31ST EDITION — 2020

BECKETT THE #1 AUTHORITY ON COLLECTIBLES

RACING COLLECTIBLES PRICE GUIDE

THE HOBBY'S MOST RELIABLE AND RELIED UPON SOURCE ™

Founder: Dr. James Beckett III
Edited by the Price Guide Staff of
BECKETT MEDIA

Manufactured in the United States of America | Published by Beckett Media LLC

Beckett Media LLC
4635 McEwen Dr.
Dallas, TX 75244
(972)991-6657
beckett.com

First Printing
ISBN: 978-1-936681-37-2

COVER IMAG

Table of Contents

How To Use This Book

Isn't it great? A book that is geared toward every type of racing collector. From the individual driver collectors to the set collectors to the die-cast collectors this book has something for each to enjoy. This Edition of *Beckett Racing Collectibles Price Guide* has been arranged to fit the collector's needs with the inclusion of a comprehensive card Price Guide, die-cast Price Guide and an alphabetical checklist. The cards and die-cast you collect, who appears on them, what they look like, where they are from, and (most important to most of you) what their current values are enumerated within. Many of the features contained in the other Beckett Price Guides have been incorporated into this volume since condition grading, terminology, and many other aspects of collecting are common to the card hobby in general. We hope you find the book both interesting and useful in your collecting pursuits.

The Beckett Guide has been successful where other attempts have failed because it is complete, current, and valid. This Price Guide contains two prices by condition for all the racing cards listed. Since the condition that most die-cast pieces are commonly sold in is Near Mint-Mint, the die-cast price guide has been arranged to provide two pricing columns. The prices for each piece reflects the current selling range for that piece. The HI column generally represents full retail selling price. The LO column generally represents the lowest price one could expect to find with extensive shopping. The prices for both the cards and die-cast were added to the listings just prior to printing and reflect not the author's opinions or desires but the going retail prices for each card or die-cast, based on the marketplace (racing shows and events, sports card shops, ads from racing publications, current mail-order catalogs, local club meetings, auction results, on-line networks, and other firsthand reportings of actually realized prices).

What is the best price guide available on the market today? Of course, card sellers prefer the price guide with the highest prices, while card buyers naturally prefer the one with the lowest prices. Accuracy, however, is the true test. Use the price guide trusted by more collectors and dealers than all the others combined. Look for the Beckett® name which stands for accuracy and integrity.

To facilitate your use of this book, read the complete introductory section on the following pages before going to the pricing pages. Every collectible field has its own terminology; we've tried to capture most of these terms and definitions in our glossary. Please read carefully the section on grading and the condition of your cards, as you cannot determine which price is appropriate for a given card without first knowing its condition.

Introduction

Did you know that monthly updates are available in the pages of *Beckett Sports Card Monthly*? You can also find daily updates on www.beckett.com. Pricing changes along with new listings for the latest releases in cards and die-casts are there as well.

Inside the pages of *BSCM*, you can find news about the latest and greatest cards to hit the market. We also answer questions from other collectors like yourself.

Log on to www.beckett.com to get daily updates on pricing and checklists via the Online Price Guides (OPG) and the latest collectible news on the frontpage.

We are not exclusive to racing collectibles, you can also find information about baseball, basketball, football, golf, hockey, soccer, tennis and wrestling collectibles on www.beckett.com.

We also publish specific sports titles for *Beckett Baseball*, *Beckett Basketball*, *Beckett Football* and *Beckett Hockey* throughout the year.

So collecting racing cards — while still pursued as a hobby with youthful exuberance by kids in the neighborhood — has also taken on the trappings of an industry, with thousands of full- and part-time card dealers, as well as vendors of supplies, clubs and conventions. In fact, each year since 1980 thousands of hobbyists have assembled for a National Sports Collectors Convention, at which hundreds of dealers have displayed their wares, seminars have been conducted, autographs penned by sports notables, and millions of cards changed hands. The Beckett Guide is the best annual guide available to the exciting world of racing cards and die-cast. Read it and use it. May your enjoyment and your card collection increase in the coming months and years.

How To Use & Condition Guide

What the Columns Mean
The LO and HI columns reflect current retail selling ranges. The HI column generally represents full retail selling price. The LO column generally represents the low-est price one could expect to find with extensive shopping.

Multipliers

Parallel sets and lightly traded insert sets are listed with multipliers to provide values of unlisted cards. Multiplier ranges (i.e. 20X to 40X HI) apply only to the HI column. Example: If base card A lists for 20 to 50 cents, and the multiplier is "20X to 40X HI," then the parallel version of card A or the insert card in question is valued at $10 to $20.

Pricing Premiums
Some cards can trade at premium price levels compared to values listed in this issue. Those include but are not limited to: cards of drivers who became hot since this issue went to press, regional stars or fan favorites in high demand locally, and memorabilia cards with unusually dramatic swatches or patches.

Stated Odds and Print Runs
Odds of pulling inserts are listed as a ratio (1:12 = one in 12 packs). If the odds vary by pack type, they are listed separately. Stated odds are provided by the manufacturer based on the entire print run and should not be viewed as a guarantee by neither Beckett Media LP nor the manufacturer.

Currency
This Price Guide reflects the North American market. All listed prices are in U.S. dollars. Based on the current exchange rate, prices in Canadian dollars are 35% to 50% higher.

Grades
Mint (MT) - No flaws. Four perfect corners, 55/45 or better centering, smooth edges, original color borders and gloss; no print spots, color or focus imperfections.
Near Mint-Mint (NRMT-MT) - Must have 60/40 or better centering, smooth edges, original color borders and gloss. One of the following very minor flaws is allowed: a slight touch of wear on one corner, barely noticeable print spots, color or focus imperfections.
Near Mint (NM) - Centering of 70/30 to 60/40. In addition, one of the following minor flaws is allowed: a slight touch of wear on two or three corners, slightly rough edges, minor print spots, color or focus imperfections.
Excellent-Mint (EXMT) - Centering no worse than 80/20. No more than two of the following flaws are allowed: two or three fuzzy corners, slightly rough edges, very minor border discoloration, minor print spots, color or focus imperfections.
Excellent (EX) - Centering no worse than 80/20 with four fuzzy corners. May also have rough edges, minor border discoloration and minor print spots, color or focus imperfections.
Very Good (VG) - Handled, but not abused. Slightly rounded corners with slight layering, slight notching on edges, moderate border discoloration, some gloss lost from the surface but no scuffing. May have hairline creases.
Good (G), Fair (F), Poor (P) - Well-worn or abused. Badly rounded and layered corners, scuffing, no original gloss, major border discol-oration and serious creases.

Price Guide Percentage by Grade

	1970-1979	1980-1987	1988-Present
MT	250-400%	200-300%	100-200%
NRMT-MT	125-200%	100%	100%
NRMT	100%	40-60%	40-60%
EXMT	40-60%	25-40%	20-30%
EX	20-40%	15-25%	10-20%
VG	10-20%	5-15%	5-10%
G/F/P	5-10%	5%	5%

Understanding Values

Determining Value

Why are some items more valuable than others? Obviously, the economic laws of supply and demand are applicable to card collecting just as they are to any other field where a commodity is bought, sold or traded in a free, unregulated market.

Supply (the number of cards available on the market) is less than the total number of cards originally produced since attrition diminishes that original quantity. Each year a percentage of cards is typically thrown away, destroyed or otherwise lost to collectors. This percentage is much, much smaller today than it was in the past because more and more people have become increasingly aware of the value of their cards.

For those who collect only Mint condition cards, the supply of older cards can be quite small indeed. Until recently, collectors were not so conscious of the need to preserve the condition of their cards. For this reason, it is difficult to know exactly how many 1972 STP cards are currently available, Mint or otherwise. It is generally accepted that there are fewer 1972 STP cards available than 1988 Maxx. If demand were equal for each of these sets, the law of supply and demand would increase the price for the least available set. Demand, however, is never equal for all sets, so price correlations can be complicated. The demand for a card is influenced by many factors. These include: (1) the age of the card; (2) the number of cards printed; (3) the driver(s) portrayed on the card; (4) the attractiveness and popularity of the set; and (5) the physical condition of the card.

In general, (1) the older the card, (2) the fewer the number of the cards printed, (3) the more famous, popular and talented the driver, (4) the more attractive and popular the set, and (5) the better the condition of the card, the higher the value of the card will be. There are exceptions to all but one of these factors: the condition of the card. Given two cards similar in all respects except condition, the one in the best condition will always be valued higher.

While those guidelines help to establish the value of a card, the countless exceptions and peculiarities make any simple, direct mathematical formula to determine card values impossible.

Regional Variation

Since the market varies from region to region, card prices of local drivers may be higher. This is known as a regional premium. How significant the premium is — and if there is any premium at all — depends on the local popularity of the driver.

The largest regional premiums usually do not apply to superstars, who often are so well-known nationwide that the prices of their key cards are too high for local dealers to realize a premium.

Lesser stars often command the strongest premiums. Their popularity is concentrated in their home region, creating local demand that greatly exceeds overall demand.

Regional premiums can apply to popular retired drivers and sometimes can be found in the areas where the drivers grew up or started racing.

A regional discount is the converse of a regional premium. Regional discounts occur when a driver has been so popular in his region for so long that local collectors and dealers have accumulat-

ed quantities of his key cards. The abundant supply may make the cards available in that area at the lowest prices anywhere.

Set Prices

A somewhat paradoxical situation exists in the price of a complete set vs. the combined cost of the individual cards in the set. In nearly every case, the sum of the prices for the individual cards is higher than the cost for the complete set. This is prevalent especially in the cards of the last few years. The reasons for this apparent anomaly stem from the habits of collectors and from the carrying costs to dealers. Today, each card in a set normally is produced in the same quantity as all other cards in its set.

Many collectors pick up only stars, superstars and particular teams. As a result, the dealer is left with a shortage of certain driver cards and an abundance of others. He therefore incurs an expense in simply "carrying" these less desirable cards in stock. On the other hand, if he sells a complete set, he gets rid of large numbers of cards at one time. For this reason, he generally is willing to receive less money for a complete set. By doing this, he recovers all of his costs and also makes a profit.

The disparity between the price of the complete set and the sum of the individual cards also has been influenced by the fact that some of the major manufacturers now are pre-collating card sets. Since "pulling" individual cards from the sets involves a specific type of labor (and cost), the singles or star card market is not affected significantly by pre-collation.

Set prices also do not include rare card varieties, unless specifically stated. Of course, the prices for sets do include one example of each type for the given set, but this is the least expensive variety.

History of Racing Cards

The history of racing cards is not an extensive story like with the other major sports. For the modern era of the racing card market only began in 1988. Before that time there were only a few sets produced and the majority of those sets were about forms of racing other than NASCAR. The early cards, 1960-1980, mainly paid tribute to Indy and Drag Racing. While the racing card market may have lagged behind the other sports in early history, it has more than kept up with them in terms of growth since 1988. In just a few short years racing cards have grown from plain photos on plain cardboard to colorful, high-tech works of art.

One of the earliest known racing card set that features racing drivers is the 1911 American Auto Drivers set. The cards were produced for the American Tobacco Company and were inserted in packs of cigarettes. Each of the 25 cards was available with a small ad for either Hassan or Mecca Cigarettes on the cardback. The unnumbered cards feature top race car drivers of the day from both North America and Europe. They represented all types of auto racing events.

There were also a few other racing or automobile focused sets produced during the first half of this century. Sets like the 1911 Turkey Reds and the 1931 Ogden's Motor Races featured the cars and events of that time period. The drivers of the cars were secondary. Other sets issued in Europe like the 1939 Churchman's King of Speed and the Will's Cigarette set featured a few racing cards but those cards were only part of multisport set. These few sets represent the trend for the majority of automobile related issues prior to World War II.

It wasn't until the post World War II era that more driver focused racing sets were introduced to the market. From 1954-1966 racing saw the production of only a few sets. Three of the sets, 1954 Stark and Wetzel Meats, 1960 Hawes Wax and the 1962 Marhoefer Meats, focused on the most popular form of racing at the time, Indy Car. As you can see from the set names, each was a promotional type set. The cards of the two meat products sets were distributed in various meat products. This makes it difficult to find Near Mint or better copies of these cards. The Hawes set was made for the Hawes Furniture Wax company by Canadian card manufacturer Parkhurst. This is the same company that produced the majority of Hockey cards issued during the 50's and early 60's. Topps and Donruss also issued a set each focused on Hot Rods and Drag racing in 1965. Donruss' issue of the 1965 Spec Sheet set comes well before the beginning of their regular production of baseball cards in 1981.

The decade of the 70's saw the production of primarily drag racing sets. More than half of the few racing sets produced during that time had a drag racing theme. All the drag racing sets were produced by Fleer and each focused on drivers of the American Hot Rod Association.

The first NASCAR related set was produced in 1972. The eleven card STP set featured full-bleed photos and unnumbered card backs that contained some biographical information on each of the drivers and the STP name and address. This set was a promotion of the STP corporation and features some of the top names in NASCAR at that time. The cards are tough to come by and usually are found in conditions less than Near Mint. This set is the only full NASCAR card set until the 1983 UNO set and the 1986 SportStars Photo-Graphics set.

From 1980 to the beginning of the modern racing card collecting era (1988), IndyCar sets dominated the market. This was primarily due to the introduction of the A & S Racing Collectables company. This manufacturer produced IndyCar sets from 1983-87. Another form of open-wheel racing also saw its first regular issued set, the 1987 World of Outlaw set. This set features the first card of NASCAR superstar Jeff Gordon.

The Modern Era

In 1988, the racing card market changed. The J.R. Maxx company decided to produce a 100-card racing set that focused on the drivers and cars of NASCAR racing. It was just part of the evolution that NASCAR was going through. The sport itself was growing in popularity and it made common sense for there to be trading cards of these growing heroes of racing. The set was to be the first mass marketed NASCAR trading card set ever issued. Maxx also signed an agreement to be the only licensed card of NASCAR. The issue of this set is considered to be the start of the modern era of racing cards. Through the marketing of these cards, racing fans became aware that there were now racing cards available of their

favorite drivers.

During the period of time from 1988-1991, other forms of racing were also flourishing from a card standpoint. There were a couple drag racing sets each of those years, a regular manufacturer of World of Outlaw cards, All World Indy began producing Indy sets and local small tracks started seeing the sale of racing cards that featured the drivers that were racing in that region.

Maxx was the only major producer of NASCAR cards from 1988-90. They were not only making a base set of cards, but were also contracting with companies like Crisco and Holly Farms to make promotional sets that featured those companies logos.

In 1991, the NASCAR card market saw the introduction to two new companies Traks and Pro Set. Pro Set was a major sports card manufacturer of the time but Traks was just getting started. Traks first set in 1991 would include the first NASCAR card of a young driver named Jeff Gordon. They would also go on to produce two promotional Dale Earnhardt sets, a Kyle Petty set and a Richard Petty set that year. Pro Set entered the racing card market from two ways NASCAR and NHRA. They produced full sets for each form of racing.

In 1993, the market would see a dramatic expansion with five new card companies coming jumping into hobby. Action Packed, Finish Line, Hi-Tech, Press Pass, and Wheels all started issuing racing sets in 1993. Action Packed not only brought its embossed printing process to racing cards but also brought the first high end retail product that racing had seen. Prior to this time boxes were generally retailed for $10-$20, but Action Packed's cost was nearly double the highest retail box prices. This did not discourage fans and collectors who were willing to purchase this new high end product. That year also saw the introduction of the parallel insert cards. The 1993 Finish Line set had a silver foil parallel version for each card. This silver parallel set was one of the most sought after and very few collectors were not working on the set at the time.

With greater competition, companies were looking for that edge that would separate their products from the rest. Many new innovations in racing cards hit the market in 1994. Finish Line introduced Phone Cards to racing collectors through inserts in their Finish Line Gold product. Press Pass introduced the first interactive game, with their Cup Chase insert cards. SkyBox introduced the first single race interactive game with their Brickyard winner redemption card. Press Pass with its VIP brand introduced signature redemption cards with its 24K Gold exchange cards. Maxx introduced the first ClearChrome cards with the 20-card subset in their Maxx Medallion product. So from nearly every manufacturer, the collectors were getting something new and different than they had ever seen before.

The market continued to grow in 1996. The hobby saw a total of 30 base brand products produced from nine different manufacturers. The market also saw the lose of Maxx in 1996. The grandfather of the modern racing card era filed bankruptcy and went out of business in the summer. Parallel inserts, Phone Cards and interactive games and race used equipment inserts were also the trend. There were very few products issued in 1996 that didn't include at least one of those four types of cards.

The year of 1997 in racing collectibles was one of both growth and decline. The die cast market exhibited growth while trying to reach more collectors with product and product line variations. The big 3 (Action/RCCA, Racing Champions and Revell) each debuted new premium lines. Action, in conjunction with Hasbro, started its Winner's Circle line to establish a presence in the mass market, Revelll also established its Revell Racing line to serve the same function. Racing Champions, through its merger with Wheels, that established a foundation that has helped to launch a new premium line in conjunction with the 50th anniversary of NASCAR.

The card market exhibited slight growth in 1997. Maxx rejoined the market after being resurrected by Upper Deck. Press Pass was bought by Wheels. Finish Line shut its doors and shutdown it's phone cards. An emphasis was placed again on high-end inserts whether it be autographed cards or cards containing "race-used" items.

Since 1997, the racing card market has seen two manufacturers depart from producing cards. In 1998, Pinnacle declared bankruptcy while in 2000 Upper Deck made the decision to cease racing card production. These actions left Press Pass as the only company producing racing cards.

Since 2001, Press Pass has been the only manufacturer for trading cards, but a few drivers have worked their way into some multisport sets along with some other sports' sets.

Press Pass, which created the first "memorabilia" cards, continued to be innovative in their usage of both autographs and memorabilia on cards. To their credit, considering their current monopoly in producing cards, they continue to search for new ways to bring the racing experience to the collector.

In 2006, Motorsports Authentics jumped into the die-cast industry by purchasing and merging Action Performance and Team Caliber. The first listings from the joint venture were tagged as Motorsports Authentics and while they looked like those of Action Performance, the packages stated otherwise. MA brought back the Action name for the 2008 and beyond die-cast listings.

In addition, both Winner's Circle and Racing Champion have produced die-cast pieces with "memorabilia" cards as part of the whole package.

An important collector shift has occurred in the last few years as the older drivers, while still popular, are making way for a new generation of drivers. Such young drivers as Tony Stewart, Matt Kenseth, Dale Earnhardt Jr, Ryan Newman, Jimmie Johnson and Kevin Harvick have quickly become fan and collector favorites.

Finding Out More

The above has been a thumbnail sketch of racing card and die-cast collecting from its inception to the present. It is difficult to tell the whole story in just a few pages. Serious collectors should subscribe to at least one of the excellent hobby periodicals. We also suggest that collectors visit their local card shop(s), attend local racing shows or events in their area and sign up for any dealer's catalogs that are available. Card and die-cast collecting is still a young and informal hobby. You can learn more about it at shops and shows and reading periodicals and catalogs. After all, smart dealers realize that spending a few minutes to teach and educate the beginners about the hobby often pays off in the long run. You should also check out www.beckett.com for more information regarding the hobby and for more up to date listings and pricing information.

2007 AAA Limited Edition

AAA distributed the individual event cards at each NASCAR race during the 2007 season. Each card is serial numbered to 5,000. The set includes one card for each of the 38 NEXTEL Cup events of 2007. Each card is a hard laminated plastic and measures approximately 4' x 8". This full-season set comes in a very nice full-color collector's box, which is hand-numbered on the outside. The outside serial number matches the serial numbers on the cards inside.

COMPLETE SET (38) 50.00 100.00
COMP.FACT.SET (38) 75.00 150.00
COMMON RAGAN 2.00 5.00

2017 Absolute

1 Dale Jarrett .40 1.00
2 Darrell Waltrip .60 1.50
3 Jeff Hammond .30 .75
4 Michael Waltrip .40 1.00
5 Ned Jarrett .30 .75
6 Wally Dallenbach .25 .60
7 Rusty Wallace .40 1.00
8 Terry Labonte .40 1.00
9 Bobby Labonte .40 1.00
10 Bill Elliott .60 1.50
11 Carl Edwards .40 1.00
12 Cale Yarborough .40 1.00
13 Derrike Cope .30 .75
14 Greg Biffle .30 .75
15 Harry Gant .30 .75
16 Jeff Burton .30 .75
17 Richard Petty .60 1.50
18 Kyle Petty .30 .75
19 Mark Martin .40 1.00
20 Kaz Grala .40 1.00
21 Junior Johnson .40 1.00
22 Hershel McGriff .25 .60
23 Ernie Irvan .40 1.00
24 Bobby Allison .30 .75
25 Donnie Allison .30 .75
26 Brett Bodine .25 .60
27 Geoff Bodine .25 .60
28 Dale Inman .30 .75
29 Joe Nemechek .25 .60
30 Rex White .25 .60
31 Jeffrey Earnhardt .40 1.00
32 Chase Elliott .50 1.25
33 Daniel Hemric .40 1.00
34 Matt Kenseth .40 1.00
35 Aric Almirola .30 .75
36 Clint Bowyer .40 1.00
37 Denny Hamlin .40 1.00
38 Dakoda Armstrong .40 1.00
39 Ryan Newman .30 .75
40 Paul Menard .25 .60
41 Michael Annett .40 1.00
42 Casey Mears .25 .60
43 Justin Allgaier .30 .75
44 Corey LaJoie .30 .75
45 Brad Keselowski .50 1.25
46 Landon Cassill .30 .75
47 John Hunter Nemechek .30 .75
48 Joey Gase .40 1.00
49 Elliott Sadler .25 .60
50 Brandon Jones .25 .60
51 Danica Patrick .75 2.00
52 Kevin Harvick .50 1.25
53 Jamie McMurray .40 1.00
54 William Byron .60 1.50
55 Trevor Bayne .40 1.00
56 Ryan Blaney .30 .75
57 Kurt Busch .30 .75
58 Cole Custer .40 1.00
59 Regan Smith .30 .75
60 David Ragan .30 .75
61 Garrett Smithley .40 1.00
62 Matt DiBenedetto .25 .60
63 Ty Dillon .40 1.00
64 Jimmie Johnson .60 1.50
65 Gray Gaulding .25 .60
66 Kasey Kahne .40 1.00
67 AJ Allmendinger .40 1.00
68 Martin Truex Jr. .30 .75
69 Todd Gilliland .60 1.50
70 Cameron Hayley .30 .75
71 Daniel Suarez .75 2.00
72 Bubba Wallace .40 1.00
73 Austin Dillon .50 1.25
74 Blake Koch .30 .75
75 Tyler Reddick .40 1.00
76 Erik Jones .60 1.50
77 Kate Dallenbach .75 2.00
78 Kyle Larson .60 1.50
79 Chris Buescher .30 .75
80 Joey Logano .40 1.00
81 Cole Whitt .30 .75
82 Kyle Busch .50 1.25
83 Ricky Stenhouse Jr. .40 1.00
84 Alex Bowman .40 1.00
85 Harrison Burton .50 1.25
86 Dale Earnhardt Jr .75 2.00
87 Julia Landauer .40 1.00
88 Noah Gragson .30 .75
89 Chad Knaus .25 .60
90 Tony Gibson .25 .60
91 Denny Hamlin .40 1.00
92 Matt Kenseth .40 1.00
93 Austin Dillon .50 1.25
94 Kyle Busch .50 1.25
95 Clint Bowyer .40 1.00
96 Danica Patrick .75 2.00
97 Kevin Harvick .50 1.25
98 Dale Earnhardt Jr .75 2.00
99 Jimmie Johnson .60 1.50
100 Kurt Busch .30 .75

2017 Absolute Spectrum Gold

*GOLD/25: 3X TO 8X BASIC CARDS

2017 Absolute Spectrum Red

*RED/99: 2X TO 5X BASIC CARDS

2017 Absolute Spectrum Silver

*SILVER/299: 1.2X TO 3X BASIC CARDS

2017 Absolute Absolute Ink

*BLUE/75-99: .5X TO 1.2X BASIC AU
*BLUE/50-65: .6X TO 1.5X BASIC AU
*BLUE/25: .8X TO 2X BASIC AU
*RED/25: .8X TO 2X BASIC AU
*RED/15: 1X TO 2.5X BASIC AU
1 Brett Bodine 2.00 5.00
2 Cale Yarborough 3.00 8.00
3 Dakoda Armstrong 3.00 8.00
4 Dale Inman 4.00 10.00
5 Dale Jarrett 5.00 12.00
6 Darrell Waltrip 5.00 12.00
7 Dave Blaney 2.00 5.00
8 Dick Berggren 2.00 5.00
9 Donnie Allison 2.50 6.00
10 Ernie Irvan 3.00 8.00
11 Geoff Bodine 2.00 5.00
12 Harry Gant 2.50 6.00
13 Hershel McGriff 2.00 5.00
14 Jack Ingram 2.00 5.00
15 Jeff Burton 2.50 6.00
16 Jeff Hammond 2.50 6.00
17 Joey Gase 3.00 8.00
18 Josh Wise 2.00 5.00
19 Junior Johnson 8.00 20.00
20 Kelley Earnhardt 10.00 25.00
21 Ken Schrader 2.00 5.00
22 Kenny Wallace 2.00 5.00
23 Kerry Earnhardt 4.00 10.00
24 Kyle Petty 2.50 6.00
25 Larry McReynolds 2.00 5.00
26 Bobby Labonte 3.00 8.00
27 Michael Waltrip 3.00 8.00
28 Mike Wallace 3.00 8.00
29 Ned Jarrett
30 Harrison Rhodes
31 Johnny Sauter
32 Rex White 2.00 5.00
33 Richard Petty 12.00 30.00
34 Kyle Larson 6.00 15.00
35 Rusty Wallace
36 Terry Labonte 3.00 8.00
37 Matt Kenseth 3.00 8.00
38 Ricky Stenhouse Jr. 3.00 8.00
39 Wally Dallenbach 2.00 5.00
40 Ward Burton 2.00 5.00

2017 Absolute Absolute Precision

*BLUE/199: .5X TO 1.2X BASIC INSERTS
*RED/149: .5X TO 1.2X BASIC INSERTS
*GOLD/99: .6X TO 1.5X BASIC INSERTS
1 Dale Earnhardt Jr 1.50 4.00
2 Joey Logano .75 2.00
3 Kyle Busch 1.00 2.50
4 Jamie McMurray .75 2.00
5 Chase Elliott 1.00 2.50
6 Martin Truex Jr. .60 1.50
7 Matt Kenseth .75 2.00
8 Austin Dillon 1.00 2.50
9 Jimmie Johnson 1.25 3.00
10 Kevin Harvick 1.00 2.50
11 Danica Patrick 1.50 4.00
12 Paul Menard .50 1.25
13 Clint Bowyer .75 2.00
14 Kasey Kahne .75 2.00
15 Richard Petty 1.25 3.00

2017 Absolute Action Packed

*BLUE/199: .5X TO 1.2X BASIC INSERTS
*RED/149: .5X TO 1.2X BASIC INSERTS
*GOLD/99: .6X TO 1.5X BASIC INSERTS
1 Jimmie Johnson 1.50 4.00
2 Kevin Harvick 1.25 3.00
3 Dale Earnhardt Jr 2.00 5.00
4 Danica Patrick 2.00 5.00
5 Brad Keselowski 1.25 3.00
6 Matt Kenseth 1.00 2.50
7 Kyle Busch 1.25 3.00
8 Joey Logano 1.00 2.50
9 Denny Hamlin 1.00 2.50
10 Kasey Kahne 1.00 2.50
11 Martin Truex Jr. .75 2.00
12 Richard Petty 1.50 4.00
14 Chase Elliott 1.25 3.00
15 Kurt Busch .75 2.00

2017 Absolute Icons

*BLUE/199: .5X TO 1.2X BASIC INSERTS
*RED/149: .5X TO 1.2X BASIC INSERTS
*GOLD/99: .6X TO 1.5X BASIC INSERTS
1 Rusty Wallace 1.00 2.50
2 Bill Elliott 1.50 4.00
3 Cale Yarborough 1.00 2.50
4 Carl Edwards 1.00 2.50
5 Dale Jarrett 1.00 2.50
6 Darrell Waltrip 1.50 4.00
7 Mark Martin 1.00 2.50
8 Michael Waltrip 1.00 2.50
9 Dale Earnhardt Jr 2.00 5.00
10 Richard Petty 1.50 4.00
11 Jimmie Johnson 1.50 4.00
12 Terry Labonte 1.00 2.50
13 Bobby Labonte 1.00 2.50
14 Ned Jarrett .75 2.00
15 Junior Johnson 1.00 2.50

2017 Absolute Memorabilia

*SILVER/99: .5X TO 1.2X BASIC MEM
*SILVER/50: .6X TO 1.5X BASIC MEM
*SILVER/25: .8X TO 2X BASIC MEM
*SILVER/15-20: 1X TO 2.5X BASIC MEM
*BLUE/49: .6X TO 1.5X BASIC MEM
*BLUE/25: .8X TO 2X BASIC MEM
*RED/25: .8X TO 2X BASIC MEM
1 AJ Allmendinger 2.50 6.00
2 Austin Dillon 3.00 8.00
3 Brad Keselowski 3.00 8.00
4 Chase Elliott 3.00 8.00
6 Dale Earnhardt Jr 5.00 12.00
8 David Ragan 2.00 5.00
10 Erik Jones 4.00 10.00
11 Jamie McMurray 2.50 6.00
12 Joey Logano 2.50 6.00
13 Kasey Kahne 2.50 6.00
16 Kyle Larson 4.00 10.00
18 Ryan Newman 2.00 5.00
20 Kaz Grala 2.50 6.00

2017 Absolute Memorabilia Signatures

*SILVER/75-99: .5X TO 1.2X BASIC MEM AU/150-325
*SILVER/75-99: .4X TO 1X BASIC MEM AU/75-105
*SILVER/35-50: .5X TO 1.2X BASIC MEM AU/75-105
*SILVER/25: .4X TO 1X BASIC MEM AU/25
*SILVER/20: .5X TO 1.2X BASIC MEM AU/25-30
*BLUE35-49: .6X TO 1.5X BASIC MEM AU/150-325
*BLUE/35-49: .5X TO 1.2X BASIC MEM AU/75-105
*BLUE/25: .6X TO 1.5X BASIC MEM AU/75-105
*BLUE/15-20: .5X TO 1.2X BASIC MEM AU/25-30
*RED/25: .8X TO 2X BASIC MEM AU/150-325
*RED/25: .6X TO 1.5X BASIC MEM AU/75-105
*RED/15: .8X TO 2X BASIC MEM AU/75-105
*RED/15: .5X TO 1.2X BASIC MEM AU/25-30
1 Danica Patrick/25
2 Alex Bowman/219 8.00 20.00
3 Aric Almirola/166 3.00 8.00
4 Bill Elliott/25 30.00 60.00
5 Brendan Gaughan/275 2.50 6.00
6 Brennan Poole/150 2.50 6.00
7 Casey Mears/227 2.50 6.00
8 Chris Buescher/317 3.00 8.00
9 Corey LaJoie/75 4.00 10.00
10 Elliott Sadler/100 3.00 8.00
11 Gray Gaulding/100 3.00 8.00
12 Jamie McMurray/105 5.00 12.00
13 Jeb Burton/25 6.00 15.00
14 Jeffrey Earnhardt/301 6.00 15.00
15 Justin Allgaier/167 3.00 8.00
16 Kaz Grala/30 8.00 20.00
17 Kyle Larson/150 15.00 40.00
18 Landon Cassill/325 3.00 8.00
19 Mark Martin/167 4.00 10.00
20 Matt DiBenedetto/100 3.00 8.00
21 Michael Annett/100
22 Reed Sorenson/100 3.00 8.00
23 Regan Smith/100 4.00 10.00
24 Ryan Reed/100 5.00 12.00
25 Ryan Sieg/317

2017 Absolute RPM

*BLUE/199: .5X TO 1.2X BASIC INSERTS
*RED/149: .5X TO 1.2X BASIC INSERTS
*GOLD/99: .6X TO 1.5X BASIC INSERTS
1 Kyle Busch 1.25 3.00
2 Chase Elliott 1.25 3.00
3 Kurt Busch .75 2.00
4 Jimmie Johnson 1.50 4.00
5 Kevin Harvick 1.25 3.00
6 Daniel Suarez 2.00 5.00
7 Brad Keselowski 1.25 3.00
8 Dale Earnhardt Jr 2.00 5.00
9 AJ Allmendinger 1.00 2.50
10 Danica Patrick 2.00 5.00
11 Matt Kenseth 1.00 2.50
12 Denny Hamlin 1.00 2.50
13 Martin Truex Jr. .75 2.00
14 Joey Logano 1.00 2.50
15 Austin Dillon 1.25 3.00

2017 Absolute Team Tandems

*SILVER/99: .5X TO 1.2X BASIC MEM
*BLUE/49: .6X TO 1.5X BASIC MEM
*RED/25: .8X TO 2X BASIC MEM
1 Clint Bowyer 4.00 10.00
Kevin Harvick
2 Kasey Kahne 4.00 10.00
Chase Elliott
3 Danica Patrick 6.00 15.00
Kurt Busch
4 Austin Dillon 4.00 10.00
Ryan Newman
5 Denny Hamlin 4.00 10.00
Kyle Busch
6 Daniel Suarez 6.00 15.00
Matt Kenseth
7 David Ragan 2.50 6.00
Landon Cassill
8 AJ Allmendinger 3.00 8.00
Chris Buescher
9 Corey LaJoie 2.50 6.00
Gray Gaulding
10 Dale Earnhardt Jr 6.00 15.00
Jimmie Johnson

2017 Absolute Tools of the Trade

*SILVER/99: .5X TO 1.2X BASIC MEM
*SILVER/25: .8X TO 2X BASIC MEM
*SILVER/15: 1X TO 2.5X BASIC MEM
*BLUE/49: .6X TO 1.5X BASIC MEM
*RED/25: .8X TO 2X BASIC MEM
1 AJ Allmendinger 2.50 6.00
2 Aric Almirola 2.00 5.00
3 Austin Dillon 3.00 8.00
6 Chase Elliott 3.00 8.00
9 Corey LaJoie 2.00 5.00
12 David Ragan 2.00 5.00
13 Denny Hamlin 2.50 6.00
14 Erik Jones 4.00 10.00
15 Gray Gaulding 1.50 4.00
16 Jamie McMurray 2.50 6.00
17 Jimmie Johnson 4.00 10.00
19 Kasey Kahne 2.50 6.00
21 Kurt Busch 2.00 5.00
23 Kyle Larson 4.00 10.00
24 Martin Truex Jr. 2.00 5.00
26 Paul Menard 1.50 4.00
29 Trevor Bayne 2.50 6.00
30 Ty Dillon 2.50 6.00
31 Alex Bowman 2.50 6.00
33 Cole Custer 2.50 6.00
34 Kaz Grala 2.50 6.00
35 Ricky Stenhouse Jr. 2.50 6.00

2017 Absolute Tools of the Trade Duals

*SILVER/99: .5X TO 1.2X BASIC MEM
*SILVER/15: 1X TO 2.5X BASIC MEM
*BLUE/49: .6X TO 1.5X BASIC MEM
*RED/25: .8X TO 2X BASIC MEM
1 AJ Allmendinger 3.00 8.00
2 Austin Dillon 4.00 10.00
3 Brad Keselowski 4.00 10.00
4 Chase Elliott 4.00 10.00
5 Clint Bowyer 3.00 8.00
6 Dale Earnhardt Jr 6.00 15.00
7 Daniel Suarez 6.00 15.00
8 David Ragan 2.50 6.00
10 Erik Jones 5.00 12.00
11 Jamie McMurray 3.00 8.00
12 Jimmie Johnson 5.00 12.00
13 Joey Logano 3.00 8.00
15 Kyle Busch 4.00 10.00
16 Kyle Larson 5.00 12.00
17 Martin Truex Jr. 2.50 6.00
18 Matt Kenseth 3.00 8.00
19 Ryan Blaney 2.50 6.00
20 Ryan Newman 2.50 6.00

2017 Absolute Tools of the Trade Trios

*SILVER/99: .5X TO 1.2X BASIC MEM
*SILVER/49: .6X TO 1.5X BASIC MEM
*SILVER/25: .8X TO 2X BASIC MEM
*BLUE/49: .6X TO 1.5X BASIC MEM
*BLUE/25: .8X TO 2X BASIC MEM
*RED/25: .8X TO 2X BASIC MEM
1 Kevin Harvick 4.00 10.00
2 Kasey Kahne 3.00 8.00
3 Jimmie Johnson 5.00 12.00
4 Dale Earnhardt Jr 6.00 15.00
5 Brad Keselowski 4.00 10.00
6 Matt Kenseth 3.00 8.00
7 Erik Jones 5.00 12.00
8 Ryan Newman 2.50 6.00
9 Clint Bowyer 3.00 8.00
11 Kyle Busch 4.00 10.00
12 Kaz Grala 3.00 8.00
13 Ty Dillon 3.00 8.00
14 Gray Gaulding 2.00 5.00
15 Corey LaJoie 2.50 6.00

1990 AC Racing Proven Winners

This 7-card black-bordered set features drivers sponsored by the AC Racing team. The cards were given away as complete sets and include six top drivers and one unnumbered checklist card. The Proven Winners name is included on the back of the checklist card. The cards were distributed as a promotion given out at many of NASCAR speedways.

COMPLETE SET (7) 25.00 60.00
1 Rusty Wallace 5.00 12.00
2 Darrell Waltrip 3.00 8.00
3 Dale Earnhardt 12.00 30.00
4 Ken Schrader 3.00 8.00
5 Ricky Rudd 3.00 8.00
6 Bobby Hillin 1.50 4.00
NNO Cover Checklist Card .75 2.00

1991 AC Racing

This 10-card set was given away as a promotion at many NASCAR speedways. The cards feature some of the top names in racing that carried the AC Racing logo on their cars.

COMPLETE SET (10) 12.50 30.00
1 Dale Earnhardt 5.00 12.00
2 Rusty Wallace 2.00 5.00
3 Darrell Waltrip 1.25 3.00
4 Ernie Irvan 1.25 3.00
5 Ricky Rudd 1.25 3.00
6 Ken Schrader .50 1.25
7 Kyle Petty 1.50 4.00
8 Rick Wilson .50 1.25
9 Hut Stricklin .50 1.25
NNO Cover .30 .75
Checklist Card

1992 AC-Delco

This 10-card set was produced and distributed by AC-Delco and GM Service Parts in 1992. The cards feature a blue bordered design and include drivers of the 1992 AC Race Team.

COMPLETE SET (10) 2.50 6.00
1 Rusty Wallace 1.25 3.00
2 Ricky Rudd .40 1.00
3 Kyle Petty 1.00 2.50
4 Darrell Waltrip .75 2.00
5 Ernie Irvan .75 2.00
6 Ken Schrader .30 .75
7 Dave Marcis .40 1.00
8 Hut Stricklin .30 .75
9 AC Delco 500 Race .20 .50
10 Cover .20 .50
Checklist Card

1992 AC Racing Postcards

This 8-card set was produced and distributed by AC Racing in 1992. The unnumbered cards are postcard sized (approximately 3-3/4" by 5-1/4") and feature an artist's rendering of a top AC Racing sponsored driver on the front. Backs are primarily black in color and include the AC Racing logo. The cards were sold as a complete set packaged in a black wrap-around cardboard package. They were also given away at the AC suite at Michigan Speedway.

COMPLETE SET (8) 4.00 15.00
1 Dale Earnhardt 3.00 8.00
2 Ernie Irvan .60 1.50
3 Kyle Petty .75 2.00
4 Ricky Rudd .30 .75
5 Ken Schrader .25 .60
6 Hut Stricklin .25 .60
7 Rusty Wallace 1.00 2.50
8 Darrell Waltrip .60 1.50

1993 AC Racing Foldouts

This 10-card set features drivers sponsored by the AC Racing team. The cards are bi-fold and measure approximately 3-1/2" by 4-5/8" when fully unfolded. Numbering was done according to the driver's car number. The cards were sold as complete sets and packaging included a gray AC Racing 1:64 scale die cast car as well.

COMPLETE SET (10) 4.00 10.00
2 Rusty Wallace .75 2.00
3 Dale Earnhardt 2.50 6.00
4 Ernie Irvan .30 .75
17 Darrell Waltrip .30 .75
24 Jeff Gordon 1.25 3.00
25 Ken Schrader .20 .50
40 Kenny Wallace .20 .50
41 Phil Parsons .20 .50
42 Kyle Petty .30 .75
NNO Cover .10 .30
Checklist Card

1992 Action Packed Allison Family

Produced by Action Packed to honor the career of the late Clifford Allison, this set was distributed in factory set form. The cards included Clifford's father Bobby and brother Davey and were sold packaged in a black folding binder with proceeds going to help The Children of Clifford Allison Trust Fund. Production was limited to 5000 numbered sets. The sets were donated by Action Packed to the Allison family. Also, there was one set of 24K gold cards produced.

COMPLETE SET (3) 16.00 40.00
NNO Bobby Allison 4.00 10.00
NNO Clifford Allison 4.00 10.00
NNO Davey Allison 5.00 12.00

1992 Action Packed Kyle Petty Prototypes

Action Packed released this three-card Kyle Petty set as a preview to its initial 1993 NASCAR set. The card numbering begins at 101 and each is clearly marked "prototype" on the cardback.

COMPLETE SET (3) 20.00 35.00
101 Kyle Petty's Car 2.50 6.00
102 Kyle Petty 6.00 15.00
103 Kyle Petty's Car 2.50 6.00

1992 Action Packed Richard Petty

This 3-card set was issued to commemorate the career of Richard Petty. The first two cards were issued together in a cello wrapper with the third card being issued separately.

COMMON CARD (RP1-RP3) 1.50 4.00
RP1 Richard Petty/100,000 2.50 6.00
RP2 Richard Petty's Car/100,000 1.00 2.50
RP3 Richard Petty/50,000 4.00 10.00

1993 Action Packed Prototypes

Action Packed produced these cards to preview its 1993 release. The cards are similar to regular issue 1993 cards, but contain the words "1993 Prototype" on the cardback along with different card numbering. The cards were released together and are often sold as a complete set.

COMPLETE SET (5) 50.00 120.00
AK1 Alan Kulwicki 12.50 30.00
BA1 Bobby Allison 6.00 15.00
DE1 Dale Earnhardt 15.00 40.00
DJ1 Dale Jarrett 6.00 15.00
JG1 Jeff Gordon 15.00 40.00

1993 Action Packed

This is the first Action Packed racing release, issued in three separate series, and features the now standard raised embossed printing process. Twenty-four pack boxes with seven cards per pack housed the first series, while series two and three contained six cards per pack. The series one set was released in early 1993 and includes five different subsets: 92 Race Winners, 92 Pole Winners, Top Ten Points, Young Guns, and King Richard Petty. Series two, released in mid-1993, is highlighted by the first Dale Earnhardt Action Packed cards. A four card sub-set of Dale Earnhardt featured braille on the back of the cards. The series two includes six different subsets: Daytona '93 (90-95), Back in Black (120-123), Back in Black Brail (124-127), The Allisons (140-149), Young Guns (150-156), and Brothers (161-164). Fall 1993 saw the release of series three featuring Rusty Wallace and Race Week in Charlotte subsets, along with six card memorial insert sets of both Davey Allison and Alan Kulwicki. 24K Gold insert cards were also distributed throughout packs of all three series.

COMPLETE SET (207) 25.00 60.00
COMP.SERIES 1 SET (84) 10.00 25.00
COMP.SERIES 2 SET (84) 8.00 20.00
COMP.SERIES 3 SET (39) 8.00 20.00
1 Alan Kulwicki WIN 2.00 5.00
2 Kyle Petty WIN .40 1.00
3 Darrell Waltrip's Car WIN .25 .60
4 Geoff Bodine WIN .25 .60
5 Davey Allison WIN 1.25 3.00
6 Rusty Wallace WIN 1.00 2.50
7 Harry Gant WIN .25 .60
8 Ernie Irvan WIN .40 1.00
9 Mark Martin WIN 1.25 3.00
10 Richard Petty Braille 1.00 2.50
11 Terry Labonte's Car .40 1.00
12 Bobby Labonte 1.00 2.50
13 Kyle Petty's Car .25 .60
14 Kyle Petty .40 1.00
15 Dale Jarrett 1.00 2.50
16 Darrell Waltrip .40 1.00
17 Darrell Waltrip's Car .25 .60
18 Ken Schrader's Car .10 .30
19 Ken Schrader .25 .60
20 Ken Schrader PW .25 .60
21 Davey Allison PW 1.25 3.00
22 Mark Martin PW 1.25 3.00
23 Kyle Petty PW .40 1.00
24 Darrell Waltrip PW .40 1.00
25 Ernie Irvan PW .40 1.00
26 Alan Kulwicki PW .60 1.50
27 Brett Bodine PW .25 .60
28 Rusty Wallace PW 1.00 2.50
29 Rick Mast PW .25 .60
30 Sterling Marlin's Car PW .25 .60
31 Richard Petty's Car Braille .40 1.00
32 Jeff Gordon 2.50 6.00

33 Ernie Irvan's Car	.25	.60
34 Ernie Irvan	.40	1.00
35 Kenny Wallace	.25	.60
36 Terry Labonte	.75	2.00
37 Geoff Bodine's Car	.10	.30
38 Geoff Bodine	.25	.60
39 Geoff Bodine	.25	.60
40 Alan Kulwicki T10	.60	1.50
41 Darrell Waltrip T10	.40	1.00
42 Kyle Petty T10	.40	1.00
43 Davey Allison T10	1.25	3.00
44 Mark Martin T10	1.00	2.50
45 Harry Gant T10	.25	.60
46 Terry Labonte T10	.40	1.00
47 Sterling Marlin T10	.25	.60
48 Rick Mast	.25	.60
49 Rick Mast w/Car	.25	.60
50 Richard Petty's Car KR	.40	1.00
51 Richard Petty KR	.40	1.00
52 Richard Petty KR	.40	1.00
53 Richard Petty KR	.40	1.00
54 Richard Petty KR	.40	1.00
55 Sterling Marlin	1.00	2.50
56 Sterling Marlin's Car	.25	.60
57 Brett Bodine	.25	.60
58 Morgan Shepherd	.25	.60
59 Morgan Shepherd's Car	.10	.30
60 Kenny Wallace YG	.25	.60
61 Jeff Gordon YG	1.50	4.00
62 Bobby Labonte YG	1.00	2.50
63 J.Gordon/Wallace/Lab.YG	1.50	4.00
64 Alan Kulwicki	.60	1.50
65 Wally Dallenbach Jr.'s Car	.10	.30
66 Wally Dallenbach Jr.	.25	.60
67 Michael Waltrip	.40	1.00
68 Michael Waltrip's Car	.25	.60
69 Hut Stricklin	.25	.60
70 Richard Petty's Car BR	.40	1.00
71 Richard Petty BR	.40	1.00
72 Richard Petty BR	.40	1.00
73 Harry Gant	.25	.60
74 Harry Gant's Car	.10	.30
75 Richard Petty BR	.40	1.00
76 Richard Petty BR	.40	1.00
77 Mark Martin	1.00	2.50
78 Mark Martin's Car	.40	1.00
79 Davey Allison's Car	.40	1.00
80 Davey Allison	1.25	3.00
81 Richard Petty	.75	2.00
82 Richard Petty's Car	.25	.60
83 Rusty Wallace	1.25	3.00
84 Rusty Wallace's Car	.40	1.00
85 Alan Kulwicki	.50	1.25
86 Jeff Gordon CRC	2.00	4.00
87 Jeff Gordon's Car	1.25	3.00
88 Dale Earnhardt	2.50	6.00
89 Dale Earnhardt's Car	1.00	2.50
90 Dale Jarrett D93	.30	.75
91 Kyle Petty D93	.15	.40
92 Richard Petty D93	.30	.75
93 Jeff Gordon D93	2.00	4.00
94 Dale Earnhardt D93	1.25	3.00
95 Dale Earnhardt D93	1.25	3.00
96 Brett Bodine	.15	.40
97 Davey Allison	1.25	2.50
98 Davey Allison's Car	.30	.75
99 Kyle Petty	.30	.75
100 Kyle Petty's Car	.15	.40
101 Kenny Wallace	.15	.40
102 Kenny Wallace's Car	.07	.20
103 Darrell Waltrip	.30	.75
104 Darrell Waltrip's Car	.15	.40
105 Rick Mast	.15	.40
106 Rick Mast's Car	.07	.20
107 Rusty Wallace	1.00	2.50
108 Rusty Wallace's Car	.30	.75
109 Mark Martin	1.50	3.00
110 Mark Martin's Car	.30	.75
111 Geoff Bodine	.15	.40
112 Geoff Bodine's Car	.07	.20
113 Wally Dallenbach Jr.	.15	.40
114 Wally Dallenbach Jr.'s Car	.07	.20
115 Dale Jarrett	.75	2.00
116 Morgan Shepherd	.15	.40
117 Morgan Shepherd's Car	.07	.20
118 Rick Wilson	.15	.40
119 Rick Wilson's car	.07	.20
120 Dale Earnhardt BB	.75	2.00
121 Dale Earnhardt BB	.75	2.00
122 Dale Earnhardt BB	.75	2.00
123 Dale Earnhardt BB	.75	2.00
124 Dale Earnhardt BR	.75	2.00
125 Dale Earnhardt BR	.75	2.00
126 Dale Earnhardt BR	.75	2.00
127 Dale Earnhardt BR	.75	2.00
128 Ernie Irvan	.30	.75
129 Ernie Irvan's Car	.15	.40
130 Sterling Marlin	.75	2.00
131 Sterling Marlin's Car	.15	.40
132 Jimmy Spencer	.15	.40
133 Jimmy Spencer's Car	.07	.20
134 Ken Schrader	.15	.40
135 Ken Schrader's Car	.07	.20
136 Michael Waltrip	.30	.75
137 Michael Waltrip's Car	.15	.40
138 Dale Earnhardt PW	1.25	3.00
139 Earnhardt WIN/Jr./Kerry	6.00	15.00
140 Allison Family TA	.75	2.00
141 Donnie Allison TA	.15	.40
142 Clifford Allison TA	.15	.40
143 Donnie Allison TA Bobby Allison	.15	.40
144 Davey Allison Family TA	.75	2.00
145 Donnie Allison Family TA	.15	.40
146 Da.Allison/Cliff./Bobby TA	.75	2.00
147 Bobby Allison TA	.15	.40
148 Donnie Allison TA	.15	.40
149 Hut Stricklin Family TA	.15	.40
150 Jeff Gordon YG	2.00	4.00
151 Kenny Wallace YG	.15	.40
152 Bobby Labonte YG	.75	2.00
153 Jeff Gordon YG	2.00	4.00
154 Kenny Wallace YG	.15	.40
155 Bobby Labonte YG	.75	2.00
156 J.Gordon Wallace Lab.YG	3.00	6.00
157 Harry Gant	.15	.40
158 Harry Gant's Car	.07	.20
159 Hut Stricklin	.15	.40
160 R.Petty Kyle Petty FS	.30	.75
161 Geoff Bodine Brett Bodine B	.15	.40
162 T.Labonte B.Labonte B	.50	1.25
163 R.Wallace Ken.Wallace B	.60	1.50
164 M.Waltrip D.Waltrip B	.30	.75
165 Ned Jarrett Dale Jarrett	.30	.75
166 Bobby Labonte	.75	2.00
167 Terry Labonte	.60	1.50
168 Terry Labonte's Car	.30	.75
169 Geoff Bodine	.07	.20
170 Wally Dallenbach Jr.	.07	.20
171 Dale Earnhardt	1.50	4.00
172 Harry Gant	.07	.20
173 Jeff Gordon	1.50	3.00
174 Bobby Hillin	.07	.20
175 Sterling Marlin	.50	1.25
176 Mark Martin	.75	2.00
177 Morgan Shepherd	.07	.20
178 Ken Schrader	.07	.20
179 Michael Waltrip	.15	.40
180 Brett Bodine	.07	.20
181 Derrike Cope	.07	.20
182 Ernie Irvan	.15	.40
183 Dale Jarrett	.60	1.50
184 Bobby Labonte	.60	1.50
185 Terry Labonte	.40	1.00
186 Kyle Petty	.15	.40
187 Ken Schrader	.07	.20
188 Jimmy Spencer	.07	.20
189 Hut Stricklin	.07	.20
190 Darrell Waltrip	.15	.40
191 Rusty Wallace RW	.30	1.00
192 Rusty Wallace RW	.30	1.00
193 Rusty Wallace RW	.30	1.00
194 Rusty Wallace's Car RW	.07	.20
195 Rusty Wallace's Car RW	.07	.20
196 Rusty Wallace in Pits RW	.07	.20
197 Rusty Wallace RW	.30	1.00
198 Dale Earnhardt WIN	.75	2.00
199 Ernie Irvan WIN	.15	.40
200 Rick Mast WIN	.07	.20
201 Ernie Irvan PS	.15	.40
202 Dale Earnhardt WIN	.75	2.00
203 Ken Schrader PS	.07	.20
204 Sterling Marlin WIN	.50	1.25
205 Jeff Gordon PS	1.00	2.50
206 Michael Waltrip WIN	.15	.40
207 Dale Earnhardt WIN	.75	2.00
KP1 Kyle Petty's Car Promo	1.25	3.00
KP2 Kyle Petty Promo	1.25	3.00
AKDA A.Kulwicki/D.Allison	7.50	20.00
AKDAG A.Kulwicki/D.Allison 24K	12.50	30.00

1993 Action Packed 24K Gold

These insert cards were randomly distributed in all three series of 1993 Action Packed cards. They are distinguishable from the regular issue cards by the "G" suffix on the card numbers as well as the 24Kt. Gold logo on the card fronts. Card #73G Rusty Wallace apparently was not included in packs but hit the secondary market at a later date, presumably after Action Packed ceased card operations.

COMPLETE SET (72)	1200.00	2400.00
COMP.SERIES 1 (17)	600.00	1200.00
COMP.SERIES 2 (21)	300.00	600.00
COMP.SERIES 3 (34)	300.00	600.00
1G Alan Kulwicki T10	20.00	50.00
2G Darrell Waltrip T10	8.00	20.00
3G Kyle Petty T10	8.00	20.00
4G Davey Allison T10	12.00	30.00
5G Mark Martin T10	15.00	40.00
6G Harry Gant T10	5.00	12.00
7G Terry Labonte T10	10.00	25.00
8G Sterling Marlin T10	10.00	25.00
9G Kenny Wallace YG	5.00	12.00
10G Jeff Gordon YG	20.00	50.00
11G Bobby Labonte YG	12.50	30.00
12G J.Gordon/Wall./Lab.YG	25.00	60.00
13G Richard Petty KR	10.00	25.00
14G Richard Petty KR	10.00	25.00
15G Richard Petty KR	10.00	25.00
16G Richard Petty KR	10.00	25.00
17G Richard Petty KR	10.00	25.00
18G Dale Earnhardt BB	12.50	30.00
19G Dale Earnhardt BB	12.50	30.00
20G Dale Earnhardt BB	12.50	30.00
21G Dale Earnhardt BB	12.50	30.00
22G Dale Earnhardt BB Braille	8.00	20.00
23G Dale Earnhardt BB Braille	8.00	20.00
24G Dale Earnhardt BB Braille	8.00	20.00
25G Dale Earnhardt BB Braille	8.00	20.00
26G Jeff Gordon YG	20.00	50.00
27G Kenny Wallace YG	4.00	10.00
28G Bobby Labonte YG	12.50	30.00
29G Jeff Gordon YG	20.00	50.00
30G Kenny Wallace YG	4.00	10.00
31G Bobby Labonte YG	12.50	30.00
32G J.Gordon/Wall./Lab.YG	20.00	50.00
33G Dale Jarrett D93	6.00	15.00
34G Kyle Petty D93	6.00	15.00
35G Richard Petty D93	8.00	20.00
36G Jeff Gordon D93	20.00	50.00
37G Dale Earnhardt D93	8.00	20.00
38G Dale Earnhardt D93	8.00	20.00
39G Alan Kulwicki	10.00	25.00
40G Alan Kulwicki	10.00	25.00
41G Alan Kulwicki	10.00	25.00
42G Alan Kulwicki	10.00	25.00
43G Alan Kulwicki	10.00	25.00
44G Alan Kulwicki	10.00	25.00
45G Davey Allison	8.00	20.00
46G Davey Allison	8.00	20.00
47G Davey Allison	8.00	20.00
48G Davey Allison	8.00	20.00
49G Davey Allison	8.00	20.00
50G Davey Allison	8.00	20.00
51G Geoff Bodine	8.00	8.00
52G Wally Dallenbach Jr.	3.00	8.00
53G Dale Earnhardt	15.00	40.00
54G Harry Gant	3.00	8.00
55G Jeff Gordon	20.00	50.00
56G Bobby Hillin	3.00	8.00
57G Sterling Marlin	10.00	25.00
58G Mark Martin	12.50	30.00
59G Morgan Shepherd	3.00	8.00
60G Kenny Wallace	3.00	8.00
61G Michael Waltrip	5.00	12.00
62G Brett Bodine	3.00	8.00
63G Derrike Cope	3.00	8.00
64G Ernie Irvan	5.00	12.00
65G Dale Jarrett	6.00	15.00
66G Bobby Labonte	10.00	25.00
67G Terry Labonte	10.00	25.00
68G Kyle Petty	5.00	12.00
69G Ken Schrader	3.00	8.00
70G Jimmy Spencer	3.00	8.00
71G Hut Stricklin	3.00	8.00
72G Darrell Waltrip	5.00	12.00
73G Rusty Wallace	5.00	12.00

1993 Action Packed Davey Allison

A special insert set devoted to the life of the late Davey Allison. The cards were randomly inserted in series three packs of 1993 Action Packed.

COMPLETE SET (6)	3.00	8.00
COMMON CARD (DA1-DA6)	.75	1.50

1993 Action Packed Alan Kulwicki

A special insert set devoted to the life of the late Alan Kulwicki. The cards were randomly inserted in series three packs of 1993 Action Packed.

COMPLETE SET (6)	3.00	8.00
COMMON CARD (AK1-AK6)	.75	1.50

1994 Action Packed Prototypes

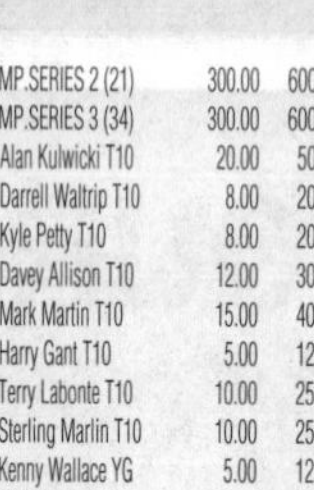

Action Packed released several prototype cards throughout the 1994 year. Two Kyle Petty cards were released for series one, five individual driver cards for series two, and four more for series three. Two prototype 24K Gold cards were also issued, but are not considered part of the basic 11-card set.

COMPLETE SET (11)	15.00	40.00
2R941 Dale Earnhardt	10.00	25.00
2R942 Jeff Gordon	6.00	15.00
2R942G Jeff Gordon 24K Gold	8.00	20.00
2R943 Kyle Petty	1.25	3.00
2R943G Kyle Petty 24K Gold	1.50	4.00
2R944 Dale Jarrett	2.50	6.00
2R945 Rusty Wallace's Car	5.00	12.00
3R941 Ricky Rudd	1.25	3.00
3R942 Richard Childress	1.25	3.00
3R944 Mark Martin	4.00	10.00
3R94S Jeff Gordon	6.00	15.00
KP1 Kyle Petty's Car	1.25	3.00
KP2 Kyle Petty	1.25	3.00

1994 Action Packed

The 1994 Action Packed set was released in three series with each pack containing six cards. Wax boxes contained 24-packs per box and color photos of popular drivers were featured on the wrapper fronts. The standard Action Packed 24K Gold insert was distributed throughout all three series with series three also including a Richard Childress Racing insert. Series one is highlighted by Race Winners, Top Ten, Young Guns, Two Timers and Pit Crew Champs subsets. Series two features Neil Bonnett and Kyle Petty subsets along with a Daytona Review. A special Kyle Petty Diamond card (#92D) was also inserted in series two, at a rate of approximatey 1:1,650, that features an authentic diamond embedded in the card front. The diamond earring Kyle Petty card is numbered of 1000. The third series is highlighted by a Rest and Relaxation subset (139-167) and a Winner subset (179-193).

COMPLETE SET (209)	20.00	50.00
COMP.SERIES 1 (66)	10.00	25.00
COMP.SERIES 2 (72)	10.00	25.00
COMP.SERIES 3 (71)	10.00	25.00
WAX BOX SERIES 1	15.00	40.00
WAX BOX SERIES 2	15.00	40.00
WAX BOX SERIES 3	20.00	50.00
1 Dale Earnhardt	2.00	5.00
2 Rusty Wallace	.75	2.00
3 Mark Martin	.75	2.00
4 Dale Jarrett	.75	2.00
5 Kyle Petty	.25	.60
6 Ernie Irvan	.25	.60
7 Morgan Shepherd	.10	.30
8 Dale Earnhardt WC Champ	2.00	5.00
9 Ken Schrader	.10	.30
10 Ricky Rudd	.40	1.00
11 Harry Gant	.25	.60
12 Jimmy Spencer	.10	.30
13 Darrell Waltrip	.25	.60
14 Jeff Gordon	1.25	3.00
15 Sterling Marlin	.40	1.00
16 Geoff Bodine	.10	.30
17 Michael Waltrip	.25	.60
18 Terry Labonte	.40	1.00
19 Bobby Labonte	.60	1.50
20 Brett Bodine	.10	.30
21 Rick Mast	.10	.30
22 Wally Dallenbach Jr.	.10	.30
23 Kenny Wallace	.10	.30
24 Hut Stricklin	.10	.30
25 Derrike Cope	.10	.30
26 Bobby Hillin	.10	.30
27 Rick Wilson	.10	.30
28 Lake Speed	.10	.30
29 Alan Kulwicki	.50	1.25
30 Jeff Gordon ROY	1.25	3.00
31 Rusty Wallace's Car WIN	.25	.60
32 Dale Earnhardt WIN	2.00	5.00
33 Mark Martin WIN	.75	2.00
34 Ernie Irvan w Crew WIN	.25	.60
35 Dale Jarrett WIN	.60	1.50
36 Morgan Shepherd WIN	.10	.30
37 Kyle Petty WIN	.25	.60
38 Ricky Rudd WIN	.40	1.00
39 Geoff Bodine WIN	.10	.30
40 Davey Allison WIN	.60	1.50
41 Dale Earnhardt's Car	.75	2.00
42 Rusty Wallace's Car	.40	1.00
43 Mark Martin's Car	.40	1.00
44 D.Jarrett K.Petty w Car	.40	1.00
45 Kyle Petty's Car	.10	.30
46 Ernie Irvan's Car	.25	.60
47 Morgan Shepherd's Car	.05	.15
48 Bill Elliott's Car	.40	1.00
49 Ken Schrader's Car	.05	.15
50 Ricky Rudd's Car	.10	.30
51 John Andretti R RC	.10	.30
52 Ward Burton R	.25	.60
53 Steve Grissom R	.10	.30
54 Joe Nemechek R	.10	.30
55 Jeff Burton R	.40	1.00
56 Loy Allen Jr. R	.10	.30
57 Lake Speed TC	.10	.30
58 Ernie Irvan w Car	.25	.60
59 Geoff Bodine TC	.10	.30
60 Dick Trickle TC	.10	.30
61 Jimmy Hensley TC	.10	.30
62 Buddy Parrott	.05	.15
63 Donnie Richeson	.05	.15
64 Steve Hmiel	.05	.15
65 Mike Hill	.05	.15
66 Doug Hewitt	.05	.15
67 Rusty Wallace	.75	2.00
68 Dale Earnhardt	2.00	5.00
69 Mark Martin	.75	2.00
70 Darrell Waltrip	.25	.60
71 Dale Jarrett	.60	1.50
72 Morgan Shepherd	.10	.30
73 Jeff Gordon	1.25	3.00
74 Ken Schrader	.10	.30
75 Brett Bodine	.10	.30
76 Harry Gant	.25	.60
77 Sterling Marlin	.40	1.00
78 Terry Labonte	.40	1.00
79 Ricky Rudd	.40	1.00
80 Geoff Bodine	.10	.30
81 Ernie Irvan	.25	.60
82 Kyle Petty	.25	.60
83 Jimmy Spencer	.10	.30
84 Hut Stricklin	.10	.30
85 Bobby Labonte	.60	1.50
86 Derrike Cope	.10	.30
87 Loy Allen Jr.	.10	.30
88 Michael Waltrip	.25	.60
89 Ted Musgrave	.10	.30
90 Lake Speed	.10	.30
91 Todd Bodine	.10	.30
92 Kyle Petty KPS	.25	.60
92D Kyle Petty Earring/1000	25.00	60.00
93 Kyle Petty BR KPS	.25	.60
94 Kyle Petty KPS	.25	.60
95 Kyle Petty w Aerosmith KPS	.25	.60
96 Kyle Petty w Family KPS	.25	.60
97 Kyle Petty w M.Waltrip KPS	.25	.60
98 Neil Bonnett David Bonnett	.25	.60
99 Dale Earnhardt Bonnett	2.00	5.00
100 Neil Bonnett Darrell Waltrip	.25	.60
101 Neil Bonnett	.40	1.00
102 Neil Bonnett	.40	1.00
103 Jeff Gordon DR	1.25	3.00
104 Dale Earnhardt DR	2.00	5.00
105 Ernie Irvan DR	.25	.60
106 Loy Allen Jr. DR	.10	.30
107 Sterling Marlin DR	.40	1.00
108 Rusty Wallace's Car	.40	1.00
109 Sterling Marlin's Car	.10	.30
110 Terry Labonte's Car	.25	.60
111 Geoff Bodine's Car	.05	.15
112 Ricky Rudd's Car	.10	.30
113 Lake Speed's Car	.05	.15
114 Ted Musgrave's Car	.05	.15
115 Mark Martin's Car	.40	1.00
116 Hut Stricklin's Car	.05	.15
117 Ken Schrader's Car	.05	.15
118 Jimmy Spencer's Car	.05	.15
119 Kyle Petty's Car	.10	.30
120 Wally Dallenbach Jr.'s Car	.05	.15
121 John Andretti's Car	.05	.15
122 Steve Grissom's Car	.05	.15
123 Ward Burton's Car	.05	.15
124 Joe Nemechek's Car	.05	.15
125 Jeff Burton's Car	.05	.15
126 Dale Earnhardt's Car	.75	2.00
127 Darrell Waltrip's Car	.10	.30
128 Dale Jarrett's Car	.40	1.00
129 Morgan Shepherd's Car	.05	.15
130 Bobby Labonte's Car	.10	.30
131 Jeff Gordon's Car	.50	1.25
132 Brett Bodine's Car	.05	.15
133 Michael Waltrip's Car	.10	.30
134 Todd Bodine's Car	.05	.15
135 Ernie Irvan's Car	.25	.60
136 Harry Gant's Car	.10	.30
137 Rick Mast's Car	.05	.15
138 Bill Elliott's Car	.40	1.00
139 Brett Bodine RR	.05	.15
140 Geoff Bodine	.10	.30
141 Todd Bodine	.05	.15
142 Jeff Burton	.10	.30
143 Derrike Cope	.10	.30
144 Wally Dallenbach Jr.	.10	.30
145 Harry Gant	.10	.30
146 Jeff Gordon	1.25	3.00
147 Steve Grissom	.10	.30
148 Ernie Irvan	.25	.60
149 Dale Jarrett	.60	1.50
150 Bobby Labonte	.60	1.50
151 Terry Labonte	.40	1.00
152 Sterling Marlin	.40	1.00
153 Mark Martin	.75	2.00
154 Rick Mast	.10	.30
155 Ted Musgrave	.10	.30
156 Joe Nemechek	.10	.30
157 Kyle Petty	.10	.30
158 Ricky Rudd	.40	1.00
159 Greg Sacks	.10	.30
160 Ken Schrader	.10	.30
161 Morgan Shepherd	.10	.30
162 Lake Speed	.10	.30
163 Jimmy Spencer	.10	.30
164 Hut Stricklin RR	.10	.30
165 Mike Wallace RR	.10	.30
166 Darrell Waltrip RR	.25	.60
167 Michael Waltrip RR	.25	.60
168 Roger Penske	.05	.15
169 Junior Johnson	.10	.30
170 Robert Yates	.05	.15
171 Joe Gibbs	.25	.60
172 Ricky Rudd	.40	1.00
173 Glen Wood Len Wood Eddie Wood	.05	.15
174 Jack Roush	.05	.15
175 Joe Hendrick(Papa) Rick Hendrick	.05	.15
176 Felix Sabates	.05	.15
177 Richard Childress	.25	.60
178 Richard Petty	.40	1.00
179 Dale Earnhardt WIN	2.00	5.00
180 Dale Earnhardt WIN	2.00	5.00
181 Ernie Irvan WIN	.10	.30
182 Ernie Irvan WIN	.10	.30
183 Rusty Wallace WIN	.75	2.00
184 Terry Labonte WIN	.40	1.00
185 Sterling Marlin WIN	.40	1.00
186 Rusty Wallace WIN	.75	2.00
187 Dale Earnhardt WIN	2.00	5.00
188 Ernie Irvan WIN	.25	.60
189 Jeff Gordon WIN	1.25	3.00
190 Rusty Wallace WIN	.75	2.00
191 Rusty Wallace WIN	.75	2.00
192 Rusty Wallace WIN	.75	2.00
193 Jimmy Spencer WIN	.10	.30
194 Ernie Irvan	.25	.60
195 Ernie Irvan	.25	.60
196 Ernie Irvan	.25	.60
197 Ernie Irvan	.25	.60
198 Ernie Irvan	.25	.60
199 Mark Martin	.75	2.00
200 Mark Martin	.75	2.00
201 Mark Martin	.75	2.00
202 Mark Martin	.75	2.00
203 Mark Martin	.75	2.00
204 R.Wallace Kenny Mike	.50	1.25
205 Todd Bodine Brett Bodine Geoff Bodine	.10	.30
206 Rusty Wallace WS	.50	1.25
207 Geoff Bodine WS	.10	.30
208 Joe Nemechek WS	.10	.30
209 Jeff Gordon WS	1.25	3.00

1994 Action Packed 24K Gold

Randomly inserted in packs over all three 1994 Action Packed series, each card includes the 24Kt. Gold logo on the card front. There were 1,000 of the Jeff Gordon card (#189G) inserted in series three. The only way the card came was autographed and the card is not included in the complete set price. Many cards in the set were also used in subsets in the regular issue. Wrapper stated odds for pulling a 24K Gold card are 1:96 packs.

COMPLETE SET (59)	600.00	1200.00
COMP.SERIES 1 (20)	250.00	500.00
COMP.SERIES 2 (25)	250.00	500.00
COMP.SERIES 3 (14)	250.00	500.00
1G Rusty Wallace	8.00	20.00
2G Dale Earnhardt	25.00	50.00
3G Mark Martin	6.00	15.00
4G Ernie Irvan	2.50	6.00
5G Dale Jarrett WIN	5.00	12.00
6G Morgan Shepherd WIN	1.50	4.00
7G Kyle Petty WIN	2.50	6.00
8G Ricky Rudd WIN	4.00	10.00
9G Geoff Bodine WIN	1.50	4.00
10G Davey Allison	8.00	20.00
11G Dale Earnhardt's Car	10.00	25.00
12G Rusty Wallace's Car	5.00	12.00
13G Mark Martin's Car	5.00	10.00
14G D.Jarrett K.Petty	6.00	15.00
15G Kyle Petty's Car	1.50	4.00
16G Ernie Irvan's Car	2.50	6.00
17G Morgan Shepherd's Car	1.50	4.00
18G Bill Elliott's Car	5.00	12.00
19G Ken Schrader's Car	1.50	4.00
20G Ricky Rudd's Car	1.50	4.00
21G Rusty Wallace	8.00	20.00
22G Dale Earnhardt	25.00	50.00
23G Mark Martin	6.00	15.00
24G Darrell Waltrip	3.00	8.00
25G Dale Jarrett	6.00	15.00
26G Morgan Shepherd	2.00	5.00
27G Jeff Gordon	12.00	30.00
28G Ken Schrader	2.00	5.00
29G Brett Bodine	2.00	5.00
30G Harry Gant	2.50	6.00
31G Sterling Marlin	4.00	10.00
32G Terry Labonte	5.00	12.00
33G Ricky Rudd	4.00	10.00
34G Geoff Bodine	2.00	5.00
35G Ernie Irvan	2.50	6.00
36G Kyle Petty	2.50	6.00
37G Jimmy Spencer	2.00	5.00
38G Hut Stricklin	2.00	5.00
39G Bobby Labonte	5.00	12.00
40G Derrike Cope	2.00	5.00
41G Loy Allen Jr.	2.00	5.00
42G Michael Waltrip	2.50	6.00
43G Ted Musgrave	2.00	5.00
44G Lake Speed	2.00	5.00
45G Todd Bodine	2.00	5.00
179G Dale Earnhardt WIN	10.00	25.00
180G Dale Earnhardt WIN	10.00	25.00
181G Ernie Irvan WIN	2.00	5.00
182G Ernie Irvan WIN	2.00	5.00
183G Rusty Wallace WIN	5.00	12.00
184G Terry Labonte WIN	5.00	12.00
185G Sterling Marlin WIN	4.00	10.00
186G Rusty Wallace WIN	5.00	12.00
187G Dale Earnhardt WIN	10.00	25.00
188G Ernie Irvan WIN	2.00	5.00
189G Jeff Gordon WIN AUTO	20.00	50.00
190G Rusty Wallace WIN	5.00	12.00
191G Rusty Wallace WIN	5.00	12.00
192G Rusty Wallace WIN	5.00	12.00
193G Jimmy Spencer WIN	2.00	5.00

1994 Action Packed Mint

*MINT CARDS: 2X TO 5X BASIC CARDS

1994 Action Packed Champ and Challenger

Action Packed issued this special set to highlight the careers of two of NASCAR's most popular drivers of 1994 -- the 1993 "Champ" Dale Earnhardt and "Challenger" Jeff Gordon. The cards were distributed in 6-card packs with 24 packs per box. Cards #1-20 have green and red borders and focus on Gordon, while cards #21-40 feature black and white borders and highlight Earnhardt's 1993 Championship season. The last two cards (#41-42) featured both Gordon and Earnhardt. Complete factory sets were sold through both the Action Packed dealer network and the Action Packed Club.

COMPLETE SET (42)	10.00	25.00

COMP.FACT.SET (42) 12.00 30.00
1 Jeff Gordon .30 .75
2 Ray Evernham .15 .40
3 Jeff Gordon .30 .75
4 Jeff Gordon .30 .75
5 Jeff Gordon .30 .75
6 Jeff Gordon .30 .75
7 Jeff Gordon in Pits .30 .75
8 Jeff Gordon in Pits .30 .75
9 Jeff Gordon .30 .75
10 Jeff Gordon .30 .75
11 Jeff Gordon .30 .75
12 Jimmy Johnson .15 .40
13 Jeff Gordon .30 .75
14 Jeff Gordon .30 .75
15 Jeff Gordon .30 .75
16 Jeff Gordon's Car .15 .40
17 Jeff Gordon's Car .15 .40
18 Jeff Gordon .30 .75
19 Jeff Gordon .30 .75
20 Jeff Gordon .30 .75
21 Dale Earnhardt .60 1.50
22 Dale Earnhardt .60 1.50
23 Dale Earnhardt .60 1.50
24 Dale Earnhardt .60 1.50
25 Dale Earnhardt .60 1.50
26 Dale Earnhardt .60 1.50
27 Dale Earnhardt .60 1.50
28 Dale Earnhardt .60 1.50
29 Dale Earnhardt .60 1.50
30 Dale Earnhardt .60 1.50
31 Dale Earnhardt .60 1.50
Neil Bonnett
32 Dale Earnhardt's Car .15 .40
33 Dale Earnhardt's Car .15 .40
34 Dale Earnhardt .60 1.50
Alan Kulwicki Cars
35 Dale Earnhardt's Car .15 .40
36 Dale Earnhardt's Car .15 .40
37 Dale Earnhardt .60 1.50
Rusty Wallace Cars
38 Dale Earnhardt .60 1.50
39 Dale Earnhardt .60 1.50
40 Dale Earnhardt .60 1.50
41 Dale Earnhardt .15 .40
Jeff Gordon Cars
42 Dale Earnhardt .60 1.50
Jeff Gordon

1994 Action Packed Champ and Challenger 24K Gold

This insert set is basically a parallel to 12-cards from the regular issue 1994 Action Packed Champ and Challenger issue. As with all Action Packed Gold cards, the 24Kt. Gold stamp appears on the card fronts, while the backs include a "G" suffix on the card numbers. Wrapper stated odds for pulling one of the popular inserts is 1:96.

COMPLETE SET (12) 200.00 400.00
1G Jeff Gordon 15.00 40.00
5G Jeff Gordon 15.00 40.00
9G Jeff Gordon 15.00 40.00
17G Jeff Gordon's Car 15.00 40.00
20G Jeff Gordon 15.00 40.00
22G Dale Earnhardt 15.00 40.00
28G Dale Earnhardt 15.00 40.00
30G Dale Earnhardt 15.00 40.00
32G Dale Earnhardt's Car 15.00 40.00
39G Dale Earnhardt 15.00 40.00
41G D.Earnhardt 15.00 40.00
J.Gordon Cars
42G D.Earnhardt 15.00 40.00
J.Gordon

1994 Action Packed Richard Childress Racing

Richard Childress, Dale Earnhardt and the Goodwrench Racing Team are the focus of this insert set from series three packs of 1994 Action Packed. The cards were issued in the same pack ratio as the regular series cards, except cards #18 and #20 which are considered tougher to find than the rest of the set.

COMPLETE SET (20) 12.00 30.00
RCR1 Richard Childress .15 .40
RCR2 Dale Earnhardt's Car .75 1.50
RCR3 Dale Earnhardt 1.25 3.00
RCR4 Dale Earnhardt 1.25 3.00
RCR5 Dale Earnhardt's Car .75 1.50
RCR6 Dale Earnhardt's Car .75 1.50
RCR7 Andy Petree .15 .40
RCR8 Eddie Lanier .15 .40
RCR9 David Smith .15 .40
RCR10 Jimmy Elledge .15 .40
RCR11 Cecil Gordon .15 .40
RCR12 Danny Lawrence .15 .40
RCR13 Danny Myers .15 .40
RCR14 Joe Dan Bailey .15 .40
RCR15 Gene DeHart .15 .40
RCR16 John Mulloy .15 .40
RCR17 Hank Jones .15 .40
RCR18 Craig Donley SP 1.50 3.00
RCR19 Jim Baldwin .15 .40
RCR20 Don Hawk SP 1.50 3.00

1994 Action Packed Badge of Honor Pins

This set of Badge of Honor Pins was issued one pin at a time as promos mailed directly to dealers and other card retailers. Each pin features a color photo of the driver mounted on a bronze colored solid-metal stick pin. The year of issue is noted below the player photo.

COMPLETE SET (4) 5.00 12.00
1 Jeff Gordon 2.50 6.00
2 Terry Labonte 1.00 2.50
3 Kyle Petty .75 2.00
4 Rusty Wallace 1.50 4.00

1994 Action Packed Coastars

Action Packed produced these cards in 1994 as 6-card panels ready to be punched-out from their backing. The cards were intended to be used as drink coasters and feature the driver's photo on front and his car on back. They are most often found intact in the original 6-card form. The cards were distributed through the Action Packed dealer network and were also made available to Action Packed Club members.

COMPLETE SET (18) 6.00 15.00
1 Geoff Bodine .20 .50
2 Dale Earnhardt 1.50 4.00
3 Bill Elliott .40 1.00
4 Harry Gant .20 .50
5 Jeff Gordon .75 2.00
6 Ernie Irvan .30 .75
7 Dale Jarrett .50 1.25
8 Bobby Labonte .50 1.25
9 Terry Labonte .40 1.00
10 Sterling Marlin .30 .75
11 Mark Martin .60 1.50
12 Joe Nemechek .20 .50
13 Kyle Petty .30 .75
14 Ricky Rudd .30 .75
15 Ken Schrader .20 .50
16 Rusty Wallace .60 1.50
17 Darrell Waltrip .30 .75
18 Michael Waltrip .30 .75

1994 Action Packed Mammoth

These oversized cards (roughly 7 1/2" x 10 1/2") are essentially a super-sized parallel version of the driver's basic issue 1994 Action Packed card. Each was sold separately, primarily through mass market retailers.

COMPLETE SET (5) 7.50 20.00
2 Rusty Wallace 2.00 5.00
3 Mark Martin 2.00 5.00
11 Harry Gant .75 2.00
14 Jeff Gordon 3.00 8.00
18 Terry Labonte 1.25 3.00

1994 Action Packed Mint Collection Jeff Gordon

This four-card set was originally done for distribution through the Home Shopping Network. Two of the cards are regular cards from the 1994 Action Packed Champ and Challenger set. The other two cards were produced with a gold leaf coating. The sets are numbered of 1,000 and come in a black slip cover case.

11 Jeff Gordon Gold Leaf 5.00 12.00
11 Jeff Gordon 2.00 5.00
19 Jeff Gordon Gold Leaf 5.00 12.00
19 Jeff Gordon 2.00 5.00

1994 Action Packed Select 24K Gold

This 10-card set was produced by Action Packed and was distributed through the Winston Cup Catalog in a separate black card display box with each card wrapped in black felt. It focuses on the 1985-1994 winners of the Winston Select. It features the first Action Packed card of Bill Elliott. Some cards reportedly made their way into packs.

COMPLETE SET (10) 30.00 80.00
W1 Darrell Waltrip 1.00 2.50
W2 Bill Elliott 1.00 2.50
W3 Dale Earnhardt 8.00 20.00
W4 Terry Labonte 1.50 4.00
W5 Rusty Wallace 3.00 8.00
W6 Dale Earnhardt 8.00 20.00
W7 Davey Allison 2.50 6.00
W8 Davey Allison 2.50 6.00
W9 Dale Earnhardt 8.00 20.00
W10 Geoff Bodine .50 1.25

1994 Action Packed Smokin' Joe's

This 13-card set was produced by Action Packed and was distributed through the Winston Cup Catalog. It features members of the Smokin' Joe's racing teams in the NASCAR, NHRA, and AMA circuits. The set includes a 24K Gold checklist.

COMPLETE SET (13) 6.00 15.00
1 Hut Stricklin .75 2.00
2 Hut Stricklin's Car .60 1.50
3 Jim Head .60 1.50
4 Jim Head's Car .40 1.00
5 Gordie Bonin .60 1.50
6 Gordie Bonin's Car .40 1.00
7 Mike Hale .60 1.50
8 Mike Hale's Bike .40 1.00
9 Kevin Magee .60 1.50
10 Kevin Magee's Bike .40 1.00
11 Mike Smith .60 1.50
12 Mike Smith's Bike .40 1.00
13 Checklist Card .60 1.50

1995 Action Packed Country

Action Packed's third Winston Cup card release for 1995 was entitled Winston Cup Country and was produced by Pinnacle Brands. The set is comprised of several series of subsets: Riding Shotgun (1-10), Shades (11-20), Motor Racing Outreach (21-25) Now and Then (26-43), Winners (44-56), Crew Chiefs (57-61), Drivers (62-85), SuperTruck Drivers (86-91), SuperTrucks (92-98) and SuperTruck Owners (99-101). The embossed cards were packed 24-foil packs to a box with 6-cards per pack and distributed to both hobby and retail outlets. Insert sets include: Silver Speed parallel, 24KT Team, 2nd Career Choice, and Team Rainbow.

COMPLETE SET (101) 12.00 30.00
1 Bobby Labonte RS .25 .60
2 Jeremy Mayfield RS .07 .20
3 Bill Elliott RS .25 .60
4 Darrell Waltrip RS .15 .40
5 Dale Earnhardt RS .60 1.50
6 Jeff Gordon RS .40 1.00
7 Ricky Rudd RS .15 .40
8 John Andretti RS .07 .20
9 Kenny Wallace RS .07 .20
10 Sterling Marlin RS .15 .40
11 Dale Earnhardt S .60 1.50
12 Rusty Wallace S .30 .75
13 Dale Jarrett S .25 .60
14 Jeff Gordon S .40 1.00
15 Sterling Marlin S .15 .40
16 Ricky Rudd S .15 .40
17 D.Earnhardt .60 1.50
Tay.Earn
18 Darrell Waltrip S .15 .40
19 Terry Labonte S .25 .60
20 Richard Petty S .25 .60
21 S.Waltrip .15 .40
D.Waltrip MRO
22 J.Gordon .40 1.00
Brooke MRO
23 L.Speed .07 .20
Rice MRO
24 B.Elliott .25 .60
Cindy MRO
25 D.Earn .60 1.50
Teresa
Helton
26 Dale Earnhardt NT .60 1.50
27 Dale Earnhardt NT .60 1.50
28 Dale Earnhardt NT .60 1.50
29 Dale Earnhardt NT .60 1.50
30 Dale Earnhardt NT .60 1.50
31 Dale Earnhardt NT .60 1.50
32 Darrell Waltrip NT .15 .40
33 Darrell Waltrip NT .15 .40
34 Darrell Waltrip NT .15 .40
35 Darrell Waltrip NT .15 .40
36 Darrell Waltrip NT .15 .40
37 Darrell Waltrip NT .15 .40
38 Rusty Wallace NT .30 .75
39 Rusty Wallace NT .30 .75
40 Rusty Wallace NT .30 .75
41 Rusty Wallace NT .30 .75
42 Rusty Wallace NT .30 .75
43 Rusty Wallace NT .30 .75
44 Mark Martin WIN .30 .75
45 D.Earnhardt .60 1.50
Teresa WIN
46 Bobby Labonte WIN .25 .60
47 Kyle Petty WIN .15 .40
48 Terry Labonte WIN .25 .60
49 Bobby Labonte WIN .25 .60
50 Jeff Gordon WIN .40 1.00
51 Jeff Gordon WIN .40 1.00
52 Dale Jarrett WIN .25 .60
53 Sterling Marlin WIN .15 .40
54 Dale Earnhardt WIN .60 1.50
55 Mark Martin WIN .30 .75
56 B.Labonte .25 .60
Gibbs WIN
57 Andy Petree .02 .10
58 Steve Hmiel .02 .10
59 Ray Evernham .02 .10
60 Tony Glover .02 .10
61 Robin Pemberton .02 .10
62 Dale Earnhardt 1.25 3.00
63 Jeff Gordon .75 2.00
64 Ted Musgrave .07 .20
65 Dale Jarrett .50 1.25
66 Bobby Hamilton .07 .20
67 Morgan Shepherd .07 .20
68 Bobby Labonte .50 1.25
69 Michael Waltrip .15 .40
70 Ricky Rudd .25 .60
71 Ken Schrader .07 .20
72 Bill Elliott .30 .75
73 Steve Grissom .07 .20
74 Derrike Cope .07 .20
75 Brett Bodine .07 .20
76 John Andretti .07 .20
77 Rick Mast .07 .20
78 Dick Trickle .07 .20
79 Ricky Craven .15 .40
80 Todd Bodine .07 .20
81 Robert Pressley .07 .20
82 Kenny Wallace .07 .20
83 Jeff Burton .25 .60
84 Jimmy Spencer .07 .20
85 Geoff Bodine .07 .20
86 Ron Hornaday Jr. STD RC .07 .20
87 Butch Miller STD .02 .10
88 Ken Schrader STD .07 .20
89 Tobey Butler STD .02 .10
90 Rick Carelli STD .02 .10
91 Scott Lagasse STD .07 .20
92 Sammy Swindell's SuperTruck .02 .10
93 Scott Lagasse's SuperTruck .02 .10
94 Mike Bliss' SuperTruck .02 .10
95 Mike Chase's SuperTruck .02 .10
96 Geoff Bodine's SuperTruck .02 .10
97 Ken Schrader's SuperTruck .02 .10
98 R.Hornaday's SuperTruck .02 .10
99 J.Gordon .40 1.00
R.Hendrick STO
100 Jim Venable STO .02 .10
101 Ken Schrader STO .07 .20
P1 Jeff Gordon Promo 2.00 5.00
P46 Bobby Labonte Promo 1.00 2.50

1995 Action Packed Country Silver Speed

COMPLETE SET (84) 75.00 150.00
*SILVER SPEEDS: 3X TO 6X BASIC CARDS

1995 Action Packed Country 24K Team

The 24KT, Micro-Etched cards feature 10 of Winston Cup's best drivers in this 14-card set. Three Dale Earnhardt and three Jeff Gordon cards highlighted a new design for Action Packed's 24K insert line. The cards were seeded at a rate of one per 72 packs.

COMPLETE SET (14) 175.00 350.00
1 Jeff Gordon 12.50 30.00
2 Jeff Gordon 12.50 30.00
3 Jeff Gordon 12.50 30.00
4 Mark Martin 10.00 25.00
5 Dale Earnhardt 20.00 50.00
6 Dale Earnhardt 20.00 50.00
7 Dale Earnhardt 20.00 50.00
8 Rusty Wallace 10.00 25.00
9 Sterling Marlin 5.00 12.00
10 Bobby Labonte 8.00 20.00
11 Bill Elliott 8.00 20.00
12 Ricky Rudd 5.00 12.00
13 Ken Schrader 2.50 6.00
14 Ted Musgrave 2.50 6.00

1995 Action Packed Country 2nd Career Choice

This 9-card insert set features some of the top Winston Cup drivers reviling what they would be doing if they weren't racing. The cards utilize holographic gold-foil printing technology. The cards were seeded at a rate of one per 24 packs.

COMPLETE SET (9) 25.00 60.00
1 Bobby Hillin .75 2.00
2 Kenny Wallace .75 2.00
3 Rusty Wallace 6.00 15.00
4 Dale Jarrett 5.00 12.00
5 Derrike Cope .75 2.00
6 Dale Earnhardt 15.00 40.00
7 Bobby Labonte 5.00 12.00
8 Sterling Marlin 2.00 5.00
9 Terry Labonte 3.00 8.00

1995 Action Packed Country Team Rainbow

This 12-card insert set takes a look at Jeff Gordon and the DuPont Rainbow Warrior team. The cards use lenticular printing technology to bring them to life. The cards were randomly inserted in hobby packs only at a rate of one per 36 packs.

COMPLETE SET (12) 75.00 150.00
1 Jeff Gordon 12.50 25.00
Brooke Gordon
2 Jeff Gordon's Car 6.00 12.00
3 Jeff Gordon w 12.50 25.00
Crew
4 Ray Evernham 6.00 12.00
5 Jeff Gordon 12.50 25.00
Brooke Gordon
6 Pit Stop 6.00 12.00
7 Jeff Gordon's Car 6.00 12.00
8 Gordon 12.50 25.00
Evernham
Hendrick
9 Jeff Gordon's Helmet 6.00 12.00
10 Victory Shout 12.50 25.00
11 Interview 12.50 25.00
12 Jeff Gordon 12.50 25.00
Ray Evernham
P1 Jeff Gordon Promo #1 3.00 6.00

1995 Action Packed Badge of Honor Pins

This set of Badge of Honor Pins was issued through both hobby and mass market retailers. Each pin features a color photo of the driver mounted on a bronze colored solid-metal stick pin which was attached to a thin pink colored backer board the size of a standard trading card. The year of issue is noted below the player photo.

COMPLETE SET (9) 6.00 15.00
1 Bill Elliott .75 2.00
2 Jeff Gordon 2.00 5.00
3 Dale Jarrett 1.00 2.50
4 Steve Kinser .50 1.25
5 Terry Labonte .75 2.00
6 Mark Martin 1.25 3.00
7 Robert Pressley .50 1.25
8 Ricky Rudd .75 2.00
9 Rusty Wallace 1.25 3.00

1995 Action Packed Hendrick Motorsports

This eight-card set was distributed through Hendrick Motorsport's merchandising trailers, as well as some Rick Hendrick's car dealerships.

COMPLETE SET (8) 2.00 5.00
1 Jeff Gordon .75 2.00
2 Ken Schrader .20 .50
3 Terry Labonte .30 .75
4 Scott Lagasse .20 .50
5 Ricky Hendrick Jr. .20 .50
6 Rick Hendrick .10 .30
Cover Card
7 Papa Joe Hendrick .10 .30
8 Jimmy Johnson .10 .30

1995 Action Packed Mammoth

This six-card set features the top names in NASCAR. The cards are approximately 7.5" X 10.5" in size. They were distributed through Action Packed dealer network. The cards came in clear poly bag packs with each pack having one card.

COMPLETE SET (6) 10.00 25.00
MM1 Dale Earnhardt 4.00 8.00
MM2 Bill Elliott .75 2.00
MM3 Rusty Wallace 1.25 3.00
MM4 Jeff Gordon 1.50 4.00
MM5 Mark Martin 1.25 3.00
MM6 Dale Earnhardt 4.00 8.00

1995 Action Packed McDonald's Bill Elliott

Originally offered during 1995 Speedweeks at Daytona, these cards were distributed through participating Florida and North Carolina area McDonald's restaurants. Three-card cello packs, as well as 21-card factory sets were produced. The set features Bill Elliott's life in and away from racing. Approximately one autograph certificate was distributed per case witch was redeemable for a signed Bill Elliott card.

COMPLETE SET (21) 8.00 16.00
COMPLETE FACT. SET (21) 10.00 20.00
MC1 Bill Elliott .50 1.00
MC2 Ernie Elliott .50 1.00
MC3 Bill Elliott .50 1.00
MC4 Bill Elliott .50 1.00
MC5 Bill Elliott .50 1.00
MC6 Bill Elliott's Car .50 1.00
MC7 Bill Elliott .50 1.00
MC8 Bill Elliott's Car .50 1.00
MC9 Bill Elliott in Car .50 1.00
MC10 Bill Elliott .50 1.00
MC11 Bill Elliott .50 1.00
MC12 Bill Elliott .50 1.00
MC13 Bill Elliott .50 1.00
MC14 Bill Elliott .50 1.00
MC15 Bill Elliott .50 1.00
MC16 Bill Elliott w .50 1.00
Car
MC17 Bill Elliott .50 1.00
MC18 Bill Elliott in Car .50 1.00
MG19 Bill Elliott .50 1.00
MG20 Bill Elliott's Transporter .50 1.00
MG21 Bill Elliott .50 1.00

1995 Action Packed Preview Promos 24K Gold

This 3-card issue promotes the 1995 Action Packed Preview set. Each of the three cards is numbered and utilizes the 24K Gold technology.

COMPLETE SET (3) 20.00 35.00
P2 Ricky Craven Promo 4.00 10.00
P3 Steve Kinser Promo 4.00 10.00
P4 Bill Elliott Promo 8.00 20.00

1995 Action Packed Preview

Action Packed's first racing issue for 1995 is also commonly called Action Packed Winston Cup Preview as the wrapper states. The cards were packaged in 6-card packs with 24 packs per box. A new Driving With Dale subset was included featuring popular drivers discussing what it's like to race against Earnhardt. The now standard Action Packed subsets of Race Winners, Pole Winners and Top Ten were also part of the regular issue. This set marks the first regular issue Bill Elliott Action Packed card. There was also a Dale Earnhardt Big Picture redemption card randomly inserted in packs. The card folds out to make a big picture of Dale Earnhardt. There were reportedly 2,500 cards produced.

COMPLETE SET (78) 10.00 25.00
1 John Andretti .07 .20
2 Brett Bodine .07 .20
3 Geoff Bodine .07 .20
4 Todd Bodine .07 .20
5 Jeff Burton .25 .60
6 Derrike Cope .07 .20
7 Dale Earnhardt 1.25 3.00
8 Bill Elliott .30 .75
9 Jeff Gordon .75 2.00
10 Steve Grissom .07 .20
11 Dale Jarrett .50 1.25
12 Steve Kinser .07 .20
13 Bobby Labonte .50 1.25
14 Terry Labonte .25 .60
15 Mark Martin .60 1.50
16 Kyle Petty .15 .40
17 Ricky Rudd .25 .60
18 Ken Schrader .07 .20
19 Jimmy Spencer .07 .20
20 Dick Trickle .07 .20
21 Kenny Wallace .07 .20
22 Mike Wallace .07 .20
23 Rusty Wallace .60 1.50
24 Darrell Waltrip .15 .40
25 Michael Waltrip .15 .40
26 Ricky Craven .07 .20
27 Steve Kinser .07 .20
28 Robert Pressley .07 .20
29 Loy Allen Jr. PW .02 .10
30 Geoff Bodine PW .02 .10
31 Chuck Bown PW .02 .10
32 Ward Burton PW .02 .10
33 Dale Earnhardt PW .60 1.50
34 Bill Elliott PW .25 .60
35 Harry Gant PW .07 .20
36 Jeff Gordon PW .40 1.00
37 David Green PW .02 .10
38 Ernie Irvan PW .07 .20
39 Sterling Marlin PW .15 .40
40 Mark Martin PW .30 .75
41 Rick Mast PW .02 .10
42 Ted Musgrave PW .02 .10
43 Ricky Rudd PW .15 .40
44 Greg Sacks PW .02 .10
45 Jimmy Spencer PW .02 .10
46 Rusty Wallace PW .30 .75
47 Geoff Bodine WIN .02 .10
48 Dale Earnhardt WIN .60 1.50
49 Bill Elliott WIN .25 .60
50 Jeff Gordon WIN .40 1.00
51 Ernie Irvan WIN .07 .20
52 Dale Jarrett WIN .25 .60
53 Terry Labonte WIN .25 .60
54 Sterling Marlin WIN .15 .40
55 Mark Martin WIN .30 .75
56 Ricky Rudd WIN .15 .40
57 Jimmy Spencer WIN .02 .10
58 Rusty Wallace WIN .30 .75
59 Dale Earnhardt WC Champ .60 1.50
60 Mark Martin T10 .30 .75
61 Rusty Wallace T10 .30 .75
62 Ken Schrader T10 .02 .10
63 Ricky Rudd T10 .15 .40
64 Morgan Shepherd T10 .02 .10
65 Terry Labonte T10 .25 .60
66 Jeff Gordon T10 .40 1.00
67 Darrell Waltrip T10 .07 .20
68 Bill Elliott T10 .25 .60
69 Bill Elliott DD .25 .60
70 Jeff Gordon DD .40 1.00
71 Ernie Irvan DD .07 .20

72 Mark Martin DD .30 .75
73 Richard Petty DD .25 .60
74 Robert Pressley DD .02 .10
75 Ricky Rudd DD .15 .40
76 Ken Schrader DD .02 .10
77 Rusty Wallace DD .30 .75
78 Darrell Waltrip DD .07 .20
BP1 Dale Earnhardt 12.50 30.00

1995 Action Packed Preview 24K Gold

Randomly inserted in 1995 Action Packed Preview packs, each card includes the now standard 24Kt. Gold logo on the card front. These Gold cards are essentially parallel versions of the corresponding driver's Driving With Dale subset card. Wrapper stated odds for pulling a 24K Gold card are 1:96.

COMPLETE SET (10) 100.00 200.00
1G Bill Elliott 10.00 25.00
2G Jeff Gordon 25.00 60.00
3G Ernie Irvan 2.50 6.00
4G Mark Martin 20.00 50.00
5G Richard Petty 8.00 20.00
6G Robert Pressley 2.50 6.00
7G Ricky Rudd 8.00 20.00
8G Ken Schrader 2.50 6.00
9G Rusty Wallace 20.00 50.00
10G Darrell Waltrip 5.00 12.00

1995 Action Packed Preview Bill Elliott

Action Packed added Bill Elliott to its stable of featured drivers in 1995. This special 6-card insert was distributed in 1995 Action Packed foil packs and includes cards of Elliott's life away from auto racing. There was also a Bill Elliott promo card issued through the Elliott Fan Club.

COMPLETE SET (6) 3.00 8.00
COMMON ELLIOTT (BE1-BE6) .60 1.50

1995 Action Packed Stars

Action Packed's second Winston Cup card release for 1995 was entitled Winston Cup Stars and was Pinnacle Brands' first NASCAR release after acquiring the rights to the Action Packed name. The set is comprised of several series of subsets: Out of the Chute (1-30), Mean Rides (31-45), Race Winners (46-53), Picture Perfect (54-59), Settles In (60-65), Cope With It (66-70), On The Other Side (71-75), Winning The War (76-81), and McDonald's Bill Elliott (82-86) featuring two cards using Pinnacle's patented lenticular printing technology. These two cards (84-85) showing Bill Elliott "morphing" into the Batman logo and the Thunderbat race car, were produced in fewer numbers than the other regular issue cards. Cards were packed 24-foil packs to a box with 6-cards per pack and distributed to both hobby and retail outlets. Insert sets include: Silver Speed parallel, 24K Gold, Dale Earnhardt Race For Eight, and Trucks That Haul (hobby pack exclusive).

COMPLETE SET (86) 10.00 25.00
COMP.SHORT SET (84) 8.00 20.00
HOBBY WAX BOX 20.00 40.00
RETAIL WAX BOX 20.00 40.00
1 Sterling Marlin OC .15 .40
2 Terry Labonte OC .25 .60
3 Mark Martin OC .60 1.50
4 Geoff Bodine OC .07 .20
5 Jeff Burton OC .25 .60
6 Ricky Rudd OC .25 .60
7 Brett Bodine OC .07 .20
8 Derrike Cope OC .07 .20
9 Ted Musgrave OC .07 .20
10 Darrell Waltrip OC .15 .40
11 Bobby Labonte OC .50 1.25
12 Morgan Shepherd OC .07 .20
13 Jimmy Spencer OC .07 .20
14 Ken Schrader OC .07 .20
15 Dale Jarrett OC .50 1.25
16 Kyle Petty OC .15 .40
17 Michael Waltrip OC .15 .40
18 Robert Pressley OC .07 .20
19 John Andretti OC .07 .20
20 Todd Bodine OC .07 .20
21 Joe Nemechek OC .07 .20
22 Bill Elliott OC .30 .75
23 Dale Earnhardt OC 1.25 3.00
24 Jeff Gordon OC .75 2.00
25 Rusty Wallace OC .60 1.50
26 Rick Mast OC .07 .20
27 Dick Trickle OC .07 .20
28 Randy LaJoie OC .07 .20
29 Steve Grissom OC .07 .20
30 Ricky Craven OC .07 .20
31 Dale Earnhardt's Car .50 1.25
32 Rusty Wallace's Car .25 .60
33 Sterling Marlin's Car .07 .20
34 Terry Labonte's Car .15 .40
35 Mark Martin's Car .25 .60
36 Bill Elliott's Car .15 .40
37 Ricky Rudd's Car .07 .20
38 Joe Nemechek's Car .02 .10
39 Darrell Waltrip's Car .07 .20
40 Jeff Gordon's Car .40 1.00
41 Jimmy Spencer's Car .02 .10
42 Ken Schrader's Car .02 .10
43 Dale Jarrett's Car .15 .40
44 Steve Kinser's Car .02 .10
45 Bobby Hamilton's Car .02 .10
46 Sterling Marlin RW .15 .40
47 Jeff Gordon RW .40 1.00
48 Terry Labonte RW .25 .60
49 Jeff Gordon RW .75 2.00
50 Sterling Marlin RW .15 .40
51 Jeff Gordon RW .75 2.00
52 Dale Earnhardt RW 1.25 3.00
53 Rusty Wallace RW .60 1.50
54 Sterling Marlin OC .15 .40
55 Sterling Marlin OC .15 .40
56 Sterling Marlin OC .15 .40
57 Sterling Marlin OC .15 .40
58 Sterling Marlin OC .15 .40
59 Sterling Marlin OC .15 .40
60 Jeff Gordon PP .40 1.00
61 Jeff Gordon PP .40 1.00
62 Jeff Gordon PP .40 1.00
63 Jeff Gordon PP .40 1.00
64 Jeff Gordon PP .40 1.00
65 Jeff Gordon PP .40 1.00
66 Derrike Cope CWI .07 .20
67 Derrike Cope CWI .07 .20
68 Derrike Cope CWI .07 .20
69 Derrike Cope CWI .07 .20
70 Derrike Cope CWI .07 .20
71 Ernie Irvan OOS .15 .40
72 Ernie Irvan OOS .15 .40
73 Ernie Irvan OOS .15 .40
74 Ernie Irvan OOS .15 .40
75 Ernie Irvan OOS .15 .40
76 Rusty Wallace WW .30 .75
77 Rusty Wallace WW .30 .75
78 Rusty Wallace WW .30 .75
79 Rusty Wallace WW .30 .75
80 Rusty Wallace WW .30 .75
81 Rusty Wallace WW .30 .75
82 Bill Elliott's Thunderbat Car .15 .40
83 Bill Elliott's Car .15 .40
84 Bill Elliott Magic Motion 2.50 6.00
85 Bill Elliott Magic Motion 2.50 6.00
86 J.Gordon .60 1.50
B.Labonte
T.Lab.
NNO Dale Earnhardt Brick. 400 3.00 8.00

1995 Action Packed Stars Silver Speed

COMPLETE SET (84) 60.00 125.00
*SILVER SPEEDS: 3X TO 8X BASIC CARDS

1995 Action Packed Stars 24K Gold

Randomly inserted in 1995 Action Packed Stars packs, each card includes the now standard 24Kt. Gold logo on the card front. These Gold cards are essentially parallel versions of the corresponding driver's regular cards with an emphasis on Jeff Gordon and Dale Earnhardt. Wrapper stated odds for pulling a 24K Gold card are 1:72.

COMPLETE SET (21) 400.00 1000.00
1G Sterling Marlin 3.00 8.00
2G Jeff Gordon 12.00 30.00
3G Terry Labonte 5.00 12.00
4G Jeff Gordon 10.00 30.00
5G Sterling Marlin 3.00 8.00
6G Jeff Gordon 12.00 30.00
7G Dale Earnhardt 20.00 50.00
8G Rusty Wallace 10.00 25.00
9G Dale Earnhardt 20.00 50.00
10G Dale Earnhardt 20.00 50.00
11G Dale Earnhardt 20.00 50.00
12G Dale Earnhardt 20.00 50.00
13G Dale Earnhardt 20.00 50.00
14G Dale Earnhardt 20.00 50.00
15G Dale Earnhardt 20.00 50.00
16G Dale Earnhardt 20.00 50.00
17G Rusty Wallace 10.00 25.00
18G Rusty Wallace 10.00 25.00
19G Jeff Gordon 15.00 30.00
20G Jeff Gordon 12.00 30.00
21G Ernie Irvan 3.00 8.00

1995 Action Packed Stars Dale Earnhardt Race for Eight

Using Pinnacle Brands' micro-etching printing technology, Action Packed produced this 8-card Dale Earnhardt insert set distributed through 1995 Action Packed Stars packs. The cards were inserted at the ratio of 1:24 packs.

COMPLETE SET (8) 25.00 60.00
DE1 Dale Earnhardt 5.00 12.00
DE2 Dale Earnhardt 5.00 12.00
DE3 Dale Earnhardt 5.00 12.00
DE4 Dale Earnhardt 5.00 12.00
DE5 Dale Earnhardt w 5.00 12.00
Teresa
DE6 Dale Earnhardt 5.00 12.00
DE7 Dale Earnhardt 5.00 12.00
DE8 Dale Earnhardt's Car 5.00 12.00

1995 Action Packed Stars Dale Earnhardt Silver Salute

The set consists of four oversized (approximately 5" by 7") cards distributed in both 1995 Action Packed Stars (1,3) and Action Packed Country (2,4). The cards commemorate Earnhardt's silver car used in the 1995 Winston Select. Two cards (1,2) were inserted at the rate of one per box, with the other two (3,4) inserted about one per case.

COMPLETE SET (4) 80.00 200.00
1 Dale Earnhardt w 8.00 20.00
Silver Car
2 Dale Earnhardt 8.00 20.00
Richard Childress
3 Dale Earnhardt's Silver Car 50.00 120.00
4 Dale 40.00 70.00
Teresa Earnhardt

1995 Action Packed Stars Trucks That Haul

NASCAR's SuperTrucks is the feature of this hobby only insert in 1995 Action Packed Stars foil packs. The cards use Pinnacle's micro-etching printing process and were inserted at the average rate of 1:36 packs.

COMPLETE SET (6) 30.00 50.00
1 J.Gordon 8.00 20.00
Hend.Truck
2 Teresa Earnhardt's Truck 4.00 10.00
3 Frank Vessels' Truck 2.00 5.00
4 Geoff Bodine's Truck 2.00 5.00
5 Richard Childress' Truck 2.00 5.00
6 Ken Schrader's Truck 2.00 5.00

1995 Action Packed Sundrop Dale Earnhardt

One card was inserted in each specially marked 12-pack of Sundrop citrus soda. Five hundred signed copies of each of the three cards were also randomly inserted in the soft drink packages. However, the autographed cards were not certified in any way and are otherwise indistinguishable from the unsigned regular cards.

COMPLETE SET (3) 12.50 30.00
SD1 Dale Earnhardt 3.00 8.00
SD2 Dale Earnhardt 3.00 8.00
SD3 D.Earnhardt 6.00 15.00
Dale Jr.

1996 Action Packed Credentials

This 105-card set was released by Pinnacle Brands. It was the first Action Packed regular issue set to feature square corners, instead of the normal rounded corners. The cards still featured the embossed technology that Action Packed is known for. The set features nine topical subsets; Jeff Gordon Defending Champion (1-5), Dale Earnhardt Seven-Time Champion (6-10), Mark Martin On the Mark (11-15), Daytona Winners (16-19), Drivers (20-54), Speed Machines (55-64), Crew Chiefs (65-69), Owners (70-83), Behind the Scenes (84-93), and Wives, Camera, Action (94-101). Cards were distributed in six card packs with 24 packs per box and 10 boxes per case. The packs carried a suggested retail price of $2.99.

COMPLETE SET (105) 10.00 25.00
1 Jeff Gordon DC .40 1.00
2 Jeff Gordon DC .40 1.00
3 Jeff Gordon DC .40 1.00
4 Jeff Gordon DC .40 1.00
5 Jeff Gordon DC .40 1.00
6 Dale Earnhardt STC .60 1.50
7 Dale Earnhardt STC .60 1.50
8 Dale Earnhardt STC .60 1.50
9 Dale Earnhardt STC .60 1.50
10 Dale Earnhardt STC .60 1.50
11 Mark Martin OTM .30 .75
12 Mark Martin OTM .30 .75
13 Mark Martin OTM .30 .75
14 Mark Martin OTM .30 .75
15 Mark Martin OTM .30 .75
16 Dale Jarrett DW .25 .60
17 Dale Earnhardt DW .60 1.50
18 Ernie Irvan DW .07 .20
19 Dale Jarrett DW .25 .60
20 Jeff Gordon .75 2.00
21 Dale Earnhardt 1.25 3.00
22 Sterling Marlin .25 .60
23 Mark Martin .60 1.50
24 Rusty Wallace .60 1.50
25 Terry Labonte .25 .60
26 Ted Musgrave .07 .20
27 Bill Elliott .30 .75
28 Ricky Rudd .25 .60
29 Bobby Labonte .50 1.25
30 Morgan Shepherd .07 .20
31 Michael Waltrip .15 .40
32 Dale Jarrett .50 1.25
33 Bobby Hamilton .07 .20
34 Derrike Cope .07 .20
35 Ernie Irvan .15 .40
36 Ken Schrader .15 .40
37 John Andretti .07 .20
38 Darrell Waltrip .15 .40
39 Brett Bodine .07 .20
40 Rick Mast .07 .20
41 Ward Burton .15 .40
42 Lake Speed .07 .20
43 Loy Allen .07 .20
44 Hut Stricklin .07 .20
45 Jimmy Spencer .07 .20
46 Mike Wallace .07 .20
47 Joe Nemechek .07 .20
48 Robert Pressley .07 .20
49 Geoff Bodine .07 .20
50 Jeremy Mayfield .15 .40
51 Jeff Burton .25 .60
52 Kenny Wallace .07 .20
53 Bobby Hillin .07 .20
54 Johnny Benson .15 .40
55 Rusty Wallace SM .30 .75
56 Terry Labonte SM .15 .40
57 Dale Earnhardt SM .60 1.50
58 Michael Waltrip SM .15 .40
59 Bobby Hamilton SM .02 .10
60 Bobby Labonte SM .25 .60
61 Darrell Waltrip SM .07 .20
62 Mark Martin SM .30 .75
63 Richard Childress SM .15 .40
64 Ken Schrader SM .07 .20
65 David Smith .02 .10
66 Ray Evernham .15 .40
67 Jimmy Makar .02 .10
68 Larry McReynolds .02 .10
69 Todd Parrott .02 .10
70 Roger Penske .02 .10
D.Miller OWN
71 Richard Childress OWN .15 .40
72 Larry McClure OWN .02 .10
73 Rick Hendrick OWN .02 .10
74 Jack Roush OWN .02 .10
75 Cale Yarborough OWN .02 .10
76 Ricky Rudd OWN .15 .40
77 Bobby Allison OWN .07 .20
78 Richard Petty OWN .25 .60
79 Darrell Waltrip OWN .07 .20
80 Joe Gibbs OWN .15 .40
81 Bill Elliott .15 .40
Charles Hardy OWN
82 Robert Yates OWN .02 .10
83 M.Kranefuss .02 .10
Carl Haas OWN
84 Andrea Nemechek BTS .02 .10
85 Kim Wallace BTS .02 .10
86 Buffy Waltrip BTS .02 .10
87 Kim Irvan BTS .02 .10
88 Kim Burton .02 .10
Paige Burton BTS
89 Rice Speed BTS .02 .10
90 Stevie Waltrip .15 .40
Darrell Waltrip BTS
91 Bill Elliott .15 .40
Cindy BTS
92 Brooke Gordon BTS .25 .60
93 Donna Labonte BTS .07 .20
94 Darrell Waltrip WCA .07 .20
95 Sterling Marlin WCA .15 .40
96 Michael Waltrip WCA .15 .40
97 K.Wallace .07 .20
Brandy
Brittany
Brooke WCA
98 Bobby Labonte WCA .25 .60
99 Jeff Gordon WCA .40 1.00
100 Jeremy Mayfield WCA .07 .20
101 Bill Elliott WCA .15 .40
102 Johnny Benson .15 .40
103 Ricky Craven .15 .40
Travis Roy
104 Dale Earnhardt CL .60 1.50
105 Jeff Gordon CL .30 .75

1996 Action Packed Credentials Silver Speed

COMPLETE SET (42) 40.00 100.00
*SILVER SPEED: 3X TO 6X BASE CARD

1996 Action Packed Credentials Fan Scan

This 9-card insert set allowed collectors to go inside a race car during a NASCAR race. Each card back included a 1-800 phone number along with a personal identification number. During selected NASCAR races, the collector could phone the number, enter the PIN, and listen to the sounds the driver is hearing inside his helmet. Advanced broadcast electronics made the technology possible. The cards were seeded one in 72 packs.

COMPLETE SET (9) 100.00 250.00
1 Dale Earnhardt 30.00 80.00
2 Dale Earnhardt's Car 15.00 40.00
3 Mark Martin 15.00 40.00
4 Jeff Gordon 20.00 50.00
5 Ted Musgrave 2.00 5.00
6 Ernie Irvan 4.00 10.00
7 Bobby Hamilton 2.00 5.00
8 Dale Jarrett 12.50 30.00
9 Jeff Burton 6.00 15.00

1996 Action Packed Credentials Leaders of the Pack

This 10-card insert set features the top Winston Cup drivers. The cards were printed on rainbow holographic foil with holographic and gold foil stamping. The cards were available in hobby only packs at a rate of one in 35.

COMPLETE SET (10) 75.00 150.00
1 Dale Earnhardt 10.00 25.00
2 Dale Earnhardt 10.00 25.00
3 Dale Earnhardt 10.00 25.00
4 Dale Earnhardt 10.00 25.00
5 Jeff Gordon 6.00 15.00
6 Jeff Gordon 6.00 15.00
7 Jeff Gordon 6.00 15.00
8 Jeff Gordon 6.00 15.00
9 Sterling Marlin 2.00 5.00
10 Sterling Marlin 2.00 5.00

1996 Action Packed Credentials Jumbos

This four-card series feature the top drivers in Winston Cup. The cards measure 5" X 7" and were available one per special retail box.

COMPLETE SET (4) 6.00 15.00
1 Dale Earnhardt 3.00 8.00
2 Jeff Gordon 2.00 5.00
3 Dale Jarrett 1.25 3.00
4 Bill Elliott .75 2.00

1996 Action Packed McDonald's

For the second year, McDonald's distributed a small card set produced by Action Packed. The 1996 set features square corners instead of Action Packed's traditional rounded ones. While the set has a strong Bill Elliott focus, like the 1995 issue, it also includes cards of other top Winston Cup drivers and their rides. The set was distributed through 4-card packs with one unnumbered checklist card per pack. Packs originally sold for 99-cents from participating McDonald's stores.

COMPLETE SET (29) 6.00 15.00
1 Bill Elliott .30 .75
2 Dale Earnhardt 1.50 4.00
3 Jeff Gordon 1.00 2.50
4 Sterling Marlin .25 .60
5 Mark Martin .75 2.00
6 Bobby Labonte .60 1.50
7 Terry Labonte .25 .60
8 Ernie Irvan .10 .30
9 Kenny Wallace .08 .25
10 Dale Jarrett .50 1.25
11 Bill Elliott's Car .08 .25
12 Dale Earnhardt's Car .60 1.50
13 Jeff Gordon's Car .40 1.00
14 Sterling Marlin's Car .08 .25
15 Mark Martin's Car .25 .60
16 Bobby Labonte's Car .10 .30
17 Terry Labonte's Car .08 .25
18 Ernie Irvan's Car .07 .15
19 Kenny Wallace's Car .07 .15
20 Dale Jarrett's Car .08 .25
21 Bill Elliott .25 .60
22 Bill Elliott .25 .60
23 Bill Elliott .25 .60
24 Bill Elliott .25 .60
25 Bill Elliott .25 .60
26 Bill Elliott .25 .60
27 Bill Elliott .25 .60
28 Bill Elliott .25 .60
NNO Bill Elliott CL .08 .25

1997 Action Packed

This 86-card set was released by Pinnacle Brands. The cards still feature the embossed technology that Action Packed is known for. The set features three topical subsets; Championship Drive (53-56), 1996 A Look Back (57-68), and Orient Express (71-84). Cards were distributed in six card packs with 24 packs per box and 10 boxes per case. The packs carried a suggested retail price of $2.99.

COMPLETE SET (86) 10.00 25.00
1 Bobby Hamilton .07 .20
2 Rusty Wallace .60 1.50
3 Dale Earnhardt 1.25 3.00
4 Sterling Marlin .25 .60
5 Terry Labonte .25 .60
6 Mark Martin .60 1.50
7 Jeremy Mayfield .15 .40
8 Jeff Gordon .75 2.00
9 Ernie Irvan .15 .40
10 Ricky Rudd .25 .60
11 Bill Elliott .30 .75
12 Jimmy Spencer .07 .20
13 Dale Jarrett .50 1.25
14 Ward Burton .15 .40
15 Michael Waltrip .15 .40
16 Ted Musgrave .07 .20
17 Darrell Waltrip .15 .40
18 Bobby Labonte .50 1.25
19 John Andretti .07 .20
20 Robert Pressley .07 .20
21 Chad Little .15 .40
22 Geoff Bodine .07 .20
23 Morgan Shepherd .07 .20
24 Mike Skinner .07 .20
25 Ricky Craven .07 .20
26 Robby Gordon RC .25 .60
27 Mark Martin's Car .25 .60
28 Jeremy Mayfield's Car .02 .10
29 Jeff Gordon's Car .30 .75
30 Ernie Irvan's Car .07 .20
31 Ricky Rudd's Car .07 .20
32 Bill Elliott's Car .15 .40
33 Jimmy Spencer's Car .02 .10
34 Dale Jarrett's Car .15 .40
35 Ward Burton's Car .02 .10
36 Michael Waltrip's Car .07 .20
37 Ted Musgrave's Car .02 .10
38 Darrell Waltrip's Car .07 .20
39 Bobby Labonte's Car .15 .40
40 John Andretti's Car .02 .10
41 Robert Pressley's Car .02 .10
42 Chad Little's Car .02 .10
43 Morgan Shepherd's Car .02 .10
44 Rusty Wallace's Car .25 .60
45 Dale Earnhardt's Car .50 1.25
46 Sterling Marlin's Car .07 .20
47 Terry Labonte's Car .15 .40
48 Geoff Bodine's Car .02 .10
49 Bobby Hamilton's Car .02 .10
50 Mike Skinner's Car .02 .10
51 Ricky Craven's Car .02 .10
52 Robby Gordon's Car .15 .40
53 Terry Labonte .25 .60
54 Dale Jarrett .50 1.25
55 Randy LaJoie .07 .20
56 David Green .07 .20
57 Randy LaJoie .07 .20
58 Bill Elliott .30 .75
59 Michael Waltrip .15 .40
60 Hut Stricklin .07 .20
61 Johnny Benson .07 .20
62 Carl Hill .07 .20
63 Dale Jarrett .50 1.25
64 Bill Elliott .30 .75
65 Elmo Langley .07 .20
66 Harry Hyde .02 .10
67 Richard Petty .25 .60
68 Johnny Benson .07 .20
69 Rusty Wallace .60 1.50
70 David Green .07 .20
71 Michael Waltrip .15 .40
72 Dale Jarrett .50 1.25
73 Rusty Wallace's Car .25 .60
74 Michael Waltrip's Car .07 .20
75 Robby Gordon's Car .15 .40
76 Sterling Marlin's Car .07 .20
77 Ernie Irvan's Car .07 .20
78 Dale Jarrett's Car .15 .40
79 David Green .07 .20
80 Ernie Irvan .15 .40
81 Johnny Benson's Car .02 .10
82 Robin Pemberton .02 .10
83 Terry Labonte's Car .15 .40
84 Dale Earnhardt's Car .50 1.25
85 Darrell Waltrip CL .07 .20
86 Bobby Hamilton CL .02 .10
P8 Jeff Gordon Promo 1.00 2.50

1997 Action Packed First Impressions

COMPLETE SET (86) 25.00 60.00
*FIRST IMPRESS: 1.2X TO 3X BASE CARDS

1997 Action Packed 24K Gold

Each card from this 14-card set is marked with the now standard 24Kt. Gold logo on the card front. The cards were randomly inserted in hobby packs at a ratio of 1:71 and inserted in retail packs at a ratio of 1:86.

COMPLETE SET (14) 150.00 300.00
1 Rusty Wallace 10.00 25.00
2 Dale Earnhardt 20.00 50.00
3 Jeff Gordon 12.50 30.00
4 Ernie Irvan 2.50 6.00
5 Terry Labonte 4.00 10.00
6 Johnny Benson 1.25 3.00
7 David Green 1.25 3.00

"When my mom was diagnosed with cancer, I wanted her to have access to the best treatments available."

SONEQUA MARTIN-GREEN
Stand Up To Cancer Ambassador

Photo By
MATT SAYLES

THAT'S WHY I'M SO PASSIONATE ABOUT EXPANDING AWARENESS OF CLINICAL TRIALS

You want the best treatments for your loved ones. My mom's cancer was treated using a therapy made possible by clinical trials. I want all people diagnosed with cancer to have access to the treatments that will make them long-term survivors, like my mom.

Cancer clinical trials may be the right option for you or a loved one. The more information you have about clinical trials, the more empowered you will be to seek out your best treatments.

Learn more at **StandUpToCancer.org/ClinicalTrials**

Stand Up To Cancer is a division of the Entertainment Industry Foundation (EIF), a 501(c)(3) charitable organization.

8 Dale Jarrett 8.00 20.00
9 Sterling Marlin 4.00 10.00
10 Michael Waltrip 2.50 6.00
11 Mark Martin 10.00 25.00
12 Bobby Hamilton 1.25 3.00
13 Ted Musgrave 1.25 3.00
14 Randy LaJoie 1.25 3.00

1997 Action Packed Chevy Madness

This 6-card set is actually the beginning of a 15-card set that was distributed in 1997 Pinnacle(13-15) and 1997 Racer's Choice(7-12). The cards feature the top Chevy drivers from the Winston Cup Series. The cards were randomly inserted into hobby packs at a ratio of 1:10 and inserted into retail packs at a ratio of 1:12.

COMPLETE SET (6) 10.00 40.00
1 Dale Earnhardt's Car 8.00 20.00
2 Darrell Waltrip's Car 1.00 2.50
3 Dave Marcis' Car .50 1.25
4 Jeff Gordon's Car 5.00 12.00
5 Sterling Marlin's Car 1.50 4.00
6 Steve Grissom's Car .50 1.25

1997 Action Packed Fifth Anniversary

This 12-card set celebrates five years of NASCAR card production by Action Packed. The set includes current and retired NASCAR stars. The cards were randomly inserted into hobby packs at a ratio of 1:128 and inserted into retail packs at a ratio of 1:153.

COMPLETE SET (12) 150.00 300.00
1 Richard Petty 2.00 15.00
2 Cale Yarborough 2.00 5.00
3 Bobby Allison 2.00 5.00
4 Ned Jarrett 2.00 5.00
5 Benny Parsons 2.00 5.00
6 Dale Earnhardt 15.00 40.00
7 Rusty Wallace 8.00 40.00
8 Jeff Gordon 10.00 25.00
9 Terry Labonte 3.00 8.00
10 Dale Jarrett 6.00 15.00
11 Mark Martin 8.00 40.00
12 Bill Elliott 4.00 10.00

1997 Action Packed Fifth Anniversary Autographs

This 5-card set is a partial parallel to the Fifth Anniversary set. It contains the first five cards from that set featuring autographs from retired NASCAR legends. The cards were randomly inserted into hobby packs at a ratio of 1:165 and inserted into retail packs at a ratio of 1:198.

COMPLETE SET (5) 75.00 150.00
1 Richard Petty 15.00 40.00
2 Cale Yarborough 6.00 15.00
3 Bobby Allison 6.00 15.00
4 Ned Jarrett 6.00 15.00
5 Benny Parsons 30.00 60.00

1997 Action Packed Ironman Champion

This 2-card set highlights Terry Labonte's run for the 1997 Winston Cup Points Championship. The cards were randomly inserted into hobby packs at a ratio of 1:192 and inserted into retail packs at a ratio of 1:230.

COMPLETE SET (2) 30.00 80.00
1 Terry Labonte 15.00 40.00
2 T.Labonte
B.Labonte 15.00 40.00

1997 Action Packed Rolling Thunder

This 14-card set features some of the top stars from NASCAR. The cards were randomly inserted into hobby packs at a ratio of 1:23 and inserted into retail packs at a ratio of 1:28.

COMPLETE SET (14) 60.00 125.00
1 Mark Martin 8.00 20.00
2 Dale Earnhardt 15.00 40.00
3 Jeff Gordon 10.00 25.00
4 Ernie Irvan 2.00 5.00
5 Terry Labonte 3.00 8.00
6 Kyle Petty 2.00 5.00
7 Darrell Waltrip 2.00 5.00
8 Mike Skinner 1.00 2.50
9 Ricky Craven 1.00 2.50
10 Dale Jarrett 6.00 15.00
11 Sterling Marlin 3.00 8.00
12 Steve Grissom 1.00 2.50
13 Bill Elliott 4.00 10.00
14 Ricky Rudd 3.00 8.00

1997 ActionVision

This 12-card set utilizes Kodak's KODAMOTION technology to provide race action replay cards. This product marks the first time that NASCAR trading cards have been marketed in this fashion. Cards were distributed in one card packs with 18 packs per box and 20 boxes per case.

COMPLETE SET (12) 12.50 30.00
1 Terry Labonte 1.50 4.00
2 Jeff Gordon Victory Lane 2.50 6.00
3 Dale Earnhardt Qualifying 4.00 10.00
4 Dale Jarrett Victory Lane 2.50 6.00
5 J.Gordon
R.Wall
T.Labonte 2.50 6.00
6 J.Gordon
T.Labonte
R.Craven 2.50 6.00
7 Rusty Wallace Pit Stop 2.00 5.00
8 Dale Earnhardt Pit Stop 4.00 10.00
9 Terry Labonte Pit Stop 1.25 3.00
10 Jeff Gordon Pit Stop 2.50 6.00
11 Dale Jarrett Pit Stop 2.00 5.00
12 Bill Elliott Talladega Crash 1.50 4.00
P1 Bobby Labonte Promo 3.00 8.00

1997 ActionVision Precious Metal

This 4-card series is the last section of a 9-card set that was started in 1997 VIP. The cards from this set contain a piece of sheet metal along with a picture of the driver and the car which is encased in a polyurethane card. Cards with multi-colored pieces of sheet metal often carry a premium over those that do not. Each of the four cards inserted into ActionVision was limited in production to 350. The cards were randomly inserted into packs at a ratio of 1:160.

COMPLETE SET (4) 200.00 400.00
*MULTI-COLOR METAL: .75X TO 1.25X
6 Dale Earnhardt 50.00 120.00
7 Dale Jarrett 15.00 40.00
8 Ernie Irvan 15.00 40.00
9 Mark Martin 30.00 80.00

1997 Alka-Seltzer Terry Labonte

This three card Terry Labonte set was available through a mail-in offer from Alka-Seltzer. The offer was posted on Alka-Seltzer's home page on the internet. The collector had to fill out a form on-line and in return would receive a free sample of cherry flavored Alka-Seltzer along with one Terry Labonte trading card.

COMPLETE SET (3) 2.50 6.00
COMMON DRIVER (1-3) .75 2.00

1993-94 Alliance Robert Pressley/Dennis Setzer

The Alliance Racing Team set was released two consecutive years by D and D Racing Images. The cards in both sets are identical except for the driver card #11. The 1993 release features Robert Pressley (#11A), while the 1994 set includes Dennis Setzer (#11B). Either set carries the same value.

COMPLETE SET (12) 4.00 6.00
1 Barbara Welch .20 .50
2 Ricky Pearson .20 .50
3 Ricky Case .20 .50
4 Jeff Fender .20 .50
5 Dick Boles .20 .50
6 Chris McPherson .20 .50
7 Clarence Ogle .20 .50
8 Eddie Pearson .20 .50
9 Owen Edwards .20 .50
10 Dennis McCarson .20 .50
11A Robert Pressley .40 1.00
11B Dennis Setzer .40 1.00
NNO Alliance Transporter CL .20 .50

2007 Americana

COMPLETE SET (100) 30.00 60.00
COMMON CARD (1-100) .40 1.00
MINOR STARS .40 1.00
SEMISTARS .60 1.50
UNLISTED STARS .75 2.00
*RETAIL: .3X TO .8X BASIC CARDS
*SILVER PROOFS: 1.5X TO 4X BASIC CARDS
*SILVER PROOFS RETAIL: 1.5X TO 4X BASIC CARDS
SILVER PROOFS #'d TO 250
*GOLD PROOFS: 2X TO 5X BASIC CARDS
*GOLD PROOFS RETAIL: 2X TO 5X BASIC CARDS
GOLD PROOFS #'d TO 100
*PLATINUM PROOFS: 3X TO 8X BASIC CARDS
*PLATINUM PROOFS RETAIL: 3X TO 8X BASIC CARDS
PLATINUM PROOFS #'d TO 25
69 Bobby Allison .75 2.00

2007 Americana Private Signings

RANDOM INSERTS IN PACKS
PRINT RUNS B/WN 5-1250 COPIES PER
NO PRICING ON QTY OF 15 OR LESS
69 Bobby Allison/100 10.00 25.00

2007 Americana Stars Material

RANDOM INSERTS IN PACKS
PRINT RUNS B/WN 10-250 COPIES PER
NO PRICING ON QTY OF 10
69 Bobby Allison Shirt/250 4.00 10.00

2007 Americana Stars Material Silver Proofs

*SILVER: .5X TO 1.2X BASIC
RANDOM INSERTS IN PACKS
PRINT RUNS B/WN 5-100 COPIES PER
NO PRICING ON QTY OF 10 OR LESS

2007 Americana Stars Material Gold Proofs

*GOLD: .75X TO 2X BASIC
RANDOM INSERTS IN PACKS
PRINT RUNS B/WN 1-35 COPIES PER
NO PRICING ON QTY OF 10 OR LESS

2007 Americana Stars Signature Material

RANDOM INSERTS IN PACKS
PRINT RUNS B/WN 5-250 COPIES PER
NO PRICING ON QTY OF 10 OR LESS
69 Bobby Allison Shirt/100 10.00 25.00

2008 Americana II Sports Legends

RANDOM INSERTS IN PACKS
STATED PRINT RUN 500 SERIAL #'d SETS
12 Richard Petty 1.50 4.00

2008 Americana II Sports Legends Material

RANDOM INSERTS IN PACKS
STATED PRINT RUN 100 SERIAL #'d SETS
12 Richard Petty/100 5.00 12.00

2008 Americana II Sports Legends Signature

RANDOM INSERTS IN PACKS
PRINT RUNS B/WN 50-100 COPIES PER
12 Richard Petty/50 20.00 50.00

2008 Americana II Sports Legends Signature Material

RANDOM INSERTS IN PACKS
STATED PRINT RUN 100 SERIAL #'d SETS
12 Richard Petty/100 25.00 50.00

1992 Arena Joe Gibbs Racing

Arena Trading Cards Inc. produced this set honoring the Interstate Batteries Joe Gibbs Racing Team. The cards were sold in complete set form and included a Hologram card featuring Dale Jarrett's Interstate Batteries car along with an unnumbered cover/checklist card.

COMPLETE SET (12) 1.25 3.00
1 Joe Gibbs .15 .40
2 Dale Jarrett .12 .30
3 Jimmy Makar .05 .15
4 Dale Jarrett's Crew .12 .30
5 Dale Jarrett's Car .05 .10
6 Dale Jarrett's Car .05 .10
7 Dale Jarrett
Jimmy Makar .12 .30
8 Dale Jarrett .12 .30
9 Joe Gibbs
Jimmy Makar .15 .40
10 Dale Jarrett's Transporter .05 .10
NNO Cover Card CL .05 .10
NNO Dale Jarrett's Car HOLO .50 1.25

1994-95 Assets

Produced by Classic, the 1994 Assets set features stars from basketball, hockey, football, baseball, and auto racing. The set was released in two series of 50 cards each. 1,994 cases were produced of each series. This standard-sized card set features a player photo with his name in silver letters on the lower left corner and the Assets logo on the upper right. The back has a color photo on the left side along with a biography on the right side of the card. A Sprint phone card is randomly inserted in each five-card pack.

COMPLETE SET (100) 6.00 15.00
5 Dale Earnhardt .75 2.00
30 Dale Earnhardt .75 2.00
68 Jeff Gordon .60 1.50
93 Jeff Gordon .60 1.50

1994-95 Assets Die Cuts

This 25-card standard-size set was randomly inserted into packs. DC1-10 were included in series one while DC11-25 were included in series two packs. These cards feature the player on the card and the ability to separate the player's photo. The back contains information about the player on the section of the card that is separable.

COMPLETE SET (25) 30.00 80.00
DC5 Dale Earnhardt 7.50 15.00
DC19 Jeff Gordon's Car 1.50 4.00

1994-95 Assets Silver Signature

This 48-card standard-size set was randomly inserted at a rate of four per box. The cards are identical to the first twenty-four cards in the each series, except that these show a silver facsimile autograph on their fronts. The first 24 cards correspond to cards 1-24 in the first series while the second 24 cards correspond to cards 51-74 in the second series.

*SILVER SIGS: 1.2X TO 3X BASIC CARDS

1994-95 Assets Phone Cards $5

These cards measure 2" by 3 1/4", have rounded corners and were randomly inserted into packs. Cards 1-5 were inserted into first series packs while 6-15 were in second series packs. The front features the player's photo, with "Five Dollars" written in cursive script along the left edge. In the bottom left corner is the Assets logo. The back gives instructions on how to use the phone card. Series one cards expired on December 1, 1995 while second series cards expired on March 31, 1996.

COMPLETE SET (15) 8.00 20.00
*PIN NUMBER REVEALED: .2X TO .5X
9 Jeff Gordon 2.50 6.00

1994-95 Assets Phone Cards One Minute

Measuring 2" by 3 1/4", these cards have rounded corners and were inserted one per pack. Cards 1-24 were in first series packs while 25-48 were included with second series packs. The front features the player's photo and on the side is how long the card is good for. The Assets logo is in the bottom left corner. The back gives instructions on how to use the phone card. The first series cards expired on December 1, 1995 while the second series cards expired on March 31, 1996. The cards with a $2 logo are worth a mulitple of the regular cards. Please refer to the values below for these cards.

COMPLETE SET (48) 7.50 20.00
*PIN NUMB.REVEALED: .2X TO .5X BASIC INS.
*TWO DOLLAR: .5X TO 1.2X BASIC INSERTS
5 Dale Earnhardt 1.50 4.00
30 Jeff Gordon 1.25 3.00

1995 Assets

This 50-card set features the top names in racing in Classic's first racing issue under the Assets brand. The cards are printed on 18pt. stock and use full-bleed printing. There are three topical subsets; Drivers (1-28),Winners (29-44), and Cars (45-50). The cards came six cards per pack, 18 packs per box and 16 boxes per case.

COMPLETE SET (50) 6.00 15.00
1 Dale Earnhardt 1.00 2.50
2 Rusty Wallace .40 1.00
3 Jeff Gordon .60 1.50
4 Kyle Petty .10 .30
5 Brett Bodine .05 .15
6 Sterling Marlin .20 .50
7 Darrell Waltrip .10 .30
8 Sterling Marlin .20 .50
9 Geoff Bodine .05 .15
10 Ricky Craven .05 .15
11 Robert Pressley .05 .15
12 Bobby Labonte .30 .75
13 Dale Jarrett .30 .75
14 Dick Trickle .05 .15
15 Jeff Burton .20 .50
16 John Andretti .05 .15
17 Ken Schrader .05 .15
18 Ernie Irvan .10 .30
19 Michael Waltrip .10 .30
20 Morgan Shepherd .05 .15
21 Ricky Rudd .20 .50
22 Steve Kinser .05 .15
23 Ted Musgrave .05 .15
24 Terry Labonte .20 .50
25 Todd Bodine .05 .15
26 Ward Burton .10 .30
27 Mark Martin .40 1.00
28 Bobby Hamilton .05 .15
29 Dale Earnhardt 1.00 2.50
30 Rusty Wallace .40 1.00
31 Jeff Gordon .60 1.50
32 Kyle Petty .10 .30
33 Geoff Bodine .05 .15
34 Sterling Marlin .20 .50
35 Darrell Waltrip .10 .30
36 Dale Jarrett .30 .75
37 Ken Schrader .05 .15
38 Ernie Irvan .10 .30
39 Ricky Rudd .20 .50
40 Terry Labonte .20 .50
41 Mark Martin .40 1.00
42 Morgan Shepherd .05 .15
43 Ward Burton .10 .30
44 Dale Earnhardt 1.00 2.50
45 Morgan Shepherd's Car .02 .10
46 Dale Earnhardt's Car .40 1.00
47 Rusty Wallace's Car .20 .50
48 Mark Martin's Car .20 .50
49 Jeff Gordon's Car .30 .75
50 Checklist .02 .10
P1 Dale Earnhardt Promo 15.00 30.00

1995 Assets Gold Signature

COMPLETE SET (50) 30.00 80.00
*GOLD SIG.: 2.5X TO 6X BASE CARDS

1995 Assets 1-Minute Phone Cards

This 20-card insert set features Winston Cup personalities on 1-minute phone cards. The cards were inserted at a rate of one per pack. The cards expired 12/31/1995. There were three parallel versions of the 1-minute set: the 1-minute gold signature, $2 phone cards and $2 gold signature phone cards. The cards in the 1-minute gold signature set expired on 12/31/1995 and were inserted at a rate of one per 26 packs. The cards in both the $2 set and the $2 signature set expired on 5/1/96. The $2 cards were inserted one per six packs, while the $2 signature cards were inserted one per 58 packs.

COMPLETE 1-MIN.SET (20) 4.00 10.00
COMP.1-MIN GOLD SIG.(20) 12.00 30.00
*1 MIN.GOLD SIG.: 1.2X TO 3X BASIC INSERTS
COMP.$2 CARD SET (20) 7.50 20.00
*$2.00 CARDS: .8X TO 2X BASIC INSERTS
COMP.$2 GOLD SIG.(20) 20.00 50.00
*$2 GOLD SIG.: 2X TO 5X BASIC INSERTS
1 Dick Trickle .05 .15
2 Bobby Labonte .30 .75
3 Brett Bodine .05 .15
4 Dale Earnhardt 1.00 2.50
5 Dale Jarrett .30 .75
6 Darrell Waltrip .10 .30
7 Ernie Irvan .10 .30
8 Geoff Bodine .05 .15
9 Jeff Gordon .60 1.50
10 John Andretti .05 .15
11 Ken Schrader .05 .15
12 Kyle Petty .10 .30
13 Mark Martin .40 1.00
14 Michael Waltrip .10 .30
15 Morgan Shepherd .05 .15
16 Ward Burton .10 .30
17 Ricky Rudd .20 .50
18 Rusty Wallace .40 1.00
19 Sterling Marlin .20 .50
20 Terry Labonte .20 .50

1995 Assets $5 Phone Cards

This 10-card insert set features the top Winston Cup personalities on $5 phone cards. Each card was worth $5 of phone time. The expiration date of the cards was 5/1/96 and the odds of pulling one from a pack were one in 18. There is also a $25 denomination that was a parallel to the $5 set. The $25 denomination also expired on 5/1/96 and they were randomly inserted at a rate of one per 288 packs.

COMPLETE $5 SET (10) 10.00 25.00
COMPLETE $25 SET (10) 25.00 60.00
*$25 CARDS: 1X TO 2.5X $5.00 CARDS
*PIN NUMBER REVEALED: HALF VALUE
1 Sterling Marlin .60 1.50
2 Dale Earnhardt 3.00 8.00
3 Darrell Waltrip .40 1.00
4 Jeff Gordon 2.00 5.00
5 Ken Schrader .20 .50
6 Kyle Petty .40 1.00
7 Mark Martin 1.25 3.00
8 Richard Petty .40 1.00
9 Rusty Wallace 1.25 3.00
10 Terry Labonte .60 1.50

1995 Assets $100 Phone Cards

This 5-card insert set features five of the top Winston Cup personalities on $100 phone cards. The cards were inserted at a rate of one per 3200 packs. Each card has a covered pin number on the back that must be revealed to use the card. The cards have an expiration date of 5/1/96. There is also a 5-card parallel version of this set in the amount of $1000. The cards are identical to the $100 except for the dollar denomination. The odds of finding a $1000 card were one per 28,800 packs. There was a $1000 Dale Earnhardt promo phone card that was distributed to dealers and the media. The card is identical to the regular issue except that it doesn't have a pin number in order to make it invalid.

COMPLETE $100 SET (5) 40.00 100.00
*$1000 CARDS: 1.5X TO 4X $100 CARDS
*USED CARDS: .1X TO .3X BASIC INSERTS
1 Ricky Rudd 3.00 8.00
2 Dale Earnhardt 15.00 40.00
3 Jeff Gordon 10.00 25.00
4 Mark Martin 6.00 15.00
5 Rusty Wallace 6.00 15.00

1995 Assets Coca-Cola 600 Die Cut Phone Cards

This 10-card insert set was an interactive game for the 1995 Coca-Cola 600 race. The cards were die cut phone cards and if you held the winner of the race, Bobby Labonte, you could then call the 1-800 number on the back of the card and enter that card's pin number for a chance to win a prize. The grand prize was a trip for two to the 1996 Coca-Cola 600. There were 3000 special 10-card winner sets produced and numerous bonus prizes offered. The expiration for the game was 12/1/1995.

COMPLETE SET (10) 10.00 25.00
*PIN NUMBER REVEALED: HALF VALUE
1 Dale Earnhardt 4.00 10.00
2 Rusty Wallace 1.50 4.00
3 Jeff Gordon 2.50 6.00
4 Bobby Labonte WIN 1.25 3.00
5 Terry Labonte .75 2.00
6 Geoff Bodine .25 .60
7 Dale Jarrett 1.25 3.00
8 Mark Martin 1.50 4.00
9 Ricky Rudd .75 2.00
10 Field Card .15 .40

1995 Assets Images Previews

This 5-card insert set was a preview for Classic's Images racing product. The cards feature micro-foil technolgoy and could be found at a rate of one per 18 Assets packs.

COMPLETE SET (5) 6.00 15.00
RI1 Dale Earnhardt 3.00 8.00
RI2 Al Unser Jr. .40 1.00
RI3 Rick Mears .20 .50
RI4 Jeff Gordon 2.00 5.00
RI5 John Force .40 1.00

1995 Assets Gold

This 50-card set measures the standard size. The fronts feature borderless player action photos with the player's name printed in gold at the bottom. The backs carry a portrait of the player with his name, career highlights, and statistics. The Dale Earnhardt card was pulled from circulation early in the product's release. It is considered a Short Print (SP) but is not included in the complete set price.

COMPLETE SET (49) 6.00 15.00
1 Dale Earnhardt SP 6.00 15.00

1995 Assets Gold Die Cuts Silver

This 20-card set was randomly inserted in packs at a rate of one in 18. The fronts feature a borderless player color action photo with a diamond-shaped top and the player's action taking place in front of the card name. The backs carry the card name, player's name and career highlights. The cards are numbered on the backs. Gold versions were inserted at a rate of one in 72 packs.

COMPLETE SET (20) 10.00 25.00
*GOLDS: .8X TO 2X SILVERS
GOLD STATED ODDS 1:72
SDC10 Dale Earnhardt 2.00 5.00

1995 Assets Gold Printer's Proofs

These parallel cards were randomly seeded at the rate of 1:18 packs. They feature the words "Printer's Proof" on the cardfronts.

*PRINT PROOF: 2X TO 5X BASIC CARDS
1 Dale Earnhardt SP 10.00 25.00

1995 Assets Gold Silver Signatures

COMP. SILVER SIG SET (50) 15.00 40.00
*SILVER SIGS: .8X TO 2X BASIC CARDS
1 Dale Earnhardt SP 5.00 15.00

1995 Assets Gold Phone Cards $2

This 47-card set was randomly inserted in packs and measures 2 1/8" by 3 3/8". The fronts feature color action player photos with the player's name below. The $2 calling value is printed vertically down the left. The backs carry the instructions on how to use the cards which expired on 7/31/96. The cards are unnumbered.

COMPLETE SET (47) 15.00 40.00
*PIN NUMBER REVEALED: HALF VALUE
1 Dale Earnhardt 2.00 5.00

1995 Assets Gold Phone Cards $5

This 16-card set measures 2 1/8" by 3 3/8" and was randomly inserted in packs. The fronts feature color action player photos with the player's name below. The $5 calling value is printed vertically down the left. The backs carry the instructions on how to use the cards which expired on 7/31/96. The cards are unnumbered. The Microlined versions are inserted at a rate of one in 18 packs versus one in six packs for the basic $5 card.

COMPLETE SET (16) 25.00 60.00
*MICROLINED: .6X TO 1.5X BASIC INSERTS
STATED ODDS 1:18
*PIN NUMBER REVEALED: HALF VALUE
12 Dale Earnhardt 3.00 8.00

1996 Assets

The 1996 Classic Assets was issued in one set totalling 50 cards. This 50-card premium set has a tremendous selection of the top athletes in the world headlines. Each card features action photos, up-to-date statistics and is printed on high-quality, foil-stamped stock. Hot Print cards are parallel cards randomly inserted in Hot Packs and are valued at a multiple of the regular cards below.

COMPLETE SET (50)	5.00	10.00
3 Todd Bodine	.05	.15
9 Dale Earnhardt	1.00	2.50
21 Sterling Marlin	.08	.25
22 Mark Martin	.30	.75
27 Ted Musgrave	.05	.15

1996 Assets Hot Prints

*HOT PRINTS: .8X TO 2X BASIC CARDS

1996 Assets A Cut Above

The even cards were randomly inserted in retail packs at a rate of one in eight, and the odd cards were inserted in clear asset packs at a rate of one in 20, this 20-card die-cut set is composed of 10 phone cards and 10 trading cards. The cards have rounded corners except for one which is cut in a straight corner design. The fronts feature a color action player cut-out superimposed over a gray background with the words "cut above" printed throughout and resembled to be cut so it displays a basketball game behind it. The backs carry a color action player photo with the player's name and a short career summary.

COMPLETE SET (20)	20.00	50.00
CA6 Mark Martin	1.25	3.00
CA17 Sterling Marlin	1.00	2.50

1996 Assets A Cut Above Phone Cards

This 10-card set, which were inserted at a rate of one in eight, measures approximately 2 1/8" by 3 3/8" have rounded corners except for one corner which is cut out and made straight. The fronts feature a color action player cut-out superimposed over a gray background with the words "cut above" printed throughout and resembled to be cut so that it displays a game going on behind the background. The backs carry the instructions on how to use the card. The cards expired on 1/31/97.

COMPLETE SET (10)	12.50	30.00
*PIN NUMBER REVEALED: HALF VALUE		
1 Dale Earnhardt	5.00	8.00

1996 Assets Crystal Phone Cards

Randomly inserted in retail packs at a rate of one in 250, this high-tech, 10-card insert set contains clear holographic phone cards worth five minutes of long distance calling time. The cards measure approximately 2 1/8" by 3 3/8" with rounded corners. The fronts display a color action double-image player cut-out on a clear crystal background with the player's name printed vertically on the side. The backs carry instructions on how to use the card. The cards expired January 31, 1997. Twenty dollar phone cards of these athletes were issued, they are valued as a multiple of the cards below.

COMPLETE SET (10)	20.00	50.00
*PIN NUMBER REVEALED: HALF VALUE		
3 Dale Earnhardt	3.00	8.00

1996 Assets Crystal Phone Cards $20

3 Dale Earnhardt	6.00	15.00

1996 Assets Phone Cards $2

COMPLETE SET (30)	12.50	30.00
*$2 CARDS: .6X TO 1.5X $1 CARDS		
*PIN NUMBER REVEALED: HALF VALUE		

1996 Assets Phone Cards $5

This 20-card set was randomly inserted in retail packs at a rate of 1 in 5. The cards measure approximately 2 1/8" by 3 3/8" with rounded corners. The fronts display color action player photos with the player's name in a red bar below. The backs carry the instructions on how to use the cards and the expiration date of 1/31/97.

COMPLETE SET (20)	30.00	80.00
*PIN NUMBER REVEALED: HALF VALUE		
6 Dale Earnhardt	2.50	6.00
10 Mark Martin	1.25	3.00

1996 Assets Phone Cards $10

This 10-card set was randomly inserted in packs at a rate of 1 in 20. The cards measure approximately 2 1/8" by 3 3/8" with rounded corners. The fronts display color action player photos with the player's name in a red bar below. The backs carry the instructions on how to use the cards and the expiration date of 1/31/97.

COMPLETE SET (10)	25.00	60.00
*PIN NUMBER REVEALED: HALF VALUE		
3 Dale Earnhardt	4.00	10.00

1996 Assets Phone Cards $20

This five card set measures approximately 2 1/8" by 3 3/8" with rounded corners and were randomly inserted in retail packs. The fronts display color action player photos with the player's name. The backs carry the instructions on how to use the cards and the expiration date of 1/31/97.

COMPLETE SET (5)	25.00	60.00
*PIN NUMBER REVEALED: HALF VALUE		
1 Dale Earnhardt	8.00	20.00

1996 Assets Phone Cards $100

This five card set, randomly inserted in packs, measures approximately 2 1/8" by 3 3/8" with rounded corners. The fronts display color action player photos with the player's name. The backs carry the instructions on how to use the cards and the expiration date of 1/31/97.

COMPLETE SET (5)	40.00	80.00
*PIN NUMBER REVEALED: HALF VALUE		
1 Dale Earnhardt	10.00	25.00

1996 Assets Silksations

Randomly inserted in retail packs at a rate of one in 100, this 10-card standard-size set features duplexed fabric-stock with top athletes. The fronts display a color action player cut-out with a two-tone background. The player's name is printed below. The backs carry a head photo of the player made to appear as if it is coming out of a square hole in gold cloth. The player's name and a short career summary are below. The cards are numbered with a "S" prefix and sequenced in alphabetical order.

COMPLETE SET (10)	40.00	80.00
3 Dale Earnhardt	10.00	25.00

1996 Assets Racing

This 50-card set was produced by Classic. The cards were printed on 18-point stock and each card front features foil stamping and dual photos. The cards were distributed via six card packs (5 regular cards and 1 phone card) with 18-packs per box and 12-boxes per case.

COMPLETE SET (50)	6.00	15.00
1 Dale Earnhardt	1.00	2.50
2 Jeff Gordon	.60	1.50
3 Ricky Rudd	.20	.50
4 Geoff Bodine	.05	.15
5 Ernie Irvan	.10	.30
6 John Andretti	.05	.15
7 Kyle Petty	.10	.30
8 Darrell Waltrip	.10	.30
9 Dale Jarrett	.40	1.00
10 Sterling Marlin	.20	.50
11 Jimmy Spencer	.05	.15
12 Loy Allen Jr.	.05	.15
13 Richard Childress	.10	.30
14 Ken Schrader	.05	.15
15 Ned Jarrett	.05	.15
16 Ward Burton	.10	.30
17 Todd Bodine	.05	.15
18 Mark Martin	.50	1.25
19 Morgan Shepherd	.05	.15
20 Bobby Labonte	.40	1.00
21 Robert Pressley	.05	.15
22 Hut Stricklin	.05	.15
23 Jerry Punch	.02	.10
24 Ricky Rudd	.20	.50
25 Ward Burton	.10	.30
26 Bobby Hamilton	.05	.15
27 Johnny Benson	.10	.30
28 Michael Waltrip	.10	.30
29 Mark Martin	.50	1.25
30 Andy Petree	.02	.10
31 Ted Musgrave	.05	.15
32 Mike Wallace	.05	.15
33 Ernie Irvan	.10	.30
34 Jeff Burton	.20	.50
35 Robert Yates	.02	.10
36 Dick Trickle	.05	.15
37 Kenny Wallace	.05	.15
38 Dale Earnhardt	1.00	2.50
39 Brett Bodine	.05	.15
40 Ricky Craven	.05	.15
41 Kyle Petty	.10	.30
42 Dale Jarrett	.40	1.00
43 Darrell Waltrip	.10	.30
44 Dale Earnhardt	1.00	2.50
45 John Andretti	.05	.15
46 Terry Labonte	.20	.50
47 Richard Petty	.20	.50
48 Ernie Irvan	.10	.30
49 Mark Martin	.50	1.25
50 Ricky Rudd	.20	.50
P1 Dale Earnhardt Promo	2.50	6.00
P2 Dale Earnhardt PC Promo	15.00	30.00

1996 Assets Racing $2 Phone Cards

This 25-card set features top drivers on $2 phone cards. Each horizontally designed card featured a driver or car photo on the front and usage instruction on the back. The expiration date for the use of the cards was 11/30/97. The cards were inserted one per pack.

COMPLETE SET (25)	5.00	12.00
1 Dale Earnhardt	1.00	2.50
2 Ward Burton	.10	.30
3 Jimmy Spencer	.05	.15
4 Geoff Bodine	.05	.15
5 Dale Jarrett	.40	1.00
6 Ernie Irvan	.10	.30
7 Ken Schrader	.05	.15
8 Ricky Craven	.05	.15
9 Mark Martin	.50	1.25
10 Dale Earnhardt's Car	.50	1.25
11 Darrell Waltrip	.10	.30
12 Sterling Marlin	.20	.50
13 Ricky Rudd	.20	.50
14 Bill Elliott	.30	.75
15 Rusty Wallace's Car	.10	.30
16 John Andretti	.05	.15
17 Ernie Irvan	.10	.30
18 Michael Waltrip	.10	.30
19 Kyle Petty	.10	.30
20 Mike Wallace	.05	.15
21 Bobby Hamilton	.05	.15
22 Dale Jarrett's Car	.20	.50
23 Ted Musgrave	.05	.15
24 Jeremy Mayfield	.10	.30
25 Ernie Irvan's Car	.05	.15

1996 Assets Racing $5 Phone Cards

This 15-card set features top drivers from the Winston Cup series. Each card carried $5 in phone time. The cards feature a horizontal design on the front and dialing instructions on the back. The phone time expired 11/30/97. The cards were seeded one in five packs.

COMPLETE SET (15)	6.00	15.00
1 Ricky Rudd	.40	1.00
2 Jeff Burton	.40	1.00
3 Mark Martin	1.00	2.50
4 Darrell Waltrip	.25	.60
5 Bill Elliott	.60	1.50
6 Dale Earnhardt	2.00	5.00
7 Brett Bodine	.10	.30
8 Ted Musgrave	.10	.30
9 Michael Waltrip	.25	.60
10 Ernie Irvan	.25	.60
11 Dale Earnhardt's Car	1.00	2.50
12 Kyle Petty	.25	.60
13 Jimmy Spencer	.10	.30
14 Robert Pressley	.10	.30
15 John Andretti	.10	.30

1996 Assets Racing $10 Phone Cards

Each card in the 10-card insert set features $10 in phone time. The cards carry a horizontal design on the front and dialing instructions on the back. The phone time expired 11/30/1997. The cards were inserted one in 15 packs.

COMPLETE SET (10)	6.00	15.00
1 John Andretti	.15	.40
2 Bobby Hamilton	.15	.40
3 Robert Pressley	.15	.40
4 Dale Earnhardt	2.50	6.00
5 Ernie Irvan	.30	.75
6 Jimmy Spencer	.15	.40
7 Kyle Petty	.30	.75
8 Mark Martin	1.25	3.00
9 Dale Earnhardt's Car	1.25	3.00
10 Ricky Rudd	.50	1.25

1996 Assets Racing $100 Cup Champion Interactive Phone Cards

This 20-card set was an interactive game. Each card from this set carried a minimum $5 phone time value. Because the game rewarded the card that featured the 1996 Winston Cup Champion and Terry Labonte was not on a regular card in the set, the field card was the winning card in the set. The field card was activated for an additional $95 worth of phone time. The phone cards were randomly seeded one in 15 packs. The phone time on each of the cards expired 11/30/1997.

COMPLETE SET (20)	25.00	60.00
1 Dale Earnhardt	4.00	10.00
2 Jeff Gordon	2.50	6.00
3 Jeff Burton	.75	2.00
4 Dale Jarrett	1.50	4.00
5 Kyle Petty	.50	1.25
6 Darrell Waltrip	.50	1.25
7 Ernie Irvan	.50	1.25
8 Sterling Marlin	.75	2.00
9 Ricky Rudd	.75	2.00
10 Rusty Wallace's Car	.50	1.25
11 Mark Martin	2.00	5.00
12 Ken Schrader	.25	.60
13 Ted Musgrave	.25	.60
14 Michael Waltrip	.50	1.25
15 Ward Burton	.50	1.25
16 Bobby Labonte	1.50	4.00
17 Kenny Wallace	.25	.60
18 Ricky Craven	.25	.60
19 Bobby Hamilton	.25	.60
20 Field Card WIN	2.00	5.00

1996 Assets Racing $1000 Cup Champion Interactive Phone Cards

This 20-card set was an interactive game. Each card from this set carried a minimum $10 phone time value. Because the game rewarded the card that featured the 1996 Winston Cup Champion and Terry Labonte was not on a regular card in the set, the field card was the winning card in the set. The field card was activated for an additional $990 worth of phone time. The $1000 phone cards were randomly seeded one in 432 packs. The phone time on each of the cards expired 11/30/1997.

COMPLETE SET (20)	50.00	120.00
1 Dale Earnhardt	8.00	20.00
2 Rick Mast	.30	.75
3 Ricky Craven	.50	1.25
4 Ward Burton	1.00	2.50
5 Ricky Rudd	1.50	4.00
6 Dale Jarrett	3.00	8.00
7 Michael Waltrip	1.00	2.50
8 Jeff Burton	1.50	4.00
9 Ken Schrader	.50	1.25
10 Mark Martin	4.00	10.00
11 Darrell Waltrip	1.00	2.50
12 Kyle Petty	1.00	2.50
13 Ernie Irvan	1.00	2.50
14 Bobby Hamilton	.50	1.25
15 Ted Musgrave	.50	1.25
16 Kenny Wallace	.50	1.25
17 Rusty Wallace's Car	1.00	2.50
18 Bobby Labonte	3.00	8.00
19 Sterling Marlin	1.50	4.00
20 Field Card WIN	12.00	30.00

1996 Assets Racing Competitor's License

Each card from this 20-card insert set features a custom holographic overlay and simulates a driver's license. The cards were randomly inserted one in 15 packs.

COMPLETE SET (20)	30.00	80.00
CL1 Ernie Irvan	1.25	3.00
CL2 Kyle Petty	1.25	3.00
CL3 Mark Martin	5.00	12.00
CL4 Dale Earnhardt	6.00	15.00
CL5 Brett Bodine	.60	1.50
CL6 Ward Burton	1.25	3.00
CL7 Sterling Marlin	2.00	5.00
CL8 Ricky Craven	.60	1.50
CL9 Ted Musgrave	.60	1.50
CL10 Darrell Waltrip	1.25	3.00
CL11 Ricky Rudd	2.00	5.00
CL12 Dale Jarrett	4.00	10.00
CL13 Geoff Bodine	.60	1.50
CL14 Michael Waltrip	1.25	3.00
CL15 Ken Schrader	.60	1.50
CL16 Bobby Hamilton	.60	1.50
CL17 Bobby Labonte	4.00	10.00
CL18 Jimmy Spencer	.60	1.50
CL19 Jeff Burton	2.00	5.00
CL20 Terry Labonte	2.00	5.00

1996 Assets Racing Race Day

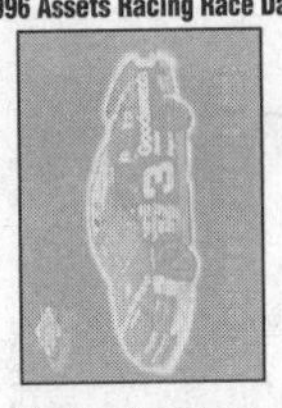

Randomly inserted one in 40 packs are these Race Day insert cards. The 10-card set features topics such as a typical day for a crew chief to an in-depth look at the superstitions and strategies behind 10 top racing teams. These cards are textured to give them a road-surface look and feel.

COMPLETE SET (10)	20.00	50.00
RD1 Morgan Shepherd's Car	.50	1.25
RD2 Rusty Wallace's Car	4.00	10.00
RD3 Dale Earnhardt's Car	8.00	20.00
RD4 Sterling Marlin's Car	1.50	4.00
RD5 Bobby Labonte's Car	3.00	8.00
RD6 Mark Martin's Car	4.00	10.00
RD7 Ernie Irvan's Car	1.00	2.50
RD8 Dale Jarrett's Car	3.00	8.00
RD9 Michael Waltrip's Car	1.00	2.50
RD10 Ricky Rudd's Car	1.50	4.00

1996 Autographed Racing

This 50-card set was the first issue by Score Board of the Autographed Racing brand. The product was packaged 5-cards per pack, 24 packs per box and 12 boxes per case. Original suggested retail on the packs was $4.99 each. The complete set consists of the top drivers on both the Winston Cup and Busch circuits. Also included were special redemption cards for officially licensed racing memorabilia at a rate of one per box.

COMPLETE SET (50)	10.00	20.00
1 Dale Earnhardt	1.00	2.50
2 Jeff Gordon	.60	1.50
3 Kyle Petty	.10	.30
4 Rick Mast	.05	.15
5 Richard Childress	.10	.30
6 Terry Labonte	.20	.50
7 Rusty Wallace's Car	.20	.50
8 Ken Schrader	.05	.15
9 Geoff Bodine	.05	.15
10 Richard Petty	.20	.50
11 Mike Skinner	.05	.15
12 Kenny Wallace	.05	.15
13 Sterling Marlin	.20	.50
14 Robert Pressley	.05	.15
15 Dale Jarrett	.40	1.00
16 Ted Musgrave	.05	.15
17 Ricky Rudd	.20	.50
18 Joe Gibbs	.10	.30
19 Morgan Shepherd	.05	.15
20 Mark Martin's Car	.20	.50
21 Hut Stricklin	.05	.15
22 Larry McReynolds	.02	.10
23 Brett Bodine	.05	.15
24 Mark Martin	.50	1.25
25 Dale Earnhardt's Car	.40	1.00
26 Elton Sawyer	.05	.15
27 Jeff Burton	.20	.50
28 Wood Brothers	.02	.10
29 David Smith	.02	.10
30 Ernie Irvan	.10	.30
31 Steve Hmiel	.02	.10
32 Mike Wallace	.05	.15
33 Dave Marcis	.10	.30
34 Michael Waltrip	.10	.30
35 Darrell Waltrip	.10	.30
36 Robin Pemberton	.02	.10
37 Loy Allen Jr.	.05	.15
38 Dick Trickle	.05	.15
39 Robert Yates	.02	.10
40 Randy LaJoie	.05	.15
41 John Andretti	.05	.15
42 Larry McClure	.02	.10
43 Bobby Labonte	.40	1.00
44 Ward Burton	.10	.30
45 Jeremy Mayfield	.10	.30
46 Ricky Craven	.05	.15
47 Jimmy Spencer	.05	.15
48 Todd Bodine	.05	.15
49 Jack Roush	.02	.10
50 Bobby Hamilton	.05	.15

1996 Autographed Racing Autographs

This 65-card insert set features hand-signed cards of the top names in racing. The cards were inserted at a rate of one in 12 packs. The cards featured red foil on the front along with the autograph. The backs carry the statement, "Congratulations. You've received an authentic 1996 Autographed Racing Autographed Card.

COMPLETE SET (65)	600.00	1000.00
1 Loy Allen Jr.	5.00	12.00
2 John Andretti	5.00	12.00
3 Paul Andrews	3.00	8.00
4 Johnny Benson	5.00	12.00
5 Brett Bodine	5.00	12.00
6 Geoff Bodine	5.00	12.00
7 Todd Bodine	5.00	12.00
8 Jeff Burton	8.00	20.00
9 Ward Burton	8.00	20.00
10 Richard Childress	10.00	25.00
11 Ricky Craven	5.00	12.00
12 Barry Dodson	3.00	8.00
13 Dale Earnhardt	125.00	250.00
14 Joe Gibbs	15.00	30.00
15 Tony Glover	4.00	10.00
16 Jeff Gordon	60.00	120.00
17 David Green	5.00	12.00
18 Bobby Hamilton	10.00	25.00
19 Doug Hewitt	3.00	8.00
20 Steve Hmiel	3.00	8.00
21 Ernie Irvan	10.00	25.00
22 Dale Jarrett	12.50	30.00
23 Ned Jarrett	10.00	25.00
24 Jason Keller	3.00	8.00
25 Bobby Labonte	12.50	30.00
26 Terry Labonte	10.00	25.00
27 Randy LaJoie	3.00	8.00
28 Jimmy Makar	3.00	8.00
29 Dave Marcis	12.50	30.00
30 Sterling Marlin	12.50	30.00
31 Mark Martin	15.00	40.00
32 Rick Mast	5.00	12.00
33 Jeremy Mayfield	10.00	25.00
34 Larry McClure	4.00	10.00
35 Mike McLaughlin	5.00	12.00
36 Larry McReynolds	5.00	12.00
37 Patty Moise	5.00	12.00
38 Brad Parrott	4.00	10.00
39 Buddy Parrott	3.00	8.00
40 Todd Parrott	3.00	8.00
41 Robin Pemberton	3.00	8.00
42 Runt Pittman	3.00	8.00
43 Charley Pressley	3.00	8.00
44 Robert Pressley	5.00	12.00
45 Dr. Jerry Punch	3.00	8.00
46 Chuck Rider	3.00	8.00
47 Jack Roush	10.00	25.00
48 Ricky Rudd	12.50	30.00
49 Elton Sawyer	5.00	12.00
50 Ken Schrader	10.00	25.00
51 Morgan Shepherd	5.00	12.00
52 Mike Skinner	5.00	12.00
53 David Smith/235	4.00	10.00
54 Jimmy Spencer	8.00	20.00
55 Hut Stricklin	5.00	12.00
56 Dick Trickle	5.00	12.00
57 Kenny Wallace	5.00	12.00
58 Mike Wallace	5.00	12.00
59 Darrell Waltrip	8.00	20.00
60 Michael Waltrip	8.00	20.00
61 Eddie Wood	3.00	8.00
62 Glen Wood	3.00	8.00
63 Kim Wood	3.00	8.00
64 Len Wood	3.00	8.00
65 Robert Yates	3.00	8.00

1996 Autographed Racing Autographs Certified Golds

This is a "Certified" parallel version to the 65-card Autograph set. Each card features gold foil stamping on the front instead of silver and each autographed card is serial numbered. The backs of the Certified cards feature the same statement as the regular autographs. Certified Gold autographs were inserted in packs at a rate of one in 24 packs.

*CERT.GOLDS: .5X TO 1.2X BASIC AUTOS		
1 Loy Allen Jr.	6.00	15.00
2 John Andretti	6.00	15.00
3 Paul Andrews	4.00	10.00
4 Johnny Benson	6.00	15.00
5 Brett Bodine	6.00	15.00
6 Geoff Bodine	6.00	15.00
7 Todd Bodine	6.00	15.00
8 Jeff Burton	12.50	30.00
9 Ward Burton	12.50	30.00
10 Richard Childress	12.50	30.00
11 Ricky Craven	6.00	15.00
12 Barry Dodson	4.00	10.00
13 Dale Earnhardt's Car	150.00	300.00
14 Joe Gibbs	15.00	40.00
15 Tony Glover	5.00	12.00
16 Jeff Gordon	60.00	150.00
17 David Green	6.00	15.00
18 Bobby Hamilton	12.50	30.00
19 Doug Hewitt	4.00	10.00
20 Steve Hmiel	4.00	10.00
21 Ernie Irvan	12.50	30.00
22 Dale Jarrett	15.00	40.00
23 Ned Jarrett	12.50	30.00
24 Jason Keller	4.00	10.00
25 Bobby Labonte	12.50	30.00
26 Terry Labonte	15.00	40.00
27 Randy LaJoie	4.00	10.00
28 Jimmy Makar	4.00	10.00
29 Dave Marcis	15.00	40.00
30 Sterling Marlin	15.00	40.00
31 Mark Martin	20.00	50.00
32 Rick Mast	6.00	15.00
33 Jeremy Mayfield	12.50	30.00
34 Larry McClure/245	5.00	12.00
35 Mike McLaughlin	6.00	15.00
36 Larry McReynolds	6.00	15.00
37 Patty Moise	6.00	15.00
38 Brad Parrott	5.00	12.00
39 Buddy Parrott	4.00	10.00
40 Todd Parrott	4.00	10.00
41 Robin Pemberton	4.00	10.00
42 Runt Pittman	4.00	10.00
43 Charley Pressley	4.00	10.00
44 Robert Pressley	6.00	15.00
45 Dr. Jerry Punch	4.00	10.00
46 Chuck Rider	4.00	10.00
47 Jack Roush	12.50	30.00
48 Ricky Rudd	15.00	40.00
49 Elton Sawyer	6.00	15.00
50 Ken Schrader	12.50	30.00
51 Morgan Shepherd	6.00	15.00
52 Mike Skinner	6.00	15.00
53 David Smith/235	5.00	12.00
54 Jimmy Spencer	10.00	25.00
55 Hut Stricklin	6.00	15.00
56 Dick Trickle	6.00	15.00
57 Kenny Wallace/275	6.00	15.00
58 Mike Wallace	6.00	15.00
59 Darrell Waltrip	10.00	25.00
60 Michael Waltrip/265	12.50	30.00
61 Eddie Wood	4.00	10.00
62 Glen Wood	4.00	10.00
63 Kim Wood/220	4.00	10.00
64 Len Wood	4.00	10.00
65 Robert Yates	4.00	10.00

1996 Autographed Racing Front Runners

This 89-card set features a double-front design. Each card has basically two front sides. The Front Runners logo on each side is stamped in silver foil. The cards are unnumbered and checklisted below in alphabetical order. Odds of finding a Front Runners card was one every two packs.

COMPLETE SET (89)	15.00	30.00
1 P.Andrews G.Bodine	.05	.15
2 B.Bodine G.Bodine	.05	.15
3 B.Bodine T.Bodine	.05	.15

4 G.Bodine T.Bodine	.05	.15
5 J.Burton J.Burton's Car	.20	.50
6 J.Burton W.Burton	.20	.50
7 J.Burton M.Martin with hat	.50	1.25
8 J.Burton M.Martin no hat	.50	1.25
9 J.Burton's Car M.Martin's Car	.10	.30
10 J.Burton T.Musgrave	.20	.50
11 J.Burton J.Roush	.20	.50
12 J.Burton's Car J.Roush	.10	.30
13 R.Childress Dale Earnhardt	1.00	2.50
14 R.Childress D.Earnhardt's Car	.40	1.00
15 R.Childress R.Petty	.20	.50
16 R.Craven R.Craven	.05	.15
17 R.Craven C.Pressley	.05	.15
18 R.Craven DuPont C.Pressley	.05	.15
19 D.Earnhardt D.Earnhardt	1.00	2.50
20 D.Earnhardt D.Earnhardt's Car	1.00	2.50
21 D.Earn.w Olympic car	1.00	2.50
22 D.Earnhardt R.Petty	1.00	2.50
23 J.Gibbs B.Labonte shades	.40	1.00
24 J.Gibbs B.Labonte w o shades	.40	1.00
25 J.Gibbs B.Labonte's Car	.10	.30
26 T.Glover S.Marlin shades	.20	.50
27 T.Glover S.Marlin w o shades	.20	.50
28 T.Glover S.Marlin's Car	.05	.15
29 B.Hamilton R.Petty	.20	.50
30 B.Hamilton profile R.Petty	.20	.50
31 S.Hmiel M.Martin with hat	.50	1.25
32 S.Hmiel M.Martin no hat	.50	1.25
33 E.Irvan E.Irvan	.10	.30
34 Irvan facing front Irvan's car	.10	.30
35 E.Irvan E.Irvan's car	.10	.30
36 E.Irvan D.Jarrett VL	.40	1.00
37 E.Irvan D.Jarrett shades	.40	1.00
38 Irvan facing front Jarr.shades	.40	1.00
39 E.Irvan facing front D.Jarrett VL	.40	1.00
40 E.Irvan's Car D.Jarrett's Car	.10	.30
41 Irvan facing front McReyn.	.10	.30
42 E.Irvan profile L.McReynolds	.10	.30
43 E.Irvan profile R.Yates	.10	.30
44 E.Irvan facing front R.Yates	.10	.30
45 E.Irvan's Car R.Yates	.05	.15
46 D.Jarrett D.Jarrett	.40	1.00
47 D.Jarrett VL D.Jarrett's Car	.40	1.00
48 D.Jarrett shades D.Jarrett's Car	.40	1.00
49 D.Jarrett VL N.Jarrett	.40	1.00
50 D.Jarrett VL T.Parrott	.40	1.00
51 D.Jarrett VL R.Yates	.40	1.00
52 D.Jarrett shades R.Yates	.40	1.00
53 D.Jarrett's Car R.Yates	.10	.30
54 B.Labonte shades B.Labonte	.40	1.00
55 B.Lab.shades B.Lab.Car	.40	1.00
56 B.Lab.no shades B.Lab.Car	.40	1.00
57 B.Labonte shades J.Makar	.40	1.00
58 B.Labonte no shades J.Makar	.40	1.00
59 Marl.no shades Marl.shades	.20	.50
60 Marlin no shades Marl.car	.20	.50
61 S.Marlin shades Marlin's Car	.20	.50
62 S.Marlin shades L.McClure	.20	.50
63 S.Marlin no shades McClure	.20	.50
65 S.Marlin shades R.Pittman	.20	.50
66 S.Marlin w o shades R.Pittman	.20	.50
66 S.Marlin's Car R.Pittman	.05	.15
67 Martin with hat Martin no hat	.50	1.25
68 Martin with hat Martin's Car	.50	1.25
69 Martin no hat Martin's Car	.50	1.25
70 M.Martin with hat T.Musgrave	.50	1.25
71 M.Martin no hat T.Musgrave	.50	1.25
72 M.Martin with hat J.Roush	.50	1.25
73 M.Martin no hat J.Roush	.50	1.25
74 M.Martin's Car J.Roush	.20	.50
75 P.Moise E.Sawyer	.05	.15
76 T.Musgrave J.Roush	.05	.15
77 R.Pemberton R.Wallace's Car	.20	.50
78 K.Petty R.Petty	.20	.50
79 C.Pressley R.Pressley	.05	.15
80 K.Wallace M.Wallace	.05	.15
81 D.Walt.with hel D.Wal.no hel	.10	.30
82 D.Wal.with hel M.Wal.shades	.10	.30
83 D.Waltrip with hel M.Waltrip	.10	.30
84 D.Walt.no hel M.Walt.shades	.10	.30
85 D.Waltrip no hel M.Waltrip	.10	.30
86 M.Waltrip M.Waltrip shades	.10	.30
87 M.Waltrip M.Waltrip's Car	.10	.30
88 M.Waltrip Wood Brothers	.10	.30
89 M.Waltrip's Car Wood Brothers	.10	.30

1996 Autographed Racing High Performance

This 20-card insert set includes the top names in racing on foil-stamped cards. The card fronts feature a driver's photo framed by a wood and marble design. The cards were inserted at a rate of one in eight packs.

COMPLETE SET (20)	20.00	50.00
HP1 Dale Earnhardt	6.00	15.00
HP2 Kyle Petty	.75	2.00
HP3 Jeremy Mayfield	.75	2.00
HP4 Sterling Marlin	1.25	3.00
HP5 Ward Burton	.75	2.00
HP6 Mark Martin	3.00	8.00
HP7 Bobby Labonte	2.50	6.00
HP8 Ricky Craven	.40	1.00
HP9 Michael Waltrip	.75	2.00
HP10 Ricky Rudd	1.25	3.00
HP11 Ted Musgrave	.40	1.00
HP12 Ken Schrader	.40	1.00
HP13 Dale Jarrett	2.50	6.00
HP14 Brett Bodine	.40	1.00
HP15 Jimmy Spencer	.40	1.00
HP16 Bobby Hamilton	.40	1.00
HP17 Darrell Waltrip	.75	2.00
HP18 Robert Pressley	.40	1.00
HP19 Ernie Irvan	.75	2.00
HP20 Geoff Bodine	.40	1.00

1996 Autographed Racing Kings of the Circuit $5 Phone Cards

This 10-card insert set highlights the careers of racing legends. Each card carries a $5 phone time value. The cards are printed on silver foil board. The backs feature dialing instructions for the phone time. The phone time on the cards expired 2/28/98. Odds of finding a Kings of the Circuit card are one in 30 packs.

COMPLETE SET (10)	12.00	30.00
KC1 Dale Jarrett	1.50	4.00
KC2 Mark Martin	2.00	5.00
KC3 Sterling Marlin	.75	2.00
KC4 Bill Elliott	1.25	3.00
KC5 Ernie Irvan	.50	1.25
KC6 Dale Earnhardt	4.00	10.00
KC7 Bill Elliott	1.25	3.00
KC8 Dale Earnhardt's Car	1.50	4.00
KC9 Rusty Wallace's Car	.75	2.00
KC10 Dale Earnhardt	4.00	10.00

1997 Autographed Racing

This 50-card set was the second issue by Score Board of the Autographed Racing brand. The product was packaged 5 cards per pack, 24 packs per box, and 10 boxes per case. The complete set consists of drivers from the Winston Cup and Busch circuits.

COMPLETE SET (50)	6.00	15.00
1 Dale Earnhardt	1.00	2.50
2 Kyle Petty	.10	.30
3 Terry Labonte	.20	.50
4 Jeff Gordon	.60	1.50
5 Michael Waltrip	.10	.30
6 Dale Jarrett	.40	1.00
7 Lake Speed	.05	.15
8 Bobby Labonte	.40	1.00
9 Robby Gordon RC	.20	.50
10 Rick Mast	.05	.15
11 Geoff Bodine	.05	.15
12 Sterling Marlin	.20	.50
13 Jeff Burton	.20	.50
14 Steve Park RC	1.00	2.00
15 Darrell Waltrip	.10	.30
16 Randy LaJoie	.05	.15
17 Mark Martin	.50	1.25
18 Bobby Hamilton	.05	.15
19 Ernie Irvan	.10	.30
20 Steve Grissom	.05	.15
21 Ted Musgrave	.05	.15
22 Jeremy Mayfield	.10	.30
23 Ricky Rudd	.20	.50
24 Ricky Craven	.05	.15
25 Hut Stricklin	.05	.15
26 Morgan Shepherd	.05	.15
27 Brett Bodine	.05	.15
28 John Andretti	.05	.15
29 Robert Pressley	.05	.15
30 Dick Trickle	.05	.15
31 Ernie Irvan's Car	.05	.15
32 Robby Gordon's Car	.10	.30
33 Bobby Hamilton's Car	.02	.10
34 Dale Jarrett's Car	.10	.30
35 Rusty Wallace's Car	.20	.50
36 Dale Earnhardt's Car	.60	1.50
37 Sterling Marlin's Car	.05	.15
38 Mark Martin's Car	.20	.50
39 Bobby Labonte's Car	.10	.30
40 Michael Waltrip's Car	.05	.15
41 D.Earnhardt J.Gordon	1.25	3.00
42 D.Jarrett E.Irvan	.30	.75
43 J.Burton R.Craven	.10	.30
44 M.Martin S.Marlin	.50	1.25
45 M.Waltrip B.Labonte	.30	.75
46 B.Hamilton K.Petty	.10	.30
47 D.Earnhardt D.Jarrett	2.00	5.00
48 D.Waltrip G.Bodine	.10	.30
49 D.Earnhardt R.Wall.Cars	.60	1.50
50 B.Labonte T.Labonte	.40	1.00

1997 Autographed Racing Autographs

This insert set features hand-signed cards from the top names in racing. It is important to note that the 56-card checklist presented below may not be complete. Some of the autographed cards distributed in packs were in the form of redemption cards or cards from the 1996 Autographed Racing product. Signed cards were randomly inserted into packs at an overall rate of 5:24.

1 John Andretti	7.50	15.00
2 Tommy Baldwin	2.00	5.00
3 Brett Bodine	3.00	8.00
4 Geoff Bodine	3.00	8.00
5 Todd Bodine	3.00	8.00
6 Jeff Burton	8.00	20.00
7 Richard Childress	7.50	15.00
8 Ricky Craven	7.50	15.00
9 Wally Dallenbach Jr.	3.00	8.00
10 Gary DeHart	2.00	5.00
11 Randy Dorton	7.50	15.00
12 Dale Earnhardt	150.00	300.00
13 Ray Evernham	7.50	15.00
14 Joe Gibbs	15.00	30.00
15 Tony Glover	2.00	5.00
16 Jeff Gordon	30.00	80.00
17 Robby Gordon	10.00	25.00
18 Andy Graves	2.00	5.00
19 Steve Grissom	3.00	8.00
20 Bobby Hamilton	10.00	25.00
21 Rick Hendrick	15.00	40.00
22 Steve Hmiel	2.00	5.00
23 Ron Hornaday Jr.	3.00	8.00
24 Ernie Irvan	10.00	25.00
25 Dale Jarrett	10.00	25.00
26 Jimmy Johnson	3.00	8.00
27 Terry Labonte	12.50	30.00
28 Bobby Labonte	6.00	15.00
29 Randy LaJoie	3.00	8.00
30 Jimmy Makar	2.00	5.00
31 Sterling Marlin	6.00	15.00
32 Dave Marcis	7.50	15.00
33 Mark Martin	15.00	40.00
34 Rick Mast	3.00	8.00
35 Jeremy Mayfield	7.50	15.00
36 Kenny Mayne	2.00	5.00
37 Larry McReynolds	7.50	15.00
38 Ted Musgrave	3.00	8.00
39 Buddy Parrott	2.00	5.00
40 Todd Parrott	2.00	5.00
41 Robin Pemberton	2.00	5.00
42 Kyle Petty	7.50	15.00
43 Shelton Pittman	2.00	5.00
44 Robert Pressley	3.00	8.00
45 Dr. Jerry Punch	2.00	5.00
46 Harry Raimer	2.00	5.00
47 Dave Rezendes	3.00	8.00
48 Greg Sacks	3.00	8.00
49 Morgan Shepherd	3.00	8.00
50 Hut Stricklin	3.00	8.00
51 Dick Trickle	3.00	8.00
52 Kenny Wallace	4.00	10.00
53 Mike Wallace	7.50	15.00
54 Darrell Waltrip	12.50	30.00
55 Michael Waltrip	7.50	15.00
56 Wood Brothers	2.00	5.00

1997 Autographed Racing Mayne Street

This 30-card insert set is named for ESPN annoucer Kenny Mayne. The card backs features his commentary on each driver. The cards were randomly inserted into hobby packs at a ratio of 1:4.

COMPLETE SET (30)	20.00	75.00
KM1 Dale Earnhardt	8.00	20.00
KM2 Kyle Petty	1.00	2.50
KM3 Terry Labonte	1.50	4.00
KM4 Jeff Gordon	5.00	12.00
KM5 Michael Waltrip	1.00	2.50
KM6 Dale Jarrett	3.00	8.00
KM7 Lake Speed	.50	1.25
KM8 Bobby Labonte	3.00	8.00
KM9 Robby Gordon	1.50	4.00
KM10 Rick Mast	.50	1.25
KM11 Geoff Bodine	.50	1.25
KM12 Sterling Marlin	1.50	4.00
KM13 Jeff Burton	1.50	4.00
KM14 Steve Park	6.00	15.00
KM15 Darrell Waltrip	1.00	2.50
KM16 Randy LaJoie	.50	1.25
KM17 Mark Martin	4.00	10.00
KM18 Bobby Hamilton	.50	1.25
KM19 Ernie Irvan	1.00	2.50
KM20 Steve Grissom	.50	1.25
KM21 Ted Musgrave	.50	1.25
KM22 Jeremy Mayfield	1.00	2.50
KM23 Ricky Rudd	1.50	4.00
KM24 Ricky Craven	.50	1.25
KM25 Hut Stricklin	.50	1.25
KM26 Morgan Shepherd	.50	1.25
KM27 Brett Bodine	.50	1.25
KM28 John Andretti	.50	1.25
KM29 Robert Pressley	.50	1.25
KM30 Dick Trickle	.50	1.25

1997 Autographed Racing Take the Checkered Flag

The 2-card set features hand-numbered cards commemorating the winner of each leg of the Winston Million. Each card contains a portion of a real checkered flag. The cards were randomly inserted into hobby packs at a ratio of 1:240.

TF1 Jeff Gordon/325	20.00	50.00
TF2 Mark Martin	15.00	40.00

2004 Bass Pro Shops Racing

1 Dale Earnhardt Jr.		
2 Martin Truex Jr.	3.00	6.00
3 D.Earnhardt Jr. M.Truex Jr.	5.00	10.00

1986 Big League Cards Alan Kulwicki Quincy's

This card was produced by Big League Cards for the Quincy's Steakhouse Racing Team and driver Alan Kulwicki. It features a color image of Kulwicki on the front along with the Big League Cards name above the photo and the year and Quincy's title below. The light blue colored cardback has contact information for the Steakhouse at the top and a brief bio on Kulwicki followed by a description of his chase for 1986 NASCAR Rookie of the Year honors. A 1985 copyright line appears on the back as well. The card was issued at the 1986 Daytona 500 primarily to media members in their media information kits.

NNO Alan Kulwicki	25.00	60.00

1998 Big League Cards Creative Images

This 10-card promotional set was produced by Big League Cards and distributed by Creative Images of Vermont. Each card was produced in the typical Big League Cards design along with a local Vermont sponsor logo in the lower right corner of the cardfront. Most of these cards were produced earlier than 1998 and often include a copyright date other than 1998. The Creative Images name, address, and phone number are included on the cardback at the bottom edge. Reportedly, only 3,000 sets were produced and they were intially offered in a mail-order advertisement for $29.95 per set.

COMPLETE SET (10)	12.00	30.00
7 Darrell Waltrip	1.50	4.00
8 Ernie Irvan	1.50	4.00
9 Mark Martin	2.50	6.00
10 Dale Jarrett	2.00	5.00
11 Bill Elliott	2.00	5.00
12 Terry Labonte	2.00	5.00
13 Ricky Rudd	1.50	4.00
13 Rusty Wallace	2.50	6.00
29 Dale Earnhardt	6.00	15.00
30 Jeff Gordon	3.00	8.00

1992 Bikers of the Racing Scene

Eagle Productions produced this set featuring participants and other personalities associated with the First Annual Winston Cup Harley Ride in September 1992. The cards feature the Winston Cup personality with their favorite Harley motorcyle. Each checklist card carries the set production number which was limited to 90,000.

COMPLETE SET (34)	3.20	8.00
1 Richard Petty	.40	1.00
2 Pre-Dawn	.05	.10
3 Richard Childress	.12	.30
4 Spook Caspers	.07	.20
5 Kirk Shelmerdine	.07	.20
6 Danny Myers	.07	.20
7 Paul Andrews	.07	.20
8 Will Lind	.07	.20
9 Jerry Huskins Randy Butner	.07	.20
10 Jimmy Cox	.07	.20
11 Danny Culler	.07	.20
12 Dennis Dawson	.07	.20
13 Bryan Dorsey	.07	.20
14 Dan Gatewood	.07	.20
15 Kevin Youngblood	.07	.20
16 John Hall	.07	.20
17 Jimmy Means	.07	.20
18 Robin Metdepenningen	.07	.20
19 Gary Nelson	.07	.20
20 Tommy Rigsbee	.07	.20
21 Jimmy Shore	.07	.20
22 Marty Tharpe	.07	.20
23 Danny West	.07	.20
24 Mike McQueen Darren Jolly	.07	.20
25 Kyle Petty	.25	.60
26 Waddell Wilson	.07	.20
27 Steve Barkdoll	.12	.30
28 Dick Brooks	.07	.20
29 Tracy Leslie	.07	.20
30 Michael Waltrip	.15	.40
31 BethBruce M.Walt R.Wils Child. D.Culler D.Tilley	.15	.40
32 Rick Wilson	.07	.20
33 Harry Gant	.10	.25
34 Checklist Card	.05	.10
P1 Rick Wilson Promo	.07	.20

2004 Blue Bonnet Bobby Labonte

This 4-card set was issued on packages of Blue Bonnet in late 2004. The 4 cards all feature Bobby Labonte with different accomplishments throughout his career. The cards were meant to be cut off of the box.

COMPLETE SET (4)	2.50	6.00
1 Bobby Labonte 21 wins	.60	1.50
2 Bobby Labonte '00 Champion	.60	1.50
3 Bobby Labonte 26 Top 10s	.60	1.50
4 Bobby Labonte career winnings	.60	1.50

1998 Burger King Dale Earnhardt

This four card set was distributed at participating Burger King's in the Southeast section of the country.

COMPLETE SET (4)	8.00	20.00
1 Dale Earnhardt's Car	1.50	4.00
2 Dale Earnhardt	3.00	8.00
3 Dale Earnhardt's Car	1.50	4.00
4 Dale Earnhardt	3.00	8.00

1992 Card Dynamics Davey Allison

This five-card set was issued in a display box and has five polished aluminum cards that feature Davey Allison. The sets were distributed by Card Dynamics and 4,000 sets were produced. There is a numbered certificate of authenticity that comes with each set.

COMP.FACT SET (5)	15.00	40.00
COMMON CARD (1-5)	4.00	10.00

1992 Card Dynamics Harry Gant

This five-card set was issued in a display box and has five polished aluminum cards that feature Harry Gant. The sets were distributed by Card Dynamics and 4,000 sets were reportedly produced. There is a numbered certificate of authenticity that comes with each set. The set was not produced in the original quantities stated on the certificate.

COMP. FACT SET (5)	6.00	15.00
COMMON CARD (1-5)	1.50	4.00

1992 Card Dynamics Gant Oil

The 1992 Gant Oil cards were produced as promotional advertising for Gant Oil Company. The cards could be purchased for $6.00 when you bought gas at one of the 28 participating Gant Oil stations through out North Carolina. There was one driver available every month over the course of the 10 month long NASCAR season (February to November). Each card has a production serial number and are made of polished aluminum. Cards are unnumbered but have been numbered below in order of release with number of cards produced following each driver's name.

COMPLETE SET (10)	25.00	60.00
1 Darrell Waltrip/4000	3.00	8.00
2 Harry Gant/4000	1.50	4.00
3 Sterling Marlin/4000	2.00	5.00
4 Rusty Wallace/4000	5.00	12.00
5 Davey Allison/5000	3.00	8.00
6 Mark Martin/4000	6.00	15.00
7 Ernie Irvan/4000	3.00	8.00
8 Kyle Petty/4000	4.00	10.00
9 Bill Elliott/5000	4.00	10.00
10 Alan Kulwicki/5000	4.00	10.00

1992 Card Dynamics Jerry Glanville

This five-card set was issued in a display box and has five polished aluminum cards that feature Jerry Glanville. The sets were distributed by Card Dynamics and 5,000 sets were reportedly produced. There is a numbered certificate of authenticity that comes with each set.

COMP. FACT SET (5)	6.00	15.00
COMMON CARD (1-5)	1.50	4.00

1992 Card Dynamics Ernie Irvan

This five-card set was issued in a display box and has five polished aluminum cards that feature Ernie Irvan. The sets were distributed by Card Dynamics and 2,000 sets were reportedly produced. There is a numbered certificate of authenticity that comes with each set. The set was not produced in the original quantities stated on the certificate.

COMP. FACT SET (5)	10.00	25.00
COMMON CARD (1-5)	2.50	6.00

1992 Card Dynamics Alan Kulwicki

This five-card set was issued in a display box and has five polished aluminum cards that feature Alan Kulwicki. The sets were distributed by Card Dynamics and 4,000 sets were reportedly produced. There is a numbered certificate of authenticity that comes with each set. The set was not produced in the original quantities stated on the certificate.

COMP. FACT SET (5) 12.00 30.00
COMMON CARD (1-5) 3.00 8.00

1992 Card Dynamics Kyle Petty

This five-card set was issued in a display box and has five polished aluminum cards that feature Kyle Petty. The sets were distributed by Card Dynamics and 4,000 sets were reportedly produced. There is a numbered certificate of authenticity that comes with each set. The set was not produced in the original quantities stated on the certificate.

COMP. FACT SET (5) 8.00 20.00
COMMON CARD (1-5) 2.00 5.00

1992 Card Dynamics Ricky Rudd

This five-card set was issued in a display box and has five polished aluminum cards that feature Ricky Rudd. The sets were distributed by Card Dynamics and 4,000 sets were reportedly produced. There is a numbered certificate of authenticity that comes with each set. The set was not produced in the original quantities stated on the certificate.

COMP. FACT SET (5) 8.00 20.00
COMMON CARD (1-5) 1.50 4.00

1992 Card Dynamics Rusty Wallace

This five-card set was issued in a display box and has five polished aluminum cards that feature Rusty Wallace. The sets were distributed by Card Dynamics and 2,000 sets were reportedly produced. There is a numbered certificate of authenticity that comes with each set. The set was not produced in the original quantities stated on the certificate.

COMP. FACT SET (5) 15.00 40.00
COMMON CARD (1-5) 4.00 10.00

1992 Card Dynamics Darrell Waltrip

This five-card set was issued in a display box and has five polished aluminum cards that feature Darrell Waltrip. The sets were distributed by Card Dynamics and 4,000 sets were reportedly produced. There is a numbered certificate of authenticity that comes with each set.

COMP.FACT SET (5) 10.00 25.00
COMMON CARD (1-5) 2.50 6.00

1992 Card Dynamics Michael Waltrip

This five-card set was issued in a display box and has five polished aluminum cards that feature Michael Waltrip. The sets were distributed by Card Dynamics and 2,000 sets were reportedly produced. There is a numbered certificate of authenticity that comes with each set. The sets were not produced in the original quantities (15,000) stated on the certificate.

COMP. FACT SET (5) 6.00 15.00
COMMON CARD (1-5) 1.25 3.00

1994 Card Dynamics Black Top Busch Series

This 10-card set was made exclusively for Black Top Racing in King, North Carolina. The set features some of the best NASCAR Winston Cup drivers to race in the Busch series. 5,000 of each card was made.

COMPLETE SET (10) 32.00 80.00
1 Bobby Labonte 2.50 6.00
2 Jeff Gordon 6.00 15.00
3 Harry Gant 1.25 3.00
4 Dale Earnhardt 10.00 25.00
5 Terry Labonte 1.50 4.00
6 Robert Pressley 1.25 3.00
7 Mark Martin 4.00 10.00
8 Alan Kulwicki 2.50 6.00
9 Ernie Irvan 1.50 4.00
10 Steve Grissom 1.00 2.50

1993 Card Dynamics Alliance Racing Daytona

This three-card set was sold to dealers who attended the Alliance Racing dealers meeting at Daytona Beach on February 11, 1993, during SpeedWeek. There were 999 of the sets produced with each one coming in a blue display box. There was a sequentially numbered certificate in each set. The promo cards were given away as door prizes at the meeting. Only 99 promo sets were produced.

COMPLETE SET (3) 12.00 30.00
1 Robert Pressley 5.00 12.00
2 Robert Pressley's Car 4.00 10.00
3 Ricky Pearson 5.00 12.00

1993-95 Card Dynamics Double Eagle Postcards

This nine-card postcard size set was released in separate series. The first series consisted of five cards and was released in 1993, the second series consisted of two cards and was released in 1994. The third series consisted of two cards and was released in 1995. Each card was produced in quantities of 500 each. The cards were made exclusively for Double Eagle Racing of Asheboro, North Carolina. The cards are unnumbered and are in order of release below. Cards 1-5 are series one cards, 6 and 7 are series two and cards 8 and 9 are series three.

COMPLETE SET (9) 200.00 500.00
1 Jeff Gordon 40.00 100.00
Baby Ruth
2 Rusty Wallace 30.00 80.00
3 Dale Earnhardt 75.00 150.00
4 Alan Kulwicki 25.00 60.00
5 Ernie Irvan 20.00 50.00
6 Harry Gant 12.50 30.00
7 Jeff Gordon 40.00 100.00
DuPont
8 Mark Martin 30.00 80.00
9 Geoff Bodine 12.50 30.00

1993 Card Dynamics Gant Oil

The 1993 Gant Oil cards were produced as promotional advertising for Gant Oil Company. The cards could be purchased for $8.00 when you bought gas at one of the participating Gant Oil stations throughout North Carolina. There was one driver available every month over the course of the 10 month long NASCAR season (February to November). Each card has a production serial number and is made of polished aluminum. There were 6,000 of each card produced.

COMPLETE SET (10) 25.00 60.00
1 Richard Petty 5.00 12.00
2 Bill Elliott 3.00 8.00
3 Rusty Wallace 5.00 12.00
4 Geoff Bodine 1.50 4.00
5 Harry Gant 1.50 4.00
6 Jeff Gordon 8.00 20.00
7 Kyle Petty 1.50 4.00
8 Dale Earnhardt 12.00 30.00
9 Dale Jarrett 3.00 8.00
10 Alan Kulwicki 4.00 10.00

1993-95 Card Dynamics North State Chevrolet

This three-card set was issued over three consecutive years, 1993-1995. The cards were made specifically for North State Chevrolet in Greensboro, North Carolina. The Dale Earnhardt card was produced in shorter quantities due to distribution through a competitior of Dale Earnhardt Chevrolet. There are 2,000 of each of the Ernie Irvan and Harry Gant. There are 650 of the Dale Earnhardt card. The cards are unnumbered, but are numbered and listed below in the order of year they were released.

COMPLETE SET (3) 125.00 250.00
1 Ernie Irvan 18.00 40.00
2 Dale Earnhardt 100.00 175.00
3 Harry Gant 18.00 40.00

1993 Card Dynamics Robert Pressley

This one-card and die-cast combination piece was sold to Alliance Fan Club members. There were 2,759 sets produced. Each piece comes in a display box and with a certificate of authenticity.

1 Robert Pressley 6.00 15.00
with die-cast car

1993 Card Dynamics Robert Pressley Postcard

This postcard was sold to Alliance Fan Club members at an open house meeting in Arden, North Carolina. There were 500 produced.

1 Robert Pressley 6.00 15.00

1993 Card Dynamics Quik Chek

The 1993 Quik Chek cards were produced as promotional advertising for Quik Chek Food and Gas Marts. The cards could be purchased for $6.00 when you bought gas at a Quik Chek. There was one driver available every month over the course of the 10 month long NASCAR season (February to November). Each card has a production serial number and was made on polished aluminum. Cards are unnumbered, but have been numbered below in order of release with number of cards produced following each drivers name.

COMPLETE SET (10) 25.00 60.00
1 Alan Kulwicki/7000 4.00 10.00
2 Harry Gant/5000 1.50 4.00
3 Richard Petty/5000 5.00 12.00
4 Bill Elliott/5000 3.00 8.00
5 Rusty Wallace/5000 5.00 12.00
6 Geoff Bodine/5000 1.50 4.00
7 Kyle Petty/5000 1.50 4.00
8 Dale Earnhardt/7000 12.00 30.00
9 Jeff Gordon/7000 8.00 20.00
10 Mark Martin/5000 5.00 12.00

1994 Card Dynamics Double Eagle Dale Earnhardt

This six-card set was made by Card Dynamics exclusively for Double Eagle Racing in Asheboro, North Carolina. The set features Dale's career from his 1979 Rookie of the Year award to his 1991 Winston Cup title. There were 5,000 of each polished aluminum card made. The cards are unnumbered but arranged below in order of the year they feature.

COMPLETE SET (6) 35.00 75.00
COMMON CARD 6.00 15.00

1994 Card Dynamics Gant Oil

The 1994 Gant Oil cards were produced as promotional advertising for Gant Oil Company. The cards could be purchased for $8.00 when you bought gas at one of the participating Gant Oil stations throughout North Carolina. There was one driver available every month over the course of the 10 month long NASCAR season (February to November). Each card has a production serial number and is made of polished aluminum. There were 6,000 of each card produced. Cards are unnumbered, but have been numbered below in order of release.

COMPLETE SET (10) 25.00 60.00
1 Harry Gant 1.50 4.00
2 Rusty Wallace 6.00 15.00
3 Ernie Irvan 2.00 5.00
4 Jeff Gordon 8.00 20.00
5 Hut Stricklin 2.00 5.00
6 Darrell Waltrip 3.00 8.00
7 Morgan Shepherd 2.00 5.00
8 Mark Martin 5.00 12.00
9 Bobby Labonte 3.00 8.00
10 Ken Schrader 1.25 3.00

1994 Card Dynamics Jeff Gordon Fan Club

This three-card set features Jeff's younger years. The three cards are made of polished aluminum and come in a display box. There were 1,200 sets made and they were sold by the Jeff Gordon Fan Club.

COMP. FACT SET (3) 20.00 50.00
COMMON CARD 7.50 20.00

1994 Card Dynamics Montgomery Motors

This six-card set was available through Montgomery Motors located in Troy, North Carolina. The cards were given away free to any person who test drove a new Ford, Lincoln or Mercury. You could also purchase the cards for $30.00 from the dealership. There were 1,000 silver leaf versions of each card made. A gold leaf parallel version of each card was also made. There were 200 of each of these and they were signed by the drivers.

COMPLETE SET (3) 40.00 100.00
1 Ernie Irvan 12.50 30.00
2 Mark Martin 15.00 40.00
3 Rusty Wallace 12.50 30.00

1994 Card Dynamics Texas Pete Joe Nemechek

This one-card and die-cast combination piece was produced in a quantity of 15,000. The pieces were available to those who sent in labels from cans of Texas Pete's Chili No Beans. The item comes in a white display box with each box sequentially numbered of 15,000 on the front. A letter of authenticity also accompanies the piece and can be found inside the box.

1 Joe Nemechek 4.00 10.00
with die-cast car

1995 Card Dynamics Allsports Postcards

These two postcards were issued through the featured driver's fan club. Your club membership was free when you ordered the postcard. There were 500 of each postcard produced. Each card was hand signed and individually numbered.

1 Steve Grissom 15.00 30.00
2 Shawna Robinson 25.00 50.00

2008 Americana Celebrity Cuts

COMPLETE SET (100) 125.00 200.00
STATED PRINT RUN 499 SERIAL #'d SETS
*CENTURY SILVER/50: .6X TO 1.5X BASE
*CENTURY GOLD/25: .75X TO 2X BASE
UNPRICED CENTURY PLATINUM #'d TO 1
8 Bobby Allison 2.00 5.00
73 Richard Petty 2.00 5.00

2008 Americana Celebrity Cuts Century Material

RANDOM INSERTS IN PACKS
PRINT RUNS B/WN 5-100 COPIES
NO PRICING ON QTY OF 5
8 Bobby Allison/100 4.00 10.00
73 Richard Petty/100 6.00 15.00

2008 Americana Celebrity Cuts Century Material Combo

RANDOM INSERTS IN PACKS
PRINT RUNS B/WN 5-50 COPIES PER
NO PRICING ON QTY OF 10 OR LESS
8 Bobby Allison/50 6.00 15.00
73 Richard Petty/50 8.00 20.00

2008 Americana Celebrity Cuts Century Signature Gold

RANDOM INSERTS IN PACKS
PRINT RUNS B/WN 1-200 COPIES PER
NO PRICING ON QTY OF 14 OR LESS
8 Bobby Allison/200 10.00 25.00
73 Richard Petty/200 25.00 50.00

2008 Americana Celebrity Cuts Century Signature Material

RANDOM INSERTS IN PACKS
PRINT RUNS B/WN 1-50 COPIES PER
NO PRICING ON QTY OF 14 OR LESS
8 Bobby Allison/50 15.00 40.00
73 Richard Petty/50 25.00 60.00

2008 Americana Celebrity Cuts Century Signature Material Prime

8 Bobby Allison/4

2016 Certified

1 Kevin Harvick .50 1.25
2 Kyle Busch .50 1.25
3 Kurt Busch .30 .75
4 Carl Edwards .40 1.00
5 Jimmie Johnson .60 1.50
6 Brad Keselowski .50 1.25
7 Joey Logano .40 1.00
8 Martin Truex Jr. .30 .75
9 Austin Dillon .50 1.25
10 Dale Earnhardt Jr. .75 2.00
11 Matt Kenseth .40 1.00
12 Denny Hamlin .40 1.00
13 Jamie McMurray .40 1.00
14 Kasey Kahne .40 1.00
15 A.J. Allmendinger .40 1.00
16 Ryan Newman .30 .75
17 Trevor Bayne .40 1.00
18 Ricky Stenhouse Jr. .40 1.00
19 Kyle Larson .60 1.50
20 Paul Menard .25 .60
21 Danica Patrick .75 2.00
22 Greg Biffle .30 .75
23 Aric Almirola .30 .75
24 Clint Bowyer .40 1.00
25 Landon Cassill .30 .75
26 Casey Mears .25 .60
27 David Ragan .30 .75
28 Michael McDowell .40 1.00
29 Regan Smith .30 .75
30 Matt DiBenedetto .25 .60
31 Michael Annett .40 1.00
32 Cole Whitt .30 .75
33 Tony Stewart .60 1.50
34 Alex Bowman .40 1.00
35 Josh Wise .25 .60
36 Bobby Labonte .40 1.00
37 David Gilliland .25 .60
38 Reed Sorenson .25 .60
39 Morgan Shepherd .40 1.00
40 Ty Dillon .40 1.00
41 Brendan Gaughan .25 .60
42 Daniel Suarez .75 2.00
43 Dylan Lupton .40 1.00
44 Jeb Burton .30 .75
45 Ryan Reed .40 1.00
46 Daniel Hemric .40 1.00
47 John Hunter Nemechek .30 .75
48 Ryan Truex .30 .75
49 Tyler Reddick .40 1.00
50 Dale Earnhardt Jr .75 2.00
51 Jimmie Johnson .60 1.50
52 Kevin Harvick .50 1.25
53 Tony Stewart .60 1.50
54 Danica Patrick .75 2.00
55 Kyle Busch .50 1.25
56 Carl Edwards .40 1.00
57 Joey Logano .40 1.00
58 Martin Truex Jr. .30 .75
59 Brad Keselowski .50 1.25
60 Matt Kenseth .40 1.00
61 Kasey Kahne .40 1.00
62 Denny Hamlin .40 1.00
63 Bill Elliott .60 1.50
64 Bobby Allison .30 .75
65 Danny Myers .60 1.50
66 Darrell Waltrip .60 1.50
67 David Pearson .40 1.00
68 Donnie Allison .30 .75
69 Ernie Irvan .40 1.00
70 Fred Lorenzen .25 .60
71 Geoff Bodine .25 .60
72 Harry Gant .30 .75
73 Jack Ingram .25 .60
74 Junior Johnson .40 1.00
75 Dave Marcis .30 .75
76 Mark Martin .40 1.00
77 Jeff Burton .30 .75
78 Ned Jarrett .30 .75
79 Glen Wood .25 .60
80 Ricky Craven .25 .60
81 Richard Petty .60 1.50
82 Rusty Wallace .40 1.00
83 Terry Labonte .40 1.00
84 Rico Abreu .50 1.25
85 Christopher Bell .50 1.25
86 William Byron .60 1.50
87 Cole Custer .40 1.00
88 Bubba Wallace .40 1.00
89 Elliott Sadler .25 .60
90 Ben Rhodes .25 .60
91 J.J. Yeley .25 .60
92 Nicole Behar .60 1.50
93 Brennan Poole .40 1.00
94 Cameron Hayley .30 .75
95 Garrett Smithley .40 1.00
96 Ahnna Parkhurst .60 1.50
97 Erik Jones .60 1.50
98 Brandon Jones .40 1.00
99 Kate Dallenbach .75 2.00
100 Collin Cabre .30 .75
101 Chase Elliott FIRE AU/99 25.00 60.00
102 Ryan Blaney FIRE AU/99 12.00 30.00
103 Brian Scott FIRE AU/99 4.00 10.00
104 Chris Buescher FIRE AU/199 4.00 10.00
105 Jeffrey Earnhardt FIRE AU/199 5.00 12.00

2016 Certified Mirror Gold

*GOLD/25: 1.5X TO 4X BASIC INSERTS

2016 Certified Mirror Silver

*SILVER: 1X TO 2.5X BASIC CARDS

2016 Certified Epix

*ORANGE/99: .5X TO 1.2X BASIC INSERTS
*SILVER/99: .5X TO 1.2X BASIC INSERTS
*RED/75: .5X TO 1.2X BASIC INSERTS
*BLUE/50: .6X TO 1.5X BASIC INSERTS
*GOLD/25: .8X TO 2X BASIC INSERTS
1 Jimmie Johnson 3.00 8.00
2 Dale Earnhardt Jr. 4.00 10.00
3 Tony Stewart 3.00 8.00
4 Kevin Harvick 2.50 6.00
5 Danica Patrick 4.00 10.00
6 Chase Elliott 2.50 6.00
7 Kasey Kahne 2.00 5.00
8 Matt Kenseth 2.00 5.00
9 Carl Edwards 2.00 5.00
10 Kyle Busch 2.50 6.00
11 Joey Logano 2.00 5.00
12 Martin Truex Jr. 1.50 4.00
13 Denny Hamlin 2.00 5.00
14 Clint Bowyer 2.00 5.00
15 Terry Labonte 2.00 5.00
16 Rusty Wallace 2.00 5.00
17 Mark Martin 2.00 5.00
18 Richard Petty 3.00 8.00
19 Harry Gant 1.50 4.00
20 David Pearson 2.00 5.00

2016 Certified Famed Fabrics

STATED PRINT RUN 199-299 SER.#'d SETS
1 Mark Martin/199 4.00 10.00
3 Tony Stewart/299 6.00 15.00

2016 Certified Gold Team

*ORANGE/99: .5X TO 1.2X BASIC INSERTS
*SILVER/99: .5X TO 1.2X BASIC INSERTS
*RED/75: .5X TO 1.2X BASIC INSERTS
*BLUE/50: .6X TO 1.5X BASIC INSERTS
*GOLD/25: .8X TO 2X BASIC INSERTS
1 Tony Stewart 3.00 8.00
2 Rusty Wallace 2.00 5.00
3 David Pearson 2.00 5.00
4 Kevin Harvick 2.50 6.00
5 Terry Labonte 2.00 5.00
6 Mark Martin 2.00 5.00
7 Richard Petty 3.00 8.00
8 Dale Earnhardt Jr 4.00 10.00
9 Junior Johnson 2.00 5.00
10 Jimmie Johnson 3.00 8.00
11 Carl Edwards 2.00 5.00
12 Kurt Busch 1.50 4.00
13 Joey Logano 2.00 5.00
14 Kasey Kahne 2.00 5.00
15 Brad Keselowski 2.50 6.00
16 Darrell Waltrip 3.00 8.00
17 Matt Kenseth 2.00 5.00
18 Kyle Busch 2.50 6.00
19 Danica Patrick 4.00 10.00
20 Clint Bowyer 2.00 5.00

2016 Certified Legends

*ORANGE/99: .5X TO 1.2X BASIC INSERTS
*SILVER/99: .5X TO 1.2X BASIC INSERTS
*RED/75: .5X TO 1.2X BASIC INSERTS
*BLUE/50: .6X TO 1.5X BASIC INSERTS
*GOLD/25: .8X TO 2X BASIC INSERTS
1 Dave Marcis 1.50 4.00
2 Richard Petty 3.00 8.00
3 Tony Stewart 3.00 8.00
4 Mark Martin 2.00 5.00
5 Rusty Wallace 2.00 5.00
6 David Pearson 2.00 5.00
7 Bill Elliott 3.00 8.00
8 Terry Labonte 2.00 5.00
9 Ned Jarrett 1.50 4.00
10 Bobby Allison 1.50 4.00
11 Darrell Waltrip 3.00 8.00
12 Donnie Allison 1.50 4.00
13 Ernie Irvan 2.00 5.00
14 Fred Lorenzen 1.25 3.00
15 Harry Gant 1.50 4.00
16 Glen Wood 1.25 3.00
17 Geoff Bodine 1.25 3.00
18 Jack Ingram 1.25 3.00
19 Jeff Burton 1.50 4.00
20 Michael Waltrip 2.00 5.00

2016 Certified Potential Signatures

1 Austin Dillon/30 10.00 25.00
2 Brandon Jones/175 4.00 10.00
3 Austin Theriault/200 3.00 8.00
4 Chase Elliott/25 40.00 80.00
5 Cameron Hayley/299 3.00 8.00
6 Christopher Bell/175 5.00 12.00
7 Collin Cabre/29 6.00 15.00
8 Daniel Hemric/125 5.00 12.00
9 Daniel Suarez/125 12.00 30.00
10 Bubba Wallace/85 5.00 12.00
12 Erik Jones/165 10.00 25.00
13 Jeb Burton/299 3.00 8.00
14 Cole Custer/287 4.00 10.00
15 John Hunter Nemechek/125 4.00 10.00
16 Kate Dallenbach/35 12.00 30.00
17 Kyle Benjamin/39 6.00 15.00
18 Garrett Smithley/299 4.00 10.00
19 Landon Cassill/49 5.00 12.00
20 Jeremy Clements/250 3.00 8.00
21 Michael Annett/99 5.00 12.00
22 Ricky Stenhouse Jr./99 5.00 12.00
23 Rico Abreu/149 6.00 15.00
24 Ruben Garcia Jr./49 4.00 10.00
25 Jesse Little/250 3.00 8.00
26 Ryan Reed/60 6.00 15.00
27 Ryan Truex/99 4.00 10.00
28 Nicole Behar/299 6.00 15.00
29 Ty Dillon/190 4.00 10.00
30 Tyler Reddick/170 4.00 10.00
31 William Byron/49 25.00 50.00
32 T.J. Bell/135 3.00 8.00
33 Alex Bowman/299 4.00 10.00
34 Paul Menard/30 5.00 12.00
35 Ahnna Parkhurst/299 10.00 25.00

2016 Certified Potential Signatures Mirror Blue

*BLUE/35-50: .6X TO 1.5X BASIC AU/165-299
*BLUE/35-50: .5X TO 1.2X BASIC AU/85-149
*BLUE/25-30: .5X TO 1.2X BASIC AU/35-60
*BLUE/15-20: .8X TO 2X BASIC AU/85-149
*BLUE/15-20: .6X TO 1.5X BASIC AU/35-60
*BLUE/15-20: .5X TO 1.2X BASIC AU/25-30

2016 Certified Potential Signatures Mirror Gold

*GOLD/25: .8X TO 2X BASIC AU/165-299
*GOLD/25: .6X TO 1.5X BASIC AU/85-149
*GOLD/15: .8X TO 2X BASIC AU/85-149
*GOLD/15: .6X TO 1.5X BASIC AU/35-60
*GOLD/15: .5X TO 1.2X BASIC AU/25-30

2016 Certified Potential Signatures Mirror Orange

*ORANGE/75-149: .5X TO 1.2X BASIC AU/165-299
*ORANGE/75-149: .4X TO 1X BASIC AU/85-149
*ORANGE/75-149: .25X TO .6X BASIC AU/25-30
*ORANGE/49-60: .6X TO 1.5X BASIC AU/165-299
*ORANGE/25-26: .8X TO 2X BASIC AU/165-299
*ORANGE/25-26: .6X TO 1.5X BASIC AU/85-149
*ORANGE/25-26: .5X TO 1.2X BASIC AU/35-60

2016 Certified Potential Signatures Mirror Red

*RED/75-99: .5X TO 1.2X BASIC AU/165-299
*RED/75-99: .4X TO 1X BASIC AU/85-149
*RED/35-50: .6X TO 1.5X BASIC AU/165-299
*RED/35-50: .4X TO 1X BASIC AU/35-60
*RED/25: .6X TO 1.5X BASIC AU/85-149
*RED/25: .5X TO 1.2X BASIC AU/35-60
*RED/25: .4X TO 1X BASIC AU/25-30

2016 Certified Potential Signatures Mirror Silver

*SILVER/80-99: .5X TO 1.2X BASIC AU/165-299
*SILVER/80-99: .4X TO 1X BASIC AU/85-149
*SILVER/80-99: .25X TO .6X BASIC AU/25-30
*SILVER/35-50: .6X TO 1.5X BASIC AU/165-299
*SILVER/35-50: .5X TO 1.2X BASIC AU/85-149
*SILVER/35-50: .4X TO 1X BASIC AU/35-60
*SILVER/25-26: .8X TO 2X BASIC AU/165-299
*SILVER/25-26: .6X TO 1.5X BASIC AU/85-149
*SILVER/25-26: .5X TO 1.2X BASIC AU/35-60
*SILVER/15: .8X TO 2X BASIC AU/85-149

2016 Certified Signatures

1 Brad Keselowski/199 8.00 20.00
2 Brendan Gaughan/285 2.50 6.00
3 Carl Edwards/33 8.00 20.00
4 Casey Mears/149 3.00 8.00
5 Danny Myers/60 10.00 25.00
6 Clint Bowyer/85 5.00 12.00
7 Danica Patrick/65 40.00 80.00
9 Greg Biffle/199 3.00 8.00
10 Jamie McMurray/54 6.00 15.00
11 Joey Logano/35 6.00 15.00
12 Josh Wise/99 3.00 8.00
13 Kasey Kahne/50 8.00 20.00
14 Kurt Busch/139 4.00 10.00
15 Martin Truex Jr./165 3.00 8.00
16 Matt Kenseth/35 6.00 15.00
17 Ryan Newman/35 5.00 12.00
18 Bill Elliott/49 10.00 25.00
19 Terry Labonte/49 6.00 15.00
20 Harry Gant/99 4.00 10.00
21 Rusty Wallace/49 6.00 15.00
22 Bobby Allison/49 5.00 12.00
23 Bobby Labonte/49 6.00 15.00
24 Dale Earnhardt Jr./25
25 Darrell Waltrip/29 12.00 30.00
26 Donnie Allison/50 5.00 12.00
27 Ernie Irvan/75 5.00 12.00
28 Jimmie Johnson/25 30.00 60.00
29 Kevin Harvick/50 8.00 20.00
30 Kyle Busch/28 10.00 25.00
31 Mark Martin/25
32 J.J. Yeley/235 2.50 6.00
33 Elliott Sadler/299 2.50 6.00
34 Geoff Bodine/299 2.50 6.00
35 Jack Ingram/49 4.00 10.00
36 Junior Johnson/35 20.00 50.00
37 Justin Allgaier/263 3.00 8.00
38 Matt Crafton/84 3.00 8.00
39 Kyle Larson/75 12.00 30.00
40 Reed Sorenson/135 3.00 8.00
41 Matt DiBenedetto/199 2.50 6.00
42 Michael Annett/99 5.00 12.00
44 Michael McDowell/299 4.00 10.00
45 Trevor Bayne/299 4.00 10.00
46 David Ragan/261 3.00 8.00
47 Aric Almirola/204 3.00 8.00
48 Paul Menard/30 5.00 12.00
49 Regan Smith/99 4.00 10.00
50 Kyle Petty/299 3.00 8.00

2016 Certified Signatures Mirror Blue

*BLUE/35-50: .6X TO 1.5X BASIC AU/165-299
*BLUE/35-50: .5X TO 1.2X BASIC AU/75-149
*BLUE/35-50: .4X TO 1X BASIC AU/35-65
*BLUE/25-30: .6X TO 1.5X BASIC AU/75-149
*BLUE/25-30: .5X TO 1.2X BASIC AU/35-65
*BLUE/15-20: .8X TO 2X BASIC AU/75-149
*BLUE/15-20: .6X TO 1.5X BASIC AU/35-65
*BLUE/15-20: .5X TO 1.2X BASIC AU/25-33

2016 Certified Signatures Mirror Gold

*GOLD/25: .8X TO 2X BASIC AU/165-299
*GOLD/25: .6X TO 1.5X BASIC AU/75-149
*GOLD/25: .5X TO 1.2X BASIC AU/35-65
*GOLD/15-20: .8X TO 2X BASIC AU/75-149
*GOLD/15-20: .6X TO 1.5X BASIC AU/35-65
*GOLD/15-20: .5X TO 1.2X BASIC AU/25-33

2016 Certified Signatures Mirror Orange

*ORANGE/100-149: .5X TO 1.2X BASIC AU/165-299
*ORANGE/100-149: .4X TO 1X BASIC AU/75-149
*ORANGE/49-60: .6X TO 1.5X BASIC AU/165-299
*ORANGE/49-60: .5X TO 1.2X BASIC AU/75-149
*ORANGE/49-60: .3X TO .8X BASIC AU/25-33
*ORANGE/25-30: .6X TO 1.5X BASIC AU/75-149
*ORANGE/25-30: .5X TO 1.2X BASIC AU/35-65
*ORANGE/15-20: 1X TO 2.5X BASIC AU/165-299
*ORANGE/15-20: .8X TO 2X BASIC AU/75-149
*ORANGE/15-20: .6X TO 1.5X BASIC AU/35-65
*ORANGE/15-20: .5X TO 1.2X BASIC AU/25-33

2016 Certified Signatures Mirror Red

*RED/75: .5X TO 1.2X BASIC AU/165-299
*RED/75: .4X TO 1X BASIC AU/75-149
*RED/35-60: .6X TO 1.5X BASIC AU/165-299
*RED/35-60: .5X TO 1.2X BASIC AU/75-149
*RED/35-60: .6X TO 1.5X BASIC AU/165-299
*RED/25-30: .6X TO 1.5X BASIC AU/75-149
*RED/25-30: .2X TO 1.2X BASIC AU/35-65
*RED/25-30: .4X TO 1X BASIC AU/25-30
*RED/20: .6X TO 1.5X BASIC AU/35-65
*RED/20: .5X TO 1.2X BASIC AU/25-30

2016 Certified Signatures Mirror Silver

*SILVER/99: .5X TO 1.2X BASIC AU/165-299
*SILVER/99: .4X TO 1X BASIC AU/75-149
*SILVER/35-55: .6X TO 1.5X BASIC AU/165-299

*SILVER/35-55: .5X TO 1.2X BASIC AU/75-149
*SILVER/35-55: .3X TO .8X BASIC AU/25-33
*SILVER/25: .8X TO 2X BASIC AU/165-299
*SILVER/25: .6X TO 1.5X BASIC AU/75-149
*SILVER/25: .5X TO 1.2X BASIC AU/35-65
*SILVER/15-20: 1X TO 2.5X BASIC AU/165-299
*SILVER/15-20: .8X TO 2X BASIC AU/75-149
*SILVER/15-20: .6X TO 1.5X BASIC AU/35-65

2016 Certified Skills

*ORANGE/99: .5X TO 1.2X BASIC INSERTS
*SILVER/99: .5X TO 1.2X BASIC INSERTS
*RED/75: .5X TO 1.2X BASIC INSERTS
*BLUE/50: .6X TO 1.5X BASIC INSERTS
*GOLD/25: .8X TO 2X BASIC INSERTS
1 Ryan Newman 1.50 4.00
2 Jimmie Johnson 3.00 8.00
3 Tony Stewart 3.00 8.00
4 Chase Elliott 2.50 6.00
5 Kyle Busch 2.50 6.00
6 Austin Dillon 2.50 6.00
7 Joey Logano 2.00 5.00
8 Greg Biffle 1.50 4.00
9 Kevin Harvick 2.50 6.00
10 Kasey Kahne 2.00 5.00
11 Kurt Busch 1.50 4.00
12 Ricky Stenhouse Jr. 2.00 5.00
13 Ryan Blaney 1.50 4.00
14 Trevor Bayne 2.00 5.00
15 Ty Dillon 2.00 5.00
16 Danica Patrick 4.00 10.00
17 Carl Edwards 2.00 5.00
18 Denny Hamlin 2.00 5.00
19 Matt Kenseth 2.00 5.00
20 Brian Scott 1.25 3.00

2016 Certified Sprint Cup Signature Swatches

*RED/75: .5X TO 1.2X BASIC MEM AU/199
*RED/75: .4X TO 1X BASIC MEM AU/75-99
*RED/35-50: .5X TO 1.2X BASIC MEM AU/75-99
*RED/35-50: .4X TO 1X BASIC MEM AU/50-60
*RED/30: .6X TO 1.5X BASIC MEM AU/75-99
*RED/20: .5X TO 1.2X BASIC MEM AU/30
*BLUE/50: .6X TO 1.5X BASIC MEM AU/199
*BLUE/50: .5X TO 1.2X BASIC MEM AU/75-99
*BLUE/25-30: .6X TO 1.5X BASIC MEM AU/75-99
*BLUE/25-30: .5X TO 1.2X BASIC MEM AU/50-60
*BLUE/15-20: .6X TO 1.5X BASIC MEM AU/50-60
*BLUE/15-20: .5X TO 1.2X BASIC MEM AU/30
*GOLD/25: .8X TO 2X BASIC MEM AU/199
*GOLD/25: .6X TO 1.5X BASIC MEM AU/75-99
*GOLD/15: .8X TO 2X BASIC MEM AU/75-99
*GOLD/15: .6X TO 1.5X BASIC MEM AU/50-60
*ORANGE/99: .5X TO 1.2X BASIC MEM AU/199
*ORANGE/50: .5X TO 1.2X BASIC MEM AU/99
*ORANGE/15: .8X TO 2X BASIC MEM AU/99
*ORANGE/15: .6X TO 1.5X BASIC MEM AU/50
*SILVER/99: .5X TO 1.2X BASIC MEM AU/199
*SILVER/25: .6X TO 1.5X BASIC MEM AU/99
1 Carl Edwards/50 8.00 20.00
2 Casey Mears/99 4.00 10.00
3 Cole Whitt/199 4.00 10.00
4 Dale Earnhardt Jr./50 30.00 60.00
5 Danica Patrick
6 Denny Hamlin/50 8.00 20.00
7 Jamie McMurray/99 6.00 15.00
8 Jimmie Johnson/30 30.00 60.00
9 Joey Logano/60 8.00 20.00
10 Kasey Kahne/50 8.00 20.00
11 Kevin Harvick/50 10.00 25.00
12 Kyle Busch/60 10.00 25.00
13 Matt Kenseth/75 6.00 15.00
14 Ryan Newman/75 5.00 12.00
15 Austin Dillon/75 8.00 20.00

2016 Certified Sprint Cup Swatches

2 Denny Hamlin 4.00 10.00
4 Matt Kenseth 4.00 10.00
5 Ricky Stenhouse Jr. 4.00 10.00
6 Mark Martin 4.00 10.00
7 Kyle Busch 5.00 12.00
9 Carl Edwards 4.00 10.00
10 Greg Biffle 4.00 10.00
13 Aric Almirola 3.00 8.00
15 Bobby Labonte 4.00 10.00
16 David Ragan 3.00 8.00
17 Jamie McMurray 4.00 10.00
18 Kyle Larson 6.00 15.00
19 Clint Bowyer 4.00 10.00
20 Jeffrey Earnhardt 4.00 10.00
21 Martin Truex Jr. 3.00 8.00
23 Casey Mears 2.50 6.00
24 Brad Keselowski 5.00 12.00
27 Chase Elliott 5.00 12.00
28 Jimmie Johnson 6.00 15.00
29 Kasey Kahne 4.00 10.00
30 Dale Earnhardt Jr. 8.00 20.00
31 Landon Cassill 4.00 10.00
32 Ryan Blaney 3.00 8.00
33 Paul Menard 2.50 6.00
35 Trevor Bayne 4.00 10.00
36 Kevin Harvick 5.00 12.00
37 Kurt Busch 3.00 8.00
38 Regan Smith 3.00 8.00
39 Brian Scott 2.50 6.00
40 Josh Wise 2.50 6.00

2016 Certified Xfinity Materials

STATED PRINT RUN 299 SER.#'d SETS
1 Erik Jones 6.00 15.00
2 Ryan Reed 4.00 10.00
3 Jeb Burton 3.00 8.00
5 Ty Dillon 4.00 10.00
6 Daniel Suarez 8.00 20.00
7 Brandon Jones 4.00 10.00
8 Brendan Gaughan 2.50 6.00
9 Bubba Wallace 4.00 10.00

2018 Certified

*ORANGE/249: .8X TO 2X BASIC CARDS
*RED/199: .8X TO 2X BASIC CARDS
*BLUE/99: 1X TO 2.5X BASIC CARDS
*GOLD/49: 1.2X TO 3X BASIC CARDS
*MIRROR GOLD/25: 1.5X TO 4X BASIC CARDS
*PURPLE/25: 1.5X TO 4X BASIC CARDS
1 Jimmie Johnson .60 1.50
2 Paul Menard .25 .60
3 Spencer Davis .25 .60
4 Kyle Busch .50 1.25
5 Brandon Jones .25 .60
6 Collin Cabre .25 .60
7 Ryan Truex .30 .75
8 Kevin Harvick .50 1.25
9 Matt Kenseth .40 1.00
10 Michael Annett .40 1.00
11 Dale Earnhardt Jr .75 2.00
12 John Hunter Nemechek .30 .75
13 Carl Edwards .40 1.00
14 Alex Bowman .40 1.00
15 Cody Coughlin .40 1.00
16 Julia Landauer .25 .60
17 Chris Buescher .30 .75
18 Daniel Hemric .40 1.00
19 Ryan Preece .40 1.00
20 Ty Dillon .40 1.00
21 Ricky Stenhouse Jr .40 1.00
22 Matt Tifft .40 1.00
23 Chase Briscoe .60 1.50
24 Cole Rouse .60 1.50
25 Spencer Gallagher .40 1.00
26 Martin Truex Jr. .30 .75
27 Ryan Reed .40 1.00
28 Michael McDowell .40 1.00
29 Chase Elliott .50 1.25
30 Austin Dillon .50 1.25
31 Jeffrey Earnhardt .40 1.00
32 Timothy Peters .25 .60
33 Mark Martin .40 1.00
34 Tony Stewart .60 1.50
35 Garrett Smithley .40 1.00
36 T.J. Bell .25 .60
37 Ryan Blaney .30 .75
38 Brennan Poole .25 .60
39 Trevor Bayne .40 1.00
40 Wendell Chavous .40 1.00
41 Reed Sorenson .25 .60
42 Cameron Hayley .25 .60
43 Aric Almirola .30 .75
44 J.J. Yeley .25 .60
45 Justin Haley .75 2.00
46 Kurt Busch .30 .75
47 Landon Cassill .30 .75
48 David Ragan .30 .75
49 A.J. Allmendinger .40 1.00
50 Clint Bowyer .40 1.00
51 Daniel Suarez .40 1.00
52 Elliott Sadler .25 .60
53 Dakoda Armstrong .40 1.00
54 Ryan Newman .30 .75
55 Jamie McMurray .30 .75
56 Jeb Burton .30 .75
57 Jack Sprague .25 .60
58 Ross Chastain .40 1.00
59 Johnny Sauter .25 .60
60 Jeremy Clements .25 .60
61 Grant Enfinger .50 1.25
62 Erik Jones .40 1.00
63 Kasey Kahne .40 1.00
64 Justin Allgaier .30 .75
65 Blake Koch .25 .60
66 Corey LaJoie .30 .75
67 Joey Gase .25 .60
68 Dylan Lupton .25 .60
69 Denny Hamlin .40 1.00
70 Nicole Behar .40 1.00
71 Casey Mears .25 .60
72 Danica Patrick .75 2.00
73 Brad Keselowski .50 1.25
74 Kyle Benjamin .25 .60
75 Joey Logano .40 1.00
76 Cole Custer .40 1.00
77 Kyle Larson .60 1.50
78 Matt DiBenedetto .25 .60
79 Cole Whitt .30 .75
80 Austin Cindric .40 1.00
81 Tony Stewart IMM .60 1.50
82 Terry Labonte IMM .60 1.50
83 Darrell Waltrip IMM .60 1.50
84 Derrike Cope IMM .30 .75
85 Carl Edwards IMM .40 1.00
86 Dale Earnhardt Jr IMM .75 2.00
87 Junior Johnson IMM .40 1.00
88 Richard Petty IMM .60 1.50
89 Marcos Ambrose IMM .40 1.00
90 Rusty Wallace IMM .40 1.00
91 Chase Elliott CAR .50 1.25
92 Martin Truex Jr. CAR .30 .75
93 Kevin Harvick CAR .50 1.25
94 Jimmie Johnson CAR .60 1.50
95 Danica Patrick CAR .75 2.00
96 Brad Keselowski CAR .50 1.25
97 Austin Dillon CAR .50 1.25
98 Ryan Blaney CAR .30 .75
99 Joey Logano CAR .40 1.00
100 Denny Hamlin CAR .40 1.00

2018 Certified Complete Materials

*RED/199: .4X TO 1X BASIC MEM/299
*RED/99: .6X TO 1.5X BASIC MEM/499
*RED/99: .5X TO 1.2X BASIC MEM/199-299
*BLUE/49: .8X TO 2X BASIC MEM/499
*BLUE/49: .6X TO 1.5X BASIC MEM/199-299
*GOLD/25: 1X TO 2.5X BASIC MEM/499
*GOLD/25: .8X TO 2X BASIC MEM/199-299
1 Jimmie Johnson/199 6.00 15.00
2 Dale Earnhardt Jr/299 8.00 20.00
3 Kevin Harvick/199 5.00 12.00
4 Chase Elliott/299 5.00 12.00
5 Ryan Blaney/499 2.50 6.00
6 William Byron/299 4.00 10.00
7 Bubba Wallace/499 3.00 8.00
8 Martin Truex Jr./199 3.00 8.00
9 Kyle Busch/199 5.00 12.00
10 Joey Logano/299 4.00 10.00

2018 Certified Cup Swatches

*RED/199: .5X TO 1.2X BASIC MEM/399-499
*RED/199: .4X TO 1X BASIC MEM/199-299
*RED/99: .5X TO 1.2X BASIC MEM/199-299
*BLUE/49: .8X TO 2X BASIC MEM/399-499
*BLUE/49: .6X TO 1.5X BASIC MEM/199-299
*GOLD/25: 1X TO 2.5X BASIC MEM/399-499
*GOLD/25: .8X TO 2X BASIC MEM/199-299
1 Alex Bowman/499 2.50 6.00
2 Aric Almirola/499 2.00 5.00
3 Austin Dillon/499 3.00 8.00
4 Brad Keselowski/499 3.00 8.00
5 Bubba Wallace/499 2.50 6.00
6 Chase Elliott/499 3.00 8.00
8 Dale Earnhardt Jr/499 5.00 12.00
9 Daniel Suarez/499 2.50 6.00
10 Denny Hamlin/299 3.00 8.00
12 Jamie McMurray/499 2.50 6.00
13 Jimmie Johnson/499 4.00 10.00
14 Joey Logano/399 2.50 6.00
15 Kasey Kahne/399 2.50 6.00
16 Kevin Harvick/499 3.00 8.00
17 Kurt Busch/499 2.00 5.00
18 Kyle Busch/199 4.00 10.00
19 Kyle Larson/499 4.00 10.00
20 Martin Truex Jr./499 2.00 5.00
21 Paul Menard/499 1.50 4.00
22 Ricky Stenhouse Jr/499 2.50 6.00
23 Ryan Blaney/499 2.00 5.00
24 Ryan Newman/499 2.00 5.00
25 Trevor Bayne/499 2.50 6.00

2018 Certified Epix

*RED/149: .4X TO 1X BASIC INSERTS/199
*BLUE/99: .5X TO 1.2X BASIC INSERTS/199
*GOLD/49: .6X TO 1.5X BASIC INSERTS/199
*MIRROR GOLD/25: .8X TO 2X BASIC INSERTS/199
*PURPLE/25: .8X TO 2X BASIC INSERTS/199
1 Kyle Busch 2.00 5.00
2 Kasey Kahne 1.50 4.00
3 Danica Patrick 3.00 8.00
4 Austin Dillon 2.00 5.00
5 Denny Hamlin 1.50 4.00
6 Chase Elliott 2.00 5.00
7 Kevin Harvick 2.00 5.00
8 Brad Keselowski 2.00 5.00
9 Richard Petty 2.50 6.00
10 Ryan Blaney 1.25 3.00
11 Dale Earnhardt Jr 3.00 8.00
12 Jimmie Johnson 2.50 6.00
13 Kyle Larson 2.50 6.00
14 Trevor Bayne 1.50 4.00
15 Joey Logano 1.50 4.00
16 Martin Truex Jr. 1.25 3.00
17 Kurt Busch 1.25 3.00
18 Carl Edwards 1.50 4.00
19 Clint Bowyer 1.50 4.00
20 Tony Stewart 2.50 6.00

2018 Certified Fresh Faces

*RED/149: .4X TO 1X BASIC INSERTS/199
*BLUE/99: .5X TO 1.2X BASIC INSERTS/199
*GOLD/49: .6X TO 1.5X BASIC INSERTS/199
*MIRROR GOLD/25: .8X TO 2X BASIC INSERTS/199
*PURPLE/25: .8X TO 2X BASIC INSERTS/199
1 Chase Elliott 2.00 5.00
2 Ryan Blaney 1.25 3.00
3 William Byron 1.50 4.00
4 Bubba Wallace 1.50 4.00
5 Alex Bowman 1.50 4.00
6 Erik Jones 1.50 4.00
7 Ricky Stenhouse Jr 1.50 4.00
8 Kaz Grala 2.00 5.00
9 Christopher Bell 1.50 4.00
10 Tyler Reddick 1.50 4.00
11 Todd Gilliland 1.25 3.00
12 Dakoda Armstrong 1.50 4.00
13 Ty Dillon 1.50 4.00
14 Austin Dillon 2.00 5.00
15 Daniel Suarez 1.50 4.00

2018 Certified Fresh Faces Signatures

*RED/149: .4X TO 1X BASIC AU/149-299
*RED/75-99: .5X TO 1.2X BASIC AU/149-299
*RED/75-99: .4X TO 1X BASIC AU/75-99
*RED/49: .5X TO 1.2X BASIC AU/75-99
*RED/25: .5X TO 1.2X BASIC AU/50
*RED/20: .5X TO 1.2X BASIC AU/25
*BLUE/49-50: .6X TO 1.5X BASIC AU/149-299
*BLUE/49-50: .5X TO 1.2X BASIC AU/75-99
*BLUE/25: .6X TO 1.5X BASIC AU/75-99
*BLUE/20: .6X TO 1.5X BASIC AU/50
*BLUE/15: .5X TO 1.2X BASIC AU/25
*GOLD/25: .8X TO 2X BASIC AU/149-299
*GOLD/25: .6X TO 1.5X BASIC AU/75-199
*GOLD/15: .6X TO 1.5X BASIC AU/50
*GOLD/15: .5X TO 1.2X BASIC AU/25
1 Alex Bowman/25 8.00 20.00
2 Austin Dillon/25 10.00 25.00
3 Brandon Jones/99 3.00 8.00
4 Brennan Poole/199 2.50 6.00
6 Cameron Hayley/249 2.50 6.00
7 Chase Briscoe/99 8.00 20.00
8 Chase Elliott/25 12.00 30.00
10 Cole Rouse/186
11 Dakoda Armstrong/149 4.00 10.00
12 Erik Jones/50 8.00 20.00
13 Garrett Smithley/85 5.00 12.00
16 Kyle Larson/25 12.00 30.00
17 Matt Tifft/199 4.00 10.00
18 Nicole Behar/85 5.00 12.00
19 Ryan Preece/99 25.00 50.00
20 Ryan Reed/199 4.00 10.00
21 Spencer Gallagher/199 4.00 10.00
23 Tyler Reddick/99 5.00 12.00
24 Cole Custer/75 5.00 12.00
25 Ryan Truex/99 4.00 10.00

2018 Certified Materials Signatures

2 Ryan Blaney/99 10.00 25.00
3 Chase Elliott/75
5 Danica Patrick/45 30.00 60.00
6 Kevin Harvick/75
9 Erik Jones/75 8.00 20.00
12 Kyle Busch/75 8.00 20.00
13 Kyle Larson/99 10.00 25.00
14 Clint Bowyer/75 6.00 15.00
15 Ryan Newman/75 5.00 12.00

2018 Certified Materials Signatures Blue

*BLUE/42: .5X TO 1.2X BASIC MEM AU/75-99
*BLUE/25: .6X TO 1.5X BASIC MEM AU/75-99
*BLUE/15-24: .8X TO 2X BASIC MEM AU/75-99
*BLUE/15-24: .6X TO 1.5X BASIC MEM AU/45
4 Dale Earnhardt Jr/49 30.00 80.00

2018 Certified Materials Signatures Gold

*GOLD/25: .6X TO 1.5X BASIC MEM AU/75-99
*GOLD/15: .8X TO 2X BASIC MEM AU/75-99
*GOLD/15: .6X TO 1.5X BASIC MEM AU/45
3 Chase Elliott/15 60.00 125.00
4 Dale Earnhardt Jr/25 40.00 100.00

2018 Certified NEXT Signatures

*RED/149: .4X TO 1X BASIC AU/210-249
*BLUE/49-50: .6X TO 1.5X BASIC AU/210-249
*GOLD/25: .8X TO 2X BASIC AU/210-249
1 Cayden Lapcevich/210 4.00 10.00
2 Chase Cabre/210 4.00 10.00
3 Hailie Deegan/210 150.00 250.00
4 Harrison Burton/249 4.00 10.00
5 Riley Herbst/210 6.00 15.00
6 Todd Gilliland/249 5.00 12.00
7 Ty Majeski/210 10.00 25.00
8 Zane Smith/210 4.00 10.00

2018 Certified Piece of the Race

*RED/199: .5X TO 1.2X BASIC MEM/399-499
*RED/125: .4X TO 1X BASIC MEM/199-299
*RED/99: .5X TO 1.2X BASIC MEM/199-499
*BLUE/49: .8X TO 2X BASIC MEM/399-499
*BLUE/49: .6X TO 1.5X BASIC MEM/199-299
*GOLD/25: 1X TO 2.5X BASIC MEM/399-499
*GOLD/25: .8X TO 2X BASIC MEM/199-299
1 Jimmie Johnson/499 4.00 10.00
2 Dale Earnhardt Jr/199 6.00 15.00
3 Kevin Harvick/499 3.00 8.00
4 Chase Elliott/499 3.00 8.00
5 Ryan Blaney/499 2.00 5.00
6 William Byron/499 2.50 6.00
7 Bubba Wallace/499 2.50 6.00
8 Martin Truex Jr./499 2.00 5.00
9 Kyle Busch/399 3.00 8.00
10 Joey Logano/499 2.50 6.00
12 Tony Stewart/499 4.00 10.00
13 Danica Patrick/499 5.00 12.00
14 Kyle Larson/199 5.00 12.00
16 Kurt Busch/399 2.00 5.00
17 Ryan Newman/499 2.00 5.00
18 Trevor Bayne/499 2.50 6.00
19 Aric Almirola/499 2.00 5.00
20 Alex Bowman/499 2.50 6.00

2018 Certified Signature Swatches

1 Alex Bowman/99 6.00 15.00
2 Aric Almirola/99 5.00 12.00
3 Austin Dillon/49 10.00 25.00
4 Cole Custer/99 6.00 15.00
6 Daniel Suarez/99 6.00 15.00
7 Denny Hamlin/99 6.00 15.00
8 Erik Jones/75 8.00 20.00
9 Jamie McMurray/149 5.00 12.00
11 Kasey Kahne/49
12 Kurt Busch/41 6.00 15.00
13 Martin Truex Jr./78 5.00 12.00
15 Paul Menard/99 4.00 10.00
16 Ryan Blaney/99 10.00 25.00
17 Ryan Newman/75 5.00 12.00
19 Trevor Bayne/99 6.00 15.00

2018 Certified Signature Swatches Blue

*BLUE/49: .6X TO 1.5X BASIC MEM AU/149
*BLUE/49: .5X TO 1.2X BASIC MEM AU/75-99
*BLUE/25-30: .6X TO 1.5X BASIC MEM AU/75-99
*BLUE/25-30: .5X TO 1.2X BASIC MEM AU/41-49
*BLUE/20: .6X TO 1.5X BASIC MEM AU/41-49
5 Dale Earnhardt Jr/49 30.00 80.00

2018 Certified Signature Swatches Gold

*GOLD/25: .8X TO 2X BASIC MEM AU/149
*GOLD/25: .6X TO 1.5X BASIC MEM AU/75-99
*GOLD/25: .5X TO 1.2X BASIC MEM AU/41-49
*GOLD/15: .8X TO 2X BASIC MEM AU/75-99
*GOLD/15: .6X TO 1.5X BASIC MEM AU/41-49
5 Dale Earnhardt Jr/25 40.00 100.00

2018 Certified Signature Swatches Red

*RED/99: .5X TO 1.2X BASIC MEM AU/149
*RED/75-99: .4X TO 1X BASIC MEM AU/75-99
*RED/35-50: .5X TO 1.2X BASIC MEM AU/75-99
*RED/35-50: .4X TO 1X BASIC MEM AU/41-49
*RED/25-31: .6X TO 1.5X BASIC MEM AU/75-99
*RED/25-31: .5X TO 1.2X BASIC MEM AU/41-49
5 Dale Earnhardt Jr/50 40.00 80.00

2018 Certified Signatures

*RED/149: .4X TO 1X BASIC AU/149-249
*RED/75-99: .5X TO 1.2X BASIC AU/149-249
*RED/75-99: .4X TO 1X BASIC AU/75-99
*RED/44-50: .5X TO 1.2X BASIC AU/75-99
*RED/25: .5X TO 1.2X BASIC AU/49-50
*RED/25: .4X TO 1X BASIC AU/25-30
*RED/20: .5X TO 1.2X BASIC AU/25-30
*BLUE/44-50: .6X TO 1.5X BASIC AU/149-249
*BLUE/44-50: .5X TO 1.2X BASIC AU/75-99
*BLUE/25: .6X TO 1.5X BASIC AU/75-99
*BLUE/15-20: .8X TO 2X BASIC AU/75-99
*BLUE/15-20: .5X TO 1.2X BASIC AU/25-30
*GOLD/25: .8X TO 2X BASIC AU/149-249
*GOLD/25: .6X TO 1.5X BASIC AU/75-99
*GOLD/15-20: .8X TO 2X BASIC AU/75-99
*GOLD/15-20: .6X TO 1.5X BASIC AU/49-50
*GOLD/15-20: .5X TO 1.2X BASIC AU/25-30
1 Aric Almirola/49 5.00 12.00
2 Brad Keselowski/99 6.00 15.00
3 Chris Buescher/199 3.00 8.00
4 Bobby Allison/99 4.00 10.00
5 Bobby Labonte/99 5.00 12.00
6 Daniel Hemric/149 4.00 10.00
7 Daniel Suarez/30 8.00 20.00
8 David Ragan/149 3.00 8.00
9 Donnie Allison/199 3.00 8.00
10 Elliott Sadler/99 3.00 8.00
11 Jeff Burton/99 4.00 10.00
13 Jeremy Clements/85 3.00 8.00
14 John Hunter Nemechek/99 8.00 20.00
16 Justin Allgaier/249 3.00 8.00
17 Kasey Kahne/25 8.00 20.00
18 Kyle Benjamin/99 8.00 20.00
19 Kyle Petty/75 4.00 10.00
20 Lake Speed/85 3.00 8.00
21 Landon Cassill/199 3.00 8.00
22 Matt DiBenedetto/199 2.50 6.00
24 Michael Annett/249 4.00 10.00
25 Michael McDowell/249 4.00 10.00
26 Morgan Shepherd/99 5.00 12.00
27 Ned Jarrett/99 4.00 10.00
29 Reed Sorenson/199 2.50 6.00
30 Ross Chastain/99 5.00 12.00
32 Wally Dallenbach/99 3.00 8.00
33 Ward Burton/99 3.00 8.00
34 Alex Bowman/25 8.00 20.00
37 Erik Jones/50 8.00 20.00

2018 Certified Signing Sessions

*RED/75: .5X TO 1.2X BASIC AU/149-199
*RED/75: .4X TO 1X BASIC AU/85-99
*RED/35-50: .5X TO 1.2X BASIC AU/85-99
*RED/35-50: .4X TO 1X BASIC AU/49-50
*RED/25-29: .5X TO 1.2X BASIC AU/49-50
*RED/25-29: .4X TO 1X BASIC AU/25-31
*RED/15-20: .5X TO 1.2X BASIC AU/25-31
*BLUE/49-50: .6X TO 1.5X BASIC AU/149-199
*BLUE/49-50: .5X TO 1.2X BASIC AU/85-99
*BLUE/25: .6X TO 1.5X BASIC AU/85-99
*BLUE/25: .5X TO 1.2X BASIC AU/49-50
*BLUE/15-20: .6X TO 1.5X BASIC AU/49-50
*BLUE/15-20: .5X TO 1.2X BASIC AU/25-31
*GOLD/25: .8X TO 2X BASIC AU/149-199
*GOLD/25: .6X TO 1.5X BASIC AU/85-99
*GOLD/15-22: .8X TO 2X BASIC AU/85-99
*GOLD/15-22: .6X TO 1.5X BASIC AU/49-50
*GOLD/15-22: .5X TO 1.2X BASIC AU/25-31
1 Carl Edwards/99 8.00 20.00
2 Clint Bowyer/49 6.00 15.00
3 Dale Earnhardt Jr/25 50.00 100.00
4 Dale Jarrett/88 5.00 12.00
5 Danica Patrick/25 50.00 100.00
6 Denny Hamlin/49 6.00 15.00
7 Ernie Irvan/85 5.00 12.00
8 Greg Biffle/199 3.00 8.00
9 Jamie McMurray/50 6.00 15.00
12 Kenny Wallace/199 2.50 6.00
15 Kyle Busch/25 25.00 50.00
17 Marcos Ambrose/99 5.00 12.00
21 Ricky Stenhouse Jr/199 4.00 10.00
23 Ryan Newman/31 6.00 15.00
24 Terry Labonte/149 8.00 20.00
26 Trevor Bayne/49 6.00 15.00

2018 Certified Skills

*RED/149: .4X TO 1X BASIC INSERTS/199
*BLUE/99: .5X TO 1.2X BASIC INSERTS/199
*GOLD/49: .6X TO 1.5X BASIC INSERTS/199
*MIRROR GOLD/25: .8X TO 2X BASIC INSERTS/199
*PURPLE/25: .8X TO 2X BASIC INSERTS/199
1 Brad Keselowski 2.00 5.00
2 Austin Dillon 2.00 5.00
3 Kevin Harvick 2.00 5.00
4 Chase Elliott 2.00 5.00
5 Aric Almirola 1.25 3.00
6 Denny Hamlin 1.50 4.00
7 Ryan Blaney 1.25 3.00
8 Clint Bowyer 1.50 4.00
9 Ricky Stenhouse Jr 1.50 4.00
10 Kyle Busch 2.00 5.00
11 Joey Logano 1.50 4.00
12 William Byron 1.50 4.00
13 Ryan Newman 1.25 3.00
14 Kurt Busch 1.25 3.00
15 Kyle Larson 2.50 6.00
16 Bubba Wallace 1.50 4.00
17 A.J. Allmendinger 1.50 4.00
18 Jimmie Johnson 2.50 6.00
19 Martin Truex Jr. 1.25 3.00
20 Alex Bowman 1.50 4.00

2018 Certified Stars

*RED/149: .4X TO 1X BASIC INSERTS/199
*BLUE/99: .5X TO 1.2X BASIC INSERTS/199
*GOLD/49: .6X TO 1.5X BASIC INSERTS/199
*MIRROR GOLD/25: .8X TO 2X BASIC INSERTS/199
*PURPLE/25: .8X TO 2X BASIC INSERTS/199
1 Chase Elliott 2.00 5.00
2 Denny Hamlin 1.50 4.00
3 Joey Logano 1.50 4.00
4 Austin Dillon 2.00 5.00
5 Trevor Bayne 1.50 4.00
6 Danica Patrick 3.00 8.00
7 Kasey Kahne 1.50 4.00
8 Ryan Newman 1.25 3.00
9 Ryan Blaney 1.25 3.00
10 A.J. Allmendinger 1.50 4.00
11 Kevin Harvick 2.00 5.00
12 Kyle Busch 2.00 5.00
13 Clint Bowyer 1.50 4.00
14 Alex Bowman 1.50 4.00
15 Brad Keselowski 2.00 5.00
16 Daniel Suarez 1.50 4.00
17 Martin Truex Jr. 1.25 3.00
18 Jimmie Johnson 2.50 6.00
19 Kyle Larson 2.50 6.00
20 Aric Almirola 1.25 3.00
21 Jamie McMurray 1.50 4.00
22 Dale Earnhardt Jr 3.00 8.00
23 Tony Stewart 2.50 6.00
24 Carl Edwards 1.50 4.00
25 Richard Petty 2.50 6.00

2018 Certified Xfinity Materials

*RED/199: .5X TO 1.2X BASIC MEM/499
*BLUE/49: .8X TO 2X BASIC MEM/499
*GOLD/25: 1X TO 2.5X BASIC MEM/499
1 Christopher Bell 2.50 6.00
2 Kaz Grala 3.00 8.00
3 Tyler Reddick 2.50 6.00
4 Cole Custer 2.50 6.00
5 Garrett Smithley 2.50 6.00

1994 Classic Dale Earnhardt 23K Gold

1 Dale Earnhardt/10000 25.00 50.00

1995 Classic National

This 20-card multi-sport set was issued by Classic to commemorate the 16th National Sports Collectors Convention in St. Louis. The set included a certificate of limited edition, with the serial number out of 9,995 sets produced. One thousand Sprint 20-minute phone cards featuring Ki-Jana Carter and Nolan Ryan were also distributed.

COMPLETE SET (20) 8.00 20.00
NC4 Dale Earnhardt 2.00 5.00

1996 Classic

This 60-card set features the top drivers and crew members and contains many of the car and sponsor changes for the 1996 season. The first 50 cards in the set were packaged like a regular set would be. The last 10 cards in the set (51-60) were more like inserts. The SP cards were reported to come anywhere from one every 9 packs to one every 36 packs. There were no stated odds on the SP cards. The set is commonly sold without the final 10 cards in the set due to the difficulty in finding those short printed cards. There were 10 cards in each pack, 36 packs per box and 12 boxes per case. There were also Hot Boxes of Classic produced. A Hot Box yielded at least 5 inserts per pack.

COMPLETE SET (60) 15.00 40.00
COMP.SET w/o SP's (50) 5.00 12.00
COMP.SP SET (10) 10.00 30.00
1 Sterling Marlin .25 .60
2 Todd Bodine .07 .20
3 Ted Musgrave .07 .20
4 Dick Trickle .07 .20
5 Jack Roush .02 .10
6 Ricky Rudd .25 .60
7 Mike Wallace .07 .20
8 Dave Marcis .15 .40
9 Robert Pressley .07 .20
10 Ned Jarrett .07 .20
11 Jeremy Mayfield .15 .40
12 Richard Petty .25 .60
13 Kyle Petty .15 .40
14 Mark Martin .40 1.00
15 Steve Hmiel .02 .10
16 Kenny Wallace .07 .20
17 Elton Sawyer .07 .20
18 Jason Keller .07 .20
19 Larry McClure .02 .10
20 Ward Burton .15 .40
21 Shelton Pittman .02 .10
22 Larry McReynolds .02 .10
23 Robert Yates .02 .10
24 Darrell Waltrip .15 .40
25 Tony Glover .02 .10
26 Michael Waltrip .15 .40
27 Len Wood .02 .10
Glen Wood
28 Morgan Shepherd .07 .20
29 Brett Bodine .07 .20
30 Mark Martin's Car .25 .60
31 Sterling Marlin's Car .07 .20
32 Dale Earnhardt's Car .60 1.50
33 Dale Jarrett's Car .15 .40
34 Bobby Hamilton's Car .02 .10
35 Michael Waltrip's Car .07 .20
36 Rusty Wallace's Car .15 .40
37 Ernie Irvan .15 .40
38 Rick Mast .07 .20
39 David Green .07 .20
40 Joe Gibbs .15 .40
41 Michael Waltrip .15 .40
42 Ted Musgrave .07 .20
43 Bobby Labonte .30 .75
44 Ward Burton .15 .40
45 Ricky Craven .07 .20

46 Ken Schrader .07 .20
47 Geoff Bodine .07 .20
48 Johnny Benson .15 .40
49 Dale Jarrett .30 .75
50 Robin Pemberton .02 .10
51 Mark Martin SP 2.00 5.00
52 Sterling Marlin SP 1.25 3.00
53 Dale Earnhardt SP 6.00 15.00
54 Michael Waltrip SP .15 .40
55 Ricky Rudd SP 1.00 2.50
56 Ernie Irvan SP .15 .40
57 Dale Jarrett SP 2.00 5.00
58 Bobby Labonte SP 2.00 5.00
59 Kyle Petty SP .15 .40
60 Darrell Waltrip SP .15 .40
HP96 Dale Earnhardt Promo 2.00 5.00
RP96 Dale Earnhardt Promo 2.50 6.00

1996 Classic Printer's Proof

COMPLETE SET (50) 75.00 150.00
*SINGLES: 8X TO 20X BASE CARDS

1996 Classic Silver

COMPLETE SET (50) 6.00 15.00
*STARS: .6X TO 1.5X BASIC CARDS

1996 Classic Images Preview

This five-card set is a preview of the '96 Images set. The cards feature top names in racing in micro-foil printing. The odds of pulling a Images Preview card was one per 30 Classic packs.

COMPLETE SET (5) 20.00 50.00
RP1 Sterling Marlin 2.50 6.00
RP2 Mark Martin 3.00 8.00
RP3 Bobby Labonte 3.00 8.00
RP4 Ricky Rudd 3.00 8.00
RP5 Dale Earnhardt's Car 8.00 20.00
R.Child.

1996 Classic Innerview

This 15-card insert set gives fans a look at the top drivers. The double foil stamped cards feature a gold facsimile signature of each driver on the front of their card. The backs feature a driver's answer to a specific question to give the fan more insight to what goes on behind-the-scenes. The cards are randomly inserted in packs at a rate of one per 50 packs.

COMPLETE SET (15) 35.00 75.00
IV1 Mark Martin 3.00 8.00
IV2 Ted Musgrave .60 1.50
IV3 Dale Earnhardt 8.00 20.00
IV4 Sterling Marlin 2.00 5.00
IV5 Kyle Petty 1.25 3.00
IV6 Mark Martin 3.00 8.00
IV7 Dale Earnhardt 8.00 20.00
IV8 Brett Bodine .60 1.50
IV9 Geoff Bodine .60 1.50
IV10 Ricky Rudd 2.00 5.00
IV11 Sterling Marlin 2.00 5.00
IV12 Bobby Labonte 3.00 8.00
IV13 Morgan Shepherd .60 1.50
IV14 Robert Pressley .60 1.50
IV15 Michael Waltrip 1.25 3.00

1996 Classic Mark Martin's Challengers

This 10-card set features some of Mark's toughest competitors. Each card has Mark's comments on the back telling what makes each driver a good competitor. The cards feature micro-foil technology and were inserted in packs at a rate of one per 15 packs.

COMPLETE SET (10) 6.00 15.00
MC1 Ted Musgrave .30 .75
MC2 Michael Waltrip .60 1.50
MC3 Dale Earnhardt's Car 2.50 6.00
MC4 Dale Jarrett 1.50 4.00
MC5 Sterling Marlin 2.00 2.50
MC6 Ken Schrader .30 .75
MC7 Geoff Bodine .30 .75
MC8 Rusty Wallace's Car .60 1.50
MC9 Bobby Labonte 1.50 4.00
MC10 Mark Martin 1.50 4.00

1996 Classic Race Chase

This 20-card insert set was an interactive game for two specific races in the 1996 season. The set is divided into subsets; cards 1-10 were for the '96 Daytona 500 and cards 11-20 were for the '96 TranSouth Financial 400. If you held the winning card for either of those two races, Dale Jarrett and Jeff Gordon respectively, you could redeem that card for a 10-card foil stamped set of the related race. You could also redeem the winning card along with a regular Classic drivers card for each of the second through tenth place finishers for a $50 phone card of a top driver and the 10-card foil stamped set. Since the winners of each of the two races were not represented in the set, the Field Card was the winner in both interactive race games. The expiration for the redemption cards was June 30, 1996.

COMPLETE SET (20) 15.00 40.00
RC1 Michael Waltrip's Car .75 2.00
RC2 Rusty Wallace's Car 1.50 4.00
RC3 Dale Earnhardt's Car 3.00 8.00
RC4 Sterling Marlin's Car 1.00 2.50
RC5 Ricky Rudd's Car 1.00 2.50
RC6 Mark Martin's Car 1.50 4.00
RC7 Bobby Labonte's Car 1.25 3.00
RC8 Ernie Irvan's Car .75 2.00
RC9 Morgan Shepherd's Car .40 1.00
RC10 Field Card WIN .40 1.00
RC11 Michael Waltrip's Car .75 2.00
RC12 Rusty Wallace's Car 1.50 4.00
RC13 Dale Earnhardt's Car 3.00 8.00
RC14 Sterling Marlin's Car 1.00 2.50
RC15 Darrell Waltrip's Car .75 2.00
RC16 Mark Martin's Car 1.50 4.00
RC17 Bobby Labonte's Car 1.25 3.00
RC18 Ernie Irvan's Car .75 2.00
RC19 Johnny Benson's Car .40 1.00
RC20 Field Card WIN .40 1.00

1995 Classic Five Sport

The 1995 Classic Five Sport set was issued in one series of 200 standard-size cards. Cards were issued in 10-card regular packs (SRP $1.99). Boxes contained 36 packs. One autographed card was guaranteed in each pack and one certified autographed card (with an embossed logo) appeared in each box. There were also memorabilia redemption cards included in some packs and were guaranteed in at least one pack per box. The cards are numbered and divided into the five sports as follows: Basketball (1-42), Football (43-92), Baseball (93-122), Hockey (123-160), Racing (161-180), Alma Maters (181-190), Picture Perfect (191-200).

COMPLETE SET (200) 6.00 15.00
161 Dale Earnhardt .75 2.00
162 John Andretti .05 .15
163 Derrike Cope .07 .20
164 Richard Childress .05 .15
165 Rusty Wallace .25 .60
166 Bobby Labonte .15 .40
167 Brett Bodine .07 .20
168 Michael Waltrip .08 .25
169 Sterling Marlin .15 .40
170 Kyle Petty .08 .25
171 Ricky Rudd .08 .25
172 Jeff Burton .08 .25
173 Dick Trickle .05 .15
174 Ernie Irvan .05 .15
175 Dale Jarrett .25 .60
176 Darrell Waltrip .08 .25
177 Geoff Bodine .05 .15
178 Ted Musgrave .05 .15
179 Morgan Shepherd .05 .15
180 Todd Bodine .05 .15

1995 Classic Five Sport Silver Die Cuts

COMPLETE SET (200) 12.00 30.00
*SILVER DC: .8X TO 2X BASIC CARDS

1995 Classic Five Sport Red Die Cuts

*RED DIE CUT: 1.2X TO 3X BASIC CARDS
RED DIE CUT STATED ODDS 1:8

1995 Classic Five Sport Printer's Proofs

*PRINTER PROOF/75: 4X TO 10X BASIC CARDS
STATED PRINT RUN 795 SETS

1995 Classic Five Sport Autographs Numbered

Cards in this set were issued primarily in 1995-96 Classic Five Sport Signings packs and are essentially a parallel verson of the basic 1995 Classic Five Sport Autographs insert. The only differences are in the hand serial numbering on the cardbacks (of 225 or 295) and the embossing crimp on the card's corner.

164 Richard Childress/225 5.00 12.00
166 Bobby Labonte/225 10.00 25.00
167 Bret Bodine/225 4.00 10.00
169 Sterling Marlin/225 8.00 20.00
170 Kyle Petty/225 4.00 10.00
171 Ricky Rudd/225 6.00 15.00
173 Dick Trickle/225 3.00 8.00
174 Ernie Irvan/225 6.00 15.00
175 Dale Jarrett/225 8.00 20.00
176 Darrell Waltrip/225 10.00 25.00
177 Geoff Bodine/225 4.00 10.00
178 Ted Musgrave/225 3.00 8.00
179 Morgan Shepherd/225 4.00 10.00
180 Todd Bodine/225 3.00 8.00
161 Dale Earnhardt/225 350.00 500.00

1995 Classic Five Sport Classic Standouts

Randomly inserted in regular packs at a rate of one in 216, this 10-card standard-size set features both the hot new stars and the established elite of all five sports. Fronts have full-color action player cutouts set against a gold and black foil background. The player's name is printed in gold foil at the top. Backs contain a full-color action shot with the player's name printed in yellow and a career highlights box. The cards are numbered with a "CS" prefix.

COMPLETE SET (10) 15.00 40.00
CS3 Dale Earnhardt 5.00 12.00

1995 Classic Five Sport Hot Box Autographs

This set of six autographed standard-sized cards were randomly inserted in Hobby Hot boxes. The cards are nearly identical to the basic Five Sports Autographs with the exception of the hand written serial number on the backs and the slightly different congratulatory message on the back that reads "...Received a Limited-Edition Autographed Card."

3 Dale Earnhardt/635 250.00 400.00

1995 Classic Five Sport On Fire

Ten of the 20-cards in this set were released in Hobby Hot Packs while the other ten were released in retail Hot packs. Fronts have full-color player cutouts set against a flame background with the On Fire logo printed at the bottom. The player's name is printed vertically in white type on the left side. backs feature biography and players's statistics.

COMPLETE SET (20) 30.00 80.00
H3 Dale Earnhardt 5.00 12.00

1995 Classic Five Sport Phone Cards $3

The five-card set of $3 Foncards were found one per 72 retail packs. The credit-card size plastic pieces have a borderless front with a full-color action player photo and the $3 emblem printed on the upper right in blue. The player's name is printed in white type vertically on the lower left. The Sprint logo appears on the bottom also. White backs carry information about how to place calls using the card.

COMPLETE SET (5) 4.00 8.00
1 Dale Earnhardt 2.00 5.00

1995 Classic Five Sport Phone Cards $4

These cards were inserted randomly into packs at a rate of one in 72 and featured the five top prospects or performers of the individual sports. The borderless fronts feature full-color action photos with the athlete's name printed in white across the bottom. The Sprint logo and $4 are printed along the top. White backs contain information about placing calls using the card.

COMPLETE SET (5) 6.00 15.00
1 Dale Earnhardt 3.00 8.00

1995 Classic Five Sport Previews

Randomly inserted in Classic hockey packs, this five-card standard-size set salutes the leaders and the up-and-coming rookies of the five sports. Borderless fronts have a full-color action shot with gold foil stamp of "preview" and the player's name, school and position printed vertically on the right side of the card. The player's sport's ball (or tire) is printed in a montage on the right. Backs have another full-color action shot and also a biography, statistics and profile. The cards are numbered with a "SP" prefix.

COMPLETE SET (5) 3.00 8.00
SP1 Dale Earnhardt 5.00 5.00

1995 Classic Five Sport Record Setters

This 10-card standard-size set was inserted in retail packs and feature the stars and rookies of the five sports. The fronts display full-bleed color action photos; the set title "Record Setters" iin prismatic block lettering appears toward the bottom. On a sepia-tone photo, the backs carry a player profile. The cards are numbered on the back with an "RS" prefix and hand-numbered out of 1250.

COMPLETE SET (10) 12.00 30.00
RS4 Dale Earnhardt 4.00 10.00

1995 Classic Five Sport Strive For Five

This interactive game card set consists of 65 cards to be used like playing cards. Collector's gained a full suit of cards to redeem prizes. The odds of finding the card in packs were one in 10. Fronts are bordered in metallic silver foil and picture the player in full-color action. The cards are numbered on both top and bottom in silver foil and the player's name is printed vertically in silver foil. Backs have green backgrounds with the game rules printed in white type.

COMPLETE SET (65) 12.00 30.00
RC1 John Andretti .20 .50
RC2 Dick Trickle .20 .50
RC3 Kyle Petty .20 .50
RC4 Bobby Labonte .40 .75
RC5 Ricky Rudd .20 .50
RC6 Darrell Waltrip .25 .60
RC7 Dale Jarrett .40 .75
RC8 Brett Bodine .20 .50
RC9 Geoff Bodine .20 .50
RC10 Ernie Irvan .25 .60
RC11 Jeff Burton .20 .50
RC12 Sterling Marlin .30 .75
RC13 Rusty Wallace .40 1.00

1995-96 Classic Five Sport Signings

COMPLETE SET (100) 6.00 15.00
79 Dale Earnhardt 1.00 2.50
80 John Andretti .07 .20
81 Rusty Wallace .30 .75
82 Bobby Labonte .20 .50
83 Michael Waltrip .10 .30
84 Sterling Marlin .20 .50
85 Brett Bodine .08 .25
86 Kyle Petty .10 .30
87 Ricky Rudd .10 .30
88 Ernie Irvan .07 .20
89 Darrell Waltrip .10 .30
90 Geoff Bodine .07 .20

1995-96 Classic Five Sport Signings Die Cuts

*DIE CUT: .8X TO 2X BASIC CARDS
STATED ODDS 1:4

1995-96 Classic Five Sport Signings Blue Signature

*BLUE SIGN: 1.5X TO 4X BASIC CARDS

1995-96 Classic Five Sport Signings Red Signature

*RED SIGN: 1.5X TO 4X BASIC CARDS

1995-96 Classic Five Sport Signings Etched in Stone

This 10-card set, printed on 16-point foil board, was randomly inserted in Hot boxes only. Hot boxes were distributed at a rate of 1:5 cases.

9 Mark Martin 3.00 8.00

1995-96 Classic Five Sport Signings Freshly Inked

This 30-card set was randomly inserted in 1995 Classic Five Sport Signings packs. The fronts features borderless player color action photos with the player's name printed in gold foil across the bottom. The backs carry an artist's drawing of the player with the player's name at the top.

COMPLETE SET (30) 12.00 30.00
STATED ODDS 1:10
FS27 John Andretti .40 1.00
FS28 Derrike Cope .40 1.00
FS29 Todd Bodine .40 1.00
FS30 Jeff Burton .60 1.50

1996 Clear Assets

The 1996 Clear Assets set was issued in one series totaling 70 cards. The set features 75 upscale acetate cards of the most collectible athletes from baseball, basketball, football, hockey and auto racing. Also included is the debut appearance by many of the top players entering the 1996 football draft. Release date was April 1996.

COMPLETE SET (70) 6.00 15.00
60 Ricky Rudd .10 .30
61 Bobby Hamilton .08 .25
62 Dale Jarrett .20 .50
63 Brett Bodine .08 .25
64 Dale Earnhardt .60 1.50
65 Sterling Marlin .15 .40
66 Mark Martin .25 .60
67 Ted Musgrave .08 .25
68 Bobby Labonte .20 .50
69 Ricky Craven .08 .25
70 Kyle Petty .15 .40

1996 Clear Assets 3X

Randomly inserted in packs at a rate of one in 100, this 10-card set is another first from Classic. The cards resemble triplexed cards with acetate in the middle and an opaque covering.

COMPLETE SET (10) 40.00 100.00
X1 Mark Martin 5.00 12.00

1996 Clear Assets A Cut Above

CA17 Sterling Marlin .60 1.50

1996 Clear Assets Phone Cards $1

COMPLETE SET (30) 5.00 12.00
*PIN NUMBER REVEALED: HALF VALUE
$1 CARDS ONE PER RETAIL PACK
*$2 CARDS: .6X TO 1.5X $1 CARDS
ONE PER HOBBY PACK
CARDS EXPIRED 10/1/97
4 Mark Martin .20 .50
19 Dale Earnhardt .75 2.00

1996 Clear Assets Phone Cards $5

Inserted at a rate of 1:10 packs, this 20-card set of acetate phone cards features many of the biggest names in sports. The Sprint phone cards carry expiration dates of 10/1/97.

COMPLETE SET (20) 12.00 30.00
*PIN NUMBER REVEALED: HALF VALUE
4 Dale Earnhardt 2.50 6.00

1996 Clear Assets Phone Cards $10

Inserted at a rate of 1:30 packs, this 10-card set of acetate phone cards features many of the biggest names in sports. The Sprint phone cards carry expiration dates of 10/1/97.

COMPLETE SET (10) 20.00 50.00
*PIN NUMBER REVEALED:HALF VALUE
3 Dale Earnhardt 5.00 12.00
8 Mark Martin 2.00 5.00

1992 Clevite Engine Builders

This 12-card promotional set features the top Winston Cup engine builders from 1985-91. The Engine Builder Award is given out each year to the engine builder who has accumulated the most points over the year. The cards are silver bordered and have a color photo on the front. Starting with Ernie Elliott in 1985, the cards are in order of the year that engine builder won the award.

COMPLETE SET (12) 6.00 15.00
1 A.E.Clevite Co. .40 1.00
2 A.E.Clevite Co. .40 1.00
3 Michigan Bearings .40 1.00
4 McCord Gaskets .40 1.00
5 A.E.Clevite Timing .40 1.00
6 Ernie Elliott .60 1.50
7 Randy Dorton .60 1.50
8 Lou LaRosa .60 1.50
9 David Evans .60 1.50
10 Rick Wetzel .60 1.50
11 Eddie Lanier .60 1.50
12 Shelton Pittman .60 1.50

1991 CM Handsome Harry

This 14-card set features one of the most popular drivers in Winston Cup history, Harry Gant. The cards feature a combination of shots of Harry in his early days and at home. Reportedly there were 25,000 sets produced. Also included is a Harry Gant promo card. The card is a cartoon and has the word PROMO in the upper right corner of the front of the card.

COMPLETE SET (14) 1.50 4.00
COMMON CARD (1-14) .15 .40
P1 Harry Gant Promo .50 1.25

1999 Coca-Cola Racing Family

These jumbo sized cards (measuring roughly 5 1/2" by 8") were issued in 1999 to promote the Coca-Cola Family of drivers. Each unnumbered card features the driver standing in front of his car along with a facsimile autograph printed across the front.

COMPLETE SET (6) 6.00 15.00
1 Jeff Burton .60 1.50
2 Dale Earnhardt 4.00 10.00
3 Bill Elliott .60 1.50
4 Dale Jarrett .75 2.00
5 Kyle Petty .40 1.00
6 Ricky Rudd .50 1.25

2000 Coca-Cola Racing Family

These cards were available as two and four card perforated sheets sold with 16oz and 12 packs of Coca-Cola. They feature the drivers of the Coca-Cola Driving Family. Prices below reflect that of single cards. Uncut sections of cards are valued at the sum of its singles.

COMPLETE SET (16) 12.50 30.00
1 Jeff Burton .50 1.25
2 Jeff Burton '99 Win .50 1.25
3 Dale Earnhardt 3.00 8.00
4 Dale Earnhardt 7T Champ 3.00 8.00
5 Bill Elliott .60 1.50
6 Dale Jarrett 1.00 2.50
7 Dale Jarrett '99 Champ 1.00 2.50
8 Bobby Labonte 1.00 2.50
9 Bobby Labonte '99 Win 1.00 2.50
10 Steve Park .50 1.25
11 Adam Petty 3.00 8.00
12 Kyle Petty .60 1.50
13 A.Petty K.Petty 3.00 8.00
14 Tony Stewart 1.25 3.00
15 Tony Stewart '99 ROY 1.25 3.00
16 Coca-Cola Racing Family 2.50 6.00

2001 Coca-Cola Econo Lodge

This set was released in 2001 and sponsored by Coke and Econo Lodge. Each card includes a scratch-off coupon on the back with a color driver photo on the front. The cards measure larger than standard size at roughly 3 1/2" by 5". Prices below reflect that of unscratched cards.

COMPLETE SET (4) 3.00 6.00
1 John Andretti .50 1.25
2 Dale Jarrett 1.00 2.50
3 Kyle Petty .60 1.50
4 Andretti Jarrett Petty .75 2.00

2005 Coca-Cola Racing Family AutoZone

COMPLETE SET (8) 10.00 20.00
1 Kurt Busch 1.50 4.00
2 Justin Diercks 1.50 4.00
3 Jeff Fultz .60 1.50
4 Kevin Harvick 2.50 6.00
5 Jeff Jefferson .60 1.50
6 Jim Pettit .60 1.50
7 Kyle Petty 1.00 2.50
8 Tony Stewart 2.50 6.00

2006 Press Pass Coca Cola AutoZone

COMPLETE SET (4) 5.00 12.00
DJ Dale Jarrett 1.00 2.50
GB Greg Biffle .75 2.00
MM Mark Martin 1.00 2.50
TS Tony Stewart 1.50 4.00

1993-96 Collector's Advantage Phone Cards

Collector's Advantage was the distributing agent for many different phone card companies, such as Planet Telecom, InterNet, Mecury Marketing, and Speed Call. Each card was produced as a promotion piece for a race day event. The cards were not numbered, nor part of a set, therefore we've cataloged them below in alphabetical order with the serial numbering and year of issue noted.

1 All-Pro Bumper to Bumper 300/4000 $6 1995 8.00 14.00
2 All-Pro Bumper to Bumper 300 Jumbo/400 $6 '95 50.00 70.00
3 Busch Lite 300/4000 $10 '96 10.00 18.00
4 Coca-Cola 600/4000 $6 '95 9.00 15.00
5 Coca-Cola 600 Jumbo/400 $6 '95 60.00 90.00
6 Goodwrench 200&400/4000 $5 '96 8.00 14.00
7 Goodwrench 200&400 Jumbo/50 $5 1996
8 Hoosier 300/4000 $6 '96 9.00 15.00
9 Hoosier 300 Jumbo/50 $6 '96
10 Hooters 500/1000 $5 '93 30.00 45.00
11 LugNut/4000 $6 '95 8.00 14.00
12 LugNut Jumbo/400 $6 '95
13 NAPA 500/4000 $5 '95 8.00 14.00
14 NAPA 500 Jumbo/50 $5 '95
15 Purolator 500/2500 $6 '95 8.00 14.00
16 Red Dog 300 Inaugural/4000 $6 1995 9.00 15.00
17 Red Dog 300 Inaugural Jumbo/400 $6 1995 50.00 80.00
18 UAW-GM 500/4000 $5 '95 8.00 14.00
19 UAW-GM 500 Jumbo/400 $6 '95 50.00 70.00

1997 Collector's Choice

The 1997 Collector's Choice set was issued in one series totaling 155 cards and featured the top names in NASCAR. The set contains the subsets: Drivers (1-50), Maximum MPH (51-100), Speedway Challenge (101-126), Team 3 (127-144) and Transitions (145-153). The cards were packaged 10 cards per pack, 36 packs per box and 12 boxes per case. Suggested retail price on a pack was 99 cents. This was the premiere issue of the Collector's Choice brand in racing by Upper Deck. Also included as an insert in packs (1:4 packs) was a game piece for Upper Deck's Meet the Stars promotion. Each game piece was a multiple choice trivia card about racing. The collector would scratch of the box next to the answer that they felt best matched the question to determine if they won. Instant win game pieces were also inserted one in 72 packs. Winning game pieces could be sent into Upper Deck for a prize drawing. The Grand Prize was a chance to meet Jeff Gordon. Prizes for 2nd through 4th were for Upper Deck Authenticated shopping sprees. The 5th prize was two special Jeff Gordon Meet the Stars cards. The blank back cards measure 5" X 7"and are titled Dynamic Debut and Magic Memories. These two cards are priced at the bottom of the base set.

COMPLETE SET (155) 5.00 12.00
1 Rick Mast .05 .15
2 Rusty Wallace .50 1.25
3 Dale Earnhardt 1.00 2.50
4 Sterling Marlin .20 .50
5 Terry Labonte .20 .50
6 Mark Martin .50 1.25
7 Geoff Bodine .05 .15
8 Hut Stricklin .05 .15
9 Lake Speed .05 .15
10 Ricky Rudd .20 .50
11 Brett Bodine .05 .15
12 Derrike Cope .05 .15
13 Bill Elliott .25 .60
14 Bobby Hamilton .05 .15
15 Wally Dallenbach .05 .15
16 Ted Musgrave .05 .15
17 Darrell Waltrip .10 .30
18 Bobby Labonte .40 1.00
19 Loy Allen .05 .15
20 Morgan Shepherd .05 .15
21 Michael Waltrip .10 .30
22 Ward Burton .10 .30
23 Jimmy Spencer .05 .15
24 Jeff Gordon .60 1.50
25 Ken Schrader .05 .15
26 Kyle Petty .10 .30
27 Bobby Hillin .05 .15
28 Ernie Irvan .10 .30
29 Jeff Purvis .05 .15
30 Johnny Benson .10 .30
31 Dave Marcis .10 .30
32 Jeremy Mayfield .10 .30
33 Robert Pressley .05 .15
34 Jeff Burton .10 .30
35 Joe Nemechek .05 .15
36 Dale Jarrett .40 1.00
37 John Andretti .05 .15
38 Kenny Wallace .05 .15
39 Elton Sawyer .05 .15
40 Dick Trickle .05 .15
41 Ricky Craven .05 .15
42 Chad Little .05 .15
43 Todd Bodine .05 .15
44 David Green .05 .15
45 Randy LaJoie .05 .15
46 Larry Pearson .05 .15
47 Jason Keller .05 .15
48 Hermie Sadler .05 .15
49 Mike McLaughlin .05 .15
50 Tim Fedewa .05 .15
51 Rick Mast's Car MM .02 .10
52 Rusty Wallace's Car MM .10 .30
53 Ricky Craven's Car MM .02 .10

54 Sterling Marlin's Car MM .05 .15
55 Terry Labonte's Car MM .10 .30
56 Mark Martin's Car MM .10 .30
57 Geoff Bodine's Car MM .02 .10
58 Hut Stricklin's Car MM .02 .10
59 Lake Speed's Car MM .02 .10
60 Ricky Rudd's Car MM .05 .15
61 Brett Bodine's Car MM .02 .10
62 Derrike Cope's Car MM .02 .10
63 Bill Elliott's Car MM .10 .30
64 Bobby Hamilton's Car MM .02 .10
65 Wally Dallenbach's Car MM .02 .10
66 Ted Musgrave's Car MM .02 .10
67 Darrell Waltrip's Car MM .05 .15
68 Bobby Labonte's Car MM .10 .30
69 Loy Allen's Car MM .02 .10
70 Morgan Shepherd's Car MM .02 .10
71 Michael Waltrip's Car MM .05 .15
72 Ward Burton's Car MM .02 .10
73 Jimmy Spencer's Car MM .02 .10
74 Jeff Gordon's Car MM .25 .60
75 Ken Schrader's Car MM .02 .10
76 Kyle Petty's Car MM .05 .15
77 Bobby Hillin's Car MM .02 .10
78 Ernie Irvan's Car MM .05 .15
79 Jeff Purvis's Car MM .02 .10
80 Johnny Benson's Car MM .02 .10
81 Dave Marcis's Car MM .05 .15
82 Jeremy Mayfield's Car MM .05 .15
83 Robert Pressley's Car MM .02 .10
84 Jeff Burton's Car MM .05 .15
85 Joe Nemechek's Car MM .02 .10
86 Dale Jarrett's Car MM .10 .30
87 John Andretti's Car MM .02 .10
88 Kenny Wallace's Car MM .02 .10
89 Elton Sawyer's Car MM .02 .10
90 Dick Trickle's Car MM .02 .10
91 Chad Little's Car MM .02 .10
92 Todd Bodine's Car MM .02 .10
93 David Green's Car MM .02 .10
94 Randy LaJoie's Car MM .02 .10
95 Larry Pearson's Car MM .02 .10
96 Jason Keller's Car MM .02 .10
97 Hermie Sadler's Car MM .02 .10
98 Mike McLaughlin's Car MM .02 .10
99 Tim Fedewa's Car MM .02 .10
100 Patty Moise's Car MM .02 .10
101 Jeff Gordon SC .30 .75
102 Rusty Wallace SC .25 .60
103 Sterling Marlin SC .10 .30
104 Terry Labonte SC .10 .30
105 Mark Martin SC .25 .60
106 Ricky Rudd SC .10 .30
107 Ted Musgrave SC .02 .10
108 Michael Waltrip SC .10 .30
109 Dale Jarrett SC .20 .50
110 Ernie Irvan SC .05 .15
111 Bill Elliott SC .10 .30
112 Ken Schrader SC .02 .10
113 Bobby Labonte SC .20 .50
114 Kyle Petty SC .05 .15
115 Ricky Craven SC .02 .10
116 Bobby Hamilton SC .02 .10
117 Johnny Benson SC .10 .30
118 Jeremy Mayfield SC .10 .30
119 Darrell Waltrip SC .05 .15
120 Junior Johnson SC .02 .10
121 Glen Wood SC .02 .10
122 Benny Parsons SC .05 .15
123 Bobby Allison SC .05 .15
124 Ned Jarrett SC .05 .15
125 Cale Yarborough SC .05 .15
126 Richard Petty SC .20 .50
127 Jeff Gordon T3 .30 .75
128 Jeff Gordon T3 .30 .75
129 Jeff Gordon's Car T3 .25 .60
130 Terry Labonte T3 .10 .30
131 Terry Labonte T3 .10 .30
132 Terry Labonte's Car T3 .10 .30
133 Ken Schrader T3 .02 .10
134 Ken Schrader T3 .02 .10
135 Ken Schrader's Car T3 .02 .10
136 Mark Martin T3 .25 .60
137 Mark Martin T3 .25 .60
138 Mark Martin's Car T3 .10 .30
139 Ted Musgrave T3 .02 .10
140 Ted Musgrave T3 .02 .10
141 Ted Musgrave's Car T3 .02 .10
142 Jeff Burton T3 .05 .15
143 Jeff Burton T3 .05 .15
144 Jeff Burton's Car T3 .02 .10
145 Rusty Wallace TRA .25 .60
146 Ricky Craven TRA .02 .10
147 Ricky Rudd TRA .10 .30
148 Bill Elliott TRA .10 .30
149 Joe Nemechek TRA .02 .10
150 Brett Bodine TRA .02 .10
151 Darrell Waltrip TRA .05 .15
152 Geoff Bodine TRA .02 .10
153 Dave Marcis TRA .05 .15
154 Jeff Gordon CL .25 .60
155 Rusty Wallace CL .10 .30
NNO Jeff Gordon 5X7 DD 2.00 5.00
NNO Jeff Gordon 5X7 MM 2.00 5.00

1997 Collector's Choice Speedecals

This 48-card insert set features driver's cars on stickers. The stickers were randomly inserted one in three packs.

COMPLETE SET (48) 10.00 20.00
S1 Rick Mast's Car .10 .25
S2 Joe Nemechek's Car .10 .25
S3 Rusty Wallace's Car .75 2.00
S4 Rusty Wallace's Helmet .75 2.00
S5 Bill Elliott's Car .40 1.00
S6 Bill Elliott's Helmet .40 1.00
S7 Sterling Marlin's Car .30 .75
S8 Sterling Marlin's Helmet .30 .75
S9 Terry Labonte's Car .30 .75
S10 Terry Labonte's Helmet .30 .75
S11 Mark Martin's Car .75 2.00
S12 Mark Martin's Helmet .75 2.00
S13 Bobby Hamilton's Car .10 .25
S14 Derrike Cope's Car .10 .25
S15 Ricky Craven's Car .10 .25
S16 Ricky Craven's Helmet .10 .25
S17 Lake Speed's Car .10 .25
S18 Morgan Shepherd's Car .10 .25
S19 Ricky Rudd's Car .30 .75
S20 Ricky Rudd's Helmet .30 .75
S21 Kyle Petty's Car .20 .50
S22 Kyle Petty's Helmet .20 .50
S23 Johnny Benson's Car .20 .50
S24 Johnny Benson's Helmet .20 .50
S25 Ernie Irvan's Car .20 .50
S26 Kenny Wallace's Car .10 .25
S27 Jeff Burton's Car .20 .50
S28 Jeff Burton's Helmet .20 .50
S29 Ken Schrader's Car .10 .25
S30 Dave Marcis's Car .20 .50
S31 Ted Musgrave's Car .10 .25
S32 Ted Musgrave's Helmet .10 .25
S33 Darrell Waltrip's Car .20 .50
S34 Darrell Waltrip's Helmet .20 .50
S35 Bobby Labonte's Car .60 1.50
S36 Bobby Labonte's Helmet .60 1.50
S37 Dale Jarrett's Car .60 1.50
S38 Dale Jarrett's Helmet .60 1.50
S39 Jeremy Mayfield's Car .20 .50
S40 Jeremy Mayfield's Car .20 .50
S41 Michael Waltrip's Car .20 .50
S42 Michael Waltrip's Helmet .20 .50
S43 Ward Burton's Car .20 .50
S44 Wally Dallenbach's Car .10 .25
S45 Wally Dallenbach's Helmet .10 .25
S46 Jimmy Spencer's Car .10 .25
S47 Jeff Gordon's Car 1.00 2.50
S48 Jeff Gordon's Helmet 1.00 2.50

1997 Collector's Choice Triple Force

This 30-card insert set features 10 groups of three cards. Each group of three cards was given a letter designation. Taking each of the three interlocking die-cut cards a collector could put them together like a puzzle. The cards together formed a photo across all three cards. The odds of pulling a Triple Force card were one in eleven packs.

COMPLETE SET (30) 30.00 80.00
A1 Dale Jarrett 3.00 8.00
A2 Ernie Irvan 1.00 2.50
A3 Dale Jarrett 3.00 8.00
B1 Ted Musgrave .50 1.25
B2 Jeff Burton 1.00 2.50
B3 Mark Martin 4.00 10.00
C1 Johnny Benson 1.00 2.50
C2 Ricky Craven .50 1.25
C3 Jeremy Mayfield 1.00 2.50
D1 Terry Labonte 1.50 4.00
D2 Terry Labonte 1.50 4.00
D3 Terry Labonte 1.50 4.00
E1 Jimmy Spencer .50 1.25
E2 Dale Jarrett 3.00 8.00
E3 Michael Waltrip 1.00 2.50
F1 Jeff Gordon 5.00 12.00
F2 Terry Labonte 1.50 4.00
F3 Ken Schrader .50 1.25
G1 Terry Labonte 1.50 4.00
G2 Jeff Gordon 5.00 12.00
G3 Jeff Gordon 5.00 12.00
H1 Bobby Hamilton .50 1.25
H2 Rusty Wallace 4.00 10.00
H3 Geoff Bodine .50 1.25
I1 Ricky Craven .50 1.25
I2 Ernie Irvan 1.00 2.50
I3 Dale Jarrett 3.00 8.00
J1 Mark Martin 4.00 10.00
J2 Rusty Wallace 4.00 10.00
J3 Johnny Benson 1.00 2.50

1997 Collector's Choice Upper Deck 500

The cards from this 90-card insert set make up pieces to a game. The cards carry driver or car photos. Each card is given a value of laps, track position, or penalty. Similar to a card game the collector plays their cards until one player has accumulated 600 laps. The cards were inserted one per pack.

COMPLETE SET (90) 8.00 20.00
UD1 Dale Earnhardt 1.00 2.50
UD2 Rusty Wallace .50 1.25
UD3 Rusty Wallace's Car .10 .30
UD4 Robin Pemberton .05 .10
UD5 Sterling Marlin .20 .50
UD6 Sterling Marlin's Car .05 .15
UD7 Terry Labonte .20 .50
UD8 Terry Labonte's Car .10 .30
UD9 Mark Martin .50 1.25
UD10 Mark Martin's Car .10 .30
UD11 Steve Hmiel .05 .10
UD12 Geoff Bodine .05 .15
UD13 Geoff Bodine's Car .05 .10
UD14 Hut Stricklin .05 .15
UD15 Hut Stricklin's Car .05 .10
UD16 Lake Speed .05 .15
UD17 Lake Speed's Car .05 .10
UD18 Ricky Rudd .20 .50
UD19 Ricky Rudd's Car .05 .15
UD20 Brett Bodine .05 .15
UD21 Brett Bodine's Car .05 .10
UD22 Derrike Cope .05 .15
UD23 Derrike Cope's Car .05 .10
UD24 Bobby Allison .05 .15
UD25 Bill Elliott .25 .60
UD26 Bill Elliott's Car .10 .30
UD27 Bobby Hamilton .05 .15
UD28 Bobby Hamilton's Car .05 .10
UD29 Richard Petty .20 .50
UD30 Wally Dallenbach .05 .15
UD31 Wally Dallenbach's Car .05 .10
UD32 Ted Musgrave .05 .15
UD33 Ted Musgrave's Car .05 .10
UD34 Darrell Waltrip .10 .30
UD35 Darrell Waltrip's Car .05 .15
UD36 Bobby Labonte .40 1.00
UD37 Bobby Labonte's Car .10 .30
UD38 Loy Allen .05 .15
UD39 Loy Allen's Car .05 .10
UD40 Morgan Shepherd .05 .15
UD41 Morgan Shepherd's Car .05 .10
UD42 Michael Waltrip .10 .30
UD43 Michael Waltrip's Car .05 .15
UD44 Ward Burton .10 .30
UD45 Ward Burton's Car .05 .15
UD46 Jimmy Spencer .05 .15
UD47 Jimmy Spencer's Car .05 .10
UD48 Jeff Gordon .60 1.50
UD49 Jeff Gordon's Car .25 .60
UD50 Ray Evernham .05 .15
UD51 Rick Hendrick .05 .10
UD52 Ken Schrader .05 .15
UD53 Ken Schrader's Car .05 .10
UD54 Kyle Petty .10 .30
UD55 Kyle Petty's Car .05 .15
UD56 Bobby Hillin .05 .15
UD57 Bobby Hillin's Car .05 .10
UD58 Ernie Irvan .10 .30
UD59 Ernie Irvan's Car .05 .15
UD60 Jeff Purvis .05 .15
UD61 Jeff Purvis's Car .05 .10
UD62 Johnny Benson .10 .30
UD63 Johnny Benson's Car .05 .10
UD64 Dave Marcis .10 .30
UD65 Dave Marcis's Car .05 .15
UD66 Jeremy Mayfield .10 .30
UD67 Jeremy Mayfield's Car .05 .15
UD68 Cale Yarborough .05 .15
UD69 Robert Pressley .05 .15
UD70 Robert Pressley's Car .05 .10
UD71 Jeff Burton .10 .30
UD72 Jeff Burton's Car .05 .15
UD73 Joe Nemechek .05 .15
UD74 Joe Nemechek's Car .05 .10
UD75 Dale Jarrett .40 1.00
UD76 Dale Jarrett's Car .10 .30
UD77 John Andretti .05 .15
UD78 John Andretti's Car .05 .10
UD79 Kenny Wallace .05 .15
UD80 Kenny Wallace's Car .05 .10
UD81 Elton Sawyer .05 .15
UD82 Elton Sawyer's Car .05 .10
UD83 Dick Trickle .05 .15
UD84 Dick Trickle's Car .05 .10
UD85 Ricky Craven .05 .15
UD86 Ricky Craven's Car .05 .10
UD87 Chad Little .05 .15
UD88 Chad Little's Car .05 .10
UD89 Rick Mast .05 .15
UD90 Rick Mast's Car .05 .10
NNO Instruction Card .05 .10

1997 Collector's Choice Victory Circle

The top 10 active career victory leaders was the focus of this 10-card insert set. The cards feature red foil stamping on the front and were inserted one in fifty packs.

COMPLETE SET (10) 50.00 120.00
VC1 Darrell Waltrip 2.00 5.00
VC2 Dale Earnhardt 15.00 40.00
VC3 Rusty Wallace 8.00 20.00
VC4 Bill Elliott 4.00 10.00
VC5 Mark Martin 8.00 20.00
VC6 Geoff Bodine 1.00 2.50
VC7 Terry Labonte 3.00 8.00
VC8 Ricky Rudd 3.00 8.00
VC9 Jeff Gordon 10.00 25.00
VC10 Ernie Irvan 2.00 5.00

1998 Collector's Choice

The 1998 Collector's Choice set was issued in one series totaling 117 cards and featured the top names in NASCAR. The set consists of five topical subsets: Speed Merchants (1-36), Rollin' Thunder (37-72), Future Stock (73-87), Perils of the Pits (88-98), and Trophy Dash (99-112). The cards were packaged 14 cards per pack and 36 packs per box. Suggested retail price on a pack was $1.29.

COMPLETE SET (117) 5.00 12.00
HOBBY BOX 20.00 50.00
RETAIL BOX 15.00 40.00
1 Morgan Shepherd .05 .15
2 Rusty Wallace .40 1.00
3 Dale Earnhardt .75 2.00
4 Sterling Marlin .15 .40
5 Terry Labonte .15 .40
6 Mark Martin .40 1.00
7 Geoff Bodine .05 .15
8 Hut Stricklin .05 .15
9 Lake Speed .05 .15
10 Ricky Rudd .15 .40
11 Brett Bodine .05 .15
12 Dale Jarrett .30 .75
13 Bill Elliott .20 .50
14 Bobby Hamilton .05 .15
15 Wally Dallenbach .05 .15
16 Ted Musgrave .05 .15
17 Darrell Waltrip .08 .25
18 Bobby Labonte .30 .75
19 Steve Grissom .05 .15
20 Rick Mast .05 .15
21 Michael Waltrip .08 .25
22 Ward Burton .08 .25
23 Jimmy Spencer .05 .15
24 Jeff Gordon .50 1.25
25 Ricky Craven .05 .15
26 Kyle Petty .08 .25
27 Kenny Wallace .05 .15
28 Ernie Irvan .08 .25
29 David Green .05 .15
30 Johnny Benson .08 .25
31 Mike Skinner .05 .15
32 Jeremy Mayfield .08 .25
33 Ken Schrader .05 .15
34 Jeff Burton .15 .40
35 Robby Gordon .05 .15
36 Derrike Cope .05 .15
37 Morgan Shepherd's Car .01 .05
38 Rusty Wallace's Car .15 .40
39 Dale Earnhardt's Car .30 .75
40 Sterling Marlin's Car .05 .15
41 Terry Labonte's Car .05 .15
42 Mark Martin's Car .15 .40
43 Geoff Bodine's Car .01 .05
44 Hut Stricklin's Car .01 .05
45 Lake Speed's Car .01 .05
46 Ricky Rudd's Car .05 .15
47 Brett Bodine's Car .01 .05
48 Dale Jarrett's Car .08 .25
49 Bill Elliott's Car .05 .15
50 Bobby Hamilton's Car .01 .05
51 Wally Dallenbach's Car .01 .05
52 Ted Musgrave's Car .01 .05
53 Darrell Waltrip's Car .05 .15
54 Bobby Labonte's Car .08 .25
55 Steve Grissom's Car .01 .05
56 Rick Mast's Car .01 .05
57 Michael Waltrip's Car .05 .15
58 Ward Burton's Car .05 .15
59 Jimmy Spencer's Car .01 .05
60 Jeff Gordon's Car .20 .50
61 Ricky Craven's Car .01 .05
62 Kyle Petty's Car .05 .15
63 Kenny Wallace's Car .01 .05
64 Ernie Irvan's Car .05 .15
65 David Green's Car .01 .05
66 Johnny Benson's Car .01 .05
67 Mike Skinner's Car .01 .05
68 Jeremy Mayfield's Car .05 .15
69 Ken Schrader's Car .01 .05
70 Jeff Burton's Car .05 .15
71 Robby Gordon's Car .01 .05
72 Derrike Cope's Car .01 .05
73 Jeff Burton FS .08 .25
74 Robby Gordon FS .01 .05
75 Mike Skinner FS .01 .05
76 Johnny Benson FS .05 .15
77 Ricky Craven FS .01 .05
78 Ward Burton FS .05 .15
79 Jeremy Mayfield FS .05 .15
80 Steve Grissom FS .01 .05
81 John Andretti FS .01 .05
82 David Green FS .01 .05
83 Bobby Labonte FS .15 .40
84 Kenny Wallace FS .01 .05
85 Mike Wallace FS .01 .05
86 Joe Nemechek FS .01 .05
87 Chad Little FS .05 .15
88 Jeff Gordon PP .25 .60
89 Terry Labonte PP .08 .25
90 Ricky Craven PP .01 .05
91 Kyle Petty PP .05 .15
92 Dale Jarrett PP .15 .40
93 Rusty Wallace PP .20 .50
94 Ricky Rudd PP .08 .25
95 Bobby Labonte PP .15 .40
96 Bobby Hamilton PP .01 .05
97 Mark Martin PP .20 .50
98 Jeff Gordon TD .25 .60
99 Mark Martin TD .20 .50
100 Terry Labonte TD .08 .25
101 Dale Jarrett TD .15 .40
102 Jeff Burton TD .08 .25
103 Dale Earnhardt TD .40 1.00
104 Bobby Hamilton TD .01 .05
105 Ricky Rudd TD .08 .25
106 Michael Waltrip TD .05 .15
107 Jeremy Mayfield TD .05 .15
108 Ted Musgrave TD .01 .05
109 Bill Elliott TD .08 .25
110 Johnny Benson TD .05 .15
111 Rusty Wallace TD .20 .50
112 Darrell Waltrip TD .05 .15
113 Checklist .01 .05
114 Checklist .01 .05
115 Checklist .01 .05
116 Checklist .01 .05
117 Checklist .01 .05

1998 Collector's Choice Star Quest

This 50-card set is a four-tier insert set that features autographed cards in its fourth tier. The Qualifier Tier (first) cards were inserted into packs at a ratio of 1:3. The Pole Tier (second) cards were inserted into packs at a ratio of 1:11. The Win Tier (third) cards were inserted into packs at a ratio of 1:71. The Championship Tier (fourth) autographed cards were inserted into packs at a ratio of 1:250.

COMP.1-STAR SET (20) 7.50 15.00
SQ1 Brett Bodine .20 .50
SQ2 Jimmy Spencer's Car .08 .25
SQ3 Mike Wallace .20 .50
SQ4 Bobby Labonte 1.25 3.00
SQ5 Morgan Shepherd .20 .50
SQ6 Derrike Cope's Car .08 .25
SQ7 Kenny Wallace .20 .50
SQ8 Chad Little .20 .50
SQ9 Hut Stricklin .20 .50
SQ10 Lake Speed's Car .08 .25
SQ11 Ricky Craven .40 1.00
SQ12 Steve Grissom .20 .50
SQ13 Dick Trickle's Car .08 .25
SQ14 Rick Mast .20 .50
SQ15 David Green's Car .08 .25
SQ16 Wally Dallenbach .20 .50
SQ17 Joe Nemechek .20 .50
SQ18 Ken Schrader's Car .08 .25
SQ19 Geoff Bodine's Car .08 .25
SQ20 Bobby Hamilton's Car .08 .25
SQ21 Mike Skinner .50 1.25
SQ22 Michael Waltrip 1.00 2.50
SQ23 Johnny Benson 1.00 2.50
SQ24 Ward Burton 1.00 2.50
SQ25 Robby Gordon's Car .25 .60
SQ26 Dale Earnhardt 10.00 25.00
SQ27 Ted Musgrave's Car .25 .60
SQ28 Jeremy Mayfield's Car .50 1.25
SQ29 Mark Martin's Car 2.00 5.00
SQ30 Sterling Marlin 1.50 4.00
SQ31 Ernie Irvan 4.00 10.00
SQ32 Ricky Rudd 6.00 15.00
SQ33 Jeff Burton 6.00 15.00
SQ34 Rusty Wallace 12.00 30.00
SQ35 Darrell Waltrip 4.00 10.00
SQ36 Jeff Gordon 20.00 50.00
SQ37 Terry Labonte 8.00 20.00
SQ38 Bill Elliott 8.00 20.00
SQ39 Dale Jarrett 10.00 25.00
SQ40 Kyle Petty 4.00 10.00
SQ41 Jeff Gordon AUTO 75.00 150.00
SQ42 Bill Elliott AUTO 25.00 50.00
SQ43 Dale Jarrett AUTO 25.00 50.00
SQ44 Kyle Petty AUTO 20.00 40.00
SQ45 Bobby Labonte AUTO 25.00 50.00
SQ46 Mark Martin AUTO 20.00 40.00
SQ47 Geoff Bodine AUTO 12.50 25.00
SQ48 Rusty Wallace AUTO 25.00 50.00
SQ49 Robby Gordon AUTO 12.50 25.00
SQ50 Ted Musgrave AUTO 12.50 25.00

1998 Collector's Choice CC600

The cards from this 90-card insert set make up pieces to a game. The cards carry driver or car photos. Each card is given a value of laps, track position, or penalty. Similar to a card game the collector plays their cards until one player has accumulated 600 laps. The cards were inserted one per pack.

COMPLETE SET (90) 5.00 12.00
CC1 Play Card .01 .05
CC2 Play Card .01 .05
CC3 Play Card .01 .05
CC4 Play Card .01 .05
CC5 Play Card .01 .05
CC6 Morgan Shepherd .05 .15
CC7 Rusty Wallace .40 1.00
CC8 Sterling Marlin .15 .40
CC9 Terry Labonte .15 .40
CC10 Mark Martin .40 1.00
CC11 Geoff Bodine .05 .15
CC12 Hut Stricklin .05 .15
CC13 Lake Speed .05 .15
CC14 Ricky Rudd .15 .40
CC15 Brett Bodine .05 .15
CC16 Dale Jarrett .30 .75
CC17 Bill Elliott .20 .50
CC18 Bobby Hamilton .05 .15
CC19 Wally Dallenbach .05 .15
CC20 Ted Musgrave .05 .15
CC21 Darrell Waltrip .10 .25
CC22 Bobby Labonte .30 .75
CC23 Steve Grissom .05 .15
CC24 Rick Mast .05 .15
CC25 Michael Waltrip .10 .25
CC26 Ward Burton .10 .25
CC27 Jimmy Spencer .05 .15
CC28 Ricky Craven .05 .15
CC29 Kyle Petty .10 .25
CC30 Kenny Wallace .05 .15
CC31 Ernie Irvan .10 .25
CC32 David Green .05 .15
CC33 Johnny Benson .10 .25
CC34 Mike Skinner .05 .15
CC35 Jeremy Mayfield .10 .25
CC36 Ken Schrader .05 .15
CC37 Jeff Burton .15 .40
CC38 Robby Gordon .05 .15
CC39 Derrike Cope .05 .15
CC40 Morgan Shepherd's Car .01 .05
CC41 Rusty Wallace's Car .15 .40
CC42 Sterling Marlin .15 .40
CC43 Mark Martin .40 1.00
CC44 Geoff Bodine .05 .15
CC45 Hut Stricklin .05 .15
CC46 Lake Speed's Car .01 .05
CC47 Ricky Rudd's Car .05 .15
CC48 Brett Bodine .05 .15
CC49 Dale Jarrett's Car .10 .25
CC50 Bill Elliott's Car .05 .15
CC51 Bobby Hamilton .05 .15
CC52 Wally Dallenbach .05 .15
CC53 Ted Musgrave's Car .01 .05
CC54 Darrell Waltrip .10 .25
CC55 Bobby Labonte's Car .10 .25
CC56 Steve Grissom's Car .01 .05
CC57 Rick Mast's Car .01 .05
CC58 Michael Waltrip .10 .25
CC59 Ward Burton .10 .25
CC60 Jimmy Spencer's Car .01 .05
CC61 Ricky Craven's Car .01 .05
CC62 Kyle Petty .10 .25
CC63 Kenny Wallace .05 .15
CC64 Ernie Irvan's Car .05 .15
CC65 David Green's Car .01 .05
CC66 Johnny Benson's Car .01 .05
CC67 Mike Skinner .05 .15
CC68 Jeremy Mayfield's Car .05 .15
CC69 Ken Schrader's Car .01 .05
CC70 Jeff Burton's Car .05 .15
CC71 Robby Gordon .05 .15
CC72 Derrike Cope .05 .15
CC73 Morgan Shepherd .05 .15
CC74 Rusty Wallace's Car .15 .40
CC75 Sterling Marlin's Car .05 .15
CC76 Mark Martin .40 1.00
CC77 Geoff Bodine's Car .01 .05
CC78 Hut Stricklin .05 .15
CC79 Lake Speed .05 .15
CC80 Ricky Rudd's Car .05 .15
CC81 Brett Bodine .05 .15
CC82 Dale Jarrett .30 .75
CC83 Bill Elliott's Car .05 .15
CC84 Bobby Hamilton .05 .15
CC85 Wally Dallenbach .05 .15
CC86 Ted Musgrave's Car .01 .05
CC87 Darrell Waltrip .10 .25
CC88 Bobby Labonte's Car .10 .25
CC89 Steve Grissom .05 .15
CC90 Rick Mast .05 .15
NNO Instruction Card .05 .10

1992 Coyote Rookies

This 14-card set features Winston Cup Rookies of the Year from 1980-1991. The first card is a checklist, then the next 12 cards are in order of ROY winner starting with Jody Ridley in 1980 and finishing with Bobby Hamilton in 1991. The final card in the set is a promo/checklist card with Jody Ridley on the front.

COMPLETE SET (14) 3.00 8.00
1 Checklist Card .10 .25
2 Jody Ridley .15 .40
3 Ron Bouchard .15 .40
4 Geoff Bodine .15 .40
5 Sterling Marlin .25 .60
6 Rusty Wallace .60 1.50
7 Ken Schrader .15 .40
8 Alan Kulwicki .50 1.25
9 Davey Allison .40 1.00
10 Ken Bouchard .15 .40
11 Dick Trickle .15 .40
12 Rob Moroso .15 .40
13 Bobby Hamilton .25 .60
14 Jody Ridley CL .15 .40

1995 Crown Jewels Promos

These Promo cards were issued to preview the 1995 Crown Jewels release. The cards are unnumbered and each was serial numbered as noted below.

PD1 Jeff Gordon Diamond/3000 15.00 35.00

PE1 Jeff Gordon Emerald/6000 10.00 25.00
PR1 Jeff Gordon Ruby/12,000 4.00 10.00

1995 Crown Jewels

The 80-card Ruby base set is Wheels Race Cards inaugural Crown Jewels brand issue. The cards, printed on 24 pt. paper stock, came five cards per pack, 24 packs per box and 12 boxes per case. There were two methods of distribution of the product; a hobby only version, that was limited to 2200 cases and a special retail version. The set includes subsets of Winston Cup Drivers (1-30), Winston Cup Driver/Owners (31-35), Winston Cup Crew Chiefs (36-40), Winston Cup Cars (41-53), Busch Drivers (54-63), Headliners (64-73) and Win Cards (74-80). Three redemption programs were included as inserts. All three, the Gemstone game cards, the Dual Jewels redemption game and the E-Race to Win cards expired 12/31/95. There were also three individual inserts randomly seeded in packs. Sterling Marlin Back-to-Back Daytona winner could be found one in 288 packs. The Chad Little Goody's 300 winner autographed card was seeded one in 576. Finally a two sided card that featured Jeff Gordon on one side and Terry Labonte on the other was randomly inserted at a rate of one in 288 packs.

COMPLETE RUBY SET (80) 8.00 20.00
COMP.E-RACE TO WIN SET (10) .25 .50
DUAL JEWELS REDEMP.CARDS .02 .10
1 Dale Earnhardt 1.25 3.00
2 Jeff Gordon .75 2.00
3 Mark Martin .60 1.50
4 Rusty Wallace .60 1.50
5 Ricky Rudd .25 .60
6 Terry Labonte .25 .60
7 Bobby Labonte .50 1.25
8 Ken Schrader .07 .20
9 Sterling Marlin .25 .60
10 Darrell Waltrip .15 .40
11 Geoff Bodine .07 .20
12 Kyle Petty .15 .40
13 Dale Jarrett .50 1.25
14 Ernie Irvan .15 .40
15 Bill Elliott .30 .75
16 Morgan Shepherd .07 .20
17 Michael Waltrip .15 .40
18 Ted Musgrave .07 .20
19 Lake Speed .07 .20
20 Jimmy Spencer .07 .20
21 Brett Bodine .07 .20
22 Joe Nemechek .07 .20
23 Steve Grissom .07 .20
24 Derrike Cope .07 .20
25 John Andretti .07 .20
26 Kenny Bernstein .07 .20
27 Joe Gibbs .15 .40
28 Larry McClure .02 .10
29 Travis Carter .02 .10
30 Junior Johnson .07 .20
31 Geoff Bodine .07 .20
32 Ricky Rudd .25 .60
33 Darrell Waltrip .15 .40
34 Joe Nemechek .07 .20
35 Bill Elliott .30 .75
36 Robin Pemberton .02 .10
37 Jimmy Makar .02 .10
38 Bill Ingle .02 .10
39 Robbie Loomis .02 .10
40 Buddy Parrott .02 .10
41 Ken Schrader's Car .02 .10
42 Bobby Labonte's Car .15 .40
43 Joe Nemechek's Car .02 .10
44 Derrike Cope's Car .02 .10
45 Brett Bodine's Car .02 .10
46 Kyle Petty's Car .07 .20
47 Hut Stricklin's Car .02 .10
48 Jimmy Spencer's Car .02 .10
49 Ricky Rudd's Transporter .02 .10
50 Kyle Petty's Transporter .02 .10
51 Darrell Waltrip's Transporter .02 .10
52 Terry Labonte's Transporter .07 .20
53 Geoff Bodine's Transporter .02 .10
54 David Green .07 .20
55 Tommy Houston .07 .20
56 Johnny Benson .15 .40
57 Chad Little .07 .20
58 Kenny Wallace .07 .20
59 Hermie Sadler .07 .20
60 Jason Keller .07 .20
61 Bobby Dotter .07 .20
62 Stevie Reeves .07 .20
63 Mike McLaughlin .07 .20
64 D.Earn Waltrip Cars CJT .60 1.50
65 Bill Elliott w Car CJT .15 .40
66 Sterling Marlin CJT .15 .40
67 Chad Little Mark Rypien CJT .07 .20
68 J.Gordon T.Labonte CJT .40 1.00
69 Ernie Irvan CJT .07 .20
70 Dale Jarrett CJT .25 .60
71 Bobby Labonte CJT .25 .60
72 Kyle Petty CJT .07 .20
73 J.Gordon T.Lab.Car CJT .30 .75
74 Sterling Marlin RW .15 .40
75 Jeff Gordon RW .40 1.00
76 Terry Labonte RW .15 .40
77 Jeff Gordon RW .40 1.00
78 Sterling Marlin RW .15 .40
79 Checklist (1-73) .02 .10
80 Checklist (74-80 Inserts) .02 .10
DT1 J.Gordon T.Labonte DT 15.00 40.00
GS1 Chad Little AUTO 15.00 40.00
SM1 Sterling Marlin BB 15.00 40.00

1995 Crown Jewels Diamond

COMPLETE SET (80) 150.00 300.00
*DIAMOND/599: 5X TO 12X RUBY

1995 Crown Jewels Emerald

COMPLETE SET (80) 125.00 250.00
*EMERALD/1199: 4X TO 10X RUBY

1995 Crown Jewels Sapphire

COMPLETE SET (80) 15.00 40.00
*SAPPHIRE: 2X TO 4X RUBYS

1995 Crown Jewels Dual Jewels

The six-card Ruby insert set features double-sided pairings of the top Winston Cup drivers. The Ruby Dual Jewel cards were inserted one per 48 packs in Crown Jewels. Emerald and Diamond parallels were produced as well and randomly inserted in packs. There was also Dual Jewels redemption game. If you had 2 Ruby, 2 Emerald, and 2 Diamond Dual Jewels redemption cards, you could redeem them for an uncut sheet of the six Dual Jewels cards in Sapphire foil stamping. The expiration of the cards was 12/31/95.

COMPLETE RUBY SET (6) 30.00 80.00
*EMERALDS: .4X TO 1X BASIC INSERTS
*DIAMONDS: .6X TO 1.5X BASIC INSERTS
UNCUT SAPPHIRE SHEET 60.00 150.00
DJ1 D.Earnhardt J.Gordon 10.00 25.00
DJ2 R.Wallace Dale Jarrett 6.00 15.00
DJ3 Bill Elliott Terry Labonte 6.00 15.00
DJ4 Mark Martin Ernie Irvan 6.00 15.00
DJ5 Kyle Petty Ricky Rudd 3.00 8.00
DJ6 D.Earnhardt Dave Marcis 6.00 15.00

1995 Crown Jewels Signature Gems

Each of the seven die-cut, micro-etched insert cards feature a top Winston Cup star. The Signature Gems cards were inserted at a rate of one per 48 packs in Crown Jewels.

COMPLETE SET (7) 30.00 80.00
UNCUT SIG.SERIES SHEET 30.00 60.00
SG1 Jeff Gordon 5.00 12.00
SG2 Rusty Wallace 4.00 10.00
SG3 Dale Earnhardt 8.00 20.00
SG4 Ernie Irvan 1.00 2.50
SG5 Ricky Rudd 1.50 4.00
SG6 Mark Martin 4.00 10.00
SG7 Bill Elliott 2.00 5.00

1996 Crown Jewels Elite Promos

These Promo cards were issued to preview the 1995 Crown Jewels release. The cards are unnumbered but have been assigned card numbers below according to its foil color.

PC1 Bobby Labonte Citrine 2.00 5.00
PD1 Bobby Labonte Diamond 2.00 5.00
PE1 Bobby Labonte Emerald 2.00 5.00
PS1 Bobby Labonte Sapphire 2.00 5.00

1996 Crown Jewels Elite

The 1996 Crown Jewels Elite set was issued in one series totalling 78 cards. Each card is printed on 24-point paper and comes with a red metallic foil stamping (red diamond in the crown logo) and a red colored background behind the driver's name. There were 1125 hobby cases produced with 16-boxes per case, 24-packs per box and 5-cards per pack. There were numerous parallel sets produced as well causing constant confusion among collectors. Finally, a special card was made to commemorate Dale Earnhardt's seven Winston Cup Championships which featured seven different gemstones on one card: amethyst, citrine, emerald, peridot, ruby, sapphire, and topaz. The card was available in base elite boxes at a rate of one in 384 packs and Treasure Chest and Diamond Tribute versions were also made. The Diamond Tribute Earnhardt 7 cards feature seven pieces of real diamond.

COMPLETE RUBY SET (78) 10.00 25.00
WAX BOX HOBBY 25.00 60.00
*RETAIL BLUE: .4X TO 1X BASIC CARDS
1 Dale Earnhardt 1.25 3.00
2 Jeff Gordon .75 2.00
3 Terry Labonte .25 .60
4 Mark Martin .60 1.50
5 Sterling Marlin .25 .60
6 Rusty Wallace .60 1.50
7 Bill Elliott .30 .75
8 Bobby Labonte .50 1.25
9 Dale Jarrett .50 1.25
10 Bobby Hamilton .07 .20
11 Ted Musgrave .07 .20
12 Darrell Waltrip .15 .40
13 Kyle Petty .15 .40
14 Ken Schrader .07 .20
15 Michael Waltrip .15 .40
16 Derrike Cope .07 .20
17 Jeff Burton .25 .60
18 Ricky Craven .07 .20
19 Steve Grissom .07 .20
20 Robert Pressley .07 .20
21 Joe Nemechek .07 .20
22 Brett Bodine .07 .20
23 Jimmy Spencer .07 .20
24 Ward Burton .15 .40
25 Jeremy Mayfield .15 .40
26 Dale Jarrett .50 1.25
27 Dale Earnhardt 1.25 3.00
28 Jeff Gordon .75 2.00
29 Jeff Gordon .75 2.00
30 Jeff Gordon .75 2.00
31 Terry Labonte .25 .60
32 Rusty Wallace .60 1.50
33 Sterling Marlin .25 .60
34 Rusty Wallace .60 1.50
35 Travis Carter .02 .10
36 Bobby Allison .02 .10
37 Robert Yates .02 .10
38 Larry Hedrick .02 .10
39 Cale Yarborough .02 .10
40 Bill Ingle .02 .10
41 David Smith .02 .10
42 Todd Parrott .02 .10
43 Charlie Pressley .02 .10
44 Donnie Wingo .02 .10
45 Eddie Wood .02 .10
46 Len Wood .02 .10
47 Donnie Richeson .02 .10
48 J.Nemechek J.Buice .02 .10
49 C.Pressley R.Craven .02 .10
50 D.Richeson B.Bodine .02 .10
51 J.Fennig D.Cope .02 .10
52 T.Parrott D.Jarrett .07 .20
53 M.Martin S.Hmiel .30 .75
54 R.Wallace Pemberton .60 1.50
55 B.Labonte J.Makar .07 .20
56 D.Earnhardt D.Smith .60 1.50
57 Dale Earnhardt's Trans. .50 1.25
58 Kyle Petty's Trans. .07 .20
59 Derrike Cope's Trans. .02 .10
60 Rusty Wallace's Trans. .15 .40
61 Bill Elliott's Trans. .15 .40
62 Dale Jarrett's Trans. .15 .40
63 Terry Labonte's Trans. .15 .40
64 Bobby Labonte's Trans. .15 .40
65 Joe Nemechek's Trans. .02 .10
66 Steve Grissom's Trans. .02 .10
67 David Green BGN .07 .20
68 Randy LaJoie BGN .07 .20
69 Curtis Markham BGN .07 .20
70 Phil Parsons BGN .07 .20
71 Chad Little BGN .07 .20
72 Jason Keller BGN .07 .20
73 Jeff Green BGN .07 .20
74 Mark Martin BGN .60 1.50
75 Steve Grissom BGN .07 .20
76 Bobby Labonte BGN .50 1.25
77 Checklist .02 .10
78 Checklist .02 .10
SD1 D.Earnhardt 7 Diam/300 100.00 200.00
SG1 D.Earnhardt 7 Gems/1500 25.00 60.00
SGTC1 Earnh.7 Gems TC/1500 25.00 60.00

1996 Crown Jewels Elite Diamond Tribute

COMPLETE SET (78) 10.00 25.00
*DIAM.TRIBUTE: .5X TO 1.2X BASE CARDS

1996 Crown Jewels Elite Diamond Tribute Citrine

COMPLETE SET (78) 75.00 150.00
*DIAM.TRIB.CITRINE/999: .4X TO 1X SAPP

1996 Crown Jewels Elite Emerald

COMPLETE SET (78) 100.00 200.00
*EMERALD/599: 3X TO 8X BASIC CARDS

1996 Crown Jewels Elite Emerald Treasure Chest

COMPLETE SET (78) 125.00 250.00
*EMERALD TCs: .5X TO 1.2X BASE EMERALD

1996 Crown Jewels Elite Sapphire Retail

COMPLETE SET (78) 40.00 100.00
*SAPPHIRE/1099: 2.5X TO 6X BASIC CARDS

1996 Crown Jewels Elite Sapphire Treasure Chest

COMPLETE SET (78) 75.00 150.00
*SAPPHIRE TC/1099: .4X TO 1X SAPPHIRE

1996 Crown Jewels Elite Treasure Chest

COMPLETE SET (78) 10.00 25.00
*TREAS.CHEST: .5X TO 1.2X BASE CARDS

1996 Crown Jewels Elite Birthstones of the Champions

Randomly inserted in packs at a rate of one in 192, this six-card set features the active Winston Cup Champions. Each card carries the actual birthstone for that driver. The cards were seeded in packs of the regular Elite product (1:192 packs) with 375 of each card made.

COMPLETE SET (6) 125.00 250.00
COMP.DIAM.TRIBUTE (6) 125.00 250.00
*DIAM.TRIBUTE: .4X TO 1X BASIC INSERTS
COMP. TREAS.CHEST (6) 150.00 300.00
*TC CARDS: .5X TO 1.2X BASIC INSERTS
BC1 Dale Earnhardt 25.00 60.00
BC2 Jeff Gordon 12.00 30.00
BC3 Rusty Wallace 12.00 30.00
BC4 Darrell Waltrip 4.00 10.00
BC5 Bill Elliott 8.00 20.00
BC6 Terry Labonte 6.00 15.00

1996 Crown Jewels Elite Dual Jewels Amethyst

Randomly inserted in packs at a rate of one in 96, this eight-card set features the top NASCAR drivers on dual sided cards. Each card has basically two front sides. The cards carry an amethyst or purple color foil stamping.

COMPLETE SET (8) 30.00 80.00
COMP.DIAM.TRIBUTE (8) 30.00 80.00
*DIAMOND TRIB: .4X TO 1X BASIC INSERTS
COMP.TREAS.CHEST (8) 40.00 100.00
*TREAS.CHEST: .5X TO 1.2X BASIC INSERTS
DJ1 D.Earnhardt J.Gordon 15.00 40.00
DJ2 D.Jarrett S.Marlin 6.00 15.00
DJ3 T.Labonte B.Labonte 5.00 12.00
DJ4 B.Elliott M.Martin 6.00 15.00
DJ5 D.Waltrip M.Waltrip 2.50 6.00
DJ6 B.Hamilton K.Petty 2.50 6.00
DJ7 R.Wallace K.Wallace 6.00 15.00
DJ8 W.Burton J.Burton 2.50 6.00

1996 Crown Jewels Elite Dual Jewels Garnet

Randomly inserted in packs at a rate of one in 48, this eight-card set features the top NASCAR drivers on dual sided cards. Each card has basically two front sides. The cards carry a garnet or reddish brown color foil stamping.

COMPLETE SET (8) 25.00 60.00
COMP. DIAMOND TRIB. (8) 25.00 60.00
*DIAMOND TRIB: .4X TO 1X BASIC INSERTS
COMP. TREAS.CHEST (8) 30.00 80.00
*TREAS.CHEST: .5X TO 1.2X BASIC INSERTS
DJ1 D.Earnhardt J.Gordon 10.00 25.00
DJ2 D.Jarrett S.Marlin 4.00 10.00
DJ3 T.Labonte B.Labonte 3.00 8.00
DJ4 B.Elliott M.Martin 4.00 10.00
DJ5 D.Waltrip M.Waltrip 2.00 6.00
DJ6 B.Hamilton K.Petty 1.50 4.00
DJ7 R.Wallace K.Wallace 4.00 10.00
DJ8 W.Burton J.Burton 1.50 4.00

1996 Crown Jewels Elite Dual Jewels Sapphire

Randomly inserted in packs at a rate of one in 192, this eight-card set features the top NASCAR drivers on dual sided cards. Each card has basically two front sides. The cards carry a sapphire or deep blue color foil stamping. There was also a Treasure Chest parallel version of each card. The parallels have a treasure chest logo on them to differentiate them from the base dual jewels cards. These cards were seeded one in 192 Treasure Chest packs.

COMPLETE SET (8) 60.00 150.00
COMP.TREAS.CHEST (8) 75.00 200.00
*TREAS.CHEST: .5X TO 1.2X BASIC INSERTS
DJ1 D.Earnhardt J.Gordon 40.00 100.00
DJ2 D.Jarrett S.Marlin 10.00 25.00
DJ3 T.Labonte B.Labonte 8.00 20.00
DJ4 B.Elliott M.Martin 10.00 25.00
DJ5 D.Waltrip M.Waltrip 4.00 10.00
DJ6 B.Hamilton K.Petty 4.00 10.00
DJ7 R.Wallace K.Wallace 10.00 25.00
DJ8 W.Burton J.Burton 4.00 10.00

1996 Crown Jewels Elite Crown Signature Amethyst

This 10-card set features the top Winston Cup drivers. The cards carry a facsimile signature across the front and carry an amethyst or purple logo. There were 480 of each card available only in Diamond Tribute boxes at a rate of one in 24 packs.

COMPLETE SET (10) 40.00 100.00
COMP.GARNET SET (10) 20.00 50.00
*GARNETS: .25X TO .6X BASIC INSERTS
COMP.PERIDOT SET (10) 20.00 50.00
*PERIDOT: .25X TO .6X BASIC INSERTS
CS1 Dale Earnhardt 12.50 30.00
CS2 Jeff Gordon 8.00 20.00
CS3 Rusty Wallace 6.00 15.00
CS4 Bill Elliott 3.00 8.00
CS5 Terry Labonte 2.50 6.00
CS6 Bobby Labonte 5.00 12.00
CS7 Ricky Craven .75 2.00
CS8 Sterling Marlin 2.50 6.00
CS9 Dale Jarrett 5.00 12.00
CS10 Mark Martin 6.00 15.00

1996 Crown Jewels Elite Diamonds in the Rough Sapphire

This five-card set pays tribute to some of the best up and coming young drivers on the Winston Cup circuit. The cards were available in Diamond Tribute boxes only at a rate of one in 48 packs.

COMPLETE SAPPHIRE SET (5) 6.00 15.00
COMP.CITRINE SET (5) 4.00 10.00
*CITRINES: .25X TO .6X BASIC INSERTS
COMP.RUBY SET (5) 4.00 10.00
*RUBYS: .25X TO .6X BASIC INSERTS
DR1 Jeff Burton 2.50 6.00
DR2 Steve Grissom 1.25 3.00
DR3 Ricky Craven 1.25 3.00
DR4 Robert Pressley 1.25 3.00
DR5 Jeremy Mayfield 2.50 6.00

1992 Dayco Series 1

The 1992 set was the first of three releases sponsored by Dayco. The cards in each set are numbered consecutively, although they are most often sold as separate series. The 1992 release features nine drivers pictured with their cars at Daytona. An unnumbered checklist/cover card rounds out the set as the tenth card.

COMPLETE SET (10) 4.00 10.00
1 Davey Allison .40 1.00
2 Rusty Wallace .60 1.50
3 Derrike Cope .25 .60
4 Ernie Irvan .40 1.00
5 Dale Jarrett .30 .75
6 Hut Stricklin .15 .40
7 Sterling Marlin .25 .60
8 Morgan Shepherd .25 .60
9 Bobby Hamilton .25 .60
NNO Cover Card Checklist .10 .25

1993 Dayco Series 2 Rusty Wallace

The 1993 Dayco set highlights the career of Rusty Wallace. The cards are numbered as a continuation of the 1992 Dayco release. Two foil cards are included as well as a checklist on the back of card #11.

COMPLETE SET (15) 3.00 8.00
11 Rusty Wallace CL .30 .75
12 Rusty Wallace Earnhardt Cars .30 .75
13 Rusty Wallace Rick Mears Cars .30 .75
14 Rusty Wallace Roger Penske .30 .75
15 Rusty Wallace .30 .75
16 Mike Wallace Kenny Wallace Rusty Wallace .30 .75
17 Rusty Wallace .30 .75
18 Rusty Wallace .30 .75
19 Rusty Wallace .30 .75
20 Rusty Wallace in Pits .30 .75
21 Rusty Wallace Buddy Parrott .30 .75
22 Rusty Wallace .30 .75
23 Rusty Wallace Buddy Parrott Don Miller .30 .75
24 Rusty Wallace FOIL .30 .75
25 Rusty Wallace's Car FOIL .30 .75

1994 Dayco Series 3

The 1994 set was the last of three releases sponsored by Dayco. The cards are numbered consecutively from series two, although they are most often sold as a separate set. The 1994 release is very similar in design to the 1992 first series and features 14-drivers pictured with their cars at Daytona. Neil Bonnett's card begins the set and includes a checklist cardback.

COMPLETE SET (15) 4.00 10.00
26 Neil Bonnett CL .40 1.00
27 Rusty Wallace .75 2.00
28 Sterling Marlin .40 1.00
29 Geoff Bodine .30 .75
30 Jeff Burton .50 1.25
31 Chuck Bown .30 .75
32 Loy Allen Jr. .30 .75
33 Harry Gant .40 1.00
34 Bobby Labonte .60 1.50
35 Hut Stricklin .30 .75
36 Ward Burton .50 1.25
37 Rick Mast .30 .75
38 Jeremy Mayfield .30 .75
39 Derrike Cope .30 .75
40 Dave Marcis .30 .75

1955 Diamond Matchbooks Stock Cars

The Diamond Match Co. produced these matchbook covers featuring Stock Car drivers of various circuits. They measure approximately 1 1/2" by 4 1/2" (when completely folded out). We've listed the drivers alphabetically. Each of the covers was produced with black ink on the text. Complete covers with matches intact are valued at approximately 1 1/2 times the prices listed below.

COMPLETE SET (3) 30.00 60.00
1 Ray Crawford Enrique Iglesias 6.00 12.00
2 Tim Flock 7.50 15.00
3 Lee Petty 12.50 25.00
4 Jack Rutherfurd 5.00 10.00
5 Phil Walters 5.00 10.00

1972-83 Dimanche/Derniere Heure

The blank-backed photo sheets in this multi-sport set measure approximately 8 1/2" by 11" and feature white-bordered color sports star photos from Dimanche Derniere Heure, a Montreal newspaper. The player's name, position and biographical information appear within the lower white margin. All text is in French. A white vinyl album was available for storing the photo sheets. Printed on the album's spine are the words, "Mes Vedettes du Sport" (My Stars of Sport).The photos are unnumbered and are checklisted below in alphabetical order according to sport or team as follows: Montreal Expos baseball players (1-117; National League baseball players (118-130); Montreal Canadiens hockey players (131-177); wrestlers (178-202); prize fighters (203-204); auto racing drivers (205-208); women's golf (209); Patof the circus clown (210); and CFL (211-278).

208 Emerson Fittipaldi 3.00 6.00
209 Alan Jones 1.50 3.00
210 Jody Scheckter 2.00 4.00
211 Patrick Tambay 1.50 3.00

2017 Donruss

1 Jimmie Johnson RK 1.00 2.50
2 Kyle Busch RK .75 2.00
3 Dale Earnhardt Jr. RK 1.25 3.00
4 Kevin Harvick RK .75 2.00
5 Clint Bowyer RK .60 1.50
6 Denny Hamlin RK .60 1.50
7 Danica Patrick RQ 1.25 3.00
8 Joey Logano RK .60 1.50
9 Brad Keselowski RK .75 2.00
10 Matt Kenseth RK .60 1.50
11 Kurt Busch RK .50 1.25
12 Carl Edwards RK .60 1.50
13 Kasey Kahne RK .60 1.50
14 Chase Elliott RK .75 2.00
15 Greg Biffle RK .50 1.25
16 Martin Truex Jr. RK .50 1.25
17 Jamie McMurray RK .60 1.50
18 Trevor Bayne RK .60 1.50
19 Ryan Newman RK .50 1.25
20 Paul Menard RK .40 1.00
21 Ryan Blaney RK .50 1.25
22 Chris Buescher RK .50 1.25
23 Austin Dillon RK .75 2.00

24 Bobby Labonte RK .60 1.50
25 Casey Mears RK .40 1.00
26 A.J. Allmendinger RK .60 1.50
27 Tony Stewart RK 1.00 2.50
28 Ty Dillon RR .60 1.50
29 Erik Jones RR 1.00 2.50
30 William Byron RR 1.00 2.50
31 Cole Custer RR .60 1.50
32 Daniel Hemric RR .60 1.50
33 Kate Dallenbach RR 1.25 3.00
34 Cameron Hayley RR .50 1.25
35 Todd Gilliland RR 1.00 2.50
36 Garrett Smithley RR .60 1.50
37A Dale Earnhardt Jr. .75 2.00
37B Dale Earnhardt Jr. SP 2.00 5.00
38A Matt Kenseth .40 1.00
38B Matt Kenseth SP 1.00 2.50
39 Brad Keselowski .50 1.25
40A Kevin Harvick .50 1.25
40B Kevin Harvick SP 1.25 3.00
41 Denny Hamlin .40 1.00
42 Austin Dillon .50 1.25
43 Joey Logano .40 1.00
44A Kyle Busch .50 1.25
44B Kyle Busch SP 1.25 3.00
45A Carl Edwards .40 1.00
45B Carl Edwards SP 1.00 2.50
46 Chase Elliott .50 1.25
47 Jimmie Johnson .60 1.50
47B Jimmie Johnson SP 1.50 4.00
48 Kurt Busch .30 .75
48B Kurt Busch SP .75 2.00
49 Martin Truex Jr. .30 .75
50A Jamie McMurray .40 1.00
50B Jamie McMurray SP 1.00 2.50
51 Kasey Kahne .40 1.00
52 Danica Patrick .75 2.00
53 Casey Mears .25 .60
54 Trevor Bayne .40 1.00
55 Clint Bowyer .40 1.00
56 Paul Menard .25 .60
57A Greg Biffle .30 .75
57B Greg Biffle SP .75 2.00
58 Ricky Stenhouse Jr. .40 1.00
59 A.J. Allmendinger .40 1.00
60A Ryan Newman .30 .75
60B Ryan Newman SP .75 2.00
61 Jeffrey Earnhardt .40 1.00
62 Chris Buescher .30 .75
63 Ryan Blaney .30 .75
64 Landon Cassill .30 .75
65 Bobby Labonte .40 1.00
66 Brian Scott .25 .60
67 Michael Annett .40 1.00
68 Matt DiBenedetto .25 .60
69 Alex Bowman .40 1.00
70 Michael McDowell .40 1.00
71 Regan Smith .30 .75
72 David Ragan .30 .75
73 Elliott Sadler .25 .60
74 Daniel Suarez .75 2.00
75 Justin Allgaier .30 .75
76 Ross Chastain .40 1.00
77 Erik Jones .60 1.50
78 Ryan Reed .40 1.00
79 Brendan Gaughan .25 .60
80 Bubba Wallace .40 1.00
81 Ty Dillon .40 1.00
82 William Byron .60 1.50
83 Christopher Bell .50 1.25
84 Matt Crafton .25 .60
85 Ben Kennedy .30 .75
86 Cameron Hayley .30 .75
87 Johnny Sauter .25 .60
88 Daniel Hemric .40 1.00
89 John Hunter Nemechek .30 .75
90 Tyler Reddick .40 1.00
91 Jimmie Johnson .60 1.50
92 Kevin Harvick .50 1.25
93 Dale Earnhardt Jr. .75 2.00
94 Danica Patrick .75 2.00
95 Kyle Busch .50 1.25
96 Martin Truex Jr. .30 .75
97 Joey Logano .40 1.00
98 Brad Keselowski .50 1.25
99 Kasey Kahne .40 1.00
100 D.Earnhardt DUALS .75 2.00
101 K.Harvick DUALS .50 1.25
102 J.Johnson DUALS .60 1.50
103 K.Busch DUALS .50 1.25
104 B.Keselowski DUALS .50 1.25
105 K.Kahne DUALS .40 1.00
106 M.Truex DUALS .30 .75
107 A.Allmndngr DUALS .40 1.00
108 T.Bayne DUALS .40 1.00
109 R.Smith DUALS .30 .75
110 D.Patrick DUALS .75 2.00
111 K.Larson DUALS .60 1.50
112 D.Hamlin DUALS .40 1.00
113 C.Bowyer DUALS .40 1.00
114 R.Newman DUALS .30 .75
115 P.Menard DUALS .25 .60
116 J.Logano DUALS .40 1.00
117 M.Kenseth DUALS .40 1.00
118 C.Elliott DUALS .50 1.25
119 G.Biffle DUALS .30 .75
120 R.Blaney DUALS .30 .75
121 Martin Truex Jr. .30 .75
122 Kevin Harvick .50 1.25
123 Kyle Busch .50 1.25
124 Matt Kenseth .40 1.00
125 Joey Logano .40 1.00
126 Chase Elliott .50 1.25
127 Brad Keselowski .50 1.25
128 Kurt Busch .30 .75
129 Denny Hamlin .40 1.00
130 Carl Edwards .40 1.00
131 Jimmie Johnson .60 1.50
132 Austin Dillon .50 1.25
133 Kyle Larson .60 1.50
134 Jamie McMurray .40 1.00
135 Chris Buescher .30 .75
136 Tony Stewart .60 1.50
137 Dale Earnhardt Jr. 84 .75 2.00
138 Junior Johnson 84 .40 1.00
139 Jimmie Johnson 84 .60 1.50
140 Michael Waltrip 84 .40 1.00
141 Chase Elliott 84 .50 1.25
142 Joey Logano 84 .40 1.00
143 Rusty Wallace 84 .40 1.00
144 Carl Edwards 84 .40 1.00
145 Daniel Suarez 84 .75 2.00
146 Denny Hamlin 84 .40 1.00
147 Kevin Harvick 84 .50 1.25
148 Austin Dillon 84 .50 1.25
149 Brad Keselowski 84 .50 1.25
150 Kasey Kahne 84 .40 1.00
151 Harry Gant 84 .30 .75
152 Danica Patrick 84 .75 2.00
153 Casey Mears 84 .25 .60
154 Clint Bowyer 84 .40 1.00
155 Greg Biffle 84 .30 .75
156 Ricky Stenhouse Jr. 84 .40 1.00
157 Kyle Busch 84 .50 1.25
158 Bobby Labonte 84 .40 1.00
159 Kyle Larson 84 .60 1.50
160 Terry Labonte 84 .40 1.00
161 A.J. Allmendinger 84 .40 1.00
162 Alex Bowman 84 .40 1.00
163 Bill Elliott 84 .60 1.50
164 Bobby Allison 84 .30 .75
165 Darrell Waltrip 84 .60 1.50
166 Dave Marcis 84 .30 .75
167 David Pearson 84 .40 1.00
168 David Ragan 84 .30 .75
169 Ernie Irvan 84 .40 1.00
170 Jamie McMurray 84 .40 1.00
171 Jeff Burton 84 .30 .75
172 Martin Truex Jr. 84 .30 .75
173 Kyle Petty 84 .30 .75
174 Mark Martin 84 .40 1.00
175 Kurt Busch 84 .30 .75
176 Ned Jarrett 84 .30 .75
177 Richard Petty 84 .60 1.50
178 Matt Kenseth 84 .40 1.00
179 Aric Almirola 84 .30 .75
180 Ryan Newman 84 .30 .75
181 William Byron 84 .60 1.50
182 Terry Labonte SP 1.00 2.50
183 Richard Petty SP 1.50 4.00
184 Bill Elliott SP 1.50 4.00
185 Ned Jarrett SP .75 2.00
186 Jeff Burton SP .75 2.00
187 Harry Gant SP .75 2.00
188 Tony Stewart SP 1.50 4.00
189 Daniel Suarez SP 2.00 5.00

2017 Donruss Artist Proof

*AP/25: 1.5X TO 4X BASIC CARDS (1-36)
*AP/25: 2.5X TO 6X BASIC CARDS (37-181)
*AP/25: 1X TO 2.5X BASIC CARDS (1-36)

2017 Donruss Blue Foil

*BLUE/299: .75X TO 2X BASIC CARDS (1-36)
*BLUE/299: 1.2X TO 3X BASIC CARDS (37-181)
*BLUE/299: .5X TO 1.2X BASIC CARDS (1-36)

2017 Donruss Gold Foil

*GOLD/499: .6X TO 1.5X BASIC CARDS (1-36)
*GOLD/499: 1X TO 2.5X BASIC CARDS (37-181)
*GOLD/499: .4X TO 1X BASIC CARDS (1-36)

2017 Donruss Gold Press Proof

*GOLD PP/99: 1X TO 2.5X BASIC CARDS (1-36)
*GOLD PP/99: 1.5X TO 4X BASIC CARDS (37-181)
*GOLD PP/99: .6X TO 1.5X BASIC CARDS (1-36)

2017 Donruss Green Foil

*GREEN/199: .75X TO 2X BASIC CARDS (1-36)
*GREEN/199: 1.2X TO 3X BASIC CARDS (37-181)
*GREEN/199: .5X TO 1.2X BASIC CARDS (1-36)

2017 Donruss Press Proof

*AP/49: 1.2X TO 3X BASIC CARDS (1-36)
*AP/49: 2X TO 5X BASIC CARDS (37-181)
*AP/49: .8X TO 2X BASIC CARDS (1-36)

2017 Donruss Call to the Hall

*CRACK ICE/999: .6X TO 1.5X BASIC INSERTS
1 Mark Martin 1.00 2.50
2 Richard Childress .75 2.00
3 Rick Hendrick .75 2.00
4 Terry Labonte 1.00 2.50
5 Bruton Smith .75 2.00
6 Bill Elliott 1.50 4.00
7 Fred Lorenzen .60 1.50
8 Jack Ingram .60 1.50
9 Rusty Wallace 1.00 2.50
10 Junior Johnson 1.00 2.50
11 Richard Petty 1.50 4.00
12 David Pearson 1.00 2.50

2017 Donruss Classics

*CRACK ICE/999: .6X TO 1.5X BASIC INSERTS
1 Dale Earnhardt Jr. 2.00 5.00
2 Jimmie Johnson 1.50 4.00
3 Matt Kenseth 1.00 2.50
4 Mark Martin 1.00 2.50
5 Richard Petty 1.50 4.00
6 Rusty Wallace 1.00 2.50
7 Bill Elliott 1.50 4.00
8 Brad Keselowski 1.25 3.00
9 Kevin Harvick 1.25 3.00
10 Bobby Labonte 1.00 2.50
11 Terry Labonte 1.00 2.50
12 Darrell Waltrip 1.50 4.00
13 Michael Waltrip 1.00 2.50
14 Kyle Petty .75 2.00
15 Tony Stewart 1.50 4.00
16 Danica Patrick 2.00 5.00

2017 Donruss Cut to The Chase

*CRACK ICE/999: .6X TO 1.5X BASIC INSERTS
DRIVERS HAVE MULT CARDS OF EQUAL VALUE
1 Martin Truex Jr. .75 2.00
2 Kevin Harvick 1.25 3.00
3 Martin Truex Jr. .75 2.00
4 Jimmie Johnson 1.50 4.00
5 Kevin Harvick 1.25 3.00
6 Joey Logano 1.00 2.50
7 Jimmie Johnson 1.50 4.00
8 Carl Edwards 1.00 2.50
9 Joey Logano 1.00 2.50
10 Jimmie Johnson 1.50 4.00

2017 Donruss Dual Rubber Relics

*GOLD/25: .75X TO 2X BASIC TIRE
1 Brad Keselowski 3.00 8.00
2 Carl Edwards 2.50 6.00
3 Chase Elliott 3.00 8.00
4 Dale Earnhardt Jr. 10.00 25.00
5 Danica Patrick 10.00 25.00
6 Denny Hamlin 2.50 6.00
7 Jimmie Johnson 4.00 10.00
8 Joey Logano 2.50 6.00
9 Kasey Kahne 2.50 6.00
10 Kevin Harvick 3.00 8.00
11 Kurt Busch 2.00 5.00
12 Kyle Busch 3.00 8.00
13 Matt Kenseth 2.50 6.00
14 Ryan Newman 2.00 5.00

2017 Donruss Elite Dominators

1 Jimmie Johnson 2.50 6.00
2 Kevin Harvick 2.00 5.00
3 Dale Earnhardt Jr. 3.00 8.00
4 Brad Keselowski 2.00 5.00
5 Kyle Busch 2.00 5.00

2017 Donruss Phenoms

*CRACK ICE/999: .6X TO 1.5X BASIC INSERTS
1 Chase Elliott 1.25 3.00
2 Ty Dillon 1.00 2.50
3 Erik Jones 1.50 4.00
4 William Byron 1.50 4.00
5 Daniel Hemric 1.00 2.50
6 Cole Custer 1.00 2.50
7 Collin Cabre .60 1.50
8 Harrison Burton 1.25 3.00
9 Todd Gilliland 1.50 4.00
10 Austin Dillon 1.25 3.00

2017 Donruss Pole Position

1 Carl Edwards 1.00 2.50
2 Martin Truex Jr. .75 2.00
3 Joey Logano 1.00 2.50
4 Chase Elliott 1.25 3.00
5 Kyle Busch 1.25 3.00
6 Jimmie Johnson 1.50 4.00
7 Brad Keselowski 1.25 3.00
8 Austin Dillon 1.25 3.00
9 Kevin Harvick 1.25 3.00
10 Matt Kenseth 1.00 2.50

2017 Donruss Retro Relics 1984

*GOLD/99: .5X TO 1.2X BASIC RELICS
*GOLD/25: .8X TO 2X BASIC TIRE
1 Alex Bowman 2.50 6.00
2 Aric Almirola 2.00 5.00
3 Bobby Labonte 2.50 6.00
4 Brad Keselowski 3.00 8.00
5 Brandon Jones 1.50 4.00
6 Brendan Gaughan 1.50 4.00
7 Brian Scott 1.50 4.00
8 Bubba Wallace 2.50 6.00
9 Carl Edwards 2.50 6.00
10 Clint Bowyer 2.50 6.00
11 Cole Custer 2.50 6.00
12 Cole Whitt 2.00 5.00
13 Dale Earnhardt Jr. 5.00 12.00
14 Daniel Hemric 2.50 6.00
15 Denny Hamlin 2.50 6.00
16 Elliott Sadler 1.50 4.00
17 Erik Jones 4.00 10.00
18 Garrett Smithley 2.50 6.00
19 J.J. Yeley 2.50 6.00
20 Jeremy Clements 1.50 4.00
21 Jimmie Johnson 4.00 10.00
22 Joey Logano 2.50 6.00
23 John Hunter Nemechek 2.00 5.00
24 Justin Allgaier 2.00 5.00
26 Kevin Harvick 3.00 8.00
27 Kurt Busch 2.00 5.00
28 Kyle Benjamin 1.50 4.00
29 Kyle Busch 3.00 8.00
30 Martin Truex Jr. 2.00 5.00
32 Ricky Stenhouse Jr. 2.50 6.00
33 Ryan Blaney 2.00 5.00
34 T.J. Bell 1.50 4.00
35 Trevor Bayne 2.50 6.00
36 Tyler Reddick 2.50 6.00

2017 Donruss Rubber Relics

*GOLD/90-99: .5X TO 1.2X BASIC TIRE
*GOLD/35-60: .6X TO 1.5X BASIC TIRE
*GOLD/25-30: .8X TO 2X BASIC TIRE
*GOLD/16-22: 1X TO 2.5X BASIC TIRE
1 Austin Dillon 3.00 8.00
2 Bobby Labonte 2.50 6.00
3 Brad Keselowski 3.00 8.00
4 Brandon Jones 1.50 4.00
5 Brendan Gaughan 1.50 4.00
6 Bubba Wallace 2.50 6.00
7 Carl Edwards 2.50 6.00
8 Carl Edwards 2.50 6.00
9 Casey Mears 1.50 4.00
10 Chase Elliott 3.00 8.00
11 Chris Buescher 2.00 5.00
12 Clint Bowyer 2.50 6.00
13 Dale Earnhardt Jr. 5.00 12.00
14 Dale Earnhardt Jr. 5.00 12.00
15 Danica Patrick 5.00 12.00
16 Daniel Suarez 5.00 12.00
17 David Ragan 2.00 5.00
18 Denny Hamlin 2.50 6.00
19 Erik Jones 4.00 10.00
20 Greg Biffle 2.00 5.00
21 Jamie McMurray 2.50 6.00
22 Jeb Burton 2.00 5.00
23 Jeffrey Earnhardt 2.50 6.00
25 Jimmie Johnson 4.00 10.00
26 Joey Logano 2.50 6.00
27 Joey Logano 2.50 6.00
28 Kasey Kahne 2.50 6.00
29 Kasey Kahne 2.50 6.00
30 Kevin Harvick 3.00 8.00
31 Kevin Harvick 3.00 8.00
32 Kurt Busch 2.00 5.00
33 Kyle Busch 3.00 8.00
34 Kyle Busch 3.00 8.00
35 Kyle Larson 4.00 10.00
36 Matt DiBenedetto 1.50 4.00
37 Matt Kenseth 2.50 6.00
38 Paul Menard 1.50 4.00
39 Ricky Stenhouse Jr. 2.50 6.00
40 Ryan Newman 2.00 5.00
41 Ryan Reed 2.50 6.00
42 Tony Stewart 4.00 10.00
43 Trevor Bayne 2.50 6.00
44 Ty Dillon 2.50 6.00

2017 Donruss Signature Series

*GOLD/25: .8X TO 2X BASIC AU
1 Ahnna Parkhurst 5.00 12.00
2 Alex Bowman 5.00 12.00
3 Alon Day 10.00 25.00
4 Aric Almirola 4.00 10.00
6 Brandon Jones 3.00 8.00
7 Brendan Gaughan 3.00 8.00
9 Bubba Wallace 5.00 12.00
10 Cameron Hayley 4.00 10.00
11 Chris Buescher 4.00 10.00
12 Cole Custer 5.00 12.00
13 Cole Whitt 4.00 10.00
14 Collin Cabre 3.00 8.00
15 Dakoda Armstrong 5.00 12.00
16 Daniel Hemric 5.00 12.00
17 Daniel Suarez 10.00 25.00
19 David Ragan 4.00 10.00
21 Elliott Sadler 3.00 8.00
22 Garrett Smithley 5.00 12.00
25 Jeffrey Earnhardt 5.00 12.00
26 John Hunter Nemechek 4.00 10.00
29 Julia Landauer 5.00 12.00
30 Justin Allgaier 4.00 10.00
32 Matt DiBenedetto 3.00 8.00
33 Matt Tifft 8.00 20.00
34 Michael Annett 5.00 12.00
35 Michael McDowell 5.00 12.00
36 Nicole Behar 5.00 12.00
37 Noah Gragson 4.00 10.00
38 Reed Sorenson 3.00 8.00
40 Ryan Reed 5.00 12.00
42 Todd Gilliland 8.00 20.00
46 William Byron 8.00 20.00
47 Robert Hight 5.00 12.00
48 Courtney Force 6.00 15.00
49 Brittany Force 6.00 15.00
50 Ashley Force 8.00 20.00

2017 Donruss Significant Signatures

*GOLD/25: .8X TO 2X BASIC AU
1 Bobby Allison 4.00 10.00
2 Bobby Labonte 5.00 12.00
3 Brad Keselowski
4 Dale Earnhardt Jr.
5 Glen Wood 3.00 8.00
6 Jack Roush 4.00 10.00
8 Kevin Harvick
9 Kurt Busch 10.00 25.00
10 Kyle Busch
11 Matt Kenseth 5.00 12.00
13 Don Garlits 4.00 10.00
14 Mario Andretti 10.00 25.00

2017 Donruss Speed

*CRACK ICE/999: .6X TO 1.5X BASIC INSERTS
1 Jimmie Johnson 1.50 4.00
2 Dale Earnhardt Jr. 2.00 5.00
3 Kevin Harvick 1.25 3.00
4 Martin Truex Jr. .75 2.00
5 Kyle Busch 1.25 3.00
6 Ryan Newman .75 2.00
7 Denny Hamlin 1.00 2.50
8 Danica Patrick 2.00 5.00
9 Trevor Bayne 1.00 2.50
10 Carl Edwards 1.00 2.50

2017 Donruss Studio Signatures

3 Casey Mears 3.00 8.00
4 Chase Elliott 30.00 60.00
5 Dale Earnhardt Jr. 50.00 100.00
6 Danica Patrick 50.00 100.00
9 Kyle Larson 12.00 30.00
10 Paul Menard 3.00 8.00
11 Ricky Stenhouse Jr. 5.00 12.00
12 Ryan Blaney 4.00 10.00
13 Ryan Newman 4.00 10.00
15 Ty Dillon

2017 Donruss Top Tier

*CRACK ICE/999: .6X TO 1.5X BASIC INSERTS
1 Martin Truex Jr. .75 2.00
2 Chase Elliott 1.25 3.00
3 Brad Keselowski 1.25 3.00
4 Kevin Harvick 1.25 3.00
5 Danica Patrick 2.00 5.00
6 Jimmie Johnson 1.50 4.00
7 Dale Earnhardt Jr. 2.00 5.00
8 Clint Bowyer 1.00 2.50
9 Denny Hamlin 1.00 2.50
10 Carl Edwards 1.00 2.50
11 Austin Dillon 1.25 3.00
12 Kurt Busch .75 2.00

2017 Donruss Track Masters

*CRACK ICE/999: .6X TO 1.5X BASIC INSERTS
1 Denny Hamlin 1.00 2.50
2 Carl Edwards 1.00 2.50
3 Dale Earnhardt Jr. 2.00 5.00
4 Kevin Harvick 1.25 3.00
5 Matt Kenseth 1.00 2.50
6 Martin Truex Jr. .75 2.00
7 Joey Logano 1.00 2.50
8 Brad Keselowski 1.25 3.00
9 Jimmie Johnson 1.50 4.00
10 Kurt Busch .75 2.00

2018 Donruss

1 Tony Stewart RK 1.00 2.50
2 Dale Earnhardt Jr. RK 1.25 3.00
3 Carl Edwards RK .60 1.50
4 Jamie McMurray RK .60 1.50
5 Brad Keselowski RK .75 2.00
6 Austin Dillon RK .75 2.00
7 Kevin Harvick RK .75 2.00
8 Kasey Kahne RK .60 1.50
9 Trevor Bayne RK .60 1.50
10 Chase Elliott RK .75 2.00
11 Denny Hamlin RK .60 1.50
12 Ryan Blaney RK .50 1.25
13 Clint Bowyer RK .60 1.50
14 Kyle Busch RK .75 2.00
15 Kurt Busch RK .50 1.25
16 Matt Kenseth RK .60 1.50
17 Joey Logano RK .60 1.50
18 Daniel Suarez RK .60 1.50
19 Ryan Newman RK .50 1.25
20 Kyle Larson RK 1.00 2.50
21 A.J. Allmendinger RK .60 1.50
22 Martin Truex Jr. RK .50 1.25
23 Alex Bowman RK .60 1.50
24 Jimmie Johnson RK 1.00 2.50
25 Danica Patrick RQ 1.25 3.00
26 William Byron RR .60 1.50
27 Bubba Wallace RR .60 1.50
28 Cole Custer RR .60 1.50
29 Christopher Bell RR .60 1.50
30 Spencer Gallagher RR .60 1.50
31 Jamie McMurray .40 1.00
32A Brad Keselowski .50 1.25
Full name
32B Brad Keselowski SP 1.25 3.00
BK
33A Austin Dillon .50 1.25
Name on right
33B Austin Dillon SP 1.25 3.00
Name centered
34A Kevin Harvick .50 1.25
Full name
34B Kevin Harvick SP 1.25 3.00
Happy
35A Kasey Kahne .40 1.00
Full name
35B Kasey Kahne SP 1.00 2.50
Kasey
36 Trevor Bayne .40 1.00
37A Chase Elliott .50 1.25
Full name
37B Chase Elliott SP 1.25 3.00
Chase
38 Denny Hamlin .40 1.00
39A Ryan Blaney .30 .75
Name on right
39B Ryan Blaney SP .75 2.00
Name centered
40A Clint Bowyer .40 1.00
Name on right
40B Clint Bowyer SP 1.00 2.50
Name centered
41A Kyle Busch .50 1.25
Name on right
41B Kyle Busch SP 1.25 3.00
Name centered
42 Kurt Busch .30 .75
43A Matt Kenseth .40 1.00
Name on right
43B Matt Kenseth SP 1.00 2.50
Name centered
44A Joey Logano .40 1.00
Full name
44B Joey Logano SP 1.00 2.50
Sliced Bread
45 Daniel Suarez .40 1.00
46A Ryan Newman .30 .75
Full name
46B Ryan Newman SP .75 2.00
Rocket Man
47A Kyle Larson .60 1.50
Name on right
47B Kyle Larson SP 1.50 4.00
Name centered
48A A.J. Allmendinger .40 1.00
Name on right
48B A.J. Allmendinger SP 1.00 2.50
Name centered
49A Martin Truex Jr. .30 .75
Name on right
49B Martin Truex Jr. SP .75 2.00
Name centered
50 Alex Bowman .40 1.00
51A Jimmie Johnson .60 1.50
Full name
51B Jimmie Johnson SP 1.50 4.00
JJ
52A Danica Patrick .75 2.00
Name on right
52B Danica Patrick SP 2.00 5.00
Name centered
53A Dale Earnhardt Jr. .75 2.00
Full name
53B Dale Earnhardt Jr. SP 2.00 5.00
Dale Jr.
54A Aric Almirola .30 .75
Name on right
54B Aric Almirola SP .75 2.00
Name centered
55 Ty Dillon .40 1.00
56A Ricky Stenhouse Jr. .40 1.00
Name on right
56B Ricky Stenhouse Jr. SP 1.00 2.50
Name centered
57A Erik Jones .40 1.00
Full name
57B Erik Jones SP 1.00 2.50
ROY
58 Paul Menard .25 .60
59 Corey LaJoie .30 .75
60 Matt DiBenedetto .25 .60
61 Landon Cassill .30 .75
62 Chris Buescher .30 .75
63 David Ragan .30 .75
64 Gray Gaulding .25 .60
65 Brendan Gaughan .25 .60
66 Casey Mears .25 .60
67 Michael McDowell .40 1.00
68 Reed Sorenson .25 .60
69 Elliott Sadler .25 .60
70 Michael Annett .40 1.00
71 Justin Allgaier .30 .75
72 Blake Koch .25 .60
73 Ryan Reed .40 1.00
74 Daniel Hemric .40 1.00
75 Dakoda Armstrong .40 1.00
76 Brandon Jones .25 .60
77 Tyler Reddick .40 1.00
78 Brennan Poole .25 .60
79 Joey Gase .25 .60
80 Matt Tifft .40 1.00
81 Kevin Harvick CAR .50 1.25
82 Jimmie Johnson CAR .60 1.50
83 Martin Truex Jr. CAR .30 .75
84 Jamie McMurray CAR .40 1.00
85 Kyle Larson CAR .60 1.50
86 Kurt Busch CAR .30 .75
87 Kyle Busch CAR .50 1.25
88 Brad Keselowski CAR .50 1.25
89 Kasey Kahne CAR .40 1.00
90 Chase Elliott CAR .50 1.25
91 Ryan Blaney CAR .30 .75
92 Denny Hamlin CAR .40 1.00
93 Austin Dillon CAR .50 1.25
94 Clint Bowyer CAR .40 1.00
95 Erik Jones CAR .40 1.00
96 Joey Logano CAR .40 1.00
97 Matt Kenseth CAR .40 1.00
98 A.J. Allmendinger CAR .40 1.00
99 Aric Almirola CAR .30 .75
100 Dale Earnhardt Jr. CAR .75 2.00
101A David Ragan RETRO .30 .75
101B Dale Earnhardt Jr. RETRO SP 2.00 5.00
102A Tony Stewart RETRO .60 1.50
Full name
102B Tony Stewart RETRO SP 1.50 4.00
Smoke
103 Carl Edwards RETRO .40 1.00
104 Richard Petty RETRO .60 1.50
105 Rusty Wallace RETRO .40 1.00
106 Dale Jarrett RETRO .40 1.00
107 Mark Martin RETRO .40 1.00
108 Terry Labonte RETRO .40 1.00
109 Bobby Labonte RETRO .40 1.00
110 Ernie Irvan RETRO .40 1.00
111 Harry Gant RETRO .30 .75
112 Bill Elliott RETRO .60 1.50
113 Kenny Wallace RETRO .25 .60
114 Kerry Earnhardt RETRO .40 1.00
115 Kyle Petty RETRO .30 .75
116 Marcos Ambrose RETRO .40 1.00
117 Michael Waltrip RETRO .40 1.00
118 Ward Burton RETRO .25 .60
119 Derrike Cope RETRO .30 .75
120 Greg Biffle RETRO .30 .75
121 Jamie McMurray RETRO .40 1.00
122 Brad Keselowski RETRO .50 1.25
123 Austin Dillon RETRO .50 1.25
124A Kevin Harvick RETRO .50 1.25
Full name
124B Kevin Harvick RETRO SP 1.25 3.00
Happy
125 Kasey Kahne RETRO .40 1.00
126 Trevor Bayne RETRO .40 1.00
127 Chase Elliott RETRO .50 1.25
128 Denny Hamlin RETRO .40 1.00
129 Ryan Blaney RETRO .30 .75
130 Clint Bowyer RETRO .40 1.00
131 Kyle Busch RETRO .50 1.25
132 Kurt Busch RETRO .30 .75
133 Matt Kenseth RETRO .40 1.00
134 Joey Logano RETRO .40 1.00
135 Daniel Suarez RETRO .40 1.00
136 Ryan Newman RETRO .30 .75
137 Kyle Larson RETRO .60 1.50
138 A.J. Allmendinger RETRO .40 1.00
139 Martin Truex Jr. RETRO .30 .75
140 Alex Bowman RETRO .40 1.00
141A Jimmie Johnson RETRO .60 1.50
Full name
141B Jimmie Johnson RETRO SP 1.50 4.00
JJ
142A Danica Patrick RETRO .75 2.00
Full name
142B Danica Patrick RETRO SP 2.00 5.00
Danica
143 Aric Almirola RETRO .30 .75
144 Ty Dillon RETRO .40 1.00

145 Ricky Stenhouse Jr. RETRO .40 1.00
146 Erik Jones RETRO .40 1.00
147 Paul Menard RETRO .25 .60
148 Corey LaJoie RETRO .30 .75
149 Landon Cassill RETRO .30 .75
150 Dale Earnhardt Jr. RETRO .75 2.00
151 Richard Petty LEG .60 1.50
152 Carl Edwards LEG .40 1.00
153 Dale Earnhardt Jr. LEG .75 2.00
154 Rusty Wallace LEG .40 1.00
155 Mark Martin LEG .40 1.00
156 Dale Jarrett LEG .40 1.00
157 Terry Labonte LEG .40 1.00
158 Bobby Labonte LEG .40 1.00
159 Bill Elliott LEG .60 1.50
160 Bobby Allison LEG .30 .75
161 Cale Yarborough LEG .40 1.00
162 Darrell Waltrip LEG .60 1.50
163 Derrike Cope LEG .30 .75
164 Donnie Allison LEG .30 .75
165 Ernie Irvan LEG .40 1.00
166 Greg Biffle LEG .30 .75
167 Harry Gant LEG .30 .75
168 Hershel McGriff LEG .25 .60
169 Jeff Burton LEG .30 .75
170 Junior Johnson LEG .40 1.00
171 Kenny Wallace LEG .25 .60
172 Kerry Earnhardt LEG .40 1.00
173 Michael Waltrip LEG .40 1.00
174 Ned Jarrett LEG .30 .75
175 Kyle Petty LEG .30 .75

2018 Donruss Artist Proofs
*AP/25: 1.5X TO 4X BASIC CARDS (1-31)
*AP/25: 2.5X TO 6X BASIC CARDS (32-175)
*AP/25: 1X TO 2.5X BASIC SP

2018 Donruss Gold Foil
*GOLD/499: .6X TO 1.5X BASIC CARDS (1-31)
*GOLD/499: 1X TO 2.5X BASIC CARDS (32-175)
*GOLD/499: .4X TO 1X BASIC SP

2018 Donruss Gold Press Proofs
*GOLD PP/99: 1X TO 2.5X BASIC CARDS (1-31)
*GOLD PP/99: 1.5X TO 4X BASIC CARDS (32-175)
*GOLD PP/99: .6X TO 1.5X BASIC SP

2018 Donruss Green Foil
*GREEN/199: .8X TO 2X BASIC CARDS (1-31)
*GREEN/199: 1.2X TO 3X BASIC CARDS (32-175)
*GREEN/199: .5X TO 1.2X BASIC SP

2018 Donruss Press Proofs
*PP/49: 1.2X TO 3X BASIC CARDS (1-31)
*PP/49: 2X TO 5X BASIC CARDS (32-175)
*PP/49: .8X TO 2X BASIC SP

2018 Donruss Red Foil
*RED/299: .8X TO 2X BASIC CARDS (1-31)
*RED/299: 1.2X TO 3X BASIC CARDS (32-175)
*RED/299: .5X TO 1.2X BASIC SP

2018 Donruss Classics
*CRACKED/999: .5X TO 1.2X BASIC INSERTS
*XPLOSION/99: .8X TO 2X BASIC INSERTS
1 Dale Earnhardt Jr. 2.00 5.00
2 Tony Stewart 1.50 4.00
3 Richard Petty 1.50 4.00
4 Darrell Waltrip 1.50 4.00
5 Jimmie Johnson 1.50 4.00
6 Kevin Harvick 1.25 3.00
7 Kyle Busch 1.25 3.00
8 Kurt Busch .75 2.00
9 Kyle Larson 1.50 4.00
10 Ryan Blaney .75 2.00
11 Rusty Wallace 1.00 2.50
12 Dale Jarrett 1.00 2.50
13 Mark Martin 1.00 2.50
14 Terry Labonte 1.00 2.50
15 Bobby Labonte 1.00 2.50
16 Ryan Newman .75 2.00
17 Michael Waltrip 1.00 2.50
18 Matt Kenseth 1.00 2.50
19 Danica Patrick 2.00 5.00
20 Tony Stewart 1.50 4.00

2018 Donruss Elite Dominators
1 Tony Stewart 2.00 5.00
2 Jimmie Johnson 2.00 5.00
3 Martin Truex Jr. 1.00 2.50
4 Joey Logano 1.25 3.00
5 Kyle Larson 2.00 5.00

2018 Donruss Elite Series
1 Tony Stewart 2.00 5.00
2 Kevin Harvick 1.50 4.00
3 Danica Patrick 2.50 6.00
4 Kyle Busch 1.50 4.00
5 Denny Hamlin 1.25 3.00

2018 Donruss Masters of the Track
*CRACKED/999: .5X TO 1.2X BASIC INSERTS
*XPLOSION/99: .8X TO 2X BASIC INSERTS
1 Jimmie Johnson 1.50 4.00
2 Richard Petty 1.50 4.00
3 Tony Stewart 1.50 4.00
4 Mark Martin 1.00 2.50
5 Dale Earnhardt Jr. 2.00 5.00
6 Terry Labonte 1.00 2.50
7 Carl Edwards 1.00 2.50
8 Darrell Waltrip 1.50 4.00

2018 Donruss NEXT in Line
*CRACKED/999: .5X TO 1.2X BASIC INSERTS
*XPLOSION/99: .8X TO 2X BASIC INSERTS
1 Cayden Lapcevich 1.00 2.50
2 Chase Cabre 1.00 2.50
3 Hailie Deegan 12.00 30.00
4 Harrison Burton 1.00 2.50
5 Riley Herbst 1.50 4.00
6 Zane Smith 1.00 2.50
7 Ty Majeski 2.50 6.00

2018 Donruss Phenoms
*CRACKED/999: .5X TO 1.2X BASIC INSERTS
*XPLOSION/99: .8X TO 2X BASIC INSERTS
1 William Byron 1.00 2.50
2 Bubba Wallace 1.00 2.50
3 Kaz Grala 1.25 3.00
4 Spencer Gallagher 1.00 2.50
5 Cody Coughlin 1.00 2.50
6 Grant Enfinger 1.25 3.00
7 Noah Gragson 1.00 2.50
8 Austin Cindric 1.00 2.50
9 Wendell Chavous 1.00 2.50

2018 Donruss Pole Position
*CRACKED/999: .5X TO 1.2X BASIC INSERTS
*XPLOSION/99: .8X TO 2X BASIC INSERTS
1 Chase Elliott 1.25 3.00
2 Kevin Harvick 1.25 3.00
3 Joey Logano 1.00 2.50
4 Kyle Larson 1.50 4.00
5 Clint Bowyer 1.00 2.50
6 Brad Keselowski 1.25 3.00
7 Dale Earnhardt Jr. 2.00 5.00
8 Matt Kenseth 1.00 2.50
9 Erik Jones 1.00 2.50
10 Kyle Busch 1.25 3.00
11 Ryan Blaney .75 2.00
12 Martin Truex Jr. .75 2.00

2018 Donruss Racing Relics
1 A.J. Allmendinger 2.50 6.00
2 Ryan Truex 2.00 5.00
3 Austin Dillon 3.00 8.00
4 Brad Keselowski 3.00 8.00
5 Brandon Jones 1.50 4.00
6 Bubba Wallace 2.50 6.00
7 Chase Elliott 3.00 8.00
8 Chris Buescher 2.00 5.00
9 Dale Earnhardt Jr. 5.00 12.00
11 Denny Hamlin 2.50 6.00
12 Greg Biffle 2.00 5.00
13 Kevin Harvick 3.00 8.00
14 Kyle Larson 4.00 10.00
15 Martin Truex Jr. 2.00 5.00
16 Reed Sorenson 1.50 4.00
17 Ryan Newman 2.00 5.00
18 Trevor Bayne 2.50 6.00
19 Tony Stewart 4.00 10.00
20 Jimmie Johnson 4.00 10.00

2018 Donruss Racing Relics Holo Gold
*GOLD/99: .5X TO 1.2X BASIC MEM
*GOLD/25: .8X TO 2X BASIC MEM
10 Danica Patrick/99 6.00 15.00

2018 Donruss Retro Relics '85
1 Kevin Harvick 3.00 8.00
2 Jimmie Johnson 4.00 10.00
4 Dale Earnhardt Jr. 5.00 12.00
5 Chase Elliott 3.00 8.00
6 Daniel Suarez 2.50 6.00
7 David Ragan 2.00 5.00
8 Denny Hamlin 2.50 6.00
9 Martin Truex Jr. 2.00 5.00
10 Greg Biffle 2.00 5.00
11 Daniel Hemric 2.50 6.00
12 Bubba Wallace 2.50 6.00
13 Brad Keselowski 3.00 8.00
14 Matt Kenseth 2.50 6.00
15 Ricky Stenhouse Jr. 2.50 6.00
16 Trevor Bayne 2.50 6.00
17 Tony Stewart 4.00 10.00
18 Carl Edwards 2.50 6.00
19 Kasey Kahne 2.50 6.00
20 Erik Jones 2.50 6.00
21 Elliott Sadler 1.50 4.00
22 Cole Whitt 2.00 5.00
23 Casey Mears 1.50 4.00
24 Brendan Gaughan 1.50 4.00
25 Aric Almirola 2.00 5.00

2018 Donruss Retro Relics '85 Holo Gold
*GOLD/75-99: .5X TO 1.2X BASIC MEM
3 Danica Patrick/99 6.00 15.00

2018 Donruss Rubber Relic Signatures
1 Brad Keselowski 8.00 20.00
2 Bubba Wallace 6.00 15.00
3 Chase Elliott 25.00 50.00
4 Clint Bowyer 6.00 15.00
5 Dale Earnhardt Jr. 25.00 50.00
6 Danica Patrick 30.00 60.00
7 Denny Hamlin
9 Joey Logano 6.00 15.00
10 Tony Stewart
11 Kevin Harvick 15.00 40.00
12 Kyle Busch 12.00 30.00
13 Kyle Larson 10.00 25.00
14 Martin Truex Jr. 5.00 12.00
15 Ryan Newman 5.00 12.00

2018 Donruss Rubber Relics
1 A.J. Allmendinger 2.50 6.00
3 Brad Keselowski 3.00 8.00
4 Brandon Jones 1.50 4.00
5 Austin Dillon 3.00 8.00
6 Chase Elliott 3.00 8.00
7 Clint Bowyer 2.50 6.00
8 Cole Custer 2.50 6.00
10 Danica Patrick 5.00 12.00
11 Erik Jones 2.50 6.00
12 Garrett Smithley 2.50 6.00
13 Collin Cabre 1.50 4.00
14 Jeffrey Earnhardt 2.50 6.00
15 Jimmie Johnson 4.00 10.00
16 Joey Logano 2.50 6.00
17 John Hunter Nemechek 2.00 5.00
18 Denny Hamlin 2.50 6.00
19 Kasey Kahne 2.50 6.00
20 Justin Allgaier 2.00 5.00
21 Kevin Harvick 3.00 8.00
22 Kurt Busch 2.00 5.00
23 Kyle Busch 3.00 8.00
24 Kyle Larson 4.00 10.00
25 Martin Truex Jr. 2.00 5.00
26 Matt DiBenedetto 1.50 4.00
27 Matt Kenseth 2.50 6.00
28 Matt Tifft 2.50 6.00
29 Michael Annett 2.50 6.00
30 Daniel Hemric 2.50 6.00
31 Ross Chastain 2.50 6.00
32 Paul Menard 1.50 4.00
33 Ricky Stenhouse Jr. 2.50 6.00
34 Ryan Blaney 2.00 5.00
35 Ryan Newman 2.00 5.00
36 Ryan Reed 2.50 6.00
37 Tony Stewart 4.00 10.00
38 Trevor Bayne 2.50 6.00
39 Ty Dillon 2.50 6.00
40 Todd Gilliland 2.00 5.00

2018 Donruss Rubber Relics Holo Gold
*GOLD/99: .5X TO 1.2X BASIC MEM
10 Danica Patrick/99 6.00 15.00

2018 Donruss Signature Series
1 Ahnna Parkhurst 5.00 12.00
2 Ben Rhodes 3.00 8.00
3 Brandon Jones 3.00 8.00
5 Cayden Lapcevich
6 Chase Cabre 5.00 12.00
9 Cole Whitt
10 Dakoda Armstrong 5.00 12.00
12 Ryan Newman 4.00 10.00
15 Hailie Deegan 100.00 200.00
16 Hannah Newhouse 12.00 30.00
18 Harrison Rhodes 4.00 10.00
19 Jeffrey Earnhardt 12.00
20 Jeremy Clements
21 Joey Gase
22 John Hunter Nemechek 4.00 10.00
23 Josh Wise 3.00 8.00
24 Julia Landauer
25 Kate Dallenbach 5.00 12.00
26 Kaz Grala 6.00 15.00
27 Matt DiBenedetto 3.00 8.00
28 Matt Kenseth 5.00 12.00
29 Matt Tifft
30 Michael McDowell
31 Mike Wallace
32 Nicole Behar 6.00 15.00
34 Riley Herbst 8.00 20.00
35 Ross Chastain
36 Ryan Preece 5.00 12.00
37 Ryan Reed 5.00 12.00
39 Ryan Truex 4.00 10.00
40 Spencer Davis 3.00 8.00
41 Spencer Gallagher 5.00 12.00
43 Timothy Peters 3.00 8.00
44 Todd Gilliland 4.00 10.00
47 Tyler Reddick 5.00 12.00
49 Zane Smith 5.00 12.00
50 Gray Gaulding 3.00 8.00

2018 Donruss Signature Series Holo Gold
*GOLD/25: .8X TO 2X BASIC AU
*GOLD/19-23: 1X TO 2.5X BASIC AU
48 William Byron/23 12.00 30.00

2018 Donruss Significant Signatures
*GOLD/25: .8X TO 2X BASIC AU
1 Bill Elliott 8.00 20.00
2 Bobby Labonte 5.00 12.00
3 Darrell Waltrip
4 Derrike Cope 4.00 10.00
6 Ernie Irvan 5.00 12.00
8 Harry Gant 4.00 10.00
9 Johnny Sauter 3.00 8.00
10 Junior Johnson
11 Kelley Earnhardt
12 Kerry Earnhardt
13 Kyle Petty
14 Mark Martin
15 Michael Waltrip 5.00 12.00
16 Morgan Shepherd
17 Ned Jarrett 4.00 10.00
18 Richard Petty
19 Terry Labonte 25.00 50.00
20 Wally Dallenbach 3.00 8.00

2018 Donruss Slingshot
SS1 Richard Petty 12.00 30.00
SS2 Carl Edwards 8.00 20.00
SS3 Tony Stewart 12.00 30.00
SS4 Dale Earnhardt Jr. 15.00 40.00

2018 Donruss Studio
*CRACKED/999: .5X TO 1.2X BASIC INSERTS
*XPLOSION/99: .8X TO 2X BASIC INSERTS
1 Jimmie Johnson 1.50 4.00
2 Kevin Harvick 1.25 3.00
3 Danica Patrick 2.00 5.00
4 Dale Earnhardt Jr. 2.00 5.00
5 Chase Elliott 1.25 3.00
6 Ryan Blaney .75 2.00
7 Trevor Bayne 1.00 2.50
8 Kyle Busch 1.25 3.00
9 Kyle Larson 1.50 4.00
10 Erik Jones 1.00 2.50
11 Martin Truex Jr. .75 2.00
12 Ricky Stenhouse Jr. 1.00 2.50
13 Brad Keselowski 1.25 3.00
14 Bubba Wallace 1.00 2.50
15 Clint Bowyer 1.00 2.50
16 Denny Hamlin 1.00 2.50
17 Corey LaJoie .75 2.00
18 Kasey Kahne 1.00 2.50
19 Ryan Newman .75 2.00
20 Tony Stewart 1.50 4.00

2018 Donruss Studio Signatures
*GOLD/25: .8X TO 2X BASIC AU
2 Aric Almirola 4.00 10.00
3 Austin Dillon 6.00 15.00
4 Daniel Suarez
5 Paul Menard 3.00 8.00
6 Ryan Blaney 8.00 20.00
7 Kasey Kahne 5.00 12.00
8 Kurt Busch 6.00 15.00
9 Jamie McMurray
10 Erik Jones 10.00 25.00

2019 Donruss
1 Jimmie Johnson RK 1.00 2.50
2 Brad Keselowski RK .75 2.00
3 Martin Truex Jr. RK .50 1.25
4 Kevin Harvick RK .75 2.00
5 Kyle Busch RK .75 2.00
6 Kurt Busch RK .50 1.25
7 Richard Petty RK 1.00 2.50
8 Dale Earnhardt Jr. RK 1.25 3.00
9 Bill Elliott RK 1.00 2.50
10 Dale Jarrett RK .60 1.50
11 Darrell Waltrip RK 1.00 2.50
12 Joey Logano RK .60 1.50
13 Rusty Wallace RK .60 1.50
14 Tony Stewart RK 1.00 2.50
15 Terry Labonte RK .60 1.50
16 Jimmie Johnson RET RR 1.00 2.50
17 Richard Petty RET RR 1.00 2.50
18 Danica Patrick RET RR 1.25 3.00
19 Terry Labonte RET RR .60 1.50
20 Dale Jarrett RET RR .60 1.50
21 Bobby Labonte RET RR .60 1.50
22 Carl Edwards RET RR .60 1.50
23 Michael Waltrip RET RR .60 1.50
24 Rusty Wallace RET RR .60 1.50
25 Darrell Waltrip RET RR 1.00 2.50
26 Austin Cindric .40 1.00
27 Corey LaJoie .30 .75
28A Mark Martin .40 1.00
28B Mark Martin SP 1.00 2.50
29A Terry Labonte .40 1.00
29B Terry Labonte SP 1.00 2.50
30 Martin Truex Jr. .30 .75
31A Chase Elliott .50 1.25
31B Bill Elliott 1.50 4.00
Chase Elliott SP
32 Trevor Bayne .40 1.00
33 Ryan Truex .30 .75
34A Richard Petty .60 1.50
34B Richard Petty SP 1.50 4.00
35 John Hunter Nemechek .30 .75
36 Jeremy Clements .25 .60
37 David Ragan .30 .75
38A Bubba Wallace .40 1.00
38B Bubba Wallace SP 1.00 2.50
39A Danica Patrick .75 2.00
39B Danica Patrick SP 2.00 5.00
40 Michael Annett .40 1.00
41 Alex Bowman .40 1.00
42 Daniel Suarez .40 1.00
43 Clint Bowyer .40 1.00
44 Ricky Stenhouse Jr .40 1.00
45 Michael McDowell .40 1.00
46 Ross Chastain .40 1.00
47 Rusty Wallace .40 1.00
48A Jimmie Johnson .60 1.50
48B Jimmie Johnson SP 1.50 4.00
49A Joey Logano .40 1.00
49B Joey Logano SP 1.00 2.50
50A Kyle Busch .50 1.25
50B Kyle Busch SP 1.25 3.00
51 Ryan Reed .40 1.00
52 Aric Almirola .30 .75
53 Erik Jones .40 1.00
54 Ryan Blaney .30 .75
55A Darrell Waltrip .60 1.50
55B Darrell Waltrip SP 1.50 4.00
56 Brad Keselowski .50 1.25
57 Daniel Hemric .40 1.00
58 Tyler Reddick .40 1.00
59 Matt Tifft .40 1.00
60A Kevin Harvick .50 1.25
60B Kevin Harvick SP 1.25 3.00
61 Ty Dillon .40 1.00
62 Jamie McMurray .40 1.00
63 Denny Hamlin .40 1.00
64 Kasey Kahne .40 1.00
65A Tony Stewart .60 1.50
65B Tony Stewart SP 1.50 4.00
66 Kurt Busch .30 .75
67 Elliott Sadler .25 .60
68 Justin Allgaier .30 .75
69A Dale Jarrett .40 1.00
69B Dale Jarrett SP 1.00 2.50
70 Kyle Larson .60 1.50
71 Christopher Bell .75 2.00
72A Dale Earnhardt Jr. .75 2.00
72B Dale Earnhardt Jr. SP 2.00 5.00
73 Austin Dillon .50 1.25
74 Matt Kenseth .40 1.00
75 Cole Custer .40 1.00
76 Brandon Jones .25 .60
77 Paul Menard .25 .60
78 Cole Whitt .30 .75
79 Chris Buescher .30 .75
80 Matt DiBenedetto .25 .60
81A Ryan Newman .30 .75
81B Ryan Newman SP .75 2.00
82 William Byron .40 1.00
83 Bill Elliott .60 1.50
84 Carl Edwards .40 1.00
85 Johnny Sauter .25 .60
86 Jimmie Johnson CAR .60 1.50
87 Martin Truex Jr. CAR .30 .75
88 Kyle Busch CAR .50 1.25
89 Kevin Harvick CAR .50 1.25
90 Brad Keselowski CAR .50 1.25
91 Joey Logano CAR .40 1.00
92 Aric Almirola CAR .30 .75
93 Kyle Larson CAR .60 1.50
94 Chase Elliott CAR .50 1.25
95 Austin Dillon CAR .50 1.25
96 Alex Bowman CAR .40 1.00
97 Ryan Blaney CAR .30 .75
98 Clint Bowyer CAR .40 1.00
99 Erik Jones CAR .40 1.00
100 Danica Patrick CAR .75 2.00
101 Danica Patrick RETRO .75 2.00
102A Dale Earnhardt Jr. RETRO .75 2.00
102B Dale Earnhardt Jr. RET SP 2.00 5.00
103 Carl Edwards RETRO .40 1.00
104A Richard Petty RETRO .60 1.50
104B Kyle Petty 1.50 4.00
Richard Petty RET SP
105 Tony Stewart RETRO .60 1.50
106A Jimmie Johnson RETRO .60 1.50
106B Jimmie Johnson RET SP 1.50 4.00
107A Kevin Harvick RETRO .50 1.25
107B Kevin Harvick RET SP 1.25 3.00
108A Chase Elliott RETRO .50 1.25
108B Chase Elliott RET SP 1.25 3.00
109A Ryan Blaney RETRO .30 .75
109B Ryan Blaney RET SP .75 2.00
110 Bubba Wallace RETRO .40 1.00
111 Martin Truex Jr. RETRO .30 .75
112 Kyle Busch RETRO .50 1.25
113 Brad Keselowski RETRO .50 1.25
114 Joey Logano RETRO .40 1.00
115 Aric Almirola RETRO .30 .75
116 Kyle Larson RETRO .60 1.50
117 Kurt Busch RETRO .30 .75
118 Austin Dillon RETRO .50 1.25
119 Alex Bowman RETRO .40 1.00
120 Clint Bowyer RETRO .40 1.00
121 Erik Jones RETRO .40 1.00
122 Denny Hamlin RETRO .40 1.00
123 Ryan Newman RETRO .30 .75
124 Paul Menard RETRO .25 .60
125 Ricky Stenhouse Jr RETRO .40 1.00
126 Daniel Suarez RETRO .40 1.00
127A Jamie McMurray RETRO .40 1.00
127B Jamie McMurray RET SP 1.00 2.50
128A William Byron RETRO .40 1.00
128B William Byron RET SP 1.00 2.50
129 Chris Buescher RETRO .30 .75
130 David Ragan RETRO .30 .75
131 Michael McDowell RETRO .40 1.00
132 Kasey Kahne RETRO .40 1.00
133 Ty Dillon RETRO .40 1.00
134 Matt DiBenedetto RETRO .25 .60
135 Trevor Bayne RETRO .40 1.00
136 Matt Kenseth RETRO .40 1.00
137 Corey LaJoie RETRO .30 .75
138 Cole Whitt RETRO .30 .75
139 Christopher Bell RETRO .75 2.00
140 Daniel Hemric RETRO .40 1.00
141 Justin Allgaier RETRO .30 .75
142 Ross Chastain RETRO .40 1.00
143 Elliott Sadler RETRO .25 .60
144 Matt Tifft RETRO .40 1.00
145 Tyler Reddick RETRO .40 1.00
146 Brandon Jones RETRO .25 .60
147 Cole Custer RETRO .40 1.00
148 Ryan Truex RETRO .30 .75
149 Austin Cindric RETRO .40 1.00
150 Ryan Reed RETRO .40 1.00
151 Michael Annett RETRO .40 1.00
152 Jeremy Clements RETRO .25 .60
153 John Hunter Nemechek RETRO .30 .75
154 Mark Martin RETRO .40 1.00
155A Dale Jarrett RETRO .40 1.00
155B Dale Jarrett RET SP 1.00 2.50
156 Rusty Wallace RETRO .40 1.00
157A Bill Elliott RETRO .60 1.50
157B Bill Elliott RET SP 1.50 4.00
158 Darrell Waltrip RETRO .60 1.50
159 Terry Labonte RETRO .60 1.50
160 Harry Gant RETRO .30 .75
161 Carl Edwards LEG .40 1.00
162 Dale Earnhardt Jr. LEG .75 2.00
163 Dale Jarrett LEG .40 1.00
164 Bobby Labonte LEG .40 1.00
165 Mark Martin LEG .40 1.00
166 Terry Labonte LEG .40 1.00
167 Rusty Wallace LEG .40 1.00
168 Bobby Allison LEG .30 .75
169 Richard Petty LEG .60 1.50
170 Darrell Waltrip LEG .60 1.50
171 Tony Stewart LEG .60 1.50
172 Bill Elliott LEG .60 1.50
173 Harry Gant LEG .30 .75
174 Ned Jarrett LEG .30 .75
175 Wally Dallenbach LEG .30 .75

2019 Donruss Black
*BLACK/199: .8X TO 2X BASIC CARDS (1-25)
*BLACK/199: 1.2X TO 3X BASIC CARDS (26-175)
*BLACK/199: .5X TO 1.2X BASIC SP

2019 Donruss Gold
*GOLD/299: .8X TO 2X BASIC CARDS (1-25)
*GOLD/299: 1.2X TO 3X BASIC CARDS (26-175)
*GOLD/299: .5X TO 1.2X BASIC SP

2019 Donruss Gold Press Proofs
*GOLD PP/99: 1X TO 2.5X BASIC CARDS (1-25)
*GOLD PP/99: 1.5X TO 4X BASIC CARDS (26-175)
*GOLD PP/99: .6X TO 1.5X BASIC SP

2019 Donruss Press Proofs
*PP/49: 1.2X TO 3X BASIC CARDS (1-25)
*PP/49: 2X TO 5X BASIC CARDS (26-175)
*PP/49: 1X TO 2.5X BASIC SP

2019 Donruss Silver
*SILVER: .6X TO 1.5X BASIC CARDS (1-31)
*SILVER: 1X TO 2.5X BASIC CARDS (32-175)
*SILVER: .4X TO 1X BASIC SP

2019 Donruss Action
*CRACKED/25: 1X TO 2.5X BASIC INSERTS
*HOLO: .5X TO 1.2X BASIC INSERTS
1 William Byron 1.00 2.50
2 Ryan Blaney .75 2.00
3 Alex Bowman 1.00 2.50
4 Joey Logano 1.00 2.50
5 Bubba Wallace 1.00 2.50
6 Erik Jones 1.00 2.50
7 Austin Dillon 1.25 3.00
8 Daniel Suarez 1.00 2.50
9 Chris Buescher .75 2.00
10 Kyle Larson 1.50 4.00
11 Ty Dillon 1.00 2.50
12 Jimmie Johnson 1.50 4.00

2019 Donruss Champion
*CRACKED/25: 1X TO 2.5X BASIC INSERTS
*HOLO: .5X TO 1.2X BASIC INSERTS

2019 Donruss Classics
*CRACKED/25: 1X TO 2.5X BASIC INSERTS
*HOLO: .5X TO 1.2X BASIC INSERTS
1 Denny Hamlin 1.00 2.50
2 Dale Earnhardt Jr. 2.00 5.00
3 Martin Truex Jr. .75 2.00
4 Jimmie Johnson 1.50 4.00
5 Danica Patrick 2.00 5.00
6 Carl Edwards 1.00 2.50
7 Mark Martin 1.00 2.50
8 Rusty Wallace 1.00 2.50
9 Kevin Harvick 1.25 3.00
10 Brad Keselowski 1.25 3.00
11 Joey Logano 1.00 2.50
12 Kyle Busch 1.25 3.00
13 Richard Petty 1.50 4.00
14 Kyle Larson 1.50 4.00
15 Chase Elliott 1.25 3.00
16 Ryan Blaney .75 2.00
17 Bubba Wallace 1.00 2.50
18 Austin Dillon 1.25 3.00
19 William Byron 1.00 2.50
20 Ryan Newman .75 2.00

2019 Donruss Decades of Speed
*CRACKED/25: 1X TO 2.5X BASIC INSERTS
*HOLO: .5X TO 1.2X BASIC INSERTS
1 Jimmie Johnson 1.50 4.00
2 Dale Earnhardt Jr. 2.00 5.00
3 Bill Elliott 1.50 4.00
4 Terry Labonte 1.00 2.50
5 Richard Petty 1.50 4.00
6 Richard Petty 1.50 4.00
7 Richard Petty 1.50 4.00
8 Ned Jarrett .75 2.00

2019 Donruss Icons
*CRACKED/25: 1X TO 2.5X BASIC INSERTS
*HOLO: .5X TO 1.2X BASIC INSERTS
1 Richard Petty 1.50 4.00
2 Jimmie Johnson 1.50 4.00
3 Dale Earnhardt Jr. 2.00 5.00
4 Darrell Waltrip 1.50 4.00
5 Mark Martin 1.00 2.50
6 Rusty Wallace 1.00 2.50
7 Dale Jarrett 1.00 2.50
8 Tony Stewart 1.50 4.00
9 Bobby Allison .75 2.00
10 Terry Labonte 1.00 2.50

2019 Donruss Originals
*CRACKED/25: 1X TO 2.5X BASIC INSERTS
*HOLO: .5X TO 1.2X BASIC INSERTS
1 Jimmie Johnson 1.50 4.00
2 Kevin Harvick 1.25 3.00
3 Denny Hamlin 1.00 2.50
4 Kyle Busch 1.25 3.00
5 Clint Bowyer 1.00 2.50
6 Chase Elliott 1.25 3.00
7 Ryan Blaney .75 2.00
8 Joey Logano 1.00 2.50
9 Brad Keselowski 1.25 3.00
10 Kyle Larson 1.50 4.00
11 Aric Almirola .75 2.00
12 Austin Dillon 1.25 3.00
13 Kurt Busch .75 2.00
14 William Byron 1.00 2.50

2019 Donruss Race Day Relics
*GOLD/25: .8X TO 2X BASIC JSY
*RED/185: .5X TO 1.2X BASIC JSY
1 Alex Bowman 2.50 6.00
2 Aric Almirola 2.00 5.00
3 Blake Koch 1.50 4.00
4 Bubba Wallace 2.50 6.00
5 Chase Elliott 3.00 8.00
6 Chris Buescher 2.00 5.00
7 Cole Whitt 2.00 5.00
8 Dale Earnhardt Jr. 5.00 12.00
9 Daniel Suarez 2.00 5.00
10 Denny Hamlin 2.50 6.00
11 Erik Jones 2.50 6.00
12 Jimmie Johnson 4.00 10.00
13 Tony Stewart 4.00 10.00
14 Ryan Blaney 2.00 5.00
15 Joey Logano 2.50 6.00
16 John Hunter Nemechek 2.00 5.00
17 Justin Allgaier 2.00 5.00
18 Kevin Harvick 3.00 8.00
19 Kyle Busch 3.00 8.00
20 Martin Truex Jr. 2.00 5.00
21 Paul Menard 1.50 4.00
22 Ross Chastain 2.50 6.00
23 Ryan Newman 2.00 5.00
24 Trevor Bayne 2.50 6.00
25 Tyler Reddick 2.50 6.00

2019 Donruss Retro Relics '86
*GOLD/25: .8X TO 2X BASIC JSY
*RED/185: .5X TO 1.2X BASIC JSY
1 Ryan Blaney 2.00 5.00
2 Elliott Sadler 1.50 4.00
3 Ty Dillon 2.50 6.00
4 Austin Dillon 3.00 8.00
5 Clint Bowyer 2.50 6.00
6 Kasey Kahne 2.50 6.00
7 David Ragan 2.00 5.00
8 Kyle Larson 4.00 10.00
9 Cameron Hayley 1.50 4.00
10 Jamie McMurray 2.50 6.00
11 Tony Stewart 4.00 10.00
12 Kyle Busch 3.00 8.00
13 Dale Earnhardt Jr. 5.00 12.00
14 Kevin Harvick 3.00 8.00
15 Kurt Busch 2.00 5.00
16 William Byron 2.50 6.00
17 Corey LaJoie 2.00 5.00
18 Jimmie Johnson 4.00 10.00
19 Brad Keselowski 3.00 8.00
20 Daniel Hemric 2.50 6.00

2019 Donruss Top Tier
*CRACKED/25: 1X TO 2.5X BASIC INSERTS
*HOLO: .5X TO 1.2X BASIC INSERTS
1 Jimmie Johnson 1.50 4.00
2 Kevin Harvick 1.25 3.00
3 Chase Elliott 1.25 3.00
4 Ryan Blaney .75 2.00
5 Bubba Wallace 1.00 2.50
6 Martin Truex Jr. .75 2.00
7 Kyle Busch 1.25 3.00
8 Denny Hamlin 1.00 2.50
9 Brad Keselowski 1.25 3.00
10 Austin Dillon 1.25 3.00

2020 Donruss
1 Chase Elliott RK .75 2.00
2 Brad Keselowski RK .75 2.00
3 Austin Dillon RK .75 2.00
4 Ryan Newman RK .50 1.25
5 Kyle Busch RK .75 2.00
6 Joey Logano RK .60 1.50
7 Richard Petty RK 1.00 2.50
8 Dale Earnhardt Jr. RK 1.25 3.00
9 Jimmie Johnson RK 1.00 2.50
10 Martin Truex Jr. RK .50 1.25
11 Tony Stewart RK 1.00 2.50
12 Denny Hamlin RK .60 1.50
13 Kyle Larson RK 1.00 2.50
14 Bubba Wallace RK .60 1.50
15 Ryan Blaney RK .50 1.25
16 Hailie Deegan RR 2.50 6.00
17 Derek Kraus RR .50 1.25
18 Sam Mayer RR .40 1.00
19 Tanner Gray RR .60 1.50
20 Max McLaughlin RR .75 2.00
21 Jesse Little RR .50 1.25
22 Brittney Zamora RR .75 2.00
23 Alex Bowman .40 1.00
24 Aric Almirola .30 .75
25 Austin Dillon .50 1.25
26 Brad Keselowski .50 1.25
27 Bubba Wallace .40 1.00
28 Chase Elliott .50 1.25
29 Chris Buescher .30 .75
30 Clint Bowyer .40 1.00
31 Corey LaJoie .30 .75
32 Daniel Hemric .40 1.00
33 Daniel Suarez .40 1.00
34 David Ragan .30 .75
35 Denny Hamlin .40 1.00
36 Erik Jones .40 1.00
37 Jamie McMurray .40 1.00
38 Jimmie Johnson .60 1.50
39 Joey Logano .40 1.00
40 Kevin Harvick .50 1.25
41 Kurt Busch .30 .75
42 Kyle Busch .50 1.25
43 Kyle Larson .60 1.50
44 Martin Truex Jr. .30 .75
45 Matt DiBenedetto .25 .60
46 Matt Tifft .40 1.00
47 Michael McDowell .40 1.00
48 Paul Menard .25 .60
49 Reed Sorenson .25 .60
50 Ricky Stenhouse Jr. .40 1.00
51 Ryan Blaney .30 .75
52 Ryan Newman .30 .75
53 Ryan Preece .25 .60
54 Ty Dillon .40 1.00
55 William Byron .40 1.00
56 Christopher Bell .40 1.00
57 Cole Custer .40 1.00
58 Tyler Reddick .40 1.00
59 Austin Cindric .40 1.00
60 Chase Briscoe .40 1.00
61 Justin Allgaier .30 .75
62 Michael Annett .40 1.00
63 Noah Gragson .25 .60
64 Justin Haley .25 .60
65 John Hunter Nemechek .30 .75
66 Gray Gaulding .25 .60
67 Ryan Sieg .25 .60
68 Jeb Burton .30 .75
69 Jeremy Clements .25 .60
70 Morgan Shepherd .40 1.00
71 Riley Herbst .30 .75
72 Ryan Truex .30 .75
73 Zane Smith .25 .60
74 Brett Moffitt .40 1.00
75 Brandon Jones .25 .60
76 Todd Gilliland .30 .75
77 Harrison Burton .50 1.25
78 Ross Chastain .40 1.00
79 Matt Crafton .30 .75
80 Darrell Waltrip .60 1.50
81 Bobby Allison .30 .75
82 Bobby Labonte .40 1.00
83 Carl Edwards .40 1.00
84 Matt Kenseth .40 1.00
85 Dale Jarrett .40 1.00
86 Danica Patrick .75 2.00
87 Bill Elliott .60 1.50
88 Greg Biffle .30 .75
89 Tony Stewart .60 1.50
90 Rusty Wallace .40 1.00
91 Kasey Kahne .40 1.00
92 Marcos Ambrose .40 1.00
93 Mark Martin .40 1.00
94 Dale Earnhardt Jr. .75 2.00
95 Michael Waltrip .40 1.00
96 Terry Labonte .40 1.00
97 Richard Petty .60 1.50
98 Jimmie Johnson CAR .60 1.50
99 Chase Elliott CAR .50 1.25
100 William Byron CAR .40 1.00
101 Denny Hamlin CAR .40 1.00
102 Kyle Busch CAR .50 1.25
103 Martin Truex Jr. CAR .30 .75
104 Ryan Blaney CAR .30 .75
105 Brad Keselowski CAR .50 1.25
106 Joey Logano CAR .40 1.00
107 Kevin Harvick CAR .50 1.25
108 Clint Bowyer CAR .40 1.00
109 Aric Almirola CAR .30 .75
110 Kyle Larson CAR .60 1.50
111 Austin Dillon CAR .50 1.25
112 Kurt Busch CAR .30 .75
113 Bubba Wallace CAR .40 1.00
114 Daniel Hemric CAR .40 1.00
115 Ryan Newman CAR .30 .75
116 Harrison Burton RETRO .50 1.25
117 Chase Briscoe RETRO .40 1.00
118 Jeremy Clements RETRO .25 .60
119 Jeff Burton RETRO .30 .75
120 Kasey Kahne RETRO .40 1.00
121 Ross Chastain RETRO .40 1.00
122 Reed Sorenson RETRO .25 .60
123 Matt Kenseth RETRO .40 1.00
124 Chris Buescher RETRO .30 .75
125 Matt Tifft RETRO .40 1.00
126 Matt DiBenedetto RETRO .25 .60
127 Cole Custer RETRO .40 1.00
128 Michael Waltrip RETRO .40 1.00
129 Richard Petty RETRO .60 1.50
130 Aric Almirola RETRO .30 .75
131 Bubba Wallace RETRO .40 1.00
132 David Ragan RETRO .30 .75
133 Ricky Stenhouse Jr. RETRO .40 1.00
134 Paul Menard RETRO .25 .60
135 Chase Elliott RETRO .50 1.25
136 Michael McDowell RETRO .40 1.00
137 Ryan Blaney RETRO .30 .75
138 Ty Dillon RETRO .40 1.00
139 Ryan Preece RETRO .25 .60
140 Kevin Harvick RETRO .50 1.25
141 Danica Patrick RETRO .75 2.00
142 Daniel Hemric RETRO .40 1.00
143 Terry Labonte RETRO .40 1.00
144 Daniel Suarez RETRO .40 1.00
145 Noah Gragson RETRO .25 .60
146 Rusty Wallace RETRO .40 1.00
147 Justin Allgaier RETRO .30 .75
148 Brad Keselowski RETRO .50 1.25
149 Erik Jones RETRO .40 1.00
150 John Hunter Nemechek RETRO .30 .75
151 Riley Herbst RETRO .30 .75
152 Mark Martin RETRO .40 1.00
153 Alex Bowman RETRO .40 1.00
154 Clint Bowyer RETRO .40 1.00
155 Darrell Waltrip RETRO .60 1.50
156 Tony Stewart RETRO .60 1.50
157 Brett Moffitt RETRO .40 1.00
158 Ryan Sieg RETRO .25 .60
159 Bill Elliott RETRO .60 1.50
160 Jimmie Johnson RETRO .60 1.50
161 Kurt Busch RETRO .30 .75
162 Kyle Larson RETRO .60 1.50
163 William Byron RETRO .40 1.00
164 Christopher Bell RETRO .40 1.00
165 Bobby Allison RETRO .30 .75
166 Bobby Labonte RETRO .40 1.00
167 Morgan Shepherd RETRO .40 1.00
168 Austin Dillon RETRO .50 1.25
169 Greg Biffle RETRO .30 .75
170 Dale Earnhardt Jr. RETRO .75 2.00
171 Carl Edwards RETRO .40 1.00
172 Joey Logano RETRO .40 1.00
173 Marcos Ambrose RETRO .40 1.00
174 Denny Hamlin RETRO .40 1.00
175 Gray Gaulding RETRO .25 .60
176 Tyler Reddick RETRO .40 1.00
177 Zane Smith RETRO .25 .60
178 Jamie McMurray RETRO .40 1.00
179 Justin Haley RETRO .25 .60
180 Martin Truex Jr. RETRO .30 .75
181 Ryan Truex RETRO .30 .75
182 Kyle Busch RETRO .50 1.25
183 Corey LaJoie RETRO .30 .75
184 Dale Jarrett RETRO .40 1.00
185 Austin Cindric RETRO .40 1.00
186 Michael Annett RETRO .40 1.00
187 Ryan Newman RETRO .30 .75
188 Jeb Burton RETRO .30 .75
189 Kurt Busch RET CAR .30 .75
190 Brad Keselowski RET CAR .50 1.25
191 Austin Dillon RET CAR .50 1.25
192 Ryan Newman RET CAR .30 .75
193 Chase Elliott RET CAR .50 1.25
194 Denny Hamlin RET CAR .40 1.00
195 Ryan Blaney RET CAR .30 .75
196 Kyle Busch RET CAR .50 1.25
197 William Byron RET CAR .40 1.00
198 Bubba Wallace RET CAR .40 1.00
199 Jimmie Johnson RET CAR .60 1.50
200 Alex Bowman RET CAR .40 1.00

2020 Donruss Blue
*BLUE/299: .8X TO 2X BASIC CARDS (1-22)
*BLUE/299: 1.2X TO 3X BASIC CARDS (23-200)

2020 Donruss Carolina Blue
*CAR BLUE: .6X TO 1.5X BASIC CARDS (1-22)
*CAR BLUE: 1X TO 2.5X BASIC CARDS (23-200)

2020 Donruss Green
*GREEN/99: 1X TO 2.5X BASIC CARDS (1-22)
*GREEN/99: 1.5X TO 4X BASIC CARDS (23-200)

2020 Donruss Orange
*ORANGE: .6X TO 1.5X BASIC CARDS (1-22)
*ORANGE: 1X TO 2.5X BASIC CARDS (23-200)

2020 Donruss Pink
*PINK/25: 1.5X TO 4X BASIC CARDS (1-22)
*PINK/25: 2.5X TO 6X BASIC CARDS (23-200)

2020 Donruss Purple
*PURPLE/49: 1.2X TO 3X BASIC CARDS (1-22)
*PURPLE/49: 2X TO 5X BASIC CARDS (23-200)

2020 Donruss Red
*RED/299: .8X TO 2X BASIC CARDS (1-22)
*RED/299: 1.2X TO 3X BASIC CARDS (23-200)

2020 Donruss Silver
*SILVER: .6X TO 1.5X BASIC CARDS (1-22)
*SILVER: 1X TO 2.5X BASIC CARDS (23-200)

2020 Donruss Action Packed
*CHECKERS: .5X TO 1.2X BASIC INSERTS
*CRACKED/25: 1.2X TO 3X BASIC INSERTS
*HOLO/199: .6X TO 1.5X BASIC INSERTS
1 Austin Dillon 1.25 3.00
2 Martin Truex Jr. .75 2.00
3 Joey Logano 1.00 2.50
4 Kevin Harvick 1.25 3.00
5 Chase Elliott 1.25 3.00
6 Jimmie Johnson 1.50 4.00
7 William Byron 1.00 2.50
8 Denny Hamlin 1.00 2.50

2020 Donruss Aero Package
*CHECKERS: .5X TO 1.2X BASIC INSERTS
*CRACKED/25: 1.2X TO 3X BASIC INSERTS
*HOLO/199: .6X TO 1.5X BASIC INSERTS
1 Denny Hamlin 1.00 2.50
2 William Byron 1.00 2.50
3 Kyle Busch 1.25 3.00
4 Kurt Busch .75 2.00
5 Kyle Larson 1.50 4.00
6 Ryan Blaney .75 2.00
7 Chase Elliott 1.25 3.00
8 Martin Truex Jr. .75 2.00
9 Brad Keselowski 1.25 3.00
10 Joey Logano 1.00 2.50
11 Austin Dillon 1.25 3.00
12 Daniel Suarez 1.00 2.50

2020 Donruss Classics
*CHECKERS: .5X TO 1.2X BASIC INSERTS
*CRACKED/25: 1.2X TO 3X BASIC INSERTS
*HOLO/199: .6X TO 1.5X BASIC INSERTS
1 Dale Earnhardt Jr. 2.00 5.00
2 Danica Patrick 2.00 5.00
3 Bobby Labonte 1.00 2.50
4 Richard Petty 1.50 4.00
5 Terry Labonte 1.00 2.50
6 Bobby Allison .75 2.00
7 Jimmie Johnson 1.50 4.00
8 Darrell Waltrip 1.50 4.00
9 Bill Elliott 1.50 4.00
10 Mark Martin 1.00 2.50
11 Rusty Wallace 1.00 2.50
12 Matt Kenseth 1.00 2.50
13 Carl Edwards 1.00 2.50
14 Greg Biffle .75 2.00
15 Kyle Petty .75 2.00
16 Jeff Burton .75 2.00

2020 Donruss Contenders
*CHECKERS: .5X TO 1.2X BASIC INSERTS
*CRACKED/25: 1.2X TO 3X BASIC INSERTS
*HOLO/199: .6X TO 1.5X BASIC INSERTS
1 Martin Truex Jr. .75 2.00
2 Kevin Harvick 1.25 3.00
3 Joey Logano 1.00 2.50
4 Kyle Busch 1.25 3.00
5 Brad Keselowski 1.25 3.00
6 Chase Elliott 1.25 3.00
7 Denny Hamlin 1.00 2.50
8 Kyle Larson 1.50 4.00
9 William Byron 1.00 2.50
10 Ryan Blaney .75 2.00
11 Alex Bowman 1.00 2.50
12 Aric Almirola .75 2.00
13 Ryan Newman .75 2.00
14 Kurt Busch .75 2.00
15 Clint Bowyer 1.00 2.50
16 Erik Jones 1.00 2.50

2020 Donruss Dominators
*CHECKERS: .5X TO 1.2X BASIC INSERTS
*CRACKED/25: 1.2X TO 3X BASIC INSERTS
*HOLO/199: .6X TO 1.5X BASIC INSERTS
1 Jimmie Johnson 1.50 4.00
2 Tony Stewart 1.50 4.00
3 Kyle Busch 1.25 3.00
4 Terry Labonte 1.00 2.50
5 Richard Petty 1.50 4.00
6 Bobby Allison .75 2.00
7 Darrell Waltrip 1.50 4.00
8 Rusty Wallace 1.00 2.50
9 Kevin Harvick 1.25 3.00
10 Mark Martin 1.00 2.50

2020 Donruss Elite Series
*CHECKERS: .5X TO 1.2X BASIC INSERTS
*CRACKED/25: 1.2X TO 3X BASIC INSERTS
*HOLO/199: .6X TO 1.5X BASIC INSERTS
1 Kyle Busch 1.25 3.00
2 Kevin Harvick 1.25 3.00
3 Ryan Newman .75 2.00
4 Jimmie Johnson 1.50 4.00
5 Chase Elliott 1.25 3.00
6 Brad Keselowski 1.25 3.00
7 Denny Hamlin 1.00 2.50
8 Austin Dillon 1.25 3.00
9 Ryan Blaney .75 2.00
10 Alex Bowman 1.00 2.50

2020 Donruss New Age
*CHECKERS: .5X TO 1.2X BASIC INSERTS
*CRACKED/25: 1.2X TO 3X BASIC INSERTS
*HOLO/199: .6X TO 1.5X BASIC INSERTS
1 William Byron 1.00 2.50
2 Ryan Blaney .75 2.00
3 Chase Elliott 1.25 3.00
4 Bubba Wallace 1.00 2.50
5 Daniel Hemric 1.00 2.50
6 Matt Tifft 1.00 2.50
7 Ross Chastain 1.00 2.50
8 Ryan Preece .60 1.50
9 Hailie Deegan 4.00 10.00
10 Thad Moffitt .60 1.50

2020 Donruss Retro Series
*CHECKERS: .5X TO 1.2X BASIC INSERTS
*CRACKED/25: 1.2X TO 3X BASIC INSERTS
*HOLO/199: .6X TO 1.5X BASIC INSERTS
1 Martin Truex Jr. .75 2.00
2 Joey Logano 1.00 2.50
3 Jimmie Johnson 1.50 4.00
4 Kevin Harvick 1.25 3.00
5 Aric Almirola .75 2.00
6 William Byron 1.00 2.50
7 Chase Elliott 1.25 3.00
8 Ryan Blaney .75 2.00
9 Brad Keselowski 1.25 3.00
10 Kyle Busch 1.25 3.00

2020 Donruss Signature Series Red
*BASE: .3X TO .8X RED AU/150-250
*BASE: .25X TO .6X BASIC AU/42-50
*BASE: .5X TO .5X BASIC AU/25
*GOLD/25: .6X TO 1.5X GOLD AU/150-250
*GOLD/25: .5X TO 1.2X GOLD AU/42-50
*GOLD/18-24: .5X TO 1.2X GOLD AU/25
1 Bill Elliott/25 15.00 40.00
2 Cody Ware/250 6.00 15.00
3 Ray Black Jr./50 8.00 20.00
4 David Ragan/200 5.00 12.00
5 Dylan Lupton/250 4.00 10.00
6 Ernie Irvan/150 4.00 10.00
7 Gray Gaulding/250 4.00 10.00
8 Harrison Rhodes/250 4.00 10.00
9 Harry Gant/250 5.00 12.00
11 Jeb Burton/250 5.00 12.00
12 Kaz Grala/250 5.00 12.00
13 Kyle Petty/44 6.00 15.00
14 Landon Cassill/250 5.00 12.00
15 Reed Sorenson/50 5.00 12.00
16 Spencer Boyd/250 5.00 12.00
17 Ty Dillon/25 10.00 25.00
18 Aric Almirola/50 6.00 15.00
19 Bobby Labonte/25 10.00 25.00
20 Bubba Wallace/43 8.00 20.00
21 Clint Bowyer/25 10.00 25.00
22 William Byron/50 8.00 20.00
23 Brett Moffitt/50 8.00 20.00
24 Kyle Larson/42 12.00 30.00
25 Morgan Shepherd/250 6.00 15.00
26 Christopher Bell/250 6.00 15.00
27 Daniel Suarez/25 10.00 25.00
28 Justin Allgaier/250 5.00 12.00
29 Martin Truex Jr./25 8.00 20.00
30 Tyler Reddick/250 6.00 15.00

2020 Donruss Top Tier
*CHECKERS: .5X TO 1.2X BASIC INSERTS
*CRACKED/25: 1.2X TO 3X BASIC INSERTS
*HOLO/199: .6X TO 1.5X BASIC INSERTS
1 Jimmie Johnson 1.50 4.00
2 Carl Edwards 1.00 2.50
3 Dale Earnhardt Jr. 2.00 5.00
4 Dale Jarrett 1.00 2.50
5 Danica Patrick 2.00 5.00
6 Kevin Harvick 1.25 3.00
7 Kyle Busch 1.25 3.00
8 Richard Petty 1.50 4.00

2019 Donruss Optic
*BLUE: 2.5X TO 6X BASIC CARDS
*HOLO: .75X TO 2X BASIC CARDS
1 Richard Petty RK .60 1.50
2 Jimmie Johnson RK .60 1.50
3 Kevin Harvick RK .50 1.25
4 Dale Earnhardt Jr. RK .75 2.00
5 Kyle Busch RK .50 1.25
6 Richard Petty RET RR .60 1.50
7 Danica Patrick RET RR .75 2.00
8 Terry Labonte RET RR .40 1.00
9 Dale Jarrett RET RR .40 1.00
10 Rusty Wallace RET RR .40 1.00
11 Dale Earnhardt Jr. .75 2.00
12 Denny Hamlin .40 1.00
13 Martin Truex Jr. .30 .75
14 Erik Jones .40 1.00
15 Kyle Busch .50 1.25
16 Kevin Harvick .50 1.25
17 Aric Almirola .30 .75
18 Brad Keselowski .50 1.25
19 Joey Logano .40 1.00
20 Kyle Larson .60 1.50
21 Kurt Busch .30 .75
22 Chase Elliott .50 1.25
23 Austin Dillon .50 1.25
24 Alex Bowman .40 1.00
25 Ryan Blaney .30 .75
26 Clint Bowyer .40 1.00
27 Jimmie Johnson .60 1.50
28 Ryan Newman .30 .75
29 Paul Menard .25 .60
30 Ricky Stenhouse Jr .40 1.00
31 Daniel Suarez .40 1.00
32 Jamie McMurray .40 1.00
33 William Byron .40 1.00
34 Chris Buescher .30 .75
35 David Ragan .30 .75
36 Bubba Wallace .40 1.00
37 Kasey Kahne .40 1.00
38 Ty Dillon .40 1.00
39 Matt Kenseth .40 1.00
40 Danica Patrick .75 2.00
41 Christopher Bell .75 2.00
42 Joe Nemechek .25 .60
43 Justin Allgaier .30 .75
44 Ross Chastain .40 1.00
45 Elliott Sadler .25 .60
46 Johnny Sauter .25 .60
47 Carl Edwards .40 1.00
48 Chase Briscoe .40 1.00
49 Cole Custer .40 1.00
50 John Hunter Nemechek .30 .75
51 Dale Jarrett .40 1.00
52 Mark Martin .40 1.00
53 Cody Coughlin .30 .75
54 Bobby Labonte .40 1.00
55 Bill Elliott .60 1.50
56 David Ragan RETRO .30 .75
57 Dale Earnhardt Jr. RETRO .75 2.00
58 Alex Bowman RETRO .40 1.00
59 Bubba Wallace RETRO .40 1.00
60 Ty Dillon RETRO .40 1.00
61 Bobby Labonte RETRO .40 1.00
62 Matt Kenseth RETRO .40 1.00
63 Chase Briscoe RETRO .40 1.00
64 Ross Chastain RETRO .40 1.00
65 Denny Hamlin RETRO .40 1.00
66 Kevin Harvick RETRO .50 1.25
67 Austin Dillon RETRO .50 1.25
68 Cole Custer RETRO .40 1.00
69 Bill Elliott RETRO .60 1.50
70 Erik Jones RETRO .40 1.00
71 Joey Logano RETRO .40 1.00
72 Ricky Stenhouse Jr RETRO .40 1.00
73 Daniel Suarez RETRO .40 1.00
74 Clint Bowyer RETRO .40 1.00
75 Justin Allgaier RETRO .30 .75
76 Carl Edwards RETRO .40 1.00
77 Elliott Sadler RETRO .25 .60
78 Kyle Busch RETRO .50 1.25
79 Aric Almirola RETRO .30 .75
80 Kyle Larson RETRO .60 1.50
81 Paul Menard RETRO .25 .60
82 Christopher Bell RETRO .75 2.00
83 John Hunter Nemechek RETRO .30 .75
84 William Byron RETRO .40 1.00
85 Chris Buescher RETRO .30 .75
86 Rusty Wallace LEG .40 1.00
87 Mark Martin LEG .40 1.00
88 Darrell Waltrip LEG .60 1.50
89 Terry Labonte LEG .40 1.00
90 Richard Petty LEG .60 1.50

2019 Donruss Optic Illusion
*HOLO: .6X TO 1.5X BASIC INSERTS
*BLUE: 1.5X TO 4X BASIC INSERTS
*RED: 1.5X TO 4X BASIC INSERTS
1 Jimmie Johnson 1.00 2.50
2 Kevin Harvick .75 2.00
3 Martin Truex Jr. .50 1.25
4 Danica Patrick 1.25 3.00
5 Chase Elliott .75 2.00
6 Ryan Blaney .50 1.25
7 Bubba Wallace .60 1.50
8 Tony Stewart 1.00 2.50
9 Kyle Busch .75 2.00
10 Denny Hamlin .60 1.50

2019 Donruss Optic Signatures Holo
1 Richard Petty/25 RK
2 Jimmie Johnson/25 RK EXCH 25.00 50.00
3 Kevin Harvick/25 RK EXCH 10.00 25.00
4 Dale Earnhardt Jr./25 RK 15.00 40.00
5 Kyle Busch/25 RK 30.00 60.00
6 Richard Petty/25 RET RR
7 Danica Patrick/75 RET RR 30.00 60.00
8 Terry Labonte/75 RET RR 15.00 40.00
9 Dale Jarrett/75 RET RR 15.00 40.00
10 Rusty Wallace/75 RET RR 5.00 12.00
11 Dale Earnhardt Jr./75 25.00 50.00
12 Denny Hamlin/75 5.00 12.00
13 Martin Truex Jr./75 8.00 20.00
14 Erik Jones/75 5.00 12.00
15 Kyle Busch/49 25.00 50.00
16 Kevin Harvick/49 8.00 20.00
17 Aric Almirola/75 4.00 10.00
18 Brad Keselowski/75 6.00 15.00
19 Joey Logano/75 5.00 12.00
20 Kyle Larson/75 8.00 20.00
21 Kurt Busch/75 4.00 10.00
22 Chase Elliott/25
23 Austin Dillon/75 6.00 15.00
24 Alex Bowman/75 5.00 12.00
25 Ryan Blaney/49 10.00 25.00
26 Clint Bowyer/75 5.00 12.00
27 Jimmie Johnson/25 EXCH 25.00 50.00
28 Ryan Newman/75 4.00 10.00
29 Paul Menard/75 3.00 8.00
30 Ricky Stenhouse Jr/75 12.00 30.00
32 Jamie McMurray/75
33 William Byron/75 15.00 40.00
34 Chris Buescher/75 4.00 10.00
35 David Ragan/75 4.00 10.00
36 Bubba Wallace/75 EXCH 5.00 12.00
37 Kasey Kahne/75 5.00 12.00
39 Matt Kenseth/75 5.00 12.00
40 Danica Patrick/49 40.00 80.00
41 Christopher Bell/75 10.00 5.00
43 Justin Allgaier/75
47 Carl Edwards/75 8.00 20.00
48 Chase Briscoe/75 5.00 12.00
49 Cole Custer/75
51 Dale Jarrett/75 15.00 40.00
52 Mark Martin/75 15.00 40.00
53 Cody Coughlin/31
54 Bobby Labonte/75 10.00 25.00
55 Bill Elliott/75 8.00 20.00
56 David Ragan/75 RETRO 4.00 10.00
57 Dale Earnhardt Jr./75 RETRO 25.00 50.00
58 Alex Bowman/75 RETRO 5.00 12.00
59 Bubba Wallace/75 RETRO EXCH 5.00 12.00
61 Bobby Labonte/75 RETRO 10.00 25.00
62 Matt Kenseth/75 RETRO 5.00 12.00
63 Chase Briscoe/75 RETRO 5.00 12.00
64 Ross Chastain/75 RETRO
65 Denny Hamlin/75 RETRO 5.00 12.00
66 Kevin Harvick/25 RETRO EXCH 10.00 25.00
67 Austin Dillon/75 RETRO 6.00 15.00
68 Cole Custer/75 RETRO
69 Bill Elliott/75 RETRO 8.00 20.00
70 Erik Jones/75 RETRO 5.00 12.00
71 Joey Logano/75 RETRO 5.00 12.00
72 Ricky Stenhouse Jr/75 RETRO 12.00 30.00
74 Clint Bowyer/75 RETRO 5.00 12.00
75 Justin Allgaier/75 RETRO
76 Carl Edwards/75 RETRO 8.00 20.00
78 Kyle Busch/49 RETRO 25.00 50.00
79 Aric Almirola/75 RETRO 4.00 10.00
80 Kyle Larson/75 RETRO 8.00 20.00
81 Paul Menard/75 RETRO 3.00 8.00
82 Christopher Bell/75 RETRO 10.00 25.00
84 William Byron/75 RETRO 15.00 40.00
85 Chris Buescher/75 RETRO 4.00 10.00
86 Rusty Wallace/75 LEG 5.00 12.00
87 Mark Martin/75 LEG 15.00 40.00
88 Darrell Waltrip/75 LEG 8.00 20.00
89 Terry Labonte/75 LEG 15.00 40.00
90 Richard Petty/25 LEG

2008 Donruss Sports Legends
This set was released on December 10, 2008. The base set consists of 144 cards and features cards of players from various sports.
COMPLETE SET (144) 40.00 100.00
8 Bobby Allison .50 1.25
109 Cale Yarborough .60 1.50
116 Al Unser .40 1.00
137 Richard Petty .75 2.00
139 Al Unser Jr. .40 1.00

2008 Donruss Sports Legends Mirror Blue
*BLUE/100: 2X TO 5X BASIC CARDS
STATED PRINT RUN 100 SER.#'d SETS

2008 Donruss Sports Legends Mirror Gold
*GOLD/25: 3X TO 8X BASIC CARDS
STATED PRINT RUN 25 SER.#'d SETS

2008 Donruss Sports Legends Mirror Red
*RED/250: 1.5X TO 4X BASIC CARDS
STATED PRINT RUN 250 SER.#'d SETS

2008 Donruss Sports Legends Museum Collection
SILVER PRINT RUN 1000 SER.#'d SETS
*GOLD/100: .6X TO 1.5X SILVER/1000
GOLD PRINT RUN 100 SER.#'d SETS
27 Al Unser 1.00 2.50
34 Cale Yarborough 1.50 4.00

2008 Donruss Sports Legends Museum Collection Signatures
STATED PRINT RUN 1-250
SERIAL #'d UNDER 25 NOT PRICED
27 Al Unser/50 10.00 25.00
34 Cale Yarborough/100 8.00 20.00

2008 Donruss Sports Legends Certified Cuts
STATED PRINT RUN 1-100
SERIAL #'d TO 1 NOT PRICED
20 Richard Petty/20 75.00 135.00

2008 Donruss Sports Legends Materials Mirror Blue
*MIRROR BLUE: .5X TO 1.2X MIRROR RED
MIRROR BLUE PRINT RUN 5-250
SERIAL #'d UNDER 15 NOT PRICED

2008 Donruss Sports Legends Materials Mirror Gold
*GOLD/25: .8X TO 2X MIRROR RED
GOLD PRINT RUN 1-25 SER.#'d SETS
SERIAL #'d UNDER 20 NOT PRICED

2008 Donruss Sports Legends Materials Mirror Red
MIRROR RED PRINT RUN 10-500
SERIAL #'d UNDER 25 NOT PRICED
*GOLD/25: .8X TO 2X MIRROR RED
UNPRICED MIRROR EMERALD PRINT RUN 1-5
UNPRICED MIRROR BLACK PRINT RUN 1
8 Bobby Allison Jeans/500 3.00 8.00
137 Richard Petty Pants/400 5.00 12.00

2008 Donruss Sports Legends Signature Connection Combos
STATED PRINT RUN 25-100
14 A.Unser/A.Unser Jr./100 20.00 40.00
16 A.Unser/R.Petty/100 25.00 60.00

2008 Donruss Sports Legends Signatures Mirror Blue
MIRROR BLUE PRINT RUN 2-250
SERIAL #'d UNDER 10 NOT PRICED
UNPRICED MIRROR EMERALD PRINT RUN 1-5
UNPRICED MIRROR BLACK PRINT RUN 1
8 Bobby Allison/26 10.00 25.00
109 Cale Yarborough/50 10.00 25.00
116 Al Unser/50 10.00 25.00
137 Richard Petty/65 25.00 50.00
139 Al Unser Jr./100 8.00 20.00

2008 Donruss Sports Legends Signatures Mirror Gold

MIRROR GOLD PRINT RUN 4-25
SERIAL #'d UNDER 10 NOT PRICED
8 Bobby Allison/15 12.00 30.00
109 Cale Yarborough/25 12.00 30.00
116 Al Unser/25 12.00 30.00
137 Richard Petty/10 30.00 80.00
139 Al Unser Jr./25 10.00 25.00

2008 Donruss Sports Legends Signatures Mirror Red

*MIRROR RED: .3X TO .8X MIRROR BLUE
MIRROR RED PRINT RUN 25-1370
109 Cale Yarborough/297 8.00 20.00
116 Al Unser/142 8.00 20.00
139 Al Unser Jr./219 6.00 15.00

2009 Element

COMPLETE SET (100) 15.00 40.00
WAX BOX HOBBY 70.00 100.00
WAX BOX RETAIL 50.00 75.00
1 Aric Almirola .30 .75
2 Greg Biffle .30 .75
3 Clint Bowyer .40 1.00
4 Jeff Burton .30 .75
5 Kurt Busch .30 .75
6 Kyle Busch .50 1.25
7 Dale Earnhardt Jr. .75 2.00
8 Carl Edwards .40 1.00
9 David Gilliland .25 .60
10 Jeff Gordon .75 2.00
11 Denny Hamlin .40 1.00
12 Kevin Harvick .50 1.25
13 Sam Hornish Jr. .30 .75
14 Jimmie Johnson .60 1.50
15 Kasey Kahne .40 1.00
16 Matt Kenseth .40 1.00
17 Travis Kvapil .25 .60
18 Bobby Labonte .40 1.00
19 Joey Logano RC 2.00 5.00
20 Mark Martin .40 1.00
21 Jamie McMurray .40 1.00
22 Casey Mears .25 .60
23 Paul Menard .25 .60
24 Juan Pablo Montoya .50 1.25
25 Joe Nemechek .25 .60
26 Ryan Newman .30 .75
27 Kyle Petty .30 .75
28 David Ragan .30 .75
29 David Reutimann .30 .75
30 Elliott Sadler .25 .60
31 Regan Smith .30 .75
32 Tony Stewart .60 1.50
33 Martin Truex Jr. .30 .75
34 Brian Vickers .25 .60
35 Michael Waltrip .40 1.00
36 Clint Bowyer NNS .40 1.00
37 Landon Cassill NNS .75 2.00
38 Bryan Clauson NNS .30 .75
39 Dale Earnhardt Jr. NNS .75 2.00
40 Carl Edwards NNS .40 1.00
41 Denny Hamlin NNS .40 1.00
42 Kevin Harvick NNS .50 1.25
43 Brad Keselowski NNS .50 1.25
44 Joey Logano NNS .75 2.00
45 Colin Braun CWTS .30 .75
46 Erik Darnell CWTS .30 .75
47 Ron Hornaday CWTS .25 .60
48 Mike Skinner CWTS .25 .60
49 Joey Logano AN .75 2.00
50 Dale Earnhardt Jr. AN .75 2.00
51 Jeff Gordon AN .75 2.00
52 Carl Edwards AN .40 1.00
53 Tony Stewart AN .60 1.50
54 Jimmie Johnson AN .60 1.50
55 Carl Edwards' Car .15 .40
56 Jimmie Johnson's Car .25 .60
57 Greg Biffle's Car .12 .30
58 Jeff Burton's Car .12 .30
59 Kevin Harvick's Car .20 .50
60 Clint Bowyer's Car .15 .40
61 Tony Stewart's Car .25 .60
62 Jeff Gordon's Car .30 .75
63 Dale Earnhardt Jr.'s Car .30 .75
64 Matt Kenseth's Car .15 .40
65 Denny Hamlin's Car .15 .40
66 Kyle Busch's Car .20 .50
67 Kasey Kahne's Car .15 .40
68 Brian Vickers' Car .10 .25
69 Kurt Busch's Car .12 .30
70 Martin Truex Jr.'s Car .12 .30
71 David Ragan's Car .12 .30
72 Sam Hornish Jr.'s Car .12 .30
73 Clint Bowyer C .40 1.00
74 Kyle Busch C .50 1.25
75 Dale Earnhardt Jr. C .75 2.00
76 Carl Edwards C .40 1.00
77 Jeff Gordon C .75 2.00
78 Joey Logano C .75 2.00
79 Jeff Burton M .30 .75
80 Carl Edwards M .40 1.00
81 Joey Logano M .75 2.00
82 Mark Martin M .40 1.00
83 Ryan Newman M .30 .75
84 Tony Stewart M .60 1.50
85 Martin Truex Jr.'s Car N .12 .30
86 Denny Hamlin's Car N .15 .40
87 Tony Stewart's Car N .25 .60
88 Matt Kenseth's Car N .15 .40
89 Kyle Busch's Car N .20 .50
90 Jeff Gordon's Car N .30 .75
91 Jimmie Johnson's Car N .25 .60
92 Brian Vickers' Car N .10 .25
93 Dale Earnhardt Jr.'s Car N .30 .75
94 Carl Edwards' Car N .15 .40
95 Ricky Carmichael RC 2.00 5.00
96 Marc Davis RC .60 1.50
97 Austin Dillon RC 3.00 8.00
98 Scott Speed RC 1.25 3.00
99 Ricky Stenhouse Jr. RC 1.00 2.50
100 Josh Wise RC .75 2.00

2009 Element Radioactive

*RADIOACTIVE: 2.5X TO 6X BASE
STATED PRINT RUN 100 SERIAL #'D SETS

2009 Element 1-2-3 Finish

STATED PRINT RUN 50 SERIAL #'d SETS
RCR Burton/Harvick/Bowyer 50.00 100.00
RFR Biffle/Kenseth/Edwards 25.00 60.00

2009 Element Big Win

STATED PRINT RUN 35 SERIAL #'d SETS
BWCE Carl Edwards 20.00 50.00
BWDE Dale Earnhardt Jr. 30.00 80.00
BWDH Denny Hamlin 15.00 40.00
BWJB Jeff Burton 15.00 40.00
BWJJ Jimmie Johnson 15.00 40.00
BWKB Kyle Busch 15.00 40.00
BWKK Kasey Kahne 15.00 40.00
BWRN Ryan Newman 10.00 25.00
BWTS Tony Stewart 20.00 50.00

2009 Element Elements of the Race Black Flag

ERBCE Carl Edwards 2.50 6.00
ERBDE Dale Earnhardt Jr. 5.00 12.00
ERBJG Jeff Gordon 5.00 12.00
ERBJJ Jimmie Johnson 4.00 10.00
ERBJM Juan Pablo Montoya 3.00 8.00
ERBKB Kyle Busch 3.00 8.00
ERBKH Kevin Harvick 3.00 8.00
ERBKK Kasey Kahne 2.50 6.00
ERBMM Mark Martin 2.50 6.00
ERBTS Tony Stewart 4.00 10.00

2009 Element Elements of the Race Blue-Yellow Flag

*BLUE-ORANGE: .8X TO 2X BLACK
STATED PRINT RUN 50 SERIAL #'d SETS

2009 Element Elements of the Race Black-White Flag

*CHECKERED: .8X TO 2X BLACK
STATED PRINT RUN 50 SERIAL #'d SETS

2009 Element Elements of the Race Checkered Flag

STATED PRINT RUN 5 SERIAL #'d SETS
NOT PRICED DUE TO SCARCITY

2009 Element Elements of the Race Red Flag

*RED: .4X TO 1X BLACK
STATED PRINT RUN 99 SERIAL #'d SETS

2009 Element Elements of the Race White Flag

*WHITE: .5X TO 1.2X BLACK
STATED PRINT RUN 75 SERIAL #'d SETS

2009 Element Elements of the Race Yellow Flag

*YELLOW: .4X TO 1X BLACK
STATED PRINT RUN 99 SERIAL #'d SETS

2009 Element Green White Checker

STATED PRINT RUN 25 SERIAL #'d SETS
GWCCB Clint Bowyer 40.00 80.00
GWCCE Carl Edwards 50.00 100.00
GWCDE Dale Earnhardt Jr. 100.00 175.00
GWCJB Jeff Burton 40.00 80.00
GWCKB Kyle Busch 40.00 80.00

2009 Element Jimmie Johnson 3-Time Champ Tires

COMMON JOHNSON 15.00 40.00
STATED PRINT RUN 48 SERIAL #'d SETS

2009 Element Kinetic Energy

COMPLETE SET (12) 12.00 30.00
STATED ODDS 1:6
KE1 Dale Earnhardt Jr. AMP 1.25 3.00
KE2 Jeff Gordon 1.00 2.50
KE3 Carl Edwards .50 1.25
KE4 Kasey Kahne .50 1.25
KE5 Kyle Busch .60 1.50
KE6 Jimmie Johnson .75 2.00
KE7 Joey Logano 1.00 2.50
KE8 Kevin Harvick .60 1.50
KE9 Dale Earnhardt Jr. NG 1.00 2.50
KE10 Jeff Burton .40 1.00
KE11 Greg Biffle .40 1.00
KE12 Jimmie Johnson .75 2.00

2009 Element Lab Report

COMPLETE SET (27) 12.00 30.00
STATED ODDS 1:2
LR1 Aric Almirola .30 .75
LR2 Greg Biffle .30 .75
LR3 Clint Bowyer .40 1.00
LR4 Jeff Burton .30 .75
LR5 Kurt Busch .30 .75
LR6 Kyle Busch .50 1.25
LR7 Landon Cassill .75 2.00
LR8 Dale Earnhardt Jr. .75 2.00
LR9 Carl Edwards .40 1.00
LR10 Jeff Gordon .75 2.00
LR11 Denny Hamlin .40 1.00
LR12 Kevin Harvick .50 1.25
LR13 Ron Hornaday .25 .60
LR14 Jimmie Johnson .60 1.50
LR15 Kasey Kahne .40 1.00
LR16 Matt Kenseth .40 1.00
LR17 Brad Keselowski .50 1.25
LR18 Bobby Labonte .40 1.00
LR19 Joey Logano .75 2.00
LR20 Mark Martin .40 1.00
LR21 Juan Pablo Montoya .50 1.25
LR22 David Ragan .30 .75
LR23 Elliott Sadler .25 .60
LR24 Regan Smith .30 .75
LR25 Tony Stewart .60 1.50
LR26 Martin Truex Jr. .30 .75
LR27 Brian Vickers .25 .60

2009 Element Missing Elements

ME1 Dale Earnhardt Jr. 1.50 4.00
ME2 Jeff Gordon 1.50 4.00
ME3 Dale Earnhardt 5.00 12.00
ME4 Thomas Edison 1.50 4.00
ME5 Albert Einstein 1.50 4.00
ME6 Henry Ford 1.50 4.00

2009 Element Missing Elements Exchange

COMPLETE SET (6) 12.00 30.00
STATED ODDS 1:12
ME1 Dale Earnhardt Jr. 1.50 4.00
ME2 Jeff Gordon 1.50 4.00
ME3 Dale Earnhardt 5.00 12.00
ME4 Thomas Edison 1.50 4.00
ME5 Albert Einstein 1.50 4.00
ME6 Henry Ford 1.50 4.00

2009 Element Nobel Prize

COMPLETE SET (6) 6.00 15.00
STATED ODDS 1:12
NP1 Carl Edwards .50 1.25
NP2 Dale Earnhardt Jr. 1.00 2.50
NP3 Kyle Petty .40 1.00
NP4 Jeff Burton .40 1.00
NP5 Joey Logano 1.00 2.50
NP6 Jimmie Johnson .75 2.00

2009 Element Taking the Checkers

STATED PRINT RUN 45 SERIAL #'d SETS
TCCB Clint Bowyer 15.00 40.00
TCCE Carl Edwards Bristol 20.00 50.00
TCCE Carl Edwards Las Vegas 20.00 50.00
TCDE Dale Earnhardt Jr. 20.00 50.00
TCDH Denny Hamlin 20.00 50.00
TCJB Jeff Burton 20.00 50.00
TCJL Joey Logano 20.00 50.00
TCKB Kyle Busch 20.00 50.00
TCKK Kasey Kahne 20.00 50.00

2009 Element Undiscovered Elements Autographs

STATED PRINT RUN 125-130
UEAD Austin Dillon/130 40.00 80.00
UEJA Justin Allgaier/130 10.00 25.00
UEJW Josh Wise/125 12.00 30.00
UEMD Marc Davis/127 15.00 40.00
UERC Ricky Carmichael/130 25.00 60.00
UERS Ricky Stenhouse Jr./130 10.00 25.00
UESS Scott Speed/130 15.00 40.00

2009 Element Undiscovered Elements Autographs Red Ink

STATED PRINT RUN 5-25
UEAD Austin Dillon 100.00 175.00
UEJA Justin Allgaier 75.00 150.00
UEJW Josh Wise JW blue/10
UEJW Josh Wise JW red/10
UEJW Josh Wise
UEMD Marc Davis 30.00 60.00
UERC Ricky Carmichael 40.00 80.00
UERS Ricky Stenhouse Jr. 40.00 80.00
UESS Scott Speed 60.00 120.00

2010 Element

COMPLETE SET (100) 15.00 40.00
WAX BOX HOBBY (24) 75.00 100.00
1 Jeff Burton .25 .60
2 Denny Hamlin .30 .75
3 Tony Stewart .50 1.25
4 Jimmie Johnson .50 1.25
5 Kyle Busch .40 1.00
6 Kurt Busch .25 .60
7 Kevin Harvick .40 1.00
8 Greg Biffle .25 .60
9 Jeff Gordon .60 1.50
10 Carl Edwards .30 .75
11 Ryan Newman .25 .60
12 Bobby Labonte .30 .75
13 Mark Martin .30 .75
14 Clint Bowyer .30 .75
15 Brad Keselowski .40 1.00
16 Dale Earnhardt Jr. .60 1.50
17 Kasey Kahne .30 .75
18 Matt Kenseth .30 .75
19 Sam Hornish Jr. .25 .60
20 Jamie McMurray .30 .75
21 Joey Logano .30 .75
22 A.J. Allmendinger .30 .75
23 Brian Vickers .20 .50
24 David Ragan .25 .60
25 David Reutimann .25 .60
26 Elliott Sadler .20 .50
27 Joe Nemechek .20 .50
28 Juan Pablo Montoya .30 .75
29 Marcos Ambrose .30 .75
30 Martin Truex Jr. .25 .60
31 Michael Waltrip .30 .75
32 Paul Menard .20 .50
33 Reed Sorenson .20 .50
34 Regan Smith .25 .60
35 Robby Gordon .20 .50
36 Scott Speed .30 .75
37 Mark Martin's Car .12 .30
38 Tony Stewart's Car .20 .50
39 Jimmie Johnson's Car .20 .50
40 Denny Hamlin's Car .12 .30
41 Jeff Gordon's Car .25 .60
42 Kurt Busch's Car .10 .25
43 Brian Vickers' Car .07 .20
44 Carl Edwards' Car .12 .30
45 Ryan Newman's Car .10 .25
46 Juan Pablo Montoya's Car .12 .30
47 Greg Biffle's Car .10 .25
48 Kyle Busch's Car .15 .40
49 Matt Kenseth's Car .12 .30
50 Clint Bowyer's Car .12 .30
51 Joey Logano's Car .12 .30
52 Dale Earnhardt Jr.'s Car .25 .60
53 Jeff Burton's Car .10 .25
54 Justin Allgaier NNS .25 .60
55 Steve Wallace NNS .25 .60
56 Brendan Gaughan NNS .20 .50
57 Michael McDowell NNS .25 .60
58 Erik Darnell NNS .20 .50
59 Danica Patrick NNS RC 4.00 10.00
60 Ricky Stenhouse Jr. NNS .30 .75
61 Marc Davis NNS .20 .50
62 Ron Hornaday CWS .20 .50
63 Mike Skinner CWS .20 .50
64 Ricky Carmichael CWS .30 .75
65 Colin Braun CWS .25 .60
66 J.R. Fitzpatrick CWS .25 .60
67 Tayler Malsam CWS .20 .50
68 Brian Vickers Car GG .07 .20
69 Kyle Busch's Car GG .15 .40
70 Jeff Gordon's Car GG .25 .60
71 Mark Martin's Car GG .12 .30
72 Tony Stewart's Car GG .20 .50
73 Jimmie Johnson's Car GG .20 .50
74 Brian Vickers' Car FE .07 .20
75 Tony Stewart's Car FE .20 .50
76 Joey Logano's Car FE .12 .30
77 Mark Martin's Car FE .12 .30
78 Jimmie Johnson's Car FE .20 .50
79 Dale Earnhardt Jr.'s Car FE .25 .60
80 Mark Martin SE .30 .75
81 Tony Stewart SE .50 1.25
82 Jimmie Johnson SE .50 1.25
83 Jeff Gordon SE .60 1.50
84 Carl Edwards SE .30 .75
85 Dale Earnhardt Jr. SE .60 1.50
86 RCR fabrication .20 .50
87 RCR wagons .15 .40
88 RCR cars .15 .40
89 RCR paint shop .20 .50
90 RCR Bowyer's hauler .12 .30
91 RCR chassis shop .20 .50
92 Denny Hamlin RR .30 .75
93 Joey Logano RR .30 .75
94 Ryan Newman RR .25 .60
95 Scott Speed RR .30 .75
96 Brian Vickers RR .20 .50
97 Tony Stewart RR .50 1.25
98 Trevor Bayne UE RC 4.00 10.00
99 Leilani Munter UE RC 1.25 3.00
100 Ryan Truex UE RC 1.25 3.00

2010 Element Blue

*SINGLES: 3X TO 8X BASIC CARDS
STATED PRINT RUN 35 SER.#'d SETS
59 Danica Patrick NNS 75.00 150.00
98 Trevor Bayne UE 30.00 80.00

2010 Element Green

COMPLETE SET (100) 175.00 300.00
*SINGLES: .6X TO 1.5X BASIC CARDS
STATED ODDS 1:6
59 Danica Patrick NNS 15.00 40.00
98 Trevor Bayne UE 15.00 40.00

2010 Element Purple

COMPLETE SET (61) 400.00 800.00
*SINGLES 1-61: 4X TO 10X BASIC
STATED PRINT RUN 25 SER.#'d SETS
59 Danica Patrick NNS 75.00 150.00

2010 Element Red Target

COMPLETE SET (100) 75.00 150.00
*SINGLES: .6X TO 1.5X BASIC CARDS
STATED ODDS 1 PER TARGET PACK
59 Danica Patrick NNS 12.00 30.00
98 Trevor Bayne UE 12.00 30.00

2010 Element 10 in '10

COMPLETE SET (10)
STATED ODDS 1:6
TT1 Mark Martin .60 1.50
TT2 Tony Stewart 1.00 2.50
TT3 Jimmie Johnson 1.00 2.50
TT4 Kasey Kahne .60 1.50
TT5 Jeff Gordon 1.25 3.00
TT6 Dale Earnhardt Jr. 1.25 3.00
TT7 Juan Pablo Montoya .60 1.50
TT8 Carl Edwards .60 1.50
TT9 Kyle Busch .75 2.00
TT10 Danica Patrick 4.00 10.00

2010 Element Finish Line Checkered Flag

STATED PRINT RUN 10 SER.#'d SETS
NOT PRICED DUE TO SCARCITY

2010 Element Finish Line Green Flag

STATED PRINT RUN 20 SER.#'d SETS
NOT PRICED DUE TO SCARCITY

2010 Element Finish Line Tires

STATED PRINT RUN 99 SER.#'d SETS
FLCE Denny Hamlin 4.00 10.00
FLJG Jeff Gordon 8.00 20.00
FLJJ Jimmie Johnson 6.00 15.00
FLJL Joey Logano 4.00 10.00
FLKK Kasey Kahne 4.00 10.00
FLMK Matt Kenseth 4.00 10.00
FLMM Mark Martin 4.00 10.00
FLTS Tony Stewart 6.00 15.00
FLKuB Kurt Busch 3.00 8.00
FLKyB Kyle Busch 5.00 12.00

2010 Element Flagship Performers Championships Black

STATED PRINT RUN 25 SER.#'d SETS
*BLUE-ORANGE/25: .4X TO 1X BLACK/25
UNPRICED CHECKERED PRINT RUN 1
UNPRICED GREEN PRINT RUN 5
*RED/25: .4X TO 1X BLACK/25
*WHITE/15: .5X TO 1.2X BLACK/25
*X/25: .4X TO 1X BLACK/25
*YELLOW/25: .4X TO 1X BLACK/25
FPCJG Jeff Gordon 10.00 25.00
FPCJJ Jimmie Johnson 8.00 20.00
FPCMK Matt Kenseth 5.00 12.00
FPCTS Tony Stewart 8.00 20.00
FPCKuB Kurt Busch 4.00 10.00

2010 Element Flagship Performers Consecutive Starts Black

BLACK STATED PRINT RUN 20
*BLUE-ORANGE/20: .4X TO 1X BLACK/20
UNPRICED CHECKERED PRINT RUN 1
UNPRICED GREEN PRINT RUN 5
*RED/20: .4X TO 1X BLACK/20
UNPRICED WHITE PRINT RUN 10
*YELLOW/20: .4X TO 1X BLACK/20
UNPRICED X PRINT RUN 10
FPSBL Bobby Labonte 5.00 12.00
FPSJB Jeff Burton 4.00 10.00
FPSJG Jeff Gordon 10.00 25.00
FPSJJ Jimmie Johnson 8.00 20.00
FPSMK Matt Kenseth 5.00 12.00
FPSRN Ryan Newman 4.00 10.00
FPSTS Tony Stewart 8.00 20.00
FPSDJr Dale Earnhardt Jr. 10.00 25.00

2010 Element Flagship Performers Wins Black

BLACK STATED PRINT RUN 20
*BLUE-ORANGE/20: .4X TO 1X BLACK/20
UNPRICED CHECKERED PRINT RUN 1
UNPRICED GREEN PRINT RUN 5
*RED/20: .4X TO 1X BLACK/20
*WHITE/15: .5X TO 1.2X BLACK/20
UNPRICED X PRINT RUN 10
*YELLOW/20: .4X TO 1X BLACK/20
FPWCE Carl Edwards 6.00 15.00
FPWJB Jeff Burton 5.00 12.00
FPWJG Jeff Gordon 12.00 30.00
FPWJJ Jimmie Johnson 10.00 25.00
FPWMK Matt Kenseth 6.00 15.00
FPWMM Mark Martin 6.00 15.00
FPWTS Tony Stewart 10.00 25.00
FPWDJr Dale Earnhardt Jr. 12.00 30.00
FPWKuB Kurt Busch 5.00 12.00
FPWKyB Kyle Busch 8.00 20.00

2010 Element Green-White-Checkers Green

STATED PRINT RUN 50 SER.#'d SETS
GWCJM Jamie McMurray 8.00 20.00
GWCKB Kurt Busch 6.00 15.00
GWCKK Kasey Kahne 8.00 20.00
GWCKyB Kyle Busch 10.00 25.00

2010 Element High Octane Vehicle

COMPLETE SET (12) 6.00 15.00
STATED ODDS 1:6
HOV1 Buck Baker's Car .60 1.50
HOV2 1951 Hudson Hornet .60 1.50
HOV3 1957 Chevrolet .60 1.50
HOV4 1969 Dodge Charger Daytona .60 1.50
HOV5 Pete Hamilton's Car .60 1.50
HOV6 1972 Chevrolet Monte Carlo .60 1.50
HOV7 David Pearson's Car .60 1.50
HOV8 Cale Yarborough's Car .60 1.50
HOV9 Dale Earnhardt's Car 3.00 8.00
HOV10 Kurt Busch's Car .50 1.25
HOV11 Denny Hamlin's Car .60 1.50
HOV12 Jimmie Johnson's Car 1.00 2.50

2010 Element Recycled Materials Green

STATED PRINT RUN 125 SER.#'d SETS
*BLUE/25: .6X TO 1.5X GREEN/125
RMCE Carl Edwards 5.00 12.00
RMJB Jeff Burton 4.00 10.00
RMJG Jeff Gordon 10.00 25.00
RMJJ Jimmie Johnson 8.00 20.00
RMJL Joey Logano 5.00 12.00
RMKH Kevin Harvick 6.00 15.00
RMKK Kasey Kahne 5.00 12.00
RMMA Marcos Ambrose 20.00 50.00
RMMM Mark Martin 5.00 12.00
RMRN Ryan Newman 4.00 10.00
RMTS Tony Stewart 8.00 20.00
RMJPM Juan Pablo Montoya 5.00 12.00
RMDEJr Dale Earnhardt Jr. 10.00 25.00

2010 Element Undiscovered Elements Autographs

STATED PRINT RUN 125 SER.#'d SETS
UEAO Alli Owens
UECW Chrissy Wallace 10.00 25.00
UEJC Jennifer Jo Cobb 15.00 40.00
UELM Leilani Munter 15.00 40.00
UEPK Parker Kligerman 10.00 25.00
UERT Ryan Truex 12.00 30.00
UETB Trevor Bayne 50.00 100.00

2010 Element Undiscovered Elements Autographs Red Ink Inscriptions

STATED PRINT RUN 25 SER.#'d SETS
UEAO Alli Owens
UECW Chrissy Wallace 30.00 60.00
UEJC Jennifer Jo Cobb 40.00 100.00
UELM Leilani Munter 30.00 60.00
UEPK Parker Kligerman 40.00 80.00
UERT Ryan Truex 40.00 80.00
UETB Trevor Bayne 100.00 200.00

2011 Element

COMPLETE SET (100) 6.00 15.00
WAX BOX HOBBY (24) 60.00 100.00
WAX BOX RETAIL (24) 50.00 75.00
1 A.J. Allmendinger .30 .75
2 Marcos Ambrose .30 .75
3 Greg Biffle .25 .60
4 Clint Bowyer .30 .75
5 Jeff Burton .25 .60
6 Kurt Busch .25 .60
7 Kyle Busch .40 1.00
8 Dale Earnhardt Jr. .60 1.50
9 Carl Edwards .30 .75
10 Bill Elliott .50 1.25
11 Jeff Gordon .60 1.50
12 Robby Gordon .20 .50
13 Denny Hamlin .30 .75
14 Kevin Harvick .40 1.00
15 Jimmie Johnson .50 1.25
16 Kasey Kahne .30 .75
17 Matt Kenseth .30 .75
18 Brad Keselowski .40 1.00
19 Travis Kvapil .20 .50
20 Bobby Labonte .30 .75
21 Joey Logano .30 .75
22 Mark Martin .30 .75
23 Jamie McMurray .30 .75
24 Juan Pablo Montoya .30 .75
25 Joe Nemechek .20 .50
26 Ryan Newman .25 .60
27 David Ragan .25 .60
28 David Reutimann .25 .60
29 Scott Speed .25 .60
30 Regan Smith .25 .60
31 Tony Stewart .50 1.25
32 Martin Truex Jr. .25 .60
33 Brian Vickers .20 .50
34 Michael Waltrip .40 1.00
35 Kurt Busch's Car .10 .25
36 Dale Earnhardt Jr.'s Car .25 .60
37 Jeff Gordon's Car .25 .60
38 Jimmie Johnson's Car .20 .50
39 Mark Martin's Car .12 .30
40 Tony Stewart's Car .20 .50
41 Kyle Busch's Car .15 .40
42 Carl Edwards' Car .12 .30
43 Kevin Harvick's Car .15 .40
44 Denny Hamlin's Car .12 .30
45 Justin Allgaier NNS .25 .60
46 Brendan Gaughan NNS .20 .50
47 Danica Patrick NNS 2.00 5.00
48 Brian Scott NNS .20 .50
49 Ricky Stenhouse Jr. NNS .30 .75
50 Steve Wallace NNS .25 .60
51 Trevor Bayne NNS .60 1.50
52 Josh Wise NNS .20 .50
53 Michael McDowell NNS .25 .60
54 James Buescher NCWTS .20 .50
55 Ricky Carmichael NCWTS .30 .75
56 Ron Hornaday NCWTS .20 .50
57 Johnny Sauter NCWTS .20 .50
58 Mike Skinner NCWTS .20 .50
59 Tayler Malsam NCWTS .20 .50
60 Justin Lofton NCWTS .20 .50
61 Austin Dillon CWTS .40 1.00
62 Brian Ickler NCWTS .25 .60
63 Jamie McMurray SS .30 .75
64 Jimmie Johnson SS .50 1.25
65 Kyle Busch SS .40 1.00
66 Kurt Busch SS .25 .60
67 Kevin Harvick SS .40 1.00
68 Denny Hamlin SS .30 .75
69 Ryan Newman SS .25 .60
70 David Reutimann SS .25 .60
71 Greg Biffle SS .25 .60
72 Carl Edwards SS .30 .75
73 Jeff Burton's Car GF .10 .25
74 Kurt Busch's Car GF .10 .25
75 Kevin Harvick's Car GF .15 .40
76 Carl Edwards' Car GF .12 .30
77 Mark Martin's Car GF .12 .30
78 Tony Stewart's Car GF .20 .50
79 Hendrick Motorsports .60 1.50
80 Roush Fenway Racing .30 .75
81 Joe Gibbs Racing .40 1.00
82 Earnhardt Ganassi Racing .30 .75
83 Penske Racing .40 1.00
84 Michael Waltrip Racing .40 1.00
85 Red Bull Racing .30 .75
86 Stewart Haas Racing .50 1.25
87 J.Johnson/D.Hamlin TP .50 1.25
88 Jamie McMurray TP .30 .75
89 Kevin Harvick TP .40 1.00
90 Jimmie Johnson TP .50 1.25
91 Matt Kenseth TP .30 .75
92 Jimmie Johnson TP .50 1.25
93 Jeff Gordon TP .60 1.50
94 Dale Earnhardt Jr. TP .60 1.50
95 Jeff Burton TP .25 .60
96 Brandon McReynolds UE RC .40 1.00
97 Logan Ruffin UE RC .40 1.00
98 Cole Whitt UE RC .60 1.50
99 Chase Elliott UE RC 5.00 12.00
100 Jessica Brunelli UE RC .50 1.25

2011 Element Black

*BLACK: 3X TO 8X BASE
STATED PRINT RUN 35 SER.#'d SETS

2011 Element Purple

*PURPLE/25: 4X TO 10X BASE
STATED PRINT RUN 25 SER.#'d SETS

2011 Element Green

COMPLETE SET (100) 20.00 50.00
*GREEN: .8X TO 2X BASE
STATED ODDS 1:6

2011 Element Red

COMPLETE SET (100) 20.00 50.00
*RED: .6X TO 1.5X BASE
STATED ODDS 1 PER TARGET PACK

2011 Element Autographs

ANNOUNCED PRINT RUN 10-125
1 Justin Allgaier/75* 5.00 12.00
2 A.J. Allmendinger/60* 6.00 15.00
3 Marcos Ambrose/75* 6.00 15.00
4 Trevor Bayne/45* 25.00 60.00
5 Greg Biffle/89* 5.00 12.00
6 Clint Bowyer/58* 6.00 15.00
7 Colin Braun/70* 5.00 12.00
8 James Buescher/75* 4.00 10.00
9 Jeff Burton/60* 5.00 12.00
10 Kurt Busch/99* 8.00 20.00
11 Kyle Busch/25*
12 Kevin Conway/70* 5.00 12.00
13 Matt DiBenedetto/45* 4.00 10.00
14 Austin Dillon/75* 15.00 40.00
15 Paige Duke/40* 15.00 30.00
16 Dale Earnhardt Jr./45* 40.00 100.00

17 Carl Edwards/60* 8.00 20.00
18 Brendan Gaughan/45* 4.00 10.00
19 Jeff Gordon/25* 60.00 120.00
20 Robby Gordon/70* 4.00 10.00
21 Denny Hamlin/40* 6.00 15.00
22 Kevin Harvick/45* 8.00 20.00
23 Ron Hornaday/45*
24 Sam Hornish Jr./100* 5.00 12.00
25 Brian Ickler/90* 5.00 12.00
26 Jimmie Johnson/15* 40.00 80.00
27 Kasey Kahne/25* 40.00 80.00
28 Matt Kenseth/60* 12.00 30.00
29 Brad Keselowski/75* 10.00 25.00
30 Travis Kvapil/70*
31 Bobby Labonte/60* 6.00 15.00
32 Scott Lagasse Jr/45* 4.00 10.00
33 Justin Lofton/35* 4.00 10.00
34 Joey Logano/25* 6.00 15.00
35 Mark Martin/15* 40.00 80.00
36 Michael McDowell/105* 5.00 12.00
37 Jamie McMurray/60* 6.00 15.00
38 Paul Menard/125* 4.00 10.00
39 Juan Pablo Montoya/35* 6.00 15.00
40 Joe Nemechek/70* 6.00 15.00
41 Ryan Newman/70* 5.00 12.00
42 Monica Palumbo/40* 15.00 40.00
43 Danica Patrick/10*
44 David Ragan/85* 5.00 12.00
45 David Reutimann/80* 5.00 12.00
46 Elliott Sadler/45* 4.00 10.00
47 Johnny Sauter/45* 4.00 10.00
48 Brian Scott/45*
49 Mike Skinner/35* 4.00 10.00
50 Regan Smith/100* 5.00 12.00
51 Scott Speed/90* 5.00 12.00
52 Ricky Stenhouse Jr./45* 6.00 15.00
53 Tony Stewart/25* 40.00 80.00
54 Martin Truex Jr./75* 5.00 12.00
55 Brian Vickers/90* 4.00 10.00
56 Steve Wallace/45* 5.00 12.00
57 Michael Waltrip/10*
58 Josh Wise/45* 4.00 10.00
59 Amanda Wright/40* 15.00 30.00

2011 Element Autographs Gold

*GOLD/25: .6X TO 1.5X BASIC AU
STATED PRINT RUN 5-25
48 Regan Smith/25 20.00 50.00
49 Scott Speed/25 15.00 40.00

2011 Element Autographs Silver

*SILVER/25-50: .5X TO 1.2X BASIC AU
STATED PRINT RUN 5-50
36 Jamie McMurray/25 12.00 30.00
40 Ryan Newman/25 15.00 40.00
43 David Reutimann/45 12.00 30.00

2011 Element Cut and Collect Exclusives

COMPLETE SET (4) 2.50 6.00
STATED ODDS 1 PER BLASTER BOX
NNO Jimmie Johnson .30 .75
NNO Jeff Gordon .40 1.00
NNO Dale Earnhardt Jr .40 1.00
NNO Danica Patrick .75 2.00

2011 Element Finish Line Green Flag

STATED PRINT RUN 25 SER.#'d SETS
FLCB Clint Bowyer 4.00 10.00
FLDE Dale Earnhardt Jr 25.00 50.00
FLDH Denny Hamlin 4.00 10.00
FLDR David Reutimann 8.00 20.00
FLJJ Jimmie Johnson 12.00 30.00
FLJM Jamie McMurray 8.00 20.00
FLKH Kevin Harvick 10.00 25.00
FLRN Ryan Newman 8.00 20.00
FLTS Tony Stewart 6.00 15.00
FLJPM Juan Pablo Montoya 4.00 10.00
FLKUB Kurt Busch 3.00 8.00
FLKYB Kyle Busch 5.00 12.00

2011 Element Finish Line Tires

STATED PRINT RUN 99 SER.#'d SETS
*FAST PASS/30: .5X TO 1.2X TIRE/99
FLCB Clint Bowyer 4.00 10.00
FLDE Dale Earnhardt Jr 15.00 40.00
FLDH Denny Hamlin 4.00 10.00
FLDR David Reutimann 8.00 20.00
FLJJ Jimmie Johnson 6.00 15.00
FLJM Jamie McMurray 8.00 20.00
FLKH Kevin Harvick 10.00 25.00
FLRN Ryan Newman 3.00 8.00
FLTS Tony Stewart 6.00 15.00
FLJPM Juan Pablo Montoya 4.00 10.00
FLKUB Kurt Busch 3.00 8.00
FLKYB Kyle Busch 5.00 12.00

2011 Element Flagship Performers 2010 Green Flag Passes Blue-Yellow

STATED PRINT RUN 50 SER.#'d SETS
FPPAA A.J. Allmendinger 4.00 10.00
FPPBK Brad Keselowski 5.00 12.00
FPPDE Dale Earnhardt Jr 8.00 20.00
FPPDR David Ragan 3.00 8.00
FPPJB Jeff Burton 6.00 15.00
FPPJL Joey Logano 4.00 10.00
FPPKK Kasey Kahne 4.00 10.00
FPPMT Martin Truex Jr. 3.00 8.00
FPPSS Scott Speed 3.00 8.00

2011 Element Flagship Performers 2010 Laps Completed Yellow

STATED PRINT RUN 50 SER.#'d SETS
FPLCE Carl Edwards 4.00 10.00
FPLDE Dale Earnhardt Jr 8.00 20.00
FPLJL Joey Logano 4.00 10.00
FPLJM Jamie McMurray 4.00 10.00
FPLKH Kevin Harvick 5.00 12.00
FPLMK Matt Kenseth 4.00 10.00
FPLMM Mark Martin 4.00 10.00
FPLTS Tony Stewart 6.00 15.00
FPLKyB Kyle Busch 5.00 12.00

2011 Element Flagship Performers Career Starts Green

STATED PRINT RUN 25 SER.#'d SETS
FPSBE Bill Elliott 8.00 20.00
FPSBL Bobby Labonte 8.00 20.00
FPSJB Jeff Burton 8.00 20.00
FPSJG Jeff Gordon 10.00 25.00
FPSMM Mark Martin 5.00 12.00
FPSMW Michael Waltrip 6.00 15.00

2011 Element Flagship Performers Career Wins White

STATED PRINT RUN 50 SER.#'d SETS
FPWBE Bill Elliott 6.00 15.00
FPWCE Carl Edwards 4.00 10.00
FPWGB Greg Biffle 6.00 15.00
FPWJB Jeff Burton 6.00 15.00
FPWJG Jeff Gordon 10.00 25.00
FPWJJ Jimmie Johnson 6.00 15.00
FPWTS Tony Stewart 6.00 15.00
FPWDEJ Dale Earnhardt Jr. 8.00 20.00
FPWKuB Kurt Busch 3.00 8.00
FPWKyB Kyle Busch 5.00 12.00

2011 Element Flagship Performers Championships Checkered

STATED PRINT RUN 25 SER.#'d SETS
FPCBE Bill Elliott 8.00 20.00
FPCJG Jeff Gordon 10.00 25.00
FPCJJ Jimmie Johnson 8.00 20.00
FPCMK Matt Kenseth 5.00 12.00
FPCTS Tony Stewart 8.00 20.00
FPCKuB Kurt Busch 4.00 10.00

2011 Element Flagship Performers Race Streak Without DNF Red

STATED PRINT RUN 50 SER.#'d SETS
FPDCE Carl Edwards 4.00 10.00
FPDDE Dale Earnhardt Jr 8.00 20.00
FPDDR David Reutimann 6.00 15.00
FPDJJ Jimmie Johnson 6.00 15.00
FPDJM Jamie McMurray 6.00 15.00
FPDMK Matt Kenseth 4.00 10.00
FPDMM Mark Martin 4.00 10.00
FPDRN Ryan Newman 3.00 8.00
FPDTS Tony Stewart 6.00 15.00

2011 Element Flagstand Swatches

STATED PRINT RUN 25 SER.#'d SETS
FSSDE Dale Earnhardt Jr. 75.00 150.00
FSSJG Jeff Gordon 100.00 200.00
FSSJJ Jimmie Johnson 100.00 200.00
FSSKB Kyle Busch 60.00 120.00
FSSKH Kevin Harvick 60.00 120.00
FSSTS Tony Stewart 75.00 150.00

2011 Element High Octane Vehicle

COMPLETE SET (12) 10.00 25.00
STATED ODDS 1:6
HOV1 Jimmie Johnson 1.00 2.50
HOV2 Denny Hamlin .60 1.50
HOV3 Justin Allgaier .50 1.25
HOV4 Carl Edwards .60 1.50
HOV5 Travis Kvapil .40 1.00
HOV6 Carl Edwards .60 1.50
HOV7 Bill Elliott 1.00 2.50
HOV8 Ron Hornaday .40 1.00
HOV9 Michael Waltrip .75 2.00
HOV10 Bill Elliott 1.00 2.50
HOV11 Greg Biffle .50 1.25
HOV12 Terry Labonte .60 1.50

2011 Element Tales from the Track

COMPLETE SET (10) 8.00 20.00
STATED ODDS 1:6
TT1 C.Yarborough Rough Landing .60 1.50
TT2 L.Petty Pothole Ahead .50 1.25
TT3 R.Petty Drag Racing King 1.00 2.50
TT4 R.Petty Auto Repair 1.00 2.50
TT5 B.Elliott Talladega Comeback 1.00 2.50
TT6 G.Bodine Intimidating Race .40 1.00
TT7 Pearson/Petty Small Step 1.00 2.50
TT8 N.Jarrett Fire on Board .50 1.25
TT9 P.Goldsmith First in Flight .40 1.00
TT10 Beauchamp/L.Petty Review .50 1.25

2011 Element Trackside Treasures Silver

STATED PRINT RUN 85 SER.#'d SETS
*HOLO/25: .5X TO 1.2X SILVER/85
TTBE Bill Elliott SM 8.00 20.00
TTBK Brad Keselowski SM 6.00 15.00
TTBV Brian Vickers SM 3.00 8.00
TTCE Carl Edwards FS 5.00 12.00
TTDP Danica Patrick SM 20.00 50.00
TTDR David Ragan SM 4.00 10.00
TTDR David Reutimann SM 6.00 15.00
TTJM Jamie McMurray SM 5.00 12.00
TTKH Kevin Harvick SM 6.00 15.00
TTKK Kasey Kahne FS 5.00 12.00
TTMT Martin Truex Jr. SM 4.00 10.00
TTMW Michael Waltrip FS 6.00 15.00
TTRN Ryan Newman FS 4.00 10.00
TTJPM Juan Pablo Montoya SM 5.00 12.00

2011 Elements Undiscovered Elements Autographs

STATED PRINT RUN 225 SER.#'d SETS
*RED INK/25: .5X TO 1.2X AUTO/225
1 Jessica Brunelli 8.00 20.00
2 Chase Elliott 75.00 150.00
3 Brandon McReynolds 6.00 15.00
4 Logan Ruffin 6.00 15.00
5 Cole Whitt 10.00 25.00

1992 Erin Maxx Trans-Am

This 100-card set was produced by Erin Maxx and features top drivers and cars of SCCA Trans-Am racing. The cards feature color photos of the driver or car on the cardfront with a small driver photo on the cardback.

COMPLETE SET (100) 6.00 15.00
1 Wayne Akers' Car .05 .15
2 Wayne Akers .08 .25
3 Bobby Archer's Car .05 .15
4 Bobby Archer .08 .25
5 Tommy Archer's Car .05 .15
6 Tommy Archer .08 .25
7 Jack Baldwin's Car .08 .25
8 Jack Baldwin .20 .50
9 Jerry Clinton's Car .05 .15
10 Jerry Clinton .08 .25
11 Jim Derhaag's Car .05 .15
12 Jim Derhaag .08 .25
13 Michael Dingman's Car .05 .15
14 Michael Dingman .08 .25
15 Ron Fellows' Car .08 .25
16 Ron Fellows .20 .50
17 Paul Gentilozzi's Car .08 .25
18 Paul Gentilozzi .20 .50
19 Scott Sharp's Car .08 .25
20 Scott Sharp .20 .50
21 Stuart Hayner's Car .05 .15
22 Stuart Hayner .08 .25
23 Phil Mahre's Car .05 .15
24 Phil Mahre .08 .25
25 Steve Mahre's Car .05 .15
26 Steve Mahre .08 .25
27 Deborah Gregg's Car .05 .15
28 Deborah Gregg .08 .25
29 Greg Pickett's Car .05 .15
30 Greg Pickett .08 .25
31 George Robinson's Car .05 .15
32 George Robinson .08 .25
33 Randy Ruhlman's Car .05 .15
34 Randy Ruhlman .08 .25
35 Trois-Rivieres .05 .15
36 Trois-Rivieres Winners .05 .15
37 R.J. Valentine's Car .05 .15
38 R.J. Valentine .08 .25
39 Tech Inspection .05 .15
40 Scott Sharp's Car .08 .25
41 Tech Pix .05 .15
42 Scott Sharp's Car .08 .25
43 Wally Owens' Car .05 .15
44 Kenwood's Tour De Force .05 .15
45 Glenn Fox's Car .05 .15
46 Glenn Fox .08 .25
47 Courtney Smith's Car .05 .15
48 Courtney Smith .08 .25
49 Checklist 1-50 .05 .15
50 Checklist 51-100 .05 .15
51 John Anderson's Car .05 .15
52 Glenn Andrew's Car .05 .15
53 Jeff Davis' Car .05 .15
54 Peter De Man's Car .05 .15
55 Rick Dittman's Car .05 .15
56 Mike Downs' Car .05 .15
57 Bill Gray's Car .05 .15
58 Ed Hinchliff's Car .05 .15
59 Steve Anderson's Car .05 .15
60 Les Lindley's Car .05 .15
61 Bruce Nesbitt's Car .05 .15
62 Frank Panzarella's Car .05 .15
63 Bob Patch's Car .05 .15
64 Mark Pielsticker's Car .05 .15
65 Andy Porterfield's Car .05 .15
66 Brian Richards' Car .05 .15
67 Don Sak's Car .05 .15
68 Craig Shafer's Car .05 .15
69 Jerry Simmons' Car .05 .15
70 Rich Sloma's Car .05 .15
73 S.Sharp .05 .15
R.Fellows
G.Pickett
74 Irv Hoerr .05 .15
D.Brassfield
G.Pickett
75 S.Sharp .05 .15
P.Gentilozzi
Hoerr
G.Robinson
L.Lindley
76 S.Sharp .05 .15
G.Pickett
P.Gentilozzi
77 Sharp .05 .15
Hoerr
Baldwin
G.Robinson
T.Gloy
78 Hoerr .05 .15
S.Sharp
Stuart Hayner
79 Hoerr .05 .15
Hayner
Gentilozzi
P.Mahre
Baldwin
80 D.Brassfield .05 .15
Sharp
Baldwin
81 Brassfield .05 .15
Fellows
Hoerr
Sharp
Baldwin
82 G.Robinson .05 .15
Baldwin
Lindley
83 Sharp .05 .15
Baldwin
Hoerr
Fellows
Brassfield
84 Lindley .05 .15
Sharp
Baldwin
85 Sharp .05 .15
Brassfield
Baldwin
Gentilozzi
Pruett
86 Sharp .05 .15
Lindley
Brassfield
87 Will Moody .05 .15
88 Brassfield .05 .15
Gentilozzi
Sharp
89 Sharp .05 .15
Fellows
Gentilozzi
Baldwin
Hoerr
90 Sharp .05 .15
Chris Kneifel
Hoerr
91 Sharp .05 .15
Chris Kneifel
Sobey
Lindley
Brassfield
92 Baldwin .05 .15
Fellows
Sharp
93 Gentilozzi .05 .15
Steve Petty
Sharp
Brassfield
Hoerr
94 Fast Five Alumni .05 .15
95 S.Sharp .05 .15
Fellows
Baldwin
96 Buz McCall .05 .15
97 '92 Class Picture .05 .15
98 '92 Grid .05 .15
99 '92 Long Beach Start .05 .15
100 Scott Sharp's Car .05 .15

1994 Ernie Irvan Fan Club

This five card set was distributed exclusively to members of the Ernie Irvan Fan Club. The black-bordered cards feature Irvan and family and were sold for $5.00 each through the Club in complete set form. Each card back contains either statistical or biographical information and are unnumbered.

COMPLETE SET (5) 2.50 6.00
1 Ernie Irvan .60 1.50
2 Ernie Irvan .60 1.50
3 Ernie Irvan .60 1.50
4 Ernie Irvan .60 1.50
5 Ernie Irvan's Car .60 1.50

2003 eTopps

COMPLETE SET (27) 75.00 150.00
PRINT RUNS STATED BELOW
PROVIDED BY TOPPS
1 Tony Stewart/3194 5.00 12.00
2 Mark Martin/3403 4.00 10.00
2B Mark Martin AU/100 30.00 60.00
3 Jamie McMurray/3000 4.00 10.00
4 Jeff Gordon/6000 6.00 15.00
5 Jimmie Johnson/2945 5.00 12.00
6 Ryan Newman/4000 5.00 12.00
7 Rusty Wallace/3126 4.00 10.00
8 Elliott Sadler/2648 3.00 8.00
10 Ricky Rudd/2164 4.00 10.00
11 Matt Kenseth/5000 5.00 12.00
12 Jeff Burton/1682 4.00 10.00
13 Bill Elliott/2392 6.00 15.00
14 Casey Mears/2389 3.00 8.00
15 Ricky Craven/1709 4.00 10.00
16 Bobby Labonte/2249 3.00 8.00
18 Sterling Marlin/2186 3.00 8.00
19 Greg Biffle/2802 3.00 8.00
20 Robby Gordon/1937 4.00 10.00
21 Kevin Harvick/4000 5.00 12.00
22 Kyle Petty/3000 4.00 10.00
23 Jerry Nadeau/3000 3.00 8.00
24 Terry Labonte2283 4.00 10.00
25 Richard Petty/3065 5.00 12.00
26 Jeremy Mayfield/2216 3.00 8.00
29 Johnny Benson/3000 3.00 8.00
30 Joe Nemechek/1910 4.00 10.00
33 Kurt Busch/3000 3.00 8.00

2005 eTopps Autographs

MM1 Mark Martin/2003 eTopps/100

1993 Finish Line Promos

Finish Line released this four-card set in its own cello wrapper. Therefore, the promo cards are often sold in complete set form.

COMPLETE SET (4) 12.50 25.00
P1 Davey Allison 5.00 10.00
P2 Jeff Gordon 6.00 15.00
P3 Terry Labonte 4.00 8.00
Bobby Labonte
P4 Cover Card .20 .50

1993 Finish Line

Pro Set produced this 180-card set for Finish Line. The set features star drivers, cars and crew members of the top Winston Cup teams from the previous season. Cards were packaged 12 per foil pack with 36 packs per box and in 23-card jumbo packs. Inserts included a Silver parallel set (one per foil pack/two per jumbo), an unnumbered Alan Kulwicki memorial card, as well as a 15-card Davey Allison set (jumbo packs only). A special hologram card featuring Davey Allison (numbered of 5000) was also produced and randomly distributed through foil packs. A factory set was also available through the Finish Line Racing Club. Each factory set came with a Finish Line binder and sheets and the Davey Allison set was also included.

COMPLETE SET (180) 8.00 20.00
WAX BOX 15.00 40.00
1 Alan Kulwicki .25 .60
2 Harry Gant .15 .40
3 Ricky Rudd .25 .60
4 Darrell Waltrip .15 .40
5 Rusty Wallace .60 1.50
6 Brett Bodine .07 .20
7 Ted Musgrave .07 .20
8 Rick Mast .07 .20
9 Hut Stricklin .07 .20
10 Todd Bodine .07 .20
11 Bobby Hillin .07 .20
12 Mark Martin's Car .25 .60
13 Wally Dallenbach Jr.'s Car .02 .10
14 Jeff Gordon's Car .40 1.00
15 Michael Waltrip's Car .07 .20
16 Richard Jackson .02 .10
17 Jack Roush .02 .10
18 Junior Johnson .07 .20
19 Glen Wood .02 .10
20 Leo Jackson .02 .10
21 George Bradshaw .02 .10
22 Rick Mast's Car .02 .10
23 Ken Wilson .02 .10
24 Don Miller .02 .10
25 Donnie Richeson .02 .10
26 Doug Richert .02 .10
27 T.Labonte .30 .75
B.Labonte
28 Robert Pressley .07 .20
29 Jeff Burton .25 .60
30 Chuck Bown .07 .20
31 Mike Wallace .07 .20
32 Derrike Cope's Car .02 .10
33 Gary Nelson .02 .10
34 Winston Kelley .02 .10
Dick Brooks
Jim Phillips
35 Danny Myers .02 .10
36 Waddell Wilson .02 .10
37 Alan Kulwicki .25 .60
38 Kyle Petty .15 .40
39 Terry Labonte .30 .75
40 Ernie Irvan .15 .40
41 Geoff Bodine .07 .20
42 Dale Jarrett .50 1.25
43 Wally Dallenbach Jr. .07 .20
44 Jimmy Means .07 .20
45 Rusty Wallace's Car .25 .60
46 Sterling Marlin's Car .07 .20
47 Morgan Shepherd's Car .02 .10
48 Davey Allison's Car .15 .40
49 Phil Parsons .07 .20
50 Bill Stavola .02 .10
51 Darrell Waltrip .15 .40
52 Chuck Rider .02 .10
53 Junie Donlavey .02 .10
54 Gary DeHart .02 .10
55 Donnie Wingo .02 .10
56 Ken Howes .02 .10
57 Robin Pemberton .02 .10
58 Jeff Hammond .02 .10
59 Butch Miller .07 .20
60 Ricky Craven .15 .40
61 Richard Petty .30 .75
62 Joey Knuckles .02 .10
63 Donnie Allison .07 .20
64 Joe Moore .02 .10
Allen Bestwick
65 Jim Bown .02 .10
66 Davey Allison .40 1.00
67 Ricky Rudd .25 .60
68 Ernie Irvan .15 .40
69 Geoff Bodine .07 .20
70 Dick Trickle .07 .20
71 Dave Marcis .07 .20
72 Rick Wilson .07 .20
73 Jimmy Spencer's Car .02 .10
74 Ken Schrader's Car .02 .10
75 Rick Wilson's Car .02 .10
76 Alan Kulwicki .25 .60
77 Joe Gibbs .15 .40
78 Felix Sabates .02 .10
79 Buddy Parrott .02 .10
80 Mike Beam .02 .10
81 Mike Hill .02 .10
82 David Green .07 .20
83 Jeff Gordon CRC 1.00 2.50
84 Tom Peck .07 .20
85 Richard Petty .30 .75
86 Dale Inman .02 .10
87 Barney Hall .02 .10
Eli Gold
88 Pete Wright .02 .10
89 Davey Allison .30 .75
90 Terry Labonte .30 .75
91 Morgan Shepherd .07 .20
92 Ted Musgrave .07 .20
93 Jimmy Hensley .07 .20
94 Geoff Bodine's Bobsled .02 .10
95 Darrell Waltrip's Car .07 .20
96 Harry Gant's Car .02 .10
97 Rick Hendrick .02 .10
98 Bill Davis .02 .10
99 Cale Yarborough .07 .20
100 Paul Andrews .02 .10
101 Ray Evernham .02 .10
102 David Fuge .02 .10
103 Ward Burton .15 .40
104 Jimmy Spencer .07 .20
105 Danny Glad .02 .10
106 David Smith .02 .10
107 Darrell Waltrip .15 .40
108 Brett Bodine .07 .20
109 Michael Waltrip .15 .40
110 Jeff Gordon 1.00 2.50
111 Dale Jarrett's Car .15 .40
112 Kenny Wallace's Car .02 .10
113 Bobby Allison .07 .20
114 Richard Petty .25 .60
115 Barry Dodson .02 .10
116 Doug Hewitt .02 .10
117 Bobby Labonte .50 1.25
118 Bobby Dotter .02 .10
119 Neil Bonnett .25 .60
120 Jimmy Fennig .02 .10
121 Kyle Petty .15 .40
122 Rusty Wallace .60 1.50
123 Michael Waltrip .15 .40
124 Ernie Irvan's Car .15 .40
125 Brett Bodine's Car .02 .10
126 Bobby Hamilton's Car .02 .10
127 Larry Hedrick .02 .10
128 Howard Comstock .02 .10
129 Robbie Loomis .02 .10
130 Steve Grissom .07 .20
131 Shelton Pittman .02 .10
132 Jimmy Johnson .02 .10
133 Mark Martin .60 1.50
134 Ken Schrader .07 .20
135 Bobby Labonte .50 1.25
136 Hut Stricklin's Car .02 .10
137 Walter Bud Moore .02 .10
138 Tony Glover .02 .10
139 Troy Beebe .02 .10
140 Tracy Leslie .02 .10
141 Will Lind .02 .10
142 Harry Gant .15 .40
143 Ken Schrader .07 .20
144 Ricky Rudd's Car .07 .20
145 Bobby Hillin's Car .02 .10
146 Billy Hagan .02 .10
147 Larry McReynolds .02 .10
148 Richard Lasater .02 .10
149 Eddie Wood .02 .10
150 Sterling Marlin .30 .75
151 Kenny Wallace .07 .20
152 Larry McClure .02 .10
153 Steve Hmiel .02 .10
154 Kenny Wallace .07 .20
155 Andy Petree .02 .10
156 Morgan Shepherd .07 .20
157 Geoff Bodine's Car .02 .10
158 Robert Yates .02 .10
159 Joe Nemechek .07 .20
160 Jack Sprague .02 .10
161 Kenny Bernstein .07 .20
162 Glen Wood Family .02 .10
163 Tommy Houston .07 .20
164 Mark Martin .60 1.50
165 Bobby Labonte's Car .07 .20
166 Leonard Wood .02 .10
167 Ted Musgrave's Car .02 .10
168 Sterling Marlin .30 .75
169 Dale Jarrett .50 1.25
170 Alan Kulwicki's Car .15 .40
171 Kyle Petty's Car .07 .20
172 Junior Johnson .07 .20
173 Dale Jarrett .30 .75
J.Gibbs
174 Jimmy Makar .02 .10
175 Tim Brewer .02 .10
176 Len Wood .02 .10
177 Ned Jarrett .07 .20
178 Roger Penske .02 .10
179 Doug Williams .02 .10
180 Hut Stricklin .07 .20
NNO Alan Kulwicki MEM 1.50 4.00
NNO Davey Allison HOLO/5000 15.00 40.00

1993 Finish Line Silver

COMPLETE SET (180) 15.00 40.00
*STARS: 1.2X TO 3X BASIC CARDS

1993 Finish Line Davey Allison

Pro Set produced this 15-card set for Finish Line to honor the 1992 Driver of the Year, Davey Allison. The cards were packaged one per 1993 Finish Line jumbo pack.

COMPLETE SET (15)	4.00	10.00
1 Davey Allison w/car	.40	1.00
2 Davey Allison	.40	1.00
3 Davey Allison w/car	.40	1.00
4 Davey Allison's Car Bobby Allison's Car	.40	1.00
5 Davey Allison Bobby Allison	.40	1.00
6 Davey Allison w/car	.40	1.00
7 Davey Allison w/car	.40	1.00
8 Davey Allison w/daughter	.40	1.00
9 Davey Allison w/car	.40	1.00
10 Davey Allison Donnie Allison Bobby Allison Neil Bonnett Hut Stricklin Mickey Gibbs	.40	1.00
11 Davey Allison w/family	.40	1.00
12 Davey Allison	.40	1.00
13 Davey Allison w/car	.40	1.00
14 Davey Allison w/son	.40	1.00
15 Davey Allison	.40	1.00

1993 Finish Line Commemorative Sheets

Produced by Pro Set for Finish Line Racing Club, this 30-sheet, blank backed set features the fronts of six 1993 Finish Line cards. The sheets measure approximately 8-1/2" by 11" and include the Finish Line logo along with sheet number. Although the sheets are individually numbered of 10,000, reportedly less than 2500 sets were actually distributed.

COMPLETE SET	30.00	75.00
1 Daytona	.75	2.00
2 Rockingham	1.50	4.00
3 Richmond	1.50	4.00
4 Atlanta	.75	2.00
5 Darlington	.75	2.00
6 Bristol	1.00	2.50
7 North Wilkesboro	1.00	2.50
8 Martinsville	1.00	2.50
9 Talladega	1.00	2.50
10 Sonoma	1.50	4.00
11 Charlotte	.75	2.00
12 Dover	1.00	2.50
13 Pocono	1.00	2.50
14 Michigan	1.50	4.00
15 Daytona	.75	2.00
16 New Hampshire	1.00	2.50
17 Pocono	1.00	2.50
18 Talladega	.75	2.00
19 Watkins Glen	1.00	2.50
20 Michigan	1.50	4.00
21 Bristol	1.50	4.00
22 Darlington	1.00	2.50
23 Richmond	1.50	4.00
24 Dover	1.00	2.50
25 Martinsville	.75	2.00
26 North Wilkesboro	1.00	2.50
27 Charlotte	.75	2.00
28 Rockingham	1.00	2.50
29 Phoenix	1.00	2.50
30 Atlanta	1.50	4.00

1994 Finish Line Promos

Finish Line produced four promo cards to preview the 1994 Finish Line release. The cards were packaged in a cello wrapper and are often sold as a complete set.

COMPLETE SET (4)	3.00	8.00
P1 Harry Gant	.75	2.00
P2 Mark Martin	1.25	3.00
P3 Rusty Wallace	1.25	3.00
P4 Cover Card	.20	.50

1994 Finish Line

For the first time Finish Line produced their own NASCAR set in 1994. The 150-card set was packaged in 12-card hobby and retail foil packs and 23-card jumbo packs. Inserts included a Silver parallel set, along with six other sets. Finish Line once again included unnumbered tribute cards that featured Jeff Gordon, Hermie Sadler, Harry Gant and a large (5" by 7") Sterling Marlin card.

COMPLETE SET (150)	6.00	15.00
WAX BOX	12.50	30.00
1 Harry Gant	.15	.40
2 Rick Mast	.07	.20
3 Wally Dallenbach Jr.'s Car	.02	.10
4 Geoff Bodine's Car	.02	.10
5 Buddy Parrott	.02	.10
6 Barney Hall	.02	.10
7 Mark Martin	.60	1.50
8 Travis Carter	.02	.10
9 Ned Jarrett	.02	.10
10 Ernie Irvan	.15	.40
11 Kyle Petty	.15	.40
12 Hut Stricklin	.07	.20
13 Jimmy Makar	.02	.10
14 John Andretti RC	.07	.20
15 Bobby Hillin	.07	.20
16 Jimmy Hensley	.07	.20
17 Terry Labonte's Car	.15	.40
18 Kenny Wallace	.07	.20
19 Ted Musgrave's Car	.02	.10
20 Dale Jarrett	.50	1.25
21 Sterling Marlin	.25	.60
22 Eli Gold	.02	.10
23 Dave Marcis	.15	.40
24 Lake Speed	.07	.20
25 Gary DeHart	.02	.10
26 Bobby Labonte	.50	1.25
27 Ken Schrader	.07	.20
28 Kyle Petty's Car	.07	.20
29 Rusty Wallace	.60	1.50
30 Steve Grissom	.07	.20
31 Ernie Irvan	.15	.40
32 Michael Waltrip	.15	.40
33 Doug Hewitt	.02	.10
34 Jimmy Means	.07	.20
35 Hut Stricklin	.07	.20
36 Jeff Gordon	.75	2.00
37 Morgan Shepherd's Car	.02	.10
38 Terry Labonte	.25	.60
39 Geoff Bodine	.07	.20
40 Darrell Waltrip's Car	.07	.20
41 Pete Wright	.02	.10
42 Morgan Shepherd	.07	.20
43 Michael Waltrip's Car	.07	.20
44 Bobby Hillin	.07	.20
45 Jeff Burton's Car	.07	.20
46 Ken Wilson	.02	.10
47 Donnie Wingo	.02	.10
48 Greg Sacks	.07	.20
49 Junior Johnson	.07	.20
50 Rick Mast	.07	.20
51 Lake Speed's Car	.02	.10
52 Ernie Irvan's Car	.07	.20
53 Rick Hendrick	.02	.10
54 Leo Jackson	.02	.10
55 Ray Evernham	.15	.40
56 Ken Schrader's Car	.02	.10
57 Neil Bonnett	.25	.60
58 Richard Petty OWN	.25	.60
59 Chuck Rider	.02	.10
60 Kyle Petty	.15	.40
61 Brett Bodine	.07	.20
62 Jimmy Spencer	.07	.20
63 Bobby Labonte's Car	.25	.60
64 Richard Petty	.25	.60
65 Ricky Rudd	.25	.60
66 Steve Hmiel	.02	.10
67 Dale Jarrett	.50	1.25
68 Brett Bodine's Car	.02	.10
69 Lake Speed	.07	.20
70 Kenny Bernstein	.07	.20
71 Larry McReynolds	.02	.10
72 Robin Pemberton	.02	.10
73 Ricky Rudd	.25	.60
74 Rusty Wallace	.60	1.50
75 Jeff Gordon	.75	2.00
76 Loy Allen Jr.	.07	.20
77 Loy Allen Jr.'s Car	.02	.10
78 Dale Jarrett	.50	1.25
79 Harry Gant	.15	.40
80 Morgan Shepherd	.07	.20
81 Mike Beam	.02	.10
82 Sterling Marlin's Car	.07	.20
83 Glen Wood	.02	.10
84 Kyle Petty	.15	.40
85 Mark Martin	.60	1.50
86 Joe Nemechek	.07	.20
87 Mike Wallace	.07	.20
88 Barry Dodson	.02	.10
89 Wally Dallenbach Jr.	.07	.20
90 Rusty Wallace	.60	1.50
91 Ricky Rudd's Car	.07	.20
92 Jack Roush	.02	.10
93 Ken Schrader	.07	.20
94 Len Wood Eddie Wood	.02	.10
95 Dale Inman	.02	.10
96 Roger Penske	.02	.10
97 Donnie Richeson	.02	.10
98 Mike Hill	.02	.10
99 Mark Martin's Car	.25	.60
100 Jerry Punch	.02	.10
101 Jimmy Hensley	.07	.20
102 Darrell Waltrip	.15	.40
103 Brett Bodine	.07	.20
104 Rusty Wallace's Car	.25	.60
105 Tony Glover	.02	.10
106 Ward Burton's Car	.02	.10
107 Ted Musgrave	.07	.20
108 Todd Bodine	.07	.20
109 Dale Jarrett's Car	.25	.60
110 Leonard Wood	.02	.10
111 Jimmy Spencer	.07	.20
112 Ernie Irvan	.15	.40
113 Jeff Burton	.25	.60
114 Jeff Hammond	.02	.10
115 Ward Burton	.15	.40
116 Ken Schrader	.07	.20
117 Butch Mock	.02	.10
118 Derrike Cope	.07	.20
119 Robert Yates	.02	.10
120 Benny Parsons	.02	.10
121 Jimmy Spencer's Car	.02	.10
122 Morgan Shepherd	.07	.20
123 Jeff Gordon's Car	.40	1.00
124 Terry Labonte	.25	.60
125 Joe Gibbs	.15	.40
126 Mark Martin	.60	1.50
127 Hut Stricklin's Car	.02	.10
128 Bobby Labonte	.50	1.25
129 Darrell Waltrip	.15	.40
130 Walter Bud Moore	.02	.10
131 Robbie Loomis	.07	.20
132 Bobby Allison	.15	.40
133 Ken Howes	.02	.10
134 Michael Waltrip	.15	.40
135 Ricky Rudd	.25	.60
136 Jimmy Johnson	.02	.10
137 Jimmy Spencer	.07	.20
138 Harry Gant	.15	.40
139 Jimmy Fennig	.02	.10
140 Derrike Cope	.07	.20
141 Geoff Bodine	.07	.20
142 Felix Sabates	.02	.10
143 Cale Yarborough	.07	.20
144 Junie Donlavey	.02	.10
145 Sterling Marlin	.25	.60
146 Richard Broome	.02	.10
147 Chuck Bown	.07	.20
148 Larry McClure	.02	.10
149 Ted Musgrave	.02	.10
150 Wally Dallenbach Jr.	.07	.20
NNO Jeff Gordon ROY	2.00	5.00
NNO Hermie Sadler ROY	.75	2.00
NNO Harry Gant Last Ride	1.00	3.00
NNO Sterling Marlin 5X7	2.00	5.00

1994 Finish Line Silver

COMPLETE SET (150)	12.00	30.00

*SILVERS: 1X TO 2.5X BASIC CARDS

1994 Finish Line Neil Bonnett

Neil Bonnett is the focus of this five-card tribute set randomly inserted in 1994 Finish Line retail packs. All five cards are unnumbered.

COMPLETE SET (5)	3.00	6.00
COMMON CARD	.75	1.50

1994 Finish Line Busch Grand National

Finish Line produced this 15-card insert set that focuses on up-and-coming drivers from Busch Series racing. The cards were randomly packed in all types of 1994 Finish Line racing packs. The odds of pulling a BGN card from a regular pack or a jumbo pack was one in eight packs.

COMPLETE SET (15)	5.00	12.00
BGN1 David Green	.30	.75
BGN2 Jeff Burton	.60	1.50
BGN3 Bobby Dotter	.30	.75
BGN4 Todd Bodine	.30	.75
BGN5 Hermie Sadler	.30	.75
BGN6 Tom Peck	.30	.75
BGN7 Tracy Leslie	.30	.75
BGN8 Ricky Craven	.50	1.25
BGN9 Chuck Bown	.30	.75
BGN10 Steve Grissom	.50	1.25
BGN11 Joe Nemechek	.50	1.25
BGN12 Robert Pressley	.50	1.25
BGN13 Rodney Combs	.30	.75
BGN14 Ward Burton	.50	1.25
BGN15 Mike Wallace	.30	.75

1994 Finish Line Down Home

This 10-card set was produced by Finish Line for insertion in its 1994 racing product. The cards focus on drivers from small towns with information about the driver as well as their hometown. The cards were randomly inserted in all types of 1994 Finish Line racing packs. The cards were seeded in packs at a rate of one in eight packs.

COMPLETE SET (10)	5.00	12.00
1 Harry Gant	.50	1.25
2 Ernie Irvan	.50	1.25
3 Dale Jarrett	1.50	4.00
4 Mark Martin	2.00	5.00
5 Kyle Petty	.50	1.25
6 Ricky Rudd	.75	2.00
7 Ken Schrader	.25	.60
8 Morgan Shepherd	.25	.60
9 Jimmy Spencer	.25	.60
10 Rusty Wallace	2.00	5.00

1994 Finish Line Gold Signature

Gold foil signatures adorn the fronts of these 5 cards randomly inserted in 1994 Finish Line hobby packs. Backs feature a short driver bio and the set title "Gold Signature Series." Odds of finding a Gold Signature card was one in 20 packs. The cards are unnumbered and have been listed below in alphabetical order.

COMPLETE SET (5)	10.00	25.00
1 Ernie Irvan	1.25	3.00
2 Dale Jarrett	4.00	10.00
3 Mark Martin	5.00	12.00
4 Kyle Petty	1.25	3.00
5 Rusty Wallace	5.00	12.00

1994 Finish Line New Stars on the Horizon

Finish Line produced this eight-card insert set that focuses on 1994 Winston Cup rookies. The cards were randomly packed in all types of 1994 Finish Line racing packs. The cards could be pulled at a rate of one in eight packs.

COMPLETE SET (8)	3.00	8.00
1 John Andretti	.60	1.50
2 Todd Bodine	.30	.75
3 Chuck Bown	.30	.75
4 Jeff Burton	.75	2.00
5 Ward Burton	.60	1.50
6 Steve Grissom	.60	1.50
7 Joe Nemechek	.60	1.50
8 Loy Allen Jr.	.30	.75

1994 Finish Line Victory Lane

Finish Line produced this 18-card insert set that focuses on 1993 race winners. The cards were inserted one per 1994 Finish Line special retail jumbo pack and one every eight regular packs. The cards were printed on silver foil card stock.

COMPLETE SET (18)	12.50	30.00
VL1 Davey Allison	1.50	4.00
VL2 Geoff Bodine	.40	1.00
VL3 Ernie Irvan	.75	2.00
VL4 Dale Jarrett	2.50	6.00
VL5 Mark Martin	3.00	8.00
VL6 Kyle Petty	.75	2.00
VL7 Morgan Shepherd	.40	1.00
VL8 Ricky Rudd	1.25	3.00
VL9 Rusty Wallace	3.00	8.00
VL10 Rusty Wallace	3.00	8.00
VL11 Ricky Rudd	1.25	3.00
VL12 Morgan Shepherd	.40	1.00
VL13 Kyle Petty	.75	2.00
VL14 Mark Martin	3.00	8.00
VL15 Dale Jarrett	2.50	6.00
VL16 Davey Allison	1.50	4.00
VL17 Geoff Bodine	.40	1.00
VL18 Ernie Irvan	.75	2.00

1994 Finish Line Gold Promos

Finish Line produced these promo cards to preview the 1994 Finish Line Gold release. The unnumbered cards were packaged in a cello wrapper and are often sold as a complete set.

COMPLETE SET (3)	3.00	8.00
P1 Jeff Gordon's Car Promo	2.50	6.00
P2 Terry Labonte Promo	1.50	4.00
P3 Cover Card Promo	.20	.50

1994 Finish Line Gold

Finish Line produced their first premium NASCAR set in 1994 -- Finish Line Gold. The 100-card set was packaged in 8-card packs with 32 packs per box in 2,500 numbered 12 box cases. Inserts included an Autograph series, Calling Cards and a Teamwork set. Finish Line produced a special Ernie Irvan hologram card (numbered of 3000) randomly inserted in packs. Three promo cards came packaged in together in a cello pack. They were distributed to dealers and members of the media.

COMPLETE SET (100)	8.00	20.00
WAX BOX	20.00	50.00
1 Joe Gibbs	.15	.40
2 Hut Stricklin's Car	.02	.10
3 Ricky Rudd's Car	.07	.20
4 Sterling Marlin	.25	.60
5 Hut Stricklin	.07	.20
6 Lake Speed	.07	.20
7 Kyle Petty	.15	.40
8 Ernie Irvan	.15	.40
9 Dale Jarrett	.50	1.25
10 Rusty Wallace	.60	1.50
11 Jeff Gordon	.75	2.00
12 Michael Waltrip	.15	.40
13 Darrell Waltrip	.15	.40
14 Mark Martin	.60	1.50
15 Morgan Shepherd	.07	.20
16 Rusty Wallace's Car	.25	.60
17 Robert Pressley	.07	.20
18 Ted Musgrave	.07	.20
19 Ken Schrader	.07	.20
20 Wally Dallenbach Jr.'s Car	.02	.10
21 Geoff Bodine	.07	.20
22 Kyle Petty	.15	.40
23 Brett Bodine's Car	.02	.10
24 Rusty Wallace	.60	1.50
25 Brett Bodine	.07	.20
26 Robert Yates	.02	.10
27 Morgan Shepherd	.07	.20
28 Jeff Gordon	.75	2.00
29 Terry Labonte	.25	.60
30 Darrell Waltrip's Car	.07	.20
31 Darrell Waltrip	.15	.40
32 Bobby Labonte's Car	.15	.40
33 Terry Labonte	.25	.60
34 Ricky Rudd	.25	.60
35 Ken Schrader	.07	.20
36 Harry Gant	.15	.40
37 Kenny Wallace	.07	.20
38 Dale Jarrett	.50	1.25
39 Geoff Bodine	.07	.20
40 Morgan Shepherd's Car	.02	.10
41 Harry Gant	.15	.40
42 Jimmy Spencer	.07	.20
43 Ernie Irvan	.15	.40
44 Ricky Craven	.15	.40
45 Lake Speed	.07	.20
46 Ernie Irvan's Car	.07	.20
47 Terry Labonte's Car	.15	.40
48 Mark Martin	.60	1.50
49 Ricky Rudd	.25	.60
50 Ted Musgrave	.07	.20
51 Sterling Marlin's Car	.07	.20
52 Harry Gant	.15	.40
53 Jimmy Spencer	.07	.20
54 Geoff Bodine	.07	.20
55 Ted Musgrave	.07	.20
56 Felix Sabates Chany Sabates	.02	.10
57 Ricky Rudd	.25	.60
58 Kyle Petty's Car	.07	.20
59 Rusty Wallace	.60	1.50
60 Jeff Gordon	.75	2.00
61 Jack Roush	.02	.10
62 Michael Waltrip	.15	.40
63 Geoff Bodine's Car	.02	.10
64 Darrell Waltrip	.15	.40
65 Jeff Gordon's Car	.40	1.00
66 Darrell Waltrip	.15	.40
67 Hut Stricklin	.07	.20
68 Rusty Wallace	.60	1.50
69 Morgan Shepherd	.07	.20
70 Sterling Marlin	.25	.60
71 Kyle Petty	.15	.40
72 Mark Martin	.60	1.50
73 Hut Stricklin	.07	.20
74 Michael Waltrip's Car	.07	.20
75 Dale Jarrett	.50	1.25
76 Ken Schrader	.07	.20
77 Terry Labonte	.25	.60
78 Hermie Sadler	.07	.20
79 Mark Martin's Car	.25	.60
80 Ernie Irvan	.15	.40
81 Mark Martin	.60	1.50
82 Brett Bodine	.07	.20
83 Richard Petty	.25	.60
84 Michael Waltrip	.15	.40
85 Kyle Petty	.15	.40
86 Lake Speed's Car	.02	.10
87 Ken Schrader's Car	.02	.10
88 Jeff Gordon	.75	2.00
89 Dale Jarrett	.50	1.25
90 Jimmy Spencer	.07	.20
91 Harry Gant	.15	.40
92 David Green	.07	.20
93 Ernie Irvan	.15	.40
94 Ricky Rudd	.25	.60
95 Dale Jarrett's Car	.15	.40
96 Lake Speed	.07	.20
97 Jimmy Spencer's Car	.02	.10
98 Morgan Shepherd	.07	.20
99 Brett Bodine	.07	.20
100 Sterling Marlin	.25	.60
NNO Ernie Irvan HOLO/3000	20.00	50.00

1994 Finish Line Gold Autographs

Nineteen drivers and crew members signed copies of their regular 1994 Finish Line Gold cards to be randomly inserted into packs (approximately one per box). The autographs were signed using a gold paint pen and limited to less than 2000 copies of each card.

COMPLETE SET (19)	150.00	300.00
6 Lake Speed	7.50	15.00
15 Morgan Shepherd	7.50	15.00
16 Buddy Parrott	4.00	8.00
17 Robert Pressley	7.50	15.00
33 Terry Labonte	12.50	30.00
37 Kenny Wallace	7.50	15.00
38 Dale Jarrett	25.00	50.00
44 Ricky Craven	10.00	25.00
51 Tony Glover	4.00	8.00
65 Ray Evernham	8.00	20.00
76 Ken Schrader	8.00	20.00
78 Hermie Sadler	7.50	15.00
80 Ernie Irvan	10.00	25.00
81 Mark Martin	15.00	40.00
84 Michael Waltrip	8.00	20.00
92 David Green	7.50	15.00
94 Ricky Rudd	15.00	30.00
95 Jimmy Makar	4.00	8.00
99 Brett Bodine	7.50	15.00

1994 Finish Line Gold Phone Cards

For the first time in racing, prepaid calling cards were inserted in card packs with this set. Each card had a phone value of $2.50 and was printed on the usual plastic stock similar to a credit card. The cards are numbered of 3,000 and carried an expiration date of 12/31/95. Phone cards with the pin number revealed are generally worth half of Mint unscratched cards.

COMPLETE SET (9)	5.00	12.00
1 Geoff Bodine/3000	.10	.30
2 Jeff Gordon/3000	1.25	3.00
3 Ernie Irvan/3000	.25	.60
4 Dale Jarrett/3000	.75	2.00
5 Mark Martin/3000	1.00	2.50
6 Kyle Petty/3000	.25	.60
7 Ricky Rudd/3000	.40	1.00
8 Rusty Wallace/3000	1.00	2.50
9 Darrell Waltrip/3000	.25	.60

1994 Finish Line Gold Teamwork

Teamwork cards were randomly inserted in 1994 Finish Line Gold at a rate of one per eight packs. Each card features a top Winston Cup NASCAR driver along with their crew chief and were printed on gold foil stock.

COMPLETE SET (10)	8.00	20.00
TG1 Rusty Wallace B.Parrott	2.50	6.00
TG2 Mark Martin S.Hmiel	2.50	6.00
TG3 Ricky Rudd Bill Ingle	1.00	2.50
TG4 Dale Jarrett Jimmy Makar	2.00	5.00
TG5 M.Shepherd L.Wood	.30	.75
TG6 Jeff Gordon R.Evernham	3.00	8.00
TG7 Ernie Irvan McReynolds	.60	1.50
TG8 Brett Bodine Don.Richeson	.30	.75
TG9 Geoff Bodine Paul Andrews	.30	.75
TG10 Darrell Waltrip Barry Dodson	.60	1.50

1994 Finish Line Phone Cards

These cards were issued in clear envelopes and sold through major retail outlets. They were the first phone cards released by Finish Line. There were 5000 of each series one card (1-5) produced and 1800 of each series two card (6-10). Finish Line made available a gold version of the Bill Elliott and the Ernie Irvan cards.

COMPLETE SET (15)	25.00	60.00
1 Bill Elliott	2.00	5.00
2 Jeff Gordon	4.00	10.00
3 Bobby Labonte	2.50	6.00
4 Sterling Marlin	1.50	4.00
5 Rusty Wallace	3.00	8.00
6 Geoff Bodine	1.25	3.00
7 Bill Elliott	2.00	5.00
8 Jeff Gordon	4.00	10.00
9 Ernie Irvan	1.25	3.00
10 Dale Jarrett	2.50	6.00
11 Mark Martin	3.00	8.00
12 Kyle Petty	1.25	3.00
13 Ricky Rudd	1.50	4.00
14 Rusty Wallace	3.00	8.00
15 Darrell Waltrip	1.25	3.00
16 Bill Elliott Gold/600	10.00	25.00
17 Ernie Irvan Gold/600	6.00	15.00

1995 Finish Line

Classic produced this 1995 set for Finish Line. The 120-card set was packaged in 10-card hobby and 10-card retail foil packs with 36-packs per box. Hobby cases were numbered sequentially to 1995. Inserts included Silver foil and Printer's Proof parallel sets, along with four others. Hobby and retail pack versions differed according to which inserts could be found. Two different Dale Earnhardt autographed cards, one for hobby and one for retail packs, were also randomly inserted. Each signed card was numbered of 250. Other than the signature the cards are the same as card #89 in the set. There was also another Dale Eanhardt certified autograph card similar to #111 in the basic set that was also serial numbered to 250, but there were no foil markings or nameplate on the front of the card.

COMPLETE SET (120) 6.00 15.00
1 Dale Earnhardt 1.25 3.00
2 Rusty Wallace .60 1.50
3 Darrell Waltrip .15 .40
4 Sterling Marlin .25 .60
5 Terry Labonte .25 .60
6 Mark Martin .60 1.50
7 Geoff Bodine .07 .20
8 Jeff Burton .25 .60
9 Jimmy Spencer .07 .20
10 Ricky Rudd .25 .60
11 Brett Bodine .07 .20
12 Bobby Allison .07 .20
13 John Andretti .07 .20
Nancy Andretti
14 Rick Hendrick .02 .10
15 Robert Gee .02 .10
16 Ted Musgrave .07 .20
17 Darrell Waltrip .15 .40
18 Dale Jarrett .50 1.25
19 Kenny Wallace .07 .20
20 David Green .07 .20
21 Morgan Shepherd .07 .20
22 Rick Mast .07 .20
23 Chad Little .07 .20
24 Jeff Gordon .75 2.00
25 Ken Schrader .07 .20
26 Steve Kinser .07 .20
Bernstein
27 Sterling Marlin .25 .60
28 Ernie Irvan .25 .60
29 Geoff Bodine .07 .20
30 Michael Waltrip .15 .40
Elizabeth Waltrip
31 Ward Burton .15 .40
32 Jeremy Mayfield .15 .40
33 Robert Pressley .07 .20
34 Rusty Wallace .50 1.50
35 Todd Bodine .07 .20
36 Paul Andrews .02 .10
37 Dale Jarrett .50 1.25
38 Morgan Shepherd .07 .20
39 Joe Nemechek .07 .20
Andrea Nemechek
40 Felix Sabates .02 .10
41 Ricky Craven .15 .40
42 Kyle Petty .15 .40
43 Richard Petty .25 .60
44 Robert Yates .02 .10
45 Hermie Sadler .07 .20
46 Johnny Benson .15 .40
47 Ken Schrader .07 .20
48 Steve Grissom .07 .20
49 Bobby Dotter .07 .20
50 Dick Trickle .07 .20
51 Ernie Irvan .15 .40
52 Kyle Petty .15 .40
53 Jeff Gordon .75 2.00
54 Mark Martin .60 1.50
55 Morgan Shepherd .07 .20
56 Ward Burton .15 .40
57 Jimmy Makar .02 .10
58 Darrell Waltrip .15 .40
59 Walter Bud Moore .02 .10
60 Rick Mast .07 .20
61 Michael Waltrip .15 .40
62 Derrike Cope .07 .20
63 Buddy Parrott .02 .10
64 Lake Speed .07 .20
65 Ray Evernham .02 .10
66 Steve Hmiel .02 .10
67 Jeff Gordon w .60 1.50
Crew
68 Brett Bodine .07 .20
69 Terry Labonte .25 .60
70 Rusty Wallace .60 1.50
71 Larry Pearson .02 .10
72 Ted Musgrave .07 .20
73 Kyle Petty .15 .40
74 John Andretti .07 .20
75 Todd Bodine .07 .20
Lynn Bodine
76 Joe Nemechek .07 .20
77 Jimmy Spencer .07 .20
78 Brett Bodine .07 .20
79 Mark Martin .60 1.50
80 Harry Gant .15 .40
81 Lake Speed .07 .20
82 Larry McReynolds .02 .10
83 Ricky Rudd .25 .60
84 Loy Allen Jr. .07 .20
85 Travis Carter .02 .10
86 Mike Wallace .07 .20
87 Geoff Bodine .07 .20
88 Dennis Setzer .07 .20
89 Dale Earnhardt 1.25 3.00
90 Mike Wallace .07 .20
91 Bobby Labonte .50 1.25
92 Ernie Irvan .15 .40
93 Jeff Burton .25 .60
94 Sterling Marlin .25 .60
95 Michael Waltrip .15 .40
96 Tim Fedewa .07 .20
97 Terry Labonte .25 .60
98 Jeremy Mayfield .15 .40
99 Bill Ingle .02 .10
100 Ken Schrader .07 .20
101 Tony Glover .02 .10
102 Todd Bodine .07 .20
103 Bobby Labonte .50 1.25
104 Richard Petty .25 .60
105 Jeff Gordon .75 2.00
106 Ricky Rudd .25 .60
107 A.G. Dillard .02 .10
108 Junior Johnson .07 .20
109 Steve Grissom .07 .20
110 Dale Jarrett .50 1.25
111 Dale Earnhardt 1.25 3.00
112 Kenny Wallace .07 .20
113 Jimmy Johnson .02 .10
114 Dave Marcis .07 .20
115 Kenny Bernstein .07 .20
116 Bobby Hamilton .07 .20
117 Steve Kinser .07 .20
118 John Andretti .07 .20
119 Derrike Cope .07 .20
120 Ricky Craven .15 .40
CE1 Dale Earnhardt Club Promo 3.00 8.00
HP1 Dale Earnhardt Promo 2.50 6.00
RP1 Dale Earnhardt Promo 2.50 6.00
89AUH D.Earn. AU/250 Red 100.00 200.00
89AUR D.Earn. AU/250 Blue 100.00 200.00
111AU D.Earn. AU/250 100.00 200.00

1995 Finish Line Printer's Proof

COMPLETE SET (120) 100.00 200.00
*PRINT.PROOF/398: 2X TO 5X BASIC CARDS

1995 Finish Line Silver

COMPLETE SET (120) 12.00 30.00
*SILVERS: 1X TO 2X BASIC CARDS

1995 Finish Line Dale Earnhardt

Randomly inserted in 1995 Finish Line packs, these 10 cards feaured Dale Earnhardt and were printed using Classic's micro-lined printing technology. Wrapper stated odds for pulling one of the cards was 1:18.

COMPLETE SET (10) 25.00 50.00
COMMON CARD (DE1-DE10) 3.00 8.00

1995 Finish Line Gold Signature

Cards from this 16-card set were randomly inserted in 1995 Finish Line retail packs. Each card was numbered one of 1995. The cards could be found at a rate of one per nine retail packs.

COMPLETE SET (16) 50.00 120.00
GS1 Jeff Gordon 8.00 20.00
GS2 Rusty Wallace 6.00 15.00
GS3 Dale Earnhardt 12.50 30.00
GS4 Sterling Marlin 2.50 6.00
GS5 Terry Labonte 2.50 6.00
GS6 Mark Martin 6.00 15.00
GS7 Geoff Bodine .75 2.00
GS8 Ken Schrader .75 2.00
GS9 Kyle Petty 1.50 4.00
GS10 Ricky Rudd 2.50 6.00
GS11 Michael Waltrip 1.50 4.00
GS12 Darrell Waltrip 1.50 4.00
GS13 Dale Jarrett 5.00 12.00
GS14 Morgan Shepherd .75 2.00
GS15 Lake Speed .75 2.00
GS16 Ted Musgrave .75 2.00

1995 Finish Line Standout Cars

Randomly inserted in hobby only packs, these 10 cards feature top driver's cars in a "Standout" format. The card's background could actually be folded to allow the card to stand-up by itself. Wrapper stated odds for pulling one of the cards is 1:9 packs.

COMPLETE SET (10) 10.00 25.00
SC1 Dale Earnhardt's Car 4.00 10.00
SC2 Mark Martin's Car 2.00 5.00
SC3 Rusty Wallace's Car 2.00 5.00
SC4 Ricky Rudd's Car .75 2.00
SC5 Morgan Shepherd's Car .25 .60
SC6 Terry Labonte's Car .75 2.00
SC7 Jeff Gordon's Car 2.50 6.00
SC8 Darrell Waltrip's Car .50 1.25
SC9 Geoff Bodine's Car .25 .60
SC10 Michael Waltrip's Car .50 1.25

1995 Finish Line Standout Drivers

Randomly inserted in retail only packs, these 10-cards feature top drivers in a "Standout" format. The card background could actually be folded to allow the card to stand-up by itself. The same ten drivers were used for both the Standout Cars and Standout Drivers insert sets. Wrapper stated odds for pulling one of the cards is 1:9 packs.

COMPLETE SET (10) 15.00 40.00
SD1 Dale Earnhardt 6.00 15.00
SD2 Mark Martin 3.00 8.00
SD3 Rusty Wallace 3.00 8.00
SD4 Ricky Rudd 1.25 3.00
SD5 Morgan Shepherd .40 1.00
SD6 Terry Labonte 1.25 3.00
SD7 Jeff Gordon 4.00 10.00
SD8 Darrell Waltrip .75 2.00
SD9 Geoff Bodine .40 1.00
SD10 Michael Waltrip .75 2.00

1995 Finish Line Coca-Cola 600

COMPLETE SET (50) 3.00 8.00
COMP.FACT.SET (65) 6.00 15.00
*SINGLES: .2X TO .5X BASE ASSETS

1995 Finish Line Coca-Cola 600 Die Cuts

COMPLETE SET (5) 1.25 3.00
C1 Dale Earnhardt .50 1.25
C2 Rusty Wallace .20 .50
C3 Jeff Gordon .30 .75
C4 Dale Jarrett .15 .40
C5 Mark Martin .20 .50

1995 Finish Line Coca-Cola 600 Winners

COMPLETE SET (10) 2.00 5.00
CC1 Darrell Waltrip .05 .15
CC2 Dale Earnhardt .50 1.25
CC3 Kyle Petty .05 .15
CC4 Darrell Waltrip .05 .15
CC5 Darrell Waltrip .05 .15
CC6 Rusty Wallace .20 .50
CC7 Davey Allison's Car .05 .15
CC8 Dale Earnhardt .50 1.25
CC9 Dale Earnhardt .50 1.25
CC10 Jeff Gordon .30 .75

1995 Finish Line Phone Card of the Month

These cards were available through the Finish Line Racing Club. The cards were printed in quantities of 1500 each.

COMPLETE SET (4) 40.00 75.00
1 Jeff Gordon/1500 12.50 25.00
2 Sterling Marlin/1500 6.00 12.00
3 Mark Martin/1500 10.00 20.00
4 Rusty Wallace/1500 10.00 20.00

1995 Finish Line Platinum 5-Unit Phone Cards

There were 500 of each of the cards in this series. The cards could be bought in different unit denomonations, 5, 10, 25, and 60. The cards were sold through the Finish Line Racing Club.

COMPLETE SET (4) 12.50 30.00
COMP. 10 UNIT SET (4) 30.00 50.00
*10U CARDS: 1X TO 1.5X 5U CARDS
COMP. 25 UNIT SET (4) 60.00 80.00
*25U CARDS: 2X TO 3X 5U CARDS
COMP. 60 UNIT SET (4) 160.00 200.00
*60U CARDS: 5X TO 7X 5U CARDS
1 Jeff Gordon 5.00 12.00
2 Mark Martin 4.00 10.00
3 Ricky Rudd 2.50 6.00
4 Rusty Wallace 4.00 10.00

1995 Finish Line SuperTrucks

The inaugural 1995 Finish Line SuperTrucks set features 80-cards that were packaged in 10-card foil packs with 36-packs per box. Sixteen-box case production was limited to 650 cases. Inserts include a Rainbow foil parallel set, along with Calling Cards, Champion's Choice, Super Signatures and Winter Heat Hot Shoes.

COMPLETE SET (80) 4.00 10.00
1 Mike Skinner RC .10 .30
2 Butch Gilliland .05 .15
3 Rick Carelli .10 .30
4 Walker Evans' Truck .02 .10
5 Joe Bessey .05 .15
6 Ken Schrader .20 .50
7 Scott Lagasse .10 .30
8 Bob Keselowski's Truck .02 .10
9 Butch Gilliland's Truck .02 .10
10 Mike Hulbert .05 .15
11 Kerry Teague .05 .15
12 Troy Beebe .05 .15
13 Walker Evans .05 .15
14 Joe Ruttman .05 .15
15 P.J. Jones .05 .15
16 Jack Sprague's Truck .02 .10
17 Jeff Gordon .60 1.50
18 Tobey Butler .05 .15
19 Jerry Glanville's Truck .02 .10
20 Roger Mears .05 .15
21 Bill Sedgwick .05 .15
22 Gary Collins .05 .15
23 Walker Evans .05 .15
24 Sammy Swindell .10 .30
25 Steve McEachern's Truck .02 .10
26 Geoff Bodine .20 .50
27 Terry Labonte .25 .60
28 Butch Miller .05 .15
29 Geoff Bodine's Truck .05 .15
30 Mike Skinner\Richard Childress .10 .30
31 Tommy Archer .05 .15
32 Steve McEachern .05 .15
33 Tobey Butler .05 .15
34 Bob Strait .05 .15
35 Jerry Glanville .05 .15
36 Mike Skinner's Truck .05 .15
37 Joe Bessey .05 .15
38 P.J. Jones .05 .15
39 Jack Sprague .05 .15
40 Tommy Archer's Truck .02 .10
41 Kerry Teague .05 .15
42 Roger Mears .05 .15
43 Ron Hornaday RC .10 .30
44 Tommy Archer .05 .15
45 Scott Lagasse .10 .30
46 Walker Evans .05 .15
47 Gary Collins' Truck .02 .10
48 Jack Sprague .05 .15
49 Bob Keselowski .05 .15
50 Geoff Bodine .20 .50
51 Ken Schrader .20 .50
52 Tobey Butler's Truck .02 .10
53 Kerry Teague's Truck .02 .10
54 Mike Skinner RC .10 .30
55 Terry Labonte .25 .60
56 Troy Beebe .05 .15
57 Richard Childress .10 .30
58 Jerry Glanville .05 .15
59 Butch Miller .05 .15
60 Terry Labonte's Truck .05 .15
61 T.J. Clark .05 .15
62 Butch Gilliland .05 .15
63 Joe Ruttman .05 .15
64 Scott Lagasse's Truck .05 .15
65 Steve McEachern .05 .15
66 Gary Collins .05 .15
67 Bob Strait .05 .15
68 Rick Carelli's Truck .02 .10
69 Sammy Swindell .10 .30
70 Ken Schrader's Truck .02 .10
71 Ron Hornaday RC .10 .30
72 T.J. Clark .05 .15
73 Geoff Bodine .20 .50
74 Mike Hulbert .05 .15
75 Ken Schrader .20 .50
76 P.J. Jones' Truck .02 .10
77 Roger Mears' Truck .02 .10
78 Bob Keselowski .05 .15
79 Rick Carelli .10 .30
80 Checklist .02 .10

1995 Finish Line SuperTrucks Rainbow Foil

COMPLETE SET (80) 25.00 50.00
*STARS: 2X TO 4X BASIC CARDS

1995 Finish Line SuperTrucks Calling Cards

Randomly packed at the rate of approximately 1:18 packs, these Calling Cards carry a phone time value of three minutes with an expiration date of 12/31/1996. Each card features a gold foil Finish Line logo on the cardfront and a serial number of 2100 on the cardback.

COMPLETE SET (10) 5.00 12.00
1 Geoff Bodine 1.00 2.50
2 Rick Carelli .60 1.50
3 Walker Evans .30 .75
4 Jerry Glanville .30 .75
5 Tobey Butler .60 1.50
6 P.J. Jones .30 .75
7 Terry Labonte 1.25 3.00
8 Roger Mears .30 .75
9 Ken Schrader 1.00 2.50
10 Mike Skinner .60 1.50

1995 Finish Line SuperTrucks Champion's Choice

Champion's Choice cards were randomly inserted in 1995 Finish Line SuperTrucks packs at the wrapper stated odds of 1:9 packs. The cards feature favorites to win SuperTrucks racing events in 1995.

COMPLETE SET (6) 4.00 10.00
CC1 Roger Mears .40 1.00
CC2 Terry Labonte 1.50 4.00
CC3 Rick Carelli .40 1.00
CC4 Ron Hornaday .60 1.50
CC5 Sammy Swindell .60 1.50
CC6 Geoff Bodine 1.00 2.50

1995 Finish Line SuperTrucks Super Signature

Super Signature Series cards were randomly inserted in 1995 Finish Line SuperTrucks packs at the wrapper stated odds of 1:9 packs. The 10-cards feature top SuperTrucks drivers printed with a gold foil signature on the cardfront.

COMPLETE SET (10) 10.00 20.00
SS1 Jeff Gordon 4.00 10.00
SS2 Richard Childress .60 1.50
SS3 Ken Schrader 2.00 4.00
SS4 Jerry Glanville .60 1.50
SS5 Mike Skinner 1.00 2.50
SS6 Tobey Butler .60 1.50
SS7 Joe Bessey .60 1.50
SS8 Scott Lagasse 1.00 2.50
SS9 P.J. Jones .60 1.50
SS10 Terry Labonte 2.00 5.00

1995 Finish Line SuperTrucks Winter Heat Hot Shoes

Winter Heat Hot Shoes cards are randomly inserted in 1995 Finish Line SuperTrucks packs at the wrapper stated odds of 1:9 packs. The four-cards feature top performers from the SuperTrucks Winter Heat events held in Tucson. The cards are printed with gold foil layering on the cardfront.

COMPLETE SET (4) 2.00 5.00
HS1 Mike Skinner .60 1.50
HS2 P.J. Jones .50 1.25
HS3 Rick Carelli .50 1.25
HS4 Ron Hornaday .60 1.50

1996 Finish Line

This 100-card set features new looks for '96 of the top Winston Cup drivers and their cars. After teaming up with Classic to produce their '95 line, Finish Line returned to making their own cards in '96. The cards were packaged 10 cards per pack, 36 packs per box and 16 boxes per case. The packs had a suggested retail price of $1.99. There were a total of 1,500 cases produced. The product was distributed through both hobby and retail channels.

COMPLETE SET (100) 4.00 10.00
1 Jeff Gordon .75 2.00
2 Ted Musgrave .07 .20
3 Rusty Wallace .60 1.50
4 Ward Burton's Car .02 .10
5 Terry Labonte .25 .60
6 Derrike Cope .07 .20
7 Steve Grissom .07 .20
8 Mark Martin .60 1.50
9 Mark Martin's Car .25 .60
10 Ricky Rudd .25 .60
11 Darrell Waltrip .15 .40
12 Jeff Burton .25 .60
13 Ernie Irvan .15 .40
14 Jeremy Mayfield .15 .40
15 Michael Waltrip's Car .07 .20
16 Hut Stricklin .07 .20
17 Brett Bodine .07 .20
18 Gary DeHart .02 .10
19 Bobby Hamilton .07 .20
20 Kyle Petty .15 .40
21 Derrike Cope's Car .02 .10
22 Dick Trickle .07 .20
23 Sterling Marlin .25 .60
24 Joe Gibbs .15 .40
25 Bobby Allison .07 .20
26 Bobby Labonte .50 1.25
27 Rusty Wallace .60 1.50
28 Rusty Wallace's Car .25 .60
29 Morgan Shepherd .07 .20
30 Geoff Bodine .07 .20
31 Ricky Craven .07 .20
32 Jimmy Spencer .07 .20
33 Ernie Irvan's Car .07 .20
34 Michael Waltrip .15 .40
35 Joe Nemechek .07 .20
36 Ward Burton .15 .40
37 John Andretti .07 .20
38 Ken Schrader .07 .20
39 Mike Wallace .07 .20
40 Bill Elliott's Car .15 .40
41 Sterling Marlin .25 .60
42 Bill Elliott .30 .75
43 Dale Jarrett .50 1.25
44 Morgan Shepherd .07 .20
45 Jimmy Spencer's Car .02 .10
46 Mike Wallace .07 .20
47 Chad Little .07 .20
48 Todd Bodine .07 .20
49 Bobby Hamilton .07 .20
50 Larry McReynolds .02 .10
51 Kenny Wallace .07 .20
52 Ricky Rudd .25 .60
53 Steve Grissom .07 .20
54 Derrike Cope .07 .20
55 Brett Bodine .07 .20
56 Darrell Waltrip .15 .40
57 Ted Musgrave .07 .20
58 Johnny Benson .07 .20
59 Geoff Bodine .07 .20
60 Mark Martin .60 1.50
61 Michael Waltrip .15 .40
62 Sterling Marlin's Car .07 .20
63 Larry McClure .02 .10
64 Jeff Burton .25 .60
65 Ward Burton .15 .40
66 Rick Mast .07 .20
67 Darrell Waltrip's Car .07 .20
68 Darrell Waltrip .15 .40
69 Bobby Labonte .50 1.25
70 Johnny Benson .07 .20
71 Todd Bodine .07 .20
72 Jimmy Makar .02 .10
73 Hut Stricklin .07 .20
74 Terry Labonte's Car .15 .40
75 Joe Nemechek .07 .20
76 Ricky Craven .07 .20
77 Bill Elliott .30 .75
78 Terry Labonte .25 .60
79 Robert Yates .02 .10
80 Ricky Rudd's Car .07 .20
81 Robin Pemberton .02 .10
82 Ray Evernham .02 .10
83 Tony Glover .02 .10
84 David Green .07 .20
85 Bobby Labonte's Car .15 .40
86 Kyle Petty .15 .40
87 Jeff Gordon .75 2.00
88 Rick Hendrick .02 .10
89 Ken Schrader .07 .20
90 Dale Jarrett's Car .15 .40
91 Felix Sabates .02 .10
92 Ernie Irvan .15 .40
93 Bill Ingle .02 .10
94 Jimmy Spencer .07 .20
95 Jeff Gordon's Car .30 .75
96 Jack Roush .02 .10
97 Steve Hmiel .02 .10
98 Johnny Benson's Car .02 .10
99 John Andretti .07 .20
100 Dale Jarrett .50 1.25

1996 Finish Line Printer's Proof

COMPLETE SET (100) 150.00 300.00
*PRINT.PROOFS: 5X TO 12X BASE CARDS

1996 Finish Line Silver

COMPLETE SET (100) 12.00 30.00
*SILVERS: 1X TO 2.5X BASE CARDS

1996 Finish Line Comin' Back Ernie Irvan

This five-card insert set features Ernie Irvan's come back from his near fatal accident at Michigan in 1994 to his return to the Winston Cup circuit. The cards use micro-foil technology and are inserted at a rate of one per 18 packs.

COMPLETE SET (5) 5.00 12.00
COMMON CARD (EI1-EI5) 1.25 3.00

1996 Finish Line Gold Signature

This 18-card insert set features the top names in Winston Cup racing. Each card has a facsimile gold signature of that specific driver across the front. The back of the card is sequentially numbered of 1996. The cards are randomly inserted in packs at a rate of one per 36.

COMPLETE SET (18) 40.00 100.00
GS1 Jeff Gordon 12.50 30.00
GS2 Sterling Marlin 4.00 10.00
GS3 Mark Martin 10.00 25.00
GS4 Rusty Wallace 10.00 25.00
GS5 Terry Labonte 4.00 10.00
GS6 Bill Elliott 5.00 12.00
GS7 Bobby Labonte 8.00 20.00
GS8 Ted Musgrave 1.25 3.00
GS9 Geoff Bodine 1.25 3.00
GS10 Bobby Hamilton 1.25 3.00
GS11 Darrell Waltrip 2.50 6.00
GS12 Michael Waltrip 2.50 6.00
GS13 Ernie Irvan 2.50 6.00

Dale Jarrett	8.00	20.00
Ken Schrader	1.25	3.00
Ricky Craven	1.25	3.00
Ricky Rudd	4.00	10.00
Kyle Petty	2.50	6.00

1996 Finish Line Man and Machine

of the 10 cards from the Man and Machine t set is printed on 16pt. stock and are fully ossed. Each card features the driver, the er and the car for the respective 10 teams in set. The cards were inserted at a rate of one per packs.

MPLETE SET (10)	6.00	15.00
Jeff Gordon	1.25	3.00
Mark Martin	1.00	2.50
3 Rusty Wallace	1.00	2.50
4 Sterling Marlin	.30	.75
5 Terry Labonte	.60	1.50
6 Ernie Irvan	.30	.75
7 Bobby Labonte	.60	1.50
8 Bill Elliott	.60	1.50
9 Derrike Cope	.15	.40
10 Johnny Benson	.15	.40

96 Finish Line Mega-Phone XL Phone Cards

s insert set offered four $25 dollar oversized ne cards. Each card is die-cut and measures by 7" and shows a horizontal picture of the er and his car. The cards were made available ough redemption cards randomly inserted in ks at a rate of one per 36 packs. There were 0 of each card made. Also, you only needed redemption card and $60 to send in to Finish e to obtain the complete four card set.

MPLETE SET (5)	20.00	50.00
eff Gordon	10.00	25.00
ill Elliott	4.00	10.00
ark Martin	8.00	20.00
usty Wallace	8.00	20.00

96 Finish Line Rise To The Top Jeff Gordon

is 10-card insert set features Jeff Gordon's se to the Top" to win the 1995 Winston Cup ampionship. Each card features micro-foil hnology and was randomly inserted at a rate of e per 18 packs.

MPLETE SET (10)	25.00	60.00
MMON GORDON (JG1-JG10)	2.50	6.00

1996 Finish Line Black Gold

e 1996 Finish Line Black Gold Limited set was sued in one series totalling 30 cards. The one-rd packs carried a suggested retail of $6.00 ch. There were 16 boxes per case, 12 packs per x and one card per pack. The cards feature a iver or his car micro photo-etched onto a metal rd front. The back is comprised of a 24pt. stock per. The two pieces, metal front and paper back, ere attached to make one card. There was an eractive game that involved one of the cards in e set. The DE - Designated Entry card allowed llectors a chance to win a 1997 Chevy Monte arlo. By sending in that card or a scratch off BGL rd (1:3 packs) that had Bobby Labonte's name n it, they were automatically entered in the awing. Bobby Labonte was the winner of the APA 500 November 8th which was the qualifier r the BGL cards to be winners. There were also o special gold inserts: Jeff Gordon and Bill lliott. These cards were randomly seeded 1:192 cks. A $25 Black Gold Megaphone XL Jumbo Die-Cut Phone card was randomly seeded 1:12 boxes. The four jumbo die-cut phone cards were printed in quantities of 2,750. Each of the jumbo phone cards carries an expiration date for the phone time of 1/1/2000.

COMPLETE SET (30)	30.00	60.00
C1 Jeff Gordon's Car	2.00	5.00
C2 Rusty Wallace's Car	1.50	4.00
C3 Sterling Marlin's Car	.50	1.25
C4 Terry Labonte's Car	.75	2.00
C5 Mark Martin's Car	1.50	4.00
C6 Ernie Irvan's Car	.40	1.00
C7 Bobby Labonte's Car	1.25	3.00
C8 Kyle Petty's Car	.40	1.00
C9 Ricky Rudd's Car	.60	1.50
C10 Bill Elliott's Car	.75	2.00
C11 Dale Jarrett's Car	1.25	3.00
C12 Darrell Waltrip's Car	.40	1.00
C13 Johnny Benson's Car	.25	.60
C14 Michael Waltrip's Car	.40	1.00
D1 Jeff Gordon	4.00	10.00
D2 Rusty Wallace	3.00	8.00
D3 DE- Designated Entry	.50	1.25
D4 Sterling Marlin	1.25	3.00
D5 Terry Labonte	1.50	4.00
D6 Mark Martin	3.00	8.00
D7 Ernie Irvan	.75	2.00
D8 Bobby Labonte	2.50	6.00
D9 Kyle Petty	.75	2.00
D10 Ricky Rudd	1.25	3.00
D11 Bill Elliott	1.50	4.00
D12 Ted Musgrave	.50	1.25
D13 Darrell Waltrip	.75	2.00
D14 Dale Jarrett	2.50	6.00
D15 Johnny Benson	.50	1.25
D16 Michael Waltrip	.50	1.25
SG1 Jeff Gordon Special Gold	25.00	60.00
SG2 Bill Elliott Special Gold	20.00	50.00
JPC1 Bill Elliott	.60	1.50
JPC2 Jeff Gordon	1.50	4.00
JPC3 Ernie Irvan	.40	1.00
JPC4 Terry Labonte	.60	1.50

1996 Finish Line Diamond Collection $5 Phone Cards

This series of cards was sold through mass retailers. The cards were issued in a black fold out case with each card front featuring a replica diamond and $5 worth of phone time.

COMPLETE SET (8)	15.00	40.00
1 Jeff Gordon	4.00	10.00
2 Bill Elliott	2.00	5.00
3 Dale Jarrett	2.50	6.00
4 Ernie Irvan	1.25	3.00
5 Mark Martin	3.00	8.00
6 Ricky Rudd	2.00	5.00
7 Terry Labonte	2.00	5.00
8 Rusty Wallace	3.00	8.00

1996 Finish Line Phone Pak

This was the first set of phone cards released in pack form. Each card carried a $2 phone value and there were 9500 of each $2 card produced. The cards were packaged three cards per pack, 15-packs per box and 16-boxes per case. A total of 800-cases were produced. Every case, box and phone card was individually numbered.There was also a parallel set of $2 signature cards. They were inserted one per pack and 5000 of each card was produced.

COMPLETE SET (40)	8.00	20.00
WAX BOX	7.50	20.00
1 John Andretti	.08	.25
2 Brett Bodine	.08	.25
3 Geoff Bodine	.08	.25
4 Todd Bodine	.08	.25
5 Jeff Burton	.30	.75
6 Ward Burton	.20	.50
7 Derrike Cope	.08	.25
8 Ricky Craven	.08	.25
9 Bill Elliott	.50	1.25
10 Bill Elliott's Car	.20	.50
11 Jeff Gordon	1.00	2.50
12 Jeff Gordon's Car	.40	1.00
13 Steve Grissom	.08	.25
14 Bobby Hamilton	.08	.25
15 Ernie Irvan	.20	.50
16 Ernie Irvan's Car	.08	.25
17 Dale Jarrett	.60	1.50
18 Bobby Labonte	.60	1.50
19 Bobby Labonte's Car	.20	.50
20 Terry Labonte	.30	.75
21 Terry Labonte's Car	.20	.50
22 Sterling Marlin	.30	.75
23 Sterling Marlin's Car	.20	.50
24 Mark Martin	.75	2.00
25 Mark Martin's Car	.30	.75
26 Ted Musgrave	.08	.25
27 Joe Nemechek	.08	.25
28 Kyle Petty	.20	.50
29 Ricky Rudd	.30	.75
30 Ricky Rudd's Car	.08	.25
31 Ken Schrader	.08	.25
32 Morgan Shepherd	.08	.25
33 Hut Stricklin	.08	.25
34 Dick Trickle	.08	.25
35 Mike Wallace	.08	.25
36 Rusty Wallace	.75	2.00
37 Rusty Wallace's Car	.30	.75
38 Michael Waltrip	.20	.50
39 Darrell Waltrip	.20	.50
40 Darrell Waltrip's Car	.08	.25
P1 Mark Martin Promo	1.25	3.00

1996 Finish Line Phone Pak $2 Signature

COMPLETE SET (40)	7.50	20.00
*$2 SIGNATURE: .6X TO 1.5X BASIC INSERTS		

1996 Finish Line Phone Pak $5

This insert series of 24 cards features $5 in phone time value. There were 570 of each of the cards produced and the odd of pulling one from a pack was 1:15. Due to the bankruptcy of Finish Line, the phone time on these cards is not valid.

COMPLETE SET (24)	10.00	25.00
1 John Andretti	.20	.50
2 Brett Bodine	.20	.50
3 Geoff Bodine	.20	.50
4 Jeff Burton	.60	1.50
5 Ward Burton	.40	1.00
6 Ricky Craven	.20	.50
7 Derrike Cope	.20	.50
8 Bill Elliott	1.00	2.50
9 Jeff Gordon	2.00	5.00
10 Bobby Hamilton	.20	.50
11 Ernie Irvan	.40	1.00
12 Dale Jarrett	1.25	3.00
13 Bobby Labonte	1.25	3.00
14 Terry Labonte	.60	1.50
15 Sterling Marlin	.60	1.50
16 Mark Martin	1.25	3.00
17 Ted Musgrave	.20	.50
18 Kyle Petty	.40	1.00
19 Ricky Rudd	.60	1.50
20 Ken Schrader	.20	.50
21 Morgan Shepherd	.20	.50
22 Rusty Wallace	1.50	4.00
23 Michael Waltrip	.40	1.00
24 Darrell Waltrip	.40	1.00

1996 Finish Line Phone Pak $10

There were 570 of each of the $10 cards. The cards were inserted at a rate of one in 30 packs. Due to the bankruptcy of Finish Line, the phone time on these cards is not valid.

COMPLETE SET (12)	12.00	30.00
1 Geoff Bodine	.40	1.00
2 Bill Elliott	2.00	5.00
3 Jeff Gordon	4.00	10.00
4 Ernie Irvan	.75	2.00
5 Bobby Labonte	2.50	6.00
6 Terry Labonte	1.25	3.00
7 Sterling Marlin	1.25	3.00
8 Mark Martin	3.00	8.00
9 Ricky Rudd	1.25	3.00
10 Ken Schrader	.40	1.00
11 Rusty Wallace	3.00	8.00
12 Darrell Waltrip	.75	2.00

1996 Finish Line Phone Pak $50

This series of insert phone cards features $50 in phone time value. The cards were inserted at a rate of one in 60 packs. Due to the bankruptcy of Finish Line, the phone time on these cards is not valid.

COMPLETE SET (8)	20.00	50.00
1 Bill Elliott	3.00	8.00
2 Jeff Gordon	6.00	15.00
3 Ernie Irvan	1.25	3.00
4 Bobby Labonte	4.00	10.00
5 Terry Labonte	2.00	5.00
6 Mark Martin	5.00	12.00
7 Ricky Rudd	2.00	5.00
8 Rusty Wallace	5.00	12.00

1996 Finish Line Phone Pak $100

There were 280 of each of the $100 phone cards. The cards were inserted one in 120 packs. Due to the bankruptcy of Finish Line, the phone time on these cards is not valid.

COMPLETE SET (6)	30.00	80.00
1 Bill Elliott	5.00	12.00
2 Jeff Gordon	10.00	25.00
3 Ernie Irvan	2.00	5.00
4 Terry Labonte	3.00	8.00
5 Mark Martin	8.00	20.00
6 Rusty Wallace	8.00	20.00

1996 Finish Line Save Mart Phone Cards

This set of three phone cards was distributed at the Save Mart Supermarkets in the Sonoma, California area in conjunction with the Save Mart Supermarkets 300 race. They were used as a promotion to get people to come in to the stores. The phone time on these cards has expired.

COMPLETE SET (3)	2.00	5.00
1 Geoff Bodine/2650	.75	2.00
2 Ernie Irvan/2650	1.00	2.50
3 Save-Mart Car/2650	.40	1.00

1997 Finish Line Phone Pak II

This was the second consecutive year for Finish Line Phone Paks. The set was divided into tiers with each carrying a different phone time value: one call 5-minute cards (#1-37), $5 cards (#39-66), $10 cards (#67-86), $50 cards (#87-94), and $100 cards (#95-100). Each card is individually serial numbered. There was also a special Wild Card insert card that could be used for a random amount of phone time. When calling to collect your prize you would find out what denomination between 5 and 60 minutes you received. The Wild Card was inserted one in 15-packs. Each one call card was numbered of 7950 and each Wild Card was numbered of 4180. The cares were packaged three cards per pack, 15-packs per box and 16-boxes per case.

COMPLETE SET (100)	150.00	300.00
COMP.SET w/o SP's (38)	4.00	10.00
39-66 $5 CARD STATED ODDS 1:7.5		
$5 CARD PRINT RUN 500 SER.#'d SETS		
$10 CARD STATED ODDS 1:15		
$10 CARD PRINT RUN 360 SER.#'d SETS		
$50 CARD STATED ODDS 1:60		
$100 CARD STATED ODDS 1:240		
1 Jeff Gordon	.75	2.00
2 Bill Elliott	.30	.75
3 Mark Martin	.60	1.50
4 Rusty Wallace	.60	1.50
5 Terry Labonte	.30	.75
6 Ernie Irvan	.15	.40
7 Ricky Rudd	.30	.75
8 Bobby Labonte	.50	1.25
9 Sterling Marlin	.30	.75
10 Darrell Waltrip	.15	.40
11 Ted Musgrave	.08	.25
12 Dale Jarrett	.50	1.25
13 Ricky Craven	.08	.25
14 Jeremy Mayfield	.15	.40
15 Eli Gold	.05	.15
16 Michael Waltrip	.15	.40
17 Jimmy Spencer	.08	.25
18 Brett Bodine	.08	.25
19 Geoff Bodine	.08	.25
20 John Andretti	.08	.25
21 Ken Schrader	.08	.25
22 Bobby Hamilton	.08	.25
23 Derrike Cope	.08	.25
24 Ward Burton	.15	.40
25 Joe Nemechek	.08	.25
26 Kenny Wallace	.08	.25
27 Mike Wallace	.08	.25
28 Morgan Shepherd	.08	.25
29 Rick Hendrick	.05	.15
30 Jack Roush	.05	.15
31 Larry McClure	.05	.15
32 Felix Sabates	.05	.15
33 Joe Gibbs	.15	.40
34 Robert Yates	.05	.15
35 Chuck Rider	.05	.15
36 L.Wood E.Wood M.Waltrip	.15	.40
37 Bill Elliott	.30	.75
38 Wild Card	.05	.15
39 Jeff Gordon $5	2.50	6.00
40 Bill Elliott $5	1.00	2.50
41 Mark Martin $5	2.00	5.00
42 Rusty Wallace $5	2.00	5.00
43 Terry Labonte $5	1.00	2.50
44 Ernie Irvan $5	.50	1.25
45 Ricky Rudd $5	1.00	2.50
46 Bobby Labonte $5	1.50	4.00
47 Sterling Marlin $5	1.00	2.50
48 Darrell Waltrip $5	.50	1.25
49 Ted Musgrave $5	.30	.75
50 Dale Jarrett $5	1.50	4.00
51 Ricky Craven $5	.30	.75
52 Jeremy Mayfield $5	.50	1.25
53 Eli Gold $5	.20	.50
54 Michael Waltrip $5	.50	1.25
55 Jimmy Spencer $5	.30	.75
56 Brett Bodine $5	.30	.75
57 Geoff Bodine $5	.30	.75
58 John Andretti $5	.30	.75
59 Ken Schrader $5	.30	.75
60 Bobby Hamilton $5	.30	.75
61 Derrike Cope $5	.30	.75
62 Ward Burton $5	.50	1.25
63 Joe Nemechek $5	.30	.75
64 Kenny Wallace $5	.30	.75
65 Mike Wallace $5	.30	.75
66 Morgan Shepherd $5	.30	.75
67 Rusty Wallace's Car $10	3.00	8.00
68 Sterling Marlin's Car $10	1.25	3.00
69 Terry Labonte's Car $10	1.50	4.00
70 Mark Martin's Car $10	3.00	8.00
71 Geoff Bodine's Car $10	.50	1.25
72 Ricky Rudd's Car $10	1.50	4.00
73 Brett Bodine's Car $10	.50	1.25
74 Ted Musgrave's Car $10	.50	1.25
75 Darrell Waltrip's Car $10	.75	2.00
76 Bobby Labonte's Car $10	2.50	6.00
77 Michael Waltrip's Car $10	.50	1.25
78 Ward Burton's Car $10	.75	2.00
79 Jimmy Spencer's Car $10	.50	1.25
80 Jeff Gordon's Car $10	4.00	10.00
81 Ricky Craven's Car $10	.50	1.25
82 Ernie Irvan's Car $10	.75	2.00
83 Johnny Benson's Car $10	.75	2.00
84 Kyle Petty's Car $10	.75	2.00
85 Dale Jarrett's Car $10	2.50	6.00
86 Bill Elliott's Car $10	1.50	4.00
87 Jeff Gordon $50	12.50	30.00
88 Bill Elliott $50	5.00	12.00
89 Mark Martin $50	10.00	25.00
90 Rusty Wallace $50	10.00	25.00
91 Terry Labonte $50	5.00	12.00
92 Ernie Irvan $50	2.50	6.00
93 Ricky Rudd $50	5.00	12.00
94 Bobby Labonte $50	7.50	20.00
95 Jeff Gordon $100	20.00	50.00
96 Bill Elliott $100	7.50	20.00
97 Mark Martin $100	15.00	40.00
98 Rusty Wallace $100	15.00	40.00
99 Terry Labonte $100	7.50	20.00
100 Ernie Irvan $100	4.00	10.00
P1 Jeff Gordon Promo	2.00	5.00

2000 Firestone Checkered Flag

COMPLETE SET (3)	2.00	5.00
1 Mario Andretti	1.25	3.00
2 Michael Andretti	.30	.75
NNO M.Andretti Mi.Andretti	1.25	3.00

1996 Flair

This 100-card set is the inaugural issue of the Flair brand by Fleer/SkyBox. The cards printed on double thick board feature top drivers from both the Winston Cup and Busch circuits. Cards also featured 100 percent etched-foil and three photos on every basic card. The cards were available through both hobby and retail outlets. The product as distributed via six box cases, with 24 packs per box and five cards per pack. Each pack carried a suggested retail of $4.99.

COMPLETE SET (100)	8.00	20.00
WAX BOX	25.00	60.00
1 John Andretti	.10	.30
2 Johnny Benson	.10	.30
3 Brett Bodine	.10	.30
4 Geoff Bodine	.10	.30
5 Jeff Burton	.40	1.00
6 Ward Burton	.25	.60
7 Derrike Cope	.10	.30
8 Ricky Craven	.10	.30
9 Wally Dallenbach	.10	.30
10 Dale Earnhardt	2.00	5.00
11 Bill Elliott	.50	1.25
12 Jeff Gordon	1.25	3.00
13 Steve Grissom	.10	.30
14 Bobby Hamilton	.10	.30
15 Ernie Irvan	.25	.60
16 Dale Jarrett	.75	2.00
17 Bobby Labonte	.75	2.00
18 Terry Labonte	.40	1.00
19 Dave Marcis	.25	.60
20 Sterling Marlin	.40	1.00
21 Mark Martin	1.00	2.50
22 Rick Mast	.10	.30
23 Jeremy Mayfield	.25	.60
24 Ted Musgrave	.10	.30
25 Joe Nemechek	.10	.30
26 Kyle Petty	.25	.60
27 Robert Pressley	.10	.30
28 Ricky Rudd	.40	1.00
29 Ken Schrader	.10	.30
30 Lake Speed	.10	.30
31 Jimmy Spencer	.10	.30
32 Hut Stricklin	.10	.30
33 Kenny Wallace	.10	.30
34 Mike Wallace	.10	.30
35 Rusty Wallace	1.00	2.50
36 Michael Waltrip	.25	.60
37 Glenn Allen Jr.	.10	.30
38 Rodney Combs	.10	.30
39 David Green	.10	.30
40 Randy LaJoie	.10	.30
41 Chad Little	.10	.30
42 Curtis Markham	.10	.30
43 Mike McLaughlin	.10	.30
44 Patty Moise	.10	.30
45 Phil Parsons	.10	.30
46 Jeff Purvis	.10	.30
47 Bobby Allison	.05	.15
48 Richard Childress	.25	.60
49 Joe Gibbs	.25	.60
50 Rick Hendrick	.05	.15
51 Richard Petty	.40	1.00
52 Jack Roush	.05	.15
53 Ray Evernham	.25	.60
54 Todd Parrott	.05	.15
55 Robin Pemberton	.05	.15
56 David Smith	.05	.15
57 John Andretti's Car	.05	.15
58 Johnny Benson's Car	.05	.15
59 Brett Bodine's Car	.05	.15
60 Geoff Bodine's Car	.05	.15
61 Jeff Burton's Car	.10	.30
62 Ward Burton's Car	.05	.15
63 Derrike Cope's Car	.05	.15
64 Ricky Craven's Car	.05	.15
65 Wally Dallenbach's Car	.05	.15
66 Dale Earnhardt's Car	.75	2.00
67 Bill Elliott's Car	.25	.60
68 Jeff Gordon's Car	.50	1.25
69 Steve Grissom's Car	.05	.15
70 Bobby Hamilton's Car	.05	.15
71 Ernie Irvan's Car	.10	.30
72 Dale Jarrett's Car	.25	.60
73 Bobby Labonte's Car	.25	.60
74 Terry Labonte's Car	.25	.60
75 Dave Marcis' Car	.10	.30
76 Sterling Marlin's Car	.10	.30
77 Mark Martin's Car	.40	1.00
78 Rick Mast's Car	.05	.15
79 Jeremy Mayfield's Car	.10	.30
80 Ted Musgrave's Car	.05	.15
81 Joe Nemechek's Car	.05	.15
82 Kyle Petty's Car	.10	.30
83 Robert Pressley's Car	.05	.15
84 Ricky Rudd's Car	.10	.30
85 Ken Schrader's Car	.05	.15
86 Lake Speed's Car	.05	.15
87 Jimmy Spencer's Car	.05	.15
88 Hut Stricklin's Car	.05	.15
89 Kenny Wallace's Car	.05	.15
90 Mike Wallace's Car	.05	.15
91 Rusty Wallace's Car	.40	1.00
92 Michael Waltrip's Car	.10	.30
93 D.Jarrett E.Irvin	.60	1.50
94 Dale Jarrett	.75	2.00
95 Bobby Labonte	.75	2.00
96 Terry Labonte	.40	1.00
97 Mark Martin	1.00	2.50
98 Mike Wallace	.10	.30
99 Jeff Gordon CL	.60	1.50
100 Rusty Wallace CL	.40	1.00
P1 Jeff Gordon Promo	5.00	10.00

1996 Flair Autographs

This 12-card insert set consist of the top names in NASCAR. Autograph redemption cards were randomly inserted in packs at a rate of one in 100. The redemption card featured one of the 12 drivers on the front and instructions on how and where to redeem it.

COMPLETE SET (12)	500.00	1000.00
1 Ricky Craven	10.00	20.00
2 Dale Earnhardt	150.00	300.00
3 Bill Elliott	20.00	50.00
4 Jeff Gordon	50.00	100.00
5 Ernie Irvan	12.50	30.00
6 Dale Jarrett	12.50	30.00
7 Bobby Labonte	12.50	30.00
8 Terry Labonte	12.50	30.00
9 Sterling Marlin.	15.00	40.00
10 Mark Martin	15.00	40.00
11 Ted Musgrave	10.00	20.00
12 Rusty Wallace	20.00	50.00

1996 Flair Center Spotlight

A card from this 10-card insert set was randomly inserted one in five packs. The cards show the cars of leading drivers with 100 percent foil designs and a glittering UV coating. Each card front shows a car with two spotlight type effects in the backgound.

COMPLETE SET (10)	25.00	60.00
1 Johnny Benson	.50	1.25
2 Dale Earnhardt	8.00	20.00
3 Bill Elliott	2.00	5.00
4 Jeff Gordon	5.00	12.00
5 Bobby Hamilton	.50	1.25
6 Bobby Labonte	3.00	8.00
7 Terry Labonte	1.50	4.00
8 Mark Martin	4.00	10.00
9 Ricky Rudd	1.50	4.00
10 Rusty Wallace	4.00	10.00

1996 Flair Hot Numbers

This 10-card insert set featues holofoil stamping and embossed printing to showcase NASCAR's top drivers. The card fronts feature a driver's photo, the driver's car number in holofoil and a facsimile of the driver's signature. Hot Number cards were inserted one in 24 packs.

COMPLETE SET (10)	50.00	100.00
1 Dale Earnhardt	10.00	25.00
2 Bill Elliott	5.00	12.00
3 Jeff Gordon	8.00	20.00
4 Ernie Irvan	3.00	8.00
5 Dale Jarrett	6.00	15.00
6 Bobby Labonte	6.00	15.00
7 Terry Labonte	4.00	10.00
8 Mark Martin	4.00	10.00
9 Ricky Rudd	4.00	10.00
10 Rusty Wallace	6.00	15.00

1996 Flair Power Performance

Cards from this die-cut 10-card set were seeded one in 12 packs. The card fronts feature a driver's photo imposed over a tachometer. The words Power Performance and the driver's name also appear on the front in holofoil stamping.

COMPLETE SET (10) 40.00 100.00
1 Ricky Craven .75 2.00
2 Dale Earnhardt 12.50 30.00
3 Bill Elliott 3.00 8.00
4 Jeff Gordon 8.00 20.00
5 Dale Jarrett 5.00 12.00
6 Terry Labonte 2.50 6.00
7 Sterling Marlin 2.50 6.00
8 Mark Martin 6.00 15.00
9 Ricky Rudd 2.50 6.00
10 Rusty Wallace 6.00 15.00

1992 Food Lion Richard Petty

This set was issued to employees of the Food Lion supermarket chain. 2,300 of these factory sets were produced and packaged in white boxes with the Food Lion logo on each box. In the summer of 1993, the remaining 400 sets were offered to the public at the cost of $34.

COMPLETE SET (116) 6.00 15.00
1 Daytona, FL February .05 .10
2 Richard Petty 1964 .30 .75
3 Richard Petty w/Car .30 .75
4 Richard Petty 1981 .30 .75
5 Rockingham, NC March .05 .10
6 Richard Petty 1971 .30 .75
7 Richard Petty 1974 .30 .75
8 Richard Petty's Car .12 .30
9 Richmond, VA March .05 .10
10 Richard Petty's Car .12 .30
11 Richard Petty .30 .75
12 Richard Petty .30 .75
13 Atlanta, GA March .05 .10
14 Richard Petty's Car .12 .30
15 Richard Petty .30 .75
16 Richard Petty's Car .12 .30
17 Darlington, SC March .05 .10
18 Richard Petty .30 .75
19 Richard Petty's Car .12 .30
20 Richard Petty's Car .12 .30
21 Bristol, TN April .05 .10
22 Richard Petty .30 .75
23 Richard Petty in Car .30 .75
24 Richard Petty w/Car .30 .75
25 N. Wilkesboro, NC April .05 .10
26 Richard Petty w/Dad .30 .75
27 Richard Petty's Car .12 .30
28 Richard Petty's Car .12 .30
29 Martinsville, VA April .05 .10
30 Richard Petty .30 .75
31 Richard Petty .30 .75
32 Richard Petty .30 .75
33 Talladega, AL May .05 .10
34 Richard Petty w/Car .30 .75
35 Richard Petty's Trailer .12 .30
36 Richard Petty 1983 .30 .75
37 Charlotte, NC May .05 .10
38 Richard Petty w/Car .30 .75
39 Richard Petty on Car .30 .75
40 Richard Petty 1977 .30 .75
41 Dover, DE May .05 .10
42 Richard Petty in Car .30 .75
43 Richard Petty .30 .75
44 Richard Petty 1984 .30 .75
45 Sonoma, CA June .05 .10
46 Richard Petty w/Car .30 .75
47 Richard Petty w/Car .30 .75
48 Richard Petty w/Car .30 .75
49 Pocono, PA June .05 .10
50 Richard Petty .30 .75
51 Richard Petty .30 .75
52 Richard Petty w/Brother .30 .75
53 Brooklyn, MI June .05 .10
54 Richard Petty .30 .75
55 Richard Petty 1981 .30 .75
56 Richard Petty w/Car .30 .75
57 Daytona, FL July .05 .10
58 Richard Petty's Car .12 .30
59 Richard Petty 1975 .30 .75
60 Richard Petty 1984 .30 .75
61 Pocono, PA July .05 .10
62 Richard Petty's Car .12 .30
63 Richard Petty .30 .75
64 Richard Petty's Car .12 .30
65 Talladega, AL July .05 .10
66 Richard Petty on Bike .30 .75
67 Richard Petty 1984 .30 .75
68 Richard Petty's Car .12 .30
69 Watkins Glen, NY Aug. .05 .10
70 Richard Petty w/Car .30 .75
71 Richard Petty .30 .75
72 Richard Petty .30 .75
73 Brooklyn, MI August .05 .10
74 Richard Petty w/Brother .30 .75
75 Richard Petty 1974 .30 .75
76 Richard Petty .30 .75
77 Bristol, TN August .05 .10
78 Richard Petty's Car .12 .30
79 Richard Petty .30 .75
80 Richard Petty in Car .30 .75
81 Darlington, SC Sept. .05 .10
82 Richard Petty's Car .12 .30
83 Richard Petty .30 .75
84 Richard Petty .30 .75
85 Richmond, VA September .05 .10
86 Richard Petty 1970 .30 .75
87 Richard Petty's Car .12 .30
88 Richard Petty w/Dodge .30 .75
89 Dover, DE September .05 .10
90 Richard Petty .30 .75
91 Richard Petty .30 .75
92 Richard Petty .30 .75
93 Martinsville, VA Sept. .05 .10
94 Richard Petty 1970 .30 .75
95 Richard Petty 1969 .30 .75
96 Richard Petty .30 .75
97 N. Wilkesboro, NC Oct. .05 .10
98 Richard Petty w/Brother .30 .75
99 Richard Petty .30 .75
100 Richard Petty .30 .75
101 Charlotte, NC October .05 .10
102 Richard Petty .30 .75
103 Richard Petty w/Car .30 .75
104 Richard Petty .30 .75
105 Rockingham, NC October .05 .10
106 Richard Petty's Car .12 .30
107 Richard Petty's Car .12 .30
108 Richard Petty Pit Stop .30 .75
109 Phoenix, AZ November .05 .10
110 Richard Petty .30 .75
111 Richard Petty .30 .75
112 Richard Petty .30 .75
113 Atlanta, GA November .05 .10
114 Richard Petty's Car .12 .30
115 Richard Petty's Transporter .12 .30
116 Richard Petty's Car .12 .30
NNO Richard Petty HOLO 75.00 200.00

1991 Galfield Press Pioneers of Racing

Reportedly 3,077 sets were produced. This set was issued in a Pioneers of Racing binder and produced by noted NASCAR historian Greg Fielden. Greg personally signed each of the binders the set came in.

COMPLETE SET (107) 40.00 100.00
1 Fireball Roberts .60 1.50
Tim Flock
2 Herb Thomas .50 1.25
Tim Flock
3 Lloyd Seay .30 .75
4 Four Abreast Start .30 .75
5 Tim Flock .50 1.25
Barney Smith
6 Carol Tillman .30 .75
7 Marshall Teague .50 1.25
Herb Thomas
8 Phil Orr .30 .75
9 Curtis Turner
Fireball Roberts
10 100,000 at 105 MPH .30 .75
11 Bill Holland .30 .75
12 Jack Smith .30 .75
13 Fonty Flock .50 1.25
14 Bob Flock .30 .75
15 Curtis Turner .50 1.25
16 Fireball Roberts
17 Fonty Flock .50 1.25
18 Daytona Beach .30 .75
19 Jim Reed 1.00 2.50
Lee Petty
20 John Fish .30 .75
21 Curtis Turner .50 1.25
Sara Christian
22 Tim Flock .50 1.25
23 Junior Johnson .60 1.50
24 Rex White .60 1.50
Fireball Roberts
25 Joe Weatherly .50 1.25
M.Panch
Ed.Dibos
26 Eddie Skinner .30 .75
27 Iggy Katona .30 .75
Johnny Mantz
28 Bill Widenhouse .30 .75
29 Buck Baker .50 1.25
Jimmie Lewallen
30 Bobby Johns .30 .75
Joe Weatherly
31 Banjo Matthews .30 .75
32 Fonty Flock .50 1.25
Jimmie Lewallen
33 Joe Guide, Jr. .30 .75
34 Larry Flynn .30 .75
35 Lakewood Speedway .30 .75
36 North Wilkesboro Speedway .30 .75
37 Fonty Flock .50 1.25
Marvin Panch
38 Herb Thomas .50 1.25
Frank Mundy
39 Bill O'Dell .30 .75
40 Jimmy Florian .30 .75
41 1959 Daytona .30 .75
42 Paul Goldsmith .50 1.25
43 Louise Smith .50 1.25
44 Frank Mundy .30 .75
45 Doug Cooper .30 .75
46 Red Vogt .30 .75
47 Raleigh Speedway .30 .75
48 Gober Sosebee .30 .75
Tommy Moon
Swayne Pritchett
49 Curtis Turner .50 1.25
50 Dick Bailey .30 .75
51 D.Kimberling .50 1.25
J.Weatherly
E.Pagan
Roberts
J.Eubanks
52 Pee Wee Jones .30 .75
Jim Reed
53 Checklist Card .30 .75
54 Marion Cox .30 .75
55 Benny Georgeson .30 .75
57 Cotton Owens .30 .75
58 Nash .50 1.25
Sager
Rambo
Brown
Guide
Roberts
Rathmann
59 Danny Letner .30 .75
60 Bob Flock .30 .75
61 Tim Flock .50 1.25
62 Tim Flock .50 1.25
Herb Thomas
63 Red Byron .30 .75
Mickey Rhodes
64 Tim Flock .50 1.25
Jim Paschal
Fonty Flock
65 Larry Frank .50 1.25
66 Herb Thomas .50 1.25
67 Hershel McGriff .30 .75
68 Fireball Roberts
69 Curtis Turner .50 1.25
70 Marshall Teague .30 .75
71 Hershel McGriff .30 .75
Frankie Schneider
72 Bobby Myers .30 .75
73 Paul Goldsmith .50 1.25
74 Herschel Buchanan .30 .75
Joe Guide Jr.
75 Buddy Shuman .30 .75
Mickey Fenn
76 Bob Welborn .30 .75
77 Axel Anderson .30 .75
78 Mar.Panch .50 1.25
T.Lund
Bob Pronger
Bob Welborn
79 June Cleveland .30 .75
80 Tim Flock .50 1.25
81 Dick Rathmann .30 .75
82 Glenn Dunnaway .30 .75
83 Herb Thomas .50 1.25
84 Cotton Owens .30 .75
85 Red Byron .30 .75
86 Fireball Roberts
87 Joe Weatherly .50 1.25
88 Tim Flock .50 1.25
89 Herb Thomas .50 1.25
90 Gwyn Staley .30 .75
Charlie Scott
91 Curtis Turner .40 1.00
Bobby Isaac
92 Paul Goldsmith .50 1.25
Jimmy Thompson
93 Fireball Roberts
Roy Jones
94 Junior Johnson .60 1.50
95 Lloyd Seay .30 .75
96 Jimmy Thompson .30 .75
97 Eduardo Dibos .30 .75
98 Raymond Parks .30 .75
99 Daytona Speedweek .30 .75
100 Tim Flock .50 1.25
101 Tim Flock .50 1.25
Joe Lee Johnson
Spud Murphy
102 Tim Flock .50 1.25
Ted Chester
103 Joe Weatherly .50 1.25
104 Red Byron .30 .75
105 Ed Livingston .30 .75
Friday Hassler
106 Doug Yates .30 .75
107 Checklist Card .30 .75

1992 Hilton G. Hill Gold True Legend

The 16-card set features drivers who raced from 1949-1971. The set includes such greats as Curtis Turner, Tiny Lund and Tim Flock. There was also approximately 20 uncut sheets produced.

COMPLETE SET (16) 4.00 10.00
1 Checklist .25 .60
2 Bowman Gray Stadium .25 .60
3 Bob Welborn .30 .75
4 Tim Flock .40 1.00
5 Curtis Turner .40 1.00
6 Bob McGinnis .30 .75
7 Tiny Lund .40 1.00
8 Bobby Myers .30 .75
9 E.H. Weddle .30 .75
10 PeeWee Jones .30 .75
11 Johnny Dodson .30 .75
12 Whitey Norman .30 .75
13 Jimmie Lewallen .30 .75
14 Jack Holloway .30 .75
15 Billy Myers .30 .75
16 Phillip Smith .30 .75

1991 Hickory Motor Speedway

This set was produced to honor the 40th Anniversary of Hickory Motor Speedway. Color and black and white photos of the short track's most famous events are featured. The cards were released in complete set form and sold at the track.

COMPLETE SET (12) 2.00 5.00
1 Opening Day Traffic .10 .30
2 Joe Littlejohn .10 .30
3 The First Race .10 .30
4 Hickory Today .10 .30
5 Jack Ingram's Car .10 .30
6 Earnhardt .10 .30
Gant
T.Houston
Shepherd
D.Jarrett
7 Max Prestwood Jr. .10 .30
8 A Packed House .10 .30
9 Dale Fischlein's Car .10 .30
10 D.Earnhardt 1.00 2.50
J.Nemechek Cars
11 Robert Huffman w Car .20 .50
NNO Cover Card .10 .30

1994-95 Highland Mint/VIP

The 1994-95 Highland Mint cards are replicas of the 1994 VIP series cards. The silver (.999 silver) and bronze cards contain 4.25 Troy Ounces of metal. Each card is individually numbered, packaged in a lucite display holder and accompanied by a certificate of authenticity. The production mintage according to Highland Mint is listed below. The actual card numbering follows that of the original cards, but we have listed and numbered them below alphabetically for convenience. A 24-karat gold-plated on .999 silver version of the Dale Earnhardt card (numbered of 500) was also produced.

1B Dale Earnhardt B/5000 50.00 100.00
1G Dale Earnhardt G/500 250.00 500.00
1S Dale Earnhardt S/1000 150.00 250.00
2B Bill Elliott B/2500 15.00 40.00
2S Bill Elliott S/500 150.00 200.00
3B Jeff Gordon B/5000 25.00 60.00
3S Jeff Gordon S/1000 150.00 225.00
4B Ernie Irvan B/5000 12.00 30.00
4S Ernie Irvan S/1000 150.00 200.00
5B Mark Martin B/5000 20.00 50.00
5S Mark Martin S/1000 150.00 200.00
6B Rusty Wallace B/5000 15.00 40.00
6S Rusty Wallace S/1000 150.00 200.00

1993 Hi-Tech Tire Test

Hi-Tech produced this set commemorating the 1992 NASCAR tire tests at the Indianapolis Motor Speedway. The ten-card set was distributed in two 5-card packs each packed 36 per box. Reportedly, production was limited to 1000 cases.

COMPLETE SET (10) 2.00 5.00
1 Dale Earnhardt's Car 1.00 2.50
2 Darrell Waltrip's Car .20 .50
3 Davey Allison's Car .30 .75
4 Rusty Wallace's Car .50 1.25
5 Ernie Irvan's Car .20 .50
6 Mark Martin's Car .50 1.25
7 Kyle Petty's Car .20 .50
8 Land Speed Record at IMS .10 .30
9 Bill Elliott's Car .30 .75
10 Brickyard 400 Logo .10 .30
P1 Rusty Wallace's Car Promo 1.00 2.50
P2 Davey Allison's Car Promo 1.00 2.50

1994 Hi-Tech Brickyard 400 Prototypes

Three cards comprise this set released by Hi-Tech to preview its 1994 Brickyard 400 set. Each card is numbered of 20,000.

COMPLETE SET (3) 3.00 8.00
1 Richard Petty w/Car 1.00 2.50
2 Jeff Gordon's Car 2.00 5.00
3 Kyle Petty's Car .75 2.00

1994 Hi-Tech Brickyard 400

For the second year, Hi-Tech produced a set commemorating the Brickyard 400. The 1994 set was expanded to 70-cards featuring action from the 1993 tire tests at IMS. The cards were packaged 8-cards per pack with 24-packs per box. Reportedly, production was limited to 2,500 12-box cases. Inserts included a Richard Petty set as well as Metamorphosis cards. The Metamorphosis card shows an IndyCar transforming into a stock car racer. It was packed approximately one per box. There was also a 70-card Artist Proof parallel version of the base set. The cards feature a 1 of 200 logo on the front to differentiate them from the base cards. The Artist Proof cards were inserted at a rate of one per box.

COMPLETE SET (70) 10.00 25.00
1 Track Action .01 .05
2 Rusty Wallace's Car .20 .50
3 Bobby Hillin's Car .01 .05
4 Morgan Shepherd's Car .05 .15
5 Dave Marcis' Car .01 .05
6 Brett Bodine in Pits .01 .05
7 Morgan Shepherd's Car .01 .05
8 Geoff Bodine's Car .01 .05
9 Dale Earnhardt's Car .50 1.25
10 Bill Elliott's Car .10 .30
11 Kenny Wallace's Car .01 .05
12 Bobby Labonte's Car .10 .30
13 Geoff Bodine's Car .01 .05
14 Mark Martin's Car .20 .50
15 Bill Elliott's Car .10 .30
16 P.J. Jones' Car .01 .05
17 John Andretti's Car .01 .05
18 Darrell Waltrip's Car .05 .15
19 Mark Martin's Car .20 .50
20 Jeff Gordon's Car .30 .75
21 Greg Sacks' Car .01 .05
22 Terry Labonte's Car .10 .30
23 Lake Speed's Car .01 .05
24 Greg Sacks' Car .01 .05
25 Geoff Bodine's Car .01 .05
26 Kenny Wallace's Car .01 .05
27 M.Martin .20 .50
J.Spencer Cars
28 Rusty Wallace's Car .20 .50
29 Mark Martin's Car .20 .50
30 Lake Speed in Car .01 .05
31 Mark Martin's Car .20 .50
32 G.Bodine .01 .05
B.Bodine Cars
33 Race Action .01 .05
34 Pit Action .01 .05
35 Action .01 .05
36 Rick Mast .05 .15
37 Rusty Wallace .40 1.00
38 Dale Earnhardt 1.00 2.50
39 Terry Labonte .20 .50
40 Mark Martin .40 1.00
41 G.Bodine .01 .05
T.Bodine
B.Bodine
42 Sterling Marlin .20 .50
43 D.K. Ulrich .01 .05
44 Bill Elliott's Car .10 .30
45 Jimmy Spencer .05 .15
46 John Andretti .05 .15
47 Geoff Bodine .05 .15
48 Darrell Waltrip .10 .30
49 Dale Jarrett .25 .60
50 Morgan Shepherd .05 .15
51 Bobby Labonte .25 .60
52 Jeff Gordon .60 1.50
53 Ken Schrader .05 .15
54 Brett Bodine .05 .15
55 Lake Speed .05 .15
56 Michael Waltrip .10 .30
57 Jimmy Horton .05 .15
58 Harry Gant .10 .30
59 Kenny Wallace .05 .15
60 Kyle Petty .10 .30
61 Rick Wilson .05 .15
62 Ted Musgrave .05 .15
63 Greg Sacks .05 .15
64 Dave Marcis .10 .30
65 Todd Bodine .05 .15
66 Bobby Hillin .05 .15
67 Derrike Cope .05 .15
68 Performance History .01 .05
69 Jeff Gordon .60 1.50
70 Checklist Card .01 .05
BYSE1 Metamorphosis Card .75 2.00

1994 Hi-Tech Brickyard 400 Artist Proofs

COMPLETE SET (70) 60.00 150.00
*ARTIST PROOFS: 6X TO 15X BASE CARDS

1994 Hi-Tech Brickyard 400 Richard Petty

Richard Petty is the focus of this Hi-Tech issue. The cards were randomly inserted in 1994 Hi-Tech Brickyard 400 packs and highlight Petty's involvement with the historic race at IMS. The cards were randomly inserted at a rate of one per 20 Hi-Tech Brickyard 400 packs.

COMPLETE SET (6) 2.50 6.00
1 Richard Petty w/Car 1.25 2.50
2 Richard Petty 's Car .40 1.00
3 Richard Petty's Car .40 1.00
4 Richard Petty w/Car .40 1.00
5 Richard Petty w/Car .40 1.00
6 Richard Petty's Car .40 1.00

1995 Hi-Tech Brickyard 400 Prototypes

Three cards comprise this set released by Hi-Tech to preview its 1995 Brickyard 400 set. Each card is numbered of 20,000. Although the cards carry a 1994 date on the copyright line, the cards preview the 1995 set.

COMPLETE SET (3) 4.00 10.00
P1 Mark Martin's Car 1.25 3.00
P2 Ernie Irvan .75 2.00
P3 Dale Earnhardt 2.50 6.00

1995 Hi-Tech Brickyard 400

In 1995, Hi-Tech again produced a card set commemorating the 1994 Brickyard 400. The cards were released in two separate complete factory sets. The tin box version contained 90 regular cards, 10 Top Ten cards and one Jeff Gordon 23K Gold card. The 90 regular cards wer printed on 18 point card stock with gold foil layering. Production was limited to 10,000 factor sets. Hi-Tech also produced the set for distribution in a wooden factory set box with a special Jeff Gordon Gold and Silver card (numbered of 1000). The wooden box version wa limited to 1000 sets. Although the cards carry th year 1994 on the copyright line, it's considered a 1995 release.

COMPLETE SET (90) 10.00 25.0
COMP.FACT.SET (101) 25.00 50.0
COMP.WOOD BOX (101) 40.00 100.0
1 Rick Mast's Car .02 .1
2 Dale Earnhardt's Car .40 1.0
3 Jeff Gordon's Car UER 00 .30 .7
4 Geoff Bodine's Car .02 .1
5 Bobby Labonte's Car .08 .2
6 Bill Elliott's Car .08 .2
7 Brett Bodine's Car .02 .1
8 Sterling Marlin's Car .05 .1
9 Mark Martin's Car .20 .5
10 Morgan Shepherd's Car .02 .1
11 Rusty Wallace's Car .20 .5
12 Greg Sacks' Car .02 .1
13 Dale Jarrett's Car .08 .2
14 Michael Waltrip's Car .05 .1
15 Dave Marcis' Car .02 .1
16 Ernie Irvan's Car .05 .15
17 Rich Bickle's Car .02 .10
18 Hut Stricklin's Car .02 .10
19 Terry Labonte's Car .08 .25
20 W. Dallenbach Jr.'s Car .02 .10
21 Ken Schrader's Car .02 .10
22 Jimmy Hensley's Car .02 .10
23 Todd Bodine's Car .02 .10
24 Danny Sullivan's Car .02 .10
25 Darrell Waltrip's Car .05 .15
26 John Andretti's Car .02 .10
27 Jeff Purvis' Car .02 .10
28 Joe Nemechek's Car .02 .10
29 Jeremy Mayfield's Car .05 .15
30 Bobby Hamilton's Car .02 .10
31 Ward Burton's Car .05 .15
32 Jimmy Spencer's Car .02 .10
33 Bobby Hillin's Car .02 .10
34 Kyle Petty's Car .05 .15
35 Ted Musgrave's Car .02 .10
36 Jeff Burton's Car .05 .15
37 Derrike Cope's Car .02 .10
38 Lake Speed's Car .02 .10
39 Harry Gant's Car .05 .15
40 Jeff Gordon Race Action .30 .75
41 Dale Earnhardt 1.00 2.50
42 Hut Stricklin's Car .02 .10
43 W. Dallenbach Jr.'s Car .02 .10
44 Joe Nemechek .05 .15
45 Rick Mast .05 .15
46 Richard Jackson Team .02 .10
47 Terry Labonte .20 .50
48 Jeremy Mayfield .08 .25
49 Bobby Hamilton .05 .15
50 Bobby Hillin .05 .15
51 Jeff Burton .20 .50
52 Kyle Petty .08 .25
53 Gordon .20 .50
G.Bod
Schr.Cars
54 Checklist .02 .10
55 John Andretti .05 .15
56 Dale Earnhardt 1.00 2.50
57 Danny Sullivan .05 .15
58 Jimmy Spencer .05 .15
59 Michael Waltrip .08 .25
60 Ken Schrader .05 .15
61 Bobby Labonte .40 1.00
62 Early-Race Action .02 .10
63 Bill Elliott's Car .08 .25
64 Todd Bodine .05 .15
65 Ted Musgrave .05 .15
66 Lake Speed .05 .15
67 Harry Gant .08 .25
68 Greg Sacks .05 .15
69 Jeff Purvis .05 .15

Mark Martin .50 1.25
Rich Bickle .05 .15
Dave Marcis .05 .15
Brett Bodine .05 .15
Geoff Bodine .05 .15
Dale Jarrett .40 1.00
Ward Burton .08 .25
Dale Earnhardt's Car .40 1.00
Darrell Waltrip .08 .25
Ernie Irvan .08 .25
Morgan Shepherd .05 .15
Jimmy Hensley .05 .15
Derrike Cope .05 .15
Rusty Wallace .50 1.25
Sterling Marlin .20 .50
Hut Stricklin .05 .15
Ernie Irvan's Car .05 .15
Dale Earnhardt 1.00 2.50
Jeff Gordon .60 1.50
Jeff Gordon's Car .30 .75
Indianapolis Motor .02 .10
J.Gordon Silver/1000 25.00 60.00
J Jeff Gordon Gold/10000 2.00 5.00

995 Hi-Tech Brickyard 400 Top Ten

e Top Ten set was issued as an insert into ory sets of 1994 Hi-Tech Brickyard 400. The cards were distributed in both the tin and oden box versions of the set and were printed nolographic foil stock. Each card was produced n three different background designs: stars, ughnut shaped, and raindrop shaped. The star kground version seems to be the toughest to l with cards carrying a 25 percent premium.

MPLETE SET (10) 7.50 20.00
1 Jeff Gordon 1.00 2.50
2 Brett Bodine .10 .25
3 Bill Elliott's Car .15 .40
4 Rusty Wallace .75 2.00
5 Dale Earnhardt 1.50 4.00
6 Darrell Waltrip .15 .40
7 Ken Schrader .10 .25
8 Michael Waltrip .15 .40
9 Todd Bodine .10 .25
10 Morgan Shepherd .10 .25

1992 Hooters Alan Kulwicki

is 15-card set is a promotional issue by the staurant chain Hooters. The cards were sold in mplete set form at many of the restaurants as ll as given away at some racing events. The rds feature Alan Kulwicki and his Hooters onsored #7 Ford Thunderbird.

MPLETE SET (15) 4.00 10.00
MMON CARD (1-14) .30 .75

1993 Hoyle Playing Cards

yle produced these three decks of playing cards early 1993. Each deck features racing stats or ce action photos from the era highlighted. All ree sets are packaged in similar boxes that differ cording to box color: 1947-59 (green), 1960-79 range) and 1980-91 (yellow). Although drivers some photos can be specifically identified, the rds are seldom sold as singles. Therefore, we t only complete set prices for the three card cks.

OMPLETE SET 1947-1959 (54) 1.25 3.00
OMPLETE SET 1960-1979 (54) 1.25 3.00
OMPLETE SET 1980-1991 (54) 1.25 3.00

1995 Images

is 100-card set is the inaugural issue for this and. The product was a joint effort between anufacturers Classic and Finish Line. The set atures the top drivers from NASCAR, NHRA, Indy ar and World of Outlaws. The cards have action otography and are printed on 18-point micro- ed foil board. The product came six-cards per ack, 24-packs per box and 16 boxes per case. ach case consisted of 8 red boxes and 8 black oxes. Certain inserts were only available in one olor box and not the other. There was also Hot oxes in which half of each pack would consist of sert cards. A Hot Box could be found 1 in every cases. Two known uncorrected errors exist in is set, card number 36 Ray Evernham doesn't ve a card number on the back of the card and ard number 78 Jeff Burton is misnumbered as umber 4.

COMPLETE SET (100) 8.00 20.00
1 Al Unser Jr. .15 .40
2 Rusty Wallace .60 1.50
3 Dale Earnhardt 1.25 3.00
4 Sterling Marlin .25 .60
5 Terry Labonte .25 .60
6 Mark Martin .40 1.00
7 Geoff Bodine .07 .20
8 Jeff Burton .25 .60
9 Lake Speed .07 .20
10 Ricky Rudd .25 .60
11 Brett Bodine .07 .20
12 Derrike Cope .07 .20
13 John Force .25 .60
14 Robby Gordon .07 .20
15 Dick Trickle .07 .20
16 Ted Musgrave .07 .20
17 Darrell Waltrip .15 .40
18 Bobby Labonte .50 1.25
19 Loy Allen Jr. .07 .20
20 Walker Evans .02 .10
21 Morgan Shepherd .07 .20
22 Joe Amato .07 .20
23 Jimmy Spencer .07 .20
24 Jeff Gordon .75 2.00
25 Ken Schrader .07 .20
26 Hut Stricklin .07 .20
27 Steve Kinser .25 .60
28 Dale Jarrett .50 1.25
29 Steve Grissom .07 .20
30 Michael Waltrip .15 .40
31 Ward Burton .15 .40
32 Roger Mears .07 .20
33 Robert Pressley .07 .20
34 Bill Seebold .02 .10
35 Mike Skinner RC .07 .20
36 Ray Evernham .02 .10
37 John Andretti .07 .20
38 Sammy Swindell .07 .20
39 Larry McReynolds .02 .10
40 Tony Glover .02 .10
41 Ricky Craven .15 .40
42 Kyle Petty .15 .40
43 Bobby Hamilton .07 .20
44 David Green .07 .20
45 Steve Hmiel .02 .10
46 Bobby Labonte .50 1.25
47 Darrell Waltrip .15 .40
48 Jeff Gordon .75 2.00
49 Al Unser Jr. .15 .40
50 Dale Earnhardt 1.25 3.00
51 P.J. Jones .07 .20
52 Ken Schrader .07 .20
53 Geoff Bodine .07 .20
54 Sterling Marlin .25 .60
55 Terry Labonte .25 .60
56 Morgan Shepherd .07 .20
57 Robert Pressley .07 .20
58 Ricky Rudd .25 .60
59 Ward Burton .15 .40
60 Rick Carelli .07 .20
61 Ted Musgrave .07 .20
62 Kenny Bernstein .07 .20
63 Jimmy Spencer .07 .20
64 Brett Bodine .07 .20
65 Mark Martin .60 1.50
66 Rusty Wallace .60 1.50
67 Lake Speed .07 .20
68 Rick Mast .07 .20
69 Dick Trickle .07 .20
70 Michael Waltrip .15 .40
71 Dave Marcis .07 .20
72 Jeff Gordon .75 2.00
73 John Andretti .07 .20
74 Derrike Cope .07 .20
75 Todd Bodine .07 .20
76 Kyle Petty .15 .40
77 Dale Jarrett .50 1.25
78 Jeff Burton .25 .60
79 Steve Grissom .07 .20
80 Ernie Irvan .15 .40
81 Bobby Labonte .50 1.25
82 Ernie Irvan .15 .40
83 Bobby Hamilton .07 .20
84 Sterling Marlin .25 .60
85 Robby Gordon .07 .20
86 Todd Bodine .07 .20
87 Joe Nemechek .07 .20
88 Mark Martin .60 1.50
89 Ricky Rudd .25 .60
90 Mike Wallace .07 .20
91 Terry Labonte .25 .60
92 Geoff Bodine .07 .20
93 Ernie Irvan .15 .40
94 Rusty Wallace .50 1.25
95 Ricky Craven .15 .40
96 John Force .25 .60
97 Dale Earnhardt 1.25 3.00
98 Jeremy Mayfield .15 .40
99 Dale Earnhardt CL .60 1.50
100 Jeff Gordon CL .40 1.00
P1 Jeff Gordon Promo 7.50 15.00

1995 Images Gold

COMPLETE SET (100) 15.00 40.00
*GOLDS: .8X TO 2X BASIC CARDS

1995 Images Circuit Champions

This 10-card insert set features eight Champions from a variety of racing circuits along with two all-time greats. The acetate cards are sequentially numbered to 675 and inserted at a rate of one per 192 packs. The cards were inserted in both the Red and Black boxes.

COMPLETE SET (10) 60.00 150.00
1 Al Unser Jr. 4.00 10.00
2 Roger Mears 2.00 5.00
3 Bill Seebold 1.00 2.50
4 John Force 6.00 15.00
5 Steve Kinser 6.00 15.00
6 Mike Skinner 2.00 5.00
7 David Green 2.00 5.00
8 Dale Earnhardt 30.00 80.00
9 Glen Wood 1.00 2.50
Leonard Wood
10 Joe Amato 2.00 5.00

1995 Images Driven

This 15-card insert set features some of the top drivers in NASCAR, NHRA, and IndyCar racing. The cards use holographic foil technology and are sequentially numbered to 1,800. The cards can be found one per 24 packs in the Red Images boxes only.

COMPLETE SET (15) 25.00 60.00
D1 Dale Earnhardt 8.00 20.00
D2 Jeff Gordon 5.00 12.00
D3 Bobby Labonte 3.00 8.00
D4 Sterling Marlin 1.50 4.00
D5 Mark Martin 2.50 6.00
D6 Kyle Petty 1.00 2.50
D7 Ricky Rudd 1.50 4.00
D8 Rusty Wallace 4.00 10.00
D9 Ken Schrader .50 1.25
D10 John Force 1.50 4.00
D11 Michael Waltrip 1.00 2.50
D12 Robby Gordon .50 1.25
D13 Terry Labonte 1.50 4.00
D14 Al Unser Jr. 1.00 2.50
D15 Darrell Waltrip 1.00 2.50

1995 Images Hard Chargers

This 10-card insert set uses holographic foil technology to bring the top NASCAR drivers to life. The cards come sequentially numbered to 2,500 and are inserted one per 24 packs in the Black Images boxes only.

COMPLETE SET (10) 20.00 50.00
HC1 Bobby Labonte 3.00 8.00
HC2 Sterling Marlin 1.50 4.00
HC3 Mark Martin 2.50 6.00
HC4 Ricky Rudd 1.50 4.00
HC5 Ken Schrader .50 1.25
HC6 Rusty Wallace 4.00 10.00
HC7 Michael Waltrip 1.00 2.50
HC8 Jeff Gordon 5.00 12.00
HC9 Dale Earnhardt 8.00 20.00
HC10 Terry Labonte 1.50 4.00

1995 Images Owner's Pride

Owners of some of the top teams in racing are featured in this 15-card insert set. The fronts of the micro-lined, foil-board cards feature a photo of the car. The backs contain a large photo of the owner. Each card is numbered 1 of 5,000 and could be found one per 18 packs. The Owner's Pride cards could be found in both the Red and Black boxes.

COMPLETE SET (15) 12.00 30.00
OP1 Travis Carter .20 .50
OP2 Richard Childress .40 1.00
OP3 A.G. Dillard .20 .50
OP4 Joe Gibbs .40 1.00
OP5 Jeff Gordon 4.00 10.00
OP6 Junior Johnson .40 1.00
OP7 Larry McClure .20 .50
OP8 Jack Roush .40 1.00
OP9 Ricky Rudd 1.25 3.00
OP10 F.Sabates .20 .50
C.Sabates
OP11 Robert Yates .40 1.00
OP12 Kenny Bernstein .40 1.00
OP13 Dale Earnhardt 6.00 15.00
OP14 Rick Hendrick .40 1.00
OP15 Roger Penske .40 1.00
Don Miller

1993-94 Images Four Sport

These 150 standard-size cards feature on their borderless fronts color player action shots with backgrounds that have been thrown out of focus. On the white background to the left, career highlights, biography and statistics are displayed. Just 6,500 of each card were produced. The set closes with Classic Headlines (128-147) and checklists (148-150). A redemption card inserted one per case entitled the collector to one set of basketball draft preview cards. This offered expired 9/30/94.

COMPLETE SET (150) 6.00 15.00
28 Matt Martin .08 .25

1995 Images Race Reflections Dale Earnhardt

The 10-card insert set is a tribute to racing great Dale Earnhardt. The innovative double foil-board cards are randomly inserted in Black boxes only at a rate of one every 32 packs.

COMPLETE SET (10) 40.00 100.00
COMMON CARD (DE1-DE10) 5.00 12.00
*FACSIMILE SIGNATURE: 1X TO 2X HI COL.

1995 Images Race Reflections Jeff Gordon

This 10-card insert set highlights much of the success Jeff Gordon enjoyed in his career through the middle of 1995. The innovative double foil-board cards are randomly inserted in Red boxes only at a rate of one every 32 packs. There is also a parallel version of each of the ten cards. The parallel features a facsimile signature on the fronts of the cards. The signature cards were randomly inserted at a rate of one every 96 packs.

COMPLETE SET (10) 40.00 100.00
COMMON CARD (JG1-JG10) 5.00 12.00
*FACSIMILE SIGNATURE: 1X TO 2X HI COL.

1994 IMS Indianapolis 500 Champions Collection

COMPLETE SET (12) 4.00 10.00
NNO Mario Andretti 1.00 2.50
NNO Emerson Fittipaldi .50 1.25
NNO A.J. Foyt .60 1.50
NNO Gordon Johncock .25 .60
NNO Arie Luyendyk .60 1.50
NNO Rick Mears .50 1.25
NNO Bobby Rahal .40 1.00
NNO Johnny Rutherford .25 .60
NNO Tom Sneva .25 .60
NNO Danny Sullivan .25 .60
NNO Al Unser Sr.
NNO Al Unser Jr. .75 2.00

2011 In The Game Canadiana Red

BLUE/50: .75X TO 2X BASIC RED
UNPRICED ONYX ANNOUNCED RUN 5
ANNOUNCED PRINT RUN 180 SETS
40 Jacques Villeneuve .60 1.50

2011 In The Game Canadiana Autographs

OVERALL AUTO/MEM ODDS THREE PER BOX
AJV1 Jacques Villeneuve 25.00 50.00
AJV2 Jacques Villeneuve 25.00 50.00

2011 In The Game Canadiana Autographs Blue

*BLUE: .75X TO 1.5X BLACK AUTOS
OVERALL AUTO ODDS ONE PER BOX

1991 IROC

The 1991 IROC set was produced by Dodge and included a short sales brochure covering the Daytona IROC automobile and the 1991 IROC race schedule. Each cardback contains an action photo along with the set title 1991 IROC. Cardfronts contain the driver's photo and career highlights surrounded by a checkered flag border. Distribution was by complete set only sealed in a cello wrapper. The cards later were illegally reprinted. The counterfeits can be distinguished by an incomplete checkered flag design along the card border. One side of the border will be missing approximately 1/4 of the checkered flag.

COMPLETE SET (12) 100.00 200.00
1 Al Unser 6.00 15.00
2 Tom Kendall 4.00 10.00
3 Bob Wollek 4.00 10.00
4 Mark Martin 15.00 40.00
5 Bill Elliott 12.00 30.00
6 Al Unser Jr. 10.00 25.00
7 Scott Pruett 4.00 10.00
8 Geoff Bodine 4.00 10.00
9 Geoff Brabham 4.00 10.00
10 Rusty Wallace 15.00 40.00
11 Dorsey Schroeder 4.00 10.00
12 Dale Earnhardt 40.00 100.00

1994-96 John Deere

Over a three year period, the John Deere tractor company used professional athletes to promote their products and included cards of these athletes in their set. These five cards were issued in 1994 (Ryan and Novacek), 1995 (Jackson and Petty) and 1996 (Larry Bird). For our cataloguing purposes we are sequencing these cards in alphabetical order. Larry Bird signed some cards for this promotion but these cards are so thinly traded that no pricing is available

COMPLETE SET (5) 15.00 40.00
4 Richard Petty 5.00 12.00

1997 Jurassic Park

This 61-card set is another uniquely themed set from Wheels. The cards feature the top names in racing and are printed on 24 point stock. Each card has a jungle-like background and is stamped in silver foil. The cards were packed 6 cards per pack and 24 packs per box.

COMPLETE SET (61) 8.00 20.00
1 Jeff Gordon 1.00 2.50
2 Dale Jarrett .60 1.50
3 Terry Labonte .30 .75
4 Mark Martin .75 2.00
5 Rusty Wallace .75 2.00
6 Bobby Labonte .60 1.50
7 Sterling Marlin .30 .75
8 Jeff Burton .30 .75
9 Ted Musgrave .08 .25
10 Michael Waltrip .20 .50
11 David Green .08 .25
12 Ricky Craven .08 .25
13 Johnny Benson .20 .50
14 Jeremy Mayfield .20 .50
15 Bobby Hamilton .08 .25
16 Kyle Petty .20 .50
17 Darrell Waltrip .20 .50
18 Wally Dallenbach .08 .25
19 Bill Elliott .40 1.00
20 Jeff Green .08 .25
21 Joe Nemechek .08 .25
22 Derrike Cope .08 .25
23 Ward Burton .20 .50
24 Chad Little .08 .25
25 Mike Skinner .08 .25
26 Todd Bodine .08 .25
27 Hut Stricklin .08 .25
28 Ken Schrader .08 .25
29 Steve Grissom .08 .25
30 Robby Gordon RC .30 .75
31 Kenny Wallace .08 .25
32 Bobby Hillin .08 .25
33 Jimmy Spencer .08 .25
34 John Andretti .08 .25
35 Steve Park RC .75 2.00
36 Michael Waltrip .20 .50
37 Dale Jarrett .60 1.50
38 Mike McLaughlin .08 .25
39 Todd Bodine .08 .25
40 Terry Labonte .30 .75
41 Jeff Fuller .08 .25
42 Phil Parsons .08 .25
43 Jason Keller .08 .25
44 Mark Martin .75 2.00
45 Randy LaJoie .08 .25
46 Joe Nemechek .08 .25
47 Loy Allen .08 .25
48 Jeff Gordon 1.00 2.50
49 Mark Martin .75 2.00
50 Mark Martin .75 2.00
51 Jeff Gordon 1.00 2.50
52 John Andretti .08 .25
53 Jimmy Makar .05 .15
54 Charley Pressley .08 .25
55 Donnie Wingo .05 .15
56 Richard Childress .20 .50
57 Andy Petree .05 .15
58 Travis Carter .05 .15
59 Joe Gibbs .20 .50
60 Checklist .05 .15
61 Checklist .05 .15
P1 Mark Martin Promo 2.00 5.00

1997 Jurassic Park Triceratops

COMPLETE SET (61) 15.00 40.00
*TRICERATOPS: .8X TO 2X BASE CARDS

1997 Jurassic Park Carnivore

This 12-card insert set features the top drivers from the NASCAR circuit. The cards are horizontal and feature the drivers' numbers in the background. The cards were randomly inserted in packs at a ratio of 1:15.

COMPLETE SET (12) 30.00 60.00
C1 Dale Earnhardt 12.50 30.00
C2 Jeff Gordon 4.00 10.00
C3 Dale Jarrett 2.50 6.00
C4 Bobby Labonte 2.50 6.00
C5 Jimmy Spencer .40 1.00
C6 Bill Elliott 1.50 4.00
C7 Terry Labonte 1.25 3.00
C8 Rusty Wallace 3.00 8.00
C9 Ward Burton .75 2.00
C10 Mark Martin 3.00 8.00
C11 Todd Bodine .40 1.00
C12 Sterling Marlin 1.25 3.00

1997 Jurassic Park Pteranodon

This 10-card insert set is printed on clear plastic and contains portrait shots of the top drivers on the NASCAR circuit. The cards were randomly inserted in packs at a ratio of 1:30.

COMPLETE SET (10) 50.00 100.00
P1 Dale Earnhardt 25.00 60.00
P2 Jeff Gordon 6.00 15.00
P3 Bobby Labonte 4.00 10.00
P4 Terry Labonte 2.00 5.00
P5 Rusty Wallace 5.00 12.00
P6 Ward Burton 1.25 3.00
P7 Sterling Marlin 2.00 5.00
P8 Mark Martin 5.00 12.00
P9 Dale Jarrett 4.00 10.00
P10 Kyle Petty 1.25 3.00

1997 Jurassic Park Raptors

This 16-card insert set features drivers on micro-etched cards. The cards were randomly inserted in packs at a ratio of 1:6.

COMPLETE SET (16) 15.00 40.00
R1 Terry Labonte 1.25 3.00
R2 Jeff Gordon 4.00 10.00
R3 Johnny Benson .75 2.00
R4 Ward Burton .75 2.00
R5 Bobby Hamilton .40 1.00
R6 Ricky Craven .40 1.00
R7 Michael Waltrip .75 2.00
R8 Bobby Labonte 2.50 6.00
R9 Dale Jarrett 2.50 6.00
R10 Bill Elliott 1.50 4.00
R11 Rusty Wallace 3.00 8.00
R12 Jimmy Spencer .40 1.00
R13 Sterling Marlin 1.25 3.00
R14 Kyle Petty .75 2.00
R15 Ken Schrader .40 1.00
R16 Robby Gordon 1.25 3.00

1997 Jurassic Park Thunder Lizard

This 10-card set features cards that are encased with actual lizard skin. The cards were randomly inserted in packs at a ratio of 1:90 with each card serial numbered of 350.

COMPLETE SET (10) 50.00 120.00
TL1 Jeff Gordon 20.00 50.00
TL2 Dale Jarrett 12.50 30.00
TL3 Bobby Labonte 12.50 30.00
TL4 Rusty Wallace 15.00 40.00
TL5 Bill Elliott 8.00 20.00
TL6 Jeff Burton 4.00 10.00
TL7 Mark Martin 15.00 40.00
TL8 Dale Earnhardt 20.00 50.00
TL9 Mike Skinner 2.00 5.00
TL10 Robby Gordon 6.00 15.00

1997 Jurassic Park T-Rex

This 10-card insert set features cards that are diecut, embossed and micro-etched. The cards were randomly inserted in packs at a ratio of 1:60.

COMPLETE SET (10) 75.00 200.00
TR1 Terry Labonte 5.00 12.00
TR2 Jeff Gordon 15.00 40.00
TR3 Dale Jarrett 10.00 25.00
TR4 Bobby Labonte 10.00 25.00
TR5 Dale Earnhardt 25.00 60.00
TR6 Rusty Wallace 12.50 30.00
TR7 Mike Skinner 1.50 4.00
TR8 Joe Nemechek 1.50 4.00
TR9 Jeremy Mayfield 3.00 8.00
TR10 Bill Elliott 6.00 15.00

1997 Jurassic Park The Ride Jeff Gordon

This diecast/card set was available through a redemption program by Wheels and through RCCA(Racing Collectibles Club of America). The set consists of five Jeff Gordon cards, one cover card, and a 1:64 Action/RCCA #24 Jeff Gordon Jurassic Park Hood Opened car..

COMPLETE SET (5) 10.00 25.00
COMMON CARD (1-5) 2.00 5.00
NNO Cover Card .40 1.00

1992 Just Racing Larry Caudill

This 30-card set features NASCAR driver Larry Caudill. The sets were sold in complete set form. Each set was boxed and sealed and came with a numbered certificate of authenticity. There were also 100 signed and numbered cards randomly inserted in the sets.

COMPLETE SET (30) 2.00 5.00
COMMON CARD (1-30) .08 .25
AUTOGRAPHED CARDS 5.00 10.00

1937 Kellogg's Pep Stamps

Kellogg's distributed these multi-sport stamps inside specially marked Pep brand cereal boxes in 1937. They were originally issued in four-stamp blocks along with an instructional type tab at the top. The tab contained the sheet number. We've noted the sheet number after each athlete's name below. Note that six athletes appear on two sheets, thereby making those six double prints. There were 24-different sheets produced. We've catalogued the unnumbered stamps below in single loose form according to sport (AR- auto racing, AV- aviation, BB- baseball, BX- boxing, FB- football, GO- golf, HO- horses, SW- swimming, TN- tennis). Stamps can often be found intact in blocks of four along with the tab. Complete blocks of stamps are valued at roughly 50 percent more than the total value of the four individual stamps as priced below. An album was also produced to house the set.

COMPLETE SET (90) 1000.00 2000.00
AR1 Billy Arnold 6 7.50 15.00
AR2 Bill Cummings 2 7.50 15.00
AR3 Ralph DePalma 14 10.00 20.00
AR4 Tommy Milton 8 7.50 15.00
AR5 Mauri Rose 10 12.50 25.00
AR6 Wilbur Shaw 24 12.50 25.00

2006 Kellogg's Racing

This 2-card set was found on boxes of Kellogg's brand snacks.

COMPLETE SET (2) 2.00 5.00
1 Kyle Busch 1.50 4.00
2 Terry Labonte .75 2.00

1996 KnightQuest

This 45-card theme set features a theme based on King Arthur's time. The drivers are the Knights and the track is their battle field. Each card is printed on 24-pt paper stock with UV coating and foil stamped in silver holographic foil. The set is made up of three subsets: Armor Knights (1-20), Conquerors (21-33) and Wizards (34-45). The cards are packaged four cards per pack, 24 cards per box and 20 boxes per case. There were 999 Hobby cases and 699 Retail cases produced. Wheels also continued its E-Race to Win redemption game for KnightQuest. The expiration of both game cards was 5/31/96.

COMPLETE SET (45) 6.00 15.00
1 Dale Earnhardt K 1.25 3.00
2 Jeff Gordon K .75 2.00
3 Sterling Marlin K .25 .60
4 Ted Musgrave K .07 .20
5 Mark Martin K .60 1.50
6 Terry Labonte K .25 .60
7 Rusty Wallace K .60 1.50
8 Morgan Shepherd K .07 .20
9 Bobby Labonte K .50 1.25
10 Ricky Rudd K .25 .60
11 Bill Elliott K .30 .75
12 Ernie Irvan K .15 .40
13 Ken Schrader K .07 .20
14 Derrike Cope K .07 .20
15 Dale Jarrett K .50 1.25
16 Geoff Bodine K .07 .20
17 Darrell Waltrip K .15 .40
18 Kyle Petty K .15 .40
19 Michael Waltrip K .15 .40
20 Brett Bodine K .07 .20
21 Jeff Gordon C .75 2.00
22 Dale Earnhardt C 1.25 3.00
23 Rusty Wallace C .60 1.50
24 Mark Martin C .60 1.50
25 Dale Earnhardt C 1.25 3.00
26 Bobby Labonte C .50 1.25
27 Kyle Petty C .15 .40
28 Terry Labonte C .25 .60
29 Bobby Labonte C .50 1.25
30 Jeff Gordon C .75 2.00
31 Jeff Gordon C .75 2.00
32 Dale Jarrett C .50 1.25
33 Sterling Marlin C .25 .60
34 Junior Johnson W .07 .20
35 Travis Carter W .02 .10
36 Bob Brannan W .02 .10
37 Tony Glover W .02 .10
38 Don Miller W .02 .10
39 Larry McReynolds W .02 .10
40 Ray Evernham W .02 .10
41 Steve Hmiel W .02 .10
42 Cecil Gordon W .02 .10
43 Andy Petree W .02 .10
44 Richard Childress W .15 .40
45 Don Hawk W .02 .10

1996 KnightQuest Black Knights

COMPLETE SET (45) 150.00 250.00
*BLACK KNIGHTS: 4X TO 10X BASE CARDS

1996 KnightQuest Red Knight Preview

COMPLETE SET (45) 12.00 30.00
*RED KNIGHTS: .8X TO 2X BASE CARDS

1996 KnightQuest Royalty

COMPLETE SET (45) 50.00 100.00
*ROYALTY: 2.5X TO 6X BASIC CARDS

1996 KnightQuest White Knights

COMPLETE SET (45) 150.00 300.00
*WHITE KNIGHTS: 5X TO 12X BASIC CARDS

1996 KnightQuest First Knights

This 10-card insert set features some of the drivers who won Poles in 1995. The cards are printed on foil board and are die-cut. Each card is sequentially numbered of 1,499 and can be found one per 36 packs. The First Knight cards were available in hobby packs.

COMPLETE SET (10) 30.00 80.00
FK1 Dale Earnhardt 8.00 20.00
FK2 Dale Jarrett 3.00 8.00
FK3 Jeff Gordon 5.00 12.00
FK4 Mark Martin 4.00 10.00
FK5 Bobby Labonte 3.00 8.00
FK6 Terry Labonte 1.50 4.00
FK7 Ricky Rudd 1.50 4.00
FK8 Ken Schrader .50 1.25
FK9 Bill Elliott 2.00 5.00
FK10 Sterling Marlin 1.50 4.00

1996 KnightQuest Knights of the Round Table

The 10-card insert set features the top 10 drivers in Winston Cup. The cards use a gold embossed printing process on 1/4 of the card to show a silhouette of the driver. The other 3/4 of the card show the driver in the car, belted up and ready to go. There are 1,199 of each card and they can be found in both hobby and retail packs at a rate of one per 72 packs.

COMPLETE SET (10) 60.00 150.00
KT1 Jeff Gordon 8.00 20.00
KT2 Dale Earnhardt 12.00 30.00
KT3 Darrell Waltrip 2.00 5.00
KT4 Mark Martin 5.00 12.00
KT5 Terry Labonte 3.00 8.00
KT6 Sterling Marlin 3.00 8.00
KT7 Bill Elliott 4.00 10.00
KT8 Rusty Wallace 5.00 12.00
KT9 Michael Waltrip 2.00 5.00
KT10 Ernie Irvan 2.00 5.00

1996 KnightQuest Kenji Momota

This four-card set features the first Japanese driver to ever race in the SuperTruck series. The cards are printed on 24-pt, UV coated paper stock. They can be found one per 48 packs. There were two different signature versions of card #KMS1. There were 1,500 signature cards produced with an English signature and 1,000 with a Japanese signature. The odds of finding a signature card was one in 480 packs. The Kenji Momota cards were available in both hobby and retail packs.

COMPLETE SET (4) 4.00 10.00
COMMON CARD (KM1-KM4) 1.25 3.00
KMS1A K.Momota Amer.AU/1500 6.00 15.00
KMS1J K.Momota Japan.AU/1000 8.00 20.00

1996 KnightQuest Protectors of the Crown

This six-card set features the active Winston Cup Champions. The cards are printed on foil board using embossed technology. Each card is numbered sequentially of 899 and can be found one per hobby 98 packs. There was also an uncut sheet available through the E-Race to Win redemption game. By being unnumbered, the cards on the uncut sheet are different than the regular Protectors of the Crown inserts.

COMPLETE SET (6) 12.00 30.00
UNCUT SHEET 15.00 40.00
PC1 Darrell Waltrip 1.00 2.50
PC2 Dale Earnhardt 5.00 12.00
PC3 Terry Labonte 1.00 2.50
PC4 Rusty Wallace 1.00 2.50
PC5 Bill Elliott 1.50 4.00
PC6 Jeff Gordon 3.00 8.00

1996 KnightQuest Santa Claus

This 5-card set features four of the top names in Winston Cup and Santa Claus. Each card has "Merry Christmas" on the front and "wishing you a Merry Christmas" on the back. Each card is numbered 1 of 1499. There is also parallel green version of each card available in retail packs.

COMPLETE RED SET (5) 25.00 60.00
*GREEN CARDS: .4X TO 1X REDS
SC1 Dale Earnhardt 10.00 25.00
SC2 Bobby Labonte 4.00 10.00
SC3 Rusty Wallace 5.00 12.00
SC4 Mark Martin 5.00 12.00
SC5 Santa Claus .30 .75

1991 Langenberg ARCA/Hot Stuff

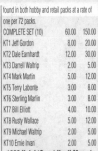

M.B. Langenberg (H.S.Promotions) produced this set under the name Hot Stuff in 1991. The cards feature drivers of the ARCA PermaTex Supercar Series and were printed on thin white stock. They were originally sold in complete set form.

COMPLETE SET (68) 5.00 10.00
1 Bob Brevak .07 .20
2 Lee Raymond .07 .20
3 Carl Miskotten III .07 .20
4 Mike Fry .07 .20
5 Scott Stovall .07 .20
6 Bobby Bowsher .15 .40
7 Brian Jaeger .07 .20
8 Bob Dotter Sr. .15 .40
9 Eric Smith .07 .20
10 Glenn Brewer .07 .20
11 Mike Wallace .60 1.50
12 Roger Blackstock .07 .20
13 Glenn Sullivan .07 .20
14 Roger Otto .07 .20
15 Craig Rubright .07 .20
16 Roy Payne .15 .40
17 Billy Simmons .07 .20
18 Graham Taylor .07 .20
19 Chris Gehrke .07 .20
20 Keith Waid .07 .20
21 Bobby Bowsher .15 .40
22 Billy Thomas .07 .20
23 Chet Blanton .07 .20
24 Dave Jensen .07 .20
25 Bill Venturini .15 .40
26 Mike Davis .07 .20
27 Ken Rowley .07 .20
28 Charlie Glotzbach .07 .20
29 Bob Keselowski .15 .40
30 Wayne Dellinger .07 .20
31 Cecil Eunice .07 .20
32 Mark Gibson .07 .20
33 Dale McDowell .07 .20
34 Bob Brevak .07 .20
35 Bobby Gerhart .07 .20
36 Frank Kimmel .07 .20
37 Jerry Cook .07 .20
38 Jerry Hufflin .07 .20
39 Brad Holman .07 .20
40 Ben Hess .15 .40
41 Jimmy Horton .15 .40
42 Richard Hinds .07 .20
43 Bill Flowers .07 .20
44 Ferrel Harris .07 .20
45 Mark Gibson .07 .20
46 Joe Booher .07 .20
47 Ken Ragan .07 .20
48 Donnie Moran .07 .20
49 Bobby Massey .07 .20
50 Checklist .07 .20
51 Dave Simko .07 .20
52 David Boggs .07 .20
53 Larry Couch .07 .20
54 Dorsey Schroeder .15 .40
55 Mark Thompson .07 .20
56 Jerry Hill .07 .20
57 Gary Weinbroer .07 .20
58 Scott Hansen .07 .20
59 Gary Hawes .07 .20
60 Tom Bigelow .07 .20
61 David Elliott .07 .20
62 '91 Daytona Action .07 .20
63 '91 Daytona Action .07 .20
64 '91 Atlanta Action .07 .20
65 '88 Dayton Pit Stop .07 .20
66 Goodyear Tire .07 .20
67 Hoosier Tire .07 .20
68 '91 ARCA Schedule .07 .20

1991 Langenberg ARTGO

This 36-card set was produced by Hot Stuff Promotions of Rockford, Illinois. The cards were sold at the ARTGO All-Star 100 race, at Rockford Speedway on July 23, 1991.

COMPLETE SET (36) 25.00 50.00
1 Matt Kenseth XRC 15.00 40.00
2 Robbie Reiser .08 .25
3 Larry Schuler .08 .25
4 Ed Holmes .08 .25
5 Al Schill .08 .25
6 Jerry Wood .08 .25
7 Todd Coon .08 .25
8 Bryan Refner .08 .25
9 Joe Shear .08 .25
10 John Zeigler .08 .25
11 Scott Hansen .08 .25
12 Kregg Hurlbert .08 .25
13 John Knaus .08 .25
14 Bill Venturini .15 .40
15 Johnny Spaw .08 .25
16 Nolan McBride .08 .25
17 Monte Gress .08 .25
18 Tom Carlson .08 .25
19 David Anspaugh .08 .25
20 John Loehman .08 .25
21 Keith Nelson .08 .25
22 Dennis Berry .08 .25
23 Dick Harrington .08 .25
24 Dave Weltmeyer .08 .25
25 Kevin Cywinski .08 .25
26 Tony Strupp .08 .25
27 Jim Weber .08 .25
28 Steve Carlson .25 1.00
29 Tracy Schuler .08 .25
30 Al Schill, Jr. .08 .25
31 M.G. Gajewski .08 .25
32 Bob Brownell .08 .25
33 Joe Shear .08 .25
34 Dennis Lampman .08 .25
35 Conrad Morgan .08 .25
36 Checklist Card .08 .25

1991 Langenberg Stock Car Champions

This 30-card set features track champions from around the country. Each card in the set carries a "Say NO! To Drugs" logo on the front with each drivers name.

COMPLETE SET (30) 3.00 8.00
1 John Knaus .10 .30
2 Steve Fraise .10 .30
3 Keith Berner .10 .30
4 Brian Ater .10 .30
5 Tom Rients .10 .30
6 Kevin Nuttleman .10 .30
7 Mel Walen .10 .30
8 Al Humphrey .10 .30
9 Chris Harat .10 .30
10 Brad Denney .10 .30
11 Richie Jensen .10 .30
12 Jay Stuart .10 .30
13 Jeff Martin .10 .30
14 Howard Willis .10 .30
15 Ronnie Thomas .10 .30
16 Babe Branscombe .10 .30
17 Tom Guithues .10 .30
18 Randy Olson .10 .30
19 Dennis Setzer .30 .75
20 Charlie Williamson .10 .30
21 Bryan Refner .10 .30
22 Fred Joehnck .10 .30
23 Roger Otto .10 .30
24 Terry Cook .10 .30
25 Roger Avants .10 .30
26 Larry Mosher .10 .30
27 Nick Kuipers .10 .30
28 Terry Lackey .10 .30
29 Vinny Annarummo .10 .30
30 Checklist Card .10 .30

1992 Langenberg ARCA/Flash

M.B. Langenberg produced this set under the name '92 Flash. The cards feature drivers of the ARCA Supercar Series and were printed on slightly thicker card stock than the 1991 release. They were originally sold in complete set form and included an unnumbered Clifford Allison card. Reportedly there were 5,000 sets produced.

COMPLETE SET (111) 8.00 20.00
1 Bill Venturini .30 .75
2 Bobby Bowsher .30 .75
3 Bob Keselowski .08 .25
4 Bob Dotter Sr. .08 .25
5 Bobby Gerhart .08 .25
6 Bob Brevak .08 .25
7 Ben Hess .08 .25
8 Glenn Brewer .08 .25
9 Mark Gibson .08 .25
10 Roy Payne .08 .25
11 Checklist .02 .10
12 Jim Clarke .08 .25
13 Bill Venturini's Car .08 .25
14 Bobby Bowsher's Car .08 .25
15 Bob Keselowski .08 .25
16 Bob Dotter Sr. .08 .25
17 Bobby Gerhart .08 .25
18 Bob Brevak .08 .25
19 Ben Hess .08 .25
20 Glenn Brewer .08 .25
21 Mark Gibson .08 .25
22 Roy Payne .08 .25
23 Bob Strait .08 .25
24 Billy Thomas .08 .25
25 Jerry Huffman .08 .25
26 Gary Hawes .08 .25
27 Keith Waid .08 .25
28 Clay Young's Car .02 .10
Craig Rubright's Car
Bob Keselowski's Car/'91 Atlanta
29 Jerry Hill .08 .25
30 Randy Huffman's Car .02 .10
31 Dale McDowell .08 .25
32 Roger Blackstock's Car .02 .10
33 Red Farmer .30 .75
34 Dave Weltmeyer .08 .25
35 H.B. Bailey .08 .25
36 Loy Allen Jr. .30 .75
37 Bill Venturini Champion .30 .75
38 Jeff McClure .08 .25
39 Lee Raymond .08 .25
40 Dave Mader .08 .25
41 Andy Genzman .08 .25
42 Rich Bickle .30 .75
43 Alan Pruitt .08 .25
44 Bob Schacht .08 .25
Bill Venturini
Bob Keselowski Cars
45 David Hall .08 .25
46 Jerry Hufflin .08 .25
47 Thad Coleman .08 .25
48 Mike Wren .08 .25
49 Eddie Bierschwale .08 .25
50 Tom Sherrill .08 .25
51 Scotty Sands .08 .25
52 1992 Daytona .02 .10
53 Stan Fox .30 .75
54 Jimmy Horton .30 .75
55 Gary Weinbroer's Car .08 .25
56 Craig Rubright .08 .25
57 Jerry Churchill .08 .25
58 Clifford Allison .30 .75
59 Rich Bickle's Car .08 .25
Roulo Brothers
60 Mike Fry's Car .08 .25
61 Jeff Purvis .30 .75
62 Ron Burchette .08 .25
63 T.W. Taylor .08 .25
64 Bob Denny .08 .25
65 Billy Bigley Jr. .08 .25
66 Charlie Baker .08 .25
67 Bobby Massey .08 .25
68 Mike Davis .08 .25
69 Graham Taylor's Car .02 .10
70 Tim Fedewa 1.25 3.00
71 Andy Hillenburg .30 .75
72 Mark Gibson Pit Stop .02 .10
73 Frank Kimmel .08 .25
74 Frank Kimmel Pit Stop .02 .10
75 David Elliott .08 .25
76 Clay Young .08 .25
77 Scott Bloomquist's Car .08 .25
78 Dennis Setzer .30 .75
79 Dave Jensen .08 .25
80 Brad Smith's Car .02 .10
81 Bob Keselowski w/Car .02 .10
82 Wayne Dellinger .08 .25
83 Bobby Woods .08 .25
84 Paul Holt Jr. .08 .25
85 Mark Thompson .08 .25
86 Tim Porter .08 .25
87 Ken Rowley's Car .02 .10
88 Jody Gara's Car .02 .10
89 Mark Harding .08 .25
90 Tim Priebe's Car .02 .10
91 James Elliott .08 .25
92 Wally Finney .08 .25
93 Richard Hampton's Car .02 .10
94 T.W. Taylor Pit Stop .02 .10
95 James Hylton's Car .02 .10
96 Rich Hayes .08 .25
97 Joe Booher .08 .25
98 Eric Smith's Car .02 .10
99 Ron Otto's Car .02 .10
100 Bob Williams .08 .25
101 Tony Schwengel's Car .08 .25
102 Dave Simko .08 .25
103 Ben Hess Pit Stop .02 .10
104 Ken Ragan .08 .25
105 Maurice Randall's Car .02 .10
106 Bob Schacht .08 .25
107 Robbie Cowart .08 .25
108 Checklist .02 .10
109 Arca Officials & Sched .02 .10
110 Hoosier Tire Midwest .02 .10
NNO Clifford Allison .75 2.00

1993 Langenberg ARCA/Flash Prototype

M.B. Langenberg produced this prototype card under the name '93 Flash. The Loy Allen card was made as a preview to the 1993 ARCA set that was never produced.

PR1 Loy Allen Jr. .80 2.00

1994 Langenberg ARCA/Flash

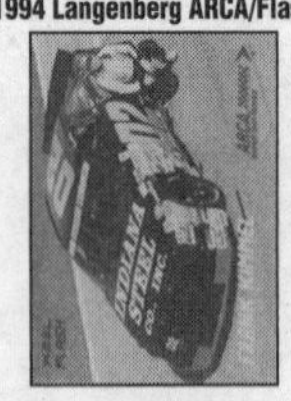

M.B. Langenberg produced this set under the name '94 M.B.L. Flash. The cards feature drivers of the ARCA Supercar Series and were printed on thin card stock with a blue-green cardback. They were originally sold in complete set form. Two promo cards were produced and distributed to advertise the series, but are not considered part of the complete regular set.

COMPLETE SET (100) 10.00 20.00
1 ARCA Cover Card .08 .25
2 Tim Steele .20 .50
3 Bob Keselowski .20 .50
4 Bobby Bowsher .20 .50
5 Frank Kimmel .08 .25
6 Bob Brevak .08 .25
7 Bob Strait .08 .25
8 Robert Ham .08 .25
9 Glenn Brewer .08 .25
10 Ken Allen .08 .25
11 Bob Dotter Sr. .08 .25
12 L.W. Miller .08 .25
13 Rick Sheppard .08 .25
14 Eric Smith .08 .25
15 Dave Weltmeyer .08 .25
16 Craig Rubright .08 .25
17 Roger Blackstock .08 .25
18 Jeff Purvis .20 .50
19 Randy Churchill .08 .25
20 Mark Thompson .08 .25
21 Jeep Pflum .08 .25
22 Curt Dickie .08 .25
23 Gary Hawes .08 .25
24 Loy Allen Jr. .20 .50
25 Brigette Anne Shirley .08 .25
26 ARCA Officials .08 .25
27 Jerry Huffman .08 .25
28 Jimmy Horton .20 .50
29 Jerry Foyt .08 .25
30 Todd Coon .08 .25
31 Ken Rowley .08 .25
32 Dave Jensen .08 .25
33 Joe Niemiroski .08 .25
34 Tony Schwengel .08 .25
35 Rick Heuser .08 .25
36 Laura Lane .08 .25
37 Gary Bradberry .20 .50
38 Alan Pruitt .08 .25
39 Danny Kelley .08 .25
40 Wally Finney .08 .25
41 Billy Bigley Jr. .20 .50
42 Bob Schacht .08 .25
43 Ken Schrader .20 .50
44 John Wilkinson .08 .25
45 Billy Thomas .08 .25
46 Donny Paul .08 .25
47 David Hall .08 .25
48 Andy Stone .08 .25
49 Bob Hill .08 .25
50 Ron Burchette .08 .25
51 Red Farmer .20 .50
52 James Hylton .20 .50
53 Mike Wallace .20 .50
54 Tom Bigelow .08 .25
55 Wayne Larson .08 .25
56 Peter Gibbons .08 .25
57 Jeff McClure .20 .50
58 Andy Farr .08 .25
59 Kerry Teague .20 .50
60 Bob Williams .08 .25
61 Bobby Gerhart .08 .25
62 Jerry Glanville .20 .50
63 Marvin Smith .08 .25
64 Dale Fischlein .08
65 Rich Bickle .20
66 Greg Caver .08
67 Randy Huffman .08
68 Bill Venturini .20
69 Dave Simko .08
70 Tim Porter .08
71 Jody Gara .08
72 Perry Tripp .08
73 Bill Venturini .20
74 John Stradtman .08
75 Scotty Sands .08
76 Rich Hayes .08
77 Tim Fedewa 1.25 3.
78 Joey Sonntag .08
79 Tom Sherrill .08
80 Delma Cowart .20
81 Jerry Hill .08
82 David Boggs .08
83 Greg Roe .08
84 Bobby Coyle .08
85 Mark Gibson .08
86 Gary Weinbroer .08
87 1994 ARCA Schedule .08
88 ARCA Pace Car CL .08
89 Checklist 21-60 .08
90 Checklist 61-100 .08
91 Tim Steele's Car .08
92 Bob Keselowski's Car .08
93 Bobby Bowsher's Car .08
94 Frank Kimmel's Car .08
95 Bob Brevak's Car .08
96 Bob Strait's Car .08
97 Robert Ham's Car .08
98 Glenn Brewer's Car .08
99 Ken Allen's Car .08
100 Jeff McClure's Car .08

2011 Leaf Legends of Sport Cu Signatures

RP5 Richard Petty 20.00 50.

1992 Limited Editions Promos

Limited Editions released this four-card set to preview its 1992 driver sets. The cards are numbered and feature a card from each of the Gant, Gordon and Glanville sets, marked promo and a card showing the other four drivers togeth

COMPLETE SET (4) 2.50 6.
1 Harry Gant .30
2 K.Wallace .40 1.
J.Hensley
T.Houston
C.Bown
3 Jerry Glanville .60 1.
4 Jeff Gordon 6.00 15.

1992 Limited Editions Chuck Bown

This is one of six Busch series driver sets produced by Limited Editions and distributed in complete set form. Each of the black bordered issues looks similar, but features a different driv Chuck Bown is the focus of this set. Promo complete sets were also produced with the word "PROMO" on the card fronts. There is no price differnce for the promo version.

COMP. FACT SET (15) 1.60 4.
COMMON CARD (1-15) .10

1992 Limited Editions Harry Ga

This set is the first in a continuing series of driv sets produced by Limited Editions. The Harry G issue differs from the others in that it contains a green border as opposed to black. The cards we distributed in a white box picturing Gant and we individually numbered of 25,000. Uncut sheets the sets were also made available to members o the Limited Editions Collector Club -- 500 numbered and signed by Gant and 2000 unsign

COMP. FACT SET (15) 2.00 5.
COMMON CARD (1-15) .10
SEMISTARS .15

1992 Limited Editions Jerry Glanville

This set is issue number five in a line of Busch series driver sets produced by Limited Editions. Each of the black bordered issues looks similar, but features a different driver. Jerry Glanville is the focus of this set.

COMPLETE SET (12) 1.50 4.00
COMMON CARD (1-12) .10 .30
JERRY GLANVILLE CARD .15 .40

1992 Limited Editions Jeff Gordon

This set is issue number six in a line of Busch series driver sets produced by Limited Editions. Each of the issues looks similar, but features a different driver. Jeff Gordon and the Baby Ruth Race Team are the focus of this set. There were 300 Jeff Gordon autographed cards randomly inserted in the sets. There was also a factory binder. Inside each binder was a promo card of Jeff Gordon, each stamped 1 of 1,000. There were also unstamped versions of the promo card. The 1,000 indicated how many binders there were.

COMPLETE SET (12) 3.00 8.00
COMMON CARD (1-12) .25 .60
AU2 Jeff Gordon AU/300 50.00 120.00

1992 Limited Editions Jimmy Hensley

This is one of six Busch series driver sets produced by Limited Editions and distributed in complete set form. Each of the black bordered issues looks similar, but focuses on a different driver. Jimmy Hensley is the focus of this set.

COMP. FACT SET (15) 1.50 4.00
COMMON CARD (1-15) .10 .30
JIMMY HENSLEY CARDS .15 .40

1992 Limited Editions Tommy Houston

This is one of six Busch series driver sets produced by Limited Editions and distributed in complete set form. Each of the black bordered issues looks similar, but features a different driver. Tommy Houston is the focus of this set.

COMP. FACT SET (15) 1.50 4.00
COMMON CARD (1-15) .10 .30
TOMMY HOUSTON CARD .15 .40

1992 Limited Editions Kenny Wallace

This is one of six Busch series driver sets produced by Limited Editions and distributed in complete set form. Each of the black bordered issues looks similar, but focuses on a different driver. Kenny Wallace is the focus of this set.

COMPLETE SET (15) 1.50 4.00
COMMON CARD (1-15) .10 .30
KENNY WALLACE CARDS .15 .40

1997 Lindberg ARCA

1 Roger Blackstock .75 2.00
2 Kenny Brown .75 2.00
3 Bob Hill .75 2.00
4 Marvin Smith .75 2.00
5 Tim Steele .75 2.00

1995 Lipton Tea Johnny Benson Jr.

Packages of Lipton Tea included one of three Johnny Benson Jr. cards produced in 1995. Each of the three cards features an artist's rendering of a Lipton Tea Racing Team action scene. The cards are unnumbered.

COMPLETE SET (3) 2.50 6.00
COMMON CARD .75 2.00

2006 Little Debbie

This 7-card set was found on boxes of Little Debbie snacks.

COMPLETE SET (7) 6.00 12.00
1 Ken Schrader's Car .75 2.00
Jimmy Watts
James Rhodes
2 Ken Schrader's Car .75 2.00
3 Ken Schrader's Car .75 2.00
4 Ken Schrader's Car .75 2.00
Chuck White
Mike Smith
5 Ken Schrader's Car .75 2.00
6 Ken Schrader's Car .75 2.00
7 Ken Schrader's Car .75 2.00

1992 Mac Tools Winner's Cup

Mac Tools produced this set honoring top performers of the NASCAR, Indycar and NHRA racing circuits. The set is titled Winners' Cup Series and mentions it as a series one issue. There was no series two set produced. The cards were packaged in two different packs. Each pack contained 10 cards and a cover card. The cards are unnumbered and have been arranged below alphabetically.

COMPLETE SET (21) 6.00 15.00
1 Bobby Allison .60 1.50
Hut Stricklin
2 Davey Allison .75 2.00
3 Dale Armstrong .30 .75
4 Ron Ayers .30 .75
5 Kenny Bernstein .50 1.25
6 Michael Brotherton .30 .75
7 Jim Crawford .30 .75
8 Mike Dunn .30 .75
9 Harry Gant .40 1.00
10 Darrell Gwynn .30 .75
11 Jerry Gwynn .30 .75
12 Ernie Irvan .75 2.00
13 Lori Johns .30 .75
14 Bobby Labonte 1.25 3.00
15 Mark Martin 1.50 4.00
16 Tom McEwen .30 .75
17 Richard Petty 1.50 4.00
18 Don Prudhomme .75 2.00
19 Kenny Wallace .50 1.25
20 Rusty Wallace 1.25 3.00
21 Checklist Card UER .20 .50

1993 Maxwell House

The 1993 Maxwell House set was produced by Kraft General Foods for distribution in Maxwell House coffee products. The cards were released in two series of 15-driver cards and one cover card each. Series one features a solid blue border, while the border on series two is a mix of light and dark blue. The cards are often sold in separate series in their original cello wrappers. Note that the copyright date for series one cards is 1992, but the cards were released in early 1993.

COMPLETE SET (32) 20.00 50.00
COMPLETE SERIES 1 (16) 8.00 25.00
COMPLETE SERIES 2 (16) 8.00 25.00
1 Bobby Labonte 3.00 8.00
2 Alan Kulwicki 1.50 4.00
3 Davey Allison 1.50 4.00
4 Harry Gant .25 .60
5 Kyle Petty .25 .60
6 Mark Martin 4.00 10.00
7 Ricky Rudd .40 1.00
8 Darrell Waltrip .25 .60
9 Ernie Irvan 1.50 4.00
10 Rusty Wallace 4.00 10.00
11 Morgan Shepherd .15 .40
12 Brett Bodine .15 .40
13 Ken Schrader .15 .40
14 Dale Jarrett 3.00 8.00
15 Richard Petty 1.50 4.00
16 Bobby Labonte 3.00 8.00
Terry Labonte
17 Davey Allison 1.50 4.00
B.Allison
18 Richard Petty 1.50 4.00
Kyle Petty
19 Rusty Wallace 4.00 10.00
K.Wallace
20 Geoff Bodine .15 .40
Brett Bodine
21 Darrell Waltrip .25 .60
Michael Waltrip
22 Dale Jarrett 3.00 8.00
Ned Jarrett
23 Sterling Marlin .25 .60
Coo Coo Marlin
24 Jeff Gordon 5.00 12.00
K.Wall
B.Labonte
25 Jeff Gordon 5.00 12.00
26 Kenny Wallace .15 .40
27 Hut Stricklin .15 .40
28 Geoff Bodine .15 .40
29 Terry Labonte 2.00 5.00
30 Bobby Hillin .15 .40
NNO Cover Card 1 .15 .40
NNO Cover Card 2 .15 .40

1988 Maxx Charlotte

This set contains cards from the second and third printings of 1988 Maxx. The Charlotte name refers to what was believed to be the location of the second and third printings, although all three printings took place at the same location. The set is often called the "First Annual Edition" by collectors. It contains numerous variations from the Myrtle Beach set. The cover cards were printed with two different starburst descriptions (pack versus factory set) in both the Charlotte and Myrtle Beach versions. During the second printing, 10 cards including the two variations of the cover card were changed. The Myrtle Beach notation was removed from the four checklist cards. The special offer price ($19.95) was changed prior to the second printing to $21.45 on the Cover Cards. The Talladega Streaks #10 card was eliminated to make room for Darrell Waltrip. Checklist #19 was changed to reflect this move. On card #26 Phil Parsons, his wife's name was included in the family section on the back of the card. It was excluded in the first printing Myrtle Beach. During the third printing of this set six cards were changed. The #59 1988 Begins card was eliminated to make room for the #59 Brett Bodine card. Checklist #69 was changed to reflect this move. The #43 Daytona International Speedway card was changed to card #47. The #47 Single File card was eliminated. Richard Petty was included in the set on, of course, card #43. Checklist #36 was updated to reflect the changes on cards #43 and #47. On the #88 Ken Bouchard card, the family section was changed to reflect the fact that he and his fiancee, Heidi, were married during the season. There was also a card #99 of Dale Earnhardt that originally wasn't released due to Maxx not getting approval from Dale. The card was later issued with a sticker on it via an insert redemption in the 1994 Maxx Medallion set. (See that set for more on the stickered version.) Then in 1996, as Maxx was going out of business, a signed version of this card was

COMPLETE SET (100) 15.00 30.00
COMP.FACT.SET (100) 40.00 80.00
WAX BOX 150.00 250.00
1A Cover Card 10 .40 1.00
1B Cover Card 100 12.00 30.00
2 Richard Petty's Car 1.50 4.00
3 J.D. McDuffie RC 1.00 2.50
4 Cale Yarborough's Car 1.00 2.50
5 Davey Allison RC 2.50 6.00
6 Rodney Combs RC 1.00 2.50
7 B.Allison/Bonn/Bodine Cars .75 2.00
8 Mickey Gibbs RC .60 1.50
9 Dale Earnhardt's Car 3.00 8.00
10 Darrell Waltrip RC 2.50 6.00
11 Sterling Marlin's Car 1.50 4.00
12 Brad Teague .40 1.00
13 Dale Earnhardt's Car 3.00 8.00
14 Rusty Wallace RC 2.50 6.00
15 Pit Row Action 1.50 4.00
16 Larry Pollard RC .40 1.00
17 Dale Earnhardt's Car 3.00 8.00
18 Benny Parsons' Car 1.00 2.50
19 Checklist #1 .40 1.00
20 Neil Bonnett RC 2.00 5.00
21 Martinsville Speedway .75 2.00
22 Bill Elliott's Car 1.50 4.00
23 Michael Waltrip's Car 1.25 3.00
24 Trevor Boys .40 1.00
25 Morgan Shepherd RC 1.50 4.00
26 Phil Parsons w/Marcia .40 1.00
27 Darrell Waltrip In Pits 1.25 3.00
28 Hut Stricklin RC 1.00 2.50
29 Richard Childress 1.50 4.00
30 Bobby Allison RC 1.25 3.00
31 R.Petty/R.Rudd Cars 1.50 4.00
32 Richmond Fairgrounds .75 2.00
33 Derrike Cope RC 1.25 3.00
34 Neil Bonnett's Car .75 2.00
35 Geoff Bodine/Benny Parsons Crash 1.00 2.50
36A CL w/o Petty 4.00 10.00
36B CL w/Petty .40 1.00
37 Larry Pearson RC 1.00 2.50
38 Dale Earnhardt's Car 3.00 8.00
39 Dave Pletcher RC .40 1.00
40 Davey Allison ROY 4.00 10.00
41 Alan Kulwicki's Car 1.00 2.50
42 Jimmy Means .40 1.00
43 Richard Petty RC 3.00 8.00
44 Dave Marcis RC 1.50 4.00
45 Tire Wars/Earnhardt's Trailer 3.00 8.00
46 Lake Speed RC 1.00 2.50
47 Daytona Int. Speedway .75 2.00
48 Mark Martin RC 2.50 6.00
49 D.Earnhardt/D.Allison Cars 3.00 8.00
50 Bill Elliott RC 2.50 6.00
51 Ken Ragan .40 1.00
52 Bobby Hillin RC 1.00 2.50
53 Alabama Int. Speedway .75 2.00
54 Dale Earnhardt's Car 3.00 8.00
55 Buddy Baker RC 1.50 4.00
56 Charlotte Motor Speedway .75 2.00
57 Rick Wilson Crash .40 1.00
58 Alan Kulwicki RC 2.00 5.00
59 Brett Bodine RC 1.50 4.00
60 Richard Petty's Car 1.50 4.00
61 Dale Jarrett RC 2.50 6.00
62 R.Wallace/G.Bodine Cars 1.25 3.00
63 Terry Labonte RC 2.50 6.00
64 Dave Marcis' Car .60 1.50
65 Greg Sacks RC 1.00 2.50
66 Jimmy Horton RC .40 1.00
67 Geoff Bodine RC 1.00 2.50
68 Rick Wilson RC 1.00 2.50
69A CL w/1988 Begins 4.00 10.00
69B CL w/Bodine .40 1.00
70 Bill Elliott FF 1.50 4.00
71 Mark Stahl .40 1.00
72 Harry Ranier .40 1.00
Lundy Shop
73 Phoenix Int. Raceway .75 2.00
74 Ken Schrader RC 3.00 8.00
75 Darrell Waltrip's Car 1.25 3.00
76 Benny Parsons RC 1.50 4.00
77 Watkins Glen Int. .75 2.00
78 Phil Barkdoll RC .40 1.00
79 Speedway Club/Charlotte .75 2.00
80 Sterling Marlin RC 2.00 5.00
81 Ken Schrader's Car 1.25 3.00
82 Riverside Int./R.Petty's Car 1.50 4.00
83 Buddy Arrington .40 1.00
84 D.Earnhardt/R.Petty Cars 3.00 8.00
85 Connie Saylor .40 1.00
86 North Wilkesboro Speedway .75 2.00
87 D.Earnhardt WC Champ 10.00 25.00
88 Ken Bouchard RC married .40 1.00
89 Davey Allison's Car 1.50 4.00
90 Cale Yarborough RC 1.50 4.00
91 Michigan Int. Speedway .75 2.00
92 Eddie Bierschwale RC .40 1.00
93 Jim Sauter RC 1.00 2.50
94 Bobby Allison/Benny Parsons cars 1.00 2.50
95 Ernie Irvan RC 1.50 4.00
96 Buddy Baker's Car .60 1.50
97 Filling the Stands/Charlotte .75 2.00
98 Michael Waltrip RC 1.50 4.00
99A Great Body Pit Row .60 1.50
99P Dale Earnhardt Promo 40.00 100.00
100 Checklist 4 no Myrtle Beach line.40 1.00

1988 Maxx Myrtle Beach

This was Maxx's first attempt at producing a mass-market racing product. The Myrtle Beach (First Edition) set contains 100 cards including a Cover Card and four checklists. The set was initially introduced at the 1988 Coca Cola 600 in Charlotte. The Myrtle Beach name was attached to this set due to the printer's notation on the four checklists. The 100 standard sized cards comprising this set were issued in complete factory sets which were made available to collectors for the price of $19.95 through an offer on the cover cards. Ten-card shrink-wrapped packs were packaged in 44-count boxes and in 1989 Maxx Combo packs which contained three 10-card '88 packs. It is important to note the combo packs contain cards from all three printings of this set. The Cover Card from this set was produced with two different descriptions located in the yellow starburst on the front of the card. The cover card in the factory sets reads "100 Collector cards...", while the cover card in the shrink-wrapped packs shows "10 Collector cards...". The scarce nature of this set is attributable to the ten variations which it contains. Reportedly 10,000 of the Myrtle Beach sets were produced. The cards listed below are the ten Myrtle Beach variations.

COMPLETE SET (100) 75.00 150.00
COMP.FACT.SET (100) 125.00 250.00
1A Cover Card 10 5.00 10.00
1B Cover Card 100 20.00 50.00
10 Talladega Streaks 20.00 50.00
19 Checklist 1 4.00 10.00
with Myrtle Beach line
26 Phil Parsons w/o Marcia 15.00 40.00
36 Checklist 2 4.00 10.00
with Myrtle Beach line
43 Daytona Int. Speedway 5.00 12.00
47 Single File/Dav.Allison's Car 5.00 12.00
59 1988 Begins Daytona 5.00 12.00
69 Checklist 3 4.00 10.00
with Myrtle Beach line
88 Ken Bouchard engaged 5.00 12.00
100 Checklist 4 4.00 10.00
with Myrtle Beach line

1989 Maxx Previews

This ten-card set was produced by Maxx to give collectors a preview of the '89 Maxx release. It consists of two Cover cards and eight unnumbered driver cards. These cards were available in '89 Maxx Combo packs. Each combo pack contained three ten-card packs of '88 Maxx and five '89 Preview cards, one of which was a cover card. These cards were collated so one pack contained one half of the Preview set and the other pack contained the other half of the set. The first Cover card features a starburst design and is considered the toughest of the two. The second Cover card features Bill Elliott's car and can be found with either a checklist back or coupon back good for 100 laps toward the 500 needed for a subscription to Grand National Scene.

COMPLETE SET (10) 6.00 15.00
1 Geoff Bodine .50 1.25
2 Bill Elliott 1.50 4.00
3 Bobby Hillin .60 1.50
4 Sterling Marlin .75 2.00
5 Mark Martin 3.00 8.00
6 Richard Petty 2.50 6.00
7 Rusty Wallace 2.00 5.00
8 Michael Waltrip 1.25 3.00
9 Cover Card A 3.00 6.00
10 Cover Card B CL .30 .75
11 Cover Card B 100-Laps .30 .75

1989 Maxx

This set consists of 220 cards featuring drivers, their cars, team owners, crew chiefs, All-Pro crew members, and all-time greats from the NASCAR circuit. It was made available as a mail order set, commonly referred to as the Toolbox set, as a hobby set, and through wax boxes with 48 12-card wax packs, containing ten regular cards, one cover card, and two sticker cards. The set price includes the corrected version of card number 5, Geoff Bodine. A Winston Cup set containing the first one hundred cards of this set was also produced. It was packaged in a yellow box with red checkerboard squares. This set is commonly known as the "Peak" set since it features a picture of Kyle Petty's Peak Antifreeze sponsored car on the box.

COMPLETE SET (220) 40.00 100.00
COMP.FACT.SET (220) 20.00 50.00
COMP.TOOL BOX SET (220) 40.00 100.00
COMP.PEAK SET (100) 30.00 80.00
WAX BOX 250.00 350.00
1 Ken Bouchard ROY .30 .75
2 Ernie Irvan 1.25 3.00
3 Dale Earnhardt RC 15.00 40.00
4 Rick Wilson .60 1.50
5A Geoff Bodine ERR 5.00 10.00
5B Geoff Bodine COR 4.00 8.00
6 Mark Martin 3.00 8.00
7 Alan Kulwicki 1.50 4.00
8 Bobby Hillin .60 1.50
9 Bill Elliott 1.50 4.00
10 Ken Bouchard .30 .75
11 Terry Labonte 1.50 4.00
12 Bobby Allison 1.00 2.50
13 Robert Gee .75 2.00
14 Harry Hyde RC .75 2.00
15 Brett Bodine .60 1.50
16 Larry Pearson .30 .75
17 Darrell Waltrip 1.25 3.00
18 Barry Dodson RC .75 2.00
19 Bill Stavola RC .75 2.00
Mickey Stavola RC
20 James Lewter RC .75 2.00
21 Neil Bonnett 1.25 3.00
22 Tim Brewer RC .75 2.00
23 Eddie Bierschwale .30 .75
24 Travis Carter RC .75 2.00
25 Ken Schrader 1.25 3.00
26 Ricky Rudd RC 4.00 10.00
27 Rusty Wallace 2.00 5.00
28 Davey Allison 2.00 5.00
29 Dale Jarrett 2.00 5.00
30 Michael Waltrip 1.25 3.00
31 Jim Sauter .60 1.50
32 Todd Parrott RC .75 2.00
33 Harry Gant RC .75 2.00
34 Rodney Combs .60 1.50
35 Tony Glover RC .75 2.00
36 Will Lind RC .75 2.00
37 Cale Yarborough 1.25 3.00
38 Kirk Shelmerdine RC .75 2.00
39 Ted Conder .75 2.00
Felix Sabates RC
40 Raymond Beadle RC .75 2.00
41 Jim Bown RC .75 2.00
42 Kyle Petty RC 3.00 8.00
43 Richard Petty 2.50 6.00
44 Jeff Hammond RC .75 2.00
45 Harry Melling RC .75 2.00
46 Butch Mock RC .75 2.00
Bob Rahilly RC
47 Doug Williams RC .75 2.00
48 Mickey Gibbs .30 .75
49 Darrell Bryant RC .75 2.00
50 Bill Elliott WC Champ 1.50 4.00
51 Walter Bud Moore .30 .75
52 Jimmy Means .30 .75
53 Billy Woodruff RC .75 2.00
54 Rusty Wallace 2.00 5.00
55 Phil Parsons .30 .75
56 Leonard Wood .75 2.00
57 Hut Stricklin .60 1.50
58 Ken Thompson RC .75 2.00
59 Gary Nelson RC .75 2.00
60 D.Earnhardt Pit Champs 6.00 15.00
61 Rick Hendrick RC 1.25 3.00
62 Barry Dodson .75 2.00
63 Roland Wlodyka RC .75 2.00
64 Danny Schiff .75 2.00
Buddy Baker
65 Gale Wilson RC .75 2.00
66 Rick Mast RC .75 2.00
67 Brad Teague .30 .75
68 Derrike Cope .75 2.00
69 Checklist 1-100 .30 .75
70 J.D. McDuffie .60 1.50
71 Dave Marcis .75 2.00
72 Eddie Evans RC .75 2.00
73 Phil Barkdoll .30 .75
74 Ernie Elliott RC .75 2.00
75 Morgan Shepherd .75 2.00
76 Dale Inman RC .75 2.00
77 Junior Johnson .75 2.00
78 David Smith RC .75 2.00
79 Jimmy Fennig RC .75 2.00
80 Jimmy Horton .30 .75
81 Mike Beam RC .75 2.00
82 Jimmy Makar RC .75 2.00
83 Lake Speed .30 .75
84 Mike Alexander RC .75 2.00
85 Dennis Connor RC .75 2.00
86 Mike Hill RC .75 2.00
87 Richard Childress .75 2.00
88 Greg Sacks .60 1.50
89 Waddell Wilson RC .75 2.00
90 Chad Little RC 1.50 4.00
91 Norman Koshimizu RC .75 2.00
92 Harold Elliott RC .75 2.00
93 Cliff Champion RC .75 2.00
94 Sterling Marlin .75 2.00
95 Trevor Boys .30 .75
96 Howard Poston (Slick) RC .75 2.00
97 Jake Elder RC .75 2.00
98 Chuck Rider RC .75 2.00
99 Connie Saylor .30 .75
100 Bill Elliott FF 1.50 4.00
101 Richard Petty's Car YR 1.00 2.50
102 D.Earn./Bonnett Cars YR 2.50 6.00
103 N.Bonnett/Kulwicki Cars YR .60 1.50
104 Motorcraft Quality Parts 500 YR.30 .75
105 Lake Speed in Pits YR .12 .30
106 Bill Elliott's Car YR .60 1.50
107 First Union 400 YR .40 1.00
108 Dale Earnhardt's Car YR 2.50 6.00
109 Winston 500 YR .40 1.00
110 Coca Cola 400 YR .30 .75
111 Harry Gant in Pits YR .75 2.00
112 Budweiser 400 YR .30 .75
113 Davey Allison's Car YR .75 2.00
114 A.Kulwi/R.Wall Cars YR .75 2.00
115 Bill Elliott/R.Wilson Cars YR .60 1.50
116 Sterling Marlin's Car YR .30 .75
117 Talladega Diehard 500 YR .40 1.00
118 Neil Bonnett's Car YR .50 1.25
119 Davey Allison's Car YR .75 2.00
120 Busch 500 YR .30 .75
121 Dale Earnhardt's Car YR 2.50 6.00
122 Geoff Bodine's Car YR .20 .50
123 Bill Elliott in Pits YR .60 1.50
124 Davey Allison's Car YR .75 2.00
125 Waltrip/Marlin/Elliott
R.Wallace Cars YR .75 2.00
126 Holly Farms 400 YR .30 .75
127 Kul/Elliott/R.Wall
D.Allis/Martin Cars YR 1.25 3.00
128 Checker 500 YR .30 .75
129 Bill Elliott in Pits YR .60 1.50
130 The Winston YR .30 .75
131 Benny Parsons/Phil Parsons 1.25 3.00
132 Tommy Houston RC .75 2.00
133 Kenny Bernstein RC 1.25 3.00
134 Jack Roush RC 1.25 3.00
135 Rob Moroso RC .75 2.00
136 Les Richter RC .75 2.00
137 Dick Beaty RC .75 2.00
138 Harold Kinder RC .75 2.00
139 Checklist 101-160 .40 1.00
140 D.Waltrip/Mich.Waltrip 1.25 3.00
141 Bobby Allison VL 1.00 2.50
142 Neil Bonnett VL 1.25 3.00
143 Neil Bonnett VL 1.25 3.00
144 D.Earnhardt w/Crew VL 6.00 15.00
145 Lake Speed VL .30 .75
146 Bill Elliott VL 1.50 4.00
147 Terry Labonte VL 1.50 4.00
148 D.Earnhardt/Teresa VL 6.00 15.00
149 Phil Parsons VL .30 .75
150 Darrell Waltrip VL 1.25 3.00
151 Bill Elliott VL 1.50 4.00
152 Rusty Wallace VL 2.00 5.00
153 Geoff Bodine VL .50 1.25
154 Rusty Wallace VL 2.00 5.00
155 Bill Elliott VL 1.50 4.00
156 Bill Elliott VL 1.50 4.00
157 Ken Schrader VL 1.25 3.00
158 Ricky Rudd VL 4.00 10.00
159 Davey Allison VL 2.00 5.00
160 Dale Earnhardt VL 4.00 10.00
161 Bill Elliott w/Crew VL 1.50 4.00
162 Davey Allison VL 2.00 5.00
163 Bill Elliott VL 1.50 4.00
164 Darrell Waltrip VL 1.25 3.00
165 Rusty Wallace VL 2.00 5.00
166 Rusty Wallace VL 2.00 5.00
167 Rusty Wallace VL 2.00 5.00
168 Alan Kulwicki VL 1.50 4.00
169 Rusty Wallace VL 2.00 5.00
170 Terry Labonte/J.Johnson VL 1.50 4.00
171 Sterling Marlin VL .75 2.00
172 Tommy Ellis RC .75 2.00
173 Billy Hagan RC .75 2.00
174 Rod Osterlund RC .75 2.00
175 Elton Sawyer RC .75 2.00
176 Robert Yates RC .75 2.00
177 Ed Berrier RC .75 2.00
178 Kenny Wallace RC 1.50 4.00
179 Joe Thurman RC .75 2.00
180 Davey Allison/B.Allison 2.00 5.00
181 Richard Petty's Car C 1.00 2.50
182 Smokey Yunick C .30 .75

183 Ralph Moody's Car C .30 .75
184 Donnie Allison C RC .75 2.00
185 Marvin Panch/Johnny Allen carsC.75 2.00
186 Fred Lorenzen C RC .75 2.00
187 Wendell Scott's Car C .12 .30
188 Curtis Turner C .75 2.00
189 Asheville-Weaverville C .30 .75
190 Junior Johnson
Chris Economaki C .75 2.00
191 Darel Dieringer's Car C .12 .30
192 Marvin Panch C .75 2.00
193 R.Petty/J.Smith Cars C 1.00 2.50
194 David Pearson C 2.50 6.00
195 Talladega '70 C .30 .75
196 Tim Flock In Car C .75 2.00
197 Fireball Roberts' Car C .50 1.25
198 Bobby Isaac C .30 .75
199 Wood Bros. '67 C .12 .30
200 Ned Jarrett C .75 2.00
201 Jack Ingram .75 2.00
202 G.Bodine/B.Bodine .60 1.50
203 Elmo Langley RC .75 2.00
204 Steve Grissom RC .75 2.00
205 Ronald Cooper RC .75 2.00
206 Tim Morgan/Larry McClure Team.30 .75
207 Ronnie Silver RC .75 2.00
208 Jimmy Spencer RC 2.00 5.00
209 Ben Hess RC .75 2.00
210 R.Wallace/Ken.Wallace 2.00 5.00
211 Bob Whitcomb RC .75 2.00
212 Billy Standridge RC .75 2.00
213 Glen Wood .30 .75
214 L.D. Ottinger RC .75 2.00
215 David Pearson RC 2.50 6.00
216 Patty Moise RC 1.25 3.00
217 Checklist 162-220 .30 .75
218 Chuck Bown RC .75 2.00
219 Jimmy Hensley RC .75 2.00
220 R.Petty/Kyle Petty 3.00 8.00

1989 Maxx Stickers

Inserted two per pack in 1989 Maxx, each sticker card features two removable sticker flags. Each flag contains a colored number representing a race car number. The sticker cards are not numbered individually, but have been assigned card numbers below in the order of the left flag number.

COMPLETE SET (20) 25.00 50.00
1 2/33 1.25 3.00
2 3/52 1.25 3.00
3 4/42 1.25 3.00
4 5/43 1.25 3.00
5 6/84 1.25 3.00
6 7/55 1.25 3.00
7 8/57 1.25 3.00
8 9/71 1.25 3.00
9 11/88 1.25 3.00
10 12/68 1.25 3.00
11 15/3 1.25 3.00
12 16/75 1.25 3.00
13 17/83 1.25 3.00
14 21/17 1.25 3.00
15 25/33 1.25 3.00
16 26/43 1.25 3.00
17 27/94 1.25 3.00
18 28/5 1.25 3.00
19 29/27 1.25 3.00
20 30/9 1.25 3.00

1989 Maxx Crisco

This 25-card set contains one Cover card, and 24 driver cards. It was produced by Maxx and distributed by Proctor and Gamble as a complete set. They were given away with a purchase of their product in selected stores throughout the country. They were kept in a floor standup display, featuring Greg Sacks, that held 96 sets. It is reported that one million sets were produced. Two weeks after these sets were shipped to Proctor and Gamble, Greg Sacks parted company with his car owner Buddy Baker and a large portion of these sets were destroyed. However, many of these sets found their way into the hobby through closeout sales.

COMPLETE SET (25) 5.00 12.00
1 Greg Sacks .30 .75
2 Darrell Waltrip .60 1.50
3 Ken Schrader .60 1.50
4 Bill Elliott .75 2.00
5 Rusty Wallace 1.00 2.50
6 Dale Earnhardt 3.00 8.00
7 Terry Labonte .75 2.00
8 Geoff Bodine .25 .60
9 Brett Bodine .30 .75
10 Davey Allison 1.00 2.50
11 Ricky Rudd 2.00 5.00
12 Kyle Petty 1.50 4.00
13 Alan Kulwicki .75 2.00
14 Neil Bonnett .60 1.50
15 Rick Wilson .30 .75
16 Harry Gant .40 1.00
17 Richard Petty 1.25 3.00
18 Phil Parsons .15 .40
19 Sterling Marlin .40 1.00
20 Bobby Hillin .30 .75
21 Michael Waltrip .60 1.50
22 Dale Jarrett 1.00 2.50
23 Morgan Shepherd .40 1.00
24 Greg Sacks w/Car .30 .75
NNO Header Card .15 .40

1990 Maxx

This 200-card set was produced in three different print runs. It was distributed in four different factory sets. The "tin box" set was sold by Maxx through a mail order offer for $29.95, and contains cards from the first printing. The cards from these sets have a glossy finish. The second of the sets was the white box Hobby set distributed to authorized Maxx dealers containing cards from the first printing. The third of the sets was the red/white box Hobby set which contains cards from the second printing. In the second printing four error cards were corrected: number 8 Bobby Hillin, number 28 Davey Allison, number 39 Kirk Shelmerdine, and number 97 Chuck Bown. The fourth of these sets was the red/yellow Hobby set which contains cards from the third printing. In the third printing three error cards were corrected:number 13 Mickey Gibbs, number 69 Checklist, and number 85 Larry McClure. Cards from all three printings of this set were also distributed in wax packs. The packs are distinguishable by the lettering on the bottom of them. Packs from the first printing have white lettering, packs from the second printing have black lettering, and packs form the third printing also have black lettering and have the roman numeral three under the lettering. It is important to note that because of the black borders on these cards they are susceptible to chipping.

COMPLETE SET (200) 10.00 25.00
COMP.FACT.WHITE (200) 12.50 30.00
COMP.FACT.RED/WHT (200) 12.50 30.00
COMP.FACT.RED/YELL (200) 12.50 30.00
1 Terry Labonte 2.00 5.00
2 Ernie Irvan 1.50 4.00
3 Dale Earnhardt 6.00 15.00
4 Phil Parsons .40 1.00
5 Ricky Rudd 1.50 4.00
6 Mark Martin 4.00 10.00
7 Alan Kulwicki 2.00 5.00
8A Bobby Hillin ERR .75 2.00
8B Bobby Hillin COR .75 2.00
9 Bill Elliott 2.00 5.00
10 Derrike Cope 1.00 2.50
11 Geoff Bodine .60 1.50
12 Bobby Allison 1.25 3.00
13A Mickey Gibbs ERR 2.50 6.00
13B Mickey Gibbs COR .75 2.00
14 A.J. Foyt 1.50 4.00
15 Morgan Shepherd 1.00 2.50
16 Larry Pearson .40 1.00
17 Darrell Waltrip 1.50 4.00
18 Cale Yarborough 1.50 4.00
19 Barry Dodson 1.00 2.50
20 Bob Whitcomb .40 1.00
21 Neil Bonnett 1.50 4.00
22 Rob Moroso .40 1.00
23 Eddie Bierschwale .40 1.00
24 Cliff Champion .40 1.00
25 Ken Schrader 1.50 4.00
26 Brett Bodine .60 1.50
27 Rusty Wallace 2.50 6.00
28A Davey Allison ERR 4.00 10.00
28B Davey Allison COR 4.00 10.00
29 Dale Jarrett 2.50 6.00
30 Michael Waltrip 1.25 3.00
31 Jim Sauter .75 2.00
32 Tony Glover .40 1.00
33 Harry Gant 1.50 4.00
34 Rodney Combs .75 2.00
35 Jimmy Fennig .40 1.00
36 Raymond Beadle .40 1.00
37 Buddy Parrott RC 1.00 2.50
38 Brandon Baker RC 1.00 2.50
39A Kirk Shelmerdine ERR 2.50 6.00
39B Kirk Shelmerdine COR 1.25 3.00
40 Jim Phillips RC 1.00 2.50
41 Jim Bown .40 1.00
42 Kyle Petty 2.00 5.00
43 Richard Petty 3.00 8.00
44 Bob Tullius RC 1.00 2.50
45 Richard Childress 1.00 2.50
46 Steve Hmiel RC 1.00 2.50
47 Ronnie Silver .40 1.00
48 Greg Sacks .75 2.00
49 Tony Spanos RC 1.00 2.50
50 Darrell Waltrip Pit Champs 1.50 4.00
51 Junie Donlavey RC 1.00 2.50
52 Jimmy Means .40 1.00
53 Mike Beam .40 1.00
54 Jack Roush 1.00 2.50
55 Felix Sabates 1.00 2.50
56 Ted Conder RC 1.00 2.50
57 Hut Stricklin .75 2.00
58 Ken Ragan .40 1.00
59 Ronald Cooper .40 1.00
60 Jeff Hammond 1.00 2.50
61 Elton Sawyer .40 1.00
62 Leo Jackson RC 1.00 2.50
63 Rick Hendrick 1.00 2.50
64 Dale Inman .40 1.00
65 Travis Carter .40 1.00
66 Dick Trickle RC 1.50 4.00
67 Brad Teague .40 1.00
68 Richard Broome RC 1.00 2.50
69A Checklist A ERR 1.40 4.00
69B Checklist A COR .40 1.00
70 J.D. McDuffie .75 2.00
71 Dave Marcis .75 2.00
72 Harry Melling .40 1.00
73 Phil Barkdoll .40 1.00
74 Leonard Wood .40 1.00
75 Rick Wilson .40 1.00
76 Gary Nelson .40 1.00
77A Ben Hess ERR 2.50 6.00
77B Ben Hess COR .40 1.00
78 Larry McReynolds RC 1.00 2.50
79 Darrell Bryant .40 1.00
80 Jimmy Horton .40 1.00
81 Kenny Bernstein 1.00 2.50
82 Doug Richert RC 1.00 2.50
83 Lake Speed .40 1.00
84 Mike Alexander .40 1.00
85A Larry McClure ERR Tim 1.25 3.00
85B Larry McClure COR 1.25 3.00
86 Robin Pemberton RC 1.00 2.50
87 Waddell Wilson .40 1.00
88 Jimmy Spencer 1.00 2.50
89 Rod Osterlund .40 1.00
90 Stan Barrett RC 1.00 2.50
91 Tommy Ellis .40 1.00
92 Danny Schiff RC 1.00 2.50
93 Buddy Baker 1.00 2.50
94 Sterling Marlin 1.00 2.50
95 Kenny Wallace 1.00 2.50
96 Tim Brewer .40 1.00
97A Chuck Bown ERR Brown 2.50 6.00
97B Chuck Bown COR Bown .60 1.50
98 Butch Miller RC 1.00 2.50
99 Connie Saylor .40 1.00
100 Darrell Waltrip FF 1.50 4.00
101 Dan Ford RC 1.00 2.50
102 Howard Poston Slick .40 1.00
103 David Evans .40 1.00
104 Harold Elliott .40 1.00
105 Ken Thompson .40 1.00
106 Robert Gee 1.00 2.50
107 James Lewter .40 1.00
108 Will Lind .40 1.00
109 Jerry Schweitz RC 1.00 2.50
110 Eddie Wood RC 1.00 2.50
111 Norman Koshimizu .40 1.00
112 Barry Dodson 1.00 2.50
113 Mike Hill .40 1.00
114 Jimmy Makar .40 1.00
115 Barry Dodson 1.00 2.50
116 Dale Earnhardt AP 6.00 15.00
117 Junior Johnson 1.00 2.50
118 Shawna Robinson RC 2.00 5.00
119 Richard Jackson RC 1.00 2.50
120 Chad Little 1.00 2.50
121 Chuck Rider .40 1.00
122 L.D. Ottinger .40 1.00
123 Dennis Connor .40 1.00
124 Ken Bouchard .40 1.00
125 Jimmy Hensley .40 1.00
126 Robert Yates 1.00 2.50
127 Doug Williams .40 1.00
128 Mark Stahl .40 1.00
129 Rick Mast .40 1.00
130 Walter Bud Moore .40 1.00
131 David Pearson 2.00 5.00
132 Paul Andrews RC 1.00 2.50
133 Tommy Houston .40 1.00
134 Jack Pennington RC 1.00 2.50
135 Billy Hagan .40 1.00
136 Joe Thurman .40 1.00
137A Bill Ingle ERR Billy 2.50 6.00
137B Bill Ingle COR Bill .60 1.50
138 Patty Moise 1.00 2.50
139 Glen Wood .40 1.00
140 Billy Standridge .40 1.00
141 Harry Hyde .40 1.00
142 Steve Grissom .40 1.00
143 Bob Rahilly .40 1.00
144 Butch Mock .40 1.00
145 Ernie Elliott .40 1.00
146 Les Richter .40 1.00
147 Dick Beaty .40 1.00
148 Harold Kinder .40 1.00
149 Elmo Langley .40 1.00
150 Dick Trickle ROY 1.50 4.00
151 Bobby Hamilton RC 1.50 4.00
152 Jack Ingram 1.00 2.50
153 Bill Stavola .40 1.00
154 Bob Jenkins RC 1.00 2.50
155 Ned Jarrett .75 2.00
156 Benny Parsons 1.50 4.00
157 Jerry Punch RC 1.00 2.50
158 Ken Squier RC 1.00 2.50
159 Chris Economaki RC 1.00 2.50
160 Jack Arute RC 1.00 2.50
161 Dick Berggren RC 1.00 2.50
162 Mike Joy RC 1.00 2.50
163 Barney Hall RC 1.00 2.50
164 Eli Gold RC 1.00 2.50
165 Dick Brooks RC 1.00 2.50
166 Winston Kelley RC 1.00 2.50
167 Darrell Waltrip YR 1.50 4.00
168 Rusty Wallace
Darrell Waltrip Cars YR 2.50 6.00
169 Sterling Marlin's Car YR 1.00 2.50
170 Pontiac 400 YR .40 1.00
171 Harry Gant YR 1.50 4.00
172 Bill Elliott/Bobby Hillin Cars YR 2.00 5.00
173 First Union 400 YR .40 1.00
174 Darrell Waltrip YR 1.50 4.00
175 Davey Allison YR 2.50 6.00
176 Sterling Marlin YR 1.00 2.50
177 Darrell Waltrip's Car YR 1.50 4.00
178 Darrell Waltrip YR 1.50 4.00
179 D.Earnhardt/Teresa YR 6.00 15.00
180 Banquet Foods 300 YR .40 1.00
181 Terry Labonte YR 2.00 5.00
182 Bill Elliott YR 2.00 5.00
183 Earnhardt/R.Wilson
Shepherd/Schrader Cars 6.00 15.00
184 Bill Elliott YR 2.00 5.00
185 DW/T.Lab/Martin/Jarrett Cars YR 4.00 10.00
186 Bud At The Glen YR .40 1.00
187 Rusty Wallace's Car YR 2.50 6.00
188 Busch 500 YR .40 1.00
189 Heinz Southern 500 YR .40 1.00
190 Rusty Wallace YR 2.50 6.00
191 Dale Earnhardt's Car YR 6.00 15.00
192 Richard Petty/Kyle Petty Cars YR 3.00 8.00
193 Richard Childress YR 1.00 2.50
194 Michael Waltrip
Phil Parsons Cars YR 1.25 3.00
195 D.Earnhardt/M.Martin Cars YR 6.00 15.00
196 Rusty Wallace's Car YR 2.50 6.00
197 Rusty Wallace in Pits YR 2.50 6.00
198 Rusty Wallace YR 2.50 6.00
199 Checklist B .40 1.00
200 Checklist C .40 1.00

1990 Maxx Glossy

COMP.GLOSSY TIN (200) 30.00 60.00
*GLOSSY: 1X TO 2.5X BASIC CARDS

1990 Maxx Bill Elliott Vortex Comics

This set was actually issued as a 4-card panel inside Vortex Comics' Legends of NASCAR Bill Elliott comic book. The cards are most often found attached as a panel of four and utilize the same card design found in the regular issue 1990 Maxx set.

COMPLETE SET (4) 1.50 4.00
COMMON CARD (E1-E4) .40 1.00
E1 Bill Elliott .40 1.00

1990 Maxx Holly Farms

This is a 30-card set produced by Maxx and distributed by Holly Farms. It consists of 30 driver cards and one prize card, which was for a contest to win a trip to the 1991 Daytona 500. It was distributed as a 30-card set packaged in cello-wrap and given only to Holly Farms employees. As part of a Holly Farms promotion, three-card packs were produced and made available to the public in exchange for proof of purchase.seals from Holly Farm products. These cards are distinguishable from regular 1990 Maxx cards by a red, yellow, and black Holly Farms logo located in the upper right hand corner of the card.

COMPLETE SET (30) 6.00 15.00
HF1 Dale Earnhardt 2.00 5.00
HF2 Bill Elliott .60 1.50
HF3 Darrell Waltrip .50 1.25
HF4 Rusty Wallace .75 2.00
HF5 Ken Schrader .50 1.25
HF6 Richard Petty 1.00 2.50
HF7 Harry Gant .50 1.25
HF8 Mark Martin 1.25 3.00
HF9 Davey Allison .75 2.00
HF10 Neil Bonnett .50 1.25
HF11 Alan Kulwicki .60 1.50
HF12 Terry Labonte .60 1.50
HF13 Ricky Rudd .50 1.25
HF14 Geoff Bodine .20 .50
HF15 Sterling Marlin .30 .75
HF16 Morgan Shepherd .30 .75
HF17 Kyle Petty .60 1.50
HF18 Michael Waltrip .40 1.00
HF19 Phil Parsons .12 .30
HF20 Dale Jarrett .75 2.00
HF21 Brett Bodine .20 .50
HF22 Lake Speed .12 .30
HF23 Ernie Irvan .50 1.25
HF24 Junior Johnson .30 .75
HF25 Cale Yarborough .50 1.25
HF26 Bobby Allison .40 1.00
HF27 Derrike Cope .30 .75
HF28 Bobby Hillin .25 .60
HF29 Benny Parsons .50 1.25
HF30 Ned Jarrett .25 .60

1991 Maxx

This 240-card set was distributed in two different factory sets and in 15-card wax packs. The front of these cards have a black outer border, two shades of blue for the inner border and the drivers' name boxed in yellow at the bottom of the card. The "Deluxe" mail order set contains 240 cards from the regular set , the 20-card Winston Acrylic set, and the 48-card Maxx Update set. The standard hobby factory set is packaged in a blue, shrink-wrapped box with Richard Petty and Bill Elliott cards visible. A special version of this set containing a Bill Elliott autograph card was available through the J.C.Penney catalog. Card number 200 incorrectly lists Davey Allison's points as 4,423 instead of 3,423, a corrected version was not produced.

COMPLETE SET (240) 10.00 25.00
COMP.FACT.SET (240) 12.50 30.00
COMP.MAIL ORDER (308) 20.00 40.00
COMP.JC PENNEY SET (241) 20.00 40.00
WAX BOX 12.50 30.00
1 Rick Mast .12 .30
2 Rusty Wallace .50 1.25
3 Dale Earnhardt 1.25 3.00
4 Ernie Irvan .30 .75
5 Ricky Rudd .30 .75
6 Mark Martin .50 1.25
7 Alan Kulwicki .40 1.00
8 Rick Wilson .12 .30
9 Bill Elliott .40 1.00
10 Derrike Cope .20 .50
11 Geoff Bodine .12 .30
12 Hut Stricklin .12 .30
13 Ken Bouchard .12 .30
14 A.J. Foyt .20 .50
15 Morgan Shepherd .20 .50
16 Joey Knuckles RC .20 .50
17 Darrell Waltrip .30 .75
18 Greg Sacks .12 .30
19 Chad Little .20 .50
20 Jimmy Hensley .12 .30
21 Dale Jarrett .30 .75
22 Sterling Marlin .20 .50
23 Eddie Bierschwale .12 .30
24 Mickey Gibbs .12 .30
25 Ken Schrader .12 .30
26 Brett Bodine .12 .30
27 Bobby Allison .25 .60
28 Davey Allison .50 1.25
29 Jeff Hammond .20 .50
30 Michael Waltrip .25 .60
31 Jim Sauter .12 .30
32 Cale Yarborough .30 .75
33 Harry Gant .20 .50
34 Jimmy Makar .12 .30
35 Robert Yates .20 .50
36 Neil Bonnett .30 .75
37 Rick Hendrick .20 .50
38 Harry Hyde .12 .30
39 Kenny Wallace .20 .50
40 Tom Kendall .12 .30
41 Larry Pearson .12 .30
42 Kyle Petty .40 1.00
43 Richard Petty .60 1.50
44 Jimmy Horton .12 .30
45 Mike Beam .12 .30
46 Walter Bud Moore .12 .30
47 Jack Pennington .12 .30
48 James Hylton .12 .30
49 Rodney Combs .12 .30
50 Bill Elliott Pit Champs .40 1.00
51 Jeff Purvis RC .20 .50
52 Jimmy Means .12 .30
53 Bobby Labonte RC 2.50 6.00
54 Richard Childress .20 .50
55 Billy Hagan .12 .30
56 Bill Ingle RC .20 .50
57 Jim Bown .12 .30
58 Ken Ragan .12 .30
59 Larry McReynolds .20 .50
60 Jack Roush .20 .50
61 Phil Parsons .12 .30
62 Harry Melling .12 .30
63 Barry Dodson .12 .30
64 Tony Glover .12 .30
65 Tommy Houston .12 .30
66 Dick Trickle .12 .30
67 Cliff Champion .12 .30
68 Bobby Hamilton .20 .50
69 Gary Nelson .12 .30
70 J.D. McDuffie .12 .30
71 Dave Marcis .15 .40
72 Ernie Elliott .12 .30
73 Phil Barkdoll .12 .30
74 Junie Donlavey .12 .30
75 Chuck Rider .12 .30
76 Ben Hess .12 .30
77 Steve Hmiel .12 .30
78 Felix Sabates .20 .50
79 Tim Brewer .12 .30
80 Tim Morgan .12 .30
81 Larry McClure .12 .30
82 Mark Stahl .12 .30
83 Lake Speed .12 .30
84 Waddell Wilson .12 .30
85 Mike Alexander .12 .30
86 Robin Pemberton .12 .30
87 Junior Johnson .20 .50
88 Leonard Wood .12 .30
89 Kenny Bernstein .12 .30
90 Buddy Baker .15 .40
91 Patty Moise .20 .50
92 Elton Sawyer .12 .30
93 Bob Whitcomb .12 .30
94 Terry Labonte .20 .50
95 Raymond Beadle .12 .30
96 Kirk Shelmerdine .12 .30
97 Chuck Bown .12 .30
98 Jimmy Spencer .20 .50
99 Bobby Hillin .12 .30
100 Rob Moroso ROY .12 .30
101 Rod Osterlund .12 .30
102 Les Richter .12 .30
103 Jimmy Fennig .12 .30
104 Doyle Ford RC .20 .50
105 Elmo Langley .12 .30
106 Richard Jackson .12 .30
107 Jimmy Cox RC .20 .50
108 Dick Beaty .12 .30
109 Kyle Petty's Car MM .40 1.00
110 Bob Tullius .12 .30
111 Buddy Parrott .12 .30
112 H.B. Bailey RC .20 .50
113 Martin/G.Bodine
Marlin/Irvan Cars MM .50 1.25
114 Billy Standridge .12 .30
115 Doug Williams .12 .30
116 Tracy Leslie RC .20 .50
117 Donnie Allison .15 .40
118 Michael Waltrip Crash MM .25 .60
119 Ed Berrier .12 .30
120 Travis Carter .12 .30
121 Dennis Connor .12 .30
122 Richard Petty
Rob Moroso Crash MM .60 1.50
123 Ward Burton RC 1.25 3.00
124 Bob Rahilly .12 .30
125 Butch Mock .12 .30
126 Robin Pemberton .12 .30
127 Michael Waltrip/D.Cope Cars MM.25 .60
128 Donnie Wingo RC .20 .50
129 Darrell Bryant .12 .30
130 Mike McLaughlin RC .20 .50
131 Robbie Loomis RC .30 .75
132 Charlie Glotzbach RC .20 .50
133 Dave Rezendes RC .20 .50
134 Davey Johnson RC .20 .50
135 Paul Andrews .12 .30
136 Daytona MM .07 .20
137 The Racestoppers .07 .20
138 Jack Ingram .20 .50
139 Joe Nemechek RC .50 1.25
140 G.Bodine/K.Petty/Irvan Cars MM.40 1.00
141 Jeffrey Ellis .20 .50
142 Butch Miller .12 .30
143 Bill Venturini RC .20 .50
144 Richard Broome .12 .30
145 Alan Kulwicki in Pits MM .40 1.00
146 Dave Mader RC .20 .50
147 Robert Pressley RC .20 .50
148 Steve Loyd RC .20 .50
149 Ricky Pearson .20 .50
150 Darrell Waltrip FF .30 .75
151 Don Bierschwale RC .20 .50
152 Leo Jackson .12 .30
153 Tommy Ellis .12 .30
154 Randy Baker RC .20 .50
155 Bill Stavola .12 .30
156 D.K. Ulrich RC .20 .50
157 L.D. Ottinger .12 .30
158 Phoenix MM .07 .20
159 Glen Wood/Eddie
Wood/Len Wood .12 .30
160 Andy Petree RC .20 .50
161 Steve Grissom .12 .30
162 Dale Inman .12 .30
163 Charlotte Speedway MM .07 .20
164 Dick Moroso RC .20 .50
165 Doug Richert .12 .30
166 Peter Sospenzo RC .20 .50
167 Chuck Bown MM .12 .30
168 Sandi Fix Miss Winston .12 .30
169 David Pearson .40 1.00
170 Derrike Cope YR .20 .50
171 Mark Martin YR .50 1.25
172 Kyle Petty YR .40 1.00
173 Dale Earnhardt YR 1.25 3.00
174 Dale Earnhardt YR 1.25 3.00
175 Davey Allison/B.Allison YR .50 1.25
176 Brett Bodine YR .12 .30
177 Geoff Bodine YR .12 .30
178 Dale Earnhardt YR 1.25 3.00
179 Dale Earnhardt YR 1.25 3.00
180 Rusty Wallace YR .50 1.25
181 Derrike Cope YR .20 .50
182 Rusty Wallace YR .50 1.25
183 Harry Gant YR .20 .50
184 Dale Earnhardt YR 1.25 3.00
185 Dale Earnhardt YR 1.25 3.00
186 Geoff Bodine YR .12 .30
187 Dale Earnhardt YR 1.25 3.00
188 Ricky Rudd YR .30 .75
189 Mark Martin YR .50 1.25
190 Ernie Irvan YR .30 .75
191 Dale Earnhardt/Teresa YR 1.25 3.00
192 Dale Earnhardt/Teresa YR 1.25 3.00
193 Bill Elliott YR .40 1.00
194 Geoff Bodine YR .12 .30
195 Mark Martin YR .50 1.25
196 Davey Allison YR .50 1.25
197 Alan Kulwicki YR .40 1.00
198 Dale Earnhardt YR 1.25 3.00
199 Morgan Shepherd YR .20 .50
200 Dale Earnhardt/Teresa YR UER 1.25 3.00
201 Jeff Burton RC 2.00 5.00
202 Larry Hedrick RC .20 .50
203 Todd Bodine RC .20 .50
204 Tom Peck RC .20 .50
205 Kirk Shelmerdine .12 .30
206 David Smith .12 .30
207 Darrell Andrews RC .20 .50
208 Danny Lawrence RC .20 .50
209 Mike Hill .12 .30
210 Norman Koshimizu .12 .30

211 James Lewter .12 .30
212 Will Lind .12 .30
213 Cecil Gordon RC .20 .50
214 Howard Poston .12 .30
215 Eddie Lanier RC .20 .50
216 Troy Martin RC .20 .50
217 Bobby Moody RC .20 .50
218 Henry Benfield RC .20 .50
219 Kirk Shelmerdine .12 .30
220 Dale Earnhardt AP 1.25 3.00
221 Jack Arute .12 .30
222 Dick Berggren .12 .30
223 Dick Brooks .12 .30
224 Chris Economaki .12 .30
225 Eli Gold .12 .30
226 Barney Hall .12 .30
227 Ned Jarrett .15 .40
228 Bob Jenkins .12 .30
229 Mike Joy .12 .30
230 Winston Kelley .12 .30
231 Benny Parsons .30 .75
232 Jim Phillips .12 .30
233 Jerry Punch .12 .30
234 Ken Squier .12 .30
235 Bobby Dotter RC .20 .50
236 Jake Elder .12 .30
237 Checklist 1-60 .07 .20
238 Checklist 61-120 .07 .20
239 Checklist 121-180 .07 .20
240 Checklist 181-240 .07 .20
P1 Bill Elliott Promo 15.00 40.00

1991 Maxx The Winston Acrylics

This 20-card set was distributed as a complete set in the '91 Maxx mail order set and was randomly inserted into '91 Maxx wax packs. They were produced on laser-etched acrylic and are relatively thin when compared to a standard card. Widespread reports show that many of the mail order sets did not contain all of the cards in this set. The cards are unnumbered and have been listed below in alphabetical order.

COMPLETE SET (20) 6.00 15.00
1 Davey Allison 1.00 2.50
2 Brett Bodine .25 .60
3 Geoff Bodine .25 .60
4 Derrike Cope .40 1.00
5 Dale Earnhardt 2.50 6.00
6 Bill Elliott .75 2.00
7 Harry Gant .40 1.00
8 Bobby Hillin .25 .60
9 Alan Kulwicki .75 2.00
10 Terry Labonte .40 1.00
11 Mark Martin 1.00 2.50
12 Phil Parsons .25 .60
13 Kyle Petty .75 2.00
14 Ricky Rudd .60 1.50
15 Ken Schrader .25 .60
16 Morgan Shepherd .40 1.00
17 Lake Speed .25 .60
18 Dick Trickle .25 .60
19 Rusty Wallace 1.00 2.50
20 Darrell Waltrip .60 1.50

1991 Maxx Update

Richard Childress

This 48-card set was distributed in 1991 Maxx "Deluxe" mail order sets and foil packs from the second printing. It was also It contains 33 corrected cards from the 1991 Maxx set and 15 updated cards of drivers such as Dale Earnhardt, Ernie Irvan, Mark Martin, Alan Kulwicki, Richard Petty, and Bobby Labonte.

COMPLETE SET (48) 4.00 10.00
1 Rick Mast .12 .30
3 Dale Earnhardt 1.25 3.00
4 Ernie Irvan .30 .75
5 Ricky Rudd .30 .75
6 Mark Martin .50 1.25
7 Alan Kulwicki .40 1.00
8 Rick Wilson .12 .30
9 Bill Elliott .40 1.00
11 Geoff Bodine .12 .30
12 Hut Stricklin .12 .30
13 Ken Bouchard .12 .30
15 Morgan Shepherd .12 .30
17 Darrell Waltrip .30 .75
22 Sterling Marlin .20 .50
25 Ken Schrader .12 .30
30 Michael Waltrip .25 .60
33 Harry Gant .20 .50
39 Kenny Wallace .20 .50
40 Tom Kendall .12 .30
42 Kyle Petty .40 1.00
43 Richard Petty .60 1.50
49 Rodney Combs .12 .30
50 Bill Elliott Pit Champs .40 1.00
53 Bobby Labonte RC 2.50 6.00
54 Richard Childress .20 .50
57 Jim Bown .12 .30
58 Ken Ragan .12 .30
66 Dick Trickle .12 .30
68 Bobby Hamilton .20 .50
73 Phil Barkdoll .12 .30
83 Lake Speed .12 .30
85 Mike Alexander .12 .30
94 Terry Labonte .20 .50
97 Chuck Bown .12 .30
98 Jimmy Spencer .20 .50
100 Rob Moroso ROY .12 .30
117 Donnie Allison .15 .40
126 Robin Pemberton .12 .30
132 Charlie Glotzbach RC .20 .50
139 Joe Nemechek RC .50 1.25
141 Jeffrey Ellis RC .20 .50
147 Robert Pressley .20 .50
150 Darrell Waltrip FF .30 .75
164 Dick Moroso RC .20 .50
165 Doug Richert .12 .30
200 Dale Earnhardt 1.25 3.00
Teresa YR
220 Dale Earnhardt AP 1.25 3.00
235 Bobby Dotter RC .20 .50

1991 Maxx Bill Elliott Team

This 30-card set features Bill Elliott and members of the Coors-Melling Racing Team. Both versions of the set are virtually identical except for the set name on the cardback and that the Elliott set does not include team owner Harry Melling. His card replaced that of Teresa Alligood. Both sets were offered through Bill Elliott's souvenir program and through Maxx's mail order program. All the cards are unnumbered, but have been assigned numbers according to the listing found on the checklist card.

COMPLETE SET (40) 4.00 10.00
1 Jim Waldrop .12 .30
2 Melvin Turner .12 .30
3 Casey Elliott .12 .30
4 Dan Elliott .12 .30
5 Bill Elliott .40 1.00
6 Diana Pugh .12 .30
7 Bill Elliott's Car .40 1.00
8 Matt Thompson .12 .30
9 Mike Thomas .12 .30
10 Wayne McCord .12 .30
11 Bill Elliott's Pit Crew .40 1.00
Pit Crew Champs
12 Charles Palmer .12 .30
13 Jerry Seabolt .12 .30
14 Denver Harris .12 .30
15 Terron Carver .12 .30
16 Mike Dalrymple .12 .30
17 Alan Palmer .12 .30
18 Michael Rinker .12 .30
19 Doug Shaak .12 .30
20 Bill Elliott .40 1.00
21 Dave Kriska .12 .30
22 Alexis Leras .12 .30
23 Mike Colt .12 .30
24 Chuck Hill .12 .30
25 Glen Blakely .12 .30
26 Tommy Cole .12 .30
27 Clinton Chumbley .12 .30
28 Mike Brandt .12 .30
29 Phil Seabolt .12 .30
30 Ron Brooks .12 .30
31 Johnny Trammell .12 .30
32 Mike Rich .12 .30
33 Mark Gaddis .12 .30
34 Gregory Trammell .12 .30
35 Wayne Hamby .12 .30
36 Dan Palmer .12 .30
37 Teresa Alligood .12 .30
Elliott Team only
38 Ernie Elliott .12 .30
39 Team Shops .40 1.00
40 Cover Checklist Card .07 .20

1991 Maxx Bill Elliott Team Coors/Melling

*COORS/MELLING: .4X TO 1X BASIC CARDS
37 Harry Melling .12 .30
Coors/Melling Team only

1991 Maxx McDonald's

This 31-card set was produced by Maxx and distributed in over 250 McDonald's locations in North Carolina and South Carolina between August 30 and October 24, 1991. Any customer purchasing a Bacon, Egg and Cheese Value Meal or a Big Mac Extra Value Meal was given a five-card cellophane pack. Each pack contained one cover card and four driver cards. It features the top 28 finishers in the 1990 NASCAR Winston Cup points race, one McDonald's All-Star Team card, and one cover card. This set contains eight error cards that were corrected in the middle of the press run. The blue portion of the McDonald's All-Star Racing Team logo is missing from the upper right hand corner of all the error cards. It is important to note that due to the nature of the distribution of these cards that a large portion became available to the hobby.

COMPLETE SET (31) 4.00 10.00
1A Dale Earnhardt ERR 2.50 6.00
1B Dale Earnhardt COR 1.50 4.00
2A Mark Martin ERR 1.00 2.50
2B Mark Martin COR .60 1.50
3A Geoff Bodine ERR .25 .60
3B Geoff Bodine COR .15 .40
4A Bill Elliott ERR .75 2.00
4B Bill Elliott COR .50 1.25
5 Morgan Shepherd .25 .60
6 Rusty Wallace .60 1.50
7 Ricky Rudd .40 1.00
8 Alan Kulwicki .50 1.25
9 Ernie Irvan .40 1.00
10 Ken Schrader .15 .40
11 Kyle Petty .50 1.25
12 Brett Bodine .15 .40
13 Davey Allison .60 1.50
14 Sterling Marlin .25 .60
15 Terry Labonte .25 .60
16 Michael Waltrip .30 .75
17 Harry Gant .25 .60
18 Derrike Cope .25 .60
19 Bobby Hillin .15 .40
20 Darrell Waltrip .40 1.00
21A Dave Marcis ERR .30 .75
21B Dave Marcis COR .20 .50
22A Dick Trickle ERR .25 .60
22B Dick Trickle COR .15 .40
23A Rick Wilson ERR .25 .60
23B Rick Wilson COR .15 .40
24A Jimmy Spencer ERR .40 1.00
24B Jimmy Spencer COR .25 .60
25 Dale Jarrett .40 1.00
26 Richard Petty .75 2.00
27 Rick Mast .15 .40
28 Hut Stricklin .15 .40
29 Jimmy Means .15 .40
30 D.Earnhardt 1.50 4.00
Martin
Elliott
NNO Cover Card .10 .25

1991 Maxx Motorsport

This 40-card set was produced by Maxx for Prospective Marketing International/Ford Motorsport Sportswear. It features the top-ten 1991 Ford race teams and the 1991 Winston Legends champion. It was made available as a sequentially numbered set in orange boxes through the Fall 1992 Ford Motorsport Sportswear and Accessories Catalog. 75,000 of these sets were produced.

COMPLETE SET (40) 6.00 6.00
1 Bill Elliott .50 1.25
2 Davey Allison .60 1.50
3 Wally Dallenbach Jr. .25 .60
4 Sterling Marlin .25 .60
5 Mark Martin .60 1.50
6 Morgan Shepherd .25 .60
7 Alan Kulwicki .50 1.25
8 Dale Jarrett .40 1.00
9 Geoff Bodine .15 .40
10 Chad Little .25 .60
11 Robert Yates .25 .60
12 Jack Roush .25 .60
13 Walter Bud Moore .15 .40
14 Harry Melling .15 .40
15 Wood Brothers .15 .40
16 Junior Johnson .25 .60
17 Chuck Little .15 .40
18 Junie Donlavey .15 .40
19 Larry McReynolds .25 .60
20 Robin Pemberton .15 .40
21 Donnie Wingo .25 .60
22 Mike Beam .15 .40
23 Ernie Elliott .15 .40
24 Paul Andrews .15 .40
25 Leonard Wood .15 .40
26 Harry Hyde .15 .40
27 Tim Brewer .15 .40
28 Davey Allison's Car .25 .60
29 Bill Elliott's Car .20 .50
30 Davey Allison's Car .25 .60
31 Wally Dallenbach Jr.'s Car .10 .25
32 Sterling Marlin's Car .10 .25
33 Mark Martin's Car .25 .60
34 Morgan Shepherd's Car .10 .25
35 Alan Kulwicki's Car .20 .50
36 Dale Jarrett's Car .15 .40
37 Geoff Bodine's Car .05 .15
38 Chad Little's Car .10 .25
39 Elmo Langley .15 .40
Cale Yarborough Cars
40 Wally Dallenbach Jr. w .10 .25
Crew

1991 Maxx Racing for Kids

These three sheets feature six cards on each that are from the 1990 Maxx set. The cards came on uncut sheets and each card has a "Special Edition Racing for Kids" logo in the upper left hand corner. The cards are a parallel to the regular version. The sheets were issued as a promotional insert in Racing For Kids magazine over three months, January, February and March 1991. We've included prices for uncut sheets below with the corresponding individual card numbers after the drivers' name.

COMPLETE SET (3) 30.00 75.00
1 Sheet 1 12.00 30.00
2 Sheet 2 8.00 20.00
3 Sheet 3 10.00 25.00

1991 Maxx Winston 20th Anniversary Foils

This 21-card set was produced to commemorate 20 years of involvement in the NASCAR circuit by the R.J. Reynolds Tobacco Company. It portrays the past Winston Cup Champions on foil-etched cards. This set was made available through multi-pack premium offers on Winston cigarettes and later through the Club Maxx mail order club. The cards are unnumbered and listed in order by year of Winston Cup win.

COMPLETE SET (21) 5.00 8.00
1 Richard Petty 1971 Car .30 .75
2 Richard Petty 1972 Car .30 .75
3 Benny Parsons 1973 Car .15 .40
4 Richard Petty 1974 Car .30 .75
5 Richard Petty 1975 Car .30 .75
6 Cale Yarborough 1976 Car .15 .40
7 Cale Yarborough 1977 Car .15 .40
8 Cale Yarborough 1978 Car .15 .40
9 Richard Petty 1979 Car .30 .75
10 Dale Earnhardt 1980 Car .60 1.50
11 Darrell Waltrip 1981 Car .15 .40
12 Darrell Waltrip 1982 Car .15 .40
13 Bobby Allison 1983 Car .12 .30
14 Terry Labonte 1984 Car .10 .25
15 Darrell Waltrip 1985 Car .15 .40
16 Dale Earnhardt 1986 Car .60 1.50
17 Dale Earnhardt 1987 Car .60 1.50
18 Bill Elliott 1988 Car .20 .50
19 Rusty Wallace 1989 Car .25 .60
20 Dale Earnhardt 1990 Car .60 1.50
NNO Checklist .05 .10

1992 Maxx All-Pro Team

This 50-card set was produced by Maxx for Gargoyle Performance Eyewear. It features every member of the 1991 All-Pro team. The set was made available through speedway vendors and through Maxx's mail order program.

COMPLETE SET (50) 2.00 4.00
1 Dale Earnhardt .75 2.00
2 Harry Gant .07 .20
3 Mark Martin .30 .75
4 Larry McReynolds .10 .25
5 Kirk Shelmerdine .05 .15
6 Tony Glover .05 .15
7 Larry Wallace .10 .25
8 Leo Jackson .05 .15
9 Eddie Lanier .05 .15
10 Harold Stott .10 .25
11 Andy Petree .05 .15
12 Will Lind .05 .15
13 Kirk Shelmerdine .05 .15
14 Doug Richert .05 .15
15 Tim Brewer .05 .15
16 Scott Robinette .05 .15
17 Darrell Andrews .05 .15
18 Todd Parrott .05 .15
19 David Smith .05 .15
20 Charley Pressley .05 .15
21 Gary Brooks .05 .15
22 Norman Koshimizu .05 .15
23 Danny Myers .05 .15
24 Henry Benfield .05 .15
25 Dan Ford .05 .15
26 Paul Andrews .05 .15
27 Mike Hill .05 .15
28 Will Lind .05 .15
29 Mike Thomas .05 .15
30 Shorty Edwards .10 .25
31 Danny Lawrence .05 .15
32 Devin Barbee .10 .25
33 Ronnie Reavis .05 .15
34 Howard Poston (Slick) .05 .15
35 Dan Ford .05 .15
36 Darrell Dunn .10 .25
37 Gale Wilson .05 .15
38 Norman Koshimizu .05 .15
39 Jerry Schweitz .05 .15
40 James Lewter .05 .15
41 Abbie Garwood .10 .25
42 Mark Osborn .10 .25
43 David Little .10 .25
44 Wayne Dalton .05 .15
45 Troy Martin .05 .15
46 Glen Bobo .10 .25
47 Bobby Moody .05 .15
48 David Munari .05 .15
NNO Dale Inman .05 .15
NNO Checklist .05 .10

1992 Maxx Bobby Hamilton

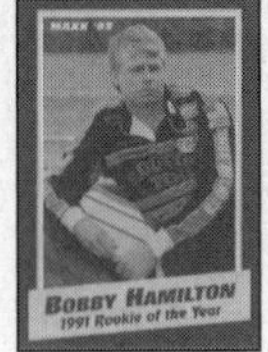

This 16-card set was produced to honor Bobby Hamilton as the Winston Cup 1992 Rookie of the Year. It was distributed as a complete set in one foil pack.

COMPLETE SET (16) 1.25 3.00
BOBBY HAMILTON CARD .10 .30

1992 Maxx Craftsman

This eight-card set was produced by Maxx and distributed by Sears. It features drivers with Craftsman sponsorship. It was only made available to those who ordered a red hobby set from the 1992 Sears Christmas Wish catalog. The unnumbered cards have been listed below alphabetically.

COMPLETE SET (8) 2.00 5.00
1 Geoff Bodine .25 .60
2 Bill Elliott .75 2.00
3 Harry Gant .30 .75
4 Bobby Hamilton .40 1.00
5 Sterling Marlin .40 1.00
6 Greg Sacks .25 .60
7 Darrell Waltrip .60 1.50
8 Rick Wilson .25 .60

1992 Maxx IMHOF

This 40-card set was produced by Maxx to honor new and previous inductees into the International Motor Sports Hall of Fame. The cards include sketches by renowned motorsports artist Jeanne Barnes. These Cards have no number orientation.

COMPLETE SET (40) 3.00 8.00
1 Checklist .07 .20
2 IMHOF Aerial View .07 .20
3 IMHOF Rotunda .07 .20
4 Gerald Dial Chairman .07 .20
5 Don Naman Exec. Dir. .07 .20
6 IMHOF Commission .07 .20
7 Groundbreaking .07 .20
8 Ribbon Cutting .07 .20
9 Jenny Gilliand Miss IMHOF .07 .20
10 Official Car Chevy .07 .20
11 Buck Baker Art .10 .30
12 Tony Bettenhausen Art .10 .30
13 Jack Brabham Art .10 .30
14 Malcolm Campbell Art .10 .30
15 Jim Clark Art .10 .30
16 Juan Manuel Fangio Art .10 .30
17 Tim Flock Art .10 .30
18 Dan Gurney Art .10 .30
19 Anton Hulman(Tony) Art .10 .30
20 Ned Jarrett Art .10 .30
21 Junior Johnson Art .10 .30
22 Parnelli Jones Art .10 .30
23 Fred Lorenzen Art .10 .30
24 Bruce McLaren Art .10 .30
25 Stirling Moss Art .10 .30
26 Barney Oldfield Art .10 .30
27 Glenn Fireball Roberts Art .10 .30
28 Wilbur Shaw Art .10 .30
29 Carroll Shelby Art .10 .30
30 Bobby Unser Art .10 .30
31 Bill Vukovich Art .10 .30
32 Smokey Yunick Art .10 .30
33 Jeanne Barnes Artist .07 .20
34 Winston Cutaway Car .07 .20
35 1919 Indy Racer .07 .20
36 Richard Petty's Car .10 .30
37 Darrell Waltrip's Car .07 .20
38 Don Garlits' Car .07 .20
39 Glenn Fireball Roberts' Car .07 .20
40 T.G. Shepherd .07 .20

1992 Maxx McDonald's

This 37-card set was produced by Maxx and distributed by McDonald's. It was made available exclusively at over 1,300 McDonald's locations throughout 15 states in August 1992. Customers could obtain four-card packs for $.99 each or by purchasing an Extra Value Meal. It features members of the 1992 McDonald's All-Star Race Team and 29 other top NASCAR Winston Cup drivers, plus the respective car owners and crew chiefs of the McDonald's All-Star Racing Team. Like its predecessor, a large amount of these cards found their way into the hobby. Each pack came with a cover card.

COMPLETE SET (37) 4.00 10.00
1 D.Earnhardt .75 2.00
D.Allison
Elliott
2 Dale Earnhardt .75 2.00
3 Davey Allison .15 .40
4 Bill Elliott .20 .50
5 Richard Childress .10 .25
6 Robert Yates .10 .25
7 Junior Johnson .10 .25
8 Kirk Shelmerdine .05 .15
9 Larry McReynolds .10 .25
10 Tim Brewer .05 .15
11 Ricky Rudd .07 .20
12 Harry Gant .07 .20
13 Ernie Irvan .15 .40
14 Mark Martin .30 .75
15 Sterling Marlin .10 .25
16 Darrell Waltrip .15 .40
17 Ken Schrader .05 .15
18 Rusty Wallace .25 .60
19 Morgan Shepherd .10 .25
20 Alan Kulwicki .20 .50
21 Geoff Bodine .05 .15
22 Michael Waltrip .12 .30
23 Hut Stricklin .05 .15
24 Dale Jarrett .12 .30
25 Terry Labonte .10 .25
26 Brett Bodine .05 .15
27 Rick Mast .05 .15
28 Bobby Hamilton .10 .25
29 Ted Musgrave .10 .25
30 Richard Petty .30 .75
31 Jimmy Spencer .10 .25
32 Chad Little .10 .25
33 Derrike Cope .10 .25
34 Dave Marcis .07 .20
35 Kyle Petty .20 .50
36 Dick Trickle .05 .15
NNO Cover Card .05 .10

1992 Maxx Motorsport

This 50-card set was produced by Maxx for Prospective Marketing International/Ford Motorsport Sportswear. It features drivers, owners, and crew chiefs from the 13 Ford race teams. This set was only made available through the 1993 Ford Motorsport Sportswear and Accessories Catalog. 50,000 of these sets were made.

COMPLETE SET (50) 2.50 6.00
1 Bill Elliott .30 .75
2 Davey Allison .25 .60
3 Alan Kulwicki .30 .75
4 Sterling Marlin .15 .40
5 Mark Martin .50 1.25
6 Geoff Bodine .10 .25
7 Brett Bodine .10 .25
8 Morgan Shepherd .15 .40
9 Dick Trickle .10 .25
10 Wally Dallenbach Jr. .10 .25
11 Jimmy Hensley .10 .25
12 Charlie Glotzbach .10 .25
13 Chad Little .15 .40
14 Junior Johnson .15 .40
15 Robert Yates .15 .40
16 Jack Roush .15 .40
17 Walter Bud Moore .10 .25
18 Kenny Bernstein .15 .40
19 Eddie Wood .10 .25
20 Bill Stavola .10 .25
21 Cale Yarborough .25 .60
22 Junie Donlavey .10 .25
23 Harry Melling .10 .25
24 Tim Brewer .10 .25
25 Larry McReynolds .15 .40
26 Paul Andrews .10 .25
27 Mike Beam .10 .25
28 Steve Hmiel .10 .25
29 Donnie Wingo .10 .25
30 Donnie Richeson .15 .40
31 Leonard Wood .10 .25
32 Ken Wilson .10 .25
33 Steve Loyd .10 .25
34 Bob Johnson .10 .25
35 Gene Roberts .15 .40
36 Bill Elliott w/Crew .30 .75
37 Davey Allison w/Crew .25 .60
38 Alan Kulwicki w/Crew .30 .75
39 Sterling Marlin w/Crew .15 .40
40 Mark Martin w/Crew .50 1.25
41 Geoff Bodine w/Crew .10 .25
42 Brett Bodine w/Crew .10 .25
43 Morgan Shepherd w/Crew .15 .40
44 Dick Trickle w/Crew .10 .25
45 Wally Dallenbach Jr. w/Crew .10 .25
46 Jimmy Hensley w/Crew .10 .25
47 Charlie Glotzbach w/Crew .10 .25
48 Chad Little w/Crew .15 .40
49 Formation Flying cars .50 1.25
50 Martin/Kulwicki/Allison/Elliott .50 1.25

1992 Maxx Red

This 300-card set was made available through hobby sets and 14-card wax packs. Special versions of the hobby sets were distributed through different retail outlets. QVC sold these sets with an autographed Bill Elliott card and Sears sold a set through its catalog that contained the 16-card Bobby Hamilton 1992 Rookie of the Year set and the 8-card Craftsman set.

COMPLETE SET (300) 12.50 30.00
COMP.FACT.SET (304) 15.00 40.00
WAX BOX 12.50 30.00
1 Rick Mast .10 .25
2 Rusty Wallace .40 1.00
3 Dale Earnhardt 1.25 3.00
4 Ernie Irvan .25 .60
5 Ricky Rudd .12 .30
6 Mark Martin .50 1.25
7 Alan Kulwicki .30 .75
8 Rick Wilson .10 .25

9 Phil Parsons .10 .25
10 Derrike Cope .15 .40
11 Bill Elliott .30 .75
12 Hut Stricklin .10 .25
13 Bobby Dotter .10 .25
14 Mike Chase RC .15 .40
15 Geoff Bodine .10 .25
16 Wally Dallenbach Jr. .10 .25
17 Darrell Waltrip .25 .60
18 Dale Jarrett .20 .50
19 Randy LaJoie RC .15 .40
20 Buddy Baker .12 .30
21 Morgan Shepherd .15 .40
22 Sterling Marlin .15 .40
23 Mike Wallace .10 .25
24 Kenny Wallace .15 .40
25 Ken Schrader .10 .25
26 Brett Bodine .10 .25
27 Jimmy Hensley .10 .25
28 Davey Allison .25 .60
29 Jeff Gordon 2.50 6.00
30 Michael Waltrip .20 .50
31 Clifford Allison RC .20 .50
32 Cecil Eunice RC .15 .40
33 Harry Gant .12 .30
34 Chuck Bown .10 .25
35 Todd Bodine .10 .25
36 H.B. Bailey .10 .25
37 Joe Nemechek .15 .40
38 Dave Rezendes .10 .25
39 Tommy Houston .10 .25
40 Tom Kendall .10 .25
41 Larry Pearson .10 .25
42 Kyle Petty .30 .75
43 Richard Petty .50 1.25
44 Bobby Labonte .40 1.00
45 Irv Hoerr RC .15 .40
46 Dick Trickle .10 .25
47 Greg Sacks .10 .25
48 James Hylton .10 .25
49 Stanley Smith .10 .25
50 Jeff Gordon ROY 2.50 6.00
51 Jeff Purvis .10 .25
52 Jimmy Means .10 .25
53 Bobby Hillin .10 .25
54 Jack Ingram .15 .40
55 Ted Musgrave .15 .40
56 Bill Sedgwick RC .15 .40
57 Jeff Burton .20 .50
58 Steve Grissom .10 .25
59 Patty Moise .15 .40
60 Elton Sawyer .10 .25
61 Bill Venturini .10 .25
62 Mike McLaughlin .10 .25
63 Ed Berrier .10 .25
64 Tracy Leslie .10 .25
65 Shawna Robinson .25 .60
66 Chad Little .15 .40
67 Ed Ferree RC .15 .40
68 Bobby Hamilton .15 .40
69 Peter Sospenzo .10 .25
70 John Paul Jr. RC .15 .40
71 Dave Marcis .12 .30
72 Jim Bown .10 .25
73 Phil Barkdoll .10 .25
74 Tom Peck .10 .25
75 Joe Ruttman .10 .25
76 Charlie Glotzbach .10 .25
77 Rich Bickle RC .15 .40
78 Larry Phillips RC .15 .40
79 David Green RC .30 .75
80 Jack Sprague RC .15 .40
81 Robert Pressley .10 .25
82 Mark Stahl .10 .25
83 Lake Speed .10 .25
84 Butch Miller .10 .25
85 Jeff Green RC .30 .75
86 Ward Burton .15 .40
87 Dorsey Schroeder RC .15 .40
88 Ricky Craven RC .60 1.50
89 Jim Sauter .10 .25
90 Troy Beebe .10 .25
91 Bobby Labonte BGN Champ .40 1.00
92 Dave Mader .10 .25
93 Mickey Gibbs .10 .25
94 Terry Labonte .15 .40
95 Eddie Bierschwale .10 .25
96 Randy Baker .10 .25
97 Tommy Ellis .10 .25
98 Jimmy Spencer .15 .40
99 Bobby Hamilton ROY .15 .40
100 Bill Elliott FF .30 .75
101 Ed McClure RC
Ted.McClure RC/J.McClure RC .15 .40
102 Richard Childress .15 .40
103 Rick Hendrick .15 .40
104 Robert Yates .15 .40
105 Leo Jackson .10 .25
106 Larry McClure .10 .25
107 Tim Morgan .10 .25
108 Jack Roush .15 .40
109 Junior Johnson .15 .40
110 Roger Penske .15 .40
111 Don Miller .10 .25
112 Walter Bud Moore .10 .25
113 Chuck Rider .10 .25
114 Bobby Allison .20 .50
115 Bob Bilby .10 .25
116 Eddie Wood .10 .25
117 Len Wood .15 .40
118 Glen Wood .10 .25
119 Billy Hagan .10 .25
120 Kenny Bernstein .15 .40
121 Butch Mock .10 .25
122 Bob Rahilly .10 .25
123 Richard Jackson .10 .25
124 George Bradshaw .10 .25
125 David Fuge RC .15 .40
126 Mark Smith RC .15 .40
127 D.K. Ulrich .10 .25
128 Ray DeWitt RC/Diane DeWitt RC.15 .40
129 Travis Carter .10 .25
130 Bill Stavola .10 .25
131 Larry Hedrick .10 .25
132 Chuck Little .10 .25
133 Bob Whitcomb .10 .25
134 Felix Sabates .15 .40
135 Cale Yarborough .25 .60
136 Dick Moroso .15 .40
137 Harry Melling .10 .25
138 Junie Donlavey .10 .25
139 Don Bierschwale .10 .25
140 Sam McMahon III RC .15 .40
141 A.J. Foyt .15 .40
142 Jeffrey Ellis .10 .25
143 Tony Glover .10 .25
144 Ken Wilson .10 .25
145 Dale Inman .10 .25
146 Steve Hmiel .10 .25
147 Morgan Shepherd Pit Champs .15 .40
148 Kirk Shelmerdine .10 .25
149 Waddell Wilson .10 .25
150 Larry McReynolds .15 .40
151 Andy Petree .10 .25
152 Tony Glover .10 .25
153 Robin Pemberton .10 .25
154 Mike Beam .10 .25
155 Jeff Hammond .15 .40
156 Richard Broome .10 .25
157 Eddie Dickerson RC .15 .40
158 Ernie Elliott .10 .25
159 Donnie Wingo .10 .25
160 Paul Andrews .10 .25
161 Tim Brewer .10 .25
162 Bill Ingle .10 .25
163 Jimmy Fennig .10 .25
164 Dewey Livengood RC .15 .40
165 Bob Johnson .10 .25
166 Clyde McLeod .10 .25
167 Buddy Parrott .10 .25
168 Doug Williams .10 .25
169 Steve Loyd .10 .25
170 Leonard Wood .10 .25
171 Gene Roberts RC .15 .40
172 Jimmy Makar .10 .25
173 Robbie Loomis .15 .40
174 David Ifft .10 .25
175 Steve Barkdoll RC .15 .40
176 Donnie Allison .12 .30
177 Dennis Connor .10 .25
178 Barry Dodson .10 .25
179 Harry Hyde .15 .40
180 Bob Labonte RC .15 .40
181 Steve Bird .10 .25
182 Jeff Hensley .10 .25
183 Ricky Pearson .10 .25
184 Scott Houston .10 .25
185 Eddie Pearson RC .15 .40
186 Tony Eury RC .30 .75
187 Donnie Richeson RC .15 .40
188 Military Cars MM .06 .15
189 Sterling Marlin's Car MM .05 .15
190 Davey Allison/Darrell
Waltrip Cars MM .10 .25
191 G.Bodine/B.Bodine Cars MM .05 .15
192 Kyle Petty's Car MM .12 .30
193 Rick Mast's Car MM .05 .10
194 Ken Schrader's Car MM .05 .10
195 Darrell Waltrip's Car MM .05 .10
196 Talladega Speedway MM .05 .15
197 Bobby Hamilton/Ted
Musgrave Cars MM .05 .15
198 Davey Allison .10 .25
Dale Jarrett Cars MM
199 Richmond International MM .05 .15
200 Mark Martin's Car MM .20 .50
201 Harry Gant's Car MM .05 .15
202 Rusty Wallace MM .40 1.00
203 Dale Earnhardt's Car MM .50 1.25
204 Robert Black .10 .25
205 Les Richter .10 .25
206 Dick Beaty .10 .25
207 Doyle Ford .10 .25
208 Buster Auton RC .15 .40
209 Bruce Roney .10 .25
210 Mike Chaplin RC .15 .40
211 Chuck Romeo RC .15 .40
212 Jimmy Cox .10 .25
213 Buddy Morrow RC .15 .40
214 Tim Earp RC .15 .40
215 Elmo Langley .10 .25
216 Jack Whittemore RC .15 .40
217 Carl Hill .10 .25
218 Art Krebs RC .15 .40
219 Gary Nelson .10 .25
220 Chris Economaki .10 .25
221 Ned Jarrett .12 .30
222 Neil Bonnett .25 .60
223 Mike Joy .10 .25
224 Dick Berggren .10 .25
225 Winston Kelley .10 .25
226 Jack Arute .10 .25
227 Jim Phillips .10 .25
228 Ken Squier .10 .25
229 Beth Bruce Ms. Winston .15 .40
230 Renee White Ms. Winston .15 .40
231 Dale Earnhardt AP 1.25 3.00
232 Harry Gant AP .12 .30
233 Mark Martin AP .50 1.25
234 Larry McReynolds AP .15 .40
235 Kirk Shelmerdine/Tony Glover AP.10 .25
236 Larry Wallace AP RC .15 .40
237 Leo Jackson/Eddie Lanier AP .15 .40
238 Harold Stott AP .15 .40
239 Andy Petree/Will Lind AP .10 .25
240 Kirk Shelmerdine AP .10 .25
241 Doug Richert/Tim Brewer AP .10 .25
242 Scott Robinette AP RC .15 .40
243 Darrell Andrews/Todd Parrott AP.10 .25
244 David Smith AP .15 .40
245 Charley Pressley/Gary Brooks AP.10 .25
246 Norman Koshimizu AP .10 .25
247 Danny Myers/Henry Benfield AP.10 .25
248 Dan Ford AP .10 .25
249 Paul Andrews/Mike Hill AP .10 .25
250 Will Lind AP .10 .25
251 Mike Thomas/Shorty Edwards AP.15 .40
252 Danny Lawrence AP .10 .25
253 Devin Barbee RC
Ronnie Reavis AP RC .15 .40
254 Howard Poston (Slick) AP .10 .25
255 Dan Ford/Darrell Dunn AP RC .15 .40
256 Gale Wilson AP .10 .25
257 Norman Koshimizu
Jerry Schweitz AP .10 .25
258 James Lewter AP .10 .25
259 Abbie Garwood RC
Mark Osborn AP RC .15 .40
260 David Little AP RC .15 .40
261 Wayne Dalton/Troy Martin AP .10 .25
262 Glen Bobo AP RC .15 .40
263 Bobby Moody/David Munari AP.10 .25
264 Ernie Irvan YR .25 .60
265 Dale Earnhardt/Teresa YR 1.25 3.00
266 Kyle Petty YR .30 .75
267 Ken Schrader YR .10 .25
268 Ricky Rudd YR .12 .30
269 Rusty Wallace YR .40 1.00
270 Darrell Waltrip YR .25 .60
271 Dale Earnhardt/Teresa YR 1.25 3.00
272 Harry Gant YR .12 .30
273 Davey Allison YR .25 .60
274 Davey Allison/Deb.Allison YR RC.25 .60
275 Ken Schrader YR .10 .25
276 Davey Allison w/Crew YR .25 .60
277 Darrell Waltrip YR .25 .60
278 Davey Allison/Yates YR .25 .60
279 Bill Elliott YR .30 .75
280 Rusty Wallace YR .40 1.00
281 Dale Earnhardt/Teresa YR 1.25 3.00
282 Ernie Irvan YR .25 .60
283 Dale Jarrett YR .20 .50
284 Alan Kulwicki YR .30 .75
285 Harry Gant YR .12 .30
286 Harry Gant YR .12 .30
287 Harry Gant YR .12 .30
288 Harry Gant YR .12 .30
289 Dale Earnhardt YR 1.25 3.00
290 Geoff Bodine YR .10 .25
291 Davey Allison YR .25 .60
292 Davey Allison/Yates YR .25 .60
293 Mark Martin YR .50 1.25
294 Dale Earnhardt YR 1.25 3.00
295 Checklist No. 1 .07 .20
296 Checklist No. 2 .07 .20
297 Checklist No. 3 .07 .20
298 Checklist No. 4 .07 .20
299 Checklist No. 5 .07 .20
300 Checklist No. 6 .07 .20
P1 Bill Elliott Promo Red 8.00 20.00

1992 Maxx Black

COMPLETE SET (300) 12.50 30.00
COMP.FACT.SET (304) 15.00 40.00
*STARS: .5X TO 1.2X RED CARDS
WAX BOX 12.50 30.00

1992 Maxx Red Update

This 30-card set was produced with the intent of being distributed on the "retail" market. It contains 30 numbered cards and two unnumbered cards, shows updated photos of drivers who changed uniforms along with a few noted personalities. It features the first Maxx cards of Joe Gibbs and Jerry Glanville.

COMPLETE SET (32) 2.50 6.00
U1 Greg Sacks .12 .30
U2 Geoff Bodine .12 .30
U3 Jeff Burton .25 .60
U4 Derrike Cope .20 .50
U5 Jerry Glanville RC .30 .75
U6 Jeff Gordon 3.00 8.00
U7 Jimmy Hensley .12 .30
U8 Ben Hess .12 .30
U9 Dale Jarrett .25 .60
U10 Chad Little .20 .50
U11 Mark Martin .60 1.50
U12 Joe Nemechek .20 .50
U13 Bob Schacht RC .20 .50
U14 Stanley Smith .12 .30
U15 Lake Speed .12 .30
U16 Dick Trickle .12 .30
U17 Kenny Wallace .20 .50
U18 Ron McCreary RC .20 .50
U19 Joe Gibbs RC .30 .75
U20 Dick Brooks .12 .30
U21 Bill Connell RC .20 .50
U22 Eli Gold .12 .30
U23 Barney Hall .12 .30
U24 Glenn Jarrett RC .20 .50
U25 Bob Jenkins .12 .30
U26 John Kernan .12 .30
U27 Benny Parsons .30 .75
U28 Pat Patterson RC .20 .50
U29 Randy Pemberton RC .20 .50
U30 Dr. Jerry Punch .12 .30
NNO Eddie Pearson RC .20 .50
NNO Geoff Bodine .12 .30

1992 Maxx Black Update

COMPLETE SET (32) 2.50 6.00
*STARS: .4X TO 1X RED UPDATES

1992 Maxx Sam Bass

This 11-card set was designed by noted motorsports artist Sam Bass. The set contains paintings of drivers such as Bobby Allison, Richard Petty, and Neil Bonnett. It is important to note this set also contains the only Tim Richmond card made by Maxx. This set was sent free to the buyers of the black mail order set.

COMPLETE SET (11) 3.00 8.00
1 Richard Petty .60 1.50
2 J.D. McDuffie .12 .30
3 Ned Jarrett .15 .40
4 Tim Richmond .15 .40
5 Harold Kinder .12 .30
6 Rob Moroso .12 .30
7 Bobby Allison .25 .60
8 Bill Elliott .40 1.00
9 Junior Johnson .20 .50
10 Neil Bonnett .30 .75
NNO Sam Bass .20 .50

1992 Maxx Texaco Davey Allison

This 20-card set was produced by Maxx and made available at over 1,200 Texaco gas stations in the eastern and southeastern region of the country in February 1992. This set features 1992 Daytona 500 winner Davey Allison and the Robert Yates Texaco Havoline Racing Team. They were available in four-card packs and could be purchased for $.99. Full sets were made available through Club Maxx in July of 1992. 2,000 of the cover cards in this set were autographed and randomly inserted into packs. A large number of these cards found their way into the hobby through factory closeouts.

COMPLETE SET (20) 2.00 5.00
1 Davey Allison .15 .40
2 Davey Allison's Car .15 .40
3 Robert Yates .10 .25
4 Larry McReynolds .10 .25
5 Davey Allison's Car w/Crew .05 .15
6 Davey Allison's Car w/Crew .05 .15
7 Davey Allison's Transporter .05 .15
8 Davey Allison's Car .05 .15
9 Robert Yates .10 .25
Larry McReynolds
10 Davey Allison .15 .40
11 Davey Allison w/Car .15 .40
12 Dav.Allison .30 .75
Earnhardt Cars
13 Davey Allison in Pits .15 .40
14 Dav.Allison .15 .40
Deb.Allison
Yates
L.McReyn.
15 Davey Allison .15 .40
Larry McReynolds
16 Davey Allison .15 .40
17 Davey Allison .15 .40
Robert Yates
18 Davey Allison .15 .40
R.Yates
L.McReynolds
19 Dav.Allison .15 .40
B.Allison
Yates
L.McReyn
20 Davey Allison w .15 .40
Crew CL
NNO Davey Allison AU 75.00 150.00

1992 Maxx The Winston

This 50-card set was produced by Maxx and documents the first ever night running of The Winston. 50,000 sets were made and it was made available through Maxx's mail order program.

COMPLETE SET (50) 3.00 8.00
1 Davey Allison .25 .60
2 Kyle Petty .30 .75
3 Ken Schrader .10 .25
4 Ricky Rudd .12 .30
5 Bill Elliott .30 .75
6 Rusty Wallace .40 1.00
7 Alan Kulwicki .30 .75
8 Ernie Irvan .25 .60
9 Richard Petty .50 1.25
10 Terry Labonte .15 .40
11 Darrell Waltrip .25 .60
12 Harry Gant .12 .30
13 Geoff Bodine .10 .25
14 Dale Earnhardt 1.25 3.00
15 Michael Waltrip .20 .50
16 Dave Mader .10 .25
17 Mark Martin .50 1.25
18 Dale Jarrett .20 .50
19 Morgan Shepherd .15 .40
20 Hut Stricklin .10 .25
21 Davey Allison's Car .10 .25
22 Kyle Petty's Car .12 .30
23 Ken Schrader's Car .05 .10
24 Ricky Rudd's Car .05 .10
25 Bill Elliott's Car .12 .30
26 Rusty Wallace's Car .15 .40
27 Alan Kulwicki's Car .12 .30
28 Ernie Irvan's Car .10 .25
29 Richard Petty's Car .20 .50
30 Terry Labonte's Car .05 .15
31 Darrell Waltrip's Car .10 .25
32 Harry Gant's Car .05 .10
33 Geoff Bodine's Car .05 .10
34 Dale Earnhardt's Car .50 1.25
35 Michael Waltrip's Car .07 .20
36 Dave Mader's Car .05 .10
37 Mark Martin's Car .20 .50
38 Dale Jarrett's Car .07 .20
39 Morgan Shepherd's Car .05 .15
40 Hut Stricklin's Car .05 .10
41 Davey Allison's Car .10 .25
42 Davey Allison.Pole Win .25 .60
43 Michael Waltrip Win .20 .50
44 Final Pace Lap .05 .15
45 First Segment .05 .15
46 Second Segment .05 .15
47 Third Segment .05 .15
48 Davey Allison .12 .30
K.Petty Cars
49 Victory Lane .05 .15
50 Davey Allison Win .25 .60

1993 Maxx

This 300-card set was distributed in complete factory set form and through 12-card wax packs. It is commonly known as the green set for the bright green border. A blue bordered parallel set was released later in the year through Club Maxx. The blue bordered set is known as the Maxx Premier Series and is priced under that title.

COMPLETE SET (300) 8.00 20.00
COMP.FACT.SET (300) 10.00 25.00
WAX BOX 15.00 40.00
1 Rick Mast .07 .20
2 Rusty Wallace .60 1.50
3 Dale Earnhardt 1.25 3.00
4 Ernie Irvan .15 .40
5 Ricky Rudd .25 .60
6 Mark Martin .60 1.50
7 Alan Kulwicki .25 .60
8 Sterling Marlin .30 .75
9 Chad Little .07 .20
10 Derrike Cope .07 .20
11 Bill Elliott .30 .75
12 Jimmy Spencer .07 .20
13 Alan Kulwicki/Bill Elliott Cars MM.07 .20
14 Terry Labonte .30 .75
15 Geoff Bodine .07 .20
16 Wally Dallenbach Jr. .07 .20
17 Darrell Waltrip .15 .40
18 Dale Jarrett .50 1.25
19 Tom Peck .07 .20
20 Alan Kulwicki's Car .07 .20
21 Morgan Shepherd .07 .20
22 Bobby Labonte .50 1.25
23 Eddie Bierschwale .02 .10
24 Jeff Gordon CRC 1.25 3.00
25 Ken Schrader .07 .20
26 Brett Bodine .07 .20
27 Hut Stricklin .07 .20
28 Davey Allison .40 1.00
29 Jimmy Horton .07 .20
30 Michael Waltrip .15 .40
31 Steve Grissom .07 .20
32 Charlie Glotzbach .07 .20
33 Harry Gant .15 .40
34 Todd Bodine .07 .20
35 Jeff Purvis .07 .20
36 Ward Burton .15 .40
37 Bill Elliott's Car .07 .20
38 Jerry O'Neill .02 .10
39 Buddy Baker .07 .20
40 Kenny Wallace .07 .20
41 Phil Parsons .07 .20
42 Kyle Petty .15 .40
43 Richard Petty .30 .75
44 Rick Wilson .07 .20
45 Jeff Burton .25 .60
46 Al Unser Jr. .15 .40
47 Bill Venturini .07 .20
48 James Hylton .02 .10
49 Stanley Smith .02 .10
50 Tommy Houston .07 .20
51 Richard Lasater .02 .10
52 Jimmy Means .07 .20
53 Mike Wallace .07 .20
54 Jack Sprague .02 .10
55 Ted Musgrave .07 .20
56 Dale Earnhardt's Car .50 1.25
57 Troy Beebe .02 .10
58 Bill Sedgwick .02 .10
59 Robert Pressley .07 .20
60 Jeff Green .07 .20
61 Kyle Petty's Car .07 .20
62 H.B. Bailey .02 .10
63 Chuck Bown .02 .10
64 Dorsey Schroeder .07 .20
65 Dave Mader .02 .10
66 Jimmy Hensley .07 .20
67 Ed Berrier .02 .10
68 Bobby Hamilton .07 .20
69 Greg Sacks .07 .20
70 Tommy Ellis .02 .10
71 Dave Marcis .07 .20
72 Tracy Leslie .02 .10
73 Phil Barkdoll .07 .20
74 Kyle Petty's Car MM .07 .20
75 Dick Trickle .07 .20
76 Butch Miller .07 .20
77 Mike Potter .02 .10
78 Shawna Robinson .40 1.00
79 Dave Rezendes .07 .20
80 Bobby Dotter .07 .20
81 Lonnie Rush Jr. .02 .10
82 Andy Belmont .07 .20
83 Lake Speed .07 .20
84 Rich Bickle .07 .20
85 Mark Martin's Car .30 .75
86 Mickey Gibbs .02 .10
87 Joe Nemechek .07 .20
88 Sterling Marlin's Car .07 .20
89 Jerry Hill .02 .10
90 Bobby Hillin .07 .20
91 Bob Schacht .02 .10
92 Kerry Teague .02 .10
93 Larry Pearson .07 .20
94 Dav.Allison/Elliott Cars MM .07 .20
95 Jim Sauter .02 .10
96 Ed Ferree .02 .10
97 Bobby Hamilton's Car .02 .10
98 Jim Bown .02 .10
99 Ricky Craven .15 .40
100 Junior Johnson .07 .20
101 Robert Yates .02 .10
102 Leo Jackson .02 .10
103 Felix Sabates .02 .10
104 Jack Roush .02 .10
105 Rick Hendrick .02 .10
106 Billy Hagen .02 .10
107 Tim Morgan .02 .10
108 Larry McClure .02 .10
109 Ted.McClure/J.McClure
Ed McClure .02 .10
110 Richard Childress .15 .40
111 Roger Penske .02 .10
112 Don Miller .02 .10
113 Bobby Labonte's Car .07 .20
114 Glen Wood .02 .10
115 Len Wood .02 .10
116 Eddie Wood .02 .10
117 Kenny Bernstein .07 .20
118 Walter Bud Moore .02 .10
119 Ray DeWitt .02 .10
120 D.K. Ulrich .02 .10
121 Davey Allison's Car .07 .20
122 Joe Gibbs .15 .40
123 Bill Stavola .02 .10
124 Mickey Stavola .02 .10
125 Richard Jackson .02 .10
126 Chuck Rider .02 .10
127 George Bradshaw .02 .10
128 Mark Smith .02 .10
129 Bobby Allison .07 .20
130 Bob Bilby .02 .10
131 Davey Allison Crash MM .07 .20
132 Larry Hedrick .02 .10
133 Harry Melling .02 .10
134 Junie Donlavey .02 .10
135 Bill Davis .02 .10
136 Cale Yarborough .07 .20
137 Frank Cicci/Scott Welliver .02 .10
138 Dick Moroso .02 .10
139 Butch Mock .02 .10
140 Bob Rahilly .02 .10
141 Don Bierschwale .02 .10
142 Paul Andrews .02 .10
143 Mike Beam .02 .10
144 Larry McReynolds .02 .10
145 Steve Barkdoll .02 .10
146 Robin Pemberton .02 .10
147 Steve Hmiel .02 .10
148 Gary DeHart .02 .10
149 Pete Wright .02 .10
150 Ricky Rudd's Car .07 .20
151 Jake Elder .02 .10
152 Mike Hill .02 .10
153 Tony Glover .02 .10
154 Andy Petree .02 .10
155 Buddy Parrott .02 .10
156 Richard Petty MM .25 .60
157 Leonard Wood .02 .10
158 Donnie Richeson .02 .10
159 Donnie Wingo .02 .10
160 Ken Howes .02 .10
161 Sandy Jones .02 .10
162 Jimmy Makar .02 .10
163 Ken Wilson .02 .10
164 Barry Dodson .02 .10
165 Doug Hewitt .02 .10
166 Howard Comstock .02 .10
167 David Fuge .02 .10
168 Jeff Gordon's Car .50 1.25
169 Robbie Loomis .02 .10
170 Jimmy Fennig .02 .10
171 Bob Johnson .02 .10
172 Doug Richert .02 .10
173 Ernie Elliott .02 .10
174 Doug Williams .02 .10
175 Tim Brewer .02 .10
176 Gil Martin .02 .10
177 Kenny Wallace's Car .02 .10
178 Ray Evernham .02 .10
179 Troy Selberg .02 .10
180 Dennis Connor .02 .10
181 Jeff Hammond .02 .10
182 Dale Inman .02 .10
183 Harry Hyde .02 .10

184 Vic Kangas .02 .10
185 Bob Labonte .02 .10
186 Ken Schrader's Car .02 .10
187 Clyde McLeod .02 .10
188 Ricky Pearson .02 .10
189 Tony Eury .25 .60
190 Alan Kulwicki WC Champ .15 .40
191 Jimmy Hensley WC ROY .07 .20
192 Larry McReynolds .02 .10
193 Bill Elliott FF .15 .40
194 Ken Schrader Pit Champs .07 .20
195 Joe Nemechek Busch Champ .07 .20
196 Ricky Craven Busch ROY .15 .40
197 Ricky Rudd IROC Champ .25 .60
198 Dick Beaty .02 .10
199 Da.All./R.Petty/Mart.Cars MM .15 .40
200 Barney Hall .02 .10
201 Eli Gold .02 .10
202 Ned Jarrett .07 .20
203 Glenn Jarrett .02 .10
204 Dick Berggren .02 .10
205 Jack Arute .02 .10
206 Bob Jenkins .02 .10
207 Benny Parsons .07 .20
208 Jerry Punch .02 .10
209 Joe Moore .02 .10
210 Jim Phillips .02 .10
211 Chris Economaki .02 .10
212 Winston Kelley .02 .10
213 Dick Brooks .02 .10
214 John Kernan .02 .10
215 Mike Joy .02 .10
216 Randy Pemberton .02 .10
217 Allen Bestwick .02 .10
218 Ken Squier .02 .10
219 Neil Bonnett .15 .40
220 Davey Allison Crash MM .07 .20
221 Larry Phillips/B.Gordon .02 .10
222 Mike Love/Charlie Cragen .02 .10
223 Steve Murgic/Ricky Icenhower .02 .10
224 Michael Ritch/Joe Kosiski .02 .10
225 Steve Hendren/Larry Phillips .02 .10
226 Darrell Waltrip MM .07 .20
227 Buster Auton .02 .10
228 Jimmy Cox .02 .10
229 Les Richter .02 .10
230 Ray Hill .02 .10
231 Doyle Ford .02 .10
232 Chuck Romeo .02 .10
233 Elmo Langley .02 .10
234 Jack Whittemore .02 .10
235 Walt Green .02 .10
236 Mike Chaplin .02 .10
237 Tim Earp .02 .10
238 Bruce Roney .02 .10
239 Carl Hill .02 .10
240 Mark Connolly .02 .10
241 Gary Miller .02 .10
242 Marlin Wright .02 .10
243 Gary Nelson .02 .10
244 Ernie Irvan's Car .15 .40
245 Richard Petty w/Car MM .25 .60
246 Harry Gant AP .07 .20
247 Tony Glover AP .02 .10
248 David Little AP .02 .10
249 Gary Brooks AP .02 .10
250 Bill Wilburn AP .02 .10
251 Jeff Clark AP .02 .10
252 Shelton Pittman AP .02 .10
253 Scott Robinson AP .02 .10
254 Glen Bobo AP .02 .10
255 James Lewter AP .02 .10
256 Jerry Schweitz AP .02 .10
257 Harold Stott AP .02 .10
258 Ryan Pemberton AP .02 .10
259 Gale Wilson AP .02 .10
260 Danny Glad AP .02 .10
261 Howard Poston (Slick) AP .02 .10
262 Brooke Sealy Ms.Winston 1.00 2.50
263 Geoff Bodine YR .07 .20
264 Davey Allison/Yates/McR.YR .15 .40
265 Bill Elliott w/Crew YR .15 .40
266 Bill Elliott YR .15 .40
267 Bill Elliott/J.Johnson YR .15 .40
268 Bill Elliott YR .15 .40
269 Alan Kulwicki w/Crew YR .15 .40
270 Davey Allison/Yates/McR.YR .15 .40
271 Mark Martin YR .30 .75
272 Davey Allison w/Crew YR .15 .40
273 Robert Yates YR .25 .60
274 Dale Earnhardt YR/Jr./Kerry 3.00 8.00
275 Harry Gant YR .07 .20
276 Ernie Irvan YR .07 .20
277 Alan Kulwicki w/Crew YR .15 .40
278 Davey Allison YR .15 .40
279 Ernie Irvan YR .07 .20
280 Darrell Waltrip YR .07 .20
281 Ernie Irvan YR .07 .20
282 Kyle Petty/Felix Sabates YR .15 .40
283 Harry Gant YR .07 .20
284 Darrell Waltrip YR .07 .20
285 Darrell Waltrip YR .07 .20
286 Rusty Wallace w/Crew YR .30 .75
287 Ricky Rudd w/Crew YR .25 .60
288 Geoff Bodine YR .07 .20
289 Geoff Bodine w/Crew YR .07 .20
290 Mark Martin YR .30 .75
291 Kyle Petty YR .15 .40
292 Davey Allison/Yates YR .15 .40
293 Bill Elliott YR .15 .40
294 Alan Kulwicki MM .15 .40
295 Checklist #1 .02 .10
296 Checklist #2 .02 .10
297 Checklist #3 .02 .10
298 Checklist #4 .02 .10
299 Checklist #5 .02 .10
300 Checklist #6 .02 .10
P1 Bill Elliott Promo 2.00 5.00

1993 Maxx Premier Series

COMPLETE SET (300) 20.00 50.00
*SINGLES: .8X TO 2X BASIC CARDS

1993 Maxx Baby Ruth Jeff Burton

This four-card set was produced by Maxx and distributed by the Baby Ruth Race Team. It features photos of Baby Ruth driver Jeff Burton.

COMPLETE SET (4) 5.00 10.00
1 Jeff Burton 1.00 2.50
2 Jeff Burton's Car 1.00 2.50
3 Jeff Burton in Pits 1.00 2.50
4 Jeff Burton 1.00 2.50
Gil Martin

1993 Maxx Club Sam Bass Chromium

This 11-card set features the art work of racing artist Sam Bass. The gold bordered cards were printed using Maxx's Chromium technology. According to reports at time of issue, 6,000 sets were produced.

COMPLETE SET (11) 15.00 40.00
1 Bobby Allison 2.00 5.00
2 Bobby Allison 2.00 5.00
3 Rusty Wallace 3.00 8.00
4 Dav.Allison 2.50 6.00
B.Allison
5 Dale Jarrett's Car 1.00 2.50
6 Rusty Wallace 3.00 8.00
7 Jeff Gordon 4.00 10.00
8 Alan Kulwicki 2.00 5.00
9 Davey Allison 2.50 6.00
10 Jeff Gordon 4.00 10.00
11 Cover Card .75 2.00

1993 Maxx Jeff Gordon

This 20-card set was produced by Maxx and was distributed only in set form through Club Maxx for $4.95 per set. It highlights his career from his early childhood to debut on the Winston Cup circuit. 1,000 Jeff Gordon autographed cards were randomly inserted into the sets at a 1:100 ratio.

COMPLETE SET (20) 7.50 20.00
COMMON CARD (1-20) .60 1.50
JEFF GORDON AUTO 40.00 100.00
NNO Jeff Gordon AU 30.00 80.00

1993 Maxx Lowes Foods Stickers

Maxx produced this sticker set for distribution through Lowes Foods Stores. The stickers were distributed over a 5-week period (one per week) and include three drivers per sticker strip. Sticker fronts feature a top Winston Cup driver along with the Maxx and Lowes logos. Backs include Lowes Food Stores coupons. The strips actually are three individual stickers attached together. We've listed and priced the stickers in complete three-sticker strips.

COMPLETE SET (5) 6.00 15.00
1 J.Spencer .75 2.00
R.Rudd
K.Wallace
2 B.Elliott 3.00 8.00
D.Waltrip
J.Gordon
3 Dav.Allison 1.25 3.00
K.Petty
B.Hamilton
4 T.Labonte 2.00 5.00
S.Marlin
B.Labonte
5 M.Shepherd .75 2.00
B.Bodine
K.Schrader

1993 Maxx Motorsport

This 50-card set was produced by Maxx and distributed by Ford Motorsports. It consists of Ford's twenty drivers and their cars, plus the cards of the late Davey Allison and Alan Kulwicki.

COMPLETE SET (50) 2.50 6.00
1 Brett Bodine .07 .20
2 Geoff Bodine .07 .20
3 Todd Bodine .07 .20
4 Derrike Cope .07 .20
5 Wally Dallenbach Jr. .07 .20
6 Bill Elliott .30 .75
7 Bobby Hamilton .07 .20
8 Jimmy Hensley .07 .20
9 Bobby Hillin .07 .20
10 P.J. Jones .07 .20
11 Bobby Labonte .40 1.00
12 Sterling Marlin .15 .40
13 Mark Martin .50 1.25
14 Rick Mast .07 .20
15 Ted Musgrave .07 .20
16 Greg Sacks .07 .20
17 Morgan Shepherd .07 .20
18 Lake Speed .07 .20
19 Jimmy Spencer .07 .20
20 Hut Stricklin .07 .20
21 Brett Bodine's Car .02 .10
22 Geoff Bodine's Car .02 .10
23 Todd Bodine's Car .02 .10
24 Derrike Cope's Car .02 .10
25 Wally Dallenbach Jr.'s Car .02 .10
26 Bill Elliott's Car .20 .50
27 Bill Hamilton's Car .02 .10
28 Jimmy Hensley's Car .02 .10
29 Bobby Hillin's Car .02 .10
30 P.J. Jones' Car .02 .10
31 Bobby Labonte's Car .20 .50
32 Sterling Marlin's Car .07 .20
33 Mark Martin's Car .25 .60
34 Rick Mast's Car .02 .10
35 Ted Musgrave's Car .02 .10
36 Greg Sacks' Car .02 .10
37 Morgan Shepherd's Car .02 .10
38 Lake Speed's Car .02 .10
39 Jimmy Spencer's Car .02 .10
40 Hut Stricklin's Car .02 .10
41 Davey Allison .40 1.00
42 Davey Allison's Car .20 .50
43 Alan Kulwicki .20 .50
44 Alan Kulwicki's Car .15 .40
45 Lee Morse .02 .10
46 Michael Kranefuss .02 .10
47 Alan Kulwicki .20 .50
Bill Elliott
48 Manufacturers' Champs .02 .10
49 Davey Allison's Car .20 .50
50 Mark Martin's Car .25 .60

1993 Maxx Premier Plus

This 212-card set was the first "super premium" racing set produced. Factory sets were available through Maxx dealers and Maxx's mail order program. It was also available in eight-card foil packs. Insert cards of the Maxx Mascot and the Maxx Rookie Contenders (1 of 20,000) were included in hobby sets and randomly inserted in foil packs. There is also a version of the Maxx Rookie Contenders card that doesn't have the 1 of 20,000 printed on it.

COMPLETE SET (212) 12.00 30.00
COMP.FACT.SET (212) 12.00 30.00
WAX BOX 15.00 40.00
1 Rick Mast .10 .30
2 Rusty Wallace 1.00 2.50
3 Dale Earnhardt 2.00 5.00
4 Ernie Irvan .25 .60
5 Ricky Rudd .40 1.00
6 Mark Martin 1.00 2.50
7 Alan Kulwicki .40 1.00
8 Sterling Marlin .50 1.25
9 Chad Little .10 .30
10 Derrike Cope .10 .30
11 Bill Elliott .50 1.25
12 Jimmy Spencer .10 .30
13 Alan Kulwicki/Elliott Cars MM .25 .60
14 Terry Labonte .50 1.25
15 Geoff Bodine .10 .30
16 Wally Dallenbach, Jr. .10 .30
17 Darrell Waltrip .25 .60
18 Dale Jarrett .75 2.00
19 Tom Peck .10 .30
20 Alan Kulwicki's Car .25 .60
21 Morgan Shepherd .10 .30
22 Bobby Labonte .75 2.00
23 Kyle Petty's Car MM .10 .30
24 Jeff Gordon CRC 1.50 4.00
25 Ken Schrader .10 .30
26 Brett Bodine .10 .30
27 Hut Stricklin .10 .30
28 Davey Allison .60 1.50
29 Dav.Allison/Elliott Cars MM .10 .30
30 Michael Waltrip .25 .60
31 Steve Grissom .10 .30
32 Ken Schrader's Car .05 .15
33 Harry Gant .25 .60
34 Todd Bodine .10 .30
35 Bobby Hamilton's Car .05 .15
36 Ward Burton .25 .60
37 Bill Elliott's Car .10 .30
38 Jerry O'Neill .05 .15
39 Jeff Gordon's Car .75 2.00
40 Kenny Wallace .10 .30
41 Phil Parsons .10 .30
42 Kyle Petty .25 .60
43 Richard Petty .50 1.25
44 Rick Wilson .10 .30
45 Jeff Burton .40 1.00
46 Al Unser Jr. .25 .60
47 Bill Venturini .05 .15
48 Richard Petty MM .40 1.00
49 Stanley Smith .05 .15
50 Tommy Houston .10 .30
51 Bobby Labonte's Car .10 .30
52 Jimmy Means .10 .30
53 Mike Wallace .10 .30
54 Jack Sprague .05 .15
55 Ted Musgrave .10 .30
56 Dale Earnhardt's Car .75 2.00
57 Da.All/R.Pet/Mart/B.Lab.Cars MM.40 1.00
58 Jim Sauter .05 .15
59 Robert Pressley .10 .30
60 Dav.Allison/K.Petty Cars MM .10 .30
61 Kyle Petty's Car .10 .30
62 Davey Allison Crash MM .10 .30
63 Chuck Bown .10 .30
64 Sterling Marlin's Car .10 .30
65 Darrell Waltrip MM .10 .30
66 Jimmy Hensley .10 .30
67 Ernie Irvan's Car .25 .60
68 Bobby Hamilton .10 .30
69 Greg Sacks .10 .30
70 Tommy Ellis .05 .15
71 Dave Marcis .10 .30
72 Tracy Leslie .05 .15
73 Ricky Craven .25 .60
74 Richard Petty w/Car MM .40 1.00
75 Dick Trickle .10 .30
76 Butch Miller .10 .30
77 Jim Bown .05 .15
78 Shawna Robinson .60 1.50
79 Davey Allison's Car .10 .30
80 Bobby Dotter .05 .15
81 Alan Kulwicki MM .25 .60
82 Kenny Wallace's Car .05 .15
83 Lake Speed .10 .30
84 Bobby Hillin .10 .30
85 Mark Martin's Car .25 .60
86 Bob Schacht .05 .15
87 Joe Nemechek .10 .30
88 Ricky Rudd's Car .10 .30
89 Junior Johnson .10 .30
90 Robert Yates .05 .15
91 Leo Jackson .05 .15
92 Felix Sabates .05 .15
93 Jack Roush .05 .15
94 Rick Hendrick .05 .15
95 Billy Hagan .05 .15
96 Tim Morgan .05 .15
97 Larry McClure .05 .15
98 Ted McClure/J.McClure
Ed McClure .05 .15
99 Richard Childress .25 .60
100 Roger Penske .05 .15
101 Don Miller .05 .15
102 Glen Wood .05 .15
103 Len Wood .05 .15
104 Eddie Wood .05 .15
105 Kenny Bernstein .10 .30
106 Walter Bud Moore .05 .15
107 Ray DeWitt .05 .15
108 D.K. Ulrich .05 .15
109 Joe Gibbs .25 .60
110 Bill Stavola .05 .15
111 Mickey Stavola .05 .15
112 Richard Jackson .05 .15
113 Chuck Rider .05 .15
114 George Bradshaw .05 .15
115 Mark Smith .05 .15
116 Bobby Allison .10 .30
117 Bob Bilby .05 .15
118 Larry Hedrick .05 .15
119 Harry Melling .05 .15
120 Junie Donlavey .05 .15
121 Bill Davis .05 .15
122 Cale Yarborough .10 .30
123 Frank Cicci/Scott Welliver .05 .15
124 Dick Moroso .05 .15
125 Butch Mock .05 .15
126 Bob Rahilly .05 .15
127 Paul Andrews .05 .15
128 Mike Beam .05 .15
129 Larry McReynolds .05 .15
130 Tim Brewer .05 .15
131 Robin Pemberton .05 .15
132 Steve Hmiel .05 .15
133 Gary DeHart .05 .15
134 Pete Wright .05 .15
135 Jake Elder .05 .15
136 Mike Hill .05 .15
137 Tony Glover .05 .15
138 Andy Petree .05 .15
139 Buddy Parrott .05 .15
140 Leonard Wood .05 .15
141 Donnie Richeson .05 .15
142 Donnie Wingo .05 .15
143 Ken Howes .05 .15
144 Sandy Jones .05 .15
145 Jimmy Makar .05 .15
146 Ken Wilson .05 .15
147 Barry Dodson .05 .15
148 Doug Hewitt .05 .15
149 Howard Comstock .05 .15
150 David Fuge .05 .15
151 Robbie Loomis .05 .15
152 Jimmy Fennig .05 .15
153 Bob Johnson .05 .15
154 Doug Richert .05 .15
155 Ernie Elliott .05 .15
156 Doug Williams .05 .15
157 Tim Brewer .05 .15
158 Ray Evernham .05 .15
159 Troy Seberg .05 .15
160 Dennis Connor .05 .15
161 Jeff Hammond .05 .15
162 Dale Inman .05 .15
163 Harry Hyde .05 .15
164 Vic Kangas .05 .15
165 Bob Labonte .05 .15
166 Clyde McLeod .05 .15
167 Ricky Pearson .05 .15
168 Tony Eury .40 1.00
169 Ricky Rudd IROC Champ .40 1.00
170 Dick Beaty .05 .15
171 Ken Schrader w/Crew .10 .30
172 Alan Kulwicki WC Champ .25 .60
173 Jimmy Hensley WC ROY .10 .30
174 Larry McReynolds .05 .15
175 Bill Elliott FF .25 .60
176 Joe Nemechek Busch Champ .10 .30
177 Ricky Craven Busch ROY .25 .60
178 Geoff Bodine YR .10 .30
179 Davey Allison YR .25 .60
180 Bill Elliott YR .25 .60
181 Bill Elliott YR .25 .60
182 Bill Elliott YR .25 .60
183 Bill Elliott/J.Johnson YR .25 .60
184 Alan Kulwicki YR .25 .60
185 Davey Allison YR .25 .60
186 Mark Martin YR .50 1.25
187 Davey Allison YR .25 .60
188 Bobby Allison YR .10 .30
189 Dale Earnhardt YR/Jr./Kerry 4.00 10.00
190 Harry Gant YR .10 .30
191 Ernie Irvan YR .10 .30
192 Alan Kulwicki YR .25 .60
193 Dav.Allison/Yates/McRey.YR .10 .30
194 Ernie Irvan YR .10 .30
195 Darrell Waltrip YR .10 .30
196 Ernie Irvan w/Crew YR .10 .30
197 Kyle Petty YR .25 .60
198 Harry Gant YR .10 .30
199 Darrell Waltrip YR .10 .30
200 Darrell Waltrip YR .10 .30
201 Rusty Wallace YR .50 1.25
202 Ricky Rudd YR .40 1.00
203 Geoff Bodine YR .10 .30
204 Geoff Bodine YR .10 .30
205 Mark Martin YR .50 1.25
206 Kyle Petty YR .25 .60
207 Davey Allison w/Crew YR .25 .60
208 Bill Elliott YR .25 .60
209 Checklist #1 .05 .15
210 Checklist #2 .05 .15
211 Checklist #3 .05 .15
212 Checklist #4 .05 .15
P1 Bill Elliott Promo 5.00 12.00
NNO Mascot Card 1.00 3.00
NNO J.Gordon/B.Lab/K.Wall 10.00 25.00

1993 Maxx Premier Plus Jumbos

These three cards commemorate special happenings in the 1992 Winston Cup season. The Alan Kulwicki and Davey Allison cards pay tribute to the two great drivers. The Dale Earnhardt card celebrates his sixth Winston Cup championship. The cards use Maxx's Chromium technology and measure 8" X 10". The Dale Earnhardt card was sold with the 1993 Maxx Premier Series set via the Maxx Club. There were 80,000 of Earnhardt card. The other two cards were sold through the club and retail outlets.

COMPLETE SET (3) 15.00 30.00
1 Davey Allison 3.00 8.00
2 Dale Earnhardt 7.50 15.00
3 Alan Kulwicki 3.00 8.00

1993 Maxx Retail Jumbos

This nine-card set was inserted in special blister retail packs that were distributed in retail outlets such as K-Mart and Wal-Mart. The jumbo cards measure 3" by 5".

COMPLETE SET (9) 5.00 12.00
1 Darrell Waltrip .50 1.25
2 Ken Schrader .25 .60
3 Phil Parsons .25 .60
4 Sterling Marlin 1.00 2.50
5 Mark Martin 2.00 5.00
6 Dale Jarrett 1.50 4.00
7 Bill Elliott 1.00 2.50
8 Derrike Cope .25 .60
9 Brett Bodine .25 .60

1993 Maxx Texaco Davey Allison

This 20-card set was produced by Maxx and made available through Texaco gas stations in the southeastern region of the country. They were distributed in four-card packs and could be purchased for $.99. 5,000 of these cards were autographed by Davey Allison and randomly inserted into packs. The signed cards are different from their base card counterparts by the placement of Davey's printed name on the cardfronts. It is printed in a different location than on the unsigned version -- typically much lower on the cardfront. Like their predecessor, a large number of sets made thier way into the hobby.

COMPLETE SET (20) 4.00 10.00
1 Davey Allison .40 1.00
2 Dav.Allison .40 1.00
Cliff.Allison
Bob.Allison
3 Robert Yates .15 .40
4 Larry McReynolds .15 .40
5 Davey Allison w .15 .40
Crew
6 Davey Allison .15 .40
Yates
McReynolds
7 Davey Allison .40 1.00
8 Dav.Allison .15 .40
R.Wallace Cars
9 Davey Allison Crash .15 .40
10 Davey Allison .15 .40
Yates
McReynolds
11 Dav.Allison .15 .40
Bob.Allison
Yates
12 Davey Allison .15 .40
Bob.Allison
13 Davey Allison .40 1.00
14 Dav.Allison .15 .40
McReynolds
Yates
15 Davey Allison in Pits .15 .40
16 Davey Allison .15 .40
17 Davey Allison's Car .15 .40
18 Davey Allison .15 .40
Bobby Hillin
19 Davey Allison .40 1.00
20 Davey Allison w .15 .40
Crew CL
AU1 Davey Allison AUTO 75.00 150.00

1993 Maxx Winnebago Motorsports

This 11-card set was produced by Maxx and distributed by Winnebago Motorsports. The cards feature drivers in non-racing photos using Winnebago vehicles.

COMPLETE SET (11) 10.00 20.00
1 Sterling Marlin 1.00 2.50
2 J.Gordon 4.00 8.00
B.Lab
Bickle
K.Wall.
3 Bobby Allison 1.00 2.50
4 Winnebago Motor. Van .40 1.00
5 Bobby Allison .75 2.00
Judy Allison
6 B.Allison .75 2.00
Child
Spenc
Schrader
Marlin
Keselowski
7 Ken Schrader .75 2.00
8 Tony Bettenhausen .75 2.00
S.Johansson
9 David Rampy's Funny Car .40 1.00
10 Bob Keselowski's Car .40 1.00
NNO Cover Card .40 1.00

1993 Maxx The Winston

This 51-card set was produced by Maxx and features drivers who raced in the 1993 Winston Select. Each set contains a special chromium Dale Earnhardt card and were originally available through Club Maxx at a price of $10 per set.

COMP.FACT.SET (51) 3.00 8.00
1 Dale Earnhardt .60 1.50
2 Mark Martin .25 .60
3 Ernie Irvan .10 .25
4 Ken Schrader .02 .10
5 Geoff Bodine .02 .10
6 Darrell Waltrip .07 .20
7 Sterling Marlin .07 .20
8 Rusty Wallace .25 .60
9 Davey Allison .20 .50
10 Brett Bodine .02 .10
11 Rick Mast .02 .10
12 Morgan Shepherd .02 .10
13 Harry Gant .07 .20
14 Bill Elliott .15 .40
15 Terry Labonte .15 .40
16 Ricky Rudd .15 .40
17 Jimmy Hensley .02 .10
18 Michael Waltrip .07 .20
19 Dale Jarrett .20 .50
20 Kyle Petty .07 .20
21 Dale Earnhardt's Car .40 1.00
22 Mark Martin's Car .15 .40
23 Ernie Irvan's Car .07 .20
24 Ken Schrader's Car .02 .10
25 Geoff Bodine's Car .02 .10
26 Darrell Waltrip's Car .02 .10
27 Sterling Marlin's Car .02 .10
28 Rusty Wallace's Car .15 .40
29 Davey Allison's Car .10 .25
30 Brett Bodine's Car .02 .10
31 Rick Mast's Car .02 .10
32 Morgan Shepherd's Car .02 .10
33 Harry Gant's Car .02 .10
34 Bill Elliott's Car .07 .20
35 Terry Labonte's Car .07 .20
36 Ricky Rudd's Car .02 .10
37 Jimmy Hensley's Car .02 .10
38 Michael Waltrip's Car .07 .20
39 Dale Jarrett's Car .10 .25
40 Kyle Petty's Car .02 .10
41 Ernie Irvan PW .10 .25
42 Sterling Marlin Win .07 .20
43 Charlotte Motor Speedway .02 .10
44 Winston Starting Lineup .02 .10
45 First Segment .02 .10

46 Second Segment .02 .10
47 Third Segment .02 .10
48 Third Segment .02 .10
49 Dale Earnhardt's Car Win .40 1.00
50 Dale Earnhardt VL .50 1.25
51 Dale Earnhardt Chromium 1.00 2.50

1994 Maxx

The 1994 Maxx set was released in two separate series with the first series also being issued as a factory set packaged with four Rookies of the Year inserts. The sets feature the now standard Maxx subsets: Memorable Moments, Year in Review and highlight cards featuring the various NASCAR award winners from 1993. Each series also included randomly packed rookies insert cards with series two also containing an assortment of autographed insert cards. Packaging for each series was similar: 10 cards per pack with 36 packs per box. Jumbo packs were produced for series one with 20-cards per pack.

COMPLETE SET (340) 10.00 25.00
COMP.FACT.SET (244) 12.00 30.00
COMP.SERIES 1 (240) 6.00 15.00
COMP.SERIES 2 (100) 4.00 10.00
WAX BOX SERIES 1 15.00 40.00
WAX BOX SERIES 2 15.00 40.00
1 Rick Mast .07 .20
2 Rusty Wallace .60 1.50
3 Dale Earnhardt 1.25 3.00
4 Jimmy Hensley .07 .20
5 Ricky Rudd .25 .60
6 Mark Martin .60 1.50
7 Alan Kulwicki .25 .60
8 Sterling Marlin .25 .60
9 P.J. Jones .07 .20
10 Geoff Bodine .07 .20
11 Bill Elliott .30 .75
12 Jimmy Spencer .07 .20
13 Jeff Gordon MM .40 1.00
14 Terry Labonte .25 .60
15 Lake Speed .07 .20
16 Wally Dallenbach Jr. .07 .20
17 Darrell Waltrip .15 .40
18 Dale Jarrett .50 1.25
19 Chad Little .15 .40
20 Bobby Hamilton .07 .20
21 Morgan Shepherd .07 .20
22 Bobby Labonte .50 1.25
23 Dale Earnhardt's Car .50 1.25
24 Jeff Gordon 1.00 2.50
25 Ken Schrader .07 .20
26 Brett Bodine .07 .20
27 Hut Stricklin .07 .20
28 Davey Allison .30 .75
29 Ernie Irvan .15 .40
30 Michael Waltrip .15 .40
31 Neil Bonnett .25 .60
32 Jimmy Horton .07 .20
33 Harry Gant .07 .20
34 Rusty Wallace's Car .15 .40
35 Mark Martin's Car .15 .40
36 Dale Jarrett's Car .15 .40
37 Loy Allen Jr. .07 .20
38 Dale Jarrett's Car MM .15 .40
39 Kyle Petty's Car .07 .20
40 Kenny Wallace .07 .20
41 Dick Trickle .07 .20
42 Kyle Petty .15 .40
43 Richard Petty .25 .60
44 Rick Wilson .07 .20
45 T.W. Taylor .02 .10
46 James Hylton .07 .20
47 Phil Parsons .07 .20
48 Ernie Irvan's Car .07 .20
49 Stanley Smith .02 .10
50 Morgan Shepherd's Car .02 .10
51 Joe Ruttman .07 .20
52 Jimmy Means .07 .20
53 Davey Allison's Car MM .15 .40
54 Bill Elliott's Car .15 .40
55 Ted Musgrave .07 .20
56 Ken Schrader's Car .02 .10
57 Bob Schacht .02 .10
58 Jim Sauter .02 .10
59 Ricky Rudd w/Car .15 .40
60 Harry Gant's Car .07 .20
61 Ken Bouchard .07 .20
62 Dave Marcis' Car .07 .20
63 Rich Bickle .07 .20
64 Darrell Waltrip's Car .07 .20
65 Jeff Gordon's Car .30 .75
66 Jeff Burton's Car .07 .20
67 Geoff Bodine's Car .02 .10
68 Greg Sacks .07 .20
69 Tom Kendall .07 .20
70 Michael Waltrip's Car .07 .20
71 Dave Marcis .07 .20
72 John Andretti RC .07 .20
73 Todd Bodine's Car .02 .10
74 Bobby Labonte's Car .15 .40
75 Todd Bodine .07 .20
76 Brett Bodine's Car .02 .10
77 Jeff Purvis .07 .20
78 Rick Mast's Car .02 .10
79 Rick Carelli RC .07 .20
80 Wally Dallenbach Jr.'s Car .02 .10
81 Jimmy Spencer's Car .02 .10
82 Bobby Hillin's Car .02 .10
83 Lake Speed's Car .02 .10
84 Richard Childress .15 .40
85 Roger Penske .07 .20
86 Don Miller .02 .10
87 Jack Roush .02 .10
88 Joe Gibbs .15 .40
89 Felix Sabates .02 .10
90 Bobby Hillin .07 .20
91 Tim Morgan .02 .10
92 Larry McClure .02 .10
93 Ted McClure
J.McClure/Ed McClure .02 .10
94 Glen Wood .02 .10
95 Len Wood .02 .10
96 Eddie Wood .02 .10
97 Junior Johnson .07 .20
98 Derrike Cope .07 .20
99 Andy Hillenburg .07 .20
100 Rick Hendrick .02 .10
101 Leo Jackson .02 .10
102 Bobby Allison .07 .20
103 Bob Bilby .02 .10
104 Bill Stavola .02 .10
105 Mickey Stavola .02 .10
106 Paul Moore (Bud) .02 .10
107 Chuck Rider .02 .10
108 Billy Hagan .02 .10
109 Bill Davis .02 .10
110 Kenny Bernstein .07 .20
111 Richard Jackson .02 .10
112 Ray DeWitt/Diane DeWitt .02 .10
113 D.K. Ulrich .02 .10
114 Cale Yarborough .07 .20
115 Junie Donlavey .02 .10
116 Larry Hedrick .02 .10
117 Robert Yates .02 .10
118 George Bradshaw .02 .10
119 Mark Smith .02 .10
120 David Fuge .02 .10
121 Harry Melling .02 .10
122 Atlanta MM .02 .10
123 Dick Moroso .02 .10
124 Butch Mock .02 .10
125 Alan Kulwicki's Trans. MM .15 .40
126 Andy Petree .02 .10
127 Buddy Parrott .02 .10
128 Steve Hmiel .02 .10
129 Howard Comstock .02 .10
130 Jimmy Makar .02 .10
131 Robin Pemberton .02 .10
132 Jeff Hammond .02 .10
133 Tony Glover .02 .10
134 Leonard Wood .02 .10
135 Mike Beam .02 .10
136 Mike Hill .02 .10
137 Gary DeHart .02 .10
138 Ray Evernham .15 .40
139 Ken Howes .02 .10
140 Jimmy Fennig .02 .10
141 Barry Dodson .02 .10
142 Ken Wilson .02 .10
143 Donnie Wingo .02 .10
144 Doug Hewitt .02 .10
145 Pete Wright .02 .10
146 Tim Brewer .02 .10
147 Donnie Richeson .02 .10
148 Sandy Jones .02 .10
149 Bob Johnson .02 .10
150 Geoff Bodine/Brett
Bodine Cars MM .02 .10
151 Doug Williams .02 .10
152 Waddell Wilson .02 .10
153 Doug Richert .02 .10
154 Larry McReynolds .02 .10
155 Dennis Connor .02 .10
156 Harry Hyde .02 .10
157 Paul Andrews .02 .10
158 Robbie Loomis .07 .20
159 Troy Selberg .02 .10
160 Dale Inman .02 .10
161 Tony Eury .25 .60
162 Dale Fischlein .02 .10
163 Steve Grissom .07 .20
164 Ricky Craven .07 .20
165 David Green .07 .20
166 Chuck Bown .07 .20
167 Joe Nemechek .07 .20
168 Ward Burton .15 .40
169 Bobby Dotter .07 .20
170 Robert Pressley .07 .20
171 Hermie Sadler .07 .20
172 Mike Wallace .07 .20
173 Tracy Leslie .07 .20
174 Tom Peck .07 .20
175 Jeff Burton .25 .60
176 Rodney Combs .07 .20
177 Talladega Speedway MM .02 .10
178 Tommy Houston .07 .20
179 Joe Bessey .07 .20
180 Tim Fedewa .07 .20
181 Jack Sprague .07 .20
182 Richard Lasater .02 .10
183 Roy Payne .07 .20
184 Shawna Robinson .30 .75
185 Larry Pearson .07 .20
186 Jim Bown .07 .20
187 Nathan Buttke .02 .10
188 Butch Miller .07 .20
189 Jason Keller RC .25 .60
190 Randy LaJoie .07 .20
191 Dave Rezendes .07 .20
192 Jeff Green .07 .20
193 Ed Berrier .02 .10
194 Troy Beebe .02 .10
195 Dennis Setzer .07 .20
196 David Bonnett .07 .20
197 Steve Grissom BGN Champ .02 .10
198 Hermie Sadler BGN ROY .02 .10
199 Rusty Wallace w/Crew .25 .60
200 Steve Hmiel .02 .10
201 Jeff Gordon WC ROY .60 1.50
202 Bill Elliott FF .25 .60
203 Davey Allison IROC Champ .15 .40
204 Jimmy Horton Crash MM .02 .10
205 Dale Jarrett/Kyle Petty Cars MM .15 .40
206 Rusty Wallace's Car MM .15 .40
207 Dale Jarrett/Gibbs YR .30 .75
208 Rusty Wallace YR .25 .60
209 Davey Allison YR .15 .40
210 Morgan Shepherd w/Crew YR .02 .10
211 Dale Earnhardt YR .60 1.50
212 Rusty Wallace YR .25 .60
213 Rusty Wallace w/Crew YR .25 .60
214 Rusty Wallace YR .25 .60
215 Ernie Irvan YR .07 .20
216 Geoff Bodine w/Crew YR .02 .10
217 Sterling Marlin YR .15 .40
218 Dale Earnhardt YR .60 1.50
219 Dale Earnhardt YR .60 1.50
220 Kyle Petty YR .07 .20
221 Ricky Rudd YR .02 .10
222 Dale Earnhardt YR .60 1.50
223 Rusty Wallace YR .25 .60
224 Dale Earnhardt YR .60 1.50
225 Dale Earnhardt YR .60 1.50
226 Mark Martin YR .25 .60
227 Mark Martin YR .25 .60
228 Mark Martin YR .25 .60
229 Mark Martin YR .25 .60
230 Rusty Wallace w/Crew YR .25 .60
231 Rusty Wallace w/Crew YR .25 .60
232 Ernie Irvan/Yates/McR.YR .15 .40
233 Rusty Wallace YR .25 .60
234 Ernie Irvan YR .07 .20
235 Rusty Wallace YR .25 .60
236 Mark Martin YR .25 .60
237 Rusty Wallace YR .25 .60
238 Dale Earnhardt WC Champ .60 1.50
239 Checklist #1 .02 .10
240 Checklist #2 .02 .10
241 Bill Elliott .30 .75
242 Harry Gant .15 .40
243 Harry Gant's Car .07 .20
244 Sterling Marlin .25 .60
245 Sterling Marlin's Car .07 .20
246 Terry Labonte .25 .60
247 Terry Labonte's Car .15 .40
248 Morgan Shepherd .07 .20
249 Morgan Shepherd's Car .02 .10
250 Ernie Irvan .15 .40
251 Ernie Irvan's Car .07 .20
252 Dale Jarrett .50 1.25
253 Dale Jarrett's Car .15 .40
254 Bobby Labonte .50 1.25
255 Bobby Labonte's Car .15 .40
256 Ken Schrader .07 .20
257 Ken Schrader's Car .02 .10
258 Mark Martin .60 1.50
259 Mark Martin's Car .15 .40
260 Michael Waltrip .15 .40
261 Michael Waltrip's Car .07 .20
262 Derrike Cope .07 .20
263 Hut Stricklin .07 .20
264 Sterling Marlin .25 .60
265 Chuck Bown .07 .20
266 Ted Musgrave .07 .20
267 Jimmy Spencer .07 .20
268 Wally Dallenbach Jr. .07 .20
269 Jeff Purvis .07 .20
270 Greg Sacks .07 .20
271 Rich Bickle .07 .20
272 Bobby Hamilton .07 .20
273 Dick Trickle's Car .02 .10
274 Hut Stricklin's Car .02 .10
275 Terry Labonte's Car .15 .40
276 Ted Musgrave's Car .02 .10
277 Greg Sacks' Car .02 .10
278 Jimmy Hensley's Car .02 .10
279 Derrike Cope's Car .02 .10
280 Bobby Hamilton's Car .02 .10
281 Ricky Rudd's Car .07 .20
282 Geoff Bodine's Car .02 .10
283 Kevin Hamlin RC .02 .10
284 Charley Pressley .02 .10
285 Jim Long .02 .10
286 Bill Ingle .02 .10
287 Peter Sospenzo .02 .10
288 Freddy Fryar .02 .10
289 Chris Hussey .02 .10
290 Mike Hillman .02 .10
291 Gordon Gibbs .02 .10
292 Ken Glen .02 .10
293 Tony Furr .02 .10
294 Pete Wright .02 .10
295 Travis Carter .02 .10
296 Gary Bechtel/Carolyn Bechtel .02 .10
297 A.G. Dillard .07 .20
298 Kenny Wallace .07 .20
299 Elton Sawyer .07 .20
300 Rodney Combs .07 .20
301 Phil Parsons .07 .20
302 Kevin Lepage RC .15 .40
303 Johnny Benson RC .25 .60
304 Mike McLaughlin .07 .20
305 Patty Moise .07 .20
306 Larry Pearson .07 .20
307 Robert Pressley .07 .20
308 Clyde McLeod .02 .10
309 Ricky Pearson .02 .10
310 Gil Martin .02 .10
311 Fil Martocci .02 .10
312 F.Cicci/S.Welliver/John Gittler .02 .10
313 John Andretti's Car MM .02 .10
314 Shawna Robinson's Car MM .15 .40
315 Mike Skinner's Car MM .02 .10
316 Loy Allen Jr. MM .02 .10
317 Bob Jenkins .02 .10
318 Buddy Baker .02 .10
319 Checklist Card 1 .02 .10
320 Checklist Card 2 .02 .10
321 Joe Nemechek WS .02 .10
322 Rusty Wallace WS .25 .60
323 Winston Select Action .02 .10
324 Winston Select Action .02 .10
325 Winston Select Action .02 .10
326 Ken Schrader 's Car WS .02 .10
327 Jeff Gordon's Car WS .30 .75
328 Jeff Gordon WS .75 2.00
329 Winston Select Action .02 .10
330 Winston Select Action .02 .10
331 Winston Select Action .02 .10
332 Geoff Bodine Crash WS .02 .10
333 Winston Select Action .02 .10
334 Irvan/D.Earnhardt/W.Burton Cars .15 .40
335 Gordon/R.Wall/Earn.Cars .40 1.00
336 Geoff Bodine/Ernie Irvan Cars .02 .10
337 Winston Select Action .02 .10
338 Geoff Bodine's Car .02 .10
339 Geoff Bodine WS .02 .10
340 Geoff Bodine WS .02 .10
P11 Bill Elliott Promo 2.00 5.00
S24 Jeff Gordon Sample 3.00 8.00
PC Bill Elliott Club Promo 4.00 10.00
PS2 Ted Musgrave Promo .75 2.00

1994 Maxx Autographs

Maxx packaged Autographed cards throughout the print run of 1994 series two and Medallion products. Although a few older Maxx issues were included, most of the cards signed were from series one 1994 Maxx and the Rookie Class of '94 insert sets. Wrapper stated odds for pulling an autographed card from series two was 1:200 packs. To pull a signed card from Maxx Medallion collectors faced wrapper stated odds of 1:18 packs. Each signed card was crimped with Maxx's corporate seal which reads "J.R. Maxx Inc. Corporate Seal 1988 North Carolina."

COMPLETE SET (37) 600.00 1000.00
1 Rick Mast 6.00 15.00
2 Steve Grissom Rookie Class 6.00 15.00
3 Joe Nemechek Rookie Class 6.00 15.00
4 John Andretti Rookie Class 6.00 15.00
5 Ricky Rudd 15.00 40.00
6 Mark Martin 15.00 40.00
7 Loy Allen Jr. Rookie Class 6.00 15.00
8 Jeremy Mayfield Rook.Class 10.00 25.00
9 Bill Elliott '91 Maxx 40.00 80.00
9 Loy Allen Jr. Rookie Class 6.00 15.00
11 Bill Elliott '92 Maxx Red 30.00 60.00
14 Terry Labonte 12.50 30.00
18 Dale Jarrett 12.50 30.00
20 Buddy Baker '92 Maxx Red 6.00 15.00
20 Buddy Baker '92 Maxx Black 6.00 15.00
22 Bobby Labonte 12.50 30.00
24 Jeff Gordon 75.00 150.00
25 Ken Schrader 6.00 15.00
33 Harry Gant 10.00 25.00
37 Loy Allen Jr. 6.00 15.00
42 Kyle Petty 20.00 40.00
47 Phil Parsons 6.00 15.00
63 Rich Bickle 6.00 15.00
94 Glen Wood 6.00 15.00
95 Len Wood 6.00 15.00
96 Eddie Wood 6.00 15.00
154 Larry McReynolds 6.00 15.00
163 Steve Grissom 6.00 15.00
167 Joe Nemechek 6.00 15.00
168 Ward Burton 10.00 25.00
170 Robert Pressley 6.00 15.00
172 Mike Wallace 6.00 15.00
175 Jeff Burton 8.00 20.00
184 Shawna Robinson 15.00 30.00
227 Mark Martin 20.00 40.00
298 Kenny Wallace 6.00 15.00
318 Buddy Baker 6.00 15.00

1994 Maxx Rookie Class of '94

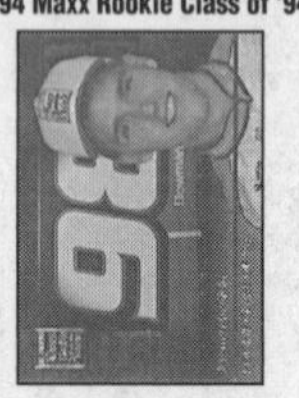

Maxx produced this set featuring the nine candidates for the 1994 Winston Cup Rookie of the Year award. The cards were distributed in 1994 Maxx series two packs at the stated odds of 1:12.

COMPLETE SET (10) 10.00 20.00
1 Jeff Burton 1.50 4.00
2 Steve Grissom 1.50 4.00
3 Joe Nemechek 1.50 4.00
4 John Andretti 1.50 4.00
5 Ward Burton 1.50 4.00
6 Mike Wallace .75 2.00
7 Loy Allen Jr. .75 2.00
8 Jeremy Mayfield 3.00 8.00
9 Billy Standridge .75 2.00
10 Checklist .75 2.00

1994 Maxx Rookies of the Year

Maxx produced this set featuring various Winston Cup Rookies of the Year awarded between 1966 and 1993. The cards were distributed in 1994 Maxx series one packs at the wrapper stated odds of 1:12 packs.

COMPLETE SET (16) 10.00 25.00
1 James Hylton .30 .75
2 Ricky Rudd 1.00 2.50
3 Dale Earnhardt 5.00 12.00
4 Geoff Bodine .30 .75
5 Sterling Marlin 1.00 2.50
6 Rusty Wallace 2.50 6.00
7 Ken Schrader .30 .75
8 Alan Kulwicki 1.00 2.50
9 Davey Allison 1.25 3.00
10 Ken Bouchard .30 .75
11 Dick Trickle .30 .75
12 Bobby Hamilton .30 .75
13 Jimmy Hensley .30 .75
14 Kenny Wallace .30 .75
15 Bobby Labonte 2.00 5.00
16 Jeff Gordon 4.00 10.00

1994 Maxx Medallion

Maxx released the Medallion set in late 1994. The first 55 cards in the set were printed on typical cardboard stock while the last 20 cards were produced on a clear plastic stock. Packs contained eight total cards; seven regular issue cards and one clear card. Boxes contained 18 packs. Maxx also included randomly packed (approximately 1:360) certificates for 1988 Dale Earnhardt cards (#99) that had been previously unreleased. Each card carried a gold sticker on the front showing the serial number of 999 and to help differentiate it from the other card #99 that was released after the bankruptcy of Maxx. Also randomly inserted in packs of Medallion were autographed cards. Pricing for those cards can be found under the 1994 Maxx Autograph listing.

COMPLETE SET (75) 12.50 25.00
COMP.SET w/o SP's (55) 3.00 8.00
WAX BOX 25.00 50.00
1 Jeff Gordon's Car .50 1.25
2 Brett Bodine's Car .05 .15
3 Bill Elliott .40 1.00
4 Rusty Wallace .75 2.00
5 Darrell Waltrip .20 .50
6 Ken Schrader .08 .25
7 Michael Waltrip's Car .08 .25
8 Todd Bodine's Car .05 .15
9 Morgan Shepherd .08 .25
10 Ricky Rudd .30 .75
11 Terry Labonte .30 .75
12 Ted Musgrave's Car .05 .15
13 Sterling Marlin's Car .08 .25
14 Lake Speed .08 .25
15 Bobby Labonte .60 1.50
16 Ernie Irvan's Car .08 .25
17 Greg Sacks' Car .05 .15
18 Jeff Burton .30 .75
19 Joe Nemechek's Car .05 .15
20 Bobby Hillin's Car .05 .15
21 Rick Mast's Car .05 .15
22 Wally Dallenbach Jr.'s Car .05 .15
23 Bobby Hamilton .08 .25
24 Kyle Petty .20 .50
25 Jeremy Mayfield's Car .20 .50
26 Derrike Cope's Car .05 .15
27 John Andretti's Car .05 .15
28 Rich Bickle's Car .05 .15
29 A.J. Foyt's Car .05 .15
30 Ward Burton .20 .50
31 Jimmy Hensley's Car .05 .15
32 Jeff Purvis .08 .25
33 Mark Martin .75 2.00
34 Hut Stricklin's Car .05 .15
35 Harry Gant .20 .50
36 Geoff Bodine's Car .05 .15
37 Dale Jarrett .60 1.50
38 Dave Marcis' Car .05 .15
39 Mike Chase .08 .25
40 Jimmy Spencer's Car .05 .15
41 NASCAR Arrives In .05 .15
42 A Warm Welcome .05 .15
43 Birthday Wishes .05 .15
44 Gentlemen Start Your Engines .05 .15
45 In Formation .05 .15
46 J.Gordon/Earnhardt Cars .60 1.50
47 Gordon's Car YL .40 1.00
48 Coming Off Turn One/Gordon's Car .20 .50
49 Jeff Gordon/G.Bodine Cars .40 1.00
50 Jeff Gordon's Car JR .40 1.00
51 Dave Marcis/Mike Chase Cars .05 .15
52 Jeff Gordon/Irvan Cars .40 1.00
53 Jeff Gordon BY 1.00 2.50
54 NASCAR World .05 .15
55 Checklist Card .05 .15
56 Jeff Gordon 3.00 8.00
57 Bobby Labonte 2.00 5.00
58 Jeff Burton's Car .50 1.25
59 Wally Dallenbach Jr.'s Car .30 .75
60 Brett Bodine .50 1.25
61 Ernie Irvan 1.00 2.50
62 Morgan Shepherd .50 1.25
63 Jimmy Spencer's Car .30 .75
64 Bill Elliott 1.25 3.00
65 Mike Wallace .50 1.25
66 Ricky Rudd 1.25 3.00
67 Ernie Irvan's Car .50 1.25
68 A.J. Foyt 1.00 2.50
69 Rusty Wallace 2.50 6.00
70 Mark Martin 2.50 6.00
71 Ted Musgrave .50 1.25
72 Ricky Rudd's Car .50 1.25
73 Kyle Petty 1.00 2.50
74 Harry Gant .50 1.25
75 Geoff Bodine's Car .30 .75
99SP D.Earnhardt 1988/999 125.00 250.00

1994 Maxx Motorsport

This 25-card set was produced by Maxx and distributed by Ford Motorsport and Club Maxx. This year's set features top Ford drivers on oversized (approximately 3-1/2" by 5") cards utilizing the metallic printing process commonly found with Maxx Premier Plus. Reportedly, 10,000 sets were produced.

COMPLETE SET (25) 4.00 8.00
1 Ernie Irvan .10 .30
2 Rusty Wallace .75 2.00
3 Mark Martin .75 2.00
4 Bill Elliott .40 1.00
5 Jimmy Spencer .07 .20
6 Ted Musgrave .07 .20
7 Geoff Bodine .07 .20
8 Brett Bodine .07 .20
9 Todd Bodine .07 .20
10 Jeff Burton .30 .75
11 Rick Mast .07 .20
12 Lake Speed .07 .20
13 Morgan Shepherd .07 .20
14 Ricky Rudd .30 .75
15 Derrike Cope .07 .20
16 Hut Stricklin .07 .20
17 Loy Allen Jr. .07 .20
18 Mike Wallace .07 .20
19 Greg Sacks .07 .20
20 Jimmy Hensley .07 .20
21 Rich Bickle .07 .20
22 Bobby Hillin .07 .20
23 Jeremy Mayfield .07 .20
24 Randy LaJoie .07 .20
25 Checklist .04 .10

1994 Maxx Premier Plus

Maxx produced the Premier Plus set for the second year in 1994. The cards were produced using a metallic chromium printing process now standard with Premier Plus. The cards closely resemble those found in series one 1994 Maxx, except for the special printing features and card numbering. An Alan Kulwicki set was produced and randomly inserted in packs. Cards could be found in eight-card packs, 36-pack boxes and complete factory sets which also included six Alan Kulwicki insert cards per set.

COMPLETE SET (200) 10.00 25.00
COMP.FACT.SET (206) 12.00 30.00
WAX BOX 15.00 40.00
1 Rick Mast .10 .30
2 Rusty Wallace 1.00 2.50
3 Dale Earnhardt 2.00 5.00
4 Jimmy Hensley .10 .30
5 Ricky Rudd .40 1.00
6 Mark Martin 1.00 2.50
7 Alan Kulwicki .40 1.00
8 Sterling Marlin .40 1.00
9 Bill Elliott FF .40 1.00
10 Geoff Bodine .10 .30
11 Bill Elliott .50 1.25
12 Jimmy Spencer .10 .30
13 Jeff Gordon MM .60 1.50
14 Terry Labonte .40 1.00
15 Lake Speed .10 .30
16 Wally Dallenbach Jr. .10 .30
17 Darrell Waltrip .25 .60
18 Dale Jarrett 1.00 2.00
19 Dale Jarrett's Car MM .25 .60
20 Bobby Hamilton .10 .30
21 Morgan Shepherd .10 .30
22 Bobby Labonte .75 2.00
23 Dale Earnhardt's Car .75 2.00
24 Jeff Gordon 1.25 3.00
25 Ken Schrader .10 .30
26 Brett Bodine .10 .30
27 Hut Stricklin .10 .30
28 Davey Allison .60 1.50
29 Ernie Irvan .25 .60
30 Michael Waltrip .25 .60
31 Davey Allison's Car MM .25 .60
32 Jimmy Horton .10 .30
33 Harry Gant .25 .60
34 Rusty Wallace's Car .40 1.00
35 Mark Martin's Car .40 1.00

36 Dale Jarrett's Car .25 .60
37 Travis Carter .05 .15
38 Hut Stricklin's Car .05 .15
39 Kyle Petty's Car .10 .30
40 Kenny Wallace .10 .30
41 Dick Trickle .10 .30
42 Kyle Petty .25 .60
43 Richard Petty .40 1.00
44 Rick Wilson .10 .30
45 Atlanta MM .05 .15
46 Jeff Gordon WC ROY 1.25 3.00
47 Phil Parsons .10 .30
48 Ernie Irvan's Car .10 .30
49 Alan Kulwicki 's Trans. MM .10 .30
50 Morgan Shepherd's Car .05 .15
51 Hermie Sadler BGN ROY .10 .30
52 Jimmy Means .10 .30
53 Steve Hmiel .05 .15
54 Bill Elliott's Car .25 .60
55 Ted Musgrave .10 .30
56 Ken Schrader's Car .05 .15
57 Geoff Bodine/Brett Bodine Cars MM .05 .15
58 Davey Allison IROC Champ .60 1.50
59 Ricky Rudd's Car .10 .30
60 Harry Gant's Car .10 .30
61 Steve Grissom BGN Champ .05 .15
62 Dave Marcis' Car .10 .30
63 New Hampshire MM .05 .15
64 Darrell Waltrip's Car .10 .30
65 Jeff Gordon's Car .50 1.25
66 Jeff Burton's Car .10 .30
67 Geoff Bodine's Car .05 .15
68 Greg Sacks .10 .30
69 Talladega Speedway MM .25 .60
70 Michael Waltrip's Car .10 .30
71 Dave Marcis .25 .60
72 Jimmy Horton Crash MM .05 .15
73 Todd Bodine's Car .05 .15
74 Bobby Labonte's Car .25 .60
75 Todd Bodine .10 .30
76 Brett Bodine's Car .05 .15
77 Neil Bonnett .40 1.00
78 Rick Mast's Car .05 .15
79 Dale Jarrett/Kyle Petty Cars MM .25 .60
80 Wally Dallenbach Jr.'s Car .05 .15
81 Jimmy Spencer's Car .05 .15
82 Bobby Hillin's Car .05 .15
83 Lake Speed's Car .05 .15
84 Richard Childress .25 .60
85 Roger Penske .05 .15
86 Don Miller .05 .15
87 Jack Roush .05 .15
88 Joe Gibbs .25 .60
89 Felix Sabates .05 .15
90 Bobby Hillin .10 .30
91 Tim Morgan .05 .15
92 Larry McClure .05 .15
93 T.McClure/J.McClure/Ed McClure .05 .15
94 Glen Wood .05 .15
95 Len Wood .05 .15
96 Eddie Wood .05 .15
97 Junior Johnson .10 .30
98 Derrike Cope .10 .30
99 Rusty Wallace w/Crew .40 1.00
100 Rick Hendrick .05 .15
101 Leo Jackson .05 .15
102 Bobby Allison .10 .30
103 Bob Bilby .05 .15
104 Bill Stavola .05 .15
105 Mickey Stavola .05 .15
106 Walter Bud Moore .05 .15
107 Chuck Rider .05 .15
108 Billy Hagan .05 .15
109 Bill Davis .05 .15
110 Kenny Bernstein .10 .30
111 Richard Jackson .05 .15
112 Ray DeWitt/Diane DeWitt .05 .15
113 D.K. Ulrich .05 .15
114 Cale Yarborough .10 .30
115 Junie Donlavey .05 .15
116 Larry Hedrick .05 .15
117 Robert Yates .05 .15
118 Rusty Wallace's Car .40 1.00
119 Andy Petree .05 .15
120 Buddy Parrott .05 .15
121 Steve Hmiel .05 .15
122 Howard Comstock .05 .15
123 Jimmy Makar .05 .15
124 Robin Pemberton .05 .15
125 Jeff Hammond .05 .15
126 Tony Glover .05 .15
127 Leonard Wood .05 .15
128 Mike Beam .05 .15
129 Mike Hill .05 .15
130 Gary DeHart .05 .15
131 Ray Evernham .25 .60
132 Ken Howes .05 .15
133 Jimmy Fennig .05 .15
134 Barry Dodson .05 .15
135 Ken Wilson .05 .15
136 Donnie Wingo .05 .15
137 Doug Hewitt .05 .15
138 Pete Wright .05 .15
139 Tim Brewer .05 .15
140 Donnie Richeson .05 .15
141 Sandy Jones .05 .15
142 Bob Johnson .05 .15
143 Doug Williams .05 .15
144 Waddell Wilson .05 .15
145 Doug Richert .05 .15
146 Larry McReynolds .05 .15
147 Paul Andrews .05 .15
148 Robbie Loomis .10 .30
149 Dale Inman .05 .15
150 Steve Grissom .10 .30
151 Ricky Craven .10 .30
152 David Green .10 .30
153 Chuck Bown .10 .30
154 Joe Nemechek .10 .30
155 Ward Burton .25 .60
156 Bobby Dotter .10 .30
157 Robert Pressley .10 .30
158 Hermie Sadler .10 .30
159 Tracy Leslie .10 .30
160 Mike Wallace .10 .30
161 Tom Peck .10 .30
162 Jeff Burton .40 1.00
163 Rodney Combs .10 .30
164 Tommy Houston .10 .30
165 Dale Earnhardt w/Crew 1.00 2.50
166 Dale Jarrett YR .25 .60
167 Rusty Wallace YR .40 1.00
168 Davey Allison YR .40 1.00
169 Morgan Shepherd w/Crew YR .05 .15
170 Dale Earnhardt YR 1.00 2.50
171 Rusty Wallace YR .40 1.00
172 Rusty Wallace w/Crew YR .40 1.00
173 Rusty Wallace YR .40 1.00
174 Ernie Irvan YR .10 .30
175 Geoff Bodine w/Crew YR .05 .15
176 Sterling Marlin YR .25 .60
177 Dale Earnhardt YR 1.00 2.50
178 Dale Earnhardt w/Crew YR 1.00 2.50
179 Kyle Petty YR .10 .30
180 Ricky Rudd YR .25 .60
181 Dale Earnhardt w/Crew YR 1.00 2.50
182 Rusty Wallace w/Crew YR .40 1.00
183 Dale Earnhardt/Childress YR 1.00 2.50
184 Dale Earnhardt YR 1.00 2.50
185 Mark Martin YR .40 1.00
186 Mark Martin YR .40 1.00
187 Mark Martin YR .40 1.00
188 Mark Martin w/Crew YR .40 1.00
189 Rusty Wallace YR .40 1.00
190 Rusty Wallace w/Crew YR .40 1.00
191 Ernie Irvan/Yates/McR.YR .25 .60
192 Rusty Wallace YR .40 1.00
193 Ernie Irvan YR .25 .60
194 Rusty Wallace YR .40 1.00
195 Mark Martin/Roush YR .40 1.00
196 Rusty Wallace YR .40 1.00
197 Checklist .05 .15
198 Checklist .05 .15
199 Checklist .05 .15
200 Checklist .05 .15
P1 Bill Elliott Promo 2.50 6.00

1994 Maxx Premier Plus Alan Kulwicki

Maxx produced these fourteen cards honoring the late Alan Kulwicki to be random inserts in 1994 Premier Plus. Wrapper stated odds for pulling a card was 1:15 packs. Six cards could also be randomly found in each Premier Plus factory set.

COMPLETE SET (14) 8.00 20.00
COMMON CARD (1-14) .75 2.00

1994 Maxx Premier Series

Maxx again offered a special Premier Series set to its Club Maxx members. The 1994 issue included 300 regular cards all featuring new photography and different card design. Eight cards that constitute the first series of the 1994 Maxx Jumbo issue were also included with each complete set.

COMPLETE SET (300) 12.50 30.00
COMP.FACT.SET (308) 15.00 40.00
1 Rick Mast .07 .20
2 Rusty Wallace .60 1.50
3 Dale Earnhardt 1.25 3.00
4 Jimmy Hensley .07 .20
5 Ricky Rudd .25 .60
6 Mark Martin .60 1.50
7 Alan Kulwicki .25 .60
8 Sterling Marlin .25 .60
9 P.J. Jones .07 .20
10 Geoff Bodine .07 .20
11 Bill Elliott .30 .75
12 Jimmy Spencer .07 .20
13 Jeff Gordon MM .40 1.00
14 Terry Labonte .25 .60
15 Lake Speed .07 .20
16 Wally Dallenbach, Jr. .07 .20
17 Darrell Waltrip .15 .40
18 Dale Jarrett .50 1.25
19 Chad Little .07 .20
20 Bobby Hamilton .07 .20
21 Morgan Shepherd .07 .20
22 Bobby Labonte .50 1.25
23 Dale Earnhardt's Car .50 1.25
24 Jeff Gordon .75 2.00
25 Ken Schrader .07 .20
26 Brett Bodine .07 .20
27 Hut Stricklin .07 .20
28 Davey Allison .15 .40
29 Ernie Irvan .15 .40
30 Michael Waltrip .15 .40
31 Neil Bonnett .25 .60
32 Jimmy Horton .07 .20
33 Harry Gant .15 .40
34 Rusty Wallace's Car .25 .60
35 Mark Martin's Car .25 .60
36 Dale Jarrett's Car .15 .40
37 Loy Allen Jr. .07 .20
38 Dale Jarrett's Car MM .15 .40
39 Kyle Petty's Car .07 .20
40 Kenny Wallace .07 .20
41 Dick Trickle .07 .20
42 Kyle Petty .15 .40
43 Richard Petty .25 .60
44 Rick Wilson .07 .20
45 T.W. Taylor .02 .10
46 James Hylton .07 .20
47 Phil Parsons .07 .20
48 Ernie Irvan's Car .15 .40
49 Stanley Smith .02 .10
50 Morgan Shepherd's Car .02 .10
51 Joe Ruttman .07 .20
52 Jimmy Means .07 .20
53 Davey Allison's Car MM .15 .40
54 Bill Elliott's Car .15 .40
55 Ted Musgrave .07 .20
56 Ken Schrader's Car .02 .10
57 Bob Schacht .02 .10
58 Jim Sauter .07 .20
59 Ricky Rudd's Car .07 .20
60 Harry Gant's Car .07 .20
61 Ken Bouchard .07 .20
62 Dave Marcis .07 .20
63 Rich Bickle .07 .20
64 Darrell Waltrip's Car .07 .20
65 Jeff Gordon's Car .30 .75
66 Jeff Burton's Car .07 .20
67 Geoff Bodine's Car .02 .10
68 Greg Sacks .07 .20
69 Tom Kendall .07 .20
70 Michael Waltrip .15 .40
71 Dave Marcis .07 .20
72 John Andretti .07 .20
73 Todd Bodine's Car .02 .10
74 Bobby Labonte's Car .07 .20
75 Todd Bodine .07 .20
76 Brett Bodine's Car .02 .10
77 Jeff Purvis .07 .20
78 Rick Mast's Car .02 .10
79 Rick Carelli .07 .20
80 Wally Dallenbach Jr.'s Car .02 .10
81 Jimmy Spencer's Car .02 .10
82 Bobby Hillin's Car .02 .10
83 Lake Speed's Car .02 .10
84 Richard Childress .15 .40
85 Roger Penske .02 .10
86 Don Miller .02 .10
87 Jack Roush .07 .20
88 Joe Gibbs .15 .40
89 Felix Sabates .02 .10
90 Bobby Hillin .07 .20
91 Tim Morgan .02 .10
92 Larry McClure .02 .10
93 Ted.McClure/J.McClure Ed McClure .02 .10
94 Glen Wood .02 .10
95 Len Wood .02 .10
96 Eddie Wood .02 .10
97 Junior Johnson .07 .20
98 Derrike Cope .07 .20
99 Andy Hillenburg .07 .20
100 Rick Hendrick .02 .10
101 Leo Jackson .02 .10
102 Bobby Allison .07 .20
103 Bob Bilby .02 .10
104 Bill Stavola .02 .10
105 Mickey Stavola .02 .10
106 Walter Bud Moore .02 .10
107 Chuck Rider .02 .10
108 Billy Hagan .02 .10
109 Bill Davis .02 .10
110 Kenny Bernstein .02 .10
111 Richard Jackson .02 .10
112 Ray DeWitt/Diane DeWitt .02 .10
113 D.K. Ulrich .02 .10
114 Cale Yarborough .07 .20
115 Junie Donlavey .02 .10
116 Larry Hedrick .02 .10
117 Robert Yates .02 .10
118 George Bradshaw .02 .10
119 Mark Smith .02 .10
120 David Fuge .02 .10
121 Harry Melling .02 .10
122 Atlanta MM .02 .10
123 Dick Moroso .02 .10
124 Butch Mock .02 .10
125 Alan Kulwicki Trans. MM .07 .20
126 Andy Petree .02 .10
127 Buddy Parrott .02 .10
128 Steve Hmiel .02 .10
129 Howard Comstock .02 .10
130 Jimmy Makar .02 .10
131 Robin Pemberton .02 .10
132 Jeff Hammond .02 .10
133 Tony Glover .02 .10
134 Leonard Wood .02 .10
135 Mike Beam .02 .10
136 Mike Hill .02 .10
137 Gary DeHart .02 .10
138 Ray Evernham .02 .10
139 Ken Howes .02 .10
140 Jimmy Fennig .02 .10
141 Barry Dodson .02 .10
142 Ken Wilson .02 .10
143 Donnie Wingo .02 .10
144 Doug Hewitt .02 .10
145 Pete Wright .02 .10
146 Tim Brewer .02 .10
147 Donnie Richeson .02 .10
148 Sandy Jones .02 .10
149 Bob Johnson .02 .10
150 Geoff Bodine/Brett Bodine Cars MM .02 .10
151 Doug Williams .02 .10
152 Waddell Wilson .02 .10
153 Doug Richert .02 .10
154 Larry McReynolds .02 .10
155 Dennis Connor .02 .10
156 Harry Hyde .02 .10
157 Paul Andrews .02 .10
158 Robbie Loomis .02 .10
159 Troy Selberg .02 .10
160 Dale Inman .02 .10
161 Tony Eury .25 .60
162 Dale Fischlein .02 .10
163 Steve Grissom .07 .20
164 Ricky Craven .15 .40
165 David Green .07 .20
166 Chuck Bown .07 .20
167 Joe Nemechek .07 .20
168 Ward Burton .07 .20
169 Bobby Dotter .07 .20
170 Robert Pressley .07 .20
171 Hermie Sadler .07 .20
172 Mike Wallace .07 .20
173 Tracy Leslie .07 .20
174 Tom Peck .07 .20
175 Jeff Burton .25 .60
176 Rodney Combs .07 .20
177 New Hampshire MM .02 .10
178 Tommy Houston .07 .20
179 Joe Bessey .07 .20
180 Tim Fedewa .07 .20
181 Jack Sprague .07 .20
182 Richard Lasater .02 .10
183 Roy Payne .02 .10
184 Shawna Robinson .30 .75
185 Larry Pearson .07 .20
186 Jim Bown .07 .20
187 Nathan Buttke .02 .10
188 Butch Miller .07 .20
189 Jason Keller RC .25 .60
190 Randy LaJoie .07 .20
191 Dave Rezendes .07 .20
192 Jeff Green .07 .20
193 Ed Berrier .07 .20
194 Troy Beebe .07 .20
195 Dennis Setzer .07 .20
196 David Bonnett .07 .20
197 Barney Hall .02 .10
198 Eli Gold .02 .10
199 Ned Jarrett .02 .10
200 Benny Parsons .07 .20
201 Jack Arute .02 .10
202 Jerry Punch .02 .10
203 Talladega Speedway MM .02 .10
204 Mike Joy .02 .10
205 Dick Brooks .02 .10
206 Winston Kelley .02 .10
207 Jim Phillips .02 .10
208 John Kernan .02 .10
209 Randy Pemberton .02 .10
210 Ken Squier .02 .10
211 Joe Moore .02 .10
212 Chris Economaki .02 .10
213 Allen Bestwick .02 .10
214 Glenn Jarrett .02 .10
215 Dick Berggren .02 .10
216 Les Richter .02 .10
217 Gary Nelson .02 .10
218 Ray Hill .02 .10
219 Carl Hill .02 .10
220 Chuck Romeo .02 .10
221 Jack Whittemore .02 .10
222 Jimmy Cox .02 .10
223 Bruce Roney .02 .10
224 Marlin Wright .02 .10
225 Mike Chaplin .02 .10
226 Tim Earp .02 .10
227 Doyle Ford .02 .10
228 Buster Auton .02 .10
229 Elmo Langley .02 .10
230 Walt Green .02 .10
231 Gary Miller .02 .10
232 Morris Metcalfe .02 .10
233 Rich Burgdoff .02 .10
234 Jimmy Horton Crash MM .02 .10
235 Steve Hmiel .02 .10
236 Troy Martin AP .02 .10
237 Gary Brooks AP .02 .10
238 Eddie Wood AP .02 .10
239 Raymond Fox III AP .02 .10
240 David Smith AP .02 .10
241 Robert Yates AP .02 .10
242 Todd Parrott AP .02 .10
243 David Munari AP .02 .10
244 James Lewter AP .02 .10
245 Norman Koshimizu AP .02 .10
246 Harold Stott AP .02 .10
247 Will Lind AP .02 .10
248 Norman Koshimizu AP .02 .10
249 Danny Lawrence AP .02 .10
250 Dan Ford AP .02 .10
251 Barry Beggarly .02 .10
252 Steve Boley/Jerry Williams .02 .10
253 Mel Walen/Larry Phillips .02 .10
254 Barry Beggarly/Charlie Cragen .02 .10
255 Robert Miller/Tony Ponder .02 .10
256 Steve Grissom BGN Champ .02 .10
257 Hermie Sadler BGN ROY .07 .20
258 Rusty Wallace w/Crew .25 .60
259 Steve Hmiel .25 .60
260 Jeff Gordon WC ROY .75 2.00
261 Bill Elliott FF .25 .60
262 Da.Allison IROC Champ .25 .60
263 Dale Jarrett/Kyle Petty Cars MM .15 .40
264 Morgan Shepherd's Car MM .02 .10
265 Rusty Wallace's Car MM .25 .60
266 Dale Jarrett YR .25 .60
267 Rusty Wallace YR .25 .60
268 Davey Allison w/Crew YR .15 .40
269 Morgan Shepherd YR .02 .10
270 Dale Earnhardt YR .60 1.50
271 Rusty Wallace YR .25 .60
272 Rusty Wallace YR .25 .60
273 Rusty Wallace YR .25 .60
274 Ernie Irvan YR .07 .20
275 Geoff Bodine YR .07 .20
276 Sterling Marlin YR .15 .40
277 Dale Earnhardt YR .60 1.50
278 Dale Earnhardt YR .60 1.50
279 Kyle Petty YR .07 .20
280 Ricky Rudd YR .15 .40
281 Dale Earnhardt YR .60 1.50
282 Rusty Wallace YR .25 .60
283 Dale Earnhardt YR .60 1.50
284 Dale Earnhardt YR .60 1.50
285 Mark Martin YR .25 .60
286 Mark Martin YR .25 .60
287 Mark Martin YR .25 .60
288 Mark Martin YR .25 .60
289 Rusty Wallace YR .25 .60
290 Rusty Wallace YR .25 .60
291 Ernie Irvan/Yates/McRey.YR .15 .40
292 Rusty Wallace YR .25 .60
293 Ernie Irvan YR .07 .20
294 Rusty Wallace YR .25 .60
295 Mark Martin YR .25 .60
296 Rusty Wallace YR .25 .60
297 D.Earnhardt WC Champ .60 1.50
298 Checklist #1 .02 .10
299 Checklist #2 .02 .10
300 Checklist #3 .02 .10
P11 Bill Elliott Club Promo 2.50 6.00

1994 Maxx Premier Series Jumbos

The Maxx Premier Series Jumbos were distributed in two series; the first eight cards with Maxx Premier Plus factory sets and the second four cards with the Premier Series binder sold through Club Maxx. The twelve cards are actually enlarged (3-1/2" by 5") copies of the corresponding driver's 1994 Premier Plus issue.

COMPLETE SET (12) 10.00 20.00
COMPLETE SERIES 1 (8) 5.00 10.00
COMPLETE SERIES 2 (4) 5.00 10.00
1 Bill Elliott .60 1.50
2 Ernie Irvan's Car .40 1.00
3 Dale Jarrett's Car .60 1.50
4 Mark Martin 1.00 2.50
5 Darrell Waltrip .60 1.50
6 Richard Petty .60 1.50
7 Alan Kulwicki .60 1.50
8 Jeff Gordon 2.00 5.00
9 Rusty Wallace's Car 1.00 2.00
10 Kyle Petty 1.00 2.00
11 Davey Allison 1.25 3.00
12 Harry Gant 1.00 2.00

1994 Maxx The Select 25

This 25-card chromium set was produced by Maxx and features the top drivers in the 1993 Winston Cup Points standings. These cards were made available in specially marked two packs of Winston Select cigarettes and through a mail-in offer which required 20 Winston Select wrappers and $14.95. This set was closed-out by the manufacturer when the cards set aside for the mail-in offer where not redeemed.

COMPLETE SET (25) 6.00 15.00
1 Dale Earnhardt 1.50 4.00
2 Rusty Wallace .60 1.50
3 Mark Martin .60 1.50
4 Dale Jarrett .50 1.25
5 Kyle Petty .20 .50
6 Ernie Irvan .20 .50
7 Morgan Shepherd .10 .30
8 Bill Elliott .30 .75
9 Ken Schrader .10 .30
10 Ricky Rudd .20 .50
11 Harry Gant .20 .50
12 Jimmy Spencer .10 .30
13 Darrell Waltrip .20 .50
14 Jeff Gordon .75 2.00
15 Sterling Marlin .20 .50
16 Geoff Bodine .10 .30
17 Michael Waltrip .10 .30
18 Terry Labonte .30 .75
19 Bobby Labonte .50 1.25
20 Brett Bodine .10 .30
21 Rick Mast .10 .30
22 Wally Dallenbach Jr. .10 .30
23 Kenny Wallace .10 .30
24 Hut Stricklin .10 .30
25 Ted Musgrave .10 .30

1994 Maxx Texaco Ernie Irvan

Maxx continued the line of Texaco cards in 1994, this year with new team driver Ernie Irvan. For the first time the cards were distributed through foil packs with eight cards per pack. Cards 20-24 were produced with gold foil layering.

COMPLETE SET (50) 2.50 6.00
1 Ernie Irvan .20 .50
2 Robert Yates .02 .10
3 Larry McReynolds .02 .10
4 Ernie Irvan's Car .02 .10
5 Ernie Irvan's Car .02 .10
6 Ernie Irvan Larry McReynolds .02 .10
7 Ernie Irvan's Car .02 .10
8 On the Pole .02 .10
9 Ernie Irvan in Pits .02 .10
10 Ernie Irvan's Car .02 .10
11 Ernie Irvan's Car .02 .10
12 Ernie Irvan .02 .10
13 Robert Yates .02 .10
14 Ernie Irvan's Car w/Crew .02 .10
15 Ernie Irvan's Transporter .02 .10
16 Ernie Irvan's Car .02 .10
17 Ernie Irvan's Car .02 .10
18 Ernie Irvan's Shop .02 .10
19 Ernie Irvan w/Car .02 .10
20 Ernie Irvan Yates McReynolds .02 .10
21 Ernie Irvan .20 .50
22 Ernie Irvan w Crew .02 .10
23 Ernie Irvan .20 .50
24 Ernie Irvan .20 .50
25 Jeremy Anderson .02 .10
26 Gary Beveridge .02 .10
27 Mike Bumgarner .02 .10
28 Gene Carrigan .02 .10
29 Jeff Clark .02 .10
30 Bret Conway .02 .10
31 Steve Foster .02 .10
32 Raymond Fox III .02 .10
33 Libby Gant .02 .10
34 Dennis Greene .02 .10
35 Michael Hanson .02 .10
36 Eric Horn .02 .10
37 Vernon Hubbard .02 .10
38 Gil Kerley .02 .10
39 Joey Knuckles .02 .10
40 Norman Koshimizu .02 .10
41 Dave Kriska .02 .10
42 Larry Lackey .02 .10
43 James Lewter .02 .10
44 Mike Long .02 .10
45 Nick Ramey .02 .10
46 Wade Thomas .02 .10
47 Terry Throneburg .02 .10
48 Doug Yates .02 .10
49 Richard Yates .02 .10
50 Checklist Card .02 .10

1995 Maxx

Two series were again produced for the 1995 Maxx base brand release. The cards were issued 10 per pack with 36-packs per foil box. Memorable Moments and Victory Lane subsets were included in series one. Several insert sets were distributed over the print run for each series as well. The first card of the Dale Earnhardt Chase the Champion series was included in Maxx one. The popular insert set was distributed by Maxx over the course of the year through five of its different product releases. Series two included a 10-card Bill Elliott Bat Chase insert set packaged approximately 2 cards every 36 packs. A promo card for each series was produced as well.

COMPLETE SET (270) 15.00 40.00
COMP.SERIES 1 (180) 8.00 20.00
COMP.SERIES 2 (90) 4.00 10.00
1 Rick Mast .07 .20
2 Rusty Wallace .60 1.50
3 Jeff Gordon's Car MM .30 .75
4 Sterling Marlin .25 .60
5 Terry Labonte .25 .60
6 Mark Martin .60 1.50
7 Geoff Bodine .07 .20
8 Jeff Burton .25 .60
9 Sterling Marlin VL .15 .40
10 Ricky Rudd .25 .60
11 Bill Elliott .30 .75
12 Derrike Cope .07 .20
13 Rusty Wallace VL .30 .75
14 Technical Tidbit .02 .10
15 Lake Speed .07 .20
16 Ted Musgrave .07 .20
17 Darrell Waltrip .15 .40
18 Dale Jarrett .50 1.25
19 Loy Allen Jr. .07 .20
20 Technical Tidbit/roof flaps .02 .10
21 Morgan Shepherd .07 .20
22 Bobby Labonte .50 1.25
23 Hut Stricklin .07 .20
24 Jeff Gordon .75 2.00
25 Ken Schrader .07 .20
26 Brett Bodine .07 .20
27 Jimmy Spencer .07 .20
28 Ernie Irvan .15 .40
29 Steve Grissom .07 .20
30 Michael Waltrip .15 .40
31 Ward Burton .15 .40
32 Dick Trickle .07 .20
33 Harry Gant .15 .40
34 Ernie Irvan/Jimmy Spencer Cars MM .07 .20
35 Richard Childress .15 .40
36 Walter Bud Moore .02 .10
37 Felix Sabates .02 .10
38 Ernie Irvan VL .07 .20
39 Kenny Wallace .07 .20
40 Bobby Hamilton .07 .20
41 Joe Nemechek .07 .20
42 Kyle Petty .15 .40
43 Richard Petty .25 .60
44 John Andretti .07 .20
45 Wally Dallenbach Jr. .07 .20
46 Ernie Irvan VL .07 .20
47 Steve Kinser .07 .20
48 Darlington VL .02 .10
49 Robert Yates .02 .10
50 Roger Penske .02 .10
51 Rusty Wallace's Car VL .15 .40
52 Glen Wood .02 .10

Card	Low	High
53 Len Wood	.02	.10
54 Eddie Wood	.02	.10
55 Jimmy Hensley	.07	.20
56 Don Miller	.02	.10
57 Tim Morgan	.02	.10
58 Terry Labonte VL	.15	.40
59 Larry McClure	.02	.10
60 Rusty Wallace VL	.30	.75
61 Jack Roush	.02	.10
62 Rick Hendrick	.02	.10
63 Talladega Speedway VL	.02	.10
64 Kenny Bernstein	.07	.20
65 Butch Mock	.02	.10
66 Chuck Rider	.02	.10
67 Cale Yarborough	.07	.20
68 Ernie Irvan VL	.07	.20
69 Teddy McClure	.02	.10
70 Joe Gibbs	.15	.40
71 Dave Marcis	.07	.20
72 Jeff Gordon VL	.40	1.00
73 Geoff Bodine VL	.07	.20
74 Richard Jackson	.02	.10
75 Todd Bodine	.07	.20
76 Junior Johnson	.07	.20
77 Greg Sacks	.07	.20
78 Bill Davis	.02	.10
79 D.K. Ulrich	.02	.10
80 Jeff Gordon VL	.40	1.00
81 Travis Carter	.02	.10
82 Bill Stavola	.02	.10
83 Rusty Wallace VL	.30	.75
84 Mickey Stavola	.02	.10
85 Leo Jackson	.02	.10
86 Larry Hedrick	.02	.10
87 Rusty Wallace VL	.30	.75
88 Gary Bechtel/Carolyn Bechtel	.02	.10
89 Rusty Wallace VL	.30	.75
90 Mike Wallace	.07	.20
91 Bobby Allison	.07	.20
92 Jimmy Spencer VL	.07	.20
93 Junie Donlavey	.02	.10
94 A.G. Dillard	.02	.10
95 Ricky Rudd VL	.15	.40
96 Andy Petree	.02	.10
97 Larry McReynolds	.02	.10
98 Jeremy Mayfield	.15	.40
99 Geoff Bodine VL	.07	.20
100 Buddy Parrott	.02	.10
101 Steve Hmiel	.02	.10
102 Jimmy Spencer VL	.07	.20
103 Ken Howes	.02	.10
104 Leonard Wood	.02	.10
105 Jeff Gordon VL	.40	1.00
106 Bill Ingle	.02	.10
107 Jimmy Fennig	.02	.10
108 Doug Hewitt	.02	.10
109 Mark Martin VL	.30	.75
110 Robin Pemberton	.02	.10
111 Ray Evernham	.02	.10
112 Geoff Bodine VL	.07	.20
113 Donnie Wingo	.02	.10
114 Pete Peterson	.02	.10
115 Rusty Wallace VL	.30	.75
116 Tony Glover	.02	.10
117 Gary DeHart	.02	.10
118 Jimmy Makar	.02	.10
119 Bill Elliott VL	.15	.40
120 Mike Beam	.02	.10
121 Kevin Hamlin	.02	.10
122 Paul Andrews	.02	.10
123 Terry Labonte VL	.15	.40
124 Chris Hussey	.02	.10
125 Mark Martin MM	.30	.75
126 Jim Long	.02	.10
127 Rusty Wallace VL	.30	.75
128 Donnie Richeson	.02	.10
129 Rusty Wallace VL	.30	.75
130 Troy Selberg	.02	.10
131 Tony Furr	.02	.10
132 Mike Hill	.02	.10
133 Geoff Bodine VL	.07	.20
134 Freddy Fryar	.02	.10
135 Philippe Lopez	.02	.10
136 Dale Jarrett VL	.15	.40
137 Jeff Hammond	.02	.10
138 Buddy Barnes	.02	.10
139 Gord/DW/T.Lab/Sch.Cars VL	.30	.75
140 Charley Pressley	.02	.10
141 Doug Richert	.02	.10
142 Terry Labonte VL	.15	.40
143 Mike Hillman	.02	.10
144 D.Cope/B.Hillin Standridge Cars MM	.02	.10
145 Robbie Loomis	.02	.10
146 Mark Martin VL	.30	.75
147 Harry Gant MM	.07	.20
148 Bobby Labonte Crash MM	.15	.40
149 David Green BGN Champ	.07	.20
150 David Green	.07	.20
151 Ricky Craven	.07	.20
152 Chad Little	.07	.20
153 Kenny Wallace	.07	.20
154 Robert Pressley	.07	.20
155 Johnny Benson	.15	.40
156 Bobby Dotter	.07	.20
157 Larry Pearson	.02	.10
158 Dennis Setzer	.07	.20
159 Tim Fedewa	.07	.20
160 Jeff Burton	.25	.60
161 Rusty Wallace's Car	.15	.40
162 Mark Martin's Car	.25	.60
163 Ernie Irvan's Car	.07	.20
164 Ken Schrader's Car	.02	.10
165 Morgan Shepherd's Car	.02	.10
166 Ricky Rudd's Car	.07	.20
167 Michael Waltrip's Car	.07	.20
168 Ted Musgrave's Car	.02	.10
169 Jeff Gordon's Car	.30	.75
170 Lake Speed's Car	.02	.10
171 Kyle Petty's Car	.07	.20
172 Sterling Marlin's Car	.07	.20
173 Terry Labonte's Car	.15	.40
174 Darrell Waltrip's Car	.07	.20
175 Dale Jarrett's Car	.15	.40
176 Rick Mast's Car	.02	.10
177 Geoff Bodine's Car	.02	.10
178 Todd Bodine's Car	.02	.10
179 Hut Stricklin's Car	.02	.10
180 Checklist Card	.02	.10
181 Lake Speed	.07	.20
182 Loy Allen Jr.	.07	.20
183 Steve Grissom	.07	.20
184 Dick Trickle	.07	.20
185 Bobby Hamilton	.07	.20
186 John Andretti	.07	.20
187 Charles Hardy	.02	.10
188 Tony Gibson	.02	.10
189 Jeremy Mayfield's Car	.07	.20
190 Jeremy Mayfield	.15	.40
191 Ken Howes	.02	.10
192 Robin Pemberton	.02	.10
193 Chris Hussey	.02	.10
194 Bill Davis	.02	.10
195 Davy Jones	.07	.20
196 Randy LaJoie	.07	.20
197 Donnie Richeson	.02	.10
198 Tony Furr	.02	.10
199 Mike Hill	.02	.10
200 Elton Sawyer	.07	.20
201 Johnny Benson, Jr.	.15	.40
202 Bobby Dotter	.07	.20
203 Andy Petree	.02	.10
204 Ricky Rudd	.25	.60
205 Ricky Rudd's Car	.07	.20
206 Darrell Waltrip	.15	.40
207 Darrell Waltrip's Car	.07	.20
208 Chad Little	.07	.20
209 Hut Stricklin's Car	.02	.10
210 Hut Stricklin	.07	.20
211 Richard Broome	.02	.10
212 Geoff Bodine	.07	.20
213 Geoff Bodine's Car	.02	.10
214 Robert Pressley	.07	.20
215 Mark Martin	.60	1.50
216 Dale Jarrett	.50	1.25
217 Joe Nemechek	.07	.20
218 Joe Nemechek's Car	.02	.10
219 Joe Nemechek	.07	.20
220 Joe Nemechek's Car	.02	.10
221 Bill Elliott	.30	.75
222 Bill Elliott's Car	.15	.40
223 Brett Bodine	.07	.20
224 Brett Bodine's Car	.02	.10
225 Junior Johnson	.07	.20
226 Jimmy Spencer	.07	.20
227 Jimmy Spencer's Car	.02	.10
228 Travis Carter	.02	.10
229 Cecil Gordon	.02	.10
230 Terry Labonte	.25	.60
231 Terry Labonte's Car	.15	.40
232 Terry Labonte	.25	.60
233 Terry Labonte's Car	.15	.40
234 Kyle Petty	.15	.40
235 Kyle Petty's Car	.07	.20
236 Jeff Gordon	.75	2.00
237 Jeff Gordon's Car	.30	.75
238 Scott Lagasse's Truck	.02	.10
239 Scott Lagasse	.07	.20
240 Bobby Labonte	.50	1.25
241 Bobby Labonte's Car	.15	.40
242 David Green's Car	.02	.10
243 Bobby Labonte	.50	1.25
244 Michael Waltrip	.15	.40
245 Michael Waltrip's Car	.07	.20
246 Michael Waltrip	.15	.40
247 Michael Waltrip's Car	.07	.20
248 Ricky Craven	.07	.20
249 Ricky Craven's Car	.02	.10
250 Ricky Craven	.07	.20
251 Ricky Craven's Car	.02	.10
252 Ken Schrader	.07	.20
253 Ken Schrader's Car	.02	.10
254 Ken Schrader	.07	.20
255 Ken Schrader's Car	.02	.10
256 Ken Schrader	.07	.20
257 Ken Schrader's Truck	.02	.10
258 Ray Evernham	.15	.40
259 Joe Gibbs	.15	.40
260 Bob Jenkins	.02	.10
261 Jeff Fuller RC	.07	.20
262 Mike McLaughlin	.07	.20
263 Kenny Wallace	.07	.20
264 Cale Yarborough	.07	.20
265 Chuck Bown	.07	.20
266 Dave Marcis	.15	.40
267 Howard Comstock	.02	.10
268 Jimmy Means	.02	.10
269 Chad Little's Car	.02	.10
270 Checklist Card	.02	.10
P1G Jeff Gordon in Pits Promo	1.00	2.50
P1R Jeff Gordon in Pits Promo Red Foil	1.50	4.00
P2 Ricky Rudd Promo	.60	1.50
P3 M.Martin/S.Hmiel Promo Sheet	1.50	4.00

1995 Maxx Autographs

This 48-card set features 1995 Maxx series one cards autographed by some of the top personalities in NASCAR. The cards were randomly inserted in 1995 Maxx series two packs. To guarantee its authenticity, each signed card was crimped with Maxx's corporate seal which reads "J.R. Maxx Inc. Corporate Seal 1988 North Carolina." Most of the Johnny Benson cards were signed on the back.

Card	Low	High
COMPLETE SET (48)	500.00	800.00
5 Terry Labonte	12.50	30.00
7 Geoff Bodine	6.00	15.00
16 Ted Musgrave	6.00	15.00
21 Morgan Shepherd	6.00	15.00
22 Bobby Labonte	12.50	30.00
24 Jeff Gordon	40.00	80.00
25 Ken Schrader	15.00	30.00
30 Michael Waltrip	8.00	20.00
41 Joe Nemechek	6.00	15.00
42 Kyle Petty	10.00	25.00
96 Andy Petree	5.00	10.00
97 Larry McReynolds	6.00	15.00
100 Buddy Parrott	5.00	10.00
101 Steve Hmiel	5.00	10.00
103 Ken Howes	5.00	10.00
104 Leonard Wood	5.00	10.00
106 Bill Ingle	5.00	10.00
108 Doug Hewitt	5.00	10.00
110 Robin Pemberton	5.00	10.00
113 Donnie Wingo	5.00	10.00
114 Pete Peterson	5.00	10.00
116 Tony Glover	5.00	10.00
117 Gary DeHart	5.00	10.00
118 Jimmy Makar	5.00	10.00
120 Mike Beam	5.00	10.00
121 Kevin Hamlin	5.00	10.00
122 Paul Andrews	5.00	10.00
124 Chris Hussey	5.00	10.00
126 Jim Long	5.00	10.00
128 Donnie Richeson	5.00	10.00
130 Troy Selberg	5.00	10.00
131 Tony Furr	5.00	10.00
132 Mike Hill	5.00	10.00
135 Philippe Lopez	5.00	10.00
137 Jeff Hammond	6.00	15.00
138 Buddy Barnes	5.00	10.00
140 Charley Pressley	5.00	10.00
141 Doug Richert	5.00	10.00
143 Mike Hillman	5.00	10.00
145 Robbie Loomis	5.00	10.00
151 Ricky Craven	10.00	25.00
152 Chad Little	10.00	25.00
154 Robert Pressley	6.00	15.00
155 Johnny Benson	6.00	15.00
156 Bobby Dotter	5.00	10.00
157 Larry Pearson	6.00	15.00
158 Dennis Setzer	6.00	15.00
159 Tim Fedewa	6.00	15.00

1995 Maxx Chase the Champion

Dale Earnhardt Chase the Champion cards were distributed over Maxx's five major racing issues of 1995: series one and two Maxx (1:36), Premier Plus (1:24), Premier Series (2 per factory set) and Medallion (1:18). The cards were consecutively numbered and include silver foil layering on the cardfront. Card number 1 was in series one packs, cards numbered 2 and 3 were in Premier Series sets, cards numbered 4 and 5 were inserts in Premier Plus packs, cards numbered 6 and 7 were inserts in series two packs, and numbers 8 through 10 were inserts in Medallion.

Card	Low	High
COMPLETE SET (10)	40.00	100.00
1 Dale Earnhardt	5.00	12.00
2 Dale Earnhardt	5.00	12.00
3 Dale Earnhardt	5.00	12.00
4 Dale Earnhardt's Car	5.00	12.00
5 Dale Earnhardt	5.00	12.00
6 Dale Earnhardt	5.00	12.00
7 D.Earnhardt T.Earnhardt	5.00	12.00
8 Dale Earnhardt	5.00	12.00
9 D.Earn Childress Teresa	5.00	12.00
10 Dale Earnhardt	5.00	12.00

1995 Maxx Bill Elliott Bat Chase

Bill Elliott's special ThunderBat paint scheme car is the focus of this ten-card set. Series two packs included two of the Bat Chase insert cards approximately every 36 packs. These sets were also made available thru Club Maxx for $5.99 in October, 1995. The sets were purchased immediately by both Club members and dealers. A glow-in-the-dark paint was used on the border of all ten cards. There was also a autographed 8" X 10" version of Bill Elliott's Thunderbat card. The card was signed in gold and was available through the Maxx Club. Each of the autographed cards were numberd to 500.

Card	Low	High
COMPLETE SET (10)	15.00	30.00
COMMON CARD (1-10)	1.00	3.00
NNO Bill Elliott's Car AU/500	40.00	80.00

1995 Maxx License to Drive

License to Drive inserts were distributed over three products with three different insertion ratios: Maxx series one (1:40), Maxx series two (2:36) and Maxx Premier Plus (1:17). The five series two cards were numbered with an LTD prefix. Crown Chrome versions of the five Premier Plus cards were also produced and inserted in Maxx Crown Chrome packs at the rate of 1:22 packs.

Card	Low	High
COMPLETE SET (15)	20.00	50.00
COMP.MAXX SERIES 1 (5)	15.00	30.00
COMP.MAXX SERIES 2 (5)	10.00	20.00
COMP.MAXX PREM.PLUS (5)	20.00	40.00
*CROWN CHROME 6-10: SAME PRICE		
1 Terry Labonte's Car	5.00	10.00
2 Harry Gant's Car	3.00	6.00
3 Sterling Marlin's Car	4.00	8.00
4 Dick Trickle's Car	2.50	5.00
5 Hut Stricklin's Car	2.50	5.00
6 Ted Musgrave's Car	3.00	6.00
7 Mark Martin's Car	6.00	12.00
8 Ward Burton's Car	4.00	8.00
9 Rick Mast's Car	3.00	6.00
10 Morgan Shepherd's Car	3.00	6.00
11 Michael Waltrip's Car	2.00	4.00
12 Darrell Waltrip's Car	2.00	4.00
13 Geoff Bodine's Car	1.50	3.00
14 Brett Bodine's Car	1.50	3.00
15 Todd Bodine's Car	1.50	3.00

1995 Maxx Over the Wall

Over the Wall inserts feature pit scenes of top Winston Cup race teams. The cards were randomly inserted in 1995 Maxx series one packs at the wrapper stated rate of 1:20 packs.

Card	Low	High
COMPLETE SET (10)	15.00	40.00
1 Jeff Gordon in Pits	4.00	10.00
2 Brett Bodine in Pits	.40	1.00
3 Hut Stricklin in Pits	.40	1.00
4 Kyle Petty in Pits	.75	2.00
5 Darrell Waltrip in Pits	.75	2.00
6 Kenny Wallace in Pits	.40	1.00
7 Ken Schrader in Pits	.40	1.00
8 Bill Elliott in Pits	1.50	4.00
9 Geoff Bodine in Pits	.40	1.00
10 Terry Labonte in Pits	1.25	3.00

1995 Maxx Stand Ups

This six-card set features drivers and cars from Winston Cup. The cards were produced using a die cut "stand-up" card design and were issued in special retail packs at the rate of one per pack.

Card	Low	High
COMPLETE SET (6)	1.25	3.00
1 Geoff Bodine	.15	.40
2 Andretti Marlin G.Bodine Cars	.15	.40
3 Jeff Burton ROY	.50	1.25
4 Ernie Irvan's Car	.15	.40
5 Rusty Wallace's Car	.30	.75
6 Richard Petty	.50	1.25

1995 Maxx SuperTrucks

SuperTrucks cards were distributed over three products with three different insertion ratios: Maxx series one (1:40), Maxx Premier Plus (1:17) and Maxx Medallion (1:2). The last 15 cards were numbered with an ST prefix. Unnumbered Crown Chrome versions of the five Premier Plus cards were also produced and inserted in Maxx Crown Chrome packs at the rate of 1:22 packs.

Card	Low	High
COMPLETE SET (20)	25.00	50.00
COMP.MAXX SET (5)	10.00	20.00
COMP.MAXX PREM. PLUS (5)	12.50	25.00
COMP.MAXX MEDALLION (10)	6.00	14.00
*CROWN CHROME CARDS SAME PRICE		
1 M.Skinner P.J.Jones Trucks	2.50	5.00
2 Rick Carelli's Truck	2.00	4.00
3 Tobey Butler C.Huartson Trucks	2.00	4.00
4 Scott Lagasse T.J.Clark Trucks	2.50	5.00
5 Rick Carelli's Truck	2.00	4.00
6 Scott Lagasse's Truck	2.50	5.00
7 Ken Schrader's Truck	5.00	10.00
8 Geoff Bodine's Truck	5.00	10.00
9 Jerry Glanville's Truck	2.50	5.00
10 Rick Carelli's Truck	2.50	5.00
11 John Nemechek's Truck	.75	1.50
12 Sammy Swindell's Truck	.75	2.00
13 Bob Strait's Truck	.75	1.50
14 Mike Chase's Truck	.75	1.50
15 Walker Evans' Truck	.75	1.50
16 Bob Brevak's Truck	.75	1.50
17 Tobey Butler's Truck	.75	1.50
18 Steve Portenga's Truck	.75	1.50
19 Jerry Churchill's Truck	.75	1.50
20 Butch Miller's Truck	.75	1.50

1995 Maxx Top 5 of 2005

Top 5 of 2005 was an exclusive insert to 1995 Maxx series two. The cards were inserted at the wrapper stated rate of 2:36 and featured drivers Maxx felt could be top contenders ten years down the road.

Card	Low	High
COMPLETE SET (5)	3.00	8.00
TOP1 Ricky Craven	.30	.75
TOP2 Bobby Labonte	2.00	5.00
TOP3 Jason Keller	.60	1.50
TOP4 David Hutio	.30	.75
TOP5 Toby Porter	.30	.75

1995 Maxx Medallion

The second year of the Medallion brand features the "Colors of NASCAR" theme. The 61-card set consists of 30 of the top NASCAR drivers and their cars. Maxx produced 999 cases of this product, which came 18 packs per box with 8 cards per pack. Randomly inserted in packs were On the Road Again, Head-to-Head, Busch Grand National, SuperTrucks, Jeff Gordon Puzzles and the final three Dale Earnhardt Chase the Champion cards. Although the BGN and Head-to-Head cards are numbered differently, as if inserts, most consider the cards part of the regular issue bringing the number of cards in the set to an even 70. Maxx also included a special Checkered Flag Chase box, one per case, that contains parallel cards printed in blue foil.

Card	Low	High
COMPLETE SET (70)	8.00	20.00
WAX BOX	20.00	50.00
1 Rick Mast	.07	.20
2 Rusty Wallace	.60	1.50
3 Sterling Marlin	.25	.60
4 Terry Labonte	.25	.60
5 Mark Martin	.60	1.50
6 Geoff Bodine	.07	.20
7 Jeff Burton	.25	.60
8 Lake Speed	.07	.20
9 Ricky Rudd	.25	.60
10 Brett Bodine	.07	.20
11 Derrike Cope	.07	.20
12 Ted Musgrave	.07	.20
13 Darrell Waltrip	.15	.40
14 Bobby Labonte	.50	1.25
15 Morgan Shepherd	.07	.20
16 Jimmy Spencer	.07	.20
17 Jeff Gordon	.75	2.00
18 Ken Schrader	.07	.20
19 Hut Stricklin	.07	.20
20 Dale Jarrett	.50	1.25
21 Michael Waltrip	.15	.40
22 Ward Burton	.15	.40
23 John Andretti	.07	.20
24 Kyle Petty	.15	.40
25 Bobby Hamilton	.07	.20
26 Todd Bodine	.07	.20
27 Bobby Hillin	.07	.20
28 Joe Nemechek	.07	.20
29 Mike Wallace	.07	.20
30 Bill Elliott	.30	.75
31 Rick Mast's Car	.02	.10
32 Rusty Wallace's Car	.25	.60
33 Sterling Marlin's Car	.07	.20
34 Terry Labonte's Car	.15	.40
35 Mark Martin's Car	.25	.60
36 Geoff Bodine's Car	.02	.10
37 Jeff Burton's Car	.07	.20
38 Lake Speed's Car	.07	.20
39 Ricky Rudd's Car	.07	.20
40 Brett Bodine's Car	.02	.10
41 Derrike Cope's Car	.02	.10
42 Ted Musgrave's Car	.02	.10
43 Darrell Waltrip's Car	.07	.20
44 Bobby Labonte's Car	.15	.40
45 Morgan Shepherd's Car	.02	.10
46 Jimmy Spencer's Car	.02	.10
47 Jeff Gordon's Car	.40	1.00
48 Ken Schrader's Car	.02	.10
49 Hut Stricklin's Car	.02	.10
50 Dale Jarrett's Car	.15	.40
51 Michael Waltrip's Car	.07	.20
52 Ward Burton's Car	.02	.10
53 John Andretti's Car	.02	.10
54 Kyle Petty's Car	.07	.20
55 Bobby Hamilton's Car	.02	.10
56 Todd Bodine's Car	.02	.10
57 Bobby Hillin's Car	.02	.10
58 Joe Nemechek's Car	.02	.10
59 Mike Wallace's Car	.02	.10
60 Bill Elliott's Car	.15	.40
61 Checklist Card	.02	.10
P1 T.Musgrave's Car Promo	1.25	3.00
BGN1 Johnny Benson	.15	.40
BGN2 Chad Little	.20	.50
BGN3 Jason Keller	.20	.50
BGN4 Mike McLaughlin	.20	.50
BGN5 Larry Pearson	.20	.50
HTH1 Ricky Craven	.20	.50
HTH2 Ricky Craven's Car	.20	.50
HTH3 Robert Pressley	.20	.50
HTH4 Robert Pressley's Car	.20	.50

1995 Maxx Medallion Blue

Card	Low	High
COMPLETE BLUE SET (70)	100.00	200.00
*BLUE FOILS: 6X TO 12X BASE CARDS		

1995 Maxx Medallion Jeff Gordon Puzzle

Nine Jeff Gordon puzzle cards were produced for and distributed through 1995 Maxx Medallion. Although wrapper stated odds are 1:40, most pack breakers reported much easier ratios on the eight regular cards (numbers 1-3,5-9), about one in four packs, and a much tougher ratio on the short printed card (number 4), about one per case. The number 4 puzzle cards were inserted into the Checkered Flag Chase boxes. Once completed, the puzzle could be returned to Maxx in exchange for a signed 8" by 10" Jeff Gordon card. Maxx reports only 999 of the cards were signed and numbered. Since Maxx has gone out of business numerous extra signed Jeff Gordon photos have surfaced. We have had multiple reports of people having the same numbered photos of 999.

Card	Low	High
COMPLETE SET (9)	8.00	20.00
1 Jeff Gordon	.75	2.00
2 Jeff Gordon	.75	2.00
3 Jeff Gordon	.75	2.00
4 Jeff Gordon SP	2.50	6.00
5 Jeff Gordon	.75	2.00
6 Jeff Gordon	.75	2.00
7 Jeff Gordon	.75	2.00
8 Jeff Gordon	.75	2.00
9 Jeff Gordon	.75	2.00
NNO Jeff Gordon AUTO/999	60.00	120.00

1995 Maxx Medallion On the Road Again

Unlike many of the 1995 Maxx inserts, On the Road Again was exclusive to one product -- Maxx Medallion. The cards were packaged approximately one every two foil packs and feature top Winston Cup race teams' transporters.

Card	Low	High
COMPLETE SET (10)	5.00	10.00
OTR1 Ken Schrader's Trans.	.40	1.00
OTR2 Jeff Gordon's Transporter	.75	2.00
OTR3 Terry Labonte's Trans.	.60	1.50
OTR4 Steve Grissom's Trans.	.40	1.00
OTR5 Bill Elliott's Transporter	.60	1.50
OTR6 Jeff Burton's Transporter	.40	1.00
OTR7 Bobby Labonte's Trans.	.60	1.50
OTR8 Lake Speed's Transporter	.40	1.00
OTR9 Derrike Cope's Transporter	.40	1.00
OTR10 Ricky Rudd's Transporter	.60	1.50

1995 Maxx Premier Plus

Maxx again used its chromium printing technology to produce a Premier Plus issue. The cards were distributed in 7-card packs with 36 packs per foil box. In additon to a few new insert sets, Premier Plus included continuations to three other Maxx insert issues. A Crown Chrome parallel release was also produced and issued in its own packs. Crown Chrome came 6-cards to a pack with 24 packs per box. A special Silver Select Dale Earnhardt card was produced and distributed only through Crown Chrome and each was numbered of 750. Maxx reportedly limited production to 9000 numbered boxes.

Card	Low	High
COMPLETE SET (183)	10.00	25.00
1 Rick Mast	.10	.30
2 Rusty Wallace	1.00	2.50
3 Scott Lagasse	.10	.30
4 Sterling Marlin	.40	1.00
5 Terry Labonte	.50	1.25
6 Mark Martin	1.00	2.50
7 Geoff Bodine	.10	.30
8 Jeff Burton	.40	1.00
9 Ricky Craven	.25	.60
10 Ricky Rudd	.40	1.00
11 Bill Elliott	.50	1.25
12 Derrike Cope	.10	.30
13 Scott Lagasse's SuperTruck	.05	.15
14 Ken Schrader's SuperTruck	.05	.15
15 Lake Speed	.10	.30

16 Ted Musgrave .10 .30
17 Darrell Waltrip .25 .60
18 Dale Jarrett .75 2.00
19 Loy Allen Jr. .10 .30
20 Steve Kinser .10 .30
21 Morgan Shepherd .10 .30
22 Bobby Labonte .75 2.00
23 Randy LaJoie .10 .30
24 Jeff Gordon 1.25 3.00
25 Ken Schrader .10 .30
26 Brett Bodine .10 .30
27 Jimmy Spencer .10 .30
28 Ernie Irvan .25 .60
29 Steve Grissom .10 .30
30 Michael Waltrip .25 .60
31 Ward Burton .25 .60
32 Dick Trickle .10 .30
33 Harry Gant .25 .60
34 Terry Labonte's Car .25 .60
35 Mark Martin's Car .40 1.00
36 Bobby Labonte's Car .40 1.00
37 Rusty Wallace's Car .40 1.00
38 Sterling Marlin's Car .10 .30
39 Kyle Petty's Car .10 .30
40 Bobby Hamilton .10 .30
41 Joe Nemechek .10 .30
42 Kyle Petty .25 .60
43 Richard Petty .40 1.00
44 Brett Bodine's Car .05 .15
45 John Andretti .10 .30
46 Todd Bodine's Car .05 .15
47 Michael Waltrip's Car .10 .30
48 Dale Jarrett's Car .40 1.00
49 Joe Nemechek's Car .05 .15
50 Morgan Shepherd's Car .05 .15
51 Bill Elliott's Car .25 .60
52 Ricky Craven's Car .05 .15
53 Kenny Wallace .10 .30
54 Bobby Hamilton's Car .05 .15
55 Jimmy Hensley .10 .30
56 Ken Schrader's Car .05 .15
57 Steve Kinser's Car .05 .15
58 Dick Trickle's Car .05 .15
59 Ricky Rudd's Car .10 .30
60 Robert Pressley's Car .05 .15
61 Ted Musgrave's Car .05 .15
62 Rick Mast's Car .05 .15
63 Darrell Waltrip's Car .10 .30
64 Jeff Gordon's Car .60 1.50
65 Jeff Burton's Car .10 .30
66 Geoff Bodine's Car .05 .15
67 Jimmy Spencer's Car .05 .15
68 Roger Penske .05 .15
69 Don Miller .05 .15
70 Jack Roush .05 .15
71 Dave Marcis .25 .60
72 Joe Gibbs .25 .60
73 Junior Johnson .10 .30
74 Rick Hendrick .05 .15
75 Todd Bodine .10 .30
76 Felix Sabates .05 .15
77 Greg Sacks .10 .30
78 Tim Morgan .05 .15
79 Larry McClure .05 .15
80 Glen Wood .05 .15
81 Len Wood .05 .15
82 Eddie Wood .05 .15
83 Leo Jackson .05 .15
84 Bobby Allison .10 .30
85 Gary Bechtel/Carolyn Bechtel .05 .15
86 Bill Stavola .05 .15
87 Mickey Stavola .05 .15
88 Walter Bud Moore .05 .15
89 Chuck Rider .05 .15
90 Mike Wallace .10 .30
91 Bill Davis .05 .15
92 Kenny Bernstein .10 .30
93 Richard Jackson .05 .15
94 D.K. Ulrich .05 .15
95 Cale Yarborough .10 .30
96 Junie Donlavey .05 .15
97 Larry Hedrick .05 .15
98 Jeremy Mayfield .25 .60
99 Robert Yates .05 .15
100 Travis Carter .05 .15
101 Butch Mock .05 .15
102 Dick Brooks .05 .15
103 Andy Petree .05 .15
104 Buddy Parrott .05 .15
105 Steve Hmiel .05 .15
106 Jimmy Makar .05 .15
107 Robin Pemberton .05 .15
108 Jeff Hammond .05 .15
109 Tony Glover .05 .15
110 Leonard Wood .05 .15
111 Mike Beam .05 .15
112 Mike Hill .05 .15
113 Gary DeHart .05 .15
114 Ray Evernham .05 .15
115 Ken Howes .05 .15
116 Bill Ingle .05 .15
117 Pete Peterson .05 .15
118 Cecil Gordon .05 .15
119 Donnie Wingo .05 .15
120 Doug Hewitt .05 .15
121 Donnie Richeson .05 .15
122 Richard Broome .05 .15
123 Kevin Hamlin .05 .15
124 Charley Pressley .05 .15
125 Larry McReynolds .05 .15
126 Paul Andrews .05 .15
127 Robbie Loomis .05 .15
128 Troy Selberg .05 .15
129 Jimmy Fennig .05 .15
130 Barry Dodson .05 .15
131 David Green .10 .30
132 Ricky Craven .10 .30
133 Chad Little .10 .30
134 Kenny Wallace .10 .30
135 Bobby Dotter .10 .30
136 Tracy Leslie .10 .30
137 Larry Pearson .10 .30
138 Dennis Setzer .10 .30
139 Robert Pressley .10 .30
140 Johnny Benson Jr. .25 .60
141 Terry Labonte .40 1.00
142 Terry Labonte's Car .25 .60
143 Ken Schrader .10 .30
144 Ken Schrader's Car .05 .15
145 Joe Nemechek .10 .30
146 Joe Nemechek's Car .05 .15
147 Jeff Gordon VL .60 1.50
148 Sterling Marlin VL .40 1.00
149 Rusty Wallace VL .40 1.00
150 Ernie Irvan VL .10 .30
151 Ernie Irvan VL .10 .30
152 Darlington VL .05 .15
153 Rusty Wallace in Pits VL .40 1.00
154 Terry Labonte VL .25 .60
155 Rusty Wallace VL .40 1.00
156 Talladega Speedway .05 .15
157 Ernie Irvan w/Crew VL .10 .30
158 Jeff Gordon VL .60 1.50
159 Geoff Bodine VL .10 .30
160 Jeff Gordon VL .60 1.50
161 Rusty Wallace VL .40 1.00
162 Rusty Wallace VL .40 1.00
163 Rusty Wallace VL .40 1.00
164 Jimmy Spencer VL .10 .30
165 Ricky Rudd w/Crew VL .40 1.00
166 Geoff Bodine VL .10 .30
167 Jimmy Spencer VL .10 .30
168 Jeff Gordon VL .60 1.50
169 Mark Martin VL .40 1.00
170 Geoff Bodine VL .10 .30
171 Rusty Wallace VL .40 1.00
172 Bill Elliott/J.Johnson VL .25 .60
173 Terry Labonte VL .25 .60
174 Rusty Wallace VL .40 1.00
175 Rusty Wallace VL .40 1.00
176 Geoff Bodine VL .10 .30
177 Dale Jarrett VL .40 1.00
178 Rockingham Race Action .05 .15
179 Terry Labonte VL .25 .60
180 Mark Martin VL .40 1.00
181 Jeff Burton ROY .40 1.00
182 Checklist #1 .05 .15
183 Checklist #2 .05 .15
P1 Darrell Waltrip Promo .60 1.50
SS1 D.Earnhardt Sil.Sel/750 20.00 50.00

1995 Maxx Premier Plus Crown Chrome

COMPLETE SET (185) 10.00 25.00
*CROWN CHROMES: .4X TO 1X PREM.PLUS

1995 Maxx Premier Plus PaceSetters

PaceSetter inserts were exclusive to the Maxx Premier Plus and Crown Chrome parallel issues. The cards were packaged approximately 1:17 packs in Premier Plus packs..

COMPLETE SET (9) 25.00 60.00
*CROWN CHROME: .4X TO 1X BASIC INSERTS
PS1 Mark Martin 5.00 12.00
PS2 Rusty Wallace 5.00 12.00
PS3 Ken Schrader .60 1.50
PS4 Ricky Rudd 2.00 5.00
PS5 Morgan Shepherd .60 1.50
PS6 Terry Labonte 2.50 6.00
PS7 Jeff Gordon 6.00 15.00
PS8 Darrell Waltrip 1.25 3.00
PS9 Bill Elliott 2.50 6.00

1995 Maxx Premier Plus Series Two Previews

Five cards were produced to preview the 1995 Maxx series two set. The cards were randomly inserted in Premier Plus packs at the rate of 1:17 packs.

COMPLETE SET (5) 4.00 10.00
*CROWN CHROME: .4X TO 1X BASIC INSERTS
PRE1 Lake Speed .75 2.00
PRE2 Jimmy Spencer .75 2.00
PRE3 Steve Grissom .75 2.00
PRE4 Dale Jarrett 1.50 4.00
PRE5 Dick Trickle .75 2.00

1995 Maxx Premier Plus Top Hats

Five cards were produced by Maxx to honor top young Winston Cup drivers. The cards were randomly inserted in Premier Plus packs at the rate of 1:17 packs. A Crown Chrome parallel version was also produced and inserted in packs at the approximate rate of 1:22. Each Top Hat card is numbered 1 of 1995.

COMPLETE SET (5) 5.00 12.00
*CROWN CHROME: .4X TO 1X BASIC INSERTS
TH1 Ted Musgrave 1.00 2.50
TH2 Ward Burton 1.50 4.00
TH3 Steve Grissom 1.00 2.50
TH4 Jimmy Spencer 1.00 2.50
TH5 Brett Bodine 1.00 2.50

1995 Maxx Premier Plus Retail Jumbos

This six-card set feature jumbo sized cards (3 1/2" X 5") of some of the best Winston Cup drivers. The cards use the Premier Plus chromium printing technology. Originally the cards were only available through Kmart stores but were later distributed via the Maxx Club. In the blister Kmart packs, Jumbo cards came one per along with two 1995 Maxx series one packs and one Texaco Ernie Irvan pack. The cards are unnumbered and checklisted below in alphabetical order.

COMPLETE SET (6) 4.00 10.00
1 Geoff Bodine .20 .50
2 Jeff Burton .60 1.50
3 Mark Martin 1.50 4.00
4 Ricky Rudd .60 1.50
5 Morgan Shepherd .20 .50
6 Rusty Wallace 1.50 4.00

1995 Maxx Premier Series

Club Maxx members had the chance to purchase the 1995 Maxx Premier Series set directly from Maxx for $64.95 plus shipping charges. Non-members could buy the set for $69.95 plus shipping. Production was limited to 45,000 numbered sets and each factory set included two Dale Earnhardt Chase the Champion cards (#2-3). These Earnhardt cards are priced in the 1995 MAXX Chase the Champion listings. A special gold foil embossed binder to house the set was offered for sale as well.

COMPLETE SET (300) 20.00 40.00
COMP.FACT.SET (302) 40.00 80.00
1 Rick Mast .15 .40
2 Rusty Wallace 1.25 3.00
3 Jeff Gordon's Car MM .60 1.50
4 Sterling Marlin .50 1.25
5 Terry Labonte .50 1.25
6 Mark Martin 1.25 3.00
7 Geoff Bodine .15 .40
8 Jeff Burton .50 1.25
9 Ricky Craven .15 .40
10 Ricky Rudd .50 1.25
11 Bill Elliott .60 1.50
12 Derrike Cope .15 .40
13 Todd Bodine's Car MM .07 .20
14 Tire Wars .07 .20
15 Lake Speed .15 .40
16 Ted Musgrave .15 .40
17 Darrell Waltrip .30 .75
18 Dale Jarrett 1.00 2.50
18 Ernie Irvan .30 .75
19 Loy Allen Jr. .15 .40
20 Steve Kinser .15 .40
21 Morgan Shepherd .15 .40
22 Bobby Labonte 1.00 2.50
23 Randy LaJoie .15 .40
24 Jeff Gordon 2.00 4.00
25 Ken Schrader .15 .40
26 Brett Bodine .15 .40
27 Jimmy Spencer .15 .40
28 Ernie Irvan .30 .75
29 Steve Grissom .15 .40
30 Michael Waltrip .30 .75
31 Ward Burton .15 .40
32 Dick Trickle .15 .40
33 Harry Gant .30 .75
34 Terry Labonte's Car .30 .75
35 Mark Martin's Car .50 1.25
36 Bobby Labonte's Car .30 .75
37 Rusty Wallace's Car .50 1.25
38 Sterling Marlin's Car .15 .40
39 Kyle Petty's Car .15 .40
40 Bobby Hamilton .15 .40
41 Joe Nemechek .15 .40
42 Kyle Petty .30 .75
43 Richard Petty .50 1.25
44 Bobby Hillin .15 .40
45 John Andretti .15 .40
46 Scott Lagasse .15 .40
47 Billy Standridge .15 .40
48 Dale Jarrett's Car .50 1.25
49 Joe Nemechek's Car .07 .20
50 Morgan Shepherd's Car .07 .20
51 Bill Elliott's Car .30 .75
52 Ricky Craven's Car .07 .20
53 Kenny Wallace .15 .40
54 John Andretti's Car .07 .20
55 Jimmy Hensley .15 .40
56 Ken Schrader's Car .07 .20
57 Scott Lagasse's SuperTruck .07 .20
58 Dick Trickle's Car .07 .20
59 Ricky Rudd's Car .15 .40
60 Robert Pressley's Car .07 .20
61 Ted Musgrave's Car .07 .20
62 Rick Mast's Car .07 .20
63 Darrell Waltrip's Car .15 .40
64 Jeff Gordon's Car .60 1.50
65 Jeff Burton's Car .15 .40
66 Geoff Bodine's Car .07 .20
67 Jimmy Spencer's Car .07 .20
68 Todd Bodine's Car .07 .20
69 Michael Waltrip's Car .15 .40
70 Brett Bodine's Car .07 .20
71 Dave Marcis .30 .75
72 Steve Kinser's Car .07 .20
73 Mike Wallace's Car .07 .20
74 Maxx Card's Car .07 .20
75 Todd Bodine .15 .40
76 Ward Burton's Car .07 .20
77 Greg Sacks .15 .40
78 Jeremy Mayfield's Car .15 .40
79 Loy Allen Jr.'s Car .07 .20
80 Roger Penske .07 .20
81 Don Miller .07 .20
82 Jack Roush .07 .20
83 Joe Gibbs .30 .75
84 Felix Sabates .07 .20
85 Tim Morgan .07 .20
86 Larry McClure .07 .20
87 Ted.McClure/J.Mc Clure/Ed McClure .07 .20
88 Glen Wood .07 .20
89 Len Wood .07 .20
90 Mike Wallace .15 .40
91 Eddie Wood .07 .20
92 Junior Johnson .15 .40
93 Rick Hendrick .07 .20
94 Leo Jackson .07 .20
95 Bobby Allison .15 .40
96 Gary Bechtel/Carolyn Bechtel .07 .20
97 Bill Stavola .07 .20
98 Jeremy Mayfield .30 .75
99 Mickey Stavola .07 .20
100 Walter Bud Moore .07 .20
101 Chuck Rider .07 .20
102 Ken Schrader's SuperTruck .07 .20
103 Bill Davis .07 .20
104 Kenny Bernstein .15 .40
105 Richard Jackson .07 .20
106 Ray DeWitt/Diane DeWitt .07 .20
107 D.K. Ulrich .07 .20
108 Cale Yarborough .15 .40
109 Junie Donlavey .07 .20
110 Larry Hedrick .07 .20
111 Robert Yates .07 .20
112 Gene Bradshaw .07 .20
113 Mark Smith .07 .20
114 David Fuge .07 .20
115 Travis Carter .07 .20
116 A.G. Dillard .07 .20
117 Butch Mock .07 .20
118 Harry Melling .07 .20
119 Dick Moroso .07 .20
120 Dick Brooks .07 .20
121 Roof Flaps .07 .20
122 Andy Petree .07 .20
123 Buddy Parrott .07 .20
124 Steve Hmiel .07 .20
125 Jimmy Makar .07 .20
126 Robin Pemberton .07 .20
127 Jeff Hammond .07 .20
128 Tony Glover .07 .20
129 Leonard Wood .07 .20
130 Mike Beam .07 .20
131 Mike Hill .07 .20
132 Gary DeHart .07 .20
133 Ray Evernham .30 .75
134 Ken Howes .07 .20
135 Bill Ingle .07 .20
136 Pete Peterson .07 .20
137 Cecil Gordon .07 .20
138 Donnie Wingo .07 .20
139 Doug Hewitt .07 .20
140 Phillippe Lopez .07 .20
141 Chris Hussey .07 .20
142 Donnie Richeson .07 .20
143 Richard Broome .07 .20
144 Kevin Hamlin .07 .20
145 Ken Glen .07 .20
146 Charley Pressley .07 .20
147 Tony Furr .07 .20
148 Larry McReynolds .07 .20
149 Dale Fischlein .07 .20
150 Paul Andrews .07 .20
151 Robbie Loomis .07 .20
152 Mike Hillman .07 .20
153 Troy Selberg .07 .20
154 Jimmy Fennig .07 .20
155 Barry Dodson .07 .20
156 Waddell Wilson .07 .20
157 Dale Inman .07 .20
158 Charlie Smith .07 .20
159 David Green .15 .40
160 David Green's Car .07 .20
161 Ricky Craven .15 .40
162 Ricky Craven's Car .07 .20
163 Chad Little .15 .40
164 Chad Little's Car .07 .20
165 Kenny Wallace .15 .40
166 Bobby Dotter .15 .40
167 Tracy Leslie .15 .40
168 Larry Pearson .15 .40
169 Dennis Setzer .15 .40
170 Robert Pressley .15 .40
171 Johnny Benson Jr. .15 .40
172 Tim Fedewa .15 .40
173 Mike McLaughlin .15 .40
174 Jim Bown .15 .40
175 Elton Sawyer .15 .40
176 Jason Keller .15 .40
177 Rodney Combs .15 .40
178 Doug Heveron .15 .40
179 Tommy Houston .15 .40
180 Kevin Lepage .15 .40
181 Dirk Stephens .15 .40
182 Stevie Reeves .15 .40
183 Phil Parsons .15 .40
184 Ernie Irvan/Jim.Spencer Cars MM.15 .40
185 Shawna Robinson .60 1.50
186 Patty Moise .15 .40
187 Terry Labonte .50 1.25
188 Terry Labonte's Car .30 .75
189 Ken Schrader .15 .40
190 Ken Schrader's Car .07 .20
191 Joe Nemechek .15 .40
192 Joe Nemechek's Car .07 .20
193 Bobby Hillin
B.Standridge Cars MM .07 .20
194 Barney Hall .15 .40
195 Eli Gold .07 .20
196 Benny Parsons .15 .40
197 Dr. Jerry Punch .07 .20
198 Buddy Baker .15 .40
199 Mike Joy .07 .20
200 Winston Kelley .07 .20
201 Jim Phillips .07 .20
202 John Kernan .07 .20
203 Randy Pemberton .15 .40
204 Bill Weber .07 .20
205 Joe Moore .07 .20
206 Mark Garrow .07 .20
207 Allen Bestwick .15 .40
208 Glenn Jarrett .07 .20
209 Pat Patterson .07 .20
210 Dr. Dick Berggren .07 .20
211 Harry Gant MM .15 .40
212 Ken Squier .07 .20
213 B.Labonte/B.Hamilton
Mast Cars MM .30 .75
214 Mike Helton .07 .20
215 Gary Nelson .07 .20
216 Ray Hill .07 .20
217 Carl Hill .07 .20
218 Brian DeHart .07 .20
219 Jack Whittemore .07 .20
220 Jimmy Cox .07 .20
221 Bruce Roney .07 .20
222 Marlin Wright .07 .20
223 David Hoots .07 .20
224 Tim Earp .07 .20
225 Doyle Ford .07 .20
226 Buster Auton .07 .20
227 Elmo Langley .07 .20
228 Walt Green .07 .20
229 Gary Miller .07 .20
230 Morris Metcalfe .07 .20
231 Rich Burgdoff .07 .20
232 J.Burton/W.Burton MM .30 .75
233 Larry McReynolds AP .07 .20
234 Troy Martin AP .07 .20
235 Dan Ford AP .07 .20
236 Bill Wilburn AP .07 .20
237 Raymond Fox III AP .07 .20
238 David Smith AP .07 .20
239 Robert Yates AP .07 .20
240 Darrell Andrews AP .07 .20
241 Glen Bobo AP .07 .20
242 James Lewter AP .07 .20
243 Norman Koshimizu AP .07 .20
244 Eric Horn AP .07 .20
245 Joe Dan Bailey AP .07 .20
246 Joe Lewis AP .07 .20
247 Danny Lawrence AP .07 .20
248 Slick Poston AP .07 .20
249 D.Cope/T.Labonte Cars MM .15 .40
250 David Rogers' Car .07 .20
251 Mark Burgtorf/David Rogers .07 .20
252 Dale Planck/John Knaus .07 .20
253 Barry Beggarly/Charlie Cragen .07 .20
254 Larry Phillips/Paul Peeples Jr. .07 .20
255 David Green BGN Champion .15 .40
256 Johnny Benson Jr. BGN ROY .15 .40
257 Jeff Gordon w/Crew 1.00 2.50
258 Ray Evernham WC
Crew Chief of the Year .07 .20
259 Jeff Burton Winston Cup ROY .15 .40
260 Bill Elliott FF .30 .75
261 Mark Martin IROC Champ .60 1.50
262 Jeff Gordon YR .75 2.00
263 Sterling Marlin YR .30 .75
264 Rusty Wallace YR .60 1.50
265 Ernie Irvan YR .15 .40
266 Ernie Irvan YR .15 .40
267 Darlington YR .07 .20
268 Rusty Wallace in Pits YR .50 1.25
269 Terry Labonte YR .30 .75
270 Rusty Wallace YR .60 1.50
271 Talladega Speedway YR .07 .20
272 Ernie Irvan w/Crew YR .15 .40
273 Jeff Gordon YR .75 2.00
274 Geoff Bodine YR .15 .40
275 Jeff Gordon YR .75 2.00
276 Rusty Wallace YR .60 1.50
277 Rusty Wallace YR .60 1.50
278 Rusty Wallace YR .60 1.50
279 Jimmy Spencer YR .15 .40
280 Ricky Rudd w/Crew YR .30 .75
281 Geoff Bodine YR .15 .40
282 Jimmy Spencer YR .15 .40
283 Jeff Gordon YR .75 2.00
284 Mark Martin/Roush YR .60 1.50
285 Geoff Bodine YR .15 .40
286 Rusty Wallace YR .60 1.50
287 Bill Elliott/J.Johnson YR .30 .75
288 Terry Labonte YR .30 .75
289 Rusty Wallace w/Crew YR .60 1.50
290 Rusty Wallace YR .60 1.50
291 Geoff Bodine YR .15 .40
292 Dale Jarrett YR .50 1.25
293 Rockingham Speedway YR .07 .20
294 Terry Labonte YR .30 .75
295 Mark Martin YR .60 1.50
296 Bobby Labonte Crash MM .30 .75
297 Phoenix Int. MM .07 .20
298 Checklist #1 .07 .20
299 Checklist #2 .07 .20
300 Checklist #3 .07 .20
P1G Jeff Burton Gold Promo .40 1.00
P1R Jeff Burton Red Promo 1.25 3.00

1995 Maxx Premier Series Update

This 15-card set is an update to the regular 300 card Premier Series set. The set is packaged in a brown box and was primarily distributed through the Maxx Club.

COMPLETE SET (15) 2.50 5.00
1 Loy Allen .15 .40
2 Elton Sawyer .15 .40
3 Hut Stricklin .15 .40
4 Ward Burton .30 .75
5 Bobby Hillin .15 .40
6 Dave Marcis .30 .75
7 Greg Sacks .15 .40
8 Jeremy Mayfield .30 .75
9 Mike Beam .07 .20
10 Ricky Craven .15 .40
11 Robert Pressley .15 .40
12 Ernie Irvan .30 .75
13 Ernie Irvan in Pits .15 .40
14 Ernie Irvan's Car .15 .40
15 Checklist .07 .20

1995 Maxx Larger than Life Dale Earnhardt

This seven-card set is a 8" X 10" version of card numbers 1-7 of the regular Chase the Champions set. The regular size card #8 from the Maxx Dale Earnhardt Chase the Champion series came along with the seven jumbo cards in a large foil pack. There were a reported 20,000 packs produced. The cards were primarily distributed through the Maxx Club.

COMPLETE SET (7) 15.00 30.00
COMMON CARD (1-7) 2.00 5.00

1996 Maxx

The 1996 Maxx set has a total of 100 cards. The 10-card packs were distributed 36-packs per foil box. The set features the topical subset Memorable Moments (numbers 34, 36, 50, 61, 70, 97 and 98) and closes with checklist cards (numbers 99-100). A wide assortment of insert cards were randomly packed as well. Sterling Marlin was featured on the 1996 Maxx series one wrapper.

COMPLETE SET (100) 6.00 15.00
1 Rick Mast .07 .20
2 Rusty Wallace .50 1.25
3 Dale Earnhardt 1.00 2.50
4 Sterling Marlin .25 .60
5 Terry Labonte .25 .60
6 Mark Martin .50 1.25
7 Geoff Bodine .07 .20
8 Jeff Burton .25 .60
9 Lake Speed .07 .20
10 Ricky Rudd .25 .60
11 Brett Bodine .07 .20
12 Derrike Cope .07 .20
13 Joe Nemechek's Car .02 .10
14 Jimmy Spencer's Car .02 .10
15 Dick Trickle .07 .20
16 Ted Musgrave .07 .20
17 Darrell Waltrip .15 .40
18 Bobby Labonte .50 1.25
19 Geoff Bodine's Car .02 .10
20 Rick Mast's Car .02 .10
21 Morgan Shepherd .07 .20
22 Bobby Labonte's Car .15 .40
23 Jimmy Spencer .07 .20
24 Jeff Gordon .60 1.50
25 Ken Schrader .07 .20
26 Hut Stricklin .07 .20
27 Darrell Waltrip's Car .02 .10
28 Dale Jarrett .50 1.25
29 Steve Grissom .07 .20
30 Michael Waltrip .15 .40
31 Kyle Petty's Car .07 .20
32 Bill Elliott's Car .15 .40
33 Robert Pressley .07 .20
34 J.Hensley/G.Sacks Cars .02 .10
35 Terry Labonte's Car .15 .40
36 Ride Across America MM .02 .10
37 John Andretti .07 .20
38 Ricky Rudd's Car .07 .20
39 Michael Waltrip's Car .07 .20
40 Bobby Hamilton's Car .02 .10
41 Ricky Craven .07 .20
42 Kyle Petty .15 .40
43 Richard Petty .25 .60
44 Bobby Hamilton .07 .20
45 Derrike Cope's Car .02 .10
46 Steve Grissom's Car .02 .10
47 John Andretti's Car .02 .10
48 Dale Jarrett's Car .15 .40
49 Ken Schrader's Car .02 .10
50 Promising Pole Pos.MM .02 .10
51 Morgan Shepherd's Car .02 .10
52 Robert Yates .02 .10
53 Rusty Wallace's Car .25 .60
54 Mark Martin's Car .25 .60
55 R.Penske/D.Miller .02 .10
56 Ricky Craven's Car .02 .10
57 Robert Pressley's Car .02 .10
58 L.Wood/K.Wood/E.Wood/G.Wood.02 .10
59 Jeff Burton's Car .07 .20
60 Richard Jackson .02 .10
61 E.Sawyer/L.Speed Cars MM .02 .10
62 Brett Bodine's Car .02 .10
63 Ted Musgrave's Car .02 .10
64 Lake Speed's Car .02 .10
65 Jack Roush .02 .10
66 Rick Hendrick .02 .10

67 Chuck Rider .02 .10
68 Charles Hardy .02 .10
69 Joe Gibbs .15 .40
70 Mark Martin's Car .25 .60
71 Junior Johnson .07 .20
72 Travis Carter .02 .10
73 Bobby Allison .07 .20
74 Johnny Benson Jr. .15 .40
75 Chad Little .07 .20
76 Jason Keller .07 .20
77 Mike McLaughlin .07 .20
78 Jeff Green .07 .20
79 Leonard Wood .02 .10
80 Ray Evernham .15 .40
81 Bill Ingle .02 .10
82 Doug Hewitt .02 .10
83 Robbie Loomis .02 .10
84 Andy Petree .02 .10
85 Larry McReynolds .02 .10
86 Steve Hmiel .02 .10
87 Joe Nemechek .07 .20
88 Jeff Gordon's Car .25 .60
89 Robin Pemberton .02 .10
90 Mike Beam .02 .10
91 Ken Howes .02 .10
92 Howard Comstock .02 .10
93 Tony Glover .02 .10
94 Bill Elliott .30 .75
95 Gary DeHart .02 .10
96 Jimmy Makar .02 .10
97 Ted Musgrave's Car .02 .10
98 D.Jarrett/E.Irvan Cars MM .15 .40
99 Checklist (1-100) .02 .10
100 Checklist (Chase Cards) .02 .10
P1 Sterling Marlin Promo .75 2.00
P2 T.Labonte Maxx Seal Promo 2.00 5.00
P3 D.Jarrett Promo Sheet 1.50 4.00
P4 Steve Grissom Promo Sheet .75 2.00

1996 Maxx Chase the Champion

For the second year, Maxx produced an insert set honoring the previous season's Winston Cup champion. The Chase the Champion cards were distributed over the course of 1996 in various Maxx racing card products. Series one packs contained card #1 at the wrapper stated rate of one in 36. Cards #2 and 3 were inserted in factory sets of '96 Maxx Premier Plus. Cards # 4, 5 and 6 were randomly inserted in packs of '96 Maxx Odyssey at a rate of one per 18 packs. Card # 8 was found in Maxx Made in America packs. Cards #7 and 9-14 were supposed to be distributed through packs of Maxx products scheduled to be released in the second half of the year. Since Maxx filed for bankruptcy those products never made it to the market. But the cards had already been printed and quantities of those cards did become available in the secondary market.

COMPLETE SET (14) 30.00 80.00
COMMON CARD 4.00 10.00

1996 Maxx Family Ties

Family Ties inserts feature a famous racing family connection on silver foil card stock. The cards were randomly inserted in packs at the rate of one in 18.

COMPLETE SET (5) 6.00 15.00
MINOR STARS 1.50 4.00
FT1 G.Bodine 1.00 2.50
B.Bodine
T.Bodine
FT2 J.Burton 1.00 2.50
W.Burton
FT3 T.Labonte 3.00 6.00
B.Labonte
FT4 R.Wall 3.00 6.00
M.Wall
K.Wallace
FT5 D.Waltrip 1.50 4.00
M.Waltrip

1996 Maxx Sterling Marlin

Randomly inserted in packs at a rate of one in 12, a redemption card was issued to be exchanged for this 5-card set devoted to Sterling Marlin. The expiration date for the exchange card was May 1, 1996.

COMPLETE SET (5) 2.00 5.00
COMMON CARD (1-5) .50 1.25

1996 Maxx On The Road Again

Transporters were again the focus of Maxx's On the Road inserts. The first five cards of the series were randomly inserted in packs at the rate of one in 18 packs.

COMPLETE SET (5) 1.50 4.00
OTRA1 Kyle Petty's Transporter .30 .75
OTRA2 BGN Transporter .30 .75
OTRA3 Rusty Wallace's Trans. .60 1.50
OTRA4 Darrell Waltrip's Trans. .30 .75
OTRA5 Winston Cup Transporter .30 .75

1996 Maxx Over the Wall

The 1995 Unocal 76/Rockingham World Championship Pit Crew Competition was the focus of this 10-card Maxx insert set. The cards included the featured pit crew's best time in the competition printed in blue foil. They were randomly inserted in Maxx packs at the rate of 1:12.

COMPLETE SET (10) 4.00 10.00
OTW1 Brett Bodine's Car .50 1.25
OTW2 Kyle Petty's Car .50 1.25
OTW3 Jeff Burton's Car 1.00 2.50
OTW4 Derrike Cope's Car .50 1.25
OTW5 Terry Labonte's Car 1.25 3.00
OTW6 Geoff Bodine's Car .50 1.25
OTW7 Bobby Labonte's Car 1.50 4.00
OTW8 Joe Nemechek's Car .50 1.25
OTW9 Ricky Rudd's Car 1.00 2.50
OTW10 Todd Bodine's Car .50 1.25

1996 Maxx Sam Bass

This eight card set consists of Four Driver's and their cars, with art work featuring Sam Bass.

COMPLETE SET (8) 3.00 8.00
1 Jeff Gordon 2.00 5.00
2 Jeff Gordon's Car .75 2.00
3 Jeff Burton .50 1.25
4 Jeff Burton's Car .25 .60
5 Ricky Craven .25 .60
6 Ricky Craven's Car .16 .40
7 Robert Pressley .25 .60
8 Robert Pressley's Car .16 .40

1996 Maxx SuperTrucks

Randomly inserted in packs at a rate of one in 12, this 10-card issue features top machines of the NASCAR SuperTrucks Series.

COMPLETE SET (10) 5.00 12.00
ST1 Mike Bliss' Truck .50 1.25
ST2 Tommy Archer's Truck .50 1.25
ST3 Rodney Combs' Truck .50 1.25
ST4 Rodney Combs Jr.'s Truck .50 1.25
ST5 Chad Little's Truck .50 1.25
ST6 Derrike Cope's Truck .50 1.25
ST7 T.J.Clark's Truck .50 1.25
ST8 Darrell Waltrip's Truck 1.00 2.50
ST9 Kenny Wallace's Truck .50 1.25
ST10 Kenji Momota's Truck .50 1.25

1996 Maxx Made in America

This 100-card set was the last Maxx product released before they went out of business.The product was thought to have been distributed by Maxx's printer. The cards feature a car or driver photo on the front with a U.S. flag in the background. There were eight cards per pack and 36 packs per box. The product was originally scheduled to have a special 1988 #99 Dale Earnhardt autograph card inserted one in 6,703 packs. We have received no confirmation that this card ever made it into packs. We have received a few reports of unsigned versions of this card being found in packs.

COMPLETE SET (100) 5.00 12.00
1 Rick Mast .07 .20
2 Rusty Wallace .60 1.50
3 Jeff Green .07 .20
4 Sterling Marlin .25 .60
5 Terry Labonte .25 .60
6 Mark Martin .60 1.50
7 Geoff Bodine .07 .20
8 Ernie Irvan's Car .07 .20
9 Lake Speed .07 .20
10 Ricky Rudd .25 .60
11 Brett Bodine .07 .20
12 Derrike Cope .07 .20
13 Joe Nemechek's Car .02 .10
14 Jimmy Spencer's Car .02 .10
15 Jeff Burton's Car .07 .20
16 Ted Musgrave .07 .20
17 Darrell Waltrip .15 .40
18 Bobby Labonte .50 1.25
19 Lake Speed's Car .02 .10
20 Rick Mast's Car .02 .10
21 Michael Waltrip .15 .40
22 Ward Burton .15 .40
23 Jimmy Spencer .02 .10
24 Jeff Gordon .75 2.00
25 Ken Schrader .07 .20
26 Jeremy Mayfield's Car .15 .40
27 Darrell Waltrip's Car .07 .20
28 Ernie Irvan .15 .40
29 Bobby Labonte .50 1.25
30 Johnny Benson's Car .02 .10
31 Kyle Petty's Car .02 .10
32 Bill Elliott's Car .15 .40
33 Robert Pressley .07 .20
34 Bobby Labonte's Car .15 .40
35 Terry Labonte's Car .15 .40
36 Ward Burton's Car .02 .10
37 John Andretti .02 .10
38 Ricky Rudd's Car .07 .20
39 Bobby Hamilton's Car .02 .10
40 Dale Jarrett's Car .15 .40
41 Ricky Craven .07 .20
42 Kyle Petty .15 .40
43 Richard Petty .25 .60
44 Bobby Hamilton .07 .20
45 Derrike Cope's Car .02 .10
46 Kenny Wallace .07 .20
47 John Andretti's Car .02 .10
48 Geoff Bodine's Car .02 .10
49 Ken Schrader's Car .02 .10
50 Morgan Shepherd's Car .02 .10
51 Michael Waltrip's Car .07 .20
52 Mike McLaughlin's Car .02 .10
53 Rusty Wallace's Car .25 .60
54 Mark Martin's Car .25 .60
55 Tim Fedewa .07 .20
56 Ricky Craven's Car .02 .10
57 Robert Pressley's Car .02 .10
58 Jason Keller's Car .02 .10
59 Tim Fedewa's Car .02 .10
60 Larry Pearson's Car .02 .10
61 Hermie Sadler .07 .20
62 Jeff Fuller's Car .02 .10
63 Ted Musgrave's Car .02 .10
64 David Green .07 .20
65 Phil Parsons' Car .02 .10
66 Sterling Marlin's Car .07 .20
67 Steve Grissom .07 .20
68 Chad Little's Car .02 .10
69 Hermie Sadler's Car .02 .10
70 Jeff Green's Car .02 .10
71 Phil Parsons .07 .20
72 Jeff Fuller .07 .20
73 Jeff Fuller's Car .02 .10
74 Chad Little .07 .20
75 Morgan Shepherd .07 .20
76 Jason Keller .07 .20
77 Mike McLaughlin .07 .20
78 Ricky Craven .07 .20
79 Ricky Craven's Car .02 .10
80 Michael Waltrip .15 .40
81 Michael Waltrip's Car .07 .20
82 Terry Labonte .25 .60
83 Terry Labonte's Car .15 .40
84 Joe Nemechek .07 .20
85 Joe Nemechek's Car .02 .10
86 Larry Pearson .07 .20
87 Joe Nemechek .07 .20
88 Dale Jarrett .50 1.25
89 Rodney Combs .07 .20
90 Bobby Labonte's Car .15 .40
91 Steve Grissom .07 .20
92 Steve Grissom's Car .02 .10
93 Kenny Wallace's Car .02 .10
94 Bill Elliott .30 .75
95 Kenny Wallace .07 .20
96 Dale Jarrett .50 1.25
97 Dale Jarrett's Car .15 .40
98 Jeremy Mayfield .15 .40
99 Jeff Burton .25 .60
100 Checklist .02 .10

1996 Maxx Made in America Blue Ribbon

Each card in this 15-card insert set features a pop-up design. The car or driver photo on the front of each card can be popped out and formed into the shape of the photo. The cards were inserted one per pack.

COMPLETE SET (15) 2.00 5.00
BR1 Derrike Cope's Car .03 .15
BR2 Ernie Irvan .25 .60
BR3 Bill Elliott .40 1.00
BR4 Ricky Craven .10 .30
BR5 Michael Waltrip .25 .60
BR6 Rusty Wallace's Car .25 .60
BR7 Bobby Labonte's Car .25 .60
BR8 John Andretti .10 .30
BR9 Ward Burton .25 .60
BR10 Ricky Rudd's Car .10 .30
BR11 Darrell Waltrip's Car .10 .30
BR12 Johnny Benson's Car .03 .15
BR13 Sterling Marlin's Car .10 .30
BR14 Chad Little's Car .03 .15
BR15 Jeff Green .10 .30

1996 Maxx Odyssey

This 100-card set features most of the top names from Winston Cup and Busch racing. The cards were printed on 18 point paper stock as opposed to Maxx's normal 14 point board. Each card front features a driver or car photo, gold foil stamping and the Racing Odyssey logo. Cards were packaged 10 cards per pack and 36 packs per box.

COMPLETE SET (100) 6.00 15.00
1 Rick Mast .05 .15
2 Rusty Wallace .50 1.25
3 Jeff Green .05 .15
4 Sterling Marlin .20 .50
5 Terry Labonte .20 .50
6 Mark Martin .50 1.25
7 Geoff Bodine .05 .15
8 Geoff Bodine's Car .02 .10
9 Lake Speed .05 .15
10 Ricky Rudd .20 .50
11 Brett Bodine .05 .15
12 Derrike Cope .05 .15
13 Joe Nemechek's Car .02 .10
14 Jimmy Spencer's Car .02 .10
15 Jeff Burton's Car .05 .15
16 Ted Musgrave .05 .15
17 Darrell Waltrip .10 .30
18 Bobby Labonte .40 1.00
19 Lake Speed's Car .02 .10
20 Rick Mast's Car .02 .10
21 Michael Waltrip .10 .30
22 Ward Burton .10 .30
23 Jimmy Spencer .05 .15
24 Jeff Gordon .60 1.50
25 Ken Schrader .05 .15
26 Jeremy Mayfield's Car .10 .30
27 Darrell Waltrip's Car .05 .15
28 Ernie Irvan .10 .30
29 Steve Grissom .05 .15
30 Johnny Benson's Car .02 .10
31 Kyle Petty's Car .05 .15
32 Bill Elliott's Car .10 .30
33 Robert Pressley .05 .15
34 Bobby Labonte's Car .10 .30
35 Terry Labonte's Car .10 .30
36 Ward Burton's Car .02 .10
37 John Andretti .05 .15
38 Ricky Rudd's Car .05 .15
39 Bobby Hamilton's Car .02 .10
40 Dale Jarrett's Car .10 .30
41 Ricky Craven .05 .15
42 Kyle Petty .10 .30
43 Richard Petty .20 .50
44 Bobby Hamilton .05 .15
45 Derrike Cope's Car .02 .10
46 Steve Grissom's Car .02 .10
47 John Andretti's Car .02 .10
48 Ernie Irvan's Car .05 .15
49 Ken Schrader's Car .02 .10
50 Morgan Shepherd's Car .02 .10
51 Michael Waltrip's Car .05 .15
52 Mike McLaughlin's Car .02 .10
53 Rusty Wallace's Car .10 .30
54 Mark Martin's Car .20 .50
55 Tim Fedewa .05 .15
56 Ricky Craven's Car .02 .10
57 Robert Pressley's Car .02 .10
58 Jason Keller's Car .02 .10
59 Tim Fedewa's Car .02 .10
60 Larry Pearson's Car .02 .10
61 Hermie Sadler .05 .15
62 Brett Bodine's Car .02 .10
63 Ted Musgrave's Car .02 .10
64 David Green .05 .15
65 Phil Parsons' Car .02 .10
66 Steve Grissom's Car .02 .10
67 Steve Grissom .05 .15
68 Chad Little's Car .02 .10
69 Hermie Sadler's Car .02 .10
70 Dale Earnhardt's Car .30 .75
71 Phil Parsons .05 .15
72 Jeff Fuller .05 .15
73 Jeff Fuller's Car .02 .10
74 Chad Little .05 .15
75 Morgan Shepherd .05 .15
76 Jason Keller .05 .15
77 Mike McLaughlin .05 .15
78 Ricky Craven .05 .15
79 Ricky Craven's Car .02 .10
80 Michael Waltrip .10 .30
81 Michael Waltrip's Car .05 .15
82 Terry Labonte .20 .50
83 Terry Labonte's Car .10 .30
84 Joe Nemechek .05 .15
85 Joe Nemechek's Car .02 .10
86 Larry Pearson .05 .15
87 Joe Nemechek .05 .15
88 Dale Jarrett .40 1.00
89 Rodney Combs .05 .15
90 Mike Skinner .05 .15
Will Lind
91 Steve Grissom .05 .15
92 Steve Grissom's Car .02 .10
93 Kenny Wallace's Car .02 .10
94 Bill Elliott .25 .60
95 Kenny Wallace .05 .15
96 Dale Jarrett .40 1.00
97 Dale Jarrett's Car .10 .30
98 Jeremy Mayfield .10 .30
99 Jeff Burton .20 .50
100 Checklist .02 .10
P1 Bobby Labonte Promo .75 2.00

1996 Maxx Odyssey Millennium

This 10-card, holographic, die-cut set features Winston Cup drivers and their cars. The cards were randomly inserted in packs at a rate of one per three packs. The series was originally intended to be the first 10 of a larger 30 card set. The rest of the cards were not released due to Maxx's bankruptcy shortly after the release of Odyssey.

COMPLETE SET (10) 5.00 12.00
MM1 Dale Earnhardt's Car 1.00 2.50
MM2 Jimmy Spencer .30 .75
MM3 Robert Pressley .30 .75
MM4 Brett Bodine's Car .20 .50
MM5 Sterling Marlin .50 1.25
MM6 Jeff Gordon 1.50 4.00
MM7 Bobby Hamilton .30 .75
MM8 Kyle Petty's Car .20 .50
MM9 Bill Elliott's Car .40 1.00
MM10 Terry Labonte's Car .40 1.00

1996 Maxx Odyssey On The Road Again

This five-card insert features the transporters that bring the race cars and equipment to and from the track. The cards were randomly inserted one in three packs.

COMPLETE SET (5) .60 1.50
OTRA1 Steve Grissom's Trans. .12 .30
OTRA2 Michael Waltrip's Trans. .15 .40
OTRA3 Sterling Marlin's Trans. .25 .60
OTRA4 Brett Bodine's Trans. .12 .30
OTRA5 Steve Grissom's Trans. .12 .30

1996 Maxx Odyssey Radio Active

This 15-card set uses die-cut printing to make pop-up cards. The set features drivers from Winston Cup, Busch and the SuperTruck series. The cards were randomly inserted in packs at a rate of one per two packs.

COMPLETE SET (15) 3.00 8.00
RA1 Derrike Cope's Car .07 .20
RA2 Ernie Irvan .30 .75
RA3 Bill Elliott .60 1.50
RA4 Ricky Craven .15 .40
RA5 Michael Waltrip .30 .75
RA6 Rusty Wallace's Car .40 1.00
RA7 Bobby Labonte's Car .30 .75
RA8 John Andretti .15 .40
RA9 Ward Burton .30 .75
RA10 Ricky Rudd's Car .30 .75
RA11 Darrell Waltrip's Car .07 .20
RA12 Johnny Benson's Car .07 .20
RA13 Sterling Marlin's Car .15 .40
RA14 Chad Little's Car .07 .20
RA15 Jeff Green .15 .40

1996 Maxx Premier Series

The 1996 Maxx Premier set was issued in one series totalling 300 cards. The cards were sold via mail-order through the Maxx Club. The product was sold in complete set form only. The set features a "Year in Review" yearbook theme and contains NASCAR Winston Cup, Busch Grand National and SuperTruck drivers, owners and crew chiefs. The cards were available with a sheet and binder combination to house the set. Cards #2 and #3 of the Chase the Champion series was available as part of this set. The seven card Superlatives set was also inserted one per factory Premier Series set. Sets originally retailed to Club members for $49.99.

COMPLETE SET (300) 25.00 50.00
1 Rick Mast .20 .50
2 Rusty Wallace 1.25 3.00
3 Dale Earnhardt 2.50 6.00
4 Sterling Marlin .60 1.50
5 Terry Labonte .60 1.50
6 Mark Martin 1.25 3.00
7 Geoff Bodine .20 .50
8 Jeff Burton .60 1.50
9 Lake Speed .20 .50
10 Ricky Rudd .60 1.50
11 Brett Bodine .20 .50
12 Derrike Cope .20 .50
13 Rockingham Rumble MM .08 .25
14 Rain, Rain; Go Away MM .08 .25
15 Dick Trickle .20 .50
16 Ted Musgrave .20 .50
17 Darrell Waltrip .40 1.00
18 Bobby Labonte 1.25 3.00
19 Loy Allen .20 .50
20 Jeremy Mayfield's Car .20 .50
21 Morgan Shepherd .20 .50
22 Randy LaJoie .20 .50
23 Jimmy Spencer .20 .50
24 Jeff Gordon 1.50 4.00
25 Ken Schrader .20 .50
26 Hut Stricklin .20 .50
27 Elton Sawyer .20 .50
28 Dale Jarrett 1.25 3.00
29 Steve Grissom .20 .50
30 Michael Waltrip .40 1.00
31 Ward Burton .20 .50
32 Chuck Brown .20 .50
33 Robert Pressley .20 .50
34 Terry Labonte's Car .40 1.00
35 Mark Martin's Car .60 1.50
36 Bobby Labonte's Car .40 1.00
37 John Andretti .20 .50
38 Rusty Wallace's Car .60 1.50
39 Loy Allen's Car .08 .25
40 Greg Sacks .20 .50
41 Ricky Craven .20 .50
42 Kyle Petty .40 1.00
43 Richard Petty .60 1.50
44 Bobby Hamilton .20 .50
45 Jeff Purvis .20 .50
46 Elton Sawyer's Car .08 .25
47 Ernie Irvan's Car .20 .50
48 Joe Nemechek's Car .08 .25
49 Morgan Shepherd's Car .08 .25
50 Bill Elliott's Car .40 1.00
51 Ricky Craven's Car .08 .25
52 Richard Petty's Car .40 1.00
53 Ken Schrader's Car .08 .25
54 Ward Burton's Car .08 .25
55 Dick Trickle's Car .08 .25
56 Ricky Rudd's Car .20 .50
57 Robert Pressley's Car .08 .25
58 Ted Musgrave's Car .08 .25
59 Rick Mast's Car .08 .25
60 Darrell Waltrip's Car .20 .50
61 Sterling Marlin's Car .20 .50
62 Geoff Bodine's Car .08 .25
63 Jimmy Spencer's Car .08 .25
64 Todd Bodine's Car .08 .25
65 Michael Waltrip's Car .20 .50
66 Brett Bodine's Car .08 .25
67 Derrike Cope's Car .08 .25
68 John Andretti's Car .08 .25
69 Steve Grissom's Car .08 .25
70 Lake Speed's Car .08 .25
71 Dave Marcis .40 1.00
72 Kyle Petty's Car .20 .50
73 Dale Earnhardt's Car 1.00 2.50
74 Ward Burton's Car .20 .50
75 Todd Bodine .20 .50
76 Mike Skinner .20 .50
77 Ron Hornaday Jr. .20 .50
78 Joe Ruttman .20 .50
79 Butch Miller .20 .50
80 Roger Penske .08 .25
81 Don Miller .08 .25
82 Larry McClure .08 .25
83 Jack Roush .08 .25
84 Joe Gibbs .40 1.00
85 Felix Sabates .08 .25
86 Gary Bechtel .08 .25
87 Joe Nemechek .20 .50
88 Ernie Irvan .40 1.00
89 Dale Jarrett's Car .40 1.00
90 Mike Wallace .20 .50
91 Len Wood .08 .25
92 Glen Wood .08 .25
93 Charles Hardy .08 .25
94 Bill Elliott .75 2.00
95 Junior Johnson .20 .50
96 Rick Hendrick .08 .25
97 Leo Jackson .08 .25
98 Jeremy Mayfield .40 1.00
99 Bobby Allison .20 .50
100 Carolyn Bechtel .08 .25
101 Michael Kranefuss .08 .25
102 Carl Haas .08 .25
103 Bud Moore .08 .25
104 Chuck Rider .08 .25
105 Eddie Wood .08 .25
106 Richard Jackson .08 .25
107 Bill Stavola .08 .25
108 Cale Yarborough .20 .50
109 Junie Donlavey .08 .25
110 Larry Hedrick .08 .25
111 Robert Yates .08 .25
112 Travis Carter .08 .25
113 Alan Dillard .08 .25
114 Butch Mock .08 .25
115 Harry Melling .08 .25
116 Bill Davis .08 .25
117 Kim Wood Hall .08 .25
118 Mike Wallace's Car .08 .25
119 Andy Petree .08 .25
120 Buddy Parrott .08 .25
121 Steve Hmiel .08 .25
122 Jimmy Makar .08 .25
123 Robin Pemberton .08 .25
124 Tony Glover .08 .25
125 Leonard Wood .08 .25
126 Larry McReynolds .08 .25
127 Gary DeHart .08 .25
128 Ray Evernham .40 1.00
129 Ken Howes .08 .25
130 Bill Ingle .08 .25
131 Pete Peterson .08 .25
132 Cecil Gordon .08 .25
133 Donnie Wingo .08 .25
134 Doug Hewitt .08 .25
135 Philippe Lopez .08 .25
136 Donnie Richeson .08 .25
137 Richard Broome .08 .25
138 Kevin Hamlin .08 .25
139 Charley Pressley .08 .25
140 Dale Fischlein .08 .25
141 Paul Andrews .08 .25
142 Robbie Loomis .08 .25
143 Troy Selberg .08 .25
144 Jimmy Fennig .08 .25
145 Barry Dodson .08 .25
146 Waddell Wilson .08 .25
147 Dale Inman .08 .25
148 Peter Sospenzo .08 .25
149 Tim Brewer .08 .25
150 Rick Ren .08 .25
151 Mike Beam .08 .25
152 Howard Comstock .08 .25
153 Jeff Hammond .08 .25
154 Chris Hussey .08 .25
155 Todd Parrott .08 .25
156 Johnny Benson's Car .08 .25
157 Chad Little's Car .08 .25
158 Mike McLaughlin's Car .08 .25
159 Jeff Green's Car .08 .25
160 Chad Little .20 .50

161 David Green .20 .50
162 Jeff Green .20 .50
163 Curtis Markham .20 .50
164 Hermie Sadler .20 .50
165 Jeff Fuller .20 .50
166 Bobby Dotter .20 .50
167 Tracy Leslie .20 .50
168 Larry Pearson .20 .50
169 Dennis Setzer .20 .50
170 Ricky Craven .40 1.00
171 Tim Fedewa .20 .50
172 Mike McLaughlin .20 .50
173 Jim Bown .20 .50
174 Elton Sawyer .20 .50
175 Jason Keller .20 .50
176 Rodney Combs .20 .50
177 Doug Heveron .20 .50
178 Tommy Houston .20 .50
179 Kevin Lapage .20 .50
180 Maxx Car .08 .25
181 Phil Parsons .20 .50
182 Ricky Craven's Car .08 .25
183 Patty Moise .20 .50
184 Kenny Wallace .20 .50
185 Terry Labonte BGN .40 1.00
186 Steve Grissom BGN .20 .50
187 Steve Grissom's Car .08 .25
188 Joe Nemechek BGN .20 .50
189 Joe Nemechek's Car .08 .25
190 Michael Waltrip BGN .40 1.00
191 Michael Waltrip's Car .20 .50
192 Ronnie Silver .08 .25
193 Barney Hall .08 .25
194 Eli Gold .08 .25
195 Benny Parsons .08 .25
196 Dr. Jerry Punch .08 .25
197 Buddy Baker .08 .25
198 Winston Kelley .08 .25
199 Jim Phillips .08 .25
200 John Kernan .08 .25
201 Randy Pemberton .08 .25
202 Bill Weber .08 .25
203 Joe Moore .08 .25
204 Bob Jenkins .08 .25
205 Allen Bestwick .08 .25
206 Glenn Jarrett .08 .25
207 Dr. Dick Berggren .08 .25
208 Mel Walen .08 .25
209 Dale Plank .08 .25
210 Jon Compagnone .08 .25
211 Paul White .08 .25
212 Ray Guss .08 .25
213 Jeff Wildung .08 .25
214 Phil Warren .08 .25
215 Mike Helton .08 .25
216 Gary Nelson .08 .25
217 Ray Hill .08 .25
218 Carl Hill .08 .25
219 Brian DeHart .08 .25
220 Jack Whittemore .08 .25
221 Jimmy Cox .08 .25
222 Bruce Roney .08 .25
223 Marlin Wright .08 .25
224 David Hoots .08 .25
225 Tim Earp .08 .25
226 Doyle Ford .08 .25
227 Buster Auton .08 .25
228 Elmo Langley .08 .25
229 Walt Green .08 .25
230 Gary Miller .08 .25
231 Morris Metcalfe .08 .25
232 Rich Burgdoff .08 .25
233 Hoss Berry .08 .25
234 Steve Peterson .08 .25
235 Jason Keller's Car .08 .25
236 Patty Moise's Car .08 .25
237 Kenny Wallace's Car .08 .25
238 Kenny Wallace's Car .08 .25
239 Curtis Markham's Car .08 .25
240 Tim Fedewa's Car .08 .25
241 Dennis Setzer's Car .08 .25
242 Terry Labonte's Car .40 1.00
243 Jeff Fuller's Car .08 .25
244 Hermie Sadler's Car .08 .25
245 Tommy Houston's Car .08 .25
246 Doug Heveron's Car .08 .25
247 Kevin Lepage's Car .08 .25
248 Tracy Leslie's Car .08 .25
249 Dirk Stephens' Car .08 .25
250 Testing in the Rain MM .08 .25
251 Larry Pearson's Car .08 .25
252 Phil Parson's Car .08 .25
253 Elton Sawyer's Car .08 .25
254 Riding the Wall MM .08 .25
255 On the Comeback Trail MM .08 .25
256 Larry Phillips WRS Champ .08 .25
257 Jeff Fuller BGN ROY .20 .50
258 Johnny Benson BGN Champ .40 1.00
259 WC Pit Crew Champs .20 .50
260 Ricky Craven .20 .50
Winston Cup Rookie of the Year
261 Bill Elliott FF .40 1.00
262 Dale Earnhardt 1.25 3.00
263 Race 1 - Daytona .08 .25
264 Race 2 - Rockingham .08 .25
265 Race 3 - Richmond .08 .25
266 Race 4 - Atlanta .08 .25
267 Race 5 - Darlington .08 .25
268 Race 6 - Bristol .08 .25
269 Race 7 - North Wilkesboro .08 .25
270 Race 8 - Martinsville .08 .25
271 Race 9 - Talladega .08 .25
272 Race 10 - Sonoma .08 .25
273 Winston Select Open .08 .25
274 Winston Select .08 .25
275 Race 11 - Charlotte .08 .25
276 Race 12 - Dover .08 .25
277 Race 13 - Pocono .08 .25
278 Race 14 - Michigan .08 .25
279 Race 15 - Daytona .08 .25
280 Race 16 - New Hampshire .08 .25
281 Race 17 - Pocono .08 .25
282 Race 18 - Talladega .08 .25
283 Race 19 - Indianapolis .08 .25
284 Race 20 - Watkins Glen .08 .25
285 Race 21 - Michigan .08 .25
286 Race 22 - Bristol .08 .25
287 Race 23 - Darlington .08 .25
288 Race 24 - Richmond .08 .25
289 Race 25 - Dover .08 .25
290 Race 26 - Martinsville .08 .25
291 Race 27 - North Wilkesboro .08 .25
292 Race 28 - Charlotte .08 .25
293 Race 29 - Rockingham .08 .25
294 Race 30 - Phoenix .08 .25
295 Race 31 - Atlanta .08 .25
296 Jeff Gordon WC Champ 1.00 2.50
297 Mike Skinner ST Champ .20 .50
298 Checklist #1 .08 .25
299 Checklist #2 .08 .25
300 Checklist #3 .08 .25
P1G Ricky Craven Gold Promo .40 1.00
P1R Ricky Craven Red Promo 1.00 2.50

1996 Maxx Premier Series Superlatives

This seven-card insert set was inserted one complete set per factory set of 1996 Maxx Premier Series. The cards take the theme of "the best" and "the most" of the 1995 NASCAR class. For example Ricky Craven is given the title "Most Likely to Succeed." Each card front features a driver and a car photo along with the driver's name and the title Maxx has honored them with.

COMPLETE SET (7) 3.00 8.00
SL1 Bill Elliott .75 2.00
SL2 Mark Martin 1.25 3.00
SL3 Bobby Labonte 1.25 3.00
SL4 Terry Labonte .60 1.50
SL5 Bobby Hamilton .20 .50
SL6 Ricky Craven .20 .50
SL7 Ken Schrader .20 .50

1996 Maxx Autographs

These three cards were intended to be inserted into Maxx Signed and Sealed. Due to Maxx's bankruptcy, the Signed and Sealed set was never distributed in a Maxx product. The exact distribution pattern of these cards is unknown.

COMPLETE SET (3) 150.00 250.00
5 Terry Labonte 50.00 100.00
24 Jeff Gordon 60.00 120.00
25 Ken Schrader 25.00 50.00

1996 Maxx Band-Aid Dale Jarrett

This four-card set features Dale Jarrett bearing his NASCAR Busch Grand National sponsor. The cards were issued in boxes of Band-Aid bandages as part of a sales promotion.

COMPLETE SET (4) .75 2.00
1 Dale Jarrett .25 .60
2 Dale Jarrett .25 .60
3 Dale Jarrett's Car .25 .60
4 D.Jarrett .25 .60
Zachary Jarrett

1996 Maxx Pepsi 500

This five-card set features past winners of the Daytona 500. The cards were originally offered in 12 packs of Pepsi during a regional promotion in the Daytona area in conjunction with the race. They were also offered through the Maxx Club.

COMPLETE SET (5) 1.50 4.00
1 Bobby Allison .40 1.00
2 Geoff Bodine .20 .50
3 Darrell Waltrip .40 1.00
4 Derrike Cope .20 .50
5 Sterling Marlin .60 1.50

1997 Maxx

This 120-card set marks Maxx's return to the hobby after a 18 month hiatus. The product was produced and distributed by Upper Deck. Cards were distributed in 10 card packs with 24 packs per box. The packs carried a suggested retail price of $1.99. According to Upper Deck this product contains 50 randomly inserted Dale Earnhardt autographed 1988 Maxx cards.

COMPLETE SET (120) 8.00 20.00
1 Morgan Shepherd .05 .15
2 Rusty Wallace .50 1.25
3 Dale Earnhardt 1.00 2.50
4 Sterling Marlin .20 .50
5 Terry Labonte .20 .50
6 Mark Martin .50 1.25
7 Geoff Bodine .05 .15
8 Hut Stricklin .05 .15
9 Lake Speed .05 .15
10 Ricky Rudd .20 .50
11 Brett Bodine .05 .15
12 Dale Jarrett .40 1.00
13 Bill Elliott .25 .60
14 Dick Trickle .05 .15
15 Wally Dallenbach .05 .15
16 Ted Musgrave .05 .15
17 Darrell Waltrip .10 .30
18 Bobby Labonte .40 1.00
19 Gary Bradberry .05 .15
20 Rick Mast .05 .15
21 Michael Waltrip .10 .30
22 Ward Burton .10 .30
23 Jimmy Spencer .05 .15
24 Jeff Gordon .60 1.50
25 Ricky Craven .05 .15
26 Chad Little .10 .30
27 Kenny Wallace .05 .15
28 Ernie Irvan .10 .30
29 Jeff Green .05 .15
30 Johnny Benson .10 .30
31 Mike Skinner .05 .15
32 Mike Wallace .05 .15
33 Ken Schrader .05 .15
34 Jeff Burton .20 .50
35 David Green .05 .15
36 Derrike Cope .05 .15
37 Jeremy Mayfield .10 .30
38 Dave Marcis .05 .15
39 John Andretti .05 .15
40 Robby Gordon RC .20 .50
41 Steve Grissom .05 .15
42 Joe Nemechek .05 .15
43 Bobby Hamilton .05 .15
44 Kyle Petty .10 .30
45 Elliott Sadler RC 1.50 4.00
46 Morgan Shepherd's Car .02 .10
47 Rusty Wallace's Car .10 .30
48 Dale Earnhardt's Car .40 1.00
49 Sterling Marlin's Car .05 .15
50 Terry Labonte's Car .10 .30
51 Mark Martin's Car .10 .30
52 Geoff Bodine's Car .02 .10
53 Hut Stricklin's Car .02 .10
54 Lake Speed's Car .02 .10
55 Ricky Rudd's Car .05 .15
56 Brett Bodine's Car .02 .10
57 Dale Jarrett's Car .10 .30
58 Bill Elliott's Car .10 .30
59 Dick Trickle's Car .02 .10
60 Wally Dallenbach's Car .02 .10
61 Ted Musgrave's Car .02 .10
62 Darrell Waltrip's Car .02 .10
63 Bobby Labonte's Car .10 .30
64 Gary Bradberry's Car .02 .10
65 Rick Mast's Car .02 .10
66 Michael Waltrip's Car .05 .15
67 Ward Burton's Car .02 .10
68 Jimmy Spencer's Car .02 .10
69 Jeff Gordon's Car .25 .60
70 Ricky Craven's Car .02 .10
71 Chad Little's Car .02 .10
72 Kenny Wallace's Car .02 .10
73 Ernie Irvan's Car .05 .15
74 Jeff Green's Car .02 .10
75 Johnny Benson's Car .02 .10
76 Mike Skinner's Car .02 .10
77 Mike Wallace's Car .02 .10
78 Ken Schrader's Car .02 .10
79 Jeff Burton's Car .02 .10
80 David Green's Car .02 .10
81 Derrike Cope's Car .02 .10
82 Jeremy Mayfield's Car .02 .10
83 Dave Marcis's Car .02 .10
84 John Andretti's Car .02 .10
85 Robby Gordon's Car .10 .30
86 Steve Grissom's Car .02 .10
87 Joe Nemechek's Car .02 .10
88 Bobby Hamilton's Car .02 .10
89 Kyle Petty's Car .05 .15
90 Elliott Sadler's Car .05 .15
91 Terry Labonte PS .10 .30
92 Robbie Gordon PS .10 .30
93 Bobby Labonte PS .20 .50
94 Ward Burton PS .10 .30
95 Bill Elliott PS .10 .30
96 Bill Elliott PS .10 .30
97 Ted Musgrave PS .05 .15
98 Rusty Wallace PS .25 .60
99 Ricky Craven PS .05 .15
100 Bobby Hamilton PS .05 .15
101 Rusty Wallace PS .25 .60
102 Ernie Irvan PS .10 .30
103 Mark Martin PS .25 .60
104 Jeff Burton PS .10 .30
105 Joe Nemechek PS .05 .15
106 Mark Martin MO .25 .60
107 Rusty Wallace MO .25 .60
108 Morgan Shepherd MO .05 .15
109 Dale Earnhardt MO .50 1.25
110 Ricky Rudd MO .10 .30
111 Lake Speed MO .05 .15
112 Sterling Marlin MO .10 .30
113 Michael Waltrip MO .10 .30
114 Terry Labonte MO .10 .30
115 Geoff Bodine MO .05 .15
116 Ken Schrader MO .05 .15
117 Dale Jarrett MO .20 .50
118 Bill Elliott MO .10 .30
119 Darrell Waltrip MO .10 .30
120 Ernie Irvan MO .10 .30
R2 Rusty Wallace Promo 1.00 2.50
NNO D.Earnhardt/50 '88 AU 600.00 900.00

1997 Maxx Chase the Champion

This 10-card set features the top drivers from the NASCAR circuit on micro-etched cards. The cards were randomly inserted in packs at a ratio of 1:5.

COMPLETE SET (10) 10.00 25.00
COMP.GOLD SET (10) 40.00 80.00
*GOLD DCs: 1X TO 2.5X BASIC INSERTS
GOLD DIE CUT STATED ODDS 1:21
C1 Jeff Gordon 4.00 10.00
C2 Mark Martin 3.00 8.00
C3 Terry Labonte 1.25 3.00
C4 Dale Jarrett 2.50 6.00
C5 Jeff Burton 1.25 3.00
C6 Bobby Labonte 2.50 6.00
C7 Ricky Rudd 1.25 3.00
C8 Michael Waltrip .75 2.00
C9 Jeremy Mayfield .75 2.00
C10 Bill Elliott 1.50 4.00

1997 Maxx Flag Firsts

This 25-card set looks back at the first victories of some of today's top NASCAR drivers. The cards were randomly inserted in packs at a ratio of 1:3.

COMPLETE SET (25) 15.00 40.00
FF1 Morgan Shepherd .40 1.00
FF2 Rusty Wallace 3.00 8.00
FF3 Dale Jarrett 2.50 6.00
FF4 Sterling Marlin 1.25 3.00
FF5 Terry Labonte 1.25 3.00
FF6 Mark Martin 3.00 8.00
FF7 Geoff Bodine .40 1.00
FF8 Ken Schrader .40 1.00
FF9 Lake Speed .40 1.00
FF10 Ricky Rudd 1.25 3.00
FF11 Brett Bodine .40 1.00
FF12 Derrike Cope .40 1.00
FF13 Kyle Petty .75 2.00
FF14 Dale Earnhardt 6.00 15.00
FF15 Bobby Hamilton .40 1.00
FF16 John Andretti .40 1.00
FF17 Darrell Waltrip .75 2.00
FF18 Bobby Labonte 2.50 6.00
FF19 Bill Elliott 1.50 4.00
FF20 Ernie Irvan .75 2.00
FF21 Jeff Burton 1.25 3.00
FF22 Ward Burton .75 2.00
FF23 Jimmy Spencer .40 1.00
FF24 Jeff Gordon 4.00 10.00
FF25 Dave Marcis .40 1.00

1997 Maxx Rookies of the Year

This 9-card set features eight of the past winners of the Maxx Winston Cup Rookie of the Year Award. It is important to note that card number MR9 Johnny Benson does not have the Maxx logo with the Rookie of the year logo in the bottom right corner like the other eight cards in the set. The cards were randomly inserted in packs at a ratio of 1:11.

COMPLETE SET (9) 8.00 20.00
MR1 Ken Bouchard .50 1.25
MR2 Dick Trickle .50 1.25
MR3 Rob Moroso .50 1.25
MR4 Bobby Hamilton .50 1.25
MR5 Jimmy Hensley .50 1.25
MR6 Jeff Gordon 5.00 12.00
MR7 Jeff Burton 1.50 4.00
MR8 Ricky Craven .50 1.25
MR9 Johnny Benson 1.00 2.50

1998 Maxx

The 1998 Maxx set was issued in one series totalling 105 cards. This product features a special "Signed, Sealed and Delivered autographed insert card of Richard Petty that earns one lucky collector a free trip to the famous Richard Petty Driving Experience. The set contains the topical subsets: Home Cookin (61-75), License to Drive (76-90), and Front Runners (91-105).

COMPLETE SET (105) 10.00 25.00
1 Jeremy Mayfield .10 .30
2 Rusty Wallace .50 1.25
3 Dale Earnhardt 1.00 2.50
4 Bobby Hamilton .05 .15
5 Terry Labonte .20 .50
6 Mark Martin .50 1.25
7 Geoff Bodine .05 .15
8 Ernie Irvan .10 .30
9 Jeff Burton .20 .50
10 Ricky Rudd .20 .50
11 Johnny Benson .10 .30
12 Dale Jarrett .40 1.00
13 Jerry Nadeau RC .20 .50
14 Steve Park .40 1.00
15 Bill Elliott .25 .60
16 Ted Musgrave .05 .15
17 Darrell Waltrip .10 .30
18 Bobby Labonte .40 1.00
19 Todd Bodine .05 .15
20 Kyle Petty .10 .30
21 Michael Waltrip .10 .30
22 Ken Schrader .05 .15
23 Jimmy Spencer .05 .15
24 Jeff Gordon .60 1.50
25 Ricky Craven .05 .15
26 John Andretti .05 .15
27 Sterling Marlin .20 .50
28 Kenny Irwin .10 .30
29 Mike Skinner .05 .15
30 Derrike Cope .05 .15
31 Jeremy Mayfield's Car .05 .15
32 Rusty Wallace's Car .20 .50
33 Dale Earnhardt's Car .40 1.00
34 Bobby Hamilton's Car .02 .10
35 Terry Labonte's Car .10 .30
36 Mark Martin's Car .20 .50
37 Geoff Bodine's Car .02 .10
38 Ernie Irvan's Car .02 .10
39 Jeff Burton's Car .10 .30
40 Ricky Rudd's Car .05 .15
41 Johnny Benson's Car .02 .10
42 Dale Jarrett's Car .10 .30
43 Jerry Nadeau's Car .10 .30
44 Steve Park's Car .10 .30
45 Bill Elliott's Car .10 .30
46 Ted Musgrave's Car .02 .10
47 Darrell Waltrip's Car .02 .10
48 Bobby Labonte's Car .10 .30
49 Todd Bodine's Car .02 .10
50 Kyle Petty's Car .02 .10
51 Michael Waltrip's Car .05 .15
52 Ken Schrader's Car .02 .10
53 Jimmy Spencer's Car .02 .10
54 Jeff Gordon's Car .25 .60
55 Ricky Craven's Car .02 .10
56 John Andretti's Car .02 .10
57 Sterling Marlin's Car .05 .15
58 Kenny Irwin's Car .05 .15
59 Mike Skinner's Car .02 .10
60 Derrike Cope's Car .02 .10
61 Jimmy Spencer's Car HC .02 .10
62 Bill Elliott's Car HC .10 .30
63 Darrell Waltrip's Car HC .02 .10
64 Jeff Gordon's Car HC .25 .60
65 John Andretti's Car HC .02 .10
66 Johnny Benson's Car HC .02 .10
67 Jeff Burton's Car HC .10 .30
68 Bobby Hamilton's Car HC .02 .10
69 Ernie Irvan's Car HC .02 .10
70 Dale Jarrett's Car HC .10 .30
71 Bobby Labonte's Car HC .10 .30
72 Terry Labonte's Car HC .10 .30
73 Kyle Petty's Car HC .02 .10
74 Ricky Rudd's Car HC .05 .15
75 Morgan Shepherd HC .02 .10
76 Kenny Irwin's Car LTD .10 .30
77 Steve Park's Car LTD .02 .10
78 Jerry Nadeau's Car LTD .10 .30
79 Todd Bodine's Car LTD .02 .10
80 Mike Skinner's Car LTD .02 .10
81 Jeremy Mayfield's Car LTD .02 .10
82 Ricky Craven's Car LTD .02 .10
83 Steve Grissom's Car LTD .02 .10
84 Brett Bodine's Car LTD .02 .10
85 Jeff Burton's Car LTD .05 .15
86 Ward Burton's Car LTD .02 .10
87 Chad Little's Car LTD .02 .10
88 David Green's Car LTD .02 .10
89 John Andretti's Car LTD .02 .10
90 Bobby Labonte's Car LTD .10 .30
91 Jeff Gordon's Car FR .25 .60
92 Dale Jarrett's Car FR .10 .30
93 Mark Martin's Car FR .20 .50
94 Jeff Burton's Car FR .05 .15
95 Dale Earnhardt's Car FR .40 1.00
96 Terry Labonte's Car FR .10 .30
97 Bobby Labonte's Car FR .10 .30
98 Bill Elliott's Car FR .10 .30
99 Rusty Wallace's Car FR .20 .50
100 Ken Schrader's Car FR .02 .10
101 Johnny Benson's Car FR .02 .10
102 Ted Musgrave's Car FR .02 .10
103 Ernie Irvan's Car FR .02 .10
104 Steve Park's Car FR .05 .15
105 Kenny Irwin's Car FR .05 .15

1998 Maxx Focus on a Champion

This 15-card set features the top contenders for the Winston Cup Championship. These cards are randomly inserted one per 24 packs.

COMPLETE SET (15) 30.00 80.00
COMP.CEL SET (15) 100.00 200.00
*CEL CARDS: 1X TO 2.5X BASIC INSERTS
FC1 Jeff Gordon 8.00 20.00
FC2 Dale Jarrett 5.00 12.00
FC3 Dale Earnhardt 12.50 30.00
FC4 Mark Martin 6.00 15.00
FC5 Jeff Burton 2.50 6.00
FC6 Kyle Petty 1.50 4.00
FC7 Terry Labonte 2.50 6.00
FC8 Bobby Labonte 5.00 12.00
FC9 Bill Elliott 3.00 8.00
FC10 Rusty Wallace 6.00 15.00
FC11 Ken Schrader .75 2.00
FC12 Johnny Benson 1.50 4.00
FC13 Ted Musgrave .75 2.00
FC14 Ernie Irvan 1.50 4.00
FC15 Kenny Irwin 1.50 4.00

1998 Maxx Swappin' Paint

This 25-card set features the cars of the top contenders for the Winston Cup Championship. These cards are randomly inserted one per three packs.

COMPLETE SET (25) 15.00 30.00
SW1 Steve Park 3.00 8.00
SW2 Terry Labonte's Car 1.00 2.50
SW3 Ernie Irvan's Car .30 .75
SW4 Bobby Hamilton .50 1.25
SW5 Derrike Cope's Car .30 .75
SW6 John Andretti's Car .30 .75
SW7 Geoff Bodine's Car .30 .75
SW8 Hut Stricklin's Car .30 .75
SW9 Jeff Burton's Car 1.00 2.50
SW10 Robert Pressley's Car .30 .75
SW11 Brett Bodine's Car .30 .75
SW12 Rick Mast's Car .30 .75
SW13 Jerry Nadeau's Car 1.00 2.50
SW14 Sterling Marlin's Car .50 1.25
SW15 Johnny Benson's Car .30 .75
SW16 Ted Musgrave's Car .30 .75
SW17 Todd Bodine's Car .30 .75
SW18 J.Mayfield 4.00 10.00
R.Wallace
SW19 Mark Martin's Car 1.50 4.00
SW20 Chad Little .50 1.25
SW21 Joe Nemechek's Car .30 .75
SW22 Dick Trickle .50 1.25
SW23 Jimmy Spencer's Car .30 .75
SW24 Kenny Irwin's Car .50 1.25
SW25 Ricky Craven's Car .30 .75

1998 Maxx Teamwork

This 10-card set features the cars and pit crews of the top contenders for the Winston Cup Championship. These cards are randomly inserted one per 11 packs.

COMPLETE SET (10) 10.00 25.00
TW1 Jeff Gordon's Car 2.50 6.00
TW2 Terry Labonte's Car 1.25 3.00
TW3 Ricky Craven's Car .40 1.00
TW4 Mark Martin's Car 2.00 5.00
TW5 Jeff Burton's Car 1.25 3.00
TW6 Ted Musgrave's Car .40 1.00
TW7 Chad Little's Car .40 1.00
TW8 Johnny Benson's Car .40 1.00
TW9 Dale Jarrett's Car 1.25 3.00
TW10 Kenny Irwin's Car .60 1.50

1998 Maxx 1997 Year In Review

The 1997 Maxx Year in Review Boxed Set was issued in one-series factory set totalling 161-base cards, four Award Winners (AW1-AW4) cards and 10 cards (PO1-PO10) featuring the top finishers.

COMPLETE FACT.SET (175) 12.00 30.00
1 Jeff Gordon .60 1.50
2 Mike Skinner .05 .15
3 Ricky Craven's Car .02 .10
4 Ward Burton's Car .05 .15
5 Hendrick Sweep .10 .30
6 Jeff Gordon's Car .25 .60
7 Mark Martin's Car .20 .50
8 Ernie Irvan's Car .05 .15
9 Dale Earnhardt's Car .50 1.25
10 Ricky Craven's Car .02 .10
11 Rusty Wallace .40 1.00
12 Terry Labonte's Car .10 .30
13 Kyle Petty's Car .05 .15
14 Ricky Rudd's Car .05 .15
15 Ernie Irvan's Car .05 .15
16 Dale Jarrett .40 1.00
17 Robby Gordon .05 .15
18 Johnny Benson's Car .02 .10
19 Geoff Bodine's Car .02 .10
20 Steve Grissom's Car .02 .10
21 Dale Jarrett .40 1.00
22 Dale Jarrett's Car .10 .30
23 Darrell Waltrip .10 .30
24 Michael Waltrip's Car .02 .10
25 Ted Musgrave's Car .02 .10
26 Jeff Burton .20 .50
27 Dale Jarrett's Car .10 .30
28 Steve Grissom's Car .02 .10
29 Jeff Gordon's Car .25 .60
30 Darrell Waltrip's Car .05 .15
31 Jeff Gordon's Car .25 .60
32 Rusty Wallace's Car .20 .50
33 Dale Earnhardt's Car .50 1.25
34 Jeremy Mayfield's Car .05 .15
35 Ted Musgrave's Car .02 .10
36 Jeff Gordon's Car .25 .60
37 Kenny Wallace .05 .15
38 Mark Martin's Car .20 .50
39 Rusty Wallace .50 1.25
40 Ricky Craven's Car .02 .10
41 Mark Martin .50 1.25
42 John Andretti .05 .15
43 Jeff Burton's Car .05 .15
44 Bill Elliott .25 .60
45 Dale Jarrett's Car .10 .30
46 Mark Martin .50 1.25
47 Mark Martin's Car .20 .50
48 Darrell Waltrip's Car .05 .15
49 Ernie Irvan's Car .05 .15
50 Alcatraz Island .02 .10
51 Jeff Gordon's Car .25 .60
52 Jeff Gordon .60 1.50
53 Dale Earnhardt's Car .50 1.25
54 Jeff Burton's Car .05 .15
55 Darrell Waltrip's Car .05 .15
56 Ricky Rudd .20 .50

57 Bobby Labonte	.40	1.00
58 Jeff Burton's Car	.05	.15
59 Bobby Labonte's Car	.10	.30
60 Dave Marcis' Car	.02	.10
61 Jeff Gordon	.60	1.50
62 Bobby Hamilton's Car	.02	.10
63 Derrike Cope's Car	.02	.10
64 Morgan Shepherd's Car	.02	.10
65 Ward Burton's Car	.05	.15
66 Ernie Irvan	.10	.30
67 Dale Jarrett	.40	1.00
68 Derrike Cope's Car	.02	.10
69 Ted Musgrave's Car	.02	.10
70 Bill Elliott's Car	.10	.30
71 Jeff Gordon	.60	1.50
72 Joe Nemechek	.05	.15
73 Ricky Rudd	.20	.50
74 Jimmy Spencer's Car	.02	.10
75 Ted Musgrave's Car	.02	.10
76 John Andretti	.05	.15
77 Mike Skinner	.05	.15
78 Terry Labonte's Car	.10	.30
79 Kyle Petty's Car	.05	.15
80 Ward Burton's Car	.05	.15
81 Jeff Burton	.20	.50
82 Ken Schrader	.05	.15
83 Hut Stricklin's Car	.02	.10
84 Rusty Wallace's Car	.20	.50
85 Dale Jarrett	.40	1.00
86 Dale Jarrett's Car	.10	.30
87 Joe Nemechek	.05	.15
88 Johnny Benson's Car	.02	.10
89 Ted Musgrave's Car	.02	.10
90 Bill Elliott's Car	.10	.30
91 Ricky Rudd	.20	.50
92 Ernie Irvan's Car	.05	.15
93 Kyle Petty's Car	.05	.15
94 Michael Waltrip's Car	.05	.15
95 Darrell Waltrip's Car	.05	.15
96 Jeff Gordon's Car	.25	.60
97 Todd Bodine	.05	.15
98 Steve Grissom's Car	.02	.10
99 Ricky Rudd	.20	.50
100 Robby Gordon's Car	.02	.10
101 Mark Martin	.50	1.25
102 Johnny Benson's Car	.02	.10
103 Rusty Wallace's Car	.20	.50
104 Bill Elliott's Car	.10	.30
105 Jeff Burton's Car	.05	.15
106 Dale Jarrett	.40	1.00
107 Kenny Wallace	.05	.15
108 Steve Grissom's Car	.02	.10
109 Geoff Bodine's Car	.02	.10
110 David Green's Car	.02	.10
111 Jeff Gordon	.60	1.50
112 Bobby Labonte	.40	1.00
113 Chad Little's Car	.05	.15
114 Dick Trickle's Car	.02	.10
115 Jeff Burton's Car	.05	.15
116 Dale Jarrett	.40	1.00
117 Bill Elliott's Car	.10	.30
118 Ted Musgrave's Car	.02	.10
119 Joe Nemechek	.05	.15
120 Kenny Irwin	.10	.30
121 Jeff Gordon	.60	1.50
122 Ken Schrader	.05	.15
123 Ernie Irvan's Car	.05	.15
124 John Andretti's Car	.02	.10
125 Geoff Bodine's Car	.02	.10
126 Mark Martin	.50	1.25
127 Mark Martin's Car	.20	.50
128 Dale Earnhardt's Car	.50	1.25
129 Robby Gordon's Car	.02	.10
130 Jeff Gordon's Car	.25	.60
131 Jeff Burton	.20	.50
132 Ward Burton's Car	.05	.15
133 Ricky Craven's Car	.02	.10
134 Bobby Hamilton's Car	.02	.10
135 Rusty Wallace's Car	.20	.50
136 Dale Jarrett	.40	1.00
137 Geoff Bodine	.05	.15
138 Terry Labonte's Car	.10	.30
139 Bobby Labonte's Car	.10	.30
140 Darrell Waltrip's Car	.05	.15
141 Terry Labonte	.20	.50
142 Ernie Irvan	.10	.30
143 Kyle Petty's Car	.05	.15
144 Mark Martin's Car	.20	.50
145 Ken Schrader's Car	.02	.10
146 Bobby Hamilton	.05	.15
147 Bobby Labonte	.40	1.00
148 Sterling Marlin's Car	.05	.15
149 Bill Elliott	.25	.60
150 Bobby Hamilton	.05	.15
151 Dale Jarrett	.40	1.00
152 Bobby Hamilton's Car	.02	.10
153 Kyle Petty's Car	.05	.15
154 Dale Jarrett's Car	.10	.30
155 Darrell Waltrip's Car	.05	.15
156 Bobby Labonte	.40	1.00
157 Geoff Bodine	.05	.15
158 Bobby Hamilton's Car	.02	.10
159 Mark Martin's Car	.20	.50
160 Chad Little's Car	.05	.15
161 Checklist	.02	.10
AW1 Jeff Gordon	1.25	3.00
AW2 Mike Skinner	.20	.50
AW3 Dale Jarrett	.75	2.00
AW4 Bill Elliott	.50	1.25
PO1 Jeff Gordon	1.25	3.00
PO2 Dale Jarrett	.75	2.00
PO3 Mark Martin	1.00	2.50
PO4 Jeff Burton	.40	1.00
PO5 Dale Earnhardt	2.00	5.00
PO6 Terry Labonte	.50	1.25
PO7 Bobby Labonte	.75	2.00
PO8 Bill Elliott	.50	1.25
PO9 Rusty Wallace	1.00	2.50
PO10 Ken Schrader	.20	.50

1998 Maxx 10th Anniversary

The 1998 Maxx 10th Anniversary set was issued in one series totalling 134 cards. The card fronts feature color photos surrounded by a white-border with the Maxx 10th Anniversary logo in the upper right corner. The set contains the topical subsets: Family Ties (91-107), Farewell Tour (108-116) and Racin' Up Wins (117-126).

COMPLETE SET (134)	10.00	25.00
1 Rusty Wallace	.60	1.50
2 Chad Little	.20	.50
3 Bobby Hamilton	.10	.30
4 Terry Labonte	.30	.75
5 Mark Martin	.75	2.00
6 Alan Kulwicki	.30	.75
7 Geoff Bodine	.10	.30
8 Brett Bodine	.10	.30
9 Ricky Rudd	.30	.75
10 Donnie Allison	.10	.30
11 Jeremy Mayfield	.20	.50
12 Jerry Nadeau RC	.20	.50
13 Jeff Burton	.30	.75
14 Bill Elliott	.40	1.00
15 Elton Sawyer	.10	.30
16 Darrell Waltrip	.20	.50
17 Bobby Labonte	.60	1.50
18 Ward Burton	.20	.50
19 Michael Waltrip	.20	.50
20 David Pearson	.20	.50
21 Bobby Allison	.20	.50
22 Jimmy Spencer	.10	.30
23 Dale Jarrett	.60	1.50
24 Jeff Gordon	1.00	2.50
25 Johnny Benson	.20	.50
26 Kevin Lepage	.10	.30
27 Davey Allison	.40	1.00
28 Kenny Irwin	.20	.50
29 Ken Schrader	.10	.30
30 Harry Gant	.20	.50
31 Cale Yarborough	.20	.50
32 Ernie Irvan	.20	.50
33 Ned Jarrett	.20	.50
34 Dale Earnhardt Jr.	1.50	4.00
35 Jeff Green	.10	.30
36 Sterling Marlin	.30	.75
37 Steve Grissom	.10	.30
38 Robert Pressley	.10	.30
39 Richard Petty	.30	.75
40 Kyle Petty	.20	.50
41 John Andretti	.10	.30
42 Benny Parsons	.10	.30
43 Buddy Baker	.10	.30
44 Neil Bonnett	.30	.75
45 Kenny Wallace	.10	.30
46 Rusty Wallace's Car	.30	.75
47 Chad Little's Car	.05	.15
48 Bobby Hamilton's Car	.05	.15
49 Terry Labonte's Car	.20	.50
50 Mark Martin's Car	.30	.75
51 Jimmy Spencer's Car	.20	.50
52 Geoff Bodine's Car	.05	.15
53 Brett Bodine's Car	.05	.15
54 Ricky Rudd's Car	.10	.30
55 Donnie Allison's Car	.05	.15
56 Jeremy Mayfield's Car	.05	.15
57 Jerry Nadeau's Car	.20	.50
58 Jeff Burton's Car	.10	.30
59 Bill Elliott's Car	.20	.50
60 Elton Sawyer	.10	.30
61 Darrell Waltrip's Car	.05	.15
62 Bobby Labonte's Car	.20	.50
63 Ward Burton's Car	.10	.30
64 Michael Waltrip's Car	.10	.30
65 David Pearson's Car	.05	.15
66 Bobby Allison's Car	.05	.15
67 Jimmy Spencer's Car	.05	.15
68 Dale Jarrett's Car	.20	.50
69 Jeff Gordon's Car	.40	1.00
70 Johnny Benson's Car	.05	.15
71 Kevin Lepage's Car	.05	.15
72 Davey Allison's Car	.20	.50
73 Kenny Irwin's Car	.10	.30
74 Ken Schrader's Car	.05	.15
75 Harry Gant's Car	.05	.15
76 Cale Yarborough's Car	.10	.30
77 Ernie Irvan's Car	.10	.30
78 Ned Jarrett's Car	.05	.15
79 Dale Earnhardt Jr.'s Car	.75	2.00
80 Jeff Green's Car	.05	.15
81 Sterling Marlin's Car	.10	.30
82 Steve Grissom's Car	.05	.15
83 Robert Pressley's Car	.05	.15
84 Richard Petty's Car	.10	.30
85 Kyle Petty's Car	.10	.30
86 John Andretti's Car	.05	.15
87 Benny Parsons's Car	.05	.15
88 Buddy Baker's Car	.05	.15
89 Neil Bonnett's Car	.05	.15
90 Kenny Wallace's Car	.05	.15
91 Donnie Allison	.10	.30
92 Bobby Allison	.20	.50
93 Davey Allison	.40	1.00
94 Richard Petty	.30	.75
95 Kyle Petty	.20	.50
96 Dale Earnhardt	1.50	4.00
97 Dale Earnhardt Jr.	1.50	4.00
98 Darrell Waltrip	.20	.50
99 Michael Waltrip	.20	.50
100 Mike Wallace	.10	.30
101 Rusty Wallace	.75	2.00
102 Kenny Wallace	.10	.30
103 Geoff Bodine	.10	.30
104 Brett Bodine	.10	.30
105 Todd Bodine	.10	.30
106 Terry Labonte	.30	.75
107 Bobby Labonte	.60	1.50
108 Richard Petty	.30	.75
109 Bobby Allison	.30	.75
110 Cale Yarborough	.10	.30
111 Benny Parsons	.10	.30
112 Buddy Baker	.10	.30
113 Davey Allison	.40	1.00
114 Harry Gant	.10	.30
115 Neil Bonnett	.30	.75
116 Alan Kulwicki	.30	.75
117 B.Elliott R.Wallace	.40	1.00
118 D.Waltrip R.Wallace	.30	.75
119 Dale Earnhardt	1.50	4.00
120 D.Allison H.Gant	.30	.75
121 B.Elliott D.Allison	.30	.75
122 Rusty Wallace	.75	2.00
123 Rusty Wallace	.75	2.00
124 Jeff Gordon	1.00	2.50
125 Jeff Gordon	1.00	2.50
126 Jeff Gordon	1.00	2.50
127 Checklist	.05	.15
128 Checklist	.05	.15
129 Checklist	.05	.15
130 Checklist	.05	.15
131 Checklist	.05	.15
132 Checklist	.05	.15
133 Checklist	.05	.15
134 Checklist	.05	.15
P1 Rusty Wallace Promo	.75	2.00

1998 Maxx 10th Anniversary Buy Back Autographs

Randomly inserted in packs at a rate of one in 288, this assorted insert set features older MAXX cards that were bought back by Upper Deck and signed by the featured driver. Each card inserted into packs was stamped with Maxx's Seal of Authenticity hologram on the back and hand serial numbered on the front. Some cards later made their into the secondary market without serial numbering but with the hologram on the backs.

1 Bobby Allison '88 #30	10.00	25.00
2 Buddy Baker '88 #55/169	12.00	30.00
3 Brett Bodine '88 #59/149	10.00	25.00
4 Geoff Bodine '88 #67	10.00	25.00
5 Derrick Cope '88 #33/149	8.00	20.00
26 Ernie Irvan '88 #95/148	15.00	40.00
27 Dale Jarrett '88 #61	20.00	50.00
29 Dave Marcis '88 #44/170	12.00	30.00
30 Benny Parsons '88 #76/153	30.00	60.00
42 Richard Petty SSD/250	15.00	40.00
43 Ken Schrader '88 #74/150	15.00	40.00
44 M.Shepherd '88 #25/149	12.00	30.00
45 Lake Speed '88 #46	12.00	30.00
47 Rusty Wallace '88 #14/297	20.00	50.00
48 Darrell Waltrip '88 #10/179	25.00	60.00
49 M.Waltrip '88 #98/149	15.00	40.00
50 C.Yarborough '88 #90/149	10.00	25.00

1998 Maxx 10th Anniversary Card of the Year

Randomly inserted in packs at a rate of one in 23, these insert cards depict highlights from the first 10 years of Maxx.

COMPLETE SET (10)	25.00	60.00
CY1 Davey Allison	3.00	8.00
CY2 K.Petty R.Petty	2.50	6.00
CY3 Rusty Wallace	5.00	12.00
CY4 Darrell Waltrip	1.50	4.00
CY5 Jeff Gordon	8.00	20.00
CY6 Richard Petty	2.50	6.00
CY7 Rusty Wallace	5.00	12.00
CY8 Dale Jarrett	5.00	12.00
CY9 Mark Martin	6.00	15.00
CY10 Jeff Gordon	8.00	20.00

1998 Maxx 10th Anniversary Champions Past

Randomly inserted in packs at a rate of one in 5, this is the first of a two-tiered insert set that features the past ten Winston Cup Champions.

COMPLETE SET (10)	15.00	40.00
*DIE CUT/1000: 1X TO 2.5X BASIC INSERTS		
CP1 Jeff Gordon	4.00	10.00
CP2 Terry Labonte	1.25	3.00
CP3 Dale Earnhardt	6.00	15.00
CP4 Alan Kulwicki	1.25	3.00
CP5 Rusty Wallace	2.50	6.00
CP6 Bill Elliott	1.50	4.00
CP7 Darrell Waltrip	.75	2.00
CP8 Bobby Allison	.75	2.00
CP9 Richard Petty	1.25	3.00
CP10 Cale Yarborough	.75	2.00

1998 Maxx 10th Anniversary Maxximum Preview

Inserted one per pack, this 25-card insert set features the Ionix technology with a unique design of top drivers who are also included in the Maxx Maxximum set.

COMPLETE SET (25)	15.00	30.00
P1 Darrell Waltrip	.40	1.00
P2 Rusty Wallace	1.25	3.00
P3 Sterling Marlin	.60	1.50
P4 Bobby Hamilton	.25	.60
P5 Terry Labonte	.60	1.50
P6 Mark Martin	1.50	4.00
P7 Geoff Bodine	.25	.60
P8 Ernie Irvan	.40	1.00
P9 Jeff Burton	.60	1.50
P10 Ricky Rudd	.60	1.50
P11 Dale Jarrett	1.25	3.00
P12 Jeremy Mayfield	.40	1.00
P13 Jerry Nadeau	.60	1.50
P14 Ken Schrader	.25	.60
P15 Kyle Petty	.40	1.00
P16 Chad Little	.40	1.00
P17 Todd Bodine	.25	.60
P18 Bobby Labonte	1.25	3.00
P19 Bill Elliott	.75	2.00
P20 Mike Skinner	.25	.60
P21 Michael Waltrip	.40	1.00
P22 John Andretti	.25	.60
P23 Jimmy Spencer	.25	.60
P24 Jeff Gordon	2.00	5.00
P25 Kenny Irwin	.40	1.00

1999 Maxx

The 1999 Maxx set was issued in one series totalling 90 cards. The set contains cards featuring NASCAR Winston Cup Drivers, NASCAR Winston Cup Cars, and Roots of Racing subset cards.

COMPLETE SET (90)	7.50	20.00
1 Jeff Gordon	.75	2.00
2 Jeff Gordon's Car	.30	.75
3 Jeff Gordon's Car RR	.30	.75
4 Jeff Burton	.25	.60
5 Jeff Burton's Car	.07	.20
6 Jeff Burton RR	.15	.40
7 Dale Jarrett	.50	1.25
8 Dale Jarrett's Car	.15	.40
9 Dale Jarrett's Car RR	.15	.40
10 Ward Burton	.15	.40
11 Ward Burton	.15	.40
12 Ward Burton	.15	.40
13 Bill Elliott	.30	.75
14 Bill Elliott's Car	.15	.40
15 Bill Elliott's Car RR	.15	.40
16 Johnny Benson	.15	.40
17 Johnny Benson	.15	.40
18 Johnny Benson	.15	.40
19 Dale Earnhardt Jr.	1.25	2.50
20 Dale Earnhardt Jr.'s Car	.40	1.00
21 D.Earnhardt Jr.'s Car RR	.40	1.00
22 Sterling Marlin	.25	.60
23 Sterling Marlin's Car	.07	.20
24 Sterling Marlin RR	.15	.40
25 Ken Schrader	.07	.20
26 Ken Schrader	.07	.20
27 Ken Schrader	.07	.20
28 Bobby Labonte	.50	1.25
29 Bobby Labonte's Car	.15	.40
30 Bobby Labonte RR	.25	.60
31 Chad Little	.15	.40
32 Chad Little	.15	.40
33 Chad Little	.15	.40
34 Jeremy Mayfield	.15	.40
35 Jeremy Mayfield's Car	.07	.20
36 Jeremy Mayfield RR	.07	.20
37 Ricky Rudd	.25	.60
38 Ricky Rudd's Car	.07	.20
39 Ricky Rudd's Car RR	.07	.20
40 John Andretti	.07	.20
41 John Andretti	.07	.20
42 John Andretti	.07	.20
43 Rusty Wallace	.60	1.50
44 Rusty Wallace's Car	.25	.60
45 Rusty Wallace RR	.30	.75
46 Darrell Waltrip	.15	.40
47 Darrell Waltrip's Car	.07	.20
48 Darrell Waltrip RR	.07	.20
49 Geoffrey Bodine	.07	.20
50 Geoffrey Bodine	.07	.20
51 Geoffrey Bodine	.07	.20
52 Mark Martin	.60	1.50
53 Mark Martin's Car	.25	.60
54 Mark Martin RR	.30	.75
55 Kenny Irwin	.15	.40
56 Kenny Irwin's Car	.07	.20
57 Kenny Irwin's Car RR	.07	.20
58 Mike Skinner	.15	.40
59 Mike Skinner	.15	.40
60 Mike Skinner	.15	.40
61 Kyle Petty	.15	.40
62 Kyle Petty's Car	.07	.20
63 Kyle Petty's Car RR	.07	.20
64 Bobby Hamilton	.07	.20
65 Bobby Hamilton	.07	.20
66 Bobby Hamilton	.07	.20
67 Jerry Nadeau	.15	.40
68 Jerry Nadeau	.15	.40
69 Jerry Nadeau	.15	.40
70 Tony Stewart CRC	1.00	2.50
71 Tony Stewart's Car	.30	.75
72 Tony Stewart RR	.40	1.00
73 Ernie Irvan	.15	.40
74 Ernie Irvan's Car	.07	.20
75 Ernie Irvan's Car RR	.07	.20
76 Steve Park	.40	1.00
77 Steve Park's Car	.07	.20
78 Steve Park RR	.25	.60
79 Kevin Lepage	.07	.20
80 Kevin Lepage	.07	.20
81 Kevin Lepage	.07	.20
82 Elliott Sadler	.15	.40
83 Elliott Sadler	.15	.40
84 Elliott Sadler	.15	.40
85 Terry Labonte	.25	.60
86 Terry Labonte's Car	.15	.40
87 Terry Labonte's Car RR	.15	.40
88 Dale Earnhardt	1.25	3.00
89 Dale Earnhardt's Car	.50	1.25
90 Jeff Gordon CL	.40	1.00

1999 Maxx FANtastic Finishes

Randomly inserted in packs at the rate of one in twelve, this 30 card set focuses on the top NASCAR drivers and the closest finishes in their Winston Cup careers.

COMPLETE SET (30)	60.00	120.00
F1 Jeff Gordon's Car	6.00	15.00
F2 Steve Park's Car	3.00	8.00
F3 Elliott Sadler's Car	1.25	3.00
F4 Bobby Hamilton's Car	.60	1.50
F5 Rusty Wallace's Car	5.00	12.00
F6 Kyle Petty's Car	1.25	3.00
F7 Kenny Irwin's Car	1.25	3.00
F8 Jerry Nadeau's Car	1.25	3.00
F9 Dale Jarrett's Car	4.00	10.00
F10 Dale Earnhardt's Car	10.00	25.00
F11 Ken Schrader's Car	.60	1.50
F12 Jeff Burton's Car	2.00	5.00
F13 Ernie Irvan's Car	1.25	3.00
F14 John Andretti's Car	.60	1.50
F15 Dale Earnhardt Jr.'s Car	8.00	20.00
F16 Bill Elliott's Car	2.50	6.00
F17 Mark Martin's Car	5.00	12.00
F18 Mike Skinner's Car	1.25	3.00
F19 Ward Burton's Car	1.25	3.00
F20 Darrell Waltrip's Car	1.25	3.00
F21 Chad Little's Car	1.25	3.00
F22 Ricky Rudd's Car	2.00	5.00
F23 Johnny Benson's Car	1.25	3.00
F24 Terry Labonte's Car	2.00	5.00
F25 Sterling Marlin's Car	2.00	5.00
F26 Kevin Lepage's Car	.60	1.50
F27 Jeremy Mayfield's Car	1.25	3.00
F28 Tony Stewart's Car	6.00	15.00
F29 Bobby Labonte's Car	4.00	10.00
F30 Michael Waltrip's Car	1.25	3.00

1999 Maxx Focus on a Champion

Randomly inserted in packs at the rate of one in 1 in 24 this set highlights the top 15 drivers who will be chasing the 1999 NASCAR Winston Cup title.

COMPLETE SET (15)	25.00	60.00
*GOLD CARDS: .8X TO 2X BASIC INSERTS		
FC1 Jeff Gordon	3.00	8.00
FC2 Dale Earnhardt	5.00	12.00
FC3 Dale Earnhardt Jr.	4.00	10.00
FC4 Mark Martin	2.50	6.00
FC5 Dale Jarrett	2.00	5.00
FC6 Jeremy Mayfield	.60	1.50
FC7 Rusty Wallace	2.50	6.00
FC8 Terry Labonte	1.00	2.50
FC9 Jeff Burton	1.00	2.50
FC10 Ernie Irvan	.60	1.50
FC11 Bill Elliott	1.25	3.00
FC12 Bobby Labonte	2.00	5.00
FC13 Jerry Nadeau	.60	1.50
FC14 Steve Park	1.50	4.00
FC15 Kenny Irwin	.60	1.50

1999 Maxx Race Ticket

Randomly inserted in packs at the rate of one in eight, these scratch off game cards give the collector a chance to instantly win a pair of tickets to a 1999 NASCAR Winston Cup race.

COMPLETE SET (30)	25.00	50.00
RT1 Jerry Nadeau's Car	.60	1.50
RT2 Jeff Burton's Car	1.00	2.50
RT3 Jeremy Mayfield's Car	.60	1.50
RT4 Dale Earnhardt Jr.'s Car	4.00	10.00
RT5 Steve Park's Car	1.50	4.00
RT6 Kenny Irwin's Car	.60	1.50
RT7 Ernie Irvan's Car	.60	1.50
RT8 Dale Jarrett's Car	2.00	5.00
RT9 Kevin Lepage's Car	.30	.75
RT10 Bill Elliott's Car	1.25	3.00
RT11 Bobby Hamilton's Car	.30	.75
RT12 Chad Little's Car	.60	1.50
RT13 Brett Bodine's Car	.30	.75
RT14 Ken Schrader's Car	.30	.75
RT15 Ricky Rudd's Car	1.00	2.50
RT16 Johnny Benson's Car	.60	1.50
RT17 John Andretti's Car	.30	.75
RT18 Tony Stewart's Car	3.00	8.00
RT19 Mark Martin's Car	2.50	6.00
RT20 Ward Burton's Car	.60	1.50
RT21 Elliott Sadler's Car	.60	1.50
RT22 Jeff Gordon's Car	3.00	8.00
RT23 Kyle Petty's Car	.60	1.50
RT24 Terry Labonte's Car	1.00	2.50
RT25 Sterling Marlin's Car	1.00	2.50
RT26 Darrell Waltrip's Car	.60	1.50
RT27 Bobby Labonte's Car	2.00	5.00
RT28 Mike Skinner's Car	.60	1.50
RT29 Michael Waltrip's Car	.60	1.50
RT30 Rusty Wallace's Car	2.50	6.00

1999 Maxx Racer's Ink

Randomly inserted in packs these cards feature authentic autographs from the top five drivers on the NASCAR Winston Cup circuit and each card was hand numbered to 250.

JG Jeff Gordon	100.00	200.00
JM Jeremy Mayfield	8.00	20.00
MM Mark Martin	25.00	60.00
RW Rusty Wallace	6.00	15.00

1999 Maxx Racing Images

Randomly inserted in packs at the rate of one in three, this 30 card set features all the new 1999 uniforms and cars with dual photos on the front of each card in Light F/X technology.

COMPLETE SET (30)	12.50	25.00
RI1 Darrell Waltrip	.30	.75
RI2 Kevin Lepage	.15	.40
RI3 Bobby Labonte	1.00	2.50
RI4 Ricky Rudd	.50	1.25
RI5 Jeff Burton	.50	1.25
RI6 Brett Bodine	.15	.40
RI7 Mike Skinner	.30	.75
RI8 John Andretti	.15	.40
RI9 Dale Jarrett	1.00	2.50
RI10 Bill Elliott	.60	1.50
RI11 Ward Burton	.30	.75
RI12 Terry Labonte	.50	1.25
RI13 Kenny Irwin	.30	.75
RI14 Ken Schrader	.15	.40
RI15 Tony Stewart	1.50	4.00
RI16 Sterling Marlin	.50	1.25
RI17 Ernie Irvan	.30	.75
RI18 Bobby Hamilton	.15	.40
RI19 Johnny Benson	.30	.75
RI20 Michael Waltrip	.30	.75
RI21 Jeremy Mayfield	.30	.75
RI22 Chad Little	.30	.75
RI23 Rusty Wallace	1.25	3.00
RI24 Jeff Gordon	1.50	4.00
RI25 Steve Park	.75	2.00
RI26 Jerry Nadeau	.30	.75
RI27 Elliott Sadler	.30	.75
RI28 Dale Earnhardt Jr.	2.00	5.00
RI29 Kyle Petty	.30	.75
RI30 Mark Martin	1.25	3.00

1998 Maxx Signed, Sealed, and Delivered

Each card in this set was signed by the featured driver and included a postmark style gold foil design on the cardfront. The cardbacks include a congratulatory message from Upper Deck along with hand serial numbering. It is not known exactly how the cards were distributed but they appeared on the market after Upper Deck stopped producing racing cards.

COMMON CARD/250	10.00	25.00
SEMISTARS/250	15.00	40.00
S1 Rusty Wallace/250	30.00	60.00
S2 Dale Jarrett/250	15.00	40.00
S3 Jeff Gordon/250	40.00	80.00
S4 Richard Petty/250	20.00	50.00
S5 Jeff Burton/250	10.00	25.00

2000 Maxx

Released as an 85-card set, Maxx is comprised of 39 regular issue driver cards, 20 Race Car cards, 16 Rookie Future cards, nine Front Row Favorites cards and one checklist. Maxx was packaged in 24-pack boxes with packs containing eight cards and carried a suggested retail price of $1.99.

COMPLETE SET (85)	10.00	25.00
1 Dale Jarrett	.50	1.25
2 Rusty Wallace	.60	1.50
3 Dale Earnhardt	1.25	3.00
4 John Andretti	.07	.20
5 Terry Labonte	.25	.60
6 Mark Martin	.60	1.50
7 Michael Waltrip	.15	.40
8 Dale Earnhardt Jr. CRC	1.00	2.50
9 Jerry Nadeau	.15	.40
10 Scott Pruett	.07	.20
11 Kevin Lepage	.07	.20
12 Bobby Hamilton	.07	.20
13 Mike Skinner	.07	.20
14 Johnny Benson	.15	.40
15 Chad Little	.15	.40
16 Kenny Wallace	.07	.20
17 Matt Kenseth CRC	.60	1.50
18 Bobby Labonte	.50	1.25
19 Joe Nemechek	.07	.20

y Stewart .75 2.00
tt Sadler .15 .40
d Burton .15 .40
Hornaday .07 .20
Gordon .75 2.00
by Gordon .07 .20
dy LaJoie .07 .20
ey Atwood .25 .60
ky Rudd .25 .60
Burton .25 .60
k Parker Jr. RC .25 .60
ling Marlin .25 .60
emy Mayfield .07 .20
ve Park .25 .60
e Petty .15 .40
ell Waltrip .15 .40
in Grubb .07 .20
m Petty 3.00 6.00
on Jarrett .07 .20
don Amick .07 .20
y Stewart's Car .30 .75
e Jarrett's Car .15 .40
ty Wallace's Car .25 .60
e Earnhardt's Car .50 1.25
n Andretti's Car .02 .10
y Labonte's Car .15 .40
k Martin's Car .25 .60
tt Kenseth's Car .25 .60
e Earnhardt Jr.'s Car .40 1.00
y Nadeau's Car .15 .40
e Petty's Car .07 .20
d Burton's Car .07 .20
emy Mayfield's Car .07 .20
ke Skinner's Car .02 .10
tt Pruett's Car .02 .10
Burton's Car .07 .20
ve Park's Car .07 .20
ky Rudd's Car .07 .20
by Labonte's Car .15 .40
Gordon's Car .30 .75
mie Johnson RF RC 5.00 12.00
rick Gilchrist RF .07 .20
hael Ritch RF .07 .20
in Harvick RF .50 1.50
ky Hendrick RF RC 1.25 3.00
dy Houston RF RC .07 .20
tt Hutter RF .07 .20
Sauter RF .07 .20
ie Skinner RF .07 .20
hony Lazzaro RF .07 .20
s Wasson RF .07 .20
g Biffle RF .25 .60
. Jones RF .07 .20
mie Sadler RF .07 .20
on Leffler RF .07 .20
t Busch RF RC 1.50 4.00
by Labonte's Car FRF .15 .40
Gordon's Car FRF .30 .75
sty Wallace's Car FRF .25 .60
rd Burton's Car FRF .07 .20
y Stewart's Car FRF .30 .75
nny Irwin's Car FRF .02 .10
ke Skinner's Car FRF .02 .10
rk Martin's Car FRF .25 .60
e Nemechek's Car FRF .02 .10
sty Wallace CL .25 .60

00 Maxx Collectible Covers

mly inserted into packs at one in 72, this 5-nsert set features swatches of authentic car s. Card backs carry a "CC" prefix followed by iver's initials.

PLETE SET (5) 30.00 80.00
Bobby Labonte 6.00 15.00
Dale Jarrett 6.00 15.00
K Matt Kenseth 8.00 20.00
V Rusty Wallace 6.00 15.00
S Tony Stewart 10.00 25.00

2000 Maxx Drive Time

mly inserted into packs at one in three, this rd insert highlights some of the top moments from 1999. Card backs carry a "DT" prefix.

COMPLETE SET (10) 6.00 15.00
DT1 Tony Stewart 1.00 2.50
DT2 Jeff Gordon 1.00 2.50
DT3 Ward Burton .20 .50
DT4 Jeff Burton .30 .75
DT5 Dale Jarrett .60 1.50
DT6 Mark Martin .75 2.00
DT7 Bobby Labonte .60 1.50
DT8 Rusty Wallace .75 2.00
DT9 Matt Kenseth .75 2.00
DT10 Ricky Rudd .30 .75

2000 Maxx Fantastic Finishes

Randomly inserted into packs at one in 11, this 10-card insert highlights some of the more interesting finishes in 1999. Card backs carry a "FF" prefix.

COMPLETE SET (10) 8.00 20.00
FF1 Dale Earnhardt 2.00 5.00
FF2 Dale Earnhardt Jr. 1.50 4.00
FF3 Terry Labonte .40 1.00
FF4 Matt Kenseth 1.00 2.50
FF5 Tony Stewart 1.25 3.00
FF6 Jeff Burton .40 1.00
FF7 Dale Jarrett .75 2.00
FF8 Bobby Labonte .75 2.00
FF9 Jeff Gordon 1.25 3.00
FF10 Mark Martin 1.00 2.50

2000 Maxx Focus On A Champion

Randomly inserted into packs at one in 23, this 5-card insert highlights the top drivers chasing the Winston Cup. Card backs carry a "FC" prefix.

COMPLETE SET (5) 12.50 30.00
FC1 Dale Jarrett 2.50 6.00
FC2 Tony Stewart 4.00 10.00
FC3 Bobby Labonte 2.50 6.00
FC4 Jeff Burton 1.25 3.00
FC5 Jeff Gordon 4.00 10.00

2000 Maxx Oval Office

Randomly inserted into packs at one in 72, this 5-card insert highlights the most elite drivers of NASCAR. Card backs carry a "OO" prefix.

COMPLETE SET (5) 30.00 80.00
OO1 Dale Jarrett 5.00 12.00
OO2 Dale Earnhardt 12.50 30.00
OO3 Jeff Gordon 8.00 20.00
OO4 Terry Labonte 2.50 6.00
OO5 Mark Martin 6.00 15.00

2000 Maxx Racer's Ink

Randomly inserted into packs at one in 144, this 16-card insert features authentic autographs from top drivers like Dale Earnhardt and Bobby Labonte as well as a signed card of the late Adam Petty. The cardbacks carry the player's initials as numbering.

COMPLETE SET (16) 600.00 1200.00
AP Adam Petty 100.00 200.00
BL Bobby Labonte 12.00 30.00
CA Casey Atwood 6.00 15.00
DE Dale Earnhardt 200.00 350.00
DJ Dale Jarrett 15.00 40.00
JA John Andretti 6.00 20.00
JB Jeff Burton 10.00 25.00
JM Jeremy Mayfield 8.00 20.00
JR Dale Earnhardt Jr. 100.00 200.00
KS Ken Schrader 6.00 20.00
KW Kenny Wallace 6.00 15.00
RW Rusty Wallace 10.00 25.00
SD Boris Said 8.00 20.00
TL Terry Labonte 12.00 30.00
TS Tony Stewart 40.00 80.00
WB Ward Burton 8.00 20.00
JG Jeff Gordon 150.00 300.00

2000 Maxx Speedway Boogie

Randomly inserted into packs at one in 11, this 10-card insert highlights the fastest drivers in NASCAR. Card backs carry a "SB" prefix.

COMPLETE SET (10) 8.00 20.00
SB1 Jeff Gordon 1.25 3.00
SB2 Matt Kenseth 1.00 2.50
SB3 Bobby Labonte .75 2.00
SB4 Terry Labonte .40 1.00
SB5 Dale Earnhardt Jr. 1.50 4.00
SB6 Dale Jarrett .75 2.00
SB7 Mark Martin 1.00 2.50
SB8 Jeff Burton .40 1.00
SB9 Ricky Rudd .40 1.00
SB10 Tony Stewart 1.25 3.00

1998 Maxximum

The 1998 Maxximum set was issued in one series totalling 100 cards. The cards feature the new card technology, Ionix, with full-bleed color photography. The set contains the topical subsets: Iron Men (1-25), Steel Chariots (26-50), Armor Clad (51-75), and Heat of Battle (76-100).

COMPLETE SET (100) 12.00 30.00
WAX BOX 30.00 60.00
1 Darrell Waltrip .30 .75
2 Rusty Wallace 1.25 3.00
3 Dale Earnhardt 2.50 6.00
4 Bobby Hamilton .15 .40
5 Terry Labonte .50 1.25
6 Mark Martin 1.25 3.00
7 Geoff Bodine .15 .40
8 Ernie Irvan .30 .75
9 Jeff Burton .50 1.25
10 Ricky Rudd .50 1.25
11 Dale Jarrett 1.00 2.50
12 Jeremy Mayfield .30 .75
13 Jerry Nadeau RC .50 1.25
14 Ken Schrader .15 .40
15 Kyle Petty .30 .75
16 Chad Little .30 .75
17 Todd Bodine .15 .40
18 Bobby Labonte 1.00 2.50
19 Bill Elliott .60 1.50
20 Mike Skinner .15 .40
21 Michael Waltrip .30 .75
22 John Andretti .15 .40
23 Jimmy Spencer .15 .40
24 Jeff Gordon 1.50 4.00
25 Kenny Irwin .30 .75
26 Darrell Waltrip's Car .07 .20
27 Rusty Wallace's Car .50 1.25
28 Dale Earnhardt's Car 1.00 2.50
29 Bobby Hamilton's Car .07 .20
30 Terry Labonte's Car .30 .75
31 Mark Martin's Car .50 1.25
32 Geoff Bodine's Car .07 .20
33 Ernie Irvan's Car .07 .20
34 Jeff Burton's Car .30 .75
35 Ricky Rudd's Car .15 .40
36 Dale Jarrett's Car .30 .75
37 Jeremy Mayfield's Car .07 .20
38 Jerry Nadeau's Car .30 .75
39 Ken Schrader's Car .07 .20
40 Kyle Petty's Car .07 .20
41 Chad Little's Car .07 .20
42 Todd Bodine's Car .07 .20
43 Bobby Labonte's Car .30 .75
44 Bill Elliott's Car .30 .75
45 Mike Skinner's Car .07 .20
46 Michael Waltrip's Car .15 .40
47 John Andretti's Car .07 .20
48 Jimmy Spencer's Car .07 .20
49 Jeff Gordon's Car .60 1.50
50 Kenny Irwin's Car .07 .20
51 Darrell Waltrip .30 .75
52 Rusty Wallace 1.25 3.00
53 Dale Earnhardt Jr. 2.00 5.00
54 Bobby Hamilton .15 .40
55 Terry Labonte .50 1.25
56 Mark Martin 1.25 3.00
57 Geoff Bodine .15 .40
58 Ernie Irvan .30 .75
59 Jeff Burton .50 1.25
60 Ricky Rudd .50 1.25
61 Dale Jarrett 1.00 1.50
62 Jeremy Mayfield .30 .75
63 Jerry Nadeau .50 1.25
64 Ken Schrader .15 .40
65 Kyle Petty .30 .75
66 Chad Little .30 .75
67 Todd Bodine .15 .40
68 Bobby Labonte 1.00 2.50
69 Bill Elliott .60 1.50
70 Mike Skinner .15 .40
71 Michael Waltrip .30 .75
72 John Andretti .15 .40
73 Jimmy Spencer .15 .40
74 Jeff Gordon 1.50 4.00
75 Kenny Irwin .30 .75
76 Darrell Waltrip's Car .07 .20
77 Rusty Wallace 1.25 3.00
78 Dale Earnhardt Jr. 2.00 5.00
79 Bobby Hamilton's Car .07 .20
80 Terry Labonte's Car .30 .75
81 Mark Martin's Car .50 1.25
82 Geoff Bodine's Car .07 .20
83 Ernie Irvan's Car .07 .20
84 Jeff Burton's Car .30 .75
85 Ricky Rudd's Car .15 .40
86 Dale Jarrett's Car .30 .75
87 Jeremy Mayfield's Car .07 .20
88 Jerry Nadeau's Car .30 .75
89 Ken Schrader's Car .07 .20
90 Kyle Petty's Car .07 .20
91 Chad Little's Car .07 .20
92 Todd Bodine's Car .07 .20
93 Bobby Labonte's Car .30 .75
94 Bill Elliott's Car .30 .75
95 Mike Skinner's Car .07 .20
96 Michael Waltrip's Car .15 .40
97 John Andretti's Car .07 .20
98 Jimmy Spencer's Car .07 .20
99 Jeff Gordon's Car .60 1.50
100 Kenny Irwin's Car .07 .20
S24 Jeff Gordon Sample 1.25 3.00

1998 Maxximum Battle Proven

Randomly inserted in packs at a rate of one in four, this die-cut insert set highlights NASCAR drivers who have each posted more than one career Winston Cup victory.

COMPLETE SET (15) 12.00 30.00
B1 Darrell Waltrip .60 1.50
B2 Dale Earnhardt 5.00 12.00
B3 Rusty Wallace 2.50 6.00
B4 Bill Elliott 1.25 3.00
B5 Jeff Gordon 3.00 8.00
B6 Mark Martin 2.50 6.00
B7 Terry Labonte 1.00 2.50
B8 Ricky Rudd 1.00 2.50
B9 Geoff Bodine .30 .75
B10 Ernie Irvan .60 1.50
B11 Dale Jarrett 2.00 5.00
B12 Kyle Petty .60 1.50
B13 Sterling Marlin .60 1.50
B14 Bobby Labonte 2.00 5.00
B15 Jeff Burton 1.00 2.50

1998 Maxximum Field Generals One Star

Sequentially numbered to 2,000, this die-cut insert set is the first of a four-tiered collection showcasing the best Winston Cup drivers.

COMPLETE SET (15) 60.00 120.00
*TWO STAR/1000: .4X TO 1X ONE STAR/200
1 Rusty Wallace 8.00 20.00
2 Jeremy Mayfield 2.00 5.00
3 Jeff Gordon 10.00 25.00
4 Terry Labonte 3.00 8.00
5 Dale Jarrett 6.00 15.00
6 Mark Martin 8.00 20.00
7 Jeff Burton 3.00 8.00
8 Kenny Irwin 2.00 5.00
9 Darrell Waltrip 2.00 5.00
10 Dale Earnhardt 15.00 40.00
11 Ernie Irvan 2.00 5.00
12 Bobby Labonte 6.00 15.00
13 Kyle Petty 2.00 5.00
14 Jimmy Spencer 1.00 2.50
15 John Andretti 1.00 2.50

1998 Maxximum Field Generals Three Star Autographs

Sequentially numbered to 100, this double die cut insert set is the third of a four-tiered collection showcasing the best Winston Cup drivers. Each Three Star card was signed by the featured driver. A Four Star parallel was also produced with each signed card being numbered of just 1.

COMPLETE SET (15) 700.00 1200.00
1 Rusty Wallace 30.00 60.00
2 Jeremy Mayfield 20.00 40.00
3 Jeff Gordon 100.00 200.00
4 Terry Labonte 30.00 60.00
5 Dale Jarrett 30.00 60.00
6 Mark Martin 40.00 80.00
7 Jeff Burton 12.00 30.00
8 Kenny Irwin 25.00 50.00
9 Darrell Waltrip 25.00 50.00
10 Dale Earnhardt 250.00 350.00
11 Ernie Irvan 25.00 50.00
12 Bobby Labonte 30.00 60.00
13 Kyle Petty 25.00 50.00
14 Jimmy Spencer 10.00 25.00
15 John Andretti 10.00 25.00

1998 Maxximum Field Generals Four Star Autographs

Sequentially numbered 1/1, this double die cut autographed insert set is the fourth of a four-tiered collection showcasing the best Winston Cup drivers.

1998 Maxximum First Class

Randomly inserted in packs at a rate of one in three, this insert focuses on 20 drivers who have established themselves to be the most successful drivers on the current Winston Cup circuit.

COMPLETE SET (20) 12.00 30.00
F1 Jeff Gordon 3.00 8.00
F2 Jimmy Spencer .30 .75
F3 John Andretti .30 .75
F4 Michael Waltrip .60 1.50
F5 Bill Elliott 1.25 3.00
F6 Bobby Labonte 2.00 5.00
F7 Kyle Petty .60 1.50
F8 Ken Schrader .30 .75
F9 Jeremy Mayfield .60 1.50
F10 Dale Jarrett 2.00 5.00
F11 Ricky Rudd 1.00 2.50
F12 Jeff Burton 1.00 2.50
F13 Ernie Irvan .60 1.50
F14 Geoff Bodine .30 .75
F15 Mark Martin 2.50 6.00
F16 Terry Labonte 1.00 2.50
F17 Bobby Hamilton .30 .75
F18 Rusty Wallace 2.50 6.00
F19 Darrell Waltrip .60 1.50
F20 Sterling Marlin .60 1.50

2000 Maxximum

Released as a 44-card set, Maxximum features top NASCAR drivers in portrait style photographs set on a card with white outlining borders and bronze foil highlights. Maxximum was packaged in 24-pack boxes with each pack containing four cards.

COMPLETE SET (44) 12.50 30.00
1 Dale Jarrett 1.00 2.50
2 Bobby Labonte 1.00 2.50
3 Mark Martin 1.25 3.00
4 Tony Stewart 1.50 4.00
5 Jeff Burton .50 1.25
6 Jeff Gordon 1.50 4.00
7 Dale Earnhardt 2.50 6.00
8 Rusty Wallace 1.00 3.00
9 Ward Burton .30 .75
10 Mike Skinner .15 .40
11 Jeremy Mayfield .15 .40
12 Terry Labonte .50 1.25
13 Bobby Hamilton .15 .40
14 Steve Park .50 1.25
15 Casey Atwood .50 1.25
16 Sterling Marlin .50 1.25
17 John Andretti .15 .40
18 Wally Dallenbach .15 .40
19 Kenny Irwin .30 .75
20 Bill Elliott .60 1.50
21 Kenny Wallace .15 .40
22 Chad Little .30 .75
23 Elliott Sadler .30 .75
24 Kevin Lepage .15 .40
25 Kyle Petty .30 .75
26 Johnny Benson .30 .75
27 Michael Waltrip .30 .75
28 Ricky Rudd .50 1.25
29 Jerry Nadeau .30 .75
30 Darrell Waltrip .30 .75
31 Dale Earnhardt Jr. CRC 2.00 5.00
32 Matt Kenseth CRC 1.25 3.00
33 Ron Hornaday .15 .40
34 Scott Pruett .15 .40
35 Robby Gordon .15 .40
36 Stacy Compton RC .30 .75
37 Randy LaJoie .15 .40
38 Jimmie Johnson RC 6.00 15.00
39 Kevin Harvick 1.25 3.00
40 Derrick Gilchrist .15 .40
41 Adam Petty 3.00 6.00
42 Kevin Grubb .15 .40
43 Hank Parker Jr. RC .50 1.25
44 Jeff Gordon CL .60 1.50

2000 Maxximum Die Cuts

COMPLETE SET (44) 60.00 120.00
*DIE CUT/250: 2X TO 5X BASE CARDS

2000 Maxximum MPH

*SINGLES/70-99: 6X TO 15X HI COL.
*SINGLES/45-69: 8X TO 20X HI COL.
*SINGLES/30-44: 10X TO 25X HI COL.
*SINGLES/20-29: 15X TO 30X HI COL.
38 Jimmie Johnson/92 40.00 80.00

2000 Maxximum Cruise Control

Randomly inserted in packs at the rate of one in four, this 10-card set is die cut along the top and bottom edges of the card. Each card is enhanced with silver foil highlights.

COMPLETE SET (10) 8.00 20.00
CC1 Terry Labonte .75 2.00
CC2 Bobby Labonte 1.50 4.00
CC3 John Andretti .25 .60
CC4 Bill Elliott 1.00 2.50
CC5 Dale Earnhardt Jr. 3.00 8.00
CC6 Matt Kenseth 2.00 5.00
CC7 Scott Pruett .25 .60
CC8 Steve Park .75 2.00
CC9 Jeff Gordon 2.50 6.00
CC10 Darrell Waltrip .50 1.25

2000 Maxximum Dialed In

Randomly inserted in packs at the rate of one in 12, this 7-card set features die cut left and right edges and driver portrait photography. Each card contains silver foil highlights.

COMPLETE SET (7) 10.00 25.00
DI1 Dale Jarrett 2.00 5.00
DI2 Tony Stewart 3.00 8.00
DI3 Jeff Gordon 3.00 8.00
DI4 Bobby Labonte 2.00 5.00
DI5 Terry Labonte 1.00 2.50
DI6 Mark Martin 2.50 6.00
DI7 Jeff Burton 1.00 2.50

2000 Maxximum Nifty Fifty

Randomly inserted in packs at the rate of one in 24, this 5-card set pays tribute to Rusty Wallace and his victory at the Food City 500 on a card die cut on all edges. Each card contains silver foil highlights.

COMPLETE SET (5) 8.00 20.00
COMMON R.WALLACE 1.50 4.00

2000 Maxximum Pure Adrenaline

Randomly inserted in packs at the rate of one in 12, this 8-card set features die cut cards along the left and right edges of the card. Drivers appear on the back while their cars appear on the front. Each card contains gold foil highlights

COMPLETE SET (8) 8.00 20.00
PA1 Tony Stewart 4.00 10.00
PA2 Ward Burton .75 2.00
PA3 Bobby Labonte 2.50 6.00
PA4 Ricky Rudd 1.25 3.00
PA5 Joe Nemechek .40 1.00
PA6 Rusty Wallace 3.00 8.00
PA7 Mike Skinner .40 1.00
PA8 Jeff Burton 1.25 3.00

2000 Maxximum Roots of Racing

Randomly inserted in packs at the rate of one in 24, this 5-card set spotlights top NASCAR drivers on a red-bordered die cut card.

COMPLETE SET (5) 8.00 20.00
R1 Dale Earnhardt 5.00 12.00
R2 Kyle Petty .60 1.50
R3 Tony Stewart 3.00 8.00
R4 Dale Jarrett 2.00 5.00
R5 Jeff Gordon 3.00 8.00

2000 Maxximum Signatures

Randomly inserted in packs at the rate of one in 23 for single autographs, one in 144 for double autographs, and one in 287 for triple autographs. Quadruple autographs are sequentially numbered to 100. Several cards were issued as exchange cards with an expiration date of 6/14/2001. Blaise Alexander did not sign for the set although he did have an exchange card inserted into packs.

BE Bill Elliott 10.00 25.00
CA Casey Atwood 8.00 20.00
DE Dale Earnhardt 250.00 400.00
DG Derrick Gilchrist 5.00 12.00
HP Hank Parker Jr. 6.00 15.00
JG Joe Gibbs 20.00 40.00
JJ Jason Jarrett 6.00 15.00
JL Justin Labonte 6.00 15.00
JM Jeremy Mayfield 8.00 20.00
JO Jimmie Johnson 40.00 100.00
KH Kevin Harvick 10.00 25.00
KI Kenny Irwin EXCH 2.00 5.00
LE Jason Leffler 6.00 15.00
MK Matt Kenseth 20.00 50.00
RG Robby Gordon 8.00 20.00
RR Ricky Rudd 8.00 20.00
RW Rusty Wallace 10.00 25.00
SC Stacy Compton 6.00 15.00
SP Scott Pruett 6.00 15.00
TS Tony Stewart 25.00 60.00
WB Ward Burton 8.00 20.00
DE2 D.Earn/D.Earnhardt Jr. 500.00 1000.00
DJ2 D.Jarrett/J.Jarrett 20.00 50.00
DN2 D.Jarrett/N.Jarrett 30.00 60.00
DR2 D.Jarrett/R.Rudd 25.00 50.00
MD2 M.Waltrip/D.Waltrip 12.00 30.00
MK2 M.Martin/M.Kenseth 75.00 200.00
RJ2 R.Wallace/J.Mayfield 12.50 30.00
TB2 T.Labonte/B.Labonte 40.00 100.00
WJ2 W.Burton/J.Burton 15.00 40.00
BTJ3 B.Labon/Stewart/Gibbs 40.00 100.00
NDJ3 Ned/D.Jarrett/J.Jarrett 30.00 80.00
RKM3 R.Wal./K.Wal./M.Wal. 15.00 40.00
TBJ3 Terry/Bobby/J.Labonte 40.00 80.00
GIB4 Stew/Leffl/B.Labn/Gibbs 75.00 150.00
ROU4 Mart/Litt/J.Brtn/Kens 100.00 200.00

2000 Maxximum Young Lions

Randomly inserted in packs at the rate of one in 24, this 10-card set focuses on younger NASCAR drivers. Each card is die cut in the shape of a lion's head and features portrait style photography.

COMPLETE SET (10) 20.00 50.00
YL1 Jason Jarrett .75 2.00
YL2 Matt Kenseth 4.00 15.00
YL3 Casey Atwood 1.00 2.50
YL4 Stacy Compton .75 2.00
YL5 Adam Petty 5.00 12.00
YL6 Lyndon Amick .75 2.00
YL7 Hank Parker Jr. 1.00 2.50
YL8 Kevin Grubb .75 2.00
YL9 Jimmie Johnson 8.00 20.00
YL10 Kevin Harvick 5.00 12.00

1995 Metallic Impressions Classic Dale Earnhardt 21-Card Tin

Metallic Impressions produced this 21-card Dale Earnhardt set for Classic Inc. The metal cards were distributed in complete set form in a tin box. Production was limited to 9,950 sets with each including a numbered certificate of authenticity. In the top of each tin box was a 21st card numbered E1. It featured Dale and car owner Richard Childress. Metallic Impressions also produced a five-card and a 10-card version of this set. The card fronts are the same as the ones in the larger 21 card set. The difference is the numbering on the back. For example in the ten card set card #5 is the same as card #9 in the 21 card set except for the number.

COMP.FACT SET (21) 12.50 25.00
DALE EARNHARDT'S CAR .50 1.25
DALE EARNHARDT .60 1.50
COMP.FACT 10 CARD SET 10.00 20.00
COMP.FACT 5 CARD SET 5.00 10.00
E1 Dale Earnhardt .60 1.50
Richard Childress

1995 Metallic Impressions Kyle Petty 10-Card Tin

This 10-card set from Metallic Impressions features Kyle Petty on the company's full color embossed metal cards. The backs have additional photos and commentary on Kyle and his many interest. The 10-card set was produced in a quantity of 19,950. Each set is accompanied by an individually numbered Certificate of Authenticity. There is also a five-card version of this set available in a tin box.

COMP.10-CARD TIN SET (10) 10.00 20.00
COMMON CARD .75 2.00
COMP.5-CARD TIN SET (5) 4.00 10.00

1995 Metallic Impressions Richard Petty

Richard Petty is the feature of this 5-card set produced by Metallic Impressions in 1995. The metal cards were distributed in complete set form in a tin box. Each card features a picture of King Richard or one of his famous cars.

COMP.FACT SET (5) 4.00 10.00
COMMON PETTY (1-5) .75 2.00

1995 Metallic Impressions Upper Deck Rusty Wallace

This set was produced in conjunction with Upper Deck. Card fronts show photos of Rusty in every aspect of race-day action. Cards are embossed in sturdy, durable metal with card edges rolled for extra durability and safety. Full-color card backs feature an additional photo, commentary and selected race results. The 20-card set comes in a specifically designed embossed collector's tin with an individually numbered Certificate of Authenticity. There were 12,500 sets produced. There is also a five card version of this set in a tin box.

COMPLETE SET (20) 10.00 25.00
COMMON CARD (1-20) .75 1.50
COMP.FIVE CARD SET 5.00 10.00

1995 Metallic Impressions Winston Cup Champions 10-Card Tin

This 10-card set issued by Metallic Impressions features 10 former Winston Cup Champions. The cards are made of embossed metal and come in a tin display box. There were 49,900 sets made.

COMP. FACT SET (10) 12.50 30.00
1 Richard Petty 1.25 3.00
2 Benny Parsons .75 2.00
3 Cale Yarborough .75 2.00
4 Dale Earnhardt 5.00 12.00
5 Darrell Waltrip 1.00 2.50
6 Bobby Allison .75 2.00
7 Terry Labonte 1.25 3.00
8 Bill Elliott 1.25 3.00
9 Rusty Wallace 2.00 5.00
10 Alan Kulwicki 1.25 3.00

1996 Metallic Impressions 25th Anniversary Winston Cup Champions

This 25-card set was produced by Metallic Impressions. The cards were available through packs of Winston cigarettes. There was one card per every two pack of cigarettes. The set was also available by trading in Winston cigarette wrappers.

COMPLETE SET (25) 16.00 40.00
1 Richard Petty .60 1.50
2 Richard Petty .60 1.50
3 Benny Parsons .30 .75
4 Richard Petty .60 1.50
5 Richard Petty .60 1.50
6 Cale Yarborough .30 .75
7 Cale Yarborough .30 .75
8 Cale Yarborough .30 .75
9 Richard Petty .60 1.50
10 Dale Earnhardt 2.50 6.00
11 Darrell Waltrip .40 1.00
12 Darrell Waltrip .40 1.00
13 Bobby Allison .40 1.00
14 Terry Labonte .60 1.50
15 Darrell Waltrip .40 1.00
16 Dale Earnhardt 2.50 6.00
17 Dale Earnhardt 2.50 6.00
18 Bill Elliott .60 1.50
19 Rusty Wallace 1.00 2.50
20 Dale Earnhardt 2.50 6.00
21 Dale Earnhardt 2.50 6.00
22 Alan Kulwicki .60 1.50
23 Dale Earnhardt 2.50 6.00
24 Dale Earnhardt 2.50 6.00
25 Jeff Gordon 1.50 4.00

1996 Metallic Impressions Avon All-Time Racing Greatest

This five-card sets was produced by Metallic Impressions for Avon. The set was originally sold through the May 1996 Avon catalog. The five NASCAR drivers featured in the set are all former Winston Cup champions. The cards are embossed metal and come in a metal tin.

COMP.FACT SET (5) 10.00 20.00
1 Dale Earnhardt 4.00 10.00
2 Darrell Waltrip 1.00 2.50
3 Bill Elliott 1.25 3.00
4 Terry Labonte 1.25 3.00
5 Rusty Wallace 2.00 5.00

1996 Metallic Impressions Dale Earnhardt Burger King

This 3-card set was prodced by Metallic Impressions and sponsored by Burger King. Each card highlights an eventful year from Dale Earnhardt's career.

COMPLETE SET (3) 6.00 15.00
1 Dale Earnhardt's Car 1987 2.00 5.00
2 Dale Earnhardt 1990 2.00 5.00
3 Dale Earnhardt's Car 1995 2.00 5.00

1996 Metallic Impressions Jeff Gordon Winston Cup Champ 10-Card Tin

Jeff Gordon is the feature of this 10-card set produced by Metallic Impressions. The metal cards were distributed in complete set form in a tin box. Each 10-card set comes with a numbered certificate of authenticity. Metallic Impressions also produced a five-card version of this set.

COMP.10-CARD TIN SET (10) 10.00 25.00
COMMON CARD 1.00 2.50
COMP.5-CARD TIN SET (10) 5.00 12.00

1996 Metallic Impressions Winston Cup Top Five

This five-card set features the Top Five finishers in the 1996 Winston Cup points race. The cards are made of embossed metal and come in a colorful tin. $1.00 from each card set sold went to benefit the continued development of Brenner Children's Hospital.

COMP. FACT SET (5) 5.00 12.00
1 Terry Labonte .60 1.50
2 Jeff Gordon 1.25 3.00
3 Dale Jarrett .75 2.00
4 Dale Earnhardt 2.00 5.00
5 Mark Martin 1.00 2.50

1996 M-Force

This 45-card set is the first issued by Press Pass under the M-Force brand name. The cards feature 38 point board, two-sided mirror foil, and a damage resistant laminent. The top drivers and cars are included in 1996 race action. The cards were packaged two cards per pack, 24 packs per box and 20 boxes per case. The product was distributed through hobby channels.

COMPLETE SET (45) 12.50 30.00
1 Rusty Wallace 1.25 3.00
2 Rusty Wallace's Car .50 1.25
3 Dale Earnhardt 2.50 6.00
4 Dale Earnhardt's Car 1.00 2.50
5 Sterling Marlin .50 1.25
6 Sterling Marlin's Car .15 .40
7 Terry Labonte .50 1.25
8 Terry Labonte's Car .30 .75
9 Mark Martin 1.25 3.00
10 Mark Martin's Car .50 1.25
11 Ricky Rudd .50 1.25
12 Ricky Rudd's Car .15 .40
13 Ted Musgrave .15 .40
14 Richard Petty .50 1.25
15 Darrell Waltrip .30 .75
16 Bobby Allison .07 .20
17 Bobby Labonte 1.00 3.00
18 Michael Waltrip .30 .75
19 Jeff Gordon 1.50 4.00
20 Jeff Gordon's Car .60 1.50
21 Ken Schrader in Car .15 .40
22 Ernie Irvan .30 .75
23 Ernie Irvan's Car .15 .40
24 Steve Grissom .15 .40
25 Johnny Benson .15 .40
26 Bobby Hamilton .15 .40
27 Bobby Hamilton's Car .07 .20
28 Ricky Craven .15 .40
29 Ricky Craven's Car .07 .20
30 Kyle Petty .30 .75
31 Kyle Petty's Car .15 .40
32 David Pearson .07 .20
33 Dale Jarrett 1.00 2.50
34 Dale Jarrett's Car .30 .75
35 Bill Elliott .60 1.50
36 Bill Elliott's Car .30 .75
37 Jeremy Mayfield .30 .75
38 Jeff Burton .50 1.25
39 Cale Yarborough .30 .75
40 Jeff Gordon 1.50 4.00
41 Mark Martin 1.25 3.00
42 Rusty Wallace 1.25 3.00
43 Bill Elliott .60 1.50
44 Ernie Irvan .30 .75
45 Dale Earnhardt's Car CL 1.00 2.50
P1 Jeff Gordon Blue Promo 2.00 5.00
P2 Jeff Gordon Green Promo 2.00 5.00
P3 Jeff Gordon Silver Promo 2.00 5.00

1996 M-Force Black

This 12-card insert set features the top drivers from Winston Cup. The fronts of the cards are embossed driver or car portraits on black foil board. The backs feature the same silver mirror foil as the base cards. The Blacks were randomly inserted one in 96 packs.

COMPLETE SET (12) 250.00 500.00
B1 Rusty Wallace 10.00 25.00
B2 Rusty Wallace's Car 4.00 10.00
B3 Dale Earnhardt 12.00 30.00
B4 Dale Earnhardt's Car 8.00 20.00
B5 Terry Labonte 4.00 10.00
B6 Mark Martin 10.00 25.00
B7 Jeff Gordon 12.50 30.00
B8 Jeff Gordon's Car 5.00 12.00
B9 Ernie Irvan 2.50 6.00
B10 Dale Jarrett 8.00 20.00
B11 Bill Elliott 5.00 12.00
B12 Jeff Gordon 12.50 30.00

1996 M-Force Sheet Metal

This 6-card insert set was the first to incorporate actual race used sheet metal into a trading card. The piece of sheet metal along with a photo of the driver is permanently encased in a clear polyurethane card. Cards containing multi-colored pieces of sheet metal carry a 25 percent premium over those that do not. The cards were seeded one in 288 packs and serial numbered of 200.

COMPLETE SET (6) 250.00 500.00
M1 Rusty Wallace 20.00 50.00
M2 Dale Earnhardt 60.00 120.00
M3 Terry Labonte 20.00 50.00
M4 Mark Martin 25.00 60.00
M5 Jeff Gordon 50.00 100.00
M6 Bill Elliott 20.00 50.00

1996 M-Force Silvers

Eighteen of the top drivers are a part of this insert set. The card fronts are embossed driver or car portraits on silver foil board. The backs of the cards feature the same silver mirror foil as the base cards. The Silvers were inserted one in eight packs.

COMPLETE SET (18) 25.00 60.00
S1 Rusty Wallace's Car 1.50 4.00
S2 Dale Earnhardt 5.00 12.00
S3 Dale Earnhardt's Car 3.00 8.00
S4 Sterling Marlin 1.50 4.00
S5 Terry Labonte 1.50 4.00
S6 Terry Labonte's Car 1.00 2.50
S7 Ricky Rudd 1.50 4.00
S8 Richard Petty 1.50 4.00
S9 Bobby Labonte 4.00 10.00
S10 Jeff Gordon's Car 2.00 5.00
S11 Bobby Hamilton's Car .25 .60
S12 Ricky Craven .50 1.25
S13 Kyle Petty 1.00 2.50
S14 Jeff Gordon 5.00 12.00
S15 Mark Martin 4.00 10.00
S16 Rusty Wallace 4.00 10.00
S17 Bill Elliott 2.00 5.00
S18 Ernie Irvan 1.00 2.50

1992 Miller Genuine Draft Rusty Wallace

This six-card set was released by the Miller Brewing company. The cards were inserted into twelve packs of Miller Genuine Draft. There were three cards in a white envelope glued inside the twelve packs. Each three cards with envelope is considered a "set." Each card features art work by Sam Bass and measures 3 5/8" X 5 3/8". The front also carries "Miller Brewing Company Reminds You to Please THINK WHEN YOU DRINK." Think when you drink is in a yellow triangle. The cards are blank backed.

COMPLETE SET (6) 6.00 15.00
COMMON CARD 1.25 3.00

1993 Miller Genuine Draft Rusty Wallace Post Cards

This five-card set was available as a send-away offer from Miller Brewing Company. The cards measure 3 1/2" X 5 1/4" and came in a white envelope. There was one cover card in each envelope.

COMPLETE SET (5) 5.00 12.00
COMMON CARD 1.25 3.00
NNO Cover Card .20 .50

2002 Miller Electric Post Cards

This 4-card set was produced for Miller Electric in 2002. The cards are approximately 4x6. Each card featured one team with each car pictured.

COMPLETE SET (4) 8.00 20.00
1 Dale Jr 5.00 12.00
S.Park
M.Waltrip
2 B.Elliott 2.50 6.00
J.Mayfield
3 K.Harvick 2.50 6.00
J.Green
R.Gordon
4 Martin 3.00 8.00
Kenseth
Busch
J.Burton

1991 Motorcraft Racing

This 1991 release features members and machines of the Motorcraft Racing teams. The cards were primarily distributed through participating Ford dealerships and are unnumbered. We have listed and numbered the cards below in alphabetical order.

COMPLETE SET (7) 4.00 10.00
1 Bob Glidden .30 .75
Morgan Shepherd Cars
2 Bob Glidden w .30 .75
Car
3 Bob Glidden's Car .30 .75
4 Bob Glidden Family Racing .75 2.00
5 Walter Bud Moore .50 1.25
6 Morgan Shepherd .75 2.00
7 Morgan Shepherd's Car .30 .75

1992 Motorcraft Racing

This 1992 release features members and machines of the Motorcraft Racing teams. The cards were primarily distributed in complete set form through participating Ford dealerships and are unnumbered. We have listed and numbered the cards below in alphabetical order.

COMPLETE SET (10) 2.50 6.00
1 Geoff Bodine .25 .60
2 Geoff Bodine's Car .10 .25
3 Geoff Bodine's Pit Crew .25 .60
4 Geoff Bodine .25 .60
Bob Glidden Cars
5 Bob Glidden .25 .60
6 Bob Glidden's Car .10 .25
7 Bob Glidden .25 .60
Etta Glidden
8 Walter Bud Moore .25 .60
9 Cover Card .15 .40
10 Motorcraft Special Events .15 .40

1993 Motorcraft Decade of Champions

This 1993 release honors Motorcraft Quality Part's ten years of motorsports sponsorship. The cards were primarily distributed in complete set form through participating Ford dealerships and are unnumbered. We have listed and numbered the cards below in alphabetical order.

COMPLETE SET (10) 2.50 6.00
1 Geoff Bodine's Car .40 1.00
2 Manny Esquerra's Truck .30 .75
3 Bob Glidden's Car .30 .75
4 Bob Glidden's Car .30 .75
5 John Jones' Car .30 .75
6 Mark Oswald's Car .30 .75
7 Ricky Rudd's Car .50 1.25
8 Morgan Shepherd's Car .40 1.00
9 Rickie Smith's Car .30 .75
NNO Cover Card .20 .50

1993 Motorcraft Manufacturers Championship

Ford produced this set to honor its 1992 NASCAR Manufacturers' Championship. Eight car and drivers are included along with a trophy card and a cover card. As is common with Motorcraft sets, the cards are unnumbered and listed below alphabetically.

COMPLETE SET (10) 4.00 6.00
1 Davey Allison .60 1.50
2 Geoff Bodine .20 .50
3 Bill Elliott .60 1.25
4 Jimmy Hensley .20 .50
5 Alan Kulwicki .40 1.00
6 Sterling Marlin .30 .75
7 Mark Martin 1.00 2.50
8 Morgan Shepherd .20 .50
9 Cover Card .20 .50
10 Trophy Card .20 .50

1994 MW Windows

This five-card set was produced for distribution at the 1994 National Association of Homebuilders Show held in Las Vegas and was sponsored by MW Windows. The cards are called the Aces Collection and feature four drivers and one checklist card picturing the four. Reportedly, production was held to 7500 complete sets. The cards are unnumbered, but have been assigned numbers below alphabetically with the checklist card last.

COMPLETE SET (5) 5.00 12.00
1 Jeff Gordon 1.50 4.00
2 Bobby Labonte 1.00 2.50
3 Terry Labonte .75 2.00
4 Ken Schrader .40 1.00
5 Gordon 1.25 3.00
B.Labonte
T.Labonte
Schrader

1995 MW Windows

This five-card set was produced for distribution at the 1995 National Association of Homebuilders Show held in Houston and was sponsored by MW Windows. The cards are titled Fast Riders and feature four drivers and one checklist card picturing the four. Reportedly, production was held to 7500 complete sets.The cards are unnumbered, but have been assigned numbers below alphabetically with the checklist card last.

COMPLETE SET (5) 4.00 10.00
1 David Green .75 2.00
2 Dale Jarrett 1.25 3.00
3 Terry Labonte 1.00 2.50
4 Michael Waltrip .75 2.00
5 T.Labonte 1.00 2.50
M.Waltrip
D.Jarrett
D.Green

2005 NAPA

COMP.UNCUT SET (2) 4.00 10.00
COMPLETE SET (2) 3.00 8.00
NNO Michael Waltrip .75 2.00
NNO Dale Earnhardt Jr. 1.50 4.00

2004 National Trading Card Day

This 53-card set (49 basic cards plus four cover cards) was given out in five separate sealed packs (one from each of the following manufacturers: Donruss, Fleer, Press Pass, Topps and Upper Deck). One of the five packs was distributed at no cost to each patron that visited a participating sports card shop on April 3rd, 2004 as part of the National Trading Card Day promotion in an effort to increase awareness of collecting sports cards. The 50-card set is composed of 16 baseball, 9 basketball, 10 football, 4 golf, 5 hockey and 4 NASCAR cards. Of note, first year cards of NBA rookie stars LeBron James and Carmelo Anthony were included respectively within the UD and Fleer packs. An early Alex Rodriguez Yankees card was also highlighted within the Fleer pack.

F1-F9 ISSUED IN FLEER PACK
T1-T12 ISSUED IN TOPPS PACK
DP1-DP6 ISSUED IN DONRUSS PACK
PP1-PP7 ISSUED IN PRESS PASS PACK
UD1-UD15 ISSUED IN UPPER DECK PACK
PP2 Jeff Gordon 1.50 4.00
PP3 Jimmie Johnson 1.25 3.00
PP4 Dale Earnhardt Jr. 1.50 4.00
PP5 Tony Stewart 1.00 2.50

2003 Nilla Wafers Team Nabisco

This set of 4-oversized (roughly 3 1/4" by 4") cards was produced by KF Holdings and issued one per Nabisco product during the 2003 season. Each card was produced with lenticular printing technology on the front and has rounded corners. The cardbacks feature a color photo of the driver, the Team Nabisco logo at the bottom and a copyright date of 2002, although the cards were released in 2003.

COMPLETE SET (4) 12.50 25.00
1 Dale Earnhardt Jr. Oreo 4.00 8.00
2 Dale Earnhardt Jr. Nilla Waf 4.00 8.00
3 Michael Waltrip 3.00 6.00
4 Earn.Jr. 4.00 8.00
Green
Harvick
M.Walt

1996 No Fear

This eight-card jumbo-sized set was issued through No Fear. It is a multi-sport set that features a posed color player shot on the front and a white back featuring a slogan by No Fear. The mode of distribution is unclear. The cards are not numbered and checklisted below in alphabetical order.

COMPLETE SET (8) 5.00 12.00
4 Robby Gordon Racing .40 1.00

1992 Pace American Canadian Tour

This 50-card set features drivers who raced in the American Canadian Tour. The cards were sold in complete set form and reportedly 30,000 sets were produced. Each set was individually numbered. The cards were produced by Pace Cards, Inc. of Stowe, Vermont.

COMPLETE SET (50) 4.80 12.00
1 Junior Hanley .05 .15
2 Robbie Crouch .05 .15
3 Beaver Dragon .05 .15
4 Kevin Lepage .05 .15
5 Derek Lynch .05 .15
6 Brad Leighton .05 .15
7 Randy MacDonald .05 .15
8 Dan Beede .05 .15
9 Roger Laperle .05 .15
10 Ralph Nason .05 .15
11 Jean-Paul Cabana .05 .15
12 Bill Zardo, Sr. .05 .15
13 Claude Leclerc .05 .15
14 Robbie Thompson .05 .15
15 Danny Knoll, Jr. .05 .15
16 Bill Zardo, Jr. .05 .15
17 John Greedy .05 .15
18 Blair Bessett .05 .15
19 Buzzie Bezanson .05 .15
20 Phil Pinkham .05 .15
21 Sylvain Metivier .05 .15
22 Andre Beaudoin .05 .15
23 Gord Bennett .05 .15
24 Donald Forte .05 .15
25 Jeff Stevens .05 .15
26 Yvon Bedard .05 .15
27 Dave Dion .05 .15
28 Rollie MacDonald .05 .15
29 Ricky Craven .40 1.00
30 Chuck Bown .05 .15
31 Bob Randall .05 .15
32 Dave Moody .05 .15
33 Stan Meserve .05 .15
34 Tom Curley .05 .15
35 Robbie Crouch .05 .15
36 Dan Beede .05 .15
37 Derek Lynch .05 .15
38 Dan Beede .05 .15
Roger Laperle
39 Randy MacDonald .05 .15
Brad Leighton
40 Randy MacDonald .05 .15
41 Robbie Thompson .05 .15
42 Bill Zardo, Sr. .05 .15
43 Claude Leclerc .05 .15
Brad Leighton
44 John Greedy .05 .15
45 Roger Laperle .05 .15
Yvon Bedard
46 Gord Bennett .05 .15
47 Beaver Dragon .05 .15
Ralph Nason
48 Yvon Bedard .05 .15
49 Jean-Paul Cabana .05 .15
Buzzie Bezanson
Slyvain Metivier
50 Randy MacDonald .05 .15
John Greedy

2016 Panini Black Friday Racing Memorabilia

*CRACKED/25: .8X TO 2X BASIC MEM
R1 Dale Earnhardt Jr 4.00 10.00
R2 Jimmie Johnson 2.50 6.00
R3 Kyle Busch 2.50 6.00
R4 Ryan Newman 2.50 6.00
R5 Chase Elliott 2.50 6.00

2010 Panini Century Sports Stamp Autographs

STATED PRINT RUN 5-100
NO PRICING ON QTY 25 OR LESS
1A Cale Yarborough/30 8.00 20.00
1B Cale Yarborough/20
47A Al Unser/35 20.00 50.00
47B Al Unser/15
48A Al Unser, Jr./36 15.00 40.00
48B Al Unser, Jr./20

2012 Panini Golden Age

COMP.SET w/o SP's (146) 15.00 40.00
SP ANNCD PRINT RUN OF 92 PER
93 Richard Petty 1.00 2.50
112 Bobby Allison .50 1.25
112SP Bobby Allison SP 6.00 15.00
122 Al Unser .50 1.25

2012 Panini Golden Age Mini Broadleaf Blue Ink

*MINI BLUE: 2.5X TO 6X BASIC

2012 Panini Golden Age Min Broadleaf Brown Ink

*MINI BROWN: .6X TO 1.5X BASIC
APPX.ODDS ONE PER PACK

2012 Panini Golden Age Min Crofts Candy Blue Ink

*MINI BLUE: 1.5X TO 4X BASIC

2012 Panini Golden Age Min Crofts Candy Red Ink

*MINI RED: 1.5X TO 4X BASIC
APPX.ODDS 1:8 HOBBY

2012 Panini Golden Age Mini Cobb Tobacco

*MINI COBB: 2.5X TO 6X BASIC

2012 Panini Golden Age Fergus Bakery Pennants Blue

ISSUED AS BOX TOPPERS
2 Bobby Allison 2.00 5
41 Richard Petty 8.00 20
46 Al Unser 2.00 5

2012 Panini Golden Age Fergus Bakery Pennants Yellow

ISSUED AS BOX TOPPERS
2 Bobby Allison 2.00 5
41 Richard Petty 8.00 20
46 Al Unser 2.00 5

2012 Panini Golden Age Histo Signatures

STATED ODDS 1:24 HOBBY
37 Al Unser 8.00 20
40 Bobby Allison 5.00 12
49 Richard Petty 20.00 50

2012 Panini Golden Age Muse Age Memorabilia

STATED ODDS 1:24 HOBBY
19 Bobby Allison Shirt 4.00 10

2013 Panini Golden Age

75 Mario Andretti .30
122 Darrell Waltrip .30

2013 Panini Golden Age Min American Caramel Blue Back

*MINI BLUE: 1.2X TO 3X BASIC

2013 Panini Golden Age Min American Caramel Red Back

*MINI RED: 2X TO 5X BASIC

2013 Panini Golden Age Min Carolina Brights Green Back

*MINI GREEN: .75X TO 2X BASIC

2013 Panini Golden Age Min Carolina Brights Purple Back

*MINI PURPLE: 2X TO 5X BASIC

2013 Panini Golden Age Min Nadja Caramels Back

*MINI NADJA: 2X TO 5X BASIC

2013 Panini Golden Age Whit

*WHITE: 3X TO 8X BASIC
NO WHITE SP PRICING AVAILABLE

2013 Panini Golden Age Delo Gum

COMPLETE SET (30) 40.00 8
9 Darrell Waltrip .75 2

2013 Panini Golden Age Histo Signatures

EXCHANGE DEADLINE 12/26/2014
DW Darrell Waltrip 6.00 15
MA Mario Andretti 10.00 25

2013 Panini Golden Age Playi Cards

COMPLETE SET (53) 50.00 10
1 Mario Andretti .75 2
32 Richard Petty 1.25 3

2016 Panini National Treasure

1 Jimmie Johnson 8.00 20
2 Dale Earnhardt Jr. 10.00 25
3 Kevin Harvick 6.00 15
4 Tony Stewart 8.00 20
5 Danica Patrick 10.00 25
6 Kyle Busch 6.00 15
7 Matt Kenseth 5.00 12
8 Joey Logano 5.00 12
9 Kasey Kahne 5.00 12
10 Martin Truex Jr. 4.00 10
11 Ricky Stenhouse Jr. 5.00 12
12 Greg Biffle 4.00 10
13 Jamie McMurray 5.00 12
14 Trevor Bayne 5.00 12
15 Casey Mears 3.00 8
16 Kurt Busch 4.00 1
17 David Ragan 4.00 10
18 Ryan Newman 4.00 10
19 Bobby Labonte 5.00 12
20 Ty Dillon 5.00 12
21 Denny Hamlin 5.00 12
22 Clint Bowyer 5.00 1
23 Carl Edwards 5.00 12
24 Brad Keselowski 6.00 15
25 Austin Dillon 6.00 15
26 Jimmie Johnson CAR 8.00 20
27 Dale Earnhardt Jr. CAR 10.00 25
28 Kevin Harvick CAR 6.00 15
29 Tony Stewart CAR 8.00 20
30 Danica Patrick CAR 10.00 25

Kyle Busch CAR 6.00 15.00
Matt Kenseth CAR 5.00 12.00
Rusty Wallace CAR 5.00 12.00
Richard Petty CAR 8.00 20.00
Terry Labonte CAR 5.00 12.00
Harry Gant LEG 4.00 10.00
Richard Petty LEG 8.00 20.00
Mark Martin LEG 5.00 12.00
Rusty Wallace LEG 5.00 12.00
Darrell Waltrip LEG 8.00 20.00
Terry Labonte LEG 5.00 12.00
Bill Elliott LEG 8.00 20.00
Bobby Allison LEG 4.00 10.00
David Pearson LEG 5.00 12.00
Junior Johnson LEG 5.00 12.00
Chase Elliott FS AU 50.00 100.00
Brian Scott FS AU 6.00 15.00
Jeffrey Earnhardt FS AU
Chris Buescher FS AU 8.00 20.00
Ryan Blaney FS AU 8.00 20.00

2016 Panini National Treasures Championship Signature Threads

Matt Kenseth 10.00 25.00
Kurt Busch 8.00 20.00

2016 Panini National Treasures Championship Signatures

SILVER: .5X TO 1.2X BASIC AU
Brad Keselowski/49 10.00 25.00
Darrell Waltrip/25 15.00 40.00
John Force/75 10.00 25.00
Richard Petty/99 25.00 50.00
Rusty Wallace/75 6.00 15.00
Terry Labonte/99 6.00 15.00

2016 Panini National Treasures Dual Driver Materials

SILVER/15: .5X TO 1.2X BASIC DUAL FIRE/25
Dale Earnhardt Jr. 10.00 25.00
Jimmie Johnson
Menard/A.Dillon 6.00 15.00
K.Harvick/T.Stewart 8.00 20.00
M.Martin/T.Bayne 5.00 12.00
C.Edwards/M.Kenseth 5.00 12.00
C.Elliott/K.Kahne 6.00 15.00
B.Keselowski/J.Logano 6.00 15.00
C.Buescher/R.Blaney 4.00 10.00
P.Menard/R.Newman 4.00 10.00
C.Buescher/R.Reed 5.00 12.00
K.Larson/J.McMurray 8.00 20.00
A.Dillon/T.Dillon 6.00 15.00

2016 Panini National Treasures Dual Signatures

B.Keselowski/J.Logano/99 20.00 40.00
K.Larson/J.McMurray/25 25.00 60.00
P.Menard/R.Newman/25 12.00 30.00
C.Elliott/K.Kahne/25 50.00 100.00
J.Johnson/D.Earnhardt Jr/24 75.00 150.00
D.Patrick/K.Harvick/26 50.00 100.00
K.Harvick/K.Busch/25
K.Busch/D.Hamlin/25 30.00 60.00
C.Edwards/M.Kenseth/50 12.00 30.00
M.Martin/T.Bayne/15
D.Earnhardt Jr/D.Waltrip/25 50.00 100.00
B.Elliott/J.McMurray/48 25.00 60.00
B.Keselowski/R.Wallace/50 15.00 40.00
T.Labonte/D.Waltrip/25 25.00 60.00
C.Elliott/J.Johnson/25 75.00 150.00
T.Labonte/B.Labonte/49 12.00 30.00
B.Force/C.Force/99 40.00 80.00
J.Force/M.Andretti/75 30.00 60.00

2016 Panini National Treasures Firesuit Materials

Carl Edwards 5.00 12.00
Chase Elliott 6.00 15.00
Clint Bowyer 5.00 12.00
Dale Earnhardt Jr. 10.00 25.00
Denny Hamlin 5.00 12.00
Jimmie Johnson 8.00 20.00
Joey Logano 5.00 12.00
Kevin Harvick 6.00 15.00
Kyle Busch 6.00 15.00
Mark Martin 5.00 12.00
Martin Truex Jr. 4.00 10.00
Matt Kenseth 5.00 12.00

2016 Panini National Treasures Jumbo Firesuit Signatures

Aric Almirola 10.00 25.00
Austin Dillon
Bobby Labonte 12.00 30.00
Carl Edwards
Clint Bowyer 12.00 30.00
Dale Earnhardt Jr.
Denny Hamlin 12.00 30.00
Greg Biffle 10.00 25.00
Joey Logano 12.00 30.00
Kurt Busch 10.00 25.00
Mark Martin 12.00 30.00
Martin Truex Jr. 10.00 25.00
Matt Kenseth 12.00 30.00
Ryan Newman 10.00 25.00
Ty Dillon 12.00 30.00

2016 Panini National Treasures Sheet Metal Materials

*SILVER/15: .5X TO 1.2X BASIC MET/25
1 Ryan Newman 4.00 10.00
2 Carl Edwards 5.00 12.00
4 Clint Bowyer 5.00 12.00
5 Dale Earnhardt Jr. 10.00 25.00
7 Denny Hamlin 5.00 12.00
8 Jimmie Johnson 8.00 20.00
9 Joey Logano 5.00 12.00
10 Kasey Kahne 5.00 12.00
11 Kevin Harvick 6.00 15.00
12 Kyle Busch 6.00 15.00
14 Martin Truex Jr. 4.00 10.00
15 Matt Kenseth 5.00 12.00

2016 Panini National Treasures Signature Firesuit Materials

1 Aric Almirola/25 8.00 20.00
2 Austin Dillon/25 12.00 30.00
3 Bobby Labonte/25 10.00 25.00
4 Carl Edwards/25 10.00 25.00
6 Clint Bowyer/25 10.00 25.00
7 Dale Earnhardt Jr./25 50.00 100.00
14 Kasey Kahne/20 10.00 25.00
16 Kurt Busch/25 8.00 20.00
18 Kyle Larson/25
19 Martin Truex Jr./25 8.00 20.00
20 Matt Kenseth/25 10.00 25.00
23 Ryan Newman/25 8.00 20.00
24 Ty Dillon/25 10.00 25.00

2016 Panini National Treasures Signature Quad Materials

1 Aric Almirola/25 10.00 25.00
2 Austin Dillon/25 15.00 40.00
4 Carl Edwards/25 12.00 30.00
8 Danica Patrick/25 50.00 100.00
9 Denny Hamlin/25 12.00 30.00
10 Greg Biffle/25 10.00 25.00
15 Kevin Harvick/25 15.00 40.00
16 Kurt Busch/20 10.00 25.00
18 Kyle Larson/25 20.00 50.00
21 Ryan Newman/25 10.00 25.00
22 Ty Dillon/25 12.00 30.00

2016 Panini National Treasures Signatures

1 Brad Keselowski/99 8.00 20.00
5 Clint Bowyer/25 10.00 25.00
6 Harry Gant/49 6.00 15.00
7 Jeff Burton/49 6.00 15.00
11 Kasey Kahne/35 8.00 20.00
14 Kyle Larson/25 15.00 40.00
16 Martin Truex Jr./49 6.00 15.00
19 Danny Chocolate Myers/99 10.00 25.00
23 Casey Mears/49 5.00 12.00

2016 Panini National Treasures Timelines

*SILVER/15: .5X TO 1.2X BASIC TIME
1 Aric Almirola 4.00 10.00
2 Austin Dillon 6.00 15.00
4 Clint Bowyer 5.00 12.00
6 Jamie McMurray 5.00 12.00
7 Joey Logano 5.00 12.00
8 Kasey Kahne 5.00 12.00
9 Kurt Busch 4.00 10.00
11 Martin Truex Jr. 4.00 10.00
12 Matt Kenseth 5.00 12.00
14 Tony Stewart 8.00 20.00
15 Ryan Newman 4.00 10.00
16 Ty Dillon 5.00 12.00
17 Brian Scott 3.00 8.00
18 Jeffrey Earnhardt 5.00 12.00
19 Chris Buescher 4.00 10.00
20 Ryan Blaney 4.00 10.00

2016 Panini National Treasures Timelines Signatures

2 Austin Dillon/25 15.00 40.00
4 Clint Bowyer/25 12.00 30.00
9 Mark Martin/25 12.00 30.00
10 Martin Truex Jr./25 10.00 25.00
13 Elliott Sadler/49 8.00 20.00
14 Ryan Newman/25 10.00 25.00
15 Ty Dillon/25 12.00 30.00

2017 Panini National Treasures

1 Jimmie Johnson 8.00 20.00
2 Kevin Harvick 6.00 15.00
3 Dale Earnhardt Jr. 10.00 25.00
4 Brad Keselowski 6.00 15.00
5 Kyle Busch 6.00 15.00
6 Denny Hamlin 5.00 12.00
7 Danica Patrick 10.00 25.00
8 Matt Kenseth 5.00 12.00
9 Austin Dillon 6.00 15.00
10 Chase Elliott 6.00 15.00
11 Joey Logano 5.00 12.00
12 Clint Bowyer 5.00 12.00
13 Ryan Newman 4.00 10.00
14 Kasey Kahne 5.00 12.00
15 Martin Truex Jr. 4.00 10.00
16 Jimmie Johnson CAR 8.00 20.00
17 Dale Earnhardt Jr. CAR 10.00 25.00
18 Kevin Harvick CAR 6.00 15.00
19 Danica Patrick CAR 10.00 25.00
20 Kyle Busch CAR 6.00 15.00
21 Bill Elliott LEG 8.00 20.00
22 Carl Edwards LEG 5.00 12.00
23 Greg Biffle LEG 4.00 10.00
24 Dale Jarrett LEG 5.00 12.00
25 Darrell Waltrip LEG 8.00 20.00
26 Jeff Burton LEG 4.00 10.00
27 Mark Martin LEG 5.00 12.00
28 Michael Waltrip LEG 5.00 12.00
29 Richard Petty LEG 8.00 20.00
30 Rusty Wallace LEG 5.00 12.00
31 Tony Stewart LEG 8.00 20.00

2017 Panini National Treasures Century Gold

*GOLD/15: .5X TO 1.2X BASIC MEM/25

2017 Panini National Treasures Century Holo Silver

*SILVER/20: .5X TO 1.2X BASIC MEM/25

2017 Panini National Treasures Championship Signatures Gold

*BASE/48-50: .25X TO .6X BASIC AU/15-20
*BASE/25: .3X TO .8X BASIC AU/15-20
*BASE/20: .4X TO 1X BASIC AU/15-20
*SILVER/25: .3X TO .8X BASIC AU/15-20
*SILVER/15-20: .4X TO 1X BASIC AU/15-20
2 Chad Knaus/15 30.00 80.00
4 Dale Jarrett/15 20.00 50.00
5 Bill Elliott/15 20.00 50.00
6 Bobby Labonte/15 12.00 30.00
7 Brad Keselowski/20 15.00 40.00
8 Cale Yarborough/15 12.00 30.00
9 Darrell Waltrip/15 20.00 50.00
10 Rusty Wallace/15 12.00 30.00
11 Tony Stewart/15 20.00 50.00

2017 Panini National Treasures Championship Swatches

*SILVER/20: .5X TO 1.2X BASIC MEM/25
*GOLD/15: .5X TO 1.2X BASIC MEM/25
1 Brad Keselowski 6.00 15.00
2 Kevin Harvick 6.00 15.00
3 Kyle Busch 6.00 15.00
5 Dale Jarrett 5.00 12.00

2017 Panini National Treasures Dual Firesuit Materials Gold

*BASE/25: .3X TO .8X GOLD MEM/15
*SILVER/20: .4X TO 1X GOLD MEM/15
1 Danica Patrick 12.00 30.00
2 Dale Earnhardt Jr. 12.00 30.00
4 Chase Elliott 8.00 20.00
5 Clint Bowyer 6.00 15.00
6 Greg Biffle 5.00 12.00
11 Martin Truex Jr. 5.00 12.00
15 Ryan Newman 5.00 12.00
17 William Byron 10.00 25.00
18 Austin Dillon 8.00 20.00
20 Aric Almirola 5.00 12.00

2017 Panini National Treasures Dual Firesuit Signatures Holo Silver

*BASE/25: .3X TO .8X SILVER MEM AU/20
*GOLD/15: .4X TO 1X SILVER MEM AU/20
1 Danica Patrick 40.00 80.00
2 Dale Earnhardt Jr. 50.00 100.00
3 A.J. Allmendinger 15.00 40.00
5 Clint Bowyer 15.00 40.00
6 Greg Biffle 12.00 30.00
8 Joey Logano 15.00 40.00
9 Kasey Kahne 15.00 40.00
10 Kyle Larson 25.00 60.00
11 Martin Truex Jr. 12.00 30.00
12 Paul Menard 10.00 25.00
13 Ricky Stenhouse Jr. 15.00 40.00
15 Ryan Newman 12.00 30.00
16 Trevor Bayne 15.00 40.00
17 William Byron
18 Austin Dillon 20.00 50.00
19 Landon Cassill 12.00 30.00
20 Aric Almirola
21 Tony Stewart 25.00 60.00

2017 Panini National Treasures Dual Sheet Metal Materials Gold

*BASE/25: .3X TO .8X GOLD MEM/15
*SILVER/20: .4X TO 1X GOLD/15
2 Chase Elliott 8.00 20.00
5 Kasey Kahne 6.00 15.00
9 Kyle Larson 10.00 25.00
12 Jimmie Johnson 10.00 25.00
13 Dale Earnhardt Jr. 12.00 30.00
14 Kevin Harvick 8.00 20.00

2017 Panini National Treasures Dual Tire Signatures Gold

*BASE/25: .3X TO .8X GOLD TIRE AU/15
*SILVER/20: .4X TO 1X GOLD TIRE AU/15
2 Denny Hamlin/15 15.00 40.00
3 Mark Martin/15 25.00 60.00
4 Danica Patrick/15 40.00 80.00
5 Austin Dillon/15 20.00 50.00
6 Jamie McMurray/15 15.00 40.00
7 Kurt Busch/15 12.00 30.00
9 William Byron/15
10 Brad Keselowski/15 20.00 50.00
11 Martin Truex Jr./15 12.00 30.00
12 Carl Edwards/15 15.00 40.00
13 Kevin Harvick/15 20.00 50.00
14 Matt Kenseth/15 15.00 40.00
15 Kyle Busch/15 25.00 60.00
16 Tony Stewart/15 25.00 60.00

2017 Panini National Treasures Jumbo Firesuit Materials Gold

*BASE/25: .3X TO .8X GOLD MEM/15
*SILVER/20: .4X TO 1X GOLD MEM/15
4 Denny Hamlin 6.00 15.00
5 Matt Kenseth 6.00 15.00
7 Jamie McMurray 6.00 15.00

2017 Panini National Treasures Jumbo Sheet Metal Materials Gold

*BASE/15: .3X TO .8X GOLD MEM/25
*SILVER/20: .4X TO 1X GOLD SHEET/15
1 Jimmie Johnson 10.00 25.00
2 Dale Earnhardt Jr. 12.00 30.00
5 Chase Elliott 8.00 20.00

2017 Panini National Treasures Jumbo Tire Signatures Gold

*BASE/99: .25X TO .6X GOLD MEM AU/25
*BASE/40-50: .3X TO .8X GOLD MEM AU/25
*BASE/40-50: .25X TO .6X GOLD MEM AU/15-20
*BASE/24-25: .3X TO .8X GOLD MEM AU/25
*SILVER/35-50: .3X TO .8X BASIC MEM AU/25
*SILVER/25: .3X TO .8X BASIC MEM AU/15-20
*SILVER/20: .4X TO 1X BASIC MEM AU/20
1 A.J. Allmendinger/15 15.00 40.00
2 Brad Keselowski/20 20.00 50.00
3 Chase Elliott/15 20.00 50.00
5 Corey LaJoie/25 10.00 25.00
6 Carl Edwards/15 15.00 40.00
9 Joey Logano/25 30.00 80.00
10 Kasey Kahne/25 12.00 30.00
11 Kevin Harvick/25 15.00 40.00
12 Kyle Busch/25 20.00 50.00
13 Martin Truex Jr./25 10.00 25.00
14 Matt Kenseth/15 15.00 40.00

2017 Panini National Treasures Legendary Material Signatures Gold

*BASE/23-25: .3X TO .8X GOLD MEM AU/15
*SILVER/19-20: .4X TO 1X GOLD MEM AU/15
1 Bill Elliott/15
6 Rusty Wallace/15 15.00 40.00
7 Terry Labonte/15 15.00 40.00
8 Derrike Cope/15 12.00 30.00
9 Michael Waltrip/15
10 Carl Edwards/15 15.00 40.00

2017 Panini National Treasures Legendary Signatures Gold

*BASE/70-99: .2X TO .5X GOLD AU/15-20
*BASE/70-99: .25X TO .6X GOLD AU/25
*BASE/50: .3X TO .8X GOLD AU/25
*BASE/30: .3X TO .8X GOLD AU/15-20
*SILVER/35-50: .3X TO .8X GOLD AU/25
*SILVER/35-50: .25X TO .6X GOLD AU/15-20
*SILVER/25: .2X TO .8X GOLD AU/15-20
*HOLO GOLD/15: .5X TO 1.2X BASIC AU/25
*HOLO GOLD/15: .4X TO 1X BASIC AU/15-20
1 Ray Evernham/25 8.00 20.00
2 Cale Yarborough/15 12.00 30.00
3 Harry Gant/25 8.00 20.00
4 Hershel McGriff/25 6.00 15.00
5 Larry McReynolds/20 8.00 20.00
6 Wally Dallenbach/25 6.00 15.00
7 Junior Johnson/25 10.00 25.00
8 Michael Waltrip/15 12.00 30.00
9 Darrell Waltrip/15 20.00 50.00
11 Terry Labonte/20
12 Rusty Wallace/15 12.00 30.00
14 Ned Jarrett/25 8.00 20.00
15 Mark Martin/25 25.00 60.00

2017 Panini National Treasures Magnificent Marks Gold

*BASE/25: .3X TO .8X GOLD AU/15
*SILVER/20: .4X TO 1X GOLD AU/15
2 Danica Patrick/15
3 Kenny Wallace/15 8.00 20.00
4 Michael Waltrip/15 12.00 30.00
5 Ray Evernham/15 10.00 25.00
6 Rusty Wallace/15 12.00 30.00
7 Chad Knaus/15 30.00 80.00
8 Cale Yarborough/15 12.00 30.00
9 Harry Gant/15 10.00 25.00

2017 Panini National Treasures Quad Materials

*GOLD/15: .5X TO 1.2X BASIC MEM/25
*SILVER/20: .5X TO 1.2X BASIC MEM/25
2 Kasey Kahne 6.00 15.00
3 Denny Hamlin 6.00 15.00
7 Ryan Newman 5.00 12.00
8 Martin Truex Jr. 5.00 12.00
11 Jamie McMurray 6.00 15.00
12 A.J. Allmendinger 6.00 15.00
13 Brad Keselowski 8.00 20.00
15 David Ragan 5.00 12.00

2017 Panini National Treasures Signatures Gold

*BASE/70-99: .25X TO .6X GOLD AU/25
*BASE/45: .25X TO .6X GOLD AU/15
*BASE/25: .3X TO .8X GOLD AU/15
*SILVER/50: .3X TO .8X GOLD AU/25
*SILVER/20: .4X TO 1X GOLD AU/15
*HOLO GOLD/15: .5X TO 1.2X GOLD AU/25
1 Brett Bodine/15
2 Dave Blaney/25 6.00 15.00
3 Jeff Burton/15 10.00 25.00
4 Joe Nemechek/25 6.00 15.00
5 Kate Dallenbach/25 20.00 50.00
7 Kelley Earnhardt/25 15.00 40.00
8 Kenny Wallace/25 6.00 15.00
9 Kerry Earnhardt/25 10.00 25.00
10 Kyle Petty/25 8.00 20.00
11 Mike Wallace/25 10.00 25.00
17 John Hunter Nemechek/25 8.00 20.00
18 Joey Gase/25 10.00 25.00
19 Jeb Burton/25 8.00 20.00

2017 Panini National Treasures Teammates Dual Materials

*SILVER/15: .5X TO 1.2X BASIC MEM/25
*SILVER/20: .5X TO 1.2X BASIC MEM/25
1 J.Johnson/C.Elliott 8.00 20.00
2 K.Kahne/D.Earnhardt Jr. 10.00 25.00
3 K.Busch/D.Patrick 10.00 25.00
4 C.Bowyer/K.Harvick 6.00 15.00
5 B.Keselowski/J.Logano 6.00 15.00
6 M.Kenseth/K.Busch 6.00 15.00
7 D.Hamlin/D.Suarez 10.00 25.00
8 R.Newman/A.Dillon 6.00 15.00
9 J.McMurray/K.Larson 8.00 20.00
10 R.Stenhouse Jr./T.Bayne 5.00 12.00

2017 Panini National Treasures Three Wide

*GOLD/15: .5X TO 1.2X BASIC MEM/25
*SILVER/20: .5X TO 1.2X BASIC MEM/25
1 Erik Jones 10.00 25.00
2 Ty Dillon 6.00 15.00
3 Daniel Suarez 12.00 30.00
5 Jimmie Johnson 10.00 25.00
7 Kevin Harvick 8.00 20.00
8 Chase Elliott 8.00 20.00
11 A.J. Allmendinger 6.00 15.00
14 David Ragan 5.00 12.00

2017 Panini National Treasures Three Wide Signatures Gold

*BASE/24-25: .3X TO .8X GOLD AU/15
*SILVER/18-20: .4X TO 1X GOLD/15
2 Chris Buescher
3 Cole Custer 15.00 40.00
4 Cole Whitt 12.00 30.00
5 Daniel Hemric 15.00 40.00
6 A.J. Allmendinger 15.00 40.00
7 Bobby Labonte 15.00 40.00
8 Dale Earnhardt Jr. 50.00 100.00
9 Greg Biffle 12.00 30.00
10 Kasey Kahne 15.00 40.00
11 Martin Truex Jr. 12.00 30.00
12 Ryan Newman 12.00 30.00
13 Joey Logano 15.00 40.00
14 Clint Bowyer 15.00 40.00
15 Chase Elliott 20.00 50.00

2017 Panini National Treasures Winning Material Signatures Gold

*BASE/25: .3X TO .8X GOLD AU/15
*SILVER/20: .4X TO 1X GOLD AU/15
1 Rusty Wallace 15.00 40.00
2 Bill Elliott
4 Kyle Busch 25.00 60.00
5 Matt Kenseth 15.00 40.00
6 Kevin Harvick 20.00 50.00
7 Kurt Busch 12.00 30.00
9 Carl Edwards 15.00 40.00
10 Brad Keselowski 20.00 50.00

2017 Panini National Treasures Winning Signatures Gold

*BASE/99: .25X TO .6X GOLD AU/25
*BASE/50: .3X TO .8X GOLD AU/25
*BASE/15: X TO X GOLD AU/15
*BASE/25: .3X TO .8X GOLD AU/15
*SILVER/40-50: .3X TO .8X GOLD AU/25
*SILVER/25: .3X TO .8X GOLD AU/15
*SILVER/20: .4X TO 1X GOLD AU/15
*HOLO GOLD/15: .5X TO 1.2X GOLD AU/25
2 Darrell Waltrip/15 20.00 50.00
3 Cale Yarborough/15 12.00 30.00
4 Rusty Wallace/15 12.00 30.00
5 Ned Jarrett/25 8.00 20.00
6 Junior Johnson/25 10.00 25.00
7 Bill Elliott/15 20.00 50.00
8 Mark Martin/25 25.00 60.00
9 Kyle Busch/15 15.00 40.00
10 Matt Kenseth/15 12.00 30.00
11 Kevin Harvick/25 12.00 30.00
13 Kurt Busch/15 10.00 25.00
14 Denny Hamlin/25 10.00 25.00
15 Carl Edwards/25 10.00 25.00

2018 Panini Prime

*GOLD/25: .5X TO 1.2X BASIC CARDS/50
1 Kyle Busch POR 2.50 6.00
2 Joey Logano POR 2.00 5.00
3 Kevin Harvick POR 2.50 6.00
4 Clint Bowyer POR 2.00 5.00
5 Kurt Busch POR 1.50 4.00
6 Brad Keselowski POR 2.50 6.00
7 Denny Hamlin POR 2.00 5.00
8 Ryan Blaney POR 1.50 4.00
9 Martin Truex Jr. POR 1.50 4.00
10 Kyle Larson POR 3.00 8.00
11 Aric Almirola POR 1.50 4.00
12 Alex Bowman POR 2.00 5.00
13 Erik Jones POR 2.00 5.00
14 Jimmie Johnson POR 3.00 8.00
15 Ricky Stenhouse Jr POR 2.00 5.00
16 Ryan Newman POR 1.50 4.00
17 Austin Dillon POR 2.50 6.00
18 Chase Elliott POR 2.50 6.00
19 William Byron POR 2.00 5.00
20 Bubba Wallace POR 2.00 5.00
21 Ty Dillon POR 2.00 5.00
22 Kasey Kahne POR 2.00 5.00
23 Trevor Bayne POR 2.00 5.00
24 Danica Patrick POR 4.00 10.00
25 Dale Earnhardt Jr POR 4.00 10.00
26 Tony Stewart POR 3.00 8.00
27 Carl Edwards POR 2.00 5.00
28 Richard Petty POR 3.00 8.00
29 Terry Labonte POR 2.00 5.00
30 Bill Elliott POR 3.00 8.00
31 Dale Jarrett POR 2.00 5.00
32 Darrell Waltrip POR 3.00 8.00
33 Rusty Wallace POR 2.00 5.00
34 Mark Martin POR 2.00 5.00
35 Kyle Busch DRI 2.50 6.00
36 Joey Logano DRI 2.00 5.00
37 Kevin Harvick DRI 2.50 6.00
38 Clint Bowyer DRI 2.00 5.00
39 Kurt Busch DRI 1.50 4.00
40 Brad Keselowski DRI 2.50 6.00
41 Denny Hamlin DRI 2.00 5.00
42 Ryan Blaney DRI 1.50 4.00
43 Martin Truex Jr. DRI 1.50 4.00
44 Kyle Larson DRI 3.00 8.00
45 Aric Almirola DRI 1.50 4.00
46 Alex Bowman DRI 2.00 5.00
47 Erik Jones DRI 2.00 5.00
48 Jimmie Johnson DRI 3.00 8.00
49 Ryan Newman DRI 1.50 4.00
50 Austin Dillon DRI 2.50 6.00
51 Chase Elliott DRI 2.50 6.00
52 William Byron DRI 2.00 5.00
53 Bubba Wallace DRI 2.00 5.00
54 Ty Dillon DRI 2.00 5.00
55 Kasey Kahne DRI 2.00 5.00
56 Trevor Bayne DRI 2.00 5.00
57 Danica Patrick DRI 4.00 10.00
58 Dale Earnhardt Jr DRI 4.00 10.00
59 Tony Stewart DRI 3.00 8.00
60 Carl Edwards DRI 2.00 5.00
61 Richard Petty DRI 3.00 8.00
62 Terry Labonte DRI 2.00 5.00
63 Bill Elliott DRI 3.00 8.00
64 Dale Jarrett DRI 2.00 5.00
65 Darrell Waltrip DRI 3.00 8.00
66 Rusty Wallace DRI 2.00 5.00
67 Mark Martin DRI 2.00 5.00
68 Kyle Busch CAR 2.50 6.00
69 Joey Logano CAR 2.00 5.00
70 Kevin Harvick CAR 2.50 6.00
71 Clint Bowyer CAR 2.00 5.00
72 Kurt Busch CAR 1.50 4.00
73 Brad Keselowski CAR 2.50 6.00
74 Denny Hamlin CAR 2.00 5.00
75 Ryan Blaney CAR 1.50 4.00
76 Martin Truex Jr. CAR 1.50 4.00
77 Kyle Larson CAR 3.00 8.00
78 Aric Almirola CAR 1.50 4.00
79 Alex Bowman CAR 2.00 5.00
80 Jimmie Johnson CAR 3.00 8.00
81 Ricky Stenhouse Jr CAR 2.00 5.00
82 Ryan Newman CAR 1.50 4.00
83 Austin Dillon CAR 2.50 6.00
84 Chase Elliott CAR 2.50 6.00
85 William Byron CAR 2.00 5.00
86 Bubba Wallace CAR 2.00 5.00
87 Ty Dillon CAR 2.00 5.00
88 Kasey Kahne CAR 2.00 5.00
89 Trevor Bayne CAR 2.00 5.00
90 Danica Patrick CAR 4.00 10.00
91 Dale Earnhardt Jr CAR 4.00 10.00
92 Tony Stewart CAR 3.00 8.00
93 Carl Edwards CAR 2.00 5.00
94 Richard Petty CAR 3.00 8.00
95 Terry Labonte CAR 2.00 5.00
96 Bill Elliott CAR 3.00 8.00
97 Dale Jarrett CAR 2.00 5.00
98 Darrell Waltrip CAR 3.00 8.00
99 Rusty Wallace CAR 2.00 5.00
100 Mark Martin CAR 2.00 5.00

2018 Panini Prime Autograph Materials

*GOLD/50: .5X TO 1.2X BASIC MEM AU/99
*GOLD/25: .6X TO 1.5X BASIC MEM AU/65-99
*GOLD/25: .5X TO 1.2X BASIC MEM AU/49-50
1 Danica Patrick/25
2 Aric Almirola/25 8.00 20.00
3 Austin Dillon/50 10.00 25.00
5 Brad Keselowski/99 8.00 20.00
6 Clint Bowyer/50 8.00 20.00
7 Cole Whitt/99 5.00 12.00
8 Corey LaJoie/99 5.00 12.00
9 Dale Earnhardt Jr/25
10 Denny Hamlin/50 8.00 20.00
12 Greg Biffle/49
13 Jamie McMurray/50 8.00 20.00
14 Kasey Kahne/99 6.00 15.00
15 Kaz Grala/15
16 Kevin Harvick/25
17 Kurt Busch/99 5.00 12.00
18 Kyle Larson/50 12.00 30.00
19 Landon Cassill/50
20 Martin Truex Jr./99 5.00 12.00
21 Matt Kenseth/99 6.00 15.00
23 Ross Chastain/65
25 Terry Labonte/50 8.00 20.00

2018 Panini Prime Clear Silhouettes

*GOLD/50: .5X TO 1.2X BASIC FIRE/99
1 Aric Almirola 2.50 6.00
2 Austin Dillon 4.00 10.00
3 Brad Keselowski 4.00 10.00
4 Bubba Wallace 3.00 8.00
5 Chase Elliott 4.00 10.00
6 Clint Bowyer 3.00 8.00
7 Dale Earnhardt Jr 6.00 15.00
8 Daniel Suarez 3.00 8.00
9 David Ragan 2.50 6.00
10 Denny Hamlin 3.00 8.00
11 Elliott Sadler 2.00 5.00
12 Erik Jones 3.00 8.00
13 Jamie McMurray 3.00 8.00
14 Joe Nemechek 2.00 5.00
15 Joey Logano 3.00 8.00
16 Justin Allgaier 2.50 6.00
17 Kaz Grala 4.00 10.00
18 Kevin Harvick 4.00 10.00
19 Kurt Busch 2.50 6.00
20 Kyle Busch 4.00 10.00
21 Kyle Larson 5.00 12.00
22 Martin Truex Jr. 2.50 6.00
23 Michael Annett 3.00 8.00
24 Paul Menard 2.00 5.00
25 Ryan Blaney 2.50 6.00
26 Ryan Newman 2.50 6.00
27 Trevor Bayne 3.00 8.00
28 Ty Dillon 3.00 8.00
29 William Byron 3.00 8.00
30 Zane Smith 3.00 8.00

2018 Panini Prime Clear Silhouettes Dual

*GOLD/50: .5X TO 1.2X BASIC MEM/99
1 Aric Almirola/99 2.50 6.00
2 Austin Dillon/99 4.00 10.00
3 Brad Keselowski/99 4.00 10.00
4 Bubba Wallace/99 3.00 8.00
CSCE Chase Elliott/99 4.00 10.00
6 Clint Bowyer/99 3.00 8.00
7 Dale Earnhardt Jr/99 6.00 15.00
8 Daniel Suarez/99 3.00 8.00
9 David Ragan/99 2.50 6.00
10 Denny Hamlin/99 3.00 8.00
11 Elliott Sadler/99 2.00 5.00
12 Erik Jones/99 3.00 8.00
13 Jamie McMurray/99 3.00 8.00
14 Joe Nemechek/25 3.00 8.00
15 Joey Logano/99 3.00 8.00
16 John Hunter Nemechek/99 2.50 6.00
17 Julia Landauer/99 2.00 5.00
18 Justin Allgaier/99 2.50 6.00
19 Kaz Grala/99 4.00 10.00
20 Kevin Harvick/99 4.00 10.00
21 Kurt Busch/99 2.50 6.00
22 Kyle Busch/99 4.00 10.00
23 Kyle Larson/99 5.00 12.00
24 Martin Truex Jr./99 2.50 6.00
25 Michael Annett/99 3.00 8.00
26 Paul Menard/99 2.00 5.00
27 Ryan Blaney/99 2.50 6.00
28 Ryan Newman/99 2.50 6.00
29 Spencer Gallagher/99 2.00 5.00
30 Tony Stewart/99 5.00 12.00

2018 Panini Prime Driver Signatures

*GOLD/50: .5X TO 1.2X BASIC AU/99
*GOLD/25: .6X TO 1.5X BASIC AU/99
*GOLD/25: .5X TO 1.2X BASIC AU/49-60
*GOLD/23: .8X TO 2X BASIC AU/99

1 Rusty Wallace/99 8.00 20.00
3 Carl Edwards/25 15.00 40.00
4 Wally Dallenbach/99 3.00 8.00
5 Dale Jarrett/50 6.00 15.00
6 Danica Patrick/25
7 Darrell Waltrip/99 8.00 20.00
8 Derrike Cope/49
9 Kurt Busch/99 4.00 10.00
10 Jack Sprague/99 3.00 8.00
11 Austin Dillon/99 6.00 15.00
12 Mark Martin/25 12.00 30.00
13 Matt Kenseth/99 5.00 12.00
14 Michael Waltrip/99 5.00 12.00
15 Ned Jarrett/50 5.00 12.00
16 Richard Petty/25
17 Bill Elliott/99 8.00 20.00
18 Terry Labonte/50 6.00 15.00
21 Greg Biffle/50
22 Kasey Kahne/99 5.00 12.00
23 Brad Keselowski/99 6.00 15.00
24 Joey Logano/60
25 Dale Earnhardt Jr/25

2018 Panini Prime Dual Material Autographs

*GOLD/50: .5X TO 1.2X BASIC MEM AU/99
*GOLD/42: .4X TO 1X BASIC MEM AU/50
*GOLD/25-34: .5X TO 1.2X BASIC MEM AU/50
*GOLD/25: .6X TO 1.5X BASIC MEM AU/99
*GOLD/15: .6X TO 1.5X BASIC MEM AU/50
1 Danica Patrick/25
2 Dale Earnhardt Jr/25
3 Austin Dillon/50 10.00 25.00
4 Denny Hamlin/99 6.00 15.00
5 Jamie McMurray/50 8.00 20.00
6 Kyle Busch/25
7 Kyle Larson/50 12.00 30.00
8 William Byron/50 15.00 40.00
9 Ryan Newman/50 6.00 15.00
10 Cole Whitt/99 5.00 12.00
11 Corey LaJoie/99 5.00 12.00
12 Ryan Blaney/50
13 Ross Chastain/99
14 Jimmie Johnson/25
15 Greg Biffle/50
16 Aric Almirola/25 8.00 20.00
17 Bubba Wallace/43
19 Ricky Stenhouse Jr/25
20 Ty Dillon/50
21 Landon Cassill/50
22 Spencer Gallagher/95 EXCH 6.00 15.00
24 Erik Jones/25

2018 Panini Prime Hats Off Headband

1 Austin Dillon/36 5.00 12.00
2 Daniel Suarez/35 4.00 10.00
3 Denny Hamlin/36 4.00 10.00
5 Jimmie Johnson/28 8.00 20.00
6 Joey Logano/36 4.00 10.00
7 Kurt Busch/36 3.00 8.00
8 Kyle Busch/36 5.00 12.00
9 Kyle Busch/34 6.00 15.00
10 Kyle Busch/30 6.00 15.00
11 Kyle Busch/30 6.00 15.00
12 Martin Truex Jr./36 3.00 8.00
13 Martin Truex Jr./34 4.00 10.00
14 Paul Menard/36 2.50 6.00
15 Ryan Newman/20 5.00 12.00
16 William Byron/26 5.00 12.00
17 William Byron/26 5.00 12.00
18 Chase Elliott/34 6.00 15.00
19 Kevin Harvick/34 6.00 15.00
20 Christopher Bell/22 6.00 15.00

2018 Panini Prime Prime Number Signatures

*GOLD/99: .5X TO 1.2X BASIC AU/49
*GOLD/99: .6X TO 1.5X BASIC AU/25
*GOLD/50: .5X TO 1.2X BASIC AU/25
1 Austin Dillon/99 6.00 15.00
2 Brad Keselowski/99 6.00 15.00
3 Chase Elliott/25
4 Clint Bowyer/99 5.00 12.00
5 Denny Hamlin/50 6.00 15.00
6 Jamie McMurray/99 5.00 12.00
7 Jimmie Johnson/25
8 Joey Logano/50
9 Kevin Harvick/25 15.00 40.00
10 Kurt Busch/99 4.00 10.00
11 Kyle Busch/25 25.00 50.00
12 Kyle Larson/99 8.00 20.00
13 Martin Truex Jr./25 6.00 15.00
14 Paul Menard/50
15 Ricky Stenhouse Jr/50
16 Ryan Blaney/50
17 Ryan Newman/99 4.00 10.00
18 Trevor Bayne/25
19 Ty Dillon/25
20 William Byron/99

2018 Panini Prime Prime Signatures

*GOLD/37-50: .6X TO 1.5X BASIC AU/90-99
*GOLD/25: .6X TO 1.5X BASIC AU/99
*GOLD/25: .5X TO 1.2X BASIC AU/49-50
1 Bill Elliott/99 8.00 20.00
3 Carl Edwards/25 15.00 40.00
4 Dale Earnhardt Jr/25
5 Dale Jarrett/50 6.00 15.00
6 Danica Patrick/25
7 Darrell Waltrip/99 8.00 20.00
8 Derrike Cope/49
9 Greg Biffle/35
10 Jack Sprague/99 3.00 8.00
11 Junior Johnson/78
12 Mark Martin/25 12.00 30.00
13 Matt Kenseth/99 5.00 12.00
14 Michael Waltrip/99 5.00 12.00
15 Ned Jarrett/90 4.00 10.00
16 Richard Petty/25
17 Rusty Wallace/99 8.00 20.00
18 Terry Labonte/50 6.00 15.00
20 Wally Dallenbach/99 3.00 8.00

2018 Panini Prime Quad Material Autographs

*GOLD/41-50: .5X TO 1.2X BASIC MEM AU/75-99
*GOLD/41-50: .4X TO 1X BASIC MEM AU/37-60
*GOLD/25-27: .6X TO 1.5X BASIC MEM AU/75-99
*GOLD/25-27: .5X TO 1.2X BASIC MEM AU/41-50
*GOLD/15: .6X TO 1.5X BASIC MEM AU/37
1 Kurt Busch/99 6.00 15.00
2 Kasey Kahne/99 8.00 20.00
3 Austin Dillon/50 12.00 30.00
4 Kevin Harvick/25
5 Clint Bowyer/60 10.00 25.00
6 Brad Keselowski/99 10.00 25.00
7 Jamie McMurray/50 10.00 25.00
8 Kyle Busch/25
9 Kyle Larson/50 15.00 40.00
10 Joey Logano/75
11 Martin Truex Jr./99 6.00 15.00
12 William Byron/50 20.00 50.00
13 Ryan Newman/50 8.00 20.00
14 Cole Whitt/99 6.00 15.00
15 Ryan Blaney/50
16 Jimmie Johnson/25
17 Chase Elliott/25 60.00 125.00
18 Aric Almirola/39 8.00 20.00
19 Bubba Wallace/43
20 Paul Menard/50
21 Ricky Stenhouse Jr/50
22 Ty Dillon/54
23 Trevor Bayne/37
24 Erik Jones/25

2018 Panini Prime Race Used Duals Firesuit

*GOLD/25: .5X TO 1.2X BASIC FIRE/50
3 Austin Dillon 5.00 12.00
4 Brad Keselowski 5.00 12.00
5 Bubba Wallace 4.00 10.00
7 Chris Buescher 3.00 8.00
9 Clint Bowyer 4.00 10.00
10 Cole Custer 4.00 10.00
11 Cole Whitt 3.00 8.00
15 David Ragan 3.00 8.00
16 Denny Hamlin 4.00 10.00
17 Elliott Sadler 2.50 6.00
19 Jamie McMurray 4.00 10.00
21 Joey Logano 4.00 10.00
22 John Hunter Nemechek 3.00 8.00
24 Kasey Kahne 4.00 10.00
25 Kevin Harvick 5.00 12.00
27 Paul Menard 2.50 6.00
28 Ryan Newman 3.00 8.00

2018 Panini Prime Race Used Duals Sheet Metal

*GOLD/25: .5X TO 1.2X BASIC SHEET/50
1 Alex Bowman 4.00 10.00
2 Aric Almirola 3.00 8.00
3 Austin Dillon 5.00 12.00
4 Brad Keselowski 5.00 12.00
5 Bubba Wallace 4.00 10.00
6 Chase Elliott 5.00 12.00
7 Chris Buescher 3.00 8.00
8 Christopher Bell 4.00 10.00
9 Clint Bowyer 4.00 10.00
10 Cole Custer 4.00 10.00
11 Cole Whitt 3.00 8.00
12 Corey LaJoie 3.00 8.00
13 Dale Earnhardt Jr 8.00 20.00
14 Daniel Suarez 4.00 10.00
15 David Ragan 3.00 8.00
16 Denny Hamlin 4.00 10.00
17 Elliott Sadler 2.50 6.00
18 Erik Jones 4.00 10.00
19 Jamie McMurray 4.00 10.00
20 Jimmie Johnson 6.00 15.00
21 Joey Logano 4.00 10.00
22 John Hunter Nemechek 3.00 8.00
23 Justin Allgaier 3.00 8.00
24 Kasey Kahne 4.00 10.00
25 Kevin Harvick 5.00 12.00
26 Kyle Busch 5.00 12.00
27 Paul Menard 2.50 6.00
28 Ryan Newman 3.00 8.00
29 Trevor Bayne 4.00 10.00
30 Tony Stewart 6.00 15.00

2018 Panini Prime Race Used Duals Tire

*GOLD/25: .5X TO 1.2X BASIC TIRE/50
1 Alex Bowman 4.00 10.00
2 Aric Almirola 3.00 8.00
3 Austin Dillon 5.00 12.00
4 Brad Keselowski 5.00 12.00
5 Bubba Wallace 4.00 10.00
6 Chase Elliott 5.00 12.00
7 Chris Buescher 3.00 8.00
8 Christopher Bell 4.00 10.00
9 Clint Bowyer 4.00 10.00
10 Cole Custer 4.00 10.00
12 Corey LaJoie 3.00 8.00
RUDDS Daniel Suarez 4.00 10.00
15 David Ragan 3.00 8.00
16 Denny Hamlin 4.00 10.00
17 Elliott Sadler 2.50 6.00
18 Erik Jones 4.00 10.00
19 Jamie McMurray 4.00 10.00
20 Jimmie Johnson 6.00 15.00
21 Joey Logano 4.00 10.00
22 John Hunter Nemechek 3.00 8.00
23 Justin Allgaier 3.00 8.00
24 Kasey Kahne 4.00 10.00
25 Kevin Harvick 5.00 12.00
26 Kyle Busch 5.00 12.00
27 Paul Menard 2.50 6.00
28 Ryan Newman 3.00 8.00
29 Trevor Bayne 4.00 10.00
30 Tony Stewart 6.00 15.00

2018 Panini Prime Race Used Firesuits

*GOLD/25: .5X TO 1.2X BASIC FIRE/50
3 Brad Keselowski 5.00 12.00
7 Clint Bowyer 4.00 10.00
12 David Ragan 3.00 8.00
16 Jamie McMurray 4.00 10.00
21 Kasey Kahne 4.00 10.00
22 Kaz Grala 5.00 12.00
27 Martin Truex Jr. 3.00 8.00
28 Matt DiBenedetto 2.50 6.00
29 Matt Kenseth 4.00 10.00
35 Ryan Reed 4.00 10.00
39 Ty Dillon 4.00 10.00

2018 Panini Prime Race Used Quads Firesuit

*GOLD/25: .5X TO 1.2X BASIC FIRE/50
1 Blake Koch 3.00 8.00
2 Brandon Jones 3.00 8.00
3 Brennan Poole 3.00 8.00
4 Chase Briscoe 8.00 20.00
6 Cole Whitt 4.00 10.00
7 Elliott Sadler 3.00 8.00
8 Joey Gase 3.00 8.00
10 Matt Tifft 5.00 12.00

2018 Panini Prime Race Used Quads Sheet Metal

*GOLD/25: .5X TO 1.2X BASIC SHEET/50
1 Blake Koch 3.00 8.00
2 Brandon Jones 3.00 8.00
3 Brennan Poole 3.00 8.00
4 Chase Briscoe 8.00 20.00
5 Christopher Bell 5.00 12.00
6 Cole Whitt 4.00 10.00
7 Elliott Sadler 3.00 8.00
8 Joey Gase 3.00 8.00
9 Justin Allgaier 4.00 10.00
10 Matt Tifft 5.00 12.00

2018 Panini Prime Race Used Sheet Metal

*GOLD/25: .5X TO 1.2X BASIC SHEET/50
2 Austin Dillon 5.00 12.00
3 Brad Keselowski 5.00 12.00
4 Bubba Wallace 4.00 10.00
5 Chase Elliott 5.00 12.00
7 Clint Bowyer 4.00 10.00
10 Dale Earnhardt Jr 8.00 20.00
11 Daniel Suarez 4.00 10.00
12 David Ragan 3.00 8.00
13 Denny Hamlin 4.00 10.00
14 Elliott Sadler 2.50 6.00
15 Erik Jones 4.00 10.00
16 Jamie McMurray 4.00 10.00
17 Jimmie Johnson 6.00 15.00
18 Joey Logano 4.00 10.00
19 John Hunter Nemechek 3.00 8.00
20 Justin Allgaier 3.00 8.00
21 Kasey Kahne 4.00 10.00
22 Kaz Grala 5.00 12.00
23 Kevin Harvick 5.00 12.00
24 Kurt Busch 3.00 8.00
25 Kyle Busch 5.00 12.00
26 Kyle Larson 6.00 15.00
29 Matt Kenseth 4.00 10.00
30 Michael Annett 4.00 10.00
31 Paul Menard 2.50 6.00
33 Ryan Blaney 3.00 8.00
34 Ryan Newman 3.00 8.00
36 Spencer Gallagher 4.00 10.00
37 Tony Stewart 6.00 15.00
38 Trevor Bayne 4.00 10.00
39 Ty Dillon 4.00 10.00
40 William Byron 4.00 10.00

2018 Panini Prime Race Used Tires

*GOLD/25: .5X TO 1.2X BASIC TIRE/50
4 Bubba Wallace 4.00 10.00
5 Chase Elliott 5.00 12.00
10 Dale Earnhardt Jr 8.00 20.00
17 Jimmie Johnson 6.00 15.00
23 Kevin Harvick 5.00 12.00
25 Kyle Busch 5.00 12.00
27 Martin Truex Jr. 3.00 8.00
33 Ryan Blaney 3.00 8.00
37 Tony Stewart 6.00 15.00
40 William Byron 4.00 10.00

2018 Panini Prime Race Used Trios Firesuit

*GOLD/25: .5X TO 1.2X BASIC FIRE/50
1 Kevin Harvick 6.00 15.00
2 Jimmie Johnson 8.00 20.00
4 Tony Stewart 8.00 20.00
6 Bubba Wallace 5.00 12.00
8 Kyle Busch 6.00 15.00
9 Brad Keselowski 6.00 15.00
10 Joey Logano 5.00 12.00
12 John Hunter Nemechek 4.00 10.00
13 Paul Menard 3.00 8.00
14 Ryan Blaney 4.00 10.00
15 Ryan Newman 4.00 10.00
16 Jamie McMurray 5.00 12.00
17 Martin Truex Jr. 4.00 10.00
20 Kasey Kahne 5.00 12.00

2018 Panini Prime Race Used Trios Sheet Metal

*GOLD/25: .5X TO 1.2X BASIC SHEET/50
1 Kevin Harvick 6.00 15.00
2 Jimmie Johnson 8.00 20.00
3 Dale Earnhardt Jr 10.00 25.00
4 Tony Stewart 8.00 20.00
5 Chase Elliott 6.00 15.00
6 Bubba Wallace 5.00 12.00
7 William Byron 5.00 12.00
8 Kyle Busch 6.00 15.00
9 Brad Keselowski 6.00 15.00
RUTJL Joey Logano 5.00 12.00
11 Denny Hamlin 5.00 12.00
12 John Hunter Nemechek 4.00 10.00
13 Paul Menard 3.00 8.00
14 Ryan Blaney 4.00 10.00
15 Ryan Newman 4.00 10.00
16 Jamie McMurray 5.00 12.00
17 Martin Truex Jr. 4.00 10.00
18 Erik Jones 5.00 12.00
19 Michael Annett 5.00 12.00
20 Kasey Kahne 5.00 12.00

2018 Panini Prime Race Used Trios Tire

*GOLD/25: .5X TO 1.2X BASIC TIRE/50
1 Kevin Harvick 6.00 15.00
2 Jimmie Johnson 8.00 20.00
4 Tony Stewart 8.00 20.00
5 Chase Elliott 6.00 15.00
6 Bubba Wallace 5.00 12.00
7 William Byron 5.00 12.00
8 Kyle Busch 6.00 15.00
10 Joey Logano 5.00 12.00
11 Denny Hamlin 5.00 12.00
12 John Hunter Nemechek 4.00 10.00
13 Paul Menard 3.00 8.00
14 Ryan Blaney 4.00 10.00
15 Ryan Newman 4.00 10.00
16 Jamie McMurray 5.00 12.00
17 Martin Truex Jr. 4.00 10.00
18 Erik Jones 5.00 12.00
19 Michael Annett 5.00 12.00
20 Kasey Kahne 5.00 12.00

2018 Panini Prime Shadowbox Signatures

*GOLD/50: .5X TO 1.2X BASIC AU/99
*GOLD/25: .5X TO 1.2X BASIC AU/50
1 Danica Patrick/25
2 Mark Martin/25 12.00 30.00
3 Dale Earnhardt Jr/25
4 Joey Logano/99
5 Kurt Busch/99 12.00 30.00
7 Carl Edwards/25 15.00 40.00
8 Matt Kenseth/99 5.00 12.00
9 Darrell Waltrip/99 8.00 20.00
10 Rusty Wallace/99 8.00 20.00
11 Kasey Kahne/99 5.00 12.00
12 Dale Jarrett/50 6.00 15.00
13 Bill Elliott/99 8.00 20.00
14 Austin Dillon/99 6.00 15.00
15 Kevin Harvick/25
16 Denny Hamlin/99 5.00 12.00
17 Clint Bowyer/99 5.00 12.00
18 Richard Petty/25
19 Jimmie Johnson/25
20 Kyle Busch/25 20.00 50.00

2018 Panini Prime Signature Swatches

*GOLD/50: .5X TO 1.2X BASIC MEM AU/99
*GOLD/25-34: .6X TO 1.5X BASIC MEM AU/99
*GOLD/25-34: .5X TO 1.2X BASIC MEM AU/39-60
*GOLD/15-22: .6X TO 1.5X BASIC MEM AU/39-60
SSCE Carl Edwards/25
2 Cole Whitt/99 5.00 12.00
SSRC Ross Chastain/99
4 Greg Biffle/49
5 Terry Labonte/60 8.00 20.00
6 Bubba Wallace/43
7 Joey Logano/60
8 Jimmie Johnson/25
9 Chase Elliott/25 50.00 100.00
10 Aric Almirola/25 8.00 20.00
11 Dale Earnhardt Jr/25
12 Jamie McMurray/99 6.00 15.00
13 Kyle Busch/25
14 Kyle Larson/99 10.00 25.00
15 Martin Truex Jr./99 5.00 12.00
16 William Byron/99 12.00 30.00
17 Ryan Blaney/39
18 Danica Patrick/25
20 Kevin Harvick/25

2018 Panini Prime Triple Material Autographs

*GOLD/37-50: .5X TO 1.2X BASIC MEM AU/99
*GOLD/37-50: .4X TO 1X BASIC MEM AU/50
*GOLD/25-28: .6X TO 1.5X BASIC MEM AU/99
*GOLD/25-28: .5X TO 1.2X BASIC MEM AU/49-60
*GOLD/15: .6X TO 1.5X BASIC MEM AU/43
1 Dale Earnhardt Jr/25
3 Matt Kenseth/99 8.00 20.00
4 Denny Hamlin/99 8.00 20.00
5 Corey LaJoie/99 6.00 15.00
6 Ross Chastain/99
7 Spencer Gallagher/49 EXCH 10.00 25.00
8 Kaz Grala/30
9 Kurt Busch/99 6.00 15.00
10 Austin Dillon/50 12.00 30.00
11 Kevin Harvick/25
12 Clint Bowyer/60 10.00 25.00
13 Brad Keselowski/99 10.00 25.00
14 Kyle Larson/50 15.00 40.00
15 Joey Logano/50
16 Martin Truex Jr./99 6.00 15.00
17 William Byron/50 20.00 50.00
18 Ryan Newman/50 8.00 20.00
19 Ryan Blaney/50
20 Chase Elliott/25 60.00 125.00
21 Aric Almirola/25 10.00 25.00
22 Bubba Wallace/43
23 Paul Menard/35
24 Ricky Stenhouse Jr/25
25 Trevor Bayne/25

2019 Panini Prime Clear Silhouettes

*GOLD/25: .6X TO 1.5X BASIC JSY/99
*GOLD/18: .8X TO 2X BASIC JSY/99
1 Jimmie Johnson/99 5.00 12.00
2 Kevin Harvick/99 4.00 10.00
3 Chase Elliott/99 4.00 10.00
4 Dale Earnhardt Jr./99 6.00 15.00
5 Tony Stewart/25 8.00 20.00
6 Clint Bowyer/99 3.00 8.00
7 Austin Dillon/99 3.00 8.00
8 Kyle Busch/99 4.00 10.00
9 Kyle Larson/99 5.00 12.00
10 Brad Keselowski/99 5.00 12.00
11 Bubba Wallace/99 3.00 8.00
12 Denny Hamlin/99 3.00 8.00
13 Joey Logano/99 3.00 8.00
14 Martin Truex Jr./99 2.50 6.00
15 Ryan Newman/99 2.50 6.00
16 Ryan Blaney/99 2.50 6.00
17 William Byron/99 3.00 8.00
18 Aric Almirola/99 2.50 6.00
19 Alex Bowman/99 3.00 8.00
20 Kurt Busch/99 2.50 6.00

2019 Panini Prime Clear Silhouettes Dual

*GOLD/25: .6X TO 1.5X BASIC JSY/99
1 Kurt Busch 2.50 6.00
2 Kyle Busch 4.00 10.00
3 Kevin Harvick 4.00 10.00
4 Aric Almirola 2.50 6.00
5 Chase Elliott 4.00 10.00
6 Denny Hamlin 3.00 8.00
7 Dale Earnhardt Jr. 6.00 15.00
8 Clint Bowyer 3.00 8.00
9 Martin Truex Jr. 2.50 6.00
10 Ty Dillon 3.00 8.00

2019 Panini Prime Dual Material Autographs

*GOLD/25: .6X TO 1.5X BASIC MEM AU/75-99
*GOLD/25: .5X TO 1.2X BASIC MEM AU/43-49
*GOLD/18: .5X TO 1.2X BASIC MEM AU/25
1 Gray Gaulding/15
2 Joey Logano/75 6.00 15.00
3 Matt Kenseth/99 6.00 15.00
7 Ty Dillon/99 EXCH 6.00 15.00
8 Trevor Bayne/99 6.00 15.00
9 Tony Stewart/25
11 Ryan Newman/49
12 Ryan Blaney/25 EXCH 8.00 20.00
13 Ross Chastain/99 EXCH 6.00 15.00
15 Erik Jones/49 8.00 20.00
17 Alex Bowman/20 12.00 30.00
19 Kevin Harvick/25 12.00 30.00
20 Kasey Kahne/99
21 Jamie McMurray/25
22 Austin Dillon/50 EXCH 10.00 25.00
23 Bubba Wallace/43 EXCH 8.00 20.00
25 Kyle Busch/25

2019 Panini Prime Hats Off Headband

1 Aric Almirola/36 3.00 8.00
2 Kevin Harvick/26 6.00 15.00
3 Kevin Harvick/36 5.00 12.00
4 Alex Bowman/28 5.00 12.00
5 Kyle Larson/36 6.00 15.00
6 Chase Elliott/25 6.00 15.00
7 William Byron/30 5.00 12.00
8 Kevin Harvick/26 6.00 15.00
9 Denny Hamlin/26 5.00 12.00
10 Austin Dillon/18 8.00 20.00
11 Clint Bowyer/31 5.00 12.00
12 Ryan Blaney/35 3.00 8.00
13 Bubba Wallace/31 5.00 12.00
14 Erik Jones/25 5.00 12.00
15 Brad Keselowski/28 6.00 15.00
16 Chase Elliott/30 6.00 15.00

2019 Panini Prime Jumbo Material Signatures Sheet Metal

1 Alex Bowman/25 10.00 25.00
4 Brad Keselowski/99 12.00 30.00
7 Clint Bowyer/25 10.00 25.00
8 Dale Earnhardt Jr./25 30.00 60.00
11 Denny Hamlin/25
12 Erik Jones/25 10.00 25.00
15 Joey Logano/25 10.00 25.00
16 Kasey Kahne/25
18 Kurt Busch/25 8.00 20.00
19 Kyle Busch/18
20 Kyle Larson/25
21 Martin Truex Jr./19 30.00 60.00
24 Ryan Newman/25
25 William Byron/24 12.00 30.00

2019 Panini Prime Jumbo Material Signatures Tire

3 Austin Dillon/50 10.00 25.00
4 Brad Keselowski/99 8.00 20.00
6 Chase Elliott/25 12.00 30.00
7 Clint Bowyer/50 8.00 20.00
11 Denny Hamlin/75
12 Erik Jones/49 8.00 20.00
13 Jamie McMurray/25 10.00 25.00
14 Jimmie Johnson/25 30.00 60.00
15 Joey Logano/75 6.00 15.00
16 Kasey Kahne/99
17 Kevin Harvick/35 10.00 25.00
18 Kurt Busch/99 5.00 12.00
19 Kyle Busch/25 12.00 30.00
21 Martin Truex Jr./25
23 Ryan Blaney/25 8.00 20.00
24 Ryan Newman/99
25 William Byron/99 6.00 15.00

2019 Panini Prime Legacy Signatures

*GOLD/25: .6X TO 1.5X BASIC AU/99
*GOLD/25: .5X TO 1.2X BASIC AU/43
1 Mark Martin/99 10.00 25.00
2 Terry Labonte/99 12.00 30.00
3 Bill Elliott/99 8.00 20.00
4 Dale Jarrett/99 5.00 12.00
5 Rusty Wallace/99 5.00 12.00
6 Darrell Waltrip/99 8.00 20.00
7 Ned Jarrett/99 4.00 10.00
8 Richard Petty/43 15.00 40.00
9 Bobby Allison/25
10 Bruton Smith/99

2019 Panini Prime NASCAR Shadowbox Signatures Car Number

*SPONSOR/25: .6X TO 1.5X CAR # AU/75-99
*SPONSOR/25: .5X TO 1.2X CAR # AU/42-50
*SPONSOR/18-24: .8X TO 2X CAR # AU/75-99
*SPONSOR/18-24: .6X TO 1.5X CAR # AU/42-50
*SPONSOR/18-24: .5X TO 1.2X CAR # AU/25
2 William Byron/99 8.00 20
3 Ty Dillon/99 EXCH 5.00 12.
5 Ryan Newman/49 5.00 12
6 Alex Bowman/88 5.00 12
8 Austin Dillon/50
9 Brad Keselowski/99 6.00 15.
10 Bubba Wallace/43 EXCH 6.00 15.
11 Chase Elliott/25
12 Clint Bowyer/50 6.00 15.
13 John Hunter Nemechek/99 4.00 10.
14 Dale Earnhardt Jr./25 30.00 60.
16 Denny Hamlin/99
17 Erik Jones/99 5.00 12.
20 Jimmie Johnson/25 30.00 60.
21 Joey Logano/75 5.00 12.
22 Kasey Kahne/99 5.00 12.
24 Kevin Harvick/25
25 Kurt Busch/99 4.00 10.
26 Kyle Busch/25 30.00 60.
27 Kyle Larson/42 10.00 25.
28 Martin Truex Jr./49 8.00 20.
30 Ross Chastain/99 EXCH 6.00 15.

2019 Panini Prime Prime Cars D Cut Signatures

*GOLD/25: .6X TO 1.5X BASIC AU/99
*GOLD/25: .5X TO 1.2X BASIC AU/43-50
*GOLD/18-24: .6X TO 1.5X BASIC AU/43-50
*GOLD/18-24: .5X TO 1.2X BASIC AU/25
1 Kurt Busch/99 4.00 10.
2 Brad Keselowski/99 6.00 15.
3 Austin Dillon/25
4 Kevin Harvick/25
5 Ryan Newman/49 5.00 12.
7 Chase Elliott/25
8 William Byron/49 10.00 25.
9 Jimmie Johnson/25 30.00 60.
10 Dale Earnhardt Jr./25 30.00 60.
11 Bubba Wallace/43 EXCH 6.00 15.
15 Clint Bowyer/50 6.00 15.
16 Gray Gaulding/15
17 Joey Logano/50 6.00 15.
18 Kyle Busch/25 30.00 60.
20 Martin Truex Jr./25 10.00 25.

2019 Panini Prime Prime Jumb Prime Colors

1 Alex Bowman/20 100.00 200.
5 Bobby Labonte/29
7 Brad Keselowski/24
9 Chase Elliott/22 40.00 80.
11 Chris Buescher/18 12.00 30.
12 Christopher Bell/15
14 Clint Bowyer/20 25.00 50.
15 Clint Bowyer/17 25.00 50.
17 Cole Custer/15
18 Dale Earnhardt Jr./16
22 Daniel Hemric/20
24 David Ragan/16
29 Erik Jones/18 15.00 40.
34 Jeb Burton/15 12.00 30.
35 Jimmie Johnson/24 25.00 60.
36 Jimmie Johnson/22 25.00 60.
42 Kasey Kahne/21 15.00 40.
44 Kevin Harvick/19
45 Kurt Busch/16
47 Kyle Busch/22 100.00 200.
49 Mark Martin/16
50 Martin Truex Jr./15
51 Martin Truex Jr./15
53 Matt DiBenedetto/16 10.00 25.
57 Michael Annett/20 15.00 40.
59 Michael McDowell/15
66 Ross Chastain/20
67 Ross Chastain/18
70 Ryan Newman/17 12.00 30.
72 Ryan Newman/17 12.00 30.
73 Ryan Preece/25 12.00 30.
74 Terry Labonte/18 60.00 125.
75 Tony Stewart/15
76 Tony Stewart/20
82 William Byron/15
83 William Byron/15

2019 Panini Prime Prime Names Die Cut Signatures

*GOLD/25: .6X TO 1.5X BASIC AU/99
*GOLD/25: .5X TO 1.2X BASIC AU/40-50
*GOLD/15: .5X TO 1.2X BASIC AU/25
1 Bill Elliott/25 12.00 30.
2 Bobby Allison/15
3 Dale Jarrett/99 5.00 12.
4 Darrell Waltrip/99 8.00 20.
5 Hailie Deegan/49 150.00 250.
7 Joe Nemechek/99 3.00 8.
8 Kenny Wallace/40
9 Kyle Petty/99
10 Michael Waltrip/99
11 Ned Jarrett/50 5.00 12.
12 Rusty Wallace/99 5.00 12.
13 Spencer Boyd/99
14 Tanner Berryhill/25
15 Danica Patrick/25 30.00 60.

5 Mark Martin/49 12.00 30.00
7 Matt Kenseth/99
8 Greg Biffle/99 4.00 10.00
0 Richard Petty/43 15.00 40.00
1 Dale Earnhardt Jr./25 30.00 60.00
2 Tony Stewart/25
3 Jimmie Johnson/25 30.00 60.00
4 Chase Elliott/25
5 Kevin Harvick/25

2019 Panini Prime Prime Number Die Cut Signatures

GOLD/25: .6X TO 1.5X BASIC AU/88-99
GOLD/25: .5X TO 1.2X BASIC AU/42-50
GOLD/15-24: .6X TO 1.5X BASIC AU/42-50
GOLD/15-24: .5X TO 1.2X BASIC AU/25
Denny Hamlin/49
Clint Bowyer/49 6.00 15.00
Ross Chastain/99 EXCH 6.00 15.00
Kyle Busch/25 30.00 60.00
Martin Truex Jr./25 10.00 25.00
1 Joey Logano/50 6.00 15.00
2 William Byron/49 10.00 25.00
3 Joe Nemechek/99 3.00 8.00
5 Kyle Larson/42 10.00 25.00
6 Bubba Wallace/43 EXCH 6.00 15.00
7 Cody Ware/99 10.00 25.00
8 Jimmie Johnson/25 30.00 60.00
9 Alex Bowman/88 5.00 12.00
0 Tanner Berryhill/25

2019 Panini Prime Quad Materials Autographs

GOLD/25: .6X TO 1.5X BASIC INSERTS/99
GOLD/25: .5X TO 1.2X BASIC INSERTS/43-50
GOLD/18-24: .6X TO 1.5X BASIC INSERTS/43-50
GOLD/18-24: .5X TO 1.2X BASIC INSERTS/25
Alex Bowman/25 12.00 30.00
Austin Dillon/50 EXCH 12.00 30.00
Brad Keselowski/99 10.00 25.00
Bubba Wallace/43 EXCH 10.00 25.00
Chase Elliott/25
Clint Bowyer/50 10.00 25.00
Dale Earnhardt Jr./25 40.00 80.00
0 Denny Hamlin/49
1 Erik Jones/49 10.00 25.00
2 Jamie McMurray/25
3 Jimmie Johnson/25 60.00 125.00
4 Kasey Kahne/99
5 Kevin Harvick/25 15.00 40.00
6 Kyle Busch/25
8 Martin Truex Jr./49 25.00 50.00
0 Ross Chastain/99 EXCH 8.00 20.00
1 Ryan Blaney/25 EXCH 10.00 25.00
2 Ryan Newman/49
4 Trevor Bayne/99 8.00 20.00
5 William Byron/50 10.00 25.00

2019 Panini Prime Race Used Duals Firesuits

GOLD/25: .5X TO 1.2X BASIC MEM/50
William Byron 4.00 10.00
Trevor Bayne 4.00 10.00
Alex Bowman 4.00 10.00
Aric Almirola 3.00 8.00
Austin Dillon 5.00 12.00
Brad Keselowski 5.00 12.00
0 Bubba Wallace 4.00 10.00
1 Chase Elliott 5.00 12.00
2 Clint Bowyer 4.00 10.00
4 Ryan Preece 2.50 6.00
5 Daniel Hemric 4.00 10.00
6 Denny Hamlin 4.00 10.00
8 Harrison Rhodes 2.50 6.00
9 Jamie McMurray 4.00 10.00
0 Jimmie Johnson 6.00 15.00
2 Ryan Blaney 3.00 8.00
3 Kaz Grala 3.00 8.00
4 Kevin Harvick 5.00 12.00
6 Kyle Busch 5.00 12.00
9 Matt Tifft 4.00 10.00
0 Ross Chastain 4.00 10.00

2019 Panini Prime Race Used Firesuits

GOLD/25: .5X TO 1.2X BASIC MEM/39-50
Greg Biffle/39 3.00 8.00
Matt Kenseth/39 4.00 10.00
Bobby Labonte/50 4.00 10.00
Richard Petty/50 6.00 15.00
Alex Bowman/50 4.00 10.00
Aric Almirola/50 3.00 8.00
Austin Dillon/50 5.00 12.00
Brad Keselowski/50 5.00 12.00
0 Bubba Wallace/50 4.00 10.00
1 Chase Elliott/50 5.00 12.00
2 Clint Bowyer/50 4.00 10.00
3 Cole Custer/50 4.00 10.00
4 Dale Earnhardt Jr./50 8.00 20.00
5 Daniel Hemric/50 4.00 10.00
6 Denny Hamlin/50 4.00 10.00
8 Harrison Rhodes/50 2.50 6.00
9 Jamie McMurray/50 4.00 10.00
20 Jimmie Johnson/50 6.00 15.00
22 Kasey Kahne/50 4.00 10.00
23 Kaz Grala/50 3.00 8.00
24 Kevin Harvick/50 5.00 12.00
26 Kyle Busch/50 5.00 12.00
29 Matt Tifft/50 4.00 10.00
30 Ross Chastain/50 4.00 10.00
31 Ryan Blaney/50 3.00 8.00
33 Ryan Preece/50 2.50 6.00
34 Terry Labonte/50 4.00 10.00
36 Trevor Bayne/50 4.00 10.00
38 William Byron/50 4.00 10.00

2019 Panini Prime Race Used Quads Firesuits

*GOLD/25: .5X TO 1.2X BASIC MEM/50
1 William Byron/50 4.00 10.00
2 Alex Bowman/25 5.00 12.00
3 Aric Almirola/50 3.00 8.00
4 Austin Dillon/50 5.00 12.00
5 Chase Elliott/50 5.00 12.00
6 Jimmie Johnson/50 6.00 15.00
7 Joey Logano/50 4.00 10.00
8 Ryan Blaney/50 3.00 8.00
9 Kevin Harvick/50 5.00 12.00
10 Kyle Busch/50 5.00 12.00

2019 Panini Prime Race Used Quads Tires

*GOLD/25: .5X TO 1.2X BASIC MEM/50
1 William Byron 4.00 10.00
2 Alex Bowman 4.00 10.00
3 Aric Almirola 3.00 8.00
4 Austin Dillon 5.00 12.00
5 Chase Elliott 5.00 12.00
6 Jimmie Johnson 6.00 15.00
7 Joey Logano 4.00 10.00
8 Ryan Blaney 3.00 8.00
9 Kevin Harvick 5.00 12.00
10 Kyle Busch 5.00 12.00

2019 Panini Prime Race Used Sheet Metal

*GOLD/25: .5X TO 1.2X BASIC MEM/50
1 Gray Gaulding 2.50 6.00
2 Greg Biffle 3.00 8.00
3 Matt Kenseth 4.00 10.00
6 Alex Bowman 4.00 10.00
7 Aric Almirola 3.00 8.00
8 Austin Dillon 5.00 12.00
9 Brad Keselowski 5.00 12.00
10 Bubba Wallace 4.00 10.00
11 Chase Elliott 5.00 12.00
12 Clint Bowyer 4.00 10.00
13 Cole Custer 4.00 10.00
14 Dale Earnhardt Jr. 8.00 20.00
15 Daniel Hemric 4.00 10.00
16 Denny Hamlin 4.00 10.00
20 Jimmie Johnson 6.00 15.00
22 Kasey Kahne 4.00 10.00
23 Kaz Grala 3.00 8.00
24 Kevin Harvick 5.00 12.00
26 Kyle Busch 5.00 12.00
29 Matt Tifft 4.00 10.00
30 Ross Chastain 4.00 10.00
31 Ryan Blaney 3.00 8.00
33 Ryan Preece 2.50 6.00
35 Tony Stewart 6.00 15.00
36 Trevor Bayne 4.00 10.00
38 William Byron 4.00 10.00
39 Carl Edwards 4.00 10.00
40 Danica Patrick 8.00 20.00

2019 Panini Prime Race Used Tires

*GOLD/25: .5X TO 1.2X BASIC MEM/50
1 Gray Gaulding/50 2.50 6.00
3 Matt Kenseth/50 4.00 10.00
5 Richard Petty/25 8.00 20.00
6 Alex Bowman/50 4.00 10.00
7 Aric Almirola/50 3.00 8.00
8 Austin Dillon/50 5.00 12.00
9 Brad Keselowski/50 5.00 12.00
10 Bubba Wallace/50 4.00 10.00
11 Chase Elliott/50 5.00 12.00
12 Clint Bowyer/50 4.00 10.00
13 Cole Custer/50 4.00 10.00
15 Daniel Hemric/50 4.00 10.00
16 Denny Hamlin/50 4.00 10.00
20 Jimmie Johnson/50 6.00 15.00
22 Kasey Kahne/50 4.00 10.00
24 Kevin Harvick/50 5.00 12.00
26 Kyle Busch/50 5.00 12.00
29 Matt Tifft/50 4.00 10.00
30 Ross Chastain/50 4.00 10.00
31 Ryan Blaney/50 3.00 8.00
33 Ryan Preece/50 2.50 6.00
35 Tony Stewart/27 8.00 20.00
36 Trevor Bayne/50 4.00 10.00
38 William Byron/50 4.00 10.00
39 Carl Edwards/50 4.00 10.00
40 Danica Patrick/50 8.00 20.00

2019 Panini Prime Race Used Trios Firesuits

*GOLD/25: .5X TO 1.2X BASIC MEM/50
1 Matt Tifft/50 4.00 10.00
3 William Byron/50 4.00 10.00
6 Alex Bowman/25 5.00 12.00
7 Aric Almirola/50 3.00 8.00
8 Austin Dillon/50 5.00 12.00
9 Brad Keselowski/50 5.00 12.00
10 Bubba Wallace/50 4.00 10.00
11 Chase Elliott/50 5.00 12.00
12 Clint Bowyer/50 4.00 10.00
14 Ryan Preece/50 2.50 6.00
15 Daniel Hemric/50 4.00 10.00
16 Kevin Harvick/50 5.00 12.00
18 Ryan Blaney/50 3.00 8.00
19 Kyle Busch/50 5.00 12.00

2019 Panini Prime Race Used Trios Sheet Metal

*GOLD/25: .5X TO 1.2X BASIC MEM/50
1 Matt Tifft 4.00 10.00
3 William Byron 4.00 10.00
8 Austin Dillon 5.00 12.00
9 Brad Keselowski 5.00 12.00
10 Bubba Wallace 4.00 10.00
12 Clint Bowyer 4.00 10.00
14 Ryan Preece 2.50 6.00
15 Daniel Hemric 4.00 10.00
16 Kevin Harvick 5.00 12.00
18 Ryan Blaney 3.00 8.00
19 Kyle Busch 5.00 12.00

2019 Panini Prime Race Used Trios Tires

*GOLD/25: .5X TO 1.2X BASIC MEM/50
1 Matt Tifft 4.00 10.00
3 William Byron 4.00 10.00
6 Alex Bowman 4.00 10.00
7 Aric Almirola 3.00 8.00
8 Austin Dillon 5.00 12.00
9 Brad Keselowski 5.00 12.00
10 Bubba Wallace 4.00 10.00
11 Chase Elliott 5.00 12.00
12 Clint Bowyer 4.00 10.00
14 Ryan Preece 2.50 6.00
15 Daniel Hemric 4.00 10.00
16 Kevin Harvick 5.00 12.00
18 Ryan Blaney 3.00 8.00
19 Kyle Busch 5.00 12.00

2019 Panini Prime Shadowbox Signatures

*GOLD/25: .6X TO 1.5X BASIC AU/75-99
*GOLD/25: .5X TO 1.2X BASIC AU/43-50
1 Danica Patrick/50 25.00 50.00
2 Bill Elliott/25 12.00 30.00
3 Carl Edwards/99 8.00 20.00
4 Clint Bowyer/50 6.00 15.00
5 Dale Earnhardt Jr./25 30.00 60.00
6 Dale Jarrett/99 5.00 12.00
7 Darrell Waltrip/99 8.00 20.00
8 Derrike Cope/25
9 Matt Kenseth/99
10 Jamie McMurray/25 8.00 20.00
11 Kasey Kahne/75 5.00 12.00
12 Mark Martin/49 12.00 30.00
13 Michael Waltrip/99
14 Richard Petty/43 15.00 40.00
15 Rusty Wallace/99 5.00 12.00
16 Greg Biffle/99 4.00 10.00
17 Jimmie Johnson/25 30.00 60.00
18 Hailie Deegan/75 100.00 200.00
19 Tony Stewart/25
20 Dale Earnhardt Jr./25 30.00 60.00

2019 Panini Prime Timeline Signatures

*NAME/25: .5X TO 1.2X BASIC MEM AU/49-50
*NAME/18-24: .8X TO 2X BASIC MEM AU/99
*NAME/18-24: .5X TO 1.2X BASIC MEM AU/25
1 Gray Gaulding/15
2 Kevin Harvick/25 12.00 30.00
3 Jimmie Johnson/25 60.00 125.00
4 Dale Earnhardt Jr./25 30.00 60.00
5 Chase Elliott/25
6 Clint Bowyer/49 8.00 20.00
7 Kyle Busch/25
8 Denny Hamlin/49
9 Joey Logano/50 8.00 20.00
10 Martin Truex Jr./25 25.00 50.00
11 Austin Dillon/25 EXCH 12.00 30.00
13 William Byron/99 6.00 15.00

2016 Panini Prizm

1A Jamie McMurray .50 1.25
1B Donnie Allison SP 1.25 3.00
2A Brad Keselowski .60 1.50
2B Rusty Wallace SP 1.50 4.00
3 Austin Dillon .60 1.50
4 Kevin Harvick .60 1.50
5A Kasey Kahne .50 1.25
5B Terry Labonte SP 1.50 4.00
6A Trevor Bayne .50 1.25
6B Mark Martin SP 1.50 4.00
7 Alex Bowman .50 1.25
8 Dale Earnhardt Jr. 1.00 2.50
9A Sam Hornish Jr. .40 1.00
9B Bill Elliott SP 2.50 6.00
10 Danica Patrick 1.00 2.50
11 Denny Hamlin .50 1.25
12 David Ragan .40 1.00
13 Casey Mears .30 .75
14 Tony Stewart .75 2.00
15 Clint Bowyer .50 1.25
16 Greg Biffle .40 1.00
17A Ricky Stenhouse Jr. .50 1.25
17B Darrell Waltrip SP 2.50 6.00
18 Kyle Busch .60 1.50
19 Carl Edwards .50 1.25
20 Matt Kenseth .50 1.25
21 Jeb Burton .40 1.00
22A Joey Logano .50 1.25
22B Bobby Allison SP 1.25 3.00
23 Bobby Labonte .50 1.25
24 Chase Elliott .60 1.50
25 Martin Truex Jr. .40 1.00
26 Ryan Blaney .40 1.00
27 Paul Menard .30 .75
28 Justin Allgaier .40 1.00
29 Landon Cassill .40 1.00
30 Kurt Busch .40 1.00
31 Ryan Newman .40 1.00
32 Jeffrey Earnhardt .50 1.25
33 Ty Dillon .50 1.25
34 Darrell Wallace Jr. .50 1.25
35 Chris Buescher .40 1.00
36 Kyle Larson .75 2.00
37 Aric Almirola .40 1.00
38 Brian Scott .30 .75
39 A.J. Allmendinger .50 1.25
40 Jimmie Johnson .75 2.00
41 Michael Annett .50 1.25
42 Matt DiBenedetto .30 .75
43A Josh Wise .30 .75
43B Richard Petty SP 2.50 6.00
44 Erik Jones .75 2.00
45 Regan Smith .40 1.00
46 Kurt Busch .40 1.00
47 Carl Edwards .50 1.25
48 Brad Keselowski .60 1.50
49 Chase Elliott 2.00 5.00
50 Austin Dillon .60 1.50
51 Matt Kenseth .50 1.25
52 Denny Hamlin .50 1.25
53 Jamie McMurray .50 1.25
54 Ryan Newman .40 1.00
55 Kevin Harvick .60 1.50
56 Kasey Kahne .50 1.25
57 Danica Patrick 1.00 2.50
58 Tony Stewart .75 2.00
59 Kyle Busch .60 1.50
60 Joey Logano .50 1.25
61 Jimmie Johnson .75 2.00
62 Martin Truex Jr. .40 1.00
63 Dale Earnhardt Jr. 1.00 2.50
64 Kevin Harvick .60 1.50
65 Jimmie Johnson .75 2.00
66 Kyle Busch .60 1.50
67 Tony Stewart .75 2.00
68 Kurt Busch .40 1.00
69 Matt Kenseth .50 1.25
70 Brad Keselowski .60 1.50
71 Terry Labonte .50 1.25
72 Richard Petty .75 2.00
73 Dale Earnhardt Jr. 1.00 2.50
74 Denny Hamlin .50 1.25
75 Tony Stewart .75 2.00
76 Kyle Busch .60 1.50
77 Joey Logano .50 1.25
78 Kevin Harvick .60 1.50
79 Kasey Kahne .50 1.25
80 Danica Patrick 1.00 2.50
81 Jimmie Johnson .75 2.00
82 Brad Keselowski .60 1.50
83 Ryan Newman .40 1.00
84 Ricky Stenhouse Jr. .50 1.25
85 Kyle Larson .75 2.00
86 Clint Bowyer .50 1.25
87 Austin Dillon .60 1.50
88 Carl Edwards .50 1.25
89 Jamie McMurray .50 1.25
90 Paul Menard .30 .75
91 Richard Petty .75 2.00
92 Richard Petty .75 2.00
93 Darrell Waltrip .75 2.00
94 David Pearson .50 1.25
95 Rusty Wallace .50 1.25
96 Bobby Allison .40 1.00
97 Bill Elliott .75 2.00
98 Terry Labonte .50 1.25
99 Ned Jarrett .40 1.00
100 Chase Drivers .75 2.00

2016 Panini Prizm Prizms

*PRIZM: 1.2X TO 3X BASIC CARDS
*PRIZM: .5X TO 1.2X BASIC SP

2016 Panini Prizm Prizms Blue Flag

*BLUE/99: 2X TO 5X BASIC CARDS

2016 Panini Prizm Prizms Green Flag

*GREEN/149: 1.5X TO 4X BASIC CARDS

2016 Panini Prizm Prizms Rainbow

57 Danica Patrick 30.00 60.00

2016 Panini Prizm Prizms Red Flag

*RED/75: 2X TO 5X BASIC CARDS

2016 Panini Prizm Prizms Red White and Blue

*RWB: 1.5X TO 4X BASIC CARDS

2016 Panini Prizm Autographs Prizms

2 Alex Bowman 4.00 10.00
3 Aric Almirola 3.00 8.00
4 Austin Dillon 5.00 12.00
6 Brandon Jones 4.00 10.00
7 Brendan Gaughan 2.50 6.00
9 Brian Scott 2.50 6.00
11 Casey Mears 2.50 6.00
12 Chris Buescher 3.00 8.00
13 Christopher Bell
14 Clint Bowyer 4.00 10.00
15 Cole Custer
17 Collin Cabre 3.00 8.00
19 Daniel Hemric 4.00 10.00
20 Daniel Suarez 10.00 25.00
21 David Gilliland 2.50 6.00
22 Darrell Wallace Jr. 4.00 10.00
26 Elliott Sadler 2.50 6.00
27 Erik Jones 30.00 60.00
28 Greg Biffle 3.00 8.00
30 Jamie McMurray 4.00 10.00
32 Jeb Burton 3.00 8.00
33 Jeffrey Earnhardt 4.00 10.00
35 John Hunter Nemechek 3.00 8.00
37 Kate Dallenbach 30.00 60.00
39 Kurt Busch 3.00 8.00
40 Kyle Benjamin 4.00 10.00
41 Kyle Larson
42 Landon Cassill 3.00 8.00
43 Martin Truex Jr. 8.00 20.00
44 Matt DiBenedetto 2.50 6.00
45 Michael Annett 4.00 10.00
48 Paul Menard 2.50 6.00
49 Regan Smith 3.00 8.00
50 Ricky Stenhouse Jr. 4.00 10.00
51 Rico Abreu 12.00 30.00
52 Ruben Garcia Jr. 2.50 6.00
53 Ryan Blaney 8.00 20.00
54 Ryan Newman 3.00 8.00
55 Ryan Reed 4.00 10.00
56 Trevor Bayne 4.00 10.00
57 Ty Dillon 4.00 10.00
58 Tyler Reddick 4.00 10.00
59 William Byron 30.00 60.00
61 Bobby Labonte 4.00 10.00
62 Carl Edwards 8.00 20.00
63 Chase Elliott 40.00 80.00
64 Denny Hamlin 8.00 20.00
65 Joey Logano 10.00 25.00
66 Kasey Kahne 8.00 20.00
67 Kyle Busch 25.00 50.00
68 Matt Kenseth 6.00 15.00
69 Danica Patrick
71 Bobby Allison 3.00 8.00
72 Kevin Harvick 12.00 30.00
73 Josh Wise 2.50 6.00
74 Dale Earnhardt Jr. 30.00 60.00
76 Danny Myers
77 Ryan Truex 3.00 8.00
78 Donnie Allison 3.00 8.00
79 Ernie Irvan 4.00 10.00
80 David Ragan 3.00 8.00
82 Ned Jarrett 3.00 8.00
83 Jimmie Johnson 30.00 60.00
84 Rusty Wallace 10.00 25.00

2016 Panini Prizm Autographs Prizms Blue Flag

69 Danica Patrick/15 200.00 300.00

2016 Panini Prizm Autographs Prizms Rainbow

69 Danica Patrick 100.00 200.00

2016 Panini Prizm Autographs Prizms Red White and Blue

*RWB/25: .8X TO 2X BASIC AU

2016 Panini Prizm Blowing Smoke

*PRIZM: .6X TO 1.5X BASIC INSERTS
1 Terry Labonte 1.00 2.50
2 Kevin Harvick 1.25 3.00
3 Kyle Busch 1.25 3.00
4 Dale Earnhardt Jr. 2.00 5.00
5 Jimmie Johnson 1.50 4.00
6 Tony Stewart 1.50 4.00
7 Rusty Wallace 1.00 2.50
8 Richard Petty 1.50 4.00
9 Carl Edwards 1.00 2.50
10 Joey Logano 1.00 2.50
11 Brad Keselowski 1.25 3.00
12 Matt Kenseth 1.00 2.50

2016 Panini Prizm Champions

*PRIZM: .6X TO 1.5X BASIC INSERTS
1 Richard Petty 2.50 6.00
2 Terry Labonte 1.50 4.00
3 Jimmie Johnson 2.50 6.00
4 Darrell Waltrip 2.50 6.00
5 Tony Stewart 2.50 6.00

2016 Panini Prizm Competitors

*PRIZMS: .6X TO1.5X BASIC INSERTS
1 Dale Earnhardt Jr. 2.00 5.00
2 Kyle Busch 1.25 3.00
3 Danica Patrick 2.00 5.00
4 Jimmie Johnson 1.50 4.00
5 Tony Stewart 1.50 4.00
6 Carl Edwards 1.00 2.50
7 Joey Logano 1.00 2.50
8 Denny Hamlin 1.00 2.50
9 Kasey Kahne 1.00 2.50

2016 Panini Prizm Firesuit Fabrics

*GREEN/99: .5X TO 1.2X BASIC FIRE/149
*GREEN/35: .4X TO 1X BASIC FIRE/50
*GREEN/25: .5X TO 1.2X BASIC FIRE/50
*RED/25: .8X TO 2X BASIC FIRE/149
1 Dale Earnhardt Jr./50 10.00 25.00
2 Jimmie Johnson/50 8.00 20.00
3 Kyle Busch/149 4.00 10.00
4 Matt Kenseth/149 3.00 8.00
5 Matt DiBenedetto/149 2.00 5.00
6 Bobby Labonte/149 3.00 8.00
7 Ricky Stenhouse Jr./149 3.00 8.00
8 Carl Edwards/149 3.00 8.00
9 Chase Elliott/50 6.00 15.00
10 Erik Jones/149 5.00 12.00
11 Denny Hamlin/149 3.00 8.00
12 Jamie McMurray/149 3.00 8.00
13 John Hunter Nemechek/149 2.50 6.00
14 Ryan Newman/149 2.50 6.00
15 Paul Menard/149 2.00 5.00
16 Jeb Burton/149 2.50 6.00
17 Aric Almirola/149 2.50 6.00
18 Kasey Kahne/50 5.00 12.00
19 Kyle Larson/149 5.00 12.00
20 Greg Biffle/149 2.50 6.00
21 Danica Patrick/50 12.00 30.00

2016 Panini Prizm Firesuit Fabrics Prizms Blue Flag

*BLUE/75: .5X TO 1.2X BASIC FIRE/149
*BLUE/15: .6X TO 1.5X BASIC FIRE/50
21 Danica Patrick/15 40.00 80.00

2016 Panini Prizm Machinery

*PRIZMS:.6 X TO 1.5X BASIC INSERTS
1 Dale Earnhardt Jr. 2.00 5.00
2 Danica Patrick 2.00 5.00
3 Jimmie Johnson 1.50 4.00
4 Tony Stewart 1.50 4.00
5 Kasey Kahne 1.00 2.50
6 Kevin Harvick 1.25 3.00
7 Matt Kenseth 1.00 2.50
8 Martin Truex Jr. .75 2.00
9 Clint Bowyer 1.00 2.50

2016 Panini Prizm Patented Penmanship Prizms

2 Dale Earnhardt Jr. 40.00 80.00
3 Jimmie Johnson 30.00 60.00
4 Kevin Harvick 10.00 25.00
5 Mark Martin 4.00 10.00
6 Terry Labonte 8.00 20.00
8 Bobby Allison 3.00 8.00
9 Richard Petty
11 Danica Patrick
12 Bill Elliott 8.00 20.00
13 Darrell Waltrip 6.00 15.00
14 Carl Edwards 10.00 25.00
15 Ernie Irvan 4.00 10.00

2016 Panini Prizm Patented Penmanship Prizms Blue Flag

11 Danica Patrick/15 75.00 150.00

2016 Panini Prizm Patented Penmanship Prizms Camo

*CAMO/94: .5X TO 1.2X BASIC AU
*CAMO/36: .6X TO 1.5X BASIC AU
*CAMO17-19: 1X TO 2.5X BASIC AU

2016 Panini Prizm Patented Penmanship Prizms Green Flag

*GREEN/75: .5X TO 1.2X BASIC AU
*GREEN/35-50: .6X TO 1.5X BASIC AU

2016 Panini Prizm Patented Penmanship Prizms Rainbow

*RAINBOW/24: .8X TO 2X BASIC AU
11 Danica Patrick 50.00 125.00

2016 Panini Prizm Patented Penmanship Prizms Red Flag

*RED/25: .8X TO 2X BASIC AU
*RED/15: 1X TO 2.5X BASIC AU

2016 Panini Prizm Patented Pennmanship Prizms Red White and Blue

*RWB/25: .8X TO 2X BASIC AU

2016 Panini Prizm Qualifying Times

*PRIZMS: .6X TO1.5X BASIC INSERTS
1 Carl Edwards 1.00 2.50
2 Kyle Busch 1.25 3.00
3 Clint Bowyer 1.00 2.50
4 Kevin Harvick 1.25 3.00
5 Matt Kenseth 1.00 2.50
6 Dale Earnhardt Jr. 2.00 5.00
7 Jimmie Johnson 1.50 4.00
8 Tony Stewart 1.50 4.00
9 Danica Patrick 2.00 5.00

2016 Panini Prizm Race Used Tire

*GREEN/99: .6X TO 1.5X BASIC TIRE
*BLUE/49: .8X TO 2X BASIC TIRE
1 Dale Earnhardt Jr. 4.00 10.00
2 Jimmie Johnson 3.00 8.00
3 Kyle Busch 2.50 6.00
4 Matt Kenseth 2.00 5.00
5 Joey Logano 2.00 5.00
6 Kevin Harvick 2.50 6.00
7 Carl Edwards 2.00 5.00
8 Brad Keselowski 2.50 6.00
9 Martin Truex Jr. 1.50 4.00
10 Ryan Newman 1.50 4.00
11 Kasey Kahne 2.00 5.00
12 Danica Patrick 6.00 15.00
13 Tony Stewart 3.00 8.00
14 Kurt Busch 1.50 4.00

2016 Panini Prizm Raising the Flag

*PRIZMS: .6X TO 1.5X BASIC INSERTS
1 Jimmie Johnson 1.50 4.00
2 Matt Kenseth 1.00 2.50
3 Kyle Busch 1.25 3.00
4 Joey Logano 1.00 2.50
5 Dale Earnhardt Jr. 2.00 5.00
6 Carl Edwards 1.00 2.50
7 Terry Labonte 1.00 2.50
8 Mark Martin 1.00 2.50
9 Tony Stewart 1.50 4.00
10 Kevin Harvick 1.25 3.00
11 Denny Hamlin 1.00 2.50
12 Kurt Busch .75 2.00

2016 Panini Prizm Winner's Circle

*PRIZM: .6X TO 1.5X BASIC INSERTS
1 Joey Logano .75 2.00
2 Jimmie Johnson 1.25 3.00
3 Kevin Harvick 1.00 2.50
4 Kevin Harvick 1.00 2.50
5 Brad Keselowski 1.00 2.50
6 Denny Hamlin .75 2.00
7 Jimmie Johnson 1.25 3.00
8 Matt Kenseth .75 2.00
9 Kurt Busch .60 1.50
10 Dale Earnhardt Jr. 1.50 4.00
11 Jimmie Johnson 1.25 3.00
12 Carl Edwards .75 2.00
13 Jimmie Johnson 1.25 3.00
14 Martin Truex Jr. .60 1.50
15 Kurt Busch .60 1.50
16 Kyle Busch 1.00 2.50
17 Dale Earnhardt Jr. 1.50 4.00
18 Kyle Busch 1.00 2.50
19 Kyle Busch 1.00 2.50
20 Kyle Busch 1.00 2.50
21 Matt Kenseth .75 2.00
22 Joey Logano .75 2.00
23 Matt Kenseth .75 2.00
24 Joey Logano .75 2.00
25 Carl Edwards .75 2.00
26 Matt Kenseth .75 2.00
27 Denny Hamlin .75 2.00
28 Matt Kenseth .75 2.00
29 Kevin Harvick 1.00 2.50
30 Joey Logano .75 2.00
31 Joey Logano .75 2.00
32 Joey Logano .75 2.00
33 Denny Hamlin .75 2.00
34 Jimmie Johnson 1.25 3.00
35 Dale Earnhardt Jr. 1.50 4.00
36 Kyle Busch 1.00 2.50

2018 Panini Prizm

1 Chase Elliott .60 1.50
2A Tony Stewart .75 2.00
2B Tony Stewart VAR 2.50 6.00
3 Kaz Grala .60 1.50
4 Trevor Bayne .50 1.25
5A Jimmie Johnson .75 2.00
5B Jimmie Johnson VAR 2.50 6.00
6 Bill Elliott .75 2.00
7 Erik Jones .50 1.25
8 Kasey Kahne .50 1.25
9 Kurt Busch .40 1.00
10 Ryan Newman .40 1.00

11 Bubba Wallace .50 1.25
12 Darrell Waltrip .75 2.00
13 Ricky Stenhouse Jr. .50 1.25
14 Paul Menard .30 .75
15 Danica Patrick 1.00 2.50
16 Ty Dillon .50 1.25
17A Dale Jarrett .50 1.25
17B Dale Jarrett VAR 1.50 4.00
18 Brad Keselowski .60 1.50
19 Harry Gant .40 1.00
20 Austin Dillon .60 1.50
21 Alex Bowman .50 1.25
22A Dale Earnhardt Jr 1.00 2.50
22B Dale Earnhardt Jr VAR 3.00 8.00
23A Carl Edwards .50 1.25
23B Carl Edwards VAR 1.50 4.00
24 Hannah Newhouse 1.25 3.00
25A Rusty Wallace .50 1.25
25B Rusty Wallace VAR 1.50 4.00
26 Denny Hamlin .50 1.25
27 Ward Burton .30 .75
28 Ryan Blaney .40 1.00
29 Kyle Busch .60 1.50
30 Hailie Deegan 2.50 6.00
31 William Byron .50 1.25
32 Tyler Reddick .50 1.25
33 Matt Kenseth .50 1.25
34 Kyle Larson .75 2.00
35 Greg Biffle .40 1.00
36 Daniel Suarez .50 1.25
37A Terry Labonte .50 1.25
37B Terry Labonte VAR 1.50 4.00
38 Chris Buescher .40 1.00
39 Christopher Bell .50 1.25
40 Martin Truex Jr. .40 1.00
41A Mark Martin .50 1.25
41B Mark Martin VAR 1.50 4.00
42 Aric Almirola .40 1.00
43 Jeff Burton .40 1.00
44 Jamie McMurray .50 1.25
45 Joey Logano .50 1.25
46 Kevin Harvick .60 1.50
47A Richard Petty .75 2.00
47B Richard Petty VAR 2.50 6.00
48 Clint Bowyer .50 1.25
49A Kyle Petty .40 1.00
49B Kyle Petty VAR 1.25 3.00
50 Marcos Ambrose .50 1.25
51 Kevin Harvick VOR .60 1.50
52 Danica Patrick VOR 1.00 2.50
53 Jimmie Johnson VOR .75 2.00
54 Chase Elliott VOR .60 1.50
55 Tony Stewart VOR .75 2.00
56 Dale Earnhardt Jr VOR 1.00 2.50
57 Bubba Wallace VOR .50 1.25
58 Ryan Blaney VOR .40 1.00
59 Denny Hamlin VOR .50 1.25
60 Martin Truex Jr. VOR .40 1.00
61 Tony Stewart SG .75 2.00
62 Kasey Kahne SG .50 1.25
63 William Byron SG .50 1.25
64 Clint Bowyer SG .50 1.25
65 Jimmie Johnson SG .75 2.00
66 Kyle Busch SG .60 1.50
67 Danica Patrick SG 1.00 2.50
68 Chase Elliott SG .60 1.50
69 Dale Earnhardt Jr SG 1.00 2.50
70 Kevin Harvick SG .60 1.50
71 Jimmie Johnson GFOR .75 2.00
72 Dale Earnhardt Jr GFOR 1.00 2.50
73 Joey Logano GFOR .50 1.25
74 Carl Edwards GFOR .50 1.25
75 Danica Patrick GFOR 1.00 2.50
76 Ryan Newman GFOR .40 1.00
77 Kevin Harvick GFOR .60 1.50
78 Ryan Blaney GFOR .40 1.00
79 Tony Stewart GFOR .75 2.00
80 Chase Elliott GFOR .60 1.50
81 Kevin Harvick EXP .60 1.50
82 Chase Elliott EXP .60 1.50
83 Dale Earnhardt Jr EXP 1.00 2.50
84 Kurt Busch EXP .40 1.00
85 Danica Patrick EXP 1.00 2.50
86 Tony Stewart EXP .75 2.00
87 Kyle Busch EXP .60 1.50
88 Brad Keselowski EXP .60 1.50
89 Jimmie Johnson EXP .75 2.00
90 Martin Truex Jr. EXP .40 1.00

2018 Panini Prizm Prizms

*PRIZMS: 1.2X TO 3X BASIC CARDS
*PRIZMS: .5X TO 1.2X BASIC VAR

2018 Panini Prizm Prizms Blue

*BLUE/99: 2X TO 5X BASIC CARDS
*BLUE/99: .6X TO 1.5X BASIC VAR

2018 Panini Prizm Prizms Camo

*CAMO: 1.5X TO 4X BASIC CARDS
*CAMO: .5X TO 1.2X BASIC VAR

2018 Panini Prizm Prizms Green

*GREEN/149: 1.5X TO 4X BASIC CARDS
*GREEN/149: .5X TO 1.2X BASIC VAR

2018 Panini Prizm Prizms Rainbow

*RAINBOW/24: 3X TO 8X BASIC CARDS
*RAINBOW/24: 1.2X TO 3X BASIC VAR

2018 Panini Prizm Prizms Red

*RED/75: 2X TO 5X BASIC CARDS
*RED/75: .6X TO 1.5X BASIC VAR

2018 Panini Prizm Prizms Red White and Blue

*RWB: 1.5X TO 4X BASIC CARDS
*RWB: .5X TO 1.2X BASIC VAR

2018 Panini Prizm Autographs Prizms

*BLUE/75: .6X TO 1.5X BASIC AU
*BLUE/35-60: .8X TO 2X BASIC AU
*BLUE/25-30: 1X TO 2.5X BASIC AU
*BLUE/15: 1.2X TO 3X BASIC AU
*GREEN/75-99: .6X TO 1.5X BASIC AU
*GREEN/35-60: .8X TO 2X BASIC AU
*GREEN/25: 1X TO 2.5X BASIC AU
*GREEN/15: 1.2X TO 3X BASIC AU
*RAINBOW/24: 1.2X TO 3X BASIC AU
*RED/35-50: .8X TO 2X BASIC AU
*RED/25: 1X TO 2.5X BASIC AU
*RED/15: 1.2X TO 3X BASIC AU
*RWB/149-199: .5X TO 1.2X BASIC AU
*RWB/75-125: .6X TO 1.5X BASIC AU
*RWB/50: .8X TO 2X BASIC AU
*RWB/25: 1X TO 2.5X BASIC AU
*RWB/15: 1.2X TO 3X BASIC AU
1 Grant Enfinger 5.00 12.00
2 Greg Biffle 3.00 8.00
3 Erik Jones 6.00 15.00
4 Joey Gase 2.50 6.00
5 Cole Custer 4.00 10.00
6 Corey LaJoie 3.00 8.00
7 Daniel Suarez 4.00 10.00
8 Ricky Stenhouse Jr. 4.00 10.00
9 Alex Bowman 4.00 10.00
11 Paul Menard 2.50 6.00
13 Aric Almirola 4.00 10.00
14 Kyle Benjamin 2.50 6.00
15 Michael Annett 4.00 10.00
17 Todd Gilliland 3.00 8.00
18 Tyler Reddick 4.00 10.00
19 Reed Sorenson 2.50 6.00
20 Bubba Wallace 4.00 10.00
21 Dakoda Armstrong 4.00 10.00
22 Daniel Hemric 4.00 10.00
23 Jeb Burton 3.00 8.00
24 Kurt Busch EXCH 3.00 8.00
25 Matt Tifft
26 Elliott Sadler 2.50 6.00
27 Ryan Reed 4.00 10.00
28 Wendell Chavous 4.00 10.00
30 Landon Cassill 3.00 8.00
31 Matt DiBenedetto 2.50 6.00
32 Cole Whitt 3.00 8.00
33 Austin Dillon 5.00 12.00
34 Cameron Hayley 2.50 6.00
35 Kyle Larson 6.00 15.00
36 Morgan Shepherd 4.00 10.00
37 Ryan Preece 12.00 30.00
38 Ryan Truex 3.00 8.00
39 Wally Dallenbach 2.50 6.00
40 Martin Truex Jr. 3.00 8.00

2018 Panini Prizm Brilliance

*PRIZMS: .6X TO 1.5X BASIC INSERTS
1 Kyle Busch 1.25 3.00
2 Denny Hamlin 1.00 2.50
3 Joey Logano 1.00 2.50
4 Jimmie Johnson 1.50 4.00
5 Kevin Harvick 1.25 3.00
6 Dale Earnhardt Jr 2.00 5.00
7 Danica Patrick 2.00 5.00
8 Tony Stewart 1.50 4.00
9 Carl Edwards 1.00 2.50
10 Daniel Suarez 1.00 2.50

2018 Panini Prizm Fireworks

*PRIZMS: .6X TO 1.5X BASIC INSERTS
1 Jimmie Johnson 1.50 4.00
2 Richard Petty 1.50 4.00
3 Dale Earnhardt Jr 2.00 5.00
4 Danica Patrick 2.00 5.00
5 Kevin Harvick 1.25 3.00
6 Chase Elliott 1.25 3.00
7 Brad Keselowski 1.25 3.00
8 Kyle Busch 1.25 3.00
9 Martin Truex Jr. .75 2.00
10 Austin Dillon 1.25 3.00
11 Denny Hamlin 1.00 2.50
12 Bubba Wallace 1.00 2.50
13 William Byron 1.00 2.50
14 Erik Jones 1.00 2.50
15 Kasey Kahne 1.00 2.50
16 Ryan Newman .75 2.00
17 Trevor Bayne 1.00 2.50
18 Terry Labonte 1.00 2.50
19 Mark Martin 1.00 2.50
20 Dale Jarrett 1.00 2.50

2018 Panini Prizm Illumination

*PRIZMS: .6X TO 1.5X BASIC INSERTS
1 Dale Earnhardt Jr 2.00 5.00
2 Jimmie Johnson 1.50 4.00
3 Tony Stewart 1.50 4.00
4 Danica Patrick 2.00 5.00
5 Carl Edwards 1.00 2.50
6 Kevin Harvick 1.25 3.00
7 Chase Elliott 1.25 3.00
8 Ryan Blaney .75 2.00
9 Bubba Wallace 1.00 2.50
10 William Byron 1.00 2.50
11 Brad Keselowski 1.25 3.00
12 Joey Logano 1.00 2.50
13 Richard Petty 1.50 4.00
14 Martin Truex Jr. .75 2.00
15 Rusty Wallace 1.00 2.50

2018 Panini Prizm Instant Impact

*PRIZMS: .6X TO 1.5X BASIC INSERTS
1 Jimmie Johnson 1.50 4.00
2 Martin Truex Jr. .75 2.00
3 Kyle Larson 1.50 4.00
4 Ryan Newman .75 2.00
5 Brad Keselowski 1.25 3.00
6 Kevin Harvick 1.25 3.00
7 Clint Bowyer 1.00 2.50
8 Joey Logano 1.00 2.50
9 Chase Elliott 1.25 3.00
10 Ryan Blaney .75 2.00
11 William Byron 1.00 2.50
12 Bubba Wallace 1.00 2.50
13 Danica Patrick 2.00 5.00
14 Alex Bowman 1.00 2.50
15 Trevor Bayne 1.00 2.50

2018 Panini Prizm National Pride

*PRIZMS: .6X TO 1.5X BASIC INSERTS
1 Jimmie Johnson 1.50 4.00
2 Dale Earnhardt Jr 2.00 5.00
3 Kevin Harvick 1.25 3.00
4 Kyle Busch 1.25 3.00
5 Chase Elliott 1.25 3.00
6 Ryan Blaney .75 2.00
7 Denny Hamlin 1.00 2.50
8 Martin Truex Jr. .75 2.00
9 Austin Dillon 1.25 3.00
10 Clint Bowyer 1.00 2.50
11 Joey Logano 1.00 2.50
12 Ryan Newman .75 2.00
13 Alex Bowman 1.00 2.50
14 William Byron 1.00 2.50
15 Bubba Wallace 1.00 2.50

2018 Panini Prizm Patented Pennmanship Prizms

1 Bobby Labonte 4.00 10.00
2 Bobby Allison 3.00 8.00
3 Dave Blaney 2.50 6.00
4 Harry Gant 3.00 8.00
6 Dale Jarrett
8 Mark Martin
9 Matt Kenseth
10 Richard Petty
11 Jimmie Johnson
12 Carl Edwards 4.00 10.00
13 Terry Labonte
14 Tony Stewart 12.00 30.00
16 Chase Elliott 20.00 40.00
17 Dale Earnhardt Jr
18 Danica Patrick
19 Derrike Cope 3.00 8.00
20 Donnie Allison 3.00 8.00

2018 Panini Prizm Patented Pennmanship Prizms Blue

*BLUE/75: .6X TO 1.5X BASIC AU
*BLUE/35-60: .8X TO 2X BASIC AU
*BLUE/25: 1X TO 2.5X BASIC AU
11 Jimmie Johnson/25 20.00 50.00

2018 Panini Prizm Patented Pennmanship Prizms Green

*GREEN/75-99: .6X TO 1.5X BASIC AU
*GREEN/50: .8X TO 2X BASIC AU
*GREEN/25: 1X TO 2.5X BASIC AU
11 Jimmie Johnson/25 20.00 50.00

2018 Panini Prizm Patented Pennmanship Prizms Rainbow

*RAINBOW/24: 1.2X TO 3X BASIC AU
11 Jimmie Johnson 25.00 60.00
17 Dale Earnhardt Jr 75.00 150.00
18 Danica Patrick 50.00 100.00

2018 Panini Prizm Patented Pennmanship Prizms Red

*RED/50: .8X TO 2X BASIC AU
*RED/25: 1X TO 2.5X BASIC AU
11 Jimmie Johnson/25 20.00 50.00

2018 Panini Prizm Patented Pennmanship Prizms Red White and Blue

*RWB/99-125: .6X TO 1.5X BASIC AU
*RWB/60: .8X TO 2X BASIC AU
*RWB/25: 1X TO 2.5X BASIC AU
*RWB/20: 1.2X TO 3X BASIC AU
11 Jimmie Johnson/25 20.00 50.00
17 Dale Earnhardt Jr/20 75.00 150.00
18 Danica Patrick/20 50.00 100.00

2018 Panini Prizm Scripted Signatures Prizms

*BLUE/75: .6X TO 1.5X BASIC AU
*BLUE/35-60: .8X TO 2X BASIC AU
*BLUE/25: 1X TO 2.5X BASIC AU
*GREEN/75-99: .6X TO 1.5X BASIC AU
*GREEN/50-60: .8X TO 2X BASIC AU
*GREEN/25: 1X TO 2.5X BASIC AU
*RED/35-50: .8X TO 2X BASIC AU
*RED/25: 1X TO 2.5X BASIC AU
1 Grant Enfinger 5.00 12.00
2 Greg Biffle 3.00 8.00
3 Erik Jones 6.00 15.00
4 Kenny Wallace 2.50 6.00
5 David Ragan 3.00 8.00
6 Trevor Bayne 4.00 10.00
7 Brandon Jones 2.50 6.00
8 Brennan Poole 2.50 6.00
9 Casey Mears 2.50 6.00
10 Chase Briscoe 6.00 15.00
11 Chris Buescher 3.00 8.00
12 Christopher Bell 5.00 12.00
13 Cody Coughlin 4.00 10.00
14 J.J. Yeley 2.50 6.00
15 Johnny Sauter 2.50 6.00
16 Justin Allgaier 3.00 8.00
17 Kaz Grala 5.00 12.00
18 Ty Dillon 4.00 10.00
19 Dale Earnhardt Jr
20 Danica Patrick
21 Ryan Blaney 3.00 8.00
22 Ryan Newman 3.00 8.00
23 William Byron 6.00 15.00
24 Austin Cindric 4.00 10.00
25 Brad Keselowski 5.00 12.00
26 Justin Haley 8.00 20.00
27 Jeff Burton 3.00 8.00
28 Clint Bowyer 4.00 10.00
29 Collin Cabre 2.50 6.00
30 Denny Hamlin 4.00 10.00
31 Ernie Irvan 4.00 10.00
32 Harrison Burton 4.00 10.00
33 Harrison Rhodes 3.00 8.00
34 Joey Logano 4.00 10.00
35 Kasey Kahne 4.00 10.00
36 Ward Burton 2.50 6.00
37 Kyle Busch 5.00 12.00
38 Martin Truex Jr. 3.00 8.00
39 Michael McDowell 4.00 10.00
40 Kevin Harvick

2018 Panini Prizm Scripted Signatures Prizms Rainbow

*RAINBOW/24: 1.2X TO 3X BASIC AU
19 Dale Earnhardt Jr 75.00 150.00
20 Danica Patrick 50.00 100.00

2018 Panini Prizm Scripted Signatures Prizms Red White and Blue

*RWB/149-199: .5X TO 1.2X BASIC AU
*RWB/75-125: .6X TO 1.5X BASIC AU
*RWB/60: .8X TO 2X BASIC AU
*RWB/25: 1X TO 2.5X BASIC AU
*RWB/20: 1.2X TO 3X BASIC AU
19 Dale Earnhardt Jr/20 75.00 150.00
20 Danica Patrick/20 50.00 100.00

2018 Panini Prizm Stars and Stripes

*PRIZMS: .6X TO 1.5X BASIC INSERTS
1 Jamie McMurray 1.00 2.50
2 Austin Dillon 1.25 3.00
3 Kevin Harvick 1.25 3.00
4 Chase Elliott 1.25 3.00
5 Aric Almirola .75 2.00
6 Denny Hamlin 1.00 2.50
7 Ryan Blaney .75 2.00
8 Clint Bowyer 1.00 2.50
9 Danica Patrick 2.00 5.00
10 Dale Earnhardt Jr 2.00 5.00
11 Kyle Busch 1.25 3.00
12 Kurt Busch .75 2.00
13 Joey Logano 1.00 2.50
14 Ryan Newman .75 2.00
15 Jimmie Johnson 1.50 4.00

2018 Panini Prizm Team Tandems

*PRIZMS: .6X TO 1.5X BASIC INSERTS
1 A.Bowman/J.Johnson 1.50 4.00
2 C.Elliott/W.Byron 1.25 3.00
3 A.Almirola/K.Harvick 1.25 3.00
4 C.Bowyer/K.Busch 1.00 2.50
5 J.McMurray/K.Larson 1.50 4.00
6 B.Kslwski/J.Logano 1.25 3.00
7 P.Menard/R.Blaney .75 2.00
8 R.Stenhouse/T.Bayne 1.00 2.50
9 D.Hamlin/K.Busch 1.25 3.00
10 D.Suarez/E.Jones 1.00 2.50

2019 Panini Prizm

1 Kurt Busch .40 1.00
2 Brad Keselowski .60 1.50
3A Austin Dillon .60 1.50
3B Austin Dillon VAR 2.00 5.00
4A Kevin Harvick .60 1.50
4B Kevin Harvick VAR 2.00 5.00
5 Ryan Newman .40 1.00
6 Daniel Hemric .50 1.25
7A Chase Elliott .60 1.50
7B Bill Elliott 2.50 6.00
Chase Elliott VAR
8 Aric Almirola .40 1.00
9 Denny Hamlin .50 1.25
10A Ryan Blaney .40 1.00
10B Ryan Blaney VAR 1.25 3.00
11 Ty Dillon .50 1.25
12 Clint Bowyer .50 1.25
13 Ross Chastain .50 1.25
14 Ricky Stenhouse Jr. .50 1.25
15A Kyle Busch .60 1.50
15B Kyle Busch VAR 2.00 5.00
16 Martin Truex Jr. .40 1.00
17 Erik Jones .50 1.25
18 Paul Menard .30 .75
19A Joey Logano .50 1.25
19B Joey Logano VAR 1.50 4.00
20 William Byron .50 1.25
21 Corey LaJoie .40 1.00
22 Michael McDowell .50 1.25
23 Matt Tifft .50 1.25
24 Chris Buescher .40 1.00
25 David Ragan .40 1.00
26 Daniel Suarez .50 1.25
27 Kyle Larson .75 2.00
28 Bubba Wallace .50 1.25
29 Ryan Preece .30 .75
30 Jimmie Johnson .75 2.00
31 Alex Bowman .50 1.25
32 Matt DiBenedetto .30 .75
33 Tanner Berryhill .30 .75
34 Noah Gragson .30 .75
35 Justin Haley .30 .75
36 Chase Briscoe .50 1.25
37 Gray Gaulding .30 .75
38 John Hunter Nemechek .40 1.00
39 Hailie Deegan 2.00 5.00
40A Richard Petty .75 2.00
40B Richard Petty VAR 2.50 6.00
41A Dale Earnhardt Jr. 1.00 2.50
41B Dale Earnhardt Jr. VAR 3.00 8.00
42A Danica Patrick 1.00 2.50
42B Danica Patrick VAR 3.00 8.00
43A Tony Stewart .75 2.00
43B Tony Stewart VAR 2.50 6.00
44 Mark Martin .50 1.25
45 Bobby Labonte .50 1.25
46 Carl Edwards .50 1.25
47 Dale Jarrett .50 1.25
48 Kasey Kahne .50 1.25
49 Terry Labonte .50 1.25
50 Rusty Wallace .50 1.25
51 Kevin Harvick ACC .60 1.50
52 Jimmie Johnson ACC .75 2.00
53 Kyle Busch ACC .60 1.50
54 Joey Logano ACC .50 1.25
55 Kurt Busch ACC .40 1.00
56 Martin Truex Jr. ACC .40 1.00
57 Ryan Blaney ACC .40 1.00
58 Chase Elliott ACC .60 1.50
59 William Byron ACC .50 1.25
60 Ryan Newman ACC .40 1.00
61 Jimmie Johnson PROM .75 2.00
62 Joey Logano PROM .50 1.25
63 Martin Truex Jr. PROM .40 1.00
64 Kevin Harvick PROM .60 1.50
65 Chase Elliott PROM .60 1.50
66 William Byron PROM .50 1.25
67 Kyle Busch PROM .60 1.50
68 Denny Hamlin PROM .50 1.25
69 Brad Keselowski PROM .60 1.50
70 Aric Almirola PROM .40 1.00
71 Chase Elliott VEL .60 1.50
72 Denny Hamlin VEL .50 1.25
73 Jimmie Johnson VEL .75 2.00
74 Joey Logano VEL .50 1.25
75 Kevin Harvick VEL .60 1.50
76 Kyle Busch VEL .60 1.50
77 Martin Truex Jr. VEL .40 1.00
78 Austin Dillon VEL .60 1.50
79 Kurt Busch VEL .40 1.00
80 Kyle Larson VEL .75 2.00
81 Jimmie Johnson PT .75 2.00
82 Kevin Harvick PT .60 1.50
83 Kyle Busch PT .60 1.50
84 Chase Elliott PT .60 1.50
85 Martin Truex Jr. PT .40 1.00
86 Denny Hamlin PT .50 1.25
87 Aric Almirola PT .40 1.00
88 Ryan Newman PT .40 1.00
89 Daniel Hemric PT .50 1.25
90 Daniel Hemric PT .50 1.25

2019 Panini Prizm Prizms Blue

*BLUE/75: 2X TO 5X BASIC CARDS
*BLUE/75: .6X TO 1.5X BASIC VAR

2019 Panini Prizm Prizms Camo

*BLUE: 1.5X TO 4X BASIC CARDS
*BLUE: .5X TO 1.2X BASIC VAR

2019 Panini Prizm Prizms Flash

*FLASH: 1.5X TO 4X BASIC CARDS
*FLASH: .5X TO 1.2X BASIC VAR

2019 Panini Prizm Prizms Green

*GREEN/99: 2X TO 5X BASIC CARDS
*GREEN/99: .6X TO 1.5X BASIC VAR

2019 Panini Prizm Prizms Rainbow

*RAINBOW/24: 3X TO 8X BASIC CARDS
*RAINBOW/24: 1X TO 2.5X BASIC VAR

2019 Panini Prizm Prizms Red

*RED/50: 2.5X TO 6X BASIC CARDS
*RED/50: .8X TO 2X BASIC VAR

2019 Panini Prizm Prizms Red White and Blue

*RWB: 1.5X TO 4X BASIC CARDS
*RWB: .5X TO 1.2X BASIC VAR

2019 Panini Prizm Prizms White Sparkle

*SPARKLE: 1.5X TO 4X BASIC CARDS
*SPARKLE: .5X TO 1.2X BASIC VAR

2019 Panini Prizm Apex

*PRIZMS: .6X TO 1.5X BASIC INSERTS
*SPARKLE: .8X TO 2X BASIC INSERTS
1 Kevin Harvick 1.25 3.00
2 Chase Elliott 1.25 3.00
3 Ryan Blaney .75 2.00
4 Danica Patrick 2.00 5.00
5 Dale Earnhardt Jr 2.00 5.00
6 Richard Petty 1.50 4.00
7 Hailie Deegan 4.00 10.00
8 William Byron 1.00 2.50
9 Kyle Busch 1.25 3.00
10 Carl Edwards 1.00 2.50
11 Martin Truex Jr. .75 2.00
12 Joey Logano 1.00 2.50
13 Denny Hamlin 1.00 2.50
14 Tony Stewart 1.50 4.00
15 Bubba Wallace 1.00 2.50

2019 Panini Prizm Autographs Prizms

*BLUE/75: .6X TO 1.5X BASIC AU
*BLUE/35-50: .8X TO 2X BASIC AU
*CAMO: .5X TO 1.2X BASIC AU
*GREEN/75-99: .6X TO 1.5X BASIC AU
*RAINBOW/24: 1X TO 2.5X BASIC AU
*RED/35-50: .8X TO 2X BASIC AU
*RED/25: 1X TO 2.5X BASIC AU
*RWB: .5X TO 1.2X BASIC AU
1 Anthony Alfredo 2.50 6.00
2 Chase Purdy 4.00 10.00
3 Christopher Bell 8.00 20.00
4 Cody Ware 8.00 20.00
5 Cole Custer 4.00 10.00
6 Corey LaJoie 3.00 8.00
7 Daniel Hemric 4.00 10.00
8 Derek Kraus 5.00 12.00
9 Gray Gaulding 2.50 6.00
10 Harrison Rhodes 2.50 6.00
11 Justin Allgaier 3.00 8.00
12 Justin Haley 2.50 6.00
13 Matt Tifft 4.00 10.00
14 Michael Annett 4.00 10.00
15 Michael McDowell 4.00 10.00
16 Noah Gragson 2.50 6.00
18 Riley Herbst 3.00 8.00
19 Ryan Preece 2.50 6.00
20 Ryan Vargas 2.50 6.00

2019 Panini Prizm Endorsements Prizms

*BLUE/75: .6X TO 1.5X BASIC AU
*BLUE/35-50: .8X TO 2X BASIC AU
*BLUE/25: 1X TO 2.5X BASIC AU
*CAMO: .5X TO 1.2X BASIC AU
*GREEN/75-99: .6X TO 1.5X BASIC AU
*GREEN/50: .8X TO 2X BASIC AU
*RAINBOW/24: 1X TO 2.5X BASIC AU
*RED/50: .8X TO 2X BASIC AU
*RED/25: 1X TO 2.5X BASIC AU
*RWB: .5X TO 1.2X BASIC AU
1 Bill Elliott 6.00 15.00
2 Carl Edwards
3 Dale Earnhardt Jr
4 Dale Jarrett 6.00 15.00
5 Danica Patrick 25.00 50.00
6 Darrell Waltrip 6.00 15.00
7 Greg Biffle
8 Harry Gant 3.00 8.00
9 Jamie McMurray 4.00 10.00
10 Jeff Burton 3.00 8.00
11 Kasey Kahne 4.00 10.00
12 Kenny Wallace 2.50 6.00
13 Mark Martin
14 Matt Kenseth 5.00 12.00
15 Michael Waltrip 4.00 10.00
16 Ned Jarrett 5.00 12.00
17 Richard Petty 12.00 30.00
18 Rusty Wallace 4.00 10.00
19 Terry Labonte 5.00 12.00
20 Tony Stewart 25.00 50.00

2019 Panini Prizm Expert Level

*PRIZMS: .6X TO 1.5X BASIC INSERTS
*SPARKLE: .8X TO 2X BASIC INSERTS
1 Jimmie Johnson 1.50 4.00
2 Joey Logano 1.00 2.50
3 Martin Truex Jr. .75 2.00
4 Kyle Busch 1.25 3.00
5 Richard Petty 1.50 4.00
6 Kevin Harvick 1.25 3.00
7 Ryan Newman .75 2.00
8 Kurt Busch .75 2.00
9 Brad Keselowski 1.25 3.00
10 Dale Earnhardt Jr 2.00 5.00

2019 Panini Prizm Fireworks

*PRIZMS: .6X TO 1.5X BASIC INSERTS
*SPARKLE: .8X TO 2X BASIC INSERTS
1 Austin Dillon 1.25 3.00
2 Danica Patrick 2.00 5.00
3 Dale Earnhardt Jr 2.00 5.00
4 Chase Elliott 1.25 3.00
5 Hailie Deegan 4.00 10.00
6 Jimmie Johnson 1.50 4.00
7 Ryan Blaney .75 2.00
8 Kevin Harvick 1.25 3.00
9 Aric Almirola .75 2.00
10 Kyle Larson 1.50 4.00
11 Kyle Busch 1.25 3.00
12 Brad Keselowski 1.25 3.00
13 William Byron 1.00 2.50
14 Ryan Newman .75 2.00
15 Clint Bowyer 1.00 2.50
16 Denny Hamlin 1.00 2.50
17 Martin Truex Jr. .75 2.00
18 Richard Petty 1.50 4.00
19 Carl Edwards 1.00 2.50
20 Tony Stewart 1.50 4.00

2019 Panini Prizm In the Groove

*PRIZMS: .6X TO 1.5X BASIC INSERTS
*SPARKLE: .8X TO 2X BASIC INSERTS
1 Jimmie Johnson 1.50 4.00
2 Kevin Harvick 1.25 3.00
3 Chase Elliott 1.25 3.00
4 Ryan Blaney .75 2.00
5 Martin Truex Jr. .75 2.00
6 Joey Logano 1.00 2.50
7 Kyle Busch 1.25 3.00
8 Brad Keselowski 1.25 3.00
9 William Byron 1.00 2.50
10 Kurt Busch .75 2.00
11 Kyle Larson 1.50 4.00
12 Austin Dillon 1.25 3.00
13 Aric Almirola .75 2.00
14 Ryan Newman .75 2.00
15 Ross Chastain 1.00 2.50

2019 Panini Prizm National Pride

1 Tony Stewart 1.50 4.0
2 Dale Earnhardt Jr 2.00 5.0
3 Chase Elliott 1.25 3.0
4 Kevin Harvick 1.25 3.0
5 Danica Patrick 2.00 5.0
6 Brad Keselowski 1.25 3.0
7 Kyle Busch 1.25 3.0
8 Denny Hamlin 1.00 2.5
9 Jimmie Johnson 1.50 4.0
10 Richard Petty 1.50 4.0
11 Carl Edwards 1.00 2.5
12 Kurt Busch .75 2.0
13 Bubba Wallace 1.00 2.5
14 Martin Truex Jr. .75 2.0
15 Austin Dillon 1.25 3.0

2019 Panini Prizm Patented Pennmanship Prizms

*BLUE/75: .6X TO 1.5X BASIC AU
*BLUE/35: .8X TO 2X BASIC AU
*BLUE/25-30: 1X TO 2.5X BASIC AU
*BLUE/18: 1.2X TO 3X BASIC AU
*CAMO: .5X TO 1.2X BASIC AU
*GREEN/99: .6X TO 1.5X BASIC AU
*GREEN/35-50: .8X TO 2X BASIC AU
*RAINBOW/24: 1X TO 2.5X BASIC AU
*RED/50: .8X TO 2X BASIC AU
*RED/25: 1X TO 2.5X BASIC AU
*RWB: .5X TO 1.2X BASIC AU
1 Bobby Allison 3.00 8.00
2 Dale Earnhardt Jr
3 Danica Patrick 25.00 50.00
4 Ernie Irvan 5.00 12.00
5 Jimmie Johnson
6 Kevin Harvick
7 Kurt Busch 3.00 8.00
8 Kyle Busch 6.00 15.00
9 Kyle Larson 6.00 15.00
10 Kyle Petty 3.00 8.00
11 Marcos Ambrose 4.00 10.00

12 Mark Martin
13 Martin Truex Jr. 3.00 8.00
14 Richard Petty 12.00 30.00
15 Ricky Stenhouse Jr.
16 Ryan Blaney 3.00 8.00
17 Ryan Newman 6.00 15.00
18 Thad Moffitt 3.00 8.00
19 Ty Dillon 4.00 10.00
20 William Byron 6.00 15.00

2019 Panini Prizm Scripted Signatures Prizms

*BLUE/75: .6X TO 1.5X BASIC AU
*BLUE/35: .8X TO 2X BASIC AU
*BLUE/25-30: 1X TO 2.5X BASIC AU
*BLUE/18: 1.2X TO 3X BASIC AU
*CAMO: .5X TO 1.2X BASIC AU
*GREEN/99: .6X TO 1.5X BASIC AU
*GREEN/35-49: .8X TO 2X BASIC AU
*RAINBOW/24: 1X TO 2.5X BASIC AU
*RAINBOW/18: 1.2X TO 3X BASIC AU
*RED/50: .8X TO 2X BASIC AU
*RED/25: 1X TO 2.5X BASIC AU
*RWB: .5X TO 1.2X BASIC AU
1 Carl Edwards
2 Chase Elliott
3 Dale Earnhardt Jr
4 Dale Jarrett 6.00 15.00
5 Hailie Deegan 30.00 60.00
7 Harrison Burton 5.00 12.00
8 Jimmie Johnson
9 Kevin Harvick
10 Kyle Busch 5.00 12.00
11 Mark Martin
12 Michael Waltrip 4.00 10.00
13 Tanner Berryhill 2.50 6.00
14 Tanner Thorson
15 Thad Moffitt 3.00 8.00
16 Tony Stewart 25.00 50.00
17 Trevor Bayne 4.00 10.00
18 Ty Dillon 4.00 10.00
19 Will Rodgers 2.50 6.00
20 Zane Smith 2.50 6.00

2019 Panini Prizm Signing Sessions Prizms

*BLUE/75: .6X TO 1.5X BASIC AU
*BLUE/35-50: .8X TO 2X BASIC AU
*BLUE/25-30: 1X TO 2.5X BASIC AU
*CAMO: .5X TO 1.2X BASIC AU
*GREEN/75-99: .6X TO 1.5X BASIC AU
*GREEN/35: .8X TO 2X BASIC AU
*GREEN/25: 1X TO 2.5X BASIC AU
*RAINBOW/24: 1X TO 2.5X BASIC AU
*RAINBOW/18: 1.2X TO 3X BASIC AU
*RED/50: .8X TO 2X BASIC AU
*RED/25: 1X TO 2.5X BASIC AU
*RED/18: 1.2X TO 3X BASIC AU
*RWB: .5X TO 1.2X BASIC AU
2 Aric Almirola 3.00 8.00
3 Austin Dillon 5.00 12.00
4 Brad Keselowski 5.00 12.00
5 Bubba Wallace 4.00 10.00
6 Chase Elliott 12.00 30.00
7 Clint Bowyer 4.00 10.00
8 Daniel Suarez 4.00 10.00
9 Denny Hamlin 4.00 10.00
10 Jimmie Johnson
11 Alex Bowman 4.00 10.00
Joey Logano
12 John Hunter Nemechek 3.00 8.00
13 Kevin Harvick
14 Kurt Busch 3.00 8.00
15 Kyle Busch 6.00 15.00
16 Kyle Larson 6.00 15.00
17 Martin Truex Jr. 3.00 8.00
18 Ryan Blaney 3.00 8.00
19 Ryan Newman 3.00 8.00
20 William Byron 6.00 15.00

2019 Panini Prizm Teammates

*PRIZMS: .6X TO 1.5X BASIC INSERTS
*SPARKLE: .8X TO 2X BASIC INSERTS
1 A.Bowman/J.Johnson 1.50 4.00
2 C.Elliott/W.Byron 1.25 3.00
3 D.Hamlin/M.Truex 1.00 2.50
4 K.Busch/M.Truex 1.25 3.00
5 B.Keselowski/J.Logano 1.25 3.00
6 D.Suarez/K.Harvick 1.25 3.00
7 A.Almirola/C.Bowyer 1.00 2.50
8 K.Busch/K.Larson 1.50 4.00
9 B.Wallace/R.Petty 1.50 4.00
10 A.Dillon/D.Hemric 1.25 3.00

2016 Panini Torque

1 David Gilliland .30 .75
2 Tony Stewart .75 2.00
3 Kevin Harvick .60 1.50
4 Jimmie Johnson .75 2.00
5 Carl Edwards .50 1.25
6 Denny Hamlin .50 1.25
7 Kyle Busch .60 1.50
8 Joey Logano .50 1.25
9 Kurt Busch .40 1.00
10 Dale Earnhardt Jr. 1.00 2.50
11 Brad Keselowski .60 1.50
12 Austin Dillon .60 1.50
13 Martin Truex Jr. .40 1.00
14 Jamie McMurray .50 1.25
15 Aric Almirola .40 1.00
16 Ricky Stenhouse Jr. .50 1.25
17 Matt Kenseth .50 1.25
18 Chase Elliott .60 1.50
19 Ryan Blaney RC .40 1.00
20 Kasey Kahne .50 1.25
21 A.J. Allmendinger .50 1.25
22 Ryan Newman .40 1.00
23 Trevor Bayne .50 1.25
24 Paul Menard .30 .75
25 Regan Smith .40 1.00
26 Kyle Larson .75 2.00
27 Brian Scott RC .30 .75
28 Casey Mears .30 .75
29 Greg Biffle .40 1.00
30 Landon Cassill .40 1.00
31 Danica Patrick 1.00 2.50
32 David Ragan .40 1.00
33 Clint Bowyer .50 1.25
34 Michael McDowell .50 1.25
35 Matt DiBenedetto .30 .75
36 Michael Annett .50 1.25
37 Chris Buescher RC .50 1.25
38 Brennan Poole RC .50 1.25
39 Cole Whitt .40 1.00
40 Josh Wise .30 .75
41 Jeffrey Earnhardt RC .50 1.25
42 Justin Allgaier .40 1.00
43 Bobby Labonte .50 1.25
44 Robert Richardson .30 .75
45 Ty Dillon .50 1.25
46 Daniel Suarez 1.00 2.50
47 Elliott Sadler .30 .75
48 Dale Earnhardt Jr. 1.00 2.50
49 Brandon Jones .50 1.25
50 Ty Dillon .50 1.25
51 Brendan Gaughan .30 .75
52 Erik Jones RC .75 2.00
53 Bubba Wallace .50 1.25
54 Ryan Reed .50 1.25
55 Jeb Burton .40 1.00
56 Kyle Busch .60 1.50
57 Chase Elliott .60 1.50
58 Austin Dillon .60 1.50
59 Joey Logano .50 1.25
60 Kasey Kahne .50 1.25
61 Brad Keselowski .60 1.50
62 Kevin Harvick .60 1.50
63 Ryan Blaney .40 1.00
64 Daniel Hemric .50 1.25
65 John Hunter Nemechek .40 1.00
66 Tyler Reddick .50 1.25
67 John Wes Townley .50 1.25
68 Rico Abreu RC .60 1.50
69 Cole Custer RC .50 1.25
70 Daniel Suarez 1.00 2.50
71 Ryan Reed .50 1.25
72 Kyle Busch .60 1.50
73 Dale Earnhardt Jr. 1.00 2.50
74 Jimmie Johnson .75 2.00
75 Kasey Kahne .50 1.25
76 Danica Patrick 1.00 2.50
77 Chase Elliott .60 1.50
78 Tony Stewart .75 2.00
79 Jamie McMurray .50 1.25
80 Kevin Harvick .60 1.50
81 Matt Kenseth .50 1.25
82 Carl Edwards .50 1.25
83 Denny Hamlin .50 1.25
84 Kyle Busch .60 1.50
85 Kurt Busch .40 1.00
86 Joey Logano .50 1.25
87 Brad Keselowski .60 1.50
88 Austin Dillon .60 1.50
89 Martin Truex Jr. .40 1.00
90 Richard Petty .75 2.00
91 Harry Gant .40 1.00
92 Bill Elliott .75 2.00
93 Bobby Allison .40 1.00
94 Darrell Waltrip .75 2.00
95 David Pearson .50 1.25
96 Richard Petty .75 2.00
97 Ernie Irvan .50 1.25
98 Mark Martin .50 1.25
99 Rusty Wallace .50 1.25
100 Terry Labonte .50 1.25

2016 Panini Torque Blue

*BLUE/125: 1X TO 2.5X BASIC CARDS

2016 Panini Torque Gold

*GOLD: .8X TO 2X BASIC CARDS

2016 Panini Torque Purple

*PURPLE/25: 2X TO 5X BASIC CARDS

2016 Panini Torque Red

*RED/99: 1.25X TO 3X BASIC CARDS

2016 Panini Torque Championship Vision

*GOLD/149: .5X TO 1.2X BASIC INSERTS
*BLUE/99: .6X TO 1.5X BASIC INSERTS
*RED/49: .8X TO 2X BASIC INSERTS
*GREEN/25: 1X TO 2.5X BASIC INSERTS
1 Richard Petty 1.25 3.00
2 Terry Labonte .75 2.00
3 Jimmie Johnson 1.25 3.00
4 Rusty Wallace .75 2.00
5 Tony Stewart 1.25 3.00
6 Kyle Busch 1.00 2.50
7 Kevin Harvick 1.00 2.50
8 Brad Keselowski 1.00 2.50
9 Kurt Busch .60 1.50
10 Matt Kenseth .75 2.00

2016 Panini Torque Clear Vision

*GOLD/149: .5X TO 1.2X BASIC INSERTS
*BLUE/99: .6X TO 1.5X BASIC INSERTS
*RED/49: .8X TO 2X BASIC INSERTS
*GREEN/25: 1X TO 2.5X BASIC INSERTS
1 Brian Scott .50 1.25
2 Tony Stewart 1.25 3.00
3 Kevin Harvick 1.00 2.50
4 Jimmie Johnson 1.25 3.00
5 Carl Edwards .75 2.00
6 Denny Hamlin .75 2.00
7 Kyle Busch 1.00 2.50
8 Joey Logano .75 2.00
9 Kurt Busch .60 1.50
10 Dale Earnhardt Jr. 1.50 4.00
11 Brad Keselowski 1.00 2.50
12 Austin Dillon 1.00 2.50
13 Martin Truex Jr. .60 1.50
14 Jamie McMurray .75 2.00
15 Ricky Stenhouse Jr. .75 2.00
16 Matt Kenseth .75 2.00
17 Chase Elliott 1.00 2.50
18 Ryan Blaney .60 1.50
19 Kasey Kahne .75 2.00
20 A.J. Allmendinger .75 2.00
21 Ryan Newman .60 1.50
22 Kyle Larson 1.25 3.00
23 Landon Cassill .60 1.50
24 Danica Patrick 1.50 4.00
25 Clint Bowyer .75 2.00
26 Cole Whitt .60 1.50
27 Jeffrey Earnhardt .75 2.00
28 Chris Buescher .60 1.50
29 Bobby Labonte .75 2.00
30 Ty Dillon .75 2.00
31 Harry Gant .60 1.50
32 Bill Elliott 1.25 3.00
33 Bobby Allison .60 1.50
34 Darrell Waltrip 1.25 3.00
35 David Pearson .75 2.00
36 Richard Petty 1.25 3.00
37 Ernie Irvan .75 2.00
38 Mark Martin .75 2.00
39 Rusty Wallace .75 2.00
40 Terry Labonte .75 2.00

2016 Panini Torque Driver Scripts

*BLUE/60-99: .5X TO 1.2X BASIC AU
*BLUE/35-50: .6X TO 1.5X BASIC AU
*GREEN/25: .8X TO 2X BASIC AU
*GREEN/15-20: 1X TO 2.5X BASIC AU
*RED/40-49: .6X TO 1.5X BASIC AU
*RED/25: .8X TO 2X BASIC AU
1 Garrett Smithley 4.00 10.00
2 Ben Rhodes 2.50 6.00
3 Jeremy Clements 3.00 8.00
4 Geoff Bodine 2.50 6.00
5 Cameron Hayley 3.00 8.00
6 Christopher Bell 5.00 12.00
7 Cole Custer 4.00 10.00
8 Collin Cabre 3.00 8.00
10 Daniel Hemric 4.00 10.00
11 Daniel Suarez 8.00 20.00
14 Ben Kennedy 3.00 8.00
17 J.J. Yeley 2.50 6.00
19 Spencer Gallagher 3.00 8.00
21 Jesse Little 3.00 8.00
22 Morgan Shepherd 4.00 10.00
23 Justin Allgaier 3.00 8.00
24 Kate Dallenbach 10.00 25.00
27 Matt Crafton 2.50 6.00
28 Nicole Behar 6.00 15.00
29 Reed Sorenson 2.50 6.00
30 Rico Abreu 5.00 12.00
31 Ruben Garcia Jr. 2.50 6.00
32 T.J. Bell 2.50 6.00
33 Tyler Reddick 4.00 10.00
34 William Byron 6.00 15.00
35 Austin Theriault 3.00 8.00

2016 Panini Torque Dual Materials

*BLUE/75-99: .5X TO 1.2X BASIC DUAL MEM/199-299
*BLUE/75-99: .4X TO 1X BASIC DUAL MEM/99-149
*BLUE/20: .5X TO 1.2X BASIC DUAL MEM/25
*GREEN/25: .8X TO 2X BASIC DUAL MEM/199-299
*GREEN/25: .6X TO 1.5X BASIC DUAL MEM/99-149
*RED/49: .6X TO 1.5X BASIC DUAL MEM/199-299
*RED/49: .5X TO 1.2X BASIC DUAL MEM/99-149
*RED/15: .5X TO 1.2X BASIC DUAL MEM/25
1 Bobby Labonte/299 2.50 6.00
2 David Ragan/199 2.00 5.00
3 Chase Elliott/149 4.00 10.00
4 Ty Dillon/199 2.50 6.00
5 Jeb Burton/249 2.00 5.00
6 Landon Cassill/299 2.00 5.00
7 Mark Martin/299 2.50 6.00
8 Ricky Stenhouse Jr./149 3.00 8.00
9 Ryan Newman/299 2.00 5.00
11 Collin Cabre/25 4.00 10.00
12 Erik Jones/299 4.00 10.00
13 Jeffrey Earnhardt/299 2.50 6.00
15 Kyle Larson/149 5.00 12.00
16 Matt DiBenedetto/149 2.00 5.00
17 Michael Annett/99 3.00 8.00
18 Ryan Reed/299 2.50 6.00
19 Trevor Bayne/149 3.00 8.00
20 Tyler Reddick/125 3.00 8.00

2016 Panini Torque Gas N Go

*GOLD/199: .6X TO 1.5X BASIC INSERTS
*SILVER/99: .8X TO 2X BASIC INSERTS
1 Brad Keselowski .75 2.00
2 Joey Logano .60 1.50
3 Ryan Newman .50 1.25
4 Carl Edwards .60 1.50
5 Matt Kenseth .60 1.50
6 Kevin Harvick .75 2.00
7 Jimmie Johnson 1.00 2.50
8 Dale Earnhardt Jr. 1.25 3.00
9 Danica Patrick 1.25 3.00
10 Tony Stewart 1.00 2.50

2016 Panini Torque Helmets

*BLUE/99: .6X TO 1.5X BASIC INSERT
*RED/49: .8X TO 2X BASIC INSERT
*GREEN/25: 1X TO 2.5X BASIC INSERTS
1 Jimmie Johnson 1.25 3.00
2 Kevin Harvick 1.00 2.50
3 Dale Earnhardt Jr. 1.50 4.00
4 Danica Patrick 1.50 4.00
5 Tony Stewart 1.25 3.00
6 Brad Keselowski 1.00 2.50
7 Chase Elliott 1.00 2.50
8 Kasey Kahne .75 2.00
9 Kyle Busch 1.00 2.50
10 Carl Edwards .75 2.00

2016 Panini Torque Metal Materials

*BLUE/99: .6X TO 1.5X BASIC METAL/249
*RED/49: .8X TO 2X BASIC METAL/249
*GREEN/25: 1X TO 2.5X BASIC METAL/249
1 Aric Almirola
2 Austin Dillon 4.00 10.00
3 Bobby Labonte 3.00 8.00
4 Brad Keselowski 4.00 10.00
5 Carl Edwards 3.00 8.00
6 Casey Mears 2.00 5.00
7 Chase Elliott 4.00 10.00
8 Clint Bowyer 3.00 8.00
9 Dale Earnhardt Jr. 6.00 15.00
10 Danica Patrick 6.00 15.00
11 Denny Hamlin 3.00 8.00
12 Joey Logano 3.00 8.00
13 Greg Biffle 2.50 6.00
14 Kasey Kahne 3.00 8.00
15 Kevin Harvick 4.00 10.00
16 Kyle Busch 4.00 10.00
17 Matt Kenseth 3.00 8.00
18 Jimmie Johnson 5.00 12.00
19 Ryan Newman 2.50 6.00
20 Trevor Bayne 3.00 8.00

2016 Panini Torque Nicknames

*GOLD/199: .6X TO 1.5X BASIC INSERTS
*SILVER/99: .8X TO 2X BASIC INSERTS
1 Harry Gant .50 1.25
2 Dale Earnhardt Jr. 1.25 3.00
3 Kevin Harvick .75 2.00
4 Tony Stewart 1.00 2.50
5 David Pearson .60 1.50
6 Richard Petty 1.00 2.50
7A Darrell Waltrip 1.00 2.50
7B Bill Elliott 1.00 2.50
9 Kyle Busch .75 2.00
10 Terry Labonte .60 1.50

2016 Panini Torque Painted to Perfection

*BLUE/99: .6X TO 1.5X BASIC INSERTS
*RED/49: .8X TO 2X BASIC INSERTS
*GREEN/25: 1X TO 2.5X BASIC INSERTS
1 Harry Gant .60 1.50
2 Rusty Wallace .75 2.00
3 Richard Petty 1.25 3.00
4 Tony Stewart 1.25 3.00
5 Kyle Busch 1.00 2.50
6 Kevin Harvick 1.00 2.50
7 Dale Earnhardt Jr. 1.50 4.00
8 Kasey Kahne .75 2.00
9 Denny Hamlin .75 2.00
10 Joey Logano .75 2.00
11 Carl Edwards .75 2.00
12 Brad Keselowski 1.00 2.50
13 Matt Kenseth .75 2.00
14 Danica Patrick 1.50 4.00
15 Ryan Newman .60 1.50
16 Clint Bowyer .75 2.00
17 Greg Biffle .60 1.50
18 Casey Mears .50 1.25
19 David Ragan .60 1.50
20 Jamie McMurray .75 2.00

2016 Panini Torque Pairings Materials

*BLUE/99: .6X TO 1.5X BASIC DUAL MEM/249
*BLUE/99: .5X TO 1.2X BASIC DUAL MEM/125-149
*RED/49: .8X TO 2X BASIC DUAL MEM/249
*RED/49: .6X TO 1.5X BASIC DUAL MEM/125-149
*RED/25: .8X TO 2X BASIC DUAL MEM/125
*GREEN/25: 1X TO 2.5X BASIC DUAL MEM/249
*GREEN/25: .8X TO 2X BASIC DUAL MEM/125-149
1 D.Earnhardt/J.Johnson 8.00 20.00
2 C.Elliott/D.Earnhardt 10.00 25.00
3 D.Earnhardt/K.Kahne 10.00 25.00
4 C.Elliott/J.Johnson 8.00 20.00
7 D.Earnhardt/R.Petty 10.00 25.00
9 D.Patrick/T.Stewart 8.00 20.00
11 C.Edwards/D.Hamlin 4.00 10.00
12 D.Hamlin/K.Busch 5.00 12.00
13 C.Edwards/K.Busch 5.00 12.00
14 K.Busch/M.Kenseth 5.00 12.00
16 A.Dillon/T.Dillon 6.00 15.00
17 K.Harvick/T.Stewart 8.00 20.00
18 B.Kselwski/J.Logano 6.00 15.00
19 P.Menard/R.Newman 3.00 8.00
20 J.McMurray/K.Larson 6.00 15.00
21 G.Biffle/T.Bayne 4.00 10.00
22 R.Stenhouse/T.Bayne 5.00 12.00
24 D.Ragan/M.DiBenedetto 4.00 10.00
25 A.Almirola/B.Scott 4.00 10.00
26 C.Bowyer/M.Annett 5.00 12.00
27 B.Elliott/J.McMurray 6.00 15.00
28 A.Dillon/P.Menard 6.00 15.00
29 A.Dillon/R.Newman 6.00 15.00
30 D.Patrick/K.Harvick 8.00 20.00

2016 Panini Torque Pole Position

*BLUE/99: .6X TO 1.5X BASIC INSERTS
*RED/49: .8X TO 2X BASIC INSERTS
*GREEN/25: 1X TO 2.5X BASIC INSERTS
1 Martin Truex Jr. .60 1.50
2 Tony Stewart 1.25 3.00
3 Kevin Harvick 1.00 2.50
4 Jimmie Johnson 1.25 3.00
5 Carl Edwards .75 2.00
6 Denny Hamlin .75 2.00
7 Kyle Busch 1.00 2.50
8 Joey Logano .75 2.00
9 Kurt Busch .60 1.50
10 Dale Earnhardt Jr. 1.50 4.00
11 Brad Keselowski 1.00 2.50
12 Austin Dillon 1.00 2.50
13 Ricky Stenhouse Jr. .75 2.00
14 Matt Kenseth .75 2.00
15 Chase Elliott 1.00 2.50
16 Kasey Kahne .75 2.00
17 Ryan Newman .60 1.50
18 Trevor Bayne .75 2.00
19 Danica Patrick 1.50 4.00
20 Clint Bowyer .75 2.00

2016 Panini Torque Quad Materials

*BLUE/99: .5X TO 1.2X QUAD MEM/149-199
*BLUE/99: .3X TO .8X QUAD MEM/48
*BLUE/99: .25X TO .6X QUAD MEM/23
*RED/49: .6X TO 1.5X BASIC QUAD MEM/149-199
*RED/49: .4X TO 1X BASIC QUAD MEM/48
*RED/49: .3X TO .8X BASIC QUAD MEM/23
*GREEN/25: .8X TO 2X BASIC QUAD MEM/149-199
*GREEN/25: .5X TO 1.2X BASIC QUAD MEM/48
*GREEN/25: .4X TO 1X BASIC QUAD MEM/23
1 Jimmie Johnson/48 8.00 20.00
2 Dale Earnhardt Jr/149 6.00 15.00
3 Chase Elliott/199 4.00 10.00
4 Ryan Reed/199 3.00 8.00
5 Paul Menard/199 2.00 5.00
6 Landon Cassill/199 2.50 6.00
7 Kevin Harvick/199 4.00 10.00
8 Kasey Kahne/199 3.00 8.00
9 Jeb Burton/23 5.00 12.00
10 Danica Patrick/149 6.00 15.00

2016 Panini Torque Race Kings

*GOLD/199: .6X TO 1.5X BASIC INSERTS
*SILVER/99: .8X TO 2X BASIC INSERTS
1 Harry Gant .50 1.25
2 Richard Petty 1.00 2.50
3 Rusty Wallace .60 1.50
4 Terry Labonte .60 1.50
5 Bill Elliott 1.00 2.50
6 Bobby Allison .50 1.25
7 Darrell Waltrip 1.00 2.50
8 David Pearson .60 1.50
9 Ernie Irvan .60 1.50
10 Mark Martin .60 1.50
11 Junior Johnson .60 1.50
12 Tony Stewart 1.00 2.50
13 Jimmie Johnson 1.00 2.50
14 Donnie Allison .50 1.25
15 Ned Jarrett .50 1.25

2016 Panini Torque Rubber Relics

*BLUE/99: .6X TO 1.5X BASIC TIRE/399
*BLUE/25: .5X TO 1.2X BASIC TIRE/49
*RED/49: .8X TO 2X BASIC TIRE/399
*GREEN/25: 1X TO 2.5X BASIC TIRE/399
1 A.J. Allmendinger/399 3.00 8.00
2 Austin Dillon/399 4.00 10.00
3 Brad Keselowski/399 4.00 10.00
4 Carl Edwards/399 3.00 8.00
5 Clint Bowyer/399 3.00 8.00
6 Dale Earnhardt Jr/49 12.00 30.00
7 Dale Earnhardt Jr/399 6.00 15.00
8 Danica Patrick/399 6.00 15.00
9 Denny Hamlin/399 3.00 8.00
10 Greg Biffle/399 2.50 6.00
12 Jimmie Johnson/399 5.00 12.00
13 Joey Logano/399 3.00 8.00
14 Kasey Kahne/399 3.00 8.00
15 Kevin Harvick/399 4.00 10.00
16 Kurt Busch/399 2.50 6.00
17 Kyle Busch/399 4.00 10.00
18 Matt Kenseth/399 3.00 8.00
19 Richard Petty/49 10.00 25.00
20 Tony Stewart/399 5.00 12.00

2016 Panini Torque Shades

*GOLD/199: .6X TO 1.5X BASIC INSERTS
*SILVER/99: .8X TO 2X BASIC INSERTS
1 Kevin Harvick .75 2.00
2 Jimmie Johnson 1.00 2.50
3 Dale Earnhardt Jr. 1.25 3.00
4 Danica Patrick 1.25 3.00
5 Tony Stewart 1.00 2.50
6 Brad Keselowski .75 2.00
7 Clint Bowyer .60 1.50
8 Kyle Busch .75 2.00
9 Kasey Kahne .60 1.50
10 Jamie McMurray .60 1.50
11 Martin Truex Jr. .50 1.25
12 Carl Edwards .60 1.50
13 Kurt Busch .50 1.25
14 Joey Logano .60 1.50
15 Denny Hamlin .60 1.50

2016 Panini Torque Silhouettes Firesuit Autographs

1 Austin Dillon/25
2 Brad Keselowski/35 8.00 20.00
3 Carl Edwards/49 6.00 15.00
4 Chase Elliott/35 30.00 60.00
5 Clint Bowyer/60 6.00 15.00
6 Dale Earnhardt Jr/25 30.00 60.00
7 Danica Patrick/20 50.00 100.00
8 Denny Hamlin/35 6.00 15.00
9 Greg Biffle/75 4.00 10.00
10 Jamie McMurray/50 6.00 15.00
11 Jimmie Johnson/25 25.00 50.00
12 Joey Logano/49 6.00 15.00
13 Kasey Kahne/50 10.00 25.00
14 Kevin Harvick/35 15.00 40.00
15 Kurt Busch/30 6.00 15.00
16 Kyle Busch/35 12.00 30.00
17 Martin Truex Jr./150 4.00 10.00
18 Matt Kenseth/30 8.00 20.00
19 Ryan Reed/91 5.00 12.00
20 Ricky Stenhouse Jr./75 5.00 12.00
21 Ryan Blaney/30 12.00 30.00
22 Ryan Newman/30 6.00 15.00
23 Josh Wise/50 4.00 10.00
24 Trevor Bayne/35 6.00 15.00
25 Ty Dillon/30 8.00 20.00

2016 Panini Torque Silhouettes Firesuit Autographs Blue

*BLUE/75: .4X TO 1X BASIC FIRE AU/75-150
*BLUE/35-50: .5X TO 1.2X BASIC FIRE AU/75-150
*BLUE/35-50: .4X TO 1X BASIC FIRE AU/35-60
*BLUE/25: .6X TO 1.5X BASIC FIRE AU/75-150
*BLUE/25: .5X TO 1.2X BASIC FIRE AU/35-60
*BLUE/25: .4X TO 1X BASIC FIRE AU/25-30
*BLUE/15-24: .6X TO 1.5X BASIC FIRE AU/35-60
*BLUE/15-24: .5X TO 1.2X BASIC FIRE AU/25-30
*BLUE/15-24: .4X TO 1X BASIC FIRE AU/15-24

2016 Panini Torque Silhouettes Sheet Metal Autographs

1 Austin Dillon/49 8.00 20.00
2 Brad Keselowski/35 8.00 20.00
3 Carl Edwards/49 6.00 15.00
4 Chase Elliott/35 30.00 60.00
5 Clint Bowyer/60 6.00 15.00
6 Dale Earnhardt Jr/25 30.00 60.00
7 Danica Patrick/20 50.00 100.00
8 Denny Hamlin/50 6.00 15.00
10 Greg Biffle/75 4.00 10.00
11 Ryan Truex/100 4.00 10.00
12 Erik Jones/75 20.00 40.00
13 Jeffrey Earnhardt/75 5.00 12.00
14 Jimmie Johnson/25 25.00 50.00
15 Joey Logano/49 6.00 15.00
16 Kasey Kahne/50 10.00 25.00
17 Kevin Harvick/35 15.00 40.00
18 Kurt Busch/30 6.00 15.00
19 Kyle Busch/35 12.00 30.00
20 Matt Kenseth/30 8.00 20.00
21 Ricky Stenhouse Jr./50 6.00 15.00
22 Ryan Blaney/50 10.00 25.00
23 Ryan Newman/30 6.00 15.00
25 Ty Dillon/30 8.00 20.00

2016 Panini Torque Silhouettes Sheet Metal Autographs Blue

*BLUE/75: .4X TO 1X BASIC SHEET AU/75-100
*BLUE/35-50: .5X TO 1.2X BASIC SHEET AU/75-100
*BLUE/35-50: .4X TO 1X BASIC SHEET AU/35-50
*BLUE/25: .5X TO 1.2X BASIC SHEET AU/35-60
*BLUE/25: .4X TO 1X BASIC SHEET AU/25-30
*BLUE/15-24: .6X TO 1.5X BASIC SHEET AU/35-60
*BLUE/15-24: .5X TO 1.2X BASIC SHEET AU/25-30
*BLUE/15-24: .4X TO 1X BASIC SHEET AU/20

2016 Panini Torque Silhouettes Sheet Metal Autographs Green

*GREEN/25: .6X TO 1.5X BASIC SHEET AU/75-100
*GREEN/25: .5X TO 1.2X BASIC SHEET AU/35-60
*GREEN/15-20: .8X TO 2X BASIC SHEET AU/75-100
*GREEN/15-20: .6X TO 1.5X BASIC SHEET AU/35-60
*GREEN/15-20: .5X TO 1.2X BASIC SHEET AU/25-30

2016 Panini Torque Silhouettes Sheet Metal Autographs Red

*RED/40: .5X TO 1.2X BASIC SHEET AU/75-100
*RED/25-30: .6X TO 1.5X BASIC SHEET AU/75-100
*RED/25-30: .5X TO 1.2X BASIC SHEET AU/35-60
*RED/15-20: .6X TO 1.5X BASIC SHEET AU/35-60
*RED/15-20: .5X TO 1.2X BASIC SHEET AU/25-30

2016 Panini Torque Special Paint

*GOLD/199: .6X TO 1.5X BASIC INSERTS
*SILVER/99: .8X TO 2X BASIC INSERTS
1 Jimmie Johnson 1.00 2.50
2 Dale Earnhardt Jr. 1.25 3.00
3 Denny Hamlin .60 1.50
4 Kyle Busch .75 2.00
5 Matt Kenseth .60 1.50
6 Joey Logano .60 1.50
7 Greg Biffle .50 1.25
8 Chase Elliott .75 2.00
9 Paul Menard .40 1.00
10 Martin Truex Jr. .50 1.25

2016 Panini Torque Superstar Vision

*GOLD/149: .5X TO 1.2X BASIC INSERTS
*BLUE/99: .6X TO 1.5X BASIC INSERTS
*RED/49: .8X TO 2X BASIC INSERTS
*GREEN/25: 1X TO 2.5X BASIC INSERTS
1 Tony Stewart 1.25 3.00
2 Jimmie Johnson 1.25 3.00
3 Dale Earnhardt Jr. 1.50 4.00
4 Danica Patrick 1.50 4.00
5 Kasey Kahne .75 2.00
6 Kyle Busch 1.00 2.50
7 Kevin Harvick 1.00 2.50
8 Chase Elliott 1.00 2.50
9 Austin Dillon 1.00 2.50
10 Ty Dillon .75 2.00
11 Brad Keselowski 1.00 2.50
12 Matt Kenseth .75 2.00
13 Ryan Newman .60 1.50
14 Clint Bowyer .75 2.00
15 Carl Edwards .75 2.00
16 Denny Hamlin .75 2.00
17 Terry Labonte .75 2.00
18 Joey Logano .75 2.00
19 Kurt Busch .60 1.50

20 Bobby Labonte .75 2.00
21 Mark Martin .75 2.00
22 Darrell Waltrip 1.25 3.00
23 Rusty Wallace .75 2.00
24 Richard Petty 1.25 3.00
25 David Pearson .75 2.00

2016 Panini Torque Victory Laps

*GOLD/199: .6X TO 1.5X BASIC INSERTS
*SILVER/99: .8X TO 2X BASIC INSERTS
1 Denny Hamlin .60 1.50
2 Dale Earnhardt Jr. 1.25 3.00
3 Kyle Busch .75 2.00
4 Jimmie Johnson 1.00 2.50
5 Carl Edwards .60 1.50
6 Matt Kenseth .60 1.50
7 Joey Logano .60 1.50
8 Richard Petty 1.00 2.50
9 Kasey Kahne .60 1.50
10 Brad Keselowski .75 2.00
11 Kevin Harvick .75 2.00
12 Clint Bowyer .60 1.50
13 Martin Truex Jr. .50 1.25
14 Kurt Busch .50 1.25
15 Rusty Wallace .60 1.50

2016 Panini Torque Winning Vision

*GOLD/149: .5X TO 1.2X BASIC INSERTS
*BLUE/99: .6X TO 1.5X BASIC INSERTS
*RED/49: .8X TO 2X BASIC INSERTS
*GREEN/25: 1X TO 2.5X BASIC INSERTS
1 Mark Martin .75 2.00
2 Tony Stewart 1.25 3.00
3 Kevin Harvick 1.00 2.50
4 Jimmie Johnson 1.25 3.00
5 Carl Edwards .75 2.00
6 Denny Hamlin .75 2.00
7 Kyle Busch 1.00 2.50
8 Joey Logano .75 2.00
9 Kurt Busch .60 1.50
10 Dale Earnhardt Jr. 1.50 4.00
11 Brad Keselowski 1.00 2.50
12 Martin Truex Jr. .60 1.50
13 Matt Kenseth .75 2.00
14 Kasey Kahne .75 2.00
15 Greg Biffle .60 1.50
16 Ryan Newman .60 1.50
17 Clint Bowyer .75 2.00
18 Jamie McMurray .75 2.00
19 Rusty Wallace .75 2.00
20 David Ragan .60 1.50
21 A.J. Allmendinger .75 2.00
22 Trevor Bayne .75 2.00
23 Casey Mears .50 1.25
24 Richard Petty 1.25 3.00
25 David Pearson .75 2.00

2017 Panini Torque

*ARTIST/75: 1.2X TO 3X BASIC CARDS
*BLUE/150: 1X TO 2.5X BASIC CARDS
*GOLD: .8X TO 2X BASIC CARDS
*SILVER/25: 2X TO 5X BASIC CARDS
*PURPLE/50: 1.5X TO 4X BASIC CARDS
*RED/100: 1.25X TO 3X BASIC CARDS
1 Jamie McMurray .50 1.25
2 Brad Keselowski .60 1.50
3 Austin Dillon .60 1.50
4 Kasey Kahne .50 1.25
5 Trevor Bayne .50 1.25
6 Denny Hamlin .50 1.25
7 Ricky Stenhouse Jr. .50 1.25
8 Kyle Busch .60 1.50
9 Gray Gaulding .30 .75
10 Matt Kenseth .50 1.25
11 Ryan Blaney .40 1.00
12 Joey Logano .50 1.25
13 Chase Elliott .60 1.50
14 Paul Menard .30 .75
15 Ryan Newman .40 1.00
16 Chris Buescher .40 1.00
17 Kyle Larson .75 2.00
18 Aric Almirola .40 1.00
19 AJ Allmendinger .50 1.25
20 Jimmie Johnson .75 2.00
21 Kevin Harvick .60 1.50
22 Danica Patrick 1.00 2.50
23 Clint Bowyer .50 1.25
24 Erik Jones .75 2.00
25 Martin Truex Jr. .40 1.00
26 Kurt Busch .40 1.00
27 Dale Earnhardt Jr 1.00 2.50
28 Greg Biffle .40 1.00
29 Ty Dillon .50 1.25
30 Richard Petty .75 2.00
31 Terry Labonte .50 1.25
32 Bill Elliott .75 2.00
33 Mark Martin .50 1.25
34 Dale Jarrett .50 1.25
35 Rusty Wallace .50 1.25
36 Daniel Suarez 1.00 2.50
37 Daniel Hemric .50 1.25
38 Elliott Sadler .30 .75
39 Ty Dillon .50 1.25
40 Michael Annett .50 1.25
41 Justin Allgaier .40 1.00
42 Blake Koch .40 1.00
43 Ryan Reed .50 1.25
44 Brad Keselowski .60 1.50
45 Joey Logano .50 1.25
46 Ryan Blaney .40 1.00
47 Brandon Jones .30 .75
48 Brennan Poole .30 .75
49 Brendan Gaughan .30 .75
50 Cole Custer .50 1.25
51 William Byron .75 2.00
52 Joey Gase .50 1.25
53 Matt Tifft .75 2.00
54 Kaz Grala .50 1.25
55 Jimmie Johnson .75 2.00
56 Danica Patrick 1.00 2.50
57 Kevin Harvick .60 1.50
58 Dale Earnhardt Jr 1.00 2.50
59 Kasey Kahne .50 1.25
60 Clint Bowyer .50 1.25
61 Chase Elliott .60 1.50
62 Trevor Bayne .50 1.25
63 Austin Dillon .60 1.50
64 AJ Allmendinger .50 1.25
65 Brad Keselowski .60 1.50
66 Gray Gaulding .30 .75
67 Denny Hamlin .50 1.25
68 Jamie McMurray .50 1.25
69 Joey Logano .50 1.25
70 Martin Truex Jr. .40 1.00
71 Ryan Newman .40 1.00
72 Matt Kenseth .50 1.25
73 Dale Earnhardt Jr 1.00 2.50
74 Jimmie Johnson .75 2.00
75 Danica Patrick 1.00 2.50
76 Kevin Harvick .60 1.50
77 Ryan Newman .40 1.00
78 Kasey Kahne .50 1.25
79 Gray Gaulding .30 .75
80 Denny Hamlin .50 1.25
81 Joey Logano .50 1.25
82 Jimmie Johnson .75 2.00
83 Kevin Harvick .60 1.50
84 Kurt Busch .40 1.00
85 Kyle Busch .60 1.50
86 Matt Kenseth .50 1.25
87 Ryan Newman .40 1.00
89 Denny Hamlin .50 1.25
90 Clint Bowyer .50 1.25
91 Jimmie Johnson .75 2.00
92 Joey Logano .50 1.25
93 Carl Edwards .50 1.25
94 Kyle Busch .60 1.50
95 Danica Patrick 1.00 2.50
96 Kevin Harvick .60 1.50
97 Dale Earnhardt Jr 1.00 2.50
98 Chase Elliott .60 1.50
99 Denny Hamlin .50 1.25
100 Ryan Newman .40 1.00

2017 Panini Torque Clear Vision

*GOLD/149: .5X TO 1.2X BASIC INSERTS
*BLUE/99: .6X TO 1.5X BASIC INSERTS
*RED/49: .8X TO 2X BASIC INSERTS
*GREEN/25: 1X TO 2.5X BASIC INSERTS
1 Jamie McMurray .75 2.00
2 Brad Keselowski 1.00 2.50
3 Austin Dillon 1.00 2.50
4 Kevin Harvick 1.00 2.50
5 Terry Labonte .75 2.00
6 Mark Martin .75 2.00
7 Ricky Stenhouse Jr. .75 2.00
8 Dale Earnhardt Jr 1.50 4.00
9 Kasey Kahne .75 2.00
10 Danica Patrick 1.50 4.00
11 Denny Hamlin .75 2.00
12 Joey Logano .75 2.00
13 Chase Elliott 1.00 2.50
14 Paul Menard .50 1.25
15 Ryan Newman .60 1.50
16 Chris Buescher .60 1.50
17 Kyle Larson 1.25 3.00
18 Kyle Busch 1.00 2.50
19 Michael Waltrip .75 2.00
20 Matt Kenseth .75 2.00
21 AJ Allmendinger .75 2.00
22 Jimmie Johnson 1.25 3.00
23 Clint Bowyer .75 2.00
24 Ward Burton .50 1.25
25 Martin Truex Jr. .60 1.50
26 Kurt Busch .60 1.50
27 Aric Almirola .60 1.50
28 Greg Biffle .60 1.50
29 Brennan Poole .50 1.25
30 Ryan Reed .75 2.00
31 Trevor Bayne .75 2.00
32 Bill Elliott 1.25 3.00
33 Ryan Blaney .60 1.50
34 Dale Jarrett .75 2.00
35 Rusty Wallace .75 2.00
36 Richard Petty 1.25 3.00
37 Brandon Jones .50 1.25
38 Elliott Sadler .50 1.25
39 Carl Edwards .75 2.00
40 Michael Annett .75 2.00
41 Justin Allgaier .60 1.50
42 Blake Koch .60 1.50
43 Daniel Suarez 1.50 4.00
44 Ty Dillon .75 2.00
45 Erik Jones 1.25 3.00
46 Daniel Hemric .75 2.00
47 Cole Custer .75 2.00
48 William Byron 1.25 3.00
49 Matt Tifft 1.25 3.00
50 Kaz Grala .75 2.00

2017 Panini Torque Driver Scripts

1 Ahnna Parkhurst 4.00 10.00
2 Alon Day 8.00 20.00
3 Bill Elliott 6.00 15.00
4 Blake Koch 3.00 8.00
5 Bobby Allison 3.00 8.00
6 Brett Bodine 2.50 6.00
7 Cale Yarborough 4.00 10.00
8 Collin Cabre 2.50 6.00
9 Dale Inman 3.00 8.00
10 Dale Jarrett 4.00 10.00
11 Darrell Waltrip 6.00 15.00
12 Dave Marcis 3.00 8.00
13 Donnie Allison 3.00 8.00
14 Ernie Irvan 4.00 10.00
15 Geoff Bodine 2.50 6.00
16 Harry Gant 3.00 8.00
17 Hershel McGriff 2.50 6.00
18 Junior Johnson 4.00 10.00
19 Ken Schrader 2.50 6.00
20 Kenny Wallace 2.50 6.00
21 Kaz Grala 4.00 10.00
22 Michael Waltrip 4.00 10.00
23 Morgan Shepherd 4.00 10.00
24 Ned Jarrett 3.00 8.00
27 Rex White 2.50 6.00
28 Richard Petty 25.00 50.00
29 Ricky Craven 2.50 6.00
30 Ward Burton 2.50 6.00
31 Rusty Wallace 4.00 10.00
32 Carl Edwards 4.00 10.00
33 Terry Labonte 4.00 10.00
34 Jeff Burton
35 Brennan Poole 2.50 6.00

2017 Panini Torque Driver Scripts Blue

*BLUE/75-99: .5X TO 1.2X BASIC AU
*BLUE/50: .6X TO 1.5X BASIC AU
*BLUE/20: 1X TO 2.5X BASIC AU

2017 Panini Torque Driver Scripts Green

*GREEN/25: .8X TO 2X BASIC AU
*GREEN: 1X TO 2.5X BASIC AU

2017 Panini Torque Driver Scripts Red

*RED/35-49: .6X TO 1.5X BASIC AU
*RED/25: .8X TO 2X BASIC AU
*RED/15: 1X TO 2.5X BASIC AU

2017 Panini Torque Dual Materials

*BLUE/99: .5X TO 1.5X BASIC FIRE/249-499
*BLUE/99: .4X TO 1X BASIC FIRE/199
*BLUE/49: .6X TO 1.5X BASIC FIRE/249-499
*BLUE/25: .5X TO 1.2X BASIC FIRE/49
*BLUE/20: .5X TO 1.2X BASIC FIRE/25
*RED/49: .6X TO 1.5X BASIC FIRE/249-499
*RED/49: .5X TO 1.2X BASIC FIRE/199
*RED/25: .8X TO 2X BASIC FIRE/249-499
*GREEN/25: .8X TO 2X BASIC FIRE/249-499
*GREEN/25: .6X TO 1.5X BASIC FIRE/199
1 Austin Dillon/499 3.00 8.00
2 Brad Keselowski/499 3.00 8.00
3 Bubba Wallace/499 2.50 6.00
4 Chase Elliott/49 5.00 12.00
5 Chris Buescher/25 4.00 10.00
6 Clint Bowyer/25 5.00 12.00
7 Dale Earnhardt Jr/199 6.00 15.00
8 Danica Patrick/199 8.00 20.00
9 Daniel Suarez/249 5.00 12.00
10 David Ragan/199 2.50 6.00
11 Denny Hamlin/49 4.00 10.00
12 Erik Jones/49 6.00 15.00
14 Joey Logano/199 3.00 8.00
15 Kasey Kahne/49 4.00 10.00
16 Kevin Harvick/199 4.00 10.00
17 Kyle Busch/499 3.00 8.00
18 Matt Kenseth/299 2.50 6.00
19 Ryan Newman/399 2.00 5.00
20 Trevor Bayne/499 2.50 6.00

2017 Panini Torque Horsepower Heroes

*GOLD/199: .6X TO 1.5X BASIC INSERTS
*SILVER/99: .8X TO 2X BASIC INSERTS
1 Jamie McMurray .60 1.50
2 Brad Keselowski .75 2.00
3 Austin Dillon .75 2.00
4 Kevin Harvick .75 2.00
5 Kasey Kahne .60 1.50
6 Trevor Bayne .60 1.50
7 Dale Earnhardt Jr 1.25 3.00
8 Danica Patrick 1.25 3.00
9 Denny Hamlin .60 1.50
10 Ty Dillon .60 1.50
11 Clint Bowyer .60 1.50
12 Matt Kenseth .60 1.50
13 Kyle Busch .75 2.00
14 Joey Logano .60 1.50
15 Ricky Stenhouse Jr. .60 1.50
16 Ryan Blaney .50 1.25
17 Chase Elliott .75 2.00
18 Paul Menard .40 1.00
19 Chris Buescher .50 1.25
20 Aric Almirola .50 1.25
21 Jimmie Johnson 1.00 2.50
22 Martin Truex Jr. .50 1.25
23 Kyle Larson 1.00 2.50
24 Kurt Busch .50 1.25
25 Erik Jones 1.00 2.50

2017 Panini Torque Jumbo Firesuit Signatures Blue

*BLUE/99: .5X TO 1.2X BASIC FIRE AU/166-167
*BLUE/75: .4X TO 1X BASIC FIRE AU/75-91
*BLUE/50: .5X TO 1.2X BASIC FIRE AU/41-57
*BLUE40-49: .5X TO 1.2X BASIC FIRE AU/41-57
*BLUE/25: .5X TO 1.2X BASIC FIRE AU/41-57
*BLUE/15: .4X TO 1X BASIC FIRE AU/19

2017 Panini Torque Jumbo Firesuit Signatures Green

*GREEN/25: .8X TO 2X BASIC FIRE AU/166-167
*GREEN/25: .6X TO 1.5X BASIC FIRE AU/75-91
*GREEN/24: .5X TO 1.2X BASIC FIRE AU/41-57
*GREEN/15: .8X TO 2X BASIC FIRE AU/75-91
*GREEN/15: .6X TO 1.5X BASIC FIRE AU/41-57

2017 Panini Torque Jumbo Firesuit Signatures Red

*RED/49: .6X TO 1.5X BASIC FIRE AU/166-167
*RED/49: .5X TO 1.2X BASIC FIRE AU/75-91
*RED/35: .4X TO 1X BASIC FIRE AU/41-57
*RED/25: .6X TO 1.5X BASIC FIRE AU/75-91
*RED/25: .5X TO 1.2X BASIC FIRE AU/41-57
*RED/20: .6X TO 1.5X BASIC FIRE AU/41-57

2017 Panini Torque Metal Materials

*BLUE/99: .5X TO 1.2X BASIC SHEET/249-499
*BLUE/99: .4X TO 1X BASIC SHEET/199
*BLUE/49: .6X TO 1.5X BASIC SHEET/249-499
*BLUE/15: .5X TO 1.2X BASIC SHEET/25
*RED/49: .6X TO 1.5X BASIC SHEET/249-499
*RED/49: .5X TO 1.2X BASIC SHEET/199
*RED/25: .8X TO 2X BASIC SHEET/249-499
*GREEN/25: .8X TO 2X BASIC SHEET/249-499
*GREEN/25: .6X TO 1.5X BASIC SHEET/99-199
1 Austin Dillon/499 3.00 8.00
2 Brandon Jones/499 1.50 4.00
3 Brendan Gaughan/499 1.50 4.00
4 Bubba Wallace/499 2.50 6.00
5 Daniel Suarez/199 6.00 15.00
6 David Gilliland/275 1.50 4.00
7 Jeb Burton/299 2.00 5.00
8 Jamie McMurray/199 3.00 8.00
9 Joey Logano/199 3.00 8.00
10 Kurt Busch/299 2.00 5.00
11 Kyle Larson/99 5.00 12.00
12 Landon Cassill/299 2.00 5.00
13 Paul Menard/299 1.50 4.00
14 Ryan Reed/149 3.00 8.00
16 Danica Patrick/49 8.00 20.00
17 Tyler Reddick/149 3.00 8.00
18 Kevin Harvick/199 4.00 10.00
19 Dale Earnhardt Jr/25 10.00 25.00
20 Jimmie Johnson/25 8.00 20.00

2017 Panini Torque Pairings Materials

*BLUE/99: .4X TO 1X BASIC FIRE/99-199
*BLUE/49: .5X TO 1.2X BASIC FIRE/75-199
*BLUE/25: .5X TO 1.2X BASIC FIRE/49
*RED/49: .5X TO 1.2X BASIC FIRE/75-199
*RED/25: .6X TO 1.5X BASIC FIRE/75-199
*GREEN/25: .6X TO 1.5X BASIC FIRE/75-199
1 Joey Logano 4.00 10.00
Brad Keselowski/199
2 Jamie McMurray 5.00 12.00
Kyle Larson/199
3 Austin Dillon 4.00 10.00
Ryan Newman/199
4 Clint Bowyer 4.00 10.00
Kevin Harvick/199
5 Danica Patrick 6.00 15.00
Kurt Busch/199
6 Kasey Kahne 5.00 12.00
Jimmie Johnson/199
7 Dale Earnhardt Jr 6.00 15.00
Chase Elliott/99
8 Ricky Stenhouse Jr. 3.00 8.00
Trevor Bayne/199
9 Denny Hamlin 3.00 8.00
Matt Kenseth/99
10 Daniel Suarez 6.00 15.00
Kyle Busch/199
11 David Ragan 2.50 6.00
Landon Cassill/199
13 Erik Jones 5.00 12.00
Martin Truex Jr./199
14 Matt Kenseth 4.00 10.00
Kyle Busch/75
15 Dale Earnhardt Jr 8.00 20.00
Jimmie Johnson/49

2017 Panini Torque Quad Materials

*BLUE/99: .5X TO 1.2X BASIC MATERIALS/299
*BLUE/99: .4X TO 1X BASIC MATERIALS/75-199
*BLUE49-50: .5X TO 1.2X BASIC MATERIALS/75-199
*BLUE/25: .5X TO 1.2X BASIC MATERIALS/49
*BLUE/15-20: .5X TO 1.2X BASIC MATERIALS/25
*BLUE/15-20: .4X TO 1X BASIC MATERIALS/15
*RED/99: .5X TO 1.2X BASIC MATERIALS/299
*RED/99: .5X TO 1.2X BASIC MATERIALS/75-199
*RED/49-50: .5X TO 1.2X BASIC MATERIALS/75-199
*RED/25: .5X TO 1.2X BASIC MATERIALS/49
*RED/15-20: .5X TO 1.2X BASIC MATERIALS/25
*RED/15: .4X TO 1X BASIC MATERIALS/20
*GREEN/25: .8X TO 2X BASIC MATERIALS/299
*GREEN/25: .6X TO 1.5X BASIC MATERIALS/75-199
*GREEN/15: .6X TO 1.5X BASIC MATERIALS/49
1 Austin Dillon/75 4.00 10.00
2 Brad Keselowski/49 5.00 12.00
4 Chris Buescher/25 4.00 10.00
5 Clint Bowyer/25 5.00 12.00
6 Dale Earnhardt Jr/99 6.00 15.00
7 Danica Patrick/20 12.00 30.00
8 Daniel Suarez/199 6.00 15.00
9 David Ragan/49 3.00 8.00
11 Erik Jones/49 6.00 15.00
12 Jamie McMurray/99 3.00 8.00
13 Jeb Burton/99 2.50 6.00
14 Jimmie Johnson/49 6.00 15.00
15 Joey Logano/99 3.00 8.00
16 Kasey Kahne/25 5.00 12.00
17 Kevin Harvick/99 4.00 10.00
18 Kurt Busch/99 2.50 6.00
19 Kyle Busch/99 4.00 10.00
20 Kyle Larson/99 5.00 12.00
21 Martin Truex Jr./299 2.00 5.00
22 Matt Kenseth/99 3.00 8.00
23 Paul Menard/99 2.00 5.00
24 Ryan Newman/199 2.50 6.00
25 Tyler Reddick/99 3.00 8.00

2017 Panini Torque Raced Relics

*BLUE/99: .5X TO 1.2X BASIC MATERIALS/399-499
*BLUE/99: .4X TO 1X BASIC MATERIALS/199
*BLUE/49: .5X TO 1.2X BASIC MATERIALS/199
*BLUE/25: .5X TO 1.2X BASIC MATERIALS/49
*RED/49: .6X TO 1.5X BASIC MATERIALS/399-499
*RED/49: .5X TO 1.2X BASIC MATERIALS/199
*RED/25: .6X TO 1.5X BASIC MATERIALS/99
*GREEN/25: .8X TO 2X BASIC MATERIALS/399-499
*GREEN/25: .6X TO 1.5X BASIC MATERIALS/199
*GREEN/20: .8X TO 2X BASIC MATERIALS/99
1 Austin Dillon/499 3.00 8.00
2 Brad Keselowski/499 3.00 8.00
3 Chase Elliott/499 3.00 8.00
4 Clint Bowyer/199 3.00 8.00
5 Dale Earnhardt Jr/399 8.00 20.00
6 Danica Patrick/99 8.00 20.00
7 Daniel Suarez/499 5.00 12.00
8 Erik Jones/49 6.00 15.00
9 Jamie McMurray/499 2.50 6.00
10 Jimmie Johnson/499 4.00 10.00
11 Joey Logano/499 2.50 6.00
12 Kasey Kahne/499 3.00 8.00
13 Kevin Harvick/499 3.00 8.00
14 Kurt Busch/499 2.00 5.00
15 Kyle Busch/499 3.00 8.00
16 Martin Truex Jr./499 2.00 5.00
17 Matt Kenseth/499 2.50 6.00
18 Ricky Stenhouse Jr./499 2.50 6.00
19 Ryan Newman/499 2.00 5.00
20 Ty Dillon/499 2.50 6.00

2017 Panini Torque Rookie Stripes

*GOLD/199: .6X TO 1.5X BASIC INSERTS
*SILVER/99: .8X TO 2X BASIC INSERTS
1 Erik Jones 1.00 2.50
2 Ty Dillon .60 1.50
3 Daniel Suarez 1.25 3.00
4 Daniel Hemric .60 1.50
5 William Byron 1.00 2.50
6 Cole Custer .60 1.50
7 Corey LaJoie .50 1.25
8 Chase Elliott .75 2.00
9 Erik Jones 1.00 2.50
10 William Byron 1.00 2.50

2017 Panini Torque Special Paint

*GOLD/199: .6X TO 1.5X BASIC INSERTS
*SILVER/99: .8X TO 2X BASIC INSERTS
1 Kasey Kahne .60 1.50
2 Danica Patrick 1.25 3.00
3 Kyle Busch .75 2.00
4 Joey Logano .60 1.50
5 Paul Menard .40 1.00
6 Ryan Newman .50 1.25
7 Chris Buescher .50 1.25
8 Aric Almirola .50 1.25
9 Jimmie Johnson 1.00 2.50
10 Dale Earnhardt Jr 1.25 3.00

2017 Panini Torque Track Vision

*GOLD/149: .5X TO 1.2X BASIC INSERTS
*BLUE/99: .6X TO 1.5X BASIC INSERTS
*RED/49: .8X TO 2X BASIC INSERTS
*GREEN/25: 1X TO 2.5X BASIC INSERTS
1 Dale Earnhardt Jr 1.50 4.00
2 Jimmie Johnson 1.25 3.00
3 Kevin Harvick 1.00 2.50
4 Danica Patrick 1.50 4.00
5 Kurt Busch .60 1.50
6 Brad Keselowski 1.00 2.50
7 Austin Dillon 1.00 2.50
8 Kyle Busch 1.00 2.50
9 Kasey Kahne .75 2.00
10 Martin Truex Jr. .60 1.50

2017 Panini Torque Trackside

*BLUE/99: .6X TO 1.5X BASIC INSERTS
*RED/49: .8X TO 2X BASIC INSERTS
*GREEN/25: 1X TO 2.5X BASIC INSERTS
1 Dale Earnhardt Jr 1.50 4.00
2 Jimmie Johnson 1.25 3.00
3 Kevin Harvick 1.00 2.50
4 Matt Kenseth .75 2.00
5 Denny Hamlin .75 2.00
6 Martin Truex Jr. .60 1.50
7 Austin Dillon 1.00 2.50
8 Chase Elliott 1.00 2.50
9 Kyle Busch 1.00 2.50
10 Richard Petty 1.25 3.00

2018 Panini Victory Lane

1 Jamie McMurray .40 1.00
2 Brad Keselowski .50 1.25
3 Austin Dillon .50 1.25
4 Kevin Harvick .50 1.25
5 Trevor Bayne .40 1.00
6 Chase Elliott .50 1.25
7 Denny Hamlin .40 1.00
8 Ryan Blaney .30 .75
9 Ty Dillon .40 1.00
10 Clint Bowyer .40 1.00
11 Ricky Stenhouse Jr. .40 1.00
12 Kyle Busch .50 1.25
13 Daniel Suarez .40 1.00
14 Erik Jones .40 1.00
15 Paul Menard .25 .60
16 Joey Logano .40 1.00
17 Ryan Newman .30 .75
18 Matt DiBenedetto .25 .60
19 Jeffrey Earnhardt .40 1.00
20 Aric Almirola .30 .75
21 Chris Buescher .30 .75
22 Kurt Busch .30 .75
23 Kyle Larson .60 1.50
24 A.J. Allmendinger .40 1.00
25 Jimmie Johnson .60 1.50
26 Cole Whitt .40 1.00
27 Matt Kenseth .40 1.00
28 Martin Truex Jr. .30 .75
29 Alex Bowman .40 1.00
30 Kasey Kahne .40 1.00
31 William Byron .40 1.00
32 Bubba Wallace .40 1.00
33 Austin Cindric .40 1.00
34 Tyler Reddick .40 1.00
35 Christopher Bell .40 1.00
36 Chase Cabre .40 1.00
37 Hailie Deegan 2.50 6.00
38 Riley Herbst .60 1.50
39 Cayden Lapcevich .40 1.00
40 Zane Smith .40 1.00
41 Martin Truex Jr. PRW .30 .75
42 Kyle Busch PRW .50 1.25
43 Kyle Busch PRW .50 1.25
44 Martin Truex Jr. PRW .30 .75
45 Brad Keselowski PRW .50 1.25
46 Martin Truex Jr. PRW .30 .75
47 Kyle Busch PRW .50 1.25
48 Kevin Harvick PRW .50 1.25
49 Matt Kenseth PRW .40 1.00
50 Martin Truex Jr. PRW .30 .75
51 Richard Petty PW .60 1.50
52 Tony Stewart PW .60 1.50
53 Dale Earnhardt Jr. PW .75 2.00
54 Richard Petty PW .60 1.50
55 Richard Petty PW .60 1.50
56 Ward Burton PW .25 .60
57 Bill Elliott PW .60 1.50
58 Dale Jarrett PW .40 1.00
59 Richard Petty PW .60 1.50
60 Bobby Allison PW .30 .75
61 Tony Stewart PW .60 1.50
62 Richard Petty PW .60 1.50
63 Dale Earnhardt Jr. PW .75 2.00
64 Carl Edwards PW .40 1.00
65 Kevin Harvick PW .50 1.25
66 Joey Logano PW .40 1.00
67 Dale Earnhardt Jr. PW .75 2.00
68 Denny Hamlin PW .40 1.00
69 Derrike Cope PW .30 .75
70 Jimmie Johnson PW .60 1.50
71 Richard Petty PW .60 1.50
72 Darrell Waltrip PW .60 1.50
73 Dale Earnhardt Jr. PW .75 2.00
74 Michael Waltrip PW .40 1.00
75 Bill Elliott PW .60 1.50
76 Terry Labonte PW .40 1.00
77 Tony Stewart PW .60 1.50
78 Jimmie Johnson PW .60 1.50
79 Ernie Irvan PW .40 1.00
80 Brad Keselowski PW .50 1.25
81 Jimmie Johnson PW .60 1.50
82 Tony Stewart PW .60 1.50
83 Ricky Stenhouse Jr. PW .40 1.00
84 Jimmie Johnson PW .60 1.50
85 Jimmie Johnson PW .60 1.50
86 Denny Hamlin PW .40 1.00
87 Joey Logano PW .40 1.00
88 Dale Earnhardt Jr. PW .75 2.00
89 Tony Stewart PW .60 1.50
90 Kurt Busch PW .30 .75
91 Jimmie Johnson PW .60 1.50
92 Jimmie Johnson PW .60 1.50
93 Dale Earnhardt Jr. PW .75 2.00
94 Dale Jarrett PW .40 1.00
95 Kevin Harvick PW .50 1.25
96 Kyle Busch PW .50 1.25
97 Bobby Allison PW .30 .75
98 Dale Earnhardt Jr. PW .75 2.00
99 Jimmie Johnson PW .60 1.50
100 Jimmie Johnson PW .60 1.50

2018 Panini Victory Lane Silver

*SILVER: 1X TO 2.5X BASIC CARDS

2018 Panini Victory Lane Celebrations

*GOLD/99: .8X TO 2X BASIC INSERTS
*RED/49: 1X TO 2.5X BASIC INSERTS
*BLUE/25: 1.2X TO 3X BASIC INSERTS
1 Carl Edwards .75 2.00
2 Jimmie Johnson 1.25 3.00
3 Kevin Harvick 1.00 2.50
4 Dale Earnhardt Jr. 1.50 4.00
5 Brad Keselowski 1.00 2.50
6 Chase Elliott 1.00 2.50
7 Tony Stewart 1.25 3.00
8 Joey Logano .75 2.00
9 Martin Truex Jr. .60 1.50
10 Kyle Busch 1.00 2.50
11 Ryan Newman .60 1.50
12 Denny Hamlin .75 2.00
13 Kurt Busch .60 1.50
14 Austin Dillon 1.00 2.50
15 Kyle Larson 1.25 3.00

2018 Panini Victory Lane Champions

*GOLD/99: .8X TO 2X BASIC INSERTS
*RED/49: 1X TO 2.5X BASIC INSERTS
*BLUE/25: 1.2X TO 3X BASIC INSERTS
1 Jimmie Johnson 1.25 3.00
2 Richard Petty 1.25 3.00
3 Bobby Allison .60 1.50
4 Darrell Waltrip 1.25 3.00
5 Tony Stewart 1.25 3.00
6 Ned Jarrett .60 1.50
7 Terry Labonte .75 2.00
8 Bill Elliott 1.25 3.00
9 Rusty Wallace .75 2.00
10 Dale Jarrett .75 2.00
11 Bobby Labonte .75 2.00
12 Brad Keselowski 1.00 2.50
13 Kevin Harvick 1.00 2.50
14 Kyle Busch 1.00 2.50
15 Martin Truex Jr. .60 1.50

2018 Panini Victory Lane Chasing the Flag

*GOLD/99: .8X TO 2X BASIC INSERTS
*RED/49: 1X TO 2.5X BASIC INSERTS
*BLUE/25: 1.2X TO 3X BASIC INSERTS
1 Danica Patrick 1.50 4.00
2 Dale Earnhardt Jr. 1.50 4.00
3 Kevin Harvick 1.00 2.50
4 Jimmie Johnson 1.25 3.00
5 Tony Stewart 1.25 3.00
6 Carl Edwards .75 2.00

7 Richard Petty 1.25 3.00
8 Kyle Busch 1.00 2.50
9 Ryan Blaney .60 1.50
10 Chase Elliott 1.00 2.50

2018 Panini Victory Lane Engineered to Perfection Materials Green

*BASE/399: .25X TO .6X GREEN MEM/99
*BASE/199: .25X TO .6X GREEN MEM/49
*BASE/99: .25X TO .6X GREEN MEM/25
*GOLD/199: .3X TO .8X GREEN MEM/99
*GOLD/99: .3X TO .8X GREEN MEM/49
*GOLD/49: .3X TO .8X GREEN MEM/25
*BLACK/25: .6X TO 1.5X GREEN MEM/99
*BLACK/25: .5X TO 1.2X GREEN MEM/49
*BLACK/18: .6X TO 1.5X GREEN MEM/49
1 A.J. Allmendinger/99 4.00 10.00
2 Brad Keselowski/99 5.00 12.00
3 Brandon Jones/99 2.50 6.00
4 Bubba Wallace/99 4.00 10.00
5 Clint Bowyer/99 4.00 10.00
6 Cole Custer/99 4.00 10.00
7 Daniel Hemric/99 4.00 10.00
8 Erik Jones/99 4.00 10.00
9 Garrett Smithley/99 4.00 10.00
10 Cole Whitt/99 3.00 8.00
11 Greg Biffle/99 3.00 8.00
12 Jamie McMurray/99 4.00 10.00
13 Joey Logano/99 4.00 10.00
14 Kasey Kahne/25 6.00 15.00
15 Kyle Busch/49 6.00 15.00
16 Martin Truex Jr./99 3.00 8.00
17 Matt DiBenedetto/49 3.00 8.00
18 Matt Kenseth/25 6.00 15.00
19 Matt Tifft/99 4.00 10.00
20 Paul Menard/99 2.50 6.00
21 Ricky Stenhouse Jr./99 4.00 10.00
22 Ryan Newman/99 3.00 8.00
23 Tony Stewart/99 6.00 15.00
24 Trevor Bayne/99 4.00 10.00
25 William Byron/25 6.00 15.00

2018 Panini Victory Lane Engineered to Perfection Triple Materials

*GOLD/199: .5X TO 1.2X BASIC MEM/299-399
*GOLD/99: .5X TO 1.2X BASIC MEM/199
*GOLD/49: .5X TO 1.2X BASIC MEM/99
*GOLD/25: .5X TO 1.2X BASIC MEM/49
*GOLD/15: .5X TO 1.2X BASIC MEM/25
*GREEN/99: .6X TO 1.5X BASIC MEM/299-399
*GREEN/49: .6X TO 1.5X BASIC MEM/199
*GREEN/25: .6X TO 1.5X BASIC MEM/99
*BLACK/25: 1X TO 2.5X BASIC MEM/299-399
*BLACK/25: .8X TO 2X BASIC MEM/199
1 Blake Koch/399 1.50 4.00
2 Brandon Jones/399 1.50 4.00
3 Chris Buescher/399 2.00 5.00
4 Daniel Hemric/399 2.50 6.00
5 Denny Hamlin/399 2.50 6.00
6 Elliott Sadler/399 1.50 4.00
7 Erik Jones/399 2.50 6.00
8 John Hunter Nemechek/399 2.00 5.00
9 Justin Allgaier/399 2.00 5.00
10 Kasey Kahne/199 3.00 8.00
11 Martin Truex Jr./399 2.00 5.00
12 Matt DiBenedetto/299 1.50 4.00
13 Matt Kenseth/99 4.00 10.00
14 Michael Annett/399 2.50 6.00
15 Ricky Stenhouse Jr./399 2.50 6.00
16 Ross Chastain/399 2.50 6.00
17 Ryan Newman/49 4.00 10.00
18 Ryan Reed/399 2.50 6.00
19 Ty Dillon/399 2.50 6.00
20 William Byron/25 6.00 15.00

2018 Panini Victory Lane Foundations

*GOLD/99: .8X TO 2X BASIC INSERTS
*RED/49: 1X TO 2.5X BASIC INSERTS
*BLUE/25: 1.2X TO 3X BASIC INSERTS
1 Dale Earnhardt Jr. 1.50 4.00
2 Tony Stewart 1.25 3.00
3 Carl Edwards .75 2.00
4 Mark Martin .75 2.00
5 Danica Patrick 1.50 4.00
6 Richard Petty 1.25 3.00
7 Darrell Waltrip 1.25 3.00
8 Rusty Wallace .75 2.00
9 Terry Labonte .75 2.00
10 Bobby Labonte .75 2.00
11 Junior Johnson .75 2.00
12 Harry Gant .60 1.50
13 Dale Jarrett .75 2.00
14 Bill Elliott 1.25 3.00
15 Bobby Allison .60 1.50

2018 Panini Victory Lane NASCAR at 70

*GOLD/99: .8X TO 2X BASIC INSERTS
*RED/49: 1X TO 2.5X BASIC INSERTS
*BLUE/25: 1.2X TO 3X BASIC INSERTS
1 Richard Petty 1.25 3.00
2 Bill Elliott 1.25 3.00
3 Rusty Wallace .75 2.00
4 Harry Gant .60 1.50
5 Bobby Labonte .75 2.00
6 Junior Johnson .75 2.00
7 Darrell Waltrip 1.25 3.00
8 Mark Martin .75 2.00
9 Jimmie Johnson 1.25 3.00
10 Dale Earnhardt Jr. 1.50 4.00

2018 Panini Victory Lane Pedal to the Metal

*BLUE/25: 1.5X TO 4X BASIC INSERTS
1 A.J. Allmendinger .60 1.50
2 Alex Bowman .60 1.50
3 Aric Almirola .50 1.25
4 Austin Dillon .75 2.00
5 Brad Keselowski .75 2.00
6 Bubba Wallace .60 1.50
7 Casey Mears .40 1.00
8 Chase Elliott .75 2.00
9 Chris Buescher .50 1.25
10 Clint Bowyer .60 1.50
11 Cole Custer .60 1.50
12 Cole Whitt .50 1.25
13 Corey LaJoie .50 1.25
14 Dale Earnhardt Jr. 1.25 3.00
15 Danica Patrick 1.25 3.00
16 Daniel Hemric .60 1.50
17 Daniel Suarez .60 1.50
18 David Ragan .50 1.25
19 Denny Hamlin .60 1.50
20 Elliott Sadler .40 1.00
21 Erik Jones .60 1.50
22 Christopher Bell .60 1.50
23 Jamie McMurray .60 1.50
24 Jeffrey Earnhardt .60 1.50
25 Jimmie Johnson 1.00 2.50
26 Joey Gase .40 1.00
27 Joey Logano .60 1.50
28 John Hunter Nemechek .50 1.25
29 Justin Allgaier .50 1.25
30 J.J. Yeley .40 1.00
31 Kasey Kahne .60 1.50
32 Kaz Grala .75 2.00
33 Kevin Harvick .75 2.00
34 Kurt Busch .50 1.25
35 Kyle Busch .75 2.00
36 Kyle Larson 1.00 2.50
37 Landon Cassill .50 1.25
38 Martin Truex Jr. .50 1.25
39 Matt DiBenedetto .40 1.00
40 Matt Kenseth .60 1.50
41 Michael Annett .60 1.50
42 Michael McDowell .60 1.50
43 Paul Menard .40 1.00
44 Ricky Stenhouse Jr. .60 1.50
45 Ryan Blaney .50 1.25
46 Ryan Newman .50 1.25
47 Spencer Gallagher .60 1.50
48 Trevor Bayne .60 1.50
49 Ty Dillon .60 1.50
50 William Byron .60 1.50
51 Jamie McMurray CAR .60 1.50
52 Brad Keselowski CAR .75 2.00
53 Austin Dillon CAR .75 2.00
54 Kevin Harvick CAR .75 2.00
55 Trevor Bayne CAR .60 1.50
56 Chase Elliott CAR .75 2.00
57 Denny Hamlin CAR .60 1.50
58 Ryan Blaney CAR .50 1.25
59 Ty Dillon CAR .60 1.50
60 Clint Bowyer CAR .60 1.50
61 Ricky Stenhouse Jr. CAR .60 1.50
62 Kyle Busch CAR .75 2.00
63 Daniel Suarez CAR .60 1.50
64 Erik Jones CAR .60 1.50
65 Joey Logano CAR .60 1.50
66 Ryan Newman CAR .50 1.25
67 Kurt Busch CAR .50 1.25
68 Kyle Larson CAR 1.00 2.50
69 A.J. Allmendinger CAR .60 1.50
70 Jimmie Johnson CAR 1.00 2.50
71 Matt Kenseth CAR .60 1.50
72 Martin Truex Jr. CAR .50 1.25
73 Alex Bowman CAR .60 1.50
74 Danica Patrick CAR 1.25 3.00
75 Dale Earnhardt Jr. CAR 1.25 3.00
76 Richard Petty 1.00 2.50
77 Darrell Waltrip 1.00 2.50
78 Bill Elliott 1.00 2.50
79 Bobby Allison .50 1.25
80 Bobby Labonte .60 1.50
81 Terry Labonte .60 1.50
82 Marcos Ambrose .60 1.50
83 Carl Edwards .60 1.50
84 Dale Jarrett .60 1.50
85 Derrike Cope .50 1.25
86 Donnie Allison .50 1.25
87 Ernie Irvan .60 1.50
88 Greg Biffle .50 1.25
89 Harry Gant .50 1.25
90 Jeff Burton .50 1.25
91 Junior Johnson .60 1.50
92 Kenny Wallace .40 1.00
93 Rusty Wallace .60 1.50
94 Kyle Petty .50 1.25
95 Mark Martin .60 1.50
96 Michael Waltrip .60 1.50
97 Morgan Shepherd .60 1.50
98 Ned Jarrett .50 1.25
99 Ward Burton .40 1.00
100 Tony Stewart 1.00 2.50

2018 Panini Victory Lane Race Day

*GOLD/99: .8X TO 2X BASIC INSERTS
*RED/49: 1X TO 2.5X BASIC INSERTS
*BLUE/25: 1.2X TO 3X BASIC INSERTS
1 Jimmie Johnson 1.25 3.00
2 Kevin Harvick 1.00 2.50
3 Chase Elliott 1.00 2.50
4 Clint Bowyer .75 2.00
5 Denny Hamlin .75 2.00
6 Kyle Busch 1.00 2.50
7 Martin Truex Jr. .60 1.50
8 Brad Keselowski 1.00 2.50
9 Danica Patrick 1.50 4.00
10 Dale Earnhardt Jr. 1.50 4.00

2018 Panini Victory Lane Race Ready Dual Materials Green

*BASE/399: .25X TO .6X GREEN MEM/99
*BASE/49: .25X TO .6X GREEN MEM/18
*GOLD/199: .3X TO .8X GREEN MEM/399
*GOLD/99: .3X TO .8X GREEN MEM/49
*GOLD/25: .3X TO .8X GREEN MEM/18
*BLACK/25: .6X TO 1.5X GREEN MEM/99
1 Brandon Jones/99 2.50 6.00
2 Clint Bowyer/99 4.00 10.00
3 Cole Custer/99 4.00 10.00
4 Dale Earnhardt Jr./99 8.00 20.00
5 Denny Hamlin/99 4.00 10.00
6 Elliott Sadler/99 2.50 6.00
7 Garrett Smithley/99 4.00 10.00
8 Tony Stewart/99 6.00 15.00
9 Joey Logano/99 4.00 10.00
10 John Hunter Nemechek/99 3.00 8.00
11 Justin Allgaier/99 3.00 8.00
12 Kyle Busch/18 10.00 25.00
13 Matt DiBenedetto/49 3.00 8.00
15 Michael Annett/99 4.00 10.00
16 Michael McDowell/99 4.00 10.00
17 Paul Menard/99 2.50 6.00
18 Ross Chastain/99 4.00 10.00
19 Ryan Reed/99 4.00 10.00
20 Ty Dillon/99 4.00 10.00

2018 Panini Victory Lane Race Ready Materials Black

*GREEN/99: .25X TO .6X BASIC MEM/25
*BASE/399: .15X TO .4X BLACK MEM/25
*BASE/99: .25X TO .6X BLACK MEM/25
*GOLD/199: .2X TO .5X BLACK MEM/25
*GOLD/48-49: .3X TO .8X BASIC MEM/25
1 A.J. Allmendinger/25 6.00 15.00
2 Daniel Suarez/25 6.00 15.00
3 Bubba Wallace/25 6.00 15.00
4 Cameron Hayley/25 4.00 10.00
5 Chase Elliott/25 8.00 20.00
6 Clint Bowyer/25 6.00 15.00
7 Collin Cabre/25 4.00 10.00
8 Dale Earnhardt Jr./25 12.00 30.00
9 Danica Patrick/25 12.00 30.00
10 Daniel Hemric/25 6.00 15.00
11 Denny Hamlin/25 6.00 15.00
12 Erik Jones/25 6.00 15.00
17 Julia Landauer/25 4.00 10.00
20 Kurt Busch/25 5.00 12.00
22 Ryan Blaney/25 5.00 12.00
23 Ryan Newman/25 5.00 12.00
24 Tony Stewart/25 10.00 25.00

2018 Panini Victory Lane Remarkable Remnants Material Autographs

*GOLD/199: .3X TO .8X BASIC MEM AU/70-150
*GOLD/75-99: .4X TO 1X BASIC MEM AU/70-150
*GOLD/49-50: .5X TO 1.2X BASIC MEM AU/70-150
*GOLD/25: .5X TO 1.5X BASIC MEM AU/59
*GREEN/75-99: .4X TO 1X BASIC MEM AU/70-150
*GREEN/49-50: .5X TO 1.2X BASIC MEM AU/70-150
*GREEN/25: .6X TO 1.5X BASIC MEM AU/99
*BLACK/25: .6X TO 1.5X BASIC MEM AU/70-150
*BLACK/18: .8X TO 2X BASIC MEM AU/70-150
1 Dale Earnhardt Jr./70
2 Jimmie Johnson/59 15.00 40.00
3 Kevin Harvick/150 12.00 30.00
4 Chase Elliott/100 15.00 40.00
5 Tony Stewart/145 8.00 20.00
6 Carl Edwards/89 8.00 20.00
7 Joey Logano/100 6.00 15.00
8 Kyle Busch/99 12.00 30.00
9 Martin Truex Jr./100 4.00 10.00
10 William Byron/126 15.00 40.00

2018 Panini Victory Lane Starting Grid

*GOLD/99: .8X TO 2X BASIC INSERTS
*RED/49: 1X TO 2.5X BASIC INSERTS
*BLUE/25: 1.2X TO 3X BASIC INSERTS
1 Jamie McMurray .75 2.00
2 Brad Keselowski 1.00 2.50
3 Austin Dillon 1.00 2.50
4 Kevin Harvick 1.00 2.50
5 Trevor Bayne .75 2.00
6 Chase Elliott 1.00 2.50
7 Denny Hamlin .75 2.00
8 Ryan Blaney .60 1.50
9 Ty Dillon .75 2.00
10 Clint Bowyer .75 2.00
11 Ricky Stenhouse Jr. .75 2.00
12 Kyle Busch 1.00 2.50
13 Daniel Suarez .75 2.00
14 Erik Jones .75 2.00
15 Paul Menard .50 1.25
16 Joey Logano .75 2.00
17 Ryan Newman .60 1.50
18 Kurt Busch .60 1.50
19 Kyle Larson 1.25 3.00
20 Bubba Wallace .75 2.00
21 A.J. Allmendinger .75 2.00
22 Jimmie Johnson 1.25 3.00
23 Matt Kenseth .75 2.00
24 Martin Truex Jr. .60 1.50
25 Alex Bowman .75 2.00

2019 Panini Victory Lane

*GOLD/25: 2.5X TO 6X BASIC CARDS
1 Kurt Busch .30 .75
2 Brad Keselowski .50 1.25
3 Austin Dillon .50 1.25
4 Kevin Harvick .50 1.25
5 Ryan Newman .30 .75
6 Daniel Hemric .40 1.00
7 Chase Elliott .50 1.25
8 Aric Almirola .30 .75
9 Denny Hamlin .40 1.00
10 Ryan Blaney .30 .75
11 Ty Dillon .40 1.00
12 Clint Bowyer .40 1.00
13 Ross Chastain .40 1.00
14 Ricky Stenhouse Jr .40 1.00
15 Kyle Busch .50 1.25
16 Martin Truex Jr. .30 .75
17 Erik Jones .40 1.00
18 Paul Menard .25 .60
19 Joey Logano .40 1.00
20 William Byron .40 1.00
21 Corey LaJoie .30 .75
22 Michael McDowell .40 1.00
23 Matt Tifft .40 1.00
24 Chris Buescher .30 .75
25 David Ragan .30 .75
26 Daniel Suarez .40 1.00
27 Kyle Larson .60 1.50
28 Bubba Wallace .40 1.00
29 Ryan Preece .25 .60
30 Jimmie Johnson .60 1.50
31 Alex Bowman .40 1.00
32 Matt DiBenedetto .25 .60
33 Tanner Berryhill .25 .60
34 Landon Cassill .30 .75
35 Cole Custer .40 1.00
36 Noah Gragson .25 .60
37 Michael Annett .40 1.00
38 Justin Allgaier .30 .75
39 Gray Gaulding .25 .60
40 Zane Smith .25 .60
41 Justin Haley .25 .60
42 Christopher Bell .75 2.00
43 John Hunter Nemechek .30 .75
44 Chase Briscoe .40 1.00
45 Richard Petty .60 1.50
46 Dale Earnhardt Jr .75 2.00
47 Danica Patrick .75 2.00
48 Mark Martin .40 1.00
49 Terry Labonte .40 1.00
50 Darrell Waltrip .60 1.50
51 Brad Keselowski PRW .50 1.25
52 Kyle Busch PRW .50 1.25
53 Ryan Blaney PRW .30 .75
54 Chase Elliott PRW .50 1.25
55 Aric Almirola PRW .30 .75
56 Chase Elliott PRW .50 1.25
57 Joey Logano PRW .40 1.00
58 Kevin Harvick PRW .50 1.25
59 Kyle Busch PRW .50 1.25
60 Joey Logano PRW .40 1.00
61 Joey Logano PC .40 1.00
62 Martin Truex Jr. PC .30 .75
63 Jimmie Johnson PC .60 1.50
64 Kyle Busch PC .50 1.25
65 Kevin Harvick PC .50 1.25
66 Brad Keselowski PC .50 1.25
67 Tony Stewart PC .60 1.50
68 Matt Kenseth PC .40 1.00
69 Bobby Labonte PC .40 1.00
70 Dale Jarrett PC .40 1.00
71 Terry Labonte PC .40 1.00
72 Rusty Wallace PC .40 1.00
73 Bill Elliott PC .60 1.50
74 Darrell Waltrip PC .60 1.50
75 Richard Petty PC .60 1.50
76 Bobby Allison PW .30 .75
77 Austin Dillon PW .50 1.25
78 Jimmie Johnson PW .60 1.50
79 Richard Petty PW .60 1.50
80 Chase Elliott PW .50 1.25
81 Dale Earnhardt Jr PW .75 2.00
82 Erik Jones PW .40 1.00
83 Darrell Waltrip PW .60 1.50
84 Jimmie Johnson PW .60 1.50
85 Kevin Harvick PW .50 1.25
86 Ricky Stenhouse Jr PW .40 1.00
87 Austin Dillon PW .50 1.25
88 Ryan Newman PW .30 .75
89 Rusty Wallace PW .40 1.00
90 Richard Petty PW .60 1.50
91 Dale Earnhardt Jr PW .75 2.00
92 Ryan Blaney PW .30 .75
93 Kyle Larson PW .60 1.50
94 Kasey Kahne PW .40 1.00
95 Richard Petty PW .60 1.50
96 Tony Stewart PW .60 1.50
97 Jimmie Johnson PW .60 1.50
98 Kyle Busch PW .50 1.25
99 Richard Petty PW .60 1.50
100 Darrell Waltrip PW .60 1.50

2019 Panini Victory Lane Dual Swatch Signatures

*GOLD/99: .5X TO 1.2X BASIC MEM AU
*GOLD/49: .6X TO 1.5X BASIC MEM AU
*RED/25: .8X TO 2X BASIC MEM AU
2 Brad Keselowski 5.00 12.00
3 Chase Briscoe 4.00 10.00
4 Christopher Bell 10.00 25.00
5 Dale Earnhardt Jr EXCH 25.00 50.00
6 Daniel Hemric 4.00 10.00
7 Denny Hamlin 4.00 10.00
8 Jamie McMurray 4.00 10.00
9 Jimmie Johnson 15.00 40.00
10 John Hunter Nemechek 3.00 8.00
11 Kevin Harvick 5.00 12.00
12 Kurt Busch 3.00 8.00
13 Kyle Larson 6.00 15.00
14 Matt Kenseth 4.00 10.00
15 Ryan Blaney 3.00 8.00

2019 Panini Victory Lane Horsepower Heroes

*BLUE/99: .8X TO 2X BASIC INSERTS
*GOLD/25: 1.2X TO 3X BASIC INSERTS
1 Jimmie Johnson 1.25 3.00
2 Kyle Busch 1.00 2.50
3 Martin Truex Jr. .60 1.50
4 Joey Logano .75 2.00
5 William Byron .75 2.00
6 Richard Petty 1.25 3.00
7 Dale Earnhardt Jr 1.50 4.00
8 Denny Hamlin .75 2.00
9 Brad Keselowski 1.00 2.50
10 Austin Dillon 1.00 2.50
11 Bubba Wallace .75 2.00
12 Danica Patrick 1.50 4.00
13 Ryan Blaney .60 1.50
14 Chase Elliott 1.00 2.50
15 Kevin Harvick 1.00 2.50

2019 Panini Victory Lane Machines

*BLUE/99: .8X TO 2X BASIC INSERTS
*GOLD/25: 1.2X TO 3X BASIC INSERTS
1 Jimmie Johnson 1.25 3.00
2 Kevin Harvick 1.00 2.50
3 Chase Elliott 1.00 2.50
4 Kyle Busch 1.00 2.50
5 Martin Truex Jr. .60 1.50
6 Ryan Blaney .60 1.50
7 Joey Logano .75 2.00
8 William Byron .75 2.00
9 Bubba Wallace .75 2.00
10 Denny Hamlin .75 2.00
11 Brad Keselowski 1.00 2.50
12 Austin Dillon 1.00 2.50
13 Kyle Larson 1.25 3.00
14 Kurt Busch .60 1.50
15 Ty Dillon .75 2.00
16 Ryan Newman .60 1.50
17 Clint Bowyer .75 2.00
18 Alex Bowman .75 2.00
19 Aric Almirola .60 1.50
20 Daniel Suarez .75 2.00

2019 Panini Victory Lane Pedal to the Metal

*GOLD/25: 1.5X TO 4X BASIC INSERTS
1 Ryan Preece .40 1.00
2 Tanner Thorson .40 1.00
3 Anthony Alfredo .40 1.00
4 Gray Gaulding .40 1.00
5 Hailie Deegan 2.50 6.00
6 Cole Custer .60 1.50
7 Daniel Hemric .60 1.50
8 Tanner Berryhill .40 1.00
9 Landon Cassill .50 1.25
10 Ryan Blaney .50 1.25
11 Daniel Suarez .60 1.50
12 William Byron .60 1.50
13 Chase Briscoe .60 1.50
14 Brad Keselowski .75 2.00
15 Paul Menard .40 1.00
16 Bubba Wallace .60 1.50
17 Kyle Larson 1.00 2.50
18 Derek Kraus .75 2.00
19 Michael McDowell .60 1.50
20 Justin Haley .40 1.00
21 Ryan Vargas .40 1.00
22 Chase Elliott .75 2.00
23 Christopher Bell 1.25 3.00
24 Chris Buescher .50 1.25
25 Aric Almirola .50 1.25
26 Matt Tifft .60 1.50
27 Martin Truex Jr. .50 1.25
28 Zane Smith .40 1.00
29 Clint Bowyer .60 1.50
30 Matt DiBenedetto .40 1.00
31 Denny Hamlin .60 1.50
32 Alex Bowman .60 1.50
33 Jimmie Johnson 1.00 2.50
34 Kurt Busch .50 1.25
35 Kyle Busch .75 2.00
36 Ricky Stenhouse Jr .60 1.50
37 Ty Dillon .60 1.50
38 Ross Chastain .60 1.50
39 Joey Logano .60 1.50
40 Michael Annett .60 1.50
41 Kevin Harvick .75 2.00
42 Erik Jones .60 1.50
43 David Ragan .50 1.25
44 Harrison Burton .75 2.00
45 Corey LaJoie .50 1.25
46 Noah Gragson .40 1.00
47 Ryan Newman .50 1.25
48 Justin Allgaier .50 1.25
49 Austin Dillon .75 2.00
50 John Hunter Nemechek .50 1.25
51 Ryan Blaney CAR .50 1.25
52 William Byron CAR .60 1.50
53 Brad Keselowski CAR .75 2.00
54 Kyle Larson CAR 1.00 2.50
55 Chase Elliott CAR .75 2.00
56 Aric Almirola CAR .50 1.25
57 Denny Hamlin CAR .60 1.50
58 Alex Bowman CAR .60 1.50
59 Kyle Busch CAR .75 2.00
60 Ty Dillon CAR .60 1.50
61 Kevin Harvick CAR .75 2.00
62 Erik Jones CAR .60 1.50
63 Austin Dillon CAR .75 2.00
64 Joey Logano CAR .60 1.50
65 Martin Truex Jr. CAR .50 1.25
66 Richard Petty LEG 1.00 2.50
67 Darrell Waltrip LEG 1.00 2.50
68 Terry Labonte LEG .60 1.50
69 Bobby Allison LEG .50 1.25
70 Bill Elliott LEG 1.00 2.50
71 Harry Gant LEG .50 1.25
72 Tony Stewart LEG 1.00 2.50
73 Dale Jarrett LEG .60 1.50
74 Mark Martin LEG .60 1.50
75 Rusty Wallace LEG .60 1.50
76 Joey Logano CHAMP .60 1.50
77 Martin Truex Jr. CHAMP .50 1.25
78 Jimmie Johnson CHAMP 1.00 2.50
79 Kyle Busch CHAMP .75 2.00
80 Kevin Harvick CHAMP .75 2.00
81 Jimmie Johnson CHAMP 1.00 2.50
82 Brad Keselowski CHAMP .75 2.00
83 Tony Stewart CHAMP 1.00 2.50
84 Jimmie Johnson CHAMP 1.00 2.50
85 Jimmie Johnson CHAMP 1.00 2.50
86 Jimmie Johnson CHAMP 1.00 2.50
87 Jimmie Johnson CHAMP 1.00 2.50
88 Jimmie Johnson CHAMP 1.00 2.50
89 Matt Kenseth CHAMP .60 1.50
90 Bobby Labonte CHAMP .60 1.50
91 Dale Jarrett CHAMP .60 1.50
92 Terry Labonte CHAMP .60 1.50
93 Rusty Wallace CHAMP .60 1.50
94 Bill Elliott CHAMP 1.00 2.50
95 Darrell Waltrip CHAMP 1.00 2.50
96 Bobby Allison CHAMP .50 1.25
97 Richard Petty CHAMP 1.00 2.50
98 Richard Petty CHAMP 1.00 2.50
99 Richard Petty CHAMP 1.00 2.50
100 Richard Petty CHAMP 1.00 2.50

2019 Panini Victory Lane Quad Swatches

*GOLD/99: .6X TO 1.5X BASIC MEM
*RED/25: 1X TO 2.5X BASIC MEM
1 Dale Earnhardt Jr 5.00 12.00
2 Jimmie Johnson 4.00 10.00
3 Kevin Harvick 3.00 8.00
4 Kyle Busch 3.00 8.00
5 Joey Logano 2.50 6.00
6 Martin Truex Jr. 2.00 5.00
7 Chase Elliott 3.00 8.00
8 Ryan Blaney 2.00 5.00
10 Bubba Wallace 2.50 6.00

2019 Panini Victory Lane Signature Swatches Gold

*GOLD/99: .5X TO 1.2X BASIC MEM AU
*GOLD/49: .6X TO 1.5X BASIC MEM AU
*GOLD/25: .8X TO 2X BASIC MEM AU
8 Hailie Deegan/99 125.00 250.00

2019 Panini Victory Lane Signature Swatches Red

*RED/25: .8X TO 2X BASIC MEM AU
8 Hailie Deegan/25 150.00 300.00

2019 Panini Victory Lane Starting Grid

*BLUE/99: .8X TO 2X BASIC INSERTS
*GOLD/25: 1.2X TO 3X BASIC INSERTS
1 Austin Dillon 1.00 2.50
2 Ricky Stenhouse Jr .75 2.00
3 Jimmie Johnson 1.25 3.00
4 Kevin Harvick 1.00 2.50
5 Ty Dillon .75 2.00
6 Tanner Berryhill .50 1.25
7 Matt Tifft .75 2.00
8 Kyle Busch 1.00 2.50
9 Bubba Wallace .75 2.00
10 William Byron .75 2.00
11 Martin Truex Jr. .60 1.50
12 Joey Logano .75 2.00
13 Aric Almirola .60 1.50
14 Ryan Preece .50 1.25
15 Clint Bowyer .75 2.00
16 Kyle Larson 1.25 3.00
17 Kurt Busch .60 1.50
18 Alex Bowman .75 2.00
19 Chase Elliott 1.00 2.50
20 Daniel Suarez .75 2.00
21 Ryan Blaney .60 1.50
22 Denny Hamlin .75 2.00
23 Brad Keselowski 1.00 2.50
24 Daniel Hemric .75 2.00
25 Ryan Newman .60 1.50

2019 Panini Victory Lane Top 10

*BLUE/99: .8X TO 2X BASIC INSERTS
*GOLD/25: 1.2X TO 3X BASIC INSERTS
1 Joey Logano .75 2.00
2 Martin Truex Jr. .60 1.50
3 Kevin Harvick 1.00 2.50
4 Kyle Busch 1.00 2.50
5 Aric Almirola .60 1.50
6 Chase Elliott 1.00 2.50
7 Denny Hamlin .75 2.00
8 Brad Keselowski 1.00 2.50
9 Kyle Larson 1.25 3.00
10 Ryan Blaney .60 1.50

2019 Panini Victory Lane Track Stars

*BLUE/99: .8X TO 2X BASIC INSERTS
*GOLD/25: 1.2X TO 3X BASIC INSERTS
1 Jimmie Johnson 1.25 3.00
2 Kevin Harvick 1.00 2.50
3 Chase Elliott 1.00 2.50
4 Kyle Busch 1.00 2.50
5 Martin Truex Jr. .60 1.50
6 Ryan Blaney .60 1.50
7 Joey Logano .75 2.00
8 William Byron .75 2.00
9 Bubba Wallace .75 2.00
10 Dale Earnhardt Jr 1.50 4.00
11 Danica Patrick 1.50 4.00
12 Denny Hamlin .75 2.00
13 Brad Keselowski 1.00 2.50
14 Austin Dillon 1.00 2.50
15 Kyle Larson 1.25 3.00

2019 Panini Victory Lane Triple Swatch Signatures

*GOLD/75-99: .5X TO 1.2X BASIC MEM AU
*GOLD/40: .6X TO 1.5X BASIC MEM AU
*RED/25: .8X TO 2X BASIC MEM AU
1 Austin Dillon 5.00 12.00
2 Chase Elliott 25.00 60.00
3 Chris Buescher 3.00 8.00
4 Clint Bowyer 4.00 10.00
5 Daniel Suarez 4.00 10.00
6 David Ragan 3.00 8.00

7 Erik Jones 4.00 10.00
8 Justin Allgaier 3.00 8.00
9 Kasey Kahne 4.00 10.00
10 Kyle Busch 12.00 30.00

2019 Panini Victory Lane Triple Swatches

*GOLD/25: .6X TO 1.5X BASIC MEM
*RED/25: 1X TO 2.5X BASIC MEM
1 Austin Dillon 3.00 8.00
2 Chris Buescher 2.00 5.00
3 Christopher Bell 5.00 12.00
4 Clint Bowyer 2.50 6.00
5 Daniel Suarez 2.50 6.00
6 Jamie McMurray 2.50 6.00
7 Kyle Busch 3.00 8.00
8 Matt Tifft 2.50 6.00
9 Michael McDowell 2.50 6.00
10 Ty Dillon 2.50 6.00
11 Ryan Newman 2.00 5.00
12 Paul Menard 1.50 4.00
13 Kurt Busch 2.00 5.00
14 John Hunter Nemechek 2.00 5.00
15 David Ragan 2.00 5.00

1992 Pepsi Richard Petty

This five-card set features the King of stock car racing, Richard Petty. The cards highlight Richard Petty's career. The cards were a promotional giveaway by Pepsi Co.

COMPLETE SET (5) 2.00 5.00
COMMON CARD .40 1.00

1993 Pepsi 400 Victory Lane

Produced and distributed by Pepsi, this five-card set honors past winners of the Pepsi 400. The cards are unnumbered and listed below alphabetically. Although no year is present on the cards, they can be distinguished from the 1994 Pepsi 400 release by the orange colored Victory Lane title on the cardfronts.

COMPLETE SET (5) 4.00 10.00
1 Bobby Allison 1.25 3.00
2 Davey Allison 2.00 5.00
3 Buddy Baker .50 1.25
4 Ernie Irvan 1.25 3.00
5 David Pearson .50 1.25

1994 Pepsi 400 Victory Lane

Pepsi again produced and distributed a Pepsi 400 commemorative set in 1994. The cards are very similar to the 1993 issue, except they include the year 1994 on the cardfronts, as well as a yellow colored Victory Lane title. The cards are unnumbered and listed below alphabetically.

COMPLETE SET (6) 4.00 8.00
1 Donnie Allison .50 1.25
2 A.J.Foyt .50 1.25
3 Richard Petty 1.25 3.00
4 Greg Sacks .50 1.25
5 Cale Yarborough .50 1.25
6 Cover .10 .30
Checklist Card

1981-82 Philip Morris

This 18-card standard-size set was included in the Champions of American Sport program and features major stars from a variety of sports. The program was issued in conjunction with a traveling exhibition organized by the National Portrait Gallery and the Smithsonian Institution and sponsored by Philip Morris and Miller Brewing Company. The cards are either reproductions of works of art (paintings) or famous photographs of the time. The cards are frequently found with a perforated edge on at least one side. The cards were actually obtained from two perforated pages in the program. There is no notation anywhere on the cards indicating the manufacturer or sponsor.

COMPLETE SET (18) 40.00 100.00
4 A.J. Foyt 3.20 8.00

1996 Pinnacle

The 1996 Pinnacle set was issued in one series totalling 96 cards. This is the first issue under the Pinnacle name brand. The cards features NASCAR's top drivers and their rides printed on 20 point board. Each card has gold foil stamping and UV coating. The set includes these sub-sets; Jeff Gordon Persistence (66-73), Sterling Marlin Sterling (74-77), Hall of Fame (78-81), and Winners (85-89). The cards come 10-cards per pack, 24 packs per box and 16 boxes per case. The packs carried a suggested retail price for $2.49 each.

COMPLETE SET (96) 6.00 15.00
*FOIL: .6X TO 1.5X BASIC CARDS
1 Rick Mast .07 .20
2 Rusty Wallace .60 1.50
3 Dale Earnhardt 1.25 3.00
4 Sterling Marlin .25 .60
5 Terry Labonte .25 .60
6 Mark Martin .60 1.50
7 Geoff Bodine .07 .20
8 Hut Stricklin .07 .20
9 Lake Speed .07 .20
10 Ricky Rudd .25 .60
11 Brett Bodine .07 .20
12 Derrike Cope .07 .20
13 Dale Jarrett .50 1.25
14 Joe Nemechek .07 .20
15 Wally Dallenbach .07 .20
16 Ted Musgrave .07 .20
17 Darrell Waltrip .15 .40
18 Bobby Labonte .50 1.25
19 Kenny Wallace .07 .20
20 Bobby Hillin Jr. .07 .20
21 Michael Waltrip .15 .40
22 Ward Burton .15 .40
23 Jimmy Spencer .07 .20
24 Jeff Gordon .75 2.00
25 Ken Schrader .07 .20
26 Morgan Shepherd .07 .20
27 Bill Elliott .30 .75
28 Ernie Irvan .15 .40
29 Bobby Hamilton .07 .20
30 Johnny Benson .15 .40
31 Kyle Petty .15 .40
32 Ricky Craven .07 .20
33 Robert Pressley .07 .20
34 John Andretti .07 .20
35 Jeremy Mayfield .15 .40
36 Rick Mast's Car .02 .10
37 Rusty Wallace's Car .25 .60
38 Dale Earnhardt's Car .50 1.25
39 Sterling Marlin's Car .07 .20
40 Terry Labonte's Car .15 .40
41 Mark Martin's Car .25 .60
42 Geoff Bodine's Car .02 .10
43 Ricky Rudd's Car .07 .20
44 Derrike Cope's Car .02 .10
45 Ted Musgrave's Car .02 .10
46 Darrell Waltrip's Car .02 .10
47 Bobby Labonte's Car .15 .40
48 Michael Waltrip's Car .07 .20
49 Ward Burton's Car .02 .10
50 Jimmy Spencer's Car .02 .10
51 Jeff Gordon's Car .30 .75
52 Ernie Irvan's Car .07 .20
53 Johnny Benson's Car .02 .10
54 Robert Pressley's Car .02 .10
55 John Andretti's Car .02 .10
56 Ricky Craven's Car .02 .10
57 Kyle Petty's Car .07 .20
58 Bobby Hamilton's Car .02 .10
59 Dave Marcis' Car .07 .20
60 Morgan Shepherd's Car .02 .10
61 Bobby Hillin's Car .02 .10
62 Kenny Wallace's Car .02 .10
63 Joe Nemechek's Car .02 .10
64 Dale Jarrett's Car .15 .40
65 Hut Stricklin's Car .02 .10
66 Jeff Gordon PER .75 2.00
67 Jeff Gordon PER .75 2.00
68 Jeff Gordon PER .75 2.00
69 Jeff Gordon PER .75 2.00
70 Jeff Gordon PER .75 2.00
71 Jeff Gordon PER .75 2.00
72 Jeff Gordon PER .75 2.00
73 Jeff Gordon PER .75 2.00
74 Sterling Marlin STE .15 .40
75 Sterling Marlin STE .15 .40
76 Sterling Marlin STE .15 .40
77 Sterling Marlin STE .15 .40
78 Joe Gibbs HOF .15 .40
79 Bobby Labonte HOF .25 .60
80 Jimmy Makar HOF .02 .10
81 Bobby Labonte's Car HOF .15 .40
82 Elmo Langley .02 .10
83 Doyle Ford .02 .10
84 Buster Auton .02 .10
85 Jeff Gordon W .75 2.00
86 Rusty Wallace W .30 .75
87 Sterling Marlin W .15 .40
88 Ernie Irvan W .07 .20
89 Rusty Wallace W .30 .75
90 Bobby Labonte's Transporter .15 .40
91 Dale Earnhardt's Transporter .50 1.25
92 Jeff Gordon's Transporter .30 .75
93 Sterling Marlin's Transporter .07 .20
94 Rusty Wallace's Transporter .25 .60
95 Jeff Gordon CL .30 .75
96 Mark Martin CL .25 .60
DS1 Bill Elliott Driver Suit 8.00 20.00

1996 Pinnacle Artist Proofs

COMPLETE SET (96) 20.00 400.00
*ARTIST PROOF: 8X TO 20X BASE CARDS

1996 Pinnacle Winston Cup Collection Dufex

COMPLETE SET (96) 40.00 80.00
*WC COLLECTION: 2.5X TO 6X BASE CARDS

1996 Pinnacle Bill's Back

Randomly inserted in hobby and retail packs at a rate of one in 360, this two-card set features NASCAR's perennial fan favorite Bill Elliott. The two card salute captures Bill's return to racing after a potentially career-ending crash. The cards are printed on all-foil dufex card stock.

COMMON CARD (1-2) 8.00 20.00

1996 Pinnacle Checkered Flag

This 15-card insert set features the top names in racing. The cards were available only through magazine packs at a rate of one in 38 packs. The card fronts feature driver photos in front of a checkered flag, rainbow hologram background. The driver's name is in a gold foil stripe across the bottom of each card..

COMPLETE SET (15) 40.00 100.00
1 Jeff Gordon 6.00 15.00
2 Rusty Wallace 5.00 12.00
3 Dale Earnhardt 10.00 25.00
4 Sterling Marlin 2.00 5.00
5 Terry Labonte 2.00 5.00
6 Mark Martin 5.00 12.00
7 Bobby Labonte 4.00 10.00
8 Dale Jarrett 4.00 10.00
9 Bill Elliott 2.50 6.00
10 Ricky Rudd 2.00 5.00
11 Michael Waltrip 1.25 3.00
12 Ricky Craven .60 1.50
13 Ernie Irvan 1.25 3.00
14 Geoff Bodine .60 1.50
15 Darrell Waltrip 1.25 3.00

1996 Pinnacle Cut Above

Randomly inserted in retail and hobby packs at a rate of one in 24, this 15-card insert set highlights the top drivers on the circuit. The photo of the driver is imposed over a background of that particular driver's uniform. The card is die-cut and uses gold foil stamping for the driver's name.

COMPLETE SET (15) 30.00 80.00
1 Jeff Gordon 6.00 15.00
2 Bill Elliott 2.50 6.00
3 Terry Labonte 2.00 5.00
4 Ernie Irvan 1.25 3.00
5 Johnny Benson 1.25 3.00
6 Ricky Rudd 2.00 5.00
7 Dale Jarrett 4.00 10.00
8 Rusty Wallace 5.00 12.00
9 Bobby Labonte 4.00 10.00
10 Mark Martin 5.00 12.00
11 Ricky Craven .60 1.50
12 Robert Pressley .60 1.50
13 Ted Musgrave .60 1.50
14 Sterling Marlin 2.00 5.00
15 Geoff Bodine .60 1.50

1996 Pinnacle Team Pinnacle

Randomly inserted in retail and hobby packs at a rate of one in 90 and magazine packs at a rate of one in 144, each of the 12 cards in this set features a double sided design. The cards display one of NASCAR's top drivers on one side and either their crew chief or owner on the flipside. The driver's side of each card features dufex printing technology.

COMPLETE SET (12) 150.00 350.00
1 Jeff Gordon 12.50 30.00
2 Rusty Wallace 10.00 25.00
3 Dale Earnhardt 20.00 50.00
4 Dale Jarrett 8.00 20.00
5 Terry Labonte 4.00 10.00
6 Mark Martin 10.00 25.00
7 Bill Elliott 5.00 12.00
8 Sterling Marlin 4.00 10.00
9 Ricky Rudd 4.00 10.00
10 Jeff Gordon 12.50 30.00
11 Dale Earnhardt 20.00 50.00
12 Dale Jarrett 8.00 20.00
P8 S.Marlin 2.50 6.00
T.Glover Promo

1996 Pinnacle Pole Position

The 1996 Pinnacle Pole Position set was issued in one series totalling 100 cards. The product was distributed only to K-Mart stores. The set contains the following topical subsets: Drivers (1-25) and The Early Years (72-81). The cards were packaged seven cards per pack, and 24 packs per box. The packs carried a suggested retail price of $1.99.

COMPLETE SET (100) 7.50 20.00
1 John Andretti .07 .20
2 Rusty Wallace .60 1.50
3 Dale Earnhardt 1.25 3.00
4 Sterling Marlin .25 .60
5 Terry Labonte .25 .60
6 Mark Martin .60 1.50
7 Geoff Bodine .07 .20
8 Hut Stricklin .07 .20
9 Kenny Wallace .07 .20
10 Ricky Rudd .25 .60
11 Kyle Petty .15 .40
12 Ernie Irvan .15 .40
13 Dale Jarrett .50 1.25
14 Bill Elliott .30 .75
15 Jeff Burton .25 .60
16 Robert Pressley .07 .20
17 Darrell Waltrip .15 .40
18 Bobby Labonte .50 1.25
19 Bobby Hamilton .07 .20
20 Johnny Benson Jr. .15 .40
21 Michael Waltrip .15 .40
22 Ward Burton .15 .40
23 Jimmy Spencer .07 .20
24 Jeff Gordon .75 2.00
25 Ken Schrader .07 .20
26 Rusty Wallace's Car .15 .40
27 Dale Earnhardt's Car .50 1.25
28 Sterling Marlin's Car .07 .20
29 Terry Labonte's Car .15 .40
30 Mark Martin's Car .15 .40
31 Ricky Rudd's Car .07 .20
32 Brett Bodine's Car .02 .10
33 Derrike Cope's Car .02 .10
34 Ted Musgrave's Car .02 .10
35 Darrell Waltrip's Car .07 .20
36 Bobby Labonte's Car .15 .40
37 Michael Waltrip's Car .07 .20
38 Ward Burton's Car .02 .10
39 Jimmy Spencer's Car .02 .10
40 Jeff Gordon's Car .30 .75
41 Ernie Irvan's Car .07 .20
42 Kyle Petty's Car .07 .20
43 Bobby Hamilton's Car .02 .10
44 Dale Jarrett's Car .15 .40
45 Johnny Benson's Car .02 .10
46 Robert Pressley's Car .02 .10
47 Ricky Craven's Car .02 .10
48 Bobby Hillin's Car .02 .10
49 Jeff Burton's Car .15 .40
50 Joe Nemechek's Car .02 .10
51 Jeff Gordon 95C .40 1.00
52 Jeff Gordon 95C .40 1.00
53 Jeff Gordon 95C .40 1.00
54 Jeff Gordon 95C .40 1.00
55 Jeff Gordon 95C .40 1.00
56 Dale Earnhardt SE .60 1.50
57 Dale Earnhardt SE .60 1.50
58 Dale Earnhardt SE .60 1.50
59 Dale Earnhardt SE .60 1.50
60 Dale Earnhardt SE .60 1.50
61 Johnny Benson Jr. RS .15 .40
62 Johnny Benson Jr. RS .15 .40
63 Johnny Benson Jr. RS .15 .40
64 Sterling Marlin WIN .15 .40
65 Rusty Wallace WIN .30 .75
66 Michael Waltrip WIN .15 .40
67 Dale Jarrett WIN .15 .40
68 Jeff Gordon WIN .50 1.25
69 Jeff Gordon WIN .50 1.25
70 Rusty Wallace WIN .30 .75
71 Sterling Marlin WIN .15 .40
72 Dale Earnhardt EY .60 1.50
73 Jeff Gordon EY .50 1.25
74 Kyle Petty EY .07 .20
75 Bobby Labonte EY .15 .40
76 Sterling Marlin EY .15 .40
77 Mark Martin EY .30 .75
78 Rusty Wallace EY .30 .75
79 Terry Labonte EY .15 .40
80 Ricky Rudd EY .15 .40
81 Darrell Waltrip EY .07 .20
82 Ray Evernham .07 .20
83 Larry McReynolds .02 .10
84 David Smith .02 .10
85 Andy Petree .02 .10
86 Richard Broome .02 .10
87 Richard Childress .15 .40
88 Larry McClure .02 .10
89 Rick Hendrick .02 .10
90 Filbert Martocci .02 .10
91 Jack Roush .02 .10
92 Joe Gibbs .15 .40
93 Robert Yates .02 .10
94 John Andretti .07 .20
95 John Andretti .07 .20
96 John Andretti .07 .20
97 John Andretti .07 .20
98 John Andretti .07 .20
99 Bill McCarthy CL .02 .10
100 Gary Miller CL .02 .10

1996 Pinnacle Pole Position Lightning Fast

COMPLETE SET (100) 50.00 120.00
*LIGHTNING FAST: 2.5X TO 6X BASE CARDS

1996 Pinnacle Pole Position Certified Strong

Randomly inserted in packs at a rate of one in 23, this 15-card set features rainbow foil hologram technology. The top drivers in NASCAR make an appearance in this set.

COMPLETE SET (15) 30.00 80.00
1 Jeff Gordon 5.00 12.00
2 Rusty Wallace 1.50 4.00
3 Dale Earnhardt 8.00 20.00
4 Sterling Marlin 1.50 4.00
5 Terry Labonte 1.50 4.00
6 Mark Martin 1.50 4.00
7 Ernie Irvan 1.50 4.00
8 Dale Jarrett 1.50 4.00
9 Jeremy Mayfield 1.00 2.50
10 Ricky Rudd 1.25 3.00
11 Bobby Labonte 1.50 4.00
12 Bobby Hamilton 1.25 3.00
13 Bill Elliott 2.50 6.00
14 Kyle Petty 1.25 3.00
15 Ricky Craven 1.25 3.00

1996 Pinnacle Pole Position No Limit

This 16-card insert set features the top cars on the NASCAR circuit. Each card was printed on silver mirror foil board and the front has a shot of the car and the words "speed limit" with the international "no" symbol over the top of it. The cards were randomly inserted in packs at a rate of one in 37. The Gold Parallel cards feature gold mirror foil board instead of the base silver. The gold cards were seeded one in 240 packs.

COMPLETE SET (16) 100.00 200.00
*GOLDS: 1.5X TO 4X BASIC INSERTS
1 Jeff Gordon 6.00 15.00
2 Rusty Wallace 2.00 5.00
3 Dale Earnhardt 10.00 25.00
4 Sterling Marlin 2.00 5.00
5 Terry Labonte 2.00 5.00
6 Mark Martin 2.00 5.00
7 Ernie Irvan 2.00 5.00
8 Robert Pressley 1.25 3.00
9 Dale Jarrett 2.00 5.00
10 Ricky Rudd 1.50 4.00
11 Bill Elliott 3.00 8.00
12 Darrell Waltrip 2.00 5.00
13 Jeff Burton 1.50 4.00
14 Jimmy Spencer 1.50 4.00
15 Bobby Labonte 2.00 5.00
16 Ken Schrader 1.25 3.00

1997 Pinnacle

This 96-card set was produced by Pinnacle Brands. The set features four topical subsets: Race Review (59-72), Texas Tornado (73-84), New Face (85-87), and Turn 4 (88-95). Cards were distributed in ten card packs with 18 packs per box and 24 boxes per case. The packs carried a suggested retail price of $2.99. A Terry Labonte 24K Gold Collector's Club promo card was issued to all members who joined the club.

COMPLETE SET (96) 6.00 15.00
1 Kyle Petty .10 .30
2 Rusty Wallace .40 1.00
3 Dale Earnhardt 1.00 2.50
4 Sterling Marlin .20 .50
5 Terry Labonte .20 .50
6 Mark Martin .50 1.25
7 Geoff Bodine .05 .15
8 Bill Elliott .25 .60
9 David Green .05 .15
10 Ricky Rudd .20 .50
11 Brett Bodine .05 .15
12 Derrike Cope .05 .15
13 Jeremy Mayfield .10 .30
14 Robby Gordon RC .20 .50
15 Steve Grissom .05 .15
16 Ted Musgrave .05 .15
17 Darrell Waltrip .10 .30
18 Bobby Labonte .40 1.00
19 Johnny Benson .10 .30
20 Bobby Hamilton .05 .15
21 Michael Waltrip .10 .30
22 Ward Burton .10 .30
23 Jimmy Spencer .05 .15
24 Jeff Gordon .60 1.50
25 Ricky Craven .05 .15
26 Mike Skinner .05 .15
27 Dale Jarrett .40 1.00
28 Ernie Irvan .10 .30
29 Jeff Green .05 .15
30 Kyle Petty's Car .05 .15
31 Rusty Wallace's Car .10 .30
32 Dale Earnhardt's Car .40 1.00
33 Sterling Marlin's Car .05 .15
34 Terry Labonte's Car .05 .15
35 Mark Martin's Car .10 .30
36 Geoff Bodine's Car .02 .10
37 Bill Elliott's Car .05 .15
38 David Green's Car .02 .10
39 Ricky Rudd's Car .05 .15
40 Brett Bodine's Car .02 .10
41 Derrike Cope's Car .02 .10
42 Jeremy Mayfield's Car .10 .30
43 Robby Gordon's Car .10 .30
44 Steve Grissom's Car .02 .10
45 Ted Musgrave's Car .02 .10
46 Darrell Waltrip's Car .05 .15
47 Bobby Labonte's Car .10 .30
48 Johnny Benson's Car .02 .10
49 Bobby Hamilton's Car .02 .10
50 Michael Waltrip's Car .05 .15
51 Ward Burton's Car .02 .10
52 Jimmy Spencer's Car .02 .10
53 Jeff Gordon's Car .25 .60
54 Ricky Craven's Car .02 .10
55 Mike Skinner's Car .02 .10
56 Dale Jarrett's Car .10 .30
57 Ernie Irvan's Car .05 .15
58 Jeff Green's Car .02 .10
59 Terry Labonte RR .10 .30
60 Dale Jarrett RR .20 .50
61 Mark Martin RR .25 .60
62 Rusty Wallace RR .25 .60
63 Bill Elliott RR .10 .30
64 Bobby Labonte RR .20 .50
65 Ernie Irvan RR .05 .15
66 Dale Earnhardt's Car RR .40 1.00
67 Ricky Rudd RR .10 .30
68 Dale Earnhardt's Car RR .40 1.00
69 Dale Earnhardt RR .50 1.25
70 Dale Earnhardt's Car RR .40 1.00
71 Sterling Marlin RR .10 .30
72 Mike Skinner RR .02 .10
73 Rusty Wallace TT .25 .60
74 Dale Jarrett TT .20 .50
75 Mark Martin TT .25 .60
76 Terry Labonte TT .10 .30
77 Bobby Labonte TT .20 .50
78 Sterling Marlin TT .10 .30
79 Kyle Petty TT .05 .15
80 Ernie Irvan TT .05 .15
81 Bobby Hamilton TT .02 .10
82 Dale Earnhardt TT .50 1.25
83 Michael Waltrip TT .05 .15
84 Dale Earnhardt TT .50 1.25
85 Jeff Green NF .02 .10
86 Mike Skinner NF .02 .10
87 David Green NF .02 .10
88 Johnny Benson's Car T4 .02 .10
89 Dale Jarrett's Car T4 .10 .30
90 Mark Martin's Car T4 .10 .30
91 Dale Earnhardt's Car T4 .40 1.00
92 Rusty Wallace's Car T4 .10 .30
93 Terry Labonte's Car T4 .05 .15
94 Darrell Waltrip's Car T4 .05 .15
95 Dale Earnhardt's Car T4 .40 1.00
96 Rusty Wallace CL .20 .50
RC1 Terry Labonte Coll.Club Promo 6.00 15.00

1997 Pinnacle Artist Proofs

COMPLETE RED SET (50) 25.00 50.00
*RED ART.PROOFS: 3X TO 8X HI COL.
*BLUE ART.PROOF: 6X TO 15X HI COL.
*PURPLE AP: 10X TO 25X HI COL.

1997 Pinnacle Trophy Collection

COMPLETE SET (96) 25.00 60.00
*TROPHY COLL: 2X TO 5X BASE CARDS

1997 Pinnacle Chevy Madness

This 3-card insert set is a continuation of the set that was started in 1997 Action Packed. The cards were randomly inserted in packs at a ratio of 1:23.

COMPLETE SET (3) 10.00 25.00
13 Dale Earnhardt's Car 8.00 20.00
14 David Green's Car .50 1.25
15 Jeff Gordon's Car 5.00 12.00

1997 Pinnacle Bobby Labonte Helmets

This 10-card set features ten helmets worn by Bobby Labonte during the 1997 Winston Cup season. Each card has a Dufex surface and features a logo from a different NFL team. The cards were randomly inserted in hobby packs at a ratio of 1:89.

COMPLETE SET (10) 6.00 15.00
1 Bobby Labonte 1.00 2.50
2 Bobby Labonte 1.00 2.50
3 Bobby Labonte 1.00 2.50
4 Bobby Labonte 1.00 2.50
5 Bobby Labonte 1.00 2.50
6 Bobby Labonte 1.00 2.50
7 Bobby Labonte 1.00 2.50
8 Bobby Labonte 1.00 2.50
9 Bobby Labonte 1.00 2.50
10 Bobby Labonte 1.00 2.50

1997 Pinnacle Spellbound

This 12-card set features 12 drivers, each of whom appears on a letter of the words, "NASCAR RACING". The cards were randomly inserted in packs at a ratio of 1:23.

COMPLETE SET (12) 15.00 40.00
*PROMOS: .2X TO .5X BASIC INSERTS
1N Terry Labonte 1.50 4.00
2A Dale Jarrett 3.00 8.00
3S Dale Earnhardt 8.00 20.00
4C Rusty Wallace 3.00 8.00
5A Mark Martin 4.00 10.00
6R Jeff Gordon 5.00 12.00
7R Bobby Hamilton .50 1.25
8A Kyle Petty 1.00 2.50
9C Ernie Irvan 1.00 2.50
10I Ricky Rudd 1.50 4.00
11N Bill Elliott 2.00 5.00
12G Bobby Labonte 3.00 8.00

1997 Pinnacle Spellbound Autographs

This five-card set features the autographs of five drivers from the regular set. Each of the drivers signed 500 cards. The Jeff Gordon card inserted in packs was actually a redemption that could be redeemed for an autographed card. An insert ratio was not given for these cards.

COMPLETE SET (5) 200.00 400.00
1N Terry Labonte 5.00 12.00
2A Dale Jarrett 5.00 12.00
3S Dale Earnhardt 125.00 250.00
6R Jeff Gordon EXCH 2.00 5.00
6RAU Jeff Gordon AUTO 30.00 60.00
11N Bill Elliott 10.00 25.00

1997 Pinnacle Team Pinnacle

This 10-card insert set features 10 top NASCAR drivers on double-sided cards with their crew chiefs. These cards have red and blue versions. Both colors have the same value. The cards were randomly inserted in packs at a ratio of 1:240.

COMPLETE SET (10) 100.00 200.00
1 Jeff Gordon 10.00 25.00
2 Rusty Wallace 6.00 15.00
3 Dale Earnhardt 15.00 40.00
4 Darrell Waltrip 2.00 5.00
5 Terry Labonte 3.00 8.00
6 Mark Martin 8.00 20.00

7 Bobby Labonte 6.00 15.00
8 Ricky Rudd 3.00 8.00
9 Dale Jarrett 6.00 15.00
10 Bill Elliott 4.00 10.00

1997 Pinnacle Certified

This 100-card set was released by Pinnacle Brands. The set features two topical subsets: War Paint (69-88) and Burning Desire (89-98). Cards were distributed in six card packs with 20 packs per box and 16 boxes per case. The packs carried a suggested retail price of $4.99.

COMPLETE SET (100) 10.00 25.00
1 Kyle Petty .40 1.00
2 Rusty Wallace 1.25 3.00
3 Dale Earnhardt 2.50 6.00
4 Sterling Marlin .60 1.50
5 Terry Labonte .60 1.50
6 Mark Martin 1.25 3.00
7 Bill Elliott .60 1.50
8 Jeremy Mayfield .40 1.00
9 Ted Musgrave .20 .50
10 Ricky Rudd .60 1.50
11 Robby Gordon RC .60 1.50
12 Johnny Benson .40 1.00
13 Bobby Hamilton .20 .50
14 Mike Skinner .20 .50
15 Dale Jarrett 1.00 2.50
16 Steve Grissom .20 .50
17 Darrell Waltrip .40 1.00
18 Bobby Labonte 1.00 2.50
19 Ernie Irvan .40 1.00
20 Jeff Green .20 .50
21 Michael Waltrip .40 1.00
22 Ward Burton .40 1.00
23 Geoff Bodine .20 .50
24 Jeff Gordon 1.50 4.00
25 Ricky Craven .20 .50
26 Jimmy Spencer .20 .50
27 Brett Bodine .20 .50
28 David Green .20 .50
29 John Andretti .20 .50
30 Ken Schrader .20 .50
31 Chad Little .40 1.00
32 Joe Nemecheck .20 .50
33 Hut Stricklin .20 .50
34 Kenny Wallace .20 .50
35 Kyle Petty's Car .07 .20
36 Rusty Wallace's Car .60 1.50
37 Dale Earnhardt's Car 1.00 2.50
38 Sterling Marlin's Car .20 .50
39 Terry Labonte's Car .40 1.00
40 Mark Martin's Car .60 1.50
41 Bill Elliott's Car .40 1.00
42 Jeremy Mayfield's Car .07 .20
43 Ted Musgrave's Car .07 .20
44 Ricky Rudd's Car .20 .50
45 Robby Gordon's Car .40 1.00
46 Johnny Benson's Car .07 .20
47 Bobby Hamilton's Car .07 .20
48 Mike Skinner's Car .07 .20
49 Dale Jarrett's Car .20 .50
50 Steve Grissom's Car .07 .20
51 Darrell Waltrip's Car .07 .20
52 Bobby Labonte's Car .40 1.00
53 Ernie Irvan's Car .20 .50
54 Jeff Green's Car .07 .20
55 Michael Waltrip's Car .20 .50
56 Ward Burton's Car .20 .50
57 Geoff Bodine's Car .07 .20
58 Jeff Gordon's Car .60 1.50
59 Ricky Craven's Car .40 1.00
60 Jimmy Spencer's Car .07 .20
61 Brett Bodine's Car .07 .20
62 David Green's Car .07 .20
63 John Andretti's Car .07 .20
64 Ken Schrader's Car .07 .20
65 Chad Little's Car .07 .20
66 Joe Nemecheck's Car .07 .20
67 Hut Stricklin's Car .07 .20
68 Kenny Wallace's Car .07 .20
69 Darrell Waltrip's Car WP .07 .20
70 Darrell Waltrip's Car WP .07 .20
71 Darrell Waltrip's Car WP .07 .20
72 Jeremy Mayfield's Car WP .07 .20
73 Jeremy Mayfield's Car WP .07 .20
74 Jeff Gordon's Car WP .60 1.50
75 Ward Burton's Car WP .07 .20
76 Dale Earnhardt's Car WP 1.00 2.50
77 Bobby Labonte's Car WP .40 1.00
78 Michael Waltrip's Car WP .20 .50
79 Robby Gordon's Car WP .40 1.00
80 Terry Labonte's Car WP .40 1.00
81 Bill Elliott's Car WP .40 1.00
82 Bobby Hamilton's Car WP .07 .20
83 Chad Little's Car WP .07 .20
84 Jeff Green's Car WP .07 .20
85 Jeff Green's Car WP .07 .20
86 Rick Mast's Car WP .07 .20
87 Ernie Irvan's Car WP .20 .50
88 Geoff Bodine's Car WP .07 .20
89 Jeff Gordon BD .75 2.00
90 Terry Labonte BD .40 1.00
91 Mark Martin BD .60 1.50
92 Dale Jarrett BD .60 1.50
93 Dale Earnhardt BD 1.25 3.00
94 Ricky Rudd BD .40 1.00
95 Rusty Wallace BD .60 1.50
96 Bobby Hamilton BD .20 .50
97 Bobby Labonte BD .60 1.50
98 Kyle Petty BD .40 1.00
P6 Mark Martin Promo 2.00 5.00
NNO Checklist 1 .07 .20
NNO Checklist 2 .07 .20

1997 Pinnacle Certified Mirror Blue

COMPLETE SET (100) 300.00 600.00
*MIRROR BLUES: 4X TO 10X HI COL.

1997 Pinnacle Certified Mirror Gold

COMPLETE SET (100) 300.00 750.00
*MIRROR GOLDS: 4X TO 10X HI COL.

1997 Pinnacle Certified Mirror Red

COMPLETE SET (100) 250.00 500.00
*MIRROR REDS: 3X TO 8X HI COL.

1997 Pinnacle Certified Red

COMPLETE SET (100) 50.00 120.00
*REDS: 1.5X TO 4X BASE CARDS

1997 Pinnacle Certified Certified Team

This 10-card insert set features some of the top stars from the Winston Cup circuit. The cards were randomly inserted in packs at a ratio of 1:19.

COMPLETE SET (10) 15.00 40.00
COMP.GOLD SET (10) 60.00 150.00
*GOLD TEAM: 1.2X TO 3X BASIC INSERTS
GOLD TEAM STATED ODDS: 1:119
1 Dale Earnhardt 6.00 15.00
2 Jeff Gordon 4.00 10.00
3 Ricky Rudd 1.50 4.00
4 Bobby Labonte 2.50 6.00
5 Terry Labonte 1.50 4.00
6 Rusty Wallace 3.00 8.00
7 Mark Martin 3.00 8.00
8 Bill Elliott 1.50 4.00
9 Dale Jarrett 2.50 6.00
10 Jeremy Mayfield 1.00 2.50

1997 Pinnacle Certified Epix

This 10-card insert set features some of the top drivers in NASCAR. The Orange colored base cards were randomly inserted in packs at a ratio of 1:15.

COMPLETE SET (10) 15.00 40.00
COMP.PURPLE SET (10) 25.00 60.00
*PURPLES: .8X TO 2X ORANGE
COMP.EMERALD SET (10) 100.00 200.00
*EMERALDS: 1.5X TO 4X ORANGE
E1 Dale Earnhardt 4.00 10.00
E2 Jeff Gordon 2.50 6.00
E3 Ricky Rudd 1.00 2.50
E4 Bobby Labonte 1.50 4.00
E5 Terry Labonte 1.00 2.50
E6 Rusty Wallace 2.00 5.00
E7 Mark Martin 2.00 5.00
E8 Darrell Waltrip .60 1.50
E9 Dale Jarrett 1.50 4.00
E10 Ernie Irvan .60 1.50

1997 Pinnacle Checkers

This nine-card set was issued through Checkers Drive-In Restaurants. The cards were distributed via single card packs. Each pack has one collector card and t-shirt offer card. You received one pack free with a purchase of a combo meal at all participating Checkers. It took 15 Checkers Racing points to get one free t-shirt. Each t-shirt offer card was worth one point.

COMPLETE SET (9) .80 2.00
1 Ricky Rudd .10 .30
2 Sterling Marlin .10 .30
3 Johnny Benson .08 .25
4 Ricky Rudd .10 .30
5 Sterling Marlin .10 .30
6 Johnny Benson .08 .25
7 Ricky Rudd .10 .30
8 Sterling Marlin .10 .30
9 Johnny Benson .08 .25

1997 Pinnacle Collectibles Club

RC1 Terry Labonte 1.50 4.00
RC2 Ricky Craven .75 2.00
RC3 Mark Martin 1.50 4.00
RC4 Jeff Gordon 3.00 8.00
RC5 Rusty Wallace 2.00 5.00
RC6 Bill Elliott 2.00 5.00

1997 Pinnacle Mint

This 30-diecut card set features the top names from the Winston Cup circuit. The cards can be used to hold the coins available in this product. Die-cut cards were distributed two per pack with the regular cards being distributed one per pack. Coins were distributed two per pack. The packs carried a suggested retail price of $2.99.

COMP. DIE CUT SET (30) 5.00 12.00
1 Terry Labonte .25 .60
2 Jeff Gordon .75 2.00
3 Dale Jarrett .40 1.00
4 Darrell Waltrip .15 .40
5 Mark Martin .60 1.50
6 Ricky Rudd .25 .60
7 Rusty Wallace .60 1.50
8 Sterling Marlin .25 .60
9 Bobby Hamilton .07 .20
10 Ernie Irvan .15 .40
11 Bobby Labonte .40 1.00
12 Johnny Benson .15 .40
13 Michael Waltrip .15 .40
14 Jimmy Spencer .07 .20
15 Ted Musgrave .07 .20
16 Geoff Bodine .07 .20
17 Bill Elliott .30 .75
18 John Andretti .07 .20
19 Ward Burton .15 .40
20 Randy LaJoie .07 .20
21 Dale Earnhardt's Car .60 1.50
22 Ricky Rudd's Car .07 .20
23 Dale Jarrett's Car .15 .40
24 Jeff Gordon's Car .40 1.00
25 Terry Labonte's Car .15 .40
26 Mark Martin's Car .25 .60
27 Bobby Labonte's Car .15 .40
28 Ernie Irvan's Car .02 .10
29 Bill Elliott's Car .15 .40
30 Johnny Benson's Car .02 .10
P1 Dale Jarrett Promo 1.25 3.00

1997 Pinnacle Mint Bronze

COMPLETE SET (30) 10.00 25.00
*BRONZE: .8X TO 2X DIE CUTS

1997 Pinnacle Mint Gold

COMPLETE SET (30) 100.00 200.00
*GOLDS: 6X TO 15X DIE CUTS

1997 Pinnacle Mint Silver

COMPLETE SET (30) 40.00 100.00
*SILVERS: 3X TO 8X DIE CUTS

1997 Pinnacle Mint Coins

This 30-coin set parallels the die cut card set. The drivers' portraits and cars are featured on the front of the coins while the Pinnacle Mint logo is featured on the back. The coins are randomly inserted in hobby packs at a ratio of 2:1 and in retail packs at a ratio of 1:1.

COMPLETE SET (30) 12.50 30.00
COMP.NICKEL SET (30) 60.00 150.00
*NICKEL-SILVER: 2X TO 5X BRONZE
NICKEL-SILVER STATED ODDS 1:20
COMP.24K GOLD (30) 250.00 500.00
*24K GOLD PLATED: 6X TO 15X BRONZE
24K GOLD STATED ODDS 1:48
1 Terry Labonte 1.00 2.50
2 Jeff Gordon 2.50 6.00
3 Dale Jarrett 1.25 3.00
4 Darrell Waltrip .50 1.25
5 Mark Martin 1.50 4.00
6 Ricky Rudd .75 2.00
7 Rusty Wallace 1.50 4.00
8 Sterling Marlin .60 1.50
9 Bobby Hamilton .25 .60
10 Ernie Irvan .50 1.25
11 Bobby Labonte 1.25 3.00
12 Johnny Benson .50 1.25
13 Michael Waltrip .50 1.25
14 Jimmy Spencer .25 .60
15 Ted Musgrave .25 .60
16 Geoff Bodine .25 .60
17 Bill Elliott 1.00 2.50
18 John Andretti .25 .60
19 Ward Burton .50 1.25
20 Randy LaJoie .25 .60
21 Dale Earnhardt's Car 2.50 6.00
22 Ricky Rudd's Car .25 .60
23 Dale Jarrett's Car .50 1.25
24 Jeff Gordon's Car 1.00 2.50
25 Terry Labonte's Car .50 1.25
26 Mark Martin's Car .60 1.50
27 Bobby Labonte's Car .50 1.25
28 Ernie Irvan's Car .10 .30
29 Bill Elliott's Car .25 .60
30 Johnny Benson's Car .10 .30

1997 Pinnacle Pepsi Jeff Gordon

This set of 3-promo cards was produced by Pinnacle and distributed through Pepsi. The cards include a color photo of either Jeff Gordon or his car on the front. The backs include a brief bio on the driver's recent career along with the Pinnacle and Pepsi logos at the bottom.

COMPLETE SET (3) 2.00 5.00
1 Jeff Gordon .75 2.00
2 Jeff Gordon's Car .60 1.50
3 Jeff Gordon .75 2.00

1998 Pinnacle Mint

The 1998 Pinnacle Mint set was issued in one series totalling 30 cards. The set offers two coins and three cards per pack. Die-cut cards were also included to provide the perfect fit to make a card-and-coin collectible. The set features 30 drivers with coins that come in brass, nickel-silver, solid silver and solid gold as well as bronze-plated proof coins, silver-plated proof coins, and gold-plated proof coins.

COMPLETE SET (30) 6.00 15.00
1 Jeff Gordon .75 2.00
2 Mark Martin .60 1.50
3 Dale Earnhardt 1.25 3.00
4 Terry Labonte .25 .60
5 Dale Jarrett .50 1.25
6 Bobby Labonte .50 1.25
7 Bill Elliott .30 .75
8 Ted Musgrave .07 .20
9 Ricky Rudd .25 .60
10 Rusty Wallace .60 1.50
12 Michael Waltrip .15 .40
13 Jeff Gordon's Car .30 .75
14 Mark Martin's Car .25 .60
15 Dale Jarrett's Car .15 .40
16 Terry Labonte's Car .15 .40
17 Dale Earnhardt's Car .50 1.25
18 Bobby Labonte's Car .15 .40
19 Bill Elliott's Car .15 .40
20 Ted Musgrave's Car .05 .15
21 Ricky Rudd's Car .07 .20
22 Rusty Wallace's Car .25 .60
23 Jeremy Mayfield's Car .07 .20
24 Michael Waltrip's Car .07 .20
25 Mark Martin MM .30 .75
26 Rusty Wallace MM .30 .75
27 Jeff Gordon MM .40 1.00
28 Dale Jarrett MM .25 .60
29 Ricky Rudd MM .15 .40
30 Ernie Irvan MM .15 .40
P1 Mark Martin Promo 1.00 2.50

1998 Pinnacle Mint Die Cuts

COMPLETE SET (30) 5.00 12.00
*DIE CUTS: .3X TO .8X BASE CARDS

1998 Pinnacle Mint Championship Mint

This two-card set depicts Jeff Gordon and his car during his 1997 Winston Cup Championship season. These cards were randomly inserted into hobby packs at a ratio of one per 41 packs and into retail packs at a ratio of one per 71 packs.

1 Jeff Gordon 7.50 20.00
2 Jeff Gordon's Car 5.00 12.00

1998 Pinnacle Mint Gold Team

COMPLETE SET (30) 125.00 250.00
*GOLD TEAM: 5X TO 12X BASE CARDS

1998 Pinnacle Mint Silver Team

COMPLETE SET (30) 60.00 150.00
*SILVER TEAM: 4X TO 10X BASE CARDS

1998 Pinnacle Mint Coins

This 30-coin set parallels the base card set. These coins were inserted into hobby packs at a ratio of 2:1 and into retail packs at a ratio of 1:1.

COMPLETE SET (30) 10.00 25.00
*GOLD-PLATED: 5X TO 12X BASE COINS
GOLD-PLATED STATED ODDS 1:199
*NICKEL-SILVER: 1.5X TO 4X BASE COINS
NICKEL-SILVER STATED ODDS 1:41
*BRONZE PROOFS: 4X TO 10X BASE COINS
BRONZE PR.PRINT RUN 500 SER.#'d SETS
*GOLD PROOFS: 10X TO 25X BASE COINS
GOLD PROOF PRINT RUN 100 SER.#'d SETS
*SILVER PROOFS: 6X TO 15X BASE COINS
SILV.PROOF PRINT RUN 250 SER.#'d SETS
*SOLID SILVERS: 6X TO 15X BASE COINS
SOLID SILVER ODDS: 1:288 HOB, 1:960 RET
UNPRICED SOLID GOLDS SER.#'d OF 1
1 Jeff Gordon 1.25 3.00
2 Mark Martin 1.00 2.50
3 Dale Earnhardt 2.00 5.00
4 Terry Labonte .40 1.00
5 Dale Jarrett .75 2.00
6 Bobby Labonte .75 2.00
7 Bill Elliott .50 1.25
8 Ted Musgrave .10 .30
9 Ricky Rudd .40 1.00
10 Rusty Wallace 1.00 2.50
11 Jeremy Mayfield .25 .60
12 Michael Waltrip .25 .60
13 Jeff Gordon's Car .50 1.25
14 Mark Martin's Car .40 1.00
15 Dale Jarrett's Car .25 .60
16 Terry Labonte's Car .25 .60
17 Dale Earnhardt's Car .75 2.00
18 Bobby Labonte's Car .25 .60
19 Bill Elliott's Car .25 .60
20 Ted Musgrave's Car .10 .25
21 Ricky Rudd's Car .10 .30
22 Rusty Wallace's Car .40 1.00
23 Jeremy Mayfield's Car .10 .30
24 Michael Waltrip's Car .10 .30
01 Mark Martin MM .50 1.25
02 Rusty Wallace MM .50 1.25
03 Jeff Gordon MM .60 1.50
04 Dale Jarrett MM .40 1.00
05 Ricky Rudd MM .25 .60
06 Ernie Irvan MM .25 .60

1998 Pinnacle Mint Championship Mint Coins

Randomly inserted in hobby packs and retail packs at a rate of 1:89 and 1:129 respectively, this set is a metal alloy insert made from the melted hood of Jeff Gordon's 1997 Talladega race car. The retail version contains traditional sized coins, one of Gordon and one of the car. Hobby packs contain a double-sized version of the coins.

COMPLETE SET (4) 60.00 150.00
1A Jeff Gordon's Car 10.00 25.00
1B Jeff Gordon's Car Jumbo 10.00 25.00
2A Jeff Gordon 20.00 50.00
2B Jeff Gordon Jumbo 20.00 50.00

1997 Pinnacle Portraits

This set was issued in packs with one oversized card along with a package of standard sized cards. Each features a color photo of the featured driver or his ride.

COMPLETE SET (50) 7.50 20.00
1 Jeff Gordon 1.25 3.00
2 Mark Martin 1.00 2.50
3 Dale Earnhardt 2.00 5.00
4 Terry Labonte .40 1.00
5 Bobby Labonte .75 2.00
6 Bill Elliott .60 1.50
7 Ricky Rudd .40 1.00
8 Dale Jarrett .75 2.00
9 Ted Musgrave .10 .30
10 Jeremy Mayfield .25 .60
11 Johnny Benson .25 .60
12 Ricky Craven .10 .30
13 Michael Waltrip .25 .60
14 Kyle Petty .25 .60
15 Ernie Irvan .25 .60
16 Bobby Hamilton .10 .30
17 Mike Skinner .10 .30
18 Rusty Wallace 1.00 2.50
19 Ken Schrader .10 .30
20 Jimmy Spencer .10 .30
21 Jeff Gordon's Car .50 1.25
22 Mark Martin's Car .40 1.00
23 Dale Earnhardt's Car .75 2.00
24 Terry Labonte's Car .25 .60
25 Bobby Labonte's Car .25 .60
26 Bill Elliott's Car .25 .60
27 Ricky Rudd's Car .10 .30
28 Dale Jarrett's Car .25 .60
29 Ted Musgrave's Car .05 .15
30 Jeremy Mayfield's Car .10 .30
31 Johnny Benson's Car .05 .15
32 Ricky Craven's Car .05 .15
33 Michael Waltrip's Car .10 .30
34 Kyle Petty's Car .10 .30
35 Ernie Irvan's Car .10 .30
36 Bobby Hamilton's Car .05 .15
37 Mike Skinner's Car .05 .15
38 Rusty Wallace's Car .40 1.00
39 Ken Schrader's Car .05 .15
40 Jimmy Spencer's Car .05 .15
41 Mark Martin SS .50 1.25
42 Terry Labonte SS .25 .60
43 Chad Little SS .10 .30
44 Dale Jarrett SS .40 1.00
45 Bill Elliott SS .25 .60
46 David Green SS .10 .30
47 Ernie Irvan SS .10 .30
48 Michael Waltrip SS .25 .60
49 Ted Musgrave SS .05 .15
50 Steve Grissom SS .05 .15

1997 Pinnacle Portraits 8x10

These oversized (roughly 8" x 10") cards were issued one per pack of the Pinnacle Portraits product. Each card was numbered with the driver's initials and the card number. A Dufex parallel version was also created and inserted at the rate of 1:9 packs.

*SINGLES: .6X TO 1.5X BASE CARDS
*DUFEX: 1X TO 2.5X BASIC INSERTS
BE1 Bill Elliott 1.00 2.50
BE2 Bill Elliott 1.00 2.50
BE3 Bill Elliott 1.00 2.50
BE4 Bill Elliott 1.00 2.50
DE1 Dale Earnhardt 3.00 8.00
DE2 Dale Earnhardt 3.00 8.00
DE3 Dale Earnhardt 3.00 8.00
DE4 Dale Earnhardt 3.00 8.00
DJ1 Dale Jarrett 1.25 3.00
DJ2 Dale Jarrett 1.25 3.00
DJ3 Dale Jarrett 1.25 3.00
DJ4 Dale Jarrett 1.25 3.00
JG1 Jeff Gordon 2.00 5.00
JG2 Jeff Gordon 2.00 5.00
JG3 Jeff Gordon 2.00 5.00
JG4 Jeff Gordon 2.00 5.00
MM1 Mark Martin 1.50 4.00
MM2 Mark Martin 1.50 4.00
MM3 Mark Martin 1.50 4.00
MM4 Mark Martin 1.50 4.00
TL1 Terry Labonte .60 1.50
TL2 Terry Labonte .60 1.50
TL3 Terry Labonte .60 1.50
TL4 Terry Labonte .60 1.50

1997 Pinnacle Precision

This 77-card set was distributed in collectible oil cans. The cards themselves are made of steel and carry a 1996 copyright date on the backs. Each can included two 2-card packs of steel cards, one koozie and one static cling decal. The cans carried a suggested retail price of $9.99.

COMPLETE SET (77) 40.00 80.00
1 Bob Brannan .08 .25
2 Rick Hendrick .08 .25
3 Jeff Gordon 1.50 4.00
4 Jeff Gordon Pit Action .75 2.00
5 Jeff Gordon's Car .75 2.00
6 Jeff Gordon 1.50 4.00
7 Ray Evernham .20 .50
8 Jeff Gordon's Car .75 2.00
9 Jeff Gordon 1.50 4.00
10 Don Hawk .08 .25
11 Richard Childress .30 .75
12 Dale Earnhardt's Transporter 1.25 3.00
13 Dale Earnhardt Pit Action 1.25 3.00
14 Dale Earnhardt's Car 1.50 4.00
15 Dale Earnhardt 2.50 6.00
16 David Smith .08 .25
17 Dale Earnhardt's Car 1.50 4.00
18 Dale Earnhardt 2.50 6.00
19 Sterling Marlin's Transporter .08 .25
20 Larry McClure .08 .25
21 Sterling Marlin .50 1.25
22 Sterling Marlin Pit Action .20 .50
23 Sterling Marlin's Car .20 .50
24 Sterling Marlin .50 1.25
25 Shelton Pittman .08 .25
26 Sterling Marlin's Car .20 .50
27 Sterling Marlin .50 1.25
28 Dale Jarrett's Transporter .30 .75
29 Robert Yates .08 .25
30 Dale Jarrett 1.00 2.50
31 Dale Jarrett Pit Action .30 .75
32 Dale Jarrett's Car .30 .75
33 Dale Jarrett 1.00 2.50
34 Todd Parrott .08 .25
35 Dale Jarrett's Car .30 .75
36 Dale Jarrett 1.00 2.50
37 Rusty Wallace's Transporter .30 .75
38 Roger Penske .08 .25
39 Rusty Wallace 1.25 3.00
40 Rusty Wallace Pit Action .30 .75
41 Rusty Wallace's Car .30 .75
42 Rusty Wallace 1.25 3.00
43 Robin Pemberton .08 .25
44 Rusty Wallace's Car .30 .75
45 Rusty Wallace 1.25 3.00
46 Steve Jones .08 .25
47 Bill Elliott .75 2.00
48 Bill Elliott .75 2.00
49 Bill Elliott Pit Action .30 .75
50 Bill Elliott's Car .30 .75
51 Bill Elliott .75 2.00
52 Mike Beam .08 .25
53 Bill Elliott's Car .30 .75
54 Bill Elliott .75 2.00
55 Terry Labonte's Transporter .30 .75
56 Rick Hendrick .08 .25
57 Terry Labonte .50 1.25
58 Terry Labonte Pit Action .30 .75
59 Terry Labonte's Car .30 .75
60 Terry Labonte .50 1.25
61 Gary DeHart .08 .25
62 Terry Labonte's Car .30 .75
63 Terry Labonte .50 1.25
64 Ricky Rudd's Transporter .20 .50
65 Ricky Rudd .50 1.25
66 Ricky Rudd .50 1.25
67 Ricky Rudd Pit Action .20 .50
68 Ricky Rudd's Car .20 .50
69 Ricky Rudd .50 1.25
70 Ricky Rudd .50 1.25
71 Ricky Rudd's Car .20 .50
72 Ricky Rudd .50 1.25
73 Bobby Labonte 1.00 2.50
74 Ricky Craven .20 .50
75 Johnny Benson .30 .75
76 Jeremy Mayfield .30 .75
77 Checklist .08 .25
P0 Bill Elliott Promo 2.00 5.00

1997 Pinnacle Precision Bronze

COMPLETE SET (77) 100.00 250.00
*BRONZES: 1X TO 2.5X BASIC CARDS

1997 Pinnacle Precision Gold

COMPLETE SET (77) 1000.00 1800.00
*GOLDS: 6X TO 15X BASIC CARDS

1997 Pinnacle Precision Silver

COMPLETE SET (77) 250.00 600.00
*SILVERS: 2.5X TO 6X BASIC CARDS

1997 Pinnacle Precision Terry Labonte Autographs

This is a 7-card Terry Labonte set that features his autograph on each card. Reportedly, only 50 of each card was signed. The cards were randomly inserted in cans at a ratio of 1:1120.

COMMON CARD 60.00 120.00

1997 Pinnacle Totally Certified Platinum Red

Randomly inserted two in every pack, this 100-card set is the base set of this product and is sequentially numbered to 2999. The difference is found in the red design element.

COMPLETE SET (100) 25.00 60.00
1 Kyle Petty .50 1.25
2 Rusty Wallace 2.00 5.00
3 Dale Earnhardt 4.00 10.00
4 Sterling Marlin .75 2.00
5 Terry Labonte .75 2.00
6 Mark Martin 2.00 5.00
7 Bill Elliott 1.00 2.50
8 Jeremy Mayfield .50 1.25
9 Ted Musgrave .30 .75
10 Ricky Rudd .75 2.00
11 Robby Gordon .75 2.00
12 Johnny Benson .50 1.25
13 Bobby Hamilton .30 .75
14 Mike Skinner .30 .75
15 Dale Jarrett 1.50 4.00
16 Steve Grissom .30 .75
17 Darrell Waltrip .30 .75

18 Bobby Labonte 1.50 4.00
19 Ernie Irvan .50 1.25
20 Jeff Green .30 .75
21 Michael Waltrip .50 1.25
22 Ward Burton .50 1.25
23 Geoff Bodine .30 .75
24 Jeff Gordon 2.50 6.00
25 Ricky Craven .30 .75
26 Jimmy Spencer .30 .75
27 Brett Bodine .30 .75
28 David Green .30 .75
29 John Andretti .30 .75
30 Ken Schrader .30 .75
31 Chad Little .30 .75
32 Joe Nemechek .30 .75
33 Hut Stricklin .30 .75
34 Kenny Wallace .30 .75
35 Kyle Petty's Car .30 .75
36 Rusty Wallace's Car .75 2.00
37 Dale Earnhardt's Car 1.50 4.00
38 Sterling Marlin's Car .30 .75
39 Terry Labonte's Car .30 .75
40 Mark Martin's Car .75 2.00
41 Bill Elliott's Car .30 .75
42 Jeremy Mayfield's Car .15 .40
43 Ted Musgrave's Car .15 .40
44 Ricky Rudd's Car .30 .75
45 Robby Gordon's Car .50 1.25
46 Johnny Benson's Car .15 .40
47 Bobby Hamilton's Car .15 .40
48 Mike Skinner's Car .15 .40
49 Dale Jarrett's Car .75 2.00
50 Steve Grissom's Car .15 .40
51 Darrell Waltrip's Car .30 .75
52 Bobby Labonte's Car .75 2.00
53 Ernie Irvan's Car .30 .75
54 Jeff Green's Car .15 .40
55 Michael Waltrip's Car .30 .75
56 Ward Burton's Car .15 .40
57 Geoff Bodine's Car .15 .40
58 Jeff Gordon's Car 1.25 3.00
59 Ricky Craven's Car .15 .40
60 Jimmy Spencer's Car .15 .40
61 Brett Bodine's Car .15 .40
62 David Green's Car .15 .40
63 John Andretti's Car .15 .40
64 Ken Schrader's Car .15 .40
65 Chad Little's Car .15 .40
66 Joe Nemechek's Car .15 .40
67 Hut Stricklin's Car .15 .40
68 Kenny Wallace's Car .15 .40
69 Darrell Waltrip WP .30 .75
70 Darrell Waltrip WP .30 .75
71 Darrell Waltrip WP .30 .75
72 Jeremy Mayfield WP .30 .75
73 Jeremy Mayfield WP .30 .75
74 Jeff Gordon WP 1.25 3.00
75 Ward Burton WP .15 .40
76 Dale Earnhardt WP 2.00 5.00
77 Bobby Labonte WP .75 2.00
78 Michael Waltrip WP .30 .75
79 Robby Gordon WP .50 1.25
80 Terry Labonte WP .50 1.25
81 Bill Elliott WP .50 1.25
82 Bobby Hamilton WP .15 .40
83 Chad Little WP .15 .40
84 Jeff Green WP .15 .40
85 Jeff Green WP .15 .40
86 Rick Mast WP .15 .40
87 Ernie Irvan WP .30 .75
88 Geoff Bodine WP .15 .40
89 Jeff Gordon BD 1.25 3.00
90 Terry Labonte BD .50 1.25
91 Mark Martin BD .75 2.00
92 Dale Jarrett BD .75 2.00
93 Dale Earnhardt BD 2.00 5.00
94 Ricky Rudd BD .50 1.25
95 Rusty Wallace BD .75 2.00
96 Bobby Hamilton BD .15 .40
97 Bobby Labonte BD .75 2.00
98 Kyle Petty BD .30 .75
99 Checklist 1 .15 .40
100 Checklist 2 .15 .40
P10 Ricky Rudd Promo 1.00 2.50

1997 Pinnacle Totally Certified Platinum Blue

COMPLETE SET (100) 60.00 120.00
*BLUES: .6X TO 1.5X REDS

1997 Pinnacle Totally Certified Platinum Gold

*GOLDS: 5X TO 12X REDS

1991-92 Pioneers of Stock Car Racing

This set was issued in two series of six-cards each. Series one was released in 1991 with series two being issued in 1992.

COMPLETE SET (12) 2.00 5.00
COMPLETE SERIES 1 (6) 1.00 2.50
COMPLETE SERIES 2 (6) 1.00 2.50
1 Rod Long .20 .50
2 Junior Johnson .20 .50
3 Bobby Myers .20 .50
4 D.Waltrip .30 .75
Walt.Wallace
Fred.Fryar
P.B.Correll
5 Curtis Crider .20 .50
6 Rod Long .20 .50
7 Billy Myers .20 .50
8 Bill Morton .20 .50
9 Gene Glover .20 .50
10 Tim Flock .20 .50
NNO Cover Card Series 1 .07 .20
NNO Cover Card Series 2 .07 .20

2004 Post Cereal

These cards were produced by KF Holdings and issued in various boxes of Post Cereals in early 2004. Note that the copyright line on the cardbacks lists the year as 2003, but the cards were released in 2004. Each was produced with lenticular technology with alternating photos of the driver and his car on the front. There was also a blue decoder lens built in to the card that could be used on the postopia.com website as part of an online game. The cardbacks feature another color photo of the driver along with basic statistics.

COMPLETE SET (7) 7.50 15.00
1 Greg Biffle .75 2.00
2 Jeff Burton .75 2.00
3 Kurt Busch .75 2.00
4 Dale Earnhardt Jr. 2.00 5.00
5 Matt Kenseth 1.25 3.00
6 Mark Martin 1.25 3.00
7 Michael Waltrip .75 2.00

1994 Power

In 1994, Pro Set produced only a Power racing set. The 150-cards include eight different subsets: Daytona Beach, Power Teams, Power Winners, Power Prospects, Stat Leaders, Power Rigs, Power Owners and MRN Radio announcers. The cards were packaged 12-cards per foil pack. A Gold parallel set was also produced and inserted one per pack along with a randomly inserted Dale Earnhardt Hologram card (numbered of 3500). Each of the last 20 cards in the set (cars subset) was also produced in a gold prism foil version inserted one per special 25-card retail blister pack.

COMPLETE SET (150) 6.00 15.00
*PRISM CARS: .6X TO 1.5X BASE CARD HI
DB1 Loy Allen Jr. DB .02 .10
DB2 Dale Earnhardt DB .50 1.25
DB3 Ernie Irvan DB .05 .15
DB4 Sterling Marlin DB .08 .25
DB5 Jeff Gordon DB .30 .75
PT6 Richard Childress PT .05 .15
PT7 Roger Penske PT .01 .05
PT8 Jack Roush PT .01 .05
PT9 Robert Yates PT .01 .05
PT10 Glen Wood PT .01 .05
PT11 Joe Gibbs PT .05 .15
PT12 Felix Sabates PT .01 .05
PT13 Ricky Rudd PT .08 .25
PT14 Junior Johnson PT .02 .10
PT15 Joe Hendrick (Papa) PT .01 .05
PW16 Dale Earnhardt PW .50 1.25
PW17 Rusty Wallace PW .25 .60
PW18 Ernie Irvan PW .05 .15
PW19 Dale Jarrett PW .20 .50
PW20 Mark Martin PW .25 .60
PW21 Morgan Shepherd PW .02 .10
PW22 Kyle Petty PW .05 .15
PW23 Ricky Rudd PW .08 .25
PW24 Geoff Bodine PW .02 .10
PW25 Davey Allison PW .15 .40
PP26 Loy Allen Jr. PP .02 .10
PP27 John Andretti PP RC .02 .10
PP28 Steve Grissom PP .02 .10
PP29 Ward Burton PP .05 .15
PP30 Mike Wallace PP .02 .10
PP31 Joe Nemechek PP .02 .10
PP32 Todd Bodine PP .02 .10
PP33 Chuck Bown PP .02 .10
PP34 Robert Pressley PP .02 .10
PP35 Jeff Burton PP .08 .25
PP36 Randy LaJoie PP .02 .10
PP37 Billy Standridge PP .01 .05
SL38 Dale Earnhardt SL .50 1.25
SL39 Rusty Wallace SL .25 .60
SL40 Terry Labonte SL .08 .25
SL41 Ricky Rudd SL .08 .25
SL42 Geoff Bodine SL .02 .10
SL43 Harry Gant SL .05 .15
SL44 Mark Martin SL .25 .60
SL45 Buddy Baker SL .02 .10
SL46 Darrell Waltrip SL .05 .15
SL47 Leonard Wood SL .01 .05
SL48 Dale Inman SL .01 .05
SL49 Tim Brewer SL .01 .05
SL50 Harry Hyde SL .01 .05
SL51 Jeff Hammond SL .01 .05
SL52 Travis Carter SL .01 .05
SL53 Buddy Parrott SL .01 .05
SL54 Rusty Wallace in Pits SL .08 .25
SL55 Brett Bodine In Pits SL .01 .05
SL56 Mark Martin in Pits SL .08 .25
SL57 Bill Elliott in Pits SL .05 .15
SL58 Michael Waltrip in Pits SL .02 .10
PR59 Dale Earnhardt's Trans. PR .20 .50
PR60 Darrell Waltrip's Trans. PR .01 .05
PR61 Ernie Irvan's Trans. PR .02 .10
PR62 Mark Martin's Trans. PR .08 .25
PR63 Rusty Wallace's Trans. PR .08 .25
PO64 Richard Petty PO .08 .25
PO65 Junior Johnson PO .02 .10
PO66 Richard Childress PO .05 .15
PO67 Walter Bud Moore PO .01 .05
PO68 Harry Melling PO .01 .05
PO69 Darrell Waltrip PO .05 .15
PO70 Eli Gold MR .01 .05
MR71 Barney Hall MR .01 .05
MR72 Dick Brooks .01 .05
Winston Kelley
Jim Phillips MR
MR73 Joe Moore .01 .05
Allen Bestwick
Fred Armstrong MR
74 Bobby Allison .05 .15
75 Kenny Bernstein .02 .10
76 Rich Bickle .02 .10
77 Brett Bodine .02 .10
78 Geoff Bodine .02 .10
79 George Bradshaw .01 .05
80 Travis Carter .01 .05
81 Richard Childress .05 .15
82 Derrike Cope .02 .10
83 Wally Dallenbach Jr. .02 .10
84 Bill Davis .01 .05
85 Junie Donlavey .01 .05
86 Harry Gant .05 .15
87 Harry Gant .05 .15
88 Joe Gibbs .05 .15
89 Jeff Gordon .30 .75
90 Jeff Gordon .30 .75
91 Bobby Hamilton .02 .10
92 Rick Hendrick .01 .05
93 Jimmy Hensley .02 .10
94 Jimmy Hensley .02 .10
95 Ernie Irvan .05 .15
96 Richard Jackson .01 .05
97 Junior Johnson .02 .10
98 Bobby Labonte .20 .50
99 Chad Little .02 .10
100 Dave Marcis .05 .15
101 Sterling Marlin .08 .25
102 Sterling Marlin .08 .25
103 Rick Mast .02 .10
104 Larry McClure .01 .05
105 Walter Bud Moore .01 .05
106 Ted Musgrave .02 .10
107 Roger Penske .01 .05
108 Kyle Petty .05 .15
109 Kyle Petty .05 .15
110 Richard Petty .08 .25
111 Chuck Rider .01 .05
112 Jack Roush .01 .05
113 Felix Sabates .01 .05
114 Greg Sacks .02 .10
115 Ken Schrader .02 .10
116 Lake Speed .02 .10
117 Jimmy Spencer .02 .10
118 Jimmy Spencer .02 .10
119 Hut Stricklin .02 .10
120 Dick Trickle .02 .10
121 Mike Wallace .02 .10
122 Rusty Wallace .25 .60
123 Rusty Wallace .25 .60
124 Roger Penske .01 .05
125 Darrell Waltrip .05 .15
126 Michael Waltrip .05 .15
127 Pete Wright .01 .05
128 Cale Yarborough .02 .10
129 Robert Yates .01 .05
130 Jeff Burton .08 .25
131 Hut Stricklin's Car .01 .05
132 Jeff Gordon's Car .15 .40
133 Geoff Bodine's Car .01 .05
134 Todd Bodine's Car .01 .05
135 Randy LaJoie's Car .01 .05
136 Derrike Cope's Car .01 .05
137 Lake Speed's Car .01 .05
138 Ward Burton's Car .01 .05
139 Mike Wallace's Car .01 .05
140 Terry Labonte's Car .05 .15
141 Sterling Marlin's Car .02 .10
142 Jimmy Spencer's Car .01 .05
143 Michael Waltrip's Car .02 .10
144 Brett Bodine's Car .01 .05
145 Rick Mast's Car .01 .05
146 Harry Gant's Car .02 .10
147 Wally Dallenbach Jr.'s Car .01 .05
148 Ernie Irvan's Car .02 .10
149 Greg Sacks' Car .01 .05
150 Darrell Waltrip's Car .02 .10
P1 Jeff Gordon Promo 2.50 6.00
DB1 Dale Earnhardt Promo 4.00 10.00
PW1 Ernie Irvan Promo 1.00 2.50
NNO D.Earnhardt HOLO/3500 15.00 40.00

1994 Power Gold

COMPLETE SET (150) 7.50 20.00
*GOLD CARDS: .8X TO 2X BASIC CARDS

1994 Power Preview

This 31-card set was issued as a preview to the Power racing set released later in the year. The cards were distributed to hobby outlets in factory set form only and included 18 silver foil stamped driver cards, 12 prism foil car cards and one gold foil Dale Earnhardt tribute card (number 31).

COMPLETE SET (31) 3.00 8.00
1 Geoff Bodine .02 .10
2 Derrike Cope .02 .10
3 Wally Dallenbach Jr. .02 .10
4 Ted Musgrave .02 .10
5 Jimmy Spencer .02 .10
6 Michael Waltrip .07 .20
7 Hut Stricklin .02 .10
8 Rusty Wallace .30 .75
9 Darrell Waltrip .07 .20
10 Dale Jarrett .25 .60
11 Ken Schrader .02 .10
12 Jeff Gordon .50 1.25
13 Ricky Rudd .15 .40
14 Kyle Petty .07 .20
15 Mark Martin .30 .75
16 Harry Gant .07 .20
17 Harry Gant .07 .20
Leo Jackson
18 Bobby Hillin .02 .10
Junie Donlavey
19 Mark Martin's Car FOIL .15 .40
20 Ted Musgrave's Car FOIL .07 .20
21 Wally Dallenbach's Car FOIL .07 .20
22 Jeff Gordon's Car FOIL .30 .75
23 Bobby Hillin's Car FOIL .07 .20
24 Geoff Bodine's Car FOIL .07 .20
25 Harry Gant's Car FOIL .07 .20
26 Kyle Petty's Car FOIL .07 .20
27 Michael Waltrip's Car FOIL
28 Hut Stricklin's Car FOIL .07 .20
29 Dale Jarrett's Car FOIL .15 .40
30 Derrike Cope's Car FOIL .07 .20
31 Dale Earnhardt WC Champ .75 2.00
P16 Harry Gant Promo .40 1.00

1997 Predator Promos

These 6-cards were issued to promote and preview the 1997 Wheels Predator product. Each card is numbered on the back and features the corresponding foil color and design for one of the many parallel sets in the product.

P1 Jeff Gordon Predator 3.00 8.00
P1 Jeff Gordon Pred.1st Slash 3.00 8.00
P2 Jeff Gordon Red Wolf 3.00 8.00
P2 Jeff Gordon Red Wolf 1st 3.00 8.00
P3 Jeff Gordon Black Wolf 3.00 8.00
P3 Jeff Gordon Black Wolf 1st Slash 3.00 8.00

1997 Predator

This 66-card set is another uniquely themed set from Wheels. The cards feature the top names in racing. There are two Double Eagle cards in this product that commemorates Terry Labonte's 1984 and 1996 Winston Cup Championship winning seasons. The Gold Double Eagle card was made available only in First Slash boxes while the Silver Double Eagle card was made available only in the Hobby boxes. The cards were packaged 5 cards per pack, 20 packs per box and 16 boxes per case. The first 375 cases off the press had the First Slash logo stamped on all of the cards in those cases.

COMPLETE SET (66) 6.00 15.00
WAX BOX 40.00 75.00
FIRST SLASH WAX BOX 50.00 90.00
RETAIL WAX BOX 35.00 70.00
1 Jeff Gordon .75 2.00
2 Terry Labonte .25 .60
3 Dale Earnhardt 1.25 3.00
4 Dale Jarrett .50 1.25
5 Mark Martin .60 1.50
6 Rusty Wallace .60 1.50
7 Sterling Marlin .25 .60
8 David Green .07 .20
9 Jeff Burton .25 .60
10 Bobby Hamilton .07 .20
11 Michael Waltrip .15 .40
12 Bobby Labonte .50 1.25
13 Ricky Craven .07 .20
14 Johnny Benson .15 .40
15 Jeremy Mayfield .15 .40
16 Hut Stricklin .07 .20
17 Kyle Petty .15 .40
18 Darrell Waltrip .15 .40
19 John Andretti .07 .20
20 Bill Elliott .30 .75
21 Robert Pressley .07 .20
22 Joe Nemechek .07 .20
23 Derrike Cope .07 .20
24 Ward Burton .15 .40
25 Chad Little .15 .40
26 Mike Skinner .07 .20
27 Jimmy Spencer .07 .20
28 Dave Marcis .07 .20
29 Wally Dallenbach .07 .20
30 Kenny Wallace .07 .20
31 Brett Bodine .07 .20
32 Ted Musgrave .07 .20
33 Robby Gordon RC .25 .60
34 Randy LaJoie .07 .20
35 Jeff Fuller .07 .20
36 Jason Keller .07 .20
37 Mike McLaughlin .07 .20
38 Bobby Labonte .50 1.25
39 Dale Jarrett .50 1.25
40 Michael Waltrip .15 .40
41 Mark Martin .60 1.50
42 Steve Park RC 1.50 4.00
43 Glenn Allen .07 .20
44 Jeff Gordon .75 2.00
45 Terry Labonte .25 .60
46 Bobby Hamilton .07 .20
47 Bobby Labonte .50 1.25
48 Ray Evernham .07 .20
49 Gary DeHart .02 .10
50 Todd Parrott .02 .10
51 Steve Hmiel .02 .10
52 Robin Pemberton .02 .10
53 Jimmy Makar .02 .10
54 Jeff Hammond .02 .10
55 Larry McReynolds .02 .10
56 Kevin Hamlin .02 .10
57 David Smith .02 .10
58 Richard Childress .15 .40
59 Joe Gibbs .15 .40
60 Rick Hendrick .02 .10
61 Robert Yates .02 .10
62 Johnny Benson .15 .40
63 Randy LaJoie .07 .20
64 Bill Elliott .30 .75
65 Ron Hornaday .07 .20
66 Checklist .02 .10
GD1 Terry Labonte 8.00 20.00
SD1 Terry Labonte 5.00 12.00

1997 Predator Black Wolf First Slash

COMPLETE SET (66) 25.00 60.00
*BLACK WOLF FS: 2.5X TO 6X BASIC CARDS

1997 Predator First Slash

COMP.FIRST SLASH (66) 8.00 20.00
*FIRST SLASH: .6X TO 1.5X BASE CARDS

1997 Predator Grizzly

COMPLETE SET (66) 40.00 80.00
*GRIZZLY: 2X TO 5X BASE CARDS
COMP.FS GRIZZLY (66) 60.00 120.00
*GRIZZLY FIRST SLASH: 3X TO 8X BASE CARDS

1997 Predator Red Wolf

COMPLETE SET (66) 75.00 150.00
*RED WOLF: 3X TO 8X BASIC CARDS
COMP.FS RED WOLF (66) 125.00 250.00
*RED WOLF FS: 5X TO 12X BASIC CARDS

1997 Predator American Eagle

This 10-card insert set features the top drivers from NASCAR. The cards are set against a background of an eagle. The cards were randomly inserted in packs at a ratio of 1:30.

COMPLETE SET (10) 40.00 80.00
COMP.FIRST SLASH (10) 50.00 100.00
*FIRST SLASH: .5X TO 1.2X BASIC INSERTS
AE1 Dale Earnhardt 12.00 30.00
AE2 Jeff Gordon 8.00 20.00
AE3 Rusty Wallace 6.00 15.00
AE4 Terry Labonte 2.50 6.00
AE5 Dale Jarrett 5.00 12.00
AE6 Sterling Marlin 2.50 6.00
AE7 Mark Martin 6.00 15.00
AE8 Bobby Labonte 5.00 12.00
AE9 Bill Elliott 3.00 8.00
AE10 Darrell Waltrip 1.50 4.00

1997 Predator Eye of the Tiger

This 8-card insert set features NASCAR top stars on horizontal cards that are foil enhanced and micro-etched. The cards were randomly inserted in packs at a ratio of 1:10.

COMPLETE SET (8) 10.00 25.00
COMP.FIRST SLASH (8) 15.00 40.00
*FIRST SLASH: .5X TO 1.2X BASIC INSERTS
ET1 Dale Earnhardt 5.00 12.00
ET2 Jeff Gordon 3.00 8.00
ET3 Rusty Wallace 2.50 6.00
ET4 Terry Labonte 1.00 2.50
ET5 Dale Jarrett 2.00 5.00
ET6 Mark Martin 2.50 6.00
ET7 Bobby Labonte 2.00 5.00
ET8 Sterling Marlin 1.00 2.50

1997 Predator Gatorback

This 10-card set is a sublevel parallel of the Gatorback Authentic insert set. The cards feature a simulated crocodile hide distinguishing it from the Gatorback Authentic cards. The cards were randomly inserted in packs at a ratio of 1:40.

COMPLETE SET (10) 40.00 80.00
COMP.FIRST SLASH (10) 50.00 100.00
*FIRST SLASH: .5X TO 1.2X BASIC INSERTS
GB1 Dale Earnhardt 15.00 40.00
GB2 Jeff Gordon 12.00 30.00
GB3 Mike Skinner 1.00 2.50
GB4 Dale Jarrett 6.00 15.00
GB5 Rusty Wallace 8.00 20.00
GB6 Bobby Labonte 6.00 15.00
GB7 Mark Martin 8.00 20.00
GB8 Sterling Marlin 3.00 8.00
GB9 Darrell Waltrip 2.00 5.00
GB10 Bill Elliott 4.00 10.00

1997 Predator Gatorback Authentic

This 10-card set is the rarest of all Predator insert sets. The cards are highlighted by actual crocodile hide imported from Australia. There are two versions of each card; the white crocodile skin cards are found only in First Slash boxes and the brown crocodile skin cards are found only in Hobby boxes. The cards were randomly inserted in packs at a ratio of 1:120.

COMPLETE SET (10) 125.00 250.00
COMP.FIRST SLASH (10) 200.00 400.00
*FIRST SLASH: .5X TO 1.2X BASIC INSERTS
GBA1 Dale Earnhardt 30.00 80.00
GBA2 Jeff Gordon 25.00 60.00
GBA3 Mike Skinner 5.00 12.00
GBA4 Dale Jarrett 15.00 40.00
GBA5 Rusty Wallace 15.00 40.00
GBA6 Bobby Labonte 15.00 40.00
GBA7 Mark Martin 20.00 50.00
GBA8 Sterling Marlin 8.00 20.00
GBA9 Darrell Waltrip 6.00 15.00
GBA10 Bill Elliott 10.00 25.00

1997 Predator Golden Eagle

This 10-card insert set features the top drivers from NASCAR. The cards are set against a background of an eagle highlighted by gold foil. The cards were randomly inserted in packs at a ratio of 1:40.

COMPLETE SET (10) 50.00 100.00
COMP.FIRST SLASH (10) 60.00 120.00
*FIRST SLASH: .5X TO 1.2X BASIC INSERTS
GE1 Dale Earnhardt 15.00 40.00
GE2 Jeff Gordon 10.00 25.00
GE3 Rusty Wallace 8.00 20.00
GE4 Terry Labonte 3.00 8.00
GE5 Dale Jarrett 6.00 15.00
GE6 Sterling Marlin 3.00 8.00
GE7 Mark Martin 8.00 20.00
GE8 Bobby Labonte 6.00 15.00
GE9 Bill Elliott 4.00 10.00
GE10 Darrell Waltrip 2.00 5.00

1993 Press Pass Davey Allison

This five-card set uses prism printing technology to highlight Davey Allison's career. There were 25,000 sets produced and were distributed through a mail in offer in the '93 Press Pass Preview set. The sets could be had for $7.95 + $3.00 shipping and handling. In 1994, Press Pass also made the sets available to members of the Press Pass Club and the Press Pass Dealer Network.

COMPLETE SET (5) 2.00 5.00
1 Davey Allison .50 1.25
2 Davey Allison .50 1.25
3 Davey Allison .50 1.25
4 Davey Allison .50 1.25
B.Allison
5 Davey Allison .50 1.25

1993 Press Pass Previews

This 34-card set was the debut set from manufacturer Press Pass. The set was released in the late summer of '93 and features some of the top names in racing. The set originally retailed for $12.95.

COMPLETE SET (34) 8.00 20.00
1 Davey Allison Foil 2.00 4.00
2 Brett Bodine .15 .40
3 Geoff Bodine .15 .40
4 Derrike Cope .15 .40
5 Harry Gant .30 .75
6 Jimmy Hensley .15 .40
7 Dale Jarrett 1.00 2.50
8 Alan Kulwicki .50 1.25
9 Sterling Marlin .60 1.50
10 Mark Martin 1.50 3.00
11 Kyle Petty .30 .75
12 Ken Schrader .15 .40
13 Morgan Shepherd .15 .40
14 Jimmy Spencer .15 .40
15 Rusty Wallace 1.25 3.00
16 Joe Gibbs .30 .75
17 J.Gordon 4.00 10.00
K.Wall.
B.Lab.
18A J.Gordon Redemp. Expired 2.50 5.00
18B Jeff Gordon Foil 5.00 12.00
19 Bobby Labonte 1.00 2.50
20 Kenny Wallace .15 .40
21 Alan Kulwicki .50 1.25
22 Rusty Wallace 1.25 3.00
23 Bobby Allison .15 .40
24 Morgan Shepherd's Car .07 .20
25 Kenny Wallace's Car .07 .20
26 Jeff Gordon's Car .75 2.00
27 Dale Jarrett's Car .30 .75
28 Bobby Labonte's Car .30 .75
29 Jimmy Spencer's Car .07 .20
30 Kyle Petty's Car .15 .40
31 Rusty Wallace's Car .50 1.25
32 Sterling Marlin's Car .15 .40
33 Harry Gant's Car .15 .40
34 Mark Martin's Car .50 1.25

1994 Press Pass

This 150-card base brand set features top drivers from both the Winston Cup and Busch circuits. The cards came 10-cards to a pack. There were two different 36-count boxes which the packs came in. There was a regular box and a Race Day box. The only difference in the two boxes was the Race Day packs gave the collector the opportunity to pull a Race Day insert card. The Race Day packs were easily identifiable due to the bright yellow star burst on the front of the pack.

COMPLETE SET (150)	8.00	20.00
WAX BOX	20.00	50.00
1 Brett Bodine	.07	.20
2 Geoff Bodine	.07	.20
3 Derrike Cope	.07	.20
4 Wally Dallenbach Jr.	.07	.20
5 Dale Earnhardt	1.25	3.00
6 Harry Gant	.15	.40
7 Jeff Gordon	.75	2.00
8 Bobby Hamilton	.07	.20
9 Jimmy Hensley	.07	.20
10 Bobby Hillin	.07	.20
11 Ernie Irvan	.15	.40
12 Dale Jarrett	.50	1.25
13 Bobby Labonte	.50	1.25
14 Terry Labonte	.25	.60
15 Dave Marcis	.07	.20
16 Sterling Marlin	.25	.60
17 Mark Martin	.60	1.50
18 Rick Mast	.07	.20
19 Jimmy Means	.07	.20
20 Ted Musgrave	.07	.20
21 Kyle Petty	.15	.40
22 Ken Schrader	.07	.20
23 Morgan Shepherd	.07	.20
24 Lake Speed	.07	.20
25 Jimmy Spencer	.07	.20
26 Hut Stricklin	.07	.20
27 Kenny Wallace	.07	.20
28 Rusty Wallace	.75	2.00
29 Darrell Waltrip	.15	.40
30 Michael Waltrip	.15	.40
31 Rusty Wallace	.30	.75
K.Wallace		
32 Mark Martin	.30	.75
Jack Roush		
33 Darrell Waltrip	.15	.40
Michael Waltrip		
34 Dale Jarrett	.15	.40
Joe Gibbs		
35 Geoff Bodine	.02	.10
Bobby Hillin		
36 Brett Bodine	.02	.10
Kenny Bernstein		
37 Derrike Cope's Car	.02	.10
38 Morgan Shepherd's Car	.02	.10
39 Bobby Hamilton's Car	.02	.10
40 Jeff Gordon's Car	.30	.75
41 Bobby Hillin's Car	.02	.10
42 Dale Jarrett's Car	.15	.40
43 Ken Schrader's Car	.02	.10
44 Bobby Labonte's Car	.07	.20
45 Jimmy Spencer's Car	.02	.10
46 Kyle Petty's Car	.07	.20
47 Rusty Wallace's Car	.25	.60
48 Geoff Bodine's Car	.02	.10
49 Michael Waltrip's Car	.07	.20
50 Dick Trickle's Car	.02	.10
51 Sterling Marlin's Car	.07	.20
52 Harry Gant's Car	.07	.20
53 Ernie Irvan's Car	.07	.20
54 Mark Martin's Car	.25	.60
55 Todd Bodine	.07	.20
56 Chuck Bown	.07	.20
57 Ward Burton	.15	.40
58 Ricky Craven	.07	.20
59 Bobby Dotter	.07	.20
60 David Green	.07	.20
61 Steve Grissom	.07	.20
62 Joe Nemechek	.07	.20
63 Shawna Robinson	.30	.75
64 Steve Grissom's Car	.02	.10
65 Joe Nemechek's Car	.02	.10
66 Bobby Dotter's Car	.02	.10
67 Ricky Craven's Car	.02	.10
68 Todd Bodine's Car	.02	.10
69 Chuck Bown's Car	.02	.10
70 Shawna Robinson's Car	.07	.20
71 David Green's Car	.02	.10
72 Hermie Sadler's Car	.02	.10
73 Bobby Allison	.07	.20
74 Kenny Bernstein	.07	.20
75 Geoff Bodine	.07	.20
76 Bill Davis	.02	.10
77 Junie Donlavey	.02	.10
78 Joe Gibbs	.15	.40
79 Rick Hendrick	.02	.10
80 Leo Jackson	.02	.10
81 Walter Bud Moore	.02	.10
82 Roger Penske	.02	.10
Don Miller		
83 Chuck Rider	.02	.10
84 Jack Roush	.02	.10
85 Felix Sabates	.02	.10
86 Bill Stavola	.02	.10
Mickey Stavola		
87 Darrell Waltrip	.15	.40
88 Glen Wood	.02	.10
Eddie Wood		
Len Wood		
89 Cale Yarborough	.07	.20
90 Robert Yates	.02	.10
91 Paul Andrews	.02	.10
92 Barry Dodson	.02	.10
93 Ray Evernham	.02	.10
94 Jimmy Fennig	.02	.10
95 Jeff Hammond	.02	.10
96 Doug Hewitt	.02	.10
97 Steve Hmiel	.02	.10
98 Ken Howes	.02	.10
99 Sandy Jones	.02	.10
100 Jimmy Makar	.02	.10
101 Larry McReynolds	.02	.10
102 Buddy Parrott	.02	.10
103 Robin Pemberton	.02	.10
104 Donnie Richeson	.02	.10
105 Doug Williams	.02	.10
106 Ken Wilson	.02	.10
107 Donnie Wingo	.02	.10
108 Leonard Wood	.02	.10
109 Allen Bestwick	.02	.10
110 Dick Brooks	.02	.10
111 Eli Gold	.02	.10
112 Barney Hall	.02	.10
113 Ned Jarrett	.02	.10
114 Winston Kelley	.02	.10
115 Joe Moore	.02	.10
116 Benny Parsons	.07	.20
117 Jim Phillips	.02	.10
118 Rusty Wallace DOY	.30	.75
119 Ken Schrader Pole Win	.02	.10
120 Steve Hmiel	.02	.10
121 Mark Martin TT	.30	.75
122 Dale Jarrett TT	.15	.40
123 Rusty Wallace TT	.30	.75
124 Jeff Gordon ROY	.40	1.00
125 Steve Grissom BGN Champ	.02	.10
126 Joe Nemechek Pop. Driver	.02	.10
127 Davey Allison HR	.25	.60
128 Donnie Allison HR	.07	.20
129 Tim Flock HR	.02	.10
130 Alan Kulwicki HR	.15	.40
131 Fred Lorenzen HR	.02	.10
132 Tiny Lund HR	.02	.10
133 David Pearson HR	.02	.10
134 Glenn Roberts(Fireball) HR	.02	.10
135 Curtis Turner HR	.02	.10
136 Geoff Bodine Art	.02	.10
137 Geoff Bodine Art	.02	.10
138 Derrike Cope Art	.02	.10
139 Speed Racer Art	.02	.10
140 Dale Jarrett Art	.15	.40
141 Mark Martin ART	.30	.75
142 Ken Schrader Art	.02	.10
143 Morgan Shepherd Art	.02	.10
144 Rusty Wallace ART	.40	1.00
145 Harry Gant Farewell	.07	.20
146 Harry Gant Farewell	.07	.20
147 Checklist #1	.02	.10
148 Checklist #2	.02	.10
149 Checklist #3	.02	.10
150 Checklist #4	.02	.10

1994 Press Pass Checkered Flags

This four-card insert set features 1993 multiple race winners. The cards use gold foil stamping and could be found one in every 12 packs.

COMPLETE SET (4)	4.00	10.00
CF1 Dale Earnhardt	2.50	6.00
CF2 Ernie Irvan	.30	.75
CF3 Mark Martin	1.25	3.00
CF4 Rusty Wallace	1.50	4.00

1994 Press Pass Cup Chase

This 30-card set was the first interactive racing game set produced. The specially stamped "Cup Chase" cards were a parallel to the first 30 cards in the set. The collector that owned the Dale Earnhardt Cup Chase card, the 1994 Winston Cup Champion, was able to redeem that card for a special Dale Earnhardt card and an uncut sheet of the 30 Cup Chase cards. An interesting note about the uncut sheet is that in the bottom right hand corner there is a black card and the sheet doesn't have the Dale Earnhardt card on it. The Cup Chase cards were inserted in packs of Press Pass at a rate of one every 18. The cards could be redeemed until March 31, 1995.

COMPLETE SET (30)	75.00	150.00
UNCUT SHEET PRIZE	40.00	100.00
CC1 Brett Bodine	.75	2.00
CC2 Geoff Bodine	.75	2.00
CC3 Derrike Cope	.75	2.00
CC4 Wally Dallenbach Jr.	.75	2.00
CC5 Dale Earnhardt W1	15.00	40.00
CC6 Harry Gant	1.50	4.00
CC7 Jeff Gordon	8.00	20.00
CC8 Bobby Hamilton	.75	2.00
CC9 Jimmy Hensley	.75	2.00
CC10 Bobby Hillin	.75	2.00
CC11 Ernie Irvan	1.50	4.00
CC12 Dale Jarrett	4.00	10.00
CC13 Bobby Labonte	4.00	10.00
CC14 Terry Labonte	2.50	6.00
CC15 Dave Marcis	.75	2.00
CC16 Sterling Marlin	2.50	6.00
CC17 Mark Martin W2	6.00	15.00
CC18 Rick Mast	.75	2.00
CC19 Jimmy Means	.75	2.00
CC20 Ted Musgrave	.75	2.00
CC21 Kyle Petty	1.50	4.00
CC22 Ken Schrader	.75	2.00
CC23 Morgan Shepherd	.75	2.00
CC24 Lake Speed	.75	2.00
CC25 Jimmy Spencer	.75	2.00
CC26 Hut Stricklin	.75	2.00
CC27 Kenny Wallace	.75	2.00
CC28 Rusty Wallace W3	6.00	15.00
CC29 Darrell Waltrip	1.50	4.00
CC30 Michael Waltrip	1.50	4.00
SPCL1 Dale Earnhardt Prize	30.00	60.00

1994 Press Pass Prospects

This five-card insert set uses Thermofoil printing technology to bring five of the top Busch Grand National drivers to collectors. The five drivers were in their rookie years on the Winston Cup circuit in 1994. The cards were randomly seeded at a rate of one per eight packs. The uncut sheet was the prize for returning the second place finisher in the Press Pass Cup Chase

COMPLETE SET (5)	2.50	6.00
UNCUT SHEET PRIZE	7.50	15.00
PP1 Chuck Bown	.40	1.00
PP2 Ward Burton	.75	2.00
PP3 Ricky Craven	.40	1.00
PP4 Steve Grissom	.75	2.00
PP5 Joe Nemechek	.75	2.00

1994 Press Pass Race Day

This 12-card insert set was issued across two Press Pass brands. The first 10 cards in the set were made available through specially marked "Race Day" boxes of Press Pass. The last two cards were randomly inserted in boxes of 1994 VIP. The cards feature drivers who took the checkered flag during 1993 and the 1994 Daytona 500 winner. The cards are printed using the holofoil technology and were randomly inserted in packs at a rate of one per 72.

COMPLETE SET (12)	25.00	60.00
RD1 Davey Allison	2.00	5.00
RD2 Geoff Bodine	.60	1.50
RD3 Ernie Irvan	1.25	3.00
RD4 Dale Jarrett	4.00	10.00
RD5 Mark Martin	5.00	12.00
RD6 Kyle Petty	1.25	3.00
RD7 Jeff Gordon	6.00	15.00
RD8 Morgan Shepherd	.60	1.50
RD9 Rusty Wallace	6.00	15.00
RD10 Dale Earnhardt	10.00	25.00
RD11 Sterling Marlin	2.00	5.00
NNO Cover Card	.30	.75

1994 Press Pass Authentics

These 8" X 10" cards are blown up versions of the five drivers' regular 1994 Press Pass cards. The cards are actually 5" X 7" and framed in a black border. The cards came in two versions: signed and unsigned. There were 1500 cards unsigned and 1000 cards signed. The signed cards were each autographed in gold pen by the driver. All cards are numbered of 2500 no matter if they were signed or unsigned. The cards were made available through the Press Pass Club and to the Press Pass dealer network. The original retail price for each piece was $25 for unsigned and $35 for signed cards.

COMPLETE SET (5)	30.00	80.00
*SIGNED CARDS: 1X TO 2.5X BASE CARDS		
1 Jeff Gordon	12.00	30.00
2 Ernie Irvan	4.00	10.00
3 Mark Martin	7.50	20.00
4 Kyle Petty	4.00	10.00
5 Rusty Wallace	7.50	20.00

1994 Press Pass Holofoils

Press Pass produced this Holofoil set featuring six popular Winston Cup drivers. The cards were sold directly to collectors in complete set form along with a certificate numbering the set one of 15,000 made. The cards contain a photo of the driver printed on holofoil card stock with driver stats on the backs.

COMPLETE SET (6)	4.00	10.00
H1 Dale Earnhardt	2.00	5.00
H2 Jeff Gordon	1.00	2.50
H3 Ernie Irvan	.40	1.00
H4 Mark Martin	.75	2.00
H5 Kyle Petty	.40	1.00
H6 Rusty Wallace	.75	2.00

1995 Press Pass Prototypes

Three cards comprise this release intended to preview the 1995 Press Pass regular set. The cards are numbered and carry the word "Prototype."

COMPLETE SET (3)	3.00	8.00
1 Kyle Petty	.76	2.00
2 Terry Labonte's Car	.75	2.00
3 Jeff Gordon	2.00	5.00

1995 Press Pass

This 145-card base brand set features top drivers from the Winston Cup and Busch Grand National circuits. The cards came 10 cards per pack, 36 packs per box and 20 boxes per case. The set is broken into 10 topical subsets: Winston Cup Drivers (1-36), Winston Cup Cars (37-54), Busch Series Drivers (55-72), Busch Series Cars (73-81), Winston Cup Owners (82-90), Winston Cup Crew Chiefs (91-99), Small Town Saturday Night (100-108), Award Winners (109-117), Heroes of Racing (118-123) SportsKings (124-126), Personal Rides (127-135), Breaking Through (136-143). Also randomly inserted at a rate of one per box in special retail boxes were autograph cards. The only two drivers cards that were autographed are the Sterling Marlin and David Green cards.

COMPLETE SET (145)	10.00	25.00
HOBBY WAX BOX	30.00	55.00
1 Loy Allen Jr.	.07	.20
2 John Andretti	.07	.20
3 Brett Bodine	.07	.20
4 Geoff Bodine	.07	.20
5 Todd Bodine	.07	.20
6 Jeff Burton	.25	.60
7 Ward Burton	.15	.40
8 Derrike Cope	.07	.20
9 Dale Earnhardt	1.25	3.00
10 Jeff Gordon	.75	2.00
11 Steve Grissom	.07	.20
12 Bobby Hamilton	.07	.20
13 Ernie Irvan	.15	.40
14 Dale Jarrett	.50	1.25
15 Bobby Labonte	.50	1.25
16 Terry Labonte	.25	.60
17 Dave Marcis	.15	.40
18 Sterling Marlin	.25	.60
19 Mark Martin	.60	1.50
20 Rick Mast	.07	.20
21 Ted Musgrave	.07	.20
22 Joe Nemechek	.07	.20
23 Kyle Petty	.15	.40
24 Ricky Rudd	.25	.60
25 Greg Sacks	.07	.20
26 Ken Schrader	.07	.20
27 Morgan Shepherd	.07	.20
28 Lake Speed	.07	.20
29 Jimmy Spencer	.07	.20
30 Hut Stricklin	.07	.20
31 Dick Trickle	.07	.20
32 Kenny Wallace	.07	.20
33 Mike Wallace	.07	.20
34 Rusty Wallace	.60	1.50
35 Darrell Waltrip	.15	.40
36 Michael Waltrip	.15	.40
Elizabeth Waltrip		
37 Morgan Shepherd's Car	.02	.10
38 Jeff Gordon's Car	.30	.75
39 Geoff Bodine's Car	.02	.10
40 Ted Musgrave's Car	.02	.10
41 Dale Earnhardt's Car	.50	1.25
42 Dale Jarrett's Car	.15	.40
43 Terry Labonte's Car	.15	.40
44 Sterling Marlin's Car	.07	.20
45 Ken Schrader's Car	.02	.10
46 Kyle Petty's Car	.07	.20
47 Rusty Wallace's Car	.25	.60
48 Michael Waltrip's Car	.07	.20
49 Brett Bodine's Car	.02	.10
50 John Andretti's Car	.02	.10
51 Ernie Irvan's Car	.07	.20
52 Ricky Rudd's Car	.07	.20
53 Mark Martin's Car	.25	.60
54 Darrell Waltrip's Car	.07	.20
55 Johnny Benson Jr.	.15	.40
56 Jim Bown	.07	.20
57 Ricky Craven	.15	.40
58 Bobby Dotter	.07	.20
59 Tim Fedewa	.07	.20
60 David Green	.07	.20
61 Tommy Houston	.07	.20
62 Jason Keller	.07	.20
63 Randy LaJoie	.07	.20
64 Tracy Leslie	.07	.20
65 Chad Little	.07	.20
66 Mark Martin	.60	1.50
67 Mike McLaughlin	.07	.20
68 Larry Pearson	.07	.20
69 Robert Pressley	.07	.20
70 Elton Sawyer	.07	.20
71 Dennis Setzer	.07	.20
72 Kenny Wallace	.07	.20
73 Dennis Setzer's Car	.02	.10
74 Chad Little's Car	.02	.10
75 Bobby Dotter's Car	.02	.10
76 Ricky Craven's Car	.02	.10
77 Mike McLaughlin's Car	.02	.10
78 Randy LaJoie's Car	.02	.10
79 David Green's Car	.02	.10
80 Larry Pearson's Car	.02	.10
81 Kenny Wallace's Car	.02	.10
82 Richard Childress	.15	.40
83 Rick Hendrick	.02	.10
84 Walter Bud Moore	.02	.10
85 Roger Penske	.02	.10
Don Miller		
86 Richard Petty	.25	.60
87 Chuck Rider	.02	.10
88 Felix Sabates	.02	.10
89 Cale Yarborough	.07	.20
90 Robert Yates	.02	.10
91 Mike Beam	.02	.10
92 Ray Evernham	.15	.40
93 Steve Hmiel	.02	.10
94 Ken Howes	.02	.10
95 Bill Ingle	.02	.10
96 Larry McReynolds	.02	.10
97 Buddy Parrott	.02	.10
98 Andy Petree	.02	.10
99 Leonard Wood	.02	.10
100 John Andretti ST	.07	.20
101 Geoff Bodine ST	.07	.20
102 Jeff Gordon ST	.40	1.00
103 Steve Kinser ST	.07	.20
104 Mark Martin ST	.30	.75
105 Joe Nemechek ST	.07	.20
106 Ken Schrader ST	.07	.20
107 Jimmy Spencer ST	.07	.20
108 Darrell Waltrip ST	.15	.40
109 Jeff Burton AW	.15	.40
110 Geoff Bodine AW	.07	.20
111 Ray Evernham AW	.07	.20
112 David Green AW	.07	.20
113 Johnny Benson AW	.15	.40
114 David Green AW	.07	.20
115 Dale Earnhardt's Car AW	.50	1.25
116 Mark Martin's Car AW	.25	.60
117 Michael Waltrip's Car AW	.60	1.50
118 Buck Baker HR	.07	.20
119 Buddy Baker HR	.07	.20
120 Harry Gant HR	.15	.40
121 J.D. McDuffie HR	.02	.10
122 Marvin Panch HR	.02	.10
123 Lennie Pond HR	.02	.10
124 Bobby Allison S	.07	.20
125 David Pearson S	.07	.20
126 Richard Petty S	.25	.60
127 Geoff Bodine PR	.07	.20
128 Harry Gant PR	.15	.40
129 Jeff Gordon PR	.40	1.00
130 Bobby Hamilton PR	.07	.20
131 Kyle Petty PR	.15	.40
132 Richard Petty PR	.25	.60
133 Ken Schrader PR	.07	.20
134 Morgan Shepherd PR	.07	.20
135 Rusty Wallace PR	.30	.75
136 Jeff Gordon BT	.40	1.00
137 Sterling Marlin BT	.15	.40
138 Jimmy Spencer BT	.07	.20
139 Johnny Benson BT	.15	.40
140 Ricky Craven BT	.15	.40
141 Elton Sawyer BT	.07	.20
142 Dennis Setzer BT	.07	.20
143 Mike Wallace BT	.07	.20
144 Checklist	.02	.10
145 Checklist	.02	.10
A18 Sterling Marlin AUTO	10.00	25.00
A60 David Green AUTO	6.00	12.00

1995 Press Pass Red Hot

COMPLETE SET (145)	25.00	60.00
*RED HOTS: 1X TO 2.5X BASE CARDS		

1995 Press Pass Checkered Flags

This eight-card set features Winston Cup drivers who won multiple races in the 1994 season. The cards are gold foil stamped and were inserted in packs at a rate of one per nine.

COMPLETE SET (8)	10.00	25.00
CF1 Geoff Bodine	.30	.75
CF2 Dale Earnhardt	5.00	12.00
CF3 Jeff Gordon	3.00	8.00
CF4 Ernie Irvan	.60	1.50
CF5 Terry Labonte	1.00	2.50
CF6 Mark Martin	2.50	6.00
CF7 Jimmy Spencer	.30	.75
CF8 Rusty Wallace	2.50	6.00

1995 Press Pass Cup Chase

This 36-card insert set is a parallel of the first 36 cards in the base Press Pass set. The cards feature a gold foil stamp "Cup Chase" to differentiate the cards. This is the second year of the interactive game from Press Pass. The rules changed in 1995 so the collector could redeem a Cup Chase card of not only the Winston Cup Champion but the winners of five specific races throughout the year: Daytona 500, Winston Select 500, Coca-Cola 600, Brickyard 400 and the MBNA 500. If you held a Cup Chase card for the winner of any of those five races, you could redeem it for a special holo-prism card of the 1994 winning driver of that specific race. If you had the Winston Cup Champion card (Jeff Gordon), you could redeem that card for the entire set of five special holoprism cards. Odds of finding a Cup Chase card was one per 24 packs. The winning cards could be redeemed until January 31, 1996.

COMPLETE SET (36)	75.00	150.00
1 Loy Allen Jr.	1.25	3.00
2 John Andretti	1.25	3.00
3 Brett Bodine	1.25	3.00
4 Geoff Bodine	1.25	3.00
5 Todd Bodine	1.25	3.00
6 Jeff Burton	2.50	6.00
7 Ward Burton	2.50	6.00
8 Derrike Cope	1.25	3.00
9 Dale Earnhardt WIN	12.50	30.00
10 Jeff Gordon WIN	10.00	25.00
11 Steve Grissom	1.25	3.00
12 Bobby Hamilton	1.25	3.00
13 Ernie Irvan	2.50	6.00
14 Dale Jarrett	4.00	10.00
15 Bobby Labonte WIN	6.00	15.00
16 Terry Labonte	2.50	6.00
17 Dave Marcis	2.50	6.00
18 Sterling Marlin WIN	4.00	10.00
19 Mark Martin WIN	8.00	20.00
20 Rick Mast	1.25	3.00
21 Ted Musgrave	1.25	3.00
22 Joe Nemechek	1.25	3.00
23 Kyle Petty	2.50	6.00
24 Ricky Rudd	3.00	8.00
25 Greg Sacks	1.25	3.00
26 Ken Schrader	1.25	3.00
27 Morgan Shepherd	1.25	3.00
28 Lake Speed	1.25	3.00
29 Jimmy Spencer	1.25	3.00
30 Hut Stricklin	1.25	3.00
31 Dick Trickle	1.25	3.00
32 Kenny Wallace	1.25	3.00
33 Mike Wallace	1.25	3.00
34 Rusty Wallace	4.00	10.00
35 Darrell Waltrip	2.50	6.00
36 Michael Waltrip	2.50	6.00

1995 Press Pass Cup Chase Prizes

This five-card insert set features the winning drivers of these 1994 races: the Daytona 500, Winston Select 500, Coca-Cola 600, Brickyard 400 and the MBNA 500. The cards were printed using holoprism technology and were made available two different ways. First, the cards were inserted as chiptoppers at a rate of one per hobby case. The cards were also the redemption prizes for the Cup Chase game winners.

COMPLETE SET (5)	30.00	80.00
CCR1 Sterling Marlin	3.00	8.00
CCR2 Dale Earnhardt	15.00	40.00
CCR3 Jeff Gordon	10.00	25.00
CCR4 Jeff Gordon	10.00	25.00
CCR5 Rusty Wallace	8.00	20.00

1995 Press Pass Race Day

This 12-card insert set features winning drivers from the 1994 Winston Cup season. The cards use holofoil technology and were inserted at a rate of one per 24 packs.

COMPLETE SET (12)	30.00	80.00
RD1 Cover Card	.30	.75
RD2 Geoff Bodine	.60	1.50
RD3 Dale Earnhardt	10.00	25.00
RD4 Jeff Gordon	6.00	15.00
RD5 Ernie Irvan	1.25	3.00
RD6 Dale Jarrett	4.00	10.00
RD7 Terry Labonte	2.00	5.00
RD8 Sterling Marlin	2.00	5.00
RD9 Mark Martin	5.00	12.00
RD10 Ricky Rudd	2.00	5.00
RD11 Jimmy Spencer	.60	1.50
RD12 Rusty Wallace	5.00	12.00

1996 Press Pass

This 120-card set is the base brand from Press Pass. It features the best drivers in stock car racing. This is the first set to ever include each of NASCAR's Winston Cup Regional Series champions. The set is also the first to show many of the driver and sponsor changes for the 1996 season. The set features the following topical subsets: Winston Cup Drivers (1-36), Winston Cup Cars (37-54), Busch Grand National Drivers (55-63), SuperTrucks Drivers (64-72), Teamwork (73-81), Daytona Winner (82-90), Shattered (91-

99), Champions (100-108), Winner's Circle (109-112) and '96 Preview (113-119). Hobby product was packaged eight cards per pack, 24 packs per box and 20 boxes per case. Also, included in Hobby only packs was a special Jeff Gordon Championship card. It pays tribute to the 1995 Winston Cup Champion. These cards are found one per 480 packs. Retail product was packed eight cards per pack, 36 packs per box and 20 boxes per case.

Card	Low	High
COMPLETE SET (120)	8.00	20.00
1 John Andretti	.07	.20
2 Brett Bodine	.07	.20
3 Geoff Bodine	.07	.20
4 Todd Bodine	.07	.20
5 Jeff Burton	.25	.60
6 Ward Burton	.15	.40
7 Derrike Cope	.07	.20
8 Ricky Craven	.07	.20
9 Dale Earnhardt	1.00	2.50
10 Bill Elliott	.30	.75
11 Jeff Gordon	.75	2.00
12 Steve Grissom	.07	.20
13 Bobby Hamilton	.07	.20
14 Ernie Irvan	.15	.40
15 Dale Jarrett	.50	1.25
16 Bobby Labonte	.50	1.25
17 Terry Labonte	.25	.60
18 Dave Marcis	.15	.40
19 Sterling Marlin	.25	.60
20 Mark Martin	.60	1.50
21 Rick Mast	.07	.20
22 Jeremy Mayfield	.15	.40
23 Ted Musgrave	.07	.20
24 Joe Nemechek	.07	.20
25 Kyle Petty	.15	.40
26 Robert Pressley	.07	.20
27 Ricky Rudd	.25	.60
28 Ken Schrader	.07	.20
29 Morgan Shepherd	.07	.20
30 Lake Speed	.07	.20
31 Hut Stricklin	.07	.20
32 Dick Trickle	.07	.20
33 Mike Wallace	.07	.20
34 Rusty Wallace	.60	1.50
35 Darrell Waltrip	.15	.40
36 Michael Waltrip	.15	.40
37 Kyle Petty's Car	.07	.20
38 Jeff Gordon's Car	.30	.75
39 Ted Musgrave's Car	.02	.10
40 Dale Earnhardt's Car	.50	1.25
41 Bobby Labonte's Car	.15	.40
42 Terry Labonte's Car	.15	.40
43 Sterling Marlin's Car	.07	.20
44 Ricky Craven's Car	.02	.10
45 Derrike Cope's Car	.02	.10
46 Bill Elliott's Car	.15	.40
47 Rusty Wallace's Car	.25	.60
48 Michael Waltrip's Car	.07	.20
49 Bobby Hamilton's Car	.02	.10
50 Dale Jarrett's Car	.15	.40
51 Ernie Irvan's Car	.07	.20
52 Ricky Rudd's Car	.07	.20
53 Mark Martin's Car	.25	.60
54 Darrell Waltrip's Car	.07	.20
55 Johnny Benson Jr.	.15	.40
56 Tim Fedewa	.07	.20
57 Jeff Fuller	.07	.20
58 Jeff Green	.07	.20
59 Jason Keller	.07	.20
60 Chad Little	.07	.20
61 Mike McLaughlin	.07	.20
62 Larry Pearson	.07	.20
63 Elton Sawyer	.07	.20
64 Mike Bliss RC	.07	.20
65 Rick Carelli	.07	.20
66 Ron Hornaday Jr.	.07	.20
67 Ernie Irvan	.15	.40
68 Butch Miller	.07	.20
69 Joe Ruttman	.07	.20
70 Bill Sedgwick	.07	.20
71 Mike Skinner	.07	.20
72 Bob Strait	.07	.20
73 Penske Miller Pember R.Wall TW	.07	.20
74 L.McClure Glover Marlin TW	.07	.20
75 R.Hendrick DeHart T.Labonte TW	.07	.20
76 M.Martin Roush Hmiel TW	.30	.75
77 Gibbs Makar B.Labonte TW	.15	.40
78 J.Gordon Hend Evern.TW	.40	1.00
79 Yates McReynolds D.Jarrett	.07	.20
80 R.Petty Loomis Hamilton	.25	.60
81 C.Hardy M.Beam B.Elliott	.07	.20
82 Bobby Allison DW	.07	.20
83 Geoff Bodine DW	.07	.20
84 Derrike Cope DW	.07	.20
85 Bill Elliott DW	.15	.40
86 Ernie Irvan DW	.07	.20
87 Dale Jarrett DW	.15	.40
88 Sterling Marlin DW	.15	.40
89 Richard Petty DW	.25	.60
90 Darrell Waltrip DW	.07	.20
91 Ricky Craven S	.07	.20
92 Bill Elliott S	.15	.40
93 Jeff Gordon S	.40	1.00
94 Bobby Labonte S	.15	.40
95 Sterling Marlin S	.15	.40
96 Mark Martin S	.30	.75
97 Kyle Petty S	.07	.20
98 Ricky Rudd S	.15	.40
99 Rusty Wallace S	.30	.75
100 J.Gordon B.Gordon WCC	.40	1.00
101 Andy Hillenburg AACA Champ	.07	.20
102 Jon Compagnone Eastern Champ	.02	.10
103 Phil Warren Mid-Atlantic Champ	.02	.10
104 Jeff Wildung Northwest Champ	.02	.10
105 Mel Walen Northern Champ	.02	.10
106 Paul White Sunbelt Champ	.02	.10
107 Dale Planck Mid-America Champ	.02	.10
108 Ray Guss Jr. Central Champ	.02	.10
109 Unocal RaceStoppers WC	.02	.10
110 Bill Brodrick WC	.02	.10
111 J.Gordon J.Benson WC	.40	1.00
112 Bill Venturini WC	.02	.10
113 Johnny Benson PRE	.15	.40
114 David Green PRE	.07	.20
115 Dale Jarrett PRE	.15	.40
116 Mike McLaughlin PRE	.07	.20
117 Morgan Shepherd PRE	.07	.20
118 Michael Waltrip PRE	.15	.40
119 Rusty Wallace's Car PRE	.25	.60
120 Checklist Card	.02	.10
P2 Terry Labonte Promo	.75	2.00
PN1 Bobby Labonte Gold Promo	2.00	5.00
PN2 Bobby Labonte Red Promo	4.00	10.00
0 Jeff Gordon Championship	12.50	30.00

1996 Press Pass Scorchers

Card	Low	High
COMPLETE SET (120)	30.00	60.00

*SCORCHERS: 1.2X TO 3X BASE CARDS

1996 Press Pass Torquers

Card	Low	High
COMPLETE SET (120)	30.00	60.00

*TORQUERS: 1.2X TO 3X BASE CARDS

1996 Press Pass Burning Rubber

This seven-card set is the first to incorporate race used equipment into trading cards. Press Pass took tires from winning race cars in the 1995 season and had them cut into pieces. These pieces were then attached to the cards that appear in this set. Each card is individually numbered to 500 and the backs contain a certificate of authenticity. The cards were inserted at a rate of one per 480 packs.

Card	Low	High
COMPLETE SET (7)	150.00	300.00
BR1 Kyle Petty's Car	12.50	30.00
BR2 Jeff Gordon's Car	25.00	50.00
BR3 Dale Earnhardt's Car	25.00	60.00
BR4 Terry Labonte's Car	10.00	25.00
BR5 Sterling Marlin's Car	12.50	30.00
BR6 Bill Elliott's Car	15.00	40.00
BR7 Mark Martin's Car	15.00	40.00

1996 Press Pass Burning Rubber Die Cast Inserts

These three cards were issued individually in 1996 Press Pass Die Cast Sets. Each set features a group of die cast racing pieces along with one of these Burning Rubber cards. Each card is numbered "1 of 1" on the cardbacks but the announced print runs were printed on the outside of the boxes that housed each set.

Card	Low	High
1 Bobby Labonte's Car/1008	30.00	60.00
2 Terry Labonte's Car/1996	30.00	60.00
3 Rusty Wallace/1996	30.00	60.00

1996 Press Pass Checkered Flags

This six-card set continues the insert theme started in 1994. The cards feature some of the tops names in NASCAR and were distributed in Wal-Mart only packs at a ratio of 1:9 packs.

Card	Low	High
COMPLETE SET (6)	8.00	20.00
CF1 Jeff Gordon	3.00	8.00
CF2 Bobby Labonte	2.00	5.00
CF3 Terry Labonte	1.00	2.50
CF4 Sterling Marlin	1.00	2.50
CF5 Mark Martin	2.50	6.00
CF6 Rusty Wallace	2.50	6.00

1996 Press Pass Cup Chase

This 37-card set is the third year in a row for Press Pass' interactive game. This is the first year that you could redeem a Cup Chase driver's card for a prize if they finish in the top 3 in any one of the five selected races. The interactive races are the February 18th Daytona 500, March 10th Purolator 500, April 14th First Union 400, May 5th Save Mart Supermarkets 300, and the June 16th UAW-GM Teamwork 500. The prize for having one of the top three finishers is a limited holographic foil card of that driver. There is also a Grand Prize awarded to those who redeem the 1996 Winston Cup Champion's Cup Chase card at the end of the season. The Grand Prize is an entire 37-card holographic foil cup chase set. Prizes could be redeemed through January 31, 1997. The Cup Chase cards are seeded one per 24 packs.

Card	Low	High
COMPLETE SET (37)	60.00	120.00
COMP.FOIL SET (37)	25.00	50.00

*FOIL NO-WIN: .4X TO 1X BASIC INSERTS
*FOIL WIN: .12X TO .3X BASIC INSERTS

Card	Low	High
1 John Andretti	.75	2.00
2 Brett Bodine	.75	2.00
3 Geoff Bodine WIN	.75	2.00
4 Todd Bodine	.75	2.00
5 Jeff Burton	2.50	6.00
6 Ward Burton	1.50	4.00
7 Derrike Cope	.75	2.00
8 Ricky Craven	.75	2.00
9 Dale Earnhardt WIN	10.00	25.00
10 Bill Elliott	3.00	8.00
11 Jeff Gordon WIN	8.00	20.00
12 Steve Grissom	.75	2.00
13 Bobby Hamilton	.75	2.00
14 Ernie Irvan	1.50	4.00
15 Dale Jarrett WIN	5.00	12.00
16 Bobby Labonte	5.00	12.00
17 Terry Labonte WIN	2.50	6.00
18 Dave Marcis	1.50	4.00
19 Sterling Marlin	2.50	6.00
20 Mark Martin WIN	6.00	15.00
21 Rick Mast	.75	2.00
22 Jeremy Mayfield	1.50	4.00
23 Ted Musgrave	.75	2.00
24 Joe Nemechek	.75	2.00
25 Kyle Petty	1.50	4.00
26 Robert Pressley	.75	2.00
27 Ricky Rudd WIN	2.50	6.00
28 Ken Schrader WIN	.75	2.00
29 Morgan Shepherd	.75	2.00
30 Lake Speed	.75	2.00
31 Hut Stricklin	.75	2.00
32 Dick Trickle	.75	2.00
33 Mike Wallace	.75	2.00
34 Rusty Wallace WIN	6.00	15.00
35 Darrell Waltrip	1.50	4.00
36 Michael Waltrip	1.50	4.00
37 Johnny Benson, Jr.	1.50	4.00

1996 Press Pass F.Q.S.

This 18-card set uses Nitrokrome technology to bring you nine of the fastest Winston Cup drivers and their cars. F.Q.S is an acronym for Fastest Qualifing Speed. Every driver's card number ends with the letter A, while each driver's car card number ends with the letter B. The cards were randomly inserted at a rate of one per 12 packs.

Card	Low	High
COMPLETE SET (18)	60.00	125.00
FQS1A Dale Earnhardt	8.00	20.00
FQS1B Dale Earnhardt's Car	3.00	8.00
FQS2A Bill Elliott	2.00	5.00
FQS2B Bill Elliott's Car	1.00	2.50
FQS3A Jeff Gordon	5.00	12.00
FQS3B Jeff Gordon's Car	2.00	5.00
FQS4A Dale Jarrett	3.00	8.00
FQS4B Dale Jarrett's Car	1.00	2.50
FQS5A Bobby Labonte	3.00	8.00
FQS5B Bobby Labonte's Car	1.00	2.50
FQS6A Terry Labonte	1.50	4.00
FQS6B Terry Labonte's Car	1.00	2.50
FQS7A Sterling Marlin	1.50	4.00
FQS7B Sterling Marlin's Car	.50	1.25
FQS8A Mark Martin	4.00	10.00
FQS8B Mark Martin's Car	1.50	4.00
FQS9A Ricky Rudd	1.50	4.00
FQS9B Ricky Rudd's Car	.50	1.25

1996 Press Pass Focused

This set is made up of ten of the top drivers in Winston Cup. Each card is produced on clear acetate stock. The cards were randomly seeded at a rate of one per 72 packs.

Card	Low	High
COMPLETE SET (10)	60.00	150.00
F1 Dale Earnhardt	15.00	40.00
F2 Bill Elliott	4.00	10.00
F3 Jeff Gordon	10.00	25.00
F4 Ernie Irvan	2.00	5.00
F5 Terry Labonte	3.00	8.00
F6 Sterling Marlin	3.00	8.00
F7 Mark Martin	8.00	20.00
F8 Kyle Petty	2.00	5.00
F9 Ricky Rudd	3.00	8.00
F10 Rusty Wallace	8.00	20.00
P1 Jeff Gordon Promo	2.00	5.00

1996 Press Pass R and N China

This 26-card set was produced by R and N China. Each card is made out of porcelain and is a replica of a 1996 Press Pass card.

Card	Low	High
COMPLETE SET (26)	125.00	250.00
1 John Andretti	3.00	8.00
5 Jeff Burton	5.00	12.00
8 Ricky Craven	3.00	8.00
9 Dale Earnhardt	30.00	60.00
11 Jeff Gordon	12.50	35.00
13 Bobby Hamilton	3.00	8.00
14 Ernie Irvan	4.00	10.00
15 Dale Jarrett	7.50	20.00
16 Bobby Labonte	7.50	20.00
17 Terry Labonte	6.00	15.00
19 Sterling Marlin	4.00	10.00
20 Mark Martin	10.00	25.00
22 Jeremy Mayfield	3.00	8.00
23 Ted Musgrave	3.00	8.00
24 Joe Nemechek	3.00	8.00
25 Kyle Petty	3.00	8.00
28 Ken Schrader	3.00	8.00
34 Rusty Wallace	10.00	25.00
35 Darrell Waltrip	4.00	10.00
36 Michael Waltrip	4.00	10.00
38 Jeff Gordon's Car	6.00	15.00
42 Terry Labonte's Car	3.00	8.00
47 Rusty Wallace's Car	4.00	10.00
50 Dale Jarrett's Car	4.00	10.00
53 Mark Martin's Car	3.00	8.00
55 Johnny Benson	3.00	8.00

1997 Press Pass

The 1997 Press Pass set was issued in one series totalling 140 cards. The set contains the topical subsets: Winston Cup Drivers (1-30), Winston Cup Cars (31-45), SuperTruck Drivers (46-54), Japan Race (55-63), BGN Drivers (64-78), Back-to-Back (79-90), Highlights (91-109), Champions (110-120), '97 Preview (121-133), and 10 Wins (1334-138). The cards were distributed to both hobby and retail. The hobby product consisted of eight card packs, 24 packs per box and 20 boxes per case. The retail boxes consisted of eight card packs, 32 packs per box and 20 boxes per case. There are two insert cards priced at the bottom of the base set listing. One is the Jeff Gordon Sam Bass Top Flight card. The card was intended to be in the 1996 VIP Top Flight set but was inserted in '97 Press Pass packs at a rate of one in 480 packs. Also a special holofoil Terry Labonte Winston Cup Champion card could be found in packs at a rate of one in 480.

Card	Low	High
COMPLETE SET (140)	10.00	25.00
1 Terry Labonte	.25	.60
2 Jeff Gordon	.75	2.00
3 Dale Jarrett	.50	1.25
4 Dale Earnhardt	1.25	3.00
5 Mark Martin	.60	1.50
6 Ricky Rudd	.25	.60
7 Rusty Wallace	.30	.75
8 Sterling Marlin	.25	.60
9 Bobby Hamilton	.07	.20
10 Ernie Irvan	.15	.40
11 Bobby Labonte	.50	1.25
12 Ken Schrader	.07	.20
13 Jeff Burton	.25	.60
14 Michael Waltrip	.15	.40
15 Ted Musgrave	.07	.20
16 Geoff Bodine	.07	.20
17 Rick Mast	.07	.20
18 Morgan Shepherd	.07	.20
19 Ricky Craven	.07	.20
20 Johnny Benson	.15	.40
21 Hut Stricklin	.07	.20
22 Jeremy Mayfield	.15	.40
23 Kyle Petty	.15	.40
24 Kenny Wallace	.07	.20
25 Darrell Waltrip	.15	.40
26 Bill Elliott	.30	.75
27 Robert Pressley	.07	.20
28 Ward Burton	.15	.40
29 Joe Nemechek	.07	.20
30 Mike Skinner	.07	.20
31 Rusty Wallace's Car	.25	.60
32 Dale Earnhardt's Car	.50	1.25
33 Sterling Marlin's Car	.07	.20
34 Terry Labonte's Car	.07	.20
35 Mark Martin's Car	.25	.60
36 Ricky Rudd's Car	.07	.20
37 Bobby Labonte's Car	.15	.40
38 Michael Waltrip's Car	.07	.20
39 Jeff Gordon's Car	.30	.75
40 Ernie Irvan's Car	.02	.10
41 Ricky Craven's Car	.02	.10
42 Kyle Petty's Car	.02	.10
43 Bobby Hamilton's Car	.02	.10
44 Dale Jarrett's Car	.15	.40
45 Bill Elliott's Car	.07	.20
46 Mike Bliss	.07	.20
47 Rick Carelli	.07	.20
48 Ron Hornaday	.07	.20
49 Butch Miller	.07	.20
50 Joe Ruttman	.07	.20
51 Bill Sedgwick	.07	.20
52 Mike Skinner	.07	.20
53 Rusty Wallace	.60	1.50
54 Darrell Waltrip	.15	.40
55 Johnny Benson's Car	.02	.10
56 Dale Earnhardt's Car	.50	1.25
57 Jeff Gordon's Car	.30	.75
58 Ernie Irvan's Car	.02	.10
59 Dale Jarrett's Car	.15	.40
60 Terry Labonte's Car	.07	.20
61 Sterling Marlin's Car	.07	.20
62 Rusty Wallace's Car	.25	.60
63 Michael Waltrip's Car	.07	.20
64 Todd Bodine	.07	.20
65 Rodney Combs	.07	.20
66 Ricky Craven	.07	.20
67 Jeff Fuller	.07	.20
68 David Green	.07	.20
69 Jeff Green	.07	.20
70 Dale Jarrett	.50	1.25
71 Jason Keller	.07	.20
72 Terry Labonte	.25	.60
73 Randy LaJoie	.07	.20
74 Chad Little	.15	.40
75 Mark Martin	.60	1.50
76 Mike McLaughlin	.07	.20
77 Larry Pearson	.15	.40
78 Michael Waltrip	.15	.40
79 Michael Waltrip	.15	.40
80 Dale Jarrett	.50	1.25
81 Bobby Labonte	.50	1.25
82 Terry Labonte	.25	.60
83 Ricky Craven	.07	.20
84 Rusty Wallace	.60	1.50
85 Ken Schrader	.07	.20
86 Mike Wallace	.07	.20
87 Jeremy Mayfield	.15	.40
88 Chad Little	.15	.40
89 Mark Martin	.60	1.50
90 Kenny Wallace	.07	.20
91 Robby Gordon RC	.25	.60
92 Jimmy Johnson	.07	.20
93 M.Waltrip David Pearson	.15	.40
94 Dale Jarrett	.50	1.25
95 Dale Earnhardt's Car	.50	1.25
96 J.Gordon D.Jarrett's Cars	.30	.75
97 T.Labonte R.Petty	.25	.60
98 Sterling Marlin	.25	.60
99 Rusty Wallace's Car	.25	.60
100 Michael Waltrip	.15	.40
101 Ernie Irvan	.15	.40
102 Dale Jarrett	.50	1.25
103 Geoff Bodine	.07	.20
104 Jeff Gordon's Car	.30	.75
105 Jeff Gordon's Car	.30	.75
106 Terry Labonte's Car	.07	.20
107 Ricky Rudd	.25	.60
108 B.Hamilton R.Petty	.25	.60
109 Bobby Labonte	.50	1.25
110 Terry Labonte	.25	.60
111 Randy LaJoie	.07	.20
112 Mark Martin	.60	1.50
113 Ron Hornaday	.07	.20
114 Kelly Tanner	.07	.20
115 Joe Kosiski	.07	.20
116 Lyndon Amick RC	.15	.40
117 Dave Dion	.07	.20
118 Tony Hirschman	.02	.10
119 Chris Raudman	.02	.10
120 Mike Cope	.07	.20
121 Kyle Petty	.15	.40
122 Rusty Wallace's Car	.25	.60
123 Michael Waltrip	.15	.40
124 Dale Jarrett	.50	1.25
125 Chad Little	.15	.40
126 Joe Nemechek	.07	.20
127 Steve Grissom	.07	.20
128 Robby Gordon	.15	.40
129 Mike Wallace	.07	.20
130 Bill Elliott's Car	.07	.20
131 Ken Schrader	.07	.20
132 Wally Dallenbach	.07	.20
133 Derrike Cope	.07	.20
134 Jeff Gordon W	.40	1.00
135 Jeff Gordon W	.40	1.00
136 Jeff Gordon W	.40	1.00
137 Jeff Gordon W	.40	1.00
138 Jeff Gordon W	.40	1.00
139 Checklist	.02	.10
140 Checklist	.02	.10
P1 Dale Jarrett Promo	.75	2.00
P2 Bobby Labonte National Promo	1.25	3.00
P3 Bobby Labonte's Car Natl.Promo	.75	2.00
SB1 Jeff Gordon Sam Bass	20.00	50.00
0 Terry Labonte WC Champ	15.00	40.00

1997 Press Pass Lasers Silver

Card	Low	High
COMPLETE SET (140)	20.00	50.00

*LASERS: 1.2X TO 3X BASIC CARDS

1997 Press Pass Oil Slicks

Card	Low	High
COMPLETE SET (140)	250.00	500.00

*OIL SLICK: 8X TO 20X BASIC CARDS

1997 Press Pass Torquers Blue

Card	Low	High
COMPLETE SET (140)	20.00	50.00

*TORQUERS: 1.2X TO 3X BASIC CARDS

1997 Press Pass Autographs

This set features autographed cards from the top stars from the Winston Cup and Busch Circuits. These cards were inserted into three Press Pass products: ActionVision, Press Pass Premium, and VIP. The cards were randomly inserted in ActionVision packs at a ratio of 1:160, Press Pass Premuim packs at a ratio of 1:72 packs, and VIP packs at a ratio of 1:60 packs. Each card is numbered on the back "#/35" but a total of 41-different cards were released over the three products. Note that card #27 was produced in two different versions.

Card	Low	High
COMPLETE SET (41)	800.00	1400.00
1 T.Labonte PPP/VIP/ACTN	12.00	30.00
2 J.Gordon PPP/VIP/ACTN	60.00	120.00
3 Dale Jarrett VIP/ACTN	8.00	20.00
4 D.Earnhardt PPP/VIP/ACTN	100.00	200.00
5 Steve Hmiel PPP/VIP	5.00	10.00
6 Ricky Rudd VIP/ACTN	12.00	30.00
7 Rusty Wallace VIP/ACTN	15.00	40.00
8 Sterling Marlin VIP/ACTN	10.00	25.00
9 Bobby Hamilton PPP/VIP	10.00	25.00
10 Bobby Labonte PPP/VIP	12.00	30.00
11 Ken Schrader PPP/VIP	6.00	15.00
12 Jeff Burton VIP/ACTN	8.00	20.00
13 Michael Waltrip PPP/VIP	8.00	20.00
14 Ted Musgrave PPP/VIP	6.00	15.00
15 Geoff Bodine PPP	6.00	15.00
16 Ricky Craven VIP	10.00	25.00
17 Johnny Benson PPP	12.00	30.00
18 Jeremy Mayfield VIP	10.00	25.00
19 Kyle Petty PPP/VIP/ACTN	12.00	30.00
20 Bill Elliott VIP/ACTN	25.00	60.00
21 Wood Brothers VIP	5.00	10.00
22 Joe Nemechek PPP	6.00	15.00
23 Wally Dallenbach PPP	4.00	10.00
24 Robby Gordon PPP/VIP	10.00	25.00
25 David Green VIP	6.00	15.00
26 Jason Keller PPP/VIP	4.00	10.00
27 Jeff Green PPP/VIP	6.00	15.00
27A R.Gordon/Green/Skin VIP	10.00	25.00
28 Mike McLaughlin PPP/VIP	4.00	10.00
29 Chad Little VIP	12.00	30.00
30 Jeff Fuller PPP/VIP	4.00	10.00
31 Todd Bodine PPP/VIP	5.00	12.00
32 Rodney Combs PPP	4.00	10.00
33 Randy LaJoie PPP/VIP	6.00	15.00
34 Ray Evernham VIP	12.00	30.00
35 Larry McReynolds PPP	5.00	12.00
36 Gary DeHart VIP	5.00	10.00
37 Mike Beam VIP	5.00	10.00
38 Darrell Waltrip VIP	15.00	40.00
39 Ward Burton VIP	10.00	25.00
40 Mike Skinner VIP	6.00	15.00

1997 Press Pass Banquet Bound

This 10-card insert set features the top drivers from 1996. The cards are printed on rainbow holofoil board and were inserted one in 12 packs.

Card	Low	High
COMPLETE SET (10)	12.50	30.00
BB1 Terry Labonte	1.25	3.00
BB2 Jeff Gordon	4.00	10.00
BB3 Dale Jarrett	2.50	6.00
BB4 Dale Earnhardt	6.00	15.00
BB5 Mark Martin	3.00	8.00
BB6 Ricky Rudd	1.25	3.00
BB7 Rusty Wallace	3.00	8.00
BB8 Sterling Marlin	1.25	3.00
BB9 Bobby Hamilton	.40	1.00
BB10 Ernie Irvan	.75	2.00

1997 Press Pass Burning Rubber

Authentic race-used tires from the top drivers are incorporated in this seven-card insert set. The cards feature an acetate, die-cut design with a photo of the driver in the center with a tire shaped piece of race used rubber surrounding it. Each was serial numbered of 400-cards made. The cards were seeded in packs at a rate of one in 480.

Card	Low	High
BR1 Rusty Wallace	10.00	25.00
BR2 Dale Earnhardt	30.00	80.00
BR3 Terry Labonte	10.00	25.00
BR4 Michael Waltrip	8.00	20.00
BR5 Jeff Gordon	20.00	50.00
BR6 Ernie Irvan	8.00	20.00
BR7 Dale Jarrett	10.00	25.00

1997 Press Pass Clear Cut

Randomly inserted in packs at a rate of one in 18, this 10-card set features drivers who won races in 1996. The cards feature a clear die-cut acetate design.

Card	Low	High
COMPLETE SET (10)	12.50	30.00
C1 Dale Earnhardt	6.00	15.00
C2 Jeff Gordon	4.00	10.00
C3 Ernie Irvan	.75	2.00
C4 Dale Jarrett	2.50	6.00
C5 Bobby Labonte	2.50	6.00
C6 Terry Labonte	1.25	3.00
C7 Mark Martin	3.00	8.00
C8 Ricky Rudd	1.25	3.00
C9 Rusty Wallace	3.00	8.00
C10 Michael Waltrip	.75	2.00

1997 Press Pass Cup Chase

This was the fourth consecutive year of the popular Press Pass' interactive game. This year if the collector owned a Cup Chase card of one of the three top finishers from any one of the 10 selected Winston Cup race events, the card could be redeemed for a limited gold NitroKrome die cut card of that driver. Card number CC20 was a Field Card to be used in the event that a Winston Cup driver not featured in the set finishes 1st, 2nd, or 3rd at one of the 10 selected races. The prize for the Field Card was one of the 19 featured drivers gold NitroKrome die cut cards drawn at random. At the end of the '97 season, the Winston Cup Champion's Cup Chase card could be redeemed for the entire 20-card gold NitroKrome die cut Cup Chase set. This set included a special card of the 1996 Winston Cup Champion Terry Labonte that was available only through the redemption. Each Cup Chase card could be redeemed for two usages throughout the entire 1997 season. Each time the card was redeemed Press Pass embossed one of the corners. After the card had been embossed twice it is no longer redeemable. The Cup Chase card of the '97 WC Champion could only be redeemed once. The deadline to claim prizes was January 30, 1998. The 10 eligible races were: Feb.16 - Daytona, March 9 - Atlanta, April 6 - Texas, May 4 - Sears Point, May 25 - Charlotte, June 22- California, August 2 - Indianapolis, August 23 - Bristol, September 28 - Martinsville, November 2 - Phoenix. There was also a die cut

parallel version of the 20-card set which could not be redeemed for prizes. The die cuts were inserted as chip toppers one per case.
COMPLETE SET (20) 50.00 100.00
COMP.DIE CUT GOLD (20) 75.00 150.00
*DIE CUT GOLD WIN: .6X TO 1.5X BASIC INS.
*DC GOLD NO-WIN: .8X TO 2X BASIC INS.
COMP.DIE CUT BLUE (20) 25.00 60.00
*DIE CUT BLUE WIN: .2X TO .5X BASIC INS.
*DC BLUE NO-WIN: .4X TO 1X BASIC INS.
CC1 Johnny Benson 1.25 3.00
CC2 Jeff Burton WIN 4.00 10.00
CC3 Ward Burton 1.25 3.00
CC4 Ricky Craven WIN 3.00 6.00
CC5 Dale Earnhardt 10.00 25.00
CC6 Bill Elliott 2.00 5.00
CC7 Jeff Gordon WIN 6.00 15.00
CC8 Bobby Hamilton WIN 2.50 5.00
CC9 Ernie Irvan WIN 3.00 6.00
CC10 Dale Jarrett WIN 4.00 10.00
CC11 Bobby Labonte WIN 4.00 10.00
CC12 Terry Labonte WIN 4.00 10.00
CC13 Sterling Marlin 2.00 5.00
CC14 Mark Martin WIN 5.00 12.00
CC15 Kyle Petty 1.25 3.00
CC16 Ricky Rudd WIN 4.00 10.00
CC17 Ken Schrader .60 1.50
CC18 Rusty Wallace WIN 5.00 12.00
CC19 Michael Waltrip 1.25 3.00
CC20 Field Card WIN .60 1.50

1997 Press Pass Victory Lane

Randomly inserted in packs at a rate of one in 18, this 18-card set was divided with nine cards being drivers and nine cards being driver's cars. The cards are number 1-9 with an A or B extension after the number. All the A cards were shots of the driver while all the B cards were shots of their cars. The A cards were available in hobby packs and the B cards were available in retail packs.

COMPLETE SET (18) 60.00 100.00
COMP.DRIVER SET (9) 45.00 75.00
COMP.CAR SET (9) 15.00 30.00
VL1A Dale Earnhardt 10.00 25.00
VL1B Dale Earnhardt's Car 4.00 10.00
VL2A Jeff Gordon 6.00 15.00
VL2B Jeff Gordon's Car 2.50 6.00
VL3A Ernie Irvan 1.25 3.00
VL3B Ernie Irvan's Car .30 .75
VL4A Dale Jarrett 4.00 10.00
VL4B Dale Jarrett's Car 1.25 3.00
VL5A Terry Labonte 2.00 5.00
VL5B Terry Labonte's Car .60 1.50
VL6A Sterling Marlin 2.00 5.00
VL6B Sterling Marlin's Car .60 1.50
VL7A Ricky Rudd 2.00 5.00
VL7B Ricky Rudd's Car .60 1.50
VL8A Rusty Wallace 5.00 12.00
VL8B Rusty Wallace's Car 2.00 5.00
VL9A Michael Waltrip 1.25 3.00
VL9B Michael Waltrip's Car .60 1.50

1998 Press Pass

The 1998 Press Pass set was issued in one series totalling 150 cards and was distributed in eight-card packs. The fronts feature color photos with silver-etched foil highlights. The set contains the topical subsets: NASCAR Winston Cup Drivers (1-27), NASCAR Winston Cup Cars (28-36), NASCAR Busch Series Drivers (37-49), NASCAR Craftsman Truck Series (50-54), 1998 NASCAR Winston Cup Previews (55-63), Teammates (64-81), Champions (82-93), NASCAR Winston Cup Crew Chiefs (94-100), and NASCAR's 50 Greatest Drivers of All-Time (101-150). A special all foil Jeff Gordon Winston Cup Champion card can be found in hobby packs at the rate of one in 480.

COMPLETE SET (150) 12.00 30.00
COMP.REGULAR SET (100) 6.00 15.00
1 Jeff Gordon .75 2.00
2 Mark Martin .60 1.50
3 Dale Jarrett .50 1.25
4 Dale Earnhardt 1.25 3.00
5 Terry Labonte .25 .60
6 Ricky Rudd .25 .60
7 Rusty Wallace .60 1.50
8 Sterling Marlin .25 .60
9 Bobby Hamilton .07 .20
10 Ernie Irvan .15 .40
11 Bobby Labonte .50 1.25
12 Ken Schrader .07 .20
13 Jeff Burton .25 .60
14 Michael Waltrip .15 .40
15 Ted Musgrave .07 .20
16 Geoff Bodine .07 .20
17 Ward Burton .15 .40
18 Ricky Craven .15 .40
19 Johnny Benson .15 .40
20 Jeremy Mayfield .15 .40
21 Kyle Petty .15 .40
22 Darrell Waltrip .15 .40
23 Bill Elliott .30 .75
24 Mike Skinner .07 .20
25 David Green .07 .20
26 Joe Nemechek .07 .20
27 Wally Dallenbach .07 .20
28 Rusty Wallace's Car .25 .60
29 Dale Earnhardt's Car .50 1.25
30 Terry Labonte's Car .15 .40
31 Mark Martin's Car .25 .60
32 Ricky Rudd's Car .07 .20
33 Bobby Labonte's Car .02 .10
34 Jeff Gordon's Car .30 .75
35 Dale Jarrett's Car .15 .40
36 Bill Elliott's Car .15 .40
37 Randy LaJoie .07 .20
38 Todd Bodine .07 .20
39 Tim Fedewa .07 .20
40 Kevin Lepage .07 .20
41 Mark Martin .60 1.50
42 Mike McLaughlin .07 .20
43 Jason Keller .07 .20
44 Steve Park .50 1.25
45 Dale Jarrett .50 1.25
46 Dale Earnhardt Jr. 2.00 4.00
47 Ricky Craven .15 .40
48 Elliott Sadler .15 .40
49 Hermie Sadler .07 .20
50 Rich Bickle .07 .20
51 Jack Sprague .07 .20
52 Joe Ruttman .07 .20
53 Mike Bliss .07 .20
54 Ron Hornaday .07 .20
55 Ernie Irvan .15 .40
56 Kenny Irwin .15 .40
57 Sterling Marlin .25 .60
58 Steve Park .50 1.25
59 Johnny Benson .15 .40
60 Todd Bodine .07 .20
61 Bobby Hamilton .07 .20
62 Ted Musgrave .07 .20
63 Jimmy Spencer .07 .20
64 Darren Jolly .02 .10
65 Jeff Knight .02 .10
66 Barry Muse .02 .10
67 Mike Belden .02 .10
68 Mike Trower .02 .10
69 Chris Anderson .02 .10
70 Patrick Donahue .02 .10
71 Brian Whitesell .02 .10
72 Ray Evernham .02 .10
73 J.J. Clodfelter .02 .10
74 Ben Leslie .02 .10
75 Dennis Ritchie .02 .10
76 Mitch Williams .02 .10
77 Lonnie Dubay .02 .10
78 Luke Shimp .02 .10
79 Butch Hylton .02 .10
80 Steve Spahr .02 .10
81 Jimmy Fennig .02 .10
82 Randy LaJoie .07 .20
83 Jack Sprague .07 .20
84 Mike Stefanik RC .07 .20
85 Butch Gilliland .07 .20
86 Mike Swaim Jr. .07 .20
87 Hal Goodson .07 .20
88 Bryan Germone .07 .20
89 Joe Kosiski .07 .20
90 Kelly Tanner .07 .20
91 Gary Scelzi .07 .20
92 Mark Martin IROC .60 1.50
93 Andy Green .02 .10
94 Jimmy Makar .02 .10
95 Ray Evernham .02 .10
96 Jimmy Fennig .02 .10
97 Larry McReynolds .02 .10
98 Todd Parrott .02 .10
99 Robin Pemberton .02 .10
100 WC Schedule CL .02 .10
101 Jeff Gordon RET 1.25 3.00
102 Mark Martin RET 1.00 2.50
103 Dale Jarrett RET .75 2.00
104 Dale Earnhardt RET 2.00 5.00
105 Rusty Wallace RET 1.00 2.50
106 Ricky Rudd RET .40 1.00
107 Bill Elliott RET .50 1.25
108 Terry Labonte RET .40 1.00
109 Ralph Earnhardt RET .25 .60
110 Richie Evans RET .10 .30
111 Red Farmer RET .10 .30
112 Ray Hendrick RET .10 .30
113 Darrell Waltrip RET .25 .60
114 Tiny Lund RET .10 .30
115 Jerry Cook RET .10 .30
116 Geoff Bodine RET .10 .30
117 Bob Welborn RET .10 .30
118 Fred Lorenzen RET .25 .60
119 Herb Thomas RET .10 .30
120 Tim Flock RET .25 .60
121 Lee Petty RET .25 .60
122 Buck Baker RET .10 .30
123 Rex White RET .10 .30
124 Ned Jarrett RET .25 .60
125 Benny Parsons RET .25 .60
126 Joe Weatherly RET .10 .30
127 David Pearson RET .25 .60
128 Bobby Isaac RET .10 .30
129 Tim Richmond RET .25 .60
130 Curtis Turner RET .10 .30
131 Alan Kulwicki RET .25 .60
132 Bobby Allison RET .25 .60
133 Cale Yarborough RET .25 .60
134 Richard Petty RET .40 1.00
135 Davey Allison RET .40 1.00
136 Glen Wood RET .10 .30
137 Harry Gant RET .25 .60
138 Junior Johnson RET .25 .60
139 Fireball Roberts RET .25 .60
140 Neil Bonnett RET .25 .60
141 Lee Roy Yarborough RET .10 .30
142 Buddy Baker RET .10 .30
143 A.J. Foyt RET .25 .60
144 Red Byron RET .10 .30
145 Cotton Owens RET .10 .30
146 Hershel McGriff RET .10 .30
147 Marvin Panch RET .10 .30
148 Jack Ingram RET .10 .30
149 Marshall Teague RET .10 .30
150 Ernie Irvan CL .15 .40
P1 Jeff Gordon Promo 2.00 5.00
P2 Mark Martin Club Promo 1.50 4.00
0 Jeff Gordon 1997 Champion 12.50 30.00

1998 Press Pass Oil Slicks

COMPLETE SET (100) 300.00 600.00
*OIL SLICK/100: 12X TO 30X BASE CARDS

1998 Press Pass Autographs

Randomly inserted in hobby packs at the rate of one in 240, this 14-card set features autographed color photos of top NASCAR drivers. Each card was individually numbered.

COMPLETE SET (14) 600.00 900.00
1 Dale Earnhardt/63 150.00 300.00
2 Jeff Gordon/60 100.00 200.00
3 Dale Jarrett 25.00 60.00
4 Terry Labonte/109 20.00 50.00
5 Mark Martin/101 30.00 60.00
6 Bobby Labonte/203 12.00 30.00
7 Jeff Burton 8.00 20.00
8 Rusty Wallace 20.00 50.00
9 Michael Waltrip/285 10.00 25.00
10 Ricky Craven 6.00 15.00
11 Ricky Rudd 15.00 40.00
12 Mike Skinner/212 6.00 15.00
13 Darrell Waltrip/158 20.00 40.00
14 Johnny Benson 10.00 25.00

1998 Press Pass Cup Chase

This was the fifth consecutive year of the popular Press Pass interactive game. This year if the collector owned a Cup Chase card of one of the three top finishers from any one of the 11 selected Winston Cup race events, the card could be redeemed for an all-foil embossed die-cut card of that driver. Card number CC20 is a Field Card. In the event that a Winston Cup driver not featured in the Cup Chase set finishes 1st, 2nd, or 3rd at one of the 11 selected races, the Field Card can be redeemed. The prize for the Field Card is one of the 19 featured drivers die-cut cards drawn at random. At the end of the '98 season, the '98 Winston Cup Champion's Cup Chase card can be redeemed for a special 20-card Cup Chase set. Each Cup Chase card can be redeemed for two uses throughout the entire '98 season. Each time the card is redeemed Press Pass embossed one of the corners. After the card has been embossed twice it is no longer redeemable. The Cup Chase card of the '97 WC Champion can only be redeemed once. Deadline to claim prizes is January 31, 1999. The 11 eligible races are February 15 - Daytona, March 8- Atlanta, April 5 - Texas, May 3 - California, June 6 - Richmond, June 28 - Sears Point, July 26 - Pocono, August 16 - Michigan, September 6 - Darlington, September 27 - Martinsville, October 25 - Phoenix.

COMPLETE SET (20) 75.00 150.00
COMP.DIE CUT SET (19) 25.00 60.00
*DIE CUT WIN: .2X TO .5X BASE INSERTS
*DIE CUT NO-WIN: .3X TO .8X BASE INS.
CC1 Johnny Benson 2.00 5.00
CC2 Jeff Burton Win 2 4.00 10.00
CC3 Ward Burton 2.00 5.00
CC4 Ricky Craven 2.00 5.00
CC5 Dale Earnhardt's Car Win 2 10.00 25.00
CC6 Bill Elliott 3.00 8.00
CC7 Jeff Gordon Win 2 Champ 10.00 25.00
CC8 Bobby Hamilton Win 2.00 5.00
CC9 Ernie Irvan 2.00 5.00
CC10 Dale Jarrett Win 2 6.00 15.00
CC11 Bobby Labonte Win 2 6.00 15.00
CC12 Terry Labonte Win 2 5.00 12.00
CC13 Sterling Marlin 2.50 6.00
CC14 Mark Martin Win 2 6.00 15.00
CC15 Kyle Petty 2.00 5.00
CC16 Ricky Rudd Win 4.00 10.00
CC17 Ken Schrader 1.25 3.00
CC18 Rusty Wallace Win 2 6.00 15.00
CC19 Michael Waltrip 2.00 5.00
CC20 Field Card Win 2 2.00 5.00

1998 Press Pass Oil Cans

Randomly inserted in packs at the rate of one in 18, this nine-card set features color photos of top NASCAR Winston Cup drivers on all foil embossed cards.

COMPLETE SET (9) 12.50 30.00
OC1 Jeff Burton 1.25 3.00
OC2 Dale Earnhardt's Car 3.00 8.00
OC3 Jeff Gordon 4.00 10.00
OC4 Dale Jarrett 1.50 4.00
OC5 Bobby Labonte 2.50 6.00
OC6 Terry Labonte 1.50 4.00
OC7 Mark Martin 3.00 8.00
OC8 Ricky Rudd 1.25 3.00
OC9 Rusty Wallace 3.00 8.00

1998 Press Pass Pit Stop

Randomly inserted in packs at the rate of one in 12, this 18-card set features color photos of the hottest teams as they make their record pit stops printed on die-cut cards with intricate foil stamping.

COMPLETE SET (18) 12.50 30.00
PS1 Rusty Wallace's Car 2.50 6.00
PS2 Dale Earnhardt's Car 5.00 12.00
PS3 Sterling Marlin's Car .75 2.00
PS4 Terry Labonte's Car 1.25 3.00
PS5 Mark Martin's Car 2.00 6.00
PS6 Ricky Rudd's Car .75 2.00
PS7 Ted Musgrave's Car .30 .75
PS8 Darrell Waltrip's Car .60 1.50
PS9 Bobby Labonte's Car 2.00 5.00
PS10 Michael Waltrip's Car .60 1.50
PS11 Ward Burton's Car .60 1.50
PS12 Jeff Gordon's Car 3.00 8.00
PS13 Kenny Irwin's Car .30 .75
PS14 John Andretti's Car .30 .75
PS15 Kyle Petty's Car .60 1.50
PS16 Dale Jarrett's Car 1.50 4.00
PS17 Bill Elliott's Car 1.50 4.00
PS18 Jeff Burton's Car .75 2.00

1998 Press Pass Shockers

Randomly inserted in hobby packs at the rate of one in 12, this 15-card set features color photos of the best NASCAR Winston Cup drivers printed on extra thick die-cut cards.

COMPLETE SET (15) 15.00 40.00
ST1A Terry Labonte 1.50 4.00
ST2A Jeff Gordon 3.00 8.00
ST3A Dale Earnhardt 5.00 12.00
ST4A Dale Jarrett 1.50 4.00
ST5A Mark Martin 2.50 6.00
ST6A Ricky Rudd 1.25 3.00
ST7A Rusty Wallace 2.50 6.00
ST8A Bill Elliott 1.50 4.00
ST9A Bobby Labonte 1.50 4.00
ST10A Kyle Petty .60 1.50
ST11A Jeff Burton 1.25 3.00
ST12A Michael Waltrip .60 1.50
ST13A Ted Musgrave .40 1.00
ST14A Mike Skinner .40 1.00
ST15A Ward Burton .60 1.50
P2 Dale Jarrett Promo 2.50 6.00

1998 Press Pass Torpedoes

Randomly inserted in packs at the rate of one in 12, this 15-card set features color photos of the hot cars of the best NASCAR Winston Cup drivers printed on extra thick die-cut cards.

COMPLETE SET (15) 25.00 50.00
ST1B Terry Labonte's Car 1.50 4.00
ST2B Jeff Gordon's Car 3.00 8.00
ST3B Dale Earnhardt's Car 5.00 12.00
ST4B Dale Jarrett's Car 1.50 4.00
ST5B Mark Martin's Car 2.50 6.00
ST6B Ricky Rudd's Car 1.25 3.00
ST7B Rusty Wallace's Car 2.50 6.00
ST8B Bill Elliott's Car 1.50 4.00
ST9B Bobby Labonte's Car 2.00 5.00
ST10B Kyle Petty's Car .40 1.00
ST11B Jeff Burton's Car 1.25 3.00
ST12B Michael Waltrip's Car .40 1.00
ST13B Ted Musgrave's Car .40 1.00
ST14B Mike Skinner's Car .40 1.00
ST15B Ward Burton's Car .75 2.00

1998 Press Pass Triple Gear 3 in 1

This nine-card set features actual pieces of race-used tires, firesuits and sheet metal from the pictured driver's car. 33-redemption cards for each driver were produced with eleven cards for each driver inserted in the following products: 1998 Press Pass, 1998 Press Pass Premium, and 1998 VIP.

STG1 Rusty Wallace 40.00 100.00
STG2 Dale Earnhardt 250.00 500.00
STG3 Terry Labonte 40.00 100.00
STG4 Mark Martin 50.00 120.00
STG5 Bobby Labonte 40.00 100.00
STG6 Jeff Gordon 200.00 400.00
STG7 Mike Skinner 25.00 60.00
STG8 Dale Jarrett 40.00 100.00
STG9 Jeff Burton 30.00 80.00

1998 Press Pass Triple Gear Burning Rubber

Randomly inserted in packs at the rate of one in 480, this nine-card set features actual pieces of race-used tires from NASCAR Winston Cup's top drivers. Each card is individually numbered to 250.

TG1 Rusty Wallace 10.00 25.00
TG2 Dale Earnhardt 30.00 60.00
TG3 Terry Labonte 10.00 25.00
TG4 Mark Martin 10.00 25.00
TG5 Bobby Labonte 10.00 25.00
TG6 Jeff Gordon 15.00 40.00
TG7 Mike Skinner 6.00 15.00
TG8 Dale Jarrett 8.00 20.00
TG9 Jeff Burton 8.00 20.00

1999 Press Pass

The 1999 Press Pass set was issued in one series totaling 136 cards. The set contains these subsets: NASCAR Winston Cup Drivers (1-27), NASCAR Winston Cup Machine (28-36), Busch Drivers (37-51), Super Truck (52-57) Young Guns (58-63), Crew Chiefs (64-72), NASCAR Series Champions (73-81), On the Pole (82-94), Winston Cup Preview (95-99). The final 36-cards of the base issue set feature a "Retro" theme and were inserted one per pack. Those cards measure slightly more narrow than a standard sized card.

COMPLETE SET (136) 12.50 30.00
WAX BOX 45.00 75.00
1 Jeff Gordon .75 2.00
2 Mark Martin .60 1.50
3 Dale Jarrett .50 1.25
4 Rusty Wallace .60 1.50
5 Bobby Labonte .50 1.25
6 Jeremy Mayfield .15 .40
7 Jeff Burton .25 .60
8 Dale Earnhardt 1.25 3.00
9 Terry Labonte .25 .60
10 Ken Schrader .07 .20
11 John Andretti .07 .20
12 Ernie Irvan .15 .40
13 Jimmy Spencer .07 .20
14 Sterling Marlin .25 .60
15 Michael Waltrip .15 .40
16 Bill Elliott .30 .75
17 Bobby Hamilton .50 1.25
18 Johnny Benson .15 .40
19 Kenny Irwin .15 .40
20 Ward Burton .15 .40
21 Darrell Waltrip .15 .40
22 Joe Nemechek .07 .20
23 Ricky Rudd .25 .60
24 Mike Skinner .07 .20
25 Robert Pressley .07 .20
26 Steve Park .40 1.00
27 Geoff Bodine .07 .20
28 Jeff Gordon's Car .30 .75
29 Mark Martin's Car .25 .60
30 Dale Jarrett's Car .15 .40
31 Rusty Wallace's Car .25 .60
32 Bobby Labonte's Car .15 .40
33 Jeremy Mayfield's Car .07 .20
34 Jeff Burton's Car .07 .20
35 Dale Earnhardt's Car .50 1.25
36 Terry Labonte's Car .15 .40
37 Dale Earnhardt Jr. 1.00 2.50
38 Matt Kenseth RC 2.50 6.00
39 Mike McLaughlin .07 .20
40 Randy LaJoie .07 .20
41 Elton Sawyer .07 .20
42 Jason Jarrett .07 .20
43 Elliott Sadler .15 .40
44 Tim Fedewa .07 .20
45 Mike Dillon .07 .20
46 Hermie Sadler .07 .20
47 Glenn Allen .07 .20
48 Dale Jarrett .50 1.25
49 Mark Martin .60 1.50
50 Jeff Burton .25 .60
51 Michael Waltrip .15 .40
52 Ron Barfield ST .07 .20
53 Ron Hornaday ST .07 .20
54 Jack Sprague ST .07 .20
55 Joe Ruttman ST .07 .20
56 Jay Sauter ST RC .07 .20
57 Rich Bickle ST .07 .20
58 Dale Earnhardt Jr. YG .60 1.50
59 Elliott Sadler YG .15 .40
60 Jason Jarrett YG .07 .20
61 Tony Stewart YG .75 2.00
62 Matt Kenseth YG 2.00 5.00
63 Adam Petty YG RC 4.00 10.00
64 Larry McReynolds .02 .10
65 Jimmy Makar .02 .10
66 Robin Pemberton .02 .10
67 Todd Parrott .02 .10
68 Ray Evernham .07 .20
69 Andy Graves .07 .20
70 Jimmy Fennig .02 .10
71 Paul Andrews .02 .10
72 Jeff Buice .02 .10
73 Dale Earnhardt Jr. Champ .60 1.50
74 Ron Hornaday Champ .07 .20
75 Mike Stefanik Champ .07 .20
76 Kevin Harvick Champ RC 4.00 10.00
77 Steve Kosiski Champ .07 .20
78 Steve Portenga Champ .07 .20
79 Jeff Gordon OTP .40 1.00
80 Rusty Wallace OTP .30 .75
81 Ward Burton OTP .15 .40
82 Ernie Irvan OTP .07 .20
83 Bobby Labonte OTP .25 .60
84 Ken Schrader OTP .07 .20
85 Kenny Irwin OTP .07 .20
86 Bobby Hamilton OTP .07 .20
87 Dale Jarrett OTP .25 .60
88 Mark Martin OTP .30 .75
89 Rick Mast OTP .07 .20
90 Jeremy Mayfield OTP .07 .20
91 Derrike Cope OTP .07 .20
92 Elliott Sadler PRE .15 .40
93 Jerry Nadeau PRE .15 .40
94 Tony Stewart PRE .75 2.00
95 Kevin Lepage PRE .07 .20
96 Ernie Irvan PRE .07 .20
97 Kenny Wallace PRE .07 .20
98 Jason Jarrett PRE .07 .20
99 Jeff Gordon PRE .40 1.00
100 Checklist .02 .10
101 Jeff Gordon RET 1.25 3.00
102 Mark Martin RET 1.00 2.50
103 Dale Jarrett RET .75 2.00
104 Rusty Wallace RET 1.00 2.50
105 Bobby Labonte RET .75 2.00
106 Jeremy Mayfield RET .25 .60
107 Jeff Burton RET .40 1.00
108 Chad Little RET .25 .60
109 Terry Labonte RET .40 1.00
110 Ken Schrader RET .10 .30
111 John Andretti RET .10 .30
112 Ernie Irvan RET .25 .60
113 Jimmy Spencer RET .10 .30
114 Sterling Marlin RET .40 1.00
115 Michael Waltrip RET .25 .60
116 Bill Elliott RET .50 1.25
117 Bobby Hamilton RET .10 .30
118 Johnny Benson RET .10 .30
119 Kenny Irwin RET .25 .60
120 Ward Burton RET .25 .60
121 Darrell Waltrip RET .25 .60
122 Joe Nemechek RET .10 .30
123 Ricky Rudd RET .40 1.00
124 Mike Skinner RET .10 .30
125 Robert Pressley RET .10 .30
126 Steve Park RET .60 1.50
127 Geoff Bodine RET .10 .30
128 Bobby Allison RET .25 .60
129 Buddy Baker RET .10 .30
130 Ned Jarrett RET .10 .30
131 David Pearson RET .25 .60
132 Richard Petty RET .40 1.00
133 Cale Yarborough RET .25 .60
134 Junior Johnson RET .10 .30
135 Benny Parsons RET .10 .30
136 Harry Gant RET .10 .30
P1 Jeff Gordon Promo 1.50 4.00
P2 Mark Martin Promo .75 2.00
P3 Terry Labonte Promo .60 1.50
0 Jeff Gordon '98 Champ/800 20.00 50.00

1999 Press Pass Autographs

Randomly inserted in packs at the rate of one in 240, each card was individually serial numbered and features an authentic autograph of a leading driver. The unnumbered cardbacks contain a congratulatory message from Press Pass along with the hand written serial number.

COMPLETE SET (21) 900.00 1500.00
1 Rich Bickle/500 5.00 12.00
2 Jeff Burton/250 10.00 25.00
3 Dale Earnhardt/75 250.00 500.00
4 Dale Earnhardt Jr./250 60.00 120.00
5 Bill Elliott/250 12.00 30.00
6 Ray Evernham/500 10.00 25.00
7 Jeff Gordon/75 125.00 250.00
8 Andy Graves/250 8.00 20.00
9 Ron Hornaday/500 8.00 20.00
10 Ernie Irvan/240 15.00 30.00
11 Kenny Irwin/249 15.00 40.00
12 Dale Jarrett/250 20.00 50.00
13 Terry Labonte/250 20.00 50.00
14 Randy LaJoie/500 5.00 12.00
15 Mark Martin/235 30.00 60.00
16 Jeremy Mayfield/250 10.00 25.00
17 Ricky Rudd/245 20.00 40.00
18 Jack Sprague/500 5.00 12.00
19 Tony Stewart/500 25.00 60.00
20 Rusty Wallace/70 60.00 120.00
21 Michael Waltrip/250 6.00 15.00

1999 Press Pass Burning Rubber

Randomly inserted in packs at the rate of one in 480, this nine card set features a piece of race-used tire. Each card was serial numbered of 250.

COMPLETE SET (9) 300.00 600.00
BR1 Terry Labonte's Car 10.00 25.00
BR2 Mark Martin's Car 12.00 30.00
BR3 Bobby Labonte's Car 10.00 25.00
BR4 Jeff Burton's Car 8.00 20.00
BR5 Dale Jarrett's Car 10.00 25.00
BR6 Ricky Rudd's Car 8.00 20.00
BR7 Jeff Gordon's Car 20.00 50.00
BR8 Rusty Wallace's Car 10.00 25.00
BR9 Dale Earnhardt's Car 25.00 60.00

1999 Press Pass Chase Cars

Randomly inserted in packs at the rate of one in twelve, this 18-card retail only set features laser gold foil stamping.

COMPLETE SET (18) 30.00 60.00
1B Dale Jarrett's Car 4.00 10.00
2B Bobby Labonte's Car 4.00 10.00
3B Mark Martin's Car 5.00 12.00
4B Jeremy Mayfield's Car .60 1.50
5B Ken Schrader's Car .60 1.50
6B Mike Skinner's Car .60 1.50
7B Dale Earnhardt's Car 10.00 25.00
8B Jeff Burton's Car 2.00 5.00
9B Ricky Rudd's Car 2.00 5.00
10B Michael Waltrip's Car 1.25 3.00
11B Jeff Gordon's Car 6.00 15.00
12B Bill Elliott's Car 2.50 6.00
13B Terry Labonte's Car 2.50 6.00
14B Ernie Irvan's Car 1.25 3.00
15B Johnny Benson's Car 1.25 3.00
16B Sterling Marlin's Car 2.00 5.00
17B Joe Nemechek's Car .60 1.50
18B Rusty Wallace's Car 5.00 12.00

1999 Press Pass Cup Chase

Randomly inserted in packs at the rate of one in 24, this 20 card set returns sporting an all new design coupled with a combination etch/emboss enhancement on foil board. Collectors could redeem their winning Cup Chase cards for a multi-level embossed die cut version of the cards printed on 24pt. stock.

COMPLETE SET (20) 125.00 250.00
COMP.DIE CUT SET (20) 30.00 80.00
*DIE CUT WIN: .12X TO .3X BASE INSERTS
*DIE CUT NO-WIN: .25X TO .6X BASE INS.
1 John Andretti 1.50 4.00
2 Johnny Benson 3.00 8.00
3 Jeff Burton WIN 2 4.00 10.00
4 Dale Earnhardt WIN 2 15.00 40.00

5 Bill Elliott	6.00	15.00
6 Jeff Gordon WIN 2	15.00	40.00
7 Bobby Hamilton	1.50	4.00
8 Ernie Irvan	3.00	8.00
9 Kenny Irwin WIN	4.00	10.00
10 Dale Jarrett WIN 2	8.00	20.00
11 Bobby Labonte WIN 2	8.00	20.00
12 Terry Labonte WIN	6.00	15.00
13 Sterling Marlin	5.00	12.00
14 Mark Martin WIN 2	8.00	20.00
15 Jeremy Mayfield WIN	5.00	12.00
16 Ricky Rudd WIN	8.00	20.00
17 Ken Schrader	1.50	4.00
18 Mike Skinner	1.50	4.00
19 Rusty Wallace WIN	12.00	30.00
20 Field Card WIN	4.00	10.00

1999 Press Pass Oil Cans

Randomly inserted in packs at the rate of one in 18, this nine card sculptured embossed set is printed on shimmering foil board.

COMPLETE SET (9)	20.00	50.00
1 Mark Martin	5.00	12.00
2 Jeff Burton	2.00	5.00
3 Bill Elliott	2.50	6.00
4 Dale Jarrett	4.00	10.00
5 Terry Labonte	2.00	5.00
6 Jeff Gordon	6.00	15.00
7 Bobby Labonte	4.00	10.00
8 Jeremy Mayfield	1.25	3.00
9 Rusty Wallace	5.00	12.00

1999 Press Pass Pit Stop

Randomly inserted in packs at the rate of one in eight, this 18 card set features some of the best cars on the Winston Cup circuit.

COMPLETE SET (18)	12.50	30.00
1 Steve Park's Car	2.00	5.00
2 Rusty Wallace's Car	3.00	8.00
3 Dale Earnhardt's Car	6.00	15.00
4 Bobby Hamilton's Car	.40	1.00
5 Terry Labonte's Car	1.25	3.00
6 Mark Martin's Car	3.00	8.00
7 Ricky Rudd's Car	1.25	3.00
8 Jeremy Mayfield's Car	.75	2.00
9 Johnny Benson's Car	.75	2.00
10 Bobby Labonte's Car	2.50	6.00
11 Michael Waltrip's Car	.75	2.00
12 Jeff Gordon's Car	4.00	10.00
13 Kenny Irwin's Car	.75	2.00
14 Mike Skinner's Car	.40	1.00
15 Ernie Irvan's Car	.75	2.00
16 Dale Jarrett's Car	2.50	6.00
17 Bill Elliott's Car	1.50	4.00
18 Jeff Burton's Car	1.25	3.00

1999 Press Pass Showman

Randomly inserted in packs at the rate of one in eight, this 36-card hobby only set showcases the NASCAR Winston cup drivers on a die-cut laser gold foil card.

COMPLETE SET (18)	25.00	60.00
1A Dale Jarrett	5.00	12.00
2A Bobby Labonte	5.00	12.00
3A Mark Martin	6.00	15.00
4A Jeremy Mayfield	1.50	4.00
5A Ken Schrader	.75	2.00
6A Mike Skinner	.75	2.00
7A Dale Earnhardt Jr.	10.00	25.00
8A Jeff Burton	2.50	6.00
9A Ricky Rudd	2.50	6.00
10A Michael Waltrip	1.50	4.00
11A Jeff Gordon	8.00	20.00
12A Bill Elliott	3.00	8.00
13A Terry Labonte	2.50	6.00
14A Ernie Irvan	1.50	4.00
15A Johnny Benson	1.50	4.00
16A Sterling Marlin	2.50	6.00
17A Joe Nemechek	.75	2.00
18A Rusty Wallace	6.00	15.00
P1 Dale Earnhardt Jr. Promo	2.00	5.00

1999 Press Pass Skidmarks

COMPLETE SET (100)	200.00	400.00
*SKIDMARKS: 4X TO 10X BASE CARDS		
*SKIDMARK RCs: 2X TO 5X BASE CARDS		

1999 Press Pass Triple Gear 3 in 1

Randomly inserted in packs, this nine card set features three pieces of authentic race-used memorabilia (tire, firesuit, and sheetmetal) on a single card. Only 33 cards of each driver produced with each being hand serial numbered on the back in red ink. Eleven of each driver's cards were inserted into 1999 Press Pass, 11 into Press Pass Premium, and 11 into Press Pass VIP.

TG1 Terry Labonte	100.00	200.00
TG2 Mark Martin	125.00	250.00
TG3 Jeff Gordon	250.00	500.00
TG4 Bobby Labonte	100.00	200.00
TG5 Rusty Wallace	100.00	200.00
TG6 Dale Jarrett	100.00	200.00
TG7 Jeff Burton	60.00	150.00
TG8 Mike Skinner	50.00	120.00
TG9 Dale Earnhardt	300.00	600.00

2000 Press Pass

This 100-card single series set was released in January, 2000. They were issued in eight card hobby and retail packs with a SRP of $2.99. The basic cards feature a driver or car portrait with their name on the left of the front. The set has the following subsets: NASCAR Crew Chiefs (28-36), 1999 Replay (37-45), Double Duty (46-54), NASCAR Busch Series (55-63), NASCAR Touring Series Champions (64-72), Shootout (73-81), Generation Now (82-90) and NASCAR 2000 Preview (91-99). There was also a commemorative Dale Jarrett card randomly inserted into packs. This card, which honored his 1999 Winston Cup Championship, is serial numbered to 800. In addition, a Dale Jarrett promotional card was distributed to dealers and hobby media several weeks prior to the product's release. The card is easy to identify by the "PROMO I of I" numbering on the back.

COMPLETE SET (100)	8.00	20.00
1 Dale Jarrett	.50	1.25
2 Bobby Labonte	.50	1.25
3 Mark Martin	.60	1.50
4 Tony Stewart	.75	2.00
5 Jeff Burton	.25	.60
6 Jeff Gordon	.75	2.00
7 Dale Earnhardt	1.25	3.00
8 Rusty Wallace	.60	1.50
9 Ward Burton	.15	.40
10 Mike Skinner	.10	.30
11 Jeremy Mayfield	.10	.30
12 Terry Labonte	.25	.60
13 Bobby Hamilton	.10	.30
14 Steve Park	.25	.60
15 Ken Schrader	.10	.30
16 Sterling Marlin	.25	.60
17 John Andretti	.10	.30
18 Wally Dallenbach Jr.	.10	.30
19 Kenny Irwin	.15	.40
20 Jimmy Spencer	.10	.30
21 Kenny Wallace	.10	.30
22 Chad Little	.15	.40
23 Elliott Sadler	.15	.40
24 Johnny Benson	.15	.40
25 Michael Waltrip	.15	.40
26 Ricky Rudd	.25	.60
27 Darrell Waltrip	.15	.40
28 Robin Pemberton	.05	.15
29 Kevin Hamlin	.05	.15
30 Jimmy Fenning	.05	.15
31 Jimmy Makar	.05	.15
32 Greg Zipadelli	.05	.15
33 Brian Whitesell	.05	.15
34 Larry McReynolds	.05	.15
35 Todd Parrott	.05	.15
36 Frank Stoddard	.05	.15
37 Jeff Gordon's Car REP	.30	.75
38 Jeff Burton REP	.15	.40
39 Dale Earnhardt Jr. REP CRC	.50	1.25
40 Bobby Labonte REP	.25	.60
41 Dale Jarrett REP	.25	.60
42 Tony Stewart REP	.40	1.00
43 Ernie Irvan REP	.15	.40
44 Tony Stewart REP	.40	1.00
45 Mark Martin REP	.30	.75
46 Dale Earnhardt Jr.'s Car DD	.40	1.00
47 Matt Kenseth's Car DD	.25	.60
48 Mike Skinner's Car DD	.05	.15
49 Mark Martin's Car DD	.25	.60
50 Ken Schrader's Car DD	.05	.15
51 Michael Waltrip's Car DD	.10	.30
52 Bobby Labonte DD	.25	.60
53 Jeff Gordon DD	.30	.75
54 Rusty Wallace DD	.30	.75
55 Tony Stewart	.75	2.00
56 Ward Burton	.15	.40
57 Joe Nemechek	.10	.30
58 Kenny Irwin	.15	.40
59 Mike Skinner	.10	.30
60 Mark Martin	.60	1.50
61 Casey Atwood	.25	.60
62 Dale Earnhardt Jr.	1.00	2.50
63 Jeff Gordon	.75	2.00
64 Matt Kenseth	.60	1.50
65 Steve Park	.25	.60
66 Elliott Sadler	.15	.40
67 Tony Stewart	.75	2.00
68 Kenny Irwin	.15	.40
69 Jeff Burton	.25	.60
70 Dale Earnhardt Jr.	1.00	2.50
71 Jeff Green	.10	.30
72 Matt Kenseth SO	.30	.75
73 Todd Bodine SO	.10	.30
74 Elton Sawyer SO	.10	.30
75 Dave Blaney SO	.10	.30
76 Jason Keller SO	.10	.30
77 Mike McLauglin SO	.10	.30
78 Randy LaJoie SO	.10	.30
79 Casey Atwood SO	.15	.40
80 Dick Trickle SO	.10	.30
81 Joe Nemechek SO	.10	.30
82 Tim Fedewa GN	.10	.30
83 Kevin Grubb GN	.10	.30
84 Jack Sprague GN	.10	.30
85 Dale Earnhardt Jr. GN	.50	1.25
86 Wayne Anderson GN	.05	.15
87 Robert Huffman GN	.05	.15
88 Tony Hirschman GN	.05	.15
89 Sean Woodside GN	.05	.15
90 Bradley Leighton GN	.05	.15
91 Raymond Guss Jr. OOP	.05	.15
92 Dave Blaney OOP	.10	.30
93 Dale Earnhardt Jr. OOP	.50	1.25
94 Matt Kenseth OOP	.30	.75
95 Jerry Nadeau OOP	.15	.40
96 Ricky Rudd OOP	.15	.40
97 Ken Schrader OOP	.10	.30
98 Michael Waltrip OOP	.15	.40
99 Mike Bliss OOP	.10	.30
100 Checklist Card	.05	.15
0 D.Jarrett 1999 Champ/800	12.50	30.00
P1 Dale Jarrett Promo	1.00	2.50

2000 Press Pass Millennium

COMPLETE SET (100)	40.00	100.00
*MILLENNIUM: 2X TO 5X BASIC CARDS		

2000 Press Pass Burning Rubber

Inserted one every 480 packs, these cards feature cutting edge technology showcasing swatches of race-used tires. Each card was serial numbered of 200 on the back. According to Press Pass no autographed Burning Rubber cards were inserted into this product, although previously planned.

BR1 Dale Jarrett	8.00	20.00
BR2 Mark Martin	10.00	25.00
BR3 Bobby Labonte	8.00	20.00
BR4 Tony Stewart	12.00	30.00
BR5 Jeff Gordon	15.00	40.00
BR6 Dale Earnhardt's Car	25.00	60.00
BR7 Rusty Wallace	8.00	20.00
BR8 Terry Labonte	8.00	20.00
BR9 Dale Earnhardt Jr.	15.00	40.00

2000 Press Pass Cup Chase

Randomly inserted in packs at a rate of one in 48 packs. Press Passâ€™ famous interactive game features a new twist in 2000. The 17-card set gives collectors the chance to redeem winning driverâ€™s cards for a full set of 17 plastic die-cut Cup Chase cards, the 16 drivers and a Dale Jarrett Champion card. Plus an opportunity to win a race-used memorabilia card of the 2000 Winston Cup champion.

COMPLETE SET (17)	125.00	250.00
CC1 John Andretti	2.50	6.00
CC2 Ward Burton WIN	6.00	15.00
CC3 Jeff Burton WIN	6.00	15.00
CC4 Dale Earnhardt	15.00	40.00
CC5 Dale Earnhardt Jr. WIN	20.00	50.00
CC6 Jeff Gordon WIN	12.50	30.00
CC7 Dale Jarrett WIN	7.50	20.00
CC8 Matt Kenseth	6.00	15.00
CC9 Bobby Labonte WIN	7.50	20.00
CC10 Terry Labonte	4.00	10.00
CC11 Mark Martin	7.50	20.00
CC12 Jeremy Mayfield	2.50	6.00
CC13 Ricky Rudd	4.00	10.00
CC14 Mike Skinner	2.50	6.00
CC15 Tony Stewart WIN	10.00	25.00
CC16 Rusty Wallace WIN	10.00	25.00
CC17 Field Card	2.00	5.00

2000 Press Pass Cup Chase Die Cut Prizes

COMPLETE SET (17)	15.00	30.00
CC1 John Andretti	.50	1.25
CC2 Ward Burton	.60	1.50
CC3 Jeff Burton	1.00	2.50
CC4 Dale Earnhardt	5.00	12.00
CC5 Dale Earnhardt Jr.	4.00	10.00
CC6 Jeff Gordon	3.00	8.00
CC7 Dale Jarrett	2.00	5.00
CC8 Matt Kenseth	2.50	6.00
CC9 Bobby Labonte	2.00	5.00
CC10 Terry Labonte	1.00	2.50
CC11 Mark Martin	2.50	6.00
CC12 Jeremy Mayfield	.50	1.25
CC13 Ricky Rudd	1.00	2.50
CC14 Mike Skinner	.50	1.25
CC15 Tony Stewart	3.00	8.00
CC16 Rusty Wallace	2.50	6.00
CC17 Dale Jarrett 2000 Champ	2.00	5.00
CCC1 Bobby Labonte Tire/650	15.00	30.00

2000 Press Pass Oil Cans

Randomly inserted in packs at a rate of one in six this all-foil multi-level embossed insert features die-cut images of nine top drivers bursting out of a can.

COMPLETE SET (9)	10.00	25.00
OC1 Tony Stewart	3.00	8.00
OC2 Terry Labonte	1.00	2.50
OC3 Rusty Wallace	2.50	6.00
OC4 Mark Martin	2.50	6.00
OC5 Jeff Burton	1.00	2.50
OC6 Jeff Gordon	3.00	8.00
OC7 Dale Earnhardt's Car	5.00	12.00
OC8 Dale Jarrett	2.00	5.00
OC9 Bobby Labonte	2.00	5.00

2000 Press Pass Pitstop

Randomly inserted in packs at a rate of one in eight. An 18-card micro-embossed die-cut insert puts collectors in the pits with the greatest teams in NASCAR.

COMPLETE SET (18)	10.00	25.00
PS1 Dale Jarrett's Car	.75	2.00
PS2 Rusty Wallace's Car	1.25	3.00
PS3 Dale Earnhardt's Car	2.50	6.00
PS4 Bobby Hamilton's Car	.15	.40
PS5 Terry Labonte's Car	.60	1.50
PS6 Mark Martin's Car	1.25	3.00
PS7 Ricky Rudd's Car	.50	1.25
PS8 Jeremy Mayfield's Car	.15	.40
PS9 Bobby Labonte's Car	1.00	2.50
PS10 Elliott Sadler's Car	.15	.40
PS11 Ward Burton's Car	.30	.75
PS12 Jeff Gordon's Car	1.50	4.00
PS13 Tony Stewart's Car	1.50	4.00
PS14 Kenny Irwin's Car	.30	.75
PS15 Mike Skinner's Car	.15	.40
PS16 Matt Kenseth's Car	1.25	3.00
PS17 Dale Earnhardt Jr.'s Car	2.00	5.00
PS18 Jeff Burton's Car	.50	1.25

2000 Press Pass Showcar Die Cuts

Inserted at a rate of one every twelve retail packs, these cards feature the cars of some of NASCAR's leading drivers on a card die-cut to resemble film cels. Card backs carry an "SC" prefix.

COMPLETE SET (18)	20.00	40.00
*NON-DIE CUTS: 1.5X TO 4X DIE CUT		
SC1 Darrell Waltrip's Car	1.00	2.50
SC2 Bobby Labonte's Car	.60	1.50
SC3 Dale Jarrett's Car	.60	1.50
SC4 Dale Earnhardt Jr.'s Car	1.50	4.00
SC5 Dale Earnhardt's Car	4.00	10.00
SC6 Jeff Burton's Car	.50	1.25
SC7 Jeff Gordon's Car	1.25	3.00
SC8 Jeremy Mayfield's Car	.40	1.00
SC9 John Andretti's Car	.40	1.00
SC10 Ken Schrader's Car	.40	1.00
SC11 Mark Martin's Car	.60	1.50
SC12 Mike Skinner's Car	.40	1.00
SC13 Ricky Rudd's Car	.50	1.25
SC14 Rusty Wallace's Car	.60	1.50
SC15 Sterling Marlin's Car	.60	1.50
SC16 Terry Labonte's Car	.60	1.50
SC17 Tony Stewart's Car	1.00	2.50
SC18 Ward Burton's Car	.50	1.25

2000 Press Pass Showman Die Cuts

Randomly inserted in packs at a rate of one in eight, frame by frame action captures eighteen of the most recognizable athletes in NASCAR.

COMPLETE SET (18)	25.00	50.00
*NON-DIE CUTS: 1.5X TO 4X DIE CUT		
NON-DIE CUT STATED ODDS 1:100		
SM1 Darrell Waltrip	1.25	3.00
SM2 Bobby Labonte	.75	2.00
SM3 Dale Jarrett	.75	2.00
SM4 Dale Earnhardt Jr.	2.00	5.00
SM5 Dale Earnhardt Jr.	2.00	5.00
SM6 Jeff Burton	.60	1.50
SM7 Jeff Gordon	1.50	4.00
SM8 Jeremy Mayfield	.50	1.25
SM9 John Andretti	.50	1.25
SM10 Ken Schrader	.50	1.25
SM11 Mark Martin	.75	2.00
SM12 Mike Skinner	.50	1.25
SM13 Ricky Rudd	.60	1.50
SM14 Rusty Wallace	.75	2.00
SM15 Sterling Marlin	.75	2.00
SM16 Terry Labonte	.75	2.00
SM17 Tony Stewart	1.25	3.00
SM18 Ward Burton	.60	1.50

2000 Press Pass Skidmarks

Randomly inserted in packs at a rate of one in 48. Revolutionary technology creates an image on a trading card using ground-up, race-used tire rubber.

COMPLETE SET (9)	50.00	120.00
SK1 Dale Jarrett	6.00	15.00
SK2 Mark Martin	6.00	15.00
SK3 Bobby Labonte	6.00	15.00
SK4 Tony Stewart	8.00	20.00
SK5 Jeff Gordon	8.00	20.00
SK6 Dale Earnhardt	12.50	30.00
SK7 Rusty Wallace	6.00	15.00
SK8 Terry Labonte	5.00	12.00
SK9 Dale Earnhardt Jr.	8.00	20.00

2000 Press Pass Techno-Retro

Cards from this set are slightly smaller than standard sized. Each measures roughly 2" by 2 1/4" and were inserted one per Press Pass pack.

COMPLETE SET (36)	7.50	20.00
TR1 John Andretti	.10	.30
TR2 Johnny Benson	.15	.40
TR3 Jeff Burton	.25	.60
TR4 Ward Burton	.15	.40
TR5 Wally Dallenbach	.10	.30
TR6 Dale Earnhardt's Car	1.25	3.00
TR7 Dale Earnhardt Jr.	1.00	2.50
TR8 Jeff Gordon	.75	2.00
TR9 Bobby Hamilton	.10	.30
TR10 Kenny Irwin	.15	.40
TR11 Dale Jarrett	.50	1.25
TR12 Bobby Labonte	.50	1.25
TR13 Terry Labonte	.25	.60
TR14 Chad Little	.15	.40
TR15 Sterling Marlin	.25	.60
TR16 Mark Martin	.60	1.50
TR17 Jeremy Mayfield	.10	.30
TR18 Joe Nemechek	.10	.30
TR19 Steve Park	.25	.60
TR20 Ricky Rudd	.25	.60
TR21 Elliott Sadler	.15	.40
TR22 Ken Schrader	.10	.30
TR23 Mike Skinner	.10	.30
TR24 Tony Stewart	.75	2.00
TR25 Rusty Wallace	.60	1.50
TR26 Darrell Waltrip	.15	.40
TR27 Michael Waltrip	.15	.40
TR28 Bobby Allison	.10	.30
TR29 Buddy Baker	.10	.30
TR30 A.J. Foyt	.15	.40
TR31 Ned Jarrett	.10	.30
TR32 Junior Johnson	.10	.30
TR33 Benny Parsons	.10	.30
TR34 Richard Petty	.25	.60
TR35 David Pearson	.15	.40
TR36 Cale Yarborough	.10	.30

2001 Press Pass

Released in late January 2001, this 100-card set features 47 driver cards, 13 racing team cards, 11 replay cards from the 2000 season, 10 touring series cards, 12 shoot out cards, 6 season preview cards, and a checklist/schedule card. Base card stock features full color photos, both action and portrait, with a border along the left side of the card stating the racer's name and a border along the bottom. On the driver cards, a small black and white car photo is placed in the lower left hand corner. A special zero card featuring Bobby Labonte was inserted in Hobby packs only. Press Pass was packaged in 36 pack boxes for Retail and 28 pack boxes for Hobby. Each pack contained eight cards.

COMPLETE SET (100)	8.00	20.00
1 Bobby Labonte	.60	1.50
2 Dale Earnhardt	1.50	4.00
3 Jeff Burton	.25	.60
4 Dale Jarrett	.60	1.50
5 Ricky Rudd	.40	1.00
6 Tony Stewart	1.00	2.50
7 Rusty Wallace	.75	2.00
8 Mark Martin	.75	2.00
9 Jeff Gordon	1.00	2.50
10 Ward Burton	.25	.60
11 Steve Park	.25	.60
12 Mike Skinner	.10	.30
13 Matt Kenseth	1.00	2.50
14 Joe Nemechek	.10	.30
15 Dale Earnhardt Jr.	1.25	3.00
16 Terry Labonte	.40	1.00
17 Ken Schrader	.10	.30
18 Sterling Marlin	.40	1.00
19 Jerry Nadeau	.25	.60
20 Jimmy Spencer	.10	.30
21 John Andretti	.10	.30
22 Jeremy Mayfield	.10	.30
23 Robert Pressley	.10	.30
24 Kenny Wallace	.10	.30
25 Kevin Lepage	.10	.30
26 Elliott Sadler	.25	.60
27 Bobby Hamilton Jr.	.10	.30
28 Dave Blaney	.10	.30
29 Wally Dallenbach Jr.	.10	.30
30 Brett Bodine	.10	.30
31 Darrell Waltrip	.25	.60
32 Stacy Compton	.10	.30
33 Kyle Petty	.25	.60
34 Scott Pruett	.10	.30
35 Jeff Green	.10	.30
36 Jason Keller	.10	.30
37 Kevin Harvick	.75	2.00
38 Todd Bodine	.10	.30
39 Elton Sawyer	.10	.30
40 Randy LaJoie	.10	.30
41 Casey Atwood	.10	.30
42 David Green	.10	.30
43 Kevin Grubb	.10	.30
44 Hank Parker Jr.	.25	.60
45 Matt Kenseth	1.00	2.50
46 Mark Martin	.75	2.00
47 Tim Fedewa	.10	.30
48 Bobby Labonte's Car	.25	.60
49 Dale Earnhardt's Car	.60	1.50
50 Jeff Burton's Car	.25	.60
51 Dale Jarrett's Car	.25	.60
52 Ricky Rudd's Car	.10	.30
53 Tony Stewart's Car	.40	1.00
54 Rusty Wallace's Car	.40	1.00
55 Mark Martin's Car	.40	1.00
56 Jeff Gordon's Car	.40	1.00
57 Ward Burton's Car	.10	.30
58 Mike Skinner's Car	.07	.20
59 Matt Kenseth's Car	.40	1.00
60 Jeremy Mayfield's Car	.07	.20
61 Jeff Burton REP	.25	.60
62 Matt Kenseth REP	1.00	2.50
63 Bobby Labonte REP	.60	1.50
64 Dale Earnhardt Jr. REP	1.25	3.00
65 Rusty Wallace REP	.60	2.00
66 Dale Jarrett REP	.60	1.50
67 Dale Earnhardt REP	1.50	4.00
68 Tony Stewart REP	1.00	2.50
69 Steve Park REP	.25	.60
70 Jerry Nadeau REP	.25	.60
71 Bobby Labonte REP	.60	1.50
72 Jeff Green	.10	.30
73 Greg Biffle	.25	.60
74 Billy Bigley Jr. RC	.10	.30
75 Garrett Evans RC	.10	.30
76 Brad Leighton	.10	.30
77 Jerry Marquis	.10	.30
78 Robert Huffman	.10	.30
79 Steve Boley	.10	.30
80 Matt Crafton RC	.25	.60
81 Steve Carlson RC	.10	.30
82 Dale Jarrett SO	.60	1.50
83 Mike Skinner SO	.10	.30
84 Rusty Wallace SO	.75	2.00
85 Terry Labonte SO	.40	1.00
86 Ricky Rudd SO	.40	1.00
87 Jeremy Mayfield SO	.10	.30
88 Jeff Gordon SO	1.00	2.50
89 Dale Earnhardt Jr. SO	1.25	3.00
90 Steve Park SO	.25	.60
91 Bobby Labonte SO	.60	1.50
92 Tony Stewart SO	1.00	2.50
93 Jeff Burton SO	.25	.60
94 Elliott Sadler PV	.25	.60
95 Bobby Hamilton Jr. PV	.10	.30
96 Ryan Newman PV RC	3.00	8.00
97 Jeff Burton PV	.25	.60
98 Mark Martin PV	.75	2.00
99 Dale Jarrett PV	.60	1.50
100 Checklist Schedule	.10	.30
P1 Bobby Labonte Promo	1.00	2.50
0 Bobby Labonte WC Champ	12.00	30.00

2001 Press Pass Millennium

COMP.MILLENNIUM (100)	50.00	125.00
*MILLENNIUM: 2X TO 5X BASIC CARDS		

2001 Press Pass Autographs

Randomly inserted in packs, this set features a portrait style color photo of the driver on the right side of the card front with a ghosted image of his car to the left. The bottom of the card has a black and silver section with the driver's name. Since the cards were not numbered, we have arranged them in alphabetical order in our checklist. This set also includes one of the last insert cards signed by Dale Earnhardt.

1 John Andretti	5.00	12.00
2 Greg Biffle	10.00	25.00
3 Billy Bigley Jr.	5.00	12.00
4 Dave Blaney	5.00	12.00
5 Brett Bodine	5.00	12.00
6 Todd Bodine	5.00	12.00
7 Steve Boley	5.00	12.00
8 Jeff Burton	12.00	30.00
9 Ward Burton	10.00	25.00
10 Stacy Compton	5.00	12.00
11 Dale Earnhardt	600.00	1000.00
12 Dale Earnhardt Jr.	50.00	100.00
13 Tim Fedewa	5.00	12.00
14 Jeff Gordon	100.00	175.00
15 David Green	5.00	12.00
16 Jeff Green	7.50	20.00
17 Mark Green	5.00	12.00
18 Kevin Grubb	5.00	12.00
19 Bobby Hamilton	10.00	25.00
20 Kevin Harvick	15.00	40.00
21 Robert Huffman	5.00	12.00
22 Dale Jarrett	20.00	50.00
23 Jason Keller	5.00	12.00
24 Matt Kenseth	30.00	60.00
25 Bobby Labonte	15.00	40.00
26 Terry Labonte	15.00	40.00
27 Randy LaJoie	5.00	12.00
28 Brad Leighton	5.00	12.00
29 Chad Little	5.00	12.00
30 Jerry Marquis	5.00	12.00
31 Mark Martin	30.00	60.00
32 Jeremy Mayfield	8.00	20.00
34 Joe Nemechek	5.00	12.00
35 Steve Park	8.00	20.00
36 Hank Parker Jr.	5.00	12.00
37 Robert Pressley	5.00	12.00
38 Ricky Rudd	15.00	40.00
39 Elton Sawyer	5.00	12.00
40 Ken Schrader	10.00	25.00
41 Mike Skinner	5.00	12.00
42 Jimmy Spencer	8.00	20.00
43 Tony Stewart	25.00	60.00
44 Dick Trickle	5.00	12.00
45 Rusty Wallace	15.00	40.00
33 Mike McLaughlin	5.00	12.00

2001 Press Pass Burning Rubber Drivers

ndomly inserted in Hobby packs at the rate of e in 480, this nine card set features a profile oto of a driver and a square swatch of a race ed tire. Card backgrounds are white, and feature "tire mark" effect through the middle.

CARS: .3X TO .8X DRIVERS
AR STATED ODDS 1:720 RETAIL
RD1 Jeff Gordon/90 25.00 60.00
RD2 Rusty Wallace/90 12.00 30.00
RD3 Dale Earnhardt/90 40.00 100.00
RD4 Dale Jarrett/90 12.00 30.00
RD5 Terry Labonte/85 12.00 30.00
RD6 Mark Martin/90 15.00 40.00
RD7 Bobby Labonte/90 8.00 20.00
RD8 Dale Earnhardt Jr./90 25.00 60.00
RD9 Tony Stewart/90 20.00 50.00

2001 Press Pass Cup Chase

Randomly inserted in packs at the rate of one in 24, this 17-card set features redemption cards with an interactive game. If the pictured driver wins any of the selected races on the back of the card, it could be redeemed (before 1/31/2002) for a complete 17-card set of holofoil die cut cards featuring both drivers and cars. The original Cup Chase insert card was also returned to the collector with a special stamp from Press Pass. These stamped cards are typically worth less than original unstamped copies.

COMPLETE SET (17) 75.00 150.00
CC1 Steve Park 4.00 10.00
CC2 Rusty Wallace 6.00 15.00
CC3 Dale Earnhardt 6.00 15.00
CC4 Jeff Gordon WIN 6.00 15.00
CC5 Terry Labonte 4.00 10.00
CC6 Ken Schrader 1.50 4.00
CC7 Dale Earnhardt Jr. 10.00 25.00
CC8 Jeff Burton WIN 4.00 10.00
CC9 Tony Stewart 6.00 15.00
CC10 Ward Burton 2.50 6.00
CC11 Jeremy Mayfield 1.50 4.00
CC12 Mike Skinner 1.50 4.00
CC13 Ricky Rudd WIN 5.00 12.00
CC14 Dale Jarrett 6.00 15.00
CC15 Matt Kenseth 6.00 15.00
CC16 Bobby Labonte 6.00 15.00
CC17 Field Card WIN .40 1.00

2001 Press Pass Cup Chase Die Cut Prizes

COMPLETE SET (17) 12.50 30.00
CC1 Steve Park 1.00 2.50
CC2 Rusty Wallace 1.50 4.00
CC3 Dale Earnhardt 5.00 12.00
CC4 Jeff Gordon 3.00 8.00
CC5 Terry Labonte 1.50 4.00
CC6 Ken Schrader 1.00 2.50
CC7 Dale Earnhardt Jr. 4.00 10.00
CC8 Jeff Burton 1.25 3.00
CC9 Tony Stewart 2.50 6.00
CC10 Ward Burton 1.00 2.50
CC11 Jeremy Mayfield 1.00 2.50
CC12 Mike Skinner .75 2.00
CC13 Ricky Rudd 1.25 3.00
CC14 Dale Jarrett 1.50 4.00
CC15 Matt Kenseth 2.00 5.00
CC16 Bobby Labonte 1.25 3.00
CC17 Bobby Labonte Champ 1.50 4.00
CCC1 Jeff Gordon Tire/400 12.00 30.00

2001 Press Pass Double Burner

Randomly seeded in Hobby packs, this nine card set features a driver portrait photo framed by a gold oval and on the left side has a swatch of a race worn firesuit and on the right, a race worn glove. Each card is sequentially numbered to 100.

DB1 Jeff Gordon 40.00 100.00
DB2 Rusty Wallace 20.00 50.00
DB3 Dale Earnhardt 100.00 200.00
DB4 Dale Jarrett 20.00 50.00
DB5 Tony Stewart 30.00 80.00
DB6 Mark Martin 20.00 50.00
DB7 Matt Kenseth 15.00 40.00
DB8 Dale Earnhardt Jr. 50.00 120.00
DB9 Bobby Labonte 20.00 50.00

2001 Press Pass Ground Zero

Randomly inserted in packs at the rate of one in 18, this nine card set features portrait style photography set against an all foil laser etched background with colors to match each driver's racing team.

COMPLETE SET (9) 40.00 100.00
GZ1 Matt Kenseth 5.00 12.00
GZ2 Rusty Wallace 4.00 10.00
GZ3 Dale Earnhardt 8.00 20.00
GZ4 Jeff Gordon 5.00 12.00
GZ5 Tony Stewart 5.00 12.00
GZ6 Mark Martin 4.00 10.00
GZ7 Dale Jarrett 3.00 8.00
GZ8 Dale Earnhardt Jr. 6.00 15.00
GZ9 Ward Burton 1.25 3.00

2001 Press Pass Showman/Showcar

Randomly inserted in packs at the rate of one in eight, this 24-card set features numbered cards from S1A to S12B. Each driver has two card versions (A and B) where the A version features two profile photos of the driver and the B version features a photo of the car. All cards are printed on rainbow holofoil and are die cut on both the left and right side of this horizontal design.

COMPLETE SET (24) 30.00 80.00
*CARS: .8X TO 2X BASE CARD HI
S1A Steve Park 1.00 2.50
S1B Steve Park's Car .50 1.25
S2A Rusty Wallace 3.00 8.00
S2B Rusty Wallace's Car 1.50 4.00
S3A Matt Kenseth 4.00 10.00
S3B Matt Kenseth's Car 2.00 5.00
S4A Jeff Gordon 4.00 10.00
S4B Jeff Gordon's Car 2.00 5.00
S5A Terry Labonte 1.50 4.00
S5B Terry Labonte's Car .75 2.00
S6A Mark Martin 3.00 8.00
S6B Mark Martin's Car 1.50 4.00
S7A Dale Earnhardt 6.00 15.00
S7B Dale Earnhardt's Car 3.00 8.00
S8A Dale Earnhardt Jr. 5.00 12.00
S8B Dale Earnhardt Jr.'s Car 2.50 6.00
S9A Bobby Labonte 2.50 6.00
S9B Bobby Labonte's Car 1.25 3.00
S10A Tony Stewart 4.00 10.00
S10B Tony Stewart's Car 2.00 5.00
S11A Dale Jarrett 2.50 6.00
S11B Dale Jarrett's Car 1.25 3.00
S12A Mike Skinner .50 1.25
S12B Mike Skinner's Car .25 .60

2001 Press Pass Total Memorabilia Power Pick

Randomly inserted in Hobby packs at the rate of one in 200, this nine card set gives collectors the opportunity to win all race used memorabilia cards of the specific driver who's number is pictured on the card. The cards expired on 1/31/2002.

TM1 Jeff Gordon .60 1.50
TM2 Rusty Wallace .40 1.00
TM3 Dale Earnhardt 1.00 2.50
TM4 Dale Jarrett .40 1.00
TM5 Tony Stewart .60 1.50
TM6 Mark Martin .40 1.00
TM7 Matt Kenseth .40 1.00
TM8 Dale Earnhardt Jr. .60 1.50
TM9 Bobby Labonte .40 1.00

2001 Press Pass Triple Burner

Randomly seeded in retail packs, this nine card set features three swatches of race used memorabilia. On the left side of the card, a swatch of race used sheet metal appears, a race used lugnut is in the middle, and on the right, a swatch of a race used tire appears. Each card is sequentially numbered to 100.

TB1 Jeff Gordon 40.00 100.00
TB2 Rusty Wallace 25.00 60.00
TB3A Dale Earnhardt lug nut 60.00 150.00
TB3B Dale Earnhardt pit board 100.00 200.00
TB4 Dale Jarrett 25.00 60.00
TB5 Tony Stewart 30.00 80.00
TB6 Mark Martin 25.00 60.00
TB7 Matt Kenseth 25.00 60.00
TB8 Dale Earnhardt Jr. 40.00 100.00
TB9 Bobby Labonte 25.00 60.00

2001 Press Pass Velocity

Randomly inserted in packs at the rate of one in eight, this nine card set features driver portrait photos centered on the top of the card in holofoil and a photo of the respective driver's car on the bottom. Names on the bottom are printed in holofoil.

COMPLETE SET (9) 15.00 40.00
VL1 Jeff Gordon 4.00 10.00
VL2 Rusty Wallace 3.00 8.00
VL3 Dale Jarrett 2.50 6.00
VL4 Matt Kenseth 4.00 10.00
VL5 Tony Stewart 4.00 10.00
VL6 Mark Martin 3.00 8.00
VL7 Jeff Burton 1.00 2.50
VL8 Dale Earnhardt Jr. 5.00 12.00
VL9 Dale Earnhardt 6.00 15.00

2001 Press Pass Vintage

Inserted in packs at the rate of one in one, this 27-card set features top NASCAR drivers on a vintage style card. Driver portrait photography is framed by a red line and cards are white bordered. Names appear along the bottom, and racing team names appear along the top.

COMPLETE SET (27) 10.00 25.00
VN1 Bobby Labonte 1.00 2.50
VN2 Dale Earnhardt 2.50 6.00
VN3 Jeff Burton .40 1.00
VN4 Dale Jarrett 1.00 2.50
VN5 Ricky Rudd .60 1.50
VN6 Tony Stewart 1.50 4.00
VN7 Rusty Wallace 1.25 3.00
VN8 Mark Martin 1.25 3.00
VN9 Jeff Gordon 1.50 4.00
VN10 Ward Burton .40 1.00
VN11 Steve Park .40 1.00
VN12 Mike Skinner .20 .50
VN13 Matt Kenseth 1.50 4.00
VN14 Joe Nemechek .20 .50
VN15 Dale Earnhardt Jr. 2.00 5.00
VN16 Terry Labonte .60 1.50
VN17 Ken Schrader .20 .50
VN18 Sterling Marlin .60 1.50
VN19 Jerry Nadeau .40 1.00
VN20 Jimmy Spencer .20 .50
VN21 John Andretti .20 .50
VN22 Jeremy Mayfield .20 .50
VN23 Robert Pressley .20 .50
VN24 Kenny Wallace .20 .50
VN25 Kevin Lepage .20 .50
VN26 Elliott Sadler .40 1.00
VN27 Bobby Hamilton .20 .50

2002 Press Pass

Issued in early 2002, this 100-card set features a mix of leading NASCAR drivers and the cars they drive. The cards were packaged in 8-card hobby and retail packs. The following subsets were included in the base set: NASCAR Busch Series drivers, Craftsman Truck Series drivers, Replays, and NASCAR Touring Series drivers. A special insert card (#0) featuring Jeff Gordon's 2001 Winston Cup Championship was randomly inserted in packs.

COMPLETE SET (100) 12.50 30.00
1 John Andretti .10 .30
2 Dave Blaney .10 .30
3 Brett Bodine .10 .30
4 Todd Bodine .10 .30
5 Ward Burton .25 .60
6 Jeff Burton .25 .60
7 Kurt Busch .40 1.00
8 Stacy Compton .10 .30
9 Ricky Craven .10 .30
10 Dale Earnhardt Jr. 1.25 3.00
11 Jeff Gordon 1.00 2.50
12 Bobby Hamilton .10 .30
13 Kevin Harvick .75 2.00
14 Ron Hornaday .10 .30
15 Dale Jarrett .60 1.50
16 Buckshot Jones .10 .30
17 Matt Kenseth .75 2.00
18 Bobby Labonte .60 1.50
19 Terry Labonte .40 1.00
20 Jason Leffler .10 .30
21 Sterling Marlin .40 1.00
22 Mark Martin .75 2.00
23 Jeremy Mayfield .10 .30
24 Jerry Nadeau .25 .60
25 Joe Nemechek .10 .30
26 Ryan Newman CRC .75 2.00
27 Steve Park .25 .60
28 Kyle Petty .25 .60
29 Ricky Rudd .40 1.00
30 Elliott Sadler .25 .60
31 Ken Schrader .10 .30
32 Mike Skinner .10 .30
33 Jimmy Spencer .10 .30
34 Tony Stewart .75 2.00
35 Rusty Wallace .60 1.50
36 Michael Waltrip .25 .60
37 Greg Biffle NBS .25 .60
38 Larry Foyt NBS RC .25 .60
39 David Green NBS .10 .30
40 Jeff Green NBS .10 .30
41 Kevin Grubb NBS .10 .30
42 Tim Fedewa NBS .10 .30
43 Kevin Harvick NBS .75 2.00
44 Jimmie Johnson NBS .75 2.00
45 Jason Keller NBS .10 .30
46 Randy LaJoie NBS .10 .30
47 Chad Little NBS .10 .30
48 Mike McLaughlin NBS .10 .30
49 Jamie McMurray NBS RC 3.00 8.00
50 Ryan Newman NBS .75 2.00
51 Hank Parker Jr. NBS .10 .30
52 Tony Raines NBS .10 .30
53 Elton Sawyer NBS .10 .30
54 Scott Wimmer NBS RC .25 .60
55 Scott Riggs CTS RC .75 2.00
56 Ricky Hendrick CTS .50 1.25
57 Jon Wood CTS RC .25 .60
58 Jack Sprague CTS .10 .30
59 Travis Kvapil CTS RC .75 2.00
60 Coy Gibbs CTS RC .25 .60
61 Matt Crafton CTS .10 .30
62 Billy Bigley CTS .10 .30
63 Ted Musgrave CTS .10 .30
64 Michael Waltrip REP .25 .60
65 Kevin Harvick REP .75 2.00
66 Jeff Gordon REP 1.00 2.50
67 Jeff Burton REP .25 .60
68 Elliott Sadler REP .25 .60
69 Steve Park REP .25 .60
70 Tony Stewart REP .75 2.00
71 Ryan Newman REP .75 2.00
72 Sterling Marlin REP .40 1.00
73 Kerry Earnhardt REP .25 .60
74 Shawna Robinson REP .25 .60
75 Dale Earnhardt Jr. REP 1.25 3.00
76 Rusty Wallace's Car .25 .60
77 Mark Martin's Car .25 .60
78 Michael Waltrip's Car .10 .30
79 Matt Kenseth's Car .40 1.00
80 Bobby Labonte's Car .25 .60
81 Tony Stewart's Car .40 1.00
82 Ward Burton's Car .07 .20
83 Jeff Gordon's Car .40 1.00
84 Ricky Rudd 's Car .10 .30
85 Kevin Harvick's Car .40 1.00
86 Sterling Marlin's Car .07 .20
87 Dale Jarrett's Car .25 .60
88 Jeff Burton's Car .07 .20
89 Steve Carlson NTS .10 .30
90 Mike Olsen NTS .10 .30
91 Kyle Berck NTS RC .10 .30
92 Mike Stefanik NTS .10 .30
93 Craig Raudman NTS RC .10 .30
94 Cam Strader NTS RC .10 .30
95 Brendan Gaughan NTS RC .40 1.00
96 Kevin Hamlin NTS .10 .30
97 Jack Sprague CTS Champ .10 .30
98 Kevin Harvick BGN Champ .75 2.00
99 Jeff Gordon WC Champ 1.00 2.50
100 Dale Earnhardt Jr. CL .50 1.50
0 Jeff Gordon 2001 WC Champ 6.00 15.00

2002 Press Pass Platinum

COMPLETE SET (100) 20.00 40.00
*PLATINUM: .6X TO 1.5X BASIC CARDS

2002 Press Pass Autographs

Inserted in packs at stated odds of one in 72 hobby packs and one in 240 retail packs, these cards feature autographs from leading NASCAR figures. Dale Earnhardt Jr. and Tony Stewart did not return their cards in time for pack inclusion and those cards could be redeemed until December 31, 2002.

1 Bobby Allison 8.00 20.00
2 John Andretti 5.00 12.00
3 Casey Atwood 6.00 15.00
4 Buddy Baker 6.00 15.00
6 Greg Biffle 6.00 15.00
7 Billy Bigley 5.00 12.00
8 Dave Blaney 6.00 15.00
8 Brett Bodine 5.00 12.00
9 Todd Bodine 5.00 12.00
10 Jeff Burton 6.00 15.00
11 Ward Burton 8.00 20.00
12 Kurt Busch 12.00 30.00
13 Richard Childress 8.00 20.00
14 Stacy Compton 5.00 12.00
15 Matt Crafton 5.00 12.00
16 Ricky Craven 4.00 10.00
17 Dale Earnhardt Jr. 50.00 100.00
18 Kerry Earnhardt 6.00 15.00
19 Tim Fedewa 5.00 12.00
20 Larry Foyt 5.00 12.00
21 Coy Gibbs 6.00 15.00
22 Jeff Gordon 75.00 150.00
23 David Green 5.00 12.00
24 Jeff Green 5.00 12.00
25 Kevin Grubb 5.00 12.00
26 Kevin Harvick 12.00 30.00
27 Ricky Hendrick 15.00 40.00
28 Ron Hornaday 5.00 12.00
29 Dale Jarrett 12.00 30.00
30 Ned Jarrett 8.00 20.00
31 Jimmie Johnson 40.00 80.00
32 Buckshot Jones 5.00 12.00
33 Jason Keller 5.00 12.00
34 Matt Kenseth 12.00 30.00
35 Travis Kvapil 6.00 15.00
36 Bobby Labonte 10.00 25.00
37 Terry Labonte 10.00 25.00
38 Randy LaJoie 5.00 12.00
39 Jason Leffler 5.00 12.00
40 Chad Little 5.00 12.00
41 Sterling Marlin 12.00 30.00
42 Mark Martin 15.00 40.00
43 Mike McLaughlin 5.00 12.00
44 Jamie McMurray 12.00 30.00
45 Ted Musgrave 5.00 12.00
46 Jerry Nadeau 15.00 40.00
47 Joe Nemechek 5.00 12.00
48 Ryan Newman 8.00 20.00
49 Steve Park 8.00 20.00
50 Hank Parker Jr. 5.00 12.00
51 Benny Parsons 8.00 20.00
52 David Pearson 8.00 20.00
53 Kyle Petty 8.00 20.00
54 Richard Petty 25.00 60.00
55 Robert Pressley 5.00 12.00
56 Tony Raines 5.00 12.00
57 Scott Riggs 6.00 15.00
58 Shawna Robinson 15.00 40.00
59 Ricky Rudd 8.00 20.00
60 Joe Ruttman 5.00 12.00
61 Elliott Sadler 8.00 20.00
62 Elton Sawyer 5.00 12.00
63 Ken Schrader 6.00 15.00
64 Mike Skinner 5.00 12.00
65 Jack Sprague 5.00 12.00
66 Tony Stewart 25.00 60.00
67 Rusty Wallace 12.00 30.00
68 Darrell Waltrip 20.00 50.00
69 Michael Waltrip 8.00 20.00
70 Scott Wimmer 6.00 15.00
71 Glen Wood 5.00 12.00
72 Jon Wood 6.00 15.00
73 Cale Yarborough 8.00 20.00

2002 Press Pass Burning Rubber Drivers

Inserted in hobby packs at stated odds of one in 480, these 12 cards feature swatches of race-used tires. Each card was issued to a stated print run of 90 serial numbered sets.

BRD1 Jeff Gordon 30.00 80.00
BRD2 Rusty Wallace 10.00 25.00
BRD3 Dale Earnhardt 50.00 100.00
BRD4 Kevin Harvick 12.00 30.00
BRD5 Dale Jarrett 12.00 30.00
BRD6 Terry Labonte 12.00 30.00
BRD7 Mark Martin 12.00 30.00
BRD8 Bobby Labonte 12.00 30.00
BRD9 Dale Earnhardt Jr. 30.00 80.00
BRD10 Tony Stewart 20.00 40.00
BRD11 Matt Kenseth 10.00 25.00
BRD12 Michael Waltrip 10.00 25.00

2002 Press Pass Cup Chase

Issued in packs at stated odds of one in 24, these cards feature leading candidates to win races in the eight key NASCAR races. These cards could be redeemed until January 31, 2003 for a complete set of Press Pass Cup Chase Prizes.

CC1 Jeff Burton 7.50 20.00
CC2 Ward Burton WIN 12.50 30.00
CC3 Dale Earnhardt Jr. WIN 12.50 30.00
CC4 Jeff Gordon WIN 12.50 30.00
CC5 Kevin Harvick WIN 12.50 30.00
CC6 Dale Jarrett 7.50 20.00
CC7 Matt Kenseth WIN 12.50 30.00
CC8 Bobby Labonte 7.50 20.00
CC9 Terry Labonte 7.50 20.00
CC10 Mark Martin WIN 12.50 30.00
CC11 Sterling Marlin WIN 12.50 30.00
CC12 Ricky Rudd 6.00 15.00
CC13 Ken Schrader 6.00 15.00
CC14 Steve Park 5.00 12.00
CC15 Tony Stewart 25.00 50.00
CC16 Rusty Wallace 12.50 30.00
CC17 Michael Waltrip 6.00 15.00
CC18 Field Card WIN 10.00 25.00

2002 Press Pass Cup Chase Prizes

COMPLETE SET (18) 12.50 30.00
CC1 Jeff Burton 1.25 3.00
CC2 Ward Burton .75 2.00
CC3 Dale Earnhardt Jr. 5.00 12.00
CC4 Jeff Gordon 4.00 10.00
CC5 Kevin Harvick 2.00 5.00
CC6 Dale Jarrett 1.50 4.00
CC7 Matt Kenseth 2.50 6.00
CC8 Bobby Labonte 1.50 4.00
CC9 Terry Labonte 1.50 4.00
CC10 Mark Martin 2.00 5.00
CC11 Mike Skinner 1.00 2.50
CC12 Ricky Rudd 1.25 3.00
CC13 Ken Schrader .75 2.00
CC14 Sterling Marlin 1.25 3.00
CC15 Tony Stewart 3.00 8.00
CC16 Rusty Wallace 2.00 5.00
CC17 Michael Waltrip 1.00 2.50
CC18 Jeff Gordon WC Champ 5.00 12.00
NNO Tony Stewart Tire 12.00 30.00

2002 Press Pass Season's Greetings

Randomly inserted into packs, these three cards wish the collectors good tidings for the holiday season. Each features a picture of Santa Claus.

SG1 Merry Christmas 4.00 10.00
SG2 Happy Holidays 4.00 10.00
SG3 Season's Greetings 4.00 10.00

2002 Press Pass Showman

Issued at hobby packs at stated odds of one in eight for drivers and retail packs at stated odds of one in eight for the car cards. These cards feature drivers who fans come out to root for on the circuit.

COMPLETE SET (12) 20.00 50.00
COMP.CAR SET (8) 10.00 25.00
*CARS: .2X TO .5X DRIVERS
CAR STATED ODDS 1:8 RETAIL
S1A Ward Burton 1.25 3.00
S2A Dale Earnhardt Jr. 6.00 15.00
S3A Jeff Gordon 5.00 12.00
S4A Kevin Harvick 4.00 10.00
S5A Dale Jarrett 3.00 8.00
S6A Steve Park 1.25 3.00
S7A Bobby Labonte 3.00 8.00
S8A Terry Labonte 2.00 5.00
S9A Michael Waltrip 1.25 3.00
S10A Ricky Rudd 1.50 4.00
S11A Tony Stewart 4.00 10.00
S12A Rusty Wallace 3.00 8.00

2002 Press Pass Top Shelf

Issued in packs at stated odds of one in 18, these nine cards feature the top group of NASCAR drivers and their helmet on a foil etched card.

COMPLETE SET (9) 25.00 60.00
TS1 Dale Earnhardt Jr. 6.00 15.00
TS2 Jeff Gordon 5.00 12.00
TS3 Kevin Harvick 4.00 10.00
TS4 Dale Jarrett 3.00 8.00
TS5 Bobby Labonte 3.00 8.00
TS6 Terry Labonte 2.00 5.00
TS7 Ricky Rudd 2.00 5.00
TS8 Tony Stewart 4.00 10.00
TS9 Rusty Wallace 3.00 8.00

2002 Press Pass Velocity

Inserted into packs at stated odds of one in eight, these nine cards feature laser etched holofoil with razed type.

COMPLETE SET (9) 10.00 25.00
VL1 Jeff Burton .60 1.50
VL2 Dale Earnhardt Jr. 3.00 8.00
VL3 Jeff Gordon 2.50 6.00
VL4 Kevin Harvick 2.00 5.00
VL5 Dale Jarrett 1.50 4.00
VL6 Bobby Labonte 1.50 4.00
VL7 Sterling Marlin 1.00 2.50
VL8 Mark Martin 2.00 5.00
VL9 Rusty Wallace 1.50 4.00

2002 Press Pass Vintage

Issued one per pack, these 36 cards feature a mix of today's leading drivers along with some NASCAR legends on a old style card with a black and white picture.

COMPLETE SET (36) 7.50 20.00
VN1 Dave Blaney .20 .50
VN2 Brett Bodine .20 .50
VN3 Jeff Burton .40 1.00
VN4 Ward Burton .40 1.00
VN5 Ricky Craven .20 .50
VN6 Dale Earnhardt Jr. 2.00 5.00
VN7 Jeff Gordon 1.50 4.00
VN8 Bobby Hamilton .20 .50
VN9 Kevin Harvick 1.25 3.00
VN10 Dale Jarrett 1.00 2.50
VN11 Matt Kenseth 1.25 3.00
VN12 Bobby Labonte 1.00 2.50
VN13 Terry Labonte .60 1.50
VN14 Sterling Marlin .60 1.50
VN15 Mark Martin 1.25 3.00
VN16 Jerry Nadeau .40 1.00
VN17 Joe Nemechek .20 .50
VN18 Steve Park .40 1.00
VN19 Ricky Rudd .60 1.50
VN20 Elliott Sadler .40 1.00
VN21 Ken Schrader .20 .50
VN22 Mike Skinner .20 .50
VN23 Jimmy Spencer .20 .50
VN24 Tony Stewart 1.25 3.00
VN25 Rusty Wallace 1.00 2.50
VN26 Michael Waltrip .40 1.00
VN27 Richard Petty .60 1.50
VN28 Bobby Allison .40 1.00
VN29 Buddy Baker .20 .50
VN30 Ned Jarrett .20 .50
VN31 Junior Johnson .20 .50
VN32 Benny Parsons .20 .50
VN33 David Pearson .20 .50
VN34 Darrell Waltrip .40 1.00
VN35 Glen Wood .20 .50
VN36 Cale Yarborough .20 .50

2003 Press Pass

This 100 card set was released in December, 2002. This set was issued in eight card packs which came either 28 packs to a hobby box or 36 packs to a retail box. Both hobby and retail boxes were packed 20 boxes to a case. There was a special card honoring Jamie McMurray's first career win randomly inserted into these packs. In addition, a "King for a Day" entry card was inserted at a stated rate of one in 28 packs.

COMPLETE SET (100) 10.00 25.00
WAX BOX HOBBY (28) 40.00 80.00
1 John Andretti .10 .30
2 Casey Atwood .10 .30
3 Dave Blaney .10 .30
4 Brett Bodine .10 .30
5 Jeff Burton .25 .60
6 Ward Burton .25 .60
7 Kurt Busch .40 1.00
8 Ricky Craven .10 .30
9 Dale Earnhardt Jr. 1.25 3.00

10 Jeff Gordon 1.00 2.50
11 Robby Gordon .10 .30
12 Jeff Green .10 .30
13 Bobby Hamilton .10 .30
14 Kevin Harvick .60 1.50
15 Dale Jarrett .60 1.50
16 Jimmie Johnson 1.00 2.50
17 Matt Kenseth .75 2.00
18 Bobby Labonte .60 1.50
19 Terry Labonte .40 1.00
20 Sterling Marlin .40 1.00
21 Mark Martin .75 2.00
22 Jeremy Mayfield .10 .30
23 Ryan Newman .75 2.00
24 Steve Park .25 .60
25 Kyle Petty .25 .60
26 Ricky Rudd .40 1.00
27 Elliott Sadler .25 .60
28 Ken Schrader .10 .30
29 Mike Skinner .10 .30
30 Jimmy Spencer .10 .30
31 Tony Stewart .75 2.00
32 Rusty Wallace .60 1.50
33 Michael Waltrip .25 .60
34 Greg Biffle NBS .25 .60
35 Kerry Earnhardt NBS .25 .60
36 Scott Wimmer NBS .25 .60
37 Johnny Sauter NBS .25 .60
38 Ricky Hendrick NBS .50 1.25
39 Hank Parker Jr. NBS .10 .30
40 Brian Vickers NBS .50 1.25
41 Scott Riggs NBS .25 .60
42 Chad Little NBS .10 .30
43 Jack Sprague NBS .10 .30
44 Jamie McMurray NBS .60 1.50
45 Casey Mears NBS .25 .60
46 Matt Crafton CTS .10 .30
47 Coy Gibbs CTS .25 .60
48 Travis Kvapil CTS .25 .60
49 Jason Leffler CTS .10 .30
50 Ted Musgrave CTS .10 .30
51 Robert Pressley CTS .10 .30
52 Joe Ruttman CTS .10 .30
53 Dennis Setzer CTS .10 .30
54 Jon Wood CTS .25 .60
55 Dale Earnhardt Jr. DS 1.25 3.00
56 Kevin Harvick DS .60 1.50
57 Elliott Sadler DS .10 .30
58 Kurt Busch DS .40 1.00
59 Jimmie Johnson DS .75 2.00
60 Jeff Gordon DS 1.00 2.50
61 Tony Stewart DS .75 2.00
62 Ryan Newman DS .75 2.00
63 Jr. 1.00 2.50
JJ
New
Sad
Ken
Bus DS
64 J.Johnson Feb.17 RR .60 1.50
65 J.Johnson Apr.28 RR .60 1.50
66 J.Johnson Dover June RR .60 1.50
67 J.Johnson Dover Sept RR .60 1.50
68 R.Newman Winston RR .60 1.50
69 R.Newman Loudon RR .60 1.50
70 Bouncing Back WCS .25 .60
71 A Man of His Word WCS .25 .60
72 Double Take WCS .40 1.00
73 Survivor WCS .10 .30
74 Rock Steady WCS .40 1.00
75 Kurt-ain Call WCS .25 .60
76 Texas Tornado WCS .25 .60
77 Screeching Halt WCS .25 .60
78 The California Kid WCS .40 1.00
79 Two of a Kind WCS .40 1.00
80 Ups and Downs WCS .25 .60
81 Pit Bulls WCS .40 1.00
82 Reversal of Fortune WCS .10 .30
83 Defending his Turf WCS .25 .60
84 Rags to Riches WCS .40 1.00
85 Jake Hobgood RC .10 .30
86 Kevin Hamlin .10 .30
87 Steve Carlson .10 .30
88 Jeff Fultz RC .10 .30
89 Eric Norris RC .10 .30
90 Andy Santerre RC .40 1.00
91 Rusty Wallace's Car OTW .25 .60
92 Mark Martin's Car OTW .40 1.00
93 Kevin Harvick's Car OTW .25 .60
94 Ryan Newman's Car OTW .40 1.00
95 Matt Kenseth's Car OTW .40 1.00
96 Tony Stewart's Car OTW .40 1.00
97 Ward Burton's Car OTW .10 .30
98 Jeff Gordon's Car OTW .40 1.00
99 Dale Earnhardt Jr.'s Car OTW .50 1.25
100 Jeff Gordon Header .50 1.25
0 Jamie McMurray First Win 6.00 15.00
NNO King for a Day Entry Card .75 2.00

2003 Press Pass Gold Holofoil

COMPLETE SET (100) 25.00 50.00
*PLATINUM: .6X TO 1.5X BASE CARDS

2003 Press Pass Samples

*SAMPLES: 2.5X TO 6X BASIC CARDS

2003 Press Pass Autographs

Inserted at a stated rate of one in 72, these 63 signed cards feature a mix of today's NASCAR drivers as well as some legendary drivers from the past. Each card's image was photographed in such a way as to make the driver appear he was signing the card from inside it. Some of these cards were available in packs of 2003 Press Pass, 2003 Press Pass Eclipse or both, and are tagged as such.

1 John Andretti E/P 8.00 20.00
2 Casey Atwood E/P 4.00 10.00
3 Buddy Baker E/P 8.00 20.00
4 Greg Biffle E/P 10.00 25.00
5 Dave Blaney E/P 4.00 10.00
6 Brett Bodine E/P 4.00 10.00
7 Jeff Burton Citgo E 8.00 20.00
8 Jeff Burton Gain E 8.00 20.00
9 Kurt Busch E/P 12.00 30.00
10 Richard Childress E/P 8.00 20.00
11 Matt Crafton E/P 4.00 10.00
12 Ricky Craven E/P 8.00 20.00
13 Bill Davis E/P 4.00 10.00
14 Kerry Earnhardt E 8.00 15.00
15 Coy Gibbs E/P 10.00 25.00
16 Jeff Gordon E/P 75.00 150.00
17 Robby Gordon E/P 4.00 10.00
18 David Green E/P 8.00 20.00
19 Jeff Green E/P 4.00 10.00
20 Mark Green E/P 4.00 10.00
21 Bobby Hamilton E/P 8.00 20.00
22 Kevin Harvick E/P 12.00 30.00
23 Ricky Hendrick E/P 8.00 20.00
24 Shane Hmiel E/P 8.00 20.00
25 Dale Jarrett E/P 20.00 50.00
26 Ned Jarrett E/P 8.00 20.00
27 Jimmie Johnson E/P 25.00 60.00
28 Junior Johnson E/P 20.00 40.00
29 Jason Keller E/P 4.00 10.00
30 Matt Kenseth E/P 10.00 25.00
31 Travis Kvapil E/P 10.00 25.00
32 Bobby Labonte E/P 8.00 20.00
33 Terry Labonte E/P 12.00 30.00
34 Randy LaJoie E/P 4.00 10.00
35 Jason Leffler E 4.00 10.00
36 Chad Little E/P 4.00 10.00
37 Mark Martin E/P 20.00 50.00
38 Jeremy Mayfield E/P 10.00 25.00
39 Jamie McMurray E/P 8.00 20.00
40 Casey Mears E/P 8.00 20.00
41 Ted Musgrave E 8.00 20.00
42 Ryan Newman E/P 8.00 20.00
43 Hank Parker Jr. E/P 8.00 20.00
44 Benny Parsons E/P 15.00 40.00
45 David Pearson E/P 20.00 30.00
46 Kyle Petty E/P 12.00 30.00
47 Richard Petty E/P 25.00 60.00
48 Tony Raines E/P 4.00 10.00
49 Scott Riggs E/P 10.00 25.00
50 Ricky Rudd E/P 20.00 50.00
51 Joe Ruttman E/P 4.00 10.00
52 Elliott Sadler E/P 10.00 25.00
53 Johnny Sauter E 8.00 20.00
54 Ken Schrader E/P 10.00 25.00
55 Dennis Setzer E/P 4.00 10.00
56 Mike Skinner E/P 8.00 20.00
57 Jimmy Spencer E/P 8.00 20.00
58 Brian Vickers E/P 8.00 20.00
59 Rusty Wallace E/P 20.00 50.00
60 Michael Waltrip E/P 10.00 25.00
61 Scott Wimmer E/P 8.00 20.00
62 Jon Wood E/P 8.00 20.00
63 Cale Yarborough E/P 8.00 20.00

2003 Press Pass Burning Rubber Cars

*CARS: .3X TO .8X DRIVERS

2003 Press Pass Burning Rubber Drivers

Inserted at a stated rate of one in 480 hobby packs, these 18 cards feature pieces of race-used tires set against a card featuring a picture of the driver. These cards were issued to a stated print run of 50 serial numbered sets.

BRD1 Jeff Gordon 40.00 80.00
BRD2 Ryan Newman 30.00 60.00
BRD3 Kevin Harvick 25.00 50.00
BRD4 Jimmie Johnson 30.00 60.00
BRD5 Rusty Wallace 25.00 50.00
BRD6 Mark Martin 25.00 50.00
BRD7 Matt Kenseth 25.00 50.00
BRD8 Bobby Labonte 20.00 40.00
BRD9 Tony Stewart 30.00 60.00
BRD10 Dale Earnhardt Jr. 40.00 80.00
BRD11 Steve Park 20.00 40.00
BRD12 Sterling Marlin 20.00 40.00
BRD13 John Andretti 15.00 30.00
BRD14 Kyle Petty 15.00 30.00
BRD15 Jimmy Spencer 15.00 30.00
BRD16 Dale Earnhardt 40.00 100.00
BRD17 Dale Jarrett 25.00 50.00
BRD18 Terry Labonte 12.00 30.00

2003 Press Pass Burning Rubber Drivers Autographs

Randomly inserted into packs, these seven cards form a partial parallel to the Burning Rubber Car insert set. These cards were signed by the driver and serial numbered to the driver's car number.

*CARS: .4X TO 1X DRIVERS
BRDJG Jeff Gordon/24
BRDJJ Jimmie Johnson/48 60.00 120.00
BRDKH Kevin Harvick/29 60.00 120.00
BRDMK Matt Kenseth/17
BRDMM Mark Martin/6
BRDRN Ryan Newman/12
BRDRW Rusty Wallace/2
BRDTS Tony Stewart/20

2003 Press Pass Cup Chase

Inserted in Press Pass packs at a rate of one in 28, these cards are part of a year-long contest which allows fans to win a special limited edition plastic Cup Chase card set. The expiration date to send in these cards was January 31, 2004.

CCR1 Jeff Burton 5.00 12.00
CCR2 Ward Burton 5.00 12.00
CCR3 Dale Earnhardt Jr. 12.50 30.00
CCR4 Jeff Gordon 12.50 30.00
CCR5 Kevin Harvick WIN 12.50 30.00
CCR6 Dale Jarrett 8.00 20.00
CCR7 Jimmie Johnson WIN 12.50 30.00
CCR8 Matt Kenseth 10.00 25.00
CCR9 Bobby Labonte 8.00 20.00
CCR10 Terry Labonte 5.00 12.00
CCR11 Mark Martin 8.00 20.00
CCR12 Ryan Newman WIN 12.50 30.00
CCR13 Jeremy Mayfield 3.00 8.00
CCR14 Sterling Marlin 5.00 12.00
CCR15 Tony Stewart 10.00 25.00
CCR16 Rusty Wallace 8.00 20.00
CCR17 Ricky Craven WIN 12.50 30.00
CCR18 Field Card WIN 12.50 30.00

2003 Press Pass Cup Chase Prizes

COMPLETE SET (18) 12.50 30.00
CCR1 Jeff Burton .75 2.00
CCR2 Ward Burton .75 2.00
CCR3 Dale Earnhardt Jr. 4.00 10.00
CCR4 Jeff Gordon 3.00 8.00
CCR5 Kevin Harvick 2.00 5.00
CCR6 Dale Jarrett 2.00 5.00
CCR7 Jimmie Johnson 2.50 6.00
CCR8 Matt Kenseth 2.50 6.00
CCR9 Bobby Labonte 2.00 5.00
CCR10 Terry Labonte 1.25 3.00
CCR11 Mark Martin 2.50 6.00
CCR12 Ryan Newman 2.50 6.00
CCR13 Jeremy Mayfield .40 1.00
CCR14 Sterling Marlin 1.25 3.00
CCR15 Tony Stewart 2.50 6.00
CCR16 Rusty Wallace 2.00 5.00
CCR17 Ricky Craven .75 2.00
CCR18 Tony Stewart Champion .75 2.00

2003 Press Pass Santa Claus

Inserted in packs at stated odds of one in 144 for S1, one in 180 for S2 and one in 720 for S3, these cards feature that sleigh-riding gentleman from the North Pole and were released in time for the 2002 Christmas season.

COMPLETE SET (3) 20.00 40.00
S1 Santa Claus 6.00 15.00
S2 Santa Claus 6.00 15.00
S3 Santa Claus 12.50 30.00

2003 Press Pass Showman

Inserted at a stated rate of one in six hobby packs, these 12 die-cut cards feature two photos, one of which is the driver and the other is that driver's race car.

COMPLETE SET (12) 10.00 25.00
*CARS: .4X TO 1X DRIVERS
CAR STATED ODDS 1:6 RETAIL
S1A Jeff Burton .75 2.00
S2A Ryan Newman 2.50 6.00
S3A Jeff Gordon 3.00 8.00
S4A Kevin Harvick 2.00 5.00
S5A Dale Jarrett 2.00 5.00
S6A Jimmie Johnson 2.50 6.00
S7A Bobby Labonte 2.00 5.00
S8A Sterling Marlin 1.25 3.00
S9A Mark Martin 2.50 6.00
S10A Ricky Rudd 1.25 3.00
S11A Tony Stewart 2.50 6.00
S12A Rusty Wallace 2.00 5.00

2003 Press Pass Snapshots

Issued at a stated rate of one per pack, this 36-card set (measuring approximately 2 3/8" by 2 3/4") features drivers and their most memorable moments of the 2002 NASCAR season.

COMPLETE SET (36) 10.00 25.00
SN1 John Andretti .20 .50
SN2 Casey Atwood .20 .50
SN3 Jeff Burton .40 1.00
SN4 Ward Burton .40 1.00
SN5 Ricky Craven .20 .50
SN6 Dale Earnhardt Jr. 2.00 5.00
SN7 Jeff Gordon 1.50 4.00
SN8 Bobby Hamilton .20 .50
SN9 Kevin Harvick 1.00 2.50
SN10 Dale Jarrett 1.00 2.50
SN11 Jimmie Johnson 1.50 4.00
SN12 Matt Kenseth 1.25 3.00
SN13 Bobby Labonte 1.00 2.50
SN14 Terry Labonte .60 1.50
SN15 Sterling Marlin .60 1.50
SN16 Mark Martin 1.25 3.00
SN17 Ryan Newman 1.25 3.00
SN18 Kurt Busch .60 1.50
SN19 Ricky Rudd .60 1.50
SN20 Elliott Sadler .40 1.00
SN21 Ken Schrader .20 .50
SN22 Mike Skinner .20 .50
SN23 Jimmy Spencer .20 .50
SN24 Tony Stewart 1.25 3.00
SN25 Rusty Wallace 1.00 2.50
SN26 Robby Gordon .20 .50
SN27 Richard Petty .60 1.50
SN28 Bobby Allison .20 .50
SN29 Buddy Baker .20 .50
SN30 Ned Jarrett .40 1.00
SN31 Junior Johnson .20 .50
SN32 Benny Parsons .40 1.00
SN33 David Pearson .40 1.00
SN34 Harry Gant .20 .50
SN35 Glen Wood .20 .50
SN36 Cale Yarborough .40 1.00

2003 Press Pass Top Shelf

Inserted at a state rate of one in eight, these 10 cards feature drivers who are highlighted on silver foil board with an embossed finish.

COMPLETE SET (10) 10.00 25.00
TS1 Dale Earnhardt Jr. 3.00 8.00
TS2 Jeff Gordon 2.50 6.00
TS3 Dale Jarrett 1.50 4.00
TS4 Jimmie Johnson 2.50 6.00
TS5 Bobby Labonte 1.50 4.00
TS6 Mark Martin 2.00 5.00
TS7 Ryan Newman 2.00 5.00
TS8 Tony Stewart 2.00 5.00
TS9 Rusty Wallace 1.50 4.00
TS10 Kevin Harvick 1.50 4.00

2003 Press Pass Velocity

Issued at a stated rate of one in 18, these nine cards feature the driver along with a background photo of his car. These cards were printed on holofoil stock.

COMPLETE SET (9) 15.00 40.00
VC1 Dale Earnhardt Jr. 8.00 20.00
VC2 Jeff Gordon 6.00 15.00
VC3 Dale Jarrett 4.00 10.00
VC4 Jimmie Johnson 6.00 15.00
VC5 Sterling Marlin 2.50 6.00
VC6 Mark Martin 5.00 12.00
VC7 Ricky Rudd 2.50 6.00
VC8 Tony Stewart 5.00 12.00
VC9 Rusty Wallace 4.00 10.00

2004 Press Pass

This 100 card set was released December 9, 2003. This set was issued in eight card packs which came 28 packs to a hobby or retail box. Both hobby and retail boxes were packed 20 boxes to a case. The SRP for both hobby and retail packs was $2.99. There was a special card honoring Ryan Newman's most wins in 2003 randomly inserted into these packs.

COMPLETE SET (100) 10.00 25.00
WAX BOX HOBBY (28) 50.00 75.00
WAX BOX RETAIL (28) 40.00 70.00
1 Greg Biffle .25 .60
2 Dave Blaney .20 .50
3 Brett Bodine .25 .60
4 Todd Bodine .25 .60
5 Jeff Burton .25 .60
6 Ward Burton .25 .60
7 Kurt Busch .25 .60
8 Ricky Craven .20 .50
9 Dale Earnhardt Jr. .60 1.50
9B Dale Earnhardt Jr. grand. 3.00 8.00
9C Matt Kenseth blue sky 3.00 8.00
10 Jeff Gordon .60 1.50
10B Jeff Gordon infield 3.00 8.00
11 Robby Gordon .20 .50
12 Kevin Harvick .40 1.00
13 Dale Jarrett .30 .75
14 Jimmie Johnson .50 1.25
15 Matt Kenseth .30 .75
16 Bobby Labonte .30 .75
17 Terry Labonte .30 .75
18 Sterling Marlin .30 .75
19 Mark Martin .30 .75
20 Jeremy Mayfield .20 .50
21 Jamie McMurray .30 .75
21B Jamie McMurray infield 2.00 5.00
22 Casey Mears .20 .50
23 Joe Nemechek .20 .50
24 Ryan Newman .25 .60
25 Kyle Petty .25 .60
26 Tony Raines .20 .50
27 Ricky Rudd .25 .60
28 Elliott Sadler .20 .50
29 Ken Schrader .20 .50
30 Jimmy Spencer .20 .50
31 Tony Stewart .50 1.25
31B Tony Stewart skyline 3.00 8.00
32 Rusty Wallace .30 .75
33 Michael Waltrip .30 .75
34 Kenny Wallace .20 .50
35 Jerry Nadeau .20 .50
36 Christian Fittipaldi RC .30 .75
37 Stacy Compton .20 .50
38 Kyle Busch RC 3.00 8.00
38B Kyle Busch infield 6.00 15.00
39 Coy Gibbs .25 .60
40 David Green .20 .50
41 Kevin Grubb .20 .50
42 Kasey Kahne 1.25 3.00
43 Scott Wimmer .30 .75
44 Chase Montgomery .20 .50
45 Regan Smith RC .40 1.00
46 Jimmy Vasser .20 .50
47 Brian Vickers .40 1.00
47B Brian Vickers grandstand 3.00 8.00
48 Jason Keller .20 .50
49 Matt Crafton .20 .50
50 Rick Crawford .20 .50
51 Carl Edwards .60 1.50
52 Tina Gordon RC .60 1.50
53 Andy Houston .20 .50
54 Travis Kvapil .20 .50
55 Dennis Setzer .20 .50
56 Jon Wood .25 .60
57 Robert Pressley .20 .50
58 Charlie Bradberry RC .25 .60
59 Jeff Jefferson RC .25 .60
60 Steve Carlson .20 .50
61 Andy Santerre .20 .50
62 Todd Szegedy RC .25 .60
63 Robert Huffman .20 .50
64 Rusty Wallace's Car OTW .12 .30
65 Mark Martin's Car OTW .12 .30
66 Dale Earnhardt Jr.'s Car OTW .25 .60
67 Ryan Newman's Car OTW .10 .25
68 Bobby Labonte's Car OTW .12 .30
68B B.Labonte's Car OTW SP 1.50 4.00
69 Tony Stewart's Car OTW .20 .50
70 Kevin Harvick's Car OTW .15 .40
71 Elliott Sadler's Car OTW .07 .20
72 Casey Mears' Car OTW .07 .20
73 Jamie McMurray's Car OTW .12 .30
74 Dale Jarrett's Car OTW .12 .30
75 Kurt Busch's Car OTW .10 .25
75B Kurt Busch's Car OTW SP 1.25 3.00
76 Penske Power WCS .30 .75
77 Figuring It Out WCS .30 .75
78 One For The Ages WCS .25 .60
79 Duking'-ing It Out WCS .30 .75
80 The Drive for Five WCS .30 .75
81 No Ordinary Joe WCS .20 .50
82 Growing Up Fast WCS .25 .60
83 Spring Reign WCS .50 1.25
84 Million-dollar Magic WCS .50 1.25
85 Quiet Confidence WCS .30 .75
86 In the Groove WCS .50 1.25
87 Two for the Road WCS .20 .50
88 Jamie McMurray RR .30 .75
89 Casey Mears RR .20 .50
90 Greg Biffle RR .25 .60
91 Dale Earnhardt Jr. DS .60 1.50
92 Jamie McMurray DS .30 .75
93 Jeff Gordon DS .60 1.50
94 Kurt Busch DS .25 .60
95 Jimmie Johnson DS blue .50 1.25
95B Jimmie Johnson DS red 2.50 6.00
96 Casey Mears DS .20 .50
97 Matt Kenseth DS .30 .75
98 Ryan Newman DS .25 .60
99 Kevin Harvick DS .40 1.00
100 Matt Kenseth Schedule .30 .75
0 Ryan Newman/600 10.00 25.00

2004 Press Pass Platinum

COMPLETE SET (100) 15.00 40.00
*PLATINUM: .6X TO 1.5X BASE CARDS

2004 Press Pass Samples

*SAMPLES: 2X TO 5X BASE CARDS

2004 Press Pass Autographs

Inserted at a stated rate of one in 84 hobby and one in 196 retail, these 55 signed cards feature a mix of today's NASCAR drivers as well as some legendary drivers from the past. Each card's image was placed on the upper left-hand side of the card's horizontal view. Some of these cards were available in packs of 2004 Press Pass, 2004 Press Pass Eclipse of both, and are tagged as such.

1 Bobby Allison P 8.00 20.00
2 Buddy Baker P 6.00 15.00
3 Greg Biffle P 8.00 20.00
4 Dave Blaney P 6.00 15.00
5 Mike Bliss P 6.00 15.00
6 Brett Bodine P 6.00 15.00
7 Todd Bodine P 6.00 15.00
8 Jeff Burton P 8.00 20.00
9 Kurt Busch P 12.00 30.00
10 Kyle Busch P 25.00 60.00
11 Richard Childress P 8.00 20.00
12 Stacy Compton P 6.00 15.00
13 Matt Crafton P 6.00 15.00
14 Ricky Craven P 10.00 25.00
15 Rick Crawford P 6.00 15.00
16 Dale Earnhardt Jr. E 50.00 100.00
17 Kerry Earnhardt E 10.00 25.00
18 Carl Edwards P 30.00 60.00
19 Christian Fittipaldi P 10.00 25.00
20 Coy Gibbs P 6.00 15.00
21 Jeff Gordon P 75.00 150.00
22 Robby Gordon E 8.00 20.00
23 Tina Gordon P 10.00 25.00
24 David Green P 6.00 15.00
25 Kevin Harvick P 12.00 30.00
26 Andy Houston P 6.00 15.00
27 Dale Jarrett P 15.00 40.00
28 Ned Jarrett P 8.00 20.00
29 Jimmie Johnson P 30.00 60.00
30 Kasey Kahne BGN P 15.00 40.00
31 Kasey Kahne NCS 20.00 50.00
32 Jason Keller P 6.00 15.00
33 Matt Kenseth P 15.00 40.00
34 Travis Kvapil P 10.00 25.00
35 Bobby Labonte P 15.00 40.00
36 Terry Labonte P 15.00 40.00
37 Damon Lusk P 6.00 15.00
38 Sterling Marlin P 10.00 25.00
39 Mark Martin P 20.00 50.00
40 Jeremy Mayfield 10.00 25.00
41 Mike McLaughlin P 6.00 15.00
42 Jamie McMurray E 10.00 25.00
43 Casey Mears E 10.00 25.00
44 Joe Nemechek P 8.00 20.00
45 Ryan Newman P 15.00 30.00
46 Benny Parsons P 10.00 25.00
47 David Pearson P 10.00 25.00
48 Kyle Petty E 10.00 25.00
49 Richard Petty P 25.00 60.00
50 Tony Raines P 6.00 15.00
51 Scott Riggs P 8.00 20.00
52 Ricky Rudd P 10.00 25.00
53 Johnny Sauter P 8.00 20.00
54 Ken Schrader P 8.00 20.00
55 Dennis Setzer P 6.00 15.00
56 Regan Smith P 6.00 15.00
57 Brian Vickers P 10.00 25.00
58 Kenny Wallace P 10.00 25.00
59 Rusty Wallace P 12.50 30.00
60 Scott Wimmer P 8.00 20.00
61 Glen Wood P 6.00 15.00
62 Jon Wood P 8.00 20.00
63 Robert Yates P 10.00 25.00
64 Cale Yarborough E 8.00 20.00

2004 Press Pass Burning Rubber Autographs

Randomly inserted in packs of 2004 Press Pass, this 8-card set featured NASCAR's hottest drivers along with a swatch of race-used tire along with an autograph. Each card was serial numbered to the driver's car number. The design looked like that of the 2004 Press Pass Burning Rubber Drivers. These were available in both hobby and retail packs of 2004 Press Pass. Some cards are not priced due to scarcity.

BRJG Jeff Gordon/24 125.00 250.00
BRJJ Jimmie Johnson/48 60.00 120.00
BRKB Kurt Busch/97
BRKH Kevin Harvick/29 60.00 120.00
BRMK Matt Kenseth/17
BRMM Mark Martin/6
BRRN Ryan Newman/12
BRRW Rusty Wallace/2

2004 Press Pass Burning Rubber Drivers

Inserted at a stated rate of one in 180 retail packs, these 18 cards feature pieces of race-used tires set against a card featuring the driver. These cards were issued to a stated print run of 70 serial numbered sets.

*CARS/140: .3X TO .8X DRIVERS/70
BRD1 Jimmie Johnson 15.00 40.00
BRD2 Matt Kenseth 12.00 30.00

D3 Kevin Harvick 10.00 25.00
D4 Jeff Gordon 15.00 40.00
D5 Kurt Busch 10.00 25.00
D6 Mark Martin 8.00 20.00
D7 Ryan Newman 10.00 25.00
D8 Bobby Labonte 10.00 25.00
D9 Rusty Wallace 10.00 25.00
D10 Dale Earnhardt Jr. 20.00 50.00
D11 Michael Waltrip 10.00 25.00
D12 Jamie McMurray 8.00 20.00
D13 Tony Stewart 12.00 30.00
D14 Casey Mears 8.00 20.00
D15 Terry Labonte 10.00 25.00
D16 Dale Jarrett 10.00 25.00
D17 Dale Earnhardt 30.00 80.00
D18 Robby Gordon 8.00 20.00

2004 Press Pass Cup Chase

ese 18 cards were issued in packs of 2004 ress Pass at a rate of 1:28 hobby and retail acks. There were 17 drivers and 1 field card. If e driver won any of the 8 races listed on the back f the card or the Nextel Cup Championship that ard was redeemable, along with $3.95 for s&h, r a complete set of 17 of the prize cards. If you ad the champion, you were also sent a special emorabilia card of his. The exchange deadline r these was January 31, 2005. Cards that were edeemable are noted below.

CR1 Matt Kenseth 12.50 25.00
CR2 Jeff Gordon WIN 20.00 40.00
CR3 Dale Earnhardt Jr. WIN 20.00 40.00
CR4 Bobby Labonte 8.00 20.00
CR5 Michael Waltrip 6.00 15.00
CR6 Kurt Busch 8.00 20.00
CR7 Jimmie Johnson WIN 8.00 20.00
CR8 Rusty Wallace 6.00 15.00
CR9 Kevin Harvick 8.00 20.00
CR10 Sterling Marlin 6.00 15.00
CR11 Tony Stewart 8.00 20.00
CR12 Mark Martin 6.00 15.00
CR13 Terry Labonte 6.00 15.00
CR14 Jeff Burton 5.00 12.00
CR15 Ryan Newman 10.00 25.00
CCR16 Elliott Sadler 6.00 15.00
CR17 Greg Biffle 6.00 15.00
CCR18 Field Card 10.00 25.00

2004 Press Pass Cup Chase Prizes

COMPLETE SET (18) 15.00 40.00
CCR1 Matt Kenseth 3.00 8.00
CCR2 Jeff Gordon 4.00 10.00
CCR3 Dale Earnhardt Jr. 4.00 10.00
CCR4 Bobby Labonte 2.00 5.00
CCR5 Michael Waltrip 1.00 2.50
CCR6 Kurt Busch 1.50 4.00
CCR7 Jimmie Johnson 3.00 8.00
CCR8 Rusty Wallace 2.00 5.00
CCR9 Kevin Harvick 2.50 6.00
CCR10 Sterling Marlin 1.50 4.00
CCR11 Tony Stewart 2.50 6.00
CCR12 Mark Martin 2.50 6.00
CCR13 Terry Labonte 1.50 4.00
CCR14 Jeff Burton 1.00 2.50
CCR15 Ryan Newman 3.00 8.00
CCR16 Elliott Sadler 1.00 2.50
CCR17 Greg Biffle 1.00 2.50
CCR18 Matt Kenseth Champion 3.00 8.00

2004 Press Pass Schedule

This 4-card set features one of NASCAR's hottest drivers with a 2004 Nextel Cup schedule on the back. These cards were packaged inside of blaster boxes, which were available at most retail stores, as a box topper. They were the standard 2 1/2" x 3 1/2".

COMPLETE SET (4) 30.00 60.00
1 Jeff Gordon 7.50 20.00
2 Jimmie Johnson 6.00 15.00
3 Dale Earnhardt Jr. 8.00 20.00
4 Tony Stewart 6.00 15.00

2004 Press Pass Season's Greetings

Inserted in packs at stated odds of one in 72, these cards feature that sleigh-riding gentleman from the North Pole and were released in time for the 2003 Christmas season.

COMPLETE SET (3) 12.50 30.00
SC1 Santa 5.00 12.00
SC2 Santa with Sleigh 5.00 12.00
SC3 Santa with Tree 5.00 12.00

2004 Press Pass Showman

Inserted at a stated rate of one in six retail packs, these 12 die-cut cards feature a photo of the featured driver.

COMPLETE SET (12) 12.50 30.00
*SHOWCAR: .4X TO 1X SHOWMAN
S1A Jeff Burton .50 1.25
S2A Kurt Busch 1.00 2.50
S3A Matt Kenseth 2.00 5.00
S4A Dale Earnhardt Jr. 2.50 6.00
S5A Jeff Gordon 2.50 6.00
S6A Dale Jarrett 1.25 3.00
S7A Jimmie Johnson 2.00 5.00
S8A Bobby Labonte 1.25 3.00
S9A Terry Labonte 1.00 2.50
S10A Mark Martin 1.50 4.00
S11A Tony Stewart 1.50 4.00
S12A Michael Waltrip .50 1.25

2004 Press Pass Snapshots

Issued at a stated rate of one per pack, this 36-card set (measuring approximately 2 3/8" by 2 3/4") features drivers and their most memorable moments of the 2003 NASCAR season along with some retired drivers with highlights from their days of racing.

COMPLETE SET (36) 8.00 20.00
SN1 Greg Biffle .40 1.00
SN2 Jeff Burton .40 1.00
SN3 Ward Burton .40 1.00
SN4 Kurt Busch .60 1.50
SN5 Ricky Craven .20 .50
SN6 Dale Earnhardt Jr. 1.50 4.00
SN7 Jeff Gordon 1.50 4.00
SN8 Robby Gordon .20 .50
SN9 Kevin Harvick 1.25 3.00
SN10 Dale Jarrett 1.00 2.50
SN11 Jimmie Johnson 1.50 4.00
SN12 Matt Kenseth 1.50 4.00
SN13 Bobby Labonte 1.00 2.50
SN14 Terry Labonte .60 1.50
SN15 Sterling Marlin .60 1.50
SN16 Mark Martin 1.25 3.00
SN17 Jamie McMurray .60 1.50
SN18 Casey Mears .40 1.00
SN19 Joe Nemechek .20 .50
SN20 Ryan Newman 1.50 4.00
SN21 Ricky Rudd .60 1.50
SN22 Elliott Sadler .40 1.00
SN23 Michael Waltrip .40 1.00
SN24 Jimmy Spencer .20 .50
SN25 Tony Stewart 1.25 3.00
SN26 Rusty Wallace 1.00 2.50
SN27 Richard Petty .60 1.50
SN28 Buddy Baker .20 .50
SN29 Harry Gant .20 .50
SN30 Ned Jarrett .40 1.00
SN31 Junior Johnson .20 .50
SN32 Benny Parsons .20 .50
SN33 David Pearson .20 .50
SN34 Bobby Allison .20 .50
SN35 Glen Wood .20 .50
SN36 Cale Yarborough .20 .50

2004 Press Pass Top Shelf

Inserted at a state rate of 1:8 in both hobby and retail packs. These 10 cards feature drivers with silver foil names plates and a holofoil embossed finish.

COMPLETE SET (10) 10.00 25.00
TS1 Matt Kenseth 2.00 5.00
TS2 Kevin Harvick 1.50 4.00
TS3 Dale Earnhardt Jr. 2.50 6.00
TS4 Ryan Newman 2.00 5.00
TS5 Jimmie Johnson 2.00 5.00
TS6 Jeff Gordon 2.50 6.00
TS7 Tony Stewart 1.50 4.00
TS8 Bobby Labonte 1.25 3.00
TS9 Terry Labonte .75 2.00
TS10 Kurt Busch .75 2.00

2004 Press Pass Velocity

Issued at a stated rate of one in 18, these nine cards feature the driver along with a background photo of his car. These cards were printed on holofoil stock.

COMPLETE SET (9) 15.00 40.00
VC1 Michael Waltrip .75 2.00
VC2 Rusty Wallace 1.50 4.00
VC3 Kevin Harvick 2.00 5.00
VC4 Mark Martin 2.00 5.00
VC5 Matt Kenseth 2.50 6.00
VC6 Jimmie Johnson 2.50 6.00
VC7 Jeff Gordon 3.00 8.00
VC8 Dale Earnhardt Jr. 3.00 8.00
VC9 Kurt Busch 1.25 3.00

2005 Press Pass

COMPLETE SET (120) 15.00 40.00
WAX BOX HOBBY (28) 50.00 80.00
WAX BOX RETAIL (24) 35.00 60.00
1 Ward Burton .25 .60
2 Joe Nemechek .20 .50
3 Rusty Wallace .30 .75
4 Terry Labonte .30 .75
5 Mark Martin .30 .75
6 Dale Earnhardt Jr. .60 1.50
7 Kasey Kahne .50 1.25
8 Scott Riggs .25 .60
9 Ryan Newman .25 .60
10 Michael Waltrip .30 .75
11 Greg Biffle .25 .60
12 Matt Kenseth .30 .75
13 Bobby Labonte .30 .75
14 Jeremy Mayfield .20 .50
15 Tony Stewart .50 1.25
16 Ricky Rudd .25 .60
17 Scott Wimmer .30 .75
18 Dave Blaney .20 .50
19 Jeff Gordon .60 1.50
20 Brian Vickers .20 .50
21 Kevin Harvick .40 1.00
22 Jeff Burton .25 .60
23 Robby Gordon .20 .50
24 Ricky Craven .20 .50
25 Boris Said .20 .50
26 Elliott Sadler .20 .50
27 Sterling Marlin .30 .75
28 Casey Mears .20 .50
29 Jamie McMurray .30 .75
30 Jeff Green .20 .50
31 Kyle Petty .25 .60
32 Jimmie Johnson .50 1.25
33 Ken Schrader .20 .50
34 Brendan Gaughan .20 .50
35 Dale Jarrett .30 .75
36 Kurt Busch .25 .60
37 Jason Leffler .20 .50
38 Ron Hornaday .20 .50
39 Kyle Busch .75 2.00
40 Mark McFarland RC .30 .75
41 Martin Truex Jr. .75 2.00
42 Tim Fedewa .20 .50
43 Jason Keller .20 .50
44 Kenny Wallace .20 .50
45 David Green .20 .50
46 Kasey Kahne .50 1.25
47 Justin Labonte .30 .75
48 Greg Biffle .25 .60
49 Andy Houston .20 .50
50 Matt Crafton .20 .50
51 Terry Cook .20 .50
52 Tina Gordon .30 .75
53 Rick Crawford .20 .50
54 Jack Sprague .20 .50
55 Dennis Setzer .20 .50
56 Jon Wood .25 .60
57 Carl Edwards .60 1.50
58 Jeff Fultz .20 .50
59 Andy Santerre .20 .50
60 Justin Diercks RC .40 1.00
61 Jeff Jefferson .20 .50
62 Tony Hirschman .20 .50
63 Mike Duncan RC .40 1.00
64 Ryan Newman's Car OTW .10 .25
65 Dale Jr's Car OTW .25 .60
66 Elliott Sadler's Car OTW .07 .20
67 Bobby Labonte's Car OTW .12 .30
68 Rusty Wallace's Car OTW .12 .30
69 Kurt Busch's Car OTW .10 .25
70 Kevin Harvick's Car OTW .15 .40
71 Dale Jarrett's Car OTW .12 .30
72 Mark Martin's Car OTW .12 .30
73 Dale Earnhardt Jr. NS .60 1.50
74 Matt Kenseth NS .30 .75
75 Dale Earnhardt Jr. NS .60 1.50
76 Jimmie Johnson NS .50 1.25
77 Kurt Busch NS .25 .60
78 Dale Earnhardt Jr. NS .60 1.50
79 Rusty Wallace NS .30 .75
80 Jeff Gordon NS .60 1.50
81 Richard Petty NS .50 1.25
82 Jimmie Johnson NS .50 1.25
83 Mark Martin .50 1.25
T.Stewart NS
84 Jeff Gordon NS .60 1.50
85 Kasey Kahne RR .50 1.25
86 Brian Vickers RR .20 .50
87 Scott Wimmer RR .30 .75
88 Brendan Gaughan RR .20 .50
89 Scott Riggs RR .25 .60
90 Martin Truex Jr. RR .75 2.00
91 Richard Petty Y .50 1.25
92 J.Hend/Grdn/JJ/T.Lab/Vick Y .60 1.50
93 Kevin Harvick Y .40 1.00
94 Dale Earnhardt Jr. Y .60 1.50
95 Jeff Gordon Y .60 1.50
96 T.Labonte/J.Labonte Y .30 .75
97 Ky.Busch/K.Busch Y .75 2.00
98 Rusty Wallace Y .30 .75
99 Michael Waltrip Y .30 .75
100 Rusty Wallace P .30 .75
101 Mark Martin P .30 .75
102 Dale Earnhardt Jr. P .60 1.50
103 Michael Waltrip P .30 .75
104 Bobby Labonte P .30 .75
105 Jeff Gordon P .60 1.50
106 Jimmie Johnson P .50 1.25
107 Ken Schrader P .20 .50
108 Dale Jarrett P .30 .75
109 Dale Earnhardt Jr's Car .25 .60
110 Elliott Sadler's Car .07 .20
111 Rusty Wallace's Car .12 .30
112 Jeff Gordon's Car .25 .60
113 Dale Earnhardt Jr's Car .25 .60
114 Jimmie Johnson's Car .20 .50
115 Mark Martin's Car .12 .30
116 Ryan Newman's Car .10 .25
117 Kurt Busch's Car .10 .25
118 Jimmie Johnson's Car .20 .50
119 WC/BGN Schedule .10 .20
120 Dale Jr/JJ/Gordon CL .40 1.00

2005 Press Pass Platinum

*PLATINUM: 2.5X TO 6X BASE

2005 Press Pass Samples

*SAMPLES: 1.5X TO 4X BASE

2005 Press Pass Autographs

1 Bobby Allison E/P 6.00 15.00
2 Greg Biffle BGN E/P 8.00 20.00
3 Greg Biffle NCS E/P 8.00 20.00
4 Mike Bliss E/P 5.00 12.00
5 Clint Bowyer E/P 10.00 25.00
6 Jeff Burton E 6.00 15.00
7 Kurt Busch E/P 10.00 25.00
8 Kyle Busch BGN E/P 15.00 40.00
9 Kyle Busch NCS E/P 15.00 40.00
10 Richard Childress E 6.00 15.00
11 Terry Cook E/P 6.00 15.00
12 Matt Crafton E/P 6.00 15.00
13 Ricky Craven E/P 8.00 20.00
14 Dale Earnhardt Jr. E 50.00 100.00
15 Kerry Earnhardt E 8.00 20.00
16 Carl Edwards E/P 20.00 50.00
17 Tim Fedewa E 5.00 12.00
18 Brendan Gaughan E/P 8.00 20.00
19 Jeff Gordon E/P 100.00 175.00
20 Tina Gordon E/P 8.00 20.00
21 David Green E/P 5.00 12.00
22 Jeff Green E/P 6.00 15.00
23 Kevin Harvick E/P 10.00 25.00
24 Ron Hornaday E/P 6.00 15.00
25 Andy Houston E/P 5.00 12.00
26 Dale Jarrett E/P 10.00 25.00
27 Jimmie Johnson E/P 25.00 60.00
28 Kasey Kahne BGN E/P 6.00 15.00
29 Kasey Kahne NCS E/P 15.00 40.00
30 Jason Keller E/P 5.00 12.00
31 Matt Kenseth BGN E/P 10.00 25.00
32 Matt Kenseth NCS E/P 8.00 20.00
33 Bobby Labonte E/P 10.00 25.00
34 Justin Labonte E/P 10.00 25.00
35 Terry Labonte E 15.00 40.00
36 Bill Lester E 8.00 20.00
37 Mark Martin E/P 20.00 50.00
38 Jeremy Mayfield E 8.00 20.00
39 Mark McFarland E 8.00 20.00
40 Jamie McMurray 8.00 20.00
41 Casey Mears 5.00 12.00
42 Joe Nemechek E/P 8.00 20.00
43 Ryan Newman E/P 6.00 15.00
44 Steve Park E/P 10.00 25.00
45 Benny Parsons E/P 25.00 60.00
46 David Pearson E/P 8.00 20.00
47 Kyle Petty E 10.00 25.00
48 Richard Petty E/P 25.00 60.00
49 Scott Riggs E/P 6.00 15.00
50 Ricky Rudd E/P 8.00 20.00
51 Boris Said E/P 5.00 12.00
52 Johnny Sauter E 6.00 15.00
53 Ken Schrader E 6.00 15.00
54 Dennis Setzer E/P 5.00 12.00
55 Jack Sprague E/P 5.00 12.00
56 Tony Stewart E/P 20.00 40.00
57 Martin Truex Jr. 10.00 25.00
58 Brian Vickers E/P 5.00 12.00
59 Kenny Wallace E/P 8.00 20.00
60 Rusty Wallace E/P 12.00 30.00
61 Michael Waltrip 8.00 20.00
62 Scott Wimmer E 6.00 15.00
63 Paul Wolfe E 6.00 15.00
64 Glen Wood E/P 5.00 12.00
65 Jon Wood E/P 8.00 15.00
66 Robert Yates E/P 6.00 15.00
67 J.J. Yeley E/P 6.00 15.00

2005 Press Pass Burning Rubber Autographs

This 8-card set was released in packs of 2005 Press Pass. Each card had a swatch of race-used tire along with a signature from the corresponding driver. Each card was serial numbered to the driver's door number. There was a late addition to the set. The Dale Earnhardt Jr. was only available in packs of 2006 Press Pass Legends.

STATED PRINT RUN 2-48
BRDE Dale Earnhardt Jr./8
BRJJ Jimmie Johnson/48 60.00 120.00
BRKH Kevin Harvick/29 60.00 120.00
BRMK Matt Kenseth/17
BRMM Mark Martin/6
BRRN Ryan Newman/12
BRRW Rusty Wallace/2
BRTS Tony Stewart/20 125.00 200.00

2005 Press Pass Burning Rubber Drivers

*CARS/130: .3X TO .8X DRIVERS/80
UNPRICED GOLD PRINT RUN 1
BRD1 Jimmie Johnson 15.00 40.00
BRD2 Matt Kenseth 12.00 30.00
BRD3 Kevin Harvick 12.50 30.00
BRD4 Jeff Gordon 25.00 60.00
BRD5 Bobby Labonte 12.50 30.00
BRD6 Rusty Wallace 12.50 30.00
BRD7 Dale Earnhardt Jr. 25.00 60.00
BRD8 Michael Waltrip 10.00 25.00
BRD9 Jamie McMurray 10.00 25.00
BRD10 Tony Stewart 20.00 50.00
BRD11 Casey Mears 8.00 20.00
BRD12 Terry Labonte 12.50 30.00
BRD13 Dale Jarrett 12.50 30.00
BRD14 Scott Riggs 8.00 20.00
BRD15 Joe Nemechek 8.00 20.00
BRD16 Ricky Rudd 10.00 25.00
BRD17 Kurt Busch 10.00 25.00
BRD18 Mark Martin 12.00 30.00

2005 Press Pass Cup Chase

CCR1 Kurt Busch Winner 15.00 30.00
CCR2 Dale Jarrett 6.00 15.00
CCR3 Jimmie Johnson Winner 15.00 30.00
CCR4 Jamie McMurray 6.00 15.00
CCR5 Elliott Sadler 6.00 15.00
CCR6 Kevin Harvick Winner 15.00 30.00
CCR7 Jeff Gordon Winner 20.00 40.00
CCR8 Tony Stewart Winner 15.00 30.00
CCR9 Bobby Labonte 6.00 15.00
CCR10 Matt Kenseth 8.00 20.00
CCR11 Greg Biffle Winner 15.00 30.00
CCR12 Michael Waltrip 6.00 15.00
CCR13 Ryan Newman 8.00 20.00
CCR14 Kasey Kahne 10.00 25.00
CCR15 Dale Earnhardt Jr. 10.00 25.00
CCR16 Mark Martin 8.00 20.00
CCR17 Rusty Wallace 6.00 15.00
CCR18 Field Card Winner 15.00 30.00

2005 Press Pass Cup Chase Prizes

COMPLETE SET (18) 15.00 30.00
CCP1 Kurt Busch 1.00 2.50
CCP2 Dale Jarrett 1.25 3.00
CCP3 Jimmie Johnson 2.50 6.00
CCP4 Jamie McMurray 1.00 2.50
CCP5 Elliott Sadler 1.00 2.50
CCP6 Kevin Harvick 2.00 5.00
CCP7 Jeff Gordon 4.00 10.00
CCP8 Tony Stewart 2.50 6.00
CCP9 Bobby Labonte 1.25 3.00
CCP10 Matt Kenseth 2.00 5.00
CCP11 Greg Biffle 1.00 2.50
CCP12 Michael Waltrip 1.25 3.00
CCP13 Ryan Newman 1.50 4.00
CCP14 Kasey Kahne 2.00 5.00
CCP15 Dale Earnhardt Jr. 4.00 10.00
CCP16 Mark Martin 1.50 4.00
CCP17 Rusty Wallace 1.50 4.00
CCP18 Kurt Busch '04 Champ 1.00 2.50
NNO Tony Stewart Firesuit 8.00 20.00

2005 Press Pass Game Face

COMPLETE SET (9) 10.00 25.00
GF1 Dale Jarrett 1.25 3.00
GF2 Jimmie Johnson 2.00 5.00
GF3 Dale Earnhardt Jr. 2.50 6.00
GF4 Kevin Harvick 1.50 4.00
GF5 Bobby Labonte 1.25 3.00
GF6 Jeff Gordon 2.50 6.00
GF7 Tony Stewart 1.50 4.00
GF8 Michael Waltrip .60 1.50
GF9 Mark Martin 1.50 4.00

2005 Press Pass Season's Greetings

1 Santa Claus Snowmobile 10.00 20.00
2 Santa Claus Daytona or Bust 6.00 12.00

2005 Press Pass Showman

COMPLETE SET (12) 20.00 50.00
STATED ODDS 1:18
*SHOWCARS: .3X TO.8X SHOWMAN
SM1 Mark Martin 2.50 6.00
SM2 Kurt Busch 1.50 4.00
SM3 Jimmie Johnson 3.00 8.00
SM4 Dale Earnhardt Jr. 4.00 10.00
SM5 Jeff Gordon 4.00 10.00
SM6 Dale Jarrett 2.00 5.00
SM7 Rusty Wallace 2.00 5.00
SM8 Kevin Harvick 2.50 6.00
SM9 Michael Waltrip 1.00 2.50
SM10 Tony Stewart 2.50 6.00
SM11 Bobby Labonte 2.00 5.00
SM12 Terry Labonte 1.50 4.00

2005 Press Pass Snapshots

COMPLETE SET (36) 10.00 25.00
STATED ODDS 1:2
SN1 Greg Biffle .30 .75
SN2 Dave Blaney .15 .40
SN3 Jeff Burton .30 .75
SN4 Kurt Busch .50 1.25
SN5 Dale Earnhardt Jr. 1.25 3.00
SN6 Carl Edwards 1.00 2.50
SN7 Brendan Gaughan .30 .75
SN8 Jeff Gordon 1.25 3.00
SN9 Jeff Green .15 .40
SN10 Kevin Harvick .75 2.00
SN11 Dale Jarrett .60 1.50
SN12 Jimmie Johnson 1.00 2.50
SN13 Kasey Kahne 1.25 3.00
SN14 Matt Kenseth 1.00 2.50
SN15 Bobby Labonte .60 1.50
SN16 Terry Labonte .50 1.25
SN17 Mark Martin .75 2.00
SN18 Jeremy Mayfield .15 .40
SN19 Joe Nemechek .15 .40
SN20 Scott Riggs .30 .75
SN21 Ricky Rudd .50 1.25
SN22 Elliott Sadler .30 .75
SN23 Ken Schrader .15 .40
SN24 Tony Stewart .75 2.00
SN25 Rusty Wallace .60 1.50
SN26 Michael Waltrip .30 .75
SN27 Bobby Allison .15 .40
SN28 Davey Allison .30 .75
SN29 Geoff Bodine .15 .40
SN30 Harry Gant .30 .75
SN31 Alan Kulwicki .30 .75
SN32 Benny Parsons .15 .40
SN33 David Pearson .15 .40
SN34 Richard Petty .75 2.00
SN35 Glen Wood .15 .40
SN36 Cale Yarborough .15 .40

2005 Press Pass Snapshots Extra

COMPLETE SET (18) 12.00 30.00
SS1 Dale Earnhardt Jr. 1.25 3.00
SS2 Jeff Gordon 1.25 3.00
SS3 Jimmie Johnson 1.00 2.50
SS4 Dale Jarrett .60 1.50
SS5 Jason Keller #2 .40 1.00
SS6 Jason Keller #3 .40 1.00
SS7 Jason Leffler .40 1.00
SS8 Jason Leffler #2 .40 1.00
SS9 Ken Schrader .40 1.00
SS10 Ken Schrader #2 .40 1.00
SS11 Davey Allison 1.25 3.00
SS12 Kenny Wallace .40 1.00
SS13 Rick Crawford .40 1.00
SS14 Alan Kulwicki 1.00 2.50
SS15 Kerry Earnhardt .60 1.50
SS16 Andy Houston .40 1.00
SS17 Kerry Earnhardt #2 .60 1.50
SS18 Jason Keller .40 1.00

2005 Press Pass Top Ten

COMPLETE SET (10) 15.00 40.00
TT1 Jeff Gordon 6.00 15.00
TT2 Jimmie Johnson 5.00 12.00
TT3 Dale Earnhardt Jr. 6.00 15.00
TT4 Tony Stewart 4.00 10.00
TT5 Matt Kenseth 5.00 12.00
TT6 Elliott Sadler 1.50 4.00
TT7 Kurt Busch 2.50 6.00
TT8 Mark Martin 4.00 10.00
TT9 Jeremy Mayfield 1.00 2.50
TT10 Ryan Newman 5.00 12.00

2005 Press Pass Velocity

COMPLETE SET (9) 15.00 40.00
V1 Dale Jarrett 1.50 4.00
V2 Jimmie Johnson 2.50 6.00
V3 Jeff Gordon 3.00 8.00
V4 Ricky Rudd 1.25 3.00
V5 Matt Kenseth 2.50 6.00
V6 Michael Waltrip .75 2.00
V7 Dale Earnhardt Jr. 3.00 8.00
V8 Mark Martin 2.50 6.00
V9 Rusty Wallace 2.00 4.00

2006 Press Pass

COMPLETE SET (120) 15.00 40.00
WAX BOX HOBBY (28) 60.00 90.00
WAX BOX RETAIL 50.00 80.00
1 Mike Bliss .20 .50
2 Joe Nemechek .20 .50
3 Martin Truex Jr. .50 1.25
4 Rusty Wallace .30 .75
5 Kyle Busch .40 1.00
6 Mark Martin .30 .75
7 Dave Blaney .20 .50
8 Robby Gordon .20 .50
9 Dale Earnhardt Jr. .60 1.50
10 Kasey Kahne .40 1.00
11 Ryan Newman .25 .60
12 Greg Biffle .25 .60
13 Matt Kenseth .30 .75
14 Bobby Labonte .30 .75
15 Jeremy Mayfield .20 .50
16 Tony Stewart .50 1.25
17 Ricky Rudd .25 .60
18 Jeff Gordon .60 1.50
19 Brian Vickers .20 .50
20 Kevin Harvick .40 1.00
21 Jeff Burton .25 .60
22 Kevin Lepage .20 .50
23 Sterling Marlin .30 .75
24 Jamie McMurray .30 .75
25 Terry Labonte .30 .75
26 Kyle Petty .25 .60
27 Jimmie Johnson .50 1.25
28 Dale Jarrett .30 .75
29 Kurt Busch .25 .60
30 Carl Edwards .30 .75
31 Johnny Sauter NBS .30 .75
32 Clint Bowyer NBS .60 1.50
33 Martin Truex Jr. NBS .50 1.25
34 J.J. Yeley NBS .50 1.25
35 Denny Hamlin NBS 1.25 3.00
36 Kenny Wallace NBS .20 .50
37 David Green NBS .20 .50
38 Tony Raines NBS .20 .50
39 Jason Keller NBS .20 .50
40 Kasey Kahne NBS .40 1.00
41 Reed Sorenson NBS .50 1.25
42 Carl Edwards NBS .30 .75
43 Mike Skinner CTS .20 .50
44 Ron Hornaday CTS .20 .50
45 Terry Cook CTS .20 .50
46 Rick Crawford CTS .20 .50
47 Jack Sprague CTS .20 .50
48 Bill Lester CTS .30 .75
49 Dennis Setzer CTS .20 .50
50 Todd Kluever CTS .60 1.50
51 Ricky Craven CTS .20 .50
52 Andy Santerre .20 .50
53 Tony Hirschman .20 .50
54 Justin Diercks .30 .75
55 Mike Duncan .20 .50
56 Jeff Fultz .20 .50
57 Jeff Jefferson .20 .50
58 Buddy Baker .25 .60
59 Jack Ingram .20 .50
60 Fred Lorenzen .25 .60
61 Lee Petty .25 .60
62 Rex White .20 .50
63 Donnie Allison .25 .60
64 Neil Bonnett .30 .75
65 Curtis Turner .25 .60
66 Fireball Roberts .30 .75
67 Kyle Busch RR .40 1.00
68 Travis Kvapil RR .20 .50
69 Carl Edwards RR .30 .75
70 Denny Hamlin RR 1.25 3.00
71 Reed Sorenson RR .50 1.25
72 Todd Kluever RR .60 1.50
73 Jimmie Johnson's Car OTW .50 1.25
74 Dale Jarrett's Car OTW .30 .75
75 Ricky Rudd's Car OTW .25 .60
76 Dale Earnhardt Jr's Car OTW .60 1.50
77 Jeff Gordon's Car OTW .60 1.50
78 Greg Biffle's Car OTW .25 .60
79 Kevin Harvick's Car OTW .40 1.00
80 Jeff Burton's Car OTW .25 .60
81 Mark Martin's Car OTW .30 .75
82 Kurt Busch's Car OTW .25 .60
83 Carl Edwards' Car OTW .30 .75
84 Rusty Wallace's Car OTW .30 .75
85 Jeff Gordon NS .60 1.50
86 Greg Biffle NS .25 .60
87 Carl Edwards NS .30 .75
88 Kevin Harvick NS .40 1.00
89 Kasey Kahne NS .40 1.00
90 Mark Martin NS .30 .75
91 Jimmie Johnson NS .50 1.25
92 Greg Biffle NS .25 .60
93 Tony Stewart NS .50 1.25
94 Tony Stewart NS .50 1.25
95 Matt Kenseth NS .30 .75
96 Kyle Busch NS .40 1.00
97 Dale Earnhardt Jr. U .60 1.50
98 Kasey Kahne U .40 1.00
99 Ryan Newman U .25 .60
100 Tony Stewart U .50 1.25
101 Carl Edwards U .30 .75
102 Martin Truex Jr. U .50 1.25
103 Jimmie Johnson U .50 1.25
104 Jeff Gordon U .60 1.50
105 Matt Kenseth U .30 .75
106 Dale Jarrett U .30 .75
107 Kevin Harvick U .40 1.00
108 Kurt Busch U .25 .60
109 Tony Stewart TT .50 1.25
110 Greg Biffle TT .25 .60
111 Jimmie Johnson TT .50 1.25
112 Rusty Wallace TT .30 .75
113 Mark Martin TT .30 .75
114 Kurt Busch TT .25 .60
115 Jeremy Mayfield TT .20 .50
116 Carl Edwards TT .30 .75
117 Matt Kenseth TT .30 .75
118 Ryan Newman TT .25 .60
119 Checklist CL .10 .30
120 Tony Stewart Schedule .50 1.25
0 Cup Chase 10 4.00 10.00
NNO Santa Claus 3.00 8.00

2006 Press Pass Blue

COMPLETE SET (120) 100.00 200.00
*BLUE: 1.2X TO 3X BASE
STATED ODDS 1 PER HOBBY PACK

2006 Press Pass Gold

COMPLETE SET (120) 125.00 250.00
*GOLD: $$1.2X TO $$3X BASE
STATED ODDS 1 PER RETAIL PACK

2006 Press Pass Platinum

COMPLETE SET (120) 250.00 500.00
*PLATINUM: 2.5X TO 6X BASE
STATED PRINT RUN 100 SERIAL #'d SETS

2006 Press Pass Autographs

STATED ODDS 1:84
1 Bobby Allison 8.00 20.00
2 Buddy Baker 6.00 15.00
3 Dave Blaney NC 6.00 15.00
4 Mike Bliss NC 6.00 15.00
5 Clint Bowyer NBS 15.00 40.00
6 Jeff Burton NCS 8.00 20.00
7 Kurt Busch NC 12.50 30.00
8 Kyle Busch NC 20.00 50.00
9 Terry Cook CTS 6.00 15.00
10 Ricky Craven CTS 8.00 20.00
11 Rick Crawford CTS 5.00 12.00
12 Kerry Earnhardt NBS 8.00 20.00
13 Carl Edwards NBS 15.00 40.00
14 Carl Edwards NCS 15.00 40.00
15 Harry Gant 8.00 20.00
16 Jeff Gordon NC 125.00 250.00
17 Robby Gordon NC 10.00 25.00
18 David Green NBS 5.00 12.00
19 Jeff Green NCS 6.00 15.00
20 Denny Hamlin NBS 20.00 50.00
21 Kevin Harvick NC 12.50 30.00
22 Ron Hornaday CTS 6.00 15.00
23 Dale Jarrett NC 15.00 40.00
24 Jimmie Johnson NC 25.00 60.00
25 Kasey Kahne NBS 20.00 50.00
26 Kasey Kahne NC 20.00 50.00
27 Jason Keller NBS 6.00 15.00
28 Matt Kenseth NC 15.00 40.00
29 Todd Kluever CTS 8.00 20.00
30 Travis Kvapil NC 10.00 25.00
31 Bobby Labonte NC 15.00 40.00
32 Justin Labonte NBS 8.00 20.00
33 Bill Lester CTS 8.00 20.00
34 Fred Lorenzen 6.00 15.00
35 Sterling Marlin NC 15.00 30.00
36 Mark Martin NC 30.00 60.00
37 Jeremy Mayfield NC 8.00 20.00
38 Jamie McMurray NC 10.00 25.00
39 Casey Mears NC 10.00 25.00
40 Joe Nemechek NC 8.00 20.00
41 Ryan Newman NC 15.00 30.00
42 Marvin Panch 5.00 12.00
43 Benny Parsons 15.00 40.00
44 David Pearson 10.00 25.00
45 Richard Petty 20.00 50.00
46 Tony Raines NBS 5.00 12.00
47 Ricky Rudd NCS 10.00 25.00
48 Boris Said NC 8.00 20.00
49 Johnny Sauter NBS 6.00 15.00
50 Ken Schrader NCS 8.00 20.00
51 Dennis Setzer CTS 6.00 15.00
52 Jack Sprague CTS 6.00 15.00
53 Tony Stewart NC 25.00 60.00
54 Martin Truex Jr. NBS 8.00 20.00
55 Brian Vickers NC 8.00 20.00
56 Rex White 5.00 12.00
57 Glen Wood 6.00 15.00
58 Jon Wood NBS 6.00 15.00
59 Cale Yarborough 10.00 25.00
60 J.J. Yeley NBS 8.00 20.00
61 Rusty Wallace

2006 Press Pass Blaster Kmart

COMPLETE SET (6) 8.00 20.00
CEC Carl Edwards .50 1.25
DEC Dale Earnhardt Jr. 1.00 2.50
JGC Jeff Gordon 1.00 2.50
KHC Kevin Harvick .60 1.50
KKC Kasey Kahne .60 1.50
TSC Tony Stewart .75 2.00

2006 Press Pass Blaster Target

COMPLETE SET (6) 8.00 20.00
CEB Carl Edwards .50 1.25
DEB Dale Earnhardt Jr. 1.00 2.50
JGB Jeff Gordon 1.00 2.50
KHB Kevin Harvick .60 1.50
KKB Kasey Kahne .60 1.50
TSB Tony Stewart .75 2.00

2006 Press Pass Blaster Wal-Mart

COMPLETE SET (6) 8.00 20.00
CEA Carl Edwards .50 1.25
DEA Dale Earnhardt Jr. 1.00 2.50
JGA Jeff Gordon 1.00 2.50
KHA Kevin Harvick .60 1.50
KKA Kasey Kahne .60 1.50
TSA Tony Stewart .75 2.00

2006 Press Pass Burning Rubber Autographs

STATED PRINT RUN 2-99
BRCE Carl Edwards/99 25.00 60.00
BRJG Jeff Gordon/24 100.00 200.00
BRJJ Jimmie Johnson/48 60.00 120.00
BRKB Kyle Busch/5
BRKH Kevin Harvick/29 60.00 120.00
BRKK Kasey Kahne/9
BRMK Matt Kenseth/17
BRMM Mark Martin/6
BRRN Ryan Newman/12
BRRW Rusty Wallace/2
BRTS Tony Stewart/20 75.00 150.00

2006 Press Pass Burning Rubber Drivers

STATED ODDS 1:112
STATED PRINT RUN 100 SERIAL #'d SETS
*CARS/370: .25X TO .6X DRIVERS/100
UNPRICED GOLD PRINT RUN 1
BRD1 Kurt Busch 8.00 20.00
BRD2 Kyle Busch 8.00 20.00
BRD3 Dale Earnhardt Jr. 15.00 40.00
BRD4 Carl Edwards 12.00 30.00
BRD5 Jeff Gordon 15.00 40.00
BRD6 Kevin Harvick 8.00 20.00
BRD7 Dale Jarrett 8.00 20.00
BRD8 Jimmie Johnson 12.00 30.00
BRD9 Kasey Kahne 10.00 25.00
BRD10 Matt Kenseth 10.00 25.00
BRD11 Bobby Labonte 10.00 25.00
BRD12 Terry Labonte 10.00 25.00
BRD13 Mark Martin 10.00 25.00
BRD14 Jamie McMurray 6.00 15.00
BRD15 Ricky Rudd 6.00 15.00
BRD16 Tony Stewart 12.00 30.00
BRD17 Martin Truex Jr. 10.00 25.00
BRD18 Rusty Wallace 10.00 25.00

2006 Press Pass Cup Chase

STATED ODDS 1:28
CCR1 Tony Stewart 8.00 20.00
CCR2 Greg Biffle 6.00 15.00
CCR3 Jimmie Johnson Winner 12.50 25.00
CCR4 Kurt Busch 6.00 12.00
CCR5 Kyle Busch Winner 8.00 20.00
CCR6 Carl Edwards 6.00 15.00
CCR7 Matt Kenseth Winner 8.00 20.00
CCR8 Jamie McMurray 6.00 12.00
CCR9 Ryan Newman 7.50 15.00
CCR10 Jeff Gordon Winner 15.00 30.00
CCR11 Ricky Rudd 4.00 8.00
CCR12 Dale Earnhardt Jr. Winner 15.00 30.00
CCR13 Dale Jarrett 6.00 12.00
CCR14 Kevin Harvick Winner 10.00 25.00
CCR15 Bobby Labonte 5.00 10.00
CCR16 Elliott Sadler 6.00 12.00
CCR17 Jeff Burton Winner 10.00 25.00
CCR18 Field Card Winner 12.50 25.00

2006 Press Pass Cup Chase Prizes

COMPLETE SET (10) 8.00 20.00
CC1 Jimmie Johnson 1.00 2.50
CC2 Matt Kenseth .60 1.50
CC3 Denny Hamlin 2.50 6.00
CC4 Kevin Harvick .75 2.00
CC5 Dale Earnhardt Jr. 1.25 3.00
CC6 Jeff Gordon 1.25 3.00
CC7 Jeff Burton .50 1.25
CC8 Kasey Kahne .75 2.00
CC9 Mark Martin .60 1.50
CC10 Kyle Busch .75 2.00
CCP1 Jimmie Johnson FS/475 15.00 40.00

2006 Press Pass Game Face

COMPLETE SET (9) 10.00 25.00
STATED ODDS 1:6
GF1 Jeff Gordon 1.25 3.00
GF2 Mark Martin .60 1.50
GF3 Ricky Rudd .50 1.25
GF4 Dale Earnhardt Jr. 1.25 3.00
GF5 Dale Jarrett .60 1.50
GF6 Jimmie Johnson 1.00 2.50
GF7 Bobby Labonte .60 1.50
GF8 Martin Truex Jr. 1.00 2.50
GF9 Jeff Burton .50 1.25

2006 Press Pass Snapshots

COMPLETE SET (36) 12.50 30.00
STATED ODDS 1:2
SN1 John Andretti .20 .50
SN2 Tony Raines .20 .50
SN3 Jeff Burton .25 .60
SN4 Bobby Labonte .30 .75
SN5 Kasey Kahne .40 1.00
SN6 Terry Cook .20 .50
SN7 Jimmie Johnson .50 1.25
SN8 Ricky Craven .20 .50
SN9 Rick Crawford .20 .50
SN10 Dave Blaney .20 .50
SN11 Dale Earnhardt Jr. .60 1.50
SN12 Dennis Setzer .20 .50
SN13 Kyle Petty .25 .60
SN14 John Andretti .20 .50
SN15 Dale Jarrett .30 .75
SN16 Kenny Wallace .20 .50
SN17 Jimmie Johnson .50 1.25
SN18 Kerry Earnhardt .30 .75
SN19 Martin Truex Jr. .50 1.25
SN20 Jason Keller .20 .50
SN21 Todd Kluever .60 1.50
SN22 Boris Said .20 .50
SN23 Bobby Labonte .30 .75
SN24 Johnny Sauter .30 .75
SN25 Mark Martin .30 .75
SN26 Ron Hornaday .20 .50
SN27 Ricky Rudd .25 .60
SN28 Ricky Craven .20 .50
SN29 Jeff Burton .25 .60
SN30 Jeff Gordon .60 1.50
SN31 Dale Jarrett .30 .75
SN32 Mike Skinner .20 .50
SN33 Dave Blaney .20 .50
SN34 Mark Martin .30 .75
SN35 Martin Truex Jr. .50 1.25
SN36 Ricky Rudd CL .25 .60

2006 Press Pass Velocity

COMPLETE SET (9) 15.00 40.00
STATED ODDS 1:12
VE1 Dale Earnhardt Jr. 1.50 4.00
VE2 Mark Martin .75 2.00
VE3 Carl Edwards .75 2.00
VE4 Jeff Gordon 1.50 4.00
VE5 Ricky Rudd .60 1.50
VE6 Tony Stewart 1.25 3.00
VE7 Martin Truex Jr. 1.25 3.00
VE8 Jimmie Johnson 1.25 3.00
VE9 Dale Jarrett .75 2.00

2007 Press Pass

This 120-card set was released December 2006. This set was issued in six card packs which came 28 packs to a hobby and 24 packs per retail box. Both hobby and retail boxes were packed 20 boxes to a case. The SRP for both hobby and retail packs was $2.99. There was a special 00 card honoring the 2006 Cup Chase drivers which was inserted into packs at a rate of one in 72. There was also an un-numbered Happy Holidays Santa card which was inserted into packs at a rate of one in 72.

COMPLETE SET (120) 15.00 40.00
WAX BOX HOBBY (28) 60.00 90.00
WAX BOX RETAIL (28) 50.00 75.00
1 Matt Kenseth .30 .75
2 Jimmie Johnson .50 1.25
3 Kevin Harvick .40 1.00
4 Kyle Busch .40 1.00
5 Denny Hamlin .40 1.00
6 Dale Earnhardt Jr. .60 1.50
7 Mark Martin .30 .75
8 Jeff Burton .25 .60
9 Jeff Gordon .60 1.50
10 Kasey Kahne .30 .75
11 Tony Stewart .50 1.25
12 Greg Biffle .25 .60
13 Carl Edwards .30 .75
14 Kurt Busch .25 .60
15 Casey Mears .20 .50
16 Clint Bowyer .30 .75
17 Ryan Newman .25 .60
18 Scott Riggs .25 .60
19 Jamie McMurray .30 .75
20 Brian Vickers .30 .75
21 Reed Sorenson .20 .50
22 Martin Truex Jr. .25 .60
23 Dale Jarrett .30 .75
24 Bobby Labonte .30 .75
25 Robby Gordon .20 .50
26 J.J. Yeley .30 .75
27 Dave Blaney .20 .50
28 Ken Schrader .20 .50
29 Joe Nemechek .20 .50
30 Sterling Marlin .30 .75
31 Kyle Petty .25 .60
32 David Stremme .20 .50
33 Tony Raines .20 .50
34 Kevin Harvick NBS .40 1.00
35 Carl Edwards NBS .30 .75
36 Denny Hamlin NBS .40 1.00
37 Clint Bowyer NBS .30 .75
38 J.J. Yeley NBS .30 .75
39 Paul Menard NBS 1.00 2.50
40 Jon Wood NBS .30 .75
41 David Green NBS .20 .50
42 Todd Kluever NBS .30 .75
43 Regan Smith NBS .60 1.50
44 Danny O'Quinn NBS .50 1.25
45 Steve Wallace NBS .30 .75
46 Ron Hornaday CTS .20 .50
47 Erik Darnell CTS .50 1.25
48 Mike Skinner CTS .20 .50
49 Bill Lester CTS .30 .75
50 Erin Crocker CTS 1.00 2.50
51 David Ragan CTS .60 1.50
52 Mike Olsen RC .50 1.25
53 Gary Lewis RC .50 1.25
54 J.R. Norris RC .60 1.50
55 Davey Allison .50 1.25
56 Buddy Baker .25 .60
57 Neil Bonnett .30 .75
58 Fred Lorenzen .25 .60
59 Marvin Panch .20 .50
60 Fireball Roberts .30 .75
61 Rusty Wallace .30 .75
62 Rex White .20 .50
63 Glen Wood .20 .50
64 Clint Bowyer RR .30 .75
65 Denny Hamlin RR .40 1.00
66 Reed Sorenson RR .20 .50
67 David Stremme RR .20 .50
68 Martin Truex Jr. RR .25 .60
69 J.J. Yeley RR .30 .75
70 Todd Kluever RR .30 .75
71 Erin Crocker RR 1.00 2.50
72 Erik Darnell RR .50 1.25
73 Jeff Gordon's Car OT .25 .60
74 Mark Martin's Car OT .12 .30
75 Matt Kenseth's Car OT .12 .30
76 Kevin Harvick's car OT .15 .40
77 Jimmie Johnson's Car OT .20 .50
78 Dale Jarrett's Car OT .12 .30
79 Tony Stewart's Car OT .20 .50
80 Denny Hamlin's Car OT .15 .40
81 Kurt Busch's Car OT .15 .40
82 Carl Edwards' Car OT .12 .30
83 Terry Labonte's Car OT .12 .30
84 Kasey Kahne's Car OT .12 .30
85 Greg Biffle NS .25 .60
86 Dale Earnhardt Jr. NS .60 1.50
87 Kurt Busch NS .25 .60
88 Carl Edwards NS .30 .75
89 Kasey Kahne NS .30 .75
90 Denny Hamlin NS .40 1.00
91 Tony Stewart NS .50 1.25
92 Kyle Busch NS .40 1.00
93 K.Harvick
D.Harvick NS .40 1.00
94 Jimmie Johnson NS .50 1.25
95 Matt Kenseth NS .30 .75
96 Jimmie Johnson U .50 1.25
97 Kevin Harvick U .40 1.00
98 Denny Hamlin U .40 1.00
99 Kurt Busch U .25 .60
100 Jeff Gordon U .60 1.50
101 Kasey Kahne U .30 .75
102 Greg Biffle U .25 .60
103 Tony Stewart U .50 1.25
104 Kyle Busch U .40 1.00
105 Matt Kenseth U .30 .75
106 Dale Earnhardt Jr. U .60 1.50
107 Jeff Burton U .25 .60
108 Matt Kenseth TT .30 .75
109 Jimmie Johnson TT .50 1.25
110 Kevin Harvick TT .40 1.00
111 Kyle Busch TT .40 1.00
112 Denny Hamlin TT .40 1.00
113 Dale Earnhardt Jr. TT .60 1.50
114 Mark Martin TT .30 .75
115 Jeff Burton TT .25 .60
116 Jeff Gordon TT .60 1.50
117 Kasey Kahne TT .30 .75
118 Schedule .15 .40
119 Juan Pablo Montoya RC 1.00 2.50
CL Jimmie Johnson CL .50 1.25
00 Cup Chase Top 10 4.00 10.00
NNO Santa Happy Holidays 2.50 6.00

2007 Press Pass Blue

COMPLETE SET (120) 25.00 60.00
*BLUE: .6X TO 1.5X BASE
STATED ODDS 1 PER HOBBY PACK

2007 Press Pass Gold

COMPLETE SET (120) 40.00 80.00
*GOLD: 1.2X TO 3X BASE

2007 Press Pass Platinum

*PLATINUM: 4X TO 10X BASE

2007 Press Pass Autographs

Inserted at a stated rate of one in 84 hobby and one in 96 retail, these 40 signed cards feature a mix of today's NASCAR Nextel Cup drivers as as Busch Series and Craftsman Truck Series drivers. Some of these cards were available in packs of 2007 Press Pass and 2007 Press Pass Eclipse or both, and are tagged as such.

UNPRICED PRESS PLATE PRINT RUN 1
1 Greg Biffle NC P 6.00 15
2 Dave Blaney NC P 6.00 15
3 Clint Bowyer NC P 12.00 30
4 Kurt Busch NC P 12.00 30
5 Kyle Busch 15.00 40
6 Jeff Burton NC P 8.00 20.
7 Terry Cook CTS P 6.00 15
8 Rick Crawford CTS P 6.00 15.
9 Erin Crocker CTS P 15.00 40.
10 Erik Darnell CTS P 5.00 12.
11 Dale Earnhardt Jr. 30.00 80.
12 Carl Edwards NC P 15.00 40.
13 Jeff Gordon 50.00 100.
14 David Green NBS P 6.00 15.
15 Jeff Green 5.00 12.
16 Denny Hamlin NC P 15.00 40.
17 Kevin Harvick NC P 12.00 30.
18 Ron Hornaday CTS P 6.00 15.0
19 Dale Jarrett 12.00 30.0
20 Jimmie Johnson 25.00 60.
21 Kasey Kahne 20.00 50.
22 Matt Kenseth NC P 12.00 30.0
23 Todd Kluever NBS P 10.00 25.0
24 Bobby Labonte NC P 10.00 25.0
25 Terry Labonte NC P 12.00 30.0
26 Burney Lamar NBS P 6.00 15.0
27 Bill Lester CTS P 8.00 20.0
28 Sterling Marlin NC P 10.00 25.0
29 Mark Martin NC P 15.00 40.0
30 Jamie McMurray NC P 10.00 25.0
31 Casey Mears NC P 10.00 25.0
32 Paul Menard 5.00 12.0
33 Joe Nemechek NC P 8.00 20.0
34 Ryan Newman NC P 8.00 20.0
35 Danny O'Quinn NBS P 6.00 15.0
36 David Ragan CTS P 8.00 20.0
37 Tony Raines NC P 6.00 15.0
38 Scott Riggs NC P 5.00 12.0
39 Johnny Sauter NBS P 8.00 20.0
40 Mike Skinner CTS P 6.00 15.0
41 Regan Smith NBS P 6.00 15.0
42 Reed Sorenson NC P 6.00 15.0
43 Tony Stewart NC P 20.00 50.0
44 David Stremme NC P 8.00 20.0
45 Martin Truex Jr. NC P 12.00 30.0
46 Brian Vickers NC P 10.00 25.0
47 Steve Wallace NBS P 12.00 30.0
48 Jon Wood NBS P 5.00 12.0
49 J.J. Yeley 8.00 20.00

2007 Press Pass Burning Rubber Autographs

STATED PRINT RUN 8-48
BRSJG Jeff Gordon/24 100.00 200.00
BRSJJ Jimmie Johnson/48 60.00 120.00
BRSKB Kurt Busch/2
BRSKH Kevin Harvick/29 50.00 100.00
BRSMK Matt Kenseth/17
BRSTS Tony Stewart/20 100.00 200.00

2007 Press Pass Burning Rubber Drivers

This 18-card set featured swatches of race-used, race-win, tires. Each card was noted as to which race the tires were used. They were inserted in packs of 2007 Press Pass Hobby packs at a rate of one in 112, and they were serial numbered to 75 copies. Each card carried a "BRD" prefix to its card number.

UNPRICED GOLD PRINT RUN 1
*TEAM/325: .3X TO .8X DRIVERS/75
BRD1 Jimmie Johnson Daytona 20.00 50.00
BRD2 Matt Kenseth California 15.00 40.00
BRD3 Tony Stewart Martinsville 20.00 50.00
BRD4 Kasey Kahne Texas 15.00 40.00
BRD5 Kevin Harvick Phoenix 15.00 40.00
BRD6 Jimmie Johnson Talladega 20.00 50.00
BRD7 Dale Earnhardt Jr. Richmond 30.00 80.00
BRD8 Greg Biffle Darlington 12.00 30.00
BRD9 Kasey Kahne Charlotte 15.00 40.00
BRD10 Denny Hamlin Pocono 6-11 12.00 30.00
BRD11 Jeff Gordon Sonoma 30.00 80.00
BRD12 Tony Stewart Daytona 20.00 50.00

BRD13 Jeff Gordon Chicago 7-9 30.00 80.00
BRD14 Kyle Busch N.Hampshire 12.00 30.00
BRD15 Denny Hamlin Pocono 7-23 12.00 30.00
BRD16 Jimmie Johnson Indianapolis 15.00 40.00
BRD17 Kevin Harvick Watkins Glen 15.00 40.00
BRD18 Jeff Burton Dover 12.00 30.00

2007 Press Pass Cup Chase

These 18 cards were issued in packs of 2007 Press Pass at a rate of one in 20 hobby, and one in 36 retail packs. There were 17 drivers and 1 field card. If the driver pictured on the front qualified for the Chase, that card was redeemable, along with $3.95 for s&h, for a complete set of 12 of the prize cards. The set included only those drivers that qualified for the Chase. If you had the champion, you were also sent a special memorabilia card of his. The exchange deadline for these was December 31, 2007. Cards that were redeemable are noted below. Redeemed cards were stamped by Press Pass and returned. The cards featured the driver's car on the card front.

CCR1 Jeff Gordon Winner 15.00 40.00
CCR2 Bobby Labonte 2.50 6.00
CCR3 Kasey Kahne 2.00 5.00
CCR4 Matt Kenseth Winner 8.00 20.00
CCR5 Tony Stewart Winner 10.00 25.00
CCR6 Ryan Newman 2.00 5.00
CCR7 Jamie McMurray 2.00 5.00
CCR8 J.Johnson Winner Champ 40.00 80.00
CCR9 Greg Biffle 2.00 5.00
CCR10 Jeff Burton Winner 6.00 15.00
CCR11 Martin Truex Jr. Winner 6.00 15.00
CCR12 Denny Hamlin Winner 8.00 20.00
CCR13 Kurt Busch Winner 8.00 20.00
CCR14 Dale Earnhardt Jr. 5.00 12.00
CCR15 Kyle Busch Winner 8.00 20.00
CCR16 Kevin Harvick Winner 8.00 20.00
CCR17 Carl Edwards Winner 8.00 20.00
CCR18 Field Card Winner 4.00 10.00

2007 Press Pass Cup Chase Prizes

COMPLETE SET (12) 6.00 15.00
ISSUED VIA MAIL REDEMPTION
CC1 Jimmie Johnson .75 2.00
CC2 Jeff Gordon 1.00 2.50
CC3 Tony Stewart .75 2.00
CC4 Carl Edwards .50 1.25
CC5 Kurt Busch .40 1.00
CC6 Denny Hamlin .60 1.50
CC7 Martin Truex Jr. .40 1.00
CC8 Matt Kenseth .50 1.25
CC9 Kyle Busch .60 1.50
CC10 Jeff Burton .40 1.00
CC11 Kevin Harvick .60 1.50
CC12 Clint Bowyer .50 1.25
CCP1 Jimmie Johnson TIRE 20.00 40.00

2007 Press Pass Race Day

This 12-card set was inserted into packs of 2007 Press Pass at a rate of one in six in both Hobby and Retail packs. The cards carried a "RD" prefix for their card numbers.

COMPLETE SET (12) 15.00 40.00
STATED ODDS 1:6
RD1 Jeff Gordon 1.25 3.00
RD2 Dale Jarrett .60 1.50
RD3 Tony Stewart 1.00 2.50
RD4 Kevin Harvick .75 2.00
RD5 Jimmie Johnson 1.00 2.50
RD6 Dale Earnhardt Jr. 1.25 3.00
RD7 Denny Hamlin .75 2.00
RD8 Jeff Burton .50 1.25
RD9 Mark Martin .60 1.50
RD10 Kasey Kahne .60 1.50
RD11 Martin Truex Jr. .50 1.25
RD12 Bobby Labonte .60 1.50

2007 Press Pass Snapshots

This 36-card insert set was found in packs of 2007 Press Pass. The cards were inserted at a rate of one in two packs.

COMPLETE SET (36) 12.50 25.00
STATED ODDS 1:2
SN1 Greg Biffle .30 .75
SN2 Dave Blaney .25 .60
SN3 Jeff Burton .30 .75
SN4 Kurt Busch .30 .75
SN5 Dale Earnhardt Jr. .75 2.00
SN6 Carl Edwards .40 1.00
SN7 Jeff Gordon .75 2.00
SN8 Robby Gordon .25 .60
SN9 Jeff Green .25 .60
SN10 Denny Hamlin .50 1.25
SN11 Kevin Harvick .50 1.25
SN12 Dale Jarrett .40 1.00
SN13 Jimmie Johnson .60 1.50
SN14 Kasey Kahne .40 1.00
SN15 Matt Kenseth .40 1.00
SN16 Bobby Labonte .40 1.00
SN17 Terry Labonte .40 1.00
SN18 Sterling Marlin .40 1.00
SN19 Mark Martin .40 1.00
SN20 Jamie McMurray .40 1.00
SN21 Joe Nemechek .25 .60
SN22 Tony Raines .25 .60
SN23 Scott Riggs .30 .75
SN24 Ken Schrader .25 .60
SN25 Reed Sorenson .25 .60
SN26 Tony Stewart .60 1.50
SN27 Martin Truex Jr. .30 .75
SN28 David Green .25 .60
SN29 Paul Menard 1.25 3.00
SN30 Danny O'Quinn .60 1.50
SN31 Regan Smith .75 2.00
SN32 Steve Wallace .40 1.00
SN33 Jon Wood .40 1.00
SN34 Rick Crawford .25 .60
SN35 Erik Darnell .60 1.50
SN36 Ron Hornaday CL .25 .60

2007 Press Pass Velocity

This 9-card set was inserted into packs of 2007 Press Pass at a rate of one in 12 packs. Each card carried a "V" prefix for its card number.

COMPLETE SET (9) 15.00 40.00
STATED ODDS 1:12
V1 Kasey Kahne .60 1.50
V2 Jimmie Johnson 1.00 2.50
V3 Matt Kenseth .60 1.50
V4 Dale Earnhardt Jr. 1.25 3.00
V5 Jeff Gordon 1.25 3.00
V6 Dale Jarrett .60 1.50
V7 Jamie McMurray .60 1.50
V8 Tony Stewart 1.00 2.50
V9 Denny Hamlin .60 1.50

2007 Press Pass K-Mart

This 6-card insert set was available in 2-card bonus packs in the 2007 Press Pass blaster boxes found at K-Mart. Each card carried a "C" suffix for its card number.

COMPLETE SET (6) 15.00 40.00
DEC Dale Earnhardt Jr. 2.00 5.00
JGC Jeff Gordon 2.00 5.00
JJC Jimmie Johnson 1.50 4.00
KHC Kevin Harvick 1.25 3.00
KKC Kasey Kahne 1.00 2.50
TSC Tony Stewart 1.50 4.00

2007 Press Pass Target

This 6-card insert set was available in 2-card bonus packs in the 2007 Press Pass blaster boxes found at Target. Each card carried a "B" suffix for its card number.

COMPLETE SET (6) 12.50 30.00
DEB Dale Earnhardt Jr. 2.00 5.00
JGB Jeff Gordon 2.00 5.00
JJB Jimmie Johnson 1.50 4.00
KHB Kevin Harvick 1.25 3.00
KKB Kasey Kahne 1.00 2.50
TSB Tony Stewart 1.50 4.00

2007 Press Pass Target Race Win Tires

This 9-card set featured swatches of race-used, race-win tires. Each card noted the date and location of the victory. These carried a "RW" prefix for the card number. These were only available inside the 2007 Press Pass box blaster packs from Target. Each card was serial numbered to 50.

RW1 Jimmie Johnson Daytona 40.00 80.00
RW2 Kevin Harvick Phoenix 30.00 60.00
RW3 Dale Earnhardt Jr. Richmond 50.00 100.00
RW4 Denny Hamlin Pocono 6-11
RW5 Kasey Kahne Michigan 50.00 100.00
RW6 Jeff Gordon Sonoma 50.00 100.00
RW7 Tony Stewart Daytona
RW8 Jeff Gordon Chicago 50.00 100.00
RW9 Matt Kenseth Bristol 40.00 80.00

2007 Press Pass Wal-Mart

This 6-card insert set was available in 2-card bonus packs in the 2007 Press Pass blaster boxes found at Wal-Mart. Each card carried an "A" suffix for its card number.

COMPLETE SET (6) 12.50 30.00
DEA Dale Earnhardt Jr. 1.50 4.00
JGA Jeff Gordon 1.50 4.00
JJA Jimmie Johnson 1.25 3.00
KHA Kevin Harvick 1.00 2.50
KKA Kasey Kahne .75 2.00
TSA Tony Stewart 1.25 3.00

2007 Press Pass Wal-Mart Autographs

This 6-card autograph set was randomly inserted in blaster box packs found only at Wal-Mart. The cards were serial numbered to 45 or 50.

STATED PRINT RUN 45-50
CE Carl Edwards/50 25.00 60.00
JG Jeff Gordon/45 50.00 120.00
KH Kevin Harvick/50 20.00 50.00
KK Kasey Kahne/45 20.00 50.00
MK Matt Kenseth/50
MM Mark Martin/50 25.00 60.00
MT Martin Truex Jr./50 20.00 50.00
TS Tony Stewart/50 40.00 100.00

2008 Press Pass

COMPLETE SET (120) 12.50 30.00
WAX BOX HOBBY (28) 60.00 100.00
WAX BOX RETAIL (24) 50.00 75.00
1 Jeff Gordon .60 1.50
2 Tony Stewart .50 1.25
3 Denny Hamlin .40 1.00
4 Matt Kenseth .30 .75
5 Carl Edwards .30 .75
6 Jimmie Johnson .50 1.25
7 Jeff Burton .25 .60
8 Kyle Busch .40 1.00
9 Clint Bowyer .30 .75
10 Kevin Harvick .40 1.00
11 Martin Truex Jr. .25 .60
12 Kurt Busch .25 .60
13 Dale Earnhardt Jr. .60 1.50
14 Ryan Newman .25 .60
15 Greg Biffle .25 .60
16 Casey Mears .20 .50
17 Bobby Labonte .30 .75
18 Juan Pablo Montoya .50 1.25
19 Jamie McMurray .30 .75
20 J.J. Yeley .30 .75
21 Mark Martin .30 .75
22 Kasey Kahne .30 .75
23 David Ragan .25 .60
24 Elliott Sadler .20 .50
25 Jeff Green .20 .50
26 Ricky Rudd .25 .60
27 Tony Raines .20 .50
28 Johnny Sauter .30 .75
29 Dave Blaney .20 .50
30 Paul Menard .20 .50
31 Scott Riggs .25 .60
32 Kyle Petty .25 .60
33 Brian Vickers .20 .50
34 Dale Jarrett .30 .75
35 Ken Schrader .25 .60
36 Michael Waltrip .30 .75
37 Carl Edwards NBS .30 .75
38 Stephen Leicht NBS .30 .75
39 Marcos Ambrose NBS .50 1.25
40 Scott Wimmer NBS .25 .60
41 Steve Wallace NBS .30 .75
42 Todd Kluever NBS .30 .75
43 Kelly Bires NBS .30 .75
44 Sam Hornish Jr. NBS .50 1.25
45 Cale Gale NBS .20 .50
46 Mike Skinner CTS .20 .50
47 Ron Hornaday CTS .20 .50
48 Todd Bodine CTS .20 .50
49 Rick Crawford CTS .20 .50
50 Jack Sprague CTS .20 .50
51 Erik Darnell CTS .25 .60
52 T.J. Bell CTS .30 .75
53 Travis Kvapil CTS .20 .50
54 Joey Clanton CTS RC .60 1.50
55 Buddy Baker .25 .60
56 Rusty Wallace .30 .75
57 Tim Flock .20 .50
58 Lee Petty .25 .60
59 Jack Ingram .20 .50
60 Tim Richmond .25 .60
61 Dale Earnhardt 2.00 5.00
62 Glen Wood .20 .50
63 Rex White .20 .50
64 Jeff Gordon's Car BFS .25 .60
65 Martin Truex Jr.'s Car BFS .10 .25
66 Dale Jarrett's Car BFS .12 .30
67 Jeff Burton's Car BFS .10 .25
68 Jimmie Johnson's Car BFS .20 .50
69 Jamie McMurray's Car BFS .12 .30
70 Mark Martin's Car BFS .12 .30
71 Ricky Rudd's Car BFS .10 .25
72 Ryan Newman's Car BFS .10 .25
73 Juan Pablo Montoya NS .50 1.25
74 D.Gilliland/R.Rudd NS .25 .60
75 K.Harvick/M.Martin Cars NS .15 .40
76 Kevin Harvick NS .40 1.00
77 Casey Mears NS .20 .50
78 Juan Pablo Montoya NS .50 1.25
79 Martin Truex Jr. NS .25 .60
80 J.Montoya/K.Harvick NS .50 1.25
81 Jimmie Johnson NS .50 1.25
82 Juan Pablo Montoya RR .50 1.25
83 David Ragan RR .25 .60
84 Paul Menard RR .20 .50
85 David Reutimann RR .25 .60
86 David Ragan NBS RR .25 .60
87 Marcos Ambrose RR .50 1.25
88 Kevin Harvick's Car U .15 .40
89 Juan Pablo Montoya's Car U .20 .50
90 Martin Truex Jr.'s Car U .10 .25
91 Jamie McMurray's Car U .12 .30
92 Jeff Gordon's Car U .25 .60
93 Jeff Burton's Car U .10 .25
94 Kyle Busch's Car U .15 .40
95 Tony Stewart's Car U .20 .50
96 Dale Jr. First Cup Start .60 1.50
97 Dale Jr. Rookie All-Star .60 1.50
98 Dale Jr. First Cup Win .60 1.50
99 Dale Jr. Best Finish .60 1.50
100 Dale Jr. Most Wins .60 1.50
101 Dale Jr. Daytona Win .60 1.50
102 Dale Jr. Talladega .60 1.50
103 Dale Jr. Daytona .60 1.50
104 Dale Jr. AMP .60 1.50
105 Dale Jr. National Guard .60 1.50
106 Dale Jr. HMS .60 1.50
107 Jimmie Johnson Top 12 .50 1.25
108 Jeff Gordon Top 12 .60 1.50
109 Tony Stewart Top 12 .50 1.25
110 Carl Edwards Top 12 .30 .75
111 Kurt Busch Top 12 .25 .60
112 Denny Hamlin Top 12 .40 1.00
113 Martin Truex Jr. Top 12 .25 .60
114 Matt Kenseth Top 12 .30 .75
115 Kyle Busch Top 12 .40 1.00
116 Jeff Burton Top 12 .25 .60
117 Kevin Harvick Top 12 .40 1.00
118 Clint Bowyer Top 12 .30 .75
119 Schedule .12 .30
120 Michael Waltrip CL .30 .75
00 Cup Chase Contenders 4.00 10.00
0 Santa Claus 2.50 6.00

2008 Press Pass Blue

COMPLETE SET (120) 25.00 60.00
*BLUE: 1.2X TO 3X BASE
STATED ODDS 1 PER RETAIL PACK

2008 Press Pass Gold

COMPLETE SET (120) 60.00 120.00
*GOLD: .8X TO 2X BASE
STATED ODDS 1 PER HOBBY PACK

2008 Press Pass Platinum

*PLATINUM: 4X TO 10X BASE
STATED PRINT RUN 100 SERIAL #'d SETS

2008 Press Pass Autographs

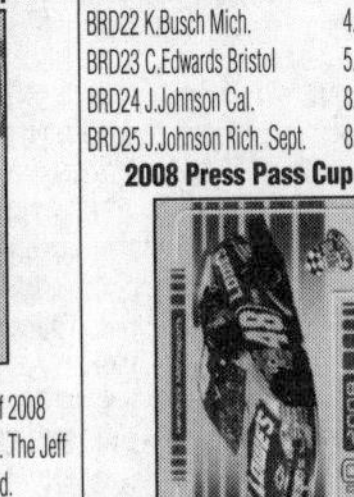

This 46-card set was released in packs of 2008 Press Pass and 2008 Press Pass Eclipse. The Jeff Gordon was released as an exchange card.

STATED ODDS 1:84 H, 1:96 R PP '08
STATED ODDS 1:20 H, 1:96 R ECLIPSE
UNPRICED PRESS PLATE PRINT RUN 1
1 A.J. Allmendinger NC P/E 8.00 20.00
2 Aric Almirola NBS P/E 6.00 15.00
3 Marcos Ambrose NBS P/E 15.00 40.00
4 T.J. Bell CTS E 5.00 12.00
5 Greg Biffle NC P/E 12.50 30.00
6 Kelly Bires NBS P/E 8.00 20.00
7 Dave Blaney NC P 8.00 20.00
8 Clint Bowyer NC P/E 15.00 40.00
9 Kurt Busch NC E 12.00 30.00
10 Kyle Busch NC P/E 20.00 50.00
11 Joey Clanton CTS P/E 5.00 15.00
12 Rick Crawford CTS E 6.00 15.00
13 Erik Darnell CTS E 8.00 20.00
14 Dale Earnhardt Jr. NC P/E 40.00 100.00
15 Jeff Gordon NC P/E 100.00 175.00
16 Denny Hamlin NC P/E 20.00 50.00
17 Kevin Harvick NC P/E 15.00 40.00
18 Ron Hornaday CTS P/E 5.00 15.00
19 Dale Jarrett NC P/E 20.00 40.00
20 Jimmie Johnson NC P 20.00 50.00
21 Kasey Kahne NC P/E 20.00 50.00
22 Matt Kenseth NC P/E 25.00 50.00
23 Todd Kluever NBS P/E 8.00 20.00
24 Travis Kvapil CTS E 6.00 15.00
25 Bobby Labonte NC P/E 15.00 30.00
26 Mark Martin NC P/E 15.00 40.00
27 Casey Mears NC P/E 12.00 30.00
28 Paul Menard NC P/E 10.00 25.00
29 Ryan Newman NC P/E 12.00 30.00
30 David Ragan NC P/E 8.00 20.00
31 Tony Raines NC P/E 5.00 15.00
32 Scott Riggs NC P/E 6.00 15.00
33 Elliott Sadler NC P/E 8.00 20.00
34 Johnny Sauter NBS E 6.00 15.00
35 Ken Schrader NC P/E 6.00 15.00
36 Mike Skinner CTS E 6.00 15.00
37 Regan Smith NC P/E 6.00 15.00
38 Reed Sorenson NC E 8.00 20.00
39 Jack Sprague CTS P/E 5.00 12.00
40 Tony Stewart NC P 50.00 100.00
41 Martin Truex Jr. NC P/E 12.00 30.00
42 Brian Vickers NC P/E 8.00 20.00
43 Michael Waltrip NC P/E 10.00 25.00
44 Scott Wimmer NBS P/E 6.00 15.00
45 Jon Wood NBS P/E 5.00 15.00
46 J.J. Yeley NC P/E 6.00 15.00

2008 Press Pass Burning Rubber Autographs

SERIAL #'d TO DRIVER'S DOOR #
STATED PRINT RUN 5-99
BRCE Carl Edwards/99 50.00 100.00
BRCM Casey Mears/25 30.00 80.00
BRDE Dale Earnhardt Jr./8
BRDH Denny Hamlin/11
BRJG Jeff Gordon/24 80.00 150.00
BRKB Kyle Busch/5
BRKH Kevin Harvick/29 50.00 100.00

2008 Press Pass Burning Rubber Drivers

STATED ODDS 1:112
STATED PRINT RUN 60 SERIAL #'d SETS
*PRIME CUT/25: 1X TO 2.5X DRIVERS
*TEAM/175: .3X TO .8X DRIVERS
BRD1 K.Harvick Daytona 6.00 15.00
BRD2 Matt Kenseth Cal. 5.00 12.00
BRD3 J.Johnson Vegas 8.00 20.00
BRD4 J.Johnson Atlanta 8.00 20.00
BRD5 Kyle Busch Bristol 6.00 15.00
BRD6 J.Johnson Martinsville 8.00 20.00
BRD7 Jeff Burton Texas 4.00 10.00
BRD8 J.Gordon Phoenix 10.00 25.00
BRD9 J.Gordon Talladega 10.00 25.00
BRD10 J.Johnson Rich. May 8.00 20.00
BRD11 Casey Mears Char. 3.00 8.00
BRD12 M.Truex Jr. Dover 4.00 10.00
BRD13 J.Gordon Pocono 10.00 25.00
BRD14 C.Edwards Mich. 5.00 12.00
BRD15 J.Montoya Infineon 8.00 20.00
BRD16 Denny Hamlin NH 6.00 15.00
BRD17 J.McMurray Daytona 5.00 12.00
BRD18 T.Stewart Chicago 8.00 20.00
BRD19 T.Stewart Indy 8.00 20.00
BRD20 K.Busch Pocono 4.00 10.00
BRD21 T.Stewart Watkins 8.00 20.00
BRD22 K.Busch Mich. 4.00 10.00
BRD23 C.Edwards Bristol 5.00 12.00
BRD24 J.Johnson Cal. 8.00 20.00
BRD25 J.Johnson Rich. Sept. 8.00 20.00

2008 Press Pass Cup Chase

COMPLETE SET (18) 75.00 150.00
STATED ODDS 1:28 H, 1:36 R
CC1 Ryan Newman 1.50 4.00
CC2 Matt Kenseth 2.00 5.00
CC3 Jeff Gordon 4.00 10.00
CC4 Dale Earnhardt Jr. 4.00 10.00
CC5 Denny Hamlin 2.50 6.00
CC6 Kevin Harvick 2.50 6.00
CC7 Clint Bowyer 2.00 5.00
CC8 Martin Truex Jr. 1.50 4.00
CC9 Juan Pablo Montoya 4.00 10.00
CC10 Jamie McMurray 2.00 5.00
CC11 Tony Stewart 3.00 8.00
CC12 Jeff Burton 1.50 4.00
CC13 Kasey Kahne 2.00 5.00
CC14 Jimmie Johnson WIN 25.00 50.00
CC15 Carl Edwards 2.00 5.00
CC16 Kurt Busch 1.50 4.00
CC17 Greg Biffle 1.50 4.00
CC18 Field Card .75 2.00

2008 Press Pass Cup Chase Prizes

COMPLETE SET (12) 6.00 15.00
ISUED VIA MAIL REDEMPTION
CC1 Jimmie Johnson .75 2.00
CC2 Carl Edwards .50 1.25
CC3 Jeff Gordon 1.00 2.50
CC4 Dale Earnhardt Jr. 1.00 2.50
CC5 Clint Bowyer .50 1.25
CC6 Denny Hamlin .60 1.50
CC7 Jeff Burton .40 1.00
CC8 Tony Stewart .75 2.00
CC9 Greg Biffle .40 1.00
CC10 Kyle Busch .60 1.50
CC11 Kevin Harvick .60 1.50
CC12 Matt Kenseth .50 1.25
CCJJ Jimmie Johnson Tire 25.00 50.00

2008 Press Pass Race Day

COMPLETE SET (12) 15.00 30.00
STATED ODDS 1:6
RD1 Tony Stewart .60 1.50
RD2 Ryan Newman .30 .75
RD3 Martin Truex Jr. .30 .75
RD4 Jeff Gordon .75 2.00
RD5 Dale Jarrett .40 1.00
RD6 Jeff Burton .30 .75
RD7 Brian Vickers .25 .60
RD8 Dale Earnhardt Jr. .75 2.00
RD9 Matt Kenseth .40 1.00
RD10 Juan Pablo Montoya .60 1.50
RD11 Carl Edwards .40 1.00
RD12 Michael Waltrip .40 1.00

2008 Press Pass Slideshow

COMPLETE SET (36) 15.00 30.00
STATED ODDS 1:2
SS1 Casey Mears .20 .50
SS2 Johnny Sauter .30 .75
SS3 Jeff Burton Orange .25 .60
SS4 Kyle Petty .25 .60
SS5 Sam Hornish Jr. .50 1.25
SS6 Jimmie Johnson Blue .50 1.25
SS7 Todd Bodine Red .20 .50
SS8 Jeff Green .20 .50
SS9 T.J. Bell .30 .75
SS10 Michael Waltrip .30 .75
SS11 Tony Raines .20 .50
SS12 Dale Earnhardt Jr. Red Red .60 1.50
SS13 Cale Gale .20 .50
SS14 Mark Martin Yellow .30 .75
SS15 Jack Sprague Blue .20 .50
SS16 Ricky Rudd .25 .60
SS17 Tony Stewart Orange .50 1.25
SS18 Ron Hornaday .20 .50
SS19 Mike Skinner Red .20 .50
SS20 Jamie McMurray .30 .75
SS21 Todd Bodine .20 .50
SS22 Martin Truex Jr. Red .25 .60
SS23 Kelly Bires .30 .75
SS24 Scott Riggs .25 .60
SS25 Ryan Newman Blue .25 .60
SS26 Todd Kluever Red .30 .75
SS27 Travis Kvapil .20 .50
SS28 Elliott Sadler .20 .50
SS29 Jack Sprague .20 .50
SS30 T.J. Bell .30 .75
SS31 Joey Clanton Yellow .30 .75
SS32 Stephen Leicht Blue .30 .75
SS33 Ron Hornaday .20 .50
SS34 Michael Waltrip Blue .30 .75
SS35 Scott Wimmer Green .25 .60
SS36 Dale Earnhardt Jr. .60 1.50

2008 Press Pass VIP National Convention Promo

COMPLETE SET (6) 12.00 30.00
1 Jimmie Johnson 1.50 4.00
2 Tony Stewart 1.50 4.00
3 Dale Earnhardt Jr. 2.00 5.00
4 Kyle Busch 1.25 3.00
5 Carl Edwards 1.00 2.50
6 Jeff Gordon 2.00 5.00

2008 Press Pass Weekend Warriors

COMPLETE SET (9) 15.00 40.00
STATED ODDS 1:12
WW1 Jeff Gordon 1.00 2.50
WW2 Tony Stewart .75 2.00
WW3 Jamie McMurray .50 1.25
WW4 Kevin Harvick .60 1.50
WW5 Dale Earnhardt Jr. 1.00 2.50
WW6 Jeff Burton .40 1.00
WW7 Martin Truex Jr. .40 1.00
WW8 Jimmie Johnson .75 2.00
WW9 Mark Martin .50 1.25

2008 Press Pass Target

COMPLETE SET (6) 8.00 20.00
STATED ODDS 2 PER TARGET BLASTER BOX
DEB Dale Earnhardt Jr. 1.25 3.00
JGB Jeff Gordon 1.25 3.00
JJB Jimmie Johnson 1.00 2.50
JMB Juan Pablo Montoya 1.00 2.50
KKB Kasey Kahne .60 1.50
TSB Tony Stewart 1.00 2.50

2008 Press Pass Target Victory Tires

RANDOMLY INSERTED IN TARGET BLASTER BOX
STATED PRINT RUN 50 SERIAL #'d SETS
TTCE C.Edwards Bristol 12.00 30.00
TTDH Denny Hamlin NH 25.00 50.00
TTJG J.Gordon Talladega 40.00 80.00
TTJJ J.Johnson Vegas 30.00 60.00
TTJM J.Montoya Infineon 25.00 50.00
TTKH K.Harvick Daytona 25.00 50.00
TTMK Matt Kenseth Cal. 25.00 50.00
TTMT M.Truex Jr. Dover 20.00 40.00
TTTS T.Stewart Indy 30.00 60.00

2008 Press Pass Wal-Mart

COMPLETE SET (6) 8.00 20.00
STATED ODDS 2 PER WAL-MART BLASTER BOX
DEA Dale Earnhardt Jr. 1.25 3.00
JGA Jeff Gordon 1.25 3.00
JJA Jimmie Johnson 1.00 2.50
JMA Juan Pablo Montoya 1.00 2.50
KKA Kasey Kahne .60 1.50
TSA Tony Stewart 1.00 2.50

2008 Press Pass Wal-Mart Autographs

RANDOM INSERTS IN WAL-MART BLASTER
STATED PRINT RUN 50 SER.#'d SETS
1 Dale Earnhardt Jr.
2 Carl Edwards 40.00 80.00
3 Jeff Gordon 125.00 200.00
4 Denny Hamlin
5 Kevin Harvick
6 Jimmie Johnson 60.00 120.00
7 Matt Kenseth 40.00 80.00
8 Mark Martin
9 Tony Stewart
10 Martin Truex Jr. 25.00 50.00

2009 Press Pass

This set was released on December 11, 2008. The second series was released on July 15.

COMPLETE SET (220) 10.00 25.00
COMP.SERIES 1 (120) 5.00 12.00
COMP.SERIES 2 (100) 5.00 12.00
WAX BOX SER.1 HOBBY (28) 60.00 90.00
WAX BOX SER.1 RETAIL (28) 50.00 75.00
WAX BOX SER.2 HOBBY (30) 60.00 90.00
WAX BOX SER.2 RETAIL (28) 50.00 75.00
1 Kyle Busch .40 1.00
2 Carl Edwards .30 .75
3 Jimmie Johnson .50 1.25
4 Dale Earnhardt Jr. .60 1.50
5 Clint Bowyer .30 .75
6 Denny Hamlin .30 .75
7 Jeff Burton .25 .60
8 Tony Stewart .50 1.25
9 Greg Biffle .25 .60
10 Jeff Gordon .60 1.50
11 Kevin Harvick .40 1.00
12 Matt Kenseth .30 .75
13 Kasey Kahne .30 .75
14 David Ragan .25 .60
15 Brian Vickers .20 .50
16 Ryan Newman .25 .60
17 Martin Truex Jr. .25 .60
18 Jamie McMurray .30 .75
19 Kurt Busch .25 .60

20 Bobby Labonte .30 .75
21 Juan Pablo Montoya .40 1.00
22 Elliott Sadler .20 .50
23 Travis Kvapil .20 .50
24 Casey Mears .20 .50
25 David Reutimann .25 .60
26 David Gilliland .20 .50
27 Mark Martin .30 .75
28 Dave Blaney .20 .50
29 Sam Hornish Jr. .25 .60
30 Regan Smith .25 .60
31 Scott Riggs .25 .60
32 Joe Nemechek .20 .50
33 Michael McDowell .30 .75
34 Kyle Petty .25 .60
35 Aric Almirola .25 .60
36 Joey Logano RC 2.50 6.00
37 Jeff Burton NNS .25 .60
38 Greg Biffle NNS .25 .60
39 Clint Bowyer NNS .30 .75
40 Landon Cassill NNS RC 1.00 2.50
41 Bryan Clauson NNS .25 .60
42 Dale Earnhardt Jr. NNS .60 1.50
43 Carl Edwards NNS .30 .75
44 Cale Gale NNS .20 .50
45 Brad Keselowski NNS .40 1.00
46 Kevin Harvick NNS .40 1.00
47 David Ragan NNS .25 .60
48 Scott Wimmer NNS .25 .60
49 Colin Braun CTS .30 .75
50 Erik Darnell CTS .25 .60
51 Rick Crawford CTS .20 .50
52 Jon Wood CTS .20 .50
53 Mike Skinner CTS .20 .50
54 Ron Hornaday CTS .20 .50
55 Jeff Gordon's Car BFS .30 .75
56 Dale Earnhardt Jr.'s Car BFS .25 .60
57 Denny Hamlin's Car BFS .12 .30
58 Carl Edwards' Car BFS .12 .30
59 Jimmie Johnson's Car BFS .20 .50
60 Mark Martin's Car BFS .12 .30
61 Kevin Harvick's Car BFS .15 .40
62 Kyle Busch's Car BFS .15 .40
63 Martin Truex Jr.'s Car BFS .10 .25
64 Matt Kenseth's Car BFS .12 .30
65 Jeff Burton's Car BFS .10 .25
66 Greg Biffle's Car BFS .10 .25
67 Dale Earnhardt Jr. NS .60 1.50
68 Ryan Newman NS .25 .60
69 Jeff Burton NS .25 .60
70 Denny Hamlin NS .30 .75
71 Carl Edwards NS .30 .75
72 Jimmie Johnson NS .50 1.25
73 Kasey Kahne NS .30 .75
74 Dale Earnhardt Jr. NS .60 1.50
75 Kurt Busch NS .25 .60
76 Jimmie Johnson NS .50 1.25
77 Kyle Busch NS .40 1.00
78 Carl Edwards NS .30 .75
79 David Ragan LF .25 .60
80 Tony Stewart LF .50 1.25
81 Carl Edwards LF .30 .75
82 Ryan Newman LF .25 .60
83 Rick Hendrick LF .25 .60
84 Casey Mears LF .20 .50
85 Clint Bowyer LF .30 .75
86 Jeff Burton LF .25 .60
87 Tony Stewart TY .25 .60
88 Tony Stewart TY .25 .60
89 Tony Stewart TY .25 .60
90 Tony Stewart TY .25 .60
91 Tony Stewart TY .25 .60
92 Tony Stewart TY .25 .60
93 Tony Stewart TY .25 .60
94 Tony Stewart TY .25 .60
95 Tony Stewart TY .25 .60
96 Tony Stewart TY .25 .60
97 Tony Stewart TY .25 .60
98 Joey Logano TTY .30 .75
99 Joey Logano TTY .30 .75
100 Joey Logano TTY .30 .75
101 Joey Logano TTY .30 .75
102 Joey Logano TTY .30 .75
103 Joey Logano TTY .30 .75
104 Joey Logano TTY .30 .75
105 Joey Logano TTY .30 .75
106 Joey Logano TTY .30 .75
107 Kyle Busch TT .40 1.00
108 Carl Edwards TT .30 .75
109 Jimmie Johnson TT .50 1.25
110 Dale Earnhardt Jr. TT .60 1.50
111 Clint Bowyer TT .30 .75
112 Denny Hamlin TT .30 .75
113 Jeff Burton TT .25 .60
114 Tony Stewart TT .50 1.25
115 Greg Biffle TT .25 .60
116 Jeff Gordon TT .60 1.50
117 Kevin Harvick TT .40 1.00
118 Matt Kenseth TT .30 .75
119 Schedule .20 .50
120 A.J. Allmendinger .30 .75
121 Marcos Ambrose CRC .30 .75
122 Greg Biffle .25 .60
123 Clint Bowyer .30 .75
124 Jeff Burton .25 .60
125 Kurt Busch .25 .60
126 Kyle Busch .40 1.00
127 Dale Earnhardt Jr. .60 1.50
128 Carl Edwards .30 .75
129 Jeff Gordon .60 1.50
130 Robby Gordon .20 .50
131 Denny Hamlin .30 .75
132 Kevin Harvick .40 1.00
133 Sam Hornish Jr. .25 .60
134 Jimmie Johnson .50 1.25
135 Kasey Kahne .30 .75
136 Matt Kenseth .30 .75
137 Brad Keselowski CRC .75 2.00
138 Bobby Labonte .30 .75
139 Joey Logano CRC .60 1.50
140 Mark Martin .30 .75
141 Jamie McMurray .30 .75
142 Casey Mears .20 .50
143 Paul Menard .20 .50
144 Juan Pablo Montoya .40 1.00
145 Ryan Newman .25 .60
146 David Ragan .25 .60
147 David Reutimann .25 .60
148 Elliott Sadler .20 .50
149 Reed Sorenson .20 .50
150 Scott Speed RC .40 1.00
151 Regan Smith .25 .60
152 Tony Stewart .50 1.25
153 Martin Truex Jr. .25 .60
154 Brian Vickers .20 .50
155 Michael Waltrip .30 .75
156 Justin Allgaier NNS RC .30 .75
157 Kyle Busch NNS .40 1.00
158 Marc Davis NNS .50 1.25
159 Dale Earnhardt Jr. NNS .60 1.50
160 Carl Edwards NNS .30 .75
161 Brendan Gaughan NNS .20 .50
162 Kevin Harvick NNS .40 1.00
163 Brad Keselowski NNS .40 1.00
164 Scott Lagasse Jr. NNS RC .40 1.00
165 Tony Stewart NNS .50 1.25
166 Colin Braun CTS .25 .60
167 Kyle Busch CTS .40 1.00
168 Ricky Carmichael CTS RC .75 2.00
169 J.R. Fitzpatrick CTS RC .30 .75
170 Ron Hornaday CTS .20 .50
171 Tayler Malsam CTS RC .30 .75
172 Mike Skinner CTS .20 .50
173 Colin Braun's Truck BS .10 .25
174 Paul Menard's Car BS .07 .20
175 Kurt Busch's Car BS .10 .25
176 Jeff Burton's Car BS .10 .25
177 David Ragan's Car BS .10 .25
178 Michael Waltrip's Car BS .12 .30
179 Talladega Superspeedway BS .20 .50
180 Dale Earnhardt Jr. FW .60 1.50
181 Jeff Gordon FW .60 1.50
182 Tony Stewart FW .50 1.25
183 Carl Edwards FW .30 .75
184 Kasey Kahne FW .30 .75
185 Brian Vickers FW .20 .50
186 Jimmie Johnson 2006 .50 1.25
187 Jimmie Johnson 2007 .50 1.25
188 Jimmie Johnson 2008 .50 1.25
189 Chad Knaus .40 1.00
190 Jimmie Johnson's Crew .50 1.25
191 Jimmie Johnson 2009 .50 1.25
192 Rick Hendrick HMS .25 .60
193 Knaus/Hendrick/Johnson HMS .50 1.25
194 Jeff Gordon HMS .60 1.50
195 Jeff Gordon HMS .60 1.50
196 Hendrick/Gordon HMS .60 1.50
197 Johnson/Hendrick HMS .50 1.25
198 Dale Jr./Hendrick HMS .60 1.50
199 Martin/Hendrick HMS .30 .75
200 Jr./JJ/Hendrick
Gordon/Martin HMS .60 1.50
201 Kurt Busch's Car A .10 .25
202 Mark Martin's Car A .12 .30
203 Kasey Kahne's Car A .12 .30
204 Denny Hamlin's Car A .12 .30
205 Tony Stewart's Car A .20 .50
206 Matt Kenseth's Car A .12 .30
207 Kyle Busch's Car A .15 .40
208 Joey Logano's Car A .25 .60
209 Jeff Gordon's Car A .25 .60
210 Jimmie Johnson's Car A .20 .50
211 Dale Earnhardt Jr's Car A .25 .60
212 Carl Edwards' Car A .12 .30
213 Tony Stewart M .50 1.25
214 Joey Logano M .60 1.50
215 Jeff Gordon M .60 1.50
216 Dale Earnhardt Jr. M .60 1.50
217 Ryan Newman M .25 .60
218 Jeff Gordon M .60 1.50
CL Jimmie Johnson CL .50 1.25
CL2 Jeff Gordon CL .60 1.50
0 Cup Chase Drivers 2.00 5.00

2009 Press Pass Blue

COMPLETE SET (220) 40.00 100.00
COMP.SER.1 (120) 20.00 50.00
COMP.SER.2 (100) 20.00 50.00
*BLUE: .6X TO 1.5 X BASE
STATED ODDS 1 PER RETAIL PACK

2009 Press Pass Final Standings

107 Kyle Busch/150 2.50 6.00
108 Carl Edwards/99 8.00 20.00
109 Jimmie Johnson/48 25.00 60.00
110 Dale Earnhardt Jr./170 8.00 20.00
111 Clint Bowyer/120 2.50 6.00
112 Denny Hamlin/135 8.00 20.00
113 Jeff Burton/125 5.00 12.00
114 Tony Stewart/140 8.00 20.00
115 Greg Biffle/110 6.00 15.00
116 Jeff Gordon/130 10.00 25.00
117 Kevin Harvick/115 10.00 25.00
118 Matt Kenseth/160 3.00 8.00

2009 Press Pass Gold

COMPLETE SET (120) 40.00 100.00
COMP.SER.1 (120) 20.00 50.00
COMP.SER.2 (100) 20.00 50.00
GOLD: .6X TO 1.5X BASE
STATED ODDS 1 PER HOBBY PACK

2009 Press Pass Gold Holofoil

GOLD HOLO: 2.5X TO 6X BASE
STATED PRINT RUN 100 SERIAL #'d SETS

2009 Press Pass Red

COMP.FACT.SET (220) 15.00 40.00
*SINGLES: .4X TO 1X BASIC CARDS

2009 Press Pass Autographs Chase Edition

STATED PRINT RUN 25 SERIAL #'d SETS
CB Clint Bowyer 25.00 60.00
CE Carl Edwards 60.00 120.00
DE Dale Earnhardt Jr. 100.00 200.00
DH Denny Hamlin 30.00 80.00
GB Greg Biffle 25.00 60.00
JB Jeff Burton 30.00 80.00
JG Jeff Gordon 100.00 200.00
JJ Jimmie Johnson 60.00 120.00
KB Kyle Busch 40.00 100.00
KH Kevin Harvick 30.00 80.00
MK Matt Kenseth 30.00 80.00
TS Tony Stewart 40.00 100.00

2009 Press Pass Autographs Gold

GOLD STATED ODDS 1:84H 1:144R
UNPRICED PRINT PLATE PRINT RUN 1
1 Justin Allgaier NS 8.00 20.00
2 A.J. Allmendinger 8.00 20.00
3 Aric Almirola 6.00 15.00
4 Marcos Ambrose 12.00 30.00
5 Greg Biffle 6.00 15.00
6 Colin Braun CWTS 6.00 15.00
7 James Buescher CWTS 10.00 25.00
8 Kurt Busch 6.00 15.00
9 Kyle Busch 10.00 25.00
10 Ricky Carmichael CWTS 20.00 50.00
11 Erik Darnell NS 6.00 15.00
12 Dale Earnhardt Jr. EXCH 100.00 200.00
13 Carl Edwards 8.00 20.00
14 JR Fitzpatrick CWTS 8.00 20.00
15 Brendan Gaughan NS
16 Robby Gordon 5.00 12.00
17 Jeff Gordon EXCH 125.00 200.00
18 Denny Hamlin 8.00 20.00
19 Kevin Harvick 10.00 25.00
20 Ron Hornaday CWTS 5.00 12.00
21 Sam Hornish Jr.
22 Jimmie Johnson EXCH 60.00 120.00
23 Matt Kenseth 8.00 20.00
24 Brad Keselowski 10.00 25.00
25 Brad Keselowski NS 10.00 25.00
26 Bobby Labonte 8.00 20.00
27 Scott Lagasse Jr. NS
28 Stephen Leicht NS 5.00 12.00
29 Joey Logano 40.00 100.00
30 Tayler Malsam CWTS 8.00 20.00
31 Mark Martin 8.00 20.00
32 Michael McDowell NS 8.00 20.00
33 Jamie McMurray 8.00 20.00
34 Paul Menard 5.00 12.00
35 Casey Mears 5.00 12.00
36 Juan Pablo Montoya 10.00 25.00
37 Joe Nemechek 5.00 12.00
38 Ryan Newman 6.00 15.00
39 David Ragan 6.00 15.00
40 David Reutimann 6.00 15.00
41 Scott Riggs 6.00 15.00
42 Elliott Sadler 5.00 12.00
43 Johnny Sauter CWTS 8.00 20.00
44 Brian Scott CWTS
45 Mike Skinner CWTS 5.00 12.00
46 Regan Smith 6.00 15.00
47 Reed Sorenson 5.00 12.00
48 Scott Speed 10.00 25.00
49 Ricky Stenhouse Jr. NS 20.00 50.00
50 Tony Stewart 50.00 100.00
51 David Stremme
52 Martin Truex Jr. 6.00 15.00
53 Brian Vickers 5.00 12.00
54 Steve Wallace NS 5.00 12.00
55 Michael Waltrip 8.00 20.00

2009 Press Pass Autographs Silver

SILVER STATED ODDS 1:84 HOB
1 A.J. Allmendinger 8.00 20.00
2 Aric Almirola 6.00 15.00
3 Greg Biffle 6.00 15.00
4 Kelly Bires 5.00 12.00
5 Clint Bowyer 8.00 20.00
6 Colin Braun 6.00 15.00
7 Jeff Burton 5.00 12.00
8 Kurt Busch 6.00 15.00
9 Kyle Busch 10.00 25.00
10 Ricky Carmichael 20.00 50.00
11 Patrick Carpentier 12.00 30.00
12 Landon Cassill 15.00 40.00
13 Bryan Clauson 6.00 15.00
14 Rick Crawford 4.00 10.00
15 Erik Darnell 5.00 12.00
16 Dale Earnhardt Jr. 50.00 100.00
17 Carl Edwards 8.00 20.00
18 Cale Gale 5.00 12.00
19 David Gilliland 5.00 12.00
20 Jeff Gordon 125.00 200.00
21 Denny Hamlin 8.00 20.00
22 Kevin Harvick 10.00 25.00
23 Ron Hornaday 5.00 12.00
24 Sam Hornish Jr. 6.00 15.00
25 Jimmie Johnson 50.00 100.00
26 Kasey Kahne 15.00 40.00
27 Matt Kenseth 8.00 20.00
28 Brad Keselowski 10.00 25.00
29 Travis Kvapil 5.00 12.00
30 Bobby Labonte 8.00 20.00
31 Joey Logano 15.00 40.00
32 Mark Martin 8.00 20.00
33 Jamie McMurray 8.00 20.00
34 Casey Mears 5.00 12.00
35 Paul Menard 5.00 12.00
36 Chase Miller 10.00 25.00
37 Juan Pablo Montoya 10.00 25.00
38 Joe Nemechek 5.00 12.00
39 Ryan Newman 6.00 15.00
40 David Ragan 6.00 15.00
41 Scott Riggs 6.00 15.00
42 Elliott Sadler 5.00 12.00
43 Mike Skinner 5.00 12.00
44 Regan Smith 6.00 15.00
45 Reed Sorenson 5.00 12.00
46 Jack Sprague 6.00 15.00
47 Martin Truex Jr. 6.00 15.00
48 Brian Vickers 5.00 12.00
49 Michael Waltrip 8.00 20.00
50 Scott Wimmer 6.00 15.00

2009 Press Pass Autographs Track Edition

STATED PRINT RUN 20-25
CE Carl Edwards/25 30.00 80.00
DE Dale Earnhardt Jr./25 100.00 200.00
JG Jeff Gordon/25 100.00 200.00
JJ Jimmie Johnson/25 40.00 100.00
JL Joey Logano/25 40.00 100.00
KB Kyle Busch/25 25.00 60.00
KH Kevin Harvick/25 30.00 80.00
KK Kasey Kahne/20 40.00 100.00
MK Matt Kenseth/25 25.00 60.00
RP Richard Petty/25 40.00 100.00

2009 Press Pass Burning Rubber Autographs

CARDS SERIAL #'d TO DRIVER'S DOOR
STATED PRINT RUN 2-48
BRSDE Dale Earnhardt Jr./8
BRSDH Denny Hamlin/11
BRSJG Jeff Gordon/24 150.00 300.00
BRSJJ Jimmie Johnson/48 60.00 120.00
BRSKH Kevin Harvick/29 60.00 120.00
BRSPC Patrick Carpentier/10
BRSKuB Kurt Busch/2
BRSKyB Kyle Busch/18

2009 Press Pass Burning Rubber Drivers

STATED ODDS 1:28
BRD1-BRD26 PRINT RUN 185
BRD27-BRD36 PRINT RUN 320
*PRIME/25: 1X TO 2.5X DRIVER/185
*PRIME/25: 1.2X TO 3X DRIVER/320
*TEAMS/250: .3X TO .8X DRIVER/185
*TEAMS/85: .6X TO 1.5X DRIVER/320
BRD1 R.Newman Daytona 3.00 8.00
BRD2 C.Edwards California 4.00 10.00
BRD3 C.Edwards Las Vegas 4.00 10.00
BRD4 Ky.Busch Atlanta 5.00 12.00
BRD5 J.Burton Bristol 3.00 8.00
BRD6 D.Hamlin Martinsville 4.00 10.00
BRD7 C.Edwards Texas 4.00 10.00
BRD8 J.Johnson Phoenix 6.00 15.00
BRD9 Ky.Busch Talladega 5.00 12.00
BRD10 C.Bowyer Richmond 4.00 10.00
BRD11 Ky.Busch Darlington 5.00 12.00
BRD12 K.Kahne Charlotte 4.00 10.00
BRD13 Ky.Busch Dover 5.00 12.00
BRD14 K.Kahne Pocono 4.00 10.00
BRD15 D.Earnhardt Jr. Michigan 8.00 20.00
BRD16 Ky.Busch Infineon 5.00 12.00
BRD17 K.Busch New Hampshire 3.00 8.00
BRD18 Ky.Busch Daytona 5.00 12.00
BRD19 Ky.Busch Chicagoland 5.00 12.00
BRD20 J.Johnson Indianapolis 6.00 15.00
BRD21 C.Edwards Pocono 4.00 10.00
BRD22 Ky.Busch Watkins Glen 5.00 12.00
BRD23 C.Edwards Michigan 4.00 10.00
BRD24 C.Edwards Bristol 4.00 10.00
BRD25 J.Johnson California 6.00 15.00
BRD26 J.Johnson Richmond 6.00 15.00
BRD27 Greg Biffle 2.50 6.00
BRD28 Greg Biffle 2.50 6.00
BRD29 Jimmie Johnson 5.00 12.00
BRD30 Tony Stewart 5.00 12.00
BRD32 Jimmie Johnson 5.00 12.00
BRD33 Carl Edwards 3.00 8.00
BRD34 Carl Edwards 3.00 8.00
BRD35 Jimmie Johnson 5.00 12.00
BRD36 Carl Edwards 3.00 8.00
BRDCH Jimmie Johnson 5.00 12.00
BRDJL J.Logano Kentucky 5.00 12.00

2009 Press Pass Chase for the Sprint Cup

COMPLETE SET (12) 5.00 12.00
ONE SET PER FACTORY SET
CC1 Mark Martin .40 1.00
CC2 Tony Stewart .60 1.50
CC3 Jimmie Johnson .60 1.50
CC4 Denny Hamlin .40 1.00
CC5 Kasey Kahne .40 1.00
CC6 Jeff Gordon .75 2.00
CC7 Kurt Busch .30 .75
CC8 Brian Vickers .25 .60
CC9 Carl Edwards .40 1.00
CC10 Ryan Newman .30 .75
CC11 Juan Pablo Montoya .50 1.25
CC12 Greg Biffle .30 .75

2009 Press Pass Cup Chase

STATED ODDS 1:28
CCR1 Jimmie Johnson CHAMP 15.00 40.00
CCR2 Denny Hamlin WIN 2.50 6.00
CCR3 Kyle Busch 2.00 5.00
CCR4 Martin Truex Jr. 1.25 3.00
CCR5 Jeff Burton 1.25 3.00
CCR6 Carl Edwards WIN 2.50 6.00
CCR7 Clint Bowyer 1.50 4.00
CCR8 Joey Logano 3.00 8.00
CCR9 Kevin Harvick 2.00 5.00
CCR10 Kurt Busch WIN 2.00 5.00
CCR11 Juan Pablo Montoya WIN 3.00 8.00
CCR12 Dale Earnhardt Jr. 3.00 8.00
CCR13 Jeff Gordon WIN 5.00 12.00
CCR14 Kasey Kahne WIN 2.50 6.00
CCR15 Matt Kenseth 1.50 4.00
CCR16 Greg Biffle WIN 2.00 5.00
CCR17 Tony Stewart WIN 4.00 10.00
CCR18 Field Card WIN 1.50 4.00

2009 Press Pass Cup Chase Prizes

COMPLETE SET (12) 6.00 15.00
ISSUED VIA MAIL REDEMPTION
CC1 Mark Martin .50 1.25
CC2 Tony Stewart .75 2.00
CC3 Jimmie Johnson .75 2.00
CC4 Denny Hamlin .50 1.25
CC5 Kasey Kahne .50 1.25
CC6 Jeff Gordon 1.00 2.50
CC7 Kurt Busch .40 1.00
CC8 Brian Vickers .30 .75
CC9 Carl Edwards .50 1.25
CC10 Ryan Newman .40 1.00
CC11 Juan Pablo Montoya .60 1.50
CC12 Greg Biffle .40 1.00
CCJJ Jimmie Johnson Tire 10.00 25.00

2009 Press Pass Daytona 500 Tires

STATED PRINT RUN 25 SER.#'d SETS
TTSS Scott Speed
TTCB Clint Bowyer
TTCE Carl Edwards 10.00 25.00
TTDH Denny Hamlin 10.00 25.00
TTJB Jeff Burton
TTJG Jeff Gordon 20.00 50.00
TTJJ Jimmie Johnson
TTJL Joey Logano
TTKH Kevin Harvick
TTKK Kasey Kahne
TTMK Matt Kenseth
TTRN Ryan Newman 8.00 20.00
TTTS Tony Stewart
TTDEJR Dale Earnhardt Jr. 20.00 50.00

2009 Press Pass Freeze Frame

COMPLETE SET (36) 15.00 40.00
STATED ODDS 1:2
FF1 Jeff Gordon 1.25 3.00
FF2 Mike Skinner .40 1.00
FF3 Kyle Busch .75 2.00
FF4 Michael McDowell .60 1.50
FF5 Jon Wood .40 1.00
FF6 Dale Earnhardt Jr. 1.25 3.00
FF7 Geoff Bodine .40 1.00
FF8 Cale Gale .40 1.00
FF9 Jimmie Johnson 1.00 2.50
FF10 Fireball Roberts .50 1.25
FF11 Bobby Labonte .60 1.50
FF12 Joey Logano 1.25 3.00
FF13 Ron Hornaday .40 1.00
FF14 Jeff Gordon 1.25 3.00
FF15 Kevin Harvick .75 2.00
FF16 Carl Edwards .60 1.50
FF17 Joe Nemechek .40 1.00
FF18 Fred Lorenzen .50 1.25
FF19 Tony Stewart 1.00 2.50
FF20 Jack Ingram .40 1.00
FF21 Dale Earnhardt Jr. 1.25 3.00
FF22 Erik Darnell .50 1.25
FF23 Dale Earnhardt 4.00 10.00
FF24 Cale Gale .40 1.00
FF25 Glen Wood .40 1.00
FF26 Kyle Petty .50 1.25
FF27 Marvin Panch .40 1.00
FF28 Scott Riggs .50 1.25
FF29 Jimmie Johnson 1.00 2.50
FF30 Pete Hamilton .40 1.00
FF31 Dale Earnhardt 4.00 10.00
FF32 Tony Stewart 1.00 2.50
FF33 Scott Riggs .50 1.25
FF34 Jon Wood .40 1.00
FF35 Landon Cassill 1.25 3.00
FF36 Rex White .40 1.00

2009 Press Pass Game Face

COMPLETE SET (9) 12.00 30.00
STATED ODDS 1:15
GF1 Dale Earnhardt Jr. 1.50 4.00
GF2 Jeff Gordon 1.50 4.00
GF3 Carl Edwards .75 2.00
GF4 Kyle Busch 1.00 2.50
GF5 Jimmie Johnson 1.25 3.00
GF6 Clint Bowyer .75 2.00
GF7 Kasey Kahne .75 2.00
GF8 Mark Martin .75 2.00
GF9 Tony Stewart 1.25 3.00

2009 Press Pass NASCAR Gallery

COMPLETE SET (12) 15.00 40.00
STATED ODDS 1:6
NG1 Mark Martin .60 1.50
NG2 Kyle Busch .75 2.00
NG3 Tony Stewart 1.00 2.50
NG4 Matt Kenseth .60 1.50
NG5 Carl Edwards .60 1.50
NG6 Kasey Kahne .60 1.50
NG7 Brian Vickers .40 1.00
NG8 Jeff Burton .50 1.25
NG9 Jeff Gordon 1.25 3.00
NG10 Kevin Harvick .75 2.00
NG11 Jimmie Johnson 1.00 2.50
NG12 Joey Logano 1.25 3.00

2009 Press Pass Pieces Race Used Memorabilia

ONE CARD PER FACTORY SET
AA A.J. Allmendinger SM 3.00 8.00
BK Brad Keselowski FS 4.00 10.00
BL Bobby Labonte S 3.00 8.00
CB Clint Bowyer PWB 3.00 8.00
CM Casey Mears FS 2.50 6.00
DE Dale Earnhardt Jr. CC 6.00 15.00
JG Jeff Gordon CC 5.00 12.00
JM Juan Pablo Montoya FS 4.00 10.00
JM Jamie McMurray FS 2.50 6.00
KB Kyle Busch CC 3.00 8.00
MK Matt Kenseth FS 3.00 8.00
MT Martin Truex Jr. FS 2.50 6.00
MW Michael Waltrip SM 3.00 8.00
RS Reed Sorenson FS 3.00 8.00
TS Tony Stewart SM 5.00 12.00

2009 Press Pass Pocket Portraits

COMPLETE SET (30) 15.00 40.00
STATED ODDS 1 PER PACK
P1 Greg Biffle .30 .75
P2 Clint Bowyer .40 1.00
P3 Jeff Burton .30 .75
P4 Kyle Busch .50 1.25
P5 Kurt Busch .30 .75
P6 Dale Earnhardt Jr. .75 2.00
P7 Carl Edwards .40 1.00
P8 Jeff Gordon .75 2.00
P9 Denny Hamlin .40 1.00
P10 Kevin Harvick .50 1.25
P11 Jimmie Johnson .60 1.50
P12 Kasey Kahne .40 1.00
P13 Matt Kenseth .40 1.00
P14 Bobby Labonte .40 1.00
P15 Joey Logano .75 2.00
P16 Mark Martin .40 1.00
P17 Jamie McMurray .40 1.00
P18 Juan Pablo Montoya .50 1.25
P19 Ryan Newman .30 .75
P20 David Ragan .30 .75
P21 Elliott Sadler .25 .60
P22 Reed Sorenson .25 .60
P23 Scott Speed .50 1.25
P24 Tony Stewart .60 1.50
P25 Brian Vickers .25 .60
P26 Michael Waltrip .40 1.00
P27 Bobby Allison .30 .75
P28 Dale Earnhardt Sr. 2.50 6.00
P29 David Pearson .40 1.00
P30 Richard Petty .60 1.50

2009 Press Pass Pocket Portraits Checkered Flag

COMPLETE SET (15) 125.00 250.00
*SINGLES: 3X TO 8X BASIC INSERTS
STATED ODDS 1:150

2009 Press Pass Pocket Portraits Hometown

COMPLETE SET (29) 20.00 50.00
*SINGLES: .6X TO 1.5X BASIC INSERTS
STATED ODDS 1:15

2009 Press Pass Pocket Portraits Smoke

COMPLETE SET (30) 60.00 120.00
*SINGLES: 1X TO 2.5X BASIC INSERTS
STATED ODDS 1:30

2009 Press Pass Pocket Portraits Target

COMPLETE SET (15) 12.00 30.00
STATED ODDS 2 PER TARGET BLASTER
PPT1 Dale Earnhardt Jr. NG .75 2.00
PPT2 Jeff Gordon .75 2.00
PPT3 Jimmie Johnson .60 1.50
PPT4 Tony Stewart .60 1.50
PPT5 Kevin Harvick .50 1.25
PPT6 Dale Earnhardt .75 2.00
PPT7 Joey Logano .75 2.00
PPT8 Brian Vickers .25 .60
PPT9 Kurt Busch .30 .75
PPT10 Denny Hamlin .40 1.00
PPT11 Mark Martin .40 1.00
PPT12 Ryan Newman .30 .75
PPT13 Greg Biffle .30 .75
PPT14 David Reutimann .30 .75
PPT15 Donnie Allison .30 .75

2009 Press Pass Pocket Portraits Wal-Mart

COMPLETE SET (15) 12.00 30.00
STATED ODDS 2 PER WAL-MART BLASTER
PPW1 Dale Earnhardt Jr. AMP .75 2.00
PPW2 Kasey Kahne .40 1.00
PPW3 Carl Edwards .40 1.00
PPW4 Kyle Busch .50 1.25
PPW5 Jeff Burton .30 .75
PPW6 Richard Petty .60 1.50
PPW7 Scott Speed .50 1.25
PPW8 Matt Kenseth .40 1.00
PPW9 Bobby Labonte .40 1.00
PPW10 David Ragan .30 .75
PPW11 Martin Truex Jr .30 .75
PPW12 Michael Waltrip .40 1.00
PPW13 Clint Bowyer .40 1.00
PPW14 AJ Allmendinger .40 1.00
PPW15 Brad Keselowski .50 1.25

2009 Press Pass Prospect Pieces

OVERALL R-U STATED ODDS 1:30H 1:112R
STATED PRINT RUN 100 SER.#'d SETS
PPBK Brad Keselowski 6.00 15.00
PPCD Colin Braun 4.00 10.00
PPJA Justin Allgaier 5.00 12.00
PPJB James Buescher 6.00 15.00
PPJF JR Fitzpatrick 6.00 15.00
PPRC Ricky Carmichael 12.00 30.00
PPTM Tayler Malsam 5.00 12.00

2009 Press Pass Prospect Pieces Autographs

STATED PRINT RUN 50 SER.#'d SETS
PPBK Brad Keselowski 30.00 80.00
PPCD Colin Braun 15.00 40.00
PPJA Justin Allgaier 25.00 60.00
PPJB James Buescher 12.00 30.00
PPJF J.R. Fitzpatrick 12.00 30.00
PPRC Ricky Carmichael 20.00 50.00
PPTM Tayler Malsam 12.00 30.00

2009 Press Pass Sponsor Swatches

OVERALL R-U STATED ODDS 1:30H 1:112R
STATED PRINT RUN 200 SER.#'d SETS
SSAA Aric Almirola 4.00 10.00
SSBL Bobby Labonte 5.00 12.00
SSBV Brian Vickers 3.00 8.00
SSCE Carl Edwards/250 5.00 12.00

SSCM Casey Mears 3.00 8.00
SSDH Denny Hamlin 5.00 12.00
SSDR David Ragan 4.00 10.00
SSGB Greg Biffle 4.00 10.00
SSJG Jeff Gordon/250 10.00 25.00
SSJJ Jimmie Johnson/250 8.00 20.00
SSJL Joey Logano/250 8.00 20.00
SSJM Jamie McMurray 5.00 12.00
SSKB Kurt Busch 4.00 10.00
SSKH Kevin Harvick/225 6.00 15.00
SSKK Kasey Kahne 5.00 12.00
SSMK Matt Kenseth/250 5.00 12.00
SSMM Mark Martin 5.00 12.00
SSMT Martin Truex Jr. 4.00 10.00
SSMW Michael Waltrip/250 5.00 12.00
SSRN Ryan Newman 4.00 10.00
SSSS Scott Speed 6.00 15.00
SSTS Tony Stewart/250 8.00 20.00
SSDR2 David Reutimann 4.00 10.00
SSJPM Juan Pablo Montoya/250 6.00 15.00
SSKB2 Kyle Busch/225 6.00 15.00
SSDEJR Dale Earnhardt Jr./250 10.00 25.00

2009 Press Pass Santa Hats

STATED PRINT RUN 50 SERIAL #'d SETS
SH1 A.J. Allmendinger 6.00 15.00
SH2 Greg Biffle 5.00 12.00
SH3 Clint Bowyer 6.00 15.00
SH4 Jeff Burton 15.00 40.00
SH5 Kyle Busch 8.00 20.00
SH6 Carl Edwards 6.00 15.00
SH7 Denny Hamlin 6.00 15.00
SH8 Kevin Harvick 8.00 20.00
SH9 Jimmie Johnson 10.00 25.00
SH10 Kasey Kahne 30.00 80.00
SH11 Bobby Labonte 6.00 15.00
SH12 Mark Martin 6.00 15.00
SH13 Regan Smith 5.00 12.00
SH14 Kyle Petty 12.00 30.00
SH15 David Ragan 5.00 12.00
SH16 Elliott Sadler 10.00 25.00
SH17 Reed Sorenson 8.00 20.00
SH18 Michael Waltrip 6.00 15.00

2009 Press Pass Tony Stewart 10 Years Firesuit

STATED PRINT RUN 300 SERIAL #'d SETS
TS1 Tony Stewart 8.00 20.00
TS2 Tony Stewart 8.00 20.00
TS3 Tony Stewart 8.00 20.00

2009 Press Pass Total Tire

STATED PRINT RUN 25 SERIAL #'d SETS
TT1 Dale Earnhardt Jr. 75.00 150.00
TT2 Jeff Gordon 75.00 150.00
TT3 Kyle Busch 15.00 40.00
TT4 Joey Logano 50.00 100.00
TT5 Jimmie Johnson 30.00 80.00
TT6 Tony Stewart 25.00 60.00

2009 Press Pass Tradin' Paint

COMPLETE SET (9) 10.00 25.00
STATED ODDS 1:12
TP1 Dale Earnhardt Jr. 1.25 3.00
TP2 Kyle Busch .75 2.00
TP3 Tony Stewart 1.00 2.50
TP4 Matt Kenseth .60 1.50
TP5 David Ragan .50 1.25
TP6 Kevin Harvick .75 2.00
TP7 Jeff Burton .50 1.25
TP8 David Reutimann .50 1.25
TP9 Jeff Gordon 1.25 3.00

2009 Press Pass Unleashed

COMPLETE SET (12) 12.00 30.00
STATED ODDS 1:6
U1 Dale Earnhardt Jr. 1.25 3.00
U2 Ryan Newman .50 1.25
U3 Carl Edwards .60 1.50
U4 Kyle Busch .75 2.00
U5 Jimmie Johnson 1.00 2.50
U6 Clint Bowyer .60 1.50
U7 Kasey Kahne .60 1.50
U8 Kyle Busch .75 2.00
U9 Jimmie Johnson 1.00 2.50
U10 Carl Edwards .60 1.50
U11 Dale Earnhardt Jr. 1.25 3.00
U12 Joey Logano 1.25 3.00

2009 Press Pass Target

COMPLETE SET (6) 10.00 25.00
STATED ODDS 2 PER BLASTER BOX
CEB Carl Edwards .75 2.00
DEB Dale Earnhardt Jr. 1.50 4.00
JGB Jeff Gordon 1.50 4.00
JJB Jimmie Johnson 1.25 3.00
KBB Kyle Busch 1.00 2.50
TSB Tony Stewart 1.25 3.00

2009 Press Pass Wal-Mart

COMPLETE SET (6) 10.00 25.00
STATED ODDS 2 PER BLASTER BOX
CEA Carl Edwards .75 2.00
DEA Dale Earnhardt Jr. 1.50 4.00
JGA Jeff Gordon 1.50 4.00
JJA Jimmie Johnson 1.25 3.00
KBA Kyle Busch 1.00 2.50
TSA Tony Stewart 1.25 3.00

2009 Press Pass Wal-Mart Signature Edition

STATED PRINT RUN 15-50
JG Jeff Gordon/15
JJ Jimmie Johnson/15
JL Joey Logano/50 75.00 150.00
JM Juan Pablo Montoya/50
KH Kevin Harvick/50

2010 Press Pass

COMPLETE SET (129) 50.00 100.00
COMP.SET w/o SPs (120) 20.00 50.00
SP STATED ODDS 1:30
WAX BOX HOBBY (30) 70.00 100.00
WAX BOX FAST PASS (30) 100.00 125.00
WAX BOX RETAIL 60.00 80.00
1 Tony Stewart CL .50 1.25
2 Mark Martin .30 .75
3 Tony Stewart .50 1.25
4 Jimmie Johnson .50 1.25
5 Denny Hamlin .30 .75
6 Kasey Kahne .30 .75
7 Jeff Gordon .60 1.50
8 Kurt Busch .25 .60
9 Brian Vickers .20 .50
10 Carl Edwards .30 .75
11 Ryan Newman .25 .60
12 Juan Pablo Montoya .30 .75
13 Greg Biffle .25 .60
14 Kyle Busch .40 1.00
15 Matt Kenseth .30 .75
16 Clint Bowyer .30 .75
17 David Reutimann .25 .60
18 Marcos Ambrose .30 .75
19 Jeff Burton .25 .60
20 Joey Logano .30 .75
21 Casey Mears .20 .50
22 Dale Earnhardt Jr .60 1.50
23 Kevin Harvick .40 1.00
24 Jamie McMurray .30 .75
25 A.J. Allmendinger .30 .75
26 Martin Truex Jr .25 .60
27 Sam Hornish Jr .25 .60
28 Elliott Sadler .20 .50
29 Reed Sorenson .20 .50
30 David Ragan .25 .60
31 Paul Menard .20 .50
32 Michael Waltrip .30 .75
33 Robby Gordon .20 .50
34 Scott Speed .30 .75
35 Joe Nemechek .20 .50
36 Brad Keselowski .40 1.00
37 Kyle Busch NNS .40 1.00
38 Carl Edwards NNS .30 .75
39 Joey Logano NNS .30 .75
40 Brad Keselowski NNS .40 1.00
41 Justin Allgaier NNS .25 .60
42 Steve Wallace NNS .25 .60
43 Brendan Gaughan NNS .20 .50
44 Michael McDowell NNS .25 .60
45 Erik Darnell NNS .20 .50
46 Stephen Leicht NNS .20 .50
47 Ricky Stenhouse Jr. NNS .30 .75
48 Marc Davis NNS .20 .50
49 Ron Hornaday CWTS .20 .50
50 Mike Skinner CWTS .20 .50
51 Brian Scott CWTS RC .25 .60
52 Colin Braun CWTS .25 .60
53 Johnny Sauter CWTS .20 .50
54 Tayler Malsam CWTS .20 .50
55 James Buescher CWTS RC .25 .60
56 Ricky Carmichael CWTS .30 .75
57 J.R. Fitzpatrick CWTS .25 .60
58 Mark Martin's Car M .15 .40
59 Greg Biffle's Car M .12 .30
60 Joey Logano's Car M .15 .40
61 Jeff Gordon's Car M .30 .75
62 Brad Keselowski's Car M .20 .50
63 Kevin Harvick's Car M .20 .50
64 Clint Bowyer's Car M .15 .40
65 Marcos Ambrose's Car M .15 .40
66 Jimmie Johnson's Car M .25 .60
67 Brian Vickers' Car M .10 .25
68 Dale Jr.'s Car M .30 .75
69 Carl Edwards' Car M .15 .40
70 Marcos Ambrose RR .30 .75
71 Brad Keselowski RR .40 1.00
72 Joey Logano RR .30 .75
73 Scott Speed RR .30 .75
74 Justin Allgaier RR .25 .60
75 Brendan Gaughan RR .20 .50
76 Michael McDowell RR .25 .60
77 Tayler Malsam RR .20 .50
78 James Buescher RR .25 .60
79 Ricky Carmichael RR .30 .75
80 J.R. Fitzpatrick RR .25 .60
81 Johnny Sauter RR .20 .50
82 Reed Sorenson's Car WN .10 .25
83 Denny Hamlin's Car WN .15 .40
84 Jeff Gordon's Car WN .30 .75
85 J.Montoya's Car WN .15 .40
86 Kurt Busch's Car WN .12 .30
87 Matt Kenseth's Car WN .15 .40
88 Kasey Kahne's Car WN .15 .40
89 Jimmie Johnson's Car WN .25 .60
90 Mark Martin's Car WN .15 .40
91 Eldora T.Stewart's Car .25 .60
92 Star-Studded Field .40 1.00
93 Tony Stewart's Car PD .25 .60
94 Red Farmer's Car PD .10 .25
95 Logano/Ky.Busch's Car PD .20 .50
96 Jimmie Johnson's Car PD .20 .50
97 Marcos Ambrose's Car PD .15 .40
98 Tony Stewart's Car PD .25 .60
99 Tony Stewart's Car PD .25 .60
100 Tony Stewart H .50 1.25
101 Juan Pablo Montoya H .30 .75
102 David Reutimann H .25 .60
103 Marcos Ambrose H .30 .75
104 Mark Martin H .30 .75
105 Kurt Busch H .25 .60
106 R.Petty/Kahne H .50 1.25
107 Kyle Busch H .40 1.00
108 Ron Hornaday H .20 .50
109 Mark Martin T12 .30 .75
110 Tony Stewart T12 .50 1.25
111 Jimmie Johnson T12 .50 1.25
112 Denny Hamlin T12 .30 .75
113 Kasey Kahne T12 .30 .75
114 Jeff Gordon T12 .60 1.50
115 Kurt Busch T12 .25 .60
116 Brian Vickers T12 .20 .50
117 Carl Edwards T12 .30 .75
118 Ryan Newman T12 .25 .60
119 Juan Pablo Montoya T12 .30 .75
120 Greg Biffle T12 .25 .60
121 Jeff Gordon SP 2.00 5.00
122 Mark Martin SP 1.00 2.50
123 Jimmie Johnson SP 1.50 4.00
124 Juan Pablo Montoya SP 1.00 2.50
125 Kurt Busch SP .75 2.00
126 Tony Stewart SP 1.50 4.00
127 Denny Hamlin SP 1.00 2.50
128 Kasey Kahne SP 1.00 2.50
129 Ryan Newman SP .75 2.00
0 Cup Chase Drivers 4.00 10.00

2010 Press Pass Blue

COMPLETE SET (120) 20.00 50.00
*BLUE: .6X TO 1.5X BASIC CARDS
STATED ODDS 1 PER RETAIL PACK

2010 Press Pass Gold

COMPLETE SET (120) 20.00 50.00
*SINGLES: .5X TO 1.2X BASIC CARDS
STATED ODDS 1 PER HOBBY PACK
18 Marcos Ambrose 2.00 5.00
65 Marcos Ambrose's Car M 1.00 2.50
70 Marcos Ambrose RR 2.00 5.00
97 Marcos Ambrose's Car PD 1.00 2.50
103 Marcos Ambrose H 2.00 5.00

2010 Press Pass Holofoil

*SINGLES(1-120): 2X TO 5X BASE
*SP SINGLES (121-129): .8X TO 2X BASE SPs
STATED PRINT RUN 100 SER.#'d SETS
18 Marcos Ambrose 12.00 30.00
65 Marcos Ambrose's Car M 5.00 12.00
70 Marcos Ambrose RR 12.00 30.00
97 Marcos Ambrose's Car PD 5.00 12.00
103 Marcos Ambrose H 12.00 30.00

2010 Press Pass Purple

COMPLETE SET (120) 500.00 1000.00
*SINGLES: 4X TO 10X BASIC CARDS
*SP SINGLES: 1.5X TO 4X BASE SPs
STATED PRINT RUN 25 SER.#'d SETS

2010 Press Pass Autographs

STATED ODDS 1:84
UNPRICED PRINT PLATE PRINT RUN 1
UNPRICED TRACK EDITION PRINT RUN 10
1 Justin Allgaier 6.00 15.00
2 A.J. Allmendinger 8.00 20.00
3 Marcos Ambrose 12.00 30.00
4 Greg Biffle 6.00 15.00
5 Clint Bowyer 8.00 20.00
6 Colin Braun 6.00 15.00
7 James Buescher 6.00 15.00
8 Jeff Burton 6.00 15.00
9 Kurt Busch 6.00 15.00
10 Kyle Busch 15.00 40.00
11 Ricky Carmichael 8.00 20.00
12 Erik Darnell 5.00 12.00
13 Marc Davis 5.00 12.00
14 Dale Earnhardt Jr. 50.00 100.00
15 Carl Edwards 8.00 20.00
16 J.R. Fitzpatrick 6.00 15.00
17 Brendan Gaughan 5.00 12.00
18 Jeff Gordon 75.00 150.00
19 Robby Gordon 5.00 12.00
20 Denny Hamlin 8.00 20.00
21 Kevin Harvick 10.00 25.00
22 Ron Hornaday 5.00 12.00
23 Sam Hornish Jr. 6.00 15.00
24 Jimmie Johnson 50.00 100.00
25 Kasey Kahne 30.00 60.00
26 Matt Kenseth 15.00 40.00
27 Brad Keselowski 10.00 25.00
28 Brad Keselowski 10.00 25.00
29 Bobby Labonte 8.00 20.00
30 Scott Lagasse Jr. 5.00 12.00
31 Stephen Leicht 5.00 12.00
32 Joey Logano 8.00 20.00
33 Mark Martin 8.00 20.00
34 Jamie McMurray 8.00 20.00
35 Casey Mears 5.00 12.00
36 Paul Menard 5.00 12.00
37 Juan Pablo Montoya 8.00 20.00
38 Joe Nemechek 5.00 12.00
39 Ryan Newman 6.00 15.00
40 David Ragan 6.00 15.00
41 David Reutimann 6.00 15.00
42 Elliott Sadler 5.00 12.00
43 Johnny Sauter 5.00 12.00
44 Brian Scott 6.00 15.00
45 Mike Skinner 5.00 12.00
46 Regan Smith 6.00 15.00
47 Reed Sorenson 5.00 12.00
48 Scott Speed 8.00 20.00
49 Ricky Stenhouse Jr. 8.00 20.00
50 Martin Truex Jr. 6.00 15.00
51 Brian Vickers 5.00 12.00
52 Steve Wallace 6.00 15.00
53 Michael Waltrip 8.00 20.00

2010 Press Pass Autographs Chase Edition

STATED PRINT RUN 25 SER.#'d SETS
1 Greg Biffle 10.00 25.00
2 Kurt Busch 10.00 25.00
3 Carl Edwards
4 Jeff Gordon 100.00 200.00
5 Denny Hamlin 12.00 30.00
6 Jimmie Johnson 60.00 120.00
7 Kasey Kahne
8 Mark Martin 12.00 30.00
9 Juan Pablo Montoya 12.00 30.00
10 Ryan Newman 10.00 25.00
11 Tony Stewart 40.00 80.00
12 Brian Vickers 8.00 20.00

2010 Press Pass Burning Rubber

STATED PRINT RUN 250 SER.#'d SETS
*GOLD/50: .6X TO 1.5X BASIC INSERTS
*GOLD/99: .5X TO 1.2X BASIC INSERTS
*PRIME CUT/25: .8X TO 2X BASIC INSERTS
BR1 Matt Kenseth 3.00 8.00
BR2 Matt Kenseth 3.00 8.00
BR3 Kyle Busch 4.00 10.00
BR4 Kyle Busch 4.00 10.00
BR5 Jimmie Johnson 5.00 12.00
BR6 Jeff Gordon 6.00 15.00
BR7 Mark Martin 3.00 8.00
BR8 Brad Keselowski 4.00 10.00
BR9 Kyle Busch 4.00 10.00
BR10 Mark Martin 3.00 8.00
BR11 Tony Stewart 5.00 12.00
BR12 David Reutimann 2.50 6.00
BR13 Tony Stewart 5.00 12.00
BR14 Mark Martin 3.00 8.00
BR15 Kasey Kahne 3.00 8.00
BR16 Joey Logano 3.00 8.00
BR17 Jimmie Johnson 5.00 12.00
BR18 Denny Hamlin 3.00 8.00
BR19 Brian Vickers 2.00 5.00
BR20 Kyle Busch 4.00 10.00
BR21 Kasey Kahne 3.00 8.00
BR22 Denny Hamlin 3.00 8.00
BR23 Mark Martin 3.00 8.00
BR24 Jimmie Johnson 5.00 12.00
BR25 Tony Stewart 5.00 12.00
BR26 Jimmie Johnson 5.00 12.00
BR27 Jimmie Johnson 5.00 12.00
BR28 Denny Hamlin 3.00 8.00
BR29 Jamie McMurray 3.00 8.00
BR30 Kurt Busch 2.50 6.00
BR31 Jimmie Johnson 5.00 12.00
BR32 Denny Hamlin 3.00 8.00

2010 Press Pass Burning Rubber Autographs

SER.#'d TO DOOR NUMBER
STATED PRINT RUN 8-48
STEDE Dale Earnhardt Jr./8
SSTEJG Jeff Gordon/24 125.00 250.00
SSTEJJ Jimmie Johnson/48 100.00 200.00
SSTEJL Joey Logano/20 50.00 100.00
SSTEKH Kevin Harvick/29 50.00 100.00
SSTEMK Matt Kenseth/17

2010 Press Pass By The Numbers

COMPLETE SET (50) 75.00 150.00
PROGRESSIVE ODDS 1:3 TO 1:600
BN1 Jeff Gordon 1.25 3.00
BN2 Kyle Busch .75 2.00
BN3 Johnson/Yarborough 25.00 50.00
BN4 Mark Martin .60 1.50
BN5 Richard Petty 1.00 2.50
BN6 Davey Allison 1.00 2.50
BN7 Petty/Earnhardt 20.00 40.00
BN8 Harry Gant .60 1.50
BN9 T.Labonte/B.Labonte .60 1.50
BN10 Dale Earnhardt 3.00 8.00
BN11 Tony Stewart 1.00 2.50
BN12 Rusty Wallace .60 1.50
BN13 Jeff Gordon 1.25 3.00
BN14 Mike Skinner .40 1.00
BN15 Jeff Burton .50 1.25
BN16 Dale Earnhardt 3.00 8.00
BN17 Darrell Waltrip 1.00 2.50
BN18 Dale Earnhardt Jr. 1.25 3.00
BN19 Elliott Sadler .40 1.00
BN20 David Pearson .60 1.50
BN21 Jeff Gordon 1.25 3.00
BN22 Carl Edwards .60 1.50
BN23 Davey Allison 1.00 2.50
BN24 Michael Waltrip .60 1.50
BN25 Richard Petty 1.00 2.50
BN26 Fred Lorenzen .40 1.00
BN27 Bobby Allison .50 1.25
BN28 Paul Menard .40 1.00
BN29 Darrell Waltrip 1.00 2.50
BN30 Joe Nemechek .40 1.00
BN31 Tony Stewart 1.00 2.50
BN32 Robby Gordon .40 1.00
BN33 Matt Kenseth .60 1.50
BN34 Regan Smith .50 1.25
BN35 Benny Parsons .60 1.50
BN36 Kevin Harvick .75 2.00
BN37 David Pearson .60 1.50
BN38 Reed Sorenson .40 1.00
BN39 Bobby Allison .50 1.25
BN40 Ron Hornaday .40 1.00
BN41 Glen Wood .40 1.00
BN42 Richard Petty 1.00 2.50
BN43 A.J. Allmendinger .60 1.50
BN44 Lee Petty .50 1.25
BN45 Bobby Allison .50 1.25
BN46 Tim Flock .40 1.00
BN47 Alan Kulwicki 1.00 2.50
BN48 Curtis Turner .40 1.00
BN49 Rex White .40 1.00
BN50 David Reutimann .50 1.25

2010 Press Pass Cup Chase

STATED ODDS 1:28
CCR1 Tony Stewart WIN 4.00 10.00
CCR2 Kurt Busch WIN 2.00 5.00
CCR3 Greg Biffle WIN 2.00 5.00
CCR4 Dale Earnhardt Jr. 3.00 8.00
CCR5 Joey Logano 1.50 4.00
CCR6 Jeff Gordon WIN 5.00 12.00
CCR7 Ryan Newman 1.25 3.00
CCR8 Kyle Busch WIN 3.00 8.00
CCR9 Carl Edwards WIN 2.50 6.00
CCR10 Brian Vickers 1.00 2.50
CCR11 Kevin Harvick WIN 3.00 8.00
CCR12 Jimmie Johnson CHAMP 12.00 30.00
CCR13 Juan Pablo Montoya 1.50 4.00
CCR14 Denny Hamlin WIN 2.50 6.00
CCR15 Clint Bowyer WIN 2.50 6.00
CCR16 Kasey Kahne 1.50 4.00
CCR17 Mark Martin 1.50 4.00
CCR18 Field Card WIN 2.50 6.00

2010 Press Pass Cup Chase Prizes

COMPLETE SET (12) 5.00 12.00
ISSUED VIA MAIL REDEMPTION
CC1 Denny Hamlin .40 1.00
CC2 Jimmie Johnson .60 1.50
CC3 Kevin Harvick .50 1.25
CC4 Kyle Busch .50 1.25
CC5 Kurt Busch .30 .75
CC6 Tony Stewart .60 1.50
CC7 Greg Biffle .30 .75
CC8 Jeff Gordon .75 2.00
CC9 Carl Edwards .40 1.00
CC10 Jeff Burton .30 .75
CC11 Matt Kenseth .40 1.00
CC12 Clint Bowyer .40 1.00

2010 Press Pass Final Standings

FS1 Jimmie Johnson/25 30.00 60.00
FS2 Mark Martin/40 15.00 40.00
FS3 Jeff Gordon/50 20.00 50.00
FS4 Kurt Busch/60 10.00 25.00
FS5 Denny Hamlin/70 8.00 20.00
FS6 Tony Stewart/80 10.00 25.00
FS7 Greg Biffle/90 8.00 20.00
FS8 Juan Pablo Montoya/100 8.00 20.00
FS9 Ryan Newman/110 8.00 20.00
FS10 Kasey Kahne/120 8.00 20.00
FS11 Carl Edwards/130 8.00 20.00
FS12 Brian Vickers/140 8.00 20.00

2010 Press Pass NASCAR Hall of Fame

STATED ODDS 1:30
*BLUE RETAIL: .4X TO 1X BASIC INSERTS
*HOLOFOIL/50: .8X TO 2X BASIC INSERTS
NHOF1 Birth of NASCAR PP 2.00 5.00
NHOF2 Driving Ambition PP 2.00 5.00
NHOF3 Revving Up PP 2.00 5.00
NHOF4 Gaining Speed PP 2.00 5.00
NHOF5 Shifting Gears PP 2.00 5.00
NHOF6 Streamline Hotel Meeting EC 2.00 5.00
NHOF7 First NASCAR Race EC 2.00 5.00
NHOF8 First Strictly Stock Race EC 2.00 5.00
NHOF9 First 500 Mile Event EC 2.00 5.00
NHOF10 First Road Course Race EC 2.00 5.00
NHOF11 First Daytona 500 ST 2.00 5.00
NHOF12 First Telecast on CBS ME 2.00 5.00
NHOF13 First Race at Charlotte ST 2.00 5.00
NHOF14 Wendell Scott Victory ME 1.50 4.00
NHOF15 14 Lap Margin of Victory ST 2.00 5.00
NHOF16 Petty's Record Season ME 2.00 5.00
NHOF17 Alabama Intnl Speedway ST 2.00 5.00
NHOF18 Last Race on Dirt ME 2.00 5.00
NHOF19 Winston Comes To NASCAR ST 2.00 5.00
NHOF20 Modern Era Begins ME 2.00 5.00
NHOF21 Bill France Sr. Bill France Sr. ST 3.00 8.00
NHOF22 First Woman at Daytona 500 ME 2.00 5.00
NHOF23 1979 Daytona 500 ST 2.00 5.00
NHOF24 Cars Downsized ME 2.00 5.00
NHOF25 Darrell Waltrip ST 2.00 5.00
NHOF26 200 MPH ME 2.00 5.00
NHOF27 Petty's 200th Win ST 2.00 5.00
NHOF28 All Races Televised ME 2.00 5.00
NHOF29 Richard Petty Retires ST 2.00 5.00
NHOF30 1992 Championship ME 2.00 5.00
NHOF31 Jeff Gordon's Car ST 2.50 6.00
NHOF32 Earnhardt Ties Petty ME 6.00 15.00
NHOF33 Introduction of SAFER Barrier ST 2.00 5.00
NHOF34 First Chase ME 2.00 5.00
NHOF35 Car of Tomorrow Debuts ST 2.00 5.00
NHOF36 Red Byron's Car ME 1.50 4.00
NHOF37 Herb Thomas' Car ST 2.00 2.50
NHOF38 Lee Petty's Car ME 2.00 4.00
NHOF39 Fireball Roberts' Car ST 2.00 5.00
NHOF40 Richard Petty's Car ME 2.00 5.00
NHOF41 Bobby Isaac's Car ST 1.50 4.00
NHOF42 D.Pearson's Car ME 1.25 3.00
NHOF43 C.Yarborough's Car ST 2.00 5.00
NHOF44 D.Waltrip's Car ME 2.00 5.00
NHOF45 Richie Evans' Car ST 1.50 4.00
NHOF46 Bobby Allison's Car ME 2.00 5.00
NHOF47 Dale Earnhardt's Car ST 6.00 15.00
NHOF48 Ron Hornaday's Truck ME 2.00 5.00
NHOF49 Kurt Busch's Car ST 1.00 2.50
NHOF50 J.Johnson's Car ME 2.00 5.00
NHOF51 Bill France Sr. PP 3.00 8.00
NHOF52 Bill France Sr. EC 3.00 8.00
NHOF53 Bill France Sr. EL 3.00 8.00
NHOF54 Bill France Sr. EC 3.00 8.00
NHOF55 Bill France Sr. PPP 3.00 8.00
NHOF56 Bill France Sr. EL 3.00 8.00
NHOF57 Bill France Sr. PPP 3.00 8.00
NHOF58 Bill France Sr. PPP 3.00 8.00
NHOF59 Bill France Sr. PPP 3.00 8.00
NHOF60 Bill France Sr. ME 3.00 8.00
NHOF61 Richard Petty PP 2.00 5.00
NHOF62 Richard Petty EC 2.00 5.00
NHOF63 Richard Petty EL 2.00 5.00
NHOF64 Richard Petty EC 2.00 5.00
NHOF65 Richard Petty PPP 2.00 5.00
NHOF66 Richard Petty EL 2.00 5.00
NHOF67 Richard Petty PPP 2.00 5.00
NHOF68 Richard Petty PPP 2.00 5.00
NHOF69 Richard Petty PPP 2.00 5.00
NHOF70 Richard Petty ME 2.00 5.00
NHOF71 Dale Earnhardt PP 6.00 15.00
NHOF72 Dale Earnhardt EC 6.00 15.00
NHOF73 Dale Earnhardt EL 6.00 15.00
NHOF74 Dale Earnhardt EC 6.00 15.00
NHOF75 Dale Earnhardt PPP 6.00 15.00
NHOF76 Dale Earnhardt EL 6.00 15.00
NHOF77 Dale Earnhardt PPP 6.00 15.00
NHOF78 Dale Earnhardt PPP 6.00 15.00
NHOF79 Dale Earnhardt PPP 6.00 15.00
NHOF80 Dale Earnhardt ME 6.00 15.00
NHOF81 Bill France Jr. PP 2.00 5.00
NHOF82 Bill France Jr. EC 2.00 5.00
NHOF83 Bill France Jr. EL 2.00 5.00
NHOF84 Bill France Jr. EC 2.00 5.00
NHOF85 Bill France Jr. PPP 2.00 5.00
NHOF86 Bill France Jr. EL 2.00 5.00
NHOF87 Bill France Jr. PPP 2.00 5.00
NHOF88 Bill France Jr. PPP 2.00 5.00
NHOF89 Bill France Jr. PPP 2.00 5.00
NHOF90 Bill France Jr. ME 2.00 5.00
NHOF91 Junior Johnson PP 1.50 4.00
NHOF92 Junior Johnson EC 1.50 4.00
NHOF93 Junior Johnson EL 1.50 4.00
NHOF94 Junior Johnson EC 1.50 4.00
NHOF95 Junior Johnson PPP 1.50 4.00
NHOF96 Junior Johnson EL 1.50 4.00
NHOF97 Junior Johnson PPP 1.50 4.00
NHOF98 Junior Johnson PPP 1.50 4.00
NHOF99 Junior Johnson PPP 1.50 4.00
NHOF100 Junior Johnson ME 1.50 4.00

2010 Press Pass Top 12 Tires

SER #'d TO DOOR NUMBER
SOME NOT PRICED DUE TO SCARCITY
BV Brian Vickers/83 10.00 25.00
CE Carl Edwards/99 15.00 30.00
DH Denny Hamlin/11
GB Greg Biffle/16
JG Jeff Gordon/24 50.00 100.00
JJ Jimmie Johnson/48 20.00 40.00
JM Juan Pablo Montoya/42 10.00 25.00
KB Kurt Busch/2
KK Kasey Kahne/9
MM Mark Martin/5
RN Ryan Newman/39 15.00 30.00
TS Tony Stewart/14

2010 Press Pass Top 12 Tires 10

STATED PRINT RUN 10 SER.#'d SETS
NOT PRICED DUE TO SCARCITY

2010 Press Pass Tradin' Paint

COMPLETE SET (9) 12.00 30.00
STATED ODDS 1:12
TP1 Jeff Gordon 1.25 3.00
TP2 Matt Kenseth .60 1.50
TP3 Kyle Busch .75 2.00
TP4 Tony Stewart 1.00 2.50
TP5 Juan Pablo Montoya .60 1.50
TP6 Carl Edwards .60 1.50
TP7 Kevin Harvick .75 2.00
TP8 Dale Earnhardt Jr. 1.25 3.00
TP9 Jimmie Johnson 1.00 2.50

2010 Press Pass Tradin' Paint Sheet Metal

STATED PRINT RUN 299 SER.#'d SETS
*GOLD/42-50: .6X TO 1.2X SHT METAL/299
*HOLO/25: .6X TO 1.5X SHEET METAL/299

TPCB Clint Bowyer 4.00 10.00
TPCE Carl Edwards 4.00 10.00
TPDE Dale Earnhardt Jr. 8.00 20.00
TPES Elliott Sadler 2.50 6.00
TPJG Jeff Gordon NG 8.00 20.00
TPJJ Jimmie Johnson 6.00 15.00
TPKB Kyle Busch 5.00 12.00
TPMK Matt Kenseth 4.00 10.00
TPRN Ryan Newman 3.00 8.00
TPRS Reed Sorenson 2.50 6.00
TPTS Tony Stewart 6.00 15.00
TPJG2 Jeff Gordon Pepsi 8.00 20.00

2010 Press Pass Unleashed

COMPLETE SET (12) 12.00 30.00
STATED ODDS 1:6
U1 Matt Kenseth .50 1.25
U2 Jeff Gordon 1.00 2.50
U3 Kyle Busch .60 1.50
U4 Brad Keselowski .60 1.50
U5 David Reutimann .40 1.00
U6 Jimmie Johnson .75 2.00
U7 Tony Stewart .75 2.00
U8 Kasey Kahne .50 1.25
U9 Joey Logano .50 1.25
U10 Mark Martin .50 1.25
U11 Jimmie Johnson .75 2.00
U12 Brian Vickers .30 .75

2010 Press Pass Target By The Numbers

COMPLETE SET (6) 25.00 50.00
BNT1 Dale Earnhardt Jr. 655 2.50 6.00
BNT2 Dale Earnhardt 406 6.00 15.00
BNT3 Joey Logano 287 1.25 3.00
BNT4 Jeff Gordon 67 2.50 6.00
BNT5 Tony Stewart 280 2.00 5.00
BNT6 Jimmie Johnson 171 2.00 5.00

2010 Press Pass Target Top Numbers Tires

TNT-BK Brad Keselowski 20.00 40.00
TNT-DE Dale Jr. NG 30.00 60.00

2010 Press Pass Wal-Mart By The Numbers

COMPLETE SET (6) 25.00 50.00
STATED ODDS 1:30

2010 Press Pass Wal-Mart Top Numbers Tires

TNW-DE Dale Jr. AMP 30.00 60.00
TNW-JL Joey Logano 20.00 40.00

2011 Press Pass

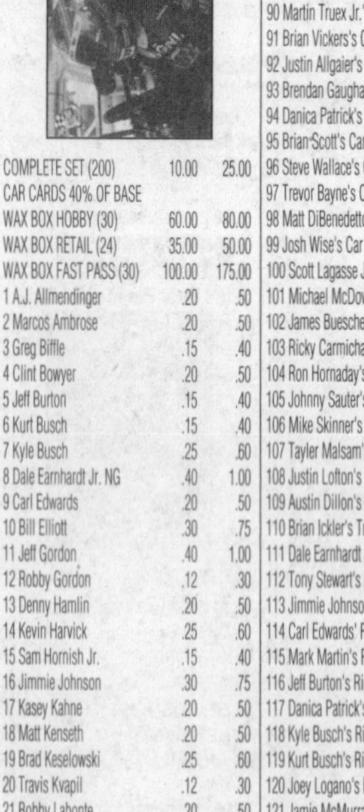

COMPLETE SET (200) 10.00 25.00
CAR CARDS 40% OF BASE
WAX BOX HOBBY (30) 60.00 80.00
WAX BOX RETAIL (24) 35.00 50.00
WAX BOX FAST PASS (30) 100.00 175.00
1 A.J. Allmendinger .20 .50
2 Marcos Ambrose .20 .50
3 Greg Biffle .15 .40
4 Clint Bowyer .20 .50
5 Jeff Burton .15 .40
6 Kurt Busch .15 .40
7 Kyle Busch .25 .60
8 Dale Earnhardt Jr. NG .40 1.00
9 Carl Edwards .20 .50
10 Bill Elliott .30 .75
11 Jeff Gordon .40 1.00
12 Robby Gordon .12 .30
13 Denny Hamlin .20 .50
14 Kevin Harvick .25 .60
15 Sam Hornish Jr. .15 .40
16 Jimmie Johnson .30 .75
17 Kasey Kahne .20 .50
18 Matt Kenseth .20 .50
19 Brad Keselowski .25 .60
20 Travis Kvapil .12 .30
21 Bobby Labonte .20 .50
22 Joey Logano .20 .50
23 Mark Martin .20 .50
24 Jamie McMurray .20 .50
25 Paul Menard .12 .30
26 Juan Pablo Montoya .20 .50
27 Joe Nemechek .12 .30
28 Ryan Newman .15 .40
29 David Ragan .15 .40
30 David Reutimann .15 .40
31 Elliott Sadler .12 .30
32 Scott Speed .15 .40
33 Regan Smith .15 .40
34 Tony Stewart .30 .75
35 Martin Truex Jr. .12 .30
36 Brian Vickers .12 .30
37 Justin Allgaier NNS .15 .40
38 Brendan Gaughan NNS .12 .30
39 Danica Patrick NNS .75 2.00
40 Brian Scott NNS .12 .30
41 Steve Wallace NNS .15 .40
42 Trevor Bayne NNS .40 1.00
43 Matt DiBenedetto NNS .12 .30
44 Josh Wise NNS .12 .30
45 Scott Lagasse Jr. NNS .12 .30
46 Michael McDowell NNS .15 .40
47 James Buescher CWTS .12 .30
48 Ricky Carmichael CWTS .20 .50
49 Ron Hornaday CWTS .12 .30
50 Johnny Sauter CWTS .12 .30
51 Mike Skinner CWTS .12 .30
52 Tayler Malsam CWTS .12 .30
53 Justin Lofton CWTS .20 .50
54 Austin Dillon CWTS .40 1.00
55 Brian Ickler CWTS .25 .60
56 A.J. Allmendinger's Car .12 .30
57 Marcos Ambrose's Car .12 .30
58 Greg Biffle's Car .10 .25
59 Clint Bowyer's Car .12 .30
60 Jeff Burton's Car .10 .25
61 Kurt Busch's Car .10 .25
62 Kyle Busch's Car .15 .40
63 Dale Earnhardt Jr.'s Car .25 .60
64 Carl Edwards' Car .12 .30
65 Bill Elliott's Car .20 .50
66 Jeff Gordon's Car .25 .60
67 Robby Gordon's Car .07 .20
68 Denny Hamlin's Car .12 .30
69 Kevin Harvick's Car .15 .40
70 Sam Hornish Jr.'s Car .10 .25
71 Jimmie Johnson's Car .20 .50
72 Kasey Kahne's Car .12 .30
73 Matt Kenseth's Car .12 .30
74 Brad Keselowski's Car .15 .40
75 Travis Kvapil's Car .07 .20
76 Bobby Labonte's Car .12 .30
77 Joey Logano's Car .12 .30
78 Mark Martin's Car .12 .30
79 Jamie McMurray's Car .12 .30
80 Paul Menard's Car .07 .20
81 Juan Pablo Montoya's Car .12 .30
82 Joe Nemechek's Car .07 .20
83 Ryan Newman's Car .10 .25
84 David Ragan's Car .10 .25
85 David Reutimann's Car .10 .25
86 Elliott Sadler's Car .07 .20
87 Scott Speed's Car .10 .25
88 Regan Smith's Car .10 .25
89 Tony Stewart's Car .20 .50
90 Martin Truex Jr.'s Car .10 .25
91 Brian Vickers's Car .07 .20
92 Justin Allgaier's Car .10 .25
93 Brendan Gaughan's Car .07 .20
94 Danica Patrick's Car .50 1.25
95 Brian Scott's Car .07 .20
96 Steve Wallace's Car .10 .25
97 Trevor Bayne's Car .25 .60
98 Matt DiBenedetto's Car .07 .20
99 Josh Wise's Car .07 .20
100 Scott Lagasse Jr.'s Car .07 .20
101 Michael McDowell's Car .10 .25
102 James Buescher's Truck .07 .20
103 Ricky Carmichael's Truck .12 .30
104 Ron Hornaday's Truck .07 .20
105 Johnny Sauter's Truck .07 .20
106 Mike Skinner's Truck .07 .20
107 Tayler Malsam's Truck .07 .20
108 Justin Lofton's Truck .07 .20
109 Austin Dillon's Truck .15 .40
110 Brian Ickler's Truck .10 .25
111 Dale Earnhardt Jr.'s Rig .25 .60
112 Tony Stewart's Rig .20 .50
113 Jimmie Johnson's Rig .20 .50
114 Carl Edwards' Rig .12 .30
115 Mark Martin's Rig .12 .30
116 Jeff Burton's Rig .10 .25
117 Danica Patrick's Rig .50 1.25
118 Kyle Busch's Rig .15 .40
119 Kurt Busch's Rig .10 .25
120 Joey Logano's Rig .12 .30
121 Jamie McMurray's Rig .12 .30
122 Scott Speed's Rig .10 .25
123 Stewart .20 .50
Waltrip's Cars Bristol CC
124 Daytona
125 Keselowski .15 .40
Burton's Cars DARL
126 Kahne .20 .50
Busch
JJ
Hamlin's Cars ATL
127 Keselowski .15 .40
Kahne
Newman's Cars CHAR
128 Rain Delay Martinsville .12 .30
129 Phoenix .12 .30
130 Kahne .12 .30
Wimmer's Cars LV
131 Jr .25 .60
Martin
Reut
Ragan's Cars TALL
132 Stew .20 .50
Biff
JJ
Kahne's Cars TEX
133 California .12 .30
134 Watkins Glen .12 .30
135 Kevin Harvick LP .25 .60
136 Jimmie Johnson LP .30 .75
137 Jamie McMurray LP .20 .50
138 Kurt Busch LP .15 .40
139 Denny Hamlin LP .20 .50
140 Ryan Newman LP .15 .40
141 Kyle Busch LP .25 .60
142 David Reutimann LP .15 .40
143 Greg Biffle LP .15 .40
144 Juan Pablo Montoya LP .20 .50
145 Justin Allgaier LP .15 .40
146 Brad Keselowski LP .25 .60
147 Carl Edwards LP .20 .50
148 Dale Earnhardt Jr. LP .40 1.00
149 Marcos Ambrose LP .20 .50
150 Johnny Sauter LP .12 .30
151 Austin Dillon LP .25 .60
152 Ron Hornaday LP .12 .30
153 Tony Stewart LP .30 .75
154 Jamie McMurray HL .20 .50
155 Danica Patrick HL .75 2.00
156 Dale Earnhardt Jr. HL .40 1.00
157 Jamie McMurray HL .20 .50
158 Kyle Busch HL .25 .60
159 Brian Vickers HL .12 .30
160 Kyle Busch HL .25 .60
161 Jeff Gordon HL .40 1.00
162 Jimmie Johnson HL .30 .75
163 Ragan .15 .40
Logano
Waltrip Cars HL
164 Jimmie Johnson HL .30 .75
165 Ambrose .12 .30
Newman
Logano Cars HL
166 Jeff Burton HL .15 .40
167 Kurt Busch HL .15 .40
168 Marcos Ambrose HL .20 .50
169 Dale Jr.'s Car NNS HL .25 .60
170 Denny Hamlin HL .20 .50
171 A.J. Allmendinger's Car GG .12 .30
172 Marcos Ambrose's Car GG .12 .30
173 Greg Biffle's Car GG .10 .25
174 Clint Bowyer's Car GG .12 .30
175 Jeff Burton's Car GG .10 .25
176 Kurt Busch's Car GG .10 .25
177 Kyle Busch's Car GG .15 .40
178 Dale Earnhardt Jr.'s Car GG .25 .60
179 Carl Edwards' Car GG .12 .30
180 Jeff Gordon's Car GG .25 .60
181 Denny Hamlin's Car GG .12 .30
182 Sam Hornish Jr.'s Car GG .10 .25
183 Jimmie Johnson's Car GG .20 .50
184 Bobby Labonte's Car GG .12 .30
185 Joey Logano's Car GG .12 .30
186 Tony Stewart's Car GG .20 .50
187 Martin Truex Jr.'s Car GG .10 .25
188 Ryan Newman's Car GG .10 .25
189 Kevin Harvick T12 .25 .60
190 Kyle Busch T12 .25 .60
191 Jeff Gordon T12 .40 1.00
192 Carl Edwards T12 .20 .50
193 Jimmie Johnson T12 .30 .75
194 Tony Stewart T12 .30 .75
195 Jeff Burton T12 .15 .40
196 Matt Kenseth T12 .20 .50
197 Denny Hamlin T12 .20 .50
198 Kurt Busch T12 .15 .40
199 Clint Bowyer T12 .20 .50
200 Greg Biffle T12 .15 .40
0 Chase Contenders 1.50 4.00

2011 Press Pass Blue Retail

*BLUE RETAIL: 3X TO 8X BASE
STATED ODDS 1:12 RETAIL

2011 Press Pass Gold

*GOLD/50: 4X TO 10X BASIC CARDS
STATED PRINT RUN 50 SER.#'d SETS

2011 Press Pass Purple

*PURPLE/25: 6X TO 15X BASIC CARDS
PURPLE PRINT RUN 25 SER.#'d SETS

2011 Press Pass Autographs Bronze

STATED PRINT RUN 5-150
1 Justin Allgaier/75 5.00 12.00
2 A.J. Allmendinger/99 6.00 15.00
3 Marcos Ambrose/73 6.00 15.00
4 Trevor Bayne/75 20.00 50.00
5 Greg Biffle/75 5.00 12.00
6 Clint Bowyer/99 6.00 15.00
7 Colin Braun/65 5.00 12.00
8 James Buescher
9 Jeff Burton/99 5.00 12.00
10 Kurt Busch/70 5.00 12.00
11 Kyle Busch/5
12 Kevin Conway/65 5.00 12.00
13 Matt DiBenedetto/75 4.00 10.00
14 Austin Dillon 12.00 30.00
15 Dale Earnhardt Jr./20 60.00 120.00
16 Carl Edwards/99 6.00 15.00
17 Brendan Gaughan 4.00 10.00
18 Jeff Gordon/20
19 Robby Gordon/20
20 Denny Hamlin/75 6.00 15.00
21 Kevin Harvick/10
22 Ron Hornaday 4.00 10.00
23 Sam Hornish Jr./75 5.00 12.00
24 Brian Ickler 5.00 12.00
25 Jimmie Johnson/5
26 Kasey Kahne/20 40.00 80.00
27 Matt Kenseth/99 6.00 15.00
28 Brad Keselowski/35 12.00 30.00
29 Travis Kvapil/99 4.00 10.00
30 Bobby Labonte/23
31 Scott Lagasse Jr. 4.00 10.00
32 Justin Lofton 4.00 10.00
33 Joey Logano/99 6.00 15.00
34 Tayler Malsam/75 4.00 10.00
35 Mark Martin/54 6.00 15.00
36 Michael McDowell 5.00 12.00
37 Jamie McMurray/99 6.00 15.00
38 Paul Menard/78 4.00 10.00
39 Juan Pablo Montoya/50 6.00 15.00
40 Joe Nemechek/99 4.00 10.00
41 Joe Nemechek/24
42 Ryan Newman/99 5.00 12.00
43 Ryan Newman/44 5.00 12.00
44 Danica Patrick/50 75.00 125.00
45 David Ragan/75 5.00 12.00
46 David Reutimann/99 5.00 12.00
47 Elliott Sadler/45 4.00 10.00
48 Johnny Sauter 4.00 10.00
49 Brian Scott/75 4.00 10.00
50 Mike Skinner 4.00 10.00
51 Regan Smith/99 5.00 12.00
52 Scott Speed/75 5.00 12.00
53 Ricky Stenhouse Jr./72
54 Tony Stewart/20
55 Martin Truex Jr./99 5.00 12.00
56 Brian Vickers/99 4.00 10.00
57 Steve Wallace 5.00 12.00
58 Michael Waltrip/99 6.00 15.00
59 Josh Wise 4.00 10.00

2011 Press Pass Autographs Gold

*GOLD/15-25: .8X TO 2X BRONZE
STATED PRINT RUN 5-25
41 Danica Patrick/15 125.00 250.00
48 Regan Smith 20.00 50.00

2011 Press Pass Autographs Silver

*SILVER/18-52: .8X TO 2X BRONZE
STATED PRINT RUN 5-52
4 Trevor Bayne 25.00 60.00
15 Paige Duke/40 25.00 50.00
43 Monica Palumbo/40 25.00 50.00
44 Danica Patrick/25 100.00 150.00
60 Amanda Wright/40 25.00 50.00

2011 Press Pass Bristol Sweep Holofoil

STATED PRINT RUN 50 SER.#'d SETS
BRKYB3 Kyle Busch 10.00 25.00

2011 Press Pass Burning Rubber Gold

STATED PRINT RUN 150 SER.#'d SETS
*HOLO/50: .5X TO 1.2X GOLD/150
*PRIME CUT/25: .6X TO 1.5X GOLD/150
BRDE Dale Jr. Daytona 10.00 25.00
BRDH D.Hamlin Martinsville Spring 5.00 12.00
BRDR D.Reutimann Chicago 6.00 12.00
BRGB G.Biffle Pocono 4.00 10.00
BRJJ J.Johnson Fontana 10.00 25.00
BRJM J.McMurray Daytona 5.00 12.00
BRJMO J.Montoya Watkins Glen 5.00 12.00
BRKH K.Harvick Talladega 6.00 15.00
BRRN R.Newman Phoenix 4.00 10.00
BRTS T.Stewart Atlanta 12.00 30.00
BRCCE C.Edwards Phoenix 5.00 12.00
BRCDH2 D.Hamlin Martinsville Fall 5.00 12.00
BRCDH1 D.Hamlin Texas Fall 5.00 12.00
BRCGB G.Biffle Kansas 4.00 10.00
BRCJJ J.Johnson Dover 10.00 25.00
BRCJM J.McMurray Charlotte 5.00 12.00
BRCTS T.Stewart California 12.00 30.00
BRJJ2 J.Johnson Las Vegas 10.00 25.00
BRJJ3 J.Johnson Bristol 10.00 25.00
BRJM2 J.McMurray Indy 5.00 12.00
BRKH2 K.Harvick Daytona 6.00 15.00
BRKUB K.Busch Atlanta 6.00 15.00
BRKYB Ky.Busch Richmond 8.00 20.00
BRCCB1 C.Bowyer New Hampshire 5.00 12.00
BRCCB2 C.Bowyer Talladega 5.00 12.00
BRCCE1 C.Edwards Miami 5.00 12.00

2011 Press Pass Cup Chase

STATED ODDS 1:30
CCR1 Denny Hamlin WIN 2.50 6.00
CCR2 Jimmie Johnson WIN 4.00 10.00
CCR3 Kevin Harvick WIN 3.00 8.00
CCR4 Kyle Busch WIN 3.00 8.00
CCR5 Kurt Busch WIN 2.00 5.00
CCR6 Tony Stewart CHAMP 8.00 20.00
CCR7 Greg Biffle 1.25 3.00
CCR8 Jeff Gordon WIN 5.00 12.00
CCR9 Carl Edwards WIN 2.50 6.00
CCR10 Jeff Burton 1.25 3.00
CCR11 Matt Kenseth WIN 2.50 6.00
CCR12 Clint Bowyer 1.50 4.00
CCR13 Dale Earnhardt Jr. WIN 5.00 12.00
CCR14 Mark Martin 1.50 4.00
CCR15 Ryan Newman WIN 2.00 5.00
CCR16 Jamie McMurray 1.50 4.00
CCR17 Kasey Kahne 2.50 6.00
CCR18 Field Card WIN 1.50 4.00

2011 Press Pass Cup Chase Prizes

COMPLETE SET (12) 5.00 12.00
ISSUED VIA MAIL REDEMPTION
CC1 Kyle Busch .50 1.25
CC2 Kevin Harvick .50 1.25
CC3 Jeff Gordon .75 2.00
CC4 Matt Kenseth .40 1.00
CC5 Carl Edwards .40 1.00
CC6 Jimmie Johnson .60 1.50
CC7 Kurt Busch .30 .75
CC8 Ryan Newman .30 .75
CC9 Tony Stewart .60 1.50
CC10 Dale Earnhardt Jr. .75 2.00
CC11 Brad Keselowski .50 1.25
CC12 Denny Hamlin .40 1.00
CCP Tony Stewart Firesuit 6.00 15.00

2011 Press Pass Flashback

COMPLETE SET (12) 8.00 20.00
STATED ODDS 1:10
FB1 Greg Biffle .50 1.25
FB2 Jeff Burton .50 1.25
FB3 Matt Kenseth .60 1.50
FB4 Dale Earnhardt Jr. 1.25 3.00
FB5 Carl Edwards .60 1.50
FB6 Kevin Harvick .75 2.00
FB7 Jeff Gordon 1.25 3.00
FB8 Jimmie Johnson 1.00 2.50
FB9 Tony Stewart 1.00 2.50
FB10 Bill Elliott 1.00 2.50
FB11 Mark Martin .60 1.50
FB12 Michael Waltrip .75 2.00

2011 Press Pass Geared Up Holofoil

HOLOFOIL PRINT RUN 20-50
*GOLD/50-100: .3X TO .8X HOLO/20-50
GUAA A.J. Allmendinger 6.00 15.00
GUBE Bill Elliott 10.00 25.00
GUBK Brad Keselowski 8.00 20.00
GUBV Brian Vickers 4.00 10.00
GUCB Clint Bowyer 6.00 15.00
GUCE Carl Edwards 6.00 15.00
GUDE Dale Earnhardt Jr. 12.00 30.00
GUDH Denny Hamlin/25 25.00 60.00
GUDP Danica Patrick 25.00 60.00
GUES Elliott Sadler 4.00 10.00
GUGB Greg Biffle/25 5.00 12.00
GUJA Justin Allgaier 5.00 12.00
GUJB Jeff Burton 5.00 12.00
GUJG Jeff Gordon 12.00 30.00
GUJJ Jimmie Johnson 10.00 25.00
GUJL Joey Logano/20 6.00 15.00
GUJM Jamie McMurray 6.00 15.00
GUKH Kevin Harvick 8.00 20.00
GUKK Kasey Kahne 6.00 15.00
GUMA Marcos Ambrose 6.00 15.00
GUMK Matt Kenseth 6.00 15.00
GUMM Mark Martin 6.00 15.00
GUMT Martin Truex Jr. 5.00 12.00
GUMW Michael Waltrip 8.00 20.00
GUPM Paul Menard 4.00 10.00
GUSH Sam Hornish Jr. 5.00 12.00
GUSS Scott Speed 5.00 12.00
GUTS Tony Stewart 10.00 25.00
GUDRA David Ragan 5.00 12.00
GUDRE David Reutimann 5.00 12.00
GUJPM Juan Pablo Montoya 6.00 15.00
GUKUB Kurt Busch 5.00 12.00
GUKYB Kyle Busch 8.00 20.00

2011 Press Pass NASCAR Hall of Fame

BOBBY ALLISON 1.00 2.50
BOBBY ALLISON ODDS 1:30 PP
NED JARRETT 1.25 3.00
NED JARRETT ODDS 1:24 ELEMENT
BUD MOORE 1.25 3.00
BUD MOORE ODDS 1:24 ECLIPSE
DAVID PEARSON 2.00 5.00
D.PEARSON ODDS 1:24 PP PREM
LEE PETTY 1.25 3.00
LEE PETTY ODDS 1:24 STEALTH
*BLUE RETAIL: .4X TO 1X BASIC INSERTS
*HOLOFOIL/50: .8X TO 2X BASIC INSERTS

2011 Press Pass Tradin' Paint

COMPLETE SET (9) 10.00 25.00
STATED ODDS 1:15
TP1 Ryan Newman .60 1.50
TP2 Kyle Busch 1.00 2.50
TP3 Dale Earnhardt Jr. 1.50 4.00
TP4 Jimmie Johnson 1.25 3.00
TP5 Jeff Gordon 1.50 4.00
TP6 Carl Edwards .75 2.00
TP7 Mark Martin .75 2.00
TP8 Tony Stewart 1.25 3.00
TP9 Dale Earnhardt Jr. NNS 1.50 4.00

2011 Press Pass Tradin' Paint Sheet Metal Holofoil

STATED PRINT RUN 50 SER.#'d SETS
*BLUE/25: .6X TO 1.5X HOLO/50
TPCE Carl Edwards 5.00 12.00
TPDE Dale Earnhardt Jr. 10.00 25.00
TPJG Jeff Gordon 10.00 25.00
TPJJ Jimmie Johnson 8.00 20.00
TPMM Mark Martin 5.00 12.00
TPRN Ryan Newman 4.00 10.00
TPTS Tony Stewart 8.00 20.00
TPKYB Kyle Busch 6.00 15.00

2011 Press Pass Winning Tickets

COMP.SET w/o SPs (46) 15.00 40.00
STATED ODDS 1:3
WT1 Jamie McMurray .60 1.50
WT2 Jimmie Johnson 1.00 2.50
WT3 Jimmie Johnson 1.00 2.50
WT4 Kurt Busch .50 1.25
WT5 Jimmie Johnson 1.00 2.50
WT6 Denny Hamlin .60 1.50
WT7 Ryan Newman .50 1.25
WT8 Denny Hamlin .60 1.50
WT9 Kevin Harvick .75 2.00
WT10 Kyle Busch .75 2.00
WT11 Denny Hamlin .60 1.50
WT12 Kyle Busch .75 2.00
WT13 Kurt Busch .50 1.25
WT14 Denny Hamlin .60 1.50
WT15 Denny Hamlin .60 1.50
WT16 Jimmie Johnson 1.00 2.50
WT17 Jimmie Johnson 1.00 2.50
WT18 Kevin Harvick .75 2.00
WT19 David Reutimann .50 1.25
WT20 Jamie McMurray .60 1.50
WT21 Greg Biffle .50 1.25
WT22 Juan Pablo Montoya .60 1.50
WT23 Kevin Harvick .75 2.00
WT24 Kyle Busch .75 2.00
WT25 Tony Stewart 1.00 2.50
WT26 Denny Hamlin .60 1.50
WT27 Clint Bowyer .60 1.50
WT28 Jimmie Johnson 1.00 2.50
WT29 Greg Biffle .50 1.25
WT30 Justin Allgaier .50 1.25
WT31 Kevin Harvick .75 2.00
WT32 Denny Hamlin .60 1.50
WT33 Brad Keselowski .75 2.00
WT34 Dale Earnhardt Jr. 1.25 3.00
WT35 Joey Logano .60 1.50
WT36 Dale Earnhardt Jr. 1.25 3.00
WT37 Carl Edwards .60 1.50
WT38 Marcos Ambrose .60 1.50
WT39 Kyle Busch .75 2.00
WT40 Kevin Harvick .75 2.00
WT41 Kyle Busch .75 2.00
WT42 Johnny Sauter .40 1.00
WT43 Austin Dillon .75 2.00
WT44 Kevin Harvick .75 2.00
WT45 Ron Hornaday .40 1.00
WT46 Kyle Busch .75 2.00
WT47 Benny Parsons SP 1.25 3.00
WT48 David Pearson SP 1.25 3.00
WT49 Richard Petty SP 2.00 5.00
WT50 Bill Elliott SP 2.00 5.00
WT51 Bill Elliott SP 2.00 5.00
WT52 Davey Allison SP 2.00 5.00
WT53 Bobby Allison SP 1.00 2.50
WT54 Darrell Waltrip SP 2.00 5.00
WT55 Jeff Gordon SP 2.50 6.00
WT56 Dale Earnhardt SP 6.00 15.00
WT57 Dale Earnhardt SP 6.00 15.00
WT58 Michael Waltrip SP 1.50 4.00
WT59 Kevin Harvick SP 1.50 4.00
WT60 Jimmie Johnson SP 2.00 5.00
WT61 Kevin Harvick SP 1.50 4.00
WT62 Jeff Gordon SP 2.50 6.00

2011 Press Pass Target Top 12 Tires

STATED PRINT RUN 25 SER.#'d SETS
T12CB Clint Bowyer 8.00 20.00
T12CE Carl Edwards
T12DH Denny Hamlin 8.00 20.00
T12JB Jeff Burton
T12JG Jeff Gordon 20.00 50.00
T12KH Kevin Harvick

2011 Press Pass Target Winning Tickets

COMPLETE SET (8) 6.00 15.00
RANDOM INSERTS IN TARGET BLASTER BOXES
WTT1 Kevin Harvick .75 2.00
WTT2 Jimmie Johnson 1.00 2.50
WTT3 Kasey Kahne .60 1.50
WTT4 Carl Edwards NNS .60 1.50
WTT5 Jamie McMurray NNS .60 1.50
WTT6 Kevin Harvick NNS .75 2.00
WTT7 Kyle Busch NNS .75 2.00
WTT8 Joey Logano NNS .60 1.50

2011 Press Pass Wal-Mart Top 12 Tires

T12KYB Kyle Busch 10.00 25.00

2011 Press Pass Wal-Mart Winning Tickets

COMPLETE SET (8) 6.00 15.00
RANDOM INSERTS IN WALMART BLASTER BOXES
WTW1 Kevin Harvick NNS .75 2.00
WTW2 Kyle Busch NNS .75 2.00
WTW3 Martin Truex Jr. .75 2.00
WTW4 Kurt Busch .75 2.00
WTW5 Brad Keselowski NNS .50 1.25
WTW6 Kyle Busch NNS .50 1.25
WTW7 Kyle Busch NNS .75 2.00
WTW8 Brad Keselowski NNS .75 2.00

2012 Press Pass

COMPLETE SET (100) 8.00 20.00
*CAR CARDS 50% OF BASE
CHASE CONTENDERS ODDS 1:60 HOB
SANTA STATED ODDS 1:150
WAX BOX HOBBY 50.00 80.00
WAX BOX RETAIL 35.00 50.00
1 A.J. Allmendinger .25 .60
2 Marcos Ambrose .25 .60
3 Trevor Bayne .25 .60
4 Greg Biffle .20 .50
5 Jeff Burton .20 .50
6 Kurt Busch .20 .50
7 Kyle Busch .30 .75
8 Landon Cassill .20 .50
9 Kevin Conway .15 .40
10 Dale Earnhardt Jr. .50 1.25
11 Carl Edwards .25 .60
12 David Gilliland .15 .40
13 Jeff Gordon .50 1.25
14 Robby Gordon .15 .40
15 Denny Hamlin .25 .60
16 Kevin Harvick .30 .75
17 Jimmie Johnson .40 1.00
18 Kasey Kahne .25 .60
19 Matt Kenseth .25 .60
20 Brad Keselowski .30 .75

21 Travis Kvapil .15 .40
22 Bobby Labonte .25 .60
23 Joey Logano .25 .60
24 Mark Martin .25 .60
25 Jamie McMurray .25 .60
26 Casey Mears .15 .40
27 Paul Menard .15 .40
28 Juan Pablo Montoya .25 .60
29 Ryan Newman .20 .50
30 David Ragan .20 .50
31 David Reutimann .20 .50
32 Regan Smith .20 .50
33 Tony Stewart .40 1.00
34 Martin Truex Jr. .20 .50
35 Brian Vickers .15 .40
36 Michael Waltrip .25 .60
37 Justin Allgaier NNS .20 .50
38 Aric Almirola NNS .20 .50
39 Trevor Bayne NNS .25 .60
40 Jennifer Jo Cobb NNS .25 .60
41 Jason Leffler NNS .15 .40
42 Danica Patrick NNS .75 2.00
43 Brian Scott NNS .15 .40
44 Reed Sorenson NNS .15 .40
45 Ricky Stenhouse Jr. NNS .25 .60
46 Kenny Wallace NNS .15 .40
47 Mike Wallace NNS .20 .50
48 Steve Wallace NNS .15 .40
49 Josh Wise NNS .15 .40
50 James Buescher CWTS .15 .40
51 Ricky Carmichael CWTS .25 .60
52 Joey Coulter CWTS .15 .40
53 Austin Dillon CWTS .30 .75
54 Brendan Gaughan CWTS .15 .40
55 Ron Hornaday CWTS .15 .40
56 Justin Lofton CWTS .15 .40
57 Johanna Long CWTS .40 1.00
58 Miguel Paludo CWTS .15 .40
59 Max Papis CWTS .15 .40
60 Timothy Peters CWTS .15 .40
61 Mark Martin's Rig .12 .30
62 Jeff Burton's Rig .10 .25
63 Jeff Gordon's Rig .25 .60
64 Kyle Busch's Rig .15 .40
65 Carl Edwards' Rig .12 .30
66 Ryan Newman's Rig .10 .25
67 Juan Pablo Montoya's Rig .12 .30
68 Dale Earnhardt Jr.'s Rig .25 .60
69 Jimmie Johnson's Rig .20 .50
70 Kurt Busch's Rig .10 .25
71 Kurt Busch FR .20 .50
72 Carl Edwards FR .25 .60
73 Juan Pablo Montoya FR .25 .60
74 David Ragan FR .20 .50
75 Dale Earnhardt Jr. FR .50 1.25
76 Jeff Gordon FR .50 1.25
77 Kasey Kahne FR .25 .60
78 Matt Kenseth FR .25 .60
79 Joey Logano FR .25 .60
80 Mark Martin FR .25 .60
81 Kevin Harvick HC .30 .75
82 Kyle Busch HC .30 .75
83 Carl Edwards HC .25 .60
84 Jimmie Johnson HC .40 1.00
85 Kurt Busch HC .20 .50
86 Jeff Gordon HC .50 1.25
87 Ryan Newman HC .20 .50
88 Paul Menard HC .15 .40
89 Ricky Stenhouse Jr. HC .25 .60
90 Justin Allgaier HC .20 .50
91 Trevor Bayne's Car HL .12 .30
92 First Wins HL .25 .60
93 Kyle Busch's Car HL .15 .40
94 Danica Patrick's Car HL .40 1.00
95 Kevin Harvick HL .30 .75
96 Jeff Gordon's Car HL .25 .60
97 Dale Earnhardt Jr. HL .50 1.25
98 Mark Martin HL .25 .60
99 Kyle Busch's Car HL .15 .40
100 Carl Edwards' Car HL .12 .30
0 2011 Chase Contenders 3.00 8.00

2012 Press Pass Blue

*BLUE: .8X TO 2X BASIC CARDS
ONE BLUE PER RETAIL PACK

2012 Press Pass Gold

COMPLETE SET (100) 30.00 80.00
*GOLD: 1.5X TO 4X BASIC CARDS
STATED ODDS 1:3 HOBBY

2012 Press Pass Blue Holofoil

*HOLOFOIL/35: 5X TO 12X BASIC CARDS
BLUE HOLOFOIL PRINT RUN 35

2012 Press Pass Purple

*PURPLE/35: 5X TO 12X BASIC CARDS
PURPLE PRINT RUN 35 SER.#'d SETS

2012 Press Pass Autographs Silver

SILVER STATED PRINT RUN 5-199
*RED/25-35: .6X TO 1.5X SILVER AU/99-199
*RED/25: .5X TO 1.2X SILVER AU/65-75
*RED/15: .4X TO 1X SILVER AU/25-35
UNPRICED BLUE PRINT RUN 5-10
UNPRICED PRINT PLATE PRINT RUN 1
OVERALL AUTOGRAPH ODDS 1:90 HOBBY
PPABK Brad Keselowski/175 8.00 20.00
PPABL Bobby Labonte/50 10.00 25.00
PPABV Brian Vickers/75 6.00 15.00
PPACB Clint Bowyer/25
PPACM Casey Mears/50 6.00 15.00
PPADE Dale Earnhardt Jr./15 50.00 100.00
PPADP Danica Patrick/150 60.00 100.00
PPAGB Greg Biffle/199 6.00 15.00
PPAJB Jeff Burton/150 6.00 15.00
PPAJG Jeff Gordon/15 50.00 100.00
PPAJM Jamie McMurray/10
PPAJY J.J. Yeley/50 6.00 15.00
PPAKH Kevin Harvick/25 15.00 40.00
PPAKK Kasey Kahne/15 12.00 30.00
PPALC Landon Cassill/130 6.00 15.00
PPAMA Marcos Ambrose/9
PPAMK Matt Kenseth/15
PPAMM Mark Martin/10
PPAPM Paul Menard/199 5.00 12.00
PPARG Robby Gordon/65 6.00 15.00
PPARN Ryan Newman/99 6.00 15.00
PPATS Tony Stewart/75 25.00 50.00
PPAAA1 A.J. Allmendinger/145 8.00 20.00
PPADR1 David Ragan/199 6.00 15.00
PPADR2 David Reutimann/135 6.00 15.00
PPAJJ1 Jimmie Johnson/15 50.00 100.00
PPAJL1 Joey Logano/15
PPAJPM Juan Pablo Montoya/5
PPAKUB Kurt Busch/20 20.00 40.00
PPAKYB Kyle Busch/20 15.00 40.00
PPATB1 Trevor Bayne/35 25.00 50.00

2012 Press Pass Burning Rubber Gold

GOLD STATED PRINT RUN 99
*HOLOFOIL/25: .6X TO 1.5X GOLD/99
*PRIME CUT/25: .8X TO 2X GOLD/99
*PURPLE/15: .8X TO 2X GOLD/99
BRBK Brad Keselowski 8.00 20.00
BRBK2 Brad Keselowski 8.00 20.00
BRBK3 Brad Keselowski 8.00 20.00
BRCE Carl Edwards 6.00 15.00
BRDH Denny Hamlin 6.00 15.00
BRDR David Ragan 5.00 12.00
BRJG Jeff Gordon 10.00 25.00
BRJG2 Jeff Gordon 10.00 25.00
BRJG3 Jeff Gordon 10.00 25.00
BRJJ Jimmie Johnson 8.00 20.00
BRKH Kevin Harvick 8.00 20.00
BRKH2 Kevin Harvick 8.00 20.00
BRKH3 Kevin Harvick 8.00 20.00
BRKH4 Kevin Harvick 8.00 20.00
BRKUB Kurt Busch 5.00 12.00
BRKYB Kyle Busch 6.00 15.00
BRKYB2 Kyle Busch 6.00 15.00
BRKYB3 Kyle Busch 6.00 15.00
BRKYB4 Kyle Busch 6.00 15.00
BRMA Marcos Ambrose 6.00 15.00
BRMK Matt Kenseth 6.00 15.00
BRMK2 Matt Kenseth 6.00 15.00
BRPM Paul Menard 4.00 10.00
BRRN Ryan Newman 5.00 15.00
BRRS Regan Smith 5.00 12.00
BRTB Trevor Bayne 6.00 15.00

2012 Press Pass Cup Chase

STATED ODDS 1:30
CCR1 Denny Hamlin WIN 2.00 5.00
CCR2 Jimmie Johnson WIN 3.00 8.00
CCR3 Kevin Harvick WIN 2.50 6.00
CCR4 Kyle Busch 1.50 4.00
CCR5 Kurt Busch 1.00 2.50
CCR6 Tony Stewart WIN 3.00 8.00
CCR7 Greg Biffle WIN 1.50 4.00
CCR8 Jeff Gordon WIN 4.00 10.00
CCR9 Carl Edwards 1.25 3.00
CCR10 Jeff Burton 1.00 2.50
CCR11 Matt Kenseth WIN 2.00 5.00
CCR12 Brad Keselowski CHAMP 10.00 25.00
CCR13 Dale Earnhardt Jr. WIN 4.00 10.00
CCR14 Mark Martin 1.25 3.00
CCR15 Ryan Newman 1.00 2.50
CCR16 Jamie McMurray 1.25 3.00
CCR17 Kasey Kahne WIN 2.00 5.00
CCR18 Field Card WIN 1.25 3.00

2012 Press Pass Cup Chase Prizes

COMPLETE SET (12) 4.00 10.00
ISSUED VIA MAIL REDEMPTION
CCP1 Denny Hamlin .40 1.00
CCP2 Jimmie Johnson .60 1.50
CCP3 Tony Stewart .60 1.50
CCP4 Brad Keselowski .50 1.25
CCP5 Greg Biffle .30 .75
CCP6 Clint Bowyer .40 1.00
CCP7 Dale Earnhardt Jr. .75 2.00
CCP8 Matt Kenseth .40 1.00
CCP9 Kevin Harvick .50 1.25
CCP10 Martin Truex .30 .75
CCP11 Kasey Kahne .40 1.00
CCP12 Jeff Gordon .75 2.00
CCP Brad Keselowski Firesuit 12.50 25.00

2012 Press Pass Four Wide Firesuit

FIRESUIT STATED PRINT RUN 25
UNPRICED GLOVE PRINT RUN 1
*SHEET METAL/15: .5X TO 1.2X FIRESUIT/25
*TIRE/10: .6X TO 1.5X FIRESUIT/25
FWCE Carl Edwards 15.00 40.00
FWDEJR Dale Earnhardt Jr. 30.00 80.00
FWDP Danica Patrick 50.00 125.00
FWJG Jeff Gordon 30.00 80.00
FWJJ Jimmie Johnson 25.00 60.00
FWJL Joey Logano 15.00 40.00
FWKB Kyle Busch 20.00 50.00
FWKH Kevin Harvick 20.00 50.00
FWKK Kasey Kahne 15.00 40.00
FWMK Matt Kenseth 15.00 40.00
FWMM Mark Martin 15.00 40.00
FWTS Tony Stewart 25.00 60.00

2012 Press Pass NASCAR Hall of Fame

126-135 ODDS 1:30 PRESS PASS HOB
136-145 ODDS 1:20 PRESS PASS IGNITE
146-150 ODDS 1:8 PRESS PASS FANFARE
EACH HAS FIVE CARDS OF EQUAL VALUE
*BLUE RETAIL: .4X TO 1X BASIC INSERTS
*HOLOFOIL/50: .8X TO 2X BASIC INSERTS
NHOF126 Cale Yarborough 1.25 3.00
NHOF127 Cale Yarborough 1.25 3.00
NHOF128 Cale Yarborough 1.25 3.00
NHOF129 Cale Yarborough 1.25 3.00
NHOF130 Cale Yarborough 1.25 3.00
NHOF131 Darrell Waltrip 2.00 5.00
NHOF132 Darrell Waltrip 2.00 5.00
NHOF133 Darrell Waltrip 2.00 5.00
NHOF134 Darrell Waltrip 2.00 5.00
NHOF135 Darrell Waltrip 2.00 5.00
NHOF136 Dale Inman 1.00 2.50
NHOF137 Dale Inman 1.00 2.50
NHOF138 Dale Inman 1.00 2.50
NHOF139 Dale Inman 1.00 2.50
NHOF140 Dale Inman 1.00 2.50
NHOF141 Richie Evans 1.00 2.50
NHOF142 Richie Evans 1.00 2.50
NHOF143 Richie Evans 1.00 2.50
NHOF144 Richie Evans 1.00 2.50
NHOF145 Richie Evans 1.00 2.50
NHOF146 Glen Wood 1.00 2.50
NHOF147 Glen Wood 1.00 2.50
NHOF148 Glen Wood 1.00 2.50
NHOF149 Glen Wood 1.00 2.50
NHOF150 Glen Wood 1.00 2.50

2012 Press Pass Power Picks Gold

1-25 INSERTED IN PP AND TOTAL MEM
26-54 INSERTED IN IGNITE
55-75 INSERTED IN REDLINE
STATED PRINT RUN 50 SER.#'d SETS
*BLUE/50: .4X TO 1X GOLD/50
UNPRICED HOLOFOIL PRINT RUN 10
SOME HAVE MULTIPLE CARDS OF SAME VALUE
1 Trevor Bayne 2.50 6.00
2 Kurt Busch 2.00 5.00
3 Kyle Busch 3.00 8.00
4 Dale Earnhardt Jr. 5.00 12.00
5 Carl Edwards 2.50 6.00
6 Jeff Gordon 5.00 12.00
7 Kevin Harvick 3.00 8.00
8 Jimmie Johnson 4.00 10.00
9 Kasey Kahne 2.50 6.00
10 Matt Kenseth 2.50 6.00
11 Brad Keselowski 3.00 8.00
12 Joey Logano 2.50 6.00
13 Mark Martin 2.50 6.00
14 Ryan Newman 2.00 5.00
15 Tony Stewart 4.00 10.00
16 Richard Petty 4.00 10.00
17 Dale Earnhardt 8.00 20.00
18 Bobby Allison 2.00 5.00
19 David Pearson 2.50 6.00
20 Cale Yarborough 2.50 6.00
21 Darrell Waltrip 4.00 10.00
22 Rusty Wallace 2.50 6.00
23 Terry Labonte 2.50 6.00
24 Ned Jarrett 2.00 5.00
25 Bill Elliott 4.00 10.00
26 A.J. Allmendinger 2.50 6.00
27 Aric Almirola 2.00 5.00
28 Greg Biffle 2.00 5.00
29 Clint Bowyer 2.50 6.00
30 Jeff Burton 2.00 5.00
31 Kurt Busch 2.00 5.00
32 Kyle Busch 3.00 8.00
33 Dale Earnhardt Jr. 5.00 12.00
34 Carl Edwards 2.50 6.00
35 Jeff Gordon 5.00 12.00
36 Jimmie Johnson 4.00 10.00
37 Kasey Kahne 2.50 6.00
38 Matt Kenseth 2.50 6.00
39 Brad Keselowski 3.00 8.00
40 Bobby Labonte 2.50 6.00
41 Joey Logano 2.50 6.00
42 Mark Martin 2.50 6.00
43 Jamie McMurray 2.50 6.00
44 Paul Menard 1.50 4.00
45 Juan Pablo Montoya 2.50 6.00
46 Ryan Newman 2.00 5.00
47 Danica Patrick 8.00 20.00
48 David Ragan 2.00 5.00
49 Tony Stewart 4.00 10.00
50 Martin Truex Jr. 2.00 5.00
51 Michael Waltrip 2.50 6.00
52 Trevor Bayne 2.50 6.00
53 Denny Hamlin 2.50 6.00
54 Danica Patrick 8.00 20.00
55 Dale Earnhardt Jr. 5.00 12.00
56 Jeff Gordon 5.00 12.00
57 Jimmie Johnson 4.00 10.00
58 Kasey Kahne 2.50 6.00
59 Tony Stewart 4.00 10.00
60 Danica Patrick 8.00 20.00
61 Danica Patrick 8.00 20.00
62 Carl Edwards 2.50 6.00
63 Kyle Busch 3.00 8.00
64 Joey Logano 2.50 6.00
65 Kevin Harvick 3.00 8.00
66 Jeff Burton 2.00 5.00
67 Matt Kenseth 2.50 6.00
68 Kurt Busch 2.00 5.00
69 Ryan Newman 2.00 5.00
70 Martin Truex Jr. 2.00 5.00
71 A.J. Allmendinger 2.50 6.00
72 Aric Almirola 2.00 5.00
73 Richard Petty 4.00 10.00
74 Dale Earnhardt 8.00 20.00
75 Brad Keselowski 3.00 8.00

2012 Press Pass Preferred Line

COMPLETE SET (9) 10.00 25.00
STATED ODDS 1:15
PL1 Joey Logano .75 2.00
PL2 Jeff Burton .60 1.50
PL3 Ryan Newman .60 1.50
PL4 Jeff Gordon 1.50 4.00
PL5 Dale Earnhardt Jr. 1.50 4.00
PL6 Danica Patrick 2.50 6.00
PL7 Tony Stewart 1.25 3.00
PL8 Carl Edwards .75 2.00
PL9 Kevin Harvick 1.00 2.50

2012 Press Pass Showman

COMPLETE SET (9) 10.00 25.00
STATED ODDS 1:15
*SHOWCAR: .3X TO .8X SHOWMAN
SM1 Dale Earnhardt Jr. 1.50 4.00
SM2 Jeff Gordon 1.50 4.00
SM3 Tony Stewart 1.25 3.00
SM4 Jimmie Johnson 1.25 3.00
SM5 Mark Martin .75 2.00
SM6 Carl Edwards .75 2.00
SM7 Kevin Harvick 1.00 2.50
SM8 Kurt Busch .60 1.50
SM9 Kyle Busch 1.00 2.50

2012 Press Pass Signature Series Race Used

UNPRICED SIG.SERIES PRINT RUN 12

2012 Press Pass Snapshots

SS1-SS65 STATED ODDS 1:3
SS66-SS75 SP STATED ODDS 1:20
SS1 A.J. Allmendinger 1.00 2.50
SS2 Marcos Ambrose 1.00 2.50
SS3 Trevor Bayne 1.00 2.50
SS4 Greg Biffle .75 2.00
SS5 Jeff Burton .75 2.00
SS6 Kurt Busch .75 2.00
SS7 Kyle Busch 1.25 3.00
SS8 Landon Cassill .75 2.00
SS9 Kevin Conway .60 1.50
SS10 Dale Earnhardt Jr. 2.00 5.00
SS11 Carl Edwards 1.00 2.50
SS12 David Gilliland .60 1.50
SS13 Jeff Gordon 2.00 5.00
SS14 Robby Gordon .60 1.50
SS15 Denny Hamlin 1.00 2.50
SS16 Kevin Harvick 1.25 3.00
SS17 Jimmie Johnson 1.50 4.00
SS18 Kasey Kahne 1.00 2.50
SS19 Matt Kenseth 1.00 2.50
SS20 Brad Keselowski 1.25 3.00
SS21 Travis Kvapil .60 1.50
SS22 Bobby Labonte 1.00 2.50
SS23 Joey Logano 1.00 2.50
SS24 Mark Martin 1.00 2.50
SS25 Jamie McMurray 1.00 2.50
SS26 Casey Mears .60 1.50
SS27 Paul Menard .60 1.50
SS28 Juan Pablo Montoya 1.00 2.50
SS29 Ryan Newman .75 2.00
SS30 David Ragan .75 2.00
SS31 David Reutimann .75 2.00
SS32 Regan Smith .75 2.00
SS33 Tony Stewart 1.50 4.00
SS34 Martin Truex Jr. .75 2.00
SS35 Brian Vickers .60 1.50
SS36 Darrell Waltrip 1.50 4.00
SS37 Michael Waltrip 1.00 2.50
SS38 J.J. Yeley .60 1.50
SS39 Justin Allgaier NNS .75 2.00
SS40 Aric Almirola NNS .75 2.00
SS41 Trevor Bayne NNS 1.00 2.50
SS42 Jennifer Jo Cobb NNS 1.00 2.50
SS43 Jason Leffler NNS .60 1.50
SS44 Danica Patrick NNS 3.00 8.00
SS45 Robert Richardson NNS .60 1.50
SS46 Brian Scott NNS .60 1.50
SS47 Reed Sorenson NNS .60 1.50
SS48 Ricky Stenhouse NNS 1.00 2.50
SS49 Kenny Wallace NNS .60 1.50
SS50 Mike Wallace NNS .75 2.00
SS51 Steve Wallace NNS .60 1.50
SS52 Josh Wise NNS .60 1.50
SS53 James Buescher CWTS .60 1.50
SS54 Ricky Carmichael CWTS 1.00 2.50
SS55 Joey Coulter CWTS .60 1.50
SS56 Austin Dillon CWTS 1.25 3.00
SS57 Brendan Gaughan CWTS .60 1.50
SS58 Ron Hornaday CWTS .60 1.50
SS59 Johanna Long CWTS 1.50 4.00
SS60 Miguel Paludo CWTS .60 1.50
SS61 Max Papis CWTS .60 1.50
SS62 Timothy Peters CWTS .60 1.50
SS63 Monica Palumbo Miss SC 1.25 3.00
SS64 Kim Coon Miss SC 1.25 3.00
SS65 Richard Petty LEG 1.50 4.00
SS66 Dale Earnhardt LEG SP 2.50 6.00
SS67 A.J. Allmendinger SP 1.25 3.00
SS68 Marcos Ambrose SP 1.25 3.00
SS69 Kyle Busch SP 1.50 4.00
SS70 Dale Earnhardt Jr. SP 2.50 6.00
SS71 Jeff Gordon SP 2.50 6.00
SS72 Denny Hamlin SP 1.25 3.00
SS73 Jimmie Johnson SP 2.00 5.00
SS74 Mark Martin SP 1.25 3.00
SS75 Tony Stewart SP 2.00 5.00

2012 Press Pass Target Snapshots

COMPLETE SET (9) 8.00 20.00
RANDOM INSERTS IN TARGET PACKS
SSTG1 A.J. Allmendinger 1.00 2.50
SSTG2 Marcos Ambrose 1.00 2.50
SSTG3 Trevor Bayne 1.00 2.50
SSTG4 Greg Biffle .75 2.00
SSTG5 Kyle Busch 1.25 3.00
SSTG6 Carl Edwards 1.00 2.50
SSTG7 Denny Hamlin 1.00 2.50
SSTG8 Matt Kenseth 1.00 2.50
SSTG9 Joey Logano 1.00 2.50

2012 Press Pass Triple Gear Tire

TIRE PRINT RUN 25 SER.#'d SETS
*SHEET METAL/15: .6X TO 1.5X TIRE/25
UNPRICED 3 IN 1 PRINT RUN 5
TGDE Dale Earnhardt 25.00 50.00
TGDEJr Dale Earnhardt Jr. 25.00 50.00
TGDP Danica Patrick 25.00 50.00
TGJG Jeff Gordon 15.00 30.00
TGJJ Jimmie Johnson 10.00 25.00
TGKH Kevin Harvick 10.00 25.00
TGKYB Kyle Busch 10.00 25.00
TGMM Mark Martin 8.00 20.00
TGTS Tony Stewart 12.00 30.00

2012 Press Pass Ultimate Collection Holofoil

HOLOFOIL STATED PRINT RUN 50
*BLUE HOLO/25: .5X TO 1.2X HOLO/50
UCCE Carl Edwards Shoes 8.00 20.00
UCDEJR Dale Earnhardt Jr. Fire. 12.00 30.00
UCDH Denny Hamlin Firesuit 6.00 15.00
UCJB Jeff Burton Firesuit 5.00 12.00
UCJG Jeff Gordon Sheet Metal 12.00 30.00
UCKK Kasey Kahne Sheet Metal 6.00 15.00
UCKUB Kurt Busch Firesuit 5.00 12.00
UCMK Matt Kenseth Gloves 8.00 20.00
UCTB Trevor Bayne Sheet Metal 8.00 20.00

2012 Press Pass Wal-Mart Snapshots

COMPLETE SET (9) 8.00 20.00
RANDOM INSERTS IN WAL-MART PACKS
SSWM1 Tony Stewart 1.50 4.00
SSWM2 Jeff Burton .75 2.00
SSWM3 Dale Earnhardt Jr. 2.00 5.00
SSWM4 Jeff Gordon 2.00 5.00
SSWM5 Kevin Harvick 1.25 3.00
SSWM6 Jimmie Johnson 1.50 4.00
SSWM7 Mark Martin 1.00 2.50
SSWM8 Ryan Newman .75 2.00
SSWM9 Regan Smith .75 2.00

2013 Press Pass

COMPLETE SET (100) 8.00 20.00
0 CARD STATED ODDS 1:270 HOB
WAX BOX HOBBY 60.00 80.00
1 Aric Almirola .20 .50
2 Marcos Ambrose .25 .60
3 Trevor Bayne .25 .60
4 Greg Biffle .20 .50
5 Dave Blaney .15 .40
6 Clint Bowyer .25 .60
7 Jeff Burton .20 .50
8 Kurt Busch .20 .50
9 Kyle Busch .30 .75
10 Kyle Busch .30 .75
11 Landon Cassill .20 .50
12 Dale Earnhardt Jr. .50 1.25
13 Dale Earnhardt Jr. .50 1.25
14 Carl Edwards .25 .60
15 David Gilliland .15 .40
16 Jeff Gordon .50 1.25
17 Jeff Gordon .50 1.25
18 Denny Hamlin .25 .60
19 Kevin Harvick .30 .75
20 Kevin Harvick .30 .75
21 Jimmie Johnson .40 1.00
22 Jimmie Johnson .40 1.00
23 Kasey Kahne .25 .60
24 Matt Kenseth .25 .60
25 Brad Keselowski .30 .75
26 Bobby Labonte .25 .60
27 Joey Logano .25 .60
28 Mark Martin .25 .60
29 Michael McDowell .20 .50
30 Jamie McMurray .25 .60
31 Casey Mears .15 .40
32 Paul Menard .15 .40
33 Juan Pablo Montoya .25 .60
34 Joe Nemechek .15 .40
35 Ryan Newman .20 .50
36 Danica Patrick .60 1.50
37 David Ragan .20 .50
38 David Reutimann .20 .50
39 Regan Smith .20 .50
40 Tony Stewart .40 1.00
41 Tony Stewart .40 1.00
42 Martin Truex Jr. .20 .50
43 Michael Waltrip .25 .60
44 Josh Wise .15 .40
45 Justin Allgaier NNS .20 .50
46 Trevor Bayne NNS .25 .60
47 Kurt Busch NNS .20 .50
48 Kyle Busch NNS .30 .75
49 Austin Dillon NNS .30 .75
50 Sam Hornish Jr. NNS .20 .50
51 Johanna Long NNS .25 .60
52 Tayler Malsam NNS .15 .40
53 Travis Pastrana NNS .25 .60
54 Danica Patrick NNS .60 1.50
55 Elliott Sadler NNS .15 .40
56 Ricky Stenhouse Jr. NNS .25 .60
57 Ryan Truex NNS .20 .50
58 Cole Whitt NNS .20 .50
59 James Buescher CWTS .15 .40
60 Ty Dillon CWTS .25 .60
61 Ron Hornaday CWTS .15 .40
62 Parker Kligerman CWTS .15 .40
63 Justin Lofton CWTS .15 .40
64 Miguel Paludo CWTS .15 .40
65 Timothy Peters CWTS .15 .40
66 Tony Stewart's Car .20 .50
67 Kyle Busch's Car .15 .40
68 Dale Earnhardt Jr.'s Car .25 .60
69 Jeff Gordon's Car .25 .60
70 Jimmie Johnson's Car .20 .50
71 Marcos Ambrose's Car .12 .30
72 Kasey Kahne's Car .12 .30
73 Denny Hamlin's Car .15 .30
74 Kevin Harvick's Car .15 .40
75 Jimmie Johnson's Car NU .20 .50
76 Mark Martin's Car NU .12 .30
77 Kyle Busch's Car NU .15 .40
78 Juan Pablo Montoya's Car NU .15 .40
79 Carl Edwards' Car NU .12 .30
80 Aric Almirola's Car NU .15 .40
81 Dale Earnhardt Jr.'s Car NU .25 .60
82 Jeff Burton's Car NU .15 .40
83 Martin Truex Jr.'s Car NU .15 .40
84 Dale Earnhardt Jr. HS .50 1.25
85 Jeff Gordon HS .50 1.25
86 Jimmie Johnson HS .40 1.00
87 Kevin Harvick HS .30 .75
88 Kasey Kahne HS .25 .60
89 Carl Edwards HS .25 .60
90 Tony Stewart HS .40 1.00
91 Danica Patrick HS .60 1.50
92 Kyle Busch HS .30 .75
93 Kevin Harvick OT .25 .60
94 Martin Truex Jr. OT .15 .40
95 Kyle Busch OT .25 .60
96 Carl Edwards OT .20 .50
97 Jeff Gordon OT .40 1.00
98 Ryan Newman OT .15 .40
99 Dale Earnhardt Jr. OT .40 1.00
100 Johnson CL/Hamlin/Stewart .25 .60
0 2012 Chase Contenders 6.00 15.00

2013 Press Pass Color Proofs Black

COMPLETE SET (100) 12.00 30.00
*BLACK: .6X TO 1.5X BASIC CARDS
ONE PER HOBBY PACK

2013 Press Pass Color Proofs Cyan

*CYAN/35: 5X TO 12X BASIC CARDS

2013 Press Pass Color Proofs Magenta

*MAGENTA: 3X TO 8X BASIC CARDS

2013 Press Pass Aerodynamic Autographs Holofoil

STATED PRINT RUN 5-20
CE Carl Edwards/20 40.00 80.00
KH Kevin Harvick/20 50.00 100.00

2013 Press Pass Burning Rubber Gold

GOLD STATED PRINT RUN 199
*BLUE/50: .6X TO 1.5X GOLD/199
*HOLOFOIL/75: .5X TO 1.2X GOLD/199
BRBK Brad Keselowski's Car 5.00 12.00
BRBK2 Brad Keselowski's Car 5.00 12.00
BRBK3 Brad Keselowski's Car 5.00 12.00
BRCB Clint Bowyer's Car 4.00 10.00
BRCB2 Clint Bowyer's Car 4.00 10.00
BRDE Dale Earnhardt Jr.'s Car 8.00 20.00
BRDE2 Dale Earnhardt Jr.'s Car 8.00 20.00
BRDH Denny Hamlin's Car 4.00 10.00
BRDH2 Denny Hamlin's Car 4.00 10.00
BRDH3 Denny Hamlin's Car 4.00 10.00
BRGB Greg Biffle's Car 3.00 8.00
BRGB2 Greg Biffle's Car 3.00 8.00
BRJG Jeff Gordon's Car 8.00 20.00
BRJJ Jimmie Johnson's Car 5.00 12.00
BRJJ2 Jimmie Johnson's Car 5.00 12.00
BRJJ3 Jimmie Johnson's Car 5.00 12.00
BRJL Joey Logano's Car 4.00 10.00
BRKB Kyle Busch's Car 5.00 12.00
BRKK Kasey Kahne's Car 4.00 10.00
BRKK2 Kasey Kahne's Car 4.00 10.00
BRMA Marcos Ambrose's Car 4.00 10.00
BRMK Matt Kenseth's Car 4.00 10.00
BRRN Ryan Newman's Car 3.00 8.00
BRTS Tony Stewart's Car 5.00 12.00
BRTS2 Tony Stewart 5.00 12.00
BRTS3 Tony Stewart's Car 5.00 12.00

2013 Press Pass Cool Persistence

COMPLETE SET (9) 8.00 20.00
STATED ODDS 1:15 HOB/RET
CP1 Mark Martin .60 1.50
CP2 Danica Patrick 1.50 4.00
CP3 Carl Edwards .60 1.50
CP4 Kevin Harvick .75 2.00
CP5 Marcos Ambrose .60 1.50
CP6 Denny Hamlin .60 1.50
CP7 Dale Earnhardt Jr. 1.25 3.00
CP8 Jeff Gordon 1.25 3.00
CP9 Jimmie Johnson 1.00 2.50

2013 Press Pass Cup Chase

STATED ODDS 1:30 HOB, 1:96 RET
CC1 Greg Biffle WIN 5.00 12.00
CC2 Jeff Burton 3.00 8.00
CC3 Kurt Busch WIN 5.00 12.00
CC4 Kyle Busch WIN 5.00 12.00
CC5 Dale Earnhardt Jr. WIN 6.00 15.00
CC6 Carl Edwards WIN 5.00 12.00
CC7 Jeff Gordon WIN 6.00 15.00
CC8 Denny Hamlin 4.00 10.00
CC9 Kevin Harvick WIN 5.00 12.00
CC10 Jimmie Johnson CHAMP 15.00 40.00
CC11 Kasey Kahne WIN 5.00 12.00
CC12 Matt Kenseth WIN 5.00 12.00
CC13 Brad Keselowski 4.00 10.00
CC14 Mark Martin 4.00 10.00
CC15 Ryan Newman WIN 5.00 12.00
CC16 Danica Patrick 5.00 12.00
CC17 Tony Stewart 5.00 12.00
CC18 Field Card WIN 6.00 15.00

2013 Press Pass Cup Chase Prizes

CCP1 Matt Kenseth .50 1.25
CCP2 Jimmie Johnson .75 2.00
CCP3 Kyle Busch .60 1.50
CCP4 Kevin Harvick .60 1.50
CCP5 Carl Edwards .50 1.25
CCP6 Joey Logano .50 1.25
CCP7 Greg Biffle .40 1.00
CCP8 Dale Earnhardt Jr. 1.00 2.50

CCP9 Kurt Busch .40 1.00
CCP10 Clint Bowyer .50 1.25
CCP11 Kasey Kahne .50 1.25
CCE12 Ryan Newman .40 1.00
CCE13 Jeff Gordon 1.00 2.50
CCPJJ Jimmie Johnson/200 FIRE

2013 Press Pass NASCAR Hall of Fame

COMPLETE SET (15) 4.00 10.00
151/152/154/157/160/163 ODDS 1:30 PP HOB
153/155/158/161/164 ODDS 1:20 ING HOB
156/159/162/165 ODDS 1:8 FANFARE
*BLUE: .4X TO 1X BASIC INSERTS
*HOLOFOIL/50: .8X TO 2X BASIC INSERTS
NHOF151 Buck Baker 1.25 3.00
NHOF152 Buck Baker 1.25 3.00
NHOF153 Buck Baker 1.25 3.00
NHOF154 Cotton Owens 1.00 2.50
NHOF155 Cotton Owens 1.00 2.50
NHOF156 Cotton Owens 1.00 2.50
NHOF157 Herb Thomas 1.00 2.50
NHOF158 Herb Thomas 1.00 2.50
NHOF159 Herb Thomas 1.00 2.50
NHOF160 Rusty Wallace 1.25 3.00
NHOF161 Rusty Wallace 1.25 3.00
NHOF162 Rusty Wallace 1.25 3.00
NHOF163 Leonard Wood 1.00 2.50
NHOF164 Leonard Wood 1.00 2.50
NHOF165 Leonard Wood 1.00 2.50

2013 Press Pass Power Picks Blue

BLUE STATED PRINT RUN 99
*GOLD/50: .5X TO 1.2X BASIC INSERTS/99
1 Trevor Bayne 2.00 5.00
2 Kurt Busch 1.50 4.00
3 Kyle Busch 2.50 6.00
4 Dale Earnhardt Jr. 4.00 10.00
5 Carl Edwards 2.00 5.00
6 Jeff Gordon 4.00 10.00
7 Kevin Harvick 2.50 6.00
8 Jimmie Johnson 3.00 8.00
9 Kasey Kahne 2.00 5.00
10 Matt Kenseth 2.00 5.00
11 Marcos Ambrose 2.00 5.00
12 Joey Logano 2.00 5.00
13 Mark Martin 2.00 5.00
14 Ryan Newman 1.50 4.00
15 Tony Stewart 3.00 8.00
16 Richard Petty 3.00 8.00
17 Dale Earnhardt 6.00 15.00
18 Danica Patrick 5.00 12.00
19 Travis Pastrana 2.00 5.00
20 Austin Dillon 2.50 6.00
21 Ty Dillon 2.00 5.00
22 Denny Hamlin 2.00 5.00
23 Terry Labonte 2.00 5.00
24 Clint Bowyer 2.00 5.00
25 Greg Biffle 1.50 4.00
26 Aric Almirola 1.50 4.00
27 Marcos Ambrose 2.00 5.00
28 Trevor Bayne 2.00 5.00
29 Greg Biffle 1.50 4.00
30 Jeff Burton 1.50 4.00
31 Kurt Busch 1.50 4.00
32 Kyle Busch 2.50 6.00
33 Dale Earnhardt Jr. 4.00 10.00
34 Carl Edwards 2.00 5.00
35 Jeff Gordon 4.00 10.00
36 Denny Hamlin 2.00 5.00
37 Kevin Harvick 2.50 6.00
38 Jimmie Johnson 3.00 8.00
39 Kasey Kahne 2.00 5.00
40 Brad Keselowski 2.50 6.00
41 Bobby Labonte 2.00 5.00
42 Joey Logano 2.00 5.00
43 Mark Martin 2.00 5.00
44 Jamie McMurray 2.00 5.00
45 Paul Menard 1.25 3.00
46 Juan Pablo Montoya 2.00 5.00
47 Ryan Newman 1.50 4.00
48 Danica Patrick 5.00 12.00
49 Ricky Stenhouse Jr. 2.00 5.00
50 Tony Stewart 3.00 8.00

2013 Press Pass Racing Champions

STATED ODDS 1:6 HOB, 1:4 RET
RC1 Matt Kenseth's Car .50 1.25
RC2 Denny Hamlin's Car .50 1.25
RC3 Tony Stewart's Car .75 2.00
RC4 Brad Keselowski's Car .60 1.50
RC5 Tony Stewart's Car .75 2.00
RC6 Ryan Newman's Car .40 1.00
RC7 Greg Biffle's Car .40 1.00
RC8 Denny Hamlin's Car .50 1.25
RC9 Kyle Busch's Car SP 5.00 12.00
RC10 Brad Keselowski's Car .60 1.50
RC11 Jimmie Johnson's Car .75 2.00
RC12 Kasey Kahne's Car .50 1.25
RC13 Jimmie Johnson's Car .75 2.00
RC14 Joey Logano's Car .50 1.25
RC15 Dale Earnhardt Jr.'s Car SP 12.50 25.00
RC16 Clint Bowyer's Car .50 1.25
RC17 Brad Keselowski's Car .60 1.50
RC18 Tony Stewart's Car SP 6.00 15.00
RC19 Kasey Kahne's Car .50 1.25
RC20 Jimmie Johnson's Car SP 6.00 15.00
RC21 Jeff Gordon's Car SP 12.50 25.00
RC22 Marcos Ambrose's Car .50 1.25
RC23 Greg Biffle's Car .40 1.00
RC24 Denny Hamlin's Car .50 1.25
RC25 Denny Hamlin's Car .50 1.25
RC26 Clint Bowyer's Car .50 1.25
RC27 Kyle Busch's Car .60 1.50
RC28 Tony Stewart's Car .75 2.00
RC29 Matt Kenseth's Car .50 1.25
RC30 Dale Earnhardt Jr.'s Car 1.00 2.50
RC31 Jimmie Johnson's Car .75 2.00
RC32 Austin Dillon's Car .60 1.50
RC33 Brad Keselowski's Car .60 1.50
RC34 Carl Edwards' Car .50 1.25
RC35 Kevin Harvick's Car .60 1.50
RC36 Joey Logano's Car .50 1.25

2013 Press Pass Signings Silver

SILVER PRINT RUN 1-100
EXCH EXPIRATION: 7/1/2013
*GOLD/15-50: .5X TO 1.2X SILVER/15-100
AA Aric Almirola/50
AD Austin Dillon NNS/65 12.00 30.00
BL Bobby Labonte/50 8.00 20.00
CB Clint Bowyer/50 10.00 25.00
CE Carl Edwards/35 10.00 25.00
CM Casey Mears/50 8.00 20.00
CW Cole Whitt NNS/65 6.00 15.00
DB Dave Blaney/50
DG David Gilliland/50
DH Denny Hamlin/99 8.00 20.00
DP1 Danica Patrick/25 60.00 120.00
ES Elliott Sadler NNS/50
GB Greg Biffle/50 6.00 15.00
JA Justin Allgaier NNS/65
JB Jeff Burton/25
JL Joey Logano/50 12.00 30.00
JM Jamie McMurray/50 8.00 20.00
JPM Juan Pablo Montoya/25
JW Josh Wise/50
KUB Kurt Busch/25
LC Landon Cassill/65 6.00 15.00
MA Marcos Ambrose/50 8.00 20.00
MK Matt Kenseth/50 10.00 25.00
MT Martin Truex Jr./100 6.00 15.00
PM Paul Menard/65 5.00 12.00
RN Ryan Newman/50
RSJ R.Stenhouse Jr. NNS/65 15.00 40.00
RT Ryan Truex NNS/65 6.00 15.00
TB Trevor Bayne/25
TD Ty Dillon CWTS/65 8.00 20.00
TP T.Pastrana NNS/15 EXCH 30.00 60.00

2013 Press Pass Remembering Davey Allison Blue

COMMON ALLISON (DA1-DA4) 6.00 15.00
DA1-DA2 INSERTED IN 2013 PRESS PASS
DA3-DA4 INSERTED IN 2013 TOTAL MEM
COMMON ALLISON (DA5-DA10) 10.00 25.00
DA5-DA10 INSERTED IN 2013 LEGENDS
BLUE INSERTED IN RETAIL PACKS ONLY
*DA1-DA4 GOLD: .6X TO 1.5X BLUE
*DA5-DA10 GOLD: .25X TO .6X BLUE
*DA1-DA2 HOLO/28: 1.2X TO 3X BLUE
*DA3-DA4 HOLO/28: 2X TO 5X BLUE
*DA5-DA10 HOLO/28: .8X TO 2X BLUE
GOLD/HOLOFOIL INSERTED IN HOBBY PACKS ONLY

2014 Press Pass

COMPLETE SET (100) 6.00 15.00
0 CARD ODDS 1:270
WAX BOX HOBBY 65.00 80.00
1 Aric Almirola .20 .50
2 Marcos Ambrose .25 .60
3 Greg Biffle .20 .50
4 Clint Bowyer .25 .60
5 Jeff Burton .20 .50
6 Kurt Busch .20 .50
7 Kyle Busch .30 .75
8 Dale Earnhardt Jr. .50 1.25
9 Dale Earnhardt Jr. .50 1.25
10 Carl Edwards .25 .60
11 David Gilliland .15 .40
12 Jeff Gordon .50 1.25
13 Jeff Gordon .50 1.25
14 Denny Hamlin .25 .60
15 Kevin Harvick .30 .75
16 Jimmie Johnson .40 1.00
17 Jimmie Johnson .40 1.00
18 Kasey Kahne .25 .60
19 Matt Kenseth .25 .60
20 Brad Keselowski .30 .75
21 Travis Kvapil .15 .40
22 Bobby Labonte .25 .60
23 Joey Logano .25 .60
24 Mark Martin .25 .60
25 Michael McDowell .20 .50
26 Jamie McMurray .25 .60
27 Casey Mears .15 .40
28 Paul Menard .15 .40
29 Juan Pablo Montoya .25 .60
30 Danica Patrick .50 1.25
31 Danica Patrick .50 1.25
32 David Ragan .20 .50
33 David Reutimann .20 .50
34 Regan Smith .20 .50
35 Scott Speed .15 .40
36 Ricky Stenhouse Jr. .25 .60
37 Tony Stewart .40 1.00
38 Tony Stewart .40 1.00
39 Martin Truex Jr .20 .50
40 Josh Wise .15 .40
41 Justin Allgaier CRC .20 .50
42 Austin Dillon CRC .30 .75
43 Kyle Larson CRC .75 2.00
44 Justin Allgaier NNS .20 .50
45 Trevor Bayne NNS .25 .60
46 Austin Dillon NNS .30 .75
47 Jeffrey Earnhardt NNS .25 .60
48 Sam Hornish Jr. NNS .20 .50
49 Parker Kligerman NNS .15 .40
50 Kyle Larson NNS .50 1.25
51 Johanna Long NNS .25 .60
52 Travis Pastrana NNS .25 .60
53 Elliott Sadler NNS .15 .40
54 Brian Scott NNS .15 .40
55 Regan Smith NNS .20 .50
56 Brad Sweet NNS .20 .50
57 Brian Vickers NNS .15 .40
58 Ryan Blaney CWTS .20 .50
59 James Buescher CWTS .15 .40
60 Jeb Burton CWTS .20 .50
61 Jennifer Jo Cobb CWTS .25 .60
62 Ty Dillon CWTS .25 .60
63 Brendan Gaughan CWTS .15 .40
64 Brennan Newberry CWTS .15 .40
65 Miguel Paludo CWTS .15 .40
66 Matt Kenseth's Car GC .15 .40
67 Dale Earnhardt Jr.'s Car GC .25 .60
68 Jeff Gordon's Car GC .25 .60
69 Jimmie Johnson's Car GC .20 .50
70 Carl Edwards' Car GC .12 .30
71 Kyle Busch's Car GC .15 .40
72 Kasey Kahne's Car GC .15 .40
73 Denny Hamlin's Car GC .15 .40
74 Danica Patrick's Car GC .25 .60
75 Greg Biffle GB .15 .40
76 Jimmie Johnson GB .30 .75
77 Kurt Busch GB .15 .40
78 Dale Earnhardt Jr. GB .40 1.00
79 Jeff Burton GB .15 .40
80 Kevin Harvick GB .20 .50
81 Dale Earnhardt Jr. HS .40 1.00
82 Jeff Gordon HS .40 1.00
83 Jimmie Johnson HS .30 .75
84 Matt Kenseth HS .20 .50
85 Kasey Kahne HS .20 .50
86 Carl Edwards HS .20 .50
87 Tony Stewart HS .30 .75
88 Danica Patrick HS .40 1.00
89 Kyle Busch HS .25 .60
90 Marcos Ambrose SS .20 .50
91 Carl Edwards SS .20 .50
92 Michael Waltrip SS .20 .50
93 Jimmie Johnson SS .30 .75
94 Kyle Busch SS .25 .60
95 Austin Dillon SS .25 .60
96 Travis Pastrana SS .20 .50
97 Danica Patrick SS .40 1.00
98 Denny Hamlin SS .20 .50
99 Dale Earnhardt Jr. SS .40 1.00
100 Dale Earnhardt Jr. CL .30 .75
0 2013 Chase Contenders 6.00 15.00

2014 Press Pass Color Proofs Black

*BLACK/70: 3X TO 8X BASIC CARDS

2014 Press Pass Color Proofs Cyan

*CYAN/35: 5X TO 12X BASIC CARDS

2014 Press Pass Color Proofs Magenta

*MAGENTA: 4X TO 10X BASIC CARDS

2014 Press Pass Gold

*GOLD: .6X TO 1.5X BASIC CARDS

2014 Press Pass Aerodynamic Autographs Holofoil

AACE Carl Edwards/20 20.00 50.00
AAMA Marcos Ambrose/20 20.00 50.00

2014 Press Pass Burning Rubber Gold

*BLUE/25: .6X TO 1.5X GOLD/75
*HOLOFOIL/50: .5X TO 1.2X GOLD/75
*MELTING/10: 1.2X TO 3X GOLD/75
BRCE Carl Edwards 5.00 12.00
BRCE2 Carl Edwards 5.00 12.00
BRDR David Ragan 4.00 10.00
BRGB Greg Biffle 4.00 10.00
BRJJ Jimmie Johnson 6.00 15.00
BRJJ2 Jimmie Johnson 6.00 15.00
BRJJ3 Jimmie Johnson 6.00 15.00
BRJJ4 Jimmie Johnson 6.00 15.00
BRJL Joey Logano 6.00 15.00
BRKH Kevin Harvick 6.00 15.00
BRKH2 Kevin Harvick 6.00 15.00
BRKK Kasey Kahne 5.00 12.00
BRKK2 Kasey Kahne 5.00 12.00
BRKYB Kyle Busch 6.00 15.00
BRKYB2 Kyle Busch 6.00 15.00
BRKYB3 Kyle Busch 6.00 15.00
BRKYB4 Kyle Busch 6.00 15.00
BRMK Matt Kenseth 5.00 12.00
BRMK2 Matt Kenseth 5.00 12.00
BRMK3 Matt Kenseth 5.00 12.00
BRMK4 Matt Kenseth 5.00 12.00
BRMK5 Matt Kenseth 5.00 12.00
BRMTJ Martin Truex Jr. 5.00 12.00
BRTS Tony Stewart 8.00 20.00

2014 Press Pass Burning Rubber Chase Edition Silver

BRCBK Brad Keselowski 6.00 15.00
BRCDH Denny Hamlin 5.00 12.00
BRCJG Jeff Gordon 10.00 25.00
BRCJJ Jimmie Johnson 8.00 20.00
BRCJJ2 Jimmie Johnson 8.00 20.00
BRCJM Jamie McMurray 5.00 12.00
BRCKH Kevin Harvick 6.00 15.00
BRCKH2 Kevin Harvick 6.00 15.00
BRCMK Matt Kenseth 5.00 12.00
BRCMK2 Matt Kenseth 5.00 12.00

2014 Press Pass Cup Chase

STATED ODDS 1:30
1 Greg Biffle 3.00 8.00
2 Kurt Busch 3.00 8.00
3 Kyle Busch 5.00 12.00
4 Dale Earnhardt Jr. 8.00 20.00
5 Carl Edwards 4.00 10.00
6 Jeff Gordon 10.00 25.00
7 Denny Hamlin 5.00 12.00
8 Jimmie Johnson 12.50 30.00
9 Kasey Kahne 6.00 12.00
10 Matt Kenseth 6.00 15.00
11 Brad Keselowski 5.00 12.00
12 Joey Logano 5.00 12.00
13 Danica Patrick 8.00 20.00
14 Ricky Stenhouse Jr. 4.00 10.00
15 Tony Stewart 6.00 15.00
16 Field Card 6.00 15.00

2014 Press Pass NASCAR Hall of Fame

NHOF 166 Tim Flock 3.00 8.00
NHOF 167 Jack Ingram 3.00 8.00
NHOF 168 Dale Jarrett 4.00 10.00
NHOF 169 Maurice Petty 3.00 8.00
NHOF 170 Fireball Roberts 3.00 8.00

2014 Press Pass Replay

OVERALL STATED ODDS 1:6
1 Jimmie Johnson SP 12.00 30.00
2 Carl Edwards .60 1.50
3 Matt Kenseth SP 6.00 15.00
4 Kasey Kahne .60 1.50
5 Kyle Busch .75 2.00
6 Jimmie Johnson 1.00 2.50
7 Kyle Busch SP 8.00 20.00
8 Matt Kenseth .60 1.50
9 Kevin Harvick .75 2.00
10 David Ragan .50 1.25
11 Matt Kenseth .60 1.50
12 Kevin Harvick .75 2.00
13 Tony Stewart 1.00 2.50
14 Jimmie Johnson 1.00 2.50
15 Greg Biffle .50 1.25
16 Martin Truex Jr .50 1.25
17 Matt Kenseth .60 1.50
18 Jimmie Johnson 1.00 2.50
19 Kasey Kahne SP 6.00 15.00
20 Kyle Busch .75 2.00
21 Joey Logano .60 1.50
22 Matt Kenseth .60 1.50
23 Kyle Busch .75 2.00
24 Carl Edwards SP 6.00 15.00

2014 Press Pass Signings Silver

*GOLD/45-75: .4X TO 1X SILVER/50-100
*GOLD/20-25: .5X TO 1.2X SILVER/50-100
*GOLD/25: .4X TO 1X SILVER/30
PPSAA Aric Almirola/50 5.00 12.00
PPSAD Austin Dillon NNS/50 25.00 50.00
PPSBL Bobby Labonte/25 8.00 20.00
PPSBS Brian Scott NNS/100
PPSCB Clint Bowyer/100
PPSCE Carl Edwards/25 8.00 20.00
PPSCM Casey Mears/50 4.00 10.00
PPSDG David Gilliland/100
PPSDR1 David Ragan/50 5.00 12.00
PPSDR2 David Reutimann/50
PPSGB Greg Biffle/100 5.00 12.00
PPSJB Jeff Burton/100 5.00 12.00
PPSJL Joey Logano/50 6.00 15.00
PPSJM Jamie McMurray/50 6.00 15.00
PPSJPM Juan Pablo Montoya/50 6.00 15.00
PPSJW Josh Wise/100 4.00 10.00
PPSKUB Kurt Busch/50 5.00 12.00
PPSMA Marcos Ambrose/35 8.00 20.00
PPSMK Matt Kenseth/50 8.00 20.00
PPSMMD Michael McDowell/100 5.00 12.00
PPSPM Paul Menard/100
PPSRS Regan Smith NNS/50 5.00 12.00
PPSRSJ Ricky Stenhouse, Jr./80 6.00 15.00
PPSSS Scott Speed/100
PPSTD Ty Dillon CWTS/50 6.00 15.00
PPSTK Travis Kvapil/50 4.00 10.00

2014 Press Pass Velocity

COMPLETE SET (9) 5.00 12.00
STATED ODDS 1:15
1 Dale Earnhardt Jr 1.25 3.00
2 Marcos Ambrose .60 1.50
3 Denny Hamlin .60 1.50
4 Kurt Busch .50 1.25
5 Jimmie Johnson 1.00 2.50
6 Matt Kenseth .60 1.50
7 Brad Keselowski .75 2.00
8 Kyle Busch .75 2.00
9 Austin Dillon .75 2.00

1994 Press Pass 24K Gold 5000 Series

1 Dale Earnhardt 75.00 150.00
2 Jeff Gordon 50.00 100.00
3 Ernie Irvan 25.00 50.00
4 Mark Martin 30.00 60.00
5 Kyle Petty 25.00 60.00
6 Rusty Wallace 30.00 60.00

2014 Press Pass American Thunder

1 A.J. Allmendinger .30 .75
2 Justin Allgaier .25 .60
3 Aric Almirola CRC .40 1.00
4 Michael Annett RC 1.25 3.00
5 Marcos Ambrose .30 .75
6 Greg Biffle .25 .60
7 Alex Bowman RC 1.25 3.00
8 Clint Bowyer .30 .75
9 Kurt Busch .25 .60
10 Kyle Busch .40 1.00
11 Austin Dillon .40 1.00
12 Dale Earnhardt Jr. .60 1.50
13 Carl Edwards .30 .75
14 David Gilliland .20 .50
15 Jeff Gordon .60 1.50
16 Denny Hamlin .30 .75
17 Kevin Harvick .40 1.00
18 Jimmie Johnson .50 1.25
19 Kasey Kahne .30 .75
20 Matt Kenseth .30 .75
21 Brad Keselowski .40 1.00
22 Parker Kligerman CRC .30 .75
23 Kyle Larson CRC 1.50 4.00
24 Joey Logano .30 .75
25 Michael McDowell .25 .60
26 Jamie McMurray .30 .75
27 Casey Mears .20 .50
28 Paul Menard .20 .50
29 Ryan Newman .25 .60
30 Danica Patrick .60 1.50
31 David Ragan .25 .60
32 Ricky Stenhouse Jr. .30 .75
33 Tony Stewart .50 1.25
34 Ryan Truex CRC .40 1.00
35 Martin Truex Jr .25 .60
36 Brian Vickers .20 .50
37 Michael Waltrip .30 .75
38 Cole Whitt CRC .60 1.50
39 Josh Wise .20 .50
40 Trevor Bayne NNS .30 .75
41 James Buescher NNS .20 .50
42 Ty Dillon NNS .30 .75
43 Jeffrey Earnhardt NNS .30 .75
44 Chase Elliott NNS 1.25 3.00
45 Brendan Gaughan NNS .20 .50
46 Dylan Kwasniewski NNS .25 .60
47 Elliott Sadler NNS .20 .50
48 Brian Scott NNS .20 .50
49 Regan Smith NNS .25 .60
50 Ptrck/Stwrt/Bsch/Hrvck BIA .60 1.50
51 Grdn/Jhnsn/Ernhrdt/Khne BIA .60 1.50
52 Bwyr/Wltrp/Vckrs BIA .30 .75
53 Bffle/Edwrds/Stnhse BIA .30 .75
54 Nwmn/Dlln/Mnrd BIA .40 1.00
55 Bsch/Knsth/Hmln BIA .40 1.00
56 J.Logano/B.Keselowski BIA .40 1.00
57 J.McMurray/K.Larson BIA .60 1.50
58 A.Almirola/M.Ambrose BIA .30 .75
59 A.Bowman/Ryan Truex BIA .75 2.00
60 P.Kligerman/C.Whitt BIA .25 .60
61 Austin Dillon's Rig .20 .50
62 Kasey Kahne's Rig .15 .40
63 Danica Patrick's Rig .30 .75
64 Tony Stewart's Rig .25 .60
65 Kyle Busch's Rig .20 .50
66 Jeff Gordon's Rig .30 .75
67 Jimmie Johnson's Rig .25 .60
68 Dale Earnhardt Jr.'s Rig .30 .75
69 Carl Edwards' Rig .15 .40
70 Dale Earnhardt Jr. CL .40 1.00

2014 Press Pass American Thunder Black and White

*B&W VETS/50: 4X TO 10X BASIC CARDS
*B&W ROOK/50: 2X TO 5X BASIC CRC/RC

2014 Press Pass American Thunder Cyan

*CYAN: 5X TO 12X BASIC CARDS

2014 Press Pass American Thunder Magenta

*MAGENTA: 5X TO 12X BASIC CARDS
RANDOM INSERTS IN RETAIL PACKS

2014 Press Pass American Thunder Autographs White

ATAAA Aric Almirola/25 6.00 15.00
ATAAB Alex Bowman/25 15.00 40.00
ATAAD Austin Dillon/35 10.00 25.00
ATAAJA A.J. Allmendinger/25 8.00 20.00
ATABG Brendan Gaughan/25 5.00 12.00
ATABS Brian Scott/25 5.00 12.00
ATABV Brian Vickers/25 5.00 12.00
ATACB Clint Bowyer/15 12.00 30.00
ATACE1 Carl Edwards/35 12.00 30.00
ATACE2 Chase Elliott/25 60.00 120.00
ATACM Casey Mears/25 5.00 12.00
ATACW Cole Whitt/25 6.00 15.00
ATADEJ Dale Earnhardt Jr./15 60.00 120.00
ATADG David Gilliland/25 5.00 12.00
ATADH Denny Hamlin/60 6.00 15.00
ATADK Dylan Kwasniewski/25 12.00 30.00
ATADP Danica Patrick/15 60.00 120.00
ATADR David Ragan/25 6.00 15.00
ATAES Elliott Sadler/25 5.00 12.00
ATAGB Greg Biffle/25 6.00 15.00
ATAJA Justin Allgaier/25 6.00 15.00
ATAJB2 James Buescher/25 5.00 12.00
ATAJE Jeffrey Earnhardt/25 12.00 30.00
ATAJG Jeff Gordon/15 75.00 150.00
ATAJJ Jimmie Johnson/15 50.00 100.00
ATAJL Joey Logano/35 8.00 20.00
ATAJM Jamie McMurray/25 8.00 20.00
ATAJW Josh Wise/25 5.00 12.00
ATAKH Kevin Harvick/35 15.00 40.00
ATAKK Kasey Kahne/15 25.00 50.00
ATAKL Kyle Larson/25 40.00 80.00
ATAKUB Kurt Busch/25 6.00 15.00
ATAKYB Kyle Busch/35 10.00 25.00
ATAMA1 Marcos Ambrose/35 8.00 20.00
ATAMA2 Michael Annett/25 20.00 50.00
ATAMK Matt Kenseth/35 12.00 30.00
ATAMM Michael McDowell/25 6.00 15.00
ATAMTJ Martin Truex Jr./25 6.00 15.00
ATAMW Michael Waltrip/25 6.00 15.00
ATAPK Parker Kligerman/25 5.00 12.00
ATAPM Paul Menard/25 5.00 12.00
ATARN Ryan Newman/35 6.00 15.00
ATARS Regan Smith/25 6.00 15.00
ATARS Ricky Stenhouse Jr./25 8.00 20.00
ATART Ryan Truex/25 5.00 12.00
ATATB Trevor Bayne/25 8.00 20.00
ATATD Ty Dillon/25 8.00 20.00
ATATS Tony Stewart/15 25.00 60.00

2014 Press Pass American Thunder Battle Armor Silver

*BLUE/25: .6X TO 1.5X SILVER/99
BAAD Austin Dillon 5.00 12.00
BABK Brad Keselowski 5.00 12.00
BACE Carl Edwards 4.00 10.00
BADP Danica Patrick 10.00 25.00
BAGB Greg Biffle 3.00 8.00
BAJG Jeff Gordon 8.00 20.00
BAJJ Jimmie Johnson 6.00 15.00
BAKH Kevin Harvick 5.00 12.00
BAKK Kasey Kahne 4.00 10.00
BAKL Kyle Larson 8.00 20.00
BATS Tony Stewart 6.00 15.00
BADEJ Dale Earnhardt Jr. 8.00 20.00
BAKUB Kurt Busch 3.00 8.00
BAKYB Kyle Busch 5.00 12.00

2014 Press Pass American Thunder Brothers In Arms Relics Silver

*BLUE/25: .5X TO 1.2X SILVER/50
BATP J.Logano/B.Keselowski 8.00 20.00
BAHMS Grdn/Jhnsn/Ernhrdt/Khne 25.00 50.00
BAJGR Bsch/Knsth/Hmln 8.00 20.00
BAMWR Bwyr/Wltrp/Vckrs 6.00 15.00
BARCR Nwmn/Dlln/Mnrd 10.00 25.00
BARFR Bffle/Edwrds/Stnhse 8.00 20.00
BARPM A.Almirola/M.Ambrose 8.00 20.00
BASHR Ptrck/Stwrt/Bsch/Hrvck 20.00 50.00
BACGRFS J.McMurray/K.Larson 10.00 25.00

2014 Press Pass American Thunder Class A Uniforms Blue

*SILVER: .3X TO .8X BLUE/99
CAUAA Aric Almirola 3.00 8.00
CAUAD Austin Dillon 5.00 12.00
CAUBK Brad Keselowski 5.00 12.00
CAUBV Brian Vickers 2.50 6.00
CAUCB Clint Bowyer 4.00 10.00
CAUCE Carl Edwards 4.00 10.00
CAUDH Denny Hamlin 4.00 10.00
CAUDP Danica Patrick 10.00 25.00
CAUDR David Ragan 3.00 8.00
CAUES Elliott Sadler 2.50 6.00
CAUGB Greg Biffle 3.00 8.00
CAUJA Justin Allgaier 4.00 10.00
CAUJG Jeff Gordon 8.00 20.00
CAUJJ Jimmie Johnson 6.00 15.00
CAUJL Joey Logano 5.00 12.00
CAUJM Jamie McMurray 4.00 10.00
CAUJW Josh Wise 2.50 6.00
CAUKH Kevin Harvick 5.00 12.00
CAUKK Kasey Kahne 4.00 10.00
CAUKL Kyle Larson 8.00 20.00
CAUMA Marcos Ambrose 4.00 10.00
CAUMK Matt Kenseth 4.00 10.00
CAUMM Michael McDowell 3.00 8.00
CAUMW Michael Waltrip 4.00 10.00
CAUPM Paul Menard 2.50 6.00
CAURN Ryan Newman 3.00 8.00
CAURS Regan Smith 3.00 8.00
CAURS Ricky Stenhouse Jr. 4.00 10.00
CAUTB Trevor Bayne
CAUTD Ty Dillon 4.00 10.00
CAUTS Tony Stewart 6.00 15.00
CAUDEJ Dale Earnhardt Jr. 8.00 20.00
CAUKYB Kyle Busch 5.00 12.00
CAUMTJ Martin Truex Jr 3.00 8.00

2014 Press Pass American Thunder Climbing the Ranks

COMPLETE SET (10) 8.00 20.00
STATED ODDS 1:10
CR1 Austin Dillon 1.25 3.00
CR2 Kyle Larson 2.00 5.00
CR3 Brian Vickers .60 1.50
CR4 Ryan Truex .75 2.00
CR5 Brian Scott .60 1.50
CR6 Parker Kligerman .60 1.50
CR7 Justin Allgaier .75 2.00
CR8 Ty Dillon 1.00 2.50
CR9 Danica Patrick 2.00 5.00
CR10 Ricky Stenhouse Jr. 1.00 2.50

2014 Press Pass American Thunder Great American Legend

COMPLETE SET (10) 6.00 15.00
STATED ODDS 1:10
GAL1 Richard Petty 1964 .75 2.00
GAL2 Richard Petty 1966 .75 2.00
GAL3 Richard Petty 1971 .75 2.00
GAL4 Richard Petty 1973 .75 2.00
GAL5 Richard Petty 1974 .75 2.00
GAL6 Richard Petty 1979 .75 2.00
GAL7 Richard Petty 1981 .75 2.00
GAL8 Richard Petty 1992 .75 2.00
GAL9 Richard Petty 2008 .75 2.00
GAL10 Richard Petty 2014 .75 2.00

2014 Press Pass American Thunder Great American Legend Autographs

GLARP Richard Petty 20.00 40.00

2014 Press Pass American Thunder Great American Legend Relics Blue

*RED/50: .4X TO 1X BLUE/50
GLMRP Richard Petty 12.00 30.00

2014 Press Pass American Thunder Great American Treads Autographs Blue

GATCE Carl Edwards/25 25.00 50.00
GATJL Joey Logano/25 25.00 50.00
GATKL Kyle Larson/25 75.00 150.00
GATMA Marcos Ambrose/25 40.00 80.00
GATRS Ricky Stenhouse Jr./25 12.00 30.00
GATKYB Kyle Busch/25 30.00 60.00

2014 Press Pass American Thunder Top Speed

COMPLETE SET (11) 8.00 20.00
STATED ODDS 1:10
TS1 Austin Dillon 1.25 3.00
TS2 Martin Truex Jr. .75 2.00
TS3 Greg Biffle .75 2.00
TS4 Carl Edwards 1.00 2.50
TS5 Ryan Newman 1.00 2.50
TS6 Brad Keselowski 1.25 3.00
TS7 Dale Earnhardt Jr. 2.00 5.00
TS8 Jeff Gordon 2.00 5.00
TS9 Ricky Stenhouse Jr. 1.00 2.50
TS10 Paul Menard .60 1.50
TS11 Marcos Ambrose 1.00 2.50

2014 Press Pass American Thunder With Honors
COMPLETE SET (9) 8.00 20.00
STATED ODDS 1:10
WH1 Earnhardt Jr./Menard 2.00 5.00
WH2 Intros .75 2.00
WH3 Parade Lap .75 2.00
WH4 Parade of Drivers .75 2.00
WH5 Presenting Colors .75 2.00
WH6 National Anthem Drivers 1.00 2.50
WH7 National Anthem Flag 2.50 6.00
WH8 Thunderbirds Flyover .75 2.00
WH9 Flyover .75 2.00

2002 Press Pass Bosch
Primarily available thru Auto Zone Stores, this four-card set was produced by Press Pass honoring the 100-year anniversary of Bosch Spark Plugs. Although the cards carry a 2001 copyright year, the set was released in 2002.
COMPLETE SET (4) 3.00 8.00
1 Ward Burton .75 2.00
2 Jeff Burton .75 2.00
3 Sterling Marlin 1.25 3.00
4 Ken Schrader .75 2.00

2002 Press Pass Brian Vickers Fan Club

This jumbo sized card was issued to members of the Brian Vickers Fan Club in 2002. Press Pass produced the card featuring a Vickers photo on the front and a bio on the back. The card is also numbered "Series 1" on the back.
SER1 Brian Vickers 7.50 15.00

1999 Press Pass Bryan

This set was sponsored by Bryan Meat Products and produced by Press Pass. Each card includes the Bryan logo. Complete sets were issued as part of a sales promotion.
COMPLETE SET (11) 3.00 6.00
1 Derrike Cope .20 .50
2 Geoffrey Bodine .20 .50
3 Todd Bodine .20 .50
4 David Green .20 .50
5 Jeff Green .20 .50
6 Dale Jarrett .60 1.50
7 Jason Jarrett .20 .50
8 Rusty Wallace .75 2.00
9 Kenny Wallace .20 .50
10 Darrell Waltrip .30 .75
11 Michael Waltrip .30 .75

2006 Press Pass Burnouts
*HOLOFOIL/100-125: .5X TO 1.2X
HT1 Kyle Busch 3.00 8.00
HT2 Jeff Gordon 5.00 12.00
HT3 Martin Truex Jr 4.00 10.00
HT4 Kevin Harvick 3.00 8.00
HT5 Denny Hamlin 10.00 25.00
HT6 Reed Sorenson 4.00 10.00
HT7 Carl Edwards 2.50 6.00
HT8 Clint Bowyer 5.00 12.00
HT9 J.J. Yeley 4.00 10.00
HT10 Jimmie Johnson 4.00 10.00
HT11 Dale Earnhardt Jr. 5.00 12.00
HT12 Kasey Kahne 3.00 8.00
HT13 Elliott Sadler 1.50 4.00
HT14 Mark Martin 2.50 6.00
HT15 Jeremy Mayfield 1.50 4.00
HT16 Terry Labonte 2.50 6.00
HT17 Matt Kenseth 2.50 6.00
HT18 Ryan Newman 2.00 5.00

2007 Press Pass Burnouts
This 6-card set was randomly inserted into retail blaster boxes only at Target. Cards 1-3 could only be found in Press Pass Eclipse and cards 4-6 could only be found in Press Pass Stealth. The cards had a swatch of race-used tire and carried a "BO" prefix for its card number. The cards were inserted one per box.
*BLUE/99: .8X TO 2X BASE
*GOLD/299: .6X TO 1.5X BASE
BO1 Jimmie Johnson 2.50 6.00
BO2 Dale Earnhardt Jr. 3.00 8.00
BO3 Kevin Harvick 2.00 5.00
BO4 Kasey Kahne 1.50 4.00
BO5 Tony Stewart 2.50 6.00
BO6 Jeff Gordon 3.00 8.00

2008 Press Pass Burnouts
COMPLETE SET (8) 40.00 100.00
BO1-BO4 ODDS 1 PER TARGET ECLIPSE BLASTER BOX
BO5-BO8 ODDS 1 PER TARGET VIP BLASTER BOX
*BLUE/99: .6X TO 1.5X BASIC
*GOLD/299: .5X TO 1.2X BASIC
BO1 Jeff Gordon 4.00 10.00
BO2 Carl Edwards 2.00 5.00
BO3 Kevin Harvick 2.50 6.00
BO4 Denny Hamlin 2.50 6.00
BO5 Tony Stewart 3.00 8.00
BO6 Juan Pablo Montoya 3.00 8.00
BO7 Jimmie Johnson 3.00 8.00
BO8 Martin Truex Jr. 1.50 4.00

2000 Press Pass Chef Boyardee

This six-card set was made available one card at a time through insertion in specially marked Chef Boyardee products. A contest was also conducted that allowed collectors to win signed copies of cards from the set. Those autographs are not cataloged since they were not certified in any way.
COMPLETE SET (6) 8.00 20.00
1 Bobby Labonte .75 2.00
2 Tony Stewart 1.25 3.00
3 Bobby Labonte .75 2.00
4 Tony Stewart 1.25 3.00
5 Joe Gibbs .75 2.00
6 B.Labonte 1.25 3.00
T.Stewart

2001 Press Pass Coca-Cola Racing Family
This 3-card set was issued by Press Pass to promote the drivers in the 2001 Coca-Cola Racing Family. Each card features two drivers on the front with a black and white cardback featuring a comprehensive bio of each driver.
COMPLETE SET (3) 3.00 8.00
1 D.Jarrett 1.00 2.50
R.Rudd
2 B.Labonte 1.50 4.00
T.Stewart
3 J.Andretti .75 2.00
K.Petty

2003 Press Pass Coca-Cola Racing Family
This 12-card set was released in 2003 through Coca-Cola products. Each card was sponsored by Coke, produced by Press Pass, and measures slightly smaller than standard size at 2 1/2" by 3". One card was given away with the purchase of 2 20-ounce bottles of Coca-Cola products at participating stores.
COMPLETE SET (12) 8.00 20.00
1 John Andretti .30 .75
2 Jeff Burton .60 1.50
3 Kurt Busch .60 1.50
4 Bill Elliott .60 1.50
5 Kevin Harvick 1.25 3.00
6 Dale Jarrett 1.25 3.00
7 Bobby Labonte 1.25 3.00
8 Steve Park .50 1.25
9 Kyle Petty .50 1.25
10 Ricky Rudd .75 2.00
11 Tony Stewart 1.50 4.00
12 Michael Waltrip .50 1.25

2003 Press Pass Coca-Cola Racing Family Regional
This set was released in 2003 through Coca-Cola products. Each card was sponsored by Coke, produced by Press Pass, and measures slightly smaller than standard size at 2 1/2" by 3". One card was seeded into specially marked cases of Coca-Cola product pimarily-in the regional Texas area.
COMPLETE SET (4) 5.00 12.00
1 Bobby Labonte 1.50 4.00
2 Dale Jarrett 1.50 4.00
3 Tony Stewart SP 2.50 6.00
4 Kevin Harvick 1.50 4.00

2003 Press Pass Coca-Cola Racing Family Scratch-off
This 6-card set was released in the Summer of 2003 as the third promotional Press Pass Coca-Cola Family Racing set of the year. The unnumbered cards feature a scratch-off area on the back which gave the collector a chance to win one of several prizes. The contest expired on September 30, 2003.
COMPLETE SET (6) 4.00 10.00
1 John Andretti .50 1.25
2 Kurt Busch 1.00 2.50
3 Kyle Petty .75 2.00
4 Ricky Rudd 1.00 2.50
5 Elliott Sadler .50 1.25
6 Michael Waltrip .75 2.00

2006 Press Pass Collectors Series Making the Show
COMPLETE SET (25) 10.00 25.00
COM.FACT.SET (26) 12.00 30.00
MS1 Mark Martin .25 .60
MS2 Jeff Gordon .50 1.25
MS3 Matt Kenseth .25 .60
MS4 Ryan Newman .20 .50
MS5 Denny Hamlin 1.00 2.50
MS6 Sterling Marlin .25 .60
MS7 Jimmie Johnson .40 1.00
MS8 J.J. Yeley .40 1.00
MS9 Jamie McMurray .25 .60
MS10 Terry Labonte .25 .60
MS11 Carl Edwards .25 .60
MS12 Dale Jarrett .25 .60
MS13 Kasey Kahne .30 .75
MS14 Martin Truex Jr. .40 1.00
MS15 Greg Biffle .20 .50
MS16 Kevin Harvick .30 .75
MS17 Tony Stewart .40 1.00
MS18 Jeff Burton .20 .50
MS19 Kyle Busch .30 .75
MS20 Scott Riggs .20 .50
MS21 Ken Schrader .15 .40
MS22 Bobby Labonte .25 .60
MS23 Dale Earnhardt Jr. .50 1.25
MS24 Kurt Busch .20 .50
MS25 Casey Mears CL .15 .40

2007 Press Pass Collector's Series Box Set
COMPLETE SET (25) 8.00 20.00
COMP.FACT.SET (26) 10.00 25.00
EACH FACT.SET CONTAINS 1 MEM.OR AUTO
SB1 Clint Bowyer .20 .50
SB2 Jeff Burton .15 .40
SB3 Kurt Busch .15 .40
SB4 Kyle Busch .25 .60
SB5 Dale Earnhardt Jr. .40 1.00
SB6 Carl Edwards .20 .50
SB7 Jeff Gordon .40 1.00
SB8 Denny Hamlin .25 .60
SB9 Kevin Harvick .25 .60
SB10 Dale Jarrett .20 .50
SB11 Jimmie Johnson .30 .75
SB12 Kasey Kahne .20 .50
SB13 Matt Kenseth .20 .50
SB14 Bobby Labonte .20 .50
SB15 Sterling Marlin .20 .50
SB16 Mark Martin .20 .50
SB17 Jamie McMurray .20 .50
SB18 Juan Pablo Montoya .60 1.50
SB19 Ryan Newman .15 .40
SB20 Ricky Rudd .15 .40
SB21 Tony Stewart .30 .75
SB22 David Stremme .12 .30
SB23 Martin Truex Jr. .15 .40
SB24 Brian Vickers .20 .50
SB25 Michael Waltrip .20 .50

2008 Press Pass Collector's Series Box Set
COMP.FACT.SET (26) 15.00 30.00
COMPLETE SET (25) 6.00 15.00
1 AU OR MEM PER FACT.SET
1 Kyle Busch .30 .75
2 Carl Edwards .25 .60
3 Jimmie Johnson .40 1.00
4 Dale Earnhardt Jr .50 1.25
5 Jeff Burton .20 .50
6 Greg Biffle .20 .50
7 Kevin Harvick .30 .75
8 Tony Stewart .40 1.00
9 Matt Kenseth .25 .60
10 Jeff Gordon .50 1.25
11 Denny Hamlin .30 .75
12 Clint Bowyer .25 .60
13 David Ragan .20 .50
14 Kasey Kahne .25 .60
15 Brian Vickers .15 .40
16 Ryan Newman .20 .50
17 Martin Truex Jr .20 .50
18 Kurt Busch .20 .50
19 Juan Pablo Montoya .40 1.00
20 Bobby Labonte .25 .60
21 David Reutimann .20 .50
22 Mark Martin .25 .60
23 Scott Riggs .20 .50
24 Kyle Petty .20 .50
25 Joe Nemechek .15 .40

2003 Press Pass Craftsman

This 30-card set featured Craftsman Truck Series drivers and were available through Craftsman Tools retailers. They were available in packs of 5 cards with the purchase of $35 in Craftsman products. Cards 20-30 are autographed and inserted in packs at a rate of one in 300.
COMP.SET w/o AUTOS (19) 5.00 12.00
1 Ricky Craven .40 1.00
2 Larry Foyt .30 .75
3 Bobby Hamilton .30 .75
4 Rick Crawford .30 .75
5 David Starr .30 .75
6 Dennis Setzer .30 .75
7 Terry Cook .30 .75
8 Bill Lester .30 .75
9 Chad Chaffin .30 .75
10 A.J. Foyt .60 1.50
11 Andy Petree .30 .75
12 Rick Crawford's Truck .20 .50
13 Dennis Setzer's Truck .20 .50
14 Terry Cook's Truck .20 .50
15 Cook .30 .75
Setzer
Starr
16 R.Craven .40 1.00
L.Foyt
17 A.J.Foyt .60 1.50
L.Foyt
18 B.Hamilton .30 .75
Chaffin
Lester
19 Checklist .20 .50
20 Ricky Craven AU 20.00 40.00
21 Larry Foyt AU 15.00 30.00
22 Bobby Hamilton AU
23 Rick Crawford AU
24 David Starr AU
25 Dennis Setzer AU
26 Terry Cook AU
27 Bill Lester AU
28 Chad Chaffin AU
29 A.J. Foyt AU
30 Andy Petree AU

2001-03 Press Pass Dale Earnhardt

Starting mid-year 2001, this set celebrated the life of Dale Earnhardt with each card featuring an event from the racing life of Earnhardt. Most Press Pass products in 2001 and 2002 included 8 or 9 cards featuring a specific theme with the following insertion ratios for 2001: DE1-DE8 1:48 VIP, DE9-DE16 1:48 Stealth, DE17-DE25 1:48 Optima. The 2002 products included: DE26-DE34 1:72 Press Pass, DE35-DE43 1:72 High Gear, DE35(B)-DE43(B) 1:72 Eclipse, DE44-DE52 1:72 Press Pass Premium, DE53-DE62 1:72 Trackside, DE63-DE70 1:72 VIP, DE71-DE79 1:72 Stealth, DE80-DE88 1:72 Optima, and DE89-DE100 1:72 2003 Press Pass.
COMMON DALE (DE1-DE79) 7.50 15.00
COMMON DALE (DE80-DE100) 10.00 25.00
*CELEBRATION FOILS: 1X TO 2.5X BASIC INS.
CELEB.FOIL PRINT RUN 250 SER.#'d SETS

2003-04 Press Pass 10th Anniversary Earnhardt
This cross brand set was produced by Press Pass in conjunction with their online poll allowing collector's to select their favorite Press Pass Dale Earnhardt cards. They were inserted in packs at a rate of 1:72 in various 2003 and 2004 products: TA1-TA12 inserted in 2003 Press Pass Eclipse, TA13-TA24 2003 Press Pass Premium, TA25-TA37 2003 Press Pass Trackside, TA38-TA50 2003 VIP, TA51-TA63 2003 Press Pass Stealth, TA64-TA76 2003 Press Pass Optima, TA77-TA88 were found in 2004 Press Pass, and TA89-TA100 in 2004 Press Pass Eclipse. The cards are reprints of the originals with a silver foil border and the backs have a description of the card and when it was issued. There is also a gold parallel version of this set.
COMMON EARN.(TA1-TA88) 4.00 10.00
*GOLD/250: .8X TO 2X BASIC INSERTS
GOLD PRINT RUN 250 SERIAL #'d SETS

2015 Press Pass Signings Gold
PPSAA Aric Almirola 3.00 8.00
PPSAB Alex Bowman RET 4.00 10.00
PPSAD Austin Dillon SP
PPSAJ A.J. Allmendinger 4.00 10.00
PPSBG Brendan Gaughan RET 4.00 10.00
PPSBS Brian Scott RET 4.00 10.00
PPSBV Brian Vickers RET 2.50 6.00
PPSCB1 Clint Bowyer 4.00 10.00
PPSCB2 Chris Buescher RET 3.00 8.00
PPSCED Carl Edwards SP 10.00 25.00
PPSCEL Chase Elliott SP
PPSCM Casey Mears RET 2.50 6.00
PPSCW Cole Whitt RET 3.00 8.00
PPSDA Dakoda Armstrong RET
PPSDE Dale Earnhardt Jr SP
PPSDG David Gilliland RET
PPSDH Denny Hamlin SP 6.00 15.00
PPSDK Dylan Kwasniewski RET
PPSDP Danica Patrick SP 60.00 100.00
PPSDR David Ragan RET
PPSDW Darrell Wallace Jr. RET 4.00 10.00
PPSES Elliott Sadler RET 3.00 8.00
PPSGB Greg Biffle 3.00 8.00
PPSJA Justin Allgaier RET
PPSJB James Buescher RET 2.50 6.00
PPSJBU Jeb Burton RET 3.00 8.00
PPSJE Jeffrey Earnhardt RET 4.00 10.00
PPSJG Jeff Gordon SP 60.00 100.00
PPSJJ Jimmie Johnson SP 40.00 80.00
PPSJJC Jennifer Jo Cobb RET 8.00 20.00
PPSJL Joey Logano SP 10.00 25.00
PPSJM Jamie McMurray 4.00 10.00
PPSJS Johnny Sauter RET 2.50 6.00
PPSJW Josh Wise RET 2.50 6.00
PPSJY J.J. Yeley RET 2.50 6.00
PPSKH Kevin Harvick SP
PPSKK Kasey Kahne SP 10.00 25.00
PPSKL Kyle Larson SP 15.00 40.00
PPSKUB Kurt Busch SP 6.00 15.00
PPSKYB Kyle Busch SP 10.00 25.00
PPSMA1 Marcos Ambrose SP 12.00 30.00
PPSMA2 Michael Annett RET 4.00 10.00
PPSMK Matt Kenseth SP 8.00 20.00
PPSMM Michael McDowell RET 3.00 8.00
PPSMT Martin Truex Jr RET
PPSMW Michael Waltrip RET SP
PPSPK Parker Kligerman RET 2.50 6.00
PPSPM Paul Menard RET 2.50 6.00
PPSRB Ryan Blaney RET SP
PPSRN Ryan Newman SP 5.00 12.00
PPSRR Ryan Reed RET 8.00 20.00
PPSRS Regan Smith RET 4.00 10.00
PPSRST Ricky Stenhouse Jr. 4.00 10.00
PPSRT Ryan Truex RET
PPSSH Sam Hornish Jr. RET 3.00 8.00
PPSTBA Trevor Bayne RET 4.00 10.00
PPSTBE Tanner Berryhill RET 6.00 15.00
PPSTD Ty Dillon SP 6.00 15.00

2015 Press Pass Signings Blue
*BLUE/75-150: .4X TO 1X GOLD AU
*BLUE/50: .5X TO 1.2X GOLD AU
*BLUE/15-25: .6X TO 1.5X GOLD AU
*BLUE/15-25: .4X TO 1X GOLD SP AU
PPSAD Austin Dillon/15 15.00 30.00

2015 Press Pass Signings Green
*GREEN/50: .5X TO 1.2X GOLD AU
*GREEN/15-25: .6X TO 1.5X GOLD AU

2015 Press Pass Signings Red
*RED/75: .4X TO 1X GOLD AU
*RED/50: .5X TO 1.2X GOLD AU
*RED/15-25: .6X TO 1.5X GOLD AU

2015 Press Pass
COMPLETE SET (100) 6.00 15.00
*CAR CARDS 50% OF BASE
1 A.J. Allmendinger .25 .60
2 Justin Allgaier .20 .50
3 Aric Almirola .20 .50
4 Michael Annett .25 .60
5 Marcos Ambrose .25 .60
6 Greg Biffle .20 .50
7 Alex Bowman .25 .60
8 Clint Bowyer .25 .60
9 Kurt Busch .20 .50
10 Kyle Busch .30 .75
11 Austin Dillon .30 .75
12 Dale Earnhardt Jr. .50 1.25
13 Carl Edwards .25 .60
14 David Gilliland .15 .40
15 Jeff Gordon .50 1.25
16 Denny Hamlin .25 .60
17 Kevin Harvick .30 .75
18 Jimmie Johnson .40 1.00
19 Kasey Kahne .25 .60
20 Matt Kenseth .25 .60
21 Brad Keselowski .30 .75
22 Kyle Larson .40 1.00
23 Joey Logano .25 .60
24 Michael McDowell .20 .50
25 Jamie McMurray .25 .60
26 Casey Mears .15 .40
27 Paul Menard .15 .40
28 Ryan Newman .20 .50
29 Danica Patrick .50 1.25
30 David Ragan .20 .50
31 Ricky Stenhouse Jr. .25 .60
32 Tony Stewart .40 1.00
33 Ryan Truex .20 .50
34 Martin Truex Jr. .20 .50
35 Brian Vickers .15 .40
36 Michael Waltrip .25 .60
37 Cole Whitt .20 .50
38 Josh Wise .15 .40
39 J.J. Yeley .15 .40
40 Dakoda Armstrong NNS .25 .60
41 Trevor Bayne NNS .25 .60
42 Tanner Berryhill NNS .15 .40
43 Chris Buescher NNS .20 .50
44 James Buescher NNS .15 .40
45 Ty Dillon NNS .25 .60
46 Jeffrey Earnhardt NNS .25 .60
47 Chase Elliott NNS .30 .75
48 Brendan Gaughan NNS .15 .40
49 Sam Hornish Jr. NNS .20 .50
50 Dylan Kwasniewski NNS .20 .50
51 Ryan Reed NNS .20 .50
52 Elliott Sadler NNS .20 .50
53 Brian Scott NNS .15 .40
54 Regan Smith NNS .25 .60
55 Ryan Blaney CWTS .20 .50
56 Jeb Burton CWTS .20 .50
57 Jennifer Jo Cobb CWTS .25 .60
58 Matt Crafton CWTS .15 .40
59 Johnny Sauter CWTS .15 .40
60 Darrell Wallace Jr. CWTS .25 .60
61 Aric Almirola H .15 .40
62 Kurt Busch H .15 .40
63 Kyle Busch H .25 .60
64 Austin Dillon H .25 .60
65 Dale Earnhardt Jr H .40 1.00
66 Carl Edwards H .20 .50
67 Jeff Gordon H .40 1.00
68 Denny Hamlin H .20 .50
69 Kevin Harvick H .25 .60
70 Jimmie Johnson H .30 .75
71 Brad Keselowski H .25 .60
72 Matt Kenseth H .20 .50
73 Kyle Larson H .30 .75
74 Joey Logano H .20 .50
75 Ryan Newman H .15 .40
76 Ty Dillon H .20 .50
77 Chase Elliott H .25 .60
78 Darrell Wallace Jr. H .20 .50
79 Dale Earnhardt Jr. CC .40 1.00
80 Brad Keselowski CC .25 .60
81 Jimmie Johnson CC .30 .75
82 Jeff Gordon CC .40 1.00
83 Joey Logano CC .20 .50
84 Carl Edwards CC .20 .50
85 Kevin Harvick CC .25 .60
86 Kyle Busch CC .25 .60
87 Matt Kenseth CC .20 .50
88 Ryan Newman CC .15 .40
89 Kasey Kahne CC .20 .50
90 Austin Dillon's Car OTW .15 .40
91 Dale Earnhardt Jr.'s Car OTW .25 .60
92 Jeff Gordon's Car OTW .25 .60
93 Jimmie Johnson's Car OTW .20 .50
94 Kevin Harvick's Car OTW .15 .40
95 Kyle Busch's Car OTW .15 .40
96 Matt Kenseth's Car OTW .12 .30
97 Kyle Larson's Car OTW .20 .50
98 Tony Stewart's Car OTW .20 .50
99 Chase Elliott's Car OTW .15 .40
100 Chase Contenders CL .30 .75

2015 Press Pass Cup Chase
COMPLETE SET (100) 15.00 40.00
*CUP CHASE: .8X TO 2X PRESS PASS

2015 Press Pass Cup Chase Blue
*BLUE/25: 6X TO 15X PRESS PASS

2015 Press Pass Cup Chase Gold
*GOLD/75: 2.5X TO 6X PRESS PASS

2015 Press Pass Cup Chase Green
*GREEN/10: 8X TO 20X PRESS PASS

2015 Press Pass Burning Rubber Gold
*BLUE/50: .5X TO 1.2X GOLD
BRAA Aric Almirola 8.00 20.00
BRDH Denny Hamlin 10.00 25.00
BRKK Kasey Kahne 10.00 25.00
BRAJA A.J. Allmendinger 10.00 25.00
BRBK1 Brad Keselowski 12.00 30.00
BRBK2 Brad Keselowski 12.00 30.00
BRBK3 Brad Keselowski 12.00 30.00
BRBK4 Brad Keselowski 12.00 30.00
BRCE1 Carl Edwards 12.00 30.00
BRCE2 Carl Edwards 12.00 30.00
BRJG1 Jeff Gordon 20.00 50.00
BRJG2 Jeff Gordon 20.00 50.00
BRJG3 Jeff Gordon 20.00 50.00
BRJJ1 Jimmie Johnson 12.00 30.00
BRJJ2 Jimmie Johnson 12.00 30.00
BRJJ3 Jimmie Johnson 15.00 40.00
BRJL1 Joey Logano 10.00 25.00
BRJL2 Joey Logano 10.00 25.00
BRJL3 Joey Logano 10.00 25.00
BRKH1 Kevin Harvick 12.00 30.00
BRKH2 Kevin Harvick 12.00 30.00
BRKUB Kurt Busch 8.00 20.00
BRKYB Kyle Busch 12.00 30.00
BRDEJ1 Dale Earnhardt Jr 20.00 50.00
BRDEJ2 Dale Earnhardt Jr 15.00 40.00
BRDEJ3 Dale Earnhardt Jr 15.00 40.00

2015 Press Pass Championship Caliber Signature Edition Gold
*BLUE/25: .75X TO 2X GOLD/50
*BLUE/15: .75X TO 2X GOLD/30
CCAD Austin Dillon/50 8.00 20.00
CCCE Carl Edwards/30 10.00 25.00
CCDH Denny Hamlin/50 8.00 20.00
CCJG Jeff Gordon/25 50.00 100.00
CCJJ Jimmie Johnson/25 30.00 80.00
CCJL Joey Logano/50 12.00 30.00
CCKH Kevin Harvick/50 12.00 30.00
CCKL Kyle Larson/25 25.00 60.00
CCMK Matt Kenseth/50 8.00 20.00
CCRN Ryan Newman/50 6.00 15.00
CCTD Ty Dillon/50 8.00 20.00
CCCE2 Chase Elliott/30 75.00 150.00
CCDEJ Dale Earnhardt Jr/25 50.00 100.00
CCKUB Kurt Busch/50 6.00 15.00
CCKYB Kyle Busch/50 10.00 25.00

2015 Press Pass Championship Caliber Single
*DUAL/25: .5X TO 1.2X SINGLE/50
CCMAD Austin Dillon 8.00 20.00
CCMBK Brad Keselowski 8.00 20.00
CCMCE Carl Edwards 6.00 15.00
CCMDH Denny Hamlin 6.00 15.00
CCMJG Jeff Gordon 15.00 40.00
CCMJJ Jimmie Johnson 10.00 25.00
CCMJL Joey Logano 6.00 15.00
CCMKH Kevin Harvick 8.00 20.00
CCMKL Kyle Larson 12.00 30.00
CCMMK Matt Kenseth 6.00 15.00
CCMRN Ryan Newman 5.00 12.00
CCMTD Ty Dillon 8.00 20.00
CCMCE2 Chase Elliott 8.00 20.00
CCMDEJ Dale Earnhardt Jr 12.00 30.00
CCMKUB Kurt Busch 5.00 12.00
CCMKYB Kyle Busch 8.00 20.00

2015 Press Pass Cuts Gold
*BLUE/25: .5X TO 1.2X GOLD/50
CCCAD Austin Dillon 8.00 20.00
CCCCE Carl Edwards 6.00 15.00
CCCCE Chase Elliott 12.00 30.00
CCCDEJ Dale Earnhardt Jr 12.00 30.00
CCCDH Denny Hamlin 6.00 15.00
CCCDP Danica Patrick 12.00 30.00
CCCJG Jeff Gordon 12.00 30.00
CCCJJ Jimmie Johnson 10.00 25.00
CCCJL Joey Logano 6.00 15.00
CCCKH Kevin Harvick 8.00 20.00
CCCKK Kasey Kahne 6.00 15.00
CCCKL Kyle Larson 10.00 25.00
CCCKYB Kyle Busch 8.00 20.00
CCCMK Matt Kenseth 6.00 15.00
CCCTD Ty Dillon 6.00 15.00
CCCTS Tony Stewart 10.00 25.00

2015 Press Pass Dale Earnhardt Tribute
COMPLETE SET (5) 8.00 20.00
DE1 In The Early Years 2.00 5.00
DE2 In The Early Years 2.00 5.00
DE3 Track Records 2.00 5.00
DE4 Championships 2.00 5.00
DE5 Legendary Relationships 2.00 5.00

2015 Press Pass Four Wide Signature Edition Gold

*BLUE/25: .6X TO 1.5X GOLD/50
*BLUE/15: .6X TO 1.5X GOLD/25-35
4WAD Austin Dillon 8.00 20.00
4WCE Chase Elliott 100.00 200.00
4WDH Denny Hamlin 10.00 25.00
4WDP Danica Patrick 60.00 120.00
4WJG Jeff Gordon 60.00 120.00
4WJJ Jimmie Johnson 60.00 120.00
4WJL Joey Logano 20.00 50.00
4WKH Kevin Harvick 30.00 80.00
4WKK Kasey Kahne 10.00 25.00
4WMA Marcos Ambrose 10.00 25.00
4WMK Matt Kenseth 15.00 40.00
4WTD Ty Dillon 15.00 40.00
4WDEJ Dale Earnhardt Jr 50.00 100.00
4WKUB Kurt Busch 8.00 20.00
4WKYB Kyle Busch 12.00 30.00

2015 Press Pass Pit Road Pieces Gold

*BLUE/25: .5X TO 1.2X GOLD/50
PPMCB Clint Bowyer 6.00 15.00
PPMCE Carl Edwards 6.00 15.00
PPMDH Denny Hamlin 6.00 15.00
PPMDP Danica Patrick 12.00 30.00
PPMGB Greg Biffle 5.00 12.00
PPMJG Jeff Gordon 12.00 30.00
PPMJJ Jimmie Johnson 10.00 25.00
PPMJL Joey Logano 8.00 20.00
PPMKK Kasey Kahne 6.00 15.00
PPMKL Kyle Larson 10.00 25.00
PPMMK Matt Kenseth 6.00 15.00
PPMRN Ryan Newman 5.00 12.00
PPMTS Tony Stewart 10.00 25.00
PPMDEJ Dale Earnhardt Jr 12.00 30.00
PPMKUB Kurt Busch 5.00 12.00
PPMBECE B.Elliott/C.Elliott 12.00 30.00

2015 Press Pass Pit Road Pieces Signature Edition Gold

*BLUE/25: .75X TO 2X GOLD/50
*BLUE/15: .5X TO 1.2X GOLD/25
PRPCB Clint Bowyer/50 6.00 15.00
PRPCE Carl Edwards/50 8.00 20.00
PRPDH Denny Hamlin/50 8.00 20.00
PRPDP Danica Patrick/20 50.00 100.00
PRPGB Greg Biffle/50 6.00 15.00
PRPJG Jeff Gordon/25 50.00 100.00
PRPJJ Jimmie Johnson/25 30.00 80.00
PRPJL Joey Logano/50 10.00 25.00
PRPKK Kasey Kahne/50 8.00 20.00
PRPKL Kyle Larson/25 25.00 60.00
PRPMK Matt Kenseth/50 8.00 20.00
PRPRN Ryan Newman/50 6.00 15.00
PRPDEJ Dale Earnhardt Jr/25 50.00 100.00
PRPKUB Kurt Busch/50 6.00 15.00
PRPBECE B.Elliott/C.Elliott/25 60.00 120.00

2015 Press Pass Signature Series Gold

SSAA Aric Almirola/50 8.00 20.00
SSBV Brian Vickers/50 6.00 15.00
SSCB Clint Bowyer/50 10.00 25.00
SSCE Carl Edwards/50 10.00 25.00
SSDP Danica Patrick/15 60.00 120.00
SSGB Greg Biffle/50 8.00 20.00
SSKH Kevin Harvick/50 15.00 40.00
SSKL Kyle Larson/25 30.00 60.00
SSMA Marcos Ambrose/50 10.00 25.00
SSMK Matt Kenseth/50 6.00 15.00
SSPM Paul Menard/50 6.00 15.00
SSRN Ryan Newman/20 10.00 25.00
SSTD Ty Dillon/35 10.00 25.00
SSCE2 Chase Elliott/25 50.00 100.00
SSKYB Kyle Busch/50 12.00 30.00

2015 Press Pass Signature Series Blue

*BLUE/25: .5X TO 1.2X GOLD/35-50
*BLUE/15: .4X TO 1X GOLD/20
SSCE2 Chase Elliott/15 75.00 150.00

2015 Press Pass Cup Chase Three Wide Gold

*BLUE/25: .5X TO 1.2X GOLD/50
3WAD Austin Dillon 8.00 20.00
3WCE Chase Elliott 12.00 30.00
3WDH Denny Hamlin 6.00 15.00
3WDP Danica Patrick 15.00 40.00
3WJG Jeff Gordon 12.00 30.00
3WJJ Jimmie Johnson 10.00 25.00
3WJL Joey Logano 10.00 25.00
3WKH Kevin Harvick 8.00 20.00
3WKK Kasey Kahne 6.00 15.00
3WMK Matt Kenseth 6.00 15.00
3WTD Ty Dillon 6.00 15.00
3WTS Tony Stewart 10.00 25.00
3WDEJ Dale Earnhardt Jr 12.00 30.00
3WKUB Kurt Busch 5.00 12.00
3WKYB Kyle Busch 8.00 20.00

2004 Press Pass Dale Earnhardt Gallery

This cross brand set was produced by Press Pass as a tribute to Dale Earnhardt. They were inserted in packs at a rate of 1:72 in various 2004 and 2005 products: DEG1-DEG9 inserted in 2004 Press Pass Premium, DEG10-DEG18 2004 Press Pass Stealth, DEG19-DEG27 2004 Press Pass Trackside, DEG28-DEG37 2004 VIP, DEG38-DEG45 2004 Press Pass Optima, DEG46-DEG54 2005 Press Pass. The cards are paintings of the Dale with a white border and the backs have a description of the painting. There is also a gold parallel version of this set.
COMMON EARNHARDT 5.00 12.00

2004 Press Pass Dale Earnhardt The Legacy Victories

COMP.TIN SET (76) 20.00 40.00
COMPLETE SET (76) 15.00 30.00
COMMON EARNHARDT .50 1.25

2005 Press Pass Dale Earnhardt Victories

COMMON EARNHARDT 4.00 10.00

2007 Press Pass Dale The Movie

COMPLETE SET (50) 15.00 30.00
COMP.FACT.SET (50) 15.00 30.00
1 Dale Earnhardt .30 .75
Racer's Perspective
2 Dale Earnhardt .30 .75
Daytona Dominance
3 Dale Earnhardt .30 .75
Legendary Racer
4 Dale Earnhardt .30 .75
Son of a Legend
5 Ralph Earnhardt .05 .15
6 Dale Earnhardt .30 .75
Picks Up Where His Father Left Off
7 Dale Earnhardt .30 .75
Darrell Waltrip
8 Dale Earnhardt .30 .75
Early Cup Racing
9 Dale Earnhardt .30 .75
First Cup Win
10 Dale Earnhardt .30 .75
First Championship
11 Dale Earnhardt .30 .75
Wrangler Sponsorship
12 Dale Earnhardt .30 .75
Great American Cowboy
13 Dale Earnhardt .30 .75
One Tough Customer
14 Dale Earnhardt .30 .75
Richard Childress
15 Dale Earnhardt .30 .75
16 Wins in 2 Years
16 Dale Earnhardt .30 .75
Wild Side
17 Danny Chocolate Myers .05 .10
18 Kelley Earnhardt .10 .25
Dale Earnhardt Jr.
19 Kerry Earnhardt .05 .10
20 Dale Earnhardt .30 .75
Steve Byrnes
21 Dale Earnhardt's Car .30 .75
Pass in the Grass
22 Dale Earnhardt .30 .75
Darrell Waltrip Rivalry
23 Dale Earnhardt's Car .30 .75
Goodwrench Era Begins
24 Dale Earnhardt .30 .75
Intimidator
25 Dale Earnhardt .30 .75
Teresa Earnhardt
Four Championships
26 Dale Earnhardt's Car .12 .30
Brian Williams
27 Dale Earnhardt .30 .75
Working on the Farm
28 Dale Earnhardt's Car .12 .30
Final Victory Talladega
29 Dale Earnhardt .30 .75
Darrell Waltrip DEI
30 Dale Earnhardt .30 .75
Taylor Nicole Earnhardt
31 Dale Earnhardt .30 .75
Dale Earnhardt Jr.
32 Dale Earnhardt .30 .75
Hands On Racer
33 Dale Earnhardt's Car .12 .30
1986 Daytona 500
34 Dale Earnhardt's Car .12 .30
1990 Daytona 500
35 Dale Earnhardt's Car .12 .30
Jeff Gordon's Car/1997 Daytona 500
36 Dale Earnhardt .30 .75
Girl with Penny
37 Dale Earnhardt's Car .12 .30
1998 Daytona 500 Final Pit Stop
38 Dale Earnhardt's Car .12 .30
1998 Daytona 500 Congratulations
39 Dale Earnhardt's Car .12 .30
1998 Daytona 500 Burnout
40 Dale Earnhardt's Car .12 .30
1998 Daytona 500 Victory Lane
41 Dale Earnhardt .30 .75
1998 Daytona 500 Celebration
42 Dale Earnhardt .30 .75
Reflections
43 Mourning A Legend .30 .75
44 Steve Park's Car .01 .05
45 Dale Earnhardt's Car/Bobby Labonte's Car/Kevin Harvick's Car/Jeff Gordon .12 .30
46 Dale Earnhardt Jr.'s Car/Kevin Harvick's Car/Michael Waltrip's Car/Jimmi .05 .10
47 Dale Earnhardt .30 .75
American Dream
48 Dale Earnhardt .30 .75
Honored Hero
49 Dale Earnhardt .30 .75
Career Milestones
50 Dale Earnhardt Statue CL .30 .75

2004 Press Pass Dale Earnhardt Jr.

COMPLETE TIN SET (74) 10.00 25.00
COMP.SET w/o TIN (72) 6.00 15.00
COMMON DALE JR. .20 .50
COMMON DALE JR./SR.
*BLUE: .8X TO 2X BASIC CARDS
*BRONZE: .8X TO 2X BASIC CARDS
*GOLD: 1X TO 2.5X BASIC CARDS

2004 Press Pass Dale Earnhardt Jr. Gallery

This 8-card set was inserted into the Press Pass Dale Earnhardt Jr. tin sets. There were two cards per sealed set. The cards featured silver foil highlights. Each card carried a "G" prefix for its card numbering.
COMPLETE SET (8) 10.00 25.00
COMMON DALE JR. 2.00 5.00

2004 Press Pass Dale Earnhardt Jr. Tins

COMPLETE SET (4) 12.50 30.00
COMMON TIN 3.00 8.00

2002 Press Pass Dale Earnhardt Jr. Firesuit

This card was sent out to collectors who were waiting on a Dale Earnhardt Jr. autograph exchange card that has yet to be redeemed. It shows Dale Jr. in his 1999 Busch Championship celebration and the swatch of firesuit is from the AC Delco uniform from that same season. Some of these were also available in 2003 Press Pass packs.
NNO Dale Earnhardt Jr. 30.00 80.00

2003 Press Pass Dale Jarrett Fan Club

DJ Dale Jarrett 15.00 30.00

2008 Press Pass Daytona 500 50th Anniversary

COMP.FACT.SET (51) 15.00 30.00
COMPLETE SET (50) 10.00 25.00
1 Lee Petty '59 .15 .40
2 Marvin Panch '61 .12 .30
3 Fireball Roberts '62 .15 .40
4 Tiny Lund '63 .12 .30
5 Richard Petty '64 .30 .75
6 Fred Lorenzen '65 .15 .40
7 Richard Petty '66 .30 .75
8 Cale Yarborough '68 .20 .50
9 Lee Roy Yarbrough '69 .12 .30
10 Pete Hamilton '70 .12 .30
11 Richard Petty '71 .30 .75
12 Richard Petty '73 .30 .75
13 Richard Petty '74 .30 .75
14 Benny Parsons '75 .20 .50
15 David Pearson '76 .20 .50
16 Cale Yarborough '77 .20 .50
17 Bobby Allison '78 .15 .40
18 Richard Petty '79 .30 .75
19 Buddy Baker '80 .15 .40
20 Richard Petty '81 .30 .75
21 Bobby Allison '82 .15 .40
22 Cale Yarborough '83 .20 .50
23 Cale Yarborough '84 .20 .50
24 Geoff Bodine '86 .12 .30
25 Bobby Allison '88 .15 .40
26 Darrell Waltrip '89 .30 .75
27 Derrike Cope '90 .20 .50
28 Ernie Irvan '91 .20 .50
29 Davey Allison '92 .30 .75
30 Dale Jarrett '93 .20 .50
31 Sterling Marlin '94 .20 .50
32 Sterling Marlin '95 .20 .50
33 Dale Jarrett '96 .20 .50
34 Jeff Gordon '97 .40 1.00
35 Dale Earnhardt '98 1.25 3.00
36 Jeff Gordon '99 .40 1.00
37 Dale Jarrett '00 .20 .50
38 Michael Waltrip '01 .20 .50
39 Ward Burton '02 .15 .40
40 Michael Waltrip '03 .20 .50
41 Dale Earnhardt Jr. '04 .40 1.00
42 Jeff Gordon '05 .40 1.00
43 Jimmie Johnson '06 .30 .75
44 Kevin Harvick '07 .25 .60
45 Lee Petty FF .15 .40
46 D.Pearson/R.Petty FF .30 .75
47 B.Allison/Do.Allison/C.Yarb. FF .20 .50
48 Dale Earnhardt FF 1.25 3.00
49 Kevin Harvick FF .25 .60
50 Checklist .20 .50
NNO '08 Winner Tire Redemption 25.00 50.00

2002 Press Pass Delphi

This 7-card promotional set was sponsored by Delphi and produced by Press Pass. Each card features a color image, of drivers Delphi sponsors, on the front and his car on the back.
COMPLETE SET (7) 8.00 20.00
D1 Joe Nemechek .60 1.25
D2 Jeff Gordon 3.00 8.00
D3 Terry Labonte 1.25 3.00
D4 Jimmie Johnson 2.50 6.00
D5 Ricky Hendrick .60 1.25
D6 Jack Sprague .60 1.25
NNO Joe Nemechek's Car .40 1.00
Cover

1999 Press Pass Dew Crew

This 4-card set was sponsored by Mountain Dew and issued as part of a sales promotion in packages of soft drinks.
COMPLETE SET (4) 4.00 10.00
1 Casey Atwood 2.00 5.00
2 Ward Burton .75 2.00
3 Terry Labonte 1.25 3.00
4 Chad Little .40 1.00

2006 Press Pass Dominator Dale Earnhardt

This 33-card set was released in November, 2006 in factory sealed tins. Each tin contained one of 3 oversized jumbo cards. The 33 cards highlighted Dale Earnhardt's career.
COMP.FACT.SET (34) 12.50 30.00
COMPLETE SET (33) 10.00 25.00
COMMON EARNHARDT .60 1.50

2006 Press Pass Dominator Dale Earnhardt Jumbo

This 3-card insert set was issued at a rate of one per tin set. Each card was oversized and featured Dale Earnhardt.
COMPLETE SET (3) 8.00 20.00
STATED ODDS 1 PER TIN
SR1 Dale Earnhardt Appeal 3.00 8.00
SR2 Dale Earnhardt 3.00 8.00
SR3 Dale Earnhardt 3.00 8.00

2006 Press Pass Dominator Dale Earnhardt Jr.

This 33-card set was released in November, 2006 in factory sealed tins. Each tin contained one of 3 oversized jumbo cards. The 33 cards highlighted Dale Earnhardt Jr.'s career.
COMP.FACT.SET (34) 12.50 30.00
COMPLETE SET (33) 10.00 25.00
COMMON DALE JR. .50 1.25

2006 Press Pass Dominator Dale Earnhardt Jr. Jumbo

This 3-card insert set was issued at a rate of one per tin set. Each card was oversized and featured Dale Earnhardt Jr.
COMPLETE SET (3) 5.00 12.00
STSTED ODDS 1 PER TIN
JR1 Dale Jr. 1.00 2.50
JR2 Dale Jr. 1.00 2.50
JR3 Dale Jr. Competitor 1.00 2.50

2006 Press Pass Dominator Jeff Gordon

This 33-card set was released in November, 2006 in factory sealed tins. Each tin contained one of 3 oversized jumbo cards. The 33 cards highlighted Jeff Gordon's career.
COMP.FACT.SET (34) 12.50 30.00
COMPLETE SET (33) 10.00 25.00
COMMON GORDON .50 1.25

2006 Press Pass Dominator Jeff Gordon Jumbo

This 3-card insert set was issued at a rate of one per tin set. Each card was oversized and featured Jeff Gordon.
COMPLETE SET (3) 5.00 12.00
STATED ODDS 1 PER TIN
JG1 Jeff Gordon 1.00 2.50
JG2 Jeff Gordon Performance 1.00 2.50
JG3 Jeff Gordon 1.00 2.50

2006 Press Pass Dominator Tins

This 3-tin set featured a 33-card set inside for the corresponding driver.
DE Dale Earnhardt 3.00 8.00
JG Jeff Gordon 2.00 5.00
JR Dale Earnhardt Jr. 2.00 5.00

2002 Press Pass Double Burner

Randomly inserted into hobby packs across most 2002 Press Pass products, this set features nine leading drivers. All cards in this set are serial numbered to 100 and include a swatch of a race used glove and firesuit. Some cards were issued via mail redemption cards which carried an expiration date of 1/31/2003.
DB1 Dale Earnhardt Jr. 100.00 200.00
DB2 Jeff Gordon 75.00 150.00
DB3 Kevin Harvick 40.00 80.00
DB4 Dale Jarrett 40.00 80.00
DB5 Bobby Labonte 40.00 80.00
DB6 Terry Labonte 30.00 60.00
DB7 Mark Martin 40.00 80.00
DB8 Tony Stewart 40.00 80.00
DB9 Rusty Wallace 40.00 80.00

2003 Press Pass Double Burner

Issued as part of a year long Press Pass insert program, these 10 cards feature race-used pieces of both firesuits and gloves embedded in a trading card. The cards were issued to a stated print run of 100 serial numbered sets but spread out over a number of their card brands in 2003. Each card was initially released as a redemption card featuring a Press Pass Authentics hologram sticker.
DB1 Jeff Gordon 50.00 120.00
DB2 Ryan Newman 15.00 40.00
DB3 Kevin Harvick 15.00 40.00
DB4 Jimmie Johnson 25.00 60.00
DB5 Rusty Wallace 20.00 50.00
DB6 Mark Martin 15.00 40.00
DB7 Matt Kenseth 20.00 50.00
DB8 Bobby Labonte 15.00 40.00
DB9 Tony Stewart 30.00 80.00
DB10 Dale Earnhardt Jr. 50.00 120.00

2003 Press Pass Double Burner Exchange

DB1 Jeff Gordon EXCH 2.00 5.00
DB2 Ryan Newman EXCH 1.00 2.50
DB3 Kevin Harvick EXCH 1.00 2.50
DB4 Jimmie Johnson EXCH 1.50 4.00
DB5 Rusty Wallace EXCH 1.00 2.50
DB6 Mark Martin EXCH 1.00 2.50
DB7 Matt Kenseth EXCH 1.00 2.50
DB8 Bobby Labonte EXCH 1.00 2.50
DB9 Tony Stewart EXCH 1.25 3.00
DB10 Dale Earnhardt Jr. EXCH 2.00 5.00

2004 Press Pass Double Burner

Issued as part of a year long Press Pass insert program, these 10 cards feature race-used pieces of both firesuits and gloves embedded in a trading card. The cards were issued to a stated print run of 100 serial numbered sets but spread out over a number of their card brands in 2004. Each card was initially released as a redemption card featuring a Press Pass Authentics hologram sticker.
DB1 Jeff Gordon 25.00 60.00
DB2 Ryan Newman 10.00 25.00
DB4 Jimmie Johnson 20.00 50.00
DB5 Rusty Wallace 12.00 30.00
DB6 Mark Martin 12.00 30.00
DB7 Matt Kenseth 12.00 30.00
DB8 Bobby Labonte 12.00 30.00
DB9 Tony Stewart 20.00 50.00
DB10 Dale Earnhardt Jr. 25.00 60.00

2004 Press Pass Double Burner Exchange

RANDOM INSERTS IN RETAIL PACKS
DB1 Jeff Gordon 1.50 4.00
DB2 Ryan Newman .75 2.00
DB3 Kevin Harvick 1.00 2.50
DB4 Jimmie Johnson 1.50 4.00
DB5 Rusty Wallace 1.25 3.00
DB6 Mark Martin 1.25 3.00
DB7 Matt Kenseth 1.00 2.50
DB8 Bobby Labonte .75 2.00
DB9 Tony Stewart 1.25 3.00
DB10 Dale Earnhardt Jr. 1.50 4.00

2005 Press Pass Double Burner

DB1 Jeff Gordon 30.00 80.00
DB2 Ryan Newman 10.00 25.00
DB3 Kevin Harvick 15.00 40.00
DB4 Jimmie Johnson 20.00 50.00
DB5 Rusty Wallace 12.00 30.00
DB6 Mark Martin 15.00 40.00
DB7 Matt Kenseth 12.00 30.00
DB8 Bobby Labonte 12.00 30.00
DB9 Tony Stewart 20.00 50.00
DB10 Dale Earnhardt Jr. 25.00 60.00
DB11 Kurt Busch 10.00 25.00
DB12 Brian Vickers 8.00 20.00

2005 Press Pass Double Burner Exchange

*EXCHANGE: .5X TO 1X BASE

2006 Press Pass Double Burner Firesuit-Glove

STATED PRINT RUN 100 SERIAL #'d SETS
AVAILABLE IN PACKS OF '06 PREMIUM
DB1 Jeff Gordon 15.00 40.00
DB2 Dale Jarrett 8.00 20.00
DB3 Matt Kenseth 8.00 20.00
DB4 Jimmie Johnson 12.00 30.00
DB5 Kevin Harvick 10.00 25.00
DB6 Dale Earnhardt Jr. 15.00 40.00
DB7 Carl Edwards 8.00 20.00
DB8 Ryan Newman 6.00 15.00
DB9 Tony Stewart 12.00 30.00

2006 Press Pass Double Burner Metal-Tire

AVAILABLE IN PACKS OF '06 PRESS PASS
DB1 Carl Edwards 10.00 25.00
DB2 Dale Earnhardt Jr. 20.00 50.00
DB3 Jeff Gordon 20.00 50.00
DB4 Dale Jarrett 10.00 25.00
DB5 Jimmie Johnson 15.00 40.00
DB6 Mark Martin 10.00 25.00
DB8 Tony Stewart 15.00 40.00
DB9 Martin Truex Jr. 15.00 40.00

2007 Press Pass Double Burner Firesuit-Glove

DB1 Matt Kenseth 12.00 30.00
DB2 Dale Earnhardt Jr. 15.00 40.00
DB3 Denny Hamlin 12.00 30.00
DB4 Jimmie Johnson 12.00 30.00
DB5 Martin Truex Jr. 10.00 25.00
DB6 Jeff Gordon 20.00 50.00
DB7 Kasey Kahne 20.00 50.00
DB8 Kurt Busch 12.00 30.00
DB9 Carl Edwards 12.00 30.00

2007 Press Pass Double Burner Metal-Tire

This 9-card set featured swatches of race-used sheet metal and race-used tires. These were available in packs of 2007 Press Pass as exchange cards, which were redeemable until December 31, 2007. Each card is serial numbered to 100 and carried a "DB" prefix for its card number.
STATED PRINT RUN 100 SERIAL #'d SETS
*EXPIRED EXCH: .08X TO .25X
DBCE Carl Edwards 12.00 30.00
DBDE Dale Earnhardt Jr. 25.00 60.00
DBDH Denny Hamlin 12.00 30.00
DBJG Jeff Gordon 20.00 50.00
DBJJ Jimmie Johnson 20.00 50.00
DBKH Kevin Harvick 12.00 30.00
DBKK Kasey Kahne 20.00 50.00
DBMK Matt Kenseth 12.00 30.00
DBRS Reed Sorenson 10.00 25.00
DBTS Tony Stewart 15.00 40.00

2008 Press Pass Double Burner Firesuit-Glove

STATED PRINT RUN 100 SERIAL #'d SETS
DBCE Carl Edwards 15.00 40.00
DBDJ Dale Jarrett 15.00 40.00
DBJG Jeff Gordon 15.00 40.00
DBJJ Jimmie Johnson 12.00 30.00
DBJM Juan Pablo Montoya 12.00 30.00
DBMK Matt Kenseth 15.00 40.00
DBMM Mark Martin 12.00 30.00
DBMT Martin Truex Jr. 10.00 25.00
DBTS Tony Stewart 20.00 50.00

2008 Press Pass Double Burner Metal-Tire

STATED PRINT RUN 100 SERIAL #'d SETS
DBCE Carl Edwards 15.00 40.00

DBDE Dale Earnhardt Jr.
DBDH Denny Hamlin 15.00 40.00
DBJG Jeff Gordon 40.00 80.00
DBJJ Jimmie Johnson 12.00 30.00
DBJM Juan Pablo Montoya 12.00 30.00
DBKK Kasey Kahne
DBMM Mark Martin 12.00 30.00
DBMT Martin Truex Jr. 10.00 25.00

2002 Press Pass Eclipse

This 50 card set was issued in four card hobby and retail packs. In addition, a special promotion included two packs and CD-Rom to keep up with the values of these cards for $9.99.

COMPLETE SET (50) 12.00 30.00
WAX BOX 40.00 100.00
1 Jeff Gordon .75 2.00
2 Tony Stewart .60 1.50
3 Ricky Rudd .30 .75
4 Sterling Marlin .40 1.00
5 Dale Jarrett .40 1.00
6 Bobby Labonte .40 1.00
7 Rusty Wallace .40 1.00
8 Dale Earnhardt Jr. 1.00 2.50
9 Kevin Harvick .50 1.25
10 Jeff Burton .40 1.00
11 Ricky Craven .25 .60
12 Matt Kenseth .60 1.50
13 Ward Burton .30 .75
14 Jerry Nadeau .25 .60
15 Bobby Hamilton .25 .60
16 Ken Schrader .25 .60
17 Elliott Sadler .25 .60
18 Terry Labonte .40 1.00
19 Dave Blaney .25 .60
20 Michael Waltrip .40 1.00
21 Kurt Busch .30 .75
22 Joe Nemechek .25 .60
23 John Andretti .30 .75
24 Todd Bodine .25 .60
25 Brett Bodine .25 .60
26 Steve Park .40 1.00
27 Kyle Petty .30 .75
28 Ryan Newman CRC 1.25 3.00
29 Jeff Gordon ACC .60 1.50
30 Jeff Gordon ACC .60 1.50
31 Jeff Gordon ACC .60 1.50
32 Jeff Gordon ACC .60 1.50
33 Jeff Gordon ACC .60 1.50
34 Bobby Labonte ACC .30 .75
35 Jeff Gordon ACC .60 1.50
36 Jeff Gordon ACC .60 1.50
37 Matt Kenseth ACC .50 1.25
38 Jeff Gordon SO .60 1.50
39 Dale Jarrett SO .30 .75
40 Dale Earnhardt Jr. SO .75 2.00
41 Stacy Compton SO .20 .50
42 Bobby Labonte SO .30 .75
43 Ryan Newman SO 1.00 2.50
44 Ricky Rudd SO .25 .60
45 Sterling Marlin SO .30 .75
46 Todd Bodine SO .20 .50
47 Jimmy Spencer SO .20 .50
48 Ricky Craven SO .20 .50
49 Kurt Busch SO .25 .60
50 Checklist .10 .25
P1 Jeff Gordon Promo 2.50 5.00

2002 Press Pass Eclipse Samples

COMPLETE SET (50) 60.00 120.00
*SAMPLES: 1.5X TO 4X BASIC CARDS

2002 Press Pass Eclipse Solar Eclipse

COMPLETE SET (50) 20.00 50.00
*SOLAR ECLIPSE: .8X TO 2X BASE CARD HI

2002 Press Pass Eclipse Father and Son Autographs

Randomly inserted into packs, these five cards feature dual signed cards of both fathers and sons who have been involved with Nascar. Each card was issued to a stated print run of 100 serial numbered sets.

FS1 A.J./Larry Foyt 40.00 100.00
FS2 Joe/Coy Gibbs 30.00 60.00
FS3 Ned/Dale Jarrett 40.00 100.00
FS4 Hank/Hank Parker Jr. 25.00 50.00
FS5 Richard/Kyle Petty 75.00 150.00

2002 Press Pass Eclipse Racing Champions

Issued at stated odds of one per hobby pack and one in two retail packs, this die-cut 36-card set was printed on plastic. The set was foil stamped and featured 2002 Winston Cup winners..

COMPLETE SET (36) 12.50 30.00
RC1 Michael Waltrip .30 .75
RC2 Steve Park .30 .75
RC3 Jeff Gordon 1.25 3.00
RC4 Kevin Harvick 1.00 2.50
RC5 Dale Jarrett .75 2.00
RC6 Elliott Sadler .30 .75
RC7 Dale Jarrett .75 2.00
RC8 Dale Jarrett .75 2.00
RC9 Bobby Hamilton .15 .40
RC10 Rusty Wallace .75 2.00
RC11 Tony Stewart 1.00 2.50
RC12 Jeff Burton .30 .75
RC13 Jeff Gordon 1.25 3.00
RC14 Jeff Gordon 1.25 3.00
RC15 Ricky Rudd .50 1.25
RC16 Tony Stewart 1.00 2.50
RC17 Dale Earnhardt Jr. 1.50 4.00
RC18 Kevin Harvick 1.00 2.50
RC19 Dale Jarrett .75 2.00
RC20 Bobby Labonte .75 2.00
RC21 Jeff Gordon 1.25 3.00
RC22 Jeff Gordon 1.25 3.00
RC23 Sterling Marlin .50 1.25
RC24 Tony Stewart 1.00 2.50
RC25 Ward Burton .30 .75
RC26 Ricky Rudd .50 1.25
RC27 Dale Earnhardt Jr. 1.50 4.00
RC28 Jeff Gordon 1.25 3.00
RC29 Sterling Marlin .50 1.25
RC30 Ricky Craven .15 .40
RC31 Dale Earnhardt Jr. 1.50 4.00
RC32 Jeff Burton .30 .75
RC33 Joe Nemechek .15 .40
RC34 Bobby Labonte .75 2.00
RC35 Robby Gordon .15 .40
RC36 Richard Petty .30 .75

2002 Press Pass Eclipse Skidmarks

Issued at a stated rate of one in 20, this nine card set features pieces of race-used tires specially treated to enhance the card design.

COMPLETE SET (9) 30.00 80.00
SK1 Terry Labonte 4.00 10.00
SK2 Dale Earnhardt Jr. 6.00 15.00
SK3 Kevin Harvick 5.00 12.00
SK4 Jeff Gordon 8.00 20.00
SK5 Bobby Labonte 4.00 10.00
SK6 Ricky Rudd 3.00 8.00
SK7 Dale Jarrett 4.00 10.00
SK8 Tony Stewart 6.00 15.00
SK9 Rusty Wallace 5.00 12.00

2002 Press Pass Eclipse Supernova

Inserted at a rate of one in eight, this 12 card set featured some of the leading drivers in Nascar.

COMPLETE SET (12) 15.00 40.00
*NUMBERED/250: 1.2X TO 3X BASIC INSERTS
SN1 Jeff Burton .75 2.00
SN2 Dale Earnhardt Jr. 2.00 5.00
SN3 Kevin Harvick 1.00 2.50
SN4 Ward Burton .60 1.50
SN5 Jeff Gordon 1.50 4.00
SN6 Dale Jarrett .75 2.00
SN7 Matt Kenseth 1.25 3.00
SN8 Bobby Labonte .75 2.00
SN9 Tony Stewart 1.25 3.00
SN10 Terry Labonte .75 2.00
SN11 Ricky Rudd .60 1.50
SN12 Rusty Wallace .75 2.00

2002 Press Pass Eclipse Under Cover Drivers

Issued at a stated rate of one in 24 hobby packs, these 12 cards feature pieces of car covers included as part of the card. These cards are the 1st time pieces of car covers were used in a set.

*GOLD/400: .4X TO 1X DRIVER/625
*GOLD CAR/300: .5X TO 1.2X DRIVER/675
*HOLOFOIL/100: .8X TO 2X DRIVER/625
CD1 Jimmie Johnson 6.00 15.00
CD2 Jerry Nadeau 3.00 8.00
CD3 Jeff Gordon 8.00 20.00
CD4 Terry Labonte 5.00 12.00
CD5 Bobby Labonte 5.00 12.00
CD6 Tony Stewart 6.00 15.00
CD7 Ken Schrader 3.00 8.00
CD8 Elliott Sadler 3.00 8.00
CD9 Ryan Newman 4.00 10.00
CD10 Ricky Craven 3.00 8.00
CD11 Michael Waltrip 5.00 12.00
CD12 Dale Earnhardt Jr. 8.00 20.00

2002 Press Pass Eclipse Under Cover Double Cover

Issued at a stated rate of one in 240 hobby or retail packs, these eight cards feature two pieces of car covers on them. Each of these cards were issued to a stated print run of 625 serial numbered sets.

COMPLETE SET (8) 150.00 300.00
DC1 J.Nadeau/J.Gordon 12.00 30.00
DC2 J.Johnson/J.Gordon 25.00 60.00
DC3 J.Gordon/T.Labonte 15.00 40.00
DC4 J.Nadeau/J.Johnson 12.50 30.00
DC5 T.Labonte/J.Johnson 12.50 30.00
DC6 T.Labonte/J.Nadeau 12.50 30.00
DC7 B.Labonte/T.Stewart 15.00 40.00
DC8 D.Earn.Jr./M.Waltrip 25.00 60.00

2002 Press Pass Eclipse Warp Speed

Inserted in packs at a stated rate of one in 12, these eight cards feature some of the fastest drivers on the Nascar circuit. These cards were issued in holo-foil board and plastic for an interesting feel.

COMPLETE SET (8) 10.00 25.00
WS1 Jeff Gordon 3.00 8.00
WS2 Dale Earnhardt Jr. 4.00 10.00
WS3 Rusty Wallace 2.00 5.00
WS4 Dale Jarrett 2.00 5.00
WS5 Tony Stewart 2.50 6.00
WS6 Kevin Harvick 2.50 6.00
WS7 Jeff Burton .75 2.00
WS8 Ricky Rudd 1.25 3.00

2003 Press Pass Eclipse

This 50-card set was issued in five card hobby and four card retail packs with a suggested retail price of $3.99. These went live in March of 2003. The cards featured a white border with silver foil highlights and a full color photo of the drive or his car.

COMPLETE SET (50) 15.00 40.00
WAX BOX HOBBY (24) 60.00 100.00
WAX BOX RETAIL (28) 30.00 80.00
1 Tony Stewart 1.25 3.00
2 Mark Martin 1.25 3.00
3 Kurt Busch .60 1.50
4 Jeff Gordon 1.50 4.00
5 Jimmie Johnson 1.25 3.00
6 Ryan Newman 1.25 3.00
7 Rusty Wallace 1.00 2.50
8 Matt Kenseth 1.25 3.00
9 Dale Jarrett 1.00 2.50
10 Ricky Rudd .60 1.50
11 Dale Earnhardt Jr. 2.00 5.00
12 Jeff Burton .50 1.25
13 Michael Waltrip .50 1.25
14 Ricky Craven .25 .60
15 Bobby Labonte 1.25 3.00
16 Jeff Green .25 .60
17 Sterling Marlin .60 1.50
18 Dave Blaney .25 .60
19 Robby Gordon .25 .60
20 Kevin Harvick 1.00 2.50
21 Kyle Petty .50 1.25
22 Elliott Sadler .50 1.25
23 Terry Labonte .60 1.50
24 Ward Burton .50 1.25
25 Jeremy Mayfield .25 .60
26 Steve Park .50 1.25
27 Jamie McMurray 1.00 2.50
28 Ryan Newman ACC 1.25 3.00
29 Matt Kenseth ACC 1.25 3.00
30 Dale Earnhardt Jr. ACC 2.00 5.00
31 Mark Martin ACC 1.25 3.00
32 Tony Stewart ACC 1.25 3.00
33 Mark Martin ACC 1.25 3.00
34 Ryan Newman ACC 1.25 3.00
35 Jeff Gordon ACC 1.50 4.00
36 Chip Ganassi ACC .25 .60
37 All-American Kid WCS .50 1.25
38 Kansas City Chiefs WCS .50 1.25
39 Holy Cow WCS .25 .60
40 Any Given Sunday WCS .50 1.25
41 Speed Demons WCS .25 .60
42 The Spin Doctor WCS .50 1.25
43 Born to Run WCS .50 1.25
44 High Five WCS .25 .60
45 CHAMP-agne Celebration WCS .50 1.25
46 Jeff Gordon HS 1.50 4.00
47 Ryan Newman HS 1.25 3.00
48 Jimmie Johnson HS 1.25 3.00
49 Dale Earnhardt Jr. HS 2.00 5.00
50 Tony Stewart HS 1.25 3.00

2003 Press Pass Eclipse Solar Eclipse

COMPLETE SET (50) 25.00 60.00
*SOLAR ECLIPSE: .6X TO 1.5X

2003 Press Pass Eclipse Double Hot Treads

This 11 card set featured a swatch of race-used tires from 2 drivers per card. The drivers were paired up with a teammate on the opposite sides of the card. Each card was inserted one per specially marked retail box and each was serial numbered to 999.

DT1 B.Labonte 8.00 20.00
T.Stewart
DT2 R.Gordon 6.00 15.00
K.Harvick
DT3 J.Andretti 4.00 10.00
K.Petty
DT4 W.Burton 4.00 10.00
K.Wallace
DT5 S.Marlin 4.00 10.00
J.McMurray
DT6 M.Kenseth 6.00 15.00
M.Martin
DT7 J.Burton 5.00 12.00
K.Busch
DT8 J.Gordon/J.Johnson 10.00 25.00
DT9 R.Newman 6.00 15.00
R.Wallace
DT10 D.Earnhardt Jr. 10.00 25.00
M.Waltrip
DT11 S.Park 6.00 12.00
M.Waltrip

2003 Press Pass Eclipse Racing Champions

Issued at stated odds of one per hobby pack and one in two retail packs, this die-cut 36-card set was printed on plastic. The set was foil stamped and featured 2003 Winston Cup winners..

COMPLETE SET (36) 15.00 40.00
STATED ODDS 1 PER PACK HOBBY
STATED ODDS 1:2 RETAIL
RC1 Tony Stewart 1.25 3.00
RC2 Jimmie Johnson 1.25 3.00
RC3 Ward Burton .50 1.25
RC4 Matt Kenseth 1.25 3.00
RC5 Sterling Marlin .60 1.50
RC6 Tony Stewart 1.25 3.00
RC7 Sterling Marlin .60 1.50
RC8 Kurt Busch .60 1.50
RC9 Matt Kenseth 1.25 3.00
RC10 Bobby Labonte 1.25 3.00
RC11 Dale Earnhardt Jr. 2.00 5.00
RC12 Jimmie Johnson 1.25 3.00
RC13 Tony Stewart 1.25 3.00
RC14 Ryan Newman 1.25 3.00
RC15 Mark Martin 1.25 3.00
RC16 Jimmie Johnson 1.25 3.00
RC17 Dale Jarrett 1.00 2.50
RC18 Matt Kenseth 1.25 3.00
RC19 Ricky Rudd .60 1.50
RC20 Michael Waltrip .50 1.25
RC21 Kevin Harvick 1.00 2.50
RC22 Ward Burton .50 1.25
RC23 Tony Stewart 1.25 3.00
RC24 Dale Jarrett 1.00 2.50
RC25 Jeff Gordon 1.50 4.00
RC26 Jeff Gordon 1.50 4.00
RC27 Matt Kenseth 1.25 3.00
RC28 Ryan Newman 1.25 3.00
RC29 Jimmie Johnson 1.25 3.00
RC30 Jeff Gordon 1.50 4.00
RC31 Dale Earnhardt Jr. 2.00 5.00
RC32 Jamie McMurray 1.00 2.50
RC33 Kurt Busch .60 1.50
RC34 Kurt Busch .60 1.50
RC35 Matt Kenseth 1.25 3.00
RC36 Kurt Busch .60 1.50

2003 Press Pass Eclipse Skidmarks

Issued at a stated rate of one in 18 for both hobby and retail packs. This 18-card set features pieces of race-used tires ground up and specially treated work as into the card design.

COMPLETE SET (18) 100.00 200.00
SM1 John Andretti 4.00 10.00
SM2 Jeff Gordon 8.00 20.00
SM3 Tony Stewart 6.00 15.00
SM4 Rusty Wallace 5.00 12.00
SM5 Ryan Newman 6.00 15.00
SM6 Kurt Busch 4.00 10.00
SM7 Mark Martin 4.00 10.00
SM8 Jimmie Johnson 6.00 15.00
SM9 Matt Kenseth 5.00 12.00
SM10 Jamie McMurray 4.00 10.00
SM11 Terry Labonte 4.00 10.00
SM12 Dale Jarrett 5.00 12.00
SM13 Kevin Harvick 5.00 12.00
SM14 Bobby Labonte 5.00 12.00
SM15 Ward Burton 4.00 10.00
SM16 Robby Gordon 5.00 12.00
SM17 Jeff Green 3.00 8.00
SM18 Jeff Burton 5.00 12.00

2003 Press Pass Eclipse Supernova

Inserted at a rate of one in eight, this 12-card set featured some of the leading drivers in Nascar.

COMPLETE SET (12) 20.00 50.00
SN1 Steve Park 1.25 3.00
SN2 Dale Earnhardt Jr. 4.00 10.00
SN3 Jeff Gordon 3.00 8.00
SN4 Kevin Harvick 2.50 6.00
SN5 Dale Jarrett 2.50 6.00
SN6 Matt Kenseth 2.50 6.00
SN7 Bobby Labonte 2.50 6.00
SN8 Jimmie Johnson 2.50 6.00
SN9 Mark Martin 2.50 6.00
SN10 Michael Waltrip 1.25 3.00
SN11 Tony Stewart 3.00 8.00
SN12 Rusty Wallace 2.50 6.00

2003 Press Pass Eclipse Teammates Autographs

Randomly inserted into packs, these seven cards feature dual signed cards of NASCAR teammates. Each card was issued to a stated print run of 25 serial numbered sets.

JAKP J.Andretti/K.Petty 30.00 80.00
JBKB J.Burton/K.Busch 50.00 120.00
JGJJ J.Gordon/J.Johnson 200.00 400.00
KHRG K.Harvick/R.Gordon 125.00 200.00
MMMK M.Martin/M.Kenseth 125.00 200.00
RNRW R.Newman/R.Wallace 125.00 200.00
SMJM S.Marlin/J.McMurray 30.00 80.00

2003 Press Pass Eclipse Under Cover Double Cover

Issued at a stated rate of one in 240 packs, these 9 cards feature pieces of car covers included as part of the card and feature a pair of teammates and a swatch for each driver. Each card was also serial numbered to 530 and feature photos of the drivers.

DC1 J.Nemechek/J.Gordon 8.00 20.00
DC2 J.Johnson/J.Gordon 12.00 30.00
DC3 T.Labonte/J.Gordon 8.00 20.00
DC4 J.Nemechek/J.Johnson 8.00 20.00
DC5 T.Labonte/J.Johnson 8.00 20.00
DC6 T.Labonte/J.Nemechek 6.00 15.00
DC7 B.Labonte/T.Stewart 8.00 20.00
DC8 K.Harvick/R.Gordon 6.00 15.00
DC9 K.Harvick/J.Green 6.00 15.00

2003 Press Pass Eclipse Under Cover Driver Autographs

Randomly inserted in hobby packs, these 5 cards feature pieces of car covers included as part of the card along with the driver's signature. Each card was also hand numbered to the driver's door number and feature photos of the driver.

*CARS: .4X TO 1X DRIVERS
UCDBL Bobby Labonte/18 75.00 150.00
UCDJG Jeff Gordon/24 150.00 300.00
UCDJJ Jimmie Johnson/48 60.00 120.00
UCDRN Ryan Newman/12
UCDTL Terry Labonte/5

2003 Press Pass Eclipse Under Cover Driver Silver

Randomly inserted in hobby packs, these 17 cards feature pieces of car covers included as part of the card. Each card was also serial numbered to 450 and feature photos of the driver and have silver foil highlights.

*GOLD/260: .6X TO 1.5X SILVER/450
*RED/100: .8X TO 2X SILVER/450
*CARS/215: .5X TO 1.2X DRIVERS SILVER
UCD1 Jeff Gordon 5.00 12.00
UCD2 Ryan Newman 4.00 8.00
UCD3 Kevin Harvick 3.00 8.00
UCD4 Jimmie Johnson 3.00 15.00
UCD5 Tony Stewart 4.00 10.00
UCD6 Bobby Labonte 3.00 8.00
UCD7 Dale Earnhardt Jr. 5.00 12.00
UCD8 Jeff Burton 2.50 6.00
UCD9 Ricky Craven 2.50 6.00
UCD10 Terry Labonte 2.50 6.00
UCD11 Michael Waltrip 2.50 6.00
UCD12 Robby Gordon 2.50 6.00
UCD13 Joe Nemechek 2.50 6.00
UCD14 Elliott Sadler 2.50 6.00
UCD15 Jeff Green 2.50 6.00
UCD16 Matt Kenseth 4.00 10.00
UCD17 Mark Martin 4.00 10.00

2003 Press Pass Eclipse Warp Speed

Inserted in packs at a stated rate of one in 12, these eight cards feature some of the fastest drivers on the Nascar circuit. These cards were issued in holo-foil board and plastic for an interesting feel. Each card had a "WS" suffix along with its card number.

COMPLETE SET (8) 12.50 30.00
WS1 Jeff Gordon 4.00 10.00
WS2 Dale Earnhardt Jr. 5.00 12.00
WS3 Rusty Wallace 2.50 6.00
WS4 Steve Park 1.25 3.00
WS5 Tony Stewart 3.00 8.00
WS6 Jimmie Johnson 3.00 8.00
WS7 Mark Martin 3.00 8.00
WS8 Michael Waltrip 1.25 3.00

2004 Press Pass Eclipse

This 50-card set was issued in five card hobby and four card retail packs with a suggested retail price of $3.99. These went live in March of 2004. The cards featured a white border with silver foil highlights and a full color photo of the drive or his car.

COMPLETE SET (90) 15.00 40.00
WAX BOX HOBBY (20) 60.00 120.00
1 Matt Kenseth 1.25 3.00
2 Jimmie Johnson 1.25 3.00
2B Jimmie Johnson -official 5.00 12.00
3 Dale Earnhardt Jr. 1.50 4.00
4 Jeff Gordon 1.50 4.00
5 Kevin Harvick 1.00 2.50
6 Ryan Newman 1.25 3.00
7 Tony Stewart 1.00 2.50
7B Tony Stewart blue sky 4.00 10.00
8 Bobby Labonte .75 2.00
9 Terry Labonte .60 1.50
10 Kurt Busch .60 1.50
11 Jeff Burton .40 1.00
12 Jamie McMurray .60 1.50
13 Rusty Wallace .75 2.00
14 Michael Waltrip .40 1.00
15 Robby Gordon .25 .60
16 Mark Martin 1.00 2.50
17 Sterling Marlin .60 1.50
18 Jeremy Mayfield .25 .60
19 Greg Biffle .40 1.00
20 Elliott Sadler .40 1.00
21 Ricky Rudd .60 1.50
22 Dale Jarrett 1.00 2.50
23 Ricky Craven .25 .60
24 Kenny Wallace .25 .60
25 Casey Mears .40 1.00
26 Ken Schrader .25 .60
27 Kyle Petty .40 1.00
28 Rusty Wallace's Car .40 1.00
29 Mark Martin's Car .40 1.00
30 Dale Earnhardt Jr.'s Car .60 1.50
31 Michael Waltrip's Car .25 .60
32 Matt Kenseth's Car .60 1.50
33 Bobby Labonte's Car .40 1.00
34 Tony Stewart's Car .40 1.00
35 Kevin Harvick's Car .40 1.00
36 Kurt Busch's Car .25 .60
37 Brian Vickers .75 2.00
38 David Green .25 .60
39 Scott Riggs .40 1.00
39B Scott Riggs blue sky 1.50 4.00
40 Kasey Kahne 1.50 4.00
41 Johnny Sauter .40 1.00
42 Scott Wimmer .40 1.00
43 Mike Bliss .25 .60
44 Stacy Compton .25 .60
45 Coy Gibbs .40 1.00
46 Ryan Newman Z 1.25 3.00
47 Dale Earnhardt Jr. Z 1.50 4.00
47B Dale Earnhardt Jr. Z SP 6.00 15.00
48 Jimmie Johnson Z 1.25 3.00
49 Matt Kenseth Z 1.25 3.00
50 Ryan Newman Z 1.25 3.00
51 Matt Kenseth Z 1.25 3.00
52 Dale Earnhardt Jr. Z 1.50 4.00
53 Jeff Gordon Z 1.50 4.00
54 Ryan Newman Z 1.25 3.00
55 Bobby Labonte P .75 2.00
55B Bobby Labonte P SP 3.00 8.00
56 Dale Earnhardt Jr. P 1.50 4.00
57 Jeff Gordon P 1.50 4.00
58 Jimmie Johnson P 1.25 3.00
59 Kevin Harvick P 1.00 2.50
60 Matt Kenseth P 1.25 3.00
61 Michael Waltrip P .40 1.00
62 Rusty Wallace P .75 2.00
63 Tony Stewart P 1.00 2.50
64 Tony Stewart WCS 1.00 2.50
65 Ryan Newman's Car WCS 1.25 3.00
66 Bobby Labonte WCS .75 2.00
67 Kurt Busch WCS .60 1.50
68 Greg Biffle WCS .40 1.00
69 Ryan Newman WCS 1.25 3.00
70 Ryan Newman WCS 1.25 3.00
71 Kevin Harvick WCS 1.00 2.50
72 Terry Labonte WCS .60 1.50
73 Dale Earnhardt Jr. LL 1.50 4.00
74 Kevin Harvick LL 1.00 2.50
75 Jeff Gordon LL 1.50 4.00
76 M.Martin 1.00 2.50
R.Wallace LL
77 Matt Kenseth LL 1.25 3.00
78 Earnhardt Jr. 1.50 4.00
Johnson LL
79 Mark Martin LL 1.00 2.50
80 Michael Waltrip LL .40 1.00
80B Michael Waltrip LL blue sky 1.50 4.00
81 Terry Labonte LL .60 1.50
82 R.Gordon 1.00 2.50
K.Harvick LL
83 Ryan Newman LL 1.25 3.00
84 Tony Stewart LL 1.00 2.50
85 Jimmie Johnson LL 1.25 3.00
86 Jamie McMurray LL .60 1.50
87 Bobby Labonte LL .75 2.00
88 Matt Kenseth SM 1.25 3.00
89 Brian Vickers SM .75 2.00
90 Travis Kvapil SM .25 .60

2004 Press Pass Eclipse Samples

COMPLETE SET (90) 60.00 120.00
*SAMPLES: 2X TO 5X BASE

2004 Press Pass Eclipse Destination WIN

This 27-card set featured 2003 race winners celebrating at the track in which they won. The cards are die-cut and produced on a plastic card stock. They were inserted at a rate of 1 in 2 packs.

COMPLETE SET (27) 12.50 30.00
1 Dale Earnhardt Jr. 1.50 4.00
2 Dale Earnhardt Jr. 1.50 4.00
3 Michael Waltrip .40 1.00
4 Dale Jarrett .75 2.00
5 Matt Kenseth 1.25 3.00
6 Bobby Labonte .75 2.00
7 Ricky Craven .25 .60
8 Kurt Busch .60 1.50
9 Ryan Newman 1.25 3.00
10 Dale Earnhardt Jr. 1.50 4.00
11 Jeff Gordon 1.50 4.00
12 Kurt Busch .60 1.50
13 Joe Nemechek .25 .60
14 Jimmie Johnson 1.25 3.00
15 Ryan Newman 1.25 3.00
16 Tony Stewart 1.00 2.50
17 Robby Gordon .25 .60
18 Greg Biffle .40 1.00
19 Jimmie Johnson 1.25 3.00
20 Ryan Newman 1.25 3.00
21 Kevin Harvick 1.00 2.50

22 Terry Labonte .60 1.50
23 Ryan Newman 1.25 3.00
24 Michael Waltrip .40 1.00
25 Tony Stewart 1.00 2.50
26 Jeff Gordon 1.50 4.00
27 Dale Earnhardt Jr. 1.50 4.00

2004 Press Pass Eclipse Hyperdrive

This 9-card set featured some of NASCAR's fastest drivers. The cards were designed to be seen on the horizontal angle with a picture of the driver and a smaller image of his car. The cards were produced on a plastic card stock. They were randomly inserted at a rate of 1 in 10 packs.

COMPLETE SET (9) 20.00 50.00
HP1 Michael Waltrip 1.00 2.50
HP2 Rusty Wallace 1.50 4.00
HP3 Tony Stewart 2.00 5.00
HP4 Ryan Newman 2.50 6.00
HP5 Dale Earnhardt Jr. 3.00 8.00
HP6 Mark Martin 2.00 5.00
HP7 Jeff Gordon 3.00 8.00
HP8 Jimmie Johnson 2.50 6.00
HP9 Matt Kenseth 2.50 6.00

2004 Press Pass Eclipse Maxim

This 12-card set featured some of NASCAR's most popular drivers. The cards were designed with a picture of the driver and some foil highlights and were produced on a plastic card stock. They were randomly inserted at a rate of 1 in 6 packs.

COMPLETE SET (12) 15.00 40.00
MX1 Matt Kenseth 2.00 5.00
MX2 Jimmie Johnson 2.00 5.00
MX3 Dale Earnhardt Jr. 2.50 6.00
MX4 Jeff Gordon 2.50 6.00
MX5 Kevin Harvick 1.50 4.00
MX6 Tony Stewart 1.50 4.00
MX7 Bobby Labonte 1.25 3.00
MX8 Kurt Busch 1.00 2.50
MX9 Michael Waltrip .60 1.50
MX10 Mark Martin 1.50 4.00
MX11 Greg Biffle .60 1.50
MX12 Dale Jarrett 1.25 3.00

2004 Press Pass Eclipse Skidmarks

Issued at a stated rate of one in 18 for both hobby and retail packs. This 18-card set features pieces of race-used tires ground up and specially treated work as into the card design. There was also a holofoil parallel.

*HOLOFOIL/500: .6X TO 1.5X BASIC INSERTS
SM1 Jeff Gordon 10.00 25.00
SM2 Kurt Busch 4.00 10.00
SM3 Jimmie Johnson 8.00 20.00
SM4 Matt Kenseth 8.00 20.00
SM5 Mark Martin 6.00 15.00
SM6 Robby Gordon 2.00 5.00
SM7 Dale Earnhardt Jr. 8.00 20.00
SM8 Terry Labonte 5.00 12.00
SM9 Kevin Harvick 6.00 15.00
SM10 Dale Jarrett 5.00 12.00
SM11 Ryan Newman 8.00 20.00
SM12 Greg Biffle 4.00 10.00
SM13 Tony Stewart 6.00 15.00
SM14 Bobby Labonte 6.00 15.00
SM15 Rusty Wallace 5.00 12.00
SM16 Sterling Marlin 4.00 10.00
SM17 Michael Waltrip 4.00 10.00
SM18 Jamie McMurray 4.00 10.00

2004 Press Pass Eclipse Teammates Autographs

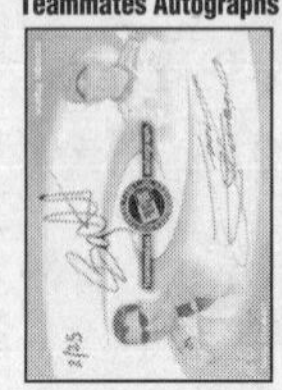

Randomly inserted into packs, these seven cards feature dual signed cards of NASCAR teammates. Each card was issued to a stated print run of 25 serial numbered sets.

1 R.Gordon/K.Harvick 100.00 200.00
2 J.Johnson/J.Gordon 300.00 600.00
3 G.Biffle/M.Martin 100.00 200.00
4 B.Labonte/T.Stewart 100.00 200.00
5 D.Jarrett/E.Sadler 40.00 100.00
6 C.Mears/J.McMurray 20.00 50.00
7 R.Newman/R.Wallace 30.00 80.00

2004 Press Pass Eclipse Under Cover Autographs

Randomly inserted in retail packs, these 8 cards feature pieces of car covers included as part of the card and a signature of the driver. Each card was also hand numbered to the driver's door number and featured an image of the driver.

STATED PRINT RUN 2-48
UCBL Bobby Labonte/18 75.00 150.00
UCDE Dale Earnhardt Jr./8
UCJG Jeff Gordon/24 150.00 300.00
UCJJ Jimmie Johnson/48 60.00 120.00
UCKH Kevin Harvick/29 60.00 120.00
UCMM Mark Martin/6
UCRN Ryan Newman/12
UCRW Rusty Wallace/2

2004 Press Pass Eclipse Under Cover Double Cover

This 9-card set featured pieces of car covers included as part of the card and feature a pair of teammates and a swatch for each driver. Each card was also serial numbered to 100 and feature photos of the drivers.

DC1 D.Earnhardt Jr. 40.00 100.00
M.Waltrip
DC2 R.Wallace 30.00 80.00
R.Newman
DC3 J.Johnson 40.00 100.00
J.Gordon
DC4 T.Labonte 25.00 60.00
J.Gordon
DC5 T.Labonte 10.00 25.00
J.Johnson
DC6 J.Nemechek 12.50 30.00
T.Labonte
DC7 J.Nemechek 20.00 50.00
J.Gordon
DC8 J.Johnson 10.00 25.00
J.Nemechek
DC9 M.Kenseth 25.00 60.00
J.Burton
DC10 B.Labonte 25.00 60.00
T.Stewart
DC11 K.Harvick 25.00 60.00
R.Gordon
DC12 K.Busch 25.00 60.00
M.Kenseth
DC13 M.Kenseth 40.00 100.00
M.Martin
DC14 M.Martin 20.00 50.00
J.Burton
DC15 J.Burton 15.00 40.00
K.Busch

2004 Press Pass Eclipse Under Cover Driver Silver

Randomly inserted in hobby packs, these 15 cards feature pieces of car covers included as part of the card. Each card was also serial numbered to 690 and feature photos of the driver and have silver foil highlights.

OVERALL UNDER COVER ODDS 1:10
STATED PRINT RUN 690 SER.#'d SETS
*CAR/170: .6X TO 1.5X SILVER/690
*GOLD/325: .5X TO 1.2X SILVER/690
*RED/100: .8X TO 2X SILVER/690
UCD1 Jimmie Johnson 6.00 15.00
UCD2 Matt Kenseth 4.00 10.00
UCD3 Kevin Harvick 4.00 10.00
UCD4 Jeff Gordon 8.00 20.00
UCD5 Kurt Busch 4.00 10.00
UCD6 Mark Martin 5.00 12.00
UCD7 Ryan Newman 4.00 10.00
UCD8 Bobby Labonte 4.00 10.00
UCD9 Rusty Wallace 5.00 12.00
UCD10 Michael Waltrip 3.00 8.00
UCD11 Robby Gordon 3.00 8.00
UCD12 Dale Earnhardt Jr. 8.00 20.00
UCD13 Terry Labonte 4.00 10.00
UCD14 Tony Stewart 6.00 15.00
UCD15 Jeff Burton 3.00 8.00

2005 Press Pass Eclipse

This 90-card set was issued in five card hobby and four card retail packs with a suggested retail price of $5.99 for hobby and $2.99 for retail. These went live in March of 2005. The cards featured a white border with silver foil highlights and a full color photo of the drive or his car. The zero card featured Kurt Busch as the 2004 Nextel Cup Champion, with two versions: gold, numbered to 200, and holofoil numbered to 50. These were found only in hobby packs.

COMPLETE SET (90) 15.00 40.00
WAX BOX HOBBY (20) 50.00 100.00
WAX BOX RETAIL (24) 35.00 60.00
1 Kurt Busch .60 1.50
2 Jimmie Johnson 1.25 3.00
3 Jeff Gordon 1.50 4.00
4 Mark Martin 1.00 2.50
5 Dale Earnhardt Jr. 1.50 4.00
6 Tony Stewart 1.00 2.50
7 Ryan Newman 1.25 3.00
8 Matt Kenseth 1.25 3.00
9 Elliott Sadler .40 1.00
10 Jeremy Mayfield .25 .60
11 Jamie McMurray .60 1.50
12 Bobby Labonte .75 2.00
13 Kasey Kahne 1.50 4.00
14 Kevin Harvick 1.00 2.50
15 Dale Jarrett .75 2.00
16 Rusty Wallace .75 2.00
17 Greg Biffle .40 1.00
18 Joe Nemechek .25 .60
19 Michael Waltrip .40 1.00
20 Sterling Marlin .60 1.50
21 Casey Mears .40 1.00
22 Ricky Rudd .60 1.50
23 Brian Vickers .75 2.00
24 Terry Labonte .60 1.50
25 Jeff Green .25 .60
26 Ken Schrader .25 .60
27 Kyle Petty .40 1.00
28 Joe Nemechek's Car S .25 .60
29 Mark Martin's Car S .40 1.00
30 Dale Earnhardt Jr's Car S .60 1.50
31 Scott Riggs' Car S .25 .60
32 Ryan Newman's Car S .40 1.00
33 Michael Waltrip's Car S .25 .60
34 Matt Kenseth's Car S .40 1.00
35 Scott Wimmer's Car S .25 .60
36 Jamie McMurray's Car S .25 .60
37 Martin Truex Jr. 1.25 3.00
38 Kyle Busch 1.00 2.50
39 Ron Hornaday .25 .60
40 Jason Leffler .25 .60
41 Jason Keller .25 .60
42 Kenny Wallace .25 .60
43 Tim Fedewa .25 .60
44 David Green .25 .60
45 Justin Labonte .60 1.50
46 Jimmie Johnson Z 1.25 3.00
47 Ryan Newman Z 1.25 3.00
48 Jeff Gordon Z 1.50 4.00
49 Jimmie Johnson Z 1.25 3.00
50 Jimmie Johnson Z 1.25 3.00
51 Kasey Kahne Z 1.50 4.00
52 Kurt Busch Z .60 1.50
53 Dale Earnhardt Jr. Z 1.50 4.00
54 Kurt Busch Z .60 1.50
55 Bobby Labonte P .75 2.00
56 Dale Earnhardt Jr. P 1.50 4.00
57 Jeff Gordon P 1.50 4.00
58 Jimmie Johnson P 1.25 3.00
59 Kevin Harvick P 1.00 2.50
60 Matt Kenseth P 1.25 3.00
61 Michael Waltrip P .40 1.00
62 Rusty Wallace P .75 2.00
63 Tony Stewart P 1.00 2.50
64 Ryan Newman's Car NS .40 1.00
65 J.Gordon 1.50 4.00
J.Johnson NS
66 Tony Stewart NS 1.00 2.50
67 Kurt Busch NS .60 1.50
68 Jimmie Johnson's Car NS .40 1.00
69 Tony Stewart NS 1.00 2.50
70 Jeff Gordon NS 1.50 4.00
71 Dale Earnhardt Jr. NS 1.50 4.00
72 J.Gordon 1.50 4.00
J.Johnson NS
73 Dale Earnhardt Jr. LL 1.50 4.00
74 Greg Biffle LL .40 1.00
75 Jeff Gordon LL 1.50 4.00
76 Brian Vickers LL .75 2.00
77 Ricky Rudd LL .60 1.50
78 Kasey Kahne LL 1.50 4.00
79 Mark Martin LL 1.00 2.50
80 Michael Waltrip LL .40 1.00
81 Terry Labonte LL .60 1.50
82 Rusty Wallace LL .75 2.00
83 Dale Jarrett LL .75 2.00
84 Tony Stewart LL 1.00 2.50
85 J.Johnson/J.Gordon LL 1.50 4.00
86 Jamie McMurray LL .60 1.50
87 Bobby Labonte LL .75 2.00
88 Kurt Busch SM .60 1.50
89 Martin Truex Jr. SM 1.25 3.00
90 Jimmie Johnson SM CL 1.25 3.00
0 Kurt Busch Gold/200 5.00 12.00
0 Kurt Busch Holofoil/50 10.00 25.00

2005 Press Pass Eclipse Samples

*SAMPLES: 1.5X TO 4X

2005 Press Pass Eclipse Destination WIN

COMPLETE SET (27) 10.00 25.00
1 Dale Earnhardt Jr. 1.25 3.00
2 Matt Kenseth 1.00 2.50
3 Dale Earnhardt Jr. 1.25 3.00
4 Jimmie Johnson 1.00 2.50
5 Kurt Busch .50 1.25
6 Elliott Sadler .30 .75
7 Rusty Wallace .60 1.50
8 Jeff Gordon 1.25 3.00
9 Jeff Gordon 1.25 3.00
10 Dale Earnhardt Jr. 1.25 3.00
11 Jimmie Johnson 1.00 2.50
12 Mark Martin .75 2.00
13 Jimmie Johnson 1.00 2.50
14 Ryan Newman 1.00 2.50
15 Jeff Gordon 1.25 3.00
16 Tony Stewart .75 2.00
17 Kurt Busch .50 1.25
18 Jeff Gordon 1.25 3.00
19 Tony Stewart .75 2.00
20 Greg Biffle .30 .75
21 Dale Earnhardt Jr. 1.25 3.00
22 Jeremy Mayfield .15 .40
23 Dale Earnhardt Jr. 1.25 3.00
24 Joe Nemechek .15 .40
25 Jimmie Johnson 1.00 2.50
26 Dale Earnhardt Jr. 1.25 3.00
27 Greg Biffle .30 .75

2005 Press Pass Eclipse Hyperdrive

COMPLETE SET (9) 12.50 30.00
HD1 Michael Waltrip .75 2.00
HD2 Bobby Labonte 1.50 4.00
HD3 Dale Jarrett 1.50 4.00
HD4 Kevin Harvick 2.00 5.00
HD5 Dale Earnhardt Jr. 3.00 8.00
HD6 Mark Martin 2.00 5.00
HD7 Jeff Gordon 3.00 8.00
HD8 Jimmie Johnson 2.50 6.00
HD9 Kurt Busch 1.25 3.00

2005 Press Pass Eclipse Maxim

COMPLETE SET (12) 15.00 40.00
MX1 Ryan Newman 2.50 6.00
MX2 Jimmie Johnson 2.50 6.00
MX3 Dale Earnhardt Jr. 3.00 8.00
MX4 Jeff Gordon 3.00 8.00
MX5 Jamie McMurray 1.25 3.00
MX6 Tony Stewart 2.00 5.00
MX7 Terry Labonte 1.25 3.00
MX8 Dale Jarrett 1.50 4.00
MX9 Michael Waltrip .75 2.00
MX10 Mark Martin 2.00 5.00
MX11 Kasey Kahne 3.00 8.00
MX12 Rusty Wallace 1.50 4.00

2005 Press Pass Eclipse Skidmarks

*HOLOFOIL/250: .6X TO 1.5X SKIDMARKS
SM1 Jeff Gordon 8.00 20.00
SM2 Kurt Busch 3.00 8.00
SM3 Jimmie Johnson 6.00 15.00
SM4 Matt Kenseth 6.00 15.00
SM5 Mark Martin 5.00 12.00
SM6 Elliott Sadler 2.00 5.00
SM7 Dale Earnhardt Jr. 8.00 20.00
SM8 Ricky Rudd 3.00 8.00
SM9 Kevin Harvick 5.00 12.00
SM10 Dale Jarrett 4.00 10.00
SM11 Ryan Newman 6.00 15.00
SM12 Kasey Kahne 8.00 20.00
SM13 Tony Stewart 5.00 12.00
SM14 Bobby Labonte 4.00 10.00
SM15 Rusty Wallace 4.00 10.00
SM16 Casey Mears 2.00 5.00
SM17 Michael Waltrip 2.00 5.00
SM18 Jamie McMurray 3.00 8.00

2005 Press Pass Eclipse Teammates Autographs

STATED PRINT RUN 25 SER.#'d SETS
1 Stewart/Leffler/Labonte 125.00 200.00
2 Busch/Martin/Kenseth 175.00 300.00
3 R.Newman/R.Wallace 75.00 150.00
4 K.Kahne/J.Mayfield
5 D.Jarrett/E.Sadler 100.00 200.00
6 J.Gordon/J.Johnson 350.00 500.00
7 B.Vickers/T.Labonte 60.00 120.00
8 Ku.Busch/C.Edwards 200.00 300.00
9 M.Kenseth/M.Martin 125.00 250.00

2005 Press Pass Eclipse Under Cover Autographs

STATED PRINT RUN 2-48
UCBL Bobby Labonte/18 75.00 150.00
UCDE Dale Earnhardt Jr./8
UCJG Jeff Gordon/24 150.00 300.00
UCJJ Jimmie Johnson/48 60.00 120.00
UCKH Kevin Harvick/29 60.00 120.00
UCMK Matt Kenseth/17
UCRN Ryan Newman/12
UCRW Rusty Wallace/2
UCTS Tony Stewart/20 125.00 200.00

2005 Press Pass Eclipse Under Cover Drivers Silver

*HOLOFOIL/100: .6X TO 1.5X SILVER/690
*RED/400: .4X TO 1X SILVER/690
*CARS/120: .5X TO 1.2X DRIVERS/690
UCD1 Jimmie Johnson 4.00 10.00
UCD2 Matt Kenseth 2.50 6.00
UCD3 Kevin Harvick 3.00 8.00
UCD4 Jeff Gordon 5.00 12.00
UCD5 Kurt Busch 2.00 5.00
UCD6 Mark Martin 2.50 6.00
UCD7 Ryan Newman 2.00 5.00
UCD8 Bobby Labonte 2.50 6.00
UCD9 Rusty Wallace 2.50 6.00
UCD10 Michael Waltrip 2.50 6.00
UCD11 Dale Earnhardt Jr. 5.00 12.00
UCD12 Terry Labonte 2.50 6.00
UCD13 Tony Stewart 4.00 10.00

2005 Press Pass Eclipse Under Cover Double Cover

DC1 D.Earnhardt Jr./M.Waltrip 8.00 20.00
DC2 R.Wallace/R.Newman 6.00 15.00
DC3 J.Johnson/J.Gordon 10.00 25.00
DC4 K.Busch/M.Martin 6.00 15.00
DC5 B.Labonte/T.Stewart 8.00 20.00
DC6 K.Busch/M.Kenseth 8.00 20.00
DC7 M.Kenseth/M.Martin 8.00 20.00
DC8 J.Johnson/T.Labonte 8.00 20.00
DC9 J.Gordon/T.Labonte 8.00 20.00

2006 Press Pass Eclipse

COMPLETE SET (90) 15.00 40.00
WAX BOX HOBBY (20) 90.00 135.00
1 Tony Stewart .60 1.50
2 Greg Biffle .30 .75
3 Carl Edwards .40 1.00
4 Mark Martin .40 1.00
5 Jimmie Johnson .60 1.50
6 Ryan Newman .30 .75
7 Matt Kenseth .40 1.00
8 Rusty Wallace .40 1.00
9 Jeremy Mayfield .25 .60
10 Jeff Gordon .75 2.00
11 Jamie McMurray .40 1.00
12 Elliott Sadler .25 .60
13 Kevin Harvick .50 1.25
14 Dale Jarrett .40 1.00
15 Joe Nemechek .25 .60
16 Brian Vickers .25 .60
17 Jeff Burton .30 .75
18 Dale Earnhardt Jr. .75 2.00
19 Kyle Busch .50 1.25
20 Ricky Rudd .30 .75
21 Casey Mears .25 .60
22 Kasey Kahne .50 1.25
23 Bobby Labonte .40 1.00
24 Dave Blaney .25 .60
25 Kyle Petty .30 .75
26 Sterling Marlin .40 1.00
27 Terry Labonte .40 1.00
28 Martin Truex Jr. NBS .60 1.50
29 Clint Bowyer NBS .75 2.00
30 Carl Edwards NBS .40 1.00
31 Reed Sorenson NBS .60 1.50
32 Denny Hamlin NBS 1.50 4.00
33 J.J. Yeley NBS .60 1.50
34 Johnny Sauter NBS .40 1.00
35 Jon Wood NBS .30 .75
36 Kasey Kahne NBS .50 1.25
37 Dale Jarrett WS .40 1.00
38 Kyle Busch WS .50 1.25
39 Ryan Newman WS .30 .75
40 Jimmie Johnson WS .60 1.50
41 Martin Truex Jr. WS .60 1.50
42 Jeff Gordon WS .75 2.00
43 Kevin Harvick WS .50 1.25
44 Kasey Kahne WS .50 1.25
45 Tony Stewart WS .60 1.50
46 Greg Biffle P .30 .75
47 Rusty Wallace P .40 1.00
47B Rusty Wallace P Blk Jacket .75 2.00
48 Brian Vickers P .25 .60
49 Kyle Petty P .30 .75
50 Tony Stewart P .60 1.50
51 Joe Nemechek P .25 .60
52 Ryan Newman NS .30 .75
53 Dale Jarrett NS .40 1.00
54 Mark Martin NS .40 1.00
55 Jimmie Johnson NS .60 1.50
56 Jeff Gordon NS .75 2.00
57 Carl Edwards NS .40 1.00
57B C.Edwards NS no cameraman .75 2.00
58 Bobby Labonte TN .40 1.00
59 Martin Truex Jr. TN .60 1.50
60 Kasey Kahne TN .50 1.25
60B Kasey Kahne TN no license 1.00 2.50
61 Greg Biffle TN .30 .75
62 Tony Stewart TN .60 1.50
63 Dale Earnhardt Jr. TN .75 2.00
64 Carl Edwards BA .40 1.00
65 NCS Top-10 BA .60 1.50
66 Rusty Wallace BA .40 1.00
67 Ryan Newman BA .30 .75
68 Mark Martin BA .40 1.00
69 Tony Stewart BA .60 1.50
70 Tony Stewart BA .60 1.50
70 Tony Stewart BA .60 1.50
71 Tony Stewart BA .60 1.50
72 Tony Stewart BA .60 1.50
73 Dale Earnhardt Jr. LL .75 2.00
74 Jeff Gordon LL .75 2.00
75 Dale Jarrett LL .40 1.00
75B Dale Jarrett LL no pic in book .75 2.00
76 Carl Edwards LL .40 1.00
77 Terry Labonte LL .40 1.00
78 Tony Stewart LL .60 1.50
79 Martin Truex Jr. LL .60 1.50
80 Rusty Wallace LL .40 1.00
81 Jimmie Johnson LL .60 1.50
82 Mark Martin LL .40 1.00
83 Kyle Busch LL .50 1.25
84 Kevin Harvick LL .50 1.25
85 Tony Stewart SM .60 1.50
86 Martin Truex Jr. SM .60 1.50
87 Kyle Busch SM .50 1.25
87B Kyle Busch SM d 1.00 2.50
88 Carl Edwards SM .40 1.00
89 Ricky Rudd SM .30 .75
90 Dale Earnhardt Jr. CL .75 2.00
0 Tony Stewart Champ 4.00 10.00

2006 Press Pass Eclipse Hyperdrive

COMPLETE SET (9) 12.50 30.00
STATED ODDS 1:10
HP1 Carl Edwards .75 2.00
HP2 Tony Stewart 1.25 3.00
HP3 Dale Earnhardt Jr. 1.50 4.00
HP4 Jimmie Johnson 1.25 3.00
HP5 Mark Martin .75 2.00
HP6 Kasey Kahne 1.00 2.50
HP7 Jeff Gordon 1.50 4.00
HP8 Martin Truex Jr. 1.25 3.00
HP9 Rusty Wallace .75 2.00

2006 Press Pass Eclipse Racing Champions

COMPLETE SET (27) 10.00 25.00
STATED ODDS 1:2
RC1 Jeff Gordon 1.00 2.50
RC2 Greg Biffle .40 1.00
RC3 Jimmie Johnson .75 2.00
RC4 Carl Edwards .50 1.25
RC5 Kevin Harvick .60 1.50
RC6 Kasey Kahne .60 1.50
RC7 Tony Stewart .75 2.00
RC8 Dale Earnhardt Jr. 1.00 2.50
RC9 Jeremy Mayfield .30 .75
RC10 Matt Kenseth .50 1.25
RC11 Kyle Busch .60 1.50
RC12 Ryan Newman .40 1.00
RC13 Dale Jarrett .50 1.25
RC14 Mark Martin .50 1.25
RC15 Tony Stewart NBS .75 2.00
RC16 Mark Martin NBS .50 1.25
RC17 Martin Truex Jr. NBS .75 2.00
RC18 Carl Edwards NBS .50 1.25
RC19 Kevin Harvick NBS .60 1.50
RC20 Reed Sorenson NBS .75 2.00
RC21 Kasey Kahne NBS .60 1.50
RC22 Matt Kenseth NBS .50 1.25
RC23 Clint Bowyer NBS 1.00 2.50
RC24 Johnny Sauter NBS .50 1.25
RC25 David Green NBS .30 .75
RC26 Ryan Newman NBS .40 1.00
RC27 Kyle Busch NBS .60 1.50

2006 Press Pass Eclipse Skidmarks

STATED ODDS 1:
*HOLOFOIL/250: .8X TO 2X BASIC INSERT
SM1 Kyle Busch 2.00 5.00
SM2 Dale Earnhardt Jr. 4.00 10.00
SM3 Bobby Labonte 1.50 4.00
SM4 Matt Kenseth 1.50 4.00
SM5 Bobby Labonte 1.50 4.00
SM6 Ryan Newman 1.25 3.00
SM7 Jimmie Johnson 2.50 6.00
SM8 Mark Martin 1.50 4.00
SM9 Dale Jarrett 1.50 4.00
SM10 Rusty Wallace 2.50 6.00
SM11 Martin Truex Jr. 2.50 6.00
SM12 Kasey Kahne 2.00 5.00
SM13 Greg Biffle 1.25 3.00
SM14 Jeff Gordon 3.00 8.00
SM15 Carl Edwards 1.50 4.00
SM16 Tony Stewart 2.50 6.00
SM17 Kevin Harvick 2.00 5.00
SM18 Jeff Burton 1.25 3.00

2006 Press Pass Eclipse Supernova

COMPLETE SET (12) 15.00 40.00
STATED ODDS 1:5
SU1 Ryan Newman .60 1.50
SU2 Jeff Gordon 1.50 4.00
SU3 Greg Biffle .60 1.50
SU4 Martin Truex Jr. 1.25 3.00
SU5 Tony Stewart 1.25 3.00
SU6 Rusty Wallace .75 2.00
SU7 Carl Edwards .75 2.00
SU8 Matt Kenseth .75 2.00
SU9 Jeff Burton .60 1.50
SU10 Dale Earnhardt Jr. 1.50 4.00
SU11 Mark Martin .75 2.00
SU12 Jimmie Johnson 1.25 3.00

2006 Press Pass Eclipse Teammates Autographs

1 G.Biffle/M.Kenseth 75.00 150.00
2 Ky.Busch/B.Vickers 30.00 80.00
3 C.Edwards/M.Martin 100.00 200.00
4 D.Jarrett/E.Sadler 75.00 150.00
5 J.Johnson/J.Gordon 200.00 400.00
6 K.Kahne/J.Mayfield 20.00 50.00
7 R.Wallace/R.Newman 20.00 50.00
8 K.Harvick/J.Burton 60.00 120.00

2006 Press Pass Eclipse Under Cover Autographs

STATED PRINT RUN 2-48
GB Greg Biffle/16
JG Jeff Gordon/24 150.00 300.00
JJ Jimmie Johnson/48 60.00 120.00

KH Kevin Harvick/29 40.00 100.00
MK Matt Kenseth/17
MM Mark Martin/6
RN Ryan Newman/12
RW Rusty Wallace/2
TS Tony Stewart/20 50.00 100.00

2006 Press Pass Eclipse Under Cover Double Cover

*HOLOFOIL/25: .6X TO 1.5X BASIC INSERTS
DC1 J.Johnson
J.Gordon 25.00 60.00
DC2 M.Martin
M.Kenseth 20.00 50.00
DC3 M.Martin
G.Biffle 15.00 40.00
DC4 R.Newman
R.Wallace 10.00 25.00
DC5 J.Gordon
T.Labonte 25.00 60.00
DC6 M.Kenseth
C.Edwards 20.00 50.00
DC7 C.Edwards
M.Martin 20.00 50.00
DC8 T.Labonte
J.Johnson 15.00 40.00
DC9 G.Biffle
C.Edwards 20.00 50.00

2006 Press Pass Eclipse Under Cover Drivers Silver

STATED PRINT RUN 400 SERIAL #'d SETS
*HOLOFOIL/100: .6X TO 1.5X SILVER
*RED/225: .5X TO 1.2X SILVER
*CARS/140: .4X TO 1X SILVER
UCD1 Matt Kenseth 8.00 20.00
UCD2 Ryan Newman 8.00 20.00
UCD3 Dale Earnhardt Jr. 10.00 25.00
UCD4 Mark Martin 8.00 20.00
UCD5 Kasey Kahne 6.00 15.00
UCD6 Bobby Labonte 6.00 15.00
UCD7 Jimmie Johnson 8.00 20.00
UCD8 Terry Labonte 6.00 15.00
UCD9 Tony Stewart 8.00 20.00
UCD10 Carl Edwards 8.00 20.00
UCD11 Jeff Gordon 10.00 25.00
UCD12 Kevin Harvick 8.00 20.00
UCD13 Rusty Wallace 8.00 20.00
UCD14 Greg Biffle 8.00 20.00

2007 Press Pass Eclipse

This 90-card set was issued in five card hobby and four card retail packs with a suggested retail price of $5.99 for hobby and $2.99 for retail. These went live in March of 2007. The cards featured a white border with silver foli highlights and a full color photo of the drive or his car. The zero card featured all 10 Cup Chase participants, these were found only in hobby packs and inserted at a rate of one in 72. Hobby boxes contained 24 - five card packs and Retail boxes contained 24 - four card packs and both were packed in 20 box cases.

COMPLETE SET (90) 15.00 40.00
WAX BOX HOBBY (24) 90.00 135.00
WAX BOX RETAIL (24) 50.00 75.00
1 Jimmie Johnson .60 1.50
2 Matt Kenseth .40 1.00
3 Denny Hamlin .50 1.25
4 Kevin Harvick .50 1.25
5A Dale Earnhardt Jr. .75 2.00
5B Dale Jr. no Target logo 1.50 4.00
6A Jeff Gordon .75 2.00
6B J.Gordon crew missing logo 1.50 4.00
7 Jeff Burton .30 .75
8 Kasey Kahne .40 1.00
9 Mark Martin .40 1.00
10 Kyle Busch .50 1.25
11 Tony Stewart .60 1.50
12 Carl Edwards .40 1.00
13 Greg Biffle .30 .75
14 Casey Mears .25 .60
15 Kurt Busch .30 .75
16 Clint Bowyer .40 1.00
17 Ryan Newman .30 .75
18 Martin Truex Jr. .30 .75
19 Scott Riggs .30 .75
20 Bobby Labonte .40 1.00
21 Elliott Sadler .25 .60
22 Reed Sorenson .25 .60
23 Jamie McMurray .40 1.00
24 Dave Blaney .25 .60
25 Joe Nemechek .25 .60
26 Jeff Green .25 .60
27 J.J. Yeley .40 1.00
28 Ken Schrader .25 .60
29 Kyle Petty .30 .75
30 David Stremme .25 .60
31 Sterling Marlin .40 1.00
32 Tony Raines .25 .60
33 Jeff Gordon TO .75 2.00
34 Kurt Busch TO .30 .75
35 Jimmie Johnson TO .60 1.50
36 Ryan Newman TO .30 .75
37 Kasey Kahne TO .40 1.00
38 Denny Hamlin TO .50 1.25
39 Kevin Harvick TO .50 1.25
40 Kasey Kahne P .40 1.00
41 Dale Earnhardt Jr. P .75 2.00
42 Scott Riggs P .30 .75
43 Jeff Burton P .30 .75
44A Kevin Harvick P .50 1.25
44B Kevin Harvick missing official 1.00 2.50
45 Kyle Busch P .50 1.25
46 Casey Mears P .25 .60
47 Jeff Gordon P .75 2.00
48 Matt Kenseth P .40 1.00
49 Matt Kenseth FP .40 1.00
50 Jimmie Johnson FP .60 1.50
51 Kevin Harvick FP .50 1.25
52 Dave Blaney FP .25 .60
53 Mark Martin FP .40 1.00
54 Joe Nemechek FP .25 .60
55 Jeff Gordon FP .75 2.00
56 Sterling Marlin NT .40 1.00
57 Denny Hamlin NT .50 1.25
58 Dale Jarrett NT .40 1.00
59A Tony Stewart NT .60 1.50
59B T.Stewart NT no table 1.25 3.00
60 Joe Nemechek NT .25 .60
61 J.J. Yeley NT .40 1.00
62 Rusty Wallace NT .40 1.00
63 Reed Sorenson NT .25 .60
64 Martin/Kahne/Burton NS .40 1.00
65 Kevin Harvick NS .50 1.25
66 Jeff Burton NS .30 .75
67 Tony Stewart NS .60 1.50
68 Kasey Kahne NS .40 1.00
69 Jimmie Johnson NS .60 1.50
70 Tony Stewart NS .60 1.50
71 Jimmie Johnson NS .60 1.50
72 Jimmie Johnson NS .60 1.50
73A Jimmie Johnson NYC .60 1.50
73B J.Johnson signs reversed 1.25 3.00
74 Matt Kenseth NYC .40 1.00
75 Denny Hamlin NYC .50 1.25
76 Kevin Harvick NYC .50 1.25
77 Dale Earnhardt Jr. NYC .75 2.00
78 Tony Stewart NYC .60 1.50
79 Jimmie Johnson SM .60 1.50
80 Denny Hamlin SM .50 1.25
81 Kevin Harvick SM .50 1.25
82 Danny O'Quinn SM .60 1.50
83 Mark Martin SM .40 1.00
84 Juan Pablo Montoya RC 1.25 3.00
85A David Gilliland RC .60 1.50
85B D.Gilliland missing sign 1.25 3.00
86 Paul Menard CRC 1.25 3.00
87 Regan Smith CRC .75 2.00
88 Mark Martin .40 1.00
89 Dale Jarrett .40 1.00
0 Cup Chase 10 4.00 10.00
CL Dale Earnhardt Jr. CL .75 2.00

2007 Press Pass Eclipse Gold

*GOLD: 8X TO 20X BASE

2007 Press Pass Eclipse Ecliptic

This 12-card set was inserted into packs of 2007 Press Pass Eclipse at a rate of one in six for both Hobby and Retail. The cards were highlighted on a combination of holofoil board and plastic to create a unique finish. The cards carried an "EC" prefix for thier card numbers.

COMPLETE SET (12) 15.00 40.00
EC1 Jimmie Johnson 1.00 2.50
EC2 Mark Martin .60 1.50
EC3 Kasey Kahne .60 1.50
EC4 Matt Kenseth .60 1.50
EC5 Jeff Gordon 1.25 3.00
EC6 Ryan Newman .50 1.25
EC7 Tony Stewart 1.00 2.50
EC8 Dale Earnhardt Jr. 1.25 3.00
EC9 Denny Hamlin .75 2.00
EC10 Jamie McMurray .60 1.50
EC11 Kevin Harvick .75 2.00
EC12 Carl Edwards .60 1.50

2007 Press Pass Eclipse Hyperdrive

This 9-card set was inserted into packs of 2007 Press Pass Eclipse at a rate of one in 12 for both Hobby and Retail. The cards were highlighted on a combination of holofoil board and plastic to create a unique finish. The cards carried an "HP" prefix for thier card numbers.

COMPLETE SET (9) 12.50 30.00
HD1 Tony Stewart 1.50 4.00
HD2 Matt Kenseth 1.00 2.50
HD3 Greg Biffle .75 2.00
HD4 Kevin Harvick 1.25 3.00
HD5 Jimmie Johnson 1.50 4.00
HD6 Kasey Kahne 1.00 2.50
HD7 Jeff Gordon 2.00 5.00
HD8 Jeff Burton .75 2.00
HD9 Dale Earnhardt Jr. 2.00 5.00

2007 Press Pass Eclipse Racing Champions

This 27-card set was inserted into packs of 2007 Press Pass Eclipse at a rate of one in two packs for both Hobby and Retail. Each card carried a "RC" prefix for its card number.

COMPLETE SET (27) 12.50 30.00
RC1 Kasey Kahne .30 .75
RC2 Kevin Harvick .40 1.00
RC3 Jimmie Johnson .50 1.25
RC4 Tony Stewart .50 1.25
RC5 Matt Kenseth .30 .75
RC6 Greg Biffle .25 .60
RC7 Jeff Gordon .60 1.50
RC8 Denny Hamlin .40 1.00
RC9 Jeff Burton .25 .60
RC10 Kurt Busch .25 .60
RC11 Kyle Busch .40 1.00
RC12 Dale Earnhardt Jr. .60 1.50
RC13 Kevin Harvick .40 1.00
RC14 Carl Edwards .30 .75
RC15 Matt Kenseth .30 .75
RC16 Jeff Burton .25 .60
RC17 Kurt Busch .25 .60
RC18 Dale Earnhardt Jr. .60 1.50
RC19 Denny Hamlin .40 1.00
RC20 Kasey Kahne .30 .75
RC21 Clint Bowyer .30 .75
RC22 Greg Biffle .25 .60
RC23 Kyle Busch .40 1.00
RC24 David Gilliland .50 1.25
RC25 Paul Menard 1.00 2.50
RC26 Tony Stewart .50 1.25
RC27 Martin Truex Jr. .25 .60

2007 Press Pass Eclipse Skidmarks

This 18-card set was inserted into packs of 2007 Press Pass Eclipse at a rate of one in 18 Hobby and Retail packs. The set utilized actual race-used tires to enhance the design elements on the card. Each card carried a "SM" prefix for its card number. There was also a Holofoil parallel which was serial numbered to 250 copies and only available in Hobby packs.

*HOLOFOIL/250: .8X TO 2X BASIC INSERT
SM1 Dale Earnhardt Jr 4.00 10.00
SM2 Reed Sorenson 3.00 8.00
SM3 Kevin Harvick 3.00 8.00
SM4 Matt Kenseth 3.00 8.00
SM5 Denny Hamlin 3.00 8.00
SM6 Jimmie Johnson 3.00 8.00
SM7 Kyle Busch 2.50 6.00
SM8 Kasey Kahne 3.00 8.00
SM9 Jeff Burton 2.50 6.00
SM10 Tony Stewart 3.00 8.00
SM11 Mark Martin 3.00 8.00
SM12 Scott Riggs 2.00 5.00
SM13 Carl Edwards 3.00 8.00
SM14 Clint Bowyer 3.00 8.00
SM15 Greg Biffle 2.00 5.00
SM16 Jeff Gordon 4.00 10.00
SM17 Ryan Newman 3.00 8.00
SM18 Martin Truex Jr. 2.50 6.00

2007 Press Pass Eclipse Teammates Autographs

This 6-card set featured double and triple signed certified autograph cards. The drivers were paired with teammates on the cards and each was serial numbered to just 25 copies. The Gordon/Johnson/Ky.Busch and the Harvick/Bowyer/Burton cards were not released in packs. They were additions that were only available in the Collector's Series Box Set that was released in October 2007.

1 Dale Jr/Truex Jr/Menard 200.00 400.00
2 Kahne/Riggs/Sadler 125.00 250.00
3 Montoya/Sorenson/Stremme 125.00 250.00
4 Hamlin/Stewart/Yeley 125.00 250.00
5 Busch/Newman 75.00 150.00
6 Biffle/Edwards/Kenseth 125.00 250.00
7 J.Gordon/J.Johnson/Ky.Busch 200.00 400.00
8 K.Harvick/C.Bowyer/J.Burton 125.00 250.00

2007 Press Pass Eclipse Under Cover Autographs

This 7-card set was inserted randomly into Hobby packs of 2007 Press Pass Eclipse. Each card featured a swatch of race-used car cover and a signature of the corresponding driver. The cards were serial numbered to the driver's door number.

STATED PRINT RUN 8-48
UCDE Dale Earnhardt Jr./8
UCGB Greg Biffle/16
UCJG Jeff Gordon/24 150.00 300.00
UCJJ Jimmie Johnson/48 60.00 120.00
UCKK Kasey Kahne/9
UCMK Matt Kenseth/17
UCRN Ryan Newman/12
UCTS Tony Stewart/20 100.00 200.00

2007 Press Pass Eclipse Under Cover Double Cover NASCAR

This 6-card set was inserted randomly into Hobby packs of 2007 Press Pass Eclipse. This set had a parallel, Under Cover Double Cover Name. Each card featured a swatch of race-used car cover under the die-cut design of the word NASCAR. The cards were serial numbered to 99.

*NAME/25: 1.2X TO 3X NASCAR
DC1 Edwards/Biffle 10.00 25.00
DC2 Sorenson/Stremme 10.00 25.00
DC3 Gordon/Johnson 25.00 50.00
DC4 Newman/Busch 12.00 30.00
DC5 Kenseth/Edwards 12.00 30.00
DC6 Dale Jr./Truex Jr. 25.00 50.00

2007 Press Pass Eclipse Under Cover Drivers

This 14-card set was inserted randomly into Hobby packs of 2007 Press Pass Eclipse. Each card featured a swatch of race-used car cover under the die-cut design of a car. The cards were serial numbered to 450.

*NAME/99: .6X TO 1.5X BASE DRIVERS
*NASCAR/270: .5X TO 1.2X BASE DRIVERS
*TEAMS/135: .5X TO 1.2X DRIVERS
*TEAMS NASCAR/25: 1X TO 2.5X DRIVER
UCD1 Dale Earnhardt Jr. 4.00 10.00
UCD2 David Stremme 1.25 3.00
UCD3 Reed Sorenson 1.25 3.00
UCD4 Matt Kenseth 2.00 5.00
UCD5 Kevin Harvick 2.50 6.00
UCD6 Greg Biffle 1.50 4.00
UCD7 Jimmie Johnson 3.00 8.00
UCD8 Ryan Newman 1.50 4.00
UCD9 Tony Stewart 3.00 8.00
UCD10 Martin Truex Jr. 1.50 4.00
UCD11 Carl Edwards 2.00 5.00
UCD12 Kasey Kahne 2.00 5.00
UCD13 Jeff Gordon 4.00 10.00
UCD14 Kurt Busch 1.50 4.00

2008 Press Pass Eclipse

COMPLETE SET (90) 15.00 40.00
WAX BOX HOBBY (24) 100.00 150.00
WAX BOX RETAIL (28) 60.00 100.00
1 Jimmie Johnson .60 1.50
2 Jeff Gordon .75 2.00
3 Clint Bowyer .40 1.00
4 Matt Kenseth .40 1.00
5A Tony Stewart .60 1.50
5B T.Stewart no bckgrn 2.50 6.00
6 Kurt Busch .30 .75
7 Jeff Burton .30 .75
8 Carl Edwards .40 1.00
9 Kevin Harvick .50 1.25
10 Martin Truex Jr. .30 .75
11 Denny Hamlin .50 1.25
12 Ryan Newman .30 .75
13 Greg Biffle .30 .75
14 Jamie McMurray .40 1.00
15 Bobby Labonte .40 1.00
16 Kasey Kahne .40 1.00
17 Juan Pablo Montoya .60 1.50
18 Reed Sorenson .25 .60
19 David Ragan .30 .75
20 Elliott Sadler .25 .60
21A Mark Martin .40 1.00
21B Mark Martin Army 1.50 4.00
22 Dave Blaney .25 .60
23 Paul Menard .25 .60
24 Kyle Petty .30 .75
25 Brian Vickers .25 .60
26 Dale Jarrett .40 1.00
27 Michael Waltrip .40 1.00
28A Jeff Gordon RM .75 2.00
28B Jeff Gordon RM red 3.00 8.00
29 Ryan Newman RM .30 .75
30 Jimmie Johnson RM .60 1.50
31 Clint Bowyer RM .40 1.00
32 Kasey Kahne RM .40 1.00
33 Kurt Busch RM .30 .75
34 Denny Hamlin RM .50 1.25
35 Dave Blaney RM .25 .60
36 Michael Waltrip RM .40 1.00
37A Jimmie Johnson track .60 1.50
37B Jimmie Johnson TO 2.50 6.00
38 Jeff Gordon TO .75 2.00
39 Denny Hamlin TO .50 1.25
40 Kurt Busch TO .30 .75
41 Ryan Newman TO .30 .75
42 Kasey Kahne TO .40 1.00
43 Martin Truex Jr. TO .30 .75
44 Clint Bowyer TO .40 1.00
45 Jeff Burton TO .30 .75
46 Clint Bowyer NS .40 1.00
47 Carl Edwards NS .40 1.00
48 Greg Biffle NS .30 .75
49 Jeff Gordon NS .75 2.00
50 Jeff Gordon NS .75 2.00
51 Jimmie Johnson NS .60 1.50
52 Jimmie Johnson NS .60 1.50
53 Jimmie Johnson NS .60 1.50
54 Rick Hendrick NS .40 1.00
55 Jeff Gordon's Car LP .30 .75
56 Jamie McMurray's Car LP .15 .40
57 Ryan Newman's Car LP .12 .30
58 Carl Edwards' Car LP .15 .40
59 Martin Truex Jr.'s Car LP .12 .30
60 David Ragan's Car LP .12 .30
61 Matt Kenseth's Car LP .15 .40
62 Jeff Burton's Car LP .12 .30
63 Mark Martin's Car LP .15 .40
64 Jimmie Johnson's Car LP .25 .60
65 Kurt Busch BTF .30 .75
66 Ryan Newman BTF .30 .75
67A Dale Earnhardt Jr. BTF .75 2.00
67B Dale Earnhardt Jr. BTF go-kart 3.00 8.00
68 Brian Vickers BTF .25 .60
69 Dario Franchitti BTF .60 1.50
70 Reed Sorenson BTF .25 .60
71 Michael Waltrip BTF .40 1.00
72 Juan Pablo Montoya BTF .60 1.50
73 Jimmie Johnson SO .60 1.50
74 T.Stewart/Montoya SO .60 1.50
75 Top 10 Drivers SO .75 2.00
76 Carl Edwards SO .40 1.00
77 Kevin Harvick SO .50 1.25
78 Tony Stewart SO .60 1.50
79 Jeff Gordon SO .75 2.00
80 Jeff Burton SO .30 .75
81 Jimmie Johnson SO .60 1.50
82 Dario Franchitti PREV RC 1.50 4.00
83 J.J.Yeley PREV .40 1.00
84 S.Hornish Jr.PREV CRC 1.50 4.00
85A Casey Mears PREV .25 .60
85B Casey Mears P Carquest 1.00 2.50
86 Dale Earnhardt Jr. PREV .75 2.00
87 Kasey Kahne PREV .40 1.00
88 Kyle Busch PREV .50 1.25
89 Patrick Carpentier PREV RC 2.00 5.00
90 Dale Earnhardt Jr. CL .75 2.00

2008 Press Pass Eclipse Gold

*GOLD: 5X TO 12X BASE
STATED PRINT RUN 25 SERIAL #'d SETS

2008 Press Pass Eclipse Escape Velocity

COMPLETE SET (12) 15.00 40.00
STATED ODDS 1:6
EV1 Jeff Gordon 1.25 3.00
EV2 Michael Waltrip .60 1.50
EV3 Juan Pablo Montoya 1.00 2.50
EV4 Tony Stewart 1.00 2.50
EV5 Jamie McMurray .60 1.50
EV6 Martin Truex Jr. .50 1.25
EV7 Jimmie Johnson 1.00 2.50
EV8 Ryan Newman .50 1.25
EV9 Kevin Harvick .75 2.00
EV10 Jeff Burton .50 1.25
EV11 Bobby Labonte .60 1.50
EV12 Dale Jarrett .60 1.50

2008 Press Pass Eclipse Hyperdrive

COMPLETE SET (9) 15.00 40.00
STATED ODDS 1:12
HP1 Tony Stewart 1.25 3.00
HP2 Mark Martin .75 2.00
HP3 Jeff Gordon 1.50 4.00
HP4 Martin Truex Jr. .60 1.50
HP5 Kevin Harvick 1.00 2.50
HP6 Kasey Kahne .75 2.00
HP7 Matt Kenseth .75 2.00
HP8 Jimmie Johnson 1.25 3.00
HP9 Jeff Burton .60 1.50

2008 Press Pass Eclipse Star Tracks

COMPLETE SET (18) 40.00 100.00
STATED ODDS 1:18
*HOLOFOIL/250: .5X TO 1.2X BASE
ST1 Dale Jarrett 1.50 4.00
ST2 Tony Stewart 2.50 6.00
ST3 Brian Vickers 1.00 2.50
ST4 Jeff Gordon 3.00 8.00
ST5 Mark Martin 1.50 4.00
ST6 Ryan Newman 1.25 3.00
ST7 Kevin Harvick 2.00 5.00
ST8 Kasey Kahne 1.50 4.00
ST9 Kurt Busch 1.25 3.00
ST10 Jimmie Johnson 2.50 6.00
ST11 Jeff Burton 1.25 3.00
ST12 Martin Truex Jr. 1.25 3.00
ST13 Matt Kenseth 1.50 4.00
ST14 Carl Edwards 1.50 4.00
ST15 Dale Earnhardt Jr. 3.00 8.00
ST16 Jamie McMurray 1.50 4.00
ST17 Juan Pablo Montoya 2.50 6.00
ST18 Michael Waltrip 1.50 4.00

2008 Press Pass Eclipse Stellar

COMPLETE SET (25) 15.00 30.00
STATED ODDS 1:2
ST1 Jimmie Johnson .75 2.00
ST2 Jeff Gordon 1.00 2.50
ST3 Carl Edwards .50 1.25
ST4 Tony Stewart .75 2.00
ST5 Kurt Busch .40 1.00
ST6 Matt Kenseth .50 1.25
ST7 Clint Bowyer .50 1.25
ST8 Jeff Burton .40 1.00
ST9 Kevin Harvick .60 1.50
ST10 Denny Hamlin .60 1.50
ST11 Martin Truex Jr. .40 1.00
ST12 Greg Biffle .40 1.00
ST13 Jamie McMurray .50 1.25
ST14 Juan Pablo Montoya .75 2.00
ST15 Kevin Harvick .60 1.50
ST16 Jeff Burton .40 1.00
ST17 Carl Edwards .50 1.25
ST18 Denny Hamlin .60 1.50
ST19 Clint Bowyer .50 1.25
ST20 Kasey Kahne .50 1.25
ST21 Matt Kenseth .50 1.25
ST22 Bobby Labonte .50 1.25
ST23 Juan Pablo Montoya .75 2.00
ST24 Mike Skinner .30 .75
ST25 Ron Hornaday .30 .75

2008 Press Pass Eclipse Teammates Autographs

STATED PRINT RUN 25 SERIAL #'d SETS
UNLESS NOTED BELOW
AV Allmendinger/Vickers/35 75.00 150.00
BN K.Busch/R.Newman/35 75.00 150.00
EG D.Earnhardt Jr./J.Gordon 500.00 750.00
EJ D.Earnhardt Jr./J.Johnson 250.00 400.00
EM D.Earnhardt Jr./C.Mears 150.00 300.00
KS K.Kahne/E.Sadler/35 75.00 150.00
BBH Bowyer/Burton/Harvick 125.00 250.00
BHS Ky.Bsch/Hmln/Stwrt/35 250.00 400.00
FMS Fran/Montoya/Sornsn 125.00 250.00
EGJM Dale Jr./Gordon/JJ/Mears 500.00 800.00

2008 Press Pass Eclipse Under Cover Autographs

STATED PRINT RUN 1-48
UCDE Dale Earnhardt Jr./8
UCJG Jeff Gordon/24 150.00 300.00
UCJJ Jimmie Johnson/48 60.00 120.00
UCKB Kurt Busch/2
UCKK Kasey Kahne/9
UCMK Matt Kenseth/17
UCMT Martin Truex Jr./1
UCRN Ryan Newman/12

2008 Press Pass Eclipse Under Cover Double Cover NASCAR

OVERALL R-U STATED ODDS 1:10
STATED PRINT RUN 99 SERIAL #'d SETS
*NAME/25: .8X TO 2X NASCAR/99
DC1 M.Martin/M.Truex Jr. 15.00 40.00
DC2 K.Harvick/J.Burton 10.00 25.00
DC3 C.Edwards/M.Kenseth 10.00 25.00
DC4 M.Kenseth/D.Ragan 12.50 30.00
DC5 Ku.Busch/R.Newman 12.50 30.00
DC6 J.Gordon/J.Johnson 25.00 60.00
DC7 C.Edwards/D.Ragan 10.00 25.00

2008 Press Pass Eclipse Under Cover Drivers

OVERALL R-U STATED ODDS 1:10
STATED PRINT RUN 250 SERIAL #'d SETS
*NAME/50: .8X TO 2X DRIVERS
*NASCAR/150: .5X TO 1.2X DRIVERS
*TEAMS/99: .6X TO 1.5X DRIVERS
*TEAM NASCAR/25: 1.2X TO 3X DRIVER
UCD1 Martin Truex Jr. 1.50 4.00
UCD2 Tony Stewart 3.00 8.00
UCD3 Kevin Harvick 2.50 6.00
UCD4 Kurt Busch 1.50 4.00
UCD5 Carl Edwards 2.00 5.00
UCD6 Mark Martin 2.00 5.00
UCD7 Ryan Newman 1.50 4.00
UCD8 Reed Sorenson 1.25 3.00
UCD9 Matt Kenseth 2.00 5.00
UCD10 David Ragan 1.50 4.00
UCD11 Jeff Burton 1.50 4.00
UCD12 Dale Jarrett 2.00 5.00
UCD13 Michael Waltrip 2.00 5.00
UCD14 Jimmie Johnson 3.00 8.00
UCD15 Jeff Gordon 4.00 10.00

2009 Press Pass Eclipse

This set was released on February 26, 2009. The base set consists of 90 cards.

COMPLETE SET (90) 20.00 50.00
WAX BOX HOBBY 60.00 100.00
WAX BOX RETAIL 50.00 80.00
1 Casey Mears .25 .60
2 Martin Truex Jr. .30 .75
3 Kurt Busch .30 .75
4 Mark Martin .40 1.00
5 David Ragan .30 .75
6 Aric Almirola .30 .75
7 Kasey Kahne .40 1.00
8 Reed Sorenson .25 .60
9 Denny Hamlin .40 1.00
10 Tony Stewart .60 1.50
11 Greg Biffle .30 .75
12 Matt Kenseth .40 1.00
13 Kyle Busch .50 1.25
14 Joey Logano RC .75 2.00
15 Jeff Gordon .75 2.00
16 Jamie McMurray .40 1.00
17 Kevin Harvick .50 1.25
18 Jeff Burton .30 .75
19 Clint Bowyer .40 1.00
20 Ryan Newman .30 .75
21 Juan Pablo Montoya .50 1.25
22 Jimmie Johnson .60 1.50
23 Michael Waltrip .40 1.00
24 Sam Hornish Jr. .30 .75
25 Joe Nemechek .25 .60
26 Scott Speed RC .50 1.25
27 Brian Vickers .25 .60
28 Dale Earnhardt Jr. .75 2.00
29 Carl Edwards .40 1.00
30 David Reutimann .30 .75
31 Jeff Gordon O .75 2.00
32 Mark Martin O .40 1.00
33 Tony Stewart O .60 1.50
34 Jimmie Johnson O .60 1.50
35 Dale Earnhardt Jr. O .75 2.00
36 Jeff Burton O .30 .75
37 Ryan Newman TO .30 .75
38 Jeff Gordon TO .75 2.00
39 Kasey Kahne TO .40 1.00
40 Jimmie Johnson TO .60 1.50
41 Kurt Busch TO .30 .75
42 Greg Biffle TO .30 .75
43 Denny Hamlin TO .40 1.00
44 Joe Nemechek TO .25 .60
45 Jimmie Johnson TO .25 .60
46 Jimmie Johnson's Car LM .25 .60
47 Kasey Kahne's Car LM .15 .40
48 Kyle Busch's Car LM .20 .50
49 Carl Edwards's Car LM .15 .40
50 Jeff Burton's Car LM .12 .30
51 Jeff Gordon's Car LM .30 .75
52 Jamie McMurray's Car LM .15 .40
53 Kevin Harvick's Car LM .20 .50
54 Dale Earnhardt Jr.'s Car LM .30 .75
55 Greg Biffle's Car LM .12 .30
56 Tony Stewart's Car LM .25 .60
57 Matt Kenseth's Car LM .15 .40
58 Jimmie Johnson BS .60 1.50
59 Carl Edwards BS .40 1.00
60 Jeff Gordon BS .75 2.00
61 Matt Kenseth BS .40 1.00
62 Tony Stewart BS .60 1.50
63 Denny Hamlin BS .40 1.00
64 Clint Bowyer BS .40 1.00
65 Kevin Harvick BS .50 1.25
66 Greg Biffle BS .30 .75
67 Dale Earnhardt Jr. BS .75 2.00
68 Kyle Busch BS .50 1.25
69 Kurt Busch BS .30 .75
70 Jimmie Johnson GC .60 1.50
71 Jeff Gordon GC .75 2.00
72 Carl Edwards GC .40 1.00
73 Tony Stewart GC .60 1.50
74 Kyle Busch GC .50 1.25
75 Greg Biffle GC .30 .75
76 Kyle Busch P .50 1.25
77 Jimmie Johnson P .60 1.50
78 Matt Kenseth P .40 1.00
79 Jamie McMurray P .40 1.00
80 David Gilliland P .25 .60
81 Aric Almirola P .30 .75
82 Greg Biffle P .30 .75
83 David Ragan P .30 .75
84 Kevin Harvick P .50 1.25
85 Jimmie Johnson NY .60 1.50
86 Dale Earnhardt Jr. NY .75 2.00
87 Regan Smith NY .30 .75
88 Jimmie Johnson NY .60 1.50
89 Carl Edwards NY .40 1.00
90 Jimmie Johnson CL .60 1.50
NNO Black Hole Instant Win 100.00 175.00

2009 Press Pass Eclipse Black and White

COMPLETE SET (90) 30.00 80.00
*BLACK AND WHITE: .8X TO 2X BASE

2009 Press Pass Eclipse Blue

COMPLETE SET (90) 30.00 80.00
*BLUE: .8X TO 2X BASIC CARDS
STATED ODDS 1:2 RETAIL

2009 Press Pass Eclipse Black Hole Firesuits
STATED PRINT RUN 50 SER.#'d SETS
BH1 Dale Earnhardt Jr. AMP 12.00 30.00
BH2 Dale Earnhardt Jr. NG 12.00 30.00
BH3 Jeff Gordon 12.00 30.00
BH4 Jimmie Johnson 10.00 25.00
BH5 Kasey Kahne 6.00 15.00
BH6 Kyle Busch 8.00 20.00

2009 Press Pass Eclipse Ecliptic Path
COMPLETE SET (18) 15.00 40.00
STATED ODDS 1:4
EP1 Matt Kenseth .60 1.50
EP2 Denny Hamlin .60 1.50
EP3 Kevin Harvick .75 2.00
EP4 Casey Mears .40 1.00
EP5 Jimmie Johnson 1.00 2.50
EP6 Juan Pablo Montoya .75 2.00
EP7 Kyle Busch .75 2.00
EP8 David Ragan .50 1.25
EP9 Carl Edwards .60 1.50
EP10 Jeff Burton .50 1.25
EP11 Scott Speed .75 2.00
EP12 Dale Earnhardt Jr. 1.25 3.00
EP13 Mark Martin .60 1.50
EP14 Jamie McMurray .60 1.50
EP15 Joey Logano 1.25 3.00
EP16 Kasey Kahne .60 1.50
EP17 Greg Biffle .50 1.25
EP18 Tony Stewart 1.00 2.50

2009 Press Pass Eclipse Solar Swatches
SSDE1 Dale Earnhardt Jr. E/10
SSDE2 Dale Earnhardt Jr. A/20 25.00 60.00
SSDE3 Dale Earnhardt Jr. R/25 25.00 60.00
SSDE4 Dale Earnhardt Jr. N/15 25.00 60.00
SSDE5 Dale Earnhardt Jr. H/20 25.00 60.00
SSDE6 Dale Earnhardt Jr. A/25 25.00 60.00
SSDE7 Dale Earnhardt Jr. R/15 25.00 60.00
SSDE8 Dale Earnhardt Jr. D/20 25.00 60.00
SSDE9 Dale Earnhardt Jr. T/25 25.00 60.00
SSDE10 Dale Earnhardt Jr. J/15 25.00 60.00
SSDE11 Dale Earnhardt Jr. R/20 25.00 60.00
SSCE1 Carl Edwards E/299 4.00 10.00
SSCE2 Carl Edwards D/299 5.00 12.00
SSCE3 Carl Edwards W/50 12.00 30.00
SSCE4 Carl Edwards A/299 4.00 10.00
SSCE5 Carl Edwards R/99 8.00 20.00
SSCE6 Carl Edwards D/250 5.00 12.00
SSCE7 Carl Edwards S/299 5.00 12.00
SSJG1 Jeff Gordon G/299 8.00 20.00
SSJG2 Jeff Gordon O/250 8.00 20.00
SSJG3 Jeff Gordon R/299 8.00 20.00
SSJG4 Jeff Gordon D/50 25.00 60.00
SSJG5 Jeff Gordon O/299 8.00 20.00
SSJG6 Jeff Gordon N/99 15.00 40.00
SSKH1 Kevin Harvick H/250 5.00 12.00
SSKH2 Kevin Harvick A/299 5.00 12.00
SSKH3 Kevin Harvick R/250 5.00 12.00
SSKH4 Kevin Harvick V/50 15.00 40.00
SSKH5 Kevin Harvick I/299 5.00 12.00
SSKH6 Kevin Harvick C/99 10.00 25.00
SSKH7 Kevin Harvick K/299 5.00 12.00
SSJJ1 Jimmie Johnson J/99 12.00 30.00
SSJJ2 Jimmie Johnson O/200 6.00 15.00
SSJJ3 Jimmie Johnson H/65 15.00 40.00
SSJJ4 Jimmie Johnson N/200 6.00 15.00
SSJJ5 Jimmie Johnson S/50 20.00 50.00
SSJJ6 Jimmie Johnson O/200 6.00 15.00
SSJJ7 Jimmie Johnson N/200 6.00 15.00
SSTS1 Tony Stewart S/99 12.00 30.00
SSTS2 Tony Stewart T/299 6.00 15.00
SSTS3 Tony Stewart E/250 6.00 15.00
SSTS4 Tony Stewart W/50 20.00 50.00
SSTS5 Tony Stewart A/250 6.00 15.00
SSTS6 Tony Stewart R/299 6.00 15.00
SSTS7 Tony Stewart T/250 6.00 15.00
SSMW1 Michael Waltrip W/299 4.00 10.00
SSMW2 Michael Waltrip A/250 4.00 10.00
SSMW3 Michael Waltrip L/299 4.00 10.00
SSMW4 Michael Waltrip T/99 8.00 20.00
SSMW5 Michael Waltrip R/299 4.00 10.00
SSMW6 Michael Waltrip I/50 12.00 30.00
SSMW7 Michael Waltrip P/299 4.00 10.00

2009 Press Pass Eclipse Solar System
COMPLETE SET (9) 12.00 30.00
STATED ODDS 1:12
SS1 Jimmie Johnson 1.25 3.00
SS2 Carl Edwards .75 2.00
SS3 Greg Biffle .60 1.50
SS4 Kevin Harvick 1.00 2.50
SS5 Clint Bowyer .75 2.00
SS6 Jeff Burton .60 1.50
SS7 Jeff Gordon 1.50 4.00
SS8 Denny Hamlin .75 2.00
SS9 Tony Stewart 1.25 3.00

2009 Press Pass Eclipse Under Cover Autographs
SERIAL #'d TO DRIVER'S DOOR NO.
STATED PRINT RUN 17-55
UCSJG Jeff Gordon/24 150.00 300.00
UCSJJ Jimmie Johnson/48 60.00 120.00
UCSJM Juan Pablo Montoya/42 50.00 100.00
UCSKH Kevin Harvick/29 60.00 120.00
UCSMK Matt Kenseth
UCSMW Michael Waltrip/55 15.00 40.00
UCSTS Tony Stewart/20 75.00 150.00

2010 Press Pass Eclipse

COMPLETE SET (90) 15.00 40.00
WAX BOX HOBBY (24) 60.00 100.00
1 Brad Keselowski .40 1.00
2 Brian Vickers .20 .50
3 Carl Edwards .30 .75
4 Clint Bowyer .30 .75
5 Dale Earnhardt Jr. .60 1.50
6 David Reutimann .25 .60
7 David Ragan .25 .60
8 Denny Hamlin .30 .75
9 Elliott Sadler .20 .50
10 Greg Biffle .25 .60
11 Jeff Gordon .60 1.50
12 Jeff Burton .25 .60
13 Jimmie Johnson .50 1.25
14 Joey Logano .30 .75
15 Juan Pablo Montoya .30 .75
16 Kasey Kahne .30 .75
17 Kevin Harvick .40 1.00
18 Kurt Busch .25 .60
19 Kyle Busch .40 1.00
20 Marcos Ambrose .30 .75
21 Mark Martin .30 .75
22 Matt Kenseth .30 .75
23 Michael Waltrip .30 .75
24 Robby Gordon .20 .50
25 Ryan Newman .25 .60
26 Tony Stewart .50 1.25
27 Danica Patrick RC 4.00 10.00
28 Kurt Busch's Car .10 .25
29 Mark Martin's Car .12 .30
30 Kasey Kahne's Car .12 .30
31 Denny Hamlin's Car .12 .30
32 Tony Stewart's Car .20 .50
33 Greg Biffle's Car .10 .25
34 Kyle Busch's Car .15 .40
35 Elliott Sadler's Car .07 .20
36 Joey Logano's Car .12 .30
37 Jeff Gordon's Car .25 .60
38 Kevin Harvick's Car .15 .40
39 Jeff Burton's Car .10 .25
40 Ryan Newman's Car .10 .25
41 Juan Pablo Montoya's Car .12 .30
42 Jimmie Johnson's Car .20 .50
43 Brian Vickers' Car .07 .20
44 Carl Edwards' Car .12 .30
45 Dale Earnhardt's Car .60 1.50
46 Richard Petty's Car .20 .50
47 Jeff Gordon Bristol .60 1.50
48 Jimmie Johnson Charlotte .50 1.25
49 Kevin Harvick Chicago .40 1.00
50 Jeff Gordon Darlington .60 1.50
51 Jeff Gordon Daytona .60 1.50
52 Jimmie Johnson Dover .50 1.25
53 Jimmie Johnson Fontana .50 1.25
54 Jeff Gordon Indianapolis .60 1.50
55 Jimmie Johnson Las Vegas .50 1.25
56 Jeff Gordon Martinsville .60 1.50
57 Greg Biffle Miami .25 .60
58 Mark Martin Michigan .30 .75
59 Jeff Burton New Hampshire .25 .60
60 Jimmie Johnson Phoenix .50 1.25
61 Jeff Gordon Sonoma .60 1.50
62 Jeff Gordon Talladega .60 1.50
63 Carl Edwards Texas .30 .75
64 Tony Stewart Watkins Glen .50 1.25
65 Jimmie Johnson Vegas .50 1.25
66 Jimmie Johnson 4X Vegas .50 1.25
67 Jimmie Johnson's Car Vegas .20 .50
68 Jimmie Johnson's Car Burnout .20 .50
69 Jimmie Johnson Vegas .50 1.25
70 Joey Logano Vegas .30 .75
71 Dale Earnhardt Jr. Vegas .60 1.50
72 Mark Martin Vegas .30 .75
73 Tony Stewart Vegas .50 1.25
74 Jeff Gordon Vegas .60 1.50
75 Ryan Newman Vegas .25 .60
76 Brian Vickers E .20 .50
77 Dale Earnhardt Jr. E .60 1.50
78 Jeff Gordon E .60 1.50
79 Jimmie Johnson E .50 1.25
80 Joey Logano E .30 .75
81 Juan Pablo Montoya E .30 .75
82 Denny Hamlin E .30 .75
83 Kyle Busch E .40 1.00
84 Tony Stewart E .50 1.25
85 A.J. Allmendinger 2010 .30 .75
86 Brad Keselowski 2010 .40 1.00
87 Kasey Kahne 2010 .30 .75
88 Mark Martin 2010 .30 .75
89 Martin Truex Jr. 2010 .25 .60
90 Matt Kenseth 2010 .30 .75

2010 Press Pass Eclipse Blue
COMPLETE SET (90) 20.00 50.00
*SINGLES: .6X TO 1.5X BASIC CARDS
STATED ODDS 1 PER RETAIL PACK
27 Danica Patrick 8.00 20.00

2010 Press Pass Eclipse Gold
COMPLETE SET (90) 20.00 50.00
*SINGLES: .6 TO 1.5X BASIC CARDS
STATED ODDS 1:2
27 Danica Patrick 8.00 20.00

2010 Press Pass Eclipse Purple
COMPLETE SET (64) 400.00 800.00
*SINGLES: 4X TO 10X BASIC CARDS
STATED PRINT RUN 25 SER.#'d SETS
27 Danica Patrick 60.00 120.00

2010 Press Pass Eclipse Cars
COMPLETE SET (9) 8.00 20.00
STATED ODDS 1:6
C1 Mark Martin's Car .50 1.25
C2 Tony Stewart's Car .75 2.00
C3 Kyle Busch's Car .60 1.50
C4 Joey Logano's Car .50 1.25
C5 Jeff Gordon's Car 1.00 2.50
C6 Juan Pablo Montoya's Car .50 1.25
C7 Jimmie Johnson's Car .75 2.00
C8 Dale Earnhardt Jr.'s Car 1.00 2.50
C9 Carl Edwards' Car .50 1.25

2010 Press Pass Eclipse Danica
COMPLETE SET (2) 15.00 30.00
STATED ODDS 1:54 RETAIL PACKS
DP1 Danica Patrick 8.00 20.00
DP2 Danica Patrick 8.00 20.00

2010 Press Pass Eclipse Decade
COMPLETE SET (8) 12.00 30.00
STATED ODDS 1:14
D1 Jimmie Johnson 1.25 3.00
D2 Jeff Gordon 1.50 4.00
D3 Tony Stewart 1.25 3.00
D4 Carl Edwards .75 2.00
D5 Kurt Busch .60 1.50
D6 Dale Earnhardt Jr. 1.50 4.00
D7 Kyle Busch 1.00 2.50
D8 Mark Martin .75 2.00

2010 Press Pass Eclipse Element Inserts
COMPLETE SET (5) 12.00 30.00
STATED ODDS 1:24
1 Jimmie Johnson 1.50 4.00
2 Jeff Gordon 2.00 5.00
3 Dale Earnhardt Jr. 2.00 5.00
4 Tony Stewart 1.50 4.00
5 Mark Martin 1.00 2.50

2010 Press Pass Eclipse Focus
COMPLETE SET (6) 15.00 40.00
STATED ODDS 1:24
F1 Dale Earnhardt Jr. 2.00 5.00
F2 Tony Stewart 1.50 4.00
F3 Jeff Gordon 2.00 5.00
F4 Mark Martin 1.00 2.50
F5 Kasey Kahne 1.00 2.50
F6 Jimmie Johnson 1.50 4.00

2010 Press Pass Eclipse Signature Series Shoes Autographs
SERIAL #'d TO DRIVER'S DOOR NO.
STATED PRINT RUN 6-29
SSSEDH Denny Hamlin/11
SSSEDR David Ragan/6
SSSEJG Jeff Gordon/24 100.00 200.00
SSSEJL Joey Logano/20 50.00 100.00
SSSEKB Kyle Busch/18 25.00 60.00
SSSEKH Kevin Harvick/29 30.00 80.00
SSSETS Tony Stewart/14 60.00 150.00

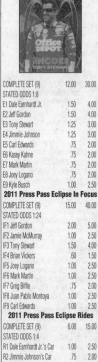

2010 Press Pass Eclipse Spellbound Swatches
OVERALL R-U ODDS 1:8
STATED PRINT RUN 99-299
EACH HAS MULTIPLE CARDS OF SAME VALUE
SSBK1 Brad Keselowski K 5.00 12.00
SSJG1 Jeff Gordon G 8.00 20.00
SSJJ1 Jimmie Johnson J 5.00 12.00
SSJL1 Joey Logano L 3.00 8.00
SSKB1 Kyle Busch B 4.00 10.00
SSMM1 Mark Martin M 4.00 10.00
SSTS1 Tony Stewart S 6.00 15.00
SSDEJ1 Dale Earnhardt Jr. E 6.00 15.00

2010 Press Pass Eclipse Spellbound Swatches Holofoil
STATED PRINT RUN 3-99
EACH HAS MULTIPLE CARDS OF SAME VALUE
SSCE1 Carl Edwards E 4.00 10.00
SSJG1 Jeff Gordon G 15.00 40.00
SSJJ1 Jimmie Johnson J 8.00 20.00
SSJL1 Joey Logano L 8.00 20.00
SSKB1 Kyle Busch B 10.00 25.00
SSRP1 Richard Petty P/43 8.00 20.00
SSTS1 Tony Stewart S 15.00 40.00
SSDEJ1 Dale Earnhardt Jr. E 8.00 20.00

2011 Press Pass Eclipse
COMPLETE SET (90) 15.00 40.00
WAX BOX HOBBY (24) 75.00 125.00
1 A.J. Allmendinger .30 .75
2 Marcos Ambrose .30 .75
3 Greg Biffle .25 .60
4 Clint Bowyer .30 .75
5 Jeff Burton .25 .60
6 Kurt Busch .25 .60
7 Kyle Busch .40 1.00
8 Dale Earnhardt Jr. .60 1.50
9 Carl Edwards .30 .75
10 Bill Elliott .50 1.25
11 Jeff Gordon .60 1.50
12 Denny Hamlin .30 .75
13 Kevin Harvick .40 1.00
14 Jimmie Johnson .50 1.25
15 Kasey Kahne .30 .75
16 Matt Kenseth .30 .75
17 Brad Keselowski .40 1.00
18 Travis Kvapil .20 .50
19 Bobby Labonte .30 .75
20 Joey Logano .30 .75
21 Mark Martin .30 .75
22 Jamie McMurray .30 .75
23 Paul Menard .20 .50
24 Juan Pablo Montoya .30 .75
25 Ryan Newman .25 .60
26 David Ragan .25 .60
27 David Reutimann .25 .60
28 Regan Smith .25 .60
29 Tony Stewart .50 1.25
30 Martin Truex Jr. .25 .60
31 Brian Vickers .20 .50
32 Michael Waltrip .40 1.00
33 David Reutimann's Car HP .10 .25
34 Jamie McMurray's Car HP .12 .30
35 Mark Martin's Car HP .12 .30
36 David Ragan's Car HP .10 .25
37 Denny Hamlin's Car HP .12 .30
38 Tony Stewart's Car HP .20 .50
39 Greg Biffle's Car HP .10 .25
40 Matt Kenseth's Car HP .12 .30
41 Kyle Busch's Car HP .15 .40
42 Joey Logano's Car HP .12 .30
43 Jeff Gordon's Car HP .25 .60
44 Jeff Burton's Car HP .10 .25
45 Clint Bowyer's Car HP .12 .30
46 Ryan Newman's Car HP .10 .25
47 Jimmie Johnson's Car HP .20 .50
48 Martin Truex Jr.'s Car HP .10 .25
49 Brian Vickers' Car HP .07 .20
50 Dale Earnhardt Jr.'s Car HP .25 .60
51 Carl Edwards' Car HP .12 .30
52 Jimmie Johnson HS .50 1.25
53 Dale Earnhardt Jr. HS .60 1.50
54 Jamie McMurray HS .30 .75
55 Denny Hamlin HS .30 .75
56 Brad Keselowski HS .40 1.00
57 Ricky Stenhouse HS .30 .75
58 Austin Dillon HS .40 1.00
59 Tony Stewart HS .50 1.25
60 Brad Keselowski HS .40 1.00
61 Tony Stewart SB .50 1.25
62 Jimmie Johnson SB .50 1.25
63 Jimmie Johnson SB .50 1.25
64 Jeff Gordon SB .60 1.50
65 Clint Bowyer SB .30 .75
66 Kevin Harvick SB .40 1.00
67 Denny Hamlin SB .30 .75
68 Kyle Busch SB .40 1.00
69 Carl Edwards SB .30 .75
70 Greg Biffle SB .25 .60
71 D.Hamlin/J.Johnson SB .50 1.25
72 Dale Earnhardt Jr. SB .60 1.50
73 Mark Martin's Car SS .12 .30
74 Denny Hamlin's Car SS .12 .30
75 Tony Stewart's Car SS .20 .50
76 Jeff Gordon's Car SS .25 .60
77 Jimmie Johnson's Car SS .20 .50
78 Carl Edwards' Car SS .12 .30
79 Joey Logano's Car SS .12 .30
80 Danica Patrick's Car SS .50 1.25
81 Jeff Burton's Car SS .10 .25
82 Clint Bowyer's Car SS .12 .30
83 Dale Earnhardt Jr.'s Car SS .25 .60
84 Kyle Busch's Car SS .15 .40
85 Kasey Kahne 2011 .30 .75
86 Kurt Busch 2011 .25 .60
87 Kevin Harvick 2011 .40 1.00
88 Marcos Ambrose 2011 .30 .75
89 Paul Menard 2011 .20 .50
90 Jeff Gordon 2011 .60 1.50

2011 Press Pass Eclipse Blue
COMPLETE SET (90) 20.00 50.00
*BLUE: 2X TO 5X BASE
STATED ODDS 1 PER RETAIL PACK

2011 Press Pass Eclipse Gold
*GOLD: 2.5X TO 6X BASE
STATED PRINT RUN 55 SER.#'d SETS
2 Marcos Ambrose 12.00 30.00
88 Marcos Ambrose 2011 12.00 30.00

2011 Press Pass Eclipse Purple
*PURPLE: 4X TO 10X BASE
STATED PRINT RUN 25 SER.#'d SETS

2011 Press Pass Eclipse Encore

COMPLETE SET (9) 12.00 30.00
STATED ODDS 1:8
E1 Dale Earnhardt Jr. 1.50 4.00
E2 Jeff Gordon 1.50 4.00
E3 Tony Stewart 1.25 3.00
E4 Jimmie Johnson 1.25 3.00
E5 Carl Edwards .75 2.00
E6 Kasey Kahne .75 2.00
E7 Mark Martin .75 2.00
E8 Joey Logano .75 2.00
E9 Kyle Busch 1.00 2.50

2011 Press Pass Eclipse In Focus
COMPLETE SET (9) 15.00 40.00
STATED ODDS 1:24
IF1 Jeff Gordon 2.00 5.00
IF2 Jamie McMurray 1.00 2.50
IF3 Tony Stewart 1.50 4.00
IF4 Brian Vickers .60 1.50
IF5 Joey Logano 1.00 2.50
IF6 Mark Martin 1.00 2.50
IF7 Greg Biffle .75 2.00
IF8 Juan Pablo Montoya 1.00 2.50
IF9 Carl Edwards 1.00 2.50

2011 Press Pass Eclipse Rides
COMPLETE SET (9) 6.00 15.00
STATED ODDS 1:4
R1 Dale Earnhardt Jr.'s Car 1.00 2.50
R2 Jimmie Johnson's Car .75 2.00
R3 Kyle Busch's Car .60 1.50
R4 Joey Logano's Car .50 1.25
R5 Brian Vickers' Car .30 .75
R6 David Reutimann's Car .40 1.00
R7 Jamie McMurray's Car .50 1.25
R8 Juan Pablo Montoya's Car .50 1.25
R9 Danica Patrick's Car 2.00 5.00

2011 Press Pass Eclipse Spellbound Swatches
OVERALL ODDS 1:8
SBBE1 Bill Elliott E/250 6.00 15.00
SBBE2 Bill Elliott L/150 6.00 15.00
SBBE3 Bill Elliott L/150 6.00 15.00
SBBE4 Bill Elliott I/100 8.00 20.00
SBBE5 Bill Elliott O/100 8.00 20.00
SBBE6 Bill Elliott T/75 8.00 20.00
SBBE7 Bill Elliott T/50 10.00 25.00
SBCE1 Carl Edwards E/250 4.00 10.00
SBCE2 Carl Edwards D/150 4.00 10.00
SBCE3 Carl Edwards W/150 4.00 10.00
SBCE4 Carl Edwards A/100 5.00 12.00
SBCE5 Carl Edwards R/100 5.00 12.00
SBCE6 Carl Edwards D/75 5.00 12.00
SBCE7 Carl Edwards S/50 6.00 15.00
SBDE1 Dale Earnhardt E/25 30.00 80.00
SBDE2 Dale Earnhardt A/25 30.00 80.00
SBDE3 Dale Earnhardt R/20 30.00 80.00
SBDE4 Dale Earnhardt N/20 30.00 80.00
SBDE5 Dale Earnhardt H/15 30.00 80.00
SBDE6 Dale Earnhardt A/15 30.00 80.00
SBDE7 Dale Earnhardt R/10
SBDE8 Dale Earnhardt D/10
SBDE9 Dale Earnhardt T/5
SBDH1 Denny Hamlin H/250 4.00 10.00
SBDH2 Denny Hamlin A/150 4.00 10.00
SBDH3 Denny Hamlin M/150 4.00 10.00
SBDH4 Denny Hamlin L/100 5.00 12.00
SBDH5 Denny Hamlin I/75 5.00 12.00
SBDH6 Denny Hamlin N/50 6.00 15.00
SBDP1 Danica Patrick P/250 12.00 30.00
SBDP2 Danica Patrick A/150 12.00 30.00
SBDP3 Danica Patrick T/150 12.00 30.00
SBDP4 Danica Patrick R/100 15.00 40.00
SBDP5 Danica Patrick I/100 15.00 40.00
SBDP6 Danica Patrick C/75 15.00 40.00
SBDP7 Danica Patrick K/50 20.00 50.00
SBDR1 David Reutimann R/125 4.00 10.00
SBDR2 David Reutimann E/125 4.00 10.00
SBDR3 David Reutimann U/100 4.00 10.00
SBDR4 David Reutimann T/100 4.00 10.00
SBDR5 David Reutimann I/75 4.00 10.00
SBDR6 David Reutimann M/75 4.00 10.00
SBDR7 David Reutimann A/50 5.00 12.00
SBDR8 David Reutimann N/50 5.00 12.00
SBDR9 David Reutimann N/25 6.00 15.00
SBJB1 Jeff Burton B/250 3.00 8.00
SBJB2 Jeff Burton U/150 3.00 8.00
SBJB3 Jeff Burton R/150 3.00 8.00
SBJB4 Jeff Burton T/100 4.00 10.00
SBJB5 Jeff Burton O/75 4.00 10.00
SBJB6 Jeff Burton N/50 5.00 12.00
SBJG1 Jeff Gordon G/250 10.00 25.00
SBJG2 Jeff Gordon O/150 10.00 25.00
SBJG3 Jeff Gordon R/150 10.00 25.00
SBJG4 Jeff Gordon D/100 12.00 30.00
SBJG5 Jeff Gordon O/75 12.00 30.00
SBJG6 Jeff Gordon N/50 15.00 40.00
SBJJ1 Jimmie Johnson J/250 6.00 15.00
SBJJ2 Jimmie Johnson O/150 6.00 15.00
SBJJ3 Jimmie Johnson H/150 6.00 15.00
SBJJ4 Jimmie Johnson N/100 8.00 20.00
SBJJ5 Jimmie Johnson S/100 8.00 20.00
SBJJ6 Jimmie Johnson O/75 8.00 20.00
SBJJ7 Jimmie Johnson N/50 10.00 25.00
SBJL1 Joey Logano L/250 4.00 10.00
SBJL2 Joey Logano O/150 4.00 10.00
SBJL3 Joey Logano G/150 4.00 10.00
SBJL4 Joey Logano A/100 5.00 12.00
SBJL5 Joey Logano N/75 5.00 12.00
SBJL6 Joey Logano O/50 6.00 15.00
SBKB1 Kyle Busch B/250 5.00 12.00
SBKB2 Kyle Busch U/150 5.00 12.00
SBKB3 Kyle Busch S/100 6.00 15.00
SBKB4 Kyle Busch C/75 6.00 15.00
SBKB5 Kyle Busch H/50 8.00 20.00
SBKH1 Kevin Harvick H/250 5.00 12.00
SBKH2 Kevin Harvick A/150 5.00 12.00
SBKH3 Kevin Harvick R/150 5.00 12.00
SBKH4 Kevin Harvick V/100 6.00 15.00
SBKH5 Kevin Harvick I/100 6.00 15.00
SBKH6 Kevin Harvick C/75 6.00 15.00
SBKH7 Kevin Harvick K/50 8.00 20.00
SBKK1 Kasey Kahne K/250 4.00 10.00
SBKK2 Kasey Kahne A/150 4.00 10.00
SBKK3 Kasey Kahne H/100 5.00 12.00
SBKK4 Kasey Kahne N/75 5.00 12.00
SBKK5 Kasey Kahne E/50 6.00 15.00
SBMK1 Matt Kenseth K/250 4.00 10.00
SBMK2 Matt Kenseth E/150 4.00 10.00
SBMK3 Matt Kenseth N/150 4.00 10.00
SBMK4 Matt Kenseth S/100 5.00 12.00
SBMK5 Matt Kenseth E/100 5.00 12.00
SBMK6 Matt Kenseth T/75 5.00 12.00
SBMK7 Matt Kenseth H/50 6.00 15.00
SBMM1 Mark Martin M/250 4.00 10.00
SBMM2 Mark Martin A/150 4.00 10.00
SBMM3 Mark Martin R/150 4.00 10.00
SBMM4 Mark Martin T/100 5.00 12.00
SBMM5 Mark Martin I/75 5.00 12.00
SBMM6 Mark Martin N/50 6.00 15.00
SBMT1 Martin Truex Jr. T/250 3.00 8.00
SBMT2 Martin Truex Jr. R/150 3.00 8.00
SBMT3 Martin Truex Jr. U/150 3.00 8.00
SBMT4 Martin Truex Jr. E/75 4.00 10.00
SBMT5 Martin Truex Jr. X/75 4.00 10.00
SBMT6 Martin Truex Jr. J/50 5.00 12.00
SBMT7 Martin Truex Jr. R/25 6.00 15.00
SBTS1 Tony Stewart S/200 6.00 15.00
SBTS2 Tony Stewart T/150 6.00 15.00
SBTS3 Tony Stewart E/150 6.00 15.00
SBTS4 Tony Stewart W/100 8.00 20.00
SBTS5 Tony Stewart A/100 8.00 20.00
SBTS6 Tony Stewart R/75 8.00 20.00
SBTS7 Tony Stewart T/50 12.00 30.00
SBDEJR1 Dale Earnhardt Jr. E/125 12.00 30.00
SBDEJR2 Dale Earnhardt Jr. A/125 12.00 30.00
SBDEJR3 Dale Earnhardt Jr. R/125 12.00 30.00
SBDEJR4 Dale Earnhardt Jr. N/125 12.00 30.00
SBDEJR5 Dale Earnhardt Jr. H/125 12.00 30.00
SBDEJR6 Dale Earnhardt Jr. A/100 12.00 30.00
SBDEJR7 Dale Earnhardt Jr. R/100 12.00 30.00
SBDEJR8 Dale Earnhardt Jr. D/75 12.00 30.00
SBDEJR9 Dale Earnhardt Jr. T/75 12.00 30.00
SBDEJR10 Dale Earnhardt Jr. J/35 15.00 40.00
SBDEJR11 Dale Earnhardt Jr. R/35 15.00 40.00

2011 Press Pass FanFare
COMPLETE SET (100) 40.00 100.00
1 A.J. Allmendinger .60 1.50
2 Marcos Ambrose .60 1.50
3 Trevor Bayne CRC 1.25 3.00
4 Greg Biffle .50 1.25
5 Clint Bowyer .60 1.50
6 Jeff Burton .50 1.25
7 Kurt Busch .50 1.25
8 Kyle Busch .75 2.00
9 Landon Cassill CRC .60 1.50
10 Kevin Conway .50 1.25
11 Dale Earnhardt Jr. 1.25 3.00
12 Carl Edwards .60 1.50
13 David Gilliland .40 1.00
14 Jeff Gordon 1.25 3.00
15 Robby Gordon .40 1.00
16 Denny Hamlin .60 1.50
17 Kevin Harvick .75 2.00
18 Jimmie Johnson 1.00 2.50
19 Kasey Kahne .60 1.50
20 Matt Kenseth .60 1.50
21 Brad Keselowski .75 2.00
22 Travis Kvapil .40 1.00
23 Bobby Labonte .60 1.50
24 Joey Logano .60 1.50
25 Mark Martin .60 1.50
26 Jamie McMurray .60 1.50
27 Casey Mears .40 1.00
28 Paul Menard .40 1.00
29 Juan Pablo Montoya .60 1.50
30 Joe Nemechek .40 1.00
31 Ryan Newman .50 1.25
32 David Ragan .50 1.25
33 David Reutimann .50 1.25
34 Regan Smith .50 1.25
35 Tony Stewart 1.00 2.50
36 Martin Truex Jr .50 1.25
37 Brian Vickers .40 1.00
38 Michael Waltrip .75 2.00
39 J.J. Yeley .40 1.00
40 Justin Allgaier .50 1.25
41 Aric Almirola .50 1.25
42 Trevor Bayne 1.25 3.00
43 Jennifer Jo Cobb RC 1.50 4.00
44 Jason Leffler .50 1.25
45 Danica Patrick 2.50 6.00
46 Robert Richardson .40 1.00
47 Elliott Sadler .40 1.00
48 Brian Scott .40 1.00
49 Reed Sorenson .40 1.00
50 Ricky Stenhouse Jr. .60 1.50
51 Ryan Truex .60 1.50
52 Kenny Wallace .40 1.00
53 Mike Wallace .60 1.50
54 Steve Wallace .50 1.25
55 Josh Wise .40 1.00
56 James Buescher .40 1.00
57 Ricky Carmichael .60 1.50
58 Joey Coulter CWTS RC .60 1.50
59 Dusty Davis .60 1.50
60 Austin Dillon .75 2.00

61 Brendan Gaughan .40 1.00
62 Craig Goess .75 2.00
63 Ron Hornaday .40 1.00
64 Justin Johnson 1.00 2.50
65 Parker Kligerman CWTS RC .60 1.50
66 Justin Lofton .40 1.00
67 Johanna Long RC 1.00 2.50
68 Miguel Paludo RC .60 1.50
69 Max Papis .75 2.00
70 Timothy Peters .40 1.00
71 Nelson Piquet Jr RC .60 1.50
72 Johnny Sauter .40 1.00
73 Brad Sweet RC .75 2.00
74 Cole Whitt RC 1.25 3.00
75 Bobby Allison .50 1.25
76 Donnie Allison .50 1.25
77 Geoffrey Bodine .40 1.00
78 Dale Earnhardt 3.00 8.00
79 Bill Elliott 1.00 2.50
80 Harry Gant .50 1.25
81 Paul Goldsmith .40 1.00
82 Ernie Irvan .50 1.25
83 Dale Jarrett .60 1.50
84 Ned Jarrett .50 1.25
85 Alan Kulwicki 1.00 2.50
86 Terry Labonte .60 1.50
87 Fred Lorenzen .50 1.25
88 Dave Marcis .50 1.25
89 Benny Parsons .60 1.50
90 David Pearson .60 1.50
91 Lee Petty .50 1.25
92 Richard Petty 1.00 2.50
93 Rusty Wallace .60 1.50
94 Darrell Waltrip 1.00 2.50
95 Cale Yarborough .60 1.50
96 Joe Gibbs .50 1.25
97 Richard Childress .60 1.50
98 Jack Roush .50 1.25
99 Chip Ganassi .50 1.25
100 Carl Edwards CL .40 1.00

2011 Press Pass FanFare Blue Die Cuts
*BLUE: .5X TO 1.2X BASE
RETAIL ONLY PARALLEL

2011 Press Pass FanFare Emerald
*EMERALD/25: 2X TO 5X BASE
STATED PRINT RUN 25 SER.#'d SETS

2011 Press Pass FanFare Holofoil Die Cuts
*HOLO: .5X TO 1.2X BASE
*HOLO SPs: .8X TO 2X BASE
HOBBY ONLY PARALLEL
SPs: 11/14/35/45/78/92/94/96/97/98

2011 Press Pass FanFare Ruby Die Cuts
*RUBY DC/15: 2.5X TO 6X BASE
STATED PRINT RUN 15 SER.#'d SETS

2011 Press Pass FanFare Silver
*SILVER: 1.5X TO 4X BASE
STATED PRINT RUN 25 SER.#'d SETS

2011 Press Pass FanFare Autographs Bronze
STATED PRINT RUN 10-250
1 Justin Allgaier/120 4.00 10.00
2 A.J. Allmendinger/50 6.00 15.00
3 Aric Almirola/115 4.00 10.00
4 Marcos Ambrose/50 6.00 15.00
5 Trevor Bayne CUP/60 15.00 40.00
6 Trevor Bayne NNS/115 15.00 40.00
7 Greg Biffle/65 5.00 12.00
8 Clint Bowyer/65 6.00 15.00
9 James Buescher/200 3.00 8.00
10 Jeff Burton/50 5.00 12.00
11 Kurt Busch/50 5.00 12.00
12 Kyle Busch/20 20.00 50.00
13 Ricky Carmichael/200 5.00 12.00
14 Landon Cassill/65 6.00 15.00
16 Jennifer Jo Cobb/250 12.00 30.00
17 Kevin Conway/65 5.00 12.00
19 Joey Coulter/250 5.00 12.00
20 Dusty Davis/120 5.00 12.00
21 Austin Dillon/245 12.00 30.00
22 Dale Earnhardt Jr./10
23 Carl Edwards/25 8.00 20.00
25 Brendan Gaughan/125 3.00 8.00
27 David Gilliland/20 5.00 12.00
28 Craig Goess/250 6.00 15.00
29 Jeff Gordon/15 60.00 100.00
30 Robby Gordon/65 4.00 10.00
31 Denny Hamlin/10 EXCH
32 Kevin Harvick/25 25.00 60.00
33 Ron Hornaday/120 3.00 8.00
34 Jimmie Johnson/15 40.00 80.00
35 Justin Johnson/250 8.00 20.00
36 Kasey Kahne/35 8.00 20.00
37 Matt Kenseth/25 8.00 20.00
38 Brad Keselowski/70 10.00 25.00
39 Parker Kligerman/250 5.00 12.00
40 Travis Kvapil/20 5.00 12.00
41 Bobby Labonte/20 12.00 30.00
43 Justin Lofton/195 5.00 12.00
44 Joey Logano/50 6.00 15.00
45 Johanna Long/250 8.00 20.00
46 Tayler Malsam/120 3.00 8.00
47 Mark Martin/10
48 Eric McClure/250 4.00 10.00
49 Jamie McMurray/65 6.00 15.00
50 Casey Mears/65 4.00 10.00
51 Paul Menard/65 4.00 10.00
52 Juan Pablo Montoya/65 6.00 15.00
53 Joe Nemechek/65 4.00 10.00
54 Ryan Newman/50 5.00 12.00
55 Miguel Paludo/250 5.00 12.00
57 Max Papis/200 6.00 15.00
58 Danica Patrick/70 50.00 100.00
59 Timothy Peters/250 3.00 8.00
60 Nelson Piquet Jr/120 5.00 12.00
61 David Ragan/65 5.00 12.00
62 David Reutimann/65 5.00 12.00
63 Robert Richardson/250 3.00 8.00
65 Elliott Sadler/60 4.00 10.00
66 Johnny Sauter/190 3.00 8.00
67 Brian Scott/120 3.00 8.00
68 Regan Smith/65 5.00 12.00
69 Reed Sorenson/120 3.00 8.00
70 Ricky Stenhouse/120 5.00 12.00
71 Tony Stewart/35 15.00 40.00
72 Brad Sweet/200 6.00 15.00
73 Martin Truex Jr./55 5.00 12.00
74 Ryan Truex/200 5.00 12.00
75 Brian Vickers/55 4.00 10.00
76 Kenny Wallace/250 3.00 8.00
77 Mike Wallace/250 5.00 12.00
78 Steve Wallace/245 4.00 10.00
79 Michael Waltrip/10
80 Cole Whitt/250 10.00 25.00
81 Josh Wise/120 3.00 8.00
82 J.J. Yeley/65 4.00 10.00

2011 Press Pass FanFare Autographs Gold
*GOLD/90-150: .4X TO 1X BRONZE/115-250
*GOLD/75: .5X TO 1.2X BRONZE/115
*GOLD/40-75: .5X TO 1.2X BRONZE/60-70
*GOLD/25-35: .5X TO 1.2X BRONZE/50-60
*GOLD/15: .5X TO 1.2X BRONZE/25-35
STATED PRINT RUN 5-150
58 Danica Patrick/50 60.00 120.00

2011 Press Pass FanFare Autographs Silver
*SILVER/45-80: .5X TO 1.2X BRNZ/115-250
*SILVER/25: .6X TO 1.5X BRONZE/115
*SILVER/25: .5X TO 1.2X BRONZE/50-70
STATED PRINT RUN 5-80
15 Richard Childress/80 12.00 30.00
18 Kim Coon/50 25.00 50.00
24 Chip Ganassi/80 15.00 40.00
26 Joe Gibbs/80 15.00 40.00
42 Jason Leffler/50 5.00 12.00
56 Monica Palumbo/50 12.00 30.00
64 Jack Roush/80 15.00 40.00

2011 Press Pass FanFare Championship Caliber
COMPLETE SET (30) 60.00 120.00
COMP.SET w/o SPs (25) 20.00 50.00
STATED ODDS 1 PER PACK
CC1 Jimmie Johnson SP 10.00 20.00
CC2 Tony Stewart 1.25 3.00
CC3 Kurt Busch .60 1.50
CC4 Matt Kenseth .75 2.00
CC5 Jeff Gordon SP 10.00 20.00
CC6 Bobby Labonte .75 2.00
CC7 Dale Jarrett .75 2.00
CC8 Terry Labonte .75 2.00
CC9 Dale Earnhardt SP 10.00 20.00
CC10 Alan Kulwicki 1.25 3.00
CC11 Rusty Wallace .75 2.00
CC12 Bill Elliott SP 5.00 12.00
CC13 Darrell Waltrip 1.25 3.00
CC14 Bobby Allison .60 1.50
CC15 Richard Petty SP 10.00 20.00
CC16 Cale Yarborough .75 2.00
CC17 Benny Parsons .75 2.00
CC18 David Pearson .75 2.00
CC19 Ned Jarrett .60 1.50
CC20 Rex White .60 1.50
CC21 Lee Petty .60 1.50
CC22 Brad Keselowski 1.00 2.50
CC23 Kyle Busch 1.00 2.50
CC24 Clint Bowyer .75 2.00
CC25 Carl Edwards .75 2.00
CC26 Kevin Harvick 1.00 2.50
CC27 Martin Truex Jr. .60 1.50
CC28 Ron Hornaday .50 1.25
CC29 Bobby Labonte .75 2.00
CC30 Ralph Earnhardt 1.25 3.00

2011 Press Pass FanFare Magnificent Materials
STATED PRINT RUN 50-225
*HOLO/20-50: .6X TO 1.5X BASIC MATERIAL
MMAA A.J. Allmendinger/199 4.00 10.00
MMMA Marcos Ambrose/175 4.00 10.00
MMTB Trevor Bayne/199 8.00 20.00
MMGB Greg Biffle/199 3.00 8.00
MMCB Clint Bowyer/199 4.00 10.00
MMJB Jeff Burton/199 3.00 8.00
MMKB Kurt Busch/199 3.00 8.00
MMKB Kyle Busch/199 5.00 12.00
MMLC Landon Cassill/199 4.00 10.00
MMKC Kevin Conway/199 3.00 8.00
MMDE Dale Earnhardt Jr./199 8.00 20.00
MMCE Carl Edwards/199 4.00 10.00
MMDG David Gilliland/199 2.50 6.00
MMJG Jeff Gordon/199 8.00 20.00
MMRG Robby Gordon/199 2.50 6.00
MMDH Denny Hamlin/199 4.00 10.00
MMKH Kevin Harvick/199 5.00 12.00
MMJJ Jimmie Johnson/199 6.00 15.00
MMKK Kasey Kahne/199 4.00 10.00
MMMK Matt Kenseth/225 4.00 10.00
MMBK Brad Keselowski/199 5.00 12.00
MMTK Travis Kvapil/199 2.50 6.00
MMBL Bobby Labonte/199 4.00 10.00
MMJL Joey Logano/199 4.00 10.00
MMMM Mark Martin/199 4.00 10.00
MMJM Jamie McMurray/199 4.00 10.00
MMCM Casey Mears/199 2.50 6.00
MMPM Paul Menard/199 2.50 6.00
MMJM Juan Pablo Montoya/199 4.00 10.00
MMJN Joe Nemechek/199 2.50 6.00
MMRN Ryan Newman/225 3.00 8.00
MMDR David Ragan/199 3.00 8.00
MMDR David Reutimann/225 3.00 8.00
MMRS Regan Smith/199 3.00 8.00
MMTS Tony Stewart/199 6.00 15.00
MMMT Martin Truex Jr./199 3.00 8.00
MMBV Brian Vickers/199 2.50 6.00
MMMW Michael Waltrip/199 5.00 12.00
MMJY J.J. Yeley/199 2.50 6.00
MMJB James Buescher/199 2.50 6.00
MMRC Ricky Carmichael/199 4.00 10.00
MMJC Joey Coulter/199 4.00 10.00
MMDD Dusty Davis/199 4.00 10.00
MMAD Austin Dillon/199 5.00 12.00
MMBG Brendan Gaughan/199 2.50 6.00
MMRH Ron Hornaday/199 2.50 6.00
MMPK Parker Kligerman/199 4.00 10.00
MMJL Justin Lofton/199 2.50 6.00
MMJL Johanna Long/199 6.00 15.00
MMTM Tayler Malsam/75 3.00 8.00
MMMP Miguel Paludo/199 4.00 10.00
MMMP Max Papis/199 5.00 12.00
MMTP Timothy Peters/199 2.50 6.00
MMNP Nelson Piquet Jr/199 4.00 10.00
MMCR Clay Rogers/199 3.00 8.00
MMJS Johnny Sauter/199 2.50 6.00
MMBS Brad Sweet/199 5.00 12.00
MMCW Cole Whitt/145 8.00 20.00
MMJA Justin Allgaier/225 3.00 8.00
MMAA Aric Almirola/199 3.00 8.00
MMTB Trevor Bayne/199 8.00 20.00
MMJC Jennifer Jo Cobb 10.00 25.00
MMJL Jason Leffler/199 3.00 8.00
MMDP Danica Patrick/199 12.00 30.00
MMRR Robert Richardson/199 2.50 6.00
MMES Elliott Sadler/199 2.50 6.00
MMBS Brian Scott/199 2.50 6.00
MMRS2 Reed Sorenson/199 2.50 6.00
MMRS Ricky Stenhouse/199 5.00 12.00
MMRT Ryan Truex/225 4.00 10.00
MMKW Kenny Wallace/199 2.50 6.00
MMMW Mike Wallace/199 4.00 10.00
MMSW Steve Wallace/199 3.00 8.00
MMJW Josh Wise/50 3.00 8.00

2011 Press Pass FanFare Magnificent Materials Dual Swatches
STATED PRINT RUN 50 SER.#'d SETS
MMDTB Trevor Bayne 12.00 30.00
MMDJB Jeff Burton 5.00 12.00
MMDKB Kyle Busch 8.00 20.00
MMDDE Dale Earnhardt Jr. 12.00 30.00
MMDCE Carl Edwards 6.00 15.00
MMDDG David Gilliland 4.00 10.00
MMDJG Jeff Gordon 12.00 30.00
MMDDH Denny Hamlin 6.00 15.00
MMDKH Kevin Harvick 8.00 20.00
MMDJJ Jimmie Johnson 10.00 25.00
MMDKK Kasey Kahne 6.00 15.00
MMDMK Matt Kenseth 6.00 15.00
MMDBK Brad Keselowski 8.00 20.00
MMDTK Travis Kvapil 4.00 10.00
MMDBL Bobby Labonte 6.00 15.00
MMDJL Joey Logano 6.00 15.00
MMDMM Mark Martin 6.00 15.00
MMDJM Jamie McMurray 6.00 15.00
MMDCM Casey Mears 4.00 10.00
MMDJM Juan Pablo Montoya 6.00 15.00
MMDJN Joe Nemechek 4.00 10.00
MMDRN Ryan Newman 5.00 12.00
MMDDR David Ragan 5.00 12.00
MMDDR David Reutimann 5.00 12.00
MMDTS Tony Stewart 10.00 25.00
MMDMT Martin Truex Jr. 5.00 12.00
MMDBV Brian Vickers 4.00 10.00
MMDMW Michael Waltrip 8.00 20.00
MMDJB James Buescher 4.00 10.00
MMDRC Ricky Carmichael 6.00 15.00
MMDJC Joey Coulter 6.00 15.00
MMDDD Dusty Davis/40 6.00 15.00
MMDAD Austin Dillon 8.00 20.00
MMDBG Brendan Gaughan 4.00 10.00
MMDRH Ron Hornaday 4.00 10.00
MMDJL Justin Lofton 4.00 10.00
MMDJL Johanna Long 10.00 25.00
MMDMP Max Papis 8.00 20.00
MMDJS Johnny Sauter 4.00 10.00
MMDBS Brad Sweet 8.00 20.00
MMDCW Cole Whitt 12.00 30.00
MMDJA Justin Allgaier 5.00 12.00
MMDAA Aric Almirola 5.00 12.00
MMDTB Trevor Bayne 12.00 30.00
MMDJC Jennifer Jo Cobb 15.00 40.00
MMDJL4 Jason Leffler 5.00 12.00
MMDDP Danica Patrick 25.00 60.00
MMDRR Robert Richardson 4.00 10.00
MMDES Elliott Sadler 4.00 10.00
MMDBS Brian Scott 4.00 10.00
MMDRS Reed Sorenson 4.00 10.00
MMSRS Ricky Stenhouse 6.00 15.00
MMDJW Josh Wise 4.00 10.00

2011 Press Pass FanFare Magnificent Materials Signatures
STATED PRINT RUN 25-99
*HOLOFOIL/25: .5X TO 1.2X AUTO/50-99
MMSEAA Aric Almirola 8.00 20.00
MMSEBG Brendan Gaughan 6.00 15.00
MMSEBS2 Brad Sweet 8.00 20.00
MMSEBS Brian Scott 6.00 15.00
MMSECE Carl Edwards/50 10.00 25.00
MMSEDD Dusty Davis/97 10.00 25.00
MMSEDE Dale Earnhardt Jr./25 60.00 120.00
MMSEDG David Gilliland 6.00 15.00
MMSEDH Denny Hamlin 10.00 25.00
MMSEDP Danica Patrick/25 75.00 150.00
MMSEES Elliott Sadler 6.00 15.00
MMSEJA Justin Allgaier 8.00 20.00
MMSEJB James Buescher 6.00 15.00
MMSEJG Jeff Gordon/25 75.00 150.00
MMSEJJ Jimmie Johnson/25 50.00 100.00
MMSEJL2 Justin Lofton/96 6.00 15.00
MMSEJL Jason Leffler 8.00 20.00
MMSEJN Joe Nemechek 6.00 15.00
MMSEJS Johnny Sauter 6.00 15.00
MMSEJW Josh Wise 6.00 15.00
MMSEKB Kyle Busch/50 12.00 30.00
MMSEKH Kevin Harvick/50 12.00 30.00
MMSEKK Kasey Kahne/25 40.00 100.00
MMSEMK Matt Kenseth/50 12.00 30.00
MMSEMM Mark Martin/25 12.00 30.00
MMSEMP Max Papis 8.00 20.00
MMSENP Nelson Piquet Jr. 10.00 25.00
MMSERC Ricky Carmichael 10.00 25.00
MMSERH Ron Hornaday 6.00 15.00
MMSERS Reed Sorenson 6.00 15.00
MMSERS2 Ricky Stenhouse Jr. 12.00 30.00
MMSERT Ryan Truex 10.00 25.00
MMSETB Trevor Bayne/50 20.00 50.00
MMSETK Travis Kvapil/50 6.00 15.00
MMSETM Tayler Malsam 6.00 15.00
MMSETS Tony Stewart/25 25.00 60.00

2011 Press Pass FanFare Promotional Memorabilia
RETAILER INCENTIVE 1 PER CASE
PMDE Dale Earnhardt Jr. 25.00 60.00
PMJG Jeff Gordon 15.00 40.00
PMJJ Jimmie Johnson 6.00 15.00

2011 Press Pass FanFare Rookie Standouts
COMPLETE SET (15) 15.00 40.00
STATED ODDS 1:3
RS1 Trevor Bayne 1.50 4.00
RS2 Joey Logano .75 2.00
RS3 Juan Pablo Montoya .75 2.00
RS4 Denny Hamlin .75 2.00
RS5 Kyle Busch SP 5.00 12.00
RS6 Kasey Kahne .75 2.00
RS7 Jamie McMurray .75 2.00
RS8 Ryan Newman .60 1.50
RS9 Kevin Harvick 1.00 2.50
RS10 Matt Kenseth .75 2.00
RS11 Tony Stewart SP 8.00 20.00
RS12 Jeff Burton .60 1.50
RS13 Jeff Gordon SP 8.00 20.00
RS14 Dale Earnhardt SP 12.50 25.00
RS15 Richard Petty SP 6.00 15.00

2012 Press Pass Fanfare
WAX BOX HOBBY 100.00 135.00
1 Aric Almirola .50 1.25
2 Marcos Ambrose .60 1.50
3 Trevor Bayne .60 1.50
4 Greg Biffle .50 1.25
5 Dave Blaney .40 1.00
6 Clint Bowyer .60 1.50
7 Jeff Burton .50 1.25
8 Kurt Busch .50 1.25
9 Kyle Busch .75 2.00
10 Kyle Busch .75 2.00
11 Landon Cassill .50 1.25
12 Dale Earnhardt Jr 1.25 3.00
13 Dale Earnhardt Jr 1.25 3.00
14 Carl Edwards .60 1.50
15 David Gilliland .40 1.00
16 Jeff Gordon 1.25 3.00
17 Jeff Gordon 1.25 3.00
18 Denny Hamlin .60 1.50
19 Kevin Harvick .75 2.00
20 Jimmie Johnson 1.00 2.50
21 Jimmie Johnson 1.00 2.50
22 Kasey Kahne .60 1.50
23 Matt Kenseth .60 1.50
24 Brad Keselowski .75 2.00
25 Bobby Labonte .60 1.50
26 Joey Logano .60 1.50
27 Mark Martin .60 1.50
28 Michael McDowell .50 1.25
29 Jamie McMurray .60 1.50
30 Casey Mears .40 1.00
31 Paul Menard .40 1.00
32 Juan Pablo Montoya .60 1.50
33 Joe Nemechek .40 1.00
34 Ryan Newman .50 1.25
35 Danica Patrick CRC 4.00 10.00
36 David Ragan .50 1.25
37 David Reutimann .50 1.25
38 Regan Smith .50 1.25
39 Tony Stewart 1.00 2.50
40 Tony Stewart 1.00 2.50
41 Martin Truex Jr .50 1.25
42 Michael Waltrip .60 1.50
43 Josh Wise CRC .40 1.00
44 Justin Allgaier NNS .50 1.25
45 Trevor Bayne NNS .60 1.50
46 Jason Bowles NNS RC .75 2.00
47 Kurt Busch NNS .50 1.25
48 Kyle Busch NNS .75 2.00
49 Austin Dillon NNS .75 2.00
50 Jeffrey Earnhardt NNS RC 1.00 2.50
51 Sam Hornish Jr. NNS .50 1.25
52 Johanna Long NNS 1.00 2.50
53 Tayler Malsam NNS .40 1.00
54 Travis Pastrana NNS 1.00 2.50
55 Danica Patrick NNS 2.00 5.00
56 Elliott Sadler NNS .40 1.00
57 Brian Scott NNS .40 1.00
58 Ricky Stenhouse Jr. NNS .60 1.50
59 Ryan Truex NNS .50 1.25
60 Kenny Wallace NNS .40 1.00
61 Cole Whitt NNS .50 1.25
62 Dakoda Armstrong CWTS RC .75 2.00
63 James Buescher CWTS .40 1.00
64 Jeb Burton CWTS RC 1.00 2.50
65 Ward Burton CWTS .40 1.00
66 Ross Chastain CWTS RC .60 1.50
67 Joey Coulter CWTS .40 1.00
68 Ty Dillon CWTS RC 1.00 2.50
69 Paulie Harraka CWTS RC .60 1.50
70 Ron Hornaday CWTS .40 1.00
71 John King CWTS RC .75 2.00
72 Parker Kligerman CWTS .40 1.00
73 Justin Lofton CWTS .40 1.00
74 Miguel Paludo CWTS .40 1.00
75 Timothy Peters CWTS .40 1.00
76 Jorge Arteaga YG RC .75 2.00
77 Ryan Blaney YG RC 1.00 2.50
78 Gray Gaulding YG RC .75 2.00
79 Darrell Wallace Jr. YG RC 1.25 3.00
80 Bobby Allison LEG .40 1.00
81 Davey Allison LEG 1.00 2.50
82 Donnie Allison LEG .50 1.25
83 Dale Earnhardt LEG 2.00 5.00
84 Bill Elliott LEG 1.00 2.50
85 Harry Gant LEG .50 1.25
86 Ernie Irvan LEG .50 1.25
87 Dale Jarrett LEG .60 1.50
88 Ned Jarrett LEG .50 1.25
89 Alan Kulwicki LEG 1.00 2.50
90 Terry Labonte LEG .60 1.50
91 Fred Lorenzen LEG .40 1.00
92 Cotton Owens LEG .40 1.00
93 Benny Parsons LEG .60 1.50
94 David Pearson LEG .60 1.50
95 Richard Petty LEG 1.00 2.50
96 Tim Richmond LEG .50 1.25
97 Rusty Wallace LEG .60 1.50
98 Darrell Waltrip LEG 1.00 2.50
99 Cale Yarborough LEG .60 1.50
100 Dale Earnhardt Jr CL .75 2.00

2012 Press Pass Fanfare Blue Foil Die Cuts
*BLUE DIE CUT: .8X TO 2X BASIC CARDS
*BLUE DC SP: 1.2X TO 3X BASIC CARDS
ONE PER RETAIL PACK
SP STATED ODDS 1:40

2012 Press Pass Fanfare Holofoil Die Cuts
*HOLOFOIL DC: .5X TO 1.2X BASIC CARDS
*HOLOFOIL DC SP: .8X TO 2X BASIC CARDS
ONE PER PACK
SP STATED ODDS 1:40

2012 Press Pass Fanfare Sapphire
*SAPPHIRE/20: 2.5X TO 6X BASIC CARDS
SAPPHIRE PRINT RUN 20 SER.#'d SETS
35 Danica Patrick 12.00 30.00

2012 Press Pass Fanfare Silver
*SILVER/25: 2X TO 5X BASIC CARDS
SILVER PRINT RUN 25 SER.#'d SETS
35 Danica Patrick 10.00 25.00

2012 Press Pass Fanfare Autographs Blue
*BLUE/25: .8X TO 2X SILVER/275-399
*BLUE/25: .6X TO 1.5X SILVER/160-199
*BLUE/20: .8X TO 2X SILVER/165
BLUE STATED PRINT RUN 1-25

2012 Press Pass Fanfare Autographs Gold
*GOLD/99-150: .5X TO 1.2X SILVER/275-399
*GOLD/99: .4X TO 1X SILVER/125-199
*GOLD/75-80: .5X TO 1.2X SILVER/125-175
*GOLD/50-75: .4X TO 1X SILVER/99
*GOLD/25: .5X TO 1.2X SILVER/50-75
*GOLD/15: .6X TO 1.5X SILVER/50
GOLD STATED PRINT RUN 1-150
JB1 Jason Bowles NNS/99 10.00 25.00
LC Landon Cassill/150 5.00 12.00
WB Ward Burton CWTS/99 4.00 10.00

2012 Press Pass Fanfare Autographs Red
*RED/75: .6X TO 1.5X SILVER/275-399
*RED/50-75: .5X TO 1.2X SILVER/150-199
*RED/25: .6X TO 1.5X SILVER/99-150
*RED/20: .8X TO 2X SILVER/99
RED STATED PRINT RUN 1-75
GB Greg Biffle/75 5.00 12.00

2012 Press Pass Fanfare Autographs Silver
STATED PRINT RUN 1-399
AA Aric Almirola/75 6.00 15.00
AD Austin Dillon NNS/165 10.00 25.00
BL Bobby Labonte/150 5.00 12.00
BS Brian Scott NNS/399 3.00 8.00
CB Clint Bowyer/150 5.00 12.00
CE Carl Edwards/75 6.00 15.00
CW Cole Whitt NNS/175 4.00 10.00
DA Dakoda Armstrong CWTS/299 5.00 12.00
DB Dave Blaney/299 4.00 10.00
DE Dale Earnhardt Jr/5
DG David Gilliland/299 2.50 6.00
DH Denny Hamlin/50 12.00 30.00
DP Danica Patrick NNS/1
DR David Ragan/299 4.00 10.00
DR David Reutimann/299 3.00 8.00
DW Darrell Wallace Jr. YG/399 6.00 15.00
ES Elliott Sadler NNS/75 4.00 10.00
GG Gray Gaulding YG/399 5.00 12.00
JA1 Justin Allgaier NNS/50 5.00 12.00
JA2 Jorge Arteaga YG/399 4.00 10.00
JB1 Jason Bowles NNS/175 5.00 12.00
JB2 James Buescher CWTS/299 2.50 6.00
JB3 Jeb Burton CWTS/299 6.00 15.00
JB4 Jeff Burton/50 5.00 12.00
JC Joey Coulter CWTS/299 2.50 6.00
JE Jeffrey Earnhardt NNS/299 8.00 20.00
JG Jeff Gordon/20 30.00 80.00
JJ Jimmie Johnson/20 30.00 60.00
JK John King CWTS/299 4.00 10.00
JL3 Justin Lofton CWTS/175 3.00 8.00
JL1 Joey Logano/5
JL2 Johanna Long NNS/175 6.00 15.00
JM Jamie McMurray/99 5.00 12.00
JN Joe Nemechek/125 3.00 8.00
JPM Juan Pablo Montoya/50 5.00 12.00
JW Josh Wise/175 3.00 8.00
KB1 Kurt Busch/175 4.00 10.00
KB2 Kurt Busch NNS/99 4.00 10.00
KB3 Kyle Busch/50 15.00 40.00
KB4 Kyle Busch NNS/99 10.00 25.00
KH Kevin Harvick/50 8.00 20.00
KK Kasey Kahne/50 15.00 40.00
KW Kenny Wallace NNS/299 2.50 6.00
LC Landon Cassill/399 3.00 8.00
MA Marcos Ambrose/50 25.00 50.00
MK Matt Kenseth/75 6.00 15.00
MM1 Mark Martin/5
MM2 Michael McDowell/299 3.00 8.00
MP Miguel Paludo CWTS/299 2.50 6.00
MW Michael Waltrip/15 10.00 25.00
PH Paulie Harraka CWTS/175 5.00 12.00
PK Parker Kligerman CWTS/299 4.00 10.00
PM Paul Menard/199 3.00 8.00
RB Ryan Blaney YG/399 6.00 15.00
RC Ross Chastain CWTS/299 4.00 10.00
RH Ron Hornaday CWTS/160 3.00 8.00
RN Ryan Newman/99 6.00 15.00
RS1 Regan Smith/175 4.00 10.00
RS2 Ricky Stenhouse Jr. NNS/175 8.00 20.00
RT Ryan Truex NNS/275 3.00 8.00
SH Sam Hornish Jr. NNS/299 3.00 8.00
TB1 Trevor Bayne/75 6.00 15.00
TB2 Trevor Bayne NNS/99 5.00 12.00
TD Ty Dillon CWTS/175 10.00 25.00
TM Tayler Malsam NNS/299 2.50 6.00
TP1 Travis Pastrana NNS/10
TP2 Timothy Peters CWTS/299 2.50 6.00
TS Tony Stewart/10
WB Ward Burton CWTS/175 3.00 8.00

2012 Press Pass Fanfare Magnificent Materials
STATED PRINT RUN 50-299
MMAA Aric Almirola/299 2.50 6.00
MMAD Austin Dillon/299 4.00 10.00
MMBK Brad Keselowski/250 4.00 10.00
MMBL Bobby Labonte/25 6.00 15.00
MMBS Brian Scott/125 2.50 6.00
MMCB Clint Bowyer/250 3.00 8.00
MMCE Carl Edwards/250 3.00 8.00
MMCM Casey Mears/75 3.00 8.00
MMCW Cole Whitt/299 2.50 6.00
MMDA Dakoda Armstrong/150 5.00 12.00
MMDB Dave Blaney/250 2.00 5.00
MMDEJR Dale Earnhardt Jr/250 8.00 20.00
MMDEJR2 Dale Earnhardt Jr/235 8.00 20.00
MMDG David Gilliland/250 3.00 8.00
MMDH Denny Hamlin/250 4.00 10.00
MMDP Danica Patrick/250 8.00 20.00
MMDP2 Danica Patrick/250 8.00 20.00
MMDR David Ragan/75 4.00 10.00
MMDR2 David Reutimann/75 4.00 10.00
MMES Elliott Sadler/75 2.50 6.00
MMGB Greg Biffle/250 2.50 6.00
MMGG Gray Gaulding/125 4.00 10.00
MMJA Justin Allgaier/250 2.50 6.00
MMJA2 Jorge Arteaga/150 4.00 10.00
MMJB Jeff Burton/250 2.50 6.00
MMJB2 Jason Bowles/125 4.00 10.00
MMJB3 James Buescher/250 2.00 5.00
MMJB4 Jeb Burton/275 5.00 12.00
MMJC Joey Coulter/99 2.50 6.00
MMJE Jeffrey Earnhardt/125 6.00 15.00
MMJG Jeff Gordon/250 6.00 15.00
MMJG2 Jeff Gordon/250 6.00 15.00
MMJJ Jimmie Johnson/125 6.00 15.00
MMJL Joey Logano/125 4.00 10.00
MMJL2 Johanna Long/250 5.00 12.00
MMJL3 Justin Lofton/250 2.00 5.00
MMJM Jamie McMurray/250 3.00 8.00
MMJN Joe Nemechek/50 3.00 8.00
MMJPM Juan Pablo Montoya/250 3.00 8.00
MMJW Josh Wise/299 2.00 5.00
MMKH Kevin Harvick/250 4.00 10.00
MMKK Kasey Kahne/125 4.00 10.00
MMKUB Kurt Busch/250 2.50 6.00
MMKUB2 Kurt Busch/75 4.00 10.00
MMKW Kenny Wallace/250 2.00 5.00
MMKYB Kyle Busch/250 4.00 10.00
MMKYB3 Kyle Busch/99 5.00 12.00
MMLC Landon Cassill/75 4.00 10.00
MMMA Marcos Ambrose/250 6.00 15.00
MMMD Maryeve Dufault/199 4.00 10.00
MMMK Matt Kenseth/299 3.00 8.00
MMMM Mark Martin/250 3.00 8.00
MMMM2 Michael McDowell/250 2.50 6.00
MMMP Miguel Paludo/150 2.50 6.00
MMMT Martin Truex Jr/250 2.50 6.00
MMMW Michael Waltrip/299 3.00 8.00
MMPH Paulie Harraka/250 3.00 8.00
MMPK Parker Kligerman/150 2.50 6.00
MMPM Paul Menard/250 2.00 5.00
MMRB Ryan Blaney/125 6.00 15.00
MMRC Ross Chastain/99 4.00 10.00
MMRH Ron Hornaday/199 2.00 5.00
MMRN Ryan Newman/250 2.50 6.00
MMRS Regan Smith/125 5.00 12.00
MMRS2 Ricky Stenhouse Jr/250 3.00 8.00
MMRT Ryan Truex/175 3.00 8.00
MMSH Sam Hornish Jr./250 2.50 6.00
MMTB Trevor Bayne/250 3.00 8.00
MMTB2 Trevor Bayne/250 3.00 8.00
MMTD Ty Dillon/199 5.00 12.00
MMTM Tayler Malsam/250 2.00 5.00
MMTP Travis Pastrana/250 4.00 10.00
MMTP2 Timothy Peters/250 2.00 5.00
MMTS Tony Stewart/250 6.00 15.00
MMTS2 Tony Stewart/250 6.00 15.00
MMWB Ward Burton/199 2.00 5.00

2012 Press Pass Fanfare Magnificent Materials Gold
*GOLD/99-125: .5X TO 1.2X MAT/199-299
*GOLD/75: .6X TO 1.5X MAT/175-275
*GOLD/50-75: .5X TO 1.2X MAT/99-150
*GOLD/50: .4X TO 1X MAT/50/75
*GOLD/75: .3X TO .8X MAT/25
GOLD STATED PRINT RUN 10-125

2012 Press Pass Fanfare Magnificent Materials Dual Swatches
*DUAL/50: .6X TO 1.5X MAT/175-299
*DUAL/50: .5X TO 1.2X MAT/99-150
*DUAL/50: .4X TO 1X MAT/50-75
*DUAL/50: .3X TO .8X MAT/25
STATED PRINT RUN 50 SER.#'d SETS

2012 Press Pass Fanfare Magnificent Materials Signatures
STATED PRINT RUN 10-99
*BLUE/25: .5X TO 1.2X AUTO/95-99
AA Aric Almirola/99 8.00 20.00
AD Austin Dillon NNS/99 20.00 40.00
CB Clint Bowyer/99 10.00 25.00
CE Carl Edwards/25 12.00 30.00
CW Cole Whitt NNS/99 8.00 20.00
DE Dale Earnhardt Jr/25 25.00 60.00
DH Denny Hamlin/99 10.00 25.00
DP Danica Patrick NNS/10
ES Elliott Sadler NNS/99 6.00 15.00
JA Justin Allgaier NNS/99 6.00 15.00
JB1 Jason Bowles NNS/99 12.00 30.00
JB2 Jeff Burton/99 8.00 20.00
JG Jeff Gordon/25 25.00 60.00
JJ Jimmie Johnson/25 20.00 50.00
JL1 Justin Lofton CWTS/99 6.00 15.00
JL2 Joey Logano/95 12.00 30.00
JL3 Johanna Long NNS/99 15.00 40.00
JW Josh Wise/99 6.00 15.00
KB Kyle Busch/25 15.00 40.00
KH Kevin Harvick/25 15.00 40.00
KK Kasey Kahne/25 12.00 30.00
MA Marcos Ambrose/99 12.00 30.00
MM Mark Martin/25 12.00 30.00
MT Martin Truex Jr/99 8.00 20.00
PH Paulie Harraka CWTS/99 10.00 25.00
PM Paul Menard/99 6.00 15.00
RH Ron Hornaday CWTS/99 6.00 15.00
RN Ryan Newman/99 6.00 15.00
RS1 Regan Smith/99 8.00 20.00
RS2 Ricky Stenhouse Jr. NNS/99 10.00 25.00
RT Ryan Truex NNS/99 8.00 20.00
TB Trevor Bayne/99 10.00 25.00
TD Ty Dillon CWTS/99 12.00 30.00
TP Travis Pastrana NNS/25 20.00 50.00
TS Tony Stewart/25 30.00 60.00
WB Ward Burton CWTS/99 6.00 15.00

2012 Press Pass Fanfare Power Rankings
STATED ODDS 1:1, SP ODDS 1:40
PR1 Greg Biffle .60 1.50
PR2 Matt Kenseth .75 2.00
PR3 Kyle Busch SP 5.00 12.00
PR4 Denny Hamlin SP 5.00 12.00
PR5 Jimmie Johnson 1.25 3.00
PR6 Dale Earnhardt Jr SP 6.00 15.00
PR7 Brad Keselowski 1.00 2.50
PR8 Kasey Kahne .75 2.00
PR9 Martin Truex Jr .60 1.50
PR10 Carl Edwards .75 2.00
PR11 Tony Stewart SP 5.00 12.00
PR12 Kevin Harvick SP 6.00 15.00
PR13 Clint Bowyer .75 2.00
PR14 Ryan Newman .60 1.50
PR15 Paul Menard .50 1.25

2012 Press Pass Fanfare Showtime
STATED ODDS 1:3
S1 Dale Earnhardt Jr's Car 1.50 4.00
S2 Jeff Gordon's Car 1.50 4.00
S3 Jimmie Johnson's Car 1.25 3.00
S4 Kasey Kahne's Car .75 2.00
S5 Tony Stewart's Car 1.25 3.00
S6 Danica Patrick's Car 2.50 6.00
S7 Carl Edwards's Car .75 2.00
S8 Kyle Busch's Car 1.00 2.50
S9 Denny Hamlin's Car .75 2.00
S10 Matt Kenseth's Car .75 2.00

2013 Press Pass Fanfare
1 Aric Almirola .50 1.25
2 Marcos Ambrose .60 1.50
3 Marcos Ambrose .60 1.50
4 Trevor Bayne .60 1.50
5 Greg Biffle .50 1.25
6 Greg Biffle .50 1.25
7 Clint Bowyer .60 1.50
8 Clint Bowyer .60 1.50
9 Jeff Burton .50 1.25
10 Jeff Burton .50 1.25
11 Kurt Busch .50 1.25
12 Kyle Busch .75 2.00
13 Kyle Busch .75 2.00
14 Dale Earnhardt Jr. 1.25 3.00
15 Dale Earnhardt Jr. 1.25 3.00
16 Carl Edwards .60 1.50
17 Carl Edwards .60 1.50
18 David Gilliland .40 1.00
19 Jeff Gordon 1.25 3.00
20 Jeff Gordon 1.25 3.00
21 Denny Hamlin .60 1.50
22 Denny Hamlin .60 1.50
23 Kevin Harvick .75 2.00
24 Kevin Harvick .75 2.00
25 Jimmie Johnson 1.00 2.50
26 Kasey Kahne .60 1.50
27 Kasey Kahne .60 1.50
28 Matt Kenseth .60 1.50
29 Matt Kenseth .60 1.50
30 Brad Keselowski .75 2.00
31 Brad Keselowski .75 2.00
32 Travis Kvapil .40 1.00
33 Bobby Labonte .60 1.50
34 Joey Logano .60 1.50
35 Joey Logano .60 1.50
36 Mark Martin .60 1.50
37 Mark Martin .60 1.50
38 Michael McDowell .50 1.25
39 Jamie McMurray .60 1.50
40 Casey Mears .40 1.00
41 Paul Menard .40 1.00
42 Paul Menard .40 1.00
43 Juan Pablo Montoya .60 1.50
44 Ryan Newman .50 1.25
45 Ryan Newman .50 1.25
46 Danica Patrick 1.50 4.00
47 Danica Patrick 1.50 4.00
48 David Ragan .50 1.25
49 David Reutimann .50 1.25
50 Regan Smith .50 1.25
51 Scott Speed .40 1.00
52 Ricky Stenhouse Jr. CRC .60 1.50
53 Ricky Stenhouse Jr. .60 1.50
54 Tony Stewart 1.00 2.50
55 Tony Stewart 1.00 2.50
56 David Stremme .40 1.00
57 Martin Truex .50 1.25
58 Martin Truex .50 1.25
59 Michael Waltrip .60 1.50
60 Josh Wise .40 1.00
61 Justin Allgaier NNS .50 1.25
62 Trevor Bayne NNS .60 1.50
63 Austin Dillon NNS .75 2.00
64 Ty Dillon NNS .40 1.00
65 Jeffrey Earnhardt NNS .60 1.50
66 Sam Hornish Jr NNS .50 1.25
67 Parker Kligerman NNS .40 1.00
68 Kyle Larson NNS RC 5.00 12.00
69 Johanna Long NNS .60 1.50
70 Hal Martin NNS RC .40 1.00
71 Travis Pastrana NNS .60 1.50
72 Nelson Piquet Jr NNS .50 1.25
73 Elliott Sadler NNS .40 1.00
74 Brian Scott NNS .40 1.00
75 Regan Smith NNS .50 1.25
76 Brad Sweet NNS .50 1.25
77 Brian Vickers NNS .40 1.00
78 Ryan Blaney CWTS .50 1.25
79 James Buescher CWTS .40 1.00
80 Jeb Burton CWTS .50 1.25
81 Jennifer Jo Cobb CWTS .60 1.50
82 Ty Dillon CWTS .60 1.50
83 Brendan Gaughan CWTS .40 1.00
84 Brennan Newberry CWTS RC .50 1.25
85 Miguel Paludo CWTS .40 1.00
86 Bobby Allison LEG .50 1.25
87 Davey Allison LEG 1.00 2.50
88 Donnie Allison LEG .50 1.25
89 Bill Elliott LEG 1.00 2.50
90 Terry Labonte LEG .60 1.50
91 David Pearson LEG .60 1.50
92 Richard Petty LEG 1.00 2.50
93 Darrell Waltrip LEG 1.00 2.50
94 Cale Yarborough LEG .60 1.50
95 Annabeth Barnes YG RC .60 1.50
96 Mackena Bell YG RC .50 1.25
97 Austin Dyne YG RC .40 1.00
98 Dylan Kwasniewski YG RC .50 1.25
99 Ben Rhodes YG RC .40 1.00
100 Patrick/Stenhouse CL 1.00 2.50

2013 Press Pass Fanfare Holofoil Die Cuts
*HOLO DIE CUT: .5X TO 1.2X BASIC CARDS
*HOLO DC SP: 1.2X TO 3X BASIC CARDS
ONE PER PACK
SP STATED ODDS 1:40

2013 Press Pass Fanfare Red Foil Die Cuts
*RED DIE CUT: .6X TO 1.5X BASIC CARDS
*RED DC SP: 1.5X TO 4X BASIC CARDS
ONE PER RETAIL PACK

2013 Press Pass Fanfare Sapphire
*SAPPHIRE/20: 2.5X TO 6X BASIC CARDS

2013 Press Pass Fanfare Silver
*SILVER/25: 2X TO 5X BASIC CARDS
STATED PRINT RUN 25 SER.#'d SETS

2013 Press Pass Fanfare Autographs Gold
AA Aric Almirola/25 8.00 20.00
BG Brendan Gaughan CWTS/125 3.00 8.00
BN Brennan Newberry CWTS/125 4.00 10.00
BS2 Brad Sweet NNS/75 5.00 12.00
BV Brian Vickers NNS/25 6.00 15.00
CM Casey Mears/50 4.00 10.00
DG David Gilliland/75 4.00 10.00
DR David Ragan/99 4.00 10.00
DR2 David Reutimann/75 5.00 12.00
DS David Stremme/99 3.00 8.00
HM Hal Martin NNS/125 3.00 8.00
JA Justin Allgaier NNS/25 8.00 20.00
JB2 James Buescher CWTS/125 3.00 8.00
JB3 Jeb Burton CWTS/125 4.00 10.00
JE Jeffrey Earnhardt NNS/75 6.00 15.00
JJC Jennifer Jo Cobb CWTS/125 5.00 12.00
JL2 Johanna Long NNS/99 5.00 12.00
JW Josh Wise/25 6.00 15.00
KL Kyle Larson NNS/125 20.00 40.00
KUB Kurt Busch/15 8.00 20.00
MM2 Michael McDowell/75 5.00 12.00
MP Miguel Paludo CWTS/125 3.00 8.00
NPJ Nelson Piquet Jr NNS/125 4.00 10.00
PK Parker Kligerman NNS/125 3.00 8.00
RB Ryan Blaney CWTS/125 4.00 10.00
SHJ Sam Hornish Jr NNS/99 4.00 10.00
TB Trevor Bayne/25 10.00 25.00
TB2 Trevor Bayne NNS/25 10.00 25.00
TD Ty Dillon NNS/25 10.00 25.00
TK Travis Kvapil/75 4.00 10.00

2013 Press Pass Fanfare Autographs Red
BG Brendan Gaughan CWTS/99 3.00 8.00
BN Brennan Newberry CWTS/99 4.00 10.00
BS2 Brad Sweet NNS/50 5.00 12.00
CM Casey Mears/25 6.00 15.00
DG David Gilliland/25 6.00 15.00
DR David Ragan/25 8.00 20.00
DR2 David Reutimann/25 8.00 20.00
DS David Stremme/25 6.00 15.00
HM Hal Martin NNS/99 3.00 8.00
JB2 James Buescher CWTS/99 3.00 8.00
JB3 Jeb Burton CWTS/99 4.00 10.00
JE Jeffrey Earnhardt NNS/50 6.00 15.00
JJC Jennifer Jo Cobb CWTS/99 5.00 12.00
JL2 Johanna Long NNS/50 6.00 15.00
KL Kyle Larson NNS/99 20.00 40.00
MP Miguel Paludo CWTS/99 3.00 8.00
PK Parker Kligerman NNS/99 3.00 8.00
RB Ryan Blaney CWTS/99 4.00 10.00
TK Travis Kvapil/25 6.00 15.00
MM2 Michael McDowell/25 8.00 20.00
NPJ Nelson Piquet Jr NNS/99 4.00 10.00
RS2 Regan Smith NNS/25 8.00 20.00
SHJ Sam Hornish Jr NNS/50 5.00 12.00

2013 Press Pass Fanfare Fan Following
FF6-FF15: ONE PER PACK
FF1-FF5 SP STATED ODDS 1:40
FF1 Dale Earnhardt Jr. SP 3.00 8.00
FF2 Jeff Gordon SP 3.00 8.00
FF3 Jimmie Johnson SP 2.50 6.00
FF4 Tony Stewart SP 2.50 6.00
FF5 Danica Patrick SP 4.00 10.00
FF6 Carl Edwards .75 2.00
FF7 Kyle Busch 1.00 2.50
FF8 Travis Pastrana .75 2.00
FF9 Kasey Kahne .75 2.00
FF10 Brad Keselowski 1.00 2.50
FF11 Kevin Harvick 1.00 2.50
FF12 Joey Logano .75 2.00
FF13 Marcos Ambrose .75 2.00
FF14 Ricky Stenhouse Jr. .75 2.00
FF15 Austin Dillon NNS 1.00 2.50

2013 Press Pass Fanfare Fan Following National Convention VIP
COMPLET SET (5) 4.00 10.00
FFN1 Dale Earnhardt Jr. 1.00 2.50
FFN2 Jeff Gordon 1.00 2.50
FFN3 Jimmie Johnson .75 2.00
FFN4 Tony Stewart .75 2.00
FFN5 Danica Patrick 1.25 3.00

2013 Press Pass Fanfare Magnificent Materials Signatures
*BLUE/25: .6X TO 1.5X BASIC JSY AU/99
*BLUE/25: .5X TO 1.2X BASIC JSY AU/50
AD Austin Dillon NNS/99 15.00 40.00
AL Aric Almirola/99 5.00 12.00
CB Clint Bowyer/99 6.00 15.00
CE Carl Edwards/99 6.00 15.00
DH Denny Hamlin/99 6.00 15.00
ES Elliott Sadler NNS/99 4.00 10.00
GB Greg Biffle/99 5.00 12.00
JA Justin Allgaier NNS/99 5.00 12.00
JB Jeff Burton/99 5.00 12.00
JE Jeffrey Earnhardt NNS/99 6.00 15.00
JG Jeff Gordon/25 60.00 120.00
JJ Jimmie Johnson/25 25.00 60.00
JL Johanna Long NNS/99 8.00 20.00
JM Jamie McMurray/99 6.00 15.00
JPM Juan Pablo Montoya/99 6.00 15.00
JW Josh Wise/99 4.00 10.00
KH Kevin Harvick/50 10.00 25.00
KK Kasey Kahne/25 10.00 25.00
KYB Kyle Busch/50 10.00 25.00
MA Marcos Ambrose/99 6.00 15.00
MK Matt Kenseth/50 8.00 20.00
MTJ Martin Truex/99 5.00 12.00
PM Paul Menard/99 4.00 10.00
RN Ryan Newman/99 5.00 12.00
RS Regan Smith/99 5.00 12.00
RS2 Regan Smith NNS/99 5.00 12.00
TD Ty Dillon CWTS/99 8.00 20.00
TP Travis Pastrana NNS/25 10.00 25.00
TS Tony Stewart/25 30.00 60.00

2013 Press Pass Fanfare Magnificent Materials Silver
SILVER PRINT RUN 40-199
*GOLD/50: .6X TO 1.5X SLVR/115-199
*GOLD/50: .5X TO 1.2X SLVR/65-98
*GOLD/50: .4X TO 1X SLVR/40
*DUAL SWTCH/50: .6X TO 1.5X SLVR/199
*JUMBO/25: .8X TO 2X SLVR/199
*JUMBO/25: .6X TO 1.5X SLVR/199
*JUMBO/25: .5X TO 1.2X SLVR/40
*MELTING/10: 1X TO 2.5X SLVR/199
AA Aric Almirola/199 2.50 6.00
AD Austin Dillon/199 4.00 10.00
BK Brad Keselowski/199 4.00 10.00
BL Bobby Labonte/199 3.00 8.00
BN Brennan Newberry/199 2.50 6.00
BS Brian Scott/115 2.00 5.00
BV Brian Vickers/199 2.00 5.00
CB Clint Bowyer/199 3.00 8.00
CE Carl Edwards/199 3.00 8.00
CM Casey Mears/199 2.00 5.00
DG David Gilliland/199 2.00 5.00
DH Denny Hamlin/199 3.00 8.00
DP Danica Patrick/199 8.00 20.00
DR David Ragan/199 2.50 6.00
DS David Stremme/199 2.00 5.00
ES Elliott Sadler/199 2.00 5.00
GB Greg Biffle/199 2.50 6.00
HM Hal Martin/199 2.00 5.00
JA Justin Allgaier/199 2.50 6.00
JB Jeff Burton/199 2.50 6.00
JC Jennifer Jo Cobb/199 3.00 8.00
JE Jeffrey Earnhardt/40 5.00 12.00
JG Jeff Gordon/199 15.00 40.00
JJ Jimmie Johnson/199 5.00 12.00
JL Joey Logano/199 3.00 8.00
JM Jamie McMurray/199 3.00 8.00
JW Josh Wise/199 2.00 5.00
KH Kevin Harvick/199 4.00 10.00
KK Kasey Kahne/199 3.00 8.00
KL Kyle Larson/199 8.00 20.00
MA Marcos Ambrose/199 3.00 8.00
MK Matt Kenseth/199 3.00 8.00
MM Mark Martin/199 3.00 8.00
MP Miguel Paludo/199 2.00 5.00
MW Michael Waltrip/199 3.00 8.00
NP Nelson Piquet Jr/199 2.50 6.00
PK Parker Kligerman/65 2.50 6.00
PM Paul Menard/199 2.00 5.00
RB Ryan Blaney/98 3.00 8.00
RN Ryan Newman/199 2.50 6.00
RS Regan Smith/199 2.50 6.00
RS Ricky Stenhouse Jr./199 3.00 8.00
SH Sam Hornish Jr./199 2.50 6.00
TB Trevor Bayne/199 3.00 8.00
TD Ty Dillon/199 3.00 8.00
TP Travis Pastrana/199 3.00 8.00
TS Tony Stewart/199 5.00 12.00
BS2 Brad Sweet/199 2.50 6.00
DEJ Dale Earnhardt Jr./199 6.00 15.00
DR2 David Reutimann/199 2.50 6.00
JB2 James Buescher/199 2.00 5.00
JL2 Johanna Long/93 4.00 10.00
JPM Juan Pablo Montoya/199 3.00 8.00
KUB Kurt Busch/199 2.50 6.00
KYB Kyle Busch/199 4.00 10.00
MM2 Michael McDowell/199 2.50 6.00
MTJ Martin Truex/199 2.50 6.00
RS2 Regan Smith/199 2.50 6.00
TB2 Trevor Bayne/199 3.00 8.00

2013 Press Pass Fanfare Rookie Stripes Memorabilia
STATED PRINT RUN 25 SER.#'d SETS
DP Danica Patrick 75.00 125.00
RS Ricky Stenhouse Jr.

2013 Press Pass Fanfare Showtime
STATED ODDS 1:3
S1 Kasey Kahne's Car .75 2.00
S2 Danica Patrick's Car 2.00 5.00
S3 Tony Stewart's Car 1.25 3.00
S4 Kyle Busch's Car 1.00 2.50
S5 Matt Kenseth's Car .75 2.00
S6 Jeff Gordon's Car 1.50 4.00
S7 Kevin Harvick's Car 1.00 2.50
S8 Jimmie Johnson's Car 1.25 3.00
S9 Dale Earnhardt Jr.'s Car 1.50 4.00
S10 Carl Edwards' Car .75 2.00

2013 Press Pass Fanfare Signature Ride Autographs
*RED/50: .4X TO 1X BASIC AU/75
*RED/25: .5X TO 1.2X BASIC AU/50-75
CB Clint Bowyer/25 8.00 20.00
CM Casey Mears/75 4.00 10.00
GB Greg Biffle/25 6.00 15.00
SS Scott Speed/25 5.00 12.00
KUB Kurt Busch/50 5.00 12.00
RSJ Ricky Stenhouse Jr./75

2013 Press Pass Fanfare Young Guns Autographs Silver
STATED PRINT RUN 225
*GOLD/149: .5X TO 1.2X SILVER/225
*RED/99: .6X TO 1.5X SILVER/225
AB Annabeth Barnes 5.00 12.00
AD Austin Dyne 3.00 8.00
BR Ben Rhodes 3.00 8.00
DK Dylan Kwasniewski 4.00 10.00
MB Mackena Bell 4.00 10.00

2010 Press Pass Five Star
STATED PRINT RUN 35 SER.#'d SETS
WAX BOX HOBBY (3) 500.00 600.00
1 Richard Petty 8.00 20.00
2 David Pearson 5.00 12.00
3 Bobby Allison 6.00 15.00
4 Jeff Gordon 10.00 25.00
5 Dale Earnhardt 25.00 60.00
6 Jimmie Johnson 15.00 40.00
7 Bill Elliott 10.00 25.00
8 Mark Martin 5.00 12.00
9 Tony Stewart 8.00 20.00
10 Kurt Busch 4.00 10.00
11 Jeff Burton 4.00 10.00
12 Davey Allison 8.00 20.00
13 Kyle Busch 6.00 15.00
14 Dale Earnhardt Jr. 10.00 25.00
15 Matt Kenseth 5.00 12.00
16 Carl Edwards 5.00 12.00
17 Denny Hamlin 5.00 12.00
18 Kevin Harvick 15.00 40.00
19 Ryan Newman 4.00 10.00
20 Kasey Kahne 5.00 12.00
21 Joey Logano 5.00 12.00
22 Danica Patrick 60.00 120.00
23 Mario Andretti 5.00 12.00
24 John Force 10.00 25.00
25 Tony Schumacher 10.00 25.00

2010 Press Pass Five Star Classic Compilations Combos Firesuit Autographs
STATED PRINT RUN 15 SER.#'d SETS
CCMHMS Gordon/JJ Martin/Dale Jr. 300.00 500.00
CCMJGR Logano/Busch/Hamlin 75.00 150.00
CCMRCR Harvick/Bowyer/Burton 125.00 200.00
CCMROU Edwards/Kens Ragan/Biffle 100.00 200.00
CCMDPDE D.Patrick D.Earnhardt Jr 125.00 250.00
CCMJJJG J.Johnson/J.Gordon 150.00 300.00
CCMDEJG D.Earnhardt Jr./J.Gordon
CCMTSDE T.Stewart/D.Earnhardt Jr 150.00300.00
CCMKKJG K.Kahne/J.Gordon 125.00 250.00
CCMLEG Petty/Pearson Yarborough/Waltrip 150.00 300.00

2010 Press Pass Five Star Classic Compilations Sheet Metal Autographs
STATED PRINT RUN 25 SER.#'d SETS
BE Bill Elliott 25.00 60.00
CE Carl Edwards 50.00 100.00
DEJ Dale Earnhardt Jr. 150.00 300.00
DP Danica Patrick 150.00 300.00
JG Jeff Gordon 150.00 300.00
JJ Jimmie Johnson 60.00 120.00
JL Joey Logano 30.00 80.00
KB Kyle Busch 50.00 100.00
KH Kevin Harvick 50.00 100.00
KK Kasey Kahne 60.00 120.00
RP Richard Petty 100.00 200.00
TS Tony Stewart 60.00 120.00

2010 Press Pass Five Star Classic Compilations Wrangler Firesuit Dual
STATED PRINT RUN 25 SER.#'d SETS
EE Dale Sr./Dale Jr. 250.00 400.00

2010 Press Pass Five Star Paramount Pieces Aluminum
STATED PRINT RUN 10-25
*GOLD/15: .5X TO 1.2X ALUM/20-25
*BLUE/15-20: .5X TO 1.2X ALUM/20-25
BE Bill Elliott/25 15.00 40.00
BK Brad Keselowski/10
CE Carl Edwards/20 15.00 40.00
DE Dale Earnhardt/25 60.00 120.00
DEJ1 Dale Earnhardt Jr./25 20.00 50.00
DEJ2 Earnhardt Jr. Wrangler/25 40.00 100.00
DH Denny Hamlin/10
DP Danica Patrick/25 20.00 50.00
JB Jeff Burton/20 10.00 25.00
JF John Force/20 15.00 40.00
JG Jeff Gordon/25 30.00 80.00
JJ Jimmie Johnson/25 25.00 60.00
JL Joey Logano/20 15.00 40.00
KBU Kyle Busch/20 12.00 30.00
KH Kevin Harvick/20 15.00 40.00
KK Kasey Kahne/25 10.00 25.00
MK Matt Kenseth/20 12.00 30.00
MM Mark Martin/25 12.00 30.00
RP Richard Petty/25 25.00 60.00
TS Tony Stewart/25 25.00 60.00

2010 Press Pass Five Star Signature Souvenirs Aluminum
STATED PRINT RUN 50 SER.#'d SETS
UNPRICED HOLOFOIL PRINT RUN 10
UNPRICED MELTING PRINT RUN 1
SSBE Bill Elliott 25.00 60.00
SSCE Carl Edwards 40.00 80.00
SSDE Dale Earnhardt Jr. 50.00 100.00
SSDP Danica Patrick 75.00 150.00
SSJF John Force 25.00 60.00
SSJG Jeff Gordon 50.00 100.00
SSJJ Jimmie Johnson 40.00 80.00
SSJL Joey Logano 20.00 50.00
SSKB Kyle Busch 25.00 60.00
SSKH Kevin Harvick 25.00 60.00
SSKK Kasey Kahne 40.00 80.00
SSMM Mark Martin 15.00 40.00
SSRP Richard Petty 40.00 80.00
SSTS Tony Stewart 40.00 80.00

2010 Press Pass Five Star Signature Souvenirs Gold
*GOLD/25: .5X TO 1.2X ALUMINUM
STATED PRINT RUN 25 SER.#'d SETS
SSDP Danica Patrick 75.00 150.00

2010 Press Pass Five Star Signatures Aluminum
STATED PRINT RUN 35-45
*GOLD/20: .5X TO 1.2X ALUMINUM
UNPRICED HOLOFOIL PRINT RUN 10
UNPRICED MELTING PRINT RUN 1
BE Bill Elliott 15.00 40.00
BK Brad Keselowski 12.00 30.00
CE Carl Edwards 10.00 25.00
DEJ Dale Earnhardt Jr. 50.00 100.00
DH Denny Hamlin 10.00 25.00
DP Danica Patrick 60.00 120.00
JB Jeff Burton 8.00 20.00
JF John Force 25.00 60.00
JG Jeff Gordon/45 50.00 100.00
JJ Jimmie Johnson 30.00 80.00
JL Joey Logano 10.00 25.00
KB Kyle Busch 12.00 30.00
KH Kevin Harvick 12.00 30.00
KK Kasey Kahne 12.00 30.00
MM Mark Martin 20.00 50.00
RP Richard Petty 15.00 40.00
TS Tony Schumacher 8.00 20.00
TST Tony Stewart 15.00 40.00

2014 Press Pass Five Star
1 Jeff Burton 8.00 20.00
2 Kurt Busch 8.00 20.00
3 Kyle Busch 12.00 30.00
4 Dale Earnhardt Jr. 20.00 50.00
5 Carl Edwards 10.00 25.00
6 Jeff Gordon 20.00 50.00
7 Denny Hamlin 10.00 25.00
8 Kevin Harvick 12.00 30.00
9 Jimmie Johnson 15.00 40.00
10 Kasey Kahne 10.00 25.00
11 Matt Kenseth 10.00 25.00
12 Brad Keselowski 12.00 30.00
13 Mark Martin 10.00 25.00
14 Danica Patrick 40.00 80.00
15 Tony Stewart 15.00 40.00
16 Justin Allgaier 8.00 20.00
17 Austin Dillon 12.00 30.00
18 Kyle Larson CRC 25.00 60.00
19 Bobby Allison 8.00 20.00
20 Davey Allison 15.00 40.00
21 John Force 15.00 40.00
22 Terry Labonte 10.00 25.00
23 Richard Petty 15.00 40.00
24 David Pearson 8.00 20.00
25 Darrell Waltrip 15.00 40.00
26 Dale Earnhardt 40.00 100.00

2014 Press Pass Five Star Holofoil
*HOLO/10: .5X TO 1.2X BASIC CARD/15

2014 Press Pass Five Star Cut Signatures
FSSJNG Jack Nicklaus/45 100.00 175.00

2014 Press Pass Five Star Paramount Pieces Gold
*HOLOFOIL/10: .5X TO 1.2X GOLD/25
PPAD Austin Dillon 10.00 25.00
PPBK Brad Keselowski 10.00 25.00
PPCB Clint Bowyer 8.00 20.00
PPCE Carl Edwards 8.00 20.00
PPDE Dale Earnhardt 25.00 60.00
PPDEJR Dale Earnhardt Jr. 15.00 40.00
PPDH Denny Hamlin 8.00 20.00
PPDP Danica Patrick 20.00 50.00
PPJB Jeff Burton 6.00 15.00
PPJF John Force 12.00 30.00
PPJG Jeff Gordon 15.00 40.00
PPJJ Jimmie Johnson 10.00 25.00
PPKH Kevin Harvick 10.00 25.00
PPKK Kasey Kahne 8.00 20.00
PPKYB Kyle Busch 10.00 25.00
PPMA Marcos Ambrose 8.00 20.00
PPMK Matt Kenseth 8.00 20.00
PPMM Mark Martin 10.00 25.00
PPRP Richard Petty 12.00 30.00
PPTL Terry Labonte 15.00 40.00
PPTP Travis Pastrana 8.00 20.00
PPTS Tony Stewart 12.00 30.00

2014 Press Pass Five Star Signature Souvenirs Gold
*HOLOFOIL/25: .5X TO 1.2X GOLD/50
EXCH EXPIRATION: 1/30/2015
SSCE Carl Edwards/50 12.00 30.00
SSDE Dale Earnhardt Jr./50 40.00 80.00
SSDH Denny Hamlin/50 12.00 30.00
SSDP Danica Patrick/50 60.00 120.00
SSJG Jeff Gordon/50 30.00 80.00
SSJJ Jimmie Johnson/50 30.00 80.00
SSKH Kevin Harvick/50 15.00 40.00
SSKK Kasey Kahne/50 12.00 30.00
SSKYB Kyle Busch/50 15.00 40.00
SSMA Marcos Ambrose/50 12.00 30.00
SSMK Matt Kenseth/50 12.00 30.00
SSTS Tony Stewart/50 EXCH 30.00 60.00

2006 Press Pass Four Wide
STATED PRINT RUN 50 SER.#'d SETS
UNPRICED FLAG PRINT RUN 1
FWBL Bobby Labonte 15.00 40.00
FWDE Dale Earnhardt Jr. 30.00 80.00
FWJG Jeff Gordon 30.00 80.00
FWJJ Jimmie Johnson 25.00 60.00
FWKH Kevin Harvick 15.00 40.00
FWMK Matt Kenseth 15.00 40.00
FWMM Mark Martin 15.00 40.00
FWRN Ryan Newman 12.00 30.00
FWRW Rusty Wallace 15.00 40.00
FWTS Tony Stewart 25.00 60.00

2007 Press Pass Four Wide
This 9-card set was issued as redemption cards in packs of 2007 Press Pass products. Each card featured swatches of race-used sheet metal, race-used tires, race-used car covers and a large piece of race used firesuit. Each card was serial numbered to 50 and carried a "FW" prefix to its card number. The exchange cards were redeemable until December 31, 2007.
STATED PRINT RUN 50 SER.#'d SETS
FWDE Dale Earnhardt Jr. 60.00 120.00
FWDH Denny Hamlin 25.00 60.00
FWJG Jeff Gordon 60.00 120.00
FWJJ Jimmie Johnson 30.00 80.00
FWKH Kevin Harvick 30.00 80.00
FWKK Kasey Kahne 30.00 80.00
FWMT Martin Truex Jr. 25.00 60.00
FWRN Ryan Newman 25.00 60.00
FWTS Tony Stewart 40.00 100.00

2007 Press Pass Four Wide Exchange

This 9-card exchange set pictured swatches of race-used sheet metal and race-used tires, race-used car covers and a large swatch of race-used firesuit. These were available in packs of 2007 Press Pass and redeemable for the actual four-piece race-used memorabilia cards. These were redeemable until December 31, 2007. Each card is serial numbered to 50 and carried a "FW" prefix for its card number. Each of these had a Press Pass Authentic hologram sticker. Cards were not returned after they were redeemed.

FWDE Dale Earnhardt Jr. 4.00 10.00
FWDH Denny Hamlin 2.00 5.00
FWJG Jeff Gordon 4.00 10.00
FWJJ Jimmie Johnson 3.00 8.00
FWKH Kevin Harvick 2.00 5.00
FWKK Kasey Kahne 3.00 8.00
FWMT Martin Truex Jr. 2.00 5.00
FWRN Ryan Newman 2.00 5.00
FWTS Tony Stewart 3.00 8.00

2008 Press Pass Four Wide

STATED PRINT RUN 50 SER.#'d SETS
FWKB Kurt Busch 40.00 100.00
FWDE1 Dale Earnhardt Jr. 100.00 200.00
FWDE2 Dale Earnhardt Jr. AMP 40.00 100.00
FWDE3 Dale Earnhardt Jr. NG 40.00 100.00
FWCE Carl Edwards 40.00 100.00
FWJG Jeff Gordon 50.00 120.00
FWDH Denny Hamlin 30.00 80.00
FWKH Kevin Harvick 30.00 80.00
FWJJ Jimmie Johnson 40.00 100.00
FWKK Kasey Kahne 30.00 80.00
FWMK Matt Kenseth 40.00 100.00
FWJM Juan Pablo Montoya 25.00 60.00
FWTS Tony Stewart 40.00 100.00
FWMT Martin Truex Jr. 30.00 80.00

2009 Press Pass Four Wide Firesuit

STATED PRINT RUN 50 SER.#'d SETS
UNPRICED AUTO PRINT RUN 5
UNPRICED FLAG PRINT RUN 1
UNPRICED SHEET METAL PRINT RUN 10
FWBV Brian Vickers 12.00 30.00
FWCB Clint Bowyer JD 20.00 50.00
FWCB2 Clint Bowyer Cheerios 20.00 50.00
FWCE Carl Edwards Aflac 20.00 50.00
FWDE Dale Earnhardt Jr. AMP 40.00 100.00
FWDE2 Dale Earnhardt Jr. NG 40.00 100.00
FWDH Denny Hamlin 25.00 60.00
FWDR David Ragan 15.00 40.00
FWGB Greg Biffle 15.00 40.00
FWJB Jeff Burton 15.00 40.00
FWJG Jeff Gordon 40.00 100.00
FWJJ Jimmie Johnson 30.00 80.00
FWJL Joey Logano 15.00 40.00
FWJM Juan Pablo Montoya 15.00 40.00
FWKB Kyle Busch 15.00 40.00
FWKH Kevin Harvick 25.00 60.00
FWKK Kasey Kahne 20.00 50.00
FWMK Matt Kenseth 20.00 50.00
FWMM Mark Martin 25.00 60.00
FWMT Martin Truex Jr. 15.00 40.00
FWMW Michael Waltrip 20.00 50.00
FWRN Ryan Newman 15.00 40.00
FWSS Scott Speed 25.00 60.00
FWTS Tony Stewart HD 40.00 100.00
FWTS2 Tony Stewart OS 40.00 100.00

2009 Press Pass Four Wide Tire

*TIRE/25: .4X TO 1X FIRESUIT/50
STATED PRINT RUN 25 SER.#'d SETS
FWDR2 David Ragan UPS 15.00 40.00
FWCE Carl Edwards Office Depot 50.00 120.00

2010 Press Pass Four Wide Firesuit

STATED PRINT RUN 25 SER.#'d SETS
UNPRICED SHOE PRINT RUN 1
UNPRICED TIRE PRINT RUN 10
*SHEET METAL/15: .5X TO 1.2X FIRESUIT/25
FWBK Brad Keselowski 50.00 100.00
FWBV Brian Vickers 40.00 80.00
FWCE Carl Edwards 50.00 100.00
FWJG Jeff Gordon 100.00 200.00
FWJJ Jimmie Johnson 40.00 100.00
FWJL Joey Logano 40.00 80.00
FWJM Juan Pablo Montoya 25.00 60.00
FWKB Kyle Busch 50.00 100.00
FWKH Kevin Harvick 40.00 100.00
FWMK Matt Kenseth 60.00 120.00
FWMM Mark Martin 60.00 120.00
FWMT Martin Truex Jr. 30.00 60.00
FWRN Ryan Newman 40.00 80.00
FWTS Tony Stewart 75.00 150.00
FWDE1 Dale Jr. AMP 75.00 150.00
FWDE2 Dale Jr. NG 75.00 150.00

2011 Press Pass Four Wide Firesuit

STATED PRINT RUN 25 SER.#'d SETS
UNPRICED AUTO PRINT RUN 5
UNPRICED GLOVE PRINT RUN 1
*SHEET METAL/15: .4X TO 1X FIRESUIT/25
UNPRICED SHOE PRINT RUN 1
UNPRICED TIRE PRINT RUN 10
FWBE Bill Elliott 30.00 80.00
FWBK Brad Keselowski 25.00 60.00
FWBV Brian Vickers 30.00 80.00
FWCE Carl Edwards 40.00 100.00
FWDE Dale Earnhardt Jr. 50.00 120.00
FWDH Denny Hamlin 25.00 60.00
FWDP Danica Patrick 50.00 120.00
FWJB Jeff Burton 25.00 60.00
FWJG Jeff Gordon 75.00 150.00
FWJJ Jimmie Johnson 75.00 150.00
FWJL Joey Logano 25.00 60.00
FWJM Jamie McMurray 40.00 100.00
FWJM Juan Pablo Montoya 25.00 60.00
FWKB Kyle Busch 30.00 80.00
FWKH Kevin Harvick 30.00 80.00
FWMK Matt Kenseth 30.00 80.00
FWMM Mark Martin 30.00 80.00
FWRN Ryan Newman 25.00 60.00
FWTS Tony Stewart 40.00 100.00

2009 Press Pass Fusion

COMPLETE SET (90) 15.00 40.00
63 Greg Biffle .15 .40
64 Kyle Busch .30 .75
65 Dale Earnhardt, Jr. .75 2.00
66 Dale Earnhardt, Sr. 1.25 3.00
67 Carl Edwards .30 .75
68 Jeff Gordon .75 2.00
69 Kevin Harvick .30 .75
70 Jimmie Johnson .50 1.25
71 Kasey Kahne .50 1.25
72 Matt Kenseth .15 .40
73 Joey Logano 1.25 3.00
74 Mark Martin .50 1.25
75 Tony Stewart .50 1.25
76 Richard Petty .50 1.25

2009 Press Pass Fusion Bronze

*BRONZE: 1X TO 2.5X BASE
STATED PRINT RUN 150 SER. #'d SETS

2009 Press Pass Fusion Gold

*GOLD: 2X TO 5X BASE
STATED PRINT RUN 50 SER. #'d SETS

2009 Press Pass Fusion Green

*GREEN: 3X TO 8X BASE
STATED PRINT RUN 25 SER. #'d SETS

2009 Press Pass Fusion Silver

*SILVER: 1.25X TO 3X BASE
STATED PRINT RUN 99 SER. #'d SETS

2009 Press Pass Fusion Cross Training

COMPLETE SET (10) 6.00 15.00
STATED ODDS 1:10
CT8 B.Gibson/R.Petty 1.50 4.00

2009 Press Pass Fusion Revered Relics Gold

STATED PRINT RUN 5-50
*HOLOFOIL/25: .5X TO 1.2X BASIC RELIC
RRCE Carl Edwards 8.00 20.00
RRJG Jeff Gordon 15.00 40.00
RRJJ Jimmie Johnson 10.00 25.00
RRJL Joey Logano 10.00 25.00
RRKB Kyle Busch 10.00 25.00
RRKH Kevin Harvick 20.00 50.00
RRKK Kasey Kahne 15.00 40.00
RRMM Mark Martin 20.00 50.00
RRTS Tony Stewart 15.00 40.00
RRDEJ Dale Earnhardt, Jr. 20.00 50.00
RRDES Dale Earnhardt, Sr. 30.00 75.00
RRGBMK G.Biffle/M.Kenseth 25.00 60.00

2009 Press Pass Fusion Revered Relics Silver

STATED PRINT RUN 15-299
RRJG Jeff Gordon/65 15.00 40.00
RRJJ Jimmie Johnson/65 10.00 25.00
RRJL Joey Logano/65 10.00 25.00
RRKH Kevin Harvick/65 20.00 50.00
RRKK Kasey Kahne/65 15.00 40.00
RRMM Mark Martin/65 20.00 50.00
RRTS Tony Stewart/65 15.00 40.00
RRDEJ Dale Earnhardt, Jr./65 20.00 50.00
RRDES Dale Earnhardt, Sr./65 30.00 75.00
RRGBMK G.Biffle/M.Kenseth/65 25.00 60.00

2001 Press Pass Excedrin Racing

This three card set was available in specially marked packages of Excedrin. The cards are black and white and feature a picture of the driver front and back.

COMPLETE SET (3) 2.50 6.00
1 David Pearson .75 2.00
2 Cale Yarborough .75 2.00
3 Darrell Waltrip .75 2.00

2000 Press Pass Gatorade Front Runner Award

This 12-card set was released by Press Pass in conjunction with Gatorade to honor the 1999 Front Runner Award winners. Three cards were issued at a time over the span of four months (June through September) to collectors that purchased two 32-ounce bottles of Gatorade at participating convenience stores.

COMPLETE SET (12) 10.00 25.00
1 Jeff Burton .40 1.00
2 Mark Martin 1.25 3.00
3 Steve Park .60 1.50
4 Tony Stewart 1.50 4.00
5 Dale Jarrett 1.00 2.50
6 Mike Skinner .20 .50
7 John Andretti .20 .50
8 Jeff Gordon 1.50 4.00
9 Terry Labonte .60 1.50
10 Bobby Labonte 1.00 2.50
11 Ward Burton .30 .75
12 Dale Earnhardt 3.00 8.00

2001 Press Pass Gatorade Front Runner Award

This set was produced by Press Pass and distributed by Gatorade. Each card honors one of the Gatorade Front Runner Award winners from the 2000 Winston Cup season.

COMPLETE SET (10) 6.00 12.00
1 Mark Martin 1.25 3.00
2 Matt Kenseth 1.25 3.00
3 Jeff Gordon 1.50 4.00
4 Jeff Burton .40 1.00
5 Ward Burton .40 1.00
6 Jeremy Mayfield .20 .50
7 Rusty Wallace 1.25 3.00
8 Mike Skinner .20 .50
9 Jerry Nadeau .40 1.00
NNO Cover Card .10 .30

2003 Press Pass Gatorade Jumbos

These cards were produced by Press Pass and sponsored and distributed by Gatorade. Each driver card includes a perforated redemption card at the bottom which could be removed and sent in for a chance to win signed merchandise. The cards with the tab measure roughly 4" by 7 1/4" and 4" by 4 3/4" with the tab removed. Prices below reflect that of cards with the contest tab intact.

COMPLETE SET (4) 5.00 12.00
1 Jimmie Johnson 1.50 4.00
2 Matt Kenseth 1.50 4.00
3 Mark Martin 1.50 4.00
4 Ryan Newman 1.50 4.00

2008 Press Pass Gillette Young Guns

COMPLETE SET (6) 10.00 25.00
1 Clint Bowyer 1.00 2.50
2 Kurt Busch .75 2.00
3 Carl Edwards 1.00 2.50
4 Denny Hamlin 1.25 3.00
5 Kasey Kahne 1.00 2.50
6 Ryan Newman .75 2.00

2006 Press Pass Goody's

This 7-card set was produced by Press Pass for Goody's Headache Powders to celebrate the first family of racing, the Pettys. These cards were distributed at Wal-Mart and other retailers in the South. These cards were distributed the summer of 2006 in 4-card packs. Each pack contained a cover card checklist.

COMPLETE SET (7) 5.00 12.00
GCC1 Richard Petty .60 1.50
GCC2 Richard Petty .60 1.50
GCC3 Kyle Petty .30 .75
GCC4 Richard Petty .60 1.50
GCC5 Kyle Petty .30 .75
GCC6 Kyle Petty .30 .75
CL Checklist CL .15 .40

2001 Press Pass Hot Treads

Issued one per High Gear, Press Pass Premier, Stealth and Trackside Special Retail box, these 20 cards feature some of the leading NASCAR drivers. As these cards are printed to different quantities, we have listed the stated print runs in our checklist.

HT1 Bobby Labonte/2405 4.00 10.00
HT2 Tony Stewart/2405 8.00 20.00
HT3 Rusty Wallace/2405 6.00 15.00
HT4 Mike Skinner/2400 4.00 10.00
HT5 Ken Schrader/2500 5.00 12.00
HT6 Dale Earnhardt/1000 15.00 40.00
HT7 Terry Labonte/1000 5.00 12.00
HT8 Joe Nemechek/1000 4.00 10.00
HT9 Dale Jarrett/1000 5.00 12.00
HT10 Ward Burton/1000 5.00 12.00
HT11 Jeff Gordon/1665 6.00 15.00
HT12 Jeremy Mayfield/1660 5.00 12.00
HT13 Mark Martin/1665 4.00 10.00
HT14 Jeff Burton/1660 5.00 12.00
HT15 Dave Blaney/1660 5.00 12.00
HT16 Dale Earnhardt Jr./2405 8.00 20.00
HT17 Steve Park/2400 4.00 10.00
HT18 Matt Kenseth/2405 5.00 12.00
HT19 Ricky Rudd/2400 5.00 12.00
HT20 Bobby Hamilton/2400 4.00 10.00

2001 Press Pass Hot Treads Rookie Rubber

Issued one per special Optima retail box, these six cards feature not only rookies on the NASCAR circuit but a piece of a race-worn tire.

COMPLETE SET (6) 25.00 60.00
RR1 Casey Atwood 4.00 10.00
RR2 Kurt Busch 6.00 15.00
RR3 Ron Hornaday 4.00 10.00
RR4 Andy Houston 4.00 10.00
RR5 Kevin Harvick 8.00 20.00
RR6 Jason Leffler 4.00 10.00

2002 Press Pass Hot Treads

Issued one per special retail box, these cards feature leading drivers and special pieces of memorabilia relating to them. They were issued 8-10 cards at a time in various 2002 Press Pass releases. The final 10-cards feature the popular Coca-Cola family of drivers.

HT1-HT8 ONE PER PRESS PASS SPEC.RETAIL
HT9-HT16 ONE PER HIGH GEAR SPEC.RETAIL
HT17-HT24 ONE PER ECLIPSE SPEC.RETAIL
HT25-HT32 ONE PER PP PREMIUM SPEC.RET.
HT33-HT42 ONE PER VIP SPEC.RETAIL
HT1 Steve Park's Car/2300 4.00 10.00
HT2 Ward Burton's Car/2300 5.00 12.00
HT3 Elliott Sadler's Car/2300 5.00 12.00
HT4 Mike Skinner's Car/2300 4.00 10.00
HT5 Tony Stewart's Car/2300 8.00 20.00
HT6 Mark Martin's Car/2300 6.00 15.00
HT7 Michael Waltrip's Car/2300 5.00 12.00
HT8 Dave Blaney's Car/2300 5.00 12.00
HT9 Kevin Harvick's Car/1555 6.00 15.00
HT10 Terry Labonte's Car/1555 6.00 15.00
HT11 Jerry Nadeau's Car/1555 4.00 10.00
HT12 Ken Schrader's Car/1555 5.00 12.00
HT13 Larry Foyt's Car/1555 4.00 10.00
HT14 Jim Johnson's Car/1555 10.00 25.00
HT15 Jeff Burton's Car/1555 5.00 12.00
HT16 Kurt Busch's Car/1555 5.00 12.00
HT17 Jeff Gordon's Car/2425 10.00 25.00
HT18 J.McMurray's Car/2425 5.00 12.00
HT19 Hank Parker Jr's Car/2425 4.00 10.00
HT20 Rusty Wallace's Car/2425 6.00 15.00
HT21 Matt Kenseth's Car/2425 6.00 15.00
HT22 Dale Jarrett's Car/2425 5.00 12.00
HT23 B.Labonte's Car/2425 5.00 12.00
HT24 Bobby Hamilton's Car/2425 4.00 10.00
HT25 Dale Jr.'s Car/2375 12.00 30.00
HT26 Sterling Marlin's Car/2375 5.00 12.00
HT27 John Andretti's Car/2375 5.00 12.00
HT28 Jimmy Spencer's Car/2375 4.00 10.00
HT29 Hut Stricklin's Car/2375 4.00 10.00
HT30 Ji.Johnson's Car/2375 10.00 25.00
HT31 R.Newman's Car/2375 5.00 12.00
HT32 Kyle Petty's Car/2375 6.00 15.00
HT33 Steve Park's Car/900 6.00 15.00
HT34 M.Waltrip's Car/900 6.00 15.00
HT35 Bobby Labonte's Car/900 6.00 15.00
HT36 Tony Stewart's Car/900 8.00 20.00
HT37 Ricky Rudd's Car/900 5.00 12.00
HT38 Kevin Harvick's Car/900 6.00 15.00
HT39 John Andretti's Car/900 5.00 12.00
HT40 Kyle Petty's Car/900 6.00 15.00
HT41 Dale Jarrett's Car/900 6.00 15.00
HT42 Jeff Burton's Car/900 5.00 12.00

2004 Press Pass Hot Treads

This 18-card set was issued randomly into retail blaster boxes of 2004 Press Pass Eclipse and 2004 Press Pass Premium. The cards featured a swatch of race-used tire. Cards HTR1-HTR9 were available in '04 Press Pass Eclipse blaster boxes and serial numbered to 1100, cards HTR10-HTR18 were available in '04 Press Pass Premium blaster boxes and were serial numbered to 1250. The set also had a silver holofoil parallel.

*HOLOFOIL/200: .8X TO 2X BASIC INSERT
SILVER PRINT RUN 200 SER.#'d SETS
HTR1 Ricky Rudd/1100 4.00 10.00
HTR2 Dale Earnhardt Jr./1100 6.00 15.00
HTR3 Jimmie Johnson/1100 4.00 10.00
HTR4 Matt Kenseth/1100 4.00 10.00
HTR5 Ryan Newman/1100 4.00 10.00
HTR6 Kevin Harvick/1100 6.00 15.00
HTR7 Bobby Labonte/1100 4.00 10.00
HTR8 Greg Biffle/1100 4.00 10.00
HTR9 Terry Labonte/1100 5.00 12.00
HTR10 Brian Vickers/1250 4.00 10.00
HTR11 Jeff Gordon/1250 6.00 15.00
HTR12 Tony Stewart/1250 4.00 10.00
HTR13 Rusty Wallace/1250 5.00 12.00
HTR14 Kurt Busch/1250 4.00 10.00
HTR15 Mark Martin/1250 5.00 12.00
HTR16 Michael Waltrip/1250 5.00 12.00
HTR17 Jamie McMurray/1250 4.00 10.00
HTR18 Dale Jarrett/1250 5.00 12.00

2005 Press Pass Hot Treads

*HOLOFOIL/100: .6X TO 1.5X HOT TREAD/900
HTR1 Dale Earnhardt Jr. 8.00 20.00
HTR2 Mark Martin 5.00 12.00
HTR3 Ryan Newman 5.00 12.00
HTR4 Matt Kenseth 6.00 15.00
HTR5 Kurt Busch 5.00 12.00
HTR6 Kasey Kahne 4.00 10.00
HTR7 Dale Jarrett 6.00 15.00
HTR8 Kevin Harvick 6.00 15.00
HTR9 Rusty Wallace 6.00 15.00
HTR10 Jeff Gordon 8.00 20.00
HTR11 Tony Stewart 6.00 15.00
HTR12 Elliott Sadler 5.00 12.00
HTR13 Jeremy Mayfield 4.00 10.00
HTR14 Martin Truex Jr. 5.00 12.00
HTR15 Michael Waltrip 5.00 12.00
HTR16 Bobby Labonte 5.00 12.00
HTR17 Jamie McMurray 5.00 12.00
HTR18 Jimmie Johnson 6.00 15.00

2007 Press Pass Hot Treads

This 6-card set was randomly inserted into retail blaster boxes only at Wal-Mart. Cards 1-3 could only be found in Press Pass Eclipse and cards 4-6 could only be found in Press Pass Stealth. The cards had a swatch of race-used tire and carried a "HT" prefix for its card number. The cards were inserted one per box.

*BLUE/99: .8X TO 2X BASE
*GOLD/299: .6X TO 1.5X BASE
HT1 Kasey Kahne 6.00 15.00
HT2 Tony Stewart 6.00 15.00
HT3 Jeff Gordon 8.00 20.00
HT4 Jimmie Johnson 6.00 15.00
HT5 Dale Earnhardt Jr. 6.00 15.00
HT6 Kevin Harvick 5.00 12.00

2008 Press Pass Hot Treads

HT1-HT4: 1 PER WALMART ECLIPSE BLASTER
HT5-HT8: 1 PER WALMART VIP BLASTER
*BLUE/99: .6X TO 1.5X BASIC INSERTS
*GOLD/299: .5X TO 1.2X BASIC INSERTS
HT1 Denny Hamlin 4.00 10.00
HT2 Juan Pablo Montoya 4.00 10.00
HT3 Jimmie Johnson 5.00 12.00
HT4 Martin Truex Jr. 4.00 10.00
HT5 Jeff Gordon 6.00 15.00
HT6 Carl Edwards 5.00 12.00
HT7 Kevin Harvick 4.00 10.00
HT8 Tony Stewart 5.00 12.00

2012 Press Pass Ignite

COMPLETE SET (70) 8.00 20.00
1 A.J. Allmendinger .30 .75
2 Aric Almirola .25 .60
3 Marcos Ambrose .30 .75
4 Trevor Bayne .30 .75
5 Greg Biffle .25 .60
6 Dave Blaney .20 .50
7 Clint Bowyer .30 .75
8 Jeff Burton .25 .60
9 Kurt Busch .25 .60
10 Kyle Busch .40 1.00
11 Landon Cassill .25 .60
12 Dale Earnhardt Jr. .60 1.50
13 Carl Edwards .30 .75
14 David Gilliland .20 .50
15 Jeff Gordon .60 1.50
16 Denny Hamlin .30 .75
17 Kevin Harvick .40 1.00
18 Jimmie Johnson .50 1.25
19 Kasey Kahne .30 .75
20 Matt Kenseth .30 .75
21 Brad Keselowski .40 1.00
22 Bobby Labonte .30 .75
23 Joey Logano .30 .75
24 Mark Martin .30 .75
25 Jamie McMurray .30 .75
26 Casey Mears .20 .50
27 Paul Menard .20 .50
28 Juan Pablo Montoya .30 .75
29 Ryan Newman .25 .60
30 Danica Patrick CRC 1.50 4.00
31 David Ragan .25 .60
32 Regan Smith .25 .60
33 Tony Stewart .50 1.25
34 Martin Truex .25 .60
35 Michael Waltrip .30 .75
36 Josh Wise CRC .20 .50
37 Justin Allgaier NNS .25 .60
38 Kurt Busch NNS .25 .60
39 Austin Dillon NNS .40 1.00
40 Sam Hornish Jr. NNS .25 .60
41 Brad Keselowski NNS .40 1.00
42 Joey Logano NNS .30 .75
43 Johanna Long NNS .50 1.25
44 Travis Pastrana NNS RC .50 1.25
45 Danica Patrick NNS 1.00 2.50
46 Elliott Sadler NNS .20 .50
47 Ricky Stenhouse Jr. NNS .30 .75
48 Kenny Wallace NNS .20 .50
49 Cole Whitt NNS .25 .60
50 Ty Dillon CWTS RC .50 1.25
51 Carl Edwards' Car TS .20 .50
52 Greg Biffle's Car TS .15 .40
53 Dale Earnhardt Jr.'s Car TS .40 1.00
54 Marcos Ambrose's Car TS .20 .50
55 Casey Mears's Car TS .12 .30
56 Jeff Gordon's Car TS .40 1.00
57 Martin Truex's Car TS .15 .40
58 Ricky Stenhouse Jr.'s Car TS .20 .50
59 Trevor Bayne's Car TS .20 .50
60 Tony Stewart's Car TS .30 .75
61 Mark Martin's Car TS .20 .50
62 Jimmie Johnson's Car TS .30 .75
63 Aric Almirola's Car TS .15 .40
64 Paul Menard's Car TS .12 .30
65 David Ragan's Car TS .15 .40
66 Matt Kenseth's Car TS .20 .50
67 Ryan Newman's Car TS .15 .40
68 A.J. Allmendinger's Car TS .20 .50
69 Brad Keselowski's Car TS .25 .60
70 Joey Logano's Car TS .20 .50

2012 Press Pass Ignite Proofs Black and White

*BLACK/50: 4X TO 10X BASIC CARDS
RANDOM INSERTS IN HOBBY PACKS
STATED PRINT RUN 50 SER.#'d SETS
30 Danica Patrick 10.00 25.00

2012 Press Pass Ignite Proofs Cyan

*CYAN: 5X TO 12X BASIC CARDS
RANDOM INSERTS IN WAL-MART PACKS
30 Danica Patrick 12.00 30.00

2012 Press Pass Ignite Proofs Magenta

*MAGENTA: 5X TO 12X BASIC CARDS
RANDOM INSERTS IN TARGET PACKS
30 Danica Patrick 12.00 30.00

2012 Press Pass Ignite Double Burner Silver

RETAIL EXCLUSIVE PRINT RUN 25
UNPRICED GUN METAL PRINT RUN 10
UNPRICED RED PRINT RUN 1
DBCE Carl Edwards 10.00 25.00
DBDE Dale Earnhardt Jr. 20.00 50.00
DBDP Danica Patrick 30.00 80.00
DBJG Jeff Gordon 20.00 50.00
DBJJ Jimmie Johnson 15.00 40.00
DBKH Kevin Harvick 12.00 30.00
DBKK Kasey Kahne 10.00 25.00
DBTP Travis Pastrana NNS 15.00 40.00
DBTS Tony Stewart
DBKYB Kyle Busch 12.00 30.00

2012 Press Pass Ignite Materials Autographs Silver

OVERALL AUTO ODDS 1:20 HOB
ANNOUNCED PRINT RUN 40-150
GUN METAL/45: .5X TO 1.2X BASIC AU/150
GUN METAL/20: .6X TO 1.5X BASIC AU/75-125*
UNPRICED RED PRINT RUN 5
IMAA Aric Almirola/125* 8.00 20.00
IMAJ A.J. Allmendinger/125* 10.00 25.00
IMBK Brad Keselowski/150* 20.00 50.00
IMBL Bobby Labonte/125* 10.00 25.00
IMCB Clint Bowyer/125* 10.00 25.00
IMCE Carl Edwards/125* 10.00 25.00
IMDE Dale Earnhardt Jr./64* 50.00 100.00
IMDH Denny Hamlin/125* 12.00 30.00
IMDP Danica Patrick/65* 75.00 125.00
IMDP2 Danica Patrick/65* 75.00 125.00
IMGB Greg Biffle/125* 8.00 20.00
IMJA Justin Allgaier/150* 8.00 20.00
IMJB Jeff Burton/125* 8.00 20.00
IMJG Jeff Gordon/65* 50.00 100.00
IMJJ Jimmie Johnson/65* 25.00 50.00
IMJL Joey Logano/150* 10.00 25.00
IMJM Jamie McMurray/150* 10.00 25.00
IMJPM Juan Pablo Montoya/150* 10.00 25.00
IMKH Kevin Harvick/125* 12.00 30.00
IMKK Kasey Kahne/65* 10.00 25.00
IMKUB Kurt Busch/125* 8.00 20.00
IMKYB Kyle Busch/125* 12.00 30.00
IMMA Marcos Ambrose/150* 12.00 30.00
IMMK Matt Kenseth/150* 10.00 25.00
IMMM Mark Martin/125* 10.00 25.00
IMMT Martin Truex/150* 8.00 20.00
IMMW Michael Waltrip/20* 15.00 40.00
IMPM Paul Menard/125* 6.00 15.00
IMRN Ryan Newman/125* 8.00 20.00
IMTB Trevor Bayne/150* 10.00 25.00
IMTP Travis Pastrana/40* 50.00 100.00
IMTS Tony Stewart/75* 30.00 60.00

2012 Press Pass Ignite Limelight

STATED ODDS 1:10 HOB
SP STATED ODDS 1:100 HOB
L1 Danica Patrick SP 15.00 40.00
L2 Tony Stewart SP 6.00 15.00
L3 Carl Edwards .50 1.25
L4 Clint Bowyer .50 1.25
L5 Jeff Gordon 1.00 2.50
L6 Brad Keselowski .60 1.50
L7 Dale Earnhardt Jr. 1.00 2.50
L8 Jimmie Johnson .75 2.00
L9 Travis Pastrana SP 6.00 15.00

2012 Press Pass Ignite Materials Silver

OVERALL MATERIAL ODDS 1:20 HOB
SILVER VETERAN PRINT RUN 99
SILVER LEGEND PRINT RUN 50
*GUN METAL/50-99: .4X TO 1X SILVER
UNPRICED RED PRINT RUN 10
IMAA Aric Almirola 5.00 12.00
IMAJ A.J. Allmendinger 6.00 15.00
IMBA Bobby Allison L 5.00 12.00
IMBK Brad Keselowski 8.00 20.00
IMBL Bobby Labonte 6.00 15.00
IMCB Clint Bowyer 6.00 15.00
IMCE Carl Edwards 6.00 15.00
IMCM Casey Mears 4.00 10.00
IMDA Davey Allison L 8.00 20.00
IMDE Dale Earnhardt L 20.00 50.00
IMDEJR1 Dale Earnhardt Jr. NG 12.00 30.00
IMDEJR2 Dale Earnhardt Jr. Dew 12.00 30.00
IMDG David Gilliland 4.00 10.00
IMDH Denny Hamlin 6.00 15.00
IMDP Danica Patrick 20.00 50.00
IMDP2 Danica Patrick NNS 15.00 40.00
IMDP3 David Pearson L 6.00 15.00
IMDR1 David Ragan 5.00 12.00
IMDR2 David Reutimann 5.00 12.00
IMGB Greg Biffle 5.00 12.00
IMJA Justin Allgaier NNS 5.00 12.00
IMJB Jeff Burton 5.00 12.00
IMJG1 Jeff Gordon DTEH 12.00 30.00
IMJG2 Jeff Gordon DuPont 12.00 30.00
IMJJ Jimmie Johnson 8.00 20.00
IMJL Joey Logano 8.00 20.00
IMJM Jamie McMurray 6.00 15.00
IMJPM Juan Pablo Montoya 6.00 15.00
IMJW Josh Wise 4.00 10.00
IMKH Kevin Harvick 8.00 20.00
IMKK Kasey Kahne 6.00 15.00
IMKUB Kurt Busch 5.00 12.00
IMKYB Kyle Busch 8.00 20.00
IMMA Marcos Ambrose 6.00 15.00
IMMK Matt Kenseth 6.00 15.00
IMMM Mark Martin 6.00 15.00
IMMT Martin Truex 5.00 12.00
IMMW Michael Waltrip 6.00 15.00
IMPM Paul Menard 4.00 10.00
IMRN Ryan Newman 5.00 12.00
IMRP Richard Petty L 10.00 25.00
IMTB Trevor Bayne 6.00 15.00
IMTB2 Trevor Bayne NNS 6.00 15.00
IMTL Terry Labonte L 8.00 20.00

IMTP Travis Pastrana NNS 8.00 20.00
IMTS1 Tony Stewart Mobil 10.00 25.00
IMTS2 Tony Stewart OD 10.00 25.00

2012 Press Pass Ignite Profile

STATED ODDS 1:10 HOB
SP STATED ODDS 1:100 HOB
P1 Ryan Newman .40 1.00
P2 Mark Martin .50 1.25
P3 Paul Menard .30 .75
P4 Danica Patrick SP 12.00 30.00
P5 Trevor Bayne .50 1.25
P6 Dale Earnhardt Jr. 1.00 2.50
P7 Jeff Gordon SP 8.00 20.00
P8 Jimmie Johnson .75 2.00
P9 Tony Stewart .75 2.00
P10 Carl Edwards SP 6.00 15.00
P11 Kyle Busch SP 8.00 20.00
P12 Matt Kenseth .50 1.25

2012 Press Pass Ignite Steel Horses

STATED ODDS 1:10 HOB
SP STATED ODDS 1:100 HOB
SH1 Dale Earnhardt Jr.'s Car 1.00 2.50
SH2 Jeff Gordon's Car 1.00 2.50
SH3 Danica Patrick's Car SP 12.00 30.00
SH4 Tony Stewart's Car .75 2.00
SH5 Kevin Harvick's Car SP 8.00 20.00
SH6 Carl Edwards' Car .50 1.25
SH7 Jimmie Johnson's Car SP 6.00 15.00
SH8 Kasey Kahne's Car .50 1.25
SH9 Kyle Busch's Car .60 1.50

2013 Press Pass Ignite

*CAR CARDS 60% OF BASE
0 DANICA DAY500 ODDS 1:200 HOB
1 Aric Almirola .25 .60
2 Marcos Ambrose .30 .75
3 Trevor Bayne .30 .75
4 Greg Biffle .25 .60
5 Clint Bowyer .30 .75
6 Jeff Burton .25 .60
7 Kurt Busch .25 .60
8 Kyle Busch .40 1.00
9 Dale Earnhardt Jr. .60 1.50
10 Carl Edwards .30 .75
11 David Gilliland .20 .50
12 Jeff Gordon .60 1.50
13 Denny Hamlin .30 .75
14 Kevin Harvick .40 1.00
15 Jimmie Johnson .50 1.25
16 Kasey Kahne .30 .75
17 Matt Kenseth .30 .75
18 Brad Keselowski .40 1.00
19 Travis Kvapil .20 .50
20 Bobby Labonte .30 .75
21 Joey Logano .30 .75
22 Mark Martin .30 .75
23 Michael McDowell .25 .60
24 Jamie McMurray .30 .75
25 Casey Mears .20 .50
26 Paul Menard .20 .50
27 Juan Pablo Montoya .30 .75
28 Ryan Newman .25 .60
29 Danica Patrick .75 2.00
30 David Ragan .25 .60
31 David Reutimann .25 .60
32 Regan Smith .25 .60
33 Scott Speed .20 .50
34 Ricky Stenhouse Jr. .25 .60
35 Tony Stewart .50 1.25
36 David Stremme .15 .40
37 Martin Truex Jr. .25 .60
38 Michael Waltrip .30 .75
39 Josh Wise .20 .50
40 Justin Allgaier .25 .60
41 Austin Dillon .40 1.00
42 Jeffrey Earnhardt .30 .75
43 Sam Hornish Jr. .25 .60
44 Travis Pastrana .30 .75
45 Elliott Sadler .20 .50
46 Regan Smith .25 .60
47 Brian Vickers .20 .50
48 James Buescher .20 .50
49 Ty Dillon .30 .75
50 Johanna Long .30 .75
51 Danica Patrick's Car TS .50 1.25
52 Jeff Gordon's Car TS .40 1.00
53 Trevor Bayne's Car TS .20 .50
54 Ryan Newman's Car TS .15 .40
55 Tony Stewart's Car TS .30 .75
56 Kasey Kahne's Car TS .20 .50
57 Denny Hamlin's Car TS .20 .50
58 Kyle Busch's Car TS .25 .60
59 Joey Logano's Car TS .20 .50
60 Matt Kenseth's Car TS .20 .50
61 Dale Earnhardt Jr.'s Car TS .40 1.00
62 Ricky Stenhouse Jr's Car TS .20 .50
63 Juan Pablo Montoya's Car TS .20 .50
64 Paul Menard's Car TS .12 .30
65 Casey Mears' Car TS .12 .30
66 Austin Dillon's Car TS .25 .60
67 Carl Edwards' Car TS .20 .50
68 Clint Bowyer's Car TS .20 .50
69 Martin Truex's Car TS .15 .40
70 Jeff Burton's Car TS .15 .40
0 Danica Patrick DAY500 6.00 15.00

2013 Press Pass Ignite Proofs Black and White

*B&W/50: 4X TO 10X BASIC CARDS

2013 Press Pass Ignite Proofs Cyan

*CYAN: 5X TO 12X BASIC CARDS
ONE PER RETAIL BLASTER BOX

2013 Press Pass Ignite Proofs Magenta

*MAGENTA: 5X TO 12X BASIC CARDS
ONE PER RETAIL BLASTER BOX

2013 Press Pass Ignite Convoy

STATED ODDS 1:10 HOB
1 Jeff Burton's Hauler .40 1.00
2 Dale Earnhardt Jr.'s Hauler 1.00 2.50
3 Jeff Gordon's Hauler 1.00 2.50
4 Marcos Ambrose's Hauler .50 1.25
5 Jimmie Johnson's Hauler .75 2.00
6 Kasey Kahne's Hauler .50 1.25
7 Ryan Newman's Hauler .40 1.00
8 Danica Patrick's Hauler 1.25 3.00
9 Tony Stewart's Hauler .75 2.00
10 Kyle Busch's Hauler .60 1.50

2013 Press Pass Ignite Double Burner Silver

STATED PRINT RUN 25 SER.#'d SETS
DBBK Brad Keselowski 12.00 30.00
DBCE Carl Edwards 10.00 25.00
DBDE Dale Earnhardt Jr. 20.00 50.00
DBDP Danica Patrick 25.00 60.00
DBJG Jeff Gordon 20.00 50.00
DBJJ Jimmie Johnson 15.00 40.00
DBKH Kevin Harvick 12.00 30.00
DBKK Kasey Kahne 10.00 25.00
DBKYB Kyle Busch 12.00 30.00
DBTS Tony Stewart 15.00 40.00

2013 Press Pass Ignite Great American Treads Autographs Blue Holofoil

STATED PRINT RUN 5-20
GATAA Aric Almirola/20 12.00 30.00
GATCB Clint Bowyer/20 15.00 40.00
GATGB Greg Biffle/20 12.00 30.00
GATJL Joey Logano/20 15.00 40.00
GATMA Marcos Ambrose/20 15.00 40.00
GATPM Paul Menard/20 10.00 25.00
GATRN Ryan Newman/20 12.00 30.00
GATRS Ricky Stenhouse Jr./20 15.00 40.00

2013 Press Pass Ignite Hot Threads Silver

OVERALL ONE MEM PER HOBBY BOX
*BLUE/99: .5X TO 1.2X SILVER
*OVERSIZE PATCH/20: 1.2X TO 3X SILVER
HTAA Aric Almirola 2.50 6.00
HTAD Austin Dillon 4.00 10.00
HTBK Brad Keselowski 4.00 10.00
HTBL Bobby Labonte 3.00 8.00
HTCB Clint Bowyer 3.00 8.00
HTCE Carl Edwards 3.00 8.00
HTDA Davey Allison 5.00 12.00
HTDEJR Dale Earnhardt Jr. 6.00 15.00
HTDG David Gilliland 2.00 5.00
HTDH Denny Hamlin 3.00 8.00
HTDP Danica Patrick 8.00 20.00
HTDR David Ragan 2.50 6.00
HTES Elliott Sadler 2.00 5.00
HTGB Greg Biffle 2.50 6.00
HTJA Justin Allgaier 2.50 6.00
HTJB Jeff Burton 2.50 6.00
HTJG Jeff Gordon 6.00 15.00
HTJG2 Jeff Gordon PP 5.00 12.00
HTJJ Jimmie Johnson 5.00 12.00
HTJL Joey Logano 3.00 8.00
HTJM Jamie McMurray 3.00 8.00
HTJPM Juan Pablo Montoya 3.00 8.00
HTJW Josh Wise 2.00 5.00
HTKH Kevin Harvick 4.00 10.00
HTKK Kasey Kahne 3.00 8.00
HTKYB Kyle Busch 4.00 10.00
HTMA Marcos Ambrose 3.00 8.00
HTMM Mark Martin 3.00 8.00
HTMMD Michael McDowell 2.50 6.00
HTMT Martin Truex Jr. 2.50 6.00
HTMW Michael Waltrip 3.00 8.00
HTPM Paul Menard 2.00 5.00
HTRN Ryan Newman 2.50 6.00
HTRS Ricky Stenhouse Jr. 3.00 8.00
HTRS Regan Smith 4.00 10.00
HTTB Trevor Bayne 5.00 12.00
HTTL Terry Labonte 3.00 8.00
HTTP Travis Pastrana 3.00 8.00
HTTS Tony Stewart 5.00 12.00

2013 Press Pass Ignite Ink Black

STATED PRINT RUN 5-99
*BLUE/20-25: .6X TO 1.5X BLACK/75-99
*BLUE/20-25: .5X TO 1.2X BLACK/50-60
IIAA Aric Almirola/75 4.00 10.00
IIAD Austin Dillon/99 12.00 30.00
IIBV Brian Vickers/99 3.00 8.00
IICB Clint Bowyer/50 6.00 15.00
IICE Carl Edwards/60 6.00 15.00
IICM Casey Mears/99 3.00 8.00
IIDE Dale Earnhardt Jr./20 40.00 80.00
IIDG David Gilliland/75 3.00 8.00
IIDR David Ragan/75 4.00 10.00
IIDR2 David Reutimann/25 6.00 15.00
IIDS David Stremme/99 3.00 8.00
IIES Elliott Sadler/75 3.00 8.00
IIGB Greg Biffle/50 5.00 12.00
IIJA Justin Allgaier/75 4.00 10.00
IIJB Jeff Burton/25 6.00 15.00
IIJE Jeffrey Earnhardt/75 6.00 15.00
IIJG Jeff Gordon/17 60.00 120.00
IIJJ Jimmie Johnson/20 25.00 50.00
IIJL Joey Logano/50 6.00 15.00
IIJM Jamie McMurray/75 5.00 12.00
IIJPM Juan Pablo Montoya/50 6.00 15.00
IIJW Josh Wise/99 3.00 8.00
IIKH Kevin Harvick/45 20.00 40.00
IIKK Kasey Kahne/25 8.00 20.00
IIKUB Kurt Busch/75 6.00 15.00
IIKYB Kyle Busch/45 12.00 30.00
IIMA Marcos Ambrose/40 6.00 15.00
IIMD Michael McDowell/99 4.00 10.00
IIMK Matt Kenseth/70 8.00 20.00
IIMT Martin Truex Jr./99 4.00 10.00
IIMW Michael Waltrip/20 8.00 20.00
IIPM Paul Menard/75 3.00 8.00
IIRN Ryan Newman/50 5.00 12.00
IIRS Regan Smith/99 4.00 10.00
IIRSJ Ricky Stenhouse Jr./75 6.00 15.00
IISH Sam Hornish Jr/75 4.00 10.00
IISS Scott Speed/99 3.00 8.00
IITB Trevor Bayne/99 6.00 15.00
IITD Ty Dillon/75 6.00 15.00
IITK Travis Kvapil/50 4.00 10.00
IITP Travis Pastrana/50 12.50 25.00
IITS Tony Stewart/35 30.00 60.00

2013 Press Pass Ignite Profile

STATED ODDS 1:10 HOB
SP STATED ODDS 1:200 HOB
1 Kyle Busch SP 8.00 20.00
2 Travis Pastrana SP 12.00 30.00
3 Carl Edwards .50 1.25
4 Jeff Gordon 1.00 2.50
5 Denny Hamlin .50 1.25
6 Kevin Harvick SP 8.00 20.00
7 Jimmie Johnson .75 2.00
8 Kasey Kahne .50 1.25
9 Matt Kenseth .50 1.25
10 Mark Martin .50 1.25
11 Kurt Busch .40 1.00
12 Danica Patrick SP 20.00 40.00
13 Ricky Stenhouse Jr. SP 10.00 25.00
14 Tony Stewart .75 2.00
15 Brad Keselowski .60 1.50

2013 Press Pass Ignite Turning Point

STATED ODDS 1:10 HOB
1 Jeff Gordon's Car 1.00 2.50
2 Austin Dillon's Car .60 1.50
3 Dale Earnhardt Jr's Car 1.00 2.50
4 Carl Edwards' Car .50 1.25
5 Jimmie Johnson's Car .75 2.00
6 Tony Stewart's Car .75 2.00
7 Danica Patrick's Car 1.25 3.00
8 Kevin Harvick's Car .60 1.50
9 Kyle Busch's Car .60 1.50
10 Marcos Ambrose's Car .50 1.25

1999 Press Pass Jeff Gordon Fan Club

JG Jeff Gordon 20.00 40.00

2005 Press Pass Legends

This 50-card set features some of NASCAR's greatest drivers along with some current superstars. They were released in September, 2005 in hobby only 5-card packs. Boxes consisted of 3 mini boxes which each factory sealed, containing 6 packs in each. An entry card for a chance to win a signed lithograph of NASCAR's 50 geatest drivers was inserted into packs at a rate of one in 18.

COMPLETE SET (50) 15.00 40.00
WAX BOX (18) 100.00 150.00
MINI BOX (6) 35.00 60.00
1 Lee Petty .40 1.00
2 Curtis Turner .40 1.00
3 Fireball Roberts .40 1.00
4 Marvin Panch .25 .60
5 Glen Wood .25 .60
6 Tiny Lund .25 .60
7 Fred Lorenzen .40 1.00
8 Rex White .25 .60
9 Cale Yarborough .40 1.00
10 Richard Petty 1.25 3.00
11 Buddy Baker .40 1.00
12 David Pearson .40 1.00
13 Bobby Allison .40 1.00
14 Jack Ingram .25 .60
15 Benny Parsons .25 .60
16 Donnie Allison .40 1.00
17 Harry Gant .40 1.00
18 Neil Bonnett .25 .60
19 Dale Earnhardt 2.00 5.00
20 Ricky Rudd .60 1.50
21 Terry Labonte .60 1.50
22 Rusty Wallace .75 2.00
23 Tim Richmond .40 1.00
24 Mark Martin 1.00 2.50
25 Dale Jarrett .75 2.00
26 Alan Kulwicki .60 1.50
27 Davey Allison .60 1.50
28 Jeff Gordon 1.50 4.00
29 Tony Stewart 1.00 2.50
30 Dale Earnhardt Jr. 1.50 4.00
31 Jimmie Johnson 1.25 3.00
32 Kasey Kahne 1.50 4.00
33 Kyle Busch CRC 1.00 2.50
34 Richard Petty C 1.25 3.00
35 Benny Parsons C .25 .60
36 Cale Yarborough C .40 1.00
37 Bobby Allison C .40 1.00
38 Rusty Wallace C .75 2.00
39 Alan Kulwicki C .60 1.50
40 Dale Earnhardt C 2.00 5.00
41 Terry Labonte C .60 1.50
42 Bobby Labonte C .75 2.00
43 Jeff Gordon C 1.50 4.00
44 Tony Stewart C 1.00 2.50
45 Matt Kenseth C 1.25 3.00
46 Kurt Busch C .60 1.50
47 L.Petty 1.25 3.00
R.Petty
K.Petty FT
48 Do.Allison .60 1.50
B.Allison
D.Allison FT
49 T.Labonte .60 1.50
B.Labonte
J.Labonte FT
50 D.Allison 1.50 4.00
Gordon
Petty CL
NNO Lithograph Entry Card 3.00 6.00

2005 Press Pass Legends Blue

*BLUE: 1X TO 2.5X BASE

2005 Press Pass Legends Gold

GOLD: 1.2X TO 3X BASE

2005 Press Pass Legends Holofoil

*HOLOFOIL: 2.5X TO 6X BASE

2005 Press Pass Legends Autographs Blue

STATED ODDS 1:18
1 Bobby Allison/700 6.00 15.00
2 Buddy Baker/720 8.00 20.00
3 Harry Gant/700 8.00 20.00
4 Fred Lorenzen/700 8.00 20.00
5 Jack Ingram/650 6.00 15.00
6 Marvin Panch/675 6.00 15.00
7 Benny Parsons/700 15.00 40.00
8 David Pearson/650 8.00 20.00
9 Richard Petty/100 40.00 80.00
10 Rex White/700 5.00 12.00
11 Glen Wood/700 6.00 15.00
12 Cale Yarborough/700 6.00 15.00

2005 Press Pass Legends Autographs Black

1 Bobby Allison/50 15.00 40.00
2 Buddy Baker/50 15.00 40.00
3 Harry Gant/50 20.00 50.00
4 Fred Lorenzen/50 20.00 50.00
5 Jack Ingram/100 15.00 40.00
6 Marvin Panch/100 15.00 40.00
7 Benny Parsons/50 25.00 60.00
8 David Pearson/100 20.00 50.00
9 Richard Petty/50 50.00 100.00
10 Rex White/50 12.00 30.00
11 Glen Wood/50 15.00 40.00
12 Cale Yarborough/50 15.00 40.00
13 Kurt Busch/50 15.00 40.00
14 Dale Earnhardt Jr./50 75.00 150.00
15 Jeff Gordon/50 75.00 150.00
16 Kevin Harvick/50 20.00 50.00
17 Dale Jarrett/50 40.00 100.00
18 Jimmie Johnson/50 50.00 120.00
19 Kasey Kahne/50 25.00 60.00
20 Matt Kenseth/50 50.00 100.00
21 Bobby Labonte/50 30.00 60.00
22 Terry Labonte/50 20.00 50.00
23 Mark Martin/50 30.00 80.00
24 Ryan Newman/50 25.00 60.00
25 Ricky Rudd/50 15.00 40.00
26 Tony Stewart/50 50.00 100.00

2005 Press Pass Legends Double Threads Bronze

*GOLD/99: .6X TO 1.5X BRONZE
*SILVER/225: .5X TO 1.2X BRONZE
DTBK K.Busch/M.Kenseth 5.00 12.00
DTEW D.Earnhardt Jr./M.Waltrip 10.00 25.00
DTGJ J.Gordon/J.Johnson 10.00 25.00
DTKV K.Kahne/B.Vickers 8.00 20.00
DTLG T.Labonte/J.Gordon 10.00 25.00
DTLL B.Labonte/T.Labonte 5.00 12.00
DTMB M.Martin/K.Busch 5.00 12.00
DTMK M.Martin/M.Kenseth 5.00 12.00
DTNW R.Newman/R.Wallace 5.00 12.00
DTSL T.Stewart/T.Labonte 8.00 20.00

2005 Press Pass Legends Greatest Moments

COMPLETE SET (18) 40.00 100.00
GM1 Benny Parsons .75 2.00
GM2 David Pearson Firecrkr.400 1.25 3.00
GM3 David Pearson Day.500 1.25 3.00
GM4 Richard Petty Day.500 4.00 10.00
GM5 Cale Yarborough 1.25 3.00
GM6 Richard Petty Firecrkr.400 4.00 10.00
GM7 Dale Earnhardt Winst.'87 6.00 15.00
GM8 B.Allison 2.00 5.00
D.Allison
GM9 Harry Gant 1.25 3.00
GM10 Davey Allison 2.00 5.00
GM11 Alan Kulwicki 2.00 5.00
GM12 Jeff Gordon 5.00 12.00
GM13 Terry Labonte 2.00 5.00
GM14 Dale Earnhardt Daytona 6.00 15.00
GM15 Dale Earnhardt Winst.'00 6.00 15.00
GM16 Kevin Harvick 3.00 8.00
GM17 Dale Earnhardt Jr. 5.00 12.00
GM18 R.Craven 2.00 5.00
K.Busch

2005 Press Pass Legends Heritage

COMPLETE SET (12) 30.00 80.00
HE1 Davey Allison 3.00 8.00
HE2 Jeff Gordon 8.00 20.00
HE3 Dale Jarrett 4.00 10.00
HE4 Alan Kulwicki 3.00 8.00
HE5 Terry Labonte 3.00 8.00
HE6 Mark Martin 5.00 12.00
HE7 David Pearson 2.00 5.00
HE8 Richard Petty 6.00 15.00
HE9 Fireball Roberts 2.00 5.00
HE10 Rusty Wallace 4.00 10.00
HE11 Michael Waltrip 2.00 5.00
HE12 Glen Wood 1.25 3.00

2005 Press Pass Legends Threads and Treads Bronze

*GOLD/99: .6X TO 1.5X BRONZE/375
*SILVER/225: .5X TO 1.2X BRONZE/375
TTDE Dale Earnhardt 15.00 40.00
TTDJ Dale Jarrett 3.00 8.00
TTJG Jeff Gordon 6.00 15.00
TTJJ Jimmie Johnson 5.00 12.00
TTJR Dale Earnhardt Jr. 6.00 15.00
TTKK Kasey Kahne 5.00 12.00
TTMM Mark Martin 3.00 8.00
TTRN Ryan Newman 2.50 6.00
TTRW Rusty Wallace 3.00 8.00
TTTL Terry Labonte 3.00 8.00
TTTS Tony Stewart 5.00 12.00

2005 Press Pass Legends Tim Richmond Racing Artifacts

COMPLETE SET (3)
TRF T.Richmond Firesuit B/375 12.50 30.00
TRF T.Richmond Firesuit S/225 15.00 40.00
TRF T.Richmond Firesuit G/99 20.00 50.00
TRG T.Richmond Glove/99 12.00 30.00
TRFG T.Richmond Fire.Glove/50 30.00 80.00

2006 Press Pass Legends

This 50-card set features some of NASCAR's greatest drivers along with some current superstars. They were released in September, 2006 in hobby only 5-card packs. Boxes consisted of 3 mini boxes which each factory sealed, containing 6 packs in each. An entry card for a chance to win a signed lithograph of NASCAR's 50 geatest drivers was inserted into packs at a rate of one in 18.

COMPLETE SET (50) 12.50 30.00
WAX BOX (18) 75.00 125.00
MINI BOX (6) 35.00 50.00
1 Tim Flock .25 .60
2 Lee Petty .30 .75
3 Marshall Teague .25 .60
4 Curtis Turner .30 .75
5 Fireball Roberts .40 1.00
6 Marvin Panch .25 .60
7 Ned Jarrett .30 .75
8 Glen Wood .25 .60
9 Tiny Lund .25 .60
10 Ralph Earnhardt .40 1.00
11 Fred Lorenzen .30 .75
12 Rex White .25 .60
13 Cale Yarborough .40 1.00
14 Richard Petty .60 1.50
15 Buddy Baker .30 .75
16 David Pearson .40 1.00
17 Bobby Allison .30 .75
18 Jack Ingram .25 .60
19 Benny Parsons .40 1.00
20 Donnie Allison .30 .75
21 Darrell Waltrip .60 1.50
22 Harry Gant .30 .75
23 Neil Bonnett .40 1.00
24 Dale Earnhardt 2.50 6.00
25 Janet Guthrie .25 .60
26 Terry Labonte .40 1.00
27 Kyle Petty .30 .75
28 Rusty Wallace .40 1.00
29 Tim Richmond .30 .75
30 Mark Martin .40 1.00
31 Dale Jarrett .40 1.00
32 Alan Kulwicki .60 1.50
33 Davey Allison .60 1.50
34 Bobby Labonte .40 1.00
35 Jeff Gordon .75 2.00
36 Tony Stewart .60 1.50
37 Dale Earnhardt Jr. .75 2.00
38 Matt Kenseth .40 1.00
39 Kurt Busch .30 .75
40 Kevin Harvick .50 1.25
41 Jimmie Johnson .60 1.50
42 Ryan Newman .30 .75
43 Kasey Kahne .50 1.25
44 Carl Edwards .40 1.00
45 Denny Hamlin CRC 1.50 4.00
46 R.Petty/J.Gordon REC Poles .75 2.00
47 Dale Sr./Dale Jr. REC 2.50 6.00
48 R.Petty/J.Gordon REC Champs .75 2.00
49 R.Petty/J.Gordon REC Top 10s .75 2.00
CL Fred Lorenzen CL .30 .75
NNO Lithograph Contest Card 1.50 4.00

2006 Press Pass Legends Blue

COMPLETE SET (50) 20.00 50.00
*BLUE: .8X TO 2X BASE

2006 Press Pass Legends Bronze

COMPLETE SET (50) 40.00 100.00
*BRONZE: 1.2X TO 3X

2006 Press Pass Legends Gold

*GOLD: 2.5X TO 6X BASE

2006 Press Pass Legends Holofoil

*HOLO: 4X TO 10X BASE

2006 Press Pass Legends Autographs Black

This 30-card set featured certified autographs signed in black ink. Most of these were serial numbered to 50, see the checklist below for the exceptions. The cards were certified by the manufacturer on thier cardbacks. The combined rate for all autographs and race-used cards was one in six packs.

1 Bobby Allison/50 15.00 40.00
2 Donnie Allison/50 15.00 40.00
3 Buddy Baker/50
4 Harry Gant/50 15.00 40.00
5 Janet Guthrie/50 15.00 40.00
6 Jack Ingram/50 12.50 30.00
7 Ned Jarrett/75 12.50 30.00
8 Fred Lorenzen/220 10.00 25.00
9 Marvin Panch/250 10.00 25.00
10 Benny Parsons/50 25.00 60.00
11 David Pearson/50 20.00 50.00
12 Richard Petty/50 30.00 60.00
13 Rusty Wallace/200 12.50 30.00
14 Darrell Waltrip/25 50.00 120.00
15 Rex White/50 15.00 40.00
16 Glen Wood/50 12.50 30.00
17 Cale Yarborough/50 15.00 40.00
19 Jeff Burton/50 15.00 40.00
20 Kurt Busch/50 20.00 50.00
21 Dale Earnhardt Jr./50 60.00 150.00
22 Carl Edwards/50 25.00 60.00
23 Jeff Gordon/50 60.00 150.00
25 Jimmie Johnson/50 40.00 100.00
26 Kasey Kahne/50 25.00 60.00
27 Matt Kenseth/50 40.00 80.00
28 Bobby Labonte/50 20.00 50.00
29 Terry Labonte/50 30.00 60.00
30 Mark Martin/50 15.00 40.00
31 Ryan Newman/50 25.00 60.00
32 Tony Stewart/50 40.00 100.00

2006 Press Pass Legends Autographs Blue

This 19-card set featured certified autographs signed in blue ink. Most of these were serial numbered to 650, see the checklist below for the exceptions. The cards were certified by the manufacturer on thier cardbacks. The combined rate for all autographs and race-used cards was one in six packs.

1 Bobby Allison/650 6.00 15.00
2 Donnie Allison/650 12.50 30.00
3 Buddy Baker/650 8.00 20.00
4 Greg Biffle/50 12.00 30.00
5 Harry Gant/600 8.00 20.00
6 Janet Guthrie/545 12.50 30.00
7 Kevin Harvick/50 25.00 60.00
8 Jack Ingram/645 6.00 15.00
9 Ned Jarrett/205 8.00 20.00
10 Fred Lorenzen/480 6.00 15.00
11 Marvin Panch/400 6.00 15.00
12 Benny Parsons/650 12.00 30.00
13 David Pearson/650 8.00 20.00
14 Richard Petty/100 25.00 60.00
15 Rusty Wallace/300 15.00 40.00
16 Darrell Waltrip/45 75.00 125.00
17 Rex White/650 6.00 15.00
18 Glen Wood/650 6.00 15.00
19 Cale Yarborough/645 6.00 15.00

2006 Press Pass Legends Champion Threads and Treads Bronze

This 7-card set features swatches of past champions' firesuit and tire. The cards had bronze foil highlights and each was serial numbered to 399. The cards carried a "CTT" prefix for thier card numbers. The overall odds were combined with other race-used cards and autographs at a rate of one in six packs.

*GOLD/99: .8X TO 2X BRONZE
*SILVER/299: .6X TO 1.5X BRONZE
CTTBL Bobby Labonte 5.00 12.00
CTTDJ Dale Jarrett 5.00 12.00
CTTJG Jeff Gordon 8.00 20.00
CTTKB Kurt Busch 5.00 12.00
CTTMK Matt Kenseth 5.00 12.00
CTTTL Terry Labonte 6.00 15.00
CTTTS Tony Stewart 8.00 20.00

2006 Press Pass Legends Champion Threads Bronze

This 7-card set features swatches of past champions' firesuits. The cards had bronze foil highlights and each was serial numbered to 399.The cards carried a "CT" prefix for thier card numbers. The overall odds were combined with other race-used cards and autographs at a rate of one in six packs.

*GOLD/50: .6X TO 1.5X BRONZE
*PATCH/25: 1.2X TO 3X BRONZE
*SILVER/199: .5X TO 1.2X BRONZE
CTBL Bobby Labonte 4.00 10.00
CTDJ Dale Jarrett 6.00 15.00
CTJG Jeff Gordon 8.00 20.00
CTKB Kurt Busch 3.00 8.00
CTMK Matt Kenseth 4.00 10.00
CTTL Terry Labonte 6.00 15.00
CTTS Tony Stewart 6.00 15.00

2006 Press Pass Legends Heritage Silver

This 15-card set was randomly inserted in packs at a rate of one in 18. These were serial numbered to 549 on their card fronts. Each carried an "HE" prefix for its card number.

COMPLETE SET (18) 50.00 120.00
*GOLD/99: .6X TO 1.5X SILVER
HE1 Richard Petty 2.50 6.00
HE2 David Pearson 1.50 4.00
HE3 Bobby Allison 1.25 3.00
HE4 Darrell Waltrip 2.50 6.00
HE5 Cale Yarborough 1.50 4.00
HE6 Dale Earnhardt 10.00 25.00
HE7 Jeff Gordon 3.00 8.00
HE8 Rusty Wallace 1.50 4.00
HE9 Lee Petty 1.25 3.00

HE10 Tony Stewart 2.50 6.00
HE11 Jimmie Johnson 2.50 6.00
HE12 Dale Earnhardt Jr. 3.00 8.00
HE13 L.Petty 2.50 6.00
R.Petty
HE14 B.Allison 2.50 6.00
D.Allison
HE15 Dale Sr. 10.00 25.00
Dale Jr.

2006 Press Pass Legends Memorable Moments Silver

This 15-card set was randomly inserted in packs at a rate of one in 12. These were serial numbered to 699 on their card fronts. Each carried an "MM" prefix for its card number.

COMPLETE SET (16) 40.00 100.00
*GOLD/99: .8X TO 2X SILVER
MM1 Bobby Allison 1.00 2.50
MM2 David Pearson Charlotte 1.25 3.00
MM3 Jeff Gordon Charlotte 2.50 6.00
MM4 Jimmie Johnson 2.00 5.00
MM5 David Pearson Darlington 1.25 3.00
MM6 Jeff Gordon Darlington 2.50 6.00
MM7 Dale Earnhardt 8.00 20.00
MM8 Jeff Gordon Darlington '97 2.50 6.00
MM9 Richard Petty N.Wilkesboro 2.00 5.00
MM10 Richard Petty N.Wilkesboro '72 2.00 5.00
MM11 Jeff Gordon N.Wilkesboro 2.50 6.00
MM12 Cale Yarborough 1.25 3.00
MM13 Curtis Turner 1.00 2.50
MM14 Matt Kenseth 1.25 3.00
MM15 Richard Petty Rockingham 2.00 5.00
MM16 Rusty Wallace 1.25 3.00

2006 Press Pass Legends Racing Artifacts Firesuit Bronze

This 9-card set featured swatches of race-used firesuits. Each card was highlighted with bronze foil and serial numbered to 399. The cards carried an "F" suffix for their card numbering. The odds were combined overall with other race-used memorabilia and autographs cards, and were inserted at a rate of one in six.

*GOLD/99: .6X TO 1.5X BRONZE
*PATCH/25: 2X TO 5X BRONZE
*SILVER/199: .5X TO 1.2X BRONZE
AKF Alan Kulwicki 10.00 25.00
BBF Buddy Baker 8.00 20.00
CYF Cale Yarborough 12.50 30.00
DAF Davey Allison 20.00 50.00
DEF Dale Earnhardt 20.00 50.00
DPF David Pearson 12.50 30.00
RWF Rusty Wallace 8.00 20.00
TLF Tiny Lund 12.50 30.00
TRF Tim Richmond 12.50 30.00

2006 Press Pass Legends Racing Artifacts Hat

This 1-card set featured a swatch of a Richard Petty's trademark cowboy hat. It was highlighted with gold foil and serial numbered to 99. The cards carried an "H" suffix for its card numbering. The odds were combined overall with other race-used memorabilia and autograph cards, and were inserted at a rate of one in six.

RPH Richard Petty 60.00 120.00

2006 Press Pass Legends Racing Artifacts Sheet Metal Bronze

This 2-card set featured swatches of race-used sheet metal. Each card was highlighted with bronze foil and serial numbered to 199. The cards carried an "SM" suffix for their card numbering. The odds were combined overall with other race-used memorabilia and autographs cards, and were inserted at a rate of one in six.

*GOLD/50: .6X TO 1.5X BRONZE
*SILVER/99: .5X TO 1.2X BRONZE
BASM Bobby Allison 12.00 30.00
BPSM Benny Parsons 12.00 30.00

2006 Press Pass Legends Racing Artifacts Tire Bronze

This 2-card set featured swatches of race-used tires. Each card was highlighted with bronze foil and serial numbered to 399. The cards carried a "T" suffix for their card numbering. The odds were combined overall with other race-used memorabilia and autographs cards, and were inserted at a rate of one in six.

*GOLD/50: .6X TO 1.5X BRONZE
*SILVER/199: .5X TO 1.2X BRONZE
DET Dale Earnhardt 10.00 25.00
RWT Rusty Wallace 10.00 25.00

2006 Press Pass Legends Triple Threads

This 9-card set featured three memorabillia swatches per card. Each card contained a swatch of race-used firesuit, glove and shoe. These were serial numbered to 50.

TTCE Carl Edwards 60.00 120.00
TTDE Dale Earnhardt Jr. 75.00 150.00
TTJG Jeff Gordon 100.00 175.00
TTJJ Jimmie Johnson
TTKH Kevin Harvick 50.00 100.00
TTMK Matt Kenseth 50.00 100.00
TTMT Martin Truex Jr. 40.00 80.00
TTRN Ryan Newman 40.00 80.00
TTTS Tony Stewart 20.00 50.00

2007 Press Pass Legends

COMPLETE SET (70) 15.00 40.00
WAX BOX 100.00 150.00
MINI BOX 30.00 60.00
1 Lee Petty .25 .60
2 Louise Smith .20 .50
3 Marshall Teague .20 .50
4 Curtis Turner .25 .60
5 Tim Flock .20 .50
6 Cotton Owens .20 .50
7 Glen Wood .20 .50
8 Marty Robbins .25 .60
9 Marvin Panch .20 .50
10 Ralph Earnhardt .30 .75
11 Fireball Roberts .30 .75
12 Rex White .20 .50
13 Tiny Lund .20 .50
14 Ned Jarrett .25 .60
15 David Pearson .30 .75
16 Fred Lorenzen .25 .60
17 Jack Ingram .20 .50
18 Richard Petty .50 1.25
19 Bobby Allison .25 .60
20 Janet Guthrie .20 .50
21 Cale Yarborough .30 .75
22 Benny Parsons .30 .75
23 Donnie Allison .25 .60
24 Harry Gant .25 .60
25 Buddy Baker .25 .60
26 Bud Moore .25 .60
27 Neil Bonnett .30 .75
28 Darrell Waltrip .50 1.25
29 Dale Earnhardt 2.00 5.00
30 Alan Kulwicki .50 1.25
31 Tim Richmond .25 .60
32 Rusty Wallace .30 .75
33 Ricky Rudd .25 .60
34 Dale Jarrett .30 .75
35 Mark Martin .30 .75
36 Davey Allison .50 1.25
37 Bobby Labonte .30 .75
38 Jeff Burton .25 .60
39 Tony Stewart .50 1.25
40 Jeff Gordon .60 1.50
41 Matt Kenseth .30 .75
42 Dale Earnhardt Jr. .60 1.50
43 Jimmie Johnson .50 1.25
44 Juan Pablo Montoya RC 1.00 2.50
45 Kevin Harvick .40 1.00
46 Ryan Newman .25 .60
47 Kurt Busch .25 .60
48 Carl Edwards .30 .75
49 Kasey Kahne .30 .75
50 Denny Hamlin .40 1.00
51 Dale Earnhardt N 2.00 5.00
52 Harry Gant N .25 .60
53 Ricky Rudd N .25 .60
54 Fred Lorenzen N .25 .60
55 Richard Petty N .50 1.25
56 Darrell Waltrip N .50 1.25
57 Fireball Roberts N .30 .75
58 Cale Yarborough N .30 .75
59 Kevin Harvick N .40 1.00
60 David Pearson N .30 .75
61 Ned Jarrett N .25 .60
62 Tiny Lund N .20 .50
63 B.Allison/Do.Allison/N.Bonnett N.30 .75
64 B.Allison/Do.Allison
C.Yarborough R .30 .75
65 D.Waltrip/D.Earnhardt R 2.00 5.00
66 B.Allison/R.Petty R .50 1.25
67 C.Yarborough/D.Waltrip R .50 1.25
68 D.Earnhardt/J.Gordon R 2.00 5.00
69 D.Pearson/R.Petty R .50 1.25
70 Buddy Baker CL .25 .60

2007 Press Pass Legends Blue

COMPLETE SET (70) 25.00 60.00
*BLUE: 1X TO 2.5X BASE
STATED PRINT RUN 999 SERIAL #'d SETS

2007 Press Pass Legends Bronze

COMPLETE SET (70) 75.00 125.00
*BRONZE: 1.5X TO 4X BASE
STATED PRINT RUN 599 SERIAL #'d SETS

2007 Press Pass Legends Gold

*GOLD: 2.5X TO 6X BASE
STATED PRINT RUN 249 SERIAL #'d SETS

2007 Press Pass Legends Holofoil

*HOLOFOIL: 4X TO 10X BASE
STATED PRINT RUN 99 SERIAL #'d SETS

2007 Press Pass Legends Autographs Black

STATED PRINT RUN 24-145
1 Bobby Allison/49 12.50 30.00
2 Donnie Allison/48 8.00 20.00
3 Buddy Baker/46 10.00 25.00
4 Harry Gant/50 10.00 25.00
5 Janet Guthrie/50 12.50 30.00
6 Jack Ingram/50 8.00 20.00
7 Ned Jarrett/50 10.00 25.00
8 Bud Moore/93 10.00 25.00
9 Cotton Owens/145 8.00 20.00
10 Marvin Panch/50 8.00 20.00
11 David Pearson/48 15.00 40.00
12 Richard Petty/48 30.00 60.00
13 Darrell Waltrip/48 25.00 60.00
14 Rex White/95 12.50 30.00
15 Glen Wood/24 8.00 20.00
16 Cale Yarborough/24 15.00 40.00

2007 Press Pass Legends Autographs Blue

STATED PRINT RUN 48-670
1 Bobby Allison/562 10.00 25.00
2 Donnie Allison/644 6.00 15.00
3 Buddy Baker/567 8.00 20.00
4 Kurt Busch/70 15.00 40.00
5 Dale Earnhardt Jr./59 50.00 120.00
6 Carl Edwards/71 15.00 40.00
7 Harry Gant/638 8.00 20.00
8 Jeff Gordon/48 50.00 120.00
9 Janet Guthrie/385 10.00 25.00
10 Denny Hamlin/59 20.00 50.00
11 Kevin Harvick/71 12.00 30.00
12 Jack Ingram/655 6.00 15.00
13 Dale Jarrett/61 15.00 40.00
14 Ned Jarrett/230 8.00 20.00
15 Jimmie Johnson/71 30.00 80.00
16 Kasey Kahne/75 15.00 40.00
17 Matt Kenseth/60 15.00 40.00
18 Mark Martin/62 20.00 50.00
19 Juan Pablo Montoya/73 25.00 60.00
20 Bud Moore/383 8.00 20.00
21 Cotton Owens/361 8.00 20.00
22 Marvin Panch/502 6.00 15.00
23 David Pearson/306 10.00 25.00
24 Richard Petty/570 15.00 40.00
25 Darrell Waltrip/182 20.00 50.00
26 Rex White/594 8.00 20.00
27 Glen Wood/670 6.00 15.00
28 Cale Yarborough/269 10.00 25.00

2007 Press Pass Legends Autographs Inscriptions Blue

STATED PRINT RUN 1-75
1 Bobby Allison 3 Daytona 500 wins/23
2 Donnie Allison Alabama Gang/23
3 Dale Jr. 8/7
4 Dale Jr. 07/1
5 Harry Gant Mr. September/23
6 Jeff Gordon 24/9
7 Guthrie 1977 Daytona 500 Top Rookie/23
8 Denny Hamlin 11/9
9 Dale Jarrett #44/9
10 Ned Jarrett #11 Dale's Dad/25
11 Matt Kenseth 03 Cup Champion/9
12 Mark Martin The Kid/9
13 Marvin Panch Pancho/75 10.00 25.00
14 Pearson Silver Fox 105 Cup Wins only/21
15 Richard Petty 43/19
16 Darrell Waltrip 11 Jaws/15
17 Cale Yarborough 3 Time Champ/20

2007 Press Pass Legends Dale Earnhardt Silver

COMPLETE SET (9) 40.00 75.00
COMMON DALE 4.00 10.00
STATED PRINT RUN 499 SERIAL #'d SETS
*GOLD/99: .6X TO 1.5X SILVER

2007 Press Pass Legends Father and Son Firesuits Bronze

OVERALL STATED AU/MEM ODDS 4:18
STATED PRINT RUN 99 SERIAL #'d SETS
*GOLD/25: .6X TO 1.5X BRONZE
*SILVER/50: .5X TO 1.2X BRONZE
BADAF B.Allison/Do.Allison 10.00 25.00
RWSWF R.Wallace/S.Wallace 15.00 40.00

2007 Press Pass Legends Legends Gallery Silver

COMPLETE SET (12) 10.00 25.00
STATED PRINT RUN 499 SERIAL #'d SETS
*GOLD/99: .8X TO 2X SILVER
LG1 Lee Petty .50 1.25
LG2 Fireball Roberts .60 1.50
LG3 Rusty Wallace .60 1.50
LG4 Rex White .40 1.00
LG5 Dale Earnhardt 4.00 10.00
LG6 Curtis Turner .50 1.25
LG7 Fred Lorenzen .50 1.25
LG8 Janet Guthrie .40 1.00
LG9 Glen Wood .40 1.00
LG10 Marshall Teague .40 1.00
LG11 Jack Ingram .40 1.00
LG12 Tim Flock .40 1.00

2007 Press Pass Legends Memorable Moments Silver

COMPLETE SET (15) 15.00 40.00
STATED PRINT RUN 499 SERIAL #'d SETS
*GOLD/169: .6X TO 1.5X SILVER/499
MM1 Darrell Waltrip B 1.25 3.00
MM2 Cale Yarborough B .75 2.00
MM3 Jeff Gordon B 1.50 4.00
MM4 Dale Earnhardt B 5.00 12.00
MM5 Rusty Wallace B .75 2.00
MM6 Richard Petty D 1.25 3.00
MM7 B.Allison/Do.Allison/C.Yarborough D .75 2.00
MM8 Dale Earnhardt D 5.00 12.00
MM9 Darrell Waltrip D 1.25 3.00
MM10 David Pearson D .75 2.00
MM11 Richard Petty D 1.25 3.00
MM12 B.Allison/Do.Allison T .60 1.50
MM13 Dale Earnhardt T 5.00 12.00
MM14 Davey Allison T 1.25 3.00
MM15 Dale Earnhardt Jr. T 5.00 12.00

2007 Press Pass Legends Racing Artifacts Firesuit Bronze

OVERALL STATED AU/MEM ODDS 4:18
STATED PRINT RUN 99-199
GOLD/25-50: .6X TO 1.5X BRONZE
*SILVER/50-99: .5X TO 1.2X BRONZE
AGF Alabama Gang/99 30.00 60.00
AKF Alan Kulwicki 12.00 30.00
BAF Bobby Allison 15.00 30.00
BBF Buddy Baker 12.00 25.00
CYF Cale Yarborough 12.00 25.00
DEF Dale Earnhardt 60.00 120.00
DPF David Pearson 10.00 25.00
DWF Darrell Waltrip 20.00 40.00
HGF Harry Gant 12.00 25.00
MRF Marty Robbins 15.00 30.00
NBF Neil Bonnett 15.00 30.00
RWF Rusty Wallace 15.00 30.00
TLF Tiny Lund 12.00 25.00
TRF Tim Richmond 12.00 25.00
DAAF Davey Allison 10.00 25.00
DOAF Donnie Allison 12.00 25.00

2007 Press Pass Legends Racing Artifacts Firesuit Patch

OVERALL STATED AU/MEM ODDS 4:18
STATED PRINT RUN 25 SER.#'d SETS
AKF Alan Kulwicki 25.00 60.00
BAF Bobby Allison 25.00 60.00
BBF Buddy Baker
CYF Cale Yarborough
DEF Dale Earnhardt 300.00 450.00
DPF David Pearson 75.00 150.00
DWF Darrell Waltrip 75.00 150.00
HGF Harry Gant
MRF Marty Robbins 75.00 150.00
NBF Neil Bonnett 75.00 125.00
RWF Rusty Wallace
TLF Tiny Lund
TRF Tim Richmond 100.00 200.00
DAAF Davey Allison 40.00 100.00
DOAF Donnie Allison

2007 Press Pass Legends Racing Artifacts Hat

OVERALL STATED AU/MEM ODDS 4:18
STATED PRINT RUN 99 SERIAL #'d SETS
RPH Richard Petty 50.00 100.00

2007 Press Pass Legends Racing Artifacts Sheet Metal Bronze

OVERALL STATED AU/MEM ODDS 4:18
STATED PRINT RUN 199 SERIAL #'d SETS
*GOLD/50: .6X TO 1.5X BRONZE
*SILVER/99: .5X TO 1.2X BRONZE
BAS Bobby Allison 10.00 25.00
BPS Benny Parsons 12.00 30.00

2007 Press Pass Legends Racing Artifacts Shirt Bronze

OVERALL STATED AU/MEM ODDS 4:18
STATED PRINT RUN 199 SERIAL #'d SETS
*GOLD/50: .6X TO 1.5X BRONZE
*SILVER/99: .5X TO 1.2X BRONZE
BMSH Bud Moore 8.00 20.00
COSH Cotton Owens 6.00 15.00

2007 Press Pass Legends Racing Artifacts Tire Bronze

OVERALL STATED AU/MEM ODDS 4:18
STATED PRINT RUN 299 SERIAL #'d SETS
*GOLD/99: .8X TO 2X BRONZE
*SILVER/199: .6X TO 1.5X BRONZE
DET Dale Earnhardt 10.00 25.00
RWT Rusty Wallace 10.00 25.00

2007 Press Pass Legends Signature Series

STATED PRINT RUN 25 SER.#'d SETS
BL Bobby Labonte 75.00 150.00
CE Carl Edwards 125.00 250.00
DH Denny Hamlin 75.00 150.00
DJ Dale Jarrett 60.00 120.00
JG Jeff Gordon 125.00 250.00
JJ Jimmie Johnson 125.00 250.00
JM Juan Pablo Montoya 60.00 120.00
KB Kurt Busch 50.00 100.00
KH Kevin Harvick 75.00 150.00
MK Matt Kenseth 100.00 200.00
MM Mark Martin 100.00 175.00
MT Martin Truex Jr. 75.00 150.00
PM Paul Menard 40.00 100.00
RN Ryan Newman 60.00 120.00
TS Tony Stewart 100.00 200.00

2007 Press Pass Legends Sunday Swatches Silver

OVERALL STATED AU/MEM ODDS 4:18
STATED PRINT RUN 99 SERIAL #'d SETS
*BRONZE/199: .3X TO .8X SILVER/99
*GOLD/50: .5X TO 1.2X SILVER/99
BVSS Brian Vickers 3.00 8.00
DESS Dale Earnhardt Jr. 6.00 15.00
DHSS Denny Hamlin 4.00 10.00
DJSS Dale Jarrett 3.00 8.00
JGSS Jeff Gordon 6.00 15.00
JJSS Jimmie Johnson 5.00 12.00
JMSS Juan Pablo Montoya 10.00 25.00
JYSS J.J. Yeley 3.00 8.00
KHSS Kevin Harvick 4.00 10.00
KKSS Kasey Kahne 3.00 8.00
MTSS Martin Truex Jr. 2.50 6.00
MWSS Michael Waltrip 3.00 8.00
PMSS Paul Menard 10.00 25.00
RSSS Reed Sorenson 2.00 5.00
TSSS Tony Stewart 5.00 12.00

2007 Press Pass Legends Victory Lane Bronze

OVERALL STATED AU/MEM ODDS 4:18
STATED PRINT RUN 199 SERIAL #'d SETS
*GOLD/25: .8X TO 2X BRONZE/199
*SILVER/99: .5X TO 1.2X BRONZE/199
VL1 Dale Earnhardt Jr. 8.00 20.00
VL2 Jeff Gordon 8.00 20.00
VL3 Jeff Gordon 8.00 20.00
VL4 Denny Hamlin 5.00 12.00
VL5 Kevin Harvick 5.00 12.00
VL6 Jimmie Johnson 6.00 15.00
VL7 Juan Pablo Montoya 12.00 30.00
VL8 Tony Stewart 6.00 15.00
VL9 Martin Truex Jr. 3.00 8.00

2008 Press Pass Legends

This set was released on October 23, 2008. The base set consists of 70 cards.

COMPLETE SET (70) 20.00 50.00
WAX BOX (18) 60.00 120.00
MINI BOX (6) 20.00 40.00
1 Bobby Allison .40 1.00
2 Donnie Allison .40 1.00
3 Davey Allison .75 2.00
4 Mario Andretti .75 2.00
5 Buddy Baker .40 1.00
6 Geoffrey Bodine .30 .75
7 Neil Bonnett .50 1.25
8 Mark Donohue .30 .75
9 Ralph Earnhardt .50 1.25
10 Dale Earnhardt 3.00 8.00
11 Red Farmer .40 1.00
12 Tim Flock .30 .75
13 Harry Gant .40 1.00
14 Pete Hamilton .30 .75
15 Jack Ingram .30 .75
16 Ned Jarrett .40 1.00
17 Dale Jarrett .50 1.25
18 Alan Kulwicki .75 2.00
19 Terry Labonte .50 1.25
20 Fred Lorenzen .40 1.00
21 Tiny Lund .30 .75
22 Rick Mears .50 1.25
23 Bud Moore .30 .75
24 Rob Moroso .30 .75
25 Cotton Owens .30 .75
26 Marvin Panch .30 .75
27 Benny Parsons .50 1.25
28 David Pearson .50 1.25
29 Lee Petty .40 1.00
30 Richard Petty .75 2.00
31 Tim Richmond .40 1.00
32 Marty Robbins .40 1.00
33 Fireball Roberts .40 1.00
34 Louise Smith .30 .75
35 Marshall Teague .30 .75
36 Curtis Turner .40 1.00
37 Bobby Unser .50 1.25
38 Al Unser .50 1.25
39 Al Unser Jr. .50 1.25
40 Darrell Waltrip .75 2.00
41 Rex White .30 .75
42 Glen Wood .30 .75
43 Cale Yarborough .50 1.25
44 Jeff Burton .40 1.00
45 Kurt Busch .40 1.00
46 Kyle Busch .60 1.50
47 Dale Earnhardt Jr. 1.00 2.50
48 Carl Edwards .50 1.25
49 Jeff Gordon 1.00 2.50
50 Kevin Harvick .60 1.50
51 Jimmie Johnson .75 2.00
52 Kasey Kahne .50 1.25
53 Matt Kenseth .50 1.25
54 Mark Martin .50 1.25
55 Tony Stewart .75 2.00
56 Martin Truex Jr. .40 1.00
57 Mario Andretti I .75 2.00
58 Dale Earnhardt I 3.00 8.00
59 Jeff Gordon I 1.00 2.50
60 Rick Mears I .50 1.25
61 David Pearson I .50 1.25
62 Richard Petty I .75 2.00
63 Al Unser I .50 1.25
64 Bobby Unser I .50 1.25
65 Al Unser Jr. I .50 1.25
66 Cale Yarborough I .50 1.25
67 AJ Allmendinger .50 1.25
68 Sam Hornish Jr. .75 2.00
69 Juan Pablo Montoya .75 2.00
70 Ralph Earnhardt CL .50 1.25

2008 Press Pass Legends Blue

COMPLETE SET (70) 75.00 150.00
*BLUE: .6X TO 1.5X BASE
STATED PRINT RUN 599 SERIAL #'d SETS

2008 Press Pass Legends Bronze

*BRONZE: 1X TO 2.5X BASE
STATED PRINT RUN 299 SERIAL #'d SETS

2008 Press Pass Legends Gold

*GOLD: 2X TO 5X BASE
STATED PRINT RUN 99 SERIAL #'d SETS

2008 Press Pass Legends Holo

*HOLO: 4X TO 10X BASE
STATED PRINT RUN 25 SERIAL #'d SETS

2008 Press Pass Legends 500 Club

COMPLETE SET (9) 15.00 40.00
STATED PRINT RUN 560 SERIAL #'d SETS
*GOLD/99: .8X TO 2X BASIC INSERTS
5C1 Richard Petty 2.50 6.00
5C2 Bobby Allison 1.25 3.00
5C3 Rick Mears 1.50 4.00
5C4 Al Unser 1.50 4.00
5C5 Cale Yarborough 1.50 4.00
5C6 Jeff Gordon 3.00 8.00
5C7 Dale Jarrett 1.50 4.00
5C8 Bobby Unser 1.50 4.00
5C9 Mario Andretti 2.50 6.00

2008 Press Pass Legends Autographs Black

STATED PRINT RUN 10-464
AU Al Unser/50 25.00 60.00
BM Bud Moore/234 8.00 20.00
BU Bobby Unser/50 20.00 50.00
CY Cale Yarborough/342 8.00 20.00
DE Dale Earnhardt Jr./37
DW Darrell Waltrip/15
FL Fred Lorenzen/464 6.00 15.00
GW Glen Wood/200 8.00 20.00
HG Harry Gant/305 6.00 15.00
KH Kevin Harvick/10
KK Kasey Kahne/10
MT Martin Truex Jr./85 10.00 25.00
NJ Ned Jarrett/128 8.00 20.00
RF Red Farmer/363 6.00 15.00
RM Rick Mears/32 20.00 50.00
RN Ryan Newman/10
RW Rex White/345 6.00 15.00
TL Terry Labonte/50 25.00 60.00
TS Tony Stewart 40.00 100.00

2008 Press Pass Legends Autographs Black Inscriptions

STATED PRINT RUN 1-98
AU Al Unser/20
BM Bud Moore/98 12.00 30.00
BU Bobby Unser/20
DW Darrell Waltrip/21
DW Darrell Waltrip/30 75.00 150.00
HG Harry Gant/24
MP Marvin Panch/20
RM Rick Mears/70 15.00 40.00
TL Terry Labonte/20

2008 Press Pass Legends Autographs Blue

STATED PRINT RUN 30-950
UNPRICED PRESS PLATE PRINT RUN 1
AU Al Unser/30 12.00 30.00
BA Bobby Allison/740 6.00 15.00
BM Bud Moore/169 6.00 15.00
BU Bobby Unser/35 25.00 60.00
CE Carl Edwards/75 50.00 100.00
CY Cale Yarborough/178 8.00 20.00
DA Donnie Allison/749 6.00 15.00
DE Dale Earnhardt Jr. EXCH
DH Denny Hamlin/75 20.00 50.00
DP David Pearson/540 8.00 20.00
DW Darrell Waltrip/36 40.00 100.00
FL Fred Lorenzen/298 6.00 15.00
GB Geoffrey Bodine/950 6.00 15.00
GW Glen Wood/531 6.00 15.00
HG Harry Gant/419 6.00 15.00
JG Jeff Gordon/75 60.00 120.00
JI Jack Ingram/737 6.00 15.00
JJ Jimmie Johnson/75 50.00 100.00
JL Joey Logano/126 75.00 150.00
KB Kyle Busch/75 25.00 60.00
KH Kevin Harvick/75 25.00 60.00
KK Kasey Kahne/75 25.00 60.00
MA Mario Andretti/173 20.00 50.00
MK Matt Kenseth/75 20.00 50.00
MM Mark Martin/75 15.00 40.00
MP Marvin Panch/741 6.00 15.00
NJ Ned Jarrett/146 8.00 20.00
PH Pete Hamilton/945 6.00 15.00
RF Red Farmer/628 8.00 20.00
RN Ryan Newman/75 8.00 20.00
RP Richard Petty/717 15.00 40.00
RW Rex White/402 6.00 15.00
TL Terry Labonte/138 15.00 40.00
TS Tony Stewart EXCH 30.00 80.00
AUJ Al Unser Jr./166 25.00 60.00

2008 Press Pass Legends Autographs Blue Inscriptions

STATED PRINT RUN 1-132
BA Bobby Allison/21
CY Cale Yarborough/20
DA Donnie Allison/20
DJ Dale Jarrett/132 25.00 60.00
DP David Pearson/9
DP David Pearson Fox/5
DP David Pearson/5
FL Fred Lorenzen/1
GB Geoff Bodine/21
GB Geoff Bodine/3
GW Glen Wood/21
JI Jack Ingram/24
JL Joey Logano/10
MA Mario Andretti/20
NJ Ned Jarrett/10
PH Pete Hamilton/21
RF Red Farmer/20
RM Rick Mears/32 15.00 40.00
RP Richard Petty/52 40.00 80.00
RW Rex White/20
AUJ Al Unser Jr./10
AUJ Al Unser Jr./21

2008 Press Pass Legends Dale Earnhardt Buyback

NOT PRICED DUE TO SCARCITY

2008 Press Pass Legends IROC Champions

COMPLETE SET (25) 40.00 100.00
STATED PRINT RUN 380 SERIAL #'d SETS
*GOLD/99: .8X TO 2X BASIC INSERTS
I1 Mark Donohue .60 1.50
I2 Bobby Unser 1.00 2.50
I3 Al Unser 1.00 2.50
I4 Mario Andretti 1.50 4.00
I5 Bobby Allison .75 2.00
I6 Cale Yarborough 1.00 2.50
I7 Harry Gant .75 2.00
I8 Al Unser Jr. 1.00 2.50
I9 Geoffrey Bodine .60 1.50
I10 Al Unser Jr. 1.00 2.50
I11 Terry Labonte 1.00 2.50
I12 Dale Earnhardt 6.00 15.00
I13 Davey Allison 1.50 4.00
I14 Mark Martin 1.00 2.50
I15 Dale Earnhardt 6.00 15.00
I16 Mark Martin 1.00 2.50
I17 Mark Martin 1.00 2.50
I18 Mark Martin 1.00 2.50
I19 Dale Earnhardt 6.00 15.00
I20 Dale Earnhardt 6.00 15.00
I21 Bobby Labonte 1.00 2.50
I22 Kevin Harvick 1.25 3.00

I23 Kurt Busch .75 2.00
I24 Mark Martin 1.00 2.50
I25 Tony Stewart 1.50 4.00

2008 Press Pass Legends Prominent Pieces Firesuit-Glove-Belt

STATED PRINT RUN 50 SERIAL #'d SETS
UNLESS NOTED
PP2DR David Ragan/25 20.00 50.00
PP2JM Juan Pablo Montoya/25
PP2KK Kasey Kahne/25
PP2MW Michael Waltrip/25 15.00 40.00
PP2PC Patrick Carpentier
PP2RN Ryan Newman/25 20.00 50.00

2008 Press Pass Legends Prominent Pieces Firesuit-Glove Bronze

STATED PRINT RUN 99 SERIAL #'d SETS
GOLD/25: .8X TO 2X BRONZE
*SILVER/25-50: .5X TO 1.2X BRONZE
PP1BV Brian Vickers 5.00 12.00
PP1CB Clint Bowyer 10.00 25.00
PP1CE Carl Edwards 12.00 30.00
PP1DH Denny Hamlin 8.00 20.00
PP1JJ Jimmie Johnson/50 15.00 40.00
PP1KB Kyle Busch/50 12.00 30.00
PP1KH Kevin Harvick/50 15.00 40.00
PP1MK Matt Kenseth/50 15.00 40.00
PP1MM Mark Martin/50 15.00 40.00
PP1TS Tony Stewart 15.00 40.00

2008 Press Pass Legends Prominent Pieces Metal-Tire-Net

STATED PRINT RUN 50 SERIAL #'d SETS
*GOLD/25: .8X TO 2X BASIC INSERT
PP4CB Clint Bowyer 10.00 25.00
PP4CE Carl Edwards 15.00 40.00
PP4DR David Ragan 10.00 25.00
PP4GB Greg Biffle 20.00 50.00
PP4JB Jeff Burton 15.00 40.00
PP4JM Jamie McMurray 10.00 25.00
PP4KH Kevin Harvick 12.00 30.00
PP4MK Matt Kenseth 12.00 30.00
PP4MT Martin Truex Jr. 40.00 100.00

2008 Press Pass Legends Prominent Pieces Metal-Tire Bronze

STATED PRINT RUN 99 SERIAL #'d SETS
*GOLD/25: .8X TO 2X BRONZE
SILVER/50: .5X TO 1.2X BRONZE
PP3BV Brian Vickers 6.00 15.00
PP3DE Dale Earnhardt Jr. 20.00 50.00
PP3JG Jeff Gordon 20.00 50.00
PP3JJ Jimmie Johnson 15.00 40.00
PP3JM Juan Pablo Montoya 5.00 12.00
PP3KK Kasey Kahne 15.00 40.00
PP3RN Ryan Newman 8.00 20.00
PP3TS Tony Stewart 15.00 40.00
PP3 DH Denny Hamlin 8.00 20.00
PP3KuB Kurt Busch 8.00 20.00
PP3KyB Kyle Busch 15.00 40.00

2008 Press Pass Legends Racing Artifacts Dual Memorabilia

STATED PRINT RUN 25 SERIAL #'d SETS
BADM Bobby Allison 20.00 50.00
DEDM Dale Earnhardt 40.00 100.00
MRDM Marty Robbins 20.00 50.00
TRDM Tim Richmond 25.00 60.00

2008 Press Pass Legends Racing Artifacts Firesuit Bronze

STATED PRINT RUN 150-180
*GOLD/25: .8X TO 2X BRONZE
*SILVER/50: .6X TO 1.5X BRONZE
AKF Alan Kulwicki/180 12.00 30.00
BAF Bobby Allison/150 6.00 15.00
BBF Buddy Baker/150 8.00 20.00
CYF Cale Yarborough/180 8.00 20.00
DEF Dale Earnhardt/180 20.00 50.00
DPF David Pearson/150 8.00 20.00
DWF Darrell Waltrip/180 10.00 25.00
HGF Harry Gant/150 8.00 20.00
MAF Mario Andretti/180 10.00 25.00
MRF Marty Robbins/150 12.00 30.00
NBF Neil Bonnett/150 6.00 15.00
RPF Richard Petty/180 15.00 40.00
TRF Tim Richmond/180 8.00 20.00
DaAF Davey Allison/150 15.00 40.00
DEF2 Dale Earnhardt/180 20.00 50.00
DoAF Donnie Allison/150 8.00 20.00
TLaF Terry Labonte/180 8.00 20.00
TLuF Tiny Lund/150 8.00 20.00

2008 Press Pass Legends Racing Artifacts Hat

STATED PRINT RUN 50 SERIAL #'d SETS
RPH Richard Petty 25.00 60.00

2008 Press Pass Legends Racing Artifacts Sheet Metal Bronze

STATED PRINT RUN 99 SERIAL #'d SETS
*GOLD/50: .6X TO 1.5X BRONZE
*SILVER/99: .5X TO 1.2X BRONZE
DES Dale Earnhardt 15.00 40.00
RMS Rob Moroso 10.00 25.00
TRS Tim Richmond 10.00 25.00

2008 Press Pass Legends Racing Artifacts Shirt Bronze

STATED PRINT RUN 199 SERIAL #'d SETS
*GOLD/50: .6X TO 1.5X BRONZE/199
*SILVER/99: .5X TO 1.2X BRONZE/199
BMSH Bud Moore 8.00 20.00
COSH Cotton Owens 6.00 15.00

2008 Press Pass Legends Racing Artifacts Tire Bronze

STATED PRINT RUN 199 SERIAL #'d SETS
*SILVER/99: .5X TO 1.2X BRONZE
*GOLD/50: .6X TO 1.5X BRONZE
DET Dale Earnhardt 15.00 40.00

2008 Press Pass Legends Signature Series Memorabilia

STATED PRINT RUN 25 SER.#'d SETS
LSCB Clint Bowyer 30.00 80.00
LSCE Carl Edwards 40.00 100.00
LSJG Jeff Gordon 100.00 200.00
LSJJ Jimmie Johnson 75.00 150.00
LSKH Kevin Harvick 30.00 80.00
LSMM Mark Martin 40.00 100.00

2008 Press Pass Legends Victory Lane Bronze

STATED PRINT RUN 99 SERIAL #'d SETS
*GOLD/25: .6X TO 1.5X BRONZE
*SILVER/50: .5X TO 1.2X BRONZE
VLDE Dale Earnhardt Jr. 25.00 60.00
VLJJ Jimmie Johnson 20.00 50.00
VLKB Kyle Busch 12.00 30.00
VLKH Kevin Harvick 12.00 30.00
VLKK Kasey Kahne 10.00 25.00
VLRN Ryan Newman 10.00 25.00
VLTS Tony Stewart 15.00 40.00

2009 Press Pass Legends

COMPLETE SET (70) 12.00 30.00
WAX BOX HOBBY 75.00 125.00
WAX BOX RETAIL 20.00 40.00
1 Bobby Allison .30 .75
2 Donnie Allison .30 .75
3 Davey Allison .60 1.50
4 Mario Andretti .40 1.00
5 Michael Andretti .40 1.00
6 Geoffrey Bodine .25 .60
7 Neil Bonnett .30 .75
8 Ralph Earnhardt .40 1.00
9 Dale Earnhardt 2.50 6.00
10 Red Farmer .30 .75
11 Bob Flock .25 .60
12 Fonty Flock .25 .60
13 Tim Flock .25 .60
14 John Force 1.25 3.00
15 Harry Gant .30 .75
16 Dale Jarrett .40 1.00
17 Ned Jarrett .30 .75
18 Alan Kulwicki .50 1.25
19 Terry Labonte .40 1.00
20 Fred Lorenzen .30 .75
21 Tiny Lund .40 1.00
22 Rick Mears .25 .60
23 Rob Moroso .25 .60
24 Benny Parsons .40 1.00
25 David Pearson .40 1.00
26 Lee Petty .30 .75
27 Richard Petty .60 1.50
28 Tim Richmond .30 .75
29 Ricky Rudd .30 .75
30 Curtis Turner .30 .75
31 Al Unser .40 1.00
32 Al Unser Jr. .40 1.00
33 Bobby Unser .40 1.00
34 Rusty Wallace .40 1.00
35 Darrell Waltrip .60 1.50
36 Rex White .25 .60
37 Glen Wood .25 .60
38 Cale Yarborough .40 1.00
39 Marco Andretti .50 1.25
40 Jeff Burton .30 .75
41 Kurt Busch .30 .75
42 Kyle Busch .50 1.25
43 Dale Earnhardt Jr. .75 2.00
44 Carl Edwards .40 1.00
45 Ashley Force 1.25 3.00
46 Jeff Gordon .75 2.00
47 Kevin Harvick .50 1.25
48 Jimmie Johnson .60 1.50
49 Kasey Kahne .40 1.00
50 Matt Kenseth .40 1.00
51 Bobby Labonte .40 1.00
52 Joey Logano RC .75 2.00
53 Mark Martin .40 1.00
54 Juan Pablo Montoya .50 1.25
55 Tony Stewart .60 1.50
56 Allison Family .60 1.50
57 Andretti Family .50 1.25
58 Earnhardt Family 2.50 6.00
59 Flock Family .25 .60
60 Force Family 1.25 3.00
61 Labonte Family .40 1.00
62 Mears Family .25 .60
63 Petty Family .60 1.50
64 Unser Family .40 1.00
65 Waltrip Family .60 1.50
66 Richard Petty 200 .60 1.50
67 Richard Petty 200 .60 1.50
68 Richard Petty 200 .60 1.50
69 Richard Petty 200 .60 1.50
70 Dale Earnhardt CL 2.50 6.00

2009 Press Pass Legends Gold

COMPLETE SET (70) 25.00 60.00
*SINGLES: .6X TO 1.5X BASIC CARDS
STATED PRINT RUN 399 SER.#'d SETS
25 David Pearson .60 1.50

2009 Press Pass Legends Holofoil

*SINGLES: 2.5X TO 6X BASIC CARDS
STATED PRINT RUN 50 SER.#'d SETS

2009 Press Pass Legends Red

COMPLETE SET (70) 40.00 80.00
*SINGLES: .8X TO 2X BASIC CARDS
STATED PRINT RUN 199 SER.#'d SETS

2009 Press Pass Legends Artifacts Firesuits Bronze

STATED PRINT RUN 199-250
*GOLD/25: .6X TO 1.5X BRONZE
*SILVER/50: .5X TO 1.2X BRONZE
AKF Alan Kulwicki 5.00 12.00
BAF Bobby Allison 3.00 8.00
CYF Cale Yarborough/250 4.00 10.00
DEF Dale Earnhardt/250 15.00 40.00
DJF Dale Jarrett/250 4.00 10.00
DPF David Pearson 4.00 10.00
DWF Darrell Waltrip/250 6.00 15.00
HGF Harry Gant/250 3.00 8.00
MAF Mario Andretti 4.00 10.00
NBF Neil Bonnett 3.00 8.00
RPF Richard Petty 8.00 20.00
RRF Ricky Rudd/250 3.00 8.00
TRF Tim Richmond 3.00 8.00
DaAF Davey Allison/250 6.00 15.00
DEF2 Dale Earnhardt IROC/250 12.00 30.00
DoAF Donnie Allison 3.00 8.00
TLaF Terry Labonte/250 4.00 10.00
TLuF Tiny Lund 4.00 10.00

2009 Press Pass Legends Artifacts Gloves Bronze

STATED PRINT RUN 99 SER.#'d SETS
*GOLD/25: .6X TO 1.5X BRONZE
*SILVER/50: .5X TO 1.2X BRONZE
MIAG Michael Andretti 8.00 20.00

2009 Press Pass Legends Artifacts Sheet Metal Bronze

STATED PRINT RUN 199 SER.#'d SETS
*GOLD/25: .6X TO 1.5X BRONZE
*SILVER/50: .5X TO 1.2X BRONZE
DES Dale Earnhardt 50.00 125.00
DWS Darrell Waltrip 6.00 15.00
RMS Rob Moroso 4.00 10.00
RPS Richard Petty 10.00 25.00
RWS Rusty Wallace 6.00 15.00
TRS Tim Richmond 10.00 25.00

2009 Press Pass Legends Artifacts Shirt Bronze

STATED PRINT RUN 99 SER.#'d SETS
*GOLD/25: .6X TO 1.5X BRONZE
*SILVER/50: .5X TO 1.2X BRONZE
JFSH John Force 12.00 30.00

2009 Press Pass Legends Artifacts Shoes Bronze

STATED PRINT RUN 99 SER.#'d SETS
*GOLD/25: .6X TO 1.5X BRONZE
*SILVER/50: .5X TO 1.2X BRONZE
JFS John Force 15.00 40.00
MAAS Mario Andretti 5.00 12.00
MIAS Michael Andretti 5.00 12.00

2009 Press Pass Legends Artifacts Tires Bronze

STATED PRINT RUN 199 SER.#'d SETS
*GOLD/25: .6X TO 1.5X BRONZE
*SILVER/50: .5X TO 1.2X BRONZE

2009 Press Pass Legends Autographs

UNPRICED PRINT PLATE PRINT RUN 1
UNPRICED ARTIFACTS AU PRINT RUN 10
1 Bobby Allison 6.00 15.00
2 Donnie Allison 6.00 15.00
3 Mario Andretti 8.00 20.00
4 Michael Andretti 8.00 20.00
5 Geoffrey Bodine 5.00 12.00
6 Red Farmer 6.00 15.00
7 Harry Gant 6.00 15.00
8 Dale Jarrett 12.00 30.00
9 Ned Jarrett 6.00 15.00
10 Fred Lorenzen 6.00 15.00
11 David Pearson 8.00 20.00
12 Richard Petty 20.00 50.00
13 Rick Mears 10.00 25.00
14 Ricky Rudd 6.00 15.00
15 Terry Labonte 10.00 25.00
16 Al Unser 8.00 20.00
17 Al Unser Jr. 8.00 20.00
18 Bobby Unser 8.00 20.00
19 Rusty Wallace 8.00 20.00
20 Darrell Waltrip 12.00 30.00
21 Rex White 5.00 12.00
22 Glen Wood 5.00 12.00
23 Cale Yarborough 8.00 20.00

2009 Press Pass Legends Autographs Gold

GOLD STATED PRINT RUN 20-155
1 Bobby Allison/45 8.00 20.00
2 Donnie Allison/105 8.00 20.00
3 Marco Andretti/155 12.00 30.00
4 Mario Andretti/25 10.00 25.00
5 Michael Andretti/30 10.00 25.00
6 Geoffrey Bodine/100 6.00 15.00
7 Kyle Busch/25 25.00 60.00
8 Dale Earnhardt Jr./40 50.00 120.00
9 Red Farmer/105 8.00 20.00
10 Ashley Force/150 25.00 60.00
11 John Force/55 25.00 60.00
12 Harry Gant/100 8.00 20.00
13 Jeff Gordon/35 75.00 150.00
14 Denny Hamlin/20 25.00 60.00
15 Kevin Harvick/40 15.00 40.00
16 Dale Jarrett/97 10.00 25.00
17 Ned Jarrett/105 8.00 20.00
18 Johnson Jimmie/35 30.00 80.00
19 Kasey Kahne EXCH 10.00 25.00
20 Matt Kenseth/55 10.00 25.00
21 Bobby Labonte/40 10.00 25.00
22 Joey Logano/30 20.00 50.00
23 Fred Lorenzen/105 8.00 20.00
24 Mark Martin/40 10.00 25.00
25 Ryan Newman/40 8.00 20.00
26 David Pearson/100 10.00 25.00
27 Richard Petty/105 25.00 60.00
28 Rick Mears/30 12.00 30.00
29 Ricky Rudd/105 8.00 20.00
30 Tony Stewart/40 15.00 40.00
31 Terry Labonte/100 15.00 40.00
32 Martin Truex Jr./55 8.00 20.00
33 Bobby Unser/30 10.00 25.00
34 Al Unser/30 10.00 25.00
35 Al Unser Jr./30 10.00 25.00
36 Rusty Wallace/105 10.00 25.00
37 Darrell Waltrip/105 12.00 30.00
38 Rex White/105 6.00 15.00
39 Glen Wood/103 6.00 15.00
40 Cale Yarborough/100 10.00 25.00

2009 Press Pass Legends Autographs Holofoil

STATED PRINT RUN 5-30
1 Bobby Allison/25 10.00 25.00
2 Donnie Allison/30 10.00 25.00
3 Marco Andretti/25 15.00 40.00
4 Mario Andretti/5
5 Michael Andretti/10
6 Geoffrey Bodine/30 8.00 20.00
7 Kyle Busch/15 25.00 60.00
8 Red Farmer/30 10.00 25.00
9 Ashley Force/30 30.00 80.00
10 John Force/10
11 Harry Gant/30 10.00 25.00
12 Jeff Gordon/10
13 Denny Hamlin/15
14 Kevin Harvick/15
15 Dale Jarrett/25 12.00 30.00
16 Ned Jarrett/25 10.00 25.00
17 Johnson Jimmie EXCH
18 Kasey Kahne EXCH
19 Bobby Labonte/15
20 Fred Lorenzen/25 10.00 25.00
21 Mark Martin/15
22 Ryan Newman/20
23 David Pearson/30 12.00 30.00
24 Richard Petty/25 20.00 50.00
25 Rick Mears/10
26 Terry Labonte/30 25.00 60.00
27 Martin Truex Jr./30 10.00 25.00
28 Bobby Unser/10
29 Al Unser/10
30 Al Unser Jr./10
31 Rusty Wallace/25 12.00 30.00
32 Darrell Waltrip/30 20.00 50.00
33 Rex White/30 8.00 20.00
34 Glen Wood/25 8.00 20.00
35 Cale Yarborough/30 12.00 30.00

2009 Press Pass Legends Autographs Inscriptions

STATED PRINT RUN 1-55
1 B.Allison 85 Wins/55 20.00 50.00
2 Do.Allison #1/55 15.00 40.00
3 G.Bodine Bo-Dyn Bobsled/30 15.00 40.00
4 G.Bodine Dutch/25 25.00 50.00
5 Dale Jr. #88/20
6 R.Farmer F97/55 10.00 25.00
7 D.Jarrett DJ/50 25.00 60.00
8 M.Kenseth '09 Day 500/25 40.00 100.00
9 J.Logano #20/15
10 F.Lorenzen Gold Boy/45 blu 20.00 50.00
11 F.Lorenzen Gold Boy/10 red
12 D.Pearson Silver Fox/55 25.00 50.00
13 R.Mears Thanks/15
14 D.Waltrip Jaws/50 25.00 60.00
15 D.Waltrip blue ink/5
16 D.Waltrip 88 face/5
17 D.Waltrip 17 face/1
18 R.White '60 Champ/55 10.00 25.00
19 G.Wood Woodchopper/55 10.00 25.00

2009 Press Pass Legends Autographs Red

STATED PRINT RUN 10-55
1 Bobby Allison/55 15.00 40.00
2 Mario Andretti/10
3 Michael Andretti/15
4 John Force/15 30.00 80.00
5 Harry Gant/55 10.00 25.00
6 Ned Jarrett/55 10.00 25.00
7 Richard Petty/55 20.00 50.00
8 Ricky Rudd/50 10.00 25.00
9 Terry Labonte/55 20.00 50.00
10 Bobby Unser/15
11 Al Unser/10
12 Al Unser Jr./15
13 Rusty Wallace/55 12.00 30.00
14 Cale Yarborough/45 12.00 30.00

2009 Press Pass Legends Family Autographs

STATED PRINT RUN 25 SER.#'d SETS
1 Allison Family 30.00 60.00
2 Andretti Family 50.00 100.00
3 Force Family 300.00 600.00
4 Jarrett Family 50.00 100.00
5 Labonte Family 60.00 120.00
6 Mears Family 50.00 100.00
7 Unser Family 60.00 120.00
8 Waltrip Family 40.00 80.00
9 Wallace Family 40.00 80.00

2009 Press Pass Legends Family Portraits

COMPLETE SET (25) 12.00 30.00
STATED PRINT RUN 550 SER.#'d SETS
*HOLOFOIL/99: 1X TO 2.5X BASIC INSERTS
FP1 Allison Family 1.00 2.50
FP2 Allison Family .50 1.25
FP3 Allison Family .50 1.25
FP4 Allison Family .50 1.25
FP5 Allison Family 1.00 2.50
FP6 Allison Family .50 1.25
FP7 Andretti Family .60 1.50
FP8 Andretti Family .75 2.00
FP9 Andretti Family .75 2.00
FP10 Earnhardt Family 4.00 10.00
FP11 Earnhardt Family 4.00 10.00
FP12 Earnhardt Family 4.00 10.00
FP13 Earnhardt Family 4.00 10.00
FP14 Earnhardt Family 4.00 10.00
FP15 Earnhardt Family 4.00 10.00
FP16 Flock Family .40 1.00
FP17 Force Family 2.00 5.00
FP18 Force Family 2.00 5.00
FP19 Labonte Family .60 1.50
FP20 Petty Family 1.00 2.50
FP21 Petty Family 1.00 2.50
FP22 Petty Family 1.00 2.50
FP23 Petty Family 1.00 2.50
FP24 Unser Family .60 1.50
FP25 Waltrip Family 1.00 2.50

2009 Press Pass Legends Family Relics Bronze

STATED PRINT RUN 99 SER.#'d SETS
FRW Wallace SheetMetal/Firesuit 5.00 12.00
FRAl Allison Firesuits 8.00 20.00
FREa Earnhardt Firesuits 20.00 50.00
FRLa Labonte Firesuit/SheetMetal/75 5.00 12.00
FRWa Waltrip Firesuits 8.00 20.00
FREa5 Earnhardt Firesuit/Shoes 10.00 25.00
FRFo2 Force Shirts 15.00 40.00
FRLa2 Labonte Gloves/Shoes/75 5.00 12.00
FRWa2 Waltrip SheetMetal/75 8.00 20.00

2009 Press Pass Legends Family Relics Gold

*SINGLES: .6X TO 1.5X BASIC INSERTS
STATED PRINT RUN 25 SER.#'d SETS
FRAn Andretti Firesuit/Glove/Shoe 10.00 25.00
FRFo Force Shoes 25.00 60.00
FREa3 Earnhardt Tires 50.00 125.00
FREa4 Earnhardt Engine Belt/Seat 50.00 125.00

2009 Press Pass Legends Family Relics Silver

*SINGLES: .5X TO 1.2X BASIC INSERTS
STATED PRINT RUN 50 SER.#'d SETS
FRAn Andretti Firesuit/Glove/Shoe 8.00 20.00
FRFo Force Shoes 20.00 50.00
FREa3 Earnhardt Tires 40.00 100.00

2009 Press Pass Legends Past and Present

COMPLETE SET (12) 12.00 30.00
STATED PRINT RUN 550 SER.#'d SETS
*HOLOFOIL/99: 1X TO 2.5X BASIC INSERTS
PP1 J.Gordon/R.Petty 1.25 3.00
PP2 Dale Sr./Dale Jr. 4.00 10.00
PP3 J.Johnson/C.Yarborough 1.00 2.50
PP4 M.Martin/H.Gant .60 1.50
PP5 J.Gordon/F.Lorenzen 1.25 3.00
PP6 R.White/M.Kenseth .60 1.50
PP7 D.Waltrip/C.Edwards 1.00 2.50
PP8 N.Jarrett/J.Gordon 1.25 3.00
PP9 R.Petty/M.Kenseth 1.00 2.50
PP10 R.Wallace/C.Edwards .60 1.50
PP11 T.Flock/J.Johnson 1.00 2.50
PP12 C.Yarborough/T.Stewart 1.00 2.50

2009 Press Pass Legends Petty 200th Win Autographs

COMMON PETTY/25 50.00 100.00
STATED PRINT RUN 25 SER.#'d SETS

2009 Press Pass Legends Prominent Pieces Bronze

STATED PRINT RUN 99-150
*GOLD/25: .6X TO 1.5X BRONZE/99/150
*OVERSIZED/25: .8X TO 2X BRONZE/99-150
*SILVER/50: .5X TO 1.2X BRONZE/99-150
PPBK Brad Keselowski/150 8.00 20.00
PPBV Brian Vickers 3.00 8.00
PPCB Clint Bowyer 5.00 12.00
PPCE Carl Edwards 5.00 12.00
PPDH Denny Hamlin 5.00 12.00
PPDR David Ragan 4.00 10.00
PPGB Greg Biffle/150 4.00 10.00
PPJB Jeff Burton 4.00 10.00
PPJG Jeff Gordon 12.00 30.00
PPJJ Jimmie Johnson 8.00 20.00
PPJL Joey Logano 12.00 30.00
PPJM Juan Pablo Montoya 6.00 15.00
PPKB Kurt Busch 4.00 10.00
PPKB Kyle Busch 6.00 15.00
PPKH Kevin Harvick 6.00 15.00
PPKK Kasey Kahne 6.00 15.00
PPMK Matt Kenseth/150 5.00 12.00
PPMM Mark Martin 5.00 12.00
PPMT Martin Truex Jr./150 4.00 10.00
PPMW Michael Waltrip/150 5.00 12.00
PPSS Scott Speed/150 4.00 10.00
PPTS Tony Stewart 8.00 20.00
PPDE1 Dale Earnhardt Jr. AMP 12.00 30.00
PPDE2 Dale Earnhardt Jr. NG 12.00 30.00

2010 Press Pass Legends

COMPLETE SET (80) 12.00 30.00
WAX BOX HOBBY (18) 100.00 140.00
MINI BOX (6) 25.00 50.00
1 Bobby Allison .30 .75
2 Davey Allison .60 1.50
3 Donnie Allison .30 .75
4 Mario Andretti .40 1.00
5 Kenny Bernstein .40 1.00
6 Geoff Bodine .25 .60
7 Neil Bonnett .30 .75
8 Jerry Cook .25 .60
9 Jeg Coughlin .30 .75
10 Dale Earnhardt 2.00 5.00
11 Ralph Earnhardt .60 1.50
12 Bill Elliott .75 2.00
13 John Force .75 2.00
14 Harry Gant .40 1.00
15 Don Garlits .40 1.00
16 Paul Goldsmith .30 .75
17 Ernie Irvan .30 .75
18 Dale Jarrett .40 1.00
19 Ned Jarrett .30 .75
20 Connie Kalitta .60 1.50
21 Alan Kulwicki .60 1.50
22 Terry Labonte .40 1.00
23 Fred Lorenzen .25 .60
24 Dave Marcis .30 .75
25 Rob Moroso .25 .60
26 Shirley Muldowney .30 .75
27 Benny Parsons .40 1.00
28 David Pearson .40 1.00
29 Lee Petty .30 .75
30 Richard Petty .60 1.50
31 Tim Richmond .30 .75
32 Doug Schumacher .40 1.00
33 Rusty Wallace .40 1.00
34 Darrell Waltrip .60 1.50
35 Cale Yarborough .40 1.00
36 Brandon Bernstein .40 1.00
37 Kyle Busch .50 1.25
38 Jeg Coughlin Jr. .25 .60
39 Brad Daugherty .25 .60
40 Dale Earnhardt Jr. .75 2.00
41 Carl Edwards .40 1.00
42 Ashley Force Hood 1.50 4.00
43 Brittany Force .75 2.00
44 Courtney Force .75 2.00
45 Jeff Gordon .75 2.00
46 Robert Hight .40 1.00
47 Jimmie Johnson .60 1.50
48 Mike Joy .25 .60
49 Kasey Kahne .40 1.00
50 Doug Kalitta .30 .75
51 Matt Kenseth .40 1.00
52 Mark Martin .40 1.00
53 Tony Schumacher .30 .75
54 Tony Stewart .60 1.50
55 D.Earnhardt/T.Labonte MM 2.00 5.00
56 J.Force/A.Force Hood MM .60 1.50
57 R.Petty/D.Pearson MM .25 .60
58 C.Yarborough/D.Allison MM .15 .40
59 R.Petty/C.Yarborough MM .25 .60
60 D.Waltrip/B.Allison MM .60 1.50
61 Richard Petty WC .60 1.50
62 David Pearson WC .40 1.00
63 Bobby Allison WC .30 .75
64 Darrell Waltrip WC .60 1.50
65 Cale Yarborough WC .40 1.00
66 Jeff Gordon WC .75 2.00
67 Dale Earnhardt WC 2.00 5.00
68 Rusty Wallace WC .40 1.00
69 Lee Petty WC .30 .75
70 Jimmie Johnson WC .60 1.50
71 Ned Jarrett WC .30 .75
72 Richard Petty C .60 1.50
73 David Pearson C .40 1.00
74 Darrell Waltrip C .60 1.50
75 Cale Yarborough C .40 1.00
76 Jeff Gordon C .75 2.00
77 Dale Earnhardt C 2.00 5.00
78 Lee Petty C .30 .75
79 Jimmie Johnson C .60 1.50
80 Ned Jarrett C .30 .75

2010 Press Pass Legends Gold

COMPLETE SET (80) 20.00 50.00
*GOLD: .8X TO 2X BASE
STATED PRINT RUN 399 SER.#'d SETS

2010 Press Pass Legends Holofoil

*HOLO: 3X TO 8X BASE
STATED PRINT RUN 50 SER.#'d SETS

2010 Press Pass Legends Red

*RED: 1X TO 2.5X BASE
STATED PRINT RUN 199 SER.#'d SETS

2010 Press Pass Legends 50 Win Club Memorabilia Gold

STATED PRINT RUN 75 SER.#'d SETS
*HOLOFOIL/25: .6X TO 1.5X GOLD/75
50BA Bobby Allison 6.00 15.00
50CY Cale Yarborough 6.00 15.00
50DE Dale Earnhardt 25.00 60.00
50DP David Pearson 8.00 20.00
50DW Darrell Waltrip 10.00 25.00
50JG Jeff Gordon 12.00 30.00
50JJ Jimmie Johnson 12.00 30.00
50RP Richard Petty 12.00 30.00
50RW Rusty Wallace 12.00 30.00

2010 Press Pass Legends Autographs Copper

STATED PRINT RUN 65-125
1 Bobby Allison 5.00 12.00
2 Donnie Allison 5.00 12.00
3 Mario Andretti 6.00 15.00
4 Brandon Bernstein 6.00 15.00
5 Kenny Bernstein 6.00 15.00
6 Geoff Bodine 4.00 10.00
7 Jerry Cook 4.00 10.00
8 Jeg Coughlin 5.00 12.00
9 Jeg Coughlin Jr. 4.00 10.00
10 Brad Daugherty 4.00 10.00
11 Bill Elliott 12.00 30.00
12 Ashley Force Hood 20.00 50.00
13 John Force 15.00 40.00

14 Harry Gant 6.00 15.00
15 Don Garlits 12.00 30.00
16 Paul Goldsmith 5.00 12.00
17 Robert Hight 6.00 15.00
18 Ernie Irvan 5.00 12.00
19 Dale Jarrett 10.00 25.00
20 Ned Jarrett 5.00 12.00
21 Mike Joy 4.00 10.00
22 Connie Kalitta 10.00 25.00
23 Doug Kalitta 5.00 12.00
24 Terry Labonte/119 10.00 25.00
25 Fred Lorenzen/65 4.00 10.00
26 Dave Marcis 5.00 12.00
27 Shirley Muldowney/122 10.00 25.00
28 David Pearson 8.00 20.00
29 Richard Petty 15.00 40.00
30 Don Schumacher 6.00 15.00
31 Tony Schumacher 8.00 20.00
32 Rusty Wallace 12.00 30.00
33 Darrell Waltrip 10.00 25.00
34 Cale Yarborough/122 6.00 15.00

2010 Press Pass Legends Autographs Gold

*GOLD/37-50: .5X TO 1.2X COPPER
STATED PRINT RUN 37-50
1 Bobby Allison
13 Brittany Force 25.00 60.00
14 Courtney Force 30.00 60.00
21 Dale Jarrett 15.00 40.00
26 Terry Labonte 25.00 60.00
34 Rusty Wallace 20.00 50.00

2010 Press Pass Legends Autographs Holofoil

STATED PRINT RUN 15-25
1 Bobby Allison 8.00 20.00
2 Donnie Allison/24 8.00 20.00
3 Mario Andretti/24 10.00 25.00
4 Brandon Bernstein 10.00 25.00
5 Kenny Bernstein 10.00 25.00
6 Geoff Bodine 6.00 15.00
7 Jeff Burton 8.00 20.00
8 Kurt Busch 8.00 20.00
9 Kyle Busch 12.00 30.00
10 Jerry Cook 6.00 15.00
11 Jeg Coughlin/24 8.00 20.00
12 Jeg Coughlin Jr. 6.00 15.00
13 Brad Daugherty/21 10.00 25.00
14 Dale Earnhardt Jr. 60.00 120.00
15 Carl Edwards 10.00 25.00
16 Bill Elliott 20.00 50.00
17 Ashley Force Hood 30.00 80.00
18 Brittany Force 30.00 80.00
19 Courtney Force 50.00 100.00
20 John Force 25.00 60.00
21 Harry Gant 10.00 25.00
22 Don Garlits 20.00 50.00
23 Paul Goldsmith/23 8.00 20.00
24 Jeff Gordon 50.00 100.00
25 Denny Hamlin 20.00 50.00
26 Kevin Harvick 40.00 80.00
27 Robert Hight 10.00 25.00
28 Ernie Irvan 8.00 20.00
29 Dale Jarrett 50.00 100.00
30 Ned Jarrett 8.00 20.00
31 Jimmie Johnson 15.00 40.00
32 Mike Joy 6.00 15.00
33 Kasey Kahne/24 30.00 80.00
34 Connie Kalitta 15.00 40.00
35 Doug Kalitta/17 12.00 30.00
36 Matt Kenseth 10.00 25.00
37 Brad Keselowski 12.00 30.00
38 Terry Labonte 100.00 175.00
39 Joey Logano 40.00 80.00
40 Fred Lorenzen/15 10.00 25.00
41 Dave Marcis 8.00 20.00
42 Mark Martin 20.00 50.00
43 Shirley Muldowney 20.00 50.00
44 Ryan Newman 8.00 20.00
45 Danica Patrick 100.00 175.00
46 David Pearson 12.00 30.00
47 Richard Petty 40.00 80.00
48 Don Schumacher 10.00 25.00
49 Tony Schumacher 20.00 50.00
50 Tony Stewart 25.00 60.00
51 Rusty Wallace/24 25.00 60.00
52 Darrell Waltrip/24 75.00 150.00
53 Cale Yarborough 10.00 25.00

2010 Press Pass Legends Autographs Silver

SILVER PRINT RUN 41-291
UNPRICED BLUE PRINT RUN 7-10
1 Brandon Bernstein/65 8.00 20.00
2 Kenny Bernstein/64 8.00 20.00
3 Geoff Bodine/41 5.00 12.00
4 Jerry Cook/242 4.00 10.00
5 Jeg Coughlin/91 6.00 15.00
6 Jeg Coughlin Jr./92 5.00 12.00
7 Brad Daugherty/290 4.00 10.00
8 Don Garlits/92 15.00 40.00
9 Paul Goldsmith/113 5.00 12.00
10 Ernie Irvan/93 6.00 15.00
11 Mike Joy/291 4.00 10.00
12 Connie Kalitta/88 12.00 30.00
13 Doug Kalitta/91 6.00 15.00
14 Dave Marcis/117 5.00 12.00
15 Shirley Muldowney/93 10.00 25.00
16 Don Schumacher 8.00 20.00
17 Tony Schumacher/94 8.00 20.00

2010 Press Pass Legends Family Autographs

STATED PRINT RUN 25 SER.#'d SETS
1 B.Allison/D.Allison
2 K.Bernstein/B.Bernstein 20.00 50.00
3 J.Coughlin Jr./J.Coughlin 25.00 60.00
4 Force/Force/Force/Force 250.00 350.00
5 N.Jarrett/D.Jarrett 25.00 60.00
6 D.Kalitta/C.Kalitta EXCH 25.00 60.00
7 T.Schumacher/D.Schumacher 40.00 80.00
8 M.Waltrip/D.Waltrip 20.00 50.00

2010 Press Pass Legends Lasting Legacies Autographs

STATED PRINT RUN 25 SER.#'d SETS
LLAF Ashley Force Hood 50.00 100.00
LLBA Bobby Allison 25.00 60.00
LLBB Brandon Bernstein 15.00 40.00
LLBE Bill Elliott 25.00 60.00
LLCY Cale Yarborough 20.00 50.00
LLDA Donnie Allison 20.00 50.00
LLDJ Dale Jarrett 50.00 100.00
LLDP David Pearson 20.00 50.00
LLDW Darrell Waltrip 25.00 60.00
LLEI Ernie Irvan 20.00 50.00
LLGB Geoff Bodine 15.00 40.00
LLHG Harry Gant 20.00 50.00
LLJF John Force 40.00 80.00
LLKB Kenny Bernstein 20.00 50.00
LLMA Mario Andretti 20.00 50.00
LLRH Robert Hight 20.00 50.00
LLRP Richard Petty 40.00 80.00
LLRW Rusty Wallace 50.00 100.00
LLSM Shirley Muldowney 40.00 80.00
LLTL Terry Labonte 125.00 250.00

2010 Press Pass Legends Lasting Legacies Copper

STATED PRINT RUN 150-175
LLAK Alan Kulwicki/150 10.00 25.00
LLBA Bobby Allison/150 2.50 6.00
LLBB Brandon Bernstein 3.00 8.00
LLBE1 Bill Elliott FS 6.00 15.00
LLBE2 Bill Elliott SM 6.00 15.00
LLCK Connie Kalitta 5.00 12.00
LLCY Cale Yarborough/150 5.00 12.00
LLDA Davey Allison 5.00 12.00
LLDA Donnie Allison 2.50 6.00
LLDE Dale Earnhardt 20.00 50.00
LLDJ Dale Jarrett/150 10.00 25.00
LLDK Doug Kalitta 4.00 10.00
LLDM Dave Marcis 6.00 15.00
LLDP David Pearson/150 3.00 8.00
LLDS Don Schumacher 3.00 8.00
LLDW Darrell Waltrip 5.00 12.00
LLEI Ernie Irvan 5.00 12.00
LLGB Geoff Bodine 5.00 12.00
LLHG Harry Gant/150 3.00 8.00
LLJC Jeg Coughlin 3.00 6.00
LLJC Jeg Coughlin Jr. 3.00 8.00
LLJF John Force 6.00 15.00
LLKB Kenny Bernstein 3.00 8.00
LLMA Mario Andretti 5.00 12.00
LLMM Mark Martin 3.00 8.00
LLNB Neil Bonnett 5.00 12.00
LLRH1 Robert Hight P 3.00 8.00
LLRH2 Robert Hight S 3.00 8.00
LLRM Rob Moroso 4.00 10.00
LLRP1 Richard Petty FS/150 5.00 12.00
LLRP2 Richard Petty SM 5.00 12.00
LLRP3 Richard Petty S 5.00 12.00
LLRW1 Rusty Wallace SM 6.00 15.00
LLRW2 Rusty Wallace FS 6.00 15.00
LLSM Shirley Muldowney 5.00 12.00
LLTL Terry Labonte/150 5.00 12.00
LLTR1 Tim Richmond FS/150 8.00 20.00
LLTR2 Tim Richmond SM 8.00 20.00
LLTS Tony Schumacher 6.00 15.00

2010 Press Pass Legends Lasting Legacies Gold

*GOLD/75: .5X TO 1.2X COPPER/150-175
STATED PRINT RUN 75 SER.#'d SETS
LLAF Ashley Force 12.00 30.00
LLDE2 Dale Earnhardt T 20.00 50.00
LLDW1 Darrell Waltrip FL 6.00 15.00
LLGB1 Geoff Bodine FL 6.00 15.00
LLRP3 Richard Petty T 6.00 15.00
LLRW1 Rusty Wallace SM 12.00 30.00
LLRW2 Rusty Wallace FS 12.00 30.00

2010 Press Pass Legends Lasting Legacies Holofoil

*HOLOFOIL/25: .6X TO 1.5X COPPER/15-175
STATED PRINT RUN 25 SER.#'d SETS
LLAF Ashley Force 15.00 40.00
LLDE1 Dale Earnhardt B 40.00 80.00
LLDE2 Dale Earnhardt FS 50.00 100.00
LLDE3 Dale Earnhardt G 50.00 100.00
LLDE4 Dale Earnhardt T 25.00 60.00
LLDG Don Garlits 25.00 60.00
LLDK Doug Kalitta 8.00 15.00
LLDM Dave Marcis 8.00 20.00
LLDW1 Darrell Waltrip FL 8.00 20.00
LLGB1 Geoff Bodine FL 8.00 20.00
LLRP2 Richard Petty SM 25.00 60.00
LLRP3 Richard Petty T 15.00 40.00
LLRP4 Richard Petty S 20.00 50.00
LLRW1 Rusty Wallace SM 15.00 40.00
LLRW2 Rusty Wallace FS 15.00 40.00
LLSM Shirley Muldowney 10.00 25.00
LLTL Terry Labonte 25.00 60.00
LLTR1 Tim Richmond FS 40.00 80.00
LLTR2 Tim Richmond SM 15.00 40.00

2010 Press Pass Legends Legendary Links Gold

STATED PRINT RUN 75 SER.#'d SETS
*HOLO/25: .5X TO 1.2X GOLD/75
LXBEDW B.Elliott/D.Waltrip 8.00 20.00
LXBEKK B.Elliott/K.Kahne 8.00 20.00
LXCYJJ C.Yarborough/J.Johnson 6.00 15.00
LXDAJG D.Allison/J.Gordon 20.00 50.00
LXDEJG D.Earnhardt/J.Gordon 40.00 100.00
LXGBMM G.Bodine/M.Martin 4.00 10.00
LXMADA M.Andretti/D.Allison 6.00 15.00
LXTSMA T.Stewart/M.Andretti 6.00 15.00
LXBEDEJ B.Elliott/D.Earnhardt Jr. 8.00 20.00

2010 Press Pass Legends Make and Model Gold

COMPLETE SET (9) 10.00 25.00
STATED PRINT RUN 299 SER.#'d SETS
*BLUE/99: .6X TO 1.5X GOLD/299
*HOLO/150: .5X TO 1.2X GOLD/299
1 T.Flock '55 Chrysler .50 1.25
2 L.Petty '59 Olds Super 88 .60 1.50
3 F.Lorenzen '65 Galaxie .50 1.25
4 R.Petty '67 Belvedere 1.25 3.00
5 R.Petty '74 Charger 1.25 3.00
6 B.Allison '75 AMC .60 1.50
7 D.Waltrip '81 Buick Regal 1.25 3.00
8 B.Elliott '85 Thunderbird 1.50 4.00
9 J.Gordon '07 Monte Carlo SS 1.50 4.00

2010 Press Pass Legends Memorable Matchups

STATED PRINT RUN 25 SER.#'d SETS
MMCYDA Yarborough/D.Alliso 8.00 20.00
MMDETL Earnhardt/T.Labnte 60.00 120.00
MMDWBA D.Waltrip/B.Allison 15.00 40.00
MMJFAF J.Force/A.Force Hood 40.00 80.00
MMRPCY R.Petty/Yarborough 8.00 20.00
MMRPDP R.Petty/D.Pearson 8.00 20.00
MMRWDW R.Wallace/D.Waltrip 15.00 40.00

2010 Press Pass Legends Memorable Matchups Autographs

STATED PRINT RUN 25 SER.#'d SETS
NNO J.Force/A.Force 60.00 120.00
NNO R.Petty/D.Pearson 40.00 80.00
NNO Yarborgh/D.Allisn/23 25.00 50.00
NNO R.Petty/Yarborgh/21 60.00 120.00
NNO D.Waltrip/B.Allison 20.00 50.00
NNO R.Wallace/D.Waltrip 40.00 80.00
NNO N.Jarrett/D.Jarrett 40.00 80.00

2010 Press Pass Legends Motorsports Masters

COMPLETE SET (20) 15.00 40.00
STATED ODDS 1:5
UNPRICED BLUE PRINT RUN 10
*GOLD/299: .5X TO 1.2X BASIC INSERTS
*HOLO/149: .6X TO 1.5X BASIC INSERTS
MMBA Bobby Allison .50 1.25
MMBE Bill Elliott 1.25 3.00
MMCE Carl Edwards .60 1.50
MMCY Cale Yarborough .60 1.50
MMDJ Dale Jarrett .60 1.50
MMDP David Pearson .60 1.50
MMDW Darrell Waltrip 1.00 2.50
MMJB Jeff Burton .50 1.25
MMJF John Force 1.25 3.00
MMJG Jeff Gordon 1.25 3.00
MMJJ Jimmie Johnson 1.00 2.50
MMKH Kevin Harvick .75 2.00
MMMA Mario Andretti .60 1.50
MMMK Matt Kenseth .60 1.50
MMMM Mark Martin .60 1.50
MMRP Richard Petty 1.00 2.50
MMRW Rusty Wallace .60 1.50
MMTS Tony Stewart 1.00 2.50
MMKUB Kurt Busch .50 1.25
MMKYB Kyle Busch .75 2.00

2010 Press Pass Legends Motorsports Masters Autographs Gold

*GOLD/47-50: .5X TO 1.2X SILVER
STATED PRINT RUN 25-50
7 Kurt Busch 6.00 15.00
14 Jeff Gordon/25 60.00 120.00
17 Jimmie Johnson/25 20.00 50.00
20 Matt Kenseth/25 60.00 120.00
25 Don Schumacher 8.00 20.00
27 Tony Stewart/25 12.00 30.00

2010 Press Pass Legends Motorsports Masters Autographs Holofoil

*HOLO/25: .6X TO 1.5X BASIC AUTO
STATED PRINT RUN 10-25
7 Kurt Busch 8.00 20.00
12 Don Garlits/23 20.00 50.00
16 Dale Jarrett 25.00 60.00
25 Don Schumacher 10.00 25.00

2010 Press Pass Legends Motorsports Masters Autographs Silver

STATED PRINT RUN 99 SER.#'d SETS
1 Bobby Allison 5.00 12.00
2 Donnie Allison 5.00 12.00
3 Mario Andretti 6.00 15.00
4 Brandon Bernstein 6.00 15.00
5 Kenny Bernstein 8.00 20.00
6 Geoff Bodine 4.00 10.00
7 Jeg Coughlin 5.00 12.00
8 Jeg Coughlin Jr./98 4.00 10.00
9 Bill Elliott 12.00 30.00
10 John Force 12.00 30.00
11 Don Garlits/98 12.00 30.00
12 Paul Goldsmith 5.00 12.00
13 Ernie Irvan 5.00 12.00
14 Dale Jarrett 6.00 15.00
15 Connie Kalitta 10.00 25.00
16 Doug Kalitta/96 5.00 12.00
17 Dave Marcis 5.00 12.00
18 Shirley Muldowney 12.00 30.00
19 David Pearson 6.00 15.00
20 Richard Petty 10.00 25.00
21 Tony Schumacher 8.00 20.00
22 Rusty Wallace 12.00 30.00
23 Darrell Waltrip 10.00 25.00
24 Cale Yarborough 6.00 15.00

2010 Press Pass Legends Prominent Pieces Copper

STATED PRINT RUN 99 SER.#'d SETS
*GOLD/50: .5X TO 1.2X COPPER/99
*HOLO/25: .6X TO 1.5X COPPER/99
*OVERSIZE/25: 1.2X TO 3X COPPER/99
PPBK Brad Keselowski 6.00 15.00
PPCE Carl Edwards 5.00 12.00
PPDP Danica Patrick 25.00 60.00
PPJG Jeff Gordon 15.00 40.00
PPJJ Jimmie Johnson 12.00 30.00
PPKH Kevin Harvick 6.00 15.00
PPKK Kasey Kahne 5.00 12.00
PPMK Matt Kenseth 5.00 12.00
PPMM Mark Martin 5.00 12.00
PPTS Tony Stewart 10.00 25.00
PPKYB Kyle Busch 6.00 15.00
PPDEJR Dale Earnhardt Jr. 15.00 40.00

2011 Press Pass Legends

COMPLETE SET (80) 12.00 30.00
CAR CARDS 40% OF BASE
WAX BOX HOBBY (18) 80.00 120.00
MINI BOX (6) 20.00 40.00
1 Bobby Allison .30 .75
2 Davey Allison .60 1.50
3 Donnie Allison .30 .75
4 Mario Andretti .40 1.00
5 Dick Berggren .25 .60
6 Geoff Bodine .25 .60
7 Richard Childress .40 1.00
8 Jerry Cook .25 .60
9 Dale Earnhardt 2.00 5.00
10 Ralph Earnhardt .60 1.50
11 Bill Elliott .60 1.50
12 John Force .60 1.50
13 Harry Gant .30 .75
14 Don Garlits .30 .75
15 Paul Goldsmith .25 .60
16 James Hylton .25 .60
17 Dale Inman .30 .75
18 Ernie Irvan .30 .75
19 Dale Jarrett .40 1.00
20 Ned Jarrett .30 .75
21 Alan Kulwicki .60 1.50
22 Terry Labonte .40 1.00
23 Fred Lorenzen .30 .75
24 Dave Marcis .30 .75
25 Shirley Muldowney .30 .75
26 Chocolate Myers .40 1.00
27 Benny Parsons .40 1.00
28 David Pearson .40 1.00
29 Lee Petty .30 .75
30 Richard Petty .60 1.50
31 Tim Richmond .30 .75
32 Ricky Rudd .30 .75
33 Ken Schrader .25 .60
34 Rusty Wallace .40 1.00
35 Darrell Waltrip .60 1.50
36 Cale Yarborough .40 1.00
37 Trevor Bayne .75 2.00
38 Kurt Busch .30 .75
39 Kyle Busch .50 1.25
40 Dale Earnhardt Jr .75 2.00
41 Carl Edwards .40 1.00
42 Jeff Gordon .75 2.00
43 Denny Hamlin .40 1.00
44 Kevin Harvick .50 1.25
45 Jimmie Johnson .60 1.50
46 Kasey Kahne .40 1.00
47 Matt Kenseth .40 1.00
48 Mark Martin .40 1.00
49 Danica Patrick 1.50 4.00
50 Tony Stewart .60 1.50
51 Michael Waltrip .50 1.25
52 Ryan Newman .30 .75
53 Jeff Burton .30 .75
54 Bobby Labonte .40 1.00
55 Richard Petty TR .60 1.50
56 John Force TR .60 1.50
57 Mario Andretti TR .40 1.00
58 David Pearson TR .40 1.00
59 Jeff Gordon TR .75 2.00
60 Cale Yarborough TR .40 1.00
61 Bobby Allison TR .30 .75
62 Darrell Waltrip TR .60 1.50
63 Dale Earnhardt TR 2.00 5.00
64 Dale Earnhardt LL 2.00 5.00
65 John Force LL .60 1.50
66 Mario Andretti LL .40 1.00
67 Cale Yarborough LL .40 1.00
68 Richard Childress LL .40 1.00
69 David Pearson LL .40 1.00
70 Jeff Gordon LL .75 2.00
71 Jimmie Johnson LL .60 1.50
72 Bobby Allison LL .30 .75
73 Benny Parsons IS .40 1.00
74 Captive Audience IS .25 .60
75 Richard Petty IS .60 1.50
76 Richard Petty IS .60 1.50
77 Ralph Earnhardt IS .60 1.50
78 Darrell Waltrip IS .60 1.50
79 Terry Labonte IS .40 1.00
80 Battle Scars IS .25 .60

2011 Press Pass Legends Gold

*GOLD: .8X TO 2X BASE
STATED PRINT RUN 250 SER.#'d SETS

2011 Press Pass Legends Holofoil

*HOLOFOIL: 4X TO 10X BASE
STATED PRINT RUN 25 SER.#'d SETS

2011 Press Pass Legends Purple

*PURPLE: 4X TO 10X BASE
STATED PRINT RUN 25 SER.#'d SETS

2011 Press Pass Legends Red

*RED: 1X TO 2.5X BASE
STATED PRINT RUN 99 SER.#'d SETS

2011 Press Pass Legends Autographs Gold

GOLD STATED PRINT RUN 5-99
LGADE Dale Earnhardt Jr./24 40.00 100.00
LGABA Bobby Allison/50 6.00 15.00
LGABA2 Bobby Allison/25 6.00 15.00
LGABE Bill Elliott/25 12.00 30.00
LGABE2 Bill Elliott/25 12.00 30.00
LGACE Carl Edwards/50 8.00 20.00
LGACM Chocolate Myers/99 10.00 25.00
LGACY Cale Yarborough/25 8.00 20.00
LGADA Donnie Allison/99 6.00 15.00
LGADA2 Donnie Allison/25 6.00 15.00
LGADB Dick Berggren/99 8.00 20.00
LGADG Don Garlits/50 15.00 40.00
LGADH Denny Hamlin/50 8.00 20.00
LGADI Dale Inman/99 6.00 15.00
LGADJ Dale Jarrett/50 12.00 30.00
LGADM Dave Marcis/50 10.00 25.00
LGADP1 David Pearson/50 8.00 20.00
LGADW Darrell Waltrip/50 12.00 30.00
LGADW2 Darrell Waltrip/25 12.00 30.00
LGAEI Ernie Irvan/50 6.00 15.00
LGAEI2 Ernie Irvan/25 6.00 15.00
LGAFL Fred Lorenzen/20 12.00 30.00
LGAGB Geoff Bodine/99 5.00 12.00
LGAHG Harry Gant/45 6.00 15.00
LGAJC Jerry Cook/50 5.00 12.00
LGAJF John Force/75 12.00 30.00
LGAJG Jeff Gordon/25 30.00 80.00
LGAJH James Hylton/50 5.00 12.00
LGAJJ Jimmie Johnson/25 50.00 100.00
LGAKH Kevin Harvick/25 10.00 25.00
LGAKK Kasey Kahne/25 15.00 40.00
LGAKS Ken Schrader/50 5.00 12.00
LGAKUB Kurt Busch/25 6.00 15.00
LGAKYB Kyle Busch/25 10.00 25.00
LGAMA Mario Andretti/50 10.00 25.00
LGAMK Matt Kenseth/25 15.00 40.00
LGAMM Mark Martin/25 8.00 20.00
LGAMP Marvin Panch/99 5.00 12.00
LGANJ Ned Jarrett/50 6.00 15.00
LGAPG Paul Goldsmith/49 5.00 12.00
LGARC Richard Childress/60 8.00 20.00
LGARR Ricky Rudd/25 6.00 15.00
LGARW Rusty Wallace/50 15.00 40.00
LGARW2 Rusty Wallace/25 8.00 20.00
LGASM Shirley Muldowney/45 15.00 40.00
LGATB Trevor Bayne/50 12.00 30.00
LGATS Tony Stewart/25 12.00 30.00

2011 Press Pass Legends Autographs Silver

STATED PRINT RUN 10-199
*BLUE/24-25: .6X TO 1.5X SILVER
LGABA Bobby Allison/99 5.00 12.00
LGABA2 Bobby Allison/50 5.00 12.00
LGABE Bill Elliott/50
LGACE Carl Edwards/125 6.00 15.00
LGACM Chocolate Myers/175 8.00 20.00
LGACY Cale Yarborough/25 6.00 15.00
LGACY2 Cale Yarborough/25 6.00 15.00
LGADA Donnie Allison/50 5.00 12.00
LGADA2 Donnie Allison/50 5.00 12.00
LGADB Dick Berggren/170 5.00 12.00
LGADG Don Garlits/99 12.00 30.00
LGADH Denny Hamlin/125 8.00 20.00
LGADI Dale Inman/125 5.00 12.00
LGADJ Dale Jarrett/99 10.00 25.00
LGADM Dave Marcis/98 8.00 20.00
LGADP1 David Pearson/125 6.00 15.00
LGADP2 Danica Patrick/35 60.00 120.00
LGADW Darrell Waltrip/99 10.00 25.00
LGADW2 Darrell Waltrip/50 10.00 25.00
LGAEI Ernie Irvan/99 5.00 12.00
LGAEI2 Ernie Irvan/50 5.00 12.00
LGAGB Geoff Bodine/199 4.00 10.00
LGAHG Harry Gant/99 5.00 12.00
LGAJC Jerry Cook/99 4.00 10.00
LGAJF John Force/140 12.00 30.00
LGAJH James Hylton/99 4.00 10.00
LGAKH Kevin Harvick/50 8.00 20.00
LGAKK Kasey Kahne/99 12.00 30.00
LGAKS Ken Schrader/125 4.00 10.00
LGAKUB Kurt Busch/50 5.00 12.00
LGAKYB Kyle Busch/50 8.00 20.00
LGAMA Mario Andretti/115 8.00 20.00
LGAMK Matt Kenseth/99 12.00 30.00
LGAMP Marvin Panch/145 4.00 10.00
LGANJ Ned Jarrett/99 5.00 12.00
LGAPG Paul Goldsmith/99 4.00 10.00
LGARC Richard Childress/148 6.00 15.00
LGARP Richard Petty/25 20.00 50.00
LGARR Ricky Rudd/75 5.00 12.00
LGARW Rusty Wallace/75 12.00 30.00
LGARW2 Rusty Wallace/50 6.00 15.00
LGASM Shirley Muldowney/99 12.00 30.00
LGATB Trevor Bayne/125 10.00 25.00
LGATL Terry Labonte/25 25.00 50.00
LGATL2 Terry Labonte/10

2011 Press Pass Legends Dual Firesuits Silver

SILVER STATED PRINT RUN 99
*GOLD/50: .5X TO 1.2X SILVER/99
*HOLO/25: .6X TO 1.5X SILVER/99
*PURPLE/15: .8X TO 2X SILVER/99
DECM D.Earnhardt/C.Myers 20.00 50.00

2011 Press Pass Legends Famed Fabrics Gold

STATED PRINT RUN 50 SER.#'d SETS
*HOLO/25: .5X TO 1.2X GOLD/50
*PURPLE/15: .5X TO 1.2X GOLD/99
HOFBA Bobby Allison 4.00 10.00
HOFBM Bud Moore 5.00 12.00
HOFCY Cale Yarborough 5.00 12.00
HOFDE Dale Earnhardt 25.00 60.00
HOFDI Dale Inman 4.00 10.00
HOFDP David Pearson 5.00 12.00
HOFDW Darrell Waltrip 8.00 20.00
HOFRP Richard Petty 8.00 20.00

2011 Press Pass Legends Lasting Legacies Autographs

STATED PRINT RUN 25 SER.#'d SETS
LLSEBA Bobby Allison 20.00 50.00
LLSEBE Bill Elliott 20.00 50.00
LLSECY Cale Yarborough 15.00 40.00
LLSEDA Donnie Allison 12.00 30.00
LLSEDB Dick Berggren 8.00 20.00
LLSEDG Don Garlits 40.00 80.00
LLSEDI Dale Inman 20.00 50.00
LLSEDJ Dale Jarrett 25.00 60.00
LLSEDM Dave Marcis 12.00 30.00
LLSEDP David Pearson 20.00 50.00
LLSEDW Darrell Waltrip 20.00 50.00
LLSEEI Ernie Irvan 12.00 30.00
LLSEGB Geoff Bodine 25.00 60.00
LLSEJF John Force 25.00 60.00
LLSEMA Mario Andretti 15.00 40.00
LLSEMP Marvin Panch 10.00 25.00
LLSERP Richard Petty 40.00 80.00
LLSERR Ricky Rudd 12.00 30.00
LLSERW Rusty Wallace 20.00 50.00
LLSESM Shirley Muldowney 15.00 40.00
LLSETL Terry Labonte 50.00 100.00

2011 Press Pass Legends Lasting Legacies Memorabilia Silver

STATED PRINT RUN 175-199
*GOLD/50: .5X TO 1.2X SILVER
*HOLO/25: .6X TO 1.5X SILVER
*PURPLE/15: .8X TO 2X SILVER
LLAK Alan Kulwicki/175 8.00 20.00
LLBA Bobby Allison/199 4.00 10.00
LLBE Bill Elliott/175 8.00 20.00
LLCM Chocolate Myers/199 5.00 12.00
LLCY Cale Yarborough/175 5.00 12.00
LLDE Dale Earnhardt/199 12.00 30.00
LLDI Dale Inman/199 4.00 10.00
LLDJ Dale Jarrett/175 5.00 12.00
LLDM Dave Marcis/175 6.00 15.00
LLDP David Pearson/199 5.00 12.00
LLDW Darrell Waltrip/175 8.00 20.00
LLEI Ernie Irvan/199 4.00 10.00
LLGB Geoff Bodine/175 3.00 8.00
LLHG Harry Gant/199 4.00 10.00
LLJF John Force/199 8.00 20.00
LLKS Ken Schrader/199 3.00 8.00
LLMA Mario Andretti/175 5.00 12.00
LLRC Richard Childress/199 5.00 12.00
LLRP Richard Petty/175 8.00 20.00
LLRR Ricky Rudd/175 4.00 10.00
LLRW Rusty Wallace/199 5.00 12.00
LLSM Shirley Muldowney/175 10.00 25.00
LLTL Terry Labonte/175 5.00 12.00
LLTR Tim Richmond/199 6.00 15.00
LLDA1 Davey Allison/199 10.00 25.00
LLDA2 Donnie Allison/175 4.00 10.00
LLDE2 Dale Earnhardt/199 15.00 40.00

2011 Press Pass Legends Motorsports Masters

COMPLETE SET (20) 10.00 25.00
*BRUSHED/199: .5X TO 1.2X BASIC INSERTS
*HOLOFOIL/50: 1X TO 2.5X BASIC INSERTS
MM1 Dale Earnhardt 3.00 8.00
MM2 Davey Allison 1.00 2.50
MM3 Bobby Allison .50 1.25
MM4 Richard Childress .60 1.50
MM5 John Force 1.00 2.50
MM6 Don Garlits .50 1.25
MM7 Paul Goldsmith .40 1.00
MM8 Dale Inman .50 1.25
MM9 Jerry Cook .40 1.00
MM10 Terry Labonte .60 1.50

MM11 Shirley Muldowney .50 1.25
MM12 David Pearson .60 1.50
MM13 Richard Petty 1.00 2.50
MM14 Ricky Rudd .50 1.25
MM15 Rusty Wallace .60 1.50
MM16 Darrell Waltrip 1.00 2.50
MM17 Cale Yarborough .60 1.50
MM18 Jeff Gordon 1.25 3.00
MM19 Jimmie Johnson 1.00 2.50
MM20 Tony Stewart 1.00 2.50

2011 Press Pass Legends Motorsports Masters Autographs Silver

SILVER STATED PRINT RUN 25-99
*GOLD/15-25: .5X TO 1.2X SILVER
UNPRICED BLUE PRINT RUN 1
MMAEBA Bobby Allison 8.00 20.00
MMAECY Cale Yarborough/60 6.00 15.00
MMAEDG Don Garlits 10.00 25.00
MMAEDI Dale Inman 6.00 15.00
MMAEDM Dave Marcis/75 10.00 25.00
MMAEDP David Pearson 6.00 15.00
MMAEDW Darrell Waltrip/50 12.00 30.00
MMAEHG Harry Gant 10.00 25.00
MMAEJC Jerry Cook 4.00 10.00
MMAEJF John Force/96 15.00 40.00
MMAEJH James Hylton 4.00 10.00
MMAEKS Ken Schrader 4.00 10.00
MMAEPG Paul Goldsmith/74 4.00 10.00
MMAERC Richard Childress 6.00 15.00
MMAERP Richard Petty/25 20.00 50.00
MMAERR Ricky Rudd/50 5.00 12.00
MMAERW Rusty Wallace/50 20.00 50.00
MMAESM Shirley Muldowney 12.00 30.00
MMAETL Terry Labonte /25 6.00 15.00

2011 Press Pass Legends Pacing The Field

COMPLETE SET (10) 8.00 20.00
*BRUSHED/199: .5X TO 1.2X BASIC INSERTS
*HOLO/50: .6X TO 1.5X BASIC INSERTS
PF1 Dale Earnhardt 3.00 8.00
PF2 Richard Petty 1.00 2.50
PF3 Ricky Rudd .50 1.25
PF4 Dave Marcis .50 1.25
PF5 Bill Elliott 1.00 2.50
PF6 Mark Martin .60 1.50
PF7 Ned Jarrett .50 1.25
PF8 Jeff Gordon 1.25 3.00
PF9 Tony Stewart 1.00 2.50
PF10 David Pearson .60 1.50

2011 Press Pass Legends Pacing The Field Autographs Silver

SILVER STATED PRINT RUN 15-50
UNPRICED BLUE PRINT RUN 9-10
PFABE Bill Elliott/40 12.00 30.00
PFADM Dave Marcis/15
PFADP David Pearson/40 8.00 20.00
PFAJG Jeff Gordon/50 50.00 100.00
PFAJJ Jimmie Johnson/25 40.00 100.00
PFAMM Mark Martin/25
PFANJ Ned Jarrett/40 6.00 15.00
PFARP Richard Petty/15 30.00 60.00
PFARR Ricky Rudd/40 6.00 15.00
PFATS Tony Stewart/25 12.00 30.00

2011 Press Pass Legends Prominent Pieces Silver

SILVER STATED PRINT RUN 99
*GOLD/50: .5X TO 1.2X SILVER/99
*HOLO/25: .6X TO 1.5X SILVER/99
*OVERSIZE/25: 1X TO 2.5X SILVER/99
*PURPLE/15: .8X TO 2X SILVER/99
PPCE Carl Edwards 6.00 15.00
PPDE Dale Earnhardt Jr 12.00 30.00
PPDP Danica Patrick 20.00 50.00
PPJG Jeff Gordon 12.00 30.00
PPJJ Jimmie Johnson 12.00 30.00
PPKH Kevin Harvick 8.00 20.00
PPKK Kasey Kahne 8.00 20.00
PPMK Matt Kenseth 6.00 15.00
PPMM Mark Martin 6.00 15.00
PPTB Trevor Bayne 10.00 25.00
PPTS Tony Stewart 10.00 25.00
PPKYB Kyle Busch 8.00 20.00

2011 Press Pass Legends Trophy Room Gold

GOLD STATED PRINT RUN 50
*HOLO/25: .5X TO 1.2X GOLD/50
*PURPLE/15: .6X TO 1.5X GOLD/50
TRBA Bobby Allison 4.00 10.00
TRCY Cale Yarborough 5.00 12.00
TRDE Dale Earnhardt 25.00 60.00
TRDP David Pearson 5.00 12.00
TRDW Darrell Waltrip 8.00 20.00
TRJF John Force 12.00 30.00
TRJG Jeff Gordon 10.00 25.00
TRMA Mario Andretti 5.00 12.00
TRRP Richard Petty 8.00 20.00

2012 Press Pass Legends

WAX BOX HOBBY (18) 90.00 150.00
1 Bobby Allison .30 .75
2 Davey Allison .60 1.50
3 Donnie Allison .30 .75
4 Mario Andretti .40 1.00
5 Dick Berggren .25 .60
6 Geoffrey Bodine .25 .60
7 Jerry Cook .25 .60
8 Scott Dixon .25 .60
9 Dale Earnhardt 1.25 3.00
10 Bill Elliott .60 1.50
11 Ray Evernham .30 .75
12 John Force .60 1.50
13 Dario Franchitti .25 .60
14 Harry Gant .30 .75
15 Don Garlits .30 .75
16 Paul Goldsmith .25 .60
17 Janet Guthrie .30 .75
18 Dale Inman .30 .75
19 Ernie Irvan .30 .75
20 Dale Jarrett .40 1.00
21 Ned Jarrett .30 .75
22 Fred Lorenzen .25 .60
23 Dave Marcis .30 .75
24 Tom McEwen .30 .75
25 Larry McReynolds .25 .60
26 Bud Moore .25 .60
27 Shirley Muldowney .30 .75
28 Benny Parsons .40 1.00
29 David Pearson .40 1.00
30 Maurice Petty .25 .60
31 Richard Petty .60 1.50
32 Don Prudhomme .30 .75
33 Ken Schrader .25 .60
34 Rusty Wallace .40 1.00
35 Darrell Waltrip .60 1.50
36 Leonard Wood .25 .60
37 Cale Yarborough .40 1.00
38 Jeff Burton .30 .75
39 Kyle Busch .50 1.25
40 Dale Earnhardt Jr .75 2.00
41 Carl Edwards .40 1.00
42 Jeff Gordon .75 2.00
43 Kevin Harvick .50 1.25
44 Jimmie Johnson .60 1.50
45 Kasey Kahne .40 1.00
46 Bobby Labonte .40 1.00
47 Terry Labonte .40 1.00
48 Mark Martin .40 1.00
49 Danica Patrick 1.25 3.00
50 Tony Stewart .60 1.50

2012 Press Pass Legends Gold

*GOLD/275: .8X TO 2X BASIC CARDS
STATED PRINT RUN 275 SER.#'d SETS

2012 Press Pass Legends Green

*GREEN: 1X TO 2.5X BASIC CARDS
RANDOM INSERTS IN RETAIL PACKS

2012 Press Pass Legends Rainbow Holofoil

*RAINBOW/50: 2X TO 5X BASIC CARDS
ONE PER SPECIAL BOX

2012 Press Pass Legends Silver Holofoil

*SILVER HOLO/25: 4X TO 10X BASIC CARDS
STATED PRINT RUN 25 SER.#'d SETS

2012 Press Pass Legends Red

*RED/99: 1X TO 2.5X BASIC CARDS
STATED PRINT RUN 99 SER.#'d SETS

2012 Press Pass Legends Autographs Gold

*BLUE/20-25: .6X TO 1.5X GOLD/25-150
*HOLOFOIL/20-75: .5X TO 1.2X GOLD AU
*SLVR/150-250: .3X TO .8X GOLD/99-150
*SLVR/150: .25X TO .6X GOLD/50-75
*SLVR/50-100: .3X TO .8X GOLD/25-75
BA Bobby Allison/50 6.00 15.00
BE Bill Elliott/50 12.00 30.00
BM Bud Moore/75 8.00 20.00
CY Cale Yarborough/25 8.00 20.00
DA Donnie Allison/99 5.00 12.00
DB Dick Berggren/99 4.00 10.00
DF Dario Franchitti/150 6.00 15.00
DG Don Garlits/75 10.00 25.00
DI Dale Inman/50 6.00 15.00
DJ Dale Jarrett/100 6.00 15.00
DM Dave Marcis/99 5.00 12.00
DP David Pearson/25 8.00 20.00
DP Don Prudhomme/150 12.00 30.00
DW Darrell Waltrip/25 12.00 30.00
EI Ernie Irvan/99 8.00 20.00
FL Fred Lorenzen/25 5.00 12.00
GB Geoffrey Bodine/99 6.00 15.00
HC Helio Castroneves/150 6.00 15.00
HG Harry Gant/99 5.00 12.00
JC Jerry Cook/99 4.00 10.00
JF John Force/50 15.00 40.00
JG Janet Guthrie/25 10.00 25.00
KS Ken Schrader/75 5.00 12.00
LM Larry McReynolds/75 5.00 12.00
LW Leonard Wood/75 5.00 12.00
MA Mario Andretti/50 12.00 30.00
NJ Ned Jarrett/25 6.00 15.00
PG Paul Goldsmith/99 6.00 15.00
PH Pete Hamilton/99 6.00 15.00
RE Ray Evernham/150 5.00 12.00
RP Richard Petty/5
RR Ricky Rudd/75 6.00 15.00
RW Rusty Wallace/75 8.00 20.00
SD Scott Dixon/150 4.00 10.00
SM Shirley Muldowney/99 10.00 25.00
TM Tom McEwen/150 10.00 25.00
WP Will Power/150 6.00 15.00

2012 Press Pass Legends Memorable Moments

STATED ODDS 1:4 HOBBY
*HOLOFOIL/99: 1X TO 2.5X BASIC INSERTS
MM1 Glen Wood with car .50 1.25
MM2 R.Petty's Car/DW's Car 1.00 2.50
MM3 First Restrictor Plate Race .40 1.00
MM4 Benny Parsons Champ .60 1.50
MM5 Bill Elliott's Car 1.00 2.50
MM6 Bobby Allison w/car .50 1.25
MM7 Richard Petty w/car 1.00 2.50
MM8 Davey Allison 1.00 2.50
MM9 Ernie Irvan's truck .50 1.25
MM10 Richard Petty w/car 1.00 2.50

2012 Press Pass Legends Pieces of History Memorabilia Gold

STATED PRINT RUN 25-99
*SILVER: .3X TO .8X GOLD
*HOLOFOIL/25: .6X TO 1.5X GOLD/99
*HOLOFOIL/25: .5X TO 1.2X GOLD/50
AK Alan Kulwicki FS/99 6.00 15.00
BA Bobby Allison FS/99 3.00 8.00
CO Cotton Owens Pants/99 4.00 10.00
DA Davey Allison FS/99 8.00 20.00
DB Dick Berggren Hat/50 3.00 8.00
DM Dave Marcis FS/99 3.00 8.00
EI Ernie Irvan FS/99 3.00 8.00
HG Harry Gant FS/99 4.00 10.00
SM Shirley Muldowney FS/99 8.00 20.00
TM Tom McEwen GLV/99 10.00 25.00
BE1 Bill Elliott FS/99 6.00 15.00
BE2 Bill Elliott SM/99 6.00 15.00
BE3 Bill Elliott Shoe/50 8.00 20.00
DE1 Dale Earnhardt FS/99 10.00 25.00
DE2 Dale Earnhardt GLV/25 15.00 40.00
DE3 Dale Earnhardt Shoe/50 12.00 30.00
DF1 Dario Franchitti FS/99 4.00 10.00
DF2 Dario Franchitti GLV/50 5.00 12.00
DJ1 Dale Jarrett GLV/50 5.00 12.00
DJ2 Dale Jarrett Shoe/50 5.00 12.00
DJ3 Dale Jarrett SB/50 5.00 12.00
DOA Donnie Allison FS/99 3.00 8.00
DP1 David Pearson FS/99 4.00 10.00
DP2 David Pearson Hat/50 5.00 12.00
DPR Don Prudhomme Shirt/99 10.00 25.00
DW1 Darrell Waltrip FS/99 6.00 15.00
DW2 Darrell Waltrip Flag/50 8.00 20.00
GB1 Geoffrey Bodine GLV/25 4.00 10.00
GB2 Geoffrey Bodine Flag/50 3.00 8.00
GB3 Geoffrey Bodine SM/99 2.50 6.00
JF1 John Force Boot/99 6.00 15.00
JF2 John Force Para/99 8.00 20.00
JF3 John Force Shirt/99 6.00 15.00
MA1 Mario Andretti FS/99 4.00 10.00
MA2 Mario Andretti Shoe/50 5.00 12.00
RP1 Richard Petty FS/99 6.00 15.00
RP2 Richard Petty GLV/50 8.00 20.00
RP3 Richard Petty Hat/50 8.00 20.00
RR1 Ricky Rudd FS/99 3.00 8.00
RR2 Ricky Rudd GLV/50 4.00 10.00
RW1 Rusty Wallace FS/99 4.00 10.00
RW2 Rusty Wallace GLV/50 5.00 12.00
RW3 Rusty Wallace Shoe/50 5.00 12.00
TL1 Terry Labonte FS/99 4.00 10.00
TL2 Terry Labonte GLV/50 5.00 12.00
TR1 Tim Richmond Shoe/50 6.00 15.00
TR2 Tim Richmond GLV/50 6.00 15.00
TR3 Tim Richmond FS/99 5.00 12.00

2012 Press Pass Legends Pieces of History Memorabilia Autographs Gold

PHSBA Bobby Allison FS 10.00 25.00
PHSBE Bill Elliott FS 20.00 50.00
PHSCY Cale Yarborough FS 12.00 30.00
PHSDI Dale Inman Shirt 12.00 30.00
PHSDJ Dale Jarrett GLV 15.00 40.00
PHSDP David Pearson Hat 12.00 30.00
PHSDW Darrell Waltrip FS 20.00 50.00
PHSJF John Force Para 25.00 60.00
PHSMA Mario Andretti FS 30.00 80.00
PHSRP Richard Petty Hat 20.00 50.00
PHSRW Rusty Wallace FS 30.00 60.00
PHSSM Shirley Muldowney FS 50.00 120.00
PHSTL Terry Labonte GLV 25.00 60.00

2012 Press Pass Legends Prominent Pieces Silver

STATED PRINT RUN 99 SER.#'d SETS
*GOLD/50: .4X TO 1X SILVER/99
*HOLOFOIL/25: .6X TO 1.5X SILVER/99
*OVERSIZED/25: .6X TO 1.5X SILVER/99
BL Bobby Labonte 5.00 12.00
CE Carl Edwards 5.00 12.00
DP Danica Patrick NNS 15.00 40.00
JG Jeff Gordon 10.00 25.00
JJ Jimmie Johnson 8.00 20.00
KB Kyle Busch 6.00 15.00
KH Kevin Harvick 6.00 15.00
KK Kasey Kahne 5.00 12.00
MK Matt Kenseth 5.00 12.00
MM Mark Martin 5.00 12.00
TS Tony Stewart 10.00 25.00
DEJ Dale Earnhardt Jr 12.00 30.00

2012 Press Pass Legends Trailblazers

STATED ODDS 1:4 HOBBY
SP STATED ODDS 1:40 HOBBY
*HOLOFOIL/99: 1X TO 2.5X BASIC INSERTS
TB1 Richard Petty SP 5.00 12.00
TB2 Darrell Waltrip 1.00 2.50
TB3 David Pearson .60 1.50
TB4 Glen Wood SP 4.00 10.00
TB5 Ned Jarrett .50 1.25
TB6 Dale Inman .50 1.25
TB7 Dale Earnhardt SP 10.00 25.00
TB8 Cale Yarborough .60 1.50
TB9 Bobby Allison .50 1.25
TB10 Cotton Owens .40 1.00
TB11 Tony Stewart 1.00 2.50
TB12 Janet Guthrie SP 4.00 10.00
TB13 Lee Petty .50 1.25
TB14 Jimmie Johnson 1.00 2.50
TB15 Danica Patrick SP 8.00 20.00

2012 Press Pass Legends Trailblazers Autographs Gold

*HOLOFOIL/25: .5X TO 1.2X GOLD/25-75
*SILVER/50-150: .3X TO .8X GOLD/25-75
TBBA Bobby Allison/50 6.00 15.00
TBCY Cale Yarborough/45 8.00 20.00
TBDI Dale Inman/50 6.00 15.00
TBDP David Pearson/25 8.00 20.00
TBDW Darrell Waltrip/5
TBGW Glen Wood/75 6.00 15.00
TBJG Janet Guthrie/50 8.00 20.00
TBNJ Ned Jarrett/25 6.00 15.00
TBRP Richard Petty/5

2013 Press Pass Legends

COMPLETE SET (60) 15.00 30.00
1 Bobby Allison .30 .75
2 Davey Allison .60 1.50
3 Donnie Allison .30 .75
4 Mario Andretti .40 1.00
5 Geoffrey Bodine .25 .60
6 Helio Castroneves .30 .75
7 Jerry Cook .25 .60
8 Scott Dixon .25 .60
9 Bill Elliott .60 1.50
10 John Force .60 1.50
11 Dario Franchitti .25 .60
12 Harry Gant .30 .75
13 Don Garlits .30 .75
14 Paul Goldsmith .25 .60
15 Janet Guthrie .30 .75
16 Ernie Irvan .30 .75
17 Dale Jarrett .40 1.00
18 Ned Jarrett .30 .75
19 Alan Kulwicki .60 1.50
20 Terry Labonte .40 1.00
21 Dave Marcis .30 .75
22 Tom McEwen .30 .75
23 Bud Moore .25 .60
24 Shirley Muldowney .30 .75
25 Travis Pastrana .40 1.00
26 David Pearson .40 1.00
27 Tony Pedregon .40 1.00
28 Lee Petty .30 .75
29 Maurice Petty .25 .60
30 Richard Petty .60 1.50
31 Tim Pistone .30 .75
32 Will Power .30 .75
33 Don Prudhomme .30 .75
34 Jim Reed .25 .60
35 Ricky Rudd .30 .75
36 Jimmy Spencer .25 .60
37 Rusty Wallace .40 1.00
38 Darrell Waltrip .60 1.50
39 Leonard Wood .25 .60
40 Cale Yarborough .40 1.00
41 Kyle Busch .50 1.25
42 Dale Earnhardt Jr. .75 2.00
43 Carl Edwards .40 1.00
44 Jeff Gordon .75 2.00
45 Kevin Harvick .50 1.25
46 Jimmie Johnson .60 1.50
47 Danica Patrick 1.00 2.50
48 Tony Stewart .60 1.50
49 Mark Martin Salute .40 1.00
50 Mark Martin Salute .40 1.00
51 Mark Martin Salute .40 1.00
52 Mark Martin Salute .40 1.00
53 Mark Martin Salute .40 1.00
54 Mark Martin Salute .40 1.00
55 Alan Kulwicki Tribute .60 1.50
56 Alan Kulwicki Tribute .60 1.50
57 Alan Kulwicki Tribute .60 1.50
58 Alan Kulwicki Tribute .60 1.50
59 Alan Kulwicki Tribute .60 1.50
60 Alan Kulwicki Tribute .60 1.50

2013 Press Pass Legends Blue

*RETAIL BLUE: 1.2X TO 3X BASIC CARDS

2013 Press Pass Legends Gold

*GOLD/149: 1X TO 2.5X BASIC CARDS

2013 Press Pass Legends Red

*RED/99: 1X TO 2.5X BASIC CARDS

2013 Press Pass Legends Alan Kulwicki Tribute Memorabilia Silver

STATED PRINT RUN 50 SER.#'d SETS
*GOLD/25: .6X TO 1.5X SILVER/50
AKMAK Alan Kulwicki 8.00 20.00

2013 Press Pass Legends Autographs Gold

LGBA Bobby Allison/50 6.00 15.00
LGBM Bud Moore/50 5.00 12.00
LGCY Cale Yarborough/75 6.00 15.00
LGDA Donnie Allison EXCH
LGDF Dario Franchitti/75 5.00 12.00
LGDG Don Garlits/75 8.00 20.00
LGDJ Dale Jarrett/25 8.00 20.00
LGDM Dave Marcis/150 EXCH 5.00 12.00
LGDP David Pearson/25 8.00 20.00
LGDP2 Don Prudhomme/50 6.00 15.00
LGEE Erica Enders/100 15.00 40.00
LGEI Ernie Irvan/100 5.00 12.00
LGGB Geoffrey Bodine/125 4.00 10.00
LGHC Helio Castroneves/75 6.00 15.00
LGHG Harry Gant/100 5.00 12.00
LGJC Jerry Cook/100 4.00 10.00
LGJF John Force/25 25.00 50.00
LGJG Janet Guthrie/75 6.00 15.00
LGJI Jack Ingram/150 4.00 10.00
LGJR Jim Reed/150 6.00 15.00
LGJS Jimmy Spencer/75 5.00 12.00
LGLM Larry McReynolds/155 4.00 10.00
LGLW Leonard Wood/50 5.00 12.00
LGMA Mario Andretti/25 12.00 30.00
LGMP Maurice Petty/150 8.00 20.00
LGNJ Ned Jarrett/25 5.00 12.00
LGPG Paul Goldsmith/75 5.00 12.00
LGRR Ricky Rudd/21 6.00 15.00
LGRW Rusty Wallace/15 12.00 30.00
LGSD Scott Dixon/75 5.00 12.00
LGSM Shirley Muldowney/50 6.00 15.00
LGTE Tom McEwen/53 8.00 20.00
LGTP2 Tom Pistone EXCH 6.00 15.00
LGTP3 Tony Pedregon/150 8.00 20.00
LGWJ Warren Johnson/150 12.00 30.00
LGWP Will Power/75 6.00 15.00

2013 Press Pass Legends Autographs Holofoil

LGBA Bobby Allison/25 6.00 15.00
LGBM Bud Moore/25 5.00 12.00
LGDF Dario Franchitti/25 5.00 12.00
LGDG Don Garlits/25 8.00 20.00
LGDM Dave Marcis 6.00 15.00
LGEE Erica Enders/25 25.00 50.00
LGEI Ernie Irvan/25 6.00 15.00
LGGB Geoffrey Bodine/25 5.00 12.00
LGHC Helio Castroneves/25 6.00 15.00
LGHG Harry Gant/25 6.00 15.00
LGJC Jerry Cook/25 5.00 12.00
LGJG Janet Guthrie/25 6.00 15.00
LGJI Jack Ingram/25 5.00 12.00
LGJR Jim Reed/25 8.00 20.00
LGJS Jimmy Spencer/25 5.00 12.00
LGLM Larry McReynolds/25 5.00 12.00
LGMA Mario Andretti/15 12.00 30.00
LGMP Maurice Petty/25 10.00 25.00
LGPG Paul Goldsmith/25 5.00 12.00
LGSD Scott Dixon/25 5.00 12.00
LGSM Shirley Muldowney/25 6.00 15.00
LGTE Tom McEwen/25 8.00 20.00
LGWJ Warren Johnson/25 20.00 40.00
LGDP2 Don Prudhomme/25 10.00 25.00
LGTP3 Tony Pedregon/25 10.00 25.00

2013 Press Pass Legends Autographs Silver

EXCH EXPIRATION: 4/30/2015
LGBE Bill Elliott/25 12.00 30.00
LGCY Cale Yarborough/210 5.00 12.00
LGDA Donnie Allison EXCH 5.00 12.00
LGDF Dario Franchitti/150 4.00 10.00
LGDJ Dale Jarrett/75 8.00 20.00
LGDM Dave Marcis EXCH 5.00 12.00
LGDP2 Don Prudhomme/100 5.00 12.00
LGDW Darrell Waltrip/50 12.00 30.00
LGHC Helio Castroneves/200 5.00 12.00
LGJS Jimmy Spencer/25 5.00 12.00
LGLW Leonard Wood/25 5.00 12.00
LGMA Mario Andretti/95 10.00 25.00
LGNJ Ned Jarrett/150 5.00 12.00
LGRR Ricky Rudd/100 5.00 12.00
LGRW Rusty Wallace/50 10.00 25.00
LGSD Scott Dixon/200 4.00 10.00
LGTE Tom McEwen/200 5.00 12.00
LGTP2 Tom Pistone/200 6.00 15.00
LGWP Will Power/200 5.00 12.00

2013 Press Pass Legends Famous Feats

STATED ODDS 1:4
*HOLOFOIL/99: 1X TO 2.5X BASIC INSERTS
FF1 Dale Jarrett .75 2.00
FF2 Bobby Allison .60 1.50
FF3 Bill Elliott 1.25 3.00
FF4 Richard Petty 1.25 3.00
FF5 David Pearson .75 2.00
FF6 Mario Andretti .75 2.00
FF7 Ernie Irvan .60 1.50
FF8 Janet Guthrie .60 1.50
FF9 Ned Jarrett .60 1.50
FF10 John Force 1.25 3.00

2013 Press Pass Legends Famous Feats Autographs Silver

FFBA Bobby Allison/25 6.00 15.00
FFBE Bill Elliott
FFDF Dario Franchitti/25 6.00 15.00
FFDG Don Garlits/25 12.00 30.00
FFDJ Dale Jarrett/25 10.00 25.00
FFDP David Pearson/25 8.00 20.00
FFEI Ernie Irvan/25 6.00 15.00
FFJG Janet Guthrie/25 8.00 20.00
FFNJ Ned Jarrett/25 6.00 15.00
FFRP Richard Petty
FFSM Shirley Muldowney/25 15.00 40.00

2013 Press Pass Legends Mark Martin Salute Memorabilia Silver

COMMON MARTIN/50 6.00 15.00
*GOLD/25: .6X TO 1.5X SILVER/50

2013 Press Pass Legends Pieces of History Memorabilia Silver

*GOLD/50: .4X TO 1X SILVER/65-75
*HOLOFOIL/25: .5X TO 1.2X SILVER/65-75
PHBA Bobby Allison 3.00 8.00
PHBE Bill Elliott 6.00 15.00
PHDF Dario Franchitti 4.00 10.00
PHDG Don Garlits 4.00 10.00
PHDJ Dale Jarrett 4.00 10.00
PHDM Dave Marcis 3.00 8.00
PHDoA Donnie Allison 3.00 8.00
PHDP David Pearson 4.00 10.00
PHDP2 Don Prudhomme 4.00 10.00
PHDW Darrell Waltrip 6.00 15.00
PHEI Ernie Irvan 3.00 8.00
PHGB Geoffrey Bodine 2.50 6.00
PHHC Helio Castroneves 5.00 12.00
PHHG Harry Gant 3.00 8.00
PHJF John Force 6.00 15.00
PHJG Janet Guthrie 3.00 8.00
PHMA Mario Andretti 4.00 10.00
PHRP Richard Petty 5.00 12.00
PHRR Ricky Rudd 3.00 8.00
PHRW Rusty Wallace 5.00 12.00
PHSD Scott Dixon 2.50 6.00
PHSM Shirley Muldowney 4.00 10.00
PHTL Terry Labonte 4.00 10.00
PHTM Tom McEwen 3.00 8.00
PHTP Tony Pedregon 4.00 10.00
PHWP Will Power/65 4.00 10.00

2013 Press Pass Legends Pieces of History Memorabilia Autographs Gold

PHSEBA Bobby Allison/25 10.00 25.00
PHSEBE Bill Elliott/25 12.00 30.00
PHSEDJ Dale Jarrett/25 12.00 30.00
PHSEDP David Pearson/24 10.00 25.00
PHSEDW Darrell Waltrip/25 15.00 40.00
PHSEGB Geoffrey Bodine/25 8.00 20.00
PHSEJF John Force/25 20.00 50.00
PHSEMA Mario Andretti/25 12.00 30.00
PHSEMM Mark Martin/25 12.00 30.00
PHSERP Richard Petty/25 30.00 60.00
PHSERR Ricky Rudd/24 10.00 25.00
PHSERW Rusty Wallace/25 15.00 40.00
PHSESM Shirley Muldowney/25 12.00 30.00
PHSETL Terry Labonte/25 12.00 30.00
PHSETM Tom McEwen/25 10.00 25.00
PHSEDP2 Don Prudhomme/23 15.00 40.00

2013 Press Pass Legends Prominent Pieces Silver

PPBK Brad Keselowski 6.00 15.00
PPCB Clint Bowyer 5.00 12.00
PPCE Carl Edwards 5.00 12.00
PPDE Dale Earnhardt Jr 10.00 25.00
PPDP Danica Patrick 15.00 30.00
PPJG Jeff Gordon 10.00 25.00
PPJJ Jimmie Johnson 8.00 20.00
PPKB Kyle Busch 6.00 15.00
PPKH Kevin Harvick 6.00 15.00
PPKK Kasey Kahne 5.00 12.00
PPMK Matt Kenseth 5.00 12.00
PPTS Tony Stewart 8.00 20.00

2013 Press Pass Legends Signature Style

STATED ODDS 1:5, SP ODDS 1:40
*HOLOFOIL/99: 1X TO 2.5X BASIC INSERTS
*HOLOFOIL/99: .3X TO .8X BASIC SP
SS1 Richard Petty 1.25 3.00
SS2 Terry Labonte .75 2.00
SS3 Bill Elliott 1.25 3.00
SS4 Ned Jarrett .60 1.50
SS6 Don Prudhomme .75 2.00
SS7 David Pearson SP 4.00 10.00
SS8 Darrell Waltrip SP 6.00 15.00
SS9 Tom Pistone SP 4.00 10.00
SS10 Don Garlits .60 1.50
SS11 Shirley Muldowney .75 2.00
SS12 Harry Gant .60 1.50
SS13 Kevin Harvick SP 5.00 12.00
SS14 Carl Edwards .75 2.00
SS15 Jimmy Spencer SP 4.00 10.00

2013 Press Pass Legends Signature Style Autographs Silver

SSBE Bill Elliott/25 12.00 30.00
SSDG Don Garlits/25 25.00 50.00
SSDP David Pearson/25 8.00 20.00
SSDW Darrell Waltrip/25 15.00 40.00
SSHG Harry Gant/25 6.00 15.00
SSJS Jimmy Spencer/25 5.00 12.00
SSNJ Ned Jarrett/25 8.00 20.00
SSRP Richard Petty
SSSM Shirley Muldowney/35 12.00 30.00
SSTL Terry Labonte/15 30.00 60.00
SSTM Tom McEwen
SSTP Tiger Tom Pistone EXCH 8.00 20.00
SSDP2 Don Prudhomme/50 10.00 25.00

2004 Press Pass Making the Show Collector's Series

COMPLETE TIN SET (28) 10.00 25.00
COMP.SET w/o MEM. (27) 8.00 20.00
MS1 Joe Nemechek .15 .40
MS2 Rusty Wallace .25 .60
MS3 Scott Wimmer .25 .60
MS4 Ward Burton .20 .50
MS5 Dale Earnhardt Jr. .50 1.25
MS6 Kasey Kahne 1.00 2.50
MS7 Scott Riggs .20 .50
MS8 Ryan Newman .20 .50
MS9 Michael Waltrip .25 .60
MS10 Greg Biffle .20 .50
MS11 Matt Kenseth .25 .60
MS12 Bobby Labonte .25 .60
MS13 Jeremy Mayfield .15 .40
MS14 Tony Stewart .40 1.00
MS15 Ricky Rudd .20 .50
MS16 Jeff Gordon .50 1.25
MS17 Brian Vickers .30 .75
MS18 Kevin Harvick .30 .75
MS19 Sterling Marlin .25 .60
MS20 Casey Mears .15 .40
MS21 Jamie McMurray .25 .60
MS22 Jeff Green .15 .40
MS23 Jimmie Johnson .40 1.00
MS24 Brendan Gaughan .15 .40
MS25 Robby Gordon .15 .40
MS26 Mark Martin .25 .60
MS27 Jeff Burton CL .20 .50

2004 Press Pass Making the Show Collector's Series Tins

NNO Dale Jr 2.00 5.00
Stewart
J.Gordon

2002 Press Pass Nabisco Albertsons

Available as a mail-in offer, this four card set features the Nabisco team of drivers and was sponsored by Albertsons Stores and Nabisco. The cardfronts feature one driver while the backs include photos of the entire team.

COMPLETE SET (4) 4.00 10.00
1 Dale Earnhardt Jr. 2.50 6.00
2 Kevin Harvick 1.50 4.00
3 Steve Park .75 2.00
4 Michael Waltrip .75 2.00

2003 Press Pass Nabisco Albertsons

For the second year, a card set was produced by Press Pass and sponsored by Team Nabisco and Albertsons stores. A complete set of five could by obtained at participating stores with the purchase of Nabisco products.

COMPLETE SET (5) 4.00 10.00
1 Dale Earnhardt Jr. 2.50 6.00
2 Jeff Green .50 1.25
3 Jason Keller .50 1.25
4 Steve Park .75 2.00
5 Michael Waltrip .75 2.00

2011 Press Pass Premium Hot Pursuit National Convention

COMPLETE SET (10) 6.00 12.00
HP1 Dale Earnhardt Jr. .60 1.50
HP2 Kevin Harvick .40 1.00
HP3 Jeff Gordon .60 1.50
HP4 Jimmie Johnson .50 1.25
HP5 Carl Edwards .30 .75
HP6 Danica Patrick 1.25 3.00
HP7 Denny Hamlin .30 .75
HP8 Tony Stewart .50 1.25
HP9 Mark Martin .30 .75
HP10 Kyle Busch .40 1.00

2004 Press Pass Nilla Wafers

These 4-cards were produced by Press Pass and issued on boxes of Nilla Wafers in early 2004. Each card was intended to be cut from the outside of the box and are priced below as neatly cut cards. Each includes a color photo on the front with a very simple black and white cardback.

COMPLETE SET (4) 5.00 12.00
1 Dale Earnhardt Jr. 1.50 4.00
2 Dale Earnhardt Jr. w/car 1.50 4.00
3 Dale Earnhardt Jr.'s Oreo Car 1.25 3.00
4 Michael Waltrip 1.00 2.50

1994 Press Pass Optima XL Prototypes

Press Pass released this set to preview its 1994 Optima XL line. Two different Rusty Wallace cards were released with the version entitled "Driver/Owner" the tougher of the two to find. A complete set is considered three cards with the easier Rusty Wallace version.

COMPLETE SET (3) 4.00 10.00
1 Kyle Petty .75 2.00
2A R.Wallace DD Name at bottom 1.25 3.00
2B R.Wallace DD Name at top 4.00 10.00
3 Jeff Gordon .60 1.50

1994 Press Pass Optima XL

This 64-card set was the first time Press Pass issued cards under the Optima XL brand name. The cards are larger than the standard card, measuring 2 1/2" x 4 11/16". There are seven topical subsets that combine to make up the entire set. Those subsets are, Spotlight (1-30), Double Duty (31-36), Trophy Case (37-42), Dale Earnhardt Racing Family (43-46), RCR Racing Family (47-49), Winston Cup Scene (50-58), News Makers (59-64). There is one known variation. The number 43 Teresa Earnhardt card was originally printed with a picture of both Teresa and Dale. Early in the production the card was changed to be a picture of Teresa. The set price only includes the common version. The cards were issued in six card packs which came 24 packs per box and 20 boxes per case. There was also a two-card insert set known as Chrome featuring Jeff Gordon and Ernie Irvan. The cards were printed embossed on silver foil and inserted one per 240 packs.

COMPLETE SET (64) 15.00 40.00
1 Brett Bodine .08 .25
2 Geoff Bodine .08 .25
3 Jeff Burton .30 .75
4 Dale Earnhardt 2.50 6.00
5 Harry Gant .20 .50
6 Jeff Gordon 1.00 2.50
7 Steve Grissom .08 .25
8 Ernie Irvan .20 .50
9 Dale Jarrett .60 1.50
10 Terry Labonte .30 .75
11 Sterling Marlin .30 .75
12 Mark Martin .75 2.00
13 Joe Nemechek .08 .25
14 Kyle Petty .20 .50
15 Ricky Rudd .30 .75
16 Greg Sacks .08 .25
17 Ken Schrader .08 .25
18 Morgan Shepherd .08 .25
19 Lake Speed .08 .25
20 Jimmy Spencer .08 .25
21 Hut Stricklin .08 .25
22 Rusty Wallace .75 2.00
23 Darrell Waltrip .20 .50
24 Michael Waltrip .20 .50
25 Ernie Irvan .20 .50
26 Jeff Gordon 1.00 2.50
27 Mark Martin .75 2.00
28 Kyle Petty .20 .50
29 Ken Schrader .08 .25
30 Rusty Wallace .75 2.00
31 Geoff Bodine DD .05 .15
32 Ernie Irvan DD .08 .25
33 Ricky Rudd DD .20 .50
34 Ken Schrader DD .05 .15
35 Rusty Wallace DD .40 1.00
36 Darrell Waltrip DD .08 .25
37 Sterling Marlin's Car TC .08 .25
38 Jeff Gordon TC .50 1.25
39 Terry Labonte's Car TC .20 .50
40 Rusty Wallace's Car TC .30 .75
41 Dale Earnhardt's Car TC .75 2.00
42 Ernie Irvan's Car TC .08 .25
43A Teresa Earnhardt 1.25 3.00
43B T.Earnhardt w/Dale 25.00 50.00
44 Kerry Earnhardt RC 1.50 4.00
45 Kelley Earnhardt RC 1.50 4.00
46 Dale Earnhardt Jr. RC 8.00 20.00
47 Richard Childress .20 .50
48 Hank Jones .05 .15
49 Andy Petree .05 .15
50 Race Day Frenzy WCS .05 .15
51 Rusty Wallace in Pits WCS .30 .75
52 E.Irvan R.Wall. Martin WCS .20 .50
53 Ricky Rudd's Car WCS .08 .25
54 Charlotte Motor Speed. WCS .05 .15
55 Steve Grissom Jeff Burton WCS .05 .15
56 Jeff Gordon WCS .50 1.25
57 Joe Nemechek in Pits WCS .05 .15
58 The Duel in the Sun WCS .05 .15
59 John Andretti NM RC .05 .15
60 Shawna Robinson NM .50 1.25
61 Loy Allen Jr. NM .05 .15
62 Jeff Gordon NM .50 1.25
63 Tommy Houston NM .05 .15
64 Geoff Bodine NM .05 .15
CC1 Jeff Gordon Chrome 15.00 40.00
CC2 Ernie Irvan Chrome 4.00 10.00

1994 Press Pass Optima XL Red Hot

COMPLETE SET (64) 30.00 80.00
*RED CARDS: 1X TO 2.5X HI COL.
43B Teresa Earnhardt w Dale 60.00 100.00
46 Dale Earnhardt Jr. 8.00 20.00

1994 Press Pass Optima XL Double Clutch

This six-card insert set features drivers who were active on both the Winston Cup and Busch circuits. The cards were inserted at a rate of one per 48 packs. All six cards could also be found in a super pack. These super packs were inserted at a rate of one per 2400 packs.

COMPLETE SET (6) 15.00 40.00
DC1 Dale Earnhardt 12.50 30.00
DC2 Ernie Irvan 1.00 2.50
DC3 Terry Labonte 1.50 4.00
DC4 Sterling Marlin 1.50 4.00
DC5 Mark Martin 4.00 10.00
DC6 Morgan Shepherd .50 1.25

1995 Press Pass Optima XL Prototypes

Press Pass released this set to preview its 1995 Optima XL set. The cards are consecutively numbered and often sold as a 3-card set.

COMPLETE SET (3) 3.00 8.00
XL1 Jeff Burton 1.00 2.50
XL2 Darrell Waltrip .75 2.00
XL3 Mark Martin 2.00 5.00

1995 Press Pass Optima XL

This 60-card set is the second edition of the oversized brand of racing cards produced by Press Pass. The cards measure 2 1/2" X 4 11/16" and use photography from the 1995 season. The set consists of seven subsets: Winston Cup Drivers (1-24), Busch Drivers (25-30), Trophy Case (31-36), Team 24 (37-42), Thunderous Thunderbirds (43-48), Monte Carlo Assault (49-54), and Optima Results (55-59). The product was distributed to both hobby and retail outlets and came six cards per pack, 36 packs per box and 12 boxes per case.

COMPLETE SET (60) 10.00 25.00
1 Brett Bodine .10 .30
2 Geoff Bodine .10 .30
3 Todd Bodine .10 .30
4 Derrike Cope .10 .30
5 Ricky Craven .10 .30
6 Dale Earnhardt 2.00 5.00
7 Bill Elliott .50 1.25
8 Jeff Gordon 1.50 3.00
9 Steve Grissom .10 .30
10 Dale Jarrett .75 2.00
11 Bobby Labonte .75 2.00
12 Terry Labonte .40 1.00
13 Sterling Marlin .40 1.00
14 Mark Martin 1.00 2.50
15 Ted Musgrave .10 .30
16 Kyle Petty .25 .60
17 Robert Pressley .10 .30
18 Ricky Rudd .40 1.00
19 Ken Schrader .10 .30
20 Morgan Shepherd .10 .30
21 Hut Stricklin .10 .30
22 Rusty Wallace 1.00 2.50
23 Darrell Waltrip .25 .60
24 Michael Waltrip .25 .60
25 Johnny Benson Jr. .25 .60
26 David Green .10 .30
27 Jeff Green .10 .30
28 Jason Keller .10 .30
29 Chad Little .10 .30
30 Larry Pearson .10 .30
31 Jeff Gordon TC .60 1.50
32 Bobby Labonte TC .40 1.00
33 Terry Labonte TC .25 .60
34 Sterling Marlin TC .25 .60
35 Mark Martin TC .50 1.25
36 Kyle Petty TC .10 .30
37 Chad Knaus .03 .15
38 Ray Evernham .25 .60
39 Mike Belden .03 .15
40 Mike Trower .03 .15
41 Andy Papathanassiou .03 .15
42 Barry Muse .03 .15
43 Ted Musgrave's Car .03 .15
44 Bill Elliott's Car .25 .60
45 Rusty Wallace's Car .40 1.00
46 Dale Jarrett's Car .25 .60
47 Ricky Rudd's Car .10 .30
48 Mark Martin's Car .40 1.00
49 Ken Schrader's Car .03 .15
50 Jeff Gordon's Car .60 1.50
51 Dale Earnhardt's Car .75 2.00
52 Bobby Labonte's Car .25 .60
53 Terry Labonte's Car .25 .60
54 Sterling Marlin's Car .10 .30
55 Bill Elliott OR .40 1.00
56 Jeff Gordon OR .60 1.50
57 Sterling Marlin OR .25 .60
58 Mark Martin OR .50 1.25
59 Ricky Rudd OR .25 .60
60 Checklist .03 .15

1995 Press Pass Optima XL Cool Blue

COMPLETE BLUE SET (60) 30.00 60.00
*COOL BLUE: .8X TO 2X BASE CARDS

1995 Press Pass Optima XL Die Cut

COMPLETE SET (60) 200.00 400.00
*DIE CUTS: 5X TO 12X BASE CARDS

1995 Press Pass Optima XL Red Hot

COMPLETE RED SET (60) 30.00 60.00
*RED HOTS: .8X TO 2X BASE CARDS

1995 Press Pass Optima XL JG/XL

This four-card insert set featuring the 1995 Winston Cup champion, Jeff Gordon, created an interesting twist as far as odds of finding the individual cards. The higher the card number the tougher the card was to pull out of a pack. Card number 1 came 1 per 36 packs, card number 2 came 1 per 72 packs, card number 3 came 1:216 packs and card number 4 came 1:864 packs.

COMPLETE SET (4) 50.00 120.00
1 Jeff Gordon (1:36) 2.50 6.00
2 Jeff Gordon (1:72) 4.00 10.00
3 Jeff Gordon (1:216) 12.50 30.00
4 Jeff Gordon (1:864) 40.00 100.00

1995 Press Pass Optima XL Stealth

This 18-card insert set features the top drivers in Winston Cup racing. Each of the 2 1/2" X 4 11/16" insert cards was printed using the embossed foil technology. There have been reports that some of the cards have been found without embossed printing but have shown no premium over the regular issues. The Stealth cards could be found 1 per 18 packs.

COMPLETE SET (18) 75.00 150.00
XLS1 Ricky Craven 1.25 3.00
XLS2 Dale Earnhardt 12.00 30.00
XLS3 Bill Elliott 5.00 12.00
XLS4 Jeff Gordon 10.00 25.00
XLS5 Ernie Irvan 2.50 6.00
XLS6 Bobby Labonte 8.00 20.00
XLS7 Terry Labonte 4.00 10.00
XLS8 Sterling Marlin 4.00 10.00
XLS9 Mark Martin 10.00 25.00
XLS10 Ted Musgrave 1.25 3.00
XLS11 Kyle Petty 2.50 6.00
XLS12 Robert Pressley 1.25 3.00
XLS13 Ricky Rudd 4.00 10.00
XLS14 Ken Schrader 1.25 3.00
XLS15 Morgan Shepherd 1.25 3.00
XLS16 Rusty Wallace 10.00 25.00
XLS17 Darrell Waltrip 2.50 6.00
XLS18 Michael Waltrip 2.50 6.00

2000 Press Pass Optima

The 2000 Press Pass Optima product was released in November 2000, and offered a 50-card base set featuring some of the best drivers in the world. Each pack contained 5 cards and carried a suggested retail price of $2.99.

COMPLETE SET (50) 8.00 20.00
1 John Andretti .07 .20
2 Johnny Benson .15 .40
3 Jeff Burton .25 .60
4 Ward Burton .15 .40
5 Dale Earnhardt 1.25 3.00
6 Dale Earnhardt Jr. CRC 1.25 3.00
7 Jeff Gordon .75 2.00
8 Bobby Hamilton .07 .20
9 Dale Jarrett .50 1.25
10 Matt Kenseth CRC .60 1.50
11 Bobby Labonte .50 1.25
12 Terry Labonte .25 .60
13 Kevin Lepage .07 .20
14 Chad Little .15 .40
15 Sterling Marlin .25 .60
16 Mark Martin .60 1.50
17 Jeremy Mayfield .07 .20
18 Jerry Nadeau .15 .40
19 Joe Nemechek .07 .20
20 Steve Park .25 .60
21 Ricky Rudd .25 .60
22 Mike Skinner .07 .20
23 Elliott Sadler .15 .40
24 Tony Stewart .75 2.00
25 Rusty Wallace .50 1.50
26 Darrell Waltrip .15 .40
27 Michael Waltrip .15 .40
28 Casey Atwood BGN .25 .60
29 Todd Bodine BGN .07 .20
30 David Green BGN .07 .20
31 Mark Green BGN .07 .20
32 Kevin Harvick BGN .60 1.50
33 Jason Keller BGN .07 .20
34 Jeff Green BGN .07 .20
35 Hermie Sadler BGN .07 .20
36 Matt Kenseth BGN .30 .75
37 Hank Parker Jr. BGN RC .25 .60
38 Randy LaJoie BGN .07 .20
39 Elton Sawyer BGN .07 .20
40 Jeff Burton WCL .15 .40
41 Ward Burton WCL .07 .20
42 Ricky Rudd WCL .15 .40
43 Dale Earnhardt Jr. WCL .60 1.50
44 Mark Martin WCL .30 .75
45 Dale Jarrett WCL .25 .60
46 Matt Kenseth WCL .30 .75
47 Bobby Labonte WCL .25 .60
48 Tony Stewart WCL .60 1.50
49 Rusty Wallace WCL .30 .75
50 Steve Park WCL CL .15 .40
P1 Matt Kenseth Promo 1.25 3.00

2000 Press Pass Optima Platinum

COMP.PLATINUM SET (50) 12.00 30.00
*PLATINUM: .6X TO 1.5X BASE CARDS

2000 Press Pass Optima Cool Persistence

Randomly inserted into packs at one in 18, this 6-card insert set features drivers that have what it takes to get to the front. Card backs carry a "CP" prefix.

COMPLETE SET (6) 8.00 20.00
CP1 Dale Earnhardt Jr. 6.00 15.00
CP2 Jeff Gordon 4.00 10.00
CP3 Dale Jarrett 2.50 6.00
CP4 Bobby Labonte 2.50 6.00
CP5 Terry Labonte 1.25 3.00
CP6 Rusty Wallace 3.00 8.00

2000 Press Pass Optima Encore

Randomly inserted into packs at one in 8, this 9-card insert set features drivers on a gold-foil stamped card. Card backs carry an "EN" prefix.

COMPLETE SET (9) 6.00 15.00
EN1 Dale Jarrett 1.25 3.00
EN2 Bobby Labonte 1.25 3.00
EN3 Mark Martin 1.50 4.00
EN4 Dale Earnhardt Jr. 3.00 8.00
EN5 Jeff Gordon 2.00 5.00
EN6 Dale Earnhardt's Car 3.00 8.00
EN7 Tony Stewart 2.00 5.00
EN8 Jeremy Mayfield .20 .50
EN9 Rusty Wallace 1.50 4.00

2000 Press Pass Optima G Force

Inserted at one per pack, this 27-card "set within a set" features rainbow-foil and a unique glossy coat. Card backs carry a "GF" prefix.

COMPLETE SET (27) 8.00 20.00
GF1 Johnny Benson .30 .75
GF2 Jeff Burton .50 1.25
GF3 Ward Burton .30 .75
GF4 Wally Dallenbach .15 .40
GF5 Dale Earnhardt's Car 2.50 6.00
GF6 Dale Earnhardt Jr. 2.50 6.00
GF7 Jeff Gordon 1.50 4.00
GF8 Bobby Hamilton .15 .40
GF9 Dale Jarrett 1.00 2.50
GF10 Matt Kenseth 1.25 3.00
GF11 Bobby Labonte 1.00 2.50
GF12 Terry Labonte .50 1.25
GF13 Kevin Lepage .15 .40
GF14 Chad Little .30 .75
GF15 Sterling Marlin .50 1.25
GF16 Mark Martin 1.25 3.00
GF17 Jeremy Mayfield .15 .40
GF18 Joe Nemechek .15 .40
GF19 Steve Park .50 1.25
GF20 Ricky Rudd .50 1.25
GF21 Elliott Sadler .30 .75
GF22 Mike Skinner .15 .40
GF23 Tony Stewart 1.50 4.00
GF24 Kenny Wallace .15 .40
GF25 Rusty Wallace 1.25 3.00
GF26 Darrell Waltrip .30 .75
GF27 David Green CL .15 .40

2000 Press Pass Optima Race Used Lugnuts Drivers

Randomly inserted into hobby packs at one in 120, this 20-card set features actual pitstop-used lugnuts. Card backs carry a "LD" prefix. Please note that the hobby version pictures the driver while the retail cards feature the car. Cards LD1-LD14 have a stated print run of 100 sets while cards LD15-LD20 have a stated print run of 55 sets.

COMPLETE SET (20) 500.00 1000.00
*CAR CARDS: .3X TO .8X DRIVERS
LD1 Dave Blaney 8.00 20.00
LD2 Jeff Burton 10.00 25.00
LD3 Ward Burton 8.00 20.00
LD4 Dale Jarrett 15.00 40.00
LD5 Terry Labonte 15.00 40.00
LD5X Terry Labonte EXCH 2.00 5.00
LD6 Kevin Lepage 6.00 15.00
LD7 Chad Little 6.00 15.00
LD8 Sterling Marlin 10.00 25.00
LD9 Mark Martin 20.00 50.00
LD10 Jeremy Mayfield 8.00 20.00
LD10X Jeremy Mayfield EXCH 1.25 3.00
LD11 Jerry Nadeau 6.00 15.00
LD12 Ricky Rudd 8.00 20.00
LD12X Ricky Rudd EXCH 1.25 3.00
LD13 Elliott Sadler 8.00 20.00
LD13X Elliott Sadler EXCH 1.00 2.50
LD14 Rusty Wallace 15.00 40.00
LD15 Dale Earnhardt/55 75.00 200.00
LD16 Dale Earnhardt Jr./55 60.00 150.00
LD17 Jeff Gordon/55 40.00 100.00
LD18 Matt Kenseth/55 20.00 50.00
LD19 Bobby Labonte/55 25.00 60.00
LD20 Tony Stewart/55 30.00 80.00

2000 Press Pass Optima On the Edge

Randomly inserted into packs at one in 24, this 6-card insert set features drivers that take it to the edge. Card backs carry an "OE" prefix.

COMPLETE SET (6) 15.00 40.00
OE1 Dale Earnhardt's Car 6.00 15.00
OE2 Dale Earnhardt Jr. 6.00 15.00
OE3 Jeff Gordon 4.00 10.00
OE4 Bobby Labonte 2.50 6.00
OE5 Matt Kenseth 3.00 8.00
OE6 Tony Stewart 4.00 10.00

2000 Press Pass Optima Overdrive

Randomly inserted into packs at one in 8, this 12-card insert set features some of the fastest drivers on a die cut gold foil based card. Card backs carry an "OD" prefix.

COMPLETE SET (12) 6.00 15.00
*SQUARE CUT: 1.5X TO 4X BASIC INSERTS
SQUARE CUT STATED ODDS 1:48
SQUARE CUT PRINT RUN 350 SER.#'D SETS
OD1 Jeff Burton .60 1.50
OD2 Casey Atwood .60 1.50
OD3 Mike Skinner .20 .50
OD4 Jeff Gordon 2.00 5.00
OD5 Dale Jarrett 1.25 3.00
OD6 Bobby Labonte 1.25 3.00
OD7 Mark Martin 1.50 4.00
OD8 Tony Stewart 2.00 5.00
OD9 Rusty Wallace 1.50 4.00
OD10 Matt Kenseth 1.50 4.00
OD11 Ward Burton .40 1.00
OD12 Ricky Rudd .60 1.50

2001 Press Pass Optima

This 50 card set, featuring the leading drivers in NASCAR was issued during 2001 and released in 5-card packs. The set includes the following subsets: Busch Grand National drivers (#28-39), and Winston Cup Leaders (#40-50). A Kevin Harvick Double Duty insert (numbered "0" and serial numbered of 550) was also inserted in packs at the rate of 1:480.

COMPLETE SET (50) 8.00 20.00
WAX BOX HOBBY 40.00 80.00
1 Dave Blaney .08 .25
2 Jeff Burton .20 .50
3 Ward Burton .20 .50
4 Kurt Busch CRC .30 .75
5 Dale Earnhardt Jr. 1.00 2.50
6 Jeff Gordon .75 2.00
7 Bobby Hamilton .08 .25
8 Kevin Harvick CRC .60 1.50
9 Dale Jarrett .50 1.25
10 Matt Kenseth .60 1.50
11 Bobby Labonte .50 1.25
12 Terry Labonte .30 .75
13 Sterling Marlin .30 .75
14 Mark Martin .60 1.50
15 Jerry Nadeau .20 .50
16 Joe Nemechek .08 .25
17 Steve Park .20 .50
18 Kyle Petty .20 .50
19 Robert Pressley .08 .25
20 Ricky Rudd .30 .75
21 Elliott Sadler .20 .50
22 Ken Schrader .08 .25
23 Mike Skinner .08 .25
24 Jimmy Spencer .08 .25
25 Tony Stewart .75 2.00
26 Rusty Wallace .60 1.50
27 Michael Waltrip .20 .50
28 Jeff Green BGN .08 .25
29 David Green BGN .08 .25
30 Kevin Grubb BGN .08 .25
31 Kevin Harvick BGN .60 1.50
32 Jimmie Johnson BGN .60 1.50
33 Jason Keller BGN .08 .25
34 Randy LaJoie BGN .08 .25
35 Chad Little BGN .08 .25
36 Mike McLaughlin BGN .08 .25
37 Ryan Newman BGN RC 2.50 6.00
38 Hank Parker Jr. BGN .20 .50
39 Elton Sawyer BGN .08 .25
40 Jeff Burton WCL .20 .50
41 Dale Earnhardt Jr. WCL 1.00 2.50
42 Jeff Gordon WCL .75 2.00
43 Kevin Harvick WCL .60 1.50
44 Dale Jarrett WCL .50 1.25
45 Mark Martin WCL .60 1.50
46 Steve Park WCL .20 .50
47 Ricky Rudd WCL .30 .75
48 Tony Stewart WCL .75 2.00
49 Rusty Wallace WCL .60 1.50
50 Bobby Labonte WCL CL .50 1.25
0 Kevin Harvick DD/550 12.00 30.00

2001 Press Pass Optima Gold

COMP.GOLD SET (50) 12.00 30.00
*GOLDS: .6X TO 1.5X BASE CARDS

2001 Press Pass Optima Cool Persistence

Issued at stated odds of one in six, these 12 cards feature drivers who stay cool under extreme race pressure.

COMPLETE SET (12) 8.00 20.00
CP1 Jeff Burton .50 1.25
CP2 Ward Burton .50 1.25
CP3 Dale Earnhardt Jr. 2.50 6.00
CP4 Jeff Gordon 2.00 5.00
CP5 Kevin Harvick 1.50 4.00
CP6 Dale Jarrett 1.25 3.00
CP7 Bobby Labonte 1.25 3.00
CP8 Terry Labonte .75 2.00
CP9 Steve Park .50 1.25
CP10 Ricky Rudd .75 2.00
CP11 Mike Skinner .25 .60
CP12 Rusty Wallace 1.50 4.00

2001 Press Pass Optima G Force

Inserted one per pack, cards from this set feature the top drivers from the base set. This is a continuation of Press Pass's concept of the "set within a set."

COMPLETE SET (27) 10.00 25.00
GF1 Jeff Burton .40 1.00
GF2 Ward Burton .40 1.00
GF3 Kurt Busch .60 1.50
GF4 Dale Earnhardt Jr. 2.00 5.00
GF5 Jeff Gordon 1.50 4.00
GF6 Bobby Hamilton .20 .50
GF7 Kevin Harvick 1.25 3.00
GF8 Dale Jarrett 1.00 2.50
GF9 Matt Kenseth 1.25 3.00
GF10 Bobby Labonte 1.00 2.50
GF11 Terry Labonte .60 1.50
GF12 Sterling Marlin .60 1.50
GF13 Mark Martin 1.25 3.00
GF14 Jeremy Mayfield .20 .50

GF15 Jerry Nadeau .40 1.00
GF16 Joe Nemechek .20 .50
GF17 Steve Park .40 1.00
GF18 Kyle Petty .40 1.00
GF19 Robert Pressley .20 .50
GF20 Ricky Rudd .60 1.50
GF21 Elliott Sadler .40 1.00
GF22 Ken Schrader .20 .50
GF23 Mike Skinner .20 .50
GF24 Jimmy Spencer .20 .50
GF25 Tony Stewart 1.50 4.00
GF26 Rusty Wallace 1.25 3.00
GF27 Michael Waltrip .40 1.00

2001 Press Pass Optima Race Used Lugnuts Drivers

Inserted in hobby packs at stated odds of one in 150, these 16 cards feature leading drivers in NASCAR. Each card also included a piece of race used lugnut that was viewable from both the front and back sides of the card. The hobby version (numbered of 100 unless noted) features a picture of the driver while the retail version (numbered of 115 unless noted) features their car.

*CARS: .4X TO 1X DRIVERS
LND0 Dale Earnhardt/45 125.00 250.00
LND1 Jeff Burton 6.00 15.00
LND2 Ward Burton 6.00 15.00
LND3 Dale Earnhardt Jr. 25.00 60.00
LND4 Jeff Gordon 25.00 60.00
LND5 Kevin Harvick 10.00 25.00
LND6 Dale Jarrett 8.00 20.00
LND7 Matt Kenseth 8.00 20.00
LND8 Terry Labonte 8.00 20.00
LND9 Bobby Labonte 10.00 25.00
LND10 Sterling Marlin 8.00 20.00
LND11 Mark Martin 12.00 30.00
LND12 Steve Park 6.00 15.00
LND13 Ricky Rudd 8.00 20.00
LND14 Tony Stewart 15.00 40.00
LND15 Rusty Wallace 10.00 25.00

2001 Press Pass Optima On the Edge

Inserted at stated odds of one in nine, these nine cards feature drivers who have a chance of winning the Winston Cup.

COMPLETE SET (9) 10.00 25.00
OE1 Dale Earnhardt Jr. 3.00 8.00
OE2 Jeff Gordon 2.50 6.00
OE3 Kevin Harvick 2.00 5.00
OE4 Dale Jarrett 1.50 4.00
OE5 Mark Martin 2.00 5.00
OE6 Steve Park .60 1.50
OE7 Ricky Rudd 1.00 2.50
OE8 Tony Stewart 2.50 6.00
OE9 Rusty Wallace 2.00 5.00

2001 Press Pass Optima Up Close

Inserted at stated odds of one in 12, these six cards feature drivers who deserve to have a closer look taken at their careers.

COMPLETE SET (6) 8.00 20.00
UC1 Dale Earnhardt Jr. 2.50 6.00
UC2 Jeff Gordon 2.00 5.00
UC3 Kevin Harvick 1.50 4.00
UC4 Dale Jarrett 1.25 3.00
UC5 Mark Martin 1.50 4.00
UC6 Rusty Wallace 1.50 4.00

2002 Press Pass Optima

This fifty card set was released in October, 2002. It was issued in five card hobby or retail packs which were packed 24 packs per box and 20 boxes per case with an SRP of $2.99 per pack. The card featuring both Jeff Gordon and Jimmie Johnson was issued in hobby packs at a stated rate of one in 480.

COMPLETE SET (50) 10.00 25.00
WAX BOX HOBBY 30.00 60.00
WAX BOX RETAIL (24) 30.00 60.00
1 Casey Atwood .10 .30
2 Dave Blaney .10 .30
3 Jeff Burton .25 .60
4 Ward Burton .25 .60
5 Kurt Busch .40 1.00
6 Ricky Craven .10 .30
7 Dale Earnhardt Jr. 1.25 3.00
8 Jeff Gordon 1.00 2.50
9 Robby Gordon .10 .30
10 Jeff Green .10 .30
11 Bobby Hamilton .10 .30
12 Kevin Harvick .75 2.00
13 Dale Jarrett .60 1.50
14 Jimmie Johnson CRC .75 2.00
15 Matt Kenseth .75 2.00
16 Bobby Labonte .60 1.50
17 Terry Labonte .40 1.00
18 Sterling Marlin .40 1.00
19 Mark Martin .75 2.00
20 Jeremy Mayfield .10 .30
21 Ryan Newman CRC .75 2.00
22 Steve Park .10 .30
23 Kyle Petty .25 .60
24 Ricky Rudd .40 1.00
25 Elliott Sadler .25 .60
26 Ken Schrader .10 .30
27 Jimmy Spencer .10 .30
28 Tony Stewart .75 2.00
29 Rusty Wallace .60 1.50
30 Michael Waltrip .25 .60
31 Greg Biffle .25 .60
32 Tony Raines .10 .30
33 Ricky Hendrick .50 1.25
34 Jason Keller .10 .30
35 Randy LaJoie .10 .30
36 Mike McLaughlin .10 .30
37 Jamie McMurray RC 1.25 3.00
38 Casey Mears RC 1.00 2.50
39 Hank Parker Jr. .10 .30
40 Scott Riggs RC .75 2.00
41 Johnny Sauter RC .25 .60
42 Jack Sprague .10 .30
43 Brian Vickers RC 1.00 2.50
44 Scott Wimmer RC .25 .60
45 Dale Earnhardt Jr. YG 1.25 3.00
46 Ryan Newman YG .75 2.00
47 Jimmie Johnson YG .75 2.00
48 Kevin Harvick YG .75 2.00
49 Kurt Busch YG .40 1.00
50 Matt Kenseth YG .75 2.00
0 J.Gordon J.Johnson 15.00 40.00

2002 Press Pass Optima Gold

*GOLDS: .6X TO 1.5X BASE CARDS

2002 Press Pass Optima Samples

*SAMPLES: 2X TO 5X BASE CARDS

2002 Press Pass Optima Cool Persistence

Inserted at a stated rate of one in six, these 12 cards features how persistence pays off for these drivers which stay cool under pressure.

COMPLETE SET (12) 10.00 25.00
CP1 Jeff Burton .60 1.50
CP2 Dale Earnhardt Jr. 3.00 8.00
CP3 Jeff Gordon 2.50 6.00
CP4 Kevin Harvick 2.00 5.00
CP5 Dale Jarrett 1.50 4.00
CP6 Jimmie Johnson 2.00 5.00
CP7 Matt Kenseth 2.00 5.00
CP8 Terry Labonte 1.00 2.50
CP9 Sterling Marlin 1.00 2.50
CP10 Mark Martin 2.00 5.00
CP11 Tony Stewart 2.00 5.00
CP12 Rusty Wallace 1.50 4.00

2002 Press Pass Optima Fan Favorite

Issued at a stated rate of one per pack, these 27 die-cut card set gives all the information needed to join these driver's fan clubs.

COMPLETE SET (27) 8.00 20.00
FF1 Casey Atwood .20 .50
FF2 Jeff Burton .40 1.00
FF3 Ward Burton .40 1.00
FF4 Kurt Busch .60 1.50
FF5 Ricky Craven .20 .50
FF6 Dale Earnhardt Jr. 2.00 5.00
FF7 Jeff Gordon 1.50 4.00
FF8 Robby Gordon .20 .50
FF9 Kevin Harvick 1.25 3.00
FF10 Dale Jarrett 1.00 2.50
FF11 Jimmie Johnson 1.25 3.00
FF12 Matt Kenseth 1.25 3.00
FF13 Bobby Labonte 1.00 2.50
FF14 Terry Labonte .60 1.50
FF15 Sterling Marlin .60 1.50
FF16 Mark Martin 1.25 3.00
FF17 Jeremy Mayfield .20 .50
FF18 Ryan Newman 1.25 3.00
FF19 Steve Park .20 .50
FF20 Kyle Petty .40 1.00
FF21 Ricky Rudd .60 1.50
FF22 Jeff Green .20 .50
FF23 Ken Schrader .20 .50
FF24 Jimmy Spencer .20 .50
FF25 Tony Stewart 1.25 3.00
FF26 Rusty Wallace 1.00 2.50
FF27 Dave Blaney .20 .50

2002 Press Pass Optima Q and A

Issued at a stated rate of one in nine, these nine cards feature racers answering frequently asked fan questions on these holo-foil etched cards.

COMPLETE SET (9) 10.00 25.00
QA1 Kurt Busch 1.00 2.50
QA2 Dale Earnhardt Jr. 3.00 8.00
QA3 Jimmie Johnson 2.00 5.00
QA4 Matt Kenseth 2.00 5.00
QA5 Bobby Labonte 1.50 4.00
QA6 Mark Martin 2.00 5.00
QA7 Ricky Rudd 1.00 2.50
QA8 Sterling Marlin 1.00 2.50
QA9 Tony Stewart 2.00 5.00

2002 Press Pass Optima Race Used Lugnuts Autographs

Randomly inserted into packs, these cards feature not only pieces of race-used lugnuts but also the drivers signature on the card. Each of these cards were signed to the driver's car number.

LNDA6 Jeff Gordon/24 200.00 350.00
LNDA7 Kevin Harvick/29 75.00 150.00
LNDA9 Jimmie Johnson/48 60.00 120.00
LNDA10 Matt Kenseth/17
LNDA11 Bobby Labonte/18 50.00 100.00
LNDA13 Mark Martin/6
LNDA14 Ryan Newman/12
LNDA17 Tony Stewart/20
LNDA18 Rusty Wallace/2

2002 Press Pass Optima Race Used Lugnuts Drivers

Issued in hobby packs at a stated rate of one in 160, these 18 cards feature pieces of race-used lugnuts placed on a car featuring a driver. With the exception of Dale Earnhardt Sr, these cards were issued to a stated press run of 100 sets.

*CARS/100: .4X TO 1X DRIVERS/100
LND1 Jeff Burton 10.00 25.00
LND2 Ward Burton 10.00 25.00
LND3 Kurt Busch 12.00 30.00
LND4 Dale Earnhardt/10
LND5 Dale Earnhardt Jr. 30.00 80.00
LND6 Jeff Gordon 30.00 80.00
LND7 Kevin Harvick 15.00 40.00
LND8 Dale Jarrett 12.00 30.00
LND9 Jimmie Johnson 20.00 50.00
LND10 Matt Kenseth 10.00 25.00
LND11 Bobby Labonte 15.00 40.00
LND12 Terry Labonte 12.00 30.00
LND13 Mark Martin 15.00 40.00
LND14 Ryan Newman 10.00 25.00
LND15 Ricky Rudd 10.00 25.00
LND16 Elliott Sadler 8.00 20.00
LND17 Tony Stewart 25.00 60.00
LND18 Rusty Wallace 15.00 40.00

2002 Press Pass Optima Up Close

Issued at a stated rate on one in 12, these six cards feature information about the "home away from homes" for these six NASCAR drivers.

COMPLETE SET (6) 8.00 20.00
UC1 Dale Jarrett 1.50 4.00
UC2 Jeff Gordon 2.50 6.00
UC3 Ryan Newman 2.00 5.00
UC4 Jimmie Johnson 2.00 5.00
UC5 Rusty Wallace 1.50 4.00
UC6 Dale Earnhardt Jr. 3.00 8.00

2003 Press Pass Optima

This fifty card set was released in October, 2003. It was issued in five card hobby or retail packs which were packed 28 packs per box with an SRP of $2.99 per pack. The base cards featured a color photo of the driver along with a smaller black and white photo of the driver.

COMPLETE SET (50) 10.00 25.00
WAX BOX HOBBY (28) 40.00 75.00
1 Greg Biffle CRC .20 .50
2 Dave Blaney .10 .25
3 Jeff Burton .20 .50
4 Ward Burton .20 .50
5 Kurt Busch .30 .75
6 Dale Earnhardt Jr. 1.00 2.50
7 Jeff Gordon .75 2.00
8 Robby Gordon .10 .25
9 Kevin Harvick .50 1.25
10 Dale Jarrett .50 1.25
11 Jimmie Johnson .60 1.50
12 Matt Kenseth .60 1.50
13 Bobby Labonte .50 1.25
14 Terry Labonte .30 .75
15 Sterling Marlin .30 .75
16 Mark Martin .60 1.50
17 Jamie McMurray CRC .50 1.25
18 Joe Nemechek .10 .25
19 Ryan Newman .60 1.50
20 Kyle Petty .20 .50
21 Ricky Rudd .30 .75
22 Elliott Sadler .20 .50
23 Jimmy Spencer .10 .25
24 Tony Stewart .60 1.50
25 Kenny Wallace .10 .25
26 Rusty Wallace .50 1.25
27 Michael Waltrip .20 .50
28 Jason Keller .10 .25
29 Stacy Compton .10 .25
30 David Green .10 .25
31 Kasey Kahne RC 5.00 12.00
32 Johnny Sauter .20 .50
33 Mike McLaughlin .10 .25
34 Chase Montgomery RC .30 .75
35 Jimmy Vasser RC .10 .25
36 Brian Vickers .40 1.00
37 Damon Lusk RC .30 .75
38 Mike Bliss .10 .25
39 Scott Wimmer .20 .50
40 Dale Earnhardt Jr. UC 1.00 2.50
41 Bobby Labonte UC .50 1.25
42 Elliott Sadler UC .20 .50
43 Kevin Harvick UC .50 1.25
44 Tony Stewart UC .60 1.50
45 Kurt Busch UC .30 .75
46 Dale Earnhardt Jr. TV .75 2.00
47 Dale Earnhardt Jr. Music .75 2.00
48 Dale Earnhardt Jr. Magazines .75 2.00
49 Dale Earnhardt Jr. Talk Shows .75 2.00
50 Ryan Newman CL .30 .75
NNO Signings Contest Card 2.00 5.00

2003 Press Pass Optima Gold

COMPLETE SET (50) 15.00 40.00
*GOLDS: .6X TO 1.5X BASE

2003 Press Pass Optima Samples

*SAMPLES: 2.5X TO 6X BASE

2003 Press Pass Optima Cool Persistence

COMPLETE SET (12) 10.00 25.00
CP1 Dale Earnhardt Jr. 2.50 6.00
CP2 Jimmie Johnson 1.50 4.00
CP3 Mark Martin 1.50 4.00
CP4 Ricky Rudd .75 2.00
CP5 Terry Labonte .75 2.00
CP6 Dale Jarrett 1.25 3.00
CP7 Bobby Labonte 1.25 3.00
CP8 Jeff Gordon 2.00 5.00
CP9 Tony Stewart 1.50 4.00
CP10 Rusty Wallace 1.25 3.00
CP11 Matt Kenseth 1.50 4.00
CP12 Kevin Harvick 1.25 3.00

2003 Press Pass Optima Fan Favorite

COMPLETE SET (27) 8.00 20.00
FF1 Jimmie Johnson 1.00 2.50
FF2 Jeff Burton .30 .75
FF3 Matt Kenseth 1.00 2.50
FF4 Joe Nemechek .15 .40
FF5 Jamie McMurray .75 2.00
FF6 Dale Earnhardt Jr. 1.50 4.00
FF7 Jeff Gordon 1.25 3.00
FF8 Robby Gordon .15 .40
FF9 Kevin Harvick .75 2.00
FF10 Dale Jarrett .75 2.00
FF11 Ward Burton .30 .75
FF12 Kyle Petty .30 .75
FF13 Kurt Busch .50 1.25
FF14 Terry Labonte .50 1.25
FF15 Ricky Craven .15 .40
FF16 Mark Martin 1.00 2.50
FF17 Greg Biffle .30 .75
FF18 Ryan Newman 1.00 2.50
FF19 Bobby Labonte .75 2.00
FF20 Ricky Rudd .50 1.25
FF21 Elliott Sadler .30 .75
FF22 Rusty Wallace .75 2.00
FF23 Tony Stewart 1.00 2.50
FF24 Michael Waltrip .30 .75
FF25 Sterling Marlin .50 1.25
FF26 Brian Vickers .60 1.50
FF27 David Green .15 .40

2003 Press Pass Optima Q and A

Issued at a stated rate of one in eight, these nine cards feature racers answering frequently asked fan questions on these holo-foil etched cards.

COMPLETE SET (9) 10.00 25.00
QA1 Tony Stewart 1.50 4.00
QA2 Ward Burton .50 1.25
QA3 Jeff Gordon 2.00 5.00
QA4 Dale Jarrett 1.25 3.00
QA5 Greg Biffle .50 1.25
QA6 Ryan Newman 1.50 4.00
QA7 Joe Nemechek .25 .60
QA8 Kurt Busch .75 2.00
QA9 Bobby Labonte 1.25 3.00

2003 Press Pass Optima Thunder Bolts Cars

Randomly inserted into retail packs, these 18 cards feature slices of race-used lugnuts on a photo of the driver's car. Each of these cards were issued to a stated print run of 95 sets with the exception of the Dale Earnhardt which had 3 and Kevin Harvick which had 20 copies produced. These were avalible only in retail packs.

STATED PRINT RUN 3-95
TBT1 Jeff Gordon's Car 25.00 60.00
TBT2 Ryan Newman's Car 20.00 50.00
TBT3 Kevin Harvick's Car/20
TBT4 Jimmie Johnson's Car 15.00 40.00
TBT5 Rusty Wallace's Car 12.50 30.00
TBT6 Mark Martin's Car 15.00 40.00
TBT7 Matt Kenseth's Car 15.00 40.00
TBT8 Bobby Labonte's Car 10.00 25.00
TBT9 Terry Labonte's Car 12.50 30.00
TBT10 Dale Earnhardt Jr.'s Car 30.00 80.00
TBT11 Dale Earnhardt's Car/3
TBT12 Jeff Burton's Car 10.00 25.00
TBT13 Ward Burton's Car 10.00 25.00
TBT14 Kurt Busch's Car 10.00 25.00
TBT15 Dale Jarrett's Car 15.00 40.00
TBT16 Tony Stewart's Car 20.00 50.00
TBT17 Sterling Marlin's Car 10.00 25.00
TBT18 Michael Waltrip's Car 10.00 25.00

2003 Press Pass Optima Thunder Bolts Drivers

Randomly inserted into retail packs, these 18 cards feature slices of race-used lugnuts on a photo of the driver's car. Each of these cards were issued to a stated print runs of 65, 60, 15 or 3 and noted below in the checklist. These were avalible only in hobby packs.

TBD1 Jeff Gordon/60 50.00 100.00
TBD2 Ryan Newman/60 40.00 80.00
TBD3 Kevin Harvick/15
TBD4 Jimmie Johnson/50 30.00 60.00
TBD5 Rusty Wallace/60 20.00 50.00
TBD6 Mark Martin/60 30.00 60.00
TBD7 Matt Kenseth/60 30.00 60.00
TBD8 Bobby Labonte/60 15.00 40.00
TBD9 Terry Labonte/60 20.00 50.00
TBD10 Dale Earnhardt Jr./65 60.00 120.00
TBD11 Dale Earnhardt/3
TBD12 Jeff Burton/65 15.00 40.00
TBD13 Ward Burton/65 15.00 40.00
TBD14 Kurt Busch/65 15.00 40.00
TBD15 Dale Jarrett/65 25.00 60.00
TBD16 Tony Stewart/65 40.00 80.00
TBD17 Sterling Marlin/65 15.00 40.00
TBD18 Michael Waltrip/65 15.00 40.00

2003 Press Pass Optima Thunder Bolts Drivers Autographs

Randomly inserted into retail packs, these 9 cards feature slices of race-used lugnuts on a photo of the driver's car along with a signature from the corresponding driver. These cards were limited and hand numbered to the driver's door number. Some of these cards are not priced due to scarcity. These were avalible only in hobby packs.

*CARS: .4X TO 1X DRIVERS
TBDBL Bobby Labonte/18 75.00 150.00
TBDJG Jeff Gordon/24 100.00 200.00
TBDJJ Jimmie Johnson/48 60.00 120.00
TBDKH Kevin Harvick/29 60.00 120.00
TBDMK Matt Kenseth/17
TBDMM Mark Martin/6
TBDRN Ryan Newman/12
TBDRW Rusty Wallace/2
TBDTL Terry Labonte/5

2003 Press Pass Optima Young Guns

Randomly inserted in packs at a rate of 1:12, this 6-card set featured some of NASCAR's young superstars. Each card number carried a prefix of "YG".

COMPLETE SET (6) 8.00 20.00
YG1 Dale Earnhardt Jr. 3.00 8.00
YG2 Elliott Sadler .60 1.50
YG3 Jamie McMurray 1.50 4.00
YG4 Kevin Harvick 1.50 4.00
YG5 Jimmie Johnson 2.00 5.00
YG6 Kurt Busch 1.00 2.50

2004 Press Pass Optima

This 100-card set was released in October, 2004. It was issued in five card hobby or retail packs which were packed 28 packs per hobby box and 24 per retail box with an SRP of $2.99 per pack. The base cards featured a color photo of the driver along with a smaller photo of the driver's face.

COMPLETE SET (100) 15.00 40.00
WAX BOX HOBBY (28) 50.00 80.00
WAX BOX RETAIL (24) 35.00 70.00
1 Greg Biffle .25 .60
2 Ward Burton .25 .60
3 Kurt Busch .40 1.00
4 Dale Earnhardt Jr. 1.00 2.50
5 Brendan Gaughan CRC .25 .60
6 Jeff Gordon 1.00 2.50
7 Robby Gordon .10 .30
8 Kevin Harvick .60 1.50
9 Dale Jarrett .50 1.25
10 Jimmie Johnson .75 2.00
11 Kasey Kahne CRC 1.25 3.00
12 Matt Kenseth .75 2.00
13 Bobby Labonte .50 1.25
14 Terry Labonte .40 1.00
15 Mark Martin .60 1.50
16 Jeremy Mayfield .10 .30
17 Jamie McMurray .40 1.00
18 Casey Mears .25 .60
19 Ryan Newman .75 2.00
20 Kyle Petty .25 .60
21 Scott Riggs CRC .25 .60
22 Elliott Sadler .25 .60
23 Boris Said .10 .30
24 Tony Stewart .60 1.50
25 Brian Vickers CRC .50 1.25
26 Rusty Wallace .50 1.25
27 Michael Waltrip .25 .60
28 Casey Atwood .10 .30
29 Mike Bliss .10 .30
30 Clint Bowyer RC 2.50 6.00
31 Stacy Compton .10 .30
32 Ron Hornaday .10 .30
33 J.J. Yeley RC 1.50 4.00
34 Johnny Sauter .25 .60
35 Kenny Wallace .10 .30
36 Joe Nemechek .10 .30
37 Martin Truex Jr. RC 2.50 6.00
38 Justin Labonte .40 1.00
39 Matt Kenseth .75 2.00
40 Terry Cook RC .50 1.25
41 Matt Crafton .10 .30
42 Carl Edwards .75 2.00
43 Tina Gordon RC .75 2.00
44 Bill Lester RC .50 1.25
45 Steve Park .25 .60
46 Dennis Setzer .10 .30
47 Jack Sprague .10 .30
48 Jon Wood .25 .60
49 Kasey Kahne YG 1.00 2.50
50 Scott Wimmer YG CRC .25 .60
51 Brian Vickers YG .50 1.25
52 Scott Riggs YG .25 .60
53 Brendan Gaughan YG .25 .60
54 Kyle Busch YG RC 2.50 6.00
55 Dale Earnhardt Jr.'s Car RV .40 1.00
56 Matt Kenseth's Car RV .40 1.00
57 Ryan Newman's Car RV .40 1.00
58 Jimmie Johnson's Car RV .40 1.00
59 Elliott Sadler's Car RV .10 .30
60 Rusty Wallace's Car RV .10 .30
61 Mark Martin's Car RV .25 .60
62 Jeff Gordon's Car RV .40 1.00
63 Kurt Busch's Car RV .10 .30
64 Kyle Petty CS .25 .60
65 Elliott Sadler CS .25 .60
66 Ward Burton CS .25 .60
67 Jeff Green CS .10 .30
68 Jeff Gordon CS 1.00 2.50
69 Dale Jarrett CS .50 1.25
70 Ricky Craven CS .10 .30
71 Terry Labonte CS .40 1.00
72 Kyle Petty CS .25 .60
73 Dale Earnhardt Jr. CP 1.00 2.50
74 Casey Mears CP .25 .60
75 Brian Vickers CP .50 1.25
76 Jeff Gordon CP 1.00 2.50
77 Jimmie Johnson CP .75 2.00
78 Kasey Kahne CP 1.00 2.50
79 Tony Stewart CP .60 1.50
80 Matt Kenseth CP w Pres.Bush 1.50 4.00
81 Rusty Wallace CP .50 1.25
82 Brendan Gaughan RR .25 .60
83 Dale Earnhardt Jr. RR 1.00 2.50
84 Brian Vickers RR .50 1.25
85 Kevin Harvick RR .60 1.50
86 Tony Stewart RR .60 1.50
87 Kasey Kahne RR 1.00 2.50
88 Dale Earnhardt Jr. SS 1.00 2.50
89 Kevin Harvick SS .60 1.50
90 Jimmie Johnson SS .75 2.00
91 Casey Mears SS .25 .60
92 Michael Waltrip SS .25 .60
93 Elliott Sadler SS .25 .60
94 Jeff Gordon SS 1.00 2.50
95 Matt Kenseth NP .75 2.00
96 Kurt Busch NP .40 1.00
97 Casey Mears NP .25 .60
98 Greg Biffle NP .25 .60
99 Jon Wood NP .25 .60
100 Jeff Gordon CL 1.00 2.50
NNO Signings Entry Dale Jr. 2.50 6.00

2004 Press Pass Optima Gold

*GOLD/100: 2.5X TO 6X BASIC CARDS

2004 Press Pass Optima Samples

*SAMPLES: 1.5X TO 4X BASE
STATED ODDS 1 PER BRC 124

2004 Press Pass Optima Cool Persistence

This 12-card set featured NASCAR's hottest stars. Cards were produced with a holographic image of the driver. They were randomly inserted at a rate of 1 in 6 packs.

COMPLETE SET (12) 12.50 30.00
STATED ODDS 1:6
CP1 Jeff Gordon 2.50 6.00
CP2 Terry Labonte 1.00 2.50
CP3 Dale Earnhardt Jr. 2.50 6.00
CP4 Mark Martin 1.50 4.00
CP5 Ricky Rudd 1.00 2.50
CP6 Jimmie Johnson 2.00 5.00
CP7 Ryan Newman 2.00 5.00
CP8 Tony Stewart 1.50 4.00
CP9 Matt Kenseth 2.00 5.00
CP10 Bobby Labonte 1.25 3.00
CP11 Dale Jarrett 1.25 3.00
CP12 Kasey Kahne 2.50 6.00

2004 Press Pass Optima Fan Favorite

This 27-card set featured NASCAR's hottest stars interacting with fans. Cards had a die-cut design and pictured fan interaction with the drivers. They were randomly inserted at a rate of 1 in 2 packs.

COMPLETE SET (27) 10.00 25.00
FF1 Greg Biffle .25 .60
FF2 Ward Burton .25 .60
FF3 Kurt Busch .40 1.00
FF4 Dale Earnhardt Jr. 1.00 2.50
FF5 Brendan Gaughan .25 .60
FF6 Jeff Gordon 1.00 2.50
FF7 Robby Gordon .15 .40
FF8 Kevin Harvick .60 1.50
FF9 Dale Jarrett .50 1.25
FF10 Jimmie Johnson .75 2.00
FF11 Kasey Kahne 1.00 2.50
FF12 Matt Kenseth .75 2.00
FF13 Bobby Labonte .50 1.25
FF14 Terry Labonte .40 1.00
FF15 Mark Martin .60 1.50
FF16 Casey Mears .25 .60
FF17 Joe Nemechek .15 .40
FF18 Ryan Newman .75 2.00
FF19 Kyle Petty .25 .60
FF20 Ricky Rudd .40 1.00
FF21 Elliott Sadler .25 .60
FF22 Tony Stewart .60 1.50
FF23 Brian Vickers .50 1.25
FF24 Rusty Wallace .50 1.25
FF25 Michael Waltrip .25 .60
FF26 Davey Allison .25 .60
FF27 Alan Kulwicki CL .25 .60

2004 Press Pass Optima G Force

This 6-card set featured NASCAR's hottest stars and their cars. The cards had silver foil highlights. They were randomly inserted at a rate of 1 in 12 packs.

COMPLETE SET (6) 12.50 30.00
GF1 Dale Earnhardt Jr. 3.00 8.00
GF2 Jeff Gordon 3.00 8.00
GF3 Tony Stewart 2.00 5.00
GF4 Michael Waltrip .75 2.00
GF5 Jimmie Johnson 2.50 6.00
GF6 Rusty Wallace 1.50 4.00

2004 Press Pass Optima Q&A

This 9-card set featured NASCAR's hottest stars. Cards had silver foild and etched highlights. They were randomly inserted at a rate of 1 in 8 packs.

COMPLETE SET (9) 12.50 30.00
QA1 Jeff Gordon 2.50 6.00
QA2 Mark Martin 1.50 4.00
QA3 Matt Kenseth 2.00 5.00
QA4 Tony Stewart 1.50 4.00
QA5 Elliott Sadler .60 1.50
QA6 Jimmie Johnson 2.00 5.00
QA7 Kurt Busch 1.00 2.50
QA8 Michael Waltrip .60 1.50
QA9 Dale Earnhardt Jr. 2.50 6.00

2004 Press Pass Optima Thunder Bolts Autographs

Randomly inserted into hobby and retail packs, these 7 cards feature slices of race-used lugnuts on a photo of the driver along with a signature from the corresponding driver. These cards were limited and hand numbered to the driver's door number. Some of these cards are not priced due to scarcity. The Dale Earnhardt Jr. was only available in packs of 2005 Press Pass Legends which was released in July of 2005.

STATED PRINT RUN 2-77
TBBG Brendan Gaughan/77 50.00 100.00
TBBL Bobby Labonte/18 75.00 150.00
TBDE Dale Earnhardt Jr./8
TBJG Jeff Gordon/24 150.00 300.00
TBKK Kasey Kahne/9
TBMK Matt Kenseth/17
TBRN Ryan Newman/12
TBRW Rusty Wallace/2

2004 Press Pass Optima Thunder Bolts Drivers

Randomly inserted into hobby packs at a rate of 1 in 68 packs, these 18 cards feature slices of race-used lugnuts on a photo of the driver's car. Each of these cards were serial numbered to 70 with the exception of Dale Earnhardt which only had 3 copies produced.

TBD1 Dale Earnhardt Jr. 30.00 80.00
TBD2 Kasey Kahne 25.00 60.00
TBD3 Tony Stewart 20.00 50.00
TBD4 Michael Waltrip 10.00 25.00
TBD5 Ryan Newman 25.00 60.00
TBD6 Kevin Harvick 15.00 40.00
TBD7 Rusty Wallace 20.00 50.00
TBD8 Matt Kenseth 20.00 50.00
TBD9 Jimmie Johnson 25.00 60.00
TBD10 Brendan Gaughan 10.00 25.00
TBD11 Bobby Labonte 15.00 40.00
TBD12 Dale Jarrett 15.00 40.00
TBD13 Jeff Gordon 40.00 100.00
TBD14 Mark Martin 20.00 50.00
TBD15 Jamie McMurray 20.00 40.00
TBD16 Kurt Busch 12.00 30.00
TBD17 Casey Mears 12.00 30.00
TBD18 Dale Earnhardt/3

2005 Press Pass Optima

COMPLETE SET (100) 12.00 30.00
WAX BOX HOBBY (28) 50.00 80.00
1 John Andretti .10 .30
2 Greg Biffle .25 .60
2B Greg Biffle Cup Chase 1.25 3.00
3 Dave Blaney .10 .30
4 Mike Bliss .10 .30
5 Jeff Burton .25 .60
6 Kurt Busch .40 1.00
6B Kurt Busch Cup Chase 2.00 5.00
7 Kyle Busch CRC .60 1.50
8 Dale Earnhardt Jr. 1.00 2.50
9 Carl Edwards CRC .75 2.00
9B Carl Edwards Cup Chase 4.00 10.00
10 Jeff Gordon 1.00 2.50
11 Kevin Harvick .60 1.50
12 Dale Jarrett .50 1.25
13 Jimmie Johnson .75 2.00
13B Jimmie Johnson Cup Chase 4.00 10.00
14 Kasey Kahne 1.00 2.50
15 Matt Kenseth .75 2.00
15B Matt Kenseth Cup Chase 4.00 10.00
16 Bobby Labonte .50 1.25
17 Sterling Marlin .40 1.00
18 Mark Martin .60 1.50
18B Mark Martin Cup Chase 3.00 8.00
19 Jeremy Mayfield .10 .30
19B Jeremy Mayfield Cup Chase .60 1.50
20 Jamie McMurray .40 1.00
21 Casey Mears .25 .60
22 Joe Nemechek .10 .30
23 Ryan Newman .75 2.00
23B Ryan Newman Cup Chase 4.00 10.00
24 Ricky Rudd .40 1.00
25 Elliott Sadler .25 .60
26 Ken Schrader .10 .30
27 Tony Stewart .60 1.50
27B Tony Stewart Cup Chase 3.00 8.00
28 Brian Vickers .50 1.25
29 Rusty Wallace .50 1.25
29B Rusty Wallace Cup Chase 2.50 6.00
30 Scott Wimmer .25 .60
31 Clint Bowyer BGN 1.00 2.50
32 Carl Edwards BGN .75 2.00
33 David Green .10 .30
34 Denny Hamlin BGN RC 3.00 8.00
35 Kasey Kahne BGN 1.00 2.50
36 Jason Keller BGN .10 .30
37 Reed Sorenson BGN RC 2.50 6.00
38 Martin Truex Jr. BGN .75 2.00
39 J.J. Yeley BGN .40 1.00
40 Terry Cook CTS .25 .60
41 Rick Crawford CTS .10 .30
42 Ron Hornaday CTS .10 .30
43 Todd Kluever CTS RC 1.25 3.00
44 Bill Lester CTS .40 1.00
45 Ken Schrader CTS .10 .30
46 Dennis Setzer CTS .10 .30
47 Mike Skinner CTS .10 .30
48 Jack Sprague CTS .10 .30
49 Martin Truex Jr. YG .75 2.00
50 Carl Edwards YG .75 2.00
51 Kasey Kahne YG 1.00 2.50
52 Reed Sorenson YG 2.00 5.00
53 Clint Bowyer YG 1.00 2.50
54 Kyle Busch YG .60 1.50
55 Dale Jarrett RR .50 1.25
56 Dale Earnhardt Jr. RR 1.00 2.50
57 Mark Martin RR .60 1.50
58 Jeff Gordon RR 1.00 2.50
59 Bobby Labonte RR .50 1.25
60 Martin Truex Jr. RR .75 2.00
61 Carl Edwards RR .75 2.00
62 Jimmie Johnson RR .75 2.00
63 Kurt Busch RR .40 1.00
64 Elliott Sadler DP .25 .60
65 Jeff Green DP .10 .30
66 Tony Stewart DP .60 1.50
67 Jimmie Johnson DP .75 2.00
68 Greg Biffle DP .25 .60
69 Ryan Newman DP .75 2.00
70 Scott Wimmer DP .25 .60
71 Casey Mears DP .25 .60
72 Mark Martin CP .60 1.50
73 Rusty Wallace CP .50 1.25
74 Dale Earnhardt Jr. CP 1.00 2.50
75 Mark Martin CP .60 1.50
76 Elliott Sadler CP .25 .60
77 Sterling Marlin CP .40 1.00
78 Jamie McMurray CP .40 1.00
79 Dale Jarrett CP .50 1.25
80 Mark Martin CP .60 1.50
81 Kurt Busch CP .40 1.00
82 Mark Martin DT .60 1.50
83 Kyle Petty DT .25 .60
84 Carl Edwards DT .75 2.00
85 Jimmie Johnson DT .75 2.00
86 Jeff Burton DT .25 .60
87 Dale Jarrett DT .50 1.25
88 Jeff Gordon's Car RTV .40 1.00
89 Tony Stewart's Car RTV .25 .60
90 Jeremy Mayfield's Car RTV .10 .30
91 Kevin Harvick's Car RTV .60 1.50
92 Jimmie Johnson's Car RTV .25 .60
93 Dale Earnhardt Jr's Car RTV .40 1.00
94 Greg Biffle's Car RTV .40 1.00
95 Jimmie Johnson R&R .75 2.00
96 Bobby Labonte R&R .50 1.25
97 Rusty Wallace R&R .50 1.25
98 Dale Jarrett R&R .50 1.25
99 Mark Martin R&R .60 1.50
100 Tony Stewart CL .60 1.50
NNO Carl Edwards Signings Entry 2.50 6.00

2005 Press Pass Optima Gold

*GOLD: 3X TO 8X BASE

2005 Press Pass Optima Samples

*SAMPLES: .6X TO 1.5X BASE

2005 Press Pass Optima Cool Persistence

COMPLETE SET (12) 12.50 30.00
STATED ODDS 1:6
CP1 Jeff Gordon 2.50 6.00
CP2 Ricky Rudd 1.00 2.50
CP3 Mark Martin 1.50 4.00
CP4 Jimmie Johnson 2.00 5.00
CP5 Rusty Wallace 1.25 3.00
CP6 Carl Edwards 2.00 5.00
CP7 Dale Jarrett 1.25 3.00
CP8 Sterling Marlin 1.00 2.50
CP9 Kevin Harvick 1.50 4.00
CP10 Jeff Burton .60 1.50
CP11 Bobby Labonte 1.25 3.00
CP12 Tony Stewart 1.50 4.00

2005 Press Pass Optima Corporate Cuts Drivers

STATED ODDS 1:168
STATED PRINT RUN 120 SERIAL #'d SETS
*CARS/160: .4X TO 1X DRIVERS
CCD1 Tony Stewart 12.00 30.00
CCD2 Bobby Labonte 10.00 25.00
CCD3 Kasey Kahne 10.00 25.00
CCD4 Jeremy Mayfield 5.00 12.00
CCD5 Greg Biffle 8.00 20.00
CCD6 Dale Jarrett 10.00 25.00
CCD7 Kurt Busch 8.00 20.00
CCD8 Mark Martin 12.00 30.00
CCD9 Matt Kenseth 12.00 30.00

2005 Press Pass Optima Fan Favorite

COMPLETE SET (27) 10.00 25.00
STATED ODDS 1:2
FF1 John Andretti .15 .40
FF2 Greg Biffle .25 .60
FF3 Dave Blaney .15 .40
FF4 Jeff Burton .25 .60
FF5 Kurt Busch .40 1.00
FF6 Kyle Busch .60 1.50
FF7 Carl Edwards .75 2.00
FF8 Jeff Gordon 1.00 2.50
FF9 Robby Gordon .15 .40
FF10 Kevin Harvick .60 1.50
FF11 Dale Jarrett .50 1.25
FF12 Jimmie Johnson .75 2.00
FF13 Kasey Kahne 1.00 2.50
FF14 Matt Kenseth .75 2.00
FF15 Bobby Labonte .50 1.25
FF16 Terry Labonte .40 1.00
FF17 Mark Martin .60 1.50
FF18 Jamie McMurray .40 1.00
FF19 Casey Mears .25 .60
FF20 Joe Nemechek .15 .40
FF21 Kyle Petty .25 .60
FF22 Ricky Rudd .40 1.00
FF23 Elliott Sadler .25 .60
FF24 Tony Stewart .60 1.50
FF25 Martin Truex Jr. .75 2.00
FF26 Rusty Wallace .50 1.25
FF27 Scott Wimmer .25 .60

2005 Press Pass Optima G Force

COMPLETE SET (6) 12.50 30.00
STATED ODDS 1:12
GF1 Martin Truex Jr. 2.50 6.00
GF2 Jimmie Johnson 2.50 6.00
GF3 Ricky Rudd 1.25 3.00
GF4 Mark Martin 2.00 5.00
GF5 Jeff Gordon 3.00 8.00
GF6 Dale Jarrett 1.50 4.00

2005 Press Pass Optima Q & A

COMPLETE SET (9) 12.50 30.00
STATED ODDS 1:8
QA1 Mark Martin 1.50 4.00
QA2 Kyle Busch 1.50 4.00
QA3 Elliott Sadler .60 1.50
QA4 Carl Edwards 2.00 5.00
QA5 Jeff Gordon 2.50 6.00
QA6 Dale Earnhardt Jr. 2.50 6.00
QA7 Tony Stewart 1.50 4.00
QA8 Kasey Kahne 2.50 6.00
QA9 Sterling Marlin 1.00 2.50

2005 Press Pass Optima Thunder Bolts Autographs

This 8-card set was available in packs of 2005 Press Pass Optima. Each card had a slice of a race-used lugnut and a signature from the corresponding driver. The cards were serial numbered to the driver's door number. There was a late addition to the set. Dale Earnhardt Jr. was only available in packs of 2006 Press Pass Legends.

STATED PRINT RUN 6-97
TBJG Jeff Gordon/24 175.00 350.00
TBJJ Jimmie Johnson/48 60.00 120.00
TBKB Kurt Busch/97 40.00 80.00
TBKK Kasey Kahne/9
TBMM Mark Martin/6
TBRN Ryan Newman/12
TBTS Tony Stewart/20 125.00 200.00
TBDE Dale Earnhardt Jr./8

2006 Press Pass Optima

This 100-card set featured top drivers from all levels of NASCAR, Nextel Cup, Busch Series and Craftman Trucks. They were released in October of 2006. Hobby packs consisted of five cards and 24 packs per box. Retail packs consisted of four cards and 28 packs per box.

COMPLETE SET (100) 15.00 40.00
WAX BOX HOBBY (28) 50.00 80.00
WAX BOX RETAIL (24) 40.00 70.00
1 Joe Nemechek .20 .50
2 Clint Bowyer CRC 1.25 3.00
3 Martin Truex Jr. CRC 1.00 2.50
4 Kurt Busch .25 .60
4B Kyle Busch Chase 2.00 5.00
5 Kyle Busch .40 1.00
6 Mark Martin .30 .75
6B Mark Martin Chase 1.50 4.00
7 Robby Gordon .20 .50
8 Dale Earnhardt Jr. .60 1.50
8B Dale Earnhardt Jr. Chase 3.00 8.00
9 Kasey Kahne .40 1.00
9B Kasey Kahne Chase 2.00 5.00
10 Scott Riggs .25 .60
11 Denny Hamlin CRC 2.50 6.00
11B Denny Hamlin Chase 6.00 15.00
12 Ryan Newman .25 .60
13 Sterling Marlin .30 .75
14 Greg Biffle .25 .60
15 Matt Kenseth .30 .75
15B Matt Kenseth Chase 1.50 4.00
16 J.J. Yeley CRC 1.00 2.50
17 Tony Stewart .50 1.25
18 Ken Schrader .20 .50
19 Jeff Gordon .60 1.50
19B Jeff Gordon Chase 3.00 8.00
20 Brian Vickers .20 .50
21 Jamie McMurray .30 .75
22 Kevin Harvick .40 1.00
22B Kevin Harvick Chase 2.00 5.00
23 Jeff Burton .25 .60
23B Jeff Burton Chase 1.25 3.00
24 David Stremme CRC .75 2.00
25 Reed Sorenson CRC 1.00 2.50
26 Casey Mears .20 .50
27 Bobby Labonte .30 .75
28 Terry Labonte .30 .75
29 Kyle Petty .25 .60
30 Jimmie Johnson .50 1.25
30B Jimmie Johnson Chase 2.50 6.00
31 Dale Jarrett .30 .75
32 Tony Raines .20 .50
33 Carl Edwards .30 .75
34 Todd Kluever NBS .60 1.50
35 Clint Bowyer NBS .60 1.50
36 Paul Menard NBS .20 .50
37 Denny Hamlin NBS 1.25 3.00
38 Kevin Harvick NBS .40 1.00
39 David Green NBS .25 .60
40 Regan Smith NBS .25 .60
41 Jon Wood NBS .25 .60
42 Danny O'Quinn Jr. NBS RC .60 1.50
43 Carl Edwards NBS .30 .75
44 Steve Wallace NBS RC 1.25 3.00
45 Burney Lamar NBS RC .75 2.00
46 Mike Skinner CTS .20 .50
47 David Ragan CTS RC 1.00 2.50
48 Rick Crawford CTS .20 .50
49 Bill Lester CTS .30 .75
50 Ron Hornaday CTS .20 .50
51 Erik Darnell CTS RC .60 1.50
52 Dale Jarrett's Car HS .12 .30
53 Jeff Gordon's Car HS .25 .60
54 Jamie McMurray's Car HS .12 .30
55 Tony Stewart's Car HS .20 .50
56 Kurt Busch's Car HS .10 .25
57 Mark Martin's Car HS .12 .30
58 Jeff Burton's Car HS .10 .25
59 Terry Labonte's Car HS .12 .30
60 Dale Earnhardt Jr.'s Car HS .25 .60
61 Jimmie Johnson's Car HS .20 .50
62 Bobby Labonte's Car HS .12 .30
63 Matt Kenseth's Car HS .12 .30
64 Jeff Gordon CP .60 1.50
65 Richard Petty CP .50 1.25
66 Jimmie Johnson CP .50 1.25
67 Mark Martin CP .30 .75
68 Dale Earnhardt Jr. CP .60 1.50
69 Kyle Petty CP .25 .60
70 Tony Stewart CP .50 1.25
71 Kasey Kahne CP .40 1.00
72 Bill Lester CP .30 .75
73 Clint Bowyer YG .60 1.50
74 Denny Hamlin YG 1.25 3.00
75 Reed Sorenson YG .50 1.25
76 David Stremme YG .40 1.00
77 Martin Truex Jr. YG .50 1.25
78 J.J. Yeley YG .50 1.25
79 Matt Kenseth RTV Dover .30 .75
80 Denny Hamlin RTV Pocono 1.25 3.00
81 Kasey Kahne RTV Michigan .40 1.00
82 Jeff Gordon RTV Sonoma .60 1.50
83 Tony Stewart RTV Daytona .50 1.25
84 Jeff Gordon RTV Chicago .60 1.50
85 Kyle Busch RTV New Hamp. .40 1.00
86 Denny Hamlin RTV Pocono 1.25 3.00
87 Jimmie Johnson RTV Indy .50 1.25
88 Kevin Harvick RTV Wat. Glen .40 1.00
89 Matt Kenseth RTV Michigan .30 .75
90 Matt Kenseth RTV Bristol .30 .75
91 Rusty Wallace 84 ROTY .30 .75
92 Rusty Wallace 1st Win '86 .30 .75
93 Rusty Wallace 89 Champ .30 .75
94 Rusty Wallace 50th Win .30 .75
95 Rusty Wallace Last Win .30 .75
96 Rusty Wallace Short Track .30 .75
97 Mark Martin VOTC .30 .75
98 Jimmie Johnson VOTC .50 1.25
99 Matt Kenseth VOTC .30 .75
CL Dale Jarrett CL .30 .75
NNO Elvis Presley Promo 2.00 5.00

2006 Press Pass Optima Gold

*GOLD: 4X TO 10X BASE
*GOLD: 2X TO 5X BASE CRCs

2006 Press Pass Optima Fan Favorite

This 27-card set featured top drivers interacting with fans These cards carried an "FF" prefix for their card numbering. They were inserted into packs at a rate of one in two packs.

COMPLETE SET (27) 12.50 30.00
STATED ODDS 1:2
FF1 Clint Bowyer 1.00 2.50
FF2 Jeff Burton .40 1.00
FF3 Kurt Busch .40 1.00
FF4 Dale Earnhardt Jr. 1.00 2.50
FF5 Carl Edwards .50 1.25
FF6 Jeff Gordon 1.00 2.50
FF7 Denny Hamlin 2.00 5.00
FF8 Kevin Harvick .60 1.50
FF9 Dale Jarrett .50 1.25
FF10 Jimmie Johnson .75 2.00
FF11 Kasey Kahne .60 1.50
FF12 Terry Labonte .50 1.25
FF13 Sterling Marlin .50 1.25
FF14 Mark Martin .50 1.25
FF15 Jamie McMurray .50 1.25
FF16 Joe Nemechek .30 .75
FF17 Ryan Newman .40 1.00
FF18 Kyle Petty .40 1.00
FF19 Scott Riggs .40 1.00
FF20 Ken Schrader .30 .75
FF21 Tony Stewart .75 2.00
FF22 Paul Menard .30 .75
FF23 David Green .30 .75
FF24 Rick Crawford .30 .75
FF25 Ron Hornaday .30 .75
FF26 Bill Lester .50 1.25
FF27 David Ragan 1.50 4.00

2006 Press Pass Optima Pole Position

This 9-card set featured drivers who sat on the pole during the past season. They were inserted in packs at a rate of one in eight. Each card carried a "PP" prefix for its card number.

COMPLETE SET (9) 12.50 30.00
STATED ODDS 1:8
PP1 Jeff Burton .50 1.25
PP2 Kurt Busch .50 1.25
PP3 Greg Biffle .50 1.25
PP4 Kasey Kahne .75 2.00
PP5 Jimmie Johnson 1.00 2.50
PP6 Kyle Busch .75 2.00
PP7 Ryan Newman .50 1.25
PP8 Denny Hamlin 2.50 6.00
PP9 Scott Riggs .50 1.25

2006 Press Pass Optima Q & A

This 12-card set featured NASCAR's hottest stars. These cards were inserted into packs at a rate of one in six. Each card carried a "QA" prefix for its card numbering.

COMPLETE SET (12) 10.00 25.00
QA1 Jimmie Johnson .75 2.00
QA2 Martin Truex Jr. .75 2.00
QA3 Kasey Kahne .60 1.50
QA4 Jeff Burton .40 1.00
QA5 Kevin Harvick .60 1.50
QA6 Kurt Busch .40 1.00
QA7 Dale Earnhardt Jr. 1.00 2.50
QA8 Reed Sorenson .75 2.00
QA9 Jamie McMurray .50 1.25
QA10 Dale Jarrett .50 1.25
QA11 Jeff Gordon 1.00 2.50
QA12 Tony Stewart .75 2.00

2006 Press Pass Optima Rookie Relics Drivers

This 15-card set featured swatches of sheet metal and tire from the corresponding drivers' rookie season. This set had a retail parallel Cars version. These were serial numbered to 50. Each card carried an "RRD" prefix for its card number.

*CARS/50: .4X TO 1X DRIVERS
RRD1 Clint Bowyer 25.00 60.00
RRD2 Denny Hamlin/40 60.00 120.00
RRD3 Reed Sorenson 25.00 60.00
RRD4 David Stremme 20.00 50.00
RRD5 Martin Truex Jr. 25.00 60.00
RRD6 J.J. Yeley 20.00 50.00
RRD7 Kyle Busch 25.00 60.00
RRD8 Kasey Kahne 60.00 120.00
RRD9 Jamie McMurray 20.00 50.00
RRD10 Ryan Newman 25.00 60.00
RRD11 Kevin Harvick 50.00 100.00
RRD12 Matt Kenseth 50.00 100.00
RRD13 Tony Stewart 50.00 100.00
RRD14 Jeff Burton 25.00 60.00
RRD15 Jeff Gordon 60.00 120.00

2005 Press Pass Panorama

This 81-card set was released in retail blaster boxes of 2005 Press Pass Optima, Press Pass Stealth, Press Pass Trackside and VIP. Cards PPP1-PPP18 were available in Press Pass Stealth. Cards PPP19-PPP36 were available in Press Pass Trackside. Cards PPP37-PPP54 were available in VIP. Cards PPP55-PPP81 were available in Press Pass Optima. When arranged properly, nine consecutive card backs made up trackside scenes.

COMPLETE SET (81) 25.00 60.00
PPP1 John Andretti .20 .50
PPP2 Jeff Burton .25 .60
PPP3 Jeff Gordon .60 1.50
PPP4 Denny Hamlin 2.00 5.00
PPP5 Dale Jarrett .30 .75
PPP6 Matt Kenseth .30 .75
PPP7 Bobby Labonte .30 .75
PPP8 Terry Labonte .30 .75
PPP9 Ricky Rudd .25 .60
PPP10 Jack Sprague .20 .50
PPP11 Kevin Harvick .40 1.00
PPP12 Jimmie Johnson .50 1.25
PPP13 Mark Martin .30 .75
PPP14 Tony Stewart .50 1.25
PPP15 Martin Truex Jr. .75 2.00
PPP16 Rusty Wallace .30 .75
PPP17 Michael Waltrip .30 .75
PPP18 J.J. Yeley .50 1.25
PPP19 Jeff Burton .25 .60
PPP20 Jeff Gordon .60 1.50
PPP21 Jimmie Johnson .50 1.25
PPP22 Bill Lester .60 1.50
PPP23 J.J. Yeley .50 1.25
PPP24 Michael Waltrip .30 .75
PPP25 Jimmie Johnson .50 1.25
PPP26 Dale Jarrett .30 .75
PPP27 Jeff Gordon .60 1.50
PPP28 Kevin Harvick .40 1.00
PPP29 Bobby Labonte .30 .75
PPP30 Jeff Gordon .60 1.50
PPP31 Ricky Rudd .25 .60
PPP32 Tony Stewart .50 1.25
PPP33 Dale Earnhardt Jr. .60 1.50
PPP34 Rusty Wallace .30 .75
PPP35 Terry Labonte .30 .75
PPP36 Jimmie Johnson .50 1.25
PPP37 Jeff Gordon .60 1.50
PPP38 Jeff Gordon .60 1.50
PPP39 Jeff Gordon .60 1.50
PPP40 Dale Jarrett .30 .75
PPP41 Dale Jarrett .30 .75
PPP42 Dale Jarrett .30 .75
PPP43 Jimmie Johnson .50 1.25
PPP44 Jimmie Johnson .50 1.25
PPP45 Rusty Wallace .30 .75
PPP46 Tony Stewart .50 1.25
PPP47 Tony Stewart .50 1.25
PPP48 Bobby Labonte .30 .75
PPP49 Bobby Labonte .30 .75
PPP50 Johnny Sauter .30 .75

PPP51 Paul Wolfe .40 1.00
PPP52 Todd Kluever 1.25 3.00
PPP53 Jack Sprague .20 .50
PPP54 Bill Lester .60 1.50
PPP55 Martin Truex Jr. .75 2.00
PPP56 Lee Petty .50 1.25
PPP57 Tony Raines .20 .50
PPP58 Dale Jarrett .30 .75
PPP59 Jimmie Johnson .50 1.25
PPP60 Kasey Kahne .50 1.25
PPP61 Rusty Wallace .30 .75
PPP62 Tony Stewart .50 1.25
PPP63 Bobby Labonte .30 .75
PPP64 Rusty Wallace .30 .75
PPP65 Martin Truex Jr. .75 2.00
PPP66 Ricky Craven .20 .50
PPP67 Ron Hornaday .20 .50
PPP68 Clint Bowyer 1.25 3.00
PPP69 Jack Sprague .20 .50
PPP70 Jason Keller .20 .50
PPP71 Johnny Sauter .30 .75
PPP72 Ricky Rudd .25 .60
PPP73 J.J. Yeley .50 1.25
PPP74 Terry Cook .20 .50
PPP75 Kerry Earnhardt .30 .75
PPP76 Denny Hamlin 2.00 5.00
PPP77 Dennis Setzer .20 .50
PPP78 Rex White .20 .50
PPP79 Buddy Baker .25 .60
PPP80 Martin Truex Jr. .75 2.00
PPP81 Dave Blaney .20 .50

1995 Press Pass Premium

This 36-card set features the top 36 Winston Cup drivers. The first issue of the Premium brand by Press Pass was printed in a quantity of 18,000 boxes. The cards use gold foil stamping and are printed on 24-point stock. The cards came 3 per pack, 36 packs per box and 8 boxes per case.

COMP.GOLD SET (36) 10.00 25.00
1 Dale Earnhardt 2.00 5.00
2 Mark Martin 1.00 2.50
3 Rusty Wallace 1.00 2.50
4 Ken Schrader .10 .30
5 Ricky Rudd .40 1.00
6 Morgan Shepherd .10 .30
7 Terry Labonte .40 1.00
8 Jeff Gordon 1.25 3.00
9 Darrell Waltrip .25 .60
10 Michael Waltrip .25 .60
11 Ted Musgrave .10 .30
12 Sterling Marlin .40 1.00
13 Kyle Petty .25 .60
14 Dale Jarrett .75 2.00
15 Geoff Bodine .10 .30
16 Brett Bodine .10 .30
17 Todd Bodine .10 .30
18 Bobby Labonte .75 2.00
19 Ernie Irvan .25 .60
20 Richard Petty .40 1.00
21 Greg Sacks .10 .30
22 Joe Nemechek .10 .30
23 Steve Grissom .10 .30
24 John Andretti .10 .30
25 Ricky Craven .10 .30
26 Steve Kinser .10 .30
27 Robert Pressley .10 .30
28 Randy LaJoie .10 .30
29 Davy Jones .10 .30
30 Mark Martin 1.00 2.50
31 Rusty Wallace 1.00 2.50
32 Ricky Rudd .40 1.00
33 Jeff Gordon 1.25 3.00
34 Kyle Petty .25 .60
35 Ken Schrader .10 .30
36 Sterling Marlin .40 1.00
P1 Kyle Petty Prototype 1.00 2.50

1995 Press Pass Premium Holofoil

COMPLETE SET (36) 20.00 50.00
*HOLOFOIL STARS: 1X TO 2.5X BASIC CARDS

1995 Press Pass Premium Red Hot

COMPLETE SET (36) 100.00 250.00
*RED HOTS: 4X TO 10X BASIC CARDS

1995 Press Pass Premium Hot Pursuit

This nine-card insert set features nine of the best drivers in Winston Cup. The cards use NitroKrome printing technology and were inserted at a rate of one per 18 packs.

COMPLETE SET (9) 25.00 60.00
HP1 Geoff Bodine .60 1.50
HP2 Dale Earnhardt 10.00 25.00
HP3 Jeff Gordon 6.00 15.00
HP4 Dale Jarrett 4.00 10.00
HP5 Mark Martin 5.00 12.00
HP6 Kyle Petty 1.25 3.00
HP7 Ricky Rudd 2.00 5.00
HP8 Ken Schrader .60 1.50
HP9 Rusty Wallace 5.00 12.00

1995 Press Pass Premium Phone Cards $5

This 9-card set is the first phone card insert issued by Press Pass. The cards featured $5 worth of phone time and were inserted at the rate of one per 36 packs. There was also a parallel 9-card set of $50 phone cards. The odds of finding one of the $50 cards was one in 864 packs. Ken Schrader, Sterling Marlin and Geoff Bodine also had autographed versions of both $5 and $50 phone cards. The odds of finding a signed phone card was one every 216 packs. Finally there were 18 $1995 Jeff Gordon phone cards produced. All 18 of the cards were signed in a special white ink pen. Odds of finding one of the $1995 phone cards was one in 36,000 packs. The phone time expired 1/31/1996.

COMPLETE $5 SET (9) 15.00 40.00
*AUTOGRAPHED $5 CARDS: 4X TO 10X
*AUTOGRAPHED $50 CARDS: 8X TO 20X
COMP. $50 SET (9) 100.00 200.00
*$50 CARDS: 1.25X TO 3X BASIC $5 CARDS
1 Geoff Bodine .40 1.00
2 Jeff Gordon 4.00 10.00
3 Dale Jarrett 2.50 6.00
4 Terry Labonte 1.25 3.00
5 Sterling Marlin 1.25 3.00
6 Mark Martin 3.00 8.00
7 Kyle Petty .75 2.00
8 Ken Schrader .40 1.00
9 Michael Waltrip .75 2.00
10 Jeff Gordon $1995 AUTO

1996 Press Pass Premium

The 1996 Press Pass Premium set issued in one series totalling 45 cards. The cards came in three card packs with a holofoil card in every pack. The set contains the topical subsets: Premium Drivers (1-32) and Premium Cars (33-45).

COMPLETE SET (45) 8.00 20.00
1 Jeff Gordon 1.25 3.00
2 Dale Earnhardt 2.00 5.00
3 Sterling Marlin .40 1.00
4 Mark Martin .75 2.50
5 Rusty Wallace 1.00 2.50
6 Terry Labonte .40 1.00
7 Ted Musgrave .10 .30
8 Bill Elliott .50 1.25
9 Ricky Rudd .40 1.00
10 Bobby Labonte .75 2.00
11 Morgan Shepherd .10 .30
12 Michael Waltrip .25 .60
13 Dale Jarrett .75 2.00
14 Bobby Hamilton .10 .30
15 Derrike Cope .10 .30
16 Geoff Bodine .10 .30
17 Ken Schrader .10 .30
18 John Andretti .10 .30
19 Darrell Waltrip .25 .60
20 Brett Bodine .10 .30
21 Ward Burton .25 .60
22 Ricky Craven .10 .30
23 Steve Grissom .10 .30
24 Joe Nemechek .10 .30
25 Robert Pressley .10 .30
26 Kyle Petty .25 .60
27 Jeremy Mayfield .25 .60
28 Jeff Burton .40 1.00
29 Ernie Irvan .25 .60
30 Wally Dallenbach .10 .30
31 Johnny Benson .25 .60
32 Chad Little .10 .30
33 Michael Waltrip's Car .10 .30
34 Jeff Gordon's Car .60 1.50
35 Dale Earnhardt's Car .75 2.00
36 Bobby Labonte's Car .25 .60
37 Terry Labonte's Car .25 .60
38 Ricky Craven's Car .03 .15
39 Bill Elliott's Car .25 .60
40 Rusty Wallace's Car .40 1.00
41 Dale Jarrett's Car .25 .60
42 Bobby Hamilton's Car .03 .15
43 Ernie Irvan's Car .10 .30
44 Ricky Rudd's Car .10 .30
45 Mark Martin's Car CL .40 1.00
P1 Bobby Labonte Promo 1.25 3.00

1996 Press Pass Premium Emerald Proofs

*EMER.PROOF/380: 4X TO 10X BASIC CARD

1996 Press Pass Premium Holofoil

COMPLETE SET (45) 12.50 30.00
*HOLOFOILS: .8X TO 2X BASIC CARDS

1996 Press Pass Premium $5 Phone Cards

Randomly inserted in packs at a rate of one in 36, this nine-card insert set features some of the best drivers in Winston Cup. Each card is worth $5 in phone time and carries an expiration of 4/30/97. There are two parallel versions of the $5 set, a $10 set and a $20 set. The cards are indentical except they carry $10 and $20 worth of phone time respectively. The $10 cards were randomly inserted in packs 1:216. The $20 cards were randomly inserted 1:864. There is also a $1,996 Mark Martin Phone Card. Any of the phone cards that have had the pin numbered scratched usually are worth .25X to .50X a mint phone card.

COMPLETE SET (9) 10.00 25.00
COMP.$10 SET (9) 15.00 40.00
*$10 CARDS: .6X TO 1.5X $5 CARDS
20.00 DOLLAR PC SET (9) 30.00 75.00
*$20 CARDS: 1.2X TO 3X $5 CARDS
1 Mark Martin 1.50 4.00
1 Johnny Benson .50 1.25
2 Ricky Craven .25 .60
3 Bill Elliott 1.00 2.50
4 Dale Jarrett 1.50 4.00
5 Bobby Labonte 1.50 4.00
6 Sterling Marlin .75 2.00
7 Mark Martin 1.50 4.00
8 Kyle Petty .50 1.25
9 Michael Waltrip .50 1.25

1996 Press Pass Premium Burning Rubber II

This seven-card set is the second edition of the race-used tire cards. The cards feature an actual tire look. There is an all-foil hub surrounded by the race-tire rubber. Tires from the 1996 Daytona race were acquired to use on the cards. The cards were inserted in both hobby and retail products. Cards BR1-BR4 could be found in hobby packs, while BR5-BR7 could be found in retail packs. The odds of finding a Burning Rubber card were 1:288 packs and each card was serial numbered of 500.

BR1 Jeff Gordon's Car 30.00 80.00
BR2 Mark Martin's Car 15.00 40.00
BR3 Dale Jarrett's Car 10.00 25.00
BR4 Ken Schrader's Car 10.00 25.00
BR5 Dale Earnhardt's Car 50.00 100.00
BR6 Rusty Wallace's Car 12.00 30.00
BR7 Ernie Irvan's Car 12.00 30.00

1996 Press Pass Premium Crystal Ball

Randomly inserted in packs at a rate of one in 18, this 12-card insert set uses die-cut printing to bring some of the top drivers into view. The cards use a crystal ball design and feature the driver in the crystal ball with his name in script across the base.

COMPLETE SET (12) 30.00 80.00
CB1 Johnny Benson 1.25 3.00
CB2 Ricky Craven .60 1.50
CB3 Dale Earnhardt 10.00 25.00
CB4 Bill Elliott 2.50 6.00
CB5 Jeff Gordon 6.00 15.00
CB6 Ernie Irvan 1.25 3.00
CB7 Dale Jarrett 4.00 10.00
CB8 Bobby Labonte 4.00 10.00
CB9 Terry Labonte 2.00 5.00
CB10 Sterling Marlin 2.00 5.00
CB11 Mark Martin 5.00 12.00
CB12 Rusty Wallace 5.00 12.00

1996 Press Pass Premium Hot Pursuit

Randomly inserted in packs at a rate of one in 18, this nine-card insert set features Press Pass' NitroKrome printing technology. The cards feature the top names in Winston Cup racing.

COMPLETE SET (9) 25.00 60.00
HP1 Dale Earnhardt UER 8.00 20.00
HP2 Bill Elliott 2.00 5.00
HP3 Jeff Gordon 5.00 12.00
HP4 Ernie Irvan 1.00 2.50
HP5 Bobby Labonte 3.00 8.00
HP6 Mark Martin 4.00 10.00
HP7 Ricky Rudd 1.50 4.00
HP8 Rusty Wallace 4.00 10.00
HP9 Michael Waltrip 1.00 2.50

1997 Press Pass Premium

The 1997 Press Pass Premium set was issued in one series totalling 45 cards. Cards were distributed in 3 card packs with 36 packs per box. The packs carried a suggested retail price of $3.29.

COMPLETE SET (45) 8.00 20.00
1 Terry Labonte .40 1.00
2 Jeff Gordon 1.25 3.00
3 Dale Jarrett .75 2.00
4 Dale Earnhardt 2.00 5.00
5 Mark Martin 1.00 2.50
6 Ricky Rudd .40 1.00
7 Rusty Wallace 1.00 2.50
8 Sterling Marlin .40 1.00
9 Bobby Hamilton .10 .30
10 Ernie Irvan .25 .60
11 Bobby Labonte .75 2.00
12 Ken Schrader .10 .30
13 Jeff Burton .40 1.00
14 Michael Waltrip .25 .60
15 Ted Musgrave .10 .30
16 Ricky Craven .10 .30
17 Johnny Benson .25 .60
18 Wally Dallenbach .10 .30
19 Jeremy Mayfield .25 .60
20 Kyle Petty .25 .60
21 Bill Elliott .50 1.25
22 Ward Burton .25 .60
23 Joe Nemechek .10 .30
24 Chad Little .25 .60
25 Darrell Waltrip .25 .60
26 Robby Gordon RC .40 1.00
27 M.Skinner .25 .60
R.Gordon
D.Green
28 Rusty Wallace's Car .40 1.00
29 Dale Earnhardt's Car .75 2.00
30 Terry Labonte's Car .25 .60
31 Mark Martin's Car .40 1.00
32 Ricky Rudd's Car .10 .30
33 Jeff Gordon's Car .50 1.25
34 Bobby Hamilton's Car .05 .15
35 Dale Jarrett's Car .25 .60
36 Bill Elliott's Car .25 .60
37 Bill Elliott .50 1.25
38 Jeff Gordon 1.25 3.00
39 Ernie Irvan .25 .60
40 Dale Jarrett .75 2.00
41 Bobby Labonte .75 2.00
42 Sterling Marlin .40 1.00
43 Mark Martin 1.00 2.50
44 Rusty Wallace 1.00 2.50
45 Checklist .05 .15
P1 Jeff Gordon Promo 2.00 5.00
P2 Dale Jarrett MO Promo 4.00 10.00
P3 Ernie Irvan MO Promo 2.50 6.00

1997 Press Pass Premium Emerald Proofs

*EMER.PROOF/380: 5X TO 12X BASE CARDS

1997 Press Pass Premium Mirrors

COMPLETE SET (45) 15.00 40.00
*MIRRORS: .8X TO 2X BASE CARDS

1997 Press Pass Premium Oil Slicks

*OIL SLICK/100: 8X TO 20X BASIC CARDS

1997 Press Pass Premium Crystal Ball

This 12-card insert set features some of the top names from NASCAR. The cards use a crystal ball design and feature the driver in the crystal ball with his name across the base. The cards were randomly inserted in packs at a ratio of 1:18.

COMPLETE SET (12) 25.00 50.00
COMP.DIE CUT SET (12) 50.00 100.00
*DIE CUTS: .6X TO 1.5X BASIC INSERTS
DIE CUT STATED ODDS 1:36
CB1 Ricky Craven .60 1.50
CB2 Dale Earnhardt's Car 4.00 10.00
CB3 Bill Elliott 2.50 6.00
CB4 Jeff Gordon 6.00 15.00
CB5 Ernie Irvan 1.25 3.00
CB6 Dale Jarrett 4.00 10.00
CB7 Bobby Labonte 4.00 10.00
CB8 Terry Labonte 2.00 5.00
CB9 Sterling Marlin 2.00 5.00
CB10 Mark Martin 5.00 12.00
CB11 Ricky Rudd 2.00 5.00
CB12 Rusty Wallace 5.00 12.00

1997 Press Pass Premium Double Burners

This five-card insert set features pieces of race-used tire rubber and race-used driver uniforms on the same card. The piece of the driver's uniform appears on the front of the card while the piece of the driver's tire appears on the back. Cards that contain multi-colored pieces of cloth carry a 25 percent premium over those that do not. The cards were randomly inserted in packs at a ratio of 1:432 and are individually numnered of 350.

COMPLETE SET (5) 200.00 400.00
DB1 Dale Earnhardt 40.00 100.00
DB2 Jeff Gordon 25.00 60.00
DB3 Terry Labonte 12.00 30.00
DB4 Rusty Wallace 12.00 30.00
DB5 Michael Waltrip 10.00 25.00

1997 Press Pass Premium Lap Leaders

This 12-card insert set features cel cards that are printed on acetate. The cards are randomly inserted in packs at a ratio of 1:12.

COMPLETE SET (12) 15.00 40.00
LL1 Dale Earnhardt 10.00 25.00
LL2 Bill Elliott 2.50 6.00
LL3 Jeff Gordon 6.00 15.00
LL4 Ernie Irvan 1.25 3.00
LL5 Dale Jarrett 4.00 10.00
LL6 Bobby Labonte 4.00 10.00
LL7 Terry Labonte 2.00 5.00
LL8 Mark Martin 5.00 12.00
LL9 Kyle Petty 1.25 3.00
LL10 Ricky Rudd 2.00 5.00
LL11 Rusty Wallace 5.00 12.00
LL12 Michael Waltrip 1.25 3.00

1998 Press Pass Premium

The 1998 Press Pass Premium set was issued in one series totalling 54 cards. The 3-card packs retail for $3.49 each. The set contains the topical subsets: NASCAR Busch Series (1-13), NASCAR Winston Cup Cars (14-27), and NASCAR Winston Cup Drivers (28-53).

COMPLETE SET (54) 12.00 30.00
1 Randy LaJoie .25 .60
2 Tim Fedewa .25 .60
3 Mike McLaughlin .25 .60
4 Elliott Sadler .25 .60
5 Tony Stewart RC 3.00 8.00
6 Jeff Burton .30 .75
7 Michael Waltrip .40 1.00
8 Dale Jarrett .40 1.00
9 Mark Martin .40 1.00
10 Jason Keller .25 .60
11 Hermie Sadler .25 .60
12 Dale Earnhardt Jr. 2.50 6.00
13 Joe Nemechek .25 .60
14 Rusty Wallace's Car .15 .40
15 Dale Earnhardt's Car 1.00 2.50
16 Bobby Hamilton's Car .10 .25
17 Terry Labonte's Car .15 .40
18 Mark Martin's Car .15 .40
19 Ricky Rudd's Car .12 .30
20 Bobby Labonte's Car .15 .40
21 Jeff Gordon's Car .30 .75
22 Johnny Benson's Car .15 .40
23 Kenny Irwin's Car .25 .60
24 John Andretti's Car .10 .25
25 Dale Jarrett's Car .15 .40
26 Bill Elliott's Car .30 .75
27 Jeff Burton's Car .12 .30
28 Jeff Gordon .75 2.00
29 Dale Jarrett .40 1.00
30 Mark Martin .40 1.00
31 Jeff Burton .30 .75
32 Dale Earnhardt 2.50 6.00
33 Terry Labonte .40 1.00
34 Bobby Labonte .40 1.00
35 Bill Elliott .75 2.00
36 Rusty Wallace .40 1.00
37 Ken Schrader .25 .60
38 Johnny Benson .40 1.00
39 Ted Musgrave .25 .60
40 Jeremy Mayfield .25 .60
41 Ernie Irvan .40 1.00
42 John Andretti .25 .60
43 Bobby Hamilton .25 .60
44 Ricky Rudd .30 .75
45 Michael Waltrip .40 1.00
46 Ricky Craven .15 .40
47 Jimmy Spencer .30 .75
48 Geoff Bodine .25 .60
49 Ward Burton .30 .75
50 Sterling Marlin .40 1.00
51 Todd Bodine .15 .40
52 Joe Nemechek .25 .60
53 Mike Skinner .25 .60
54 Kenny Irwin CL .60 1.50
P1 Jeff Gordon Promo 2.00 5.00
0 Dale Earnhardt Daytona 15.00 40.00

1998 Press Pass Premium Reflectors

COMPLETE SET (54) 75.00 150.00
*REFLECTOR VETS: 2X TO 5X BASE CARDS
*REFLECTOR RCs: .6X TO 1.5X BASE CARDS

1998 Press Pass Premium Flag Chasers

Randomly inserted in packs at a rate of one in 2, this 27-card insert set features multi-dimensional all-foil, die-cut cards with intricate micro-etching of the top NASCAR Winston Cup drivers and cars.

COMPLETE SET (27) 15.00 40.00
COMP.REF. SET (27) 150.00 300.00
*REFLECTORS: 3X TO 8X BASIC INSERTS
FC1 Jeff Gordon 3.00 8.00
FC2 Steve Park 1.00 2.50
FC3 Dale Jarrett 2.00 5.00
FC4 Mark Martin 2.50 6.00
FC5 Jeff Burton 1.00 2.50
FC6 Rusty Wallace 2.50 6.00
FC7 Ricky Rudd 1.00 2.50
FC8 Terry Labonte 1.00 2.50
FC9 Bobby Labonte 1.50 4.00
FC10 Ernie Irvan .60 1.50
FC11 Johnny Benson .60 1.50
FC12 Michael Waltrip .60 1.50
FC13 Bill Elliott 1.25 3.00
FC14 Ken Schrader .30 .75
FC15 Wally Dallenbach .30 .75
FC16 Kenny Irwin .60 1.50
FC17 Ricky Craven .30 .75
FC18 Mike Skinner .30 .75
FC19 Rusty Wallace's Car 1.00 2.50
FC20 Dale Earnhardt's Car 2.00 5.00
FC21 Terry Labonte's Car .60 1.50
FC22 Ricky Rudd's Car .30 .75
FC23 Bobby Labonte's Car .60 1.50
FC24 Jeff Gordon's Car 1.25 3.00
FC25 Dale Jarrett's Car .60 1.50
FC26 Bill Elliott's Car .60 1.50
FC27 Jeff Burton's Car .30 .75

1998 Press Pass Premium Rivalries

Randomly inserted in packs at a rate of one in 6, this 12-card insert set celebrates NASCAR's 50th anniversary with inter-locking die-cut cards that depict the top six driver duels from NASCAR's premier division.

COMPLETE SET (12) 20.00 50.00
1A Jeff Burton 1.25 3.00
1B Jeff Gordon 4.00 10.00
2A David Pearson .40 1.00
2B Richard Petty .75 2.00
3A Dale Earnhardt 6.00 15.00
3B Rusty Wallace 3.00 8.00
4A Cale Yarborough .40 1.00
4B Bobby Allison .40 1.00
5A Mark Martin 3.00 8.00
5B Dale Jarrett 2.50 6.00
6A Jeff Gordon's Car 1.50 4.00
6B Dale Earnhardt's Car 2.50 6.00

1998 Press Pass Premium Steel Horses

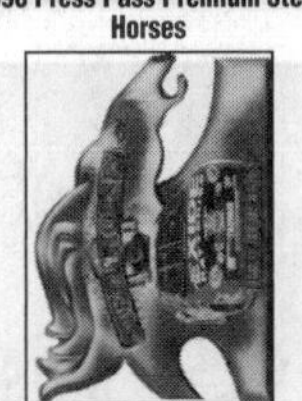

Randomly inserted in packs at a rate of one in 12, this 12-card insert set highlights the top NASCAR Winston Cup cars in an all-foil, die-cut, embossed and etched set.

COMPLETE SET (12) 20.00 50.00
SH1 Rusty Wallace's Car 4.00 10.00
SH2 Dale Earnhardt's Car 8.00 20.00
SH3 Terry Labonte's Car 2.50 6.00
SH4 Mark Martin's Car 4.00 10.00
SH5 Ricky Rudd's Car 1.25 3.00
SH6 Bobby Labonte's Car 2.50 6.00
SH7 Jeff Gordon's Car 5.00 12.00
SH8 Kenny Irwin's Car 1.25 3.00
SH9 Sterling Marlin's Car 1.25 3.00
SH10 Dale Jarrett's Car 2.50 6.00
SH11 Bill Elliott's Car 2.50 6.00
SH12 Jeff Burton's Car 1.25 3.00

1998 Press Pass Premium Triple Gear Firesuit

Randomly inserted in packs at a rate of one in 432, this 9-card insert set features authentic pieces of the drivers' firesuits. These cards are numbered to 150.

TGF1 Rusty Wallace 20.00 50.00
TGF2 Dale Earnhardt 60.00 150.00
TGF3 Terry Labonte 20.00 50.00
TGF4 Mark Martin 25.00 60.00
TGF5 Bobby Labonte 20.00 50.00
TGF6 Jeff Gordon 50.00 120.00
TGF7 Mike Skinner 15.00 40.00
TGF8 Dale Jarrett 20.00 50.00
TGF9 Jeff Burton 15.00 40.00

1999 Press Pass Premium

This 54-card set was issued by Press Pass as a premium hobby product with three cards per pack. The set features cards of most of the leading NASCAR drivers and a few of their cars. A parallel reflector set was issued at the rate of one every eight packs and is valued at a multiple of the regular cards. A special Jeff Gordon Daytona card was randomly inserted in packs and is listed at the end of these listings.

COMPLETE SET (54) 12.50 30.00
1 John Andretti .15 .40
2 Johnny Benson .30 .75
3 Geoff Bodine .15 .40
4 Jeff Burton .50 1.25
5 Ward Burton .30 .75
6 Dale Earnhardt 2.50 6.00
7 Bill Elliott .60 1.50
8 Jeff Gordon 1.50 4.00
9 Bobby Hamilton .15 .40
10 Ernie Irvan .30 .75
11 Kenny Irwin .30 .75
12 Dale Jarrett 1.00 2.50
13 Bobby Labonte 1.00 3.00
14 Terry Labonte .50 1.25
15 Chad Little .30 .75
16 Sterling Marlin .50 1.25
17 Mark Martin 1.25 3.00
18 Jeremy Mayfield .30 .75
19 Joe Nemechek .15 .40
20 Steve Park .75 2.00
21 Ricky Rudd .50 1.25
22 Elliott Sadler .30 .75
23 Tony Stewart CRC 2.00 5.00
24 Mike Skinner .15 .40
25 Jimmy Spencer .15 .40
26 Rusty Wallace 1.25 3.00
27 Michael Waltrip .30 .75
28 Jeff Gordon's Car .60 1.50
29 Mark Martin's Car .50 1.25
30 Dale Jarrett's Car .30 .75
31 Rusty Wallace's Car .50 1.25
32 Jeff Burton's Car .30 .75
33 Bobby Labonte's Car .30 .75
34 Jeremy Mayfield's Car .07 .20
35 Dale Earnhardt's Car 1.00 2.50

36 Terry Labonte's Car .30 .75
37 Mike Skinner's Car .07 .20
38 John Andretti's Car .07 .20
39 Kenny Irwin's Car .15 .40
40 Joe Nemechek .15 .40
41 Dale Earnhardt Jr. 2.00 5.00
42 Tim Fedewa .15 .40
43 Jeff Gordon 1.50 4.00
44 Ken Schrader .15 .40
45 Terry Labonte .50 1.25
46 Matt Kenseth RC 3.00 8.00
47 Randy LaJoie .15 .40
48 Mark Martin 1.25 3.00
49 Mike McLaughlin .15 .40
50 Michael Waltrip .30 .75
51 Hermie Sadler .15 .40
52 Jason Keller .15 .40
53 Todd Bodine .15 .40
54 Jason Jarrett CL .30 .75
P1 Dale Earnhardt Jr. Promo 2.00 5.00
0 Jeff Gordon Daytona 12.00 30.00

1999 Press Pass Premium Reflectors

COMPLETE SET (54) 100.00 200.00
*REFLECTORS: 2X TO 5X BASE CARDS
*REFLECTOR RCs: 1X TO 2.5X BASE CARDS

1999 Press Pass Premium Badge of Honor

These cards were inserted one every two packs. The card back resembles a shield with the drivers car number on it. There is also a non-die-cut reflector set issued to these cards which are issued one every 24 packs.

COMPLETE SET (28) 15.00 40.00
COMP.REFLECT.SET (28) 200.00 400.00
*REFLECTORS: 3X TO 8X BASIC INSERTS
BH1 Rusty Wallace 2.50 6.00
BH2 Dale Earnhardt Jr. 4.00 10.00
BH3A Michael Waltrip .60 1.50
BH3B Jimmy Spencer .30 .75
BH4 Terry Labonte 1.00 2.50
BH5 Mark Martin 2.50 6.00
BH6 Ricky Rudd 1.00 2.50
BH7 Jeremy Mayfield .60 1.50
BH8 Johnny Benson .60 1.50
BH9 Bobby Labonte 2.50 6.00
BH10 Jeff Gordon 3.00 8.00
BH11 Kenny Irwin .60 1.50
BH12 Mike Skinner .30 .75
BH13 Ernie Irvan .60 1.50
BH14 Dale Jarrett 2.00 5.00
BH15 Bill Elliott 1.25 3.00
BH16 Jeff Burton 1.00 2.50
BH17 Chad Little .60 1.50
BH18 Kevin Lepage .30 .75
BH19 Dale Earnhardt's Car 2.50 6.00
BH20 Terry Labonte's Car .50 1.25
BH21 Mark Martin's Car 1.25 3.00
BH22 Jeremy Mayfield's Car .30 .75
BH23 Bobby Labonte's Car 1.25 3.00
BH24 Jeff Gordon's Car 1.50 4.00
BH25 Dale Jarrett's Car 1.00 2.50
BH26 Dale Earnhardt Jr.'s Car 2.00 5.00
BH27 Jeff Burton's Car .50 1.25

1999 Press Pass Premium Burning Desire

This six card insert set was issued with progressing insert ratios, the odds are noted next to each driver. This set also featured race used rubber on the card.

COMPLETE SET (6) 50.00 120.00
FD1B Jeff Gordon 1:240 10.00 25.00
FD2B Dale Earnhardt Jr. 1:192 10.00 25.00
FD3B Jeremy Mayfield 1:144 3.00 8.00
FD4B Jeff Burton 1:72 3.00 8.00
FD5B Dale Jarrett 1:36 4.00 10.00
FD6B Tony Stewart 1:18 5.00 12.00

1999 Press Pass Premium Extreme Fire

This six card insert set was issued with progressing insert ratios, the odds are noted next to each driver. This set also featured race used rubber on the card.

COMPLETE SET (6) 40.00 100.00
FD1A Jeff Gordon 1:240 10.00 25.00
FD2A Dale Earnhardt 1:192 12.50 30.00
FD3A Rusty Wallace 1:144 7.50 15.00
FD4A Mark Martin 1:72 6.00 15.00
FD5A Terry Labonte 1:36 3.00 8.00
FD6A Bobby Labonte 1:18 3.00 8.00

1999 Press Pass Premium Race Used Firesuit

Inserted at the rate of one every 432 packs these nine cards feature pieces of the racing firesuits worn by various drivers. The Jeff Gordon Firesuit was not available at time of issue but was only available via a mail redemption card. The stated print run was 250 serial numbered sets.

COMPLETE SET (9) 400.00 800.00
F1 Jeff Gordon 40.00 100.00
F2 Rusty Wallace 15.00 40.00
F3 Dale Earnhardt 60.00 150.00
F4 Bobby Labonte 12.00 30.00
F5 Terry Labonte 12.00 30.00
F6 Mark Martin 20.00 50.00
F7 Mike Skinner 10.00 25.00
F8 Dale Jarrett 15.00 40.00
F9 Jeff Burton 12.00 30.00

1999 Press Pass Premium Steel Horses

Inserted one every 12 packs, these 12 cards feature pictures of some of the leading cars on the NASCAR circuit. Each card was produced in a die-cut shape of a galloping horse.

COMPLETE SET (12) 20.00 50.00
SH1 Rusty Wallace's Car 5.00 12.00
SH2 Dale Earnhardt's Car 10.00 25.00
SH3 Mike Skinner's Car .60 1.50
SH4 Terry Labonte's Car 2.00 5.00
SH5 Mark Martin's Car 5.00 12.00
SH6 Dale Earnhardt Jr.'s Car 8.00 20.00
SH7 Jeremy Mayfield's Car 1.25 3.00
SH8 Bobby Labonte's Car 5.00 12.00
SH9 Jeff Gordon's Car 6.00 15.00
SH10 Dale Jarrett's Car 4.00 10.00
SH11 Bill Elliott's Car 2.50 6.00
SH12 Jeff Burton's Car 2.00 5.00

2000 Press Pass Premium

2000 Press Pass Premium was released as a 72-card three tier base set. Contenders (numbers 1-45) were inserted at three in one, Champs and Challengers (numbers 46-63) were inserted at one in three, and Premium Choice (numbers 64-72) were inserted at one in 12. This set also features a "ZERO" card which pays tribute to the 2000 Daytona 500 winner. Press Pass Premium was packaged at 24-packs per box, 4-cards per pack, and packs carried a suggested retail price of $3.99.

COMPLETE SET (72) 40.00 100.00
COMP.SET w/o SP'S (45) 6.00 15.00
1 Steve Park .60 1.50
2 Rusty Wallace 1.50 4.00
3 Bobby Hamilton .20 .50
4 Terry Labonte .60 1.50
5 Mark Martin 1.50 4.00
6 Michael Waltrip .40 1.00
7 Jeremy Mayfield .20 .50
8 Kevin Lepage .20 .50
9 Bobby Labonte 1.25 3.00
10 Tony Stewart 2.00 5.00
11 Elliott Sadler .40 1.00
12 Ward Burton .40 1.00
13 Jeff Gordon 2.00 5.00
14 Jerry Nadeau .40 1.00
15 Jimmy Spencer .20 .50
16 Ricky Rudd .60 1.50
17 Mike Skinner .20 .50
18 Joe Nemechek .20 .50
19 Sterling Marlin .60 1.50
20 Kenny Irwin .40 1.00
21 John Andretti .20 .50
22 Kenny Wallace .20 .50
23 Geoffrey Bodine .20 .50
24 Darrell Waltrip .40 1.00
25 Dale Jarrett 1.25 3.00
26 Chad Little .40 1.00
27 Jeff Burton .60 1.50
28 Rusty Wallace's Car .60 1.50
29 Jeremy Mayfield's Car .08 .25
30 Terry Labonte's Car .40 1.00
31 Mark Martin's Car .60 1.50
32 Joe Nemechek's Car .08 .25
33 Matt Kenseth CRC .60 1.50
34 Bobby Labonte's Car .40 1.00
35 Tony Stewart's Car .75 2.00
36 Jeff Gordon's Car .75 2.00
37 Sterling Marlin's Car .20 .50
38 Ricky Rudd's Car .20 .50
39 Jeff Burton's Car .20 .50
40 Dave Blaney .20 .50
41 Mike Bliss .20 .50
42 Scott Pruett RC .20 .50
43 Dale Earnhardt Jr. CRC 2.50 6.00
44 Matt Kenseth 1.50 4.00
45 Stacy Compton CL .20 .50
46 Dale Jarrett 1.50 4.00
47 Jeff Gordon 2.50 6.00
48 Terry Labonte .75 2.00
49 Dale Earnhardt 4.00 10.00
50 Rusty Wallace 2.00 5.00
51 Darrell Waltrip .50 1.25
52 Mark Martin 2.00 5.00
53 Dale Earnhardt Jr. 3.00 8.00
54 Jeremy Mayfield .25 .60
55 Matt Kenseth 2.00 5.00
56 Bobby Labonte 1.50 4.00
57 Tony Stewart 2.50 6.00
58 Ward Burton .50 1.25
59 Ricky Rudd .75 2.00
60 Mike Skinner .25 .60
61 John Andretti .25 .60
62 Scott Pruett .25 .60
63 Jeff Burton .75 2.00
64 Dale Earnhardt 5.00 12.00
65 Jeff Gordon 3.00 8.00
66 Dale Earnhardt Jr. 4.00 10.00
67 Tony Stewart 3.00 8.00
68 Dale Jarrett 2.00 5.00
69 Mark Martin 2.50 6.00
70 Bobby Labonte 2.00 5.00
71 Jeff Burton 1.25 3.00
72 Ward Burton .60 1.50
0 Dale Jarrett Daytona Win 20.00 50.00
P1 Bobby Labonte Promo 1.00 2.50

2000 Press Pass Premium Reflectors

COMP.SET w/o SP'S (45) 12.50 30.00
*REFLECTORS 1-45: .8X TO 2X BASE CARDS
*REFLECTORS 46-63: 1.5X TO 4X BASE CARDS
*REFLECTORS 64-72: 2X TO 5X BASE CARDS

2000 Press Pass Premium In The Zone

Randomly inserted in packs at one in 12, this 12-card set showcases NASCAR's most intense drivers on all-foil cards enhanced with micro-etching. Card backs carry an "IZ" prefix.

COMPLETE SET (12) 15.00 40.00
IZ1 Tony Stewart 3.00 8.00
IZ2 Bobby Labonte 2.00 5.00
IZ3 Sterling Marlin 1.00 2.50
IZ4 Jeff Gordon 3.00 8.00
IZ5 Matt Kenseth 2.50 6.00
IZ6 Jeff Burton 1.00 2.50
IZ7 Mark Martin 2.50 6.00
IZ8 Dale Jarrett 2.00 5.00
IZ9 Dale Earnhardt Jr. 4.00 10.00
IZ10 Ward Burton .60 1.50
IZ11 Rusty Wallace 2.50 6.00
IZ12 Terry Labonte 1.00 2.50

2000 Press Pass Premium Performance Driven

Randomly seeded in packs at one in 24, this 6-card set features some of NASCAR's highest performance drivers. Card fronts contain a color portrait shot of the driver set against a black and white action shot of the respective car. Each card is all-foil and is enhanced with micro-etching. Card backs carry a "PD" prefix.

COMPLETE SET (6) 15.00 40.00
PD1 Dale Jarrett 3.00 8.00
PD2 Jeff Gordon 5.00 12.00
PD3 Tony Stewart 5.00 12.00
PD4 Dale Earnhardt Jr. 6.00 15.00
PD5 Mark Martin 4.00 10.00
PD6 Dale Earnhardt 10.00 25.00

2000 Press Pass Premium Race Used Firesuit

Inserted at the rate of one every 480 packs these nine cards feature pieces of the racing firesuits worn by various drivers.

F1 Dale Earnhardt Jr. 25.00 60.00
F2 Rusty Wallace 15.00 40.00
F3 Dale Earnhardt 60.00 150.00
F4 Jeff Gordon 25.00 60.00
F5 Terry Labonte 15.00 40.00
F6 Bobby Labonte 15.00 40.00
F7 Tony Stewart 20.00 50.00
F8 Dale Jarrett 15.00 40.00
F9 Jeff Burton 12.00 30.00

2001 Press Pass Premium

This product was released in April 2001, and featured an 81-card base set that was broken into tiers as follows: 50 Base Veterans (3:1), 19 Champs and Challengers (1:3), and 12 Premium Choice cards (1:12). Each pack contained 4-cards and carried a suggested retail price of $2.99.

COMPLETE SET (81) 60.00 120.00
WAX BOX HOBBY 75.00 125.00
1 John Andretti .25 .60
2 Jeff Burton .50 1.25
3 Dale Earnhardt 4.00 10.00
4 Ward Burton .50 1.25
5 Dale Earnhardt Jr. 3.00 8.00
6 Jeff Gordon 2.50 6.00
7 Bobby Hamilton .25 .60
8 Dale Jarrett 1.00 2.50
9 Buckshot Jones .25 .60
10 Matt Kenseth 1.50 4.00
11 Bobby Labonte 1.50 4.00
12 Jerry Nadeau .50 1.25
13 Sterling Marlin .75 2.00
14 Mark Martin 1.50 4.00
15 Jeremy Mayfield .25 .60
16 Robert Pressley .25 .60
17 Joe Nemechek .25 .60
18 Steve Park .50 1.25
19 Kyle Petty .50 1.25
20 Ricky Rudd .75 2.00
21 Elliott Sadler .50 1.25
22 Ken Schrader .25 .60
23 Mike Skinner .25 .60
24 Dave Blaney .25 .60
25 Tony Stewart 2.00 5.00
26 Rusty Wallace 1.50 4.00
27 Michael Waltrip .50 1.25
28 Steve Park .50 1.25
29 Rusty Wallace 1.50 4.00
30 Dale Earnhardt 4.00 10.00
31 Terry Labonte .75 2.00
32 Dale Earnhardt Jr. 2.50 6.00
33 Michael Waltrip .50 1.25
34 Bobby Labonte 1.50 4.00
35 Tony Stewart 2.00 5.00
36 Jeff Gordon 2.50 6.00
37 Ricky Rudd .75 2.00
38 Mike Skinner .25 .60
39 Joe Nemechek .25 .60
40 Ken Schrader .25 .60
41 Sterling Marlin .75 2.00
42 Kyle Petty .50 1.25
43 Kevin Harvick CRC 1.50 4.00
44 Dale Jarrett 1.00 2.50
45 Casey Atwood .25 .60
46 Kurt Busch CRC .75 2.00
47 Ron Hornaday .25 .60
48 Andy Houston .25 .60
49 Kevin Harvick 1.50 4.00
50 Jason Leffler CL .25 .60
51 Dale Earnhardt CC 4.00 10.00
52 Jeff Gordon CC 2.50 6.00
53 Dale Jarrett CC 1.50 4.00
54 Bobby Labonte CC 1.50 4.00
55 Terry Labonte CC 1.00 2.50
56 Rusty Wallace CC 2.00 5.00
57 Jeff Burton CC .60 1.50
58 Ward Burton CC .60 1.50
59 Dale Earnhardt Jr. CC 3.00 8.00
60 Bobby Hamilton CC .30 .75
61 Matt Kenseth CC 2.00 5.00
62 Sterling Marlin CC 1.00 2.50
63 Mark Martin CC 2.00 5.00
64 Jeremy Mayfield CC .30 .75
65 Steve Park CC .60 1.50
66 Ricky Rudd CC 1.00 2.50
67 Mike Skinner CC .30 .75
68 Tony Stewart CC 2.50 6.00
69 Michael Waltrip CC .60 1.50
70 Terry Labonte PC 1.50 4.00
71 Mike Skinner PC .75 2.00
72 Dale Earnhardt Jr. PC 6.00 15.00
73 Jeff Gordon PC 5.00 12.00
74 Dale Jarrett PC 3.00 8.00
75 Sterling Marlin PC 2.00 5.00
76 Bobby Labonte PC 3.00 8.00
77 Dale Earnhardt PC 8.00 20.00
78 Mark Martin PC 5.00 10.00
79 Ricky Rudd PC 1.25 3.00
80 Tony Stewart PC 5.00 12.00
81 Rusty Wallace PC 4.00 10.00
0 Michael Waltrip Daytona 6.00 15.00
00 Jeff Gordon No Bull 5 8.00 20.00

2001 Press Pass Premium Gold

COMP.SET w/o SP's (50) 20.00 50.00
*GOLD 1-50: .8X TO 2X BASE CARDS
*GOLD 51-69: 1.2X TO 3X BASE CARDS
*GOLD 70-81: 2X TO 5X BASE CARDS

2001 Press Pass Premium In The Zone

Randomly inserted into packs at the rate of one in 12, this twelve card insert set features drivers that are determined to "go the distance". Card backs carry an "IZ" prefix.

COMPLETE SET (12) 20.00 50.00
IZ1 Jeff Burton .75 2.00
IZ2 Dale Earnhardt Jr. 5.00 12.00
IZ3 Dale Earnhardt 6.00 15.00
IZ4 Sterling Marlin 1.25 3.00
IZ5 Jeff Gordon 4.00 10.00
IZ6 Dale Jarrett 1.50 4.00
IZ7 Matt Kenseth 2.50 6.00
IZ8 Bobby Labonte 2.50 6.00
IZ9 Mike Skinner .40 1.00
IZ10 Mark Martin 2.50 6.00
IZ11 Ricky Rudd 1.25 3.00
IZ12 Rusty Wallace 2.50 6.00

2001 Press Pass Premium Performance Driven

Randomly inserted into packs at the rate of one in 24, this nine card insert set features drivers that are performance driven. Card backs carry a "PD" prefix.

COMPLETE SET (9) 40.00 100.00
PD1 Sterling Marlin 2.00 5.00
PD2 Dale Earnhardt Jr. 8.00 20.00
PD3 Dale Earnhardt 10.00 25.00
PD4 Jeff Gordon 6.00 15.00
PD5 Bobby Labonte 4.00 10.00
PD6 Mark Martin 4.00 10.00
PD7 Ricky Rudd 2.00 5.00
PD8 Tony Stewart 5.00 12.00
PD9 Rusty Wallace 4.00 10.00

2001 Press Pass Premium Race Used Firesuit Drivers

Randomly inserted into hobby packs at the rate of one in 480, this nine card insert set features swatches of actual race-used firesuits. Card backs carry a "FD" prefix. The hobby version pictures the driver and each was serial numbered of 100. The retail version features their cars and each was serial numbered of 120.

*CARS/110: .3X TO .8X DRIVERS/100
FD0 Dale Earnhardt Jr. 40.00 100.00
FD1 Jeff Gordon 40.00 100.00
FD2 Mark Martin 20.00 50.00
FD3 Dale Earnhardt 75.00 150.00
FD4 Matt Kenseth 15.00 40.00
FD5 Bobby Labonte 20.00 50.00
FD6 Mike Skinner 8.00 20.00
FD7 Tony Stewart 20.00 40.00
FD8 Rusty Wallace 20.00 50.00

2002 Press Pass Premium

This 81-card set was released in May, 2002. This set was issued in four card hobby or retail packs which came 24 packs to a box and 20 boxes to a case with an SRP of $3.99 per pack. In addition, a special card honoring Ward Burton's Daytona 500 win was inserted at approximately a one per case rate.

COMPLETE SET (81) 30.00 80.00
COMP.SET w/o SP's (50) 10.00 25.00
WAX BOX HOBBY (24) 50.00 90.00
WAX BOX RETAIL (24) 40.00 80.00
1 John Andretti .15 .40
2 Brett Bodine .15 .40
3 Jeff Burton .30 .75
4 Ward Burton .30 .75
5 Kurt Busch .50 1.25
6 Ricky Craven .15 .40
7 Dale Earnhardt Jr. 1.50 4.00
8 Jeff Gordon 1.25 3.00
9 Jeff Green .15 .40
10 Bobby Hamilton .15 .40
11 Kevin Harvick 1.00 2.50
12 Dale Jarrett .75 2.00
13 Jimmie Johnson CRC 1.00 2.50
14 Buckshot Jones .15 .40
15 Matt Kenseth 1.00 2.50
16 Bobby Labonte .75 2.00
17 Terry Labonte .50 1.25
18 Sterling Marlin .50 1.25
19 Mark Martin 1.00 2.50
20 Jeremy Mayfield .15 .40
21 Jerry Nadeau .30 .75
22 Joe Nemechek .15 .40
23 Ryan Newman CRC 1.00 2.50
24 Kyle Petty .30 .75
25 Ricky Rudd .50 1.25
26 Elliott Sadler .30 .75
27 Ken Schrader .15 .40
28 Mike Skinner .15 .40
29 Jimmy Spencer .15 .40
30 Tony Stewart 1.00 2.50
31 Hut Stricklin .15 .40
32 Rusty Wallace .75 2.00
33 Michael Waltrip .30 .75
34 Jimmie Johnson's Car .50 1.25
35 Ryan Newman's Car .50 1.25
36 Dale Earnhardt Jr.'s Car .60 1.50
37 Jeff Burton's Car .15 .40
38 Jeff Gordon's Car .50 1.25
39 Kevin Harvick's Car .50 1.25
40 Dale Jarrett's Car .30 .75
41 Matt Kenseth's Car .50 1.25
42 Sterling Marlin's Car .15 .40
43 Mark Martin's Car .50 1.25
44 Tony Stewart's Car .50 1.25
45 Ricky Rudd's Car .15 .40
46 Jeff Gordon SW 1.25 3.00
47 Michael Waltrip SW .30 .75
48 Tony Stewart SW 1.00 2.50
49 Jimmie Johnson SW 1.00 2.50
50 Tony Stewart CL .50 1.25
51 Jeff Gordon CH 2.50 6.00
52 Dale Jarrett CH 1.50 4.00
53 Bobby Labonte CH 1.50 4.00
54 Terry Labonte CH 1.00 2.50
55 Rusty Wallace CH 1.50 4.00
56 Jeff Burton CH .60 1.50
57 Ward Burton CH .30 .75
58 Kurt Busch CH 1.00 2.50
59 Ricky Craven CH .30 .75
60 Dale Earnhardt Jr. CH 3.00 8.00
61 Kevin Harvick CH 2.00 5.00
62 Jimmie Johnson CH 2.00 5.00
63 Matt Kenseth CH 2.00 5.00
64 Sterling Marlin CH 1.00 2.50
65 Mark Martin CH 2.00 5.00
66 Ryan Newman CH 2.00 5.00
67 Ricky Rudd CH 1.00 2.50
68 Tony Stewart CH 2.00 5.00
69 Michael Waltrip CH .60 1.50
70 Jeff Burton PC 1.25 3.00
71 Dale Earnhardt Jr. PC 5.00 12.00
72 Jeff Gordon PC 4.00 10.00
73 Kevin Harvick PC 3.00 8.00
74 Dale Jarrett PC 2.50 6.00
75 Jimmie Johnson PC 3.00 8.00
76 Bobby Labonte PC 2.50 6.00
77 Terry Labonte PC 1.50 4.00
78 Sterling Marlin PC 1.50 4.00
79 Mark Martin PC 3.00 8.00
80 Tony Stewart PC 3.00 8.00
81 Rusty Wallace PC 2.50 6.00
0 Ward Burton Daytona Win 8.00 20.00

2002 Press Pass Premium Red Reflectors

COMPLETE SET (81) 100.00 200.00
COMP.SET w/o SP's (50) 15.00 40.00
*1-50 RED REF: .8X TO 2X HI COL.
*51-69 RED REF: 1X TO 2.5X HI COL.
*70-81 RED REF: 1X TO 2.5X HI COL.

2002 Press Pass Premium Samples

*SAMPLES: 2X TO 5X BASIC CARDS

2002 Press Pass Premium In The Zone

Issued in packs at a stated rate of one in 12, these holofoil gold double-etched 12 cards feature information on how leading NASCAR drivers make it to the finish line.

COMPLETE SET (12) 15.00 40.00
IZ1 Jeff Burton .75 2.00
IZ2 Ward Burton .75 2.00
IZ3 Dale Earnhardt Jr. 4.00 10.00
IZ4 Jeff Gordon 3.00 8.00
IZ5 Kevin Harvick 2.50 6.00
IZ6 Dale Jarrett 2.00 5.00
IZ7 Matt Kenseth 2.50 6.00
IZ8 Bobby Labonte 2.00 5.00
IZ9 Sterling Marlin 1.25 3.00
IZ10 Mark Martin 2.50 6.00
IZ11 Tony Stewart 2.50 6.00
IZ12 Rusty Wallace 2.00 5.00

2002 Press Pass Premium Performance Driven

Issued at a stated rate of one in 24, these nine silver foil double-etched cards feature information on how NASCAR drivers are motivated to succeed.

COMPLETE SET (9) 20.00 50.00
PD1 Dale Earnhardt Jr. 6.00 15.00
PD2 Jeff Gordon 5.00 12.00
PD3 Kevin Harvick 4.00 10.00
PD4 Dale Jarrett 3.00 8.00
PD5 Bobby Labonte 3.00 8.00
PD6 Mark Martin 4.00 10.00
PD7 Ricky Rudd 2.00 5.00
PD8 Tony Stewart 4.00 10.00
PD9 Rusty Wallace 3.00 8.00

2002 Press Pass Premium Race Used Firesuit Drivers

Inserted at a stated rate of one in 480 hobby packs, these 12 cards feature swatches of race-used firesuits. Each of these cards were issued to a stated print run of 80 serial numbered sets.

*CARS/90: .3X TO .8X DRIVERS/80
FD1 Jeff Gordon 20.00 50.00
FD2 Mark Martin 15.00 40.00
FD3 Matt Kenseth 15.00 40.00
FD4 Bobby Labonte 15.00 40.00
FD5 Dale Jarrett 15.00 40.00
FD6 Tony Stewart 20.00 50.00
FD7 Rusty Wallace 20.00 50.00
FD8 Terry Labonte 20.00 50.00
FD9 Sterling Marlin 15.00 40.00
FD10 Ken Schrader 12.00 30.00
FD11 Dale Earnhardt 60.00 150.00
FD12 Dale Earnhardt Jr. 25.00 60.00

2003 Press Pass Premium

This 81-card set was released in April, 2003. This set was issued in five card hobby or retail packs which came 24 packs to a hobby box and 28 packs to a retail box with an SRP of $3.99

per pack. Cards 51-68 were short printed and came in packs at a rate of one in three and cards 69-81 were also short printed and they were inserted at a rate of one in 12. In addition, a special card honoring Michael Waltrip's Daytona 500 win was inserted at approximately a one per case rate.

COMPLETE SET (81) 75.00 125.00
COMP.SET w/o SPs (50) 10.00 25.00
WAX BOX HOBBY (24) 60.00 100.00
WAX BOX RETAIL (28) 40.00 75.00
1 John Andretti .15 .40
2 Todd Bodine .15 .40
3 Jeff Burton .30 .75
4 Ward Burton .30 .75
5 Kurt Busch .50 1.25
6 Ricky Craven .15 .40
7 Dale Earnhardt Jr. 1.50 4.00
8 Jeff Gordon 1.25 3.00
9 Robby Gordon .15 .40
10 Jeff Green .15 .40
11 Kevin Harvick .75 2.00
12 Dale Jarrett .75 2.00
13 Jimmie Johnson 1.00 2.50
14 Matt Kenseth 1.00 2.50
15 Bobby Labonte .75 2.00
16 Terry Labonte .50 1.25
17 Sterling Marlin .50 1.25
18 Mark Martin 1.00 2.50
19 Jerry Nadeau .30 .75
20 Joe Nemechek .15 .40
21 Ryan Newman 1.00 2.50
22 Steve Park .30 .75
23 Kyle Petty .30 .75
24 Ricky Rudd .50 1.25
25 Elliott Sadler .30 .75
26 Mike Skinner .15 .40
27 Tony Stewart 1.00 2.50
28 Kenny Wallace .15 .40
29 Rusty Wallace .75 2.00
30 Michael Waltrip .30 .75
31 Greg Biffle CRC .30 .75
32 Jamie McMurray CRC .75 2.00
33 Casey Mears CRC .30 .75
34 Jeff Burton's Car .15 .40
35 Kurt Busch's Car .30 .75
36 Dale Earnhardt Jr.'s Car .60 1.50
37 Jeff Gordon's Car .50 1.25
38 Kevin Harvick's Car .30 .75
39 Dale Jarrett's Car .30 .75
40 Jimmie Johnson's Car .50 1.25
41 Elliott Sadler's Car .15 .40
42 Matt Kenseth's Car .50 1.25
43 Mark Martin's Car .50 1.25
44 Michael Waltrip's Car .15 .40
45 Greg Biffle's Car .10 .30
46 Dale Earnhardt Jr. 1.50 4.00
47 Robby Gordon .15 .40
48 Dale Earnhardt Jr. 1.50 4.00
49 Jeff Green .15 .40
50 Dale Jr. 1.50 4.00
Park
Waltrip CL
51 Terry Labonte CC 1.00 2.50
52 Rusty Wallace CC 1.50 4.00
53 Jeff Gordon CC 2.50 6.00
54 Dale Jarrett CC 1.50 4.00
55 Bobby Labonte CC 1.50 4.00
56 Tony Stewart CC 2.00 5.00
57 Jeff Burton CC .50 1.25
58 Kurt Busch CC 1.00 2.50
59 Dale Earnhardt Jr. CC 3.00 8.00
60 Kevin Harvick CC 1.50 4.00
61 Jimmie Johnson CC 3.00 8.00
62 Matt Kenseth CC 2.50 6.00
63 Sterling Marlin CC 1.00 2.50
64 Mark Martin CC 2.00 5.00
65 Ryan Newman CC 3.00 8.00
66 Steve Park CC .50 1.25
67 Ward Burton CC .50 1.25
68 Michael Waltrip CC .50 1.25
69 Kurt Busch PC 1.50 4.00
70 Dale Earnhardt Jr.PC 5.00 12.00
71 Jeff Gordon PC 4.00 10.00
72 Dale Jarrett PC 2.50 6.00
73 Jimmie Johnson PC 3.00 8.00
74 Bobby Labonte PC 2.50 6.00
75 Mark Martin PC 3.00 8.00
76 Ryan Newman PC 3.00 8.00
77 Steve Park PC 1.00 2.50
78 Tony Stewart PC 3.00 8.00
79 Rusty Wallace PC 2.50 6.00
80 Michael Waltrip PC 1.00 2.50
81 Jeff Burton PC 1.00 2.50
0 Michael Waltrip 8.00 20.00

2003 Press Pass Premium Red Reflectors

COMP.SET w/o SPs (50) 20.00 50.00
*RED REFLECT.1-50: .8X TO 2X BASE CARD HI
*RED REFLECT.51-68: 1X TO 2.5X BASE CARD
*RED REFLECT.69-81: 1X TO 2.5X BASE CARD

2003 Press Pass Premium Samples

*SINGLES: 2X TO 5X BASE CARD HI

2003 Press Pass Premium Hot Threads Drivers Autographs

Randomly inserted in hobby packs, these 9 cards feature race-used swatches of driver's firesuits along with a signature of the corresponding driver. These cards were limited and hand numbered to the driver's door number. Some cards are not priced due to scarcity.

STATED PRINT RUN 2-48
*CARS: .4X TO 1X DRIVERS
HTTBL Bobby Labonte/18 60.00 120.00
HTTJG Jeff Gordon/24 175.00 350.00
HTTJJ Jimmie Johnson/48 75.00 150.00
HTTKH Kevin Harvick/29 75.00 150.00
HTTMK Matt Kenseth/17
HTTMM Mark Martin/6
HTTRN Ryan Newman/12
HTTRW Rusty Wallace/2
HTTTL Terry Labonte/5

2003 Press Pass Premium Hot Threads Drivers

Inserted at a stated rate of one in 72 hobby packs, these 15 cards feature race-used swatches of driver's firesuits. Each of these cards were issued to a stated print run of 285 serial numbered sets with the exception of Ward Burton and Terry Labonte which only had 100 copies produced. Please note the premiums on the multi-color swatches.

*CAR/160: .4X TO 1X DRIVER/285
*CAR/475: .25X TO .6X DRIVER/100
HTD0 Dale Earnhardt/285 25.00 60.00
HTD1 Jeff Gordon/285 12.00 30.00
HTD2 Ryan Newman/285 6.00 15.00
HTD3 Kevin Harvick/285 8.00 20.00
HTD4 Jimmie Johnson/285 10.00 25.00
HTD5 Rusty Wallace/285 8.00 20.00
HTD6 Mark Martin/285 8.00 20.00
HTD7 Matt Kenseth/285 8.00 20.00
HTD8 Bobby Labonte/285 8.00 20.00
HTD9 Tony Stewart/285 10.00 25.00
HTD10 Dale Earnhardt Jr./285 12.00 30.00
HTD11 Dale Jarrett/285 8.00 20.00
HTD12 Sterling Marlin/285 6.00 15.00
HTD13 Ward Burton/100 8.00 20.00
HTD14 Terry Labonte/100 12.00 30.00

2003 Press Pass Premium In the Zone

Issued in packs at a stated rate of one in 12, these holofoil gold double-etched 12 cards feature information on how leading NASCAR drivers make it to the finish line.

COMPLETE SET (12) 20.00 40.00
IZ1 Dale Earnhardt Jr. 3.00 8.00
IZ2 Jeff Gordon 2.50 6.00
IZ3 Dale Jarrett 1.50 4.00
IZ4 Jimmie Johnson 2.00 5.00
IZ5 Matt Kenseth 2.00 5.00
IZ6 Mark Martin 2.00 5.00
IZ7 Ryan Newman 2.00 5.00
IZ8 Steve Park .60 1.50
IZ9 Ricky Rudd 1.00 2.50
IZ10 Tony Stewart 2.00 5.00
IZ11 Rusty Wallace 1.50 4.00
IZ12 Michael Waltrip .60 1.50

2003 Press Pass Premium Performance Driven

Issued at a stated rate of one in 24, these nine silver foil double-etched cards feature information on how NASCAR drivers are motivated to succeed.

COMPLETE SET (9) 20.00 50.00
PD1 Dale Earnhardt Jr. 5.00 12.00
PD2 Jeff Gordon 4.00 10.00
PD3 Jimmie Johnson 3.00 8.00
PD4 Mark Martin 3.00 8.00
PD5 Kurt Busch 1.50 4.00
PD6 Steve Park 1.00 2.50
PD7 Tony Stewart 3.00 8.00
PD8 Rusty Wallace 2.50 6.00
PD9 Michael Waltrip 1.00 2.50

2004 Press Pass Premium

This 81-card set was released in May, 2004. This set was issued in five card hobby or four card retail packs which came 20 packs to a hobby box and 24 packs to a retail box with an SRP of $3.99 per pack. Cards 51-69 were short printed and came in packs at a rate of one in three and cards 70-81 were also short printed and they were inserted at a rate of one in 10. In addition, a special card honoring Dale Earnhardt Jr.'s Daytona 500 win was inserted at approximately a one per case rate.

COMPLETE SET (81) 40.00 80.00
COMP.SET w/o SP's (50) 10.00 25.00
WAX BOX HOBBY (20) 60.00 120.00
WAX BOX RETAIL (24) 40.00 75.00
1 Dale Earnhardt Jr. 1.25 3.00
2 Tony Stewart .75 2.00
3 Kevin Harvick .75 2.00
4 Jimmie Johnson 1.00 2.50
5 Joe Nemechek .20 .50
6 Elliott Sadler .40 .75
7 Jeff Gordon 1.25 3.00
8 Matt Kenseth 1.00 2.50
9 Dale Jarrett .60 1.50
10 Bobby Labonte .60 1.50
11 Greg Biffle .40 .75
12 Casey Mears .40 .75
13 Kurt Busch .50 1.25
14 Ward Burton .40 .75
15 Ricky Rudd .50 1.25
16 Terry Labonte .50 1.25
17 Kyle Petty .40 .75
18 Ricky Craven .20 .50
19 Jeremy Mayfield .20 .50
20 Rusty Wallace .60 1.50
21 Ryan Newman 1.00 2.50
22 Jeff Green .20 .50
23 Robby Gordon .20 .50
24 Jamie McMurray .50 1.25
25 Sterling Marlin .50 1.25
26 Michael Waltrip .40 .75
27 Ken Schrader .20 .50
28 Jeff Burton .40 .75
29 Mark Martin .75 2.00
30 Kevin Lepage .20 .50
31 Brendan Gaughan CRC .40 .75
32 Kasey Kahne CRC 1.50 4.00
33 Scott Riggs CRC .40 .75
34 Johnny Sauter .40 .75
35 Brian Vickers CRC .60 1.50
36 Scott Wimmer CRC .40 .75
37 Rusty Wallace's Car .40 .75
38 Mark Martin's Car .40 .75
39 Dale Earnhardt Jr's Car .50 1.25
40 Michael Waltrip's Car .20 .50
41 Matt Kenseth's Car .50 1.25
42 Jeff Gordon's Car .50 1.25
43 Kevin Harvick's Car .40 .75
44 Jimmie Johnson's Car .50 1.25
45 Kurt Busch's Car .20 .50
46 Dale Earnhardt Jr. NS 1.25 3.00
47 Elliott Sadler NS .40 .75
48 Dale Jarrett NS .60 1.50
49 Greg Biffle NS .40 .75
50 Tony Stewart CL .75 2.00
51 Terry Labonte CC 1.00 2.50
52 Rusty Wallace CC 1.25 3.00
53 Jeff Gordon CC 2.50 6.00
54 Dale Jarrett CC 1.25 3.00
55 Bobby Labonte CC 1.25 3.00
56 Tony Stewart CC 1.50 4.00
57 Matt Kenseth CC 2.00 5.00
58 Jimmie Johnson CC 2.00 5.00
59 Dale Earnhardt Jr. CC 2.50 6.00
60 Kevin Harvick CC 1.50 4.00
61 Ryan Newman CC 2.00 5.00
62 Jeff Burton CC .60 1.50
63 Jamie McMurray CC 1.00 2.50
64 Michael Waltrip CC .60 1.50
65 Robby Gordon CC .40 1.00
66 Elliott Sadler CC .60 1.50
67 Sterling Marlin CC 1.00 2.50
68 Greg Biffle CC .60 1.50
69 Ward Burton CC .60 1.50
70 Michael Waltrip PC 1.25 3.00
71 Rusty Wallace PC 2.00 5.00
72 Tony Stewart PC 2.50 6.00
73 Bobby Labonte PC 2.00 5.00
74 Matt Kenseth PC 3.00 8.00
75 Jimmie Johnson PC 3.00 8.00
76 Dale Jarrett PC 2.00 5.00
77 Kevin Harvick PC 2.50 6.00
78 Robby Gordon PC .75 2.00
79 Jeff Gordon PC 4.00 10.00
80 Dale Earnhardt Jr. PC 4.00 10.00
81 Kurt Busch PC 1.50 4.00
0 Dale Earnhardt Jr. Daytona 8.00 20.00

2004 Press Pass Premium Samples

*SAMPLES: 2X TO 5X BASIC

2004 Press Pass Premium Asphalt Jungle

This 6-card set featured some of racing's hottest drivers. The cards were designed to be viewed at a horizontal angle and they pictured the driver with his car in the background. They were inserted at a rate of 1 in 10 packs.

COMPLETE SET (6) 12.50 30.00
A1 Tony Stewart 2.00 5.00
A2 Jeff Gordon 3.00 8.00
A3 Ryan Newman 3.00 8.00
A4 Jimmie Johnson 3.00 8.00
A5 Dale Earnhardt Jr. 3.00 8.00
A6 Kevin Harvick 2.00 5.00

2004 Press Pass Premium Hot Threads Autographs

This 9-card set was available in packs of 2004 Press Pass Premium. Each card had a swatch of a race-used firesuit and a signature from the corresponding driver. The cards were serial numbered to the driver's door number. There was a late addition to the set. Dale Earnhardt Jr. was only available in packs of 2006 Press Pass Legends.

HTDE Dale Earnhardt Jr./8
HTJG Jeff Gordon/24 175.00 350.00
HTJJ Jimmie Johnson/48 75.00 150.00
HTKH Kevin Harvick/29 75.00 150.00
HTMK Matt Kenseth/17
HTMM Mark Martin/6
HTRN Ryan Newman/12
HTRW Rusty Wallace/2
HTTS Tony Stewart/20 125.00 200.00

2004 Press Pass Premium Hot Threads Drivers Bronze

Randomly inserted into hobby packs, these 16 cards feature race-used swatches of driver's firesuits. Each of these cards was issued to a stated print run of 125 serial numbered sets. These cards also had the word "Bronze" on the front to distinguish the level. Please note there was also a retail version of the Bronze level. The difference between them was the driver's car number ghosted in the background behind the swatch on the retail version.

*RETAIL/125: .4X TO 1X BRONZE/125
*GOLD/50: .6X TO 1.5X BRONZE/125
*SILVER/75: .5X TO 1.2X BRONZE/125
HTD1 Jimmie Johnson 10.00 25.00
HTD2 Matt Kenseth 6.00 15.00
HTD3 Kevin Harvick 8.00 20.00
HTD4 Jeff Gordon 15.00 40.00
HTD5 Kurt Busch 5.00 12.00
HTD6 Mark Martin 6.00 15.00
HTD7 Ryan Newman 5.00 12.00
HTD8 Bobby Labonte 6.00 15.00
HTD9 Rusty Wallace 6.00 15.00
HTD10 Tony Stewart 10.00 25.00
HTD11 Dale Earnhardt Jr. 12.00 30.00
HTD12 Dale Jarrett 6.00 15.00
HTD13 Sterling Marlin 6.00 15.00
HTD14 Terry Labonte 6.00 15.00
HTD15 Michael Waltrip 6.00 15.00
HTD16 Dale Earnhardt 30.00 80.00

2004 Press Pass Premium In the Zone

This 6-card set featured some of racing's hottest drivers. The card fronts featured an image of the driver and had gold holofoil highlights. They were inserted at a rate of 1 in 6 packs. There was also a serial numbered parallel set.

COMPLETE SET (12) 12.50 30.00
IZ1 Bobby Labonte 1.50 4.00
IZ2 Dale Earnhardt Jr. 3.00 8.00
IZ3 Dale Jarrett 1.50 4.00
IZ4 Jeff Gordon 3.00 8.00
IZ5 Jimmie Johnson 2.50 6.00
IZ6 Terry Labonte 1.25 3.00
IZ7 Matt Kenseth 2.50 6.00
IZ8 Michael Waltrip 1.00 2.50
IZ9 Ricky Rudd 1.25 3.00
IZ10 Rusty Wallace 1.50 4.00
IZ11 Ryan Newman 2.50 6.00
IZ12 Tony Stewart 2.00 5.00

2004 Press Pass Premium Performance Driven

This 9-card set featured some of racing's hottest drivers. The card fronts featured an image of the driver and his car with silver holofoil highlights. They were inserted at a rate of 1 in 20 packs.

COMPLETE SET (9) 15.00 40.00
PD1 Tony Stewart 4.00 10.00
PD2 Ryan Newman 5.00 12.00
PD3 Rusty Wallace 3.00 8.00
PD4 Ricky Rudd 2.50 6.00
PD5 Kurt Busch 2.50 6.00
PD6 Jimmie Johnson 5.00 12.00
PD7 Jeff Gordon 6.00 15.00
PD8 Dale Jarrett 3.00 8.00
PD9 Dale Earnhardt Jr. 6.00 15.00

2005 Press Pass Premium

This 81-card set was released in May, 2005. This set was issued in five card hobby or four card retail packs which came 20 packs to a hobby box and 24 packs to a retail box with an SRP of $3.99 per pack. Cards 51-69 were short printed and came in packs at a rate of one in three and cards 70-81 were also short printed and they were inserted at a rate of one in 10. In addition, a special card honoring Jeff Gordon's Daytona 500 win was inserted at a rate of approximately one per case.

COMP.SET w/o SPs (1-50) 15.00 40.00
WAX BOX HOBBY (20) 50.00 80.00
WAX BOX RETAIL (24) 35.00 60.00
1 John Andretti .25 .60
2 Greg Biffle .40 1.00
3 Jeff Burton .40 1.00
4 Kurt Busch .60 1.50
5 Dale Earnhardt Jr. 1.50 4.00
6 Carl Edwards CRC 1.25 3.00
7 Jeff Gordon 1.50 4.00
8 Jeff Green .25 .60
9 Kevin Harvick 1.00 2.50
10 Dale Jarrett .75 2.00
11 Jimmie Johnson 1.25 3.00
12 Kasey Kahne 1.50 4.00
13 Matt Kenseth 1.25 3.00
14 Bobby Labonte .75 2.00
15 Terry Labonte .60 1.50
16 Jason Leffler .25 .60
17 Kevin Lepage .25 .60
18 Sterling Marlin .60 1.50
19 Mark Martin 1.00 2.50
20 Jeremy Mayfield .25 .60
21 Jamie McMurray .60 1.50
22 Casey Mears .60 1.50
23 Joe Nemechek .25 .60
24 Ryan Newman 1.25 3.00
25 Kyle Petty .40 1.00
26 Scott Riggs .40 1.00
27 Ricky Rudd .60 1.50
28 Elliott Sadler .40 1.00
29 Ken Schrader .25 .60
30 Tony Stewart 1.00 2.50
31 Brian Vickers .75 2.00
32 Rusty Wallace .75 2.00
33 Michael Waltrip .40 1.00
34 Scott Wimmer .40 1.00
35 Kyle Busch CRC 1.00 2.50
36 Travis Kvapil CRC .25 .60
37 Kurt Busch's Car M .25 .60
38 Jimmie Johnson's Car M .40 1.00
39 Rusty Wallace's Car M .25 .60
40 Jeff Gordon's Car M .60 1.50
41 Tony Stewart's Car M .25 .60
42 Michael Waltrip's Car M .25 .60
43 Kevin Harvick's Car M .25 .60
44 Dale Jarrett's Car M .75 2.00
45 Robby Gordon's Car M .25 .60
46 Tony Stewart S 1.00 2.50
47 Michael Waltrip S .40 1.00
48 Jimmie Johnson S 1.25 3.00
49 Dale Jarrett S .75 2.00
50 Tony Stewart CL 1.00 2.50
51 Terry Labonte CC 2.00 5.00
52 Rusty Wallace CC 2.50 6.00
53 Jeff Gordon CC 5.00 12.00
54 Dale Jarrett CC 2.50 6.00
55 Bobby Labonte CC 2.50 6.00
56 Tony Stewart CC 3.00 8.00
57 Matt Kenseth CC 4.00 10.00
58 Kurt Busch CC 2.00 5.00
59 Jimmie Johnson CC 4.00 10.00
60 Mark Martin CC 3.00 8.00
61 Dale Earnhardt Jr. CC 5.00 12.00
62 Ryan Newman CC 4.00 10.00
63 Jeremy Mayfield CC .75 2.00
64 Jamie McMurray CC 2.00 5.00
65 Kasey Kahne CC 5.00 12.00
66 Kevin Harvick CC 3.00 8.00
67 Joe Nemechek CC .75 2.00
68 Ricky Rudd CC 2.00 5.00
69 Jeff Burton CC 1.25 3.00
70 Jeff Burton PC 1.50 4.00
71 Dale Earnhardt Jr. PC 6.00 15.00
72 Jeff Gordon PC 6.00 15.00
73 Ryan Newman PC 5.00 12.00
74 Jimmie Johnson PC 5.00 12.00
75 Ricky Rudd PC 2.50 6.00
76 Bobby Labonte PC 3.00 8.00
77 Mark Martin PC 4.00 10.00
78 Kevin Harvick PC 4.00 10.00
79 Tony Stewart PC 4.00 10.00
80 Rusty Wallace PC 3.00 8.00
81 Kurt Busch PC 2.50 6.00
0 Jeff Gordon Daytona 8.00 20.00
LEG1 Davey Allison Promo 3.00 8.00

2005 Press Pass Premium Samples

COMPLETE SET (50) 75.00 150.00
*SAMPLES: 1.5X TO 4X BASE

2005 Press Pass Premium Asphalt Jungle

COMPLETE SET (6) 15.00 30.00
AJ1 Jimmie Johnson 2.50 6.00
AJ2 Mark Martin 2.00 5.00
AJ3 Jeff Gordon 3.00 8.00
AJ4 Bobby Labonte 1.50 4.00
AJ5 Tony Stewart 2.00 5.00
AJ6 Rusty Wallace 1.50 4.00

2005 Press Pass Premium Hot Threads Autographs

STATED PRINT RUN 2-48
HTBL Bobby Labonte/18 75.00 150.00
HTBV Brian Vickers/25 60.00 120.00
HTDE Dale Earnhardt Jr./8
HTJG Jeff Gordon/24 175.00 350.00
HTJJ Jimmie Johnson/48 75.00 150.00
HTKK Kasey Kahne/9
HTMK Matt Kenseth/17
HTRW Rusty Wallace/2
HTTL Terry Labonte/5
HTTS Tony Stewart/20 125.00 200.00

2005 Press Pass Premium Hot Threads Drivers

*CARS/85: .5X TO 1.2X DRIVERS/275
HTD1 Kurt Busch 2.50 6.00
HTD2 Jimmie Johnson 5.00 12.00
HTD3 Jeff Gordon 6.00 15.00
HTD4 Dale Earnhardt Jr. 6.00 15.00
HTD5 Tony Stewart 5.00 12.00
HTD6 Ryan Newman 2.50 6.00
HTD7 Matt Kenseth 3.00 8.00
HTD8 Kevin Harvick 4.00 10.00
HTD9 Bobby Labonte 3.00 8.00
HTD10 Rusty Wallace 3.00 8.00
HTD11 Dale Jarrett 3.00 8.00
HTD12 Terry Labonte 3.00 8.00
HTD13 Michael Waltrip 3.00 8.00
HTD14 Sterling Marlin 3.00 8.00

2005 Press Pass Premium In the Zone

COMPLETE SET (12) 15.00 30.00
*ELITE EDIT/250: 1X TO 2.5X IN THE ZONE
IZ1 Michael Waltrip .75 2.00
IZ2 Rusty Wallace 1.50 4.00
IZ3 Tony Stewart 2.00 5.00
IZ4 Ryan Newman 2.50 6.00
IZ5 Jeff Burton .75 2.00
IZ6 Kevin Harvick 2.00 5.00
IZ7 Jimmie Johnson 2.50 6.00
IZ8 Dale Jarrett 1.50 4.00
IZ9 Jeff Gordon 3.00 8.00
IZ10 Dale Earnhardt Jr. 3.00 8.00
IZ11 Matt Kenseth 2.50 6.00
IZ12 Bobby Labonte 1.50 4.00

2005 Press Pass Premium Performance Driven

COMPLETE SET (9) 25.00 50.00
PD1 Dale Earnhardt Jr. 5.00 12.00
PD2 Dale Jarrett 2.50 6.00
PD3 Kevin Harvick 3.00 8.00
PD4 Jeff Gordon 5.00 12.00
PD5 Jimmie Johnson 4.00 10.00
PD6 Bobby Labonte 2.50 6.00
PD7 Jeff Burton 1.25 3.00
PD8 Rusty Wallace 2.50 6.00
PD9 Tony Stewart 3.00 8.00

2006 Press Pass Premium

This 81-card set was released in May, 2005. This set was issued in five card hobby or four card retail packs which came 20 packs to a hobby box and 24 packs to a retail box with an SRP of $3.99 per pack. Cards 53-71 were short printed and came in packs at a rate of one in three and cards 72-83 were also short printed and they were inserted at a rate of one in 10. In addition, a special card honoring Jimmie Johnson's Daytona 500 win was inserted at a rate of approximately one per case.

COMPLETE SET (83) 90.00 150.00
COMP.SET w/o SPs (45) 10.00 25.00
WAX BOX HOBBY (20) 60.00 90.00
WAX BOX RETAIL (24) 50.00 80.00
1 Greg Biffle .40 1.00
2 Dave Blaney .30 .75
3 Jeff Burton .40 1.00
4 Kurt Busch .40 1.00
5 Kyle Busch .60 1.50
6 Dale Earnhardt Jr. 1.00 2.50
7 Carl Edwards .50 1.25
8 Jeff Gordon 1.00 2.50
9 Jeff Green .30 .75
10 Kevin Harvick .60 1.50
11 Dale Jarrett .50 1.25
12 Jimmie Johnson .75 2.00
13 Kasey Kahne .60 1.50
14 Matt Kenseth .50 1.25
15 Bobby Labonte .50 1.25
16 Terry Labonte .50 1.25
17 Sterling Marlin .50 1.25
18 Mark Martin .50 1.25
19 Jeremy Mayfield .30 .75
20 Casey Mears .30 .75
21 Joe Nemechek .30 .75
22 Ryan Newman .40 1.00
23 Kyle Petty .40 1.00
24 Tony Raines .30 .75
25 Scott Riggs .40 1.00
26 Elliott Sadler .30 .75
27 Ken Schrader .30 .75
28 Tony Stewart .75 2.00
29 Brian Vickers .30 .75
30 Clint Bowyer CRC 4.00 10.00
31 Denny Hamlin CRC 8.00 20.00
32 Brent Sherman RC 2.50 6.00
33 Reed Sorenson CRC 3.00 8.00
34 David Stremme CRC 2.50 6.00
35 Martin Truex Jr. CRC 3.00 8.00
36 J.J. Yeley CRC 3.00 8.00
37 Jeff Gordon's Car M .40 1.00
38 Jeff Burton's Car M .15 .40
39 Matt Kenseth's Car M .20 .50

40 Greg Biffle's Car M .15 .40
41 Carl Edwards' Car M .20 .50
42 Dale Jarrett's Car M .20 .50
43 Mark Martin's Car M .20 .50
44 Kevin Harvick's Car M .25 .60
45 Jimmie Johnson's Car M .30 .75
46 Mark Martin NS .50 1.25
47 Tony Stewart NS .75 2.00
48 Jeff Gordon NS 1.00 2.50
49 Elliott Sadler NS .30 .75
50 Denny Hamlin NS 2.00 5.00
51 Jeff Burton NS .40 1.00
52 M.Truex 1.00 2.50
C.Bowyer
R.Sorenson CL
53 Bobby Labonte CC 1.00 2.50
54 Dale Jarrett CC 1.00 2.50
55 Tony Stewart CC 1.50 4.00
56 Kurt Busch CC .75 2.00
57 Jeff Gordon CC 2.00 5.00
58 Matt Kenseth CC 1.00 2.50
59 Terry Labonte CC 1.00 2.50
60 Carl Edwards C 1.00 2.50
61 Jimmie Johnson C 1.50 4.00
62 Kasey Kahne C 1.25 3.00
63 Dale Earnhardt Jr. C 2.00 5.00
64 Greg Biffle C .75 2.00
65 Mark Martin C 1.00 2.50
66 Jeff Burton C .75 2.00
67 Kyle Busch C 1.25 3.00
68 Kevin Harvick C 1.25 3.00
69 Casey Mears C .60 1.50
70 Sterling Marlin C 1.00 2.50
71 Elliott Sadler C .60 1.50
72 Mark Martin PC 1.50 4.00
73 Jimmie Johnson PC 2.50 6.00
74 Martin Truex Jr. PC 2.50 6.00
75 Tony Stewart PC 2.50 6.00
76 Jeff Gordon PC 3.00 8.00
77 Dale Jarrett PC 1.50 4.00
78 Ryan Newman PC 1.25 3.00
79 Carl Edwards PC 1.50 4.00
80 Dale Earnhardt Jr. PC 3.00 8.00
81 Matt Kenseth PC 1.50 4.00
82 Kasey Kahne PC 2.00 5.00
83 Jeff Burton PC 1.25 3.00
0 Jimmie Johnson Daytona 6.00 15.00

2006 Press Pass Premium Asphalt Jungle

COMPLETE SET (6) 10.00 25.00
STATED ODDS 1:9
AJ1 Dale Earnhardt Jr. 1.25 3.00
AJ2 Mark Martin .60 1.50
AJ3 Jeff Gordon 1.25 3.00
AJ4 Tony Stewart 1.00 2.50
AJ5 Jimmie Johnson 1.00 2.50
AJ6 Dale Jarrett .60 1.50

2006 Press Pass Premium Hot Threads Autographs

STATED PRINT RUN 2-48
HTJJ Jimmie Johnson/48 75.00 150.00
HTKH Kevin Harvick/29 50.00 120.00
HTTS Tony Stewart/20 100.00 200.00

2006 Press Pass Premium Hot Threads Drivers

*CARS/165: .4X TO 1X DRIVERS
HTD1 Tony Stewart 20.00 50.00
HTD2 Matt Kenseth 15.00 40.00
HTD3 Dale Earnhardt Jr. 25.00 60.00
HTD4 Carl Edwards 15.00 40.00
HTD5 Jimmie Johnson 20.00 50.00
HTD6 Kevin Harvick 10.00 25.00
HTD7 Dale Jarrett 12.00 30.00
HTD8 Kasey Kahne 20.00 50.00
HTD9 Terry Labonte 8.00 20.00
HTD10 Ryan Newman 15.00 40.00
HTD11 Jeff Gordon 40.00 80.00
HTD12 Denny Hamlin 25.00 60.00
HTD13 Brian Vickers 12.50 30.00
HTD14 Kyle Busch 15.00 40.00
HTD15 Reed Sorenson 6.00 15.00

2006 Press Pass Premium In the Zone

COMPLETE SET (12) 15.00 40.00
*RED/250: X TO X BASIC INSERTS
IZ1 Dale Earnhardt Jr. 2.00 5.00
IZ2 Carl Edwards 1.00 2.50
IZ3 Dale Jarrett 1.00 2.50
IZ4 Tony Stewart 1.50 4.00
IZ5 Matt Kenseth 1.00 2.50
IZ6 Kurt Busch .75 2.00
IZ7 Jimmie Johnson 1.50 4.00
IZ8 Kevin Harvick 1.25 3.00
IZ9 Martin Truex Jr. 1.50 4.00
IZ10 Jeff Gordon 2.00 5.00
IZ11 Mark Martin 1.00 2.50
IZ12 Bobby Labonte 1.00 2.50

2007 Press Pass Premium

This 81-card set was released in April, 2007. This set was issued in five card hobby or four card retail packs which came 20 packs to a hobby box with an SRP of $4.99 per pack and 24 packs to a retail box with an SRP of $2.99 per pack. Cards 71-76, Daytona Dominators, were short-printed and inserted at a rate of one in three packs. Cards 77-82, Fan Favorites, were short-printed and inserted in packs at a rate of one in 10 packs. The RCs and CRCs, 83-90, were also short-printed and inserted into packs at a rate of one in 20 packs. In addition, a special card honoring Kevin Harvick's Daytona 500 win was inserted at a rate of one in 60 packs. A 2007 Press Pass Stealth Chrome preview card of Juan Pablo Montoya was also inserted as a box topper in every hobby box.

COMPLETE SET (90) 40.00 100.00
COMP.SET W/O SPs (70) 15.00 40.00
WAX BOX HOBBY (20) 60.00 100.00
WAX BOX RETAIL (24) 50.00 75.00
1 Jimmie Johnson CL .40 1.00
2 Mark Martin .25 .60
3 Clint Bowyer .25 .60
4 Martin Truex Jr. .20 .50
5 Kurt Busch .20 .50
6 Kyle Busch .30 .75
7 Dale Earnhardt Jr. .50 1.25
8 Kasey Kahne .25 .60
9 Scott Riggs .20 .50
10 Denny Hamlin .30 .75
11 Ryan Newman .20 .50
12 Joe Nemechek .15 .40
13 Sterling Marlin .25 .60
14 Greg Biffle .20 .50
15 Matt Kenseth .25 .60
16 J.J. Yeley .25 .60
17 Elliott Sadler .15 .40
18 Tony Stewart .40 1.00
19 Ken Schrader .15 .40
20 Dave Blaney .15 .40
21 Jeff Gordon .50 1.25
22 Casey Mears .15 .40
23 Kevin Harvick .30 .75
24 Jeff Burton .20 .50
25 David Stremme .15 .40
26 Reed Sorenson .15 .40
27 Bobby Labonte .25 .60
28 Dale Jarrett .25 .60
29 Kyle Petty .20 .50
30 Jimmie Johnson .40 1.00
31 Jeff Green .15 .40
32 Brian Vickers .25 .60
33 Carl Edwards .25 .60
34 Kasey Kahne's Car M .25 .60
35 Jeff Gordon's Car M .50 1.25
36 Kevin Harvick's Car M .30 .75
37 Tony Stewart's Car M .40 1.00
38 Kurt Busch's Car M .20 .50
39 Denny Hamlin's Car M .30 .75
40 Reed Sorenson's Car M .15 .40
41 Dale Jarrett's Car M .25 .60
42 Matt Kenseth's Car M .25 .60
43 Martin Truex Jr.'s Car M .20 .50
44 Carl Edwards' Car M .25 .60
45 Jimmie Johnson's Car M .40 1.00
46 Tony Stewart SW .40 1.00
47 D.Gilliland .40 1.00
R.Rudd SW
48 Tony Stewart SW .40 1.00
49 Jeff Gordon SW .50 1.25
50 Jack Sprague SW .15 .40
51 Kevin Harvick SW .30 .75
52 Dale Earnhardt Jr. RTTC .50 1.25
53 Denny Hamlin RTTC .30 .75
54 Tony Stewart RTTC .40 1.00
55 Carl Edwards RTTC .25 .60
56 Matt Kenseth RTTC .25 .60
57 Jeff Gordon RTTC .50 1.25
58 Kasey Kahne RTTC .25 .60
59 Jimmie Johnson RTTC .40 1.00
60 Greg Biffle RTTC .20 .50
61 Elliott Sadler RTTC .15 .40
62 Jimmie Johnson MD .40 1.00
63 Joe Nemechek MD .15 .40
64 Kyle Petty MD .20 .50
65 Dale Earnhardt Jr. MD .50 1.25
66 D.Stremme .25 .60
J.Yeley MD
67 Tony Stewart MD .40 1.00
68 Mark Martin MD .25 .60
69 Jeff Gordon MD .50 1.25
70 J.J. Yeley MD .25 .60
71 Jimmie Johnson DD .60 1.50
72 Jeff Gordon DD .75 2.00
73 Dale Earnhardt Jr. DD .75 2.00
74 Dale Jarrett DD .40 1.00
75 Michael Waltrip DD .40 1.00
76 Tony Stewart DD .60 1.50
77 Dale Earnhardt Jr. FF 1.00 2.50
78 Jeff Gordon FF 1.00 2.50
79 Kasey Kahne FF .50 1.25
80 Tony Stewart FF .75 2.00
81 Mark Martin FF .50 1.25
82 Jimmie Johnson FF .75 2.00
83 A.J. Allmendinger RD RC 2.00 5.00
84 David Gilliland RD RC 1.50 4.00
85 Paul Menard RD CRC 3.00 8.00
86 Juan Pablo Montoya RD RC 3.00 8.00
87 David Ragan RD CRC 2.00 5.00
88 David Reutimann RD RC 1.25 3.00
89 Regan Smith RD CRC 2.00 5.00
90 Jon Wood RD CRC 1.00 2.50
0 Kevin Harvick Daytona 4.00 10.00
P1 Juan Pablo Montoya Stealth 8.00 20.00
NNO Press Pass Inc. .10 .25

2007 Press Pass Premium Red

*R1-R70 RED/15: 8X TO 20X BASIC CARDS
STATED PRINT RUN 15 SERIAL #'d SETS
UNPRICED R71-R90 PRINT RUN 5

2007 Press Pass Premium Concrete Chaos

This 6-card set was inserted into packs of 2007 Press Pass Premium at a rate of one in nine. The card numbers had a "CC" prefix.

COMPLETE SET (6) 10.00 25.00
CC1 Jeff Gordon 1.25 3.00
CC2 Dale Earnhardt Jr. 1.25 3.00
CC3 Jimmie Johnson 1.00 2.50
CC4 Tony Stewart 1.00 2.50
CC5 Dale Jarrett .60 1.50
CC6 Mark Martin .60 1.50

2007 Press Pass Premium Hot Threads Autographs

STATED PRINT RUN 2-48
HTBL Bobby Labonte/43 50.00 100.00
HTJG Jeff Gordon/24 175.00 350.00
HTJJ Jimmie Johnson/48 75.00 150.00
HTMK Matt Kenseth/17 75.00 150.00
HTTS Tony Stewart/20 50.00 100.00

2007 Press Pass Premium Hot Threads Drivers

This 16-card set was randomly inserted into packs of 2007 Press Pass Premium. Each card has a swatch of the corresponding driver's race-worn firesuit.The cards were serial numbered to 145 and they were highlighted with silver foil.

STATED ODDS 1:40
STATED PRINT RUN 145 SERIAL #'d SETS
*TEAM/160: .3X TO .8X DRIVER/145
*PATCH/20: 1.5X TO 4X BASIC THREAD
HTD1 Kasey Kahne 4.00 10.00
HTD2 Martin Truex Jr. 3.00 8.00
HTD3 Ryan Newman 3.00 8.00
HTD4 Reed Sorenson 2.50 6.00
HTD5 Tony Stewart 6.00 15.00
HTD6 Denny Hamlin 5.00 12.00
HTD7 Kurt Busch 3.00 8.00
HTD8 Jeff Gordon 10.00 25.00
HTD9 Bobby Labonte 4.00 10.00
HTD10 J.J. Yeley 4.00 10.00
HTD11 Dale Earnhardt Jr. 8.00 20.00
HTD12 Matt Kenseth 4.00 10.00
HTD13 Kyle Busch 5.00 12.00
HTD14 Carl Edwards 4.00 10.00
HTD15 Jimmie Johnson 6.00 15.00
HTD16 Juan Pablo Montoya 6.00 15.00

2007 Press Pass Premium Performance Driven

This 12-card set was inserted into packs of 2007 Press Pass Premium at a rate of one in five packs. The cards carried a "PD" prefix for their card numbering. This set had a hobby only parallel whichg was serial numbered to 250.

COMPLETE SET (12) 15.00 40.00
*RED/250: .6X TO 1.5X BASIC INSERTS
PD1 Bobby Labonte .75 2.00
PD2 Kasey Kahne .75 2.00
PD3 Dale Earnhardt Jr. 1.50 4.00
PD4 Denny Hamlin 1.00 2.50
PD5 Michael Waltrip .75 2.00
PD6 Jimmie Johnson 1.25 3.00
PD7 Kurt Busch .60 1.50
PD8 Tony Stewart 1.25 3.00
PD9 Dale Jarrett .75 2.00
PD10 Jeff Gordon 1.50 4.00
PD11 Mark Martin .75 2.00
PD12 Juan Pablo Montoya 2.50 6.00

2008 Press Pass Premium

COMPLETE SET (90) 30.00 60.00
COMP.SET w/o SP's (72) 10.00 25.00
ROOKIE DEBUT STATED ODDS 1:20
WAX BOX HOBBY (20) 75.00 100.00
WAX BOX RETAIL (24) 50.00 75.00
1 Dale Earnhardt Jr. CL .75 2.00
2 Regan Smith .30 .75
3 Clint Bowyer .40 1.00
4 Martin Truex Jr. .30 .75
5 Kurt Busch .30 .75
6 Casey Mears .25 .60
7 David Ragan .30 .75
8 Mark Martin .40 1.00
9 Kasey Kahne .40 1.00
10 Denny Hamlin .50 1.25
11 Ryan Newman .30 .75
12 Paul Menard .25 .60
13 Greg Biffle .30 .75
14 Matt Kenseth .40 1.00
15 Kyle Busch .50 1.25
16 Elliott Sadler .25 .60
17 Tony Stewart .60 1.50
18 Dave Blaney .25 .60
19 Jeff Gordon .75 2.00
20 Jamie McMurray .40 1.00
21 Travis Kvapil .25 .60
22 Kevin Harvick .50 1.25
23 Jeff Burton .30 .75
24 David Gilliland .25 .60
25 Reed Sorenson .25 .60
26 Juan Pablo Montoya .60 1.50
27 Bobby Labonte .40 1.00
28 Dale Jarrett .40 1.00
29 Jimmie Johnson .60 1.50
30 Michael Waltrip .40 1.00
31 Scott Riggs .30 .75
32 Brian Vickers .25 .60
33 A.J. Allmendinger .40 1.00
34 Dale Earnhardt Jr. .75 2.00
35 J.J. Yeley .40 1.00
36 Carl Edwards .40 1.00
37 Dale Earnhardt Jr.'s Car M .30 .75
38 Kevin Harvick's Car M .20 .50
39 Michael Waltrip's Car M .15 .40
40 Martin Truex Jr.'s Car M .12 .30
41 Jimmie Johnson's Car M .25 .60
42 Denny Hamlin's Car M .20 .50
43 Jeff Gordon's Car M .30 .75
44 Kyle Busch's Car M .20 .50
45 Juan Pablo Montoya's Car M .25 .60
46 Mark Martin's Car M .15 .40
47 Tony Stewart's Car M .25 .60
48 Dale Jarrett's Car M .15 .40
49 D.Earnhardt Jr. SW Shootout .75 2.00
50 J.Johnson SW .60 1.50
51 D.Earnhardt Jr. SW Duel .75 2.00
52 D.Hamlin SW .50 1.25
53 T.Stewart SW .60 1.50
54 Kurt Busch EOP .30 .75
55 Jimmie Johnson EOP .60 1.50
56 Carl Edwards EOP .40 1.00
57 Dale Earnhardt Jr. EOP .75 2.00
58 Matt Kenseth EOP .40 1.00
59 Jeff Gordon EOP .75 2.00
60 Kasey Kahne EOP .40 1.00
61 Tony Stewart EOP .60 1.50
62 Martin Truex Jr. EOP .30 .75
63 Kyle Busch EOP .50 1.25
64 Juan Pablo Montoya EOP .60 1.50
65 Denny Hamlin EOP .50 1.25
66 Kevin Harvick EOP .50 1.25
67 J.J. Yeley MD .40 1.00
68 Tony Stewart MD .60 1.50
69 Jimmie Johnson MD .60 1.50
70 Carl Edwards MD .40 1.00
71 Dale Earnhardt Jr. MD .75 2.00
72 Juan Pablo Montoya MD .60 1.50
73 Mark Martin F .60 1.50
74 Jimmie Johnson F 1.00 2.50
75 Dale Earnhardt Jr. F 1.25 3.00
76 Clint Bowyer F .60 1.50
77 Reed Sorenson F .60 1.50
78 Carl Edwards F .60 1.50
79 Jeff Gordon F 1.25 3.00
80 Kyle Busch F .75 2.00
81 Greg Biffle F .50 1.25
82 Jeff Gordon OD 2.00 5.00
83 Jimmie Johnson OD 1.50 4.00
84 Dale Earnhardt Jr. OD 2.00 5.00
85 Tony Stewart OD 1.50 4.00
86 Carl Edwards OD 1.00 2.50
87 Patrick Carpentier RD RC 5.00 12.00
88 Dario Franchitti RD RC 4.00 10.00
89 Sam Hornish Jr. RD CRC 4.00 10.00
90 Michael McDowell RD RC 4.00 10.00
0 Ryan Newman Daytona 6.00 15.00

2008 Press Pass Premium Clean Air

COMPLETE SET (12) 12.50 30.00
STATED ODDS 1:5
CA1 Jeff Gordon 1.00 2.50
CA2 Martin Truex Jr. .40 1.00
CA3 Michael Waltrip .50 1.25
CA4 Dale Earnhardt Jr. 1.00 2.50
CA5 Mark Martin .50 1.25
CA6 Kevin Harvick .60 1.50
CA7 Matt Kenseth .50 1.25
CA8 Kasey Kahne .50 1.25
CA9 Jeff Burton .40 1.00
CA10 Jimmie Johnson .75 2.00
CA11 Bobby Labonte .50 1.25
CA12 Tony Stewart .75 2.00

2008 Press Pass Premium Going Global

COMPLETE SET (6) 15.00 40.00
STATED ODDS 1:9
*RED/250: .8X TO 2X BASIC INSERTS
GG1 Dale Earnhardt Jr. 1.25 3.00
GG2 Patrick Carpentier .75 2.00
GG3 Tony Stewart 1.00 2.50
GG4 Juan Pablo Montoya 1.00 2.50
GG5 Jeff Gordon 1.25 3.00
GG6 Dario Franchitti 1.00 2.50

2008 Press Pass Premium Hot Threads Autographs

STATED PRINT RUN 1-55
HTJG Jeff Gordon/24 75.00 150.00
HTKH Kevin Harvick/29 50.00 100.00
HTMK Matt Kenseth/17 50.00 120.00
HTMW Michael Waltrip/55 30.00 80.00

2008 Press Pass Premium Hot Threads Drivers

STATED ODDS 1:40
STATED PRINT RUN 120 SERIAL #'d SETS
*TEAM/120: .4X TO 1X DRIVER/120
HTD1 Kevin Harvick 5.00 12.00
HTD2 Martin Truex Jr. 3.00 8.00
HTD3 Brian Vickers 2.50 6.00
HTD4 Jimmie Johnson 6.00 15.00
HTD5 Denny Hamlin 5.00 12.00
HTD6 Juan Pablo Montoya 6.00 15.00
HTD7 Dale Jarrett 4.00 10.00
HTD8 Carl Edwards 4.00 10.00
HTD9 Jeff Gordon 8.00 20.00
HTD10 Ryan Newman 3.00 8.00
HTD11 Dario Franchitti 6.00 15.00
HTD12 Kurt Busch 3.00 8.00
HTD13 Mark Martin 4.00 10.00
HTD14 Paul Menard 2.50 6.00
HTD15 Reed Sorenson 2.50 6.00
HTD16 Matt Kenseth 4.00 10.00
HTD17 Tony Stewart 6.00 15.00
HTD18 Dale Earnhardt Jr. AMP 8.00 20.00
HTD19 Dale Earnhardt Jr. NG 8.00 20.00

2008 Press Pass Premium Target

COMPLETE SET (6) 12.50 30.00
STATED ODDS 2 PER TARGET BLASTER BOX
TA1 Matt Kenseth .75 2.00
TA2 Denny Hamlin 1.00 2.50
TA3 Kevin Harvick 1.00 2.50
TA4 Tony Stewart 1.25 3.00
TA5 Dale Earnhardt Jr. 1.50 4.00
TA6 Juan Pablo Montoya 1.25 3.00

2008 Press Pass Premium Team Signed Baseballs

GAN Franchitti/Montoya/Sorenson 125.00 200.00
GIB Ky.Busch/Hamlin/Stewart 200.00 350.00
HMS Dale Jr./Gordon/JJ/Mears 300.00 500.00
ROU Edwards/Kenseth
McMurray/Ragan 150.00 250.00
EGAN Franchitti/Montoya
Sorenson Entry 2.00 5.00
EGIB Ky.Busch/Hamlin/Stewart Entry 3.00 8.00
EHMS Dale Jr./Gordon/JJ/Mears Entry 5.00 12.00
EROU Edwards/Kenseth
McMurray/Ragan Entry 3.00 8.00

2008 Press Pass Premium Wal-Mart

COMPLETE SET (6) 12.50 30.00
STATED ODDS 2 PER WALMART BLASTER BOX
WM1 Dale Earnhardt Jr. 1.50 4.00
WM2 Jimmie Johnson 1.25 3.00
WM3 Kasey Kahne .75 2.00
WM4 Carl Edwards .75 2.00
WM5 Jeff Gordon 1.50 4.00
WM6 Martin Truex Jr. .60 1.50

2009 Press Pass Premium

COMPLETE SET (90) 40.00 80.00
COMP.SET w/o SPs (80) 12.00 30.00
ROOKIE STATED ODDS 1:20
WAX BOX HOBBY (20) 75.00 100.00
WAX BOX RETAIL (24) 50.00 75.00
1 Dale Earnhardt Jr. CL .75 2.00
2 David Reutimann .30 .75
3 Casey Mears .25 .60
4 Martin Truex Jr. .30 .75
5 Kurt Busch .30 .75
6 Mark Martin .40 1.00
7 David Ragan .30 .75
8 Robby Gordon .25 .60
9 Aric Almirola .30 .75
10 Kasey Kahne .40 1.00
11 Denny Hamlin .40 1.00
12 David Stremme .25 .60
13 Tony Stewart .60 1.50
14 Greg Biffle .30 .75
15 Matt Kenseth .40 1.00
16 Kyle Busch .50 1.25
17 Elliott Sadler .25 .60
18 Jeff Gordon .75 2.00
19 Jamie McMurray .40 1.00
20 Travis Kvapil .25 .60
21 Kevin Harvick .50 1.25
22 Jeff Burton .30 .75
23 Clint Bowyer .40 1.00
24 Ryan Newman .30 .75
25 Juan Pablo Montoya .50 1.25
26 Reed Sorenson .25 .60
27 A.J. Allmendinger .40 1.00
28 Jimmie Johnson .60 1.50
29 Michael Waltrip .40 1.00
30 Sam Hornish Jr. .30 .75
31 Brian Vickers .25 .60
32 Dale Earnhardt Jr. .75 2.00
33 Bobby Labonte .40 1.00
34 Paul Menard .25 .60
35 Carl Edwards .40 1.00
36 Mark Martin's Car M .15 .40
37 David Ragan's Car M .12 .30
38 Denny Hamlin's Car M .15 .40
39 Tony Stewart's Car M .25 .60
40 Matt Kenseth's Car M .15 .40
41 Kyle Busch's Car M .20 .50
42 Elliott Sadler's Car M .10 .25
43 Jeff Gordon's Car M .30 .75
44 Jeff Burton's Car M .12 .30
45 Clint Bowyer's Car M .15 .40
46 Ryan Newman's Car M .12 .30
47 Juan Pablo Montoya's Car M .20 .50
48 Jimmie Johnson's Car M .25 .60
49 Dale Earnhardt Jr.'s Car M .30 .75
50 Carl Edwards' Car M .15 .40
51 Casey Mears' Car M .25 .60
52 Kevin Harvick SW .50 1.25
53 Martin Truex Jr. SW .30 .75
54 Jeff Gordon SW .75 2.00
55 Kyle Busch SW .50 1.25
56 Tony Stewart SW .60 1.50
57 Ryan Newman MD .30 .75
58 Tony Stewart MD .60 1.50
59 David Ragan MD .30 .75
60 Carl Edwards MD .40 1.00
61 Jimmie Johnson D .60 1.50
62 Dale Earnhardt Jr. D .75 2.00
63 Jeff Gordon D .75 2.00
64 A.J. Allmendinger D .40 1.00
65 Tony Stewart D .60 1.50
66 Carl Edwards D .40 1.00
67 Jeff Burton D .30 .75
68 Mark Martin D .40 1.00
69 Juan Pablo Montoya D .50 1.25
70 Kevin Harvick D .50 1.25
71 Kasey Kahne D .40 1.00
72 Ryan Newman D .30 .75
73 Jeff Gordon SG .75 2.00
74 Bobby Labonte SG .40 1.00
75 Jeff Burton SG .30 .75
76 Tony Stewart SG .60 1.50
77 Dale Earnhardt Jr. SG .75 2.00
78 Matt Kenseth SG .40 1.00
79 Elliott Sadler SG .25 .60
80 Jimmie Johnson SG .60 1.50
81 Jeff Gordon FL 3.00 8.00
82 Jimmie Johnson FL 2.50 6.00
83 Mark Martin FL 1.50 4.00
84 Tony Stewart FL 2.50 6.00
85 Bobby Labonte FL 1.50 4.00
86 Jeff Burton FL 1.25 3.00
87 Dale Earnhardt Jr. FL 3.00 8.00
88 Joey Logano RC 4.00 10.00
89 Marcos Ambrose CRC 2.00 5.00
90 Scott Speed RC 2.50 6.00
0 Matt Kenseth Daytona 500 4.00 10.00

2009 Press Pass Premium Hot Threads

OVERALL R-U ODDS 1:20
STATED PRINT RUN 50-325
*MULTICOLOR/25: 1X TO 2.5X THREAD/299-325
HTBV1 Brian Vickers Black/299 2.50 6.00
HTBV2 Brian Vickers Blue/99 3.00 8.00
HTCE1 Carl Edwards Black/325 4.00 10.00
HTCE2 Carl Edwards Green/99 5.00 12.00
HTDH1 Denny Hamlin Purple/299 4.00 10.00
HTDH2 Denny Hamlin Black/99 5.00 12.00
HTDR1 David Ragan Yellow/299 3.00 8.00
HTDR2 David Ragan Brown/99 4.00 10.00
HTGB1 Greg Biffle Black/299 3.00 8.00
HTGB2 Greg Biffle White/99 4.00 10.00
HTJG1 Jeff Gordon Blue/325 8.00 20.00
HTJG2 Jeff Gordon Red/99 10.00 25.00
HTJJ2 Jimmie Johnson Blue/325 6.00 15.00
HTJJ1 Jimmie Johnson Black/99 8.00 20.00
HTJL2 Joey Logano Black/325 6.00 15.00
HTJL1 Joey Logano White/99 8.00 20.00
HTKB Kurt Busch Blue/299 3.00 8.00
HTKH1 Kevin Harvick Yellow/325 5.00 12.00
HTKH2 Kevin Harvick Red/99 8.00 20.00
HTKK2 Kasey Kahne Red/299 6.00 15.00
HTKK1 Kasey Kahne Black/99 5.00 12.00
HTMK1 Matt Kenseth Yellow/325 4.00 10.00
HTMK2 Matt Kenseth Black/99 5.00 12.00
HTMT1 Martin Truex Jr. Black/299 3.00 8.00
HTMT2 Martin Truex Jr. Red/99 4.00 10.00
HTMW Michael Waltrip Blue/299 4.00 10.00
HTPM1 Paul Menard Black/299 2.50 6.00
HTPM2 Paul Menard Yellow/99 3.00 8.00
HTRS1 Reed Sorenson Red/299 2.50 6.00
HTRS2 Reed Sorenson Black/50 3.00 8.00
HTSS Scott Speed Black/299 4.00 10.00
HTTS2 Tony Stewart Red/325 8.00 20.00
HTTS1 Tony Stewart White/99 8.00 20.00
HTDE1 Earnhardt Jr. AMP Grn/325 12.00 30.00
HTDE2 Earnhardt Jr. AMP White/99 15.00 40.00
HTDE1 Earnhardt Jr. NG Blue/325 10.00 25.00
HTDE2 Earnhardt Jr. NG White/99 12.00 30.00
HTJaM1 Jamie McMurray Blue/299 4.00 10.00
HTJaM2 Jamie McMurray Yellow/99 5.00 12.00
HTKyB1 Kyle Busch Brown/325 5.00 12.00
HTKyB2 Kyle Busch Yellow/99 6.00 15.00

2009 Press Pass Premium Hot Threads Autographs

SERIAL #'d TO DRIVER'S DOOR NUMBER
STATED PRINT RUN 8-55
KH Kevin Harvick/29 40.00 80.00
KK Kasey Kahne/9
MK Matt Kenseth/17
MW Michael Waltrip/55 40.00 80.00
DE1 Dale Earnhardt Jr. AMP/8
DE2 Dale Earnhardt Jr. NG/8
KyB Kyle Busch/5

2009 Press Pass Premium Signatures

STATED ODDS 1:20
1 A.J. Allmendinger 6.00 15.00
2 Aric Almirola 5.00 12.00
3 Marcos Ambrose 6.00 15.00
4 Greg Biffle 6.00 15.00
5 Clint Bowyer 6.00 15.00
6 Jeff Burton 5.00 12.00
7 Kurt Busch 5.00 12.00
8 Kyle Busch 12.00 30.00
9 Dale Earnhardt Jr. 50.00 100.00
10 Carl Edwards 6.00 15.00
11 Jeff Gordon 60.00 150.00
12 Robby Gordon 4.00 10.00
13 Denny Hamlin EXCH
14 Kevin Harvick 8.00 20.00
15 Sam Hornish Jr. 5.00 12.00
16 Jimmie Johnson 50.00 100.00
17 Kasey Kahne 6.00 15.00
18 Matt Kenseth 6.00 15.00
19 Travis Kvapil 4.00 10.00

20 Bobby Labonte 6.00 15.00
21 Joey Logano 10.00 25.00
22 Mark Martin 10.00 25.00
23 Jamie McMurray 5.00 12.00
24 Casey Mears 4.00 10.00
25 Paul Menard 4.00 10.00
26 Ryan Newman 6.00 15.00
27 David Ragan 5.00 12.00
28 David Reutimann 5.00 12.00
29 Scott Riggs 5.00 12.00
30 Elliott Sadler 4.00 10.00
31 Regan Smith 5.00 12.00
32 Reed Sorenson 4.00 10.00
33 Scott Speed 5.00 12.00
34 Tony Stewart 10.00 25.00
35 David Stremme EXCH 4.00 10.00
36 Martin Truex Jr. 5.00 12.00
37 Brian Vickers 4.00 10.00
38 Michael Waltrip 6.00 15.00

2009 Press Pass Premium Signatures Gold

*GOLD/25: .8X TO 2X BASIC SIGNATURE
STATED PRINT RUN 25 SER.#'d SETS
9 Dale Earnhardt Jr. 125.00 200.00
21 Mark Martin 30.00 80.00
33 Tony Stewart 20.00 50.00

2009 Press Pass Premium Top Contenders

COMPLETE SET (12) 20.00 50.00
STATED ODDS 1:10
*GOLD: .8X TO 2X BASIC INSERTS
TC1 Dale Earnhardt Jr. 3.00 8.00
TC2 Kevin Harvick 2.00 5.00
TC3 Kasey Kahne 1.50 4.00
TC4 Tony Stewart 2.50 6.00
TC5 Denny Hamlin 1.50 4.00
TC6 Jeff Gordon 3.00 8.00
TC7 Carl Edwards 1.50 4.00
TC8 Kyle Busch 2.00 5.00
TC9 Jimmie Johnson 2.50 6.00
TC10 Jeff Burton 1.25 3.00
TC11 Clint Bowyer 1.50 4.00
TC12 Matt Kenseth 1.50 4.00

2009 Press Pass Premium Win Streak

COMPLETE SET (15) 10.00 25.00
STATED ODDS 1:4
WS1 Jimmie Johnson 1.25 3.00
WS2 Carl Edwards .75 2.00
WS3 Jeff Gordon 1.50 4.00
WS4 Dale Earnhardt Jr. 1.50 4.00
WS5 Kevin Harvick 1.00 2.50
WS6 Tony Stewart 1.25 3.00
WS7 Kyle Busch 1.00 2.50
WS8 Kasey Kahne .75 2.00
WS9 Matt Kenseth .75 2.00
WS10 Jeff Burton .60 1.50
WS11 Denny Hamlin .75 2.00
WS12 Joey Logano 1.50 4.00
WS13 David Ragan .60 1.50
WS14 Greg Biffle .60 1.50
WS15 Clint Bowyer .75 2.00

2009 Press Pass Premium Win Streak Victory Lane

STATED ODDS 1:90
WSVL-CB Clint Bowyer 8.00 20.00
WSVL-CE Carl Edwards 10.00 25.00
WSVL-DE Dale Earnhardt Jr. 15.00 40.00
WSVL-DH Denny Hamlin 6.00 15.00
WSVL-DR David Ragan 5.00 12.00
WSVL-GB Greg Biffle 6.00 15.00
WSVL-JB Jeff Burton 10.00 25.00
WSVL-JG Jeff Gordon 25.00 60.00
WSVL-JJ Jimmie Johnson 25.00 60.00
WSVL-JL Joey Logano 6.00 15.00
WSVL-KB Kyle Busch 20.00 50.00
WSVL-KH Kevin Harvick 15.00 40.00
WSVL-KK Kasey Kahne 15.00 40.00
WSVL-MK Matt Kenseth 12.00 30.00
WSVL-TS Tony Stewart 15.00 40.00

2010 Press Pass Premium

COMPLETE SET (100) 75.00 150.00
COMP.SET w/o SPs (90) 15.00 40.00
SP STATED ODDS 1:15
WAX BOX HOBBY (20) 75.00 125.00
1 Mark Martin .40 1.00
2 Tony Stewart .60 1.50
3 Jimmie Johnson .60 1.50
4 Denny Hamlin .40 1.00
5 Kasey Kahne .40 1.00
6 Jeff Gordon .75 2.00
7 Kurt Busch .30 .75
8 Brian Vickers .25 .60
9 Carl Edwards .40 1.00
10 Ryan Newman .30 .75
11 Juan Pablo Montoya .40 1.00
12 Greg Biffle .30 .75
13 Kyle Busch .50 1.25
14 Matt Kenseth .40 1.00
15 Clint Bowyer .40 1.00
16 David Reutimann .30 .75
17 Marcos Ambrose .40 1.00
18 Jeff Burton .30 .75
19 Joey Logano .40 1.00
20 Dale Earnhardt Jr. .75 2.00
21 Kevin Harvick .50 1.25
22 Jamie McMurray .40 1.00
23 AJ Allmendinger .40 1.00
24 Martin Truex Jr. .30 .75
25 Sam Hornish Jr. .30 .75
26 Elliott Sadler .25 .60
27 David Ragan .30 .75
28 Bobby Labonte .40 1.00
29 Paul Menard .25 .60
30 Michael Waltrip .40 1.00
31 Scott Speed .40 1.00
32 Joe Nemechek .25 .60
33 Brad Keselowski .50 1.25
34 Regan Smith .30 .75
35 Travis Kvapil .25 .60
36 Kyle Busch's Car M .20 .50
37 Dale Earnhardt Jr.'s Car M .30 .75
38 Jeff Gordon's Car M .30 .75
39 Jimmie Johnson's Car M .25 .60
40 Mark Martin's Car M .15 .40
41 Tony Stewart's Car M .25 .60
42 Kasey Kahne's Car M .15 .40
43 Carl Edwards' Car M .15 .40
44 Kurt Busch's Car M .12 .30
45 Brian Vickers' Car M .10 .25
46 Joey Logano's Car M .15 .40
47 Juan Pablo Montoya's Car M .15 .40
48 Kevin Harvick's Car M .20 .50
49 Mark Martin ITC .40 1.00
50 Tony Stewart ITC .60 1.50
51 Jimmie Johnson ITC .60 1.50
52 Kasey Kahne ITC .40 1.00
53 Jeff Gordon ITC .75 2.00
54 Dale Earnhardt Jr. ITC .75 2.00
55 Tony Stewart SU .60 1.50
56 Jimmie Johnson SU .60 1.50
57 Jeff Gordon SU .75 2.00
58 Carl Edwards SU .40 1.00
59 Joey Logano SU .40 1.00
60 Dale Earnhardt Jr. SU .75 2.00
61 Kevin Harvick SU .50 1.25
62 Ryan Newman SU .30 .75
63 David Ragan SU .30 .75
64 Juan Pablo Montoya SU .40 1.00
65 Clint Bowyer SU .40 1.00
66 Jeff Burton SU .30 .75
67 Jeff Gordon's Car LP .30 .75
68 Jimmie Johnson's Car LP .25 .60
69 Mark Martin's Car LP .15 .40
70 Tony Stewart's Car LP .25 .60
71 Jeff Burton's Car LP .12 .30
72 Dale Earnhardt Jr.'s Car LP .30 .75
73 Matt Kenseth's Car PG .15 .40
74 Clint Bowyer's Car PG .15 .40
75 Kasey Kahne's Car PG .15 .40
76 Tony Stewart's Car PG .25 .60
77 Jimmie Johnson's Car PG .25 .60
78 Jeff Gordon's Car PG .30 .75
79 Jeff Burton's Car PG .12 .30
80 Kevin Harvick PT .50 1.25
81 Mark Martin PT .40 1.00
82 Jimmie Johnson PT .60 1.50
83 Tony Stewart PT .60 1.50
84 Brian Vickers DL .25 .60
85 Brian Vickers DL .25 .60
86 Brian Vickers/Scott Speed DL .40 1.00
87 Brian Vickers DL .25 .60
88 Brian Vickers DL .25 .60
89 Brian Vickers DL .25 .60
90 Scott Speed DL .40 1.00
91 Danica Patrick's Car M SP 5.00 12.00
92 Tony Stewart's Car M SP 1.25 3.00
93 Dale Earnhardt Jr.'s Car M SP 1.50 4.00
94 Kevin Conway SP 3.00 8.00
95 Carl Edwards LP SP 2.00 5.00
96 Brian Vickers DL SP 1.25 3.00
97 Mark Martin SU SP 2.00 5.00
98 Brian Vickers SU SP 1.25 3.00
99 Danica Patrick SU SP RC 6.00 15.00
100 Jamie McMurray PT SP 2.00 5.00

2010 Press Pass Premium Purple

*PURPLE: 2.5X TO 6X BASE
STATED PRINT RUN 25 SER.#'d SETS

2010 Press Pass Premium Allies

COMPLETE SET (10) 15.00 40.00
STATED ODDS 1:6
A1 Jimmie Johnson/Jeff Gordon 1.25 3.00
A2 Tony Stewart/Dale Earnhardt Jr. 1.25 3.00
A3 Jeff Burton/Mark Martin .60 1.50
A4 Kurt Busch/Sam Hornish Jr. .50 1.25
A5 Matt Kenseth/Kevin Harvick .75 2.00
A6 Dale Earnhardt Jr./Juan Pablo Montoya 1.25 3.00
A7 Tony Stewart/Ryan Newman 1.00 2.50
A8 Michael Waltrip/David Reutimann .60 1.50
A9 Tony Stewart/Kevin Harvick 1.00 2.50
A10 Kyle Busch/Denny Hamlin .75 2.00

2010 Press Pass Premium Allies Signatures

UNPRICED DUAL AU PRINT RUN 5

2010 Press Pass Premium Danica Patrick

COMPLETE SET (4) 15.00 40.00
COMMON DANICA 5.00 12.00

2010 Press Pass Premium Hot Threads

STATED PRINT RUN 299 SER.#'d SETS
*HOLO/99: .5X TO 1.2X BASIC INSERTS
*MULTICOLOR/25: .8X TO 2X BASIC INSERT
*TWO COLOR/125: .6X TO 1.5X BASIC INSERT
HTBV Brian Vickers 2.50 6.00
HTCB Clint Bowyer 4.00 10.00
HTCE Carl Edwards 4.00 10.00
HTDH Denny Hamlin 4.00 10.00
HTDP Danica Patrick 20.00 50.00
HTJB Jeff Burton 3.00 8.00
HTJG Jeff Gordon 8.00 20.00
HTJJ Jimmie Johnson 6.00 15.00
HTJL Joey Logano 4.00 10.00
HTKH Kevin Harvick 5.00 12.00
HTKK Kasey Kahne 4.00 10.00
HTRN Ryan Newman 3.00 8.00
HTDE1 Dale Earnhardt Jr. AMP 12.00 30.00
HTDE2 Dale Earnhardt Jr. NG 12.00 30.00
HTKuB Kurt Busch 3.00 8.00
HTKyB Kyle Busch 5.00 12.00
HTTS1 Tony Stewart OD 6.00 15.00
HTTS2 Tony Stewart OS 6.00 15.00

2010 Press Pass Premium Hot Threads Patches

STATED PRINT RUN 25-39
HTPCE Carl Edwards/30 60.00 120.00
HTPDE Dale Earnhardt Jr. NG/32 60.00 120.00
HTPDP Danica Patrick/25 125.00 250.00
HTPJG Jeff Gordon/39 100.00 200.00
HTPJJ Jimmie Johnson28 30.00 80.00
HTPRN Ryan Newman/35 30.00 80.00
HTPTS1 Tony Stewart OD/36 30.00 80.00
HTPTS2 Tony Stewart OS/35 30.00 80.00

2010 Press Pass Premium Iron On Patch

COMPLETE SET (4) 10.00 25.00
STATED ODDS 1 PER BLASTER BOX
1 Jeff Gordon 1.25 3.00
2 Dale Earnhardt Jr. 1.25 3.00
3 Tony Stewart 1.00 2.50
4 Danica Patrick 5.00 12.00

2010 Press Pass Premium Pairings Firesuits

STATED PRINT RUN 25 SER.#'d SETS
PFBL K.Busch/J.Logano 60.00 120.00
PFGJ J.Gordon/J.Johnson 75.00 150.00
PFKE K.Kahne/C.Edwards 125.00 250.00
PFMP M.Martin/D.Patrick 75.00 150.00
PFPE D.Patrick/Earnhardt Jr. 100.00 200.00

2010 Press Pass Premium Rivals

COMPLETE SET (8) 12.00 30.00
STATED ODDS 1:10
R1 Dale Earnhardt Jr./Jeff Gordon 1.50 4.00
R2 Kevin Harvick/Greg Biffle 1.00 2.50
R3 Tony Stewart/Juan Pablo Montoya 1.25 3.00
R4 Kevin Harvick/Juan Pablo Montoya 1.00 2.50
R5 Jeff Gordon/Jimmie Johnson 1.50 4.00
R6 Jeff Gordon/Matt Kenseth 1.50 4.00
R7 Clint Bowyer/Martin Truex Jr. .75 2.00
R8 Richard Petty/David Pearson 1.25 3.00

2010 Press Pass Premium Signatures

STATED ODDS 1:20
PSAA A.J. Allmendinger 6.00 15.00
PSMA Marcos Ambrose 15.00 40.00
PSGB Greg Biffle 5.00 12.00
PSCB Clint Bowyer 6.00 15.00
PSJB Jeff Burton 5.00 12.00
PSKUB Kurt Busch 5.00 12.00
PSKYB Kyle Busch 8.00 20.00
PSDE Dale Earnhardt Jr. 50.00 100.00
PSCE Carl Edwards 6.00 15.00
PSJG Jeff Gordon 75.00 150.00
PSRG Robby Gordon 4.00 10.00
PSDH Denny Hamlin 6.00 15.00
PSKH Kevin Harvick 8.00 20.00
PSSH Sam Hornish Jr. 5.00 12.00
PSJJ Jimmie Johnson 40.00 80.00
PSKK Kasey Kahne 6.00 15.00
PSMK Matt Kenseth 6.00 15.00
PSBK Brad Keselowski 8.00 20.00
PSBL Bobby Labonte 6.00 15.00
PSJL Joey Logano 6.00 15.00
PSMM Mark Martin 6.00 15.00
PSJM Jamie McMurray 6.00 15.00
PSPM Paul Menard 4.00 10.00
PSJPM Juan Pablo Montoya 6.00 15.00
PSRN Ryan Newman 5.00 12.00
PSDP Danica Patrick 275.00 400.00
PSDR David Ragan 5.00 12.00
PSDR David Reutimann 5.00 12.00
PSES Elliott Sadler 4.00 10.00
PSRS Regan Smith 5.00 12.00
PSSS Scott Speed 6.00 15.00
PSTS Tony Stewart 40.00 80.00
PSMT Martin Truex Jr. 5.00 12.00
PSBV Brian Vickers 4.00 10.00
PSMW Michael Waltrip 6.00 15.00

2010 Press Pass Premium Signatures Red Ink

STATED PRINT RUN 19-150
PSAA A.J. Allmendinger/24
PSBK Brad Keselowski/24 25.00 50.00
PSBL Bobby Labonte/24 20.00 50.00
PSBV Brian Vickers/24 20.00 50.00
PSCB Clint Bowyer/25 25.00 50.00
PSCE Carl Edwards/24 30.00 60.00
PSDH Denny Hamlin/24 50.00 100.00
PSDP Danica Patrick/25 150.00 300.00
PSDR David Ragan/24 15.00 40.00
PSDR David Reutimann/24 15.00 40.00
PSES Elliott Sadler/19
PSGB Greg Biffle/25 25.00 50.00
PSJB Jeff Burton/24 30.00 60.00
PSJL Joey Logano/24 30.00 60.00
PSJM Jamie McMurray/25 30.00 60.00
PSKH Kevin Harvick/23 30.00 60.00
PSKK Kasey Kahne/25 100.00 200.00
PSMA Marcos Ambrose/23
PSMK Matt Kenseth/20
PSMM Mark Martin/24 75.00 150.00
PSMT Martin Truex Jr./24 25.00 50.00
PSMW Michael Waltrip/24 15.00 40.00
PSPM Paul Menard/24 12.00 30.00
PSRG Robby Gordon/25 12.00 30.00
PSRN Ryan Newman/25 30.00 60.00
PSRS Regan Smith/24 12.00 30.00
PSSH Sam Hornish Jr./150 8.00 20.00
PSSS Scott Speed/24 12.00 30.00
PSTS Tony Stewart/50 50.00 100.00
PSJPM Juan Pablo Montoya/24 20.00 50.00
PSKUB Kurt Busch/25 30.00 60.00
PSKYB Kyle Busch/24 30.00 60.00

2011 Press Pass Premium

COMPLETE SET (100) 50.00 100.00
COMP.SET w/o SPs (90) 10.00 25.00
0 CARD STATED ODDS 1:240
SP VARIATION STATED ODDS 1:20
WAX BOX HOBBY (20) 75.00 100.00
WAX BOX RETAIL (24) 50.00 75.00
1 A.J. Allmendinger .40 1.00
2 Marcos Ambrose .40 1.00
3A Trevor Bayne CRC 2.00 5.00
3B Trevor Bayne SP 5.00 12.00
4 Greg Biffle .30 .75
5 Clint Bowyer .40 1.00
6A Jeff Burton .30 .75
6B Jeff Burton SP 1.50 4.00
7A Kurt Busch .30 .75
7B Kurt Busch SP 1.50 4.00
8A Kyle Busch .50 1.25
8B Kyle Busch SP 2.50 6.00
9A Dale Earnhardt Jr. .75 2.00
9B Dale Earnhardt Jr. SP 4.00 10.00
10A Carl Edwards .40 1.00
10B Carl Edwards SP 2.00 5.00
11 Bill Elliott .60 1.50
12 David Gilliland .25 .60
13A Jeff Gordon .75 2.00
13B Jeff Gordon SP 4.00 10.00
14 Robby Gordon .25 .60
15 Denny Hamlin .40 1.00
16A Kevin Harvick .50 1.25
16B Kevin Harvick SP 2.50 6.00
17 Jimmie Johnson .60 1.50
18A Kasey Kahne .40 1.00
18B Kasey Kahne SP 2.00 5.00
19 Matt Kenseth .40 1.00
20 Brad Keselowski .50 1.25
21 Travis Kvapil .25 .60
22 Bobby Labonte .40 1.00
23 Joey Logano .40 1.00
24 Mark Martin .40 1.00
25 Jamie McMurray .40 1.00
26 Casey Mears .25 .60
27 Paul Menard .25 .60
28 Juan Pablo Montoya .40 1.00
29 Ryan Newman .30 .75
30 David Ragan .30 .75
31 David Reutimann .30 .75
32 Regan Smith .30 .75
33A Tony Stewart .60 1.50
33B Tony Stewart SP 3.00 8.00
34 Martin Truex Jr. .30 .75
35 Brian Vickers .25 .60
36 J.J. Yeley .25 .60
37 Kyle Busch's Car M .20 .50
38 Dale Earnhardt Jr.'s Car M .30 .75
39 Jeff Gordon's Car M .30 .75
40 Jimmie Johnson's Car M .25 .60
41 Mark Martin's Car M .15 .40
42 Tony Stewart's Car M .25 .60
43 Kasey Kahne's Car M .15 .40
44 Carl Edwards' Car M .15 .40
45 Kurt Busch's Car M .12 .30
46 Brian Vickers' Car M .10 .25
47 Denny Hamlin's Car M .15 .40
48 Kevin Harvick's Car M .20 .50
49 Dale Earnhardt Jr. D500 .75 2.00
50 Jeff Gordon D500 .75 2.00
51 Kevin Harvick D500 .50 1.25
52 Matt Kenseth D500 .40 1.00
53 Jamie McMurray D500 .40 1.00
54 Trevor Bayne D500 .75 2.00
55 Brian Vickers SU .25 .60
56 Trevor Bayne SU .75 2.00
57 Kurt Busch SU .30 .75
58 Kyle Busch SU .50 1.25
59 Dale Earnhardt Jr. SU .75 2.00
60 Carl Edwards SU .40 1.00
61 Jeff Gordon SU .75 2.00
62 Denny Hamlin SU .40 1.00
63 Kevin Harvick SU .50 1.25
64 Jimmie Johnson SU .60 1.50
65 Kasey Kahne SU .40 1.00
66 Tony Stewart SU .60 1.50
67 Dale Earnhardt Jr.'s Car DP .30 .75
68 Jeff Gordon's Car DP .30 .75
69 Jamie McMurray's Car DP .15 .40
70 Kevin Harvick's Car DP .20 .50
71 Jimmie Johnson's Car DP .25 .60
72 Mark Martin's Car DP .15 .40
73 Greg Biffle PP .30 .75
74 Jeff Burton PP .30 .75
75 Kurt Busch PP .30 .75
76 Kyle Busch PP .50 1.25
77 Carl Edwards PP .40 1.00
78 Denny Hamlin PP .40 1.00
79 Brad Keselowski PP .50 1.25
80 Kurt Busch PT .30 .75
81 Kurt Busch PT .30 .75
82 Jeff Burton PT .30 .75
83 Michael Waltrip PT .50 1.25
84 Tony Stewart PT .60 1.50
85 Trevor Bayne PT .75 2.00
86 Martin Truex Jr. SI .30 .75
87 Matt Kenseth SI .40 1.00
88 Brian Vickers SI .25 .60
89 Danica Patrick SI 1.50 4.00
90 Joey Logano SI .40 1.00
0 Dale Earnhardt 10.00 25.00
CTLDE Dale Earnhardt FS/25 40.00 100.00

2011 Press Pass Premium Purple

*PURPLE: 2.5X TO 6X BASE
STATED PRINT RUN 25 SER.#'d SETS
3 Trevor Bayne 20.00 50.00

2011 Press Pass Premium Crystal Ball

COMPLETE SET (10) 15.00 40.00
STATED ODDS 1:10
CB1 Jamie McMurray .75 2.00
CB2 Jimmie Johnson 1.25 3.00
CB3 Dale Earnhardt Jr. 1.50 4.00
CB4 Jeff Gordon 1.50 4.00
CB5 Denny Hamlin .75 2.00
CB6 Danica Patrick 3.00 8.00
CB7 Tony Stewart 1.25 3.00
CB8 Carl Edwards .75 2.00
CB9 Kyle Busch 1.00 2.50
CB10 Trevor Bayne 1.50 4.00

2011 Press Pass Premium Double Burner

STATED PRINT RUN 25 SER.#'d SETS
DBCE Carl Edwards 8.00 20.00
DBDEJ Dale Earnhardt Jr. 40.00 100.00
DBDP Danica Patrick 40.00 100.00
DBJG Jeff Gordon 40.00 100.00
DBJJ Jimmie Johnson 25.00 60.00
DBKK Kasey Kahne 40.00 100.00
DBKUB Kurt Busch 6.00 15.00
DBKYB Kyle Busch 12.00 30.00
DBMM Mark Martin 8.00 20.00
DBTS Tony Stewart 20.00 50.00

2011 Press Pass Premium Hot Pursuit 3D

COMPLETE SET (10) 12.00 30.00
STATED ODDS 1:5
HP1 Dale Earnhardt Jr. 1.25 3.00
HP2 Kevin Harvick .75 2.00
HP3 Jeff Gordon 1.25 3.00
HP4 Jimmie Johnson 1.00 2.50
HP5 Carl Edwards .60 1.50
HP6 Danica Patrick 2.50 6.00
HP7 Denny Hamlin .60 1.50
HP8 Tony Stewart 1.00 2.50
HP9 Mark Martin .60 1.50
HP10 Kyle Busch .75 2.00

2011 Press Pass Premium Hot Threads

STATED PRINT RUN 150 SER.#'d SETS
*FAST PASS/25: .6X TO 1.5X BASIC/150
*MULTICLR/25: .6X TO 1.5X BASIC/150
*SECONDARY/99: .5X TO 1.2X BASIC/150
*SECONDARY/25: .6X TO 1.5X BASIC/150
HTJB Jeff Burton 2.50 6.00
HTBK Brad Keselowski 4.00 10.00
HTBV Brian Vickers 2.00 5.00
HTCE Carl Edwards 3.00 8.00
HTDH Denny Hamlin 3.00 8.00
HTDJR Dale Earnhardt Jr. 6.00 15.00
HTDP Danica Patrick 12.00 30.00
HTDR David Ragan 2.50 6.00
HTJG Jeff Gordon 6.00 15.00
HTJJ Jimmie Johnson 10.00 25.00
HTJL Joey Logano 3.00 8.00
HTJM Jamie McMurray 3.00 8.00
HTJPM Juan Pablo Montoya 3.00 8.00
HTKB1 Kurt Busch 2.50 6.00
HTKB2 Kyle Busch 4.00 10.00
HTKH Kevin Harvick 4.00 10.00
HTKK Kasey Kahne 3.00 8.00
HTMK Matt Kenseth 3.00 8.00
HTMM Mark Martin 3.00 8.00
HTPM Paul Menard 2.00 5.00
HTRN Ryan Newman 2.50 6.00
HTTS Tony Stewart 5.00 12.00

2011 Press Pass Premium Hot Threads Patches

STATED PRINT RUN 8-25
NNO Kyle Busch/12
HTPBK Brad Keselowski/13
HTPCE Carl Edwards/25 30.00 60.00
HTPDEJ Dale Earnhardt Jr./20 40.00 80.00
HTPDP Danica Patrick/15 50.00 120.00
HTPJG Jeff Gordon/10
HTPJJ Jimmie Johnson/25 30.00 60.00
HTPKK Kasey Kahne/14
HTPMM Mark Martin/8
HTPTS Tony Stewart/10

2011 Press Pass Premium Pairings Firesuits

STATED PRINT RUN 25 SER.#'d SETS
UNPRICED AUTO PRINT RUN 5
PPDEJJG Earnhardt Jr./Gordon 40.00 100.00
PPBKKB Keselowski/Ku.Bsch 20.00 50.00
PPBVKK B.Vickers/K.Kahne
PPCETB C.Edwards/T.Bayne 25.00 60.00
PPJJMM J.Johnson/M.Martin 12.00 30.00
PPKBDH K.Busch/D.Hamlin 10.00 25.00

2011 Press Pass Premium Signatures

STATED PRINT RUN 17-287
PSAJ A.J. Allmendinger/200 5.00 12.00
PSBE Bill Elliott/198 10.00 25.00
PSBK Brad Keselowski/173* 8.00 20.00
PSBL Bobby Labonte/200 5.00 12.00
PSBV Brian Vickers/173* 3.00 8.00
PSCB Clint Bowyer/189* 5.00 12.00
PSCE Carl Edwards/160 5.00 12.00
PSCM Casey Mears/100 3.00 8.00
PSDEJ Dale Earnhardt Jr./22
PSDG David Gilliland/100 3.00 8.00
PSDH Denny Hamlin/66 5.00 12.00
PSDP Danica Patrick/17
PSDR1 David Ragan/200 4.00 10.00
PSDR2 David Reutimann/178 4.00 10.00
PSGB Greg Biffle/287 4.00 10.00
PSJB Jeff Burton/91* 4.00 10.00
PSJG Jeff Gordon/17*
PSJJ Jimmie Johnson/22
PSJL Joey Logano/146* 5.00 12.00
PSJM Juan Pablo Montoya/150* 5.00 12.00
PSJM Jamie McMurray/90* 5.00 12.00
PSJY J.J. Yeley/102 3.00 8.00
PSKB1 Kurt Busch/195* 4.00 10.00
PSKB2 Kyle Busch/32 15.00 40.00
PSKC Kevin Conway/50 4.00 10.00
PSKH Kevin Harvick/256* 6.00 15.00
PSKK Kasey Kahne/37* 25.00 60.00
PSMK Matt Kenseth/189 5.00 12.00
PSMM Mark Martin/48* 5.00 12.00
PSMTJ Martin Truex Jr./200 4.00 10.00
PSMW Michael Waltrip/100 6.00 15.00
PSPM Paul Menard/200 3.00 8.00
PSRG Robby Gordon/100 3.00 8.00
PSRN Ryan Newman/149* 4.00 10.00
PSRS Regan Smith/200 8.00 20.00
PSTB Trevor Bayne/164* 10.00 25.00
PSTK Travis Kvapil/197 3.00 8.00
PSTS Tony Stewart/36* 25.00 60.00

2011 Press Pass Premium Signatures Red Ink

ANNOUNCED PRINT RUN 4-100
PSJB Jeff Burton/51* 5.00 12.00
PSJL Joey Logano/43* EXCH 6.00 15.00
PSJM Jamie McMurray/100* 6.00 15.00
PSKH Kevin Harvick/20*
PSKK Kasey Kahne/24* 30.00 80.00
PSMM Mark Martin/26* 6.00 15.00
PSTB Trevor Bayne/15*
PSTS Tony Stewart/30* 40.00 80.00

2003 Press Pass Race Exclusives

These cards were issued one at a time for select race winners in 2003. Each card follows the forma or even parallels a regular issue 2003 card with the addition of a race winning date and mention printed on the front. All cards were originally sealed in a Beckett Graded Services card holder, but not graded.

1 Michael Waltrip 3.00 8.00
9 Dale Earnhardt Jr. 6.00 15.00

2012 Press Pass Redline
PLETE SET (50) 25.00 50.00
BOX HOBBY 100.00 135.00
Allmendinger .50 1.25
Almirola .40 1.00
cos Ambrose .50 1.25
vor Bayne .50 1.25
Biffle .40 1.00
e Blaney .30 .75
t Bowyer .50 1.25
Burton .40 1.00
t Busch .40 1.00
le Busch .60 1.50
ndon Cassill .40 1.00
le Earnhardt Jr. 1.00 2.50
rl Edwards .50 1.25
avid Gilliland .30 .75
ff Gordon 1.00 2.50
nny Hamlin .50 1.25
vin Harvick .60 1.50
mmie Johnson .75 2.00
sey Kahne .50 1.25
att Kenseth .50 1.25
ad Keselowski .60 1.50
bby Labonte .50 1.25
rry Labonte .50 1.25
ey Logano .50 1.25
ark Martin .50 1.25
ichael McDowell .40 1.00
mie McMurray .50 1.25
sey Mears .30 .75
ul Menard .30 .75
an Pablo Montoya .50 1.25
yan Newman .40 1.00
anica Patrick CRC 2.50 6.00
avid Ragan .40 1.00
egan Smith .40 1.00
ny Stewart .75 2.00
artin Truex Jr. .40 1.00
ichael Waltrip .50 1.25
J. Yeley .30 .75
stin Allgaier NNS .40 1.00
urt Busch NNS .40 1.00
yle Busch NNS .60 1.50
stin Dillon NNS .60 1.50
avis Pastrana NNS .75 2.00
anica Patrick NNS 2.00 5.00
liott Sadler NNS .30 .75
D. Gibbs OWN .30 .75
e Gibbs OWN .40 1.00
ck Roush OWN .40 1.00
chard Petty LEG .75 2.00
ale Earnhardt LEG 1.50 4.00

12 Press Pass Redline Black
ACK/99: 1X TO 2.5X BASIC CARDS
ED PRINT RUN 99 SER.#'d SETS

012 Press Pass Redline Cyan
AN/50: 1.2X TO 3X BASIC CARDS
ED PRINT RUN 50 SER.#'d SETS

2 Press Pass Redline Magenta
GENTA/15: 3X TO 8X BASIC CARDS
ED PRINT RUN 15 SER.#'d SETS

2012 Press Pass Redline Full Throttle Dual Relic Red
ED PRINT RUN 25-75
VER/25: .5X TO 1.2X RED/50-75
VER/15: .4X TO 1X RED/25
Clint Bowyer/75 4.00 10.00
Carl Edwards/75 5.00 12.00
Denny Hamlin/75 5.00 12.00
Danica Patrick Cup/50 12.00 30.00
Justin Allgaier/50 4.00 10.00
Jeff Burton/75 4.00 10.00
Jeff Gordon/75 10.00 25.00
Jimmie Johnson/75 6.00 15.00
Joey Logano/75 6.00 15.00
Kevin Harvick/25 10.00 25.00
A Marcos Ambrose/25 8.00 20.00
K Matt Kenseth/75 5.00 12.00
M Mark Martin/75 5.00 12.00
Ryan Newman/75 4.00 10.00
Trevor Bayne/25 8.00 20.00
Tony Stewart/75 8.00 20.00
B Kyle Busch/75 5.00 12.00
EJR Dale Earnhardt Jr/75 10.00 25.00

12 Press Pass Redline Hall of Fame Relic Autographs Red
TED PRINT RUN 47-50
LD/24-25: .5X TO 1.2X RED/47-50
BA Bobby Allison/50 8.00 20.00
CY Cale Yarborough/50 10.00 25.00
DP David Pearson/50 10.00 25.00
DW Darrell Waltrip/50 12.00 30.00
RP Richard Petty/47 30.00 60.00

2 Press Pass Redline Intensity
DOM INSERTS IN PACKS
yle Busch .75 2.00
ale Earnhardt Jr. 1.25 3.00
arl Edwards .60 1.50
eff Gordon 1.25 3.00
I5 Kevin Harvick .75 2.00
I6 Jimmie Johnson 1.00 2.50
I7 Travis Pastrana SP 6.00 15.00
I8 Danica Patrick SP 15.00 40.00
I9 Tony Stewart SP 12.00 30.00

2012 Press Pass Redline Muscle Car Sheet Metal Red
STATED PRINT RUN 10-75
*SILVER/25: .5X TO 1.2X RED/75
*SILVER/20: .4X TO 1X RED/45
MCCE Carl Edwards/75 5.00 12.00
MCDH Denny Hamlin/75 5.00 12.00
MCJJ Jimmie Johnson/75 6.00 15.00
MCJL Joey Logano/75 6.00 15.00
MCKH Kevin Harvick/75 6.00 15.00
MCKK Kasey Kahne/75 5.00 12.00
MCMA Marcos Ambrose/75 5.00 12.00
MCMK Matt Kenseth/75 5.00 12.00
MCMM Mark Martin/75 5.00 12.00
MCDP1 Danica Patrick Cup/75 12.00 30.00
MCDP2 Danica Patrick NNS/75 12.00 30.00
MCJG1 Jeff Gordon/10
MCJG2 Jeff Gordon/45 12.00 30.00
MCKYB Kyle Busch/75 5.00 12.00
MCTS1 Tony Stewart/75 8.00 20.00
MCTS2 Tony Stewart/75 8.00 20.00
MCDEJ1 Dale Earnhardt Jr/75 10.00 25.00
MCDEJ2 Dale Earnhardt Jr/75 10.00 25.00

2012 Press Pass Redline Performance Driven
RANDOM INSERTS IN PACKS
PD1 Kyle Busch SP 8.00 20.00
PD2 Dale Earnhardt Jr. 1.25 3.00
PD3 Carl Edwards SP 6.00 15.00
PD4 Jeff Gordon 1.25 3.00
PD5 Jimmie Johnson 1.00 2.50
PD6 Matt Kenseth .60 1.50
PD7 Brad Keselowski .75 2.00
PD8 Danica Patrick SP 12.00 30.00
PD9 Tony Stewart 1.00 2.50

2012 Press Pass Redline Pieces of the Action Red
RED STATED PRINT RUN 25-75
*GOLD/25: .6X TO 1.5X RED/75
*SILVER/15-50: .5X TO 1.2X RED/25-75
PACE Carl Edwards/75 5.00 12.00
PADP Danica Patrick Cup/75 12.00 30.00
PAJG Jeff Gordon/75 10.00 25.00
PAJJ Jimmie Johnson/75 6.00 15.00
PAKH Kevin Harvick/75 6.00 15.00
PAKK Kasey Kahne/25 8.00 20.00
PATP Travis Pastrana/75 6.00 15.00
PATS Tony Stewart/75 8.00 20.00
PAKYB Kyle Busch/75 5.00 12.00
PADEJR Dale Earnhardt Jr/75 10.00 25.00

2012 Press Pass Redline Relic Autographs Red
RED PRINT RUN 19-75
*GOLD/25: .6X TO 1.5X RED/50-75
*SILVER/36-50: .5X TO 1.2X RED/62-75
*SILVER/23-25: .6X TO 1.5X RED/50
EXCH EXPIRATION: 7/5/2013
RLRCE Carl Edwards/75 8.00 20.00
RLRJB Jeff Burton/62 6.00 15.00
RLRJG Jeff Gordon/50 40.00 80.00
RLRJJ Jimmie Johnson/75 30.00 60.00
RLRJL Joey Logano/75 8.00 20.00
RLRKH Kevin Harvick/75 10.00 25.00
RLRKK Kasey Kahne/75 12.00 30.00
RLRMA Marcos Ambrose/75 10.00 25.00
RLRMK Matt Kenseth/75 8.00 20.00
RLRMM Mark Martin/75 12.00 30.00
RLRTB Trevor Bayne/75 8.00 20.00
RLRTP Travis Pastrana/50 12.00 30.00
RLRTS Tony Stewart/75 15.00 40.00
RLRDEJ Dale Earnhardt Jr./50 40.00 80.00
RLRDP1 Danica Patrick/19 80.00 150.00
RLRDP2 Danica Patrick NNS/25 50.00 100.00
RLRKYB Kyle Busch/75 10.00 25.00

2012 Press Pass Redline Relics Red
RED STATED PRINT RUN 25-75
*SILVER/25: .6X TO 1.5X RED/75
*SILVER/15: .5X TO 1.2X RED/25
RLCE Carl Edwards/75 4.00 10.00
RLDH Denny Hamlin/75 4.00 10.00
RLJB Jeff Burton/75 3.00 8.00
RLJG Jeff Gordon/75 8.00 20.00
RLJJ Jimmie Johnson/75 5.00 12.00
RLJL Joey Logano/75 5.00 12.00
RLKH Kevin Harvick/25 8.00 20.00
RLKK Kasey Kahne/25 6.00 15.00
RLMA Marcos Ambrose/25 6.00 15.00
RLMK Matt Kenseth/75 4.00 10.00
RLMM Mark Martin/75 4.00 10.00
RLTB Trevor Bayne/25 6.00 15.00
RLTP Travis Pastrana/75 5.00 12.00
RLTS Tony Stewart/75 6.00 15.00
RLDP1 Danica Patrick/25 20.00 50.00
RLDP2 Danica Patrick NNS/75 12.00 30.00
RLKYB Kyle Busch/75 5.00 12.00
RLDEJR Dale Earnhardt Jr/75 8.00 20.00

2012 Press Pass Redline Rookie Year Relic Autographs Red
RED STATED PRINT RUN 19-50
*GOLD/25: .6X TO 1.5X RED/45-50
EXCH EXPIRATION: 7/5/2013
RYJB Jeff Burton/50 6.00 15.00
RYJG Jeff Gordon/50 EXCH 50.00 100.00
RYJJ Jimmie Johnson/50 30.00 60.00
RYJL Joey Logano/49 10.00 25.00
RYKH Kevin Harvick/50 12.00 30.00
RYKK Kasey Kahne/50 12.00 30.00
RYMA Mark Martin/45 8.00 20.00
RYRP Richard Petty/50 25.00 50.00
RYTL Terry Labonte/50 8.00 20.00
RYTS Tony Stewart/50 15.00 40.00
RYDP1 Danica Patrick/19 75.00 150.00
RYKYB Kyle Busch/50 10.00 25.00
RYDEJR Dale Earnhardt Jr./50 40.00 80.00

2012 Press Pass Redline RPM
RANDOM INSERTS IN PACKS
RPM1 Kyle Busch's Car .60 1.50
RPM2 Dale Earnhardt Jr.'s Car SP 10.00 25.00
RPM3 Carl Edwards's Car .50 1.25
RPM4 Jeff Gordon's Car SP 10.00 25.00
RPM5 Denny Hamlin's Car .50 1.25
RPM6 Jimmie Johnson's Car SP 8.00 20.00
RPM7 Kasey Kahne's Car .50 1.25
RPM8 Matt Kenseth's Car .50 1.25
RPM9 Brad Keselowski's Car .60 1.50
RPM10 Mark Martin's Car .50 1.25
RPM11 Danica Patrick's Car 2.50 6.00
RPM12 Tony Stewart's Car SP 8.00 20.00

2012 Press Pass Redline Signatures Red
RED STATED PRINT RUN 10-50
*GOLD/20-25: .5X TO 1.2X RED/45-50
*GOLD/15: .5X TO 1.2X RED/25-31
EXCH EXPIRATION: 7/15/2013
RSAA Aric Almirola/49 5.00 12.00
RSAJ1 Allmendinger Shell/45 6.00 15.00
RSAJ2 Allmendinger Pennzoil/25 8.00 20.00
RSBK Brad Keselowski/50 10.00 25.00
RSBL Bobby Labonte/50 6.00 15.00
RSBO Bob Osborne CC/50 5.00 12.00
RSCB Clint Bowyer/50 5.00 12.00
RSCE1 Carl Edwards Subway/50 6.00 15.00
RSCE2 Carl Edwards Fastenal/25 8.00 20.00
RSCK Chad Knaus CC/50 8.00 20.00
RSDEJ1 Dale Earnhardt Jr. NG/31 25.00 60.00
RSDP1 Danica Patrick/25 50.00 100.00
RSDP2 Danica Patrick NNS/10
RSGB Greg Biffle/48 5.00 12.00
RSJA Justin Allgaier NNS/50 5.00 12.00
RSJB Jeff Burton/50 5.00 12.00
RSJD J.D. Gibbs OWN/49 6.00 15.00
RSJG1 J.Gordon DTEH/30 EXCH 40.00 80.00
RSJJ1 J.Johnson Lowe's/30 EXCH 25.00 50.00
RSJL1 Joey Logano HD/50 8.00 20.00
RSJL2 Joey Logano DG/25 10.00 25.00
RSJM Jamie McMurray/50 6.00 15.00
RSJPM Juan Pablo Montoya/50 6.00 15.00
RSJR Jack Roush OWN/50 10.00 25.00
RSJW Josh Wise/49 4.00 10.00
RSKH1 Kevin Harvick JJ/50 8.00 20.00
RSKH2 K.Harvick Rheem/25 10.00 25.00
RSKK Kasey Kahne/25 8.00 20.00
RSKUB Kurt Busch/50 5.00 12.00
RSKYB Kyle Busch/50 10.00 25.00
RSMA Marcos Ambrose/50 6.00 15.00
RSMK Matt Kenseth/25 6.00 15.00
RSMM Mark Martin/50 6.00 15.00
RSMT Martin Truex Jr./50 5.00 12.00
RSMW Michael Waltrip/50 5.00 12.00
RSPM Paul Menard/50 4.00 10.00
RSRC Richard Childress/50 5.00 12.00
RSRN Ryan Newman/50 5.00 12.00
RSRS Regan Smith/50 5.00 12.00
RSSA Steve Addington CC/50 6.00 15.00
RSSL Steve Letarte CC/50 5.00 12.00
RSSW Shane Wilson CC/50 4.00 10.00
RSTB Trevor Bayne/50 6.00 15.00
RSTS1 Tony Stewart OD/50 10.00 25.00
RSTS2 Tony Stewart Mobil/25 12.00 30.00

2012 Press Pass Redline V8 Relics Red
RED STATED PRINT RUN 25
V8CE Carl Edwards 10.00 25.00
V8DP Danica Patrick NNS 20.00 50.00
V8JG Jeff Gordon 20.00 50.00
V8JJ Jimmie Johnson 10.00 25.00
V8KH Kevin Harvick 12.00 30.00
V8KK Kasey Kahne 10.00 25.00
V8MK Matt Kenseth 10.00 25.00
V8TS Tony Stewart 15.00 40.00
V8KYB Kyle Busch 12.00 30.00
V8DEJR Dale Earnhardt Jr 20.00 40.00

2013 Press Pass Redline
1 Aric Almirola .40 1.00
2 Aric Almirola .40 1.00
3 Marcos Ambrose .50 1.25
4 Marcos Ambrose .50 1.25
5 Trevor Bayne .50 1.25
6 Greg Biffle .40 1.00
7 Clint Bowyer .50 1.25
8 Clint Bowyer .50 1.25
9 Jeff Burton .40 1.00
10 Jeff Burton .40 1.00
11 Kurt Busch .40 1.00
12 Kyle Busch .60 1.50
13 Kyle Busch .60 1.50
14 Dale Earnhardt Jr. 1.00 2.50
15 Carl Edwards .50 1.25
16 Carl Edwards .50 1.25
17 Jeff Gordon 1.00 2.50
18 Jeff Gordon 1.00 2.50
19 Denny Hamlin .50 1.25
20 Denny Hamlin .50 1.25
21 Kevin Harvick .60 1.50
22 Kevin Harvick .60 1.50
23 Jimmie Johnson .75 2.00
24 Jimmie Johnson .75 2.00
25 Kasey Kahne .50 1.25
26 Kasey Kahne .50 1.25
27 Matt Kenseth .50 1.25
28 Matt Kenseth .50 1.25
29 Brad Keselowski .60 1.50
30 Bobby Labonte .50 1.25
31 Joey Logano .50 1.25
32 Joey Logano .50 1.25
33 Mark Martin .50 1.25
34 Jamie McMurray .50 1.25
35 Jamie McMurray .50 1.25
36 Paul Menard .30 .75
37 Juan Pablo Montoya .50 1.25
38 Ryan Newman .40 1.00
39 Ryan Newman .40 1.00
40 Danica Patrick 1.25 3.00
41 Regan Smith .40 1.00
42 Ricky Stenhouse Jr. .50 1.25
43 Tony Stewart .75 2.00
44 Tony Stewart .75 2.00
45 Martin Truex .40 1.00
46 Michael Waltrip .50 1.25
47 Justin Allgaier .40 1.00
48 Austin Dillon .60 1.50
49 Travis Pastrana .50 1.25
50 Ty Dillon .50 1.25

2013 Press Pass Redline Black
*BLACK/99: 1X TO 2.5X BASIC CARDS

2013 Press Pass Redline Cyan
*CYAN/50: 1.2X TO 3X BASIC CARDS

2013 Press Pass Redline Magenta
*MAGENTA/15: 3X TO 8X BASIC CARDS

2013 Press Pass Redline Career Wins Relic Autographs Red
RED STATED PRINT RUN 15-50
*GOLD/17-25: .5X TO 1.2X RED/25-50
CWBA Bobby Allison/15 15.00 40.00
CWBE Bill Elliott/25 15.00 40.00
CWDP David Pearson/50 12.00 30.00
CWDW Darrell Waltrip/25 15.00 40.00
CWJJ Jimmie Johnson/48 20.00 50.00
CWRP Richard Petty/43 40.00 80.00
CWRW Rusty Wallace/27 25.00 60.00
CWTS Tony Stewart/50 20.00 50.00

2013 Press Pass Redline Dark Horse Relic Autographs Red
*GOLD/20-25: .5X TO 1.2X RED
DHCB Clint Bowyer/50 8.00 20.00
DHDP Danica Patrick/25 90.00 150.00
DHJM Jamie McMurray/50 8.00 20.00
DHMA Marcos Ambrose/47 10.00 25.00
DHMT Martin Truex/50 8.00 20.00
DHRS Ricky Stenhouse Jr./40 8.00 20.00
DHTD Ty Dillon/75 10.00 25.00
DHTP Travis Pastrana/15 25.00 50.00

2013 Press Pass Redline Dynamic Duals Dual Relic Red
STATED PRINT RUN 50-75
*SILVER/25: .5X TO 1.2X RED/50-75
DDAD Austin Dillon/75 6.00 15.00
DDCE Carl Edwards/75 5.00 12.00
DDDEJR Dale Earnhardt Jr./50 10.00 25.00
DDDH Denny Hamlin/75 5.00 12.00
DDDP Danica Patrick/50 12.00 30.00
DDGB Greg Biffle/75 4.00 10.00
DDJB Jeff Burton/75 4.00 10.00
DDJG Jeff Gordon/50 10.00 25.00
DDJJ Jimmie Johnson/50 8.00 20.00
DDKH Kevin Harvick/50 6.00 15.00
DDKK Kasey Kahne/50 5.00 12.00
DDKYB Kyle Busch/50 5.00 12.00
DDMK Matt Kenseth/75 5.00 12.00
DDMM Mark Martin/75 5.00 12.00
DDRN Ryan Newman/75 4.00 10.00
DDTD Ty Dillon/75 5.00 12.00
DDTP Travis Pastrana/75 5.00 12.00
DDTS Tony Stewart/50 8.00 20.00

2013 Press Pass Redline Intensity
STATED ODDS 1:2
1 Jeff Burton .60 1.50
2 Dale Earnhardt Jr. 1.50 4.00
3 Jeff Gordon 1.50 4.00
4 Kevin Harvick 1.00 2.50
5 Jimmie Johnson 1.25 3.00
6 Kasey Kahne .75 2.00
7 Ryan Newman .60 1.50
8 Danica Patrick 2.00 5.00
9 Tony Stewart 1.25 3.00
10 Kyle Busch 1.00 2.50

2013 Press Pass Redline Muscle Car Sheet Metal Red
STATED PRINT RUN 50 SER.#'d SETS
*SILVER/25: .5X TO 1.2X RED/50
MCMAA Aric Almirola 4.00 10.00
MCMAD Austin Dillon 6.00 15.00
MCMBK Brad Keselowski 6.00 15.00
MCMBL Bobby Labonte 5.00 12.00
MCMCB Clint Bowyer 5.00 12.00
MCMCE Carl Edwards 5.00 12.00
MCMDEJR Dale Earnhardt Jr. 10.00 25.00
MCMDP Danica Patrick 12.00 30.00
MCMJB Jeff Burton 4.00 10.00
MCMJG Jeff Gordon 10.00 25.00
MCMJJ Jimmie Johnson 8.00 20.00
MCMKH Kevin Harvick 6.00 15.00
MCMKK Kasey Kahne 5.00 12.00
MCMKUB Kurt Busch 4.00 10.00
MCMKYB Kyle Busch 5.00 12.00
MCMMK Matt Kenseth 6.00 15.00
MCMRN Ryan Newman 4.00 10.00
MCMTD Ty Dillon 5.00 12.00
MCMTP Travis Pastrana 5.00 12.00
MCMTS Tony Stewart 8.00 20.00

2013 Press Pass Redline Pieces of the Action Red
RED PRINT RUN 75 SER.#'d SETS
*GOLD/25: .5X TO 1.2X RED/75
*SILVER/50: .4X TO 1X RED/75
PABK Brad Keselowski 6.00 15.00
PACE Carl Edwards 5.00 12.00
PADE Dale Earnhardt Jr. 10.00 25.00
PADP Danica Patrick 15.00 40.00
PAJG Jeff Gordon 10.00 25.00
PAJJ Jimmie Johnson 8.00 20.00
PAKH Kevin Harvick 6.00 15.00
PAKK Kasey Kahne 5.00 12.00
PATS Tony Stewart 8.00 20.00
PAKYB Kyle Busch 6.00 15.00

2013 Press Pass Redline Redline Racers
STATED ODDS 1:2
SP STATED ODDS 1:20
1 Kyle Busch 1.00 2.50
2 Travis Pastrana .75 2.00
3 Carl Edwards .75 2.00
4 Jeff Gordon 1.50 4.00
5 Denny Hamlin .75 2.00
6 Kevin Harvick 1.00 2.50
7 Jimmie Johnson 1.25 3.00
8 Kasey Kahne .75 2.00
9 Matt Kenseth .75 2.00
10 Mark Martin .75 2.00
11 Dale Earnhardt Jr. SP 10.00 25.00
12 Danica Patrick SP 12.00 30.00
13 Ricky Stenhouse Jr. SP 8.00 20.00
14 Tony Stewart SP 8.00 20.00
15 Brad Keselowski SP 6.00 15.00

2013 Press Pass Redline Relic Autographs Red
*GOLD/18-25: .5X TO 1.2X RED/39-50
*SILVER/39-50: .5X TO 1.2X RED/75-99
*SILVER/25: .6X TO 1.5X RED/88
*SILVER/17-26: .5X TO 1.2X RED/45-50
RRSEAA Aric Almirola/99 8.00 20.00
RRSECE Carl Edwards/99 8.00 20.00
RRSEDEJ Dale Earnhardt Jr./88 30.00 60.00
RRSEDH Denny Hamlin/99 10.00 25.00
RRSEDP Danica Patrick/10
RRSEJG Jeff Gordon/95 30.00 80.00
RRSEJJ Jimmie Johnson/48 25.00 50.00
RRSEKH Kevin Harvick/75 10.00 25.00
RRSEKK Kasey Kahne/75 10.00 25.00
RRSEKYB Kyle Busch/50 15.00 40.00
RRSEMA Marcos Ambrose/50 12.00 30.00
RRSERN Ryan Newman/95 8.00 20.00
RRSERS Ricky Stenhouse Jr./45 10.00 25.00
RRSETP Travis Pastrana/60 10.00 25.00
RRSETS Tony Stewart/50 25.00 50.00

2013 Press Pass Redline Remarkable Relic Autographs Red
*GOLD/25-28: .5X TO 1.2X RED/43-50
RMRBA Bobby Allison/20 12.00 30.00
RMRBE Bill Elliott/24 15.00 40.00
RMRDJ Dale Jarrett/88 10.00 25.00
RMRDP David Pearson/21 15.00 40.00
RMRDW Darrell Waltrip/25 15.00 40.00
RMRRP Richard Petty/43 20.00 50.00
RMRRR Ricky Rudd/50 6.00 15.00
RMRRW Rusty Wallace/25 15.00 40.00
RMRTL Terry Labonte/44 12.00 30.00

2013 Press Pass Redline RPM
STATED ODDS 1:2
1 Brad Keselowski's Car .75 2.00
2 Jeff Gordon's Car 1.25 3.00
3 Dale Earnhardt Jr.'s Car 1.25 3.00
4 Carl Edwards' Car .60 1.50
5 Jimmie Johnson's Car 1.00 2.50
6 Tony Stewart's Car 1.00 2.50
7 Danica Patrick's Car 1.50 4.00
8 Kevin Harvick's Car .75 2.00
9 Kyle Busch's Car .75 2.00
10 Marcos Ambrose's Car .60 1.50

2013 Press Pass Redline Signatures Red
*BLUE/41-78: .5X TO 1.2X RED/75-99
*BLUE/25: .6X TO 1.5X RED/75
*BLUE/25: .5X TO 1.2X RED/43-50
*BLUE/15: .4X TO 1X RED/25
*HOLO/31: .5X TO 1.2X RED/95
*HOLO/15-27: .6X TO 1.5X RED/75-99
RSAA1 Aric Almirola/43 5.00 12.00
RSBL Bobby Labonte/99 6.00 15.00
RSCB Clint Bowyer/75 5.00 12.00
RSCE1 Carl Edwards/25 8.00 20.00
RSDEJR1 Dale Earnhardt Jr./50 30.00 60.00
RSDH1 Denny Hamlin/25 8.00 20.00
RSGB Greg Biffle/99 4.00 10.00
RSJA Justin Allgaier/95 4.00 10.00
RSJB Jeff Burton/31 8.00 20.00
RSJG1 Jeff Gordon/24 60.00 100.00
RSJG2 Jeff Gordon/24 60.00 100.00
RSJJ1 Jimmie Johnson/48 25.00 50.00
RSJMCM1 Jamie McMurray/25 8.00 20.00
RSJPM Juan Pablo Montoya/99 5.00 12.00
RSKH1 Kevin Harvick/29 10.00 25.00
RSKK1 Kasey Kahne/25 12.00 30.00
RSKUB Kurt Busch/99 4.00 10.00
RSKYB1 Kyle Busch/75 8.00 20.00
RSMK1 Matt Kenseth/99 6.00 15.00
RSMK2 Matt Kenseth/25 10.00 25.00
RSMM Mark Martin/75 10.00 25.00
RSMT Martin Truex/75 4.00 10.00
RSMW Michael Waltrip/70 5.00 12.00
RSPM Paul Menard/95 3.00 8.00
RSRN1 Ryan Newman/20 6.00 15.00
RSRS Regan Smith/99 4.00 10.00
RSRSJR Ricky Stenhouse Jr./35 6.00 15.00
RSTP Travis Pastrana/25 20.00 40.00
RSTS1 Tony Stewart/20 30.00 60.00

2013 Press Pass Redline V8 Relics Red
STATED PRINT RUN 25 SER.#'d SETS
V8BK Brad Keselowski 10.00 25.00
V8CE Carl Edwards 8.00 20.00
V8DE Dale Earnhardt Jr. 15.00 40.00
V8JB Jeff Burton 6.00 15.00
V8JG Jeff Gordon 30.00 60.00
V8JL Joey Logano 8.00 20.00
V8KH Kevin Harvick 10.00 25.00
V8KK Kasey Kahne 12.00 30.00
V8KYB Kyle Busch 10.00 25.00
V8MK Matt Kenseth 10.00 25.00
V8TS Tony Stewart 12.00 30.00

2013 Press Pass Redline Relics Red
STATED PRINT RUN 50 SER.#'d SETS
*SILVER/25: .5X TO 1.2X RED/50
RRBK Brad Keselowski 6.00 15.00
RRCB Clint Bowyer 5.00 12.00
RRCE Carl Edwards 5.00 12.00
RRDEJR1 Dale Earnhardt Jr. 10.00 25.00
RRDH Denny Hamlin 5.00 12.00
RRDP Danica Patrick 12.00 30.00
RRJB Jeff Burton 4.00 10.00
RRJG1 Jeff Gordon 8.00 20.00
RRJG2 Jeff Gordon 8.00 20.00
RRJJ Jimmie Johnson 8.00 20.00
RRJL Joey Logano 5.00 12.00
RRJM Jamie McMurray 5.00 12.00
RRJPM Juan Pablo Montoya 5.00 12.00
RRKH Kevin Harvick 6.00 15.00
RRKK Kasey Kahne 5.00 12.00
RRKYB Kyle Busch 6.00 15.00
RRMM Mark Martin 5.00 12.00
RRMT Martin Truex 4.00 10.00
RRPM Paul Menard 3.00 8.00
RRRN Ryan Newman 4.00 10.00
RRRS Ricky Stenhouse Jr. 5.00 12.00
RRRS Regan Smith 4.00 10.00
RRTP Travis Pastrana 5.00 12.00
RRTS Tony Stewart 8.00 20.00

2014 Press Pass Redline
1 A.J. Allmendinger .50 1.25
2 Justin Allgaier .40 1.00
3 Aric Almirola .40 1.00
4 Marcos Ambrose .50 1.25
5 Marcos Ambrose .50 1.25
6 Michael Annett RC 1.25 3.00
7 Greg Biffle .40 1.00
8 Alex Bowman RC 1.25 3.00
9 Clint Bowyer .50 1.25
10 Clint Bowyer .50 1.25
11 Kurt Busch .40 1.00
12 Kyle Busch .60 1.50
13 Kyle Busch .60 1.50
14 Austin Dillon .60 1.50
15 Austin Dillon .60 1.50
16 Dale Earnhardt Jr. 1.00 2.50
17 Dale Earnhardt Jr. 1.00 2.50
18 Carl Edwards .50 1.25
19 Carl Edwards .50 1.25
20 David Gilliland .30 .75
21 Jeff Gordon 1.00 2.50
22 Jeff Gordon 1.00 2.50
23 Denny Hamlin .50 1.25
24 Denny Hamlin .50 1.25
25 Kevin Harvick .60 1.50
26 Jimmie Johnson .75 2.00
27 Jimmie Johnson .75 2.00
28 Kasey Kahne .50 1.25
29 Kasey Kahne .50 1.25
30 Matt Kenseth .50 1.25
31 Matt Kenseth .50 1.25
32 Brad Keselowski .60 1.50
33 Kyle Larson CRC 1.00 2.50
34 Joey Logano .50 1.25
35 Joey Logano .50 1.25
36 Michael McDowell .40 1.00
37 Jamie McMurray .50 1.25
38 Jamie McMurray .50 1.25
39 Casey Mears .30 .75
40 Paul Menard .30 .75
41 Ryan Newman .40 1.00
42 Ryan Newman .40 1.00
43 Danica Patrick 1.00 2.50
44 Danica Patrick 1.00 2.50
45 David Ragan .40 1.00
46 Ricky Stenhouse Jr. .50 1.25
47 Ricky Stenhouse Jr. .50 1.25
48 Tony Stewart .75 2.00
49 Tony Stewart .75 2.00
50 Ryan Truex .40 1.00
51 Martin Truex Jr. .40 1.00
52 Brian Vickers .30 .75
53 Michael Waltrip .50 1.25
54 Cole Whitt .40 1.00
55 Josh Wise .30 .75
56 Dakoda Armstrong .50 1.25
57 Trevor Bayne .50 1.25
58 James Buescher .30 .75
59 Ty Dillon .50 1.25
60 Ty Dillon .50 1.25
61 Jeffrey Earnhardt .50 1.25
62 Chase Elliott 2.00 5.00
63 Brendan Gaughan .30 .75
64 Sam Hornish Jr. .40 1.00
65 Dylan Kwasniewski .40 1.00
66 Elliott Sadler .30 .75
67 Brian Scott .30 .75
68 Regan Smith .40 1.00
69 Ryan Blaney .40 1.00
70 Jeb Burton .40 1.00
71 Jennifer Jo Cobb .50 1.25
72 Matt Crafton .30 .75
73 Johnny Sauter .30 .75
74 Darrell Wallace Jr. .50 1.25
75 Bill Elliott .75 2.00
76 Terry Labonte .50 1.25
77 Dale Jarrett .60 1.50
78 Richard Petty .75 2.00
79 Rusty Wallace .50 1.25
80 Darrell Waltrip .75 2.00

2014 Press Pass Redline Black
*BLACK/75: 1.2X TO 3X BASIC CARDS

2014 Press Pass Redline Blue Foil
*BLUE: 2.5X TO 6X BASIC CARDS
INSERTED IN RETAIL PACKS

2014 Press Pass Redline Cyan
*CYAN/50: 1.5X TO 4X BASIC CARDS

2014 Press Pass Redline Dynamic Duals Relic Autographs Red
*BLUE/25: .5X TO 1.2X BASIC RELIC/50
*BLUE/15: .5X TO 1.2X BASIC RELIC/25
*BLUE/10: .8X TO 2X BASIC RELIC/50
*BLUE/10: .5X TO 1.2X BASIC RELIC/15
*GOLD/25: .5X TO 1.2X BASIC RELIC/50
*GOLD/10: .8X TO 2X BASIC RELIC/50
*GOLD/10: .6X TO 1.5X BASIC RELIC/25
DDAD Austin Dillon/50 12.00 30.00
DDCE Carl Edwards/50 EXCH 10.00 25.00
DDCE Chase Elliott/25 50.00 100.00
DDDH Denny Hamlin/50 10.00 25.00
DDDP Danica Patrick/15
DDJG Jeff Gordon/15 75.00 135.00
DDJJ Jimmie Johnson/15 25.00 60.00

DDJL Joey Logano/15 15.00 40.00
DDKH Kevin Harvick/25 15.00 40.00
DDKK Kasey Kahne/25 12.00 30.00
DDKL Kyle Larson/50 30.00 80.00
DDMA Marcos Ambrose/15 15.00 40.00
DDMK Matt Kenseth/50 10.00 25.00
DDDEJ Dale Earnhardt Jr./15 90.00 150.00
DDKUB Kurt Busch/15 12.00 30.00
DDKYB Kyle Busch/50 12.00 30.00

2014 Press Pass Redline First Win Relic Autographs Red

*GOLD/15: .8X TO 2X RED/25
RRFWCE Chase Elliott 50.00 100.00

2014 Press Pass Redline Full Throttle Relics Red

*GOLD/25: .5X TO 1.2X RED/50
*BLUE/10: .8X TO 2X RED/50
FTAB Alex Bowman 10.00 25.00
FTAD Austin Dillon 5.00 12.00
FTCW Cole Whitt 3.00 8.00
FTJA Justin Allgaier 3.00 8.00
FTKL Kyle Larson 12.00 30.00
FTMA Michael Annett 5.00 12.00
FTPK Parker Kligerman 2.50 6.00
FTRT Ryan Truex 3.00 8.00

2014 Press Pass Redline Head to Head Red

*GOLD/25: .6X TO 1.5X RED/75
*BLUE/10: 1X TO 2.5X RED/75
HTHADDE A.Dillon/D.Earnhardt Jr. 10.00 25.00
HTHDPKK D.Patrick/K.Kahne 10.00 25.00
HTHJGKH J.Gordon/K.Harvick 10.00 25.00
HTHJJTS J.Johnson/T.Stewart 8.00 20.00
HTHKBKL K.Busch/K.Larson 8.00 20.00

2014 Press Pass Redline Intensity

COMPLETE SET (10) 8.00 20.00
I1 Kyle Busch 1.00 2.50
I2 Austin Dillon 1.00 2.50
I3 Dale Earnhardt Jr. 1.50 4.00
I4 Jeff Gordon 1.50 4.00
I5 Kevin Harvick 1.00 2.50
I6 Jimmie Johnson 1.25 3.00
I7 Kasey Kahne .75 2.00
I8 Matt Kenseth .75 2.00
I9 Danica Patrick 3.00 8.00
I10 Tony Stewart 1.25 3.00

2014 Press Pass Redline Muscle Car Sheet Metal Red

*GOLD/25-50: .5X TO 1.2X RED/50-75
*BLUE/10-25: .6X TO 1.5X RED/50-75
MCMAD Austin Dillon/75 5.00 12.00
MCMBK Brad Keselowski/50 6.00 15.00
MCMCB Clint Bowyer/50 5.00 12.00
MCMDH Denny Hamlin/75 4.00 10.00
MCMDP Danica Patrick/75 10.00 25.00
MCMGB Greg Biffle/50 4.00 10.00
MCMJG Jeff Gordon/75 10.00 25.00
MCMJJ Jimmie Johnson/75 6.00 15.00
MCMJL Joey Logano/50 5.00 12.00
MCMKH Kevin Harvick/50 6.00 15.00
MCMKK Kasey Kahne/75 4.00 10.00
MCMMK Matt Kenseth/75 3.00 8.00
MCMTD Ty Dillon/50 5.00 12.00
MCMTS Tony Stewart/75 6.00 15.00
MCMCE1 Carl Edwards/75 4.00 10.00
MCMCE2 Chase Elliott/75 15.00 40.00
MCMDEJ Dale Earnhardt Jr./75 10.00 25.00
MCMKUB Kurt Busch/50 4.00 10.00
MCMKYB Kyle Busch/75 5.00 12.00

2014 Press Pass Redline Pieces of the Action Red

*GOLD/25: .6X TO 1.5X RED/75
*BLUE/10: .8X TO 2X RED/75
PACE Carl Edwards 5.00 12.00
PADH Denny Hamlin 5.00 12.00
PADP Danica Patrick 15.00 40.00
PAJG Jeff Gordon 12.00 30.00
PAJJ Jimmie Johnson 8.00 20.00
PAJL Joey Logano 5.00 12.00
PAKH Kevin Harvick 6.00 15.00
PAKK Kasey Kahne 5.00 12.00
PAMA Marcos Ambrose 5.00 12.00
PAMK Matt Kenseth 5.00 12.00
PATS Tony Stewart 8.00 20.00
PADEJ Dale Earnhardt Jr. 10.00 25.00
PAKYB Kyle Busch 6.00 15.00

2014 Press Pass Redline Redline Racers

COMPLETE SET (15) 8.00 20.00
RR1 Kurt Busch .60 1.50
RR2 Kyle Busch 1.00 2.50
RR3 Austin Dillon 1.00 2.50
RR4 Dale Earnhardt Jr. 1.50 4.00
RR5 Carl Edwards .75 2.00
RR6 Jeff Gordon 1.50 4.00
RR7 Denny Hamlin .75 2.00
RR8 Kevin Harvick 1.00 2.50
RR9 Jimmie Johnson 1.25 3.00
RR10 Kasey Kahne .75 2.00
RR11 Matt Kenseth .75 2.00
RR12 Kyle Larson 1.50 4.00
RR13 Joey Logano .75 2.00
RR14 Danica Patrick 4.00 10.00
RR15 Tony Stewart 1.25 3.00

2014 Press Pass Redline Relic Autographs Red

*GOLD/25: .5X TO 1.2X RED/50
*GOLD/15: .5X TO 1.2X RED/25
RRSEAA Aric Almirola/25 10.00 25.00
RRSECB Clint Bowyer/50 10.00 25.00
RRSECE1 Carl Edwards/50 EXCH 10.00 25.00
RRSECE2 Chase Elliott/25 50.00 125.00
RRSECM Casey Mears/25 8.00 20.00
RRSEDEJ Dale Earnhardt Jr./15 75.00 125.00
RRSEDH Denny Hamlin/50 10.00 25.00
RRSEDP Danica Patrick/15 75.00 135.00
RRSEGB Greg Biffle/50 8.00 20.00
RRSEJG Jeff Gordon/15 75.00 135.00
RRSEJJ Jimmie Johnson/15 60.00 100.00
RRSEJL Joey Logano/15 20.00 50.00
RRSEJM Jamie McMurray/25 12.00 30.00
RRSEKH Kevin Harvick/25 15.00 40.00
RRSEKK Kasey Kahne/25 12.00 30.00
RRSEKUB Kurt Busch/25 10.00 25.00
RRSEKYB Kyle Busch/50 12.00 30.00
RRSEMA Marcos Ambrose/25 12.00 30.00
RRSEMC Matt Crafton/50 6.00 15.00
RRSEMK Matt Kenseth/50 10.00 25.00
RRSEMTJ Martin Truex Jr./50 8.00 20.00
RRSEPM Paul Menard/50 6.00 15.00
RRSERB Ryan Blaney/25 10.00 25.00
RRSERN Ryan Newman/25 10.00 25.00
RRSERS Regan Smith/50 8.00 20.00
RRSERSJ Ricky Stenhouse Jr./50 10.00 25.00
RRSETB Trevor Bayne/25 12.00 30.00
RRSETD Ty Dillon/25 10.00 25.00

2014 Press Pass Redline Relics Red

*GOLD/50: .5X TO 1.2X RED/75
*BLUE/25: .6X TO 1.5X RED/75
RRAA Aric Almirola 2.50 6.00
RRBG Brendan Gaughan 2.00 5.00
RRBK Brad Keselowski 4.00 10.00
RRBS Brian Scott 2.00 5.00
RRBV Brian Vickers 2.00 5.00
RRCB Clint Bowyer 3.00 8.00
RRCM Casey Mears 2.00 5.00
RRDH Denny Hamlin 3.00 8.00
RRDK Dylan Kwasniewski 2.50 6.00
RRDP Danica Patrick 10.00 25.00
RRDR David Ragan 2.50 6.00
RRES Elliott Sadler 2.00 5.00
RRGB Greg Biffle 2.50 6.00
RRJG Jeff Gordon 6.00 15.00
RRJJ Jimmie Johnson 5.00 12.00
RRJL Joey Logano 5.00 12.00
RRJM Jamie McMurray 3.00 8.00
RRJS Johnny Sauter 2.00 5.00
RRJW Josh Wise 2.00 5.00
RRKH Kevin Harvick 4.00 10.00
RRKK Kasey Kahne 3.00 8.00
RRMA Marcos Ambrose 3.00 8.00
RRMC Matt Crafton 2.00 5.00
RRMK Matt Kenseth 3.00 8.00
RRMM Michael McDowell 2.50 6.00
RRMW Michael Waltrip 3.00 8.00
RRPM Paul Menard 2.00 5.00
RRRB Ryan Blaney 2.50 6.00
RRRN Ryan Newman 2.50 6.00
RRRS Regan Smith 2.50 6.00
RRTB Trevor Bayne 3.00 8.00
RRTD Ty Dillon 3.00 8.00
RRTS Tony Stewart 5.00 12.00
RRAJA A.J. Allmendinger 3.00 8.00
RRCE1 Carl Edwards 3.00 8.00
RRCE2 Chase Elliott 10.00 25.00
RRDEJ Dale Earnhardt Jr. 8.00 20.00
RRKUB Kurt Busch 2.50 6.00
RRKYB Kyle Busch 4.00 10.00
RRMTJ Martin Truex Jr. 2.50 6.00
RRRSJ Ricky Stenhouse Jr. 3.00 8.00

2014 Press Pass Redline Remarkable Relic Autographs Red

*GOLD/25: .5X TO 1.2X RED/50
RMRBE Bill Elliott 15.00 40.00
RMRDJ Dale Jarrett 12.00 30.00
RMRDW Darrell Waltrip 8.00 20.00
RMRRP Richard Petty 15.00 40.00
RMRRW Rusty Wallace 10.00 25.00
RMRTL Terry Labonte 10.00 25.00

2014 Press Pass Redline RPM

COMPLETE SET (10) 5.00 12.00
RPM1 Kyle Busch's Car 1.00 2.50
RPM2 Dale Earnhardt Jr.'s Car 1.50 4.00
RPM3 Jeff Gordon's Car 1.50 4.00
RPM4 Denny Hamlin's Car .75 2.00
RPM5 Kevin Harvick's Car 1.00 2.50
RPM6 Jimmie Johnson's Car 1.25 3.00
RPM7 Brad Keselowski's Car 1.00 2.50
RPM8 Kyle Larson's Car 1.50 4.00
RPM9 Danica Patrick's Car 1.50 4.00
RPM10 Tony Stewart's Car 1.25 3.00

2014 Press Pass Redline Signatures Red

*GOLD/50: .4X TO 1X RED AU/60-65
*GOLD/25: .5X TO 1.2X RED AU/25
*GOLD/25: .5X TO 1.2X RED AU/50-65
RSAA Aric Almirola/50 5.00 12.00
RSAB Alex Bowman/50 10.00 25.00
RSAD Austin Dillon/50 8.00 20.00
RSAJA A.J. Allmendinger/60 6.00 15.00
RSBE Bill Elliott/25 12.00 30.00
RSBG Brendan Gaughan/50 4.00 10.00
RSBS Brian Scott/50 4.00 10.00
RSCB Clint Bowyer/65 6.00 15.00
RSCE1 Carl Edwards/30 EXCH 8.00 20.00
RSCE2 Chase Elliott/25 50.00 100.00
RSCM Casey Mears/50 4.00 10.00
RSCW Cole Whitt/60 5.00 12.00
RSDA Dakoda Armstrong/60 6.00 15.00
RSDEJ Dale Earnhardt Jr./15 60.00 120.00
RSDG David Gilliland/60 4.00 10.00
RSDH Denny Hamlin/30 8.00 20.00
RSDJ Dale Jarrett/25 10.00 25.00
RSDK Dylan Kwasniewski/50 5.00 12.00
RSDP Danica Patrick/15 75.00 150.00
RSDR David Ragan/60 5.00 12.00
RSDW Darrell Waltrip/25 12.00 30.00
RSDWJ Darrell Wallace Jr./50 6.00 15.00
RSES Elliott Sadler/50 4.00 10.00
RSGB Greg Biffle/65 5.00 12.00
RSJA Justin Allgaier/60 5.00 12.00
RSJB1 James Buescher/50 4.00 10.00
RSJB2 Jeb Burton/60 5.00 12.00
RSJC Jennifer Jo Cobb/60 12.00 30.00
RSJE Jeffrey Earnhardt/50 6.00 15.00
RSJG Jeff Gordon/15 60.00 120.00
RSJJ Jimmie Johnson/15 50.00 100.00
RSJL Joey Logano/15 12.00 30.00
RSJM Jamie McMurray/25 6.00 15.00
RSJS Johnny Sauter/60 4.00 10.00
RSJW Josh Wise/60 4.00 10.00
RSKH Kevin Harvick/25 20.00 40.00
RSKK Kasey Kahne/25 8.00 20.00
RSKL Kyle Larson/50 30.00 60.00
RSKUB Kurt Busch/25 6.00 15.00
RSKYB Kyle Busch/25 10.00 25.00
RSMA1 Marcos Ambrose/15 10.00 25.00
RSMA2 Michael Annett/50
RSMC Matt Crafton/25 5.00 12.00
RSMK Matt Kenseth/30 8.00 20.00
RSMM Michael McDowell/50 5.00 12.00
RSMTJ Martin Truex Jr./65 5.00 12.00
RSMW Michael Waltrip/50 6.00 15.00
RSPK Parker Kligerman/50 4.00 10.00
RSPM Paul Menard/65 4.00 10.00
RSRB Ryan Blaney/35 6.00 15.00
RSRN Ryan Newman/65 6.00 15.00
RSRP Richard Petty/25 12.00 30.00
RSRS Regan Smith/25 6.00 15.00
RSRSJ Ricky Stenhouse Jr./65 5.00 12.00
RSRT Ryan Truex/60 5.00 12.00
RSRW Rusty Wallace/25 8.00 20.00
RSTB Trevor Bayne/50
RSTD Ty Dillon/25 8.00 20.00
RSTL Terry Labonte/25 15.00 30.00

2004 Press Pass Rookie Class

This 6-card set was available in retail packs of 2004 VIP. They were inserted into the '04 VIP retail blaster boxes at a rate of 1 per box. The cards featured 6 of the top upcoming drivers making their Nextel Cup debuts in 2004.

COMPLETE SET (6) 8.00 20.00
RC1 Kasey Kahne 3.00 8.00
RC2 Johnny Sauter 1.00 2.50
RC3 Brian Vickers 1.50 4.00
RC4 Brendan Gaughan 1.50 4.00
RC5 Scott Riggs 1.00 2.50
RC6 Scott Wimmer 1.00 2.50

2009 Press Pass Showcase

COMP.SET w/o RCs (50) 60.00 120.00
WAX BOX HOBBY (1) 225.00 300.00
1 Juan Pablo Montoya 1.25 3.00
2 Martin Truex Jr. .75 2.00
3 Dale Earnhardt Jr. 2.00 5.00
4 Jeff Gordon 2.00 5.00
5 Jimmie Johnson 1.50 4.00
6 Mark Martin 1.00 2.50
7 Kyle Busch 1.25 3.00
8 Denny Hamlin 1.00 2.50
9 Kurt Busch .75 2.00
10 Sam Hornish Jr. .75 2.00
11 David Stremme .60 1.50
12 Brian Vickers .60 1.50
13 Clint Bowyer 1.00 2.50
14 Jeff Burton .75 2.00
15 Kevin Harvick 1.25 3.00
16 Casey Mears .60 1.50
17 A.J. Allmendinger 1.00 2.50
18 Kasey Kahne 1.00 2.50
19 Elliott Sadler .60 1.50
20 Reed Sorenson .60 1.50
21 Greg Biffle .75 2.00
22 Carl Edwards 1.00 2.50
23 Matt Kenseth 1.00 2.50
24 Jamie McMurray 1.00 2.50
25 David Ragan .75 2.00
26 Ryan Newman .75 2.00
27 Tony Stewart 1.50 4.00
28 Montoya/Truex Jr. CC 1.25 3.00
29 Martin/JJ/Gordon/Jr. CC 2.00 5.00
30 Logano/Kyle/Hamlin CC 2.50 6.00
31 Hornish/Kurt/Stremme CC .75 2.00
32 Vickers/Speed CC 1.25 3.00
33 Mears/Burt/Harv/Bowyer CC 1.25 3.00
34 Sadl/Soren/Kahne/Allmen CC 1.00 2.50
35 Ragan/Biff/Kens/Edw/McM CC 1.00 2.50
36 Stewart/Newman CC 1.50 4.00
37 Dale Earnhardt Jr. EE 2.00 5.00
38 Jeff Gordon EE 2.00 5.00
39 Jimmie Johnson EE 1.50 4.00
40 Mark Martin EE 1.00 2.50
41 Kevin Harvick EE 1.25 3.00
42 Carl Edwards EE 1.00 2.50
43 Tony Stewart EE 1.50 4.00
44 Kasey Kahne EE 1.00 2.50
45 Kyle Busch EE 1.25 3.00
46 Matt Kenseth EE 1.00 2.50
47 Kurt Busch EE .75 2.00
48 Jeff Burton EE .75 2.00
49 Richard Petty EE 1.50 4.00
50 Dale Earnhardt EE 6.00 15.00
51 J.Logano JSY AU RC 25.00 60.00
52 S.Speed JSY AU RC 15.00 40.00
53 B.Keselowski JSY AU CRC 30.00 60.00

2009 Press Pass Showcase 2nd Gear

*2ND GEAR: 1X TO 2.5X BASE
STATED PRINT RUN 125 SER.#'d SETS
JSY AU STATED PRINT RUN 50
51 J.Logano JSY AU 60.00 120.00
52 S.Speed JSY AU 20.00 50.00
53 B.Keselowski JSY AU 40.00 80.00

2009 Press Pass Showcase 3rd Gear

*3RD GEAR: 1.2X TO 3X BASE
STATED PRINT RUN 50 SER.#'d SETS
JSY AU STATED PRINT RUN 25
51 J.Logano JSY AU 75.00 150.00
52 S.Speed JSY AU 30.00 60.00
53 B.Keselowski JSY AU 75.00 150.00

2009 Press Pass Showcase 4th Gear

*4TH GEAR/15: 2.5X TO 6X BASE
1-50 STATED PRINT RUN 15
51-53 UNPRICED JSY AU PRINT RUN 5

2009 Press Pass Showcase Classic Collections Firesuit

STATED PRINT RUN 25 SER.#'d SETS
CCF1 Dale Jr./Gordon/JJ 75.00 150.00
CCF2 Dale Jr./Gordon 50.00 100.00
CCF3 Dale Jr./Johnson 20.00 50.00
CCF4 Gordon/Johnson 25.00 60.00
CCF5 Logano/Kyle/Hamlin 25.00 60.00
CCF6 Vickers/Speed 15.00 40.00
CCF7 Mears/Burt/Harv/Bowyer 20.00 50.00
CCF8 Ragan/Biff/Kens/Edw/McM 40.00 80.00
CCF9 Stewart/Newman 25.00 60.00
CCF10 M.Waltrip/Reutimann 20.00 50.00

2009 Press Pass Showcase Classic Collections Sheet Metal

STATED PRINT RUN 45 SER.#'d SETS
CCS1 Dale Jr./Gordon/JJ 30.00 80.00
CCS2 Dale Jr./Gordon 25.00 60.00
CCS3 Dale Jr./Johnson 15.00 40.00
CCS4 Gordon/Johnson 25.00 60.00
CCS5 Logano/Kyle/Hamlin 20.00 50.00
CCS6 Vickers/Speed 12.00 30.00
CCS7 Mears/Burt/Harv/Bowyer 25.00 60.00
CCS8 Ragan/Biff/Kens/Edw/McM 30.00 80.00
CCS9 Stewart/Newman 15.00 40.00
CCS10 M.Waltrip/Reutimann 10.00 25.00

2009 Press Pass Showcase Classic Collections Tire

STATED PRINT RUN 99 SER.#'d SETS
CCT1 Dale Jr./Gordon/JJ 25.00 60.00
CCT2 Dale Jr./Gordon 15.00 40.00
CCT3 Dale Jr./Johnson 15.00 40.00
CCT4 Gordon/Johnson 15.00 40.00
CCT5 Logano/Kyle/Hamlin 15.00 40.00
CCT6 Vickers/Speed 8.00 20.00
CCT7 Mears/Burt/Harv/Bowyer 12.00 30.00
CCT8 Ragan/Biff/Kens/Edw/McM 12.00 30.00
CCT9 Stewart/Newman 12.00 30.00
CCT10 M.Waltrip/Reutimann 8.00 20.00

2009 Press Pass Showcase Classic Collections Ink

STATED PRINT RUN 45 SER.#'d SETS
UNPRICED INK MELTING PRINT RUN 1
*GOLD/25: .5X TO 1.2X BASIC INK
1 Montoya/Truex Jr. 20.00 50.00
2 Martin/JJ/Gordon/Jr. 400.00 600.00
3 Logano/Kyle/Hamlin 75.00 150.00
4 M.Waltrip/Reutimann 15.00 40.00
5 Hornish/Kurt/Stremme 25.00 60.00
6 Vickers/Speed 15.00 40.00
7 Mears/Burt/Harv/Bowyer 40.00 80.00
8 Sadl/Soren/Kahne/Allmen 40.00 100.00
9 Ragan/Biff/Kens/Edw/McM 60.00 120.00
10 Stewart/Newman 40.00 80.00

2009 Press Pass Showcase Elite Exhibit Triple Memorabilia

STATED PRINT RUN 99 SER.#'d SETS
UNPRICED MELTING PRINT RUN 5
*GOLD/45: .6X TO 1.6X BASE
*GREEN/25: .8X TO 2X BASE
EECE Carl Edwards 6.00 15.00
EEJG Jeff Gordon 15.00 40.00
EEJJ Jimmie Johnson 10.00 25.00
EEJL Joey Logano 20.00 50.00
EEKB Kyle Busch 8.00 20.00
EEKH Kevin Harvick 8.00 20.00
EEKK Kasey Kahne 6.00 15.00
EEMK Matt Kenseth 6.00 15.00
EETS Tony Stewart 10.00 25.00
EEDEJ Dale Earnhardt Jr. 12.00 30.00

2009 Press Pass Showcase Elite Exhibit Ink

STATED PRINT RUN 45 SER.#'d SETS
*GOLD/25: .5X TO 1.2X BASIC INK
EXCH EXPIRATION: 8/1/2010
1 Kyle Busch 25.00 60.00
2 Dale Earnhardt Jr. 30.00 80.00
3 Carl Edwards 20.00 50.00
4 Jeff Gordon 75.00 150.00
5 Kevin Harvick 15.00 40.00
6 Jimmie Johnson 20.00 50.00
7 Kasey Kahne 25.00 60.00
8 Matt Kenseth 15.00 40.00
9 Joey Logano 40.00 80.00
10 Richard Petty 25.00 60.00
11 Tony Stewart 30.00 80.00
12 Darrell Waltrip 25.00 60.00

2009 Press Pass Showcase Prized Pieces Firesuit

STATED PRINT RUN 25 SER.#'d SETS
PPFCE Carl Edwards 15.00 40.00
PPFDE Dale Earnhardt 175.00 300.00
PPFGB Greg Biffle 12.00 30.00
PPFJB Jeff Burton 40.00 100.00
PPFJG Jeff Gordon 100.00 200.00
PPFJJ Jimmie Johnson 60.00 120.00
PPFJL Joey Logano 75.00 150.00
PPFJM Juan Pablo Montoya 20.00 50.00
PPFKB Kyle Busch 75.00 150.00
PPFKH Kevin Harvick 60.00 120.00
PPFKK Kasey Kahne 50.00 100.00
PPFTS Tony Stewart 75.00 150.00
PPFDEJ Dale Earnhardt Jr. AMP 75.00 150.00
PPFDEJ2 Dale Earnhardt Jr. NG 75.00 150.00

2009 Press Pass Showcase Prized Pieces Sheet Metal

STATED PRINT RUN 45 SER.#'d SETS
PPSCE Carl Edwards 25.00 60.00
PPSDE Dale Earnhardt
PPSGB Greg Biffle 8.00 20.00
PPSJB Jeff Burton 20.00 50.00
PPSJG Jeff Gordon 20.00 50.00
PPSJJ Jimmie Johnson 25.00 60.00
PPSJL Joey Logano 20.00 50.00
PPSJM Juan Pablo Montoya 12.00 30.00
PPSKB Kyle Busch 25.00 60.00
PPSKH Kevin Harvick 12.00 30.00
PPSKK Kasey Kahne 12.00 30.00
PPSTS Tony Stewart 15.00 40.00
PPSDEJ Dale Earnhardt Jr. AMP 20.00 50.00
PPSDEJ2 Dale Earnhardt Jr. NG 20.00 50.00

2009 Press Pass Showcase Prized Pieces Tire

TIRE PRINT RUN 99 SER.#'d SETS
PPTCE Carl Edwards 5.00 12.00
PPTDE Dale Earnhardt/25 75.00 150.00
PPTGB Greg Biffle 4.00 10.00
PPTJB Jeff Burton 10.00 25.00
PPTJG Jeff Gordon 25.00 60.00
PPTJJ Jimmie Johnson 8.00 20.00
PPTJL Joey Logano 10.00 25.00
PPTJM Juan Pablo Montoya 6.00 15.00
PPTKB Kyle Busch 6.00 15.00
PPTKH Kevin Harvick 12.00 30.00
PPTKK Kasey Kahne 5.00 12.00
PPTTS Tony Stewart 20.00 50.00
PPTDEJ Dale Earnhardt Jr. AMP 10.00 25.00
PPTDEJ2 Dale Earnhardt Jr. NG 10.00 25.00

2009 Press Pass Showcase Prized Pieces Ink Tire

STATED PRINT RUN 45 SER.#'d SETS
*SHEET METAL/25: .5X TO 1.2X TIRE
1 Kyle Busch 40.00 80.00
2 Dale Earnhardt Jr. 100.00 200.00
3 Carl Edwards 50.00 100.00
4 Jeff Gordon 75.00 150.00
5 Kevin Harvick 50.00 100.00
6 Jimmie Johnson 40.00 100.00
7 Kasey Kahne 75.00 150.00
8 Matt Kenseth 50.00 100.00
9 Tony Stewart 75.00 150.00

2010 Press Pass Showcase

COMPLETE SET (51) 300.00 600.00
COMP.SET w/o SPs (50) 125.00 250.00
WAX BOX HOBBY (3) 175.00 250.00
1 Mark Martin 1.00 2.50
2 Tony Stewart OD 1.50 4.00
3 Jimmie Johnson 1.50 4.00
4 Denny Hamlin 1.00 2.50
5 Kasey Kahne 1.00 2.50
6 Jeff Gordon 2.00 5.00
7 Kurt Busch .75 2.00
8 Brian Vickers .60 1.50
9 Carl Edwards 1.00 2.50
10 Ryan Newman .75 2.00
11 Juan Pablo Montoya 1.00 2.50
12 Greg Biffle .75 2.00
13 Kyle Busch 1.25 3.00
14 Matt Kenseth 1.00 2.50
15 Clint Bowyer 1.00 2.50
16 David Reutimann .75 2.00
17 Marcos Ambrose 4.00 10.00
18 Jeff Burton .75 2.00
19 Joey Logano 1.00 2.50
20 Dale Earnhardt Jr. NG 2.00 5.00
21 Kevin Harvick 1.25 3.00
22 Jamie McMurray 1.00 2.50
23 A.J. Allmendinger 1.00 2.50
24 Martin Truex Jr. .75 2.00
25 David Ragan .75 2.00
26 Scott Speed 1.00 2.50
27 Brad Keselowski 1.25 3.00
28 Grdn/Jhn/Mrtn/Stew CC 2.00 5.00
29 Petty/Andr/DW/Yarbr CC 1.50 4.00
30 Jr./Grdn/Ptrck/Stew CC 8.00 20.00
31 Dale Jr./D.Patrick CC 8.00 20.00
32 Jr./Jhnsn/Grdn/Mrtn CC 2.00 5.00
33 Hrvick/Brtn/Bwyer CC 1.25 3.00
34 Edwr/Knsth/Biff/Rgn CC 1.00 2.50
35 Ky.Bs/Hmln/Lgano CC 1.25 3.00
36 Ku.Bs/Kesel/Hrnsh CC 1.25 3.00
37 Dale Earnhardt Jr. EE 2.00 5.00
38 Jeff Gordon EE 2.00 5.00
39 Jimmie Johnson EE 1.50 4.00
40 Mark Martin EE 1.00 2.50
41 Kevin Harvick EE 1.25 3.00
42 Carl Edwards EE 1.00 2.50
43 Tony Stewart EE 1.50 4.00
44 Kasey Kahne EE 1.00 2.50
45 Kyle Busch EE 1.25 3.00
46 Matt Kenseth EE 1.00 2.50
47 Kurt Busch EE .75 2.00
48 Jeff Burton EE .75 2.00
49 Joey Logano EE 1.00 2.50
50 Brad Keselowski EE 1.25 3.00
51 D.Patrick PP SM AU RC/75 125.00 250.00

2010 Press Pass Showcase Gold

*SINGLES: 1X TO 2.5X BASIC CARDS
STATED PRINT RUN 125 SER.#'d SETS
51 D.Patrick PP FS AU/25 250.00 350.00

2010 Press Pass Showcase Green

*GREEN/50: 1.2X TO 3X BASIC CARDS
STATED PRINT RUN 50 SER.#'d SETS

2010 Press Pass Showcase Melting

*1-50 MELTING/15: 2.5X TO 6X BASIC CARDS
MELTING PRINT RUN 15

2010 Press Pass Showcase Classic Collections Firesuit Green

STATED PRINT RUN 25 SER.#'d SETS
CCI500 Petty/Andrt/DW/Yarb 25.00 50.00
CCIFAN Jr./Gord/Dnca/Stew 30.00 80.00
CCIHMS Jr./JJ/Gordon/Martin 50.00 100.00
CCIJGR Ky.Bsch/Hmln/Logno 15.00 40.00
CCIJRM Dale Jr./Danica 30.00 80.00
CCIRCR Harvick/Burton/Bowyer 25.00 5
CCIRFR Edwrd/Knsth/Bif/Rgn 30.00 6
CCIWIN Gordn/JJ/Martn/Stewrt 25.00 6

2010 Press Pass Showcase Classic Collections Sheet Me

STATED PRINT RUN 75-99
*GOLD/25-45: .5X TO 1.2X BASIC INSERTS
CCIFAN Jr./Grdn/Danca/Stew 40.00 10
CCIHMS Jr./JJ/Gordon/Martin 30.00 8
CCIJGR Ky.Bsch/Hmln/Lgno 15.00 4
CCIJRM Dale Jr./Danica 25.00 6
CCIRCR Harvick/Burtn/Bwyer 15.00 4
CCIRFR Edwrd/Knsth/Bit/Rgn 20.00 5
CCIRPM Khne/Sdlr/Allm/Mend/75 25.00 5
CCIWIN Gordon/JJ/Martin/Stwrt 30.00 8

2010 Press Pass Showcase El Exhibit Ink

STATED PRINT RUN 20-45
*GOLD/20-25: .6X TO 1.5X BASIC AU/45
EEIBK Brad Keselowski/20 15.00 4
EEICB Marcos Ambrose/20 20.00 5
EEICE Carl Edwards/45 12.00 3
EEIDE Dale Earnhardt Jr./45 40.00 10
EEIDH Denny Hamlin/20 15.00 4
EEIDP Danica Patrick/45 125.00 2
EEIJB Jeff Burton/20 15.00 4
EEIJG Jeff Gordon/45 60.00 12
EEIJJ Jimmie Johnson/45 25.00 6
EEIJL Joey Logano/45 10.00 2
EEIKH Kevin Harvick/45 12.00 3
EEIKK Kasey Kahne/45 25.00 6
EEIMK Matt Kenseth/25 30.00 6
EEIMM Mark Martin/45 10.00 2
EEIRN Ryan Newman/20 12.00 3
EEITS Tony Stewart/45 15.00 4
EEIKB1 Kurt Busch/20 15.00 4
EEIKB2 Kyle Busch/45 12.00 3

2010 Press Pass Showcase El Exhibit Triple Memorabilia

STATED PRINT RUN 99 SER.#'d SETS
EEMCB Clint Bowyer 6.00 1
EEMCE Carl Edwards 6.00 1
EEMDE Dale Earnhardt 30.00 8
EEMDH Denny Hamlin 6.00 1
EEMDP Danica Patrick 30.00 8
EEMJB Jeff Burton 5.00 1
EEMJG Jeff Gordon 12.00 3
EEMJJ Jimmie Johnson 10.00 2
EEMJL Joey Logano 6.00 1
EEMKH Kevin Harvick 8.00 2
EEMKK Kasey Kahne 6.00 1
EEMMK Matt Kenseth 6.00 1
EEMMM Mark Martin 6.00 1
EEMRN Ryan Newman 15.00 4
EEMTS Tony Stewart 10.00 2
EEMDEJ Dale Earnhardt Jr. 12.00 3
EEMKB1 Kurt Busch 5.00 1
EEMKB2 Kyle Busch 8.00 2

2010 Press Pass Showcase El Exhibit Triple Memorabilia G

*SINGLES: .5X TO 1.2X BASIC INSERTS
STATED PRINT RUN 45 SER.#'d SETS
EEMDE Dale Earnhardt/25 40.00 10
EEMJF John Force/15
EEMRP Richard Petty/15
EEMRW Rusty Wallace 25.00 6

2010 Press Pass Showcase El Exhibit Triple Memorabilia Gre

*SINGLES: .6X TO 1.5X BASIC INSERTS
STATED PRINT RUN 25 SER.#'d SETS
EEMDE Dale Earnhardt/10
EEMJF John Force/10
EEMRP Richard Petty
EEMRW Rusty Wallace 30.00 8

2010 Press Pass Showcase Pri Pieces Firesuit Green

STATED PRINT RUN 25 SER.#'d SETS
PPMCE Carl Edwards 25.00 6
PPMDE Dale Earnhardt/10
PPMDP Danica Patrick 25.00 5
PPMJB Jeff Burton 40.00 8
PPMJG Jeff Gordon 50.00 10
PPMJJ Jimmie Johnson 75.00 15
PPMJL Joey Logano 40.00 8
PPMJL Richard Petty/10
PPMJM Juan Pablo Montoya 25.00 6
PPMJP John Force 40.00 8
PPMKB Kyle Busch 40.00 10
PPMKH Kevin Harvick 15.00 4
PPMKK Kasey Kahne 75.00 15
PPMMA Mario Andretti 15.00 4
PPMTS Tony Stewart 50.00 10
PPMMCB Clint Bowyer 25.00 6
PPMDEJR Dale Earnhardt Jr. 60.00 12

2010 Press Pass Showcase Pri Pieces Firesuit Ink Gold

STATED PRINT RUN 25 SER.#'d SETS
PPICB Clint Bowyer 20.00 5
PPICE Carl Edwards 75.00 15
PPIDP Danica Patrick 300.00 4
PPIDW Darrell Waltrip 30.00 8

B Jeff Burton 40.00 80.00
F John Force Shirt 60.00 120.00
G Jeff Gordon 125.00 250.00
J Jimmie Johnson 100.00 200.00
L Joey Logano 20.00 50.00
H Kevin Harvick 40.00 80.00
K Kasey Kahne 60.00 120.00
MA Mario Andretti 50.00 100.00
K Matt Kenseth 50.00 100.00
MM Mark Martin 100.00 175.00
N Ryan Newman 40.00 80.00
P Richard Petty 60.00 120.00
S Rusty Wallace 25.00 60.00
L Terry Labonte 75.00 150.00
S Tony Stewart 60.00 120.00
B1 Kurt Busch 40.00 80.00
B2 Kyle Busch 75.00 150.00
DEJR Dale Earnhardt Jr. 150.00 250.00

10 Press Pass Showcase Prized Pieces Sheet Metal Ink Silver

TED PRINT RUN 45 SER.#'d SETS
B Clint Bowyer 20.00 50.00
E Carl Edwards 40.00 80.00
P Danica Patrick/50 125.00 200.00
W Darrell Waltrip 30.00 60.00
B Jeff Burton 25.00 50.00
F John Force Parachute 30.00 80.00
G Jeff Gordon 100.00 200.00
J Jimmie Johnson 50.00 100.00
L Joey Logano 30.00 60.00
H Kevin Harvick 30.00 80.00
K Kasey Kahne 30.00 60.00
K Matt Kenseth 30.00 60.00
M Mark Martin 30.00 80.00
N Ryan Newman 20.00 50.00
P Richard Petty 50.00 100.00
S Rusty Wallace 15.00 40.00
L Terry Labonte 40.00 80.00
S Tony Stewart 40.00 80.00
B1 Kurt Busch 25.00 60.00
B2 Kyle Busch 30.00 80.00
DEJR Dale Earnhardt Jr. 75.00 150.00

10 Press Pass Showcase Prized Pieces Sheet Metal

TED PRINT RUN 45-99
CE Carl Edwards 12.00 30.00
DE Dale Earnhardt/45 50.00 100.00
DEJR Dale Earnhardt Jr. 20.00 50.00
DP Danica Patrick 20.00 50.00
JB Jeff Burton 8.00 20.00
JG Jeff Gordon 20.00 50.00
JJ Jimmie Johnson 15.00 40.00
JL Richard Petty/45 20.00 50.00
JL Joey Logano 10.00 25.00
JM Juan Pablo Montoya 10.00 25.00
KB Kyle Busch 12.00 30.00
KH Kevin Harvick 12.00 30.00
KK Kasey Kahne 12.00 30.00
MCB Clint Bowyer 8.00 20.00
RW Rusty Wallace 8.00 20.00
TS Tony Stewart 15.00 40.00

10 Press Pass Showcase Prized Pieces Sheet Metal Gold

NGLES: .5X TO 1.2X BASIC INSERTS
TED PRINT RUN 45 SER.#'d SETS
DE Dale Earnhardt/15
JL Richard Petty/15
JP John Force 25.00 60.00

2010 Press Pass Showcase Racing's Finest

MPLETE SET (12) 50.00 100.00
TED PRINT RUN 499 SER.#'d SETS
LD/125: .5X TO 1.2X BASIC INSERTS
REEN/50: .6X TO 1.5X BASIC INSERTS
ELTING/15: 1X TO 2.5X BASIC INSERTS
1 Dale Earnhardt 8.00 20.00
2 Richard Petty 2.50 6.00
3 John Force 3.00 8.00
4 Mario Andretti 1.50 4.00
5 Rusty Wallace 1.50 4.00
6 Benny Parsons 1.50 4.00
7 Darrell Waltrip 2.50 6.00
8 Davey Allison 2.50 6.00
9 Cale Yarborough 1.50 4.00
10 Jeff Gordon 3.00 8.00
11 Tony Stewart 2.50 6.00
12 Jimmie Johnson 2.50 6.00

2010 Press Pass Showcase Racing's Finest Ink

STATED PRINT RUN 15-25
RFICY Cale Yarborough/15 10.00 25.00
RFIDW Darrell Waltrip/15 25.00 50.00
RFIJF John Force/25 25.00 60.00
RFIMA Mario Andretti/25 20.00 50.00
RFIRP Richard Petty/25 40.00 80.00
RFITL Terry Labonte/15 50.00 100.00

2011 Press Pass Showcase

COMP.SET w/o SPs (60) 125.00 250.00
WAX BOX HOBBY (3) 100.00 175.00
1 Dale Earnhardt Jr 2.00 5.00
2 Jeff Gordon 2.00 5.00
3 Jimmie Johnson 1.50 4.00
4 Tony Stewart 1.50 4.00
5 Kevin Harvick 1.25 3.00
6 Mark Martin 1.00 2.50
7 Kurt Busch .75 2.00
8 Ryan Newman .75 2.00
9 Jeff Burton .75 2.00
10 Carl Edwards 1.00 2.50
11 Greg Biffle .75 2.00
12 Clint Bowyer 1.00 2.50
13 Kyle Busch 1.25 3.00
14 Denny Hamlin 1.00 2.50
15 Kasey Kahne 1.00 2.50
16 Matt Kenseth 1.00 2.50
17 Martin Truex Jr .75 2.00
18 Brian Vickers .60 1.50
19 Marcos Ambrose 1.00 2.50
20 Joey Logano 1.00 2.50
21 Jamie McMurray 1.00 2.50
22 Juan Pablo Montoya 1.00 2.50
23 David Ragan .75 2.00
24 Bill Elliott 1.50 4.00
25 A.J. Allmendinger 1.00 2.50
26 Bobby Labonte 1.00 2.50
27 Dale Earnhardt HOF 5.00 12.00
28 Richard Petty HOF 1.50 4.00
29 Bobby Allison HOF .75 2.00
30 David Pearson HOF 1.00 2.50
31 Lee Petty HOF .75 2.00
32 Ned Jarrett HOF .75 2.00
33 Bud Moore HOF 1.00 2.50
34 Dale Earnhardt Jr EE 2.00 5.00
35 Tony Stewart EE 1.50 4.00
36 Jeff Gordon EE 2.00 5.00
37 Jimmie Johnson EE 1.50 4.00
38 Kurt Busch EE .75 2.00
39 Carl Edwards EE 1.00 2.50
40 Matt Kenseth EE 1.00 2.50
41 Kasey Kahne EE 1.00 2.50
42 Denny Hamlin EE 1.00 2.50
43 Jimmie Johnson M 1.50 4.00
44 Jeff Gordon M 2.00 5.00
45 Mark Martin M 1.00 2.50
46 Carl Edwards M 1.00 2.50
47 Tony Stewart M 1.50 4.00
48 Kyle Busch M 1.25 3.00
49 Dale Earnhardt Jr M 2.00 5.00
50 Kevin Harvick M 1.25 3.00
51 Dale Earnhardt M 5.00 12.00
52 Danica Patrick M 4.00 10.00
53 Jr./Jhnsn/Grdn/Mrtin 2.00 5.00
54 Busch/Hamlin/Logano 1.25 3.00
55 Edwrds/Kens/Biffle/Rgn 1.00 2.50
56 J.McMurray/J.Montoya 1.00 2.50
57 Menard/Harv/Burtn/Bwyr 1.25 3.00
58 K.Kahne/B.Vickers 1.00 2.50
59 R.Newman/T.Stewart 1.50 4.00
60 K.Busch/B.Keselowski 1.25 3.00
61 Trevor Bayne SM CRC 30.00 60.00

2011 Press Pass Showcase Gold

*SINGLES: 1X TO 2.5X BASE
STATED PRINT RUN 125 SER.#'d SETS
61 Trevor Bayne FS 50.00 100.00

2011 Press Pass Showcase Green

*GREEN/25: 1.5X TO 4X BASIC CARDS
STATED PRINT RUN 25 SER.#'d SETS

2011 Press Pass Showcase Champions

COMPLETE SET (11) 40.00 100.00
STATED PRINT RUN 499 SER.#'d SETS
*GOLD/125: .5X TO 1.2X BASIC INSERTS
UNPRICED MELTING PRINT RUN 1
CH1 Jimmie Johnson 2.50 6.00
CH2 Richard Petty 2.50 6.00
CH3 Tony Stewart 2.50 6.00
CH4 Jeff Gordon 3.00 8.00
CH5 Kurt Busch 1.25 3.00
CH6 Matt Kenseth 1.50 4.00
CH7 Bobby Labonte 1.50 4.00
CH8 Dale Jarrett 1.50 4.00
CH9 Terry Labonte 1.50 4.00
CH10 Bill Elliott 2.50 6.00
CH11 Dale Earnhardt 8.00 20.00

2011 Press Pass Showcase Champions Ink

STATED PRINT RUN 25 SER.#'d SETS
CHIBE Bill Elliott 25.00 60.00
CHIBL Bobby Labonte 15.00 40.00
CHIDJ Dale Jarrett 15.00 40.00
CHIJG Jeff Gordon 40.00 100.00
CHIJJ Jimmie Johnson 40.00 100.00
CHIMK Matt Kenseth 30.00 80.00
CHIRP Richard Petty
CHITL Terry Labonte 20.00 50.00
CHITS Tony Stewart 30.00 80.00
CHIKUB Kurt Busch 15.00 40.00

2011 Press Pass Showcase Champions Memorabilia Firesuit

STATED PRINT RUN 99 SER.#'d SETS
UNPRICED MELTING PRINT RUN 5
CHMBE Bill Elliott 6.00 15.00
CHMDE Dale Earnhardt 15.00 40.00
CHMDJ Dale Jarrett 12.00 30.00
CHMJG Jeff Gordon 12.00 30.00
CHMJJ Jimmie Johnson 10.00 25.00
CHMKB Kurt Busch 6.00 15.00
CHMMK Matt Kenseth 6.00 15.00
CHMRP Richard Petty 8.00 20.00
CHMTS Tony Stewart 10.00 25.00

2011 Press Pass Showcase Champions Memorabilia Firesuit Gold

*GOLD/45: .6X TO 1.5X FIRESUIT/99
GOLD PRINT RUN 45 SER.#'d SETS
CHMTL Terry Labonte 25.00 60.00

2011 Press Pass Showcase Classic Collections Ink

STATED PRINT RUN 25 SER.#'d SETS
CCMEGR Earnhardt-Ganassi Racing 20.00 50.00
CCMHMS Hendrick Motorsports 150.00 300.00
CCMJGR Joe Gibbs Racing 30.00 60.00
CCMMWR Michael Waltrip Racing 20.00 50.00
CCMPEN Penske Racing 20.00 50.00
CCMRBR Red Bull Racing Team 20.00 50.00
CCMRCR Richard Childress Racing 50.00 100.00
CCMRFR Roush Fenway Racing
CCMRPM Richard Petty Motorsports 20.00 50.00
CCMSHR Stewart-Haas Racing 50.00 100.00

2011 Press Pass Showcase Classic Collections Sheet Metal

SHEET METAL PRINT RUN 99
*FIRESUIT/45: .6X TO 1.5X METAL/99
UNPRICED FS PATCH PRINT RUN 5
CCMEGR Earnhardt Gan. Rac. 6.00 15.00
CCMHMS Hendrick Motors. 20.00 50.00
CCMJGR Joe Gibbs Racing 8.00 20.00
CCMMWR Michael Waltrip Rac. 8.00 20.00
CCMPEN Penske Racing 8.00 20.00
CCMRBR Red Bull Team 8.00 20.00
CCMRCR Richard Childress Rac. 8.00 20.00
CCMRFR Roush Fenway Rac. 6.00 15.00
CCMRPM Richard Petty Motors. 6.00 15.00
CCMSHR StewartHaas Racing 8.00 20.00

2011 Press Pass Showcase Elite Exhibit Ink

STATED PRINT RUN 50 SER.#'d SETS
EEICE Carl Edwards 10.00 25.00
EEIDH Denny Hamlin 15.00 40.00
EEIDP Danica Patrick 75.00 150.00
EEIJB Jeff Burton 8.00 20.00
EEIJG Jeff Gordon 20.00 50.00
EEIJJ Jimmie Johnson 30.00 80.00
EEIJL Joey Logano 12.00 30.00
EEIKH Kevin Harvick 15.00 40.00
EEIKK Kasey Kahne 15.00 40.00
EEIMK Matt Kenseth 15.00 40.00
EEIMM Mark Martin 10.00 25.00
EEITS Tony Stewart 25.00 60.00
EEIDEJ Dale Earnhardt Jr 40.00 100.00
EEIKUB Kurt Busch 12.00 30.00
EEIKYB Kyle Busch 12.00 30.00

2011 Press Pass Showcase Elite Exhibit Ink Gold

*GOLD: .6X TO 1.5X BASIC INSERTS
STATED PRINT RUN 25 SER.#'d SETS
EEIDP Danica Patrick 100.00 200.00
EEIJG Jeff Gordon 60.00 120.00
EEIJJ Jimmie Johnson 50.00 100.00
EEIDEJ Dale Earnhardt Jr 60.00 120.00

2011 Press Pass Showcase Masterpieces Ink

STATED PRINT RUN 45 SER.#'d SETS
MPICE Carl Edwards 10.00 25.00
MPIDH Denny Hamlin 15.00 40.00
MPIDP Danica Patrick 60.00 120.00
MPIJB Jeff Burton 8.00 20.00
MPIJG Jeff Gordon 75.00 150.00
MPIJJ Jimmie Johnson 30.00 80.00
MPIJL Joey Logano 10.00 25.00
MPIKH Kevin Harvick 12.00 30.00
MPIKK Kasey Kahne 25.00 60.00
MPIMK Matt Kenseth 20.00 50.00
MPIMM Mark Martin 10.00 25.00
MPIRN Ryan Newman 8.00 20.00
MPITS Tony Stewart 25.00 60.00
MPIDEJ Dale Earnhardt Jr 50.00 120.00
MPIKYB Kyle Busch 20.00 50.00

2011 Press Pass Showcase Masterpieces Ink Gold

*GOLD: .6X TO 1.5X BASIC INSERTS
STATED PRINT RUN 25 SER.#'d SETS
MPIDP Danica Patrick 75.00 150.00
MPIJG Jeff Gordon 100.00 200.00
MPIJJ Jimmie Johnson 50.00 100.00
MPIDEJ Dale Earnhardt Jr 75.00 150.00

2011 Press Pass Showcase Masterpieces Memorabilia

STATED PRINT RUN 99 SER.#'d SETS
*GOLD/45: .6X TO 1.5X MEMORAB/99
UNPRICED MELTING PRINT RUN 5
MPMBK Brad Keselowski 6.00 15.00
MPMBV Brian Vickers 3.00 8.00
MPMCE Carl Edwards 5.00 12.00
MPMDE Dale Earnhardt 25.00 60.00
MPMDH Denny Hamlin 5.00 12.00
MPMDP Danica Patrick 20.00 50.00
MPMJB Jeff Burton 4.00 10.00
MPMJG Jeff Gordon 15.00 40.00
MPMJJ Jimmie Johnson 8.00 20.00
MPMJL Joey Logano 5.00 12.00
MPMKH Kevin Harvick 6.00 15.00
MPMKK Kasey Kahne 5.00 12.00
MPMMK Matt Kenseth 5.00 12.00
MPMMM Mark Martin 5.00 12.00
MPMRN Ryan Newman 4.00 10.00
MPMTS Tony Stewart 8.00 20.00
MPMDEJ Dale Earnhardt Jr 15.00 40.00
MPMKYB Kyle Busch 6.00 15.00

2011 Press Pass Showcase Prized Pieces Firesuit

STATED PRINT RUN 50-99
UNPRICED MELTING PRINT RUN 5
*GOLD/25-45: 1X TO 2.5X FIRESUIT
PPMBK Brad Keselowski/99 6.00 15.00
PPMCE Carl Edwards/99 5.00 12.00
PPMDE Dale Earnhardt/50 25.00 60.00
PPMDH Denny Hamlin/99 5.00 12.00
PPMDP Danica Patrick/99 20.00 50.00
PPMJG Jeff Gordon/99 15.00 40.00
PPMJJ Jimmie Johnson/99 8.00 20.00
PPMJL Joey Logano/99 5.00 12.00
PPMKH Kevin Harvick/99 6.00 15.00
PPMKK Kasey Kahne/99 5.00 12.00
PPMMM Mark Martin/99 5.00 12.00
PPMRP Richard Petty/99 12.00 30.00
PPMTL Terry Labonte/50 6.00 15.00
PPMTS Tony Stewart/99 8.00 20.00
PPMDEJ Dale Earnhardt Jr/99 15.00 40.00
PPMKUB Kurt Busch/99 4.00 10.00
PPMKYB Kyle Busch/99 6.00 15.00

2011 Press Pass Showcase Prized Pieces Firesuit Ink

PPIBE Bill Elliott 20.00 50.00
PPIBV Brian Vickers 15.00 40.00
PPICE Carl Edwards 30.00 80.00
PPIDH Denny Hamlin 25.00 60.00
PPIDP Danica Patrick 125.00 200.00
PPIJG Jeff Gordon 50.00 120.00
PPIJJ Jimmie Johnson 40.00 100.00
PPIJL Joey Logano 30.00 80.00
PPIJM Jamie McMurray 20.00 50.00
PPIKH Kevin Harvick 25.00 60.00
PPIKK Kasey Kahne 30.00 80.00
PPIMM Mark Martin 25.00 60.00
PPIRP Richard Petty 40.00 100.00
PPITL Terry Labonte 40.00 100.00
PPITS Tony Stewart 40.00 100.00
PPIDEJ Dale Earnhardt Jr 50.00 120.00
PPIJPM Juan Pablo Montoya 20.00 50.00
PPIKUB Kurt Busch 20.00 50.00
PPIKYB Kyle Busch 30.00 80.00

2011 Press Pass Showcase Prized Pieces Sheet Metal Ink

STATED PRINT RUN 45 SER.#'d SETS
PPIBE Bill Elliott 15.00 40.00
PPIBV Brian Vickers 15.00 40.00
PPICE Carl Edwards 25.00 60.00
PPIDH Denny Hamlin 25.00 60.00
PPIDP Danica Patrick 100.00 200.00
PPIJG Jeff Gordon 60.00 120.00
PPIJJ Jimmie Johnson 40.00 100.00
PPIJL Joey Logano 30.00 80.00
PPIJM Jamie McMurray 20.00 50.00
PPIKH Kevin Harvick 25.00 60.00
PPIKK Kasey Kahne 25.00 60.00
PPIMM Mark Martin 20.00 50.00
PPIRP Richard Petty 30.00 80.00
PPITL Terry Labonte 40.00 100.00
PPITS Tony Stewart 40.00 100.00
PPIDEJ Dale Earnhardt Jr 40.00 100.00
PPIJPM Juan Pablo Montoya 15.00 40.00
PPIKUB Kurt Busch 15.00 40.00
PPIKYB Kyle Busch 40.00 100.00

2011 Press Pass Showcase Showroom

COMPLETE SET (10) 40.00 100.00
STATED PRINT RUN 499 SER.#'d SETS
*GOLD/125: .5X TO 1.2X SHOWROOM/499
UNPRICED MELTING PRINT RUN 1
SR1 Jimmie Johnson 2.50 6.00
SR2 Jeff Gordon 3.00 8.00
SR3 Mark Martin 1.50 4.00
SR4 Carl Edwards 1.50 4.00
SR5 Tony Stewart 2.50 6.00
SR6 Kyle Busch 2.00 5.00
SR7 Dale Earnhardt Jr 3.00 8.00
SR8 Danica Patrick 6.00 15.00
SR9 Kasey Kahne 1.50 4.00
SR10 Dale Earnhardt 8.00 20.00

2011 Press Pass Showcase Showroom Memorabilia Sheet Metal

STATED PRINT RUN 45 SER.#'d SETS
SRMCE Carl Edwards 6.00 15.00
SRMDP Danica Patrick 15.00 40.00
SRMJG Jeff Gordon 15.00 40.00
SRMJJ Jimmie Johnson 10.00 25.00
SRMKK Kasey Kahne 6.00 15.00
SRMMM Mark Martin 6.00 15.00
SRMTS Tony Stewart 10.00 25.00
SRMDEJ Dale Earnhardt Jr 15.00 40.00
SRMKYB Kyle Busch 8.00 20.00

2011 Press Pass Showcase Showroom Memorabilia Sheet Metal Gold

*GOLD/25: .6X TO 1.5X BASIC
STATED PRINT RUN 25 SER.#'d SETS
SRMDE Dale Earnhardt 75.00 150.00

2012 Press Pass Showcase

*DRIVER SUBSETS: 1X BASIC CARD
WAX BOX HOBBY 100.00 175.00
1 Marcos Ambrose 1.00 2.50
2 Trevor Bayne 1.00 2.50
3 Greg Biffle .75 2.00
4 Clint Bowyer 1.00 2.50
5 Jeff Burton .75 2.00
6 Kurt Busch .75 2.00
7 Kyle Busch 1.25 3.00
8 Dale Earnhardt Jr 2.00 5.00
9 Carl Edwards 1.00 2.50
10 Jeff Gordon 2.00 5.00
11 Denny Hamlin 1.00 2.50
12 Kevin Harvick 1.25 3.00
13 Jimmie Johnson 1.50 4.00
14 Kasey Kahne 1.00 2.50
15 Matt Kenseth 1.00 2.50
16 Bobby Labonte 1.00 2.50
17 Joey Logano 1.00 2.50
18 Mark Martin 1.00 2.50
19 Ryan Newman .75 2.00
20 Tony Stewart 1.50 4.00
21 Martin Truex Jr .75 2.00
22 Travis Pastrana NNS 1.50 4.00
23 Danica Patrick NNS 3.00 8.00
24 Bobby Allison .75 2.00
25 Dale Earnhardt 3.00 8.00
26 Bill Elliott 1.50 4.00
27 Dale Jarrett 1.00 2.50
28 Terry Labonte 1.00 2.50
29 David Pearson 1.00 2.50
30 Richard Petty 1.50 4.00
31 Rusty Wallace 1.00 2.50
32 Darrell Waltrip 1.50 4.00
33 Cale Yarborough 1.00 2.50
34 Kyle Busch EE 1.25 3.00
35 Dale Earnhardt Jr EE 2.00 5.00
36 Carl Edwards EE 1.00 2.50
37 Jeff Gordon EE 2.00 5.00
38 Kevin Harvick EE 1.25 3.00
39 Jimmie Johnson EE 1.50 4.00
40 Kasey Kahne EE 1.00 2.50
41 Danica Patrick EE 3.00 8.00
42 Tony Stewart EE 1.50 4.00
43 David Pearson DM 1.00 2.50
44 Richard Petty DM 1.50 4.00
45 Jeff Gordon DM 2.00 5.00
46 Dale Earnhardt DM 3.00 8.00
47 Carl Edwards DM 1.00 2.50
48 Danica Patrick DM 3.00 8.00
49 Kyle Busch DM 1.25 3.00
50 Jimmie Johnson DM 1.50 4.00
51 Tony Stewart DM 1.50 4.00
52 Jr./Khne/Grdn/JJ CC 2.00 5.00
53 Stwrt/Patrick/Nwmn CC 3.00 8.00
54 Knsth/Edwrds/Biffle CC 1.00 2.50
55 J.Brtn/Hrvick/Menrd CC 1.25 3.00
56 Hmln/Ky.Bsch/Lgno CC 1.25 3.00
57 McMurray/Montoya CC 1.00 2.50
58 Kesel/Allmendinger CC 1.25 3.00
59 Ambrose/Almirola CC 1.00 2.50
60 Mrtn/Trx/Wtrp/Bwyr CC 1.00 2.50
61 Danica Patrick RS FS AU/50 100.00 175.00

2012 Press Pass Showcase Gold

*1-60 GOLD/125: .8X TO 2X BASIC CARDS
GOLD STATED PRINT RUN 25-125
61 D.Patrick RS Shoe AU/25 100.00 200.00

2012 Press Pass Showcase Red

*RED/25: 1.5X TO 4X BASIC CARDS
RED STATED PRINT RUN 25

2012 Press Pass Showcase Champions Memorabilia

STATED PRINT RUN 99 SER.#'d SETS
*GOLD/50: .5X TO 1.2X BASIC INSERT/99
CHDE Dale Earnhardt 12.00 30.00
CHJG Jeff Gordon 8.00 20.00
CHJJ Jimmie Johnson 6.00 15.00
CHRP Richard Petty 6.00 15.00
CHTL Terry Labonte 4.00 10.00
CHTS Tony Stewart 8.00 20.00

2012 Press Pass Showcase Champions Showcase

STATED PRINT RUN 499 SER.#'d SETS
*GOLD/125: .6X TO 1.5X BASIC INSERTS
CH1 Richard Petty 2.00 5.00
CH2 Jeff Gordon 2.50 6.00
CH3 Tony Stewart 2.00 5.00
CH4 Jimmie Johnson 2.00 5.00
CH5 Terry Labonte 1.25 3.00
CH6 David Pearson 1.25 3.00
CH7 Darrell Waltrip 2.00 5.00
CH8 Dale Earnhardt 4.00 10.00
CH9 Cale Yarborough 1.25 3.00
CH10 Bill Elliott 2.00 5.00

2012 Press Pass Showcase Champions Showcase Ink

STATED PRINT RUN 50 SER.#'d SETS
*GOLD/25: .5X TO 1.2X BASIC AU/50
CHSDP David Pearson 10.00 25.00
CHSJG Jeff Gordon 40.00 80.00
CHSJJ Jimmie Johnson 30.00 60.00
CHSRP Richard Petty 15.00 40.00
CHSTL Terry Labonte 10.00 25.00
CHSTS Tony Stewart EXCH

2012 Press Pass Showcase Classic Collections Memorabilia

STATED PRINT RUN 50-99
*GOLD/25-50: .6X TO 1.5X BASIC INSERTS
CCMEGR McMurray/Montoya 5.00 12.00
CCMHMS Dale Jr./Khne/Grdn/JJ 12.00 30.00
CCMJGR Hmln/Ky.Bsch/Lgno 10.00 25.00
CCMMWR Mrtn/Trx/Wltrp/Bwyr 8.00 20.00
CCMPEN Kesel/Allmendinger 6.00 15.00
CCMRCR J.Burtn/Hrvick/Menrd 6.00 15.00
CCMRFR Knsth/Edwrds/Biffle 10.00 25.00
CCMRPM Ambrose/Almirola 6.00 15.00
CCMSHR Stwrt/Patrick/Nwmn 15.00 40.00

2012 Press Pass Showcase Elite Exhibit Ink

STATED PRINT RUN 10-50
*GOLD/25: .5X TO 1.2X BASIC AU/50
EEICE Carl Edwards/25 12.00 30.00
EEIDE Dale Earnhardt Jr/25 40.00 100.00
EEIDH Denny Hamlin/50 8.00 20.00
EEIDP Danica Patrick NNS/23 60.00 120.00
EEIJG Jeff Gordon/25 50.00 100.00
EEIJJ Jimmie Johnson/25 25.00 50.00
EEIJL Joey Logano/50 12.00 30.00
EEIKH Kevin Harvick/50 12.00 30.00
EEIKK Kasey Kahne/50 15.00 40.00
EEIMK Matt Kenseth/50 10.00 25.00
EEIMM Mark Martin/50 15.00 40.00
EEITB Trevor Bayne/50 10.00 25.00
EEITP Travis Pastrana NNS/25 20.00 50.00
EEITS Tony Stewart/25 30.00 80.00
EEIKYB Kyle Busch/50 12.00 30.00

2012 Press Pass Showcase Masterpieces Ink

STATED PRINT RUN 7-50
EXCH EXPIRATION: 8/1/2013
MPICE Carl Edwards/50 12.00 30.00
MPIDE Dale Earnhardt Jr/50 40.00 80.00
MPIDH Denny Hamlin/50 12.00 30.00
MPIDP Danica Patrick NNS/50 60.00 120.00
MPIJG Jeff Gordon/50 50.00 100.00
MPIJJ Jimmie Johnson/50 40.00 80.00
MPIJL Joey Logano/50 12.00 30.00
MPIKH Kevin Harvick/50 15.00 40.00
MPIKK Kasey Kahne/50 20.00 50.00
MPIMM Mark Martin/50 25.00 50.00
MPIRP Richard Petty/50 20.00 50.00
MPITB Trevor Bayne/50 12.00 30.00
MPITP Travis Pastrana NNS/7
MPITS Tony Stewart/50 20.00 50.00
MPIKYB Kyle Busch/50 15.00 40.00

2012 Press Pass Showcase Masterpieces Ink Gold

*GOLD/25: .5X TO 1.2X BASIC AU/50
GOLD STATED PRINT RUN 25
MPITP Travis Pastrana NNS 25.00 50.00

2012 Press Pass Showcase Masterpieces Memorabilia

STATED PRINT RUN 50-99
*GOLD/50: .5X TO 1.2X BASIC INSERT/99
MPCE Carl Edwards/99 6.00 15.00
MPDE Dale Earnhardt/50 20.00 50.00
MPDEJR Dale Earnhardt Jr/99 12.00 30.00
MPDH Denny Hamlin/99 8.00 20.00
MPDP Danica Patrick Nationwide/99 20.00 50.00
MPJB Jeff Burton/99 5.00 12.00
MPJG Jeff Gordon/99 12.00 30.00
MPJJ Jimmie Johnson/99 10.00 25.00
MPJL Joey Logano/99 6.00 15.00
MPKH Kevin Harvick/99 8.00 20.00
MPKK Kasey Kahne/99 6.00 15.00
MPKYB Kyle Busch/99 8.00 20.00
MPMK Matt Kenseth/99 6.00 15.00
MPMM Mark Martin/99 6.00 15.00
MPRN Ryan Newman/99 5.00 12.00
MPRP Richard Petty/99 10.00 25.00
MPTB Trevor Bayne/99 6.00 15.00
MPTP Travis Pastrana/99 8.00 20.00
MPTS Tony Stewart/99 10.00 25.00

2012 Press Pass Showcase Prized Pieces

STATED PRINT RUN 11-99
*GOLD/50: .5X TO 1.2X BASIC INSERT/99
PPCE Carl Edwards/99 5.00 12.00
PPDE Dale Earnhardt Jr/88 12.00 30.00
PPDH Denny Hamlin/11
PPDP Danica Patrick NNS/99 12.00 30.00
PPJB Jeff Burton/31 6.00 15.00
PPJG1 Jeff Gordon/24 15.00 40.00
PPJG2 Jeff Gordon/24 15.00 40.00
PPJL Joey Logano/20 15.00 40.00
PPKH Kevin Harvick/99 10.00 25.00
PPKK Kasey Kahne/99 8.00 20.00
PPMA Marcos Ambrose/99 5.00 12.00
PPMK Matt Kenseth/99 5.00 12.00
PPMM Mark Martin/99 8.00 20.00
PPRN Ryan Newman/99 4.00 10.00
PPTP Travis Pastrana/99 8.00 20.00
PPTS Tony Stewart/14
PPDE2 Dale Earnhardt Jr/99 12.00 30.00
PPKYB Kyle Busch/99 6.00 15.00

2012 Press Pass Showcase Prized Pieces Ink

STATED PRINT RUN 25-50
*GOLD/25: .5X TO 1.2X BASIC INK/50
PPICE Carl Edwards/50 12.00 30.00
PPIDE Dale Earnhardt Jr/50 40.00 80.00
PPIDP Danica Patrick NNS/25 60.00 120.00
PPIKH Kevin Harvick/50 15.00 40.00
PPIKK Kasey Kahne/50 20.00 50.00
PPIMA Marcos Ambrose/50 12.00 30.00
PPIMK Matt Kenseth/50 12.00 30.00
PPIMM Mark Martin/50 25.00 50.00
PPIRN Ryan Newman/50 10.00 25.00
PPITB Trevor Bayne/50 12.00 30.00
PPITP Travis Pastrana NNS/50 20.00 50.00
PPIKYB Kyle Busch/50 15.00 40.00

2012 Press Pass Showcase Showroom

STATED PRINT RUN 499 SER.#'d SETS
*GOLD/125: .6X TO 1.5X BASIC INSERT/499
SR1 Dale Earnhardt Jr's Car 2.50 6.00
SR2 Jeff Gordon's Car 2.50 6.00
SR3 Tony Stewart's Car 2.00 5.00
SR4 Jimmie Johnson's Car 2.00 5.00
SR5 Danica Patrick's Car 4.00 10.00
SR6 Carl Edwards' Car 1.25 3.00

SR7 Kevin Harvick's Car 1.50 4.00
SR8 Richard Petty's Car 2.00 5.00
SR9 Kyle Busch's Car 1.50 4.00
SR10 Kasey Kahne's Car 1.25 3.00

2012 Press Pass Showcase Showroom Memorabilia

STATED PRINT RUN 99 SER.#'d SETS
*GOLD/50: .5X TO 1.2X BASIC MEM/99
SRCE Carl Edwards' Car 4.00 10.00
SRDP Danica Patrick's Car 10.00 25.00
SRJG Jeff Gordon's Car 8.00 20.00
SRJJ Jimmie Johnson's Car 6.00 15.00
SRKH Kevin Harvick's Car 5.00 12.00
SRKK Kasey Kahne's Car 4.00 10.00
SRRP Richard Petty's Car 6.00 15.00
SRTS Tony Stewart's Car 8.00 20.00
SRKYB Kyle Busch's Car 5.00 12.00
SRDEJR Dale Earnhardt Jr's Car 10.00 25.00

2013 Press Pass Showcase

1-60 STATED PRINT RUN 349
1 Marcos Ambrose 1.00 2.50
2 Trevor Bayne 1.00 2.50
3 Greg Biffle .75 2.00
4 Clint Bowyer 1.00 2.50
5 Jeff Burton .75 2.00
6 Kurt Busch .75 2.00
7 Kyle Busch 1.25 3.00
8 Dale Earnhardt 2.00 5.00
9 Carl Edwards 1.00 2.50
10 Jeff Gordon 2.00 5.00
11 Denny Hamlin 1.00 2.50
12 Kevin Harvick 1.25 3.00
13 Jimmie Johnson 1.50 4.00
14 Kasey Kahne 1.00 2.50
15 Matt Kenseth 1.00 2.50
16 Brad Keselowski 1.25 3.00
17 Bobby Labonte 1.00 2.50
18 Joey Logano 1.00 2.50
19 Mark Martin 1.00 2.50
20 Jamie McMurray 1.00 2.50
21 Paul Menard .60 1.50
22 Juan Pablo Montoya 1.00 2.50
23 Ryan Newman .75 2.00
24 Travis Pastrana 1.00 2.50
25 Danica Patrick 2.50 6.00
26 Tony Stewart 1.50 4.00
27 Martin Truex .75 2.00
28 Marcos Ambrose EE 1.00 2.50
29 Jeff Burton EE .75 2.00
30 Kurt Busch EE .75 2.00
31 Kyle Busch EE 1.25 3.00
32 Dale Earnhardt EE 2.00 5.00
33 Carl Edwards EE 1.00 2.50
34 Jeff Gordon EE 2.00 5.00
35 Denny Hamlin EE 1.00 2.50
36 Kevin Harvick EE 1.25 3.00
37 Jimmie Johnson EE 1.50 4.00
38 Kasey Kahne EE 1.00 2.50
39 Matt Kenseth EE 1.00 2.50
40 Joey Logano EE 1.00 2.50
41 Mark Martin EE 1.00 2.50
42 Danica Patrick EE 2.50 6.00
43 Tony Stewart EE 1.50 4.00
44 Travis Pastrana EE 1.00 2.50
45 Jeff Gordon SS 2.00 5.00
46 Jimmie Johnson SS 1.50 4.00
47 Tony Stewart SS 1.50 4.00
48 Ryan Newman SS .75 2.00
49 Dale Earnhardt SS 2.00 5.00
50 Mark Martin SS 1.00 2.50
51 Bobby Labonte SS 1.00 2.50
52 Kyle Busch SS 1.25 3.00
53 Danica Patrick SS 2.50 6.00
54 Marcos Ambrose SS 1.00 2.50
55 Grdn/Khne/Jr./Jhnsn 2.00 5.00
56 Stwrt/Ptrck/Nwmn 2.50 6.00
57 Stnhse/Edwrds/Bffle 1.00 2.50
58 Brtn/Hrvck/Mnrd 1.25 3.00
59 Knsth/Hmln/Busch 1.25 3.00
60 Mrtn/Truex/Wltrp/Bwyr 1.00 2.50
61 Stenhouse Jr. RS FS AU/75 15.00 40.00

2013 Press Pass Showcase Blue

*BLUE/25: 1.5X TO 4X BASIC CARDS

2013 Press Pass Showcase Gold

*GOLD/99: .8X TO 2X BASIC CARDS
61 Stenhouse Jr. RS FS AU/50 25.00 50.00

2013 Press Pass Showcase Green

*GREEN/20: 2X TO 5X BASIC CARDS

2013 Press Pass Showcase Purple

*PURPLE/13: 2.5X TO 6X BASIC CARDS

2013 Press Pass Showcase Classic Collections Memorabilia Silver

*GOLD/25: .6X TO 1.5X BASIC MEM/75
CCMEGR J.McMurray/J.P.Montoya 6.00 15.00
CCMHMS Grdn/Khne/Ernhrdt/Jhnsn 15.00 40.00
CCMJGR Knsth/Hmln/Busch 8.00 20.00
CCMMWR Mrtn/Truex/Wltrp/Bwyr 5.00 12.00
CCMRCR Brtn/Hrvck/Mnrd 6.00 15.00
CCMRFR Stnhse/Edwrds/Bffle 5.00 12.00
CCMRPM A.Almirola/M.Ambros 8.00 20.00
CCMSHR Stwrt/Ptrck/Nwmn 10.00 25.00

2013 Press Pass Showcase Elite Exhibit Ink Blue

EEICE Carl Edwards/30
EEIDEJR Dale Earnhardt Jr/30 40.00 100.00
EEIDH Denny Hamlin/30 10.00 25.00
EEIDP Danica Patrick/30 60.00 120.00
EEIJB Jeff Burton/30 8.00 20.00
EEIJG Jeff Gordon/30 50.00 100.00
EEIJJ Jimmie Johnson/30 25.00 50.00
EEIJL Joey Logano/30 10.00 25.00
EEIKH Kevin Harvick/30 12.00 30.00
EEIKK Kasey Kahne/30 25.00 50.00
EEIKUB Kurt Busch/30 12.00 30.00
EEIKYB Kyle Busch/30
EEIMA Marcos Ambrose/30 10.00 25.00
EEIMK Matt Kenseth/30 12.00 30.00
EEIMM Mark Martin/30 15.00 40.00
EEITP Travis Pastrana/30 15.00 40.00
EEITP1 Tony Stewart/30 25.00 50.00
EEITP2 Tony Stewart/20 25.00 50.00

2013 Press Pass Showcase Jumbo Autographs

1 Junior Johnson

2013 Press Pass Showcase Masterpieces Ink

EXCH EXPIRATION: 12/30/2014
MPICE Carl Edwards/25 EXCH 15.00 40.00
MPIDEJR Dale Earnhardt Jr/25 30.00 80.00
MPIDH Denny Hamlin/35 15.00 40.00
MPIDP Danica Patrick/25 75.00 150.00
MPIJB Jeff Burton/25 12.00 30.00
MPIJG Jeff Gordon/25 75.00 125.00
MPIJJ Jimmie Johnson/25 30.00 60.00
MPIJL Joey Logano/35 15.00 40.00
MPIKH Kevin Harvick/25 20.00 50.00
MPIKK Kasey Kahne/25 15.00 40.00
MPIKYB Kyle Busch/25 20.00 50.00
MPIMK Matt Kenseth/35 15.00 40.00
MPIRN Ryan Newman/35 12.00 30.00
MPITP Travis Pastrana/25 15.00 40.00
MPITS Tony Stewart/25 25.00 60.00

2013 Press Pass Showcase Masterpieces Memorabilia

GOLD/25: .6X TO 1.5X BASIC MEM/75
MPCE Carl Edwards 5.00 12.00
MPDEJR Dale Earnhardt Jr 10.00 25.00
MPDH Denny Hamlin 5.00 12.00
MPDP Danica Patrick 12.00 30.00
MPJB Jeff Burton 4.00 10.00
MPJG Jeff Gordon 10.00 25.00
MPJJ Jimmie Johnson 8.00 20.00
MPKH Kevin Harvick 6.00 15.00
MPKK Kasey Kahne 5.00 12.00
MPKYB Kyle Busch 6.00 15.00
MPMK Matt Kenseth 5.00 12.00
MPMM Mark Martin 5.00 12.00
MPRN Ryan Newman 4.00 10.00
MPTP Travis Pastrana 5.00 12.00
MPTS Tony Stewart 8.00 20.00

2013 Press Pass Showcase Prized Pieces

*BLUE/20: .8X TO 2X BASIC MEM/99
*BLUE/20: .5X TO 1.2X BASIC MEM/52
*GOLD/25: .6X TO 1.5X BASIC MEM/99
*GOLD/25: .4X TO 1X BASIC MEM/52
PPMAD Austin Dillon/99 6.00 15.00
PPMBK Brad Keselowski/99 10.00 25.00
PPMCE Carl Edwards/99 5.00 12.00
PPMDEJR Dale Earnhardt Jr/99 10.00 25.00
PPMDH Denny Hamlin/99 5.00 12.00
PPMJG Jeff Gordon/99 10.00 25.00
PPMJJ Jimmie Johnson/99 8.00 20.00
PPMJL Joey Logano/99 5.00 12.00
PPMKH Kevin Harvick/99 6.00 15.00
PPMKK Kasey Kahne/99 5.00 12.00
PPMKUB Kurt Busch/99 4.00 10.00
PPMKYB Kyle Busch/99 6.00 15.00
PPMMA Marcos Ambrose/99 5.00 12.00
PPMMK Matt Kenseth/99 5.00 12.00
PPMMM Mark Martin/99 5.00 12.00
PPMMW Michael Waltrip/99 5.00 12.00
PPMRN Ryan Newman/99 4.00 10.00
PPMTB Trevor Bayne/99 5.00 12.00
PPMTD Ty Dillon/52 8.00 20.00
PPMTS Tony Stewart/99 8.00 20.00

2013 Press Pass Showcase Prized Pieces Ink

*GOLD/25: .5X TO 1.2X INK/49-50
EXCH EXPIRATION: 12/30/2014
PPIAD Austin Dillon/50 8.00 20.00
PPICE Carl Edwards/25 EXCH 12.00 30.00
PPIDEJR Dale Earnhardt Jr/10
PPIDH Denny Hamlin/50 10.00 25.00
PPIJG Jeff Gordon/25 50.00 100.00
PPIJJ Jimmie Johnson/25 30.00 60.00
PPIJL Joey Logano/50 15.00 40.00
PPIKH Kevin Harvick/25 15.00 40.00
PPIKK Kasey Kahne/25 12.00 30.00
PPIKYB Kyle Busch/25 15.00 40.00
PPIMA Marcos Ambrose/50 10.00 25.00
PPIMK Matt Kenseth/50 10.00 25.00
PPIRN Ryan Newman/25 10.00 25.00
PPITB Trevor Bayne/49 10.00 25.00
PPITD Ty Dillon/50 10.00 25.00
PPITS Tony Stewart/25 30.00 80.00

2013 Press Pass Showcase Prized Pieces Ink Blue

PPIDEJR Dale Earnhardt Jr/25 25.00 60.00
PPIKK Kasey Kahne/30 12.00 30.00

2013 Press Pass Showcase Rookie Contenders

*GOLD/50: .6X TO 1.5X BASIC INSERT/299
*GREEN/25: 1X TO 2.5X BASIC INSERT/299
*PURPLE/13: 1.2X TO 3X BASIC INSERT/299
1 Danica Patrick 5.00 12.00
2 Ricky Stenhouse Jr. 2.50 6.00

2013 Press Pass Showcase Rookie Contenders Memorabilia Gold

RCMDP Danica Patrick 20.00 50.00
RCMRS Ricky Stenhouse, Jr. 15.00 40.00

2013 Press Pass Showcase Studio Showcase

*BLUE/40: 1X TO 2.5X BASIC INSERT/299
*GOLD/50: 1X TO 2.5X BASIC INSERT/299
*GREEN/25: 1.2X TO 3X BASIC INSERT/299
*PURPLE/13: 2X TO 5X BASIC INSERT/299
1 Trevor Bayne 1.25 3.00
2 Greg Biffle 1.00 2.50
3 Kyle Busch 1.50 4.00
4 Dale Earnhardt Jr. 2.50 6.00
5 Carl Edwards 1.25 3.00
6 Jeff Gordon 2.50 6.00
7 Denny Hamlin 1.25 3.00
8 Jeff Burton 1.00 2.50
9 Jimmie Johnson 2.00 5.00
10 Kasey Kahne 1.25 3.00
11 Joey Logano 1.25 3.00
12 Tony Stewart 2.00 5.00
13 Marcos Ambrose 1.25 3.00
14 Matt Kenseth 1.25 3.00
15 Danica Patrick 3.00 8.00

2013 Press Pass Showcase Series Standouts Memorabilia

*BLUE/80: .4X TO 1X BASIC MEM/75
*BLUE/50: .5X TO 1.2X BASIC MEM/75
*BLUE/20: .8X TO 2X BASIC MEM/75
*GOLD/25: .6X TO 1.5X BASIC MEM/75
SSMBL Bobby Labonte 5.00 12.00
SSMDEJR Dale Earnhardt Jr 10.00 25.00
SSMDP Danica Patrick 12.00 30.00
SSMJG Jeff Gordon 10.00 25.00
SSMJJ Jimmie Johnson 8.00 20.00
SSMKYB Kyle Busch 6.00 15.00
SSMMA Marcos Ambrose 5.00 12.00
SSMMM Mark Martin 5.00 12.00
SSMRN Ryan Newman 4.00 10.00
SSMTS Tony Stewart 8.00 20.00

2013 Press Pass Showcase Showroom

*BLUE/40: 1X TO 2.5X BASIC INSERT/299
*GOLD/50: 1X TO 2.5X BASIC INSERT/299
*GREEN/20: 1.5X TO 4X BASIC INSERT/299
*PURPLE/13: 2X TO 5X BASIC INSERT/299
1 Dale Earnhard Jr's Car 2.50 6.00
2 Jimmie Johnson's Car 2.00 5.00
3 Jeff Gordon's Car 2.50 6.00
4 Kasey Kahne's Car 1.25 3.00
5 Kyle Busch's Car 1.50 4.00
6 Brad Keselowski's Car 1.50 4.00
7 Carl Edwards' Car 1.25 3.00
8 Kevin Harvick's Car 1.50 4.00
9 Danica Patrick's Car 3.00 8.00
10 Matt Kenseth's Car 1.25 3.00

2013 Press Pass Showcase Signature Patches

ANNOUNCED TOTAL PRINT RUNS 2-21
EXCH EXPIRATION: 12/30/2014
SSPAD Austin Dillon/21* 75.00 150.00
SSPCE Carl Edwards/19* 125.00 200.00
SSPKYB Kyle Busch/15* 125.00 200.00

2013 Press Pass Showcase Studio Showcase Ink

SSIDEJR Dale Earnhardt Jr 50.00 100.00
SSIDH Denny Hamlin/20 10.00 25.00
SSIGB Greg Biffle 8.00 20.00
SSIJG Jeff Gordon EXCH 50.00 100.00
SSIJJ Jimmie Johnson 25.00 50.00
SSIJL Joey Logano 10.00 25.00
SSIKK Kasey Kahne 25.00 50.00
SSIKYB Kyle Busch 12.00 30.00
SSIMA Marcos Ambrose 10.00 25.00
SSITB Trevor Bayne 10.00 25.00
SSITS Tony Stewart 25.00 50.00

1998 Press Pass Signings

This 39-card set contains the autographs of the top drivers and crew chiefs on the Winston Cup and Busch circuits. These cards were inserted into 1998 Press Pass Premium at a ratio of one per 48 packs, 1998 Press Pass Stealth at a ratio of one per 72 packs and 1998 VIP at a ratio of one per 60 packs. Some cards were also hand serial numbered on the back.

COMPLETE SET (39) 700.00 1200.00
1 Jeff Gordon/400 P/V/S 60.00 120.00
2 Dale Jarrett P/V/S 12.00 30.00
3 Dale Earnhardt/402 P/V/S 75.00 150.00
4 Terry Labonte P/V/S 12.00 30.00
5 Ricky Rudd P/V/S 10.00 25.00
6 John Andretti V/S 6.00 15.00
7 Sterling Marlin /S 10.00 30.00
8 Bobby Hamilton V/S 8.00 20.00
9 Ernie Irvan V/S 8.00 20.00
10 Bobby Labonte P/V/S 10.00 25.00
11 Ken Schrader P 6.00 15.00
12 Jeff Burton P/V 8.00 20.00
13 Michael Waltrip P/S 10.00 25.00
14 Ted Musgrave V/S 6.00 15.00
15 Geoff Bodine V/S 6.00 15.00
16 Ward Burton V/S 8.00 20.00
17 Ricky Craven P 8.00 20.00
18 Johnny Benson V/S 8.00 20.00
20 Wally Dallenbach V 6.00 15.00
21 Tony Stewart S 40.00 80.00
22 Bill Elliott P/V/S 10.00 25.00
23 Mike Skinner P/V/S 6.00 15.00
24 David Green P 6.00 15.00
25 Joe Nemechek P/V 6.00 15.00
26 Kenny Irwin S 12.00 30.00
27 Steve Park P/V/S 8.00 20.00
28 Robin Pemberton P/V 4.00 10.00
29 Larry McReynolds P/V/S 6.00 15.00
30 Jimmy Makar P/V 4.00 10.00
31 Ray Evernham P/V/S 10.00 25.00
32 Todd Parrott P/V/S 4.00 10.00
33 Randy LaJoie P/V/S 6.00 15.00
34 Robert Pressley V/S 6.00 15.00
35 Tim Fedewa P/V 6.00 15.00
36 Kevin Lepage P/V 6.00 15.00
37 Mike McLaughlin V/S 6.00 15.00
38 Jason Keller P/V 6.00 15.00
39 D.Earnhardt Jr. P/V/S 75.00 150.00
40 Jimmy Spencer V/S 6.00 15.00

1998 Press Pass Signings Gold

1 Jeff Gordon PPP/VIP 75.00 150.00
2 Dale Jarrett PPP/VIP 25.00 50.00
3 Dale Earnhardt PPP/VIP 250.00 450.00
3B Dale Earnhardt/10
4 Terry Labonte PPP/VIP 25.00 50.00
10 Bobby Labonte VIP 15.00 40.00
12 Jeff Burton PPP/VIP 15.00 40.00
13 Michael Waltrip PPP/VIP 15.00 40.00
22 Bill Elliott PPP/VIP 40.00 80.00
40 Jimmy Spencer VIP 12.00 30.00

1999 Press Pass Signings

Inserted in Press Pass Premium packs at stated odds of one in 48, these cards feature authentic autographs of past and present NASCAR personalities. Most cards were hand serial numbered on the back and each features silver foil highlights on the front. They are often confused with the 2000 Press Pass Signings since that year's cards also featured a 1999 copyright line year. The real 1999 Signings inserts feature the words "Press Pass Signings" vertically in the background of the driver photo. Also note that additional Signings cards, including Dale Earnhardt Jr. and Matt Kenseth, were released with the 2003 VIP Tin factory set. Those Signings cards feature different serial numbering and most were signed in black ink or a very dark blue ink instead of the basic bright blue ink.

1 Glenn Allen/1500 6.00 15.00
2 Bobby Allison/500 10.00 25.00
3 John Andretti/370 6.00 15.00
4 Buddy Baker/1500 6.00 15.00
5A Johnny Benson/750 6.00 15.00
5B Johnny Benson/620 6.00 15.00
6A Dave Blaney Blue/750 6.00 15.00
6B Dave Blaney Black/500 6.00 15.00
7 Brett Bodine/750 6.00 15.00
8 Todd Bodine/500 6.00 15.00
9A Jeff Burton/250 10.00 25.00
9B Jeff Burton/500 8.00 20.00
10 Ward Burton/500 10.00 25.00
11 Derrike Cope/500 8.00 20.00
12 Wally Dallenbach/500 6.00 15.00
13 Mike Dillon/500 6.00 15.00
14 Dale Earnhardt/400 175.00 350.00
15A Dale Earnhardt Jr./875 30.00 60.00
16 Tim Fedewa/690 6.00 15.00
17 Jeff Fuller/500 4.00 10.00
18 Harry Gant/1450 6.00 15.00
19 Jeff Gordon/400 50.00 120.00
20 David Green/770 6.00 15.00
21 Jeff Green/750 6.00 15.00
22 Bobby Hamilton/480 10.00 25.00
23 Ernie Irvan/225 20.00 50.00
24 Kenny Irwin/380 20.00 50.00
25A Dale Jarrett Blue/600 12.50 30.00
25B Dale Jarrett Black/60 20.00 50.00
26 Jason Jarrett/1500 6.00 15.00
27A Ned Jarrett/400 8.00 20.00
27B Ned Jarrett Blue/355 8.00 20.00
28 Jason Keller/500 6.00 15.00
29A Matt Kenseth Blue/500 15.00 40.00
29B Matt Kenseth Black/155 30.00 60.00
30 Bobby Labonte/500 12.50 30.00
31 Terry Labonte/400 12.50 30.00
32 Randy LaJoie/750 6.00 15.00
33 Kevin Lepage/500 6.00 15.00
34 Chad Little/500 8.00 20.00
35A Jimmy Makar Blue/700 5.00 12.00
35B Jimmy Makar Black/500 5.00 12.00
36 Sterling Marlin/750 12.50 30.00
37 Mark Martin/430 15.00 40.00
38A Jeremy Mayfield Blue/490 8.00 20.00
38B Jeremy Mayfield Black/500 8.00 20.00
39A Mike McLaughlin Blue/750 6.00 15.00
39B Mike McLaughlin Black/475 6.00 15.00
40A Larry McReynolds Blue/750 8.00 20.00
40B Larry McReynolds Black/500 8.00 20.00
41 Joe Nemechek 6.00 15.00
42 Steve Park/900 8.00 20.00
43A Todd Parrott Blue/975 4.00 10.00
43B Todd Parrott Black/500 4.00 10.00
44 Robin Pemberton/750 4.00 10.00
45 Andy Petree/375 6.00 15.00
46 Robert Pressley/1000 6.00 15.00
47 Ricky Rudd/550 15.00 30.00
48A Elliott Sadler Blue/650 6.00 15.00
48B Elliott Sadler Black/250 6.00 15.00
49 Hermie Sadler/500 6.00 15.00
50 Elton Sawyer 6.00 15.00
51 Ken Schrader/1575 6.00 15.00
52A Mike Skinner Blue/350 6.00 15.00
52B Mike Skinner Black/395 6.00 15.00
53 Jimmy Spencer/650 8.00 20.00
54 Jack Sprague/750 6.00 15.00
55 Tony Stewart/500 20.00 50.00
56 Rusty Wallace 12.50 30.00
57 Darrell Waltrip/175 20.00 50.00
58 Michael Waltrip/500 8.00 20.00

1999 Press Pass Signings Gold

Inserted in packs at stated odds of one in 480, these cards feature authentic autographs of leading drivers. Each card features gold foil highlights on the front, was hand serial numbered on the back, and signed in gold ink unless noted below. They are often confused with the 2000 Press Pass Signings since that year's cards also featured a 1999 copyright line year. The real 1999 Signings inserts feature the words "Press Pass Signings" vertically in the background of the driver photo. Some cards were also issued in 2003 as part of the Press Pass VIP holiday tin factory set.

1 Ward Burton/70 25.00 60.00
2 Derrike Cope/100 15.00 40.00
3 Dale Earnhardt/100 300.00 500.00
4A D.Earnhardt Jr. Gold/85 60.00 120.00
4B D.Earnhardt Jr. Blue/125 60.00 120.00
5 Jeff Gordon/100 50.00 120.00
6 Bobby Hamilton/100 20.00 50.00
7 Jeff Hammond/100 20.00 50.00
8 Ernie Irvan/105 20.00 50.00
9 Dale Jarrett/100 30.00 60.00
10 Jason Keller/95 15.00 40.00
11 Matt Kenseth/100 40.00 80.00
12 Bobby Labonte/100 20.00 50.00
13 Terry Labonte/100 40.00 80.00
14 Jimmy Makar Blue/700 15.00 40.00
15 Mark Martin/100 30.00 80.00
16 Jeremy Mayfield/110 15.00 40.00
17 Mike McLaughlin/100 15.00 40.00
18 Larry McReynolds/100 15.00 40.00
19 Joe Nemechek/100 15.00 40.00
20 Todd Parrott/100 15.00 40.00
21 Robin Pemberton/100 15.00 40.00
22 Ricky Rudd/100 25.00 60.00
23 Elliott Sadler/65 25.00 60.00
24 Mike Skinner/100 15.00 40.00
25 Jimmy Spencer/100 10.00 25.00
26 Tony Stewart/100 40.00 80.00
27 Frank Stoddard/100 15.00 40.00
28 Rusty Wallace Blue/100 40.00 80.00
29 Darrell Waltrip/100 10.00 25.00

2000 Press Pass Signings

Randomly inserted in packs at a rate of one in 240. This autograph program featured over 60-current and past drivers. Each card features the autograph in a large area below the photo with the set name and driver's name vertically on the left. The cardbacks feature a 1999 copyright date line but were issued as a 2000 year set so they are often sold or mistaken to be the 1999 release. The cards were spread throughout all of the 2000 Press Pass products. Unlike previous years these cards were not serial numbered.

1 Bobby Allison 8.00 20.00
2 John Andretti 7.50 20.00
3 Casey Atwood 10.00 25.00
4 Buddy Baker 8.00 20.00
5 Dave Blaney 5.00 12.00
6 Brett Bodine 5.00 12.00
7 Todd Bodine 5.00 12.00
8 Jeff Burton 8.00 20.00
9 Ward Burton 10.00 25.00
10 Richard Childress 7.50 20.00
11 Stacy Compton 5.00 12.00
12 Wally Dallenbach 5.00 12.00
13 Bill Davis 3.00 8.00
14 Dale Earnhardt 100.00 200.00
15 Dale Earnhardt Jr. 50.00 100.00
16 Jimmy Elledge 3.00 8.00
17 Tim Fedewa 5.00 12.00
18 Jimmy Fennig 3.00 8.00
19 A.J. Foyt 20.00 50.00
20 Jeff Gordon 60.00 120.00
21 David Green 5.00 12.00
22 Jeff Green 5.00 12.00
23 Mark Green 5.00 12.00
24 Kevin Grubb 5.00 12.00
25 Bobby Hamilton 10.00 25.00
26 Jeff Hammond 5.00 12.00
27 Dale Jarrett 12.00 30.00
28 Ned Jarrett 7.50 20.00
29 Jason Keller 5.00 12.00
30 Matt Kenseth 15.00 40.00
31 Terry Labonte 12.00 30.00
32 Randy LaJoie 5.00 12.00
33 Kevin Lepage 5.00 12.00
34 Chad Little 7.50 20.00
35 Jimmy Makar 4.00 8.00
36 Sterling Marlin 8.00 20.00
37 Mark Martin 25.00 60.00
38 Jeremy Mayfield 10.00 25.00
39 Larry McReynolds 3.00 8.00
40 Joe Nemechek 5.00 12.00
41 Steve Park 10.00 25.00
42 Hank Parker Jr. 5.00 12.00
43 Todd Parrott 4.00 8.00
44 Benny Parsons 25.00 60.00
45 David Pearson 15.00 40.00
46 Robin Pemberton 4.00 8.00
47 Robert Pressley 5.00 12.00
48 Scott Pruett 5.00 12.00
49 Tony Raines 5.00 12.00
50 Ricky Rudd 12.00 30.00
51 Elliott Sadler 5.00 12.00
52 Hermie Sadler 5.00 12.00
53 Elton Sawyer 7.50 20.00
54 Ken Schrader 7.50 20.00
55 Mike Skinner 5.00 12.00
56 Peter Sospenzo 4.00 8.00
57 Tony Stewart 25.00 60.00
58 Frank Stoddard 4.00 8.00
59 Dick Trickle 5.00 12.00
60 Kenny Wallace 10.00 25.00
61 Darrell Waltrip 20.00 50.00
62 Michael Waltrip 10.00 25.00
63 Greg Zipadelli 4.00 8.00

2000 Press Pass Signings Gold

1 Bobby Allison/100 12.50 30.00
2 John Andretti/100 12.50 30.00
3 Buddy Baker/100 12.50 30.00
4 Dave Blaney/100 8.00 20.00
5 Brett Bodine/100 8.00 20.00
6 Jeff Burton/100 15.00 40.00
7 Ward Burton/100 15.00 40.00
8 Stacy Compton/100 8.00 20.00
9 Dale Earnhardt/100 200.00 400.00
10 Dale Earnhardt Jr./100 60.00 120.00
11 A.J. Foyt/100 30.00 80.00
12 Jeff Gordon/100 100.00 200.
13 Bobby Hamilton/100 25.00 60.
14 Dale Jarrett/100 30.00 60.
15 Ned Jarrett/100 12.50 30.
16 Matt Kenseth/50 50.00 100.
17 Bobby Labonte/100
18 Terry Labonte/100 40.00 80.
19 Chad Little/100 12.50 30.
20 Mark Martin/100 75.00 150.
21 Jeremy Mayfield/100 15.00 40.
22 Joe Nemechek/100 8.00 20.
23 Steve Park/100 15.00 40.
24 Benny Parsons/100 50.00 100.
25 David Pearson/100 25.00 60.
26 Robert Pressley/100 8.00 20.
27 Ricky Rudd/100 20.00 50.
28 Elliott Sadler/100 15.00 40.
29 Mike Skinner/100 8.00 20.
30 Tony Stewart/100 60.00 120.
31 Kenny Wallace/50 15.00 40.
32 Darrell Waltrip/100 30.00 80.
33 Michael Waltrip/100 20.00 50.

2001 Press Pass Signings

Issued in various 2001 Press Pass products at different odds, these cards feature authentic autographs along with silver foil layering on the fronts. A few cards were issued as exchange car in packs that carried one of three different expiration dates: July 31, 2002, September 11, 2002 or October 30, 2002.

STATED ODDS 1:48 PREMIUM HOB/RET
STATED ODDS 1:96 OPTIMA HOB,1:120 RET
ODDS 1:96 STEALTH HOB, 1:120 RET
ODDS 1:120 TRACKSIDE HOB, 1:240 RET
STATED ODDS 1:72 VIP HOB, 1:120 RET
1 John Andretti P/T/N/S 8.00 20.
2 Casey Atwood P/N/S 5.00 12.
3 Greg Biffle V/S 6.00 15.
4 Dave Blaney P/T/N/S 6.00 15.
5 Brett Bodine P/T/N/S 5.00 12.
6 Todd Bodine T/S 5.00 12.
7 Jeff Burton P/T/N 10.00 25.
8 Ward Burton P/T/N/S 8.00 20.
9 Kurt Busch P/T/N/S 8.00 20.
10 Stacy Compton T/N/S 5.00 12.
11 Ricky Craven P/T/N/S 8.00 20.
12 Dale Earnhardt Jr. P/S/T/N 40.00 100.
13 Tim Fedewa P/N/S 5.00 12.
14 A.J. Foyt V/S 12.50 30.
15 Jeff Gordon T/N/S 50.00 120.
16 David Green S 5.00 12.
17 Jeff Green P/V 5.00 12.
18 Mark Green V 5.00 12.
19 Kevin Grubb P/N/S 5.00 12.
20 Bobby Hamilton P 10.00 25.
21 Kevin Harvick BGN P/N/S 10.00 25.
22 Kevin Harvick WC V/S 12.00 30.
23 Ron Hornaday T/N/S 5.00 12.
24 Dale Jarrett P/T/N/S 8.00 20.
25 Buckshot Jones V/S 8.00 20.
26 Jason Keller V/S 5.00 12.
27 Matt Kenseth P/T/N/S 8.00 20.
28 Bobby Labonte P/T/N/S 12.00 30.
29 Terry Labonte T/N/S 10.00 25.
30 Randy LaJoie V/S 5.00 12.
31 Jason Leffler S 5.00 12.
32 Chad Little V/S 5.00 12.
33 Sterling Marlin P/N/S 12.00 30.
34 Mark Martin P/T/N/S 20.00 50.
35 Jeremy Mayfield P/S 8.00 20.
36 Mike McLaughlin P/N/S 5.00 12.
37 Jerry Nadeau V/S 8.00 20.
38 Joe Nemecheck P/T/N/S 5.00 12.
39 Ryan Newman P/N/S 6.00 15.
40 Steve Park P/T/N/S EXCH 15.00 40.
41 Hank Parker Jr. V/S 5.00 12.
42 Kyle Petty P/T/N/S 10.00 25.
43 Richard Petty V/S 20.00 50.
44 Robert Pressley P/T/N/S 5.00 12.
45 Tony Raines P/N/S 5.00 12.
46 Ricky Rudd P/T/N/S 10.00 25.
47 Elliott Sadler P/N/S 10.00 25.
48 Elton Sawyer V/S 5.00 12.
49 Ken Schrader P/T/N/S 8.00 20.
50 Jimmy Spencer P/T/N/S 8.00 20.
51 Tony Stewart P/T/V 25.00 50.
52 Rusty Wallace P/T/N/S 10.00 25.
53 Darrell Waltrip P/T/N/S 8.00 20.

Michael Waltrip V/S 10.00 25.00
Robert Yates T 8.00 20.00
Greg Zipadelli 5.00 12.00

2001 Press Pass Signings Gold

ohn Andretti P/T/N/S 15.00 40.00
Casey Atwood P/T/N/S 15.00 40.00
Dave Blaney P/T/S 12.00 30.00
Brett Bodine P/T/N/S 12.00 30.00
Todd Bodine V/S 12.00 30.00
Jeff Burton T/N/S 20.00 50.00
Ward Burton P/T/N/S 20.00 50.00
Kurt Busch P/T/N/S 25.00 60.00
Stacy Compton T/N/S 12.00 30.00
Ricky Craven P/T/N/S 20.00 50.00
Dale Earnhardt Jr. 75.00 150.00
A.J. Foyt V/S 20.00 50.00
Jeff Gordon S 100.00 200.00
Kevin Harvick WC V/S 40.00 100.00
Ron Hornaday T/N/S 12.00 30.00
Dale Jarrett P/T/N/S 20.00 50.00
Buckshot Jones V/S 15.00 40.00
Matt Kenseth P/T/N/S 25.00 60.00
Bobby Labonte S 15.00 40.00
Terry Labonte T/N/S 25.00 60.00
Jason Leffler S 12.00 30.00
Sterling Marlin T/N/S 25.00 60.00
Mark Martin P/T/N/S 30.00 80.00
Jeremy Mayfield S 20.00 50.00
Jerry Nadeau V/S 12.00 30.00
Joe Nemecheck P/T/N/S 12.00 30.00
Kyle Petty P/T/N/S 15.00 40.00
Robert Pressley P/T/N/S 12.00 30.00
Ricky Rudd P/T/N/S 20.00 50.00
Elliott Sadler T/N/S 15.00 40.00
Ken Schrader P/T/N/S 15.00 40.00
Jimmy Spencer P/T/N/S 12.00 30.00
Tony Stewart P/T/N/S 40.00 100.00
Rusty Wallace P/T/N/S 25.00 60.00
Darrell Waltrip P/T/N/S 30.00 80.00
Michael Waltrip V/S 15.00 40.00

2001 Press Pass Signings Transparent

Jeff Burton V/S 15.00 40.00
Ward Burton P/T/N/S 12.00 30.00
Dale Earnhardt Jr. 60.00 120.00
Dale Jarrett P/T/N/S 12.00 30.00
Matt Kenseth P/T/N/S 15.00 40.00
Bobby Labonte S 20.00 50.00
Mark Martin P/T/N/S 20.00 50.00
Jeremy Mayfield S 10.00 25.00
Kyle Petty P/T/N/S 12.00 30.00
Ricky Rudd P/T/N/S 12.00 30.00
Tony Stewart V/S 30.00 80.00
Rusty Wallace P/T/N/S 20.00 50.00
Darrell Waltrip P/T/N/S 20.00 50.00

2002 Press Pass Signings

sued at different rates depending on the product ese cards were inserted in, these 74-cards clude an authentic autograph of the featured iver. We have notated next to the driver's name hich product(s) their autographs appeared in. lease note that some of the cards were not ready r inclusion in packs and those cards could be deemed until June 30,2003. The Dale Earnhardt ., was the most notable of the redemptions.

TATED ODDS 1:48H, 1:72R PP PREMIUM
TATED ODDS 1:120H, 1:240R TRACKSIDE
TATED ODDS 1:72 HOBBY VIP
TATED ODDS 1:96 H, 1:240R STEALTH

John Andretti O/P/S/T/N 6.00 12.00
Buddy Baker O/P/S/T/N 6.00 15.00
Kyle Berck O/P/S/T/N 5.00 12.00
Greg Biffle O/S/N 8.00 20.00
Dave Blaney O/P/S/T/N 6.00 15.00
Brett Bodine O/P/S/N 5.00 12.00
Todd Bodine O/P/S/T/N 5.00 12.00
Jeff Burton O/S/T/N 6.00 15.00
Ward Burton O/P/S/T/N 6.00 15.00
0 Kurt Busch O/P/S/T/N 10.00 25.00
1 Steve Carlson O/P/S/T/N 5.00 12.00
2 Matt Crafton O/P/S/T/N 5.00 12.00
3 Ricky Craven O/S/N 5.00 12.00
4 Dale Earnhardt Jr. P/T 50.00 100.00
5 Kerry Earnhardt O/P/S/T/N 6.00 15.00
6 Larry Foyt O/P/S/T/N 5.00 12.00
7 Coy Gibbs O/P/S/T/N 5.00 12.00
8 Jeff Gordon O/P/S/T/N 40.00 100.00
9 Robby Gordon O/P/S/T/N 6.00 15.00
0 David Green O/P/S/T/N 5.00 12.00
1 Jeff Green O/P/S/T/N 5.00 12.00
2 Mark Green O/P/S/N 5.00 12.00
3 Bobby Hamilton O/P/S/T/N 8.00 20.00
4 Kevin Hamlin O/P/S/T/N 5.00 12.00
5 Jeff Hammond 6.00 15.00
6 Kevin Harvick O/P/S/T/N 12.00 30.00
7 Dale Jarrett O/P/S/T/N 10.00 25.00
8 Ned Jarrett O/S/T/N 6.00 15.00
9 Jimmie Johnson O/P/S/T/N 25.00 60.00
0 Junior Johnson O/P/S/T/N 12.00 30.00
1 Buckshot Jones O/P/S/T/N 5.00 12.00
32 Jason Keller O/P/S/N 5.00 12.00
33 Matt Kenseth O/P/S/T/N 6.00 15.00
34 Travis Kvapil O/P/S/T/N 6.00 15.00
35 Bobby Labonte O/P/S/T/N 12.00 30.00
36 Terry Labonte O/S/T/N 10.00 25.00
37 Randy Lajoie O/P/S/T/N 5.00 12.00
38 Jason Leffler O/P/S/T/N 5.00 12.00
39 Chad Little O/P/S/N 5.00 12.00
40 Sterling Marlin O/P/S/T/N 8.00 20.00
41 Mark Martin O/P/S/T/N 20.00 50.00
42 Jeremy Mayfield O/P/S/T/N 8.00 20.00
43 Mike McLaughlin O/S/N 5.00 12.00
44 Jamie McMurray O/P/S/T/N 8.00 20.00
45 Casey Mears O/S/N 8.00 20.00
46 Ted Musgrave O/P/S/T/N 5.00 12.00
47 Jerry Nadeau O/P/S/T/N 5.00 12.00
48 Ryan Newman O/P/S/T/N 6.00 15.00
49 Hank Parker Jr. O/P/S/T/N 5.00 12.00
50 Benny Parsons O/P/S/T/N 10.00 25.00
51 David Pearson O/P/S/T/N 15.00 40.00
52 Kyle Petty O/P/S/T/N 6.00 15.00
53 Richard Petty O/P/S/T/N 25.00 60.00
54 Craig Raudman O/P/S/T/N 5.00 12.00
55 Ricky Rudd O/P/S/T/N 6.00 15.00
56 Joe Ruttman O/P/S/T/N 5.00 12.00
57 Elliott Sadler O/P/S/T/N 5.00 12.00
58 Johnny Sauter O/P/S/N 5.00 12.00
59 Ken Schrader O/P/S/T/N 5.00 12.00
60 Dennis Setzer O/P/S/N 5.00 12.00
61 Mike Skinner O/S/N 5.00 12.00
62 Jimmy Spencer O/P/S/T/N 5.00 12.00
63 Jack Sprague O/P/S/T/N 5.00 12.00
64 Mike Stefanik O/P/S/T/N 5.00 12.00
65 Tony Stewart O 20.00 50.00
66 Cam Strader O/P/S/T/N 5.00 12.00
67 Hut Stricklin O/P/S/T/N 5.00 12.00
68 Rusty Wallace O/P/S/N 6.00 15.00
69 Michael Waltrip O/P/S/T/N 8.00 20.00
70 Scott Wimmer O/P/S/T/N 5.00 12.00
71 Glen Wood O/P/S/T/N 5.00 12.00
72 Jon Wood O/P/S/T/N 5.00 12.00
73 Cale Yarborough O/P/S/T/N 8.00 20.00

2002 Press Pass Signings Gold

1 Bobby Allison O/P/S/T/N 15.00 40.00
2 John Andretti O/P/S/T/N 10.00 25.00
3 Buddy Baker O/P/S/T/N 15.00 40.00
4 Kyle Berck O/P/S/N 10.00 25.00
5 Greg Biffle O/S/N 15.00 40.00
6 Dave Blaney O/P/S/T/N 12.00 30.00
7 Brett Bodine O/P/S/T/N 10.00 25.00
8 Todd Bodine O/P/S/T/N 10.00 25.00
9 Jeff Burton O/S/T/N 15.00 40.00
10 Ward Burton O/P/S/T/N 12.00 30.00
11 Kurt Busch O/P/S/T/N 15.00 40.00
12 Steve Carlson O/P/S/T/N 10.00 25.00
13 Matt Crafton O/P/S/T/N 10.00 25.00
14 Dale Earnhardt Jr. 75.00 150.00
15 Kerry Earnhardt O/P/S/T/N 12.00 30.00
16 Larry Foyt O/P/S/T/N 8.00 20.00
17 Coy Gibbs P/S/T/N 10.00 25.00
18 Jeff Gordon O/P/S/T/N 50.00 100.00
19 David Green O/P/S/T/N 10.00 25.00
20 Jeff Green O/P/S/T/N 10.00 25.00
21 Mark Green O/P/S/T/N 10.00 25.00
22 Bobby Hamilton O/P/S/T/N 12.00 30.00
23 Kevin Hamlin O/P/S/T/N 10.00 25.00
24 Kevin Harvick O/P/S/T/N 25.00 60.00
25 Dale Jarrett O/P/S/T/N 15.00 40.00
26 Ned Jarrett O/P/S/T/N 15.00 40.00
27 Jimmie Johnson O/P/S/T/N 50.00 100.00
28 Junior Johnson O/P/S/T/N 25.00 50.00
29 Buckshot Jones O/P/S/T/N 10.00 25.00
30 Jason Keller O/P/S/T/N 10.00 25.00
31 Matt Kenseth O/P/S/T/N 15.00 40.00
32 Travis Kvapil O/P/S/T/N 10.00 25.00
33 Bobby Labonte O/P/S/T/N 15.00 40.00
34 Terry Labonte O/S/T/N 20.00 50.00
35 Randy Lajoie O/P/S/T/N 10.00 25.00
36 Jason Leffler O/P/S/T/N 10.00 25.00
37 Chad Little P/S/T/N 10.00 25.00
38 Sterling Marlin O/P/S/T/N 15.00 40.00
39 Mark Martin O/P/S/T/N 25.00 60.00
40 Jeremy Mayfield O/P/S/T/N 12.00 30.00
41 Jamie McMurray O/P/S/T/N 12.00 30.00
42 Casey Mears O/S/N 12.00 30.00
43 Ted Musgrave O/P/S/T/N 10.00 25.00
44 Jerry Nadeau O/P/S/T/N 8.00 20.00
45 Ryan Newman O/P/S/T/N 15.00 40.00
46 Hank Parker Jr. O/S/T/N 10.00 25.00
47 Benny Parsons O/P/S/T/N 12.00 30.00
48 David Pearson O/P/S/T/N 25.00 50.00
49 Kyle Petty O/P/S/T/N 20.00 50.00
50 Richard Petty O/P/S/T/N 30.00 80.00
51 Craig Raudman O/P/S/T/N 10.00 25.00
52 Ricky Rudd O/P/S/T/N 12.00 30.00
53 Joe Ruttman P/S/T/N 10.00 25.00
54 Elliott Sadler O/S/N 10.00 25.00
55 Johnny Sauter P/S/T/N 12.00 30.00
56 Ken Schrader O/P/S/T/N 10.00 25.00
57 Dennis Setzer O/P/S/T/N 10.00 25.00
58 Mike Skinner O/S/N 10.00 25.00
59 Jimmy Spencer O/P/S/T/N 12.00 30.00
60 Jack Sprague O/P/S/T/N 10.00 25.00
61 Mike Stefanik O/P/S/T/N 10.00 25.00
62 Cam Strader O/P/S/T/N 10.00 25.00
63 Hut Stricklin O/P/S/T/N 10.00 25.00
64 Rusty Wallace O/P/S/T/N 20.00 50.00
65 Darrell Waltrip O/P/S/T/N 20.00 50.00
66 Michael Waltrip O/P/S/T/N 15.00 40.00
67 Scott Wimmer P/S/T/N 15.00 40.00
68 Glen Wood O/P/S/T/N 10.00 25.00
69 Jon Wood O/P/S/T/N 10.00 25.00
70 Cale Yarborough O/P/S/T/N 15.00 40.00

2002 Press Pass Signings Transparent

1 Dale Earnhardt Jr. 50.00 120.00
2 Jeff Gordon O/P/S/T/N 60.00 120.00
3 Kevin Harvick O/P/S/T/N 20.00 50.00
4 Dale Jarrett O/P/S/T/N 20.00 50.00
5 Matt Kenseth O
6 Bobby Labonte O/P/S/T/N 12.00 30.00
7 Ryan Newman O/P/S/T/N 12.00 30.00
8 Ricky Rudd O/P/S/T/N 10.00 25.00
9 Tony Stewart O/P/S/T/N 25.00 60.00
10 Rusty Wallace O/P/S/T/N 25.00 60.00

2003 Press Pass Signings

This 75-card set featured certified autographs from some of NASCAR's hottest stars as well as some of the retired greats. Some of these cards were found in packs of 2003 Press Pass, 2003 Press Pass Stealth, 2003 Press Pass Trackside, 2003 VIP or a combination of these and are tagged as such. The stated odd were 1 in 48 packs in Press Pass Premium, and 1 in 84 packs in Press Pass Stealth,Press Pass Trackside and VIP. The card fronts have a designated white space at the bottom for the autographs.

1 Bobby Allison O/S/T/N 12.00 30.00
2 John Andretti O/P/S/T/N 6.00 15.00
3 Buddy Baker O/S/T/N 6.00 15.00
4 Stanton Barrett O/S/T/N 5.00 12.00
5 Greg Biffle O/P/S/T/N 6.00 15.00
6 Chris Bingham O/S 6.00 15.00
7 Dave Blaney O/P/S/T/N 5.00 12.00
8 Mike Bliss O/S/T/N 5.00 12.00
9 Brett Bodine O/P/S/T/N 5.00 12.00
10 Jeff Burton O/S/N 6.00 15.00
11 Ward Burton O/P/S/T/N 6.00 15.00
12 Kurt Busch O/P/S/T/N 10.00 25.00
13 Steve Carlson O/P/S/T/N 5.00 12.00
14 Matt Crafton O/S/N 5.00 12.00
15 Ricky Craven O/P/S/T/N 6.00 15.00
16 Rick Crawford O/S/N 5.00 12.00
17 Dale Jr. O/S/N/04PP 40.00 100.00
18 Kerry Earnhardt O/S 8.00 20.00
19 Carl Edwards O/S/N 25.00 50.00
20 Christian Fittipaldi O/S/T/N 5.00 12.00
21 Jeff Fultz O/P/S/T/N 5.00 12.00
22 Coy Gibbs O/S/T/N 5.00 12.00
23 Jeff Gordon O/P/S/T/N 60.00 120.00
24 Robby Gordon O/P/S/T/N 6.00 15.00
25 Tina Gordon O/S/N 6.00 15.00
26 David Green O/P/S/T/N 5.00 12.00
27 Jeff Green P/T 5.00 12.00
28 Kevin Hamlin O/P/S/T/N 5.00 12.00
29 Kevin Harvick O/P/S/T/N 10.00 25.00
30 Shane Hmiel O/S/N 6.00 15.00
31 Jake Hobgood O/P/S/T/N 5.00 12.00
32 Andy Houston O/S/T/N 5.00 12.00
33 Dale Jarrett O/P/S/T/N 10.00 25.00
34 Ned Jarrett O/S/T/N 8.00 20.00
35 J.Johnson O/P/S/T/N 40.00 80.00
36 Kasey Kahne O 8.00 20.00
37 Jason Keller O/P/S/T/N 5.00 12.00
38 Matt Kenseth O/P/S/T/N 10.00 25.00
39 Travis Kvapil O/P/S/T/N 6.00 15.00
40 Bobby Labonte O/P/S/T/N 10.00 25.00
41 Terry Labonte O/P/S/T/N 15.00 40.00
42 Randy LaJoie O/P/S/T/N 5.00 12.00
43 Damon Lusk O/S/T/N 5.00 12.00
44 Steadman Marlin O/S/T/N 5.00 12.00
45 Sterling Marlin O/P/S/T/N 6.00 15.00
46 Mark Martin O/P/S/T/N 15.00 40.00
47 Jeremy Mayfield O/P/S/T/N 8.00 20.00
48 Jamie McMurray O/S/T/N 6.00 15.00
49 Casey Mears O/S/T/N 6.00 15.00
50 Chase Montgomery O/S/N 5.00 12.00
51 Jerry Nadeau O/S/T/N 8.00 20.00
52 Joe Nemechek O/S/T/N 6.00 15.00
53 Ryan Newman O/P/S/T/N 6.00 15.00
54 Eric Norris O/S/T/N 6.00 15.00
55 Steve Park P/T 15.00 40.00
56 Benny Parsons O/S/T/N 10.00 25.00
57 David Pearson O/S/T/N 8.00 20.00
58 Kyle Petty O/S/T/N 8.00 20.00
59 Richard Petty O/S/T/N 25.00 50.00
60 Tony Raines O/S/T/N 5.00 12.00
61 Scott Riggs O/P/S/T/N 6.00 15.00
62 Ricky Rudd O/P/S/T/N 6.00 15.00
63 Andy Santerre O/P/S/T/N 5.00 12.00
64 Johnny Sauter O/P/S/T/N 5.00 12.00
65 Ken Schrader O/S/T/N 6.00 15.00
66 Mike Skinner O/P/S/T/N 6.00 15.00
67 Regan Smith O/S/N 5.00 12.00
68 Jimmy Spencer O/P/S/T/N 6.00 15.00
69 Jack Sprague O/S/N 5.00 12.00
70 Tony Stewart O/S/N 25.00 60.00
71 Jimmy Vasser O/S/N 5.00 12.00
72 Brian Vickers O/S/T/N 5.00 12.00
73 Rusty Wallace O/P/S/T/N 10.00 25.00
74 Michael Waltrip O/P/S/T/N 8.00 20.00
75 Scott Wimmer O/P/S/T/N 6.00 15.00
76 Glen Wood O/S/T/N 5.00 12.00
77 Jon Wood O/S/N 5.00 12.00
78 Cale Yarborough O/S/T/N 8.00 20.00
79 Robert Yates O/S/T/N 10.00 25.00

2003 Press Pass Signings Gold

1 Bobby Allison O/S/T/N 20.00 50.00
2 John Andretti O/P/S/T 12.00 30.00
3 Buddy Baker O/S/T/N 12.00 30.00
4 Stanton Barrett O/S/T/N 12.00 30.00
5 Greg Biffle O/P/S/T/N 15.00 40.00
6 Chris Bingham O/S 12.00 30.00
7 Dave Blaney O/P/S/T/N 12.00 30.00
8 Mike Bliss O/S/T/N 10.00 25.00
9 Brett Bodine O/P/S/T/N 10.00 25.00
10 Jeff Burton O/S/N 15.00 40.00
11 Ward Burton O/S/T/N 15.00 40.00
12 Kurt Busch O/S/T/N 15.00 40.00
13 Steve Carlson O/P/S/T/N 10.00 25.00
14 Matt Crafton O/S/N 12.00 30.00
15 Ricky Craven O/P/S/T/N 12.00 30.00
16 Rick Crawford O/S/N 10.00 25.00
17 Dale Jr. O/S/N/04PP 50.00 120.00
18 Kerry Earnhardt O/S 20.00 50.00
19 Carl Edwards O/S/N 50.00 100.00
20 Christian Fittipaldi O/S/T/N 12.00 30.00
21 Jeff Fultz O/P/S/T/N 10.00 25.00
22 Coy Gibbs O/S/T/N 10.00 25.00
23 Jeff Gordon O/P/S/T/N 75.00 150.00
24 Robby Gordon O/P/S/T/N 15.00 40.00
25 Tina Gordon O/S/N 15.00 40.00
26 David Green O/S/T/N 10.00 25.00
27 Jeff Green O/P/S/T 10.00 25.00
28 Kevin Hamlin O/P/S/T/N 10.00 25.00
29 Kevin Harvick O/P/S/T/N 25.00 50.00
30 Shane Hmiel O/S/N 20.00 50.00
31 Jake Hobgood O/P/S/T/N 10.00 25.00
32 Andy Houston O/S/T/N 10.00 25.00
33 Dale Jarrett O/P/S/T/N 30.00 80.00
34 Ned Jarrett O/S/T/N 12.00 30.00
35 J.Johnson O/P/S/T/N 50.00 120.00
36 Kasey Kahne O 50.00 120.00
37 Jason Keller O/P/S/T/N 12.00 30.00
38 Matt Kenseth O/P/S/T/N 40.00 80.00
39 Travis Kvapil O/P/S/T/N 15.00 40.00
40 Bobby Labonte O/P/S/T/N 20.00 50.00
41 Terry Labonte O/P/S/T/N 30.00 80.00
42 Randy LaJoie O/P/S/T/N 10.00 25.00
43 Damon Lusk O/S/T/N 10.00 25.00
44 Steadman Marlin O/S/T/N 12.00 30.00
45 Sterling Marlin O/P/S/T/N 15.00 40.00
46 Mark Martin O/P/S/T/N 25.00 60.00
47 Jeremy Mayfield O/P/S/T/N 15.00 40.00
48 Jamie McMurray O/S/T/N 15.00 40.00
49 Casey Mears O/S/T/N 20.00 50.00
50 Chase Montgomery O/S/N 12.00 30.00
51 Jerry Nadeau O/P/S/T/N 15.00 40.00
52 Joe Nemechek O/S/T/N 12.00 30.00
53 Ryan Newman O/P/S/T/N 15.00 40.00
54 Eric Norris O/S/T/N 12.00 30.00
55 Steve Park O/P/S/T 60.00 120.00
56 Benny Parsons O/P/S/T/N 25.00 60.00
57 David Pearson O/S/T/N 25.00 60.00
58 Kyle Petty O/P/S/T/N 12.00 30.00
59 Richard Petty O/S/T/N 40.00 80.00
60 Tony Raines O/S/T/N 10.00 25.00
61 Scott Riggs O/P/S/T/N 12.00 30.00
62 Ricky Rudd O/P/S/T/N 12.00 30.00
63 Elliott Sadler O 10.00 25.00
64 Andy Santerre O/P/S/T/N 12.00 30.00
65 Johnny Sauter O/P/S/T/N 12.00 30.00
66 Ken Schrader O/S/T/N 12.00 30.00
67 Mike Skinner O/P/S/T/N 12.00 30.00
68 Regan Smith O/S/N 10.00 25.00
69 Jimmy Spencer O/P/S/T/N 12.00 30.00
70 Jack Sprague O/S/N 10.00 25.00
71 Tony Stewart O/S/N 60.00 120.00
72 Brian Vickers O/S/T/N 10.00 25.00
73 Kenny Wallace 15.00 40.00
74 Rusty Wallace O/S 25.00 60.00
75 Michael Waltrip O/P/S/T/N 20.00 50.00
76 Scott Wimmer O/P/S/T/N 12.00 30.00
77 Glen Wood O/S/T/N 10.00 25.00
78 Jon Wood O/S/N 12.00 30.00
79 Cale Yarborough O/S/T/N 15.00 40.00
80 Robert Yates O/S/T/N 10.00 25.00

2003 Press Pass Signings Transparent

1 Kurt Busch O/S/T/N 15.00 40.00
2 Jeff Gordon O/P/S/T/N 60.00 120.00
3 Kevin Harvick O/P/S/T/N 20.00 50.00
4 Dale Jarrett O/P/S/T/N 20.00 50.00
5 Jimmie Johnson O/P/S/T/N 30.00 80.00
6 Bobby Labonte O/P/S/T/N 20.00 50.00
7 Ryan Newman O/P/S/T/N 15.00 40.00
8 Tony Stewart O/S/N 30.00 80.00

2004 Press Pass Signings

This 70-card set featured certified autographs from some of NASCAR's hottest stars as well as some of the retired greats. Some of these cards were found in packs of 2004 Press Pass Optima, 2004 Press Pass Premium, 2004 Press Pass Stealth, 2004 Press Pass Trackside, 2004 VIP or a combination of these and are tagged as such. The stated odd were 1 in 48 packs in Press Pass Premium, and 1 in 84 packs in Press Pass Stealth,Press Pass Trackside and VIP.

1 Bobby Allison O/P/S/T/N 6.00 15.00
2 Greg Biffle BGN T/N 8.00 20.00
3 Greg Biffle NC O/S/T/N 8.00 20.00
4 Dave Blaney O/N 5.00 12.00
5 Mike Bliss T/N 5.00 12.00
6 Clint Bowyer S/T/N 8.00 20.00
7 Charlie Bradberry T/N 5.00 12.00
8 Jeff Burton O/T/N 6.00 15.00
9 Kurt Busch S/T/N 8.00 20.00
10 Kyle Busch O/P/S/T/N 15.00 40.00
11 Steve Carlson P/S/T/N 5.00 12.00
12 Stacy Compton T/N 5.00 12.00
13 Terry Cook O 6.00 15.00
14 Matt Crafton T/N 5.00 12.00
15 Ricky Craven O/P/S/T/N 8.00 20.00
16 Rick Crawford O 6.00 15.00
17 Dale Earnhardt Jr. O/T/N 30.00 80.00
18 Carl Edwards O/P/S/T/N 15.00 40.00
19 Tim Fedewa O/T/N 6.00 15.00
20 B.Gaughan O/P/S/T/N 8.00 20.00
21 Jeff Gordon O/P/S/T/N 50.00 100.00
22 Robby Gordon O/T/N 8.00 20.00
23 Tina Gordon O 8.00 20.00
24 David Green O/P/S/T/N 5.00 12.00
25 Jeff Green O/N 6.00 15.00
26 Kevin Harvick O/P/S/T/N 10.00 25.00
27 Ron Hornaday T/N 8.00 20.00
28 Robert Huffman P/S/T/N 5.00 12.00
29 Dale Jarrett O/P/S/T/N 6.00 15.00
30 Ned Jarrett 6.00 15.00
31 Jeff Jefferson S/T/N 5.00 12.00
32 Jimmie Johnson O/P/S/T/N 20.00 50.00
33 Kasey Kahne BGN O/S/T/N 12.00 30.00
34 Kasey Kahne NCS O/S/T/N 12.00 30.00
35 Jason Keller O/S/T/N 5.00 12.00
36 Matt Kenseth BGN O/N 12.00 30.00
37 M.Kenseth NCS O/P/S/T/N 12.00 30.00
38 Bobby Labonte O/P/S/T/N 10.00 25.00
39 Terry Labonte O/S/T/N 8.00 20.00
40 Sterling Marlin O/P/S/T/N 8.00 20.00
41 Mark Martin O/T/N 15.00 40.00
42 Jeremy Mayfield O/S/T/N 8.00 20.00
43 Jamie McMurray O 6.00 15.00
44 Casey Mears O/P/S/T 8.00 20.00
45 Paul Menard V 6.00 15.00
46 Joe Nemechek O 8.00 20.00
47 Ryan Newman O/P/S/T/N 6.00 15.00
48 Steve Park O 15.00 40.00
49 Benny Parsons P/S/T/N 8.00 20.00
50 David Pearson P/S/T/N 8.00 20.00
51 Kyle Petty O/P/S/T/N 8.00 20.00
52 Richard Petty O/P/S/T/N 20.00 50.00
53 Scott Riggs O/S/T/N 6.00 15.00
54 Ricky Rudd O/P/S/T/N 8.00 20.00
55 Andy Santerre P/S/T/N 5.00 12.00
56 Johnny Sauter NCS T/N 6.00 15.00
57 Dennis Setzer P/S/T/N 5.00 12.00
59 Tony Stewart O/P/S/T 25.00 60.00
59 Jack Sprague O 5.00 12.00
60 Todd Szegedy S/T/N 5.00 12.00
61 Martin Truex Jr. O 12.00 30.00
62 Kenny Wallace T/N 8.00 20.00
63 Rusty Wallace O/S/T/N 10.00 25.00
64 Michael Waltrip O/P/S/T/N 8.00 20.00
65 Scott Wimmer O/P/S/T/N 6.00 15.00
66 Glen Wood O/P/S/T/N 5.00 12.00
67 Jon Wood O/P/S/T/N 6.00 15.00
68 Cale Yarborough O/P/S/T/N 8.00 20.00
69 Robert Yates P/S/T/N 5.00 12.00
70 J.J. Yeley T/N 8.00 20.00

2004 Press Pass Signings Gold

1 Bobby Allison O/P/S/T/N 15.00 40.00
2 Greg Biffle BGN S/T/N 20.00 50.00
3 Greg Biffle NC O/S/T/N 20.00 50.00
4 Dave Blaney O/N 20.00 50.00
5 Mike Bliss T/N 12.00 30.00
6 Clint Bowyer S/T/N 15.00 40.00
7 Charlie Bradberry T/N 12.00 30.00
8 Jeff Burton O/T/N 20.00 50.00
9 Kurt Busch O/S/T/N 20.00 50.00
10 Kyle Busch O/P/S/T/N 30.00 80.00
11 Steve Carlson P/S/T/N 12.00 30.00
12 Stacy Compton T/N 12.00 30.00
13 Matt Crafton T/N 15.00 40.00
14 Ricky Craven O/P/S/T/N 20.00 50.00
15 Rick Crawford O 15.00 40.00
16 Dale Jr. O/P/S/T/N 50.00 120.00
17 Carl Edwards O/P/S/T/N 30.00 80.00
18 Tim Fedewa O 15.00 40.00
19 B.Gaughan O/P/S/T/N 20.00 50.00
20 Jeff Gordon O/P/S/T/N 75.00 150.00
21 Robby Gordon O/T/N 20.00 50.00
22 David Green O/P/S/T/N 12.00 30.00
23 Jeff Green O/N 15.00 40.00
24 Kevin Harvick O/P/S/T/N 30.00 80.00
25 Ron Hornaday T/N 20.00 50.00
26 Robert Huffman P/S/T/N 12.00 30.00
27 Dale Jarrett O/P/S/T/N 20.00 50.00
28 Jeff Jefferson S/T/N 12.00 30.00
29 Jimmie Johnson O/P/S/T/N 60.00 120.00
30 Kasey Kahne BGN O/S/T/N 20.00 50.00
31 Kasey Kahne NC O/S/T/N 20.00 50.00
32 Jason Keller O/S/T/N 12.00 30.00
33 Matt Kenseth BGN O/N 25.00 60.00
34 M.Kenseth NCS O/P/S/T/N 30.00 80.00
35 Bobby Labonte O/P/S/T/N 20.00 50.00
36 Terry Labonte O/S/T/N 40.00 100.00
37 Sterling Marlin O/P/S/T/N 20.00 50.00
38 Mark Martin O/T/N 25.00 60.00
39 Jeremy Mayfield O/S/T/N 20.00 50.00
40 Jamie McMurray O/T/N 25.00 60.00
41 Casey Mears O/P/S/T/N 20.00 50.00
42 Paul Menard V 20.00 50.00
43 Ryan Newman/20 O/P/S/T/N 20.00 50.00
44 Steve Park O 20.00 50.00
45 Benny Parsons P/S/T/N 20.00 50.00
46 David Pearson P/S/T/N 20.00 50.00
47 Kyle Petty O/P/S/T/N 20.00 50.00
48 Richard Petty O/P/S/T/N 40.00 80.00
49 Scott Riggs O/S/T/N 20.00 50.00
50 Ricky Rudd O/P/S/T/N 20.00 50.00
51 Andy Santerre P/S/T/N 12.00 30.00
52 Johnny Sauter BGN T/N 15.00 40.00
53 Johnny Sauter NCS T/N 15.00 40.00
54 Dennis Setzer P/S/T/N 12.00 30.00
55 Tony Stewart O/P/S/T/N 40.00 100.00
56 Todd Szegedy S/T/N 12.00 30.00
57 Martin Truex Jr. O 75.00 150.00
58 Kenny Wallace T/N 20.00 50.00
59 Rusty Wallace O/P/S/T/N 30.00 60.00
60 Michael Waltrip O/P/S/T/N 20.00 50.00
61 Scott Wimmer O/S/T/N 15.00 40.00
62 Glen Wood O/P/S/T/N 12.00 30.00
63 Jon Wood O/P/S/T/N 15.00 40.00
64 Cale Yarborough O/P/S/T/N 20.00 50.00
65 Robert Yates O/P/S/T/N 10.00 25.00
66 J.J. Yeley T/N 15.00 40.00

2004 Press Pass Signings Transparent

This 11-card set featured certified autographs from some of NASCAR's hottest stars. Some of these cards were found in packs of 2004 Press Pass Optima, 2004 Press Pass Premium, 2004 Press Pass Stealth, 2004 Press Pass Trackside or a combination of these and are tagged as such. The cards were randomly inserted in packs and hand numbered of 100. The cards were produced on a transparent plactic stock.

1 Jeff Gordon O/P/S/T 50.00 100.00
2 Kevin Harvick O/P/S/T 20.00 50.00
3 Jimmie Johnson O/P/S/T 30.00 80.00
4 Matt Kenseth O/P/S/T 25.00 60.00
5 Bobby Labonte O/P/S/T 15.00 40.00
6 Ryan Newman O/S/T 12.00 30.00
7 Richard Petty O/P/S/T 40.00 80.00
8 Ricky Rudd O/P/T 15.00 40.00
9 Tony Stewart O/S/T 25.00 60.00
10 Rusty Wallace O/P/S/T 25.00 60.00
11 Michael Waltrip O/P/S/T 15.00 40.00

2005 Press Pass Signings

1 Bobby Allison P/S 6.00 15.00
2 John Andretti S 5.00 12.00
3 Dave Blaney 5.00 12.00
4 Clint Bowyer 6.00 15.00
5 Kurt Busch P/S 6.00 15.00
6 Kyle Busch 10.00 25.00
7 Richard Childress P/S 6.00 15.00
8 Terry Cook P/S 5.00 12.00
9 Ricky Craven 8.00 20.00
10 Rick Crawford 5.00 12.00
11 Justin Diercks P/S 6.00 15.00
12 Mike Duncan P/S 5.00 12.00
13 Dale Earnhardt Jr. 30.00 80.00
14 Carl Edwards BGN 15.00 40.00
15 Carl Edwards NC 15.00 40.00
16 Jeff Fultz P/S 5.00 12.00
17 Harry Gant P/S 6.00 15.00
18 Jeff Gordon P/S 40.00 100.00
19 David Green 5.00 12.00
20 Jeff Green P/S 5.00 12.00
21 Denny Hamlin 10.00 25.00
22 Kevin Harvick P/S 10.00 25.00
23 Tony Hirschman P/S 5.00 12.00
24 Dale Jarrett P/S 10.00 25.00
25 Jeff Jefferson P/S 5.00 12.00
26 Jimmie Johnson P/S 25.00 60.00
27 Kasey Kahne BGN S 10.00 25.00
28 Kasey Kahne NC P/S 10.00 25.00
29 Matt Kenseth BGN
30 Matt Kenseth NC P/S 10.00 25.00
31 Travis Kvapil 8.00 20.00
32 Bobby Labonte 10.00 25.00
33 Justin Labonte P/S 6.00 15.00
34 Terry Labonte 10.00 25.00
35 Bill Lester S 5.00 12.00
36 Fred Lorenzen P/S 8.00 20.00
37 Sterling Marlin 8.00 20.00
38 Mark Martin P/S 15.00 40.00
39 Jeremy Mayfield S 8.00 20.00
40 Jamie McMurray 8.00 20.00
41 Casey Mears 8.00 20.00
42 Joe Nemechek P/S 6.00 15.00
43 Ryan Newman P/S 6.00 15.00
44 Benny Parsons P/S 10.00 25.00
45 David Pearson P/S 8.00 20.00
46 Richard Petty P/S 20.00 50.00
47 Scott Riggs P/S 5.00 12.00
48 Ricky Rudd P/S 8.00 20.00
49 Boris Said S 6.00 15.00
50 Andy Santerre P/S 5.00 12.00
51 Dennis Setzer P/S 5.00 12.00
52 Reed Sorenson 8.00 20.00
53 Jack Sprague P/S 5.00 12.00
54 David Stremme 8.00 20.00
55 Tony Stewart P/S 25.00 60.00
56 Brian Vickers S 8.00 20.00
57 Kenny Wallace 8.00 20.00
58 Rusty Wallace 8.00 20.00
59 Michael Waltrip P/S 8.00 20.00
60 Rex White P/S 5.00 12.00
61 Scott Wimmer P/S 5.00 12.00
62 Glen Wood P/S 5.00 12.00
63 Jon Wood S 5.00 12.00
64 Cale Yarborough P/S 6.00 15.00
65 J.J. Yeley 6.00 15.00

2005 Press Pass Signings Gold

STATED PRINT RUN 50 SER.#'d SETS

1 Bobby Allison P/S 10.00 25.00
2 John Andretti S 10.00 25.00
3 Clint Bowyer 8.00 20.00
4 Kurt Busch P/S 12.00 30.00
5 Kyle Busch NC 15.00 40.00
6 Richard Childress P/S 10.00 25.00
7 Terry Cook P/S 10.00 25.00
8 Ricky Craven 12.00 30.00
9 Rick Crawford 10.00 25.00
10 Justin Diercks P/S 12.00 30.00

11 Mike Duncan P/S 10.00 25.00
12 Kerry Earnhardt 15.00 40.00
13 Carl Edwards BGN 30.00 80.00
14 Carl Edwards NC 30.00 80.00
15 Jeff Fultz P/S 10.00 25.00
16 Harry Gant P/S 12.00 30.00
17 Jeff Gordon P/S 75.00 150.00
18 David Green 10.00 25.00
19 Jeff Green P/S 10.00 25.00
20 Denny Hamlin 20.00 50.00
21 Kevin Harvick P/S 20.00 50.00
22 Tony Hirschman P/S 10.00 25.00
23 Dale Jarrett P/S 20.00 50.00
24 Jeff Jefferson P/S 10.00 25.00
25 Jimmie Johnson P/S 40.00 100.00
26 Kasey Kahne BGN S 15.00 40.00
27 Kasey Kahne NC P/S 15.00 40.00
28 Matt Kenseth P/S 25.00 60.00
29 Travis Kvapil 12.00 30.00
30 Bobby Labonte 20.00 50.00
31 Justin Labonte P/S 12.00 30.00
32 Terry Labonte 15.00 40.00
33 Bill Lester S 12.00 30.00
34 Fred Lorenzen P/S 12.00 30.00
35 Sterling Marlin 25.00 50.00
36 Mark Martin P/S 25.00 50.00
37 Jeremy Mayfield S 15.00 40.00
38 Jamie McMurray 15.00 40.00
39 Casey Mears 15.00 40.00
40 Joe Nemechek P/S 12.00 30.00
41 Ryan Newman P/S 12.00 30.00
42 Benny Parsons P/S 20.00 50.00
43 David Pearson P/S 15.00 40.00
44 Richard Petty P/S 25.00 60.00
45 Scott Riggs P/S 10.00 25.00
46 Ricky Rudd P/S 15.00 40.00
47 Boris Said S 12.00 30.00
48 Andy Santerre P/S 10.00 25.00
49 Dennis Setzer P/S 10.00 25.00
50 Reed Sorenson 15.00 40.00
51 Jack Sprague P/S 10.00 25.00
52 Tony Stewart P/S 40.00 100.00
53 David Stremme 12.00 30.00
54 Martin Truex Jr. 15.00 40.00
55 Brian Vickers S 12.00 30.00
56 Kenny Wallace 12.00 30.00
57 Rusty Wallace 20.00 50.00
58 Michael Waltrip P/S 15.00 40.00
59 Rex White P/S 10.00 25.00
60 Scott Wimmer P/S 10.00 25.00
61 Glen Wood P/S 10.00 25.00
62 Jon Wood S 10.00 25.00
63 Cale Yarborough P/S 12.00 30.00
64 J.J. Yeley 12.00 30.00

2005 Press Pass Signings Platinum

PLATINUM STATED PRINT RUN 100
SOME CARDS WERE RELEASED w/o SERIAL #'s
1 Bobby Allison P/S 10.00 25.00
2 John Andretti S 8.00 20.00
3 Dave Blaney 10.00 25.00
4 Kurt Busch P/S 15.00 40.00
5 Kyle Busch 12.00 30.00
6 Richard Childress P/S 10.00 25.00
7 Terry Cook P/S 8.00 20.00
8 Rick Crawford 10.00 25.00
9 Justin Diercks P/S 10.00 25.00
10 Mike Duncan P/S 8.00 20.00
11 Dale Earnhardt Jr. 50.00 100.00
12 Kerry Earnhardt 10.00 25.00
13 Carl Edwards BGN 15.00 40.00
14 Carl Edwards NC 25.00 60.00
15 Jeff Fultz P/S 8.00 20.00
16 Harry Gant P/S 10.00 25.00
17 Jeff Gordon P/S 40.00 100.00
18 David Green 8.00 20.00
19 Jeff Green P/S 8.00 20.00
20 Denny Hamlin 20.00 50.00
21 Kevin Harvick P/S 15.00 40.00
22 Tony Hirschman P/S 8.00 20.00
23 Dale Jarrett P/S 12.00 30.00
24 Jeff Jefferson P/S 8.00 20.00
25 Jimmie Johnson P/S 40.00 80.00
26 Kasey Kahne BGN S 15.00 40.00
27 Kasey Kahne NC P/S 15.00 40.00
28 Matt Kenseth NC P/S 25.00 60.00
29 Bobby Labonte 12.00 30.00
30 Justin Labonte P/S 10.00 25.00
31 Terry Labonte 25.00 60.00
32 Bill Lester S 8.00 20.00
33 Fred Lorenzen P/S 12.00 30.00
34 Sterling Marlin 15.00 40.00
35 Mark Martin P/S 15.00 40.00
36 Jeremy Mayfield S 10.00 25.00
37 Jamie McMurray 12.00 30.00
38 Joe Nemechek P/S 8.00 20.00
39 Ryan Newman P/S 8.00 20.00
40 Benny Parsons P/S 25.00 60.00
41 David Pearson P/S 12.00 30.00
42 Richard Petty P/S 20.00 50.00
43 Scott Riggs P/S 8.00 20.00
44 Ricky Rudd P/S 12.00 30.00
45 Boris Said S 8.00 20.00
46 Andy Santerre P/S 8.00 20.00
47 Dennis Setzer P/S 8.00 20.00
48 Reed Sorenson 8.00 20.00
49 Jack Sprague P/S 8.00 20.00
50 Tony Stewart P/S 30.00 60.00
51 David Stremme 10.00 25.00
52 Brian Vickers S 8.00 20.00
53 Michael Waltrip P/S 12.00 30.00
54 Rex White P/S 8.00 20.00
55 Scott Wimmer P/S 8.00 20.00
56 Glen Wood P/S 8.00 20.00
57 Jon Wood S 8.00 20.00
58 Cale Yarborough P/S 10.00 25.00

2006 Press Pass Signings

*RED INK: .6X TO 1.5X BASIC AUTO
STATED ODDS 1:20 PREMIUM HOBBY
STATED ODDS 1:20 STEALTH HOBBY
STATED ODDS 1:96 STEALTH RETAIL
1 Bobby Allison P/S 8.00 20.00
2 Donnie Allison S 5.00 12.00
3 Buddy Baker P/S 5.00 12.00
4 Greg Biffle NC S 8.00 20.00
5 Dave Blaney NC S 6.00 15.00
6 Clint Bowyer NC S 10.00 25.00
7 Jeff Burton NC S 8.00 20.00
8 Kurt Busch NC S 12.50 30.00
9 Kyle Busch NC S 20.00 50.00
10 Terry Cook CTS P/S 6.00 15.00
11 Rick Crawford CTS S 5.00 12.00
12 Erin Crocker CTS P/S 10.00 25.00
13 Erik Darnell CTS S 8.00 20.00
14 Dale Earnhardt Jr. NC S 30.00 80.00
15 Carl Edwards 12.00 30.00
16 Harry Gant P/S 5.00 12.00
17 Jeff Gordon NC P/S 100.00 175.00
18 Robby Gordon NC S 8.00 20.00
19 David Green NBS P/S 5.00 12.00
20 Jeff Green 5.00 12.00
21 Denny Hamlin V 15.00 40.00
22 Kevin Harvick NC P/S 12.50 30.00
23 Ron Hornaday CTS P/S 5.00 12.00
24 Jack Ingram P/S 6.00 15.00
25 Dale Jarrett NC P/S 15.00 40.00
26 Jimmie Johnson NC P/S 25.00 60.00
27 Kasey Kahne NC P/S 12.00 30.00
28 Matt Kenseth NC P/S 15.00 40.00
29 Todd Kluever NBS S 8.00 20.00
30 Bobby Labonte NC S 15.00 40.00
31 Terry Labonte NC S 15.00 40.00
32 Bill Lester CTS S 8.00 20.00
33 Fred Lorenzen P/S 6.00 15.00
34 Sterling Marlin NC S 15.00 30.00
35 Mark Martin NC S 25.00 50.00
36 Jeremy Mayfield NC S 8.00 20.00
37 Mark McFarland NBS S 8.00 20.00
38 Jamie McMurray 10.00 25.00
39 Casey Mears NC P/S 10.00 25.00
40 Paul Menard 12.50 30.00
41 Joe Nemechek NC P/S 6.00 15.00
42 Ryan Newman NC S 6.00 15.00
43 Danny O'Quinn CTS S 12.00 30.00
44 Marvin Panch P/S 5.00 12.00
45 Benny Parsons P/S 15.00 40.00
46 David Pearson S 10.00 25.00
47 Richard Petty P/S 15.00 40.00
48 Tony Raines NC P/S 5.00 12.00
49 Scott Riggs NC P/S 6.00 15.00
50 Elliott Sadler NC S 12.00 30.00
51 Johnny Sauter V 8.00 20.00
52 Ken Schrader NC S 8.00 20.00
53 Brent Sherman NC S 8.00 20.00
54 Mike Skinner CTS P/S 5.00 12.00
55 Regan Smith NBS S 6.00 15.00
56 Reed Sorenson V 10.00 25.00
57 David Stremme NC P/S 10.00 25.00
58 Tony Stewart NC P/S 25.00 60.00
59 Martin Truex Jr. NC P/S 10.00 25.00
60 Brian Vickers NC S 8.00 20.00
61 Rex White P/S 5.00 12.00
62 Glen Wood P/S 6.00 15.00
63 Jon Wood NBS P/S 6.00 15.00
64 Cale Yarborough P/S 10.00 25.00
65 J.J. Yeley 10.00 25.00
NNO Entry Card 1.50 4.00

2006 Press Pass Signings Gold

STATED PRINT RUN 50 SER.#'d SETS
1 Bobby Allison P/S 15.00 40.00
2 Donnie Allison S 10.00 25.00
3 Buddy Baker P/S 10.00 25.00
4 Greg Biffle NC S 20.00 50.00
5 Dave Blaney NC S 12.00 30.00
6 Clint Bowyer NC S 20.00 50.00
7 Jeff Burton NC S 20.00 50.00
8 Kurt Busch NC S 40.00 80.00
9 Kyle Busch NC S 60.00 120.00
10 Terry Cook CTS P/S 12.00 30.00
11 Rick Crawford CTS S 10.00 25.00
12 Erin Crocker CTS P/S
13 Erik Darnell CTS S 15.00 40.00
14 Dale Earnhardt Jr. NC S 40.00 100.00
16 Harry Gant P/S 12.00 30.00
17 Jeff Gordon NC P/S 50.00 120.00
18 Robby Gordon NC S 20.00 50.00
19 David Green NBS P/S 10.00 25.00
20 Jeff Green 10.00 25.00
21 Denny Hamlin V 30.00 80.00
22 Kevin Harvick NC P/S 40.00 80.00
23 Ron Hornaday CTS P/S 10.00 25.00
24 Jack Ingram P/S 15.00 40.00
25 Dale Jarrett NC P/S 30.00 80.00
26 Jimmie Johnson NC P/S 40.00 100.00
27 Kasey Kahne NC P/S 30.00 80.00
28 Matt Kenseth NC P/S 20.00 50.00
29 Todd Kluever NBS S 20.00 50.00
30 Bobby Labonte NC S 30.00 80.00
31 Terry Labonte NC S 20.00 50.00
32 Bill Lester CTS S 20.00 50.00
33 Fred Lorenzen P/S 12.00 30.00
34 Sterling Marlin NC S 20.00 50.00
35 Mark Martin NC S 60.00 120.00
36 Jeremy Mayfield NC S 15.00 40.00
37 Mark McFarland NBS S 15.00 40.00
39 Casey Mears NC P/S 20.00 50.00
40 Paul Menard 25.00 60.00
41 Joe Nemechek NC P/S 12.00 30.00
42 Ryan Newman NC S 12.00 30.00
43 Danny O'Quinn CTS S 15.00 40.00
44 Marvin Panch P/S 10.00 25.00
45 Benny Parsons P/S 25.00 60.00
46 David Pearson S 20.00 50.00
47 Richard Petty P/S 30.00 80.00
48 Tony Raines NC P/S 10.00 25.00
49 Scott Riggs NC P/S 8.00 20.00
50 Elliott Sadler NC S 40.00 100.00
51 Johnny Sauter V 15.00 40.00
52 Ken Schrader NC S 15.00 40.00
53 Brent Sherman NC S 12.00 30.00
54 Mike Skinner CTS P/S 12.00 30.00
55 Regan Smith NBS S 12.00 30.00
56 Reed Sorenson V 25.00 60.00
57 David Stremme NC P/S 30.00 80.00
58 Tony Stewart NC P/S 60.00 120.00
59 Martin Truex Jr. NC P/S 20.00 50.00
60 Brian Vickers NC S 15.00 40.00
61 Rex White P/S 12.00 30.00
62 Glen Wood P/S 12.00 30.00
63 Jon Wood NBS P/S 12.00 30.00
64 Cale Yarborough P/S 20.00 50.00

2006 Press Pass Signings Silver

STATED PRINT RUN 100 SER.#'d SETS
1 Bobby Allison P/S 12.50 30.00
2 Donnie Allison S 12.00 30.00
3 Buddy Baker P/S 10.00 25.00
4 Greg Biffle NC S 12.00 30.00
6 Clint Bowyer NC S 15.00 40.00
7 Jeff Burton NC S 15.00 40.00
8 Kurt Busch NC S 30.00 60.00
9 Kyle Busch NC S 25.00 50.00
10 Terry Cook CTS P/S 8.00 20.00
11 Rick Crawford CTS S 6.00 15.00
12 Erin Crocker CTS P/S 12.00 30.00
13 Erik Darnell CTS S 10.00 25.00
14 Dale Earnhardt Jr. NC S 50.00 120.00
15 Carl Edwards 25.00 60.00
16 Harry Gant P/S 6.00 15.00
17 Jeff Gordon/50 P/S 75.00 150.00
18 Robby Gordon NC S 12.50 30.00
19 David Green NBS P/S 6.00 15.00
20 Jeff Green V 15.00 40.00
21 Denny Hamlin V 12.00 30.00
22 Kevin Harvick NC P/S 25.00 60.00
23 Ron Hornaday CTS P/S 6.00 15.00
24 Jack Ingram P/S 8.00 20.00
25 Dale Jarrett NC P/S 20.00 50.00
26 Jimmie Johnson NC P/S 30.00 80.00
27 Kasey Kahne NC P/S 20.00 50.00
28 Matt Kenseth NC P/S 25.00 60.00
29 Todd Kluever NBS S 15.00 40.00
31 Terry Labonte NC S 20.00 50.00
32 Bill Lester CTS S 12.00 30.00
33 Fred Lorenzen P/S 10.00 25.00
34 Sterling Marlin NC S 20.00 40.00
35 Mark Martin NC S 40.00 80.00
36 Jeremy Mayfield NC S 10.00 25.00
37 Mark McFarland NBS S 10.00 25.00
38 Jamie McMurray 15.00 40.00
39 Casey Mears NC P/S 12.50 30.00
41 Joe Nemechek NC P/S 8.00 20.00
42 Ryan Newman NC S 8.00 20.00
43 Danny O'Quinn CTS S 12.00 30.00
44 Marvin Panch P/S 6.00 15.00
45 Benny Parsons P/S 30.00 60.00
46 David Pearson S 12.50 30.00
47 Richard Petty P/S 20.00 50.00
48 Tony Raines NC P/S 6.00 15.00
49 Scott Riggs NC P/S 8.00 20.00
50 Elliott Sadler NC S 15.00 40.00
52 Ken Schrader NC S 10.00 25.00
53 Brent Sherman NC S 12.00 30.00
54 Mike Skinner CTS P/S 6.00 15.00
55 Regan Smith NBS S 8.00 20.00
56 Reed Sorenson V 15.00 40.00
57 David Stremme NC P/S 12.00 30.00
58 Tony Stewart NC P/S 40.00 80.00
59 Martin Truex Jr. NC P/S 15.00 40.00
60 Brian Vickers NC S 15.00 40.00
61 Rex White P/S 6.00 15.00
62 Glen Wood P/S 8.00 20.00
63 Jon Wood NBS P/S 8.00 20.00
64 Cale Yarborough P/S 12.50 30.00

2007 Press Pass Signings

This 39-card set was available in packs of 2007 Press Pass Premium, Press Pass Stealth, 2007 Traks and 2007 VIP products. The cards were certified by the manufacturer. There were three parallel sets, some of which were just partial parallels. In Premium the cards were inserted at a rate of one in 20 hobby packs. The Juan Pablo Montoya without sunglasses was only released in the Collector's Series Box Set.

STATED ODDS 1:20 PREMIUM H
STATED ODDS 1:96 PREMIUM R
STATED ODDS 1:20 STEALTH CHROME
STATED ODDS 1:96 STEALTH R
STATED ODDS 1:84 TRAKS H
STATED ODDS 1:96 TRAKS R
UNPRICED PRESS PLATE PRINT RUN 1
GL Gary Lewis 6.00 15.00
1 Bobby Allison P/S 8.00 20.00
2 Donnie Allison P/S 8.00 20.00
3 A.J. Allmendinger NC S/T 8.00 20.00
4 Aric Almirola NBS T 8.00 20.00
5 Marcos Ambrose NBS S/T 12.00 30.00
6 Buddy Baker P/S 6.00 15.00
7 Greg Biffle NC T 8.00 20.00
8 Dave Blaney NC 5.00 12.00
9 Todd Bodine CTS S/T 6.00 15.00
10 Clint Bowyer NC P/S/T 12.50 30.00
11 Jeff Burton NC P/S/T 8.00 20.00
12 Kurt Busch NC S/T 10.00 25.00
13 Kyle Busch NC P/S/T 20.00 50.00
14 Rick Crawford CTS P/S/T 5.00 12.00
15 Erik Darnell CTS P/S/T 6.00 15.00
16 Kertus Davis NBS S/T 5.00 12.00
17 Dale Jr. NC P/S/T 30.00 80.00
18 Carl Edwards NC S/T 12.50 30.00
19 Cale Gale NBS S/T 6.00 15.00
20 Harry Gant P/S 6.00 15.00
21 David Gilliland NC P/S/T 6.00 15.00
22 Jeff Gordon NC P/S/T 50.00 100.00
23 Jeff Green NC P/S/T 5.00 12.00
24 Janet Guthrie P/S 8.00 20.00
25 Denny Hamlin NC S/T 30.00 60.00
26 Kevin Harvick NC P/S/T 12.50 30.00
27 Eric Holmes T
28 Ron Hornaday CTS P/S/T 5.00 12.00
29 Sam Hornish Jr. NBS T 12.50 25.00
30 Jack Ingram P/S 5.00 12.00
31 Dale Jarrett NC S/T 12.50 30.00
32 Jimmie Johnson NC P/S/T 25.00 60.00
33 Kasey Kahne NC P/S/T 12.00 30.00
34 Matt Kenseth NC P/S/T 15.00 40.00
35 Kraig Kinser CTS S/T 8.00 20.00
36 Todd Kluever NBS S/T 10.00 25.00
37 Travis Kvapil CTS S/T 5.00 12.00
38 Bobby Labonte NC P/S/T 12.50 30.00
39 Stephen Leicht 8.00 20.00
40 Greg Lewis T 6.00 15.00
41 Fred Lorenzen P/S 6.00 15.00
42 Sterling Marlin NC P/S/T 10.00 25.00
43 Mark Martin NC P/S/T 25.00 60.00
44 Jamie McMurray NC S/T 8.00 20.00
45 Casey Mears NC T 8.00 20.00
46 Paul Menard NC P/S/T 5.00 12.00
47 Junior Miller T 10.00 25.00
48 Juan Montoya NC P/S/T 40.00 80.00
49 J.P. Montoya w/o glasses NC 50.00 100.00
50 Joe Nemechek NC S/T 5.00 12.00
51 Ryan Newman NC S/T 6.00 15.00
52 J.R. Norris T
53 Mike Olsen T 6.00 15.00
54 Marvin Panch P/S 6.00 15.00
55 David Pearson P/S 8.00 20.00
56 Timothy Peters NBS S/T 6.00 15.00
57 Richard Petty P/S 20.00 50.00
58 David Ragan NC S/T 10.00 25.00
59 Tony Raines NC 6.00 15.00
60 David Reutimann NC S/T 6.00 15.00
61 Scott Riggs NC P/S/T 6.00 15.00
62 Elliott Sadler NC P/S/T 10.00 25.00
63 Johnny Sauter NC S/T 6.00 15.00
64 Tim Schendel T 6.00 15.00
65 Ken Schrader NC S/T 6.00 15.00
66 Regan Smith NC S/T 6.00 15.00
67 Reed Sorenson NC T 10.00 25.00
68 Mike Stefanik T 10.00 25.00
69 Tony Stewart NC P/S/T 25.00 60.00
70 David Stremme NC T 10.00 25.00
71 Martin Truex Jr. NC P/S/T 15.00 40.00
72 Brian Vickers NC S/T 8.00 20.00
73 Rusty Wallace P/S 12.50 30.00
74 Steve Wallace 8.00 20.00
75 Michael Waltrip NC S/T 10.00 25.00
76 Rex White P/S 6.00 15.00
77 Scott Wimmer NBS S/T 6.00 15.00
78 Glen Wood P/S 5.00 12.00
79 Jon Wood NBS S/T 5.00 12.00
80 Jon Wood NC S/T 6.00 15.00
81 Cale Yarborough P/S 8.00 20.00
82 J.J. Yeley NC P/S/T 10.00 25.00

2007 Press Pass Signings Blue

STATED PRINT RUN 25 SER.#'d SETS
1 A.J. Allmendinger NC 20.00 50.00
2 Clint Bowyer NC 25.00 60.00
3 Jeff Burton NC 25.00 60.00
4 Kurt Busch NC 20.00 50.00
5 Kyle Busch NC 20.00 50.00
6 Dale Earnhardt Jr. NC 40.00 100.00
7 David Gilliland NC 20.00 50.00
8 Jeff Gordon NC 60.00 120.00
9 Jeff Green NC
10 Denny Hamlin NC 20.00 50.00
11 Kevin Harvick NC 20.00 50.00
12 Dale Jarrett NC
13 Jimmie Johnson NC 30.00 80.00
14 Kasey Kahne NC 12.00 30.00
15 Matt Kenseth NC 20.00 50.00
16 Bobby Labonte NC 15.00 40.00
17 Sterling Marlin NC 15.00 40.00
18 Mark Martin NC 30.00 80.00
19 Jamie McMurray NC
20 Paul Menard NC 15.00 40.00
21 Juan Pablo Montoya NC 60.00 120.00
22 Joe Nemechek NC
23 Ryan Newman NC 15.00 40.00
24 David Ragan NC 30.00 80.00
25 David Reutimann NC 12.00 30.00
26 Scott Riggs NC 20.00 50.00
27 Elliott Sadler NC 15.00 40.00
28 Johnny Sauter NC
29 Ken Schrader NC 15.00 40.00
30 Regan Smith NC 15.00 40.00
31 Tony Stewart NC 75.00 150.00
32 Martin Truex Jr. NC 40.00 80.00
33 Brian Vickers NC
34 Michael Waltrip NC
35 J.J. Yeley NC

2007 Press Pass Signings Blue Daytona

STATED PRINT RUN 150 SER.#'d SETS
1 Bobby Allison P 10.00 25.00
2 Buddy Baker P 8.00 20.00
3 Fred Lorenzen 8.00 20.00
4 Marvin Panch 8.00 20.00
5 David Pearson 10.00 25.00
6 Richard Petty 25.00 60.00
7 Cale Yarborough 10.00 25.00

2007 Press Pass Signings Gold

STATED PRINT RUN 20-50
1 A.J. Allmendinger NC S/T 8.00 20.00
2 Aric Almirola NBS T 15.00 40.00
3 Marcos Ambrose NBS S/T 50.00 100.00
4 Greg Biffle NC T 15.00 40.00
5 Dave Blaney NC 12.50 30.00
6 Todd Bodine CTS S/T 12.50 30.00
7 Clint Bowyer NC P/S/T 25.00 60.00
8 Jeff Burton NC P/S/T 20.00 50.00
9 Kurt Busch NC S/T 30.00 60.00
10 Kyle Busch NC P/S/T 30.00 80.00
11 Rick Crawford CTS P/S/T 12.50 30.00
12 Erik Darnell CTS P/S/T 15.00 40.00
13 Kertus Davis NBS S/T 10.00 25.00
14 Dale Jr. NC P/S/T 50.00 100.00
15 Carl Edwards NC S/T 20.00 50.00
16 Cale Gale NBS S/T 8.00 20.00
17 David Gilliland NC P/S/T 25.00 60.00
18 Jeff Gordon NC P/S/T 60.00 120.00
19 Jeff Green NC P/S/T 12.50 30.00
20 Denny Hamlin NC P/S/T 50.00 100.00
21 Kevin Harvick NC P/S/T 30.00 80.00
22 Ron Hornaday CTS P/S/T 12.50 30.00
23 Sam Hornish Jr. NBS T 20.00 50.00
24 Dale Jarrett NC S/T 20.00 50.00
25 Jimmie Johnson NC P/S/T 30.00 80.00
26 Kasey Kahne/20 NC/P/S/T 60.00 120.00
27 Matt Kenseth NC P/S/T 20.00 50.00
28 Kraig Kinser CTS S/T 30.00 60.00
29 Todd Kluever NBS S/T 15.00 40.00
30 Travis Kvapil CTS S/T 20.00 50.00
31 Bobby Labonte NC P/S/T 30.00 80.00
32 Stephen Leicht 15.00 30.00
33 Sterling Marlin NC P/S/T 20.00 50.00
34 Mark Martin NC P/S/T 50.00 100.00
35 Jamie McMurray NC S/T 30.00 60.00
36 Casey Mears NC T 12.00 30.00
37 Paul Menard NC P/S/T 10.00 25.00
38 Juan Montoya NC P/S/T 25.00 60.00
39 J.P. Montoya NC without glasses 60.00 120.00
40 Joe Nemechek NC S/T 12.50 30.00
41 Ryan Newman NC S/T 20.00 50.00
42 Timothy Peters NBS S/T 12.50 30.00
43 Tony Raines 15.00 30.00
44 David Ragan NC S/T 20.00 50.00
45 David Reutimann NC S/T 10.00 25.00
46 Scott Riggs NC P/S/T 12.50 30.00
47 Elliott Sadler NC S/T 20.00 50.00
48 Johnny Sauter NC S/T 20.00 50.00
49 Ken Schrader NC S/T 12.50 30.00
50 Regan Smith NC S/T 20.00 50.00
51 Reed Sorenson NC T
52 Tony Stewart NC P/S/T 60.00 120.00
53 David Stremme NC T 30.00 60.00
54 Martin Truex NC P/S/T 30.00 60.00
55 Brian Vickers NC S/T 20.00 50.00
56 Michael Waltrip NC S/T 30.00 60.00
57 Scott Wimmer NBS S/T 15.00 40.00
58 Jon Wood NC S/T 15.00 40.00
59 J.J. Yeley NC P/S/T 20.00 50.00

2007 Press Pass Signings Silver

STATED PRINT RUN 100 SER.#'d SETS
1 Aric Almirola NBS T 12.00 30.00
2 Marcos Ambrose NBS S/T 30.00 60.00
3 Greg Biffle NC T 12.00 30.00
4 Dave Blaney NC P/S/T 8.00 20.00
5 Todd Bodine CTS S/T 10.00 25.00
6 Clint Bowyer NC P/S/T 10.00 25.00
7 Jeff Burton NC P/S/T 15.00 40.00
8 Kurt Busch NC S/T 20.00 50.00
9 Kyle Busch NC P/S/T 25.00 60.00
10 Rick Crawford CTS P/S/T 8.00 20.00
11 Erik Darnell CTS P/S/T 10.00 25.00
12 Kertus Davis NBS S/T 10.00 25.00
13 Dale Earnhardt Jr. NC P/S/T 30.00 80.00
14 Carl Edwards NC S/T
15 Cale Gale NBS S/T 8.00 20.00
16 David Gilliland NC P/S/T 15.00 40.00
17 Jeff Gordon NC P/S/T 60.00 120.00
18 Jeff Green NC P/S/T 8.00 20.00
19 Denny Hamlin NC S/T 25.00 60.00
20 Kevin Harvick NC P/S/T 20.00 50.00
21 Ron Hornaday CTS P/S/T 8.00 20.00
22 Sam Hornish Jr. NBS T 15.00 40.00
23 Dale Jarrett NC S/T 15.00 40.00
24 Jimmie Johnson NC P/T 40.00 80.00
25 Kasey Kahne NC/45 P/S/T 15.00 40.00
26 Matt Kenseth NC P/S/T 20.00 50.00
27 Kraig Kinser CTS S/T 15.00 40.00
28 Todd Kluever NBS S/T 15.00 40.00
29 Travis Kvapil CTS S/T
30 Bobby Labonte NC P/S/T 25.00 60.00
31 Stephen Leicht 10.00 25.00
32 Sterling Marlin NC P/S/T 12.00 30.00
33 Mark Martin NC P/S/T 40.00 80.00
34 Jamie McMurray NC S/T 20.00 50.00
35 Casey Mears NC T 10.00 25.00
36 Paul Menard NC P/S/T 12.00 30.00
37 Juan Montoya NC P/S/T 40.00 80.00
38 J.P. Montoya no glasses NC 60.00 120.00
39 Joe Nemechek NC S/T 8.00 20.00
40 Ryan Newman NC S/T 15.00 40.00
41 Timothy Peters NBS S/T 8.00 20.00
42 David Ragan NC S/T 8.00 20.00
43 Tony Raines NC 8.00 20.00
44 David Reutimann NC S/T 8.00 20.00
45 Scott Riggs NC P/S/T 10.00 25.00
46 Elliott Sadler NC S/T 15.00 40.00
47 Johnny Sauter NC S/T 15.00 40.00
48 Ken Schrader NC S/T 8.00 20.00
49 Regan Smith NC S/T 8.00 20.00
50 Reed Sorenson NC T 15.00 40.00
51 Tony Stewart NC P/S/T 40.00 80.00
52 David Stremme NC T 12.00 30.00
53 Martin Truex Jr. NC P/S/T 15.00 40.00
54 Michael Waltrip NC S/T 15.00 40.00
55 Scott Wimmer NBS S/T 10.00 25.00
56 Jon Wood NC S/T 10.00 25.00
57 J.J. Yeley NC P/S/T 12.00 30.00

2008 Press Pass Signings

STATED ODDS PREMIUM 1:20
STATED ODDS STEATH CHROME 1:20
STATED ODDS SPEEDWAY 1:84
UNPRICED PRESS PLATE PRINT RUN 1
1 Bobby Allison 4.00 10.00
2 Donnie Allison 4.00 10.00
3 A.J. Allmendinger 5.00 12.00
4 Aric Almirola 4.00 10.00
5 Marcos Ambrose 8.00 20.00
6 Buddy Baker 4.00 10.00
7 Dave Blaney 3.00 8.00
8 Clint Bowyer 5.00 12.00
9 Colin Braun 4.00 10.00
10 Kurt Busch 4.00 10.00
11 Kyle Busch 15.00 40.00
12 Patrick Carpentier 8.00 20.00
13 Landon Cassill 4.00 10.00
14 Bryan Clauson 5.00 12.00
15 Rick Crawford 3.00 8.00
16 Erik Darnell 4.00 10.00
17 Dale Jr. AMP 40.00 100.00
18 Dale Jr. NG 40.00 100.00
19 Carl Edwards 12.00 30.00
20 Cale Gale 3.00 8.00
21 Harry Gant 4.00 10.00
22 David Gilliland 3.00 8.00
23 Jeff Gordon 60.00 120.00
24 Janet Guthrie 5.00 12.00
25 Denny Hamlin 6.00 15.00
26 Kevin Harvick 6.00 15.00
27 Ron Hornaday 3.00 8.00
28 Sam Hornish Jr. 8.00 20.00
29 Jack Ingram 3.00 8.00
30 Dale Jarrett 5.00 12.00
31 Jimmie Johnson 8.00 20.00
32 Kasey Kahne 5.00 12.00
33 Matt Kenseth 5.00 12.00
34 Brad Keselowski 10.00 25.00
35 Travis Kvapil 3.00 8.00
36 Bobby Labonte 5.00 12.00
37 Joey Logano 12.00 30.00
38 Fred Lorenzen 4.00 10.00
39 Mark Martin 5.00 12.00
40 Michael McDowell 10.00 25.00
41 Jamie McMurray 5.00 12.00
42 Casey Mears 3.00 8.00
43 Paul Menard 4.00 10.00
44 Juan Pablo Montoya 10.00 25.00
45 Joe Nemechek 4.00 10.00
46 Ryan Newman 4.00 10.00
47 Marvin Panch 4.00 10.00
48 David Pearson 6.00 15.00
49 Richard Petty 20.00 50.00
50 David Ragan 4.00 10.00
51 David Reutimann 4.00 10.00
52 Elliott Sadler 3.00 8.00
53 Mike Skinner 3.00 8.00
54 Regan Smith 4.00 10.00
55 Reed Sorenson 3.00 8.00
56 Jack Sprague 3.00 8.00
57 Tony Stewart 25.00 60.00
58 Martin Truex Jr. 4.00 10.00
59 Brian Vickers 3.00 8.00
60 Michael Waltrip 5.00 12.00
61 Rex White 4.00 10.00
62 Scott Wimmer 5.00 12.00
63 Glen Wood 4.00 10.00
64 Cale Yarborough 5.00 12.00
65 J.J. Yeley 5.00 12.00

2008 Press Pass Signings Blue

STATED PRINT RUN 8-100
1 Bobby Allison/100 8.00 20.00
2 A.J. Allmendinger/25 20.00 50.00
3 Dave Blaney/25 12.00 30.00
4 Clint Bowyer/25 20.00 50.00
5 Kurt Busch/25 15.00 40.00
6 Kyle Busch/25 75.00 150.00
7 Dale Earnhardt Jr./8
8 Jeff Gordon/25 175.00 300.00
9 Denny Hamlin/25 40.00 100.00
10 Kevin Harvick/25 30.00 80.00
11 Sam Hornish Jr./25 25.00 60.00
12 Dale Jarrett/25 30.00 80.00
13 Jimmie Johnson/25 60.00 120.00
14 Kasey Kahne/25 30.00 80.00
15 Matt Kenseth/25 40.00 100.00
16 Bobby Labonte/25 30.00 80.00
17 Mark Martin/25 30.00 80.00
18 Michael McDowell/25 20.00 50.00
19 Jamie McMurray/25 20.00 50.00
20 Paul Menard/25 8.00 20.00

21 Joe Nemechek/25 12.00 30.00
22 Ryan Newman/25 15.00 40.00
23 David Pearson/100 10.00 25.00
24 Richard Petty/100 30.00 80.00
25 David Ragan/25 15.00 40.00
26 David Reutimann/25 15.00 40.00
27 Elliott Sadler/25 12.00 30.00
28 Regan Smith/25 15.00 40.00
29 Reed Sorenson/25 12.00 30.00
30 Tony Stewart/25 75.00 150.00
31 Brian Vickers/25 12.00 30.00
32 Michael Waltrip/25 12.00 30.00
33 Rex White/100 6.00 15.00
34 Cale Yarborough/100 8.00 20.00
35 J.J. Yeley/25 20.00 50.00

2008 Press Pass Signings Gold

STATED PRINT RUN 50 SER.#'d SETS
1 A.J. Allmendinger 12.00 30.00
2 Aric Almirola 10.00 25.00
3 Marcos Ambrose 20.00 50.00
4 Greg Biffle 40.00 80.00
5 Kelly Bires 12.00 30.00
6 Dave Blaney 8.00 20.00
7 Clint Bowyer 30.00 60.00
8 Kurt Busch 10.00 25.00
9 Kyle Busch 40.00 100.00
10 Patrick Carpentier 15.00 40.00
11 Landon Cassill 25.00 60.00
12 Bryan Clauson 12.00 30.00
13 Rick Crawford 8.00 20.00
14 Erik Darnell 10.00 25.00
15 Dale Earnhardt Jr. AMP/25 125.00 250.00
16 Dale Earnhardt Jr. NG/25 125.00 250.00
17 Carl Edwards 40.00 80.00
18 Dario Franchitti 20.00 50.00
19 Cale Gale 8.00 20.00
20 David Gilliland 8.00 20.00
21 Jeff Gordon 100.00 200.00
22 Denny Hamlin 12.00 30.00
23 Kevin Harvick 15.00 40.00
24 Ron Hornaday 8.00 20.00
25 Sam Hornish Jr. 10.00 25.00
26 Dale Jarrett 50.00 100.00
27 Jimmie Johnson 30.00 80.00
28 Kasey Kahne 30.00 80.00
29 Matt Kenseth 40.00 80.00
30 Brad Keselowski 25.00 60.00
31 Travis Kvapil 8.00 20.00
32 Bobby Labonte 12.00 30.00
33 Joey Logano 30.00 80.00
34 Mark Martin 40.00 80.00
35 Michael McDowell 20.00 50.00
36 Jamie McMurray 12.00 30.00
37 Casey Mears 8.00 20.00
38 Paul Menard 8.00 20.00
39 Chase Miller 15.00 40.00
40 Juan Pablo Montoya 30.00 60.00
41 Joe Nemechek 8.00 20.00
42 Ryan Newman 8.00 20.00
43 David Ragan 10.00 25.00
44 David Reutimann 10.00 25.00
45 Scott Riggs 10.00 25.00
46 Elliott Sadler 8.00 20.00
47 Mike Skinner 8.00 20.00
48 Regan Smith 10.00 25.00
49 Reed Sorenson 8.00 20.00
50 Tony Stewart 50.00 100.00
51 Martin Truex Jr. 10.00 25.00
52 Brian Vickers 8.00 20.00
53 Michael Waltrip 12.00 30.00
54 Scott Wimmer 10.00 25.00
55 J.J. Yeley 12.00 30.00

2008 Press Pass Signings Silver

*SILVER/100: .5X TO 1.2X BASIC AU
STATED PRINT RUN 100 SER.#'d SETS
4 Greg Biffle 20.00 50.00
5 Kelly Bires 6.00 15.00
16 Dale Earnhardt Jr. AMP/50 60.00 120.00
17 Dale Earnhardt Jr. NG/50 40.00 100.00
18 Carl Edwards 8.00 20.00
19 Dario Franchitti 8.00 20.00
22 Denny Hamlin 30.00 60.00
38 Chase Miller 10.00 25.00

2009 Press Pass Signings Gold

STATED ODDS 1:20 STEALTH CHROME
UNPRICED GREEN PRINT RUN 10-15
UNPRICED PRINT PLATE PRINT RUN 1
1 Justin Allgaier 6.00 15.00
2 A.J. Allmendinger 5.00 12.00
3 Aric Almirola 5.00 12.00
4 Marcos Ambrose 6.00 15.00
5 Greg Biffle 5.00 12.00
6 Clint Bowyer 6.00 15.00
7 Colin Braun 5.00 12.00
8 Kyle Busch 8.00 20.00
9 Erik Darnell 4.00 10.00
10 Marc Davis 10.00 25.00
11 Dale Earnhardt Jr.
12 Brendan Gaughan 4.00 10.00
13 Jeff Gordon 75.00 150.00
14 Robby Gordon 4.00 10.00
15 Denny Hamlin 6.00 15.00
16 Kevin Harvick
17 Ron Hornaday 4.00 10.00
18 Sam Hornish Jr. 5.00 12.00
19 Jimmie Johnson 20.00 50.00
20 Kasey Kahne 20.00 50.00
21 Matt Kenseth 6.00 15.00
22 Brad Keselowski SC 8.00 20.00
23 Brad Keselowski NNS 8.00 20.00
24 Scott Lagasse Jr. 8.00 20.00
25 Stephen Leicht 4.00 10.00
26 Joey Logano 20.00 50.00
27 Tayler Malsam 8.00 20.00
28 Mark Martin
29 Michael McDowell 6.00 15.00
31 Casey Mears
32 Paul Menard 4.00 10.00
33 Juan Pablo Montoya 8.00 20.00
34 Joe Nemechek 4.00 10.00
35 Ryan Newman 5.00 12.00
36 David Ragan 5.00 12.00
37 David Reutimann
38 Scott Riggs 5.00 12.00
39 Elliott Sadler 4.00 10.00
40 Brian Scott 5.00 12.00
41 Mike Skinner 4.00 10.00
42 Regan Smith 5.00 12.00
43 Reed Sorenson 4.00 10.00
44 Scott Speed 8.00 20.00
45 Tony Stewart 50.00 100.00
46 Martin Truex Jr. 5.00 12.00
47 Brian Vickers
48 Michael Waltrip 6.00 15.00
56 Ricky Carmichael
JB James Buescher
JRF J.R. Fitzpatrick

2009 Press Pass Signings Orange

*ORANGE/65: .5X TO 1.2X GOLD
*ORANGE/25: .8X TO 2X GOLD
ORANGE STATED PRINT RUN 25-65
11 Dale Earnhardt Jr. 60.00 120.00
13 Jeff Gordon/25 100.00 175.00
16 Kevin Harvick 75.00 150.00
19 Jimmie Johnson/25 50.00 120.00
20 Kasey Kahne/25 100.00 200.00
26 Joey Logano/25 40.00 100.00
28 Mark Martin/25 50.00 100.00
36 David Ragan 6.00 15.00
45 Tony Stewart/25 75.00 150.00

2009 Press Pass Signings Purple

*PURPLE/45: .6X TO 1.5X GOLD
PURPLE STATED PRINT RUN 15-45
11 Dale Earnhardt Jr./45 100.00 200.00
16 Kevin Harvick/45 100.00 175.00
19 Jimmie Johnson/45 25.00 60.00
20 Kasey Kahne/45
26 Joey Logano/45

2010 Press Pass Signings Gold

GOLD STATED PRINT RUN 10-50
1 Justin Allgaier/50 8.00 20.00
2 A.J. Allmendinger/25 10.00 25.00
3 Marcos Ambrose/45 20.00 50.00
4 Trevor Bayne/40 60.00 120.00
5 Greg Biffle/35 8.00 20.00
6 Kelly Bires/50
7 Clint Bowyer/50
8 Colin Braun/50
9 James Buescher/40 8.00 20.00
10 Jeff Burton/50
11 Kurt Busch/50
12 Kyle Busch/30 12.00 30.00
13 Ricky Carmichael/40 10.00 25.00
14 Kevin Conway/25 15.00 40.00
15 Matt DiBenedetto/40 15.00 40.00
16 Austin Dillon/50 30.00 60.00
17 Dale Earnhardt Jr./50
18 Carl Edwards/25 10.00 25.00
19 Brendan Gaughan/40 6.00 15.00
20 Jeff Gordon/15
21 Robby Gordon/50 6.00 15.00
22 Denny Hamlin/25 10.00 25.00
23 Kevin Harvick/15
24 Ron Hornaday/40 6.00 15.00
25 Sam Hornish Jr./50
26 Brian Ickler/40 15.00 40.00
27 Jimmie Johnson/50
28 Kasey Kahne/15
29 Matt Kenseth/25 30.00 80.00
30 Brad Keselowski/50
31 Travis Kvapil/50
32 Bobby Labonte/50
33 Scott Lagasse Jr./50 8.00 20.00
34 Justin Lofton/39 10.00 25.00
35 Joey Logano/25 10.00 25.00
36 Tayler Malsam/50
37 Mark Martin/15
38 Jamie McMurray/50 10.00 25.00
39 Paul Menard/50
40 Juan Pablo Montoya/40 10.00 25.00
41 Joe Nemechek/50
42 Ryan Newman/15
43 Danica Patrick/15
44 David Ragan/50 8.00 20.00
45 David Reutimann/25
46 Elliott Sadler/50
47 Johnny Sauter/40 6.00 15.00
48 Brian Scott/40 8.00 20.00
49 Mike Skinner/40 6.00 15.00
50 Regan Smith/50 8.00 20.00
51 Scott Speed/50 10.00 25.00
52 Ricky Stenhouse Jr./40 10.00 25.00
53 Tony Stewart/50
54 Martin Truex Jr./50 8.00 20.00
55 Brian Vickers/35 6.00 15.00
56 Steve Wallace/50 8.00 20.00
57 Michael Waltrip/10
58 Josh Wise/35 10.00 25.00

2010 Press Pass Signings Silver

SILVER PRINT RUN 20-99
UNPRICED BLUE PRINT RUN 10
UNPRICED RED PRINT RUN 5-15
1 Justin Allgaier/75 5.00 12.00
2 A.J. Allmendinger
3 Marcos Ambrose/75 10.00 25.00
4 Trevor Bayne/75 50.00 100.00
5 Greg Biffle/75 5.00 12.00
6 Kelly Bires
7 Clint Bowyer
8 Colin Braun 5.00 12.00
9 James Buescher
10 Jeff Burton/30 30.00 60.00
11 Kurt Busch/44 5.00 12.00
12 Kyle Busch/50 8.00 20.00
13 Ricky Carmichael/75 6.00 15.00
14 Kevin Conway/65 10.00 25.00
15 Matt DiBenedetto/74 10.00 25.00
16 Austin Dillon/75 15.00 40.00
17 Dale Earnhardt Jr
18 Carl Edwards/50 6.00 15.00
19 Brendan Gaughan
20 Jeff Gordon/25 75.00 150.00
21 Robby Gordon/81 4.00 10.00
22 Denny Hamlin/45 8.00 20.00
23 Kevin Harvick/30 30.00 60.00
24 Ron Hornaday/75 4.00 10.00
25 Sam Hornish Jr./75 5.00 12.00
26 Brian Ickler/75 10.00 25.00
27 Jimmie Johnson/20
28 Kasey Kahne/25 60.00 120.00
29 Matt Kenseth/50 15.00 40.00
30 Brad Keselowski/45 8.00 20.00
31 Travis Kvapil/65 4.00 10.00
32 Bobby Labonte/80 6.00 15.00
33 Scott Lagasse Jr. 4.00 10.00
34 Justin Lofton/75
35 Joey Logano 6.00 15.00
36 Tayler Malsam/75 4.00 10.00
37 Jamie McMurray/90 6.00 15.00
38 Paul Menard/90 4.00 10.00
39 Juan Pablo Montoya 6.00 15.00
40 Joe Nemechek
41 Ryan Newman/44 5.00 12.00
42 Danica Patrick/25 60.00 120.00
43 David Ragan/75 5.00 12.00
44 David Reutimann/50 5.00 12.00
45 Elliott Sadler/24 4.00 10.00
46 Johnny Sauter
47 Brian Scott
48 Mike Skinner 4.00 10.00
49 Regan Smith/80 5.00 12.00
50 Scott Speed/80 6.00 15.00
51 Ricky Stenhouse Jr.
52 Tony Stewart/20
53 Martin Truex Jr./90 5.00 12.00
54 Brian Vickers/75 4.00 10.00
55 Steve Wallace/75 5.00 12.00
56 Michael Waltrip 6.00 15.00
57 Josh Wise/70 6.00 15.00

2011 Press Pass Signings Brushed Metal

STATED PRINT RUN 15-70
*HOLO/20-26: .5X TO 1.2X BRUSHED METAL
UNPRICED B&W PRINT RUN 5-10
UNPRICED PRINT PLATE PRINT RUN 1
PPSAA1 A.J. Allmendinger/60 6.00 15.00
PPSAA2 Aric Almirola/50 5.00 12.00
PPSAD Austin Dillon/25 25.00 50.00
PPSBE Bill Elliott/25 10.00 25.00
PPSBG Brendan Gaughan/50 4.00 10.00
PPSBK Brad Keselowski/47 10.00 25.00
PPSBL Bobby Labonte/28
PPSBS1 Brian Scott/49 4.00 10.00
PPSBS2 Brad Sweet/50 8.00 20.00
PPSBV Brian Vickers/50 4.00 10.00
PPSCB Clint Bowyer/60 6.00 15.00
PPSCE Carl Edwards/70 6.00 15.00
PPSCG Craig Goess/50 8.00 20.00
PPSCM Casey Mears/59 4.00 10.00
PPSDD Dusty Davis/49 6.00 15.00
PPSDE Dale Earnhardt Jr./20 50.00 100.00
PPSDG David Gilliland/60 4.00 10.00
PPSDP Danica Patrick/15 EXCH
PPSDR1 David Ragan/60 5.00 12.00
PPSDR2 David Reutimann/60 5.00 12.00
PPSGB Greg Biffle/50 5.00 12.00
PPSJA Justin Allgaier/50 5.00 12.00
PPSJB2 James Buescher/50 4.00 10.00
PPSJC1 Jennifer Jo Cobb/50 15.00 40.00
PPSJC2 Joey Coulter/50 8.00 20.00
PPSJG Jeff Gordon/25 75.00 125.00
PPSJJ1 Jimmie Johnson/30 40.00 80.00
PPSJJ2 Justin Johnson/50 10.00 25.00
PPSJL1 Joey Logano/48 6.00 15.00
PPSJL2 Jason Leffler/50 5.00 12.00
PPSJL3 Justin Lofton/49 4.00 10.00
PPSJL4 Johanna Long/50 10.00 25.00
PPSJM Jamie McMurray/60 6.00 15.00
PPSJPM Juan Pablo Montoya/50 6.00 15.00
PPSJS Johnny Sauter/50 4.00 10.00
PPSJW Josh Wise/50 4.00 10.00
PPSJY J.J. Yeley/60 4.00 10.00
PPSKC Kevin Conway/55 5.00 12.00
PPSKH Kevin Harvick/50 8.00 20.00
PPSKK Kasey Kahne/25 30.00 80.00
PPSKW Kenny Wallace/50 4.00 10.00
PPSKyB Kyle Busch/70 8.00 20.00
PPSLC Landon Cassill/55 6.00 15.00
PPSMA1 Marcos Ambrose/60 6.00 15.00
PPSMK Matt Kenseth/50 6.00 15.00
PPSMM Mark Martin/25 40.00 80.00
PPSMP2 Max Papis/50 8.00 20.00
PPSMT Martin Truex Jr./60 5.00 12.00
PPSMW Michael Waltrip/30 8.00 20.00
PPSMW2 Mike Wallace/50 6.00 15.00
PPSNP Nelson Piquet Jr./49
PPSPM Paul Menard/60 4.00 10.00
PPSRC Ricky Carmichael/50 6.00 15.00
PPSRG Robby Gordon/30 4.00 10.00
PPSRH Ron Hornaday/50 4.00 10.00
PPSRN Ryan Newman/50 5.00 12.00
PPSRR Robert Richardson/50 4.00 10.00
PPSRS1 Regan Smith/60 5.00 12.00
PPSRS2 Reed Sorenson/50 4.00 10.00
PPSRS3 Ricky Stenhouse Jr./50 6.00 15.00
PPSSW Steve Wallace/49 5.00 12.00
PPSTB1 Trevor Bayne/50 12.00 30.00
PPSTK Travis Kvapil/60 4.00 10.00
PPSTM Tayler Malsam/50
PPSTS Tony Stewart/25 25.00 60.00

2008 Press Pass Speedway

COMPLETE SET (100) 15.00 40.00
WAX BOX HOBBY (36) 60.00 100.00
WAX BOX RETAIL (24) 50.00 75.00
1 Aric Almirola CRC .25 .60
2 Clint Bowyer .30 .75
3 Jeff Burton .25 .60
4 Dale Earnhardt Jr. .60 1.50
5 Jeff Gordon .60 1.50
6 Kevin Harvick .40 1.00
7 Jimmie Johnson .50 1.25
8 Casey Mears .20 .50
9 Paul Menard .20 .50
10 Scott Riggs .25 .60
11 Martin Truex Jr. .25 .60
12 Kurt Busch .25 .60
13 Patrick Carpentier RC .60 1.50
14 Dario Franchitti RC .50 1.25
15 Sam Hornish Jr. CRC .50 1.25
16 Kasey Kahne .30 .75
17 Bobby Labonte .30 .75
18 Juan Pablo Montoya .50 1.25
19 Ryan Newman .25 .60
20 Elliott Sadler .20 .50
21 Greg Biffle .25 .60
22 Carl Edwards .30 .75
23 David Gilliland .20 .50
24 Matt Kenseth .30 .75
25 Travis Kvapil .20 .50
26 Jamie McMurray .30 .75
27 David Ragan .25 .60
28 Dave Blaney .20 .50
29 Kyle Busch .40 1.00
30 Denny Hamlin .40 1.00
31 Dale Jarrett .30 .75
32 David Reutimann .25 .60
33 Tony Stewart .50 1.25
34 Brian Vickers .20 .50
35 Michael Waltrip .30 .75
36 J.J. Yeley .30 .75
37 Clint Bowyer NNS .30 .75
38 Cale Gale NNS .20 .50
39 Brad Keselowski NNS RC .60 1.50
40 Scott Wimmer NNS .25 .60
41 Bryan Clauson NNS RC .30 .75
42 Dario Franchitti NNS .50 1.25
43 Chase Miller NNS RC .40 1.00
44 Marcos Ambrose NNS .50 1.25
45 Carl Edwards NNS .30 .75
46 David Ragan NNS .25 .60
47 Kyle Busch NNS .40 1.00
48 David Reutimann NNS .25 .60
49 Ron Hornaday CTS .25 .60
50 Jack Sprague CTS .20 .50
51 Colin Braun CTS RC .25 .60
52 Rick Crawford CTS .20 .50
53 Erik Darnell CTS .25 .60
54 Mike Skinner CTS .20 .50
55 Tony Eury Jr. RC .75 2.00
56 Chad Knaus .40 1.00
57 Steve Letarte RC .50 1.25
58 Greg Zipadelli .60 1.50
59 Kevin Harvick SH .40 1.00
60 Ryan Newman SH .25 .60
61 Jeff Gordon SH .60 1.50
62 Dale Earnhardt Jr. SH .60 1.50
63 Aric Almirola SH .25 .60
64 Mark Martin SH .30 .75
65 Elliott Sadler SH .20 .50
66 Martin Truex Jr. SH .25 .60
67 Kevin Harvick UTH .40 1.00
68 Dale Earnhardt Jr. UTH .60 1.50
69 Bobby Labonte UTH .30 .75
70 Jeff Burton UTH .25 .60
71 Jimmie Johnson UTH .50 1.25
72 Ryan Newman UTH .25 .60
73 Jeff Gordon UTH .60 1.50
74 Martin Truex Jr. UTH .25 .60
75 Tony Stewart UTH .50 1.25
76 Denny Hamlin's Car RSG .15 .40
77 Dale Earnhardt Jr.'s Car RSG .25 .60
78 Jeff Gordon's Car RSG .25 .60
79 Carl Edwards's Car RSG .12 .30
80 Martin Truex Jr.'s Car RSG .10 .25
81 Tony Stewart's Car RSG .20 .50
82 Martin Truex Jr.'s Car WS .10 .25
83 Kyle Busch's Car WS .15 .40
84 Tony Stewart's Car WS .20 .50
85 Jeff Gordon's Car WS .25 .60
86 Jamie McMurray's Car WS .12 .30
87 Jeff Burton's Car WS .10 .25
88 Jimmie Johnson's Car WS .20 .50
89 Brian Vickers' Car WS .07 .20
90 Carl Edwards' Car WS .12 .30
91 Dale Earnhardt Jr.'s Car H .25 .60
92 D.Franchitti/J.Montoya H .50 1.25
93 R.Newman/K.Busch Cars H .10 .25
94 Kyle Busch H .40 1.00
95 Carl Edwards H .30 .75
96 Burton/Harvick/Bowyer Cars H .15 .40
97 Dale Jarrett Fans H .30 .75
98 Ryan Newman H .25 .60
99 Kyle Busch H .40 1.00
100 Jeff Burton CL .25 .60

2008 Press Pass Speedway Gold

COMPLETE SET (100) 25.00 60.00
*GOLDS: 1X TO 2.5X BASE
STATED ODDS 1 PER PACK

2008 Press Pass Speedway Holofoil

*HOLOFOIL: 6X TO 15X BASE
STATED PRINT RUN 50 SERIAL #'d SETS

2008 Press Pass Speedway Blur

COMPLETE SET (9) 15.00 40.00
STATED ODDS 1:12
B1 Jimmie Johnson 1.25 3.00
B2 Matt Kenseth .75 2.00
B3 Dale Earnhardt Jr. 1.50 4.00
B4 Ryan Newman .60 1.50
B5 Jeff Gordon 1.50 4.00
B6 Martin Truex Jr. .60 1.50
B7 Clint Bowyer .75 2.00
B8 Tony Stewart 1.25 3.00
B9 Kevin Harvick 1.00 2.50

2008 Press Pass Speedway Cockpit

COMPLETE SET (27) 12.00 30.00
STATED ODDS 1:2
CP1 Dave Blaney .20 .50
CP2 Clint Bowyer .30 .75
CP3 Jeff Burton .25 .60
CP4 Kurt Busch .25 .60
CP5 Kyle Busch .40 1.00
CP6 Dario Franchitti .50 1.25
CP7 Jeff Gordon .60 1.50
CP8 Kevin Harvick .40 1.00
CP9 Dale Jarrett .30 .75
CP10 Jimmie Johnson .50 1.25
CP11 Matt Kenseth .30 .75
CP12 Bobby Labonte .30 .75
CP13 Mark Martin .30 .75
CP14 Jamie McMurray .30 .75
CP15 Casey Mears .20 .50
CP16 Paul Menard .20 .50
CP17 Ryan Newman .25 .60
CP18 Kyle Petty .25 .60
CP19 David Reutimann .25 .60
CP20 Elliott Sadler .20 .50
CP21 Regan Smith .25 .60
CP22 Reed Sorenson .20 .50
CP23 Tony Stewart .50 1.25
CP24 Martin Truex Jr. .25 .60
CP25 Brian Vickers .20 .50
CP26 Michael Waltrip .30 .75
CP27 JJ Yeley .30 .75

2008 Press Pass Speedway Corporate Cuts Drivers

STATED PRINT RUN 80 SERIAL #'d SETS
*TEAM/165: .3X TO .8X DRIVERS
CDAA Aric Almirola 5.00 12.00
CDCE Carl Edwards 6.00 15.00
CDDF Dario Franchitti 4.00 10.00
CDDH Denny Hamlin 10.00 25.00
CDDJ Dale Jarrett 8.00 20.00
CDDR David Ragan 5.00 12.00
CDJM Jamie McMurray 5.00 12.00
CDJPM Juan Pablo Montoya 5.00 12.00
CDKH Kevin Harvick 10.00 25.00
CDKuB Kurt Busch 5.00 12.00
CDKyB Kyle Busch 10.00 25.00
CDMK Matt Kenseth 6.00 15.00
CDMM Mark Martin 6.00 15.00
CDMT Martin Truex Jr. 5.00 12.00
CDMW Michael Waltrip 5.00 12.00
CDRN Ryan Newman 6.00 15.00
CDTS Tony Stewart 15.00 40.00

2008 Press Pass Speedway Corporate Cuts Drivers Patches

STATED PRINT RUN 7-26
CDAA Aric Almirola/26 15.00 40.00
CDMM Mark Martin/29 40.00 80.00
CDMT Martin Truex Jr./17 25.00 60.00
CDRN Ryan Newman/15 40.00 80.00

2008 Press Pass Speedway Garage Graphs

CK Chad Knaus 15.00 40.00
GZ Greg Zipadelli 8.00 20.00
SL Steve Letarte 8.00 20.00
TE Tony Eury Jr. 12.00 30.00

2008 Press Pass Speedway Garage Graphs Duals

EE D.Earnhardt Jr./T.Eury Jr. 75.00 150.00
GL J.Gordon/S.Letarte EXCH 75.00 150.00
JK J.Johnson/C.Knaus EXCH 100.00 200.00
SZ T.Stewart/G.Zipadelli EXCH 60.00 120.00

2008 Press Pass Speedway Test Drive

COMPLETE SET (12) 12.00 30.00
STATED ODDS 1:6
TD1 Jeff Gordon 1.00 2.50
TD2 Kurt Busch .40 1.00
TD3 Mark Martin .50 1.25
TD4 Tony Stewart .75 2.00
TD5 Martin Truex Jr. .40 1.00
TD6 Ryan Newman .40 1.00
TD7 Dale Earnhardt Jr. 1.00 2.50
TD8 Jeff Burton .40 1.00
TD9 Michael Waltrip .50 1.25
TD10 Carl Edwards .50 1.25
TD11 Jimmie Johnson .75 2.00
TD12 Kasey Kahne .50 1.25

2008 Press Pass Starting Grid

SG1 Kyle Busch .25 .60
SG2 Carl Edwards .20 .50
SG3 Jimmie Johnson .30 .75
SG4 Dale Earnhardt Jr. .40 1.00
SG5 Jeff Burton .15 .40
SG6 Greg Biffle .15 .40
SG7 Kevin Harvick .25 .60
SG8 Tony Stewart .30 .75
SG9 Matt Kenseth .20 .50
SG10 Jeff Gordon .40 1.00
SG11 Denny Hamlin .25 .60
SG12 Clint Bowyer .20 .50
SG13 David Ragan .15 .40
SG14 Kasey Kahne .20 .50
SG15 Brian Vickers .12 .30
SG16 Ryan Newman .15 .40
SG17 Martin Truex Jr. .15 .40
SG18 Kurt Busch .15 .40
SG19 Juan Pablo Montoya .30 .75
SG20 Bobby Labonte .20 .50
SG21 David Reutimann .15 .40
SG22 Mark Martin .20 .50
SG23 Scott Riggs .15 .40
SG24 Kyle Petty .15 .40
SG25 Joe Nemechek .12 .30

1998 Press Pass Stealth

The 1998 Press Pass Stealth set was issued in one series totalling 60 cards. The set features silver foil stamping and UV coating and highlighted with a shimmering metal effect specially produced on the NASCAR Winston Cup Series. The set contains the topical subset: Teammates (45-59).

COMPLETE SET (60) 12.50 30.00
1 Dale Earnhardt's Car .75 2.00
2 Dale Earnhardt's Car
3 Richard Childress .30 .75
4 Jeff Burton .25 .60
5 Jeff Burton's Car .10 .25
6 Jack Roush .25 .60
7 Bill Elliott .60 1.50
8 Bill Elliott's Car .25 .60
9 Joe Garone .12 .30
10 Jeff Gordon .60 1.50
11 Jeff Gordon's Car .25 .60
12 Ray Evernham .25 .60
13 Kenny Irwin .50 1.25
14 Kenny Irwin's Car .20 .50
15 Robert Yates .25 .60

16 Dale Jarrett .30 .75
17 Dale Jarrett's Car .12 .30
18 Todd Parrott .20 .50
19 Bobby Labonte .30 .75
20 Bobby Labonte's Car .12 .30
21 Jimmy Makar .20 .50
22 Terry Labonte .30 .75
23 Terry Labonte's Car .12 .30
24 Andy Graves .12 .30
25 Mark Martin .30 .75
26 Mark Martin's Car .12 .30
27 Jimmy Fennig .12 .30
28 Ricky Rudd .25 .60
29 Ricky Rudd's Car .10 .25
30 Bill Ingle .12 .30
31 Rusty Wallace .30 .75
32 Rusty Wallace's Car .12 .30
33 Robin Pemberton .12 .30
34 Michael Waltrip .30 .75
35 Michael Waltrip's Car .12 .30
36 Glen Wood .12 .30
37 Dale Earnhardt Jr. 2.00 5.00
38 Jason Keller .20 .50
39 Randy LaJoie .20 .50
40 Mark Martin .30 .75
41 Mike McLaughlin .20 .50
42 Elliott Sadler .20 .50
43 Hermie Sadler .20 .50
44 Tony Stewart RC 2.50 6.00
45 Dale Jarrett TM .30 .75
46 Kenny Irwin TM .50 1.25
47 Jeff Gordon TM .60 1.50
48 Terry Labonte TM .30 .75
49 Jeremy Mayfield TM .20 .50
50 Rusty Wallace TM .30 .75
51 Jeff Burton TM .25 .60
52 Ted Musgrave TM .20 .50
53 Chad Little TM .20 .50
54 Johnny Benson TM .30 .75
55 Mark Martin TM .30 .75
56 Sterling Marlin TM .30 .75
57 Joe Nemechek TM .20 .50
58 Mike Skinner TM .20 .50
59 Dale Earnhardt's Car TM .75 2.00
60 Dale Earnhardt Jr. CL 2.00 5.00
P1 Jeff Gordon Promo 2.00 5.00
0 J.Gordon Champ Bnz 1:110 4.00 10.00
0 J.Gordon Champ Slv 1:220 8.00 20.00
0 J.Gordon Champ Gld 1:440 15.00 40.00

1998 Press Pass Stealth Fusion

COMPLETE SET (60) 15.00 40.00
*FUSION VETS: 1.2X TO 3X BASE CARDS
*FUSION RCs: .6X TO 1.5X BASE CARDS

1998 Press Pass Stealth Awards

Randomly inserted in progressive odds at a rate of 1:22 through 1:420, this insert set honors those drivers who have proven their excellence and risen to the top in 6 key categories: Most Laps Completed (1:22), All Charged Up (1:68), Top Rookie (1:90), Most Money Won (1:120), Most Poles (1:200), and Most Wins (1:420).

COMPLETE SET (7) 100.00 200.00
1 Jeremy Mayfield 1:22 1.25 3.00
2 Jeff Burton 1:68 2.50 6.00
3 Kenny Irwin 1:90 2.00 5.00
4 Mark Martin 1:120 6.00 15.00
5 Jeff Gordon 1:200 8.00 20.00
6 Mark Martin 1:420 15.00 40.00
7 Jeff Gordon 1:420 25.00 60.00

1998 Press Pass Stealth Fan Talk

Randomly inserted in packs at a rate of one in 10, this all-foil, micro-etched insert set gives fans their chance to say why their favorite driver is the best in the business.

COMPLETE SET (9) 10.00 25.00
COMP.DIE CUT SET (9) 40.00 80.00
*DIE CUTS: .6X TO 1.5X BASIC INSERTS
1 Dale Earnhardt 6.00 15.00
2 Bill Elliott 1.25 3.00
3 Jeff Gordon 3.00 8.00
4 Dale Jarrett 2.00 5.00
5 Bobby Labonte 2.00 5.00
6 Terry Labonte 1.00 2.50
7 Mark Martin 2.50 6.00
8 Ricky Rudd 1.00 2.50
9 Rusty Wallace 2.50 6.00

1998 Press Pass Stealth Octane

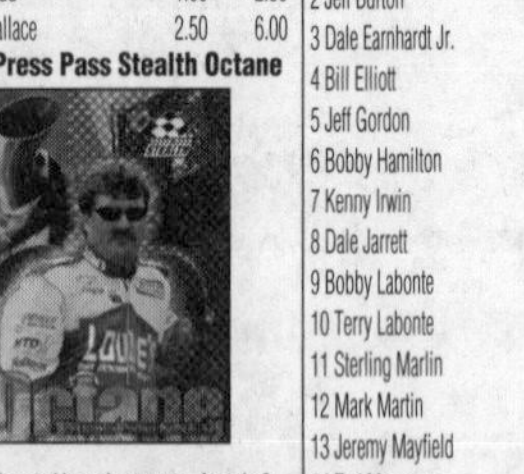

Randomly inserted in packs at a rate of one in 2, this insert offers a "set within a set" that features the top 18 NASCAR Winston Cup drivers and their rides on all-foil, micro-etched cards.

COMPLETE SET (36) 15.00 30.00
COMP.DIE CUT SET (36) 50.00 120.00
*DIE CUTS: 1.2X TO 3X BASIC INSERTS
1 John Andretti .25 .60
2 John Andretti's Car .10 .30
3 Johnny Benson .50 1.25
4 Johnny Benson's Car .10 .30
5 Jeff Burton .75 2.00
6 Jeff Burton's Car .25 .60
7 Ward Burton .50 1.25
8 Ward Burton's Car .25 .60
9 Dale Earnhardt's Car 1.50 4.00
10 Dale Earnhardt's Car 1.50 4.00
11 Bill Elliott 1.00 2.50
12 Bill Elliott's Car .50 1.25
13 Jeff Gordon 2.50 6.00
14 Jeff Gordon's Car 1.00 2.50
15 Ernie Irvan .50 1.25
16 Ernie Irvan's Car .25 .60
17 Dale Jarrett 1.50 4.00
18 Dale Jarrett's Car .50 1.25
19 Bobby Labonte 1.50 4.00
20 Bobby Labonte's Car .50 1.25
21 Terry Labonte .75 2.00
22 Terry Labonte's Car .50 1.25
23 Sterling Marlin .75 2.00
24 Sterling Marlin's Car .50 1.25
25 Mark Martin 2.00 5.00
26 Mark Martin's Car .75 2.00
27 Jeremy Mayfield .25 .60
28 Jeremy Mayfield's Car .10 .30
29 Ricky Rudd .75 2.00
30 Ricky Rudd's Car .25 .60
31 Mike Skinner .25 .60
32 Mike Skinner's Car .10 .30
33 Jimmy Spencer .25 .60
34 Jimmy Spencer's Car .10 .30
35 Rusty Wallace 2.00 5.00
36 Rusty Wallace's Car .75 2.00

1998 Press Pass Stealth Race Used Gloves

Randomly inserted in packs at a rate of one in 400, this eight-card insert set features a piece of race-used gloves from top NASCAR Winston Cup drivers like Jeff Gordon and Mark Martin. These cards are numbered to 205. Cards with multi-colored cloth carry a 25 percent premium.

G1 Rusty Wallace 10.00 25.00
G2 Jeff Burton 8.00 20.00
G3 Terry Labonte 10.00 25.00
G4 Mark Martin 12.00 30.00
G5 Bobby Labonte 10.00 25.00
G6 Jeff Gordon 20.00 50.00
G7 Dale Jarrett 10.00 25.00
G8 Dale Earnhardt 30.00 80.00

1998 Press Pass Stealth Stars

Randomly inserted in packs at a rate of one in 6, this 18-card insert set features NASCAR Winston Cup superstars on all-foil.

COMPLETE SET (18) 15.00 40.00
COMP.DIE CUT SET (18) 100.00 200.00
*DIE CUTS: 1.2X TO 3X BASIC INSERTS
1 Johnny Benson .40 1.00
2 Jeff Burton 1.25 3.00
3 Dale Earnhardt Jr. 5.00 12.00
4 Bill Elliott 1.50 4.00
5 Jeff Gordon 4.00 10.00
6 Bobby Hamilton .40 1.00
7 Kenny Irwin .75 2.00
8 Dale Jarrett 2.50 6.00
9 Bobby Labonte 2.50 6.00
10 Terry Labonte 1.25 3.00
11 Sterling Marlin 1.25 3.00
12 Mark Martin 3.00 8.00
13 Jeremy Mayfield .40 1.00
14 Ted Musgrave .40 1.00
15 Ricky Rudd 1.25 3.00
16 Jimmy Spencer .40 1.00
17 Rusty Wallace 3.00 8.00
18 Michael Waltrip .75 2.00

1999 Press Pass Stealth

This sixty card set features a mix of drivers, crew chiefs, cars and equipment needed to run on the NASCAR circuit. With three cards in each group the card backs formed a panoramic picture of the team hauler.

COMPLETE SET (60) 10.00 25.00
1 Jeff Burton .40 1.00
2 Jeff Burton's Car .10 .30
3 Frank Stoddard .05 .15
4 Ward Burton .25 .60
5 Ward Burton's Car .10 .30
6 Tommy Baldwin .05 .15
7 Dale Earnhardt 2.00 5.00
8 Dale Earnhardt's Car .75 2.00
9 Kevin Hamlin .05 .15
10 Jeff Gordon 1.25 3.00
11 Jeff Gordon's Car .50 1.25
12 Rick Hendrick .05 .15
13 Dale Jarrett .75 2.00
14 Dale Jarrett's Car .25 .60
15 Todd Parrott .05 .15
16 Bobby Labonte .75 2.00
17 Bobby Labonte's Car .25 .60
18 Jimmy Makar .05 .15
19 Terry Labonte .40 1.00
20 Terry Labonte's Car .25 .60
21 John Hendrick .05 .15
22 Mark Martin 1.00 2.50
23 Mark Martin's Car .40 1.00
24 Jack Roush .05 .15
25 Jeremy Mayfield .25 .60
26 Jeremy Mayfield's Car .10 .30
27 Michael Kranefuss .05 .15
28 Mike Skinner .10 .30
29 Mike Skinner's Car .05 .15
30 Larry McReynolds .05 .15
31 Tony Stewart CRC 1.50 4.00
32 Tony Stewart's Car .50 1.25
33 Joe Gibbs .25 .60
34 Rusty Wallace 1.00 2.50
35 Rusty Wallace's Car .40 1.00
36 Robin Pemberton .05 .15
37 Casey Atwood RC 1.00 2.50
38 Dave Blaney RC .10 .30
39 Dale Earnhardt Jr. 1.50 4.00
40 Jeff Gordon 1.25 3.00
41 Jeff Green .10 .30
42 Jason Keller .10 .30
43 Matt Kenseth RC 3.00 8.00
44 Randy LaJoie .10 .30
45 Mark Martin 1.00 2.50
46 Mike McLaughlin .10 .30
47 Elton Sawyer .10 .30
48 Michael Waltrip .25 .60
49 Caterpillar Stop Watch TT .05 .15
50 Dupont Air Gun TT .05 .15
51 Exide Car Jack TT .05 .15
52 Quality Care Gas Can TT .05 .15
53 Goodwrench Tool Cart TT .05 .15
54 Home Depot Ratchet TT .05 .15
55 Interstate Generator TT .05 .15
56 Kelloggs Tires TT .05 .15
57 Miller Lite Headphones TT .05 .15
58 Jeremy Mayfield's Car .05 .15
59 Lowes Lugnuts TT .05 .15
60 Valvoline Springs TT CL .05 .15
P1 Tony Stewart Promo 1.00 2.50

1999 Press Pass Stealth Fusion

COMPLETE SET (60) 15.00 40.00
*FUSION: 1X TO 2.5X BASIC CARDS
*FUSION RC's: .6X TO 1.5X BASIC CARDS

1999 Press Pass Stealth Big Numbers

Randomly inserted in packs at the rate of one in six, this eighteen card set is all foiled and etched featuring the top performers in NASCAR.

COMPLETE SET (18) 20.00 50.00
*DIE CUTS: 1X TO 2.5X BASIC INSERTS
DIE CUT STATED ODDS 1:18
BN1 Ward Burton .50 1.25
BN2 Jeff Burton .75 2.00
BN3 Dale Earnhardt 4.00 10.00
BN4 Dale Earnhardt Jr. 3.00 8.00
BN5 Dale Earnhardt Jr. 3.00 8.00
BN6 Mike Skinner .25 .60
BN7 Jeff Gordon 2.50 6.00
BN8 Jeff Gordon 2.50 6.00
BN9 Bobby Hamilton .25 .60
BN10 Dale Jarrett 1.50 4.00
BN11 Bobby Labonte 1.50 4.00
BN12 Terry Labonte .75 2.00
BN13 Sterling Marlin .75 2.00
BN14 Mark Martin 2.00 5.00
BN15 Jeremy Mayfield .50 1.25
BN16 Tony Stewart 2.50 6.00
BN17 Rusty Wallace 2.00 5.00
BN18 Michael Waltrip .50 1.25

1999 Press Pass Stealth Headlines

Randomly inserted in packs at increasing ratios this set features a interactive heat transfer technology. Collectors would touch the black screen to reveal the "Stealth Headline."

COMPLETE SET (9) 40.00 100.00
SH1 Jeff Gordon 10.00 25.00
SH2 Dale Earnhardt 12.50 30.00
SH3 Dale Earnhardt Jr. 8.00 20.00
SH4 Mark Martin 5.00 12.00
SH5 Rusty Wallace 5.00 12.00
SH6 Tony Stewart 3.00 8.00
SH7 Dale Earnhardt Jr. 4.00 10.00
SH8 Dale Jarrett 2.50 6.00
SH9 Terry Labonte 2.00 5.00

1999 Press Pass Stealth Octane SLX

Randomly inserted in packs at the rate of one in two these cards feature a mix of leading NASCAR drivers and the cars they drive.

COMPLETE SET (36) 12.50 30.00
*DIE CUTS: .8X TO 2X BASIC INSERTS
DIE CUT STATED ODDS 1:11
O1 John Andretti .15 .40
O2 Ward Burton .30 .75
O3 Jeff Burton .50 1.25
O4 Dale Earnhardt Jr. 2.00 5.00
O5 Dale Earnhardt Jr. 2.00 5.00
O6 Jeff Gordon 1.50 4.00
O7 Jeff Gordon 1.50 4.00
O8 Bobby Hamilton .15 .40
O9 Ernie Irvan .15 .40
O10 Dale Jarrett 1.00 2.50
O11 Terry Labonte .50 1.25
O12 Bobby Labonte 1.00 2.50
O13 Sterling Marlin .50 1.25
O14 Mark Martin 1.25 3.00
O15 Jeremy Mayfield .30 .75
O16 Joe Nemechek .15 .40
O17 Ricky Rudd .50 1.25
O18 Ken Schrader .30 .75
O19 Mike Skinner .15 .40
O20 Jimmy Spencer .15 .40
O21 Tony Stewart 1.50 4.00
O22 Elliott Sadler .15 .40
O23 Michael Waltrip .30 .75
O24 Dale Earnhardt Jr.'s Car .75 2.00
O25 Dale Earnhardt Jr.'s Car .75 2.00
O26 Jeff Gordon's Car .60 1.50
O27 Jeff Burton's Car .15 .40
O28 Dale Earnhardt's Car 1.00 2.50
O29 Tony Stewart's Car .60 1.50
O30 Bobby Labonte's Car .30 .75
O31 Terry Labonte's Car .30 .75
O32 Ward Burton's Car .15 .40
O33 Elliott Sadler's Car .10 .20
O34 Jeff Gordon's Car .60 1.50
O35 Dale Jarrett's Car .30 .75
O36 Mark Martin's Car .50 1.25

1999 Press Pass Stealth Race Used Gloves

Randomly inserted in packs at the rate of one in 480, these cards feature a swatch of race used glove.

G1 Jeff Burton/150 12.00 30.00
G2 Jeff Gordon/24 75.00 150.00
G3 Dale Earnhardt's Car/30 200.00 400.00
G4 Dale Jarrett/25 50.00 120.00
G5 Bobby Labonte/150 15.00 40.00
G6 Terry Labonte/150 15.00 40.00
G7 Mark Martin/150 20.00 50.00
G8 Tony Stewart/150 40.00 100.00
G9 Rusty Wallace/150 15.00 40.00

1999 Press Pass Stealth SST Cars

Randomly inserted in packs at the rate of one in 23, these cards come partially covered with a black peel off, remove the peel off to find a smaller picture of the driver's ride.

COMPLETE SET (9) 15.00 40.00
SS1 Dale Earnhardt Jr.'s Car 1.50 4.00
SS2 Dale Earnhardt's Car 2.00 5.00
SS3 Jeff Gordon's Car 1.25 3.00
SS4 Dale Jarrett's Car .75 2.00
SS5 Bobby Labonte's Car .75 2.00
SS6 Terry Labonte's Car .40 1.00
SS7 Mark Martin's Car 1.00 2.50
SS8 Tony Stewart's Car 1.25 3.00
SS9 Rusty Wallace's Car 1.00 2.50

1999 Press Pass Stealth SST Drivers

Randomly inserted in packs at the rate of one in 95, these cards come partially covered with a black peel off, remove the peel to find a smaller picture of the driver.

COMPLETE SET (9) 30.00 80.00
SS1 Dale Earnhardt Jr. 3.00 8.00
SS2 Dale Earnhardt's Car 2.50 6.00
SS3 Jeff Gordon 2.50 6.00
SS4 Dale Jarrett 1.50 4.00
SS5 Bobby Labonte 1.50 4.00
SS6 Terry Labonte .75 2.00
SS7 Mark Martin 2.00 5.00
SS8 Tony Stewart 2.50 6.00
SS9 Rusty Wallace 2.00 5.00

2000 Press Pass Stealth

Released in October 2000, Stealth features a 72-card base set divided up into three subsets. Card numbers 1-54 are from the Winston Cup, numbers 55-63 are BGN, and numbers 64-72 are Fan Favorites. Three cards were released for each racing team, and when the backs are laid together, they form the image of a race pit scene. Stealth was packaged in 24-pack boxes with packs containing six cards and carried a suggested retail price of 2.99.

COMPLETE SET (72) 6.00 15.00
1 Steve Park .20 .50
2 Steve Park's Car .07 .20
3 Paul Andrews .07 .20
4 Rusty Wallace .20 .50
5 Rusty Wallace's Car .07 .20
6 Robin Pemberton .07 .20
7 Dale Earnhardt 1.25 3.00
8 Dale Earnhardt's Car .50 1.25
9 Kevin Hamlin .07 .20
10 Terry Labonte .20 .50
11 Terry Labonte's Car .07 .20
12 Gary DeHart .07 .20
13 Mark Martin .20 .50
14 Mark Martin's Car .07 .20
15 Jimmy Fennig .07 .20
16 Dale Earnhardt Jr. CRC .50 1.25
17 Dale Earnhardt Jr.'s Car .20 .50
18 Tony Eury .15 .40
19 Jeremy Mayfield .12 .30
20 Jeremy Mayfield's Car
0.10 836650402

2000 Press Pass Stealth

21 Peter Sospenzo .07 .20
22 Matt Kenseth CRC .60 1.50
23 Matt Kenseth's Car .25 .60
24 Robbie Reiser .15 .40
25 Bobby Labonte .20 .50
26 Bobby Labonte's Car .07 .20
27 Jimmy Makar .12 .30
28 Tony Stewart .30 .75
29 Tony Stewart's Car .12 .30
30 Greg Zipadelli .15 .40
31 Ward Burton .15 .40
32 Ward Burton's Car .05 .15
33 Tommy Baldwin .15 .40
34 Jeff Gordon .40 1.00
35 Jeff Gordon's Car .15 .40
36 Robbie Loomis .15 .40
37 Jerry Nadeau .15 .40
38 Jerry Nadeau's Car .05 .15
39 Tony Furr .07 .20
40 Ricky Rudd .15 .40
41 Ricky Rudd's Car .05 .10
42 Mike McSwain .05 .10
43 Mike Skinner .12 .30
44 Mike Skinner's Car .05 .10
45 Larry McReynolds .15 .40
46 Dale Jarrett .20 .50
47 Dale Jarrett's Car .07 .20
48 Todd Parrott .12 .30
49 Chad Little .12 .30
50 Chad Little's Car .05 .10
51 Jeff Hammond .15 .40
52 Jeff Burton .15 .40
53 Jeff Burton's Car .05 .15
54 Frank Stoddard .07 .20
55 Casey Atwood BGN .20 .50
56 Jeff Green BGN .07 .20
57 Matt Kenseth BGN .60 1.50
58 Todd Bodine BGN .07 .20
59 Randy LaJoie BGN .07 .20
60 Jason Keller BGN .07 .20
61 David Green BGN .07 .20
62 Kevin Harvick BGN .60 1.50
63 Elton Sawyer BGN .07 .20
64 Bobby Labonte FF .20 .50
65 Jeff Gordon FF .40 1.00
66 Tony Stewart FF .30 .75
67 Terry Labonte FF .20 .50
68 Dale Jarrett FF .20 .50
69 Ricky Rudd FF .15 .40
70 Dale Earnhardt Jr. FF .50 1.25
71 Rusty Wallace FF .20 .50
72 Casey Atwood CL .20 .50

2000 Press Pass Stealth Behind the Numbers

Randomly inserted in packs at the rate of one in 12, this 9-card set features heat transfer technology that upon touch of a finger, reveals information about the driver.

COMPLETE SET (9) 15.00 40.00
BN1 Matt Kenseth 3.00 8.00
BN2 Dale Earnhardt Jr. 2.50 6.00
BN3 Mark Martin 1.00 2.50
BN4 Rusty Wallace 1.00 2.50
BN5 Dale Jarrett 1.00 2.50
BN6 Tony Stewart 1.50 4.00
BN7 Jeff Gordon 2.00 5.00
BN8 Terry Labonte 1.00 2.50
BN9 Bobby Labonte 1.00 2.50

2000 Press Pass Stealth Fusion

Randomly inserted in packs at the rate of one in one, this 36-card set is billed as the set within a set. Each card is die cut and features full color photography of drivers and their cars.

COMPLETE SET (36) 10.00 25.00
*FUSION RED: .6X TO 1.5X BASIC INSERTS
RED STATED ODDS 1:8
*FUSION GREEN: 1.2X TO 3X BASIC INSERTS
GREEN STATED ODDS 1:18
GREEN PRINT RUN 1000 SER.#'d SETS
FS1 Dale Jarrett .40 1.00
FS2 Dale Jarrett's Car .15 .40
FS3 Dale Jarrett .40 1.00
FS4 Bobby Labonte .40 1.00
FS5 Bobby Labonte's Car .15 .40
FS6 Bobby Labonte .40 1.00
FS7 Rusty Wallace .40 1.00
FS8 Rusty Wallace's Car .15 .40
FS9 Rusty Wallace .40 1.00
FS10 Mark Martin .40 1.00
FS11 Mark Martin's Car .15 .40
FS12 Mark Martin .40 1.00
FS13 Jeff Gordon .75 2.00
FS14 Jeff Gordon's Car .30 .75
FS15 Jeff Gordon .75 2.00
FS16 Dale Earnhardt Jr. 1.00 2.50
FS17 Dale Earnhardt Jr.'s Car .40 1.00
FS18 Dale Earnhardt Jr. 1.00 2.50
FS19 Matt Kenseth 1.25 3.00
FS20 Matt Kenseth's Car .50 1.25
FS21 Matt Kenseth 1.25 3.00
FS22 Tony Stewart .60 1.50
FS23 Tony Stewart .25 .60
FS24 Tony Stewart .60 1.50
FS25 Jeff Burton .30 .75
FS26 Jeff Burton's Car .12 .30
FS27 Jeff Burton .30 .75
FS28 Jeremy Mayfield .25 .60
FS29 Jeremy Mayfield .10 .25
FS30 Jeremy Mayfield .25 .60
FS31 Ward Burton .30 .75
FS32 Ward Burton .12 .30
FS33 Ward Burton .30 .75
FS34 Tony Stewart .60 1.50
FS35 Tony Stewart's Car .25 .60
FS36 Tony Stewart .60 1.50

2000 Press Pass Stealth Intensity

Randomly inserted in packs at the rate of one in 18, this 9-card set features multiple driver photos on an all foil micro-etched card stock.

COMPLETE SET (9) 20.00 50.00
IN1 Dale Jarrett 1.00 2.50
IN2 Mark Martin 1.00 2.50
IN3 Bobby Labonte 1.00 2.50
IN4 Tony Stewart 1.50 4.00
IN5 Jeff Gordon 2.00 5.00
IN6 Dale Earnhardt's Car 2.50 6.00
IN7 Rusty Wallace 1.00 2.50
IN8 Mike Skinner .60 1.50
IN9 Dale Earnhardt Jr. 2.50 6.00

2000 Press Pass Stealth Profile

Randomly inserted in packs progressively from one in 10 to one in 419, this 10-card set features an all-foil micro-etched card stock and portrait photos of drivers.

COMPLETE SET (10) 75.00 150.00
PR1 Dale Jarrett 2.00 5.00
PR2 Ward Burton 1.25 3.00
PR3 Tony Stewart 6.00 15.00
PR4 Bobby Labonte 3.00 8.00
PR5 Rusty Wallace 2.00 6.00
PR6 Mark Martin 2.00 6.00
PR7 Matt Kenseth 6.00 15.00
PR8 Dale Earnhardt Jr. 8.00 20.00
PR9 Jeff Gordon 25.00 60.00
PR10 Dale Earnhardt 30.00 80.00

2000 Press Pass Stealth Race Used Gloves

Randomly inserted in packs at the rate of one in 480, this 12-card set features authentic swatches of race-worn gloves. Stated print runs are placed next to the driver's name.

COMPLETE SET (12)
G1 Bobby Labonte/100 15.00 40.00
G2 Rusty Wallace/100 15.00 40.00
G3 Dale Earnhardt/100 50.00 120.00
G4 Jeff Burton/100 12.00 30.00
G5 Terry Labonte/100 15.00 40.00
G6 Mark Martin/50 20.00 50.00
G7 Jeff Gordon/100 40.00 100.00
G8 Dale Earnhardt Jr./50 75.00 150.00
G9 Matt Kenseth/100 15.00 40.00
G10 Mike Skinner/100 10.00 25.00
G11 Dale Jarrett/50 25.00 60.00
G12 Tony Stewart/100 20.00 50.00

2000 Press Pass Stealth SST
Randomly inserted in packs at the rate of one in eight, this 12-card set features embossed photos on an all foil card stock.
COMPLETE SET (12) 15.00 40.00
SST1 Dale Jarrett .60 1.50
SST2 Bobby Labonte .60 1.50
SST3 Mark Martin .60 1.50
SST4 Jeff Gordon 1.25 3.00
SST5 Tony Stewart 1.00 2.50
SST6 Jeff Burton .50 1.25
SST7 Matt Kenseth 2.00 5.00
SST8 Rusty Wallace .60 1.50
SST9 Ward Burton .50 1.25
SST10 Terry Labonte .60 1.50
SST11 Ricky Rudd .50 1.25
SST12 Dale Earnhardt Jr. 1.50 4.00

2001 Press Pass Stealth
Issued in 2001, this 72 card set features a mix between the leading NASCAR drivers and cards of the cars they drive. The cards were issued in 6-card packs.
COMPLETE SET (72) 12.50 30.00
WAX BOX HOBBY 40.00 75.00
1 Steve Park .30 .75
2 Steve Park's Car .30 .75
3 Steve Park .30 .75
4 Rusty Wallace .75 2.50
5 Rusty Wallace's Car .30 .75
6 Rusty Wallace .75 2.50
7 Terry Labonte .50 1.25
8 Terry Labonte's Car .30 .75
9 Terry Labonte .50 1.25
10 Mark Martin 1.00 2.50
11 Mark Martin's Car .30 .75
12 Mark Martin 1.00 2.50
13 Dale Earnhardt Jr. 1.50 4.00
14 Dale Earnhardt Jr.'s Car .60 1.50
15 Dale Earnhardt Jr. 1.50 4.00
16 Michael Waltrip .30 .75
17 Michael Waltrip's Car .15 .40
18 Michael Waltrip .30 .75
19 Bobby Labonte .75 2.00
20 Bobby Labonte's Car .30 .75
21 Bobby Labonte .75 2.00
22 Tony Stewart 1.25 3.00
23 Tony Stewart's Car .50 1.25
24 Tony Stewart 1.25 3.00
25 Ward Burton .30 .75
26 Ward Burton's Car .15 .40
27 Ward Burton .30 .75
28 Jeff Gordon 1.25 3.00
29 Jeff Gordon's Car .50 1.25
30 Jeff Gordon 1.25 3.00
31 Ricky Rudd .50 1.25
32 Ricky Rudd's Car .30 .75
33 Ricky Rudd .50 1.25
34 Kevin Harvick CRC 1.25 3.00
35 Kevin Harvick's Car .50 1.25
36 Kevin Harvick 1.25 3.00
37 Mike Skinner .15 .40
38 Mike Skinner's Car .05 .15
39 Mike Skinner .15 .40
40 Dale Jarrett .75 2.00
41 Dale Jarrett's Car .30 .75
42 Dale Jarrett .75 2.00
43 Jeff Burton .30 .75
44 Jeff Burton's Car .15 .40
45 Jeff Burton .30 .75
46 Greg Biffle BGN .30 .75
47 David Green BGN .15 .40
48 Jeff Green BGN .15 .40
49 Kevin Grubb BGN .15 .40
50 Kevin Harvick BGN 1.25 3.00
51 Randy LaJoie BGN .15 .40
52 Chad Little BGN .15 .40
53 Hank Parker Jr. BGN .30 .75
54 Elton Sawyer BGN .15 .40
55 Jeff Gordon WIN 1.00 2.50
56 Jeff Gordon WIN 1.00 2.50
57 Jeff Gordon WIN 1.00 2.50
58 Jeff Gordon WIN 1.00 2.50
59 Jeff Gordon WIN 1.00 2.50
60 Jeff Gordon WIN 1.00 2.50
61 Jeff Gordon WIN 1.00 2.50
62 Jeff Gordon WIN 1.00 2.50
63 Jeff Gordon WIN 1.00 2.50
64 Steve Park SST .30 .75
65 Jeff Gordon SST 1.25 3.00
66 Dale Earnhardt Jr. SST 1.50 4.00
67 Mark Martin SST 1.00 2.50
68 Kevin Harvick SST 1.25 3.00
69 Dale Jarrett SST .75 2.00
70 Tony Stewart SST 1.25 3.00
71 Rusty Wallace SST 1.00 2.50
72 Michael Waltrip SST CL .15 .40

2001 Press Pass Stealth Holofoils
COMPLETE SET (72) 50.00 100.00
*HOLOFOILS: .8X TO 2X BASE CARDS

2001 Press Pass Stealth Behind The Numbers
Randomly inserted into packs, these six cards feature leading drivers printed on a hexagon shaped card that can folded to form one of three different images. The stated odds were 1:48 packs.
COMPLETE SET (6) 30.00 80.00
BN1 Kevin Harvick 8.00 20.00
BN2 Mark Martin 6.00 15.00
BN3 Dale Jarrett 5.00 12.00
BN4 Terry Labonte 3.00 8.00
BN5 Tony Stewart 8.00 20.00
BN6 Rusty Wallace 6.00 15.00

2001 Press Pass Stealth Fusion
Randomly inserted into packs, these nine cards feature top drivers printed on holofoil card stock. The stated odds were 1:12 packs.
COMPLETE SET (9) 20.00 50.00
F1 Dale Earnhardt Jr. 6.00 15.00
F2 Jeff Gordon 5.00 12.00
F3 Dale Jarrett 3.00 8.00
F4 Bobby Labonte 3.00 8.00
F5 Terry Labonte 2.00 5.00
F6 Mark Martin 4.00 10.00
F7 Steve Park 1.25 3.00
F8 Tony Stewart 5.00 12.00
F9 Rusty Wallace 4.00 10.00

2001 Press Pass Stealth Lap Leaders
Issued one per pack, these 36-die cut cards feature 18-drivers who led NASCAR races along with 18-cards featuring their rides. Each card was created with a clear plastic parallel with the 18-drivers issued at the rate of 1:8 hobby packs and the cars 1:8 retail packs.
COMPLETE SET (36) 8.00 20.00
*CLEAR CARS: 1X TO 2.5X BASIC INSERTS
CLEAR CAR STATED ODDS 1:8 RETAIL
*CLEAR DRIVER: 1X TO 2.5X BASIC INSERTS
CLEAR DRIVER STATED ODDS 1:8 HOBBY
LL1 Steve Park .30 .75
LL2 Rusty Wallace 1.00 2.50
LL3 Terry Labonte .50 1.25
LL4 Dale Earnhardt Jr. 1.50 4.00
LL5 Michael Waltrip .30 .75
LL6 Matt Kenseth 1.00 2.50
LL7 Bobby Labonte .75 2.00
LL8 Tony Stewart 1.25 3.00
LL9 Ward Burton .30 .75
LL10 Jeff Gordon 1.25 3.00
LL11 Ricky Rudd .50 1.25
LL12 Kevin Harvick 1.25 3.00
LL13 Mike Skinner .15 .40
LL14 Joe Nemechek .15 .40
LL15 Sterling Marlin .50 1.25
LL16 Bobby Hamilton .15 .40
LL17 Dale Jarrett .75 2.00
LL18 Jeff Burton .30 .75
LL19 Steve Park's Car .30 .75
LL20 Rusty Wallace's Car .30 .75
LL21 Terry Labonte's Car .30 .75
LL22 Dale Earnhardt Jr.'s Car .60 1.50
LL23 Michael Waltrip's Car .15 .40
LL24 Matt Kenseth's Car .50 1.25
LL25 Bobby Labonte's Car .30 .75
LL26 Tony Stewart's Car .50 1.25
LL27 Ward Burton's Car .15 .40
LL28 Jeff Gordon's Car .50 1.25
LL29 Ricky Rudd's Car .30 .75
LL30 Kevin Harvick's Car .50 1.25
LL31 Mike Skinner's Car .05 .15
LL32 Joe Nemechek's Car .05 .15
LL33 Sterling Marlin's Car .05 .15
LL34 Bobby Hamilton's Car .05 .15
LL35 Dale Jarrett's Car .30 .75
LL36 Jeff Burton's Car .15 .40

2001 Press Pass Stealth Profile
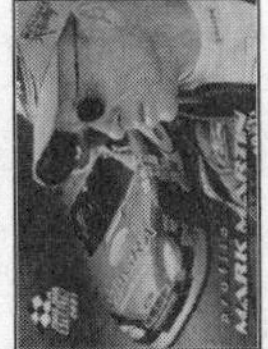
Randomly inserted into packs, these six cards feature leading NASCAR drivers laser etched on holofoil cardstock. The cards were randomly inserted in packs regressively with odds of 1:10 (#PR6) to 1:120 (#PR1).
COMPLETE SET (6) 15.00 40.00
STATED ODDS 1:10 TO 1:120 REGRESSIVE
PR1 Mark Martin 1.25 3.00
PR2 Kevin Harvick 4.00 10.00
PR3 Tony Stewart 2.00 5.00
PR4 Rusty Wallace 1.25 3.00
PR5 Jeff Gordon 2.50 6.00
PR6 Dale Earnhardt Jr. 3.00 8.00

2001 Press Pass Stealth Race Used Glove Drivers
Inserted into hobby packs at stated odds of one in 230, these 12 cards feature race-worn pieces of racing gloves. The print runs are notated next to each driver in our checklist.
*CARS/50-170: .4X TO 1X DRIVER/50-170
CAR/50-170 ODDS 1:480 RETAIL
RGD1 Jeff Gordon/50 30.00 60.00
RGD2 Rusty Wallace/120 15.00 40.00
RGD3 Michael Waltrip/170 10.00 25.00
RGD4 Tony Stewart/120 20.00 50.00
RGD5 Terry Labonte/120 10.00 25.00
RGD6 Mark Martin/50 15.00 40.00
RGD7 Matt Kenseth/120 12.00 30.00
RGD8 Dale Earnhardt Jr./50 30.00 80.00
RGD9 Jeff Burton/170 8.00 20.00
RGD10 Bobby Labonte/120 10.00 25.00
RGD11 Kevin Harvick/120 15.00 40.00
RGD12 Mike Skinner/170 8.00 20.00

2002 Press Pass Stealth

This 72 card set was released in September, 2002. These cards were issued in six card hobby or retail packs which came 24 packs per box with 20 boxes per case. When the three cards featuring either the driver or the team are placed together, a picture of the team's transporter is visible as if a puzzle was joined together.
COMPLETE SET (72) 10.00 25.00
WAX BOX HOBBY 40.00 75.00
WAX BOX RETAIL (24) 30.00 60.00
1 Rusty Wallace .60 1.50
2 Rusty Wallace's Car .25 .60
3 Rusty Wallace .60 1.50
4 Terry Labonte .40 1.00
5 Terry Labonte's Car .10 .30
6 Terry Labonte .40 1.00
7 Mark Martin .75 2.00
8 Mark Martin's Car .30 .75
9 Mark Martin .75 2.00
10 Dale Earnhardt Jr. 1.25 3.00
11 Dale Earnhardt Jr.'s Car .50 1.25
12 Dale Earnhardt Jr. 1.25 3.00
13 Ryan Newman CRC .75 2.00
14 Ryan Newman's Car .30 .75
15 Ryan Newman .75 2.00
16 Matt Kenseth .75 2.00
17 Matt Kenseth's Car .30 .75
18 Matt Kenseth .75 2.00
19 Bobby Labonte .60 1.50
20 Bobby Labonte's Car .25 .60
21 Bobby Labonte .60 1.50
22 Tony Stewart .75 2.00
23 Tony Stewart's Car .30 .75
24 Tony Stewart .75 2.00
25 Ward Burton .25 .60
26 Ward Burton's Car .10 .30
27 Ward Burton .25 .60
28 Jeff Gordon 1.00 2.50
29 Jeff Gordon's Car .40 1.00
30 Jeff Gordon 1.00 2.50
31 Kevin Harvick .75 2.00
32 Kevin Harvick's Car .30 .75
33 Kevin Harvick .75 2.00
34 Sterling Marlin .40 1.00
35 Sterling Marlin's Car .10 .30
36 Sterling Marlin .40 1.00
37 Jimmie Johnson CRC .75 2.00
38 Jimmie Johnson's Car .30 .75
39 Jimmie Johnson .75 2.00
40 Dale Jarrett .60 1.50
41 Dale Jarrett's Car .25 .60
42 Dale Jarrett .60 1.50
43 Jeff Burton .25 .60
44 Jeff Burton's Car .10 .30
45 Jeff Burton .25 .60
46 Greg Biffle .25 .60
47 Mike McLaughlin .10 .30
48 Randy LaJoie .10 .30
49 Chad Little .10 .30
50 Hank Parker Jr. .10 .30
51 Jamie McMurray RC 1.25 3.00
52 Jimmie Johnson's Car SST .30 .75
53 Kevin Harvick's Car SST .30 .75
54 Dale Jarrett's Car SST .25 .60
55 Dale Earnhardt Jr.'s Car SST .50 1.25
56 Matt Kenseth's Car SST .30 .75
57 Jeff Burton's Car SST .10 .30
58 Mark Martin's Car SST .30 .75
59 Rusty Wallace's Car SST .25 .60
60 Jeff Gordon's Car SST .40 1.00
61 Tony Stewart's Car SST .30 .75
62 Bobby Labonte's Car SST .25 .60
63 Robby Gordon's Car SST .05 .15
64 Dale Earnhardt Jr. WW 1.25 3.00
65 Kevin Harvick WW .75 2.00
66 Bobby Labonte WW .60 1.50
67 Terry Labonte WW .40 1.00
68 Mark Martin WW .75 2.00
69 Jimmie Johnson WW .75 2.00
70 Tony Stewart WW .75 2.00
71 Jeff Gordon WW 1.00 2.50
72 R.Wallace .30 .75
R.Newman CL

2002 Press Pass Stealth Gold
COMPLETE SET (72) 15.00 40.00
*GOLDS: .8X TO 2X BASIC CARDS

2002 Press Pass Stealth Samples
*SAMPLES: 2X TO 5X BASE CARDS

2002 Press Pass Stealth Behind the Numbers
Issued at stated odds ranging from one in 48 (card #BN9) to one in 240 (#BN1), these nine cards feature cards which celebrate the accomplishments and milestones of the featured drivers.
BN1 Kevin Harvick 10.00 25.00
BN2 Mark Martin 10.00 25.00
BN3 Dale Jarrett 10.00 25.00
BN4 Terry Labonte 6.00 15.00
BN5 Tony Stewart 4.00 10.00
BN6 Rusty Wallace 4.00 10.00
BN7 Jimmie Johnson 4.00 10.00
BN8 Bobby Labonte 3.00 8.00
BN9 Jeff Gordon 4.00 10.00

2002 Press Pass Stealth EFX

Issued at stated odds of one in eight, these 12 cards feature information on how NASCAR drivers stay cool while racing during summertime. Each card was printed with an all-foil design.
COMPLETE SET (12) 10.00 25.00
FX1 Ricky Rudd .60 1.50
FX2 Sterling Marlin .75 2.00
FX3 Rusty Wallace 1.25 3.00
FX4 Dale Earnhardt Jr. 2.50 6.00
FX5 Jeff Gordon 2.00 5.00
FX6 Kevin Harvick 1.50 4.00
FX7 Tony Stewart 1.50 4.00
FX8 Dale Jarrett 1.25 3.00
FX9 Jeff Burton .50 1.25
FX10 Ryan Newman 1.50 4.00
FX11 Jimmie Johnson 1.50 4.00
FX12 Terry Labonte .75 2.00

2002 Press Pass Stealth Fusion

Cards from this set were issued at a stated rate of one in 12 packs. They feature information on how a driver learns to become an elite NASCAR driver in this all holo, gold-foil stamped insert set.
COMPLETE SET (12) 15.00 40.00
F1 Jeff Burton .60 1.50
F2 Dale Earnhardt Jr. 3.00 8.00
F3 Jeff Gordon 2.50 6.00
F4 Kevin Harvick 2.00 5.00
F5 Dale Jarrett 1.50 4.00
F6 Jimmie Johnson 2.00 5.00
F7 Bobby Labonte 1.50 4.00
F8 Sterling Marlin 1.00 2.50
F9 Mark Martin 2.00 5.00
F10 Ryan Newman 2.00 5.00
F11 Tony Stewart 2.00 5.00
F12 Rusty Wallace 1.50 4.00

2002 Press Pass Stealth Lap Leaders
Inserted at a stated rate of one per pack, this 27-car die-cut set features NASCAR drivers who have led races for at least one lap.
COMPLETE SET (27) 8.00 20.00
LL1 John Andretti .15 .40
LL2 Casey Atwood .15 .40
LL3 Jeff Burton .30 .75
LL4 Ward Burton .30 .75
LL5 Kurt Busch .40 1.00
LL6 Dale Earnhardt Jr. 1.50 4.00
LL7 Jeff Gordon 1.25 3.00
LL8 Robby Gordon .15 .40
LL9 Jeff Green .15 .40
LL10 Bobby Hamilton .15 .40
LL11 Kevin Harvick 1.00 2.50
LL12 Dale Jarrett .75 2.00
LL13 Jimmie Johnson 1.00 2.50
LL14 Matt Kenseth 1.00 2.50
LL15 Bobby Labonte .75 2.00
LL16 Terry Labonte .50 1.25
LL17 Sterling Marlin .50 1.25
LL18 Mark Martin 1.00 2.50
LL19 Jeremy Mayfield .15 .40
LL20 Ryan Newman 1.00 2.50
LL21 Kyle Petty .30 .75
LL22 Ricky Rudd .40 1.00
LL23 Ken Schrader .15 .40
LL24 Mike Skinner .15 .40
LL25 Jimmy Spencer .15 .40
LL26 Tony Stewart 1.00 2.50
LL27 Rusty Wallace .75 2.00

2002 Press Pass Stealth Profile
Issued at a stated rate of one in 24, this nine-card plastic set features personal information about leading NASCAR drivers.
COMPLETE SET (9) 20.00 50.00
P1 Jeff Gordon 5.00 12.00
P2 Mark Martin 4.00 10.00
P3 Tony Stewart 4.00 10.00
P4 Kevin Harvick 4.00 10.00
P5 Matt Kenseth 4.00 10.00
P6 Jimmie Johnson 4.00 10.00
P7 Ryan Newman 4.00 10.00
P8 Dale Jarrett 3.00 8.00
P9 Bobby Labonte 3.00 8.00

2002 Press Pass Stealth Race Used Glove Drivers
Inserted into hobby packs at a stated rate of one in 480, these 16 cards feature race-used glove swatches set against a photo of the driver. These cards were issued to a stated print run of 50 serial numbered sets.
*CAR/65: .25X TO .6X DRIVER/50
GLD1 Jeff Gordon 30.00 80.00
GLD2 Rusty Wallace 15.00 40.00
GLD3 Tony Stewart 25.00 60.00
GLD4 Terry Labonte 15.00 40.00
GLD5 Mark Martin 15.00 40.00
GLD6 Matt Kenseth 10.00 25.00
GLD7 Dale Earnhardt Jr. 30.00 80.00
GLD8 Jeff Burton 10.00 25.00
GLD9 Bobby Labonte 15.00 40.00
GLD10 Kevin Harvick 12.00 30.00
GLD11 Mike Skinner 8.00 20.00
GLD12 Ryan Newman 10.00 25.00
GLD13 Jimmie Johnson 20.00 50.00
GLD14 Dale Jarrett/10
GLD15 Ken Schrader 10.00 25.00
GLD16 Dale Earnhardt/10

2003 Press Pass Stealth

This 72 card set was released in September, 2003. These cards were issued in six card hobby or retail packs which came 28 packs per box with an SRP of $2.99. When the three cards featuring either the driver or the team are placed together, the card backs feature a picture of the team's car as if a puzzle was joined together. As a bonus there was a Dale Earnhardt Sunday Money card numbered 0/0 inserted at a rate of 1 in 480 packs.
COMPLETE SET (72) 10.00 25.00
WAX BOX HOBBY (28) 45.00 80.00
1 Rusty Wallace .60 1.50
2 Rusty Wallace's Car .25 .60
3 Rusty Wallace .60 1.50
4 Terry Labonte .40 1.00
5 Terry Labonte's Car .10 .30
6 Terry Labonte .40 1.00
7 Mark Martin .75 2.00
8 Mark Martin's Car .25 .60
9 Mark Martin .75 2.00
10 Dale Earnhardt Jr. 1.25 3.00
11 Dale Earnhardt Jr.'s Car .50 1.25
12 Dale Earnhardt Jr. 1.25 3.00
13 Michael Waltrip .25 .60
14 Michael Waltrip's Car .05 .15
15 Michael Waltrip .25 .60
16 Matt Kenseth .75 2.00
17 Matt Kenseth's Car .25 .60
18 Matt Kenseth .75 2.00
19 Bobby Labonte .60 1.50
20 Bobby Labonte's Car .25 .60
21 Bobby Labonte .60 1.50
22 Tony Stewart .75 2.00
23 Tony Stewart's Car .25 .60
24 Tony Stewart .75 2.00
25 Ricky Rudd .25 .60
26 Ricky Rudd's Car .10 .30
27 Ricky Rudd .40 1.00
28 Ward Burton .25 .60
29 Ward Burton's Car .05 .15
30 Ward Burton .25 .60
31 Jeff Gordon 1.00 2.50
32 Jeff Gordon's Car .40 1.00
33 Jeff Gordon 1.00 2.50
34 Jimmie Johnson .75 2.00
35 Jimmie Johnson's Car .25 .60
36 Jimmie Johnson .75 2.00
37 Dale Jarrett .60 1.50
38 Dale Jarrett's Car .25 .60
39 Dale Jarrett .60 1.50
40 Kurt Busch .40 1.00
41 Kurt Busch's Car .10 .30
42 Kurt Busch .40 1.00
43 Jeff Burton .25 .60
44 Jeff Burton's Car .05 .15
45 Jeff Burton .25 .60
46 Scott Wimmer BGN .25 .60
47 David Green BGN .10 .30
48 Kerry Earnhardt BGN .25 .60
49 Kevin Grubb BGN .10 .30
50 Jason Keller BGN .10 .30
51 Mike McLaughlin BGN .10 .30
52 Johnny Sauter BGN .25 .60
53 Jimmy Vasser BGN RC .10 .30
54 Brian Vickers BGN .50 1.25
55 Rusty Wallace SST .60 1.50
56 Terry Labonte SST .40 1.00
57 Dale Earnhardt Jr. SST 1.25 3.00
58 Kerry Earnhardt SST .25 .60
59 Michael Waltrip SST .25 .60
60 Bobby Labonte SST .60 1.50
61 Ward Burton SST .25 .60
62 Jeff Gordon SST 1.00 2.50
63 Jimmie Johnson SST .75 2.00
64 Jeff Gordon SF 1.00 2.50
65 Ricky Rudd SF .40 1.00
66 Dale Jarrett SF .60 1.50
67 Jimmie Johnson SF .75 2.00
68 Terry Labonte SF .40 1.00
69 Mark Martin SF .75 2.00
70 Tony Stewart SF .75 2.00
71 Rusty Wallace SF .60 1.50
72 Dale Jr. .75 2.00
M.Kenseth CL
0 Dale Earnhardt Sunday Money 10.00 25.00

2003 Press Pass Stealth Red
*REDS: .8X TO 2X BASIC

2003 Press Pass Stealth Samples
*SAMPLES: 2.5X TO 6X BASE CARDS

2003 Press Pass Stealth EFX
Issued at stated odds of one in eight, these 12 cards feature information on how NASCAR drivers stay cool while racing during summertime. Each card was printed with an all-foil design.
FX1 Jeff Burton .50 1.25
FX2 Greg Biffle .50 1.25
FX3 Dale Earnhardt Jr. 2.50 6.00
FX4 Jeff Gordon 2.00 5.00
FX5 Ryan Newman 1.50 4.00
FX6 Jimmie Johnson 1.50 4.00
FX7 Bobby Labonte 1.25 3.00
FX8 Terry Labonte .75 2.00
FX9 Ricky Rudd .75 2.00
FX10 Tony Stewart 1.50 4.00
FX11 Rusty Wallace 1.25 3.00
FX12 Michael Waltrip .50 1.25

2003 Press Pass Stealth Fusion

Cards from this set were issued at a stated rate of one in 12 packs. They feature information on how a driver learns to become an elite NASCAR driver in this all holo, gold-foil stamped insert set.
FU1 Jeff Burton .60 1.50
FU2 Casey Mears .60 1.50
FU3 Dale Earnhardt Jr. 3.00 8.00
FU4 Jeff Gordon 2.50 6.00
FU5 Kevin Harvick 2.00 5.00
FU6 Jamie McMurray 1.00 2.50
FU7 Jimmie Johnson 2.00 5.00
FU8 Bobby Labonte 1.50 4.00
FU9 Mark Martin 2.00 5.00
FU10 Ricky Rudd 1.00 2.50
FU11 Rusty Wallace 1.50 4.00
FU12 Michael Waltrip .60 1.50

2003 Press Pass Stealth Gear Gripppers Drivers

Issued at a stated rate of one in 180 retail packs, these 18 cards feature pieces of race-used gloves set upon cards featuring the drivers of leading NASCAR teams. These cards were issued to a state print run of 75 serial numbered sets. The Dale Earnhardt card was issued to a stated print run of 3 sets and the Michael Waltrip was numbered to 30.
STATED PRINT RUN 3-75
*CAR/150: .25X TO .6X DRIVER/75
*CAR/30: .4X TO 1X DRIVER/30
GGD1 Jeff Gordon 20.00 50.00
GGD2 Ryan Newman 8.00 20.00
GGD3 Kevin Harvick 12.00 30.00
GGD4 Jimmie Johnson 15.00 40.00
GGD5 Rusty Wallace 12.00 30.00
GGD6 Mark Martin 12.00 30.00
GGD7 Ken Schrader 8.00 20.00
GGD8 Tony Stewart 15.00 40.00
GGD9 Terry Labonte 12.00 30.00
GGD10 Dale Earnhardt Jr. 20.00 50.00
GGD11 Dale Earnhardt/3
GGD12 Michael Waltrip/30 12.00 30.00
GGD13 Jeff Burton 10.00 25.00
GGD14 Dale Jarrett 12.00 30.00
GGD15 Joe Nemechek 8.00 20.00
GGD16 Ward Burton 8.00 20.00
GGD17 Ricky Craven 8.00 20.00
GGD18 Bobby Labonte 12.00 30.00

2003 Press Pass Stealth Gear Grippers Drivers Autographs
This 8-card set was randomly inserted hobby packs. These cards feature pieces of race-used gloves set upon cards featuring the drivers along with the their signature. These cards were limited and hand numbered to the corresponding driver's door number. Some of these cards are not priced due to scarcity.
*CARS: .4X TO 1X DRIVERS
JG Jeff Gordon/24 175.00 350.00
JJ Jimmie Johnson/48 50.00 120.00
KH Kevin Harvick/29 30.00 80.00
MK Matt Kenseth/17
MM Mark Martin/6
RN Ryan Newman/12
RW Rusty Wallace/2
TL Terry Labonte/5

2003 Press Pass Stealth No Boundaries
Issued at a stated rate of one per pack, this 25-card set features the interaction fans have with their favorite leading NASCAR drivers.
NB1 Kevin Grubb .20 .50
NB2 Kerry Earnhardt .40 1.00
NB3 Jason Keller .20 .50
NB4 Mike McLaughlin .20 .50
NB5 Johnny Sauter .40 1.00
NB6 Regan Smith .20 .50
NB7 Jimmy Vasser .20 .50
NB8 Scott Wimmer .40 1.00
NB9 Greg Biffle .40 1.00

NB10 Jeff Burton .40 1.00
NB11 Dale Earnhardt Jr. 2.00 5.00
NB12 Jeff Gordon 1.50 4.00
NB13 Kevin Harvick 1.25 3.00
NB14 Dale Jarrett 1.00 2.50
NB15 Matt Kenseth 1.25 3.00
NB16 Jimmie Johnson 1.25 3.00
NB17 Bobby Labonte 1.00 2.50
NB18 Terry Labonte .60 1.50
NB19 Mark Martin 1.25 3.00
NB20 Jamie McMurray .60 1.50
NB21 Casey Mears .40 1.00
NB22 Ricky Rudd .60 1.50
NB23 Jimmy Spencer .20 .50
NB24 Rusty Wallace 1.00 2.50
NB25 Michael Waltrip .40 1.00

2003 Press Pass Stealth Profile

Issued at a stated rate of one in 24, this nine-card plastic set features personal information about leading NASCAR drivers.

PR1 Dale Earnhardt Jr. 5.00 12.00
PR2 Jeff Gordon 4.00 10.00
PR3 Dale Jarrett 2.50 6.00
PR4 Jimmie Johnson 3.00 8.00
PR5 Bobby Labonte 2.50 6.00
PR6 Mark Martin 3.00 8.00
PR7 Ryan Newman 3.00 8.00
PR8 Rusty Wallace 2.50 6.00

2003 Press Pass Stealth Supercharged

Issued at stated odds ranging from one in 48 (card #SC9) to one in 168 (#BN1), these nine cards feature cards which celebrate the accomplishments and milestones of the featured drivers.

SC1 Jeff Gordon 20.00 50.00
SC2 Jimmie Johnson 12.50 25.00
SC3 Dale Earnhardt Jr. 12.50 30.00
SC4 Rusty Wallace 7.50 15.00
SC5 Michael Waltrip 4.00 10.00
SC6 Mark Martin 5.00 10.00
SC7 Ward Burton 4.00 8.00
SC8 Kerry Earnhardt 4.00 8.00
SC9 Terry Labonte 5.00 10.00

2004 Press Pass Stealth

Press Pass Stealth was released in May of 2004. This 100-card set featured NASCAR's hottest drivers. Photography from this set was taken during Speedweeks at Daytona in February and this was the first time drivers were pictured with their new teams for 2004. Cards were packaged 4 to a pack in both hobby and retail. Hobby boxes contained 28 packs while retail had only 24 packs, but both were packed 20 boxes to a case. The SRP for both hobby and retail was $2.99 per pack.

COMPLETE SET (100) 12.50 30.00
WAX BOX HOBBY (28) 40.00 70.00
WAX BOX RETAIL (24) 40.00 70.00
1 Kurt Busch .40 1.00
2 Kurt Busch's Car .15 .40
3 Kurt Busch .40 1.00
4 Dale Jarrett .50 1.25
5 Dale Jarrett's Car .25 .60
6 Dale Jarrett .50 1.25
7 Jimmie Johnson .75 2.00
8 Jimmie Johnson's Car .25 .60
9 Jimmie Johnson .75 2.00
10 Jamie McMurray .40 1.00
11 Jamie McMurray's Car .15 .40
12 Jamie McMurray .40 1.00
13 Sterling Marlin .40 1.00
14 Sterling Marlin's Car .15 .40
15 Sterling Marlin .40 1.00
16 Robby Gordon .15 .40
17 Robby Gordon's Car .15 .40
18 Robby Gordon .15 .40
19 Kevin Harvick .60 1.50
20 Kevin Harvick's Car .25 .60
21 Kevin Harvick .60 1.50
22 Brian Vickers CRC .50 1.25
23 Brian Vickers' Car .25 .60
24 Brian Vickers .50 1.25
25 Jeff Gordon 1.00 2.50
26 Jeff Gordon's Car .40 1.00
27 Jeff Gordon 1.00 2.50
28 Ricky Rudd .40 1.00
29 Ricky Rudd's Car .15 .40
30 Ricky Rudd .40 1.00
31 Tony Stewart .60 1.50
32 Tony Stewart's Car .25 .60
33 Tony Stewart .60 1.50
34 Michael Waltrip .25 .60
35 Michael Waltrip's Car .15 .40
36 Michael Waltrip .25 .60
37 Matt Kenseth .75 2.00
38 Matt Kenseth's Car .25 .60
39 Matt Kenseth .75 2.00
40 Bobby Labonte .50 1.25
41 Bobby Labonte's Car .25 .60
42 Bobby Labonte .50 1.25
43 Greg Biffle .25 .60
44 Greg Biffle's Car .15 .40
45 Greg Biffle .25 .60
46 Ryan Newman .75 2.00
47 Ryan Newman's Car .25 .60
48 Ryan Newman .75 2.00
49 Scott Riggs CRC .25 .60
50 Scott Riggs' Car .15 .40
51 Scott Riggs .25 .60
52 Dale Earnhardt Jr. 1.00 2.50
53 Dale Earnhardt Jr.'s Car .40 1.00
54 Dale Earnhardt Jr. 1.00 2.50
55 Mark Martin .60 1.50
56 Mark Martin's Car .25 .60
57 Mark Martin .60 1.50
58 Terry Labonte .40 1.00
59 Terry Labonte's Car .15 .40
60 Terry Labonte .40 1.00
61 Rusty Wallace .50 1.25
62 Rusty Wallace's Car .25 .60
63 Rusty Wallace .50 1.25
64 Mike Bliss .15 .40
65 Kyle Busch RC 3.00 8.00
66 Paul Wolfe RC .75 2.00
67 Jason Keller .15 .40
68 Paul Menard RC .75 2.00
69 Billy Parker Jr. RC 1.00 2.50
70 David Green .15 .40
71 Martin Truex Jr. RC 2.50 6.00
72 J.J. Yeley RC 1.50 4.00
73 Jeff Burton WW .25 .60
74 Mark Martin WW .60 1.50
75 Matt Kenseth WW .75 2.00
76 Kevin Harvick WW .60 1.50
77 Johnny Sauter WW .15 .40
78 Kasey Kahne WW CRC 1.25 3.00
79 Greg Biffle WW .25 .60
80 Joe Nemechek WW .15 .40
81 Robby Gordon WW .15 .40
82 Robby Gordon SST .15 .40
83 Dale Earnhardt Jr. SST 1.00 2.50
84 Michael Waltrip SST .25 .60
85 Matt Kenseth SST .75 2.00
86 Jeff Gordon SST 1.00 2.50
87 Kevin Harvick SST .60 1.50
88 Jimmie Johnson SST .75 2.00
89 Dale Jarrett SST .50 1.25
90 Kurt Busch SST .40 1.00
91 Rusty Wallace SF .50 1.25
92 Jamie McMurray SF .40 1.00
93 Kevin Harvick SF .60 1.50
94 Jimmie Johnson SF .75 2.00
95 Kurt Busch SF .40 1.00
96 Tony Stewart SF .60 1.50
97 Matt Kenseth SF .75 2.00
98 Michael Waltrip SF .25 .60
99 Dale Earnhardt Jr. SF 1.00 2.50
100 Kevin Harvick CL .60 1.50

2004 Press Pass Stealth Samples

*SAMPLES: 2X TO 5X BASE
STATED ODDS 1 PER BRC119

2004 Press Pass Stealth X-Ray

COMPLETE SET (100) 400.00 800.00
*RCs: 3X TO 8X BASE CARDS
STATED PRINT RUN 100 SERIAL #'d SETS

2004 Press Pass Stealth EFX

Randomly inserted in packs at a rate of 1:10, this 12-card set featured some of NASCAR's hottest drivers. The cards had holofoil designs with gold foil stamping. The cards had an "EF" prefix for their numbering on the cardbacks.

EF1 Dale Earnhardt Jr. 2.50 6.00
EF2 Jeff Gordon 2.50 6.00
EF3 Jimmie Johnson 2.00 5.00
EF4 Tony Stewart 1.50 4.00
EF5 Ryan Newman 2.00 5.00
EF6 Kurt Busch 1.00 2.50
EF7 Mark Martin 1.50 4.00
EF8 Rusty Wallace 1.25 3.00
EF9 Michael Waltrip .75 2.00
EF10 Brian Vickers 1.25 3.00
EF11 Ricky Rudd 1.00 2.50
EF12 Matt Kenseth 2.00 5.00

2004 Press Pass Stealth Fusion

Randomly inserted in packs at a rate of 1:24. These cards had a lenticular design and had a prefix of "FU" for their card numbering on the cardbacks.

COMPLETE SET (9) 20.00 50.00
FU1 Jeff Gordon 6.00 15.00
FU2 Terry Labonte 2.50 6.00
FU3 Dale Earnhardt Jr. 6.00 15.00
FU4 Michael Waltrip 2.00 5.00
FU5 Ryan Newman 5.00 12.00
FU6 Rusty Wallace 3.00 8.00
FU7 Kurt Busch 2.50 6.00
FU8 Mark Martin 4.00 10.00
FU9 Bobby Labonte 3.00 8.00

2004 Press Pass Stealth Gear Grippers Autographs

Randomly inserted in hobby packs only, this 7-card set featured a swatch of race-used glove from the corresponding driver and his signature. The cards were serial numbered to the respective driver's door number. These cards had a "HT" prefix for the card numbering on their cardbacks. The Dale Earnhardt Jr. was not released until July 2005 in packs of Press Pass Legends. The Bobby Labonte was also released late and was randomly inserted into the 2005 Box Blaster sets.

HTDE Dale Earnhardt Jr./8
HTJG Jeff Gordon/24 175.00 350.00
HTJJ Jimmie Johnson/48 75.00 150.00
HTKH Kevin Harvick/29 75.00 150.00
HTMK Matt Kenseth/17
HTMM Mark Martin/6
HTRN Ryan Newman/12
HTRW Rusty Wallace/2
HTBL Bobby Labonte/18 75.00 150.00

2004 Press Pass Stealth Gear Grippers Drivers

Randomly inserted into hobby packs only at a rate of 1:168. This 18-card set featured a swatch of the corresponding driver's race-used glove and a photo of him. The cards carried a "GGD" prefix for their card numbering on the cardbacks.

*RETAIL/120: 3X TO .8X HOBBY/80
GGD1 Jimmie Johnson 15.00 40.00
GGD2 Matt Kenseth 10.00 25.00
GGD3 Kevin Harvick 12.00 30.00
GGD4 Jeff Gordon 20.00 50.00
GGD5 Kurt Busch 8.00 20.00
GGD6 Ryan Newman 8.00 20.00
GGD7 Bobby Labonte 10.00 25.00
GGD8 Rusty Wallace 10.00 25.00
GGD9 Dale Earnhardt Jr. 25.00 60.00
GGD10 Michael Waltrip 10.00 25.00
GGD11 Jeff Burton 8.00 20.00
GGD12 Dale Jarrett 10.00 25.00
GGD13 Terry Labonte 10.00 25.00
GGD14 Robby Gordon 6.00 15.00
GGD15 Ward Burton 8.00 20.00
GGD16 Tony Stewart 15.00 40.00
GGD17 Mark Martin 10.00 25.00
GGD18 Greg Biffle 8.00 20.00

2004 Press Pass Stealth No Boundaries

Randomly inserted into packs only at a rate of 1:2. This 27-card set featured an embossed die-cut design printed on foil cards. The set featured some of NASCAR's hottest drivers and some young prospects. The cards carried an "NB" prefix for their card numbering on the cardbacks.

NB1 Clint Bowyer 1.50 4.00
NB2 Kyle Busch 1.50 4.00
NB3 David Green .30 .75
NB4 Mike Bliss .30 .75
NB5 Damon Lusk .30 .75
NB6 Paul Menard 1.25 3.00
NB7 Billy Parker Jr. 1.25 3.00
NB8 Martin Truex Jr. 2.50 6.00
NB9 J.J. Yeley 1.50 4.00
NB10 Ward Burton .50 1.25
NB11 Dale Earnhardt Jr. 2.00 5.00
NB12 Jeff Gordon 2.00 5.00
NB13 Kevin Harvick 1.25 3.00
NB14 Dale Jarrett 1.00 2.50
NB15 Jimmie Johnson 1.50 4.00
NB16 Matt Kenseth 1.50 4.00
NB17 Bobby Labonte 1.00 2.50
NB18 Terry Labonte .75 2.00
NB19 Mark Martin 1.25 3.00
NB20 Scott Riggs .50 1.25
NB21 Joe Nemechek .30 .75
NB22 Ryan Newman 1.50 4.00
NB23 Ricky Rudd .75 2.00
NB24 Elliott Sadler .50 1.25
NB25 Rusty Wallace 1.00 2.50
NB26 Michael Waltrip .50 1.25
NB27 Scott Wimmer .50 1.25

2004 Press Pass Stealth Profile

Randomly inserted into packs only at a progressive rate of 1:14 to 1:112. The individual card odds released by Press Pass are listed net to the driver's name in the checklist provided. This 12-card set featured foild cards with gold foil highlights. The cards carried a "P" prefix for their card numbering on the cardbacks.

P1 Jeff Gordon 1:112 12.50 30.00
P2 Jimmie Johnson 1:112 10.00 25.00
P3 Dale Earnhardt Jr. 1:112 10.00 25.00
P4 Kurt Busch 1:112 8.00 20.00
P5 Matt Kenseth 1:48 5.00 12.00
P6 Jamie McMurray 1:48 4.00 10.00
P7 Tony Stewart 1:48 5.00 12.00
P8 Scott Riggs 1:48 4.00 10.00
P9 Greg Biffle 1:14 3.00 8.00
P10 Bobby Labonte 1:14 3.00 8.00
P11 Michael Waltrip 1:14 3.00 8.00
P12 Dale Jarrett 1:14 3.00 8.00

2005 Press Pass Stealth

COMPLETE SET (100) 12.50 30.00
WAX BOX HOBBY (28) 40.00 70.00
WAX BOX RETAIL (24) 35.00 60.00
1 Sterling Marlin .40 1.00
2 Kasey Kahne 1.00 2.50
3 Jamie McMurray .40 1.00
4 Sterling Marlin's Car .15 .40
5 Kasey Kahne's Car .40 1.00
6 Jamie McMurray's Car .10 .25
7 Sterling Marlin .40 1.00
8 Kasey Kahne 1.00 2.50
9 Jamie McMurray .40 1.00
10 Ryan Newman .75 2.00
11 Rusty Wallace .50 1.25
12 Scott Wimmer .25 .60
13 Ryan Newman's Car .25 .60
14 Rusty Wallace's Car .15 .40
15 Scott Wimmer's Car .10 .25
16 Ryan Newman .75 2.00
17 Rusty Wallace .50 1.25
18 Scott Wimmer .25 .60
19 Dale Jarrett .50 1.25
20 Ricky Rudd .40 1.00
21 Matt Kenseth .75 2.00
22 Dale Jarrett's Car .15 .40
23 Ricky Rudd's Car .15 .40
24 Matt Kenseth's Car .25 .60
25 Dale Jarrett .50 1.25
26 Ricky Rudd .40 1.00
27 Matt Kenseth .75 2.00
28 Greg Biffle .25 .60
29 Kurt Busch .40 1.00
30 Terry Labonte .40 1.00
31 Greg Biffle's Car .10 .25
32 Kurt Busch's Car .15 .40
33 Terry Labonte's Car .15 .40
34 Greg Biffle .25 .60
35 Kurt Busch .40 1.00
36 Terry Labonte .40 1.00
37 Jeff Burton .25 .60
38 Dale Earnhardt Jr. 1.00 2.50
39 Jimmie Johnson .75 2.00
40 Jeff Burton's Car .10 .25
41 Dale Earnhardt Jr.'s Car .40 1.00
42 Jimmie Johnson's Car .25 .60
43 Jeff Burton .25 .60
44 Dale Earnhardt Jr. 1.00 2.50
45 Jimmie Johnson .75 2.00
46 Jason Leffler .15 .40
47 Kevin Harvick .60 1.50
48 Jeff Gordon 1.00 2.50
49 Jason Leffler's Car .10 .25
50 Kevin Harvick's Car .25 .60
51 Jeff Gordon's Car .40 1.00
52 Jason Leffler .15 .40
53 Kevin Harvick .60 1.50
54 Jeff Gordon 1.00 2.50
55 Tony Stewart .60 1.50
56 Michael Waltrip .25 .60
57 Bobby Labonte .50 1.25
58 Tony Stewart's Car .25 .60
59 Michael Waltrip's Car .10 .25
60 Bobby Labonte's Car .15 .40
61 Tony Stewart .60 1.50
62 Michael Waltrip .25 .60
63 Bobby Labonte .50 1.25
64 Tim Fedewa .15 .40
65 Clint Bowyer 1.00 2.50
66 David Stremme 1.00 2.50
67 Kasey Kahne 1.00 2.50
68 J.J. Yeley .40 1.00
69 Justin Labonte .40 1.00
70 Tony Raines .15 .40
71 David Green .15 .40
72 Kenny Wallace .15 .40
73 Terry Cook .25 .60
74 Mike Skinner .15 .40
75 Rick Crawford .15 .40
76 Kerry Earnhardt .25 .60
77 Ken Schrader .15 .40
78 Ron Hornaday .15 .40
79 Todd Kluever RC 1.25 3.00
80 Bill Lester .15 .40
81 Dennis Setzer .15 .40
82 Rusty Wallace H .50 1.25
83 Dale Earnhardt Jr. H 1.00 2.50
84 Michael Waltrip H .25 .60
85 Bobby Labonte H .50 1.25
86 Tony Stewart H .60 1.50
87 Jeff Gordon H 1.00 2.50
88 Kevin Harvick H .60 1.50
89 Jimmie Johnson H .75 2.00
90 Kurt Busch H .40 1.00
91 Tony Stewart SF .60 1.50
92 Bobby Labonte SF .50 1.25
93 Rusty Wallace SF .50 1.25
94 Matt Kenseth SF .75 2.00
95 Ricky Rudd SF .40 1.00
96 Jimmie Johnson SF .75 2.00
97 Jeff Gordon SF 1.00 2.50
98 Michael Waltrip SF .25 .60
99 Kevin Harvick SF .60 1.50
100 Jeff Gordon CL 1.00 2.50

2005 Press Pass Stealth Samples

*SAMPLES: 2X TO 5X BASE

2005 Press Pass Stealth X-Ray

*X-RAY: 3X TO 8X BASE

2005 Press Pass Stealth EFX

COMPLETE SET (12) 15.00 40.00
EFX1 Jeff Gordon 2.50 6.00
EFX2 Jimmie Johnson 2.00 5.00
EFX3 Dale Jarrett 1.25 3.00
EFX4 Michael Waltrip .60 1.50
EFX5 Tony Stewart 1.50 4.00
EFX6 Martin Truex Jr. 2.00 5.00
EFX7 Terry Labonte 1.00 2.50
EFX8 Bobby Labonte 1.25 3.00
EFX9 Kevin Harvick 1.50 4.00
EFX10 Jeff Burton .60 1.50
EFX11 Rusty Wallace 1.25 3.00
EFX12 Matt Kenseth 2.00 5.00

2005 Press Pass Stealth Fusion

COMPLETE SET (12) 50.00 100.00
FU1 Jeff Gordon 1:112 15.00 40.00
FU2 Jimmie Johnson 1:112 10.00 25.00
FU3 Ryan Newman 1:112 8.00 20.00
FU4 Michael Waltrip 1:112 6.00 15.00
FU5 Terry Labonte 1:48 4.00 10.00
FU6 Rusty Wallace 1:48 4.00 10.00
FU7 Tony Stewart 1:48 4.00 10.00
FU8 Matt Kenseth 1:48 4.00 10.00
FU9 Dale Jarrett 1:14 2.50 6.00
FU10 Kevin Harvick 1:14 2.50 6.00
FU11 Jeff Burton 1:14 2.00 5.00
FU12 Bobby Labonte 1:14 2.50 6.00

2005 Press Pass Stealth Gear Grippers Autographs

This 8-card set was available in packs of 2005 Press Pass Stealth. Each card had a swatch of a race-used glove and a signature from the corresponding driver. The cards were serial numbered to the driver's door number. There was a late addition to the set. Tony Stewart was only available in packs of 2006 Press Pass Legends.

GGBV Brian Vickers/25 100.00 200.00
GGDE Dale Earnhardt Jr./8
GGJG Jeff Gordon/24 175.00 350.00
GGKH Kevin Harvick/29 75.00 150.00
GGMM Mark Martin/6
GGMW Michael Waltrip/15
GGTL Terry Labonte/5
GGTS Tony Stewart/20 125.00 200.00

2005 Press Pass Stealth Gear Grippers Drivers

STATED ODDS 1:168 HOBBY
STATED PRINT RUN 75 SERIAL #'d SETS
*CARS/90: .3X TO .8X DRIVERS
GGD1 Jamie McMurray 6.00 15.00
GGD2 Matt Kenseth 6.00 15.00
GGD3 Kevin Harvick 8.00 20.00
GGD4 Jeff Gordon 12.00 30.00
GGD5 Kurt Busch 5.00 12.00
GGD6 Ryan Newman 5.00 12.00
GGD7 Bobby Labonte 6.00 15.00
GGD8 Rusty Wallace 6.00 15.00
GGD9 Michael Waltrip 6.00 15.00
GGD10 Jeff Burton 5.00 12.00
GGD11 Dale Jarrett 6.00 15.00
GGD12 Terry Labonte 6.00 15.00
GGD13 Tony Stewart 10.00 25.00
GGD14 Scott Riggs 5.00 12.00
GGD15 Brian Vickers 4.00 10.00
GGD16 Joe Nemechek 4.00 10.00
GGD17 Greg Biffle 5.00 12.00
GGD18 Dale Earnhardt Jr. 12.00 30.00

2005 Press Pass Stealth No Boundaries

COMPLETE SET (27) 15.00 40.00
NB1 Michael Waltrip .60 1.50
NB2 Rusty Wallace 1.25 3.00
NB3 Tony Stewart 1.50 4.00
NB4 Ken Schrader .40 1.00
NB5 Ricky Rudd 1.00 2.50
NB6 Kyle Petty .60 1.50
NB7 Ryan Newman 2.00 5.00
NB8 Joe Nemechek .40 1.00
NB9 Bobby Labonte 1.25 3.00
NB10 Matt Kenseth 2.00 5.00
NB11 Jimmie Johnson 2.00 5.00
NB12 Dale Jarrett 1.25 3.00
NB13 Kevin Harvick 1.25 3.00
NB14 Jeff Gordon 2.50 6.00
NB15 Dale Earnhardt Jr. 2.50 6.00
NB16 Kurt Busch 1.00 2.50
NB17 Jeff Burton .60 1.50
NB18 John Andretti .40 1.00
NB19 J.J. Yeley 1.00 2.50
NB20 Jon Wood .60 1.50
NB21 Kenny Wallace .40 1.00
NB22 Martin Truex Jr. 2.00 5.00
NB23 Justin Labonte 1.00 2.50
NB24 Denny Hamlin 2.50 6.00
NB25 David Green .40 1.00
NB26 Tim Fedewa .40 1.00
NB27 Clint Bowyer 2.50 6.00

2005 Press Pass Stealth Profile

COMPLETE SET (9) 20.00 50.00
PR1 Jeff Gordon 8.00 20.00
PR2 Jimmie Johnson 6.00 15.00
PR3 Dale Earnhardt Jr. 8.00 20.00
PR4 Jeff Burton 2.00 5.00
PR5 Mark Martin 5.00 12.00
PR6 Rusty Wallace 4.00 10.00
PR7 Kevin Harvick 4.00 10.00
PR8 Bobby Labonte 4.00 10.00
PR9 Tony Stewart 5.00 12.00

2006 Press Pass Stealth

This 97-card set was released in late June 2006. Cards 91-97 featured the drivers competing in the Nextel Cup for the first time. Each of these Cup Rookie Cards were short-printed and inserted into hobby packs at a rate of one in 20. Each of these cards featured the RC logo. The basic card design featured thick cardstock with gold foil Stealth logos and colorfoil design highlights. Hobby boxes contained 20-five card packs. The SRP for packs were $4.99.

COMPLETE SET (97) 50.00 100.00
COMP.SET w/o SPs (90) 15.00 40.00
WAX BOX HOBBY (20) 60.00 90.00
1 Greg Biffle .25 .60
2 Dave Blaney .20 .50
3 Jeff Burton .25 .60
4 Kurt Busch .25 .60
5 Kyle Busch .40 1.00
6 Dale Earnhardt Jr. .60 1.50
7 Carl Edwards .30 .75
8 Jeff Gordon .60 1.50
9 Robby Gordon .20 .50
10 Jeff Green .20 .50
11 Kevin Harvick .40 1.00
12 Dale Jarrett .30 .75
13 Jimmie Johnson .50 1.25
14 Kasey Kahne .40 1.00
15 Matt Kenseth .30 .75
16 Terry Labonte .30 .75
17 Bobby Labonte .30 .75
18 Sterling Marlin .30 .75
19 Mark Martin .30 .75
20 Jamie McMurray .30 .75
21 Casey Mears .20 .50
22 Joe Nemechek .20 .50
23 Ryan Newman .25 .60
24 Kyle Petty .25 .60
25 Tony Raines .20 .50
26 Scott Riggs .25 .60
27 Elliott Sadler .20 .50
28 Tony Stewart .50 1.25
29 Brian Vickers .20 .50
30 A.J. Foyt IV NBS RC .60 1.50
31 David Green NBS .20 .50
32 Todd Kluever NBS .60 1.50
33 Mark McFarland NBS .20 .50
34 Paul Menard NBS .20 .50
35 Danny O'Quinn NBS RC .60 1.50
36 Clint Bowyer NBS .60 1.50
37 Greg Biffle NBS .25 .60
38 Jon Wood NBS .25 .60
39 Kevin Harvick's Rig .20 .50
40 Jimmie Johnson's Rig .25 .60
41 Matt Kenseth's Rig .15 .40
42 Jeff Burton's Rig .12 .30
43 Martin Truex Jr.'s Rig .25 .60
44 Dale Jarrett's Rig .15 .40
45 Jeff Gordon's Rig .30 .75
46 Carl Edwards' Rig .15 .40
47 Dale Earnhardt Jr.'s Rig .30 .75
48 17/6/16/26/99 TM .30 .75
49 Stewart 1.25 3.00
Hamlin
Yeley TM
50 Harvick .60 1.50
Burton
Bowyer TM
51 Kahne .40 1.00
Mayfield
Riggs TM
52 Truex Jr. .60 1.50
Dale Jr. TM
53 Mears .50 1.25
Stremme
Sorenson TM
54 24/44/48/25/5 TM .60 1.50
55 Busch .25 .60
Newman TM

56 Jarrett .30 .75
Sadler TM
57 Dale Earnhardt Jr. F .60 1.50
58 Jeff Gordon F .60 1.50
59 Dale Jarrett F .30 .75
60 Tony Stewart F .50 1.25
61 Martin Truex Jr. F .50 1.25
62 Carl Edwards F .30 .75
63 Terry Labonte F .30 .75
64 Kasey Kahne F .40 1.00
65 Jimmie Johnson F .50 1.25
66 Kevin Harvick F .40 1.00
67 Bobby Labonte F .30 .75
68 Mark Martin F .30 .75
69 Kevin Harvick DD .40 1.00
70 Kasey Kahne DD .40 1.00
71 Dale Earnhardt Jr. DD .60 1.50
72 Carl Edwards DD .30 .75
73 Denny Hamlin DD 1.25 3.00
74 Matt Kenseth DD .30 .75
75 J.J. Yeley DD .50 1.25
76 Clint Bowyer DD .60 1.50
77 Reed Sorenson DD .50 1.25
78 Brian Vickers DD .20 .50
79 Tony Stewart DD .50 1.25
80 Kyle Busch DD .40 1.00
81 Greg Biffle DD .25 .60
82 Dale Earnhardt '79 RS 2.00 5.00
83 Dale Earnhardt '79 RS 2.00 5.00
84 Dale Earnhardt '79 RS 2.00 5.00
85 Dale Earnhardt '79 RS 2.00 5.00
86 Dale Earnhardt '79 RS 2.00 5.00
87 Dale Earnhardt '79 RS 2.00 5.00
88 Dale Earnhardt '79 RS 2.00 5.00
89 Dale Earnhardt '79 RS 2.00 5.00
90 Johnson .60 1.50
Gordon CL
91 Clint Bowyer CRC 2.50 6.00
92 Denny Hamlin CRC 5.00 12.00
93 Brent Sherman CRC 1.50 4.00
94 Reed Sorenson CRC 2.00 5.00
95 David Stremme CRC 1.50 4.00
96 Martin Truex Jr. CRC 2.00 5.00
97 J.J. Yeley CRC 2.00 5.00

2006 Press Pass Stealth X-Ray

*X-RAY: 2.5X TO 6X BASE

2006 Press Pass Stealth Corporate Cuts

This 14-card set featured a swatch of a sponsor shirt worn by the driver pictured on the front during the 2005 Nextel Cup season. Each card is serial numbered to 250 copies. The card number carried a 'CCD' prefix.These were available in 2006 Press Pass Stealth Hobby and Retail packs. They were inserted along with Gear Grippers at a combined rate of one in 40 hobby packs and a combined rate of one in 112 retail packs.

COMPLETE SET (14)
COMMON DRIVERS 4.00 10.00
SEMISTARS 5.00 12.00
UNLISTED STARS 6.00 15.00
STATED ODDS 1:40 HOBBY
STATED ODDS 1:112 RETAIL
STATED PRINT RUN 250 SERIAL #'d SETS
CCD1 Greg Biffle 4.00 10.00
CCD2 Jeremy Mayfield 3.00 8.00
CCD3 Dale Earnhardt Jr. 10.00 25.00
CCD4 Carl Edwards 5.00 12.00
CCD5 Reed Sorenson 8.00 20.00
CCD6 Dale Jarrett 5.00 12.00
CCD7 David Stremme 6.00 15.00
CCD8 Kasey Kahne 6.00 15.00
CCD9 Matt Kenseth 5.00 12.00
CCD10 Tony Stewart 8.00 20.00
CCD11 Kurt Busch 4.00 10.00
CCD12 Clint Bowyer 5.00 12.00
CCD13 Ryan Newman 4.00 10.00
CCD14 Jeff Burton 4.00 10.00

2006 Press Pass Stealth EFX

This 12-card set was inserted into packs of Press Pass Stealth at a rate of one in 14 to one in 112 packs progressively. The individual odds are listed below next to each card. The cards featured the top drivers on the Nextel Cup circuit and used holofoil technology to highlight the cards. Each card carried an 'EFX' prefix on the card numbers.

COMPLETE SET (12) 20.00 50.00
STATED ODDS 1:14 TO 1:112 PROGRESSIVE
EFX1 Tony Stewart 1:112 3.00 8.00
EFX2 Dale Earnhardt Jr. 1:112 4.00 10.00
EFX3 Jeff Gordon 1:112 4.00 10.00
EFX4 Jimmie Johnson 1:112 3.00 8.00
EFX5 Martin Truex Jr. 1:48 2.00 5.00
EFX6 Mark Martin 1:48 1.25 3.00
EFX7 Dale Jarrett 1:48 1.25 3.00
EFX8 Carl Edwards 1:48 1.25 3.00
EFX9 Terry Labonte 1:14 1.00 2.50
EFX10 Greg Biffle 1:14 .75 2.00
EFX11 Matt Kenseth 1:14 1.00 2.50
EFX12 Kyle Busch 1:14 1.25 3.00

2006 Press Pass Stealth Gear Grippers Autographs

This 9-card set featured a swatch of a race-used glove along with the corresponding driver's signature. Each card was hand numbered to the driver's door number. These were inserted into hobby packs only. Some of these cards are not priced due to scarcity.

CB Clint Bowyer/7
CM Casey Mears/42 75.00 150.00
DE Dale Earnhardt Jr./8
DH Denny Hamlin/11
JG Jeff Gordon/24 175.00 350.00
KH Kevin Harvick/29 75.00 150.00
MK Matt Kenseth/17
MM Mark Martin/6
RN Ryan Newman/12
TS Tony Stewart/20 125.00 200.00

2006 Press Pass Stealth Gear Grippers Drivers

This 18-card set featured a swatch of a driver's glove that had been worn during a race by the corresponding driver on the card. Each card was serial numbered to 99. These cards were only found in hobby packs of Press Pass Stealth and inserted at a combined rate of one in 40 along with the Corporate Cuts insert. Each card carried a 'GGD' prefix for its card number.

*CARS/99: .3X TO .8X DRIVERS
GGD1 Jeff Gordon 30.00 80.00
GGD2 Ryan Newman 10.00 25.00
GGD3 Dale Jarrett 12.00 30.00
GGD4 J.J. Yeley 8.00 20.00
GGD5 Tony Stewart 25.00 60.00
GGD6 Dale Earnhardt Jr. 30.00 80.00
GGD7 Matt Kenseth 15.00 40.00
GGD8 Kevin Harvick 12.00 30.00
GGD9 Denny Hamlin 8.00 20.00
GGD10 Kasey Kahne 15.00 40.00
GGD11 Reed Sorenson 8.00 20.00
GGD12 Casey Mears 8.00 20.00
GGD13 Jimmie Johnson 25.00 60.00
GGD14 Clint Bowyer 10.00 25.00
GGD15 Mark Martin 10.00 25.00
GGD16 Martin Truex Jr. 12.00 30.00
GGD17 Carl Edwards 15.00 40.00
GGD18 Jeff Burton 10.00 25.00

2006 Press Pass Stealth Hot Pass

This 27-card set featured the top drivers in NASCAR. Each card was designed to look like a "Hot Pass" ticket from the track. The cards carried an 'HP' prefix for the card number. These were inserted in packs at a rate of one in two.

COMPLETE SET (27) 15.00 40.00
HP1 Greg Biffle .50 1.25
HP2 Dave Blaney .40 1.00
HP3 Clint Bowyer 1.25 3.00
HP4 Jeff Burton .50 1.25
HP5 Kurt Busch .50 1.25
HP6 Kyle Busch .75 2.00
HP7 Dale Earnhardt Jr. 1.25 3.00
HP8 Carl Edwards .60 1.50
HP9 Jeff Gordon 1.25 3.00
HP10 Robby Gordon .40 1.00
HP11 Denny Hamlin 2.50 6.00
HP12 Kevin Harvick .75 2.00
HP13 Dale Jarrett .60 1.50
HP14 Jimmie Johnson 1.00 2.50
HP15 Kasey Kahne .75 2.00
HP16 Matt Kenseth .60 1.50
HP17 Bobby Labonte .60 1.50
HP18 Mark Martin .60 1.50
HP19 Jeremy Mayfield .40 1.00
HP20 Joe Nemechek .40 1.00
HP21 Ryan Newman .50 1.25
HP22 Tony Raines .40 1.00
HP23 Ken Schrader .40 1.00
HP24 David Stremme .75 2.00
HP25 Tony Stewart 1.00 2.50
HP26 Martin Truex Jr. 1.00 2.50
HP27 J.J. Yeley 1.00 2.50

2006 Press Pass Stealth Profile

This 9-card set features some of the top drivers in NASCAR. The cards focus on the driver's home state. The cards have the state cut into the card along with their profile. These cards were inserted into packs at a rate of one in 10. Each card carried a 'P' prefix for its card number.

COMPLETE SET (9) 20.00 50.00
P1 Dale Earnhardt Jr. 2.00 5.00
P2 Mark Martin 1.00 2.50
P3 Jeff Gordon 2.00 5.00
P4 Kasey Kahne 1.25 3.00
P5 Dale Jarrett 1.00 2.50
P6 Jimmie Johnson 1.50 4.00
P7 Tony Stewart 1.50 4.00
P8 Martin Truex Jr. 1.50 4.00
P9 Kevin Harvick 1.25 3.00

2006 Press Pass Stealth Retail

This 97-card set was released in late June 2006. Cards 91-97 featured the drivers competing in the Nextel Cup for the first time. Each of these Cup Rookie Cards were short-printed and inserted into retail packs at a rate of one in 6. Each of these cards featured the RC logo. The basic card design featured thick cardstock with silver foil Stealth logos. Retail boxes contained 24-four card packs. The SRP for packs were $2.99.

COMPLETE SET (97) 40.00 80.00
COMP.SET w/o SPs (90) 15.00 40.00
*1-90 RETAIL: .3X TO .8X BASIC CARDS
WAX BOX RETAIL (24) 40.00 70.00
91 Clint Bowyer CRC 2.50 6.00
92 Denny Hamlin CRC 5.00 12.00
93 Brent Sherman CRC 1.50 4.00
94 Reed Sorenson CRC 2.00 5.00
95 David Stremme CRC 1.50 4.00
96 Martin Truex Jr. CRC 2.00 5.00
97 J.J. Yeley CRC 2.00 5.00

2007 Press Pass Stealth Chrome

COMPLETE SET (90) 20.00 50.00
WAX BOX HOBBY (24) 80.00 110.00
1 Greg Biffle .30 .75
2 Clint Bowyer .40 1.00
3 Jeff Burton .30 .75
4 Kurt Busch .30 .75
5 Kyle Busch .50 1.25
6A Dale Earnhardt Jr. .75 2.00
6B Dale Jr. L1 dots 1.50 4.00
6C Dale Jr. L2 dots w/line 3.00 8.00
7 Carl Edwards .40 1.00
8A Jeff Gordon .75 2.00
8B J.Gordon L1 no dots 1.50 4.00
8C Gordon L2 no dots no ext 3.00 8.00
9 Denny Hamlin .50 1.25
10 Kevin Harvick .50 1.25
11 Dale Jarrett .40 1.00
12 Jimmie Johnson .60 1.50
13 Kasey Kahne .40 1.00
14 Matt Kenseth .40 1.00
15 Bobby Labonte .40 1.00
16 Mark Martin .40 1.00
17 Jamie McMurray .40 1.00
18 Casey Mears .25 .60
19 Ryan Newman .30 .75
20 Scott Riggs .30 .75
21 Ricky Rudd .30 .75
22 Elliott Sadler .25 .60
23 Reed Sorenson .25 .60
24 Tony Stewart .60 1.50
25 Martin Truex Jr. .30 .75
26 Brian Vickers .40 1.00
27 J.J. Yeley .40 1.00
28 Michael Waltrip .40 1.00
29 A.J. Allmendinger RC .75 2.00
30 David Gilliland RC .60 1.50
31 Paul Menard CRC 1.25 3.00
32A Juan Pablo Montoya RC 1.25 3.00
32B J.Montoya L1 2 yellw crnrs 2.50 6.00
32C J.Montoya L2 yell no NNCS 5.00 12.00
33 David Ragan CRC .75 2.00
34 David Reutimann RC .50 1.25
35 Regan Smith CRC .75 2.00
36 Jon Wood CRC .40 1.00
37 Marcos Ambrose NBS RC 1.50 4.00
38 Clint Bowyer NBS .40 1.00
39 Carl Edwards NBS .40 1.00
40 Kevin Harvick NBS .50 1.25
41 Stephen Leicht NBS RC 1.00 2.50
42 David Ragan NBS .75 2.00
43 David Reutimann NBS .50 1.25
44 Reed Sorenson NBS .25 .60
45 Steve Wallace NBS .40 1.00
46 Mark Martin's Rig .15 .40
47 Dale Earnhardt Jr.'s Rig .75 2.00
48 Kasey Kahne's Rig .15 .40
49 Denny Hamlin's Rig .20 .50
50 Matt Kenseth's Rig .15 .40
51 Tony Stewart's Rig .25 .60
52 Jeff Gordon's Rig .30 .75
53 Dale Jarrett's Rig .15 .40
54 Jimmie Johnson's Rig .25 .60
55 Martin Truex Jr.'s Crew PC .12 .30
56 Kurt Busch's Crew GC .12 .30
57 Dale Jr.'s Crew PC .30 .75
58 Greg Biffle's Crew GC .12 .30
59 Tony Stewart's Crew GC .25 .60
60 Jeff Gordon's Crew GC .30 .75
61 Jeff Burton's Crew GC .12 .30
62 Bobby Labonte's Crew GC .15 .40
63A Jimmie Johnson's Crew GC .25 .60
63B Johnson's Car GC L1 yell 1.25 3.00
64 Clint Bowyer .50 1.25
Kevin Harvick
Jeff Burton
65 Denny Hamlin .60 1.50
Tony Stewart
J.J. Yeley
66 David Gilliland .60 1.50
Ricky Rudd
67 Ryan Newman .30 .75
Kurt Busch
68 Joe Nemechek .75 2.00
Mark Martin
Sterling Marlin
Regan Smith
69 Carl Edwards .75 2.00
Greg Biffle
Matt Kenseth
Jamie McMurray
David Ragan
70 Reed Sorenson 1.25 3.00
Juan Pablo Montoya
David Stremme
71 Martin Truex Jr. 1.25 3.00
Dale Earnhardt Jr.
Paul Menard
72 Casey Mears .75 2.00
Kyle Busch
Jimmie Johnson
Jeff Gordon
73 J.J. Yeley DD .40 1.00
74 David Ragan DD .75 2.00
75 Denny Hamlin DD .50 1.25
76 David Reutimann DD .50 1.25
77A K.Harvick DD w/wsil strp .50 1.25
77B Harvick DD L1 w/sil/w strp 1.00 2.50
78 David Gilliland DD .60 1.50
79 Carl Edwards DD .40 1.00
80 Greg Biffle DD .30 .75
81 Reed Sorenson DD .25 .60
82 Dale Earnhardt Jr. PO .75 2.00
83 Jimmie Johnson PO .60 1.50
84A Kasey Kahne PO .40 1.00
84B K.Kahne PO L1 no logo .75 2.00
85 Matt Kenseth PO .40 1.00
86 Kevin Harvick PO .50 1.25
87 Tony Stewart PO .60 1.50
88 Jeff Burton PO .30 .75
89 Jeff Gordon PO .75 2.00
90 Dale Earnhardt Jr. CL .75 2.00

2007 Press Pass Stealth Chrome Exclusives

*EXCLUSIVES: 4X TO 10X BASE
STATED PRINT RUN 99 SERIAL #'d SETS

2007 Press Pass Stealth Chrome Platinum

*PLATINUM/25: 8X TO 10X BASE
STATED PRINT RUN 25 SER.#'d SETS

2007 Press Pass Stealth

COMPLETE SET (90) 12.50 30.00
WAX BOX RETAIL (28) 50.00 75.00
1 Greg Biffle .20 .50
2 Clint Bowyer .25 .60
3 Jeff Burton .20 .50
4 Kurt Busch .20 .50
5 Kyle Busch .30 .75
6 Dale Earnhardt Jr. .50 1.25
7 Carl Edwards .25 .60
8 Jeff Gordon .50 1.25
9 Denny Hamlin .30 .75
10 Kevin Harvick .30 .75
11 Dale Jarrett .25 .60
12 Jimmie Johnson .40 1.00
13 Kasey Kahne .25 .60
14 Matt Kenseth .25 .60
15 Bobby Labonte .25 .60
16 Mark Martin .25 .60
17 Jamie McMurray .25 .60
18 Casey Mears .15 .40
19 Ryan Newman .20 .50
20 Scott Riggs .20 .50
21 Ricky Rudd .20 .50
22 Elliott Sadler .15 .40
23 Reed Sorenson .15 .40
24 Tony Stewart .40 1.00
25 Martin Truex Jr. .20 .50
26 Brian Vickers .25 .60
27 J.J. Yeley .25 .60
28 Michael Waltrip .25 .60
29 A.J. Allmendinger RC .50 1.25
30 David Gilliland RC .40 1.00
31 Paul Menard CRC .75 2.00
32 Juan Pablo Montoya RC .75 2.00
33 David Ragan CRC .50 1.25
34 David Reutimann RC .30 .75
35 Regan Smith CRC .50 1.25
36 Jon Wood CRC .25 .60
37 Marcos Ambrose NBS RC 1.00 2.50
38 Clint Bowyer NBS .25 .60
39 Carl Edwards NBS .25 .60
40 Kevin Harvick NBS .30 .75
41 Stephen Leicht NBS RC .60 1.50
42 David Ragan NBS .50 1.25
43 David Reutimann NBS .30 .75
44 Reed Sorenson NBS .15 .40
45 Steve Wallace NBS .25 .60
46 Mark Martin's Rig .15 .40
47 Dale Earnhardt Jr.'s Rig .30 .75
48 Kasey Kahne's Rig .15 .40
49 Denny Hamlin's Rig .20 .50
50 Matt Kenseth's Rig .15 .40
51 Tony Stewart's Rig .25 .60
52 Jeff Gordon's Rig .30 .75
53 Dale Jarrett's Rig .15 .40
54 Jimmie Johnson's Rig .25 .60
55 Martin Truex Jr.'s Crew PC .12 .30
56 Kurt Busch's Crew GC .12 .30
57 Dale Jr.'s Crew PC .30 .75
58 Greg Biffle's Crew GC .12 .30
59 Tony Stewart's Crew GC .25 .60
60 Jeff Gordon's Crew GC .30 .75
61 Jeff Burton's Crew GC .12 .30
62 Bobby Labonte's Crew GC .15 .40
63 Jimmie Johnson's Crew GC .25 .60
64 Clint Bowyer .30 .75
Kevin Harvick
Jeff Burton
65 Denny Hamlin .40 1.00
Tony Stewart
J.J. Yeley
66 David Gilliland .40 1.00
Ricky Rudd
67 Ryan Newman .20 .50
Kurt Busch
68 Joe Nemechek .50 1.25
Mark Martin
Sterling Marlin
Regan Smith
69 Carl Edwards .50 1.25
Greg Biffle
Matt Kenseth
Jamie McMurray
David Ragan
70 Reed Sorenson .75 2.00
Juan Pablo Montoya
David Stremme
71 Martin Truex Jr. .75 2.00
Dale Earnhardt Jr.
Paul Menard
72 Casey Mears .50 1.25
Kyle Busch
Jimmie Johnson
Jeff Gordon
73 J.J. Yeley DD .25 .60
74 David Ragan DD .50 1.25
75 Denny Hamlin DD .30 .75
76 David Reutimann DD .30 .75
77 Kevin Harvick DD .30 .75
78 David Gilliland DD .40 1.00
79 Carl Edwards DD .25 .60
80 Greg Biffle DD .20 .50
81 Reed Sorenson DD .15 .40
82 Dale Earnhardt Jr. PO .50 1.25
83 Jimmie Johnson PO .40 1.00
84 Kasey Kahne PO .25 .60
85 Matt Kenseth PO .25 .60
86 Kevin Harvick PO .30 .75
87 Tony Stewart PO .40 1.00
88 Jeff Burton PO .20 .50
89 Jeff Gordon PO .50 1.25
90 Dale Earnhardt Jr. CL .50 1.25

2007 Press Pass Stealth Battle Armor Autographs

STATED PRINT RUN 8-48
BASDE Dale Earnhardt Jr./8
BASJG Jeff Gordon/24
BASJJ Jimmie Johnson/48 60.00 120.00
BASMK Matt Kenseth/17
BASRN Ryan Newman/12
BASTS Tony Stewart/20 60.00 120.00

2007 Press Pass Stealth Battle Armor Drivers

STATED ODDS 1:40 HOBBY
STATED PRINT RUN 150 SERIAL #'d SETS
*TEAM/85: .4X TO 1X DRIVER/150
BAD1 Jeff Gordon 10.00 25.00
BAD2 Greg Biffle 4.00 10.00
BAD3 Denny Hamlin 6.00 15.00
BAD4 David Ragan 10.00 25.00
BAD5 Ryan Newman 4.00 10.00
BAD6 Dale Earnhardt Jr. 10.00 25.00
BAD7 Carl Edwards 5.00 12.00
BAD8 Jimmie Johnson 8.00 20.00
BAD9 Jeff Burton 4.00 10.00
BAD10 Tony Stewart 8.00 20.00
BAD11 Kurt Busch 4.00 10.00
BAD12 Casey Mears 3.00 8.00
BAD13 Matt Kenseth 5.00 12.00
BAD14 Kyle Busch 6.00 15.00
BAD16 Dale Jarrett 5.00 12.00
BAD17 Martin Truex Jr. 4.00 10.00
BAD18 Juan Pablo Montoya 15.00 40.00
BAD19 Mark Martin 5.00 12.00
BAD20 Reed Sorenson 3.00 8.00
BAD21 J.J. Yeley 5.00 12.00
BAD22 David Reutimann 3.00 8.00
BAD23 Bobby Labonte 5.00 12.00
BAD24 David Stremme 3.00 8.00

2007 Press Pass Stealth Fusion

COMPLETE SET (9) 12.50 30.00
STATED ODDS 1:10
F1 Dale Jarrett .75 2.00
F2 Jeff Gordon 1.50 4.00
F3 Tony Stewart 1.25 3.00
F4 Michael Waltrip .75 2.00
F5 Jimmie Johnson 1.25 3.00
F6 Denny Hamlin 1.00 2.50
F7 Dale Earnhardt Jr. 1.50 4.00
F8 Juan Pablo Montoya 2.50 6.00
F9 Kevin Harvick 1.00 2.50

2007 Press Pass Stealth Mach 07

COMPLETE SET (12) 40.00 100.00
STATED ODDS 1:14-1:112 PROGRESSIVE
M7-1 Dale Earnhardt Jr. 10.00 25.00
M7-2 Jeff Gordon 12.50 30.00
M7-3 Tony Stewart 5.00 12.00
M7-4 Juan Pablo Montoya 5.00 12.00
M7-5 Kasey Kahne 5.00 12.00
M7-6 Jimmie Johnson 6.00 15.00
M7-7 Kevin Harvick 5.00 12.00
M7-8 Denny Hamlin 4.00 10.00
M7-9 Mark Martin 4.00 10.00
M7-10 Jeff Burton 3.00 8.00
M7-11 Bobby Labonte 3.00 8.00
M7-12 Dale Jarrett 3.00 8.00

2007 Press Pass Stealth Maximum Access

COMPLETE SET (27) 15.00 40.00
STATED ODDS 1:2
MA1 A.J. Allmendinger 1.25 3.00
MA2 Greg Biffle .50 1.25
MA3 Clint Bowyer .60 1.50
MA4 Jeff Burton .50 1.25
MA5 Kyle Busch .75 2.00
MA6 Dale Earnhardt Jr. 1.25 3.00
MA7 Carl Edwards .60 1.50
MA8 Jeff Gordon 1.25 3.00
MA9 David Gilliland 1.00 2.50
MA10 Denny Hamlin .75 2.00
MA11 Kevin Harvick .75 2.00
MA12 Dale Jarrett .60 1.50
MA13 Jimmie Johnson 1.00 2.50
MA14 Kasey Kahne .60 1.50
MA15 Matt Kenseth .60 1.50
MA16 Bobby Labonte .60 1.50
MA17 Mark Martin .60 1.50
MA18 Casey Mears .40 1.00
MA19 Paul Menard 2.00 5.00
MA20 Juan Pablo Montoya 2.00 5.00
MA21 Ryan Newman .50 1.25
MA22 David Ragan 1.25 3.00
MA23 Ricky Rudd .50 1.25
MA24 Reed Sorenson .40 1.00
MA25 Tony Stewart 1.00 2.50
MA26 Martin Truex Jr. .50 1.25
MA27 Brian Vickers .60 1.50

2007 Press Pass Stealth Maximum Access Autographs

STATED PRINT RUN 25 SER.#'d SETS
MA1 A.J. Allmendinger 25.00 60.00
MA2 Greg Biffle
MA3 Clint Bowyer 50.00 100.00
MA4 Jeff Burton
MA5 Kyle Busch
MA6 Dale Earnhardt Jr. 100.00 200.00
MA7 Carl Edwards 20.00 50.00
MA8 Jeff Gordon 100.00 200.00
MA9 David Gilliland 60.00 120.00
MA10 Denny Hamlin 75.00 150.00
MA11 Kevin Harvick 40.00 80.00
MA12 Dale Jarrett 40.00 80.00
MA13 Jimmie Johnson 60.00 120.00
MA14 Kasey Kahne 75.00 150.00
MA15 Matt Kenseth 50.00 100.00
MA16 Bobby Labonte 40.00 80.00
MA17 Mark Martin 60.00 120.00
MA18 Casey Mears
MA19 Paul Menard 25.00 60.00
MA20 Juan Pablo Montoya 20.00 50.00
MA21 Ryan Newman 40.00 80.00
MA22 David Ragan 25.00 60.00
MA23 Ricky Rudd 60.00 120.00
MA24 Reed Sorenson
MA25 Tony Stewart 50.00 100.00
MA26 Martin Truex Jr. 20.00 50.00
MA27 Brian Vickers 25.00 60.00

2008 Press Pass Stealth Chrome

COMPLETE SET (90) 15.00 40.00
WAX BOX HOBBY 75.00 125.00
1 Greg Biffle .30 .75
2 Dave Blaney .25 .60
3 Clint Bowyer .40 1.00
4 Jeff Burton .30 .75
5 Kurt Busch .30 .75
6 Scott Riggs .30 .75
7 Patrick Carpentier RC 3.00 8.00
8 Dale Earnhardt Jr. .75 2.00
9 Carl Edwards .40 1.00
10 Dario Franchitti RC 2.50 6.00
11A Jeff Gordon .75 2.00
11B Jeff Gordon blue 3.00 8.00
12 Denny Hamlin .50 1.25
13 Kevin Harvick .50 1.25
14 Sam Hornish Jr. .60 1.50
15 Dale Jarrett .40 1.00
16 Jimmie Johnson .60 1.50
17A Kasey Kahne .40 1.00
17B K.Kahne no KK logo 1.50 4.00
18 Matt Kenseth .40 1.00
19 Travis Kvapil .25 .60
20 Bobby Labonte .40 1.00
21 Mark Martin .40 1.00
22 Jeremy Mayfield .25 .60
23 Jamie McMurray .40 1.00
24 Casey Mears .25 .60
25 Paul Menard .25 .60
26 Juan Pablo Montoya .60 1.50
27 Ryan Newman .30 .75
28 Kyle Petty .30 .75
29 David Ragan .30 .75
30 Elliott Sadler .25 .60
31 Reed Sorenson .25 .60
32 Tony Stewart .60 1.50
33 Martin Truex Jr. .30 .75
34 Brian Vickers .25 .60
35 Michael Waltrip .40 1.00
36 J.J. Yeley .40 1.00
37 Clint Bowyer NNS .40 1.00
38 Bryan Clauson NNS RC 1.50 4.00
39 Carl Edwards NNS .40 1.00
40 Dario Franchitti NNS .60 1.50
41 Cale Gale NNS .25 .60

42 Kevin Harvick NNS .50 1.25
43 Brad Keselowski NNS RC 3.00 8.00
44 Tony Stewart NNS .60 1.50
45 Scott Wimmer NNS .30 .75
46 Martin Truex Jr.'s Rig C .12 .30
47 Mark Martin's Rig C .15 .40
48 Ryan Newman's Rig C .12 .30
49 Matt Kenseth's Rig C .15 .40
50 Tony Stewart's Rig C .25 .60
51 Kevin Harvick's Rig C .20 .50
52 Jeff Burton's Rig C .12 .30
53 Dale Earnhardt Jr.'s Rig C .30 .75
54 Carl Edwards' Rig C .15 .40
55 Mark Martin's Car GC .15 .40
56 Casey Mears's Car GC .10 .25
57 Denny Hamlin's Car GC .20 .50
58 Greg Biffle's Car GC .12 .30
59 Tony Stewart's Car GC .25 .60
60 Jeff Gordon's Car GC .30 .75
61 Jeff Burton's Car GC .12 .30
62 Juan Pablo Montoya's Car GC .25 .60
63A Jimmie Johnson's Car GC .25 .60
63B JJ's Car GC no chngr 2.50 6.00
64 Montoya/Fran/Sornsn .60 1.50
65 Almirl/Mart/Trx/Men/Smth .40 1.00
66 Kahne/Sadler/Carpent .75 2.00
67 JJ/Gordon/Jr./Mears .75 2.00
68 Hamlin/Stewrt/Ky.Bsch .60 1.50
69A Burton/Bowyer/Harvick .50 1.25
69B Burtn/Bowyr/Harvck VAR 2.00 5.00
70 Bif/McM/Edwrd/Kens/Ragn .40 1.00
71 Vickers/Allmendinger .40 1.00
72 Kvapil/Gilliland .25 .60
73 Greg Biffle DO .30 .75
74 Clint Bowyer DO .40 1.00
75 Kyle Busch DO .50 1.25
76 Carl Edwards DO .40 1.00
77 Dario Franchitti DO .60 1.50
78 Kevin Harvick DO .50 1.25
79 Matt Kenseth DO .40 1.00
80 David Ragan DO .30 .75
81A Tony Stewart DO .60 1.50
81B Tony Stewart DO 20s 2.50 6.00
82 Clint Bowyer PM .40 1.00
83A Dale Earnhardt Jr. PM .75 2.00
83B Dale Jr. PM one trophy 3.00 8.00
84 Jeff Gordon PM .75 2.00
85 Denny Hamlin PM .50 1.25
86 Kevin Harvick PM .50 1.25
87 Ryan Newman PM .30 .75
88 Tony Stewart PM .60 1.50
89 Martin Truex Jr. PM .30 .75
90 Jimmie Johnson PM .60 1.50

2008 Press Pass Stealth Chrome Exclusives

*EXCLUSIVES: 4X TO 10X BASE
STATED PRINT RUN 25 SERIAL #'d SETS

2008 Press Pass Stealth Chrome Exclusives Gold

*EXCLUSIVES GOLD: 3X TO 8X BASE
STATED PRINT RUN 99 SERIAL #'d SETS

2008 Press Pass Stealth

COMPLETE SET (89) 15.00 40.00
WAX BOX 50.00 75.00
1 Greg Biffle .25 .60
2 Dave Blaney .20 .50
3 Clint Bowyer .30 .75
4 Jeff Burton .25 .60
5 Kurt Busch .25 .60
6 Scott Riggs .25 .60
7 Patrick Carpentier RC 2.00 5.00
8 Dale Earnhardt Jr. .60 1.50
9 Carl Edwards .30 .75
10 Dario Franchitti RC 1.50 4.00
11 Jeff Gordon .60 1.50
12 Denny Hamlin .40 1.00
13 Kevin Harvick .40 1.00
14 Sam Hornish Jr. .50 1.25
15 Dale Jarrett .30 .75
16 Jimmie Johnson .50 1.25
17 Kasey Kahne .30 .75
18 Matt Kenseth .30 .75
19 Travis Kvapil .20 .50
20 Bobby Labonte .30 .75
21 Mark Martin .30 .75
22 Jeremy Mayfield .20 .50
23 Jamie McMurray .30 .75
24 Casey Mears .20 .50
25 Paul Menard .20 .50
26 Juan Pablo Montoya .50 1.25
27 Ryan Newman .25 .60
28 Kyle Petty .25 .60
29 David Ragan .25 .60
30 Elliott Sadler .20 .50
31 Reed Sorenson .20 .50
32 Tony Stewart .50 1.25
33 Martin Truex Jr. .25 .60
34 Brian Vickers .20 .50
35 Michael Waltrip .30 .75
36 J.J. Yeley .30 .75
37 Clint Bowyer NNS .30 .75
38 Bryan Clauson NNS RC 1.00 2.50
39 Carl Edwards NNS .30 .75
40 Dario Franchitti NNS .50 1.25
41 Cale Gale NNS .20 .50
42 Kevin Harvick NNS .40 1.00
43 Brad Keselowski NNS RC 2.00 5.00
44 Tony Stewart NNS .50 1.25
45 Scott Wimmer NNS .25 .60
46 Martin Truex Jr.'s Rig C .10 .25
47 Mark Martin's Rig C .12 .30
48 Ryan Newman's Rig C .10 .25
49 Matt Kenseth's Rig C .12 .30
50 Tony Stewart's Rig C .20 .50
51 Kevin Harvick's Rig C .15 .40
52 Jeff Burton's Rig C .10 .25
53 Dale Earnhardt Jr.'s Rig C .25 .60
54 Carl Edwards' Rig C .12 .30
55 Mark Martin's Rig C .12 .30
56 Casey Mears's Car GC .07 .20
57 Denny Hamlin's Car GC .15 .40
58 Greg Biffle's Car GC .10 .25
59 Tony Stewart's Car GC .20 .50
60 Jeff Gordon's Car GC .25 .60
61 Jeff Burton's Car GC .10 .25
62 Juan Pablo Montoya's Car GC .20 .50
63 Jimmie Johnson's Car GC .20 .50
64 Montoya/Franchitti/Sorenson .50 1.25
65 Almirola/Mart./Truex/Men./Smith .30 .75
66 Kahne/Sadler/Carpentier .60 1.50
67 JJ/Gordon/Dale Jr./Mears .60 1.50
68 Hamlin/Stewart/Ky.Busch .50 1.25
69 Burton/Bowyer/Harvick .40 1.00
70 Bif./McM./Edwards/Kens./Ragan .30 .75
71 Vickers/Allmendinger .30 .75
73 Greg Biffle DO .25 .60
74 Clint Bowyer DO .30 .75
75 Kyle Busch DO .40 1.00
76 Carl Edwards DO .30 .75
77 Dario Franchitti DO .50 1.25
78 Kevin Harvick DO .40 1.00
79 Matt Kenseth DO .30 .75
80 David Ragan DO .25 .60
81 Tony Stewart DO .50 1.25
82 Clint Bowyer PM .30 .75
83 Dale Earnhardt Jr. PM .60 1.50
84 Jeff Gordon PM .60 1.50
85 Denny Hamlin PM .40 1.00
86 Kevin Harvick PM .40 1.00
87 Ryan Newman PM .25 .60
88 Tony Stewart PM .50 1.25
89 Martin Truex Jr. PM .25 .60
90 Jimmie Johnson PM .50 1.25

2008 Press Pass Stealth Battle Armor Autographs

SERIAL #'d TO DRIVERS DOOR NUMBER
STATED PRINT RUN 8-48
BASDH Denny Hamlin/11
BASJG Jeff Gordon/24 175.00 350.00
BASJJ Jimmie Johnson/48 60.00 120.00
BASKH Kevin Harvick/29 50.00 100.00
BASKK Kasey Kahne/9
BASMK Matt Kenseth/17
BASMM Mark Martin/8
BASTS Tony Stewart/20

2008 Press Pass Stealth Battle Armor Drivers

STATED ODDS 1:40
STATED PRINT RUN 120 SERIAL #'d SETS
*TEAMS/115: .4X TO 1X DRIVERS/120
BAD1 Elliott Sadler 3.00 8.00
BAD2 Michael Waltrip 4.00 10.00
BAD3 Jeff Gordon 15.00 40.00
BAD4 Patrick Carpentier 4.00 10.00
BAD5 Carl Edwards 10.00 25.00
BAD6 Kasey Kahne 10.00 25.00
BAD7 Juan Pablo Montoya 6.00 15.00
BAD8 Ryan Newman 4.00 10.00
BAD9 Reed Sorenson 4.00 10.00
BAD10 Mark Martin 8.00 20.00
BAD11 Dario Franchitti 8.00 20.00
BAD12 Kurt Busch 4.00 10.00
BAD13 Martin Truex Jr. 4.00 10.00
BAD14 Matt Kenseth 8.00 20.00
BAD15 Jimmie Johnson 10.00 25.00
BAD16 Kyle Busch 10.00 25.00
BAD17 Kevin Harvick 8.00 20.00
BAD18 Denny Hamlin 6.00 15.00
BAD19 Dale Jarrett 6.00 15.00
BAD20 Tony Stewart 15.00 40.00
BAD21 Jeff Burton 4.00 10.00
BAD22 Casey Mears 3.00 8.00
BAD23 Dale Earnhardt Jr. 12.00 30.00

2008 Press Pass Stealth Mach 08

PROGRESSIVE ODDS 1:14-1:112
M8-1 Jeff Gordon 15.00 40.00
M8-2 Dale Earnhardt Jr. 12.00 30.00
M8-3 Tony Stewart 12.00 30.00
M8-4 Jimmie Johnson 10.00 25.00
M8-5 Mark Martin 4.00 10.00
M8-6 Martin Truex Jr. 2.50 6.00
M8-7 Kevin Harvick 5.00 12.00
M8-8 Juan Pablo Montoya 2.50 6.00
M8-9 Ryan Newman 2.50 6.00
M8-10 Jeff Burton 3.00 8.00
M8-11 Dario Franchitti 3.00 8.00
M8-12 Dale Jarrett 4.00 10.00

2008 Press Pass Stealth Maximum Access

COMPLETE SET (27) 10.00 25.00
STATED ODDS 1:2
MA1 A.J. Allmendinger .60 1.50
MA2 Greg Biffle .50 1.25
MA3 Dave Blaney .40 1.00
MA4 Clint Bowyer .60 1.50
MA5 Jeff Burton .50 1.25
MA6 Kurt Busch .50 1.25
MA7 Kyle Busch .75 2.00
MA8 Dale Earnhardt Jr. 1.25 3.00
MA9 Carl Edwards .60 1.50
MA10 Jeff Gordon 1.25 3.00
MA11 Denny Hamlin .75 2.00
MA12 Kevin Harvick .75 2.00
MA13 Dale Jarrett .60 1.50
MA14 Jimmie Johnson 1.00 2.50
MA15 Matt Kenseth .60 1.50
MA16 Bobby Labonte .60 1.50
MA17 Mark Martin .60 1.50
MA18 Jamie McMurray .60 1.50
MA19 Casey Mears .40 1.00
MA20 Juan Pablo Montoya 1.00 2.50
MA21 Ryan Newman .50 1.25
MA22 David Ragan .50 1.25
MA23 Reed Sorenson .40 1.00
MA24 Tony Stewart 1.00 2.50
MA25 Martin Truex Jr. .50 1.25
MA26 Brian Vickers .40 1.00
MA27 Michael Waltrip .60 1.50

2008 Press Pass Stealth Maximum Access Autographs

STATED PRINT RUN 25 SER.#'d SETS
MA1 A.J. Allmendinger 20.00 50.00
MA2 Greg Biffle 40.00 80.00
MA3 Dave Blaney 30.00 60.00
MA4 Clint Bowyer 50.00 100.00
MA5 Jeff Burton 30.00 60.00
MA6 Kurt Busch 20.00 50.00
MA7 Kyle Busch 150.00 250.00
MA8 Dale Earnhardt Jr. 250.00 400.00
MA9 Carl Edwards 100.00 200.00
MA10 Jeff Gordon 250.00 400.00
MA11 Denny Hamlin 50.00 100.00
MA12 Kevin Harvick 50.00 100.00
MA13 Dale Jarrett 60.00 120.00
MA14 Jimmie Johnson 75.00 150.00
MA15 Matt Kenseth 60.00 120.00
MA16 Bobby Labonte 60.00 120.00
MA17 Mark Martin 40.00 80.00
MA18 Jamie McMurray 30.00 60.00
MA19 Casey Mears 30.00 60.00
MA20 Juan Pablo Montoya 50.00 100.00
MA21 Ryan Newman 50.00 100.00
MA22 David Ragan 40.00 80.00
MA23 Reed Sorenson
MA24 Tony Stewart 30.00 80.00
MA25 Martin Truex Jr. 50.00 100.00
MA26 Brian Vickers 40.00 80.00
MA27 Michael Waltrip 40.00 80.00

2008 Press Pass Stealth Synthesis

COMPLETE SET (9) 10.00 25.00
STATED ODDS 1:10
S1 Jimmie Johnson .75 2.00
S2 Clint Bowyer .50 1.25
S3 Jeff Burton .40 1.00
S4 Tony Stewart .75 2.00
S5 Matt Kenseth .50 1.25
S6 Bobby Labonte .50 1.25
S7 Dale Earnhardt Jr. 1.00 2.50
S8 Michael Waltrip .50 1.25
S9 Jeff Gordon 1.00 2.50

2008 Press Pass Stealth Target

RANDOM INSERTS IN TARGET PACKS
TA7 Dale Earnhardt Jr 1.50 4.00
TA8 Jimmie Johnson 1.25 3.00
TA9 Kasey Kahne .75 2.00
TA10 Carl Edwards .75 2.00
TA11 Jeff Gordon 1.50 4.00
TA12 Martin Truex Jr .60 1.50

2008 Press Pass Stealth Wal-Mart

RANDOM INSERTS IN WAL-MART PACKS
WM7 Matt Kenseth .75 2.00
WM8 Denny Hamlin 1.00 2.50
WM9 Kevin Harvick 1.00 2.50
WM10 Tony Stewart 1.25 3.00
WM11 Dale Earnhardt Jr 1.50 4.00
WM12 Juan Pable Montoya 1.25 3.00

2009 Press Pass Stealth Chrome

COMPLETE SET (90) 15.00 40.00
WAX BOX (24) 60.00 100.00
1 A.J. Allmendinger .40 1.00
2 Aric Almirola .30 .75
3 Marcos Ambrose CRC .40 1.00
4 Greg Biffle .30 .75
5 Clint Bowyer .40 1.00
6 Jeff Burton .30 .75
7 Kurt Busch .30 .75
8 Kyle Busch .50 1.25
9A Dale Earnhardt Jr. .75 2.00
9B Dale Jr. no hat 2.50 6.00
9C Dale Jr. no hat lines 8.00 20.00
10 Carl Edwards .40 1.00
11A Jeff Gordon .75 2.00
11B J.Gordon no glasses 2.50 6.00
11C Gordon L2 blu bckgrnd 8.00 20.00
12 Robby Gordon .25 .60
13 Denny Hamlin .40 1.00
14 Kevin Harvick .50 1.25
15 Sam Hornish Jr. .30 .75
16 Jimmie Johnson .60 1.50
17 Kasey Kahne .40 1.00
18 Matt Kenseth .40 1.00
19 Brad Keselowski CRC 1.00 2.50
20 Joey Logano RC 2.50 6.00
21 Mark Martin .40 1.00
22 Jamie McMurray .40 1.00
23 Casey Mears .25 .60
24 Paul Menard .25 .60
25 Juan Pablo Montoya .50 1.25
26 David Ragan .30 .75
27 David Reutimann .30 .75
28 Scott Riggs .30 .75
29 Elliott Sadler .25 .60
30 Reed Sorenson .25 .60
31 Scott Speed RC 1.50 4.00
32A Tony Stewart .60 1.50
32B T.Stewart Off.Depot 2.00 5.00
33 David Stremme .25 .60
34 Martin Truex Jr. .30 .75
35 Brian Vickers .25 .60
36 Michael Waltrip .40 1.00
37 Brad Keselowski NNS .50 1.25
38 Brendan Gaughan NNS .25 .60
39 Justin Allgaier NNS RC 1.50 4.00
40 Scott Lagasse Jr. NNS RC .50 1.25
41 Marc Davis NNS RC .60 1.50
42 Steve Wallace NNS .25 .60
43 Jeff Burton NNS .40 1.00
44 Carl Edwards NNS .40 1.00
45 David Ragan NNS .30 .75
46 Kevin Harvick NNS .50 1.25
47 Joey Logano NNS .75 2.00
48 Greg Biffle NNS .30 .75
49 Tony Stewart's Rig C .25 .60
50 Kyle Busch's Rig C .20 .50
51 Jeff Gordon's Rig C .30 .75
52 Kevin Harvick's Rig C .20 .50
43 Jeff Burton NNS .30 .75
53 Dale Earnhardt Jr.'s Rig C .30 .75
54 Carl Edwards' Rig C .15 .40
55 Martin Truex Jr.'s Car GC .12 .30
56 Greg Biffle's Car GC .12 .30
57 Elliott Sadler's Car GC .10 .25
58A Joey Logano's Car GC .30 .75
58B J.Logano w/o tire 1.00 2.50
59 Jeff Gordon's Car GC .30 .75
60 Kevin Harvick's Car GC .20 .50
61 Jimmie Johnson's Car GC .25 .60
62 Brian Vickers' Car GC .10 .25
63 Dale Earnhardt Jr.'s Car GC .30 .75
64 Dale Earnhardt Jr. DO .75 2.00
65 David Ragan DO .30 .75
66 Greg Biffle DO .30 .75
67 Kyle Busch DO .50 1.25
68 Joey Logano DO .75 2.00
69 Clint Bowyer DO .40 1.00
70 Kevin Harvick DO .50 1.25
71A Carl Edwards DO .40 1.00
71B C.Edwards Scotts left 1.25 3.00
72 Michael Waltrip DO .40 1.00
73 Jeff Gordon S .75 2.00
74A Jimmie Johnson S .60 1.50
74B J.Johnson S w/hat 2.00 5.00
74C Johnson L2 w/hat Mrtns 6.00 15.00
75 Kurt Busch S .30 .75
76 Carl Edwards S .40 1.00
77 Greg Biffle S .30 .75
78 Jimmie Johnson S .60 1.50
79 Dale Earnhardt Jr. S .75 2.00
80 Jeff Gordon S .75 2.00
81 Kyle Busch S .50 1.25
82 Robby Gordon S .25 .60
83 Kyle Busch S .50 1.25
84 Marcos Ambrose S .40 1.00
85 Casey Mears SM .25 .60
86 Mark Martin SM .40 1.00
87 A.J. Allmendinger SM .40 1.00
88 Reed Sorenson SM .25 .60
89 Tony Stewart SM .60 1.50
90 Jimmie Johnson CL .60 1.50

2009 Press Pass Stealth Chrome Brushed Metal

*BRUSHED METAL: 5X TO 12X BASE
*BRUSHED METAL RCs: 2.5X TO 6X BASE
STATED PRINT RUN 25 SER.#'d SETS
3 Marcos Ambrose 25.00 60.00

2009 Press Pass Stealth Chrome Gold

*GOLD/99: 2.5X TO 6X BASE
*GOLD ROOKIE/99: 1.2X TO 3X BASE RC
STATED PRINT RUN 99 SER.#'d SETS
3 Marcos Ambrose 15.00 40.00

2009 Press Pass Stealth

COMPLETE SET (90) 12.00 30.00
WAX BOX (24) 50.00 75.00
1 A.J. Allmendinger .30 .75
2 Aric Almirola .25 .60
3 Marcos Ambrose CRC .30 .75
4 Greg Biffle .25 .60
5 Clint Bowyer .30 .75
6 Jeff Burton .25 .60
7 Kurt Busch .25 .60
8 Kyle Busch .40 1.00
9A Dale Earnhardt Jr. .60 1.50
9B Dale Jr. no hat 2.50 6.00
10 Carl Edwards .30 .75
11A Jeff Gordon .60 1.50
11B J.Gordon no hat 2.50 6.00
12 Robby Gordon .20 .50
13 Denny Hamlin .30 .75
14 Kevin Harvick .40 1.00
15 Sam Hornish Jr. .25 .60
16 Jimmie Johnson .50 1.25
17 Kasey Kahne .30 .75
18 Matt Kenseth .30 .75
19 Brad Keselowski CRC .75 2.00
20 Joey Logano RC 2.00 5.00
21 Mark Martin .30 .75
22 Jamie McMurray .30 .75
23 Casey Mears .20 .50
24 Paul Menard .20 .50
25 Juan Pablo Montoya .40 1.00
26 David Ragan .25 .60
27 David Reutimann .25 .60
28 Scott Riggs .25 .60
29 Elliott Sadler .20 .50
30 Reed Sorenson .20 .50
31 Scott Speed RC 1.25 3.00
32A Tony Stewart .50 1.25
32B T.Stewart Off.Depot 2.00 5.00
33 David Stremme .20 .50
34 Martin Truex Jr. .25 .60
35 Brian Vickers .20 .50
36 Michael Waltrip .30 .75
37 Brad Keselowski NNS .40 1.00
38 Brendan Gaughan NNS .20 .50
39 Justin Allgaier NNS RC 1.25 3.00
40 Scott Lagasse Jr. NNS RC .40 1.00
41 Marc Davis NNS RC .50 1.25
42 Steve Wallace NNS .20 .50
43 Jeff Burton NNS .25 .60
44 Carl Edwards NNS .30 .75
45 David Ragan NNS .25 .60
46 Kevin Harvick NNS .40 1.00
47 Joey Logano NNS .60 1.50
48 Greg Biffle NNS .25 .60
49 Tony Stewart's Rig C .20 .50
50 Kyle Busch's Rig C .15 .40
51 Jeff Gordon's Rig C .25 .60
52 Kevin Harvick's Rig C .15 .40
53 Dale Earnhardt Jr.'s Rig C .25 .60
54 Carl Edwards' Rig C .12 .30
55 Martin Truex Jr.'s Car GC .10 .25
56 Greg Biffle's Car GC .10 .25
57 Elliott Sadler's Car GC .07 .20
58A Joey Logano's Car GC .25 .60
58B J.Logano w/o tire 1.00 2.50
59 Jeff Gordon's Car GC .25 .60
60 Kevin Harvick's Car GC .15 .40
61 Jimmie Johnson's Car GC .20 .50
62 Brian Vickers' Car GC .07 .20
63 Dale Earnhardt Jr.'s Car GC .25 .60
64 Dale Earnhardt Jr. DO .60 1.50
65 David Ragan DO .25 .60
66 Greg Biffle DO .25 .60
67 Kyle Busch DO .40 1.00
68 Joey Logano DO .60 1.50
69 Clint Bowyer DO .30 .75
70 Kevin Harvick DO .40 1.00
71A Carl Edwards DO .30 .75
71B C.Edwards Scotts left 1.25 3.00
72 Michael Waltrip DO .30 .75
73 Jeff Gordon S .60 1.50
74A Jimmie Johnson S .50 1.25
74B J.Johnson S w/hat 2.00 5.00
75 Kurt Busch S .25 .60
76 Carl Edwards S .30 .75
77 Greg Biffle S .25 .60
78 Jimmie Johnson S .50 1.25
79 Dale Earnhardt Jr. S .60 1.50
80 Jeff Gordon S .60 1.50
81 Kyle Busch S .40 1.00
82 Robby Gordon S .20 .50
83 Kyle Busch S .40 1.00
84 Marcos Ambrose S .30 .75
85 Casey Mears SM .20 .50
86 Mark Martin SM .30 .75
87 A.J. Allmendinger SM .30 .75
88 Reed Sorenson SM .20 .50
89 Tony Stewart SM .50 1.25
90 Jimmie Johnson CL .50 1.25

2009 Press Pass Stealth Battle Armor

STATED PRINT RUN 3-425
BABL1 Bobby Labonte Red/9
BABL2 Bobby Labonte White/85 6.00 15.00
BABV1 Brian Vickers Blue/210 2.50 6.00
BABV2 Brian Vickers Silver/25 6.00 15.00
BACE1 Carl Edwards Black/185 4.00 10.00
BACE2 Carl Edwards White/115 5.00 12.00
BACE3 C.Edwards Green-Orange/50 6.00 15.00
BADE1A Dale Jr. AMP Blue/3
BADE1B Dale Jr. AMP Red/25 20.00 60.00
BADE1C Dale Jr. AMP White/299 8.00 20.00
BADE2A Dale Jr. NG Blue/20 20.00 60.00
BADE2B Dale Jr. NG White/35 15.00 40.00
BADH1 Denny Hamlin Black/420 4.00 10.00
BADH2 Denny Hamlin Blue/30 8.00 20.00
BADR David Ragan Brown/320 3.00 8.00
BAGB1 Greg Biffle Red/125 4.00 10.00
BAGB2 Greg Biffle White/425 3.00 8.00
BAGB3 Greg Biffle Yellow/50 5.00 12.00
BAJB1 Jeff Burton Black/90 4.00 10.00
BAJB2 Jeff Burton Yellow/25 8.00 20.00
BAJG1 Jeff Gordon Blue/135 10.00 25.00
BAJG2 Jeff Gordon Orange/135 10.00 25.00
BAJG3 Jeff Gordon White/40 15.00 40.00
BAJJ1 Jimmie Johnson Black/135 8.00 20.00
BAJJ2 Jimmie Johnson Blue/199 6.00 15.00
BAJJ3 Jimmie Johnson White/25 15.00 40.00
BAJL1 Joey Logano Black/240 4.00 10.00
BAJL2 Joey Logano Orange/70 10.00 25.00
BAJL3 Joey Logano White/4
BAJM1 Jamie McMurray Blue/29 4.00 10.00
BAJM2 Jamie McMurray Yellow/75 6.00 15.00
BAKB1 Kyle Busch Brown/50 8.00 20.00
BAKB2 Kyle Busch Yellow/250 5.00 12.00
BAKH1 Kevin Harvick Red/99 6.00 15.00
BAKH2 Kevin Harvick Yellow/65 8.00 20.00
BAKK Kasey Kahne Red/210 4.00 10.00
BAMK1 Matt Kenseth Black/150 5.00 12.00
BAMK2 Matt Kenseth Yellow/220 4.00 10.00
BAMT1 Martin Truex Jr. Black/25 8.00 20.00
BAMT2 Martin Truex Jr. Red/20 8.00 20.00
BAMT3 Martin Truex Jr. White/10
BASP Scott Speed Silver/265 5.00 12.00
BATS1 Tony Stewart Black/210 6.00 15.00
BATS2 Tony Stewart Red/170 6.00 15.00

2009 Press Pass Stealth Battle Armor Autographs

SERIAL #'d TO DRIVER'S DOOR NO.
STATED PRINT RUN 8-48
BASDH Denny Hamlin/11
BASGB Greg Biffle/16
BASJJ Jimmie Johnson/48 60.00 120.00
BASKB Kyle Busch/18
BASMK Matt Kenseth/17
BASDE1 Dale Earnhardt Jr. AMP/8
BASDE2 Dale Earnhardt Jr. NG/8

2009 Press Pass Stealth Battle Armor Multi-Color

BABL Bobby Labonte/130 8.00 20.00
BABV Brian Vickers/170 5.00 12.00
BACE Carl Edwards/160 8.00 20.00
BADE1 Dale Jr. AMP/185 12.00 30.00
BADE2 Dale Jr. NG/110 15.00 40.00
BADH Denny Hamlin/160 8.00 20.00
BADR David Ragan/160 6.00 15.00
BAGB Greg Biffle/160 5.00 12.00
BAJB Jeff Burton/160 6.00 15.00
BAJG Jeff Gordon/170 15.00 40.00
BAJJ Jimmie Johnson/150 12.00 30.00
BAJL Joey Logano/130 8.00 20.00
BAJM Jamie McMurray/160 8.00 20.00
BAKB Kyle Busch/160 10.00 25.00
BAKH Kevin Harvick/150 10.00 25.00
BAKK Kasey Kahne/150 8.00 20.00
BAMK Matt Kenseth/165 8.00 20.00
BAMT Martin Truex Jr./170 6.00 15.00
BASP Scott Speed/160 5.00 12.00
BATS Tony Stewart/160 12.00 30.00

2009 Press Pass Stealth Confidential Classified Bronze

COMPLETE SET (25) 10.00 25.00
STATED ODDS 1:2
*GOLD/25: 2.5X TO 6X BRONZE
*SILVER: .8X TO 2X BRONZE
PC1 Dale Earnhardt Jr. .75 2.00
PC2 Denny Hamlin .40 1.00
PC3 Casey Mears .25 .60
PC4 Carl Edwards .40 1.00
PC5 Scott Speed .50 1.25
PC6 Mark Martin .40 1.00
PC7 Kyle Busch .50 1.25
PC8 Jamie McMurray .40 1.00
PC9 Jeff Burton .30 .75
PC10 Ryan Newman .30 .75
PC11 Jimmie Johnson .60 1.50
PC12 Matt Kenseth .40 1.00
PC13 Joey Logano .75 2.00
PC14 Kevin Harvick .50 1.25
PC15 Paul Menard .25 .60
PC16 Jeff Gordon .75 2.00
PC17 Sam Hornish Jr. .30 .75
PC18 Martin Truex Jr. .30 .75
PC19 Tony Stewart .60 1.50
PC20 Clint Bowyer .40 1.00
PC21 Greg Biffle .30 .75
PC22 Brian Vickers .25 .60
PC23 David Stremme .25 .60
PC24 David Ragan .30 .75
PC25 Kurt Busch .30 .75

2009 Press Pass Stealth Mach 09

COMPLETE SET (12) 20.00 50.00
STATED ODDS 1:6
M1 Tony Stewart 1.00 2.50
M2 Kevin Harvick .75 2.00
M3 Kasey Kahne .60 1.50
M4 Joey Logano 1.25 3.00
M5 Jimmie Johnson 1.00 2.50
M6 Carl Edwards .60 1.50
M7 Clint Bowyer .60 1.50
M8 Jeff Gordon 1.25 3.00
M9 Martin Truex Jr. .50 1.25
M10 Matt Kenseth .60 1.50
M11 Dale Earnhardt Jr. 1.25 3.00
M12 David Ragan .50 1.25

2010 Press Pass Stealth

COMPLETE SET (90) 15.00 40.00
WAX BOX HOBBY 70.00 100.00
WAX BOX RETAIL 50.00 80.00
1 A.J. Allmendinger .30 .75
2 Marcos Ambrose .30 .75
3 Greg Biffle .25 .60
4 Clint Bowyer .30 .75
5 Jeff Burton .25 .60
6 Kurt Busch .25 .60
7 Kyle Busch .40 1.00
8 Dale Earnhardt Jr. .60 1.50
9 Carl Edwards .30 .75
10 Jeff Gordon .60 1.50
11 Robby Gordon .20 .50
12 Denny Hamlin .30 .75

13 Kevin Harvick .40 1.00
14 Sam Hornish Jr. .25 .60
15 Jimmie Johnson .50 1.25
16 Kasey Kahne .30 .75
17 Matt Kenseth .30 .75
18 Brad Keselowski .40 1.00
19 Travis Kvapil .20 .50
20 Bobby Labonte .30 .75
21 Joey Logano .30 .75
22 Mark Martin .30 .75
23 Jamie McMurray .30 .75
24 Paul Menard .20 .50
25 Juan Pablo Montoya .30 .75
26 Joe Nemechek .20 .50
27 Ryan Newman .25 .60
28 David Ragan .25 .60
29 David Reutimann .25 .60
30 Elliott Sadler .20 .50
31 Regan Smith .25 .60
32 Scott Speed .30 .75
33 Tony Stewart .50 1.25
34 Martin Truex Jr. .25 .60
35 Brian Vickers .20 .50
36 Michael Waltrip .30 .75
37 Justin Allgaier NNS .25 .60
38 Colin Braun NNS .25 .60
39 James Buescher NNS RC .25 .60
40 Brendan Gaughan NNS .20 .50
41 Danica Patrick NNS RC 3.00 8.00
42 Brian Scott NNS .25 .60
43 Ricky Stenhouse Jr. NNS .30 .75
44 Steve Wallace NNS .25 .60
45 Scott Lagasse Jr. NNS .20 .50
46 Josh Wise NNS .30 .75
47 Trevor Bayne NNS RC 2.00 5.00
48 John Wes Townley NNS RC .20 .50
49 Dale Earnhardt Jr. NNS .60 1.50
50 Matt DiBenedetto NNS RC .50 1.25
51 Jeff Gordon's Car MV .25 .60
52 Dale Earnhardt Jr.'s Car MV .25 .60
53 Kevin Harvick's Car MV .15 .40
54 Danica Patrick's Car MV 2.00 5.00
55 Jimmie Johnson's Car MV .20 .50
56 Mark Martin's Car MV .12 .30
57 Kyle Busch's Car MV .15 .40
58 Kasey Kahne's Car MV .12 .30
59 Kurt Busch's Car MV .10 .25
60 Carl Edwards DO .30 .75
61 Kyle Busch DO .40 1.00
62 Brad Keselowski DO .40 1.00
63 Kevin Harvick DO .40 1.00
64 Joey Logano DO .30 .75
65 Denny Hamlin DO .30 .75
66 Tony Stewart DO .50 1.25
67 Dale Earnhardt Jr. DO .60 1.50
68 Brian Vickers DO .20 .50
69 Kasey Kahne DO .30 .75
70 Mark Martin CP .30 .75
71 Kyle Busch CP .40 1.00
72 Jeff Gordon CP .60 1.50
73 Jeff Burton CP .25 .60
74 Carl Edwards CP .30 .75
75 Kevin Harvick CP .40 1.00
76 Bobby Labonte CP .30 .75
77 Dale Earnhardt Jr. CP .60 1.50
78 Ryan Newman CP .25 .60
79 Joey Logano CP .30 .75
80 Denny Hamlin CP .30 .75
81 Clint Bowyer CP .30 .75
82 David Reutimann CP .25 .60
83 Marcos Ambrose UR .30 .75
84 Joey Logano UR .30 .75
85 A.J. Allmendinger UR .30 .75
86 Brad Keselowski UR .40 1.00
87 Martin Truex Jr. UR .25 .60
88 Justin Allgaier UR .25 .60
89 Brian Scott UR .25 .60
90 Jamie McMurray UR .30 .75

2010 Press Pass Stealth Black and White

COMPLETE SET (90) 40.00 80.00
*SINGLES: .6X TO 1.5X BASIC CARDS
STATED ODDS 1 PER PACK

2010 Press Pass Stealth Purple

*SINGLES: 4X TO 10X BASIC CARDS
STATED PRINT RUN 25 SER.#'d SETS
41 Danica Patrick NNS 40.00 100.00
54 Danica Patrick's Car MV 40.00 80.00

2010 Press Pass Stealth Battle Armor Silver

STATED PRINT RUN 180-275
*FAST PASS/25: 1X TO 2.5X SILVER/180-275
*HOLOFOIL/25: .8X TO 2X SILVER/180-275
BABK Brad Keselowski/275 5.00 12.00
BABV Brian Vickers 2.50 6.00
BACE Carl Edwards 4.00 10.00
BADH Denny Hamlin 4.00 10.00
BADP Danica Patrick 15.00 40.00
BAGB Greg Biffle 3.00 8.00
BAJB Jeff Burton 3.00 8.00
BAJG Jeff Gordon 10.00 25.00
BAJJ Jimmie Johnson 6.00 15.00
BAJL Joey Logano 4.00 10.00
BAJM Jamie McMurray 4.00 10.00
BAKH Kevin Harvick/275 5.00 12.00
BAKK Kasey Kahne/275 4.00 10.00
BAMA Marcos Ambrose 4.00 10.00
BAMM Mark Martin/180 4.00 10.00
BAMT Martin Truex Jr. 3.00 8.00
BAMW Michael Waltrip 4.00 10.00
BARN Ryan Newman 3.00 8.00
BADE1 Dale Earnhardt Jr. 8.00 20.00
BADE2 Dale Earnhardt Jr. 10.00 25.00
BADR1 David Ragan/275 3.00 8.00
BADR2 David Reutimann 3.00 8.00
BAJPM Juan Pablo Montoya 4.00 10.00
BAKB1 Kyle Busch 5.00 12.00
BATS1 Tony Stewart 6.00 15.00
BATS2 Tony Stewart 6.00 15.00

2010 Press Pass Stealth Earnhardt Retail

COMPLETE SET (3) 8.00 20.00
STATED ODDS 1 PER BLASTER BOX
DE1 Dale Earnhardt Jr. 3.00 8.00
DE2 Dale Earnhardt 4.00 10.00
DE3 Dale Jr./Dale Sr. 4.00 10.00

2010 Press Pass Stealth Mach 10

COMPLETE SET (9) 12.00 30.00
STATED ODDS 1:6
MT1 Tony Stewart .75 2.00
MT2 Juan Pablo Montoya .50 1.25
MT3 Carl Edwards .50 1.25
MT4 Ryan Newman .40 1.00
MT5 Matt Kenseth .50 1.25
MT6 AJ Allmendinger .50 1.25
MT7 Kevin Harvick .60 1.50
MT8 Kasey Kahne .50 1.25
MT9 Danica Patrick 4.00 10.00

2010 Press Pass Stealth Power Players

COMPLETE SET (9) 15.00 40.00
STATED ODDS 1:6
PP1 Jimmie Johnson 1.00 2.50
PP2 Mark Martin .60 1.50
PP3 Kurt Busch .50 1.25
PP4 Denny Hamlin .60 1.50
PP5 Jeff Gordon 1.25 3.00
PP6 Kyle Busch .75 2.00
PP7 Danica Patrick 5.00 12.00
PP8 Jeff Burton .50 1.25
PP9 Clint Bowyer .60 1.50

2010 Press Pass Stealth Weekend Warriors Silver

STATED PRINT RUN 99-199
*HOLO/25: .8X TO 2X BASIC INSERTS
WWDE Dale Earnhardt Jr. AMP/99 30.00 60.00
WWJL Joey Logano/199 15.00 40.00
WWKB Kyle Busch/199 10.00 25.00
WWKH Kevin Harvick/199 15.00 40.00
WWTS Tony Stewart/199 20.00 50.00

2010 Press Pass Stealth National Convention

VIP1 Dale Earnhardt Jr. 1.50 4.00
VIP2 Jeff Gordon 1.50 4.00
VIP3 Tony Stewart 1.25 3.00
VIP4 Jimmie Johnson 1.25 3.00
VIP5 Kevin Harvick 1.00 2.50
VIP6 Danica Patrick 6.00 15.00

2011 Press Pass Stealth

COMPLETE SET (100) 12.00 30.00
WAX BOX HOBBY (24) 75.00 100.00
WAX BOX RETAIL (24) 50.00 75.00
1 Dale Earnhardt Jr. .60 1.50
2 Dale Earnhardt Jr.'s Car .25 .60
3 Dale Earnhardt Jr.'s Crew .25 .60
4 Jeff Gordon .60 1.50
5 Jeff Gordon's Car .25 .60
6 Jeff Gordon's Crew .25 .60
7 Jimmie Johnson .50 1.25
8 Jimmie Johnson's Car .20 .50
9 Jimmie Johnson's Crew .20 .50
10 Tony Stewart .50 1.25
11 Tony Stewart's Car .20 .50
12 Tony Stewart's Crew .20 .50
13 Mark Martin .30 .75
14 Mark Martin's Car .12 .30
15 Mark Martin's Crew .12 .30
16 Kevin Harvick .40 1.00
17 Kevin Harvick's Car .15 .40
18 Kevin Harvick's Crew .15 .40
19 Kasey Kahne .30 .75
20 Kasey Kahne's Car .12 .30
21 Kasey Kahne's Crew .12 .30
22 Kurt Busch .25 .60
23 Kurt Busch's Car .10 .25
24 Kurt Busch's Crew .10 .25
25 Carl Edwards .30 .75
26 Carl Edwards's Car .12 .30
27 Carl Edwards's Crew .12 .30
28 Kyle Busch .40 1.00
29 Kyle Busch's Car .15 .40
30 Kyle Busch's Crew .15 .40
31 Jeff Burton .25 .60
32 Jeff Burton's Car .10 .25
33 Jeff Burton's Crew .10 .25
34 Ryan Newman .25 .60
35 Ryan Newman's Car .10 .25
36 Ryan Newman's Crew .10 .25
37 A.J. Allmendinger .30 .75
38 Marcos Ambrose .30 .75
39 Trevor Bayne CRC .60 1.50
40 Greg Biffle .25 .60
41 Clint Bowyer .30 .75
42 Bill Elliott .50 1.25
43 Denny Hamlin .30 .75
44 Matt Kenseth .30 .75
45 Brad Keselowski .40 1.00
46 Bobby Labonte .30 .75
47 Joey Logano .30 .75
48 Jamie McMurray .30 .75
49 Paul Menard .20 .50
50 Juan Pablo Montoya .30 .75
51 David Ragan .25 .60
52 David Reutimann .25 .60
53 Martin Truex Jr. .25 .60
54 Brian Vickers .20 .50
55 Justin Allgaier NNS .25 .60
56 Aric Almirola NNS .25 .60
57 Trevor Bayne NNS .60 1.50
58 James Buescher NNS .20 .50
59 Jason Leffler NNS .25 .60
60 Danica Patrick NNS 1.25 3.00
61 Elliott Sadler NNS .20 .50
62 Brian Scott NNS .20 .50
63 Jennifer Jo Cobb NNS 2.00 5.00
64 Reed Sorenson NNS .20 .50
65 Ricky Stenhouse NNS .30 .75
66 Kenny Wallace NNS .20 .50
67 Mike Wallace NNS .30 .75
68 Steve Wallace NNS .25 .60
69 Josh Wise NNS .20 .50
70 D.Earnhardt Jr.'s Pit Box CC .25 .60
71 T.Bayne's Pit Box CC .25 .60
72 B.Vickers' Pit Box CC .07 .20
73 M.Martin's Pit Box CC .12 .30
74 K.Kahne's Pit Box CC .12 .30
75 C.Bowyer's Pit Box CC .12 .30
76 J.Gordon's Pit Box CC .25 .60
77 D.Hamlin's Pit Box CC .12 .30
78 Paul Menard C .20 .50
79 Martin Truex Jr. C .20 .50
80 Carl Edwards C .30 .75
81 Greg Biffle C .25 .60
82 Jimmie Johnson C .50 1.25
83 Jeff Gordon C .60 1.50
84 Joey Logano C .30 .75
85 Marcos Ambrose C .30 .75
86 Tony Stewart C .50 1.25
87 Dale Earnhardt Jr. C .60 1.50
88 D.Hamlin/Ky.Busch .40 1.00
89 T.Stewart/R.Newman .50 1.25
90 K.Busch/B.Keselowski .40 1.00
91 C.Edwards/M.Kenseth .30 .75
92 K.Kahne/B.Vickers .30 .75
93 Dale Earnhardt Jr.'s Crew .25 .60
94 Tony Stewart's Crew .20 .50
95 Juan Pablo Montoya's Crew .12 .30
96 A.J. Allmendinger's Crew .12 .30
97 Jamie McMurray's Crew .12 .30
98 Kyle Busch's Crew .15 .40
99 Jimmie Johnson's Crew .20 .50
100 Jeff Gordon's Crew .25 .60
0 POW Flag 10.00 25.00

2011 Press Pass Stealth Black and White

*B&W: 4X TO 10X BASE
STATED PRINT RUN 25 SER.#'d SETS
63 Jennifer Jo Cobb NNS 12.00 30.00

2011 Press Pass Stealth Holofoil

*HOLOFOIL/99: 2X TO 5X BASE
STATED PRINT RUN 99 SER.#'d SETS
63 Jennifer Jo Cobb NNS 8.00 20.00

2011 Press Pass Stealth Purple

*PURPLE: 4X TO 10X BASE
STATED PRINT RUN 25 SER.#'d SETS
63 Jennifer Jo Cobb NNS 12.00 30.00

2011 Press Pass Stealth Afterburner

STATED PRINT RUN 99 SER.#'d SETS
*GOLD/25: .5X TO 1.2X BASIC INSERTS
ABCE Carl Edwards 6.00 15.00
ABDE Dale Earnhardt Jr. 15.00 40.00
ABDP Danica Patrick 20.00 50.00
ABJG Jeff Gordon 12.00 30.00
ABJJ Jimmie Johnson 10.00 25.00
ABJL Joey Logano 6.00 15.00
ABKH Kevin Harvick 8.00 20.00
ABKK Kasey Kahne 6.00 15.00
ABKYB Kyle Busch 8.00 20.00
ABMK Matt Kenseth 6.00 15.00
ABMM Mark Martin 6.00 15.00
ABTS Tony Stewart 12.00 30.00

2011 Press Pass Stealth Flyover

COMPLETE SET (6) 10.00 25.00
STATED ODDS 1:24
FO1 T-38 Talons 2.50 6.00
FO2 F-15 Eagles 2.50 6.00
FO3 F-16 Air Force Thunderbirds 2.50 6.00
FO4 B-52 Stratofortress 2.50 6.00
FO5 A-10 Warthog 2.50 6.00
FO6 KC-135 Stratotanker 2.50 6.00

2011 Press Pass Stealth In Flight Report

COMPLETE SET (9) 12.00 30.00
STATED ODDS 1:6
IF1 Dale Earnhardt Jr. 1.50 4.00
IF2 Jimmie Johnson 1.25 3.00
IF3 Mark Martin .75 2.00
IF4 Kevin Harvick 1.00 2.50
IF5 Carl Edwards .75 2.00
IF6 Kyle Busch 1.00 2.50
IF7 Ryan Newman .60 1.50
IF8 Brad Keselowski 1.00 2.50
IF9 Danica Patrick 3.00 8.00

2011 Press Pass Stealth Metal of Honor Silver Star

STATED PRINT RUN 99 SER.#'d SETS
*HONOR/50: .5X TO 1.2X SILVER STAR
*PURPLE/25: .6X TO 1.5X SILVER STAR
BAAJ A.J. Allmendinger 5.00 12.00
BABK Brad Keselowski 6.00 15.00
BABV Brian Vickers 3.00 8.00
BACB Clint Bowyer 5.00 12.00
BACE Carl Edwards 5.00 12.00
BADE Dale Earnhardt Jr. 10.00 25.00
BADH Denny Hamlin 5.00 12.00
BADP Danica Patrick 20.00 50.00
BADR David Ragan 4.00 10.00
BAGB Greg Biffle 4.00 10.00
BAJB Jeff Burton 4.00 10.00
BAJG Jeff Gordon 10.00 25.00
BAJJ Jimmie Johnson 8.00 20.00
BAJL Joey Logano 5.00 12.00
BAJM Jamie McMurray 5.00 12.00
BAKH Kevin Harvick 6.00 15.00
BAKK Kasey Kahne 5.00 12.00
BAMK Matt Kenseth 5.00 12.00
BAMM Mark Martin 5.00 12.00
BAMT Martin Truex Jr. 4.00 10.00
BAPM Paul Menard 3.00 8.00
BARN Ryan Newman 4.00 10.00
BATB Trevor Bayne 10.00 25.00
BATS Tony Stewart 8.00 20.00
BADR2 David Reutimann 4.00 10.00
BAJPM Juan Pablo Montoya 5.00 12.00
BAKUB Kurt Busch 4.00 10.00
BAKYB Kyle Busch 6.00 15.00

2011 Press Pass Stealth Supersonic

COMPLETE SET (9) 15.00 40.00
STATED ODDS 1:12
SS1 Jeff Gordon 2.00 5.00
SS2 Tony Stewart 1.50 4.00
SS3 Kasey Kahne 1.00 2.50
SS4 Kurt Busch .75 2.00
SS5 Jeff Burton .75 2.00
SS6 Marcos Ambrose 1.00 2.50
SS7 Dale Earnhardt Jr. 2.00 5.00
SS8 Joey Logano 1.00 2.50
SS9 Jamie McMurray 1.00 2.50

2011 Press Pass Stealth U.S. Military

COMPLETE SET (5) 20.00 50.00
STATED ODDS 1:48
USAF Air Force 5.00 12.00
USAR Army 5.00 12.00
USCG Coast Guard 5.00 12.00
USMC Marines 5.00 12.00
USNA Navy 5.00 12.00

1999 Press Pass Tony Stewart Fan Club

NNO Tony Stewart 15.00 30.00

2002 Press Pass Tony Stewart Fan Club

NNO Tony Stewart 15.00 30.00

2003 Press Pass Top Prospects Memorabilia

This 24-card set featured 6 of NASCAR's young prospects. Each driver had 4 versions: a swatch of glove numbered to 100, a swatch of shoe numbered to 200, a swatch of sheet metal numbered to 250 and a swatch of tire numbered to 400. These cards were available in: 2003 Press Pass Optima at a rate of 1 in 130, 2003 Press Pass Stealth at a rate of 1 in 124 packs and 2003 Press Pass Trackside at a rate of 1 in 168.

BVG Brian Vickers Glove/100 20.00 50.00
BVM Brian Vickers Metal/250 20.00 50.00
BVS Brian Vickers Shoe/200 20.00 50.00
BVT Brian Vickers Tire/400 10.00 25.00
CBG Chad Blount Glove/100 6.00 15.00
CBM Chad Blount Metal/250 6.00 15.00
CBS Chad Blount Shoe/200 6.00 15.00
CBT Chad Blount Tire/400 5.00 12.00
SHG Shane Hmiel Glove/100 12.50 30.00
SHM Shane Hmiel Metal/250 12.50 30.00
SHS Shane Hmiel Shoe/200 12.50 30.00
SHT Shane Hmiel Tire/400 10.00 25.00
SMG Stead.Marlin Glove/100 8.00 20.00
SMM Stead.Marlin Metal/250 8.00 20.00
SMS Stead.Marlin Shoe/200 8.00 20.00
SMT Stead.Marlin Tire/400 6.00 15.00
SRG Scott Riggs Glove/100 8.00 20.00
SRM Scott Riggs Metal/250 8.00 20.00
SRS Scott Riggs Shoe/200 6.00 15.00
SRT Scott Riggs Tire/400 6.00 15.00
SWG Scott Wimmer Glove/100 8.00 20.00
SWM Scott Wimmer Metal/250 8.00 20.00
SWS Scott Wimmer Shoe/200 8.00 20.00
SWT Scott Wimmer Tire/400 6.00 15.00

2004 Press Pass Top Prospects Memorabilia

This 22-card set featured race-used swatches of the top young drivers in NASCAR. There were sheet metal and tire cards available in 2004 Press Pass Trackside at a rate of 1 in 84 packs, and they were serial numbered to 200 (sheet metal) and 350 (tire). There were glove and shoe swatches available in 2004 Press Pass Optima at a rate of 1 in 84 packs, and they were serial numbered to 100 (glove) and 150 (shoe).

GLOVE/SHOE STATED ODDS 1:98 '04 OPTIMA
GLOVE PRINT RUN 100 SERIAL #'d SETS
SHEET METAL PRINT RUN 200 SERIAL #'d SETS
SHOE PRINT RUN 150 SERIAL #'d SETS
TIRE PRINT RUN 350 SERIAL #'d SETS
CBT Clint Bowyer Tire 5.00 12.00
CBSM Clint Bowyer Metal 6.00 15.00
KBG Kyle Busch Glove 25.00 60.00
KBT Kyle Busch Tire 20.00 50.00
KBSM Kyle Busch Metal 30.00 80.00
THG Tracy Hines Glove 10.00 25.00
THS Tracy Hines Shoe 8.00 20.00
KKG Kasey Kahne Glove 25.00 60.00
KKS Kasey Kahne Shoe 20.00 50.00
KKT Kasey Kahne Tire 12.00 30.00
KKSM Kasey Kahne Metal 10.00 25.00
PMG Paul Menard Glove 6.00 15.00
PMS Paul Menard Shoe 6.00 15.00
PMT Paul Menard Tire 5.00 12.00
PMSM Paul Menard Metal 6.00 15.00
BPSM Billy Parker Metal 12.50 30.00
MTT Martin Truex Jr. Tire 15.00 40.00
MTSM Martin Truex Jr. Metal
PWT Paul Wolfe Tire 6.00 15.00
PWSM Paul Wolfe Metal 8.00 20.00
JYT J.J. Yeley Tire 10.00 25.00
JYSM J.J. Yeley Metal 12.00 30.00

2005 Press Pass Top Prospects Memorabilia

CEG Carl Edwards Glove 25.00 60.00
CES Carl Edwards Shoe 10.00 25.00
CESM Carl Edwards Metal 40.00 80.00
CET Carl Edwards Tire 12.50 30.00
DHS Denny Hamlin Shoe 15.00 40.00
DHSM Denny Hamlin Metal 8.00 20.00
DHT Denny Hamlin Tire 12.00 30.00
DSG David Stremme Glove 15.00 40.00
DST David Stremme Tire 10.00 25.00
JLG Justin Labonte Glove 10.00 25.00
JLSM Justin Labonte Metal 10.00 25.00
JLT Justin Labonte Tire 6.00 15.00
JWG Jon Wood Glove 8.00 20.00
JWS Jon Wood Shoe 6.00 15.00
JWSM Jon Wood Metal 8.00 20.00
MTG Martin Truex Jr. Glove 15.00 40.00
MTS Martin Truex Jr. Shoe 12.00 30.00
MTSM Martin Truex Jr. Metal 20.00 50.00
MTT Martin Truex Jr. Tire 8.00 20.00
RSG Reed Sorenson Glove 12.00 30.00
RSSM Reed Sorenson Metal 15.00 40.00
RST Reed Sorenson Tire 6.00 15.00

2006 Press Pass Top Prospects Gloves

This 6-card set featured swatches of race-used gloves from some of NASCAR's hottest prospects. Each card was serial numbered to 199 and carried a "G" suffix for its card number.

BLG Burney Lamar 8.00 20.00
DOG Danny O'Quinn 10.00 25.00
ECG Erin Crocker 12.50 30.00
RSG Regan Smith 8.00 20.00
SWG Steve Wallace 10.00 25.00
TKG Todd Kluever 12.50 30.00

2006 Press Pass Top Prospects Sheet Metal

This 6-card set featured swatches of race-used sheet metal from some of NASCAR's hottest prospects. Each card was serial numbered to 199 and carried an "M" suffix for its card number.

BLM Burney Lamar 10.00 25.00
DOM Danny O'Quinn 6.00 15.00
ECM Erin Crocker 15.00 40.00
RSM Regan Smith 10.00 25.00
SWM Steve Wallace 5.00 12.00
TKM Todd Kluever 5.00 12.00

2006 Press Pass Top Prospects Shoes

This 6-card set featured swatches of race-used shoes from some of NASCAR's hottest prospects. Each card was serial numbered to 199 and carried an "S" suffix for its card number.

BLS Burney Lamar 8.00 20.00
DOS Danny O'Quinn 10.00 25.00
ECS Erin Crocker 12.50 30.00
RSS Regan Smith 8.00 20.00
SWS Steve Wallace 8.00 20.00
TKS Todd Kluever 15.00 40.00

2006 Press Pass Top Prospects Tires Autographs

This 4-card set featured swatches of race-used tires from some of NASCAR's hottest prospects along with signatures. Each card was serial numbered to 25 and carried a "T" suffix for its card number.

STATED PRINT RUNS 25 SER.#'d SETS
ECT Erin Crocker 40.00 80.00
MMT Mark McFarland 30.00 60.00
RST Regan Smith
SWT Steve Wallace
TKT Todd Kluever 50.00 100.00

2006 Press Pass Top Prospects Tires Gold

BLT Burney Lamar 10.00 25.00
DOT Danny O'Quinn 5.00 12.00
ECT Erin Crocker 8.00 20.00
MMT Mark McFarland 8.00 20.00
RST Regan Smith/199
SWT Steve Wallace/199 12.50 30.00
TKT Todd Kluever 5.00 12.00

2006 Press Pass Top Prospects Tires Silver

This 5-card set featured swatches of race-used tires from some of NASCAR's hottest prospects. Most cards were serial numbered to 500 and carried a "T" suffix for its card number.

BLT Burney Lamar 8.00 20.00
DOT Danny O'Quinn 4.00 10.00
ECT Erin Crocker 6.00 15.00
MMT Mark McFarland 6.00 15.00
TKT Todd Kluever 10.00 25.00

2007 Press Pass Top Prospects Gloves

STATED PRINT RUN 200 SERIAL #'d SETS
AAG Aric Almirola 8.00 20.00
MAG Marcos Ambrose 10.00 25.00
SHG Shane Huffman 10.00 25.00
DREG David Reutimann 10.00 25.00

2007 Press Pass Top Prospects Sheet Metal

STATED PRINT RUN 350 SERIAL #'d SETS
AASM Aric Almirola 6.00 15.00
MASM Marcos Ambrose 5.00 12.00
SHSM Shane Huffman 5.00 12.00
DRASM David Ragan 5.00 12.00
DRESM David Reutimann 5.00 12.00

2007 Press Pass Top Prospects Sheet Metal-Tire

STATED PRINT RUN 75 SERIAL #'d SETS
AAST Aric Almirola 10.00 25.00
MAST Marcos Ambrose 30.00 80.00
SHST Shane Huffman 20.00 40.00
DRAST David Ragan 25.00 50.00
DREST David Reutimann 25.00 50.00

2007 Press Pass Top Prospects Shoes

STATED PRINT RUN 200 SERIAL #'d SETS
AAS Aric Almirola 8.00 20.00
MAS Marcos Ambrose 6.00 15.00
SHS Shane Huffman 5.00 12.00
DRAS David Ragan 5.00 12.00
DRES David Reutimann 5.00 12.00

2007 Press Pass Top Prospects Tire Autographs

STATED PRINT RUN 25 SER.#'d SETS
AAA Aric Almirola 40.00 80.00
MAA Marcos Ambrose 30.00 80.00
SHA Shane Huffman 40.00 80.00
SLA Stephen Leicht 40.00 80.00
DRAA David Ragan 50.00 100.00
DREA David Reutimann 50.00 100.00
SHOA Sam Hornish Jr. 20.00 50.00

2007 Press Pass Top Prospects Tires Silver

STATED PRINT RUN 250 SERIAL #'d SETS
*GOLD/99: .5X TO 1.2X SILVER
AAT Aric Almirola 8.00 20.00
DGT David Gilliland 8.00 20.00
MAT Marcos Ambrose 8.00 12.00
SHT Shane Huffman 8.00 20.00
SLT Stephen Leicht 8.00 20.00
DRaT David Ragan 8.00 20.00
DReT David Reutimann 8.00 20.00
SHoT Sam Hornish Jr. 8.00 20.00

2008 Press Pass Top Prospects Gloves

STATED PRINT RUN 175 SERIAL #'d SETS
BCG Bryan Clauson 8.00 20.00
BKG Brad Keselowski 10.00 25.00
CBG Colin Braun 8.00 20.00
CMG Chase Miller 6.00 15.00
LCG Landon Cassill 8.00 20.00

2008 Press Pass Top Prospects Metal-Tire

STATED PRINT RUN 75 SERIAL #'d SETS
BCST Bryan Clauson 10.00 25.00
BKST Brad Keselowski 12.00 30.00
CBST Colin Braun 12.00 30.00

CMST Chase Miller 10.00 25.00
LCST Landon Cassill 12.00 30.00

2008 Press Pass Top Prospects Sheet Metal

STATED PRINT RUN 175 SERIAL #'d SETS
BCSM Bryan Clauson 10.00 25.00
BKSM Brad Keselowski 20.00 50.00
CBSM Colin Braun 10.00 25.00
CMSM Chase Miller 8.00 20.00
LCSM Landon Cassill 10.00 25.00

2008 Press Pass Top Prospects Shoes

STATED PRINT RUN 175 SERIAL #'d SETS
BKS Brad Keselowski 10.00 25.00
CBS Colin Braun 8.00 20.00
CMS Chase Miller 6.00 15.00
LCS Landon Cassill 8.00 20.00

2008 Press Pass Top Prospects Tires

STATED PRINT RUN 330 SERIAL #'d SETS
*GOLD/100: .5X TO 1.2X BASIC
BCT Bryan Clauson 5.00 12.00
BKT Brad Keselowski 8.00 20.00
CBT Colin Braun 6.00 15.00
CMT Chase Miller 3.00 8.00
KBT Kelly Bires 5.00 12.00
LCT Landon Cassill 6.00 15.00

2008 Press Pass Top Prospects Tires Autographs

STATED PRINT RUN 25 SER.#'d SETS
BCAT Bryan Clauson 30.00 60.00
BKAT Brad Keselowski 50.00 100.00
CBAT Colin Braun 40.00 80.00
CMAT Chase Miller 30.00 60.00
KBAT Kelly Bires 25.00 50.00
LCAT Landon Cassill 40.00 80.00

2006 Press Pass Top 25 Drivers & Rides

This 50-card set was released at retail locations and carried an SRP of $9.99. It featured the top 25 Nextel Cup drivers. Each driver had a car card produced along with a driver card. This set was packaged in black & yellow blister packs with Top 25 Drivers & Rides printed on it. This set contained a first year card of Brent Sherman.

COMPLETE SET (50) 10.00 20.00
COMP.FACT SET (50) 10.00 20.00
COMP.DRIVERS SET (25) 6.00 12.00
COMP.CARS SET (25) 4.00 8.00
C1 Martin Truex Jr.'s Car .15 .40
C2 Kurt Busch's Car .07 .20
C3 Kyle Busch's Car .12 .30
C4 Mark Martin's Car .10 .25
C5 Clint Bowyer's Car .20 .50
C6 Dale Earnhardt Jr.'s Car .20 .50
C7 Kasey Kahne's Car .12 .30
C8 Denny Hamlin's Car .40 1.00
C9 Ryan Newman's Car .07 .20
C10 Greg Biffle's Car .07 .20
C11 Matt Kenseth's Car .10 .25
C12 J.J. Yeley's Car .15 .40
C13 Tony Stewart's Car .15 .40
C14 Jeff Gordon's Car .20 .50
C15 Kevin Harvick's Car .12 .30
C16 Jeff Burton's Car .07 .20
C17 Elliott Sadler's Car .05 .15
C18 David Stremme's Car .12 .30
C19 Reed Sorenson's Car .15 .40
C20 Casey Mears' Car .10 .25
C21 Bobby Labonte's Car .10 .25
C22 Jimmie Johnson's Car .15 .40
C23 Brent Sherman's Car .12 .30
C24 Dale Jarrett's Car .10 .25
C25 Carl Edwards' Car .10 .25
D1 Martin Truex Jr. .40 1.00
D2 Kurt Busch .20 .50
D3 Kyle Busch .30 .75
D4 Mark Martin .25 .60
D5 Clint Bowyer .50 1.25
D6 Dale Earnhardt Jr. .50 1.25
D7 Kasey Kahne .30 .75
D8 Denny Hamlin 1.00 2.50
D9 Ryan Newman .20 .50
D10 Greg Biffle .20 .50
D11 Matt Kenseth .25 .60
D12 J.J. Yeley .40 1.00
D13 Tony Stewart .40 1.00
D14 Jeff Gordon .50 1.25
D15 Kevin Harvick .30 .75
D16 Jeff Burton .20 .50
D17 Elliott Sadler .15 .40
D18 David Stremme .30 .75
D19 Reed Sorenson .40 1.00
D20 Casey Mears .15 .40
D21 Bobby Labonte .25 .60
D22 Jimmie Johnson .40 1.00
D23 Brent Sherman .30 .75
D24 Dale Jarrett .25 .60
D25 Carl Edwards .25 .60

2002 Press Pass Total Memorabilia Power Pick

Issued in packs at stated odds of 1:200 across all 2002 Press Pass brands, these nine cards were redemptions that were to be used for a chance to win complete runs of all 2002 Press Pass memorabilia cards for the featured driver. The collector would have to mail this card to Press Pass for a chance to be a winner. Five winners per driver were awarded. The expiration date for the contest was January 31, 2003.

TM0 Dale Earnhardt 5.00 12.00
TM1 Dale Earnhardt Jr. 4.00 10.00
TM2 Jeff Gordon 3.00 8.00
TM3 Kevin Harvick 3.00 6.00
TM4 Dale Jarrett 2.00 5.00
TM5 Bobby Labonte 2.00 5.00
TM6 Terry Labonte 1.50 4.00
TM7 Mark Martin 2.50 6.00
TM8 Tony Stewart 2.50 6.00
TM9 Rusty Wallace 2.00 5.00

2003 Press Pass Total Memorabilia Power Pick

Inserted at a stated rate of one in 200, these 10 cards are contest cards which allowed collectors to enter a drawing to win all the memorabilia cards of a driver which were issued in 2002. Out of all the entries, only five winners will be selected for each driver.

TM1 Jeff Gordon 8.00 20.00
TM2 Ryan Newman 6.00 15.00
TM3 Kevin Harvick 5.00 12.00
TM4 Jimmie Johnson 6.00 15.00
TM5 Rusty Wallace 6.00 15.00
TM6 Mark Martin 6.00 15.00
TM7 Matt Kenseth 6.00 15.00
TM8 Bobby Labonte 5.00 12.00
TM9 Tony Stewart 6.00 15.00
TM10 Dale Earnhardt Jr. 8.00 20.00

2004 Press Pass Total Memorabilia Power Pick

This 10-card set was randomly inserted in packs across all brands of Press Pass hobby and retail products in 2004. Each card was issued as an entry card for a chance to win an entire run of each of the specified driver's memorabilia cards issued in 2004 by Press Pass. There were 5 winners drawn for each of the 10 drivers. The entry deadline was January 31, 2005.

TM1 Jeff Gordon 12.50 25.00
TM2 Ryan Newman 4.00 10.00
TM3 Kevin Harvick 4.00 10.00
TM4 Jimmie Johnson 5.00 12.00
TM5 Rusty Wallace 3.00 8.00
TM6 Mark Martin 4.00 10.00
TM7 Matt Kenseth 4.00 10.00
TM8 Bobby Labonte 4.00 10.00
TM9 Tony Stewart 4.00 10.00
TM10 Dale Earnhardt Jr. 10.00 20.00

2005 Press Pass Total Memorabilia Power Pick

TM1 Jeff Gordon 6.00 15.00
TM2 Ryan Newman 5.00 12.00
TM3 Kevin Harvick 5.00 12.00
TM4 Jimmie Johnson 5.00 12.00
TM5 Rusty Wallace 5.00 12.00
TM6 Mark Martin 5.00 12.00
TM7 Matt Kenseth 5.00 12.00
TM8 Bobby Labonte 5.00 12.00
TM9 Tony Stewart 5.00 12.00
TM10 Dale Earnhardt Jr. 6.00 15.00
TM11 Brian Vickers 5.00 12.00
TM12 Kurt Busch 5.00 12.00

2000 Press Pass Trackside

Released as a 72-card set, Trackside Racing featured top Winston Cup drivers on cards 1-27, top race winners on cards 28-36, Busch Series drivers on cards 37-45, crew chiefs on cards 46-54, Wood Brother's milestones on cards 55-63, and track scenes on cards 64-72. Boxes contained 24 packs with six cards per pack and carried a suggested retail price of 2.99.

COMPLETE SET (72) 10.00 25.00
1 Steve Park .25 .60
2 Dale Earnhardt 1.25 3.00
3 Bobby Hamilton .12 .30
4 Terry Labonte .25 .60
5 Michael Waltrip .15 .40
6 Dale Earnhardt Jr. CRC 1.00 2.50
7 Jeff Gordon .75 2.00
8 Jerry Nadeau .15 .40
9 Mike Skinner .12 .30
10 Joe Nemechek .12 .30
11 Sterling Marlin .25 .60
12 Kenny Irwin .15 .40
13 Bobby Labonte .50 1.25
14 Tony Stewart .75 2.00
15 Ward Burton .15 .40
16 Johnny Benson Jr. .15 .40
17 John Andretti .12 .30
18 Dave Blaney .12 .30
19 Rusty Wallace .60 1.50
20 Mark Martin .60 1.50
21 Jeremy Mayfield .12 .30
22 Matt Kenseth CRC .60 1.50
23 Chad Little .15 .40
24 Ricky Rudd .25 .60
25 Darrell Waltrip .15 .40
26 Dale Jarrett .50 1.25
27 Jeff Burton .25 .60
28 Jeff Burton's Car .12 .30
29 Dale Earnhardt Jr.'s Car .40 1.00
30 Jeff Gordon's Car .30 .75
31 Rusty Wallace's Car .25 .60
32 Mark Martin's Car .25 .60
33 Bobby Labonte's Car .15 .40
34 Dale Jarrett's Car .15 .40
35 Tony Stewart's Car .30 .75
36 Dale Earnhardt's Car .50 1.25
37 Jeff Green BGN .12 .30
38 Elton Sawyer BGN .12 .30
39 Casey Atwood BGN .25 .60
40 Todd Bodine BGN .12 .30
41 Ricky Hendrick BGN RC 1.25 3.00
42 Justin Labonte BGN .12 .30
43 Hank Parker Jr. BGN RC .25 .60
44 Kenny Irwin BGN .15 .40
45 Mark Green BGN .12 .30
46 Robin Pemberton .07 .20
47 Peter Sospenso .07 .20
48 Jimmy Makar .07 .20
49 Greg Zipadelli .07 .20
50 Tommy Baldwin .07 .20
51 Larry McReynolds .07 .20
52 Jimmy Elledge .07 .20
53 Ryan Pemberton .07 .20
54 Todd Parrott .07 .20
55 Glen Wood WBM .07 .20
56 Cale Yarborough WBM .12 .30
57 A.J. Foyt WBM .15 .40
58 David Pearson WBM .15 .40
59 David Pearson WBM .15 .40
60 Buddy Baker WBM .12 .30
61 Dale Jarrett WBM .25 .60
62 Elliott Sadler WBM .15 .40
63 Wood Brothers WBM .07 .20
64 Grand Stands .07 .20
65 Infield .07 .20
66 Rigs .07 .20
67 Garage .07 .20
68 Pit Row .07 .20
69 Around the Track .07 .20
70 Pre-Race Activities .07 .20
71 Flags .07 .20
72 Checklist .07 .20
P1 Mark Martin Promo .75 2.00
NNO Jeff Burton Power Pick 2.50 6.00
NNO Chad Little Power Pick 2.00 5.00
NNO Mark Martin Power Pick 3.00 8.00
NNO Scott Pruett Power Pick 2.00 5.00

2000 Press Pass Trackside Die Cuts

COMPLETE SET (45) 20.00 50.00
*DIE CUTS: .8X TO 2X BASE CARDS

2000 Press Pass Trackside Golden

COMPLETE SET (72) 500.00 1000.00
*GOLDEN: 15X TO 30X BASE CARDS

2000 Press Pass Trackside Dialed In

Randomly inserted in packs at the rate of one in eight, this 12-card set features top NASCAR drivers on a holofoil die-cut card in the shape of the gauges in a NASCAR race car.

COMPLETE SET (12) 20.00 50.00
DI1 Dale Jarrett .60 1.50
DI2 Bobby Labonte .60 1.50
DI3 Mark Martin .60 1.50
DI4 Jeff Gordon 1.25 3.00
DI5 Tony Stewart 1.00 2.50
DI6 Jeff Burton .50 1.25
DI7 Matt Kenseth 2.00 5.00
DI8 Rusty Wallace .60 1.50
DI9 Dale Earnhardt 4.00 10.00
DI10 Terry Labonte .60 1.50
DI11 Ricky Rudd .50 1.25
DI12 Dale Earnhardt Jr. 1.50 4.00

2000 Press Pass Trackside Generation.now

Randomly inserted in packs at the rate of one in 18, this six card set features top young NASCAR drivers on an all holofoil card. Card backs carry a "GN" prefix.

COMPLETE SET (6) 12.50 30.00
GN1 Matt Kenseth 2.50 6.00
GN2 Dale Earnhardt Jr. 2.00 5.00
GN3 Casey Atwood .75 2.00
GN4 Elliott Sadler .50 1.25
GN5 Tony Stewart 1.25 3.00
GN6 Jeff Gordon 1.50 4.00

2000 Press Pass Trackside Panorama

Randomly inserted in packs, the last 9 cards of this set are short-printed. Cards P1-P27 are inserted at the rate of one in one, and cards P28-P36 are inserted at the rate of one in 12. These cards are smaller than the base set, measuring 2" X 3 1/2", and contain wide angle action photography.

COMPLETE SET (36) 25.00 50.00
P1 Steve Park .60 1.50
P2 John Andretti .40 1.00
P3 Bobby Hamilton .40 1.00
P4 Terry Labonte .60 1.50
P5 Michael Waltrip .60 1.50
P6 Brett Bodine .40 1.00
P7 Jeremy Mayfield .40 1.00
P8 Johnny Benson Jr. .60 1.50
P9 Kevin Lepage .40 1.00
P10 Elliott Sadler .40 1.00
P11 Ward Burton .50 1.25
P12 Jerry Nadeau .50 1.25
P13 Jimmy Spencer .50 1.25
P14 Ricky Rudd .50 1.25
P15 Mike Skinner .40 1.00
P16 Scott Pruett .40 1.00
P17 Joe Nemechek .40 1.00
P18 Robert Pressley .40 1.00
P19 Sterling Marlin .60 1.50
P20 Kenny Irwin 1.00 2.50
P21 Casey Atwood .60 1.50
P22 Kenny Wallace .40 1.00
P23 Geoffrey Bodine .40 1.00
P24 Darrell Waltrip 1.00 2.50
P25 Wally Dallenbach .40 1.00
P26 Dave Blaney .40 1.00
P27 Chad Little CL .40 1.00
P28 Dale Earnhardt 4.00 10.00
P29 Jeff Burton .50 1.25
P30 Rusty Wallace .60 1.50
P31 Jeff Gordon 1.25 3.00
P32 Dale Jarrett .60 1.50
P33 Matt Kenseth 2.00 5.00
P34 Bobby Labonte .60 1.50
P35 Mark Martin .60 1.50
P36 Tony Stewart 1.00 2.50

2000 Press Pass Trackside Pit Stoppers

Randomly inserted in packs at the rate of one in 240, this 13-card set features swatches of race-used pit-stop signs. Each card was serial numbered of 200-sets produced.

COMPLETE SET (13) 500.00 800.00
PS1 Ward Burton 12.50 30.00
PS2 Rusty Wallace 15.00 40.00
PS3 Dale Earnhardt 40.00 100.00
PS4 Bobby Labonte 12.50 30.00
PS5 Terry Labonte 12.50 30.00
PS6 Mark Martin 12.00 30.00
PS7 Tony Stewart 20.00 50.00
PS8 Elliott Sadler 10.00 25.00
PS9 Dave Blaney 10.00 25.00
PS10 Jeremy Mayfield 10.00 25.00
PS11 Matt Kenseth 20.00 50.00
PS12 Jeff Burton 10.00 25.00
PS13 Dale Earnhardt Jr. 30.00 80.00

2000 Press Pass Trackside Runnin N' Gunnin

Randomly inserted in packs at the rate of one in six, this 9-card set features top NASCAR racers on a holofoil card. Each card features the driver on one half and his car on the other.

COMPLETE SET (9) 10.00 25.00
RG1 Tony Stewart .75 2.00
RG2 Dale Earnhardt Jr. 1.25 3.00
RG3 Rusty Wallace .50 1.25
RG4 Mark Martin .50 1.25
RG5 Terry Labonte .50 1.25
RG6 Jeff Gordon 1.00 2.50
RG7 Jeff Burton .40 1.00
RG8 Dale Jarrett .50 1.25
RG9 Bobby Labonte .50 1.25

2000 Press Pass Trackside Too Tough To Tame

Randomly inserted in packs at the rate of one in 24, this 9-card set showcases nine top NASCAR drivers. Cards are all holofoil and picture both the driver and his car.

COMPLETE SET (9) 25.00 60.00
TT1 Dale Jarrett 1.25 3.00
TT2 Mark Martin 1.25 3.00
TT3 Bobby Labonte 1.25 3.00
TT4 Tony Stewart 2.00 5.00
TT5 Jeff Gordon 2.50 6.00
TT6 Dale Earnhardt 8.00 20.00
TT7 Rusty Wallace 1.25 3.00
TT8 Terry Labonte 1.25 3.00
TT9 Dale Earnhardt Jr. 3.00 8.00

2001 Press Pass Trackside

This is the second year that Press Pass has issued a set using the Trackside brand name. The base set consists of 63 cards and there are also two subsets:Teammates (cards numbered 64-81) and Charity Spotlight (cards numbered 82-89).

COMPLETE SET (90) 12.50 30.00
WAX BOX HOBBY 30.00 60.00
WAX BOX RETAIL 30.00 60.00
1 Dale Earnhardt Jr. 1.00 2.50
2 Jeff Gordon .75 2.00
3 Dale Earnhardt 1.25 3.00
4 Bobby Hamilton .08 .25
5 Kevin Harvick CRC .60 1.50
6 Terry Labonte .30 .75
7 Jerry Nadeau .20 .50
8 Joe Nemechek .08 .25
9 Steve Park .20 .50
10 Mike Skinner .08 .25
11 Michael Waltrip .20 .50
12 Ron Hornaday .08 .25
13 Bobby Labonte .50 1.25
14 Ken Schrader .08 .25
15 Tony Stewart .75 2.00
16 Todd Bodine .08 .25
17 Jeff Burton .20 .50
18 Kurt Busch CRC .30 .75
19 Ricky Craven .08 .25
20 Andy Houston .08 .25
21 Dale Jarrett .50 1.25
22 Matt Kenseth .60 1.50
23 Mark Martin .60 1.50
24 Jeremy Mayfield .08 .25
25 Robert Pressley .08 .25
26 Ricky Rudd .30 .75
27 Elliott Sadler .20 .50
28 Jimmy Spencer .08 .25
29 Rusty Wallace .60 1.50
30 John Andretti .08 .25
31 Casey Atwood .08 .25
32 Dave Blaney .08 .25
33 Ward Burton .20 .50
34 Stacy Compton .08 .25
35 Buckshot Jones .08 .25
36 Jason Leffler .08 .25
37 Sterling Marlin .30 .75
38 Kyle Petty .20 .50
39 Steve Park's Car .20 .50
40 Rusty Wallace's Car .20 .50
41 Terry Labonte's Car .20 .50
42 Mark Martin's Car .20 .50
43 Dale Earnhardt Jr.'s Car .60 1.50
44 Michael Waltrip's Car .08 .25
45 Matt Kenseth's Car .20 .50
46 Bobby Labonte's Car .20 .50
47 Tony Stewart's Car .30 .75
48 Jeff Gordon's Car .30 .75
49 Dale Jarrett's Car .20 .50
50 Jeff Burton's Car .08 .25
51 Jeff Green .08 .25
52 Elton Sawyer .08 .25
53 Kevin Harvick .60 1.50
54 Hank Parker Jr. .20 .50
55 Mark Green .08 .25
56 Chad Little .08 .25
57 Greg Biffle .20 .50
58 David Green .08 .25
59 Jason Keller .08 .25
60 Randy LaJoie .08 .25
61 Mike McLaughlin .08 .25
62 Jeff Purvis .08 .25
63 Tim Fedewa .08 .25
64 Kevin Harvick TM .60 1.50
65 Mike Skinner TM .08 .25
66 Bobby Labonte TM .50 1.25
67 Tony Stewart TM .75 2.00
68 Ricky Rudd TM .30 .75
69 Dale Jarrett TM .50 1.25
70 Rusty Wallace TM .60 1.50
71 Jeremy Mayfield TM .08 .25
72 Joe Nemechek TM .08 .25
73 Bobby Hamilton TM .08 .25
74 Sterling Marlin TM .30 .75
75 Jason Leffler TM .08 .25
76 Kyle Petty TM .20 .50
77 Buckshot Jones TM .08 .25
78 Andy Houston TM .08 .25
79 Ricky Craven TM .08 .25
80 Terry Labonte TM .30 .75
81 Jerry Nadeau TM .20 .50
82 Kyle Petty CS .20 .50
83 Ricky Craven CS .08 .25
84 Ward Burton CS .20 .50
85 Jeff Gordon CS .75 2.00
86 Dale Jarrett CS .50 1.25
87 Joe Nemechek CS .08 .25
88 Tony Stewart CS .75 2.00
89 Rusty Wallace CS .60 1.50
90 Checklist .02 .10

2001 Press Pass Trackside Die Cuts

COMPLETE SET (90) 30.00 80.00
*DIE CUTS: .8X TO 2X BASE CARDS

2001 Press Pass Trackside Golden

COMPLETE SET (63) 750.00 1500.00
*GOLDEN: 10X TO 25X BASE CARDS

2001 Press Pass Trackside Dialed In

Randomly inserted into packs at one in 8, this 12-card insert features illuminating dial settings enhanced by a special UV coating. Card backs carry a "D" prefix.

COMPLETE SET (12) 12.50 30.00
D1 Steve Park .75 2.00
D2 Rusty Wallace 2.50 6.00
D3 Dale Earnhardt 5.00 12.00
D4 Jeff Gordon 3.00 8.00
D5 Terry Labonte 1.25 3.00
D6 Mark Martin 2.50 6.00
D7 Bobby Labonte 2.00 5.00
D8 Dale Earnhardt Jr. 4.00 10.00
D9 Sterling Marlin 1.25 3.00
D10 Jeff Burton .75 2.00
D11 Dale Jarrett 2.00 5.00
D12 Michael Waltrip .75 2.00

2001 Press Pass Trackside Mirror Image

Randomly inserted into packs at one in 18, this 9-card insert features driver photos with special cracked-ice etching. Card backs carry a "MI" prefix.

COMPLETE SET (9) 15.00 40.00
MI1 Dale Jarrett 2.00 5.00
MI2 Rusty Wallace 2.50 6.00
MI3 Dale Earnhardt 5.00 12.00
MI4 Tony Stewart 3.00 8.00
MI5 Jeff Gordon 3.00 8.00
MI6 Mark Martin 2.50 6.00
MI7 Ricky Rudd 1.25 3.00
MI8 Dale Earnhardt Jr. 4.00 10.00
MI9 Terry Labonte 1.25 3.00

2001 Press Pass Trackside Pit Stoppers Drivers

Randomly inserted into hobby packs at a rate of one in 480, this 12-card insert features pieces of actual pit stop signs. Card backs carry a "PSD" prefix. This version pictures the driver.

*CARS: .25X TO .6X DRIVERS
PSD1 Dale Earnhardt Jr./100 40.00 100.00
PSD2 Tony Stewart/100 25.00 60.00
PSD3 Dale Earnhardt/10
PSD4 Ward Burton 8.00 20.00
PSD5 Rusty Wallace/30 40.00 100.00
PSD6 Terry Labonte 20.00 50.00
PSD7 Bobby Labonte/65 15.00 40.00
PSD8 Dave Blaney 8.00 20.00
PSD9 Matt Kenseth/100 12.00 30.00
PSD10 Steve Park/100 8.00 20.00
PSD11 Michael Waltrip/75 12.00 30.00
PSD12 Joe Nemechek 10.00 25.00

2001 Press Pass Trackside Runnin N' Gunnin

Randomly inserted into packs at one in 6, this 9-card insert features drivers that do plenty of "running and gunning" on the track. Card backs carry a "RG" prefix.

COMPLETE SET (9) 12.50 30.00
RG1 Ricky Rudd .75 2.00
RG2 Dale Earnhardt Jr. 2.50 6.00
RG3 Rusty Wallace 1.50 4.00
RG4 Mark Martin 1.50 4.00
RG5 Terry Labonte .75 2.00
RG6 Jeff Gordon 2.00 5.00
RG7 Tony Stewart 2.00 5.00
RG8 Kevin Harvick 1.50 4.00
RG9 Bobby Labonte 1.25 3.00

2002 Press Pass Trackside

This 90-card set was released in June, 2002. This set was issued in six card packs which came 24 packs to a box and 20 boxes to a case. The pack SRP was $2.99.

COMPLETE SET (90) 12.50 30.00
WAX BOX HOBBY 30.00 60.00
1 Dale Earnhardt Jr. 1.25 3.00
2 Jeff Gordon 1.00 2.50
3 Robby Gordon .10 .30
4 Jeff Green .10 .30
5 Bobby Hamilton .10 .30
6 Kevin Harvick .75 2.00
7 Jimmie Johnson CRC .75 2.00
8 Terry Labonte .40 1.00
9 Jerry Nadeau .25 .60
10 Steve Park .25 .60
11 Mike Skinner .10 .30
12 Michael Waltrip .25 .60
13 Bobby Labonte .60 1.50
14 Ken Schrader .10 .30
15 Tony Stewart .75 2.00
16 Dave Blaney .10 .30
17 Brett Bodine .10 .30
18 Jeff Burton .25 .60
19 Kurt Busch .40 1.00
20 Ricky Craven .10 .30
21 Dale Jarrett .60 1.50
22 Matt Kenseth .75 2.00
23 Mark Martin .75 2.00
24 Ryan Newman CRC .75 2.00
25 Ricky Rudd .40 1.00
26 Elliott Sadler .25 .60
27 Rusty Wallace .60 1.50
28 John Andretti .10 .30
29 Shawna Robinson .25 .60
30 Ward Burton .25 .60
31 Buckshot Jones .10 .30
32 Sterling Marlin .40 1.00
33 Jeremy Mayfield .10 .30
34 Kyle Petty .25 .60
35 Jimmy Spencer .10 .30
36 Hut Stricklin .10 .30
37 Ricky Hendrick NBS .50 1.25
38 Randy LaJoie NBS .10 .30
39 Mike McLaughlin NBS .10 .30
40 Johnny Sauter NBS RC .25 .60
41 Hank Parker Jr. NBS .10 .30
42 Scott Riggs NBS RC .75 2.00
43 Kerry Earnhardt NBS .25 .60
44 Jack Sprague NBS .10 .30
45 Scott Wimmer NBS RC .25 .60
46 Matt Crafton CTS .10 .30
47 Coy Gibbs CTS RC .25 .60
48 Travis Kvapil CTS RC .75 2.00
49 Ted Musgrave CTS .10 .30
50 Robert Pressley CTS .10 .30
51 Jon Wood CTS RC .25 .60
52 Dale Earnhardt Jr. RD 1.25 3.00
53 Jeff Gordon RD 1.00 2.50
54 Kevin Harvick RD .75 2.00
55 Dale Jarrett RD .60 1.50
56 Jimmie Johnson RD .75 2.00
57 Ryan Newman RD .75 2.00
58 Tony Stewart RD .75 2.00
59 Rusty Wallace RD .60 1.50
60 Ricky Rudd RD .40 1.00
61 Mark Martin RD .75 2.00
62 Bobby Labonte RD .60 1.50
63 Terry Labonte RD .40 1.00
64 Rusty Wallace's Car .25 .60
65 Terry Labonte's Car .10 .30
66 Mark Martin's Car .40 1.00
67 Dale Earnhardt Jr.'s Car .50 1.25
68 Michael Waltrip's Car .10 .30
69 Matt Kenseth's Car .40 1.00
70 Bobby Labonte's Car .25 .60
71 Tony Stewart's Car .40 1.00
72 Jeff Gordon's Car .40 1.00
73 Dale Earnhardt Jr. TM 1.25 3.00
74 Michael Waltrip TM .25 .60
75 Steve Park TM .25 .60
76 Kurt Busch TM .40 1.00
77 Matt Kenseth TM .75 2.00

78 Mark Martin TM .75 2.00
79 Jeff Burton TM .25 .60
80 Tony Stewart TM .75 2.00
81 Bobby Labonte TM .60 1.50
82 Jeff Gordon TM 1.00 2.50
83 Jimmie Johnson TM .75 2.00
84 Terry Labonte TM .40 1.00
85 Jerry Nadeau TM .25 .60
86 Dale Jarrett TM .60 1.50
87 Ricky Rudd TM .40 1.00
88 Rusty Wallace TM .60 1.50
89 Ryan Newman TM .75 2.00
90 Dale Jr. .75 2.00
K.Earnhardt CL

2002 Press Pass Trackside Golden

*GOLDEN: 12X TO 30X BASE CARD HI

2002 Press Pass Trackside Samples

*SAMPLES: 2X TO 5X BASE CARDS

2002 Press Pass Trackside Dialed In

Issued at a stated rate of one in eight, these 12 cards feature some on NASCAR's best drivers on cards which are illuminated by mirror-foil and enhanced etching.

COMPLETE SET (12) 12.50 30.00
DI1 Jeff Burton .60 1.50
DI2 Dale Earnhardt, Jr. 3.00 8.00
DI3 Jeff Gordon 2.50 6.00
DI4 Kevin Harvick 2.00 5.00
DI5 Dale Jarrett 1.50 4.00
DI6 Jimmie Johnson 2.00 5.00
DI7 Bobby Labonte 1.50 4.00
DI8 Terry Labonte 1.00 2.50
DI9 Sterling Marlin 1.00 2.50
DI10 Mark Martin 2.00 5.00
DI11 Tony Stewart 2.00 5.00
DI12 Rusty Wallace 1.50 4.00

2002 Press Pass Trackside Generation Now

Inserted at a stated rate of one in 36, this eight card set features leading drivers on cards which have been etched, printed on foil and also gold foil stamped.

COMPLETE SET (8) 25.00 50.00
GN1 Kevin Harvick 4.00 10.00
GN2 Tony Stewart 4.00 10.00
GN3 Dale Earnhardt Jr. 6.00 15.00
GN4 Jimmie Johnson 4.00 10.00
GN5 Ryan Newman 4.00 10.00
GN6 Matt Kenseth 4.00 10.00
GN7 Kurt Busch 2.00 5.00
GN8 Elliott Sadler 1.25 3.00

2002 Press Pass Trackside License to Drive

Inserted at a stated rate of one per pack, these 36 cards feature the development of leading NASCAR drivers.

COMPLETE SET (36) 10.00 25.00
*DIE CUTS: .6X TO 1.5X BASIC INSERTS
1 John Andretti .20 .50
2 Dave Blaney .20 .50
3 Brett Bodine .20 .50
4 Jeff Burton .40 1.00
5 Ward Burton .40 1.00
6 Kurt Busch .60 1.50
7 Ricky Craven .20 .50
8 Dale Earnhardt Jr. 2.00 5.00
9 Jeff Gordon 1.50 4.00
10 Robby Gordon .20 .50
11 Jeff Green .20 .50
12 Bobby Hamilton .20 .50
13 Kevin Harvick 1.25 3.00
14 Dale Jarrett 1.00 2.50
15 Jimmie Johnson 1.25 3.00
16 Buckshot Jones .20 .50
17 Matt Kenseth 1.25 3.00
18 Bobby Labonte 1.00 2.50
19 Terry Labonte .60 1.50
20 Sterling Marlin .60 1.50
21 Mark Martin 1.25 3.00
22 Jeremy Mayfield .20 .50
23 Jerry Nadeau .40 1.00
24 Ryan Newman 1.25 3.00
25 Steve Park .40 1.00
26 Kyle Petty .40 1.00
27 Ricky Rudd .60 1.50
28 Elliott Sadler .40 1.00
29 Ken Schrader .20 .50
30 Mike Skinner .20 .50
31 Jimmy Spencer .20 .50
32 Tony Stewart 1.25 3.00
33 Hut Stricklin .20 .50
34 Rusty Wallace 1.00 2.50
35 Michael Waltrip .40 1.00
36 Checklist .08 .25

2002 Press Pass Trackside Mirror Image

Inserted at a stated rate of one in 18, these nine cards feature questions about who might mirror the success of each driver.

COMPLETE SET (9) 20.00 50.00
MI1 Dale Earnhardt Jr. 4.00 10.00
MI2 Jeff Gordon 3.00 8.00
MI3 Kevin Harvick 2.50 6.00
MI4 Dale Jarrett 2.00 5.00
MI5 Bobby Labonte 2.00 5.00
MI6 Terry Labonte 1.25 3.00
MI7 Mark Martin 2.50 6.00
MI8 Tony Stewart 2.50 6.00
MI9 Rusty Wallace 2.00 5.00

2002 Press Pass Trackside Pit Stoppers Cars

Inserted at a stated rate of one in 240 retail packs, these 15 cards feature swatches of race-used pit signs set against a photo of the featured driver's car. Each card was issued to a different print run total as noted below.

PSC1 Bobby Labonte's Car/350 8.00 20.00
PSC2 Tony Stewart's Car/350 15.00 40.00
PSC3 Steve Park's Car/300 8.00 20.00
PSC4 D.Earnhardt Jr.'s Car/50 30.00 80.00
PSC5 Kevin Harvick's Car/200 10.00 25.00
PSC6 Ryan Newman's Car/350 8.00 20.00
PSC7 Terry Labonte's Car/350 8.00 20.00
PSC8 Rusty Wallace's Car/350 10.00 25.00
PSC9 Ricky Craven's Car/200 6.00 15.00
PSC10 Ken Schrader's Car/200 6.00 15.00
PSC11 Ster.Marlin's Car/250 8.00 20.00
PSC12 Jim.Spencer's Car/350 6.00 15.00
PSC13 Matt Kenseth's Car/60 15.00 40.00
PSC14 Ward Burton's Car/125 8.00 20.00
PSC15 Dale Earnhardt's Car/20 100.00 200.00

2002 Press Pass Trackside Pit Stoppers Drivers

Inserted at a stated rate of one in 480 hobby packs, these 15 cards feature swatches of race-used pit signs set against a photo of the featured driver. Each card was issued to a different print run as noted below.

PSD1 Bobby Labonte/150 10.00 25.00
PSD2 Tony Stewart/150 20.00 50.00
PSD3 Steve Park/150 10.00 25.00
PSD4 Dale Earnhardt Jr./50 30.00 80.00
PSD5 Kevin Harvick/100 12.00 30.00
PSD6 Ryan Newman/175 10.00 25.00
PSD7 Terry Labonte/175 10.00 25.00
PSD8 Rusty Wallace/175 12.00 30.00
PSD9 Ricky Craven/100 8.00 20.00
PSD10 Ken Schrader/150 8.00 20.00
PSD11 Sterling Marlin/150 10.00 25.00
PSD12 Jimmy Spencer/175 8.00 20.00
PSD13 Matt Kenseth/60 10.00 25.00
PSD14 Ward Burton/100 10.00 25.00
PSD15 Dale Earnhardt/20

2002 Press Pass Trackside Rookie Thunder Autographs

NNO Jimmie Johnson
Ryan Newman
Blue/12
NNO Jimmie Johnson
Ryan Newman
Silver/48
NNO Jimmie Johnson 60.00 120.00
Ryan Newman
Gold/75

2002 Press Pass Trackside Runnin N' Gunnin

Issued at a stated rate of one in six, these nine cards feature drivers who never let you see them sweat.

COMPLETE SET (9) 10.00 25.00
RG1 Dale Earnhardt Jr. 2.50 6.00
RG2 Jeff Gordon 2.00 5.00
RG3 Kevin Harvick 1.50 4.00
RG4 Bobby Labonte 1.25 3.00
RG5 Matt Kenseth 1.50 4.00
RG6 Dale Jarrett 1.25 3.00
RG7 Ricky Rudd .75 2.00
RG8 Tony Stewart 1.50 4.00
RG9 Rusty Wallace 1.25 3.00

2003 Press Pass Trackside

This 90-card set was released in June, 2003. This set was issued in six card packs which came 24 packs to a box. The pack SRP was $2.99. There was a King for a Day entry card, inserted in packs at a rate of 1 per box, which was for a chance to spend a day at a Richard Petty Driving School.

COMPLETE SET (81) 10.00 25.00
WAX BOX HOBBY (28) 40.00 75.00
1 Greg Biffle CRC .25 .60
2 Jeff Burton .25 .60
3 Kurt Busch .40 1.00
4 Dale Jarrett .60 1.50
5 Matt Kenseth .75 2.00
6 Mark Martin .75 2.00
7 Ricky Rudd .40 1.00
8 Elliott Sadler .25 .60
9 Dave Blaney .10 .30
10 John Andretti .10 .30
11 Ward Burton .25 .60
12 Sterling Marlin .40 1.00
13 Jeremy Mayfield .10 .30
14 Jamie McMurray CRC .60 1.50
15 Casey Mears CRC .25 .60
16 Ryan Newman .75 2.00
17 Kenny Wallace .10 .30
18 Rusty Wallace .60 1.50
19 Dale Earnhardt Jr. 1.25 3.00
20 Jeff Gordon 1.00 2.50
21 Robby Gordon .10 .30
22 Jeff Green .10 .30
23 Kevin Harvick .75 2.00
24 Jimmie Johnson .75 2.00
25 Bobby Labonte .60 1.50
26 Terry Labonte .40 1.00
27 Joe Nemechek .10 .30
28 Steve Park .25 .60
29 Tony Stewart .75 2.00
30 Michael Waltrip .25 .60
31 Ricky Craven .10 .30
32 Jerry Nadeau .25 .60
33 Mike Skinner .10 .30
34 Stanton Barrett BGN RC .10 .30
35 Mike Bliss BGN .10 .30
36 Stacy Compton BGN .10 .30
37 Kerry Earnhardt BGN .25 .60
38 Coy Gibbs BGN .25 .60
39 Damon Lusk BGN RC .10 .30
40 Chad Blount BGN RC .40 1.00
41 Shane Hmiel BGN RC 1.25 3.00
42 Jason Keller BGN .10 .30
43 Randy LaJoie BGN .10 .30
44 Scott Riggs BGN .25 .60
45 Brian Vickers BGN .50 1.25
46 Matt Crafton CTS .10 .30
47 Rick Crawford CTS RC .10 .30
48 Carl Edwards CTS RC 4.00 10.00
49 Andy Houston CTS .10 .30
50 Travis Kvapil CTS .25 .60
51 Jason Leffler CTS .10 .30
52 Robert Pressley CTS .10 .30
53 Dennis Setzer CTS .10 .30
54 Jon Wood CTS .25 .60
55 R.Wallace .60 1.50
K.Wallace FA
56 B.Bodine .10 .30
T.Bodine FA
57 J.Burton .25 .60
W.Burton FA
58 Ster.Marlin .40 1.00
Stead.Marlin FA RC
59 D.Jarrett .60 1.50
N.Jarrett FA
60 K.Petty .75 2.00
R.Petty FA
61 Rusty Wallace in Pits .25 .60
62 Dale Earnhardt Jr. in Pits .50 1.25
63 Ryan Newman in Pits .30 .75
64 Kerry Earnhardt in Pits .10 .30
65 Michael Waltrip in Pits .10 .30
66 Greg Biffle in Pits .10 .30
67 Bobby Labonte in Pits .25 .60
68 Kevin Harvick in Pits .30 .75
69 Robby Gordon in Pits .10 .30
70 Elliott Sadler in Pits .10 .30
71 Dale Jarrett in Pits .25 .60
72 Jeff Burton in Pits .10 .30
73 K.Wallace .25 .60
W.Burton TM
74 T.Stewart .75 2.00
B.Labonte TM
75 E.Sadler .60 1.50
D.Jarrett TM
76 R.Wallace .75 2.00
R.Newman TM
77 J.Andretti .25 .60
K.Petty TM
78 Mart .75 2.00
J.Bur
Bif
Kens
Bus TM
79 J.Johnson 1.00 2.50
J.Gordon TM
80 Mears .60 1.50
McMurray
Marlin TM
81 Rusty Wallace CL .60 1.50
NNO King for a Day Yellow 1.00 2.50

2003 Press Pass Trackside Golden

*GOLDEN: 10X TO 25X BASE

2003 Press Pass Trackside Gold Holofoil

COMPLETE SET (81) 15.00 40.00
*SINGLES: .6X TO 1.5X BASE CARD HI

2003 Press Pass Trackside Samples

*SAMPLES: 2.5X TO 6X BASIC

2003 Press Pass Trackside Dialed In

Issued at a stated rate of one in eight, these 12 cards feature some on NASCAR's best drivers on cards which are illuminated by mirror-foil and enhanced etching. These cards also featured a "DI" prefix on the card numbers.

COMPLETE SET (12) 12.50 30.00
DI1 Kerry Earnhardt .50 1.25
DI2 Dale Earnhardt Jr. 2.50 6.00
DI3 Jeff Gordon 2.00 5.00
DI4 Dale Jarrett 1.25 3.00
DI5 Jimmie Johnson 1.50 4.00
DI6 Bobby Labonte 1.25 3.00
DI7 Terry Labonte .75 2.00
DI8 Ricky Rudd .75 2.00
DI9 Ryan Newman 1.50 4.00
DI10 Tony Stewart 1.50 4.00
DI11 Rusty Wallace 1.25 3.00
DI12 Michael Waltrip .50 1.25

2003 Press Pass Trackside Hat Giveaway

Randomly inserted in packs at a rate of one per box. This 30-card set of entry cards were good for a chance to win an autographed hat of the corresponding driver. The sweepstakes ended on January 31, 2004.

PPH1 John Andretti .75 2.00
PPH2 Greg Biffle 1.50 4.00
PPH3 Brett Bodine .75 2.00
PPH4 Jeff Burton 1.50 4.00
PPH5 Kurt Busch 2.50 6.00
PPH6 Ricky Craven .75 2.00
PPH7 Jeff Gordon 6.00 15.00
PPH8 Robby Gordon .75 2.00
PPH9 Jeff Green .75 2.00
PPH10 Kevin Harvick 5.00 12.00
PPH11 Dale Jarrett 4.00 10.00
PPH12 Jimmie Johnson 5.00 12.00
PPH13 Matt Kenseth 5.00 12.00
PPH14 Bobby Labonte 4.00 10.00
PPH15 Sterling Marlin 2.50 6.00
PPH16 Mark Martin 5.00 12.00
PPH17 Jeremy Mayfield .75 2.00
PPH18 Jamie McMurray 4.00 10.00
PPH19 Casey Mears 1.50 4.00
PPH20 Jerry Nadeau 1.50 4.00
PPH21 Ryan Newman 5.00 12.00
PPH22 Steve Park 1.50 4.00
PPH23 Kyle Petty 1.50 4.00
PPH24 Ricky Rudd 2.50 6.00
PPH25 Elliott Sadler 1.50 4.00
PPH26 Mike Skinner .75 2.00
PPH27 Tony Stewart 5.00 12.00
PPH28 Kenny Wallace .75 2.00
PPH29 Rusty Wallace 4.00 10.00
PPH30 Michael Waltrip 1.50 4.00

2003 Press Pass Trackside Hot Pursuit

Inserted at a stated rate of one in 28 packs, these 8 cards feature the some of NASCAR's leading drivers. Each card carried a prefix of "HP" as part of the card number.

COMPLETE SET (8) 15.00 30.00
STATED ODDS 1:28
HP1 Kerry Earnhardt .75 2.00
HP2 Dale Earnhardt Jr. 4.00 10.00
HP3 Jimmie Johnson 2.50 6.00
HP4 Kevin Harvick 2.50 6.00
HP5 Ryan Newman 2.50 6.00
HP6 Tony Stewart 2.50 6.00
HP7 Michael Waltrip .75 2.00
HP8 Elliott Sadler .75 2.00

2003 Press Pass Trackside License to Drive

Inserted at a stated rate of one per pack, these 27 cards feature the development of leading NASCAR drivers.

COMPLETE SET (27) 10.00 20.00
STATED ODDS 1 PER PACK
LD1 Greg Biffle .30 .75
LD2 Todd Bodine .15 .40
LD3 Ward Burton .30 .75
LD4 Dale Earnhardt Jr. 1.50 4.00
LD5 Jeff Gordon 1.25 3.00
LD6 Brett Bodine .15 .40
LD7 Ricky Craven .15 .40
LD8 Bobby Labonte .75 2.00
LD9 Robby Gordon .15 .40
LD10 Jeff Burton .30 .75
LD11 Elliott Sadler .30 .75
LD12 Jerry Nadeau .30 .75
LD13 Ryan Newman 1.00 2.50
LD14 Steve Park .30 .75
LD15 Ricky Rudd .50 1.25
LD16 Ken Schrader .15 .40
LD17 Jimmy Spencer .15 .40
LD18 Tony Stewart 1.00 2.50
LD19 Rusty Wallace .75 2.00
LD20 Michael Waltrip .30 .75
LD21 Mike Skinner .15 .40
LD22 Kyle Petty .30 .75
LD23 Kevin Grubb .15 .40
LD24 Steadman Marlin .15 .40
LD25 Damon Lusk .15 .40
LD26 Scott Wimmer .30 .75
LD27 Jimmy Vasser CL .15 .40

2003 Press Pass Trackside Mirror Image

Inserted at a stated rate of one in 18, these nine cards feature questions about who might mirror the success of each driver.

COMPLETE SET (9) 12.50 30.00
MI1 Kerry Earnhardt .60 1.50
MI2 Dale Earnhardt Jr. 3.00 8.00
MI3 Jeff Gordon 2.50 6.00
MI4 Mark Martin 2.00 5.00
MI5 Bobby Labonte 1.50 4.00
MI6 Terry Labonte 1.00 2.50
MI7 Tony Stewart 2.00 5.00
MI8 Rusty Wallace 1.50 4.00
MI9 Michael Waltrip .60 1.50

2003 Press Pass Trackside Pit Stoppers Drivers

Randomly inserted in hobby packs at a rate of one in 180, these 18 cards feature swatches of race-used pit signs set against a photo of the featured driver. Each card was issued to a a stated print run of 100 with the exceptions of Dale Earnhardt of 3 and Matt Kenseth of 17.

*CARS/175: .3X TO .8X DRIVERS/100
PSD1 Jeff Gordon 20.00 50.00
PSD2 Terry Labonte 10.00 25.00
PSD3 Kevin Harvick 10.00 25.00
PSD4 Jimmie Johnson 15.00 40.00
PSD5 Rusty Wallace 12.00 30.00
PSD6 Bobby Labonte 10.00 25.00
PSD7 Tony Stewart 15.00 40.00
PSD8 Ryan Newman 8.00 20.00
PSD10 Sterling Marlin 8.00 20.00
PSD11 Ward Burton 8.00 20.00
PSD12 Michael Waltrip 10.00 25.00
PSD13 Robby Gordon 8.00 20.00
PSD14 Jeff Green 6.00 15.00
PSD15 Jamie McMurray 8.00 20.00
PSD17 Steve Park 6.00 15.00
PSD18 Dale Earnhardt Jr. 20.00 50.00

2003 Press Pass Trackside Pit Stoppers Drivers Autographs

Randomly inserted in hobby packs, these 8 cards feature swatches of race-used pit signs set against a photo of the featured driver along with a his signature. The cards were limited and hand numbered to the driver's door number. Some of the cards are not priced due to scarcity.

STATED PRINT RUN 2-48
*CARS: .4X TO 1X DRIVERS
PSDBL Bobby Labonte/18 60.00 120.00
PSDJJ Jimmie Johnson/48 60.00 120.00
PSDKH Kevin Harvick/29 40.00 100.00
PSDMK Matt Kenseth/17
PSDMM Mark Martin/6
PSDRN Ryan Newman/12
PSDRW Rusty Wallace/2
PSDTL Terry Labonte/5

2003 Press Pass Trackside Runnin n' Gunnin

Issued at a stated rate of one in six, these 12 cards feature drivers who never let you see them sweat.

COMPLETE SET (12) 7.50 20.00
RG1 Kerry Earnhardt .40 1.00
RG2 Dale Earnhardt, Jr. 2.00 5.00
RG3 Jeff Gordon 1.50 4.00
RG4 Dale Jarrett 1.00 2.50
RG5 Bobby Labonte 1.00 2.50
RG6 Jimmie Johnson 1.25 3.00
RG7 Ricky Rudd .60 1.50
RG8 Rusty Wallace 1.00 2.50
RG9 Michael Waltrip .40 1.00
RG10 Ryan Newman 1.25 3.00
RG11 Kevin Harvick 1.25 3.00
RG12 Matt Kenseth 1.25 3.00

2004 Press Pass Trackside

This 120-card set was released in June, 2004. This set was issued in six card packs which came 28 packs to a box. The pack SRP was $2.99. The set had 6 short-printed background variations as noted in the checklist below.

COMPLETE SET (120) 15.00 40.00
WAX BOX HOBBY (28) 40.00 70.00
WAX BOX RETAIL (24) 40.00 70.00
1 Brendan Gaughan CRC .30 .75
1B Brendan Gaughan -logo on wall 1.25 3.00
2 Kasey Kahne CRC 1.50 4.00
3 Sterling Marlin .50 1.25
4 Jamie McMurray .50 1.25
5 Casey Mears .30 .75
6 Ryan Newman 1.00 2.50
7 Rusty Wallace .60 1.50
8 Scott Wimmer CRC .30 .75
9 Kyle Petty .30 .75
10 Jeremy Mayfield .15 .40
11 Jeff Green .15 .40
12 Greg Biffle .30 .75
13 Kurt Busch .50 1.25
14 Jeff Burton .30 .75
15 Dale Jarrett .60 1.50
16 Matt Kenseth 1.00 2.50
17 Mark Martin .75 2.00
18 Elliott Sadler .30 .75
19 Dale Earnhardt Jr. 1.25 3.00
20 Jeff Gordon 1.25 3.00
20B J.Gordon dark background 5.00 12.00
21 Robby Gordon .15 .40
22 Kevin Harvick .75 2.00
23 Jimmie Johnson 1.00 2.50
24 Bobby Labonte .60 1.50
25 Terry Labonte .50 1.25
26 Joe Nemechek .15 .40
27 Scott Riggs CRC .30 .75
28 Tony Stewart .75 2.00
29 Brian Vickers CRC .60 1.50
30 Michael Waltrip .30 .75
31 Kyle Busch RC 4.00 10.00
32 Stacy Compton .15 .40
33 Kenny Wallace .15 .40
34 Paul Menard RC 1.00 2.50
35 Jason Keller .15 .40
36 J.J. Yeley RC 2.00 5.00
37 Ron Hornaday .15 .40
38 Billy Parker Jr. RC 1.25 3.00
39 Martin Truex Jr. RC 3.00 8.00
39B Martin Truex Jr. no official 5.00 12.00
40 Casey Atwood .15 .40
41 Tim Fedewa .15 .40
42 Clint Bowyer RC 3.00 8.00
43 Matt Crafton .15 .40
44 Rick Crawford .15 .40
45 Tina Gordon RC 1.00 2.50
46 Andy Houston .15 .40
47 Steve Park .15 .40
48 Jon Wood .30 .75
49 Terry Cook RC .60 1.50
50 Jack Sprague .15 .40
51 Dennis Setzer .15 .40
52 Rusty Wallace's Car HS .30 .75
52B Rusty Wallace's Car HS SP 1.25 3.00
53 Dale Earnhardt Jr.'s Car HS .50 1.25
54 Kasey Kahne's Car HS .50 1.25
55 Ryan Newman's Car HS .50 1.25
56 Michael Waltrip's Car HS .15 .40
57 Greg Biffle's Car HS .15 .40
58 Bobby Labonte's Car HS .30 .75
59 Kevin Harvick's Car HS .30 .75
60 Robby Gordon's Car HS .15 .40
61 Elliott Sadler's Car HS .15 .40
62 Dale Jarrett's Car HS .30 .75
63 Jimmie Johnson's Car HS .40 1.00
64 J.Green .30 .75
K.Petty TM
65 T.Stewart .75 2.00
B.Labonte TM
66 D.Jarrett .60 1.50
E.Sadler TM
67 Rusty 1.00 2.50
Gaughan
Newman TM
68 Burt 1.00 2.50
Kens
Mart
Busch
Bif. TM
69 J.Johnson 1.25 3.00
J.Gordon TM
70 Mears .50 1.25
McMurray
Marlin TM
70B Mears 2.00 5.00
McMry
Marln TM blimp
71 R.Gord .75 2.00
K.Harv
Jo.Sauter TM
72 Dale Jr. 1.25 3.00
M.Waltrip TM
73 J.Nemechek .30 .75
S.Riggs TM
74 S.Wimmer .30 .75
D.Blaney TM
75 J.Mayfield 1.25 3.00
K.Kahne TM
76 Rick Hendrick H .15 .40
77 Geoff Bodine H .15 .40
78 Tim Richmond H .15 .40
79 B.Parsons .30 .75
D.Waltrip H
80 Ken Schrader H .15 .40
81 Jack Sprague H .15 .40
82 Ricky Craven H .15 .40
83 Jerry Nadeau H .30 .75
84 R.Hendrick .75 2.00
Ky.Busch H
85 Jimmie Johnson H 1.00 2.50
86 Joe Nemechek H .15 .40
87 Brian Vickers H .60 1.50
88 Ricky Rudd H .50 1.25
89 Jeff Gordon H 1.25 3.00
90 Terry Labonte H .50 1.25
91 Brian Vickers LD .60 1.50
92 Kyle Busch LD .75 2.00
93 Kasey Kahne LD 1.25 3.00
94 Casey Atwood LD .15 .40
95 Jon Wood LD .30 .75
96 Kurt Busch LD .50 1.25
97 Billy Parker Jr. LD .60 1.50
98 Casey Mears LD .30 .75
99 Martin Truex Jr. LD 1.50 4.00
100 Dale Earnhardt Jr. TT 1.25 3.00
101 Greg Biffle TT .30 .75
102 Kevin Harvick TT .75 2.00
103 Ryan Newman TT 1.00 2.50
104 Casey Mears TT .30 .75
105 Tony Stewart TT .75 2.00
106 Bobby Labonte TT .60 1.50
107 Sterling Marlin TT .50 1.25
108 J.Gordon 1.25 3.00
J.J.
Vickers TT
109 Dale Earnhardt Jr. F 1.25 3.00
110 Michael Waltrip F .30 .75
111 Jeff Gordon F 1.25 3.00
112 Jimmie Johnson F 1.00 2.50
113 Mark Martin F .75 2.00
114 Rusty Wallace F .60 1.50
115 Kevin Harvick F .75 2.00
115B Kevin Harvick F blue sky 3.00 8.00
116 Tony Stewart F .75 2.00
117 Matt Kenseth F 1.00 2.50
118 Ryan Newman F 1.00 2.50
119 Bobby Labonte F .60 1.50
120 J.Gordon 1.25 3.00
J.Johnson CL

2004 Press Pass Trackside Golden

*GOLDEN: 2.5X TO 6X BASE

2004 Press Pass Trackside Samples

*SAMPLES: 1.5X TO 4X BASIC

2004 Press Pass Trackside Dialed In

Issued at a stated rate of one in eight, these 12 cards feature some on NASCAR's best drivers on cards which are illuminated by mirror-foil and enhanced etching. These cards also featured a "DI" prefix on the card numbers.

COMPLETE SET (12) 12.50 30.00
DI1 Jimmie Johnson 3.00 8.00
DI2 Dale Earnhardt Jr. 4.00 10.00
DI3 Jeff Gordon 4.00 10.00
DI4 Michael Waltrip 1.25 3.00
DI5 Jamie McMurray 1.50 4.00
DI6 Tony Stewart 2.50 6.00
DI7 Sterling Marlin 1.50 4.00
DI8 Bobby Labonte 2.00 5.00
DI9 Kurt Busch 1.50 4.00
DI10 Brian Vickers 2.00 5.00
DI11 Casey Mears 1.25 3.00
DI12 Rusty Wallace 2.00 5.00

2004 Press Pass Trackside Hat Giveaway

Randomly inserted in packs at a rate of 1 in 28 packs. This 39-card set of entry cards were good for a chance to win an autographed hat of the corresponding driver. The sweepstakes ended on January 31, 2005.

COMPLETE SET (39)
PPH1 Greg Biffle 1.50 4.00
PPH2 Dave Blaney 1.00 2.50
PPH3 Jeff Burton 1.50 4.00
PPH4 Ward Burton 1.50 4.00
PPH5 Kurt Busch 2.50 6.00
PPH6 Dale Earnhardt Jr. 6.00 15.00
PPH7 Brendan Gaughan 1.50 4.00
PPH8 Jeff Gordon 8.00 20.00
PPH9 Jeff Green 1.00 2.50
PPH10 Kevin Harvick 4.00 10.00
PPH11 Ron Hornaday 1.00 2.50
PPH12 Dale Jarrett 3.00 8.00
PPH13 Jimmie Johnson 5.00 12.00
PPH14 Kasey Kahne 6.00 15.00
PPH15 Bobby Labonte 3.00 8.00
PPH16 Terry Labonte 2.50 6.00
PPH17 Kevin Lepage 1.00 2.50
PPH18 Sterling Marlin 2.50 6.00
PPH19 Mark Martin 4.00 10.00
PPH20 Jeremy Mayfield 1.00 2.50
PPH21 Jamie McMurray 2.50 6.00
PPH22 Casey Mears 1.50 4.00
PPH23 Joe Nemechek 1.00 2.50
PPH24 Ryan Newman 5.00 12.00
PPH25 Scott Riggs 1.50 4.00
PPH26 Ricky Rudd 2.50 6.00
PPH27 Elliott Sadler 1.50 4.00
PPH28 Johnny Sauter 1.50 4.00
PPH29 Ken Schrader 1.00 2.50
PPH30 Tony Stewart 4.00 10.00
PPH31 Brian Vickers 3.00 8.00
PPH32 Rusty Wallace 3.00 8.00
PPH33 Michael Waltrip 1.50 4.00
PPH34 Scott Wimmer 1.50 4.00
PPH35 Martin Truex Jr. 6.00 15.00
PPH36 Ricky Craven 1.00 2.50
PPH37 Robby Gordon 1.00 2.50
PPH38 Matt Kenseth 5.00 12.00
PPH39 Kyle Petty 1.50 4.00

2004 Press Pass Trackside Hot Pass

Inserted at a stated rate of 1 in 2 packs, these 27 cards feature the some of NASCAR's leading drivers. Each card carried a prefix of "HP" as part of the card number. The cards were also designed to look like a pit pass for the track. A few drivers have a Nextel Cup and Busch Series version and are noted in the checklist below.

COMPLETE SET (27) 12.50 30.00
*NATIONAL: 1X TO 2.5X BASE
HP1 Greg Biffle .50 1.25
HP2 Jeff Burton .50 1.25
HP3 Ward Burton .50 1.25
HP4 Ricky Craven .30 .75
HP5 Dale Earnhardt Jr. 2.00 5.00
HP6 Brendan Gaughan .50 1.25
HP7 Jeff Gordon 2.00 5.00
HP8 Robby Gordon .30 .75
HP9 Jimmie Johnson 1.50 4.00
HP10 Bobby Labonte 1.00 2.50
HP11 Terry Labonte .75 2.00
HP12 Ryan Newman 1.50 4.00
HP13 Kyle Petty .50 1.25
HP14 Ricky Rudd .75 2.00
HP15 Elliott Sadler .50 1.25
HP16 Tony Stewart 1.25 3.00
HP17 Rusty Wallace 1.00 2.50
HP18 Michael Waltrip .50 1.25
HP19 Scott Wimmer BGN .50 1.25
HP20 Greg Biffle BGN .50 1.25
HP21 Kevin Harvick BGN 1.25 3.00
HP22 Kasey Kahne BGN 2.50 6.00
HP23 Kenny Wallace BGN .30 .75
HP24 Tim Fedewa BGN .30 .75
HP25 Johnny Sauter BGN .50 1.25
HP26 Robby Gordon BGN .30 .75
HP27 J.J. Yeley BGN 2.00 5.00

2004 Press Pass Trackside Hot Pursuit

Inserted at a stated rate of one in 28 packs, these 9 cards feature the some of NASCAR's leading drivers. Each card carried a prefix of "HP" as part of the card number.

COMPLETE SET (9) 12.50 30.00
HP1 Dale Earnhardt Jr. 4.00 10.00
HP2 Jimmie Johnson 4.00 10.00
HP3 Michael Waltrip 1.25 3.00
HP4 Jeff Gordon 5.00 12.00
HP5 Rusty Wallace 2.50 6.00
HP6 Matt Kenseth 4.00 10.00
HP7 Casey Mears 1.25 3.00
HP8 Dale Jarrett 2.50 6.00
HP9 Kevin Harvick 3.00 8.00

2004 Press Pass Trackside Pit Stoppers Drivers

Randomly inserted in hobby packs at a rate of one in 168, these 17 cards feature swatches of race-used pit signs set against a photo of the featured driver. Each card was issued to a a stated print run of 95 with the exceptions of Kevin Harvick of 40 and Matt Kenseth of 20.

STATED ODDS 1:168
STATED PRINT RUN 20-95
*CARS/150: .4X TO 1X DRIVERS
PSD1 Jeff Gordon 15.00 40.00
PSD2 Terry Labonte 10.00 25.00
PSD3 Kevin Harvick/40 12.00 30.00
PSD4 Jimmie Johnson 12.00 30.00
PSD5 Rusty Wallace 10.00 25.00
PSD6 Bobby Labonte 8.00 20.00
PSD7 Tony Stewart 12.00 30.00
PSD8 Ryan Newman 6.00 15.00
PSD9 Dale Earnhardt 25.00 60.00
PSD10 Sterling Marlin 6.00 15.00
PSD11 Jeff Burton 8.00 20.00
PSD12 Michael Waltrip 8.00 20.00
PSD13 Jamie McMurray 6.00 15.00
PSD14 Matt Kenseth/20 30.00 80.00
PSD15 Dale Earnhardt Jr. 15.00 40.00
PSD16 Scott Riggs 6.00 15.00
PSD17 Joe Nemechek 6.00 15.00

2004 Press Pass Trackside Pit Stoppers Autographs

Randomly inserted in hobby packs, these 8 cards feature swatches of race-used pit signs set against a photo of the featured driver along with a his signature. The cards were limited and hand numbered to the driver's door number. Some of the cards are not priced due to scarcity.

STATED PRINT RUN 2-29
PSBL Bobby Labonte/18 75.00 150.00
PSDE Dale Earnhardt Jr./8
PSKH Kevin Harvick/29 60.00 120.00
PSMK Matt Kenseth/17
PSRN Ryan Newman/12
PSRW Rusty Wallace/2
PSSR Scott Riggs/10
PSTS Tony Stewart/20 125.00 200.00

2004 Press Pass Trackside Runnin n' Gunnin

Issued at a stated rate of one in six, these 12 cards feature drivers who never let you see them sweat.

COMPLETE SET (12) 10.00 25.00
RG1 Dale Earnhardt Jr. 1.50 4.00
RG2 Jeff Gordon 1.50 4.00
RG3 Jimmie Johnson 1.25 3.00
RG4 Michael Waltrip .40 1.00
RG5 Bobby Labonte .75 2.00
RG6 Tony Stewart 1.00 2.50
RG7 Scott Riggs .40 1.00
RG8 Greg Biffle .40 1.00
RG9 Terry Labonte .60 1.50
RG10 Rusty Wallace .75 2.00
RG11 Jamie McMurray .60 1.50
RG12 Matt Kenseth 1.25 3.00

2005 Press Pass Trackside

COMPLETE SET (100) 15.00 30.00
WAX BOX HOBBY (28) 40.00 70.00
WAX BOX RETAIL (24) 35.00 60.00
1 Jeff Burton .30 .75
2 Dale Earnhardt Jr. 1.25 3.00
2B Dale Earnhardt Jr. no car 2.50 6.00
3 Jeff Gordon 1.25 3.00
4 Kevin Harvick .75 2.00
5 Jimmie Johnson 1.00 2.50
6 Bobby Labonte .60 1.50
7 Terry Labonte .50 1.25
8 Joe Nemechek .20 .50
9 Scott Riggs .30 .75
10 Tony Stewart .75 2.00
11 Brian Vickers .60 1.50
12 Kyle Busch CRC .75 2.00
13 Jeff Green .20 .50
14 Kasey Kahne 1.25 3.00
14B Kasey Kahne -white t-shirt 2.50 6.00
15 Travis Kvapil CRC .30 .75
16 Sterling Marlin .50 1.25
17 Jeremy Mayfield .20 .50
18 Jamie McMurray .50 1.25
19 Casey Mears .30 .75
20 Ryan Newman 1.00 2.50
21 Kyle Petty .30 .75
22 Ken Schrader .20 .50
23 Rusty Wallace .60 1.50
24 Scott Wimmer .30 .75
25 John Andretti .20 .50
26 Greg Biffle .30 .75
27 Kurt Busch .50 1.25
28 Carl Edwards CRC 1.00 2.50
28B Carl Edwards no wire 2.00 5.00
29 Dale Jarrett .60 1.50
30 Matt Kenseth 1.00 2.50
31 Mark Martin .75 2.00
32 Ricky Rudd .50 1.25
33 Elliott Sadler .30 .75
34 Clint Bowyer 1.25 3.00
35 Justin Labonte .50 1.25
36 David Green .20 .50
37 Denny Hamlin RC 3.00 8.00
38 Jon Wood .30 .75
39 Paul Wolfe .30 .75
40 Johnny Sauter .30 .75
41 Reed Sorenson RC 2.50 6.00
41B Reed Sorenson no reflect. 6.00 15.00
42 Jason Keller .20 .50
43 Martin Truex Jr. 1.00 2.50
44 Kenny Wallace .20 .50
45 J.J. Yeley .50 1.25
46 Terry Cook .20 .50
47 Ricky Craven .20 .50
48 Rick Crawford .20 .50
49 Kerry Earnhardt .30 .75
50 Todd Kluever RC 1.50 4.00
51 Ken Schrader .20 .50
52 Ron Hornaday .20 .50
53 Dennis Setzer .20 .50
54 Jack Sprague .20 .50
55 Rusty Wallace's Car HS .20 .50
56 Kasey Kahne's Car HS .50 1.25
57 Ryan Newman's Car HS .30 .75
58 Michael Waltrip's Car HS .10 .25
59 Bobby Labonte's Car HS .20 .50
60 Tony Stewart's Car HS .30 .75
61 Jeff Gordon's Car HS .50 1.25
61B J.Gordon's Car HS -orange spots 1.00 2.50
62 Kevin Harvick's Car HS .30 .75
63 Joe Nemechek's Car HS .10 .25
64 Elliott Sadler's Car HS .10 .25
65 Jimmie Johnson's Car HS .30 .75
66 Dale Jarrett's Car HS .20 .50
67 J.Green .30 .75
K.Petty TM
68 Stewart .75 2.00
Leffler
B.Labonte TM
69 D.Jarrett .60 1.50
E.Sadler
TM
70 J.Gordon 1.25 3.00
J.Johnson TM
71 Mears .50 1.25
Marlin
McMurray TM
72 Blaney .75 2.00
J.Burton
Harvick TM
73 Riggs .30 .75
Said
Nemechek TM
74 K.Kahne 1.25 3.00
J.Mayfield TM
75 T.Labonte .75 2.00
Vickers
Ky.Busch TM
76 K.Busch .75 2.00
K.Busch FA
77 R.Wallace .60 1.50
K.Wallace FA
78 T.Labonte .50 1.25
J.Labonte FA
79 R.Petty .75 2.00
K.Petty FA
80 B.Labonte .60 1.50
T.Labonte FA
81 J.Wood .30 .75
G.Wood FA
82 Dale Earnhardt Jr. GP 1.25 3.00
83 Jeff Gordon GP 1.25 3.00
84 Jeff Burton GP .30 .75
85 Kevin Harvick GP .75 2.00
86 Jimmie Johnson GP 1.00 2.50
86B J.Johnson GP -Chevy logo 2.00 5.00
87 Bobby Labonte GP .60 1.50
88 Tony Stewart GP .75 2.00
89 Michael Waltrip GP .30 .75
90 Dale Jarrett GP .60 1.50
91 Ricky Rudd GP .50 1.25
92 Rusty Wallace GP .60 1.50
93 Matt Kenseth GP 1.00 2.50
94 Dale Earnhardt Jr. F 1.25 3.00
95 Jeff Gordon F 1.25 3.00
96 Jimmie Johnson F 1.00 2.50
97 Tony Stewart F .75 2.00
98 Rusty Wallace F .60 1.50
99 Dale Jarrett F .60 1.50
100 Dale Earnhardt Jr. CL 1.25 3.00

2005 Press Pass Trackside Golden

*GOLDEN: 2.5X TO 6X BASE

2005 Press Pass Trackside Dialed In

COMPLETE SET (9) 10.00 25.00
DI1 Jimmie Johnson 2.50 6.00
DI2 Kevin Harvick 2.00 5.00
DI3 Jeff Gordon 3.00 8.00
DI4 Michael Waltrip .75 2.00
DI5 Tony Stewart 2.00 5.00
DI6 Bobby Labonte 1.50 4.00
DI7 Matt Kenseth 2.50 6.00
DI8 Dale Jarrett 1.50 4.00
DI9 Rusty Wallace 1.50 4.00

2005 Press Pass Trackside Hat Giveaway

COMPLETE SET (46)
PPH1 John Andretti .75 2.00
PPH2 Dave Blaney .75 2.00
PPH3 Jeff Burton 1.50 4.00
PPH4 Kurt Busch 2.50 6.00
PPH5 Kyle Busch 4.00 10.00
PPH6 Dale Earnhardt Jr. 6.00 15.00
PPH7 Carl Edwards 4.00 10.00
PPH8 Jeff Gordon 6.00 15.00
PPH9 Jeff Green .75 2.00
PPH10 Kevin Harvick 4.00 10.00
PPH11 Dale Jarrett 3.00 8.00
PPH12 Jimmie Johnson 5.00 12.00
PPH13 Kasey Kahne 6.00 15.00
PPH14 Matt Kenseth 5.00 12.00
PPH15 Travis Kvapil 1.50 4.00
PPH16 Terry Labonte 2.50 6.00
PPH17 Bobby Labonte 3.00 8.00
PPH18 Jason Leffler .75 2.00
PPH19 Kevin Lepage .75 2.00
PPH20 Jeremy Mayfield .75 2.00
PPH21 Jamie McMurray 2.50 6.00
PPH22 Casey Mears 1.50 4.00
PPH23 Joe Nemechek .75 2.00
PPH24 Ryan Newman 5.00 12.00
PPH25 Kyle Petty 1.50 4.00
PPH26 Scott Riggs 1.50 4.00
PPH27 Ricky Rudd 2.50 6.00
PPH28 Elliott Sadler 1.50 4.00
PPH29 Boris Said .75 2.00
PPH30 Ken Schrader .75 2.00
PPH31 Tony Stewart 4.00 10.00
PPH32 Brian Vickers 3.00 8.00
PPH33 Rusty Wallace 3.00 8.00
PPH34 Michael Waltrip 1.50 4.00
PPH35 Scott Wimmer 1.50 4.00
PPH36 Martin Truex Jr. 5.00 12.00
PPH37 Boston Reid 5.00 12.00
PPH38 Reed Sorenson 6.00 15.00
PPH39 David Green .75 2.00
PPH40 Kenny Wallace .75 2.00
PPH41 Rick Crawford .75 2.00
PPH42 Blake Feese 5.00 12.00
PPH43 Sterling Marlin 2.50 6.00
PPH44 Greg Biffle 1.50 4.00
PPH45 Mark Martin 4.00 10.00
PPH46 Mike Bliss .75 2.00

2005 Press Pass Trackside Hot Pass

COMPLETE SET (27) 12.50 30.00
*NATIONAL: .4X TO 1X BASE
1 John Andretti .30 .75
2 Jeff Burton .50 1.25
3 Dale Earnhardt Jr. 2.00 5.00
4 Jeff Gordon 2.00 5.00
5 Jeff Green .30 .75
6 Kevin Harvick 1.25 3.00
7 Dale Jarrett 1.00 2.50
8 Jimmie Johnson 1.50 4.00
9 Matt Kenseth 1.50 4.00
10 Bobby Labonte 1.00 2.50
11 Terry Labonte .75 2.00
12 Ryan Newman 1.50 4.00
13 Mark Martin 1.25 3.00
14 Ricky Rudd .75 2.00
15 Ken Schrader .30 .75
16 Tony Stewart 1.25 3.00
17 Rusty Wallace 1.00 2.50
18 Michael Waltrip .50 1.25
19 Denny Hamlin 2.00 5.00
20 Kasey Kahne 2.00 5.00
21 Kenny Wallace .30 .75
22 Tim Fedewa .30 .75
23 Jason Keller .30 .75
24 Martin Truex Jr. 1.50 4.00
25 David Green .30 .75
26 David Stremme 2.00 5.00
27 J.J. Yeley .75 2.00

2005 Press Pass Trackside Hot Pursuit

COMPLETE SET (9) 20.00 50.00
HP1 Kevin Harvick 3.00 8.00
HP2 Jimmie Johnson 4.00 10.00
HP3 Matt Kenseth 4.00 10.00
HP4 Jeff Gordon 5.00 12.00
HP5 Rusty Wallace 2.50 6.00
HP6 Ryan Newman 4.00 10.00
HP7 Ricky Rudd 2.00 5.00
HP8 Tony Stewart 3.00 8.00
HP9 Bobby Labonte 2.50 6.00

2005 Press Pass Trackside Pit Stoppers Autographs

STATED PRINT RUN 2-48
PSDE Dale Earnhardt Jr./8
PSJG Jeff Gordon/24 150.00 300.00
PSJJ Jimmie Johnson/48 60.00 120.00
PSRN Ryan Newman/12
PSRW Rusty Wallace/2
PSSR Scott Riggs/10
PSTS Tony Stewart/20 125.00 200.00

2005 Press Pass Trackside Pit Stoppers Drivers

STATED ODDS 1:168 HOBBY
STATED PRINT RUN 85 SERIAL #'d SETS
*CARS/85: .4X TO 1X DRIVER/85
PSD1 Jeff Gordon 10.00 25.00
PSD2 Terry Labonte 5.00 12.00
PSD3 Jimmie Johnson 8.00 20.00
PSD4 Rusty Wallace 5.00 12.00
PSD5 Tony Stewart 8.00 20.00
PSD6 Ryan Newman 4.00 10.00
PSD7 Sterling Marlin 5.00 12.00
PSD8 Michael Waltrip 5.00 12.00
PSD9 Jamie McMurray 5.00 12.00
PSD10 Matt Kenseth 5.00 12.00
PSD11 Scott Riggs 4.00 10.00
PSD12 Joe Nemechek 3.00 8.00
PSD13 Bobby Labonte 5.00 12.00
PSD14 Dale Earnhardt Jr. 10.00 25.00

2005 Press Pass Trackside Runnin n' Gunnin

COMPLETE SET (12) 10.00 25.00
RG1 Dale Earnhardt Jr. 2.00 5.00
RG2 Jeff Gordon 2.00 5.00
RG3 Jimmie Johnson 1.50 4.00
RG4 Ryan Newman 1.50 4.00
RG5 Bobby Labonte 1.00 2.50
RG6 Tony Stewart 1.25 3.00
RG7 Matt Kenseth 1.50 4.00
RG8 Dale Jarrett 1.00 2.50
RG9 Terry Labonte .75 2.00
RG10 Rusty Wallace 1.00 2.50
RG11 Kevin Harvick 1.25 3.00
RG12 Jeff Burton .50 1.25

2002 Press Pass Triple Burner

Randomly inserted into retail packs across several Press Pass products, this set features nine leading drivers' cars. All cards in this set are serial numbered to 100 and include three different swatches: race used lugnut, sheet metal and tire.

TB1 Dale Earnhardt Jr. 25.00 60.00
TB2 Jeff Gordon 40.00 100.00
TB3 Kevin Harvick 25.00 60.00
TB4 Dale Jarrett 30.00 80.00
TB5 Bobby Labonte 30.00 80.00
TB6 Terry Labonte 30.00 80.00
TB7 Mark Martin 30.00 80.00
TB8 Tony Stewart 40.00 100.00
TB9 Rusty Wallace 30.00 80.00

2003 Press Pass Triple Burner

These 10-cards are also part of a continuing Press Pass year long insert program. It kicked off with the 2003 Press Pass set in which 14-copies of each card were released. Each card contains race-used pieces of tires, sheet metal and lugnuts. They were intially issued as redemption cards and included a Press Pass Authentics hologram seal of authenticity.

STATED PRINT RUN 100 SER.#'d SETS
*EXPIRED EXCH: .1X TO .3X
TB1 Jeff Gordon 40.00 100.00
TB2 Ryan Newman 20.00 50.00
TB3 Kevin Harvick 25.00 60.00
TB4 Jimmie Johnson 30.00 80.00
TB5 Rusty Wallace 30.00 80.00
TB6 Mark Martin 30.00 80.00
TB7 Matt Kenseth 25.00 60.00
TB8 Bobby Labonte 25.00 60.00
TB9 Tony Stewart 30.00 80.00
TB10 Dale Earnhardt Jr. 40.00 100.00

2004 Press Pass Triple Burner

This 10-card set was available via redemption cards inserted into hobby packs of 2004 Press Pass brand products. Each card was originally issued as an exchange card redeemable for the specified driver's card. Each card has a swatch of his race-used tire, a swatch of his race-used sheet metal and a slice of his race-used lugnut. The cards were serial numbered to 100. The exchange cards had a deadline of January 31, 2005.

*EXPIRED EXCH: .1X TO .3X
TB1 Jeff Gordon 75.00 150.00
TB2 Ryan Newman 50.00 100.00
TB3 Kevin Harvick 40.00 80.00
TB4 Jimmie Johnson 50.00 100.00
TB5 Rusty Wallace 40.00 80.00
TB6 Mark Martin 40.00 80.00
TB7 Matt Kenseth 40.00 80.00
TB8 Bobby Labonte 30.00 60.00
TB9 Tony Stewart 40.00 80.00
TB10 Dale Earnhardt Jr. 75.00 150.00

2005 Press Pass Triple Burner

INSERTED IN HOBBY PACKS ONLY
STATED PRINT RUN 100 SERIAL #'d SETS
*EXPIRED EXCH: .1X TO .3X
TB1 Jeff Gordon 30.00 80.00
TB2 Ryan Newman 25.00 60.00
TB3 Kevin Harvick 25.00 60.00
TB4 Jimmie Johnson 25.00 60.00
TB5 Rusty Wallace 25.00 60.00
TB6 Mark Martin 15.00 40.00
TB7 Matt Kenseth 25.00 60.00
TB8 Bobby Labonte 25.00 60.00
TB9 Tony Stewart 25.00 60.00
TB10 Dale Earnhardt Jr. 30.00 80.00
TB11 Kurt Busch 25.00 60.00
TB12 Brian Vickers 20.00 50.00

2005 Press Pass UMI Cup Chase

This 11-card set features the 10 drivers from the 2005 Cup Chase along with a checklist card featuring all 10 drivers from the Cup Chase photo shoot. This set was available with purchase of the 2005 UMI Nextel Cup Series Yearbook and the 2006 UMI Preview and Press Guide.

COMP.FACT.SET (11) 15.00 30.00
1 Cup Chase Drivers CL 2.00 5.00
2 Tony Stewart 1.50 4.00
3 Greg Biffle .60 1.50
4 Rusty Wallace 1.25 3.00
5 Jimmie Johnson 2.00 5.00
6 Kurt Busch 1.00 2.50
7 Mark Martin 1.50 4.00
8 Jeremy Mayfield .40 1.00
9 Matt Kenseth 2.00 5.00
10 Carl Edwards 2.00 5.00
11 Ryan Newman 2.00 5.00

2003 Press Pass Victory Lap

This 15-card set featured drivers who won Winston Cup Championships. These sets were given away as subscription premiums with UMI Publications.

COMPLETE SET (15) 10.00 25.00
1 Header CL .20 .50
2 Richard Petty 1.25 3.00
3 Benny Parsons .50 1.25
4 Cale Yarborough .50 1.25
5 Dale Earnhardt 2.50 6.00
6 Darrell Waltrip .50 1.25
7 Bobby Allison .50 1.25
8 Terry Labonte .75 2.00
9 Rusty Wallace 1.00 2.50
10 Alan Kulwicki .50 1.25
11 Jeff Gordon 2.00 5.00
12 Dale Jarrett 1.00 2.50
13 Bobby Labonte 1.00 2.50
14 Tony Stewart 1.25 3.00
15 Matt Kenseth 1.50 4.00

1992 Pro Line Portraits Collectibles Autographs

These standard-size cards were inserted in 1992 Pro Line foil packs. The fronts display full-bleed color photos, while the backs carry extended quotes on a silver panel. The cards are unnumbered and checklisted below in alphabetical order.

2 Dale Jarrett 20.00 50.00

1991 Pro Set Prototypes

This Prototype set was released by Pro Set in its own cello wrapper and features the Bobby Allison Racing Team. Although the cards are unnumbered, they have been assigned numbers below according to alphabetical order. They are often sold as a complete set.

COMPLETE SET (4) 1.25 3.00
P1 Bobby Allison .75 2.00
P2 Hut Stricklin .40 1.00
P3 Hut Stricklin's Car .40 1.00
P4 Cover Card .25 .60

1991 Pro Set

This was Pro Set's first NASCAR release in a run of sets produced by the company from 1991-1994. The set features star drivers, cars and crew members of the top Winston Cup teams. Three cards containing errors were corrected in a later printing and a 37-card Legends insert was also included with the release. The cards were packaged 12 per foil pack with 36 packs per box. One thousand signed cards of Bobby Allison (card number 38) were also randomly inserted as was a special hologram card featuring the Winston Cup Trophy (numbered of 5000). The Allison cards were signed using a black fine line Sharpie pen.

COMPLETE SET (143) 10.00 25.00
WAX BOX 15.00 30.00
1 Rick Mast .12 .30
2 Richard Jackson .12 .30
3 Bob Johnson RC .20 .50
4 Rick Mast w/car .07 .20
5 Rusty Wallace .50 1.25
6 Rusty Wallace .50 1.25
7 Jimmy Makar .12 .30
8 Rusty Wallace's Car .30 .75
9 Ernie Irvan's Car .20 .50
10 Don Miller RC .20 .50
11 Bill Venturini RC .20 .50
12 Roger Penske RC .30 .75
13 Ernie Irvan .30 .75
14 Ernie Irvan .30 .75
15 Larry McClure .12 .30
16 Tony Glover .12 .30
17 Ricky Rudd .30 .75
18A Rick Hendrick ERR .30 .75
18B Rick Hendrick COR .20 .50
19 Waddell Wilson .12 .30
20 Ricky Rudd's Car .20 .50
21 Mark Martin .50 1.25
22 Jack Roush .20 .50
23 Robin Pemberton .12 .30
24 Steve Hmiel .12 .30
25 Mark Martin's Car .30 .75
26 Rick Wilson .12 .30
27 Beth Bruce Ms. Winston .12 .30
28 Harry Hyde .12 .30
29 Rick Wilson's Car .07 .20
30 Bob Whitcomb .12 .30
31 Buddy Parrott .12 .30
32 Derrike Cope's Car .12 .30
33 Geoff Bodine .12 .30
34 Junior Johnson .20 .50
35 Tim Brewer .12 .30
36 Geoff Bodine's Car .07 .20

Hut Stricklin .12 .30
A Bobby Allison ERR .40 1.00
B Bobby Allison COR .25 .60
Hut Stricklin's Car .07 .20
Morgan Shepherd .20 .50
Walter Bud Moore .12 .30
Morgan Shepherd's Car .12 .30
Dale Jarrett .30 .75
Dale Jarrett's Car .20 .50
Junior Johnson .20 .50
Mike Beam .12 .30
Sterling Marlin's Car .12 .30
Mickey Gibbs .12 .30
Barry Dodson .12 .30
Ken Schrader .12 .30
Rick Hendrick .20 .50
Richard Broome .12 .30
Doug Williams .12 .30
Kyle Petty .40 1.00
5 Ned Jarrett .30 .75
Dale Jarrett
5 Cale Yarborough .30 .75
7 Terry Labonte .20 .50
8 Chuck Rider .12 .30
9 Bill Ingle .20 .50
0 Michael Waltrip's Car .15 .40
1 Ken Schrader's Car .07 .20
2 Jimmy Fennig .12 .30
3 Harry Gant .20 .50
4 Andy Petree RC .20 .50
5 Richard Petty .60 1.50
6 Dale Inman .12 .30
7 Robbie Loomis RC .30 .75
8 Richard Petty's Car .40 1.00
9 Jimmy Means .12 .30
0 Jimmy Means' Car .07 .20
1 Dave Marcis .15 .40
2 Dave Marcis' Car .10 .25
3 Lake Speed .12 .30
74 Geoff Bodine .12 .30
75 George Bradshaw RC .20 .50
76 Joe Ruttman RC .20 .50
77 Butch Mock .12 .30
78 Bob Rahilly .12 .30
79 Joe Ruttman's Car .12 .30
80 Terry Labonte .20 .50
81 Steve Loyd RC .20 .50
82 Terry Labonte's Car .12 .30
83 Jimmy Spencer .12 .30
84 Travis Carter .12 .30
85 Jimmy Spencer's Car .12 .30
86 Bobby Hillin .12 .30
87 Kyle Petty .40 1.00
88 Felix Sabates .20 .50
89 Gary Nelson .12 .30
90 Wally Dallenbach Jr. RC .20 .50
91 Danny Glad RC .20 .50
92 Paul Andrews .12 .30
93 Alan Kulwicki .40 1.00
94 Alan Kulwicki's Car .25 .60
95 Chad Little .20 .50
96 Jeff Hammond .20 .50
97 Kenny Bernstein .20 .50
98 Brett Bodine's Car .07 .20
99 Mark Martin .50 1.25
100 Lake Speed's Car .07 .20
101 Wayne Bumgarner RC .20 .50
102 Brett Bodine .12 .30
103 Ted Musgrave RC .30 .75
104 Ted Musgrave's Car .20 .50
105 Larry Pearson .12 .30
106 Larry Hedrick RC .20 .50
107 Robert Harrington RC .20 .50
108 Len Wood .12 .30
109 Eddie Wood .12 .30
110 Leonard Wood .12 .30
111 Buddy Baker .15 .40
112 Dick Moroso RC .20 .50
113 Dick Moroso .20 .50
David Ifft
114 J.D. McDuffie .12 .30
115 Stanley Smith RC .20 .50
116 Eddie Bierschwale .12 .30
117 Darrell Waltrip .30 .75
118 Darrell Waltrip w/car .20 .50
119 Darrell Waltrip's Car .20 .50
120 Chuck Little .20 .50
Alfred Allen RC
121 Greg Sacks .12 .30
122 Junie Donlavey .12 .30
123 Leo Jackson .12 .30
124 Bill Stavola .12 .30
125 Renee White Ms. Winston .12 .30
126 Geoff Bodine .12 .30
127 Ken Schrader .12 .30
128 Ricky Rudd .30 .75
129 Harry Gant .20 .50
130 Richard Petty .60 1.50
131 Bobby Hamilton's Car .12 .30
132 Felix Sabates .20 .50
Gary Nelson
133 Alan Kulwicki .40 1.00
134 Alan Kulwicki Army Car .25 .60
135 Winston Showcar .07 .20
136 Greg Sacks Navy Car .07 .20
137 Mickey Gibbs Air Force Car .07 .20
138 Buddy Baker Marines Car .10 .25
139 D.Marcis Coast Guard Car .10 .25
140 T. Wayne Robertson RC .20 .50
141 Ricky Rudd .30 .75
142 Brett Bodine .12 .30
143A Phil Parsons ERR .20 .50
143B Phil Parsons COR .12 .30
AU38 Bobby Allison ERR AUTO 40.00 80.00
NNO Winston Cup HOLO/5000 8.00 20.00

1991 Pro Set Legends

Pro Set produced this 37-card set as an insert into its 1991 Winston Cup Racing packs.The cards seemed to have been produced in the same quantities as the regular issue and are often sold together as a set. Donnie Allison's card (number L11) contains an error that was later corrected.

COMPLETE SET (37) 2.00 5.00
L1 Dick Brooks .12 .30
L2 Buck Baker .20 .50
L3 Fred Lorenzen .20 .50
L4 Ned Jarrett .15 .40
L5 Dick Hutcherson .12 .30
L6 Marilyn Green .12 .30
L7 Harold Kinder .12 .30
L8 Coo Coo Marlin .20 .50
L9 Ralph Seagraves .12 .30
L10 Paul Bud Moore .12 .30
L11A Donnie Allison ERR .15 .40
L11B Donnie Allison COR .15 .40
L12 Glen Wood .12 .30
L13 Marvin Panch .20 .50
L14 Cale Yarborough .30 .75
L15 Neil Castles (Soapy) .12 .30
L16 Maurice Petty .30 .75
L17 Junior Johnson .20 .50
L18 Tim Flock .20 .50
L19 Smokey Yunick .12 .30
L20 Larry Frank .12 .30
L21 Cotton Owens .12 .30
L22 Ralph Moody Jr. .20 .50
L23 Bob Welborn .12 .30
L24 Neil Bonnett .30 .75
L25 Edwin Matthews (Banjo) .12 .30
L26 Sam McQuagg .12 .30
L27 Jim Paschal .12 .30
L28 David Pearson .40 1.00
L29 Tom Pistone .12 .30
L30 Jack Smith .12 .30
L31 Bobby Allison .25 .60
L32 Charles Ellington .12 .30
L33 Paul Goldsmith .12 .30
L34 Pete Hamilton .12 .30
L35 Rex White .20 .50
L36 Elmo Langley .12 .30
L37 Benny Parsons .30 .75

1991 Pro Set Petty Family Prototypes

Pro Set issued four cards to preview the release of the 1991 Pro Set Petty Family set. The unnumbered cards came in their own cello wrapper and are often sold as a complete set.

COMPLETE SET (4) 1.50 4.00
P1 Lee Petty's Car .30 .75
P2 Maurice Petty .75 2.00
P3 Richard Petty's Car .60 1.50
P4 Cover Card .20 .50

1991 Pro Set Petty Family

Pro Set produced this 50-card set in factory set form. It highlights the careers of Richard and the rest of the Petty racing family. The set was released again in 1992 as part of a special Petty Gift Pack containing a custom card album.

COMP. FACT SET (50) 3.00 8.00
1 Maurice Petty Art .30 .75
R.Petty ART
Lee Petty ART
2 1949 Reaper Shed .30 .75
3 Lee Petty's Car 1949 .05 .15
4 Lee Petty's Car 1949 .05 .15
5 Lee Petty w .15 .40
Car 1950
6 Lee Petty's Car 1951 .05 .15
7 Lee Petty's Car 1952 .05 .15
8 Lee Petty's Car 1953 .05 .15
9 L.Petty .30 .75
Richard Petty
M.Petty
10 Lee Petty's Car 1955 .05 .15
11 Lee Petty's Car 1956 .05 .15
12 Lee Petty's Car 1957 .05 .15
13 Richard Petty 1958 .30 .75
14 Lee Petty .05 .15
Johnny Beauchamp Cars
15 L.Petty .30 .75
Richard Petty
M.Petty
16 Richard Petty's Car 1961 .12 .30
17 Richard Petty 1962 .30 .75
18 Richard Petty .12 .30
Lee Petty Cars 1963
19 Richard Petty's Car 1964 .12 .30
20 Richard Petty's Car 1965 .12 .30
21 Richard Petty's Car 1966 .12 .30
22 Richard Petty 1967 .30 .75
23 Richard Petty's Car 1968 .12 .30
24 Richard Petty's Car 1969 .12 .30
25 Maurice Petty Art .15 .40
26 Maurice Petty .15 .40
Buddy Baker
27 Richard Petty's Car 1972 .12 .30
28 Petty Family .30 .75
29 Maurice Petty 1974 .15 .40
30 Petty Family .30 .75
31 Richard Petty's Trans. .12 .30
32 Richard Petty's Car 1977 .12 .30
33 Richard Petty's Car 1978 .12 .30
34 Richard Petty .30 .75
Kyle Petty Art
35 Richard Petty .12 .30
Kyle Petty Cars
36 Richard Petty .12 .30
Kyle Petty Cars
37 Petty Family .30 .75
38 Richard Petty's Car 1983 .12 .30
39 Kyle Petty's Car 1984 .07 .20
40 Dick Brooks' Car .01 .05
41 Richard Petty's Car 1986 .12 .30
42 Richard Petty's Car 1987 .12 .30
43 Richard Petty's Car 1989 .12 .30
44 Petty Enterprises .30 .75
45 Lee Petty .15 .40
46 Maurice Petty .15 .40
47 Richard Petty .30 .75
48 Kyle Petty .20 .50
49 Richard Petty .30 .75
Maurice Petty
50 Richard Petty Museum .30 .75

1991 Pro Set Pro Files

These cards measure the standard size. The fronts have full-bleed color photos, with facsimile autographs inscribed across the bottom of the pictures. Reportedly only 150 of each were produced and approximately 100 of each were handed out as part of a contest on the Pro Files TV show. Each week viewers were invited to send in their names and addresses to a Pro Set post office box. All subjects in the set made appearances on the TV show. The show was hosted by Craig James and Tim Brant and was aired on Saturday nights in Dallas and sponsored by Pro Set. The cards were subtitled "Signature Series". The cards are unnumbered and are listed in alphabetical order by subject in the checklist below. All of the cards were facsimile autographed except for Anne Smith who signed all of her cards personally.

COMPLETE SET (13) 120.00 300.00
11 Rusty Wallace 10.00 25.00

1992 Pro Set Prototypes

This Prototype set was released by Pro Set in its own cello wrapper. Although the cards are unnumbered, they have been assigned numbers below according to alphabetical order.

COMPLETE SET (4) 2.00 5.00
P1 Dale Earnhardt 1.50 4.00
P2 Sterling Marlin .50 1.25
P3 Morgan Shepherd .30 .75
P4 Cover Card .10 .30

1992 Pro Set

This was Pro Set's second NASCAR release. The set features star drivers, cars and crew members of the top Winston Cup teams from the previous season. Six cards containing errors were corrected in a later printing and a 32-card Legends insert was also included with the release. The Club only factory set, of which 6,000 were made, contained the corrected cards. Cards were packaged 12 per foil pack with 36 packs per box. A special hologram card featuring a Dale Earnhardt Winston Cup Champion logo (numbered of 5000) was produced and randomly distributed through packs. The card originally had a white border, but was later changed to black creating the variation.

COMPLETE SET (248) 10.00 25.00
COMP.FACT.SET (280) 15.00 40.00
1 Dale Earnhardt 1.25 3.00
2 Alan Kulwicki .30 .75
3 Steve Grissom .10 .25
4 Jimmy Hensley .10 .25
5 Tommy Houston .10 .25
6 Bobby Labonte .40 1.00
7 Joe Nemechek .15 .40
8 Robert Pressley .10 .25
9 Kenny Wallace .15 .40
10 Mike Wallace .10 .25
11 Rick Mast's Transporter .05 .10
12 Rusty Wallace's Transporter .15 .40
13 Geoff Bodine .10 .25
14 Ricky Rudd's Transporter .05 .10
15 Alan Kulwicki's Transporter .12 .30
16 Derrike Cope's Transporter .05 .15
17 Harry Gant's Transporter .05 .10
18 Kyle Petty's Transporter .12 .30
19 Dave Marcis' Transporter .05 .10
20 Ernie Irvan w/crew .25 .60
21 Terry Labonte's Transporter .05 .15
22 Jimmy Spencer's Transporter .05 .15
23 Michael Waltrip .20 .50
24 Dale Jarrett .20 .50
25 Derrike Cope's Car .05 .15
26 Kirk Shelmerdine .10 .25
27 Mike Wallace's Car .05 .10
28 Terry Labonte .15 .40
29 Joe Ruttman .10 .25
30 Kyle Petty .30 .75
31 Ricky Craven RC .60 1.50
32 Clifford Allison RC .20 .50
33 Shawna Robinson .25 .60
34 Dorsey Schroeder RC .15 .40
35 Terry Labonte .15 .40
36 Phil Parsons' Car .05 .10
37 Jimmy Means' Car .05 .10
38 Dave Marcis' Car .05 .10
39 Richard Childress .15 .40
40 Hut Stricklin's Transporter .05 .10
41 Davey Allison's Transporter .10 .25
42 Rick Mast .10 .25
43 Richard Petty .50 1.25
44 Kyle Petty .30 .75
45 Richard Petty .50 1.25
46 Chad Little's Transporter .05 .15
47 Jimmy Means .10 .25
48 Dave Marcis .12 .30
49 Harry Gant .12 .30
50 Lake Speed .10 .25
51 Jimmy Spencer .15 .40
52 Bobby Hillin .10 .25
53 Chad Little .15 .40
54 Eddie Bierschwale .10 .25
55 Jack Sprague RC .15 .40
56 Dick Trickle w/car .10 .25
57 Charlie Glotzbach .10 .25
58 Phil Barkdoll .10 .25
59 Dale Earnhardt's Car .50 1.25
60 Ernie Irvan .25 .60
61 Mark Martin's Car .20 .50
62 Geoff Bodine's Car .05 .10
63 Bobby Hamilton's Car .05 .15
64A Dorsey Schroeder's Car ERR .05 .15
64B Dorsey Schroeder's Car COR .05 .15
65 Jimmy Spencer's Car .05 .15
66 Geoff Bodine .10 .25
67A Hut Stricklin Chevy Hat .10 .25
67B Hut Stricklin No Chevy Hat .10 .25
68 Mickey Gibbs .10 .25
69 Wally Dallenbach Jr. .10 .25
70 Ted Musgrave .15 .40
71 Mark Martin .50 1.25
72 Larry Pearson .10 .25
73 Greg Sacks .10 .25
74 Phil Parsons .10 .25
75 Rick Wilson .10 .25
76 Dick Trickle's Car .05 .10
77 Greg Sacks' Car .05 .10
78 Ted Musgrave's Car .05 .15
79 Junior Johnson .15 .40
80 Tony Glover .10 .25
81 Tim Brewer .10 .25
82 Sterling Marlin .15 .40
83 Jeff Hammond .15 .40
84 Leonard Wood .10 .25
85 Andy Petree .10 .25
86 Robin Pemberton .10 .25
87 Robbie Loomis .15 .40
88 Buddy Baker .12 .30
89 J.D.McDuffie w/car .10 .25
90 Steve Hmiel .10 .25
91 Jimmy Makar .10 .25
92 Michael Waltrip's Transporter .07 .20
93 Darrell Waltrip .25 .60
94 Ricky Rudd .12 .30
95 Ernie Irvan .25 .60
96 Mark Martin .50 1.25
97 Darrell Waltrip .25 .60
98 Ken Schrader .10 .25
99 Rusty Wallace .40 1.00
100 Alan Kulwicki .30 .75
101 Geoff Bodine .10 .25
102 Michael Waltrip .20 .50
103 Hut Stricklin .10 .25
104 Ken Schrader .10 .25
105 Dale Jarrett .20 .50
106 Jim Sauter .10 .25
107 Rusty Wallace's Car .15 .40
108 Ernie Irvan's Car .10 .25
109 Ricky Rudd's Car .05 .10
110 Hut Stricklin's Car .05 .10
111 Michael Waltrip's Car .07 .20
112 Harry Gant's Car .05 .10
113 Kyle Petty's Car .12 .30
114 Richard Petty's Car .20 .50
115 Rusty Wallace .40 1.00
116 Terry Labonte's Car .05 .15
117 Stanley Smith .10 .25
118 Eddie Dickerson RC .15 .40
119 Doug Williams .10 .25
120 Donnie Wingo .10 .25
121 Steve Loyd .10 .25
122 David Ifft .10 .25
123 Dick Trickle's Transporter .05 .10
124 Richard Petty's Transporter .20 .50
125 Ward Burton .15 .40
126 Morgan Shepherd .15 .40
127 Todd Bodine .10 .25
128 Jeff Gordon 2.50 6.00
129 Bill Ingle .10 .25
130A Waddell Wilson ERR .10 .25
130B Waddell Wilson COR .10 .25
131 Doug Richert .10 .25
132 Dale Inman .10 .25
133 Ricky Rudd .12 .30
134 Morgan Shepherd .15 .40
135 Jeff Burton .20 .50
136 Tommy Ellis .10 .25
137 Allen Bestwick .15 .40
138 Barry Dodson .10 .25
139 Bobby Hamilton's Trans. .05 .15
140 Beth Bruce Ms.Winston .15 .40
141 Bill Venturini .10 .25
142 Bob Johnson .10 .25
143 Bob Rahilly .10 .25
144 Bobby Allison .20 .50
145 Bobby Dotter .10 .25
146 Brett Bodine .10 .25
147 Buddy Parrott .10 .25
148 Butch Miller .10 .25
149 Cale Yarborough .25 .60
150 Rick Mast's Car .05 .10
151 Cecil Gordon .10 .25
152 Alan Kulwicki's Car .12 .30
153 Chad Little .15 .40
154 Dick Trickle's Car .05 .10
155 Ted Musgrave's Car .05 .15
156 Brett Bodine's Car .05 .15
157 Chuck Bown .10 .25
158 Chad Little's Car .05 .15
159 Chuck Rider .10 .25
160 Morgan Shepherd's Car .05 .15
161 Dale Earnhardt 1.25 3.00
162 Sterling Marlin's Car .05 .15
163 Danny Myers .10 .25
164A David Fuge ERR RC .15 .40
164B David Fuge COR RC .15 .40
165 Ken Schrader's Car .05 .10
166 Dave Rezendes .10 .25
167 David Evans .10 .25
168 Dick Brooks .10 .25
169A Felix Sabates ERR .15 .40
169B Felix Sabates COR .15 .40
170 Gene Roberts RC .15 .40
171 Jack Pennington .10 .25
172 Dale Earnhardt's Transporter .50 1.25
173 Ken Wilson .10 .25
174 Sterling Marlin's Transporter .05 .15
175 Renee White Ms.Winston .15 .40
176 Rodney Combs .10 .25
177 Sterling Marlin .15 .40
178 Michael Waltrip's Car .07 .20
179 Winston Kelley .10 .25
180 Brett Bodine .10 .25
181 Wally Dallenbach Jr.'s Car .05 .15
182 Dale Earnhardt 1.25 3.00
183 Davey Allison .25 .60
184 Mark Martin's Transporter .20 .50
185 Donnie Richeson RC .15 .40
186 Eddie Wood .15 .40
Len Wood RC
187 Eli Gold .10 .25
188 Red Farmer .10 .25
Tommy Allison Jr.
189 Gary Nelson .10 .25
190 Harry Gant .12 .30
191 Jack Ingram .15 .40
192 Jay Smith RC .15 .40
193 Phil Parsons' Transporter .05 .10
194 Joey Knuckles .10 .25
Ryan Pemberton
195 L.D. Ottinger .10 .25
196 Mark Cronquist RC .15 .40
197 Elton Sawyer .15 .40
Patty Moise
198 Mike Beam .10 .25
199 Neil Bonnett .25 .60
200 Butch Mock .10 .25
Bob Rahilly
Dick Trickle's Car
201 Paul Andrews .10 .25
202 Ernie Irvan's Transporter .10 .25
203 Robert Yates .15 .40
204 Richard Broome .10 .25
205 Wally Dallenbach Jr.'s Trans. .05 .10
206 Tracy Leslie .10 .25
207 Will Lind .10 .25
208 Barney Hall .10 .25
209 Darrell Waltrip's Car .10 .25
210 Danny Lawrence .10 .25
211 Davey Allison .25 .60
212 Dennis Connor .10 .25
213 Dick Rahilly RC .15 .40
214 Gary DeHart RC .15 .40
215 N.Bonnett/Baker/Joy ANN .25 .60
216 James Hylton .10 .25
217 Jimmy Fennig .10 .25
218 Jimmy Horton .10 .25
219 Keith Almond .10 .25
220 Marc Reno RC .15 .40
221 Shelton Pittman .10 .25
222 Brett Bodine's Transporter .05 .10
223 Davey Allison w/crew .25 .60
224 Dale Earnhardt w/crew 1.25 3.00
225 Geoff Bodine's Transporter .05 .10
226 Walter Smith RC .15 .40
227 NASCAR Softball Team .05 .15
228 Troy Beebe .10 .25
229 Davey Allison's Car .10 .25
230 David Green RC .30 .75
231 Dewey Livengood RC .15 .40
232 Ed Berrier .10 .25
233 Eddie Lanier .10 .25
234 Irv Hoerr RC .15 .40
235 Jim Phillips .10 .25
236 Larry McReynolds .15 .40
237 Joe Moore .10 .25
238 Jimmy Means' Transporter .05 .10
239 David Smith .10 .25
240 Morgan Shepherd's Pit Crew .15 .40
241 Harry Gant DOY .12 .30
242 Mark Martin Busch Pole .50 1.25
243 Larry McReynolds .15 .40
244 Tom Peck .10 .25
245 Darrell Waltrip's Transporter .10 .25
246 Travis Carter .10 .25
247 Morgan Shepherd's Trans. .05 .15
248A Walter Bud Moore ERR Paul .10 .25
248B Walter Bud Moore COR .10 .25
NNO Earnhardt HOLO/5000 WHT 25.00 60.00
NNO Earnhardt HOLO/5000 BLK 25.00 60.00

1992 Pro Set Legends

Pro Set produced this 32-card set as an insert into its 1992 Winston Cup Racing packs.The cards seemed to have been produced in the same quantities as the regular issue and are often sold together as a set. Dick Hutcherson's card (number L4) contains a wrong photo that was later corrected.

COMPLETE SET (32) 2.00 5.00
L1 Buck Baker .10 .30
L2 Fred Lorenzen .10 .30
L3 Ned Jarrett .10 .30
L4A Dick Hutcherson ERR .15 .40
L4B Dick Hutcherson COR .15 .40
L5 Coo Coo Marlin .07 .20
L6 Paul Bud Moore .07 .20
L7 Donnie Allison .10 .30
L8 Marvin Panch .07 .20
L9 Neil Castles (Soapy) .07 .20
L10 Maurice Petty .10 .30
L11 Tim Flock .07 .20
L12 Smokey Yunick .07 .20
L13 Larry Frank .07 .20
L14 Cotton Owens .07 .20
L15 Ralph Moody Jr. .07 .20
L16 Bob Welborn .07 .20
L17 Marilyn Green .07 .20
L18 Edwin Matthews (Banjo) .07 .20
L19 Sam McQuagg .07 .20
L20 Jim Paschal .07 .20
L21 David Pearson .10 .30
L22 Tom Pistone .07 .20
L23 Jack Smith .07 .20
L24 Charles Ellington .07 .20
L25 Pete Hamilton .07 .20
L26 Rex White .07 .20
L27 Elmo Langley .07 .20
L28 Benny Parsons .10 .30
L29 Harold Kinder .07 .20
L30 Cale Yarborough .10 .30
L31 Junior Johnson .10 .30
L32 Bobby Allison .20 .50

1992 Pro Set Maxwell House

Pro Set produced this 30-card set for Maxwell House. The cards were distributed in six-card packs through Maxwell House filter packs. There were two different title cards available in those packs. An offer to obtain a complete set at $5.00 with 2 proofs of purchase or $15.00 without the POPs was also included in the promotion. The set features drivers from the top NASCAR teams with a special emphasis on Sterling Marlin and the Maxwell House Racing Team. The first 100 people who responded to the mail-in offer received a special set of cards autographed by Sterling Marlin or Junior Johnson.

COMPLETE SET (30) 3.00 8.00
1 Title Card .08 .25
2 Sterling Marlin .15 .40
3 Sterling Marlin .15 .40
4 Junior Johnson .08 .25
5 Sterling Marlin's Car .08 .25
6 Sterling Marlin's Trans. .08 .25
7 Mike Beam .08 .25
8 Sterling Marlin's Car .08 .25
9 Ricky Rudd .15 .40
10 Davey Allison .40 1.00
11 Harry Gant .15 .40
12 Ernie Irvan .15 .40
13 Mark Martin .60 1.50
14 Darrell Waltrip .15 .40
15 Ken Schrader .08 .25
16 Rusty Wallace .60 1.50
17 Morgan Shepherd .08 .25
18 Alan Kulwicki .25 .60
19 Geoff Bodine .08 .25
20 Michael Waltrip .15 .40
21 Hut Stricklin .08 .25
22 Dale Jarrett .50 1.25
23 Terry Labonte .30 .75
24 Brett Bodine .08 .25
25 Richard Petty .25 .60
26 Kyle Petty .15 .40
27 Jimmy Spencer .08 .25
28 Rick Mast .08 .25
29 Wally Dallenbach Jr. .08 .25
30 Sterling Marlin w .15 .40
Car

1992 Pro Set Racing Club

Cards from this set were issued over the course of the 1992 and 1993 race seasons and distributed to members of the Pro Set Racing Club. The cards include an RCC prefix on the numbers and feature drivers and events from both NASCAR Winston Cup and NHRA racing. Finish Line's Racing Club also distributed the cards in complete set form.

COMPLETE SET (8) 6.00 15.00
1 Kenny Bernstein's Car .75 2.00
2 Charlotte Motor Speedway .50 1.25
3 Clifford Allison 1.25 3.00
4 Clifford Allison 1.25 3.00

5 J.Amato .75 2.00
C.Pedregon
W.Johnson
6 Richard Petty's Car .75 2.00
7 Fastest NHRA Drivers .50 1.25
8 The Winston 1993 .50 1.25

1992 Pro Set Rudy Farms

Pro Set produced this 20-card set for Rudy Farms stores. The cards were distributed in Rudy Farms Sandwiches via a 3-card cello packs. The set features cards from the regular issue Pro Set release that have been re-numbered. The five card Legends series is considered part of the 20-card regular set. The Legends cards are numbered 1-5. We have added the L prefix to make it easier to read. An album was also produced for distribution with complete sets. The 5 card Legends set was also available through a proofs-of-purchase mail-in offer from R.B Rice sausage.

COMPLETE SET (20) 18.00 30.00
R.B. RICE SET (5) 3.00 8.00
1 Ricky Rudd .75 2.00
2 Davey Allison 1.00 2.50
3 Harry Gant .75 2.00
4 Ernie Irvan .75 2.00
5 Mark Martin 1.50 4.00
6 Sterling Marlin .75 2.00
7 Darrell Waltrip .75 2.00
8 Ken Schrader .40 1.00
9 Rusty Wallace 1.50 4.00
10 Morgan Shepherd .40 1.00
11 Alan Kulwicki .75 2.00
12 Geoff Bodine .40 1.00
13 Michael Waltrip .40 1.00
14 Kyle Petty .75 2.00
15 Richard Petty 1.00 2.50
L1 Ned Jarrett .40 1.00
L2 David Pearson .40 1.00
L3 Cale Yarborough .75 2.00
L4 Junior Johnson .40 1.00
L5 Bobby Allison .75 2.00

1992 Pro Set Tic Tac Hut Stricklin

Pro Set produced this 6-card set for Tic Tac. The cards were distributed in 2-card cello packs through Tic Tac four packs. The set focuses on Hut Stricklin and the associate sponsored Tic Tac Racing Team.

COMPLETE SET (6) 2.00 4.00
1 Hut Stricklin .40 1.00
2 Bobby Allison .40 1.00
3 Jimmy Fennig .20 .50
4 Keith Almond .20 .50
5 Hut Stricklin's Car .20 .50
6 Hut Stricklin .40 1.00

1994 Quality Care Glidden/Speed

Ford produced this set as a continuation of their Motorcraft Racing issues released previously. Unlike the red colored Motorcraft cards, this set is designed primarily in blue to follow the paint scheme of the Quality Care Racing Teams. Lake Speed and Bob Glidden are the two featured drivers. The cards are unnumbered and listed alphabetically below.

COMPLETE SET (10) 2.50 6.00
1 Bob Glidden .40 1.00
2 Bob Glidden's Car .25 .50
3 Bob Glidden's Car .25 .50
4 Walter Bud Moore .25 .50
5 Lake Speed's Pit Crew .25 .50
6 Lake Speed .40 1.00
7 Lake Speed's Car .25 .50
8 Lake Speed's Car .25 .50
9 Lake Speed .25 .50
Bob Glidden Cars
10 Cover Card .25 .50

1996 Racer's Choice

This 110-card set was the first time Pinnacle issued a set under the Racer's Choice brand name. The black bordered cards feature top Winston Cup stars and their cars. The cards were packaged eight cards per pack; 36 packs per box and 20 boxes per case. Suggested retail price on a pack was 99 cents. Also randomly inserted in the bottom of hobby boxes was a 5" X 7" Jeff Gordon 1995 Championship card. The card features the dufex printing technology and could be found one in every three boxes.

COMPLETE SET (110) 6.00 15.00
WAX BOX HOBBY 20.00 40.00
WAX BOX RETAIL 15.00 30.00
1 Rick Mast .05 .15
2 Rusty Wallace .50 1.25
3 Dale Earnhardt 1.00 2.50
4 Sterling Marlin .20 .50
5 Terry Labonte .20 .50
6 Mark Martin .50 1.25
7 Ward Burton .10 .30
8 Joe Nemechek .05 .15
9 Jeff Gordon .60 1.50
10 Ted Musgrave .05 .15
11 Michael Waltrip .10 .30
12 Johnny Benson, Jr. .10 .30
13 Bill Elliott .25 .60
14 Bobby Labonte .40 1.00
15 Ricky Rudd .20 .50
16 Dale Jarrett .40 1.00
17 Bobby Hamilton .05 .15
18 Ken Schrader .05 .15
19 Derrike Cope .05 .15
20 Brett Bodine .05 .15
21 Darrell Waltrip .10 .30
22 John Andretti .05 .15
23 Jeremy Mayfield .10 .30
24 Ernie Irvan .10 .30
25 Lake Speed .05 .15
26 Rusty Wallace's Car .10 .30
27 Dale Earnhardt's Car .40 1.00
28 Sterling Marlin's Car .05 .15
29 Terry Labonte's Car .10 .30
30 Mark Martin's Car .10 .30
31 Jimmy Spencer's Car .02 .10
32 Dale Jarrett's Car .10 .30
33 Ricky Rudd's Car .05 .15
34 Derrike Cope's Car .02 .10
35 Ward Burton's Car .02 .10
36 Ted Musgrave's Car .02 .10
37 Darrell Waltrip's Car .05 .15
38 Bobby Labonte's Car .10 .30
39 Michael Waltrip w/car .05 .15
40 Jeff Gordon's Car .25 .60
41 Ernie Irvan's Car .05 .15
42 Johnny Benson, Jr.'s Car .02 .10
43 Brett Bodine's Car .02 .10
44 Ricky Craven's Car .02 .10
45 Bobby Hamilton's Car .02 .10
46 Morgan Shepherd's Car .02 .10
47 Joe Nemechek's Car .02 .10
48 Bill Elliott's Car .10 .30
49 Jeremy Mayfield's Car .10 .30
50 John Andretti's Car .02 .10
51 Jeff Gordon WCC .30 .75
52 Jeff Gordon WCC .30 .75
53 Jeff Gordon WCC .30 .75
54 Jeff Gordon WCC .30 .75
55 Jeff Gordon WCC .30 .75
56 Dale Earnhardt I .50 1.25
57 Dale Earnhardt I .50 1.25
58 Dale Earnhardt I .50 1.25
59 Dale Earnhardt I .50 1.25
60 Dale Earnhardt I .50 1.25
61 Ted Musgrave HC .02 .10
62 Ted Musgrave HC .02 .10
63 Ted Musgrave HC .02 .10
64 Ted Musgrave HC .02 .10
65 Ted Musgrave HC .02 .10
66 Bobby Labonte OF .10 .30
67 Bobby Labonte OF .10 .30
68 Bobby Labonte OF .10 .30
69 Bobby Labonte OF .10 .30
70 Bobby Labonte OF .10 .30
71 Sterling Marlin PH .10 .30
72 Sterling Marlin PH .10 .30
73 Sterling Marlin PH .10 .30
74 Sterling Marlin PH .10 .30
75 Sterling Marlin PH .10 .30
76 John Andretti's Car .02 .10
77 Joe Nemechek's Car .02 .10
78 Michael Waltrip's Car .05 .15
79 Doyle Ford .02 .10
80 Jimmy Cox .02 .10
81 Elmo Langley .02 .10
82 Rusty Wallace RW .25 .60
83 Jeff Gordon RW .30 .75
84 Dale Earnhardt RW .50 1.25
85 Mark Martin RW .25 .60
86 Mark Martin RW .25 .60
87 Ward Burton RW .02 .10
88 Ricky Rudd RW .10 .30
89 Dale Earnhardt RW .50 1.25
90 Jeff Gordon BC .30 .75
91 Dale Jarrett BC .10 .30
92 Dale Earnhardt BC .50 1.25
93 Mark Martin BC .25 .60
94 Bobby Labonte BC .10 .30
95 Terry Labonte BC .10 .30
96 Ricky Rudd BC .10 .30
97 Ken Schrader BC .02 .10
98 Bill Elliott BC .10 .30
99 Sterling Marlin BC .10 .30
100 John Andretti BC .02 .10
101 Rick Mast BC .02 .10
102 Ted Musgrave BC .02 .10
103 David Green BC .02 .10
104 Hut Stricklin BC .02 .10
105 Darrell Waltrip BC .05 .15
106 Johnny Benson Jr. R .10 .30
107 Johnny Benson Jr. R .10 .30
108 Johnny Benson Jr. R .10 .30
109 Mark Martin CL .25 .60
110 Jeff Gordon CL .30 .75
J52 Jeff Gordon 5x7 2.50 6.00
P9 Jeff Gordon Promo 2.00 5.00
P99 Sterling Marlin Promo .75 2.00

1996 Racer's Choice Speedway Collection Artist's Proofs

COMPLETE SET (110) 125.00 250.00
*ARTIST PROOFS: 3X TO 8X BASE CARDS

1996 Racer's Choice Racer's Review

Cards in this set are a partial parallel to cards #51-75 from the base set. Each features a new card number and a dufex foil cardfront along with a "Racer's Review" logo.

RANDOM INSERTS IN PACKS
1 Jeff Gordon 1.50 4.00
2 Jeff Gordon 1.50 4.00
3 Jeff Gordon 1.50 4.00
4 Jeff Gordon 1.50 4.00
5 Jeff Gordon 1.50 4.00
Danielle Randall
Jim Brochhausen
6 Dale Earnhardt I 2.50 6.00
Don Hawk
7 Dale Earnhardt Jr. 2.50 6.00
8 Dale Earnhardt Jr. 2.50 6.00
9 Dale Earnhardt Jr. 2.50 6.00
10 Dale Earnhardt Jr. 2.50 6.00
11 Bobby Labonte .60 1.50
12 Bobby Labonte .60 1.50
13 Bobby Labonte .60 1.50
Donna Labonte
14 Bobby Labonte .60 1.50
15 Bobby Labonte .60 1.50
16 Sterling Marlin .60 1.50
17 Sterling Marlin .60 1.50
Clifton Marlin
Paula Marlin
Sutherlin Marlin
Steadman Marlin
18 Sterling Marlin .60 1.50
19 Sterling Marlin .60 1.50
Tony Glover
20 Sterling Marlin .60 1.50

1996 Racer's Choice Speedway Collection

COMPLETE SET (110) 15.00 40.00
*SPEEDWAY COLL: 1.5X TO 4X BASE CARDS

1996 Racer's Choice Top Ten

This 10-card insert set features the drivers who finished in the Top Ten in the 1995 Winston Cup points standings. The cards were printed on foil board and use micro-etched highlights. Top Ten cards were randomly inserted in packs at a rate of one in 69 regular packs and of one in 35 jumbo packs.

COMPLETE SET (10) 30.00 80.00
1 Jeff Gordon 6.00 15.00
2 Dale Earnhardt 10.00 25.00
3 Sterling Marlin 2.00 5.00
4 Mark Martin 2.00 5.00
5 Rusty Wallace 2.00 5.00
6 Terry Labonte 2.00 5.00
7 Ted Musgrave 1.25 3.00
8 Bill Elliott 3.00 8.00
9 Ricky Rudd 1.50 4.00
10 Bobby Labonte 2.00 5.00
P2 Dale Earnhardt Promo 4.00 10.00

1996 Racer's Choice Up Close with Dale Earnhardt

This 7-card insert set could be found in hobby only packs. The cards feature Winston Cup great Dale Earnhardt. The cards were randomly inserted in hobby packs at a rate of one in 31.

COMPLETE SET (7) 15.00 40.00
DALE EARNHARDT CARD (1-7) 2.50 6.00

1996 Racer's Choice Up Close with Jeff Gordon

This 7-card insert set features 1995 Winston Cup Champion Jeff Gordon.The cards were seeded in retail packs at a rate of one in 31.

COMPLETE SET (7) 12.00 30.00
JEFF GORDON CARD (1-7) 2.00 5.00

1996 Racer's Choice Sundrop

One card was inserted in each specially marked 12-packs of Sundrop citrus soda. The cards come in an opaque wrapper attached to the cardboard packaging of the 12-packs. There were signed copies of each of the three cards also randomly inserted in the soft drink packages. The autographed cards were not certified in any way and are otherwise indistinguishable from the unsigned regular cards. Many dealers have left the signed cards in the opaque wrappers to distinguish the origin of the card.

COMPLETE SET (3) 6.00 15.00
COMMON CARD (SD1-SD3) 2.00 5.00

1997 Racer's Choice

This 106-card set was produced by Pinnacle Brands. The white bordered cards feature the top Winston Cup stars and their cars. Cards were distributed in eight card packs with 36 pack in a box. The packs carried a suggested retail price of $.99.

COMPLETE SET (106) 6.00 15.00
1 Morgan Shepherd .05 .15
2 Rusty Wallace .50 1.25
3 Dale Earnhardt 1.00 2.50
4 Sterling Marlin .20 .50
5 Terry Labonte .20 .50
6 Mark Martin .50 1.25
7 Geoff Bodine .05 .15
8 Hut Stricklin .05 .15
9 Chad Little .10 .30
10 Ricky Rudd .20 .50
11 Brett Bodine .05 .15
12 Derrike Cope .05 .15
13 Jeremy Mayfield .10 .30
14 Robby Gordon RC .20 .50
15 Steve Grissom .05 .15
16 Ted Musgrave .05 .15
17 Darrell Waltrip .10 .30
18 Bobby Labonte .40 1.00
19 John Andretti .05 .15
20 Bobby Hamilton .05 .15
21 Michael Waltrip .10 .30
22 Ward Burton .10 .30
23 Jimmy Spencer .05 .15
24 Jeff Gordon .60 1.50
25 Ricky Craven .05 .15
26 Kyle Petty .10 .30
27 Dale Earnhardt 1.00 2.50
28 Ernie Irvan .10 .30
29 Joe Nemechek .05 .15
30 Johnny Benson .10 .30
31 Mike Skinner .05 .15
32 Dale Jarrett .40 1.00
33 Ken Schrader .05 .15
34 Bill Elliott .25 .60
35 David Green .05 .15
36 Morgan Shepherd's Car .02 .10
37 Rusty Wallace's Car .10 .30
38 Dale Earnhardt's Car .40 1.00
39 Sterling Marlin's Car .05 .15
40 Terry Labonte's Car .10 .30
41 Mark Martin's Car .10 .30
42 Geoff Bodine's Car .02 .10
43 Hut Stricklin's Car .02 .10
44 Chad Little's Car .02 .10
45 Ricky Rudd's Car .05 .15
46 Brett Bodine's Car .02 .10
47 Derrike Cope's Car .02 .10
48 Jeremy Mayfield's Car .02 .10
49 Robby Gordon's Car .10 .30
50 Steve Grissom's Car .02 .10
51 Ted Musgrave's Car .02 .10
52 Darrell Waltrip's Car .02 .10
53 Bobby Labonte's Car .10 .30
54 John Andretti's Car .02 .10
55 Bobby Hamilton's Car .02 .10
56 Michael Waltrip's Car .05 .15
57 Ward Burton's Car .02 .10
58 Jimmy Spencer's Car .02 .10
59 Geoff Bodine's Car .02 .10
60 Ricky Craven's Car .02 .10
61 Kyle Petty's Car .02 .10
62 Dale Earnhardt's Car .40 1.00
63 Ernie Irvan's Car .02 .10
64 Joe Nemechek's Car .02 .10
65 Johnny Benson's Car .02 .10
66 Mike Skinner's Car .02 .10
67 Dale Jarrett's Car .10 .30
68 Ken Schrader's Car .02 .10
69 Bill Elliott's Car .10 .30
70 David Green's Car .02 .10
71 Gary Nelson SS .02 .10
72 Robert Yates SS .02 .10
73 Robin Pemberton SS .02 .10
74 Kyle Petty SS .10 .30
75 Geoff Bodine SS .05 .15
76 Earl Barban SS .02 .10
77 Jeremy Mayfield SS .10 .30
78 Steve Grissom SS .05 .15
79 Mike Skinner SS .05 .15
80 Richard Childress SS .10 .30
81 Chocolate Meyers SS .02 .10
82 Ward Burton SS .10 .30
83 Chad Little SS .10 .30
84 Buddy Parrott SS .02 .10
85 Jimmy Cox SS .02 .10
86 Richard Petty SS .05 .15
87 Mike Skinner R .05 .15
88 David Green R .05 .15
89 Robby Gordon R .10 .30
90 Dale Earnhardt TR .50 1.25
91 Rusty Wallace TR .25 .60
92 Sterling Marlin TR .05 .15
93 Terry Labonte TR .10 .30
94 Mark Martin TR .25 .60
95 Ricky Rudd TR .10 .30
96 Ted Musgrave TR .05 .15
97 Johnny Benson TR .10 .30
98 Bobby Labonte TR .20 .50
99 Bobby Hamilton TR .05 .15
100 Michael Waltrip TR .10 .30
101 Ward Burton TR .10 .30
102 Ricky Craven TR .05 .15
103 Ernie Irvan TR .10 .30
104 Dale Earnhardt TR .50 1.25
105 Dale Jarrett TR .20 .50
106 Dale Earnhardt CL .50 1.25
P5 Terry Labonte Promo 1.00 2.50

1997 Racer's Choice Showcase Series

COMPLETE SET (106) 40.00 80.00
*SHOWCASE SERIES: 2.5X TO 6X BASE CARDS

1997 Racer's Choice Busch Clash

This 14-card insert highlights those NASCAR drivers who have appeared in the Busch Clash. The cards were randomly inserted in hobby packs at a ratio of 1:47 and in magazine packs at a ratio of 1:23.

COMPLETE SET (14) 50.00 120.00
1 Dale Earnhardt 12.50 30.00
2 Terry Labonte 2.50 6.00
3 Johnny Benson 1.50 4.00
4 Ward Burton 1.50 4.00
5 Mark Martin 6.00 15.00
6 Ricky Craven .75 2.00
7 Ernie Irvan 1.50 4.00
8 Jeff Gordon 8.00 20.00
9 Ted Musgrave .75 2.00
10 Jeremy Mayfield 1.50 4.00
11 Dale Earnhardt 12.50 30.00
12 Dale Jarrett 5.00 12.00
13 Bobby Labonte 5.00 12.00
14 Rusty Wallace 6.00 15.00

1997 Racer's Choice Chevy Madness

This 6-card set is the continuation of the set that started in 1997 Action Packed and ended in 1997 Pinnacle. The cards were randomly inserted in hobby packs at a ratio of 1:17 and in magazine packs at a ratio of 1:8.

COMPLETE SET (6) 12.50 30.00
7 Jeff Gordon 4.00 10.00
8 Dale Earnhardt 6.00 15.00
9 Ricky Craven .40 1.00
10 Robby Gordon 1.25 3.00
11 Jeff Green .40 1.00
12 Terry Labonte 1.25 3.00

1997 Racer's Choice High Octane

This 15-card set features the top 15 drivers from the Winston Cup circuit.The cards were randomly inserted in hobby packs at a ratio of 1:23 and in magazine packs at a ratio of 1:12.

COMPLETE SET (15) 50.00 100.00
COMP.GLOW SET (15) 100.00 200.00
*GLOW: .6X TO 1.5X BASIC INSERTS
1 Terry Labonte 1.50 4.00
2 Dale Earnhardt 10.00 25.00
3 Jeff Gordon 6.00 15.00
4 Dale Jarrett 1.50 4.00
5 Mark Martin 1.50 4.00
6 Rusty Wallace 1.50 4.00
7 Bill Elliott 3.00 8.00
8 Bobby Labonte 1.50 4.00
9 Ernie Irvan 1.50 4.00
10 Kyle Petty 1.25 3.00
11 Ricky Rudd 1.25 3.00
12 Johnny Benson 1.50 4.00
13 Ward Burton 1.25 3.00
14 Ted Musgrave 1.00 2.50
15 Derrick Cope 1.25 3.00

1997 Race Sharks

This 45-card set is another uniquely themed set from Wheels. The cards feature the top names in racing. The cards are printed on 36 point paper. Each card has a wave like background and is stamped in silver foil. The cards were packaged three cards per pack, 24 packs per box and 16 boxes per case. There were a total of 1250 numbered cases. The first 375 cases off the press had the First Bite logo stamped on all the cards in those cases.

COMPLETE SET (45) 5.00 12.00
1 Dale Earnhardt 1.25 3.00
2 Jeff Gordon .75 2.00
3 Dale Jarrett .50 1.25
4 Terry Labonte .25 .60
5 Rusty Wallace .60 1.50
6 Mark Martin .60 1.50
7 Sterling Marlin .25 .60
8 Bill Elliott .30 .75
9 Bobby Labonte .50 1.25
10 Bobby Hamilton .07 .20
11 Darrell Waltrip .15 .40
12 Michael Waltrip .15 .40
13 Mike Wallace .07 .20
14 Kyle Petty .15 .40
15 Ken Schrader .07 .20
16 Ricky Craven .07 .20
17 Derrike Cope .07 .20
18 Jeff Burton .25 .60
19 Ward Burton .15 .40
20 Robert Pressley .07 .20
21 Joe Nemechek .07 .20
22 Brett Bodine .07 .20
23 Jimmy Spencer .07 .20
24 Chad Little .07 .20
25 Bobby Labonte .50 1.25
26 Terry Labonte .25 .60
27 Mark Martin .60 1.50
28 Jeff Green .07 .20
29 David Green .07 .20
30 Dale Jarrett .50 1.25
31 Joe Gibbs .15 .40
32 Richard Childress .15 .40
33 Bobby Allison .07 .20
34 Dale Jarrett .50 1.25
35 Jeff Gordon .75 2.00
36 Jeff Gordon .75 2.00
37 Rusty Wallace .60 1.50
38 Sterling Marlin .25 .60
39 Rusty Wallace .60 1.50
40 Jeff Gordon .75 2.00
41 Dale Jarrett .50 1.
42 Rusty Wallace .60 1.
43 Jeff Gordon .75 2.
44 Checklist .02
45 Checklist .02
P1 Jeff Gordon Promo 2.50 6.

1997 Race Sharks First Bite

COMP.FIRST BITE SET (45) 6.00 15.
*FIRST BITE: .6X TO 1.5X BASE CARDS

1997 Race Sharks Great White

COMPLETE SET (45) 15.00 40.
*GREAT WHITE: 1.2X TO 3X BASE CARDS

1997 Race Sharks Hammerhead

COMPLETE SET (45) 40.00 80.
*HAMMERHEAD: 2.5X TO 6X HI COL.

1997 Race Sharks Hammerhead First Bite

COMP.FIRST BITE (45) 50.00 100.
*FIRST BITE: .5X TO 1.2X HAMMERHEAD

1997 Race Sharks Tiger Shark

COMPLETE SET (45) 60.00 150.
*TIGER SHARKS: 3X TO 8X HI COL.

1997 Race Sharks Great White Shark's Teeth

This 10-card insert set features the dominant drivers on the NASCAR circuit. Each card also features a real Shark's tooth embedded in the ca[rd]. The odds of pulling one of these cards is one in 96 packs. The First Bite versions of the Great White cards featured white sharks teeth as opposed to gray colored sharks teeth on the regular Great Whites.

COMPLETE SET (10) 150.00 300.00
COMP.FIRST BITE (10) 200.00 400.00
*FIRST BITE: .5X TO 1.2X BASIC INSERTS
GW1 Dale Earnhardt 40.00 100.00
GW2 Jeff Gordon 25.00 60.00
GW3 Terry Labonte 10.00 25.00
GW4 Dale Jarrett 10.00 25.00
GW5 Rusty Wallace 12.00 30.00
GW6 Mark Martin 6.00 15.00
GW7 Bobby Labonte 8.00 20.00
GW8 Bill Elliott 10.00 25.00
GW9 Sterling Marlin 8.00 20.00
GW10 Ricky Craven 6.00 15.00

1997 Race Sharks Shark Attack

Just when you thought it was safe to go back into your favorite hobby store. That was the slogan Wheels used to promote their Race Sharks product. The 10-card Shark Attack set featured micro-etched cards and a simulated embossed shark's tooth. The cards were randomly seeded one in 48 packs.

COMPLETE SET (10) 60.00 120.00
COMP.FIRST BITE (10) 75.00 150.00
*FIRST BITE: .5X TO 1.2X SHARK ATTACK
COMP.FB PREVIEW (10) 10.00 25.00
*FB PREVIEWS: .1X TO .2X SHARK ATTACK
SA1 Dale Earnhardt 15.00 40.00
SA2 Jeff Gordon 10.00 25.00
SA3 Dale Jarrett 6.00 15.00
SA4 Rusty Wallace 8.00 20.00
SA5 Terry Labonte 3.00 8.00
SA6 Sterling Marlin 3.00 8.00
SA7 Michael Waltrip 2.00 5.00
SA8 Kyle Petty 2.00 5.00
SA9 Ward Burton 2.00 5.00
SA10 Jeff Burton 3.00 8.00

1997 Race Sharks Shark Tooth Signatures

This 25-card set features autographs of Winston Cup and Busch Grand National drivers, crew chiefs, owners and other racing personalities. The cards were inserted one per 24 packs.

*FIRST BITE/400: .5X TO 1.2X BASIC AU
ST1 Dale Earnhardt/300 150.00 300.00
ST2 Jeff Gordon/400 50.00 100.00
ST3 Dale Jarrett/600 10.00 25.00
ST4 Terry Labonte/600 12.50 30.00
ST5 Sterling Marlin/600 10.00 25.00

ill Elliott/600 15.00 40.00
Ricky Craven/800 6.00 15.00
Robert Pressley/800 6.00 15.00
Jeff Burton/800 8.00 20.00
Ward Burton/800 8.00 20.00
Bobby Labonte/800 10.00 25.00
Joe Nemechek/800 3.00 8.00
Chad Little/800 6.00 15.00
David Green/800 6.00 15.00
Jeff Green/800 6.00 15.00
Joe Gibbs/400 20.00 50.00
Todd Parrott/1000 6.00 15.00
Jeff Hammond 6.00 15.00
Charlie Pressley/1000 3.00 6.00
Joey Knuckles 3.00 6.00
David Smith/1000 3.00 6.00
Brad Parrott 6.00 15.00
Eddie Dickerson/1200 3.00 6.00
Randy Dorton/1200 6.00 15.00
Jimmy Johnson/1200 3.00 6.00

997 Race Sharks Tiger Shark First Bite

P.FIRST BITE (45) 100.00 200.00
ST BITE: .5X TO 1.2X TIGER SHARK

991 Racing Concepts Shawna Robinson

s nine-card set features one of the most ular female drivers ever to race NASCAR, wna Robinson. The set was distributed ugh Sparky's and were originally sold with ts 1-6 and a Sparky's coupon that could be eemed for one of the cards, 7-9, with purchase.

MPLETE SET (9) 5.00 12.00
over Card .15 .40
hawna Robinson .60 1.50
hawna Robinson .60 1.50
Shawna Robinson .60 1.50
Shawna Robinson .60 1.50
Shawna Robinson .60 1.50
Dwight Huffman
Dennis Combs
Shawna Robinson .60 1.50
Shawna Robinson .75 2.00
David Pearson
Shawna Robinson .60 1.50

1992 Redline Graphics Short Track

edline Graphics produced this set featuring race ction scenes from various short track races. The ards primarily picture exciting crashes caught by he photographer.

COMPLETE SET (30) 4.00 8.00
Cover Card .10 .30
Late Model Sandwich .25 .60
Elko Speedway .10 .30
Window Shot #1 .10 .30
Window Shot #2 .10 .30
Veteran and Rookie .10 .30
Lift Off .10 .30
Orbit .10 .30
Landing .10 .30
10 Aftermath .10 .30
11 Inside Move .10 .30
12 Three Deep .10 .30
13 Roof Dance .10 .30
14 The Ride Continues .10 .30
15 Finally Over .10 .30
16 Miraculous .10 .30
17 High Speed Wipeout .10 .30
18 Front Stretch Mishap .10 .30
19 Prelude to Defeat .10 .30
20 Oh No! .20 .50
21 Fabulous Race .20 .50
22 Raceway Park .10 .30
23 Champion .10 .30
24 Hobby Crash .10 .30
25 Show Car .20 .50
26 Parking Lot .10 .30
27 Ouch! .10 .30
28 Father and Son .20 .50
29 Infamous Turn Four .10 .30
30 Checklist .10 .30

1992 Redline Racing Harry Gant

This set is one of four issues produced in 1992 by Redline Racing entitled My Life in Racing. The set focuses on the life of Harry Gant with text written in story form on the cardbacks. The four driver sets were packaged together in factory set form 24-sets per display box. Each set includes a colorful factory box and was limited to a production run of 25,000.

COMP. FACT SET (30) 3.00 8.00
COMMON CARD (1-30) .10 .30
P1 Harry Gant Prototype .60 1.50

1992 Redline Racing Rob Moroso

This set is one of four issues produced in 1992 by Redline Racing entitled My Life in Racing. The set focuses on the life and tragic death of Rob Moroso with text written in story form on the cardbacks. The four driver sets were packaged together in factory set form 24-sets per display box. Each set includes a colorful factory set box was limited to a production run of 25,000.

COMP. FACT SET (30) 2.50 6.00
COMMON CARD (1-30) .10 .30
P1 Rob Moroso Prototype .40 1.00

1992 Redline Racing Ken Schrader

This set is one of four issues produced in 1992 by Redline Racing entitled My Life in Racing. The set focuses on the life of Ken Schrader with text written in story form on the cardbacks. The four driver sets were packaged together in factory set form 24-sets per display box. Each set includes a colorful factory box and was limited to a production run of 25,000.

COMP. FACT SET (30) 2.50 6.00
COMMON CARD (1-30) .08 .25
P1 Ken Schrader Prototype .60 1.50

1992 Redline Racing Cale Yarborough

This set is one of four issues produced in 1992 by Redline Racing entitled My Life in Racing. The set focuses on the life of Cale Yarborough with text written in story form on the cardbacks. The four sets were packaged together in factory set form 24-sets per display box. Each set includes a colorful factory box and was limited to a production run of 25,000.

COMP. FACT SET (30) 2.50 6.00
COMMON CARD (1-30) .08 .25
P1 Cale Yarborough Prototype .60 1.50

1992 Redline Standups

Redline Racing and Photo File of New York produced this unique set in 1992. Each card could be folded in such a way as to stand-up independently. The cards were packed one per foil pack (48-packs per box) and contain a full bleed color photo on the front. Another photo and brief driver stats are on the cardback with the set name and die cut photo of the driver's car on the stand-up support piece. Uncut sheets of the 36-card set have also been made available.

COMPLETE SET (36) 5.00 12.00
1 Rick Mast .07 .20
2 Dave Marcis .07 .20
3 Richard Petty .25 .60
4 Bobby Labonte .60 1.50
5 Jimmy Means .07 .20
6 Mark Martin .75 2.00
7 Alan Kulwicki .25 .60
8 Rick Wilson .07 .20
9 Bill Elliott .40 1.00
10 Derrike Cope .07 .20
11 Geoff Bodine .07 .20
12 Jack Ingram .07 .20
13 Dick Trickle .07 .20
14 Jeff Burton .15 .40
15 Morgan Shepherd .07 .20
16 Tom Peck .07 .20
17 Darrell Waltrip .15 .40
18 Jimmy Spencer .07 .20
19 Chad Little .07 .20
20 Bobby Hillin .07 .20
21 Dale Jarrett .60 1.50
22 Sterling Marlin .15 .40
23 Bobby Hamilton .07 .20
24 Kyle Petty .15 .40
25 Ken Schrader .07 .20
26 Brett Bodine .07 .20
27 Chuck Bown .07 .20
28 Kenny Wallace .07 .20
29 Joe Nemechek .07 .20
30 Terry Labonte .40 1.00
31 Steve Grissom .07 .20
32 Jimmy Hensley .07 .20
33 Harry Gant .15 .40
34 Harry Gant .15 .40
35 Bobby Labonte .60 1.50
36 Doyle Ford .07 .20

1992 RSS Motorsports Haulers

RSS Motorsports released these cards in complete set form. They feature transporter drivers for top NASCAR race teams. Jerry Schweitz is included in the set twice with the second card bearing a "promotional card" logo on the cardback. The checklist card contains two misnumbered cards.

COMPLETE SET (30) 1.25 3.00
1 Richard Bostick Jr. .05 .15
2 Jerry Seabolt .05 .15
3 Ken J. Hartley .05 .15
4 George R. Colwell .05 .15
5 Carroll Hoss Berry .05 .15
6 Terry Hall .05 .15
7 Robin Metdepenningen .05 .15
8 Buster Auton .05 .15
9 Henry Benfield .05 .15
10 Gale W. Wilson .05 .15
11 Peter Jellen .05 .15
12 Tommy Rigsbee .05 .15
13 Harold Hughes .05 .15
14 Gene Starnes .05 .15
15 Bill McCarthy .05 .15
16 Bryan Dorsey .05 .15
17 Dennis Ritchie .05 .15
18 Joe Lewis .05 .15
19 Mike Powell .05 .15
20 Steve Foster .05 .15
21 Jerry Schweitz .05 .15
22 Ted Harrison .05 .15
23 Norman Koshimizu .05 .15
24 Charlie Hyde .05 .15
25 Mike Culbertson .05 .15
26 Jim Baldwin .05 .15
27 Bart Creasman .05 .15
28 Jerry Schweitz Promo .05 .15
29 Checklist Card UER .05 .15
30 Cover Card .05 .15

1997 SB Motorsports

This 100-card set captures the top names in Winston Cup racing, including drivers, owners, crew chiefs, crew members and announcers. Each card carries complete updated stats through the 1996 racing season. The cards were packaged six per pack with 36 packs per box and 16 boxes per case. SB stands for manufacturer Score Board.

COMPLETE SET (100) 6.00 15.00
1 Dale Earnhardt 1.00 2.50
2 Jeff Gordon .60 1.50
3 Terry Labonte .25 .60
4 Dale Jarrett .40 1.00
5 Robby Gordon RC .25 .60
6 Mark Martin .50 1.25
7 Ricky Rudd .25 .60
8 Richard Petty .25 .60
9 Ken Schrader .07 .20
10 Ernie Irvan .15 .40
11 Sterling Marlin .25 .60
12 Bobby Labonte .40 1.00
13 Ted Musgrave .07 .20
14 Bobby Hamilton .07 .20
15 Jimmy Spencer .07 .20
16 Michael Waltrip .15 .40
17 Jeff Burton .25 .60
18 Rick Mast .07 .20
19 Geoff Bodine .07 .20
20 Ricky Craven .07 .20
21 Morgan Shepherd .07 .20
22 Johnny Benson .15 .40
23 Jeremy Mayfield .15 .40
24 Wally Dallenbach .07 .20
25 Brett Bodine .07 .20
26 Larry Hedrick .02 .10
27 Ned Jarrett .02 .10
28 Darrell Waltrip .15 .40
29 Hut Stricklin .07 .20
30 Richard Petty .25 .60
31 Kyle Petty .15 .40
32 Robert Yates .02 .10
33 Mike Skinner .07 .20
34 Robin Pemberton .02 .10
35 Ray Evernham .07 .20
36 Larry McReynolds .02 .10
37 Mike Wallace .07 .20
38 Steve Park RC 1.00 2.00
39 Steve Grissom .07 .20
40 Dale Jarrett .40 1.00
41 Dale Earnhardt 1.00 2.50
42 Mark Martin .50 1.25
43 Ricky Rudd .25 .60
44 Wood Brothers .02 .10
45 Robby Gordon's Car .15 .40
46 Rusty Wallace's Car .25 .60
47 Dale Earnhardt's Car .40 1.00
48 Sterling Marlin's Car .07 .20
49 Mark Martin's Car .25 .60
50 Dale Earnhardt's Car CL .40 1.00
51 Bobby Labonte's Car .15 .40
52 Michael Waltrip's Car .07 .20
53 Ernie Irvan's Car .02 .10
54 Darrell Waltrip's Car .02 .10
55 Dale Jarrett's Car .15 .40
56 Dave Rezendes .07 .20
57 Sterling Marlin .25 .60
58 Ken Schrader .07 .20
59 Richard Childress .15 .40
60 Wood Brothers .02 .10
61 Tony Glover .02 .10
62 Steve Hmiel .02 .10
63 The Rainbow Warriors .02 .10
64 Steve Grissom .07 .20
65 Larry McClure .02 .10
66 Ernie Irvan .15 .40
67 Jerry Punch .07 .20
68 Shelton Pittman .02 .10
69 Jack Roush .02 .10
70 Geoff Bodine .07 .20
71 Robert Pressley .07 .20
72 John Andretti .07 .20
73 Ward Burton .15 .40
74 Dick Trickle .07 .20
75 Dave Marcis .07 .20
76 Kenny Wallace .07 .20
77 Todd Bodine .07 .20
78 Gary DeHart .02 .10
79 Ron Hornaday .07 .20
80 David Green .07 .20
81 Randy Dorton .02 .10
82 Kellogg's Crew .02 .10
83 Johnny Benson .15 .40
84 Jeremy Mayfield .15 .40
85 Mike Skinner .07 .20
86 #25 Hendrick Team .02 .10
87 Bobby Labonte .40 1.00
88 Jimmy Johnson .07 .20
89 Jimmy Spencer .07 .20
90 Michael Waltrip .15 .40
91 Morgan Shepherd .07 .20
92 Dale Earnhardt 1.00 2.50
93 Dale Jarrett .40 1.00
94 Rick Hendrick .02 .10
95 Mark Martin .50 1.25
96 Ricky Rudd .25 .60
97 Ernie Irvan .15 .40
98 Sterling Marlin .25 .60
99 Kyle Petty .15 .40
100 Sterling Marlin's Car CL .02 .10

1997 SB Motorsports Autographs

Five drivers from the Winston Cup circuit hand-signed insert cards for the 1997 SB Motorsports product. The cards were inserted at the rate of 1:576 Packs. Each card was sequentially hand-numbered on the front and did not contain a card number.

COMPLETE SET (5) 450.00 800.00
1 Dale Earnhardt/500 150.00 300.00
2 Jeff Gordon/250 50.00 100.00
3 Robby Gordon/500 10.00 25.00
4 Dale Jarrett 20.00 50.00
5 Terry Labonte 12.50 30.00

1997 SB Motorsports Race Chat

This 10-card insert set features quotes on the backs of each card from drivers, owners, and crew chiefs about the driver featured on the card. The quotes give insight as to how they feel about racing and their competitors. The cards were seeded one in 35 packs.

COMPLETE SET (10) 20.00 50.00
RC1 Dale Earnhardt 10.00 25.00
RC2 Ricky Craven .75 2.00
RC3 Ernie Irvan 1.50 4.00
RC4 Dale Jarrett 4.00 10.00
RC5 Sterling Marlin 2.50 6.00
RC6 Mark Martin 5.00 12.00
RC7 Johnny Benson 1.50 4.00
RC8 Ricky Rudd 2.50 6.00
RC9 Bobby Labonte 4.00 10.00
RC10 Kyle Petty 1.50 4.00

1997 SB Motorsports Winston Cup Rewind

The 31-card insert set commemorates highlights from each Winston Cup events of 1996. The cards were randomly inserted in packs at a rate of one in 8 packs.

COMPLETE SET (31) 25.00 60.00
WC1 Dale Jarrett 2.00 5.00
WC2 Dale Earnhardt's Car 2.00 5.00
WC3 Ted Musgrave .40 1.00
WC4 Johnny Benson .75 2.00
WC5 Ward Burton .75 2.00
WC6 Mark Martin 2.50 6.00
WC7 Robert Pressley .40 1.00
WC8 Ricky Craven .40 1.00
WC9 Sterling Marlin 1.25 3.00
WC10 Wally Dallenbach .40 1.00
WC11 Dale Jarrett 2.00 5.00
WC12 Bobby Labonte 2.00 5.00
WC13 Geoff Bodine .40 1.00
WC14 Bobby Hamilton .40 1.00
WC15 Dave Marcis .40 1.00
WC16 Ernie Irvan .75 2.00
WC17 Ricky Rudd 1.25 3.00
WC18 Jeremy Mayfield .75 2.00
WC19 Dale Jarrett 2.00 5.00
WC20 Dale Earnhardt's Car 2.00 5.00
WC21 Jeff Burton 1.25 3.00
WC22 Mark Martin 2.50 6.00
WC23 Hut Stricklin .40 1.00
WC24 Ernie Irvan .75 2.00
WC25 Bobby Labonte 2.00 5.00
WC26 Bobby Hamilton .40 1.00
WC27 Ted Musgrave .40 1.00
WC28 Ricky Craven .40 1.00
WC29 Ricky Rudd 1.25 3.00
WC30 Bobby Hamilton .40 1.00
WC31 Terry Labonte's Car/1996 1.25 3.00

1994 Score Board National Promos

Distributed during the 1994 National Sports Collectors Convention, this 20-card standard-size multi-sport set features four subsets: Salute to 1994 Draft Stars (1-5), Centers of Attention (6-9), Texas Heroes (10-13, 20), and Salute to Racing's Greatest (14-18). The borderless fronts feature color action cutouts on multi-colored metallic backgrounds. The players name, position, and team name appear randomly placed on arcs. The borderless backs feature a color head shot on a ghosted backgound. The players name and biography appear at the top with the player's stats and profile at the bottom. The cards are numbered on the back with an "NC" prefix. The sets were given away to attendees at Classic's National Convention Party. Each set included a certificate of authenticity, giving the set serial number out of a total of 9,900 sets produced. There were five different checklist cards created using the fronts of other cards in the set. The complete set price includes only one of the checklist cards.

COMPLETE SET (20) 20.00 40.00
14 Dale Earnhardt/1979-1981 1.50 4.00
15 Dale Earnhardt/1982-1984 1.50 4.00
16 Dale Earnhardt/1985-1987 1.50 4.00
17 Dale Earnhardt/1988-1990 1.50 4.00
18 Dale Earnhardt/1991-1993 1.50 4.00
20B Dale Earnhardt CL 1.25 3.00

1996 Score Board Dale Earnhardt

COMPLETE SET (10) 8.00 20.00
COMMON DALE EARNHARDT 1.00 2.50

1997 Score Board IQ

This set contains 50 cards and was distributed in 2-card packs, with 30 packs in each box. The IQ notation is used by Score Board stands for "Insert Quality".

COMPLETE SET (50) 10.00 25.00
1 Dale Earnhardt 2.00 5.00
2 Jeff Gordon 1.25 3.00
3 Terry Labonte .40 1.00
4 Dale Jarrett .75 2.00
5 Michael Waltrip .25 .60
6 Mark Martin 1.00 2.50
7 Dale Jarrett .75 2.00
8 Bobby Labonte .75 2.00
9 Robby Gordon RC .40 1.00
10 Rick Mast .10 .30
11 Geoff Bodine .10 .30
12 Sterling Marlin .40 1.00
13 Jeff Burton .40 1.00
14 Ward Burton .25 .60
15 Darrell Waltrip .25 .60
16 Ken Schrader .10 .30
17 Kyle Petty .25 .60
18 Bobby Hamilton .10 .30
19 Ernie Irvan .25 .60
20 Steve Grissom .10 .30
21 Ted Musgrave .10 .30
22 Jeremy Mayfield .25 .60
23 Ricky Rudd .40 1.00
24 Ricky Craven .10 .30
25 Hut Stricklin .10 .30
26 Jeff Gordon 1.25 3.00
27 Dale Earnhardt 2.00 5.00
28 Dale Jarrett .75 2.00
29 Terry Labonte .40 1.00
30 Richard Childress .25 .60
31 Rick Hendrick .10 .30
32 Richard Petty .40 1.00
33 Robert Yates .05 .15
34 Joe Gibbs .25 .60
35 Ray Evernham .25 .60
36 Larry McReynolds .05 .15
37 Jeff Gordon 1.25 3.00
38 Dale Earnhardt 2.00 5.00
39 Rusty Wallace's Car .40 1.00
40 Dale Earnhardt's Car .75 2.00
41 Sterling Marlin's Car .10 .30
42 Mark Martin's Car .40 1.00
43 Bobby Labonte's Car .25 .60
44 Michael Waltrip's Car .10 .30
45 Jeff Gordon's Car .50 1.25
46 Ernie Irvan's Car .10 .30
47 Robby Gordon's Car .25 .60
48 Bobby Hamilton's Car .05 .15
49 Dale Jarrett's Car .25 .60
50 T.Lab .60 1.50
J.Gordon
Craven
P1 Dale Jarrett Promo .60 1.50

1997 Score Board IQ $10 Phone Cards

These cards feature a foil-stamped design and each card carries $10 of phone time. They are inserted one per ten packs.

COMPLETE SET (10) 10.00 25.00
PC1 Dale Earnhardt 3.00 8.00
PC2 Rusty Wallace's Car .60 1.50
PC3 Bobby Labonte 1.25 3.00
PC4 Dale Earnhardt's Car 1.25 3.00
PC5 Sterling Marlin .60 1.50
PC6 Mark Martin 1.50 4.00
PC7 Michael Waltrip .40 1.00
PC8 Dale Jarrett 1.25 3.00
PC9 Ricky Rudd .60 1.50
PC10 Ernie Irvan .40 1.00

1997 Score Board IQ Jeff Gordon

COMPLETE SET (5) 4.00 10.00
COMMON GORDON .75 2.00

1997 Score Board IQ Remarques

These cards feature the original artwork of renowed artist Sam Bass. Ten of his more famous artworks were reprinted on canvas stock in order to create these cards. These cards are serial numbered from 101 to 570 and are autographed by Bass. These cards are inserted one per 65 packs.

COMPLETE SET (10) 150.00 300.00
COMP.BASS FINISHED (10) 250.00 500.00
*BASS FINISHED: .6X TO 1.5X BASIC INSERTS
SB1 Dale Earnhardt 30.00 80.00
SB2 Jeff Gordon 20.00 50.00
SB3 Richard Childress 4.00 10.00
SB4 Ernie Irvan 4.00 10.00
SB5 Rusty Wallace's Car 6.00 15.00
SB6 Darrell Waltrip 4.00 10.00
SB7 Richard Petty 6.00 15.00
SB8 Bobby Labonte 12.50 30.00
SB9 Alan Kulwicki 4.00 10.00
SB10 Terry Labonte 6.00 15.00

1997 Score Board Seven-Eleven Phone Cards

This 4-card set was sponsored and distributed by 7-11 Stores, licensed through Score Board, and features phone time by Frontier Communications. Each card features the driver's image on the front along with his ride and the phone card instructions on the back.

COMPLETE SET (4) 5.00 12.00
1 Dale Earnhardt 3.00 8.00
2 Sterling Marlin 1.00 2.50
3 Dale Jarrett 1.25 3.00
4 Michael Waltrip .75 2.00

1995 Select Promos

Pinnacle Brands distributed these cards as a cello wrapped set to preview its 1995 Select release. Four of the cards are promo versions of regular issue cards, along with a promo Jeff Gordon Dream Machines card. A sixth (cover) card was included as well.

COMPLETE SET (6) 8.00 20.00
12 Jeff Gordon 2.00 5.00
24 Kyle Petty .60 1.50
128 Loy Allen Jr. .40 1.00
136 Geoff Bodine .40 1.00
DM8 Jeff Gordon's Car 6.00 15.00
Dream Machine
NNO Cover Card .10 .30

1995 Select

This 150-card set is the first racing set produced from manufacturer Pinnacle. The cards came eight cards per pack, 24 packs per box and 24 boxes per case. There were 2,950 numbered cases produced. The set features six topical subsets: Owners (73-90), Crew Chief (91-108), In the Blood (109-117), Young Stars (118-128), Idols (129-134), Pole Sitters (135-136). In the original set the only card with ties to Dale Earnhardt was card number 41, a picture of his car. In the middle of 1995 Dale signed a spokesperson agreement with Pinnacle. Pinnacle then issued a special Select number 151 card Dale to complete the set. This card was distributed to dealers that ordered the Select product. The card is not part of the regular set price. Also randomly inserted in the bottom of the boxes were a Jeff Gordon Jumbo and a Jumbo Geoff Bodine Magic Motion card. These two cards are priced at the bottom of the listing.

COMPLETE SET (150) 10.00 25.00
1 Loy Allen Jr. .08 .25
2 John Andretti .08 .25
3 Brett Bodine .08 .25
4 Geoff Bodine .08 .25
5 Todd Bodine .08 .25
6 Jeff Burton .30 .75
7 Ward Burton .20 .50
8 Derrike Cope .08 .25
9 Wally Dallenbach Jr. .08 .25
10 Dave Marcis .20 .50
11 Harry Gant .20 .50
12 Jeff Gordon 1.00 2.50
13 Steve Grissom .08 .25
14 Bobby Hamilton .08 .25
15 Ernie Irvan .20 .50
16 Dale Jarrett .60 1.50
17 Bobby Labonte .60 1.50
18 Terry Labonte .30 .75
19 Sterling Marlin .30 .75
20 Mark Martin .75 2.00
21 Rick Mast .08 .25
22 Ted Musgrave .08 .25
23 Joe Nemechek .08 .25
24 Kyle Petty .20 .50
25 Ricky Rudd .30 .75
26 Greg Sacks .08 .25
27 Ken Schrader .08 .25
28 Morgan Shepherd .08 .25
29 Lake Speed .08 .25
30 Jimmy Spencer .08 .25

31 Hut Stricklin .08 .25
32 Kenny Wallace .08 .25
33 Mike Wallace .08 .25
34 Rusty Wallace .75 2.00
35 Darrell Waltrip .20 .50
36 Michael Waltrip .20 .50
37 Morgan Shepherd's Car .05 .15
38 Jeff Gordon's Car .50 1.25
39 Geoff Bodine's Car .05 .15
40 Ted Musgrave's Car .05 .15
41 Dale Earnhardt's Car .50 1.25
42 Dale Jarrett's Car .20 .50
43 Terry Labonte's Car .20 .50
44 Sterling Marlin's Car .08 .25
45 Ken Schrader's Car .05 .15
46 Kyle Petty's Car .08 .25
47 Rusty Wallace's Car .30 .75
48 Michael Waltrip's Car .08 .25
49 Brett Bodine's Car .05 .15
50 Lake Speed's Car .05 .15
51 Ernie Irvan's Car .08 .25
52 Ricky Rudd's Car .08 .25
53 Mark Martin's Car .08 .25
54 Darrell Waltrip's Car .08 .25
55 Johnny Benson Jr. .20 .50
56 Jim Bown .08 .25
57 Ricky Craven .08 .25
58 Bobby Dotter .08 .25
59 Tim Fedewa .08 .25
60 David Green .08 .25
61 Tommy Houston .08 .25
62 Jason Keller .08 .25
63 Randy LaJoie .08 .25
64 Tracy Leslie .08 .25
65 Chad Little .08 .25
66 Mark Martin .75 2.00
67 Mike McLaughlin .08 .25
68 Larry Pearson .08 .25
69 Robert Pressley .08 .25
70 Elton Sawyer .08 .25
71 Dennis Setzer .08 .25
72 Kenny Wallace .08 .25
73 Richard Petty OWN .30 .75
74 Leo Jackson OWN .05 .15
75 Bobby Allison OWN .08 .25
76 Richard Childress OWN .20 .50
77 Geoff Bodine OWN .08 .25
78 Joe Gibbs OWN .20 .50
79 Kenny Bernstein OWN .08 .25
80 Bill Davis OWN .05 .15
81 Cale Yarborough OWN .08 .25
82 Rick Hendrick OWN .05 .15
83 Roger Penske .05 .15
Don Miller OWN
84 Chuck Rider OWN .05 .15
85 Ricky Rudd OWN .20 .50
86 Jack Roush OWN .05 .15
87 Felix Sabates OWN .05 .15
88 Darrell Waltrip OWN .20 .50
89 Glen Wood .05 .15
Eddie Wood
Len Wood OWN
90 Robert Yates OWN .05 .15
91 Paul Andrews .05 .15
92 Ray Evernham .05 .15
93 Jeff Hammond .05 .15
94 Steve Hmiel .05 .15
95 Ken Howes .05 .15
96 Jimmy Makar .05 .15
97 Larry McReynolds .05 .15
98 Buddy Parrott .05 .15
99 Leonard Wood .05 .15
100 Andy Petree .05 .15
101 Jimmy Fennig .05 .15
102 Mike Beam .05 .15
103 Tony Glover .05 .15
104 Doug Hewitt .05 .15
105 Donnie Richeson .05 .15
106 Bill Ingle .05 .15
107 Donnie Wingo .05 .15
108 Robin Pemberton .05 .15
109 Richard Petty .30 .75
K.Petty IB
110 Geoff Bodine .08 .25
Todd Bodine
Brett Bodine IB
111 R.Wallace .40 1.00
Kenny
Mike IB
112 Davey Allison .30 .75
B.Allison IB
113 D.Waltrip .20 .50
M.Waltrip IB
114 B.Labonte .30 .75
T.Labonte IB
115 Dale Jarrett .30 .75
Ned Jarrett IB
116 David Pearson .08 .25
Larry Pearson IB
117 Jeff Burton .20 .50
Ward Burton IB
118 Jeff Gordon YS .50 1.25
119 Jeff Burton YS .20 .50
120 Loy Allen Jr. YS .08 .25
121 Todd Bodine YS .08 .25
122 John Andretti YS .08 .25
123 Joe Nemechek YS .08 .25
124 Kenny Wallace YS .08 .25
125 Bobby Labonte YS .30 .75
126 Ricky Craven YS .08 .25
127 Johnny Benson YS .20 .50
128 Chad Little YS .08 .25
129 R.Petty .40 1.00
M.Martin I
130 David Pearson .08 .25
Ken Schrader I
131 B.Allison .20 .50
K.Petty I
132 C.Yarborough .20 .50
R.Rudd I
133 Junior Johnson .20 .50
Darrell Waltrip I
134 A.Kulwicki .20 .50
G.Bodine I
135 Ernie Irvan PS .20 .50
136 Geoff Bodine PS .08 .25
137 Ted Musgrave PS .08 .25
138 Ricky Rudd PS .20 .50
139 Chuck Bown PS .08 .25
140 Rusty Wallace PS .40 1.00
141 Jeff Gordon PS .50 1.25
142 Rick Mast PS .08 .25
143 Mark Martin PS .40 1.00
144 Loy Allen Jr. PS .08 .25
145 Harry Gant PS .20 .50
146 Jimmy Spencer PS .08 .25
147 Checklist .05 .15
148 Checklist .05 .15
149 Checklist .05 .15
150 Checklist .05 .15
151S Dale Earnhardt 4.00 10.00
NNO Jeff Gordon YS Jumbo 6.00 15.00
NNO G.Bodine Magic Motion 2.50 6.00

1995 Select Flat Out

COMPLETE SET (150) 50.00 120.00
*FLAT OUT: 2.5X TO 6X BASE CARDS

1995 Select Dream Machines

This 12-card insert set features of the top Winston Cup Driver's cars. The cards are printed on an all-foil board and use Dufex technology. Dream Machine cards were randomly inserted one per 48 packs.

COMPLETE SET (12) 40.00 100.00
DM1 Geoff Bodine's Car 1.00 2.50
DM2 Rusty Wallace's Car 8.00 20.00
DM3 Mark Martin's Car 8.00 20.00
DM4 Ken Schrader's Car 1.00 2.50
DM5 Ricky Rudd's Car 3.00 8.00
DM6 Morgan Shepherd's Car 1.00 2.50
DM7 Ernie Irvan's Car 2.00 5.00
DM8 Jeff Gordon's Car 10.00 25.00
DM9 Michael Waltrip's Car 2.00 5.00
DM10 Darrell Waltrip's Car 2.00 5.00
DM11 Kyle Petty's Car 2.00 5.00
DM12 Terry Labonte's Car 3.00 8.00

1995 Select Skills

Some of Winston Cup racing's top drivers are featured in this 18-card insert set. The cards feature all-foil, Gold Rush printing technology and were randomly seeded one per 12 packs.

COMPLETE SET (18) 30.00 60.00
SS1 Rusty Wallace 5.00 12.00
SS2 Mark Martin 5.00 12.00
SS3 Jeff Gordon 6.00 15.00
SS4 Ernie Irvan 1.25 3.00
SS5 Terry Labonte 2.00 5.00
SS6 Ricky Rudd 2.00 5.00
SS7 Kyle Petty 1.25 3.00
SS8 Ken Schrader .60 1.50
SS9 Morgan Shepherd .60 1.50
SS10 Geoff Bodine .60 1.50
SS11 Ted Musgrave .60 1.50
SS12 Michael Waltrip 1.25 3.00
SS13 John Andretti .60 1.50
SS14 Todd Bodine .60 1.50
SS15 Sterling Marlin 2.00 5.00
SS16 Darrell Waltrip 1.25 3.00
SS17 Jimmy Spencer .60 1.50
SS18 Harry Gant 1.25 3.00

2017 Select

*RWB/299: .8X TO 2X BASIC CARDS
*BLUE/199: 1X TO 2.5X BASIC CARDS
*RED/99: 1.2X TO 3X BASIC CARDS
*WHITE/50: 1.5X TO 4X BASIC CARDS
*WHITE/50: .8X TO 2X BASIC SP
*TIE DYE/24: 2X TO 5X BASIC CARDS
*TIE DYE/24: 1X TO 2.5X BASIC SP
*SILVER: .6X TO 1.5X BASIC CARDS
*PURPLE: .6X TO 1.5X BASIC CARDS
1 Jimmie Johnson .75 2.00
2 Jimmie Johnson .75 2.00
3 Matt Tifft .75 2.00
4 Matt Tifft .75 2.00
5 Ryan Blaney .40 1.00
6 Ryan Blaney .40 1.00
7 Brad Keselowski .60 1.50
8 Brad Keselowski .60 1.50
9 Brad Keselowski .60 1.50
10 Brad Keselowski .60 1.50
11 Daniel Suarez 1.00 2.50
12 Daniel Suarez 1.00 2.50
13 David Ragan .40 1.00
14 Erik Jones .75 2.00
15 Erik Jones .75 2.00
16 Gray Gaulding .30 .75
17 Kurt Busch .40 1.00
18 Kurt Busch .40 1.00
19 Trevor Bayne .50 1.25
20 Trevor Bayne .50 1.25
21 Ty Dillon .50 1.25
22 AJ Allmendinger .50 1.25
23 Blake Koch .40 1.00
24 Kasey Kahne .50 1.25
25 Kasey Kahne .50 1.25
26 Kasey Kahne .50 1.25
27 Kasey Kahne .50 1.25
28 Kasey Kahne .50 1.25
29 Kasey Kahne .50 1.25
30 Landon Cassill .40 1.00
31 Martin Truex Jr. .40 1.00
32 Martin Truex Jr. .40 1.00
33 Martin Truex Jr. .40 1.00
34 William Byron .75 2.00
35 Aric Almirola .40 1.00
36 Aric Almirola .40 1.00
37 Joey Logano .50 1.25
38 Joey Logano .50 1.25
39 Joey Logano .50 1.25
40 Danica Patrick 1.00 2.50
41 Danica Patrick 1.00 2.50
42 Danica Patrick 1.00 2.50
43 Danica Patrick 1.00 2.50
44 Brennan Poole .30 .75
45 Brandon Jones .30 .75
46 Ricky Stenhouse Jr. .50 1.25
47 Ricky Stenhouse Jr. .50 1.25
48 Paul Menard .30 .75
49 Kyle Busch .60 1.50
50 Kyle Busch .60 1.50
51 Kyle Busch .60 1.50
52 Chase Elliott .60 1.50
53 Chase Elliott .60 1.50
54 Chase Elliott .60 1.50
55 Chase Elliott .60 1.50
56 Jamie McMurray .50 1.25
57 Jamie McMurray .50 1.25
58 Jamie McMurray .50 1.25
59 Ryan Newman .40 1.00
60 Ryan Newman .40 1.00
61 Clint Bowyer .50 1.25
62 Austin Dillon .60 1.50
63 Austin Dillon .60 1.50
64 Dale Earnhardt Jr. 1.00 2.50
65 Dale Earnhardt Jr. 1.00 2.50
66 Dale Earnhardt Jr. 1.00 2.50
67 Corey LaJoie .40 1.00
68 Joey Gase .50 1.25
69 Matt Kenseth .50 1.25
70 Matt Kenseth .50 1.25
71 Tyler Reddick .50 1.25
72 Ryan Sieg .40 1.00
73 Chris Buescher .40 1.00
74 Chris Buescher .40 1.00
75 Daniel Hemric .50 1.25
76 Michael Annett .50 1.25
77 Ryan Reed .50 1.25
78 Kevin Harvick .60 1.50
79 Kevin Harvick .60 1.50
80 Kevin Harvick .60 1.50
81 Ross Chastain .50 1.25
82 Matt DiBenedetto .30 .75
83 Matt DiBenedetto .30 .75
84 Cole Custer .50 1.25
85 Cole Custer .50 1.25
86 Kaz Grala .50 1.25
87 Dakoda Armstrong .50 1.25
88 Elliott Sadler .30 .75
89 Elliott Sadler .30 .75
90 Justin Allgaier .40 1.00
91 Denny Hamlin .50 1.25
92 Harrison Rhodes .40 1.00
93 John Hunter Nemechek .40 1.00
94 John Hunter Nemechek .40 1.00
95 Kyle Larson .75 2.00
96 Kyle Larson .75 2.00
97 Kyle Larson .75 2.00
98 Reed Sorenson .30 .75
99 Bubba Wallace .50 1.25
100 Brendan Gaughan .30 .75
101 Trevor Bayne PP SP 1.00 2.50
102 Daniel Suarez PP SP 2.00 5.00
103 Martin Truex Jr. PP SP .75 2.00
104 Matt DiBenedetto PP SP .60 1.50
105 Ryan Newman PP SP .75 2.00
106 Jamie McMurray PP SP 1.00 2.50
107 Matt Kenseth PP SP 1.00 2.50
108 Austin Dillon PP SP 1.25 3.00
109 Corey LaJoie PP SP .75 2.00
110 Kasey Kahne PP SP 1.00 2.50
111 Ricky Stenhouse Jr. PP SP 1.00 2.50
112 Denny Hamlin PP SP 1.00 2.50
113 Kurt Busch PP SP .75 2.00
114 Kevin Harvick PP SP 1.25 3.00
115 AJ Allmendinger PP SP 1.00 2.50
116 Landon Cassill PP SP .75 2.00
117 Jimmie Johnson PP SP 1.50 4.00
118 Kyle Busch PP SP 1.25 3.00
119 Paul Menard PP SP .60 1.50
120 Brad Keselowski PP SP 1.25 3.00
121 Clint Bowyer PP SP 1.00 2.50
122 Ryan Blaney PP SP .75 2.00
123 Chase Elliott PP SP 1.25 3.00
124 Dale Earnhardt Jr. PP SP 2.00 5.00
125 Danica Patrick PP SP 2.00 5.00
126 Chris Buescher PP SP .75 2.00
127 Joey Logano PP SP 1.00 2.50
128 Aric Almirola PP SP .75 2.00
129 David Ragan PP SP .75 2.00
130 Kyle Larson PP SP 1.50 4.00
131 Bill Elliott HP SP 1.50 4.00
132 Darrell Waltrip HP SP 1.50 4.00
133 Greg Biffle HP SP .75 2.00
134 Carl Edwards HP SP 1.00 2.50
135 Bobby Labonte HP SP 1.00 2.50
136 Terry Labonte HP SP 1.00 2.50
137 Rusty Wallace HP SP 1.00 2.50
138 Richard Petty HP SP 1.50 4.00
139 Dale Jarrett HP SP 1.00 2.50
140 Mark Martin HP SP 1.00 2.50

2017 Select Endorsements

*BLUE/75-199: .5X TO 1.2X BASIC AU
*BLUE/43-50: .6X TO 1.5X BASIC AU
*BLUE/25: .8X TO 2X BASIC AU
*BLUE/18-20: 1X TO 2.5X BASIC AU
*RED/99: .5X TO 1.2X BASIC AU
*RED/49: .6X TO 1.5X BASIC AU
*RED/25: .8X TO 2X BASIC AU
*RED/15: 1X TO 2.5X BASIC AU
1 Adam Stevens 12.00 30.00
2 Alan Gustafson 4.00 10.00
3 Billy Scott 4.00 10.00
4 Dale Inman 3.00 8.00
5 Dick Berggren 2.50 6.00
6 Paul Wolfe 3.00 8.00
7 Rodney Childers 4.00 10.00
8 Slugger Labbe 8.00 20.00
9 Mike Bugarewicz 6.00 15.00
10 Bill Elliott 6.00 15.00
11 Bobby Labonte 4.00 10.00
12 Mark Martin 12.00 30.00
13 Terry Labonte 4.00 10.00
14 Richard Petty 8.00 20.00
15 Dale Jarrett 4.00 10.00
16 Cale Yarborough 4.00 10.00
17 Darrell Waltrip 6.00 15.00
18 Harry Gant 3.00 8.00
19 Hershel McGriff 2.50 6.00
20 Ned Jarrett 3.00 8.00
22 Danica Patrick 40.00 80.00
24 Kevin Harvick
25 Matt Kenseth 4.00 10.00
26 Rusty Wallace 4.00 10.00
27 Dale Earnhardt Jr.
28 Casey Mears 2.50 6.00
29 Daniel Suarez 8.00 20.00
30 William Byron 30.00 60.00

2017 Select Select Stars

*WHITE/50: .8X TO 2X BASIC INSERTS
*TIE DYE/24: 1X TO 2.5X BASIC INSERTS
1 Richard Petty 1.25 3.00
2 Jimmie Johnson 1.25 3.00
3 Carl Edwards .75 2.00
4 Terry Labonte .75 2.00
5 Mark Martin .75 2.00
6 Kasey Kahne .75 2.00
7 Kevin Harvick 1.00 2.50
8 Clint Bowyer .75 2.00
9 Rusty Wallace .75 2.00
10 Matt Kenseth .75 2.00
11 Danica Patrick 1.50 4.00
12 Dale Jarrett .75 2.00
13 Kyle Busch 1.00 2.50
14 Brad Keselowski 1.00 2.50
15 Dale Earnhardt Jr. 1.50 4.00
16 Kurt Busch .60 1.50
17 Austin Dillon 1.00 2.50
18 Trevor Bayne .75 2.00
19 AJ Allmendinger .75 2.00
20 Greg Biffle .60 1.50
21 Bill Elliott 1.25 3.00
22 Bobby Labonte .75 2.00
23 Darrell Waltrip 1.25 3.00
24 Jamie McMurray .75 2.00
25 Martin Truex Jr. .60 1.50

2017 Select Select Swatches

*BLUE/75-199: .5X TO 1.2X BASIC METAL
*BLUE/49-50: .6X TO 1.5X BASIC METAL
*BLUE/30: .8X TO 2X BASIC METAL
*BLUE/20: 1X TO 2.5X BASIC METAL
*RED/75-99: .5X TO 1.2X BASIC METAL
*RED/50: .6X TO 1.5X BASIC METAL
*RED/25: .8X TO 2X BASIC METAL
*RED/15: 1X TO 2.5X BASIC METAL
1 Alex Bowman 2.50 6.00
2 Aric Almirola 2.00 5.00
3 Austin Dillon 3.00 8.00
4 Brad Keselowski 3.00 8.00
5 Casey Mears 1.50 4.00
6 Chase Elliott 3.00 8.00
7 Chris Buescher 2.00 5.00
8 Clint Bowyer 2.50 6.00
9 Cole Custer 2.50 6.00
10 Cole Whitt 2.00 5.00
11 Corey LaJoie 2.00 5.00
12 Dale Earnhardt Jr. 5.00 12.00
13 Danica Patrick 5.00 12.00
14 Daniel Hemric 2.50 6.00
15 Daniel Suarez 5.00 12.00
16 David Ragan 2.00 5.00
17 Denny Hamlin 2.50 6.00
18 Erik Jones 4.00 10.00
19 Gray Gaulding 1.50 4.00
20 Greg Biffle 2.00 5.00
21 Jamie McMurray 2.50 6.00
22 Jeffrey Earnhardt 2.50 6.00
23 Jimmie Johnson 4.00 10.00
24 Joey Logano 2.50 6.00
25 Josh Wise 1.50 4.00
26 Kasey Kahne 2.50 6.00
27 Kevin Harvick 3.00 8.00
28 Kurt Busch 2.00 5.00
29 Kyle Busch 3.00 8.00
30 Kyle Larson 4.00 10.00
31 Landon Cassill 2.00 5.00
32 Martin Truex Jr. 2.00 5.00
33 Matt DiBenedetto 1.50 4.00
34 Matt Kenseth 2.50 6.00
35 Michael Annett 2.50 6.00
36 Paul Menard 1.50 4.00
37 Reed Sorenson 1.50 4.00
38 Regan Smith 2.00 5.00
39 Ricky Stenhouse Jr. 2.50 6.00
40 Ryan Blaney 2.00 5.00
41 Ryan Newman 2.00 5.00
42 Trevor Bayne 2.50 6.00
43 Ty Dillon 2.50 6.00
44 William Byron 4.00 10.00
45 AJ Allmendinger 2.50 6.00
46 Mark Martin 2.50 6.00
47 Bobby Labonte 2.50 6.00
48 Elliott Sadler 1.50 4.00
49 Ryan Reed 2.50 6.00
50 Jeb Burton 2.00 5.00

2017 Select Sheet Metal

*BLUE/75-199: .5X TO 1.2X BASIC METAL
*BLUE/35-50: .6X TO 1.5X BASIC METAL
*BLUE/20: 1X TO 2.5X BASIC METAL
*RED/75-99: .5X TO 1.2X BASIC METAL
*RED/49-50: .6X TO 1.5X BASIC METAL
*RED/25: .8X TO 2X BASIC METAL
*RED/15: 1X TO 2.5X BASIC METAL
1 Austin Dillon 3.00 8.00
2 Brad Keselowski 3.00 8.00
3 Chase Elliott 3.00 8.00
4 Clint Bowyer 2.50 6.00
5 Dale Earnhardt Jr. 5.00 12.00
6 Danica Patrick 6.00 15.00
7 Daniel Suarez 5.00 12.00
8 Denny Hamlin 2.50 6.00
9 Erik Jones 4.00 10.00
10 Gray Gaulding 1.50 4.00
11 Jamie McMurray 2.50 6.00
12 Jimmie Johnson 4.00 10.00
13 Joey Logano 2.50 6.00
14 Kasey Kahne 2.50 6.00
15 Kevin Harvick 3.00 8.00
16 Kurt Busch 2.00 5.00
17 Kyle Busch 3.00 8.00
18 Kyle Larson 4.00 10.00
19 Martin Truex Jr. 2.00 5.00
20 Matt Kenseth 2.50 6.00
21 Paul Menard 1.50 4.00
22 Ryan Blaney 2.00 5.00
23 Ryan Newman 2.00 5.00
24 Trevor Bayne 2.50 6.00
25 Ty Dillon 2.50 6.00

2017 Select Signature Paint Schemes

1 Brad Keselowski 6.00 15.00
2 Kyle Busch 12.00 30.00
3 Dale Earnhardt Jr. 10.00 25.00
4 Denny Hamlin 5.00 12.00
5 Jamie McMurray 5.00 12.00
6 Chase Elliott 25.00 50.00
7 Clint Bowyer 5.00 12.00
8 Joey Logano 5.00 12.00
9 Kasey Kahne 5.00 12.00
10 Kurt Busch 4.00 10.00
11 Kyle Larson 25.00 50.00
12 Martin Truex Jr. 4.00 10.00
13 Paul Menard 3.00 8.00
14 Ryan Blaney 4.00 10.00
16 Ty Dillon 5.00 12.00
18 Austin Dillon EXCH 12.00 30.00
19 Greg Biffle 4.00 10.00
20 Trevor Bayne 5.00 12.00

2017 Select Signature Swatches

1 Alex Bowman 10.00 25.00
3 Austin Dillon EXCH 12.00 30.00
4 Brad Keselowski 6.00 15.00
6 Chase Elliott 25.00 50.00
7 Chris Buescher 4.00 10.00
8 Clint Bowyer 5.00 12.00
10 Cole Whitt 4.00 10.00
11 Corey LaJoie 4.00 10.00
12 Dale Earnhardt Jr. 30.00 60.00
13 Danica Patrick 50.00 100.00
14 Daniel Hemric 5.00 12.00
15 Daniel Suarez 40.00 80.00
16 David Ragan 4.00 10.00
17 Denny Hamlin 5.00 12.00
18 Erik Jones 20.00 40.00
19 Gray Gaulding 3.00 8.00
20 Greg Biffle 4.00 10.00
21 Jamie McMurray 5.00 12.00
23 Jimmie Johnson 25.00 50.00
24 Joey Logano 5.00 12.00
25 Josh Wise 3.00 8.00
26 Kasey Kahne 5.00 12.00
27 Kevin Harvick 10.00 25.00
28 Kurt Busch 4.00 10.00
29 Kyle Busch 12.00 30.00
30 Kyle Larson 15.00 30.00
31 Landon Cassill 4.00 10.00
32 Martin Truex Jr. 4.00 10.00
33 Matt DiBenedetto 3.00 8.00
34 Matt Kenseth 5.00 12.00
35 Michael Annett 5.00 12.00
36 Paul Menard 3.00 8.00
37 Reed Sorenson 3.00 8.00
38 Regan Smith 4.00 10.00
39 Ricky Stenhouse Jr. 5.00 12.00
40 Ryan Blaney 4.00 10.00
41 Ryan Newman 4.00 10.00
42 Trevor Bayne 5.00 12.00
43 Ty Dillon 5.00 12.00
44 William Byron 40.00 80.00
45 Carl Edwards 5.00 12.00
47 Bobby Labonte
48 Elliott Sadler 3.00 8.00
49 Ryan Reed 5.00 12.00

2017 Select Signatures

*BLUE/99-199: .5X TO 1.2X BASIC AU
*BLUE/49-50: .6X TO 1.5X BASIC AU
*BLUE/25: .8X TO 2X BASIC AU
*RED99: .5X TO 1.2X BASIC AU
*RED/50: .6X TO 1.5X BASIC AU
*RED/25: .8X TO 2X BASIC AU
1 Ahnna Parkhurst 6.00 15
2 Alon Day 8.00 20
4 Bobby Allison 3.00 8
5 Kaz Grala 4.00 10.
7 Brett Bodine 2.50 6.
8 Ryan Reed 4.00 10.
9 Cameron Hayley 3.00 8.
11 Collin Cabre 2.50 6.
13 Dave Marcis 8.00 20.
14 Derrike Cope 3.00 8.
15 Donnie Allison 3.00 8.
16 Ernie Irvan 4.00 10.
17 Geoff Bodine 2.50 6.
19 Brandon Jones 2.50 6.
21 Jeff Burton 3.00 8.
22 Julia Landauer 4.00 10.
24 Justin Allgaier 3.00 8.
25 Kate Dallenbach 8.00 20.
26 Kelley Earnhardt 30.00 60.
27 Ken Schrader 2.50 6.
28 Kenny Wallace 2.50 6.
29 Joey Gase 12.00 30.
30 Kerry Earnhardt 4.00 10.
32 Matt Tifft 6.00 15.
33 Michael Waltrip 4.00 10.
34 Mike Wallace
35 Brendan Gaughan 2.50 6.
36 Noah Gragson 3.00 8.
37 Tony Gibson 2.50 6.
38 AJ Allmendinger 4.00 10.
39 Rex White 2.50 6.
40 Garrett Smithley 4.00 10.
41 Elliott Sadler 2.50 6.
42 Alex Bowman
43 Spencer Davis 3.00 8.
45 Timothy Peters 2.50 6.
46 Todd Gilliland
47 Ty Majeski 10.00 25.
48 Carl Edwards 8.00 20.
49 Tyler Reddick
50 William Byron

2017 Select Speed Merchants

*WHITE/50: .8X TO 2X BASIC INSERTS
*TIE DYE/24: 1X TO 2.5X BASIC INSERTS
1 Martin Truex Jr. .75 2.0
2 Ricky Stenhouse Jr. 1.00 2.5
3 Daniel Suarez 2.00 5.0
4 Kasey Kahne 1.00 2.5
5 Brad Keselowski 1.25 3.0
6 Matt Kenseth 1.00 2.5
7 Joey Logano 1.00 2.50
8 Kurt Busch .75 2.0
9 Kyle Larson 1.50 4.0
10 Paul Menard .60 1.50
11 Jimmie Johnson 1.50 4.00
12 Clint Bowyer 1.00 2.50
13 Austin Dillon 1.25 3.00
14 Trevor Bayne 1.00 2.50
15 Kevin Harvick 1.25 3.00
16 Dale Earnhardt Jr. 2.00 5.00
17 Jamie McMurray 1.00 2.50
18 Ryan Newman .75 2.00
19 Ryan Blaney .75 2.00
20 Denny Hamlin 1.00 2.50
21 Danica Patrick 2.00 5.00
22 Chase Elliott 1.25 3.00
23 Aric Almirola .75 2.00
24 Kyle Busch 1.25 3.00
25 AJ Allmendinger 1.00 2.50

2017 Select Up Close and Personal

*WHITE/50: .8X TO 2X BASIC INSERTS
*TIE DYE/24: 1X TO 2.5X BASIC INSERTS
1 Joey Logano 1.00 2.50
2 Dale Earnhardt Jr. 2.00 5.00
3 AJ Allmendinger 1.00 2.50
4 Brad Keselowski 1.25 3.00
5 Chase Elliott 1.25 3.00
6 Kevin Harvick 1.25 3.00
7 Jimmie Johnson 1.50 4.00
8 Ryan Newman .75 2.00
9 Clint Bowyer 1.00 2.50
10 Kurt Busch .75 2.00

1994 Signature Rookies Tetrad Titans

Randomly inserted in packs, these 12 standard-size cards feature borderless color player action shots on their fronts. The player's name appears in gold-foil lettering near the bottom. The words "1 of 10,000" appear in vertical gold-foil lettering within a simulated marble column near the left edge. On a ghosted background drawing of a Greek temple, the back carries the player's name, position, team, height and weight, and career highlights. The cards of this multisport set are numbered on the back in Roman numerals.

COMPLETE SET (12) 3.00 8.00
119 Bobby Allison .20 .50

1994 Signature Rookies Tetrad Titans Autographs

Randomly inserted in packs, these 12 standard-size autographed cards comprise a parallel set to the regular 1994 Tetrad Titans set. Aside from the autographs (some cards issued as redemptions in packs) and each card's numbering out of 1,050 produced (except the 2,500 signed O.J. cards), they are identical in design to their regular issue counterparts. The cards of this multisport set are numbered on the back in Roman numerals.

COMPLETE SET (12) 125.00 250.00
119 Bobby Allison/1050 6.00 15.00

1994 SkyBox

This 27-card set is the first NASCAR issue by manufacturer SkyBox. The cards are oversized 4 1/2" X 2 1/2" and feature some of the top names in Winston Cup racing. The set includes a Anatomy of a Pit Stop subset (14-17). Card number 27, the SkyBox Winston Cup car that Dick Trickle drove in a few races, was redeemable for a card of the 1994 Brickyard 400 Winner. You could send that card in with $1.50 and receive a card of Jeff Gordon holding the Brickyard 400 trophy (expiration date 12/31/1995). This card is not included in the set price.

COMPLETE FACT.SET (27) 6.00 15.00
1 Dale Earnhardt 2.00 5.00
2 Darrell Waltrip's Car .15 .40
3 Ernie Irvan's Car .15 .40
4 Jeff Gordon's Car 1.00 3.00
5 Terry Labonte's Car .30 .75
6 Wally Dallenbach Jr.'s Car .07 .20
7 Kyle Petty's Car .15 .40
8 Lake Speed's Car .07 .20
9 Mark Martin's Car .60 1.50
10 Morgan Shepherd's Car .07 .20
11 Ricky Rudd's Car .15 .40
12 Rusty Wallace's Car .50 1.25
13 Sterling Marlin's Car .15 .40
14 Anatomy of a Pit Stop .07 .20
15 Anatomy of a Pit Stop .07 .20
16 Anatomy of a Pit Stop .07 .20
17 Anatomy of a Pit Stop .07 .20
18 Bare Frame .07 .20
19 Chevy Engine .07 .20
20 Jacked up Body .07 .20
21 Finished Body .07 .20
22 Sanding Body .07 .20
23 Finished Race Car .07 .20
24 Geoff Bodine Todd Bodine Cars .07 .20
25 Darrell Waltrip M.Waltrip Cars .15 .40
26 John Andretti's Cars .07 .20
NNO Exp. Exchange D.Trickle .15 .40
NNO Brickyard Exch Jeff Gordon 2.50 5.00

1997 SkyBox Profile

This 80-card set was Fleer/Skybox's first NASCAR release under the SkyBox brand name. The product was highlighted by a autographed card redemption program. Cards were distributed in five card packs with 24 packs per box and 6 or 12 boxes per case. The packs carried a suggested retail price of $4.99.

COMPLETE SET (80) 8.00 20.00
1 John Andretti .10 .30
2 Johnny Benson .25 .60
3 Derrike Cope .10 .30
4 Ricky Craven .10 .30
5 Dale Earnhardt 2.00 5.00
6 Bill Elliott .50 1.25
7 Jeff Gordon 1.25 3.00
8 Robby Gordon RC .40 1.00
9 Steve Grissom .10 .30
10 David Green .10 .30
11 Bobby Hamilton .10 .30
12 Bobby Hillin .10 .30
13 Ernie Irvan .25 .60
14 Dale Jarrett .75 2.00
15 Bobby Labonte .75 2.00
16 Terry Labonte .40 1.00
17 Dave Marcis .10 .30
18 Sterling Marlin .40 1.00
19 Mark Martin 1.00 2.50
20 Rick Mast .10 .30
21 Jeremy Mayfield .25 .60
22 Ted Musgrave .10 .30
23 Joe Nemechek .10 .30
24 Ricky Rudd .40 1.00
25 Ken Schrader .10 .30
26 Morgan Shepherd .10 .30
27 Hut Stricklin .10 .30
28 Dick Trickle .10 .30
29 Kenny Wallace .10 .30
30 Rusty Wallace 1.00 2.50
31 Michael Waltrip .25 .60
32 Richard Childress OWN .25 .60
33 Richard Petty OWN .10 .30
34 Rick Hendrick OWN .03 .15
35 Robert Yates OWN .03 .15
36 Joe Gibbs OWN .25 .60
37 Cale Yarborough OWN .03 .15
38 Jack Roush OWN .03 .15
39 Ray Evernham CC .10 .30
40 Larry McReynolds CC .03 .15
41 Gary DeHart CC .03 .15
42 Todd Parrott CC .03 .15
43 Marc Reno CC .03 .15
44 Steve Hmiel MG CC .03 .15
45 Robin Pemberton CC .03 .15
46 Todd Bodine .10 .30
47 Jason Keller .10 .30
48 Randy LaJoie .10 .30
49 Phil Parsons .10 .30
50 Steve Park RC 3.00 6.00
51 Buckshot Jones RC .10 .30
52 Jeff Fuller .10 .30
53 Tracy Leslie .10 .30
54 Elton Sawyer .10 .30
55 Jeff Green .10 .30
56 Mike McLaughlin .10 .30
57 Ron Barfield .10 .30
58 Glen Allen Jr. .10 .30
59 Kevin Lepage .10 .30
60 Rodney Combs .10 .30
61 Tim Fedewa .10 .30
62 Rusty Wallace's Car .40 1.00
63 Dale Earnhardt's Car .75 2.00
64 Sterling Marlin's Car .10 .30
65 Terry Labonte's Car .25 .60
66 Mark Martin's Car .40 1.00
67 Ricky Rudd's Car .10 .30
68 Bobby Labonte's Car .40 1.00
69 Michael Waltrip's Car .10 .30
70 Jeff Gordon's Car .50 1.25
71 Ernie Irvan's Car .03 .15
72 Ken Schrader's Car .03 .15
73 Derrike Cope's Car .03 .15
74 Jeremy Mayfield's Car .03 .15
75 Robby Gordon's Car .25 .60
76 Bobby Hamilton's Car .03 .15
77 Dale Jarrett's Car .40 1.00
78 Bill Elliott's Car .25 .60
79 David Green's Car .03 .15
80 Checklist .03 .15
D1 Jeff Gordon Daytona 15.00 40.00
P1 Jeff Gordon Promo .75 2.00

1997 SkyBox Profile Autographs

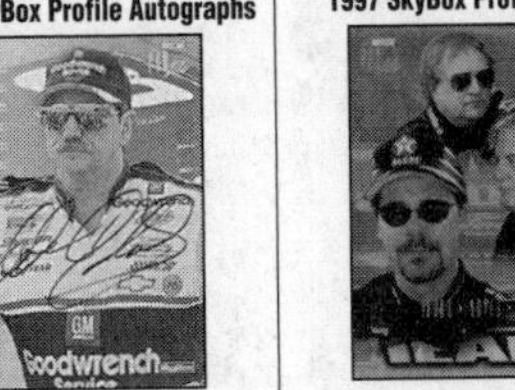

This 47-card insert set contains autograph redemption cards from each driver in this set. 11,100 cards total were set aside to be redeemed in this program. Each Winston Cup and Busch driver signed 200 cards, with the exception of Randy LaJoie who signed 500. The cards were randomly inserted in packs at a ratio of 1:24.

COMPLETE SET (47) 750.00 1500.00
1 John Andretti 10.00 20.00
2 Johnny Benson 10.00 20.00
3 Derrike Cope 7.50 15.00
4 Ricky Craven 7.50 15.00
5 Dale Earnhardt 150.00 300.00
6 Bill Elliott 30.00 80.00
7 Jeff Gordon 75.00 150.00
8 Robby Gordon 8.00 20.00
9 Steve Grissom 7.50 15.00
10 David Green 7.50 15.00
11 Bobby Hamilton 10.00 25.00
12 Bobby Hillin 7.50 15.00
13 Ernie Irvan 12.50 30.00
14 Dale Jarrett 25.00 60.00
15 Bobby Labonte 12.50 30.00
16 Terry Labonte 15.00 40.00
17 Dave Marcis 10.00 20.00
18 Sterling Marlin 12.50 30.00
19 Mark Martin 40.00 80.00
20 Rick Mast 7.50 15.00
21 Jeremy Mayfield 10.00 20.00
22 Ted Musgrave 7.50 15.00
23 Joe Nemechek 7.50 15.00
24 Ricky Rudd 12.50 30.00
25 Ken Schrader 10.00 20.00
26 Morgan Shepherd 7.50 15.00
27 Hut Stricklin 7.50 15.00
28 Dick Trickle 7.50 15.00
29 Kenny Wallace 7.50 15.00
30 Rusty Wallace 25.00 60.00
31 Michael Waltrip 8.00 20.00
46 Todd Bodine 7.50 15.00
47 Jason Keller 7.50 15.00
48 Randy LaJoie/500* 7.50 15.00
49 Phil Parsons 7.50 15.00
50 Steve Park 10.00 20.00
51 Buckshot Jones 10.00 20.00
52 Jeff Fuller 7.50 15.00
53 Tracy Leslie 7.50 15.00
54 Elton Sawyer 7.50 15.00
55 Jeff Green 7.50 15.00
56 Mike McLaughlin 7.50 15.00
57 Ron Barfield 7.50 15.00
58 Glen Allen 7.50 15.00
59 Kevin Lepage 7.50 15.00
60 Rodney Combs 7.50 15.00
61 Tim Fedewa 7.50 15.00

1997 SkyBox Profile Break Out

This 9-card insert set features young drivers who could become stars in NASCAR. The cards were randomly inserted in packs at a ratio of 1:4.

COMPLETE SET (9) 6.00 15.00
B1 Jeff Gordon 4.00 10.00
B2 Robby Gordon 1.25 3.00
B3 Ron Barfield .40 1.00
B4 Johnny Benson .75 2.00
B5 Steve Park 8.00 20.00
B6 Ricky Craven .40 1.00
B7 Bobby Labonte 2.50 6.00
B8 Jeremy Mayfield .75 2.00
B9 David Green .40 1.00

1997 SkyBox Profile Pace Setters

This 9-card insert set covers those drivers whose performances have secured their spots in the record books. The cards were randomly inserted in packs at a ratio of 1:10.

COMPLETE SET (9) 25.00 60.00
E1 Dale Earnhardt 12.50 30.00
E2 Terry Labonte 2.50 6.00
E3 Bill Elliott 3.00 8.00
E4 Ricky Rudd 2.50 6.00
E5 Jeff Gordon 8.00 20.00
E6 Dale Jarrett 5.00 12.00
E7 Michael Waltrip 1.50 4.00
E8 Rusty Wallace 6.00 15.00
E9 Mark Martin 6.00 15.00

1997 SkyBox Profile Team

This 9-card set features the strongest teams in NASCAR. Each card front pictures the driver, crew chief and car owner. The cards were randomly inserted in packs at a ratio of 1:100.

COMPLETE SET (9) 200.00 400.00
T1 Terry Labonte 8.00 20.00
T2 Jeff Gordon 25.00 60.00
T3 Dale Jarrett 15.00 40.00
T4 Dale Earnhardt 30.00 80.00
T5 Mark Martin 20.00 50.00
T6 Ricky Rudd 8.00 20.00
T7 Ernie Irvan 5.00 12.00
T8 Bill Elliott 10.00 25.00
T9 Rusty Wallace 20.00 50.00

1992 Slim Jim Bobby Labonte

Produced for and distributed by Slim Jim, the Bobby Labonte set includes 27 car and driver cards with one cover/checklist card and one bi-fold autograph card. The autograph card (number 13) is not signed but is a bi-fold card intended to be large enough unfolded for the driver to sign. The back of the checklist card included an offer to purchase additional sets at $5 each with 5 proofs of purchases from Slim Jim products. Regardless, the Slim Jim Bobby Labonte set is thought to be one of the toughest individual driver card sets to find.

COMPLETE SET (29) 7.50 20.00
1 Cover Checklist Card .40 1.00
2 Bobby Labonte's Car .40 1.00
3 Bobby Labonte .75 2.00
4 Bobby Labonte's Car .40 1.00
5 Bob Labonte Sr. .40 1.00
6 Bobby Labonte's Car .40 1.00
7 Bobby Labonte Terry Labonte .75 2.00
8 Bobby Labonte .75 2.00
9 Bobby Labonte in Pits .40 1.00
10 Bobby Labonte's Car .40 1.00
11 Bobby Labonte .75 2.00
12 Bobby Labonte's Car .40 1.00
13 Bobby Labonte Auto.Card .40 1.00
14 Bobby Labonte in Pits .40 1.00
15 Bobby Labonte .75 2.00
16 Bobby Labonte's Car Steve Grissom's Car Dale Earnhardt's Car .40 1.00
17 Bobby Labonte .75 2.00
18 Bobby Labonte in Pits .40 1.00
19 Bobby Labonte's Car .40 1.00
20 Bobby Labonte's Car Chad Little's Car .40 1.00
21 Bobby Labonte .75 2.00
22 Bobby Labonte's Car .40 1.00
23 Bobby Labonte Donna Labonte .40 1.00
24 Bobby Labonte Bob Labonte Sr. .40 1.00
25 Bobby Labonte .75 2.00
26 Bobby Labonte's Car .40 1.00
27 Bobby Labonte's Car .40 1.00
28 Bobby Labonte w Car .40 1.00
29 Bobby Labonte w Car .40 1.00

1994 Slim Jim David Green

Similar to the 1992 set, the 1994 release was produced for and distributed by Slim Jim. New driver David Green is the set's focus that includes 16 driver and car cards with one checklist card and one bi-fold autograph card. The autograph card (number 48) is not signed but is a bi-fold card intended to be large enough unfolded for the driver to sign. Cards from the Slim Jim David Green set are numbered consecutively after the 1992 Bobby Labonte set.

COMPLETE SET (18) 6.00 12.00
31 Checklist Card .20 .50
32 David Green .40 1.00
33 David Green in Pits .20 .50
34 David Green .40 1.00
35 David Green .40 1.00
36 David Green Action .20 .50
37 David Green's Car .20 .50
38 David Green .40 1.00
39 Eddie Lowery .20 .50
40 Curt Cloutier .20 .50
41 Charlie Smith .20 .50
42 David Green .40 1.00
43 David Green Steve Grissom .20 .50
44 David Green's Car .20 .50
45 David Green .40 1.00
46 David Green .20 .50
47 David Green Hermie Sadler Cars .20 .50
48 David Green Bi-Fold .40 1.00

1995 SP

This 150-card set is the inaugural SP brand issue from Upper Deck. The set is made up of seven sub-sets: Cup Contenders (1-30), Drivers (31-74), Cars (75-116), Premier Prospects (117-120), Owners (121-135) and Crew Chiefs (136-150). The product came seven cards per pack, 32 packs per box and six boxes per case. The original suggested retail price per pack was $3.99 and the product was available only through hobby outlets. At the time it was announced that SP Racing was the lowest produced SP product across the 5 major sports that have that brand. Also, SP was delayed a month from its original release date so that it could include a special Comebacks Hologram insert card of Ernie Irvan and Michael Jordan. The Comebacks card could be found one per 192 packs.

COMPLETE SET (150) 10.00 25.00
1 Rick Mast CC .10 .30
2 Rusty Wallace CC 1.00 2.50
3 Sterling Marlin CC .40 1.00
4 Terry Labonte CC .40 1.00
5 Mark Martin CC 1.00 2.50
6 Geoff Bodine CC .10 .30
7 Jeff Burton CC .40 1.00
8 Lake Speed CC .10 .30
9 Ricky Rudd CC .40 1.00
10 Brett Bodine CC .10 .30
11 Derrike Cope CC .10 .30
12 Bobby Hamilton CC .10 .30
13 Ted Musgrave CC .10 .30
14 Darrell Waltrip CC .25 .60
15 Bobby Labonte CC .75 2.00
16 Morgan Shepherd CC .10 .30
17 Joe Nemechek CC .10 .30
18 Jeff Gordon CC 1.25 3.00
19 Ken Schrader CC .10 .30
20 Hut Stricklin CC .10 .30
21 Dale Jarrett CC .75 2.00
22 Steve Grissom CC .10 .30
23 Michael Waltrip CC .25 .60
24 Ward Burton CC .10 .30
25 Todd Bodine CC .10 .30
26 Robert Pressley CC .10 .30
27 Bill Elliott CC .50 1.25
28 John Andretti CC .10 .30
29 Ricky Craven CC .10 .30
30 Kyle Petty CC .25 .60
31 Rick Mast .10 .30
32 Rusty Wallace 1.00 2.50
33 Rusty Wallace 1.00 2.50
34 Sterling Marlin .40 1.00
35 Sterling Marlin .40 1.00
36 Terry Labonte .40 1.00
37 Mark Martin 1.00 2.50
38 Mark Martin 1.00 2.50
39 Geoff Bodine .10 .30
40 Jeff Burton .40 1.00
41 Lake Speed .10 .30
42 Ricky Rudd .40 1.00
43 Brett Bodine .10 .30
44 Derrike Cope .10 .30
45 Bobby Hamilton .10 .30
46 Dick Trickle .10 .30
47 Ted Musgrave .10 .30
48 Darrell Waltrip .25 .60
49 Bobby Labonte .75 2.00
50 Morgan Shepherd .10 .30
51 Chuck Bown .10 .30
52 Jeff Purvis .10 .30
53 Jimmy Hensley .10 .30
54 Jimmy Spencer .10 .30
55 Jeff Gordon 1.25 3.00
56 Jeff Gordon 1.25 3.00
57 Ken Schrader .10 .30
58 Hut Stricklin .10 .30
59 Randy LaJoie .10 .30
60 Dale Jarrett .75 2.00
61 Steve Grissom .10 .30
62 Michael Waltrip .25 .60
63 Ward Burton .25 .60
64 Todd Bodine .10 .30
65 Robert Pressley .10 .30
66 Jeremy Mayfield .25 .60
67 Mike Wallace .10 .30
68 Bill Elliott .50 1.25
69 John Andretti .10 .30
70 Chad Little .10 .30
71 Joe Nemechek .10 .30
72 Dave Marcis .25 .60
73 Ricky Craven .10 .30
74 Kyle Petty .25 .60
75 Rick Mast's Car .05 .15
76 Rusty Wallace's Car .40 1.00
77 Rusty Wallace's Car .40 1.00
78 Sterling Marlin's Car .10 .30
79 Terry Labonte's Car .25 .60
80 Mark Martin's Car .40 1.00
81 Geoff Bodine's Car .05 .15
82 Jeff Burton's Car .10 .30
83 Lake Speed's Car .05 .15
84 Ricky Rudd's Car .10 .30
85 Brett Bodine's Car .05 .15
86 Derrike Cope's Car .05 .15
87 Bobby Hamilton's Car .05 .15
88 Dick Trickle's Car .05 .15
89 Ted Musgrave's Car .05 .15
90 Darrell Waltrip's Car .10 .30
91 Bobby Labonte's Car .40 1.00
92 Morgan Shepherd's Car .05 .15
93 Chad Little's Car .05 .15
94 Jeff Purvis' Car .05 .15
95 Jimmy Hensley's Car .05 .15
96 Jimmy Spencer's Car .05 .15
97 Jeff Gordon's Car .60 1.50
98 Ken Schrader's Car .05 .15
99 Hut Stricklin's Car .05 .15
100 Jeff Gordon's Car .60 1.50
101 Dale Jarrett's Car .40 1.00
102 Steve Grissom's Car .05 .15
103 Michael Waltrip's Car .10 .30
104 Ward Burton's Car .10 .30
105 Todd Bodine's Car .05 .15
106 Robert Pressley's Car .05 .15
107 Jeremy Mayfield's Car .10 .30
108 Mike Wallace's Car .05 .15
109 Bill Elliott's Car .25 .60
110 Bill Elliott's Car .25 .60
111 John Andretti's Car .05 .15
112 Kenny Wallace's Car .05 .15
113 Joe Nemechek's Car .05 .15
114 Dave Marcis's Car .10 .30
115 Ricky Craven's Car .05 .15
116 Kyle Petty's Car .10 .30
117 Ricky Craven PP .10 .30
118 Robert Pressley PP .10 .30
119 Randy LaJoie PP .10 .30
120 Davy Jones PP .10 .30
121 Rick Hendrick OWN .05 .15
122 Jack Roush OWN .05 .15
123 R.Penske R.Wallace OWN .40 1.00
124 Joe Gibbs OWN .25 .60
125 Felix Sabates OWN .05 .15
126 Bobby Allison OWN .10 .30
127 Richard Petty OWN .40 1.00
128 Cale Yarborough OWN .10 .30
129 Robert Yates OWN .05 .15
130 Darrell Waltrip OWN .25 .60
131 Bill Elliott OWN .50 1.25
132 Geoff Bodine OWN .10 .30
133 Junior Johnson OWN .10 .30
134 Ricky Rudd OWN .40 1.00
135 Glen Wood OWN .05 .15
136 Robin Pemberton .05 .15
137 Steve Hmiel .05 .15
138 Larry McReynolds .05 .15
139 Robbie Loomis .05 .15
140 Ray Evernham .25 .60
141 Howard Comstock .05 .15
142 Gary DeHart .05 .15
143 Paul Andrews .05 .15
144 Bill Ingle .05 .15
145 Jimmy Makar .05 .15
146 Barry Dodson .05 .15
147 Jimmy Fennig .05 .15
148 Leonard Wood .05 .15
149 Pete Peterson .05 .15
150 Ken Howes .05 .15
JG1 Jeff Gordon Promo 2.00 5.00
CB1 E.Irvan Michael Jordan 8.00 20.00

1995 SP Die Cuts

COMPLETE SET (150) 30.00 75.00
*DIE CUT STARS: 1.25X TO 3X BASIC CARDS

1995 SP Back-To-Back

This three-card insert set features the only three drivers to win back-to-back Daytona 500's. The cards feature a forward and reverse image on holographic board. Richard Petty won the event seven times including '73 and '74. Cale Yarborough was a four time winner including '83 and '84. Sterling Marlin's made the set for his '94 and '95 trips to the winner's circle. The cards were randomly inserted at a ratio of 1:81 packs.

COMPLETE SET (3) 10.00 25.00
BB1 Richard Petty 5.00 12.00
BB2 Cale Yarborough 4.00 10.00
BB3 Sterling Marlin 5.00 12.00

1995 SP Speed Merchants

The 30-card set uses HoloView technology to feature the top drivers and up and coming stars in Winston Cup racing. The cards were seeded one per five packs. There was also a die cut parallel version of the Speed Merchant cards. The die cut cards were randomly inserted one per 74 packs.

COMPLETE SET (30) 25.00 60.00
*DIE CUTS: 2X TO 5X BASIC INSERTS
SM1 Kyle Petty 1.25 3.00
SM2 Rusty Wallace 3.00 8.00
SM3 Bill Elliott 2.50 6.00
SM4 Sterling Marlin 2.00 5.00
SM5 Terry Labonte 2.00 5.00
SM6 Mark Martin 3.00 8.00
SM7 Geoff Bodine .60 1.50
SM8 Jeff Burton 2.00 5.00
SM9 Steve Grissom .60 1.50
SM10 Ricky Rudd 2.00 5.00
SM11 Brett Bodine .60 1.50
SM12 Derrike Cope .60 1.50
SM13 Ward Burton 1.25 3.00
SM14 Mike Wallace .60 1.50
SM15 Robert Pressley .60 1.50
SM16 Ted Musgrave .60 1.50
SM17 Darrell Waltrip 1.25 3.00
SM18 Bobby Labonte 4.00 10.00
SM19 Ricky Craven .60 1.50
SM20 Davy Jones .60 1.50
SM21 Morgan Shepherd .60 1.50
SM22 Randy LaJoie .60 1.50
SM23 Jeremy Mayfield 1.25 3.00
SM24 Jeff Gordon 4.00 10.00
SM25 Ken Schrader .60 1.50
SM26 Todd Bodine .60 1.50
SM27 John Andretti .60 1.50
SM28 Dale Jarrett 2.50 6.00
SM29 Greg Sacks .60 1.50
SM30 Michael Waltrip 1.25 3.00

1996 SP

The 1996 SP hobby set was issued in one series totalling 84 cards. The set contains the topical subsets: Driver Cards (1-42), Cup Contenders (43-74) and RPM (75-84). The 7-card packs retailed for $4.39 each. There were 20 packs per box and 12 boxes per case. The product was distributed through hobby channels only. Also, included as an insert in packs was a card titled Driving Aces. The card is a double sided card with Dale Earnhardt on one side and Jeff Gordon on the other. This card was inserted in packs at a rate of one in 257 and is priced at the bottom of this set.

COMPLETE SET (84) 12.00 30.00
WAX BOX 30.00 60.00
1 Rick Mast .10 .30
2 Rusty Wallace 1.00 2.50
3 Dale Earnhardt 1.50 4.00
4 Sterling Marlin .40 1.00
5 Terry Labonte .40 1.00
6 Mark Martin 1.00 2.50
7 Geoff Bodine .10 .30
8 Hut Stricklin .10 .30
9 Lake Speed .10 .30

10 Ricky Rudd .40 1.00
11 Brett Bodine .10 .30
12 Derrike Cope .10 .30
13 Bill Elliott .50 1.25
14 Bobby Hamilton .10 .30
15 Wally Dallenbach .10 .30
16 Ted Musgrave .10 .30
17 Darrell Waltrip .25 .60
18 Bobby Labonte .75 2.00
19 Loy Allen .10 .30
20 Morgan Shepherd .10 .30
21 Michael Waltrip .25 .60
22 Ward Burton .25 .60
23 Jimmy Spencer .10 .30
24 Jeff Gordon 1.25 3.00
25 Ken Schrader .10 .30
26 Kyle Petty .25 .60
27 Bobby Hillin .10 .30
28 Ernie Irvan .25 .60
29 Steve Grissom .10 .30
30 Johnny Benson .25 .60
31 Dave Marcis .10 .30
32 Jeremy Mayfield .25 .60
33 Robert Pressley .10 .30
34 Jeff Burton .40 1.00
35 Joe Nemechek .10 .30
36 Dale Jarrett .75 2.00
37 John Andretti .10 .30
38 Kenny Wallace .10 .30
39 Mike Wallace .10 .30
40 Dick Trickle .10 .30
41 Ricky Craven .10 .30
42 Chad Little .10 .30
43 Jeff Gordon CC .75 2.00
44 Sterling Marlin CC .10 .30
45 Mark Martin CC .60 1.50
46 Rusty Wallace CC .60 1.50
47 Terry Labonte CC .25 .60
48 Ted Musgrave CC .05 .15
49 Bill Elliott CC .25 .60
50 Ricky Rudd CC .25 .60
51 Bobby Labonte CC .50 1.25
52 Morgan Shepherd CC .05 .15
53 Michael Waltrip CC .25 .60
54 Dale Jarrett CC .50 1.25
55 Bobby Hamilton CC .05 .15
56 Derrike Cope CC .05 .15
57 Geoff Bodine CC .05 .15
58 Ken Schrader CC .05 .15
59 John Andretti CC .05 .15
60 Darrell Waltrip CC .10 .30
61 Brett Bodine CC .05 .15
62 Kenny Wallace CC .05 .15
63 Ward Burton CC .10 .30
64 Lake Speed CC .05 .15
65 Ricky Craven CC .05 .15
66 Jimmy Spencer CC .05 .15
67 Steve Grissom CC .05 .15
68 Joe Nemechek CC .05 .15
69 Ernie Irvan CC .10 .30
70 Kyle Petty CC .10 .30
71 Johnny Benson CC .10 .30
72 Jeff Burton CC .25 .60
73 Dave Marcis CC .05 .15
74 Jeremy Mayfield CC .10 .30
75 Michael Waltrip RPM .25 .60
76 Dale Jarrett RPM .50 1.25
77 Johnny Benson RPM .10 .30
78 Ricky Craven RPM .05 .15
79 Rusty Wallace RPM .60 1.50
80 Jeff Gordon RPM .75 2.00
81 Terry Labonte RPM .25 .60
82 Sterling Marlin RPM .10 .30
83 Mark Martin RPM .60 1.50
84 Ernie Irvan RPM .10 .30
S1 Rusty Wallace Promo 1.50 4.00
KR1 D.Earnhardt 40.00 100.00
J.Gordon Aces

1996 SP Driving Force

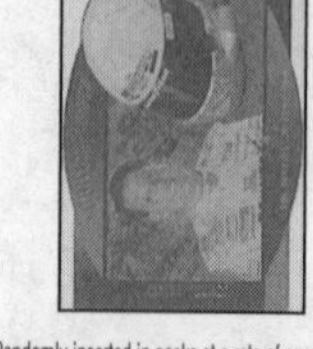

Randomly inserted in packs at a rate of one in 30, this 10-card set features the top up and coming drivers on the NASCAR circuit. The die-cut cards incorporate a driver's photo and a picture of the driver's helmet on the front.

COMPLETE SET (10) 20.00 50.00
DF1 Johnny Benson 2.50 6.00
DF2 Jeremy Mayfield 2.50 6.00
DF3 Brett Bodine 1.25 3.00
DF4 Robert Pressley 1.25 3.00
DF5 Jeff Burton 4.00 10.00
DF6 Ricky Craven 1.25 3.00
DF7 Wally Dallenbach 1.25 3.00
DF8 Bobby Labonte 8.00 20.00
DF9 Kenny Wallace 1.25 3.00
DF10 Bobby Hamilton 1.25 3.00

1996 SP Holoview Maximum Effects

This 25-card insert set features holoview printing technology to bring your favorite driver to life. The cards put the driver's photo in motion and were randomly inserted one in six packs. There is also a parallel die-cut version of this set inserted one in 73 packs.

COMPLETE SET (25) 50.00 120.00
COMP. DIE-CUT SET (25) 200.00 500.00
*DIE CUTS: 1.5X TO 4X BASIC INSERTS
ME1 Jeff Gordon 10.00 25.00
ME2 Rusty Wallace 8.00 20.00
ME3 Dale Earnhardt 12.50 30.00
ME4 Sterling Marlin 3.00 8.00
ME5 Terry Labonte 3.00 8.00
ME6 Mark Martin 8.00 20.00
ME7 Geoff Bodine 1.00 2.50
ME8 Johnny Benson 2.00 5.00
ME9 Derrike Cope 1.00 2.50
ME10 Ricky Rudd 3.00 8.00
ME11 Ricky Craven 1.00 2.50
ME12 John Andretti 1.00 2.50
ME13 Ken Schrader 1.00 2.50
ME14 Ernie Irvan 2.00 5.00
ME15 Steve Grissom 1.00 2.50
ME16 Ted Musgrave 1.00 2.50
ME17 Darrell Waltrip 2.00 5.00
ME18 Bobby Labonte 6.00 15.00
ME19 Kyle Petty 2.00 5.00
ME20 Bobby Hamilton 1.00 2.50
ME21 Kenny Wallace 1.00 2.50
ME22 Dale Jarrett 6.00 15.00
ME23 Bill Elliott 4.00 10.00
ME24 Jeremy Mayfield 2.00 5.00
ME25 Jeff Burton 3.00 8.00

1996 SP Racing Legends

This cross brand insert set features the final five cards from the 25 card series. The cards were randomly inserted in packs at a rate of one in 15.

COMPLETE SET (5) 15.00 40.00
RL21 Rusty Wallace 6.00 15.00
RL22 Bill Elliott 3.00 8.00
RL23 Mark Martin 6.00 15.00
RL24 Jeff Gordon 8.00 20.00
RL25 Header .40 1.00

1996 SP Richard Petty/STP 25th Anniversary

Randomly inserted in packs at a rate of one in 47, this nine-card set provides a historical perspective on the 25 year relationship between two of the biggest names in racing. The cards use an intricate die cut process to make them unique.

COMPLETE SET (9) 40.00 100.00
COMMON CARD (RP1-RP9) 5.00 12.00

1997 SP

This 126-card set was produced by Upper Deck. It was distributed in packs in three tiers. The cards are designated by flags on their borders. The single flag cards are randomly inserted in packs at a ratio of 6:1. The double flag cards are randomly inserted in packs at a ratio of 1:3. The triple flag cards are randomly inserted in packs at a ratio of 1:7. The double flag and triple flag tiers contain 21 cards each. Cards were distributed in seven card packs with 20 packs per box and 12 boxes per cases. 1000 cases of this product were produced.

COMPLETE SET (126) 100.00 200.00
COMP.SINGLE FLAG (84) 6.00 15.00
1 Morgan Shepherd .10 .30
2 Rusty Wallace 1.00 2.50
3 Dale Earnhardt 3F 15.00 40.00
4 Sterling Marlin .40 1.00
5 Terry Labonte .40 1.00
6 Mark Martin 2F 5.00 12.00
7 Geoff Bodine .10 .30
8 Hut Stricklin .10 .30
9 Lake Speed .10 .30
10 Ricky Rudd .40 1.00
11 Brett Bodine .10 .30
12 Dale Jarrett .75 2.00
13 Bill Elliott .50 1.25
14 Bobby Hamilton .10 .30
15 Wally Dallenbach .10 .30
16 Ted Musgrave .10 .30
17 Darrell Waltrip 3F 2.50 6.00
18 Bobby Labonte .75 2.00
19 Loy Allen .10 .30
20 Rick Mast .10 .30
21 Michael Waltrip 2F 1.25 3.00
22 Ward Burton 2F 1.25 3.00
23 Jimmy Spencer .10 .30
24 Jeff Gordon 3F 12.00 30.00
25 Ricky Craven 3F 1.25 3.00
26 Kyle Petty .25 .60
27 Bobby Hillin .25 .60
28 Ernie Irvan .25 .60
29 Robert Pressley .10 .30
30 Johnny Benson 2F 1.25 3.00
31 Dave Marcis .25 .60
32 Jeremy Mayfield .25 .60
33 Ken Schrader 2F .60 1.50
34 Jeff Burton .40 1.00
35 Chad Little .25 .60
36 Derrike Cope .10 .30
37 John Andretti .10 .30
38 Kenny Wallace .10 .30
39 Dick Trickle .10 .30
40 David Green 3F 1.25 3.00
41 Mike Wallace .10 .30
42 Joe Nemechek .10 .30
43 Morgan Shepherd's Car .05 .15
44 Rusty Wallace's Car .40 1.00
45 Dale Earnhardt's Car 3F 6.00 15.00
46 Sterling Marlin's Car .10 .30
47 Terry Labonte's Car 2F 1.25 3.00
48 Mark Martin's Car .40 1.00
49 Geoff Bodine's Car .05 .15
50 Hut Stricklin's Car .05 .15
51 Lake Speed's Car .05 .15
52 Ricky Rudd's Car 2F .60 1.50
53 Brett Bodine's Car .05 .15
54 Dale Jarrett's Car .25 .60
55 Bill Elliott's Car 3F 2.50 6.00
56 Bobby Hamilton's Car 2F .30 .75
57 Wally Dallenbach's Car .05 .15
58 Ted Musgrave's Car .05 .15
59 Darrell Waltrip's Car .10 .30
60 Bobby Labonte's Car .25 .60
61 Loy Allen's Car .05 .15
62 Rick Mast's Car .05 .15
63 Michael Waltrip's Car .10 .30
64 Ward Burton's Car .10 .30
65 Jimmy Spencer's Car 2F .30 .75
66 Jeff Gordon's Car .60 1.50
67 Ricky Craven's Car .05 .15
68 Kyle Petty's Car 3F .60 1.50
69 Bobby Hillin's Car .05 .15
70 Ernie Irvan's Car .10 .30
71 Robert Pressley's Car 3F .60 1.50
72 Johnny Benson's Car .10 .30
73 Dave Marcis's Car .10 .30
74 Jeremy Mayfield's Car .10 .30
75 Ken Schrader's Car .05 .15
76 Jeff Burton's Car .25 .60
77 Chad Little's Car .05 .15
78 Derrike Cope's Car 2F .30 .75
79 John Andretti's Car .05 .15
80 Kenny Wallace's Car .05 .15
81 Dick Trickle's Car .05 .15
82 David Green's Car 3F .60 1.50
83 Mike Wallace .10 .30
84 Joe Nemechek .10 .30
85 Rusty Wallace 3F 8.00 20.00
86 Sterling Marlin 2F 2.00 5.00
87 Terry Labonte 3F 5.00 12.00
88 Mark Martin 2F 5.00 12.00
89 Geoff Bodine .10 .30
90 Lake Speed .10 .30
91 Ricky Rudd 3F 4.00 10.00
92 Dale Jarrett 2F 4.00 10.00
93 Bill Elliott 2F 2.50 6.00
94 Bobby Hamilton .10 .30
95 Wally Dallenbach .10 .30
96 Ted Musgrave .10 .30
97 Darrell Waltrip .25 .60
98 Bobby Labonte 2F 4.00 10.00
99 Michael Waltrip .25 .60
100 Ward Burton .25 .60
101 Jimmy Spencer .10 .30
102 Jeff Gordon 2F 6.00 15.00
103 Ricky Craven .10 .30
104 Kyle Petty 3F 2.50 6.00
105 Ernie Irvan 2F 1.25 3.00
106 Johnny Benson .25 .60
107 Jeremy Mayfield .25 .60
108 Ken Schrader 3F 1.25 3.00
109 Jeff Burton .40 1.00
110 Derrike Cope .10 .30
111 John Andretti .10 .30
112 Kenny Wallace .10 .30
113 Rusty Wallace 3F 8.00 20.00
114 Sterling Marlin .40 1.00
115 Terry Labonte 3F 5.00 12.00
116 Mark Martin 3F 8.00 20.00
117 Ricky Rudd 2F 2.00 5.00
118 Dale Jarrett 3F 6.00 15.00
119 Bill Elliott .50 1.25
120 Bobby Labonte 2F 4.00 10.00
121 Jimmy Spencer 2F .60 1.50
122 Jeff Gordon 3F 12.00 30.00
123 Kyle Petty .25 .60
124 Ernie Irvan 3F 2.50 6.00
125 Ricky Craven 2F .60 1.50
126 Ken Schrader .10 .30
S24 Jeff Gordon Sample 1.50 4.00

1997 SP Super Series

COMP.SINGLE FLAG (84) 90.00 150.00
*SINGLE FLAGS: 4X TO 10X HI COL.
*DOUBLE FLAGS 2X TO 5X HI COL.
*TRIPLE FLAGS 2.5X TO 6X HI COL.

1997 SP Race Film

This 10-card insert set features film technology to capture race moments. Each card is numbered of 400. The cards were randomly inserted in packs at a ratio of 1:63.

COMPLETE SET (10) 60.00 120.00
RD1 Jeff Gordon 12.50 30.00
RD2 Rusty Wallace 10.00 25.00
RD3 Dale Earnhardt 15.00 40.00
RD4 Sterling Marlin 4.00 10.00
RD5 Terry Labonte 4.00 10.00
RD6 Mark Martin 10.00 25.00
RD7 Dale Jarrett 8.00 20.00
RD8 Ernie Irvan 2.50 6.00
RD9 Bill Elliott 5.00 12.00
RD10 Ricky Rudd 4.00 10.00

1997 SP SPx Force Autographs

This 4-card set features Upper Deck's holoview technology. Each of the four drivers signed 100 cards each. The cards were randomly inserted in packs at a ratio of 1:480.

COMPLETE SET (4) 300.00 500.00
SF1 Jeff Gordon 125.00 250.00
SF2 Rusty Wallace 60.00 120.00
SF3 Ricky Craven 40.00 80.00
SF4 Terry Labonte 50.00 100.00

1998 SP Authentic

The 1998 SP Authentic set was issued in one series totalling 84 cards. The 5-card packs retail for a suggested price of $4.99 each. The set contains the topical subset: Victory Lap (69-84).

COMPLETE SET (84) 15.00 40.00
1 Jeremy Mayfield .30 .75
2 Rusty Wallace 1.25 3.00
3 Dale Earnhardt 2.50 6.00
4 Bobby Hamilton .15 .40
5 Terry Labonte .50 1.25
6 Mark Martin 1.25 3.00
7 Geoff Bodine .15 .40
8 Hut Stricklin .15 .40
9 Jeff Burton .50 1.25
10 Ricky Rudd .50 1.25
11 Johnny Benson .30 .75
12 Dale Jarrett 1.00 2.50
13 Jerry Nadeau RC .50 1.25
14 Steve Park 1.00 2.50
15 Bill Elliott .60 1.50
16 Ted Musgrave .15 .40
17 Darrell Waltrip .30 .75
18 Bobby Labonte 1.00 2.50
19 Todd Bodine .15 .40
20 Kyle Petty .30 .75
21 Michael Waltrip .30 .75
22 Ken Schrader .15 .40
23 Jimmy Spencer .15 .40
24 Jeff Gordon 1.50 4.00
25 Ricky Craven .15 .40
26 John Andretti .15 .40
27 Sterling Marlin .50 1.25
28 Kenny Irwin .30 .75
29 Mike Skinner .15 .40
30 Derrike Cope .15 .40
31 Ernie Irvan .30 .75
32 Joe Nemechek .15 .40
33 Kenny Wallace .15 .40
34 Ward Burton .30 .75
35 Jeremy Mayfield's Car .15 .40
36 Rusty Wallace's Car .50 1.25
37 Dale Earnhardt's Car 1.00 2.50
38 Bobby Hamilton's Car .07 .20
39 Terry Labonte's Car .30 .75
40 Mark Martin's Car .50 1.25
41 Geoff Bodine's Car .07 .20
42 Hut Stricklin's Car .07 .20
43 Jeff Burton's Car .15 .40
44 Ricky Rudd's Car .15 .40
45 Johnny Benson's Car .07 .20
46 Dale Jarrett's Car .30 .75
47 Jerry Nadeau's Car .30 .75
48 Steve Park's Car .30 .75
49 Bill Elliott's Car .30 .75
50 Ted Musgrave's Car .07 .20
51 Darrell Waltrip's Car .15 .40
52 Bobby Labonte's Car .30 .75
53 Todd Bodine's Car .07 .20
54 Kyle Petty's Car .15 .40
55 Michael Waltrip's Car .15 .40
56 Ken Schrader's Car .07 .20
57 Jimmy Spencer's Car .07 .20
58 Jeff Gordon's Car .60 1.50
59 Ricky Craven's Car .07 .20
60 John Andretti's Car .07 .20
61 Sterling Marlin's Car .15 .40
62 Kenny Irwin's Car .15 .40
63 Mike Skinner's Car .07 .20
64 Derrike Cope's Car .07 .20
65 Ernie Irvan's Car .15 .40
66 Joe Nemechek's Car .07 .20
67 Kenny Wallace's Car .07 .20
68 Ward Burton's Car .15 .40
69 Darrell Waltrip VL .30 .75
70 Rusty Wallace VL 1.25 3.00
71 Bill Elliott VL .60 1.50
72 Jeff Gordon VL 1.50 4.00
73 Geoff Bodine VL .15 .40
74 Terry Labonte VL .50 1.25
75 Mark Martin VL 1.25 3.00
76 Ricky Rudd VL .50 1.25
77 Ernie Irvan VL .30 .75
78 Dale Jarrett VL 1.00 2.50
79 Kyle Petty VL .30 .75
80 Sterling Marlin VL .50 1.25
81 Dave Marcis VL .30 .75
82 Bobby Labonte VL 1.00 2.50
83 Ken Schrader VL .15 .40
84 Jimmy Spencer VL .15 .40
SPA2 Rusty Wallace Sample 1.50 4.00

1998 SP Authentic Behind the Wheel

Randomly inserted in packs at a rate of one in 4, this is the first of a three-tiered insert set that features 20 of the top NASCAR Winston Cup drivers, with each level boasting its own special insert ratio and foil treatment. Level 1 features a silver foil.

COMPLETE SET (20) 20.00 50.00
COMP.GOLD SET (20) 50.00 100.00
*GOLDS: .8X TO 2X BASIC INSERTS
GOLD STATED ODDS 1:12
*DIE CUTS: 5X TO 12X BASIC INSERTS
DIE CUTS PRINT RUN 100 SER.#'D SETS
BW1 Jeff Gordon 4.00 10.00
BW2 Dale Jarrett 2.50 6.00
BW3 Mark Martin 3.00 8.00
BW4 Jeff Burton 1.25 3.00
BW5 Terry Labonte 1.25 3.00
BW6 Bobby Labonte 2.50 6.00
BW7 Bill Elliott 1.50 4.00
BW8 Rusty Wallace 3.00 8.00
BW9 Ken Schrader .40 1.00
BW10 Johnny Benson .75 2.00
BW11 Ted Musgrave .40 1.00
BW12 Jeremy Mayfield .75 2.00
BW13 Ernie Irvan .75 2.00
BW14 Kyle Petty .75 2.00
BW15 Bobby Hamilton .40 1.00
BW16 Ricky Rudd 1.25 3.00
BW17 Michael Waltrip .75 2.00
BW18 Ricky Craven .40 1.00
BW19 Kenny Irwin .75 2.00
BW20 Steve Park 2.50 6.00

1998 SP Authentic Mark of a Legend

Randomly inserted in packs at a rate of one in 168, this five card insert set features autographs from all-time NASCAR greats.

COMPLETE SET (5) 150.00 250.00
M1 Richard Petty/220 30.00 60.00
M2 David Pearson 20.00 50.00
M3 Benny Parsons 20.00 50.00
M4 Ned Jarrett 15.00 40.00
M5 Cale Yarborough/220 15.00 40.00

1998 SP Authentic Sign of the Times

Randomly inserted in packs at a rate of one in 24, this is the first of a two-tiered insert set that contains autographs from today's top NASCAR stars including Jeff Gordon, Mark Martin and Rusty Wallace. Each card features the driver's car along with a large box in the lower right that features the signature. The basic inserts feature blue foil. Some cards were initially issued as redemptions in packs that carried an expiration date of 6/30/1999.

COMPLETE SET (10) 100.00 200.00
S1 Rusty Wallace's Car 10.00 25.00
S2 Ted Musgrave's Car 5.00 12.00
S3 Ricky Craven's Car 5.00 12.00
S4 Sterling Marlin's Car 8.00 20.00
S5 John Andretti's Car 5.00 12.00
S6 Michael Waltrip's Car 10.00 25.00
S7 Darrell Waltrip's Car 8.00 20.00
S8 Jeremy Mayfield's Car 6.00 15.00
S9 Kenny Irwin's Car 12.00 30.00
S10 Bobby Hamilton's Car 6.00 15.00

1998 SP Authentic Sign of the Times Red

Randomly inserted in packs at a rate of one in 96, this is the second of a two-tiered insert set that contains autographs from today's top NASCAR stars including Jeff Gordon, Mark Martin and Rusty Wallace. Each card features the driver's car along with a large box in the lower right that features the signature. The red foil version also included hand numbering on the backs. Some cards were initially issued as redemptions in packs that carried an expiration date of 6/30/1999.

COMPLETE SET (10) 400.00 800.00
ST1 Jeff Gordon's Car/45 150.00 300.00
ST2 Ernie Irvan's Car 15.00 40.00
ST3 Dale Earnhardt's Car 250.00 350.00
ST4 Kyle Petty's Car 15.00 40.00
ST5 Terry Labonte's Car/47 50.00 100.00
ST6 Mark Martin's Car 30.00 60.00
ST7 Dale Jarrett's Car/239 30.00 60.00
ST8 Jeff Burton's Car 10.00 25.00
ST9 Bobby Labonte's Car 12.50 30.00
ST10 Ricky Rudd's Car 15.00 40.00

1998 SP Authentic Traditions

Randomly inserted in packs at a rate of one in 288, this five card insert set features two authentic autographs: one from a NASCAR legend, and one from a current NASCAR superstar. Some cards were initially issued as redemptions in packs that carried an expiration date of 7/15/1999.

COMPLETE SET (5) 800.00 1200.00
T1 R.Petty/D.Earnhardt 350.00 500.00
T2 D.Pearson/J.Gordon 200.00 350.00
T3 B.Parsons/T.Labonte 100.00 200.00
T4 N.Jarrett/D.Jarrett 100.00 175.00
T5 C.Yarborough/R.Wallace 60.00 120.00

1999 SP Authentic

This 83 card set produced by Upper Deck was issued in four card packs. Cards numbered from 73 through 83 were produced in shorter supply than the other cards with 73 through 82 having a print run of 1000 cards and 83 having a print run of 500 signed cards. Card number 83 was also an exchange card that expired on May 25, 2000.

COMPLETE SET (83) 150.00 300.00
COMP.SET w/o SP's (72) 12.50 30.00
1 Jeff Gordon 1.50 4.00
2 Dale Earnhardt 2.50 6.00
3 Tony Stewart CRC 2.00 5.00
4 Dale Jarrett 1.00 2.50
5 Bobby Labonte 1.00 2.50
6 Ken Schrader .15 .40
7 Jerry Nadeau .30 .75
8 Mike Skinner .15 .40
9 Kyle Petty .30 .75
10 Johnny Benson .30 .75
11 Kenny Irwin .30 .75
12 Ward Burton .30 .75
13 Kevin Lepage .15 .40
14 Ernie Irvan .30 .75
15 Jeff Burton .50 1.25
16 Rusty Wallace 1.25 3.00
17 Jeremy Mayfield .30 .75
18 Elliott Sadler .30 .75
19 Bill Elliott .60 1.50
20 Mark Martin 1.25 3.00
21 Michael Waltrip .30 .75
22 Robert Pressley .15 .40
23 Ricky Rudd .50 1.25
24 Geoffrey Bodine .15 .40
25 John Andretti .15 .40
26 Darrell Waltrip .30 .75
27 Steve Park .75 2.00
28 Chad Little .30 .75
29 Bobby Hamilton .15 .40
30 Dale Earnhardt Jr. 2.00 5.00
31 Jason Keller .15 .40
32 Kenny Irwin's Car .08 .20
33 Geoffrey Bodine's Car .08 .20
34 Robert Pressley's Car .08 .20
35 Kevin Lepage's Car .08 .20
36 Tony Stewart's Car .60 1.50
37 Dale Earnhardt Jr's Car .75 2.00
38 Ernie Irvan's Car .15 .40
39 Jeff Burton's Car .15 .40
40 Chad Little's Car .08 .20
41 Rusty Wallace's Car .50 1.25
42 Steve Park's Car .30 .75
43 Mike Skinner's Car .08 .20
44 Jeremy Mayfield's Car .15 .40
45 Elliott Sadler's Car .08 .20
46 Bill Elliott's Car .30 .75
47 Darrell Waltrip's Car .15 .40
48 John Andretti's Car .08 .20
49 Kyle Petty's Car .08 .20
50 Johnny Benson's Car .15 .40
51 Jeff Gordon's Car .60 1.50
52 Dale Jarrett's Car .30 .75
53 Dale Earnhardt's Car 1.00 2.50
54 Terry Labonte's Car .30 .75
55 Bobby Labonte's Car .30 .75
56 Jerry Nadeau's Car .15 .40
57 Ricky Rudd's Car .15 .40
58 Bobby Hamilton's Car .08 .20
59 Michael Waltrip's Car .15 .40
60 Ken Schrader's Car .08 .20
61 Mark Martin's Car .50 1.25
62 Mark Martin CLASS .60 1.50
63 Darrell Waltrip CLASS .15 .40
64 Rusty Wallace CLASS .60 1.50
65 Jeff Gordon CLASS .75 2.00
66 Dale Earnhardt Jr. CLASS 1.00 2.50
67 Bobby Labonte CLASS .50 1.25
68 Jeremy Mayfield CLASS .15 .40
69 Terry Labonte CLASS .50 1.25
70 Jeff Burton CLASS .30 .75
71 Dale Jarrett CLASS .50 1.25
72 Dale Earnhardt Jr. CL 1.00 2.50
73 Bobby Labonte SP 5.00 12.00
74 Ward Burton SP 2.50 6.00
75 Jeremy Mayfield SP 2.50 6.00
76 Mark Martin SP 6.00 15.00
77 Rusty Wallace SP 6.00 15.00
78 Jeff Burton SP 3.00 8.00
79 Dale Earnhardt SP 12.50 30.00
80 Dale Jarrett SP 5.00 12.00
81 Tony Stewart SP 7.50 20.00
82 Jeff Gordon SP 7.50 20.00
83 D.Earnhardt Jr. SP AU/500 60.00 120.00

1999 SP Authentic Overdrive

*SINGLES 1-72: 3X TO 8X BASIC CARDS
1-72 STATED PRINT RUN 200 SER.#'d SETS
74 Ward Burton SP/22 25.00 60.00
78 Jeff Burton SP/99 25.00 60.00
80 Dale Jarrett SP/88 40.00 100.00
81 Tony Stewart SP/20 100.00 250.00
82 Jeff Gordon SP/24 125.00 300.00

1999 SP Authentic Cup Challengers

Inserted one every 23 packs, these cards feature 10 of the leading contenders for the Winston Cup title.

COMPLETE SET (10) 30.00 60.00
CC1 Jeff Gordon 6.00 15.00
CC2 Dale Jarrett 4.00 10.00
CC3 Jeff Burton 2.00 5.00
CC4 Rusty Wallace 5.00 12.00
CC5 Mark Martin 5.00 12.00
CC6 Jeremy Mayfield 1.25 3.00
CC7 Ward Burton 1.25 3.00
CC8 Bobby Labonte 4.00 10.00
CC9 Tony Stewart 6.00 15.00
CC10 Elliott Sadler 1.25 3.00

1999 SP Authentic Driving Force

Inserted one every 11 packs, these cards feature 11 drivers who are considered among the keys to bringing more fans to the NASCAR races.

COMPLETE SET (11) 20.00 40.00
DF1 Bobby Labonte 2.00 5.00
DF2 Terry Labonte 1.00 2.50
DF3 Jeremy Mayfield .60 1.50
DF4 Mark Martin 2.50 6.00
DF5 Rusty Wallace 2.50 6.00
DF6 Jeff Burton 1.00 2.50
DF7 Dale Earnhardt 5.00 12.00
DF8 Jeff Gordon 3.00 8.00
DF9 Dale Earnhardt Jr. 4.00 10.00
DF10 Elliott Sadler .60 1.50
DF11 Tony Stewart 3.00 8.00

1999 SP Authentic In the Driver's Seat

Inserted one every four packs, these nine cards feature racers who are considered the shapers of NASCAR. Card number DS6 was not produced.

COMPLETE SET (9)	12.50	30.00
DS1 Dale Earnhardt	3.00	8.00
DS2 Jeremy Mayfield	.40	1.00
DS3 Rusty Wallace	1.50	4.00
DS4 Tony Stewart	2.00	5.00
DS5 Bobby Labonte	1.25	3.00
DS7 Dale Earnhardt Jr.	2.50	6.00
DS8 Mark Martin	1.50	4.00
DS9 Jeff Burton	.60	1.50
DS10 Jeff Gordon	2.00	5.00

1999 SP Authentic Sign of the Times

Inserted one every 11 packs, these 26 cards feature signatures of NASCAR drivers. Several cards were issued via mail exchange cards.

COMPLETE SET (26)	500.00	1000.00
BE Bill Elliott	12.00	30.00
BH Bobby Hamilton	8.00	20.00
BL Bobby Labonte	12.00	30.00
CL Chad Little	6.00	15.00
DE Dale Earnhardt	200.00	350.00
DJ Dale Jarrett	12.00	30.00
EI Ernie Irvan	8.00	20.00
GB Geoffrey Bodine	6.00	15.00
JA John Andretti	6.00	15.00
JB Jeff Burton	6.00	15.00
JG Jeff Gordon	100.00	175.00
JM Jeremy Mayfield	6.00	15.00
JN Jerry Nadeau	8.00	20.00
KL Kevin Lepage	4.00	10.00
KP Kyle Petty	8.00	20.00
KS Ken Schrader	6.00	15.00
MM Mark Martin	40.00	80.00
MS Mike Skinner	6.00	15.00
RW Rusty Wallace	12.00	30.00
SM Sterling Marlin	8.00	20.00
SP Steve Park	8.00	20.00
TL Terry Labonte	12.00	30.00
TS Tony Stewart	20.00	40.00
WB Ward Burton	6.00	15.00
DEJ Dale Earnhardt Jr.	75.00	150.00
JBN Johnny Benson	5.00	12.00

2000 SP Authentic

Released as a 90-card set, SP Authentic features 45 regular cards, 30 SP Performance cards, and 15 SP Supremacy cards. SP Authentic was packaged in 24-pack boxes with four cards per pack and carried a suggested retail price of $3.99. Cards numbered from 46 through 75 had a stated print run of 2500 sets while cards numbered from 76 through 90 had a stated print run on 1000 sets.

COMPLETE SET (90)	60.00	120.00
COMP.SET w/o SP's (45)	10.00	25.00
WAX BOX	175.00	300.00
1 Bobby Labonte	1.00	2.50
2 Mark Martin	1.25	3.00
3 Ward Burton	.30	.75
4 Jeff Burton	.50	1.25
5 Dale Earnhardt	2.50	6.00
6 Rusty Wallace	1.00	3.00
7 Dale Jarrett	1.00	2.50
8 Ricky Rudd	.50	1.25
9 Jeremy Mayfield	.15	.40
10 Tony Stewart	2.00	5.00
11 Terry Labonte	.50	1.25
12 Jeff Gordon	1.50	4.00
13 Bill Elliott	.50	1.50
14 Justin Labonte	.15	.40
15 Chad Little	.30	.75
16 Mike Skinner	.15	.40
17 Sterling Marlin	.50	1.25
18 Johnny Benson	.30	.75
19 Dale Earnhardt Jr. CRC	2.00	5.00
20 Steve Park	.50	1.25
21 Matt Kenseth CRC	1.25	3.00
22 John Andretti	.15	.40
23 Bobby Hamilton	.15	.40
24 Kevin Lepage	.15	.40
25 P.J. Jones	.15	.40
26 Michael Waltrip	.30	.75
27 Joe Nemechek	.15	.40
28 Kenny Irwin	.30	.75
29 Elliott Sadler	.30	.75
30 Jerry Nadeau	.30	.75
31 Kyle Petty	.30	.75
32 Stacy Compton RC	.30	.75
33 Robby Gordon	.15	.40
34 Darrell Waltrip	.30	.75
35 Scott Pruett	.15	.40
36 Todd Bodine	.15	.40
37 Randy LaJoie	.15	.40
38 Jason Leffler	.15	.40
39 Jimmie Johnson RC	8.00	20.00
40 Kurt Busch RC	3.00	8.00
41 Kevin Grubb	.15	.40
42 Hank Parker Jr. RC	.50	1.25
43 Jason Keller	.15	.40
44 Kevin Harvick	1.25	3.00
45 Casey Atwood	.50	1.25
46 Chad Little PER	1.25	3.00
47 Mike Skinner PER	.75	2.00
48 Johnny Benson PER	1.25	3.00
49 Kenny Wallace PER	.75	2.00
50 John Andretti PER	.75	2.00
51 Bobby Hamilton PER	.75	2.00
52 Kevin Lepage PER	.75	2.00
53 Michael Waltrip PER	1.25	3.00
54 Joe Nemechek PER	.75	2.00
55 Kenny Irwin PER	1.25	3.00
56 Elliott Sadler PER	1.25	3.00
57 Robert Pressley PER	.75	2.00
58 Dick Trickle PER	.75	2.00
59 Stacy Compton PER	1.25	3.00
60 Robby Gordon PER	.75	2.00
61 Jason Leffler PER	.75	2.00
62 Justin Labonte PER	.75	2.00
63 Jason Jarrett PER	.75	2.00
64 Jerry Nadeau PER	1.25	3.00
65 Jay Sauter PER	.75	2.00
66 Lyndon Amick PER	.75	2.00
67 Jimmie Johnson PER	12.00	30.00
68 Michael Ritch PER	.75	2.00
69 Tony Raines PER RC	1.25	3.00
70 Darrell Waltrip PER	1.25	3.00
71 Kevin Grubb PER	.75	2.00
72 Hank Parker Jr. PER	2.00	5.00
73 Jason Keller PER	.75	2.00
74 Kevin Harvick PER	6.00	15.00
75 Casey Atwood PER	2.00	5.00
76 Bobby Labonte SUP	5.00	12.00
77 Mark Martin SUP	6.00	15.00
78 Ward Burton SUP	1.50	4.00
79 Jeff Burton SUP	3.00	8.00
80 Dale Earnhardt SUP	10.00	25.00
81 Rusty Wallace SUP	6.00	15.00
82 Dale Jarrett SUP	5.00	12.00
83 Ricky Rudd SUP	3.00	8.00
84 Jeremy Mayfield SUP	1.50	4.00
85 Tony Stewart SUP	10.00	25.00
86 Terry Labonte SUP	3.00	8.00
87 Jeff Gordon SUP	7.50	20.00
88 Bill Elliott SUP	3.00	8.00
89 Dale Earnhardt Jr. SUP	10.00	25.00
90 Matt Kenseth SUP	8.00	20.00
P88 Dale Jarrett Promo	1.00	2.50

2000 SP Authentic Overdrive Gold

*1-45 SINGLES/70-99: 8X TO 20X HI COL.
*1-45 SINGLES/45-69: 12.5X TO 25X HI COL.
*1-45 SINGLES/30-44: 15X TO 30X HI COL.
*1-45 SINGLES/20-29: 20X TO 40X HI COL.
*46-75 SINGLES/70-99: 2X TO 5X HI COL.
*46-75 SINGLES/45-69: 2.5X TO 6X HI COL.
*46-75 SINGLES/30-44: 5X TO 10X HI COL.
*46-75 SINGLES/20-29: 7.5X TO 15X HI COL.
*76-90 SINGLES/70-99: 1X TO 2.5X HI COL.
*76-90 SINGLES/20-29: 4X TO 8X HI COL.

39 Jimmie Johnson/92	125.00	200.00
40 Kurt Busch/99	20.00	50.00

2000 SP Authentic Overdrive Silver

*SILVERS 1-45: 4X TO 10X BASE CARDS
*SILVERS 46-75: .8X TO 2X BASE CARDS
*SILVERS 76-90: .4X TO 1X BASE CARDS

39 Jimmie Johnson	15.00	40.00
40 Kurt Busch	6.00	15.00
67 Jimmie Johnson PER	10.00	25.00

2000 SP Authentic Dominance

Randomly inserted in packs at the rate of one in 24, this 6-card set spotlights the most dominating NASCAR drivers. The cards contain foil highlights.

COMPLETE SET (6)	20.00	50.00
D1 Tony Stewart	8.00	20.00
D2 Dale Earnhardt Jr.	8.00	20.00
D3 Matt Kenseth	5.00	12.00
D4 Rusty Wallace	5.00	12.00
D5 Jeremy Mayfield	.60	1.50
D6 Jeff Burton	2.00	5.00

2000 SP Authentic Driver's Seat

Randomly inserted in packs at the rate of one in four, this 10-card set features close up shots of the racer in his car. Each card contains silver foil highlights.

COMPLETE SET (10)	8.00	20.00
DS1 Dale Jarrett	1.25	3.00
DS2 Bobby Labonte	1.25	3.00
DS3 Mark Martin	1.50	4.00
DS4 Tony Stewart	2.50	6.00
DS5 Jeff Burton	.60	1.50
DS6 Jeff Gordon	2.00	5.00
DS7 Matt Kenseth	1.50	4.00
DS8 Rusty Wallace	1.50	4.00
DS9 Ward Burton	.40	1.00
DS10 Mike Skinner	.20	.50

2000 SP Authentic High Velocity

Randomly inserted in packs at the rate of one in 12, this 7-card set features portrait photos of drivers and action photos of their cars. Each card contains silver foil highlights.

COMPLETE SET (8)	4.00	10.00
HV1 Ricky Rudd	.60	1.50
HV2 Bill Elliott	.75	2.00
HV3 Darrell Waltrip	.40	1.00
HV4 Terry Labonte	.60	1.50
HV5 Kyle Petty	.40	1.00
HV6 Jeremy Mayfield	.20	.50
HV7 Sterling Marlin	.60	1.50
HV8 Casey Atwood	.60	1.50

2000 SP Authentic Power Surge

Randomly inserted in packs at the rate of one in 24, this 7-card set highlights NASCAR drivers who take their cars to the limit week after week.

COMPLETE SET (7)	25.00	60.00
PS1 Dale Earnhardt	10.00	25.00
PS2 Jeff Gordon	6.00	15.00
PS3 Tony Stewart	8.00	20.00
PS4 Dale Earnhardt Jr.	8.00	20.00
PS5 Matt Kenseth	5.00	12.00
PS6 Mark Martin	5.00	12.00
PS7 Dale Jarrett	4.00	10.00

2000 SP Authentic Race for the Cup

Randomly inserted in packs at the rate of one in 12, this 10-card set features top NASCAR contenders.

COMPLETE SET (10)	8.00	20.00
R1 Jeff Gordon	2.00	5.00
R2 Dale Jarrett	1.25	3.00
R3 Ward Burton	.40	1.00
R4 Jeff Burton	.60	1.50
R5 Mark Martin	1.50	4.00
R6 Bobby Labonte	1.25	3.00
R7 Tony Stewart	2.50	6.00
R8 Rusty Wallace	1.50	4.00
R9 Ricky Rudd	.60	1.50
R10 Jeremy Mayfield	.20	.50

2000 SP Authentic Sign of the Times

Randomly inserted in packs at the rate of one in 11, this set features authentic autographs from some of NASCAR's finest. Some cards were released through exchange cards inserted into packs. Most drivers signed the cards with a blue felt tip pen while a few can be found with either blue or black ink. The basic inserts were printed with bronze colored ink wording on the fronts and feature a silver hologram Upper Deck logo on the back. A Gold parallel set was also produced with each card hand serial numbered of 25. The Gold version was printed with gold ink on the front and a gold hologram on back.

AH Andy Houston	5.00	12.00
BB Brett Bodine	5.00	12.00
BE Bill Elliott	15.00	40.00
BH Bobby Hamilton	8.00	20.00
BI Greg Biffle	8.00	20.00
CL Chad Little	5.00	12.00
CR Rick Crawford	6.00	15.00
DE Dale Earnhardt	200.00	400.00
DG Derrick Gilchrist	5.00	12.00
DJ Dale Jarrett	8.00	20.00
DM Dave Marcis	6.00	15.00
DT Dick Trickle	5.00	12.00
EI Ernie Irvan	8.00	20.00
ES Elliott Sadler	8.00	20.00
GB Geoff Bodine	5.00	12.00
GW Gus Wasson	5.00	12.00
HE Hermie Sadler	5.00	12.00
HI Bobby Hillin	5.00	12.00
HS Hut Stricklin	5.00	12.00
JA John Andretti	5.00	12.00
JB Jeff Burton	8.00	20.00
JG Jeff Gordon	60.00	120.00
JI Jimmie Johnson	50.00	100.00
JK Jason Keller	5.00	12.00
JM Jeremy Mayfield	6.00	15.00
JN Jerry Nadeau	6.00	15.00
JO Joe Nemechek	5.00	12.00
JR Dale Earnhardt Jr.	50.00	100.00
JS Jamie Skinner SP	12.00	30.00
JY Jay Sauter	5.00	12.00
KB Kurt Busch	8.00	20.00
KH Kevin Harvick	12.00	30.00
KL Kevin Lepage	5.00	12.00
LA Lyndon Amick	8.00	20.00
MC Mike McLaughlin	6.00	15.00
MH Matt Hutter	5.00	12.00
MK Matt Kenseth	10.00	25.00
MM Mark Martin	50.00	100.00
MS Mike Skinner	5.00	12.00
PJ P.J. Jones	5.00	12.00
PR Scott Pruett	5.00	12.00
RB Rich Bickle	5.00	12.00
RG Robby Gordon	6.00	15.00
RH Ron Hornaday	5.00	12.00
RL Randy LaJoie	5.00	12.00
RM Rick Mast	5.00	12.00
RP Robert Pressley	5.00	12.00
RW Rusty Wallace	15.00	40.00
SA Elton Sawyer	5.00	12.00
SC Stacy Compton	5.00	12.00
SM Sterling Marlin	8.00	20.00
SP Steve Park	6.00	15.00
TB Todd Bodine	5.00	12.00
TF Tim Fedewa	5.00	12.00
TL Terry Labonte	8.00	20.00
TR Tony Raines	5.00	12.00
WA Mike Wallace	6.00	15.00
WD Wally Dallenbach	5.00	12.00

2000 SP Authentic Sign of the Times Gold

Randomly inserted in packs, this set parallels the base Sign of the Times set on cards that feature a Gold colored background. Each card was sequentially hand numbered to 25 and includes a gold hologram Upper Deck logo on the back

*GOLD/25: 1.5X TO 4X BASIC AUTO

BH Bobby Hamilton	40.00	100.00
DE Dale Earnhardt	500.00	1000.00
JG Jeff Gordon	250.00	400.00
JI Jimmie Johnson	150.00	250.00
JR Dale Earnhardt Jr.	250.00	450.00
KH Kevin Harvick	75.00	150.00
MK Matt Kenseth	75.00	150.00

2008 SP Legendary Cuts Mystery Cut Signatures

EXCHANGE DEADLINE 12/31/2010

1996 SPx

This is the inaugural racing issue of Upper Deck's popular SPx brand. The 25-card set features holoview technology and has a die cut design. The one-card packs retailed for $3.49 each. There were 28 packs per box and 12 boxes per case. Randomly inserted in packs were special cards of Terry Labonte and Jeff Gordon. The Terry Labonte card commemorated his record breaking 514 consecutive starts. These cards were seeded one in 47 packs. The Jeff Gordon card was a tribute to the hottest young star in racing. His card was seeded one in 71 packs. There were also autograph cards of both drivers. The Terry Labonte seeded in packs was actually an autograph redemption card. This card was available one in 395 packs. The Jeff Gordon card was an autographed version of the tribute card and was also seeded one in 395 packs. There was also a Jeff Gordon Sample card that was issued as a promo.

COMPLETE SET (25)	15.00	40.00
1 Jeff Gordon	3.00	8.00
2 Rusty Wallace	2.50	6.00
3 Dale Earnhardt	5.00	12.00
4 Sterling Marlin	1.00	2.50
5 Terry Labonte	1.00	2.50
6 Mark Martin	2.50	6.00
7 Jeff Burton	1.00	2.50
8 Bobby Hamilton	.40	1.00
9 Lake Speed	.40	1.00
10 Ricky Rudd	1.00	2.50
11 Brett Bodine	.40	1.00
12 Derrike Cope	.40	1.00
13 Jeremy Mayfield	.60	1.50
14 Ricky Craven	.40	1.00
15 Johnny Benson	.60	1.50
16 Ted Musgrave	.40	1.00
17 Darrell Waltrip	.60	1.50
18 Bobby Labonte	2.00	5.00
19 Steve Grissom	.40	1.00
20 Kyle Petty	.60	1.50
21 Michael Waltrip	.60	1.50
22 Ernie Irvan	.60	1.50
23 Dale Jarrett	2.00	5.00
24 Bill Elliott	1.25	3.00
25 Ken Schrader	.40	1.00
C1 Terry Labonte COMM	5.00	12.00
C1A Terry Labonte AU	8.00	20.00
T1 Jeff Gordon Tribute	10.00	25.00
T1A Jeff Gordon AU	40.00	80.00
S1 Jeff Gordon Sample	2.00	5.00

1996 SPx Gold

COMPLETE SET (25)	60.00	150.00

*GOLDS: 1X TO 2.5X BASE CARDS

1996 SPx Elite

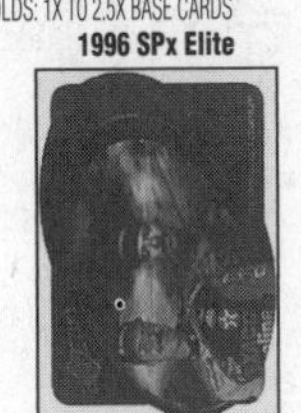

Randomly inserted in packs at a rate of one in 23, this five-card set features some of the top names in racing. The cards use the same holoview technology as the base SPx cards.

COMPLETE SET (5)	25.00	60.00
E1 Jeff Gordon	10.00	25.00
E2 Dale Jarrett	6.00	15.00
E3 Terry Labonte	3.00	8.00
E4 Rusty Wallace	8.00	20.00
E5 Ernie Irvan	2.00	5.00

1997 SPx

This 25-card set features the top names from the Winston Cup circuit. It is important to note that a significant percentage of base cards that were pulled from packs contain minor surface foil damage on the left side on each card. This has made the supply of Mint cards very small. Cards were distributed in three cards packs with 18 packs per box and 12 boxes per case. The packs carried a suggested retail price of $4.99.

COMPLETE SET (25)	15.00	40.00
1 Robby Gordon RC	.60	1.50
2 Rusty Wallace	1.50	4.00
3 Dale Earnhardt	3.00	8.00
4 Sterling Marlin	.60	1.50
5 Terry Labonte	.60	1.50
6 Mark Martin	1.50	4.00
7 Geoff Bodine	.20	.50
8 Dale Jarrett	1.25	3.00
9 Ernie Irvan	.40	1.00
10 Ricky Rudd	.60	1.50
11 Mike Skinner	.20	.50
12 Johnny Benson	.40	1.00
13 Kyle Petty	.40	1.00
14 John Andretti	.20	.50
15 Jeff Burton	.60	1.50
16 Ted Musgrave	.20	.50
17 Darrell Waltrip	.40	1.00
18 Bobby Labonte	1.25	3.00
19 Bobby Hamilton	.20	.50
20 Bill Elliott	.75	2.00
21 Michael Waltrip	.40	1.00
22 Ken Schrader	.20	.50
23 Jimmy Spencer	.20	.50
24 Jeff Gordon	2.00	5.00
25 Ricky Craven	.20	.50
S2 Rusty Wallace Promo	1.25	3.00

1997 SPx Blue

COMPLETE SET (25)	20.00	50.00

*BLUES: .6X TO 1.5X BASIC CARDS

1997 SPx Gold

COMPLETE SET (25)	250.00	500.00

*GOLDS: 5X TO 12X BASIC CARDS

1997 SPx Silver

COMPLETE SET (25)	40.00	100.00

*SILVERS: 1.2X TO 3X BASIC CARDS

1997 SPx SpeedView Autographs

This 10-card insert set features the top driver on the Winston Cup Circuit. Each card is autographed and has three photos of the driver on the front of the card. The cards were randomly inserted in packs at a ratio of 1:175.

COMPLETE SET (10)	175.00	350.00
SV1 Jeff Gordon	50.00	120.00
SV2 Rusty Wallace	15.00	30.00
SV3 Bill Elliott	10.00	25.00
SV4 Sterling Marlin	8.00	20.00
SV5 Terry Labonte	25.00	60.00
SV6 Mark Martin	15.00	40.00
SV7 Dale Jarrett	12.50	30.00
SV8 Ernie Irvan	8.00	20.00
SV9 Bobby Labonte	12.50	30.00
SV10 Ricky Rudd	8.00	20.00

1997 SPx Tag Team

This five- card insert set features the top pairs of teammates in NASCAR. The cards were randomly inserted in packs at a ratio of 1:55.

COMPLETE SET (5)	50.00	120.00
TT1 T.Labonte J.Gordon	15.00	40.00
TT2 D.Jarrett E.Irvan	7.50	20.00
TT3 M.Martin J.Burton	10.00	25.00
TT4 J.Gordon R.Craven	15.00	40.00
TT5 R.Petty K.Petty	6.00	15.00

1997 SPx Tag Team Autographs

This five-card insert set is a parallel of the base Tag team set. Each card from this set is signed by both drivers featured on the card. The cards were randomly inserted in packs at a ratio of 1:2,500.

COMPLETE SET (5)	350.00	600.00
TA1 T.Labonte/J.Gordon	100.00	200.00
TA2 D.Jarrett/E.Irvan	25.00	60.00
TA3 M.Martin/J.Burton	25.00	60.00
TA4 J.Gordon/R.Craven	75.00	150.00
TA5 R.Petty/K.Petty	50.00	100.00

1996 Speedflix

The 1996 Speedflix Racing set was issued in one series totalling 87 cards. The set includes the following subsets: Black Lighting (51-54), Champion In Motion (55-62), Back on Track (63-66), Relentless Opponent (67-70), Championship Form (71-74), Million Dollar Bill (75-78), and Winning Style (79-82). The cards use lenticular animation to bring movement to every card. The cards were packaged 5 cards per pack in both hobby and retail packs. Jumbo packs had eight cards per pack.

COMPLETE SET (87)	10.00	25.00
WAX BOX	30.00	60.00
1 Rusty Wallace	.50	1.25
2 Sterling Marlin	.20	.50
3 Terry Labonte	.20	.50
4 Bill Elliott	.25	.60
5 John Andretti	.05	.15
6 Bobby Hamilton	.05	.15
7 Darrell Waltrip	.10	.30
8 Michael Waltrip	.10	.30
9 Jeff Gordon	.60	1.50
10 Dale Jarrett	.40	1.00
11 Johnny Benson Jr.	.10	.30
12 Rick Mast	.05	.15
13 Geoff Bodine	.05	.15
14 Ward Burton	.10	.30
15 Kenny Wallace	.05	.15
16 Jeff Gordon	.60	1.50
17 Dale Earnhardt	1.00	2.50
18 Rusty Wallace	.50	1.25
19 Sterling Marlin	.20	.50
20 Mark Martin	.50	1.25
21 Ricky Rudd	.20	.50
22 Darrell Waltrip	.10	.30
23 Bobby Labonte	.40	1.00
24 Dale Jarrett	.40	1.00
25 Ricky Craven	.05	.15
26 Johnny Benson Jr.	.10	.30
27 Joe Nemechek	.05	.15
28 Ernie Irvan	.10	.30
29 Jeff Burton	.20	.50
30 Terry Labonte	.20	.50
31 Bobby Hillin Jr.	.05	.15
32 John Andretti	.05	.15
33 Mike Wallace	.05	.15
34 Kyle Petty	.10	.30
35 Lake Speed	.05	.15
36 Rusty Wallace's Car in pits	.10	.30
37 Dale Earnhardt's Car in pits	.40	1.00
38 Sterling Marlin's Car in pits	.05	.15
39 Terry Labonte's Car in pits	.10	.30
40 Mark Martin's Car in pits	.10	.30
41 Ricky Rudd's Car in pits	.05	.15
42 Bill Elliott's Car in pits	.10	.30
43 Ernie Irvan's Car in pits	.05	.15
44 Jeff Gordon's Car in pits	.25	.60
45 Bobby Labonte's Car in pits	.10	.30
46 Terry Labonte DT	.10	.30
47 Dale Jarrett DT	.10	.30
48 Michael Waltrip DT	.10	.30
49 Kenny Wallace DT	.02	.10
50 Mark Martin DT	.10	.30
51 Dale Earnhardt BL	.50	1.25
52 Dale Earnhardt BL	.50	1.25
53 Dale Earnhardt BL	.50	1.25
54 Dale Earnhardt BL	.50	1.25
55 Jeff Gordon CM	.25	.60
56 Jeff Gordon CM	.25	.60
57 Jeff Gordon CM	.25	.60
58 Jeff Gordon CM	.25	.60
59 Jeff Gordon CM	.25	.60
60 Jeff Gordon CM	.25	.60
61 Jeff Gordon CM	.25	.60
62 Jeff Gordon CM	.25	.60
63 Ernie Irvan BT	.05	.15
64 Ernie Irvan BT	.05	.15
65 Ernie Irvan BT	.05	.15
66 Ernie Irvan BT	.05	.15
67 Mark Martin RO	.10	.30
68 Mark Martin RO	.10	.30
69 Mark Martin RO	.10	.30
70 Mark Martin RO	.10	.30
71 Rusty Wallace CF	.10	.30
72 Rusty Wallace CF	.10	.30
73 Rusty Wallace CF	.10	.30
74 Rusty Wallace CF	.10	.30
75 Bill Elliott MDB	.10	.30
76 Bill Elliott MDB	.10	.30
77 Bill Elliott MDB	.10	.30
78 Bill Elliott MDB	.10	.30
79 Ricky Rudd WS	.10	.30
80 Ricky Rudd WS	.10	.30
81 Ricky Rudd WS	.10	.30
82 Ricky Rudd WS	.10	.30
83 Dale Earnhardt W	.50	1.25
84 Jeff Gordon W	.30	.75
85 Dale Earnhardt W	.50	1.25
86 Jeff Gordon CL	.30	.75
87 Mark Martin CL	.10	.30
P1 Dale Jarrett Promo	1.50	4.00

1996 Speedflix Artist Proof's

COMPLETE SET (87)	125.00	250.00

*ARTIST PROOFS: 5X TO 12X BASE CARDS

1996 Speedflix Clear Shots

This 12-card insert set features almost clear lenticular technology. It mixes an acetate card with lenticular technology. The cards were inserted in jumbo packs at a rate of one in 31.

COMPLETE SET (12) 80.00 175.00
1 Dale Earnhardt 20.00 50.00
2 Jeff Gordon 12.50 30.00
3 Sterling Marlin 4.00 10.00
4 Rusty Wallace 10.00 25.00
5 Bobby Labonte 8.00 20.00
6 Terry Labonte 4.00 10.00
7 Dale Jarrett 8.00 20.00
8 Mark Martin 10.00 25.00
9 Bill Elliott 5.00 12.00
10 Ernie Irvan 2.50 6.00
11 Ted Musgrave 1.25 3.00
12 Johnny Benson Jr. 2.50 6.00

1996 Speedflix In Motion

This 10-card insert set shows off the helmets of the top drivers on the Winston Cup circuit. The helmets are featured in multi-phase lenticular animation. In Motion cards were seeded one in 48 packs.

COMPLETE SET (10) 40.00 100.00
1 Dale Earnhardt's Helmet 6.00 15.00
2 Jeff Gordon's Helmet 4.00 10.00
3 Sterling Marlin's Helmet 1.25 3.00
4 Rusty Wallace's Helmet 1.25 3.00
5 Geoff Bodine's Helmet 1.00 2.50
6 Terry Labonte's Helmet 1.25 3.00
7 Darrell Waltrip's Helmet 1.25 3.00
8 Mark Martin's Helmet 1.25 3.00
9 Ted Musgrave's Helmet .75 2.00
10 Bill Elliott's Helmet 2.00 5.00

1996 Speedflix ProMotion

This 12-card insert set allows collectors to see their favorites on the move. The cards use multi-phase lenticular animation to show drivers getting in and out of their cars. ProMotion cards were randomly inserted one per nine packs.

COMPLETE SET (12) 25.00 60.00
1 Dale Earnhardt 8.00 20.00
2 Jeff Gordon 5.00 12.00
3 Sterling Marlin 1.50 4.00
4 Rusty Wallace 4.00 10.00
5 Michael Waltrip 1.00 2.50
6 Terry Labonte 1.50 4.00
7 Dale Jarrett 3.00 8.00
8 Mark Martin 4.00 10.00
9 Bill Elliott 2.00 5.00
10 Darrell Waltrip 1.00 2.50
11 Bobby Hamilton .50 1.25
12 Johnny Benson Jr. 1.00 2.50

1996 Sported/Match

This 15-card set was produced by the British company Howitt Printing and features cards that "pop-up" when pulled. The basic card front for the first ten cards features a photo of the player against a black background with the title "Sported! World Class Winners" running vertically along the right-side of the card. The final five-cards feature a blue background with the title "Match World Class Winners" running vertically along the right side of the card. When the cards are pulled open, they reveal some statistics and the player's greatest Sported!or Match moment.

COMPLETE SET (15) 10.00 25.00
1 Damon Hill .40 1.00
Racing

2007 Sportkings

2 Mario Andretti 6.00 15.00
22 Nigel Mansell 4.00 10.00

2007 Sportkings Mini

*MINIS: 1X TO 2X BASIC
ONE PER PACK
ANNOUNCED PRINT RUN 93 SETS

2007 Sportkings Autograph Silver

RANDOM INSERTS IN PACKS
ANNOUNCED PRINT RUN B/WN 95-99 PER
AMA Mario Andretti 25.00 50.00
ANM Nigel Mansell 35.00 60.00

2007 Sportkings Autograph Gold

*GOLD: 1.2X TO 2X BASIC
RANDOM INSERTS IN PACKS
ANNOUNCED PRINT RUN 10 SETS

2007 Sportkings Autograph Memorabilia Silver

RANDOM INSERTS IN PACKS
ANNOUNCED PRINT RUN 40 SETS
AMMA Mario Andretti Uniform 60.00 100.00
AMNM Nigel Mansell Metal Wing 60.00 100.00

2007 Sportkings Autograph Memorabilia Gold

*GOLD/10: 1.2X TO 2X SILVER/40
ANNOUNCED PRINT RUN 10 SETS
AMMA Mario Andretti Uniform 90.00 150.00
AMNM Nigel Mansell Wing 90.00 150.00

2007 Sportkings Decades Silver

ANNOUNCED PRINT RUN 20 SETS
*GOLD: .5X TO 1.2X BASIC
GOLD ANNOUNCED PRINT RUN 10 SETS
RANDOM INSERTS IN PACKS
D03 Yaz/Andretti/Clemente 50.00 100.00

2007 Sportkings Patch Silver

ANNOUNCED PRINT RUN 20 SETS
P28-P30 ANNOUNCED PRINT RUN 4 PER
NO P28-P30 PRICING DUE TO SCARCITY
*GOLD: .6X TO 1.2X BASIC
GOLD ANNOUNCED PRINT RUN 10 SETS
GOLD P28-P30 ANCD. PRINT RUN 1 PER
GOLD P28-P30 NO PRICING AVAILABLE
RANDOM INSERTS IN PACKS
P10 Mario Andretti Suit 15.00 40.00

2007 Sportkings Patch Gold

P10 Mario Andretti Uniform 25.00 50.00

2007 Sportkings Single Memorabilia Silver

RANDOM INSERTS IN PACKS
ANNOUNCED PRINT RUN 90 SETS
SM3, SM13 ANNOUNCED PRINT RUN 4 PER
NO SM3, SM13 PRICING DUE TO SCARCITY
SM10 Mario Andretti Uniform 10.00 25.00
SM15 Nigel Mansell Wing 8.00 20.00

2008 Sportkings

FIVE CARDS PER BOX
75 Ayrton Senna 4.00 8.00

2008 Sportkings Mini

*MINI: 1X TO 2X BASIC
ONE PER BOX

2008 Sportkings Single Memorabilia Silver

RANDOM INSERTS IN PACKS
2 Ayrton Senna 20.00 50.00

2008 Sportkings Triple Memorabilia Silver

RANDOM INSERTS IN PACKS
11 Senna/Mansell/Andretti 40.00 80.00

2009 Sportkings

COMPLETE SET (52) 250.00 450.00
COMMON CARD (109-160) 5.00 12.00
SEMISTARS 6.00 15.00
UNLISTED STARS 8.00 20.00
115 Mark Martin 6.00 15.00
160 Rusty Wallace 8.00 20.00

2009 Sportkings Autograph Silver

ANNOUNCED PRINT RUN B/WN 15-70 PER
UNPRICED GOLD PRINT RUN 10
RW1 Rusty Wallace/35* 40.00 80.00
RW2 Rusty Wallace/35* 40.00 80.00
MMA1 Mark Martin/25* 40.00 80.00
MMA2 Mark Martin/25* 40.00 80.00

2009 Sportkings Autograph Memorabilia Silver

ANNOUNCED PRINT RUN B/WN 15-40 PER
UNPRICED GOLD PRINT RUN 10
RANDOM INSERTS IN PACKS
RW1 Rusty Wallace Firesuit/35* 40.00 80.00
RW2 Rusty Wallace Firesuit/35* 40.00 80.00
MMA1 Mark Martin Car/30* 30.00 60.00
MMA2 Mark Martin Car/30* 30.00 60.00

2009 Sportkings Decades Silver

ANNOUNCED PRINT RUN 19 SETS
UNPRICED GOLD PRINT RUN 1
RANDOM INSERTS IN PACKS
3 Taylor/Wallace/Schmidt 40.00 80.00

2009 Sportkings Double Memorabilia Silver

ANNOUNCED PRINT RUN B/WN 1-19
UNPRICED GOLD PRINT RUN 1
RANDOM INSERTS IN PACKS
7 R.Wallace/M.Martin/19* 25.00 50.00

2009 Sportkings Mini

*MINI: .6X TO 1.5X BASIC CARDS
STATED ODDS ONE PER BOX
UNPRICED SILVER PRINT RUN 7 SETS
UNPRICED GOLD PRINT RUN 3 SETS

2009 Sportkings Patch Silver

ANNOUNCED PRINT RUN B/WN 4-19
UNPRICED GOLD PRINT RUN 1 SET
RANDOM INSERTS IN PACKS
9 Rusty Wallace/19* 40.00 80.00

2009 Sportkings Single Memorabilia Silver

ANNOUNCED PRINT RUN B/WN 4-29
UNPRICED GOLD PRINT RUN B/WN 1-4
RANDOM INSERTS IN PACKS
10 Mark Martin Car/29* 15.00 40.00
18 Rusty Wallace Uni/29* 12.00 30.00

2009 Sportkings National Convention VIP Promo

COMPLETE SET (7)
1 Lendl/Esposito/Wallace/Shamrock/Barry/Tyson 4.00 10.00
4 West/Nelson/Perry/Martin/Fats/Rice 5.00 12.00

2012 Sportkings

244 Mauri Rose 4.00 10.00
245 Kyle Petty 4.00 10.00

2012 Sportkings Mini

*MINI: .5X TO 1.2X BASIC CARDS
RANDOM INSERT IN PACKS

2012 Sportkings Premium Back

*SINGLES: .5X TO 1.2X BASIC CARDS
STATED ODDS ONE PER PACK

2012 Sportkings Autograph Memorabilia Silver

ANNOUNCED PRINT RUN 15-50
AMKP1 Kyle Petty 15.00 30.00
AMKP2 Kyle Petty 15.00 30.00

2012 Sportkings Autographs Silver

ANNOUNCED PRINT RUN 15-130
AKP1 Kyle Petty 12.00 25.00
AKP2 Kyle Petty 12.00 25.00

2012 Sportkings Quad Memorabilia Silver

ANNOUNCED PRINT RUN 30
QM3 Holy/Brunsn/Grahm/Petty 30.00 60.00

2012 Sportkings Single Memorabilia Silver

ANNOUNCED PRINT RUN 90
SM22 Kyle Petty 7.50 15.00

2012 Sportkings Triple Memorabilia Silver

ANNOUNCED PRINT RUN 30
TM5 Robinson/Petty/Sayers 15.00 30.00

1997 SportsCom FanScan

This series of cards was produced by SportsCom, Inc. Each was to be used similar to a phone card except that the phone call would be connected to the featured driver's team radios during a Winston Cup race, just like a scanner. Each card featured 10-minutes worth of time that expired on 12/31/1997. However, the holder could also purchase additional time at the rate of $1.49 per minute thereafter.

COMPLETE SET (12) 7.50 20.00
1 Jeff Burton .60 1.50
2 Dale Earnhardt 2.50 6.00
3 Jeff Gordon 1.50 4.00
4 Bobby Hamilton .30 .75
5 Ernie Irvan .60 1.50
6 Dale Jarrett 1.00 2.50
7 Sterling Marlin .60 1.50
8 Mark Martin 1.25 3.00
9 Ted Musgrave .30 .75
10 Richard Petty .75 2.00
11 Ken Schrader .40 1.00
12 Rusty Wallace 1.25 3.00

1998 SportsCom FanScan

Each card in this set was to be used similar to a phone card except that the phone call would be connected to the featured driver's team radios during a Winston Cup race, just like a scanner. Each card featured 20-Units (3-minutes = 1-unit) worth of time that expired on 3/31/1998. However, the holder could also purchase additional time at the rate of $1.49 per minute thereafter.

COMPLETE SET (9) 6.00 15.00
1 Dale Earnhardt 2.50 6.00
2 Jeff Gordon 1.50 4.00
3 Ernie Irvan .60 1.50
4 Dale Jarrett 1.00 2.50
5 Sterling Marlin .60 1.50
6 Mark Martin 1.25 3.00
7 Ken Schrader .40 1.00
8 Rusty Wallace 1.25 3.00
9 Darrell Waltrip .40 1.00

1999 SportsCom FanScan

This series marks the second year of cards produced by SportsCom, Inc. Each was to be used similar to a phone card except that the phone call would be connected to the featured driver's team radios during a Winston Cup race, just like a scanner. Each card featured 7-minutes worth of time that expired on 3/31/1999. However, the holder could also purchase additional time at the rate of $1.49 per minute thereafter.

COMPLETE SET (9) 6.00 15.00
1 Dale Earnhardt 2.50 6.00
2 Jeff Gordon 1.50 4.00
3 Ernie Irvan .60 1.50
4 Dale Jarrett 1.00 2.50
5 Sterling Marlin .60 1.50
6 Mark Martin 1.25 3.00
7 Ken Schrader .40 1.00
8 Rusty Wallace 1.25 3.00
9 Darrell Waltrip .40 1.00

1926 Sport Company of America

This 151-card set encompasses athletes from a multitude of different sports. There are 49-cards representing baseball and 14-cards for football. Each includes a black-and-white player photo within a fancy frame border. The player's name and sport are printed at the bottom. The backs carry a short player biography and statistics. The cards originally came in a small glassine envelope along with a coupon that could be redeemed for sporting equipment and are often still found in this form. The cards are unnumbered and have been checklisted below in alphabetical order within sport. We've assigned prefixes to the card numbers which serves to group the cards by sport (BB- baseball, FB- football).

RC1 Earl Cooper 20.00 40.00
RC2 Ralph De Palma 30.00 60.00
RC3 Ralph De Palo 20.00 40.00
RC4 Harry Hartz 20.00 40.00
RC5 Benny Hill 20.00 40.00
RC6 Bob McDonough 20.00 40.00
RC7 Tommy Milton 20.00 40.00
RC8 Barney Oldfield 30.00 60.00
OT1 Benny Hill 25.00 50.00
Auto Racing

1977-79 Sportscaster Series 1

COMPLETE SET (24) 17.50 35.00
101 Roger De Coster .25 .50

1977-79 Sportscaster Series 2

COMPLETE SET (24) 30.00 60.00
215 24 Hours at Le Mans 1.00 2.00

1977-79 Sportscaster Series 4

COMPLETE SET (24) 15.00 30.00
401 Clay Regazzoni .50 1.00
417 Alberto Ascari .25 .50

1977-79 Sportscaster Series 5

COMPLETE SET (24) 12.50 25.00
507 Tourist Trophy .25 .50
521 James Hunt .75 1.50
524 World Championship for Sidecars .25 .50

1977-79 Sportscaster Series 6

COMPLETE SET (24) 12.50 25.00
602 Indianapolis .75 1.50
603 Jacky Ickx .75 1.50
622 World Drivers Championship 1976 1.00 2.00

1977-79 Sportscaster Series 7

COMPLETE SET (24) 15.00 30.00
724 World Drivers Championship .25 .50

1977-79 Sportscaster Series 8

COMPLETE SET (24) 12.50 25.00
802 Juan Manuel Fangio .75 1.50
824 Niki Lauda 1.25 2.50

1977-79 Sportscaster Series 9

COMPLETE SET (24) 15.00 30.00
915 Stirling Moss 1.00 2.00

1977-79 Sportscaster Series 10

COMPLETE SET (24) 17.50 35.00
1001 European Circuits .75 1.50
1002 Rudolf Caracciola .25 .50
1009 Mario Andretti 5.00 10.00

1977-79 Sportscaster Series 11

COMPLETE SET (25) 20.00 40.00
1102 Joseph Siffert .50 1.00
1115 Richard Petty 10.00 20.00

1977-79 Sportscaster Series 12

COMPLETE SET (24) 12.50 25.00
1201 Graham Hill 2.50 5.00
1202 Michel Rougerie .25 .50
1220 Jim Clark 2.00 4.00

1977-79 Sportscaster Series 13

COMPLETE SET (24) 12.50 25.00
1316 The European F2 Trophy .25 .50

1977-79 Sportscaster Series 14

COMPLETE SET (24) 17.50 35.00
1407 500 CC WCH .25 .50

1977-79 Sportscaster Series 16

COMPLETE SET (24) 15.00 30.00
1604 Bobby and Al Unser 4.00 8.00
1622 Patrick Pons .25 .50

1977-79 Sportscaster Series 17

COMPLETE SET (24) 10.00 20.00
1716 1973 WCH 2.00 4.00

1977-79 Sportscaster Series 18

COMPLETE SET (24) 12.50 25.00
1803 Janet Guthrie 1.50 3.00
1817 French GP .25 .50
1819 Parnelli Jones 1.50 3.00

1977-79 Sportscaster Series 19

COMPLETE SET (24) 25.00 50.00
1910 1972 WCH 3.00 6.00
1917 A.J. Foyt 5.00 10.00

1977-79 Sportscaster Series 20

COMPLETE SET (24) 7.50 15.00
2003 The Monte-Carlo Rally .25 .50

1977-79 Sportscaster Series 21

COMPLETE SET (24) 15.00 30.00
2102 Karting In Europe .25 .50
2103 The Campbells .75 1.50
2122 Monaco GP .75 1.50

1977-79 Sportscaster Series 22

COMPLETE SET (24) 15.00 30.00
2207 WCH 1975 1.25 2.50

1977-79 Sportscaster Series 23

COMPLETE SET (24) 20.00 40.00
2307 2 CV-Cross .25 .50
2312 WCH 1969 2.00 4.00
2314 Jean-Pierre Wimille .25 .50

1977-79 Sportscaster Series 24

COMPLETE SET (24) 10.00 20.00
2408 The 1976 Continental Circus .25 .50
2420 Targa Florio .25 .50

1977-79 Sportscaster Series 25

COMPLETE SET (24) 10.00 20.00
2509 WCH 1970 .25 .50

1977-79 Sportscaster Series 26

COMPLETE SET (24) 15.00 30.00
2613 Jean-Pierre Beltoise .25 .50

1977-79 Sportscaster Series 27

COMPLETE SET (24) 12.50 25.00
2711 French Enduro .25 .50
2713 1974 WCH 3.00 6.00

1977-79 Sportscaster Series 28

COMPLETE SET (24) 10.00 20.00
2801 Cale Yarborough 4.00 8.00
2805 Sidecar-Cross .25 .50
2807 Jay Springsteen .25 .50

1977-79 Sportscaster Series 29

COMPLETE SET (24) 17.50 35.00
2913 1967 WCH .75 1.50

1977-79 Sportscaster Series 31

COMPLETE SET (24) 12.50 25.00
3121 Jean Behra .50 1.00

1977-79 Sportscaster Series 32

COMPLETE SET (24) 17.50 35.00
3219 1971 WCH 2.00 4.00

1977-79 Sportscaster Series 33

COMPLETE SET (24) 10.00 20.00
3309 1968 WCH 2.00 4.00

1977-79 Sportscaster Series 36

COMPLETE SET (24) 15.00 30.00
3602 Driving on Wet Surfaces .25 .50
3603 Jacques Laffite .75 1.50

1977-79 Sportscaster Series 40

COMPLETE SET (24) 10.00 20.00
4016 Hill Climbs .25 .50
4022 Pedro Rodriguez .50 1.00
4023 Honda Endurance 1976 .25 .50

1977-79 Sportscaster Series 42

COMPLETE SET (24) 15.00 30.00
4203 Car Driving On Ice .25 .50

1977-79 Sportscaster Series 43

COMPLETE SET (24) 12.50 25.00
4320 The First Races .25 .50

1977-79 Sportscaster Series 44

COMPLETE SET (24) 12.50 25.00
4412 The 1977 WCH 1.50 3.00

1977-79 Sportscaster Series 45

Card number 11 is not in our checklist. Any information on this missing card is greatly appreciated.

COMPLETE SET (24) 20.00 40.00
4501 The Ford-Cosworth 1.50 3.00
4519 The Controlled Skid .25 .50

1977-79 Sportscaster Series 46

COMPLETE SET (24) 12.50 25.00
4608 Mike Hawthorn .50 1.00

1977-79 Sportscaster Series 47

COMPLETE SET (24) 17.50 35.00
4703 Emerson Fittipaldi 4.00 8.00

1977-79 Sportscaster Series 48

COMPLETE SET (24) 10.00 20.00
4819 Denis Hulme .50 1.00

1977-79 Sportscaster Series 49

COMPLETE SET (24) 20.00 40.00
4903 Indianapolis 500 1.00 2.00

1977-79 Sportscaster Series 50

COMPLETE SET (24) 15.00 30.00
5023 John Surtees .50 1.00

1977-79 Sportscaster Series 51

COMPLETE SET (24) 20.00 40.00
5104 28 Lost .25 .50
Pryce, Lafitte
Auto Racing
5119 Jody Scheckter 1.50 3.00

1977-79 Sportscaster Series 52

COMPLETE SET (24) 10.00 20.00
5217 Tom Pryce .50 1.00
5218 Clay Regazzoni .50 1.00

1977-79 Sportscaster Series 53

COMPLETE SET (24) 15.00 30.00
5301 Alan Jones .75 1.50
5324 BRM .50 1.00

1977-79 Sportscaster Series 54

COMPLETE SET (24) 15.00 30.00
5402 Dragsters .75 1.50
5416 Brooklands .25 .50

1977-79 Sportscaster Series 56

COMPLETE SET (24) 37.50 75.00
5602 The Monza Autodrome 1.00 2.00
5621 Francois Cevert 1.00 2.00

1977-79 Sportscaster Series 57

COMPLETE SET (24) 40.00 80.00
5716 The Formula 1 1.00 2.00
5719 Jack Brabham 2.00 4.00

1977-79 Sportscaster Series 58

COMPLETE SET (24) 25.00 50.00
5822 Amedeo Gordini 1.00 2.00

1977-79 Sportscaster Series 59

COMPLETE SET (24) 50.00 100.00
5907 Jackie Stewart 2.50 6.00
5916 Enzo Ferrari 2.50 5.00

1977-79 Sportscaster Series 60

COMPLETE SET (24) 37.50 75.00
6009 Nino Farina 1.00 2.00

1977-79 Sportscaster Series 62

COMPLETE SET (24) 40.00 80.00
6215 Bill Ivy 1.00 2.00
6220 John Watson 1.00 2.00
6221 Dragsters 1.00 2.00

1977-79 Sportscaster Series 63

COMPLETE SET (24) 30.00 60.00
6312 Shirley Muldowney 4.00 8.00
6321 SPA-Francorchamps 1.00 2.00

1977-79 Sportscaster Series 64

COMPLETE SET (24) 25.00 50.00
6410 The Flags in a Race 1.00 2.00

1977-79 Sportscaster Series 65

COMPLETE SET (24) 40.00 80.00
6511 By Split Seconds 2.00 4.00
6513 The 1978 WCH 6.00 12.00

1977-79 Sportscaster Series 66

COMPLETE SET (24) 37.50 75.00
6621 Silverstone 1.00 2.00

1977-79 Sportscaster Series 67

COMPLETE SET (24) 40.00 80.00
6716 Lotus 5.00 10.00
6717 Carlos Reutemann 1.00 2.00

1977-79 Sportscaster Series 68

COMPLETE SET (24) 40.00 80.00
6812 Colin Chapman 2.50 5.00
6817 Patrick Tambay 1.00 2.00

1977-79 Sportscaster Series 69

COMPLETE SET (24) 40.00 80.00
6910 Ronnie Peterson 1.00 2.00
6918 Hans Joachim Stuck 1.00 2.00

1977-79 Sportscaster Series 70

COMPLETE SET (24) 30.00 60.00
7002 Racing Tires 1.00 2.00
7024 Lancia 1.00 2.00

1977-79 Sportscaster Series 71

COMPLETE SET (24) 40.00 80.00
7113 Vittorio Brambilla 1.00 2.00

1977-79 Sportscaster Series 72

COMPLETE SET (24) 50.00 100.00
7204 Gunnar Nilsson 1.00 2.00
7222 Joakim Bonnier 1.00 2.00

1977-79 Sportscaster Series 74

COMPLETE SET (24) 200.00 400.00
7408 Bruno Giacomelli 1.00 2.00
7412 Sandro Munari 1.00 2.00
7415 Safety in a 4.00 8.00

1977-79 Sportscaster Series 75

COMPLETE SET (24) 30.00 60.00
7503 The Canam 1.00 2.00
7510 United States GP 1.00 2.00

1977-79 Sportscaster Series 77

COMPLETE SET (24) 150.00 300.00
7711 Gigi Villoresi 1.00 2.00
7723 Gilles Villeneuve 2.50 5.00

1977-79 Sportscaster Series 78

COMPLETE SET (24) 150.00 300.00
7813 Timo Makinen 1.00 2.00

1977-79 Sportscaster Series 79

COMPLETE SET (24) 60.00 120.00
7901 Patrick Depailler 1.00 2.00
7906 Jochen Rindt 1.00 2.00
7917 Suzuki 1.00 2.00
7918 Giacomo Agostini 1.00 2.00

1977-79 Sportscaster Series 80

COMPLETE SET (24) 62.50 125.00
8003 Rick Mears 7.50 15.00

1977-79 Sportscaster Series 81

COMPLETE SET (24) 62.50 125.00
8112 The Lotus 79 5.00 10.00

1977-79 Sportscaster Series 82

COMPLETE SET (24) 50.00 100.00
8210 The Ligier Team 2.00 4.00
8218 British Grand Prix 2.00 4.00

1977-79 Sportscaster Series 83

COMPLETE SET (24) 62.50 125.00
8303 Paul Newman 12.50 25.00
8322 Lord Hesketh 2.00 4.00

1977-79 Sportscaster Series 85

COMPLETE SET (24) 62.50 125.00
8505 Brian Redman 2.00 4.00

1977-79 Sportscaster Series 86

COMPLETE SET (24) 50.00 100.00
8604 Frank Williams 2.00 4.00
8614 The Brabham Stable 2.00 4.00
8616 Benihana Grand Prix 2.00 4.00
8621 Daytona Speedway 3.00 6.00

1977-79 Sportscaster Series 87

This series contains two cards numbered 4.

COMPLETE SET (24) 60.00 120.00
8716 Lingo 1 2.00 4.00
8722 The Matra Formula 1 2.00 4.00

1977-79 Sportscaster Series 88

COMPLETE SET (24) 50.00 100.00
8809 Pocono Raceway 2.00 4.00
8821 The Tyrrell Stable 2.00 4.00

1977-79 Sportscaster Series 101

COMPLETE SET (24) 62.50 125.00
10106 The Jyvaskyla 2.00 4.00
10118 The Mille Miglia 2.00 4.00

1977-79 Sportscaster Series 102

COMPLETE SET (24) 75.00 150.00
10222 The McLaren Stable 2.50 5.00

1977-79 Sportscaster Series 103

COMPLETE SET (24) 87.50 175.00
10315 Jean-Pierre Jarier 2.50 5.00

1989 Sports Illustrated for Kids I

Since its debut issue in January 1989, SI for Kids has included a perforated sheet of nine standard-size cards bound into each magazine. The cards were consecutively numbered 1-324 through December 1991. The athletes featured represent an extremely wide spectrum of sports. Each card features color photos with variously colored borders. The borders are as follows: aqua (1-108), green (109-207), woodgrain (208-216), red (217-315), marble (316-324). The player's name is printed in a white bar at the top, while his or her sport appears at the bottom. The backs carry biographical information, career highlights, and a trivia question with answer. The cards' magazine issue date appears on the back in very small type. Although originally distributed in sheet form, the cards are frequently traded as singles. Thus, they are priced individually. The value of an intact sheet is equal to the sum of the nine cards plus a premium of up to 20%.

41 Mario Andretti 1.00 2.50
Auto Racing
54 Lyn St. James .40 1.00
Auto Racing

1990 Sports Illustrated for Kids I

187 Danny Sullivan .20 .50
Auto Racing
196 Lori Johns .20 .50
Auto Racing

1991 Sports Illustrated for Kids I

257 Al Unser Jr. .30 .75
Auto Racing
290 Rick Mears .30 .75
Auto Racing

1992 Sports Illustrated for Kids II

Since its debut issue in January 1989, SI for Kids has included a perforated sheet of nine standard-size cards bound into each magazine. In January 1992, the card numbers started over again at 1. This listing comprises the cards contained from that magazine through the last 2000 issue. The athletes featured represent an extremely wide spectrum of sports. Each card features color photos with borders of various designs and colors. The borders are as follows: navy (1-9, 19-99), clouds (10-18, 55-63, 226-234), marble (100-108, 208-216, 316-324), pink (109-207), purple (217-225), blue (235-315), gold/silver (325-486), clouds (487-495) and gold/silver (496-621). The athlete's name is printed at the top while his or her sport appears at the bottom. The backs carry biographical information, career highlights, and a trivia question with answer. The cards' magazine issue date appears on the back in very small type. Although originally distributed in sheet form, the cards are frequently traded as singles. Thus, they are priced individually. The value of an intact sheet is equal to the sum of the nine cards plus a premium of up to 20 percent. The cards labeled as "MC" were issued in SI for Kids as part of a milk promotion.

48 Darrell Waltrip .75 2.00
Auto Racing
66 Richard Petty 1.50 4.00
Auto Racing

1993 Sports Illustrated for Kids II

114 Nigel Mansell .30 .75
Auto Racing

1994 Sports Illustrated for Kids II

255 Joe Amato .10 .30
Auto Racing

1996 Sports Illustrated for Kids II

480 Dale Jarrett .40 1.00
Auto Racing

1997 Sports Illustrated for Kids II

602 Jeff Gordon 1.50 4.00
Auto Racing

1998 Sports Illustrated for Kids II

728 Eddie Cheever .10 .30
Auto Racing
735 Jeff Gordon 1.25 3.00
Auto Racing

1999 Sports Illustrated for Kids II

801 John Force .40 1.00
Drag Racing
828 Ron Hornaday .10 .30
Auto Racing

2001 Sports Illustrated for Kids

Since its debut issue in January 1989, SI for Kids has included a perforated sheet of nine standard-size cards bound into each magazine. In December 2000, for the second time, the card numbers started over again at 1. The athletes featured represent an extremely wide spectrum of sports. The athlete's name is printed at the top while his or her sport appears at the bottom. The backs carry biographical information, career highlights, and a trivia question with answer. The cards' magazine issue date appears on the back in very small type. Although originally distributed in sheet form, the cards are frequently traded as singles. Thus, they are priced individually. The value of an intact sheet is equal to the sum of the nine cards plus a premium of up to 20 percent.

COMPLETE SET (108) 25.00 50.00
78 Dale Jarrett .40 1.00
Nascar

2002 Sports Illustrated for Kids

126 Dale Earnhardt Jr. 2.00 5.00
Nascar
148 Michael Schumacher .30 .75
Auto Racing
160 Jeff Gordon 1.25 3.00
Racing
196 Helio Castroneves .20 .50
Auto Racing

2003 Sports Illustrated for Kids

Since its debut issue in January 1989, SI for Kids has included a perforated sheet of nine standard-size cards bound into each magazine. In January 2001, for the second time, the card numbers started over at 1. Listed below are the cards issued in magazines that carry 2003 cover dates. The athletes featured represent an extremely wide spectrum of sports. Although originally distributed in sheet form, the cards are frequently traded as singles. Thus, they are priced individually. The value of an intact sheet is equal to the sum of the nine cards plus a premium of up to 20 percent.

243 Jimmie Johnson's Car .15 .40
Auto Racing
306 Gil De Ferran Racing .15 .40
324 Matt Kenseth Racing .75 2.00

2004 Sports Illustrated for Kids

ONE NINE-CARD SHEET PER MAGAZINE
414 Buddy Rice Auto Racing .07 .20

2005 Sports Illustrated for Kids

459 Kurt Busch NASCAR .40 1.00
495 Jeff Gordon NASCAR 1.50 4.00
519 Dan Wheldon IndyCar 1.25 3.00

2006 Sports Illustrated for Kids

9 Tony Stewart NASCAR .25 .60
69 Kasey Kahne's Car NASCAR .20 .50
85 Sam Hornish's Car Racing .10 .30

2007 Sports Illustrated for Kids

ONE NINE-CARD SHEET PER MAGAZINE
117 Colin McRae Racing .10 .30
125 Brad Coleman Auto Racing .08 .25
153 Denny Hamlin NASCAR .08 .25

2008 Sports Illustrated for Kids

269 Kyle Busch Racing .20 .50
287 Scott Dixon Racing .08 .25

2009 Sports Illustrated for Kids

360 Lewis Hamilton Racing
402 Danica Patrick Racing

2010 Sports Illustrated for Kids

470 Jimmie Johnson Racing
490 Denny Hamlin Racing

2011 Sports Illustrated for Kids

27 Sebastian Vettel Racing
69 Kevin Harvick Racing

2012 Sports Illustrated for Kids

117 Tony Stewart Racing
162 Dario Franchitti Racing
189 Dale Earnhardt Jr. Racing

2008 Sports Illustrated Swimsuit Danica Patrick

COMPLETE SET (10) 75.00 150.00
COMMON CARD (DP1-DP10) 8.00 20.00
STATED ODDS 1:4

2008 Sports Illustrated Swimsuit Editor's Choice

EC5 Danica Patrick

2008 Sports Illustrated Swimsuit Material

COMMON CARD 15.00 30.00
STATED ODDS 1:16
PRAVER JEWEL ODDS 1:6 CASES
DPM Danica Patrick 75.00 125.00

2009 Sports Illustrated Swimsuit Danica Patrick

COMPLETE SET (10) 50.00 100.00
COMMON CARD (D1-D10) 6.00 15.00
STATED ODDS 1:4

2009 Sports Illustrated Swimsuit Materials

STATED ODDS 1:8
DP1M Danica Patrick 75.00 150.00
DP2M Danica Patrick 75.00 150.00

1991 Sports Legends Bobby Allison

K and M Cards produced this set honoring Bobby Allison as part of a continuing Sports Legends card series. The set was issued in factory set form in an oversized box numbered as series three. The cards in each series look very similar with just the driver's name on the cardfronts.

COMP. FACT SET (30) 2.00 5.00
COMMON CARD (BA1-BA30) .12 .30
P1 Bobby Allison Prototype .40 1.00
Donnie Allison
Neil Bonnett
Red Border
P2 Bobby Allison Prototype .40 1.00
Donnie Allison
Neil Bonnett
Yellow Border

1991 Sports Legends Donnie Allison

K and M Cards produced this set honoring Donnie Allison as part of a continuing Sports Legends card series. The set was issued in factory set form in an oversized box numbered as series four. The cards in each series look very similar with just the driver's name on the cardfronts. The Donnie Allison cards were printed with a red border.

COMPLETE SET (30) 2.00 5.00
DA1 Donnie Allison w/car .05 .10
DA2 Donnie Allison .07 .20
DA3 Kenny Allison .05 .15
DA4 Ronald Allison w/car .01 .05
DA5 Donald Allison .05 .15
DA6 Hut Stricklin .05 .15
DA7 Donnie Allison .07 .20
DA8 Donnie Allison .07 .20
DA9 Donnie Allison .07 .20
DA10 Donnie Allison .07 .20
DA11 Donnie Allison .07 .20
DA12 Donnie Allison .12 .30
Bobby Allison
DA13 Donnie Allison's Car .05 .10
DA14 Donnie Allison .07 .20
DA15 Donnie Allison w/car .07 .20
DA16 Donnie Allison .05 .15
B.Allison
N.Bonnett Cars
DA17 Donnie Allison .15 .40
B.Allison
N.Bonnett
DA18 Donnie Allison .07 .20
DA19 Donnie Allison w/car .07 .20
DA20 Donnie Allison .12 .30
B.Allison
DA21 Donnie Allison .15 .40
B.Allison
N.Bonnett
DA22 Donnie Allison .12 .30
B.Allison
DA23 Donnie Allison .07 .20
DA24 Donnie Allison .12 .30
B.Allison
DA25 Donnie Allison .07 .20
DA26 Donnie Allison w/car .07 .20
DA27 Donnie Allison .12 .30
B.Allison
DA28 Donnie Allison's Car .05 .10
DA29 Donnie Allison .07 .20
DA30 Donnie Allison .07 .20

1991 Sports Legends Neil Bonnett

K and M Cards produced this set honoring Neil Bonnett as part of a continuing Sports Legends card series. The set was issued in factory set form in an oversized box numbered as series five. The cards in each series look very similar with just the driver's name on the cardfronts. The Neil Bonnett cards were printed with a red border.

COMP. FACT SET (30) 2.00 5.00
NB1 Neil Bonnett w/car .15 .40
NB2 Neil Bonnett .15 .40
NB3 Neil Bonnett .15 .40
NB4 Neil Bonnett w/car .15 .40
NB5 Neil Bonnett .15 .40
NB6 Neil Bonnett w/car .15 .40
NB7 Neil Bonnett .05 .15
C.Yarborough Cars
NB8 Neil Bonnett .15 .40
NB9 Neil Bonnett .15 .40
NB10 Neil Bonnett
NB11 Neil Bonnett .15 .40
Donnie Allison
B.Allison
NB12 Neil Bonnett w/car .15 .40
NB13 Neil Bonnett w .15 .40
Crew
NB14 Neil Bonnett .15 .40
NB15 Neil Bonnett .15 .40
NB16 Neil Bonnett w/cars .15 .40
NB17 Neil Bonnett .15 .40
NB18 Neil Bonnett's Car .05 .15
NB19 Neil Bonnett .15 .40
NB20 Neil Bonnett .15 .40
NB21 Neil Bonnett's Car .05 .15
NB22 Neil Bonnett .15 .40
NB23 Neil Bonnett .15 .40
NB24 Neil Bonnett .15 .40
NB25 Neil Bonnett .15 .40
NB26 Neil Bonnett w/car .15 .40
NB27 Neil Bonnett .15 .40
NB28 Neil Bonnett .15 .40
David Bonnett
NB29 Neil Bonnett w/car .15 .40
NB30 Neil Bonnett .15 .40

1991 Sports Legends Harry Hyde

K and M Cards produced this set honoring Harry Hyde as part of a continuing Sports Legends card series. The set was issued in factory set form in an oversized box numbered as series eight. The cards in each series look very similar with just the driver's name on the cardfronts. The Harry Hyde cards were printed with a red border.

COMP. FACT SET (30) 2.00 5.00
HH1 Harry Hyde .07 .20
Tim Richmond
HH2 Tim Richmond .07 .20
HH3 Harry Hyde .05 .15
HH4 Tim Richmond's Car .05 .10
HH5 Harry Hyde .10 .25
Rick Hendrick
HH6 Harry Hyde .05 .15
Tim Richmond
HH7 Ken Schrader's Car .01 .05
HH8 Harry Hyde .05 .15
HH9 Harry Hyde .05 .15
Tim Richmond
HH10 Harry Hyde .07 .20
Tim Richmond
HH11 Harry Hyde .07 .20
Buddy Baker
HH12 Harry Hyde .05 .15
HH13 Bobby Unser w/car .15 .40
HH14 Harry Hyde .05 .15
HH15 Bobby Isaac's Car .01 .05
HH16 Harry Hyde .07 .20
Buddy Baker
HH17 Bobby Isaac's Car .01 .05
HH18 Harry Hyde w/car .01 .05
HH19 Harry Hyde .05 .15
HH20 Harry Hyde .05 .15
Buddy Baker
HH21 Harry Hyde .05 .15
HH22 Harry Hyde w/car .05 .15
HH23 Harry Hyde w/car .05 .15
HH24 Bobby Isaac's Car .01 .05
HH25 Harry Hyde .05 .15
Jesse Baird
HH26 Harry Hyde w/car .05 .15
HH27 Harry Hyde .05 .15
HH28 Harry Hyde w/car .05 .15
HH29 Harry Hyde w/car .05 .15
HH30 Harry Hyde .05 .15
P1 Harry Hyde Prototype .15 .40

1991 Sports Legends Dale Jarrett

K and M Cards produced this set honoring Dale Jarrett as part of a continuing Sports Legends card series. The set was issued in factory set form in an oversized box numbered as series ten. The cards in each series look very similar with just the driver's name on the cardfronts. The Dale Jarrett cards were printed with a dark blue border.

COMP. FACT SET (30) 2.50 6.00
DJ1 Dale Jarrett .07 .20
DJ2 Dale Jarrett .07 .20
N.Jarrett
DJ3 Dale Jarrett's Car .05 .10
DJ4 Dale Jarrett w/car .07 .20
DJ5 Dale Jarrett .07 .20
N.Jarrett
DJ6 Dale Jarrett w .07 .20
Crew
DJ7 Dale Jarrett w/car .07 .20
DJ8 Dale Jarrett .05 .10
Dav.Allison Cars
DJ9 Dale Jarrett w .07 .20
Crew
DJ10 Dale Jarrett .07 .20
N.Jarrett
DJ11 Dale Jarrett .07 .20
DJ12 Dale Jarrett w/car .07 .20
DJ13 Dale Jarrett .07 .20
DJ14 Dale Jarrett .07 .20
DJ15 Dale Jarrett .07 .20
DJ16 Dale Jarrett's Car .05 .10
DJ17 Dale Jarrett .07 .20
C.Yarborough
DJ18 Dale Jarrett w/car .07 .20
DJ19 Dale Jarrett's Car .05 .10
DJ20 Dale Jarrett's Car .05 .10
DJ21 Dale Jarrett .07 .20
DJ22 Dale Jarrett .07 .20
DJ23 Dale Jarrett .07 .20
DJ24 Dale Jarrett w/car .07 .20
DJ25 Dale Jarrett Crash .07 .20
DJ26 Dale Jarrett .07 .20
A.Petree
DJ27 Dale Jarrett's Car .05 .10
DJ28 Dale Jarrett .07 .20
DJ29 Dale Jarrett w/car .07 .20
DJ30 Dale Jarrett .07 .20
P1 Dale Jarrett Prototype .40 1.00

1991 Sports Legends Ned Jarrett

K and M Cards produced this set honoring Ned Jarrett as the first in a continuing Sports Legends card series. The set was issued in factory set form in an oversized box numbered as series one. The cards in each series look very similar with just the driver's name on the cardfronts. The Ned Jarrett cards were printed with a yellow border.

COMP. FACT SET (30) 2.00 5.00
NJ1 Ned Jarrett .07 .20
NJ2 Ned Jarrett .07 .20
NJ3 Ned Jarrett .15 .40
Glenn
Dale
NJ4 Ned Jarrett .15 .40
Dale Jarrett
NJ5 Ned Jarrett .07 .20
Ronald Reagan
NJ6 Ned Jarrett .07 .20
NJ7 Ned Jarrett .07 .20
NJ8 Ned Jarrett .07 .20
NJ9 Ned Jarrett .07 .20
NJ10 Ned Jarrett .07 .20
NJ11 Ned Jarrett .07 .20
NJ12 Ned Jarrett .07 .20
NJ13 Ned Jarrett .07 .20
NJ14 Ned Jarrett w/car .07 .20
NJ15 Ned Jarrett's Car .05 .10
NJ16 Ned Jarrett w/car .07 .20
NJ17 Ned Jarrett .07 .20
Bud Allman
NJ18 Ned Jarrett w/car .07 .20
NJ19 Ned Jarrett w/car .07 .20
NJ20 Ned Jarrett .07 .20
Curtis Turner Cars
NJ21 Ned Jarrett .07 .20
NJ22 Ned Jarrett w .07 .20
Family
NJ23 Ned Jarrett .07 .20
NJ24 Ned Jarrett .07 .20
NJ25 Ned Jarrett .07 .20
NJ26 Ned Jarrett .07 .20
NJ27 Ned Jarrett .07 .20
Dale Jarrett
NJ28 Ned Jarrett .07 .20
Barney Hall
NJ29 Ned Jarrett .07 .20
NJ30 Ned Jarrett .07 .20

1991 Sports Legends Rob Moroso

K and M Cards produced this set honoring Rob Moroso as part of a continuing Sports Legends card series. The set was issued in factory set form in an oversized box numbered as series six. The Rob Moroso cards were printed with a different design than most other Sports Legends sets. The cards feature Moroso's name in a black and gold strip running across the bottom of the cardfront. A special art print card portraying Moroso was inserted into 3,000 of the sets.

COMPLETE SET (30) 2.00 5.00
COMMON CARD (RM1-RM30) .07 .20
P1 Rob Moroso Prototype .40 1.00

1991 Sports Legends Phil Parsons

K and M Cards produced this set honoring Phil Parsons as part of a continuing Sports Legends card series. The set was issued in factory set form in an oversized box numbered as series nine. The cards in each series look very similar with just the driver's name on the cardfronts. The Phil Parsons cards were printed with a red border.

COMP. FACT SET (30) 2.00 5.00
PP1 Phil Parsons w/car .05 .15
PP2 Phil Parsons .05 .15
PP3 Phil Parsons .05 .15
PP4 Phil Parsons' Car .01 .05
PP5 Phil Parsons .05 .15
PP6 Phil Parsons .05 .15
PP7 Phil Parsons .05 .15
PP8 Phil Parsons .05 .15
PP9 Phil Parsons' Car .01 .05
PP10 Phil Parsons w/car .05 .15
PP11 Phil Parsons' Car .01 .05
PP12 Phil Parsons' Car .01 .05
PP13 Phil Parsons' Car .01 .05
PP14 Phil Parsons' Car .01 .05
PP15 Phil Parsons' Car .01 .05
PP16 Phil Parsons .05 .15
PP17 Phil Parsons .05 .15
PP18 Phil Parsons .25 .60
Earnhardt Cars
PP19 Phil Parsons' Car .01 .05
PP20 Phil Parsons .05 .15
PP21 Phil Parsons' Car .01 .05
PP22 Phil Parsons w .05 .15
Crew
PP23 Phil Parsons .05 .15
PP24 Phil Parsons .05 .15
PP25 Phil Parsons .15 .40
B.Parsons
PP26 Phil Parsons .05 .15
PP27 Phil Parsons .05 .15
PP28 Phil Parsons .05 .15
PP29 Phil Parsons' Car .01 .05
PP30 Phil Parsons .05 .15
P1 Phil Parsons Prototype .60 1.50

1991 Sports Legends Wendell Scott

K and M Cards produced this set honoring Wendell Scott as part of a continuing Sports Legends card series. The set was issued in factory set form in an oversized box numbered as series thirteen. The cards in each series look very similar with just the driver's name on the cardfronts. The Wendell Scott cards were printed with a yellow border.

COMP. FACT SET (30) 2.00 5.00
WS1 Wendell Scott w/car .05 .15
WS2 Wendell Scott's Car .01 .05
WS3 Wendell Scott .05 .15
WS4 Wendell Scott .05 .15
WS5 Wendell Scott .05 .15
WS6 Wendell Scott w/car .05 .15
WS7 Wendell Scott .05 .15
WS8 Wendell Scott .05 .15
WS9 Wendell Scott .05 .15
WS10 Wendell Scott .05 .15
WS11 Wendell Scott .05 .15
WS12 Wendell Scott's Car .01 .05
WS13 Wendell Scott .05 .15
WS14 Wendell Scott .15 .40
C.Yarborough
WS15 Wendell Scott .05 .15
WS16 Wendell Scott .05 .15
WS17 Wendell Scott .05 .15
WS18 Wendell Scott .05 .15
WS19 Wendell Scott .05 .15
WS20 Wendell Scott .05 .15
WS21 Wendell Scott .05 .15
Richard Pryor
WS22 Wendell Scott w/car .05 .15
WS23 Wendell Scott .05 .15
WS24 Wendell Scott .05 .15
WS25 Wendell Scott w/Car/1969 .05 .15
WS26 Wendell Scott w/Car .05 .15
Danville, VA
WS27 Wendell Scott .05 .15
1988 Championships
WS28 Wendell Scott .05 .15
WS29 Wendell Scott .05 .15
WS30 Wendell Scott .05 .15

1991 Sports Legends Hut Stricklin

K and M Cards produced this set honoring Hut Stricklin as part of a continuing Sports Legends card series. The set was issued in factory set form in an oversized box numbered as series twelve. The Hut Stricklin cards were printed with a different design than most other Sports Legends sets. The cards feature Stricklin's name in a white and blue strip running across the bottom of the cardfront.

COMP. FACT SET (30) 2.00 5.00
HS1 Hut Stricklin w/car .05 .15
HS2 Hut Stricklin .05 .15
HS3 Hut Stricklin .05 .15
HS4 Hut Stricklin .05 .15
HS5 Hut Stricklin .05 .15
HS6 Hut Stricklin .05 .15
HS7 Hut Stricklin .10 .25
Dav.Allison Cars
HS8 Hut Stricklin .05 .15
HS9 Hut Stricklin .05 .15
HS10 Hut Stricklin .05 .15
HS11 Hut Stricklin w/car .05 .15
HS12 Hut Stricklin w/car .05 .15
HS13 Hut Stricklin w/car .05 .15
HS14 Hut Stricklin w/car .05 .15
HS15 Hut Stricklin's Car .07 .20
HS16 Hut Stricklin w/car .05 .15
HS17 Hut Stricklin .05 .15
HS18 Hut Stricklin w/car .05 .15
HS19 Hut Stricklin w .05 .15
Crew
HS20 Hut Stricklin .05 .15
HS21 Hut Stricklin w/car .05 .15
HS22 Hut Stricklin's Car .01 .05
HS23 Hut Stricklin .05 .15
HS24 Hut Stricklin .05 .15
HS25 Hut Stricklin .05 .15
HS26 Hut Stricklin .05 .15
HS27 Hut Stricklin .05 .15
HS28 Hut Stricklin .05 .15
Kenny All.
Donald Allis.
HS29 Hut Stricklin .05 .15
HS30 Hut Stricklin's Car .01 .05
P1 Hut Stricklin Prototype .60 1.50

1991 Sports Legends Herb Thomas

K and M Cards produced this set honoring Herb Thomas as the second in a continuing Sports Legends card series. The set was issued in factory set form in an oversized box numbered as series two. The cards in each series look very similar with just the driver's name on the cardfronts. The Herb Thomas cards were printed with a light blue border.

COMP. FACT SET (30) 2.00 5.00
HT1 Herb Thomas w/car .05 .15
HT2 Herb Thomas' Car .01 .05
HT3 Herb Thomas .05 .15
HT4 Herb Thomas w/car .05 .15
HT5 Herb Thomas .05 .15
Slick Smith
Iggy Katona Cars
HT6 Herb Thomas' Car .01 .05
HT7 Herb Thomas .05 .15
HT8 Herb Thomas .05 .15
Marshall Teague Cars
HT9 Herb Thomas .05 .15
HT10 H.Thomas .15 .40
Buc.Baker
L.Petty
Lewallan
R.Liguori Cars
HT11 Herb Thomas' Car .01 .05
HT12 Herb Thomas .01 .05
Gene Comstock Cars
HT13 Herb Thomas .01 .05
Matt Gowen
F.Flock Cars
HT14 Herb Thomas w/car .05 .15
HT15 Herb Thomas' Car .01 .05
HT16 Herb Thomas' Car .01 .05
HT17 Herb Thomas' Car .01 .05
HT18 Herb Thomas' Car .01 .05
HT19 Herb Thomas' Car .01 .05
HT20 Herb Thomas' Car .01 .05
HT21 Herb Thomas w .05 .15
Crew
HT22 Herb Thomas in Pits .05 .15
HT23 Herb Thomas' Car .01 .05
HT24 Herb Thomas .05 .10
Buck Baker Cars
HT25 Herb Thomas .01 .05
Ralph Liguori Cars
HT26 Herb Thomas .05 .15
HT27 Herb Thomas .05 .10
T.Lund Cars
HT28 Herb Thomas' Car .01 .05
HT29 Herb Thomas w/car .05 .15
HT30 Herb Thomas .05 .15
P1 Herb Thomas Prototype .15 .40

1991 Sports Legends Cale Yarborough

K and M Cards produced this set honoring Cale Yarborough as part of a continuing Sports Legends card series. The set was issued in factory set form in an oversized box numbered as series eleven. The cards in each series look very similar with just the driver's name on the cardfronts. The Cale Yarborough cards were printed with an orange border.

COMP. FACT SET (30) 2.00 5.00
COMMON CARD (CY1-CY30) .07 .20
P1 Cale Yarborough Prototype .75 2.00

1992 Sports Legends Buck Baker

K and M Cards produced this set honoring Buck Baker as part of a continuing Sports Legends card series. The set was issued in factory set form in an oversized box numbered as series fifteen. The Buck Baker cards were printed with a design featuring his name in a red strip running across the bottom of the card front.

COMP. FACT SET (30) 2.00 5.00
COMMON CARD (BB1-BB30) .07 .20
P1 Buck Baker Prototype .40 1.00

1992 Sports Legends Alan Kulwicki

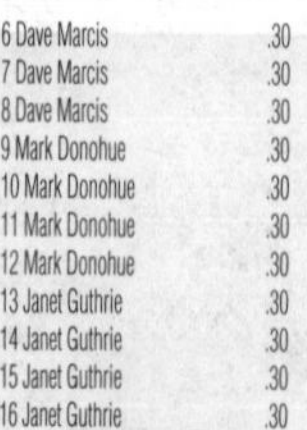

K and M Cards produced this set honoring Alan Kulwicki as part of a continuing Sports Legends card series. The set was issued in factory set form in an oversized box numbered as series seven. The cards in each series look very similar with just the driver's name on the cardfronts. The Alan Kulwicki cards were printed with an orange border.

COMP. FACT SET (30)	3.00	8.00
COMMON CARD (AK1-AK30)	.15	.40
P1 Alan Kulwicki Prototype	.75	2.00

1992 Sports Legends Fred Lorenzen

Produced in 1992 by K and M Cards, this Fred Lorenzen commemorative set was issued in factory set form. The cardfronts feature a photo of Lorenzen with backs containing text relating to the photo. The cards are numbered on back inside an outline of a trophy and checkered flag.

COMPLETE SET (16)	2.00	4.00
COMMON CARD (1-16)	.08	.25

1992 Sports Legends Rusty Wallace

K and M Cards produced this set honoring Rusty Wallace as part of a continuing Sports Legends card series. The set was issued in factory set form in an oversized box numbered as series fourteen. The cards in each series look very similar with just the driver's name on the cardfronts.

COMPLETE SET (30)	2.50	6.00
COMMON CARD (1-30)	.10	.30
P1 Rusty Wallace Prototype	1.00	2.50

1985 SportStars Photo-Graphics Stickers

SportStars Photo-Graphics Inc. produced this set on sticker card stock. The backs are blank and the fronts feature both a driver and car photo. They look very similar to the 1986 SportStars release, but are much smaller, measuring approximately 2" by 3."

COMPLETE SET (8)	40.00	75.00
NNO Mario Andretti	4.00	10.00
NNO A.J.Foyt	4.00	10.00
NNO David Pearson ERR	4.00	10.00
NNO David Pearson COR	4.00	10.00
NNO Richard Petty	5.00	12.00
NNO Al Unser Sr.	3.00	8.00
NNO Darrell Waltrip	4.00	10.00
NNO Cale Yarborough	3.00	8.00

1986 SportStars Photo-Graphics

This 13-card set was produced by SportStars, Inc. The cards are a little larger than standard size, measuring 2 3/4" X 3 1/2". The cards have a white border and picture both the driver and his car. The backs contain only driver name, birth date and place, hometown and current car. The also have a "SportStars Photo-GRAPHICS" copyright on the back. Four of the cards appear to be in shorter supply than the others: Bodine, Earnhardt, Gant, and Richmond. All the cards are unnumbered and appear below numbered in alphabetical order. The list represents the 13 known regular versions. Some variations of these cards exist.

COMPLETE SET (13)	400.00	800.00
1 Bobby Allison	6.00	15.00
2 Geoff Bodine SP	50.00	100.00
3 Neil Bonnett	20.00	50.00
4 Dale Earnhardt SP	125.00	250.00
5 Bill Elliott	10.00	25.00
6 A.J. Foyt NASCAR	10.00	25.00
7 A.J. Foyt Indy	15.00	40.00
8 Harry Gant SP	40.00	80.00
9 Terry Labonte	25.00	60.00
10 Richard Petty	15.00	40.00
11 Tim Richmond SP	75.00	135.00
12 Darrell Waltrip	6.00	15.00
13 Cale Yarborough	6.00	15.00

1992 SportStars Racing Collectibles

This 16-card set features four top drivers from the mid to late '70's. Card number 1 was inserted loosely in Racing Collectibles magazines and given to dealers who sold the magazine. The other cards came as a stitched in insert in the magazines.

COMPLETE SET (16)	4.00	10.00
1 Joe Weatherly	.30	.75
2 Joe Weatherly	.30	.75
3 Joe Weatherly	.30	.75
4 Joe Weatherly	.30	.75
5 Dave Marcis	.30	.75
6 Dave Marcis	.30	.75
7 Dave Marcis	.30	.75
8 Dave Marcis	.30	.75
9 Mark Donohue	.30	.75
10 Mark Donohue	.30	.75
11 Mark Donohue	.30	.75
12 Mark Donohue	.30	.75
13 Janet Guthrie	.30	.75
14 Janet Guthrie	.30	.75
15 Janet Guthrie	.30	.75
16 Janet Guthrie	.30	.75

2006 Stanley Tools Promo

COMPLETE SET (6)	4.00	10.00
COMP.SHEET	5.00	12.00
1 Erin Crocker	2.50	6.00
2 Kasey Kahne	.50	1.25
3 Jeremy Mayfield	.25	.60
4 Scott Riggs	.30	.75
5 Kasey Kahne First Win	.50	1.25
6 Stanley Header Card	.20	.50
6 Stanley Tools Cover Card	.20	.50

1993 Stove Top

Issued in two different three-card packs in Stove Top Stuffing packages, the cards feature an artist's rendering of a NASCAR driver on the cardfronts. Cardbacks include a driver career summary and stats. The cards are unnumbered and listed below alphabetically.

COMPLETE SET (6)	2.40	6.00
1 Jeff Gordon	1.00	2.50
2 Bobby Hamilton	.20	.50
3 Bobby Labonte	.60	1.50
4 Kenny Wallace	.20	.50
5 Rusty Wallace	.75	2.00
6 Michael Waltrip	.30	.75

1972 STP

STP Corporation produced and distributed these cards as a promotion in 1972. These are some of the earliest known NASCAR cards and, thus, are highly sought after by collectors. Cards were printed on white stock with blue lettering on the cardbacks which contain the STP name and address. Photos are full-bleed and the cards are unnumbered.

COMPLETE SET (11)	350.00	700.00
1 Bobby Allison	40.00	100.00
2 Buddy Baker	30.00	80.00
3 Dick Brooks	25.00	60.00
4 Charlie Glotzbach	25.00	60.00
5 James Hylton	25.00	60.00
6 Elmo Langley	25.00	60.00
7 Fred Lorenzen	30.00	80.00
8 Fred Lorenzen w/Car	30.00	80.00
9 Dave Marcis	30.00	80.00
10 Benny Parsons	40.00	100.00
11 Richard Petty	60.00	150.00

1991 STP Richard Petty

Using nine cards from the Richard Petty 20th anniversary set, Traks produced this 10-card issue for First Brands Corp. and STP. A cover/checklist card was added as the tenth card in the set.

COMPLETE SET (10)	4.00	10.00
1 Richard Petty	.60	1.50
2 Richard Petty's Car	.25	.60
3 Richard Petty	.60	1.50
4 Richard Kyle Petty in Pits	.60	1.50
5 Richard Petty's Car	.25	.60
6 Richard Petty	.60	1.50
7 Richard Petty's Car	.25	.60
8 Richard Petty w Car	.60	1.50
9 Richard Petty	.60	1.50
10 Checklist	.07	.20

1992 STP Daytona 500

Pro Set produced this 10-card set for First Brands (STP). The set commemorates Richard Petty's final entry in the Daytona 500. It was made available through redeeming the proof-of-purchase from any STP product.

COMPLETE SET (10)	4.00	10.00
1 Richard Petty	.50	1.25
2 Richard Petty in Car	.50	1.25
3 Green Flag	.40	1.00
4 Richard Petty's Car	.50	1.25
5 Richard Petty in Pits	.50	1.25
6 Daytona 500 Fans	.40	1.00
7 Richard Petty in Pits	.40	1.00
8 Davey Allison	.60	1.50
9 Richard Petty	.50	1.25
10 Checklist	.20	.50

1996 STP 25th Anniversary

Cards were distributed through a mail in offer on cases of STP. The six-card set features a cover card and five cards with the different paint schemes that Bobby Hamilton, driver of the Richard Petty's STP pontiac, ran under during the 1996 Winston Cup season.

COMPLETE SET (6)	2.00	5.00
COMMON CARD	.40	1.00
NNO Cover Card	.08	.25

1991 Sunbelt Racing Legends

COMPLETE SET (11)	2.00	5.00
1 Richard Petty	.50	1.25
2 Rusty Wallace	.40	1.00
3 Dale Earnhardt	1.00	2.50
4 Davey Allison	.40	1.00
5 Ricky Rudd	.25	.60
6 Mark Martin	.40	1.00
7 Darrell Waltrip	.25	.60
8 Harry Gant	.15	.40
9 Bill Elliott	.30	.75
10 Checklist Card	.05	.15
NNO Cover Card	.05	.15

1991 Superior Racing Metals

This 12-card set features some of the best names in Winston Cup racing. The cards were sold through mail and through Superior Performance's dealer network. The cards feature the were the first metal cards ever produced to feature a Winston Cup driver. The cards are unnumbered and listed below in alphabetical order.

COMPLETE SET (12)	50.00	120.00
1 Derrike Cope	3.00	8.00
2 Bill Elliott	6.00	15.00
3 Harry Gant	3.00	8.00
4 Bobby Hamilton	3.00	8.00
5 Ernie Irvan	5.00	12.00
6 Sterling Marlin	3.00	8.00
7 Mark Martin	8.00	20.00
8 Phil Parsons	2.00	5.00
9 Kyle Petty	6.00	15.00
10 Richard Petty	15.00	30.00
11 Ken Schrader	2.00	5.00
12 Darrell Waltrip	5.00	12.00

2001 Super Shots Hendrick Motorsports

This set was issued by Super Shots to commemorate the 100th win of Hendrick Motorsports. Each card features a current or past Hendrick Racing driver who contributed to the feat with the final two being devoted to the Hendrick family and a list of all 100-wins. The final card is a double sized jumbo card featuring the entire Hendrick Racing Team. Each factory boxed set could also have been upgraded to include one of 8 different banner memorabilia cards or a Jeff Gordon Raced-Used Tire card.

COMP.FACT.SET (22)	10.00	25.00
H1 Geoff Bodine	.30	.75
H2 Tim Richmond	.30	.75
H3 Darrell Waltrip w Michael	.50	1.25
H4 Ken Schrader	.50	1.25
H5 Darrell Waltrip	.50	1.25
H6 Ricky Rudd	.50	1.25
H7 Terry Labonte	.60	1.50
H8 Jeff Gordon	1.00	2.50
H9 Jeff Gordon	1.00	2.50
H10 Jeff Gordon	1.00	2.50
H11 Jeff Gordon	1.00	2.50
H12 Terry Labonte	.60	1.50
H13 Terry Labonte	.60	1.50
H14 T.Labonte J.Gordon Craven	.75	2.00
H15 Jeff Gordon	1.00	2.50
H16 Terry Labonte	.60	1.50
H17 Jeff Gordon	1.00	2.50
H18 Jerry Nadeau	.30	.75
H19 Jeff Gordon	1.00	2.50
H20 Papa Joe, John, Rick Hendrick	.30	.75
H21 100-Win list	.20	.50
HR22 Race Team Jumbo	.50	1.25
NNO Jeff Gordon Tire	15.00	40.00

2001 Super Shots Hendrick Motorsports Silver

COMP.FACT.SET (24)	150.00	250.00

*SILVERS: 2X TO 5X BASIC CARDS

2001 Super Shots Hendrick Motorsports Victory Banners

These 8-cards were issued one per factory boxed set of 2001 Super Shots Hendrick Motorsports. Each card was serial numbered of 775 and includes a swatch taken from the 100th Victory Banner displayed in victory lane at Michigan on June 10, 2001. Silver factory sets included both of the final two silver foil Banner cards.

COMPLETE SET (8)	60.00	150.00
HRB1 Jerry Nadeau	5.00	12.00
HRB2 Jeff Gordon	12.50	30.00
HRB3 Terry Labonte	6.00	15.00
HRB4 Ricky Rudd	6.00	15.00
HRB5 Darrell Waltrip	6.00	15.00
HRB6 Ken Schrader	5.00	12.00
HRB7 Tim Richmond	5.00	12.00
HRB8 Geoff Bodine	5.00	12.00
HSB1 J.Gordon T.Labonte/500	30.00	60.00
HSB2 Hendrick Race Team/500	15.00	40.00

2001 Super Shots Hendrick Motorsports Autographs

HSA1 Jeff Gordon/71	75.00	150.00
HSA2 Jerry Nadeau/72	10.00	20.00
HSA3 Terry Labonte/71	20.00	40.00
HSA4 Darrell Waltrip/71	25.00	50.00
HSA5 Ken Schrader/72	10.00	20.00
HSA6 Ricky Rudd/71	10.00	20.00

2001 Super Shots Race Used Tire Jumbos

These cards were issued by Super Shots, Inc. in 2001. Each is an oversized jumbo card featuring a swatch of race used tire from the featured driver.

RW1 Rusty Wallace/1000	10.00	20.00
JGG1 Jeff Gordon Gold/2001	8.00	20.00
JGS1 Jeff Gordon's Car Silver/2001	6.00	15.00

2001 Super Shots Sears Point CHP

These cards were produced by Super Shots for the California Highway Patrol and were given away at Sears Point Raceway to commemorate the NASCAR race that season.

COMPLETE SET (6)	3.00	8.00
SP1 Sears Point Raceway	.20	.50
SP2 Bobby Labonte's Car	.50	1.25
SP3 Tony Stewart's Car	.75	2.00
SP4 Jeff Gordon's Car	.75	2.00
SP5 Kevin Harvick's Car	.60	1.50
SP6 Dale Jarrett's Car	.50	1.25

2002 Super Shots California Speedway

For the second year in a row a set of 6-cards was produced by Super Shots for the California Speedway. The cards were also sponsored by the California Highway Patrol and each features a driver's car from the race with the final card showing the track itself.

COMPLETE SET (6)	3.00	7.00
CS1 Kevin Harvick's Car	.60	1.50
CS2 Bobby Labonte's Car	.50	1.25
CS3 Ward Burton's Car	.30	.75
CS4 Tony Stewart's Car	.75	2.00
CS5 Rusty Wallace's Car	.50	1.25
CS6 California Speedway	.20	.50

2004 Super Shots CHP Sonoma

COMPLETE SET (5)	6.00	15.00
1 Jeff Gordon	2.50	6.00
2 Jimmie Johnson	2.00	5.00
3 Kasey Kahne	2.50	6.00
4 Terry Labonte	1.00	2.50
5 Jamie McMurray	1.00	2.50

1991 Texas World Speedway

This 10-card set was released by Texas World Speedway in conjunction with the reopening of the track in 1991. The cards feature a turquoise-blue border and some of the top names in racing. The Tim Richmond card was one of the first produced after his death in 1988 and was the best selling card in the set. There were a reported 50,000 sets produced.

COMPLETE SET (10)	1.25	3.00
1 Benny Parsons	.15	.40
2 Buddy Baker	.07	.20
3 Bobby Isaac	.05	.15
4 Cale Yarborough	.15	.40
5 Richard Petty	.30	.75
6 Tim Richmond	.07	.20
7 Richard Petty Bill France	.30	.75
8 Cale Yarborough	.15	.40
9 Darrell Waltrip	.15	.40
NNO Cover Card	.05	.10

1989-90 TG Racing Masters of Racing

The 1989-90 Masters of Racing set was produced and distributed by TG Racing which used its extensive photo files to produce a history of stock car racing on cards. The 1989 issue (numbers 1-152) was broken down into four series of 38-cards each, with each series featuring a different colored border. The set was sold by series (originally $7.95 each) directly to the card hobby. Part two (numbers 153-262) of the Masters of Racing was released in the summer of 1990 under the title White Gold. The 1990 set was sold in complete factory set form only, not by series. A special Masters of Racing album was produced as well to house the cards.

COMPLETE SET (262)	60.00	150.00
COMP.SERIES 1 (152)	60.00	120.00
COMP.SERIES 2 (110)	12.00	30.00
1 Cover Card	.20	.50
2 Red Byron	.30	.75
3 Red Byron's Car	.20	.50
4 Starting Lineup	.20	.50
5 Speedy Thompson	.30	.75
6 Speedy Thompson	.20	.50
7 Buck Baker	.60	1.50
8 Buck Baker w/car	.60	1.50
9 Buck Baker/S.Thompson Carl Kiekhaefer	.60	1.50
10 Henley Gray	.30	.75
11 Henley Gray's Car	.20	.50
12 Ralph Earnhardt	1.00	2.50
13 The Wreck	.20	.50
14 Paul Goldsmith	.60	1.50
15 Paul Goldsmith w/car	.60	1.50
16 Bill Seifert	.30	.75
17 Bill Seifert w/car	.30	.75
18 Edwin Matthews w/car	.30	.75
19 Edwin Matthews w/car	.30	.75
20 Johnny Thompson w/car	.30	.75
21 Johnny Thompson w/car	.30	.75
22 Glenn Roberts(Fireball)	1.25	3.00
23 Glenn Roberts(Fireball) w/car	1.25	3.00
24 Glenn Roberts(Fireball)	1.25	3.00
25 Lennie Pond	.30	.75
26 Lennie Pond w/car	.30	.75
27 256 Wins	.30	.75
28 Sam McQuagg	.30	.75
29 Sam McQuagg w/car	.30	.75
30 Gober Sosebee	.30	.75
31 Gober Sosebee's Car	.20	.50
32 Larry Frank	.60	1.50
33 Larry Frank w/car	.60	1.50
34 Eddie Pagan	.30	.75
35 Curtis Crider	.30	.75
36 Curtis Crider w/car	.30	.75
37 Tiny Lund/Fireball Roberts' Cars	.30	.75
38 Checklist	.20	.50
39 Cover Card/D.Pearson's Car E.Brooks' Car	.20	.50
40 Lloyd Dane	.30	.75
41 David Pearson w/car	.60	1.50
42 David Pearson w/car	.60	1.50
43 David Pearson	.60	1.50
44 Roy Tyner's Car	.20	.50
45 David Ezell	.30	.75
46 Lee Roy Yarborough	.60	1.50
47 Lee Roy Yarborough w/car	.60	1.50
48 Marshall Teague	.30	.75
49 Night Time	.20	.50
50 Jabe Thomas	.30	.75
51 Dirt Track	.20	.50
52 Billy Carden	.30	.75
53 Billy Carden's Car	.20	.50
54 Ed Samples	.30	.75
55 Ed Samples' Car	.20	.50
56 Jack Smith w/car	.30	.75
57 Jack Smith w/car	.30	.75
58 Ralph Moody Jr. w/car	.30	.75
59 D.Pearson/R.Petty/J.Johnson Cars	1.00	2.50
60 David Pearson	.60	1.50
61 Tiny Lund	.60	1.50
62 Tiny Lund w/car	.60	1.50
63 Tiny Lund w/car	.60	1.50
64 Marvin Panch	.60	1.50
65 The 5 Heroes	.20	.50
66 Wilkesboro 1962	.20	.50
67 Marvin Panch w/car	.60	1.50
68 Cotton Owens	.30	.75
69 Cotton Owens w/car	.30	.75
70 Tommy Gale w/car	.30	.75
71 Tiny Lund	1.50	4.00
72 Red Fox/Cotton Owens Cars	.20	.50
73 Johnny Allen	.60	1.50
74 Johnny Allen w/car	.60	1.50
75 L.R.Yarborough/J.Johnson Herb Nab	1.00	2.50
76 Checklist/Cotton Owens	.20	.50
77 Cover Card/Junior Johnson	.20	.50
78 Walter Ballard	.30	.75
79 Walter Ballard's Car	.20	.50
80 Darel Dieringer	.30	.75
81 Darel Dieringer's Car	.20	.50
82 Ray Erickson	.30	.75
83 Ray Erickson w/car	.30	.75
84 Dick Hutcherson w/car	.30	.75
85 Dick Hutcherson's Car	.20	.50
86 Ramo Stott	.30	.75
87 Ramo Stott w/car	.30	.75
88 Don White	.30	.75
89 Don White's Car	.20	.50
90 D.Hutcherson/D.White/R.Stott	.30	.75
91 Glen Wood	.30	.75
92 Rex White w/car	.30	.75
93 Rex White's Car	.20	.50
94 Jimmie Lewallen	.30	.75
95 Jimmie Lewallen w/car	.20	.50
96 Darel Dieringer/Junior Johnson	1.00	2.50
97 Banks Simpson	.30	.75
98 Paul Lewis w/car	.30	.75
99 Glen Wood/R.White's Car	.30	.75
100 Junior Johnson	1.25	3.00
101 Junior Johnson's Car	.60	1.50
102 Junior Johnson w/car	1.25	3.00
103 Joe Millikan	.30	.75
104 J.Johnson/Ray Fox w/cars	.60	1.50
105 Bobby Myers/Billy Myers	.30	.75
106 Reino Tulonen w/car	.30	.75
107 World 600	.20	.50
108 Coo Coo Marlin	.60	1.50
109 Coo Coo Marlin w/car	.60	1.50
110 Bobby Myers	.30	.75
111 Billy Myers	.30	.75
112 Billy Myers	.30	.75
113 Bobby Myers	.30	.75
114 Checklist	.20	.50
115 Cover Card/Lund/Isaac	.20	.50
116 Buddy Arrington	.30	.75
117 Buddy Arrington's Car	.20	.50
118 Bill Blair w/car	.30	.75
119 Bill Blair w/car	.30	.75
120 Earl Brooks w/car	.30	.75
121 Earl Brooks w/car	.30	.75
122 Charlie Glotzbach	.30	.75
123 Charlie Glotzbach w/car	.30	.75
124 Charlie Glotzbach w/car	.30	.75
125 Gene Cline w/car	.30	.75
126 Nelson Stacy	.30	.75
127 Nelson Stacy w/car	.30	.75
128 Jim Reed	.30	.75
129 Jim Reed w/car	.30	.75
130 Charlie Glotzbach w/car	.30	.75
131 Bobby Isaac's Car	.30	.75
132 Neil Castles' Car	.20	.50
133 Buddy Arrington's Car	.20	.50
134 Fireball Roberts in Pits	.60	1.50
135 Neil Castles	.30	.75
136 Neil Castles' Car	.20	.50
137 Red Farmer	.30	.75
138 Red Farmer's Car	.20	.50
139 Big Winner	.30	.75
140 Pete Hamilton	.30	.75
141 Pete Hamilton w/car	.20	.50
142 Gwyn Staley	.30	.75
143 Fred Lorenzen	.60	1.50
144 Gwyn Staley/Enoch Staley Charlie Combs	.30	.75
145 Bobby Isaac w/car	.60	1.50
146 G.C. Spencer	.30	.75
147 Bob Derrington	.30	.75
148 Earl Brooks/Lorenzen Nelson Stacy Cars	.20	.50
149 Fred Lorenzen	.60	1.50
150 Fred Lorenzen w/car	.60	1.50
151 Fred Lorenzen w/car	.60	1.50
152 Checklist	.20	.50
153 Cover Card/Red Byron's Car	.07	.20
154 Bob Flock	.10	.30
155 Bob Flock/Red Byron's Cars	.07	.20
156 Fonty Flock	.20	.50
157 Fonty Flock's Car	.10	.30
158 Tim Flock	.20	.50
159 Tim Flock w/car	.20	.50
160 Fonty/Tim/Bob/Carl Flock	.20	.50
161 James Hylton	.10	.30
162 James Hylton's Car	.07	.20
163 James Hylton	.10	.30
164 Perk Brown	.10	.30
165 Perk Brown's Car	.07	.20
166 Joe Frasson	.10	.30
167 Joe Frasson's Car	.07	.20
168 Jack Handle w/car	.10	.30
169 Louise Smith	.20	.50
170 Louise Smith	.20	.50
171 L.Petty/L.Smith/Guthrie/Lella Lomb/Christ.Beckers	.40	1.00
172 Marshall Teague	.20	.50
173 Marshall Teague w/car	.20	.50
174 George Follmer	.10	.30
175 George Follmer's Car	.07	.20
176 George Follmer w/car	.10	.30
177 Bob Wellborn/Rex White Jim Reed Cars	.07	.20
178 Bob Burcham w/car	.10	.30
179 Tommy Moon	.10	.30
180 Wendell Scott	.40	1.00
181 Wendell Scott's Car	.20	.50
182 Wendell Scott/D.Pearson Cars	.20	.50
183 Dick Linder	.10	.30
184 Larry Shurter	.10	.30
185 Johnny Halford	.10	.30
186 Johnny Halford's Car	.07	.20
187 J.Paschal/F.Flock J.Eubanks' Cars	.07	.20
188 Butch Lindley	.10	.30
189 Butch Lindley's Car	.07	.20
190 Checklist	.07	.20
191 Donnie Allison	.40	1.00
192 Donnie Allison's Car	.20	.50
193 Donnie Allison's Car	.20	.50

194 Bob Welborn .10 .30
195 Hershel McGriff .10 .30
196 Hershel McGriff .10 .30
197 Hershel McGriff's Car .07 .20
198 Roscoe Pappy Hough .10 .30
199 Roscoe Pappy Hough's Car .07 .20
200 Ned Jarrett .20 .50
201 Ned Jarrett w/car .20 .50
202 Ned Jarrett w/car .20 .50
203 Ned Jarrett w/car .20 .50
204 Joe Eubanks .10 .30
205 Joe Eubanks's Car .07 .20
206 Richard Brickhouse .10 .30
207 Richard Brickhouse's Car .07 .20
208 Tom Pistone .20 .50
209 Tom Pistone's Car .10 .30
210 Buddy Shuman .10 .30
211 M.Teague/B.Flock
Ed Samples/B.Shuman .10 .30
212 Jody Ridley .10 .30
213 Jody Ridley's Car .07 .20
214 Lee Petty .40 1.00
215 Lee Petty's Car .20 .50
216 Maurice Petty .20 .50
217 Maurice Petty .20 .50
218 Al Holbert .10 .30
219 Al Holbert's Car .07 .20
220 Dick Brooks .10 .30
221 Dick Brooks/Pete Hamilton Cars.07 .20
222 Dick Brooks' Car .07 .20
223 Dick Rathmann w/car .10 .30
224 Dick Rathmann's Car .07 .20
225 Jim Vandiver .10 .30
226 Jim Vandiver's Car .07 .20
227 Gene White .10 .30
228 Checklist .07 .20
229 Dick May .10 .30
230 Dick May's Car .07 .20
231 Herb Thomas .20 .50
232 Herb Thomas/M.Teague .20 .50
233 Donald Thomas .10 .30
234 Fans' Race/1950
North Wilkesboro .07 .20
235 Jim Paschal .10 .30
236 Jim Paschal w/car .10 .30
237 Jim Paschal w/car .10 .30
238 Jim Paschal's Car .07 .20
239 Frank Mundy .10 .30
240 Frank Mundy .10 .30
241 Frankie Schneider .10 .30
242 Joe Lee Johnson .10 .30
243 Joe Lee Johnson w/car .10 .30
244 Dink Widenhouse .10 .30
245 Dink Widenhouse's Car .07 .20
246 Dave Marcis .20 .50
247 Dave Marcis' Car .10 .30
248 Bill Rexford .10 .30
249 Bill Rexford w/car .10 .30
250 Cale Yarborough .20 .50
251 Cale Yarborough .20 .50
252 Cale Yarborough w/car .20 .50
253 Cale Yarborough w/car .20 .50
254 Cale Yarborough w/car .20 .50
255 Cale Yarborough's Car .10 .30
256 Elmo Langley .20 .50
257 Elmo Langley's Car .10 .30
258 Ray Hendrick .10 .30
259 Ray Hendrick/Perk Brown .10 .30
260 Ron Bouchard .10 .30
261 Ron Bouchard w/car .10 .30
262 Checklist/Dave Marcis .07 .20
P39 Cover Card/D.Pearson's Car
E.Brooks' Car Promo .40 1.00

1991 TG Racing Tiny Lund

T.G.Racing released this 55-card set highlighting the career of Tiny Lund. The cards were sold in complete set form. Reportedly 20,000 sets were produced.

COMP. FACT SET (55) 4.00 10.00
1 Tiny Lund Art .10 .25
2 Tiny Lund .10 .25
3 Tiny Lund .10 .25
4 Tiny Lund .10 .25
5 Tiny Lund .10 .25
6 Tiny Lund's Car .05 .10
7 Tiny Lund's Car .05 .10
8 Tiny Lund .10 .25
9 Tiny Lund's Car .05 .10
10 Tiny Lund w/Car .10 .25
11 Tiny Lund/Tom Pistone .10 .25
12 Tiny Lund w/Car .10 .25
13 Tiny Lund .10 .25
14 Tiny Lund/Louis Vogt .10 .25
15 Tiny Lund .10 .25
16 Tiny Lund/Fred Lorenzen Cars .10 .25
17 Tiny Lund w/Car .10 .25
18 Tiny Lund/F.Roberts
N.Jarrett/F.Lorenzen .10 .25
19 Carnegie Medal .05 .10
20 Tiny Lund .10 .25
21 Tiny Lund .10 .25
22 Tiny Lund .10 .25
23 Tiny Lund .10 .25
24 Tiny Lund/Tom Pistone Cars .05 .10
25 Lund/Hutcher/C.Yar.
N.Jarrett/Bud.Baker/Buck Baker .15 .40
26 Tiny Lund/Bud.Baker
Brooks Robinson .10 .25
27 Tiny Lund/Fred Lorenzen Cars .05 .10
28 Tiny Lund's Car .05 .10
29 Tiny Lund .10 .25
30 Tiny Lund .10 .25
31 Tiny Lund .10 .25
32 Tiny Lund/Bud.Baker
Paul Bud Moore .10 .25
33 Tiny Lund .10 .25
34 Tiny Lund .10 .25
35 Tiny Lund/Buck Baker .10 .25
36 Tiny Lund's Car .05 .10
37 Tiny Lund/Pistone/B.France Sr. .10 .25
38 Tiny Lund/Seiichi Suzuki .10 .25
39 Tiny Lund .10 .25
40 Tiny Lund .10 .25
41 Tiny Lund .10 .25
42 Tiny Lund/Bob Baskowitz .10 .25
43 Tiny Lund .10 .25
44 Tiny Lund .10 .25
45 Tiny Lund .10 .25
46 Tiny Lund/Andy Granatelli .10 .25
47 Tiny Lund .10 .25
48 Tiny Lund .10 .25
49 Tiny Lund w/Car .10 .25
50 Tiny Lund .10 .25
51 Tiny Lund/Marty Robbins .10 .25
52 Tiny Lund .10 .25
53 1976 Marquee .05 .10
54 The Batter's Box .10 .25
55 Tiny Lund's Car CL .10 .25
P1 Tiny Lund Prototype .50 1.25

1991 TG Racing David Pearson

T.G.Racing released this six-card set highlighting the career of David Pearson. The cards were sold in complete set form.

COMP. FACT SET (6) 10.00 25.00
COMMON CARD (1-6) 2.00 5.00

1991 TG Racing Wendell Scott

T.G.Racing released this six-card set highlighting the career of Wendell Scott. The cards were sold in complete set form.

COMP. FACT SET (6) 3.00 8.00
COMMON CARD (1-6) .60 1.50

1991-92 TG Racing Masters of Racing Update

TG Racing reprinted the original Masters of Racing set in this "Update" form. This set was released in complete factory set form in a colorful box. Three cards were added to the original set and all cards contain a blue border as opposed to the various border colors of the original cards. Although the cards are marked 1991 on the copyright line, they are considered a 1992 release. Four promo cards were produced to promote the set. They are not considered part of the complete set price.

COMP.FACT SET.(265) 10.00 25.00
1 Cover Card .05 .10
2 Red Byron .20 .50
3 Red Byron's Car .07 .20
4 Starting Lineup .07 .20
5 Speedy Thompson .20 .50
6 Speedy Thompson .20 .50
7 Buck Baker .20 .50
8 Buck Baker w/Car .20 .50
9 Buck Baker/S.Thompson
Carl Kiekhaefer .07 .20
10 Henley Gray .20 .50
11 Henley Gray's Car .07 .20
12 Ralph Earnhardt .40 1.00
13 The Wreck .07 .20
14 Paul Goldsmith .12 .30
15 Paul Goldsmith w/Car .12 .30
16 Bill Seifert .20 .50
17 Bill Seifert w/Car .20 .50
18 Edwin Matthews w/Car .12 .30
19 Edwin Matthews w/Car .12 .30
20 Johnny Thompson w/Car .20 .50
21 Johnny Thompson w/Car .20 .50
22 Glenn Roberts(Fireball) .30 .75
23 Glenn Roberts(Fireball) w/Car .30 .75
24 Glenn Roberts(Fireball) .30 .75
25 Lennie Pond .20 .50
26 Lennie Pond w/Car .20 .50
27 256 Wins .40 1.00
28 Sam McQuagg .12 .30
29 Sam McQuagg w/Car .12 .30
30 Gober Sosebee .20 .50
31 Gober Sosebee's Car .07 .20
32 Larry Frank .12 .30
33 Larry Frank w/Car .12 .30
34 Eddie Pagan .20 .50
35 Curtis Crider .20 .50
36 Curtis Crider w/Car .20 .50
37 Tiny Lund/Fireball Roberts' Cars.12 .30
38 Checklist .07 .20
39 Cover Card/D.Pearson's Car
E.Brooks' Car .15 .40
40 Lloyd Dane .12 .30
41 David Pearson w/Car .40 1.00
42 David Pearson w/Car .40 1.00
43 David Pearson .40 1.00
44 Roy Tyner's Car .07 .20
45 David Ezell .20 .50
46 Lee Roy Yarborough .20 .50
47 Lee Roy Yarborough w/Car .20 .50
48 Marshall Teague .20 .50
49 Night Time .40 1.00
50 Jabe Thomas .20 .50
51 Dirt Track .07 .20
52 Billy Carden .20 .50
53 Billy Carden's Car .07 .20
54 Ed Samples .20 .50
55 Ed Samples' Car .07 .20
56 Jack Smith w/Car .12 .30
57 Jack Smith w/Car .12 .30
58 Ralph Moody Jr. w/Car .20 .50
59 D.Pearson/R.Petty/J.Johnson Cars.15 .40
60 David Pearson .40 1.00
61 Tiny Lund .20 .50
62 Tiny Lund w/Car .20 .50
63 Tiny Lund w/Car .20 .50
64 Marvin Panch .20 .50
65 The 5 Heroes .07 .20
66 Wilkesboro 1962 .07 .20
67 Marvin Panch w/Car .20 .50
68 Cotton Owens .20 .50
69 Cotton Owens w/Car .12 .30
70 Tommy Gale w/Car .20 .50
71 Tiny Lund .20 .50
72 Red Fox/Cotton Owens Cars .05 .10
73 Johnny Allen .20 .50
74 Johnny Allen w/Car .20 .50
75 L.R.Yarborough/J.Johnson
Herb Nab .20 .50
76 Checklist/Cotton Owens .12 .30
77 Cover Card/Junior Johnson .07 .20
78 Walter Ballard .20 .50
79 Walter Ballard's Car .07 .20
80 Darel Dieringer .12 .30
81 Darel Dieringer's Car .05 .10
82 Ray Erickson .20 .50
83 Ray Erickson w/Car .20 .50
84 Dick Hutcherson w/Car .12 .30
85 Dick Hutcherson's Car .05 .10
86 Ramo Stott .20 .50
87 Ramo Stott w/Car .20 .50
88 Don White .20 .50
89 Don White's Car .07 .20
90 D.Hutcherson/D.White/R.Stott .20 .50
91 Glen Wood .12 .30
92 Rex White w/Car .20 .50
93 Rex White's Car .07 .20
94 Jimmie Lewallen .12 .30
95 Jimmie Lewallen w/Car .12 .30
96 Darel Dieringer/Junior Johnson .20 .50
97 Banks Simpson .20 .50
98 Paul Lewis w/Car .20 .50
99 Glen Wood/R.White's Car .07 .20
100 Junior Johnson .20 .50
101 Junior Johnson's Car .07 .20
102 Junior Johnson w/Car .20 .50
103 Joe Millikan .20 .50
104 J.Johnson/Ray Fox w/Cars .20 .50
105 Bobby Myers/Billy Myers .20 .50
106 Reino Tulonen w/Car .20 .50
107 World 600 .07 .20
108 Coo Coo Marlin .12 .30
109 Coo Coo Marlin w/Car .12 .30
110 Ray Fox .20 .50
111 Billy Myers .20 .50
112 Billy Myers .20 .50
113 Ray Fox .20 .50
114 Checklist .07 .20
115 Cover Card/Lund/Isaac .07 .20
116 Buddy Arrington .12 .30
117 Buddy Arrington's Car .05 .10
118 Bill Blair w/Car .12 .30
119 Bill Blair w/Car .12 .30
120 Earl Brooks w/Car .20 .50
121 Earl Brooks w/Car .20 .50
122 Charlie Glotzbach .20 .50
123 Charlie Glotzbach w/Car .20 .50
124 Charlie Glotzbach w/Car .20 .50
125 Gene Cline w/Car .20 .50
126 Nelson Stacy .20 .50
127 Nelson Stacy w/Car .20 .50
128 Jim Reed .12 .30
129 Jim Reed w/Car .12 .30
130 Charlie Glotzbach w/Car .20 .50
131 Bobby Isaac's Car .05 .10
132 Neil Castles' Car .05 .10
133 Buddy Arrington's Car .05 .10
134 Fireball Roberts in Pits .30 .75
135 Neil Castles .12 .30
136 Neil Castles' Car .05 .10
137 Red Farmer .20 .50
138 Red Farmer's Car .07 .20
139 Big Winner .20 .50
140 Pete Hamilton .12 .30
141 Pete Hamilton w/Car .12 .30
142 Gwyn Staley .20 .50
143 Fred Lorenzen .20 .50
144 Gwyn Staley/Enoch Staley
Charlie Combs .20 .50
145 Bobby Isaac w/Car .20 .50
146 G.C. Spencer .12 .30
147 Bob Derrington .20 .50
148 Earl Brooks/Lorenzen
Nelson Stacy Cars .07 .20
149 Fred Lorenzen .20 .50
150 Fred Lorenzen w/Car .20 .50
151 Fred Lorenzen w/Car .20 .50
152 Checklist .07 .20
153 Cover Card/Red Byron's Car .07 .20
154 Bob Flock .20 .50
155 Bob Flock/Red Byron's Cars .07 .20
156 Fonty Flock .20 .50
157 Fonty Flock's Car .07 .20
158 Tim Flock .20 .50
159 Tim Flock w/Car .20 .50
160 Fonty/Tim/Bob/Carl Flock .20 .50
161 James Hylton .12 .30
162 James Hylton's Car .05 .10
163 James Hylton .12 .30
164 Perk Brown .20 .50
165 Perk Brown's Car .07 .20
166 Joe Frasson .20 .50
167 Joe Frasson's Car .07 .20
168 Jack Handle w/Car .20 .50
169 Louise Smith .12 .30
170 Louise Smith .12 .30
171 L.Petty/L.Smith/Guthrie/Lella
Lomb/Christ.Beckers .30 .75
172 Frank Warren .20 .50
173 Frank Warren's Car .07 .20
174 George Follmer .20 .50
175 George Follmer's Car .07 .20
176 George Follmer w/Car .20 .50
177 Bob Wellborn/Rex White
Jim Reed Cars .07 .20
178 Bob Burcham w/Car .20 .50
179 Tommy Moon .20 .50
180 Wendell Scott .12 .30
181 Wendell Scott's Car .05 .10
182 Wendell Scott/D.Pearson Cars .15 .40
183 Dick Linder .20 .50
184 Larry Shurter .20 .50
185 Johnny Halford .20 .50
186 Johnny Halford's Car .07 .20
187 J.Paschal/F.Flock
J.Eubanks' Cars .07 .20
188 Butch Lindley .20 .50
189 Butch Lindley's Car .07 .20
190 Checklist .07 .20
191 Donnie Allison .20 .50
192 Donnie Allison's Car .07 .20
193 Donnie Allison's Car .07 .20
194 Bob Welborn .12 .30
195 Hershel McGriff .20 .50
196 Hershel McGriff .20 .50
197 Hershel McGriff's Car .07 .20
198 Roscoe Pappy Hough .20 .50
199 Roscoe Pappy Hough's Car .07 .20
200 Ned Jarrett .15 .40
201 Ned Jarrett w/Car .15 .40
202 Ned Jarrett w/Car .15 .40
203 Ned Jarrett w/Car .15 .40
204 Joe Eubanks .20 .50
205 Joe Eubanks's Car .07 .20
206 Richard Brickhouse .20 .50
207 Richard Brickhouse's Car .07 .20
208 Tom Pistone .12 .30
209 Tom Pistone's Car .05 .10
210 Buddy Shuman .20 .50
211 M.Teague/B.Flock
Ed Samples/B.Shuman .20 .50
212 Jody Ridley .20 .50
213 Jody Ridley's Car .07 .20
214 Lee Petty .30 .75
215 Lee Petty's Car .12 .30
216 Maurice Petty .30 .75
217 Maurice Petty .30 .75
218 Al Holbert .20 .50
219 Al Holbert's Car .07 .20
220 Dick Brooks .12 .30
221 Dick Brooks/Pete Hamilton Cars.05 .10
222 Dick Brooks' Car .05 .10
223 Dick Rathmann w/Car .12 .30
224 Dick Rathmann's Car .05 .10
225 Jim Vandiver .20 .50
226 Jim Vandiver's Car .07 .20
227 Gene White .20 .50
228 Checklist .07 .20
229 Dick May .20 .50
230 Dick May's Car .07 .20
231 Herb Thomas .12 .30
232 Herb Thomas/M.Teague .20 .50
233 Donald Thomas .20 .50
234 Fans' Race .07 .20
235 Jim Paschal .12 .30
236 Jim Paschal w/Car .12 .30
237 Jim Paschal w/Car .12 .30
238 Jim Paschal's Car .05 .10
239 Frank Mundy .12 .30
240 Frank Mundy .12 .30
241 Frankie Schneider .20 .50
242 Joe Lee Johnson .12 .30
243 Joe Lee Johnson w/Car .12 .30
244 Dink Widenhouse .20 .50
245 Dink Widenhouse's Car .07 .20
246 Dave Marcis .15 .40
247 Dave Marcis' Car .05 .15
248 Bill Rexford .12 .30
249 Bill Rexford w/Car .12 .30
250 Cale Yarborough .30 .75
251 Cale Yarborough .30 .75
252 Cale Yarborough w/Car .30 .75
253 Cale Yarborough w/Car .30 .75
254 Cale Yarborough w/Car .30 .75
255 Cale Yarborough's Car .12 .30
256 Elmo Langley .12 .30
257 Elmo Langley's Car .05 .10
258 Ray Hendrick .20 .50
259 Ray Hendrick/Perk Brown .20 .50
260 Ron Bouchard .20 .50
261 Ron Bouchard w/Car .20 .50
262 Bobby Myers .20 .50
263 Bobby Myers .20 .50
264 Dave Marcis CL .15 .40
265 Tommy Moon w/Car .20 .50
P1 Larry Frank Promo .60 1.50
P2 Charlie Glotzbach Promo 1.00 2.50
P3 Charlie Owens Promo .60 1.50
P4 Donald Thomas Promo 1.00 2.50

1994 Tide Ricky Rudd

Proctor and Gamble produced and released this set featuring Ricky Rudd and the Tide Racing Team. The ten-card set was given away wherever the Tide showcar was on display during the 1995 Winston Cup season and was released in complete set form.

COMPLETE SET (10) 3.20 8.00
1 Ricky Rudd w/Car .30 .75
2 Ricky Rudd's Car .30 .75
3 Ricky Rudd .50 1.25
4 Ricky Rudd .30 .75
Bill Ingle
5 Ricky Rudd in Pits .30 .75
6 Ricky Rudd .50 1.25
7 Ricky Rudd's Transporter .30 .75
8 Ricky Rudd .30 .75
Linda Rudd
9 Ricky Rudd .30 .75
Linda Rudd
10 Ricky Rudd .30 .75
Linda Rudd

1996 Tide

COMPLETE SET (10) 2.50 6.00
1 Darrell Waltrip 1987 .40 1.00
2 Darrell Waltrip 1988 .40 1.00
3 Darrell Waltrip 1989 .40 1.00
4 Darrell Waltrip 1990 .40 1.00
5 Darrell Waltrip 1991 .40 1.00
6 Darrell Waltrip 1992 .40 1.00
7 Darrell Waltrip 1993 .40 1.00
8 Ricky Rudd 1994 .30 .75
9 Ricky Rudd 1995 .30 .75
10 Ricky Rudd 1996 .30 .75

1991 Tiger Tom Pistone

This is a 15 card set consisting of 3 color and 12 black and white cards produced by "If Its Racing". The set covers Tom's career from 1954 to his victory in a legends race at Hickory Speedway in 1987.

COMPLETE SET (15) 1.50 4.00
1 Tom Pistone .10 .25
2 Tom Pistone .10 .25
3 Tom Pistone .10 .25
4 Tom Pistone .10 .25
5 Tom Pistone .10 .25
6 Tom Pistone .10 .25
7 Tom Pistone .10 .25
Andy Granatelli
8 Tom Pistone .10 .25
9 Tom Pistone .10 .25
10 Tom Pistone .10 .25
11 Tom Pistone .10 .25
12 Tom Pistone .10 .25
13 Tom Pistone .50 1.25
Richard Petty
14 Tom Pistone .15 .40
Tiny Lund
15 Tom Pistone .10 .25
P1 Tom Pistone Promo .60 1.50

2006 Topps Allen and Ginter

This 350-card set was release in August, 2006. The set was issued in seven-card hobby packs with an $4 SRP. Those packs came 24 to a box and there were 12 boxes in a case. In addition, there were also six-card retail packs issued and those packs came 24 packs to a box and 20 boxes to a case. There were some subsets included in this set including Rookies (251-265); Retired Greats (266-290); Managers (291-300); Modern Personalities (301-314); Reprinted Allen and Ginters (316-319); Famous People of the Past (326-349).

COMPLETE SET (350) 60.00 120.00
COMP.SET w/o SP's (300) 15.00 40.00
SP STATED ODDS 1:2 HOBBY, 1:2 RETAIL
SP CL: 5/15/25/35/45/50-59/65/85/105/115
SP CL: 125/135/145/150-159/165/175/185
SP CL: 205/215/235/245/251/255-256/265
SP CL: 285/295/305/315/325/335/345
FRAMED ORIGINALS ODDS 1:3227 H, 1:3227 R
305 Danica Patrick SP 8.00 20.00

2006 Topps Allen and Ginter Mini

*MINI 1-350: 1X TO 2.5X BASIC
*MINI 1-350: 1X TO 2.5X BASIC RC's
APPX.15 MINIS PER 24-CT SEALED BOX
*MINI SP 1-350: .6X TO 1.5X BASIC SP
*MINI SP 1-350: .6X TO 1.5X BASIC SP RC's
MINI SP ODDS 1:13 H, 1:13 R
COMMON CARD (351-375) 20.00 50.00
SEMISTARS 351-375 30.00 60.00
UNLISTED STARS 351-375 30.00 60.00
351-375 RANDOM WITHIN RIP CARDS
OVERALL PLATE ODDS 1:865 H, 1:865 R
PLATE PRINT RUN 1 SET PER COLOR
BLACK-CYAN-MAGENTA-YELLOW ISSUED
NO PLATE PRICING DUE TO SCARCITY

2006 Topps Allen and Ginter Mini A and G Back

*A & G BACK: 2X TO 5X BASIC
*A & G BACK: 1.5X TO 4X BASIC RC's
STATED ODDS 1:5 H, 1:5 R
*A & G BACK SP: 1X TO 2.5X BASIC SP
*A & G BACK SP: 1X TO 2.5X BASIC SP RC's
SP STATED ODDS 1:65 H, 1:65 R

2006 Topps Allen and Ginter Mini Black

*BLACK: 4X TO 10X BASIC
*BLACK: 2.5X TO 6X BASIC RC's
STATED ODDS 1:10 H, 1:10 R
*BLACK SP: 1.5X TO 4X BASIC SP
*BLACK SP: 1.5X TO 4X BASIC SP RC's
SP STATED ODDS 1:130 H, 1:130 R

2006 Topps Allen and Ginter Mini No Card Number

*NO NBR: 6X TO 15X BASIC
*NO NBR: 4X TO 10X BASIC RC's
*NO NBR: 2X TO 5X BASIC SP
*NO NBR: 2X TO 5X BASIC SP RC's
STATED ODDS 1:60 H, 1:168 R
STATED PRINT RUN 50 SETS
CARDS ARE NOT SERIAL-NUMBERED
PRINT RUN INFO PROVIDED BY TOPPS

2006 Topps Allen and Ginter Autographs

GROUP A ODDS 1:2467 H, 1:3850 R
GROUP B ODDS 1:14,500 H, 1:32,000 R
GROUP C ODDS 1:2200 H, 1:4300 R
GROUP D ODDS 1:548 H, 1:1090 R
GROUP E ODDS 1:473 H, 1:1000 R
GROUP F ODDS 1:250 H, 1:520 R
GROUP G ODDS 1:158 H, 1:299 R
GROUP A PRINT RUN 50 CARDS PER
GROUP A BONDS PRINT RUN 25 CARDS
GROUP B PRINT RUN 75 CARDS PER
GROUP C PRINT RUN 100 CARDS PER
GROUP D PRINT RUN 200 CARDS PER
GROUP A-D ARE NOT SERIAL-NUMBERED
A-D PRINT RUNS PROVIDED BY TOPPS
NO BONDS PRICING DUE TO SCARCITY
DP Danica Patrick C/100 * 400.00 600.00

2007 Topps Allen and Ginter

This 350-card set was released in August, 2007. The set was issued in both hobby and retail versions. The hobby packs, which had an $4 SRP, consisted of eight-cards which came 24 packs to a box and 12 boxes to a case. Similar to the 2006 set, many non-baseball players were interspersed throughout this set. There were also a group of short-printed cards, which were inserted at a stated rate of one in two hobby or retail packs. In addition, some original 19th century Allen and Ginter cards were repurchased for this product and those original cards (featuring both sports and non-sport subjects) were inserted at a stated rate of one in 17, 072 hobby and one in 34, 654 retail packs.

COMPLETE SET (350) 60.00 120.00
COMP.SET w/o SP's (300) 20.00 50.00
SP STATED ODDS 1:2 HOBBY, 1:2 RETAIL
SP CL: 5/43/48/58/63/107/110/119/130/137
SP CL: 152/159/178/193/194/203/219/222
SP CL: 224/243/263/301/302/303/306/307
SP CL: 308/309/310/316/317/318/319/320
SP CL: 321/322/325/326/327/330/331/334
SP CL: 335/336/339/340/345/348/349/350
FRAMED ORIGINALS ODDS 1:17,072 HOBBY
FRAMED ORIGINALS ODDS 1:34,654 RETAIL
19 Mario Andretti .30 .75

2007 Topps Allen and Ginter Autographs

GROUP A ODDS 1:64,496 H, 1:122200 R
GROUP B ODDS 1:3261 H, 1:6522 R
GROUP C ODDS 1:13,987 H, 1:27,642 R
GROUP D ODDS 1:288 H, 1:578 R
GROUP E ODDS 1:6789 H, 1:13,578 R
GROUP F ODDS 1:162 H, 1:324 R
GROUP G ODDS 1:680 H, 1:1362 R
GROUP A PRINT RUN 25 CARDS PER
GROUP B PRINT RUN 100 CARDS PER
GROUP C PRINT RUN 120 CARDS PER
GROUP D PRINT RUN 200 CARDS PER
GROUP A-D ARE NOT SERIAL-NUMBERED
A-D PRINT RUNS PROVIDED BY TOPPS
NO PUJOLS PRICING DUE TO SCARCITY
EXCH DEADLINE 7/31/2009
MGA Mario Andretti D/200 * 40.00 80.00

2007 Topps Allen and Ginter Mini

*MINI 1-350: 1X TO 2.5X BASIC
*MINI 1-350: .6X TO 1.5X BASIC RC's
APPX. ONE MINI PER PACK
*MINI SP 1-350: .6X TO 1.5X BASIC SP
*MINI SP 1-350: .6X TO 1.5X BASIC SP RC's
MINI SP ODDS 1:13 H, 1:13 R
COMMON CARD (351-390) 15.00 40.00
351-390 RANDOM WITHIN RIP CARDS
OVERALL PLATE ODDS 1:788 HOBBY
PLATE PRINT RUN 1 SET PER COLOR
BLACK-CYAN-MAGENTA-YELLOW ISSUED
NO PLATE PRICING DUE TO SCARCITY

2007 Topps Allen and Ginter Mini A and G Back

*A & G BACK: 1.25X TO 3X BASIC
*A & G BACK: .75X TO 2X BASIC RC's
STATED ODDS 1:5 H, 1:5 R
*A & G BACK SP: .75X TO 2X BASIC SP
*A & G BACK SP: .75X TO 2X BASIC SP RC's
SP STATED ODDS 1:65 H, 1:65 R

2007 Topps Allen and Ginter Mini Black

*BLACK: 2X TO 5X BASIC
*BLACK: 1.5X TO 4X BASIC RC's
STATED ODDS 1:10 H, 1:10 R
*BLACK SP: 1.5X TO 4X BASIC SP
*BLACK SP: 1.5X TO 4X BASIC SP RC's
SP STATED ODDS 1:130 H, 1:130 R

2007 Topps Allen and Ginter Mini Black No Number

*BLK NO NBR: 2.5X TO 6X BASIC
*BLK NO NBR: 2X TO 5X BASIC RC's
*BLK NO NBR: 1.5X TO 4X BASIC SP
*BLK NO NBR: 1.5X TO 4X BASIC SP RC's
RANDOM INSERTS IN PACKS

2007 Topps Allen and Ginter Mini No Card Number

*NO NBR: 10X TO 25X BASIC
*NO NBR: 6X TO 15X BASIC RC's
*NO NBR: 2.5X TO 6X BASIC SP
*NO NBR: 2.5X TO 6X BASIC SP RC's
STATED ODDS 1:106 H, 1:108 R
STATED PRINT RUN 50 SETS
CARDS ARE NOT SERIAL-NUMBERED
PRINT RUN INFO PROVIDED BY TOPPS

2007 Topps Allen and Ginter N43

STATED ODDS 1:3 HOBBY BOX LOADER
MA Mario Andretti 1.00 2.50

2008 Topps Allen and Ginter

COMP.SET w/o FUKU.(350) 30.00 60.00
COMP.SET w/o SPs (300) 15.00 40.00
COMMON CARD (1-300) .15 .40
COMMON RC (1-300) .40 1.00
COMMON SP (301-350) 1.25 3.00
SP STATED ODDS 1:2 HOBBY
FRAMED ORIG.ODDS 1:26,500 HOBBY
59 Nicky Hayden .25 .60

2008 Topps Allen and Ginter Autographs
GROUP A ODDS 1:277 HOBBY
GROUP B ODDS 1:256 HOBBY
GROUP C ODDS 1:135 HOBBY
GRP A PRINT RUNS B/W 90-240 COPIES PER
CARDS ARE NOT SERIAL-NUMBERED
PRINT RUNS PROVIDED BY TOPPS
EXCHANGE DEADLINE 7/31/2010
NH Nicky Hayden A/240 * 20.00 50.00

2008 Topps Allen and Ginter Mini
*MINI 1-300: .75X TO 2X BASIC
*MINI 1-300 RC: .5X TO 1.2X BASIC RC's
APPX. ONE MINI PER PACK
*MINI SP 300-350: .75X TO 2X BASIC SP
MINI SP ODDS 1:13 HOBBY
351-390 RANDOM WITHIN RIP CARDS
OVERALL PLATE ODDS 1:961 HOBBY
PLATE PRINT RUN 1 SET PER COLOR
BLACK-CYAN-MAGENTA-YELLOW ISSUED
NO PLATE PRICING DUE TO SCARCITY

2008 Topps Allen and Ginter Mini A and G Back
*A & G BACK: 1X TO 2.5X BASIC
*A & G BACK RCs: .6X TO 1.5X BASIC RCs
STATED ODDS 1:5 HOBBY
*A & G BACK SP: 1X TO 2.5X BASIC SP
SP STATED ODDS 1:65 HOBBY

2008 Topps Allen and Ginter Mini Black
*BLACK: 1.5X TO 4X BASIC
*BLACK RCs: .75X TO 2X BASIC RCs
STATED ODDS 1:10 HOBBY
*BLACK SP: 1.2X TO 3X BASIC SP
SP STATED ODDS 1:130 HOBBY

2008 Topps Allen and Ginter Mini No Card Number
*NO NBR: 10X TO 25X BASIC
*NO NBR RCs: 4X TO 10X BASIC RCs
*NO NBR: 1.5X TO 4X BASIC SP
STATED ODDS 1:151 HOBBY
STATED PRINT RUN 50 SETS
CARDS ARE NOT SERIAL-NUMBERED
PRINT RUN INFO PROVIDED BY TOPPS

2008 Topps Allen and Ginter Relics
GROUP A ODDS 1:280 HOBBY
GROUP B ODDS 1:71 HOBBY
GROUP C ODDS 1:20 HOBBY
RELIC AU ODDS 1:26,431 HOBBY
GROUP A B/W 100-250 COPIES PER
CARDS ARE NOT SERIAL NUMBERED
PRINT RUN INFO PROVIDED BY TOPPS
NH Nicky Hayden A/250 * 10.00 25.00

2009 Topps Allen and Ginter Autographs
GROUP A ODDS 1:2730 HOBBY
GROUP B ODDS 1:51 HOBBY
CARDS ARE NOT SERIAL-NUMBERED
PRINT RUNS PROVIDED BY TOPPS
NO PHELPS PRICING DUE TO SCARCITY
EXCHANGE DEADLINE 6/30/2012
BY B.Yates/239 * B 5.00 12.00

2009 Topps Allen and Ginter Relics
GROUP A ODDS 1:100 HOBBY
GROUP B ODDS 1:215 HOBBY
GROUP D ODDS 1:17 HOBBY
GROUP C ODDS 1:39 HOBBY
CARDS ARE NOT SERIAL-NUMBERED
PRINT RUNS PROVIDED BY TOPPS
BY Brock Yates/250 * A 8.00 20.00

2011 Topps Allen and Ginter
COMPLETE SET (350) 50.00 100.00
COMP.SET w/o SP's (300) 12.50 30.00
COMMON CARD (1-300) .15 .40
COMMON RC (1-300) .40 1.00
COMMON SP (301-350) 1.25 3.00
SP ODDS 1:2 HOBBY
135 Kyle Petty .15 .40

2011 Topps Allen and Ginter Glossy
ISSUED VIA TOPPS ONLINE STORE
STATED PRINT RUN 999 SER.#'d SETS
135 Kyle Petty .75 2.00

2011 Topps Allen and Ginter Autographs
STATED ODDS 1:68 HOBBY
DUAL AUTO ODDS 1:56,000 HOBBY
EXCHANGE DEADLINE 6/30/2014
KPE Kyle Petty 10.00 25.00

2011 Topps Allen and Ginter Code Cards
*MINI 1-300: 1.5X TO 4X BASIC
*MINI 1-300 RC: .75X TO 2X BASIC RC's
OVERALL CODE ODDS 1:8 HOBBY

2011 Topps Allen and Ginter Mini
*MINI 1-300: .75X TO 2X BASIC
*MINI 1-300 RC: .5X TO 1.2X BASIC RC's
*MINI SP 301-350: .5X TO 1.2X BASIC SP
MINI SP ODDS 1:13 HOBBY
COMMON CARD (351-400) 10.00 25.00
351-400 RANDOM WITHIN RIP CARDS
STATED PLATE ODDS 1:751 HOBBY
PLATE PRINT RUN 1 SET PER COLOR
BLACK-CYAN-MAGENTA-YELLOW ISSUED
NO PLATE PRICING DUE TO SCARCITY

2011 Topps Allen and Ginter Mini A and G Back
*A & G BACK: 1X TO 2.5X BASIC
*A & G BACK RCs: .6X TO 1.5X BASIC RCs
A & G BACK ODDS 1:5 HOBBY
*A & G BACK SP: .6X TO 1.5X BASIC SP
A & G BACK SP ODDS 1:65 HOBBY

2011 Topps Allen and Ginter Mini Black
*BLACK: 2X TO 5X BASIC
*BLACK RCs: .75X TO 2X BASIC RCs
BLACK ODDS 1:10 HOBBY
BLACK SP ODDS 1:130 HOBBY
*BLACK SP: .75X TO 2X BASIC SP

2011 Topps Allen and Ginter Mini No Card Number
*NO NBR: 8X TO 20X BASIC
*NO NBR RCs: 3X TO 8X BASIC RCs
*NO NBR SP: 1.2X TO 3X BASIC SP
STATED ODDS 1:142 HOBBY

2011 Topps Allen and Ginter Relics
STATED ODDS 1:10 HOBBY
EXCHANGE DEADLINE 6/30/2014
KPE Kyle Petty 10.00 25.00

2012 Topps Allen and Ginter
COMPLETE SET (350) 30.00 60.00
COMP.SET w/o SP's (300) 15.00 40.00
SP ODDS 1:2 HOBBY
61 Richard Petty .50 1.25
237 Al Unser Sr. .25 .60

2012 Topps Allen and Ginter Mini
*MINI 1-300: .75X TO 2X BASIC
*MINI 1-300 RC: .5X TO 1.2X BASIC RC's
*MINI SP 301-350: .5X TO 1.2X BASIC SP
MINI SP ODDS 1:13 HOBBY
351-400 RANDOM WITHIN RIP CARDS
STATED PLATE ODDS 1:564 HOBBY
PLATE PRINT RUN 1 SET PER COLOR
NO PLATE PRICING DUE TO SCARCITY

2012 Topps Allen and Ginter Mini A and G Back
*A & G BACK: 1X TO 2.5X BASIC
*A & G BACK RCs: .6X TO 1.5X BASIC RCs
A & G BACK ODDS 1:5 HOBBY
*A & G BACK SP: .6X TO 1.5X BASIC SP
A & G BACK SP ODDS 1:65 HOBBY

2012 Topps Allen and Ginter Mini Black
*BLACK: 1.5X TO 4X BASIC
*BLACK RCs: .6X TO 1.5X BASIC RCs
BLACK ODDS 1:10 HOBBY
*BLACK SP: 1X TO 2.5X BASIC SP
BLACK SP ODDS 1:130 HOBBY

2012 Topps Allen and Ginter Mini Gold Border
*GOLD: .5X TO 1.2X BASIC
*GOLD RCs: .5X TO 1.2X BASIC RCs
COMMON SP (301-350) .40 1.00
SP SEMIS .60 1.50
SP UNLISTED 1.00 2.50

2012 Topps Allen and Ginter Mini No Card Number
*NO NBR: 5X TO 12X BASIC
*NO NBR RCs: 2X TO 5X BASIC RCs
*NO NBR SP: 1.2X TO 3X BASIC SP
STATED ODDS 1:111 HOBBY
ANNC'D PRINT RUN OF 50 SETS

2012 Topps Allen and Ginter Autographs
STATED ODDS 1:51 HOBBY
EXCHANGE DEADELINE 06/30/2015
AUS Al Unser Sr. 6.00 15.00
RPT Richard Petty 15.00 40.00

2012 Topps Allen and Ginter Relics
STATED ODDS 1:10 HOBBY
EXCHANGE DEADELINE 06/30/2015
AUS Al Unser Sr. 4.00 10.00
RPE Richard Petty 4.00 10.00

2013 Topps Allen and Ginter
COMPLETE SET (350) 20.00 50.00
COMP.SET w/o SP's (300) 12.00 30.00
SP ODDS 1:2 HOBBY
35 Kevin Harvick .60 1.50
184 Mike Joy .25 .60

2013 Topps Allen and Ginter Autographs
STATED ODDS 1:49 HOBBY
EXCHANGE DEADLINE 07/31/2016
KH Kevin Harvick 10.00 25.00
MJO Mike Joy 6.00 15.00

2013 Topps Allen and Ginter Autographs Red Ink
STATED ODDS 1:931 HOBBY
PRINT RUNS B/WN 10-409 SER.#'d SETS
NO PRICING ON MOST DUE TO SCARCITY
EXCHANGE DEADLINE 07/31/2013

2013 Topps Allen and Ginter Framed Mini Relics
VERSION A ODDS 1:29 HOBBY
VERSION B ODDS 1:27 HOBBY
KH Kevin Harvick 5.00 12.00
MJ Mike Joy 3.00 8.00

2013 Topps Allen and Ginter Mini
*MINI 1-300: .75X TO 2X BASIC
*MINI 1-300 RC: .5X TO 1.2X BASIC RC's
*MINI SP 301-350: .5X TO 1.2X BASIC SP
MINI SP ODDS 1:13 HOBBY
351-400 RANDOM WITHIN RIP CARDS
STATED PLATE ODDS 1:594 HOBBY
PLATE PRINT RUN 1 SET PER COLOR
BLACK-CYAN-MAGENTA-YELLOW ISSUED
NO PLATE PRICING DUE TO SCARCITY

2013 Topps Allen and Ginter Mini A and G Back
*A & G BACK: 1X TO 2.5X BASIC
*A & G BACK RCs: .6X TO 1.5X BASIC RCs
A & G BACK ODDS 1:5 HOBBY
*A & G BACK SP: .6X TO 1.5X BASIC SP
A & G BACK SP ODDS 1:65 HOBBY

2013 Topps Allen and Ginter Mini Black
*BLACK: 1.5X TO 4X BASIC
*BLACK RCs: 1X TO 2.5X BASIC RCs
BLACK ODDS 1:10 HOBBY
*BLACK SP: 1X TO 2.5X BASIC SP
BLACK SP ODDS 1:130 HOBBY

2013 Topps Allen and Ginter Mini No Card Number
*NO NBR: 4X TO 10X BASIC
*NO NBR RCs: 2.5X TO 6X BASIC RCs
*NO NBR SP: 1.2X TO 3X BASIC SP
STATED ODDS 1:102 HOBBY
ANNC'D PRINT RUN OF 50 SETS

2009 Topps American Heritage Heroes Presidential Medal of Freedom
COMPLETE SET (25) 8.00 20.00
STATED ODDS 1:4
MOF16 Richard Petty .60 1.50

2012 Total Memorabilia
COMP.SET w/o SPs (50) 15.00 40.00
WAX BOX HOBBY 100.00 125.00
1A Marcos Ambrose w/car .60 1.50
1B Marcos Ambrose SP 1.50 4.00
2 Trevor Bayne .60 1.50
3 Greg Biffle .50 1.25
4 Clint Bowyer .60 1.50
5 Jeff Burton .50 1.25
6A Kyle Busch .75 2.00
6B Kyle Busch SP 2.00 5.00
7A Dale Earnhardt Jr. NG 1.25 3.00
7B Dale Earnhardt Jr. SP DMD 3.00 8.00
8A Carl Edwards w/car .60 1.50
8B Carl Edwards SP sitting 1.50 4.00
9 David Gilliland .40 1.00
10A Jeff Gordon DTEH 1.25 3.00
10B Jeff Gordon SP Dupont 3.00 8.00
11 Robby Gordon .40 1.00
12 Denny Hamlin .60 1.50
13A Kevin Harvick JJ .75 2.00
13B Kevin Harvick SP Rheem 2.00 5.00
14A Jimmie Johnson w/car 1.00 2.50
14B Jimmie Johnson SP 2.50 6.00
15A Kasey Kahne Red Bull .60 1.50
15B Kasey Kahne SP Farmer's 1.50 4.00
16 Matt Kenseth .60 1.50
17 Brad Keselowski .75 2.00
18 Travis Kvapil .40 1.00
19 Bobby Labonte .60 1.50
20 Joey Logano .60 1.50
21 Mark Martin .60 1.50
22 Jamie McMurray .60 1.50
23 Casey Mears .40 1.00
24 Paul Menard .40 1.00
25 Juan Pablo Montoya .60 1.50
26 Joe Nemechek .40 1.00
27A Ryan Newman .50 1.25
27B Ryan Newman SP w/hlmt 1.25 3.00
28 Regan Smith .50 1.25
29A Tony Stewart 1.00 2.50
29B Tony Stewart SP w/hlmt 2.50 6.00
30 Martin Truex Jr. .50 1.25
31 Brian Vickers .40 1.00
32 Michael Waltrip .60 1.50
33 Josh Wise CRC .40 1.00
34A Danica Patrick NNS 2.50 6.00
34B Danica Patrick SP w/hlmt 20.00 40.00
35 Ricky Stenhouse Jr. NNS .60 1.50
36 Austin Dillon CWTS .75 2.00
37 Dale Earnhardt LEG 2.00 5.00
38 Terry Labonte LEG .60 1.50
39 Richard Petty LEG 1.00 2.50
40 Richard Childress OWN .50 1.25
41 Chip Ganassi OWN .40 1.00
42 J.D. Gibbs OWN .40 1.00
43 Joe Gibbs OWN .50 1.25
44 Rick Hendrick OWN .50 1.25
45 Jack Roush OWN .50 1.25
46 Steve Addington CC .40 1.00
47 Chad Knaus CC .40 1.00
48 Steve Letarte CC .40 1.00
49 Bob Osborne CC .40 1.00
50 Shane Wilson CC .40 1.00
0 Tony Stewart Champ 2.50 6.00

2012 Total Memorabilia Black and White
*B&W/99: 1X TO 2.5X BASIC CARDS
BLACK AND WHITE PRINT RUN 99
34 Danica Patrick NNS 10.00 25.00

2012 Total Memorabilia Gold
GOLD/275: .6X TO 1.5X BASIC CARDS
GOLD PRINT RUN 275 SER.#'d SETS
34 Danica Patrick NNS 6.00 15.00

2012 Total Memorabilia Red Retail
*RED/250: 1X TO 2.5X BASIC CARDS
RED PRINT RUN 250 SER.#'d SETS
34 Danica Patrick NNS 10.00 25.00

2012 Total Memorabilia Hot Rod Relics Silver
SILVER PRINT RUN 99 SER.#'d SETS
*GOLD/50: .5X TO 1.2X SILVER/99
*HOLO/10: .8X TO 2X SILVER/99
HRRCE Carl Edwards 5.00 12.00
HRRDP Danica Patrick 15.00 40.00
HRRJG Jeff Gordon 10.00 25.00
HRRJJ Jimmie Johnson 10.00 25.00
HRRKH Kevin Harvick 6.00 15.00
HRRKK Kasey Kahne 8.00 20.00
HRRMK Matt Kenseth 5.00 12.00
HRRMM Mark Martin 5.00 12.00
HRRTS Tony Stewart 10.00 25.00
HRRDEJ Dale Earnhardt Jr. 12.00 30.00
HRRKYN Kyle Busch 8.00 20.00

2012 Total Memorabilia Memory Lane
ONE PER HOBBY PACK
ML1 Tony Stewart 1.00 2.50
ML2 Ryan Newman .50 1.25
ML3 Juan Pablo Montoya .60 1.50
ML4 Martin Truex Jr. .50 1.25
ML5 Matt Kenseth .60 1.50
ML6 Jimmie Johnson 1.00 2.50
ML7 Dale Earnhardt Jr. 1.25 3.00
ML8 Michael Waltrip .60 1.50
ML9 Bobby Labonte .60 1.50

2012 Total Memorabilia Rising Stars
ONE PER HOBBY PACK
RS1 Harrison Burton 1.25 3.00
RS2 Ty Dillon 2.50 6.00
RS3 Shelby Blackstock 1.25 3.00
RS4 Jack Roush Jr. 1.50 4.00
RS5 Max Gresham 1.25 3.00
RS6 Maryeve Dufault 2.00 5.00
RS7 Amber Cope 1.50 4.00
RS8 Angela Cope 1.50 4.00

2012 Total Memorabilia Rising Stars Autographed Memorabilia Silver
SILVER STATED PRINT RUN 125
*GOLD/99: .4X TO 1X SILVER/125
*HOLO/25: .5X TO 1.2X SILVER/125
RSHB Harrison Burton 10.00 25.00
RSJR Jack Roush Jr. 10.00 25.00
RSMD Maryeve Dufault 15.00 40.00
RSMG Max Gresham 10.00 25.00
RSSB Shelby Blackstock 10.00 25.00
RSTD Ty Dillon 15.00 40.00
RSAC1 Amber Cope 12.00 30.00
RSAC2 Angela Cope 12.00 30.00

2012 Total Memorabilia Single Swatch Silver
SINGLE SILVER PRINT RUN 199-299
*GOLD/99: .5X TO 1.2X SILVER/199-299
*HOLOFOIL/50: .6X TO 1.5X SILVER/199-299
*MELTING/10: 1.2X TO 3X SILVER/199-299
*JUMBO GOLD/50: 1X TO 2.5X SLVR/199-299
*JUMBO HOLO/10: 1.5X TO 4X SLVR/199-299
*DUAL GOLD/75: .5X TO 1.2X SLVR/199-299
*DUAL HOLO/25: .8X TO 2X SLVR/199-299
*DUAL SLVR/99: .5X TO 1.2X SLVR/199-299
*TRIPLE GOLD/50: .8X TO 2X SLVR/199-299
*TRIPLE HOLO/25: 1X TO 2.5X SLVR/199-299
*TRIPLE SLVR/99: .6X TO 1.5X SLVR/199-299
*QUAD GOLD/25: 1.2X TO 3X SLVR/199-299
*QUAD HOLO/10: 2X TO 5X SLVR/199-299
*QUAD SLVR/50: 1X TO 2.5X SLVR/199-299
TMAA A.J. Allmendinger/299 3.00 8.00
TMAD Austin Dillon/199 4.00 10.00
TMBK Brad Keselowski/199 4.00 10.00
TMBL Bobby Labonte/199 3.00 8.00
TMBO Bob Osborne/199 2.00 5.00
TMCE Carl Edwards/199 3.00 8.00
TMDH Denny Hamlin/199 3.00 8.00
TMDP Danica Patrick/199 10.00 25.00
TMGB Greg Biffle/199 2.50 6.00
TMJB Jeff Burton/199 2.50 6.00
TMJD J.D. Gibbs/199 2.00 5.00
TMJJ Jimmie Johnson/199 6.00 15.00
TMJL Joey Logano/299 3.00 8.00
TMJM Jamie McMurray/299 3.00 8.00
TMJR Jack Roush/199 2.50 6.00
TMKH Kevin Harvick/199 4.00 10.00
TMKK Kasey Kahne/199 3.00 8.00
TMMA Marcos Ambrose/299 3.00 8.00
TMMK Matt Kenseth/199 3.00 8.00
TMMM Mark Martin/199 3.00 8.00
TMMT Martin Truex Jr./199 2.50 6.00
TMPM Paul Menard/199 2.00 5.00
TMRC Richard Childress/199 2.50 6.00
TMRN Ryan Newman/299 2.50 6.00
TMTB Trevor Bayne/199 3.00 8.00
TMTL Terry Labonte/199 3.00 8.00
TMTS Tony Stewart/199 6.00 15.00
TMDEJ Dale Earnhardt Jr./199 8.00 20.00
TMDR2 David Ragan/299 2.50 6.00
TMJG1 Jeff Gordon/199 6.00 15.00
TMJG2 Joe Gibbs/199 2.50 6.00
TMJPM Juan Pablo Montoya/299 3.00 8.00
TMKYB Kyle Busch/199 4.00 10.00
TMRS1 Regan Smith/199 2.50 6.00
TMRS2 Ricky Stenhouse Jr./199 3.00 8.00

2012 Total Memorabilia Tandem Treasures Dual Memorabilia Silver
SILVER PRINT RUN 99 SER.#'d SETS
*GOLD/75: .4X TO 1X SILVER/99
*HOLOFOIL/25: .5X TO 1.2X SILVER/99
TTADTD A.Dillon/T.Dillon 15.00 40.00
TTCOPE A.Cope/A.Cope 12.00 30.00
TTDEKK Earnhardt Jr./K.Kahne 10.00 25.00
TTJGKK J.Gordon/K.Kahne 10.00 25.00
TTKBJD Ky.Busch/J.D.Gibbs 6.00 15.00
TTKBJG Ky.Busch/J.Gibbs 6.00 15.00
TTKHRC K.Harvick/R.Childress 6.00 15.00
TTKHSW K.Harvick/S.Wilson 6.00 15.00
TTTSDP T.Stewart/D.Patrick 15.00 40.00
TTTSSA T.Stewart/S.Addington 8.00 20.00

2013 Total Memorabilia
COMPLETE SET (50) 12.00 30.00
WAX BOX HOBBY 90.00 125.00
1 Aric Almirola .40 1.00
2 Marcos Ambrose .50 1.25
3 Trevor Bayne .50 1.25
4 Greg Biffle .40 1.00
5 Clint Bowyer .50 1.25
6 Jeff Burton .40 1.00
7 Kurt Busch .40 1.00
8 Kyle Busch .60 1.50
9 Kyle Busch .60 1.50
10 Landon Cassill .40 1.00
11 Dale Earnhardt Jr. 1.00 2.50
12 Dale Earnhardt Jr. 1.00 2.50
13 Carl Edwards .50 1.25
14 Jeff Gordon 1.00 2.50
15 Jeff Gordon 1.00 2.50
16 Denny Hamlin .50 1.25
17 Kevin Harvick .60 1.50
18 Kevin Harvick .60 1.50
19 Jimmie Johnson .75 2.00
20 Jimmie Johnson .75 2.00
21 Kasey Kahne .50 1.25
22 Kasey Kahne .50 1.25
23 Matt Kenseth .50 1.25
24 Brad Keselowski .60 1.50
25 Bobby Labonte .50 1.25
26 Joey Logano .50 1.25
27 Mark Martin .50 1.25
28 Jamie McMurray .50 1.25
29 Paul Menard .30 .75
30 Juan Pablo Montoya .50 1.25
31 Joe Nemechek .30 .75
32 Ryan Newman .40 1.00
33 Danica Patrick 1.25 3.00
34 Tony Stewart .75 2.00
35 Martin Truex Jr. .40 1.00
36 Michael Waltrip .50 1.25
37 Josh Wise .30 .75
38 Justin Allgaier .40 1.00
39 Austin Dillon .60 1.50
40 Sam Hornish Jr. .40 1.00
41 Danica Patrick 1.25 3.00
42 Elliott Sadler .30 .75
43 Ricky Stenhouse Jr. .50 1.25
44 Josh Berry RS RC .60 1.50
45 Chris Buescher RS RC .40 1.00
46 Tim George Jr. RS RC .50 1.25
47 Kyle Larson RS RC 4.00 10.00
48 Nicole Lyons RS RC .75 2.00
49 Bryan Ortiz RS RC .75 2.00
50 Brad Keselowski CL .60 1.50

2013 Total Memorabilia Black and White
*B&W/99: 1.2X TO 3X BASIC CARDS

2013 Total Memorabilia Gold
*GOLD/275: .8X TO 2X BASIC CARDS

2013 Total Memorabilia Red
*RED: 1X TO 2.5X BASIC CARDS
RANDOM INSERTS IN RETAIL PACKS

2013 Total Memorabilia Burning Rubber Chase Edition Silver
STATED PRINT RUN 175 SER.#'d SETS
*GOLD/75: .5X TO 1.2X SILVER/175
*HOLOFOIL/50: .6X TO 1.5X SILVER/175
BRCBK Brad Keselowski's Car 5.00 12.00
BRCBK2 Brad Keselowski's Car 5.00 12.00
BRCCB Clint Bowyer's Car 4.00 10.00
BRCDH Denny Hamlin's Car 4.00 10.00
BRCJG Jeff Gordon's Car 8.00 20.00
BRCJJ Jimmie Johnson's Car 5.00 12.00
BRCJJ2 Jimmie Johnson's Car 5.00 12.00
BRCKC Kevin Harvick's Car 5.00 12.00
BRCMK Matt Kenseth 4.00 10.00
BRCMK2 Matt Kenseth 4.00 10.00

2013 Total Memorabilia Hot Rod Relics Silver
SILVER PRINT RUN 99 SER.#'d SETS
*GOLD/50: .5X TO 1.2X SILVER/99
*HOLOFOIL/10: .8X TO 2X SILVER/99
HRRCE Carl Edwards 5.00 12.00
HRRDEJR Dale Earnhardt Jr. 10.00 25.00
HRRDP Danica Patrick 12.00 30.00
HRRJG Jeff Gordon 10.00 25.00
HRRJJ Jimmie Johnson 8.00 20.00
HRRKB Kyle Busch 6.00 15.00
HRRKH Kevin Harvick 6.00 15.00
HRRKK Kasey Kahne 5.00 12.00
HRRMM Mark Martin 5.00 12.00
HRRTS Tony Stewart 8.00 20.00

2013 Total Memorabilia Memory Lane
COMPLETE SET (10) 5.00 12.00
ONE PER HOBBY PACK
ML1 Dale Earnhardt Jr. 1.00 2.50
ML2 Juan Pablo Montoya .50 1.25
ML3 Johanna Long .50 1.25
ML4 Jeff Gordon 1.00 2.50
ML5 Kevin Harvick .60 1.50
ML6 Austin Dillon .60 1.50
ML7 Ty Dillon .50 1.25
ML8 Richard Petty .75 2.00
ML9 Mark Martin .50 1.25
ML10 Davey Allison .75 2.00

2013 Total Memorabilia Rising Stars Autographs Silver
STATED PRINT RUN 125
*GOLD/99: .5X TO 1.2X SILVER AU/125
*HOLOFOIL/25: .8X TO 2X SLVR AU/125
RSABO Bryan Ortiz 10.00 25.00
RSACB Chris Buescher 5.00 12.00
RSAJB Josh Berry 8.00 20.00
RSAKL Kyle Larson 30.00 60.00
RSANL Nicole Lyons 10.00 25.00
RSATG Tim George Jr. 6.00 15.00

2013 Total Memorabilia Single Swatch Silver
ANNOUNCED PRINT RUN 312-475
*DUAL GOLD/99-199: .5X TO 1.2X SILVER
*HOLOFIL/99: .6X TO 1.5X SILVER
TMAA Aric Almirola/475* 2.50 6.00
TMAD Austin Dillon/475* 4.00 10.00
TMBL Bobby Labonte/475* 3.00 8.00
TMCB Clint Bowyer/475* 3.00 8.00
TMCE Carl Edwards/475* 3.00 8.00
TMCM Casey Mears/475* 2.00 5.00
TMCW Cole Whitt/475* 3.00 8.00
TMDE Dale Earnhardt Jr./475* 6.00 15.00
TMDG David Gilliland/475* 2.00 5.00
TMDH Denny Hamlin/475* 3.00 8.00
TMDP Danica Patrick/475* 8.00 20.00
TMDP2 Danica Patrick/475* 8.00 20.00
TMDR David Ragan/312* 2.50 6.00
TMDR2 David Reutimann/319* 2.50 6.00
TMGB Greg Biffle/438* 2.50 6.00
TMJA Justin Allgaier/475* 2.50 6.00
TMJB Jeff Burton/475* 2.50 6.00
TMJG Jeff Gordon/475* 6.00 15.00
TMJJ Jimmie Johnson/475* 5.00 12.00
TMJM Jamie McMurray/475* 3.00 8.00
TMJPM Juan Pablo Montoya/475* 3.00 8.00
TMJW Josh Wise/475* 2.00 5.00
TMJY J.J. Yeley/475* 2.00 5.00
TMKB Kyle Busch/475* 4.00 10.00
TMKH Kevin Harvick/475* 4.00 10.00
TMKK Kasey Kahne/475* 3.00 8.00
TMMA Marcos Ambrose/475* 3.00 8.00
TMMM Mark Martin/475* 3.00 8.00
TMMT Martin Truex Jr./466* 2.50 6.00
TMMW Michael Waltrip/475* 3.00 8.00
TMPM Paul Menard/385* 2.00 5.00
TMRN Ryan Newman/475* 2.50 6.00
TMTB Trevor Bayne/475* 4.00 10.00
TMTP Travis Pastrana/475* 3.00 8.00
TMTS Tony Stewart/475* 5.00 12.00

2013 Total Memorabilia Smooth Operators
COMPLETE SET (10) 5.00 12.00
ONE PER HOBBY PACK
SO1 Tony Stewart .75 2.00
SO2 Dale Earnhardt Jr. 1.00 2.50
SO3 Martin Truex Jr. .40 1.00
SO4 Jimmie Johnson .75 2.00
SO5 Kevin Harvick .60 1.50
SO6 Mark Martin .50 1.25
SO7 Jeff Burton .40 1.00
SO8 Greg Biffle .40 1.00
SO9 Carl Edwards .50 1.25
SO10 Kasey Kahne .50 1.25

2014 Total Memorabilia
1 Aric Almirola .40 1.00
2 Marcos Ambrose .50 1.25
3 Greg Biffle .40 1.00
4 Clint Bowyer .50 1.25
5 Kurt Busch .40 1.00
6 Kyle Busch .60 1.50
7 Dale Earnhardt Jr. 1.00 2.50
8 Carl Edwards .50 1.25
9 Jeff Gordon 1.00 2.50
10 Denny Hamlin .50 1.25
11 Kevin Harvick .60 1.50
12 Jimmie Johnson .75 2.00
13 Kasey Kahne .50 1.25
14 Matt Kenseth .50 1.25
15 Brad Keselowski .60 1.50
16 Bobby Labonte .50 1.25
17 Joey Logano .50 1.25
18 Mark Martin .50 1.25
19 Jamie McMurray .50 1.25
20 Casey Mears .30 .75
21 Paul Menard .30 .75
22 Ryan Newman .40 1.00
23 Danica Patrick 1.00 2.50
24 David Ragan .40 1.00
25 Ricky Stenhouse Jr. .50 1.25
26 Tony Stewart .75 2.00
27 Martin Truex Jr. .40 1.00
28 Brian Vickers .30 .75
29 Michael Waltrip .50 1.25
30 Josh Wise .30 .75
31 Justin Allgaier .40 1.00
32 Austin Dillon .60 1.50
33 Kyle Larson CRC 2.00 5.00
34 Trevor Bayne .50 1.25
35 Parker Kligerman NNS .30 .75
36 Elliott Sadler .30 .75
37 Brian Scott .30 .75
38 Regan Smith .40 1.00
39 Ryan Blaney .40 1.00
40 James Buescher .30 .75
41 Jeb Burton .40 1.00
42 Ty Dillon .50 1.25
43 Brendan Gaughan .30 .75
44 Tanner Berryhill RS RC .50 1.25
45 Ryan Gifford RS RC .50 1.25
46 Drew Herring RS RC .40 1.00
47 Daniel Suarez RS RC .40 1.00
48 Kevin Swindell RS RC .50 1.25
49 Ricky Stenhouse Jr. ROY .50 1.25
50 Jimmie Johnson CHAMP .75 2.00

2014 Total Memorabilia Black and White
*B&W/99: 1.2X TO 3X BASIC CARDS

2014 Total Memorabilia Gold
*GOLD/175: 1X TO 2.5X BASIC CARDS

2014 Total Memorabilia Red
*RED: 1X TO 2.5X BASIC CARDS

2014 Total Memorabilia Acceleration
ONE PER HOBBY PACK
AC1 Tony Stewart .75 2.00
AC2 Jimmie Johnson .75 2.00
AC3 Carl Edwards .50 1.25
AC4 Martin Truex Jr. .40 1.00
AC5 Dale Earnhardt Jr. 1.00 2.50
AC6 Jeff Gordon 1.00 2.50
AC7 Brad Keselowski .60 1.50
AC8 Kyle Busch .60 1.50
AC9 Danica Patrick 1.00 2.50
AC10 Clint Bowyer .50 1.25

2014 Total Memorabilia Champions Collection Gold
*BLUE/25: .6X TO 1.5X GOLD/50
CCAD Austin Dillon 6.00 15.00
CCJJ Jimmie Johnson 10.00 25.00

2014 Total Memorabilia Clear Cuts Blue
*MELTING/25: .5X TO 1.2X BLUE/175
CCUCE Carl Edwards 6.00 15.00
CCUDP Danica Patrick 12.00 30.00
CCUJG Jeff Gordon 12.00 30.00
CCUJJ Jimmie Johnson 10.00 25.00
CCUKK Kasey Kahne 6.00 15.00
CCUDEJ Dale Earnhardt Jr. 12.00 30.00

2014 Total Memorabilia Dirt Track Treads Silver
*BLUE/25: .6X TO 1.5X SILVER/99
*GOLD/50: .5X TO 1.2X SILVER/99
DTTAD Austin Dillon's Truck 12.00 30.00
DTTBG Brendan Gaughan's Truck 6.00 15.00
DTTJB Jeb Burton's Truck 8.00 20.00

DTTKL Kyle Larson's Truck 12.00 30.00
DTTTD Ty Dillon's Truck 10.00 25.00

2014 Total Memorabilia Dual Swatch Gold

*MELTING/25: .8X TO 2X GOLD/150
*SILVER/275: .3X TO .8X GOLD/150
*SILVER/275: .2X TO .5X GOLD/65
TMAA Aric Almirola 3.00 8.00
TMAD Austin Dillon 4.00 10.00
TMBK Brad Keselowski 5.00 12.00
TMBV Brian Vickers 2.50 6.00
TMCB Clint Bowyer 4.00 10.00
TMCE Carl Edwards 4.00 10.00
TMDE Dale Earnhardt Jr. 8.00 20.00
TMDH Denny Hamlin 4.00 10.00
TMDP Danica Patrick 8.00 20.00
TMGB Greg Biffle 3.00 8.00
TMJA Justin Allgaier 3.00 8.00
TMJB2 James Buescher 2.50 6.00
TMJG Jeff Gordon 8.00 20.00
TMJJ Jimmie Johnson 6.00 15.00
TMJL Joey Logano 4.00 10.00
TMJM Jamie McMurray 4.00 10.00
TMJW Josh Wise 2.50 6.00
TMKK Kasey Kahne 4.00 10.00
TMKL Kyle Larson/65 12.00 30.00
TMKuB Kurt Busch 3.00 8.00
TMKyB Kyle Busch 5.00 12.00
TMMA Marcos Ambrose 4.00 10.00
TMMK Matt Kenseth 4.00 10.00
TMMM Mark Martin 5.00 12.00
TMMT Martin Truex Jr. 3.00 8.00
TMMW Michael Waltrip 4.00 10.00
TMPM Paul Menard 2.50 6.00
TMRS Regan Smith 3.00 8.00
TMRSJ Ricky Stenhouse Jr. 4.00 10.00
TMTB Trevor Bayne 4.00 10.00
TMTD Ty Dillon 4.00 10.00
TMTS Tony Stewart 6.00 15.00

2014 Total Memorabilia Hall of Fame Plaques

COMPLETE SET (24) 15.00 30.00
*HOLOFOIL: .5X TO 1.2X BASIC INSERTS
ONE PER PACK
HI1 Bill France Sr. .60 1.50
HI2 Richard Petty 1.25 3.00
HI3 Bill France Jr. Holofoil .60 1.50
HI5 Junior Johnson .60 1.50
HI6 David Pearson .60 1.50
HI7 Bobby Allison .60 1.50
HI8 Lee Petty .60 1.50
HI9 Ned Jarrett .75 2.00
HI10 Bud Moore .50 1.25
HI11 Cale Yarborough .60 1.50
HI12 Darrell Waltrip Holofoil .75 2.00
HI13 Dale Inman .50 1.25
HI14 Richie Evans .50 1.25
HI15 Glen Wood .60 1.50
HI16 Buck Baker .50 1.25
HI17 Cotton Owens .50 1.25
HI18 Herb Thomas .50 1.25
HI19 Rusty Wallace .75 2.00
HI20 Leonard Wood .50 1.25
HI21 Tim Flock .50 1.25
HI22 Jack Ingram .50 1.25
HI23 Dale Jarrett Holofoil .75 2.00
HI24 Maurice Petty .60 1.50
HI25 Fireball Roberts .60 1.50

2014 Total Memorabilia Rising Stars Autographed Memorabilia Silver

*BLUE/25: .6X TO 1.5X SILVER/125
*GOLD/99: .5X TO 1.2X SILVER/125
RSADH Drew Herring 5.00 12.00
RSADS Daniel Suarez 5.00 12.00
RSAKS Kevin Swindell 6.00 15.00
RSARG Ryan Gifford 6.00 15.00
RSATB Tanner Berryhill 6.00 15.00

2014 Total Memorabilia Triple Swatch Blue

*BLUE/99: .5X TO 1.2X GOLD/150
TMES Elliott Sadler 3.00 8.00

1991 Track Pack Yesterday's Heroes

This 48-card set features some of the greatest names to ever run the NASCAR circuit. The set includes David Pearson, Ned Jarrett and Benny Parsons to name a few. The cards are listed in alphabetical order.

COMPLETE SET (48) 6.00 15.00
1 Cover Card .12 .30
2 Bill Blair .20 .50
3 Neil Bonnett .50 1.25
4 Dick Brooks .20 .50
5 Neil Castles .20 .50
6 Neil Castles .20 .50
7 Richard Childress .30 .75
8 Lloyd Dane .20 .50
9 Tim Flock .30 .75
10 Larry Frank .20 .50
11 Dick Hutcherson .20 .50
12 Ned Jarrett .25 .60
13 Joe Lee Johnson .20 .50
14 Elmo Langley .20 .50
15 Jimmie Lewallen .20 .50
16 Fred Lorenzen .30 .75
17 CooCoo Marlin .30 .75
18 Banjo Matthews .20 .50
19 Banjo Matthews .20 .50
20 Sam McQuagg .20 .50
21 Ralph Moody .30 .75
22 Ralph Moody .30 .75
23 Bud Moore .20 .50
24 Frank Mundy .20 .50
25 Benny Parsons .50 1.25
26 Jim Paschal .20 .50
27 David Pearson .60 1.50
28 David Pearson .60 1.50
29 Tom Pistone .20 .50
30 Dick Rathmann .20 .50
31 Jim Reed .20 .50
32 Bill Rexford .20 .50
33 Jim Roper .20 .50
34 Jack Smith .20 .50
35 Jack Smith .20 .50
36 Louise Smith .20 .50
37 G.C. Spencer .20 .50
38 G.C. Spencer .20 .50
39 Herb Thomas .20 .50
40 Bob Welborn .20 .50
41 Bob Welborn .20 .50
42 Rex White .30 .75
43 Glen Wood .20 .50
44 Glen Wood .20 .50
45 Cale Yarborough .50 1.25
46 Cale Yarborough .50 1.25
47 Smokey Yunick .20 .50
48 Checklist Card .12 .30

1991 Traks Promos

This 6-card set was issued to promote the 1991 Traks set. Each card is essentially identical to the base issue card except for the card numbering on back.

COMPLETE SET (6) 20.00 35.00
P1 Ernie Irvan 2.00 5.00
P2 Mark Martin 3.00 8.00
P3 Kyle Petty 2.50 6.00
P4 Richard Petty The King 4.00 10.00
P5 Richard Lee Petty 4.00 10.00
P6 Richard Petty 4.00 10.00

1991 Traks

In addition to a 200-card factory set, the premier edition Traks set was distributed in 15-card packs with 30 packs per box in late 1991. The set features the top Busch and Winston Cup drivers along with owners and other racing team members. Traks also included the first regular issue NASCAR card of Jeff Gordon (number 1). The set was available in a factory wooden box version. These were distributed through some of the television shopping channels. 1,000 sets were produced.

COMPLETE SET (200) 15.00 40.00
COMP.FACT.SET (200) 15.00 40.00
WAX BOX 30.00 60.00
1 Jeff Gordon RC 5.00 12.00
2 Rusty Wallace .75 2.00
3A Dale Earnhardt ERR 2.00 5.00
3B Dale Earnhardt COR 2.00 5.00
4 Ernie Irvan .50 1.25
5 Ricky Rudd .50 1.25
6 Mark Martin .75 2.00
7 Alan Kulwicki .60 1.50
8 Rick Wilson .20 .50
9 Troy Beebe RC .30 .75
10 Ernie Irvan w/Car .50 1.25
11 McClure Family .20 .50
12 Hut Stricklin .20 .50
13 High Speed Chaos .10 .25
14 Bobby Hillin .20 .50
15 Morgan Shepherd .30 .75
16 Eddie Lanier RC .30 .75
17 Jeff Hammond .30 .75
18 Mike Wallace RC .50 1.25
19 Chad Little .30 .75
20 Bobby Hillin .20 .50
21 Dale Jarrett .50 1.25
22 Sterling Marlin .30 .75
23 Danny Myers RC .30 .75
24 Barry Dodson .20 .50
25 Ken Schrader .20 .50
26 Neil Bonnett .50 1.25
27A Mike Colyer ERR RC .30 .75
27B Mike Colyer COR RC .30 .75
28 Davey Allison .75 2.00
29 Phil Parsons .20 .50
30 Michael Waltrip .40 1.00
31 Steve Grissom .20 .50
32 Dale Jarrett .50 1.25
33 Harry Gant .30 .75
34 Todd Bodine RC .30 .75
35 Chuck Rider .20 .50
36 Kenny Wallace .30 .75
37 Roger Penske RC .50 1.25
38 Jimmy Makar .20 .50
39 Don Miller RC .30 .75
40 Felix Sabates .30 .75
41 Kyle Petty's Transporter .60 1.50
42 Kyle Petty .60 1.50
43 Richard Petty 1.00 2.50
44 Dale Inman .20 .50
45 Bob Bilby RC .30 .75
46 Robert Yates .30 .75
47 Kyle Petty .60 1.50
48 Sprague Turner RC .30 .75
49 Doug Richert .20 .50
50 Mark Martin .75 2.00
51 Mike McLaughlin RC .30 .75
52 Butch Miller .20 .50
53 Harold Elliott .20 .50
54 Richard Childress .30 .75
55 Ted Musgrave w/Car .50 1.25
56 Tommy Ellis .20 .50
57 Kirk Shelmerdine .20 .50
58 Larry McClure .20 .50
59 Robert Pressley RC .30 .75
60 Tim Morgan .20 .50
61 Dick Trickle .20 .50
62 Leonard Wood .20 .50
63 Chuck Bown .20 .50
64 Glen Wood .20 .50
65 Steve Loyd RC .30 .75
66 Cale Yarborough .50 1.25
67 J.Johnson R.Hendrick .30 .75
68 Ricky Rudd's Car .50 1.25
69 Travis Carter .20 .50
70 Tony Glover .20 .50
71 Dave Marcis .25 .60
72 Waddell Wilson .20 .50
73 Alan Kulwicki's Car .60 1.50
74 Jimmy Fennig .20 .50
75 Michael Waltrip .40 1.00
76 Ken Wilson RC .30 .75
77 David Smith .20 .50
78 Junior Johnson .30 .75
79 Dave Rezendes RC .30 .75
80 Tony Furr RC .30 .75
81 Ted Conder .20 .50
82 Mike Beam .20 .50
83 Walter Bud Moore .20 .50
84 Terry Labonte .30 .75
85 Richard Petty w/Car 1.00 2.50
86 Donnie Wingo RC .30 .75
87 Joe Nemechek RC .75 2.00
88 Elton Sawyer Patty Moise .30 .75
89 Doug Williams .20 .50
90 Jimmy Martin RC .30 .75
91 Richard Broome .30 .75
92 Greg Moore RC .30 .75
93 Hank Jones RC .30 .75
94 Terry Labonte .30 .75
95 Will Lind .20 .50
96 Tom Peck RC .30 .75
97 Morgan Shepherd .30 .75
98 Jimmy Spencer .30 .75
99 Leo Jackson .20 .50
100 Max Helton RC .30 .75
101 Bruce Roney RC .30 .75
102 Keith Almond RC .30 .75
103A Dale Earnhardt ERR 2.00 5.00
103B Dale Earnhardt COR 2.00 5.00
104 Bob Tomlinson RC .30 .75
105 Benny Ertel RC .30 .75
106 Tommy Houston .20 .50
107 Cecil Gordon RC .30 .75
108 David Green RC .50 1.25
109 Robin Pemberton .20 .50
110 David Green's Car .50 1.25
111 John Mulloy RC .30 .75
112 Harry Gant .30 .75
113 Ed Whitaker RC .30 .75
114 Bobby Moody RC .30 .75
115 Steve Hmiel .20 .50
116 Red Farmer RC .30 .75
117 Eddie Jones RC .30 .75
118 B.Stavola/M.Stavola .20 .50
119 David Ifft RC .30 .75
120 Dick Moroso RC .30 .75
121 Eddie Wood .20 .50
122 Len Wood .20 .50
123 Lou LaRosa RC .30 .75
124 Rusty Wallace .75 2.00
125 Rob Moroso .20 .50
126 Ned Jarrett .25 .60
127 Ken Schrader .20 .50
128 Tom Higgins RC .30 .75
129 Frank Edwards .30 .75
130 Steve Waid RC .30 .75
131A Jim Phillips ERR .20 .50
131B Jim Phillips COR .20 .50
132 John Ervin RC .30 .75
133A Winston Kelley ERR .20 .50
133B Winston Kelley COR .20 .50
134A Allen Bestwick RC ERR .50 1.25
134B Allen Bestwick RC COR .50 1.25
135A Dick Brooks ERR .20 .50
135B Dick Brooks COR .20 .50
136 Ricky Rudd Winner .50 1.25
137A Eli Gold ERR .20 .50
137B Eli Gold COR .20 .50
138 Joe Hendrick (Papa) RC .50 1.25
139 Barney Hall .20 .50
140 Tim Brewer .20 .50
141 George Bradshaw RC .30 .75
142 John Wilson RC .30 .75
143 Robbie Loomis RC .50 1.25
144 Benny Parsons .50 1.25
145 Jack Steele RC .30 .75
146 Gary Nelson .20 .50
147 Ed Brasefield RC .30 .75
148 Lake Speed .20 .50
149 Bill Brodrick RC .30 .75
150 Robert Black RC .30 .75
151 Carl Hill RC .30 .75
152 Jimmy Means .20 .50
153 Mark Garrow RC .30 .75
154 Lynda Petty RC .30 .75
155 D.K. Ulrich RC .30 .75
156 Davey Allison .75 2.00
157 Jimmy Cox RC .30 .75
158 Clyde Booth RC .30 .75
159 John Kernan RC .30 .75
160 Marlin Wright RC .30 .75
161 Scott Houston RC .30 .75
162 Wayne Bumgarner RC .30 .75
163 Jeff Hensley RC .30 .75
164 Bill Davis RC .30 .75
165 Bob Jenkins .20 .50
166 Scott Cluka RC .30 .75
167 Sterling Marlin .30 .75
168 Tommy Allison RC .30 .75
169 Hubert Hensley RC .30 .75
170 Steve Bird RC .30 .75
171 John Hall RC .30 .75
172A L.D. Ottinger ERR .20 .50
172B L.D. Ottinger COR .20 .50
173 K.Petty Sabates Nelson .60 1.50
174 Andy Petree RC .30 .75
175 Joe Moore RC .30 .75
176 Shelton Pittman RC .30 .75
177 Ricky Pearson RC .30 .75
178 Ed Berrier .20 .50
179 Rusty Wallace .75 2.00
180 Richard Yates RC .30 .75
181 Frank Cicci RC Scott Welliver RC .30 .75
182 Clyde McLeod RC .30 .75
183 A.G. Dillard RC .30 .75
184 Larry McReynolds .30 .75
185 Joey Knuckles RC .30 .75
186A Teresa Earnhardt RC ERR .60 1.50
186B Teresa Earnhardt RC COR .60 1.50
187 Rick Hendrick .30 .75
188 Jerry Punch .20 .50
189A Tim Petty RC ERR .30 .75
189B Tim Petty RC COR .30 .75
190A Dale Earnhardt ERR 2.00 5.00
190B Dale Earnhardt COR 2.00 5.00
191 Checklist #1 .10 .25
192 Checklist #2 .10 .25
193 Checklist #3 .10 .25
194 Checklist #4 .10 .25
195 Checklist #5 .10 .25
196 Checklist #6 .10 .25
197 Checklist #7 .10 .25
198 Checklist #8 .10 .25
199 Patriotic Statement .10 .25
200 Richard Petty The King 1.00 2.50

1991 Traks Mello Yello Kyle Petty

Traks issued a special set to commemorate Kyle Petty and the Mello Yello race team in 1991. A cover/checklist card (number 13) was also included.

COMPLETE SET (13) 4.00 10.00
COMMON CARD (1-13) .40 1.00

1991 Traks Mom-n-Pop's Biscuits Dale Earnhardt

In conjunction with Traks, Mom-n-Pop's produced this set for distribution in its microwavable sandwich products in 1991. The cards were cello packed with one card and one cover card per pack. Dale Earnhardt is the featured driver due to Mom-n-Pop's associate sponsorship of the RCR racing team. The "Biscuits" cards look very similar to the "Ham" cards produced the same year. A numbered (of 20,000) uncut sheet version of the 6-cards was also produced and offered through packs of 1993 Wheels Mom-n-Pop's cards at $20.00 for the pair of Biscuit and Ham sheets.

COMPLETE SET (6) 5.00 12.00
COMMON CARD (1-6) 1.00 2.50

1991 Traks Mom-n-Pop's Ham Dale Earnhardt

In conjunction with Traks, Mom-n-Pop's produced this set for distribution in its country ham products in 1991. The cards were cello packed with one card and one cover card per pack. Dale Earnhardt is the featured driver due to Mom-n-Pop's associate sponsorship of the RCR racing team. The "Ham" cards look very similar to the "Biscuit" cards produced the same year. A numbered (of 20,000) uncut sheet version of the 6-cards was also produced and offered through packs of 1993 Wheels Mom-n-Pop's cards at $20.00 for the pair of Biscuit and Ham sheets.

COMPLETE SET (6) 5.00 12.00
COMMON CARD (1-6) 1.00 2.50

1991 Traks Richard Petty

The Richard Petty 20th anniversary set was Traks' first racing card release. The issue chronicles Petty's life in racing and was distributed in 12-card packs. It was also distributed as a factory set. Cards 1-25 were packaged in a replica model of Petty's 1972 Plymouth and cards 26-50 were packaged in a replica model of his 1991 Pontiac.

COMPLETE SET (50) 4.00 8.00
COMPLETE FACT.SET (50) 5.00 10.00
WAX BOX 5.00 12.00
1 Richard Petty .25 .60
2 Richard Petty's Car .10 .25
3 Richard Petty's Car .10 .25
4 Richard Petty w Car .25 .60
5 Richard Petty's Car .10 .25
6 Richard Petty w Car .25 .60
7 Richard Petty's Car .10 .25
8 Richard Petty w Car .25 .60
9 Richard Petty .25 .60
10 Richard Petty in Pits .25 .60
11 Richard Petty w Car .25 .60
12 Richard Petty's Car .10 .25
13 Richard Petty's Car .10 .25
14 Richard Petty .25 .60
15 Richard Petty's Car .10 .25
16 Richard Petty's Car .10 .25
17 Richard Petty's Car .10 .25
18 Richard Petty .25 .60
19 Richard Petty .25 .60
20 Richard Petty's Car .10 .25
21 Richard Petty w Car .25 .60
22 Richard Petty Earn D.Waltrip Cars .50 1.25
23 Richard Petty in Pits .25 .60
24 Richard Petty's Car .10 .25
25 Richard Petty's Car .10 .25
26 Richard Petty's Car .10 .25
27 Richard Petty .25 .60
28 Richard Petty's Car .10 .25
29 Richard Petty .25 .60
30 Richard Petty in Pits .25 .60
31 Richard Petty's Car .10 .25
32 Richard Petty w Car .25 .60
33 Richard Petty in Pits .25 .60
34 Richard Petty's Car .10 .25
35 Richard Petty's Car .10 .25
36 Richard Petty .25 .60
37 Richard Petty w Car .25 .60
38 Richard Petty in Pits .25 .60
39 Richard Petty .25 .60
40 Richard Petty's Car .10 .25
41 Richard Petty w Car .25 .60
42 Richard Petty in Pits .25 .60
43 Richard Petty .25 .60
44 Richard Petty .25 .60
45 Richard Petty's Car .10 .25
46 Richard Petty .25 .60
47 Richard Petty .25 .60
48 Richard Petty .25 .60
49 Richard Petty w Car .25 .60
50 Richard Petty w Car .25 .60

1992 Traks

In addition to a 200-card factory set, the 1992 Traks set was distributed in 12-card packs with 30 packs per box. The set features the top Busch and Winston Cup drivers along with owners and other racing team members. Variations on several cards exist with the versions differing according to either pack or factory set distribution. Traks also included randomly packed autographed insert cards.

COMPLETE SET (200) 8.00 20.00
COMP.FACT.SET (200) 10.00 25.00
1 Rick Mast .05 .15
2 Rusty Wallace .50 1.25
3 Dale Earnhardt 1.25 3.00
4 Ernie Irvan .10 .30
5 Ricky Rudd .20 .50
6 Mark Martin .50 1.25
7 Alan Kulwicki .20 .50
8 Rick Wilson .05 .15
9 Phil Parsons .05 .15
10 Ricky Craven RC .02 .10
11 Bobby Labonte .40 1.00
12 Hut Stricklin .05 .15
13 Sam Bass .02 .10
14 Bobby Allison .10 .30
15 R.Wallace/Mike/Kenny .25 .60
16 Race Stoppers .02 .10
17 Darrell Waltrip .10 .30
18 Dale Jarrett .40 1.00
19 Cale Yarborough .10 .30
20 Doyle Ford .02 .10
21 Morgan Shepherd .05 .15
22 Sterling Marlin .25 .60
23 Kenny Wallace Barry Dodson .02 .10
24 Kenny Wallace .05 .15
25 Ken Schrader .05 .15
26 Brett Bodine .05 .15
27 Ward Burton .10 .30
28 Davey Allison .30 .75
29A Andy Hillenburg RC .05 .15
29B Andy Hillenburg RC .05 .15
30 Michael Waltrip .10 .30
31 Steve Grissom .05 .15
32 Dale Jarrett .40 1.00
33 Harry Gant .10 .30
34 Todd Bodine .05 .15
35 Robert Yates .02 .10
36 Kenny Wallace .05 .15
37 Roger Penske .02 .10
38 Mark Martin .50 1.25
39 Don Miller .02 .10
40 Chany Sabates Felix Sabates .02 .10
41 Troy Beebe .02 .10
42 Kyle Petty .10 .30
43 Richard Petty .30 .75
44 Bobby Labonte .40 1.00
45 Butch Miller .05 .15
46 Chuck Rider .02 .10
47 Dale Inman .02 .10
48 Jack Sprague RC .05 .15
49 Doug Richert .02 .10
50 Jimmy Makar .02 .10
51 Mike McLaughlin .05 .15
52 Jimmy Means .05 .15
53 Waddell Wilson .02 .10
54 Richard Childress .10 .30
55 Ted Musgrave .05 .15
56 Darrell Waltrip .10 .30
57 Kirk Shelmerdine .02 .10
58 Larry McClure .02 .10
59 Robert Pressley .05 .15
60 Dale Earnhardt in Pits .30 .75
61 Dick Trickle .05 .15
62 Leonard Wood .02 .10
63 Chuck Bown .05 .15
64 Elmo Langley .02 .10
65 Barry Dodson .02 .10
66 Chad Little .10 .30
67 Elton Sawyer .05 .15
68 Ed McClure .02 .10
69A Kyle Petty .10 .30
69B Kyle Petty .10 .30
69C Kyle Petty .10 .30
70 Tony Glover .02 .10
71 Dave Marcis .10 .30
72A R.Wallace/Dickerson WL .25 .60
72B R.Wallace/Dickerson BL .25 .60
73 Alan Kulwicki .20 .50
74 Jimmy Fennig .02 .10
75 Michael Waltrip .10 .30
76 Ken Wilson .05 .15
77 David Smith .02 .10
78 Junior Johnson .05 .15
79 Dave Rezendes .05 .15
80 Bruce Roney .02 .10
81 Eddie Lanier .02 .10
82 Mike Beam .02 .10
83 Walter Bud Moore .02 .10
84 Terry Labonte .25 .60
85 Richard Petty .30 .75
86 Donnie Wingo .02 .10
87 Joe Nemechek .05 .15
88 Greg Moore .02 .10
89 Doug Williams .02 .10
90 Jimmy Martin .02 .10
91 Richard Broome .02 .10
92 H.Stricklin/B.Allison .05 .15
93 Hank Jones .02 .10
94 Terry Labonte .25 .60
95 Will Lind .02 .10
96 Tom Peck .05 .15
97 Morgan Shepherd .05 .15
98 Jimmy Spencer .05 .15
99 Jeff Burton .20 .50
100 Max Helton .02 .10
101 Jeff Gordon 1.50 4.00
102 Keith Almond .02 .10
103 Dale Earnhardt 1.25 3.00
104 Ernie Irvan .10 .30
105 Greg Wilson .02 .10
106 Tommy Houston .05 .15
107 Ed Whitaker .02 .10
108 David Green .05 .15
109 Robin Pemberton .02 .10
110 Mike Colyer .02 .10
111 Jerry McClure .02 .10
112 Cecil Gordon .02 .10
113A Jimmy Johnson .02 .10
113B Jimmy Johnson .02 .10
114 Neil Bonnett .10 .30
115 Steve Hmiel .02 .10
116 Charles Farmer .02 .10
117 Eddie Jones .02 .10
118 M.Stavola/B.Stavola .02 .10
119 Leo Jackson .02 .10
120 Dick Moroso .02 .10
121 Eddie Wood .02 .10
122 Len Wood .02 .10
123 Lou LaRosa .02 .10
124A Rusty Wallace .50 1.25
124B Rusty Wallace .50 1.25
125 Bobby Hillin .05 .15
126 Ned Jarrett .05 .15
127 Ken Schrader .05 .15
128 Travis Carter .02 .10
129 Frank Edwards .02 .10
130 Tom Higgins Steve Waid .02 .10
131 Jim Phillips Winston Kelley Dick Brooks .02 .10
132 John Ervin .02 .10
133A Harry Gant .10 .30
133B Harry Gant .10 .30
133C Harry Gant .10 .30
134 Allen Bestwick .02 .10
135 Barney Hall .02 .10
136 R.Rudd/R.hendrick .10 .30
137 Eli Gold .02 .10
138 Joe Hendrick (Papa) .02 .10

139 John Wilson .02 .10
140 Tim Brewer .02 .10
141 George Bradshaw .02 .10
142 Kyle Petty .10 .30
143 Robbie Loomis .05 .15
144 Benny Parsons .05 .15
145 Danny Myers .02 .10
146 H.Gant/E.Whitaker .10 .30
147 Jeff Hammond .02 .10
148 Donnie Richeson .02 .10
149 Bill Brodrick .02 .10
150 Robert Black .02 .10
151 Carl Hill .02 .10
152 Mike Wallace .05 .15
153 Mark Garrow .02 .10
154 Lynda Petty .02 .10
155A Musgrave/Ulrich ERR .02 .10
155B Musgrave/Ulrich COR .02 .10
156 Davey Allison .50 1.25
157 Jimmy Cox .02 .10
158 Clyde Booth .02 .10
159 Bob Bilby .02 .10
160 Marlin Wright .02 .10
161 Gary Nelson .02 .10
162 Jake Elder .02 .10
163 Jeff Hensley .02 .10
164 Bill Davis .02 .10
165 Tracy Leslie .05 .15
166 Tommy Ellis .02 .10
167 Sterling Marlin .25 .60
168 Tony Eury .40 1.00
169 Teddy McClure .02 .10
170 Steve Bird .02 .10
171A Paul Andrews .02 .10
171B Paul Andrews .02 .10
172 Brad Parrott .02 .10
173A Eddie Dickerson .02 .10
173B Eddie Dickerson .02 .10
174 Andy Petree .02 .10
175 Dale Earnhardt w/Crew .40 1.00
176A Shelton Pittman .02 .10
176B Shelton Pittman .02 .10
177 R.Pearson/R.Pressley .02 .10
178 Ed Berrier .02 .10
179A Rusty Wallace WL .50 1.25
179B Rusty Wallace BL .50 1.25
180 Richard Yates .02 .10
181 S.Welliver/F.Cicci .02 .10
182 Clyde McLeod .02 .10
183 A.G. Dillard .05 .15
184 Larry McReynolds .02 .10
185 Joey Knuckles .02 .10
186 Rodney Combs .05 .15
187 Rick Hendrick .02 .10
188 Jerry Punch .02 .10
189 Tim Morgan .02 .10
190 Dale Earnhardt 1.25 3.00
191 S.Marlin/D.Waltrip Crash .05 .15
192 Safe and Sure CL .02 .10
193 Dale Earnhardt's Car CL .10 .30
194 Rick Mast's Car CL .02 .10
195 Follow the Signs CL .02 .10
196 Kyle Petty's Car CL .05 .15
197 Thread the Needle CL .02 .10
198 Darrell Waltrip's Car CL .05 .15
199 Rick Wilson's Car CL .02 .10
200 Richard Petty/Lynda .25 .60
P1 Benny Parsons Prototype 1.50 4.00
P2 Kyle Petty Prototype 2.00 5.00
P3 Richard Petty Prototype 8.00 20.00
P4 Rusty Wallace Prototype 4.00 10.00

1992 Traks Autographs

This set was distributed randomly throughout 1992 Traks packs. A maximum of 5000 cards were signed by each driver and many cards can be found, as well, without signatures. The Ricky Rudd card is considered a short print signed due to the seemingly large number of available copies unsigned. Unsigned cards typically sell for a fraction of autographed issues. The set is highlighted by a dual signed Dale Earnhardt and Richard Petty card (number A1).

COMPLETE SET (10) 250.00 400.00
A1 D.Earnhardt/R.Petty 150.00 300.00
A2 Rusty Wallace 20.00 50.00
A3 Harry Gant 6.00 15.00
A4 Ernie Irvan 8.00 20.00
A5 Ricky Rudd SP 12.50 30.00
A6 Kyle Petty 8.00 20.00
A7 Jeff Gordon 30.00 60.00
A8 Bobby Labonte 12.00 30.00
A9 Benny Parsons 15.00 40.00
NNO Cover Card 4.00 10.00

1992 Traks Alliance Robert Pressley

The 1992 Traks Alliance Racing Team Robert Pressley set is very similar to the 1993-94 Alliance Robert Pressley and Dennis Setzer issues. The Traks version includes the Traks logo on the cardfronts along with a black border.

COMPLETE SET (12) 4.00 8.00
1 Cover .25 .60
Checklist Card
2 Robert Pressley .25 .60
3 Robert Pressley's Transporter .25 .60
4 Robert Pressley's Transporter .25 .60
5 Robert Pressley's Cars .25 .60
6 Robert Pressley .60 1.50
7 Robert Pressley's Car .25 .60
8 Robert Pressley's Car .25 .60
9 Robert Pressley's Pit Crew .25 .60
10 Robert Pressley .60 1.50
11 Ricky Pearson .25 .60
12 Robert Pressley's Transporter .25 .60

1992 Traks ASA

To commemorate the 25th anniversary of the American Speed Association, Traks released a special 50-card boxed set featuring many past greats of the ASA circuit as well as then current drivers.

COMPLETE SET (51) 2.00 5.00
1 Josh DuVall .07 .20
2 Glenn Allen Jr. .07 .20
3 Mike Eddy Crew .07 .20
4 Mike Eddy .07 .20
5 Pat Schauer .07 .20
6 Tim Fedewa .10 .30
7 Tom Jones .07 .20
8 Tony Raines .07 .20
9 Jay Sauter .07 .20
10 Jeff Neal .07 .20
11 Terry Baldry .07 .20
12 Dennis Lampman .07 .20
13 Rusty Wallace w/car .40 1.00
14 Johnny Benson Jr. .20 .50
15 Bob Senneker Crew .07 .20
16 Bob Senneker .07 .20
17 Dean South .07 .20
18 John Wilson .07 .20
19 Bruce VanderLaan .07 .20
20 Dave Jackson .07 .20
21 Chris Weiss .07 .20
22 Tim Fedewa .10 .30
23 Butch Fedewa .07 .20
24 Gary St.Amant .07 .20
25 Bud St. Amant .07 .20
26 Dave Jackson .07 .20
27 Glenn Allen Sr. .07 .20
28 Tom Harrington Car .07 .20
29 Dennis Vogel Car .07 .20
30 Field of Dreams .07 .20
31 Mario Caputo (Chip) .07 .20
32 Kenny Wallace .10 .30
33 Dick Trickle .10 .30
34 Butch Miller .07 .20
35 Scott Hansen .07 .20
36 Alan Kulwicki w/Car .30 .75
37 Jim Sauter Car .07 .20
38 Bobby Allison w/car .15 .40
39 Davey Allison w/car .40 1.00
40 Jimmy Fennig .07 .20
41 Mark Martin .40 1.25
42 Darrell Waltrip w/car. .07 .20
43 Harold Fair Sr. .07 .20
44 Kenny Adams .07 .20
45 Kent Stauffer .07 .20
46 Dave Taylor .07 .20
47 Terry Baker .07 .20
48 Howie Lettow .07 .20
49 Harold Alan Fair Jr. .07 .20
50 Ted Musgrave .10 .30
NNO Souvenir Order Form Card .07 .20

1992 Traks Baby Ruth Jeff Gordon

For the first of two years, Traks released a special set featuring the Baby Ruth sponsored Busch Series race team in 1992 with Jeff Gordon as the focus. Gordon is featured on two cards with the others devoted to his car and crew.

COMPLETE SET (4) 4.00 10.00
1 Jeff Gordon 2.00 4.00
2 Jeff Gordon 2.00 4.00
3 Jeff Gordon's Car .50 1.00
4 Jeff Gordon's Crew .50 1.00

1992 Traks Country Star Racing

This 13-card set features Dick Trickle and the number 2 Country Star sponsored car he drove on the Busch Grand National circuit. The set was released both as a subset to the Country Star Collection set and as an individual set.

COMPLETE SET (13) 2.40 6.00
1 Dick Trickle .30 .75
2 Dick Trickle .30 .75
3 Ted Conder .20 .50
4 Dick Trickle .30 .75
Ken Schrader
5 Mark Connolly .20 .50
6 Dick Trickle .30 .75
7 Danny Dias .20 .50
8 Dick Trickle .30 .75
9 Tucker .20 .50
Benton
Kloiber
Timmer.
Connolly
R.Richert
10 Dick Trickle .30 .75
11 Brian Grinstead .20 .50
12 Ad Card .20 .50
NNO Checklist Card .20 .50

1992 Traks Goody's

Drivers of the 1992 Goody's 300 are featured on this 25-card Traks release. The set was distributed in its own box through hobby outlets and includes most of the top drivers of 1992.

COMPLETE SET (25) 10.00 25.00
1 Bobby Labonte .75 2.00
2 Kenny Wallace .30 .75
3 Robert Pressley .20 .50
4 Chuck Bown .20 .50
5 Jimmy Hensley .20 .50
6 Todd Bodine .20 .50
7 Tommy Houston .20 .50
8 Steve Grissom .20 .50
9 Jeff Gordon 5.00 12.00
10 Jeff Burton .40 1.00
11 David Green .60 1.50
12 Tracy Leslie .20 .50
13 Butch Miller .20 .50
14 Dave Rezendes .20 .50
15 Ward Burton .30 .75
16 Ed Berrier .20 .50
17 Harry Gant .25 .60
18 Dale Jarrett .40 1.00
19 Dale Earnhardt 2.50 6.00
20 Ernie Irvan .50 1.25
21 Davey Allison .50 1.25
22 Morgan Shepherd .30 .75
23 Michael Waltrip .40 1.00
24 Ken Schrader .20 .50
25 Richard Petty 1.00 2.50

1992 Traks Kodak Ernie Irvan

The Kodak Film Racing team and Ernie Irvan were the focus of this 25-card Traks release. The cards were distributed in specially marked 2-packs of Kodak Gold Plus film, as well as in complete factory sets. Five cards (numbers 1,6,11,16,21,25) were also produced with gold foil embossing on the card fronts for distribution in the factory sets. An offer for uncut press sheets featuring the five gold cards was also included. Many of the cards are very similar to ones included in the Ernie Irvan team set also issued in 1992.

COMPLETE SET (25) 15.00 25.00
1A Ernie Irvan 1.25 2.50
R.Petty
1B Ernie Irvan 2.00 4.00
R.Petty Gold
2 Teddy McClure .50 1.00
3 Tim Morgan .50 1.00
4 Robert Larkins .50 1.00
5 Shelton Pittman .50 1.00
6A Ernie Irvan 1.25 2.50
6B Ernie Irvan Gold 2.00 4.00
7 Larry McClure .50 1.00
8 Jerry McClure .50 1.00
9 Tony Glover .50 1.00
10 Clint Ballard .50 1.00
11A Ernie Irvan's Car .50 1.00
11B Ernie Irvan's Car Gold 1.00 2.00
12 Jerry Puckett .50 1.00
13 Ernie Irvan's Car .50 1.00
14 Zeke Lester .50 1.00
15 Randall Helbert .50 1.00
16A Ernie Irvan 1.25 2.50
16B Ernie Irvan Gold 2.00 4.00
17 Bill Marsh .50 1.00
18 Johnny Townsend .50 1.00
19 McClure Bros. .50 1.00
20 Ernie Irvan w .50 1.00
Crew
21A Ernie Irvan in Pits 1.25 2.50
21B Ernie Irvan in Pits Gold 2.00 4.00
22 George Gardner .50 1.00
23 Power Builders .50 1.00
24 Ed McClure .50 1.00
25 Ernie Irvan w/Car CL .50 1.00

1992 Traks Mom-n-Pop's Ham Dale Earnhardt

Produced by Traks, Mom-n-Pop's distributed this set in its country ham products in 1992. The cards were cello packed with one card and one cover card per pack. Dale Earnhardt is the featured driver due to Mom-n-Pop's associate sponsorship of the RCR racing team. A special "Pig" card (5000 made) was produced as well and randomly inserted in packs. The card was printed with a gold foil border and features a ghosted holographic image of Earnhardt's signature to prevent counterfeiting. Mom-n-Pop's Ham Christmas packaging distributed in North and South Carolina included the special card. A numbered (of 20,000) uncut sheet version of the 6-cards was also produced and offered through packs of 1993 Wheels Mom-n-Pop's cards.

COMPLETE SET (6) 10.00 20.00
1 Dale Earnhardt w/Crew 2.00 4.00
2 Dale Earnhardt's Car 2.00 4.00
3 Dale Earnhardt 2.00 4.00
R.Childress
4 Dale Earnhardt in Pits 2.00 4.00
5 Dale Earnhardt 2.00 4.00
6 Dale Earnhardt 2.00 4.00
NNO Dale Earnhardt w/Pig 12.00 30.00

1992 Traks Benny Parsons

Benny Parsons and his career in racing is the focus of this 50-card release distributed to the hobby in 1992. 25,000 sets were printed and individually serial numbered with a certificate included with each boxed set.

COMP. FACT SET (50) 2.00 5.00
COMMON CARD (1-50) .07 .20

1992 Traks Racing Machines

Traks produced the Racing Machines series to highlight the cars, rigs and race action of NASCAR racing. The 100-card set was distributed in 12-card packs. Cases were numbered up to a maximum of 2500 10-box cases with 36 packs per box. A special 20-card bonus set was also inserted two cards per pack as well as one set per Racing Machines factory set. Four prototype cards were issued for the release, but are not considered part of the complete set.

COMPLETE SET (100) 8.00 20.00
COMP.FACT.SET (120) 10.00 25.00
WAX BOX 10.00 25.00
1 Dale Earnhardt's Transp. .50 1.25
2 Rusty Wallace's Car .30 .75
3 Dale Earnhardt's Car .60 1.50
4 Ernie Irvan's Car .07 .20
5 R.Rudd/K.Schrader Cars .07 .20
6 Mark Martin's Car .30 .75
7 Alan Kulwicki in Pits .07 .20
8 Dick Trickle's Car .02 .10
9 D.Earn/Rudd/Gant Cars .60 1.50
10 Ernie Irvan's Transp. .07 .20
11 Rick Mast's Car .02 .10
12 Hut Stricklin's Car .02 .10
13 Kyle Petty's Car .07 .20
14 Sterling Marlin's Car .07 .20
15 Geoff Bodine's Transp. .02 .10
16 Wally Dallenbach Jr.'s Car .02 .10
17 Darrell Waltrip in Pits .07 .20
18 Richard Petty's Transp. .07 .20
19 Richard Petty in Pits .07 .20
20 Ken Schrader's Transp. .02 .10
21 Morgan Shepherd in Pits .02 .10
22 Sterling Marlin's Transp. .07 .20
23 Darrell Waltrip's Transp. .07 .20
24 Rusty Wallace w/truck .40 1.00
25 Ken Schrader's Car .02 .10
26 Bobby Hamilton's Transp. .02 .10
27 Round and Round .02 .10
28 Davey Allison's Car .15 .40
29 Harry Gant's Transp. .02 .10
30 Michael Waltrip's Car
31 Steve Grissom's Car .02 .10
32 Steve Grissom's Car .02 .10
33 Harry Gant in Pits .02 .10
34 D.Earnhardt/D.Allison Cars .75 2.00
35 Davey Allison's Transp. .15 .40
36 Michael Waltrip's Car
37 Darrell Waltrip's Car .07 .20
38 Hut Stricklin In Pits UER .02 .10
40 J.Gordon/D.Allison Cars .75 2.00
41 Sterling Marlin in Pits .07 .20
42 Kyle Petty's Car .07 .20
43 Richard Petty's Car .07 .20
44 Dale Earnhardt Race Action .60 1.50
45 Sterling Marlin in Pits .07 .20
46 Kyle Petty's Transp. .07 .20
47 Rick Mast's Car .02 .10
48 Ken Schrader in Pits .02 .10
49 Morgan Shepherd's Trans. .02 .10
50 Brett Bodine w/car .07 .20
51 Alan Kulwicki's Car .07 .20
52 Wally Dallenbach Jr. in Pits .02 .10
53 Mark Martin's Transp. .20 .50
54 Dale Earnhardt in Pits .60 1.50
55 Richard Petty's Transp. .07 .20
56 Pre-Race Pageantry .02 .10
57 Bobby Labonte in Pits .20 .50
58 Rusty Wallace/R.Rudd Cars .20 .50
59 Robert Pressley's Car .02 .10
60 H.Gant/B.Labonte Cars .20 .50
61 Rick Mast's Transp. .02 .10
62 Lightning Fast .02 .10
63 Chuck Bown's Car .02 .10
64 Rusty Wallace's Motorhome .20 .50
65 Dav.Allison/M.Waltrip Cars .15 .40
66 Ted Musgrave's Transp. .02 .10
67 Bobby Hamilton in Pits .02 .10
68 Bobby Hamilton's Car .02 .10
69 Ernie Irvan in Pits .07 .20
70 Lake Speed Crash .02 .10
71 Dave Marcis' Car .07 .20
72 Michael Waltrip's Transp.
73 Mark Martin in Pits .30 .75
74 Sterling Marlin's Transp. .07 .20
75 H.Gant/B.Bodine Cars .02 .10
76 Mark Martin in Pits .30 .75
77 Alan Kulwicki's Transp. .07 .20
78 Rusty Wallace in Pits .30 .75
79 Dick Trickle's Transp. .02 .10
80 Richard Petty Action .07 .20
81 Rusty Wallace's Transp. .20 .50
82 Terry Labonte w/car .30 .75
83 Michael Waltrip's Car
84 Dale Earnhardt Race Action .60 1.50
85 Jimmy Hensley's Transp. .02 .10
86 Terry Labonte's Transp. .20 .50
87 Kyle Petty's Car .07 .20
88 Wally Dallenbach Jr.'s Trans. .02 .10
89 Dale Earnhardt in Pits .60 1.50
90 Jimmy Hensley's Car .02 .10
91 D.Earnhardt/Houston Cars .50 1.25
92 S.Marlin/R.Rudd Cars .07 .20
93 Dav.Allison/Shepherd Cars .15 .40
94 Terry Labonte Crash .20 .50
95 Ernie Irvan in Pits .07 .20
96 Derrike Cope's Transp. .02 .10
97 Richard Petty in Pits CL .07 .20
98 B.Lab/T.Lab/R.Wll/Irv Cars CL .20 .50
99 Davey Allison's Car CL .15 .40
100 D.Earnhardt/R.Petty Cars CL .50 1.25
P1 D.Earnhardt's Trans. Promo 4.00 10.00
P26 B.Hamilton's Trans. Promo 1.00 2.50
P51 A.Kulwicki's Car Promo 2.00 5.00
P76 M.Martin in Pits Promo 2.50 6.00

1992 Traks Racing Machines Bonus

Inserted two per pack in 1992 Traks Racing Machines packs and one complete set per regular factory set, the cards feature top drivers and cars in the style of regular issue 1992 Traks cards.

COMPLETE SET (20) 2.50 5.00
1B Charlotte Under Lights .01 .05
2B Barry Dodson .01 .05
3B Dale Earnhardt's Car .60 1.50
4B Jimmy Spencer .02 .10
5B Gary DeHart .01 .05
6B Steve Loyd .01 .05
7B Harry Gant MAC Team .07 .20
8B Dick Trickle .02 .10
9B Bobby Dotter's Car .01 .05
10B Ricky Craven .20 .50
11B Junior Johnson .02 .10
12B Joe Nemechek w/car .02 .10
13B Terry Labonte w/car .30 .75
14B Kenny Wallace .02 .10
15B Jimmy Hensley .02 .10
16B M.Martin .30 .75
Dallenbach Jr. Cars
17B Mike Wallace .02 .10
18B Jeff Burton .20 .50
Ward Burton
19B Tom Peck w/car .02 .10
20B Jeff Gordon Baby Boomer 2.00 4.00

1992 Traks Team Sets

This 200-card release was actually distributed as eight separate 25-card team sets. Cards from the eight sets were consecutively numbered though to form a complete set of 200. Each team set was sold in a cardboard rack-style pack shaped like that team's race car.

COMPLETE SET (200) 20.00 40.00
COMPLETE EARNHARDT (25) 5.00 10.00
COMPLETE D.ALLISON (25) 3.00 6.00
COMPLETE K.PETTY (25) 2.50 5.00
COMPLETE M.WALTRIP (25) 2.50 5.00
COMPLETE IRVAN (25) 2.50 5.00
COMPLETE D.WALTRIP (25) 2.50 5.00
COMPLETE STRICKLIN (25) 2.00 5.00
COMPLETE R.PETTY (25) 2.50 5.00
1 Dale Earnhardt's Car .20 .50
2 Dale Earnhardt .75 2.00
3 D.Earnhardt/Dav.Allison Cars .20 .50
4 Dale Earnhardt's Car .20 .50
5 Kirk Shelmerdine .10 .30
6 David Smith .10 .30
7 Will Lind .10 .30
8 Danny Myers .10 .30
9 Hank Jones .10 .30
10 Eddie Lanier .10 .30
11 Danny Lawrence .10 .30
12 Cecil Gordon .10 .30
13 Dale Earnhardt/Childress .20 .50
14 Richard Childress .10 .30
15 Dale Earnhardt w/crew .20 .50
16 Dale Earnhardt's Cars .75 2.00
17 Dale Earnhardt .75 2.00
18 Dale Earnhardt .75 2.00
19 Dale Earnhardt's Car .20 .50
20 Dale Earnhardt's Car .20 .50
21 Dale Earnhardt .75 2.00
22 Dale Earnhardt's Planes .20 .50
23 Dale Earnhardt .75 2.00
24 Dale Earnhardt's Cars .20 .50
25 Dale Earnhardt's Car CL .20 .50
26 Davey Allison .40 1.00
27 Robert Yates .10 .30
28 Davey Allison's Car .20 .50
29 Davey Allison in Pits .20 .50
30 Ryan Pemberton .10 .30
31 Richard Yates .10 .30
32 Larry McReynolds .10 .30
33 Gary Beveridge .10 .30
34 Joey Knuckles .10 .30
35 Tommy Allison .10 .30
36 Mike Bumgarner .10 .30
37 Terry Throneburg .10 .30
38 Eric Horn .10 .30
39 Gil Kerley .10 .30
40 Raymond Fox III .10 .30
41 Norman Koshimizu .10 .30
42 Davey Allison .40 1.00
43 Motor Minds .10 .30
44 Davey Allison .40 1.00
45 James Lewter .10 .30
46 Vernon Hubbard .10 .30
47 Devin Barbee .10 .30
48 Doug Yates .10 .30
49 Davey Allison/McReyn/Yates .40 1.00
50 Davey Allison CL .40 1.00
51 Kyle Petty .20 .50
52 Felix Sabates .10 .30
53 Felix Sabates .10 .30
54 Gary Nelson .10 .30
55 Kyle Petty .20 .50
56 John Wilson .10 .30
57 Larry Barnes Jr. .10 .30
58 Jerry Windell .10 .30
59 Barry Cook .10 .30
60 Scott Palmer .10 .30
61 Charles Lane .10 .30
62 Richard Bostick .10 .30
63 Earl Ramey/Doug Hess .10 .30
64 Scott Grant/Jerry Brady .10 .30
65 Jim Sutton .10 .30
66 Steve Knipe .10 .30
67 Dick Seidenspinner .10 .30
68 Donnie Richeson .10 .30
69 Jim Long .10 .30
70 Mike Ford .10 .30
71 Len Sherrill .10 .30
72 Glenn Funderburke .10 .30
73 Rick Brakefield .10 .30
74 Kyle Petty .20 .50
75 Kyle Petty's Car CL .10 .30
76 Michael Waltrip .20 .50
77 Michael Waltrip/C.Rider .10 .30
78 Chuck Rider .10 .30
79 Michael Waltrip's Car .10 .30
80 Lowrance Harry .10 .30
81 Richmond Gage .10 .30
82 Michael Waltrip in Pits .10 .30
83 Bill Ingle .10 .30
84 Engine Room .10 .30
85 Mark Cronquist .10 .30
86 Mike Windsor/Jeff Rumple .10 .30
87 Jon Leibensperger .10 .30
88 Jeff Dixon/Paul Chencutt
Bryan Smith .10 .30
89 Jeff Dixon .10 .30
90 Assembly Room .10 .30
91 Barry Swift .10 .30
92 Ray Hall .10 .30
93 Tim Lancaster .10 .30
94 Tommy Rigsbee .10 .30
95 Michael Waltrip .20 .50
96 Ronnie Silver .10 .30
97 Jeff Chandler .10 .30
98 BGN Team .10 .30
99 Michael Waltrip's Transporter .10 .30
100 Michael Waltrip's Car CL .10 .30
101 Earnhardt/D.Allison
Irvan/B.Lab/K.Petty Cars .20 .50
102 Ernie Irvan's Car .10 .30
103 Tim Morgan .10 .30
104 Larry McClure .10 .30
105 Teddy McClure .10 .30
106 Ed McClure .10 .30
107 Shelton Pittman .10 .30
108 Ernie Irvan .30 .75
109 Ernie Irvan's Car .10 .30
110 Johnny Townsend .10 .30
111 Tony Glover .10 .30
112 Jerry McClure .10 .30
113 Zeke Lester .10 .30
114 Bill Marsh .10 .30
115 Randall Helbert .10 .30
116 Clint Ballard .10 .30
117 Robert Latonis .10 .30
118 George Gardner .10 .30
119 Ernie Irvan .30 .75
120 Morgan/McClure Brothers .10 .30
121 Ernie Irvan's Car .10 .30
122 Power Builders .10 .30
123 Jerry Puckett .10 .30
124 Ernie Irvan w/crew .30 .75
125 Ernie Irvan w/car CL .30 .75
126 Western Auto Store .10 .30
127 Darrell Waltrip .20 .50
128 Joe Carver Sr. .10 .30
129 Jeff Hammond .10 .30
130 Darrell Waltrip's Car .10 .30
131 Bobby Waltrip .10 .30
132 Clifford Smith .10 .30
133 Keith Sawyer .10 .30
134 Doug Richert .10 .30
135 Jake Elder .10 .30
136 Carolyn Waltrip .10 .30
137 Ronnie Hoover .10 .30
138 Darrell Waltrip in Pits .10 .30
139 Billy Hodges .10 .30
140 Scott Mercer/David Menear .10 .30
141 Lisa Sigmon .10 .30
142 Darrell Waltrip .20 .50
143 Jeff Hammond .10 .30
144 Bob Sutton .10 .30
145 Gregg Buchanan .10 .30
146 Tom McCrimmon .10 .30
147 Robbie Hancock/Greg Carpenter .10 .30
148 Glen Skillman/Joe Parlato .10 .30
149 Ron McLeod/Danny Shull .10 .30
150 Darrell Waltrip's Transporter CL .10 .30
151 Hut Stricklin .10 .30
152 Hut Stricklin .20 .50
153 Hut Stricklin's Car .10 .30
154 Hut Stricklin in Pits .10 .30
155 Hut Stricklin's Trans
Mike Culbertson .10 .30
156 Keith Armond .10 .30
157 Jimmy Fennig .10 .30
158 Carolyn Freeman .10 .30
159 Brad Parrott .10 .30
160 Mike Basinger .10 .30
161 Glen Bobo .10 .30

162 Chris Meade .10 .30
163 Mike Boling .10 .30
164 Mike Culbertson .10 .30
165 Tom Bagen .10 .30
166 Tracie Honeycutt/Lou Ann Kropp.10 .30
167 Kenny Freeman/Glen Bobo .10 .30
168 Horsepower .10 .30
169 C.B.Lee/Mike Basinger .10 .30
170 Bobby Allison's Car .10 .30
171 Bob Bilby .10 .30
172 Nathan Sams .10 .30
173 Frank Plessinger .10 .30
174 Tom Kincaid .10 .30
175 Bobby Allison CL .20 .50
176 Richard Petty .30 .75
177 Mike Cheek .10 .30
178 Roger Pierce .10 .30
179 Johnny Cline/Jeff Chamberlain .10 .30
180 Wade Thornburg/Buddy Pugh/Stafford Wood/Jim.Walker .10 .30
181 Dale Inman .10 .30
182 Ken Perkins .10 .30
183 Petty Power .10 .30
184 Richard Petty w/crew .30 .75
185 Richard Petty w/crew .30 .75
186 Robbie Loomis .20 .50
187 Martha Bonkemeyer .10 .30
188 Kerry Lawrence .10 .30
189 From the Ground Up .10 .30
190 Wade Thornburg .10 .30
191 Stafford Wood .10 .30
192 Lynda Petty .10 .30
193 Bob Riffle .10 .30
194 David Walker .10 .30
195 R.Petty/Louise Loftin .30 .75
196 Randy Cox .10 .30
197 Lance Hill .10 .30
198 Jimmy Martin .10 .30
199 Richie Barsz .10 .30
200 Richard Petty King CL .30 .75

1993 Traks

The 1993 Traks set was released in 12-card packs with 30 packs per box. The set is divided into two series, although released together in packs. The series two Silver cards (last 50-cards) were much more difficult to pull from packs than series one, thus the difference in value. 1993 marked the first year of the now traditional Traks First Run parallel issue set. The 1-150 First Runs were packaged two cards per pack.

COMPLETE SET (200) 12.50 30.00
COMP.SET w/o SP's (150) 5.00 12.00
COMP.SILVER SET (50) 12.50 25.00
WAX BOX SERIES 1 15.00 30.00
UNCUT SILVER SHEET 15.00 30.00
1 Rick Mast's Car .02 .10
2 Rusty Wallace Win .30 .75
3 Terry Labonte's Car .15 .40
4 Ernie Irvan's Car .07 .20
5 Neil Bonnett .25 .60
6 Mark Martin .50 1.50
7 Alan Kulwicki .25 .60
8 Sterling Marlin's Car .07 .20
9 Mike Wallace .07 .20
10 Tommy Allison .02 .10
11 Mike Beam .02 .10
12 Jimmy Spencer .07 .20
13 Dick Trickle .07 .20
14 Terry Labonte .30 .75
15 Four Wide .02 .10
16 Wally Dallenbach, Jr. .07 .20
17 Benny Parsons .07 .20
18 Dale Jarrett's Car .15 .40
19 Tom Peck .07 .20
20 Bobby Hamilton's Car .02 .10
21 Morgan Shepherd .07 .20
22 Bobby Labonte .50 1.25
23 Troy Selburg .02 .10
24 Jeff Gordon's Car .50 1.25
25 Rusty Wallace's Car CL .15 .40
26 Brett Bodine .07 .20
27 Alan Kulwicki Early Ride .15 .40
28 Davey Allison .40 1.00
29 Buddy Parrott .02 .10
30 Michael Waltrip .15 .40
31 Steve Grissom's Car .02 .10
32 M.Martin/K.Schrader Cars .15 .40
33 Harry Gant .15 .40
34 Todd Bodine's Car .02 .10
35 Shawna Robinson .40 1.00
36 Kenny Bernstein .07 .20
37 Jeff Burton .25 .60
38 Len Wood .02 .10
39 Jeff Gordon CRC 1.00 2.50
40 Bobby Hillin .07 .20
41 Phil Parsons' Car .02 .10
42 Ward Burton .15 .40
43 Goodwrench 500 .02 .10
44 Rick Wilson .07 .20
45 Joe Nemechek .07 .20
46 Al Unser Jr.'s Car .15 .40
47 Ken Schrader .07 .20
48 Pete Wright .02 .10
49 Robert Yates .02 .10
50 Checklist #2/Dale Inman .02 .10
51 Steve Hmiel .02 .10
52 Jimmy Means's Car .02 .10
53 Bruce Roney .02 .10
54 Tim Fedewa RC .07 .20
55 Ted Musgrave .07 .20
56 Mark Martin's Car .15 .40
57 Jason Keller's Car .02 .10
58 Rusty Wallace .60 1.50
59 B.Stavola/M.Stavola .02 .10
60 Mark Martin's Busch Car .15 .40
61 Tim Brewer .02 .10
62 Donnie Richeson .02 .10
63 Chuck Bown .07 .20
64 Larry Hedrick .02 .10
65 Nemechek/Craven/T.Bodine .15 .40
66 Gary DeHart .02 .10
67 Mark Martin .60 1.50
68 Greg Sacks' Car .02 .10
69 Davey Allison/Yates .40 1.00
70 Harry Gant's Car .02 .10
71 Walter Bud Moore .02 .10
72 Andy Hillenburg .07 .20
73 Ray Evernham .07 .20
74 Sterling Marlin .30 .75
75 Checklist #3 .02 .10
76 Ned Jarrett .07 .20
77 Miller 400 .02 .10
78 Mark Martin's Car .15 .40
79 Glen Wood/Leonard Wood .02 .10
80 Hermie Sadler RC .07 .20
81 Jerry Glanville .07 .20
82 Alan Kulwicki First Win .15 .40
83 Lake Speed's Car .02 .10
84 Al Unser Jr. .15 .40
85 Ward Burton/Todd Bodine .07 .20
86 Larry McReynolds .02 .10
87 Greg Sacks .07 .20
88 Ken Schrader's Car .02 .10
89 Ken Howes .02 .10
90 Bobby Hillin's Car .02 .10
91 Don Miller .02 .10
92 Joe Ruttman .07 .20
93 Bill Brodrick .02 .10
94 David Green .07 .20
95 Joey Knuckles .02 .10
96 Derrike Cope .07 .20
97 Bill Davis .07 .20
98 Derrike Cope's Car .02 .10
99 Ricky Craven .15 .40
100 Davey Allison .40 1.00
101 Junior Johnson .07 .20
102 Carl Hill .02 .10
103 Dick Trickle's Car .02 .10
104 Dave Marcis .07 .20
105 Larry Pearson's Car .02 .10
106 Rick Mast .07 .20
107 Eli Gold .02 .10
108 D.K. Ulrich .02 .10
109 Mark Martin's Car .15 .40
110 Hanes 500 .02 .10
111 Jimmy Johnson .02 .10
112 Buster Auton .02 .10
113 Waddell Wilson .02 .10
114 Eddie Wood .02 .10
115 Clyde McLeod .02 .10
116 Rick Hendrick .02 .10
117 Bobby Dotter's Car .02 .10
118 Jimmy Hensley .07 .20
119 McClure Boys/T.Morgan .02 .10
120 Dave Rezendes .02 .10
121 Jack Sprague's Car .02 .10
122 Tony Glover .02 .10
123 Cale Yarborough .07 .20
124 Jimmy Means .07 .20
125 Michael Waltrip's Transporter CL.02 .10
126 Roy Payne .02 .10
127 Davey Allison .40 1.00
128 Davey Allison's Car .15 .40
129 Doug Richert .02 .10
130 Robert Pressley .07 .20
131 Ken Wilson .02 .10
132 Motorcraft 500 .02 .10
133 Jay Luckwaldt .02 .10
134 Donnie Wingo .02 .10
135 Billy Hagan .02 .10
136 Ricky Rudd's Car .07 .20
137 Jack Roush .02 .10
138 Joe Gibbs .15 .40
139 Robbie Loomis .02 .10
140 Jimmy Fennig .02 .10
141 Chuck Rider .02 .10
142 Alan Kulwicki On Pole .15 .40
143 Red Farmer .02 .10
144 Jim Bown .02 .10
145 Rusty Wallace in Pits .15 .40
146 Ricky Pearson .02 .10
147 Coca Cola 600 .02 .10
148 P.Rimer/V.Elliott/L.Shrowder .02 .10
149 Bobby Allison .07 .20
150 Checklist #6 .02 .10
151 Jeff Gordon 4.00 10.00
152 Sterling Marlin .75 2.00
153 Jeff Burton .60 1.50
154 Jimmy Spencer .25 .60
155 Ted Musgrave .25 .60
156 Ricky Craven .50 1.25
157 Harry Gant .50 1.25
158 Tracy Leslie .12 .30
159 Wally Dallenbach, Jr. .25 .60
160 Jack Sprague .12 .30
161 Mark Martin 2.00 5.00
162 Shawna Robinson 1.00 2.50
163 Tommy Houston .25 .60
164 Rusty Wallace 2.00 5.00
165 Chuck Bown .25 .60
166 Joe Nemechek .25 .60
167 Ken Schrader .25 .60
168 Rick Hendrick .12 .30
169 Larry Pearson .25 .60
170 Rick Mast .25 .60
171 Robert Yates .12 .30
172 Hermie Sadler RC .25 .60
173 Morgan Shepherd .25 .60
174 Mike Wallace .25 .60
175 Checklist #7/Tom Peck .12 .30
176 Bobby Labonte 1.25 3.00
177 Lake Speed .25 .60
178 Davey Allison/B.Allison 1.25 3.00
179 Derrike Cope .25 .60
180 Walter Bud Moore .12 .30
181 Rusty Wallace 2.00 5.00
182 Ward Burton .50 1.25
183 Bobby Dotter .12 .30
184 Terry Labonte .75 2.00
185 Todd Bodine .25 .60
186 Michael Waltrip .50 1.25
187 Roy Payne .12 .30
188 Junior Johnson .25 .60
189 Jack Roush .12 .30
190 Davey Allison 1.50 4.00
191 David Green .25 .60
192 Greg Sacks .25 .60
193 Steve Grissom .25 .60
194 Robert Pressley .25 .60
195 Dick Trickle .25 .60
196 Alan Kulwicki MEM 1.00 2.50
197 Al Unser Jr. .50 1.25
198 Brett Bodine .25 .60
199 Chuck Rider .12 .30
200 Davey Allison 1.50 4.00
P1 Jeff Gordon Promo 4.00 10.00
P2 Rusty Wallace Promo 2.00 5.00

1993 Traks First Run

COMPLETE SET (200) 60.00 125.00
COMP.SET w/o SP's (150) 10.00 25.00
COMP.SILVER SET (50) 50.00 100.00
*FIRST RUN 1-150: 1.5X TO 4X HI COL.
*FIRST RUN 151-200: 2X TO 5X HI COLUMN

1993 Traks Kodak Ernie Irvan

Once again, in 1993, Traks released a commemorate set featuring the Kodak Film Racing Team and driver Ernie Irvan. The cards are oversized (3-3/4" by 5-1/4") with a design very similar to the 1992 set. All six cards were issued with gold foil borders in a cardboard factory set type package. Reportedly 4,000 of these sets were produced and most of them were given away at Kodak's hospitality tent at Daytona.

COMPLETE FACT.SET (6) 6.00 15.00
1 Ernie Irvan w Car 2.00 4.00
2 Inside Out 1.00 2.00
3 Ernie Irvan w Crew 2.00 4.00
4 Ernie Irvan in Pits 1.00 2.00
5 Ernie Irvan 2.00 4.00
6 Ernie Irvan's Car 1.00 2.00

1993 Traks Preferred Collector

This 20-card set was made available through the Traks Club. The cards feature some of the top drivers in NASCAR Winston Cup racing. The backs list stats for the driver's career and the 1992 season. President George Bush is featured on card number 15 with Richard Petty.

COMPLETE SET (20) 6.00 15.00
1 Michael Waltrip .25 .60
2 Brett Bodine .20 .50
3 Terry Labonte .40 1.00
4 Kyle Petty .25 .60
5 Alan Kulwicki .40 1.00
6 Mark Martin .75 2.00
7 Morgan Shepherd .20 .50
9 Darrell Waltrip .25 .60
10 Hut Stricklin .20 .50
11 Rusty Wallace .50 1.25
12 Ken Schrader .20 .50
13 Dale Jarrett .50 1.25
14 Ernie Irvan .40 1.00
15 Richard Petty George Bush .40 1.00
16 Richard Petty .40 1.00
17 Harry Gant .25 .60
18 Jimmy Hensley .20 .50
19 Dick Trickle .20 .50
20 Davey Allison .40 1.00

1993 Traks Trivia

The 1993 Traks Trivia set was released to retail outlets in a blister type packaging in complete set form. The 50-cards contain photos of NASCAR drivers on front with small photos on back along with six racing trivia questions.

COMP. FACT SET (50) 5.00 10.00
1 Mark Martin .20 .50
2 Jeff Gordon .60 1.50
3 Rusty Wallace .20 .50
4 Davey Allison .20 .50
5 Jeff Purvis .05 .15
6 Mark Martin .20 .50
7 Jimmy Hensley .05 .15
8 Sterling Marlin .10 .30
9 Alan Kulwicki .20 .50
10 Davey Allison's Helmet .10 .30
11 Rusty Wallace .20 .50
12 Jimmy Spencer .05 .15
13 Joe Nemechek .05 .15
14 Terry Labonte .10 .30
15 Harry Gant .05 .15
16 Wally Dallenbach Jr. .05 .15
17 Al Unser Jr. .10 .30
18 Davey Allison B.Allison .20 .50
19 Mark Martin .20 .50
20 Lake Speed .05 .15
21 Morgan Shepherd .05 .15
22 Bobby Labonte .05 .15
23 Mark Martin .20 .50
24 Jeff Gordon .60 1.50
25 Ken Schrader .05 .15
26 Brett Bodine .05 .15
27 Morgan Shepherd's Car .05 .15
28 Davey Allison .20 .50
29 Rusty Wallace .20 .50
30 Michael Waltrip .10 .30
31 Bobby Labonte .05 .15
32 Mark Martin .20 .50
33 Harry Gant .05 .15
34 Davey Allison w/Crew .20 .50
35 Alan Kulwicki .20 .50
36 Jeff Gordon .60 1.50
37 Mark Martin .20 .50
38 Jeff Gordon's Car .25 .60
39 Rusty Wallace .20 .50
40 Davey Allison J.Glanville .20 .50
41 Mark Martin .20 .50
42 Dave Marcis .05 .15
43 Ken Schrader .05 .15
44 Greg Sacks .05 .15
45 Jeff Gordon .60 1.50
46 Bobby Hillin .05 .15
47 Ted Musgrave .05 .15
48 Bobby Allison .05 .15
49 Derrike Cope .05 .15
50 Rick Mast .05 .15

1994 Traks

1994 Traks was released in two series of 100-cards each through 12-card packs. Boxes contained 30-packs. Series one cards were produced with gold foil layering while series two included silver foil. There were a couple of uncorrected error cards in the second series. The Ned Jarrett card was supposed to be number 134 but all of them were issued with the number 123 on the back. Also, the Tracy Leslie card was supposed to be number 148 but all of them were issued with the number 127 on the back. That means there are two different number 123's and two different number 127's. Club only factory sets were also produced with a 5-card Cartoons insert set per factory issue. A First Run factory set (400 sets made) was produced for sale to Club members at $35.00 as well that included a Cartoons set autographed by the card's artist.

COMPLETE SET (200) 10.00 25.00
COMP.SERIES 1 (100) 4.00 10.00
COMP.SERIES 2 (100) 4.00 10.00
WAX BOX SERIES 1 20.00 40.00
WAX BOX SERIES 2 20.00 40.00
1 Rick Mast .07 .20
2 Rusty Wallace .60 1.50
3 Sterling Marlin .25 .60
4 Ward Burton's Car .02 .10
5 Terry Labonte .25 .60
6 Mark Martin .60 1.50
7 Alan Kulwicki .25 .60
8 Jeff Burton .25 .60
9 Mike Wallace .07 .20
10 Jeff Gordon's Car .40 1.00
11 Junior Johnson .07 .20
12 Bobby Allison .07 .20
13 Dale Jarrett .50 1.25
14 Sterling Marlin's Car .07 .20
15 Lake Speed .07 .20
16 Ted Musgrave .07 .20
17 Ricky Rudd .25 .60
18 Joe Gibbs .15 .40
19 Davey Allison .40 1.00
20 Buddy Parrott .02 .10
21 Morgan Shepherd .07 .20
22 Bobby Labonte .50 1.25
23 Ken Schrader .07 .20
24 Jeff Gordon .75 2.00
25 Neil Bonnett CL .07 .20
26 Brett Bodine .07 .20
27 Larry McReynolds .02 .10
28 Ernie Irvan .15 .40
29 Neil Bonnett .25 .60
30 Michael Waltrip .15 .40
31 Steve Grissom .07 .20
32 Bruce Roney .02 .10
33 Harry Gant .15 .40
34 Derrike Cope .07 .20
35 Shawna Robinson .30 .75
36 Jeff Gordon .75 2.00
37 Mark Martin's Car .25 .60
38 Jimmy Hensley .07 .20
39 Ricky Craven .07 .20
40 Robert Yates .02 .10
41 Dennis Setzer .07 .20
42 Kenny Bernstein .07 .20
43 Wally Dallenbach, Jr. .07 .20
44 David Green .07 .20
45 Ernie Irvan .15 .40
46 Sterling Marlin .25 .60
47 Joe Bessey .07 .20
48 Bobby Labonte .50 1.25
49 Michael Waltrip's Car .07 .20
50 Neil Bonnett CL .07 .20
51 Morgan Shepherd's Car .02 .10
52 Jimmy Means .07 .20
53 Loy Allen Jr.'s Car .02 .10
54 Steve Hmiel .02 .10
55 Ricky Rudd .25 .60
56 Jimmy Spencer .07 .20
57 Roger Penske .02 .10
58 Ken Schrader .07 .20
59 Bobby Labonte's Car .25 .60
60 Mark Martin .60 1.50
61 Derrike Cope's Car .02 .10
62 Rusty Wallace .60 1.50
63 Chuck Bown .07 .20
64 Cale Yarborough .07 .20
65 Dale Jarrett .50 1.25
66 Ernie Irvan .15 .40
67 Todd Bodine .07 .20
68 Loy Allen Jr. .07 .20
69 Morgan Shepherd .07 .20
70 Terry Labonte's Car .15 .40
71 Dave Marcis .15 .40
72 Rusty Wallace's Car .25 .60
73 Harry Gant .15 .40
74 Bobby Dotter .07 .20
75 Ken Schrader B.Bodine Cars CL .02 .10
76 Robert Pressley .07 .20
77 Leo Jackson .02 .10
78 Brett Bodine .07 .20
79 Ward Burton .15 .40
80 Rusty Wallace .60 1.50
81 Andy Hillenburg .07 .20
82 Mark Martin .60 1.50
83 Ray Evernham .15 .40
84 Ricky Rudd's Car .07 .20
85 Joe Nemechek .07 .20
86 Jeff Gordon .75 2.00
87 Ken Wilson .02 .10
88 Carl Hill .02 .10
89 Hermie Sadler BGN Rookie of the Year .07 .20
90 Bobby Hillin .07 .20
91 Ernie Irvan .15 .40
92 Larry Pearson .07 .20
93 Kenny Wallace .07 .20
94 Ernie Irvan's Car .07 .20
95 Jack Roush .02 .10
96 Terry Labonte .25 .60
97 Greg Sacks .07 .20
98 Jimmy Makar .02 .10
99 Harry Gant .15 .40
100 Mark Martin's Car CL .25 .60
101 Ernie Irvan .15 .40
102 Rusty Wallace .60 1.50
103 Dale Jarrett .50 1.25
104 Mike McLaughlin .07 .20
105 Billy Hagan .02 .10
106 Jeff Gordon .75 2.00
107 Jeremy Mayfield RC .75 2.00
108 Dale Jarrett's Car .25 .60
109 Sterling Marlin's Car .07 .20
110 John Andretti RC .07 .20
111 Kyle Petty .15 .40
112 Sterling Marlin's Car .07 .20
113 Mark Martin .60 1.50
114 Bobby Allison .07 .20
115 Jimmy Hensley .07 .20
116 Harry Gant .15 .40
117 Mike Beam .02 .10
118 Terry Labonte .25 .60
119 Eddie Wood .02 .10
120 Rodney Combs .07 .20
121 Morgan Shepherd .07 .20
122 Mike Wallace's Car .02 .10
123 Bobby Labonte .50 1.25
124 Gary DeHart .02 .10
125 Ricky Rudd's Car CL .07 .20
126 Sterling Marlin .25 .60
127 Ward Burton .15 .40
128 Chuck Bown .07 .20
129 Elton Sawyer .07 .20
130 Ricky Rudd .25 .60
131 Ken Schrader .07 .20
132 Jimmy Fennig .02 .10
133 Brett Bodine .07 .20
134 Ned Jarrett UER Numbered 123 .02 .10
135 Ernie Irvan .15 .40
136 Larry Hedrick .02 .10
137 Kyle Petty .15 .40
138 Todd Bodine's Car .02 .10
139 Todd Bodine .07 .20
140 Harry Gant's BGN Car .07 .20
141 Bobby Allison .07 .20
142 Charley Pressley .02 .10
143 Loy Allen Jr. .07 .20
144 Mark Martin .60 1.50
145 Lake Speed's Car .02 .10
146 Dale Jarrett .50 1.25
147 Dave Marcis .15 .40
148 Tracy Leslie UER Numbered 127 .07 .20
149 Lake Speed .07 .20
150 Ernie Irvan's Car CL .07 .20
151 Ted Musgrave .07 .20
152 Terry Labonte .25 .60
153 Len Wood .07 .20
154 Michael Waltrip .15 .40
155 Tim Fedewa .07 .20
156 Glen Wood Leonard Wood .02 .10
157 Rusty Wallace .60 1.50
158 Tony Glover .02 .10
159 Chuck Bown .07 .20
160 Ernie Irvan's Car .07 .20
161 Jeff Burton .25 .60
162 Buster Auton .02 .10
163 Ernie Irvan .15 .40
164 Jim Bown .07 .20
165 Derrike Cope .07 .20
166 Harry Gant .15 .40
167 Ken Howes .02 .10
168 Ken Schrader's BGN Car .02 .10
169 Robbie Loomis .07 .20
170 Mike Wallace .07 .20
171 Jeff Gordon .75 2.00
172 Richard Jackson .02 .10
173 Rick Mast .07 .20
174 Jason Keller RC .25 .60
175 Race Action CL .02 .10
176 Mark Martin .60 1.50
177 Greg Sacks .07 .20
178 Elmo Langley .02 .10
179 Doug Richert .02 .10
180 Dick Trickle .07 .20
181 Donnie Richeson .02 .10
182 Sterling Marlin .25 .60
183 Joe Nemechek .07 .20
184 Kenny Wallace .07 .20
185 Kyle Petty .15 .40
186 Wally Dallenbach Jr. .07 .20
187 Rusty Wallace's Car .25 .60
188 Morgan Shepherd .07 .20
189 Waddell Wilson .02 .10
190 Ricky Craven's BGN Car .07 .20
191 Ricky Rudd .25 .60
192 Donnie Wingo .02 .10
193 Rusty Wallace .60 1.50
194 Chuck Bown's Car .02 .10
195 Robert Pressley .07 .20
196 Troy Selberg .02 .10
197 Ted Musgrave's Car .02 .10
198 Ernie Irvan .15 .40
199 Benny Parsons .07 .20
200 Jeff Gordon in Pits CL .40 1.00
P1 Ernie Irvan's Car Prototype .40 1.00
P2 Mark Martin T10 Prototype 2.00 5.00

1994 Traks First Run

COMPLETE SET (200) 15.00 40.00
COMP.SERIES 1 (100) 10.00 20.00
COMP.SERIES 2 (100) 10.00 20.00
*FIRST RUN CARDS: 1.25X TO 2.5X BASIC CARDS

1994 Traks Autographs

Randomly inserted in both series one and two packs, these inserts are a specially designed card with each signed by the featured driver. A 13th card (cover/checklist card) was also inserted. A maximum of 3500 of each card was signed.

COMPLETE SET (13) 75.00 150.00
A1 Todd Bodine 5.00 12.00
A2 J.Burton/W.Burton 10.00 25.00
A3 Harry Gant 6.00 15.00
A4 Jeff Gordon 30.00 80.00
A5 Steve Grissom 5.00 12.00
A6 Ernie Irvan 8.00 20.00
A7 Sterling Marlin 10.00 25.00
A8 Mark Martin 12.00 30.00
A9 Joe Nemechek 6.00 15.00
A10 Robert Pressley 5.00 12.00
A11 Ken Schrader 6.00 15.00
A12 Rusty Wallace 12.50 30.00
NNO Cover Card CL 1.50 4.00

1994 Traks Winners

The Traks Winners cards are a Holofoil stamped issue randomly inserted in series two packs of 1994 Traks racing. The cards feature early 1994 race winners that also had cards in Traks series one.

COMPLETE SET (25) 10.00 25.00
W1 Sterling Marlin .50 1.25
W2 Rusty Wallace 1.25 3.00
W3 Ernie Irvan .30 .75
W4 Ernie Irvan .30 .75
W5 Terry Labonte .50 1.25
W6 Rusty Wallace 1.25 3.00
W7 Ernie Irvan .30 .75
W8 Jeff Gordon 1.50 4.00
W9 Rusty Wallace 1.25 3.00
W10 Terry Labonte .50 1.25
W11 Joe Nemechek .15 .40
W12 Harry Gant .30 .75
W13 Terry Labonte .50 1.25
W14 Mark Martin 1.25 3.00
W15 Ricky Craven .15 .40
W16 David Green .15 .40
W17 Hermie Sadler .15 .40
W18 Derrike Cope .15 .40
W19 Ricky Craven .15 .40

W20 Mike Wallace	.15	.40
W21 Jeff Gordon	1.50	4.00
W22 Jeff Gordon	1.50	4.00
W23 Ken Schrader	.15	.40
W24 Rusty Wallace	1.25	3.00
W25 Elton Sawyer	.15	.40

1994 Traks Auto Value

In conjunction with Auto Value stores, Traks issued a set featuring 50 NASCAR drivers and racing personalities and one cover/checklist card. The cards were released in packs and were free with the purchase of a specific dollar purchase or purchase of certain items. The packs could also be purchased outright. Reportedly, 84,456 of these sets were produced.

COMPLETE SET (51)	5.00	12.00
1 Sterling Marlin	.20	.50
2 Brett Bodine	.08	.25
3 Robert Pressley	.08	.25
4 Ted Musgrave	.08	.25
5 Harry Gant	.15	.40
6 Ward Burton	.08	.25
7 Michael Waltrip	.15	.40
8 Jimmy Spencer	.08	.25
9 Dale Jarrett	.60	1.50
10 Jack Roush	.08	.25
11 Steve Grissom	.08	.25
12 Morgan Shepherd	.08	.25
13 Ricky Rudd	.15	.40
14 Chuck Bown	.08	.25
15 Neil Bonnett	.20	.50
16 Rick Hendrick	.08	.25
17 Lake Speed	.08	.25
18 Todd Bodine	.08	.25
19 Jeff Burton	.08	.25
20 Greg Sacks	.08	.25
21 Rusty Wallace	.75	2.00
22 Rick Mast	.08	.25
23 Loy Allen Jr.	.08	.25
24 Chuck Rider	.08	.25
25 Jeff Gordon	1.25	2.50
26 Bobby Hillin	.08	.25
27 Bobby Labonte	.60	1.50
28 Dick Trickle	.08	.25
29 Terry Labonte	.40	1.00
30 Joe Nemechek	.08	.25
31 Wally Dallenbach Jr.	.08	.25
32 Bobby Allison	.08	.25
33 Mark Martin	.75	2.00
34 Alan Kulwicki	.25	.60
35 Jimmy Hensley	.08	.25
36 Walter Bud Moore	.08	.25
37 Davey Allison	.40	1.00
38 Dave Marcis	.08	.25
39 Derrike Cope	.08	.25
40 Ned Jarrett	.08	.25
41 Ken Schrader	.08	.25
42 Junior Johnson	.08	.25
43 Ernie Irvan	.25	.60
44 Jimmy Means	.08	.25
45 Robert Yates	.08	.25
46 Roger Penske	.08	.25
47 Joe Gibbs	.08	.25
48 Derrike Cope's Car / Ted Musgrave's Car	.08	.25
49 Rusty Wallace's Car / Ken Schrader's Car	.20	.50
50 Ricky Rudd's Car	.08	.25
NNO Checklist Card	.15	.40

1994 Traks Cartoons

The Traks Cartoons set was produced for and distributed with 1994 Traks factory sets and First Run factory sets offered to Traks Club members. The cards are oversized and measure approximately 8" X 10". First Run factory sets included a numbered Cartoons set signed the card's artist, Bill Stanford.

COMPLETE SET (5)	4.00	15.00
C1 Mark Martin	2.50	6.00
C2 Rusty Wallace	2.50	6.00
C3 Sterling Marlin	1.00	2.50
C4 Kyle Petty	.60	1.50
C5 Jeff Gordon	3.00	8.00

1994 Traks Preferred Collector

This is the second 20-card set made available only to Traks club members. The cards continue in numbering where the 1993 series left off. The cards feature some of the top drivers in NASCAR Winston Cup racing. The backs include stats for the driver's career and the 1993 season. The last two cards in the set are tributes to Davey Allison and Alan Kulwicki.

COMPLETE SET (20)	6.00	15.00
21 Rusty Wallace	.75	2.00
22 Harry Gant	.20	.50
23 Sterling Marlin	.40	1.00
24 Mark Martin	.75	2.00
25 Ted Musgrave	.10	.30
26 Greg Sacks	.10	.30
27 Ken Schrader	.10	.30
28 Morgan Shepherd	.10	.30
29 Lake Speed	.10	.30
30 Jimmy Spencer	.10	.30
31 Dick Trickle	.10	.30
32 Terry Labonte	.40	1.00
33 Jeff Gordon	1.00	2.50
34 Ernie Irvan	.20	.50
35 Bobby Labonte	.60	1.50
36 Brett Bodine	.10	.30
37 Neil Bonnett	.20	.50
38 Derrike Cope	.10	.30
39 Alan Kulwicki	.40	1.00
40 Davey Allison	.50	1.25

1994 Traks Hermie Sadler

Traks produced this individual set to commemorate the new Virginia is for Lovers Racing Team. The cards were distributed primarily through souvenir trailers and feature driver Hermie Sadler.

COMPLETE SET (10)	1.50	3.00
1 Hermie Sadler	.25	.60
2 Don Beverley	.10	.30
3 Hermie Sadler's Car	.10	.30
4 Hermie Sadler	.25	.60
5 Bobby King	.10	.30
6 Hermie Sadler's Car	.10	.30
7 Hermie Sadler	.25	.60
8 Hermie Sadler w/Crew	.10	.30
9 Hermie Sadler BGN ROY	.10	.30
10 Hermie Sadler's Transporter	.10	.30

1995 Traks

1995 Traks was released in one single series set of 75-cards through 12-card packs. Boxes contained 36-packs and production was limited to 2500 20-box cases. Dale Earnhardt was included in the set for the first time since 1992. The cards were released with an autographed Richard Petty promo card inserted along with other inserts: First Run parallel, Behind the Scenes, On the Rise, Race Scapes, Racing Machines, Series Stars and Challengers. Each insert set was also produced with a First Run parallel version. The Racing Machines and Series Stars First Run parallels were only available as part of the prizes for winners of the Challengers interactive game. A random insert in packs was a autographed Richard Petty card. The cards were inserted at a rate of one in 600 packs.

COMPLETE SET (75)	6.00	15.00
1 Geoff Bodine	.05	.15
2 John Andretti	.05	.15
3 Harry Gant	.05	.15
4 Jeff Gordon	.60	1.50
5 Elton Sawyer	.20	.50
6 Sterling Marlin	.20	.50
7 Johnny Benson Jr.	.08	.25
8 Ward Burton	.08	.25
9 Ernie Irvan	.08	.25
10 Steve Grissom	.05	.15
11 Dennis Setzer	.05	.15
12 Greg Sacks	.05	.15
13 Rusty Wallace	.50	1.25
14 Brett Bodine	.05	.15
15 Loy Allen Jr.	.05	.15
16 Ted Musgrave	.05	.15
17 Jeremy Mayfield	.08	.25
18 Dale Jarrett	.40	1.00
19 Steve Kinser	.05	.15
20 Chad Little	.05	.15
21 Dave Marcis	.05	.15
22 Kyle Petty	.08	.25
23 Ricky Rudd	.20	.50
24 Hermie Sadler	.05	.15
25 Mike Wallace	.05	.15
26 Jeff Gordon	.60	1.50
27 Dale Earnhardt	1.00	2.50
28 Ricky Craven	.05	.15
29 David Green	.05	.15
30 Mark Martin	.50	1.25
31 Rick Mast	.05	.15
32 Joe Nemechek	.05	.15
33 Todd Bodine	.05	.15
34 Kyle Petty	.08	.25
35 Tommy Houston	.05	.15
36 Robert Pressley	.05	.15
37 Morgan Shepherd	.05	.15
38 Dick Trickle	.05	.15
39 Jeff Burton	.20	.50
40 Geoff Bodine	.05	.15
41 Terry Labonte	.20	.50
42 Ken Schrader	.05	.15
43 Dale Jarrett	.40	1.00
44 Kenny Wallace	.05	.15
45 Bobby Hamilton	.05	.15
46 Rusty Wallace	.50	1.25
47 Brett Bodine	.05	.15
48 Mark Martin	.50	1.25
49 Michael Waltrip	.08	.25
50 Ward Burton	.08	.25
51 Kyle Petty	.08	.25
52 Jeff Gordon	.60	1.50
53 Mark Martin	.50	1.25
54 Geoff Bodine	.05	.15
55 Ken Schrader	.05	.15
56 Jeff Burton	.20	.50
57 Randy LaJoie	.05	.15
58 Jeff Gordon	.60	1.50
59 Ernie Irvan	.08	.25
60 Dale Jarrett	.40	1.00
61 Terry Labonte	.20	.50
62 Mark Martin	.50	1.25
63 Ricky Rudd	.20	.50
64 Ken Schrader	.05	.15
65 Morgan Shepherd	.05	.15
66 Rusty Wallace	.50	1.25
67 Derrike Cope	.05	.15
68 Jeff Gordon	.60	1.50
69 Michael Waltrip	.08	.25
70 Todd Bodine	.05	.15
71 Sterling Marlin	.20	.50
72 Sterling Marlin	.20	.50
73 Ricky Rudd	.20	.50
74 Ernie Irvan	.08	.25
75 Rusty Wallace	.50	1.25
P26 J.Gordon Proto.First Run	1.50	4.00
NNO Richard Petty AU	25.00	60.00

1995 Traks First Run

COMPLETE SET (75)	10.00	25.00
*FIRST RUN: .8X TO 2X BASIC CARDS		

1995 Traks Behind The Scenes

Behind the Scenes was produced by Traks as an insert in its 1995 Traks packs. The cards focus on non-drivers that make the sport of racing run. A parallel First Run version of each card was also produced. Wrapper stated odds of pulling a Behind the Scenes card is approximately two per pack. The hobby version was printed with silver holofoil while the retail version featured flat silver foil.

COMPLETE SET (25)	2.00	4.00
*FIRST RUN: 1.2X TO 3X BASIC INSERTS		
*RETAIL SILVER: .4X TO 1X HOBBY		
BTS1 Steve Hmiel	.08	.25
BTS2 Rick Hendrick	.08	.25
BTS3 Joe Gibbs	.08	.25
BTS4 Chuck Rider	.08	.25
BTS5 Buddy Parrott	.08	.25
BTS6 Jack Roush	.08	.25
BTS7 Larry McReynolds	.08	.25
BTS8 Roger Penske	.08	.25
BTS9 Robbie Loomis	.08	.25
BTS10 G.Wood/L.Wood	.08	.25
BTS11 Paul Andrews	.08	.25
BTS12 Robert Yates	.08	.25
BTS13 Cale Yarborough	.08	.25
BTS14 Jimmy Johnson	.08	.25
BTS15 Tony Glover	.08	.25
BTS16 Ray Evernham	.08	.25
BTS17 Eddie Wood	.08	.25
BTS18 Andy Petree	.08	.25
BTS19 Carl Hill	.08	.25
BTS20 Richard Jackson	.08	.25
BTS21 Bruce Roney	.08	.25
BTS22 Junior Johnson	.08	.25
BTS23 Leo Jackson	.08	.25
BTS24 Len Wood	.08	.25
BTS25 Kenny Bernstein	.08	.25
P1 Steve Hmiel Prototype	.40	1.00

1995 Traks Challengers

Challengers is a 15-card interactive game randomly packed in 1995 Traks packs. Production was limited to less than 2000 of each card and the top prize was a complete First Run set of all 1995 Traks cards. Contest winners were required to redeem the cards of both the top Challenger and Rookie Challenger points drivers according to Traks' point rating system. Jeff Gordon was the Challengers winner and the Rookie Challengers winner was Ricky Craven. The original expiration date of November 1995 was extended to April 15, 1996.

COMPLETE SET (15)	40.00	80.00
COMP. FIRST RUN SET	40.00	100.00
*FIRST RUN: .5X TO 1.2X BASIC INSERTS		
C1 Jeff Gordon WIN	8.00	20.00
C2 Kyle Petty	1.25	3.00
C3 Ken Schrader	.75	2.00
C4 Terry Labonte	2.50	6.00
C5 Ricky Rudd	2.50	6.00
C6 Rusty Wallace	6.00	15.00
C7 Dale Jarrett	5.00	12.00
C8 Mark Martin	6.00	15.00
C9 Geoff Bodine	.75	2.00
C10 Sterling Marlin	2.50	6.00
C11 Morgan Shepherd	.75	2.00
C12 Steve Kinser	.75	2.00
C13 Ricky Craven WIN	.75	2.00
C14 Robert Pressley	.75	2.00
C15 Randy LaJoie	.75	2.00

1995 Traks On The Rise

On the Rise inserts focus on the top future stars of the Winston Cup and Busch racing circuits. The cards were packed approximately one per pack in 1995 Traks hobby and retail. A First Run parallel of each card was also randomly issued through packs. Jeff Burton's card was also released as a prototype. The hobby version was printed with silver holofoil while the retail version featured flat silver foil.

COMPLETE SET (20)	2.50	5.00
*FIRST RUN: 1X TO 2.5X BASIC INSERTS		
OTR1 Johnny Benson Jr.	.15	.40
OTR2 Steve Kinser	.10	.25
OTR3 Mike Wallace	.10	.25
OTR4 Larry Pearson	.10	.25
OTR5 Bobby Dotter	.10	.25
OTR6 Dennis Setzer	.10	.25
OTR7 David Green	.10	.25
OTR8 Steve Grissom	.10	.25
OTR9 Hermie Sadler	.10	.25
OTR10 Mike McLaughlin	.10	.25
OTR11 Joe Nemechek	.10	.25
OTR12 John Andretti	.10	.25
OTR13 Ted Musgrave	.10	.25
OTR14 Jeff Burton	.30	.75
OTR15 Ward Burton	.15	.40
OTR16 Kenny Wallace	.10	.25
OTR17 Ricky Craven	.10	.25
OTR18 Robert Pressley	.10	.25
OTR19 Chad Little	.10	.25
OTR20 Bobby Labonte	.60	1.50
P1 Jeff Burton Prototype	.50	1.25

1995 Traks Race Scapes

Traks Race Scapes inserts were produced with art renderings of race scenes on the cardfront and checklists on the cardbacks. The cards were packed approximately one in every three packs of 1995 Traks.

COMPLETE SET (10)	.50	1.25
RS1 Checklist 1	.05	.15
RS2 Checklist 2	.05	.15
RS3 Checklist 3	.05	.15
RS4 Checklist 4	.05	.15
RS5 Checklist 5	.05	.15
RS6 Checklist 6	.05	.15
RS7 Checklist 7	.05	.15
RS8 Checklist 8	.05	.15
RS9 Contest Rules	.05	.15
RS10 1995 Winston Cup Schedule	.05	.15

1995 Traks Racing Machines

Traks Racing Machines inserts feature top Winston Cup cars printed on prism foil card stock. The cards were inserted at the wrapper stated rate of approximately 1:30 packs. A First Run parallel of each card was also produced as a prize to winners of the Challengers interactive contest.

COMPLETE SET (20)	30.00	60.00
*FIRST RUNS: .3X TO .8X BASIC INSERTS		
RM1 Todd Bodine's Car	.60	1.50
RM2 Sterling Marlin's Car	2.00	5.00
RM3 Geoff Bodine's Car	.60	1.50
RM4 Bobby Hamilton's Car	.60	1.50
RM5 Ricky Rudd's Car	2.00	5.00
RM6 Terry Labonte's Car	2.00	5.00
RM7 Jeff Gordon's Car	6.00	15.00
RM8 Morgan Shepherd's Car	.60	1.50
RM9 Mark Martin's Car	5.00	12.00
RM10 Rusty Wallace's Car	5.00	12.00
RM11 Rick Mast's Car	.60	1.50
RM12 Dale Jarrett's Car	4.00	10.00
RM13 Dick Trickle's Car	.60	1.50
RM14 Ken Schrader's Car	.60	1.50
RM15 Michael Waltrip's Car	1.00	2.50
RM16 Steve Kinser's Car	.60	1.50
RM17 Ted Musgrave's Car	.60	1.50
RM18 Kyle Petty's Car	1.00	2.50
RM19 Jeff Burton's Car	2.00	5.00
RM20 Bobby Labonte's Car	4.00	10.00

1995 Traks Series Stars

Traks Series Stars inserts feature top Winston Cup drivers printed on foil card stock. Each card was covered with a removable static cling "fan" sticker to protect the cardfront. The cards were inserted at the wrapper stated rate of approximately 1:30 packs. A First Run parallel of each card was also produced and available only as a prize to winners of the Challengers interactive contest.

COMPLETE SET (20)	25.00	60.00
*FIRST RUN: .3X TO .8X BASIC INSERTS		
SS1 Ken Schrader	.60	1.50
SS2 Terry Labonte	2.00	5.00
SS3 Morgan Shepherd	.60	1.50
SS4 Rusty Wallace	5.00	12.00
SS5 Mark Martin	5.00	12.00
SS6 Derrike Cope	.60	1.50
SS7 Sterling Marlin	2.00	5.00
SS8 Jeff Gordon	6.00	15.00
SS9 Harry Gant	.60	1.50
SS10 Geoff Bodine	.60	1.50
SS11 Ernie Irvan	1.00	2.50
SS12 Brett Bodine	.60	1.50
SS13 Michael Waltrip	1.00	2.50
SS14 Dick Trickle	.60	1.50
SS15 Ted Musgrave	.60	1.50
SS16 Ricky Rudd	2.00	5.00
SS17 Kyle Petty	1.00	2.50
SS18 Rick Mast	.60	1.50
SS19 Dale Earnhardt	10.00	25.00
SS20 Dale Jarrett	4.00	10.00

1995 Traks Auto Value

In conjunction with Auto Value stores, Traks issued a set featuring 50 NASCAR drivers and racing personalities for the second straight year. The cards were distributed through Auto Value stores in cello packs.

COMPLETE SET (51)	6.00	15.00
1 Jeff Gordon	2.00	5.00
2 Steve Grissom	.10	.30
3 Randy LaJoie	.10	.30
4 Junior Johnson	.10	.30
5 Jeff Burton	.30	.75
6 Geoff Bodine	.10	.30
7 Kyle Petty	.20	.50
8 Robert Pressley	.10	.30
9 Greg Sacks	.10	.30
10 Morgan Shepherd	.10	.30
11 John Andretti	.10	.30
12 Paul Andrews	.10	.30
13 Brett Bodine	.10	.30
14 Steve Hmiel	.10	.30
15 Ernie Irvan	.20	.50
16 Joe Gibbs	.20	.50
17 Ray Evernham	.20	.50
18 Ricky Craven	.10	.30
19 Derrike Cope	.10	.30
20 Ward Burton	.20	.50
21 Todd Bodine	.10	.30
22 Bobby Hamilton	.10	.30
23 Rick Hendrick	.10	.30
24 Dale Jarrett	.40	1.00
25 Bobby Labonte	.40	1.00
26 Steve Kinser	.10	.30
27 Dave Marcis	.20	.50
28 Sterling Marlin	.30	.75
29 Mark Martin	.50	1.25
30 Rick Mast	.10	.30
31 Jeremy Mayfield	.20	.50
32 Michael Waltrip	.20	.50
33 Ted Musgrave	.10	.30
34 Robert Yates	.10	.30
35 Cale Yarborough	.10	.30
36 Buddy Parrott	.10	.30
37 Mike Wallace	.10	.30
38 Joe Nemechek	.10	.30
39 Larry McReynolds	.10	.30
40 Roger Penske	.10	.30
41 Dick Trickle	.10	.30
42 Kenny Wallace	.10	.30
43 Jack Roush	.10	.30
44 Ken Schrader	.10	.30
45 Rusty Wallace	.50	1.25
46 Kenny Bernstein	.10	.30
47 Terry Labonte	.30	.75
48 Race Action	.10	.30
49 Race Action	.10	.30
50 Race Aciton	.10	.30
NNO Checklist	.10	.30

1995 Traks 5th Anniversary

Traks introduced a new premium brand under the name of 5th Anniversary in 1995. The release was distributed in 8-card packs with 24-packs per box. Each case contained eight boxes of Traks 5th Anniversary and four boxes of Gold. Reportedly, production was limited to 1000 cases. Insert sets include Clear Contenders and Retrospective.

COMPLETE SET (80)	8.00	20.00
1 Mark Martin	.60	1.50
2 Steve Grissom	.07	.20
3 Dale Earnhardt	1.25	3.00
4 Jeff Gordon	.75	2.00
5 Ricky Rudd	.25	.60
6 Geoff Bodine	.07	.20
7 Sterling Marlin	.25	.60
8 Johnny Benson Jr.	.15	.40
9 Rusty Wallace	.60	1.50
10 John Andretti	.07	.20
11 Derrike Cope	.07	.20
12 Ernie Irvan	.15	.40
13 Ted Musgrave	.07	.20
14 Chad Little	.07	.20
15 Kyle Petty	.15	.40
16 Brett Bodine	.07	.20
17 Ricky Craven	.15	.40
18 David Green	.07	.20
19 Terry Labonte	.25	.60
20 Dale Jarrett	.50	1.25
21 Ward Burton	.15	.40
22 Mike Wallace	.07	.20
23 Morgan Shepherd	.07	.20
24 Robert Pressley	.07	.20
25 Todd Bodine	.07	.20
26 Joe Nemechek	.07	.20
27 Rick Mast	.07	.20
28 Ken Schrader	.07	.20
29 Kenny Wallace	.07	.20
30 Jeff Burton	.25	.60
31 Michael Waltrip	.15	.40
32 Dick Trickle	.07	.20
33 Bobby Labonte	.50	1.25
34 Bobby Hamilton	.07	.20
35 Hut Stricklin	.07	.20
36 Sterling Marlin	.25	.60
37 Ricky Rudd	.25	.60
38 Jeff Gordon	.75	2.00
39 Terry Labonte	.25	.60
40 Mark Martin	.60	1.50
41 Dale Jarrett	.50	1.25
42 Rusty Wallace	.60	1.50
43 Todd Bodine's Car	.02	.10
44 Sterling Marlin's Car	.07	.20
45 Geoff Bodine's Car	.02	.10
46 Bobby Hamilton's Car	.02	.10
47 Ricky Rudd's Car	.07	.20
48 Terry Labonte's Car	.15	.40
49 Jeff Gordon's Car	.40	1.00
50 Morgan Shepherd's Car	.02	.10
51 Mark Martin's Car	.25	.60
52 Rusty Wallace's Car	.25	.60
53 Michael Waltrip's Car	.07	.20
54 Dale Jarrett's Car	.15	.40
55 Dick Trickle's Car	.02	.10
56 Rick Mast's Car	.02	.10
57 Ricky Craven's Car	.02	.10
58 Joe Nemechek's Car	.02	.10
59 Ted Musgrave's Car	.02	.10
60 Kyle Petty's Car	.07	.20
61 Jeff Burton's Car	.07	.20
62 Bobby Hamilton's Car	.02	.10
63 Steve Grissom's Car	.02	.10
64 Robert Pressley's Car	.02	.10
65 Jack Roush	.02	.10
66 Steve Hmiel	.02	.10
67 Robert Yates	.02	.10
68 Gary DeHart	.02	.10
69 Cale Yarborough	.07	.20
70 Larry McClure	.02	.10
71 Robin Pemberton	.02	.10
72 Ed McClure	.02	.10
73 Larry McReynolds	.02	.10
74 Andy Petree	.02	.10
75 Joe Gibbs	.15	.40
76 Tony Glover	.02	.10
77 Rick Hendrick	.02	.10
78 Jimmy Makar	.02	.10
79 Paul Andrews	.02	.10
80 Ray Evernham	.02	.10
P1 Ray Evernham Promo	.40	1.00
P2 Sterling Marlin's Car Promo	.50	1.25
P3 Mark Martin Promo	1.25	3.00
P4 Mark Martin Promo/4000	2.00	5.00

1995 Traks 5th Anniversary Gold

COMPLETE SET (80)	15.00	40.00
*GOLDS: .6X TO 1.5X BASIC CARDS		
GOLD ISSUED IN ELITE PACKS		

1995 Traks 5th Anniversary Red

*RED: .8X TO 2X BASIC CARDS
ISSUED IN SPECIAL FACTORY SET

1995 Traks 5th Anniversary Clear Contenders

Clear Contenders were randomly inserted in packs of Traks 5th Anniversary Gold. Wrapper stated insertion ratio is 1:3 packs. The cards feature 10 of the top NASCAR drivers on clear plastic card stock.

COMPLETE SET (10)	12.00	30.00
C1 Dale Earnhardt	5.00	12.00
C2 Mark Martin	2.50	6.00
C3 Jeff Gordon	3.00	8.00
C4 Sterling Marlin	1.00	2.50
C5 Ted Musgrave	.30	.75
C6 Rusty Wallace	2.50	6.00
C7 Bobby Labonte	2.00	5.00
C8 Michael Waltrip	.60	1.50
C9 Terry Labonte	1.00	2.50
C10 Morgan Shepherd	.30	.75

1995 Traks 5th Anniversary Jumbos

This 10-card set features the top drivers in Winston Cup. The cards are a jumbo sized card (3"X5") and were inserted in the bottom of Anniversary boxes at a rate of one per three boxes. There was also a Gold parallel version of the jumbo cards. The cards were inserted at a rate of one per case. There were 100 of each gold card made.

COMPLETE SET (10)	10.00	25.00
*GOLD/100: 1.2X TO 3X BASIC INSERTS		
E1 Jeff Gordon	2.50	6.00
E2 Terry Labonte	.75	2.00
E3 Rusty Wallace	2.00	5.00
E4 Morgan Shepherd	.25	.60
E5 Ted Musgrave	.25	.60
E6 Dale Earnhardt	4.00	10.00
E7 Sterling Marlin	.75	2.00
E8 Michael Waltrip	.50	1.25
E9 Bobby Labonte	1.50	4.00
E10 Mark Martin	2.00	5.00

1995 Traks 5th Anniversary Limited Production

1 Mark Martin	2.00	5.00
2 Jeff Gordon	4.00	10.00
3 Sterling Marlin	1.25	3.00
4 Rusty Wallace	2.00	5.00
5 Bobby Labonte	1.50	4.00

1995 Traks 5th Anniversary Retrospective

Retrospective cards were randomly inserted in 1995 Traks 5th Anniversary Gold packs only. Wrapper stated insertion ratio is 1:3 packs. The 15-cards were printed on holofoil prism card stock and feature a photo of the driver's first Traks card on the back.

COMPLETE SET (15)	8.00	20.00
R1 Mark Martin	1.25	3.00
R2 Dale Earnhardt	2.50	6.00
R3 Jeff Gordon	1.50	4.00
R4 Ricky Rudd	.50	1.25
R5 Sterling Marlin	.50	1.25
R6 Rusty Wallace	1.25	3.00
R7 Dale Jarrett	1.00	2.50
R8 Terry Labonte	.50	1.25
R9 Kyle Petty	.30	.75
R10 Ken Schrader	.15	.40
R11 Ernie Irvan	.30	.75
R12 Geoff Bodine	.15	.40
R13 Morgan Shepherd	.15	.40
R14 Cale Yarborough	.15	.40
R15 Richard Petty	.40	1.00

1995 Traks Valvoline

Traks produced this set for Valvoline in celebration of 100-years of auto racing. The cards were available in factory set form directly from Valvoline with the purchase of a case of oil or any Valvoline oil change. Each set was packaged in a tin replica Mark Martin race car and offered for sale at $12.95. The black-bordered cards feature an art rendering of a great race car from racing's

past with one representative car from each year.
COMP.FACT SET (101) 7.50 20.00
1 J.Frank Duryea's Car .05 .15
2 A.L.Riker's Car .05 .15
3 Bollee Jamin .05 .15
4 George Heath's Car .05 .15
5 Camille Jenatzy's Car .05 .15
6 Fernand Charron's Car .05 .15
7 Henri Fournier's Car .05 .15
8 Barney Oldfield's Car .05 .15
9 H.T.Thomas' Car .05 .15
10 George Heath's Car .05 .15
11 B.F.Dingley's Car .05 .15
12 Joseph Tracy's Car .05 .15
13 Scipion Borghese's Car .05 .15
14 Louis Wagner's Car .05 .15
15 Carl Fisher's Car .05 .15
16 Bob Burman's Car .05 .15
17 Ray Harroun's Car .05 .15
18 Joe Dawson's Car .05 .15
19 Jules Goux's Car .05 .15
20 Rene Thomas' Car .05 .15
21 Ralph dePalma's Car .05 .15
22 Dario Resta's Car .05 .15
23 WWI Ambulance .05 .15
24 Dodge 4 Staff Car .05 .15
25 Albert Guyot's Car .05 .15
26 Gaston Chevrolet's Car .05 .15
27 Tommy Milton's Car .05 .15
28 Jimmy Murphy's Car .05 .15
29 Albert Guyot's Car .05 .15
30 Jean Chassagne's Car .05 .15
31 Dave Lewis' Car .05 .15
32 Jules Goux's Car .05 .15
33 Robert Benoist's Car .05 .15
34 Louis Meyer's Car .05 .15
35 Ray Keech's Car .05 .15
36 Billy Arnold's Car .05 .15
37 Lou Schneider's Car .05 .15
38 Fred Frame's Car .05 .15
39 Henry Birkin's Car .05 .15
40 Bill Cummings' Car .05 .15
41 Malcolm Campbell's Car .05 .15
42 Louis Meyer's Car .05 .15
43 Bernd Rosemeyer's Car .05 .15
44 Louis Meyer's Car .05 .15
45 Wilbur Shaw's Car .05 .15
46 Ted Horn's Car .05 .15
47 Floyd Davis .05 .15
Mauri Rose's Car
48 Daimler Dingo .05 .15
49 Willys Jeep .05 .15
50 Red Ball Express .05 .15
51 M-4 Sherman Tank .05 .15
52 George Robson's Car .05 .15
53 Mauri Rose's Car .05 .15
54 Johnny Mauro's Car .05 .15
55 Red Byron's Car .05 .15
56 Johnnie Parsons' Car .05 .15
57 Lee Walerd's Car .05 .15
58 Alberto Ascari's Car .05 .15
59 Bill Vukovich's Car .05 .15
60 Lee Petty's Car .08 .25
61 Bob Sweikert's Car .05 .15
62 Fireball Roberts' Car .08 .25
63 Juan Manuel Fangio's Car .05 .15
64 Jimmy Bryan's Car .05 .15
65 Lee Petty's Car .08 .25
66 Jim Rathmann's Car .05 .15
67 A.J.Foyt's Car .20 .50
68 Joe Weatherly's Car .05 .15
69 Parnelli Jones' Car .08 .25
70 Ken Miles' Car .05 .15
71 Jim Clark's Car .05 .15
72 Don Garlits' Car .08 .25
73 Richard Petty's Car .30 .75
74 David Pearson's Car .08 .25
75 Mario Andretti's Car .20 .50
76 Ferrari 512S Roadster .05 .15
77 Don Garlits' Car .08 .25
78 Ronnie Sox's Car .05 .15
79 Gordon Johncock's Car .08 .25
80 Don Prudhomme's Car .08 .25
81 Bobby Allison's Car
82 Buddy Baker's Car .08 .25
83 A.J.Foyt's Car .20 .50
84 Tom Sneva's Car .08 .25
85 Richard Petty's Car .30 .75
86 Benny Parsons' Car .08 .25
87 Bobby Unser's Car
88 Gordon Johncock's Car .08 .25
89 Cale Yarborough's Car .08 .25
90 Joe Amato's Car .05 .15
91 Ron Bouchard's Car .05 .15
92 Shirley Muldowney's Car .20 .50
93 Al Unser's Car .20 .50
94 Neil Bonnett's Car .20 .50
95 Ken Schrader's Car .08 .25
96 Bobby Rahal's Car .08 .25
97 Rusty Wallace's Car .60 1.50
98 Al Unser Jr.'s Car .20 .50
99 Mark Martin's Car .60 1.50
100 Jeff Gordon's Car .75 2.00
NNO Checklist .05 .15
Cover Card

1996 Traks Review and Preview

This 50-card set features top drivers from the Winston Cup circuit. The cards use gold foil stamping and UV coating. The product was packaged 12 boxes per case, 24 packs per box and eight cards per pack.

COMPLETE SET (50) 6.00 15.00
1 Sterling Marlin .25 .60
2 Bobby Hamilton .07 .20
3 Ted Musgrave .07 .20
4 Robert Pressley .07 .20
5 Mark Martin .50 1.25
6 Dale Jarrett .40 1.00
7 Joe Nemechek .07 .20
8 Kyle Petty .15 .40
9 Ward Burton .15 .40
10 Ernie Irvan .15 .40
11 Mark Martin .50 1.25
12 Kyle Petty .15 .40
13 Johnny Benson .15 .40
14 Ward Burton .15 .40
15 Jeff Gordon .60 1.50
16 John Andretti .07 .20
17 Sterling Marlin .25 .60
18 Ted Musgrave .07 .20
19 Ernie Irvan .15 .40
20 Jeff Burton .25 .60
21 Ricky Craven .07 .20
22 Dale Jarrett .40 1.00
23 Morgan Shepherd .07 .20
24 Ken Schrader .07 .20
25 Robert Pressley .07 .20
26 Bobby Hamilton .07 .20
27 Geoff Bodine .07 .20
28 Michael Waltrip .15 .40
29 Joe Nemechek .07 .20
30 Steve Grissom .07 .20
31 Morgan Shepherd .07 .20
32 Sterling Marlin .25 .60
33 Hut Stricklin .07 .20
34 Rick Mast .07 .20
35 Kyle Petty .15 .40
36 Mark Martin .60 1.50
37 Dale Earnhardt 1.00 2.50
38 Derrike Cope .07 .20
39 Dale Jarrett .40 1.00
40 Brett Bodine .07 .20
41 Ernie Irvan .15 .40
42 Ken Schrader .07 .20
43 Ted Musgrave .07 .20
44 Ernie Irvan .15 .40
45 Geoff Bodine .07 .20
46 Mike Wallace .07 .20
47 Checklist I .15 .40
48 Checklist II .07 .20
Ernie Irvan's Car on front
49 Checklist III .07 .20
50 Checklist IV .07 .20
Geoff Bodine's Car on front
P1 Sterling Marlin Promo .40 1.00
P2 Mark Martin's Car Promo .50 1.25

1996 Traks Review and Preview First Run

COMPLETE SET (50) 10.00 25.00
*FIRST RUN: .8X TO 2X BASIC CARDS

1996 Traks Review and Preview Magnets

COMPLETE SET (50) 25.00 60.00
*MAGNETS: 3X TO 8X BASIC CARDS

1996 Traks Review and Preview Liquid Gold

Inserted at a rate of one per 24 packs, the Liquid Gold cards feature top names in Winston Cup racing. The cards have vibrant colors and gold accents.

COMPLETE SET (20) 15.00 40.00
LG1 Dale Jarrett 3.00 8.00
LG2 Ernie Irvan 1.25 3.00
LG3 Mark Martin 4.00 10.00
LG4 Jeff Burton 2.00 5.00
LG5 Bobby Hamilton .60 1.50
LG6 Morgan Shepherd .60 1.50
LG7 John Andretti .60 1.50
LG8 Steve Grissom .60 1.50
LG9 Rick Mast .60 1.50
LG10 Mike Wallace .60 1.50
LG11 Derrike Cope .60 1.50
LG12 Robert Pressley .60 1.50
LG13 Ward Burton 1.25 3.00
LG14 Kyle Petty 1.25 3.00
LG15 Ricky Craven .60 1.50
LG16 Sterling Marlin 2.00 5.00
LG17 Geoff Bodine .60 1.50
LG18 Jeff Gordon 5.00 12.00
LG19 Brett Bodine .60 1.50
LG20 Ted Musgrave .60 1.50

1996 Traks Review and Preview Triple-Chase

This 20-card insert set is the base set that features the top drivers in Winston Cup. The cards were inserted one per pack. There are two parallel versions: Gold and Holofoil. The Gold cards feature gold foil stamping and are inserted at a rate of one per three packs. The Holofoil cards feature holofoil highlights and were inserted one per 48 packs.

COMPLETE SET (20) 2.00 5.00
COMP.HOLO.SET (20) 40.00 80.00
*HOLOFOILS: 6X TO 15X BASIC INSERTS
COMP.GOLD SET (20) 3.00 8.00
*GOLDS: .6X TO 1.5X BASIC INSERTS
TC1 Sterling Marlin .25 .60
TC2 Ted Musgrave .07 .20
TC3 Mark Martin .40 1.00
TC4 Morgan Shepherd .07 .20
TC5 Michael Waltrip .15 .40
TC6 Dale Jarrett .40 1.00
TC7 Bobby Hamilton .07 .20
TC8 Todd Bodine .07 .20
TC9 Geoff Bodine .07 .20
TC10 Kyle Petty .15 .40
TC11 Ernie Irvan .15 .40
TC12 Steve Grissom .07 .20
TC13 Robert Pressley .07 .20
TC14 Ricky Craven .07 .20
TC15 Sterling Marlin's Car .07 .20
TC16 Mark Martin's Car .15 .40
TC17 Ernie Irvan's Car .02 .10
TC18 Kyle Petty's Car .02 .10
TC19 Ted Musgrave's Car .02 .10
TC20 Dale Jarett's Car .07 .20

2006 TRAKS

COMPLETE SET (110) 20.00 50.00
WAX BOX HOBBY (28) 40.00 70.00
WAX BOX RETAIL (24) 40.00 70.00
1 Greg Biffle .30 .75
2 Dave Blaney .25 .60
3 Clint Bowyer CRC 1.50 4.00
4 Jeff Burton .30 .75
5 Kurt Busch .30 .75
6 Kyle Busch .50 1.25
7 Dale Earnhardt Jr. .75 2.00
8 Carl Edwards .40 1.00
9 Jeff Gordon .75 2.00
10 Robby Gordon .25 .60
11 Jeff Green .25 .60
12 Denny Hamlin CRC 3.00 8.00
13 Kevin Harvick .50 1.25
14 Dale Jarrett .40 1.00
15 Jimmie Johnson .60 1.50
16 Kasey Kahne .50 1.25
17 Matt Kenseth .40 1.00
18 Bobby Labonte .40 1.00
19 Terry Labonte .40 1.00
20 Sterling Marlin .40 1.00
21 Mark Martin .40 1.00
22 Jeremy Mayfield .25 .60
23 Casey Mears .25 .60
24 Joe Nemechek .25 .60
25 Ryan Newman .30 .75
26 Kyle Petty .30 .75
27 Scott Riggs .30 .75
28 Elliott Sadler .25 .60
29 Ken Schrader .25 .60
30 Brent Sherman RC 1.00 2.50
31 Reed Sorenson CRC 1.25 3.00
32 Tony Stewart .60 1.50
33 David Stremme CRC 1.00 2.50
34 Martin Truex Jr. CRC 1.25 3.00
35 Brian Vickers .25 .60
36 J.J. Yeley CRC 1.25 3.00
37 Martin Truex Jr.'s Car .25 .60
38 Kurt Busch's Car .12 .30
39 Mark Martin's Car .15 .40
40 Dale Earnhardt Jr.'s Car .30 .75
41 Kasey Kahne's Car .20 .50
42 Denny Hamlin's Car .60 1.50
43 Ryan Newman's Car .12 .30
44 Greg Biffle's Car .12 .30
45 Matt Kenseth's Car .15 .40
46 Tony Stewart's Car .25 .60
47 Jeff Gordon's Car .30 .75
48 Kevin Harvick's Car .20 .50
49 Jeff Burton's Car .12 .30
50 Elliott Sadler's Car .10 .25
51 Bobby Labonte's Car .15 .40
52 Jimmie Johnson's Car .25 .60
53 Dale Jarrett's Car .15 .40
54 Carl Edwards' Car .15 .40
55 A.J. Foyt IV NBS RC .75 2.00
56 David Green NBS .25 .60
57 Todd Kluever NBS .75 2.00
58 Mark McFarland NBS .25 .60
59 Paul Menard NBS .25 .60
60 Danny O'Quinn NBS RC .75 2.00
61 Johnny Sauter NBS .40 1.00
62 Regan Smith NBS .30 .75
63 Jon Wood NBS .30 .75
64 Rick Crawford CTS .25 .60
65 Erin Crocker CTS RC 3.00 8.00
66 Erik Darnell CTS RC .75 2.00
67 Ron Hornaday CTS .25 .60
68 Mark Martin CTS .40 1.00
69 Mike Skinner CTS .25 .60
70 Bobby Allison .30 .75
71 Davey Allison .60 1.50
72 Donnie Allison .30 .75
73 Buddy Baker .30 .75
74 Dale Earnhardt 2.50 6.00
75 Harry Gant .30 .75
76 Jack Ingram .25 .60
77 Alan Kulwicki .60 1.50
78 Tiny Lund .25 .60
79 Marvin Panch .25 .60
80 Benny Parsons .40 1.00
81 David Pearson .40 1.00
82 Lee Petty .30 .75
83 Richard Petty .60 1.50
84 Tim Richmond .30 .75
85 Fireball Roberts .40 1.00
86 Curtis Turner .30 .75
87 Rusty Wallace .40 1.00
88 Rex White .25 .60
89 Glen Wood .25 .60
90 Cale Yarborough .40 1.00
91 Chip Ganassi Racing Hdqtrs .40 1.00
92 Dale Earnhardt Inc. Hdqtrs 1.00 2.50
93 Evernham Motorsports Hdqtrs .40 1.00
94 Hendrick Motorsports Hdqtrs .40 1.00
95 Joe Gibbs Racing Hdqtrs .40 1.00
96 Penske Racing Hdqtrs .40 1.00
97 Richard Childress Racing Hdqtrs .40 1.00
98 Robert Yates Racing Hdqtrs .40 1.00
99 Roush Racing Hdqtrs .40 1.00
100 Martin Truex Jr.'s Car PS .25 .60
101 Mark Martin's Car PS .15 .40
102 Sterling Marlin's Car PS .15 .40
103 Greg Biffle's Car PS .12 .30
104 Matt Kenseth's Car PS .15 .40
105 Kevin Harvick's Car PS .50 1.25
106 Jeff Burton's Car PS .12 .30
107 Elliott Sadler's Car PS .10 .25
108 Dale Jarrett's Car PS .15 .40
109 Carl Edwards' Car PS .15 .40
110 Checklist CL .15 .40

2006 TRAKS Autographs

STATED ODDS 1:56
*AUTO/100: .5X TO 1.2X BASIC AU
*AUTO/25: .6X TO 1.5X BASIC AUTO
*AUTO/25: .4X TO 1X BASIC AUTO SP
1 Greg Biffle NC 10.00 25.00
2 Dave Blaney NC 6.00 15.00
3 Clint Bowyer NC 15.00 40.00
4 Jeff Burton NC 10.00 25.00
5 Kurt Busch NC 10.00 25.00
6 Kyle Busch NC SP 20.00 50.00
7 Erin Crocker CTS 15.00 40.00
8 Dale Earnhardt Jr. NC SP 75.00 150.00
9 Carl Edwards 20.00 50.00
10 Jeff Gordon NC SP 200.00 350.00
11 Robby Gordon NC 8.00 20.00
12 David Green NBS 7.50 15.00
13 Denny Hamlin 30.00 60.00
14 Kevin Harvick NC SP 30.00 60.00
15 Ron Hornaday CTS 7.50 15.00
16 Dale Jarrett NC SP 20.00 50.00
17 Jimmie Johnson NC SP 60.00 120.00
18 Kasey Kahne NC 20.00 50.00
19 Matt Kenseth NC SP 12.50 30.00
20 Todd Kluever NBS 10.00 25.00
21 Bobby Labonte NC 12.00 30.00
22 Terry Labonte NC 15.00 40.00
23 Sterling Marlin NC 12.50 30.00
24 Mark Martin NC SP 60.00 120.00
25 Jeremy Mayfield NC SP 12.50 30.00
26 Casey Mears NC SP
27 Joe Nemechek NC 8.00 20.00
28 Ryan Newman NC SP 20.00 40.00
29 Tony Raines NC 7.50 15.00
30 Scott Riggs NC SP 10.00 25.00
31 Elliott Sadler NC 15.00 40.00
32 Johnny Sauter NBS 7.50 15.00
33 Mike Skinner CTS 7.50 15.00
34 Reed Sorenson NC 12.50 30.00
35 David Stremme NC 12.50 30.00
36 Tony Stewart NC 25.00 60.00
37 Martin Truex Jr. NC 12.00 30.00
38 Brian Vickers NC 10.00 25.00
39 Jon Wood NBS 7.50 15.00
40 J.J. Yeley NC 12.50 30.00

2006 TRAKS Stickers

COMPLETE SET (36) 10.00 20.00
STATED ODDS 1 PER PACK
1 Martin Truex Jr. .40 1.00
01 Joe Nemechek .15 .40
2 Kurt Busch .20 .50
5 Kyle Busch .30 .75
6 Mark Martin .25 .60
7 Robby Gordon .15 .40
07 Clint Bowyer .50 1.25
8 Dale Earnhardt Jr. .50 1.25
9 Kasey Kahne .30 .75
10 Scott Riggs .20 .50
11 Denny Hamlin 1.00 2.50
12 Ryan Newman .20 .50
14 Sterling Marlin .25 .60
16 Greg Biffle .20 .50
17 Matt Kenseth .25 .60
18 J.J. Yeley .40 1.00
19 Jeremy Mayfield .15 .40
20 Tony Stewart .40 1.00
21 Ken Schrader .15 .40
22 Dave Blaney .15 .40
24 Jeff Gordon .50 1.25
25 Brian Vickers .15 .40
26 Jamie McMurray .25 .60
29 Kevin Harvick .30 .75
31 Jeff Burton .20 .50
38 Elliott Sadler .15 .40
40 David Stremme .30 .75
41 Reed Sorenson .40 1.00
42 Casey Mears .15 .40
43 Bobby Labonte .25 .60
44 Terry Labonte .25 .60
45 Kyle Petty .20 .50
48 Jimmie Johnson .40 1.00
66 Jeff Green .15 .40
88 Dale Jarrett .25 .60
99 Carl Edwards .25 .60

2007 Traks

COMPLETE SET (100) 12.50 30.00
WAX BOX HOBBY (24) 50.00 80.00
WAX BOX RETAIL (24) 40.00 75.00
1 Greg Biffle .20 .50
2 Jeff Burton .20 .50
3 Kyle Busch .30 .75
4 Kurt Busch .20 .50
5 Dale Earnhardt Jr. .50 1.25
6 Carl Edwards .25 .60
7 Robby Gordon .15 .40
8 Jeff Gordon .50 1.25
9 Denny Hamlin .30 .75
10 Kevin Harvick .30 .75
11 Dale Jarrett .25 .60
12 Jimmie Johnson .40 1.00
13 Kasey Kahne .25 .60
14 Matt Kenseth .25 .60
15 Bobby Labonte .25 .60
16 Sterling Marlin .25 .60
17 Jamie McMurray .25 .60
18 Casey Mears .15 .40
19 Joe Nemechek .15 .40
20 Ryan Newman .20 .50
21 Kyle Petty .20 .50
22 Tony Raines .15 .40
23 Scott Riggs .20 .50
24 Ricky Rudd .20 .50
25 Johnny Sauter .25 .60
26 Ken Schrader .15 .40
27 Reed Sorenson .15 .40
28 Tony Stewart .40 1.00
29 Martin Truex Jr. .20 .50
30 Brian Vickers .25 .60
31 Michael Waltrip .25 .60
32 A.J. Allmendinger RC .50 1.25
33 Paul Menard CRC .75 2.00
34 Juan Pablo Montoya RC .75 2.00
35 David Ragan CRC .50 1.25
36 Regan Smith CRC .50 1.25
37 Aric Almirola NBS RC .60 1.50
38 Marcos Ambrose NBS RC 1.00 2.50
39 Kertus Davis NBS RC .50 1.25
40 Cale Gale NBS RC .40 1.00
41 Sam Hornish Jr. NBS RC .60 1.50
42 Shane Huffman NBS RC .60 1.50
43 Todd Kluever NBS .25 .60
44 Stephen Leicht NBS RC .60 1.50
45 Timothy Peters NBS RC .40 1.00
46 Steve Wallace NBS .25 .60
47 Scott Wimmer NBS .25 .60
48 Jon Wood NBS .25 .60
49 Todd Bodine CTS .15 .40
50 Rick Crawford CTS .15 .40
51 Erik Darnell CTS .40 1.00
52 Ron Hornaday CTS .15 .40
53 Travis Kvapil CTS .15 .40
54 Mike Skinner CTS .15 .40
55 T.J. Bell CTS RC .40 1.00
56 Carl Edwards' Car CTG .10 .25
57 Dale Jarrett's Car CTG .10 .25
58 Jeff Gordon's Car CTG .20 .50
59 Kasey Kahne's Car CTG .10 .25
60 Ryan Newman CTG .20 .50
61 Tony Stewart's Car CTG .15 .40
62 Jimmie Johnson CTG .15 .40
63 Darrell Waltrip CTG .40 1.00
64 David Stremme MG .15 .40
65 M.Martin .50 1.25
R.Smith MG
66 Kasey Kahne MG .25 .60
67 Kurt Busch MG .20 .50
68 David Reutimann MG .30 .75
69 Juan Pablo Montoya MG .75 2.00
70 Elliott Sadler MG .15 .40
71 Jimmie Johnson MG .40 1.00
72 Kyle Busch MG .30 .75
73 Dale Earnhardt Jr. MG .50 1.25
74 Jeff Gordon MG .50 1.25
75 Tony Stewart GP .40 1.00
76 Dale Jarrett GP .25 .60
77 Martin Truex Jr. GP .20 .50
78 Kevin Harvick GP .30 .75
79 Dale Earnhardt Jr. GP .50 1.25
80 Bobby Labonte GP .25 .60
81 Jimmie Johnson GP .40 1.00
82 Martin Truex Jr.'s Car NFS .20 .50
83 Dale Jr.'s Car NFS .50 1.25
84 Kasey Kahne's Car NFS .25 .60
85 Matt Kenseth's Car NFS .25 .60
86 Tony Stewart's Car NFS .40 1.00
87 Jeff Gordon's Car NFS .50 1.25
88 Kevin Harvick's Car NFS .30 .75
89 Jimmie Johnson's Car NFS .40 1.00
90 Ricky Rudd's Car NFS .20 .50
91 Jeff Burton FT .20 .50
92 Kurt Busch FT .20 .50
93 Dale Earnhardt Jr. FT .50 1.25
94 Jeff Gordon FT .50 1.25
95 Denny Hamlin FT .30 .75
96 Jimmie Johnson FT .40 1.00
97 Kasey Kahne FT .25 .60
98 Matt Kenseth FT .25 .60
99 Tony Stewart FT .40 1.00
100 Dale Jarrett CL .25 .60
NNO Entry Card 1.25 3.00
NNO Astor Shockington 1.50 4.00
NNO Jack Diesel 1.50 4.00
NNO Jimmy Dash 1.50 4.00

2007 Traks Gold

COMPLETE SET (100) 25.00 50.00
*GOLD: .8X TO 2X BASE
STATED ODDS 1 PER HOBBY PACK

2007 Traks Holofoil

*HOLOFOIL: 4X TO 10X BASE
STATED PRINT RUN 50 SERIAL #'d SETS

2007 Traks Corporate Cuts Driver

STATED ODDS 1:112
STATED PRINT RUN 99 SERIAL #'d SETS
*TEAM/180: .4X TO 1X DRIVER
CCD1 Reed Sorenson 4.00 10.00
CCD2 Kasey Kahne 6.00 15.00
CCD3 David Ragan 5.00 12.00
CCD4 Dale Jarrett 6.00 15.00
CCD5 Matt Kenseth 6.00 15.00
CCD6 Denny Hamlin 6.00 15.00
CCD7 David Stremme 4.00 10.00
CCD8 Kurt Busch 6.00 15.00
CCD9 Ryan Newman 4.00 10.00
CCD10 Carl Edwards 6.00 15.00
CCD11 Greg Biffle 5.00 12.00
CCD12 Dale Earnhardt Jr. 8.00 20.00
CCD13 Tony Stewart 6.00 15.00
CCD14 Michael Waltrip 5.00 12.00
CCD15 Mark Martin 6.00 15.00
CCD16 J.J. Yeley 4.00 10.00
CCD17 Juan Pablo Montoya 6.00 15.00
CCD18 David Reutimann 5.00 12.00

2007 Traks Driver's Seat

COMPLETE SET (27) 12.50 30.00
*VARIATIONS: 1.5X TO 4X BASIC
VARIATION STATED ODDS 1:210
VARIATION HAS DOOR #
IN PLACE OF LAP #
DS1 David Stremme .40 1.00
DS2 Jeff Gordon 1.25 3.00
DS3 Martin Truex Jr. .50 1.25
DS4 Tony Stewart 1.00 2.50
DS5 Ryan Newman .50 1.25
DS6 Mark Martin .60 1.50
DS7 Bobby Labonte .60 1.50
DS8 Jimmie Johnson 1.00 2.50
DS9 Kasey Kahne .60 1.50
DS10 Brian Vickers .60 1.50
DS11 Matt Kenseth .60 1.50
DS12 Kevin Harvick .75 2.00
DS13 Sterling Marlin .60 1.50
DS14 Dale Earnhardt Jr. 1.25 3.00
DS15 David Gilliland 1.00 2.50
DS16 Greg Biffle .50 1.25
DS17 Casey Mears .40 1.00
DS18 Kurt Busch .50 1.25
DS19 Michael Waltrip .60 1.50
DS20 Jeff Burton .50 1.25
DS20B Jeff Burton door # 2.00 5.00
DS21 Juan Pablo Montoya 2.00 5.00
DS22 Dale Jarrett .60 1.50
DS23 Johnny Sauter .60 1.50
DS24 Carl Edwards .60 1.50
DS25 J.J. Yeley .60 1.50
DS26 Ricky Rudd .50 1.25
DS27 Ken Schrader .40 1.00

2007 Traks Hot Pursuit

COMPLETE SET (12) 10.00 25.00
STATED ODDS 1:6
HP1 Jeff Gordon 1.50 4.00
HP2 Kyle Busch 1.00 2.50
HP3 Tony Stewart 1.25 3.00
HP4 Martin Truex Jr. .60 1.50
HP5 Mark Martin .75 2.00
HP6 Carl Edwards .75 2.00
HP7 Jimmie Johnson 1.25 3.00
HP8 Kasey Kahne .75 2.00
HP9 Juan Pablo Montoya 2.50 6.00
HP10 Dale Earnhardt Jr. 1.50 4.00
HP11 Matt Kenseth .75 2.00
HP12 Kevin Harvick 1.00 2.50

2007 Traks Track Time

COMPLETE SET (9) 12.50 30.00
STATED ODDS 1:12
TT1 Dale Earnhardt Jr. 1.50 4.00
TT2 Juan Pablo Montoya 2.50 6.00
TT3 Kevin Harvick 1.00 2.50
TT4 Jimmie Johnson 1.25 3.00
TT5 Dale Jarrett .75 2.00
TT6 Jeff Gordon 1.50 4.00
TT7 David Gilliland 1.25 3.00
TT8 Tony Stewart 1.25 3.00
TT9 Martin Truex Jr. .60 1.50

2007 Traks Target Exclusives

COMPLETE SET (6) 5.00 12.00
STATED ODDS 2 PER TARGET BLASTER BOX
DEA Dale Earnhardt Jr. .60 1.50

JGA Jeff Gordon .60 1.50
JJA Jimmie Johnson .50 1.25
KHA Kevin Harvick .40 1.00
KKA Kasey Kahne .30 .75
TSA Tony Stewart .50 1.25

2007 Traks Wal-Mart Exclusives

COMPLETE SET (6) 5.00 12.00
STATED ODDS 2 PER WAL-MART BLASTER BOX
DEB Dale Earnhardt Jr. .60 1.50
JGB Jeff Gordon .60 1.50
JJB Jimmie Johnson .50 1.25
KHB Kevin Harvick .40 1.00
KKB Kasey Kahne .30 .75
TSB Tony Stewart .50 1.25

2007 Traks Driver's Seat National

COMPLETE SET (27) 10.00 25.00
DS1 David Stremme .30 .75
DS2 Jeff Gordon 1.00 2.50
DS3 Martin Truex Jr. .40 1.00
DS4 Tony Stewart .75 2.00
DS5 Ryan Newman .40 1.00
DS6 Mark Martin .50 1.25
DS7 Bobby Labonte .50 1.25
DS8 Jimmie Johnson .75 2.00
DS9 Kasey Kahne .50 1.25
DS10 Brian Vickers .50 1.25
DS11 Matt Kenseth .50 1.25
DS12 Kevin Harvick .60 1.50
DS13 Sterling Marlin .50 1.25
DS14 Dale Earnhardt Jr. 1.00 2.50
DS15 David Gilliland .75 2.00
DS16 Greg Biffle .40 1.00
DS17 Casey Mears .30 .75
DS18 Kurt Busch .40 1.00
DS19 Michael Waltrip .50 1.25
DS20 Jeff Burton .40 1.00
DS21 Juan Pablo Montoya 1.50 4.00
DS22 Dale Jarrett .50 1.25
DS23 Johnny Sauter .50 1.25
DS24 Carl Edwards .50 1.25
DS25 J.J. Yeley .50 1.25
DS26 Ricky Rudd .40 1.00
DS27 Ken Schrader .30 .75

1994 UDA Commemorative Cards

1 Jeff Gordon/5000 6.00 15.00
2 Rusty Wallace/5000 5.00 12.00

1997 UDA Jeff Gordon Commemorative Cards

NNO 1995 Coming Home a Winner/2400 6.00 15.00
NNO 1995 Mid-Season Points Leader/2373 6.00 15.00
NNO 1996 Points Champ/2500 6.00 15.00

1997 UDA Commemorative Cards

COMPLETE SET
RW Rusty Wallace Career 3.00 8.00
EI1 Ernie Irvan Career 2.50 6.00
EI2 1995 Ernie Irvan Comeback 2.50 6.00

1996 Ultra

This 200-card set is the first NASCAR set produced by Fleer. The set was distributed in 10-card packs with a suggested retail of $2.49 each. The set contains the following topical subsets: Busch Drivers (120-139), Car Owners (140-148), Award Winners (149-156), Road Warriors (157-166) and Race Action (167-200).

COMPLETE SET (200) 10.00 25.00
WAX BOX 40.00 80.00
1 Jeff Gordon .75 2.00
2 Jeff Gordon .75 2.00
3 Jeff Gordon's Car .30 .75
4 Ray Evernham .02 .10
5 Dale Earnhardt 1.25 3.00
6 Dale Earnhardt 1.25 3.00
7 Dale Earnhardt's Car .50 1.25
8 Andy Petree .02 .10
9 Mark Martin .60 1.50
10 Mark Martin .60 1.50
11 Mark Martin's Car .15 .40
12 Steve Hmiel .02 .10
13 Sterling Marlin .25 .60
14 Sterling Marlin .25 .60
15 Sterling Marlin's Car .07 .20
16 Tony Glover .02 .10
17 Rusty Wallace .60 1.50
18 Rusty Wallace .60 1.50
19 Rusty Wallace's Car .15 .40
20 Robin Pemberton .02 .10
21 Terry Labonte .25 .60
22 Terry Labonte .25 .60
23 Terry Labonte's Car .07 .20
24 Gary DeHart .02 .10
25 Ted Musgrave .07 .20
26 Ted Musgrave .07 .20
27 Ted Musgrave's Car .02 .10
28 Howard Comstock .02 .10
29 Bobby Labonte .50 1.25
30 Bobby Labonte .50 1.25
31 Bobby Labonte's Car .15 .40
32 Jimmy Makar .02 .10
33 Bill Elliott .30 .75
34 Bill Elliott .30 .75
35 Bill Elliott's Car .15 .40
36 Mike Beam .02 .10
37 Ricky Rudd .25 .60
38 Ricky Rudd .25 .60
39 Ricky Rudd's Car .07 .20
40 Bill Ingle .02 .10
41 Bobby Hamilton .07 .20
42 Bobby Hamilton .07 .20
43 Bobby Hamilton's Car .02 .10
44 Michael Waltrip .15 .40
45 Michael Waltrip .15 .40
46 Michael Waltrip's Car .07 .20
47 Dale Jarrett .50 1.25
48 Dale Jarrett .50 1.25
49 Dale Jarrett's Car .15 .40
50 Morgan Shepherd .07 .20
51 Morgan Shepherd .07 .20
52 Morgan Shepherd's Car .02 .10
53 Derrike Cope .07 .20
54 Derrike Cope .07 .20
55 Derrike Cope's Car .02 .10
56 Geoff Bodine .07 .20
57 Geoff Bodine .07 .20
58 Geoff Bodine's Car .02 .10
59 Ken Schrader .07 .20
60 Ken Schrader .07 .20
61 Ken Schrader's Car .02 .10
62 John Andretti .07 .20
63 John Andretti .07 .20
64 John Andretti's Car .02 .10
65 Tim Brewer .02 .10
66 Brett Bodine .07 .20
67 Brett Bodine .07 .20
68 Brett Bodine's Car .02 .10
69 Rick Mast .07 .20
70 Rick Mast .07 .20
71 Rick Mast's Car .02 .10
72 Ward Burton .15 .40
73 Ward Burton .15 .40
74 Ward Burton's Car .02 .10
75 Lake Speed .07 .20
76 Lake Speed .07 .20
77 Lake Speed's Car .02 .10
78 Ricky Craven .07 .20
79 Ricky Craven .07 .20
80 Ricky Craven's Car .02 .10
81 Dick Trickle .07 .20
82 Dick Trickle .07 .20
83 Dick Trickle's Car .02 .10
84 Steve Grissom .07 .20
85 Steve Grissom .07 .20
86 Steve Grissom's Car .02 .10
87 Jimmy Spencer .07 .20
88 Jimmy Spencer .07 .20
89 Jimmy Spencer's Car .02 .10
90 Kyle Petty .15 .40
91 Kyle Petty .15 .40
92 Kyle Petty's Car .07 .20
93 Robert Pressley .07 .20
94 Robert Pressley .07 .20
95 Robert Pressley's Car .02 .10
96 Joe Nemechek .07 .20
97 Joe Nemechek .07 .20
98 Joe Nemechek's Car .02 .10
99 Jeremy Mayfield .15 .40
100 Jeremy Mayfield .15 .40
101 Jeremy Mayfield's Car .07 .20
102 Jeff Burton .25 .60
103 Jeff Burton .25 .60
104 Jeff Burton's Car .07 .20
105 Todd Bodine .07 .20
106 Todd Bodine .07 .20
107 Todd Bodine's Car .02 .10
108 Mike Wallace .07 .20
109 Mike Wallace .07 .20
110 Mike Wallace's Car .02 .10
111 Dave Marcis .15 .40
112 Dave Marcis .15 .40
113 Dave Marcis' Car .07 .20
114 Hut Stricklin .07 .20
115 Hut Stricklin .07 .20
116 Hut Stricklin's Car .02 .10
117 Ernie Irvan .15 .40
118 Ernie Irvan .15 .40
119 Ernie Irvan's Car .07 .20
120 Johnny Benson, Jr. .15 .40
121 Johnny Benson, Jr.'s Car .02 .10
122 Chad Little .07 .20
123 Chad Little's Car .02 .10
124 Mike McLaughlin .07 .20
125 Mike McLaughlin's Car .02 .10
126 Jeff Green .07 .20
127 Jeff Green's Car .02 .10
128 Jason Keller .07 .20
129 Jason Keller's Car .02 .10
130 Larry Pearson .07 .20
131 Larry Pearson's Car .02 .10
132 Phil Parsons .07 .20
133 Phil Parsons' Car .02 .10
134 Tim Fedewa .07 .20
135 Tim Fedewa's Car .02 .10
136 Elton Sawyer .07 .20
137 Elton Sawyer's Car .02 .10
138 Patty Moise .07 .20
139 Patty Moise's Car .02 .10
140 Rick Hendrick .02 .10
141 Richard Childress .15 .40
142 Jack Roush .02 .10
143 Larry McClure .02 .10
144 Roger Penske .02 .10
145 Joe Gibbs .15 .40
146 Richard Petty .25 .60
147 Bobby Allison .07 .20
148 Glen Wood .02 .10
149 Ricky Craven A .07 .20
150 Andy Petree A .02 .10
151 Ray Evernham A .02 .10
152 Jeff Gordon A .40 1.00
153 Johnny Benson, Jr. A .15 .40
154 Chad Little A .07 .20
155 Bill Elliott A .15 .40
156 Ernie Irvan A .15 .40
157 Jeff Gordon's Helmet .60 1.50
158 Geoff Bodine's Helmet .02 .10
159 Ted Musgrave's Helmet .02 .10
160 Derrike Cope's Helmet .02 .10
161 Rusty Wallace's Helmet .15 .40
162 Kyle Petty's Helmet .07 .20
163 Morgan Shepherd's Helmet .02 .10
164 Ricky Rudd's Helmet .15 .40
165 Mark Martin's Helmet .15 .40
166 Bobby Labonte's Helmet .15 .40
167 Daytona 500 Race Action .02 .10
168 Jeff Gordon's Car RW .30 .75
169 Terry Labonte RW .15 .40
170 J.Gordon B.Lab T.Lab.RW .40 1.00
171 Bobby Labonte's Car RW .15 .40
172 J.Gordon Brooke RW .60 1.50
173 Dale Earnhardt RW .60 1.50
174 Rusty Wallace's Car RW .15 .40
175 Dale Earnhardt's Car RW .50 1.25
176 D.Earnhardt M.Martin's Car .15 .40
177 Bobby Labonte's Car RW .15 .40
178 Kyle Petty RW .07 .20
179 UAW GM Teamwork 500 Race Action .02 .10
180 Bobby Labonte RW .25 .60
181 Jeff Gordon's Car Race Act. .15 .40
182 Jeff Gordon's Car Race Act. .15 .40
183 Dale Jarrett RW .15 .40
184 Ken Schrader's Car RW .02 .10
185 Dale Earnhardt Teresa .60 1.50
186 Mark Martin's Car RW .15 .40
187 Dale Earnhardt's Car RW .50 1.25
188 Terry Labonte's Car RW .07 .20
189 Mountain Dew Southern 500 Race Action .02 .10
190 Rusty Wallace's Car RW .15 .40
191 Jeff Gordon in Pits RW .30 .75
192 Dale Earnhardt RW .60 1.50
193 Mark Martin RW .30 .75
194 Joe Nemechek's Car .02 .10
195 Ward Burton RW .07 .20
196 Ricky Rudd RW .15 .40
197 Dale Earnhardt in Pits RW .50 1.25
198 David Green w Car .07 .20
199 Sterling Marlin RW .15 .40
200 D.Earn Gordon R.Wall.Race Act. .15 .40
P1 Jeff Gordon Promo Sheet 1.50 3.00
NNO Checklist #1 .02 .10
NNO Checklist #2 .02 .10

1996 Ultra Autographs

This 37-card insert set features the top drivers on the Winston Cup circuit. The autographed cards have a front and back design that looks like a card in the regular set but the front of the card has a silver foil seal stating "Mark of Authenticity" in a circle surrounding the Ultra logo. The Ultra logo is also different than the one used on the regular card fronts. The back has the words "Certified Autograph Card" and carries no number. An autograph redemption card was inserted one per 24 packs. This redemption card would have to be sent in to Fleer to obtain the actual autograph card. The autograph redemptions expired on 12/31/96.

COMPLETE SET (37) 500.00 1000.00
1 John Andretti 7.50 20.00
2 Johnny Benson 7.50 20.00
3 Brett Bodine 6.00 12.00
4 Geoff Bodine 6.00 12.00
5 Todd Bodine 6.00 15.00
6 Ward Burton 8.00 20.00
7 Derrike Cope 6.00 12.00
8 Ricky Craven 6.00 12.00
9 Dale Earnhardt 150.00 300.00
10 Bill Elliott 30.00 60.00
11 Jeff Gordon 40.00 100.00
12 Ernie Irvan 10.00 25.00
13 Dale Jarrett 20.00 50.00
14 Jason Keller 6.00 12.00
15 Bobby Labonte 12.50 30.00
16 Terry Labonte 12.50 30.00
17 Chad Little 7.50 20.00
18 Dave Marcis 7.50 20.00
19 Sterling Marlin 10.00 25.00
20 Mark Martin 12.50 30.00
21 Rick Mast 6.00 12.00
22 Jeremy Mayfield 7.50 20.00
23 Mike McLaughlin 6.00 12.00
24 Patty Moise 7.50 20.00
25 Ted Musgrave 6.00 12.00
26 Joe Nemechek 6.00 12.00
27 Kyle Petty 10.00 25.00
28 Richard Petty 25.00 60.00
29 Ricky Rudd 10.00 25.00
30 Elton Sawyer 6.00 12.00
31 Ken Schrader 7.50 20.00
32 Morgan Shepherd 6.00 12.00
33 Lake Speed 6.00 12.00
34 Jimmy Spencer 6.00 12.00
35 Dick Trickle 6.00 12.00
36 Rusty Wallace 12.50 30.00
37 Michael Waltrip 8.00 20.00

1996 Ultra Champions Club

Randomly inserted in packs at a rate of one in six, this five-card set features former NASCAR Winston Cup Champions. The cards are printed on silver foil board and show both a picture of the driver and the current car they were driving.

COMPLETE SET (5) 5.00 12.00
1 Rusty Wallace 1.25 3.00
2 Dale Earnhardt 2.50 6.00
3 Bill Elliott .60 1.50
4 Terry Labonte .50 1.25
5 Jeff Gordon 1.50 4.00

1996 Ultra Flair Preview

This 10-card insert set pinpoints NASCAR's top drivers of '95 in a preview of Fleer's super-premium Flair product line. Randomly inserted in packs at a rate of one in 12 packs, each of these cards features 100 percent etched foil processing.

COMPLETE SET (10) 35.00 75.00
1 Jeff Gordon 5.00 12.00
2 Dale Earnhardt 8.00 20.00
3 Sterling Marlin 1.50 4.00
4 Mark Martin 4.00 10.00
5 Rusty Wallace 4.00 10.00
6 Terry Labonte 1.50 4.00
7 Ted Musgrave .50 1.25
8 Bill Elliott 2.00 5.00
9 Ricky Rudd 1.50 4.00
10 Bobby Labonte 3.00 8.00

1996 Ultra Golden Memories

This nine-card insert set highlights the '95 season's most memorable moments. The silver foil board the cards are printed on uses a checkered flag type background behind every front photo. The cards were randomly inserted in packs at a rate of one in six.

COMPLETE SET (9) 6.00 15.00
1 Ernie Irvan .50 1.25
2 Ward Burton .50 1.25
3 Sterling Marlin .75 2.00
4 Dale Earnhardt 4.00 10.00
5 Ken Schrader .25 .60
6 Terry Labonte .75 2.00
7 Bobby Labonte 1.50 4.00
8 Terry Labonte .75 2.00
9 John Andretti .25 .60

1996 Ultra Season Crowns

Randomly inserted in packs at a rate of one in four, this 15-card insert set features statistical leaders in areas such as wins, poles, most laps led and top 5 finishers from '95.

COMPLETE SET (15) 15.00 40.00
1 Terry Labonte .60 1.50
2 Jeff Gordon 2.00 5.00
3 Dale Earnhardt 3.00 8.00
4 Jeff Gordon 2.00 5.00
5 Dale Earnhardt 3.00 8.00
6 Mark Martin 1.50 4.00
7 Jeff Gordon 2.00 5.00
8 Mark Martin 1.50 4.00
9 Dale Earnhardt 3.00 8.00
10 Jeff Gordon 2.00 5.00
11 Jeff Gordon 2.00 5.00
12 D.Earnhardt J.Gordon Cars 1.25 3.00
13 Chad Little .20 .50
14 David Green .20 .50
15 Dale Earnhardt 3.00 8.00

1996 Ultra Thunder and Lightning

This 10-card insert set features teams generating thunder on the tracks and lightning in the pits. The cards use multi-colored foil backgrounds to bring out the colors of NASCAR Winston Cup cars. The cards could be found at a rate of one per four packs.

COMPLETE SET (10) 5.00 12.00
1 Brett Bodine's Car .10 .30
2 Brett Bodine's Car .10 .30
3 Jeff Gordon's Car 1.00 2.50
4 Jeff Gordon's Car 1.00 2.50
5 Dale Earnhardt's Car 1.50 4.00
6 Dale Earnhardt's Car 1.50 4.00
7 Sterling Marlin's Car .25 .60
8 Sterling Marlin's Car .25 .60
9 Bobby Labonte's Car .50 1.25
10 Bobby Labonte's Car .50 1.25

1996 Ultra Update

The 1996 Ultra Update set was issued in one series totalling 100 cards. The 10-card packs retail for $2.49 each. The set contains the topical subsets: NASCAR Winston Cup Drivers (1-33), NASCAR Busch Grand National Drivers (34-43), Hot Start (44-46), NASCAR Winston Cup Cars (47-79), Precious Metals (80-83) and Fresh Start (84-98). The cards feature a large Ultra logo in gold foil as the backdrop. The set updates the first Ultra issue of 1996 by providing shots of driver changes and sponsor changes. There were 24 packs per box and six boxes per case.

COMPLETE SET (100) 8.00 20.00
1 John Andretti .07 .20
2 Johnny Benson Jr. .15 .40
3 Brett Bodine .07 .20
4 Geoff Bodine .07 .20
5 Jeff Burton .25 .60
6 Ward Burton .15 .40
7 Derrike Cope .07 .20
8 Ricky Craven .07 .20
9 Wally Dallenbach Jr. .07 .20
10 Dale Earnhardt 1.25 3.00
11 Bill Elliott .30 .75
12 Jeff Gordon .75 2.00
13 Steve Grissom .07 .20
14 Bobby Hamilton .07 .20
15 Ernie Irvan .15 .40
16 Dale Jarrett .40 1.00
17 Bobby Labonte .40 1.00
18 Terry Labonte .25 .60
19 Dave Marcis .15 .40
20 Sterling Marlin .25 .60
21 Mark Martin .40 1.00
22 Rick Mast .07 .20
23 Jeremy Mayfield .15 .40
24 Ted Musgrave .07 .20
25 Joe Nemechek .07 .20
26 Kyle Petty .15 .40
27 Robert Pressley .07 .20
28 Ricky Rudd .25 .60
29 Ken Schrader .07 .20
30 Hut Stricklin .07 .20
31 Kenny Wallace .07 .20
32 Rusty Wallace .50 1.25
33 Michael Waltrip .15 .40
34 Glenn Allen Jr. .07 .20
35 Rodney Combs .07 .20
36 David Green .07 .20
37 Randy LaJoie .07 .20
38 Chad Little .07 .20
39 Curtis Markham .07 .20
40 Mike McLaughlin .07 .20
41 Patty Moise .07 .20
42 Phil Parsons .07 .20
43 Jeff Purvis .07 .20
44 Dale Jarrett HS .15 .40
45 Dale Earnhardt HS .60 1.50
46 Jeff Gordon HS .40 1.00
47 John Andretti's Car .02 .10
48 Johnny Benson's Car .02 .10
49 Brett Bodine's Car .02 .10
50 Geoff Bodine's Car .02 .10
51 Jeff Burton's Car .07 .20
52 Ward Burton's Car .02 .10
53 Derrike Cope's Car .02 .10
54 Ricky Craven's Car .02 .10
55 Wally Dallenbach's Car .02 .10
56 Dale Earnhardt's Car .50 1.25
57 Bill Elliott's Car .15 .40
58 Jeff Gordon's Car .30 .75
59 Steve Grissom's Car .02 .10
60 Bobby Hamilton's Car .02 .10
61 Ernie Irvan's Car .07 .20
62 Dale Jarrett's Car .15 .40
63 Bobby Labonte's Car .15 .40
64 Terry Labonte's Car .15 .40
65 Dave Marcis' Car .07 .20
66 Sterling Marlin's Car .07 .20
67 Mark Martin's Car .25 .60
68 Rick Mast's Car .02 .10
69 Jeremy Mayfield's Car .15 .40
70 Ted Musgrave's Car .02 .10
71 Joe Nemechek's Car .02 .10
72 Kyle Petty's Car .07 .20
73 Robert Pressley's Car .02 .10
74 Ricky Rudd's Car .07 .20
75 Ken Schrader's Car .02 .10
76 Hut Stricklin's Car .02 .10
77 Kenny Wallace's Car .02 .10
78 Rusty Wallace's Car .15 .40
79 Michael Waltrip's Car .07 .20
80 Bill Elliott's Car PM .15 .40
81 T.Labonte's Silver Car PM .15 .40
82 Bobby Hamilton's 25th Anniversary Car PM .02 .10
83 B.Bodine's Gold Car PM .02 .10
84 W.Dallenbach J.Means .02 .10
85 J.Burton B.Parrott .07 .20
86 D.Jarrett T.Parrott .15 .40
87 H.Stricklin P.Lopez .02 .10
88 M.Waltrip E.Wood L.Wood .15 .40
89 Morgan Shepherd .02 .10
90 Kenny Wallace .07 .20
91 Ernie Irvan .15 .40
92 Rick Mast .07 .20
93 Geoff Bodine .07 .20
94 R.Rudd R.Broome .15 .40
95 B.Bodine D.Richeson .02 .10
96 D.Earnhardt D.Smith .60 1.50
97 Derrike Cope .02 .10
98 Johnny Benson .15 .40
99 Checklist (1-100) .02 .10
100 Checklist (inserts) .02 .10
P1 Ernie Irvan Promo .40 1.00

1996 Ultra Update Autographs

This 12-card insert set features the top names in NASCAR. The cards found in packs were redemption cards. These cards could be sent in to receive an autographed card of the driver who appeared on the front of the card. The redemption cards were seeded one in 100 packs.

COMPLETE SET (12) 400.00 800.00
1 Ricky Craven 6.00 12.00
2 Dale Earnhardt 175.00 350.00
3 Bill Elliott 30.00 60.00
4 Jeff Gordon 75.00 150.00
5 Ernie Irvan 10.00 25.00
6 Dale Jarrett 20.00 50.00
7 Bobby Labonte 12.50 30.00
8 Terry Labonte 12.50 30.00
9 Sterling Marlin 10.00 25.00
10 Mark Martin 15.00 40.00
11 Ted Musgrave 6.00 12.00
12 Rusty Wallace 20.00 50.00

1996 Ultra Update Proven Power

Randomly inserted in packs at a rate of one in 72, this 15-card set uses a reflective graphic design and 100 percent foil treatments to showcase the point leaders from the 1995 and 1996 seasons.

COMPLETE SET (15) 125.00 225.00
1 Ricky Craven 2.00 5.00
2 Dale Earnhardt 30.00 80.00
3 Bill Elliott 8.00 20.00
4 Jeff Gordon 20.00 50.00
5 Bobby Hamilton 2.00 5.00
6 Dale Jarrett 10.00 25.00
7 Bobby Labonte 10.00 25.00
8 Terry Labonte 6.00 15.00
9 Sterling Marlin 6.00 15.00
10 Mark Martin 10.00 25.00
11 Jeremy Mayfield 4.00 10.00
12 Ted Musgrave 2.00 5.00
13 Ricky Rudd 6.00 15.00
14 Ken Schrader 2.00 5.00
15 Rusty Wallace 12.50 30.00

1996 Ultra Update Rising Star

Randomly inserted in packs at a rate of one in four, this five-card set focuses on the newest drivers on the Winston Cup circuit. The cards use gold foil and thermo-embossed black ink to make the card have a tire like texture.

COMPLETE SET (5) 2.00 5.00
1 John Andretti .40 1.00
2 Johnny Benson Jr. .75 2.00
3 Jeff Burton .75 2.00
4 Ricky Craven .40 1.00
5 Jeremy Mayfield .75 2.00

1996 Ultra Update Winner

Randomly inserted in packs at a rate of one in three, this 18-card set honors at least one winner from every track in the 1995 season. The cards feature a portrait of the winning driver on the front with track info and dates on the back.

COMPLETE SET (18) 12.00 30.00
1 Jeff Gordon 1.50 4.00
2 Terry Labonte .50 1.25
3 Bobby Labonte .75 2.00
4 Jeff Gordon 1.50 4.00
5 Sterling Marlin .50 1.25
6 Kyle Petty .30 .75
7 Dale Earnhardt 2.50 6.00
8 Rusty Wallace 1.00 2.50
9 Bobby Labonte .75 2.00
10 Jeff Gordon 1.50 4.00
11 Mark Martin .75 2.00
12 Ricky Rudd .50 1.25
13 Dale Jarrett .75 2.00
14 Terry Labonte .50 1.25
15 Ward Burton .30 .75
16 Dale Earnhardt 2.50 6.00
17 Sterling Marlin .50 1.25
18 Mark Martin .75 2.00

1996 Ultra Boxed Set

This 15-card set was issued by Fleer. The set was issued in a gray and black checkered box and features the top names in Winston Cup racing. The sets were primarily sold through retail mail order catalogs.

COMP. FACT SET (15) 7.50 15.00
1 Jeff Gordon 1.00 2.50
2 Dale Earnhardt 2.00 4.00
3 Sterling Marlin .40 1.00
4 Mark Martin .75 2.00
5 Rusty Wallace .75 2.00
6 Terry Labonte .50 1.25
7 Ted Musgrave .15 .40
8 Bill Elliott .50 1.25
9 Ricky Rudd .40 1.00
10 Bobby Labonte .60 1.50
11 Morgan Shepherd .15 .40
12 Michael Waltrip .25 .60
13 Dale Jarrett .60 1.50
14 Bobby Hamilton .15 .40
15 Derrike Cope .15 .40

1997 Ultra

This 100-card set features the same popular design Fleer used for the Baseball and Football Ultra lines. The cards use full-bleed photography with UV coating and foil stamping along with the driver's name written in script across the front of each card. The card contains an image of each driver and a still shot of his car superimposed over an action photo of the vehicle. There were 3,000 cases produced. The cards were packaged nine cards per pack, 24 packs per box and six boxes per case. There were three specially themed insert cards. Card number C1 is Terry Labonte, NASCAR Winston Cup Champion. The card was inserted at a rate of one in 180 packs. 500 of these cards were inserted into packs that carried an autograph redemption. Card number P1 is Bill Elliott, 1996 Most Popular Driver. This card was seeded one in 12 packs. Also, Johnny Benson, NASCAR Rookie of the Year, appears on card number R1. The Benson cards were randomly inserted one in 72 packs.

COMPLETE SET (100) 6.00 15.00
1 John Andretti .07 .20
2 Johnny Benson .15 .40
3 Brett Bodine .07 .20
4 Geoff Bodine .07 .20
5 Jeff Burton .25 .60

6 Ward Burton .15 .40
7 Derrike Cope .07 .20
8 Ricky Craven .07 .20
9 Wally Dallenbach .07 .20
10 Dale Earnhardt 1.25 3.00
11 Bill Elliott .30 .75
12 Jeff Gordon .75 2.00
13 Bobby Hamilton .07 .20
14 Bobby Hillin .07 .20
15 Ernie Irvan .15 .40
16 Dale Jarrett .50 1.25
17 Bobby Labonte .50 1.25
18 Terry Labonte .25 .60
19 Dave Marcis .15 .40
20 Sterling Marlin .25 .60
21 Mark Martin .60 1.50
22 Rick Mast .07 .20
23 Jeremy Mayfield .15 .40
24 Ted Musgrave .07 .20
25 Joe Nemechek .07 .20
26 Kyle Petty .15 .40
27 Robert Pressley .07 .20
28 Ricky Rudd .25 .60
29 Ken Schrader .07 .20
30 Morgan Shepherd .07 .20
31 Lake Speed .07 .20
32 Jimmy Spencer .07 .20
33 Hut Stricklin .07 .20
34 Dick Trickle .07 .20
35 Kenny Wallace .07 .20
36 Rusty Wallace .60 1.50
37 Michael Waltrip .15 .40
38 Robby Gordon's Car .15 .40
39 Terry Labonte's Car .15 .40
40 Dale Jarrett's Car .15 .40
41 Jeff Gordon's Car .30 .75
42 Mark Martin's Car .25 .60
43 Dale Earnhardt's Car .50 1.25
44 Ricky Rudd's Car .07 .20
45 Sterling Marlin's Car .07 .20
46 Rusty Wallace's Car .25 .60
47 Bobby Hamilton's Car .02 .10
48 Bill Elliott's Car .15 .40
49 Bobby Labonte's Car .15 .40
50 Jeremy Mayfield's Car .15 .40
51 Johnny Benson's Car .02 .10
52 Ted Musgrave's Car .02 .10
53 Ricky Craven's Car .02 .10
54 Ernie Irvan's Car .07 .20
55 Michael Waltrip's Car .07 .20
56 Jeff Burton's Car .07 .20
57 Jimmy Spencer's Car .02 .10
58 Bobby Allison .07 .20
59 Richard Childress .15 .40
60 Joe Gibbs .15 .40
61 Rick Hendrick .02 .10
62 Richard Petty .25 .60
63 Jack Roush .02 .10
64 Robert Yates .02 .10
65 Cale Yarborough .07 .20
66 Steve Hmiel .02 .10
67 Mike Beam .02 .10
68 David Smith .02 .10
69 Eddie Len Wood .02 .10
70 Ray Evernham .15 .40
71 Todd Parrott .02 .10
72 Larry McReynolds .02 .10
73 Tech Talk - Tires .02 .10
74 Tech Talk - Fuel Cell .02 .10
75 Tech Talk - Roof Flaps .02 .10
76 Tech Talk - Motor .02 .10
77 Tech Talk - Seat .02 .10
78 Tech Talk - Rear Spoiler .02 .10
79 Tech Talk - Generator .02 .10
80 Tech Talk - Jack Stob .02 .10
81 Tech Talk - Track Bar Hole .02 .10
82 Todd Bodine .07 .20
83 David Green .07 .20
84 Jeff Green .07 .20
85 Jason Keller .07 .20
86 Randy LaJoie .07 .20
87 Chad Little .07 .20
88 Curtis Markham .07 .20
89 Phil Parsons .07 .20
90 Larry Pearson .07 .20
91 Jeff Purvis .07 .20
92 Mike McLaughlin .07 .20
93 Patty Moise .07 .20
94 Glenn Allen .07 .20
95 Kevin Lepage .07 .20
96 Rodney Combs .07 .20
97 Tim Fedewa .07 .20
98 Dennis Setzer .07 .20
99 Checklist .02 .10
100 Checklist .02 .10
C1 Terry Labonte 8.00 20.00
C1A Terry Labonte Auto 60.00 120.00
P1 Bill Elliott 1.00 2.50
R1 Johnny Benson 2.50 6.00
S1 Mark Martin Sample 1.25 3.00

1997 Ultra AKA

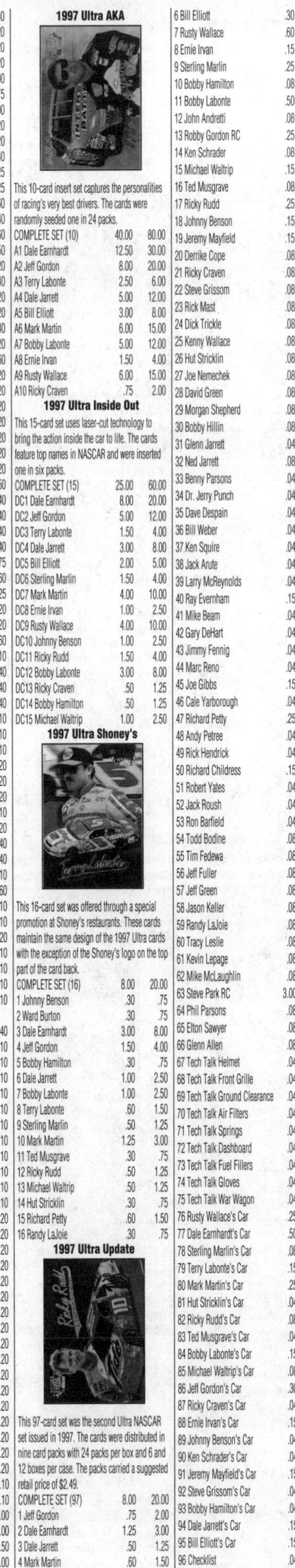

This 10-card insert set captures the personalities of racing's very best drivers. The cards were randomly seeded one in 24 packs.

COMPLETE SET (10) 40.00 80.00
A1 Dale Earnhardt 12.50 30.00
A2 Jeff Gordon 8.00 20.00
A3 Terry Labonte 2.50 6.00
A4 Dale Jarrett 5.00 12.00
A5 Bill Elliott 3.00 8.00
A6 Mark Martin 6.00 15.00
A7 Bobby Labonte 5.00 12.00
A8 Ernie Irvan 1.50 4.00
A9 Rusty Wallace 6.00 15.00
A10 Ricky Craven .75 2.00

1997 Ultra Inside Out

This 15-card set uses laser-cut technology to bring the action inside the car to life. The cards feature top names in NASCAR and were inserted one in six packs.

COMPLETE SET (15) 25.00 60.00
DC1 Dale Earnhardt 8.00 20.00
DC2 Jeff Gordon 5.00 12.00
DC3 Terry Labonte 1.50 4.00
DC4 Dale Jarrett 3.00 8.00
DC5 Bill Elliott 2.00 5.00
DC6 Sterling Marlin 1.50 4.00
DC7 Mark Martin 4.00 10.00
DC8 Ernie Irvan 1.00 2.50
DC9 Rusty Wallace 4.00 10.00
DC10 Johnny Benson 1.00 2.50
DC11 Ricky Rudd 1.50 4.00
DC12 Bobby Labonte 3.00 8.00
DC13 Ricky Craven .50 1.25
DC14 Bobby Hamilton .50 1.25
DC15 Michael Waltrip 1.00 2.50

1997 Ultra Shoney's

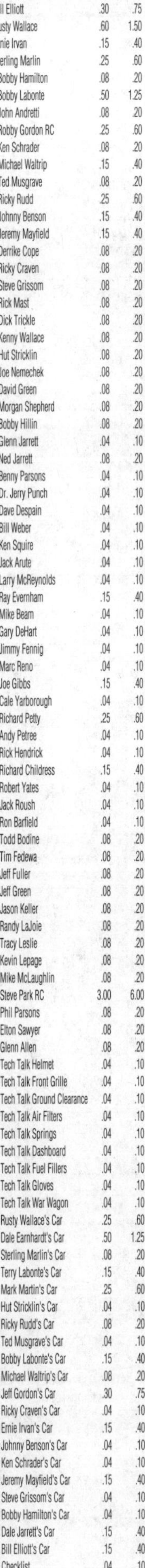

This 16-card set was offered through a special promotion at Shoney's restaurants. These cards maintain the same design of the 1997 Ultra cards with the exception of the Shoney's logo on the top part of the card back.

COMPLETE SET (16) 8.00 20.00
1 Johnny Benson .30 .75
2 Ward Burton .30 .75
3 Dale Earnhardt 3.00 8.00
4 Jeff Gordon 1.50 4.00
5 Bobby Hamilton .30 .75
6 Dale Jarrett 1.00 2.50
7 Bobby Labonte 1.00 2.50
8 Terry Labonte .60 1.50
9 Sterling Marlin .50 1.25
10 Mark Martin 1.25 3.00
11 Ted Musgrave .30 .75
12 Ricky Rudd .50 1.25
13 Michael Waltrip .50 1.25
14 Hut Stricklin .30 .75
15 Richard Petty .60 1.50
16 Randy LaJoie .30 .75

1997 Ultra Update

This 97-card set was the second Ultra NASCAR set issued in 1997. The cards were distributed in nine card packs with 24 packs per box and 6 and 12 boxes per case. The packs carried a suggested retail price of $2.49.

COMPLETE SET (97) 8.00 20.00
1 Jeff Gordon .75 2.00
2 Dale Earnhardt 1.25 3.00
3 Dale Jarrett .50 1.25
4 Mark Martin .60 1.50
5 Terry Labonte .25 .60
6 Bill Elliott .30 .75
7 Rusty Wallace .60 1.50
8 Ernie Irvan .15 .40
9 Sterling Marlin .25 .60
10 Bobby Hamilton .08 .20
11 Bobby Labonte .50 1.25
12 John Andretti .08 .20
13 Robby Gordon RC .25 .60
14 Ken Schrader .08 .20
15 Michael Waltrip .15 .40
16 Ted Musgrave .08 .20
17 Ricky Rudd .25 .60
18 Johnny Benson .15 .40
19 Jeremy Mayfield .15 .40
20 Derrike Cope .08 .20
21 Ricky Craven .08 .20
22 Steve Grissom .08 .20
23 Rick Mast .08 .20
24 Dick Trickle .08 .20
25 Kenny Wallace .08 .20
26 Hut Stricklin .08 .20
27 Joe Nemechek .08 .20
28 David Green .08 .20
29 Morgan Shepherd .08 .20
30 Bobby Hillin .08 .20
31 Glenn Jarrett .04 .10
32 Ned Jarrett .08 .20
33 Benny Parsons .04 .10
34 Dr. Jerry Punch .04 .10
35 Dave Despain .04 .10
36 Bill Weber .04 .10
37 Ken Squire .04 .10
38 Jack Arute .04 .10
39 Larry McReynolds .04 .10
40 Ray Evernham .15 .40
41 Mike Beam .04 .10
42 Gary DeHart .04 .10
43 Jimmy Fennig .04 .10
44 Marc Reno .04 .10
45 Joe Gibbs .15 .40
46 Cale Yarborough .04 .10
47 Richard Petty .25 .60
48 Andy Petree .04 .10
49 Rick Hendrick .04 .10
50 Richard Childress .15 .40
51 Robert Yates .04 .10
52 Jack Roush .04 .10
53 Ron Barfield .04 .10
54 Todd Bodine .08 .20
55 Tim Fedewa .08 .20
56 Jeff Fuller .08 .20
57 Jeff Green .08 .20
58 Jason Keller .08 .20
59 Randy LaJoie .08 .20
60 Tracy Leslie .08 .20
61 Kevin Lepage .08 .20
62 Mike McLaughlin .08 .20
63 Steve Park RC 3.00 6.00
64 Phil Parsons .08 .20
65 Elton Sawyer .08 .20
66 Glenn Allen .08 .20
67 Tech Talk Helmet .04 .10
68 Tech Talk Front Grille .04 .10
69 Tech Talk Ground Clearance .04 .10
70 Tech Talk Air Filters .04 .10
71 Tech Talk Springs .04 .10
72 Tech Talk Dashboard .04 .10
73 Tech Talk Fuel Fillers .04 .10
74 Tech Talk Gloves .04 .10
75 Tech Talk War Wagon .04 .10
76 Rusty Wallace's Car .25 .60
77 Dale Earnhardt's Car .50 1.25
78 Sterling Marlin's Car .08 .20
79 Terry Labonte's Car .15 .40
80 Mark Martin's Car .25 .60
81 Hut Stricklin's Car .04 .10
82 Ricky Rudd's Car .08 .20
83 Ted Musgrave's Car .04 .10
84 Bobby Labonte's Car .15 .40
85 Michael Waltrip's Car .08 .20
86 Jeff Gordon's Car .30 .75
87 Ricky Craven's Car .04 .10
88 Ernie Irvan's Car .15 .40
89 Johnny Benson's Car .04 .10
90 Ken Schrader's Car .04 .10
91 Jeremy Mayfield's Car .15 .40
92 Steve Grissom's Car .04 .10
93 Bobby Hamilton's Car .04 .10
94 Dale Jarrett's Car .15 .40
95 Bill Elliott's Car .15 .40
96 Checklist .04 .10
97 Checklist .04 .10

1997 Ultra Update Autographs

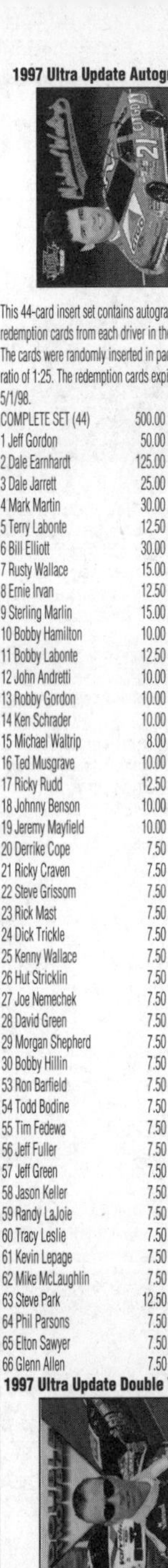

This 44-card insert set contains autograph redemption cards from each driver in the base set. The cards were randomly inserted in packs at a ratio of 1:25. The redemption cards expired on 5/1/98.

COMPLETE SET (44) 500.00 1000.00
1 Jeff Gordon 50.00 120.00
2 Dale Earnhardt 125.00 250.00
3 Dale Jarrett 25.00 50.00
4 Mark Martin 30.00 60.00
5 Terry Labonte 12.50 30.00
6 Bill Elliott 30.00 60.00
7 Rusty Wallace 15.00 30.00
8 Ernie Irvan 12.50 30.00
9 Sterling Marlin 15.00 40.00
10 Bobby Hamilton 10.00 25.00
11 Bobby Labonte 12.50 30.00
12 John Andretti 10.00 25.00
13 Robby Gordon 10.00 25.00
14 Ken Schrader 10.00 25.00
15 Michael Waltrip 8.00 20.00
16 Ted Musgrave 10.00 25.00
17 Ricky Rudd 12.50 30.00
18 Johnny Benson 10.00 25.00
19 Jeremy Mayfield 10.00 25.00
20 Derrike Cope 7.50 15.00
21 Ricky Craven 7.50 15.00
22 Steve Grissom 7.50 15.00
23 Rick Mast 7.50 15.00
24 Dick Trickle 7.50 15.00
25 Kenny Wallace 7.50 15.00
26 Hut Stricklin 7.50 15.00
27 Joe Nemechek 7.50 15.00
28 David Green 7.50 15.00
29 Morgan Shepherd 7.50 15.00
30 Bobby Hillin 7.50 15.00
53 Ron Barfield 7.50 15.00
54 Todd Bodine 7.50 15.00
55 Tim Fedewa 7.50 15.00
56 Jeff Fuller 7.50 15.00
57 Jeff Green 7.50 15.00
58 Jason Keller 7.50 15.00
59 Randy LaJoie 7.50 15.00
60 Tracy Leslie 7.50 15.00
61 Kevin Lepage 7.50 15.00
62 Mike McLaughlin 7.50 15.00
63 Steve Park 12.50 30.00
64 Phil Parsons 7.50 15.00
65 Elton Sawyer 7.50 15.00
66 Glenn Allen 7.50 15.00

1997 Ultra Update Double Trouble

This eight-card insert set features top drivers on both the Winston Cup and Busch circuits. The cards were randomly inserted in packs at a stated ratio of 1:4.

COMPLETE SET (8) 4.00 10.00
DT1 Mark Martin 2.50 6.00
DT2 Dick Trickle .30 .75
DT3 Bobby Labonte 2.00 5.00
DT4 Ricky Craven .30 .75
DT5 Michael Waltrip .60 1.50
DT6 Dale Jarrett 2.00 5.00
DT7 Terry Labonte 1.00 2.50
DT8 Joe Nemechek .30 .75

1997 Ultra Update Driver View

This 10-card insert set offers an up-close view, with laser cut cards, into the window net of some of the top Winston Cup stars. The cards were randomly inserted in packs at a ratio of 1:8.

COMPLETE SET (10) 15.00 40.00
D1 Jeff Gordon 5.00 12.00
D2 Dale Jarrett 3.00 8.00
D3 Bill Elliott 2.00 5.00
D4 Bobby Labonte 3.00 8.00
D5 Sterling Marlin 1.50 4.00
D6 Dale Earnhardt 8.00 20.00
D7 Mark Martin 4.00 10.00
D8 Terry Labonte 1.50 4.00
D9 Ricky Rudd 1.50 4.00
D10 Bobby Hamilton .50 1.25

1997 Ultra Update Elite Seats

This 10-card set features ten of the top drivers on the Winston Cup circuit on special 40-point stock cards. The cards were randomly inserted in packs at a ratio of 1:12.

COMPLETE SET (10) 25.00 60.00
E1 Jeff Gordon 5.00 12.00
E2 Dale Earnhardt 8.00 20.00
E3 Bill Elliott 2.00 5.00
E4 Ernie Irvan 1.00 2.50
E5 Ricky Rudd 1.50 4.00
E6 Dale Jarrett 3.00 8.00
E7 Terry Labonte 1.50 4.00
E8 Mark Martin 4.00 10.00
E9 Rusty Wallace 4.00 10.00
E10 Ricky Craven .50 1.25

1983 UNO Racing

This 30-card promotional set features UNO sponsored cars from 1980-83 and the drivers who drove them. The cards usually have a photo of the driver standing next to the UNO car on the front of the card. The back of the card has the UNO logo and looks like a card from an UNO card game. The sets were originally distributed via give aways.

COMPLETE SET (30) 100.00 200.00
1 Tim Richmond 2.50 6.00
2 Neil Bonnett 4.00 10.00
3 Tim Richmond 2.50 6.00
4 Lake Speed 1.50 6.00
5 D.K. Ulrich 1.50 4.00
6 Tim Richmond 2.50 6.00
7 Buddy Baker Ron Bouchard 4.00 10.00
8 Tim Richmond 2.50 6.00
9 Tim Richmond 2.50 6.00
10 Tim Richmond 2.50 6.00
11 Buddy Baker 5.00 12.00
12 Tim Richmond 2.50 6.00
13 Kyle Petty 3.00 8.00
14 Lake Speed 1.50 4.00
15 Tim Richmond 2.50 6.00
16 Kyle Petty 3.00 8.00
17 Tim Richmond 2.50 6.00
18 Tim Richmond 2.50 6.00
19 Kyle Petty 3.00 8.00
20 Buddy Baker 5.00 12.00
21 Buddy Baker 5.00 12.00
22 Tim Richmond 2.50 6.00
23 Richard Petty 15.00 40.00
24 Tim Richmond 2.50 6.00
25 Buddy Baker 5.00 12.00
26 Tim Richmond 2.50 6.00
27 Dale Earnhardt 50.00 100.00
28 Darrell Waltrip 4.00 10.00
29 Bobby Allison 5.00 12.00
30 Buddy Baker 5.00 12.00

1995 Upper Deck

Issued in two series over the first half of 1995, Upper Deck released both products through 10-card packs with 36-packs per box. Both series included several insert sets including the popular Predictor redemption cards and one Silver or Gold parallel card in every pack. Series one hobby packs featured a Jeff Gordon Salute card randomly inserted (1:108 packs) and the retail version a Sterling Marlin Salute (1:108 packs). A special Sterling Marlin Back-to-Back Salute card was randomly seeded in series two retail packs (1:108). As with most Upper Deck issues, subsets abound. Series one included Championship Pit Crew, Star Rookies, Images of '95 and Next in Line. Series two featured New for '95, Did You Know, Speedway Legends and more Star Rookies.

COMPLETE SET (300) 12.50 30.00
COMP.SERIES 1 SET (150) 8.00 20.00
COMP.SERIES 2 SET (150) 6.00 15.00
WAX BOX HOBBY SER.1 20.00 50.00
WAX BOX HOBBY SER.2 20.00 50.00
1 Rusty Wallace .60 1.50
2 Jeff Gordon .75 2.00
3 Bill Elliott .30 .75
4 Kyle Petty .15 .40
5 Darrell Waltrip .15 .40
6 Ernie Irvan .15 .40
7 Dale Jarrett .50 1.25
8 Mark Martin .60 1.50
9 Michael Waltrip .15 .40
10 Rick Mast .07 .20
11 Sterling Marlin .25 .60
12 Chad Little .07 .20
13 Geoff Bodine .07 .20
14 Ricky Rudd .25 .60
15 Lake Speed .07 .20
16 Ted Musgrave .07 .20
17 Morgan Shepherd .07 .20
18 Bobby Labonte .50 1.25
19 Ken Schrader .07 .20
20 Brett Bodine .07 .20
21 Jimmy Spencer .07 .20
22 Harry Gant .15 .40
23 Dick Trickle .07 .20
24 Derrike Cope .07 .20
25 Kenny Wallace .07 .20
26 Jeff Burton .25 .60
27 Chuck Bown .07 .20
28 John Andretti .07 .20
29 Loy Allen Jr. .07 .20
30 Hut Stricklin .07 .20
31 Steve Grissom .07 .20
32 Ward Burton .15 .40
33 Robert Pressley .07 .20
34 Joe Nemechek .07 .20
35 Wally Dallenbach Jr. .07 .20
36 Jeff Purvis .07 .20
37 Terry Labonte .25 .60
38 Jimmy Hensley .07 .20
39 Dave Marcis .07 .20
40 Todd Bodine .07 .20
41 Greg Sacks .07 .20
42 Mike Wallace .07 .20
43 Jeremy Mayfield .15 .40
44 Rusty Wallace w Car .30 .75
45 Jeff Gordon w Car .40 1.00
46 Bill Elliott w Car .15 .40
47 Kyle Petty with Car .15 .40
48 Darrell Waltrip with Car .15 .40
49 Ernie Irvan w Car .15 .40
50 Dale Jarrett with Car .25 .60
51 Mark Martin w Car .30 .75
52 Michael Waltrip with Car .15 .40
53 Rick Mast with Car .07 .20
54 Sterling Marlin with Car .15 .40
55 Chad Little with Car .07 .20
56 Geoff Bodine with Car .07 .20
57 Ricky Rudd with Car .15 .40
58 Lake Speed with Car .07 .20
59 Ted Musgrave with Car .07 .20
60 Morgan Shepherd with Car .07 .20
61 Bobby Labonte with Car .25 .60
62 Ken Schrader with Car .07 .20
63 Brett Bodine with Car .07 .20
64 Jimmy Spencer with Car .07 .20
65 Harry Gant with Car .15 .40
66 Dick Trickle with Car .07 .20
67 Jeremy Mayfield with Car .07 .20
68 Kenny Wallace with Car .07 .20
69 Rusty Wallace's Car .25 .60
70 Jeff Gordon's Car .30 .75
71 Bill Elliott's Car .15 .40
72 Kyle Petty's Car .07 .20
73 Darrell Waltrip's Car .07 .20
74 Ernie Irvan's Car .07 .20
75 Dale Jarrett's Car .15 .40
76 Mark Martin's Car .25 .60
77 Michael Waltrip's Car .07 .20
78 Rick Mast's Car .02 .10
79 Sterling Marlin's Car .07 .20
80 Chad Little's Car .02 .10
81 Geoff Bodine's Car .02 .10
82 Ricky Rudd's Car .07 .20
83 Lake Speed's Car .02 .10
84 Ted Musgrave's Car .02 .10
85 Morgan Shepherd's Car .02 .10
86 Bobby Labonte's Car .25 .60
87 Ken Schrader's Car .02 .10
88 Brett Bodine's Car .02 .10
89 Jimmy Spencer's Car .02 .10
90 Harry Gant's Car .07 .20
91 Dick Trickle's Car .02 .10
92 Derrike Cope's Car .02 .10
93 Kenny Wallace's Car .02 .10
94 Jeff Burton's Car .07 .20
95 Chuck Bown's Car .02 .10
96 John Andretti's Car .02 .10
97 Loy Allen Jr.'s Car .02 .10
98 Hut Stricklin's Car .02 .10
99 Steve Grissom's Car .02 .10
100 Ward Burton's Car .07 .20
101 Robert Pressley's Car .02 .10
102 Joe Nemechek's Car .02 .10
103 Wally Dallenbach Jr.'s Car .02 .10
104 Jeff Purvis' Car .02 .10
105 Terry Labonte's Car .15 .40
106 Jimmy Hensley's Car .02 .10
107 Dave Marcis' Car .07 .20
108 Todd Bodine's Car .02 .10
109 Greg Sacks' Car .02 .10
110 Mike Wallace's Car .02 .10
111 Jeremy Mayfield's Car .07 .20
112 Rick Mast's Car NIL .02 .10
113 Sterling Marlin's Car NIL .07 .20
114 Bobby Labonte's Car NIL .25 .60
115 Geoff Bodine NIL .07 .20
116 Ricky Rudd's Car NIL .07 .20
117 Lake Speed's Car NIL .02 .10
118 Ted Musgrave's Car NIL .02 .10
119 Morgan Shepherd's Car NIL .02 .10
120 Ward Burton's Car NIL .07 .20
121 Ken Schrader's Car NIL .02 .10
122 Brett Bodine's Car NIL .02 .10
123 Jimmy Spencer's Car NIL .02 .10
124 Dick Trickle's Car NIL .02 .10
125 Derrike Cope's Car NIL .02 .10
126 Kenny Wallace NIL .07 .20
127 John Andretti .07 .20
128 Ward Burton .15 .40
129 Steve Grissom .07 .20
130 Jeremy Mayfield .15 .40
131 Jeff Burton .25 .60
132 Joe Nemechek .07 .20
133 Michael Jordan CPC 2.50 6.00
134 Reggie Jackson CPC .15 .40
135 Joe Montana CPC 2.00 5.00
136 Ken Griffey Jr. CPC 2.00 5.00
137 Rusty Wallace's Car .25 .60
138 Jeff Gordon's Car .30 .75
139 Bill Elliott's Car .15 .40
140 Kyle Petty's Car .07 .20
141 Darrell Waltrip's Car .07 .20
142 Ernie Irvan's Car .07 .20
143 Dale Jarrett's Car .15 .40
144 Mark Martin's Car .25 .60
145 Michael Waltrip's Car .07 .20
146 Ford Engine .02 .10
147 Chevy Engine .02 .10
148 Pontiac Engine .02 .10
149 Rusty Wallace CL .15 .40
150 Rusty Wallace CL .15 .40
151 Richard Petty SL .25 .60
152 Cale Yarborough SL .07 .20
153 Junior Johnson SL .07 .20
154 Harry Gant SL .15 .40
155 Bobby Allison SL .07 .20
156 David Pearson SL .07 .20
157 Ned Jarrett SL .02 .10
158 Glen Wood SL .02 .10
159 Benny Parsons SL .07 .20
160 Smokey Yunick SL .02 .10
161 Rusty Wallace DYK .30 .75
162 Terry Labonte DYK .15 .40
163 Jeff Gordon DYK .40 1.00
164 Mark Martin DYK .30 .75
165 Dale Jarrett DYK .25 .60
166 Geoff Bodine DYK .07 .20
167 Ricky Rudd DYK .15 .40
168 Jeff Burton DYK .07 .20
169 Sterling Marlin DYK .15 .40
170 Darrell Waltrip DYK .15 .40
171 Bobby Labonte DYK .25 .60
172 Ken Schrader DYK .07 .20
173 Kyle Petty DYK .15 .40
174 John Andretti DYK .07 .20
175 Ted Musgrave DYK .07 .20
176 Randy LaJoie SR .07 .20
177 Steve Kinser SR .07 .20
178 Robert Pressley SR .07 .20
179 Ricky Craven SR .07 .20
180 Davy Jones SR .07 .20
181 Rick Mast .07 .20
182 Rusty Wallace .60 1.50
183 Rusty Wallace .60 1.50
184 Sterling Marlin .25 .60
185 Terry Labonte .25 .60
186 Terry Labonte .25 .60
187 Mark Martin .60 1.50
188 Mark Martin .60 1.50
189 Geoff Bodine .07 .20
190 Jeff Burton .25 .60
191 Lake Speed .07 .20
192 Ricky Rudd .25 .60
193 Brett Bodine .07 .20
194 Derrike Cope .07 .20
195 Dick Trickle .07 .20
196 Ted Musgrave .07 .20
197 Darrell Waltrip .15 .40
198 Bobby Labonte .50 1.25
199 Morgan Shepherd .07 .20
200 Randy LaJoie .07 .20
201 Jimmy Spencer .07 .20
202 Jeff Gordon .75 2.00
203 Ken Schrader .07 .20
204 Steve Kinser .07 .20
205 Loy Allen Jr. .07 .20
206 Dale Jarrett .50 1.25
207 Ernie Irvan .15 .40
208 Steve Grissom .07 .20
209 Michael Waltrip .15 .40
210 Ward Burton .15 .40

211 Jimmy Hensley .07 .20
212 Robert Pressley .07 .20
213 John Andretti .07 .20
214 Greg Sacks .07 .20
215 Ricky Craven .07 .20
216 Kyle Petty .15 .40
217 Jeff Purvis .07 .20
218 Gary Bradberry RC .07 .20
219 Dave Marcis .07 .20
220 Todd Bodine .07 .20
221 Davy Jones .07 .20
222 Kenny Wallace .07 .20
223 Joe Nemechek .07 .20
224 Mike Wallace .07 .20
225 Bill Elliott .30 .75
226 Chad Little .07 .20
227 Jeremy Mayfield .15 .40
228 Rick Mast SD .07 .20
229 Rusty Wallace SD .30 .75
230 Sterling Marlin SD .15 .40
231 Terry Labonte SD .15 .40
232 Mark Martin SD .30 .75
233 Geoff Bodine SD .07 .20
234 Jeff Burton SD .15 .40
235 Lake Speed SD .07 .20
236 Ricky Rudd SD .15 .40
237 Brett Bodine SD .07 .20
238 Derrike Cope SD .07 .20
239 Dick Trickle SD .07 .20
240 Ted Musgrave SD .07 .20
241 Darrell Waltrip SD .15 .40
242 Bobby Labonte SD .25 .60
243 Morgan Shepherd SD .07 .20
244 Randy LaJoie SD .07 .20
245 Jimmy Spencer SD .07 .20
246 Jeff Gordon SD .40 1.00
247 Ken Schrader SD .07 .20
248 Steve Kinser SD .07 .20
249 Loy Allen Jr. SD .07 .20
250 Dale Jarrett SD .25 .60
251 Steve Grissom SD .07 .20
252 Michael Waltrip SD .15 .40
253 Ward Burton SD .15 .40
254 Jimmy Hensley SD .07 .20
255 Robert Pressley SD .07 .20
256 John Andretti SD .07 .20
257 Greg Sacks SD .07 .20
258 Ricky Craven SD .07 .20
259 Kyle Petty SD .15 .40
260 Gary Bradberry SD .07 .20
261 Dave Marcis SD .07 .20
262 Todd Bodine SD .07 .20
263 Davy Jones SD .07 .20
264 Kenny Wallace SD .07 .20
265 Joe Nemechek SD .07 .20
266 Mike Wallace SD .07 .20
267 Bill Elliott SD .15 .40
268 Chad Little SD .07 .20
269 Jeremy Mayfield SD .07 .20
270 Rusty Wallace's Car .25 .60
271 Sterling Marlin's Car .07 .20
272 Terry Labonte's Car .15 .40
273 Geoff Bodine's Car .02 .10
274 Jeff Burton's Car .07 .20
275 Brett Bodines Car .02 .10
276 Dick Trickle's Car .02 .10
277 Ted Musgrave's Car .02 .10
278 Darrell Waltrip's Car .07 .20
279 Bobby Labonte's Car .07 .20
280 Randy LaJoie's Car .02 .10
281 Jeff Gordon's Car .30 .75
282 Ken Schrader's Car .02 .10
283 Steve Kinser's Car .02 .10
284 Loy Allen Jr.'s Car .02 .10
285 Dale Jarrett's Car .15 .40
286 Steve Grissom's Car .02 .10
287 Jimmy Hensley's Car .02 .10
288 Robert Pressley's Car .02 .10
289 John Andretti's Car .02 .10
290 Greg Sacks' Car .02 .10
291 Ricky Craven's Car .02 .10
292 Kyle Petty's Car .07 .20
293 Jeff Purvis' Car .02 .10
294 Gary Bradberry's Car .02 .10
295 Dave Marcis' Car .07 .20
296 Davy Jones' Car .02 .10
297 Kenny Wallace's Car .02 .10
298 Joe Nemechek's Car .02 .10
299 Bill Elliott's Car .15 .40
300 Checklist (151-300) .02 .10
UD1 Sterling Marlin Salute 8.00 20.00
UD2 Jeff Gordon Salute 12.50 30.00
UD2A Jeff Gordon Salute AU 30.00 80.00
UD3 Sterling Marlin BB Salute 6.00 15.00
RW1 Rusty Wallace Promo .75 2.00
PR1 Rusty Wallace Promo .75 2.00
PR2 Rusty Wallace Promo .75 2.00

1995 Upper Deck Gold Signature/Electric Gold

COMPLETE GOLD SET (300) 350.00 700.00
COMP.GOLD SIG.SET (150) 200.00 400.00
COMP. ELE.GOLD SET (150) 150.00 300.00
*GOLD STARS: 8X TO 20X BASE CARDS

1995 Upper Deck Silver Signature/Electric Silver

COMPLETE SILVER SET (300) 25.00 60.00
*SILVERS: .8X TO 2X BASE CARDS

1995 Upper Deck Autographs

Randomly inserted in series two 1995 Upper Deck, the Autograph inserts were seeded approximately 1:300 packs. Reportedly, over 5000 total cards were signed for inclusion in packs.

COMPLETE SET (30) 700.00 1200.00
181 Rick Mast 8.00 20.00
182 Rusty Wallace 10.00 25.00
186 Terry Labonte 15.00 40.00
187 Mark Martin 15.00 40.00
189 Geoff Bodine 8.00 20.00
190 Jeff Burton 12.50 30.00
191 Lake Speed 8.00 20.00
195 Dick Trickle 8.00 20.00
196 Ted Musgrave 8.00 20.00
197 Darrell Waltrip 20.00 50.00
199 Morgan Shepherd 8.00 20.00
201 Jimmy Spencer 12.50 30.00
202 Jeff Gordon 100.00 200.00
205 Loy Allen Jr. 8.00 20.00
206 Dale Jarrett 25.00 60.00
207 Ernie Irvan 20.00 40.00
208 Steve Grissom 8.00 20.00
209 Michael Waltrip 8.00 20.00
210 Ward Burton 20.00 40.00
212 Robert Pressley 8.00 20.00
213 John Andretti 8.00 20.00
214 Greg Sacks 8.00 20.00
215 Ricky Craven 12.50 30.00
216 Kyle Petty 25.00 50.00
219 Dave Marcis 12.50 30.00
220 Todd Bodine 8.00 20.00
222 Kenny Wallace 8.00 20.00
223 Joe Nemechek 8.00 20.00
224 Mike Wallace 8.00 20.00
225 Bill Elliott 30.00 60.00

1995 Upper Deck Illustrations

Illustrations cards were randomly inserted in Upper Deck series two hobby packs at the rate of 1:15 packs. The cards feature portraits of ten legendary drivers painted by noted artists Jeanne Barnes and Jim Aukland.

COMPLETE SET (10) 12.00 30.00
I1 Smokey Yunick .25 .60
I2 Bobby Allison .50 1.25
I3 Junior Johnson .50 1.25
I4 Cale Yarborough .50 1.25
I5 David Pearson .50 1.25
I6 Benny Parsons .50 1.25
I7 Ned Jarrett .50 1.25
I8 Bill Elliott 2.00 5.00
I9 Jeff Gordon 5.00 12.00
I10 Rusty Wallace 4.00 10.00

1995 Upper Deck Jumbos

Upper Deck issued the Oversized box inserts in two 5-card series. The cards could be found packaged one per at the bottom of each foil box of either series one or two 1995 Upper Deck. The cards are essentially an enlarged (5" X 7") version of a regular issue Upper Deck card. Complete series of 5-cards were offered on some Upper Deck packs in exchange for 15 wrappers and $3 per series.

COMPLETE SET (10) 15.00 40.00
OS1 Rusty Wallace 5.00 12.00
OS2 Kyle Petty 1.25 3.00
OS3 Jeff Gordon 6.00 15.00
OS4 Mark Martin 5.00 12.00
OS5 Ernie Irvan 1.25 3.00
OS6 Ken Schrader .60 1.50
OS7 Bill Elliott 2.50 6.00
OS8 Geoff Bodine .60 1.50
OS9 Ricky Rudd 2.00 5.00
OS10 Terry Labonte 2.00 5.00

1995 Upper Deck Predictor Race Winners

Upper Deck included its popular Predictor redemption cards in both series racing products. Series one packs included randomly inserted (1:18 packs) Predictor Race Winners cards. If the featured driver won any of the 31 Winston Cup races of 1995, the card (along with $3) could be exchanged for a special parallel set. A longshot card was included to cover races that none of the nine other driver cards won. The winning cards are designated below and often carry a slight premium since they were exchangeable. The parallel prize cards differ only on the cardbacks. Each prize card has a short driver biography as opposed to contest rules.The redemption game expired 2/1/96. Upper Deck produced a special Predictor Race Winner set for both the 1995 Daytona 500 and Coca-Cola 600 at Charlotte. The cards feature a gold foil stamp with the race date and use the same rules as the regular issue Predictor cards, except that the featured driver would have to win that specific race. The longshot wound up being the winning card for both races.

COMPLETE SET (10) 25.00 60.00
COMP. WIN PRIZE SET (10) 7.50 15.00
*PRIZE CARDS: .15X TO .4X BASIC INSERTS
COMP.DAYTONA 500 (10) 25.00 60.00
*DAYTONA 500: .4X TO 1X BASIC INSERTS
COMP.COCA-COLA 600 (10) 25.00 60.00
*COCA-COLA 600: .4X TO 1X BASIC INSERTS
P1 Rusty Wallace WIN 4.00 10.00
P2 Mark Martin WIN 4.00 10.00
P3 Ricky Rudd 1.50 4.00
P4 Jeff Gordon WIN 5.00 12.00
P5 Bill Elliott 2.00 5.00
P6 Geoff Bodine .50 1.25
P7 Dale Jarrett WIN 3.00 8.00
P8 Terry Labonte WIN 1.50 4.00
P9 Jimmy Spencer .50 1.25
P10 Long Shot WIN .25 .60

1995 Upper Deck Predictor Series Points

Upper Deck included its popular Predictor redemption cards in both series one and two racing products. Series two packs included randomly inserted (1:17 packs) Predictor Series Points cards. If the featured driver won the 1995 Winston Cup Points Championship, the card (along with $3) could be exchanged for a special parallel set. A longshot card was included to cover drivers not featured on individual cards. The winning card, Jeff Gordon, is designated below and often carries a slight premium since it was the only exchangeable card for the contest. The parallel prize cards differ only on the cardbacks. Each prize card has a short driver biography as opposed to contest rules.The redemption game expired 2/1/96.

COMPLETE SET (10) 12.00 30.00
COMP. WIN PRIZE SET (10) 7.50 15.00
*PRIZE CARDS: .2X TO .5X BASIC INSERTS
PP1 Rusty Wallace 3.00 8.00
PP2 Sterling Marlin 1.25 3.00
PP3 Terry Labonte 1.25 3.00
PP4 Mark Martin 3.00 8.00
PP5 Bobby Labonte 2.50 6.00
PP6 Jeff Gordon WIN 4.00 10.00
PP7 Dale Jarrett 2.50 6.00
PP8 Kyle Petty .75 2.00
PP9 Bill Elliott 1.50 4.00
PP10 Long Shot .20 .50

1995 Upper Deck Jeff Gordon Phone Cards

This set was sold to both hobby and retail outlets. The cards were sold in complete set form with each card in the set carrying five minutes of phone time.

COMPLETE SET (5) 5.00 12.00
COMMON CARD (1-5) 1.25 3.00

1995 Upper Deck Rusty Wallace Phone Cards

This set was sold to both hobby and retail outlets. The unnumbered cards were sold in complete set form with each card in the set carrying five minutes of phone time.

COMPLETE SET (5) 4.00 10.00
COMMON CARD (1-5) .75 2.00

1996 Upper Deck

The 1996 Upper Deck set totals 150 cards. This is the second year of Upper Deck Motorsports. The set features the following topical subsets: Drivers (1-40), Scrapbook (41-80), Precision Performers (81-120) and The History Book (121-150). The product was available through both hobby and retail channels. There were 12 boxes per case with each box containing 28 packs. 10 cards came per pack and had a suggested retail of $1.99. In addition to numerous insert sets, Upper Deck produced two special Jeff Gordon single card inserts highlighting his championship 1995 season. Each of the cards features a die-cut design and light F/X printing. The cards were randomly inserted at the rate of 1:108 packs.

COMPLETE SET (150) 7.50 20.00
1 Rick Mast .07 .20
2 Rusty Wallace .60 1.50
3 Sterling Marlin .25 .60
4 Terry Labonte .25 .60
5 Mark Martin .60 1.50
6 Geoff Bodine .07 .20
7 Jeff Burton .25 .60
8 Lake Speed .07 .20
9 Ricky Rudd .25 .60
10 Brett Bodine .07 .20
11 Derrike Cope .07 .20
12 Bobby Hamilton .07 .20
13 Dick Trickle .07 .20
14 Ted Musgrave .07 .20
15 Darrell Waltrip .15 .40
16 Bobby Labonte .50 1.25
17 Morgan Shepherd .07 .20
18 Chad Little .07 .20
19 Jeff Purvis .07 .20
20 Loy Allen Jr. .07 .20
21 Jimmy Spencer .07 .20
22 Jeff Gordon .75 2.00
23 Ken Schrader .07 .20
24 Hut Stricklin .07 .20
25 Ernie Irvan .15 .40
26 Dale Jarrett .50 1.25
27 Steve Grissom .07 .20
28 Michael Waltrip .15 .40
29 Ward Burton .15 .40
30 Todd Bodine .07 .20
31 Robert Pressley .07 .20
32 Jeremy Mayfield .15 .40
33 Mike Wallace .07 .20
34 Bill Elliott .30 .75
35 John Andretti .07 .20
36 Kenny Wallace .07 .20
37 Joe Nemechek .07 .20
38 Dave Marcis .15 .40
39 Ricky Craven .07 .20
40 Kyle Petty SB .07 .20
41 Rick Mast SB .02 .10
42 Rusty Wallace SB .30 .75
43 Sterling Marlin SB .15 .40
44 Terry Labonte SB .15 .40
45 Mark Martin SB .30 .75
46 Geoff Bodine SB .02 .10
47 Jeff Burton SB .07 .20
48 Lake Speed SB .02 .10
49 Ricky Rudd SB .15 .40
50 Brett Bodine SB .02 .10
51 Derrike Cope SB .02 .10
52 Bobby Hamilton SB .02 .10
53 Dick Trickle SB .02 .10
54 Ted Musgrave SB .02 .10
55 Darrell Waltrip SB .07 .20
56 Bobby Labonte SB .25 .60
57 Morgan Shepherd SB .02 .10
58 Ernie Irvan SB .07 .20
59 Ernie Irvan SB .07 .20
60 Ernie Irvan SB .07 .20
61 Jimmy Spencer SB .02 .10
62 Jeremy Mayfield SB .15 .40
63 Mike Wallace SB .02 .10
64 Ken Schrader SB .02 .10
65 Hut Stricklin SB .02 .10
66 Dale Jarrett SB .25 .60
67 Steve Grissom SB .02 .10
68 Michael Waltrip SB .15 .40
69 Ward Burton SB .07 .20
70 Todd Bodine SB .02 .10
71 Robert Pressley SB .02 .10
72 Jeff Gordon SB .40 1.00
73 Jeff Gordon SB .40 1.00
74 Bill Elliott SB .15 .40
75 John Andretti SB .02 .10
76 Kenny Wallace SB .02 .10
77 Joe Nemechek SB .02 .10
78 Dave Marcis SB .07 .20
79 Ricky Craven SB .02 .10
80 Kyle Petty PP .07 .20
81 Rick Mast PP .02 .10
82 Rusty Wallace PP .30 .75
83 Sterling Marlin PP .15 .40
84 Terry Labonte PP .15 .40
85 Mark Martin PP .30 .75
86 Geoff Bodine PP .02 .10
87 Jeff Burton PP .07 .20
88 Lake Speed PP .02 .10
89 Ricky Rudd PP .15 .40
90 Brett Bodine PP .02 .10
91 Derrike Cope PP .02 .10
92 Bobby Hamilton PP .02 .10
93 Dick Trickle PP .02 .10
94 Ted Musgrave PP .02 .10
95 Darrell Waltrip PP .07 .20
96 Bobby Labonte PP .25 .60
97 Morgan Shepherd PP .02 .10
98 Jeff Gordon PP .40 1.00
99 Mark Martin PP .30 .75
100 Michael Waltrip PP .15 .40
101 Jimmy Spencer PP .02 .10
102 Jeff Gordon PP .40 1.00
103 Ken Schrader PP .02 .10
104 Hut Stricklin PP .02 .10
105 Ernie Irvan PP .07 .20
106 Dale Jarrett PP .25 .60
107 Steve Grissom PP .02 .10
108 Michael Waltrip PP .15 .40
109 Ward Burton PP .07 .20
110 Todd Bodine PP .02 .10
111 Robert Pressley PP .02 .10
112 Jeremy Mayfield PP .15 .40
113 Mike Wallace PP .02 .10
114 Bill Elliott PP .15 .40
115 John Andretti PP .02 .10
116 Kenny Wallace PP .02 .10
117 Joe Nemechek PP .02 .10
118 Dave Marcis PP .07 .20
119 Ricky Craven PP .02 .10
120 Kyle Petty HB .07 .20
121 Rick Hendrick HB .02 .10
122 Jack Roush HB .02 .10
123 Roger Penske HB .02 .10
124 Joe Gibbs HB .15 .40
125 Felix Sabates HB .02 .10
126 Bobby Allison HB .07 .20
127 Richard Petty HB .25 .60
128 Cale Yarborough HB .07 .20
129 Robert Yates HB .07 .20
130 Darrell Waltrip HB .07 .20
131 Bill Elliott HB .15 .40
132 Geoff Bodine HB .02 .10
133 Sterling Marlin HB .15 .40
134 Ricky Rudd HB .15 .40
135 Dave Marcis HB .07 .20
136 Rusty Wallace HB .30 .75
137 Ernie Irvan HB .07 .20
138 Jeff Gordon HB .40 1.00
139 Richard Petty HB .25 .60
140 Ned Jarrett HB .07 .20
141 Benny Parsons HB .07 .20
142 Rusty Wallace HB .30 .75
143 Jeff Burton HB .07 .20
144 Smokey Yunick HB .07 .20
145 Junior Johnson HB .07 .20
146 Ken Schrader HB .07 .20
147 Harry Gant HB .07 .20
148 Rusty Wallace HB .30 .75
149 Kyle Petty HB .07 .20
150 Jeff Gordon HB .40 1.00
C1 Jeff Gordon Tribute 10.00 25.00
C2 Jeff Gordon Tribute 10.00 25.00
JG1 Jeff Gordon Promo 2.00 5.00

1996 Upper Deck All-Pro

This 10-card set features the members of the Upper Deck All-Pro team. The cards could be found on average one per every 36 packs of 1996 Upper Deck series one.

COMPLETE SET (10) 25.00 60.00
AP1 Jeff Gordon 5.00 12.00
AP2 Terry Labonte 3.00 8.00
AP3 Ray Evernham 1.00 2.50
AP4 Rick Hendrick .50 1.25
AP5 Rusty Wallace 4.00 10.00
AP6 Robin Pemberton .50 1.25
AP7 Mark Martin 4.00 10.00
AP8 Ted Musgrave 1.00 2.50
AP9 Steve Hmiel .50 1.25
AP10 Jack Roush .50 1.25

1996 Upper Deck Predictor Poles

This 10-card interactive game set features nine drivers plus one Longshot card. The object to the game was to find a card for a driver who won any of the 31 pole positions for a 1996 race. If you had a winning card it was redeemable for a special version of all 10 Retail Predictors. The cards came only in retail packs at a rate of one per 12 packs. The expiration date to redeem winning cards was 2/1/1997. The Prize set was a 10-card set featuring the same fronts as the game cards. The difference is on the back. The cards are numbered RP1-RP10 just like the game cards but instead of having "How to play Predictor" game rules each card has a brief bio on that particular driver.

COMPLETE SET (10) 10.00 25.00
COMP.PRIZE SET (10) 5.00 12.00
*PRIZE CARDS: .2X TO .5X BASIC INSERTS
RP1 Jeff Gordon WIN 4.00 10.00
RP2 Mark Martin WIN 3.00 8.00
RP3 Rusty Wallace 3.00 8.00
RP4 Ernie Irvan WIN .75 2.00
RP5 Bobby Labonte 2.50 6.00
RP6 Bill Elliott 1.50 4.00
RP7 Sterling Marlin 1.25 3.00
RP8 Ricky Rudd 1.25 3.00
RP9 Rick Mast .40 1.00
RP10 Longshot WIN .20 .50

1996 Upper Deck Predictor Wins

This 10-card interactive game set features nine drivers plus one Longshot card. The object to the game was to have a card for a driver who won any of the 31 races in 1996. If you had a winning card it was redeemable for a special version of all 10 Hobby Predictors. The cards came only in hobby packs at a rate of one per 12 packs. The winning cards expired for redemption on 2/1/1997. The Prize set was a 10-card set featuring the same fronts as the game cards. The difference is on the back. The cards are numbered HP1-HP10 just like the game cards but instead of having "How to play Predictor" game rules each card has a brief bio on that particular driver.

COMPLETE SET (10) 12.00 30.00
COMP.PRIZE SET (10) 6.00 15.00
*PRIZE CARDS: .2X TO .5X BASIC INSERTS
HP1 Jeff Gordon WIN 4.00 10.00
HP2 Rusty Wallace WIN 3.00 8.00
HP3 Sterling Marlin WIN 1.25 3.00
HP4 Bobby Labonte 2.50 6.00
HP5 Mark Martin 3.00 8.00
HP6 Ricky Rudd 1.25 3.00
HP7 Terry Labonte WIN 1.25 3.00
HP8 Kyle Petty .40 1.00
HP9 Dale Jarrett WIN 2.50 6.00
HP10 Longshot WIN .20 .50

1996 Upper Deck Racing Legends

This 10-card set salutes the legends of racing as well as potential future legends. The set was available across brand lines in 1996. The cards are randomly inserted one per 24 packs.

COMPLETE SET (10) 10.00 25.00
RLC1 Richard Petty 2.50 6.00
RLC2 Cale Yarborough 2.00 5.00
RLC3 Bobby Allison 1.00 2.50
RLC4 Ned Jarrett 1.00 2.50
RLC5 Dave Marcis 1.00 2.50
RLC6 Junior Johnson 1.00 2.50
RLC7 David Pearson 2.00 5.00
RLC8 Harry Gant 2.00 5.00
RLC9 Darrell Waltrip 2.00 5.00
RLC10 Cover Card 1.00 2.50

1996 Upper Deck Virtual Velocity

This 15-card die-cut set features some of the top drivers in Winston Cup racing. The cards are die cut and feature light F/X processing. The cards were inserted at a rate of one per six packs. A parallel gold version was done of each card and was inserted at a rate of one per 72 packs.

COMPLETE SET (15) 12.00 30.00
COMP.GOLD SET (15) 75.00 150.00
*GOLDS: 1.5X TO 4X BASIC INSERTS
VV1 Jeff Gordon 3.00 8.00
VV2 Rusty Wallace 2.50 6.00
VV3 Geoff Bodine .30 .75
VV4 Sterling Marlin 1.00 2.50
VV5 Terry Labonte 1.00 2.50
VV6 Mark Martin 2.50 6.00
VV7 Bill Elliott 1.25 3.00
VV8 Darrell Waltrip .60 1.50
VV9 Ted Musgrave .30 .75
VV10 Ricky Rudd 1.00 2.50
VV11 Morgan Shepherd .30 .75
VV12 John Andretti .30 .75
VV13 Bobby Labonte 2.00 5.00
VV14 Michael Waltrip .60 1.50
VV15 Kyle Petty .30 .75

2012 Upper Deck All-Time Greats

STATED PRINT RUN 99 SER. #'d SETS
54 Richard Petty 4.00 10.00
55 Richard Petty 4.00 10.00
56 Richard Petty 4.00 10.00
57 Richard Petty 4.00 10.00
58 Richard Petty 4.00 10.00

2012 Upper Deck All-Time Greats Bronze

*BRONZE/65: .5X TO 1.2X BASIC CARDS

2012 Upper Deck All-Time Greats Silver

*SILVER/35: .6X TO 1.5X BASIC CARDS

2012 Upper Deck All-Time Greats Athletes of the Century Booklet Autographs

STATED PRINT RUN 5-35
ACRP Richard Petty/30 40.00 80.00

2012 Upper Deck All-Time Greats Letterman Autographs

PRINT RUN 7-140
LRP Richard Petty/25 30.00 60.00

2012 Upper Deck All-Time Greats Shining Moments Autographs

PRINT RUN 2-30
SMRP1 Richard Petty/20 30.00 60.00
SMRP2 Richard Petty/20 30.00 60.00
SMRP3 Richard Petty/20 30.00 60.00
SMRP4 Richard Petty/20 30.00 60.00
SMRP5 Richard Petty/20 30.00 60.00

2012 Upper Deck All-Time Greats Signatures

PRINT RUN 3-70
GARP1 Richard Petty/20 30.00 60.00
GARP2 Richard Petty/20 30.00 60.00
GARP3 Richard Petty/20 30.00 60.00
GARP4 Richard Petty/20 30.00 60.00
GARP5 Richard Petty/20 30.00 60.00

2012 Upper Deck All-Time Greats Signatures Silver

*SILVER: X TO X BASIC CARDS
PRINT RUN 2-25

2012 Upper Deck All-Time Greats SPx All-Time Forces Autographs

PRINT RUN 1-30
ATFRP Richard Petty/30

1998 Upper Deck Diamond Vision

This 15-card set focuses on 15 of the top drivers in NASCAR utilizing motion technology. The Jeff Gordon Reeltime card was randomly inserted in packs at a ratio of 1:500. Cards were distributed in one card packs with 16 packs per box and 12 boxes per case. The packs carried a suggested retail price of $7.99.

COMPLETE SET (15) 25.00 60.00
*SIG.MOVES: 1.2X TO 3X HI COL.
1 Jeff Gordon 3.00 8.00
2 Rusty Wallace 2.50 6.00
3 Dale Earnhardt 5.00 12.00
4 Sterling Marlin 1.00 2.50
5 Terry Labonte 1.00 2.50
6 Mark Martin 2.50 6.00
7 Dale Jarrett 2.00 5.00
8 Bill Elliott 1.25 3.00
9 Ernie Irvin .60 1.50
10 Ricky Rudd 1.00 2.50
11 Jeff Burton .60 1.50
12 Ricky Craven .60 1.50
13 Bobby Labonte 2.00 5.00
14 Kyle Petty .60 1.50
15 Robby Gordon .40 1.00
RT1 Jeff Gordon RT 50.00 100.00

1998 Upper Deck Diamond Vision Vision of a Champion

This 4-card insert set features four past Winston Cup champions. The cards were randomly inserted in packs at a ratio of 1:40.

COMPLETE SET (4) 60.00 150.00
VC1 Rusty Wallace 10.00 25.00
VC2 Dale Earnhardt 20.00 50.00
VC3 Jeff Gordon 12.50 30.00
VC4 Terry Labonte 4.00 10.00

2011 Upper Deck Goodwin Champions
COMP.SET w/o VAR (210) 40.00 80.00
COMP.SET w/o SP's (150) 10.00 25.00
COMMON SP (151-190) 1.00 2.50
151-190 SP ODDS 1:3 HOBBY
COMMON SP (191-210) 1.50 4.00
191-210 SP ODDS 1:12 HOBBY
COMMON VARIATION SP 4.00 10.00
186 Amber Cope/Angela Cope SP 1.00 2.50

2011 Upper Deck Goodwin Champions Autographs
Please note that the Dwayne De Rosario card in this set was issued in the 2014 Upper Deck Goodwin Champions product.
GROUP A ODDS 1:1577 HOBBY
GROUP B ODDS 1:729 HOBBY
GROUP C ODDS 1:339 HOBBY
GROUP D ODDS 1:246 HOBBY
GROUP E ODDS 1:72 HOBBY
GROUP F ODDS 1:35 HOBBY
OVERALL AUTO ODDS 1:20 HOBBY
EXCHANGE DEADLINE 6/7/2013
AA Amber Cope/Angela Cope F 8.00 20.00

2012 Upper Deck Goodwin Champions
COMP.SET w/o VAR (210) 25.00 50.00
COMP.SET w/o SP's (150) 10.00 25.00
151-190 SP ODDS 1:3 HOBBY, BLASTER
191-210 SP ODDS 1:12 HOBBY, BLASTER
62 Richard Petty .40 1.00
98 Maryeve Dufault .30 .75

2012 Upper Deck Goodwin Champions Mini
*1-150 MINI: 1X TO 2.5X BASIC CARDS
1-150 MINI STATED ODDS 1:2 HOBBY, BLASTER
211-231 MINI ODDS 1:2 HOBBY, BLASTER

2012 Upper Deck Goodwin Champions Mini Foil
*1-150 MINI FOIL: 2.5X TO 6X BASIC
1-150 MINI FOIL ANNCD. PRINT RUN 99
*211-231 MINI FOIL: 1X TO 2.5X BASIC MINI
211-231 MINI FOIL ANNCD. PRINT RUN 199

2012 Upper Deck Goodwin Champions Mini Green
*1-150 MINI GREEN: 1.25X TO 3X BASIC
*211-231 MINI GREEN: .6X TO 1.5X BASIC MINI
TWO MINI GREEN PER HOBBY BOX
ONE MINI GREEN PER BLASTER

2012 Upper Deck Goodwin Champions Mini Green Blank Back
UNPRICED DUE TO SCARCITY

2012 Upper Deck Goodwin Champions Autographs
GROUP A ODDS 1:1,977
GROUP B ODDS 1:353
GROUP C ODDS 1:264
GROUP D ODDS 1:185
GROUP E ODDS 1:82
GROUP F ODDS 1:36
OVERALL AUTO ODDS 1:20
EXCHANGE DEADLINE 7/12/2014
AMD Maryeve Dufault F 8.00 20.00
ARP Richard Petty C 20.00 50.00

2013 Upper Deck Goodwin Champions
COMP. SET w/o VAR (210) 25.00 60.00
COMP. SET w/o SPs (150) 8.00 20.00
151-190 SP ODDS 1:3 HOBBY,BLASTER
191-210 SP ODDS 1:12 HOBBY,BLASTER
OVERALL VARIATION ODDS 1:320 H, 1:1,200 B
GROUP A ODDS 1:4,800
GROUP B ODDS 1:2,400
GROUP C ODDS 1:1,400
58 Mario Andretti .25 .60
88A Richard Petty .40 1.00
88B Richard Petty Horizontal SP A
131 Danica Patrick .60 1.50
195 Frank Lockhart SP 1.50 4.00

2013 Upper Deck Goodwin Champions Autographs
OVERALL ODDS 1:20
GROUP A ODDS 1:7,517
GROUP B ODDS 1:1,224
GROUP C ODDS 1:489
GROUP D ODDS 1:142
GROUP E ODDS 1:206
GROUP F ODDS 1:28
ADP Danica Patrick D 50.00 100.00
AMA Mario Andretti D 10.00 25.00

2013 Upper Deck Goodwin Champions Memorabilia
OVERALL ODDS 1:12
GROUP A ODDS 1:23,082
GROUP B ODDS 1:5,970
GROUP C ODDS 1:104
GROUP D ODDS 1:22
GROUP E ODDS 1:37
MDP Danica Patrick E 8.00 20.00

2013 Upper Deck Goodwin Champions Mini
*1-150 MINI: 1X TO 2.5X BASIC CARDS
7 MINIS PER HOBBY BOX, 4 MINIS PER BLASTER

2013 Upper Deck Goodwin Champions Mini Canvas
*1-150 MINI CANVAS: 2.5X TO 6X BASIC CARDS
1-150 MINI CANVAS ANNCD. PRINT RUN 99
*211-225 MINI CANVAS: 1X TO 2.5 BASIC MINI
211-225 MINI CANVAS ANNCD. PRINT RUN 198

2013 Upper Deck Goodwin Champions Mini Green
STATED ODDS 1:12 HOBBY, 1:15 BLASTER
STATED SP ODDS 1:60 HOBBY, 1:72 BLASTER

2013 Upper Deck Goodwin Champions Sport Royalty Autographs
OVERALL ODDS 1:1,161
GROUP A ODDS 1:7,473
GROUP B ODDS 1:4,171
GROUP C ODDS 1:2,050
SRARP Richard Petty C 20.00 50.00

1997 Upper Deck Hot Wheels Kyle Petty
This 5-card set was produced by Upper Deck and made available by Toys 'R Us through a special point-of-purchase offer that would enable a collector to get the set of cards after buying $5.00 worth of Hot Wheels products.
COMPLETE SET (5) 2.00 5.00
HW1 Kyle Petty .40 1.00
HW2 Kyle Petty's Car .40 1.00
HW3 Kyle Petty's Car .40 1.00
HW4 Kyle Petty .40 1.00
HW5 Kyle Petty's Car .40 1.00

1999 Upper Deck Holiday Santa Suit

Cards from this set were mailed out during the 1999 year end holiday season to Upper Deck dealers and other customers. Each card features a driver dressed as Santa along with a swatch cut from the Santa suit that the driver wore for the photo shoot.
HH3 Rusty Wallace 10.00 20.00

1996 Upper Deck Jeff Gordon Profiles
This 20-card set features highlights from Jeff Gordon's racing career. The cards are 5" X 7" and were available through special retail outlets as well as hobby shops.
COMPLETE SET (20) 6.00 15.00
COMMON CARD (1-20) .40 1.00

1999 Upper Deck MVP ProSign

These Autographs were signed for the cancelled 1999 Upper Deck MVP product but placed in packs of 2000 SP Authentic at the rate of 1:40
BB Brett Bodine 6.00 15.00
DJR Dale Jarrett Silver 30.00 60.00
DWH Darrell Waltrip Gold 20.00 40.00
DWR Darrell Waltrip Silver 20.00 40.00
JB Johnny Benson 6.00 15.00
JGH Jeff Gordon Gold 300.00 500.00
JGR Jeff Gordon Silver 300.00 500.00
JJH Jason Jarrett Gold 10.00 25.00
JJR Jason Jarrett Silver 10.00 25.00
JR Dale Earnhardt Jr. 50.00 100.00
KP Kyle Petty 15.00 30.00
KSH Ken Schrader Gold 8.00 20.00
KSR Ken Schrader Silver 8.00 20.00
MKH Matt Kenseth Gold 30.00 80.00
MKR Matt Kenseth Silver 20.00 50.00
MW Mike Wallace 7.50 20.00
TSH Tony Stewart Gold 25.00 60.00
TSR Tony Stewart Silver 20.00 50.00

2000 Upper Deck MVP
Released early in 2000, this 102 card set was issued in 10-card packs which came 28 packs per box with an SRP of $1.59 per pack. This set is evenly mixed between NASCAR drivers and the cars they drive.
COMPLETE SET (102) 8.00 20.00
1 Dale Jarrett .40 1.00
2 Rusty Wallace .50 1.25
3 Dale Earnhardt 1.00 2.50
4 John Andretti .05 .15
5 Terry Labonte .20 .50
6 Mark Martin .50 1.25
7 Ken Schrader .05 .15
8 Mike McLaughlin .05 .15
9 Boris Said RC .05 .15
10 Kyle Petty .10 .30
11 Kevin Lepage .05 .15
12 Bobby Hamilton .05 .15
13 Mike Skinner .05 .15
14 Johnny Benson .10 .30
15 Chad Little .05 .15
16 Kenny Wallace .05 .15
17 John Nemechek .05 .15
Joe TRIB
18 Bobby Labonte .40 1.00
19 Jerry Nadeau .10 .30
20 Tony Stewart .60 1.50
21 Elliott Sadler .10 .30
22 Ward Burton .10 .30
23 Ernie Irvan .10 .30
24 Jeff Gordon .60 1.50
25 Bill Elliott .25 .60
26 Ricky Craven .05 .15
27 Michael Waltrip .10 .30
28 Geoffrey Bodine .05 .15
29 Jeff Burton .20 .50
30 Robert Pressley .05 .15
31 Sterling Marlin .20 .50
32 Jeremy Mayfield .05 .15
33 Steve Park .20 .50
34 Matt Kenseth CRC .50 1.25
35 Darrell Waltrip .10 .30
36 Dave Marcis .05 .15
37 Michael Waltrip .10 .30
38 Jason Jarrett .05 .15
39 Ricky Rudd .20 .50
40 Casey Atwood .20 .50
41 Jason Keller .05 .15
42 Rick Mast .05 .15
43 Bobby Hamilton Jr. RC .10 .30
44 Randy LaJoie .05 .15
45 Dick Trickle .05 .15
46 Adam Petty 1.50 4.00
47 Hank Parker Jr. RC .20 .50
48 Tony Stewart's Car .25 .60
49 Robert Pressley's Car .02 .10
50 Dick Trickle's Car .02 .10
51 Elliott Sadler's Car .02 .10
52 Dave Marcis's Car .02 .10
53 Kenny Wallace's Car .02 .10
54 Johnny Benson's Car .02 .10
55 Geoffrey Bodine's Car .02 .10
56 Ward Burton's Car .05 .15
57 Bobby Hamilton Jr.'s Car .02 .10
58 Mark Martin's Car .20 .50
59 Hank Parker Jr.'s Car .05 .15
60 Jason Jarrett's Car .02 .10
61 Jason Keller's Car .02 .10
62 Dale Jarrett's Car .10 .30
63 Rusty Wallace's Car .20 .50
64 Jeff Burton's Car .10 .30
65 Jeff Gordon's Car .25 .60
66 Jeremy Mayfield's Car .02 .10
67 Kevin Lepage's Car .02 .10
68 Bill Elliott's Car .10 .30
69 Darrell Waltrip's Car .05 .15
70 Steve Park's Car .10 .30
71 Chad Little's Car .05 .15
72 Terry Labonte's Car .10 .30
73 Adam Petty's Car .60 1.50
74 Kyle Petty's Car .05 .15
75 Bobby Labonte's Car .10 .30
76 Matt Kenseth's Car .20 .50
77 Ernie Irvan's Car .05 .15
78 Tony Stewart's Car .25 .60
79 Casey Atwood's Car .10 .30
80 Michael Waltrip's Car .05 .15
81 Ricky Rudd's Car .05 .15
82 Mike Skinner's Car .02 .10
83 Ken Schrader's Car .02 .10
84 Bobby Hamilton's Car .02 .10
85 D.Jarrett .40 1.00
N.Jarrett
86 John Andretti's Car .02 .10
87 Dale Earnhardt's Car .40 1.00
88 Mike McLaughlin's Car .02 .10
89 Jerry Nadeau's Car .10 .30
90 Randy LaJoie's Car .02 .10
91 Sterling Marlin's Car .05 .15
92 Dale Jarrett .40 1.00
93 Dale Earnhardt Jr. .75 2.00
94 Boris Said RC .05 .15
95 Terry Labonte .20 .50
96 Darrell Waltrip .10 .30
97 Ricky Rudd .20 .50
98 Dale Earnhardt Jr.'s Car .30 .75
99 Matt Kenseth .50 1.25
100 Wally Dallenbach .05 .15
101 Tony Stewart CL .30 .75
102 Jeff Gordon CL .30 .75

2000 Upper Deck MVP Gold Script
COMPLETE SET (102) 250.00 500.00
*GOLD SCRIPT: 10X TO 25X BASE CARDS

2000 Upper Deck MVP Silver Script
COMPLETE SET (102) 15.00 40.00
*SILVER SCRIPTS: .8X TO 2X BASE CARDS

2000 Upper Deck MVP Super Script
*SINGLES/70-99: 15X TO 40X BASE CARDS
*SINGLES/45-69: 20X TO 50X BASE CARDS
*SINGLES/30-44: 40X TO 80X BASE CARDS
*SINGLES/20-29: 40X TO 80X BASE CARDS

2000 Upper Deck MVP Cup Quest 2000
Issued at stated odds of one in seven, these 10 cards honor the drivers with the best chance of finishing the year as Winston Cup champion.
COMPLETE SET (10) 10.00 25.00
CQ1 Dale Earnhardt 2.50 6.00
CQ2 Dale Earnhardt Jr. 2.00 5.00
CQ3 Terry Labonte .50 1.25
CQ4 Ward Burton .30 .75
CQ5 Tony Stewart 1.50 4.00
CQ6 Jeff Burton .50 1.25
CQ7 Dale Jarrett 1.00 2.50
CQ8 Bobby Labonte 1.00 2.50
CQ9 Jeff Gordon 1.50 4.00
CQ10 Mark Martin 1.25 3.00

2000 Upper Deck MVP Legends in the Making
Inserted at stated odds of one in 13, these 10 cards feature drivers who have the best chance to become legendary figures in NASCAR history.
LM1 Jeff Gordon 2.00 5.00
LM2 Matt Kenseth 1.50 4.00
LM3 Bobby Labonte 1.25 3.00
LM4 Terry Labonte .60 1.50
LM5 Dale Earnhardt Jr. 2.50 6.00
LM6 Dale Jarrett 1.25 3.00
LM7 Mark Martin 1.50 4.00
LM8 Jeff Burton .60 1.50
LM9 Casey Atwood .60 1.50
LM10 Tony Stewart 2.00 5.00

2000 Upper Deck MVP Magic Numbers
Inserted at stated odds of one in 391, these five cards feature not only the drivers pictured but a real piece of a race-driven NASCAR car on them.
MBL Bobby Labonte's Car 15.00 40.00
MDJ Dale Jarrett's Car 15.00 40.00
MMK Matt Kenseth's Car 15.00 40.00
MRW Rusty Wallace's Car 15.00 40.00
MTS Tony Stewart's Car 20.00 50.00

2000 Upper Deck MVP Magic Numbers Autographs
Randomly inserted in packs, these cards parallel the Magic Number insert set. These cards are serial numbered to the car number and have been autographed by the honored driver.
MABL B.Labonte's Car/18 125.00 250.00
MADJ Dale Jarrett's Car/88 40.00 80.00
MAMK M.Kenseth's Car/17 200.00 350.00
MARW Rusty Wallace's Car/2
MATS Tony Stewart's Car/20 125.00 250.00

2000 Upper Deck MVP NASCAR Gallery
Inserted in packs at stated odds of one in 27, these nine cards focus on the most collectible drivers in NASCAR.
NG1 Terry Labonte 1.00 2.50
NG2 Tony Stewart 3.00 8.00
NG3 Mark Martin 2.50 6.00
NG4 Jeff Burton 1.00 2.50
NG5 Dale Earnhardt Jr. 4.00 10.00
NG6 Matt Kenseth 2.50 6.00
NG7 Dale Jarrett 2.00 5.00
NG8 Casey Atwood 1.00 2.50
NG9 Jeff Gordon 3.00 8.00
NG10 Bobby Labonte 2.00 5.00

2000 Upper Deck MVP NASCAR Stars
Inserted at stated odds of one in five, these 11 cards highlight the sport's top drivers.
COMPLETE SET (11) 10.00 25.00
NS1 Tony Stewart 1.25 3.00
NS2 Jeff Gordon 1.25 3.00
NS3 Dale Earnhardt 2.00 5.00
NS4 Jeff Burton .40 1.00
NS5 Dale Jarrett .75 2.00
NS6 Mark Martin 1.00 2.50
NS7 Bobby Labonte .75 2.00
NS8 Terry Labonte .40 1.00
NS9 Matt Kenseth 1.00 2.50
NS10 Casey Atwood .40 1.00
NS11 Dale Earnhardt Jr. 1.50 4.00

2000 Upper Deck MVP ProSign

Inserted at stated odds of one in 144, these 15 cards feature autographs of leading drivers. All these cards were released at redemptions and had a redemption deadline of October 7, 2000. Bobby Labonte did not return his cards so none of his cards were signed.
PSBL Bobby Labonte EXCH 3.00 8.00
PSCA Casey Atwood 10.00 25.00
PSDJ Dale Jarrett 10.00 25.00
PSDW Darrell Waltrip 8.00 20.00
PSJA John Andretti 6.00 15.00
PSJB Jeff Burton 8.00 20.00
PSJG Jeff Gordon 100.00 200.00
PSJM Jeremy Mayfield 8.00 20.00
PSJR Dale Earnhardt Jr. 60.00 120.00
PSKS Ken Schrader 6.00 15.00
PSMK Matt Kenseth 8.00 20.00
PSMM Mark Martin 15.00 40.00
PSRW Rusty Wallace 8.00 20.00
PSTS Tony Stewart 25.00 60.00
PSWB Ward Burton 8.00 20.00

2000 Upper Deck Racing

Released as a 45-card base set, 2000 Upper Deck features all rainbow holofoil cards with gold foil highlights and featured close up portrait style photography. Upper Deck was packaged in 24-pack boxes with packs containing four cards and carried a suggested retail price of $2.99.
COMPLETE SET (45) 10.00 25.00
1 Dale Jarrett .75 2.00
2 Bobby Labonte .75 2.00
3 Mark Martin 1.00 2.50
4 Tony Stewart 1.25 3.00
5 Jeff Burton .40 1.00
6 Jeff Gordon 1.25 3.00
7 Dale Earnhardt 2.00 5.00
8 Rusty Wallace 1.00 2.50
9 Ward Burton .25 .60
10 Mike Skinner .10 .30
11 Jeremy Mayfield .10 .30
12 Terry Labonte .40 1.00
13 Bobby Hamilton .10 .30
14 Steve Park .40 1.00
15 Race Day .05 .15
16 Sterling Marlin .40 1.00
17 John Andretti .10 .30
18 Wally Dallenbach .10 .30
19 Kenny Irwin .25 .60
20 Bill Elliott .50 1.25
21 Kenny Wallace .10 .30
22 Chad Little .25 .60
23 Elliott Sadler .25 .60
24 Kevin Lepage .10 .30
25 Kyle Petty .25 .60
26 Johnny Benson .25 .60
27 Michael Waltrip .25 .60
28 Ricky Rudd .40 1.00
29 Jerry Nadeau .25 .60
30 Darrell Waltrip .25 .60
31 Dale Earnhardt Jr. CRC 1.50 4.00
32 Matt Kenseth CRC 1.00 2.50
33 Jason Keller .10 .30
34 Scott Pruett RC .10 .30
35 Robby Gordon .10 .30
36 Stacy Compton RC .25 .60
37 Randy LaJoie .10 .30
38 Jimmie Johnson RC 5.00 12.00
39 Kevin Harvick 1.00 2.50
40 Power Pit .05 .15
41 Garage Work .05 .15
42 Short Tracks .05 .15
43 Hank Parker Jr. RC .40 1.00
44 Casey Atwood .40 1.00
45 Tony Stewart CL .60 1.50

2000 Upper Deck Racing Brickyard's Best
Randomly inserted in packs at the rate of one in 95, this eight card set features swatches of a tire that was used in the Inaugural Brickyard 400 race in 1994.
COMPLETE SET (8) 75.00 150.00
BB1 Rusty Wallace 8.00 20.00
BB2 Mark Martin 8.00 20.00
BB3 Bill Elliott 8.00 20.00
BB4 Darrell Waltrip 8.00 20.00
BB5 Dale Jarrett 8.00 20.00
BB6 Jeff Gordon 12.00 30.00
BB7 Ernie Irvan 6.00 15.00
BB8 Kyle Petty 6.00 15.00

2000 Upper Deck Racing Dale Earnhardt Tribute
COMPLETE SET (25) 20.00 50.00
COMMON CARD (DE1-DE25) 1.50 4.00

2000 Upper Deck Racing Dale Earnhardt Jr. Tribute
COMPLETE SET (25) 15.00 40.00
COMMON CARD (DEJ1-DEJ25) 1.25 3.00

2000 Upper Deck Racing High Groove
Randomly inserted in packs at the rate of one in 12, this six card set features top NASCAR drivers in a holographic foil card. Each card pictures the driver in the upper left hand corner and a large action shot of the car.
COMPLETE SET (6) 15.00 40.00
HG1 Jeff Burton 1.00 2.50
HG2 Dale Earnhardt Jr. 4.00 10.00
HG3 Matt Kenseth 2.50 6.00
HG4 Tony Stewart 3.00 8.00
HG5 Dale Earnhardt 5.00 12.00
HG6 Jeff Gordon 3.00 8.00

2000 Upper Deck Racing Record Pace
Randomly inserted in packs at the rate of one in three, this 9-card set features the driver with action shots of his car on an all rainbow holofoil card.
COMPLETE SET (9) 12.50 30.00
RP1 Jeff Burton .60 1.50
RP2 Bobby Labonte 1.25 3.00
RP3 Dale Earnhardt 3.00 8.00
RP4 Mark Martin 1.50 4.00
RP5 Jeff Gordon 2.00 5.00
RP6 Dale Earnhardt Jr. 2.50 6.00
RP7 Dale Jarrett 1.25 3.00
RP8 Matt Kenseth 1.50 4.00
RP9 Tony Stewart 2.00 5.00

2000 Upper Deck Racing Road Signs
Randomly seeded in packs at the rate of one in 72, this 26-card set features authentic autographs of NASCAR drivers. Due to the tragic death of Adam Petty, his exchange cards were redeemable for autographs of other drivers from all 2000 Upper Deck Racing products.
RSAP Adam Petty EXCH 15.00 40.00
RSBL Bobby Labonte 12.50 30.00
RSCA Casey Atwood 6.00 15.00
RSDE Dale Earnhardt 350.00 500.00
RSDJ Dale Jarrett 12.50 30.00
RSES Elliott Sadler 10.00 25.00
RSJG Jeff Gordon 100.00 200.00
RSJR Dale Earnhardt Jr. 60.00 120.00
RSKH Kevin Harvick 12.00 30.00
RSKS Ken Schrader 8.00 20.00
RSLA Lyndon Amick 6.00 15.00
RSMK Matt Kenseth 30.00 60.00
RSMM Mark Martin 20.00 50.00
RSRH Ron Hornaday 6.00 15.00
RSRR Ricky Rudd 10.00 25.00
RSRW Rusty Wallace 10.00 25.00
RSTS Tony Stewart SP 175.00 300.00
RSWB Ward Burton 8.00 20.00

2000 Upper Deck Racing Speeding Ticket
Randomly inserted in packs at the rate of one in 12, this six card set features top drivers on an all rainbow holofoil insert card with gold foil highlights.
COMPLETE SET (6) 15.00 40.00
ST1 Jeff Gordon 3.00 8.00
ST2 Bobby Labonte 2.00 5.00
ST3 Dale Earnhardt Jr. 4.00 10.00
ST4 Tony Stewart 3.00 8.00
ST5 Dale Earnhardt 5.00 12.00
ST6 Dale Jarrett 2.00 5.00

2000 Upper Deck Racing Tear Aways
Randomly inserted in packs at the rate of one in 750, this 14-card set features swatches of race used windshield tear-aways.
COMPLETE SET (4) 75.00 150.00
TACA Casey Atwood 8.00 20.00
TADJ Dale Jarrett 10.00 25.00
TAMK Matt Kenseth 10.00 25.00
TARW Rusty Wallace 12.50 30.00

2000 Upper Deck Racing Thunder Road
Randomly inserted in packs at the rate of one in 12, this six card set features portrait shots of drivers with their cars in the background. Cards are all holographic foil with bronze foil highlights.
COMPLETE SET (6) 12.50 30.00
TR1 Kyle Petty .60 1.50
TR2 Rusty Wallace 2.50 6.00
TR3 Mark Martin 2.50 6.00
TR4 Ricky Rudd 1.00 2.50
TR5 Jeff Gordon 3.00 8.00
TR6 Tony Stewart 3.00 8.00

2000 Upper Deck Racing Tony Stewart Tribute
COMPLETE SET (25) 12.00 30.00
COMMON CARD (TS1-TS25) .75 2.00

2000 Upper Deck Racing Trophy Dash
Randomly inserted in packs at the rate of one in 72, this nine card set features both veterans and young stars on an all holofoil card stock.
COMPLETE SET (9) 50.00 120.00
TD1 Terry Labonte 2.50 6.00
TD2 Dale Earnhardt Jr. 10.00 25.00
TD3 Bobby Labonte 5.00 12.00
TD4 Matt Kenseth 6.00 15.00
TD5 Jeff Burton 2.50 6.00
TD6 Dale Earnhardt 12.50 30.00
TD7 Jeff Gordon 8.00 20.00
TD8 Dale Jarrett 5.00 12.00
TD9 Tony Stewart 8.00 20.00

2000 Upper Deck Racing Winning Formula
Randomly inserted in packs at the rate of one in 23, this six card set focuses on the top young drivers of the 2000 Winston Cup Series. Cards are issued in split format with a driver portrait on the right side and his car on the left.
COMPLETE SET (6) 25.00 60.00
WF1 Bobby Labonte 4.00 10.00
WF2 Mark Martin 5.00 12.00
WF3 Dale Earnhardt 10.00 25.00
WF4 Dale Jarrett 4.00 10.00
WF5 Tony Stewart 6.00 15.00
WF6 Jeff Gordon 6.00 15.00

2000 Upper Deck Racing CHP

This was a four card set produced for the California Highway Patrol and was given out at the California Speedway for the 2000 season.
COMPLETE SET (4) 2.00 4.00
1 Rusty Wallace .75 2.00
2 Jeremy Mayfield .25 .60
3 Mark Martin .75 2.00
4 California Speedway .12 .30

1996 Upper Deck Road To The Cup
The 1996 Upper Deck Road To The Cup set was issued in one series totalling 150 cards. The 12-

card packs had a suggested retail of $1.99 each. The set contains the topical subsets: Drivers (RC1-RC50), Screamin' Steel (RC51-RC90), Changin' Gears (RC91-RC120), Award Winner (RC121-RC135), Truckin' 96 (RC136-RC145) and Role Models (RC146-RC150). It is the first Upper Deck set to include Dale Earnhardt. In honor getting Dale inked Upper Deck went back and made a number 301 card for its 1995 Upper Deck set. The card was seeded one in 95 packs. Also, they produced a Dale Earnhardt Tribute Card. This card was randomly inserted one in 190 packs. There is also a single insert of a Jeff Gordon Commemorative card. This card was inserted one in 72 packs and features 2-D technology.

COMPLETE SET (150) 10.00 25.00
RC1 Jeff Gordon .75 2.00
RC2 Sterling Marlin .25 .60
RC3 Mark Martin .60 1.50
RC4 Rusty Wallace .60 1.50
RC5 Terry Labonte .25 .60
RC6 Ted Musgrave .07 .20
RC7 Bill Elliott .30 .75
RC8 Ricky Rudd .25 .60
RC9 Bobby Labonte .50 1.25
RC10 Morgan Shepherd .07 .20
RC11 Michael Waltrip .15 .40
RC12 Dale Jarrett .50 1.25
RC13 Bobby Hamilton .07 .20
RC14 Derrike Cope .07 .20
RC15 Geoff Bodine .07 .20
RC16 Ken Schrader .07 .20
RC17 John Andretti .07 .20
RC18 Darrell Waltrip .15 .40
RC19 Brett Bodine .07 .20
RC20 Kenny Wallace .07 .20
RC21 Ward Burton .15 .40
RC22 Lake Speed .07 .20
RC23 Ricky Craven .07 .20
RC24 Jimmy Spencer .07 .20
RC25 Steve Grissom .07 .20
RC26 Joe Nemechek .07 .20
RC27 Ernie Irvan .15 .40
RC28 Kyle Petty .15 .40
RC29 Johnny Benson .15 .40
RC30 Jeff Burton .25 .60
RC31 Mike Wallace .07 .20
RC32 Dave Marcis .15 .40
RC33 Hut Stricklin .07 .20
RC34 Bobby Hillin .07 .20
RC35 Elton Sawyer .07 .20
RC36 Loy Allen .07 .20
RC37 Rick Mast .07 .20
RC38 Jeff Purvis .07 .20
RC39 Robert Pressley .07 .20
RC40 Wally Dallenbach .07 .20
RC41 Jeremy Mayfield .15 .40
RC42 Dale Earnhardt 1.25 3.00
RC43 Chad Little .07 .20
RC44 Mike McLaughlin .07 .20
RC45 Jason Keller .07 .20
RC46 Randy LaJoie .07 .20
RC47 Tim Fedewa .07 .20
RC48 Jeff Fuller .07 .20
RC49 David Green .07 .20
RC50 Patty Moise .07 .20
RC51 Jeff Gordon's Car .30 .75
RC52 Mark Martin's Car .25 .60
RC53 Rusty Wallace's Car .25 .60
RC54 Terry Labonte's Car .15 .40
RC55 Ted Musgrave's Car .02 .10
RC56 Bill Elliott's Car .15 .40
RC57 Ricky Rudd's Car .07 .20
RC58 Bobby Labonte's Car .15 .40
RC59 Morgan Shepherd's Car .02 .10
RC60 Michael Waltrip's Car .07 .20
RC61 Dale Jarrett's Car .15 .40
RC62 Bobby Hamilton's Car .02 .10
RC63 Derrike Cope's Car .02 .10
RC64 Geoff Bodine's Car .02 .10
RC65 Ken Schrader's Car .02 .10
RC66 John Andretti's Car .02 .10
RC67 Darrell Waltrip's Car .07 .20
RC68 Brett Bodine's Car .02 .10
RC69 Rick Mast's Car .02 .10
RC70 Ward Burton's Car .02 .10
RC71 Lake Speed's Car .02 .10
RC72 Ricky Craven's Car .02 .10
RC73 Jimmy Spencer's Car .02 .10
RC74 Chad Little's Car .02 .10
RC75 Joe Nemechek's Car .02 .10
RC76 Robert Pressley's Car .02 .10
RC77 Kyle Petty's Car .07 .20
RC78 Jeremy Mayfield's Car .07 .20
RC79 Jeff Burton's Car .07 .20
RC80 Mike Wallace's Car .02 .10
RC81 Dave Marcis's Car .07 .20
RC82 Hut Stricklin's Car .02 .10
RC83 Bobby Hillin's Car .02 .10
RC84 Elton Sawyer's Car .02 .10
RC85 Loy Allen's Car .02 .10
RC86 Kenny Wallace's Car .02 .10
RC87 Jeff Purvis's Car .02 .10
RC88 Ernie Irvan's Car .02 .10
RC89 Wally Dallenbach's Car .02 .10
RC90 Johnny Benson's Car .02 .10
RC91 Mark Martin .60 1.50
RC92 Rusty Wallace .60 1.50
RC93 Ricky Rudd .25 .60
RC94 Bobby Labonte .50 1.25
RC95 Morgan Shepherd .07 .20
RC96 Michael Waltrip .15 .40
RC97 Dale Jarrett .50 1.25
RC98 Bobby Hamilton .07 .20
RC99 Geoff Bodine .07 .20
RC100 Ken Schrader .07 .20
RC101 Darrell Waltrip .15 .40
RC102 Brett Bodine .07 .20
RC103 Rick Mast .07 .20
RC104 Ward Burton .15 .40
RC105 Lake Speed .07 .20
RC106 Jimmy Spencer .07 .20
RC107 Steve Grissom .07 .20
RC108 Joe Nemechek .07 .20
RC109 Robert Pressley .07 .20
RC110 Kyle Petty .15 .40
RC111 Jeremy Mayfield .15 .40
RC112 Jeff Burton .25 .60
RC113 Mike Wallace .07 .20
RC114 Dave Marcis .15 .40
RC115 Hut Stricklin .07 .20
RC116 Dick Trickle .07 .20
RC117 Loy Allen .07 .20
RC118 Kenny Wallace .07 .20
RC119 Wally Dallenbach .07 .20
RC120 Johnny Benson .15 .40
RC121 Jeff Gordon .75 2.00
RC122 Rick Hendrick .02 .10
RC123 Ray Evernham .02 .10
RC124 Jeff Gordon .75 2.00
RC125 Sterling Marlin .25 .60
RC126 Mark Martin .60 1.50
RC127 Rusty Wallace .60 1.50
RC128 Terry Labonte .25 .60
RC129 Ted Musgrave .07 .20
RC130 Bill Elliott .30 .75
RC131 Ricky Rudd .25 .60
RC132 Bobby Labonte .50 1.25
RC133 Ricky Craven .07 .20
RC134 Bobby Hamilton .07 .20
RC135 Johnny Benson .15 .40
RC136 Ernie Irvan .15 .40
RC137 Geoff Bodine .07 .20
RC138 Geoff Bodine .07 .20
RC139 Todd Bodine .07 .20
RC140 Jimmy Hensley .07 .20
RC141 Darrell Waltrip .15 .40
RC142 Kenny Wallace .07 .20
RC143 Derrike Cope .07 .20
RC144 Ted Musgrave .07 .20
RC145 Mike Wallace .07 .20
RC146 Ricky Craven .07 .20
RC147 Jeff Burton .25 .60
RC148 Jeff Gordon .75 2.00
RC149 Jimmy Hensley .07 .20
RC150 Bobby Hamilton .07 .20
301 Dale Earnhardt 12.50 30.00
DE1 Dale Earnhardt 10.00 25.00
JG1 Jeff Gordon 2-D 8.00 20.00

1996 Upper Deck Road To The Cup Autographs

Randomly inserted in hobby packs only at a rate of one in 16, this 29-card insert set features authentic signatures from top NASCAR drivers. Card number H7 was supposed to be Bill Elliott. Due to a crash at Talladega on April 28, 1996, Bill was unable to sign his cards and was dropped from the set.

COMPLETE SET (29) 400.00 700.00
H1 Jeff Gordon 50.00 100.00
H2 Sterling Marlin 15.00 40.00
H3 Mark Martin 15.00 40.00
H4 Rusty Wallace 12.50 30.00
H5 Terry Labonte 12.50 30.00
H6 Ted Musgrave 7.50 15.00
H8 Ricky Rudd 10.00 25.00
H9 Bobby Labonte 12.50 30.00
H10 Morgan Shepherd 7.50 15.00
H11 Michael Waltrip 8.00 20.00
H12 Dale Jarrett 12.50 30.00
H13 Bobby Hamilton 10.00 25.00
H14 Derrike Cope 7.50 15.00
H15 Geoff Bodine 7.50 15.00
H16 Ken Schrader 7.50 15.00
H17 John Andretti 7.50 15.00
H18 Darrell Waltrip 15.00 30.00
H19 Brett Bodine 7.50 15.00
H20 Kenny Wallace 7.50 15.00
H21 Ward Burton 8.00 20.00
H22 Lake Speed 7.50 15.00
H23 Ricky Craven 7.50 15.00
H24 Jimmy Spencer 7.50 15.00
H25 Steve Grissom 7.50 15.00
H26 Joe Nemechek 7.50 15.00
H27 Ernie Irvan 10.00 25.00
H28 Kyle Petty 10.00 25.00
H29 Johnny Benson 10.00 25.00
H30 Jeff Burton 8.00 20.00

1996 Upper Deck Road To The Cup Diary of a Champion

Randomly inserted in packs at a rate of one in six, this 10-card insert set captures moments of "a day in the life of Jeff Gordon" both on and off the track.

COMPLETE SET (10) 6.00 15.00
COMMON CARD (DC1-DC10) 1.00 2.50

1996 Upper Deck Road To The Cup Game Face

This 10-card insert set was available only in special retail packs. Each card includes the Game Face logo and was inserted one per pack.

COMPLETE SET (10) 4.00 10.00
GF1 Jeff Gordon 1.50 4.00
GF2 Rusty Wallace 1.25 3.00
GF3 Ernie Irvan .30 .75
GF4 Dale Jarrett 1.00 2.50
GF5 Terry Labonte .50 1.25
GF6 Mark Martin 1.25 3.00
GF7 Kyle Petty .30 .75
GF8 Bobby Labonte 1.00 2.50
GF9 Bill Elliott .60 1.50
GF10 Ricky Rudd .50 1.25

1996 Upper Deck Road To The Cup Jumbos

This five-card set was available through a wrapper redemption offer. The cards measure 5" X 7" and feature some of the top names in Winston Cup.

COMPLETE SET (5) 3.00 8.00
WC1 Jeff Gordon 1.25 3.00
WC2 Rusty Wallace 1.00 2.50
WC3 Ernie Irvan .25 .60
WC4 Dale Jarrett .75 2.00
WC5 Bill Elliott .50 1.25

1996 Upper Deck Road To The Cup Leaders of the Pack

Randomly inserted in packs at a rate of one in 35, this five-card insert set features the top motorsports drivers according to miles and/or laps led.

COMPLETE SET (5) 10.00 25.00
LP1 Jeff Gordon 5.00 12.00
LP2 Rusty Wallace 4.00 10.00
LP3 Ernie Irvan 1.00 2.50
LP4 Dale Jarrett 3.00 8.00
LP5 Terry Labonte 1.50 4.00

1996 Upper Deck Road To The Cup Predictor Points

Randomly inserted in packs at a rate of one in 22. In this 10-card insert set, the Terry Labonte card was the winning card and was redeemable for a special Championship Journal Redemption set.

COMPLETE SET (10) 12.00 30.00
*PRIZE CARDS: .25X TO .6X BASIC INSERTS
PP1 Jeff Gordon 4.00 10.00
PP2 Sterling Marlin 1.25 3.00
PP3 Mark Martin 3.00 8.00
PP4 Rusty Wallace 3.00 8.00
PP5 Terry Labonte WIN 1.25 3.00
PP6 Ted Musgrave .40 1.00
PP7 Bill Elliott 1.50 4.00
PP8 Dale Jarrett 2.50 6.00
PP9 Bobby Labonte 2.50 6.00
PP10 Longshot .20 .50

1996 Upper Deck Road To The Cup Predictor Top 3

Randomly inserted in packs at a rate of one in 22. In this 10-card insert set, if the drivers whose helmets are pictured on the card finish in first, second and third in any order of any race in the 1996 season, that card was redeemable for a special 15-card set. The expiration date to return these cards was February 10,1997.

COMPLETE SET (10) 15.00 40.00
T1 J.Gordon 1.50 4.00
R.Wallace
T.Labonte
T2 T.Labonte 1.25 3.00
D.Jarrett
S.Marlin
T3 Gordon 1.50 4.00
Irvan
Long.WIN
T4 R.Wall. 1.25 3.00
D.Waltrip
Longshot
T5 Martin 1.25 3.00
R.Wallace
B.Labonte
T6 Marlin 7.50 15.00
Gordon
LS WIN
T7 J.Gordon 1.50 4.00
M.Martin
J.Benson
T8 R.Rudd 1.25 3.00
M.Martin
B.Elliott
T9 Martin 1.25 3.00
Musgrave
Longshot
T10 R.Wallace 1.25 3.00
T.Lab.
K.Petty

1996 Upper Deck Road To The Cup Predictor Top 3 Prizes

This 15-card set is the redemption prize for any of the winning Top 3 Predictor game cards. The cards feature individual drivers unlike the game which featured three driver's helmets per card. The cards are done in gold foil and have a portrait shot of the driver impossed over the top of the foil.

COMPLETE SET (15) 10.00 25.00
R1 Jeff Gordon 2.50 6.00
R2 Rusty Wallace 2.00 5.00
R3 Ernie Irvan .50 1.25
R4 Sterling Marlin .75 2.00
R5 Terry Labonte .75 2.00
R6 Mark Martin 2.00 5.00
R7 Darrell Waltrip .50 1.25
R8 Bobby Labonte 1.50 4.00
R9 Dale Jarrett 1.50 4.00
R10 Ricky Rudd .75 2.00
R11 Bill Elliott 1.00 2.50
R12 Ted Musgrave .25 .60
R13 Kyle Petty .50 1.25
R14 Johnny Benson .50 1.25
R15 Longshot .10 .30

1996 Upper Deck Road To The Cup Racing Legends

Randomly inserted in packs at a rate of one in 23, this 10-card insert set is a cross-brand chase set featuring active and retired motorsport drivers. The first ten cards from the Racing Legends series were inserted in 1996 Upper Deck.

COMPLETE SET (10) 20.00 50.00
RL11 Terry Labonte 3.00 8.00
RL12 Bobby Labonte 6.00 15.00
RL13 Sterling Marlin 3.00 8.00
RL14 Ernie Irvan 2.00 5.00
RL15 Dale Jarrett 6.00 15.00
RL16 Kyle Petty 2.00 5.00
RL17 Geoff Bodine 1.00 2.50
RL18 Ricky Rudd 3.00 8.00
RL19 Ken Schrader 1.00 2.50
RL20 Header .50 1.25

1997 Upper Deck Road To The Cup

This 150-card set features six topical subsets: Heroes of the Hardtop (1-45), Power Plants (46-89), Inside Track (90-104), Haulin' (105-120), Alternators (121-142), and Thunder Struck(143-150). Cards were distributed in ten card packs with 28 packs per box and 12 boxes per case. The packs carried a suggested retail price of $2.49.

COMPLETE SET (150) 8.00 20.00
1 Terry Labonte .25 .60
2 Jeff Gordon .75 2.00
3 Dale Jarrett .50 1.25
4 Dale Earnhardt 1.25 3.00
5 Mark Martin .60 1.50
6 Ricky Rudd .25 .60
7 Rusty Wallace .60 1.50
8 Sterling Marlin .25 .60
9 Bobby Hamilton .07 .20
10 Ernie Irvan .15 .40
11 Bobby Labonte .50 1.25
12 Bill Elliott .30 .75
13 Kyle Petty .15 .40
14 Ken Schrader .07 .20
15 Jeff Burton .25 .60
16 Michael Waltrip .15 .40
17 Jimmy Spencer .07 .20
18 Ted Musgrave .07 .20
19 Geoff Bodine .07 .20
20 Rick Mast .07 .20
21 Morgan Shepherd .07 .20
22 Ricky Craven .07 .20
23 Johnny Benson .15 .40
24 Hut Stricklin .07 .20
25 Lake Speed .07 .20
26 Brett Bodine .07 .20
27 Wally Dallenbach .07 .20
28 Jeremy Mayfield .15 .40
29 Kenny Wallace .07 .20
30 Darrell Waltrip .15 .40
31 John Andretti .07 .20
32 Robert Pressley .07 .20
33 Ward Burton .15 .40
34 Joe Nemechek .07 .20
35 Derrike Cope .07 .20
36 Dick Trickle .07 .20
37 Dave Marcis .15 .40
38 Steve Grissom .07 .20
39 Mike Wallace .07 .20
40 Chad Little .07 .20
41 Gary Bradberry .07 .20
42 David Green .07 .20
43 Bobby Hillin .07 .20
44 Terry Labonte's Car .15 .40
45 Jeff Gordon's Car .30 .75
46 Dale Jarrett's Car .15 .40
47 Mark Martin's Car .25 .60
48 Ricky Rudd's Car .07 .20
49 Rusty Wallace's Car .25 .60
50 Sterling Marlin's Car .07 .20
51 Bobby Hamilton's Car .02 .10
52 Ernie Irvan's Car .07 .20
53 Bobby Labonte's Car .15 .40
54 Bill Elliott's Car .15 .40
55 Kyle Petty's Car .07 .20
56 Ken Schrader's Car .02 .10
57 Jeff Burton's Car .07 .20
58 Michael Waltrip's Car .07 .20
59 Jimmy Spencer's Car .02 .10
60 Ted Musgrave's Car .02 .10
61 Geoff Bodine's Car .02 .10
62 Rick Mast's Car .02 .10
63 Morgan Shepherd's Car .02 .10
64 Ricky Craven's Car .02 .10
65 Johnny Benson's Car .02 .10
66 Hut Stricklin's Car .02 .10
67 Lake Speed's Car .02 .10
68 Brett Bodine's Car .02 .10
69 Wally Dallenbach's Car .02 .10
70 Jeremy Mayfield's Car .15 .40
71 Kenny Wallace's Car .02 .10
72 Darrell Waltrip's Car .07 .20
73 John Andretti's Car .02 .10
74 Robert Pressley's Car .02 .10
75 Ward Burton's Car .02 .10
76 Joe Nemechek's Car .02 .10
77 Derrike Cope's Car .02 .10
78 Dick Trickle's Car .02 .10
79 Dave Marcis's Car .07 .20
80 Steve Grissom's Car .02 .10
81 Mike Wallace's Car .02 .10
82 Chad Little's Car .02 .10
83 Gary Bradberry's Car .02 .10
84 David Green's Car .02 .10
85 Bobby Hillin's Car .02 .10
86 Terry Labonte .25 .60
87 Jeff Gordon .75 2.00
88 Dale Jarrett .50 1.25
89 Mark Martin .60 1.50
90 Ricky Rudd .25 .60
91 Rusty Wallace .60 1.50
92 Sterling Marlin .25 .60
93 Bobby Hamilton .07 .20
94 Ernie Irvan .15 .40
95 Bobby Labonte .50 1.25
96 Bill Elliott .30 .75
97 Kyle Petty .15 .40
98 Ken Schrader .07 .20
99 Jeff Burton .25 .60
100 Ted Musgrave .07 .20
101 Ricky Craven .07 .20
102 Johnny Benson .15 .40
103 Darrell Waltrip .15 .40
104 John Andretti .07 .20
105 Derrike Cope .07 .20
106 Terry Labonte's Trans. .15 .40
107 Jeff Gordon's Trans. .25 .60
108 Dale Jarrett's Trans. .15 .40
109 Jeff Burton's Trans. .07 .20
110 Ricky Rudd's Trans. .07 .20
111 Sterling Marlin's Trans. .07 .20
112 Rick Mast's Trans. .02 .10
113 Michael Waltrip's Trans. .07 .20
114 Ken Schrader's Trans. .02 .10
115 Steve Grissom's Trans. .02 .10
116 Kyle Petty's Trans. .07 .20
117 Darrell Waltrip's Trans. .07 .20
118 Bobby Labonte's Trans. .15 .40
119 Bill Elliott's Trans. .15 .40
120 Chad Little's Trans. .02 .10
121 Dale Earnhardt's Trans. .50 1.25
122 Brett Bodine's Trans. .02 .10
123 Geoff Bodine's Trans. .02 .10
124 Rusty Wallace .60 1.50
125 Sterling Marlin .25 .60
126 Bobby Hamilton .07 .20
127 Ernie Irvan .15 .40
128 Bobby Labonte .50 1.25
129 Kyle Petty .15 .40
130 Ken Schrader .07 .20
131 Ted Musgrave .07 .20
132 Rick Mast .07 .20
133 Morgan Shepherd .07 .20
134 Ricky Craven .07 .20
135 Hut Stricklin .07 .20
136 Lake Speed .07 .20
137 Brett Bodine .07 .20
138 Wally Dallenbach .07 .20
139 Darrell Waltrip .15 .40
140 Robert Pressley .07 .20
141 Joe Nemechek .07 .20
142 Derrike Cope .07 .20
143 Steve Grissom .07 .20
144 Mike Wallace .07 .20
145 Chad Little .07 .20
146 David Green .07 .20
147 Mark Martin .60 1.50
148 Ricky Rudd .25 .60
149 Gary Bradberry .07 .20
150 John Andretti .07 .20

1997 Upper Deck Road To The Cup Cup Quest

This 10-card insert set features the top stars from the Winston Cup circuit. Each card in the basic insert set was printed with a green background and serial numbered of 5000.

COMP.GREEN CUP QUEST (10) 25.00 60.00
COMP.WHITE CUP QUEST (10) 60.00 120.00
*WHITE CUP QUEST: .8X TO 2X GREEN
WHITE PRINT RUN 1000 SER.#'d SETS
COMP.CHECKERED (10) 750.00 1500.00
*CHECKERED: 6X TO 15X GREEN
CHECKERED PRINT RUN 100 SER.#'d SETS
CQ1 Terry Labonte 1.50 4.00
CQ2 Jeff Gordon 5.00 12.00
CQ3 Dale Earnhardt 8.00 20.00
CQ4 Dale Jarrett 3.00 8.00
CQ5 Rusty Wallace 4.00 10.00
CQ6 Ernie Irvan 1.00 2.50
CQ7 Mark Martin 4.00 10.00
CQ8 Sterling Marlin 1.50 4.00
CQ9 Bobby Hamilton .50 1.25
CQ10 Ricky Rudd 1.50 4.00

1997 Upper Deck Road To The Cup Million Dollar Memoirs

This 20-card set features five of top driver on the Winston Cup circuit. Each driver has four cards in the set. The cards were randomly inserted in packs at a ratio of 1:23.

COMPLETE SET (20) 60.00 150.00
MM1 Terry Labonte 2.50 6.00
MM2 Terry Labonte 2.50 6.00
MM3 Terry Labonte 2.50 6.00
MM4 Terry Labonte 2.50 6.00
MM5 Jeff Gordon 8.00 20.00
MM6 Jeff Gordon 8.00 20.00
MM7 Jeff Gordon 8.00 20.00
MM8 Jeff Gordon 8.00 20.00
MM9 Rusty Wallace 6.00 15.00
MM10 Rusty Wallace 6.00 15.00
MM11 Rusty Wallace 6.00 15.00
MM12 Rusty Wallace 6.00 15.00
MM13 Dale Jarrett 5.00 12.00
MM14 Dale Jarrett 5.00 12.00
MM15 Dale Jarrett 5.00 12.00
MM16 Dale Jarrett 5.00 12.00
MM17 Bill Elliott 3.00 8.00
MM18 Bill Elliott 3.00 8.00
MM19 Bill Elliott 3.00 8.00
MM20 Bill Elliott 3.00 8.00

1997 Upper Deck Road To The Cup Million Dollar Memoirs Autographs

COMPLETE SET (20) 500.00 1000.00
MM1 Terry Labonte 12.50 30.00
MM2 Terry Labonte 12.50 30.00
MM3 Terry Labonte 12.50 30.00
MM4 Terry Labonte 12.50 30.00
MM5 Jeff Gordon 60.00 120.00
MM6 Jeff Gordon 60.00 120.00
MM7 Jeff Gordon 60.00 120.00
MM8 Jeff Gordon 60.00 120.00
MM9 Rusty Wallace 12.50 30.00
MM10 Rusty Wallace 12.50 30.00
MM11 Rusty Wallace 12.50 30.00
MM12 Rusty Wallace 12.50 30.00
MM13 Dale Jarrett 12.50 30.00
MM14 Dale Jarrett 12.50 30.00
MM15 Dale Jarrett 12.50 30.00
MM16 Dale Jarrett 12.50 30.00
MM17 Bill Elliott 12.00 30.00
MM18 Bill Elliott 12.00 30.00
MM19 Bill Elliott 12.00 30.00
MM20 Bill Elliott 12.00 30.00

1997 Upper Deck Road To The Cup Piece of the Action

This 9-card set features pieces of a driver's seat, safety harness and window net incorporated into a trading card. The cards were seeded one in 1117 packs.

COMPLETE SET (9) 250.00 500.00
HS1 Rusty Wallace Window Net 8.00 20.00
HS2 Rusty Wallace Shoul.Harness 8.00 20.00
HS3 Rusty Wallace Seat Cover 8.00 20.00
HS4 Jeff Gordon Window Net 12.00 30.00
HS5 Jeff Gordon Should.Harness 12.00 30.00
HS6 Jeff Gordon Seat Cover 12.00 30.00
HS7 Dale Jarrett Window Net 8.00 20.00
HS8 Dale Jarrett Should.Harness 8.00 20.00
HS9 Dale Jarrett Seat Cover 8.00 20.00

1997 Upper Deck Road To The Cup Predictor Plus

This 30-card set features a scratch-off redemption game that gave collectors three chances to win. Each card has three scratch off areas that correspond to Starting Position, Laps Led, and Finish Position. There were three levels of prizes available for the winning cards. The cards featuring drivers that were winners in one of the three categories could be redeemed for a cel card of that driver. The cards that were winners in two categories could be redeemed for a complete set of die cut cel cards. Finally, the cards that were winners in all three areas could be redeemed for a complete set of cel cards and a complete base set of 1997 Upper Deck Road to the Cup. The prices below are for unscratched cards. These cards expired on 1/30/98. The cards were randomly inserted in packs at a ratio of 1:11.

COMPLETE SET (30) 40.00 80.00
*CEL PRIZES: 1X TO 2.5X BASIC INSERTS
*DIE CUT PRIZES: 1.2X TO 3X BASIC INSERTS
1 Terry Labonte .60 1.50
2 Jeff Gordon 2.00 5.00
3 Dale Jarrett 1.25 3.00
4 Sterling Marlin WIN .60 1.50
5 Ricky Craven .20 .50
6 Ernie Irvan WIN .40 1.00
7 Rusty Wallace 1.50 4.00
8 Mark Martin 1.50 4.00
9 Terry Labonte .60 1.50
10 Bill Elliott .75 2.00
11 Jeff Gordon WIN 2.00 5.00
12 Geoff Bodine WIN 3 .20 .50
13 Dale Jarrett WIN 1.25 3.00
14 Rusty Wallace 1.50 4.00
15 Jeremy Mayfield .40 1.00
16 Mark Martin 1.50 4.00
17 Ken Schrader WIN .20 .50
18 Jimmy Spencer WIN .20 .50
19 Ted Musgrave .20 .50
20 Darrell Waltrip .40 1.00
21 Jeff Burton .60 1.50
22 Ward Burton WIN .40 1.00
23 Ricky Rudd WIN .60 1.50
24 Johnny Benson WIN .40 1.00
25 Kyle Petty WIN .40 1.00
26 Bobby Hamilton WIN 3 .20 .50
27 Terry Labonte .60 1.50
28 Jeff Gordon 2.00 5.00
29 Bobby Labonte WIN 2 1.25 3.00
30 Bill Elliott WIN .75 2.00

1997 Upper Deck Road To The Cup Premiere Position

This 48-card card insert set showcases drivers who won the pole in one of 24 races in the 1996 season and early 1997 season. Each card features a die cut. The cards were randomly inserted in packs at a ratio of 1:5.

COMPLETE SET (48) 75.00 150.00
PP1 Terry Labonte 1.25 3.00
PP2 Jeff Gordon 4.00 10.00
PP3 Johnny Benson .75 2.00
PP4 Dale Earnhardt 6.00 15.00
PP5 Terry Labonte 1.25 3.00

PP6 Terry Labonte 1.25 3.00
PP7 Ricky Craven .40 1.00
PP8 Rusty Wallace 3.00 8.00
PP9 Ernie Irvan .75 2.00
PP10 Sterling Marlin 1.25 3.00
PP11 Jeff Gordon 4.00 10.00
PP12 Jeff Gordon 4.00 10.00
PP13 Bobby Hamilton .40 1.00
PP14 Rusty Wallace 3.00 8.00
PP15 Ricky Craven .40 1.00
PP16 Ernie Irvan .75 2.00
PP17 Mark Martin 3.00 8.00
PP18 Rusty Wallace 3.00 8.00
PP19 Jeremy Mayfield .75 2.00
PP20 Jeff Gordon 4.00 10.00
PP21 Jeff Gordon 4.00 10.00
PP22 Dale Jarrett 2.50 6.00
PP23 Jeff Burton 1.25 3.00
PP24 Dale Jarrett 2.50 6.00
PP25 Mark Martin 3.00 8.00
PP26 Rusty Wallace 3.00 8.00
PP27 Dale Jarrett 2.50 6.00
PP28 Jeff Gordon 4.00 10.00
PP29 Mark Martin 3.00 8.00
PP30 Ernie Irvan .75 2.00
PP31 Bobby Hamilton .40 1.00
PP32 Jeff Gordon 4.00 10.00
PP33 Bobby Labonte 2.50 6.00
PP34 Terry Labonte 1.25 3.00
PP35 Dale Jarrett 2.50 6.00
PP36 Ricky Rudd 1.25 3.00
PP37 Bobby Labonte 2.50 6.00
PP38 Bobby Hamilton .40 1.00
PP39 Bobby Labonte 2.50 6.00
PP40 Bobby Labonte 2.50 6.00
PP41 Mark Martin 3.00 8.00
PP42 Jeff Gordon 4.00 10.00
PP43 Terry Labonte 1.25 3.00
PP44 Rusty Wallace 3.00 8.00
PP45 Dale Jarrett 2.50 6.00
PP46 Dale Jarrett 2.50 6.00
PP47 Dale Jarrett 2.50 6.00
PP48 Jeff Burton 1.25 3.00

1998 Upper Deck Road To The Cup

The 1998 Upper Deck Road to the Cup set consists of 120 standard size cards. The fronts feature full bleed photos of the driver or the driver's car. A silver band lines the left side of the card where the driver's name and Upper Deck logo are found. The set contains the subsets: Taurus Time (46-60), Days of Daytona (61-75), Young Guns (76-85), Viva Las Vegas (86-100), Double Barrel (101-115), and Checklists (116-120).

COMPLETE SET (120) 15.00 35.00
WAX BOX 25.00 60.00
1 Kevin Lepage .10 .30
2 Rusty Wallace 1.00 2.50
3 Dale Jarrett 2.00 5.00
4 Bobby Hamilton's Car .05 .15
5 Terry Labonte .40 1.00
6 Mark Martin's Car .40 1.00
7 Geoff Bodine's Car .05 .15
8 Hut Stricklin .10 .30
9 Jeff Burton's Car .10 .30
10 Ricky Rudd .40 1.00
11 Brett Bodine's Car .05 .15
12 Jeremy Mayfield .25 .60
13 Jerry Nadeau RC .40 1.00
14 Loy Allen's Car .05 .15
15 Bill Elliott's Car .25 .60
16 Jeff Green .10 .30
17 Darrell Waltrip .25 .60
18 Bobby Labonte's Car .25 .60
19 David Green .10 .30
20 Dale Jarrett .75 2.00
21 Michael Waltrip .25 .60
22 Ward Burton .25 .60
23 Jimmy Spencer .10 .30
24 Jeff Gordon 1.25 3.00
25 Randy LaJoie's Car .05 .15
26 Johnny Benson .25 .60
27 Gary Bradberry .10 .30
28 Kenny Irwin .25 .60
29 Dave Marcis .25 .60
30 Derrike Cope .10 .30
31 Mike Skinner .10 .30
32 Ron Hornaday .10 .30
33 Ken Schrader .10 .30
34 Rick Mast .10 .30
35 Todd Bodine .10 .30
36 Ernie Irvan .25 .60
37 Dick Trickle's Car .05 .15
38 Robert Pressley .10 .30
39 Wally Dallenbach .10 .30
40 Sterling Marlin's Car .10 .30
41 Steve Grissom .10 .30
42 Joe Nemechek's Car .05 .15
43 John Andretti .10 .30
44 Kyle Petty's Car .10 .30
45 Kenny Wallace .10 .30
46 Rusty Wallace's Car .40 1.00
47 Mark Martin's Car .40 1.00
48 Geoff Bodine's Car .05 .15
49 Ricky Rudd's Car .10 .30
50 Jeremy Mayfield's Car .10 .30
51 Jerry Nadeau's Car .25 .60
52 Chad Little's Car .05 .15
53 Michael Waltrip's Car .10 .30
54 Jimmy Spencer's Car .05 .15
55 Johnny Benson's Car .10 .30
56 Kenny Irwin's Car .10 .30
57 Kenny Wallace's Car .05 .15
58 Dale Jarrett's Car .25 .60
59 Bill Elliott's Car .25 .60
60 Jeff Burton's Car .10 .30
61 NASCAR Gold Car .05 .15
62 Jimmy Spencer's Car .05 .15
63 Rusty Wallace's Car .40 1.00
64 Jeremy Mayfield .25 .60
65 Geoff Bodine's Car .05 .15
66 Jeff Gordon 1.25 3.00
67 John Andretti .10 .30
68 Bobby .75 2.00
Terry Labonte
69 Terry Labonte's Car .25 .60
70 Bobby Labonte's Car .25 .60
71 Chad Little's Car .05 .15
72 Sterling Marlin's Car .10 .30
73 Dave Marci's Car .10 .30
74 Jerry Nadeau's Car .25 .60
75 Dale Earnhardt 2.00 5.00
76 Kenny Irwin .25 .60
77 Jerry Nadeau's Car .25 .60
78 Todd Bodine .10 .30
79 Johnny Benson's Car .10 .30
80 John Andretti .10 .30
81 Jeremy Mayfield .25 .60
82 Kevin Lepage .10 .30
83 Dale Earnhardt Jr.'s Car .50 1.25
84 Randy LaJoie .10 .30
85 Mike Skinner's Car .05 .15
86 Rusty Wallace's Car .40 1.00
87 Ernie Irvan's Car .10 .30
88 Jeff Gordon's Car .50 1.25
89 Jeff Burton .40 1.00
90 Dale Jarrett's Car .25 .60
91 Bill Elliott's Car .25 .60
92 Jeremy Mayfield's Car .10 .30
93 Johnny Benson's Car .10 .30
94 Dale Earnhardt Jr.'s Car .50 1.25
95 Kyle Petty's Car .10 .30
96 Rick Mast's Car .05 .15
97 Terry Labonte's Car .25 .60
98 Ricky Rudd .40 1.00
99 Chad Little's Car .05 .15
100 Mark Martin's Car .40 1.00
101 Mark Martin 1.00 2.50
102 Dale Jarrett .75 2.00
103 Joe Nemechek .10 .30
104 Dave Marcis .25 .60
105 Hermie Sadler .10 .30
106 Michael Waltrip .25 .60
107 Dick Trickle .10 .30
108 Jeff Burton .40 1.00
109 Derrike Cope .10 .30
110 John Andretti .10 .30
111 Mike Wallace .10 .30
112 Robert Pressley .10 .30
113 Elliott Sadler .25 .60
114 Randy LaJoie .10 .30
115 Tony Stewart RC 6.00 15.00
116 Checklist (1-50) .05 .15
117 Checklist (51-100) .05 .15
118 Checklist (101-AN25) .05 .15
119 Checklist (AN26-CS18) .05 .15
120 Checklist (CQ1-W5) .05 .15

1998 Upper Deck Road To The Cup 50th Anniversary

Randomly inserted in packs at a rate of one in four, this 50-card insert set, highlights the top names in NASCAR from the past 50 years. The card fronts feature color photography surrounded by a blue border.

COMPLETE SET (50) 15.00 40.00
AN1 Bill France Sr. .10 .30
AN2 Daytona Beach .10 .30
AN3 Jim Roper's Car .10 .30
AN4 Tim Flock .25 .60
AN5 Hudson Hornet .10 .30
AN6 Fireball Roberts .25 .60
AN7 Smokey Yunick .25 .60
AN8 Buck Baker .25 .60
AN9 Ned Jarrett .25 .60
AN10 Richard Petty .50 1.25
AN11 Junior Johnson .25 .60
AN12 David Pearson .25 .60
AN13 Ned Jarrett .25 .60
AN14 Richard Petty .50 1.25
AN15 Ford Turino .10 .30
AN16 Buddy Baker's Car .10 .30
AN17 Richard Petty's Car .25 .60
AN18 David Pearson .25 .60
AN19 Winston Show Car .10 .30
AN20 Bobby Allison .25 .60
AN21 Richard Petty .50 1.25
AN22 Benny Parsons .25 .60
AN23 NASCAR Silver Anniversary .10 .30
AN24 Junior Johnson .25 .60
AN25 Cale Yarborough .25 .60
AN26 David Pearson .25 .60
AN27 Richard Petty .50 1.25
AN28 Bobby Allison's Car .10 .30
AN29 Rusty Wallace's Car .75 2.00
AN30 Darrell Waltrip's Car .25 .60
AN31 Bobby Hillin's Car .10 .30
AN32 Cale Yarborough's Car .10 .30
AN33 Benny Parsons's Car .10 .30
AN34 Ernie Irvan's Car .25 .60
AN35 Darrell Waltrip .50 1.25
AN36 Richard Petty's Car .25 .60
AN37 Bill Elliott's Car .50 1.25
AN38 Davey Allison .50 1.25
AN39 Davey Allison .50 1.25
Bobby Allison
AN40 Rusty Wallace 2.00 5.00
AN41 Richard Petty .50 1.25
AN42 Alan Kulwicki .50 1.25
AN43 Jeff Gordon 2.50 6.00
AN44 Terry Labonte .75 2.00
AN45 Terry Labonte .75 2.00
AN46 Suzuka Speedway .10 .30
AN47 Jeff Gordon 2.50 6.00
AN48 Jeremy Mayfield's Car .25 .60
AN49 Dale Earnhardt 4.00 10.00
AN50 Las Vegas Speedway .10 .30

1998 Upper Deck Road To The Cup 50th Anniversary Autographs

Randomly inserted in hobby packs only, this 10-card insert set is limited and hand-numbered to 50. Each card offers an autograph from a top name in NASCAR's 50-year history. The card fronts feature color photography surrounded by a blue or red border.

COMPLETE SET (10) 600.00 1000.00
AN13 Ned Jarrett 30.00 50.00
AN14 Richard Petty 25.00 60.00
AN18 David Pearson 30.00 50.00
AN25 Cale Yarborough 30.00 50.00
AN35 Darrell Waltrip 35.00 60.00
AN39 Bobby Allison 30.00 50.00
AN40 Rusty Wallace 60.00 120.00
AN44 Terry Labonte 60.00 120.00
AN47 Jeff Gordon 100.00 200.00
AN49 Dale Earnhardt 200.00 400.00

1998 Upper Deck Road To The Cup Cover Story

Randomly inserted in packs at a rate of one in 11, this 16-card insert set features hand-picked photos and in-depth prose from the editors of Tuff Stuff magazine and Winston Cup Scene.

COMPLETE SET (16) 15.00 40.00
CS1 Ernie Irvan .50 1.25
CS2 Terry Labonte .75 2.00
CS3 Darrell Waltrip .50 1.25
CS4 Kyle Petty .50 1.25
CS5 Rusty Wallace 2.00 5.00
CS6 Alan Kulwicki .50 1.25
CS7 Bill Elliott .50 1.25
CS8 Jeff Gordon 2.50 6.00
CS9 WC Grand National Scene .10 .30
CS10 Dale Earnhardt 4.00 10.00
CS11 Ernie Irvan .50 1.25
CS12 Rusty Wallace 2.00 5.00
CS13 Jeff Gordon 2.50 6.00
CS14 Indianapolis Motor Speed. .10 .30
CS15 Gordon 2.50 6.00
Labonte
Craven
CS16 J.Gordon 2.50 6.00
D.Waltrip

1998 Upper Deck Road To The Cup Cup Quest Turn 1

Sequentially numbered to 4,000, this is the first tier of a five-tiered insert set focused on the top ten drivers contending for this year's Winston Cup title.

COMPLETE SET (10) 20.00 50.00
COMP.TURN 2 SET (10) 30.00 80.00
*TURN 2: .6X TO 1.5X BASIC INSERTS
TURN 2 PRINT RUN 2000 SER.#'D SETS
COMP.TURN 3 SET (10) 60.00 150.00
*TURN 3 CARDS: 1.2X TO 3X BASIC INSERTS
TURN 3 PRINT RUN 1000 SER.#'D SETS
*TURN 4: 4X TO 10X BASIC INSERTS
TURN 4 PRINT RUN 100 SER.#'D SETS
CQ1 Jeff Gordon's Car 6.00 15.00
CQ2 Rusty Wallace's Car 5.00 12.00
CQ3 Kenny Irwin's Car 1.50 4.00
CQ4 Jeremy Mayfield's Car 1.50 4.00
CQ5 Terry Labonte's Car 3.00 8.00
CQ6 Mark Martin's Car 5.00 12.00
CQ7 Bobby Labonte's Car 3.00 8.00
CQ8 Dale Jarrett's Car 3.00 8.00
CQ9 Jeff Burton's Car 1.50 4.00
CQ10 Ernie Irvan's Car 1.50 4.00

1998 Upper Deck Road To The Cup Winning Materials

Randomly inserted in packs at a rate of one in 999, this 5-card insert set special cards with authentic race-used pieces of the engine, along with an actual piece of a driver's race-worn fire suit.

COMPLETE SET (5) 200.00 400.00
W1 Rusty Wallace 15.00 40.00
W2 Jeremy Mayfield 12.50 30.00
W3 Dale Jarrett 15.00 40.00
W4 Bobby Labonte 15.00 40.00
W5 Jeff Burton 15.00 40.00

1999 Upper Deck Road to the Cup

The 1999 Upper Deck Road to the Cup product was released in late 1999, and featured a 90-card base set that was broken into tiers as follows: 30 Veteran Drivers, 30 Car cards, and 15 Fan Favorites, and 15 Happy Hour cards.

COMPLETE SET (90) 10.00 25.00
WAX BOX 30.00 60.00
1 Kenny Irwin .15 .40
2 Dale Jarrett .50 1.25
3 Terry Labonte .25 .60
4 Geoff Bodine .07 .20
5 John Andretti .07 .20
6 Tony Stewart CRC 1.00 2.50
7 Ricky Rudd .25 .60
8 Jeremy Mayfield .15 .40
9 Chad Little .15 .40
10 Darrell Waltrip .15 .40
11 Bobby Labonte .50 1.25
12 Ken Schrader .07 .20
13 Sterling Marlin .25 .60
14 Mike Skinner .07 .20
15 Kevin Lepage .07 .20
16 Jeff Burton .25 .60
17 Elliott Sadler .15 .40
18 Mark Martin .60 1.50
19 Bill Elliott .30 .75
20 Steve Park .40 1.00
21 Jerry Nadeau .15 .40
22 Rusty Wallace .60 1.50
23 Bobby Hamilton .07 .20
24 Jeff Gordon .75 2.00
25 Randy LaJoie .07 .20
26 Dale Earnhardt 1.25 3.00
27 Ernie Irvan .15 .40
28 Johnny Benson .15 .40
29 Kyle Petty .15 .40
30 Dale Earnhardt Jr. 1.00 2.50
31 Jeremy Mayfield's Car .07 .20
32 Terry Labonte's Car .15 .40
33 John Andretti's Car .02 .10
34 Kyle Petty's Car .07 .20
35 Darrell Waltrip's Car .02 .10
36 Geoff Bodine's Car .02 .10
37 Dale Earnhardt Jr.'s Car .40 1.00
38 Bobby Labonte's Car .15 .40
39 Ken Schrader's Car .02 .10
40 Johnny Benson's Car .02 .10
41 Sterling Marlin's Car .07 .20
42 Ernie Irvan's Car .07 .20
43 Jeff Gordon's Car .30 .75
44 Mike Skinner's Car .02 .10
45 Kevin Lepage's Car .02 .10
46 Jeff Burton's Car .07 .20
47 Ricky Rudd's Car .07 .20
48 Dale Jarrett's Car .15 .40
49 Kenny Irwin's Car .07 .20
50 Randy LaJoie's Car .02 .10
51 Elliott Sadler's Car .02 .10
52 Steve Park's Car .15 .40
53 Chad Little's Car .02 .10
54 Jerry Nadeau's Car .07 .20
55 Bobby Hamilton's Car .02 .10
56 Bill Elliott's Car .15 .40
57 Mark Martin's Car .25 .60
58 Tony Stewart's Car .30 .75
59 Rusty Wallace's Car .25 .60
60 Dale Earnhardt's Car .50 1.25
61 Jeff Gordon FF .40 1.00
62 Terry Labonte FF .15 .40
63 Dale Jarrett FF .40 1.00
64 Darrell Waltrip FF .07 .20
65 Bill Elliott FF .15 .40
66 Tony Stewart FF .60 1.50
67 Dale Earnhardt Jr. FF .75 2.00
68 Ernie Irvan FF .07 .20
69 Kyle Petty FF .07 .20
70 Bobby Labonte FF .40 1.00
71 Kenny Irwin FF .07 .20
72 Jeremy Mayfield FF .07 .20
73 Ricky Rudd FF .15 .40
74 Mark Martin FF .50 1.25
75 Rusty Wallace FF .50 1.25
76 Jeremy Mayfield HH .07 .20
77 Jeff Gordon HH .40 1.00
78 Mark Martin HH .50 1.25
79 Kenny Irwin HH .07 .20
80 Rusty Wallace HH .50 1.25
81 Dale Jarrett HH .40 1.00
82 Bobby Labonte HH .40 1.00
83 Jerry Nadeau HH .15 .40
84 Tony Stewart HH .60 1.50
85 Ernie Irvan HH .07 .20
86 Steve Park HH .25 .60
87 Kevin Lepage HH .02 .10
88 Elliott Sadler HH .15 .40
89 Terry Labonte HH .15 .40
90 Dale Earnhardt Jr. CL .50 1.25

1999 Upper Deck Road to the Cup A Day in the Life

Randomly inserted in packs at the rate of one in six, this 10-card insert set details a day in the life of Jeff Gordon. Card backs carry a "JG" prefix.

COMPLETE SET (10) 5.00 12.00
COMMON GORDON (JG1-JG10) .50 1.25

1999 Upper Deck Road to the Cup NASCAR Chronicles

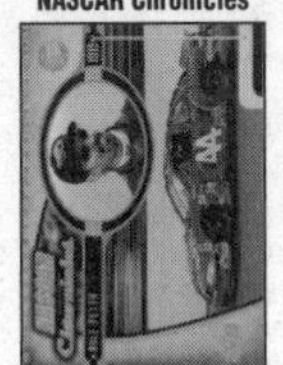

Randomly inserted in packs at the rate of one in two, This twenty card set features the journeys the top drivers have taken to make it to the NASCAR Winston Cup Circuit. Card backs carry a "NC" prefix.

COMPLETE SET (20) 15.00 40.00
NC1 Bobby Labonte 1.50 4.00
NC2 Jeff Gordon 2.50 6.00
NC3 Rusty Wallace 2.00 5.00
NC4 Terry Labonte .75 2.00
NC5 Kyle Petty .50 1.25
NC6 Kevin Lepage .25 .60
NC7 Jeff Burton .75 2.00
NC8 Jeremy Mayfield .50 1.25
NC9 Elliott Sadler .50 1.25
NC10 Mark Martin 2.00 5.00
NC11 Dale Earnhardt 3.00 8.00
NC12 Kenny Irwin .50 1.25
NC13 Bill Elliott 1.00 2.50
NC14 Dale Earnhardt Jr. 3.00 8.00
NC15 John Andretti .25 .60
NC16 Ricky Rudd .75 2.00
NC17 Dale Jarrett 1.50 4.00
NC18 Jerry Nadeau .50 1.25
NC19 Tony Stewart 2.50 6.00
NC20 Steve Park 1.25 3.00

1999 Upper Deck Road to the Cup Road to the Cup Bronze Level 1

Randomly inserted in packs at the rate of one in twelve. This set features ten drivers who competed for the NASCAR Winston Cup Championship. The cardbacks carry a "RTTC" prefix and the Level 1 cards featured bronze foil printing on the cardfronts and were not die cut. There were two die cut parallel sets produced as well: Level 2 Silver (1:23 packs) and Level 3 Gold (1:48 packs).

COMP.LEVEL 1 SET (10) 20.00 40.00
COMP.LEVEL 2 SILVER (10) 30.00 60.00
*LEVEL 2 SILVERS: .6X TO 1.5X LEVEL 1
COMP.LEVEL 3 GOLD (10) 50.00 100.00
*LEVEL 3 GOLDS: 1X TO 2.5X LEVEL 1
RTTC1 Jeff Gordon 5.00 12.00
RTTC2 Mark Martin's Car 1.50 4.00
RTTC3 Rusty Wallace 4.00 10.00
RTTC4 Terry Labonte 1.50 4.00
RTTC5 Bobby Labonte 3.00 8.00
RTTC6 Jeremy Mayfield 1.00 2.50
RTTC7 Jeff Burton 1.50 4.00
RTTC8 Dale Jarrett 3.00 8.00
RTTC9 Ricky Rudd 1.50 4.00
RTTC10 Dale Earnhardt Jr. 6.00 15.00

1999 Upper Deck Road to the Cup Signature Collection

Randomly inserted in packs at the rate of one in 999, this set features actual autographs of top NASCAR drivers. The cards look similar to the Victory Circle Signature Collection but can be differentiated by the circular shaped player image and the inclusion of a Road to the Cup logo on the cardfronts. The cardbacks carry the driver's initials as numbering. Cards of some drivers were released later without the "Road to the Cup" logo on the fronts.

DE Dale Earnhardt
DJ Dale Jarrett
JB Jeff Burton 8.00 20.00
JG Jeff Gordon 100.00 200.00
KP Kyle Petty
MM Mark Martin 40.00 80.00
RW Rusty Wallace 12.50 30.00
SP Steve Park 12.50 30.00
TS Tony Stewart 15.00 40.00
DEJR Dale Earnhardt Jr. 50.00 100.00

1999 Upper Deck Road to the Cup Signature Collection Checkered Flag

These Autographs were signed for the cancelled 1999 Upper Deck Road to the Cup Checkered Flag product but placed in packs of 2000 SP Authentic at the rate of 1:40. Each card looks nearly identical to the basic 1999 Upper Deck Road to the Cup Signature Collection cards except for the inclusion of both the Victory Circle and Checkered Flag (CF) logos on the cardfronts.

BL Bobby Labonte 12.50 30.00
DE Dale Earnhardt 250.00 500.00
JB Jeff Burton 10.00 25.00
JG Jeff Gordon 100.00 175.00
MS Mike Skinner 8.00 20.00
RW Rusty Wallace 12.00 30.00
TS Tony Stewart 15.00 40.00
DEJR Dale Earnhardt Jr. 50.00 100.00
JM Jeremy Mayfield

1999 Upper Deck Road to the Cup Tires of Daytona

Randomly inserted in packs at the rate of one in 525, This set features a piece of a race-used tire from a Winston Cup car raced at Daytona. Card backs carry a "T" prefix.

COMPLETE SET (5) 175.00 350.00
T1 Jeff Gordon 40.00 80.00
T2 Rusty Wallace 25.00 50.00
T3 Jeremy Mayfield 20.00 40.00
T4 Mark Martin 30.00 60.00
T5 Jeff Burton 12.50 30.00

1999 Upper Deck Road to the Cup Tires of Daytona Autographed

Randomly inserted in packs, this set features a piece of a race-used tire from a Winston Cup car raced at Daytona, and is autographed to the driver's car number. Card backs carry a "TS" prefix. Most cards were issued mail redemption cards that carried an expiration date of 7/1/2000.

TS1 Jeff Gordon/24 300.00 500.00
TS2 Mark Martin/6
TS3 Rusty Wallace/2
TS4 Jeremy Mayfield/12

1999 Upper Deck Road to the Cup Upper Deck Profiles

Randomly inserted in packs at the rate of one in eleven, this fifteen card set gets up close and personal with 15 of NASCAR's Winston Cup drivers. Card backs carry a "P" prefix.

COMPLETE SET (15) 40.00 80.00
P1 Jeremy Mayfield 1.25 3.00
P2 Terry Labonte 2.00 5.00
P3 Dale Earnhardt 10.00 25.00
P4 Jerry Nadeau 1.25 3.00
P5 Dale Jarrett 4.00 10.00
P6 Steve Park 3.00 8.00
P7 Mark Martin 5.00 12.00
P8 Bobby Labonte 4.00 10.00
P9 Kenny Irwin 1.25 3.00
P10 Dale Earnhardt Jr. 8.00 20.00
P11 Tony Stewart 6.00 15.00
P12 Elliott Sadler 1.25 3.00
P13 Rusty Wallace 5.00 12.00
P14 Jeff Burton 2.00 5.00
P15 Jeff Gordon 6.00 15.00

1997 Upper Deck Team Hot Wheels Pro Racing

ISSUED IN 1:64 HW RACING DIE CAST
M1 Terry Labonte .50 1.25
M2 Sterling Marlin .30 .75
M4 Bobby Hamilton .20 .50
M9 Jeff Burton .25 .60
M11 Mark Martin .50 1.25
M12 Ricky Rudd .25 .60
M13 Kyle Petty .25 .60
M14 Johnny Benson .20 .50
M15 Hut Stricklin .20 .50
M16 Michael Waltrip .30 .75

2002 Upper Deck Twizzlers

9 Kevin Harvick 1.25 3.00
10 Kevin Harvick 1.25 3.00

1998 Upper Deck UD Authentics

RW Rusty Wallace 10.00 25.00

1997 Upper Deck Victory Circle

The 1997 Upper Deck set was issued in one series totalling 120 cards. The set contains the topical subsets: Driver (1-50), Momentum (51-100) Local Legends (101-115) and Track Facts (116-120). The cards were packaged 10 cards per pack, 28 packs per box and 12 boxes per case. Each pack carried a suggested retail price of $2.49.

COMPLETE SET (120) 8.00 20.00
1 Rick Mast .07 .20
2 Rusty Wallace .60 1.50
3 Dale Earnhardt 1.25 3.00
4 Sterling Marlin .25 .60
5 Terry Labonte .25 .60
6 Mark Martin .60 1.50
7 Geoff Bodine .07 .20
8 Hut Stricklin .07 .20
9 Lake Speed .07 .20
10 Ricky Rudd .25 .60
11 Brett Bodine .07 .20
12 Derrike Cope .07 .20
13 Bill Elliott .30 .75
14 Bobby Hamilton .07 .20
15 Wally Dallenbach .07 .20
16 Ted Musgrave .07 .20
17 Darrell Waltrip .15 .40
18 Bobby Labonte .50 1.25
19 Loy Allen .07 .20
20 Morgan Shepherd .07 .20
21 Michael Waltrip .15 .40
22 Ward Burton .15 .40
23 Jimmy Spencer .07 .20
24 Jeff Gordon .75 2.00
25 Ken Schrader .07 .20
26 Kyle Petty .15 .40
27 Bobby Hillin .07 .20
28 Ernie Irvan .15 .40
29 Jeff Purvis .07 .20
30 Johnny Benson .15 .40
31 Dave Marcis .15 .40
32 Jeremy Mayfield .15 .40
33 Robert Pressley .07 .20
34 Jeff Burton .25 .60
35 Joe Nemechek .07 .20
36 Dale Jarrett .50 1.25
37 John Andretti .07 .20
38 Kenny Wallace .07 .20

39 Elton Sawyer	.07	.20
40 Dick Trickle	.07	.20
41 Ricky Craven	.07	.20
42 Chad Little	.07	.20
43 Todd Bodine	.07	.20
44 David Green	.07	.20
45 Randy LaJoie	.07	.20
46 Larry Pearson	.07	.20
47 Jason Keller	.07	.20
48 Hermie Sadler	.07	.20
49 Mike McLaughlin	.07	.20
50 Tim Fedewa	.07	.20
51 Rick Mast's Car	.02	.10
52 Rusty Wallace's Car	.25	.60
53 Ricky Craven's Car	.02	.10
54 Sterling Marlin's Car	.07	.20
55 Terry Labonte's Car	.15	.40
56 Mark Martin's Car	.25	.60
57 Geoff Bodine's Car	.02	.10
58 Hut Stricklin's Car	.02	.10
59 Lake Speed's Car	.02	.10
60 Ricky Rudd's Car	.07	.20
61 Brett Bodine's Car	.02	.10
62 Derrike Cope's Car	.02	.10
63 Bill Elliott's Car	.15	.40
64 Bobby Hamilton's Car	.02	.10
65 Wally Dallenbach's Car	.02	.10
66 Ted Musgrave's Car	.02	.10
67 Darrell Waltrip's Car	.07	.20
68 Bobby Labonte's Car	.15	.40
69 Loy Allen's Car	.02	.10
70 Morgan Shepherd's Car	.02	.10
71 Michael Waltrip's Car	.07	.20
72 Ward Burton's Car	.02	.10
73 Jimmy Spencer's Car	.02	.10
74 Jeff Gordon's Car	.30	.75
75 Ken Schrader's Car	.02	.10
76 Kyle Petty's Car	.07	.20
77 Bobby Hillin's Car	.02	.10
78 Ernie Irvan's Car	.07	.20
79 Jeff Purvis's Car	.02	.10
80 Johnny Benson's Car	.02	.10
81 Dave Marcis's Car	.07	.20
82 Jeremy Mayfield's Car	.15	.40
83 Robert Pressley's Car	.02	.10
84 Jeff Burton's Car	.07	.20
85 Joe Nemechek's Car	.02	.10
86 Dale Jarrett's Car	.15	.40
87 John Andretti's Car	.02	.10
88 Kenny Wallace's Car	.02	.10
89 Elton Sawyer's Car	.15	.40
90 Dick Trickle's Car	.02	.10
91 Chad Little's Car	.02	.10
92 Todd Bodine's Car	.02	.10
93 David Green's Car	.02	.10
94 Randy LaJoie's Car	.02	.10
95 Larry Pearson's Car	.02	.10
96 Jason Keller's Car	.02	.10
97 Hermie Sadler's Car	.02	.10
98 Mike McLaughlin's Car	.02	.10
99 Tim Fedewa's Car	.02	.10
100 Patty Moise's Car	.02	.10
101 Dale Jarrett	.50	1.25
102 Ricky Rudd	.25	.60
103 Rusty Wallace	.60	1.50
104 Sterling Marlin	.25	.60
105 Geoff Bodine	.07	.20
106 John Andretti	.07	.20
107 Jeremy Mayfield	.15	.40
108 Terry Labonte	.25	.60
109 Mark Martin	.60	1.50
110 Derrike Cope	.07	.20
111 Jeff Gordon	.75	2.00
112 Ricky Craven	.07	.20
113 Ted Musgrave	.07	.20
114 Joe Nemechek	.07	.20
115 Bill Elliott	.30	.75
116 Kenny Wallace	.07	.20
117 Darrell Waltrip	.15	.40
118 Bobby Labonte	.50	1.25
119 North Wilkesboro Speedway	.02	.10
120 North Wilkesboro Speedway	.02	.10

1997 Upper Deck Victory Circle Championship Reflections

Randomly inserted in packs at a rate of one in 4, this 10-card set highlights the top ten finishers in the point standings for the 1996 Winston Cup season.

COMPLETE SET (10)	10.00	25.00
CR1 Terry Labonte	.75	2.00
CR2 Jeff Gordon	2.50	6.00
CR3 Dale Jarrett	1.50	4.00
CR4 Dale Earnhardt	4.00	10.00
CR5 Mark Martin	2.00	5.00
CR6 Ricky Rudd	.75	2.00
CR7 Rusty Wallace	2.00	5.00
CR8 Sterling Marlin	.75	2.00
CR9 Bobby Hamilton	.25	.60
CR10 Ernie Irvan	.50	1.25

1997 Upper Deck Victory Circle Crowning Achievement

Randomly inserted in packs at a rate of one in 35, this five-card set takes a look back at Terry Labonte's record breaking season. The cards used a double die-cut design.

COMPLETE SET (5)	15.00	40.00
T.LABONTE CARD (CA1-CA5)	3.00	8.00

1997 Upper Deck Victory Circle Driver's Seat

Randomly inserted in packs at a rate of one in 69, this 10-card set takes cel technology and applies it to racing cards. The cards are best viewed when held up to light.

COMPLETE SET (10)	50.00	120.00
DS1 Dale Earnhardt	20.00	50.00
DS2 Jeff Gordon	12.50	30.00
DS3 Terry Labonte	4.00	10.00
DS4 Ken Schrader	1.25	3.00
DS5 Sterling Marlin	4.00	10.00
DS6 Mark Martin	10.00	25.00
DS7 Rusty Wallace	10.00	25.00
DS8 Bobby Labonte	8.00	20.00
DS9 Ernie Irvan	2.50	6.00
DS10 Dale Jarrett	8.00	20.00

1997 Upper Deck Victory Circle Generation Excitement

This five-card set highlights some of the up and coming stars of NASCAR's Winston Cup circuit. The cards were inserted one in 11 packs.

COMPLETE SET (5)	6.00	15.00
GE1 Jeff Gordon	4.00	10.00
GE2 Bobby Hamilton	.40	1.00
GE3 Johnny Benson	.75	2.00
GE4 Ricky Craven	.40	1.00
GE5 Bobby Labonte	2.50	6.00

1997 Upper Deck Victory Circle Piece of the Action

This 9-card set features pieces of a driver's gloves, shoes, and firesuit incorporated into a trading card. The cards were seeded one in 699 packs.

COMPLETE SET (9)	100.00	200.00
FS1 Jeff Gordon Firesuit	12.00	30.00
FS2 Jeff Gordon Glove	12.00	30.00
FS3 Jeff Gordon Shoe	12.00	30.00
FS4 Rusty Wallace Firesuit	8.00	20.00
FS5 Rusty Wallace Glove	8.00	20.00
FS6 Rusty Wallace Shoe	8.00	20.00
FS7 Dale Jarrett Firesuit	8.00	20.00
FS8 Dale Jarrett Glove	8.00	20.00
FS9 Dale Jarrett Shoe	8.00	20.00

1997 Upper Deck Victory Circle Predictor

This 10-card is an interactive predictor game. Each card has a specific goal stamped on the front. If that driver accomplishes that goal anytime during the 1997 Winston Cup season that card may be redeemed for a 10 card prize set. These cards expired on 2/1/1998. The predictor cards were inserted one per 21 packs.

COMPLETE SET (10)	20.00	50.00
COMP.PRIZE CEL SET (10)	40.00	100.00
*PRIZE CARDS: .8X TO 2X BASIC INSERTS		
PE1 Jeff Gordon WIN	6.00	15.00
PE2 Rusty Wallace WIN	5.00	12.00
PE3 Dale Jarrett WIN	4.00	10.00
PE4 Sterling Marlin	2.00	5.00
PE5 Terry Labonte	2.00	5.00
PE6 Mark Martin WIN	5.00	12.00
PE7 Bobby Labonte WIN	4.00	10.00
PE8 Ernie Irvan WIN	1.25	3.00
PE9 Bill Elliott	2.50	6.00
PE10 Ricky Rudd	2.00	5.00

1997 Upper Deck Victory Circle Victory Lap

Randomly inserted in packs at a rate of one in 109, this 10-card set is a hobby only insert. The cards feature die-cut technology and a checkered flag design. Each of the drivers in this set visited victory lane in 1996. The cards were inserted one per 109 packs.

COMPLETE SET (10)	150.00	300.00
VL1 Dale Earnhardt	40.00	100.00
VL2 Jeff Gordon	25.00	60.00
VL3 Bobby Labonte	15.00	40.00
VL4 Dale Jarrett	15.00	40.00
VL5 Ernie Irvan	5.00	12.00
VL6 Sterling Marlin	8.00	20.00
VL7 Ricky Rudd	8.00	20.00
VL8 Geoff Bodine	2.50	6.00
VL9 Bobby Hamilton	2.50	6.00
VL10 Rusty Wallace	20.00	50.00

1998 Upper Deck Victory Circle

The 1998 Upper Deck Victory Circle set was issued in one series totalling 135 cards. The set contains the topical subsets: Season Highlights (91-105), Freeze Frame (106-120), and Hard Chargers (121-135).

COMPLETE SET (150)	15.00	40.00
1 Morgan Shepherd	.08	.25
2 Rusty Wallace	.75	2.00
3 Dale Earnhardt	1.50	4.00
4 Sterling Marlin	.30	.75
5 Terry Labonte	.30	.75
6 Mark Martin	.75	2.00
7 Geoff Bodine	.08	.25
8 Hut Stricklin	.08	.25
9 Lake Speed	.08	.25
10 Ricky Rudd	.30	.75
11 Brett Bodine	.08	.25
12 Dale Jarrett	.60	1.50
13 Bill Elliott	.40	1.00
14 Dick Trickle	.08	.25
15 Wally Dallenbach	.08	.25
16 Ted Musgrave	.08	.25
17 Darrell Waltrip	.20	.50
18 Bobby Labonte	.60	1.50
19 Gary Bradberry	.08	.25
20 Rick Mast	.08	.25
21 Michael Waltrip	.20	.50
22 Ward Burton	.20	.50
23 Jimmy Spencer	.08	.25
24 Jeff Gordon	1.00	2.50
25 Ricky Craven	.08	.25
26 Chad Little	.08	.25
27 Kenny Wallace	.08	.25
28 Ernie Irvan	.20	.50
29 Steve Park	.60	1.50
30 Johnny Benson	.20	.50
31 Mike Skinner	.08	.25
32 Mike Wallace	.08	.25
33 Ken Schrader	.08	.25
34 Jeff Burton	.30	.75
35 David Green	.08	.25
36 Derrike Cope	.08	.25
37 Jeremy Mayfield	.20	.50
38 Dave Marcis	.20	.50
39 John Andretti	.08	.25
40 Robby Gordon	.08	.25
41 Steve Grissom	.08	.25
42 Joe Nemechek	.08	.25
43 Bobby Hamilton	.08	.25
44 Kyle Petty	.20	.50
45 Kenny Irwin	.20	.50
46 Morgan Shepherd's Car	.05	.15
47 Rusty Wallace's Car	.30	.75
48 Dale Earnhardt's Car	.60	1.50
49 Sterling Marlin's Car	.08	.25
50 Terry Labonte's Car	.20	.50
51 Mark Martin's Car	.30	.75
52 Geoff Bodine's Car	.05	.15
53 Hut Stricklin's Car	.05	.15
54 Lake Speed's Car	.05	.15
55 Ricky Rudd's Car	.08	.25
56 Brett Bodine's Car	.05	.15
57 Dale Jarrett's Car	.20	.50
58 Bill Elliott's Car	.20	.50
59 Dick Trickle's Car	.05	.15
60 Wally Dallenbach's Car	.05	.15
61 Ted Musgrave's Car	.05	.15
62 Darrell Waltrip's Car	.20	.50
63 Bobby Labonte's Car	.20	.50
64 Gary Bradberry's Car	.05	.15
65 Rick Mast's Car	.05	.15
66 Michael Waltrip's Car	.08	.25
67 Ward Burton's Car	.08	.25
68 Jimmy Spencer's Car	.05	.15
69 Jeff Gordon's Car	.40	1.00
70 Ricky Craven's Car	.05	.15
71 Chad Little's Car	.08	.25
72 Kenny Wallace's Car	.05	.15
73 Ernie Irvan's Car	.08	.25
74 Steve Park's Car	.20	.50
75 Johnny Benson's Car	.05	.15
76 Mike Skinner's Car	.05	.15
77 Mike Wallace's Car	.05	.15
78 Ken Schrader's Car	.05	.15
79 Jeff Burton's Car	.08	.25
80 David Green's Car	.05	.15
81 Derrike Cope's Car	.05	.15
82 Jeremy Mayfield's Car	.08	.25
83 Dave Marcis's Car	.08	.25
84 John Andretti's Car	.05	.15
85 Robby Gordon's Car	.05	.15
86 Steve Grissom's Car	.05	.15
87 Joe Nemechek's Car	.05	.15
88 Bobby Hamilton's Car	.05	.15
89 Kyle Petty's Car	.08	.25
90 Kenny Irwin's Car	.08	.25
91 Mike Skinner	.08	.25
92 J.Gordon T.Labonte Craven	.60	1.50
93 Jeff Gordon	1.00	2.50
94 Robby Gordon	.08	.25
95 Dale Jarrett	.60	1.50
96 Jeff Burton	.30	.75
97 Mark Martin	.75	2.00
98 Mark Martin	.75	2.00
99 Joe Nemechek	.08	.25
100 Jeff Gordon	1.00	2.50
101 Mike Skinner	.08	.25
102 John Andretti	.08	.25
103 Ricky Rudd	.30	.75
104 Todd Bodine	.08	.25
105 Jeff Gordon	1.00	2.50
106 Mark Martin	.75	2.00
107 Geoff Bodine	.08	.25
108 Kenny Irwin	.20	.50
109 Dave Marcis	.20	.50
110 Rusty Wallace	.75	2.00
111 Ricky Rudd	.30	.75
112 Bobby Labonte	.60	1.50
113 Ernie Irvan	.20	.50
114 Kenny Wallace	.08	.25
115 Mike Skinner	.08	.25
116 Dale Jarrett	.60	1.50
117 Mark Martin	.75	2.00
118 Terry Labonte	.30	.75
119 Jeff Gordon	1.00	2.50
120 Jeff Gordon	1.00	2.50
121 Derrike Cope	.08	.25
122 Jeremy Mayfield	.20	.50
123 Robby Gordon	.08	.25
124 Ricky Craven	.08	.25
125 Ernie Irvan	.20	.50
126 Terry Labonte	.30	.75
127 Johnny Benson	.20	.50
128 Mike Skinner	.08	.25
129 Kyle Petty	.20	.50
130 Wally Dallenbach	.08	.25
131 Rick Mast	.08	.25
132 Morgan Shepherd	.08	.25
133 Michael Waltrip	.20	.50
134 Ted Musgrave	.08	.25
135 Ricky Rudd	.30	.75
136 Ricky Craven	.08	.25
137 Geoff Bodine	.08	.25
138 Morgan Shepherd	.08	.25
139 Ted Musgrave	.08	.25
140 Mark Martin	.75	2.00
141 Darrell Waltrip	.20	.50
142 Rusty Wallace	.75	2.00
143 Jeff Burton	.20	.50
144 Bill Elliott	.40	1.00
145 Ricky Rudd	.30	.75
146 Terry Labonte	.30	.75
147 Bobby Labonte	.60	1.50
148 Steve Grissom	.08	.25
149 Dale Jarrett	.60	1.50
150 Ernie Irvan	.20	.50

1998 Upper Deck Victory Circle 32 Days of Speed

Randomly inserted in packs at the rate of one in four, this 32-card set features color photos of one of the drivers from each of the 32 NASCAR Winston Cup races.

COMPLETE SET (32)	20.00	40.00
*GOLD CARDS: 8X TO 20X BASIC INSERTS		
GOLD PRINT RUN 97 SER.#'D SETS		
D1 Mike Skinner	.15	.40
D2 Jeff Gordon	1.50	4.00
D3 Rusty Wallace	1.25	3.00
D4 Robby Gordon	.15	.40
D5 Dale Jarrett	1.00	2.50
D6 Jeff Burton	.50	1.25
D7 Rusty Wallace	1.25	3.00
D8 Kenny Wallace	.15	.40
D9 Mark Martin	1.25	3.00
D10 Mark Martin	1.25	3.00
D11 Jeff Gordon	1.50	4.00
D12 Ricky Rudd	.50	1.25
D13 Bobby Hamilton	.15	.40
D14 Ernie Irvan	.30	.75
D15 Joe Nemechek	.15	.40
D16 John Andretti	.15	.40
D17 Ken Schrader	.15	.40
D18 Dale Jarrett	1.00	2.50
D19 Ricky Rudd	.50	1.25
D20 Todd Bodine	.15	.40
D21 Johnny Benson	.30	.75
D22 Kenny Wallace	.15	.40
D23 Bobby Labonte	1.00	2.50
D24 Bill Elliott	.60	1.50
D25 Ken Schrader	.15	.40
D26 Mark Martin	1.25	3.00
D27 Ward Burton	.30	.75
D28 Bobby Labonte	1.00	2.50
D29 Terry Labonte	.50	1.25
D30 Bobby Hamilton	.15	.40
D31 Bobby Hamilton	.15	.40
D32 Jeff Gordon	1.50	4.00

1998 Upper Deck Victory Circle Autographs

Randomly inserted in packs, this five-card set features autographed color photos of favorite NASCAR Winston Cup drivers printed on unique die-cut cards. Each card was individually hand-serial numbered to 250.

COMPLETE SET (5)	250.00	500.00
AG1 Jeff Gordon	50.00	100.00
AG2 Jeff Burton	10.00	25.00
AG3 Dale Jarrett	25.00	60.00
AG4 Mark Martin	40.00	80.00
AG5 Terry Labonte	20.00	50.00

1998 Upper Deck Victory Circle Piece of the Engine

Randomly inserted in packs at the rate of one in 999, this five-card set features color photos of drivers with an actual race-used piece of the engine from the top cars in NASCAR contained in the card. There were two cards of each driver produced. Cards PE6-PE10 feature a race date the engine piece was used.

COMPLETE SET (10)	300.00	700.00
PE1 Darrell Waltrip	15.00	40.00
PE2 Rusty Wallace	20.00	50.00
PE3 Dale Jarrett	20.00	50.00
PE4 Ernie Irvan	15.00	40.00
PE5 Bobby Labonte	15.00	40.00
PE6 Darrell Waltrip	15.00	40.00
PE7 Rusty Wallace	20.00	50.00
PE8 Dale Jarrett	20.00	50.00
PE9 Ernie Irvan	15.00	40.00
PE10 Bobby Labonte	15.00	40.00

1998 Upper Deck Victory Circle Point Leaders

Randomly inserted in packs at the rate of one in 13, this 20-card set features color photos of drivers who finished in the top 20 in the final point standings for the season.

COMPLETE SET (20)	50.00	100.00
PL1 Jeff Gordon	5.00	12.00
PL2 Dale Jarrett	3.00	8.00
PL3 Mark Martin	4.00	10.00
PL4 Jeff Burton	1.50	4.00
PL5 Dale Earnhardt	8.00	20.00
PL6 Terry Labonte	1.50	4.00
PL7 Bobby Labonte	3.00	8.00
PL8 Bill Elliott	2.00	5.00
PL9 Rusty Wallace	4.00	10.00
PL10 Ken Schrader	.50	1.25
PL11 Johnny Benson	1.00	2.50
PL12 Ted Musgrave	.50	1.25
PL13 Jeremy Mayfield	1.00	2.50
PL14 Ernie Irvan	1.00	2.50
PL15 Kyle Petty	1.00	2.50
PL16 Bobby Hamilton	.50	1.25
PL17 Ricky Rudd	1.50	4.00
PL18 Michael Waltrip	1.00	2.50
PL19 Ricky Craven	.50	1.25
PL20 Jimmy Spencer	.50	1.25

1998 Upper Deck Victory Circle Predictor Plus

Randomly inserted in packs at the rate of one in 23, this 20-card set features scratch-off game cards which enabled the collector to win prizes if the driver pictured on the card achieved the goals displayed after scratching off the special cars on the card.

COMPLETE SET (20)	30.00	60.00
*CEL REDEMPT: .5X TO 1.25X BASIC INS.		
1 Ernie Irvan	1.25	3.00
2 Rusty Wallace	5.00	12.00
3 Dale Jarrett	4.00	10.00
4 Sterling Marlin	2.00	5.00
5 Terry Labonte	2.00	5.00
6 Mark Martin	5.00	12.00
7 Geoff Bodine	.60	1.50
8 Hut Stricklin	.60	1.50
9 Lake Speed	.60	1.50
10 Ricky Rudd	2.00	5.00
11 Brett Bodine	.60	1.50
12 Bill Elliott	2.50	6.00
13 Kyle Petty	1.25	3.00
14 Jeff Burton	2.00	5.00
15 Jeremy Mayfield	1.25	3.00
16 Ricky Craven	.60	1.50
17 Ted Musgrave	.60	1.50
18 Bobby Labonte	4.00	10.00
19 Mike Skinner	.60	1.50
20 Johnny Benson	1.25	3.00

1998 Upper Deck Victory Circle Sparks of Brilliance

Randomly inserted in packs at the rate of one in 84, this ten-card set features color photos of top drivers with their accomplishments on the track during the 1997 season.

COMPLETE SET (10)	200.00	400.00
SB1 Jeff Gordon	8.00	20.00
SB2 Rusty Wallace	4.00	10.00
SB3 Dale Earnhardt	25.00	60.00
SB4 Ernie Irvan	4.00	10.00
SB5 Terry Labonte	4.00	10.00
SB6 Mark Martin	4.00	10.00
SB7 Bobby Labonte	4.00	10.00
SB8 Ricky Rudd	3.00	8.00
SB9 Dale Jarrett	4.00	10.00
SB10 Jeff Burton	3.00	8.00

1999 Upper Deck Victory Circle

The 1999 Upper Deck Victory Circle set was issued in one series totalling 89 cards. The set contains the two subsets: 55 Veterans and 34 Car cards.

COMPLETE SET (89)	10.00	25.00
WAX BOX	30.00	60.00
1 Dale Jarrett	.50	1.25
2 Derrike Cope	.07	.20
3 Jeff Gordon	.75	2.00
4 Ricky Rudd	.25	.60
5 Bobby Labonte	.50	1.25
6 Mark Martin	.60	1.50
7 Jeremy Mayfield	.15	.40
8 Terry Labonte	.25	.60
9 Rusty Wallace	.60	1.50
10 Geoff Bodine	.07	.20
11 Ward Burton	.15	.40
12 Brett Bodine	.07	.20
13 Jeff Green	.07	.20
14 Dale Earnhardt Jr.	1.00	2.50
15 Jerry Nadeau	.15	.40
16 Kenny Irwin	.15	.40
17 Bill Elliott	.30	.75
18 Ernie Irvan	.15	.40
19 Darrell Waltrip	.15	.40
20 John Andretti	.07	.20
21 Kyle Petty	.15	.40
22 Steve Park	.40	1.00
23 Jeff Burton	.25	.60
24 Ken Schrader	.07	.20
25 Johnny Benson	.15	.40
26 Dave Marcis	.07	.20
27 Wally Dallenbach	.07	.20
28 Michael Waltrip	.15	.40
29 Bobby Hamilton	.07	.20
30 Sterling Marlin	.25	.60
31 Chad Little	.15	.40
32 Dick Trickle	.07	.20
33 Joe Nemechek	.07	.20
34 Mike Skinner	.07	.20
35 Kenny Wallace	.07	.20
36 Robert Pressley	.07	.20
37 Steve Grissom	.07	.20
38 Kevin Lepage	.07	.20
39 Mike Wallace	.07	.20
40 Rick Mast	.07	.20
41 Jeff Gordon's Car	.30	.75
42 Rusty Wallace's Car	.25	.60
43 Bill Elliott's Car	.15	.40
44 Johnny Benson's Car	.02	.10
45 Mark Martin's Car	.25	.60
46 Sterling Marlin's Car	.07	.20
47 Darrell Waltrip's Car	.02	.10
48 Jerry Nadeau's Car	.15	.40
49 Terry Labonte's Car	.15	.40
50 Dale Earnhardt Jr.'s Car	.40	1.00
51 Ernie Irvan's Car	.02	.10
52 Dale Jarrett's Car	.15	.40
53 Jeff Green's Car	.02	.10
54 Jeff Burton's Car	.07	.20
55 Geoff Bodine's Car	.02	.10
56 Chad Little's Car	.07	.20
57 Brett Bodine's Car	.02	.10
58 Jeremy Mayfield's Car	.07	.20
59 Steve Park's Car	.07	.20
60 Kenny Irwin's Car	.07	.20
61 Derrike Cope's Car	.02	.10
62 Kevin Lepage's Car	.02	.10
63 Bobby Hamilton's Car	.02	.10
64 Ken Schrader's Car	.02	.10
65 Kyle Petty's Car	.07	.20
66 John Andretti's Car	.02	.10
67 Ricky Rudd's Car	.07	.20
68 Bobby Labonte's Car	.15	.40
69 Michael Waltrip's Car	.07	.20
70 Joe Nemechek's Car	.02	.10
71 Kenny Wallace's Car	.02	.10
72 Mike Skinner's Car	.02	.10
73 Robert Pressley's Car	.02	.10
74 Ward Burton's Car	.07	.20
75 Mark Martin	.60	1.50
76 Jeff Gordon	.75	2.00
77 Jeremy Mayfield	.07	.20
78 Rusty Wallace	.60	1.50
79 Mark Martin's Car	.25	.60
80 Jeff Gordon	.75	2.00
81 Rusty Wallace	.60	1.50
82 Steve Park	.40	1.00
83 Dale Earnhardt	1.25	3.00
84 Jeff Gordon	.75	2.00
85 Dale Earnhardt Jr.	1.00	2.50
86 Elliott Sadler	.15	.40
87 Mike McLaughlin	.07	.20
88 Tony Stewart	.75	2.00
89 Rusty Wallace CL	.30	.75

1999 Upper Deck Victory Circle UD Exclusives

COMPLETE SET (89)	400.00	800.00
*EXCLUSIVES: 10X TO 25X BASE CARD HI		

1999 Upper Deck Victory Circle Income Statement

Randomly inserted into packs at one in 2, this 15-card insert set features some of the top money-makers from 1999. Card backs carry an "IS" prefix

COMPLETE SET (15)	10.00	25.00
IS1 Jeff Gordon	2.00	5.00
IS2 Bobby Labonte	1.25	3.00
IS3 Bill Elliott	.75	2.00
IS4 Rusty Wallace	1.50	4.00
IS5 Jeff Burton	.60	1.50
IS6 Kenny Irwin	.40	1.00
IS7 Jeremy Mayfield	.40	1.00
IS8 Dale Jarrett	1.25	3.00
IS9 Ken Schrader	.20	.50
IS10 Mark Martin	1.50	4.00
IS11 Ricky Rudd	.60	1.50
IS12 John Andretti	.20	.50
IS13 Ernie Irvan	.40	1.00
IS14 Terry Labonte	.60	1.50
IS15 Dale Earnhardt Jr.	2.50	6.00

1999 Upper Deck Victory Circle Magic Numbers

Randomly inserted into packs at the rate of one in 999, this set features actual race-used numbers peeled off from the side of the top cars in NASCAR. Card backs carry a "M" prefix.

COMPLETE SET (4)	250.00	400.00
M1 Mark Martin	10.00	25.00
M2 Bobby Labonte	10.00	25.00
M3 Dale Jarrett	15.00	40.00
M4 Rusty Wallace	10.00	25.00

1999 Upper Deck Victory Circle Magic Numbers Autographs

Randomly inserted into packs, this set features authentic autographs as well as actual race-used numbers peeled off from the side of the top cars in NASCAR. Card backs carry a "M" prefix. Print runs are listed in our checklist.

M1 Mark Martin/6
M2 Bobby Labonte/18 300.00 400.00
M3 Dale Jarrett/88 125.00 200.00
M4 Rusty Wallace/2

1999 Upper Deck Victory Circle Signature Collection

Randomly inserted into packs at one in 100, this 20-card insert set features authentic signatures from NASCAR's top drivers. The cards look similar to the Road to the Cup Signature Collection but can be differentiated by the rectangular shaped player image and the lack of a Victory Circle logo on the cardfronts. The cardbacks carry the player's initials as numbering.

BL Bobby Labonte 10.00 25.00
DE Dale Earnhardt
DJ Dale Jarrett 20.00 50.00
DW Darrell Waltrip 15.00 40.00
EI Ernie Irvan 12.50 30.00
ES Elliott Sadler 6.00 15.00
JA John Andretti 10.00 25.00
JB Jeff Burton 8.00 20.00
JG Jeff Gordon 75.00 150.00
JM Jeremy Mayfield 10.00 25.00
JN Jerry Nadeau 12.50 30.00
KI Kenny Irwin 15.00 40.00
KP Kyle Petty 12.50 30.00
MM Mark Martin 25.00 50.00
MW Michael Waltrip 10.00 25.00
RR Ricky Rudd 20.00 40.00
RW Rusty Wallace 12.50 30.00
SP Steve Park 10.00 25.00
TL Terry Labonte 12.50 30.00
DEJ Dale Earnhardt Jr. 50.00 100.00

1999 Upper Deck Victory Circle Speed Zone

Randomly inserted into packs at one in 2, this 15-card insert set features drivers that feel the need for speed. Card backs carry a "SZ" prefix.

COMPLETE SET (15) 15.00 30.00
SZ1 Bobby Labonte 1.25 3.00
SZ2 Mark Martin 1.50 4.00
SZ3 Jeff Gordon 2.00 5.00
SZ4 Ernie Irvan .40 1.00
SZ5 Bill Elliott .75 2.00
SZ6 Rusty Wallace 1.50 4.00
SZ7 Jeff Burton .60 1.50
SZ8 Dale Jarrett 1.25 3.00
SZ9 Terry Labonte .60 1.50
SZ10 Dale Earnhardt Jr. 2.50 6.00
SZ11 Steve Park 1.00 2.50
SZ12 Jeremy Mayfield .40 1.00
SZ13 John Andretti .20 .50
SZ14 Bobby Hamilton .20 .50
SZ15 Ken Schrader .20 .50

1999 Upper Deck Victory Circle Track Masters

Randomly inserted into packs at one in 11, this 15-card insert set features drivers that have "mastered" almost every track in the Northern Hemisphere. Card backs carry a "TM" prefix.

COMPLETE SET (15) 40.00 80.00
TM1 Jeff Gordon 6.00 15.00
TM2 Dale Jarrett 4.00 10.00
TM3 Ernie Irvan 1.25 3.00
TM4 Sterling Marlin 2.00 5.00
TM5 Rusty Wallace 5.00 12.00
TM6 Mark Martin 5.00 12.00
TM7 Jeff Burton 2.00 5.00
TM8 Bobby Hamilton .60 1.50
TM9 Terry Labonte 2.00 5.00
TM10 Jeremy Mayfield 1.25 3.00
TM11 Bobby Labonte 4.00 10.00
TM12 Bill Elliott 2.50 6.00
TM13 Darrell Waltrip 1.25 3.00
TM14 John Andretti .60 1.50
TM15 Dale Earnhardt Jr. 8.00 20.00

1999 Upper Deck Victory Circle Victory Circle

Randomly inserted into packs at one in 23, this 9-card insert set features top drivers on die cut card stock. Card backs carry a "V" prefix.

COMPLETE SET (9) 40.00 80.00
V1 Dale Earnhardt 12.50 30.00
V2 Bobby Labonte 5.00 12.00
V3 Terry Labonte 2.50 6.00
V4 Jeff Burton 2.50 6.00
V5 Mark Martin 6.00 15.00
V6 Dale Jarrett 5.00 12.00
V7 Jeremy Mayfield 1.50 4.00
V8 Jeff Gordon 8.00 20.00
V9 Rusty Wallace 6.00 15.00

2000 Upper Deck Victory Circle

This 85 card set was issued in 10 card packs, with 24 packs per box and a SRP of $2.99 per pack. This set features a mix of leading drivers and their cars.

COMPLETE SET (85) 10.00 25.00
1 Hank Parker Jr. RC .30 .75
2 Todd Bodine .08 .25
3 Rick Mast .08 .25
4 Rusty Wallace .75 2.00
5 Jason Jarrett .08 .25
6 Michael Waltrip .20 .50
7 Ken Schrader .08 .25
8 Steve Park .30 .75
9 Dale Earnhardt 1.50 4.00
10 Jeremy Mayfield .08 .25
11 Mike Skinner .08 .25
12 Jason Keller .08 .25
13 Lyndon Amick .08 .25
14 Johnny Benson .20 .50
15 Jeff Burton .30 .75
16 Jeff Gordon 1.00 2.50
17 Kenny Wallace .08 .25
18 Bobby Labonte .60 1.50
19 Kevin Lepage .08 .25
20 Geoffrey Bodine .08 .25
21 Bill Elliott .40 1.00
22 Tony Stewart 1.00 2.50
23 Kyle Petty .20 .50
24 Darrell Waltrip .20 .50
25 Mark Martin .75 2.00
26 John Andretti .08 .25
27 Brett Bodine .08 .25
28 Ward Burton .20 .50
29 Casey Atwood .30 .75
30 Ernie Irvan .20 .50
31 Matt Kenseth CRC .75 2.00
32 Bobby Hamilton .08 .25
33 Mike McLaughlin .08 .25
34 Dale Jarrett .60 1.50
35 Sterling Marlin .30 .75
36 Elliott Sadler .20 .50
37 Dale Earnhardt Jr. CRC 1.25 3.00
38 Terry Labonte .30 .75
39 Chad Little .08 .25
40 Kenny Irwin .20 .50
41 Ricky Rudd .30 .75
42 Derrike Cope .08 .25
43 Ned Jarrett .08 .25
44 Dick Trickle .08 .25
45 Wally Dallenbach .08 .25
46 Adam Petty 2.00 5.00
47 David Green .08 .25
48 Robert Pressley .08 .25
49 Ricky Craven .08 .25
50 Bobby Hamilton Jr. RC .20 .50
51 Randy LaJoie .08 .25
52 Ward Burton's Car .08 .25
53 Bobby Labonte's Car .20 .50
54 Casey Atwood's Car .20 .50
55 Dale Earnhardt's Car .60 1.50
56 Dale Earnhardt Jr.'s Car .50 1.25
57 Dale Jarrett's Car .20 .50
58 Jeff Burton's Car .20 .50
59 Jeff Gordon's Car .40 1.00
60 Mark Martin's Car .30 .75
61 Matt Kenseth's Car .30 .75
62 Rusty Wallace's Car .30 .75
63 Terry Labonte's Car .20 .50
64 Tony Stewart's Car .40 1.00
65 Jeff Gordon's Car .40 1.00
66 Jeff Gordon's Car .40 1.00
67 Tony Stewart's Car .40 1.00
68 Casey Atwood's Car .20 .50
69 Dale Jarrett's Car .20 .50
70 Dale Earnhardt's Car .60 1.50
71 Rusty Wallace's Car .30 .75
72 Bobby Labonte's Car .20 .50
73 Jeff Gordon's Car .40 1.00
74 Jeff Burton's Car .20 .50
75 Mark Martin's Car .30 .75
76 Ernie Irvan's Car .08 .25
77 Adam Petty's Car .75 2.00
78 Dale Earnhardt Jr.'s Car .50 1.25
79 Darrell Waltrip's Car .08 .25
80 Tony Stewart's Car .40 1.00
81 Johnny Benson .20 .50
82 John Andretti .08 .25
83 Matt Kenseth .75 2.00
84 Terry Labonte's Car .20 .50
85 Tony Stewart CL .50 1.25

2000 Upper Deck Victory Circle Exclusives Level 2 Gold

*SINGLES/70-99: 10X TO 25X HI COL.
*SINGLES/45-69: 12X TO 30X HI COL.
*SINGLES/30-44: 25X TO 50X HI COL.
*SINGLES/20-29: 40X TO 80X HI COL.

2000 Upper Deck Victory Circle Exclusives Level 1 Silver

COMPLETE SET (85) 60.00 150.00
*EXCLUSIVES L1: 4X TO 10X BASE CARDS

2000 Upper Deck Victory Circle A Day in the Life

Inserted at stated odds of one in 11, these six cards follow Dale Earnhardt Jr. as he prepares for a race day.

COMPLETE SET (6) 10.00 25.00
COMMON DALE JR. (JR1-JR6) 2.00 5.00
COMP.LTD SET (6) 75.00 150.00
*LTD CARDS: 3X TO 6X BASIC INSERTS
LTD STATED ODDS 1:287

2000 Upper Deck Victory Circle Income Statement

Inserted in packs at stated odds of one in nine, these 10 die-cut cards feature NASCAR's top drivers and their top payouts during the 1999 season.

COMPLETE SET (10) 8.00 20.00
COMP.LTD SET (10) 15.00 40.00
*LTD CARDS: .8X TO 2X BASIC INSERTS
LTD STATED ODDS 1:23
IS1 Jeff Gordon 1.25 3.00
IS2 Jeff Burton .40 1.00
IS3 Bobby Labonte .75 2.00
IS4 Dale Jarrett .75 2.00
IS5 Tony Stewart 1.25 3.00
IS6 Mark Martin 1.00 2.50
IS7 Ward Burton .25 .60
IS8 Rusty Wallace 1.00 2.50
IS9 Matt Kenseth 1.00 2.50
IS10 Casey Atwood .40 1.00

2000 Upper Deck Victory Circle Signature Collection

Inserted in packs at stated odds of one in 143, these 10-cards feature autographs from top drivers. A Gold foil parallel set for some cards was also produced. The cards were all released as redemptions and needed to be sent in by October 1, 2000.

CA Casey Atwood 6.00 15.00
DJ Dale Jarrett 10.00 25.00
DW Darrell Waltrip
JB Jeff Burton 8.00 20.00
JG Jeff Gordon 60.00 120.00
JM Jeremy Mayfield 6.00 15.00
MK Matt Kenseth 8.00 20.00
RW Rusty Wallace 8.00 20.00
TS Tony Stewart 15.00 40.00
WB Ward Burton 6.00 15.00

2000 Upper Deck Victory Circle Signature Collection Gold

2 Ward Burton/22 20.00 50.00
4 Dale Jarrett/88 15.00 40.00
5 Tony Stewart/20 50.00 100.00
6 Darrell Waltrip/66 20.00 50.00

2000 Upper Deck Victory Circle PowerDeck

Issued in packs at different odds, these six cards capture NASCAR action on digital trading cards. Stated odds for card one thru four are 1:23, and cards five and six are 1:287.

PD1 Dale Earnhardt 12.00 30.00
PD2 Dale Earnhardt Jr. 5.00 12.00
PD3 Rusty Wallace 2.00 5.00
PD4 Tony Stewart 3.00 8.00
PD5 Jeff Gordon 8.00 20.00
PD6 Dale Earnhardt Jr. 10.00 25.00

2000 Upper Deck Victory Circle Victory Circl

Inserted at stated odds of one in seven, these nine die-cut cards showcase drivers who won races in 1999.

COMP.LTD SET (9) 50.00 120.00
*LTD CARDS: 3X TO 6X HI COL.
LTD STATED ODDS 1:71
V1 Bobby Labonte .75 2.00
V2 Matt Kenseth 1.00 2.50
V3 Rusty Wallace 1.00 2.50
V4 Jeff Burton .40 1.00
V5 Casey Atwood .40 1.00
V6 Dale Jarrett .75 2.00
V7 Mark Martin 1.00 2.50
V8 Terry Labonte .40 1.00
V9 Dale Earnhardt Jr. 1.50 4.00

2000 Upper Deck Victory Circle Winning Material Autographed Victory Hat

Randomly inserted into packs, this insert set features pieces of caps worn by Drivers in victory circle along with an autograph. Cards are numberd to 30.

HBL Bobby Labonte
HJB Jeff Burton 30.00 80.00
HMM Mark Martin 75.00 200.00
HRW Rusty Wallace 75.00 150.00

2000 Upper Deck Victory Circle Winning Material Combination

Randomly inserted into packs, these four cards feature pieces of race-worn firesuits along with race-used tires. These cards are serial numbered to 50.

CDJ Dale Jarrett 25.00 60.00
CMK Matt Kenseth 25.00 60.00
CMM Mark Martin 40.00 100.00
CRW Rusty Wallace 30.00 80.00

2000 Upper Deck Victory Circle Winning Material Firesuit

Inserted into packs at stated odds of one in 287, these five cards feature pieces of race-worn firesuits.

FSDJ Dale Jarrett 15.00 40.00
FSMK Matt Kenseth 15.00 40.00
FSMM Mark Martin 10.00 25.00
FSRW Rusty Wallace 12.00 30.00
FSWB Ward Burton 12.50 30.00

2000 Upper Deck Victory Circle Winning Material Tire

Inserted into packs at stated odds of one in 989, these 10 cards feature pieces of race-used tires.

TBL Bobby Labonte 15.00 40.00
TCA Casey Atwood 10.00 25.00
TDJ Dale Jarrett 15.00 40.00
TJG Jeff Gordon 25.00 60.00
TJR Dale Earnhardt Jr. 75.00 150.00
TMK Matt Kenseth 15.00 40.00
TMM Mark Martin 15.00 40.00
TRW Rusty Wallace 15.00 40.00
TTS Tony Stewart 20.00 50.00

2011 Upper Deck World of Sports

COMPLETE SET (400) 75.00 150.00
COMP.SET w/o SPs (300) 25.00 60.00
298 Angela Cope .60 1.50
299 Amber Cope .60 1.50

1995 US Air Greg Sacks

US Air produced and distributed this set featuring Greg Sacks and the US Air Racing Team. The five black bordered cards are not numbered and listed below alphabetically.

COMPLETE SET (5) 2.00 5.00
1 Tony Furr .40 1.00
2 Greg Sacks' Car .40 1.00
3 Greg Sacks in Pits .40 1.00
4 Greg Sacks UER .60 1.50
5 D.K. Ulrich .40 1.00

1992 U.S. Playing Card

This set is actually a deck of playing cards featuring the Junior Johnson Race Team and driver Bill Elliott. While the majority of the cards from the set show only a playing card design, a few include photos of Johnson and Elliott. The cardbacks feature Bill Elliott's car.

COMP. FACT SET (56) 1.25 3.00
COMMON CARD (1-56) .01 .05
BILL ELLIOTT CARDS .20 .50

2007 Valvoline Racing

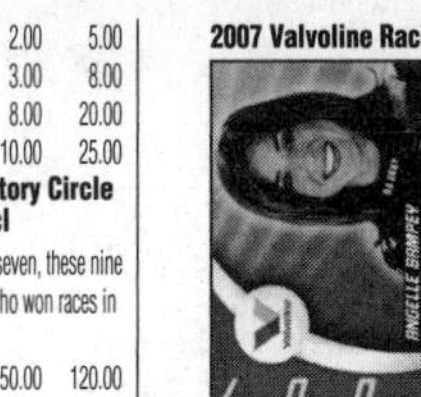

COMP.FACT SET (25) 7.50 15.00
COMPLETE SET (25) 6.00 12.00
NNO S.Payne/S.Riggs/A.Brown .60 1.50
NNO Jay Payne .30 .75
NNO Ron Kisher .30 .75
NNO Shelly Payne .30 .75
NNO Ron Capps .50 1.25
NNO Angelle Sampey 1.00 2.50
NNO Richie Stevens Jr. .30 .75
NNO Antron Brown .60 1.50
NNO Gary Scelzi .30 .75
NNO Scott Riggs .25 .60
NNO Scott Riggs' Car .25 .60
NNO Kasey Kahne .30 .75
NNO Elliott Sadler .20 .50
NNO Tony Schumacher .50 1.25
NNO Jack Beckman .30 .75
NNO Bob Newberry .30 .75
NNO Steve Francis .30 .75
NNO Conventional Valvoline .12 .30
NNO Durablend Valvoline .12 .30
NNO Maxlife Valvoline .12 .30
NNO Maxlife Synthetic Valvoline .12 .30
NNO Synpower Valvoline .12 .30
NNO VR1 Racing Valvoline .12 .30
NNO FAQs 1 .12 .30
NNO FAQs 2 .12 .30

2002 Velveeta Jeff Burton

These 3-card set was sponsored by Kraft and issued as part of boxes of Velveeta Shells and Cheese. Each card was to be cut from the box of product. The cards measure roughly 2 1/2" by 3 1/2" when cleanly cut.

COMPLETE SET (3) 5.00 10.00
COMMON CARD (1-3) 1.50 4.00

1994 VIP

This 100-card set was the first issued by card maker Press Pass under the VIP brand name. The cards are printed on 24-point stock and are foil stamped on both sides. There are four topical subsets: Portraits (73-81), Alabama Gang (82-84), Heroes of Racing (85-90), Master Mechanics (91-99). The Portraits subset features nine water color paintings for racing artist Jeanne Barnes. There were reportedly 3,500 cases made. Each case contained 20 boxes, with 36 packs per box and 6 cards per pack.

COMPLETE SET (100) 10.00 25.00
WAX BOX 30.00 60.00
1 Loy Allen Jr. .10 .30
2 Brett Bodine .10 .30
3 Geoff Bodine .10 .30
4 Todd Bodine .10 .30
5 Chuck Bown .10 .30
6 Jeff Burton .40 1.00
7 Ward Burton .25 .60
8 Derrike Cope .10 .30
9 Wally Dallenbach Jr. .10 .30
10 Dale Earnhardt 2.00 5.00
11 Harry Gant .25 .60
12 Jeff Gordon 1.25 3.00
13 Steve Grissom .10 .30
14 Bobby Hamilton .10 .30
15 Jimmy Hensley .10 .30
16 Ernie Irvan .25 .60
17 Dale Jarrett .75 2.00
18 Bobby Labonte .75 2.00
19 Terry Labonte .40 1.00
20 Sterling Marlin .40 1.00
21 Mark Martin 1.00 2.50
22 Rick Mast .10 .30
23 Ted Musgrave .10 .30
24 Joe Nemechek .10 .30
25 Kyle Petty .25 .60
26 Ricky Rudd .40 1.00
27 Greg Sacks .10 .30
28 Ken Schrader .10 .30
29 Morgan Shepherd .10 .30
30 Lake Speed .10 .30
31 Jimmy Spencer .10 .30
32 Hut Stricklin .10 .30
33 Mike Wallace .10 .30
34 Rusty Wallace 1.00 2.50
35 Darrell Waltrip .25 .60
36 Michael Waltrip .25 .60
37 Morgan Shepherd w/Car .05 .15
38 Jeff Gordon w/Car 1.25 3.00
39 Geoff Bodine w/Car .05 .15
40 Ted Musgrave w/Car .05 .15
41 Derrike Cope w/Car .05 .15
42 Dale Earnhardt w/Car 2.00 5.00
43 Dale Jarrett w/Car .75 2.00
44 Terry Labonte w/Car .40 1.00
45 Ken Schrader w/Car .05 .15
46 Bobby Labonte w/Car .75 2.00
47 Kyle Petty w/Car .10 .30
48 Rusty Wallace's Car .25 .60
49 Michael Waltrip w/Car .10 .30
50 Brett Bodine w/Car .05 .15
51 Ernie Irvan w/Car .10 .30
52 Ricky Rudd w/Car .25 .60
53 Mark Martin w/Car 1.00 2.50
54 Darrell Waltrip w/Car .10 .30
55 Johnny Benson RC .40 1.00
56 Ricky Craven .10 .30
57 Bobby Dotter .10 .30
58 David Green .10 .30
59 Tracy Leslie .10 .30
60 Chad Little .10 .30
61 Mike McLaughlin .10 .30
62 Larry Pearson .10 .30
63 Tom Peck .10 .30
64 Robert Pressley .10 .30
65 Dennis Setzer .10 .30
66 Kenny Wallace .10 .30
67 Tom Peck's Car .05 .15
68 Bobby Dotter w/Car .05 .15
69 Ricky Craven w/Car .05 .15
70 Mike McLaughlin w/Car .05 .15
71 David Green w/Car .05 .15
72 Hermie Sadler's Car .05 .15
73 Harry Gant ART .10 .30
74 Jeff Gordon ART .60 1.50
75 Ernie Irvan ART .10 .30
76 Dale Earnhardt ART .40 1.00
77 Sterling Marlin ART .25 .60
78 Mark Martin ART .40 1.00
79 Kyle Petty ART .10 .30
80 Morgan Shepherd ART .05 .15
81 Rusty Wallace ART .40 1.00
82 Bobby Allison RF .10 .30
83 Donnie Allison RF .10 .30
84 Red Farmer RF .05 .15
85 Ned Jarrett HR .05 .15
86 Junior Johnson HR .10 .30
87 Ralph Moody HR .05 .15
88 Benny Parsons HR .10 .30
89 Wendell Scott HR .10 .30
90 Cale Yarborough HR .10 .30
91 Paul Andrews MM .05 .15
92 Barry Dodson MM .05 .15
93 Jeff Hammond MM .05 .15
94 Steve Hmiel MM .05 .15
95 Jimmy Makar MM .05 .15
96 Larry McReynolds MM .05 .15
97 Buddy Parrott MM .05 .15
98 Robin Pemberton MM .05 .15
99 Andy Petree MM .05 .15
100 Checklist .05 .15
P1 Jeff Gordon's Car Prototype 2.00 5.00
P2 Ernie Irvan Prototype 1.25 3.00
P3 Harry Gant Prototype .75 2.00
P4 Rusty Wallace Prototype 2.00 5.00

1994 VIP Driver's Choice

The nine-card insert set features the drivers, as chosen by their peers, as the most likely to win the 1994 Winston Cup Championship. The cards were seeded one per eight packs.

COMPLETE SET (9) 10.00 25.00
DC1 Dale Earnhardt 5.00 12.00
DC2 Ernie Irvan .60 1.50
DC3 Dale Jarrett 2.00 5.00
DC4 Sterling Marlin 1.00 2.50
DC5 Mark Martin 2.50 6.00
DC6 Kyle Petty .60 1.50
DC7 Ken Schrader .30 .75
DC8 Morgan Shepherd .30 .75
DC9 Rusty Wallace 2.50 6.00

1994 VIP Gold Signature

This seven-card set was originally inserted in packs of VIP via redemption cards. Inserted at a rate of one per 240 packs was a redemption card that had a driver's facsimile signature in a gold foil stamping across the front. There were only 1,500 of each of the seven redemption cards. This redemption card was then used to receive a 24K Gold Signature card. The prices below are for the 24K Gold Signature cards and not the redemption card.

COMPLETE SET (7) 125.00 250.00
EC1 Dale Earnhardt 25.00 60.00
EC2 Harry Gant 3.00 8.00
EC3 Jeff Gordon 15.00 40.00
EC4 Ernie Irvan 3.00 8.00
EC5 Mark Martin 12.50 30.00
EC6 Kyle Petty 3.00 8.00
EC7 Rusty Wallace 12.50 30.00
SEC1 Super Exchange Expired .75 2.00

1994 VIP Member's Only

Although these two cards do not carry the VIP logo, they utilize the same design as the 1994 VIP set. They were distributed directly to participants of Press Pass' Member's Only collecting club. The cards are unnumbered and carry a blue foil "Member's Only" logo.

COMPLETE SET (2) 6.00 15.00
1 Geoff Bodine 2.00 5.00
2 Mark Martin 4.00 10.00

1995 VIP Promos

Press Pass produced this set to preview its 1995 VIP set. Each of the four cards can be found with either Red or Gold foil layering on the cardfront. While the Gold cards are not numbered, the Red foil versions are individually numbered of 6000 produced.

COMPLETE SET (4) 1.00 2.50
*RED CARDS: 1.2X TO 3X GOLDS
1G Dale Jarrett Gold .40 1.00
2G Bobby Labonte Gold .40 1.00
3G Michael Waltrip Gold .20 .50
4G Derrike Cope Gold .20 .50

1995 VIP

This 64-card set represents the second year for the VIP brand. The cards feature top personalities from NASCAR racing. Each card is gold-foil stamped and is printed on 24-point stock.There are four topical subsets: Heroes of Racing (46-50), Track Dominators (51-54), Master Mechanics (55-59), SuperTruck (60-63). The cards came packed six cards per pack. There were 24 packs per box and 16 boxes per case.

COMPLETE SET (64) 10.00 25.00
WAX BOX 45.00 80.00
1 John Andretti .10 .30
2 Brett Bodine .10 .30
3 Geoff Bodine .10 .30
4 Todd Bodine .10 .30
5 Jeff Burton .40 1.00
6 Ward Burton .25 .60
7 Derrike Cope .10 .30
8 Ricky Craven .10 .30
9 Dale Earnhardt 2.00 5.00
10 Bill Elliott .50 1.25
11 Jeff Gordon 1.25 3.00
12 Steve Grissom .10 .30
13 Bobby Hamilton .10 .30
14 Dale Jarrett .75 2.00
15 Bobby Labonte .75 2.00
16 Terry Labonte .40 1.00
17 Randy LaJoie .10 .30
18 Sterling Marlin .40 1.00
19 Mark Martin 1.00 2.50
20 Ted Musgrave .10 .30
21 Joe Nemechek .10 .30
22 Kyle Petty .25 .60
23 Robert Pressley .10 .30
24 Ricky Rudd .40 1.00
25 Ken Schrader .10 .30
26 Morgan Shepherd .10 .30
27 Dick Trickle .10 .30
28 Rusty Wallace 1.00 2.50
29 Darrell Waltrip .25 .60
30 Michael Waltrip .25 .60
31 Jeff Gordon 1.25 3.00
32 Sterling Marlin .40 1.00
33 Mark Martin 1.00 2.50
34 Kyle Petty .25 .60
35 Ricky Rudd .40 1.00
36 Ken Schrader .10 .30
37 Johnny Benson Jr. .25 .60
38 Rodney Combs .10 .30
39 Bobby Dotter .10 .30

40 David Green .10 .30
41 Chad Little .10 .30
42 Mike McLaughlin .10 .30
43 Larry Pearson .10 .30
44 Dennis Setzer .10 .30
45 Kenny Wallace .10 .30
46 Bobby Allison HR .10 .30
47 Ernie Irvan HR .25 .60
48 Elmo Langley HR .05 .15
49 Richard Petty HR .40 1.00
50 Tim Richmond HR .10 .30
51 Bill Elliott TD .40 1.00
52 Sterling Marlin TD .40 1.00
53 Mark Martin TD .50 1.25
54 Darrell Waltrip TD .25 .60
55 Jeff Andrews MM .05 .15
56 Danny Glad MM .05 .15
57 Charlie Siegars MM .05 .15
58 Rick Wetzel MM .05 .15
59 Gregg Wilson MM .05 .15
60 Geoff Bodine's Truck .05 .15
61 Jeff Gordon's Truck .40 1.00
62 Ken Schrader's Truck .05 .15
63 Mike Skinner's Truck .05 .15
64 Checklist .05 .15

1995 VIP Cool Blue

COMPLETE SET (64) 15.00 40.00
*COOL BLUE: .8X TO 2X BASE CARDS

1995 VIP Emerald Proofs

COMPLETE SET (64) 250.00 500.00
*EMER.PROOFS: 5X TO 12X HI COL.

1995 VIP Red Hot

COMPLETE SET (64) 15.00 40.00
*RED HOTS: .8X TO 2X BASIC CARDS

1995 VIP Autographs

This 24-card insert set consists of autographed regular VIP cards. The only way to tell the difference in one of these cards and one signed at a show or a track, is that the ones from packs don't have the UV coating. Press Pass does this intentionally to make them easier for the drivers to sign and to differentiate the insert cards. There were more than 30,000 signed cards inserted in the VIP packs at a rate of one per 24 packs. Each card was not signed in equal quantities.

COMPLETE SET (24) 175.00 350.00
7 Derrike Cope 6.00 15.00
8 Ricky Craven 6.00 15.00
11 Jeff Gordon 40.00 100.00
13 Bobby Hamilton 10.00 25.00
18 Sterling Marlin 8.00 20.00
19 Mark Martin 15.00 40.00
20 Ted Musgrave 6.00 15.00
22 Kyle Petty 15.00 40.00
25 Ken Schrader 10.00 25.00
37 Johnny Benson 10.00 25.00
38 Rodney Combs 6.00 15.00
39 Bobby Dotter 6.00 15.00
40 David Green 6.00 15.00
41 Chad Little 8.00 20.00
42 Mike McLaughlin 6.00 15.00
43 Larry Pearson 6.00 15.00
44 Dennis Setzer 6.00 15.00
45 Kenny Wallace 6.00 15.00
47 Ernie Irvan HR 10.00 25.00
55 Jeff Andrews MM 5.00 10.00
56 Danny Glad MM 5.00 10.00
57 Charlie Siegars MM 5.00 10.00
58 Rick Wetzel MM 5.00 10.00
59 Gregg Wilson MM 5.00 10.00

1995 VIP Fan's Choice

This nine-card insert set features the top nine Winston Cup drivers as voted by the Press Pass VIP Club members. The cards are printed on either gold or silver foil board. Fan's Choice Silver cards could be found at a rate of one per six packs. Gold cards were packed at the rate of 1:30 packs.

COMPLETE SET (9) 10.00 25.00
*GOLDS: 1X TO 2.5X BASIC INSERTS
FC1 Dale Earnhardt 6.00 15.00
FC2 Bill Elliott 1.50 4.00
FC3 Jeff Gordon 4.00 10.00
FC4 Terry Labonte 1.25 3.00
FC5 Sterling Marlin 1.25 3.00
FC6 Mark Martin 3.00 8.00
FC7 Ricky Rudd 1.25 3.00
FC8 Ken Schrader .40 1.00
FC9 Rusty Wallace 3.00 8.00

1995 VIP Helmets

This nine-card insert set uses Nitrokrome technology along with etched foil printed on silver or gold foil to bring out the color in some of the best Winston Cup drivers' helmets. The Silver cards were randomly inserted in packs at a rate of one per 18 with Gold cards packed at 1:90.

COMPLETE SET (9) 20.00 50.00
*GOLDS: .6X TO 1.5X BASIC INSERTS
H1 Geoff Bodine 1.25 3.00
H2 Jeff Burton 4.00 10.00
H3 Derrike Cope 1.25 3.00
H4 Jeff Gordon 12.50 30.00
H5 Kyle Petty 2.50 6.00
H6 Ricky Rudd 4.00 10.00
H7 Richard Petty 1960s 4.00 10.00
H8 Richard Petty 1980s 4.00 10.00
H9 Richard Petty 1990s 4.00 10.00

1995 VIP Reflections

This five-card insert set features the artwork of Jeanne Barnes. The card fronts show a portrait of the driver as if you were looking at him from head on. The card backs show a portrait of the driver as if you were standing behind him. The cards are printed on both silver and gold foil board with Silver cards inserted at a rate of one per 72 packs. Gold cards were packaged 1:360 packs.

COMPLETE SET (5) 25.00 60.00
*GOLDS: 1.2X TO 3X BASIC INSERTS
R1 Ricky Craven 1.00 2.50
R2 Jeff Gordon 10.00 25.00
R3 Sterling Marlin 3.00 8.00
R4 Mark Martin 8.00 20.00
R5 Rusty Wallace 8.00 20.00

1996 VIP

The 1996 VIP set was issued in one series totalling 54 cards. The cards are packaged six cards per pack, 24 packs per box and 16 boxes per case. Each base set card was printed on 24 point board and has gold foil stamping and UV coating.

COMPLETE SET (54) 8.00 20.00
1 John Andretti .10 .30
2 Johnny Benson .25 .60
3 Geoff Bodine .10 .30
4 Jeff Burton .40 1.00
5 Ward Burton .25 .60
6 Ricky Craven .10 .30
7 Wally Dallenbach .10 .30
8 Dale Earnhardt 2.00 5.00
9 Bill Elliott .50 1.25
10 Jeff Gordon 1.25 3.00
11 Bobby Hamilton .10 .30
12 Ernie Irvan .25 .60
13 Dale Jarrett .75 2.00
14 Bobby Labonte .75 2.00
15 Terry Labonte .40 1.00
16 Sterling Marlin .40 1.00
17 Mark Martin 1.00 2.50
18 Jeremy Mayfield .25 .60
19 Ted Musgrave .10 .30
20 Joe Nemechek .10 .30
21 Kyle Petty .25 .60
22 Robert Pressley .10 .30
23 Ricky Rudd .40 1.00
24 Ken Schrader .10 .30
25 Morgan Shepherd .10 .30
26 Mike Skinner .10 .30
27 Rusty Wallace 1.00 2.50
28 Darrell Waltrip .25 .60
29 Michael Waltrip .25 .60
30 Jeff Gordon 1.25 3.00
31 Mark Martin .75 2.00
32 David Green .10 .30
33 Jeff Green .10 .30
34 Jason Keller .10 .30
35 Chad Little .25 .60
36 Mike McLaughlin .10 .30
37 Jeff Gordon's Car .50 1.25
38 Dale Earnhardt's Car .75 2.00
39 Bill Elliott's Car .25 .60
40 Rusty Wallace's Car .40 1.00
41 Dale Jarrett's Car .25 .60
42 Bobby Hamilton's Car .05 .15
43 Ernie Irvan's Car .10 .30
44 Ricky Rudd's Car .10 .30
45 Mark Martin's Car .40 1.00
46 Ray Evernham .25 .60
47 Steve Hmiel .05 .15
48 Larry McReynolds .05 .15
49 David Smith .05 .15
50 Jeff Andrews .05 .15
51 Danny Glad .05 .15
52 Charlie Siegars .05 .15
53 Rick Wetzel .05 .15
54 Checklist .05 .15
P1 Mark Martin Promo 2.00 5.00
P2 Kyle Petty Club Promo 2.00 5.00

1996 VIP Emerald Proofs

COMPLETE SET (54) 200.00 400.00
*EMER.PROOFS: 4X TO 10X BASE CARDS

1996 VIP Torquers

COMPLETE SET (54) 10.00 25.00
*TORQUERS: .6X TO 1.5X BASE CARDS

1996 VIP Autographs

This 26-card set features desirable autographs from NASCAR's biggest stars. More than 25,000 autographs were inserted in packs of VIP at a rate of one per 24 packs.

COMPLETE SET (26) 400.00 800.00
1 Jeff Andrews 4.00 8.00
2 Johnny Benson 10.00 25.00
3 Geoff Bodine 6.00 15.00
4 Jeff Burton 6.00 15.00
5 Ricky Craven 6.00 15.00
6 Dale Earnhardt 100.00 200.00
7 Danny Glad 4.00 8.00
8 Jeff Gordon 50.00 100.00
9 David Green 4.00 10.00
10 Jeff Green 4.00 10.00
11 Steve Hmiel 4.00 8.00
12 Ernie Irvan 10.00 25.00
13 Jason Keller 4.00 10.00
14 Bobby Labonte 12.00 30.00
15 Chad Little 10.00 25.00
16 Sterling Marlin 10.00 25.00
17 Jeremy Mayfield 10.00 25.00
18 Mike McLaughlin 6.00 15.00
19 Ted Musgrave 6.00 15.00
20 Joe Nemechek 6.00 15.00
21 Robert Pressley 6.00 15.00
22 Charlie Siegars 4.00 8.00
23 Mike Skinner 4.00 10.00
24 David Smith 4.00 8.00
25 Rusty Wallace 12.00 30.00
26 Michael Waltrip 8.00 20.00
27 Rick Wetzel 4.00 8.00

1996 VIP Dale Earnhardt Firesuit

Randomly inserted in packs at a rate of one in 384, this two-card set incorporates a piece of Dale Earnhardt's uniform in each card. There were four different color variations Gold foil 1:512, Silver foil 1:384 in Wal-mart only packs, Blue foil 1:2048, and Green 1:6144.

DE1B Dale Earnhardt B 30.00 80.00
DE1S Dale Earnhardt S 30.00 80.00
DE1GL Dale Earnhardt GLD 30.00 80.00
DE1GR Dale Earnhardt GRN 40.00 100.00
DE2B Dale Earnhardt B 30.00 80.00
DE2S Dale Earnhardt S 30.00 80.00
DE2GL Dale Earnhardt GLD 30.00 80.00
DE2GR Dale Earnhardt GRN 40.00 100.00

1996 VIP Head Gear

Randomly inserted in packs at a rate of one in 16, this nine-card set features today's top Winston Cup talent with their helmets in an all-foil design. There was also a die cut version of each Head Gear card and they were inserted at a rate of one in 96 packs.

COMPLETE SET (9) 20.00 50.00
COMP.DIE CUT SET (9) 60.00 120.00
*DIE CUTS: .8X TO 2X BASIC INSERTS
HG1 Ricky Craven .60 1.50
HG2 Dale Earnhardt 10.00 25.00
HG3 Jeff Gordon 6.00 15.00
HG4 Ernie Irvan 1.25 3.00
HG5 Mark Martin 5.00 12.00
HG6 Ricky Rudd 2.00 5.00
HG7 Rusty Wallace 5.00 12.00
HG8 Darrell Waltrip 1.25 3.00
HG9 Michael Waltrip 1.25 3.00

1996 VIP Sam Bass Top Flight

Randomly inserted in packs at a rate of one in 48, this five-card set features art work from renowned racing artist Sam Bass. The cards come with a silver foil border. There is also a gold foil version inserted at a rate of one in 144 packs.

COMPLETE SET (5) 20.00 50.00
*GOLDS: .8X TO 2X BASIC INSERTS
SB1 Dale Earnhardt 10.00 25.00
SB2 Bill Elliott 3.00 8.00
SB3 Terry Labonte 2.00 5.00
SB4 Mark Martin 2.00 5.00
SB5 Rusty Wallace 2.00 5.00

1996 VIP War Paint

Randomly inserted in packs at a rate of one in 12, this 18-card set features the Winston Cup cars with wildest paint jobs mixed with all-foil NitroKrome technology.

COMPLETE SET (18) 25.00 60.00
COMP.GOLD SET (18) 50.00 120.00
*GOLDS: .8X TO 2X BASIC INSERTS
WP1 Rusty Wallace's Car 3.00 8.00
WP2 Dale Earnhardt's Car 6.00 15.00
WP3 Sterling Marlin's Car 1.00 2.50
WP4 Terry Labonte's Car 2.00 5.00
WP5 Mark Martin's Car 3.00 8.00
WP6 Ricky Rudd's Car 1.00 2.50
WP7 Ted Musgrave's Car .50 1.25
WP8 Darrell Waltrip's Car 1.00 2.50
WP9 Bobby Labonte's Car 2.00 5.00
WP10 Michael Waltrip's Car .50 1.25
WP11 Ward Burton's Car 1.00 2.50
WP12 Jeff Gordon's Car 4.00 10.00
WP13 Ernie Irvan's Car 1.00 2.50
WP14 Ricky Craven's Car .50 1.25
WP15 Kyle Petty's Car 1.00 2.50
WP16 Bobby Hamilton's Car .50 1.25
WP17 Dale Jarrett's Car 2.00 5.00
WP18 Bill Elliott's Car 2.00 5.00

1997 VIP

This 50-card set features stars from the top three NASCAR divisions (Winston Cup, Busch Grand National and Truck racing) and was distributed in seven-card packs with a suggested retail price of $3.99. The set was printed on extra thick 24 pt. card stock with two different foil stampings on the front.

COMPLETE SET (50) 8.00 20.00
1 Johnny Benson .25 .60
2 Geoff Bodine .10 .30
3 Jeff Burton .40 1.00
4 Ward Burton .25 .60
5 Ricky Craven .10 .30
6 Dale Earnhardt 2.00 5.00
7 Bill Elliott .60 1.50
8 Jeff Gordon 1.25 3.00
9 Robby Gordon RC .40 1.00
10 Bobby Hamilton .10 .30
11 Ernie Irvan .25 .60
12 Dale Jarrett .75 2.00
13 Bobby Labonte .75 2.00
14 Terry Labonte .40 1.00
15 Sterling Marlin .40 1.00
16 Mark Martin 1.00 2.50
17 Ted Musgrave .10 .30
18 Joe Nemechek .10 .30
19 Kyle Petty .25 .60
20 Ricky Rudd .40 1.00
21 Ken Schrader .10 .30
22 Mike Skinner .10 .30
23 Rusty Wallace 1.00 2.50
24 Darrell Waltrip .25 .60
25 Michael Waltrip .25 .60
26 David Green .10 .30
27 Chad Little .10 .30
28 Todd Bodine .10 .30
29 Tim Fedewa .10 .30
30 Jeff Fuller .10 .30
31 Jeff Green .10 .30
32 Jason Keller .10 .30
33 Randy LaJoie .10 .30
34 Kevin Lepage .10 .30
35 Mark Martin 1.00 2.50
36 Mike McLaughlin .10 .30
37 Rich Bickle .10 .30
38 Mike Bliss .10 .30
39 Rick Carelli .10 .30
40 Ron Hornaday .10 .30
41 Kenny Irwin RC 2.00 4.00
42 Tammy Jo Kirk .05 .15
43 Butch Miller .10 .30
44 Joe Ruttman .10 .30
45 Jack Sprague .10 .30
46 Jeff Burton .25 .60
47 Dale Jarrett .75 2.00
48 Mark Martin 1.00 2.50
49 Bruton Smith .05 .15
Eddie Gossage
50 Checklist .05 .15
P1 Dale Jarrett Promo 1.50 4.00

1997 VIP Explosives

COMPLETE SET (50) 15.00 40.00
*EXPLOSIVE: .8X TO 2X BASIC CARDS

1997 VIP Oil Slicks

COMPLETE SET (50) 300.00 600.00
*OIL SLICKS: 8X TO 20X BASIC CARDS

1997 VIP Head Gear

Randomly inserted in packs at the rate of one in 16, this nine-card set features the hottest drivers and driver helmets on the Winston Cup circuit and are printed on cards with an all foil NitroKrome embossed design.

COMPLETE SET (9) 15.00 40.00
COMP.DIE CUT SET (9) 40.00 75.00
*DIE CUT: .6X TO 1.5X BASIC INSERTS
HG1 Dale Earnhardt 6.00 15.00
HG2 Bill Elliott 2.00 5.00
HG3 Jeff Gordon 4.00 10.00
HG4 Ernie Irvan .75 2.00
HG5 Mark Martin 3.00 8.00
HG6 Kyle Petty .75 2.00
HG7 Ricky Rudd 1.25 3.00
HG8 Rusty Wallace 3.00 8.00
HG9 Michael Waltrip .75 2.00

1997 VIP Knights of Thunder

Randomly inserted in packs at the rate of one in 30, this six-card set features reproductions of original artworks of leading drivers by Race Artist, Sam Bass.

COMPLETE SET (6) 20.00 50.00
COMP. GOLD SET (6) 60.00 150.00
*GOLDS: 1X TO 2.5X BASIC INSERTS
KT1 Dale Earnhardt 10.00 25.00
KT2 Jeff Gordon 6.00 15.00
KT3 Dale Jarrett 4.00 10.00
KT4 Bobby Labonte 4.00 10.00
KT5 Terry Labonte 2.00 5.00
KT6 Rusty Wallace 5.00 12.00

1997 VIP Precious Metal

Randomly inserted in packs at the rate of one in 384, this set features color photos on authentic race-used sheet metal from top drivers and incorporated into a thick laminated card. Each card is individually numbered to 500 and comes with a certificate of authenticity.

COMPLETE SET (5) 125.00 250.00
*MULTI-COLOR METAL: .75X TO 1.25X
SM1 Jeff Gordon 40.00 100.00
SM2 Bobby Labonte 15.00 40.00
SM3 Bill Elliott 20.00 50.00
SM4 Terry Labonte 15.00 40.00
SM5 Rusty Wallace 15.00 40.00

1997 VIP Ring of Honor

Randomly inserted in packs at the rate of one in 10, this 12-card set features color photos of top NASCAR tracks and drivers who have tamed them. The set is printed on thick card stock and clear acetate.

COMPLETE SET (12) 15.00 40.00
COMP.DIE-CUT SET (12) 30.00 60.00
*DIE CUTS: .6X TO 1.5X BASIC INSERTS
RH1 Rusty Wallace's Car 4.00 10.00
RH2 Dale Earnhardt's Car 8.00 20.00
RH3 Sterling Marlin's Car 1.50 4.00
RH4 Terry Labonte's Car 1.50 4.00
RH5 Mark Martin's Car 4.00 10.00
RH6 Ricky Rudd's Car 1.50 4.00
RH7 Bobby Labonte's Car 3.00 8.00
RH8 Jeff Gordon's Car 5.00 12.00
RH9 Ernie Irvan's Car 1.00 2.50
RH10 Bobby Hamilton's Car .50 1.25
RH11 Dale Jarrett's Car 3.00 8.00
RH12 Bill Elliott's Car 2.50 6.00

1998 VIP

The 1998 VIP set was issued in one series totalling 50 cards. The card fronts feature full bleed color photography with two channels of etched foil stamping. The set contains the topical subsets: Winston Drivers (1-27), Busch Drivers (28-36), Winston Cars (37-46), and Las Vegas Motor Speedway (47-50).

COMPLETE SET (50) 12.00 30.00
WAX BOX 40.00 80.00
1 John Andretti .25 .60
2 Johnny Benson .40 1.00
3 Geoff Bodine .25 .60
4 Jeff Burton .30 .75
5 Ward Burton .30 .75
6 Dale Earnhardt 2.50 6.00
7 Bill Elliott .75 2.00
8 Jeff Gordon .75 2.00
9 Bobby Hamilton .25 .60
10 Ernie Irvan .40 1.00
11 Kenny Irwin .60 1.50
12 Dale Jarrett .40 1.00
13 Bobby Labonte .40 1.00
14 Terry Labonte .40 1.00
15 Sterling Marlin .40 1.00
16 Mark Martin .40 1.00
17 Jeremy Mayfield .25 .60
18 Ted Musgrave .25 .60
19 Joe Nemechek .25 .60
20 Steve Park .25 .60
21 Robert Pressley .25 .60
22 Ricky Rudd .30 .75
23 Ken Schrader .25 .60
24 Mike Skinner .25 .60
25 Jimmy Spencer .30 .75
26 Rusty Wallace .40 1.00
27 Michael Waltrip .40 1.00
28 Dale Earnhardt Jr. 2.50 6.00
29 Tim Fedewa .25 .60
30 Jason Keller .25 .60
31 Randy LaJoie .25 .60
32 Mark Martin .40 1.00
33 Mike McLaughlin .25 .60
34 Elliott Sadler .25 .60
35 Hermie Sadler .25 .60
36 Tony Stewart RC 3.00 8.00
37 Jeff Burton's Car .12 .30
38 Dale Earnhardt's Car 1.00 2.50
39 Bill Elliott's Car .30 .75
40 Jeff Gordon's Car .30 .75
41 Dale Jarrett's Car .15 .40
42 Bobby Labonte's Car .15 .40
43 Terry Labonte's Car .15 .40
44 Chad Little's Car .10 .25
45 Mark Martin's Car .15 .40
46 Rusty Wallace's Car .15 .40
47 Mark Martin .40 1.00
48 Dale Jarrett .40 1.00
49 Roush Racing .40 1.00
50 Mark Martin CL .15 .40
P1 Jeremy Mayfield Promo 1.00 2.50

1998 VIP Explosives

COMPLETE SET (50) 20.00 50.00
*EXPLOSIVE VETS: 1X TO 2.5X BASE CARDS
*EXPLOSIVE RCs: .6X TO 1.5X BASE CARDS

1998 VIP Driving Force

Randomly inserted in packs at a rate of one in 10, this 18-card insert set features NASCAR's stock cars printed on all-foil cards.

COMPLETE SET (18) 20.00 50.00
COMP.DIE CUT SET (18) 40.00 100.00
*DIE CUTS: .6X TO 1.5X BASIC INSERTS
DF1 John Andretti's Car .60 1.50
DF2 Johnny Benson's Car 1.00 2.50
DF3 Jeff Burton's Car .75 2.00
DF4 Ward Burton's Car .75 2.00
DF5 Dale Earnhardt's Car 6.00 15.00
DF6 Bill Elliott's Car 2.00 5.00
DF7 Jeff Gordon's Car 2.00 5.00
DF8 Bobby Hamilton's Car .60 1.50
DF9 Kenny Irwin's Car 1.50 4.00
DF10 Dale Jarrett's Car 1.00 2.50
DF11 Bobby Labonte's Car 1.00 2.50
DF12 Terry Labonte's Car 1.00 2.50
DF13 Sterling Marlin's Car 1.00 2.50
DF14 Mark Martin's Car 1.00 2.50
DF15 Jeremy Mayfield's Car .60 1.50
DF16 Ricky Rudd's Car .75 2.00
DF17 Ken Schrader's Car .60 1.50
DF18 Rusty Wallace's Car 1.00 2.50

1998 VIP Head Gear

Randomly inserted in packs at a rate of one in 16, this 9-card insert set was printed on all-foil and customed sculptured to resemble a driver's helmet.

COMPLETE SET (9) 15.00 40.00
COMP.DIE CUT SET (9) 25.00 60.00
*DIE CUTS: .6X TO 1.5X BASIC INSERTS
HG1 Jeff Burton .75 2.00
HG2 Dale Earnhardt 6.00 15.00
HG3 Bill Elliott 2.00 5.00
HG4 Jeff Gordon 2.00 5.00
HG5 Dale Jarrett 1.00 2.50
HG6 Bobby Labonte 1.00 2.50
HG7 Terry Labonte 1.00 2.50
HG8 Mark Martin 1.00 2.50
HG9 Rusty Wallace 1.00 2.50

1998 VIP Lap Leaders

Randomly inserted in packs at a rate of one in 20, this 9-card insert features the top NASCAR rides on micro-embossed, super thick all-foil board.

COMPLETE SET (9) 15.00 40.00
COMP.ACETATE SET (9) 30.00 80.00
*ACETATES: .8X TO 2X BASIC INSERTS
LL1 Jeff Burton's Car 1.00 2.50
LL2 Dale Earnhardt's Car 6.00 15.00
LL3 Jeff Gordon's Car 4.00 10.00
LL4 Dale Jarrett's Car 2.00 5.00
LL5 Bobby Labonte's Car 2.00 5.00
LL6 Terry Labonte's Car 2.00 5.00
LL7 Mark Martin's Car 3.00 8.00
LL8 Jeremy Mayfield's Car 1.00 2.50
LL9 Rusty Wallace's Car 3.00 8.00

1998 VIP NASCAR Country

Randomly inserted in packs at a rate of one in 10, this 9-card insert set helps celebrate NASCAR's 50th Anniversary. The cards feature the top NASCAR Winston Cup drivers teamed up with today's top country music.

COMPLETE SET (9) 12.50 30.00
COMP.DIE CUT SET (9) 30.00 80.00
*DIE CUTS: .8X TO 2X BASIC INSERTS
NC1 Dale Earnhardt 6.00 15.00
NC2 Bill Elliott 1.50 4.00
NC3 Jeff Gordon 4.00 10.00
NC4 Dale Jarrett 2.50 6.00
NC5 Bobby Labonte 2.50 6.00
NC6 Terry Labonte 1.25 3.00
NC7 Mark Martin 3.00 8.00
NC8 Ricky Rudd 1.25 3.00
NC9 Rusty Wallace 3.00 8.00

1998 VIP Triple Gear Sheet Metal

Randomly inserted in packs at a rate of one in 384, this 9-card insert set offers race-used sheet metal from the top NASCAR Winston Cup teams. Cards with multi-color pieces of sheet metal commonly carry a premium over those that do not. These cards are numbered to 225.

TGS1 Rusty Wallace 8.00 20.00
TGS2 Dale Earnhardt 60.00 120.00

TGS3 Terry Labonte 8.00 20.00
TGS4 Mark Martin 8.00 20.00
TGS5 Bobby Labonte 8.00 20.00
TGS6 Jeff Gordon 50.00 100.00
TGS7 Mike Skinner 5.00 12.00
TGS8 Dale Jarrett 8.00 20.00
TGS9 Jeff Burton 6.00 15.00

1999 VIP

This 50 card set was issued in six card hobby packs. The set features a mix of cards of drivers and the cars they drive.

COMPLETE SET (50) 12.50 30.00
1 John Andretti .10 .30
2 Johnny Benson .25 .60
3 Chad Little .25 .60
4 Jeff Burton .40 1.00
5 Ward Burton .25 .60
6 Derrike Cope .10 .30
7 Dale Earnhardt 2.00 5.00
8 Jeff Gordon 1.25 3.00
9 David Green .10 .30
10 Bobby Hamilton .10 .30
11 Kenny Irwin .25 .60
12 Dale Jarrett .75 2.00
13 Bobby Labonte .75 2.00
14 Terry Labonte .40 1.00
15 Sterling Marlin .40 1.00
16 Mark Martin 1.00 2.50
17 Jeremy Mayfield .25 .60
18 Joe Nemechek .10 .30
19 Steve Park .60 1.50
20 Ricky Rudd .40 1.00
21 Elliott Sadler .25 .60
22 Ken Schrader .10 .30
23 Mike Skinner .10 .30
24 Jimmy Spencer .10 .30
25 Tony Stewart CRC 1.50 4.00
26 Rusty Wallace 1.00 2.50
27 Michael Waltrip .25 .60
28 Casey Atwood RC 1.00 2.50
29 Dave Blaney RC .10 .30
30 Dale Earnhardt Jr. 1.50 4.00
31 Jeff Gordon BGN 1.25 3.00
32 Jason Keller .10 .30
33 Matt Kenseth RC 3.00 8.00
34 Randy LaJoie .10 .30
35 Mark Martin BGN 1.00 2.50
36 Mike McLaughlin .10 .30
37 Elton Sawyer .10 .30
38 Jimmy Spencer BGN .10 .30
39 Dick Trickle .10 .30
40 Jeff Burton's Car .05 .15
41 Dale Earnhardt's Car .75 2.00
42 Jeff Gordon's Car .50 1.25
43 Dale Jarrett's Car .25 .60
44 Bobby Labonte's Car .25 .60
45 Terry Labonte's Car .25 .60
46 Mark Martin's Car .40 1.00
47 Jeremy Mayfield's Car .10 .30
48 Tony Stewart's Car .50 1.25
49 Rusty Wallace's Car .40 1.00
50 J.Burton M.Martin CL .50 1.25
P1 Mark Martin Promo .75 2.00

1999 VIP Explosives

COMPLETE SET (50) 30.00 60.00
*EXPLOSIVES: 1X TO 2.5X BASE CARD HI
*EXPLOSIVE RCs: .6X TO 1.5X BASE CARD HI

1999 VIP Explosives Lasers

COMPLETE SET (50) 150.00 300.00
*EXP.LASERS: 5X TO 12X BASE CARD HI
*EXP.LASER RCs: 3X TO 8X BASE CARD HI

1999 VIP Double Take

Inserted one every 29 packs, these six cards feature a "transformation" of leading drivers in their finest moments.

COMPLETE SET (6) 25.00 60.00
DT1 Jeff Gordon 8.00 20.00
DT2 Rusty Wallace 6.00 15.00
DT3 Tony Stewart 8.00 20.00
DT4 Dale Earnhardt Jr. 10.00 25.00
DT5 Terry Labonte 2.50 6.00
DT6 Mark Martin 6.00 15.00

1999 VIP Head Gear

This nine card set inserted one every 10 packs, features up close shots of nine helmets and the drivers who wear them.

COMPLETE SET (9) 12.50 30.00
HG1 Jeff Gordon 3.00 8.00
HG2 Rusty Wallace 2.50 6.00
HG3 Tony Stewart 3.00 8.00
HG4 Dale Earnhardt Jr. 4.00 10.00
HG5 Terry Labonte 1.00 2.50
HG6 Mark Martin 2.50 6.00
HG7 Bobby Labonte 2.00 5.00
HG8 Dale Jarrett 2.00 5.00
HG9 Jeff Burton 1.00 2.50

1999 VIP Head Gear Plastic

COMPLETE SET (10) 25.00 60.00
*PLASTIC: .6X TO 1.5X BASIC INSERTS
HG10 Dale Earnhardt Jr. 7.50 20.00

1999 VIP Lap Leaders

These nine cards, inserted one every 20 packs, feature all plastic foil stamped cards on nine of the leading NASCAR drivers.

COMPLETE SET (9) 30.00 80.00
LL1 Jeff Gordon 6.00 15.00
LL2 Rusty Wallace 5.00 12.00
LL3 Dale Earnhardt 10.00 25.00
LL4 Dale Earnhardt Jr. 8.00 20.00
LL5 Terry Labonte 2.00 5.00
LL6 Mark Martin 5.00 12.00
LL7 Bobby Labonte 4.00 10.00
LL8 Dale Jarrett 4.00 10.00
LL9 Jeff Burton 2.00 5.00

1999 VIP Out of the Box

Issued one every nine packs, these 12 cards feature all-foil gold stamped highlights of 12 driver's careers.

COMPLETE SET (12) 12.50 30.00
OB1 Jeff Gordon 3.00 8.00
OB2 Ricky Rudd 1.00 2.50
OB3 Dale Earnhardt's Car 2.00 5.00
OB4 Dale Earnhardt Jr. 4.00 10.00
OB5 Terry Labonte 1.00 2.50
OB6 Mark Martin 2.50 6.00
OB7 Bobby Labonte 2.00 5.00
OB8 Dale Jarrett 2.00 5.00
OB9 Jeff Burton 1.00 2.50
OB10 Rusty Wallace 2.50 6.00
OB11 Tony Stewart 3.00 8.00
OB12 Ward Burton .60 1.50

1999 VIP Rear View Mirror

Issued at a stated rate of one in six packs, these nine cards feature a drivers rear view mirror perspective.

COMPLETE SET (9) 10.00 25.00
RM1 Jeff Gordon 2.50 6.00
RM2 Dale Jarrett 1.50 4.00
RM3 Dale Earnhardt 4.00 10.00
RM4 Dale Earnhardt Jr. 3.00 8.00
RM5 Jeff Burton .75 2.00
RM6 Mark Martin 2.00 5.00
RM7 Terry Labonte .75 2.00
RM8 Rusty Wallace 2.00 5.00
RM9 Tony Stewart 2.50 6.00

1999 VIP Sheet Metal

Issued one every 384 packs, these nine cards features pieces of race used sheet metal from six different drivers.

*MULTI-COLOR METAL: .75X TO 1.25X
SM1 Rusty Wallace 12.00 30.00
SM2 Dale Earnhardt's Car 50.00 100.00
SM3 Jeff Gordon 20.00 50.00
SM4 Terry Labonte 12.00 30.00
SM5 Mark Martin 15.00 40.00
SM6 Tony Stewart 20.00 50.00
SM7 Dale Jarrett 12.00 30.00
SM8 Bobby Labonte 12.00 30.00

1999 VIP Vintage Performance

These cards were inserted in Retail boxes as a box topper at a rate of one per retail box. They were sealed in a cellophane rapper.

COMPLETE SET (9) 8.00 20.00
1 Dale Jarrett 1.25 3.00
2 Rusty Wallace 1.50 4.00
3 Mark Martin 1.50 4.00
4 Jeff Gordon 2.00 5.00
5 Jeff Burton .60 1.50
6 Bobby Labonte 1.25 3.00
7 Jeremy Mayfield .40 1.00
8 Dale Earnhardt's Car 1.25 3.00
9 Terry Labonte .60 1.50

2000 VIP

Released as a 50-card set, Press Pass VIP features 18 Driver cards, eight Winston Cup 2000 Victory cards, three Big Payoff cards, six A Decade of Firsts cards, nine 50 Win Club cards, four Back to Back Championship cards and one checklist. VIP was packaged in 28-pack boxes with packs containing six cards and carried a suggested retail price of $2.99.

COMPLETE SET (50) 12.50 30.00
1 Bobby Labonte .30 .75
2 Mark Martin .30 .75
3 Ward Burton .25 .60
4 Dale Earnhardt 2.00 5.00
5 Rusty Wallace .30 .75
6 Jeff Burton .25 .60
7 Ricky Rudd .25 .60
8 Dale Jarrett .30 .75
9 Terry Labonte .30 .75
10 Jeremy Mayfield .20 .50
11 Tony Stewart .50 1.25
12 Jeff Gordon .60 1.50
13 Chad Little .20 .50
14 Johnny Benson .30 .75
15 Mike Skinner .20 .50
16 Sterling Marlin .30 .75
17 Dale Earnhardt Jr. CRC .75 2.00
18 Matt Kenseth CRC 1.00 2.50
19 Dale Jarrett V .30 .75
20 Bobby Labonte V .30 .75
21 Jeff Burton V .25 .60
22 Ward Burton V .25 .60
23 Rusty Wallace V .30 .75
24 Dale Earnhardt Jr. V .75 2.00
25 Mark Martin V .30 .75
26 Jeff Gordon V .60 1.50
27 Tony Stewart V .50 1.25
28 Dale Jarrett NB .30 .75
29 Jeff Gordon NB .60 1.50
30 Jeff Burton NB .25 .60
31 Rusty Wallace DF .30 .75
32 Jeff Gordon DF .60 1.50
33 Jeff Burton DF .25 .60
34 Jeff Gordon DF .60 1.50
35 Mark Martin DF .30 .75
36 Tony Stewart DF .50 1.25
37 David Pearson 50 W .50 1.25
38 Darrell Waltrip 50 W .50 1.25
39 Bobby Allison 50 W .25 .60
40 Cale Yarborough 50 W .30 .75
41 Dale Earnhardt's Car 50 W 2.00 5.00
42 Junior Johnson 50 W .30 .75
43 Ned Jarrett 50 W .25 .60
44 Rusty Wallace 50 W .30 .75
45 Jeff Gordon 50 W .60 1.50
46 Cale Yarborough DT .30 .75
47 Darrell Waltrip DT .50 1.25
48 Dale Earnhardt's Car DT 2.00 5.00
49 Jeff Gordon DT .60 1.50
50 Winston Cup CL .12 .30
P1 Dale Earnhardt Jr. Promo 4.00 10.00

2000 VIP Explosives

COMPLETE SET (50) 40.00 80.00
*EXPLOSIVES 1X TO 2.5X BASE CARDS

2000 VIP Explosives Lasers

COMPLETE SET (50) 200.00 400.00
*EXP.LASERS 4X TO 10X BASE CARDS

2000 VIP Head Gear

Randomly inserted in packs at the rate of one in 10, this 6-card set showcases the custom markings of some of NASCAR's driver's helmets.

COMPLETE SET (6) 12.50 30.00
*EXPLOSIVES .8X TO 2X BASIC INSERTS
EXPLOSIVES STATED ODDS 1:30
*EXP.LAS.DIE CUT: 1.2X TO 3X BASIC INS.
EXP.LASER DIE CUT ODDS 1:60
HG1 Jeff Gordon 1.25 3.00
HG2 Rusty Wallace .60 1.50
HG3 Tony Stewart 1.00 2.50
HG4 Dale Earnhardt Jr. 1.50 4.00
HG5 Terry Labonte .60 1.50
HG6 Dale Jarrett .60 1.50

2000 VIP Lap Leaders

Randomly inserted in packs at the rate of one in five, this 12-card set features top NASCAR drivers for whom it is common to come around the last turn leading the pack.

COMPLETE SET (12) 10.00 25.00
*EXPLOSIVES .8X TO 2X BASIC INSERTS
EXPLOSIVES STATED ODDS 1:15
*EXP.LASERS 1X TO 2.5X BASIC INSERTS
EXP.LASERS STATED ODDS 1:20 HOB
LL1 Jeff Gordon 2.00 5.00
LL2 Tony Stewart 2.00 5.00
LL3 Bobby Labonte 1.25 3.00
LL4 Jeff Burton .60 1.50
LL5 Dale Jarrett 1.25 3.00
LL6 Rusty Wallace 1.50 4.00
LL7 Mark Martin 1.50 4.00
LL8 Mike Skinner .20 .50
LL9 Terry Labonte .60 1.50
LL10 Ward Burton .40 1.00
LL11 Ricky Rudd .60 1.50
LL12 Jeremy Mayfield .20 .50

2000 VIP Making the Show

Randomly inserted in packs at the rate of one in one, this 24-card set features drivers that qualify week after week on an all foil die cut card.

COMPLETE SET (24) 6.00 15.00
MS1 Bobby Labonte 1.00 2.50
MS2 Chad Little .30 .75
MS3 Elliott Sadler .15 .40
MS4 Dale Earnhardt Jr. 2.00 5.00
MS5 Dale Jarrett 1.00 2.50
MS6 Jeff Burton .50 1.25
MS7 Jeff Gordon 1.50 4.00
MS8 Jeremy Mayfield .15 .40
MS9 Joe Nemechek .15 .40
MS10 Johnny Benson .30 .75
MS11 Kenny Irwin .15 .40
MS12 Mark Martin 1.25 3.00
MS13 Matt Kenseth 1.25 3.00
MS14 Mike Skinner .15 .40
MS15 Ricky Rudd .50 1.25
MS16 Kenny Wallace .15 .40
MS17 Rusty Wallace 1.25 3.00
MS18 Sterling Marlin .50 1.25
MS19 Steve Park .15 .40
MS20 Terry Labonte .50 1.25
MS21 Tony Stewart 1.50 4.00
MS22 Michael Waltrip .30 .75
MS23 Ward Burton .30 .75
MS24 Wally Dallenbach CL .25 .60

2000 VIP Rear View Mirror

Randomly inserted in packs at the rate of one in 20, this 6-card set focuses on on top drivers. Each card is printed on all foil card stock with enhanced foil stamping.

COMPLETE SET (6) 30.00 80.00
*EXPLOSIVE: .8X TO 2X BASIC INSERTS
EXPLOSIVE STATED ODDS 1:60
*EXP.LASER DCs: 1X TO 2.5X BASIC INSERTS
EXP.LASER DIE CUT STATED ODDS 1:130
RM1 Bobby Labonte 4.00 10.00
RM2 Rusty Wallace 5.00 12.00
RM3 Dale Earnhardt 10.00 25.00
RM4 Dale Earnhardt Jr. 8.00 20.00
RM5 Mark Martin 5.00 12.00
RM6 Tony Stewart 6.00 15.00

2000 VIP Sheet Metal

Randomly inserted in packs at the rate of one in 384, this 9-card set contains a swatch of race used sheet metal from nine of NASCAR's top drivers.

*MULTI-COLOR METAL: 1X TO 1.5X
SM1 Ward Burton 10.00 25.00
SM2 Jeff Burton 12.00 30.00
SM3 Dale Earnhardt 100.00 200.00
SM4 Terry Labonte 12.00 30.00
SM5 Mark Martin 12.00 30.00
SM6 Tony Stewart 25.00 60.00
SM7 Dale Earnhardt Jr. 50.00 100.00
SM8 Bobby Labonte 12.00 30.00
SM9 Jeff Gordon 5.00 100.00
SM10 Dale Earnhardt Jr. 50.00 100.00

2000 VIP Under the Lights

Randomly inserted in packs at the rate of one in 15, this 8-card set features NASCAR night vision on this all foil insert card.

COMPLETE SET (8) 12.50 30.00
*EXPLOSIVES: .8X TO 2X BASIC INSERTS
EXPLOSIVES STATED ODDS 1:45
*EXP.LASERS: 1.5X TO 4X BASIC INSERTS
EXPLOSIVE LASER ODDS 1:90 HOBBY
EXP.LASER PRINT RUN 250 SER.#'d SETS
UL1 Jeff Gordon 3.00 8.00
UL2 Dale Jarrett 2.00 5.00
UL3 Bobby Labonte 2.00 5.00
UL4 Dale Earnhardt Jr. 4.00 10.00
UL5 Tony Stewart 3.00 8.00
UL6 Rusty Wallace 2.50 6.00
UL7 Mark Martin 2.50 6.00
UL8 Mike Skinner .30 .75

2001 VIP

This 50 card set features four sub sets, 18 NASCAR Winston Cup Drivers 1-18, nine Sunday Money 2001 cards 19-27, 11 Rookie Thunder cards 28-38, and 11 All Stars cards 39-49, with one checklist card 50. VIP was available in hobby and retail stores in 24 pack boxes or retail only in a specially packed box containing one Hot Treads card.

COMPLETE SET (50) 12.50 30.00
WAX BOX HOBBY 50.00 90.00
WAX BOX RETAIL 35.00 75.00
1 Bobby Labonte 1.00 2.50
2 Mark Martin 1.25 3.00
3 Ward Burton .40 1.00
4 Steve Park .40 1.00
5 Rusty Wallace 1.25 3.00
6 Jeff Burton .40 1.00
7 Ricky Rudd .75 2.00
8 Dale Jarrett 1.00 2.50
9 Terry Labonte .75 2.00
10 Kevin Harvick CRC 1.25 3.00
11 Tony Stewart 1.50 4.00
12 Jeff Gordon 1.50 4.00
13 Michael Waltrip .40 1.00
14 Ken Schrader .20 .50
15 Mike Skinner .20 .50
16 Sterling Marlin .75 2.00
17 Dale Earnhardt Jr. 2.00 5.00
18 Jeremy Mayfield .20 .50
19 Michael Waltrip SM .40 1.00
20 Steve Park SM .40 1.00
21 Jeff Gordon SM 1.50 4.00
22 Kevin Harvick SM 1.25 3.00
23 Dale Jarrett SM 1.00 2.50
24 Elliott Sadler SM .40 1.00
25 Bobby Hamilton SM .20 .50
26 Rusty Wallace SM 1.25 3.00
27 Tony Stewart SM 1.50 4.00
28 Ricky Rudd RT .75 2.00
29 Sterling Marlin RT .75 2.00
30 Rusty Wallace RT 1.25 3.00
31 Ken Schrader RT .20 .50
32 Bobby Hamilton RT .20 .50
33 Jeff Gordon RT 1.50 4.00
34 Jeff Burton RT .40 1.00
35 Ricky Craven RT .20 .50
36 Mike Skinner RT .20 .50
37 Tony Stewart RT 1.50 4.00
38 Matt Kenseth RT 1.50 4.00
39 Terry Labonte AS .75 2.00
40 Sterling Marlin AS .75 2.00
41 Rusty Wallace AS 1.25 3.00
42 Michael Waltrip AS .40 1.00
43 Jeff Gordon AS 1.50 4.00
44 Jimmy Spencer AS .20 .50
45 Dale Earnhardt Jr. AS 2.00 5.00
46 Mark Martin AS 1.25 3.00
47 Jeremy Mayfield AS .20 .50
48 Tony Stewart AS 1.50 4.00
49 Ricky Craven AS .20 .50
50 Jeff Gordon CL .75 2.00

2001 VIP Explosives

COMPLETE SET (50) 25.00 60.00
*EXPLOSIVES: 1X TO 2.5X BASE CARDS

2001 VIP Explosives Lasers

COMPLETE SET (50) 150.00 400.00
*EXP.LASERS/420: 3X TO 8X HI COL.

2001 VIP Driver's Choice

Randomly inserted into packs at one in 18, this 8-card insert highlights each driver's car of choice. Card backs carry a "DC" prefix.

COMPLETE SET (8) 15.00 40.00
COMP.TRANS SET (8) 75.00 150.00
*TRANS: .6X TO 1.5X BASIC INSERTS
TRANS STATED ODDS 1:48
COMP.PREC.METAL (8) 150.00 300.00
*PREC.METAL/100: 1.5X TO 4X BASIC INSERTS
PREC.METAL STATED ODDS 1:480 HOBBY
PREC.METAL PRINT RUN 100 SER.#'D SETS
DC1 Jeff Gordon 2.50 6.00
DC2 Dale Jarrett 1.25 3.00
DC3 Bobby Labonte 1.25 3.00
DC4 Dale Earnhardt Jr. 3.00 8.00
DC5 Tony Stewart 2.00 5.00
DC6 Rusty Wallace 1.25 3.00
DC7 Kevin Harvick 4.00 10.00
DC8 Michael Waltrip 1.25 3.00

2001 VIP Head Gear

Randomly inserted into packs at one in 16, this 6-card insert features driver profile images as well as head shots. Card backs carry a "HG" prefix.

COMPLETE SET (6) 12.50 30.00
COMP.DIE CUT SET (6) 50.00 120.00
*DIE CUTS: 1.5X TO 4X BASIC INSERTS
DIE CUT STATED ODDS 1:60
HG1 Jeff Gordon 5.00 12.00
HG2 Rusty Wallace 4.00 10.00
HG3 Kevin Harvick 4.00 10.00
HG4 Dale Earnhardt Jr. 6.00 15.00
HG5 Sterling Marlin 1.50 4.00
HG6 Dale Jarrett 3.00 8.00

2001 VIP Making the Show

This 24-card "set within a set" features some of the best drivers in NASCAR. These cards were issued at one per pack.

COMPLETE SET (24) 8.00 20.00
1 Steve Park .40 1.00
2 Rusty Wallace 1.25 3.00
3 Terry Labonte .75 2.00
4 Mark Martin 1.25 3.00
5 Dale Earnhardt Jr. 2.00 5.00
6 Jeremy Mayfield .20 .50
7 Michael Waltrip .40 1.00
8 Matt Kenseth 1.50 4.00
9 Bobby Labonte 1.00 2.50
10 Tony Stewart 1.50 4.00
11 Ward Burton .40 1.00
12 Jeff Gordon 1.50 4.00
13 Jimmy Spencer .20 .50
14 Ricky Rudd .75 2.00
15 Kevin Harvick 1.25 3.00
16 Mike Skinner .20 .50
17 Joe Nemechek .20 .50
18 Ken Schrader .20 .50
19 Sterling Marlin .75 2.00
20 Kyle Petty .40 1.00
21 Bobby Hamilton .20 .50
22 Todd Bodine .20 .50
23 Dale Jarrett 1.00 2.50
24 Jeff Burton CL .40 1.00

2001 VIP Mile Masters

Randomly inserted into packs at one in 6, this 12-card insert highlights drivers that have logged thousands of miles throughout their career. Card backs carry a "MM" prefix.

COMPLETE SET (12) 15.00 40.00
*PREC.METAL/325: 1.2X TO 3X BASIC INSERTS
PREC.METAL STATED ODDS 1:100 HOBBY
PREC.METAL PRINT RUN 325 SER.#'d SETS
COMP.TRANS SET (12) 25.00 60.00
*TRANS: .8X TO 2X BASIC INSERTS
TRANS STATED ODDS 1:18
MM1 Jeff Gordon 1.50 4.00
MM2 Tony Stewart 1.25 3.00
MM3 Michael Waltrip .75 2.00
MM4 Dale Earnhardt Jr. 2.00 5.00
MM5 Dale Jarrett .75 2.00
MM6 Rusty Wallace .75 2.00
MM7 Ward Burton .75 2.00
MM8 Mike Skinner .50 1.25
MM9 Terry Labonte .75 2.00
MM10 Jeff Burton .60 1.50
MM11 Ricky Rudd .60 1.50
MM12 Kevin Harvick 2.50 6.00

2001 VIP Rear View Mirror

Randomly inserted into packs at one in 24, this 6-card insert features a special in-car driver shot on an embossed foil-based card. Card backs carry a "RV" prefix.

COMPLETE SET (6) 15.00 40.00
COMP.DIE CUT SET (6) 80.00 200.00
*DIE CUTS: 2X TO 5X BASIC INSERTS
DIE CUT STATED ODDS 1:120
RV1 Bobby Labonte 3.00 8.00
RV2 Rusty Wallace 4.00 10.00
RV3 Kevin Harvick 4.00 10.00
RV4 Dale Earnhardt Jr. 6.00 15.00
RV5 Ricky Rudd 2.00 5.00
RV6 Tony Stewart 5.00 12.00

2001 VIP Sheet Metal Drivers

Randomly inserted into hobby packs at one in 420, this 12-card insert features an actual swatch of race-used sheet metal. Card backs carry a "SD" prefix. Please note that each card was individually serial numbered to 75.

*CARS: .3X TO .8X DRIVERS
CARS STATED ODDS 1:544 RETAIL
CARS PRINT RUN 120 SER.#'d SETS
SD1 Steve Park 12.00 30.00
SD2 Ward Burton 12.00 30.00
SD3 Dale Earnhardt 60.00 120.00
SD4 Tony Stewart 30.00 80.00
SD5 Terry Labonte 20.00 50.00
SD6 Dale Jarrett 20.00 50.00
SD7 Bobby Labonte 20.00 50.00
SD8 Dale Earnhardt Jr. 50.00 120.00
SD9 Jeff Gordon 30.00 80.00
SD10 Michael Waltrip 15.00 40.00
SD11 Kevin Harvick 15.00 40.00
SD12 Matt Kenseth 15.00 40.00

2002 VIP

This 50-card set was issued in either four-card hobby or retail packs. Each card was printed with gold foil layering.

COMPLETE SET (50)	8.00	20.00
WAX BOX HOBBY	40.00	80.00
WAX BOX RETAIL	30.00	60.00
1 Steve Park	.25	.60
2 Rusty Wallace	.60	1.50
3 Terry Labonte	.40	1.00
4 Mark Martin	.75	2.00
5 Dale Earnhardt Jr.	1.50	3.00
6 Ryan Newman CRC	.75	2.00
7 Matt Kenseth	.75	2.00
8 Bobby Labonte	.60	1.50
9 Tony Stewart	.75	2.00
10 Ward Burton	.25	.60
11 Jeff Gordon	1.25	2.50
12 Ricky Rudd	.40	1.00
13 Kevin Harvick	.75	2.00
14 Sterling Marlin	.40	1.00
15 John Andretti	.10	.30
16 Jimmie Johnson CRC	.75	2.00
17 Dale Jarrett	.60	1.50
18 Jeff Burton	.25	.60
19 Ward Burton SG	.25	.60
20 Matt Kenseth SG	.75	2.00
21 Tony Stewart SG	.75	2.00
22 Sterling Marlin SG	.40	1.00
23 Jimmie Johnson SG	.75	2.00
24 Matt Kenseth SG	.75	2.00
25 Bobby Labonte SG	.60	1.50
26 Dale Earnhardt Jr. SG	1.50	3.00
27 Tony Stewart SG	.75	2.00
28 Jeff Gordon AS	1.25	2.50
29 Kevin Harvick AS	.75	2.00
30 Ryan Newman AS	.75	2.00
31 Rusty Wallace AS	.60	1.50
32 Tony Stewart AS	.75	2.00
33 Dale Earnhardt Jr. AS	1.50	3.00
34 Jimmie Johnson AS	.75	2.00
35 Jeff Burton AS	.25	.60
36 Mark Martin AS	.75	2.00
37 Terry Labonte SA	.40	1.00
38 Sterling Marlin SA	.40	1.00
39 Ricky Rudd SA	.40	1.00
40 Mark Martin PP	.75	2.00
41 Cale Yarborough PP	.10	.30
42 Ward Burton PP	.25	.60
43 Bobby Allison PP	.10	.30
44 Rusty Wallace PP	.60	1.50
45 Junior Johnson PP	.10	.30
46 D.Jarrett/D.Pearson PP	.60	1.50
47 D.Pearson/D.Jarrett PP	.25	.60
48 Jeff Gordon PP	1.25	2.50
49 Richard Petty PP	.40	1.00
50 J.Gordon/J.Johnson CL	.60	1.50

2002 VIP Explosives

COMPLETE SET (50) 20.00 50.00
*EXPLOSIVES: 1X TO 2.5X BASE CARD HI

2002 VIP Explosives Lasers

*EXPLOS.LASERS: 4X TO 10X BASE CARD HI

2002 VIP Samples

*SAMPLES: 2.5X TO 6X BASIC CARDS

2002 VIP Driver's Choice

Issued at a stated rate of one in 18, these nine cards feature information on where the leading drivers prefer to race.

COMPLETE SET (9)	15.00	40.00
*TRANSPARENT: .8X TO 2X BASIC INSERTS		
TRANSPARENT STATED ODDS 1:48		
*TRANS.LTD: 1.2X TO 3X BASIC INSERTS		
TRANS.LTD PRINT RUN 100 SER.#'d SETS		
DC1 Jeff Gordon	5.00	12.00
DC2 Dale Jarrett	3.00	8.00
DC3 Bobby Labonte	3.00	8.00
DC4 Dale Earnhardt Jr.	6.00	15.00
DC5 Tony Stewart	4.00	10.00
DC6 Rusty Wallace	3.00	8.00
DC7 Kevin Harvick	4.00	10.00
DC8 Mark Martin	4.00	10.00
DC9 Jimmie Johnson	4.00	10.00

2002 VIP Head Gear

Inserted at stated odds of one in 12, these nine cards feature information on how drivers gear up for race day. Each card features a driver photo set against a background of his race day helmet.

COMPLETE SET (9)	12.50	30.00
*DIE CUTS: 1X TO 2.5X BASIC INSERTS		
HG1 Jeff Gordon	4.00	10.00
HG2 Rusty Wallace	2.50	6.00
HG3 Kevin Harvick	3.00	8.00
HG4 Dale Earnhardt Jr.	5.00	12.00
HG5 Ward Burton	1.00	2.50
HG6 Dale Jarrett	2.50	6.00
HG7 Tony Stewart	3.00	8.00
HG8 Terry Labonte	1.50	4.00
HG9 Mark Martin	3.00	8.00

2002 VIP Making the Show

Inserted at a stated rate of one per pack, this 24 card set features information on how these drivers made it onto the NASCAR circuit. Each card was produced in a die-cut design.

COMPLETE SET (24)	8.00	20.00
MS1 Steve Park	.40	1.00
MS2 Rusty Wallace	1.00	2.50
MS3 Mike Skinner	.20	.50
MS4 Terry Labonte	.60	1.50
MS5 Mark Martin	1.25	3.00
MS6 Dale Earnhardt Jr.	2.00	5.00
MS7 Ryan Newman	1.25	3.00
MS8 Matt Kenseth	1.25	3.00
MS9 Bobby Labonte	1.00	2.50
MS10 Jeremy Mayfield	.20	.50
MS11 Tony Stewart	1.25	3.00
MS12 Ward Burton	.40	1.00
MS13 Jeff Gordon	1.50	4.00
MS14 Ricky Rudd	.60	1.50
MS15 Kevin Harvick	1.25	3.00
MS16 Robby Gordon	.20	.50
MS17 Ken Schrader	.20	.50
MS18 Sterling Marlin	.60	1.50
MS19 John Andretti	.20	.50
MS20 Kyle Petty	.40	1.00
MS21 Jimmie Johnson	1.25	3.00
MS22 Dale Jarrett	1.00	2.50
MS23 Jeff Burton	.40	1.00
MS24 Ricky Rudd CL	.60	1.50

2002 VIP Mile Masters

Inserted at a stated rate of one in six, these 12 cards feature drivers who are masters on the race track. Each card was produced on holofoil card stock.

COMPLETE SET (12)	12.50	30.00
*TRANSPARENT: .8X TO 2X BASIC INSERTS		
*TRANS.LTD: 1.2X TO 3X BASIC INSERTS		
MM1 Jeff Gordon	3.00	8.00
MM2 Tony Stewart	2.50	6.00
MM3 Jimmie Johnson	2.50	6.00
MM4 Dale Earnhardt Jr.	4.00	10.00
MM5 Dale Jarrett	2.00	5.00
MM6 Rusty Wallace	2.00	5.00
MM7 Ryan Newman	2.50	6.00
MM8 Mark Martin	2.50	6.00
MM9 Terry Labonte	1.25	3.00
MM10 Jeff Burton	.75	2.00
MM11 Ricky Rudd	1.00	2.50
MM12 Kevin Harvick	2.50	6.00

2002 VIP Race Used Sheet Metal Cars

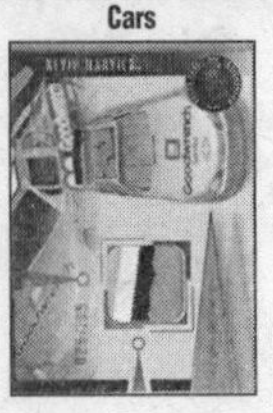

SC12 Jimmie Johnson's Car	25.00	60.00
SC14 Dale Jarrett's Car	15.00	40.00
SC15 Dale Earnhardt Jr.'s Car	60.00	120.00
SC16 Dale Earnhardt's Car		

2002 VIP Race Used Sheet Metal Drivers

Issued at a stated rate of one in 220 packs, these 16 cards feature a genuine piece of race-used sheet metal set upon a card with the picture of the featured driver. These cards were issued to a stated print run of 130 sets. The Dale Earnhardt Sr. card was issued to a stated print run of 50 sets.

SD1 Jeff Gordon	40.00	100.00
SD2 Kevin Harvick	15.00	40.00
SD3 Bobby Labonte	15.00	40.00
SD4 Terry Labonte	15.00	40.00
SD5 Ryan Newman	20.00	50.00
SD6 Steve Park	12.50	30.00
SD7 Ken Schrader	12.50	30.00
SD8 Tony Stewart	20.00	50.00
SD9 Mark Martin	20.00	50.00
SD10 Matt Kenseth	15.00	40.00
SD11 Rusty Wallace	15.00	40.00
SD12 Jimmie Johnson	25.00	60.00
SD13 Ward Burton	12.50	30.00
SD14 Dale Jarrett	15.00	40.00
SD15 Dale Earnhardt Jr.	60.00	120.00
SD16 Dale Earnhardt/50	200.00	400.00

2002 VIP Rear View Mirror

Inserted at a stated rate of one in 24, these six cards feature gold foil embossing and honor the very best drivers on the NASCAR circuit.

COMPLETE SET (6)	15.00	40.00
*DIE CUTS: .8X TO 2X BASIC INSERTS		
RM1 Bobby Labonte	3.00	8.00
RM2 Rusty Wallace	3.00	8.00
RM3 Kevin Harvick	4.00	10.00
RM4 Mark Martin	4.00	10.00
RM5 Jeff Gordon	5.00	12.00
RM6 Tony Stewart	4.00	10.00

2003 VIP

This 50-card set was issued in either five-card hobby or retail packs and packed in 28 pack boxes. This set was released in July of 2003. The SRP for packs was $2.99. Each card was printed with gold foil layering.

COMPLETE SET (50)	10.00	25.00
WAX BOX HOBBY (28)	40.00	80.00
WAX BOX RETAIL (24)	40.00	70.00
1 Jeff Burton	.25	.60
2 Ward Burton	.25	.60
3 Kurt Busch	.40	1.00
4 Dale Earnhardt Jr.	1.25	3.00
5 Jeff Gordon	1.00	2.50
6 Kevin Harvick	.60	1.50
7 Dale Jarrett	.60	1.50
8 Jimmie Johnson	.75	2.00
9 Matt Kenseth	.75	2.00
10 Bobby Labonte	.60	1.50
11 Terry Labonte	.40	1.00
12 Mark Martin	.75	2.00
13 Joe Nemechek	.10	.30
14 Ryan Newman	.75	2.00
15 Ricky Rudd	.40	1.00
16 Tony Stewart	.75	2.00
17 Rusty Wallace	.60	1.50
18 Michael Waltrip	.25	.60
19 Michael Waltrip SG	.25	.60
20 Dale Jarrett SG	.60	1.50
21 Matt Kenseth SG	.75	2.00
22 Bobby Labonte SG	.60	1.50
23 Ricky Craven SG	.10	.30
24 Kurt Busch SG	.40	1.00
25 Ryan Newman SG	.75	2.00
26 Dale Earnhardt Jr. SG	1.25	3.00
27 Jeff Gordon SG	1.00	2.50
28 Jimmie Johnson AS	.75	2.00
29 Ryan Newman AS	.75	2.00
30 Jeff Gordon AS '01	1.00	2.50
31 Dale Earnhardt Jr. AS	1.25	3.00
32 Terry Labonte AS	.40	1.00
33 Mark Martin AS	.75	2.00
34 Jeff Gordon AS '97	1.00	2.50
35 Michael Waltrip AS	.25	.60
36 Jeff Gordon AS '95	1.00	2.50
37 Cale Yarborough LEG	.25	.60
38 David Pearson LEG	.25	.60
39 Benny Parsons LEG	.25	.60
40 Bobby Allison LEG	.25	.60
41 Ned Jarrett LEG	.25	.60
42 Richard Petty LEG	.40	1.00
43 Buddy Baker LEG	.25	.60
44 Harry Gant LEG	.25	.60
45 Glen Wood LEG	.10	.30
46 Ryan Newman HR	.75	2.00
47 Bobby Labonte HR	.60	1.50
48 Jimmie Johnson HR	.75	2.00
49 Rusty Wallace HR	.60	1.50
50 Dale Jarrett HR	.60	1.50

2003 VIP Explosives

COMPLETE SET (50) 15.00 40.00
*EXPLOSIVES: 1X TO 2.5X BASE CARDS

2003 VIP Laser Explosive

LASERS: 4X TO 10X BASE CARDS
STATED ODDS 1:20

2003 VIP Samples

*SAMPLES: 2.5X TO 6X BASE

2003 VIP Tin

COMP.FACT.TIN SET (51)	25.00	40.00
COMPLETE SET (50)	10.00	25.00
*SINGLES: .4X TO 1X BASIC CARDS		

2003 VIP Driver's Choice

Issued at a stated rate of one in 12, these nine cards feature information on where the leading drivers prefer to race.

COMPLETE SET (9)	12.50	30.00
*DIE CUTS: 1.2X TO 3X BASIC INSERTS		
DIE CUTS STATED ODDS 1:60		
*NATIONAL: 1X TO 2.5X BASE		
DC1 Jimmie Johnson	2.00	5.00
DC2 Dale Earnhardt Jr.	3.00	8.00
DC3 Jeff Gordon	2.50	6.00
DC4 Dale Jarrett	1.50	4.00
DC5 Ward Burton	.60	1.25
DC6 Terry Labonte	1.00	2.50
DC7 Mark Martin	2.00	5.00
DC8 Rusty Wallace	1.50	4.00
DC9 Michael Waltrip	.60	1.25

2003 VIP Head Gear

Inserted at stated odds of one in 24, these six cards feature information on how drivers gear up for race day. Each card features a driver photo set against a background of his race day helmet.

*DIE CUTS: .8X TO 2X BASIC INSERTS		
DIE CUTS STATED ODDS 1:72		
*NATIONAL: 1X TO 2.5X BASE		
HG1 Jimmie Johnson	3.00	8.00
HG2 Dale Earnhardt Jr.	5.00	12.00
HG3 Jeff Gordon	4.00	10.00
HG4 Dale Jarrett	2.50	6.00
HG5 Rusty Wallace	2.50	6.00
HG6 Mark Martin	3.00	8.00

2003 VIP Lap Leaders

This 9-card set was randomly inserted in packs at a rate of one in 18 packs. These cards featured holofoil etched technology.

COMPLETE SET (9)	20.00	40.00
*TRANS: .8X TO 2X BASIC INSERTS		
TRANS STATED ODDS 1:48		
*TRANS LTD: 2X TO 5X BASIC INSERTS		
TRANS LTD STATED ODDS 1:120		
TRANS LTD PRINT RUN 250 SERIAL #'d SETS		
*NATIONAL: 1X TO 2.5X BASE		
LL1 Jeff Gordon	3.00	8.00
LL2 Dale Earnhardt Jr.	5.00	12.00
LL3 Bobby Labonte	2.50	6.00
LL4 Rusty Wallace	2.50	6.00
LL5 Jimmie Johnson	3.00	8.00
LL6 Mark Martin	3.00	8.00
LL7 Michael Waltrip	1.00	2.50
LL8 Dale Jarrett	2.50	6.00
LL9 Kerry Earnhardt	1.00	2.50

2003 VIP Making the Show

Inserted at a stated rate of one per pack, this 24 card set features information on how these drivers made it onto the NASCAR circuit. Each card was produced in a die-cut design.

MS1 Rusty Wallace	1.00	2.50
MS2 Terry Labonte	.60	1.50
MS3 Mark Martin	1.25	3.00
MS4 Dale Earnhardt Jr.	2.00	5.00
MS5 Kerry Earnhardt	.40	1.00
MS6 Michael Waltrip	.40	1.00
MS7 Greg Biffle	.40	1.00
MS8 Bobby Labonte	1.00	2.50
MS9 Jeremy Mayfield	.20	.50
MS10 Tony Stewart	1.25	3.00
MS11 Ricky Rudd	.60	1.50
MS12 Ward Burton	.40	1.00
MS13 Kenny Wallace	.20	.50
MS14 Jeff Gordon	1.50	4.00
MS15 Kevin Harvick	1.00	2.50
MS16 Elliott Sadler	.40	1.00
MS17 Casey Mears	.40	1.00
MS18 Jamie McMurray	.60	1.50
MS19 Kyle Petty	.40	1.00
MS20 Jimmie Johnson	1.25	3.00
MS21 Ken Schrader	.20	.50
MS22 Todd Bodine	.20	.50
MS23 Dale Jarrett	1.00	2.50
MS24 Jeff Burton CL	.40	1.00

2003 VIP Mile Masters

Inserted at a stated rate of one in six, these 12 cards feature drivers who are masters on the race track. Each card was produced on holofoil card stock.

COMPLETE SET (12)	10.00	25.00
*TRANS: .8X TO 2X BASIC INSERTS		
TRANS STATED ODDS 1:18		
*TRANS LTD: 3X TO 8X BASIC INSERTS		
TRANS LTD STATED ODDS 1:72		
TRANS LTD PRINT RUN 325 SERIAL #'d SETS		
*NATIONAL: 1X TO 2.5X BASE		
MM1 Kerry Earnhardt	.60	1.50
MM2 Dale Earnhardt Jr.	2.50	6.00
MM3 Jeff Gordon	2.00	5.00
MM4 Dale Jarrett	1.25	3.00
MM5 Jimmie Johnson	1.50	4.00
MM6 Bobby Labonte	1.25	3.00
MM7 Terry Labonte	.75	2.00
MM8 Mark Martin	1.50	4.00
MM9 Ricky Rudd	.75	2.00
MM10 Tony Stewart	1.50	4.00
MM11 Rusty Wallace	1.25	3.00
MM12 Michael Waltrip	.60	1.50

2003 VIP Tradin' Paint Cars

TPT4 Jimmie Johnson's Car	15.00	40.00
TPT10 Dale Earnhardt Jr.'s Car	25.00	60.00

2003 VIP Tradin' Paint Drivers

Randomly inserted in retail packs at a rate of one in 144, these 18 cards feature a genuine piece of race-used sheet metal set upon a card showing the driver. These cards were issued to a stated print run of 110 sets with the exception of Mark Martin who was limited to just 65 copies.

TPD1 Jeff Gordon	20.00	50.00
TPD2 Ryan Newman	15.00	40.00
TPD3 Kevin Harvick	25.00	50.00
TPD4 Jimmie Johnson	20.00	50.00
TPD5 Dale Jarrett	8.00	20.00
TPD6 Mark Martin/65	40.00	80.00
TPD7 Matt Kenseth	30.00	60.00
TPD8 Bobby Labonte	20.00	40.00
TPD9 Tony Stewart	30.00	60.00
TPD10 Dale Earnhardt Jr.	40.00	80.00
TPD11 Jeff Burton	15.00	30.00
TPD12 Kurt Busch	20.00	40.00
TPD13 Dale Earnhardt		
TPD14 Robby Gordon	15.00	30.00
TPD15 Michael Waltrip	20.00	40.00
TPD16 Ward Burton	15.00	30.00
TPD17 Rusty Wallace	25.00	50.00
TPD18 Terry Labonte	25.00	50.00

2003 VIP Tradin' Paint Driver Autographs

Randomly inserted in retail packs, these 8 cards feature a genuine piece of race-used sheet metal set upon a card showing the featured driver along with his signature. These cards were limited and hand numbered to the corresponding driver's door number. Some of these cards are not priced due to scarcity.

STATED PRINT RUN 2-48		
*CARS: .4X TO 1X DRIVERS		
BL Bobby Labonte/18	60.00	120.00
JJ Jimmie Johnson/48	60.00	120.00
KH Kevin Harvick/29	60.00	120.00
MK Matt Kenseth/17		
MM Mark Martin/6		
RN Ryan Newman/12		
RW Rusty Wallace/2		
TL Terry Labonte/5		

2004 VIP

This 90-card set was issued in either five-card hobby or retail packs in 28 pack boxes. This set was released in August of 2004. The SRP for packs was $2.99. Each card was printed with gold foil layering.

COMPLETE SET (90)	10.00	25.00
WAX BOX HOBBY (20)	40.00	80.00
WAX BOX RETAIL (24)	35.00	70.00
1 Jeff Burton	.30	.75
2 Ward Burton	.30	.75
3 Kurt Busch	.60	1.25
4 Dale Earnhardt Jr.	1.25	3.00
5 Jeff Gordon	1.25	3.00
6 Kevin Harvick	.75	2.00
7 Dale Jarrett	.60	1.50
8 Jimmie Johnson	1.00	2.50
9 Matt Kenseth	1.00	2.50
10 Bobby Labonte	.60	1.50
11 Terry Labonte	.60	1.25
12 Mark Martin	.75	2.00
13 Joe Nemechek	.20	.50
14 Ryan Newman	1.00	2.50
15 Ricky Rudd	.60	1.25
16 Tony Stewart	.75	2.00
17 Rusty Wallace	.60	1.50
18 Michael Waltrip	.30	.75
19 Greg Biffle	.30	.75
20 Kasey Kahne CRC	1.50	4.00
21 Robby Gordon	.20	.50
22 Kyle Petty	.30	.75
23 Scott Wimmer CRC	.30	.75
24 Jeremy Mayfield	.20	.50
25 Casey Mears	.20	.50
26 Jamie McMurray	.60	1.25
27 Brian Vickers CRC	.60	1.50
28 Dale Earnhardt Jr.'s Car R	.50	1.25
29 Michael Waltrip's Car R	.20	.50
30 Kevin Harvick's Car R	.30	.75
31 Rusty Wallace's Car R	.30	.75
32 Casey Mears' Car R	.20	.50
33 Jamie McMurray's Car R	.20	.50
34 Ryan Newman's Car R	.60	1.25
35 Scott Wimmer's Car R	.20	.50
36 Tony Stewart's Car R	.30	.75
37 Bobby Labonte's Car R	.30	.75
38 Jeff Gordon's Car R	.60	1.25
39 Jimmie Johnson's Car R	.60	1.25
40 Ricky Rudd's Car R	.20	.50
41 Kasey Kahne's Car R	.60	1.25
42 Jeff Burton's Car R	.20	.50
43 Dale Earnhardt Jr. SG	1.25	3.00
44 Matt Kenseth SG	1.00	2.50
45 Matt Kenseth SG	1.00	2.50
46 Dale Earnhardt Jr. SG	1.25	3.00
47 Jimmie Johnson SG	1.00	2.50
48 Kurt Busch SG	.60	1.25
49 Elliott Sadler SG	.30	.75
50 Rusty Wallace SG	.60	1.50
51 Jeff Gordon SG	1.25	3.00
52 Jeff Gordon SG	1.25	3.00
53 Dale Earnhardt Jr. SG	1.25	3.00
54 Mark Martin SG	.75	2.00
55 Dale Earnhardt Jr. HR	1.25	3.00
56 Jeff Gordon HR	1.25	3.00
57 Jimmie Johnson HR	1.00	2.50
58 Terry Labonte HR	.60	1.25
59 Sterling Marlin HR	.60	1.25
60 Tony Stewart HR	.75	2.00
61 Rusty Wallace HR	.60	1.50
62 Dale Jarrett HR	.60	1.50
63 Ryan Newman HR	1.00	2.50
64 Bobby Allison L	.30	.75
65 Davey Allison L	.60	1.25
66 Benny Parsons L	.30	.75
67 Buddy Baker L	.30	.75
68 Alan Kulwicki L	.60	1.25
69 Neil Bonnett L	.20	.50
70 Glen Wood L	.30	.75
71 Harry Gant L	.30	.75
72 Richard Petty L	.60	1.25
73 Elliott Sadler BTN	.30	.75
74 Jeff Gordon BTN	1.25	3.00
75 Tony Stewart BTN	.75	2.00
76 Scott Wimmer BTN	.30	.75
77 Dale Earnhardt Jr. BTN	1.25	3.00
78 Johnny Sauter BTN	.30	.75
79 Ryan Newman BTN	1.00	2.50
80 Jimmie Johnson BTN	1.00	2.50
81 Bobby Labonte BTN	.60	1.50
82 Richard Petty ATW	.60	1.25
83 David Pearson ATW	.30	.75
84 Bobby Allison ATW	.30	.75
85 Darrell Waltrip ATW	.60	1.25
86 Cale Yarborough ATW	.30	.75
87 Dale Earnhardt ATW	2.00	5.00
88 Jeff Gordon ATW	1.25	3.00
89 Rusty Wallace ATW	.60	1.50
90 Dale Earnhardt Jr. CL	1.25	3.00
0 Dale Earnhardt SM	10.00	25.00

2004 VIP Driver's Choice

Issued at a stated rate of one in 10, these six cards feature information on where the leading drivers prefer to race.

COMPLETE SET (6)	6.00	15.00
*DIE CUTS: .8X TO 2X BASIC		
DC1 Jimmie Johnson	2.00	5.00
DC2 Dale Earnhardt Jr.	2.50	6.00
DC3 Jeff Gordon	2.50	6.00
DC4 Rusty Wallace	1.25	3.00
DC5 Sterling Marlin	1.00	2.50
DC6 Michael Waltrip	.60	1.50

2004 VIP Head Gear

Inserted at stated odds of 1 in 5, these 12 cards feature information on how drivers gear up for race day. Each card features a driver photo set against a background of his race day helmet.

COMPLETE SET (12)	10.00	25.00
STATED ODDS 1:5		
*TRANSPARENT: .8X TO 2X BASIC		
HG1 Dale Earnhardt Jr.	2.50	6.00
HG2 Jeff Gordon	2.50	6.00
HG3 Kevin Harvick	1.50	4.00
HG4 Jimmie Johnson	2.00	5.00
HG5 Kasey Kahne	2.50	6.00
HG6 Matt Kenseth	2.00	5.00
HG7 Joe Nemechek	.40	1.00
HG8 Ricky Rudd	1.00	2.50
HG9 Elliott Sadler	.60	1.50
HG10 Tony Stewart	1.50	4.00
HG11 Rusty Wallace	1.25	3.00
HG12 Michael Waltrip	.60	1.50

2004 VIP Lap Leaders

This 9-card set was randomly inserted in packs at a rate of 1 in 8 packs. These cards featured holofoil etched technology.

COMPLETE SET (9)	12.50	30.00
STATED ODDS 1:8		
*TRANSPARENT: .8X TO 2X BASIC		
LL1 Mark Martin	2.00	5.00
LL2 Dale Earnhardt Jr.	3.00	8.00
LL3 Kasey Kahne	3.00	8.00
LL4 Ryan Newman	2.50	6.00

LL5 Michael Waltrip .75 2.00
LL6 Tony Stewart 2.00 5.00
LL7 Jeff Gordon 3.00 8.00
LL8 Bobby Labonte 1.50 4.00
LL9 Rusty Wallace 1.50 4.00

2004 VIP Making the Show

Inserted at a stated rate of 1 in 2 packs, this 27-card set features information on how these drivers made it onto the NASCAR circuit. Each card was produced in a die-cut design.

COMPLETE SET (27) 10.00 25.00
MS1 Joe Nemechek .25 .60
MS2 Rusty Wallace .75 2.00
MS3 Scott Wimmer .40 1.00
MS4 Ward Burton .40 1.00
MS5 Dale Earnhardt Jr. 1.50 4.00
MS6 Kasey Kahne 1.50 4.00
MS7 Scott Riggs .40 1.00
MS8 Ryan Newman 1.25 3.00
MS9 Michael Waltrip .40 1.00
MS10 Greg Biffle .40 1.00
MS11 Matt Kenseth 1.25 3.00
MS12 Bobby Labonte .75 2.00
MS13 Jeremy Mayfield .25 .60
MS14 Tony Stewart 1.00 2.50
MS15 Ricky Rudd .60 1.50
MS16 Jeff Gordon 1.50 4.00
MS17 Brian Vickers .75 2.00
MS18 Kevin Harvick 1.00 2.50
MS19 Sterling Marlin .60 1.50
MS20 Casey Mears .40 1.00
MS21 Jamie McMurray .60 1.50
MS22 Jeff Green .25 .60
MS23 Jimmie Johnson 1.25 3.00
MS24 Brendan Gaughan .40 1.00
MS25 Robby Gordon .25 .60
MS26 Mark Martin 1.00 2.50
MS27 Jeff Burton CL .40 1.00

2004 VIP Samples

*SAMPLES: 2X TO 5X BASE

2004 VIP Tradin' Paint Autographs

Randomly inserted in retail packs, these 4 cards feature a genuine piece of race-used sheet metal set upon a card showing the featured driver along with his signature. These cards were limited and hand numbered to the corresponding driver's door number. Some of these cards are not priced due to scarcity. The Jimmie Johnson and Jeff Gordon were not released until July 2005 in packs of Press Pass Legends. The Scott Wimmer was not released until October 2004 in the boxed sets of 2004 Press Pass Making the Show Collector's Series. The card went into products un-numbered, but it was confirmed by Press Pass that 22 copies exist.

TPBV Brian Vickers/25 100.00 200.00
TPDE Dale Earnhardt Jr./8
TPJG Jeff Gordon/24 175.00 350.00
TPJJ Jimmie Johnson/48 60.00 120.00
TPKH Kevin Harvick/29 75.00 150.00
TPMM Mark Martin/6
TPTS Tony Stewart/20
TPSW Scott Wimmer/22 50.00 100.00

2004 VIP Tradin' Paint Silver

Randomly inserted in retail packs, these 18 cards feature a genuine piece of race-used sheet metal set upon a card showing the driver. These cards were issued to a stated print run of 70 sets with the exception of Joe Nemechek who was limited to just 50 copies. Each card has the word "Silver" printed on the front near the serial number to note the level. Please note there are 2 other levels of this insert.

*BRONZE/50-70: .4X TO 1X SILVER/50-130
*GOLD/50: .5X TO 1.2X SILVER/70
*GOLD/50: .4X TO 1X SILVER/50
TPD1 Dale Earnhardt Jr. 50.00 100.00
TPD2 Jeff Gordon 50.00 100.00
TPD3 Jimmie Johnson 25.00 60.00
TPD4 Tony Stewart 25.00 60.00
TPD5 Ryan Newman 12.00 30.00
TPD6 Kevin Harvick 15.00 40.00
TPD7 Matt Kenseth 12.00 30.00
TPD8 Bobby Labonte 12.00 30.00
TPD9 Rusty Wallace 15.00 40.00
TPD10 Kurt Busch 10.00 25.00
TPD11 Robby Gordon 10.00 25.00
TPD12 Dale Jarrett 15.00 40.00
TPD13 Joe Nemechek/50 10.00 25.00
TPD14 Jeff Burton 10.00 25.00
TPD15 Scott Wimmer 8.00 20.00
TPD16 Brian Vickers 10.00 25.00
TPD17 Mark Martin 20.00 50.00
TPD18 Michael Waltrip 12.00 30.00

2005 VIP

2005 VIP was issued five cards per hobby pack and four cards per pack.

COMPLETE SET (90) 15.00 40.00
WAX BOX HOBBY (20) 40.00 70.00
WAX BOX RETAIL (24) 35.00 60.00
1 Greg Biffle .30 .75
2 Jeff Burton .30 .75
3 Kurt Busch .50 1.25
4 Kyle Busch CRC .75 2.00
5 Dale Earnhardt Jr. 1.25 3.00
6 Carl Edwards CRC 1.00 2.50
7 Jeff Gordon 1.25 3.00
8 Robby Gordon .20 .50
9 Kevin Harvick .75 2.00
10 Dale Jarrett .60 1.50
11 Jimmie Johnson 1.00 2.50
12 Kasey Kahne 1.25 3.00
13 Matt Kenseth 1.00 2.50
14 Travis Kvapil CRC .30 .75
15 Bobby Labonte .60 1.50
16 Terry Labonte .50 1.25
17 Mark Martin .75 2.00
18 Sterling Marlin .50 1.25
19 Jeremy Mayfield .20 .50
20 Jamie McMurray .50 1.25
21 Casey Mears .30 .75
22 Joe Nemechek .20 .50
23 Ryan Newman 1.00 2.50
24 Kyle Petty .30 .75
25 Ricky Rudd .50 1.25
26 Elliott Sadler .30 .75
27 Tony Stewart .75 2.00
28 Brian Vickers .60 1.50
29 Rusty Wallace .60 1.50
30 Scott Wimmer .30 .75
31 Rusty Wallace's Car R .30 .75
32 Jamie McMurray's Car R .20 .50
33 Dale Earnhardt Jr's Car R .50 1.25
34 Matt Kenseth's Car R .50 1.25
35 Bobby Labonte's Car R .30 .75
36 Kurt Busch's Car R .20 .50
37 Ricky Rudd's Car R .20 .50
38 Scott Wimmer's Car R .10 .30
39 Tony Stewart's Car R .30 .75
40 Elliott Sadler's Car R .10 .30
41 Jeff Burton's Car R .10 .30
42 Jimmie Johnson's Car R .50 1.25
43 Jeff Gordon SG 1.25 3.00
44 Greg Biffle SG .30 .75
45 Jimmie Johnson SG 1.00 2.50
46 Carl Edwards SG 1.00 2.50
47 Kevin Harvick SG .75 2.00
48 Jeff Gordon SG 1.25 3.00
49 Greg Biffle SG .30 .75
50 Kurt Busch SG .50 1.25
51 Jeff Gordon SG 1.25 3.00
52 Greg Biffle SG .30 .75
53 Kasey Kahne SG 1.25 3.00
54 Jimmie Johnson SG 1.00 2.50
55 Kasey Kahne HR 1.25 3.00
56 Ryan Newman HR 1.00 2.50
57 Martin Truex Jr. HR 1.00 2.50
58 Mark Martin HR .75 2.00
59 Ryan Newman HR 1.00 2.50
60 Mark Martin HR .75 2.00
61 Elliott Sadler HR .30 .75
62 Brian Vickers HR .60 1.50
63 Jeff Gordon HR 1.25 3.00
64 Terry Labonte F .50 1.25
65 Terry Labonte F .50 1.25
66 Terry Labonte F .50 1.25
67 Mark Martin F .75 2.00
68 Mark Martin F .75 2.00
69 Mark Martin F .75 2.00
70 Rusty Wallace F .60 1.50
71 Rusty Wallace F .60 1.50
72 Rusty Wallace F .60 1.50
73 Dale Earnhardt Jr. BN 1.25 3.00
74 Jeff Gordon BN 1.25 3.00
75 Terry Labonte BN .50 1.25
76 Jimmie Johnson BN 1.00 2.50
77 Mark Martin BN .75 2.00
78 Tony Stewart BN .75 2.00
79 Rusty Wallace BN .60 1.50
80 Bobby Labonte BN .60 1.50
81 Dale Jarrett BN .60 1.50
82 Jeff Burton BN .30 .75
83 Bobby Labonte ATML .60 1.50
84 Rusty Wallace ATML .60 1.50
85 Jeff Gordon ATML 1.25 3.00
86 Tony Stewart ATML .75 2.00
87 Mark Martin ATML .75 2.00
88 Jeff Burton ATML .30 .75
89 Dale Jarrett ATML .60 1.50
90 Wallace .75 2.00
Martin
T.Labonte CL

2005 VIP Samples

*SAMPLES: 1.5X TO 4X BASE

2005 VIP Driver's Choice

COMPLETE SET (6) 12.50 30.00
*DIE CUTS: 1X TO 2.5X BASE
DC1 Jimmie Johnson 2.00 5.00
DC2 Dale Earnhardt Jr. 2.50 6.00
DC3 Jeff Gordon 2.50 6.00
DC4 Rusty Wallace 1.25 3.00
DC5 Sterling Marlin 1.00 2.50
DC6 Tony Stewart 1.50 4.00

2005 VIP Head Gear

COMPLETE SET (12) 12.50 30.00
*TRANSPARENT: 1X TO 2.5X BASE
1 Jeff Burton .60 1.50
2 Jeff Gordon 2.50 6.00
3 Kevin Harvick 1.50 4.00
4 Jimmie Johnson 2.00 5.00
5 Kasey Kahne 2.50 6.00
6 Matt Kenseth 2.00 5.00
7 Joe Nemechek .40 1.00
8 Carl Edwards 2.00 5.00
9 Elliott Sadler .60 1.50
10 Tony Stewart 1.50 4.00
11 Rusty Wallace 1.25 3.00
12 Dale Jarrett 1.25 3.00

2005 VIP Lap Leaders

COMPLETE SET (9) 15.00 40.00
STATED ODDS 1:8
*TRANSPARENT: .8X TO 2X BASIC
1 Mark Martin 2.00 5.00
2 Dale Earnhardt Jr. 3.00 8.00
3 Kasey Kahne 3.00 8.00
4 Elliott Sadler .75 2.00
5 Matt Kenseth 2.50 6.00
6 Tony Stewart 2.00 5.00
7 Jeff Gordon 3.00 8.00
8 Bobby Labonte 1.50 4.00
9 Rusty Wallace 1.50 4.00

2005 VIP Making The Show

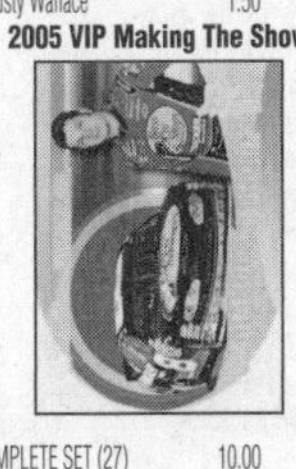

COMPLETE SET (27) 10.00 25.00
1 Joe Nemechek .30 .75
2 Rusty Wallace 1.00 2.50
3 Scott Wimmer .50 1.25
4 Martin Truex Jr. 1.50 4.00
5 Dale Earnhardt Jr. 2.00 5.00
6 Kasey Kahne 2.00 5.00
7 Scott Riggs .50 1.25
8 Ryan Newman 1.50 4.00
9 Matt Kenseth 1.50 4.00
10 Greg Biffle .50 1.25
11 John Andretti .30 .75
12 Bobby Labonte 1.00 2.50
13 Jeremy Mayfield .30 .75
14 Tony Stewart 1.25 3.00
15 Boris Said .30 .75
16 Jeff Gordon 2.00 5.00
17 Brian Vickers 1.00 2.50
18 Kevin Harvick 1.25 3.00
19 Sterling Marlin .75 2.00
20 Casey Mears .50 1.25
21 Jamie McMurray .75 2.00
22 Jeff Green .30 .75
23 Jimmie Johnson 1.50 4.00
24 Jason Leffler .30 .75
25 Mike Bliss .30 .75
26 Mark Martin 1.25 3.00
27 Jeff Burton .50 1.25

2005 VIP Tradin' Paint Autographs

STATED PRINT RUN 6-48
DE Dale Earnhardt Jr./8
JJ Jimmie Johnson/48 60.00 120.00
KH Kevin Harvick/29 75.00 150.00
KK Kasey Kahne/9
MK Matt Kenseth/17
MM Mark Martin/6
TS Tony Stewart/20

2005 VIP Tradin' Paint Drivers

STATED ODDS 1:100
STATED PRINT RUN 90 SERIAL #'d SETS
*CARS/110: .3X TO .8X DRIVERS
TPD1 Dale Earnhardt Jr. 12.00 30.00
TPD2 Jeff Gordon 12.00 30.00
TPD3 Jimmie Johnson 10.00 25.00
TPD4 Tony Stewart 10.00 25.00
TPD5 Terry Labonte 6.00 15.00
TPD6 Kevin Harvick 8.00 20.00
TPD7 Matt Kenseth 6.00 15.00
TPD8 Bobby Labonte 6.00 15.00
TPD9 Rusty Wallace 6.00 15.00
TPD10 Kurt Busch 5.00 12.00
TPD11 Kasey Kahne 10.00 25.00
TPD12 Dale Jarrett 6.00 15.00
TPD13 Joe Nemechek 4.00 10.00
TPD14 Scott Riggs 5.00 12.00
TPD15 Scott Wimmer 6.00 15.00
TPD16 Brian Vickers 4.00 10.00
TPD17 Mark Martin 6.00 15.00

2006 VIP

COMPLETE SET (96) 15.00 40.00
COMP.SET w/o SPs (90) 10.00 25.00
CRC STATED ODDS 1:6
WAX BOX HOBBY (20) 50.00 80.00
WAX BOX RETAIL (24) 40.00 70.00
1 Greg Biffle .25 .60
2 Jeff Burton .25 .60
3 Kurt Busch .25 .60
4 Kyle Busch .40 1.00
5 Dale Earnhardt Jr. .60 1.50
6 Carl Edwards .30 .75
7 Jeff Gordon .60 1.50
8 Robby Gordon .20 .50
9 Kevin Harvick .40 1.00
10 Dale Jarrett .30 .75
11 Jimmie Johnson .50 1.25
12 Kasey Kahne .40 1.00
13 Matt Kenseth .30 .75
14 Bobby Labonte .30 .75
15 Terry Labonte .30 .75
16 Mark Martin .30 .75
17 Sterling Marlin .30 .75
18 Jamie McMurray .30 .75
19 Casey Mears .20 .50
20 Joe Nemechek .20 .50
21 Ryan Newman .25 .60
22 Kyle Petty .25 .60
23 Scott Riggs .25 .60
24 Elliott Sadler .20 .50
25 Ken Schrader .20 .50
26 Tony Stewart .50 1.25
27 Brian Vickers .20 .50
28 Jeff Gordon's Car R .25 .60
29 Kurt Busch's Car R .10 .25
30 Dale Jarrett's Car R .12 .30
31 Kevin Harvick's Car R .15 .40
32 Mark Martin's Car R .12 .30
33 Martin Truex Jr.'s Car R .20 .50
34 Matt Kenseth's Car R .12 .30
35 Jimmie Johnson's Car R .20 .50
36 Carl Edwards' Car R .12 .30
37 Kasey Kahne's Car R .15 .40
38 Jeff Burton's Car R .10 .25
39 Tony Stewart's Car R .20 .50
40 Jimmie Johnson SG .50 1.25
41 Matt Kenseth SG .30 .75
42 Jimmie Johnson SG .50 1.25
43 Kasey Kahne SG .40 1.00
44 Kurt Busch SG .25 .60
45 Tony Stewart SG .50 1.25
46 Kasey Kahne SG .40 1.00
47 Kevin Harvick SG .40 1.00
48 Jimmie Johnson SG .50 1.25
49 Dale Earnhardt Jr. SG .60 1.50
50 Greg Biffle SG .25 .60
51 Kasey Kahne SG .40 1.00
52 Jimmie Johnson BTN .50 1.25
53 Dale Jarrett BTN .30 .75
54 Dale Earnhardt Jr. BTN .60 1.50
55 Tony Stewart BTN .50 1.25
56 Carl Edwards BTN .30 .75
57 Jeff Burton BTN .25 .60
58 Terry Labonte BTN .30 .75
59 Mark Martin BTN .30 .75
60 Jeff Gordon BTN .60 1.50
61 Jamie McMurray BTN .30 .75
62 Kasey Kahne BTN .40 1.00
63 Greg Biffle BTN .25 .60
64 Kurt Busch BTN .25 .60
65 Ryan Newman RF .25 .60
66 Kasey Kahne RF .40 1.00
67 Jeff Gordon RF .60 1.50
68 Greg Biffle RF .25 .60
69 Kurt Busch RF .25 .60
70 Dale Jarrett RF .30 .75
71 Jimmie Johnson RF .50 1.25
72 Tony Stewart RF .50 1.25
73 Martin Truex Jr. AS .50 1.25
74 Kasey Kahne AS .40 1.00
75 Scott Riggs AS .25 .60
76 Kyle Petty AS .25 .60
77 Kyle Busch AS .40 1.00
78 Kevin Harvick AS .40 1.00
79 Jimmie Johnson AS .50 1.25
80 Dale Jarrett IF .30 .75
81 Bobby Labonte IF .30 .75
82 Mark Martin IF .30 .75
83 Dale Earnhardt Jr. IF .60 1.50
84 Jimmie Johnson IF .50 1.25
85 Carl Edwards IF .30 .75
86 Casey Mears IF .20 .50
87 Kevin Harvick IF .40 1.00
88 Jeff Gordon IF .60 1.50
89 Kurt Busch IF .25 .60
90 Clint Bowyer CRC 1.50 4.00
91 Denny Hamlin CRC 3.00 8.00
92 Reed Sorenson CRC 1.25 3.00
93 David Stremme CRC 1.00 2.50
94 Martin Truex Jr. CRC 1.25 3.00
95 J.J. Yeley CRC 1.25 3.00
CL Jeff Gordon CL .60 1.50

2006 VIP Head Gear

COMPLETE SET (12) 12.50 30.00
*TRANSPARENT: .8X TO 2X BASIC INSERTS
HG1 Terry Labonte .50 1.25
HG2 Jimmie Johnson .75 2.00
HG3 Kasey Kahne .60 1.50
HG4 Dale Jarrett .50 1.25
HG5 Denny Hamlin 2.00 5.00
HG6 Mark Martin .50 1.25
HG7 Jeff Gordon 1.00 2.50
HG8 Tony Stewart .75 2.00
HG9 Kurt Busch .40 1.00
HG10 Kevin Harvick .60 1.50
HG11 Bobby Labonte .50 1.25
HG12 Jeff Burton .40 1.00

2006 VIP Lap Leader

COMPLETE SET (9) 10.00 25.00
*TRANSPARENT: .8X TO 2X BASIC INSERTS
LL1 Tony Stewart .60 1.50
LL2 Mark Martin .40 1.00
LL3 Dale Earnhardt Jr. .75 2.00
LL4 Kasey Kahne .50 1.25
LL5 Jimmie Johnson .60 1.50
LL6 Dale Jarrett .40 1.00
LL7 Jeff Gordon .75 2.00
LL8 Kurt Busch .30 .75
LL9 Jeff Burton .30 .75

2006 VIP Making the Show

COMPLETE SET (25) 15.00 40.00
MS1 Mark Martin .30 .75
MS2 Jeff Gordon .60 1.50
MS3 Matt Kenseth .30 .75
MS4 Ryan Newman .25 .60
MS5 Denny Hamlin 1.25 3.00
MS6 Sterling Marlin .30 .75
MS7 Jimmie Johnson .50 1.25
MS8 J.J. Yeley .50 1.25
MS9 Jamie McMurray .30 .75
MS10 Terry Labonte .30 .75
MS11 Carl Edwards .30 .75
MS12 Dale Jarrett .30 .75
MS13 Kasey Kahne .40 1.00
MS14 Martin Truex Jr. .50 1.25
MS15 Greg Biffle .25 .60
MS16 Kevin Harvick .40 1.00
MS17 Tony Stewart .50 1.25
MS18 Jeff Burton .25 .60
MS19 Kyle Busch .40 1.00
MS20 Scott Riggs .25 .60
MS21 Ken Schrader .20 .50
MS22 Bobby Labonte .30 .75
MS23 Dale Earnhardt Jr. .60 1.50
MS24 Kurt Busch .25 .60
MS25 Casey Mears .20 .50

2006 VIP Rookie Stripes

RS1 Clint Bowyer 20.00 50.00
RS2 Denny Hamlin 50.00 100.00
RS3 Reed Sorenson 20.00 50.00
RS4 David Stremme 15.00 40.00
RS5 Martin Truex Jr. 25.00 60.00
RS6 J.J. Yeley 20.00 50.00

2006 VIP Rookie Stripes Autographs

RSCB Clint Bowyer 75.00 150.00
RSDH Denny Hamlin 200.00 350.00
RSDS David Stremme 50.00 100.00

2006 VIP Tradin' Paint Autographs

STATED PRINT RUN 8-48
TPDE Dale Earnhardt Jr./8
TPJG Jeff Gordon/24 175.00 350.00
TPJJ Jimmie Johnson/48 75.00 150.00
TPKK Kasey Kahne/9
TPTS Tony Stewart/20 150.00 250.00

2006 VIP Tradin' Paint Drivers Silver

*GOLD/50: .5X TO 1.2X SILVER/80
*CARS/145: .3X TO .8X SLVR DRIV/80
TPD1 Clint Bowyer 6.00 15.00
TPD2 Kurt Busch 5.00 12.00
TPD3 Kyle Busch 8.00 20.00
TPD4 Dale Earnhardt Jr. 12.00 30.00
TPD5 Carl Edwards 6.00 15.00
TPD6 Jeff Gordon 12.00 30.00
TPD7 Kevin Harvick 8.00 20.00
TPD8 Denny Hamlin 6.00 15.00
TPD9 Dale Jarrett 6.00 15.00
TPD10 Jimmie Johnson 10.00 25.00
TPD11 Kasey Kahne 8.00 20.00
TPD12 Brian Vickers 4.00 10.00
TPD13 Bobby Labonte 6.00 15.00
TPD14 Jeff Burton 5.00 12.00
TPD15 Ryan Newman 5.00 12.00
TPD16 Reed Sorenson 5.00 12.00
TPD17 Tony Stewart 10.00 25.00
TPD18 Terry Labonte 6.00 15.00

2007 VIP

COMPLETE SET (90) 20.00 50.00
COMP.SET w/o SPs (83) 12.50 30.00
WAX BOX HOBBY (20) 50.00 80.00
WAX BOX RETAIL (24) 45.00 75.00
1 Martin Truex Jr. CL .25 .60
2 Greg Biffle .25 .60
3 Clint Bowyer .30 .75
4 Jeff Burton .25 .60
5 Kurt Busch .25 .60
6 Kyle Busch .40 1.00
7 Dale Earnhardt Jr. .60 1.50
8 Carl Edwards .30 .75
9 Jeff Gordon .60 1.50
10 Jeff Green .20 .50
11 Denny Hamlin .40 1.00
12 Kevin Harvick .40 1.00
13 Dale Jarrett .30 .75
14 Jimmie Johnson .50 1.25
15 Kasey Kahne .30 .75
16 Matt Kenseth .30 .75
17 Bobby Labonte .30 .75
18 Sterling Marlin .30 .75
19 Mark Martin .30 .75
20 Jamie McMurray .30 .75
21 Casey Mears .20 .50
22 Joe Nemechek .20 .50
23 Kyle Petty .25 .60
24 Tony Raines .20 .50
25 Ricky Rudd .25 .60
26 Reed Sorenson .20 .50
27 Tony Stewart .50 1.25
28 David Stremme .20 .50
29 Martin Truex Jr. .25 .60
30 Brian Vickers .30 .75
31 Michael Waltrip .30 .75
32 J.J. Yeley .30 .75
33 Richard Childress PB .30 .75
34 Ray Evernham PB .25 .60
35 Joe Gibbs PB .25 .60
36 Rick Hendrick PB .25 .60
37 Jack Roush PB .25 .60
38 Robert Yates PB .25 .60
39 Chip Ganassi PB .25 .60
40 Ken Schrader's Car R .07 .20
41 Tony Stewart's Car R .20 .50
42 Kurt Busch's Car R .10 .25
43 Jeff Gordon's Car R .25 .60
44 Michael Waltrip Racing AN .12 .30
45 Joe Gibbs Racing AN .10 .25
46 Roush Racing AN .10 .25
47 Bill Davis Racing AN .07 .20
48 Evernham Motorsports AN .10 .25
49 Martin Truex Jr.'s Car SV .10 .25
50 Dale Earnhardt Jr.'s Car SV .25 .60
51 Sterling Marlin's Car SV .12 .30
52 Tony Stewart's Car SV .20 .50
53 Jeff Gordon's Car SV .25 .60
54 Jamie McMurray's Car SV .12 .30
55 Jimmie Johnson's Car SV .20 .50
56 Ricky Rudd's Car SV .10 .25
57 Brian Vickers' Car SV .12 .30
58 Dale Jarrett's Car SV .12 .30
59 Kevin Harvick Red C .40 1.00
60 Jimmie Johnson Red C .50 1.25
61 Mark Martin Red C .30 .75
62 Jeff Burton Red C .25 .60
63 Tony Stewart Red C .50 1.25
64 Johnny Sauter Red C .30 .75
65 Matt Kenseth Red C .30 .75
66 Ryan Newman Red C .25 .60
67 Dale Earnhardt Jr. Red C .60 1.50
68 Martin Truex Jr. Red C .25 .60
69 Kevin Harvick Daytona AP .40 1.00
70 Matt Kenseth Cal. AP .30 .75
71 Jimmie Johnson Vegas AP .50 1.25
72 Jimmie Johnson Atl. AP .50 1.25
73 Kyle Busch Bristol AP .40 1.00
74 Jimmie Johnson Mart. AP .50 1.25
75 Jeff Burton Texas AP .25 .60
76 Jeff Gordon Phx. AP .60 1.50

77 Jeff Gordon Tall. AP .60 1.50
78 Jimmie Johnson Rich. AP .50 1.25
79 Jeff Gordon Darl. AP .60 1.50
80 Casey Mears Char. AP .20 .50
81 Martin Truex Jr. Dover AP .25 .60
82 Jeff Gordon Pocono AP .60 1.50
83 Carl Edwards Mich. AP .30 .75
84 A.J. Allmendinger SP RC .75 2.00
85 David Gilliland SP RC .60 1.50
86 Paul Menard SP CRC 1.25 3.00
87 Juan Pablo Montoya SP RC 1.25 3.00
88 David Ragan SP CRC .75 2.00
89 David Reutimann SP RC .50 1.25
90 Regan Smith SP CRC .75 2.00

2007 VIP Gear Gallery

COMPLETE SET (12) 15.00 40.00
STATED ODDS 1:4
*TRANSPARENT: .6X TO 1.5X BASIC
GG1 Ryan Newman .60 1.50
GG2 Kevin Harvick 1.00 2.50
GG3 Dale Jarrett .75 2.00
GG4 Jeff Gordon 1.50 4.00
GG5 Juan Pablo Montoya 2.50 6.00
GG6 Ricky Rudd .60 1.50
GG7 Mark Martin .75 2.00
GG8 Michael Waltrip .75 2.00
GG9 Tony Stewart 1.25 3.00
GG10 Jimmie Johnson 1.25 3.00
GG11 David Gilliland 1.25 3.00
GG12 Kyle Busch .30 .75

2007 VIP Get A Grip Autographs

STATED PRINT RUN 8-42
GGDE Dale Earnhardt Jr./8
GGJM Juan Pablo Montoya/42 60.00 120.00
GGJY J.J. Yeley/18
GGKH Kevin Harvick/29 75.00 150.00
GGKK Kasey Kahne/9
GGMK Matt Kenseth/17

2007 VIP Get A Grip Drivers

OVERALL R-U STATED ODDS 1:40
STATED PRINT RUN 70 SERIAL #'d SETS
*TEAMS/70: .5X TO 1X DRIVERS
GGD1 Mark Martin 10.00 25.00
GGD2 Carl Edwards 10.00 25.00
GGD3 Michael Waltrip 6.00 15.00
GGD4 Jamie McMurray 6.00 15.00
GGD5 Regan Smith 4.00 10.00
GGD6 Ryan Newman 6.00 15.00
GGD7 Juan Pablo Montoya 12.00 30.00
GGD8 Kasey Kahne 12.00 30.00
GGD9 Elliott Sadler 10.00 25.00
GGD10 Matt Kenseth 10.00 25.00
GGD11 Dale Jarrett 10.00 25.00
GGD12 Tony Stewart 12.00 30.00
GGD13 Jeff Gordon 15.00 40.00
GGD14 Joe Nemechek 4.00 10.00
GGD15 Scott Riggs 4.00 10.00
GGD16 Reed Sorenson 6.00 15.00
GGD17 Denny Hamlin 10.00 25.00
GGD18 Kevin Harvick 10.00 25.00
GGD19 Dave Blaney 4.00 10.00
GGD20 David Stremme 6.00 15.00
GGD21 Clint Bowyer 10.00 25.00
GGD22 Brian Vickers 8.00 20.00
GGD23 Kyle Busch 10.00 25.00
GGD24 David Ragan 8.00 20.00
GGD25 Jeff Burton 8.00 20.00
GGD26 A.J. Allmendinger 10.00 25.00
GGD27 Dale Earnhardt Jr. 15.00 40.00
GGD28 Martin Truex Jr. 10.00 25.00
GGD29 Jimmie Johnson 12.00 30.00

2007 VIP Pedal To The Metal

OVERALL R-U ODDS 1:40 HOBBY
OVERALL R-U ODDS 1:112 RETAIL
STATED PRINT RUN 50 SERIAL #'d SETS
PM1 Tony Stewart 20.00 50.00
PM2 Elliott Sadler 25.00 50.00
PM3 Dale Earnhardt Jr. 30.00 80.00
PM4 Michael Waltrip 20.00 40.00
PM5 Kasey Kahne 20.00 50.00
PM6 Carl Edwards 15.00 40.00
PM7 Jamie McMurray 20.00 40.00
PM8 Jeff Gordon 30.00 80.00
PM9 Kevin Harvick 20.00 50.00

2007 VIP Rookie Stripes

OVERALL R-U ODDS 1:40 HOB, 1:112 RET
STATED PRINT RUN 100 SER.#'d SETS
RS1 A.J. Allmendinger 15.00 40.00
RS2 Paul Menard 15.00 40.00
RS3 Juan Pablo Montoya 30.00 60.00
RS4 David Ragan 25.00 50.00
RS5 David Reutimann 12.00 30.00
RS6 Regan Smith 12.00 30.00

2007 VIP Rookie Stripes Autographs

STATED PRINT RUN 25 SER.#'d SETS
RSAJ A.J. Allmendinger 40.00 80.00
RSJM Juan Pablo Montoya 100.00 175.00
RSPM Paul Menard 40.00 80.00
RSRS Regan Smith 50.00 100.00
RSDRA David Ragan 50.00 100.00
RSDRE David Reutimann 40.00 80.00

2007 VIP Sunday Best

COMPLETE SET (25) 15.00 40.00
STATED ODDS 1:2
SB1 Clint Bowyer .40 1.00
SB2 Jeff Burton .30 .75
SB3 Kurt Busch .30 .75
SB4 Kyle Busch .50 1.25
SB5 Dale Earnhardt Jr. .75 2.00
SB6 Carl Edwards .40 1.00
SB7 Jeff Gordon .75 2.00
SB8 Denny Hamlin .50 1.25
SB9 Kevin Harvick .50 1.25
SB10 Dale Jarrett .40 1.00
SB11 Jimmie Johnson .60 1.50
SB12 Kasey Kahne .40 1.00
SB13 Matt Kenseth .40 1.00
SB14 Bobby Labonte .40 1.00
SB15 Sterling Marlin .40 1.00
SB16 Mark Martin .40 1.00
SB17 Jamie McMurray .40 1.00
SB18 Juan Pablo Montoya 1.25 3.00
SB19 Ryan Newman .30 .75
SB20 Ricky Rudd .30 .75
SB21 Tony Stewart .60 1.50
SB22 David Stremme .25 .60
SB23 Martin Truex Jr. .30 .75
SB24 Brian Vickers .40 1.00
SB25 Michael Waltrip .40 1.00

2007 VIP Trophy Club

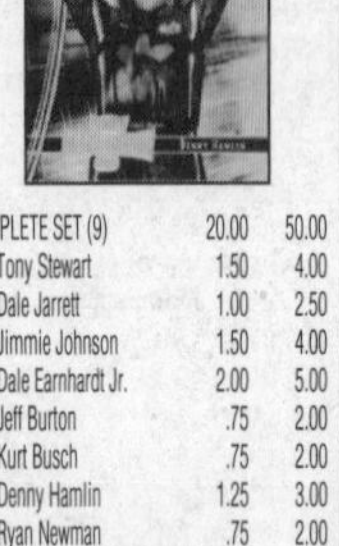

COMPLETE SET (9) 20.00 50.00
TC1 Tony Stewart 1.50 4.00
TC2 Dale Jarrett 1.00 2.50
TC3 Jimmie Johnson 1.50 4.00
TC4 Dale Earnhardt Jr. 2.00 5.00
TC5 Jeff Burton .75 2.00
TC6 Kurt Busch .75 2.00
TC7 Denny Hamlin 1.25 3.00
TC8 Ryan Newman .75 2.00
TC9 Jeff Gordon 2.00 5.00

2008 VIP

COMPLETE SET (90) 15.00 40.00
WAX BOX HOBBY 50.00 75.00
WAX BOX RETAIL 40.00 70.00
1 A.J. Allmendinger .40 1.00
2 Aric Almirola CRC .30 .75
3 Greg Biffle .30 .75
4 Clint Bowyer .40 1.00
5 Jeff Burton .30 .75
6 Kurt Busch .30 .75
7 Kyle Busch .50 1.25
8 Patrick Carpentier RC .75 2.00
9 Dale Earnhardt Jr. .75 2.00
10 Carl Edwards .40 1.00
11 David Gilliland .25 .60
12 Jeff Gordon .75 2.00
13 Denny Hamlin .50 1.25
14 Kevin Harvick .50 1.25
15 Sam Hornish Jr. CRC .60 1.50
16 Jimmie Johnson .60 1.50
17 Kasey Kahne .40 1.00
18 Matt Kenseth .40 1.00
19 Bobby Labonte .40 1.00
20 Mark Martin .40 1.00
21 Michael McDowell .60 1.50
22 Jamie McMurray .40 1.00
23 Casey Mears .25 .60
24 Juan Pablo Montoya .60 1.50
25 Joe Nemechek .25 .60
26 Ryan Newman .30 .75
27 Kyle Petty .30 .75
28 David Ragan .30 .75
29 David Reutimann .30 .75
30 Scott Riggs .30 .75
31 Elliott Sadler .25 .60
32 Regan Smith .30 .75
33 Tony Stewart .60 1.50
34 Martin Truex Jr. .30 .75
35 Michael Waltrip .40 1.00
36 J.J. Yeley .40 1.00
37 Richard Childress PB .40 1.00
38 Joe Gibbs PB .40 1.00
39 Rick Hendrick PB .40 1.00
40 Chip Ganassi PB .40 1.00
41 Ray Evernham PB .40 1.00
42 Jack Roush PB .40 1.00
43 Michael Waltrip's Car SB .15 .40
44 Jimmie Johnson's Car SB .25 .60
45 Clint Bowyer's Car SB .15 .40
46 Kyle Busch's Car SB .20 .50
47 Scott Riggs's Car SB .12 .30
48 Dale Earnhardt Jr.'s Car SB .30 .75
49 Jeff Burton's Car SB .12 .30
50 Jeff Gordon's Car SB .30 .75
51 Bobby Labonte's Car SB .15 .40
52 David Reutimann's Car SB .12 .30
53 Martin Truex Jr.'s Car SB .12 .30
54 Tony Stewart's Car SB .25 .60
55 Greg Biffle Red .30 .75
56 Jimmie Johnson Red .60 1.50
57 Elliott Sadler Red .25 .60
58 A.J. Allmendinger Red .40 1.00
59 Sam Hornish Jr. Red .60 1.50
60 Kyle Busch Red .50 1.25
61 Kasey Kahne Red .40 1.00
62 Dale Jarrett Red .40 1.00
63 Kasey Kahne Red .40 1.00
64 Greg Biffle Red .30 .75
65 Ryan Newman Daytona AP .30 .75
66 Carl Edwards California AP .40 1.00
67 Carl Edwards Las Vegas AP .40 1.00
68 Kyle Busch Atlanta AP .50 1.25
69 Jeff Burton Bristol AP .30 .75
70 Denny Hamlin Martinsville AP .50 1.25
71 Carl Edwards Texas AP .40 1.00
72 Jimmie Johnson Phoenix AP .60 1.50
73 Kyle Busch Talladega AP .50 1.25
74 Clint Bowyer Richmond AP .40 1.00
75 Kyle Busch Darlington AP .50 1.25
76 Kasey Kahne Charlotte AP .40 1.00
77 Kyle Busch Dover AP .50 1.25
78 Ryan Newman's Car R .30 .75
79 Greg Biffle's Car R .30 .75
80 Matt Kenseth's Car R .30 .75
81 Tony Stewart's Car R .60 1.50
82 Jimmie Johnson BTS .60 1.50
83 Kurt Busch BTS .30 .75
84 Reed Sorenson BTS .25 .60
85 Kyle Petty BTS .30 .75
86 Tony Stewart BTS .60 1.50
87 Michael Waltrip BTS .40 1.00
88 Ryan Newman BTS .30 .75
89 Juan Pablo Montoya BTS .60 1.50
90 Tony Stewart CL .60 1.50
0 Joey Logano/499 15.00 30.00

2008 VIP All Access

COMPLETE SET (25) 12.00 30.00
STATED ODDS 1:2
AA1 Aric Almirola .40 1.00
AA2 Clint Bowyer .50 1.25
AA3 Jeff Burton .40 1.00
AA4 Kyle Busch .60 1.50
AA5 Dale Earnhardt Jr. 1.00 2.50
AA6 Jeff Gordon 1.00 2.50
AA7 David Gilliland .30 .75
AA8 Denny Hamlin .60 1.50
AA9 Kevin Harvick .60 1.50
AA10 Jimmie Johnson .75 2.00
AA11 Kasey Kahne .50 1.25
AA12 Matt Kenseth .50 1.25
AA13 Travis Kvapil .30 .75
AA14 Bobby Labonte .50 1.25
AA15 Michael McDowell .75 2.00
AA16 Jamie McMurray .50 1.25
AA17 Casey Mears .30 .75
AA18 Ryan Newman .40 1.00
AA19 David Reutimann .40 1.00
AA20 Scott Riggs .40 1.00
AA21 Regan Smith .40 1.00
AA22 Tony Stewart .75 2.00
AA23 Martin Truex Jr. .40 1.00
AA24 Michael Waltrip .50 1.25
AA25 J.J. Yeley .50 1.25

2008 VIP Gear Gallery

COMPLETE SET (12) 12.00 30.00
STATED ODDS 1:4
*TRANSPARENT: .6X TO 1.5X
GG1 Clint Bowyer .60 1.50
GG2 Kevin Harvick .75 2.00
GG3 Ryan Newman .50 1.25
GG4 Martin Truex Jr. .50 1.25
GG5 Jimmie Johnson 1.00 2.50
GG6 Carl Edwards .60 1.50
GG7 Tony Stewart 1.00 2.50
GG8 Kyle Busch .75 2.00
GG9 Matt Kenseth .60 1.50
GG10 Jeff Gordon 1.25 3.00
GG11 Dale Earnhardt Jr. 1.25 3.00
GG12 Kasey Kahne .60 1.50

2008 VIP Gear Gallery Memorabilia

OVERALL R-U ODDS 1:40
STATED PRINT RUN 50 SERIAL #'d SETS
GGCB Clint Bowyer Firesuit 10.00 25.00
GGCE Carl Edwards Net 15.00 40.00
GGDE Dale Earnhardt Jr. Tire 30.00 80.00
GGJG Jeff Gordon Metal 30.00 80.00
GGJJ Jimmie Johnson Shoes 25.00 60.00
GGKH Kevin Harvick Net 25.00 60.00
GGKK Kasey Kahne Shirt 25.00 60.00
GGMK Matt Kenseth Glove 15.00 40.00
GGMT Martin Truex Jr. Tear-off 15.00 40.00
GGRN Ryan Newman Belt 12.00 30.00
GGTS Tony Stewart Firesuit 20.00 50.00
GGKyB Kyle Busch Metal 20.00 50.00

2008 VIP Get a Grip Drivers

OVERALL R-U ODDS 1:40
STATED PRINT RUN 99 SERIAL #'d SETS
*TEAMS/99: .4X TO 1X DRIVERS/99
GGD1 Martin Truex Jr. 4.00 10.00
GGD2 Jeff Gordon 10.00 25.00
GGD3 Greg Biffle 4.00 10.00
GGD4 Kasey Kahne 5.00 12.00
GGD5 David Reutimann 4.00 10.00
GGD6 Brian Vickers 3.00 8.00
GGD7 Carl Edwards 5.00 12.00
GGD8 Juan Pablo Montoya 8.00 20.00
GGD9 Jamie McMurray 5.00 12.00
GGD10 Michael Waltrip 5.00 12.00
GGD11 Mark Martin 5.00 12.00
GGD12 Jimmie Johnson 8.00 20.00
GGD13 Denny Hamlin 6.00 15.00
GGD14 Jeff Burton 4.00 10.00
GGD15 Casey Mears 3.00 8.00

2008 VIP Get a Grip Autographs

SERIAL #'d TO DRIVER'S DOOR #
STATED PRINT RUN 1-88
GGSCB Clint Bowyer/7
GGSDE Dale Earnhardt Jr./88 60.00 120.00
GGSJG Jeff Gordon/24 125.00 250.00
GGSKK Kasey Kahne/9
GGSMK Matt Kenseth/17
GGSMT Martin Truex Jr./1
GGSRN Ryan Newman/12

2008 VIP National Promos

1 Jimmie Johnson 1.50 4.00
2 Tony Stewart 1.50 4.00
3 Dale Earnhardt Jr. 2.00 5.00
4 Kyle Busch 1.25 3.00
5 Carl Edwards 1.00 2.50
6 Jeff Gordon 6.00 15.00

2008 VIP Rookie Stripes

OVERALL R-U ODDS 1:40
STATED PRINT RUN 100 SER.#'d SETS
RS1 Patrick Carpentier 20.00 50.00
RS2 Dario Franchitti 15.00 40.00
RS3 Sam Hornish, Jr. 15.00 40.00
RS4 Michael McDowell 12.00 30.00
RS5 Regan Smith 15.00 40.00

2008 VIP Rookie Stripes Autographs

STATED PRINT RUN 25 SER.#'d SETS
RSMM Michael McDowell 30.00 80.00
RSPC Patrick Carpentier 40.00 100.00
RSRS Regan Smith 25.00 60.00
RSSH Sam Hornish, Jr. 25.00 60.00

2008 VIP Triple Grip

OVERALL R-U ODDS 1:40
STATED PRINT RUN 25 SERIAL #'d SETS
TG1 Dale Earnhardt Jr./Jeff Gordon/Jimmie Johnson 100.00 200.00
TG2 Clint Bowyer/Jeff Burton/Kevin Harvick 75.00 150.00
TG3 Greg Biffle/Carl Edwards/Matt Kenseth 75.00 150.00
TG4 Dario Franchitti/Juan Pablo Montoya/Reed Sorenson 40.00 80.00

2008 VIP Trophy Club

COMPLETE SET (9) 15.00 40.00
STATED ODDS 1:7
*TRANSPARENT: .6X TO 1.5X BASIC
TC1 Greg Biffle .75 2.00
TC2 Matt Kenseth 1.00 2.50
TC3 Jimmie Johnson 1.50 4.00
TC4 Martin Truex Jr. .75 2.00
TC5 Ryan Newman .75 2.00
TC6 Dale Earnhardt Jr. 2.00 5.00
TC7 Carl Edwards 1.00 2.50
TC8 Jeff Burton .75 2.00
TC9 Jeff Gordon 2.00 5.00

2009 VIP

COMPLETE SET (90) 15.00 40.00
WAX BOX HOBBY (24) 60.00 100.00
WAX BOX RETAIL (28) 50.00 75.00
1 A.J. Allmendinger .40 1.00
2 Marcos Ambrose CRC .40 1.00
3 Greg Biffle .30 .75
4 Clint Bowyer .40 1.00
5 Jeff Burton .30 .75
6 Kurt Busch .30 .75
7 Kyle Busch .50 1.25
8 Dale Earnhardt Jr. .75 2.00
9 Carl Edwards .40 1.00
10 Jeff Gordon .75 2.00
11 Robby Gordon .25 .60
12 Denny Hamlin .40 1.00
13 Kevin Harvick .50 1.25
14 Sam Hornish Jr. .30 .75
15 Jimmie Johnson .60 1.50
16 Kasey Kahne .40 1.00
17 Matt Kenseth .40 1.00
18 Brad Keselowski CRC 1.25 3.00
19 Bobby Labonte .40 1.00
20 Joey Logano RC .75 2.00
21 Mark Martin .40 1.00
22 Casey Mears .25 .60
23 Paul Menard .25 .60
24 Juan Pablo Montoya .50 1.25
25 Ryan Newman .30 .75
26 David Ragan .30 .75
27 David Reutimann .30 .75
28 Elliott Sadler .25 .60
29 Regan Smith .30 .75
30 Reed Sorenson .25 .60
31 Scott Speed RC .50 1.25
32 Tony Stewart .60 1.50
33 David Stremme .25 .60
34 Martin Truex Jr. .30 .75
35 Brian Vickers .25 .60
36 Michael Waltrip .40 1.00
37 David Ragan's Car RR .12 .30
38 Denny Hamlin's Car RR .15 .40
39 Kyle Busch's Car RR .20 .50
40 Joey Logano's Car RR .30 .75
41 Jeff Gordon's Car RR .30 .75
42 Jeff Burton's Car RR .12 .30
43 Ryan Newman's Car RR .12 .30
44 Juan Pablo Montoya's Car RR .20 .50
45 Jimmie Johnson's Car RR .25 .60
46 Michael Waltrip's Car RR .15 .40
47 Dale Earnhardt Jr.'s Car RR .30 .75
48 Carl Edwards' Car RR .15 .40
49 David Ragan M .30 .75
50 Jeff Gordon M .75 2.00
51 Kurt Busch M .30 .75
52 Greg Biffle M .30 .75
53 Jeff Burton M .30 .75
54 Kevin Harvick M .50 1.25
55 Matt Kenseth M .40 1.00
56 Dale Earnhardt Jr. M .75 2.00
57 Jimmie Johnson M .60 1.50
58 Juan Pablo Montoya M .50 1.25
59 Joey Logano M .75 2.00
60 Michael Waltrip M .40 1.00
61 Jimmie Johnson Red .60 1.50
62 Sam Hornish Jr. Red .30 .75
63 Joey Logano Red .75 2.00
64 Jimmie Johnson Red .60 1.50
65 Kyle Busch Red .50 1.25
66 Jeff Gordon Red .75 2.00
67 Ryan Newman Red .30 .75
68 Matt Kenseth Red .40 1.00
69 Tony Stewart Red .60 1.50
70 Darrell Waltrip AS .60 1.50
71 Dale Earnhardt AS 2.50 6.00
72 Rusty Wallace AS .40 1.00
73 Dale Earnhardt AS 2.50 6.00
74 Davey Allison AS .60 1.50
75 Geoffrey Bodine AS .25 .60
76 Dale Earnhardt Jr. AS .75 2.00
77 Jeff Gordon AS .75 2.00
78 Jimmie Johnson AS .60 1.50
79 Dale Jarrett AS .40 1.00
80 Kasey Kahne AS .40 1.00
81 Tony Stewart AS .60 1.50
82 Martin Truex Jr. BTS .30 .75
83 Kevin Harvick BTS .50 1.25
84 Brian Vickers BTS .25 .60
85 Jimmie Johnson BTS .60 1.50
86 Jeff Gordon BTS .75 2.00
87 Scott Speed BTS .50 1.25
88 Dale Earnhardt Jr. BTS .75 2.00
89 Brian Vickers BTS .25 .60
90 Dale Earnhardt Jr. CL .50 1.25

2009 VIP Purple

*PURPLE/25: 6X TO 15X BASIC INSERTS
STATED PRINT RUN 25 SER.#'d SETS

2009 VIP After Party

COMPLETE SET (12) 12.00 30.00
STATED ODDS 1:6
*TRANSPARENT: .6X TO 1.5X BASIC INSERTS
AP1 Matt Kenseth Daytona .75 2.00
AP2 Matt Kenseth California .75 2.00
AP3 Kyle Busch Las Vegas 1.00 2.50
AP4 Kurt Busch Atlanta .60 1.50
AP5 Kyle Busch Bristol 1.00 2.50
AP6 Jimmie Johnson Martinsville 1.25 3.00
AP7 Jeff Gordon Texas 1.50 4.00
AP8 Mark Martin Phoenix .75 2.00
AP9 Brad Keselowski Talladega 1.00 2.50
AP10 Kyle Busch Richmond 1.00 2.50
AP11 Mark Martin Darlington .75 2.00
AP12 David Reutimann Charlotte .60 1.50

2009 VIP Get A Grip

STATED PRINT RUN 120 SER.#'d SETS
GGBV Brian Vickers 4.00 10.00
GGCB Clint Bowyer 6.00 15.00
GGCE Carl Edwards 6.00 15.00
GGCM Casey Mears 4.00 10.00
GGDE Dale Earnhardt Jr./100 25.00 60.00
GGDH Denny Hamlin 6.00 15.00
GGDR David Ragan 5.00 12.00
GGDR David Reutimann
GGES Elliott Sadler 4.00 10.00
GGGB Greg Biffle 5.00 12.00
GGJB Jeff Burton 5.00 12.00
GGJG Jeff Gordon/100 12.00 30.00
GGJJ Jimmie Johnson 10.00 25.00
GGJL Joey Logano/100 10.00 25.00
GGJM Juan Montoya 8.00 20.00
GGKB Kyle Busch 8.00 20.00
GGKH Kevin Harvick 8.00 20.00
GGKK Kasey Kahne 6.00 15.00
GGMK Matt Kenseth/100 6.00 15.00
GGMT Martin Truex Jr. 5.00 12.00
GGPM Paul Menard 4.00 10.00
GGRN Ryan Newman 5.00 12.00
GGSS Scott Speed 8.00 20.00
GGTS Tony Stewart 10.00 25.00

2009 VIP Get A Grip Autographs

SERIAL #'d TO DRIVER'S DOOR NO.
STATED PRINT RUN 6-39
GGSJB Jeff Burton/31 30.00 80.00
GGSKH Kevin Harvick/29 30.00 80.00
GGSRN Ryan Newman/39 30.00 80.00

2009 VIP Guest List

COMPLETE SET (25) 10.00 25.00
STATED ODDS 1:3
GG1 Kyle Busch .50 1.25
GG2 Jeff Burton .30 .75
GG3 A.J. Allmendinger .40 1.00
GG4 Tony Stewart .60 1.50
GG5 Elliott Sadler .25 .60
GG6 Martin Truex Jr. .30 .75
GG7 Jeff Gordon .75 2.00
GG8 Brian Vickers .25 .60
GG9 Michael Waltrip .40 1.00
GG10 Kasey Kahne .40 1.00
GG11 David Reutimann .30 .75
GG12 Clint Bowyer .40 1.00
GG13 Sam Hornish Jr. .30 .75
GG14 Carl Edwards .40 1.00
GG15 Bobby Labonte .40 1.00
GG16 David Stremme .25 .60
GG17 Jimmie Johnson .60 1.50
GG18 Paul Menard .25 .60
GG19 Casey Mears .25 .60
GG20 Kevin Harvick .50 1.25
GG21 Mark Martin .40 1.00
GG22 Dale Earnhardt Jr. .75 2.00
GG23 Joey Logano .75 2.00
GG24 Denny Hamlin .40 1.00
GG25 Ryan Newman .30 .75

2009 VIP Hardware

STATED ODDS 1:8
*TRANSPARENT: .8X TO 2X BASIC INSERTS
H1 Dale Earnhardt Jr. Daytona 2.00 5.00
H2 Kasey Kahne Charlotte 1.00 2.50
H3 Jeff Gordon Texas 2.00 5.00
H4 Greg Biffle Dover .75 2.00
H5 Kevin Harvick Richmond 1.25 3.00
H6 Kyle Busch Las Vegas 1.25 3.00
H7 Tony Stewart Brickyard 1.50 4.00
H8 Carl Edwards Bristol 1.00 2.50
H9 Juan Pablo Montoya Infineon 1.25 3.00

2009 VIP Leadfoot

STATED PRINT RUN 150 SER.#'d SETS
LFBV Brian Vickers 3.00 8.00
LFCE Carl Edwards 5.00 12.00
LFDE Dale Earnhardt Jr. 10.00 25.00
LFDH Denny Hamlin 5.00 12.00
LFGB Greg Biffle 4.00 10.00
LFJB Jeff Burton 4.00 10.00
LFJG Jeff Gordon 10.00 25.00
LFJJ Jimmie Johnson 8.00 20.00
LFJL Joey Logano 12.00 30.00
LFJM Jamie McMurray 5.00 12.00

LFJM Juan Montoya 6.00 15.00
LFKB Kyle Busch 6.00 15.00
LFKH Kevin Harvick 6.00 15.00
LFKK Kasey Kahne/10
LFMK Matt Kenseth 5.00 12.00
LFMT Martin Truex Jr. 4.00 10.00
LFMW Michael Waltrip 5.00 12.00
LFPM Paul Menard 3.00 8.00
LFRN Ryan Newman 4.00 10.00
LFSS Scott Speed 6.00 15.00
LFTS Tony Stewart 8.00 20.00
LFDRa David Ragan 4.00 10.00
LFDRe David Reutimann 4.00 10.00

2009 VIP Race Day Gear

STATED PRINT RUN 25 SER.#'d SETS
RDGJG Dale Earnhardt Jr. 40.00 100.00
RDGJG Jeff Gordon 40.00 100.00
RDGJJ Jimmie Johnson 30.00 80.00
RDGKB Kyle Busch 12.00 30.00
RDGTS Tony Stewart 30.00 80.00

2009 VIP Rookie Stripes

STATED PRINT RUN 100 SER.#'d SETS
RS1 Joey Logano 15.00 40.00
RS2 Scott Speed 10.00 25.00
RS3 Brad Keselowski 10.00 25.00
RS4 Marcos Ambrose 8.00 20.00

2009 VIP Rookie Stripes Autographs

STATED PRINT RUN 25 SER.#'d SETS
RSBK Brad Keselowski 90.00 150.00
RSJL Joey Logano
RSMA Marcos Ambrose
RSSS Scott Speed 20.00 50.00

2009 VIP National Promos

COMPLETE SET (6) 10.00 25.00
1 Kyle Busch .75 2.00
2 Jeff Gordon 1.25 3.00
3 Jimmie Johnson 1.00 2.50
4 Joey Logano 1.25 3.00
5 Tony Stewart 1.00 2.50
6 Dale Earnhardt Jr. SP 5.00 12.00

1996 Viper Promos

Wheels produced this 3-card promo set to advertise its new Viper card line. The cards were distributed mounted in a simulated snake skin binder.

COMPLETE SET (3) 10.00 25.00
P1 Bobby Labonte 2.00 5.00
P2 Rusty Wallace 3.00 8.00
P3 Jeff Gordon 5.00 12.00

1996 Viper

This 78-card set features many of the top names in Winston Cup. The cards use the theme of the snake with the Viper logo appearing in the top left hand corner of each card. Cards are printed on 24-point stock. There are both hobby and retail boxes of Viper. Each box contains 24-packs with five cards per pack. Each card in the first 325 cases printed carried a special First Strike logo. These First Strike cards parallel the base set and inserts and were packaged separately in specially marked boxes and packs.

COMPLETE SET (78) 10.00 25.00
1 Dale Earnhardt 1.50 4.00
2 Jeff Gordon 1.00 2.50
3 Sterling Marlin .30 .75
4 Mark Martin .75 2.00
5 Terry Labonte .30 .75
6 Rusty Wallace .75 2.00
7 Bill Elliott .40 1.00
8 Bobby Labonte .60 1.50
9 Ward Burton .20 .50
10 Bobby Hamilton .10 .25
11 Dale Jarrett .60 1.50
12 Ted Musgrave .10 .25
13 Darrell Waltrip .20 .50
14 Kyle Petty .20 .50
15 Ken Schrader .10 .25
16 Michael Waltrip .20 .50
17 Derrike Cope .10 .25
18 Jeff Burton .30 .75
19 Ricky Craven .10 .25
20 Steve Grissom .10 .25
21 Robert Pressley .10 .25
22 Joe Nemechek .10 .25
23 Jeremy Mayfield .20 .50
24 Mike Wallace .10 .25
25 Johnny Benson .20 .50
26 Jimmy Spencer .10 .25
27 Tony Glover .05 .15
28 Steve Hmiel .05 .15
29 Mike Beam .05 .15
30 Larry McReynolds .05 .15
31 Robin Pemberton .05 .15
32 Jimmy Makar .05 .15
33 Richard Childress .20 .50
34 Joe Gibbs .20 .50
35 Jack Roush .05 .15
36 Roger Penske .05 .15
37 Mark Martin .75 2.00
38 Bobby Labonte .60 1.50
39 Terry Labonte .30 .75
40 Jeff Gordon 1.00 2.50
41 Rusty Wallace .75 2.00
42 Jeff Gordon 1.00 2.50
43 Dale Earnhardt 1.50 4.00
44 Mark Martin .75 2.00
45 Mark Martin .75 2.00
46 Ward Burton .20 .50
47 Chad Little .20 .50
48 Mike McLaughlin .10 .25
49 Jason Keller .10 .25
50 David Green .10 .25
51 Larry Pearson .20 .50
52 Jeff Fuller .10 .25
53 David Green .10 .25
54 Hermie Sadler .10 .25
55 Bobby Dotter .10 .25
56 Terry Labonte .30 .75
57 Mark Martin .75 2.00
58 Dale Jarrett .60 1.50
59 Michael Waltrip .20 .50
60 Joe Nemechek .10 .25
61 Ken Schrader .10 .25
62 Mike Wallace .10 .25
63 Randy Porter .10 .25
64 Mike Skinner .10 .25
65 Joe Ruttman .10 .25
66 Ron Hornaday .10 .25
67 Butch Miller .10 .25
68 Rick Carelli .10 .25
69 Bill Sedgwick .10 .25
70 Tobey Butler .10 .25
71 Steve Portenga .10 .25
72 Bob Keselowski .10 .25
73 Ken Schrader .10 .25
74 Johnny Benson .20 .50
75 Mike Chase .10 .25
76 Checklist .05 .15
77 Checklist .05 .15
78 Cover Card .05 .15
R3 Dale Earnhardt Promo 2.00 5.00
R3FS Dale Earnhardt FS Promo 2.50 6.00

1996 Viper First Strike

COMPLETE SET (78) 20.00 50.00
*FIRST STRIKE: 1X TO 2.5X BASE CARDS

1996 Viper Red Cobra

COMPLETE SET (78) 15.00 40.00
*RED COBRA: 1.25X TO 3X BASE CARDS

1996 Viper Black Mamba

COMPLETE SET (78) 150.00 300.00
*BLACK MAMBA: 4X TO 10X HI COL.
R3B Dale Earnhardt Black 25.00 60.00

1996 Viper Black Mamba First Strike

COMPLETE SET (78) 400.00 600.00
*FIRST STRIKE: .8X TO 2X BLACK MAMBA

1996 Viper Green Mamba

COMPLETE SET (78) 250.00 450.00
*GREEN MAMBA: .4X TO 1X BLACK MAMBA

1996 Viper Copperhead Die Cuts

COMPLETE SET (78) 60.00 150.00
*COPPERHEAD: 2.5X TO 6X HI COLUMN

1996 Viper Busch Clash

This 16-card set features drivers who captured a pole in 1995. The cards have many of the drivers holding the traditional Busch Pole plaque. The cards were inserted at a rate of one in eight packs. There was also a First Strike version available in First Strike boxes at a rate of one in eight packs.

COMPLETE SET (16) 30.00 75.00
COMP.FIRST STRIKE (16) 50.00 100.00
*FIRST STRIKE: .6X TO 1.5X BASIC INSERTS
B1 Terry Labonte 2.00 5.00
B2 John Andretti .60 1.50
B3 Hut Stricklin .60 1.50
B4 David Green .60 1.50
B5 Jeff Gordon 6.00 15.00
B6 Darrell Waltrip 1.25 3.00
B7 Dale Jarrett 4.00 10.00
B8 Sterling Marlin 2.00 5.00
B9 Rick Mast .60 1.50
B10 Dave Marcis .60 1.50
B11 Mark Martin 5.00 12.00
B12 Ken Schrader .60 1.50
B13 Ted Musgrave .60 1.50
B14 Dale Earnhardt 10.00 25.00
B15 Bobby Labonte 4.00 10.00
B16 Bill Elliott 2.50 6.00

1996 Viper Cobra

This 10-card insert set ten of the top 15 finishers in the 1995 Winston Cup points race. The cards are randomly inserted one per 48 packs. The First Strike version featured the same odds and were inserted only in First Strike boxes.

COMPLETE SET (10) 75.00 125.00
*FIRST STRIKE: .5X TO 1.2X BASIC INSERTS
C1 Dale Earnhardt 25.00 60.00
C2 Jeff Gordon 15.00 40.00
C3 Bobby Labonte 10.00 25.00
C4 Mark Martin 12.50 30.00
C5 Sterling Marlin 5.00 12.00
C6 Rusty Wallace 12.50 30.00
C7 Terry Labonte 5.00 12.00
C8 Bill Elliott 6.00 15.00
C9 Bobby Hamilton 1.50 4.00
C10 Dale Jarrett 10.00 25.00

1996 Viper Dale Earnhardt

This set was available through a redemption of a winning viper venom card. The set features seven time Winston Cup Champion Dale Earnhardt and comes in a simulated snake skin case.

COMPLETE SET (3) 15.00 40.00
COMMON CARD 7.50 20.00

1996 Viper Diamondback

This eight-card insert set features a patch of simulated rattlesnake skin next to the picture of the driver on the fronts of the cards. The cards are randomly inserted in packs one per 72 packs. Each card is sequentially numbered of 1,499. The First Strike version were cards inserted into specially marked boxes of Viper First Strike. The cards are a parallel to the base inserts.

COMPLETE SET (8) 60.00 175.00
COMP.FIRST STRIKE (8) 100.00 200.00
*FIRST STRIKE: .6X TO 1.5X BASIC INSERTS
D1 Jeff Gordon 10.00 25.00
D2 Dale Earnhardt 10.00 25.00
D3 Bobby Labonte 6.00 15.00
D4 Mark Martin 4.00 10.00
D5 Terry Labonte 3.00 8.00
D6 Rusty Wallace 4.00 10.00
D7 Sterling Marlin 3.00 8.00
D8 Bill Elliott 4.00 10.00

1996 Viper Diamondback Authentic

This eight-card insert set features authentic diamondback rattlesnake skin attached to each horizontally-oriented card. The cards are inserted at a rate of one per 120 packs and are sequentially numbered of 749. There was also a parallel First Strike version that was available in specially marked Viper First Strike boxes.

COMPLETE SET (8) 100.00 200.00
COMP.CALIFORNIA SET (8) 250.00 500.00
*CALIFORNIA: 1X TO 2X BASIC INSERTS
COMP. FIRST STRIKE (8) 150.00 300.00
*FIRST STRIKE: .5X TO 1.2X BASIC INSERTS
DA1 Jeff Gordon 15.00 40.00
DA2 Dale Earnhardt 25.00 60.00
DA3 Sterling Marlin 5.00 12.00
DA4 Bobby Labonte 10.00 25.00
DA5 Rusty Wallace 12.50 30.00
DA6 Terry Labonte 5.00 12.00
DA7 Mark Martin 12.50 30.00
DA8 Bill Elliott 6.00 15.00

1996 Viper King Cobra

This 10-card set is a jumbo sized parallel to the Viper Cobra insert set. The cards measure 3" X 5" and were inserted into boxes of Viper at a rate of one per three boxes. Each card is sequentially numbered of 699. The First Strike version is a parallel to the base cards and comes in specially marked Viper First Strike boxes.

COMPLETE SET (10) 75.00 125.00
*FIRST STRIKE: .6X TO 1.5X BASIC INSERTS
KC1 Dale Earnhardt 25.00 60.00
KC2 Jeff Gordon 15.00 40.00
KC3 Dale Jarrett 10.00 25.00
KC4 Bill Elliott 6.00 15.00
KC5 Terry Labonte 5.00 12.00
KC6 Bobby Hamilton 1.50 4.00
KC7 Rusty Wallace 12.50 30.00
KC8 Mark Martin 12.50 30.00
KC9 Bobby Labonte 10.00 25.00
KC10 Sterling Marlin 5.00 12.00

1996 Viper Dale Earnhardt Cobra Mom-n-Pop's

COMPLETE SET (3) 10.00 25.00
COMMON CARD (1-3) 4.80 12.00

1997 Viper

This 82-card set features many of the top names in Winston Cup. The cards use the theme of the snake with the Viper logo appearing in the top left hand corner of each card. There are both hobby and retail boxes of Viper. Each hobby box contains 24 packs with six cards per pack. Each retail box contains 30 packs with five cards per pack. There were 200 Eastern cases and 1,000 Western cases produced. The difference in these cases is the Diamondback Authentic cards. The Eastern cases contain cards that were not produced from Western Diamondback snake skin, but facsimile skin. Each 16-box hobby case contains 12 regular boxes and four First Strike boxes. Each card in the First Strike boxes carried a special First Strike logo.

COMPLETE SET (82) 8.00 20.00
1 Jeff Gordon .75 2.00
2 Dale Jarrett .50 1.25
3 Terry Labonte .25 .60
4 Mark Martin .60 1.50
5 Rusty Wallace .60 1.50
6 Bobby Labonte .50 1.25
7 Sterling Marlin .25 .60
8 Jeff Burton .25 .60
9 Ted Musgrave .07 .20
10 Michael Waltrip .15 .40
11 David Green .07 .20
12 Ricky Craven .07 .20
13 Johnny Benson .15 .40
14 Jeremy Mayfield .15 .40
15 Bobby Hamilton .07 .20
16 Kyle Petty .15 .40
17 Darrell Waltrip .15 .40
18 Wally Dallenbach .07 .20
19 Bill Elliott .30 .75
20 Robert Pressley .07 .20
21 Joe Nemechek .07 .20
22 Derrike Cope .07 .20
23 Ward Burton .15 .40
24 Chad Little .07 .20
25 Mike Skinner .07 .20
26 Brett Bodine .07 .20
27 Hut Stricklin .07 .20
28 Dave Marcis .15 .40
29 Ken Schrader .07 .20
30 Steve Grissom .07 .20
31 Robby Gordon RC .25 .60
32 Kenny Wallace .07 .20
33 Bobby Hillin, Jr. .07 .20
34 Jimmy Spencer .07 .20
35 Dick Trickle .07 .20
36 John Andretti .07 .20
37 Steve Park RC 2.00 4.00
38 Jeff Burton .25 .60
39 Michael Waltrip .15 .40
40 Dale Jarrett .50 1.25
41 Mike McLaughlin .07 .20
42 Todd Bodine .07 .20
43 Bobby Labonte .50 1.25
44 Jeff Fuller .07 .20
45 Kyle Petty .15 .40
46 Jason Keller .07 .20
47 Mark Martin .60 1.50
48 Randy LaJoie .07 .20
49 Joe Nemechek .07 .20
50 Glenn Allen .07 .20
51 Jeff Gordon .75 2.00
52 Rusty Wallace .60 1.50
53 Dale Jarrett .50 1.25
54 Jeff Burton .25 .60
55 Dale Jarrett .50 1.25
56 Jeff Hammond .02 .10
57 Andy Petree .02 .10
58 Robbie Loomis .02 .10
59 Mike Beam .02 .10
60 Buddy Parrott .02 .10
61 Roger Penske .02 .10
62 Bill Davis .02 .10
63 Travis Carter .02 .10
64 Chuck Rider .02 .10
65 Felix Sabates .02 .10
66 Larry Hedrick .02 .10
67 Rusty Wallace's Car .25 .60
68 Dale Earnhardt's Car .50 1.25
69 Terry Labonte's Car .15 .40
70 Mark Martin's Car .25 .60
71 Brett Bodine's Car .02 .10
72 Bobby Labonte's Car .15 .40
73 Jimmy Spencer's Car .02 .10
74 Jeff Gordon's Car .30 .75
75 Mike Skinner's Car .02 .10
76 Robby Gordon's Car .15 .40
77 Wally Dallenbach's Car .02 .10
78 Kyle Petty's Car .07 .20
79 Dale Jarrett's Car .15 .40
80 Bill Elliott's Car .15 .40
81 Checklist .02 .10
82 Checklist .02 .10
P1 Dale Jarrett Promo .60 1.50
P2 Jeff Gordon Promo 1.00 2.50

1997 Viper Black Racer

COMPLETE SET (82) 50.00 100.00
*BLACK RACERS: 2.5X TO 6X HI COL.

1997 Viper Black Racer First Strike

COMP.FIRST STRIKE (82) 75.00 150.00
*FIRST STRIKE: .5X TO 1.2X BASIC INSERTS

1997 Viper First Strike

COMPLETE SET (82) 12.00 30.00
*FIRST STRIKE: .5X TO 1.2X BASE CARDS

1997 Viper Anaconda Jumbos

This 13-card insert set features oversized cards featuring the top stars of the Winston Cup circuit. The cards were randomly inserted as chiptoppers at a ratio of one per two hobby boxes.

COMPLETE SET (13) 50.00 100.00
A1 Terry Labonte 2.50 6.00
A2 Jeff Gordon 8.00 20.00
A3 Dale Jarrett 5.00 12.00
A4 Bobby Labonte 5.00 12.00
A5 Dale Earnhardt 12.50 30.00
A6 Rusty Wallace 6.00 15.00
A7 Darrell Waltrip 1.50 4.00
A8 Joe Nemechek .75 2.00
A9 Jeremy Mayfield 1.50 4.00
A10 Bill Elliott 3.00 8.00
A11 Jeff Burton 2.50 6.00
A12 Mark Martin 6.00 15.00
A13 Kyle Petty 1.50 4.00

1997 Viper Cobra

This 10-card insert set is highlighted by micro-etched cards that are die cut. The cards were randomly inserted in hobby packs at a ratio of 1:24.

COMPLETE SET (10) 20.00 50.00
COMP.FIRST STRIKE (10) 50.00 100.00
*FIRST STRIKE: .5X TO 1.2X BASIC INSERTS
C1 Dale Earnhardt 8.00 20.00
C2 Jeff Gordon 4.00 10.00
C3 Bobby Labonte 2.50 6.00
C4 Terry Labonte 1.25 3.00
C5 Rusty Wallace 3.00 8.00
C6 Bill Elliott 1.50 4.00
C7 Sterling Marlin 1.25 3.00
C8 Mark Martin 3.00 8.00
C9 Dale Jarrett 2.50 6.00
C10 Kyle Petty .75 2.00

1997 Viper Diamondback

The 10-card insert set features a patch of simulated rattlesnake skin next to the picture of the driver on the fronts of the cards. The First Strike version of these cards were inserted into specially marked boxes of Viper First Strike. The cards were randomly inserted in hobby and First Strike packs at a ratio of 1:48 and inserted in retail packs at a ratio of 1:30.

COMPLETE SET (10) 60.00 120.00
COMP.FIRST STRIKE (10) 75.00 150.00
*FIRST STRIKE: .5X TO 1.2X BASIC INSERTS
DB1 Jeff Gordon 10.00 25.00
DB2 Dale Jarrett 6.00 15.00
DB3 Bobby Labonte 6.00 15.00
DB4 Rusty Wallace 8.00 20.00
DB5 Bill Elliott 4.00 10.00
DB6 Jeff Burton 3.00 8.00
DB7 Mark Martin 8.00 20.00
DB8 Dale Earnhardt 15.00 40.00
DB9 Mike Skinner 1.00 2.50
DB10 Robby Gordon 3.00 8.00

1997 Viper Diamondback Authentic

This 10-card insert set features authentic diamondback rattlesnake skin attached to each card. The First Strike version of these cards were inserted into specially marked boxes of Viper First Strike. There are four different versions of each card: Western, Eastern, Western First Strike and Eastern First Strike. The cards were randomly inserted in hobby and First Strike packs at a ratio of 1:96 and inserted in retail packs at a ratio of 1:90.

COMPLETE SET (10) 100.00 250.00
COMP.FIRST STRIKE (10) 200.00 400.00
*FIRST STRIKE: .5X TO 1.2X BASIC INSERTS
COMP.EASTERN SET (10) 250.00 500.00
*EASTERN DIAM: .5X TO 1.2X BASIC INSERTS
COMP.EASTERN FS (10) 300.00 600.00
*EAST.FIRST STRIKE: .8X TO 2X BASIC INS.
DBA1 Jeff Gordon 15.00 40.00
DBA2 Dale Jarrett 8.00 20.00
DBA3 Bobby Labonte 8.00 20.00
DBA4 Rusty Wallace 10.00 25.00
DBA5 Bill Elliott 8.00 20.00
DBA6 Jeff Burton 6.00 15.00
DBA7 Mark Martin 10.00 25.00
DBA8 Dale Earnhardt 25.00 60.00
DBA9 Mike Skinner 5.00 12.00
DBA10 Robby Gordon 6.00 15.00

1997 Viper King Cobra

This 10-card insert set features oversized, die-cut cards portraiting the top stars of the Winston Cup circuit. The cards were randomly inserted as chiptoppers at a ratio of one per two First Strike boxes.

COMPLETE SET (10) 75.00 150.00
KC1 Dale Earnhardt 20.00 50.00
KC2 Jeff Gordon 10.00 25.00
KC3 Bobby Labonte 6.00 15.00
KC4 Terry Labonte 3.00 8.00
KC5 Rusty Wallace 8.00 20.00
KC6 Bill Elliott 4.00 10.00
KC7 Sterling Marlin 3.00 8.00
KC8 Mark Martin 8.00 20.00
KC9 Dale Jarrett 6.00 15.00
KC10 Kyle Petty 2.00 5.00

1997 Viper Sidewinder

This 16-card insert set features stars from Winston Cup series on die-cut cards. The First Strike version of these cards were inserted into specially marked boxes of Viper First Strike. The cards were randomly inserted in hobby, First Strike and retail packs at a ratio of 1:6.

COMPLETE SET (16) 15.00 40.00
COMP.FIRST STRIKE (10) 20.00 50.00
*FIRST STRIKE: .5X TO 1.2X BASIC INSERTS
S1 Terry Labonte 1.50 4.00
S2 Jeff Gordon 5.00 12.00
S3 Johnny Benson 1.00 2.50
S4 Ward Burton 1.00 2.50
S5 Bobby Hamilton .50 1.25
S6 Ricky Craven .50 1.25
S7 Michael Waltrip 1.00 2.50
S8 Bobby Labonte 3.00 8.00
S9 Dale Jarrett 3.00 8.00
S10 Bill Elliott 2.00 5.00
S11 Rusty Wallace 4.00 10.00
S12 Jimmy Spencer .50 1.25
S13 Sterling Marlin 1.50 4.00
S14 Kyle Petty 1.00 2.50
S15 Ken Schrader .50 1.25
S16 Robby Gordon 1.50 4.00

1997 Viper Snake Eyes

This 12-card insert set features stars from Winston Cup series on horizontal cards. The First Strike version of these cards were inserted into specially marked boxes of Viper First Strike. The cards were randomly inserted in hobby, First Strike and retail packs at a ratio of 1:12.

COMPLETE SET (12) 25.00 60.00
COMP.FIRST STRIKE (12) 40.00 80.00
*FIRST STRIKE: .5X TO 1.2X BASIC INSERTS
SE1 Dale Earnhardt 10.00 25.00
SE2 Jeff Gordon 6.00 15.00
SE3 Dale Jarrett 4.00 10.00
SE4 Bobby Labonte 4.00 10.00
SE5 Jimmy Spencer .60 1.50
SE6 Bill Elliott 2.50 6.00
SE7 Terry Labonte 2.00 5.00
SE8 Rusty Wallace 5.00 12.00
SE9 Jeff Burton 2.00 5.00
SE10 Mark Martin 5.00 12.00
SE11 Brett Bodine .60 1.50
SE12 Sterling Marlin 2.00 5.00

1996 Visions

The 1996 Classic Visions set consists of 150 standard-size cards. The fronts feature full-bleed color action player photos. The player's position and name are presented in blue foil, while the Classic logo and set title "96 Visions" are stamped in gold foil. The back carries a second color photo, college statistics, biography, and a player fact.

COMPLETE SET (150) 6.00 15.00
108 Dale Earnhardt's Car .30 .75
109 Dale Jarrett .20 .50
110 Mark Martin .25 .60
111 Ernie Irvan .08 .25
112 Ricky Rudd .08 .25
113 Bobby Labonte .20 .50
114 Rusty Wallace's Car .15 .40
115 Michael Waltrip .08 .25
116 Sterling Marlin .15 .40
117 Dick Trickle .05 .15
118 John Andretti .05 .15
119 Darrell Waltrip .08 .25
120 Kyle Petty .08 .25
124 Dale Earnhardt .75 2.00
127 Mark Martin .25 .60

1996 Visions Signings

The 1996 Visions Signings set consists of 100 standard-size cards. The fronts feature full-bleed color action player photos. The player's position and name are stamped in prismatic foil along with the Classic logo and set title "96 Visions Signings." This set contains standouts from five sports grouped together in this order: basketball, football, hockey, baseball and racing. Cards were distributed in six-card packs. Release date was June 1996. The main allure to this product, in addition to the conventional inserts, were autographed memorabilia redemption cards inserted one per 10 packs.

COMPLETE SET (100) 6.00 15.00
88 Dale Jarrett .20 .50
89 Mark Martin .25 .60
90 Ernie Irvan .08 .25
91 Ricky Rudd .15 .40
92 Bobby Labonte .20 .50
93 Michael Waltrip .08 .25
94 Sterling Marlin .15 .40
95 Dick Trickle .05 .15
96 Darrell Waltrip .08 .25
97 Kyle Petty .08 .25
98 John Andretti .05 .15
99 Rusty Wallace's Car .15 .40
100 Dale Earnhardt's Car .30 .75

1996 Visions Signings Artistry

This 10-card insert set was printed on thick 24-point stock. Cards were inserted at a rate of 1:60 Vision Signings packs.

COMPLETE SET (10) 20.00 50.00
3 Dale Earnhardt 5.00 12.00
9 Mark Martin 2.00 5.00

1996 Visions Signings Autographs Silver

Certified autographed cards were inserted in Visions Signings packs at an overall rate of 1:12. Some players signed only silver cards while others signed gold and silver foil cards. The Silver cards were individually serial numbered as noted below. We've listed the unnumbered cards alphabetically.

35 Ernie Irvan/265 2.50 6.00
42 Mark Martin/315 12.50 30.00
63 Ricky Rudd/285 6.00 15.00
74 Dick Trickle/285 2.00 5.00
78 Michael Waltrip/285 3.00 8.00

1992 Wheels Kyle Petty

This 14-card set features Kyle Petty and the Mello Yello team. The cards were packaged in a rack display blister with the Title Card appearing on the front of the package. There were 30,000 silver foil stamped sets made. The original suggested retail was $12. Each of the card backs featured artwork from Sam Bass. There was a gold parallel version of the set that was produced in a quantity of 12,000. The gold version originally retailed for $15.

COMPLETE SET (14) 2.50 6.00
*GOLD CARDS: 1X TO 2X SILVERS
1 Title Card .20 .50
2 Kyle Petty .30 .75
3 Felix Sabates .20 .50
4 Robin Pemberton .20 .50
5 Kyle Petty's Car .20 .50
6 Kyle Petty .30 .75
7 Kyle Petty .30 .75
8 Kyle Petty .30 .75
9 Kyle Petty .30 .75
10 Kyle Petty in Pits .20 .50
11 Kyle Petty's Car .20 .50
12 Kyle Petty's Car .20 .50
13 Kyle Petty .30 .75
14 Kyle Petty's Car Art .20 .50

1992 Wheels Dale Earnhardt Tribute Hologram

This single Dale Earnhardt holographic card comes in a snap-it deluxe card holder. It is packaged in a blister pack along with a AuthenTicket. There are four different versions; silver, gold, platinum and gold facsimile autographed. In each version the AuthenTicket is serial numbered.

1A Dale Earnhardt Facsimile Signature 6.00 15.00
1G Dale Earnhardt Gold 2.00 5.00
1P Dale Earnhardt Platinum 2.50 6.00
1S Dale Earnhardt Silver 2.00 5.00

1992 Wheels Bill Elliott Tribute Hologram

This single Bill Elliott holographic card comes in a snap-it deluxe card holder. It is packaged in a blister pack along with a AuthenTicket. There were three different versions: silver, gold, and platinum.

1G Bill Elliott Gold 1.25 3.00
1P Bill Elliott Platinum 1.50 4.00
1S Bill Elliott Silver 1.25 3.00

1992 Wheels Harry Gant Tribute Hologram

This single Harry Gant holographic card comes in a snap-it deluxe card holder. It is packaged in a blister pack along with a AuthenTicket. There are four different versions; silver, gold, platinum and silver facsimile autographed.

1A Harry Gant Facsimile Autograph 4.00 10.00
1G Harry Gant Gold 1.25 3.00
1P Harry Gant Platinum 1.50 4.00
1S Harry Gant Silver 1.25 3.00

1992 Wheels Rusty Wallace

This 14-card set features Rusty Wallace and the Miller Genuine Draft team. The cards were packaged in a rack display blister with the Title Card appearing on the front of the package. There were 35,000 silver foil stamped sets made. The original suggested retail was $12. Each of the card backs featured artwork from Tim Bruce. There was a gold parallel version of the set that was produced in a quantity of 15,000. The gold set originally retailed for $15.

COMPLETE SET (14) 3.00 8.00
*GOLD CARDS: 1X TO 2X SILVERS
1 Title Card .30 .75
2 Rusty Wallace .40 1.00
3 Roger Penske .30 .75
4 Buddy Parrott .30 .75
5 Rusty Wallace's Car .30 .75
6 Rusty Wallace .40 1.00
7 Bill Wilburn .30 .75
8 Rusty Wallace w Crew .30 .75
9 Rusty Wallace Mike Wallace Kenny Wallace .40 1.00
10 Rusty Wallace .40 1.00
11 Rusty Wallace .40 1.00
12 Rusty Wallace .40 1.00
13 Rusty Wallace .40 1.00
14 Rusty Wallace Art .30 .75

1993 Wheels Mom-n-Pop's Dale Earnhardt

The 1993 Dale Earnhardt Mom-n-Pop's set was produced by Wheels and features photos of Dale's wins during the first half of 1993. The cards were packed one card and one cover card per cello pack in various ham, biscuit and sandwich products. A coupon was included as well offering complete sets and uncut sheets of previous year's sets.

COMPLETE SET (6) 6.00 12.00
COMMON CARD (1-6) 1.00 2.50

1993 Wheels Rookie Thunder Promos

This Promo set previews the 1993 Wheels Rookie Thunder release. The cards are numbered as a group and are often sold as complete sets.

COMPLETE SET (5) 5.00 12.00
P1 Richard Petty .75 2.00
P2 Jeff Gordon 2.50 6.00
P3 Kenny Wallace .40 1.00
P4 Bobby Labonte 1.25 3.00
P5 Davey Allison 1.25 3.00

1993 Wheels Rookie Thunder

This 100-card set features Rookie of the Year drivers from 1958-1993. The cards were printed on 24-pt stock and feature UV coating. The cards were packaged eight card per pack, 30 packs per box and 20 boxes per case.

COMPLETE SET (100) 6.00 15.00
1 Shorty Rollins .01 .05
2 Richard Petty .10 .30
3 David Pearson .02 .10
4 Woodie Wilson .01 .05
5 Tom Cox .01 .05
6 Billy Wade .01 .05
7 Doug Cooper .01 .05
8 Sam McQuagg .01 .05
9 James Hylton .01 .05
10 Donnie Allison .02 .10
11 Dick Brooks .01 .05
12 Bill Dennis .01 .05
13 Walter Ballard .01 .05
14 Larry Smith .01 .05
15 Lennie Pond .01 .05
16 Earl Ross .01 .05
17 Bruce Hill .01 .05
18 Skip Manning .01 .05
19 Ricky Rudd .10 .30
20 Ronnie Thomas .01 .05
21 Jody Ridley .02 .10
22 Ron Bouchard .01 .05
23 Geoff Bodine .02 .10
24 Sterling Marlin .15 .40
25 Rusty Wallace .25 .60
26 Ken Schrader .02 .10
27 Alan Kulwicki .10 .30
28 Davey Allison .20 .50
29 Ken Bouchard .02 .10
30 Dick Trickle .02 .10
31 Jimmy Hensley .02 .10
32 Jeff Gordon CRC .50 1.25
33 Bobby Labonte .20 .50
34 Kenny Wallace .02 .10
35 Rich Bickle .02 .10
36 Joe Nemechek .02 .10
37 Jeff Gordon .50 1.25
38 Ricky Craven .07 .20
39 Hermie Sadler RC .02 .10
40 Tim Fedewa .02 .10
41 Joe Bessey .02 .10
42 Roy Payne .01 .05
43 Nathan Buttke .01 .05
44 Ricky Rudd .10 .30
45 Geoff Bodine .02 .10
46 Rusty Wallace .25 .60
47 Ken Schrader .02 .10
48 Alan Kulwicki .07 .20
49 Davey Allison .20 .50
50 Jeff Gordon .50 1.25
51 Jeff Gordon .50 1.25
52 Bobby Labonte .20 .50
53 Kenny Wallace .02 .10
54 Kenny Wallace .02 .10
55 Dick Brooks .01 .05
56 Davey Allison .20 .50
57 Alan Kulwicki .10 .30
58 Alan Kulwicki .10 .30
59 Alan Kulwicki .10 .30
60 Rusty Wallace's Car .07 .20
61 Richard Petty .10 .30
62 Jeff Gordon w/Car .50 1.25
63 Kenny Wallace .02 .10
64 Bobby Labonte .20 .50
65 Rusty Wallace .25 .60
66 Rusty Wallace .25 .60
67 Rusty Wallace .25 .60
68 Rusty Wallace .25 .60
69 Hermie Sadler RC .02 .10
70 Jeff Gordon .50 1.25
71 Jeff Gordon .50 1.25
72 Bobby Labonte .20 .50
73 Bobby Labonte .20 .50
74 Kenny Wallace .02 .10
75 Kenny Wallace .02 .10
76 Ricky Craven .07 .20
77 Joe Nemechek .02 .10
78 Bobby Labonte .20 .50
79 Richard Petty .10 .30
80 Richard Petty .10 .30
81 Bobby Labonte .20 .50
82 Jeff Gordon .50 1.25
83 Kenny Wallace .02 .10
84 Davey Allison .20 .50
85 Davey Allison .20 .50
86 Alan Kulwicki .07 .20
87 Rusty Wallace .25 .60
88 Ricky Rudd .10 .30
89 Ricky Rudd .10 .30
90 Rusty Wallace .25 .60
91 Geoff Bodine .02 .10
92 Bobby Labonte .20 .50
93 Jeff Gordon's Car .25 .60
94 Bobby Labonte in Pits .07 .20
95 Richard Petty David Pearson Cars .07 .20
96 Richard Petty .10 .30
97 Jeff Gordon .50 1.25
98 Jeff Gordon Ken Schrader .50 1.25
99 Richard Petty .10 .30
100 Davey Allison .20 .50

1993 Wheels Rookie Thunder Platinum

COMPLETE SET (100) 15.00 40.00
*PLATINUM: 1X TO 2.5X BASIC CARDS

1993 Wheels Rookie Thunder SPs

This seven-card insert set features some of the top names in NASCAR history. The cards are similar in design to the base set cards but with the only visable difference being on the bottom front of the cards is a lighting strike background instead of the blue marblized background of the regular cards. The SP cards could be found one per box.

COMPLETE SET (7) 10.00 25.00
SP1 Terry Labonte 1.25 3.00
SP2 Davey Allison B.Allison 2.00 5.00
SP3 Davey Allison 2.00 5.00
SP4 Alan Kulwicki 1.25 3.00
SP5 Alan Kulwicki 1.25 3.00
SP6 Richard Petty 1.25 3.00
SP7 Richard Petty 1.25 3.00

1994 Wheels Harry Gant Promos

This Promo set was produced to advertise the 1994 Wheels Harry Gant set. The cards are individually numbered and often sold as a set of five.

COMPLETE SET (5) 1.50 4.00
P1 Harry Gant First Daytona Race .40 1.00
P2 Harry Gant Rookie Contender .40 1.00
P3 Harry Gant Staying Focused .40 1.00
P4 Harry Gant All Business .40 1.00
P5 Harry Gant Harley Harry .40 1.00

1994 Wheels Harry Gant

This 80-card set pays tribute to racing great Harry Gant. The cards are a retrospective of Harry's career, plus the last 15 cards in the set are of other racing personalities holding a sign "I love Harry." The cards were packaged six cards per pack, 24 packs per box and 20 boxes per case. There were 1,500 cases produced. Randomly inserted in boxes were a 4" X 6" Signature card and a 4" X 6" Signature Hologram card. There were 3,300 of the Signature card produced and 1,000 of the Signature Hologram card produced. The odds of finding the Signature card was one in nine boxes. The odds of finding the Signature Hologram card was one in 30 boxes. Five promo cards were produced as well (numbers P1-P5).

COMPLETE SET (80) 5.00 12.00
1 Harry Gant .10 .25
2 Harry Gant .10 .25
3 Harry Gant .10 .25
4 Harry Gant .10 .25
5 Harry Gant .10 .25
6 Harry Gant .10 .25
7 Harry Gant's Bike .07 .20
8 Harry Gant's Car .07 .20
9 Harry Gant .10 .25
10 Harry Gant .10 .25
11 Harry Gant .10 .25
12 Harry Gant D.Trickle .10 .25
13 Harry Gant .10 .25
14 Harry Gant .10 .25
15 Harry Gant .10 .25
16 Harry Gant .10 .25
17 Harry Gant .10 .25
18 Harry Gant .10 .25
19 Harry Gant .10 .25
20 Harry Gant .10 .25
21 Harry Gant Ned Jarrett .10 .25
22 Harry Gant Peggy Gant .10 .25
23 Harry Gant .10 .25
24 Harry Gant Hal Needham Burt Reynolds .10 .25
25 Harry Gant Hal Needham .10 .25
26 Harry Gant Hal Needham .10 .25
27 Harry Gant .10 .25
28 Harry Gant .10 .25
29 Harry Gant w Car .10 .25
30 Harry Gant Donna Gant Debbie Gant .10 .25
31 Harry Gant Peggy Gant .10 .25
32 Harry Gant .10 .25
33 Harry Gant .10 .25
34 Harry Gant .10 .25
35 Harry Gant .10 .25
36 Harry Gant Peggy Gant .10 .25
37 Harry Gant .10 .25
38 Harry Gant .10 .25
39 Harry Gant .10 .25
40 Harry Gant .10 .25
41 Harry Gant Peggy Gant .10 .25
42 Harry Gant .10 .25
43 Harry Gant .10 .25
44 Harry Gant .10 .25
45 Harry Gant .10 .25
46 Harry Gant .10 .25
47 Harry Gant .10 .25
48 Harry Gant Peggy Gant .10 .25
49 Harry Gant .10 .25
50 Harry Gant .10 .25
51 Harry Gant .10 .25
52 Harry Gant .10 .25
53 Harry Gant .10 .25
54 Harry Gant .10 .25
55 Harry Gant .10 .25
56 Harry Gant .10 .25
57 Harry Gant .10 .25
58 Harry Gant .10 .25
59 Harry Gant .10 .25
60 Harry Gant .10 .25
61 Harry Gant .10 .25
62 Harry Gant .10 .25
63 Harry Gant .10 .25
64 Harry Gant .10 .25
65 Harry Gant .10 .25
66 Jeff Gordon .75 2.00
67 Ernie Irvan .15 .40
68 Sterling Marlin .25 .60
69 Derrike Cope .10 .25
70 Bobby Labonte .50 1.25
71 Larry Hedrick .07 .20
72 Benny Parsons .07 .20
73 Rusty Wallace .60 1.50
74 Mark Martin .60 1.50
75 Kyle Petty .15 .40
76 Ray Cooper .07 .20
77 Andy Petree .07 .20
78 Eddie Masencup .07 .20
79 Brian Buchauer .07 .20
80 Johnny Hayes .07 .20
1994 J.Gordon Harry Gant set 5.00 10.00
HGS1 H.Gant 4X6 AUTO/3300 6.00 15.00
NNO H.Gant 4X6 HOLO/1000 6.00 15.00

1994 Wheels Harry Gant Gold

COMPLETE GOLD SET (80) 15.00 30.00
*GOLDS: 1.5X TO 3X BASIC CARDS

1994 Wheels Harry Gant Down On The Farm

This five-card insert set gives a close look at Harry on his farm in Taylorsville, North Carolina. The cards are randomly inserted at a rate of one per box.

COMPLETE SET (5) 5.00 12.00
COMMON CARD (SP1-SP5) 1.00 3.00

1996 Wheels Dale Earnhardt Mom-n-Pop's

This three-card set features seven-time Winston Cup champion Dale Earnhardt. The cards were produced by Wheels and were inserted into Mom-n-Pop's products.

COMPLETE SET (3) 7.50 15.00
COMMON CARD (MPC1-MPC3) 2.50 5.00

1998 Wheels

The 1998 Wheels set was issued in one series totalling 100 cards. The set contains the topical subsets: NASCAR Winston Cup Drivers (1-30), NASCAR Winston Cup Cars (31-45), NASCAR Busch Series Drivers (46-59), NASCAR Busch Series Cars (60-63), NASCAR Craftsman Truck Series Drivers (64-68), NASCAR Winston Cup Crew Chiefs (69-75), NASCAR Winston Cup Owners (76-81), Daytona 500 Winners (82-90), and Team Members (91-100).

COMPLETE SET (100) 8.00 20.00
1 John Andretti .07 .20
2 Johnny Benson .15 .40
3 Geoff Bodine .07 .20
4 Todd Bodine .07 .20
5 Jeff Burton .25 .60
6 Ward Burton .15 .40
7 Ricky Craven .07 .20
8 Wally Dallenbach .07 .20
9 Dale Earnhardt 1.25 3.00
10 Bill Elliott .30 .75
11 Jeff Gordon .75 2.00
12 David Green .07 .20
13 Bobby Hamilton .07 .20
14 Ernie Irvan .15 .40
15 Kenny Irwin .15 .40
16 Dale Jarrett .50 1.25
17 Bobby Labonte .50 1.25
18 Terry Labonte .25 .60
19 Sterling Marlin .25 .60
20 Mark Martin .60 1.50
21 Jeremy Mayfield .15 .40
22 Ted Musgrave .07 .20
23 Joe Nemechek .07 .20
24 Steve Park .50 1.25
25 Ricky Rudd .25 .60
26 Ken Schrader .07 .20
27 Mike Skinner .07 .20
28 Jimmy Spencer .07 .20
29 Rusty Wallace .60 1.50
30 Michael Waltrip .15 .40
31 John Andretti's Car .02 .10
32 Johnny Benson's Car .02 .10
33 Jeff Burton's Car .07 .20
34 Dale Earnhardt's Car .50 1.25
35 Bill Elliott's Car .15 .40
36 Jeff Gordon's Car .30 .75
37 Kenny Irwin's Car .07 .20
38 Dale Jarrett's Car .15 .40
39 Bobby Labonte's Car .15 .40
40 Terry Labonte's Car .15 .40
41 Sterling Marlin's Car .07 .20
42 Mark Martin's Car .25 .60
43 Jeremy Mayfield's Car .07 .20
44 Ricky Rudd's Car .07 .20
45 Rusty Wallace's Car .25 .60
46 Jeff Burton .25 .60
47 Dale Earnhardt Jr. 1.25 3.00
48 Tim Fedewa .07 .20
49 Dale Jarrett .50 1.25
50 Jason Jarrett RC .07 .20
51 Jason Keller .07 .20
52 Randy LaJoie .07 .20
53 Mark Martin .60 1.50
54 Mike McLaughlin .07 .20
55 Joe Nemechek .07 .20
56 Elliott Sadler .15 .40
57 Hermie Sadler .07 .20
58 Tony Stewart RC 3.00 8.00
59 Michael Waltrip .15 .40
60 Dale Earnhardt Jr.'s Car .50 1.25
61 Randy LaJoie's Car .02 .10
62 Elliott Sadler's Car .02 .10
63 Tony Stewart's Car .75 2.00
64 Rich Bickle .07 .20
65 Mike Bliss .07 .20
66 Ron Hornaday .07 .20
67 Joe Ruttman .07 .20
68 Jack Sprague .07 .20
69 Ray Evernham .07 .20
70 Jimmy Fenning .02 .10
71 Andy Graves .02 .10
72 Jimmy Makar .02 .10
73 Larry McReynolds .02 .10
74 Todd Parrott .02 .10
75 Robin Pemberton .02 .10
76 Richard Childress .15 .40
77 Bill Elliott .30 .75
78 Joe Gibbs .15 .40
79 John Hendrick .02 .10
80 Jack Roush .07 .20
81 Ricky Rudd .25 .60
82 Geoff Bodine .07 .20
83 Dale Earnhardt 1.25 3.00
84 Bill Elliott .30 .75
85 Jeff Gordon .75 2.00
86 Ernie Irvan .15 .40
87 Dale Jarrett .50 1.25
88 Fred Lorenzen .07 .20
89 Sterling Marlin .25 .60
90 Richard Petty .25 .60
91 Craig Lund .02 .10
92 Chocolate Myers .02 .10
93 Jack Lewis .02 .10
94 Steve Muse .02 .10
95 Jerry Hailey .02 .10
96 Mike Moore .02 .10
97 David Rogers .02 .10
98 Larry McReynolds .02 .10
99 Dale Earnhardt's Car .50 1.25
100 Checklist .02 .10
P1 Mark Martin Promo 1.25 3.00
0 Mark Martin Las Vegas 15.00 40.00

1998 Wheels Golden

COMPLETE SET (100) 600.00 1000.00
*GOLDEN STARS: 15X TO 40X HI COL.
*GOLDEN RCs: 8X TO 20X

1998 Wheels 50th Anniversary

Randomly inserted in packs at a rate of one in 2, this 27-card insert set celebrates NASCAR's 50th anniversary. This "set within a set" shows off the most talented drivers and their cars in NASCAR Winston Cup racing. Each card is intricately die-cut and includes a customized micro-etched foil treatment.

COMPLETE SET (27) 12.00 30.00
A1 Johnny Benson .50 1.25
A2 Jeff Burton .75 2.00
A3 Dale Earnhardt 4.00 10.00
A4 Bill Elliott 1.00 2.50
A5 Jeff Gordon 2.50 6.00
A6 Kenny Irwin .50 1.25
A7 Dale Jarrett 1.50 4.00
A8 Bobby Labonte 1.50 4.00
A9 Terry Labonte .75 2.00
A10 Sterling Marlin .75 2.00
A11 Mark Martin 2.00 5.00
A12 Ricky Rudd .75 2.00
A13 Jimmy Spencer .25 .60
A14 Rusty Wallace 2.00 5.00
A15 Michael Waltrip .50 1.25
A16 Johnny Benson's Car .10 .30
A17 Jeff Burton's Car .25 .60
A18 Dale Earnhardt's Car 1.50 4.00
A19 Bill Elliott's Car .50 1.25
A20 Jeff Gordon's Car 1.00 2.50
A21 Kenny Irwin's Car .25 .60
A22 Dale Jarrett's Car .50 1.25
A23 Bobby Labonte's Car .50 1.25
A24 Terry Labonte's Car .50 1.25
A25 Sterling Marlin's Car .25 .60
A26 Mark Martin's Car .75 2.00
A27 Rusty Wallace's Car .75 2.00

1998 Wheels Autographs

Randomly inserted in packs at a rate of one in 240, this 14-card insert set features autographs from top NASCAR drivers and aspiring rookies. No more than 200 individually numbered and autographed cards were issued per driver.

COMPLETE SET (14) 400.00 750.00
1 Dale Earnhardt 200.00 400.00
2 Jeff Gordon/200 75.00 150.00
3 Dale Jarrett/200 25.00 60.00
4 Terry Labonte/150 20.00 50.00
5 Bobby Labonte/200 12.50 30.00
6 Jimmy Spencer/200 10.00 25.00
7 Jeff Burton/200 8.00 20.00
8 Geoff Bodine/200 6.00 15.00
9 Michael Waltrip/200 10.00 25.00
10 Ricky Craven/200 10.00 25.00
11 Ricky Rudd/200 10.00 25.00
12 Mike Skinner/200 6.00 15.00
13 Kenny Irwin/200 20.00 40.00
14 Johnny Benson/200 10.00 25.00

1998 Wheels Custom Shop

Randomly inserted in packs at the rate of one in 192, redemption cards for this set allowed the collector to customize his own card by selecting one of three fronts and three backs for each card. The collector then received his custom-made card by return mail with his chosen front and back selection.

COMPLETE SET (3) 40.00 80.00
*PRIZE CARDS: .4X TO 1X BASIC INSERTS
CSDJ Dale Jarrett 10.00 25.00
CSJG Jeff Gordon 15.00 40.00
CSRW Rusty Wallace 12.50 30.00

1998 Wheels Double Take

Randomly inserted in packs at a rate of one in 72, this 9-card insert set is a first-time offer that features technology that allows you to change the exposure of the card front. Watch your favorite NASCAR Winston Cup driver magically transform into his NASCAR ride.

COMPLETE SET (9) 75.00 150.00
E1 Jeff Burton 2.50 6.00
E2 Dale Earnhardt 12.50 30.00
E3 Bill Elliott 3.00 8.00
E4 Jeff Gordon 8.00 20.00
E5 Dale Jarrett 5.00 12.00
E6 Bobby Labonte 5.00 12.00
E7 Terry Labonte 2.50 6.00
E8 Mark Martin 6.00 15.00
E9 Rusty Wallace 6.00 15.00

1998 Wheels Green Flags

Randomly inserted in packs at a rate of one in 8, this 18-card insert set showcases NASCAR's fiercest cars in an etched, all-foil, emerald green foil set.

COMPLETE SET (18) 25.00 60.00
GF1 John Andretti's Car .60 1.50
GF2 Johnny Benson's Car .60 1.50
GF3 Jeff Burton's Car 1.25 3.00
GF4 Dale Earnhardt's Car 8.00 20.00
GF5 Bill Elliott's Car 2.50 6.00
GF6 Jeff Gordon's Car 5.00 12.00
GF7 Bobby Hamilton's Car .60 1.50
GF8 Kenny Irwin's Car 1.25 3.00
GF9 Dale Jarrett's Car 2.50 6.00
GF10 Bobby Labonte's Car 2.50 6.00

Terry Labonte's Car 2.50 6.00
Sterling Marlin's Car 1.25 3.00
Mark Martin's Car 4.00 10.00
Ricky Rudd's Car 1.25 3.00
Mike Skinner's Car .60 1.50
Jimmy Spencer's Car .60 1.50
Rusty Wallace's Car 4.00 10.00
Michael Waltrip's Car .60 1.50

1998 Wheels Jackpot

...mly inserted in packs at a rate of one in 12, ...-card insert set recognizes NASCAR's ...on Cup's biggest winners over the past five ... on embossed all-foil technology.

...PLETE SET (9) 15.00 40.00
...le Earnhardt 8.00 20.00
...ll Elliott 2.00 5.00
...ff Gordon 5.00 12.00
...le Jarrett 3.00 8.00
...bby Labonte 3.00 8.00
...rry Labonte 1.50 4.00
...remy Mayfield 1.00 2.50
...ky Rudd 1.50 4.00
...sty Wallace 4.00 10.00

1999 Wheels

...00 card set featuring all foil stamping ...sts of the following subsets: 37-54 Busch ...s, 55-72 Winston Cup cars, 73-81 Teams, ...' Crew Chiefs, 88-93 Truck Series drivers, ...0 Top Prospects.

...PLETE SET (100) 10.00 25.00
...n Andretti .07 .20
...nny Benson .15 .40
...ffrey Bodine .07 .20
... Burton .25 .60
...rd Burton .15 .40
...rike Cope .07 .20
...ny Wallace .07 .20
...lly Dallenbach .07 .20
...e Earnhardt 1.25 3.00
...ll Elliott .30 .75
...avid Green .07 .20
...ff Gordon .75 2.00
...obby Hamilton .07 .20
...nie Irvan .15 .40
...enny Irwin .15 .40
...ale Jarrett .50 1.25
...obby Labonte .50 1.25
...erry Labonte .25 .60
...evin Lepage .07 .20
...had Little .15 .40
...erling Marlin .25 .60
...ark Martin .60 1.50
...remy Mayfield .15 .40
...ed Musgrave .07 .20
...rry Nadeau .15 .40
...e Nemechek .07 .20
...teve Park .40 1.00
...cky Rudd .25 .60
...liott Sadler .15 .40
...en Schrader .07 .20
...ike Skinner .07 .20
...mmy Spencer .07 .20
...ony Stewart CRC 1.00 2.50
...usty Wallace .60 1.50
...arrell Waltrip .15 .40
...ichael Waltrip .15 .40
...asey Atwood BGN RC .40 1.00
...odd Bodine BGN .07 .20
...ale Earnhardt Jr. BGN 1.00 2.50
...m Fedewa BGN .07 .20
...eff Fuller BGN .07 .20
...eff Gordon BGN .75 2.00
...eff Green BGN .07 .20
...ave Blaney BGN RC .07 .20
...ason Keller BGN .07 .20
...att Kenseth BGN RC 2.50 6.00
...andy LaJoie BGN .07 .20
...ark Martin BGN .60 1.50
...ike McLaughlin BGN .07 .20
...on Sawyer BGN .07 .20
...mmy Spencer BGN .07 .20
52 Kevin Grubb BGN RC .07 .20
53 Mark Green BGN RC .07 .20
54 Glenn Allen BGN .07 .20
55 Rusty Wallace's Car .25 .60
56 Dale Earnhardt's Car .50 1.25
57 Terry Labonte's Car .15 .40
58 Mark Martin's Car .25 .60
59 Bobby Labonte's Car .15 .40
60 Jeff Gordon's Car .30 .75
61 Dale Jarrett's Car .15 .40
62 Bill Elliott's Car .15 .40
63 Jeff Burton's Car .07 .20
64 Derrike Cope's Car .02 .10
65 Dale Earnhardt Jr.'s Car .40 1.00
66 Mike Skinner's Car .02 .10
67 Joe Nemechek's Car .02 .10
68 Tony Stewart's Car .30 .75
69 Wally Dallenbach's Car .02 .10
70 Ricky Rudd's Car .07 .20
71 Chad Little's Car .07 .20
72 Jeff Gordon's Car .30 .75
73 Robin Pemberton TC .02 .10
74 Rusty Wallace TC .60 1.50
75 Roger Penske TC .02 .10
76 Jimmy Makar TC .02 .10
77 Bobby Labonte TC .50 1.25
78 Joe Gibbs TC .15 .40
79 Todd Parrott TC .02 .10
80 Dale Jarrett TC .50 1.25
81 Robert Yates TC .02 .10
82 Larry McReynolds TC .02 .10
83 Tony Furr TC .02 .10
84 Frank Stoddard TC .02 .10
85 Greg Zipadelli TC .02 .10
86 Jeff Hammond TC .02 .10
87 Sammy Johns TC .02 .10
88 Kevin Harvick CTS RC 4.00 10.00
89 Jay Sauter CTS RC .07 .20
90 Jack Sprague CTS .07 .20
91 Greg Biffle CTS RC 3.00 8.00
92 Mike Bliss CTS .07 .20
93 Mike Stefanik CTS .07 .20
94 Dave Blaney TP .07 .20
95 Tony Stewart .75 2.00
96 Dale Earnhardt Jr. TP 1.00 2.50
97 Elliott Sadler TP .15 .40
98 Matt Kenseth TP 2.00 5.00
99 Casey Atwood TP 1.25 3.00
100 Justin Labonte TP CL RC .07 .20
P1 Bobby Labonte Promo .75 2.00
P2 Jeff Gordon Promo 1.25 3.00

1999 Wheels Golden

COMPLETE SET (100) 400.00 800.00
*GOLDEN VETERANS: 20X TO 50X
*GOLDEN RCs: 10X TO 25X

1999 Wheels Autographs

Randomly inserted in packs at the rate of one in 240 these cards feature authentic autographs of leading NASCAR figures. Each driver signed a different number of cards. We have noted below the print run of all cards that were hand serial numbered on the backs. Additionally, some cards were also issued without serial numbering in the 2003 VIP Tin factory sets.

1 Glenn Allen/300 6.00 15.00
2 John Andretti/100 6.00 15.00
3 Johnny Benson/200 6.00 15.00
4 Jeff Burton/150 8.00 20.00
5 Derrike Cope/295 6.00 20.00
6 Dale Earnhardt Jr./75 75.00 150.00
7 Jeff Fuller/350 6.00 20.00
8 Jeff Gordon/75 75.00 150.00
9 Dale Jarrett/100 20.00 50.00
10 Bobby Labonte/250 12.00 30.00
11 Terry Labonte/250 15.00 40.00
12 Kevin Lepage/250 6.00 20.00
13 Chad Little/350 6.00 20.00
14 Mike McLaughlin/200 6.00 20.00
15 Mark Martin/100 30.00 60.00
16 Todd Parrott/500 8.00 20.00
17 Robin Pemberton 6.00 20.00
18 Robert Pressley/196 6.00 20.00
19 Ricky Rudd/100 10.00 25.00
20 Ken Schrader/199 10.00 25.00
21 Jimmy Spencer 8.00 20.00
22 Tony Stewart/350 20.00 40.00
23 Frank Stoddard 6.00 20.00
24 Michael Waltrip/200 10.00 25.00
25 Jeff Buice

1999 Wheels Circuit Breaker

Randomly inserted in packs at the rate of one in 24, this nine-card set of the top record-setters of the sport is printed on plastic and foil stamped.

COMPLETE SET (9) 25.00 60.00
CB1 Terry Labonte 1.25 3.00
CB2 Bobby Labonte 1.25 3.00
CB3 Dale Earnhardt 8.00 20.00
CB4 Mark Martin 1.25 3.00
CB5 Jeff Gordon 2.50 6.00
CB6 Ricky Rudd 1.00 2.50
CB7 Rusty Wallace 1.25 3.00
CB8 Dale Jarrett 1.25 3.00
CB9 Mark Martin 1.25 3.00

1999 Wheels Custom Shop

Randomly inserted in packs at the rate of one in 192, this redemption set was redesigned to let the collector choose the material used (paper, foil, or plastic) in addition to design.

COMPLETE SET (5) 75.00 175.00
*PRIZE CARDS: .4X TO 1X BASIC INSERTS
CS1 Bobby Labonte 10.00 25.00
CS2 Jeff Gordon 15.00 40.00
CS3 Dale Earnhardt Jr. 15.00 40.00
CS4 Mark Martin 12.50 30.00
CS5 Rusty Wallace 10.00 25.00

1999 Wheels Dialed In

Randomly inserted in packs at the rate of one in twelve, this all-foil, die-cut, micro-etched nine card set featured drivers who are among the best in the Winston Cup circuit.

COMPLETE SET (9) 25.00 60.00
DI1 Jeff Gordon 2.50 6.00
DI2 Rusty Wallace 1.25 3.00
DI3 Dale Earnhardt's Car 8.00 20.00
DI4 Dale Earnhardt Jr. 6.00 15.00
DI5 Terry Labonte 1.25 3.00
DI6 Mark Martin 1.25 3.00
DI7 Bobby Labonte 1.25 3.00
DI8 Dale Jarrett 1.25 3.00
DI9 Jeff Burton 1.25 3.00

1999 Wheels Flag Chasers Daytona Seven

Randomly inserted in packs at the rate of one in 565, this five-card set features progessive ratios for the different color flag swatches.

COMPLETE SET (5) 250.00 600.00
BLACK/WHITE/YELLOW PRICED BELOW
BLACK/WHITE/YELLOW ODDS 1:3424
BLACK/WHITE/YELLOW SERIAL #'D TO 69
GREEN/RED PRICED BELOW
GREEN/RED STATED ODDS 1:3634
RED/GREEN CARDS SER.#'D TO 65
*BLUE-YELLOW: 1X TO 2X BASIC INSERTS
BLUE-YELLOW STATED ODDS 1:5250
BLUE-YELLOW CARDS SER.#'D TO 45
*CHECKERED: .8X TO 2X BASIC INSERTS
CHECKERED STATED ODDS 1:6562
CHECKERED CARDS SERIAL #'D TO 36
DS1 Jeff Gordon 40.00 100.00
DS2 Dale Earnhardt 40.00 100.00
DS3 Rusty Wallace 30.00 80.00
DS4 Mark Martin 30.00 80.00
DS5 Terry Labonte 30.00 80.00

1999 Wheels High Groove

Randomly inserted in packs at the rate of one in eight, this nine card set pairs cards of famed tracks with the drivers who excel on those tracks.

COMPLETE SET (9) 12.50 30.00
HG1 Bobby Labonte 2.50 6.00
HG2 Ernie Irvan .75 2.00
HG3 Jeff Gordon 4.00 10.00
HG4 Dale Earnhardt's Car 2.50 6.00
HG5 Mark Martin 3.00 8.00
HG6 Rusty Wallace 3.00 8.00
HG7 Jeff Gordon 4.00 10.00
HG8 Dale Jarrett 2.50 6.00
HG9 Mark Martin 3.00 8.00

1999 Wheels Runnin and Gunnin

Inserted in packs at the rate of one per pack for the basic paper version and one in twelve packs for the foil version; this 36-card set features leading personalities from NASCAR.

COMPLETE SET (36) 12.50 30.00
COMP.FOIL SET (36) 100.00 200.00
*FOIL CARDS: 2.5X TO 6X BASIC INSERTS
RG1 Mark Martin 2.00 5.00
RG2 Rusty Wallace 2.00 5.00
RG3 Dale Earnhardt's Car 1.50 4.00
RG4 Terry Labonte .75 2.00
RG5 Dale Jarrett 1.50 4.00
RG6 Bill Elliott 1.00 2.50
RG7 Mike Skinner .25 .60
RG8 Bobby Labonte 1.50 4.00
RG9 Jeff Gordon 2.50 6.00
RG10 Michael Waltrip .50 1.25
RG11 Jeff Burton .75 2.00
RG12 Ernie Irvan .50 1.25
RG13 Dale Earnhardt Jr. 3.00 8.00
RG14 Ward Burton .50 1.25
RG15 Wally Dallenbach .25 .60
RG16 Ricky Rudd .75 2.00
RG17 Jeremy Mayfield .50 1.25
RG18 Tony Stewart 2.50 6.00
RG19 Johnny Benson .50 1.25
RG20 Geoffrey Bodine .25 .60
RG21 Derrike Cope .25 .60
RG22 Bobby Hamilton .25 .60
RG23 Matt Kenseth 1.25 3.00
RG24 Chad Little .50 1.25
RG24B Kevin Lepage .25 .60
RG25 Sterling Marlin .75 2.00
RG26 David Green .25 .60
RG27 Ted Musgrave .25 .60
RG28 Joe Nemechek .25 .60
RG29 Jeff Gordon 2.50 6.00
RG30 Ken Schrader .25 .60
RG31 Darrell Waltrip .50 1.25
RG32 John Andretti .25 .60
RG33 Jimmy Spencer .25 .60
RG34 Elliott Sadler .50 1.25
RG35 Kenny Irwin .50 1.25

2003 Wheels American Thunder

This 50-card set was released in May, 2003. These cards were found in 5-card hobby packs with 24 pack boxes with pack SRP of $5.99 and 4-card retail packs with 28 pack boxes with an SRP of $2.99.

COMPLETE SET (50) 12.50 25.00
WAX BOX HOBBY (24) 60.00 100.00
WAX BOX RETAIL (28) 50.00 100.00
1 John Andretti .15 .40
2 Jeff Burton .30 .75
3 Ward Burton .30 .75
4 Kurt Busch .50 1.25
5 Dale Earnhardt Jr. 1.50 4.00
6 Jeff Gordon 1.25 3.00
7 Jeff Green .15 .40
8 Kevin Harvick .75 2.00
9 Dale Jarrett .75 2.00
10 Jimmie Johnson 1.00 2.50
11 Matt Kenseth 1.00 2.50
12 Bobby Labonte .75 2.00
13 Terry Labonte .50 1.25
14 Sterling Marlin .50 1.25
15 Mark Martin 1.00 2.50
16 Jamie McMurray CRC 1.00 2.50
17 Ryan Newman 1.00 2.50
18 Steve Park .30 .75
19 Tony Stewart 1.00 2.50
20 Rusty Wallace .75 2.00
21 Michael Waltrip .30 .75
22 Jeff Gordon SS 1.25 3.00
23 Dale Jarrett SS .75 2.00
24 Bobby Labonte SS .75 2.00
25 Terry Labonte SS .50 1.25
26 Tony Stewart SS 1.00 2.50
27 Rusty Wallace SS .75 2.00
28 Bobby Labonte DT .75 2.00
29 Steve Park DT .30 .75
30 Ryan Newman DT 1.00 2.50
31 Dale Jarrett DT .75 2.00
32 Tony Stewart DT 1.00 2.50
33 Michael Waltrip DT .30 .75
34 Jimmie Johnson DT 1.00 2.50
35 Jeff Burton DT .30 .75
36 Mark Martin DT 1.00 2.50
37 Dale Earnhardt Jr. CC 1.50 4.00
38 Mark Martin CC 1.00 2.50
39 Michael Waltrip CC .30 .75
40 Matt Kenseth CC 1.00 2.50
41 Bobby Labonte CC .75 2.00
42 Ryan Newman CC 1.00 2.50
43 Jeff Gordon CC 1.25 3.00
44 Steve Park CC .30 .75
45 Ward Burton CC .30 .75
46 Dale Jr.'s Transporter .60 1.50
47 M.Waltrip's Transporter .10 .30
48 J.Johnson's Transporter .50 1.25
49 M.Martin's Transporter .50 1.25
50 D.Jarrett's Transporter CL .30 .75
P1 Jeff Gordon Promo 3.00 6.00

2003 Wheels American Thunder Born On

*BORN ON: 5X TO 12X BASIC CARDS

2003 Wheels American Thunder Holofoil

COMPLETE SET (50) 15.00 40.00
*HOLOFOIL: .8X TO 2X BASIC CARDS

2003 Wheels American Thunder Samples

*SAMPLES: 2X TO 5X BASE CARD HI

2003 Wheels American Thunder American Eagle

This 9-card set was randomly inserted in packs at a rate of one in 18. The feature foil etched cards of NASCAR's leading drivers. The cards carried an "AE" prefix for their card numbers.

COMPLETE SET (9) 20.00 40.00
*GOLDEN: 2.5X TO 6X AMERICAN EAGLE
STATED PRINT RUN 100 SERIAL #'d SETS
AE1 Rusty Wallace 2.50 6.00
AE2 Tony Stewart 3.00 8.00
AE3 Ryan Newman 3.00 8.00
AE4 Matt Kenseth 3.00 8.00
AE5 Jeff Gordon 4.00 10.00
AE6 Jimmie Johnson 3.00 8.00
AE7 Bobby Labonte 2.50 6.00
AE8 Kurt Busch 1.50 4.00
AE9 Ward Burton 1.00 2.50

2003 Wheels American Thunder American Muscle

This 11-card set was randomly inserted in packs at a rate of one in 12. The feature foil etched cards of NASCAR's leading drivers. The cards carried an "AM" prefix for their card numbers.

COMPLETE SET (11) 15.00 40.00
STATED ODDS 1:12
AM1 Dale Earnhardt Jr. 4.00 10.00
AM2 Jeff Gordon 3.00 8.00
AM3 Kevin Harvick 2.00 5.00
AM4 Jimmie Johnson 2.50 6.00
AM5 Bobby Labonte 2.00 5.00
AM6 Mark Martin 2.50 6.00
AM7 Ryan Newman 2.50 6.00
AM8 Steve Park .75 2.00
AM9 Tony Stewart 2.50 6.00
AM10 Rusty Wallace 2.00 5.00
AM11 Michael Waltrip .75 2.00

2003 Wheels American Thunder Cool Threads

This 8-card set was randomly inserted in packs. They feature swatches of shirtsworn by drivers during races. The cards carried a "CT" prefix for their card numbers and were serial numbered to 285.

STATED PRINT RUN 285 SERIAL #'d SETS
CT1 Jeff Burton 6.00 15.00
CT2 Kevin Harvick 8.00 20.00
CT3 Ryan Newman 6.00 15.00
CT4 Kenny Wallace 5.00 12.00
CT5 Mark Martin 8.00 20.00
CT6 Jeff Gordon 12.00 30.00
CT7 Dale Jarrett 6.00 15.00
CT8 Jamie McMurray 5.00 12.00

2003 Wheels American Thunder Dale Earnhardt Retrospective

This 9-card set featured cards with images of reprinted Dale Earnhardt Wheels cards on them. These cards were randoimly inserted in packs at a rate of one in 72.

COMMON EARNHARDT (AT1-AT9) 10.00 25.00
STATED ODDS 1:72
*FOIL: .8X TO 2X BASIC EARNHARDT
FOIL STATED PRINT RUN 250 SERIAL #'d SETS

2003 Wheels American Thunder Head to Toe

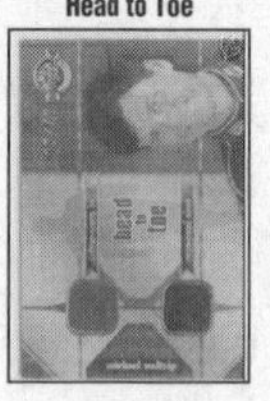

This 10-card set featured swatches of race-used hats and shoes. Each card was serial numbered to 40 and carried an "HT" prefix for its card number.

STATED PRINT RUN 40 SERIAL #'d SETS
HT1 Jeff Burton 20.00 50.00
HT2 Ricky Craven 20.00 50.00
HT3 Matt Kenseth 15.00 40.00
HT4 Sterling Marlin 20.00 50.00
HT5 Mark Martin 20.00 50.00
HT6 Mike Skinner 15.00 40.00
HT7 Tony Stewart 40.00 80.00
HT8 Rusty Wallace 20.00 50.00
HT9 Michael Waltrip 15.00 40.00
HT10 Joe Nemechek 15.00 40.00

2003 Wheels American Thunder Heads Up Goodyear

This 17-card set featured a swatch of a Goodyear hat worn during speedweeks at Daytona. Each card is serial numbered to 90 and features an "HUG" prefix on the card number.

STATED PRINT RUN 90 SERIAL #'d SETS
HUG1 Jeff Burton 10.00 25.00
HUG2 Robby Gordon 8.00 20.00
HUG3 Kevin Harvick 15.00 40.00
HUG4 Dale Jarrett 12.00 30.00
HUG5 Matt Kenseth 12.00 30.00
HUG6 Ryan Newman 12.00 30.00
HUG7 Steve Park 10.00 25.00
HUG8 Rusty Wallace 15.00 40.00
HUG9 Jeremy Mayfield 8.00 20.00
HUG10 Ward Burton 10.00 25.00
HUG11 Mark Martin 12.00 30.00
HUG12 Mike Skinner 8.00 20.00
HUG13 Dave Blaney 8.00 20.00
HUG14 Kurt Busch 10.00 25.00
HUG15 Ricky Rudd 10.00 25.00
HUG16 Ricky Craven 8.00 20.00
HUG17 Terry Labonte 12.00 30.00

2003 Wheels American Thunder Heads Up Manufacturer

This 34-card set featured a swatch of a Manufacturers hat worn during speedweeks at Daytona. Each card is serial numbered to 90 and features an "HUM" prefix on the card number.

STATED PRINT RUN 90 SERIAL #'d SETS
HUM1 John Andretti 8.00 20.00
HUM2 Brett Bodine 8.00 20.00
HUM3 Jeff Burton 10.00 25.00
HUM4 Jeff Gordon 25.00 60.00
HUM5 Robby Gordon 8.00 20.00
HUM6 Jeff Green 8.00 20.00
HUM7 Kevin Harvick 15.00 40.00
HUM8 Dale Jarrett 12.00 30.00
HUM9 Jimmie Johnson 20.00 50.00
HUM10 Matt Kenseth 12.00 30.00
HUM11 Bobby Labonte 12.00 30.00
HUM12 Jamie McMurray 10.00 25.00
HUM13 Casey Mears 8.00 20.00
HUM14 Jerry Nadeau 8.00 20.00
HUM15 Ryan Newman 12.00 30.00
HUM16 Steve Park 10.00 25.00
HUM17 Kyle Petty 10.00 25.00
HUM18 Elliott Sadler 8.00 20.00
HUM19 Rusty Wallace 15.00 40.00
HUM20 Jeremy Mayfield 8.00 20.00
HUM21 Tony Stewart 15.00 40.00
HUM22 Ward Burton 10.00 25.00
HUM23 Michael Waltrip 10.00 25.00
HUM24 Greg Biffle 10.00 25.00
HUM25 Mark Martin 15.00 40.00
HUM26 Sterling Marlin 12.00 30.00
HUM27 Kenny Wallace 8.00 20.00
HUM28 Mike Skinner 8.00 20.00
HUM29 Dave Blaney 8.00 20.00
HUM30 Kurt Busch 10.00 25.00
HUM31 Ricky Rudd 10.00 25.00
HUM32 Ricky Craven 8.00 20.00
HUM33 Terry Labonte 12.00 30.00
HUM34 Joe Nemechek 8.00 20.00

2003 Wheels American Thunder Heads Up Team

This 31-card set featured a swatch of a the driver's team hat worn during speedweeks at Daytona. Each card is serial numbered to either 60 or 90 and is noted below in the checklist and features an "HUT" prefix on the card number.

RANDOM INSERTS IN PACKS
HUT1 John Andretti/90 8.00 20.00
HUT2 Jeff Burton/90 10.00 25.00
HUT3 Jeff Gordon/60 30.00 80.00
HUT4 Robby Gordon/60 10.00 25.00
HUT5 Jeff Green/60 10.00 25.00
HUT6 Kevin Harvick/60 15.00 40.00
HUT7 Dale Jarrett/90 12.00 30.00
HUT8 Jimmie Johnson/90 20.00 50.00
HUT9 Matt Kenseth/90 15.00 40.00
HUT10 Bobby Labonte/60 15.00 40.00
HUT11 Jamie McMurray/60 12.00 30.00
HUT12 Casey Mears/60 10.00 25.00
HUT13 Ryan Newman/90 12.00 30.00
HUT14 Steve Park/90 10.00 25.00
HUT15 Kyle Petty/90 10.00 25.00
HUT16 Elliott Sadler/60 12.00 30.00
HUT17 Rusty Wallace/60 20.00 50.00
HUT18 Jeremy Mayfield/60 10.00 25.00
HUT19 Tony Stewart/60 15.00 40.00
HUT20 Ward Burton/90 10.00 25.00
HUT21 Michael Waltrip/60 12.00 30.00
HUT22 Greg Biffle/90 10.00 25.00
HUT23 Mark Martin/90 15.00 40.00
HUT24 Sterling Marlin/90 12.00 30.00
HUT25 Mike Skinner/60 10.00 25.00
HUT26 Dale Earnhardt Jr./60 30.00 80.00
HUT27 Dave Blaney/60 10.00 25.00
HUT28 Kurt Busch/60 12.00 30.00
HUT29 Ricky Rudd/90 10.00 25.00
HUT30 Terry Labonte/90 12.00 30.00
HUT31 Joe Nemechek/60 10.00 25.00

2003 Wheels American Thunder Heads Up Winston

This 34-card set featured a swatch of a Winston hat worn during speedweeks at Daytona. Each card is serial numbered to 90 and features an "HUW" prefix on the card number.

STATED PRINT RUN 90 SERIAL #'d SETS
HUW1 John Andretti 8.00 20.00
HUW2 Brett Bodine 8.00 20.00
HUW3 Jeff Burton 10.00 25.00
HUW4 Jeff Gordon 20.00 50.00
HUW5 Robby Gordon 8.00 20.00
HUW6 Jeff Green 8.00 20.00
HUW7 Kevin Harvick 15.00 40.00
HUW8 Dale Jarrett 15.00 40.00
HUW9 Jimmie Johnson 25.00 60.00
HUW10 Matt Kenseth 12.00 30.00
HUW11 Bobby Labonte 15.00 40.00
HUW12 Jamie McMurray 10.00 25.00
HUW13 Casey Mears 8.00 20.00
HUW14 Jerry Nadeau 10.00 25.00
HUW15 Ryan Newman 15.00 40.00
HUW16 Steve Park 10.00 25.00
HUW17 Kyle Petty 12.00 30.00
HUW18 Elliott Sadler 12.00 30.00
HUW19 Rusty Wallace 20.00 50.00
HUW20 Jeremy Mayfield 8.00 20.00
HUW21 Tony Stewart 20.00 50.00
HUW22 Ward Burton 10.00 25.00
HUW23 Michael Waltrip 12.00 30.00
HUW24 Greg Biffle 12.00 30.00
HUW25 Mark Martin 15.00 40.00
HUW26 Sterling Marlin 12.00 30.00

HUW27 Kenny Wallace 8.00 20.00
HUW28 Mike Skinner 8.00 20.00
HUW29 Dave Blaney 8.00 20.00
HUW30 Kurt Busch 10.00 25.00
HUW31 Ricky Rudd 10.00 25.00
HUW32 Ricky Craven 8.00 20.00
HUW33 Terry Labonte 15.00 40.00
HUW34 Joe Nemechek 8.00 20.00

2003 Wheels American Thunder Post Mark

This 18-card set was printed on clear plastic and was about the size of a postage stamp. They were inserted into packs at a rate of one in eight. These cards carried a "PM" prefix for their card numbers.

COMPLETE SET (18) 25.00 50.00
STATED ODDS 1:8
PM1 Jeff Burton .75 2.00
PM2 Ward Burton .75 2.00
PM3 Kurt Busch 1.25 3.00
PM4 Dale Earnhardt Jr. 4.00 10.00
PM5 Jeff Gordon 3.00 8.00
PM6 Jeff Green .40 1.00
PM7 Kevin Harvick 2.00 5.00
PM8 Dale Jarrett 2.00 5.00
PM9 Jimmie Johnson 2.50 6.00
PM10 Matt Kenseth 2.50 6.00
PM11 Bobby Labonte 2.00 5.00
PM12 Jamie McMurray 2.00 5.00
PM13 Mark Martin 2.50 6.00
PM14 Ryan Newman 2.50 6.00
PM15 Steve Park .75 2.00
PM16 Tony Stewart 2.50 6.00
PM17 Rusty Wallace 2.00 5.00
PM18 Michael Waltrip .75 2.00

2003 Wheels American Thunder Pushin Pedal

Randomly inserted in packs, these 14 cards featured swatches of race-used shoes. The cards were serial numbered to 285 with the exceptions of Robby Gordon of 300, Mike Skinner and Ricky Craven of 175.

UNLESS NOTED PRINT RUN 285 SETS
PP1 Jeff Burton 8.00 20.00
PP2 Jeff Gordon 20.00 50.00
PP3 Robby Gordon/300 8.00 20.00
PP4 Matt Kenseth 12.50 30.00
PP5 Mark Martin 12.50 30.00
PP6 Mike Skinner/175 8.00 20.00
PP7 Tony Stewart 15.00 40.00
PP8 Rusty Wallace 10.00 25.00
PP9 Michael Waltrip 8.00 20.00
PP10 Ricky Craven/175 8.00 20.00
PP11 Jimmie Johnson 15.00 40.00
PP12 Sterling Marlin 10.00 25.00
PP13 Terry Labonte 10.00 25.00
PP14 Joe Nemechek 6.00 15.00

2003 Wheels American Thunder Rookie Class

This 11-card set was interactive with the actual performance of the specified drivers. If the card was a winner it could be redeemed for a prize set.

COMPLETE SET (11) 10.00 25.00
RANDOM INSERTS IN PACKS
RC1 Ryan Newman WIN 3.00 8.00
RC2 Greg Biffle WIN 3.00 8.00
RC3 Jamie McMurray WIN 2.50 6.00
RC4 Casey Mears 1.00 2.50
RC5 Jack Sprague .60 1.50
RC6 Scott Riggs 1.00 2.50
RC7 Chad Blount .60 1.50
RC8 Coy Gibbs WIN 2.50 6.00
RC9 Damon Lusk WIN 1.50 4.00
RC10 Chase Montgomery .75 2.00
RC11 Regan Smith .60 1.50

2003 Wheels American Thunder Rookie Class Prizes

COMP.SET WINSTON CUP (5) 5.00 12.00
COMP.SET BUSCH SERIES (6) 4.00 10.00
*PRIZE FOIL: .25X TO .6X BASIC INSERTS
NNO Jamie McMurray Tire/600 8.00 20.00

2003 Wheels American Thunder Rookie Thunder

This 36-card set was randomly inserted in packs at a rate of one per pack. Each card carried a prefix of "RT" for the card number.

COMPLETE SET (36) 8.00 20.00
STATED ODDS 1 PER PACK
RT1 John Andretti .25 .60
RT2 Greg Biffle .50 1.25
RT3 Brett Bodine .25 .60
RT4 Jeff Burton .50 1.25
RT5 Ward Burton .50 1.25
RT6 Kurt Busch .75 2.00
RT7 Ricky Craven .25 .60
RT8 Dale Earnhardt Jr. 2.50 6.00
RT9 Jeff Gordon 2.00 5.00
RT10 Robby Gordon .25 .60
RT11 Jeff Green .25 .60
RT12 Kevin Harvick 1.25 3.00
RT13 Dale Jarrett 1.25 3.00
RT14 Jimmie Johnson 1.50 4.00
RT15 Matt Kenseth 1.50 4.00
RT16 Bobby Labonte 1.25 3.00
RT17 Terry Labonte .75 2.00
RT18 Sterling Marlin .75 2.00
RT19 Mark Martin 1.50 4.00
RT20 Casey Mears .50 1.25
RT21 Jamie McMurray 1.25 3.00
RT22 Jerry Nadeau .50 1.25
RT23 Joe Nemechek .25 .60
RT24 Ryan Newman 1.50 4.00
RT25 Steve Park .50 1.25
RT26 Kyle Petty .50 1.25
RT27 Ricky Rudd .75 2.00
RT28 Elliott Sadler .50 1.25
RT29 Ken Schrader .25 .60
RT30 Mike Skinner .25 .60
RT31 Jack Sprague .25 .60
RT32 Tony Stewart 1.50 4.00
RT33 Kenny Wallace .25 .60
RT34 Rusty Wallace 1.25 3.00
RT35 Michael Waltrip .50 1.25
RT36 Checklist .25 .60

2003 Wheels American Thunder Thunder Road

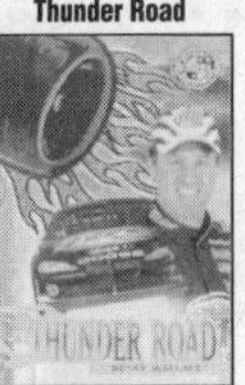

This 18-card set featured race-used tires incorporated into the card design. They were inserted in packs at a rate of one in 18. Each card carried a "TR" prefix in its card numbers.

COMPLETE SET (18) 75.00 150.00
STATED ODDS 1:18
TR1 Dale Earnhardt Jr. 10.00 25.00
TR2 Jeff Gordon 8.00 20.00
TR3 Tony Stewart 6.00 15.00
TR4 Rusty Wallace 5.00 12.00
TR5 Ryan Newman 6.00 15.00
TR6 Kurt Busch 4.00 10.00
TR7 Mark Martin 6.00 15.00
TR8 Jimmie Johnson 6.00 15.00
TR9 Matt Kenseth 6.00 15.00
TR10 Michael Waltrip 2.50 6.00
TR11 Steve Park 2.50 6.00
TR12 Jamie McMurray 5.00 12.00
TR13 Kevin Harvick 5.00 12.00
TR14 Bobby Labonte 5.00 12.00
TR15 Ward Burton 2.50 6.00
TR16 Robby Gordon 1.00 2.50
TR17 Jeff Green 1.00 2.50
TR18 Jeff Burton 2.50 6.00

2003 Wheels American Thunder Triple Hat

This 14-card set featured three swatches of hats that were worn during Daytona Speedweeks. The cards are serial numbered to 25.

STATED PRINT RUN 25 SERIAL #'d SETS
TH1 Steve Park 12.00 30.00
TH2 Rusty Wallace 15.00 40.00
TH3 Jeff Burton 15.00 40.00
TH4 Jamie McMurray 12.00 30.00
TH5 Michael Waltrip 15.00 40.00
TH6 Bobby Labonte 15.00 40.00
TH7 Jeff Gordon 60.00 100.00
TH8 Kevin Harvick 25.00 50.00
TH9 Jimmie Johnson 50.00 100.00
TH10 Dale Jarrett 25.00 50.00
TH11 Sterling Marlin 15.00 40.00
TH12 Tony Stewart 30.00 60.00
TH13 Ricky Rudd 12.00 30.00
TH14 Greg Biffle 15.00 40.00

2004 Wheels American Thunder

This 90-card set was released in September, 2004. These cards were found in 5-card hobby packs with 20 pack boxes with pack SRP of $5.99 and 4-card retail packs with 28 pack boxes with an SRP of $2.99. There was also a zero card of Air Force One in honor of President George W. Bush's trip to the Daytona 500 in February. The stated odds for this card was 1 in 72 packs.

COMPLETE SET (90) 15.00 40.00
WAX BOX HOBBY (20) 60.00 120.00
1 Jeff Burton .30 .75
2 Kurt Busch .50 1.25
3 Ricky Craven .20 .50
4 Dale Earnhardt Jr. 1.25 3.00
5 Jeff Gordon 1.25 3.00
6 Robby Gordon .20 .50
7 Jeff Green .20 .50
8 Kevin Harvick .75 2.00
9 Dale Jarrett .60 1.50
10 Jimmie Johnson 1.00 2.50
11 Kasey Kahne CRC 1.50 4.00
12 Matt Kenseth 1.00 2.50
13 Bobby Labonte .60 1.50
14 Terry Labonte .50 1.25
15 Sterling Marlin .50 1.25
16 Mark Martin .75 2.00
17 Jeremy Mayfield .20 .50
18 Jamie McMurray .50 1.25
19 Casey Mears .20 .50
20 Joe Nemechek .20 .50
21 Ryan Newman 1.00 2.50
22 Ricky Rudd .50 1.25
23 Elliott Sadler .30 .75
24 Tony Stewart .75 2.00
25 Brian Vickers CRC .60 1.50
26 Rusty Wallace .60 1.50
27 Michael Waltrip .30 .75
28 Brendan Gaughan CRC .30 .75
29 Scott Riggs CRC .30 .75
30 Scott Wimmer CRC .30 .75
31 Jimmie Johnson's Rig Rt. 66 .50 1.25
32 Sterling Marlin's Rig Rt. 66 .20 .50
33 Dale Earnhardt Jr.'s Rig Rt. 66 .50 1.25
34 Jeff Gordon's Rig Rt. 66 .50 1.25
35 Rusty Wallace's Rig Rt. 66 .30 .75
36 Michael Waltrip's Rig Rt. 66 .20 .50
37 Matt Kenseth AS 1.00 2.50
38 Ryan Newman AS 1.00 2.50
39 Tony Stewart AS .75 2.00
40 Michael Waltrip AS .30 .75
41 Dale Earnhardt Jr. AS 1.25 3.00
42 Jeff Gordon AS 1.25 3.00
43 Kasey Kahne AS 1.25 3.00
44 Elliott Sadler AS .30 .75
45 Rusty Wallace AS .60 1.50
46 Rusty Wallace's Car HR .30 .75
47 Dale Earnhardt's Car HR .50 1.25
48 Scott Rigg's Car HR .20 .50
49 Michael Waltrip's Car HR .20 .50
50 Bobby Labonte's Car HR .30 .75
51 Scott Wimmer's Car HR .20 .50
52 Jeff Gordon's Car HR .50 1.25
53 Mark Martin's Car HR .30 .75
54 Jimmie Johnson's Car HR .50 1.25
55 Michael Waltrip DT .30 .75
56 Rusty Wallace DT .60 1.50
57 Ricky Rudd DT .50 1.25
58 Elliott Sadler DT .30 .75
59 Bobby Labonte DT .60 1.50
60 Matt Kenseth DT 1.00 2.50
61 Kevin Harvick DT .75 2.00
62 Dale Earnhardt Jr. DT 1.25 3.00
63 Kurt Busch DT .50 1.25
64 Kasey Kahne RR 1.25 3.00
65 Jeff Gordon RR 1.25 3.00
66 Jamie McMurray RR .50 1.25
67 Michael Waltrip RR .30 .75
68 Bobby Labonte RR .60 1.50
69 Dale Earnhardt Jr. RR 1.25 3.00
70 Mark Martin RR .75 2.00
71 Ricky Craven RR .20 .50
72 Jimmie Johnson RR 1.00 2.50
73 Elliott Sadler RR .30 .75
74 Brian Vickers RR .60 1.50
75 Kevin Harvick RR .75 2.00
76 Jeff Gordon CC 1.25 3.00
77 Dale Earnhardt Jr. CC 1.25 3.00
78 Tony Stewart CC .75 2.00
79 Rusty Wallace CC .60 1.50
80 Terry Labonte CC .50 1.25
81 Michael Waltrip CC .30 .75
82 Jeff Burton CC .30 .75
83 Dale Jarrett CC .60 1.50
84 Jimmie Johnson CC 1.00 2.50
85 Kasey Kahne RT 1.25 3.00
86 Brian Vickers RT .60 1.50
87 Scott Wimmer RT .30 .75
88 Brendan Gaughan RT .30 .75
89 Scott Riggs RT .30 .75
90 Kahne 1.25 3.00
Busch
McMurray CL
0 Daytona 500 Air Force One 2.00 5.00
NNO American Chopper Promo .75 2.00

2004 Wheels American Thunder Samples

*SAMPLES: 2X TO 5X BASE

2004 Wheels American Thunder American Eagle

This 12-card set was randomly inserted in packs at a rate of 1 in 6. The feature foil etched cards of NASCAR's leading drivers. The cards carried an "AE" prefix for their card numbers.

COMPLETE SET (12) 12.50 30.00
STATED ODDS 1:6
*GOLDEN/250: 1.5X TO 4X AMERICAN
AE1 Jeff Burton .60 1.50
AE2 Jeff Gordon 2.50 6.00
AE3 Dale Jarrett 1.25 3.00
AE4 Jimmie Johnson 2.00 5.00
AE5 Bobby Labonte 1.25 3.00
AE6 Terry Labonte 1.00 2.50
AE7 Greg Biffle .60 1.50
AE8 Jamie McMurray 1.00 2.50
AE9 Ricky Rudd 1.00 2.50
AE10 Brian Vickers 1.25 3.00
AE11 Rusty Wallace 1.25 3.00
AE12 Michael Waltrip .60 1.50

2004 Wheels American Thunder American Muscle

This 9-card set was randomly inserted in packs at a rate of 1 in 10. The feature foil etched cards of NASCAR's leading drivers. The cards carried an "AM" prefix for their card numbers.

COMPLETE SET (9) 12.50 30.00
AM1 Dale Earnhardt Jr. 3.00 8.00
AM2 Kevin Harvick 2.00 5.00
AM3 Jimmie Johnson 2.50 6.00
AM4 Jeff Gordon 3.00 8.00
AM5 Rusty Wallace 1.50 4.00
AM6 Tony Stewart 2.00 5.00
AM7 Kasey Kahne 3.00 8.00
AM8 Bobby Labonte 1.50 4.00
AM9 Kurt Busch 1.25 3.00

2004 Wheels American Thunder Cool Threads

This 15-card set was randomly inserted in packs. They feature swatches of shirts worn by drivers during races. The cards carried a "CT" prefix for their card numbers and were serial numbered to 525.

CT1 Jeff Burton 6.00 15.00
CT2 Dale Earnhardt Jr. 20.00 40.00
CT3 Jeff Gordon 10.00 25.00
CT4 Kevin Harvick 8.00 20.00
CT5 Dale Jarrett 8.00 20.00
CT6 Matt Kenseth 8.00 20.00
CT7 Sterling Marlin 8.00 20.00
CT8 Mark Martin 10.00 25.00
CT9 Jamie McMurray 8.00 20.00
CT10 Casey Mears 8.00 20.00
CT11 Joe Nemechek 8.00 20.00
CT12 Ryan Newman 8.00 20.00
CT13 Scott Riggs 8.00 20.00
CT14 Kenny Wallace 8.00 20.00
CT15 Michael Waltrip 8.00 20.00

2004 Wheels American Thunder Cup Quest

COMPLETE SET (12) 30.00 60.00
CQ1 Jimmie Johnson 6.00 15.00
CQ2 Dale Earnhardt Jr. 8.00 20.00
CQ3 Jeff Gordon 10.00 25.00
CQ4 Tony Stewart 5.00 12.00
CQ5 Bobby Labonte 4.00 10.00
CQ6 Ryan Newman 6.00 15.00
CQ7 Dale Jarrett 4.00 10.00
CQ8 Mark Martin 5.00 12.00
CQ9 Michael Waltrip 2.50 6.00
CQ10 Terry Labonte 3.00 8.00
CQ11 Jeff Burton 2.50 6.00
CQ12 Ricky Rudd 3.00 8.00

2004 Wheels American Thunder Head to Toe

This 9-card set featured swatches of race-used hats and shoes. Each card was serial numbered to 100, unless noted in the checklist below and carried an "HT" prefix for its card number.

HT1 Jeff Burton/50 10.00 25.00
HT2 Ward Burton 10.00 25.00
HT3 Dale Earnhardt Jr. 50.00 100.00
HT4 Jeff Gordon/50 75.00 150.00
HT5 Matt Kenseth 25.00 60.00
HT6 Terry Labonte 15.00 40.00
HT7 Mark Martin/50 25.00 60.00
HT8 Joe Nemechek 10.00 25.00
HT9 Scott Riggs 10.00 25.00

2004 Wheels American Thunder Post Mark

This 27-card set was printed on clear plastic and was about the size of a postage stamp. They were inserted into packs at a rate of 1 in 2. These cards carried a "PM" prefix for their card numbers.

COMPLETE SET (27) 10.00 25.00
STATED ODDS 1:2
PM1 Ward Burton .40 1.00
PM2 Joe Nemechek .25 .60
PM3 Rusty Wallace .75 2.00
PM4 Terry Labonte .60 1.50
PM5 Mark Martin 1.00 2.50
PM6 Dale Earnhardt Jr. 1.50 4.00
PM7 Scott Riggs .40 1.00
PM8 Ryan Newman 1.25 3.00
PM9 Michael Waltrip .40 1.00
PM10 Greg Biffle .40 1.00
PM11 Matt Kenseth 1.25 3.00
PM12 Bobby Labonte .75 2.00
PM13 Tony Stewart 1.00 2.50
PM14 Ricky Rudd .60 1.50
PM15 Scott Wimmer .40 1.00
PM16 Jeff Gordon 1.50 4.00
PM17 Brian Vickers .75 2.00
PM18 Kevin Harvick 1.00 2.50
PM19 Robby Gordon .25 .60
PM20 Casey Mears .25 .60
PM21 Jamie McMurray .60 1.50
PM22 Jeff Green .25 .60
PM23 Kyle Petty .40 1.00
PM24 Jimmie Johnson 1.25 3.00
PM25 Brendan Gaughan .40 1.00
PM26 Jeff Burton .40 1.00
PM27 Kasey Kahne CL 1.50 4.00

2004 Wheels American Thunder Pushin Pedal

Randomly inserted in packs, these 15 cards featured swatches of race-used shoes. The cards were serial numbered to 275 unless noted in the checklist below..

PP1 Greg Biffle 6.00 15.00
PP2 Jeff Burton/200 8.00 20.00
PP3 Ward Burton 8.00 20.00
PP4 Kurt Busch 8.00 20.00
PP5 Dale Earnhardt Jr. 15.00 40.00
PP6 Jeff Gordon/200 20.00 50.00
PP7 Robby Gordon 6.00 15.00
PP8 Kevin Harvick 10.00 25.00
PP9 Jimmie Johnson 10.00 25.00
PP10 Matt Kenseth 10.00 25.00
PP11 Terry Labonte 8.00 20.00
PP12 Mark Martin/200 10.00 25.00
PP13 Joe Nemechek 6.00 15.00
PP14 Scott Riggs 6.00 15.00
PP15 Tony Stewart 10.00 25.00

2004 Wheels American Thunder Thunder Road

This 18-card set featured race-used tires incorporated into the card design. They were inserted in packs at a rate of one in 18. Each card carried a "TR" prefix in its card numbers.

TR1 Rusty Wallace 4.00 10.00
TR2 Terry Labonte 3.00 8.00
TR3 Mark Martin 5.00 12.00
TR4 Dale Earnhardt Jr. 8.00 20.00
TR5 Ryan Newman 6.00 15.00
TR6 Michael Waltrip 2.00 5.00
TR7 Robby Gordon 1.25 3.00
TR8 Matt Kenseth 6.00 15.00
TR9 Bobby Labonte 4.00 10.00
TR10 Tony Stewart 5.00 12.00
TR11 Ricky Rudd 3.00 8.00
TR12 Jeff Gordon 8.00 20.00
TR13 Brian Vickers 4.00 10.00
TR14 Sterling Marlin 3.00 8.00
TR15 Jamie McMurray 4.00 10.00
TR16 Jimmie Johnson 6.00 15.00
TR17 Dale Jarrett 4.00 10.00
TR18 Jeff Burton 2.00 5.00

2004 Wheels American Thunder Triple Hat

This 35-card set features three swatches of hats that were worn during Daytona Speedweeks. The cards are serial numbered to 160.

TH1 Kurt Busch 6.00 15.00
TH2 Ricky Craven 5.00 12.00
TH3 Jeff Gordon 20.00 50.00
TH4 Jeff Green 5.00 12.00
TH5 Dale Jarrett 8.00 20.00
TH6 Jimmie Johnson 15.00 40.00
TH7 Kasey Kahne 8.00 20.00
TH8 Matt Kenseth 8.00 20.00
TH9 Bobby Labonte 8.00 20.00
TH10 Terry Labonte 10.00 25.00
TH11 Sterling Marlin 6.00 15.00
TH12 Mark Martin 10.00 25.00
TH13 Jamie McMurray 6.00 15.00
TH14 Casey Mears 5.00 12.00
TH15 Joe Nemechek 5.00 12.00
TH16 Kyle Petty 6.00 15.00
TH17 Scott Riggs 5.00 12.00
TH18 Ricky Rudd 6.00 15.00
TH19 Elliott Sadler 6.00 15.00
TH20 Johnny Sauter 5.00 12.00
TH21 Tony Stewart 15.00 40.00
TH22 Brian Vickers 5.00 12.00
TH23 Rusty Wallace 10.00 25.00
TH24 Michael Waltrip 8.00 20.00
TH25 Scott Wimmer 5.00 12.00
TH26 Greg Biffle 6.00 15.00
TH27 Jeff Burton 6.00 15.00
TH28 Ward Burton 6.00 15.00
TH29 Brendan Gaughan 5.00 12.00
TH30 Kevin Lepage 5.00 12.00
TH31 Jeremy Mayfield 6.00 15.00
TH32 Ken Schrader 6.00 15.00
TH33 Dale Earnhardt Jr. 20.00 50.00
TH34 Robby Gordon 5.00 12.00
TH35 Ryan Newman 6.00 15.00

2005 Wheels American Thunder

COMPLETE SET (90) 15.00 40.00
WAX BOX HOBBY (20) 60.00 100.00
WAX BOX RETAIL (24) 50.00 80.00
1 John Andretti .20 .50
2 Greg Biffle .30 .75
3 Jeff Burton .30 .75
4 Kurt Busch .50 1.25
5 Kyle Busch CRC .75 2.00
6 Dale Earnhardt Jr. 1.25 3.00
7 Carl Edwards CRC 1.00 2.50
8 Jeff Gordon 1.25 3.00
9 Robby Gordon .20 .50
10 Kevin Harvick .75 2
11 Dale Jarrett .60 1
12 Jimmie Johnson 1.00 2
13 Kasey Kahne 1.25 3.
14 Matt Kenseth 1.00 2
15 Travis Kvapil CRC .30
16 Bobby Labonte .60 1
17 Terry Labonte .50 1
18 Jason Leffler .20
19 Sterling Marlin .50 1
20 Mark Martin .75 2.
21 Jeremy Mayfield .20
22 Jamie McMurray .50 1
23 Casey Mears .30
24 Joe Nemechek .20
25 Ricky Rudd .50 1
26 Elliott Sadler .30
27 Tony Stewart .75 2
28 Brian Vickers .60 1
29 Rusty Wallace .60 1
30 Scott Wimmer .30
31 Jimmie Johnson's Rig Rt. 66 .30
32 Mark Martin's Rig RT. 66 .30
33 Jeff Burton's Rig Rt. 66 .20
34 Jeff Gordon's Rig Rt. 66 .50 1
35 Kevin Harvick's Rig Rt. 66 .30
36 Dale Earnhardt Jr's Rig Rt. 66 .50 1
37 Mark Martin AS .75 2
38 Dale Earnhardt Jr. AS 1.25 3
39 Matt Kenseth AS 1.00 2
40 Jeff Gordon AS 1.25 3
41 Martin Truex Jr. AS 1.00 2
42 Dale Jarrett AS .60 1
43 Tony Stewart AS .75 2.
44 Bobby Labonte AS .60 1
45 Rusty Wallace AS .60 1
46 Kevin Harvick's Car HR .30
47 Rusty Wallace's Car HR .30
48 Elliott Sadler's Car HR .20
49 Mark Martin's Car HR .30
50 Tony Stewart's Car HR .30
51 Dale Jarrett's Car HR .30
52 Jeff Gordon's Car HR .50 1
53 Jimmie Johnson's Car HR .30
54 Kasey Kahne DT 1.25 3
55 Carl Edwards DT 1.00 2
56 Rusty Wallace DT .60 1
57 Dale Earnhardt Jr. DT 1.25 3
58 Tony Stewart DT .75 2
59 Bobby Labonte DT .60 1
60 Jimmie Johnson DT 1.00 2
61 Kyle Busch DT .75 2
62 Ricky Rudd DT .50 1
63 Jeff Gordon DT 1.25 3
64 Carl Edwards RR 1.00 2
65 Jeff Gordon RR 1.25 3
66 Jeremy Mayfield RR .20
67 Jimmie Johnson RR 1.00 2
68 Bobby Labonte RR .60 1
69 Dale Earnhardt Jr. RR 1.25 3
70 Mark Martin RR .75 2
71 Jeff Burton RR .30
72 Dale Jarrett RR .60 1
73 Tony Stewart RR .75 2
74 Kyle Busch RR .75 2
75 Martin Truex Jr. RR 1.00 2
76 Jamie McMurray CC .50 1
77 Dale Earnhardt Jr. CC 1.25 3
78 Kasey Kahne CC 1.25 3
79 John Andretti CC .20
80 Martin Truex Jr. CC 1.00 2
81 Scott Wimmer CC .30
82 Travis Kvapil CC .30
83 Ricky Rudd CC .50 1
84 Jimmie Johnson CC 1.00 2
85 Kyle Busch RT .75 2
86 Travis Kvapil RT .30
87 Carl Edwards RT 1.00 2
88 Reed Sorenson RT RC 2.50 6
89 Denny Hamlin RT RC 3.00 8
90 C.Edwards/Ky.Busch CL 1.00 2

2005 Wheels American Thunde Samples

COMPLETE SET (90) 75.00 150
*SAMPLES: 1.5X TO 4X BASE
STATED ODDS 1 PER BRC 135

2005 Wheels American Thunde American Eagle

COMPLETE SET (12) 12.50 30
STATED ODDS 1:6
*GOLDEN EAGLE/250: 1.5X TO 4X AMERICAN

ff Burton .60 1.50
le Earnhardt Jr. 2.50 6.00
le Jarrett 1.25 3.00
sty Wallace 1.25 3.00
bby Labonte 1.25 3.00
artin Truex Jr. 2.00 5.00
ff Gordon 2.50 6.00
e Nemechek .40 1.00
cky Rudd 1.00 2.50
Mark Martin 1.50 4.00
immie Johnson 2.00 5.00
Greg Biffle .60 1.50

)5 Wheels American Thunder American Muscle

LETE SET (9) 15.00 40.00
Mark Martin 2.00 5.00
evin Harvick 2.00 5.00
immie Johnson 2.50 6.00
eff Gordon 3.00 8.00
arl Edwards 2.50 6.00
ale Earnhardt Jr. 3.00 8.00
reg Biffle .75 2.00
lliott Sadler .75 2.00
urt Busch 1.25 3.00

)5 Wheels American Thunder Cool Threads

eff Gordon 12.00 30.00
asey Mears 4.00 10.00
terling Marlin 5.00 12.00
ale Earnhardt Jr. 12.00 30.00
att Kenseth 5.00 12.00
ark Martin 5.00 12.00
cott Riggs 4.00 10.00
e Nemechek 4.00 10.00
urt Busch 5.00 12.00
Jamie Mcmurray 5.00 12.00
Kevin Harvick 6.00 15.00
Dale Jarrett 6.00 15.00
Ryan Newman 6.00 15.00

)5 Wheels American Thunder Double Hat

ohn Andretti 6.00 15.00
Mike Bliss 6.00 15.00
arl Edwards 8.00 20.00
obby Labonte 8.00 20.00
erry Labonte 10.00 25.00
son Leffler 5.00 12.00
evin Lepage 5.00 12.00
yan Newman 6.00 15.00
oris Said 6.00 15.00

)5 Wheels American Thunder Head to Toe

arl Edwards 10.00 25.00
reg Biffle 4.00 10.00
urt Busch 4.00 10.00
ale Earnhardt Jr. 10.00 25.00
erry Labonte 5.00 12.00
ony Stewart 8.00 20.00
obby Labonte 5.00 12.00
oe Nemechek 3.00 8.00
cott Riggs 4.00 10.00
Jeff Gordon 10.00 25.00
Matt Kenseth 5.00 12.00
Mark Martin 5.00 12.00
Jimmie Johnson/60 10.00 25.00

)5 Wheels American Thunder License to Drive

LETE SET (9) 12.50 30.00
Edwards 3.00 8.00
is Kvapil 1.00 2.50
on Leffler .60 1.50
d Stremme 3.00 8.00
tin Truex Jr. 3.00 8.00
Yeley 1.50 4.00
t Bowyer 4.00 10.00
ny Hamlin 3.00 8.00
Wood 1.00 2.50

)5 Wheels American Thunder Medallion

LETE SET (27) 10.00 25.00
John Andretti .25 .60
Kyle Busch 1.00 2.50
MD3 Rusty Wallace .75 2.00
MD4 Terry Labonte .60 1.50
MD5 Mark Martin 1.00 2.50
MD6 Joe Nemechek .25 .60
MD7 Casey Mears .40 1.00
MD8 Tony Raines .25 .60
MD9 Dale Jarrett .75 2.00
MD10 Bobby Labonte .75 2.00
MD11 Tony Stewart 1.00 2.50
MD12 Ricky Rudd .60 1.50
MD13 Sterling Marlin .60 1.50
MD14 Jeff Gordon 1.50 4.00
MD15 Kevin Harvick 1.00 2.50
MD16 Robby Gordon .25 .60
MD17 Johnny Sauter .40 1.00
MD18 Jeff Green .25 .60
MD19 Kyle Petty .40 1.00
MD20 Jimmie Johnson 1.25 3.00
MD21 Mike Bliss .25 .60
MD22 Jeff Burton .40 1.00
MD23 Elliott Sadler .40 1.00
MD24 Kenny Wallace .25 .60
MD25 Paul Wolfe .40 1.00
MD26 Kasey Kahne 1.50 4.00
MD27 Scott Wimmer CL .40 1.00

2005 Wheels American Thunder Pushin Pedal

PP1 Greg Biffle 4.00 10.00
PP2 Kurt Busch 4.00 10.00
PP3 Dale Earnhardt Jr. 10.00 25.00
PP4 Terry Labonte 5.00 12.00
PP5 Kevin Harvick 6.00 15.00
PP6 Joe Nemechek 5.00 12.00
PP7 Scott Riggs 3.00 8.00
PP8 Tony Stewart 8.00 20.00
PP9 Carl Edwards 10.00 25.00
PP10 Bobby Labonte 5.00 12.00
PP11 Mark Martin 5.00 12.00
PP12 Jeff Gordon 10.00 25.00
PP13 Jimmie Johnson/60 10.00 25.00
PP14 Matt Kenseth 5.00 12.00

2005 Wheels American Thunder Single Hat

SH1 Jeff Burton 6.00 15.00
SH2 Martin Truex Jr. 6.00 15.00

2005 Wheels American Thunder Thunder Road

TR1 Rusty Wallace 4.00 10.00
TR2 Terry Labonte 3.00 8.00
TR3 Mark Martin 5.00 12.00
TR4 Dale Earnhardt Jr. 8.00 20.00
TR5 Kurt Busch 3.00 8.00
TR6 Kasey Kahne 8.00 20.00
TR7 Kyle Busch 5.00 12.00
TR8 Travis Kvapil 2.00 5.00
TR9 Bobby Labonte 4.00 10.00
TR10 Tony Stewart 6.00 15.00
TR11 Ricky Rudd 3.00 8.00
TR12 Jeff Gordon 8.00 20.00
TR13 Carl Edwards 6.00 15.00
TR14 Sterling Marlin 3.00 8.00
TR15 Martin Truex Jr. 6.00 15.00
TR16 Jimmie Johnson 6.00 15.00
TR17 Dale Jarrett 4.00 10.00
TR18 Jeff Burton 2.00 5.00

2005 Wheels American Thunder Triple Hat

TH1 Greg Biffle 8.00 20.00
TH2 Kurt Busch 6.00 15.00
TH3 Kyle Busch 8.00 20.00
TH4 Dale Earnhardt Jr. 20.00 50.00
TH5 Jeff Gordon 20.00 50.00
TH6 Jeff Green 5.00 12.00
TH7 Kevin Harvick 10.00 25.00
TH8 Dale Jarrett 10.00 25.00
TH9 Jimmie Johnson 20.00 50.00
TH10 Kasey Kahne 10.00 25.00
TH11 Matt Kenseth 10.00 25.00
TH12 Travis Kvapil 6.00 15.00
TH13 Sterling Marlin 6.00 15.00
TH14 Mark Martin 8.00 20.00
TH15 Jeremy Mayfield 6.00 15.00
TH16 Jamie McMurray 6.00 15.00
TH17 Casey Mears 6.00 15.00
TH18 Joe Nemechek 8.00 20.00
TH19 Kyle Petty 8.00 20.00
TH20 Scott Riggs 5.00 12.00
TH21 Ricky Rudd 6.00 15.00
TH22 Elliott Sadler 6.00 15.00
TH23 Tony Stewart 20.00 50.00
TH24 Brian Vickers 6.00 15.00
TH25 Rusty Wallace 8.00 20.00
TH26 Scott Wimmer 5.00 12.00

2006 Wheels American Thunder

This 96-card set was released in September, 2006. These cards were found in 5-card hobby packs with 20 pack boxes with pack SRP of $5.99 and 4-card retail packs with 24 pack boxes with an SRP of $2.99. The six Cup Rookie Cards were each randomly inserted into packs and serial numbered to 350. Each of the contained an autograph. The David Stremme was issued in packs as a redemption, but the actual cards were ready and shipped from Press Pass by the time the product went live. The checklist card had "CL" for its card number.

COMP.SET w/o SPs (90) 12.50 30.00
CRC STATED PRINT RUN 350 SERIAL #'d SETS
WAX BOX HOBBY (20) 75.00 125.00
WAX BOX RETAIL (24) 40.00 75.00
1 Greg Biffle .25 .60
2 Dave Blaney .20 .50
3 Jeff Burton .25 .60
4 Kurt Busch .25 .60
5 Kyle Busch .40 1.00
6 Dale Earnhardt Jr. .60 1.50
7 Carl Edwards .30 .75
8 Jeff Gordon .60 1.50
9 Robby Gordon .20 .50
10 Jeff Green .20 .50
11 Kevin Harvick .40 1.00
12 Dale Jarrett .30 .75
13 Jimmie Johnson .50 1.25
14 Kasey Kahne .40 1.00
15 Matt Kenseth .30 .75
16 Bobby Labonte .30 .75
17 Terry Labonte .30 .75
18 Sterling Marlin .30 .75
19 Mark Martin .30 .75
20 Jeremy Mayfield .20 .50
21 Jamie McMurray .30 .75
22 Casey Mears .20 .50
23 Joe Nemechek .20 .50
24 Ryan Newman .25 .60
25 Kyle Petty .25 .60
26 Tony Raines .20 .50
27 Scott Riggs .25 .60
28 Elliott Sadler .20 .50
29 Ken Schrader .20 .50
30 Tony Stewart .50 1.25
31 Matt Kenseth DT .30 .75
32 Dale Earnhardt Jr. DT .60 1.50
33 Terry Labonte DT .30 .75
34 Jimmie Johnson DT .50 1.25
35 Tony Stewart DT .50 1.25
36 Carl Edwards DT .30 .75
37 Jeff Gordon DT .60 1.50
38 Kyle Busch DT .40 1.00
39 Mark Martin DT .30 .75
40 Jamie McMurray DT .30 .75
41 Jeff Burton DT .25 .60
42 Bobby Labonte DT .30 .75
43 Jeff Gordon's Car HR .60 1.50
44 Mark Martin's Car HR .30 .75
45 Dale Jarrett's Car HR .30 .75
46 Jeff Burton's Car HR .25 .60

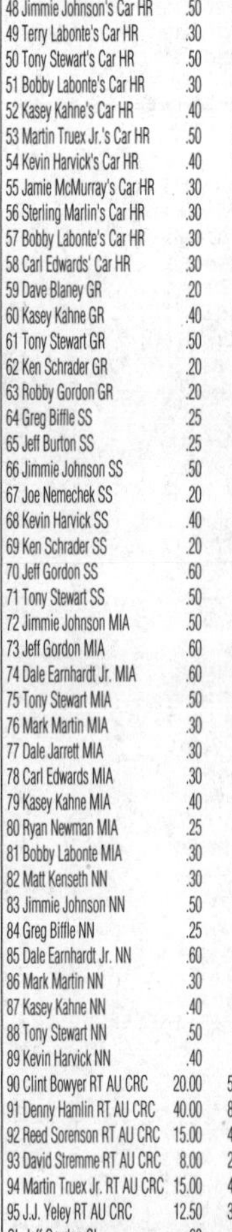

47 Dale Earnhardt Jr.'s Car HR .60 1.50
48 Jimmie Johnson's Car HR .50 1.25
49 Terry Labonte's Car HR .30 .75
50 Tony Stewart's Car HR .50 1.25
51 Bobby Labonte's Car HR .30 .75
52 Kasey Kahne's Car HR .40 1.00
53 Martin Truex Jr.'s Car HR .50 1.25
54 Kevin Harvick's Car HR .40 1.00
55 Jamie McMurray's Car HR .30 .75
56 Sterling Marlin's Car HR .30 .75
57 Bobby Labonte's Car HR .30 .75
58 Carl Edwards' Car HR .30 .75
59 Dave Blaney GR .20 .50
60 Kasey Kahne GR .40 1.00
61 Tony Stewart GR .50 1.25
62 Ken Schrader GR .20 .50
63 Robby Gordon GR .20 .50
64 Greg Biffle SS .25 .60
65 Jeff Burton SS .25 .60
66 Jimmie Johnson SS .50 1.25
67 Joe Nemechek SS .20 .50
68 Kevin Harvick SS .40 1.00
69 Ken Schrader SS .20 .50
70 Jeff Gordon SS .60 1.50
71 Tony Stewart SS .50 1.25
72 Jimmie Johnson MIA .50 1.25
73 Jeff Gordon MIA .60 1.50
74 Dale Earnhardt Jr. MIA .60 1.50
75 Tony Stewart MIA .50 1.25
76 Mark Martin MIA .30 .75
77 Dale Jarrett MIA .30 .75
78 Carl Edwards MIA .30 .75
79 Kasey Kahne MIA .40 1.00
80 Ryan Newman MIA .25 .60
81 Bobby Labonte MIA .30 .75
82 Matt Kenseth NN .30 .75
83 Jimmie Johnson NN .50 1.25
84 Greg Biffle NN .25 .60
85 Dale Earnhardt Jr. NN .60 1.50
86 Mark Martin NN .30 .75
87 Kasey Kahne NN .40 1.00
88 Tony Stewart NN .50 1.25
89 Kevin Harvick NN .40 1.00
90 Clint Bowyer RT AU CRC 20.00 50.00
91 Denny Hamlin RT AU CRC 40.00 80.00
92 Reed Sorenson RT AU CRC 15.00 40.00
93 David Stremme RT AU CRC 8.00 20.00
94 Martin Truex Jr. RT AU CRC 15.00 40.00
95 J.J. Yeley RT AU CRC 12.50 30.00
CL Jeff Gordon CL .60 1.50

2006 Wheels American Thunder American Muscle

This 9-card set was randomly inserted in packs at a rate of 1 in 10. The feature foil etched cards of NASCAR's leading drivers. The cards carried an "AM" prefix for their card numbers.

COMPLETE SET (9) 12.50 30.00
AM1 Mark Martin .60 1.50
AM2 Jeff Gordon 1.25 3.00
AM3 Tony Stewart 1.00 2.50
AM4 Dale Jarrett .60 1.50
AM5 Martin Truex Jr. 1.00 2.50
AM6 Jeff Burton .50 1.25
AM7 Dale Earnhardt Jr. 1.25 3.00
AM8 Terry Labonte .60 1.50
AM9 Jimmie Johnson 1.00 2.50

2006 Wheels American Thunder American Racing Idol

This 12-card set was randomly inserted in packs at a rate of 1 in 6. The feature foil etched cards of NASCAR's leading drivers. The cards carried an "RI" prefix for their card numbers.

COMPLETE SET (12) 15.00 40.00
*GOLDEN/250: 1.2X TO 3X BASIC INSERTS
RI1 Jimmie Johnson 1.25 3.00
RI2 Terry Labonte .75 2.00
RI3 Dale Earnhardt Jr. 1.50 4.00
RI4 Jeff Burton .60 1.50
RI5 Mark Martin .75 2.00
RI6 Jeff Gordon 1.50 4.00
RI7 Kasey Kahne 1.00 2.50
RI8 Kevin Harvick 1.00 2.50
RI9 Dale Jarrett .75 2.00
RI10 Tony Stewart 1.25 3.00
RI11 Matt Kenseth .75 2.00
RI12 Martin Truex Jr. 1.25 3.00

2006 Wheels American Thunder Cool Threads

This 15-card set was randomly inserted in packs. They feature swatches of shirts worn by drivers during races. The cards carried a "CT" prefix for their card numbers and were serial numbered to 329.

CT1 Reed Sorenson 4.00 10.00
CT2 Scott Riggs 5.00 12.00
CT3 Martin Truex Jr. 10.00 25.00
CT4 Dale Earnhardt Jr. 15.00 40.00
CT5 Casey Mears 6.00 15.00
CT6 Kurt Busch 10.00 25.00
CT7 Jeff Gordon 15.00 40.00
CT8 Kasey Kahne 6.00 15.00
CT9 David Stremme 6.00 15.00
CT10 Ryan Newman 5.00 12.00
CT11 Jeremy Mayfield 6.00 15.00
CT12 Kevin Harvick 6.00 15.00
CT13 Mark Martin 6.00 15.00
CT14 Matt Kenseth 6.00 15.00
CT15 Dale Jarrett 6.00 15.00

2006 Wheels American Thunder Double Hat

This 27-card set features two swatches of hats that were worn during Daytona Speedweeks. The cards are serial numbered to 99.

DH1 Greg Biffle 4.00 10.00
DH2 Clint Bowyer 5.00 12.00
DH3 Jeff Burton 4.00 10.00
DH4 Kurt Busch 4.00 10.00
DH5 Dale Earnhardt Jr. 10.00 25.00
DH6 Carl Edwards 5.00 12.00
DH7 Jeff Gordon 10.00 25.00
DH8 Denny Hamlin 10.00 25.00
DH9 Kevin Harvick 6.00 15.00
DH10 Dale Jarrett 5.00 12.00
DH11 Jimmie Johnson 8.00 20.00
DH12 Kasey Kahne 6.00 15.00
DH13 Matt Kenseth 5.00 12.00
DH14 Mark Martin 5.00 12.00
DH15 Jeremy Mayfield 3.00 8.00
DH16 Jamie McMurray 5.00 12.00
DH17 Casey Mears 3.00 8.00
DH18 Ryan Newman 4.00 10.00
DH19 Tony Raines 3.00 8.00
DH20 Scott Riggs 4.00 10.00
DH21 Elliott Sadler 3.00 8.00
DH22 Reed Sorenson 4.00 10.00
DH23 Tony Stewart 10.00 25.00
DH24 David Stremme 3.00 8.00
DH25 Martin Truex Jr. 4.00 10.00
DH26 Brian Vickers 3.00 8.00
DH27 J.J. Yeley 4.00 10.00

2006 Wheels American Thunder Grandstand

This 27-card set was designed to look like a ticket stub and was about 2 1/2" by 3". They were inserted into packs at a rate of 1 in 2. These cards carried a "GS" prefix for their card numbers.

COMPLETE SET (27) 10.00 25.00
GS1 Jeff Burton .40 1.00
GS2 Kurt Busch .40 1.00
GS3 Kyle Busch .60 1.50
GS4 Dale Earnhardt Jr. 1.00 2.50
GS5 Carl Edwards .50 1.25
GS6 Jeff Gordon 1.00 2.50
GS7 Denny Hamlin 2.00 5.00
GS8 Kevin Harvick .60 1.50
GS9 Dale Jarrett .50 1.25
GS10 Jimmie Johnson .75 2.00
GS11 Kasey Kahne .60 1.50
GS12 Matt Kenseth .50 1.25
GS13 Terry Labonte .50 1.25
GS14 Bobby Labonte .50 1.25
GS15 Sterling Marlin .50 1.25
GS16 Mark Martin .50 1.25
GS17 Casey Mears .30 .75
GS18 Jamie McMurray .50 1.25
GS19 Ryan Newman .40 1.00
GS20 Scott Riggs .40 1.00
GS21 Tony Stewart .75 2.00
GS22 Martin Truex Jr. .75 2.00
GS23 David Green .30 .75
GS24 Burney Lamar 1.25 3.00
GS25 Rick Crawford .30 .75
GS26 Ron Hornaday .30 .75
GS27 Bill Lester CL .50 1.25

2006 Wheels American Thunder Head to Toe

This 15-card set featured swatches of race-used hats and shoes. Each card was serial numbered to 99, unless noted in the checklist below and carried an "HT" prefix for its card number.

HT1 Scott Riggs 6.00 15.00
HT2 Ryan Newman 12.00 30.00
HT3 David Stremme 8.00 20.00
HT4 Tony Stewart 20.00 50.00
HT5 Reed Sorenson 10.00 25.00
HT6 Jeremy Mayfield 6.00 15.00
HT7 Martin Truex Jr. 10.00 25.00
HT8 Casey Mears 6.00 15.00
HT9 Dale Earnhardt Jr. 50.00 100.00
HT10 Kevin Harvick 15.00 40.00
HT11 Matt Kenseth 12.00 30.00
HT12 Jimmie Johnson/35 75.00 125.00
HT13 Mark Martin 12.00 30.00
HT14 Jeff Gordon 50.00 100.00
HT15 Carl Edwards 15.00 40.00

2006 Wheels American Thunder Pushin' Pedal

Randomly inserted in packs, these 15 cards featured swatches of race-used shoes. The cards were serial numbered to 199 unless noted in the checklist below.

PP1 Dale Earnhardt Jr. 25.00 60.00
PP2 Scott Riggs 6.00 15.00
PP3 David Stremme 5.00 12.00
PP4 Tony Stewart 12.00 30.00
PP5 Ryan Newman 10.00 25.00
PP6 Casey Mears 8.00 20.00
PP7 Kevin Harvick 12.00 30.00
PP8 Reed Sorenson 10.00 25.00
PP9 Jeremy Mayfield 6.00 15.00
PP10 Martin Truex Jr. 10.00 25.00
PP11 Mark Martin 8.00 20.00
PP12 Carl Edwards 12.00 30.00
PP13 Jeff Gordon 15.00 40.00
PP14 Jimmie Johnson/35 60.00 120.00
PP15 Bobby Labonte 8.00 20.00

2006 Wheels American Thunder Single Hat

This 8-card set features a swatch of hat that was worn during Daytona Speedweeks. The cards are serial numbered to 99.

SH1 Dave Blaney 6.00 15.00
SH2 Jeff Green 6.00 15.00
SH3 Bobby Labonte 10.00 25.00
SH4 Terry Labonte 10.00 25.00
SH5 Sterling Marlin 10.00 25.00
SH6 Joe Nemechek 6.00 15.00
SH7 Kyle Petty 10.00 25.00
SH8 Ken Schrader 10.00 25.00

2006 Wheels American Thunder Thunder Road

This 18-card set featured race-used tires incorporated into the card design. They were inserted in packs at a rate of one in 18. Each card carried a "TR" prefix in its card numbers.

TR1 Jamie McMurray 2.00 5.00
TR2 Dale Earnhardt Jr. 4.00 10.00
TR3 Bobby Labonte 2.00 5.00
TR4 Jimmie Johnson 3.00 8.00
TR5 Kevin Harvick 2.50 6.00
TR6 Tony Stewart 3.00 8.00
TR7 Martin Truex Jr. 3.00 8.00
TR8 Sterling Marlin 2.00 5.00
TR9 Dale Jarrett 2.00 5.00
TR10 Jeff Gordon 4.00 10.00
TR11 Mark Martin 2.00 5.00
TR12 Terry Labonte 2.00 5.00
TR13 Scott Riggs 1.50 4.00
TR14 Kasey Kahne 2.50 6.00
TR15 Jeff Burton 1.50 4.00
TR16 Kurt Busch 1.50 4.00
TR17 Matt Kenseth 2.00 5.00
TR18 Carl Edwards 2.00 5.00

2006 Wheels American Thunder Thunder Strokes

This 13-card set was inserted into packs of Wheels American Thunder. Each card was serial numbered to 100 copies, with the exception of the Martin Truex card which was serial numbered to 400. These autographed cards were certified authentic by the manufacturer and was stated on the card backs.

1 Clint Bowyer 20.00 50.00
2 Kurt Busch 8.00 20.00
3 Dale Earnhardt Jr. 60.00 120.00
4 Bobby Labonte 20.00 50.00
5 Sterling Marlin 15.00 40.00
6 Mark Martin 30.00 80.00
7 Casey Mears 12.50 30.00
8 Scott Riggs 12.50 30.00
9 Reed Sorenson 15.00 40.00
10 David Stremme 12.50 30.00
11 Martin Truex Jr./400 15.00 40.00
12 Danny O'Quinn 15.00 40.00
13 Erin Crocker 20.00 50.00

2007 Wheels American Thunder

COMPLETE SET (90)
COMP.SET w/o SPs (83) 12.50 30.00
RT AU INSCRIPTIONS 50 SERIAL #'d SETS
UNLESS NOTED BELOW
WAX BOX HOBBY 60.00 120.00
WAX BOX RETAIL 50.00 100.00
1 Jeff Gordon CL .75 2.00
2 Greg Biffle .30 .75
3 Jeff Burton .30 .75
4 Clint Bowyer .40 1.00
5 Kurt Busch .30 .75
6 Kyle Busch .50 1.25
7 Dale Earnhardt Jr. .75 2.00
8 Carl Edwards .40 1.00
9 Jeff Gordon .75 2.00
10 Jeff Green .25 .60
11 Denny Hamlin .50 1.25
12 Kevin Harvick .50 1.25
13 Dale Jarrett .40 1.00
14 Jimmie Johnson .60 1.50
15 Kasey Kahne .40 1.00
16 Matt Kenseth .40 1.00
17 Bobby Labonte .40 1.00
18 Sterling Marlin .40 1.00
19 Mark Martin .40 1.00
20 Jamie McMurray .40 1.00
21 Casey Mears .25 .60
22 Joe Nemechek .25 .60
23 Ryan Newman .30 .75
24 Kyle Petty .30 .75
25 Tony Raines .25 .60
26 Scott Riggs .30 .75
27 Ricky Rudd .30 .75
28 Elliott Sadler .25 .60
29 Johnny Sauter .40 1.00
30 Ken Schrader .25 .60
31 Reed Sorenson .25 .60
32 David Stremme .25 .60
33 Tony Stewart .60 1.50
34 Martin Truex Jr. .30 .75
35 Brian Vickers .40. 1.00
36 Michael Waltrip .40 1.00
37 Mark Martin's Car DT .15 .40
38 Martin Truex Jr.'s Car DT .12 .30
39 Dale Earnhardt Jr.'s Car DT .30 .75
40 Ryan Newman's Car DT .12 .30
41 Sterling Marlin's Car DT .15 .40
42 Greg Biffle's Car DT .12 .30
43 Matt Kenseth's Car DT .15 .40
44 Tony Stewart's Car DT .25 .60
45 Jeff Gordon's Car DT .30 .75
46 Jamie McMurray's Car DT .15 .40
47 Jeff Burton's Car DT .12 .30
48 Jimmie Johnson's Car DT .25 .60
49 Carl Edwards' Car HR .15 .40
50 Jeff Gordon's Car HR .30 .75
51 Martin Truex Jr.'s Car HR .12 .30
52 Tony Stewart's Car HR .25 .60
53 Kevin Harvick's Car HR .20 .50
54 Jimmie Johnson's Car HR .25 .60
55 Ricky Rudd's Car HR .12 .30
56 Denny Hamlin's Car HR .20 .50
57 Dale Earnhardt Jr.'s Car HR .30 .75
58 Brian Vickers' Car HR .15 .40
59 Bobby Labonte's Car HR .15 .40
60 Jeff Gordon RW .75 2.00
61 Tony Stewart RW .60 1.50
62 Ryan Newman RW .30 .75
63 Ricky Rudd RW .30 .75
64 Carl Edwards RW .40 1.00
65 Elliott Sadler RW .25 .60
66 Kevin Harvick RW .50 1.25
67 Greg Biffle BP .30 .75
68 Tony Stewart BP .60 1.50
69 Michael Waltrip BP .40 1.00
70 Jeff Gordon BP .75 2.00
71 Jeff Burton BP .30 .75
72 Jamie McMurray BP .40 1.00

73 Sterling Marlin HC .40 1.00
74 Tony Stewart HC .60 1.50
75 Reed Sorenson HC .25 .60
76 Jeff Gordon HC .75 2.00
77 Kurt Busch HC .30 .75
78 J.J. Yeley HC .40 1.00
79 Bobby Labonte HC .40 1.00
80 Dale Earnhardt Jr. HC .75 2.00
81 Jeff Burton HC .30 .75
82 Ricky Rudd HC .30 .75
83 Kyle Busch HC .50 1.25
84A Allmendinger RT AU/345 RC 10.00 25.00
84B Allmendinger RT AU Dinger 12.00 30.00
85 D.Gilliland RT AU RC 25.00 50.00
86A P.Menard RT AU/365 CRC 8.00 20.00
87A J.Montoya RT AU/300 RC 20.00 50.00
87B J.Montoya RT AU JPM 30.00 80.00
88 D.Ragan RT AU/305 CRC 15.00 30.00
89A Reutimann RT AU/310 RC 10.00 25.00
89B D.Reutimann RT AU Bea 12.00 30.00
90A R.Smith RT AU/310 CRC 8.00 20.00
90B R.Smith RT AU Army 15.00 40.00

2007 Wheels American Thunder American Dreams

COMPLETE SET (12) 15.00 40.00
STATED ODDS 1:6
*GOLD/250: 1.5X TO 4X BASIC INSERTS
AD1 Kevin Harvick .75 2.00
AD2 Matt Kenseth .60 1.50
AD3 Jimmie Johnson 1.00 2.50
AD4 Kyle Busch .75 2.00
AD5 Jeff Burton .50 1.25
AD6 Jeff Gordon 1.25 3.00
AD7 Casey Mears .40 1.00
AD8 Martin Truex Jr. .50 1.25
AD9 Carl Edwards .60 1.50
AD10 Dale Earnhardt Jr. 1.25 3.00
AD11 Juan Pablo Montoya 2.00 5.00
AD12 Tony Stewart 1.00 2.50

2007 Wheels American Thunder American Muscle

COMPLETE SET (9) 12.50 30.00
STATED ODDS 1:10
AM1 Mark Martin .60 1.50
AM2 Tony Stewart 1.00 2.50
AM3 Matt Kenseth .60 1.50
AM4 Jimmie Johnson 1.00 2.50
AM5 Kyle Busch .75 2.00
AM6 Martin Truex Jr. .50 1.25
AM7 Kevin Harvick .75 2.00
AM8 Ricky Rudd .50 1.25
AM9 Jeff Gordon 1.25 3.00

2007 Wheels American Thunder Cool Threads

OVERALL R-U ODDS 1:10
STATED PRINT RUN 299 SERIAL #'d SETS
CT1 A.J. Allmendinger 4.00 10.00
CT2 Michael Waltrip 4.00 10.00
CT3 Mark Martin 4.00 10.00
CT4 Brian Vickers 4.00 10.00
CT5 Dale Jarrett 8.00 20.00
CT6 Dale Earnhardt Jr. 10.00 25.00
CT7 Martin Truex Jr. 4.00 10.00
CT8 Casey Mears 4.00 10.00
CT9 Ryan Newman 6.00 15.00
CT10 Carl Edwards 8.00 20.00
CT11 Reed Sorenson 4.00 10.00
CT12 Kurt Busch 4.00 10.00
CT13 Jeff Gordon 10.00 25.00
CT14 Juan Pablo Montoya 6.00 15.00
CT15 Matt Kenseth 10.00 25.00
CT16 Jimmie Johnson 10.00 25.00

2007 Wheels American Thunder Double Hat

OVERALL R-U ODDS 1:10
STATED PRINT RUN 99 SERIAL #'d SETS
DH1 Tony Raines 6.00 15.00
DH2 Ricky Rudd 12.50 30.00
DH3 Regan Smith 8.00 20.00
DH4 Brian Vickers 6.00 15.00
DH5 Jamie McMurray 6.00 15.00
DH6 Jeff Burton 8.00 20.00
DH7 Tony Stewart 12.50 30.00

2007 Wheels American Thunder Head to Toe

OVERALL R-U ODDS 1:10
STATED PRINT RUN 99 SERIAL #'d SETS
HT1 Michael Waltrip 10.00 25.00
HT2 Tony Stewart 20.00 50.00
HT3 Martin Truex Jr. 15.00 40.00
HT4 Kasey Kahne 20.00 50.00
HT5 Dale Earnhardt Jr. 25.00 60.00
HT6 Dale Jarrett 15.00 40.00
HT7 David Ragan 10.00 25.00
HT8 Elliott Sadler 12.50 30.00
HT9 J.J. Yeley 10.00 25.00
HT10 Paul Menard 4.00 10.00
HT11 Scott Riggs 8.00 20.00
HT12 David Stremme 10.00 25.00
HT13 Matt Kenseth 12.00 30.00
HT14 Jeff Gordon 25.00 60.00

2007 Wheels American Thunder Pushin' Pedal

OVERALL R-U ODDS 1:10
STATED PRINT RUN 99 SERIAL #'d SETS
PP1 Dale Earnhardt Jr. 10.00 25.00
PP2 Tony Stewart 8.00 20.00
PP3 Dale Jarrett 5.00 12.00
PP4 Denny Hamlin 6.00 15.00
PP5 Michael Waltrip 5.00 12.00
PP6 Jamie McMurray 5.00 12.00
PP7 J.J. Yeley 5.00 12.00
PP8 Carl Edwards 6.00 15.00
PP9 Martin Truex Jr. 4.00 10.00
PP10 Regan Smith 5.00 12.00
PP11 David Reutimann 4.00 10.00
PP12 Bobby Labonte 5.00 12.00
PP13 Juan Pablo Montoya 8.00 20.00
PP14 Jimmie Johnson 8.00 20.00
PP15 Reed Sorenson 4.00 10.00
PP16 Jeff Gordon 10.00 25.00

2007 Wheels American Thunder Single Hat

OVERALL R-U ODDS 1:10
STATED PRINT RUN 99 SERIAL #'d SETS
SH1 A.J. Allmendinger 10.00 25.00
SH2 Joe Nemechek 6.00 15.00

2007 Wheels American Thunder Starting Grid

STATED ODDS 1:2
SG1 Jeff Burton .30 .75
SG2 Dale Earnhardt Jr. .75 2.00
SG3 Jeff Gordon .75 2.00
SG4 Dale Jarrett .40 1.00
SG5 Jimmie Johnson .60 1.50
SG6 Sterling Marlin .40 1.00
SG7 Jamie McMurray .40 1.00
SG8 Martin Truex Jr. .30 .75
SG9 Brian Vickers .40 1.00
SG10 Michael Waltrip .40 1.00
SG11 Mark Martin .40 1.00
SG12 Cale Gale .60 1.50
SG13 Todd Kluever .40 1.00
SG14 Scott Wimmer .40 1.00
SG15 T.J. Bell .60 1.50
SG16 Kelly Bires .60 1.50
SG17 Todd Bodine .25 .60
SG18 Joey Clanton .40 1.00
SG19 Rick Crawford .25 .60
SG20 Erik Darnell .60 1.50
SG21 Ron Hornaday .25 .60
SG22 Kraig Kinser .60 1.50
SG23 Travis Kvapil .25 .60
SG24 Mike Skinner .25 .60
SG25 Jack Sprague .25 .60

2007 Wheels American Thunder Thunder Road

STATED ODDS 1:18
TR1 Jimmie Johnson 6.00 15.00
TR2 Michael Waltrip 4.00 10.00
TR3 Martin Truex Jr. 4.00 10.00
TR4 Jamie McMurray 4.00 10.00
TR5 Ryan Newman 4.00 10.00
TR6 Dale Jarrett 4.00 10.00
TR7 Jeff Gordon 8.00 20.00
TR8 Kevin Harvick 5.00 12.00
TR9 Bobby Labonte 4.00 10.00
TR10 Dale Earnhardt Jr. 8.00 20.00
TR11 Denny Hamlin 5.00 12.00
TR12 Jeff Burton 4.00 10.00
TR13 Brian Vickers 4.00 10.00
TR14 Matt Kenseth 6.00 15.00
TR15 Kasey Kahne 6.00 15.00
TR16 Sterling Marlin 4.00 10.00
TR17 Tony Stewart 6.00 15.00
TR18 Juan Pablo Montoya 8.00 20.00

2007 Wheels American Thunder Thunder Strokes

STATED ODDS 1:20
1 Aric Almirola 8.00 20.00
2 Marcos Ambrose 20.00 50.00
3 Greg Biffle 10.00 25.00
4 Dave Blaney 8.00 20.00
5 Todd Bodine 8.00 20.00
6 Clint Bowyer 15.00 40.00
7 Kurt Busch 12.50 30.00
8 Kyle Busch 20.00 50.00
9 Rick Crawford 6.00 15.00
10 Erik Darnell 6.00 15.00
11 Kertus Davis 8.00 20.00
12 Dale Earnhardt Jr. 50.00 100.00
13 Carl Edwards 15.00 40.00
14 Jeff Gordon 100.00 200.00
15 Jeff Green 6.00 15.00
16 David Gilliland 12.50 30.00
17 Denny Hamlin 12.00 30.00
18 Kevin Harvick 15.00 40.00
19 Sam Hornish Jr. 15.00 40.00
20 Dale Jarrett 15.00 40.00
21 Jimmie Johnson 25.00 60.00
22 Matt Kenseth 25.00 60.00
23 Todd Kluever 8.00 20.00
24 Travis Kvapil 6.00 15.00
25 Bobby Labonte 15.00 40.00
26 Stephen Leicht 10.00 25.00
27 Sterling Marlin
28 Mark Martin 30.00 60.00
29 Casey Mears 10.00 25.00
30 Joe Nemechek 8.00 20.00
31 Ryan Newman 10.00 25.00
32 Timothy Peters 6.00 15.00
33 Tony Raines 6.00 15.00
34 Johnny Sauter 5.00 12.00
35 Ken Schrader 8.00 20.00
36 Reed Sorenson 10.00 25.00
37 Tony Stewart 25.00 60.00
38 David Stremme 10.00 25.00
39 Martin Truex Jr. 8.00 20.00
40 Brian Vickers 10.00 25.00
41 Steve Wallace 10.00 25.00
42 Michael Waltrip 12.50 30.00
43 Jon Wood 6.00 15.00
44 J.J. Yeley 10.00 25.00

2007 Wheels American Thunder Triple Hat

OVERALL R-U ODDS 1:10
STATED PRINT RUN 99 SERIAL #'d SETS
TH1 Greg Biffle 10.00 25.00
TH2 Dave Blaney 6.00 15.00
TH3 Clint Bowyer 10.00 25.00
TH4 Kurt Busch 10.00 25.00
TH5 Kyle Busch 10.00 25.00
TH6 Dale Earnhardt Jr. 40.00 80.00
TH7 Carl Edwards 10.00 25.00
TH8 Jeff Gordon 40.00 80.00
TH9 David Gilliland 8.00 20.00
TH10 Denny Hamlin 10.00 25.00
TH11 Kevin Harvick 12.00 30.00
TH12 Dale Jarrett 10.00 25.00
TH13 Jimmie Johnson 20.00 50.00
TH14 Kasey Kahne 12.00 30.00
TH15 Matt Kenseth 10.00 25.00
TH16 Bobby Labonte 10.00 25.00
TH17 Mark Martin 12.00 30.00
TH18 Casey Mears 10.00 25.00
TH19 Paul Menard 8.00 20.00
TH20 Juan Pablo Montoya 10.00 25.00
TH21 Ryan Newman 10.00 25.00
TH22 Kyle Petty 10.00 25.00
TH23 David Ragan 6.00 15.00
TH24 David Reutimann 10.00 25.00
TH25 Scott Riggs 6.00 15.00
TH26 Elliott Sadler 8.00 20.00
TH27 Ken Schrader 8.00 20.00
TH28 Reed Sorenson 8.00 20.00
TH29 David Stremme 6.00 15.00
TH30 Martin Truex Jr. 8.00 20.00
TH31 Michael Waltrip 10.00 25.00
TH32 J.J. Yeley 6.00 15.00

2008 Wheels American Thunder

COMPLETE SET (90) 60.00 120.00
COMP.SET w/o SPs (85) 12.00 30.00
WAX BOX HOBBY 80.00 120.00
WAX BOX RETAIL 60.00 80.00
1 Jeff Gordon .75 2.00
2 A.J. Allmendinger .40 1.00
3 Greg Biffle .30 .75
4 Dave Blaney .25 .60
5 Clint Bowyer .40 1.00
6 Jeff Burton .30 .75
7 Kurt Busch .30 .75
8 Kyle Busch .50 1.25
9 Dale Earnhardt Jr. .75 2.00
10 Carl Edwards .40 1.00
11 David Gilliland .25 .60
12 Jeff Gordon .75 2.00
13 Denny Hamlin .50 1.25
14 Kevin Harvick .50 1.25
15 Jimmie Johnson .60 1.50
16 Kasey Kahne .40 1.00
17 Matt Kenseth .40 1.00
18 Travis Kvapil .25 .60
19 Bobby Labonte .40 1.00
20 Mark Martin .40 1.00
21 Jamie McMurray .40 1.00
22 Casey Mears .25 .60
23 Paul Menard .25 .60
24 Juan Pablo Montoya .60 1.50
25 Joe Nemechek .25 .60
26 Ryan Newman .30 .75
27 Kyle Petty .30 .75
28 David Ragan .30 .75
29 David Reutimann .30 .75
30 Scott Riggs .30 .75
31 Elliott Sadler .25 .60
32 Regan Smith .30 .75
33 Tony Stewart .60 1.50
34 Martin Truex Jr. .30 .75
35 Brian Vickers .25 .60
36 Michael Waltrip .40 1.00
37 Truex Jr./Menard/Martin RM .15 .40
38 Ragan/Kenseth/McMurray/Edwards RM .15 .40
39 Sorenson/Montoya/Franchitti RM .25 .60
40 Kahne/Sadler/Carpentier RM .30 .75
41 Dale Jr./Gordon/J.J./Mears RM .30 .75
42 Busch/Stewart/Hamlin RM .25 .60
43 Waltrip/Reutimann RM .15 .40
44 Busch/Newman/Hornish Jr. RM .25 .60
45 Bowyer/Harvick/Burton RM .20 .50
46 Chip Ganassi Racing .15 .40
47 Dale Earnhardt Inc. 1.00 2.50
48 Gillette Evernham Motorsports .15 .40
49 Hendrick Motorsports .15 .40
50 Joe Gibbs Racing .15 .40
51 Michael Waltrip Racing .15 .40
52 Penske Racing .12 .30
53 Petty Enterprises .25 .60
54 Roush Fenway Racing .15 .40
55 Kyle Busch FR .50 1.25
56 Jeff Gordon FR .75 2.00
57 Dale Earnhardt Jr. FR .75 2.00
58 Greg Biffle FR .30 .75
59 Jimmie Johnson FR .60 1.50
60 Jeff Burton FR .30 .75
61 Travis Kvapil FR .25 .60
62 David Ragan FR .30 .75
63 Clint Bowyer FR .40 1.00
64 Brian Vickers GG .25 .60
65 Kasey Kahne GG .40 1.00
66 David Reutimann GG .30 .75
67 Greg Biffle GG .30 .75
68 David Ragan GG .30 .75
69 Paul Menard GG .25 .60
70 Dale Earnhardt Jr. GG .75 2.00
71 David Gilliland GG .25 .60
72 Kyle Busch GG .50 1.25
73 Dave Blaney GG .25 .60
74 Dale Earnhardt Jr. PV .75 2.00
75 Jeff Gordon PV .75 2.00
76 Michael Waltrip PV .40 1.00
77 Kasey Kahne PV .40 1.00
78 Tony Stewart PV .60 1.50
79 Kevin Harvick PV .50 1.25
80 Matt Kenseth PV .40 1.00
81 Jimmie Johnson PV .60 1.50
82 Elliott Sadler PV .25 .60
83 J.Johnson/Pres.G.W.Bush OO .60 1.50
84 T.Stewart/Pres.G.W.Bush OO .60 1.50
85 M.Kenseth/Pres.G.W.Bush OO .40 1.00
86 A.Almirola FL AU/306 CRC 15.00 40.00
87 P.Carpentier FL AU/309 25.00 60.00
88 D.Franchitti FL AU 15.00 40.00
89 S.Hornish Jr. FL AU/362 15.00 40.00
90 M.McDowell FL AU/362 12.00 30.00

2008 Wheels American Thunder American Dreams

COMPLETE SET (12) 12.00 30.00
STATED ODDS 1:6
*GOLD/250: 1.2X TO 3X BASIC
AD1 Dale Earnhardt Jr. 1.00 2.50
AD2 Tony Stewart .75 2.00
AD3 Kasey Kahne .50 1.25
AD4 Kyle Busch .60 1.50
AD5 Jeff Gordon 1.00 2.50
AD6 Martin Truex Jr. .40 1.00
AD7 Jeff Burton .40 1.00
AD8 Denny Hamlin .60 1.50
AD9 Kevin Harvick .60 1.50
AD10 Mark Martin .50 1.25
AD11 Jimmie Johnson .75 2.00
AD12 Greg Biffle .40 1.00

2008 Wheels American Thunder Campaign Buttons

COMPLETE SET (6) 15.00 40.00
STATED ODDS 1 PER BLASTER BOX
*BLUE: .4X TO 1X BASE
*GOLD: .4X TO 1X BASE
CE Carl Edwards 4.00 10.00
JG Jeff Gordon 5.00 12.00
JJ Jimmie Johnson 4.00 10.00
KB Kyle Busch 3.00 8.00
KK Kasey Kahne 3.00 8.00
TS Tony Stewart 4.00 10.00

2008 Wheels American Thunder Campaign Trail

COMPLETE SET (18) 60.00 120.00
STATED ODDS 1:18
CT1 Kyle Busch 2.00 5.00
CT2 Martin Truex Jr. 1.25 3.00
CT3 Jimmie Johnson 2.50 6.00
CT4 Clint Bowyer 1.50 4.00
CT5 David Reutimann 1.25 3.00
CT6 Dale Earnhardt Jr. 3.00 8.00
CT7 Kevin Harvick 2.00 5.00
CT8 Scott Riggs 1.25 3.00
CT9 Jeff Burton 1.25 3.00
CT10 Tony Stewart 2.50 6.00
CT11 Casey Mears 1.00 2.50
CT12 Denny Hamlin 2.00 5.00
CT13 J.J. Yeley 1.50 4.00
CT14 Michael McDowell 2.50 6.00
CT15 Jeff Gordon 3.00 8.00
CT16 Kasey Kahne 1.50 4.00
CT17 Michael Waltrip 1.50 4.00
CT18 Joey Logano 6.00 15.00

2008 Wheels American Thunder Cool Threads

OVERALL MEM ODDS 1:10
CT1 Jamie McMurray/285 4.00 10.00
CT2 Kasey Kahne/325 4.00 10.00
CT3 Michael Waltrip/285 4.00 10.00
CT4 Brian Vickers/285 4.00 10.00
CT5 David Reutimann/285 4.00 10.00
CT6 Carl Edwards/325 5.00 12.00
CT7 Kevin Harvick/325 5.00 12.00
CT8 Mark Martin/325 5.00 12.00
CT9 Martin Truex Jr./325 4.00 10.00
CT10 Aric Almirola/285 4.00 10.00
CT11 Regan Smith/285 4.00 10.00
CT12 David Ragan/325 4.00 10.00

2008 Wheels American Thunder Delegates

COMPLETE SET (25) 15.00 40.00
STATED ODDS 1:2
D1 A.J. Allmendinger .75 2.00
D2 Aric Almirola .60 1.50
D3 Clint Bowyer .75 2.00
D4 Jeff Burton .60 1.50
D5 Kurt Busch .60 1.50
D6 Dale Earnhardt Jr. 1.50 4.00
D7 Jeff Gordon 1.50 4.00
D8 Jimmie Johnson 1.25 3.00
D9 Mark Martin .75 2.00
D10 Michael McDowell 1.25 3.00
D11 Casey Mears .50 1.25
D12 Joe Nemechek .50 1.25
D13 David Reutimann .60 1.50
D14 Scott Riggs .60 1.50
D15 Regan Smith .60 1.50
D16 Tony Stewart 1.25 3.00
D17 Landon Cassill 1.50 4.00
D18 Bryan Clauson .75 2.00
D19 Cale Gale .50 1.25
D20 Joey Logano 4.00 10.00
D21 Scott Wimmer .60 1.50
D22 Rick Crawford .50 1.25
D23 Erik Darnell .60 1.50
D24 Ron Hornaday .50 1.25
D25 Jack Sprague .50 1.25

2008 Wheels American Thunder Double Hat

OVERALL MEM ODDS 1:10
STATED PRINT RUN 99 SERIAL #'d SETS
DH1 A.J. Allmendinger 4.00 10.00
DH2 Jeff Burton 8.00 20.00
DH3 David Gilliland 4.00 10.00
DH4 Denny Hamlin 10.00 25.00
DH5 Sam Hornish Jr. 8.00 20.00
DH6 Travis Kvapil 4.00 10.00
DH7 Jamie McMurray 6.00 15.00
DH8 Ryan Newman 8.00 20.00
DH9 David Reutimann 8.00 20.00
DH10 Regan Smith 4.00 10.00
DH11 Brian Vickers 5.00 12.00

2008 Wheels American Thunder Future Leaders Nicknames Autographs

STATED PRINT RUN 3-53
86 Almirola Dream Big/53 25.00 50.00
87 Carpentier 2008 Rookie/20
87 Carpentier number 10/14
87 Carpentier Flying French Man/15
87 Carpentier number 10 Valvoline/3

2008 Wheels American Thunder Head to Toe

OVERALL MEM ODDS 1:10
STATED PRINT RUN 99-150
HT1 Tony Stewart/150 6.00 15.00
HT2 Jamie McMurray/99 4.00 10.00
HT3 Greg Biffle/99 3.00 8.00
HT4 David Ragan/99 3.00 8.00
HT5 Michael Waltrip/99 4.00 10.00
HT6 Dale Jarrett/125 4.00 10.00
HT7 David Reutimann/99 3.00 8.00
HT8 Carl Edwards/125 4.00 10.00
HT9 Jeff Gordon/99 8.00 20.00
HT10 Dale Earnhardt Jr./150 8.00 20.00
HT11 Elliott Sadler/99 2.50 6.00
HT12 Martin Truex Jr./99 3.00 8.00
HT13 Matt Kenseth/125 4.00 10.00
HT14 Juan Pablo Montoya/99 6.00 15.00
HT15 Kasey Kahne/125 4.00 10.00
HT16 Denny Hamlin/125 5.00 12.00

2008 Wheels American Thunder Motorcade

COMPLETE SET (9) 12.00 30.00
STATED ODDS 1:10
M1 Jeff Gordon 1.25 3.00
M2 Michael Waltrip .60 1.50
M3 Jimmie Johnson 1.00 2.50
M4 Bobby Labonte .60 1.50
M5 Ryan Newman .50 1.25
M6 Clint Bowyer .60 1.50
M7 Tony Stewart 1.00 2.50
M8 Dale Earnhardt Jr. 1.25 3.00
M9 Matt Kenseth .60 1.50

2008 Wheels American Thunder Pushin' Pedal

OVERALL MEM ODDS 1:10
STATED PRINT RUNS 99-150
PP 1 Tony Stewart/150 5.00 12.00
PP 2 Jamie McMurray 3.00 8.00
PP 3 Greg Biffle 2.50 6.00
PP 4 David Ragan 2.50 6.00
PP 5 Michael Waltrip 3.00 8.00
PP 6 Dale Jarrett 3.00 8.00
PP 7 David Reutimann 2.50 6.00
PP 8 Carl Edwards 3.00 8.00
PP 9 Jeff Gordon 6.00 15.00
PP 10 Dale Earnhardt Jr./150 6.00 15.00
PP 11 Elliott Sadler 2.00 5.00
PP 12 Martin Truex Jr. 2.50 6.00
PP 13 Matt Kenseth 3.00 8.00
PP 14 Juan Pablo Montoya 5.00 12.00
PP 15 Kasey Kahne 3.00 8.00
PP 16 Denny Hamlin 4.00 10.00

2008 Wheels American Thund Trackside Treasury Autograp

STATED ODDS 1:20
AA A.J. Allmendinger 6.00
AA Aric Almirola 8.00
BL Bobby Labonte 12.00
BV Brian Vickers 8.00
CB Colin Braun 10.00
CB Clint Bowyer 15.00
CG Cale Gale 6.00
CM Casey Mears 10.00
DB Dave Blaney 6.00
DG David Gilliland 8.00
DH Denny Hamlin 20.00
DR David Ragan 12.00
ED Erik Darnell 8.00
ES Elliott Sadler 10.00
GB Greg Biffle 15.00
JB Jeff Burton 12.00
JG Jeff Gordon 60.00
JJ Jimmie Johnson 25.00
JL Joey Logano 15.00
JM Juan Pablo Montoya 12.00
JM Jamie McMurray 8.00
JN Joe Nemechek 6.00
JS Jack Sprague 6.00
JY J.J. Yeley 6.00
KB Kelly Bires 6.00
KB Kurt Busch 12.00
KB Kyle Busch 12.00
KH Kevin Harvick 20.00
MA Marcos Ambrose 25.00
MK Matt Kenseth 15.00
MM Mark Martin 15.00
MS Mike Skinner 6.00
MT Martin Truex Jr. 8.00
MW Michael Waltrip 10.00
PM Paul Menard 8.00
RC Rick Crawford 6.00
RH Ron Hornaday 6.00
RN Ryan Newman 8.00
RS Regan Smith 8.00
RS Reed Sorenson 8.00
SR Scott Riggs 6.00
SW Scott Wimmer 6.00
TK Travis Kvapil 6.00
TS Tony Stewart 60.00

2008 Wheels American Thund Trackside Treasury Autograp Gold

STATED PRINT RUN 25 SER.#'d SETS
AA A.J. Allmendinger 8.00
AA Aric Almirola
BL Bobby Labonte 20.00
BV Brian Vickers 10.00
CB Colin Braun 12.00
CB Clint Bowyer
CG Cale Gale 10.00
CM Casey Mears 12.00
DB Dave Blaney 8.00
DG David Gilliland 12.00
DH Denny Hamlin 25.00
DR David Ragan 20.00
ED Erik Darnell 10.00
ES Elliott Sadler 15.00
GB Greg Biffle 25.00
JB Jeff Burton 15.00
JG Jeff Gordon 100.00
JJ Jimmie Johnson 75.00
JL Joey Logano 175.00
JM Juan Pablo Montoya
JM Jamie McMurray 12.00
JN Joe Nemechek 10.00
JS Jack Sprague 12.00
JY J.J. Yeley 12.00
KB Kelly Bires 12.00
KB Kurt Busch 15.00
KB Kyle Busch 50.00
KH Kevin Harvick 25.00
MA Marcos Ambrose 50.00
MK Matt Kenseth 60.00
MM Mark Martin 15.00
MS Mike Skinner 12.00
MT Martin Truex Jr. 20.00
MW Michael Waltrip 12.00
PM Paul Menard 12.00
RC Rick Crawford 12.00
RH Ron Hornaday 12.00
RN Ryan Newman 10.00
RS Regan Smith
RS Reed Sorenson 12.00
SR Scott Riggs 12.00

SW Scott Wimmer 12.00 30.00
TK Travis Kvapil 10.00 25.00
TS Tony Stewart 60.00 120.00

2008 Wheels American Thunder Triple Hat

OVERALL MEM ODDS 1:10
TH1 Greg Biffle/99 8.00 20.00
TH2 Dave Blaney/99 6.00 15.00
TH3 Clint Bowyer/125 10.00 25.00
TH4 Kurt Busch/99 6.00 15.00
TH5 Kyle Busch/125 10.00 25.00
TH6 Patrick Carpentier/99 10.00 25.00
TH7 Dale Earnhardt Jr./125 20.00 50.00
TH8 Carl Edwards/125 15.00 40.00
TH9 Jeff Gordon/125 20.00 50.00
TH10 Kevin Harvick/125 15.00 40.00
TH11 Dale Jarrett/99 10.00 25.00
TH12 Jimmie Johnson/125 10.00 25.00
TH13 Kasey Kahne/99 15.00 40.00
TH14 Matt Kenseth/125 12.00 30.00
TH15 Bobby Labonte/99 6.00 15.00
TH16 Mark Martin/125 15.00 40.00
TH17 Casey Mears/99 8.00 20.00
TH18 Paul Menard/99 6.00 15.00
TH19 Juan Montoya/125 8.00 20.00
TH20 Kyle Petty/99 10.00 25.00
TH21 David Ragan/99 8.00 20.00
TH22 Elliott Sadler/99 10.00 25.00
TH23 Reed Sorenson/99 8.00 20.00
TH24 Tony Stewart/125 15.00 40.00
TH25 Martin Truex Jr./125 10.00 25.00
TH26 Michael Waltrip/125 8.00 20.00
TH27 J.J. Yeley/99 8.00 20.00

2003 Wheels Autographs

Issued at a stated rate of one in 60, these 52 cards feature most of the leading drivers on the NASCAR circuit.

1 John Andretti AT/HG 6.00 15.00
2 Casey Atwood AT/HG 10.00 25.00
3 Greg Biffle Blue BGN HG 10.00 25.00
4 Greg Biffle Red WC AT 10.00 25.00
5 Dave Blaney AT/HG 6.00 15.00
6 Brett Bodine AT/HG 6.00 15.00
7 Todd Bodine AT 6.00 15.00
8 Jeff Burton Citgo AT 8.00 20.00
9 Jeff Burton Gain AT 8.00 20.00
10 Ward Burton AT 10.00 25.00
11 Kurt Busch AT/HG 12.50 30.00
12 Matt Crafton AT/HG 6.00 15.00
13 Ricky Craven AT/HG 10.00 25.00
14 Kerry Earnhardt AT 12.50 30.00
15 Coy Gibbs AT/HG 8.00 20.00
16 Jeff Gordon AT/HG 50.00 120.00
17 Robby Gordon AT/HG 8.00 20.00
18 David Green AT/HG 6.00 15.00
19 Jeff Green AT/HG 6.00 15.00
20 Mark Green AT/HG 6.00 15.00
21 Bobby Hamilton AT/HG 10.00 25.00
22 Kevin Harvick AT/HG 8.00 20.00
23 Ricky Hendrick AT/HG 15.00 40.00
24 Shane Hmiel AT/HG 15.00 30.00
25 Dale Jarrett AT/HG 15.00 40.00
26 Jimmie Johnson AT/HG 25.00 60.00
27 Jason Keller AT/HG 6.00 15.00
28 Matt Kenseth AT/HG 15.00 40.00
29 Travis Kvapil AT/HG 10.00 25.00
30 Bobby Labonte AT/HG 15.00 40.00
31 Terry Labonte AT/HG 15.00 40.00
32 Randy LaJoie AT/HG 6.00 15.00
33 Jason Leffler AT/HG 6.00 15.00
34 Chad Little AT/HG 6.00 15.00
35 Sterling Marlin AT 12.50 30.00
36 Mark Martin AT/HG 20.00 50.00
37 Jeremy Mayfield AT/HG 15.00 40.00
38 Jamie McMurray Havoline AT 10.00 25.00
39 Jamie McMurray Williams AT/HG 10.00 25.00
40 Casey Mears Phillips 66 AT/HG 10.00 25.00
41 Casey Mears Target AT 10.00 25.00
42 Ted Musgrave AT/HG 10.00 25.00
43 Jerry Nadeau AT 10.00 25.00
44 Joe Nemechek AT/HG 6.00 15.00
45 Ryan Newman AT/HG 15.00 30.00
46 Hank Parker Jr. AT/HG 6.00 15.00
47 Kyle Petty AT/HG 12.50 30.00
48 Tony Raines AT/HG 6.00 15.00
49 Scott Riggs AT/HG 10.00 25.00
50 Ricky Rudd AT/HG 12.50 30.00
51 Joe Ruttman AT/HG 6.00 15.00
52 Elliott Sadler AT/HG 10.00 25.00
53 Johnny Sauter AT/HG 8.00 20.00
54 Ken Schrader AT/HG 8.00 20.00
55 Dennis Setzer AT/HG 6.00 15.00
56 Mike Skinner AT/HG 10.00 25.00
57 Jimmy Spencer AT/HG 6.00 15.00
58 Brian Vickers AT/HG 10.00 25.00
59 Rusty Wallace AT/HG 12.50 30.00
60 Michael Waltrip 10.00 25.00
61 Scott Wimmer AT/HG 10.00 25.00
62 Jon Wood AT/HG 8.00 20.00

2004 Wheels Autographs

These 59 cards were signed by the drivers pictured on them and inserted in packs at a rate of one in 60. They were certified by the manufacturer on the card backs.

1 Bobby Allison HG 8.00 20.00
2 Greg Biffle HG 10.00 25.00
3 Dave Blaney HG 6.00 15.00
4 Mike Bliss HG 6.00 15.00
5 Brett Bodine HG 8.00 20.00
6 Todd Bodine HG 8.00 20.00
7 Clint Bowyer AT 8.00 20.00
8 Jeff Burton HG 8.00 20.00
9 Ward Burton HG 10.00 25.00
10 Kurt Busch HG 12.50 30.00
11 Kyle Busch HG 20.00 50.00
12 Terry Cook AT 8.00 20.00
13 Stacy Compton HG 8.00 20.00
14 Matt Crafton HG 8.00 20.00
15 Ricky Craven HG 10.00 25.00
16 Rick Crawford HG 8.00 20.00
17 Dale Earnhardt Jr. AT 50.00 100.00
18 Kerry Earnhardt HG 15.00 40.00
19 Carl Edwards HG 10.00 25.00
20 Tim Fedewa AT 8.00 20.00
21 Christian Fittipaldi HG 8.00 20.00
22 Brendan Gaughan AT 10.00 25.00
23 Coy Gibbs HG 8.00 20.00
24 Jeff Gordon HG 100.00 200.00
25 Robby Gordon AT 10.00 25.00
26 Tina Gordon HG 8.00 20.00
27 David Green HG 8.00 20.00
28 Jeff Green AT 8.00 20.00
29 Kevin Harvick HG 12.50 30.00
30 Andy Houston HG 6.00 15.00
31 Dale Jarrett HG 15.00 40.00
32 Ned Jarrett HG 8.00 20.00
33 Jimmie Johnson HG 25.00 60.00
34 Kasey Kahne HG 15.00 40.00
35 Jason Keller HG 8.00 20.00
36 Matt Kenseth HG 6.00 15.00
37 Travis Kvapil HG 10.00 25.00
38 Bobby Labonte HG 6.00 15.00
39 Terry Labonte HG 6.00 15.00
40 Damon Lusk HG 6.00 15.00
41 Sterling Marlin HG 12.50 30.00
42 Mark Martin HG 20.00 50.00
43 Jeremy Mayfield HG 10.00 25.00
44 Mike McLaughlin HG 6.00 15.00
45 Jamie McMurray HG 10.00 25.00
46 Casey Mears HG 10.00 25.00
47 Joe Nemechek HG 8.00 20.00
48 Ryan Newman HG 15.00 30.00
49 Billy Parker Jr. AT 10.00 25.00
50 Benny Parsons HG 15.00 40.00
51 David Pearson HG 12.00 30.00
52 Kyle Petty HG 15.00 40.00
53 Richard Petty HG 20.00 50.00
54 Tony Raines HG 6.00 15.00
55 Scott Riggs HG 8.00 20.00
56 Ricky Rudd HG 10.00 25.00
57 Elliott Sadler AT 6.00 15.00
58 Johnny Sauter HG 12.00 30.00
59 Ken Schrader HG 8.00 20.00
60 Dennis Setzer HG 8.00 20.00
61 Regan Smith HG 8.00 20.00
62 Jack Sprague AT 8.00 20.00
63 Tony Stewart AT 25.00 60.00
64 Martin Truex Jr. 10.00 25.00
65 Brian Vickers HG 10.00 25.00
66 Kenny Wallace HG 10.00 25.00
67 Rusty Wallace HG 6.00 15.00
68 Michael Waltrip AT 10.00 25.00
69 Scott Wimmer HG 10.00 25.00
70 Glen Wood HG 8.00 20.00
71 Jon Wood HG 8.00 20.00
72 Cale Yarborough HG 8.00 20.00
73 J.J. Yeley AT 12.50 30.00

2005 Wheels Autographs

These 67 cards were signed by the drivers pictured on them and inserted in packs at a rate of one in 60 in both Wheels American Thunder and Wheels High Gear packs. They were certified by the manufacturer on the card backs.

1 Bobby Allison 8.00 20.00
2 Greg Biffle BGN 10.00 25.00
3 Greg Biffle NC 10.00 25.00
4 Mike Bliss 8.00 20.00
5 Clint Bowyer 10.00 25.00
6 Kurt Busch 12.00 30.00
7 Kyle Busch BGN 20.00 50.00
8 Kyle Busch NC 20.00 50.00
9 Terry Cook 8.00 20.00
10 Matt Crafton 8.00 20.00
11 Ricky Craven 10.00 25.00
12 Rick Crawford 6.00 15.00
13 Dale Earnhardt Jr. 50.00 100.00
14 Kerry Earnhardt 10.00 25.00
15 Tim Fedewa 8.00 20.00
16 Brendan Gaughan 10.00 25.00
17 Jeff Gordon 75.00 150.00
18 Robby Gordon 10.00 25.00
19 Tina Gordon 10.00 25.00
20 David Green 8.00 20.00
21 Jeff Green 8.00 20.00
22 Kevin Harvick 12.00 30.00
23 Ron Hornaday 8.00 20.00
24 Andy Houston 8.00 20.00
25 Dale Jarrett 15.00 40.00
26 Jimmie Johnson 25.00 60.00
27 Kasey Kahne BGN 20.00 50.00
28 Kasey Kahne NC 20.00 50.00
29 Jason Keller 8.00 20.00
30 Matt Kenseth BGN 15.00 40.00
31 Matt Kenseth NC 15.00 40.00
32 Bobby Labonte 15.00 40.00
33 Justin Labonte 10.00 25.00
34 Terry Labonte 15.00 40.00
35 Sterling Marlin 12.00 30.00
36 Mark Martin 20.00 50.00
37 Jeremy Mayfield 10.00 25.00
38 Mark McFarland 8.00 20.00
39 Jamie McMurray 10.00 25.00
40 Casey Mears 10.00 25.00
41 Joe Nemechek 10.00 25.00
42 Ryan Newman 12.00 30.00
43 Steve Park 20.00 50.00
44 Benny Parsons 30.00 60.00
45 David Pearson 10.00 25.00
46 Kyle Petty 8.00 20.00
47 Richard Petty 20.00 50.00
48 Scott Riggs 8.00 20.00
49 Ricky Rudd 12.00 30.00
50 Boris Said 10.00 25.00
51 Johnny Sauter 10.00 25.00
52 Ken Schrader CTS 10.00 25.00
53 Ken Schrader NC 10.00 25.00
54 Dennis Setzer 8.00 20.00
55 Jack Sprague 6.00 15.00
56 Tony Stewart 40.00 80.00
57 Martin Truex Jr. 10.00 25.00
58 Brian Vickers 10.00 25.00
59 Kenny Wallace 8.00 20.00
60 Rusty Wallace 12.00 30.00
61 Michael Waltrip 10.00 25.00
62 Scott Wimmer 8.00 20.00
63 Paul Wolfe 10.00 25.00
64 Glen Wood 6.00 15.00
65 Jon Wood 8.00 20.00
66 Cale Yarborough 8.00 20.00
67 J.J. Yeley 10.00 30.00

2006 Wheels Autographs

These 53 cards were signed by the drivers pictured on them and inserted in packs at a rate of one in 40 in both Wheels American Thunder and Wheels High Gear packs. They were certified by the manufacturer on the card backs.

STATED ODDS 1:40
1 Bobby Allison 8.00 20.00
2 Donnie Allison 12.00 30.00
3 Buddy Baker 6.00 15.00
4 Greg Biffle 10.00 25.00
5 Dave Blaney 6.00 15.00
6 Clint Bowyer NBS 15.00 40.00
7 Jeff Burton NC 8.00 20.00
8 Kurt Busch NC 10.00 25.00
9 Kyle Busch NC 15.00 40.00
10 Terry Cook CTS 6.00 15.00
11 Ricky Craven CTS 8.00 20.00
12 Rick Crawford 5.00 12.00
13 Kerry Earnhardt 8.00 20.00
14 Carl Edwards NBS 10.00 25.00
15 Carl Edwards NC 10.00 25.00
16 Harry Gant 6.00 15.00
17 Jeff Gordon NC 125.00 250.00
18 Robby Gordon 8.00 20.00
19 David Green NBS 6.00 15.00
20 Jeff Green 6.00 15.00
21 Denny Hamlin NBS 30.00 60.00
22 Kevin Harvick NC 12.00 30.00
23 Ron Hornaday CTS 6.00 15.00
24 Jack Ingram 5.00 12.00
25 Dale Jarrett NC 6.00 15.00
26 Jimmie Johnson NC 30.00 60.00
27 Kasey Kahne NBS 20.00 50.00
28 Kasey Kahne NC 20.00 50.00
29 Jason Keller NBS 5.00 12.00
30 Matt Kenseth NBS 10.00 25.00
31 Matt Kenseth NC 12.00 30.00
32 Todd Kluever CTS 5.00 12.00
33 Travis Kvapil NC 5.00 12.00
34 Bobby Labonte NC 15.00 40.00
35 Justin Labonte NBS 10.00 25.00
36 Bill Lester CTS 10.00 25.00
37 Fred Lorenzen 8.00 20.00
38 Sterling Marlin NC 10.00 25.00
39 Mark Martin NC 40.00 80.00
40 Jeremy Mayfield NC 10.00 25.00
41 Jamie McMurray NC 10.00 25.00
42 Casey Mears NC 6.00 15.00
43 Joe Nemechek NC 6.00 15.00
44 Ryan Newman NC 6.00 15.00
45 Marvin Panch 6.00 15.00
46 Benny Parsons 30.00 60.00
47 David Pearson 10.00 25.00
48 Richard Petty 25.00 60.00
49 Tony Raines NBS 5.00 12.00
50 Ricky Rudd 10.00 25.00
51 Boris Said NC 5.00 12.00
52 Johnny Sauter 5.00 12.00
53 Ken Schrader CTS 6.00 15.00
54 Dennis Setzer 5.00 12.00
55 Mike Skinner 5.00 12.00
56 Reed Sorenson NBS 5.00 12.00
57 Jack Sprague CTS 6.00 15.00
58 Tony Stewart NC 25.00 60.00
59 Brian Vickers NC 5.00 12.00
60 Rusty Wallace 12.00 30.00
61 Rex White 6.00 15.00
62 Scott Wimmer NC 5.00 12.00
63 Glen Wood 5.00 12.00
64 Jon Wood NBS 5.00 12.00
65 Cale Yarborough 8.00 20.00
66 Robert Yates 6.00 15.00
67 J.J. Yeley 6.00 15.00

2007 Wheels Autographs

These 42 cards were signed by the drivers pictured on them and inserted in packs at a rate of one in 40 in 2007 Wheels High Gear Hobby packs, and one in 96 in Retail packs of 2007 Wheels High Gear. They were certified by the manufacturer on the card backs. They were available in packs of Wheels High Gear and Wheels American Thunder, or both, and are noted below.

STATED ODDS WHG 1:40 HOB, 1:96 RET
UNPRICED PRESS PLATE PRINT RUN 1
1 Greg Biffle NC HG 10.00 25.00
2 Dave Blaney NC HG 6.00 15.00
3 Clint Bowyer NC HG 10.00 30.00
4 Jeff Burton NC HG 8.00 20.00
5 Kurt Busch NC HG 10.00 30.00
6 Kyle Busch NC HG 15.00 40.00
7 Rick Crawford 5.00 12.00
8 Erin Crocker CTS HG 15.00 40.00
9 Erik Darnell CTS HG 5.00 12.00
10 Dale Earnhardt Jr. NC HG 50.00 100.00
11 Carl Edwards NC HG 20.00 50.00
12 David Green NBS HG
13 Jeff Green NC HG 5.00 12.00
14 Denny Hamlin NC HG 12.00 30.00
15 Kevin Harvick NC HG 12.00 30.00
16 Ron Hornaday CTS HG 5.00 12.00
17 Jimmie Johnson NC HG 25.00 60.00
18 Kasey Kahne NC HG 20.00 50.00
19 Matt Kenseth NC HG 15.00 40.00
20 Todd Kluever NBS HG 8.00 20.00
21 Bobby Labonte NC HG 15.00 40.00
22 Terry Labonte NC HG 15.00 40.00
23 Burney Lamar NBS HG 6.00 15.00
24 Bill Lester CTS HG 6.00 15.00
25 Mark Martin NC HG 20.00 50.00
26 Jamie McMurray NC HG 8.00 20.00
27 Casey Mears NC HG 10.00 25.00
28 Paul Menard NBS HG 6.00 15.00
29 Joe Nemechek NC HG 6.00 15.00
30 Ryan Newman NC HG 15.00 30.00
31 Danny O'Quinn NBS HG 6.00 15.00
32 Tony Raines NC HG 5.00 12.00
33 David Ragan CTS HG 8.00 20.00
34 Mike Skinner CTS HG 5.00 12.00
35 Reed Sorenson NC HG 10.00 25.00
36 Regan Smith NBS HG 6.00 15.00
37 David Stremme NC HG 12.00 30.00
38 Tony Stewart NC HG 25.00 60.00
39 Martin Truex Jr. NC HG 15.00 40.00
40 Brian Vickers NC HG 8.00 20.00
41 Steve Wallace NBS HG 8.00 20.00
42 Jon Wood NBS HG 5.00 12.00
43 J.J. Yeley NC HG 8.00 20.00

2008 Wheels Autographs

STATED ODDS 1:40
UNPRICED PRESS PLATE PRINT RUN 1
1 A.J. Allmendinger NC HG 10.00 25.00
2 Marcos Ambrose NBS HG 20.00 40.00
3 Greg Biffle NC HG 10.00 25.00
4 Kelly Bires CTS HG 6.00 15.00
5 Dave Blaney NC HG 6.00 15.00
6 Clint Bowyer NC HG 12.00 30.00
7 Kurt Busch NC HG 12.00 30.00
8 Joey Clanton CTS HG 6.00 15.00
9 Rick Crawford CTS HG 6.00 15.00
10 Dale Earnhardt Jr. NC HG 60.00 150.00
11 Jeff Gordon NC HG 50.00 100.00
12 Denny Hamlin NC HG 15.00 40.00
13 Kevin Harvick NC HG 15.00 40.00
14 Ron Hornaday CTS HG 6.00 15.00
15 Dale Jarrett NC HG 8.00 20.00
16 Jimmie Johnson NC HG 25.00 60.00
17 Kasey Kahne NC HG 20.00 50.00
18 Matt Kenseth NC HG 12.00 30.00
19 Travis Kvapil CTS HG 6.00 15.00
20 Bobby Labonte NC HG 15.00 30.00
21 Mark Martin NC HG 15.00 40.00
22 Ryan Newman NC HG 10.00 25.00
23 David Ragan NC HG 8.00 20.00
24 Tony Raines NC HG 6.00 15.00
25 Scott Riggs NC HG 8.00 20.00
26 Elliott Sadler NC HG 10.00 25.00
27 Johnny Sauter NC HG 6.00 15.00
28 Ken Schrader NC HG 6.00 15.00
29 Regan Smith NC HG 6.00 15.00
30 Jack Sprague CTS HG 6.00 15.00
31 Tony Stewart NC HG 25.00 60.00
32 David Stremme NC HG 10.00 25.00
33 Martin Truex Jr. NC HG 8.00 20.00
34 Brian Vickers NC HG 10.00 25.00
35 Michael Waltrip NC HG 10.00 25.00
36 Scott Wimmer NBS HG 6.00 15.00
37 Jon Wood NC HG 6.00 15.00
38 J.J. Yeley NC HG 6.00 15.00

2008 Wheels Autographs Chase Edition

STATED PRINT RUN 25 SER.#'d SETS
1 Clint Bowyer NC 50.00 100.00
2 Kurt Busch NC 40.00 80.00
3 Jeff Gordon NC 150.00 300.00
4 Denny Hamlin NC 50.00 100.00
5 Kevin Harvick NC 60.00 120.00
6 Jimmie Johnson NC 75.00 150.00
7 Matt Kenseth NC 60.00 120.00
8 Tony Stewart NC 75.00 150.00
9 Martin Truex Jr. NC 60.00 120.00

2009 Wheels Autographs

STATED ODDS 1:24
UNPRICED PRESS PLATE PRINT RUN 1
2 Aric Almirola 6.00 15.00
3 Greg Biffle 6.00 15.00
4 Kelly Bires 5.00 12.00
5 Clint Bowyer 8.00 20.00
6 Colin Braun 6.00 15.00
7 Jeff Burton 6.00 15.00
8 Kurt Busch 6.00 15.00
9 Kyle Busch blue 10.00 25.00
10 Kyle Busch brown/25 50.00 100.00
11 Patrick Carpentier 8.00 20.00
12 Landon Cassill 15.00 40.00
13 Bryan Clauson 6.00 15.00
14 Rick Crawford 5.00 12.00
15 Erik Darnell 6.00 15.00
16 Dale Earnhardt Jr. black 30.00 80.00
17 Dale Earnhardt Jr. red/25 100.00 200.00
18 Carl Edwards green 8.00 20.00
19 Carl Edwards green/25 100.00 175.00
20 Cale Gale 5.00 12.00
21 David Gilliland 5.00 12.00
22 Jeff Gordon red/25 150.00 300.00
23 Jeff Gordon blue 75.00 150.00
24 Denny Hamlin purple/25 40.00 100.00
25 Denny Hamlin blue 8.00 20.00
26 Kevin Harvick blue 10.00 25.00
27 Kevin Harvick blue/50 15.00 40.00
28 Kevin Harvick yellow/25 12.00 30.00
29 Ron Hornaday 5.00 12.00
30 Sam Hornish Jr. 5.00 12.00
31 Jimmie Johnson black/25 60.00 120.00
32 Jimmie Johnson blue 40.00 100.00
33 Kasey Kahne black/25 60.00 120.00
34 Kasey Kahne blue/25 60.00 120.00
35 Kasey Kahne blue 50.00 100.00
36 Matt Kenseth yellow/25 75.00 150.00
37 Matt Kenseth blue 8.00 20.00
38 Brad Keselowski 10.00 25.00
39 Travis Kvapil 5.00 12.00
40 Bobby Labonte 8.00 20.00
41 Joey Logano black/25 75.00 150.00
42 Joey Logano blue/25 75.00 150.00
43 Joey Logano blue 15.00 40.00
44 Mark Martin 8.00 20.00
45 Jamie McMurray 8.00 20.00
46 Casey Mears 5.00 12.00
47 Paul Menard 5.00 12.00
48 Chase Miller 5.00 12.00
49 Juan Pablo Montoya 10.00 25.00
50 Joe Nemechek 5.00 12.00
51 David Ragan blue 6.00 15.00
52 David Ragan red/25 40.00 100.00
53 Scott Riggs 6.00 15.00
54 Elliott Sadler 5.00 12.00
55 Mike Skinner 5.00 12.00
56 Regan Smith 6.00 15.00
57 Reed Sorenson 5.00 12.00
58 Jack Sprague 6.00 15.00
59 Martin Truex Jr. 6.00 15.00
60 Brian Vickers 5.00 12.00
61 Michael Waltrip 8.00 20.00
62 Scott Wimmer 6.00 15.00
80 A.J. Allmendinger 8.00 20.00

2010 Wheels Autographs

STATED ODDS 1:24
UNPRICED PRINT PLATE PRINT RUN 10
UNPRICED SPECIAL INK PRINT RUN 10
UNPRICED TARGET PRINT RUN 10
1 Justin Allgaier 6.00 15.00
2 A.J. Allmendinger 8.00 20.00
3 Aric Almirola 6.00 15.00
4 Marcos Ambrose 15.00 40.00
5 Greg Biffle 6.00 15.00
6 Clint Bowyer 8.00 20.00
7 Colin Braun 6.00 15.00
8 Kurt Busch 6.00 15.00
9 Kyle Busch 25.00 60.00
10 Ricky Carmichael 12.00 30.00
11 Erik Darnell 5.00 12.00
12 Marc Davis 5.00 12.00
13 Dale Earnhardt Jr. 50.00 100.00
14 Carl Edwards 10.00 25.00
15 J.R. Fitzpatrick 6.00 15.00
16 Brendan Gaughan 5.00 12.00
17 Jeff Gordon
18 Robby Gordon 5.00 12.00
19 Denny Hamlin 15.00 40.00
20 Kevin Harvick 10.00 25.00
21 Ron Hornaday 5.00 12.00
22 Sam Hornish Jr. 6.00 15.00
23 Jimmie Johnson 50.00 100.00
24 Kasey Kahne 50.00 100.00
25 Matt Kenseth 8.00 20.00
26 Brad Keselowski 10.00 25.00
27 Brad Keselowski 10.00 25.00
28 Bobby Labonte 8.00 20.00
29 Scott Lagasse Jr. 5.00 12.00
30 Stephen Leicht 5.00 12.00
31 Joey Logano 25.00 50.00
32 Tayler Malsam 5.00 12.00
33 Mark Martin 8.00 20.00
34 Jamie McMurray 8.00 20.00
35 Casey Mears 5.00 12.00
36 Paul Menard 5.00 12.00
37 Juan Pablo Montoya 8.00 20.00
38 Joe Nemechek 5.00 12.00
39 Ryan Newman 20.00 50.00
40 David Ragan 6.00 15.00
41 David Reutimann 6.00 15.00
42 Elliott Sadler 5.00 12.00
43 Mike Skinner 5.00 12.00
44 Regan Smith 6.00 15.00
45 Reed Sorenson 5.00 12.00
46 Scott Speed 8.00 20.00
47 Ricky Stenhouse Jr. 8.00 20.00
48 Tony Stewart 40.00 80.00
49 Martin Truex Jr. 6.00 15.00
50 Brian Vickers 5.00 12.00
51 Steve Wallace 6.00 15.00
52 Michael Waltrip 8.00 20.00

1994 Wheels High Gear Promos

Wheels released this three-card set as a promotional tool for its 1994 High Gear set. All three cards may be found with either silver or gold foil layering.

COMPLETE SILVER SET (3) 6.00 15.00
*GOLD CARDS: .8X TO 2X SILVERS
P1 Jeff Gordon Silver 3.00 8.00
P2 Rusty Wallace Silver 3.00 5.00
P3 Kyle Petty Silver 2.00 4.00

1994 Wheels High Gear

This 200-card set was issued in two 100-card series. The cards are printed on 24-pt paper stock, and use UV coating and silver foil stamping. The set features top Winston Cup and Busch Grand National drivers along with crew chiefs, owner, and mechanics. There are five topical subsets; Awards (70-74), Winners (75-87), Busch Clash (88-99), Earnhardt Family (179-186), Winners (187-200). There were 3,000 numbered cases of the first series and 1,000 numbered cases of the second series. Cards came packaged six cards per pack; 24 packs per box and 24 boxes per case. In series one High Gear boxes there was a possibility of pulling a Jeff Gordon Busch Clash signature card. There were 1,500 of these cards and each was individually numbered of 1,500 on the back in black pen. They were randomly inserted in packs of series one at a rate of 1:1152 packs. In series two boxes and boxes of High Gear Day One, there was a Mark Martin "Feel the Heat" autographed card. There were 1,000 of these cards, inserted in packs at a rate of one per 1152 packs.

COMPLETE SET (200) 20.00 50.00
COMP.SERIES 1 (100) 6.00 15.00
COMP.SERIES 2 (100) 15.00 40.00
WAX BOX SERIES 1 20.00 50.00
WAX BOX SERIES 2 40.00 80.00
1 Dale Earnhardt 1.25 3.00
2 Rusty Wallace .60 1.50
3 Mark Martin .60 1.50
4 Ken Schrader .07 .20
5 Ernie Irvan .15 .40
6 Geoff Bodine .07 .20
7 Harry Gant .15 .40
8 Ricky Rudd .25 .60
9 Sterling Marlin .25 .60
10 Rick Mast .07 .20
11 Michael Waltrip .15 .40
12 Terry Labonte .25 .60
13 Bobby Labonte .50 1.25

14 Dick Trickle	.07	.20
15 Rick Wilson	.07	.20
16 Kenny Wallace	.07	.20
17 Hut Stricklin	.07	.20
18 Wally Dallenbach, Jr.	.07	.20
19 Jimmy Hensley	.07	.20
20 Ted Musgrave	.07	.20
21 Bobby Hillin	.07	.20
22 Dave Marcis	.15	.40
23 Derrike Cope	.07	.20
24 Neil Bonnett	.25	.60
25 Lake Speed	.07	.20
26 Robert Yates	.02	.10
27 Leo Jackson	.02	.10
28 Richard Petty	.25	.60
29 Junior Johnson	.07	.20
30 Rick Hendrick	.02	.10
31 Bobby Allison	.07	.20
32 Felix Sabates	.02	.10
33 Richard Childress	.15	.40
34 Bill Davis	.02	.10
35 Cale Yarborough	.07	.20
36 Jack Roush	.02	.10
37 Chuck Rider	.02	.10
38 Andy Petree	.02	.10
39 Buddy Parrott	.02	.10
40 Jimmy Makar	.02	.10
41 Mike Hill	.02	.10
42 Mike Beam	.02	.10
43 Charley Pressley	.02	.10
44 Ray Evernham	.02	.10
45 Larry McReynolds	.02	.10
46 Steve Hmiel	.02	.10
47 Ricky Craven	.07	.20
48 David Green	.07	.20
49 Bobby Dotter	.07	.20
50 Robert Pressley	.07	.20
51 Joe Bessey	.07	.20
52 Tim Fedewa	.07	.20
53 Mike McLaughlin	.07	.20
54 Roy Payne	.07	.20
55 Larry Pearson	.07	.20
56 Mike Wallace	.07	.20
57 Tracy Leslie	.07	.20
58 Tom Peck	.07	.20
59 Hermie Sadler	.07	.20
60 Chuck Bown	.07	.20
61 Todd Bodine	.07	.20
62 Shawna Robinson	.30	.75
63 Randy LaJoie	.07	.20
64 Ward Burton	.15	.40
65 Jeff Burton	.25	.60
66 Joe Nemechek	.07	.20
67 Steve Grissom	.07	.20
68 Harry Gant	.15	.40
69 Tommy Houston	.07	.20
70 Rusty Wallace's Pit Crew	.15	.40
71 Rusty Wallace DOY	.30	.75
72 Steve Grissom	.02	.10
73 Jeff Gordon WC ROY	.75	2.00
74 Hermie Sadler	.07	.20
75 Dale Jarrett WIN	.15	.40
76 Rusty Wallace WIN	.25	.60
77 Davey Allison WIN	.15	.40
78 Morgan Shepherd WIN	.02	.10
79 Dale Earnhardt WIN	.60	1.50
80 Rusty Wallace WIN	.25	.60
81 Rusty Wallace WIN	.25	.60
82 Rusty Wallace WIN	.25	.60
83 Ernie Irvan WIN	.07	.20
84 Geoff Bodine WIN	.02	.10
85 Dale Earnhardt WIN	.60	1.50
86 Kyle Petty WIN	.07	.20
87 Ricky Rudd WIN	.15	.40
88 Kyle Petty BC	.07	.20
89 Mark Martin BC	.30	.75
90 Ken Schrader BC	.02	.10
91 Rusty Wallace BC	.30	.75
92 Dale Earnhardt BC	.60	1.50
93 Brett Bodine BC	.02	.10
94 Geoff Bodine BC	.02	.10
95 Ernie Irvan BC	.07	.20
96 Bobby Labonte BC	.15	.40
97 Jeff Gordon BC	.40	1.00
98 Harry Gant BC	.07	.20
99 P.J. Jones BC	.02	.10
100 D.Allison Kulwicki Tribute	.40	1.00
101 Jeff Gordon	.75	2.00
102 Todd Bodine	.07	.20
103 Wally Dallenbach Jr.	.07	.20
104 Sterling Marlin	.25	.60
105 Terry Labonte	.25	.60
106 Mark Martin	.60	1.50
107 Geoff Bodine	.07	.20
108 Jeff Burton	.25	.60
109 Ward Burton	.15	.40
110 Mike Wallace	.07	.20
111 Derrike Cope	.07	.20
112 Chuck Bown	.07	.20
113 Robert Pressley	.07	.20
114 John Andretti RC	.07	.20
115 Lake Speed	.07	.20
116 Ted Musgrave	.07	.20
117 Darrell Waltrip	.15	.40
118 Dale Jarrett	.50	1.25
119 Loy Allen Jr.	.07	.20
120 Bobby Hamilton	.07	.20
121 Morgan Shepherd	.07	.20
122 Kyle Petty	.15	.40
123 Hut Stricklin	.07	.20
124 Joe Nemechek	.07	.20
125 Jimmy Hensley	.07	.20
126 Brett Bodine	.07	.20
127 Jimmy Spencer	.07	.20
128 Ernie Irvan	.15	.40
129 Steve Grissom	.07	.20
130 Greg Sacks	.07	.20
131 Tony Glover	.02	.10
132 Barry Dodson	.02	.10
133 Pete Wright	.02	.10
134 Chris Hussey	.02	.10
135 Gary DeHart	.02	.10
136 Doug Hewitt	.02	.10
137 Paul Andrews	.02	.10
138 Bill Ingle	.02	.10
139 Jimmy Fennig	.02	.10
140 Jeff Hammond	.02	.10
141 Donnie Richeson	.02	.10
142 Leonard Wood	.02	.10
143 Robbie Loomis	.02	.10
144 Larry Hedrick	.02	.10
145 Billy Hagan	.02	.10
146 Travis Carter	.02	.10
147 Roger Penske	.02	.10
148 Richard Jackson	.02	.10
149 Larry McClure	.02	.10
150 Bill Stavola	.02	.10
151 Mickey Stavola	.02	.10
152 Eddie Wood	.02	.10
153 Glen Wood	.02	.10
154 Len Wood	.02	.10
155 Ricky Rudd	.25	.60
156 Butch Mock	.02	.10
157 D.K. Ulrich	.02	.10
158 Joe Gibbs	.15	.40
159 Don Miller	.02	.10
160 Eddie Masencup	.02	.10
161 Mike Colyer	.02	.10
162 Hank Jones	.02	.10
163 Harry Gant	.15	.40
164 Kenny Wallace	.07	.20
165 Terry Labonte	.25	.60
166 Morgan Shepherd	.07	.20
167 Chad Little	.07	.20
168 Ernie Irvan	.15	.40
169 Shawna Robinson	.30	.75
170 Mike McLaughlin	.07	.20
171 Elton Sawyer	.07	.20
172 Dirk Stephens	.02	.10
173 Ken Schrader	.07	.20
174 Dennis Setzer	.07	.20
175 Mark Martin	.60	1.50
176 Jim Bown	.07	.20
177 Bobby Labonte	.50	1.25
178 Ed Whitaker	.02	.10
179 Tony Eury	.25	.60
180 Earnhardt Kids Dale Jr.	5.00	12.00
181 Kelley Earnhardt RC	3.00	8.00
182 Kerry Earnhardt RC	2.50	6.00
183 Dale Earnhardt Jr. RC	12.00	30.00
184 Teresa Earnhardt	.60	1.50
185 Don Hawk	.02	.10
186 Dale Earnhardt WIN	.60	1.50
187 Rusty Wallace WIN	.25	.60
188 Dale Earnhardt WIN	.60	1.50
189 Mark Martin WIN	.25	.60
190 Mark Martin WIN	.25	.60
191 Mark Martin WIN	.25	.60
192 Mark Martin WIN	.25	.60
193 Rusty Wallace WIN	.25	.60
194 Rusty Wallace WIN	.25	.60
195 Ernie Irvan WIN	.07	.20
196 Rusty Wallace WIN	.25	.60
197 Ernie Irvan WIN	.07	.20
198 Rusty Wallace WIN	.25	.60
199 Mark Martin WIN	.25	.60
200 Rusty Wallace WIN	.25	.60
MMS1 Mark Martin AU/1000	15.00	40.00
NNO Jeff Gordon BC AU/1500	20.00	50.00

1994 Wheels High Gear Day One

COMPLETE SET (100)	20.00	50.00
*DAY ONES: .6X to 1.5X SER.2 HI COL.		
180 Earnhardt Kids Dale Jr.	6.00	15.00
183 Dale Earnhardt Jr.	15.00	40.00

1994 Wheels High Gear Day One Gold

COMPLETE SET (100)	50.00	125.00
*GOLD CARDS: 1.2X TO 3X BASIC DAY ONE		
180 Earnhardt Kids Dale Jr.	15.00	30.00
183 Dale Earnhardt Jr.	30.00	60.00

1994 Wheels High Gear Gold

COMPLETE SET (200)	60.00	150.00
COMP.SERIES 1 SET (100)	20.00	50.00
COMP.SERIES 2 SET (100)	40.00	100.00
*GOLDS: 1.2X TO 3X BASE CARDS		
*GOLD SPs 1/6/71/81/91: 2X TO 5X		
183 Dale Earnhardt Jr.	15.00	40.00

1994 Wheels High Gear Dominators

This 7-card insert set features Jumbo size cards (4" by 6") of the top drivers in Winston Cup racing. The cards were distributed as box inserts in High Gear series one and two, along with High Gear Day One. Cards D1-D3 were available in series one boxes at a rate of one in six. Card D4 was available in High Gear Day One boxes at a rate of one in eight. Cards D5-D7 were available in series two boxes at a rate of one in six. There are 3,000 of each of the cards D1-D3, while there are 1,750 of the cards D4-D7.

COMPLETE SET (7)	60.00	120.00
COMP.SERIES 1 (3)	30.00	60.00
COMP.SERIES 2 (3)	30.00	60.00
D1 Mark Martin/3000	6.00	15.00
D2 Rusty Wallace/3000	6.00	15.00
D3 Dale Earnhardt/3000	20.00	40.00
D4 Ernie Irvan/1750	6.00	15.00
D5 Jeff Gordon/1750	12.50	30.00
D6 Mark Martin/1750	8.00	20.00
D7 Harry Gant/1750	6.00	15.00

1994 Wheels High Gear Legends

This six-card insert set features some of the greatest names in racing history. The cards were issued in series one, series two and High Gear Day One boxes. Series one boxes offered cards LS1-LS3 at an average of one Legends card per box. Series two and High Gear Day One boxes offered cards LS4-LS6 at a rate of one per box (24 packs).

COMPLETE SET (6)	12.00	25.00
COMP.SERIES 1 (3)	5.00	10.00
COMP.SERIES 2 (3)	7.00	15.00
LS1 Cale Yarborough	2.00	4.00
LS2 David Pearson	2.00	4.00
LS3 Bobby Allison	2.00	4.00
LS4 Richard Petty	4.00	8.00
LS5 Benny Parsons	2.00	4.00
LS6 Ned Jarrett	2.00	4.00

1994 Wheels High Gear Mega Gold

This 12-card insert set features 12 of the best drivers in Winston Cup. Cards are on all gold board and could be found at a rate of one per 12 packs. There was also a special Dale Earnhardt 7-Time Champion card. This card is the same as the regular card except that the entire card is embossed and comes with a 7-Time Champion seal on the front. The sets were also sold on QVC. There were 3,900 sets offered, including the 7-time Dale Earnhardt card for $99. An uncut sheet of all 13 cards was available. There are two different versions of uncut sheets also. The common version is a blank back sheet. The more difficult versions has complete card backs.

COMPLETE SET (12)	25.00	60.00
MG1 Dale Earnhardt	8.00	20.00
MG1S Dale Earnhardt 7T Champ	12.00	30.00
MG2 Ernie Irvan	1.25	3.00
MG3 Rusty Wallace	5.00	12.00
MG4 Mark Martin	5.00	12.00
MG5 Jeff Gordon	6.00	15.00
MG6 Ken Schrader	.60	1.50
MG7 Geoff Bodine	.60	1.50
MG8 Ricky Rudd	2.00	5.00
MG9 Kyle Petty	1.25	3.00
MG10 Terry Labonte	2.00	5.00
MG11 Darrell Waltrip	1.25	3.00
MG12 Michael Waltrip	1.25	3.00

1994 Wheels High Gear Power Pak Teams

There are three individually boxed driver's team sets that are part of the Power Pak Teams: 21-card Dale Earnhardt, 34-card Harry Gant and 41-card Rusty Wallace sets. Each team set is individually boxed and features that driver and their team. There was also a gold parallel version of each of the sets. There were 800 cases produced. There were 36 sets in each case and the cases were packaged in the following ratios: 15 Dale Earnhardt sets, 10 Rusty Wallace sets, 5 Harry Gant sets, 3 Gold Dale Earnhardt sets, 2 Gold Rusty Wallace sets and 1 Gold Harry Gant set.

COMP.EARNHARDT SET (21)	8.00	20.00
COMP.GANT SET (34)	4.00	10.00
COMP.WALLACE SET (41)	5.00	12.00
COMP.GOLD EARNHARDT (21)	20.00	40.00
COMP.GOLD GANT (34)	10.00	20.00
COMP.GOLD WALLACE (41)	12.50	25.00
*GOLD CARDS: .8X TO 2X		
E1 Richard Childress	.30	.75
E2 Andy Petree	.30	.75
E3 Dale Earnhardt	1.50	4.00
E4 Dale Earnhardt Richard Childress	1.50	4.00
E5 Dale Earnhardt Andy Petree	1.50	4.00
E6 David Smith	.30	.75
E7 Danny Meyers	.30	.75
E8 Danny Lawrence	.30	.75
E9 Eddie Lanier	.30	.75
E10 Jimmy Elledge	.30	.75
E11 Joe Dan Bailey	.30	.75
E12 Jim Baldwin	.30	.75
E13 Craig Donley	.30	.75
E14 John Mulloy	.30	.75
E15 Gene Dehart	.30	.75
E16 Jim Cook Hal Carter	.30	.75
E17 RCR Enterprises Office	.30	.75
E18 Dale Earnhardt in Pits	.30	.75
E19 Dale Earnhardt w/Crew	1.50	4.00
E20 Dale Earnhardt's Car	.30	.75
E21 Dale Earnhardt's Car CL	.30	.75
G1 Harry Gant	.40	1.00
G2 Leo Jackson	.25	.60
G3 Charley Pressley	.25	.60
G4 Billy Abernathy	.25	.60
G5 Ricky Viers	.25	.60
G6 David Rogers	.25	.60
G7 Jimmy Penland	.25	.60
G8 Allen Hester	.25	.60
G9 Jay Guy	.25	.60
G10 Ellis Frazier	.25	.60
G11 Hoss Berry	.25	.60
G12 Eddie Masencup	.25	.60
G13 Shaun Woods	.25	.60
G14 Renee Forrest	.25	.60
G15 Phil Banks	.25	.60
G16 Joe Schmaling	.25	.60
G17 Bruce Morris	.25	.60
G18 Dean Johnson	.25	.60
G19 DeWayne Felkel	.25	.60
G20 Jim Presnell	.25	.60
G21 Jan McDougald	.25	.60
G22 Marc Parks	.25	.60
G23 Jerry Vess	.25	.60
G24 Teddy Blackwell	.25	.60
G25 Roger Chastain	.25	.60
G26 Brad Turner	.25	.60
G27 Kent Mashburn	.25	.60
G28 Harry Gant in Pits	.25	.60
G29 Harry Gant	.40	1.00
G30 Harry Gant in Pits	.25	.60
G31 Harry Gant's Car	.25	.60
G32 Harry Gant's Car	.25	.60
G33 Harry Gant's Car	.25	.60
G34 Harry Gant's Car CL	.25	.60
W1 Roger Penske	.25	.60
W2 Rusty Wallace	.50	1.25
W3 Don Miller	.25	.60
W4 Dick Paysor	.25	.60
W5 Buddy Parrott	.25	.60
W6 Todd Parrott	.25	.60
W7 Brad Parrott	.25	.60
W8 Bill Wilburn	.25	.60
W9 Scott Robinson	.25	.60
W10 Paul VanderLaan	.25	.60
W11 Gary Brooks	.25	.60
W12 Earl Barban Jr.	.25	.60
W13 Jeff Thousand	.25	.60
W14 Nick Ollila	.25	.60
W15 Angela Crawford	.25	.60
W16 Stella Paysor	.25	.60
W17 Lori Wetzel	.25	.60
W18 Dave Hoffert	.25	.60
W19 Robert Pressley PT (personal trainer)	.25	.60
W20 Dennis Beaver	.25	.60
W21 Jerry Branz	.25	.60
W22 David Munari	.25	.60
W23 Rocky Owenby Barry Poovey	.25	.60
W24 Jamie Freeze Mike Wingate	.25	.60
W25 Steve Triplett James Shoffner	.25	.60
W26 Phil Ditmars Eric Durchman	.25	.60
W27 Ronnie Phillips Billy Woodruff	.25	.60
W28 Matt King Jimmy Zamrzla	.25	.60
W29 Mark Campbell	.25	.60
W30 David Evans	.25	.60
W31 Tony Lambert David Little	.25	.60
W32 David Kenny Dave Roberts	.25	.60
W33 Bo Schlager Mark Armstrong	.25	.60
W34 Rusty Wallace Buddy Parrott	.50	1.25
W35 Rusty Wallace	.50	1.25
W36 Rusty Wallace in Pits	.25	.60
W37 Rusty Wallace	.50	1.25
W38 Rusty Wallace w/Car	.25	.60
W39 Rusty Wallace	.50	1.25
W40 Rusty Wallace's Car	.25	.60
W41 Rusty Wallace's Car CL	.25	.60

1994 Wheels High Gear Rookie Shootout Autographs

This seven-card insert set features seven of the drivers that were competing for the '94 Winston Cup Rookie of the Year. Cards RS1-RS3 were available in series one boxes. There were 1,500 of each of the three cards and they were randomly seeded at one card per 384 packs. Cards RS4-RS7 were available in series two High Gear boxes and series two High Gear Day One boxes. There were 1,000 of each of the four cards and they were randomly inserted at a rate of one card per 288 packs.

COMPLETE SET (7)	60.00	120.00
RS1 Steve Grissom AUTO/1500	6.00	15.00
RS2 Ward Burton AUTO/1500	6.00	15.00
RS3 Jeff Burton AUTO/1500	8.00	20.00
RS4 Joe Nemechek AUTO/1000	8.00	20.00
RS5 Mike Wallace AUTO/1000	8.00	20.00
RS6 Loy Allen Jr. AUTO/1000	6.00	15.00
RS7 John Andretti AUTO/1000	8.00	20.00

1994 Wheels High Gear Rookie Thunder Update

This 5-card insert set features four former Rookies of the Year. The cards were an update to the 93 Wheels Rookie Thunder set. The cards were packaged in three card cellophane packs and you got one pack in the top of 1994 High Gear series one boxes. There was one checklist and two cards in each pack. The four driver cards came in two versions, a base version and a platinum parallel version.

COMPLETE SET (5)	8.00	20.00
*PLATINUM: 1X TO 2.5X BASIC CARDS		
101 Hermie Sadler	1.00	2.00
102 Jeff Gordon	3.00	6.00
103 Bobby Hamilton	1.00	2.00
104 Dale Earnhardt	6.00	12.00
NNO Checklist Card	.25	.50

1995 Wheels High Gear Promos

This three-card set was issued to promote the 1995 High Gear release by Wheels. The cards are numbered and often sold in complete set form.

COMPLETE SET (3)	4.00	10.00
P1 Rusty Wallace	1.50	3.00
P2 Jeff Gordon	2.00	5.00
P3 Mark Martin	1.50	4.00

1995 Wheels High Gear

This 100-card set features top drivers from both Winston Cup and Busch Circuits. The cards are printed on 24-point paper and display silver foil stamping and UV coating. There were 1,000 cases produced. Each case contained 20 boxes, with 24 packs per box and six cards per pack. There were also two randomly inserted autograph cards. Terry Labonte was featured on an "IceMan" card and Steve Kinser was featured on "The Outlaw" card. The autograph cards were randomly inserted at a rate of one per 480 packs. The set also included two subsets; Split Shift (61-68), and Race Winner (86-97).

COMPLETE SET (100)	8.00	20.00
COMP.E-RACE TO WIN SET (10)	.25	.50
1 Dale Earnhardt	1.25	3.00
2 Rusty Wallace	.60	1.50
3 Mark Martin	.60	1.50
4 Ricky Rudd	.25	.60
5 Morgan Shepherd	.07	.20
6 Jeff Gordon	.75	2.00
7 Darrell Waltrip	.15	.40
8 Terry Labonte	.25	.60
9 Michael Waltrip	.15	.40
10 Ted Musgrave	.07	.20
11 Geoff Bodine	.07	.20
12 Ken Schrader	.07	.20
13 Bill Elliott	.30	.75
14 Lake Speed	.07	.20
15 Sterling Marlin	.25	.60
16 Rick Mast	.07	.20
17 Kyle Petty	.15	.40
18 Ernie Irvan	.15	.40
19 Dale Jarrett	.50	1.25
20 Brett Bodine	.07	.20
21 Bobby Labonte	.50	1.25
22 Todd Bodine	.07	.20
23 Jeff Burton	.25	.60
24 Joe Nemechek	.07	.20
25 Steve Grissom	.07	.20
26 Derrike Cope	.07	.20
27 John Andretti	.07	.20
28 Mike Wallace	.07	.20
29 Ward Burton	.15	.40
30 Loy Allen Jr.	.07	.20
31 Richard Childress	.15	.40
32 Roger Penske	.02	.10
33 Jack Roush	.02	.10
34 Rick Hendrick	.02	.10
35 Ricky Rudd OWN	.25	.60
36 Robert Yates	.02	.10
37 Junior Johnson	.07	.20
38 Bobby Allison	.07	.20
39 Felix Sabates	.02	.10
40 Cale Yarborough	.07	.20
41 Andy Petree	.02	.10
42 Charlie Pressley	.02	.10
43 Ray Evernham	.07	.20
44 Larry McReynolds	.02	.10
45 Steve Hmiel	.02	.10
46 Robbie Loomis	.02	.10
47 Paul Andrews	.02	.10
48 Jeff Hammond	.02	.10
49 Doug Hewitt	.02	.10
50 Gary Dehart	.02	.10
51 Kenny Wallace	.07	.20
52 Ricky Craven	.07	.20
53 Dennis Setzer	.07	.20
54 Johnny Benson	.15	.40
55 David Green	.07	.20
56 Hermie Sadler	.07	.20
57 Elton Sawyer	.07	.20
58 Chad Little	.07	.20
59 Larry Pearson	.07	.20
60 Mike McLaughlin	.07	.20
61 Terry Labonte SS	.15	.40
62 Mike Wallace SS	.02	.10
63 Mark Martin SS	.30	.75
64 Kenny Wallace SS	.02	.10
65 Ken Schrader SS	.02	.10
66 Bobby Labonte SS	.25	.60
67 Joe Nemechek SS	.02	.10
68 Harry Gant SS	.07	.20
69 Johnny Benson BGN ROY	.15	.40
70 David Green BGN Champ	.02	.10
71 Dale Earnhardt's Car	.50	1.25
72 Rusty Wallace's Car	.25	.60
73 Mark Martin's Car	.25	.60
74 Ken Schrader's Car	.02	.10
75 Ricky Rudd's Car	.07	.20
76 Morgan Shepherd's Car	.02	.10
77 Terry Labonte's Car	.15	.40
78 Jeff Gordon's Car	.30	.75
79 Darrell Waltrip's Car	.07	.20
80 Bill Elliott's Car	.15	.40
81 Sterling Marlin's Car	.07	.20
82 Lake Speed's Car	.02	.10
83 Ted Musgrave's Car	.02	.10
84 Michael Waltrip's Car	.07	.20
85 Geoff Bodine's Car	.02	.10
86 Dale Earnhardt RW	.60	1.50
87 Rusty Wallace RW	.30	.75
88 Mark Martin RW	.30	.75
89 Ricky Rudd RW	.15	.40
90 Terry Labonte RW	.15	.40
91 Jeff Gordon RW	.40	1.00
92 Bill Elliott RW	.15	.40
93 Sterling Marlin RW	.15	.40
94 Geoff Bodine RW	.02	.10
95 Dale Jarrett RW	.25	.60
96 Ernie Irvan RW	.07	.20
97 Jimmy Spencer RW	.02	.10
98 Jeff Gordon in Pits	.30	.75
99 Jeff Burton ROY	.25	.60
100 Bill Elliott FF	.15	.40
SKS1 Steve Kinser AU/1500	10.00	20.00
TLS1 Terry Labonte AU/1500	12.50	30.00
NNO E-Race to Win Unscratched	.02	.10
NNO E-Race to Win Winner	.02	.10

1995 Wheels High Gear Day One

COMPLETE SET (100)	10.00	25.00
*DAY ONE: .6X TO 1.5X HIGH GEAR		

1995 Wheels High Gear Day One Gold

COMPLETE SET (100)	25.00	60.00
*DAY ONE GOLD: 1X TO 2.5X BASE DAY ONES ONE PER PACK		

1995 Wheels High Gear Gold

COMPLETE SET (100)	15.00	40.00
*GOLDS: 1X TO 2.5X BASIC CARDS		

1995 Wheels High Gear Busch Clash

This 16-card insert set features the drivers who qualified for the 1995 Busch Clash. Each card was printed in silver foil as well as a gold foil parallel. The silver cards use MicroEtch printing technology and were inserted at the ratio of 1:8 packs.

COMPLETE SILVER SET (16)	20.00	50.00
*GOLD: .8X TO 2X BASIC INSERT		
UNCUT GOLD SHEET	20.00	40.00
BC1 Loy Allen Jr.	.50	1.25
BC2 Geoff Bodine	.50	1.25
BC3 Ted Musgrave	.50	1.25
BC4 Bill Elliott	2.00	5.00
BC5 Ernie Irvan	1.00	2.50
BC6 Rusty Wallace	4.00	10.00
BC7 Jeff Gordon	5.00	12.00
BC8 Dale Earnhardt	8.00	20.00
BC9 Rick Mast	.50	1.25
BC10 Mark Martin	4.00	10.00
BC11 Jimmy Spencer	.25	.60
BC12 Ward Burton	1.00	2.50
BC13 Ricky Rudd	1.50	4.00
BC14 Sterling Marlin	1.50	4.00
BC15 Greg Sacks	.50	1.25
BC16 David Green	.50	1.25

1995 Wheels High Gear Dominators

is four-card insert set features top Winston Cup ivers on 3 1/2" by 5" cards. The cards are mbered of 1,750 on the backs of the card. They me in a white envelope and were inserted in xes at a rate of one per seven boxes. The Rusty allace (D1) was available in Day One boxes and e other three (D2-D4) were found in regular High ear boxes. A four card uncut sheet of the ominators was also produced. There was also a ini-Dominator version of each of the four cards. ese cards were a standard size replica of the mbo card. The cards were distributed the same their larger versions and were inserted 1:168 cks.

OMPLETE SET (4) 30.00 80.00
NCUT 4 CARD SHEET 50.00 100.00
MINI.DOMI: 10X TO 25X BASE CARD HI
INI DOMINATOR STATED ODDS 1:168
1 Rusty Wallace/1750 10.00 25.00
2 Terry Labonte/1750 4.00 10.00
3 Dale Earnhardt/1750 20.00 50.00
4 Geoff Bodine/1750 1.25 3.00

1995 Wheels High Gear Legends

his three-card insert set features three of the all me legends of Stock Car racing. The cards are rinted on silver foil board and were inserted one er 24 packs.

OMPLETE SET (3) 4.00 10.00
1 Junior Johnson 1.50 4.00
2 Fred Lorenzen 1.50 4.00
3 Red Farmer 1.50 4.00

1998 Wheels High Gear

he 1998 High Gear set was issued in one series otalling 72 cards. The cards feature color photos rinted on 24 pt.-board with multi-level foil tamping. The set contains the topical subsets: ASCAR Winston Cup Drivers (1-27), NASCAR Winston Cup Cars (28-36), NASCAR Busch Series Drivers (37-41), NASCAR Craftsman Truck Drivers 42-45), Awards (46-54), '98 Preview (55-63), nd Carmeleon (64-71).

OMPLETE SET (72) 8.00 20.00
1 Jeff Gordon .75 2.00
2 Dale Jarrett .50 1.25
3 Mark Martin .60 1.50
4 Jeff Burton .25 .60
5 Dale Earnhardt 1.25 3.00
6 Terry Labonte .25 .60
7 Bobby Labonte .50 1.25
8 Bill Elliott .30 .75
9 Rusty Wallace .60 1.50
10 Ken Schrader .07 .20
11 Johnny Benson .15 .40
12 Ted Musgrave .07 .20
13 Jeremy Mayfield .15 .40
14 Ernie Irvan .15 .40
15 Kyle Petty .15 .40
16 Bobby Hamilton .07 .20
17 Ricky Rudd .25 .60
18 Michael Waltrip .15 .40
19 Ricky Craven .07 .20
20 Jimmy Spencer .07 .20
21 Ward Burton .15 .40
22 Sterling Marlin .25 .60
23 Darrell Waltrip .15 .40
24 Joe Nemechek .07 .20
25 Mike Skinner .07 .20
26 David Green .07 .20
27 Wally Dallenbach Jr. .07 .20
28 Rusty Wallace's Car .25 .60
29 Dale Earnhardt's Car .50 1.25
30 Terry Labonte's Car .15 .40
31 Mark Martin's Car .25 .60
32 Bobby Labonte's Car .25 .60
33 Jeff Gordon's Car .30 .75
34 Dale Jarrett's Car .15 .40
35 Bill Elliott's Car .15 .40
36 Jeff Burton's Car .07 .20
37 Randy LaJoie .07 .20
38 Todd Bodine .07 .20
39 Steve Park .50 1.25
40 Phil Parsons .07 .20
41 Elliott Sadler .15 .40
42 Rich Bickle .07 .20
43 Jack Sprague .07 .20
44 Joe Ruttman .07 .20
45 Ron Hornaday Jr. .07 .20
46 Mark Martin .60 1.50
47 Brian Whitesell .02 .10
48 Dale Earnhardt's Car .50 1.25
49 Mike Skinner .07 .20
50 Jeff Gordon .75 2.00
51 Jeff Burton .25 .60
52 Jimmy Fenning .02 .10
53 Charlie Siegars .02 .10
54 Dale Jarrett .50 1.25
55 Johnny Benson .15 .40
56 Todd Bodine .07 .20
57 Robert Pressley .07 .20
58 Bobby Hamilton .07 .20
59 Ernie Irvan .15 .40
60 Kenny Irwin .15 .40
61 Sterling Marlin .25 .60
62 Steve Park .50 1.25
63 John Andretti .07 .20
64 Dale Earnhardt's Car .50 1.25
65 Terry Labonte's Car .15 .40
66 Ricky Rudd's Car .07 .20
67 Bobby Labonte's Car .25 .60
68 Michael Waltrip's Car .07 .20
69 Jeff Gordon's Car .30 .75
70 Darrell Waltrip's Car .07 .20
71 Bill Elliott's Car .15 .40
72 Checklist .02 .10
P1 Bobby Labonte Promo 1.50 4.00

1998 Wheels High Gear First Gear

COMPLETE SET (72) 12.00 30.00
*FIRST GEAR: .6X TO 1.5X BASIC CARDS

1998 Wheels High Gear MPH

COMPLETE SET (72) 300.00 600.00
*MPH CARDS: 10X TO 25X BASE CARDS

1998 Wheels High Gear Pure Gold

Randomly inserted in packs at the rate of one in six, this nine-card set commemorates NASCAR's 50th anniversary and features color photos of the best all-time drivers printed on all-foil cards.

COMPLETE SET (9) 10.00 25.00
PG1 Dale Earnhardt 5.00 12.00
PG2 Richard Petty .60 1.50
PG3 Jeff Gordon 3.00 8.00
PG4 Terry Labonte 1.00 2.50
PG5 Mark Martin 2.50 6.00
PG6 Darrell Waltrip .60 1.50
PG7 Ned Jarrett .30 .75
PG8 Bill Elliott 1.25 3.00
PG9 Rusty Wallace 2.50 6.00

1998 Wheels High Gear Autographs

Randomly inserted in packs at the rate of one in 192, this set features autographed cards of top NASCAR Winston Cup drivers with a certificate of authenticity printed on the back. All of the cards except Jimmy Spencer feature hand written serial numbering on the backs as noted below. The Jimmy Spencer card was actually released in 2003 through the VIP Tin factory set program. The unnumbered cards are checklisted below in alphabetical order.

COMPLETE SET (23) 750.00 1250.00
1 Johnny Benson/250 10.00 25.00
2 Jeff Burton/250 10.00 25.00
3 Ward Burton/250 8.00 20.00
4 Ricky Craven/200 6.00 15.00
5 Wally Dallenbach/250 6.00 15.00
6 Dale Earnhardt/50 250.00 400.00
7 Bill Elliott/250 25.00 60.00
8 Jeff Gordon/50 150.00 300.00
9 Bobby Hamilton/250 10.00 25.00
10 Ernie Irvan/225 12.50 30.00
11 Dale Jarrett/200 20.00 50.00
12 Bobby Labonte/250 12.50 30.00
13 Terry Labonte/150 25.00 60.00
14 Mark Martin/100 40.00 80.00
15 Jeremy Mayfield/250 12.50 30.00
16 Ted Musgrave/250 6.00 15.00
17 Joe Nemechek/250 6.00 15.00
18 Kyle Petty/200 12.50 30.00
19 Ken Schrader/250 8.00 20.00
20 Mike Skinner/250 6.00 15.00
21 Jimmy Spencer 10.00 25.00
22 Darrell Waltrip/250 15.00 40.00
23 Michael Waltrip/250 10.00 25.00

1998 Wheels High Gear Custom Shop

Randomly inserted in packs at the rate of one in 192, redemption cards for this five-card set allowed the collector to customize his own card by selecting one of three fronts and three backs for each card. The collector then received his custom-made card by return mail with his chosen front and back selection.

COMPLETE SET (5) 100.00 200.00
*PRIZE CARDS: .4X TO 1X BASIC INSERTS
CS1 Dale Earnhardt EXCH 30.00 80.00
CS2 Jeff Gordon EXCH 20.00 50.00
CS3 Mark Martin EXCH 12.50 30.00
CS4 Terry Labonte EXCH 8.00 20.00
CS5 Dale Jarrett EXCH 12.50 30.00

1998 Wheels High Gear Jammers

Randomly inserted in packs at the rate of one in two, this 27-card set features color photos printed on die-cut, foil stamped cards.

COMPLETE SET (27) 10.00 25.00
GJ1 Rusty Wallace 2.00 5.00
GJ2 Dale Earnhardt's Car 1.50 4.00
GJ3 Sterling Marlin .75 2.00
GJ4 Terry Labonte .75 2.00
GJ5 Mark Martin 2.00 5.00
GJ6 Ricky Rudd .75 2.00
GJ7 Ted Musgrave .25 .60
GJ8 Darrell Waltrip .50 1.25
GJ9 Bobby Labonte 1.50 4.00
GJ10 Michael Waltrip .50 1.25
GJ11 Ward Burton .50 1.25
GJ12 Jeff Gordon 2.50 6.00
GJ13 Bobby Hamilton .25 .60
GJ14 Kyle Petty .50 1.25
GJ15 Dale Jarrett 1.50 4.00
GJ16 Bill Elliott 1.00 2.50
GJ17 Jeff Burton .75 2.00
GJ18 Wally Dallenbach .25 .60
GJ19 Jimmy Spencer .25 .60
GJ20 Ken Schrader .25 .60
GJ21 Johnny Benson .50 1.25
GJ22 David Green .25 .60
GJ23 Mike Skinner .25 .60
GJ24 Joe Nemechek .25 .60
GJ25 Jeremy Mayfield .50 1.25
GJ26 Ricky Craven .25 .60
GJ27 Morgan Shepherd .25 .60

1998 Wheels High Gear High Groove

Randomly inserted in packs at the rate of one in 10, this nine-card set features color photos of cars belonging to top drivers printed on die-cut, foil stamped cards.

COMPLETE SET (9) 12.00 30.00
HG1 Rusty Wallace's Car 2.00 5.00
HG2 Dale Earnhardt's Car 4.00 10.00
HG3 Terry Labonte's Car 1.25 3.00
HG4 Mark Martin's Car 2.00 5.00
HG5 Jeff Gordon's Car 2.50 6.00
HG6 Bobby Labonte's Car 2.00 5.00
HG7 Dale Jarrett's Car 1.25 3.00
HG8 Bill Elliott's Car 1.25 3.00
HG9 Jeff Burton's Car .60 1.50

1998 Wheels High Gear Man and Machine Drivers

Randomly inserted in hobby packs only at the rate of one in 20, this nine-card set features color portraits of top drivers printed on interlocking all-foil cards made to be matched with the retail only version of this set containing color photos of their cars.

COMPLETE SET (9) 30.00 75.00
COMP.CAR SET (9) 15.00 40.00
*CARS: .25X TO .6X DRIVERS
MM1 Jeff Gordon 5.00 12.00
MM2 Mark Martin 4.00 10.00
MM3 Dale Jarrett 3.00 8.00
MM4 Jeff Burton 1.50 4.00
MM5 Terry Labonte 1.50 4.00
MM6 Bobby Labonte 3.00 8.00
MM7 Dale Earnhardt 8.00 20.00
MM8 Bill Elliott 2.00 5.00
MM9 Rusty Wallace 4.00 10.00

1998 Wheels High Gear Top Tier

Randomly inserted in packs, this eight-card set features color photos of the top eight 1997 NASCAR Winston Cup finishers printed on all-foil cards. The insertion ratios are printed after the driver's name.

COMPLETE SET (8) 25.00 60.00
TT1 Jeff Gordon 1:384 15.00 40.00
TT2 Dale Jarrett 1:192 12.50 30.00
TT3 Mark Martin 1:100 6.00 15.00
TT4 Jeff Burton 1:60 2.50 6.00
TT5 Dale Earnhardt 1:40 10.00 25.00
TT6 Terry Labonte 1:40 2.00 5.00
TT7 Bobby Labonte 1:20 2.00 5.00
TT8 Bill Elliott 1:20 1.50 4.00

1999 Wheels High Gear

The 1999 High Gear set was issued in one series totalling 72 cards. They were issued in six card hobby packs or five card retail packs. The set contains the topical subsets: NASCAR Winston Cup Drivers (1-27), NASCAR Winston Cup Cars (28-36), NASCAR Busch Drivers (37-45), Awards (46-54), '99 Preview (55-63), and Carmeleon (64-71).

COMPLETE SET (72) 10.00 25.00
WAX BOX HOBBY 50.00 100.00
WAX BOX RETAIL 20.00 50.00
1 Jeff Gordon .75 2.00
2 Mark Martin .60 1.50
3 Dale Jarrett .50 1.25
4 Rusty Wallace .60 1.50
5 Jeff Burton .25 .60
6 Bobby Labonte .50 1.25
7 Jeremy Mayfield .15 .40
8 Dale Earnhardt 1.25 3.00
9 Terry Labonte .25 .60
10 Bobby Hamilton .07 .20
11 John Andretti .07 .20
12 Ken Schrader .07 .20
13 Sterling Marlin .25 .60
14 Jimmy Spencer .07 .20
15 Chad Little .07 .20
16 Ward Burton .15 .40
17 Michael Waltrip .15 .40
18 Bill Elliott .30 .75
19 Ernie Irvan .15 .40
20 Johnny Benson .07 .20
21 Mike Skinner .07 .20
22 Ricky Rudd .25 .60
23 Robert Pressley .07 .20
24 Kenny Irwin .07 .20
25 Geoff Bodine .07 .20
26 Joe Nemechek .07 .20
27 Steve Park .40 1.00
28 Rusty Wallace's Car .25 .60
29 Dale Earnhardt's Car .50 1.25
30 Terry Labonte's Car .15 .40
31 Mark Martin's Car .25 .60
32 Bobby Labonte's Car .15 .40
33 Jeff Gordon's Car .30 .75
34 Dale Jarrett's Car .15 .40
35 Bill Elliott's Car .15 .40
36 Jeff Burton's Car .07 .20
37 Dale Earnhardt Jr. 1.00 2.50
38 Matt Kenseth RC 2.50 6.00
39 Mike McLaughlin .07 .20
40 Randy LaJoie .07 .20
41 Mark Martin .60 1.50
42 Jason Jarrett .07 .20
43 Michael Waltrip .15 .40
44 Tim Fedewa .07 .20
45 Tony Stewart .75 2.00
46 Jeff Gordon .75 2.00
47 Bill Elliott .30 .75
48 Dale Earnhardt's Car .50 1.25
49 Kenny Irwin .15 .40
50 Mark Martin .60 1.50
51 Jeff Burton .25 .60
52 Ray Evernham .07 .20
53 Bobby Hamilton .07 .20
54 Jeff Gordon .75 2.00
55 Ward Burton .15 .40
56 Geoff Bodine .07 .20
57 Darrell Waltrip .15 .40
58 Jeff Gordon .75 2.00
59 Kenny Wallace .07 .20
60 Ted Musgrave .07 .20
61 Tony Stewart .75 2.00
62 Elliott Sadler .15 .40
63 Jerry Nadeau .15 .40
64 Dale Earnhardt's Car .50 1.25
65 Terry Labonte's Car .15 .40
66 Bobby Labonte's Car .15 .40
67 Kenny Irwin's Car .02 .10
68 Rusty Wallace's Car .25 .60
69 Jeff Gordon's Car .30 .75
70 Dale Jarrett's Car .15 .40
71 Ernie Irvan's Car .02 .10
72 Jeff Gordon CL .40 1.00
P1 Jeff Gordon Promo 1.00 2.50

1999 Wheels High Gear First Gear

COMPLETE SET (72) 25.00 50.00
*FIRST GEAR: 1X TO 2.5X BASIC CARDS

1999 Wheels High Gear MPH

COMPLETE SET (72) 250.00 500.00
*MPH VETS: 10X TO 25X BASE CARDS
*MPH RCs: 3X TO 8X BASE CARDS

1999 Wheels High Gear Autographs

Randomly inserted in packs at the rate of one in 100, this 25-card set features autographed color photos of top NASCAR Winston Cup drivers with a certificate of authenticity. The cards are checklisted below in alphabetical order.

COMPLETE SET (25) 800.00 1200.00
1 John Andretti/350 5.00 12.00
2 Johnny Benson/350 10.00 25.00
3 Geoffrey Bodine/350 5.00 12.00
4 Ward Burton/350 6.00 15.00
5 Jeff Burton/350 6.00 15.00
6 Dale Earnhardt/55 250.00 400.00
7 Dale Earnhardt Jr./350 60.00 120.00
8 Bill Elliott/350 15.00 40.00
9 Jeff Gordon/100 75.00 150.00
10 Bobby Hamilton/350 6.00 15.00
11 Ernie Irvan/350 8.00 20.00
12 Kenny Irwin 15.00 40.00
13 Dale Jarrett/350 15.00 40.00
14 Bobby Labonte/250 8.00 20.00
15 Terry Labonte/100 10.00 25.00
16 Chad Little/350 8.00 20.00
17 Sterling Marlin/350 6.00 15.00
18 Mark Martin/200 25.00 60.00
19 Jeremy Mayfield/350 8.00 20.00
20 Joe Nemechek/350 6.00 15.00
21 Robert Pressley/350 6.00 15.00
22 Ricky Rudd/350 10.00 25.00
23 Ken Schrader/350 6.00 15.00
24 Mike Skinner/350 8.00 20.00
25 Jimmy Spencer/350 6.00 15.00
26 Michael Waltrip/350 8.00 20.00

1999 Wheels High Gear Custom Shop

Randomly inserted in packs at the rate of one in 200, redemption cards for this five-card set allowed the collector to customize his own card by selecting one of three fronts and three backs for each card. The collector then received his custom-made card by return mail with his chosen front and back selection.

COMPLETE SET (5) 125.00 250.00
*PRIZE CARDS: .4X TO 1X BASIC INSERTS
CSDE Dale Earnhardt EXCH 20.00 50.00
CSJG Jeff Gordon EXCH 15.00 40.00
CSJR Dale Earnhardt Jr. EXCH 15.00 40.00
CSMM Mark Martin EXCH 10.00 25.00
CSTL Terry Labonte EXCH 10.00 25.00

1999 Wheels High Gear Flag Chasers

This five card insert set features pieces of racing flags used in 1998 races. They were issued in different colors with the following insert ratios: Green: 1:2600 (numbered to 65), Yellow 1:2450 (numbered to 69); Blue-Yellow 1:3900 (numbered to 45); Black 1:2450 (numbered to 69); Red 1:2600 (numbered to 65); White 1:2450 (numbered to 69) and Checkered 1:5000 (numbered to 36). Overall ratio for flag insertion was one in 400 packs.

BLACK/WHITE/YELLOW PRICED BELOW
*GREEN/RED: .3X TO .8X BASIC INSERTS
*BLUE-YELLOW: .6X TO 1.5X BASIC INS.
*CHECKERED: 1X TO 2X BASIC INSERTS
FC1 Jeff Gordon 60.00 120.00
FC2 Mark Martin 50.00 100.00
FC3 Terry Labonte 30.00 80.00
FC4 Rusty Wallace 40.00 100.00
FC5 Dale Earnhardt 75.00 150.00

1999 Wheels High Gear Gear Shifters

Randomly inserted in packs at the rate of one in two, this 27-card set features color photos printed on die-cut, foil stamped cards.

COMPLETE SET (27) 15.00 30.00
GS1 Jeff Gordon 2.50 6.00
GS2 Mark Martin 2.00 5.00
GS3 Dale Jarrett 1.50 4.00
GS4 Rusty Wallace 2.00 5.00
GS5 Jeff Burton .75 2.00
GS6 Bobby Labonte 1.50 4.00
GS7 Jeremy Mayfield .50 1.25
GS8 Dale Earnhardt 4.00 10.00
GS9 Terry Labonte .75 2.00
GS10 Bobby Hamilton .25 .60
GS11 John Andretti .25 .60
GS12 Ken Schrader .25 .60
GS13 Sterling Marlin .75 2.00
GS14 Jimmy Spencer .25 .60
GS15 Chad Little .25 .60
GS16 Ward Burton .50 1.25
GS17 Michael Waltrip .50 1.25
GS18 Bill Elliott 1.00 2.50
GS19 Ernie Irvan .50 1.25
GS20 Johnny Benson .25 .60
GS21 Mike Skinner .25 .60
GS22 Ricky Rudd .75 2.00
GS23 Darrell Waltrip .50 1.25
GS24 Kenny Irwin .25 .60
GS25 Geoffrey Bodine .25 .60
GS26 Robert Pressley .25 .60
GS27 Steve Park CL 1.25 3.00

1999 Wheels High Gear Hot Streaks

Randomly inserted in packs at the rate of one in ten, this six-card gold foil set focuses on the legendary streaks of NASCAR drivers.

COMPLETE SET (6) 10.00 25.00
HS1 Jeff Gordon 3.00 8.00
HS2 Terry Labonte 1.00 2.50
HS3 Dale Earnhardt's Car 2.00 5.00
HS4 Ricky Rudd 1.00 2.50
HS5 Mark Martin 2.50 6.00
HS6 Dale Jarrett 2.00 5.00

1999 Wheels High Gear Man and Machine Drivers

Randomly inserted in Hobby packs at the rate of one in ten, this nine-card set features color portraits of top drivers and their machines in an interlocking set. (Hobby: 1A-9A, Retail: 1B-9B)

COMPLETE SET (9) 15.00 40.00
COMP.CAR SET (9) 12.50 30.00
*CARS: .3X TO .8X DRIVERS
MM1A Jeff Gordon 3.00 8.00
MM2A Mark Martin 2.50 6.00
MM3A Dale Jarrett 2.00 5.00
MM4A Jeff Burton 1.00 2.50
MM5A Terry Labonte 1.00 2.50
MM6A Bobby Labonte 2.00 5.00
MM7A Jeremy Mayfield .60 1.50
MM8A Jimmy Spencer .30 .75
MM9A Rusty Wallace 2.50 6.00

1999 Wheels High Gear Top Tier

Randomly inserted in packs, this eight-card set features color photos of the top eight 1998 NASCAR Winston Cup finishers printed on all-foil cards. The insertion ratios are printed after the driver's name.

COMPLETE SET (8) 30.00 80.00
TT1 Jeff Gordon 1:400 15.00 40.00
TT2 Mark Martin 1:200 8.00 20.00
TT3 Dale Jarrett 1:100 4.00 10.00
TT4 Rusty Wallace 1:80 4.00 10.00
TT5 Jeff Burton 1:40 1.25 3.00
TT6 Bobby Labonte 1:40 2.50 6.00
TT7 Jeremy Mayfield 1:20 1.25 3.00
TT8 Dale Earnhardt's Car 1:20 4.00 10.00

2000 Wheels High Gear

The 2000 High Gear set was released as a 72-card set that featured 72 of NASCAR's top stars on extra thick, 24-point stock. Released in both Hobby and Retail packs, this product carried a suggested retail price of $3.99 for 6-card Hobby packs, and $2.99 for 4-card Retail packs.

COMPLETE SET (72) 12.50 30.00
WAX BOX HOBBY 60.00 100.00
WAX BOX RETAIL 40.00 80.00
1 Dale Jarrett .50 1.25
2 Bobby Labonte .50 1.25
3 Mark Martin .60 1.50
4 Jeff Gordon .75 2.00
5 Tony Stewart .75 2.00
6 Jeff Burton .30 .75
7 Dale Earnhardt 1.25 3.00
8 Rusty Wallace .60 1.50
9 Ward Burton .20 .50
10 Mike Skinner .10 .30
11 Jeremy Mayfield .10 .30
12 Terry Labonte .30 .75
13 Bobby Hamilton .10 .30
14 Ken Schrader .10 .30
15 Sterling Marlin .30 .75
16 Steve Park .30 .75
17 Kenny Irwin .20 .50
18 John Andretti .10 .30
19 Jimmy Spencer .10 .30
20 Ricky Rudd .30 .75
21 Wally Dallenbach .10 .30
22 Kenny Wallace .10 .30
23 Kevin Lepage .10 .30
24 Chad Little .20 .50
25 Elliott Sadler .20 .50
26 Darrell Waltrip .20 .50
27 Michael Waltrip .20 .50
28 Rusty Wallace's Car .30 .75
29 Ward Burton's Car .10 .30
30 Mark Martin's Car .30 .75
31 Bobby Labonte's Car .20 .50
32 Tony Stewart's Car .40 1.00
33 Jeff Gordon's Car .30 .75
34 Mike Skinner's Car .07 .20
35 Dale Jarrett's Car .20 .50
36 Jeff Burton's Car .10 .30
37 Dale Earnhardt Jr. 1.00 2.50
38 Matt Kenseth .60 1.50
39 Jeff Green .10 .30
40 Elton Sawyer .10 .30
41 Jeff Gordon .75 2.00
42 Randy LaJoie .10 .30
43 Dave Blaney .10 .30
44 Mike McLaughlin .10 .30
45 Casey Atwood .30 .75
46 Jeff Gordon .75 2.00
47 Tony Stewart .75 2.00
48 Jeff Gordon .75 2.00
49 Bobby Labonte .50 1.25
50 Jeff Burton .30 .75
51 Bobby Labonte .50 1.25
52 Bobby Labonte .50 1.25
53 Todd Parrott .07 .20
54 Doug Yates .07 .20
55 Rusty Wallace's Car .30 .75
56 Kenny Wallace's Car .07 .20
57 Elliott Sadler's Car .07 .20
58 Mark Martin's Car .30 .75
59 Jeff Gordon's Car .30 .75
60 Bobby Labonte's Car .20 .50
61 Tony Stewart's Car .40 1.00
62 John Andretti's Car .07 .20
63 Dale Jarrett's Car .20 .50
64 Dave Blaney .10 .30
65 Dale Earnhardt Jr. 1.00 2.50
66 Matt Kenseth .60 1.50
67 Jerry Nadeau .20 .50
68 Michael Waltrip .20 .50
69 Kenny Irwin .20 .50
70 Joe Nemechek .10 .30
71 John Andretti .10 .30
72 Jeff Fuller CL .10 .30
2000 T.Stewart High Gear 2.00 5.00

2000 Wheels High Gear First Gear

COMPLETE SET (72) 25.00 50.00
*FIRST GEAR: 1X TO 2.5X BASE CARDS

2000 Wheels High Gear MPH

COMPLETE SET (72) 75.00 150.00
*MPH CARDS: 6X TO 12X BASE CARDS

2000 Wheels High Gear Autographs

Randomly inserted into packs at one in 100, this insert set features authentic autographs from drivers like Dale Earnhardt and Matt Kenseth. The unnumbered cards are listed below in alphabetical order for convenience. Please note that the copyright year on the backs is 1999, but the cards were issued in 2000. Finally, some cards were only issued in 2003 in the VIP Tin factory sets.

COMPLETE SET (28) 500.00 1000.00
1 John Andretti 10.00 25.00
2 Casey Atwood 10.00 25.00
3 Dave Blaney 6.00 15.00
4 Mike Bliss 5.00 10.00
5 Brett Bodine 5.00 10.00
6 Geoffrey Bodine 6.00 15.00
7 Todd Bodine 5.00 10.00
8 Jeff Burton 10.00 25.00
9 Dale Earnhardt 175.00 350.00
10 Dale Earnhardt Jr. 50.00 100.00
11 Tim Fedewa 5.00 10.00
12 Kevin Grubb 5.00 10.00
13 Bobby Hamilton 10.00 25.00
14 Dale Jarrett 20.00 50.00
15 Jason Keller 6.00 15.00
16 Matt Kenseth 30.00 60.00
17 Bobby Labonte 12.50 30.00
18 Terry Labonte 15.00 40.00
19 Randy LaJoie 5.00 10.00
20 Chad Little 6.00 15.00
21 Jeremy Mayfield 10.00 25.00
22 Mike McLaughlin 5.00 10.00
23 Ricky Rudd 10.00 25.00
24 Elliott Sadler 6.00 15.00
25 Mike Skinner 6.00 15.00
26 Tony Stewart 25.00 60.00
27 Kenny Wallace 5.00 10.00
28 Michael Waltrip 12.50 30.00

2000 Wheels High Gear Custom Shop

Randomly inserted in packs at one in 200, this 5-card insert allowed collectors to "custom-design" their own all-foil etched card from combinations of fronts and backs showcasing five of NASCAR's hottest drivers. Card backs are numbered using the driver's initials, and carry a "CS" prefix. The cards expired on March 31, 2001.

*PRIZE CARDS: .4X TO 1X BASIC INSERTS
CSDE Dale Earnhardt Jr. EXCH 20.00 50.00
CSDJ Dale Jarrett EXCH 10.00 25.00
CSJG Jeff Gordon EXCH 20.00 50.00
CSMK Mark Martin EXCH 10.00 25.00
CSTS Tony Stewart EXCH 12.00 30.00

2000 Wheels High Gear Flag Chasers

Randomly inserted in packs at one in 400, this 5-card insert features some of NASCAR'S top drivers and real pieces of all seven flags that were used during the 1999 NASCAR Winston Cup season. Card backs carry a "FC" prefix.

COMPLETE SET (5) 250.00 500.00
BLCK/WHT/YELL/GRN/RED PRICED BELOW
BLK/WHT/YEL/GRN/REDS #'D TO 75
*BLUE-YELLOW: .6X TO 1.5X BASIC INS.
BLUE-YELLOW CARDS #'D TO 45
*CHECKERED: 1X TO 2X BASIC INSERTS
CHECKERED STATED ODDS 1:5000
CHECKERED CARDS #'D TO 35
*CHECKERED W/BLUE ORNG: 1.5X TO 2.5X
FC1 Dale Jarrett 30.00 80.00
FC2 Jeff Gordon 50.00 120.00
FC3 Dale Earnhardt 75.00 150.00
FC4 Mark Martin 30.00 80.00
FC5 Tony Stewart 25.00 60.00

2000 Wheels High Gear Gear Shifters

Randomly inserted in packs at one in two, this 27-card insert features most of the best drivers in NASCAR. Card backs carry a "GS" prefix.

COMPLETE SET (27) 10.00 25.00
GS1 Dale Jarrett 1.25 3.00
GS2 Mark Martin 1.50 4.00
GS3 Bobby Labonte 1.25 3.00
GS4 Tony Stewart 2.00 5.00
GS5 Jeff Burton .75 2.00
GS6 Jeff Gordon 2.00 5.00
GS7 Dale Earnhardt 3.00 8.00
GS8 Rusty Wallace 1.50 4.00
GS9 Ward Burton .50 1.25
GS10 Terry Labonte .75 2.00
GS11 Mike Skinner .30 .75
GS12 Jeremy Mayfield .30 .75
GS13 Matt Kenseth 1.50 4.00
GS14 Bobby Hamilton .30 .75
GS15 Dave Blaney .30 .75
GS16 Sterling Marlin .75 2.00
GS17 John Andretti .30 .75
GS18 Kenny Irwin .50 1.25
GS19 Kevin Lepage .30 .75
GS20 Steve Park .75 2.00
GS21 Darrell Waltrip .50 1.25
GS22 Kenny Wallace .30 .75
GS23 Dale Earnhardt Jr. 2.50 6.00
GS24 Elliott Sadler .50 1.25
GS25 Michael Waltrip .50 1.25
GS26 Casey Atwood .75 2.00
GS27 Ricky Rudd .75 2.00

2000 Wheels High Gear Man and Machine Drivers

Randomly inserted in Hobby packs at the rate of one in ten, this nine-card set features color portraits of top drivers and their machines in an interlocking set.

COMPLETE SET (9) 15.00 30.00
*CARS: .3X TO .8X DRIVERS
CAR STATED ODDS 1:10 RETAIL
MM1A Tony Stewart 4.00 10.00
MM2A Dale Earnhardt Jr. 5.00 12.00
MM3A Rusty Wallace 3.00 8.00
MM4A Mark Martin 3.00 8.00
MM5A Terry Labonte 1.50 4.00
MM6A Jeff Gordon 4.00 10.00
MM7A Jeff Burton 1.50 4.00
MM8A Dale Jarrett 2.50 6.00
MM9A Bobby Labonte 2.50 6.00

2000 Wheels High Gear Sunday Sensation

Randomly inserted in packs at one in 18, this 9-card insert features nine all plastic cards of superstars that make Monday morning's headlines. Card backs carry an "OC" prefix.

COMPLETE SET (9) 20.00 40.00
OC1 Tony Stewart 5.00 12.00
OC2 Terry Labonte 2.00 5.00
OC3 Rusty Wallace 4.00 10.00
OC4 Mark Martin 4.00 10.00
OC5 Jeff Burton 2.00 5.00
OC6 Jeff Gordon 5.00 12.00
OC7 Dale Earnhardt's Car 8.00 20.00
OC8 Dale Jarrett 3.00 8.00
OC9 Bobby Labonte 3.00 8.00

2000 Wheels High Gear Top Tier

Randomly inserted in packs one in 20, this 9-card die-cut insert features the top nine drivers of the 1999 NASCAR Winston Cup season. Card backs carry a "TT" prefix.

COMPLETE SET (9) 25.00 50.00
TT1 Dale Jarrett 4.00 10.00
TT2 Bobby Labonte 4.00 10.00
TT3 Mark Martin 5.00 12.00
TT4 Jeff Gordon 5.00 12.00
TT5 Tony Stewart 6.00 15.00
TT6 Jeff Burton 2.50 6.00
TT7 Dale Earnhardt 10.00 25.00
TT8 Rusty Wallace 5.00 12.00
TT9 Ward Burton 1.50 4.00

2000 Wheels High Gear Vintage

Issued one per special retail box, these three cards feature some of the leading drivers on the NASCAR circuit.

COMPLETE SET (3) 6.00 15.00
V1 Dale Jarrett 2.00 5.00
V2 Mark Martin 2.50 6.00
V3 Tony Stewart 3.00 8.00

2000 Wheels High Gear Winning Edge

Randomly inserted in packs at one in ten, this 9-card insert features foil-etched cards that highlight some of the attention-getting moves of top drivers. Card backs carry a "WE" prefix.

COMPLETE SET (9) 15.00 30.00
WE1 Dale Jarrett 2.50 6.00
WE2 Mark Martin 3.00 8.00
WE3 Bobby Labonte 2.50 6.00
WE4 Tony Stewart 4.00 10.00
WE5 Jeff Gordon 4.00 10.00
WE6 Dale Earnhardt 6.00 15.00
WE7 Rusty Wallace 3.00 8.00
WE8 Terry Labonte 1.50 4.00
WE9 Dale Earnhardt Jr. 5.00 12.00

2001 Wheels High Gear

The 2001 Wheels High Gear product was released in March 2001, and featured a 72-card base set and is broken into subset as follows: 27 Veterans (1-27), 6 NASCAR Winston Cup Machines (28-33), 12 NASCAR Busch Series (34-45), 6 NASCAR Winston Cup Carmeleons (46-51), 6 2000 Highlights (52-57), 6 Contingency Awards (58-63), and 9 NASCAR Winston Cup Previews (64-72). Each pack contained 4-cards and carried a suggested retail price of $2.99.

COMPLETE SET (72) 12.50 30.00
1 Bobby Labonte .30 .75
2 Dale Earnhardt 2.00 5.00
3 Dale Jarrett .30 .75
4 Jeff Burton .25 .60
5 Tony Stewart .50 1.25
6 Rusty Wallace .30 .75
7 Ricky Rudd .25 .60
8 Mark Martin .30 .75
9 Ward Burton .30 .75
10 Mike Skinner .20 .50
11 Matt Kenseth 1.00 2.50
12 Steve Park .30 .75
13 Dale Earnhardt Jr. .75 2.00
14 Robert Pressley .12 .30
15 Ken Schrader .20 .50
16 Sterling Marlin .30 .75
17 Terry Labonte .30 .75
18 Joe Nemechek .12 .30
19 Kenny Wallace .20 .50
20 Bobby Hamilton .20 .50
21 John Andretti .12 .30
22 Jimmy Spencer .25 .60
23 Jerry Nadeau .25 .60
24 Jeremy Mayfield .20 .50
25 Dave Blaney .12 .30
26 Elliott Sadler .25 .60
27 Tony Stewart WCM .50 1.25
28 Ward Burton WCM .30 .75
29 Matt Kenseth WCM 1.00 2.50
30 Ricky Rudd WCM .25 .60
31 Dale Jarrett WCM .30 .75
32 Rusty Wallace WCM .30 .75
33 Kevin Grubb BGN .12 .30
34 Hank Parker Jr. BGN .12 .30
35 Todd Bodine BGN .12 .30
36 Jeff Green BGN .12 .30
37 Jason Keller BGN .12 .30
38 Kevin Harvick BGN 1.00 2.50
39 Randy LaJoie BGN .12 .30
40 Matt Kenseth BGN 1.00 2.50
41 Elton Sawyer BGN .12 .30
42 David Green BGN .12 .30
43 Jason Leffler BGN .12 .30
44 Casey Atwood BGN .30 .75
45 Ken Schrader's Car .07 .20
46 Ward Burton's Car .12 .30
47 Sterling Marlin's Car .12 .30
48 Bobby Labonte's Car .12 .30
49 Mark Martin's Car .12 .30
50 Elliott Sadler's Car .10 .25
51 Terry Labonte's Car .12 .30
52 Rusty Wallace HL .30 .75
53 Jerry Nadeau HL .25 .60
54 Steve Park HL .30 .75
55 Matt Kenseth HL 1.00 2.50
56 Dale Earnhardt Jr. HL .75 2.00
57 Bobby Labonte HL .30 .75
58 Rusty Wallace CA .30 .75
59 Matt Kenseth CA 1.00 2.50
60 Jeff Burton CA .25 .60
61 Dale Earnhardt CA 2.00 5.00
62 Jimmy Makar CA .20 .50
63 Rusty Wallace CA .30 .75
64 Elliott Sadler WCP .25 .60
65 Bobby Hamilton WCP .20 .50
66 Ryan Newman WCP RC 5.00 12.00
67 Jeff Burton WCP .25 .60
68 Sterling Marlin WCP .30 .75
69 Mark Martin WCP .30 .75
70 Dale Jarrett WCP .30 .75
71 Ricky Craven WCP .12 .30
72 2001 WC Schedule .12 .30

2001 Wheels High Gear First Gear

COMPLETE SET (72) 40.00 100.00
*FIRST GEAR: 1X TO 2.5X BASE HI

2001 Wheels High Gear MPH

COMP.MPH SET (72) 300.00 600.00
*MPH CARDS: 4X TO 10X BASE HI

2001 Wheels High Gear Autographs

Randomly inserted into packs, this 33-card set features authentic signatures from drivers like Jeff Gordon and Dale Earnhardt. Card backs are unnumbered.

1 John Andretti
2 Dave Blaney 6.00 15.00
3 Brett Bodine 6.00 15.00
4 Todd Bodine 6.00 15.00
5 Jeff Burton 8.00 20.00
6 Ward Burton 10.00 25.00
7 Stacy Compton 6.00 15.00
8 Dale Earnhardt 850.00 1100.00
9 Dale Earnhardt Jr. 75.00 150.00
10 Jeff Gordon 75.00 150.00
11 David Green 6.00 15.00
12 Jeff Green 6.00 15.00
13 Mark Green 6.00 15.00
14 Bobby Hamilton 10.00 25.00
15 Kevin Harvick 12.50 30.00
16 Dale Jarrett 20.00 50.00
17 Jason Keller 6.00 15.00
18 Matt Kenseth 15.00 40.00
19 Terry Labonte 15.00 40.00
20 Chad Little 8.00 20.00
21 Jeremy Mayfield 8.00 20.00
22 Sterling Marlin 12.50 30.00
23 Mark Martin 40.00 80.00
24 Joe Nemechek 6.00 15.00
25 Hank Parker Jr. 6.00 15.00
26 Robert Pressley 6.00 15.00
27 Ricky Rudd 12.50 30.00
28 Elton Sawyer 6.00 15.00
29 Ken Schrader 6.00 15.00
30 Mike Skinner 8.00 20.00
31 Tony Stewart 25.00 60.00
32 Dick Trickle 6.00 15.00
33 Rusty Wallace 20.00 50.00

2001 Wheels High Gear Custom Shop

Randomly inserted into packs at the rate of one in 200, this 5-card insert set features an interactive card that allows the collector to custom-design their own foil-based card. He would select one of 3-different front and back card designs and Press Pass would build the card to his specifications.

*PRIZE CARDS: .4X TO 1X BASIC INSERTS
CSBL Bobby Labonte EXCH 8.00 20.00
CSDEJ Dale Earnhardt Jr. EXCH 15.00 40.00
CSJG Jeff Gordon EXCH 15.00 40.00
CSMK Matt Kenseth EXCH 8.00 20.00
CSTS Tony Stewart EXCH 10.00 25.00

2001 Wheels High Gear Flag Chasers

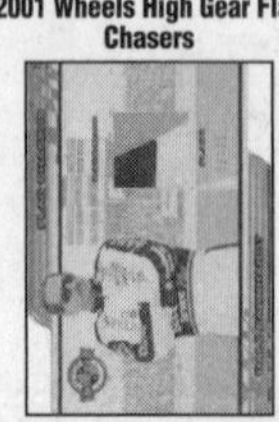

Randomly inserted into packs at the average rate of one in 325, this set features swatches of actual race-used flags. Card backs carry a "FC" prefix.

COMPLETE SET (5) 250.00 500.00
BLACK PRICED BELOW
BLACK CARDS #'D TO 75
*GREEN/RED/WHITE/YELLOW: .4X TO 1X
GREEN/RED/WHITE/YELLOW CARDS #'D TO 75
*BLUE-YELLOW: .4X TO 1X BASIC INSERTS
BLUE-YELLOW CARDS #'D TO 45
*CHECKERED CARDS: .6X TO 1.5X
CHECKERED CARDS #'D TO 35
*CHECKERED W/BLUE ORANGE 2X TO 5X
FC1 Bobby Labonte 20.00 50.00
FC2 Tony Stewart 15.00 40.00
FC3 Dale Earnhardt 50.00 100.00
FC4 Matt Kenseth 25.00 60.00
FC5 Dale Earnhardt Jr. 40.00 100.00

2001 Wheels High Gear Gear Shifters

Randomly inserted into packs at the rate of one in 2, this 27-card "set within a set" features the best drivers in NASCAR. Card backs carry a "GS" prefix.

COMPLETE SET (27) 12.50 30.00
GS1 Bobby Labonte 1.25 3.00
GS2 Dale Earnhardt 3.00 8.00
GS3 Dale Jarrett 1.25 3.00
GS4 Jeff Burton .50 1.25
GS5 Tony Stewart 2.00 5.00
GS6 Rusty Wallace 1.50 4.00
GS7 Ricky Rudd .75 2.00
GS8 Mark Martin 1.50 4.00
GS9 Ward Burton .50 1.25
GS10 Elliott Sadler .50 1.25
GS11 Mike Skinner .25 .60
GS12 Matt Kenseth 1.50 4.00
GS13 Steve Park .50 1.25
GS14 Dale Earnhardt Jr. 2.50 6.00
GS15 Robert Pressley .25 .60
GS16 Ken Schrader .25 .60
GS17 Sterling Marlin .75 2.00
GS18 Terry Labonte .75 2.00
GS19 Joe Nemechek .25 .60
GS20 Kenny Wallace .25 .60
GS21 Bobby Hamilton .25 .60
GS22 John Andretti .25 .60
GS23 Jimmy Spencer .25 .60
GS24 Jerry Nadeau .50 1.25
GS25 Jeremy Mayfield .25 .60
GS26 Dave Blaney .25 .60
GS27 Bobby Labonte 1.25 3.00

2001 Wheels High Gear Hot Streaks

Randomly inserted into packs at the rate of one in 10, this 9-card insert set features drivers that know how to have repeat success. Card backs carry a "HS" prefix.

COMPLETE SET (9) 20.00 50.00
HS1 Tony Stewart 4.00 10.00
HS2 Bobby Labonte 2.50 6.00
HS3 Dale Earnhardt 6.00 15.00
HS4 Mark Martin 3.00 8.00
HS5 Dale Jarrett 2.50 6.00
HS6 Ricky Rudd 1.50 4.00
HS7 Matt Kenseth 3.00 8.00
HS8 Dale Earnhardt Jr. 5.00 12.00
HS9 Jeff Burton 1.00 2.50

2001 Wheels High Gear Man and Machine Drivers

Randomly inserted into packs at the rate of one in 10, this 18-card insert set is broken into two subsets: MM1A-MM9A were issued in hobby packs (drivers), and cards MM1B-MM9B issued into retail packs (machines).

COMP.DRIVERS SET (9) 20.00 50.00
COMP.CAR SET (9) 15.00 40.00
*CARS: .3X TO .8X DRIVERS
MM1A Tony Stewart 4.00 10.00
MM2A Bobby Labonte 2.50 6.00
MM3A Rusty Wallace 3.00 8.00
MM4A Mark Martin 3.00 8.00
MM5A Dale Jarrett 2.50 6.00
MM6A Dale Earnhardt 6.00 15.00
MM7A Dale Earnhardt Jr. 5.00 12.00
MM8A Jeff Burton 1.00 2.50
MM9A Ward Burton 1.00 2.50

2001 Wheels High Gear Sunday Sensation

Randomly inserted into packs at the rate of one in 18, this plastic 9-card insert set features drivers that usually make Monday's headlines. Card backs carry a "SS" prefix.

COMPLETE SET (9) 15.00 40.00
SS1 Dale Jarrett 1.00 2.50
SS2 Rusty Wallace 1.00 2.50
SS3 Matt Kenseth 3.00 8.00
SS4 Steve Park 1.00 2.50
SS5 Tony Stewart 1.50 4.00
SS6 Dale Earnhardt 6.00 15.00
SS7 Bobby Labonte 1.00 2.50
SS8 Ward Burton 1.00 2.50
SS9 Jeff Burton .75 2.00

2001 Wheels High Gear Top Tier

Randomly inserted into packs at the rate of one in 20, this insert set features the top six drivers from the 2001 season. Card backs carry a "TT" prefix.

COMPLETE SET (6) 12.50 30.00
COMP.HOLOFOIL SET (6) 60.00 150.00
*HOLOFOILS: 1.5X TO 4X BASIC INSERTS
HOLOFOIL STATED ODDS 1:450
HOLOFOIL PRINT RUN 250 SER.#'D SETS
TT1 Bobby Labonte 1.25 3.00
TT2 Dale Earnhardt 8.00 20.00
TT3 Jeff Burton 1.00 2.50
TT4 Dale Jarrett 1.25 3.00
TT5 Ricky Rudd 1.00 2.50
TT6 Tony Stewart 2.00 5.00

2002 Wheels High Gear

The 2002 Wheels High Gear product was released in February 2002, and featured a 72-card base set broken into subsets as follows: 27 Veterans (1-27), 6 NASCAR Winston Cup Machines (28-33), 12 NASCAR Busch Series (34-45), 6 NASCAR Winston Cup Carmeleons (46-54), 6 2001 Highlights (55-60), 4 Contingency Awards (61-64), 2 Champ (65 and 66), and 4 NASCAR Winston Cup Previews (68-70). Each pack contained 4-cards and carried a suggested retail price of $2.99.

COMPLETE SET (72) 12.00 30.00
WAX BOX HOBBY (20) 50.00 90.00
WAX BOX RETAIL (16) 40.00 80.00
1 Dave Blaney .15 .40
2 Jeff Burton .30 .75
3 Ward Burton .30 .75
4 Kurt Busch .50 1.25
5 Ricky Craven .15 .40
6 Dale Earnhardt Jr. 1.50 4.00
7 Jeff Gordon 1.25 3.00
8 Bobby Hamilton .15 .40
9 Kevin Harvick 1.00 2.50
10 Dale Jarrett .75 2.00
11 Matt Kenseth 1.00 2.50
12 Bobby Labonte .75 2.00
13 Terry Labonte .50 1.25
14 Sterling Marlin .50 1.25
15 Mark Martin 1.00 2.50
16 Jerry Nadeau .30 .75
17 Joe Nemechek .15 .40
18 Steve Park .30 .75
19 Kyle Petty .30 .75
20 Robert Pressley .15 .40
21 Ricky Rudd .50 1.25
22 Elliott Sadler .30 .75
23 Ken Schrader .15 .40
24 Jimmy Spencer .15 .40
25 Tony Stewart 1.00 2.50
26 Rusty Wallace .75 2.00
27 Michael Waltrip .30 .75
28 Jeff Gordon's Car .50 1.25
29 Kevin Harvick's Car .50 1.25
30 Dale Jarrett's Car .30 .75
31 Ricky Rudd's Car .15 .40
32 Tony Stewart's Car .50 1.25
33 Rusty Wallace's Car .30 .75
34 Jeff Green BGN .15 .40
35 David Green BGN .15 .40
36 Kevin Grubb BGN .15 .40
37 Kevin Harvick BGN 1.00 2.50
38 Jimmie Johnson BGN 1.00 2.50
39 Jason Keller BGN .15 .40
40 Randy LaJoie BGN .15 .40
41 Chad Little BGN .15 .40
42 Jamie McMurray BGN RC 4.00 10.00
43 Ryan Newman BGN 1.00 2.50
44 Hank Parker Jr. BGN .15 .40
45 Elton Sawyer BGN .15 .40
46 Dale Earnhardt Jr.'s Car .75 2.00
47 Jeff Gordon's Car .50 1.25
48 Kevin Harvick's Car .50 1.25
49 Dale Jarrett's Car .30 .75
50 Bobby Labonte's Car .30 .75
51 Ricky Rudd's Car .15 .40
52 Ken Schrader's Car .08 .25
53 Jimmy Spencer's Car .15 .40
54 Tony Stewart's Car .50 1.25
55 Dale Earnhardt Jr. HL 1.50 4.00
56 Jeff Gordon HL 1.25 3.00
57 Kevin Harvick HL 1.00 2.50
58 Sterling Marlin HL .50 1.25
59 Steve Park HL .30 .75
60 Michael Waltrip HL .30 .75
61 Jeff Gordon CA 1.25 3.00
62 Jeff Gordon CA 1.25 3.00
63 Sterling Marlin CA .50 1.25
64 Kevin Harvick CA 1.00 2.50
65 Jeff Gordon WC Champ 1.25 3.00
66 Kevin Harvick BGN Champ 1.00 2.50
67 Ryan Newman PRE 1.00 2.50
68 Robby Gordon PRE .15 .40
69 Jeff Green PRE .15 .40
70 Jimmie Johnson PRE 1.00 2.50
71 Jeff Gordon WC Sched. .60 1.50
72 Kevin Harvick CL .50 1.25
P1 Power Pick Entry Card .08 .25

2002 Wheels High Gear First Gear

COMPLETE FIRST GEAR (72) 40.00 100.00
*FIRST GEAR: 1X TO 2.5X BASIC CARDS

2002 Wheels High Gear MPH

COMP.MPH SET (72) 200.00 400.00
*MPH CARDS: 5X TO 12X BASIC CARDS

2002 Wheels High Gear Autographs

This set features autographs of NASCAR drivers from Winston Cup, Busch, and Craftsman Truck series inserted at a rate of 1:60 hobby packs and 1:240 retail packs. The cards were not numbered and have been listed below alphabetically. The Dale Earnhardt Jr. was not released in the 2002 product, he was released in 2004 Wheels High Gear.

1 Bobby Allison 12.00 30.00
2 Casey Atwood 10.00 25.00
3 Buddy Baker 6.00 15.00
4 Greg Biffle 10.00 25.00
5 Dave Blaney 6.00 15.00
6 Brett Bodine 6.00 15.00
7 Todd Bodine 6.00 15.00
8 Jeff Burton 5.00 12.00
9 Ward Burton 10.00 25.00
10 Kurt Busch 12.00 30.00
11 Richard Childress 8.00 20.00
12 Stacy Compton 6.00 15.00
13 Matt Crafton 6.00 15.00

14 Dale Earnhardt Jr.	200.00	400.00
15 Larry Foyt	6.00	15.00
16 Coy Gibbs	8.00	20.00
17 Jeff Gordon	100.00	200.00
18 David Green	6.00	15.00
19 Jeff Green	6.00	15.00
20 Bobby Hamilton	10.00	25.00
21 Kevin Harvick	12.00	30.00
22 Ricky Hendrick	15.00	40.00
23 Ron Hornaday	6.00	15.00
24 Dale Jarrett	15.00	40.00
25 Ned Jarrett	6.00	15.00
26 Jimmie Johnson	40.00	80.00
27 Jason Keller	6.00	15.00
28 Matt Kenseth	15.00	40.00
29 Travis Kvapil	8.00	20.00
30 Bobby Labonte	10.00	25.00
31 Terry Labonte	15.00	40.00
32 Randy LaJoie	6.00	15.00
33 Chad Little	6.00	15.00
34 Sterling Marlin	15.00	40.00
35 Mark Martin	20.00	50.00
36 Mike McLaughlin	6.00	15.00
37 Jamie McMurray	8.00	20.00
38 Ted Musgrave	6.00	15.00
39 Jerry Nadeau	8.00	20.00
40 Joe Nemechek	6.00	15.00
41 Ryan Newman	8.00	20.00
42 Benny Parsons	30.00	60.00
43 David Pearson	15.00	40.00
44 Kyle Petty	12.00	30.00
45 Richard Petty	25.00	60.00
46 Robert Pressley	6.00	15.00
47 Tony Raines	6.00	15.00
48 Scott Riggs	10.00	25.00
49 Ricky Rudd	15.00	40.00
50 Joe Ruttman	6.00	15.00
51 Elton Sawyer	6.00	15.00
52 Ken Schrader	8.00	20.00
53 Mike Skinner	6.00	15.00
54 Jack Sprague	6.00	15.00
55 Tony Stewart	25.00	60.00
56 Rusty Wallace	12.00	30.00
57 Darrell Waltrip	20.00	50.00
58 Michael Waltrip	10.00	25.00
59 Scott Wimmer	10.00	25.00
60 Jon Wood	8.00	20.00
61 Cale Yarborough	12.00	30.00
62 Robert Yates	6.00	15.00

2002 Wheels High Gear Custom Shop

Randomly inserted into packs at the rate of one in 200, this 5-card insert set features an interactive card that allows the collector to custom-design their own foil-based card. Card backs carry a "CS" prefix along with the driver's initials.

CSDJ Dale Jarrett EXCH	8.00	20.00
CSJG Jeff Gordon EXCH	20.00	40.00
CSKH Kevin Harvick EXCH	8.00	20.00
CSRN Ryan Newman EXCH	8.00	20.00
CSTS Tony Stewart EXCH	12.50	30.00

2002 Wheels High Gear Flag Chasers

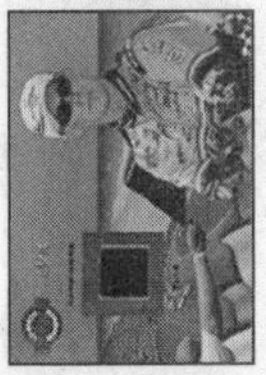

Randomly inserted into packs at the average rate of one in 400, this set features swatches of actual race-used flags. Several different parallels were produced with each version being serial numbered. Card backs carry a "FC" prefix.

WHITE CARDS #'D TO 130
*YELLOW/110: .4X TO 1X WHITE/130
*BLACK/GREEN/RED/90: .4X TO 1X WHT/130
*BLUE-YELL/40: .8X TO 2X WHITE/130
*CHECKER/35: 1X TO 2.5X WHITE/130
*CHECK.BLUE ORNG/10: 2X TO 5X WHT/130

FC1 Dale Earnhardt Jr.	12.00	30.00
FC2 Jeff Gordon	12.00	30.00
FC3 Kevin Harvick	8.00	20.00
FC4 Dale Jarrett	8.00	20.00
FC5 Tony Stewart	10.00	25.00

2002 Wheels High Gear High Groove

This die cut card features foil stamping and photos of the driver and his car. They were inserted at a rate of 1:2.

COMPLETE SET (27)	12.00	30.00
HG1 Dave Blaney	.25	.60
HG2 Jeff Burton	.50	1.25
HG3 Ward Burton	.50	1.25
HG4 Kurt Busch	.75	2.00
HG5 Ricky Craven	.25	.60
HG6 Dale Earnhardt Jr.	2.50	6.00
HG7 Jeff Gordon	2.00	5.00
HG8 Bobby Hamilton	.25	.60
HG9 Kevin Harvick	1.50	4.00
HG10 Dale Jarrett	1.25	3.00
HG11 Matt Kenseth	1.50	4.00
HG12 Bobby Labonte	1.25	3.00
HG13 Terry Labonte	.75	2.00
HG14 Sterling Marlin	.75	2.00
HG15 Mark Martin	1.50	4.00
HG16 Jerry Nadeau	.50	1.25
HG17 Joe Nemechek	.25	.60
HG18 Steve Park	.50	1.25
HG19 Kyle Petty	.50	1.25
HG20 Robert Pressley	.25	.60
HG21 Ricky Rudd	.75	2.00
HG22 Elliott Sadler	.50	1.25
HG23 Ken Schrader	.25	.60
HG24 Jimmy Spencer	.25	.60
HG25 Tony Stewart	1.50	4.00
HG26 Rusty Wallace	1.25	3.00
HG27 Michael Waltrip	.50	1.25

2002 Wheels High Gear Hot Streaks

Inserted at a rate of 1:10, this 9-card set features top drivers from 2001. Each card was printed on holofoil card stock.

COMPLETE SET (9)	15.00	40.00
HS1 Jeff Burton	1.00	2.50
HS2 Dale Earnhardt Jr.	5.00	12.00
HS3 Jeff Gordon	4.00	10.00
HS4 Kevin Harvick	3.00	8.00
HS5 Dale Jarrett	2.50	6.00
HS6 Steve Park	1.00	2.50
HS7 Ricky Rudd	1.50	4.00
HS8 Tony Stewart	3.00	8.00
HS9 Rusty Wallace	2.50	6.00

2002 Wheels High Gear Man and Machine Drivers

Randomly inserted into packs at the rate of one in 10, this insert was divided into two different sets: MM1A-MM9A were issued in hobby packs (drivers), and cards MM1B-MM9B issued into retail packs (machines). Each card was die-cut so that both the driver and car version would fit together like a puzzle.

COMPLETE SET (9)	15.00	40.00
*CARS: .4X TO 1X DRIVERS		
MM1A Dale Earnhardt Jr.	2.50	6.00
MM2A Jeff Gordon	2.00	5.00
MM3A Kevin Harvick	1.25	3.00
MM4A Dale Jarrett	1.00	2.50
MM5A Bobby Labonte	1.00	2.50
MM6A Steve Park	1.00	2.50
MM7A Ricky Rudd	.75	2.00
MM8A Tony Stewart	1.50	4.00
MM9A Rusty Wallace	1.00	2.50

2002 Wheels High Gear Sunday Sensation

Randomly inserted into packs at the rate of one in 18, this foil laser-etched 9-card insert set features drivers that usually make Monday's headlines. The cardbacks carry an "SS" prefix.

COMPLETE SET (9)	15.00	40.00
SS1 Ward Burton	1.25	3.00
SS2 Jeff Burton	1.25	3.00
SS3 Ricky Rudd	2.00	5.00
SS4 Jeff Gordon	5.00	12.00
SS5 Kevin Harvick	4.00	10.00
SS6 Dale Jarrett	3.00	8.00
SS7 Sterling Marlin	2.00	5.00
SS8 Tony Stewart	4.00	10.00
SS9 Rusty Wallace	3.00	8.00

2002 Wheels High Gear Top Tier

Randomly inserted into packs at the rate of one in 20, this insert set features the top six drivers from the 2001 season. Each card was printed on clear plastic card stock. Cardbacks carry a "TT" prefix.

COMPLETE SET (6)	15.00	40.00
*NUMBERED: 1.2X TO 3X BASIC INSERTS		
FOIL CARDS SERIAL #'d OF 250		
TT1 Jeff Gordon	5.00	12.00
TT2 Tony Stewart	4.00	10.00
TT3 Sterling Marlin	2.50	6.00
TT4 Ricky Rudd	2.00	5.00
TT5 Dale Jarrett	3.00	8.00
TT6 Bobby Labonte	3.00	8.00

2003 Wheels High Gear

This set was released in January 2003. These cards were issued in 6-card hobby packs with an SRP of $3.99. They came 20-packs to a box and 20-boxes to a case. The retail version was issued four cards per pack with an $2.99 SRP and packaged 28-packs to a box and 20-boxes to a case. There was a special 0 card honoring Tony Stewart as the 2002 NASCAR champion and those cards were inserted at a stated rate of one in 400 packs. In addition, two cards (one hobby and the other retail only) featuring Kerry Earnhardt were issued in packs with a "KE" prefix, those cards were issued at a stated rate of one in 70 packs.

COMPLETE SET (72)	12.50	30.00
WAX BOX HOBBY (20)	50.00	80.00
1 John Andretti	.15	.40
2 Dave Blaney	.15	.40
3 Brett Bodine	.15	.40
4 Jeff Burton	.30	.75
5 Ward Burton	.30	.75
6 Kurt Busch	.50	1.25
7 Ricky Craven	.15	.40
8 Dale Earnhardt Jr.	1.50	4.00
9 Robby Gordon	.15	.40
10 Jeff Gordon	1.25	3.00
11 Jeff Green	.15	.40
12 Kevin Harvick	.75	2.00
13 Dale Jarrett	.75	2.00
14 Jimmie Johnson	1.00	2.50
15 Matt Kenseth	1.00	2.50
16 Bobby Labonte	.75	2.00
17 Terry Labonte	.50	1.25
18 Sterling Marlin	.50	1.25
19 Mark Martin	1.00	2.50
20 Ryan Newman	1.00	2.50
21 Steve Park	.30	.75
22 Kyle Petty	.30	.75
23 Ricky Rudd	.50	1.25
24 Elliott Sadler	.30	.75
25 Ken Schrader	.15	.40
26 Mike Skinner	.15	.40
27 Jimmy Spencer	.15	.40
28 Tony Stewart	1.00	2.50
29 Rusty Wallace	.75	2.00
30 Michael Waltrip	.30	.75
31 Ryan Newman's Car	.50	1.25
32 Ward Burton's Car	.30	.75
33 Jimmie Johnson's Car	.50	1.25
34 Tony Stewart's Car	.50	1.25
35 Matt Kenseth's Car	.50	1.25
36 Dale Jarrett's Car	.30	.75
37 Tony Raines	.15	.40
38 Kerry Earnhardt	.30	.75
39 Johnny Sauter	.30	.75
40 Hank Parker Jr.	.15	.40
41 Greg Biffle CRC	.30	.75
42 Scott Riggs	.30	.75
43 Brian Vickers	.60	1.50
44 Scott Wimmer	.30	.75
45 Jason Keller	.15	.40
46 Jamie McMurray	.75	2.00
47 Jack Sprague	.15	.40
48 Randy LaJoie	.15	.40
49 Jeff Gordon's Car CM	.50	1.25
50 Dale Jarrett's Car CM	.30	.75
51 Ken Schrader's Car CM	.08	.20
52 Dale Earnhardt Jr.'s Car CM	.60	1.50
53 Ricky Rudd's Car CM	.15	.40
54 Tony Stewart's Car CM	.50	1.25
55 Rusty Wallace's Car CM	.30	.75
56 Kevin Harvick's Car CM	.30	.75
57 Bobby Labonte's Car CM	.30	.75
58 The Fab Four	.30	.75
59 Man Of Steel	.30	.75
60 On The Mark WCS	.30	.75
61 Contenders and Pretenders WCS	.50	1.25
62 Southern Comfort WCS	.50	1.25
63 Feeling Like A New Man WCS	.50	1.25
64 Tony Stewart NA	.75	2.00
65 Ryan Newman NA	.75	2.00
66 Jeff Green NA	.15	.40
67 Scott Riggs NA	.30	.75
68 Ryan Newman NA	.75	2.00
69 Greg Biffle NA	.30	.75
70 Elliott Sadler PREV	.30	.75
71 Kevin Harvick PREV	.60	1.50
72 Tony Stewart CL	.60	1.50
KE1 Kerry Earnhardt HOBBY	5.00	12.00
KE2 Kerry Earnhardt RETAIL	6.00	15.00
0 Tony Stewart Champion	8.00	20.00

2003 Wheels High Gear First Gear

COMPLETE SET (72)	25.00	50.00
*FIRST GEAR: .8X TO 2X BASE CARDS		

2003 Wheels High Gear MPH

*MPH: 5X TO 12X BASE CARDS

2003 Wheels High Gear Samples

*SAMPLES: 2X TO 5X BASE CARDS

2003 Wheels High Gear Custom Shop

Issued at a stated rate of one in 200, these five cards feature some of the most popular drivers on the Winston Cup circuit. Collectors were able to use these redemption cards by choosing from a variety of front and back designs to create their own custom card. The expiration date for the exchange cards is 6/30/2004.

COMPLETE SET (5)	60.00	120.00
*PRIZE CARDS: .5X TO 1.2X BASIC INSERTS		
45-DIFFERENT PRIZES ISSUED VIA MAIL		
CSDE Dale Earnhardt Jr. EXCH	20.00	40.00
CSJG Jeff Gordon EXCH	15.00	30.00
CSJJ Jimmie Johnson EXCH	12.50	25.00
CSRN Ryan Newman EXCH	12.50	25.00
CSTS Tony Stewart EXCH	12.50	25.00

2003 Wheels High Gear Dale Earnhardt Retrospective

Issued at a stated rate of one in 72, these nine cards feature a look back at some of the most popular High Gear Dale Earnhardt cards ever issued. A Foil parallel set was also issued and serial numbered to 250.

COMMON EARNHARDT	10.00	25.00
*FOILS: .8X TO 2X BASIC INSERTS		

2003 Wheels High Gear Flag Chasers Black

Randomly inserted into packs, these cards feature a race-used black flag piece embedded into a card. These cards were issued to a stated print run of 90 serial numbered sets. Six other flag colors were also produced as parallels of each card in varying quantities as noted below.

*BLUE/YELL/45: .6X TO 1.5X BLACK/90
*CHECKERED/25: .8X TO 2X BLACK/90
*GREEN/90: .4X TO 1X BLACK/90
*RED/90: .4X TO 1X BLACK/90
*WHITE/90: .4X TO 1X BLACK/90
*YELLOW/90: .4X TO 1X BLACK/90
POWER PICK ENTRY CARD ODDS 1:20

FC1 Dale Earnhardt Jr.	8.00	20.00
FC2 Jeff Gordon	6.00	15.00
FC3 Jimmie Johnson	5.00	12.00
FC4 Ryan Newman	2.50	6.00
FC5 Tony Stewart	5.00	12.00
FC6 Matt Kenseth	8.00	20.00
FC7 Jamie McMurray	5.00	12.00
FC8 Kurt Busch	2.50	6.00
FC9 Mark Martin	3.00	8.00
FC10 Ward Burton	3.00	8.00
NNO Power Pick Entry Card	1.50	4.00

2003 Wheels High Gear Full Throttle

Issued at a stated rate of one in six, these nine cards feature high-speed competitors in this set made of clear plastic stock.

COMPLETE SET (9)	10.00	25.00
FT1 Kevin Harvick	1.25	3.00
FT2 Jeff Gordon	2.00	5.00
FT3 Ryan Newman	1.50	4.00
FT4 Jimmie Johnson	1.50	4.00
FT5 Dale Jarrett	1.25	3.00
FT6 Rusty Wallace	1.25	3.00
FT7 Dale Earnhardt Jr.	2.50	6.00
FT8 Tony Stewart	1.50	4.00
FT9 Matt Kenseth	1.50	4.00

2003 Wheels High Gear High Groove

Issued at a stated rate of one in two, these 27 cards feature some of the leading drivers in NASCAR. Each card was die-cut and features a photo of the driver and his car.

COMPLETE SET (27)	10.00	25.00
HG1 Dave Blaney	.25	.60
HG2 Jeff Burton	.50	1.25
HG3 Ward Burton	.50	1.25
HG4 Kurt Busch	.75	2.00
HG5 Ricky Craven	.25	.60
HG6 Dale Earnhardt Jr.	2.50	6.00
HG7 Jeff Gordon	2.00	5.00
HG8 Robby Gordon	.25	.60
HG9 Jeff Green	.25	.60
HG10 Kevin Harvick	1.25	3.00
HG11 Dale Jarrett	1.25	3.00
HG12 Jimmie Johnson	1.50	4.00
HG13 Matt Kenseth	1.50	4.00
HG14 Bobby Labonte	1.25	3.00
HG15 Terry Labonte	.75	2.00
HG16 Sterling Marlin	.75	2.00
HG17 Mark Martin	1.50	4.00
HG18 Ryan Newman	1.50	4.00
HG19 Steve Park	.50	1.25
HG20 Kyle Petty	.50	1.25
HG21 Ricky Rudd	.75	2.00
HG22 Elliott Sadler	.50	1.25
HG23 Ken Schrader	.25	.60
HG24 Jimmy Spencer	.25	.60
HG25 Tony Stewart	1.50	4.00
HG26 Rusty Wallace	1.25	3.00
HG27 Michael Waltrip	.50	1.25

2003 Wheels High Gear Hot Treads

Randomly inserted in retail packs only, these 19 cards feature leading NASCAR drivers. These cards were issued to a stated print run of 425 serial numbered sets.

HT0 Michael Waltrip	5.00	12.00
HT1 John Andretti	4.00	10.00
HT2 Jeff Burton	5.00	12.00
HT3 Ward Burton	5.00	12.00
HT4 Kurt Busch	6.00	15.00
HT5 Jeff Gordon	10.00	25.00
HT6 Kevin Harvick	6.00	15.00
HT7 Jimmie Johnson	8.00	20.00
HT8 Matt Kenseth	5.00	12.00
HT9 Bobby Labonte	6.00	15.00
HT10 Sterling Marlin	5.00	12.00
HT11 Mark Martin	6.00	15.00
HT12 Jamie McMurray	4.00	10.00
HT13 Ryan Newman	5.00	12.00
HT14 Steve Park	4.00	10.00
HT15 Kyle Petty	5.00	12.00
HT16 Tony Stewart	8.00	20.00
HT17 Rusty Wallace	6.00	15.00
HT18 Dale Earnhardt Jr.	10.00	25.00

2003 Wheels High Gear Man

Issued at a stated rate of one in 10 hobby packs, these nine foil-embossed die-cut cards feature photos of leading drivers. A "Machine" version of each card was produced for retail packs. Collectors could interlock both the Man and Machine cards similar to a puzzle.

COMPLETE SET (9)	15.00	40.00
*MACHINE: .4X TO 1X MAN CARDS		
MACHINE STATED ODDS 1:10 RETAIL		
MM1A Jimmie Johnson	2.50	6.00
MM2A Kevin Harvick	2.00	5.00
MM3A Rusty Wallace	2.00	5.00
MM4A Tony Stewart	2.50	6.00
MM5A Ryan Newman	2.50	6.00
MM6A Dale Earnhardt Jr.	4.00	10.00
MM7A Dale Jarrett	2.00	5.00
MM8A Bobby Labonte	2.00	5.00
MM9A Jeff Gordon	3.00	8.00

2003 Wheels High Gear Sunday Sensation

Issued at a stated rate of one in 18, these nine silver foil micro-etched cards feature both NASCAR drivers and the tracks they won races on in 2002.

COMPLETE SET (9)	25.00	60.00
SS1 Matt Kenseth	4.00	10.00
SS2 Sterling Marlin	2.00	5.00
SS3 Mark Martin	4.00	10.00
SS4 Jeff Gordon	5.00	12.00
SS5 Jimmie Johnson	4.00	10.00
SS6 Ryan Newman	4.00	10.00
SS7 Tony Stewart	4.00	10.00
SS8 Ward Burton	1.25	3.00
SS9 Dale Earnhardt Jr.	6.00	15.00

2003 Wheels High Gear Top Tier

Issued at a stated rate of one in 12, these six cards feature the top drivers from the 2002 NASCAR season. Each was printed on special holofoil card stock.

COMPLETE SET (6)	8.00	20.00
TT1 Tony Stewart	2.00	5.00
TT2 Mark Martin	2.00	5.00
TT3 Kurt Busch	1.00	2.50
TT4 Jeff Gordon	2.50	6.00
TT5 Jimmie Johnson	2.00	5.00
TT6 Ryan Newman	2.00	5.00

2004 Wheels High Gear

This set was released in late January 2004. These cards were issued in 5-card hobby packs with an SRP of $2.99. They came 20-packs to a box and 20-boxes to a case. The retail version was issued four cards per pack with an $2.99 SRP and packaged 28-packs to a box and 20-boxes to a case. There was a special 0 card honoring Matt Kenseth as the 2003 NASCAR champion and those cards were inserted at a stated rate of one in 480 packs.

COMPLETE SET (72)	12.50	30.00
WAX BOX HOBBY (20)	50.00	90.00
1 Greg Biffle	.30	.75
2 Dave Blaney	.20	.50
3 Jeff Burton	.30	.75
4 Kurt Busch	.50	1.25
5 Ricky Craven	.20	.50
6 Dale Earnhardt Jr.	1.25	3.00
7 Robby Gordon	.20	.50
8 Jeff Gordon	1.25	3.00
9 Kevin Harvick	.75	2.00
10 Dale Jarrett	.60	1.50
11 Jimmie Johnson	1.00	2.50
12 Matt Kenseth	1.00	2.50
13 Bobby Labonte	.60	1.50
14 Terry Labonte	.50	1.25
15 Sterling Marlin	.50	1.25
16 Mark Martin	.75	2.00
17 Jamie McMurray	.50	1.25
18 Casey Mears	.30	.75
19 Joe Nemechek	.20	.50
20 Ryan Newman	1.00	2.50
21 Kyle Petty	.30	.75
22 Ricky Rudd	.50	1.25
23 Elliott Sadler	.30	.75
24 Jimmy Spencer	.20	.50
25 Tony Stewart	.75	2.00
26 Rusty Wallace	.60	1.50
27 Michael Waltrip	.30	.75
28 Terry Labonte C	.30	.75
29 Dale Earnhardt Jr.'s Car C	.50	1.25
30 Kurt Busch's Car C	.10	.25
31 Bobby Labonte's Car C	.30	.75
32 Elliott Sadler's Car C	.10	.25
33 Ricky Rudd's Car C	.20	.50
34 Jeff Gordon's Car C	.50	1.25
35 Robby Gordon's Car C	.10	.25
36 Jimmie Johnson's Car C	.50	1.25
37 David Green	.20	.50
38 Brian Vickers	.60	1.50
39 Scott Riggs CRC	.30	.75
40 Kasey Kahne	1.25	3.00
41 Scott Wimmer	.30	.75
42 Coy Gibbs	.30	.75
43 Mike Bliss	.20	.50
44 Johnny Sauter	.30	.75
45 Kyle Busch RC	4.00	10.00
46 Matt Kenseth NA	1.00	2.50
47 Jamie McMurray NA	.50	1.25
48 Ryan Newman NA	1.00	2.50
49 Matt Kenseth NA	1.00	2.50
50 Dale Earnhardt Jr. NA	1.25	3.00
51 Jimmie Johnson NA	1.00	2.50
52 Jeff Gordon NA	1.25	3.00
53 Brian Vickers NA	.60	1.50
54 David Stremme NA RC	2.00	5.00
55 Rusty Wallace's Car	.30	.75
56 Bobby Labonte's Car	.30	.75
57 Jimmie Johnson's Car	.50	1.25
58 Kevin Harvick's Car	.30	.75
59 Jeff Gordon's Car	.50	1.25
60 Matt Kenseth's Car	.50	1.25
61 Dale Earnhardt Jr. HL	1.25	3.00
62 Rusty Wallace HL	.60	1.50
63 Ryan Newman HL	1.00	2.50
64 Kurt Busch HL	.50	1.25
65 Bobby Labonte HL	.60	1.50
66 Michael Waltrip HL	.30	.75
67 Jamie McMurray's Car PREV	.20	.50
68 Kurt Busch's Car PREV	.50	1.25
69 Joe Nemechek's Car PREV	.10	.25
70 Scott Wimmer's Car PREV	.20	.50
71 Scott Riggs' Car PREV	.20	.50
72 Jimmie Johnson CL	1.00	2.50
0 Matt Kenseth Champ	6.00	15.00

2004 Wheels High Gear MPH

COMPLETE SET (72)	400.00	800.00
*VETERANS: 5X TO 12X HI COL.		
*RCs: 4X TO 10X HI COL.		

2004 Wheels High Gear Samples

COMPLETE SET (72)	75.00	150.00
*SAMPLES: 2X TO 5X BASE		
STATED ODDS 1 PER BRC 115		

2004 Wheels High Gear Custom Shop

Issued at a stated rate of one in 200, these five cards feature some of the most popular drivers on the Winston Cup circuit. Collectors were able to use these redemption cards by choosing from a variety of front and back designs to create their own custom card.

CSDE Dale Earnhardt Jr.	20.00	40.00
CSJG Jeff Gordon	20.00	40.00
CSJJ Jimmie Johnson	15.00	30.00
CSKH Kevin Harvick	12.50	25.00
CSTS Tony Stewart	12.50	25.00

2004 Wheels High Gear Dale Earnhardt Jr.

This 6-card set featured Dale Earnhardt Jr. in 6 different cards and were available only in specially marked blister boxes.

COMPLETE SET (6) 15.00 40.00
DJR1 Dale Earnhardt Jr. 3.00 6.00
DJR2 Dale Earnhardt Jr. 3.00 6.00
DJR3 Dale Earnhardt Jr. 3.00 6.00
DJR4 Dale Earnhardt Jr. 3.00 6.00
DJR5 Dale Earnhardt Jr. 3.00 6.00
DJR6 Dale Earnhardt Jr. 3.00 6.00

2004 Wheels High Gear Flag Chasers Black

Randomly inserted into packs, these cards feature a race-used black flag piece embedded into a card. These cards were issued to a stated print run of 100 serial numbered sets. Six other flag colors were also produced as parallels of each card in varying quantities as noted below.

BLACK STATED PRINT RUN 100
ENTRY CARD STATED ODDS 1:20
*BLUE/50: .5X TO 1.2X BLACK/100
*CHECKERED/35: .8X TO 2X BLACK/100
*GREEN/100: .4X TO 1X BLACK/100
*RED/100: .4X TO 1X BLACK/100
*WHITE/100: .4X TO 1X BLACK/100
*YELLOW/100: .4X TO 1X BLACK/100
FC1 Jimmie Johnson 15.00 40.00
FC2 Kevin Harvick 10.00 25.00
FC3 Bobby Labonte 10.00 25.00
FC4 Michael Waltrip 8.00 20.00
FC5 Tony Stewart 15.00 40.00
FC6 Jeff Gordon 20.00 50.00
FC7 Dale Earnhardt Jr. 20.00 50.00
FC8 Ryan Newman 8.00 20.00
FC9 Matt Kenseth 8.00 20.00
NNO Entry Card 1.25 3.00

2004 Wheels High Gear Full Throttle

Issued at a stated rate of one in 18, these six cards feature high-speed competitors in this set made of clear plastic stock.

COMPLETE SET (6) 12.50 30.00
FT1 Jimmie Johnson 3.00 8.00
FT2 Jeff Gordon 4.00 10.00
FT3 Ryan Newman 3.00 8.00
FT4 Tony Stewart 2.50 6.00
FT5 Matt Kenseth 3.00 8.00
FT6 Kevin Harvick 2.50 6.00

2004 Wheels High Gear High Groove

Issued at a stated rate of one per pack, these 27 cards feature some of the leading drivers in NASCAR. Each card was die-cut and features a photo of the driver and his car.

COMPLETE SET (27) 8.00 20.00
HG1 Greg Biffle .40 1.00
HG2 Jeff Burton .40 1.00
HG3 Kurt Busch .60 1.50
HG4 Ricky Craven .25 .60
HG5 Dale Earnhardt Jr. 1.50 4.00
HG6 Jeff Gordon 1.50 4.00
HG7 Robby Gordon .25 .60
HG8 Kevin Harvick 1.00 2.50
HG9 Dale Jarrett .75 2.00
HG10 Jimmie Johnson 1.25 3.00
HG11 Matt Kenseth 1.25 3.00
HG12 Bobby Labonte .75 2.00
HG13 Terry Labonte .60 1.50
HG14 Sterling Marlin .60 1.50
HG15 Mark Martin 1.00 2.50
HG16 Jamie McMurray .60 1.50
HG17 Casey Mears .40 1.00
HG18 Joe Nemechek .25 .60
HG19 Ryan Newman 1.25 3.00
HG20 Kyle Petty .40 1.00
HG21 Ricky Rudd .60 1.50
HG22 Elliott Sadler .40 1.00
HG23 Dave Blaney .25 .60
HG24 Jimmy Spencer .25 .60
HG25 Tony Stewart 1.00 2.50
HG26 Rusty Wallace .75 2.00
HG27 Michael Waltrip .40 1.00

2004 Wheels High Gear Man

Issued at a stated rate of one in 10 hobby packs, these nine foil-embossed die-cut cards feature photos of leading drivers. A "Machine" version of each card was produced for retail packs. Collectors could interlock both the Man and Machine cards similar to a puzzle.

COMPLETE SET (9) 15.00 40.00
*MACHINE: .4X TO 1X MAN
MM1A Tony Stewart 2.00 5.00
MM2A Kurt Busch 1.00 2.50
MM3A Jeff Gordon 3.00 8.00
MM4A Michael Waltrip .60 1.50
MM5A Kevin Harvick 2.00 5.00
MM6A Jimmie Johnson 2.50 6.00
MM7A Matt Kenseth 2.50 6.00
MM8A Dale Jarrett 1.25 3.00
MM9A Dale Earnhardt Jr. 3.00 8.00

2004 Wheels High Gear Sunday Sensation

Issued at a stated rate of one in 18, these nine silver foil micro-etched cards feature both NASCAR drivers and the tracks they won races on in 2003.

COMPLETE SET (9) 10.00 25.00
SS1 Michael Waltrip .50 1.25
SS2 Matt Kenseth 1.50 4.00
SS3 Dale Earnhardt Jr. 2.00 5.00
SS4 Jimmie Johnson 1.50 4.00
SS5 Tony Stewart 1.25 3.00
SS6 Ryan Newman 1.50 4.00
SS7 Kevin Harvick 1.25 3.00
SS8 Ryan Newman 1.50 4.00
SS9 Jeff Gordon 2.00 5.00

2004 Wheels High Gear Top Ten

Issued at a stated rate of one in 12, these nine cards feature the top drivers from the 2003 NASCAR season. Each was printed on special holofoil card stock.

COMPLETE SET (9) 12.50 30.00
TT1 Matt Kenseth 3.00 8.00
TT2 Jimmie Johnson 3.00 8.00
TT3 Dale Earnhardt Jr. 4.00 10.00
TT4 Jeff Gordon 4.00 10.00
TT5 Kevin Harvick 2.50 6.00
TT6 Ryan Newman 3.00 8.00
TT7 Tony Stewart 2.50 6.00
TT8 Bobby Labonte 2.00 5.00
TT9 Terry Labonte 1.50 4.00

2004 Wheels High Gear Winston Victory Lap Tribute

This 6-card set was randomly inserted in packs at a rate of one in 48. The card feature some of the most memorable drivers who won Winston Cup Championships.

COMPLETE SET (6) 40.00 100.00
*GOLDS: 1X TO 2.5X BASIC INSERTS
GOLD PRINT RUN 100 SER.#'d SETS
WVL1 Jeff Gordon 8.00 20.00
WVL2 Terry Labonte 6.00 15.00
WVL3 Richard Petty 8.00 20.00
WVL4 Dale Earnhardt 12.50 30.00
WVL5 Darrell Waltrip 6.00 15.00
WVL6 Cale Yarborough 5.00 12.00

2005 Wheels High Gear

This set was released in late January 2005. These cards were issued in 5-card hobby packs with an SRP of $2.99. They came 20-packs to a box and 20-boxes to a case. The retail version was issued four cards per pack with an $2.99 SRP and packaged 28-packs to a box and 20-boxes to a case. There was a special 0 card honoring Kurt Busch as the 2004 NASCAR champion and those cards were inserted at a stated rate of one in 480 packs.

COMPLETE SET (90) 12.50 30.00
WAX BOX HOBBY (20) 50.00 80.00
WAX BOX RETAIL (24) 35.00 60.00
1 Joe Nemechek .20 .50
2 Rusty Wallace .60 1.50
3 Mark Martin .75 2.00
4 Dale Earnhardt Jr. 1.25 3.00
5 Kasey Kahne 1.25 3.00
6 Scott Riggs .30 .75
7 Ryan Newman 1.00 2.50
8 Michael Waltrip .30 .75
9 Greg Biffle .30 .75
10 Matt Kenseth 1.00 2.50
11 Bobby Labonte .60 1.50
12 Jeremy Mayfield .20 .50
13 Tony Stewart .75 2.00
14 Ricky Rudd .50 1.25
15 Scott Wimmer .30 .75
16 Jeff Gordon 1.25 3.00
17 Brian Vickers .60 1.50
18 Kevin Harvick .75 2.00
19 Elliott Sadler .30 .75
20 Sterling Marlin .50 1.25
21 Casey Mears .30 .75
22 Jamie McMurray .50 1.25
23 Jimmie Johnson 1.00 2.50
24 Ken Schrader .20 .50
25 Brendan Gaughan .30 .75
26 Dale Jarrett .60 1.50
27 Kurt Busch .50 1.25
28 Martin Truex Jr. 1.00 2.50
29 Kyle Busch .75 2.00
30 Jason Leffler .20 .50
31 Greg Biffle .30 .75
32 David Green .20 .50
33 Ron Hornaday .20 .50
34 Jason Keller .20 .50
35 Tim Fedewa .20 .50
36 Kasey Kahne 1.25 3.00
37 Tony Stewart's Car C .30 .75
38 Rusty Wallace's Car C .20 .50
39 Elliott Sadler's Car C .08 .20
40 Kasey Kahne's Car C .50 1.25
41 Kevin Harvick's Car C .30 .75
42 Dale Jarrett's Car C .20 .50
43 Bobby Labonte's Car C .20 .50
44 Ryan Newman's Car C .08 .20
45 Ricky Rudd's Car C .20 .50
46 Kurt Busch A .50 1.25
47 Martin Truex Jr. A 1.00 2.50
48 Tony Stewart A .75 2.00
49 Kasey Kahne A 1.25 3.00
50 Ryan Newman A 1.00 2.50
51 Matt Kenseth A 1.00 2.50
52 Dale Earnhardt Jr. A 1.25 3.00
53 Jeff Gordon A 1.25 3.00
54 Jimmie Johnson A 1.00 2.50
55 Jimmie Johnson's Car .30 .75
56 Matt Kenseth's Car .30 .75
57 Ryan Newman's Car .30 .75
58 Tony Stewart's Car .30 .75
59 Jeff Gordon's Car .50 1.25
60 Michael Waltrip's Car .08 .20
61 Dale Earnhardt Jr.'s Car .50 1.25
62 Jamie McMurray's Car .20 .50
63 Mark Martin's Car .30 .75
64 Matt Kenseth NI 1.00 2.50
65 Dale Earnhardt Jr. NI 1.25 3.00
66 Jeff Gordon NI 1.25 3.00
67 Dale Earnhardt Jr. NI 1.25 3.00
68 Jamie McMurray NI .50 1.25
69 Tony Stewart NI .75 2.00
70 Jimmie Johnson NI 1.00 2.50
71 Rusty Wallace NI .60 1.50
72 Dale Earnhardt Jr. NI 1.25 3.00
73 Jimmie Johnson IF 1.00 2.50
74 Kasey Kahne IF 1.25 3.00
75 Dale Earnhardt Jr. IF 1.25 3.00
76 Michael Waltrip IF .30 .75
77 Jeff Gordon IF 1.25 3.00
78 Tony Stewart IF .75 2.00
79 Martin Truex Jr. RS 1.00 2.50
80 Jeff Gordon RS 1.25 3.00
81 Elliott Sadler RS .30 .75
82 Ryan Newman RS 1.00 2.50
83 Jimmie Johnson RS 1.00 2.50
84 Dale Earnhardt Jr. RS 1.25 3.00
85 Rusty Wallace P .60 1.50
86 Kyle Busch P .50 1.25
87 Jason Leffler P .20 .50
88 Dale Jarrett P .60 1.50
89 Terry Labonte P .50 1.25
90 Kenseth Busch Martin CL 1.00 2.50
0 Kurt Busch '04 Champion 6.00 15.00
NNO Flag Chasers Entry Card 1.50 4.00

2005 Wheels High Gear MPH

*MPH: 4X TO 10X BASE

2005 Wheels High Gear Samples

*SAMPLES: 1.5X TO 4X BASE

2005 Wheels High Gear Flag Chasers Black

Randomly inserted into packs, these cards feature a race-used black flag piece embedded into a card. These cards were issued to a stated print run of 55 serial numbered sets. Six other flag colors were also produced as parallels of each card in varying quantities as noted below. The overall stated odds were 1 in 144 packs.

*BLUE-YELLOW/25: .6X TO 1.5X BLACK
*GREEN/55: .4X TO 1X BLACK
*RED/55: .4X TO 1X BLACK
*WHITE/55: .4X TO 1X BLACK
*YELLOW/55: .4X TO 1X BLACK
FC1 Kasey Kahne 30.00 80.00
FC2 Rusty Wallace 20.00 50.00
FC3 Tony Stewart 20.00 50.00
FC4 Jimmie Johnson 25.00 60.00
FC5 Ryan Newman 25.00 60.00
FC6 Kevin Harvick 20.00 50.00
FC7 Dale Earnhardt Jr. 40.00 100.00
FC8 Jeff Gordon 30.00 80.00
FC9 Mark Martin 25.00 60.00

2005 Wheels High Gear Flag to Flag

Issued at a stated rate of one in two packs, these 27 cards feature some of the leading drivers in NASCAR. Each card was die-cut and features a photo of the driver and his car.

COMPLETE SET (27) 10.00 25.00
FF1 Greg Biffle .40 1.00
FF2 Ward Burton .40 1.00
FF3 Dale Earnhardt Jr. 1.50 4.00
FF4 Brendan Gaughan .40 1.00
FF5 Jeff Gordon 1.50 4.00
FF6 Jeff Green .25 .60
FF7 Kevin Harvick 1.00 2.50
FF8 Dale Jarrett .75 2.00
FF9 Jimmie Johnson 1.25 3.00
FF10 Kasey Kahne 1.25 3.00
FF11 Matt Kenseth 1.25 3.00
FF12 Bobby Labonte .75 2.00
FF13 Terry Labonte .60 1.50
FF14 Mark Martin 1.00 2.50
FF15 Jeremy Mayfield .40 1.00
FF16 Jamie McMurray .60 1.50
FF17 Casey Mears .40 1.00
FF18 Joe Nemechek .25 .60
FF19 Ryan Newman 1.25 3.00
FF20 Kyle Petty .40 1.00
FF21 Ricky Rudd .60 1.50
FF22 Elliott Sadler .40 1.00
FF23 Ken Schrader .25 .60
FF24 Tony Stewart 1.00 2.50
FF25 Brian Vickers .75 2.00
FF26 Rusty Wallace .75 2.00
FF27 Michael Waltrip .40 1.00

2005 Wheels High Gear Full Throttle

Issued at a stated rate of one in 12, these six cards feature high-speed competitors in this set made of clear plastic stock. Each card carried a "FT" prefix for its card number.

COMPLETE SET (6) 10.00 25.00
FT1 Dale Earnhardt Jr. 2.50 6.00
FT2 Tony Stewart 1.50 4.00
FT3 Kevin Harvick 1.50 4.00
FT4 Jeff Gordon 2.50 6.00
FT5 Dale Jarrett 1.25 3.00
FT6 Jimmie Johnson 2.00 5.00

2005 Wheels High Gear Man

Issued at a stated rate of one in five hobby packs, these nine foil-embossed cards feature photos of leading drivers. A "Machine" version of each card was produced for retail packs. Each card carried an "MMA" prefix for its card number.

COMPLETE SET (9) 10.00 25.00
*MACHINE: 1X TO 2.5X MAN
MMA1 Michael Waltrip .50 1.25
MMA2 Terry Labonte .75 2.00
MMA3 Jamie McMurray .75 2.00
MMA4 Dale Earnhardt Jr. 2.00 5.00
MMA5 Jimmie Johnson 1.50 4.00
MMA6 Kasey Kahne 2.00 5.00
MMA7 Jeff Gordon 2.00 5.00
MMA8 Tony Stewart 1.25 3.00
MMA9 Rusty Wallace 1.00 2.50

2005 Wheels High Gear Top Tier

Issued at a stated rate of one in nine, these ten cards feature the top drivers from the 2004 NASCAR season. Each was printed on special holofoil card stock.

COMPLETE SET (10) 12.50 30.00
TT1 Kurt Busch 1.00 2.50
TT2 Jimmie Johnson 2.00 5.00
TT3 Jeff Gordon 2.50 6.00
TT4 Mark Martin 1.50 4.00
TT5 Dale Earnhardt Jr. 2.50 6.00
TT6 Tony Stewart 1.50 4.00
TT7 Ryan Newman 2.00 5.00
TT8 Matt Kenseth 2.00 5.00
TT9 Elliott Sadler .60 1.50
TT10 Jeremy Mayfield .60 1.50

2006 Wheels High Gear

This set was released in late January 2006. These cards were issued in 5-card hobby packs with an SRP of $3.99. They came 20-packs to a box and 20-boxes to a case. The retail version was issued four cards per pack with an $2.99 SRP and packaged 24-packs to a box and 20-boxes to a case. There was a special 0 card honoring Tony Stewart as the 2005 NASCAR champion and those cards were inserted at a stated rate of one in 72 packs. The Daytona Variation cards were also included in packs at a rate of one in 14. The four cards included are past Daytona 500 winners and they feature a logo on the card. Jeff Gordon's variation is card number 16 and Sterling Marlin's variation is number 26.

COMPLETE SET (90) 15.00 40.00
WAX BOX HOBBY (20) 60.00 120.00
WAX BOX RETAIL (24)
1 Tony Stewart .60 1.50
2 Greg Biffle .30 .75
3 Carl Edwards .40 1.00
4 Mark Martin .40 1.00
5 Jimmie Johnson .60 1.50
6 Ryan Newman .30 .75
7 Matt Kenseth .40 1.00
8 Rusty Wallace 1.25 3.00
9 Jeremy Mayfield .25 .60
10 Jeff Gordon .75 2.00
11 Jamie McMurray .40 1.00
12 Elliott Sadler .25 .60
13 Kevin Harvick .50 1.25
14 Dale Jarrett .40 1.00
14B Dale Jarrett Daytona 1.50 4.00
15 Joe Nemechek .25 .60
16 Brian Vickers .25 .60
16B Jeff Gordon Daytona 3.00 8.00
17 Jeff Burton .30 .75
18 Dale Earnhardt Jr. .75 2.00
18B Dale Earnhardt Jr. Daytona 3.00 8.00
19 Kyle Busch .50 1.25
20 Ricky Rudd .30 .75
21 Casey Mears .25 .60
22 Kasey Kahne .50 1.25
23 Bobby Labonte .40 1.00
24 Kyle Petty .30 .75
25 Sterling Marlin .40 1.00
26 Ken Schrader .25 .60
26B Sterling Marlin Daytona 1.50 4.00
27 Robby Gordon .25 .60
28 Martin Truex Jr. NBS .60 1.50
29 Clint Bowyer NBS .75 2.00
30 Reed Sorenson NBS .60 1.50
31 Carl Edwards NBS .40 1.00
32 Denny Hamlin NBS 1.50 4.00
33 Johnny Sauter NBS .40 1.00
34 David Green NBS .25 .60
35 Jason Keller NBS .25 .60
36 J.J. Yeley NBS .60 1.50
37 Dennis Setzer CTS .25 .60
38 Ron Hornaday CTS .25 .60
39 Mike Skinner CTS .25 .60
40 Ken Schrader CTS .25 .60
41 Ricky Craven CTS .25 .60
42 Terry Cook CTS .25 .60
43 Todd Kluever CTS .75 2.00
44 Rick Crawford CTS .25 .60
45 Bill Lester CTS .40 1.00
46 Rusty Wallace's Car C .15 .40
47 Dale Earnhardt Jr.'s Car C .30 .75
48 Kasey Kahne's Car C .20 .50
49 Matt Kenseth's Car C .15 .40
50 Carl Edwards' Car C .15 .40
51 Tony Stewart's Car C .25 .60
52 Kevin Harvick's Car C .20 .50
53 Dale Jarrett's Car C .15 .40
54 Jeff Burton's Car C .12 .30
55 Tony Stewart NA .60 1.50
56 Kyle Busch NA .50 1.25
57 Martin Truex Jr. NA .60 1.50
58 Carl Edwards NA .40 1.00
59 Ryan Newman NA .30 .75
60 Tony Stewart NA .60 1.50
61 Tony Stewart NA .60 1.50
62 Tony Stewart NA .60 1.50
63 Ryan Newman NA .30 .75
64 Carl Edwards CM .40 1.00
65 Tony Stewart CM .60 1.50
66 Dale Jarrett CM .40 1.00
67 Jeff Gordon CM .75 2.00
68 Jimmie Johnson CM .60 1.50
69 Jeff Burton CM .30 .75
70 Reed Sorenson PREV CRC .60 1.50
71 Sterling Marlin PREV .40 1.00
72 Bobby Labonte PREV .40 1.00
73 David Stremme PREV CRC .50 1.25
74 Mark Martin PREV .40 1.00
75 Mark McFarland PREV .25 .60
76 Mark Martin FF .40 1.00
77 Dale Jarrett FF .40 1.00
78 Jimmie Johnson FF .60 1.50
79 Dale Earnhardt Jr. FF .75 2.00
80 Jeff Gordon FF .75 2.00
81 Kasey Kahne FF .50 1.25
82 Tony Stewart FF .60 1.50
83 Martin Truex Jr. FF .60 1.50
84 Rusty Wallace FF .40 1.00
85 Kasey Kahne NI .50 1.25
86 Jeff Green NI .25 .60
87 Ryan Newman NI .30 .75
88 Tony Stewart NI .60 1.50
89 R. Wallace M. Martin NI .40 1.00
90 Jeff Gordon CL .75 2.00
0 Tony Stewart Champ 4.00 10.00
NNO Daytona Power Pick 2.00 5.00

2006 Wheels High Gear MPH

*MPH: 4X TO 10X BASE

2006 Wheels High Gear Flag Chasers Black

Randomly inserted into packs, these cards feature a race-used black flag piece embedded into a card. These cards were issued to a stated print run of 110 serial numbered sets. The overall odds for Flag Chasers are 1 in 40 packs. Six other flag colors were also produced as parallels of each card in varying quantities as noted below.

*BLUE-YELLOW/65: .6X TO 1.5X BLACK
*GREEN/110: .4X TO 1X BLACK
*RED/110: .4X TO 1X BLACK
*WHITE/110: .4X TO 1X BLACK
*YELLOW/110: .4X TO 1X BLACK
FC1 Carl Edwards 5.00 12.00
FC2 Jeff Gordon 10.00 25.00
FC3 Dale Earnhardt Jr. 10.00 25.00
FC4 Tony Stewart 8.00 20.00
FC5 Kasey Kahne 6.00 15.00
FC6 Ryan Newman 4.00 10.00
FC7 Kevin Harvick 6.00 15.00
FC8 Dale Jarrett 5.00 12.00
FC9 Jimmie Johnson 8.00 20.00

2006 Wheels High Gear Flag to Flag

Issued at a stated rate of one in two packs, these 27 cards feature some of the leading drivers in NASCAR. Each card was die-cut and features a photo of the driver and his car.

COMPLETE SET (27) 12.50 30.00
FF1 Greg Biffle .40 1.00
FF2 Jeff Burton .40 1.00
FF3 Casey Mears .30 .75
FF4 Kyle Busch .60 1.50
FF5 Dale Earnhardt Jr. 1.00 2.50
FF6 Carl Edwards .50 1.25
FF7 Jeff Gordon 1.00 2.50
FF8 Robby Gordon .30 .75
FF9 Kevin Harvick .60 1.50
FF10 Dale Jarrett .50 1.25
FF11 Jimmie Johnson .75 2.00
FF12 Kasey Kahne .60 1.50
FF13 Matt Kenseth .50 1.25
FF14 Bobby Labonte .50 1.25
FF15 Sterling Marlin .50 1.25
FF16 Mark Martin .50 1.25
FF17 Jeremy Mayfield .30 .75
FF18 Jamie McMurray .50 1.25
FF19 Ryan Newman .40 1.00
FF20 Kyle Petty .40 1.00
FF21 Scott Riggs .40 1.00
FF22 Elliott Sadler .30 .75
FF23 Ken Schrader .30 .75
FF24 Tony Stewart .75 2.00
FF25 Martin Truex Jr. .75 2.00
FF26 Brian Vickers .30 .75
FF27 Rusty Wallace .50 1.25

2006 Wheels High Gear Full Throttle

Issued at a stated rate of one in 12, these six cards feature high-speed competitors in this set made of clear plastic stock.

COMPLETE SET (6) 12.50 30.00
FT1 Martin Truex Jr. 1.50 4.00
FT2 Jimmie Johnson 1.50 4.00
FT3 Jeff Gordon 2.00 5.00
FT4 Dale Earnhardt Jr. 2.00 5.00
FT5 Mark Martin 1.00 2.50
FT6 Tony Stewart 1.50 4.00

2006 Wheels High Gear Man & Machine Cars

COMPLETE SET (9) 40.00 80.00
*MACHINE: .8X TO 2X MAN

2006 Wheels High Gear Man & Machine Drivers

Issued at a stated rate of one in five hobby packs, these nine foil-embossed cards feature photos of leading drivers. A "Machine" version of each card was produced for retail packs. Each card carried an "MMA" prefix for its card number.

COMPLETE SET (9) 12.50 25.00
MMA1 Tony Stewart 1.25 3.00
MMA2 Jeff Gordon 1.50 4.00
MMA3 Jimmie Johnson 1.25 3.00
MMA4 Dale Earnhardt Jr. 1.50 4.00
MMA5 Mark Martin .75 2.00
MMA6 Dale Jarrett .75 2.00
MMA7 Martin Truex Jr. 1.25 3.00
MMA8 Jeff Burton .60 1.50
MMA9 Ricky Rudd .60 1.50

2006 Wheels High Gear Top Tier

Issued at a stated rate of one in nine, these ten cards feature the top drivers from the 2005 NASCAR season. Each was printed on special holofoil card stock.

COMPLETE SET (9) 15.00 40.00
TT1 Tony Stewart 2.00 5.00
TT2 Greg Biffle 1.00 2.50
TT3 Carl Edwards 1.25 3.00
TT4 Mark Martin 1.25 3.00
TT5 Jimmie Johnson 2.00 5.00
TT6 Ryan Newman 1.00 2.50
TT7 Matt Kenseth 1.25 3.00
TT8 Rusty Wallace 1.25 3.00
TT9 Jeremy Mayfield .75 2.00

2007 Wheels High Gear

This 90-card base set featured six additional variations and two short-printed cards, none of which were included in the base set price. The variations were inserted in both Hobby and Retail packs at a rate of one in 60. The variations are card #3 Denny Hamlin with a blurred background, #5 Dale Earnhardt Jr. with red in the background in place of blue, #6 Jeff Gordon with the #24 missing from the pit wagon in the background, #71 kevin Harvick CM with the warning signs behind him reversed, the running sign is above the guy getting hit with the projectile and falling sign, #73 Jimmie Johnson with the ink colors reversed on the magazine cover, "Take That" is in yellow, #88 Juan Pablo Montoya with the green infield pictured in the background. The zero card short print is Jimmie Johnson '06 Champion, which was inserted in packs at a rate of one in 60 in both Hobby and Retail. The other short print is the NNO Daytona Entry Card which was inserted at a rate of one in 20 in both Hobby and Retail packs. It was a entry for a chance to win a signed flag and helmet acquired during Daytona's Speedweeks. The promotion ended October 31, 2007 and the winner was notified by November 15, 2007.

COMPLETE SET (90) 15.00 40.00
WAX BOX HOBBY (20) 60.00 80.00
WAX BOX RETAIL (24) 45.00 70.00
1 Jimmie Johnson .50 1.25
2 Matt Kenseth .30 .75
3A Denny Hamlin .40 1.00
3B Denny Hamlin blurred 2.00 5.00
4 Kevin Harvick .40 1.00
5A Dale Earnhardt Jr. blue .60 1.50
5B Dale Earnhardt Jr. red 3.00 8.00
6A Jeff Gordon .60 1.50
6B Jeff Gordon -yellow 24 3.00 8.00
7 Jeff Burton .25 .60
8 Kasey Kahne .30 .75
9 Mark Martin .30 .75
10 Kyle Busch .40 1.00
11 Tony Stewart .50 1.25
12 Greg Biffle .25 .60
13 Carl Edwards .30 .75
14 Casey Mears .20 .50
15 Kurt Busch .25 .60
16 Clint Bowyer .30 .75
17 Ryan Newman .25 .60
18 Martin Truex Jr. .25 .60
19 Scott Riggs .25 .60
20 Bobby Labonte .30 .75
21 Elliott Sadler .20 .50
22 Reed Sorenson .20 .50
23 Jamie McMurray .30 .75
24 Joe Nemechek .20 .50
25 Jeff Green .20 .50
26 J.J. Yeley .30 .75
27 Robby Gordon .20 .50
28 Ken Schrader .20 .50
29 David Stremme .20 .50
30 Sterling Marlin .30 .75
31 Tony Raines .20 .50
32 Kevin Harvick NBS .40 1.00
33 Carl Edwards NBS .30 .75
34 Denny Hamlin NBS .40 1.00
35 Paul Menard NBS 1.00 2.50
36 Jon Wood NBS .30 .75
37 Danny O'Quinn NBS .50 1.25
38 Regan Smith NBS .60 1.50
39 Steve Wallace NBS .30 .75
40 Ron Hornaday CTS .20 .50
41 Rick Crawford CTS .20 .50
42 Mike Skinner CTS .20 .50
43 Erik Darnell CTS .50 1.25
44 Bill Lester CTS .30 .75
45 David Ragan CTS .60 1.50
46 Eric Holmes RC .60 1.50
47 Mike Olsen .50 1.25
48 Mike Stefanik .20 .50
49 Junior Miller RC .60 1.50
50 Tim Schendel RC .60 1.50
51 Gary Lewis RC .50 1.25
52 J.R. Norris RC .60 1.50
53 Rip Michels RC .60 1.50
54 Tony Stewart NA .50 1.25
55 Kasey Kahne NA .30 .75
56 Jimmie Johnson NA .50 1.25
57 Kasey Kahne NA .30 .75
58 Matt Kenseth NA .30 .75
59 Kevin Harvick NA .40 1.00
60 Denny Hamlin NA .40 1.00
61 Kasey Kahne NA .30 .75
62 Tony Stewart NA .50 1.25
63 Tony Stewart NA .50 1.25
64 Kevin Harvick NA .40 1.00
65 Denny Hamlin NA .40 1.00
66 Denny Hamlin CM .40 1.00
67 Kasey Kahne CM .30 .75
68 Ryan Newman CM .25 .60
69 Reed Sorenson CM .20 .50
70 Matt Kenseth CM .30 .75
71A Kevin Harvick CM .40 1.00
71B K.Harvick CM mixed signs 2.00 5.00
72 Scott Riggs CM .25 .60
73A J.Johnson NI red take .50 1.25
73B J.Johnson NI ylw take 2.50 6.00
74 Carl Edwards NI .30 .75
75 Kasey Kahne NI .30 .75
76 Kevin Harvick NI .40 1.00
77 Jeff Gordon NI .60 1.50
78 Clint Bowyer's Car C .12 .30
79 Kasey Kahne's Car C .12 .30
80 Ryan Newman's Car C .10 .25
81 Tony Stewart's Car C .20 .50
82 Jeff Gordon's Car C .25 .60
83 Kevin Harvick's Car C .12 .30
84 Greg Biffle's Car C .10 .25
85 Kyle Busch's Car C .15 .40
86 David Gilliland RC .50 1.25
87 Paul Menard CRC 1.50 4.00
88A Juan Pablo Montoya RC 1.00 2.50
88B J.Montoya infield 6.00 15.00
89 Jon Wood CRC 1.50 4.00
CL Jeff Gordon CL .60 1.50
NNO Daytona Entry Card 1.00 2.50
0 Jimmie Johnson Champion 4.00 10.00

2007 Wheels High Gear Final Standings Gold

FS23 Jamie McMurray/25 15.00 40.00
FS24 Joe Nemechek/27 6.00 15.00
FS25 Jeff Green/28 6.00 15.00
FS26 J.J. Yeley/29
FS27 Robby Gordon/30
FS28 Ken Schrader/31 6.00 15.00
FS29 David Stremme/33 8.00 20.00
FS30 Sterling Marlin/34 15.00 30.00
FS31 Tony Raines/35 8.00 20.00

2007 Wheels High Gear MPH

*MPH: 4X TO 10X BASIC

2007 Wheels High Gear Driven

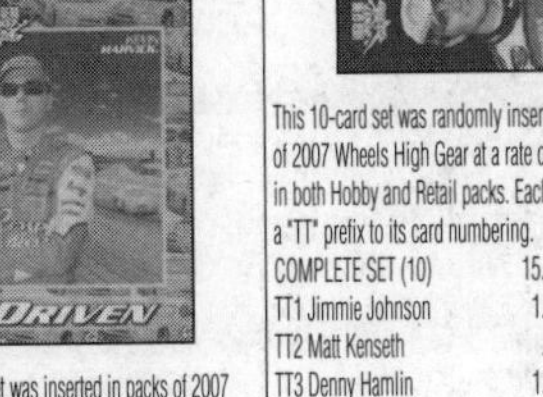

This 27-card set was inserted in packs of 2007 Wheels High Gear at a rate of one in two in both Hobby and Retail packs. The cards carried a "DR" prefix for their card numbers.

COMPLETE SET (27) 12.50 30.00
DR1 Mark Martin .50 1.25
DR2 Jeff Burton .40 1.00
DR3 Reed Sorenson .30 .75
DR4 Jimmie Johnson .75 2.00
DR5 Robby Gordon .30 .75
DR6 Martin Truex Jr. .40 1.00
DR7 Kevin Harvick .60 1.50
DR8 Matt Kenseth .50 1.25
DR9 Denny Hamlin .60 1.50
DR10 Greg Biffle .40 1.00
DR11 Ryan Newman .40 1.00
DR12 Tony Stewart .75 2.00
DR13 Clint Bowyer .50 1.25
DR14 Jeff Gordon 1.00 2.50
DR15 Jamie McMurray .50 1.25
DR16 Bobby Labonte .50 1.25
DR17 Kurt Busch .40 1.00
DR18 Dale Earnhardt Jr. 1.00 2.50
DR19 J.J. Yeley .50 1.25
DR20 Carl Edwards .50 1.25
DR21 Kasey Kahne .50 1.25
DR22 Ken Schrader .30 .75
DR23 David Stremme .30 .75
DR24 Sterling Marlin .50 1.25
DR25 Jeff Green .30 .75
DR26 Dave Blaney .30 .75
DR27 Tony Raines .30 .75

2007 Wheels High Gear Flag Chasers Black

Randomly inserted into packs, these cards feature a race-used black flag piece embedded into a card. These cards were issued to a stated print run of 89 serial numbered sets. The overall odds for Flag Chasers are one in 40 Hobby and one in 112 Retail packs. Six other flag colors were also produced as parallels of each card in varying quantities.

*BLUE-YELLOW/50: .6X TO 1.5X BLACK
*GREEN/89: .4X TO 1X BLACK
*RED/89: .4X TO 1X BLACK
*WHITE/89: .4X TO 1X BLACK
*YELLOW/89: .4X TO 1X BLACK
FC1 Dale Earnhardt Jr. 20.00 50.00
FC2 Carl Edwards 8.00 20.00
FC3 Kevin Harvick 15.00 40.00
FC4 Tony Stewart 15.00 40.00
FC5 Jimmie Johnson 10.00 25.00
FC6 Denny Hamlin 8.00 20.00
FC7 Mark Martin 15.00 40.00
FC8 Jeff Gordon 20.00 50.00
FC9 Kasey Kahne 20.00 50.00
FC10 Matt Kenseth 12.00 30.00

2007 Wheels High Gear Full Throttle

This 9-card set was randomly inserted in packs of 2007 Wheels High Gear at a rate of one in six for both Hobby and Retail packs. Each card carried a "FT" prefix for its card number.

COMPLETE SET (9) 12.50 30.00
FT1 Jeff Gordon 1.25 3.00
FT2 Reed Sorenson .40 1.00
FT3 Kevin Harvick .75 2.00
FT4 Dale Earnhardt Jr. 1.25 3.00
FT5 Kasey Kahne .60 1.50
FT6 Jimmie Johnson 1.00 2.50
FT7 Mark Martin .60 1.50
FT8 Tony Stewart 1.00 2.50
FT9 Martin Truex Jr. .50 1.25

2007 Wheels High Gear Top Tier

This 10-card set was randomly inserted in packs of 2007 Wheels High Gear at a rate of one in four in both Hobby and Retail packs. Each card carried a "TT" prefix to its card numbering.

COMPLETE SET (10) 15.00 40.00
TT1 Jimmie Johnson 1.25 3.00
TT2 Matt Kenseth .75 2.00
TT3 Denny Hamlin 1.00 2.50
TT4 Kevin Harvick 1.00 2.50
TT5 Dale Earnhardt Jr. 1.50 4.00
TT6 Jeff Gordon 1.50 4.00
TT7 Jeff Burton .60 1.50
TT8 Kasey Kahne .75 2.00
TT9 Mark Martin .75 2.00
TT10 Kyle Busch 1.00 2.50

2008 Wheels High Gear

COMPLETE SET (90) 15.00 40.00
WAX BOX HOBBY (20) 60.00 90.00
WAX BOX RETAIL (24) 50.00 75.00
1A Jimmie Johnson .40 1.00
1B J.Johnson Yellow 48 2.00 5.00
2 Jeff Gordon .50 1.25
3 Clint Bowyer .25 .60
4 Matt Kenseth .25 .60
5 Kyle Busch .30 .75
6 Tony Stewart .40 1.00
7 Kurt Busch .20 .50
8 Jeff Burton .20 .50
9 Carl Edwards .25 .60
10 Kevin Harvick .30 .75
11 Martin Truex Jr. .20 .50
12 Denny Hamlin .30 .75
13 Ryan Newman .20 .50
14 Greg Biffle .20 .50
15 Jamie McMurray .25 .60
16 Bobby Labonte .25 .60
17 Kasey Kahne .25 .60
18 Juan Pablo Montoya .40 1.00
19 Reed Sorenson .15 .40
20 David Ragan .20 .50
21 Elliott Sadler .15 .40
22 Mark Martin .25 .60
23 Paul Menard .15 .40
24 Kyle Petty .20 .50
25 Brian Vickers .15 .40
26 Dale Jarrett .25 .60
27 Michael Waltrip .25 .60
28 Marcos Ambrose NBS .40 1.00
29 Kelly Bires NBS .25 .60
30 Clint Bowyer NBS .25 .60
31 Jeff Burton NBS .20 .50
32 Carl Edwards NBS .25 .60
33 Denny Hamlin NBS .30 .75
34 Kevin Harvick NBS .30 .75
35 Steve Wallace NBS .25 .60
36 Scott Wimmer NBS .20 .50
37 Todd Bodine CTS .15 .40
38 Rick Crawford CTS .15 .40
39 Erik Darnell CTS .20 .50
40 Ron Hornaday CTS .15 .40
41 Mike Skinner CTS .15 .40
42 Jack Sprague CTS .15 .40
43 Kevin Harvick DD .30 .75
44 Kevin Harvick DD .30 .75
45 Jack Sprague DD .15 .40
46 Matt Kenseth's Car C .10 .25
47A Tony Stewart's Car C .15 .40
47B Stewart's Car C Purple .75 2.00
48 Clint Bowyer's Car C .10 .25
49 Jeff Burton's Car C .07 .20
50 Kyle Petty's Car C .07 .20
51 Kevin Harvick's Car C .12 .30
52 Jeff Gordon's Car C .20 .50
53 Dale Jarrett's Car C .10 .25
54 Carl Edwards' Car C .10 .25
55 Jimmie Johnson NA .40 1.00
56 Jeff Gordon NA .50 1.25
57 Juan Pablo Montoya NA .40 1.00
58 Jeff Gordon NA .50 1.25
59 Matt Kenseth NA .25 .60
60A Jeff Gordon NA .50 1.25
60B Jeff Gordon CA hat 2.50 6.00
61 Jimmie Johnson NA .40 1.00
62 Jeff Gordon NA .50 1.25
63 Denny Hamlin NA .30 .75
64 Martin Truex Jr.'s Car EL .07 .20
65 Kurt Busch's Car EL .07 .20
66 Matt Kenseth's Car EL .10 .25
67 Jeff Gordon's Car EL .20 .50
68 Kevin Harvick's Car EL .12 .30
69 Jeff Burton's Car EL .07 .20
70 Reed Sorenson's Car EL .05 .15
71 Jimmie Johnson's Car EL .15 .40
72A Carl Edwards' Car EL .10 .25
72B Edwards' Car EL no car .50 1.25
73 Juan Pablo Montoya NI .40 1.00
74 Kasey Kahne NI .25 .60
75 Tony Stewart NI .40 1.00
76 Casey Mears NI .15 .40
77 Clint Bowyer NI .25 .60
78 Jimmie Johnson NI .40 1.00
79 Jeff Burton NI .20 .50
80 Dale Earnhardt Jr. P .50 1.25
81 Dale Earnhardt Jr. P .50 1.25
82A Dale Earnhardt Jr. P .50 1.25
82B Earnhardt Jr. P w/o heli 2.50 6.00
83 Dale Earnhardt Jr. P .50 1.25
84 Dale Earnhardt Jr. P .50 1.25
85A Dale Earnhardt Jr. P .50 1.25
85B Earnhardt Jr. P w/o can 2.50 6.00
86 Dario Franchitti's Car P .15 .40
87 Sam Hornish Jr.'s Car P .15 .40
88 Patrick Carpentier's Car P .20 .50
89 Kyle Busch's Car P .12 .30
90 Dale Earnhardt Jr. CL .50 1.25
0 Jimmie Johnson Champ 4.00 10.00
NNO Daytona Entry Card 1.50 4.00
NNO Ride Along Entry Card 1.25 3.00

2008 Wheels High Gear Final Standings

STATED PRINT RUN 1-44
F21 Elliott Sadler/25 6.00 15.00
F22 Mark Martin/27 12.50 25.00
F23 Paul Menard/34 6.00 15.00
F24 Kyle Petty/35 5.00 12.00
F25 Brian Vickers/38 4.00 10.00
F26 Dale Jarrett/41 20.00 40.00
F27 Michael Waltrip/44 6.00 15.00

2008 Wheels High Gear MPH

*MPH: 3X TO 8X BASE
STATED PRINT RUN 100 SERIAL #'d SETS

2008 Wheels High Gear Driven

COMPLETE SET (27) 8.00 20.00
STATED ODDS 1:2
DR1 Jimmie Johnson .60 1.50
DR2 Tony Stewart .60 1.50
DR3 Kurt Busch .30 .75
DR4 Clint Bowyer .40 1.00
DR5 David Ragan .30 .75
DR6 Kyle Petty .30 .75
DR7 Elliott Sadler .25 .60
DR8 Bobby Labonte .40 1.00
DR9 Kevin Harvick .50 1.25
DR10 Mark Martin .40 1.00
DR11 Dale Jarrett .40 1.00
DR12 Kasey Kahne .40 1.00
DR13 Dave Blaney .25 .60
DR14 Greg Biffle .30 .75
DR15 Martin Truex Jr. .30 .75
DR16 Michael Waltrip .40 1.00
DR17 Reed Sorenson .25 .60
DR18 Denny Hamlin .50 1.25
DR19 Matt Kenseth .40 1.00
DR20 Jeff Burton .30 .75
DR21 Ryan Newman .30 .75
DR22 Jeff Gordon .75 2.00
DR23 Brian Vickers .25 .60
DR24 Jamie McMurray .40 1.00
DR25 Carl Edwards .40 1.00
DR26 Juan Pablo Montoya .60 1.50
DR27 A.J. Allmendinger .40 1.00

2008 Wheels High Gear Flag Chasers Black

OVERALL FLAG CHASERS STATED ODDS 1:40
STAED PRINT RUN 89 SERIAL #'d SETS
*BLUE-YELLOW/50: 1X TO 2.5X BLACK
*CHECKERED/20: 1X TO 2.5X BLACK
*GREEN/60: .6X TO 1.5X BLACK
*RED/89: .4X TO 1X BLACK
*WHITE/65: .5X TO 1.2X BLACK
*YELLOW/89: .4X TO 1X BLACK
FC1 Mark Martin 6.00 15.00
FC2 Tony Stewart 8.00 20.00
FC3 Jeff Gordon 12.00 30.00
FC4 Kevin Harvick 8.00 20.00
FC5 Juan Pablo Montoya 6.00 15.00
FC6 Jimmie Johnson 10.00 25.00
FC7 Carl Edwards 6.00 15.00
FC8 Kasey Kahne 6.00 15.00
FC9 Matt Kenseth 6.00 15.00

2008 Wheels High Gear Full Throttle

COMPLETE SET (9) 12.50 30.00
STATED ODDS 1:6
FT1 Jeff Gordon 1.00 2.50
FT2 Mark Martin .50 1.25
FT3 Kevin Harvick .60 1.50
FT4 Juan Pablo Montoya .75 2.00
FT5 Carl Edwards .50 1.25
FT6 Jeff Burton .40 1.00
FT7 Jimmie Johnson .75 2.00
FT8 Martin Truex Jr. .40 1.00
FT9 Tony Stewart .75 2.00

2008 Wheels High Gear Last Lap

STATED PRINT RUN 10 SERIAL #'d SETS
NOT PRICED DUE TO SCARCITY

2008 Wheels High Gear The Chase

COMPLETE SET (12) 15.00 40.00
STATED ODDS 1:4
TC1 Jimmie Johnson 1.00 2.50
TC2 Jeff Gordon 1.25 3.00
TC3 Clint Bowyer .60 1.50
TC4 Matt Kenseth .60 1.50
TC5 Kyle Busch .75 2.00
TC6 Tony Stewart 1.00 2.50
TC7 Kurt Busch .50 1.25
TC8 Jeff Burton .50 1.25
TC9 Carl Edwards .60 1.50
TC10 Kevin Harvick .75 2.00
TC11 Martin Truex Jr. .50 1.25
TC12 Denny Hamlin .75 2.00

2009 Wheels Main Event

COMPLETE SET (90) 100.00 200.00
COMP.SET w/o SPs (86) 12.00 30.00
WAX BOX HOBBY (20) 75.00 100.00
WAX BOX RETAIL 60.00 90.00
1 Dale Earnhardt Jr. AMP .75 2.00
2 Jeff Gordon .75 2.00
3 Tony Stewart OD .60 1.50
4 Jimmie Johnson .60 1.50
5 Kyle Busch .50 1.25
6 Kasey Kahne .40 1.00
7 Carl Edwards .40 1.00
8 Matt Kenseth .40 1.00
9 Ryan Newman .30 .75
10 Kevin Harvick .50 1.25
11 Jeff Burton .30 .75
12 Kurt Busch .30 .75
13 Greg Biffle .30 .75
14 Dale Earnhardt Jr. NG .75 2.00
15 Denny Hamlin .40 1.00
16 Mark Martin .40 1.00
17 Clint Bowyer .40 1.00
18 Brian Vickers .25 .60
19 Juan Pablo Montoya .50 1.25
20 Tony Stewart OS .60 1.50
21 Martin Truex Jr. .30 .75
22 Casey Mears .25 .60
23 Jamie McMurray .40 1.00
24 David Ragan .30 .75
25 David Reutimann .30 .75
26 Reed Sorenson .25 .60
27 Bobby Labonte .40 1.00
28 Elliott Sadler .25 .60
29 A.J. Allmendinger .40 1.00
30 Michael Waltrip .40 1.00
31 Robby Gordon .25 .60
32 Paul Menard .25 .60
33 Sam Hornish Jr. .30 .75
34 David Stremme .25 .60
35 Regan Smith .30 .75
36 Joe Nemechek .25 .60
37 Jr./Gordn/JJ/Mrtin WH .75 2.00
38 Kens/Carl/Rgn/McM/Bif WH .40 1.00
39 Mears/Harv/Burt/Bwyr WH .50 1.25
40 Hamlin/KyBusch/Logno WH .75 2.00
41 Allmen/Sorn/Kahn/Sadl WH .40 1.00
42 Hornish/Busch/Stremme WH .30 .75
43 Dale Earnhardt Jr. DS .75 2.00
44 Tony Stewart DS .60 1.50
45 Mark Martin DS .40 1.00
46 Jimmie Johnson DS .60 1.50
47 Carl Edwards DS .40 1.00
48 Kyle Busch DS .50 1.25
49 C.Knaus/J.Johnson PB .60 1.50
50 S.Letarte/J.Gordon PB .75 2.00
51 Addington RC/Ky.Bsch PB .50 1.25
52 P.Tryson RC/K.Busch PB .30 .75
53 Osborne RC/Edwards PB .40 1.00
54 G.Zipadelli/J.Logano PB .75 2.00
55 Carl Edwards AI .40 1.00
56 Matt Kenseth AI .40 1.00
57 Jimmie Johnson's Car AI .25 .60
58 Jeff Gordon's Car AI .30 .75
59 Kyle Busch AI .50 1.25
60 Kurt Busch AI .30 .75
61 Mark Martin AI .40 1.00
62 Tony Stewart's Car AI .25 .60
63 David Reutimann AI .30 .75
64 Matt Kenseth J .40 1.00
65 Kyle Busch J .50 1.25
66 Kurt Busch J .30 .75
67 Jeff Gordon J .75 2.00
68 Mark Martin J .40 1.00
69 Tony Stewart J .60 1.50
70 David Reutimann J .30 .75
71 Jimmie Johnson J .60 1.50
72 Brian Vickers J .25 .60
73 Mark Martin PF .40 1.00
74 Jeff Gordon PF .75 2.00
75 Tony Stewart PF .60 1.50
76 Jimmie Johnson PF .60 1.50
77 Brian Vickers PF .25 .60
78 Kasey Kahne PF .40 1.00
79 Carl Edwards PF .40 1.00
80 Kurt Busch PF .30 .75
81 Doyle Brunson PP .40 1.00
82 Phil Hellmuth PP .40 1.00
83 Gus Hansen PP .40 1.00
84 Phil Ivey PP .40 1.00
85 Chris Jesus Ferguson PP .40 1.00
86 Dennis Phillips PP .40 1.00
87 Joey Logano AU RC 10.00 25.00
88 Scott Speed AU RC 6.00 15.00
89 Brad Keselowski AU CRC 12.00 30.00
90 Marcos Ambrose AU CRC 20.00 50.00
NNO CONTEST CARD 4.00 10.00

2009 Wheels Main Event Fast Pass Purple

*SINGLES: 4X TO 10X BASIC CARDS
STATED PRINT RUN 25 SER.#'d SETS

2009 Wheels Main Event Foil

*SINGLES: 3X TO 8X BASIC CARDS
STATED ODDS 1:20

2009 Wheels Main Event Hat Dance Double

STATED PRINT RUN 99 SER.#'d SETS
HDAA Aric Almirola 5.00 12.00
HDAJ A.J. Allmendinger 6.00 15.00
HDBL Bobby Labonte 6.00 15.00
HDBV Brian Vickers 4.00 10.00
HDDS David Stremme 4.00 10.00
HDJG Jeff Gordon 12.00 30.00
HDJM Jamie McMurray 6.00 15.00
HDMA Marcos Ambrose 6.00 15.00
HDMM Mark Martin 6.00 15.00
HDPM Paul Menard 4.00 10.00
HDRG Robby Gordon 4.00 10.00
HDRS Reed Sorenson 4.00 10.00
HDDR2 David Reutimann 5.00 12.00
HDJPM Juan Pablo Montoya 8.00 20.00
HDRS2 Regan Smith 5.00 12.00

2009 Wheels Main Event Hat Dance Triple

STATED PRINT RUN 99 SER.#'d SETS
HDCB Clint Bowyer 5.00 12.00
HDCE Carl Edwards 5.00 12.00
HDCM Casey Mears 3.00 8.00
HDDH Denny Hamlin 5.00 12.00
HDDR David Ragan 4.00 10.00
HDES Elliott Sadler 3.00 8.00
HDGB Greg Biffle 4.00 10.00
HDJB Jeff Burton 4.00 10.00
HDJJ Jimmie Johnson 8.00 20.00
HDJL Joey Logano 15.00 40.00
HDKB Kurt Busch 4.00 10.00
HDKH Kevin Harvick 6.00 15.00
HDKK Kasey Kahne 5.00 12.00
HDMK Matt Kenseth 5.00 12.00
HDMT Martin Truex Jr. 4.00 10.00
HDMW Michael Waltrip 5.00 12.00
HDRN Ryan Newman 4.00 10.00
HDSH Sam Hornish Jr. 4.00 10.00
HDSS Scott Speed 6.00 15.00
HDTS Tony Stewart 8.00 20.00
HDKYB Kyle Busch 6.00 15.00
HDDEJR Dale Earnhardt Jr. AMP 10.00 25.00

2009 Wheels Main Event Marks Clubs

STATED ODDS 1:20
1 Justin Allgaier 6.00 15.00
2 A.J. Allmendinger 6.00 15.00
3 Aric Almirola 5.00 12.00
4 Greg Biffle 5.00 12.00
5 Clint Bowyer 6.00 15.00
6 Colin Braun
7 James Buescher 4.00 10.00
8 Kurt Busch 5.00 12.00
9 Kyle Busch 20.00 50.00
10 Ricky Carmichael 15.00 40.00
11 Chris Jesus Ferguson 20.00 40.00
12 Erik Darnell
13 Marc Davis 10.00 25.00
14 Dennis Phillips 15.00 40.00
15 Doyle Brunson 40.00 80.00
16 Dwayne Bigger BBB 12.00 30.00
17 Dale Earnhardt Jr. 60.00 120.00
18 Carl Edwards 6.00 15.00
19 J.R. Fitzpatrick
20 Brendan Gaughan
21 Jeff Gordon 100.00 200.00
22 Robby Gordon 4.00 10.00
23 Gus Hansen 20.00 40.00
24 Denny Hamlin 6.00 15.00
25 Kevin Harvick 8.00 20.00
26 Ron Hornaday 4.00 10.00

27 Sam Hornish Jr. 5.00 12.00
28 Jimmie Johnson 30.00 60.00
29 Kasey Kahne
30 Matt Kenseth 6.00 15.00
32 Bobby Labonte 6.00 15.00
33 Scott Lagasse Jr. 8.00 20.00
34 Stephen Leicht 4.00 10.00
35 Tayler Malsam 6.00 15.00
36 Mark Martin 6.00 15.00
37 Michael McDowell 6.00 15.00
38 Jamie McMurray 6.00 15.00
39 Casey Mears
40 Paul Menard 4.00 10.00
41 Juan Pablo Montoya
42 Joe Nemechek
43 Ryan Newman 5.00 12.00
44 Phil Hellmuth 15.00 40.00
45 Phil Ivey 30.00 60.00
46 David Ragan 5.00 12.00
47 David Reutimann 5.00 12.00
48 Johnny Sauter 6.00 15.00
49 Brian Scott 5.00 12.00
50 Mike Skinner
51 Regan Smith 5.00 12.00
52 Reed Sorenson 4.00 10.00
53 Ricky Stenhouse Jr. 15.00 40.00
54 Tony Stewart 20.00 50.00
55 Martin Truex Jr. 5.00 12.00
56 Brian Vickers 4.00 10.00
57 Steve Wallace 4.00 10.00
58 Michael Waltrip 6.00 15.00

2009 Wheels Main Event Marks Diamonds

STATED PRINT RUN 6-50
1 Justin Allgaier/50 8.00 20.00
3 Aric Almirola/50 6.00 15.00
4 Greg Biffle/50 6.00 15.00
6 Colin Braun/50 6.00 15.00
7 James Buescher/50 5.00 12.00
8 Kurt Busch/50 6.00 15.00
10 Ricky Carmichael/50 12.00 30.00
11 Chris Jesus Ferguson/50 25.00 50.00
12 Erik Darnell/50 6.00 15.00
13 Marc Davis/50 12.00 30.00
14 Dennis Phillips/50 25.00 50.00
19 J.R. Fitzpatrick/50 8.00 20.00
20 Brendan Gaughan/50 5.00 12.00
23 Gus Hansen/50 20.00 40.00
26 Ron Hornaday/50 5.00 12.00
27 Sam Hornish Jr./50 6.00 15.00
32 Bobby Labonte /50 8.00 20.00
33 Scott Lagasse Jr./50 10.00 25.00
34 Stephen Leicht/50 5.00 12.00
35 Tayler Malsam/50 8.00 20.00
37 Michael McDowell/50 8.00 20.00
38 Jamie McMurray/50 8.00 20.00
40 Paul Menard/50 4.00 10.00
41 Juan Pablo Montoya/50 10.00 25.00
42 Joe Nemechek/50 5.00 12.00
45 Phil Ivey/50 30.00 60.00
46 David Ragan/50 6.00 15.00
48 Johnny Sauter/50 8.00 20.00
49 Brian Scott/50 6.00 15.00
51 Regan Smith/50 6.00 15.00
52 Reed Sorenson/50 5.00 12.00
53 Ricky Stenhouse Jr./50 12.00 30.00
57 Steve Wallace/50 5.00 12.00

2009 Wheels Main Event Playing Cards Red

COMPLETE SET (54) 10.00 25.00
STATED ODDS 1 PER PACK
*BLUE: .4X TO 1X RED
2C Mike Skinner .15 .40
3C Ricky Carmichael .60 1.50
4C Marc Davis .40 1.00
5C Carl Edwards .25 .60
6C David Stremme .15 .40
7C Robby Gordon .15 .40
8C Elliott Sadler .15 .40
9C David Ragan .20 .50
10C Brad Keselowski .30 .75
JC Mark Martin .25 .60
QC Kurt Busch .20 .50
KC Matt Kenseth .25 .60
AC Jimmie Johnson .40 1.00
2D Tayler Malsam .20 .50
3D Colin Braun .20 .50
4D Justin Allgaier .25 .60
5D Dale Earnhardt Jr. .50 1.25
6D Sam Hornish Jr. .20 .50
7D Scott Speed .30 .75
8D Bobby Labonte .25 .60
9D Jamie McMurray .25 .60
10D Juan Pablo Montoya .30 .75
JD Denny Hamlin .25 .60
QD Jeff Burton .20 .50
KD Carl Edwards .25 .60
AD Tony Stewart .40 1.00
2H Ron Hornaday .15 .40
3H Scott Lagasse Jr. .30 .75
4H Kevin Harvick .30 .75
5H Kyle Busch .30 .75
6H Marcos Ambrose .25 .60
7H Michael Waltrip .25 .60
8H Reed Sorenson .15 .40
9H Casey Mears .15 .40
10H Brian Vickers .15 .40
JH Joey Logano .50 1.25
QH Kevin Harvick .30 .75
KH Kasey Kahne .25 .60
AH Jeff Gordon .50 1.25
2S J.R. Fitzpatrick .25 .60
3S Brendan Gaughan .15 .40
4S Tony Stewart .40 1.00
5S Regan Smith .20 .50
6S Paul Menard .15 .40
7S A.J. Allmendinger .25 .60
8S David Reutimann .20 .50
9S Martin Truex Jr. .20 .50
10S Clint Bowyer .25 .60
JS Greg Biffle .20 .50
QS Ryan Newman .20 .50
KS Kyle Busch .30 .75
AS Dale Earnhardt Jr. .50 1.25
JO Wheels Main Event Joker .15 .40
JO2 Wheels Main Event Logo .15 .40

2009 Wheels Main Event Poker Chips

COMPLETE SET (12) 25.00 60.00
STATED ODDS 1 PER BLASTER BOX
1 Dale Earnhardt Jr. 2.00 5.00
2 Dale Earnhardt 6.00 15.00
3 Jeff Gordon 2.00 5.00
4 Tony Stewart 1.50 4.00
5 Kasey Kahne 1.00 2.50
6 Jimmie Johnson 1.50 4.00
7 Kevin Harvick 1.25 3.00
8 Mark Martin 1.00 2.50
9 Carl Edwards 1.00 2.50
10 Kurt Busch .75 2.00
11 Matt Kenseth 1.00 2.50
12 Brad Keselowski 1.25 3.00

2009 Wheels Main Event High Rollers

COMPLETE SET (12) 10.00 25.00
HR1 Dale Earnhardt Jr. 1.25 3.00
HR2 Tony Stewart 1.00 2.50
HR3 Kasey Kahne .60 1.50
HR4 Matt Kenseth .60 1.50
HR5 Jeff Gordon 1.25 3.00
HR6 Carl Edwards .60 1.50
HR7 Jeff Burton .50 1.25
HR8 Clint Bowyer .60 1.50
HR9 Kevin Harvick .75 2.00
HR10 Mark Martin .60 1.50
HR11 Jimmie Johnson 1.00 2.50
HR12 Ryan Newman .50 1.25

2009 Wheels Main Event Renegade Rounders Wanted

COMPLETE SET (9) 25.00 60.00
STATED ODDS 1:10
RR1 Carl Edwards 2.00 5.00
RR2 Scott Speed 2.50 6.00
RR3 Martin Truex Jr. 1.50 4.00
RR4 Clint Bowyer 2.00 5.00
RR5 Kevin Harvick 2.50 6.00
RR6 Kyle Busch 2.50 6.00
RR7 Ryan Newman 1.50 4.00
RR8 Kasey Kahne 2.00 5.00
RR9 David Ragan 1.50 4.00

2009 Wheels Main Event Reward Holofoil

STATED PRINT RUN 50 SER.#'d SETS
RWCB Clint Bowyer 6.00 15.00
RWCE Carl Edwards 6.00 15.00
RWDR David Ragan 5.00 12.00
RWJL Joey Logano 15.00 40.00
RWKB Kyle Busch 8.00 20.00
RWKH Kevin Harvick 8.00 20.00
RWKK Kasey Kahne 6.00 15.00
RWMT Martin Truex Jr. 5.00 12.00
RWRN Ryan Newman 5.00 12.00
RWSS Scott Speed 8.00 20.00

2009 Wheels Main Event Stop and Go Swatches Lugnut

STATED PRINT RUN 88 SER.#'d SETS
SGLDEJ Dale Earnhardt Jr. 20.00 50.00

2009 Wheels Main Event Stop and Go Swatches Pit Banner

STATED PRINT RUN 125-175
*HOLOFOIL/75: .5X TO 1.2X BASIC INSERTS
*RED/25: .6X TO 1.5X BASIC INSERTS
SGBBK Brad Keselowski 6.00 15.00
SGBBV Brian Vickers/125 3.00 8.00
SGBCB Clint Bowyer/125 5.00 12.00
SGBCE Carl Edwards 5.00 12.00
SGBDH Denny Hamlin 5.00 12.00
SGBDR David Ragan/125 4.00 10.00
SGBDR David Reutimann/125 4.00 10.00
SGBJB Jeff Burton/125 4.00 10.00
SGBJG Jeff Gordon 12.00 30.00
SGBJJ Jimmie Johnson 8.00 20.00
SGBKB Kurt Busch/125 4.00 10.00
SGBKH Kevin Harvick 5.00 12.00
SGBKK Kasey Kahne 5.00 12.00
SGBMW Michael Waltrip/125 5.00 12.00
SGBRN Ryan Newman/125 4.00 10.00
SGBSS Scott Speed/125 6.00 15.00
SGBTS1 Tony Stewart OD 8.00 20.00
SGBTS2 Tony Stewart OS 8.00 20.00

2009 Wheels Main Event Stop and Go Swatches Pit Sign

STATED PRINT RUN 75-175
UNPRICED GREEN PRINT RUN 5-10
*HOLO/50-75: .5X TO 1.2X BASIC SIGN
*RED/25: .6X TO 1.5X BASIC SIGN
SGSBK Brad Keselowski/175 6.00 15.00
SGSBV Brian Vickers/75 3.00 8.00
SGSDR David Reutimann/125 4.00 10.00
SGSJPM Juan Pablo Montoya/125 6.00 15.00
SGSMT Martin Truex Jr./125 4.00 10.00
SGSMW Michael Waltrip/125 5.00 12.00
SGSSS Scott Speed/125 6.00 15.00

2009 Wheels Main Event Stop and Go Swatches Pit Stackers

STATED PRINT RUN 120 SER.#'d SETS
*HOLOFOIL/75: .5X TO 1.2X BASIC INSERTS
*RED/25: .6X TO 1.5X BASIC INSERTS
SGWDR David Reutimann 4.00 10.00
SGWJM Juan Pablo Montoya 6.00 15.00
SGWMT Martin Truex Jr. 4.00 10.00
SGWMW Michael Waltrip 5.00 12.00

2009 Wheels Main Event Stop and Go Swatches Wheel Covers

STATED PRINT RUN 175 SER.#'d SETS
*HOLOFOIL/75: .5X TO 1.5X BASIC INSERTS
*RED/25: .6X TO 1.5X BASIC INSERTS
SGCJG Jeff Gordon 8.00 20.00

2010 Wheels Main Event

COMPLETE SET (100) 50.00 100.00
COMP.SET w/o SP's (90) 10.00 25.00
WAX BOX HOBBY (20) 75.00 100.00
WAX BOX FAST PASS (20) 175.00 250.00
WAX BOX RETAIL (24) 50.00 75.00
1 A.J. Allmendinger .30 .75
2 Marcos Ambrose .30 .75
3 Greg Biffle .25 .60
4 Clint Bowyer .30 .75
5 Jeff Burton .25 .60
6 Kurt Busch .25 .60
7 Kyle Busch .40 1.00
8 Kevin Conway RC .50 1.25
9 Dale Earnhardt Jr. .60 1.50
10 Carl Edwards .30 .75
11 Jeff Gordon .60 1.50
12 Robby Gordon .20 .50
13 Denny Hamlin .30 .75
14 Kevin Harvick .40 1.00
15 Jimmie Johnson .50 1.25
16 Kasey Kahne .30 .75
17 Matt Kenseth .30 .75
18 Brad Keselowski .40 1.00
19 Travis Kvapil .20 .50
20 Bobby Labonte .30 .75
21 Joey Logano .30 .75
22 Mark Martin .30 .75
23 Jamie McMurray .30 .75
24 Paul Menard .20 .50
25 Juan Pablo Montoya .30 .75
26 Joe Nemechek .20 .50
27 Ryan Newman .25 .60
28 David Ragan .25 .60
29 David Reutimann .25 .60
30 Elliott Sadler .20 .50
31 Regan Smith .25 .60
32 Scott Speed .30 .75
33 Tony Stewart .50 1.25
34 Martin Truex Jr. .25 .60
35 Brian Vickers .20 .50
36 Michael Waltrip .30 .75
37 Jeff Burton's Car RR .10 .25
38 Carl Edwards' Car RR .12 .30
39 Kurt Busch's Car RR .10 .25
40 Kevin Harvick's Car RR .15 .40
41 Mark Martin's Car RR .12 .30
42 Dale Earnhardt Jr.'s Car RR .25 .60
43 Tony Stewart's Car RR .20 .50
44 Jimmie Johnson's Car RR .20 .50
45 Jeff Gordon's Car RR .25 .60
46 Dale Earnhardt Jr.'s Car RS .25 .60
47 Jeff Gordon's Car RS .25 .60
48 Jimmie Johnson's Car RS .20 .50
49 Tony Stewart's Car RS .20 .50
50 Martin Truex Jr.'s Car RS .10 .25
51 Matt Kenseth's Car RS .12 .30
52 Kasey Kahne's Car RS .12 .30
53 Kyle Busch's Car RS .15 .40
54 Clint Bowyer's Car RS .12 .30
55 Jamie McMurray SS .30 .75
56 Juan Pablo Montoya SS .30 .75
57 Kyle Busch SS .40 1.00
58 Jeff Gordon SS .60 1.50
59 Carl Edwards SS .30 .75
60 Kurt Busch SS .25 .60
61 Kevin Harvick SS .40 1.00
62 Tony Stewart SS .50 1.25
63 Jimmie Johnson SS .50 1.25
64 McMurray/Dale Jr. M .60 1.50
65 Gordon/Johnson M .60 1.50
66 Edwards/Keselowski M .40 1.00
67 Busch/Keselowski M .40 1.00
68 Hamlin/Burton M .30 .75
69 McMurray/Harvick M .40 1.00
70 Jamie McMurray PF .30 .75
71 Jimmie Johnson PF .50 1.25
72 Kurt Busch PF .25 .60
73 Denny Hamlin PF .30 .75
74 Ryan Newman PF .25 .60
75 Kevin Harvick PF .40 1.00
76 Josh Wise US .30 .75
77 Josh Wise US .30 .75
78 Josh Wise US .30 .75
79 Josh Wise US .30 .75
80 Josh Wise US .30 .75
81 Josh Wise US .30 .75
82 Justin Allgaier UC .25 .60
83 James Buescher UC RC .25 .60
84 Brian Scott UC RC .25 .60
85 Trevor Bayne UC RC 2.00 5.00
86 Steve Wallace UC .25 .60
87 Ron Hornaday UC .20 .50
88 Johnny Sauter UC .20 .50
89 Ricky Carmichael UC .30 .75
90 Austin Dillon UC .60 1.50
91 Danica Patrick SP RC 6.00 15.00
92 Dale Earnhardt Jr. SP 2.50 6.00
93 Tony Stewart SP 2.00 5.00
94 Jeff Gordon SP 2.50 6.00
95 Jimmie Johnson SP 2.00 5.00
96 Mark Martin SP 1.25 3.00
97 Carl Edwards SP 1.25 3.00
98 Kyle Busch SP 1.50 4.00
99 Kevin Harvick SP 1.50 4.00
100 Clint Bowyer SP 1.25 3.00

2010 Wheels Main Event Blue

*SINGLES (1-90): 1X TO 2.5X BASIC
*SP (91-100): .5X TO 1.2X BASIC SPs
STATED ODDS 1:10 HOBBY

2010 Wheels Main Event Purple

*SINGLES: 4X TO 10X BASE
STATED PRINT RUN 25 SER.#'d SETS

2010 Wheels Main Event American Muscle

COMPLETE SET (12) 10.00 25.00
STATED ODDS 1:6
AM1 Kurt Busch .50 1.25
AM2 Mark Martin .60 1.50
AM3 Tony Stewart 1.00 2.50
AM4 Matt Kenseth .60 1.50
AM5 Jeff Gordon 1.25 3.00
AM6 Kevin Harvick .75 2.00
AM7 Jeff Burton .50 1.25
AM8 Clint Bowyer .60 1.50
AM9 Jimmie Johnson 1.00 2.50
AM10 Martin Truex Jr. .50 1.25
AM11 Dale Earnhardt Jr. 1.25 3.00
AM12 Carl Edwards .60 1.50

2010 Wheels Main Event Marks Autographs

OVERALL AU STATED ODDS 1:20
STATED PRINT RUN 14-96
1 Justin Allgaier/81 4.00 10.00
2 A.J. Allmendinger/74 5.00 12.00
3 Marcos Ambrose/96 10.00 25.00
4 Trevor Bayne/71 30.00 80.00
5 Greg Biffle/86 4.00 10.00
6 Clint Bowyer/96 5.00 12.00
7 Colin Braun/71 4.00 10.00
8 James Buescher/91 4.00 10.00
9 Jeff Burton/54 5.00 12.00
10 Kurt Busch/91 4.00 10.00
11 Kyle Busch/56 15.00 40.00
12 Ricky Carmichael/91 5.00 12.00
13 Kevin Conway/76 8.00 20.00
14 Matt DiBenedetto/74 8.00 20.00
15 Austin Dillon/96 15.00 40.00
16 Paige Duke/50 12.00 30.00
17 Dale Earnhardt Jr./22 60.00 120.00
18 Carl Edwards/73 5.00 12.00
19 Brendan Gaughan/71 3.00 8.00
20 Jeff Gordon/25 60.00 120.00
21 Robby Gordon/19 8.00 20.00
22 Denny Hamlin/40 10.00 25.00
23 Kevin Harvick/14
24 Ron Hornaday/56 4.00 10.00
25 Sam Hornish Jr./50 5.00 12.00
26 Brian Ickler/74 8.00 20.00
28 Kasey Kahne/35 10.00 25.00
29 Matt Kenseth/71 5.00 12.00
30 Brad Keselowski/91 6.00 15.00
31 Travis Kvapil/76 3.00 8.00
32 Bobby Labonte/61 6.00 15.00
33 Scott Lagasse Jr./71 3.00 8.00
34 Justin Lofton/74 5.00 12.00
35 Joey Logano/49 10.00 25.00
36 Tayler Malsam/76 3.00 8.00
37 Mark Martin/14
38 Michael McDowell/74 4.00 10.00
39 Jamie McMurray/61 6.00 15.00
40 Paul Menard/35 6.00 15.00
41 Juan Pablo Montoya/35 10.00 25.00
42 Joe Nemechek/50 4.00 10.00
43 Ryan Newman/50 10.00 25.00
44 Monica Palumbo/50 15.00 40.00
45 Danica Patrick/25 125.00 250.00
46 David Ragan/76 4.00 10.00
47 David Reutimann/76 4.00 10.00
48 Elliott Sadler/50 4.00 10.00
49 Johnny Sauter/66 4.00 10.00
50 Brian Scott/71 4.00 10.00
51 Mike Skinner/76 3.00 8.00
52 Regan Smith/71 4.00 10.00
53 Scott Speed/50 6.00 15.00
54 Ricky Stenhouse Jr./71 5.00 12.00
55 Tony Stewart/29 15.00 40.00
56 Martin Truex Jr./50 5.00 12.00
57 Brian Vickers/71 3.00 8.00
58 Steve Wallace/71 4.00 10.00
59 Michael Waltrip/19 12.00 30.00
60 Josh Wise/76 5.00 12.00
61 Amanda Wright/50 12.00 30.00

2010 Wheels Main Event Marks Autographs Blue

1 Justin Allgaier/35 6.00 15.00
2 A.J. Allmendinger/52 6.00 15.00
3 Marcos Ambrose/50 20.00 50.00
4 Trevor Bayne/30 40.00 100.00
5 Greg Biffle/50 5.00 12.00
6 Clint Bowyer/50 6.00 15.00
7 Colin Braun/30 6.00 15.00
8 James Buescher/35 6.00 15.00
9 Jeff Burton/15 8.00 20.00
10 Kurt Busch/35 6.00 15.00
11 Kyle Busch/15 25.00 60.00
12 Ricky Carmichael/33 8.00 20.00
13 Kevin Conway/25 15.00 40.00
14 Matt DiBenedetto/35 12.00 30.00
15 Austin Dillon/30 30.00 60.00
16 Paige Duke/25 20.00 50.00
18 Carl Edwards/25 10.00 25.00
19 Brendan Gaughan/30 5.00 12.00
22 Denny Hamlin/20 10.00 25.00
24 Ron Hornaday/25 6.00 15.00
25 Sam Hornish Jr./25 8.00 20.00
26 Brian Ickler/35 12.00 30.00
29 Matt Kenseth/25 10.00 25.00
30 Brad Keselowski/25 12.00 30.00
31 Travis Kvapil/25 6.00 15.00
32 Bobby Labonte/25 10.00 25.00
33 Scott Lagasse Jr./30 5.00 12.00
34 Justin Lofton/35 8.00 20.00
35 Joey Logano/20 10.00 25.00
36 Tayler Malsam/35 5.00 12.00
38 Michael McDowell/50 5.00 12.00
39 Jamie McMurray/25 10.00 25.00
40 Paul Menard/15 6.00 15.00
42 Joe Nemechek/25 6.00 15.00
43 Ryan Newman/20 10.00 25.00
44 Monica Palumbo/25 25.00 60.00
46 David Ragan/50 5.00 12.00
47 David Reutimann/50 5.00 12.00
48 Elliott Sadler/25 6.00 15.00
49 Johnny Sauter/25 6.00 15.00
50 Brian Scott/30 6.00 15.00
51 Mike Skinner/35 5.00 12.00
52 Regan Smith/30 6.00 15.00
53 Scott Speed/25 10.00 25.00
54 Ricky Stenhouse Jr./30 8.00 20.00
55 Tony Stewart/15 15.00 40.00
56 Martin Truex Jr./25 8.00 20.00
57 Brian Vickers/30 5.00 12.00
58 Steve Wallace/30 6.00 15.00
60 Josh Wise/35 8.00 20.00
61 Amanda Wright/25 20.00 50.00

2010 Wheels Main Event Marks Autographs Red

STATED PRINT RUN 5-25
1 Justin Allgaier/25 8.00 20.00
4 Trevor Bayne/25 100.00 200.00
15 Austin Dillon/25 40.00 80.00
16 Paige Duke/25 20.00 50.00
33 Scott Lagasse Jr./25 6.00 15.00
36 Tayler Malsam/25 6.00 15.00
52 Regan Smith/25 8.00 20.00

2010 Wheels Main Event Dog Tags

COMPLETE SET (4) 6.00 15.00
STATED ODDS 1 PER BLASTER BOX
DE Dale Earnhardt 2.50 6.00
JG Jeff Gordon 1.00 2.50
JJ Jimmie Johnson .75 2.00
JR Dale Earnhardt Jr. 1.00 2.50

2010 Wheels Main Event Dual Firesuit

STATED PRINT RUN 200 SER.#'d SETS
*PURPLE/20: .4X TO 1X
KHDH K.Harvick/D.Harvick 10.00 25.00

2010 Wheels Main Event Fight Card

COMPLETE SET (25) 8.00 20.00
STATED ODDS 1 PER HOBBY PACK
*CHECKERED: .8X TO 2X BASIC INSERTS
*FULL COLOR: .4X TO 1X BASIC INSERTS
*GOLD/25: 2X TO 5X BASIC INSERTS
FC1 A.J. Allmendinger .40 1.00
FC2 Marcos Ambrose .40 1.00
FC3 Greg Biffle .30 .75
FC4 Clint Bowyer .40 1.00
FC5 Jeff Burton .30 .75
FC6 Kurt Busch .30 .75
FC7 Kyle Busch .50 1.25
FC8 Dale Earnhardt Jr. .75 2.00
FC9 Carl Edwards .40 1.00
FC10 Jeff Gordon .75 2.00
FC11 Denny Hamlin .40 1.00
FC12 Kevin Harvick .50 1.25
FC13 Jimmie Johnson .60 1.50
FC14 Kasey Kahne .40 1.00
FC15 Matt Kenseth .40 1.00
FC16 Brad Keselowski .50 1.25
FC17 Joey Logano .40 1.00
FC18 Mark Martin .40 1.00
FC19 Jamie McMurray .40 1.00
FC20 Juan Pablo Montoya .40 1.00
FC21 Ryan Newman .30 .75
FC22 David Ragan .30 .75
FC23 David Reutimann .30 .75
FC24 Tony Stewart .60 1.50
FC25 Danica Patrick 3.00 8.00

2010 Wheels Main Event Head to Head

STATED PRINT RUN 150 SER.#'d SETS
*BLUE/75: .6X TO 1.5X BASIC INSERTS
*RED/25: 1.2X TO 3X BASIC INSERTS
HHCEMK Carl Edwards/Matt Kenseth 3.00 8.00
HHDEDP Dale Earnhardt Jr.
Danica Patrick 15.00 40.00
HHDEJG Dale Earnhardt
Jr./Jeff Gordon 6.00 15.00
HHDRMT David Reutimann
Martin Truex Jr. 6.00 15.00
HHJBDH Jeff Burton/Denny Hamlin 3.00 8.00
HHJGJJ Jeff Gordon/Jimmie Johnson 6.00 15.00
HHJJMM Jimmie Johnson
Mark Martin 5.00 12.00
HHJMJP Jamie McMurray
Juan Pablo Montoya 3.00 8.00
HHKBBK Kurt Busch/Brad Keselowski 4.00 10.00
HHKBDH Kyle Busch/Denny Hamlin 4.00 10.00
HHKBJL Kyle Busch/Joey Logano 4.00 10.00
HHKHJB Kevin Harvick/Jeff Burton 4.00 10.00
HHKHJL Kevin Harvick/Joey Logano 4.00 10.00
HHKKCE Kasey Kahne/Carl Edwards 3.00 8.00
HHKKJG Kasey Kahne/Jeff Gordon 6.00 15.00
HHMMJG Mark Martin/Jeff Gordon 6.00 15.00
HHMTMA Martin Truex Jr.
Marcos Ambrose 12.00 30.00
HHSSBV Scott Speed/Brian Vickers 5.00 12.00
HHTSDE Tony Stewart
Dale Earnhardt Jr. 6.00 15.00
HHTSRN Tony Stewart/Ryan Newman 5.00 12.00

2010 Wheels Main Event Tale of the Tape

COMPLETE SET (9) 10.00 25.00
STATED ODDS 1:8
TT1 Joey Logano .60 1.50
TT2 Brian Vickers .40 1.00
TT3 Kyle Busch .75 2.00
TT4 Denny Hamlin .60 1.50
TT5 Carl Edwards .60 1.50
TT6 Mark Martin .60 1.50
TT7 Tony Stewart 1.00 2.50
TT8 Jimmie Johnson 1.00 2.50
TT9 Jeff Gordon 1.25 3.00

2010 Wheels Main Event Upper Cuts

UCBK B.Keselowski FS/199 6.00 15.00
UCCE C.Edwards PS/150 5.00 12.00
UCDE Dale Jr. Shirt/199 10.00 25.00
UCDH D.Harvick FS/150 10.00 25.00
UCDR D.Reutimann PS/150 5.00 12.00
UCJG J.Gordon Shirt/199 10.00 25.00
UCJM J.McMurray PS/150 5.00 12.00
UCKK K.Kahne Confetti/199 6.00 15.00
UCMK M.Kenseth Net/115 8.00 20.00
UCMT M.Truex Jr. PS/150 6.00 15.00
UCTS T.Stewart Banner/150 8.00 20.00
UCJM2 J.McMurray FS/199 6.00 15.00
UCKK2 K.Kahne Seat Belt/199 6.00 15.00
UCJPM2 J.P.Montoya PS/150 5.00 12.00

2010 Wheels Main Event Upper Cuts Blue

BLUE STATED PRINT RUN 25-99
*RED/15-25: .5X TO 1.2X BLUE/50-75
UCBK B.Keselowski FS/99 8.00 20.00
UCBV B.Vickers Helmet/25 40.00 80.00
UCCB C.Bowyer Stacker/50 8.00 20.00
UCCE C.Edwards PS 6.00 15.00
UCDE Dale Jr. Shirt 12.00 30.00
UCDH D.Harvick FS 12.00 30.00
UCDR D.Reutimann PS 6.00 15.00
UCJB J.Burton Stacker/50 6.00 15.00
UCJG J.Gordon Shirt 12.00 30.00
UCJJ J.Johnson Window/50 12.00 30.00
UCJM J.McMurray PS 6.00 15.00
UCJM2 J.McMurray FS 8.00 20.00
UCJPM Montoya Shifter Boot/50 6.00 15.00
UCJPM2 J.P.Montoya PS 6.00 15.00
UCKH K.Harvick Stacker/50 6.00 15.00
UCKK K.Kahne Confetti 8.00 20.00
UCKK2 K.Kahne Belt 8.00 20.00
UCMK M.Kenseth Net/25 12.00 30.00
UCMT M.Truex Jr. PS 8.00 20.00
UCTS T.Stewart Banner 10.00 25.00

2010 Wheels Main Event Upper Cuts Knock Out Patches

STATED PRINT RUN 25 SER.#'d SETS
UCKOBK Brad Keselowski 40.00 100.00
UCKOBV Brian Vickers 20.00 50.00
UCKOCE Carl Edwards 40.00 100.00
UCKODE Dale Earnhardt Jr. 50.00 120.00
UCKODH Denny Hamlin 30.00 80.00
UCKODP Danica Patrick 100.00 200.00
UCKOJB Jeff Burton 15.00 40.00
UCKOJG Jeff Gordon 60.00 120.00
UCKOJJ Jimmie Johnson 40.00 100.00
UCKOJL Joey Logano 30.00 80.00
UCKOJM Jamie McMurray 30.00 80.00
UCKOJPM Juan Pablo Montoya 25.00 60.00
UCKOKH Kevin Harvick 25.00 60.00

UCKOKK Kasey Kahne 60.00 120.00
UCKOKUB Kurt Busch 25.00 60.00
UCKOKYB Kyle Busch 25.00 60.00
UCKOMA Marcos Ambrose 30.00 80.00
UCKOMM Mark Martin 40.00 100.00
UCKOMT Martin Truex Jr. 15.00 40.00
UCKORN Ryan Newman 20.00 50.00
UCKOTS Tony Stewart 40.00 100.00

2010 Wheels Main Event Wheel to Wheel

STATED PRINT RUN 25 SER.#'d SETS
WWCEMK Carl Edwards/Matt Kenseth 15.0040.00
WWDETS Dale Earnhardt Jr.
Tony Stewart 15.00 40.00
WWJGDE Jeff Gordon
Dale Earnhardt Jr. 20.00 50.00
WWJJJG Jimmie Johnson
Jeff Gordon 20.00 50.00
WWJMJP Jamie McMurray
Juan Pablo Montoya 10.00 25.00
WWKBBK Kurt Busch
Brad Keselowski 12.00 30.00
WWKBDH Kyle Busch/Denny Hamlin
WWKBJL Kyle Busch/Joey Logano 10.00 25.00
WWTSRN Tony Stewart/Ryan Newman 12.0030.00

2011 Wheels Main Event

COMPLETE SET (90) 12.00 30.00
WAX BOX HOBBY (20) 75.00 100.00
WAX BOX RETAIL (24) 50.00 75.00
1 A.J. Allmendinger .30 .75
2 Marcos Ambrose .30 .75
3 Trevor Bayne CRC 1.50 4.00
4 Greg Biffle .25 .60
5 Clint Bowyer .30 .75
6 Jeff Burton .25 .60
7 Kurt Busch .25 .60
8 Kyle Busch .40 1.00
9 Landon Cassill .30 .75
10 Dale Earnhardt Jr. .60 1.50
11 Carl Edwards .30 .75
12 David Gilliland .20 .50
13 Jeff Gordon 2.50 6.00
14 Robby Gordon .20 .50
15 Denny Hamlin .30 .75
16 Kevin Harvick .40 1.00
17 Jimmie Johnson .50 1.25
18 Kasey Kahne .30 .75
19 Matt Kenseth .30 .75
20 Brad Keselowski .40 1.00
21 Travis Kvapil .20 .50
22 Bobby Labonte .30 .75
23 Joey Logano .30 .75
24 Mark Martin .30 .75
25 Jamie McMurray .30 .75
26 Casey Mears .20 .50
27 Paul Menard .20 .50
28 Juan Pablo Montoya .30 .75
29 Ryan Newman .25 .60
30 David Ragan .25 .60
31 David Reutimann .25 .60
32 Regan Smith .25 .60
33 Tony Stewart .50 1.25
34 Martin Truex Jr. .25 .60
35 Brian Vickers .20 .50
36 Michael Waltrip .40 1.00
37 Justin Allgaier NNS .25 .60
38 Aric Almirola NNS .25 .60
39 Trevor Bayne NNS .60 1.50
40 Jennifer Jo Cobb NNS RC .75 2.00
41 Jason Leffler NNS .25 .60
42 Danica Patrick NNS 1.25 3.00
43 Reed Sorenson NNS .20 .50
44 Ricky Stenhouse Jr. NNS .30 .75
45 Kenny Wallace NNS .20 .50
46 Mike Wallace NNS .30 .75
47 Steve Wallace NNS .25 .60
48 Josh Wise NNS .20 .50
49 James Buescher CWTS .20 .50
50 Ricky Carmichael CWTS .30 .75
51 Austin Dillon CWTS .40 1.00
52 Ron Hornaday CWTS .30 .75
53 Miguel Paludo CWTS .30 .75
54 Timothy Peters CWTS .20 .50
55 Nelson Piquet Jr. CWTS RC .30 .75
56 Johnny Sauter CWTS .20 .50
57 Brendan Gaughan CWTS .20 .50
58 Joey Coulter CWTS RC .30 .75
59 Max Papis CWTS .40 1.00
60 Brad Sweet CWTS RC .40 1.00
61 Dale Earnhardt Jr. LF .60 1.50
62 Carl Edwards LF .30 .75
63 Matt Kenseth LF .30 .75
64 Juan Pablo Montoya LF .30 .75
65 David Ragan LF .25 .60
66 Jeff Gordon LF .60 1.50
67 Kasey Kahne LF .30 .75
68 Brad Keselowski LF .40 1.00
69 Kurt Busch LF .25 .60
70 Dale Earnhardt Jr.'s Car SO .25 .60
71 Jeff Gordon's Car SO .25 .60
72 Kevin Harvick's Car SO .15 .40
73 Tony Stewart's Car SO .20 .50
74 Jeff Burton's Car SO .10 .25
75 Greg Biffle's Car SO .10 .25
76 Clint Bowyer's Car SO .12 .30
77 Jimmie Johnson's Car SO .20 .50
78 Mark Martin's Car SO .12 .30
79 Kasey Kahne SS .30 .75
80 Jimmie Johnson SS .50 1.25
81 Tony Stewart SS .50 1.25
82 Mark Martin SS .30 .75
83 Kurt Busch SS .25 .60
84 Ryan Newman SS .25 .60
85 Carl Edwards SS .30 .75
86 Kyle Busch SS .40 1.00
87 Denny Hamlin SS .30 .75
88 Matt Kenseth SS .30 .75
89 Brian Vickers SS .20 .50
90 Joey Logano SS .30 .75

2011 Wheels Main Event Black and White

*B&W: 1.2X TO 3X BASE
STATED ODDS 1:20
3 Trevor Bayne 2.00 5.00

2011 Wheels Main Event Blue

*BLUE/75: 2X TO 5X BASE
3 Trevor Bayne 3.00 8.00

2011 Wheels Main Event Red

*RED/20: 4X TO 10X BASE
3 Trevor Bayne 6.00 15.00

2011 Wheels Main Event All Stars

COMPLETE SET (21) 10.00 25.00
STATED ODDS 1:4
*BRUSHED/199: 1.2X TO 3X BASIC INSERT
*HOLO/50: 2X TO 5X BASIC INSERTS
A1 Carl Edwards .50 1.25
A2 Kyle Busch .60 1.50
A3 David Reutimann .40 1.00
A4 Tony Stewart .75 2.00
A5 Greg Biffle .40 1.00
A6 Matt Kenseth .50 1.25
A7 Denny Hamlin .50 1.25
A8 David Ragan .40 1.00
A9 Kevin Harvick .60 1.50
A10 Ryan Newman .40 1.00
A11 Jimmie Johnson .75 2.00
A12 Juan Pablo Montoya .50 1.25
A13 Kurt Busch .40 1.00
A14 Dale Earnhardt Jr. 1.00 2.50
A15 Jeff Gordon 1.00 2.50
A16 Clint Bowyer .50 1.25
A17 Jamie McMurray .50 1.25
A18 Brad Keselowski .60 1.50
A19 Mark Martin .50 1.25
A20 Regan Smith .40 1.00
A21 Kasey Kahne .50 1.25

2011 Wheels Main Event Gloves Off Silver

STATED PRINT RUN 99 SER.#'d SETS
*HOLO/25: .5X TO 1.2X SILVER/99
GODP Danica Patrick 15.00 40.00
GOJG Jeff Gordon 15.00 40.00
GOJJ Jimmie Johnson 12.00 30.00
GOJL Joey Logano 12.00 30.00
GOKB Kyle Busch 10.00 25.00
GOKH Kevin Harvick 8.00 20.00
GOMK Matt Kenseth 8.00 20.00
GOMM Mark Martin 8.00 20.00
GOTB Trevor Bayne 8.00 20.00

2011 Wheels Main Event Headliners Silver

SILVER STATED PRINT RUN 50-99
*HOLO/25: .6X TO 1.5X SILVER/99
*HOLO/25: .5X TO 1.2X SILVER/50
HLCE Carl Edwards/99 4.00 10.00
HLDE Dale Earnhardt Jr./99 10.00 25.00
HLDH Denny Hamlin/50 5.00 12.00
HLDP Danica Patrick/99 12.00 30.00
HLJB Jeff Burton/50 4.00 10.00
HLJG Jeff Gordon/99 10.00 25.00
HLJJ Jimmie Johnson/99 6.00 15.00
HLJL Joey Logano/99 10.00 25.00
HLKH Kevin Harvick/99 5.00 12.00
HLKK Kasey Kahne/99 4.00 10.00
HLKUB Kurt Busch/99 4.00 10.00
HLKYB Kyle Busch/99 6.00 15.00
HLMA Marcos Ambrose/50 5.00 12.00
HLMK Matt Kenseth/50 4.00 10.00
HLMM Mark Martin/99 5.00 12.00
HLRN Ryan Newman/50 4.00 10.00
HLTB Trevor Bayne/50 8.00 20.00
HLTS Tony Stewart/99 6.00 15.00

2011 Wheels Main Event Joe Gibbs Racing 20th Anniversary

COMPLETE SET (6) 6.00 15.00
STATED ODDS 1:20
*BRUSHED/199: .6X TO 1.5X BASIC INSERTS
*HOLO/50: 1X TO 2.5X BASIC INSERTS
JGR1 Dale Jarrett 1.00 2.50
JGR2 Bobby Labonte 1.00 2.50
JGR3 Tony Stewart 1.50 4.00
JGR4 Joe Gibbs .75 2.00
JGR5 2011 Team 1.25 3.00
JGR6 Joe Gibbs .75 2.00

2011 Wheels Main Event Lead Foot Silver

SILVER STATED PRINT RUN 99
*HOLO/25: .5X TO 1.2X SILVER/99
LFBK Brad Keselowski 6.00 15.00
LFCE Carl Edwards 8.00 20.00
LFDE Dale Earnhardt Jr. 12.00 30.00
LFDR David Ragan 6.00 15.00
LFJG Jeff Gordon 15.00 40.00
LFJM Juan Pablo Montoya 6.00 15.00
LFKK Kasey Kahne 10.00 25.00
LFMK Matt Kenseth 8.00 20.00

2011 Wheels Main Event Marks Autographs Gold

*GOLD/25: .6X TO 1.5X SILVER
GOLD STATED PRINT RUN 10-25
MEAA Aric Almirola/25 8.00 20.00
MEAA A.J. Allmendinger/25 10.00 25.00
MEAD Austin Dillon/25 30.00 60.00
MEBG Brendan Gaughan/25 6.00 15.00
MEBK Brad Keselowski/25 15.00 40.00
MEBL Bobby Labonte/15 10.00 25.00
MEBS Brian Scott/25 6.00 15.00
MEBV Brian Vickers/25 6.00 15.00
MECB Clint Bowyer/25 10.00 25.00
MECE Carl Edwards/25 10.00 25.00
MEDE Dale Earnhardt Jr./10
MEDH Denny Hamlin/25 10.00 25.00
MEDP Danica Patrick/25 125.00 200.00
MEDR David Ragan/25 8.00 20.00
MEDR David Reutimann/25 8.00 20.00
MEGB Greg Biffle/25 8.00 20.00
MEJA Justin Allgaier/25 8.00 20.00
MEJB James Buescher/25 6.00 15.00
MEJB Jeff Burton/25 8.00 20.00
MEJC Jennifer Jo Cobb/25 25.00 60.00
MEJC Joey Coulter/25 8.00 20.00
MEJG Jeff Gordon/10
MEJJ Jimmie Johnson/10
MEJL Joey Logano/15 20.00 50.00
MEJL Jason Leffler/10
MEJL Johanna Long/25 15.00 40.00
MEJM Jamie McMurray/25 10.00 25.00
MEJM Juan Pablo Montoya/10
MEJW Josh Wise/25 6.00 15.00
MEJY J.J. Yeley/15
MEKC Kim Coon/25 25.00 50.00
MEKH Kevin Harvick/15 20.00 50.00
MEKK Kasey Kahne/25 25.00 60.00
MEKW Kenny Wallace/25 6.00 15.00
MELC Landon Cassill/25 10.00 25.00
MEMA Marcos Ambrose/25 25.00 60.00
MEMK Matt Kenseth/25 20.00 50.00
MEMM Mark Martin/10
MEMP Miguel Paludo/25 10.00 25.00
MEMP Max Papis/25 12.00 30.00
MEMT Martin Truex Jr./25 15.00 40.00
MEMW Michael Waltrip/10
MEMW Mike Wallace/25 10.00 25.00
MEPM Paul Menard/25 6.00 15.00
MERC Ricky Carmichael/25 10.00 25.00
MERG Robby Gordon/25 6.00 15.00
MERH Ron Hornaday/25 6.00 15.00
MERN Ryan Newman/25 8.00 20.00
MERR Robert Richardson/25 6.00 15.00
MERS Reed Sorenson/25 6.00 15.00
MERS Ricky Stenhouse Jr./25 10.00 25.00
MERS Regan Smith/25 8.00 20.00
MESW Steve Wallace/25 8.00 20.00
METB Trevor Bayne/25 6.00 15.00
METK Travis Kvapil/15
METP Timothy Peters/25 6.00 15.00
METS Tony Stewart/25 15.00 40.00
MEKUB Kurt Busch/25 8.00 20.00
MEKYB Kyle Busch/15 20.00 50.00

2011 Wheels Main Event Marks Autographs Silver

SILVER STATED PRINT RUN 15-65
MEAA Aric Almirola/65 5.00 12.00
MEAA A.J. Allmendinger/50 6.00 15.00
MEAD Austin Dillon/64 20.00 40.00
MEBG Brendan Gaughan
MEBK Brad Keselowski/50 10.00 25.00
MEBL Bobby Labonte /30 6.00 15.00
MEBS Brian Scott/55 4.00 10.00
MEBV Brian Vickers/50 4.00 10.00
MECB Clint Bowyer/45 6.00 15.00
MECE Carl Edwards/50 6.00 15.00
MEDE Dale Earnhardt Jr./15
MEDH Denny Hamlin/50 6.00 15.00
MEDP Danica Patrick/35 75.00 150.00
MEDR David Ragan/65 5.00 12.00
MEDR David Reutimann/50 5.00 12.00
MEGB Greg Biffle/50 5.00 12.00
MEJA Justin Allgaier/65 5.00 12.00
MEJB James Buescher
MEJB Jeff Burton/50 5.00 12.00
MEJC Jennifer Jo Cobb/65 15.00 40.00
MEJC Joey Coulter
MEJG Jeff Gordon/15
MEJJ Jimmie Johnson/15 40.00 100.00
MEJL Jason Leffler
MEJL Joey Logano/30 15.00 40.00
MEJL Johanna Long
MEJM Jamie McMurray/50 6.00 15.00
MEJM Juan Pablo Montoya/15
MEJW Josh Wise/64 4.00 10.00
MEJY J.J. Yeley
MEKC Kim Coon
MEKH Kevin Harvick/30 15.00 40.00
MEKK Kasey Kahne/50 15.00 40.00
MEKW Kenny Wallace/48 4.00 10.00
MELC Landon Cassill/50 6.00 15.00
MEMA Marcos Ambrose/50 12.00 30.00
MEMK Matt Kenseth/50 12.00 30.00
MEMM Mark Martin/15
MEMP Miguel Paludo
MEMP Max Papis
MEMT Martin Truex Jr./50 10.00 25.00
MEMW Michael Waltrip/15
MEMW Mike Wallace/65 6.00 15.00
MEPM Paul Menard/65 4.00 10.00
MERC Ricky Carmichael/65 8.00 20.00
MERG Robby Gordon/44 4.00 10.00
MERH Ron Hornaday
MERN Ryan Newman/48 5.00 12.00
MERR Robert Richardson/65 4.00 10.00
MERS Reed Sorenson/65 4.00 10.00
MERS Ricky Stenhouse Jr./65 6.00 15.00
MERS Regan Smith/50 5.00 12.00
MESW Steve Wallace
METB Trevor Bayne/50 4.00 10.00
METK Travis Kvapil/30 4.00 10.00
METP Timothy Peters
METS Tony Stewart/50 10.00 25.00
MEKUB Kurt Busch/45 5.00 12.00
MEKYB Kyle Busch/30 8.00 20.00

2011 Wheels Main Event Materials Holofoil

MEMCB Clint Bowyer 8.00 20.00
MEMCE Carl Edwards 15.00 40.00

2011 Wheels Main Event Materials Silver

STATED PRINT RUN 50-99
MEMBV Brian Vickers 6.00 15.00
MEMDE Dale Earnhardt Jr. 10.00 25.00
MEMDR David Reutimann 5.00 12.00
MEMJB Jeff Burton 6.00 15.00
MEMJG Jeff Gordon 10.00 25.00
MEMJJ Jimmie Johnson 10.00 25.00
MEMJL Joey Logano 8.00 20.00
MEMJM Jamie McMurray/50 8.00 20.00
MEMJM Juan Pablo Montoya 6.00 15.00
MEMKH Kevin Harvick 10.00 25.00
MEMKK Kasey Kahne/50 10.00 25.00
MEMKUB Kurt Busch 8.00 20.00
MEMKYB Kyle Busch 8.00 20.00
MEMMT Martin Truex Jr. 6.00 15.00
MEMMW Michael Waltrip 6.00 15.00
MEMTB Trevor Bayne 15.00 40.00

2011 Wheels Main Event Rear View

COMPLETE SET (10) 10.00 25.00
STATED ODDS 1:10
*BRUSHED/199: 1X TO 2.5X BASIC INSERTS
*HOLO/50: 1.5X TO 4X BASIC INSERTS
R1 Dale Earnhardt Jr. 1.25 3.00
R2 Jeff Gordon 1.25 3.00
R3 Jimmie Johnson 1.00 2.50
R4 Tony Stewart 1.00 2.50
R5 Mark Martin .60 1.50
R6 Carl Edwards .60 1.50
R7 Kyle Busch .75 2.00
R8 Kevin Harvick .75 2.00
R9 Kurt Busch .50 1.25
R10 Matt Kenseth .60 1.50

1998 Wheels Terry Labonte Fan Club

NNO Terry Labonte 10.00 20.00

1991 Winner's Choice New England Drivers

Winner's Choice, Inc. produced this set in 1991 featuring popular New England area drivers of various race circuits. The black-bordered cards look very similar to 1991 Winner's Choice Modifieds cards and include a color driver or car photo surrounded by a checkered flag frame. The cards were packaged and sold in complete factory set form.

COMPLETE SET (120) 5.00 12.00
1 Cover Card .02 .10
2 Tony Hirschman .07 .20
3 Mike Hirschman's Car .02 .10
4 Mike Rowe .07 .20
5 Mike Rowe's Car .02 .10
6 Steve Knowlton .07 .20
7 Steve Knowlton's Car .02 .10
8 Bobby Dragon .07 .20
9 Bobby Dragon's Car .02 .10
10 Tony Sylvester .07 .20
11 Tony Sylvester's Car .02 .10
12 Dave Dion .07 .20
13 Dave Dion's Car .02 .10
14 Mike Weeden .07 .20
15 Mike Weeden's Car .02 .10
16 Bobby Gahan .07 .20
17 Bobby Gahan's Car .02 .10
18 Dean Ferri .07 .20
19 Dean Ferri's Car .02 .10
20 Lloyd Gillie .07 .20
21 Lloyd Gillie's Car .02 .10
22 Joey Kourafas .07 .20
23 Joey Kourafas' Car .02 .10
24 Jimmy Field .07 .20
25 Jimmy Field's Car .02 .10
26 Mike Johnson .07 .20
27 Mike Johnson's Car .02 .10
28 Dick McCabe .07 .20
29 Dick McCabe's Car .02 .10
30 Rick Miller .07 .20
31 Rick Miller's Car .02 .10
32 Joe Bessey .15 .40
33 Joe Bessey's Car .07 .20
34 Donny Ling Jr. .07 .20
35 Donny Ling Jr.'s Car .02 .10
36 Jamie Aube .07 .20
37 Jamie Aube's Car .02 .10
38 Ron Lamell Jr. .07 .20
39 Ron Lamell Jr.'s Car .02 .10
40 Checklist Card .02 .10
41 Mike Maietta .07 .20
42 Mike Maietta's Car .02 .10
43 Tom Bolles .07 .20
44 Tom Bolles' Car .02 .10
45 Tom Rowe .07 .20
46 Tom Rowe's Car .02 .10
47 Kelly Moore .07 .20
48 Kelly Moore's Car .02 .10
49 Bobby Gada .07 .20
50 Bobby Gada's Car .02 .10
51 Pete Rondeau .07 .20
52 Pete Rondeau's Car .02 .10
53 Dale Shaw .07 .20
54 Dale Shaw's Car .02 .10
55 Mike Olsen .07 .20
56 Mike Olsen's Car .02 .10
57 Bob Randall .07 .20
58 Bob Randall's Car .02 .10
59 Billy Clark .07 .20
60 Billy Clark's Car .02 .10
61 Tracy Gordon .07 .20
62 Tracy Gordon's Car .02 .10
63 Paul Richardson .07 .20
64 Paul Richardson's Car .02 .10
65 Glenn Cusack .07 .20
66 Glenn Cusack's Car .02 .10
67 Barney McRae .07 .20
68 Barney McRae's Car .02 .10
69 Pete Fiandaca .07 .20
70 Pete Fiandaca's Car .02 .10
71 Jeff Spraker .07 .20
72 Jeff Spraker's Car .02 .10
73 Stub Fadden .07 .20
74 Stub Fadden's Car .02 .10
75 Bruce Haley .07 .20
76 Bruce Haley's Car .02 .10
77 Pete Silva .07 .20
78 Pete Silva's Car .02 .10
79 Paul Johnson .07 .20
80 Paul Johnson's Car .02 .10
81 Checklist Card .02 .10
82 Dave Davis .07 .20
83 Dave Davis' Car .02 .10
84 Jimmy Burns .07 .20
85 Jimmy Burns' Car .02 .10
86 Bub Bilodeau .07 .20
87 Bub Bilodeau's Car .02 .10
88 Dave Darveau .07 .20
89 Dave Darveau's Car .02 .10
90 Glenn Sullivan .07 .20
91 Glenn Sullivan's Car .02 .10
92 Ricky Harrison .07 .20
93 Ricky Harrison's Car .02 .10
94 Billy Holbrook .07 .20
95 Billy Holbrook's Car .02 .10
96 John Marsh .07 .20
97 John Marsh's Car .02 .10
98 Ricky Craven .75 2.00
99 Ricky Craven's Car .40 1.00
100 Mike Stefanik .15 .40
101 Mike Stefanik's Car .07 .20
102 Bob Brunell .07 .20
103 Bob Brunell's Car .02 .10
104 Al Hammond .07 .20
105 Al Hammond's Car .02 .10
106 Babe Branscombe .07 .20
107 Babe Branscombe's Car .02 .10
108 Jeff Zuideman .07 .20
109 Jeff Zuideman's Car .02 .10
110 Jeff Barry .07 .20
111 Jeff Barry's Car .02 .10
112 Jerry Marquis .07 .20
113 Jerry Marquis' Car .02 .10
114 Art Tappen .07 .20
115 Art Tappen's Car .02 .10
116 Mike Rowe .07 .20
Tom Rowe
117 Mike Maietta .07 .20
Mike Maietta Jr
118 Bentley Warren .07 .20
119 Bentley Warren's Car .02 .10
120 Checklist Card .02 .10

1991 Winner's Choice Ricky Craven

One of Winner's Choice's first card sets, this issue focuses on the career of up-and-coming driver Ricky Craven. The cards were released in complete factory set form with Craven pictured on the set box. A contest entry card was included with each set exchangeable for a chance to win Ricky Craven's 1990 Rookie of the Year driver's suit.

COMPLETE FACT.SET (31) 10.00 20.00
1 Ricky Craven .30 .75
2 Ricky Craven w/Car .30 .75
3 Ricky Craven w/Car .30 .75
4 Ricky Craven w/Car .30 .75
5 Ricky Craven's Car .12 .30
6 Ricky Craven .30 .75
7 Ricky Craven w/Car .30 .75
8 Ricky Craven w/Car .30 .75
9 Ricky Craven's Car .12 .30
10 Ricky Craven's Car .12 .30
11 Ricky Craven w/Car .30 .75
12 Ricky Craven's Car .12 .30
13 Ricky Craven .30 .75
14 Ricky Craven w/Car .30 .75
15 Ricky Craven .30 .75
16 Ricky Craven .30 .75
Cathleen Craven
17 Richard Petty .60 1.50
R.Craven
18 Ricky Craven .30 .75
19 Ricky Craven .30 .75
Chuck Bown Cars
20 Ricky Craven .30 .75
21 Ricky Craven .30 .75
22 Ricky Craven .30 .75
Cathleen Craven
23 Ricky Craven .30 .75
24 Ricky Craven w/Crew .30 .75
25 Ricky Craven .30 .75
26 Ricky Craven's Car .12 .30
27 Ricky Craven's Car .12 .30
28 Ricky Craven .30 .75
29 Ricky Craven .30 .75
30 Ricky Craven .30 .75
NNO Contest Entry Card .07 .20

1992 Winner's Choice Busch

Winner's Choice released a full 150-card set featuring the top drivers of the Winston Cup Busch Series. The cards were distributed in factory set form, as well as through 12-card foil packs. Randomly inserted autographed cards were included in some foil packs.

COMPLETE SET (150) 10.00 25.00
COMP.FACT.SET (150) 10.00 25.00
1 Cover Card .02 .10
2 Ricky Craven .30 .75
3 Ricky Craven .30 .75
4 Ricky Craven's Car .20 .50
5 Dick McCabe .08 .25
6 Dick McCabe's Car .02 .10
7 Billy Clark .08 .25
8 Billy Clark's Car .20 .50
9 Jamie Aube .08 .25
10 Jamie Aube's Car .02 .10
11 Kelly Moore .08 .25
12 Kelly Moore's Car .02 .10
13 Joey Kourafas .08 .25
14 Joey Kourafas' Car .02 .10
15 Tony Hirschman .08 .25
16 Tony Hirschman's Car .02 .10
17 Tony Hirschman .08 .25
18 Stub Fadden .08 .25
19 Stub Fadden's Car .02 .10
20 Mike Rowe .08 .25
21 Mike Rowe's Car .02 .10
22 Dale Shaw .08 .25
23 Dale Shaw's Car .02 .10
24 Dave Dion .08 .25
25 Dave Dion's Car .02 .10
26 Joe Bessey .20 .50
27 Joe Bessey's Car .08 .25
28 Bobby Gada .08 .25
29 Bobby Gada's Car .20 .50
30 Jeff Barry .08 .25
31 Jeff Barry's Car .02 .10
32 Ken Bouchard .20 .50
33 Peter Daniels .08 .25
34 Peter Daniels' Car .02 .10
35 Barney McRae .08 .25
36 Barney McRae's Car .20 .50
37 Mike Olsen .08 .25
38 Mike Olsen's Car .02 .10
39 Bob Brunell .08 .25
40 Bob Brunell's Car .20 .50
41 Donny Ling Jr. .08 .25
42 Donny Ling Jr.'s Car .02 .10
43 Dean Ferri .08 .25
44 Dean Ferri's Car .02 .10
45 Jeff Spraker .08 .25
46 Jeff Spraker's Car .02 .10
47 Rick Miller .08 .25
48 Rick Miller's Car .02 .10
49 Lloyd Gillie .08 .25
50 Lloyd Gillie's Car .02 .10
51 Checklist Card .02 .10
52 Curtis Markham .20 .50
53 Curtis Markham's Car .08 .25
54 Ron Lamell .08 .25
55 Ron Lamell's Car .02 .10
56 Bobby Dragon .08 .25
57 Bobby Dragon's Car .20 .50
58 Mike Weeden .08 .25
59 Mike Weeden's Car .02 .10
60 Babe Branscombe .08 .25
61 Babe Branscombe's Car .20 .50
62 Kenny Wallace .30 .75
63 Kenny Wallace's Car .20 .50
64 Robert Pressley .20 .50
65 Robert Pressley's Car .08 .25
66 Chuck Bown .20 .50
67 Chuck Bown's Car .08 .25
68 Joe Nemechek .30 .75
69 Joe Nemechek's Car .20 .50
70 Todd Bodine .30 .75
71 Todd Bodine's Car .20 .50
72 Tom Peck .08 .25
73 Tom Peck's Car .02 .10
74 Steve Grissom .20 .50
75 Steve Grissom's Car .08 .25
76 Jeff Gordon 8.00 20.00
77 Jeff Gordon's Car 3.00 8.00
78 Jeff Burton 1.00 2.50
79 Jeff Burton's Car .50 1.25
80 David Green .30 .75
81 David Green's Car .20 .50
82 Butch Miller .08 .25
83 Butch Miller's Car .20 .50
84 Dave Rezendes .08 .25
85 Dave Rezendes' Car .02 .10
86 Ward Burton .75 2.00
87 Ward Burton's Car .30 .75
88 Ed Berrier .08 .25
89 Ed Berrier's Car .02 .10
90 Troy Beebe .08 .25
91 Troy Beebe's Car .02 .10
92 Ed Ferree .08 .25
93 Ed Ferree's Car .02 .10
94 Jim Bown .08 .25
95 Jim Bown's Car .02 .10
96 Tony Siscone .08 .25
97 Tony Siscone's Car .02 .10
98 Shawna Robinson 3.00 6.00
99 Shawna Robinson's Car .30 .75
100 Checklist Card .02 .10
101 Mike Maietta .08 .25
102 Mike Maietta's Car .02 .10
103 Tracy Gordon .08 .25
104 Tracy Gordon's Car .02 .10
105 Tony Papale .08 .25
106 Tony Papale's Car .02 .10
107 Jerry Marquis .08 .25
108 Jerry Marquis' Car .02 .10
109 Dave St. Clair .08 .25

110 Dave St. Clair's Car .02 .10
111 Steve Nelson .08 .25
112 Steve Nelson's Car .02 .10
113 Glenn Cusack .08 .25
114 Glenn Cusack's Car .02 .10
115 Jeff Zuideman .08 .25
116 Jeff Zuideman's Car .02 .10
117 Ed Carroll .08 .25
118 Ed Carroll's Car .02 .10
119 Tom Rosati .08 .25
120 Tom Rosati's Car .02 .10
121 Jim McCallum .08 .25
122 Jim McCallum's Car .02 .10
123 Eddy Carroll Jr. .08 .25
124 Eddy Carroll Jr.'s Car .02 .10
125 Bob Randall .08 .25
126 Bob Randall's Car .20 .50
127 Pete Fiandaca .08 .25
128 Pete Fiandaca's Car .02 .10
129 Bobby Gahan .08 .25
130 Bobby Gahan's Car .20 .50
131 Scott Bachand .08 .25
132 Scott Bachand's Car .02 .10
133 Tom Bolles .08 .25
134 Tom Bolles' Car .02 .10
135 Pete Silva .08 .25
136 Pete Silva's Car .02 .10
137 Jimmy Field .08 .25
138 Jimmy Field's Car .02 .10
139 Tony Sylvester .08 .25
140 Tony Sylvester's Car .02 .10
141 Mike Johnson .08 .25
142 Mike Johnson's Car .02 .10
143 Mike Maietta Jr. .08 .25
144 Mike Maietta Jr.'s Car .02 .10
145 Jimmy Hensley .08 .25
146 Jimmy Hensley's Car .02 .10
147 Sam Ard .08 .25
148 Sam Ard's Car .02 .10
149 Mike Greenwell .08 .25
150 Checklist Card .02 .10

1992 Winner's Choice Busch Autographs

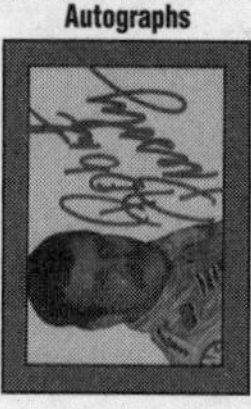

These four-cards were randomly inserted in 1992 Winner's Choice Busch foil packs. Gold borders and Gold paint pen signatures highlight the cardfronts. Reportedly, 500 of each card was autographed. The cards are unnumbered and arranged below alphabetically.

COMPLETE SET (4) 80.00 160.00
1 Chuck Bown/500 25.00 40.00
2 Ricky Craven/500 25.00 40.00
3 Robert Pressley/500 25.00 40.00
4 Kenny Wallace/500 25.00 40.00

1992 Winner's Choice Mainiac

Winner's Choice Race Cards produced this set in 1992 featuring drivers from various tracks in Maine. The cardfronts include a black and white driver photo inside a maroon colored border. The 50-cards were sold in complete set form through Winner's Choice and area tracks.

COMPLETE SET (50) 3.00 6.00
1 Cover Card .05 .15
2 Steve Reny .05 .15
3 Paul Pierce .05 .15
4 Ralph Hanson .05 .15
5 Billy Penfold .05 .15
6 Kim Gray .05 .15
7 Jimmy Burns .05 .15
8 Mary LeBlanc .05 .15
9 Doug Ripley .05 .15
10 Bob Libby .05 .15
11 Steve Chicoine .05 .15
12 Kenny Wright .05 .15
13 Mark Cyr .05 .15
14 Barry Babb .05 .15
15 David Wilcox .05 .15
16 Steve Blood .05 .15
17 Forest Peaslee .05 .15
18 Jamie Peaslee .05 .15
19 Chuck LaChance .05 .15
20 Steve Nelson .05 .15
21 Gary Smith .05 .15
22 Jerry Babb .05 .15
23 Bob Young .05 .15
24 Ray Penfold .05 .15
25 Andy Santerre .60 1.50
26 Dave McLaughlin .05 .15
27 Jon Lizotte .05 .15
28 Mike Kimball .05 .15
29 Benji Rowe .05 .15
30 John Phippen Jr. .05 .15
31 Casey Nash .05 .15
32 Joe Bowser .05 .15
33 Gene Wasson Jr. .05 .15
34 Gary Bellefleur Jr. .05 .15
35 Dick Belisle .05 .15
36 Cary Martin .05 .15
37 Lloyd Poland .05 .15
38 Moe Belanger .05 .15
39 Andy Lude .05 .15
40 Ron Benjamin .05 .15
41 Tania Schafer .05 .15
42 Bobby Babb .05 .15
43 Brad Hammond .05 .15
44 Ken Beasley .05 .15
45 Danny Grover .05 .15
46 Buster Grover .05 .15
47 Mark Billings .05 .15
48 Elaine Grover .05 .15
49 Gabe Gaboury .05 .15
50 Checklist Card .05 .15

1989 Winners Circle

One of the most sought after stock car racing sets, the 1989 Winners Circle set was primarily distributed to kids as part of a drug awareness program in North Carolina. The cards were also given out at many race tracks including the Richmond International Speedway in February, 1989. The 45 black-bordered cards feature star drivers from the early days of NASCAR. The checklist was intended to be card number 13, but is actually numbered "A." Reportedly only 150 of the 1A card of Lee Petty were produced. The set price doesn't include this card. A card album to house the set was also made available. Counterfeits have also been reported.

COMPLETE SET (45) 350.00 700.00
1A Lee Petty ERR 250.00 400.00
1B Lee Petty COR 30.00 60.00
2 Fred Lorenzen 25.00 50.00
3 Tom Pistone 10.00 20.00
4 Tiny Lund 15.00 30.00
5 Paul Goldsmith 10.00 20.00
6 Dick Hutcherson 7.50 15.00
7 Louise Smith 10.00 20.00
8 Charlie Glotzbach 7.50 15.00
9 Bob Welborn 7.50 15.00
10 Bob Flock 7.50 15.00
11 Fonty Flock 10.00 20.00
12 Tim Flock 10.00 20.00
13 Checklist 3.00 8.00
14 Ethel Mobley 10.00 20.00
15 Cotton Owens 7.50 15.00
16 David Pearson 10.00 20.00
17 Glen Wood 10.00 20.00
18 Bobby Isaac 15.00 30.00
19 Joe Lee Johnson 7.50 15.00
20 G.C. Spencer 7.50 15.00
21 Jack Smith 7.50 15.00
22 Frank Mundy 7.50 15.00
23 Bill Rexford 7.50 15.00
24 Dick Rathmann 7.50 15.00
25 Bill Blair 7.50 15.00
26 Darel Dieringer 7.50 15.00
27 Speedy Thompson 7.50 15.00
28 Donald Thomas 7.50 15.00
29 Marvin Panch 10.00 20.00
30 Buddy Shuman 7.50 15.00
31 Neil Castles 7.50 15.00
32 Buck Baker 10.00 20.00
33 Curtis Turner 10.00 20.00
34 Larry Frank 10.00 20.00
35 Lee Roy Yarborough 10.00 20.00
36 Ralph Liguori 7.50 15.00
37 Wendell Scott 15.00 30.00
38 Jim Paschal 7.50 15.00
39 Johnny Allen 10.00 20.00
40 Jimmie Lewallen 7.50 15.00
41 Maurice Petty 10.00 20.00
42 Nelson Stacy 7.50 15.00
43 Glenn Roberts(Fireball) 20.00 40.00
44 Edwin Matthews (Banjo) 7.50 15.00
45 Pete Hamilton 7.50 15.00

1995 Western Steer Earnhardt Next Generation

This 4-card set features Dale Earnhardt and three of his kids Kerry, Kelly, and Dale Jr. The cards were distributed by Western Steer and were produced using lenticular 3-D technology. There are three regular size cards and one Jumbo card. Reportedly, a total of 2500 sets were produced. There is also a black binder that was available to hold all four of the cards. The cards were available through the WSMP restaurants, Sports Image souvenir trailers and mail order.

COMPLETE SET (4) 15.00 30.00
1 D.Earnhardt 2.50 5.00
Kerry Earnhardt
2 D.Earnhardt 2.50 5.00
Kelley Earnhardt
3 D.Earnhardt 7.50 15.00
D.Earnhardt Jr.
JUM Earnhardt Family 4.00 8.00

1995 Zenith

This is the inaugural set of Pinnacle's Zenith Racing brand. The 83-card set consists of five different subsets: Hot Guns (1-33), Mean Rides (34-58), End of the Day (59-68), Joe Gibbs Racing (69-75), and Championship Quest (78-83). The product came six cards per pack, with 24 packs per box and 16 boxes per case. The suggested retail price of a pack was $3.99.

COMPLETE SET (83) 8.00 20.00
1 Rick Mast HG .10 .30
2 Rusty Wallace HG .75 2.00
3 Dale Earnhardt HG 1.50 4.00
4 Sterling Marlin HG .40 1.00
5 Hut Stricklin HG .10 .30
6 Mark Martin HG .75 2.00
7 Geoff Bodine HG .10 .30
8 Jeff Burton HG .40 1.00
9 Lake Speed HG .10 .30
10 Ricky Rudd HG .40 1.00
11 Brett Bodine HG .10 .30
12 Derrike Cope HG .10 .30
13 Jeremy Mayfield HG .25 .60
14 Joe Nemechek HG .10 .30
15 Dick Trickle HG .10 .30
16 Ted Musgrave HG .10 .30
17 Darrell Waltrip HG .25 .60
18 Bobby Labonte HG .60 1.50
19 Bobby Hillin HG .10 .30
20 Morgan Shepherd HG .10 .30
21 Kenny Wallace HG .10 .30
22 Jimmy Spencer HG .10 .30
23 Jeff Gordon HG 1.00 2.50
24 Ken Schrader HG .10 .30
25 Terry Labonte HG .40 1.00
26 Todd Bodine HG .10 .30
27 Dale Jarrett HG .60 1.50
28 Steve Grissom HG .10 .30
29 Michael Waltrip HG .25 .60
30 Bobby Hamilton HG .10 .30
31 Robert Pressley HG .10 .30
32 Ricky Craven HG .10 .30
33 John Andretti HG .10 .30
34 Rick Mast's Transporter .05 .15
35 Rusty Wallace's Transporter .40 1.00
36 Dale Earnhardt's Transporter .75 2.00
37 Sterling Marlin's Transporter .10 .30
38 Terry Labonte's Transporter .10 .30
39 Mark Martin's Transporter .40 1.00
40 Geoff Bodine's Transporter .05 .15
41 Jeremy Mayfield's Trans. .10 .30
42 Ricky Rudd's Transporter .10 .30
43 Brett Bodine's Transporter .05 .15
44 Jimmy Spencer's Transporter .05 .15
45 Dick Trickle's Transporter .05 .15
46 Ted Musgrave's Transporter .05 .15
47 Darrell Waltrip's Transporter .10 .30
48 Bobby Labonte's Transporter .25 .60
49 Morgan Shepherd's Trans. .05 .15
50 Bill Elliott's Transporter .10 .30
51 Jeff Gordon's Transporter .40 1.00
52 Robert Pressley's Transporter .05 .15
53 Dale Jarrett's Transporter .25 .60
54 Michael Waltrip's Transporter .10 .30
55 Jeff Burton's Transporter .10 .30
56 John Andretti's Transporter .05 .15
57 Kyle Petty's Transporter .10 .30
58 Bobby Hamilton's Transporter .05 .15
59 Kenny Wallace EOD .10 .30
60 John Andretti EOD .10 .30
61 Ted Musgrave EOD .10 .30
62 Jimmy Spencer EOD .10 .30
63 Bobby Labonte EOD .60 1.50
64 Jeff Gordon EOD 1.00 2.50
65 Robert Pressley EOD .10 .30
66 Bobby Hillin EOD .10 .30
67 Bobby Hamilton EOD .10 .30
68 Brett Bodine EOD .10 .30
69 Cruz Pedregon JG .10 .30
70 Cruz Pedregon JG .10 .30
71 Cory McClenathan JG .10 .30
72 Cory McClenathan JG .10 .30
73 Jim Yates JG .05 .15
74 Jim Yates JG .05 .15
75 Bobby Labonte JG .60 1.50
76 Dale Earnhardt CL .75 2.00
77 Jeff Gordon CL .50 1.25
78 Jeff Gordon CQ 1.25 3.00
79 Jeff Gordon CQ 1.25 3.00
80 Jeff Gordon CQ 1.25 3.00
81 Jeff Gordon CQ 1.25 3.00
82 Jeff Gordon CQ 1.25 3.00
83 Jeff Gordon CQ 1.25 3.00
P3 Dale Earnhardt HG Promo 5.00 12.00

1995 Zenith Helmets

The 10 cards in this set were randomly inserted in Zenith Racing at a rate of one per 72 packs. The cards feature the helmets of some of Winston Cup's top drivers captured in all-foil Dufex printing technology.

COMPLETE SET (10) 50.00 120.00
1 Dale Earnhardt 12.00 30.00
2 Rusty Wallace 6.00 15.00
3 Jeff Gordon 8.00 20.00
4 Mark Martin 6.00 15.00
5 Bill Elliott 3.00 8.00
6 Bobby Labonte 5.00 12.00
7 Sterling Marlin 3.00 8.00
8 Ted Musgrave 1.00 2.50
9 Terry Labonte 3.00 8.00
10 Ricky Rudd 3.00 8.00
P8 Ted Musgrave Promo 1.50 4.00

1995 Zenith Tribute

This two-card insert set pays tribute to racing superstars: Dale Earnhardt and Jeff Gordon. The cards were inserted at a rate of one per 120 packs. The cards use all-foil Dufex printing technology to picture these two racing greats.

1 Dale Earnhardt 8.00 20.00
2 Jeff Gordon 8.00 20.00

1995 Zenith Winston Winners

This 25-card set is a retrospective look at the winners of the first 25 Winston Cup races of the 1995 season. The cards feature all-gold foil card stock and could be found at a rate of one in six packs of Zenith Racing.

COMPLETE SET (25) 25.00 60.00
1 Sterling Marlin 1.50 4.00
2 Jeff Gordon 4.00 10.00
3 Terry Labonte 1.50 4.00
4 Jeff Gordon 4.00 10.00
Evernham
5 Sterling Marlin 1.50 4.00
6 Jeff Gordon 4.00 10.00
7 Dale Earnhardt 6.00 15.00
8 Rusty Wallace 3.00 8.00
9 Mark Martin 3.00 8.00
10 Dale Earnhardt 6.00 15.00
T.Earnhardt
11 Bobby Labonte 2.50 6.00
12 Kyle Petty 1.00 2.50
13 Terry Labonte 1.50 4.00
14 Bobby Labonte 2.50 6.00
15 Jeff Gordon 4.00 10.00
16 Jeff Gordon 4.00 10.00
17 Dale Jarrett 2.50 6.00
18 Sterling Marlin 1.50 4.00
19 Dale Earnhardt 6.00 15.00
20 Mark Martin 3.00 8.00
21 Bobby Labonte 2.50 6.00
22 Terry Labonte 1.50 4.00
23 Jeff Gordon 4.00 10.00
24 Dale Earnhardt 6.00 15.00
25 Jeff Gordon 4.00 10.00

1995 Zenith Z-Team

This 12 card set features the top Winston Cup drivers. The full body driver's photo is located on a Z-Team pedestal with a prismatic and metallic background that contains various colors. The Z-Team cards were inserted at a rate of one per 48 packs in Zenith Racing.

COMPLETE SET (12) 75.00 150.00
1 Dale Earnhardt 15.00 40.00
2 Jeff Gordon 10.00 25.00
3 Bobby Labonte 6.00 15.00
4 Terry Labonte 4.00 10.00
5 Sterling Marlin 4.00 10.00
6 Ken Schrader 1.25 3.00
7 Michael Waltrip 2.50 6.00
8 Ricky Rudd 4.00 10.00
9 Ted Musgrave 1.25 3.00
10 Morgan Shepherd 1.25 3.00
11 Rusty Wallace 8.00 20.00
12 Mark Martin 8.00 20.00

1996 Zenith

This 100-card set is the second issue of the Zenith brand by Pinnacle. The set is made up of 10 different subsets and includes the top drivers for NASCAR racing. Topical subsets include Road Pilots (1-34), Heavenly View (35-49), Sunrise (50-64), Black by Design (65-68), Tribute (69,70), Rookie of the Year (71,72), Championship Style (73-80), Trilogy (81-85), Robert Yates Racing (86-90), and Winners (91-98). A Dale Earnhardt commemorative card was inserted at the rate of 1:6025 with each being hand serial numbered of 94. The cards were packaged six cards per pack, 24 packs per box and 16 boxes per case. Suggested retail price for a pack was $3.99.

COMPLETE SET (100) 15.00 40.00
1 Dale Earnhardt 2.00 5.00
2 Jeff Gordon 1.25 3.00
3 Sterling Marlin .40 1.00
4 Terry Labonte .40 1.00
5 Ricky Rudd .40 1.00
6 Mark Martin 1.00 2.50
7 Bill Elliott .50 1.25
8 Ernie Irvan .25 .60
9 Rusty Wallace 1.00 2.50
10 Dale Jarrett .75 2.00
11 Geoff Bodine .10 .30
12 Derrike Cope .10 .30
13 Michael Waltrip .25 .60
14 Brett Bodine .10 .30
15 Ted Musgrave .10 .30
16 Hut Stricklin .10 .30
17 Rick Mast .10 .30
18 Darrell Waltrip .25 .60
19 Bobby Labonte .75 2.00
20 Jeff Burton .25 .60
21 Jeremy Mayfield .25 .60
22 Ken Schrader .10 .30
23 Johnny Benson .25 .60
24 Lake Speed .10 .30
25 John Andretti .10 .30
26 Robert Pressley .10 .30
27 Kyle Petty .25 .60
28 Ricky Craven .25 .60
29 Bobby Hamilton .10 .30
30 Joe Nemechek .10 .30
31 Morgan Shepherd .10 .30
32 Bobby Hillin .10 .30
33 Jimmy Spencer .10 .30
34 Ward Burton .25 .60
35 Dale Earnhardt's Car HV .75 2.00
36 Jeff Gordon's Car HV .50 1.25
37 Sterling Marlin's Car HV .10 .30
38 Mark Martin's Car HV .40 1.00
39 Terry Labonte's Car HV .25 .60
40 Bobby Labonte's Car HV .25 .60
41 Darrell Waltrip's Car HV .10 .30
42 Ernie Irvan's Car HV .10 .30
43 Dale Jarrett's Car HV .25 .60
44 Bobby Hamilton's Car HV .05 .15
45 Bill Elliott's Car HV .25 .60
46 Joe Nemechek's Car HV .05 .15
47 Ted Musgrave's Car HV .05 .15
48 Kyle Petty's Car HV .10 .30
49 Michael Waltrip's Car HV .10 .30
50 Dale Earnhardt S 1.00 2.50
51 Jeff Gordon S .60 1.50
52 Mark Martin S .50 1.25
53 Ricky Rudd S .25 .60
54 Terry Labonte S .25 .60
55 Kyle Petty S .10 .30
56 Bobby Hillin S .05 .15
57 Ted Musgrave S .05 .15
58 Ken Schrader S .05 .15
59 John Andretti S .05 .15
60 Dale Jarrett S .40 1.00
61 Johnny Benson S .10 .30
62 Michael Waltrip S .25 .60
63 Bobby Labonte S .40 1.00
64 Ernie Irvan S .10 .30
65 Dale Earnhardt BD 1.00 2.50
66 Dale Earnhardt BD 1.00 2.50
67 Dale Earnhardt BD 1.00 2.50
68 Dale Earnhardt BD 1.00 2.50
69 Dale Earnhardt T 1.00 2.50
70 Terry Labonte T .25 .60
71 Ricky Craven ROY .05 .15
72 Ricky Craven ROY .05 .15
73 Jeff Gordon CS .50 1.25
74 Jeff Gordon CS .50 1.25
75 Jeff Gordon CS .50 1.25
76 Jeff Gordon CS .50 1.25
77 Jeff Gordon CS .50 1.25
78 Jeff Gordon CS .50 1.25
79 Jeff Gordon CS .50 1.25
80 Jeff Gordon CS .50 1.25
81 Kenny Wallace TRI .05 .15
82 Kenny Wallace TRI .05 .15
83 Kenny Wallace TRI .05 .15
84 Kenny Wallace TRI .05 .15
85 Kenny Wallace TRI .05 .15
86 Robert Yates RYR .05 .15
87 Ernie Irvan RYR .10 .30
88 Larry McReynolds RYR .05 .15
89 Dale Jarrett RYR .40 1.00
90 Todd Parrott RYR .05 .15
91 Jeff Gordon W .60 1.50
92 Jeff Gordon W .60 1.50
93 Terry Labonte W .25 .60
94 Rusty Wallace W .50 1.25
95 Sterling Marlin W .25 .60
96 Rusty Wallace W .50 1.25
97 Dale Jarrett W .40 1.00
98 Jeff Gordon .60 1.50
Brooke W
99 Jeff Gordon CL .50 1.25
100 Bill Elliott CL .25 .60
WC1 Dale Earnhardt 7W/94 150.00 300.00

1996 Zenith Artist Proofs

COMPLETE SET (100) 300.00 600.00
*ARTIST PROOFS: 4X TO 10X BASE CARD HI

1996 Zenith Champion Salute

This 26-card insert set pays tribute to the past 25 years of NASCAR Winston Cup racing. Each card features a photo of the drivers championship ring. The rings include a real diamond chip mounted on the surface of the card. The cards were randomly inserted 1:90.

COMPLETE SET (26) 300.00 600.00
1 Jeff Gordon 15.00 40.00
2 Dale Earnhardt 25.00 60.00
3 Dale Earnhardt 25.00 60.00
4 Alan Kulwicki 3.00 8.00
5 Dale Earnhardt 25.00 60.00
6 Dale Earnhardt 25.00 60.00
7 Rusty Wallace 12.50 30.00
8 Bill Elliott 6.00 15.00
9 Dale Earnhardt 25.00 60.00
10 Dale Earnhardt 25.00 60.00
11 Darrell Waltrip 3.00 8.00
12 Terry Labonte 5.00 12.00
13 Bobby Allison 1.50 4.00
14 Darrell Waltrip 3.00 8.00
15 Darrell Waltrip 3.00 8.00
16 Dale Earnhardt 25.00 60.00
17 Richard Petty 3.00 8.00
18 Cale Yarborough 1.50 4.00
19 Cale Yarborough 1.50 4.00
20 Cale Yarborough 1.50 4.00
21 Richard Petty 3.00 8.00
22 Richard Petty 3.00 8.00
23 Benny Parsons 1.50 4.00
24 Richard Petty 3.00 8.00
25 Richard Petty 3.00 8.00
26 Richard Childress 1.50 4.00
P12 Bobby Allison Promo 2.00 5.00

1996 Zenith Highlights

This 15-card insert set features top drivers in Winston Cup racing. The cards are die-cut, foil stamped and randomly seeded 1:11 packs.

COMPLETE SET (15) 30.00 80.00
1 Dale Earnhardt 8.00 20.00
2 Jeff Gordon 5.00 12.00
3 Sterling Marlin 1.50 4.00
4 Mark Martin 4.00 10.00
5 Ricky Rudd 1.50 4.00
6 Darrell Waltrip 1.00 2.50
7 Geoff Bodine .50 1.25
8 Bobby Labonte 3.00 8.00
9 Terry Labonte 1.50 4.00
10 Michael Waltrip 1.00 2.50
11 Ken Schrader .50 1.25
12 Jimmy Spencer .50 1.25
13 Kyle Petty 1.00 2.50
14 Ernie Irvan 1.00 2.50
15 Bill Elliott 2.00 5.00

1986 Ace Drag

This set was made in West Germany for the British company Ace. The cards are actually part of a Trump card game featuring drag racing photos on the cardfront with a playing card back and rounded corners. The playing card deck contains 32-cards with one cover/rule card. Drivers are not specifically indentified on the cards, but are included below as noted.

COMPLETE SET (33) 4.00 10.00
A1 Funny Car .10 .30
A2 Funny Car .10 .30
A3 Funny Car .10 .30
A4 Funny Car .20 .50
B1 Stock Car .20 .50
B2 Stock Car .20 .50
B3 Stock Car .10 .30
B4 GT Dragster .20 .50
C1 Sling Shot .10 .30
C2 Sling Shot .10 .30
C3 Sling Shot .10 .30
C4 Sling Shot .10 .30
D1 Top Alcohol .10 .30
D2 Top Alcohol .10 .30
D3 Top Alcohol .10 .30
D4 Top Alcohol .20 .50
E1 Sportsman Pro .10 .30
E2 Sportsman Pro .10 .30
E3 Sportsman Pro .10 .30
E4 Sportsman Pro .10 .30
F1 Top Fuel Funny Car .10 .30
F2 Top Fuel Funny Car .20 .50
F3 Top Fuel Funny Car .10 .30
F4 Top Fuel Funny Car .10 .30
G1 Dragster Truck .10 .30
G2 Dragster Truck .10 .30
G3 Dragster Truck .10 .30
G4 Dragster Truck .10 .30
H1 Dragster Truck .10 .30
H2 Dragster Truck .10 .30
H3 Dragster Truck .10 .30
H4 Dragster Truck .10 .30
NNO Cover Card .10 .30

1994 Action Packed NHRA

Action Packed expanded their auto racing card line in 1994 with their first set featuring popular drivers of NHRA. The card fronts feature a ghosted white background with gold lettering for the driver's name. Packaging included 6-card packs and 24-pack boxes with popular driver's photos on the wrapper fronts. 24Kt. Gold insert cards were randomly distributed in packs.

COMPLETE SET (42) 7.50 20.00
COMP.FACT.SET (42) 7.50 20.00
1 Eddie Hill .60 1.50
2 Scott Kalitta .30 .75
3 Kenny Bernstein .60 1.50
4 Mike Dunn .20 .50
5 Rance McDaniel .20 .50
6 Cory McClenathan .30 .75
7 Joe Amato .30 .75
8 Ed McCulloch .20 .50
9 Doug Herbert .20 .50
10 Tommy Johnson Jr. .20 .50
11 Eddie Hill's Car .30 .75
12 Scott Kalitta's Car .10 .30
13 Kenny Bernstein's Car .30 .75
14 Mike Dunn's Car .10 .30
15 Rance McDaniel's Car .10 .30
16 Cory McClenathan's Car .10 .30
17 Joe Amato's Car .10 .30
18 Ed McCulloch's Car .10 .30
19 Doug Herbert's Car .10 .30
20 Tommy Johnson Jr.'s Car .10 .30
21 John Force 1.50 3.00
22 Chuck Etchells .20 .50
23 Cruz Pedregon .30 .75
24 Al Hofmann .20 .50
25 Tom Hoover .20 .50
26 Warren Johnson .20 .50
27 Kurt Johnson .20 .50
28 Scott Geoffrion .20 .50
29 Larry Morgan .20 .50
30 Mark Pawuk .20 .50
31 Tom McEwen .20 .50
32 Shirley Muldowney .60 1.50
33 Darrell Gwynn .20 .50
34 Don Garlits .60 1.50
35 Bob Glidden's Car .10 .30
36 Don Prudhomme .60 1.50
37 Cory McClenathan's Car .10 .30
38 Pat Austin's Car .10 .30
39 John Force's Car .75 2.00

40 Jim Epler's Car .10 .30
41 Warren Johnson's Car .10 .30
42 Warren Johnson's Car .10 .30
DR1 Eddie Hill Promo 1.50 4.00

1994 Action Packed NHRA 24K Gold

Randomly inserted in 1994 Action Packed Drag racing packs, each card includes the now standard 24Kt. Gold logo on the card front. These Gold cards are essentially parallel versions of the corresponding driver's regular issue. Wrapper stated odds for pulling a 24K Gold card are 1:96.

COMPLETE SET (6) 100.00 200.00
31G Tom McEwen 12.00 30.00
32G Shirley Muldowney 12.00 30.00
33G Darrell Gwynn 8.00 20.00
34G Don Garlits 25.00 50.00
35G Bob Glidden Car 10.00 25.00
36G Don Prudhomme 15.00 40.00

1994 Action Packed Winston Drag Racing 24K Gold

This three-card set was produced by Action Packed and distributed through the Winston Cup Catalog and by Action Packed dealers. The cards were printed using Action Packed's 24K Gold process and feature NHRA stars John Force, Eddie Hill, and Warren Johnson.

COMPLETE SET (3) 12.00 30.00
1 John Force 6.00 15.00
2 Eddie Hill 4.00 10.00
3 Warren Johnson 3.00 8.00

1995 Action Packed NHRA

The 1995 Action Packed NHRA set was one of the first racing sets to be released after Action Packed became a Pinnacle brand. The set focuses on the top stars of NHRA with subsets on three of the more popular drivers: Joe Amato, Kenny Bernstein, and John Force. The standard packaging of 6-cards per pack and 24-packs per box was used with a four-tier insert card program: Silver Streak parallel, Autographs, Junior Dragster Champs, and 24K Gold.

COMPLETE SET (42) 6.00 15.00
1 Scott Kalitta's Car .15 .40
2 Larry Dixon's Car .15 .40
3 Cory McClenathan's Car .20 .50
4 Connie Kalitta's Car .20 .50
5 Joe Amato's Car .15 .40
6 Kenny Bernstein's Car .30 .75
7 Mike Dunn's Car .15 .40
8 Pat Austin's Car .15 .40
9 Tommy Johnson Jr.'s Car .15 .40
10 Shelly Anderson's Car .15 .40
11 John Force's Car .40 1.00
12 Cruz Pedregon's Car .20 .50
13 Al Hofmann's Car .15 .40
14 Chuck Etchells's Car .15 .40
15 K.C. Spurlock's Car .15 .40
16 Gordie Bonin's Car .15 .40
17 Jim Epler's Car .15 .40
18 Dean Skuza's Car .15 .40
19 Gary Bolger's Car .15 .40
20 Kenji Okazaki's Car .15 .40
21 Darrell Alderman's Car .15 .40
22 Scott Geoffrion's Car .15 .40
23 Warren Johnson's Car .15 .40
24 Jim Yates' Car .15 .40
25 Kurt Johnson's Car .15 .40
26 Joe Amato .30 .75
27 Joe Amato's Car .20 .50
28 Joe Amato's Car .20 .50
29 Joe Amato .30 .75
30 Kenny Bernstein .40 1.00
31 Kenny Bernstein's Car .30 .75
32 Kenny Bernstein's Car .30 .75
33 Kenny Bernstein's Car .30 .75
34 Kenny Bernstein's Car .30 .75
35 Kenny Bernstein's Car .30 .75
36 John Force 1.00 2.50
37 John Force's Car .40 1.00
38 John Force's Car .40 1.00
39 John Force's Car .40 1.00
40 John Force's Car .40 1.00
41 Eddie Hill .40 1.00
42 Joe Gibbs .30 .75
P11 John Force's Car Prototype 2.00 5.00

1995 Action Packed NHRA Silver Streak

COMPLETE SET (42) 40.00 80.00
*SINGLES: 2X TO 5X BASE CARDS

1995 Action Packed NHRA Autographs

This 16-card insert set features the top drivers in the NHRA signatures. Each card is hand numbered of 500. The Kenny Bernstein and John Force cards were numbered of 125. The cards were available one per 24 packs.

COMPLETE SET (16) 300.00 600.00
1 Scott Kalitta/500 25.00 50.00
2 Larry Dixon/500 10.00 25.00
3 Cory McClenathan/500 12.00 30.00
6 K.Bernstein/125 90.00 150.00
7 Mike Dunn/500 10.00 25.00
9 Tommy Johnson/500 10.00 25.00
10 Shelly Anderson/500 10.00 25.00
11 John Force/125 100.00 175.00
12 Cruz Pedregon/500 15.00 40.00
13 Al Hofmann/500 10.00 25.00
21 Darrell Alderman/500 10.00 25.00
22 Scott Geoffrion/500 10.00 25.00
23 Warren Johnson/500 10.00 25.00
24 Jim Yates/500 10.00 25.00
25 Kurt Johnson/500 10.00 25.00
41 Eddie Hill/500 15.00 40.00

1995 Action Packed NHRA 24K Gold

Randomly inserted in 1995 Action Packed NHRA packs, each card includes the standard 24Kt. Gold logo on the card front. These Gold cards are essentially parallel versions of the Kenny Bernstein and John Force subset cards. Wrapper stated odds for pulling a 24K Gold card are 1:96.

COMPLETE SET (11) 125.00 250.00
30 Kenny Bernstein 10.00 25.00
31 Kenny Bernstein 10.00 25.00
32 Kenny Bernstein 10.00 25.00
33 Kenny Bernstein 10.00 25.00
34 Kenny Bernstein 10.00 25.00
35 Kenny Bernstein 10.00 25.00
36 John Force 15.00 40.00
37 John Force 15.00 40.00
38 John Force 15.00 40.00
39 John Force 15.00 40.00
40 John Force 15.00 40.00

1995 Action Packed NHRA Jr. Dragster Champs

Randomly inserted in 1995 Action Packed NHRA packs, this set provides a preview of future NHRA hopefuls -- Junior National Championship winners. Cards were packed approximately one per 48 foil packs.

COMPLETE SET (8) 20.00 40.00
1 Richard Thompson 3.00 6.00
2 Chris Bear 3.00 6.00
3 Richard Coury Jr. 3.00 6.00
4 Jamie Lynn Innes 3.00 6.00
5 James Antonnette 3.00 6.00
6 Barrie Wagers 3.00 6.00
7 Michelle Banach 3.00 6.00
8 Mark Lowry 3.00 6.00

1993 Advanced Images Quick Eight Racing

This set was produced by Advanced Images and licensed through the Quick Eight Racing Association. Each card features a driver's car image with a black border on the front. The cardbacks include a checkered flag border with detailed driver information.

COMPLETE SET (25) 5.00 12.00
1 Ken Regenthal's Car .30 .75
2 Rick Moore's Car .30 .75
3 James Smith Jr.'s Car .30 .75
4 Mike Elliott's Car .30 .75
5 Ken Regenthal's Car .30 .75
6 Dale Brinsfield's Car .30 .75
7 Paul Dunlap's Car .30 .75
8 Steve Sechler's Car .30 .75
9 Dennis Houck's Car .30 .75
10 Tom Stewart's Car .30 .75
11 Barry Blackwell's Car .30 .75
12 Dallas Cornelius's Car .30 .75
13 Danny Crouse's Car .30 .75
14 Charles Harris's Car .30 .75
15 John McClain's Car .30 .75
16 Don Plemmons's Car .30 .75
17 Sonny Tindall's Car .30 .75
18 Sam Snyder's Car .30 .75
19 Kenneth Tripp's Car .30 .75
20 Jerry Williams's Car .30 .75
21 Herb Atkins's Car .30 .75
22 Buzz Varner's Car .30 .75
23 Gary McKee's Car .30 .75
24 Rex Michael Shelton's Car .30 .75
25 Kenny Farrell's Car .30 .75

1990 Big Time Drag

This 21-card set features some of drag racings most popular cars. There is everything from Tom Hoover's Showtime Funny Car to Roger Gustin's Jet Funny Car. There were 1,500 sets produced. The cards are listed below in alphabetical order

COMPLETE SET (21) 12.00 30.00
1 Bob Bealieu .60 1.50
2 Charles Carpenter's Car .60 1.50
3 Jim Druer .60 1.50
4 Artie Farmer .60 1.50
5 Gordy Foust's Car .60 1.50
6 Roger Gustin's Car .60 1.50
7 Al Hanna's Car .60 1.50
8 Tom Hoover's Car .80 2.00
9 Tom Jacobson's Car .60 1.50
10 Donnie Little .60 1.50
11 Jeff Littleton's Car .60 1.50
12 Jerry Moreland's Car .60 1.50
13 Rocky Pirrone .60 1.50
14 Dick Rosberg .60 1.50
15 Lou Sattelmaier's Car .60 1.50
16 Paul Strommen's Car .60 1.50
17 Ken Thurm's Car .60 1.50
18 William Townes .60 1.50
19 Roy Trevino's Car .60 1.50
20 Bob Vandergriff .60 1.50
21 Norm Wizner's Car .60 1.50

1990 Big Time Drag Stickers

This 21-card sticker set is a parallel to the 1990 Big Time Drag set. The same photos were used in each set. There were 500 sticker sets produced.

COMPLETE SET (21) 40.00 75.00
1 Bob Bealieu 1.50 4.00
2 Charles Carpenter's Car 1.50 4.00
3 Jim Druer 1.50 4.00
4 Artie Farmer 1.50 4.00
5 Gordy Foust's Car 1.50 4.00
6 Roger Gustin's Car 1.50 4.00
7 Al Hanna's Car 1.50 4.00
8 Tom Hoover's Car 2.00 5.00
9 Tom Jacobson's Car 1.50 4.00
10 Donnie Little 1.50 4.00
11 Jeff Littleton's Car 1.50 4.00
12 Jerry Moreland's Car 1.50 4.00
13 Rocky Pirrone 1.50 4.00
14 Dick Rosberg 1.50 4.00
15 Lou Sattelmaier's Car 1.50 4.00
16 Paul Strommen's Car 1.50 4.00
17 Ken Thurm's Car 1.50 4.00
18 William Townes 1.50 4.00
19 Roy Trevino's Car 1.50 4.00
20 Bob Vandergriff 1.50 4.00
21 Norm Wizner's Car 1.50 4.00

1991 Big Time Drag

Big Time Drag Cards, Inc. of Roseville, Michigan produced this 96-card set in complete factory set form. The first 24-cards highlight the careers of Don Garlits and Norm Day. The final card is an unnumbered cover card.

COMPLETE SET (96) 12.50 25.00
1 Don Garlits w Car .50 1.25
2 Don Garlits w Car .50 1.25
3 Don Garlits' Car .50 1.25
4 Don Garlits' Car .50 1.25
5 Don Garlits' Car .50 1.25
6 Don Garlits' Car .50 1.25
7 Don Garlits' Car .50 1.25
8 Don Garlits' Car .50 1.25
9 Don Garlits' Car .50 1.25
10 Don Garlits' Car .50 1.25
11 Don Garlits' Car .50 1.25
12 Don Garlits' Car .50 1.25
13 Norm Day Cover Card .02 .20
14 Norm Day's Car .10 .30
15 Norm Day's Car .10 .30
16 Norm Day's Car .10 .30
17 Norm Day's Car .10 .30
18 Norm Day .20 .50
19 Norm Day's Car .10 .30
20 Norm Day W Crew .20 .50
21 Don Garlits' Car .50 1.25
22 Norm Day's Car .10 .30
23 Norm Day's Car .10 .30
24 Norm Day's Car .10 .30
25 Tom Hoover's Car .20 .50
26 Jerry Caminito's Car .10 .30
27 Wyatt Radke's Car .10 .30
28 Cruz Pedregon's Car .20 .50
29 Wayne Torkelson's Car .10 .30
30 Whit Bazemore's Car .10 .30
31 Bruce Larson's Car .10 .30
32 Joe Amato's Car .50 1.25
33 Bunny Burkett .10 .30
34 Joe Amato's Car .50 1.25
35 Della Woods w Car .10 .30
36 Della Woods' Car .10 .30
37 Al Dapozzo's Car .10 .30
38 Richard Hartman's Car .10 .30
39 Richard Hartman .10 .30
40 Bruce Larson's Car .10 .30
41 Bob Vanscriver's Car .10 .30
42 Jerry Caminito Wyatt Radke Cars .10 .30
43 Wayne Bailey's Car .10 .30
44 T.Hoover B.Larson Cars .20 .50
45 Jim Feurer's Car .10 .30
46 Jim Feurer's Car .10 .30
47 Blake Wiggins' Car .10 .30
48 Randy Moore .10 .30
49 Randy Moore's Car .10 .30
50 Carolyn Melendy's Car .10 .30
51 Sonny Leonard's Motor .02 .20
52 Wally Bell's Car .10 .30
53 Gary Grahner's Car .10 .30
54 Bill Kuhlmann's Car .10 .30
55 Tom Jacobson's Car .10 .30
56 Ken Thurm's Car .10 .30
57 Al Hanna's Car .10 .30
58 Donnie Little's Car .10 .30
59 Lou Sattelmaier's Car .10 .30
60 Gordy Foust's Car .10 .30
61 Charles Carpenter's Car .10 .30
62 Tom Hoover's Car .20 .50
63 Roy Trevino's Car .10 .30
64 Jim Feurer w Car .10 .30
65 Paul Strommen's Car .10 .30
66 Roger Gustin's Car .10 .30
67 Jack Joyce's Car .10 .30
68 Jerry Moreland's Car .10 .30
69 Jeff Littleton's Car .10 .30
70 Norm Wizner's Car .10 .30
71 Kenneth Tripp Jr.'s Car .10 .30
72 Tim McAmis' Car .10 .30
73 Tom McEwen's Car .20 .50
74 Tom McEwen's Car .20 .50
75 Tom Hoover's Car .20 .50
76 Ken Karsten Jr.'s Car .10 .30
77 Johnny West's Car .10 .30
78 Brian Gahm's Car .10 .30
79 Wally Bell's Car .10 .30
80 Roger Gustin's Car .10 .30
81 Bob Bunker's Car .10 .30
82 Terry Leggett's Car .10 .30
83 Mike Ashley's Car .10 .30
84 Al Hanna's Car .10 .30
85 Whit Bazemore's Car .10 .30
86 Wally Bell's Car .10 .30
87 Aggi Hendriks' Car .10 .30
88 Bruce Larson's Car .10 .30
89 Darrell Amberson's Car .10 .30
90 Bob Vanscriver's Car .10 .30
91 John H. Rocca's Car .10 .30
92 Wayne Bailey .10 .30
93 K.S. Pittman's Car .10 .30
94 Jack Ostrander's Car .10 .30
95 Bob Vandergriff's Car .10 .30
NNO Cover Card .02 .20

1994 Card Dynamics Joe Amato

This three-card set features the five-time Winston Top Fuel Champion. The cards are made of polished aluminum and come in a display box. There were 10,000 sets made. Each set comes with a certificate of authenticity.

COMPLETE SET (3) 5.00 12.00
COMMON CARD 2.00 5.00

1994 Card Dynamics Kenny Bernstein

This three-card set features the "King of Speed." The cards are made of polished aluminum and come in a display box. There were 10,000 sets made. Each set comes with a certificate of authenticity.

COMPLETE SET (3) 5.00 12.00
COMMON CARD 2.00 5.00

1994 Card Dynamics Eddie Hill

This three-card set features the 1994 Winston Top Fuel Champion. The cards are made of polished aluminum and come in a display box. There were 10,000 sets made. Each set comes with a certificate of authenticity.

COMPLETE SET (3) 5.00 12.00
COMMON CARD 2.00 5.00

1994 Card Dynamics Don Prudhomme

This three-card set features drag racing legend Don "The Snake" Prudhomme. The cards are made of polished aluminum and come in a display box. There were 10,000 sets made. Each set comes with a certificate of authenticity.

COMPLETE SET (3) 5.00 12.00
COMMON CARD 2.00 5.00

1989 Checkered Flag IHRA

Checkered Flag Inc. produced sets in 1989 and 1990 featuring drivers and cars of the International Hot Rod Association. The cards were sold in complete factory set form. The 1989 set features black borders and horizontally oriented car cards with a few individual driver cars. The final card, number 100, is a checklist.

COMPLETE SET (100) 15.00 25.00
1 Richard Holcomb's Car .10 .30
2 Richard Holcomb's Car .10 .30
3 Usif Lawson's Car .10 .30
4 Scott Weis' Car .10 .30
5 Butch Kemodle's Car .10 .30
6 Paul Hall's Car .10 .30
7 Bogie Kell's Car .10 .30
8 Kurt Neighbor's Car .10 .30
9 Gary Rettell's Car .10 .30
10 Steve Litton's Car .10 .30
11 Melinda Green's Car .10 .30
12 Don DeFluiter's Car .10 .30
13 Mark Thomas' Car .10 .30
14 Gary Rettell's Car .10 .30
15 Bob Gilbertson's Car .10 .30
16 Greg Moss .20 .50
17 Dan Nimmo's Car .10 .30
18 Phil Sebring's Car .10 .30
19 Dennis Ramey .20 .50
20 Dennis Ramey's Car .10 .30
21 Ted Osborne's Car .10 .30
22 Mark Osborne's Car .10 .30
23 Garley Daniels' Car .10 .30
24 Danny Estep's Car .10 .30
25 Tim Freeman's Car .10 .30
26 George Supinski's Car .10 .30
27 Dave Northrop's Car .10 .30
28 Jerry Taylor's Car .10 .30
29 Mike Davis' Car .10 .30
30 Jim Yates' Car .10 .30
31 Harold Denton .20 .50
32 Harold Denton's Car .10 .30
33 Ed Dixon's Car .10 .30
34 Ed Dixon .20 .50
35 Terry Adams .20 .50
36 Terry Adams' Car .10 .30
37 Harold Robinson's Car .10 .30
38 Larry Morgan's Car .10 .30
39 Tim Nabors' Car .10 .30
40 Steve Schmidt's Car .10 .30
41 Neil Moyer's Car .10 .30
42 Joe Sway's Car .10 .30
43 John Nobile's Car .10 .30
44 John Nobile's Car .10 .30
45 Shirl Greer's Car .10 .30
46 Shirl Greer's Car .10 .30
47 Dave Miller's Car .10 .30
48 Dave Miller's Car .10 .30
49 Billy Ewing's Car .10 .30
50 Clay Broadwater's Car .10 .30
51 Gary Litton's Car .10 .30
52 Keith Jackson's Car .10 .30
53 Whit Bazemore .20 .50
54 Craig Cain's Car .10 .30
55 Esua Speed's Car .10 .30
56 Ed Hoover's Car .10 .30
57 Ed Hoover's Car .10 .30
58 Kenneth Tripp Jr.'s Car .10 .30
59 Kenneth Tripp Sr.'s Car .10 .30
60 Billy DeWitt's Car .10 .30
61 Billy DeWitt .20 .50
62 Scotty Cannon's Car .10 .30
63 Scotty Cannon .20 .50
64 Michael Martin .20 .50
65 Michael Martin's Car .10 .30
66 Gordy Hmiel's Car .10 .30
67 Gordy Hmiel's Car .10 .30
68 Sam Snyder's Car .10 .30
69 Terry Housley's Car .10 .30
70 Jim Ray's Car .10 .30
71 John Ieppert's Car .10 .30
72 Frankie Foster's Car .10 .30
73 Buddy McGowan's Car .10 .30
74 Brian Gahm's Car .10 .30
75 Bob Dickson's Car .10 .30
76 Walter Henry's Car .10 .30
77 Gene Fryer's Car .10 .30
78 Terry Leggett's Car .10 .30
79 Blake Wiggins' Car .10 .30
80 Tim Nabors' Car .10 .30
81 Ernest Wrenn's Car .10 .30
82 Donnie Little's Car .10 .30
83 Mike Ashley's Car .10 .30
84 Ron Miller's Car .10 .30
85 Danny Bastianelli's Car .10 .30
86 Tracy Eddins' Car .10 .30
87 Kurt Neighbor's Car .10 .30
88 Greg Moss' Car .10 .30
89 Greg Moss' Car .10 .30
90 Bogie Kell's Car .10 .30
91 Jerry Gulley's Car .10 .30
92 Ernest Wrenn's Car .10 .30
93 Don DeFluiter .20 .50
94 Blake Wiggins .20 .50
95 Barry Shirley's Car .10 .30
96 Ken Regenthal's Car UER .10 .30
97 Donnie Little's Car .10 .30
98 Rick Hord's Car .10 .30
99 Ricky Bowie's Car .10 .30
100 Checklist Card .10 .30

1990 Checkered Flag IHRA

Checkered Flag Race Cards Inc. produced sets in 1989 and 1990 featuring drivers and cars of the International Hot Rod Association. The cards were sold in complete factory set form. The 1990 set features white borders and horizontally oriented car cards. The final card, #100, is a checklist. An unnumbered cover card was produced as well featuring an order form to purchase additional sets at $17.50 each.

COMPLETE SET (101) 8.00 16.00
1 Mike Ashley's Car .07 .20
2 Ronnie Sox's Car .20 .50
3 Scotty Cannon's Car .20 .50
4 Jeff Littleton's Car .07 .20
5 Gordy Foust's Car .07 .20
6 Donnie Little's Car .07 .20
7 Bob Vandergriff's Car .07 .20
8 Terry Leggett's Car .07 .20
9 Ken Regenthal's Car .20 .50
10 Ed Hoover's Car .07 .20
11 Stanley Barker's Car .07 .20
12 Tim McAmis' Car .07 .20
13 Sam Snyder's Car .07 .20
14 Brian Gahm's Car .07 .20
15 Blake Wiggins' Car .07 .20
16 Ken Karsten Jr.'s Car .07 .20
17 Eddie Harris' Car .07 .20
18 Carolyn Melendy's Car .07 .20
19 Stuart Norman's Car .07 .20
20 Terry Leggett's Car .07 .20
21 Ron Iannotti's Car .07 .20
22 Michael Martin's Car .07 .20
23 Jeff Ensslin's Car .07 .20
24 Tim McAmis' Car .07 .20
25 Al Billes' Car .07 .20
26 Gordy Hmiel's Car .07 .20
27 Manny DeJesus' Car .07 .20
28 Brian Gahm's Car .07 .20
29 Ray Ervin's Car .07 .20
30 Wally Stroupe's Car .07 .20
31 Chuck VanVallis' Car .07 .20
32 Ken Karsten Jr.'s Car .07 .20
33 Ed Hoover's Car .07 .20
34 Ronnie Sox w Car .25 .60
35 Scotty Cannon's Car .20 .50
36 Bob Vandergriff's Car .07 .20
37 Mike Ashley's Car .07 .20
38 Gordy Foust's Car .07 .20
39 Blake Wiggins' Car .07 .20
40 Ken Regenthal's Car .07 .20
41 Tracy Eddins' Car .07 .20
42 Steve Litton's Car .07 .20
43 Mark Thomas' Car .07 .20
44 Johnny West's Car .07 .20
45 Jerry Gulley's Car .07 .20
46 Bob Gilbertson's Car .07 .20
47 Dan Nimmo's Car .07 .20
48 Ronnie Midyette's Car .07 .20
49 Phil Sebring's Car .07 .20
50 Art Hendey's Car .07 .20
51 Bogie Kell's Car .07 .20
52 Greg Moss' Car .07 .20
53 Gary Litton's Car .07 .20
54 Ricky Bowie's Car .07 .20
55 Frank Kramberger's Car .07 .20
56 Keith Jackson's Car .07 .20
57 Clay Broadwater's Car .07 .20
58 Tommy Mauney's Car .07 .20
59 Ed Dixon's Car .07 .20
60 David Drongowski's Car .07 .20
61 Carlton Phillips' Car .07 .20
62 Harold Denton's Car .07 .20
63 Charlie Garrett's Car .07 .20
64 Joe Sway's Car .07 .20
65 Tim Nabors' Car .07 .20
66 Tommy Mauney's Car .07 .20
67 Terry Adams' Car .07 .20
68 Harold Denton's Car .07 .20
69 Terry Housley's Car .07 .20
70 Doug Kirk's Car .07 .20
71 Ed Dixon's Car .07 .20
72 Terry Walters' Car .07 .20
73 Neil Moyer's Car .07 .20
74 Harold Robinson's Car .07 .20
75 Jack Revelle's Car .07 .20
76 Don Kohler's Car .07 .20
77 Michael Brotherton's Car .20 .50
78 Richard Holcomb's Car .07 .20
79 Wayne Bailey's Car .07 .20
80 Fred Farndon's Car .07 .20
81 Chris Karamesines' Car .20 .50
82 John Carey's Car .07 .20
83 Melvin Eaves' Car .07 .20
84 Carroll Smoot's Car .07 .20
85 Gene Fryer's Car .07 .20
86 Craig Cain's Car .07 .20
87 Joe Groves' Car .07 .20
88 Ron Miller's Car .07 .20
89 Buddy McGowan's Car .07 .20
90 Randy Daniels' Car .07 .20
91 Mark Osborne's Car .07 .20
92 Tim Freeman's Car .07 .20
93 Ted Osborne's Car .07 .20
94 Danny Estep's Car .07 .20
95 Bruce Abbott's Car .07 .20
96 Aggi Hendriks' Car .07 .20
97 Tim Butler's Car .07 .20
98 Bob Vanscriver's Car .07 .20
99 Usif Lawson's Car .07 .20
100 Checklist Card .07 .20
NNO Cover Card .07 .20

1965 Donruss Spec Sheet

Donruss produced this 66-card set sponsored by Hot Rod magazine for distribution in gum wax packs. The cards primarily feature top cars from a wide variety of drag racing and show events, but also cover road racing and IndyCar. The most noteworthy card, #49, features Bobby Unser and his Pikes Peak Hill Climb championship.

COMPLETE SET (66) 125.00 250.00
1 Bill Burke Mel Chastain's Car 2.50 6.00
2 Fred Larson's Car 2.00 4.00
3 Sam Parriott's Car 2.00 4.00
4 Jack Lufkin's Car 2.50 6.00
5 1925 T-Roadster 2.00 4.00
6 Show Winner 2.00 4.00
7 Ageless Street Rod 2.00 4.00
8 315 Horsepower 2.00 4.00
9 Bob and Bill Summers' Car 2.00 4.00
10 Hot Rod Fever 2.00 4.00
11 East African Safari 2.00 4.00
12 Beauty and Comfort 2.00 4.00
13 Record Runs 2.00 4.00
14 Ted Wingate's Car 2.00 4.00
15 Six Pots 2.00 4.00
16 Howard Peck's Car 2.50 6.00
17 What a Machine 2.00 4.00
18 Al Eckstrand's Car 2.50 6.00
19 Kurtis Roadster 2.00 4.00
20 World's Fastest 2.00 4.00
21 Super Super Stock 2.00 4.00
22 Hot Rod Dictionary 2.00 4.00
23 Well Dressed Mill 2.00 4.00
24 Custom Pick-Up 2.00 4.00
25 Bob-Tailed T 2.00 4.00
26 Jess Van Deventer's Car 2.00 4.00
27 Offy Engine 2.00 4.00
28 334 Cubic Inches 2.00 4.00
29 Jack Williams' Car 2.00 4.00
30 Abandoned 2.00 4.00
31 Salt Flats 2.00 4.00
32 LeRoi Tex Smith's Car 2.00 4.00
33 Modified Sport Car 2.00 4.00
34 Instant Roadster 2.00 4.00
35 1923 Dodge 2.00 4.00
36 L.A. Roadsters 2.00 4.00
37 Howard Brown's Car 2.00 4.00
38 A Real Winner 2.00 4.00
39 Steve LaBonge's Car 2.00 4.00
40 Mark 27 2.00 4.00
41 Owners Pride 2.00 4.00
42 Roman Red 2.00 4.00
43 Tom McMullen's Car 2.00 4.00
44 Hot Rod Dictionary 2.00 4.00
45 Detailed Custom 2.00 4.00
46 306 Streamliner 2.00 4.00
47 The Wedge 2.00 4.00
48 The Oakland Lational 2.00 4.00
49 Bobby Unser's Car 2.50 6.00
50 Tony Nancy's Car 2.00 4.00
51 Hot Rod Dictionary 2.00 4.00

52 Bob Herda's Car 2.00 4.00
53 Bobby Unser w Car 2.50 6.00
54 National Championship 2.00 4.00
55 Hot Rod Dictionary 2.00 4.00
56 John Mazmanian's Car 2.00 4.00
57 1964 Indianapolis 500 2.00 4.00
58 Hot Rod Dictionary 2.00 4.00
59 Connie Kalitta's Car 2.50 6.00
60 Off the Line 2.00 4.00
61 Chuck Griffith's Car 2.00 4.00
62 National Drags 2.00 4.00
63 '35 Custom 2.00 4.00
64 Tom Spaulding's Car 2.00 4.00
65 Hot Rod Dictionary 2.00 4.00
66 Hot Rod Dictionary 2.00 4.00

1993 Finish Line NHRA Prototypes

This Prototype set was released by Finish Line in its own cello wrapper. Although the cards are unnumbered, they have been assigned numbers below according to alphabetical order.

COMPLETE SET (4) 2.00 5.00
1 Scott Geoffrion .60 1.50
2 Cory McClenathan's Car .60 1.50
3 Cruz Pedregon .75 2.00
4 Cover Card .10 .30

1993 Finish Line NHRA

For the first time Finish Line produced their own card set with this 1993 NHRA release. The set features star drivers, cars and crew members of the top NHRA teams of the previous season. The cards were packaged 12 per foil pack with 36 packs per box and 25-cards per jumbo pack. Insert sets included a 17-card Speedways issue and a 9-card Autographs set.

COMPLETE SET (133) 4.00 10.00
1 Joe Amato .07 .20
2 Joe Amato .07 .20
3 Joe Amato's Car .02 .10
4 Shelly Anderson .07 .20
5 Dale Armstrong .02 .10
6 Pat Austin .02 .10
7 Pat Austin's Car .01 .05
8 Walt Austin Pat Austin .02 .10
9 Lee Beard .02 .10
10 Kenny Bernstein .20 .60
11 Kenny Bernstein's Car .07 .20
12 Kenny Bernstein .20 .60
13 Jim Brissette .02 .10
14 Michael Brotherton .02 .10
15 Michael Brotherton's Car .01 .05
16 Fuzzy Carter .02 .10
17 Wes Cerny .02 .10
18 Dannielle DePorter .02 .10
19 Darrell Gwynn .07 .20
20 Jim Head .02 .10
21 Doug Herbert .02 .10
22 Eddie Hill .20 .60
23 Eddie Hill .20 .60
24 Eddie Hill's Car .07 .20
25 Tommy Johnson Jr. .07 .20
26 Tom Johnson Sr. Tommy Jr. Wendy Johnson .07 .20
27 Kim LaHaie .02 .10
28 Cory McClenathan .20 .60
29 Cory McClenathan .20 .60
30 Cory McClenathan's Car .07 .20
31 Ed McCulloch .02 .10
32 Ed McCulloch's Car .01 .05
33 John Medlen .02 .10
34 Jack Ostrander .02 .10
35 Jim Prock .02 .10
36 Don Prudhomme .20 .60
37 Don Prudhomme's Car .07 .20
38 Tim Richards .02 .10
39 Al Segrini .02 .10
40 Gene Snow .07 .20
41 Ken Veney .02 .10
42 Tom Anderson .02 .10
43 Whit Bazemore .02 .10
44 Gary Bolger .02 .10
45 Jerry Caminito .02 .10
46 Austin Coil .02 .10
47 Gary Densham .02 .10
48 Chuck Etchells .02 .10
49 Chuck Etchells' Car .01 .05
50 Jim Epler .02 .10
51 Gary Evans .02 .10
52 Bernie Fedderly .02 .10
53 John Force .50 1.25
54 John Force .50 1.25
55 John Force's Car .20 .60
56 Richard Hartman .02 .10
57 Al Hofmann .07 .20
58 Al Hofmann .07 .20
59 Al Hofmann's Car .02 .10
60 Tom Hoover .07 .20
61 Tom Hoover's Car .02 .10
62 Gordon Mineo .02 .10
63 Mike Green .02 .10
64 Mark Oswald .02 .10
65 Cruz Pedregon .20 .60
66 Cruz Pedregon .20 .60
67 Cruz Pedregon's Car .07 .20
68 Bill Schultz .02 .10
69 Johnny West .02 .10
70 Del Worsham .02 .10
71 Chuck Worsham .02 .10
72 Bruce Allen .02 .10
73 Bruce Allen's Car .01 .05
74 Greg Anderson Kurt Johnson .02 .10
75 Don Beverley .02 .10
76 Gary Brown .02 .10
77 Kenny Delco .02 .10
78 Jerry Eckman .02 .10
79 Jerry Eckman .02 .10
80 Jerry Eckman's Car .01 .05
81 Alban Gauthier's Car .01 .05
82 Scott Geoffrion .02 .10
83 Scott Geoffrion .02 .10
84 Scott Geoffrion's Car .01 .05
85 Bob Glidden .07 .20
86 Bob Glidden's Car .02 .10
87 Etta Glidden W Crew .07 .20
88 Jerry Haas .02 .10
89 Dave Hutchens Mike Sullivan .02 .10
90 Frank Iaconio .02 .10
91 Bill Jenkins .02 .10
92 Warren Johnson .07 .20
93 Warren Johnson .07 .20
94 Warren Johnson's Car .02 .10
95 Joe Lepone Jr. .02 .10
96 Larry Morgan .02 .10
97 Larry Morgan's Car .01 .05
98 Bill Orndorff .02 .10
99 Mark Pawuk .02 .10
100 Paul Rebeschi Jr. .02 .10
101 David Reher Buddy Morrison .02 .10
102 Gordie Rivera .02 .10
103 Tom Roberts .02 .10
104 Harry Scribner .02 .10
105 Rickie Smith .02 .10
106 Jim Yates .02 .10
107 James Bernard w Bike .01 .05
108 Bryon Hines .02 .10
109 Steve Johnson w/Bike .01 .05
110 John Mafaro .02 .10
111 John Myers .02 .10
112 David Schultz .02 .10
113 John Smith w Bike .01 .05
114 Blaine Johnson .02 .10
115 Bob Newberry .02 .10
116 Steve Johns .02 .10
117 Greg Stanfield .02 .10
118 Chad Guilford .02 .10
119 Edmond Richardson .02 .10
120 Jeg Coughlin Jr. .02 .10
121 Pat Austin's Car .01 .05
122 Bill Barney .02 .10
123 Anthony Bartone's Car .01 .05
124 David Nickens .02 .10
125 Buster Couch .02 .10
126 Steve Evans .02 .10
127 Bob Frey .02 .10
128 Dave McClelland .02 .10
129 Larry Minor .02 .10
130 Wally Parks .02 .10
131 Shirley Muldowney .20 .60
132 Del Worsham's Car .01 .05
133 Larry Meyer .02 .10

1993 Finish Line NHRA Autographs

Finish Line produced this nine-card set with each card individually signed by the featured driver. The cards were randomly inserted in 1993 Finish Line foil and jumbo packs.

COMPLETE SET (9) 100.00 180.00
1 Joe Amato 15.00 30.00
2 Cory McClenathan 15.00 30.00
3 Kenny Bernstein 20.00 40.00
4 Cruz Pedregon 20.00 40.00
5 John Force 40.00 80.00
6 Al Hofmann 10.00 25.00
7 Warren Johnson 10.00 25.00
8 Scott Geoffrion 8.00 20.00
9 Jerry Eckman 8.00 20.00

1993 Finish Line NHRA Speedways

NHRA race tracks are the focus of this 17-card insert set produced by Finish Line. The cards were randomly packed in 1993 Finish Line NHRA foil and jumbo packs.

COMPLETE SET (17) 1.50 3.00
T1 Pomona Raceway .10 .20
T2 Firebird International .10 .20
T3 Houston Raceway Park .10 .20
T4 Gainesville Raceway .10 .20
T5 Rockingham Dragway .10 .20
T6 Atlanta Dragway .10 .20
T7 Memphis International .10 .20
T8 Old Bridge Township .10 .20
T9 National Trail Raceway .10 .20
T10 Saniar Int'l Dragway .10 .20
T11 Bandimere Speedway .10 .20
T12 Sears Point Int'l .10 .20
T13 Seattle International .10 .20
T14 Brainerd Int'l Raceway .10 .20
T15 Indianapolis Raceway .10 .20
T16 Maple Grove Raceway .10 .20
T17 Texas Motorplex .10 .20

1970 Fleer Dragstrips

Fleer produced this 10-card set primarily as backers for their Dragstrips stickers. With each 5-cent wax pack, collector's received one of these cards and a group of automotive stickers. The cards are oversized (approximately 2-1/2" by 4-1/2") and blankbacked as are the sticker sheets. The black and white cards feature uncaptioned photos of top racers with an emphasis on Andy Granatelli and the STP IndyCar race team. We've assigned card numbers according to alphabetical order.

COMPLETE SET (10) 175.00 300.00
STICKER INSERTS 5.00 10.00
1 Darel Dieringer's Car 15.00 25.00
2 Don Garlits' Car 60.00 100.00
3 Andy Granatelli 20.00 35.00
4 Dan Gurney's Car 20.00 35.00
5 Graham Hill's Car 20.00 35.00
6 Parnelli Jones' Car w Andy Gran. 30.00 50.00
7 Joe Leonard's Car 15.00 25.00
8 Joe Leonard's Car w Andy Gran. 15.00 25.00
9 Ken Miles Lloyd Ruby's Car 15.00 25.00
10 Art Pollard's Car 15.00 25.00

1971 Fleer AHRA Drag Champs

This is the first of three consecutive sets Fleer released featuring stars of AHRA drag racing. Wax packs contained five-cards and one stick of gum. There were three different wrappers produced, each featuring a different drag racer. Although virtually all of the 63-cards feature racing cars in action, three cards were devoted to the top champions in each drag racing category. An American and Canadian version was produced with the American cards printed on white card stock and are unnumbered. The Canadian set was numbered (listed below in that order) and printed on a cream colored paper stock.

COMPLETE SET (63) 200.00 350.00
*CANADIAN CARDS: SAME VALUE
1 Arlen Vanke's Car 3.00 6.00
2 John Wiebe's Car 4.00 8.00
3 Terry Hedrick's Car 3.00 6.00
4 Steve Carbone's Car 3.00 6.00
5 Leroy Goldstein's Car 3.00 6.00
6 Pat Foster's Car 3.00 6.00
7 Don Schumacher's Car 3.00 6.00
8 Don Gay Roy Gay's Car 4.00 8.00
9 Dick Harrell's Car 3.00 6.00
10 Bill Jenkins' Car 3.00 6.00
11 Kenny Safford's Car 3.00 6.00
12 John Elliot's Car 3.00 6.00
13 Pat Minick's Car 3.00 6.00
14 Arnie Behling's Car 3.00 6.00
15 Gene Snow's Car 4.00 8.00
16 Jay Howell's Car 3.00 6.00
17 Norm Tanner's Car 3.00 6.00
18 Don Garlits' Car 4.00 8.00
19 Ray Alley's Car 3.00 6.00
20 K.S. Pittman's Car 3.00 6.00
21 Ed Miller's Car 3.00 6.00
22 Funny Car Champs 4.00 8.00
23 Chris Karamesines' Car 4.00 8.00
24 Super Stock Champs 4.00 8.00
25 Jim Nicoll's Car 4.00 8.00
26 Dick Landy's Car 3.00 6.00
27 Shirley Shahan's Car 3.00 6.00
28 John McFadde's Car 3.00 6.00
29 Leonard Hughes' Car 3.00 6.00
30 Eddie Schartman's Car 3.00 6.00
31 Ed Terry's Car 3.00 6.00
32 Hubert Platt's Car 3.00 6.00
33 Gary Kimball's Car 3.00 6.00
34 Gary Watson's Car 3.00 6.00
35 Rich Sironian's Car 3.00 6.00
36 Richard Tharp's Car 3.00 6.00
37 Jake Johnston's Car 3.00 6.00
38 Ronnie Sox's Car 4.00 8.00
39 Charles Therwanger's Car 3.00 6.00
40 Don Grotheer's Car 3.00 6.00
41 Pete Robinson's Car 3.00 6.00
42 Ron O'Donnell's Car 3.00 6.00
43 Dick Loehr's Car 3.00 6.00
44 Tom Hoover's Car 4.00 8.00
45 Dale Young's Car 3.00 6.00
46 Warren Gunter's Car 3.00 6.00
47 Bruce Larson's Car 3.00 6.00
48 Paula Murphy's Car 3.00 6.00
49 Bob Murray's Car 3.00 6.00
50 Jim Liberman's Car 3.00 6.00
51 Sam Auxier Jr.'s Car 3.00 6.00
52 Duane Ong's Car 3.00 6.00
53 Preston Davis' Car 3.00 6.00
54 Top Fuel Champs 4.00 8.00
55 Jimmy King's Car 3.00 6.00
56 Ron Martin's Car 3.00 6.00
57 Jerry Mallicoat Tom Chamblis' Car 3.00 6.00
58 Jerry Miller's Car 3.00 6.00
59 Tommy Ivo's Car 3.00 6.00
60 Bill Hielscher's Car 3.00 6.00
61 Tony Nancy's Car 3.00 6.00
62 Fritz Callier's Car 3.00 6.00
63 Don Nicholson's Car 3.00 6.00

1971 Fleer Stick Shift

Similar to the 1970 Dragstrips release, Fleer Stick Shift cards were issued primarily as backers for Stick Shift race stickers. With each 10-cent wax pack, collector's received one of these cards and a group of race stickers. The cards are oversized (approximately 2-1/2" by 4-1/2") and blankbacked as are the sticker sheets. The black and white cards feature captioned photos of cars and racers. Although only nine cards can be confirmed, the set is thought to consist of ten cards. Any additions to this list are appreciated.

COMPLETE SET (9) 400.00 750.00
STICKER INSERTS 5.00 10.00
1 Kelly Brown's Dragster 40.00 80.00
2 Dragster at Lion's Drag Strip 40.00 80.00
3 Plymouth Superbird 40.00 80.00
4 Plymouth GTX 40.00 80.00
5 Dan Ongais Driving the Winningest Car 50.00 100.00
6 Don Burns real crowd pleaser 40.00 80.00
7 Don Prudhomme 75.00 150.00
8 Chris Karamesines 60.00 120.00
9 Don Garlits 75.00 150.00

1972 Fleer AHRA Drag Nationals

For the second consecutive year, Fleer released a set featuring stars of AHRA drag racing. Wax packs contained five-cards and one stick of gum and the set size was increased to 70-cards. There is some speculation that based on the odd set size, some cards may have been printed in shorter supply than others. Again, most of the cards feature drag racing cars in action, but a larger number (versus the 1971 set) were devoted to top drivers as well. An American and Canadian version was produced with the American cards printed on white card stock, while the Canadian set was printed on a cream colored paper stock.

COMPLETE SET (70) 275.00 450.00
AMERICAN/CANADIAN SAME VALUE
1 Don Garlits' Car 5.00 10.00
2 Don Garlits 6.00 12.00
3 Don Garlits' Car 5.00 10.00
4 Phil Schofield's Car 4.00 8.00
5 Charlie Thurwanger's Car 4.00 8.00
6 Bill Leavitt's Car 4.00 8.00
7 Fritz Callier's Car 4.00 8.00
8 Richard Tharp's Car 5.00 10.00
9 John Wiebe's Car 4.00 8.00
10 Steve Carbone 4.00 8.00
11 Kenny Sanford's Car 4.00 8.00
12 Jim Hayter's Car 4.00 8.00
13 Herb McCandless' Car 4.00 8.00
14 Don Grother's Car 4.00 8.00
15 Mike Fons' Car 4.00 8.00
16 Ronnie Sox's Car 5.00 10.00
17 Joe Rundle's Car 4.00 8.00
18 Bill Jenkins' Car 4.00 8.00
19 Dick Landy's Car 4.00 8.00
20 Don Carlton's Car 4.00 8.00
21 Mart Higginbotham 4.00 8.00
22 Gene Snow 5.00 10.00
23 Butch Maas' Car 4.00 8.00
24 Dale Pulde&Mickey Thompson's Car 5.00 10.00
25 Gary Watson's Car 4.00 8.00
26 Tom McEwen 5.00 10.00
27 Don Prudhomme 6.00 12.00
28 Gary Cochran 4.00 8.00
29 Tom Hoover 5.00 10.00
30 Gene Snow's Car 5.00 10.00
31 Steve Carbone's Car 4.00 8.00
32 John Paxton's Car 4.00 8.00
33 John Wiebe 4.00 8.00
34 Dennis Baca's Car 4.00 8.00
35 Tripp Shumake's Car 4.00 8.00
36 Mart Higginbotham's Car 4.00 8.00
37 Chris Karamesines 5.00 10.00
38 Gary Cochran's Car 4.00 8.00
39 Don Cook's Car 4.00 8.00
40 Vic Brown's Car 4.00 8.00
41 Chris Karamesines' Car 5.00 10.00
42 Ronnie Sox Buddy Martin 5.00 10.00
43 Tom Hoover's Car 5.00 10.00
44 Gary Burgin's Car 4.00 8.00
45 John Lombardo's Car 4.00 8.00
46 Don Prudhomme's Car 5.00 10.00
47 Tom McEwen's Car 5.00 10.00
48 Leroy Goldstein's Car 4.00 8.00
49 Russell Long's Car 4.00 8.00
50 Don Moody's Car 4.00 8.00
51 Don Schumacher's Car 4.00 8.00
52 Doug Rose's Car 4.00 8.00
53 Larry Christopherson's Car 4.00 8.00
54 Tom Grove's Car 4.00 8.00
55 Jim Dunn's Car 4.00 8.00
56 Jim King's Car 4.00 8.00
57 Butch Leal's Car 4.00 8.00
58 Bill Jenkins' Car 4.00 8.00
59 Don Moody's Car 4.00 8.00
60 Clare Sanders' Car 4.00 8.00
61 Jim Nicoll's Car 4.00 8.00
62 Cecil Lankford's Car 4.00 8.00
63 Jim Walther's Car 4.00 8.00
64 Ralph Gould's Car 4.00 8.00
65 Dale Pulde&Mickey Thompson's Car 5.00 10.00
66 Dave Beebe's Car 4.00 8.00
67 Joe Lee's Car 4.00 8.00
68 Doug Rose's Car 4.00 8.00
69 Dale Pulde&Mickey Thompson's Car 5.00 10.00
70 Gary Watson's Car 4.00 8.00

1973 Fleer AHRA Race USA

Race USA was Fleer's final AHRA release. Wax packs again contained five-cards and one stick of gum and two different wrappers were produced. The set size again was increased to 74-cards. There is some speculation that based on the odd set size, some cards may have been printed in shorter supply than others. Many of the cards feature drag racing cars in action, but several focus on the top drivers as well.

COMPLETE SET (74) 275.00 450.00
1 Tom McEwen 5.00 10.00
2 Tom McEwen's Car 5.00 10.00
3 Tom McEwen's Car 5.00 10.00
4 Don Prudhomme 6.00 12.00
5 Don Prudhomme 6.00 12.00
6 Don Prudhomme's Car 5.00 10.00
7 Mike Randall's Car 4.00 8.00
8 Bill Leavitt's Car 4.00 8.00
9 Richard Tharp's Car 4.00 8.00
10 Bob Lambeck's Car 4.00 8.00
11 Butch Leal's Car 4.00 8.00
12 Dick Landy 4.00 8.00
13 Dick Landy's Car 4.00 8.00
14 Gary Kimball&Larry Kimballs' Car 4.00 8.00
15 Tom Hoover's Car 5.00 10.00
16 Tom Hoover w Car 5.00 10.00
17 Don Nicholson's Car 4.00 8.00
18 Ken Holthe's Car 4.00 8.00
19 Don Grotheer's Car 4.00 8.00
20 Eddie Shartman's Car 4.00 8.00
21 Wayne Gapp's Car 4.00 8.00
22 Keyy Brown's Car 4.00 8.00
23 Cogo Eads' Car 4.00 8.00
24 Gene Dunlap's Car 4.00 8.00
25 Mart Higginbotham's Car 4.00 8.00
26 Steve Carbone's Car 4.00 8.00
27 Don Cook's Car 4.00 8.00
28 Gary Cochran's Car 4.00 8.00
29 Mike Burkart's Car 4.00 8.00
30 Tom Akin's Car 4.00 8.00
31 Don Garlits DOY 5.00 10.00
32 Larry Christopherson w car 4.00 8.00
33 Larry Christopherson's Car 4.00 8.00
34 Ronnie Sox' Car 5.00 10.00
35 Ronnie Sox Buddy Martin 5.00 10.00
36 Don Schumacher's Car 4.00 8.00
37 Joe Satmary's Car 4.00 8.00
38 Joe Satmary's Car 4.00 8.00
39 Scott Shafiroff's Car 4.00 8.00
40 Pat Foster's Car 4.00 8.00
41 Chris Karamesines' Car 5.00 10.00
42 Dave Russell's Car 4.00 8.00
43 Twig Zigler 4.00 8.00
44 Ronnie Martin's Car 5.00 10.00
45 Mickey Thompson w Car 4.00 8.00
46 Dale Pulde's Car 4.00 8.00
47 Henry Harrison's Car 4.00 8.00
48 Ed McCulloch's Car 5.00 10.00
49 Ed McCulloch's Car 5.00 10.00
50 John Wiebe 5.00 10.00
51 Gary Watson's Car 4.00 8.00
52 Arlen Vanke's Car 4.00 8.00
53 Duane Jacobsen's Car 4.00 8.00
54 Ronnie Runyon's Car 4.00 8.00
55 Jerry Baker's Car 4.00 8.00
56 Barrie Poole's Car 4.00 8.00
57 Bobby Yowell's Car 4.00 8.00
58 Don Garlits 6.00 12.00
59 Don Garlits' Car 5.00 10.00
60 Don Garlits' Car 5.00 10.00
61 Jeg Coughlin's Car 4.00 8.00
62 Mike Sullivan's Car 4.00 8.00
63 Jon Petrie's Car 4.00 8.00
64 Bob Riffle's Car 4.00 8.00
65 Dave Hough's Car 4.00 8.00
66 The Mob Dragster 4.00 8.00
67 The Mob Dragster 4.00 8.00
68 Jeb Allen's Car 4.00 8.00
69 Jim Nicoll's Car 5.00 10.00
70 Ed Sigmon's Car 4.00 8.00
71 Gene Snow 5.00 10.00
72 Gene Snow's Car 5.00 10.00
73 Jake Johnston's Car 4.00 8.00
74 Chip Woodall's Car 4.00 8.00

1997 Hi-Tech NHRA Prototypes

COMPLETE SET (5)
PR1 Kenny Bernstein .60 1.50
PR2 John Force 2.50 6.00
PR3 Warren Johnson 1.00 2.50
PR4 Angelle Seeling .60 1.50
PR5 Tony Pedregon 1.00 2.50

1997 Hi-Tech NHRA

COMPLETE SET (40) 12.50 30.00
COMMON DRIVERS .25 .60
SEMISTARS .40 1.00
UNLISTED STARS .50 1.25
HT1 NHRA Header Card .20 .50
HT2 Joe Amato .30 .75
HT3 Shelly Anderson .30 .75
HT4 Kenny Bernstein .30 .75
HT5 Larry Dixon .50 1.25
HT6 Mike Dunn .20 .50
HT7 Eddie Hill .25 .60
HT8 Connie Kalitta .20 .50
HT9 Scott Kalitta .60 1.50
HT10 Cory McClenathan .50 1.25
HT11 Cristen Powell .20 .50
HT12 Gary Scelzi .30 .75
HT13 Randy Anderson .20 .50
HT14 Whit Bazemore .60 1.50
HT15 Gary Densham .30 .75
HT16 John Force 1.25 3.00
HT17 Al Hofmann .20 .50
HT18 Dean Skuza .30 .75
HT19 Mark Oswald .20 .50
HT20 Cruz Pedregon .30 .75
HT21 Tony Pedregon .50 1.25
HT22 Ron Capps .50 1.25
HT23 Del Worsham .60 1.50
HT24 Darrell Alderman .20 .50
HT25 Mike Edwards .20 .50
HT26 Scott Geoffrion .20 .50
HT27 Bob Glidden .20 .50
HT28 Chuck Harris .20 .50
HT29 Kurt Johnson .60 1.50
HT30 Warren Johnson .50 1.25
HT31 Tom Martino .20 .50
HT32 Steve Schmidt .20 .50
HT33 Jim Yates .30 .75
HT34 Hector Arana .20 .50
HT35 Matt Hines .50 1.25
HT36 Steve Johnson .20 .50
HT37 John Myers .20 .50
HT38 Dave Schultz .30 .75
HT39 Angelle Seeling 1.00 2.50
HT40 John Smith .20 .50

1997 Hi-Tech NHRA Autographs

GROUP A ODDS 1:360
GROUP B ODDS 1:180
1 Joe Amato B 10.00 25.00
2 Kenny Bernstein B 10.00 25.00
3 Ron Capps A 30.00 60.00
4 Larry Dixon A 25.00 50.00
5 John Force A 90.00 150.00
6 Eddie Hill A 12.50 30.00
7 Kurt Johnson A 15.00 40.00
8 Warren Johnson A 20.00 40.00

1997 Hi-Tech NHRA Christmas Tree

STATED ODDS 1:180
XM1 Joe Amato 4.00 10.00
XM2 Kenny Bernstein 4.00 10.00
XM3 John Force 8.00 20.00
XM4 Eddie Hill 3.00 8.00
XM5 Warren Johnson 6.00 15.00
XM6 Scott Kalitta 8.00 20.00
XM7 Tony Pedregon 6.00 15.00
XM8 Dave Schultz 4.00 10.00
XM9 Jim Yates 4.00 10.00

1997 Hi-Tech NHRA Funny Car

COMPLETE SET (11) 5.00 12.00
FC1 Funny Car Header Card .20 .50
FC2 Whit Bazemore .60 1.50
FC3 Gary Densham .30 .75
FC4 John Force 1.25 3.00
FC5 Al Hofmann .20 .50
FC6 Dean Skuza .30 .75
FC7 Mark Oswald .20 .50
FC8 Cruz Pedregon .30 .75
FC9 Del Worsham .60 1.50
FC10 Tony Pedregon .50 1.25
FC11 Ron Capps .50 1.25

1997 Hi-Tech NHRA John Force

COMPLETE SET (8) 8.00 20.00
COMMON FORCE 1.25 3.00

1997 Hi-Tech NHRA Pro Stock

COMPLETE SET (9) 2.50 6.00
PS1 Pro Stock Header Card .20 .50
PS2 Darrell Alderman .20 .50
PS3 Mike Edwards .20 .50
PS4 Scott Geoffrion .20 .50
PS5 Kurt Johnson .60 1.50
PS6 Warren Johnson .50 1.25
PS7 Steve Schmidt .20 .50
PS8 Jim Yates .30 .75
PS9 Tom Martino .20 .50

1997 Hi-Tech NHRA Pro Stock Bike

COMPLETE SET (7) 2.00 6.00
PB1 Pro Stock Bike Header Card .20 .50
PB2 Matt Hines .50 1.25
PB3 John Myers .20 .50
PB4 Dave Schultz .30 .75
PB5 Angelle Seeling 1.00 2.50
PB6 John Smith .20 .50
PB7 Steve Johnson .20 .50

1997 Hi-Tech NHRA Top Fuel

COMPLETE SET (12) 3.00 8.00
TF1 Top Fuel Header Card .20 .50
TF2 Joe Amato .30 .75
TF3 Shelly Anderson .30 .75
TF4 Kenny Bernstein .30 .75
TF5 Larry Dixon .50 1.25
TF6 Mike Dunn .20 .50
TF7 Eddie Hill .25 .60
TF8 Connie Kalitta .20 .50
TF9 Scott Kalitta .60 1.50
TF10 Cory McClenathan .50 1.25
TF11 Cristen Powell .20 .50
TF12 Gary Scelzi .30 .75

993-97 Kustom Kards Bunny Burkett

ıine-card set was produced by Kustom Kards eatures Bunny and the cars she has driven gh the years. Cards from this set were buted by her team through trackside souvenir s and autoshow appearances. Each features a border and features a card number made up year, her initials, and the final overall card ber which we've included below.

PLETE SET (9) 3.00 8.00
MON CARD (1-9) .40 1.00

1989 Mega Drag

a Promotions Inc. of Florida released this set id-1989 featuring the top names in drag ıg. The cards were sold in factory set form ctly from Mega at the original price of $19.95 $3 shipping. A series two set was planned never materialized.

MPLETE SET (110) 100.00 200.00
arrell Gwynn 1.50 3.00
arrell Gwynn's Car 1.25 2.50
ddie Hill 2.00 4.00
ddie Hill's Car 2.00 4.00
ddie Hill's Car 2.00 4.00
e Amato 2.00 4.00
e Amato's Car 1.25 2.50
ike Dunn 1.25 2.50
ike Dunn's Car 1.00 2.25
Morris Johnson Jr. 1.25 2.50
Morris Johnson Jr.'s Car 1.00 2.25
Ed McCulloch 1.25 2.50
Ed McCulloch's Car 1.00 2.25
Mike Troxel 1.25 2.50
Mike Troxel's Car 1.00 2.25
Dale Pulde 1.50 3.00
Jerry Haas 1.25 2.50
Jerry Haas' Car 1.00 2.25
Bruce Allen 1.25 2.50
Bruce Allen's Car 1.00 2.25
Shirley Muldowney 2.00 4.00
Shirley Muldowney's Car 2.00 4.00
Bill Kuhlman 1.25 2.50
Bill Kuhlman's Car 1.00 2.25
Rickie Smith 1.25 2.50
Rickie Smith's Car 1.00 2.25
Jim Feurer's Car 1.00 2.25
Denny Lucas 1.25 2.50
Denny Lucas' Car 1.00 2.25
Bruce Larson 1.25 2.50
Bruce Larson's Car 1.00 2.25
Tony Christian 1.25 2.50
Tony Christian's Car 1.00 2.25
John Martin 1.25 2.50
5 John Martin's Car 1.00 2.25
Frank Bradley 1.25 2.50
Frank Bradley's Car 1.00 2.25
Gary Ormsby 1.25 2.50
9 Gary Ormsby's Car 1.00 2.25
Kenny Koretsky 1.25 2.50
Kenny Koretsky's Car 1.00 2.25
Scott Geoffrion 1.25 2.50
3 Scott Geoffrion's Car 1.00 2.25
4 Earl Whiting 1.25 2.50
5 Earl Whiting's Car 1.00 2.25
6 Jerry Caminito 1.25 2.50
7 Jerry Caminito's Car 1.00 2.25
8 Darrell Alderman 1.50 3.00
9 Darrell Alderman's Car 1.25 2.50
0 Roland Leong 1.25 2.50
1 Roland Leong's Car 1.00 2.25
2 Gordie Rivera 1.25 2.50
63 Gordie Rivera's Car 1.00 2.25
64 R.C. Sherman's Car 1.00 2.25
65 Frank Manzo 1.25 2.50
66 Frank Manzo's Car 1.00 2.25
67 Frank Iaconio 1.25 2.50
68 Frank Iaconio's Car 1.00 2.25
69 Don Campanello 1.25 2.50
60 Don Campanello's Car 1.00 2.25
61 Bob Newberry's Car 1.00 2.25
62 Nick Nikolis 1.25 2.50
63 Nick Nikolis' Car 1.00 2.25
64 John Speelman's Car 1.00 2.25
65 Chuck Etchells 1.50 3.00
66 Chuck Etchells' Car 1.25 2.50
67 Paul Smith 1.25 2.50
68 Paul Smith's Car 1.00 2.25
69 Mark Pawuk 1.25 2.50
70 Mark Pawuk's Car 1.00 2.25
71 Arnie Karp 1.25 2.50
72 Arnie Karp's Car 1.00 2.25
73 Frank Sanchez 1.25 2.50
74 Frank Sanchez's Car 1.00 2.25
75 Lori Johns 1.50 3.00
76 Lori Johns' Car 1.25 2.50
77 Bubba Sewell's Car 1.00 2.25
78 Della Woods 1.25 2.50
79 Della Woods' Car 1.00 2.25
80 Brian Raymer's Car 1.00 2.25
81 Tim Grose 1.25 2.50
82 Tim Grose's Car 1.00 2.25
83 Tom Conway's Car 1.00 2.25
84 Darrell Amberson 1.25 2.50
85 Darrell Amberson's Car 1.00 2.25
86 Jim Head 1.25 2.50
87 Jim Head 's Car 1.00 2.25
88 Doc Halladay 1.25 2.50
89 Doc Halladay's Car 1.00 2.25
90 Dal Denton's Car 1.00 2.25
91 Dick LaHaie 1.25 2.50
92 Dick LaHaie's Car 1.00 2.25
93 Don Coonce 1.25 2.50
94 Don Coonce's Car 1.00 2.25
95 Jerry Eckman 1.25 2.50
96 Jerry Eckman's Car 1.00 2.25
97 Harold Lewelling's Car 1.00 2.25
98 Domenic Santucci Sr.'s Car 1.00 2.25
99 Al Hanna's Car 1.00 2.25
100 Gene Snow 1.50 3.00
101 Gene Snow's Car 1.25 2.50
102 Joe Lepone Jr. 1.25 2.50
103 Joe Lepone Jr.'s Car 1.00 2.25
104 Hank Enders 1.25 2.50
105 Hank Enders' Car 1.00 2.25
106 Lee Dean's Car 1.00 2.25
107 Dennis Piranio's Car 1.00 2.25
108 Don Garlits 2.00 4.00
109 Don Garlits' Car 2.00 4.00
110 Checklist 1.00 2.25

1976 Nabisco Sugar Daddy 1

This set of 25 tiny (approximately 1 1/16" by 2 3/4") cards features action scenes from a variety of popular sports from around the world. One card was included in specially marked Sugar Daddy and Sugar Mama candy bars. The set is referred to as "Sugar Daddy Sports World - Series 1" on the backs of the cards. The cards are in color with a relatively wide white border around the front of the cards.

COMPLETE SET (25) 40.00 80.00
4 Auto Racing 5.00 10.00

2007 NHRA Powerade Countdown to the Championship

COMPLETE SET (17) 5.00 12.00
1 Brandon Bernstein .50 1.25
2 Larry Dixon .50 1.25
3 Rod Fuller .20 .50
4 Tony Schumacher .50 1.25
5 Ron Capps .50 1.25
6 Robert Hight .60 1.50
7 Tony Pedregon .60 1.50
8 Gary Scelzi .30 .75
9 Greg Anderson .25 .60
10 Dave Connolly .25 .60
11 Jeg Coughlin .30 .75
12 Allen Johnson .20 .50
13 Chip Ellis .20 .50
14 Andrew Hines .20 .50
15 Peggy Llewellyn .25 .60
16 Matt Smith .20 .50
NNO Cover Card .20 .50

2005 Press Pass NHRA

COMP.FACT.SET (51) 15.00 40.00
COMPLETE SET (50) 12.50 30.00
1 David Baca RC .50 1.25
2 Brandon Bernstein RC 1.00 2.50
3 Dave Grubnic RC .50 1.25
4 Doug Herbert .50 1.25
5 Doug Kalitta RC .50 1.25
6 Scott Kalitta .50 1.25
7 Morgan Lucas RC .40 1.00
8 Cory McLenathan RC .25 .60
9 Clay Millican RC .40 1.00
10 Tony Schumacher RC 1.00 2.50
11 Scott Weis .15 .40
12 Tony Bartone .50 1.25
13 Whit Bazemore .50 1.25
14 Phil Burkart Jr. RC .40 1.00
15 Ron Capps .50 1.25
16 John Force Green 2.00 5.00
17 John Force Red 2.00 5.00
18 J.Force 2.00 5.00
A.Force RC
19 Bob Gilbertson .15 .40
20 Robert Hight RC .40 1.00
21 Eric Medlen RC 1.25 3.00
22 Cruz Pedregon 1.00 2.50
23 Frank Pedregon RC .40 1.00
24 Tony Pedregon 1.00 2.50
25 Gary Scelzi .50 1.25
26 Tim Wilkerson RC .40 1.00
27 Del Worsham .15 .40
28 Bruce Allen .15 .40
29 Greg Anderson .50 1.25
30 Dave Connolly RC .40 1.00
31 Jeg Coughlin Jr. .50 1.25
32 Mike Edwards .15 .40
33 Vieri Gaines RC .25 .60
34 Allen Johnson RC .40 1.00
35 Kurt Johnson .50 1.25
36 Warren Johnson RC .40 1.00
37 Kenny Koretsky .25 .60
38 Ron Krisher RC .40 1.00
39 Larry Morgan .15 .40
40 Jason Line RC .40 1.00
41 Richie Stevens RC .40 1.00
42 Jim Yates .15 .40
43 Antron Brown RC .60 1.50
44 Andrew Hines RC .50 1.25
45 Steve Johnson .40 1.00
46 Angelle Sampey 1.00 2.50
47 Geno Scali RC .40 1.00
48 Karen Stoffer RC .25 .60
49 GT Tonglet RC .40 1.00
50 Craig Treble RC .40 1.00

2005 Press Pass NHRA Autographs

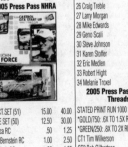

1 John Force 60.00 120.00
2 Tony Schumacher 30.00 60.00
3 Doug Kalitta 12.00 30.00
4 Scott Kalitta 60.00 120.00
5 Scott Weis 6.00 15.00
6 Dave Grubnic 8.00 20.00
7 Cory McClenathan 12.00 30.00
8 Doug Herbert 6.00 15.00
9 Clay Millican 8.00 20.00
10 Morgan Lucas 10.00 25.00
11 Gary Scelzi 15.00 40.00
12 Whit Bazemore 8.00 20.00
13 Tim Wilkerson 12.00 30.00
14 Ron Capps 15.00 40.00
15 Frank Pedregon 8.00 20.00
16 Tony Bartone 8.00 20.00
17 Greg Anderson 10.00 25.00
18 Jason Line 12.00 30.00
19 Jeg Coughlin Jr. 6.00 15.00
20 Kenny Koretsky 6.00 15.00
21 Richie Stevens
22 Vieri Gaines 10.00 25.00
23 Bob Gilbertson 8.00 20.00
24 Angelle Sampey 6.00 15.00
25 Antron Brown 25.00 50.00
26 Craig Treble 6.00 15.00
27 Larry Morgan 8.00 20.00
28 Mike Edwards 10.00 25.00
29 Geno Scali 10.00 25.00
30 Steve Johnson 10.00 25.00
31 Karen Stoffer 10.00 25.00
32 Eric Medlen 100.00 250.00
33 Robert Hight 10.00 25.00
34 Melanie Troxel 8.00 20.00

2005 Press Pass NHRA Cool Threads Red

STATED PRINT RUN 1000 SER.#'d SETS
*GOLD/750: .6X TO 1.5X RED/1000
*GREEN/250: .8X TO 2X RED
CT1 Tim Wilkerson 6.00 15.00
CT2 Bob Gilbertson 6.00 15.00
CT3 Tony Bartone 6.00 15.00
CT4 Greg Anderson 8.00 20.00
CT5 Jason Line 6.00 15.00
CT6 Kenny Koretsky 6.00 15.00
CT7 Del Worsham 6.00 15.00
CT8 Phil Burkart 6.00 15.00
CT9 John Force 8.00 20.00
CT10 Eric Medlen 8.00 20.00
CT11 Robert Hight 8.00 20.00

1991 Pro Set NHRA

This was Pro Set's first NHRA release in a run of sets produced by the company from 1991-1993. The set features star drivers, cars and crew members of the top NHRA teams. The cards were packaged 10 per foil pack with 36 packs per box. Signed cards of Don Garlits, number 105, that were UV coated and autographed in silver ink were also randomly inserted.

COMPLETE SET (130) 8.00 20.00
1 Joe Amato .30 1.00
2 Gary Ormsby .05 .15
3 Dick LaHaie .05 .15
4 Lori Johns .08 .25
5 Gene Snow .08 .25
6 Eddie Hill .30 1.00
7 Frank Bradley .05 .15
8 Kenny Bernstein .30 1.00
9 Frank Hawley .05 .15
10 Shirley Muldowney .30 1.00
11 Chris Karamesines .08 .25
12 Jim Head .05 .15
13 Don Prudhomme .08 .25
14 Tommy Johnson Jr. .08 .25
15 Michael Brotherton .05 .15
16 Darrell Gwynn .08 .25
17 John Force RC .60 1.50
18 Ed McCulloch .05 .15
19 Bruce Larson .05 .15
20 Mark Oswald .05 .15
21 Jim White .05 .15
22 K.C. Spurlock .05 .15
23 Tom Hoover .08 .25
24 Richard Hartman .05 .15
25 Scott Kalitta .30 1.00
26 Jerry Caminito .05 .15
27 Al Hofmann .05 .15
28 Glenn Mikres .05 .15
29 Chuck Etchells .05 .15
30 John Myers .05 .15
31 Paula Martin .05 .15
32 Mike Dunn .05 .15
33 Connie Kalitta .08 .25
34 Darrell Alderman .05 .15
35 Bob Glidden .08 .25
36 Jerry Eckman .05 .15
37 Larry Morgan .05 .15
38 Warren Johnson .08 .25
39 Rickie Smith .05 .15
40 Mark Pawuk .05 .15
41 Bruce Allen .05 .15
42 Joe Lepone Jr. .05 .15
43 Kenny Delco .05 .15
44 Scott Geoffrion .05 .15
45 Gordie Rivera .05 .15
46 Jerry Haas .05 .15
47 Buddy Ingersoll .05 .15
48 Jim Yates .05 .15
49 Butch Leal .05 .15
50 Joe Amato's Car .05 .15
51 Gary Ormsby's Car .02 .10
52 Dick LaHaie's Car .02 .10
53 Lori Johns' Car .02 .10
54 Gene Snow's Car .05 .15
55 Eddie Hill's Car .08 .25
56 Frank Bradley's Car .02 .10
57 Kenny Bernstein's Car .08 .25
58 Frank Hawley's Car .02 .10
59 Shirley Muldowney's Car .08 .25
60 Chris Karamesines' Car .05 .15
61 Jim Head's Car .02 .10
62 Don Prudhomme's Car .05 .15
63 Tommy Johnson Jr.'s Car .05 .15
64 Michael Brotherton's Car .02 .10
65 Darrell Gwynn's Car .05 .15
66 John Force's Car .30 1.00
67 Ed McCulloch's Car .02 .10
68 Bruce Larson's Car .02 .10
69 Mark Oswald's Car .02 .10
70 Jim White's Car .02 .10
71 K.C. Spurlock's Car .02 .10
72 Tom Hoover's Car .05 .15
73 Richard Hartman's Car .02 .10
74 Scott Kalitta's Car .02 .10
75 Jerry Caminito's Car .02 .10
76 Al Hofmann's Car .02 .10
77 Glenn Mikres' Car .02 .10
78 Chuck Etchells' Car .02 .10
79 Whit Bazemore's Car .02 .10
80 Paula Martin's Car .02 .10
81 David Schultz .02 .10
82 Darrell Alderman's Car .02 .10
83 Bob Glidden's Car .05 .15
84 Jerry Eckman's Car .02 .10
85 Larry Morgan's Car .02 .10
86 Warren Johnson's Car .08 .25
87 Rickie Smith's Car .02 .10
88 Mark Pawuk's Car .02 .10
89 Bruce Allen's Car .02 .10
90 Joe Lepone Jr.'s Car .02 .10
91 Kenny Delco's Car .02 .10
92 Scott Geoffrion's Car .02 .10
93 Gordie Rivera's Car .02 .10
94 Jerry Haas' Car .02 .10
95 Buddy Ingersoll's Car .02 .10
96 Jim Yates' Car .02 .10
97 Butch Leal's Car .02 .10
98 Buster Couch .05 .15
99 Fuzzy Carter .05 .15
100 Austin Coil .05 .15
101 Tim Richards .05 .15
102 Bob Glidden Family .05 .15
103 Kenny Bernstein Funny Car .08 .25
104 Don Prudhomme Funny Car .08 .25
105 Don Garlits .30 1.00
106 Dale Armstrong .05 .15
107 Tom McEwen .08 .25
108 Dave McClelland .05 .15
109 Steve Evans .05 .15
110 Bob Frey .05 .15
111 Deb Brittsan Miss Winston .05 .15
112 Safety Safari .02 .10
113 Gary Densham .05 .15
114 Frank Iaconio .05 .15
115 Don Beverly .05 .15
116 Lee Beard .05 .15
117 Wyatt Radke .05 .15
118 John Medlen .05 .15
119 Gary Brown .05 .15
120 Bernie Fedderly .05 .15
121 Rahn Tobler .05 .15
122 Del Worsham .05 .15
123 Kim LaHaie .05 .15
124 Larry Meyer .05 .15
125 Freddie Neely .05 .15
126 Dan Pastorini .08 .25
127 Bill Jenkins .05 .15
128 Wally Parks .05 .15
129 Connie Kalitta's Car .05 .15
130 Whit Bazemore .05 .15
AU105 Don Garlits AUTO 45.00 75.00

1992 Pro Set NHRA

This was Pro Set's second NHRA release. The set features star drivers, cars and crew members of the top NHRA teams of the previous season. The cards were packaged 12 per foil pack with 36 packs per box. 1,500 factory sets were also produced for distribution to Pro Set Racing Club members. A special hologram card featuring a Pro Set Racing logo (numbered of 5000) was produced and randomly distributed through packs. The card originally had a white border, but was later changed to black creating a variation.

COMPLETE SET (200) 6.00 15.00
COMP.FACT. SET (200) 6.00 14.00
1 Joe Amato .07 .20
2 Kenny Bernstein .20 .60
3 Don Prudhomme .30 .75
4 Frank Hawley .01 .05
5 Eddie Hill .20 .60
6 Tom McEwen .07 .20
7 Gene Snow .07 .20
8 Dick LaHaie .02 .10
9 Cory McClenathan .07 .20
10 Jim Head .02 .10
11 Tommy Johnson Jr. .07 .20
12 Pat Austin .07 .20
13 Scott Kalitta .20 .60
14 Cruz Pedregon .20 .60
15 Doug Herbert .07 .20
16 Gary Ormsby .07 .20
17 Paula Martin 's Car .01 .05
18 Frank Bradley .02 .10
19 Jack Ostrander .02 .10
20 Jim Dunn .02 .10
21 Connie Kalitta .20 .60
22 Pat Dakin .02 .10
23 Jim Murphy's Car .01 .05
24 Bobby Baldwin .02 .10
25 Kenny Koretsky .01 .05
26 Russ Collins .01 .05
27 Shirley Muldowney .20 .60
28 Kim LaHaie .01 .05
29 Gene Snow .20 .60
30 Eddie Hill .20 .60
31 Don Prudhomme .20 .60
32 Kenny Bernstein .20 .60
33 Joe Amato .20 .60
34 Del Worsham .02 .10
35 John Force .50 1.25
36 Tom Gilbertson .01 .05
37 Gary Ritter .01 .05
38 Johnny West .01 .05
39 Mark Sievers .01 .05
40 Jim Epler .02 .10
41 Ron Sutherland .01 .05
42 Wyatt Radke .02 .10
43 Freddie Neely .02 .10
44 Gordon Mineo .02 .10
45 Paula Martin .02 .10
46 Glenn Mikres .01 .05
47 John Force .50 1.25
48 Jim White .02 .10
49 Ed McCulloch .07 .20
50 Mark Oswald .02 .10
51 Al Hofmann .07 .20
52 Tom Hoover .07 .20
53 Richard Hartman .02 .10
54 Jerry Caminito .02 .10
55 Chuck Etchells .07 .20
56 Gary Densham .02 .10
57 Whit Bazemore .01 .05
58 Gary Bolger .02 .10
59 Jim Murphy .01 .05
60 Al Hofmann .07 .20
61 Del Worsham .02 .10
62 Mark Oswald .02 .10
63 Ed McCulloch .07 .20
64 Mike Dunn .02 .10
65 Warren Johnson .07 .20
66 Larry Morgan .02 .10
67 Scott Geoffrion .02 .10
68 Bob Glidden .20 .60
69 Jerry Eckman .02 .10
70 Bruce Allen .02 .10
71 Jim Yates .07 .20
72 Rickie Smith .02 .10
73 Butch Leal .02 .10
74 Joe Lepone Jr. .02 .10
75 Gary Brown .01 .05
76 Harry Scribner .01 .05
77 Paul Rebeschi Jr. .01 .05
78 Joseph Folgore .01 .05
79 Steve Schmidt .02 .10
80 Brad Klein .01 .05
81 Gordie Rivera .02 .10
82 Don Beverly .01 .05
83 Jerry Haas .01 .05
84 Frank Iaconio .02 .10
85 Vincent Khoury .01 .05
86 Kenny Delco .01 .05
87 Ray Franks .02 .10
88 Daryl Thompson .01 .05
89 Mark Pawuk .02 .10
90 Jerry Eckman .02 .10
91 Bob Glidden .20 .60
92 Scott Geoffrion .02 .10
93 Larry Morgan .02 .10
94 Warren Johnson .07 .20
95 Buddy Ingersoll .01 .05
96 Steve Johnson w/Bike .02 .10
97 Paul Gast's Bike .01 .05
98 James Bernard's Bike .01 .05
99 John Myers' Bike .07 .20
100 David Schultz's Bike .07 .20
101 Joe Amato's Car .07 .20
102 Kenny Bernstein .07 .20
103 Don Prudhomme .07 .20
104 Michael Brotherton's Car .01 .05
105 Eddie Hill .07 .20
106 Tom McEwen's Car .01 .05
107 Gene Snow's Car .01 .05
108 Kim LaHaie's Car .01 .05
109 Cory McClenathan's Car .01 .05
110 Jim Head's Car .01 .05
111 Tommy Johnson Jr.'s Car .01 .05
112 Pat Austin's Car .01 .05
113 Scott Kalitta's Car .07 .20
114 Ed McCulloch's Car .01 .05
115 Doug Herbert's Car .01 .05
116 Frank Bradley's Car .01 .05
117 John Force .50 1.25
118 Cruz Pedregon's Car .07 .20
119 Mark Oswald's Car .01 .05
120 Del Worsham's Car .01 .05
121 Al Hofmann's Car .01 .05
122 Tom Hoover's Car .01 .05
123 Richard Hartman's Car .01 .05
124 Jerry Caminito's Car .01 .05
125 Chuck Etchells' Car .01 .05
126 Gary Densham's Car .01 .05
127 Whit Bazemore's Car .01 .05
128 Gary Bolger's Car .01 .05
129 Gordon Mineo's Car .01 .05
130 Freddie Neely's Car .01 .05
131 Jerry Haas' Car .01 .05
132 Joe Lepone Jr.'s Car .01 .05
133 Gordie Rivera's Car .01 .05
134 Gary Brown's Car .01 .05
135 Harry Scribner's Car .01 .05
136 Warren Johnson's Car .01 .05
137 Larry Morgan's Car .01 .05
138 Scott Geoffrion's Car .01 .05
139 Rickie Smith's Car .01 .05
140 Bob Glidden's Car .07 .20
141 Frank Iaconio's Car .01 .05
142 Jerry Eckman's Car .01 .05
143 Jim Yates' Car .01 .05
144 Bruce Allen's Car .01 .05
145 Mark Pawuk's Car .01 .05
146 Kenny Delco's Car .01 .05
147 Kurt Johnson .01 .05
148 Mike Sullivan .01 .05
Dave Hutchens
149 Tom Anderson .01 .05
150 Bernie Fedderly .01 .05
151 John Davis .01 .05
152 Fuzzy Carter .01 .05
153 Dale Armstrong .01 .05
154 Tim Richards .01 .05
155 Ken Veney .01 .05
156 Jim Prock .01 .05
157 Austin Coil .01 .05
158 Chuck Worsham .01 .05
159 Richard Hartman .01 .05
Ray Strasser
160 Tom Roberts .01 .05
161 George Hoover .01 .05
162 Bill Schultz .01 .05
163 Larry Meyer .01 .05
164 John Medlen .01 .05
165 Walt Austin .01 .05
166 Greg Anderson .01 .05
167 Rusty Glidden .01 .05
Etta Glidden
168 Bill Orndorff .01 .05
169 Dave Butner .01 .05
170 Buddy Morrison .01 .05
David Reher
171 Rich Purdy .01 .05
172 Morris Johnson Jr. .01 .05
173 Lee Beard .01 .05
174 Rahn Tobler .01 .05
175 Dannielle DePorter .01 .05
176 Chris Karamesines .01 .05
177 Michael Brotherton .01 .05
178 Bill Jenkins .01 .05
179 Darrell Gwynn .07 .20
180 Larry Minor .01 .05
181 Buster Couch .01 .05
182 Don Garlits .20 .60
183 Dave McClelland .01 .05
184 Steve Evans .01 .05
185 Bob Frey .01 .05
186 Brock Yates .01 .05
187 Wally Parks .01 .05
188 John Mullin .01 .05
189 NHRA Softball Team .01 .05
190 Safety Safari .01 .05
191 Deb Brittsan Miss Winston .01 .05
192 Gary Evans .01 .05
193 Jim Brissette .01 .05
194 Blaine Johnson's Car .01 .05
195 Pat Austin's Car .01 .05
196 David Nickens' Car .01 .05
197 Jeff Taylor's Car .01 .05
198 John Calvert's Car .01 .05
199 John Asta's Car .01 .05
200 Scott Richardson's Car .01 .05
NNO Trophy HOLO White 30.00 80.00
NNO Trophy HOLO Black 30.00 80.00

1992 Pro Set Kenny Bernstein

Pro Set produced this set to highlight the careers of Kenny Bernstein and his crew. The cards were primarily distributed through Bernstein's souvenir outlets

COMPLETE SET (7) 1.50 4.00
1 Kenny Bernstein .20 .50
2 Kenny Bernstein w .20 .50
Crew
3 Dale Armstrong .12 .30
4 Wes Cerny .12 .30
5 Kenny Bernstein .20 .50
6 Kenny Bernstein's Car .07 .20
NNO Cover Card .07 .20

1965 Topps Hot Rods

Topps produced this 66-card set for distribution in 5-cent gum wax packs. The cards feature a wide range of cars from hot rods and racers to custom and dream cars. Three different cardback variations exist. All 66-cards were produced on gray card stock, while only 44 different cards exist with white backs. The 22-card yellow back variations seem to be the toughest to find. They were issued in the "Win-A-Card" Milton Bradley board game distributed in 1968. That game also included cards from Topps' 1967 football card and 1968 baseball card sets.

COMPLETE SET (66) 200.00 325.00

1983 A and S Racing Indy

A and S Racing Collectables produced IndyCar sets from 1983-87. The 1983 set featured 51-cards sold in complete set form and includes the first card of driver Al Unser Jr. There was no card number 13 produced -- the checklist card was unnumbered and blankbacked.

COMPLETE SET (51) 15.00 30.00
1 Rick Mears .75 2.00
2 Dennis Firestone .15 .40
3 Chip Mead .15 .40
4 Chris Kneifel .15 .40
5 Chip Ganassi .15 .40
6 Howdy Holmes .15 .40
7 Steve Krisloff UER .15 .40
8 Pancho Carter .15 .40
9 Chet Fillip .15 .40
10 Phil Caliva .15 .40
11 Geoff Brabham .15 .40
12 Jerry Sneva .15 .40
14 Herm Johnson .15 .40
15 Spike Gehlhausen .15 .40
16 Steve Chassey .15 .40
17 Pete Halsmer .15 .40
18 Kevin Cogan .15 .40
19 Teo Fabi .15 .40
20 Greg Leffler .15 .40
21 Johnny Rutherford .75 2.00
22 Tony Bettenhausen .15 .40
23 Tom Frantz .15 .40
24 George Snider .15 .40
25 Michael Chandler .15 .40
26 Danny Sullivan .30 .75
27 Doug Heveron .15 .40
28 Roger Mears .15 .40
29 Josele Garza .15 .40
30 Mike Mosley .15 .40
31 Scott Brayton .30 .75
32 Jerry Karl .15 .40
33 Mario Andretti 1.25 3.00
34 Bobby Rahal .30 .75
35 Gordon Smiley .15 .40
36 Derek Daly .15 .40
37 Phil Krueger .15 .40
38 John Mahler .15 .40
39 Bill Alsup .15 .40
40 John Paul Jr. .15 .40
41 Jim Buick .15 .40
42 Jim Hickman .15 .40
43 Al Unser Jr. .75 2.00
44 Hector Rebaque .15 .40
45 Bill Tempero .15 .40
46 Dick Ferguson .15 .40
47 Tom Sneva .30 .75
48 Al Unser .75 2.00
49 Gordon Johncock .30 .75
50 Dick Simon .15 .40
51 Gary Bettenhausen .15 .40
NNO Checklist .15 .40

1984 A and S Racing Indy

The 1984 A and S Racing Indy set features 50 of the top drivers on the IndyCar circuit, along with one checklist card (#13). An offer to purchase 1983 complete sets for $8.50 was included on the checklist card. The cards are very similar in appearance to the other A and S Indy sets produced from 1983-87.

COMPLETE SET (51) 15.00 30.00
1 Al Unser .60 1.50
2 Phil Krueger .15 .40
3 Howdy Holmes .15 .40
4 Roger Mears .15 .40
5 Johnny Rutherford .60 1.50
6 Michael Chandler .15 .40
7 Pancho Carter .15 .40
8 Dick Ferguson .15 .40
9 Phil Caliva .15 .40
10 Rick Mears .60 1.50
11 Pete Halsmer .15 .40
12 Derek Daly .15 .40
13 Checklist .15 .40
14 Steve Chassey .15 .40
15 Josele Garza .15 .40
16 Mario Andretti .75 2.00
17 Chris Kneifel .15 .40
18 Al Loquasto .15 .40
19 Dennis Firestone .15 .40
20 Teo Fabi .15 .40
21 George Snider .15 .40
22 Patrick Bedard .15 .40
23 Gary Bettenhausen .15 .40
24 Dick Simon .15 .40
25 Tom Sneva .30 .75
26 Herm Johnson .15 .40
27 Scott Brayton .30 .75
28 Bill Tempero .15 .40
29 Danny Ongais .15 .40
30 John Paul Jr. .15 .40
31 Tom Bagley .15 .40
32 Gordon Johncock .30 .75
33 Desire Wilson .15 .40
34 Greg Leffler .15 .40
35 Chip Ganassi .15 .40
36 Michael Andretti .60 1.50
37 Doug Heveron .15 .40
38 Steve Krisloff .15 .40
39 Geoff Brabham .15 .40
40 Bill Alsup .15 .40
41 Kevin Cogan .15 .40
42 Chuck Ciprich .15 .40
43 Mike Mosley .15 .40
44 Chip Mead .15 .40
45 Tony Bettenhausen .15 .40
46 Jerry Karl .15 .40
47 Al Unser Jr. .60 1.50
48 Chet Fillip .15 .40
49 Bill Vukovich Jr. .15 .40
50 Bobby Rahal .60 1.50
51 Tom Bigelow .15 .40

1985 A and S Racing Indy

The top IndyCar drivers are featured on cards from the 1985 A and S Racing Indy set. The set was originally released in complete set form only. A checklist card, number 13, was produced along with an unnumbered card featuring announcer Don Hein. The checklist card features an offer to purchase 1983-1985 complete sets directly from A and S. An autographed uncut card sheet was offered to collectors as well at a cost of $110. The Jacques Villeneuve card in this set is the uncle of the 1995 PPG series winner.

COMPLETE SET (52) 15.00 30.00
1 Mario Andretti 1.25 2.00
2 Roberto Guerrero .25 .60
3 Derek Daly .15 .40
4 John Paul Jr. .15 .40
5 Chet Fillip .15 .40
6 Al Holbert .15 .40
7 Stan Fox .15 .40
8 Steve Chassey .15 .40
9 Chip Ganassi .15 .40
10 Mike Mosley .15 .40
11 Michael Chandler .15 .40
12 Bobby Rahal .50 1.25
13 Checklist .15 .40
14 Johnny Parsons Jr. .15 .40
15 Howdy Holmes .15 .40
16 Geoff Brabham .15 .40
17 Pete Halsmer .15 .40
18 Dick Ferguson .15 .40
19 Gary Bettenhausen .15 .40
20 Gordon Johncock .25 .60
21 Roger Mears .15 .40
22 Ed Pimm .15 .40
23 Emerson Fittipaldi .25 .60
24 Al Unser Jr. .50 1.25
25 Rick Mears .50 1.25
26 Bill Alsup .15 .40
27 Spike Gehlhausen .15 .40
28 Teo Fabi .15 .40
29 Herm Johnson .15 .40
30 Tom Sneva .25 .60
31 Dick Simon .15 .40
32 Tom Gloy .15 .40
33 Dale Coyne .15 .40
34 Patrick Bedard .15 .40
35 Al Unser .50 1.25
36 Jerry Karl .15 .40
37 Chris Kneifel .15 .40
38 George Snider .15 .40
39 Tony Bettenhausen .15 .40
40 Johnny Rutherford .50 1.25
41 Scott Brayton .25 .60
42 Michael Andretti .50 1.25
43 Randy Lewis .15 .40
44 Phil Krueger .15 .40
45 Pancho Carter .15 .40
46 Dennis Firestone .15 .40
47 Kevin Cogan .15 .40
48 Jacques Villeneuve .15 .40
49 Arie Luyendyk .25 .60
50 Mario Andretti .60 1.50
Michael Andretti
51 Al Unser Jr. .50 1.25
Al Unser
NNO Don Hein .15 .40

1986 A and S Racing Indy

A and S Racing released this 50-card set in complete set form. The cards feature the top IndyCar personalities and very closely resemble the other Indy sets released by the company between 1983-87. The last card in the set features a checklist and an offer to purchase 1983-1986 complete sets directly from A and S. An autographed uncut card sheet was again offered to collectors as well at a cost of $110.

COMPLETE SET (50) 15.00 30.00
1 Al Unser .50 1.25
2 Mario Andretti .75 2.00
3 Spike Gehlhausen .15 .40
4 Josele Garza .15 .40
5 Emerson Fittipaldi .25 .60
6 Ed Pimm .15 .40
7 Dale Coyne .15 .40
8 Roberto Guerrero .25 .60
9 Pancho Carter .15 .40
10 Al Unser Jr. .50 1.25
11 Pete Halsmer .15 .40
12 George Snider .15 .40
13 Gasoline Alley .15 .40
14 Michael Roe .15 .40
15 Dick Simon .15 .40
16 Johnny Rutherford .50 1.25
17 Steve Chassey .15 .40
18 Geoff Brabham .15 .40
19 Tom Bigelow .15 .40
20 Herm Johnson .15 .40
21 Arie Luyendyk .25 .60
22 Chet Fillip .15 .40
23 John Paul Jr. .15 .40
24 Chip Ganassi .15 .40
25 Scott Brayton .25 .60
26 Phil Krueger .15 .40
27 Kevin Cogan .15 .40
28 Johnny Parsons Jr. .15 .40
29 Dennis Firestone .15 .40
30 Bobby Rahal .50 1.25
31 Jim Crawford .15 .40
32 Tom Sneva .25 .60
33 Derek Daly .15 .40
34 Dick Ferguson .15 .40
35 Gordon Johncock .25 .60
36 Scott Brayton .25 .60
Pancho Carter
37 Arie Luyendyk ROY .25 .60
38 Danny Sullivan T10 .15 .40
39 Emerson Fittipaldi T10 .15 .40
40 Rick Mears T10 .25 .60
41 Jacques Villeneuve .15 .40
42 Rupert Keegan .15 .40
43 Michael Andretti .50 1.25
44 Howdy Holmes .15 .40
45 Rick Mears .50 1.25
46 Tony Bettenhausen .15 .40
47 Gary Bettenhausen .15 .40
48 Raul Boesel .15 .40
49 Danny Sullivan .25 .60
50 Checklist .15 .40

1987 A and S Racing Indy

A and S Racing released this 50-card set in complete set form. The cards feature the top Indy Car personalities and very closely resemble the other Indy sets released by the company between 1983-87. Card number 13 features a checklist along with an offer to purchase 1983-1987 complete sets directly from A and S. Fifty uncut card sheets signed by all drivers were again offered to collectors at a cost of $110.

COMPLETE SET (50) 12.50 25.00
1 Bobby Rahal .40 1.00
2 Mario Andretti .50 1.25
Carnegie
3 Steve Chassey .15 .40
4 Tom Sneva .25 .60
5 Geoff Brabham .15 .40
6 Emerson Fittipaldi .25 .60
7 Dale Coyne .15 .40
8 Gary Bettenhausen .15 .40
9 Al Unser .40 1.00
10 Rick Mears' Record .25 .60
11 Roberto Moreno .15 .40
12 Scott Brayton .25 .60
13 Checklist .15 .40
14 A.J. Foyt .40 1.00
15 Phil Krueger .15 .40
16 Jan Lammers .15 .40
17 Ed Pimm .15 .40
18 Michael Andretti w Car .40 1.00
19 George Snider .15 .40
20 Mario Andretti w Car .50 1.25
21 Spike Gehlhausen .15 .40
22 Johnny Rutherford .40 1.00
23 Mike Nish .15 .40
24 Kevin Cogan .15 .40
25 Josele Garza .15 .40
26 Tony Bettenhausen .15 .40
27 Rick Miaskiewicz .15 .40
28 Pancho Carter .15 .40
29 Arie Luyendyk .25 .60
30 Al Unser Jr. .40 1.00
31 Dennis Firestone .15 .40
32 Raul Boesel .15 .40
33 Dominic Dobson .15 .40
34 Danny Sullivan .25 .60
35 Derek Daly .15 .40
36 Ian Ashley .15 .40
37 Randy Lewis .15 .40
38 Jim Crawford .15 .40
39 Rick Mears .40 1.00
40 Johnny Parsons Jr. .15 .40
41 Dick Simon .15 .40
42 Jacques Villeneuve .15 .40
43 Roberto Guerrero .25 .60
44 Desire Wilson .15 .40
45 Michael Andretti .25 .60
Sullivan
Mears
46 Dominic Dobson ROY .15 .40
47 Bobby Rahal WIN .25 .60
48 Mario Andretti Win .50 1.25
49 Johnny Rutherford WIN .25 .60
50 Tony Bettenhausen .15 .40
Gary Bettenhausen

1986 Ace Formula One

This set was made in West Germany for the British company Ace. The cards actually resemble a deck of playing cards with Formula One driver photos on the cardfront with a red playing card type back. The cards are unnumbered and listed below alphabetically. A German version of the set was also produced entitled Top Ace. There is no price difference between the two versions.

COMPLETE SET (33) 2.50 6.00
A1 Alfa Romeo 185T .08 .25
A2 Arrows BMW A8 .08 .25
A3 Brabham BMW BT54 .08 .25
A4 Ferrari 156/85 .08 .25
B1 Ligier Renault JS25 .08 .25
B2 McLaren TAG .08 .25
Porsche
B3 Osella Alfa Romeo FA1F .08 .25
B4 Renault RE60 .08 .25
C1 Lotus Renault 97T .08 .25
C2 Minardi Motori Moderni M185 .08 .25
C3 RAM Hart 03 .08 .25
C4 Spirit Hart 101B .08 .25
D1 Toleman Hart .08 .25
D2 Tyrrell Cosworth 012 .08 .25
D3 Williams Honda FW10 .08 .25
D4 Zakspeed 841 .08 .25
E1 Alfa Romeo 184T .08 .25
E2 Arrows BMW A7 .08 .25
E3 ATS BMW D7 .08 .25
E4 Brabham BMW BT53 .08 .25
F1 Ferrari 126C4 .08 .25
F2 Ligier Renault JS23 .08 .25
F3 RAM Hart 02 .08 .25
F4 Williams Honda FW09B .08 .25
G1 Lotus Renault 95T .08 .25
G2 McLaren TAG .08 .25
Porsche
G3 Renault RE50 .08 .25
G4 Toleman Hart TG184 .08 .25
H1 Brabham BMW BT52B .08 .25
H2 Lotus Renault 94T .08 .25
H3 Renault RE40 .08 .25
H4 Ferrari 126C3 .08 .25
NNO Cover Card .08 .25

1986 Ace Indy

This set was made in West Germany for the British company Ace. The cards are actually part of a Trump card game featuring IndyCar photos on the cardfront with a playing card back and rounded corners. The playing card deck contains 32-cards with one cover/rule card. Drivers are not specifically indentified on the cards, but are included below as noted.

COMPLETE SET (33) 3.00 8.00
A1 Amway Special .25 .60
A2 Pennzoil Special .25 .60
A3 Kraco Special .25 .60
A4 Gilmore Special .25 .60
B1 Living Well Special .25 .60
B2 Intersport March .15 .40
B3 Budweiser Lola .25 .60
B4 Bryd's Valpack March .15 .40
C1 Scheid Tyre Special Buick .15 .40
C2 STP Special .07 .20
C3 Veedol Special .15 .40
C4 Sunoco Special .15 .40
D1 Rislone Special .07 .20
D2 STP Eagle Special .15 .40
D3 McLaren Special .15 .40
D4 Wynn's Special Offy .15 .40
E1 Lightning Special .07 .20
E2 Thermo King Special .07 .20
E3 A.J.Foyt Gilmore Special .25 .60
E4 Eagle Chevrolet .07 .20
F1 True Value Special .07 .20
F2 Valvoline Special .07 .20
F3 Advan Special .07 .20
F4 Valvoline Spirit Honda .07 .20
G1 Lacatop Special .07 .20
G2 Vermont March Special .07 .20
G3 Gilmore Karco Special .25 .60
G4 Marlboro BRM Special .07 .20
H1 Nova Indy 47 .07 .20
H2 Indy Midget .07 .20
H3 Indy Midget .07 .20
H4 Clubmann Indy Stocker .07 .20
NNO Cover Card .07 .20

1987 Ace Formula One

This set was made in West Germany for the British company Ace. The cards actually resemble a deck of playing cards with Formula One driver photos on the cardfront with a blue playing card type back. The set contains 32 individual driver cards with one cover card picturing Alain Prost. The cards are unnumbered and listed below alphabetically.

COMPLETE SET (33) 3.00 8.00
1 Michele Alboreto .07 .20
2 Philippe Alliot .07 .20
3 Rene Arnoux .07 .20
4 Allen Berg .07 .20
5 Gerhard Berger .15 .40
6 Thierry Boutsen .07 .20
7 Martin Brundle .07 .20
8 Alex Caffi .07 .20
9 Ivan Capelli .07 .20
10 Eddie Cheever .07 .20
11 Christian Danner .07 .20
12 Andrea deCesaris .07 .20
13 Johnny Dumfries .07 .20
14 Teo Fabi .07 .20
15 Piercarlo Ghinzani .07 .20
16 Stefan Johansson .07 .20
17 Alan Jones .07 .20
18 Jacques Laffite .07 .20
19 Nigel Mansell .25 .60
20 Satoro Nakajma .07 .20
21 Alessandro Nannini .07 .20
22 Jonathan Palmer .07 .20
23 Riccardo Patrese .15 .40
24 Nelson Piquet .15 .40
25 Alain Prost .15 .40
26 Keke Rosberg .15 .40
27 Huub Rothengatter .07 .20
28 Ayrton Senna .50 1.25
29 Philippe Streiff .07 .20
30 Marc Surer .07 .20
31 Patrick Tambay .07 .20
32 Derek Warwick .07 .20
33 Cover Card .07 .20
Alain Prost

1990 Action Packed Indy Prototypes

Action Packed prepared these four prototype cards to demonstrate their printing technology to the racing card industry. Each card features the standard gold foil border along with an embossed driver photo on the cardfront. Backs carry a short driver biography and 1989 race results. The four cards are skip numbered.

COMPLETE SET (4) 150.00 300.00
1 Emerson Fittipaldi 40.00 75.00
6 Mario Andretti 75.00 125.00
22 Rick Mears 40.00 75.00
23 Pancho Carter 30.00 60.00

1956 Adventure R749

The Adventure series produced by Gum Products in 1956, contains a wide variety of subject matter. Cards in the set measure the standard size. The color drawings are printed on a heavy thickness of cardboard and have large white borders. The backs contain the card number, the caption, and a short text. The most expensive cards in the series of 100 are those associated with sports (Louis, Tunney, etc.). In addition, card number 86 (Schmelling) is notorious and sold at a premium price because of the Nazi symbol printed on the card. Although this set is considered by many to be a topical or non-sport set, several boxers are featured (cards 11, 22, 31-35, 41-44, 76-80, 86-90). One of the few cards of Boston-area legend Harry Agannis is in this set. The sports-related cards are in greater demand than the non-sport cards. These cards came in one-card penny packs where were packed 240 to a box.

COMPLETE SET (100) 225.00 450.00
38 Dirt Track Hot-Rodders 1.50 3.00

1991 All World Indy

All World, in cooperation with A and S Racing, produced an Indy Car set in both 1991 and '92. The 1991 issue contained 100-cards featuring individual driver cards, race by race highlight cards of the previous season and All-Time Greats and Past Champion subset cards. Foil packs contained nine cards and factory sets were produced. Signed cards from this set were randomly inserted in 1992 All World packs, although they have no distinguishing characteristics to differentiate them from regular issue cards. An offer to purchase past A and S Racing sets was also included in packs.

COMPLETE SET (100) 2.00 5.00
COMP.FACT.SET (100) 2.50 6.00
1 Al Unser Jr. .08 .25
2 Bill Vukovich III .02 .10
3 Tero Palmroth .02 .10
4 John Andretti .05 .15
5 Mario Andretti .20 .50
6 Tony Bettenhausen .02 .10
7 Tom Sneva .05 .15
8 Willy T. Ribbs .02 .10
9 Bobby Rahal .05 .15
10 Danny Sullivan .05 .15
11 Buddy Lazier .02 .10
12 Stan Fox .02 .10
13 Checklist 1 UER .02 .10
14 Dean Hall .02 .10
15 Arie Luyendyk .05 .15
16 Eddie Cheever .05 .15
17 Scott Goodyear .02 .10
18 Jon Beekhuis .02
19 Jeff Wood .02
20 Emerson Fittipaldi .05
21 Pancho Carter W/Family .02
22 Mike Groff .02
23 Rocky Moran .02
24 Roberto Guerrero .08
25 Michael Andretti .08
26 Didier Theys .02
27 Geoff Brabham .02
28 Randy Lewis .02
29 Michael Greenfield .02
30 Rick Mears .08
31 Gary Bettenhausen .02
32 Raul Boesel .02
33 Michael Andretti .08
John Andretti
34 Dominic Dobson .02
35 Al Unser .08
36 Kevin Cogan .02
37 Wally Dallenbach Jr. .02
38 Jim Crawford .02
39 Scott Brayton .05
40 Hiro Matsushita .02
41 Jeff Andretti .02
42 '90 Indy Standings .02
43 Emerson Fittipaldi Win .05
44 Arie Luyendyk Win .05
45 Al Unser Jr. WIN .08
46 Eddie Cheever ROY .05
47 Guido Dacco .02
48 Tony Bettenhausen .02
Gary Bettenhausen
49 Steve Chassey .02
50 Derek Daly .02
51 Scott Pruett .02
52 Phil Krueger .02
53 Bernard Jourdain .02
54 Johnny Rutherford .05
55 Ludwig Heimrath Jr. .02
56 Scott Atchison .02
57 John Jones .02
58 Scott Harrington .02
59 Davy Jones .02
60 Steve Saleen .02
61 Gordon Johncock .02
62 Dale Coyne .02
63 Bill Vukovich III .02
64 Bernard Jourdain .02
Scott Pruett
65 Emerson Fittipaldi WIN .05
66 Michael Andretti Win .08
67 Danny Sullivan WIN .05
68 Jim Hurtubise .02
69 Sheldon Kinser .02
70 Al Holbert .02
71 Sam Hanks ATG .02
72 Duane Carter Sr. ATG .02
73 Tony Bettenhausen Sr. ATG .02
74 Rick Mears Winner .08
75 Al Unser Jr. .08
Bobby Rahal
76 Checklist 2 UER .02
77 '90 Phoenix Race .02
78 '90 Long Beach Race .02
79 '90 Indy 500 Mile Race .02
80 '90 Milwaukee Race .02
81 '90 Detroit Race .02
82 '90 Portland Race .02
83 '90 Cleveland Race .02
84 '90 Meadowlands Race .02
85 '90 Toronto Race .02
86 '90 Michigan 500 Race .02
87 '90 Denver Race .02
88 '90 Vancouver Race .02
89 '90 Mid Ohio Race .02
90 '90 Elkhart Lake Race .02
91 '90 Nazareth Race .02
92 '90 Laguna Seca Race .02
93 Johnny Rutherford PPGC .05
94 Rick Mears PPGC .08
95 Al Unser PPGC .05
96 Mario Andretti PPGC .20
97 Bobby Rahal PPGC .05
98 Danny Sullivan .05
99 Emerson Fittipaldi PPGC .05
100 Al Unser Jr. PPGC .08
P1 Al Unser Jr. Promo 1.50 4.00
P2 Al Unser Jr.'s Car Promo 1.00 2.50

1992 All World Indy

All World, in cooperation with A and S Racing,

...duced an Indy Car set in both 1991 and '92. ...1992 issue again contained 100-cards ...uring individual driver cards and Where are ...y Now, Careers, and All-Time Greats subset ...s. Foil packs contained nine cards and factory ...s were produced as well. Autographed cards ...n the 1991 All World Indy set were randomly ...ded throughout the run of 1992 packs. ...portedly, 100 cards were signed by 40 different ...vers. The cards cannot otherwise be ...tinguished from regular issue 1991 cards and, ...refore, generally do not carry a significant ...emium over other signed cards. An offer to ...rchase uncut sheets of the set for $19.95 was ...cluded on the wrapper.

...MPLETE SET (100) 2.00 5.00
...MP.FACT.SET (100) 2.50 6.00
Michael Andretti .08 .25
Mike Groff .02 .10
Dean Hall .02 .10
Gary Bettenhausen .02 .10
Willy T. Ribbs .02 .10
Scott Pruett .02 .10
Scott Goodyear .02 .10
Bobby Rahal .08 .25
Eddie Cheever .05 .15
Phil Krueger .02 .10
Arie Luyendyk .05 .15
Michael Greenfield .02 .10
Checklist .02 .10
Stan Fox .02 .10
John Andretti .05 .15
Guido Dacco .02 .10
Kevin Cogan .02 .10
Danny Sullivan .05 .15
Mark Dismore .02 .10
Emerson Fittipaldi .05 .15
Al Unser Jr. .08 .25
Didier Theys .02 .10
Geoff Brabham .02 .10
Buddy Lazier .02 .10
Mario Andretti .20 .50
Dale Coyne .02 .10
Roberto Guerrero .08 .25
Dominic Dobson .02 .10
Johnny Parsons Jr. .02 .10
Al Unser .05 .15
31 Tony Bettenhausen .02 .10
32 Scott Brayton .05 .15
33 Gordon Johncock .05 .15
34 Tero Palmroth .02 .10
35 Dennis Vitolo .02 .10
36 Bernard Jourdain .02 .10
37 Hiro Matsushita .02 .10
38 Ted Prappas .02 .10
39 Jeff Wood .02 .10
40 Jeff Andretti .02 .10
41 Rick Mears .08 .25
42 Pancho Carter .05 .15
43 Jim Crawford .02 .10
44 Randy Lewis .02 .10
45 Buddy Lazier .02 .10
Bob Lazier
46 Michael Andretti .08 .25
47 Jeff Andretti .05 .15
48 John Andretti .05 .15
49 Andretti Family .08 .25
50 Andretti Trifecta .08 .25
51 Norman Schwartzkopf .05 .15
Carter
Unser Sr.
Ruther.
52 Rich Vogler .02 .10
53 Al Loquasto .02 .10
54 Checklist .02 .10
55 Rodger Ward ATG .02 .10
56 Louis Meyer ATG .02 .10
57 Wally Dallenbach Sr. ATG .02 .10
58 Johnnie Parsons ATG .02 .10
59 Troy Ruttman ATG .02 .10
60 Parnelli Jones ATG .05 .15
61 Eddie Sachs ATG .02 .10
62 Johnny Boyd ATG .02 .10
63 Lloyd Ruby ATG .02 .10
64 Bill Vukovich Jr. ATG .02 .10
65 George Snider .02 .10
66 Gene Hartley .02 .10
67 Howdy Holmes .02 .10
68 Lee Kunzman .02 .10
69 Larry Rice .02 .10
70 Mario Andretti C .20 .50
71 Arie Luyendyk C .10 .25
72 Gordon Johncock C .05 .15
73 Scott Goodyear C .02 .10
74 Pancho Carter C .02 .10
75 Jim Crawford C .02 .10
76 John Andretti C .05 .15
77 Johnny Rutherford C .05 .15
78 Danny Sullivan C .05 .15
79 Michael Andretti C .08 .25
80 Emerson Fittipaldi C .05 .15
81 Bobby Rahal C .05 .15
82 Steve Chassey C .02 .10
83 Checklist .02 .10
84 Al Unser Jr. .08 .25
85 Roberto Guerrero .08 .25
86 Eddie Cheever .05 .15
87 Tom Sneva .02 .10
88 Scott Pruett .02 .10
89 Phil Krueger .02 .10
90 Rick Mears .05 .15
91 Al Unser .05 .15
92 Tony Bettenhausen .02 .10
93 Dominic Dobson .02 .10
94 Scott Brayton .05 .15
95 Randy Lewis .02 .10
96 Geoff Brabham .02 .10
97 Mike Groff .02 .10
98 Gary Bettenhausen .02 .10
99 Didier Theys .02 .10
100 Kevin Cogan .02 .10

1968 American Oil Winners Circle

This set of 12 perforated game cards measures approximately 2 5/8" by 2 1/8". There are "left side" and "right side" game cards which had to be matched to win a car or a cash prize. The "right side" game cards have a color drawing of a sports personality in a circle on the left, surrounded by laurel leaf twigs, and a short career summary on the right. There is a color bar on the bottom of the game piece carrying a dollar amount and the words "right side". The "left side" game cards carry a rectangular drawing of a sports personality or a photo of a Camaro or a Corvette. A different color bar with a dollar amount and the words "left side" are under the picture. On a dark blue background, the "right side" backs carry the rules of the game, and the "left side" cards show a "Winners Circle". The cards are unnumbered and checklisted below in alphabetical order.

COMPLETE SET (12) 75.00 150.00
6 Parnelli Jones 2.50 5.00
Left side

1911 American Tobacco Auto Drivers

This 25-card set was produced for The American Tobacco Company. Each card includes a small ad for either Hassan or Mecca Cigarettes on the cardback. All 25 cards were produced with both ad back variations. The cards measure 2 1/2 x 1 3/4 and came with square corners. The cards are unnumbered and feature top race car drivers of the day from both North America and Europe representing all types of auto racing events. They were packaged one card per 10 cigarette pack and two per 20 cigarette pack. The cards were inserted in cigarette packs starting on March 27th, 1911 and ending on March 31st, 1911. Special thanks to Jon Hardgrove for providing much of this information.

COMPLETE SET (25) 90.00 800.00
1 David Bruce-Brown 15.00 25.00
2 Bob Burman 15.00 25.00
3 Louis Chevrolet 30.00 50.00
4 Walter Christie 15.00 25.00
5 Demoget 15.00 25.00
6 Ralph dePalma 30.00 50.00
7 Bert Dingley 15.00 25.00
8 Arthur Duray 15.00 25.00
9 Henri Fournier 15.00 25.00
10 Harry E. Grant 15.00 25.00
11 Victor Hemery 15.00 25.00
12 Camille Jenatzy UER 15.00 25.00
13 Vincenzo Lancia 15.00 25.00
14 Herbert Lyttle 15.00 25.00
15 Fred Marriott 15.00 25.00
16 Harry Mitchner 15.00 25.00
17 R. Mulford 15.00 25.00
18 Felice Nazarro 15.00 25.00
19 Barney Oldfield 30.00 50.00
20 George H. Robertson 15.00 25.00
21 Joe Seymour 15.00 25.00
22 Lewis P. Strang 15.00 25.00
23 Francois Szisz 15.00 25.00
24 Joseph Tracy UER 15.00 25.00
25 Louis Wagner 15.00 25.00

1987 A Question of Sport UK

These cards are part of a British board game "A Question of Sport" in which participants attempt to name an athlete by seeing a picture of them. These white bordered, full color cards measure 2 1/4" by 3 1/2" and have a back that contains only the player's name on a green background. The copyright on the box is 1986, but the game was released in early 1987. We've arranged the unnumbered cards alphabetically below.

COMPLETE SET (240) 20.00 40.00
153 Nigel Mansell .50 1.25
187 Nelson Piquet .40 1.00
190 Alain Prost .40 1.00
201 Ayrton Senna(portrait image) .75 2.00
202 Ayrton Senna(photo of car) .50 1.25

1990 A Question of Sport Jr. UK

These cards are part of a British board game "A Question of Sport Jr." in which participants attempt to name an athlete by seeing a picture of them. These white bordered, full color cards measure 2" by 3 1/4" and have a back that contains the player's name, the set title "Junior QS" and a card number in the lower right hand corner. The set is skip-numbered.

81 Nigel Mansell .40 1.00

1992 A Question of Sport UK

These cards are part of a British board game "A Question of Sport" in which participants attempt to name an athlete by seeing a picture of them. These white bordered, full color cards measure 2 1/4" by 3 1/2" and have a back that contains only the player's name. We've arranged the unnumbered cards alphabetically below.

COMPLETE SET (80) 20.00 50.00
49 Nigel Mansell .75 2.00
57 Nelson Piquet .20 .50
61 Alain Prost .20 .50
68 Ayrton Senna 2.00 5.00

1994 A Question of Sport UK

These cards are part of a British board game "A Question of Sport" in which participants attempt to name an athlete by seeing a picture of them. These white bordered, full color cards measure 2 1/4" by 3 1/2" and have a back that contains only the player's name surrounded by a blue border on white card stock. We've arranged the unnumbered cards alphabetically below.

COMPLETE SET (79) 20.00 50.00
28 Graham Hill .60 1.50
29 Damon Hill .20 .50
64 Michael Schumacher 1.20 3.00

1996 A Question of Sport Who Am I

This 100-card multi-sport set was from a game exclusively sold in England. Each front of the game cards features a blue and yellow border with a small color photo of the featured athlete on the top half. The player's name is listed below in light blue after a series of written clues about the player's identity. The only notable basketball player is Magic Johnson. The cards are not numbered and are checklisted below in alphabetical order.

COMPLETE SET (100) 30.00 75.00
9 Gerhard Berger .20 .50
12 Martin Brundle .20 .50
44 Damon Hill .60 1.50
58 Nigel Mansell 1.60 4.00
76 Alain Prost .60 1.50
81 Michael Schumacher 1.60 4.00
88 Jackie Stewart 1.00 2.50

1980 Avalon Hill USAC Race Game

This 33-card set was part of a board game. The cards feature the Indy drivers who raced in the 1980 Indianapolis 500. An interesting note is the appearance of NASCAR Winston Cup driver Tim Richmond. He finished 9th in the race. The cards are numbered in order of finish in the race.

COMPLETE SET (33) 75.00 125.00
1 Johnny Rutherford 2.50 6.00
2 Tom Sneva 1.50 4.00
3 Gary Bettenhausen 1.50 4.00
4 Gordon Johncock 1.50 4.00
5 Rick Mears 1.50 4.00
6 Pancho Carter 1.50 4.00
7 Danny Ongais 1.50 4.00
8 Tom Bigelow 1.25 3.00
9 Tim Richmond 3.00 8.00
10 Greg Leffler 1.25 3.00
11 Billy Engelhart 1.25 3.00
12 Billy Vukovich 1.25 3.00
13 Don Whittington 1.25 3.00
14 A.J.Foyt 3.00 8.00
15 George Snider 1.25 3.00
16 Dennis Firestone 1.25 3.00
17 Jerry Sneva 1.25 3.00
18 Hurley Haywood 1.25 3.00
19 Bobby Unser 1.50 4.00
20 Mario Andretti 4.00 10.00
21 Jerry Karl 1.25 3.00
22 Dick Simon 1.25 3.00
23 Roger Rager 1.25 3.00
24 Jim McElreath 1.25 3.00
25 Gordon Smiley 1.25 3.00
26 Johnny Parsons 1.25 3.00
27 Al Unser 2.50 6.00
28 Tom Bagley 1.25 3.00
29 Spike Gehlhausen 1.25 3.00
30 Bill Ehittington 1.25 3.00
31 Dick Ferguson 1.25 3.00
32 Mike Mosley 1.25 3.00
33 Larry Cannon 1.25 3.00

1986 BOSCH Indy

Bosch Spark Plugs produced this set featuring top IndyCar drivers. Each card is unnumbered and features a driver photo and car photo on the cardfront. Cardbacks contain driver career information and stats.

COMPLETE SET (8) 100.00 200.00
1 Mario Andretti 25.00 50.00
2 Emerson Fittipaldi 12.00 30.00
3 Bruno Giacomelli 8.00 20.00
4 Howdy Holmes 8.00 20.00
5 Rick Mears 12.00 30.00
6 Danny Sullivan 12.00 30.00
7 Al Unser, Jr. 12.00 30.00
8 Al Unser, Sr. 12.00 30.00

1932 Briggs Chocolate

This set was issued by C.A. Briggs Chocolate company in 1932. The cards feature 31-different sports with each card including an artist's rendering of a sporting event. Although players are not named, it is thought that most were modeled after famous athletes of the time. The cardbacks include a written portion about the sport and an offer from Briggs for free baseball equipment for building a compete set of cards.

21 Auto Racing 75.00 200.00

1991 Carms Formula One

Carms Sports Cards of Nova Scotia produced this set featuring the top drivers of Formula One racing. Most drivers have three cards: a portrait, a car photo, and a driver photo in his car. The last card in the set is a cover card complete with ordering information for additional sets. Cards were sold in factory set form with Ayrton Senna's car featured on the box.

COMPLETE SET (105) 12.50 30.00
1 Ayrton Senna 2.00 4.00
2 Ayrton Senna's Car .75 2.00
3 Ayrton Senna 2.00 4.00
4 Gerhard Berger .30 .75
5 Gerhard Berger's Car .20 .50
6 Gerhard Berger .30 .75
7 Saturo Nakajima .20 .50
8 Saturo Nakajima's Car .08 .25
9 Saturo Nakajima .20 .50
10 Stefano Modena .20 .50
11 Stefano Modena's Car .08 .25
12 Stefano Modena .20 .50
13 Nigel Mansell .75 2.00
14 Nigel Mansell's Car .30 .75
15 Nigel Mansell .75 2.00
16 Riccardo Patrese .30 .75
17 Riccardo Patrese's Car .20 .50
18 Riccardo Patrese .30 .75
19 Martin Brundle .20 .50
20 Martin Brundle's Car .08 .25
21 Martin Brundle .20 .50
22 Mark Blundell .20 .50
23 Mark Blundell's Car .08 .25
24 Mark Blundell .20 .50
25 Michele Alboreto .20 .50
26 Michele Alboreto's Car .08 .25
27 Michele Alboreto .20 .50
28 Alex Caffi .20 .50
29 Alex Caffi's Car .08 .25
30 Alex Caffi .20 .50
31 Mika Hakkinen .20 .50
32 Mika Hakkinen's Car .08 .25
33 Mika Hakkinen .20 .50
34 Julian Bailey .20 .50
35 Julian Bailey's Car .08 .25
36 Julian Bailey .20 .50
37 Olivier Grouillard .20 .50
38 Olivier Grouillard's Car .08 .25
39 Olivier Grouillard .20 .50
40 Mauricio Gugelmin .20 .50
41 Mauricio Gugelmin's Car .08 .25
42 Mauricio Gugelmin .20 .50
43 Ivan Capelli .20 .50
44 Ivan Capelli's Car .08 .25
45 Ivan Capelli .20 .50
46 Gabriele Tarquini .20 .50
47 Gabriele Tarquini's Car .08 .25
48 Gabriele Tarquini .20 .50
49 Stefan Johansson .30 .75
50 Stefan Johansson's Car .20 .50
51 Stefan Johansson .30 .75
52 Roberto Moreno .20 .50
53 Roberto Moreno's Car .08 .25
54 Roberto Moreno .20 .50
55 Nelson Piquet .20 .50
56 Nelson Piquet's Car .08 .25
57 Nelson Piquet .20 .50
58 Emanuele Pirro .20 .50
59 Emanuele Pirro's Car .08 .25
60 Emanuele Pirro .20 .50
61 J.J. Lehto .20 .50
62 J.J. Lehto's Car .08 .25
63 J.J. Lehto .20 .50
64 Pierluigi Martini .20 .50
65 Pierluigi Martini's Car .08 .25
66 Pierluigi Martini .20 .50
67 Gianni Morbidelli .20 .50
68 Gianni Morbidelli's Car .08 .25
69 Gianni Morbidelli .20 .50
70 Thierry Boutsen .20 .50
71 Thierry Boutsen's Car .08 .25
72 Thierry Boutsen .20 .50
73 Erik Comas .20 .50
74 Erik Comas' Car .08 .25
75 Erik Comas .20 .50
76 Alain Prost .30 .75
77 Alain Prost's Car .20 .50
78 Alain Prost .30 .75
79 Jean Alesi .20 .50
80 Jean Alesi's Car .08 .25
81 Jean Alesi .20 .50
82 Eric Bernard .20 .50
83 Eric Bernard's Car .08 .25
84 Eric Bernard .20 .50
85 Aguri Suzuki .20 .50
86 Aguri Suzuki's Car .08 .25
87 Aguri Suzuki .20 .50
88 Pedro Matos Chaves .20 .50
89 Pedro Matos Chaves' Car .08 .25
90 Bertrand Gachot .20 .50
91 Bertrand Gachot's Car .08 .25
92 Bertrand Gachot .20 .50
93 Andrea deCesaris .20 .50
94 Andrea deCesaris' Car .08 .25
95 Andrea deCesaris .20 .50
96 Nicola Larini .20 .50
97 Nicola Larini's Car .08 .25
98 Nicola Larini .20 .50
99 Eric Van de Poele .20 .50
100 Eric Van de Poele's Car .08 .25
101 Mario Andretti .75 2.00
102 Mario Andretti's Car .30 .75
103 Gilles Villeneuve .75 2.00
104 Gilles Villeneuve's Car .30 .75
105 Cover Card .08 .25

1997 CART Schedule Cards

This set was proedcued for the 1997 CART season with each glossy card featuring a CART 97 logo on the front along with a color image of the driver. The backs of these cards contain the 1997 CART schedule with no manufacturer identification. The cards are unnumbered and appear in alphabetical order.

COMPLETE SET (6) 1.25 3.00
1 Michael Andretti .50 1.25
2 Mark Blundell .20 .50
3 Gil De Ferran .25 .60
4 Christian Fittipaldi .25 .60
5 Max Papis .20 .50
6 Jimmy Vasser .30 .75

1939 Churchman's Kings of Speed

This European tobacco issue is part of a bigger 50 card set. The set was issued by Imperial Tobacco Company and carries the theme speed. There were 13 car cards as part of the set. Other subsets were Aviators, Motorcycle racers, Bicycle racers, Boatsmen, Winter Olympians and Summer Olympians. The cards measure 1 3/8" X 2 5/8" and feature artwork of the drivers for card fronts. The backs give a bio of the driver pictured.

COMPLETE SET (13) 20.00 35.00
11 Captain G.E.T. Eyston 1.25 3.00
12 John Cobb 1.25 3.00
13 Major Goldie Gardner 1.25 3.00
14 Ab Jenkins 1.25 3.00
15 Birabongse Bira Prince of Siam 1.25 3.00
16 Rudolf Caracciola 1.25 3.00
17 Charlie Dodson 1.25 3.00
18 Louis Gerard 1.25 3.00
19 Percy Maclure 1.25 3.00
20 Raymond Mays 1.25 3.00
21 Tazio Nuvolari 1.25 3.00
22 Richard Seaman 1.25 3.00
23 J.P. Wakefield 1.25 3.00

1992 Collect-A-Card Andretti Racing

This Collect-A-Card set highlights the racing careers of Andretti family members Mario, Michael, Jeff and John. The cards were issued in 10-card packs as well as complete factory sets. Packs included randomly inserted 24K Gold autograph cards (250 of each made) of each of the four drivers. Factory sets included a special Hologram card featuring the CART/PPG IndyCar World Series Championship trophy.

COMPLETE SET (100) 1.50 4.00
1 Checklist Card .05 .10
2 Mario Andretti's Car .05 .15
3 Mario Andretti's Car .05 .15
4 Mario Andretti .15 .40
5 Mario Andretti's Car .05 .15
6 Mario Andretti's Car .05 .15
7 Jeff Andretti .05 .15
8 John Andretti .05 .15
9 Mario Andretti's Car .05 .15
10 Mario Andretti in Car .05 .15
11 Mario Andretti's Car .05 .15
12 Mario Andretti in Car .05 .15
13 Mario Andretti .15 .40
Aldo Andretti
14 Mario Andretti in car .15 .40
15 Mario Andretti .15 .40
16 Mario Andretti's Car .05 .15
17 Mario Andretti's Car .05 .15
18 Mario Andretti's Car .05 .15
19 Mario Andretti's Car .05 .15
20 Mario Andretti's Car .05 .15
21 Mario Andretti's Car .05 .15
22 Mario Andretti's Car .05 .15
23 Mario Andretti's Car .05 .15
24 Mario Andretti in Car .05 .15
25 Mario Andretti's Car .05 .15
26 John Andretti's Car .01 .05
27 John Andretti's Car .01 .05
28 John Andretti's Car .01 .05
29 John Andretti's Car .01 .05
30 John Andretti .05 .15
31 John Andretti .05 .15
32 John .15 .40
Michael
Mario Andretti Car
33 John Andretti's Car .01 .05
34 John Andretti's Car .01 .05
35 John Andretti in Car .01 .05
36 John Andretti's Car .01 .05
37 John Andretti's Car .01 .05
38 John Andretti's Car .01 .05
39 John Andretti .05 .15
40 John Andretti's Car .01 .05
41 Mario Andretti .05 .15
A.J. Foyt Cars
42 Michael Andretti .15 .40
Mario Andretti
Al Unser Jr.
43 Michael Andretti .15 .40
Mario Andretti
44 Michael Andretti .10 .25
45 Michael Andretti's Car .05 .10
46 Michael Andretti's Car .05 .10
47 Michael Andretti .10 .25
48 Michael Andretti's Car .05 .10
49 Michael Andretti's Car .05 .10
50 Michael Andretti's Car .05 .10
51 Mario Andretti's Car .05 .15
52 Mario Andretti's Car .05 .15
53 Mario Andretti's Car .05 .15
54 Michael Andretti's Car .05 .10
55 Mario Andretti .15 .40
56 Mario Andretti's Car .05 .15
57 Mario Andretti .15 .40
58 Michael Andretti's Car .05 .10
59 Mario Andretti's Car .05 .15
60 Mario Andretti .15 .40
61 Mario Andretti's Car .05 .15
62 Mario Andretti's Car .05 .15
63 Michael Andretti's Car .05 .10
64 Michael Andretti's Car .05 .10
65 Mario Andretti's Car .05 .15
66 Jeff Andretti .05 .15
67 Michael Andretti's Car .05 .10
68 Michael Andretti .10 .25
Carl Haas
69 Mario .15 .40
Michael
Jeff Andretti
70 Mario Andretti's Car .05 .15
71 Mario Andretti .15 .40
72 Mario Andretti .15 .40
Johncock
D.Gurney Cars
73 Mario Andretti's Car .05 .15
74 Jeff Andretti's Car .01 .05
75 Mario .15 .40
Jeff
John
Michael Andretti Cars
76 Mar.Andretti .15 .40
Mich.Andretti
J. Andretti
77 Michael Andretti in Pits .10 .25
78 Mario Andretti .15 .40
A.J. Foyt
Rick Mears
79 Michael Andretti .10 .25
80 Mario Andretti's Car .05 .15
81 Mario Andretti in Car .05 .15
82 Jeff Andretti's Car .01 .05
83 Mario Andretti's Transporter .05 .15
84 Jeff Andretti .05 .15
85 Michael Andretti .20 .50
Paul Newman
86 1990 Indianapolis .15 .40
87 Jeff Andretti .05 .15
88 Michael .05 .15
Mario Andretti Car
89 Mario Andretti's Car .05 .15
90 Mario Andretti .15 .40
91 Michael .15 .40
Jeff
Mario Andretti Car
92 Jeff Andretti's Car .01 .05
93 Mario Andretti .15 .40
Jeff Andretti in Car
94 Jeff Andretti's Car .01 .05
95 Jeff Andretti's Car .01 .05
96 Mario Andretti Collage .15 .40
97 Mario Andretti .15 .40
Michael
Jeff Andretti
98 Mario Andretti .15 .40
99 Michael Andretti .10 .25
100 Checklist Card .05 .10
NNO PPG Cup HOLO .50 1.00

1955-56 Diamond Matchbooks Indy

The Diamond Match Co. produced these matchbook covers featuring Indy 500 drivers. They measure approximately 1 1/2" by 4 1/2" (when completely folded out). We've listed the drivers alphabetically. Each of the covers was produced with black and red ink with a black and white image of the driver in his car. The driver's name appears above the image and the notation "Indianapolis 500" along with the year is printed below the image. A Champion Spark Plugs ad can be found in the middle of the cover and a sponsorship logo or ad is usually found on the back. Most of the drivers are current participants for the 1955 and 1956 races while others feature recent past race winners. Complete covers with matches intact are valued at approximately 1 1/2 times the prices listed below.

COMPLETE SET (7) 100.00 175.00
1 Freddie Agabashian 1955 6.00 12.00
2 Keith Andrews 1955 6.00 12.00
3 Duane Carter 1955 6.00 12.00
4 Art Cross 1955 6.00 12.00
5 Jimmy Davies 1955 6.00 12.00
6 Pat Flaherty 1956 Winner 6.00 12.00
7 Andy Linden 1955 6.00 12.00
8 Jack McGrath 1955 6.00 12.00
9 Pat O'Connor 1955 6.00 12.00
10 Johnnie Parsons 1955 6.00 12.00
11 Dick Rathmann 1956 6.00 12.00
12 Jim Rathmann 1956 6.00 12.00
13 Jimmy Reece 1955 6.00 12.00
14 Bob Sweikert 1955 Winner 6.00 12.00
15 Johnny Thomson 1955 6.00 12.00
16 Lee Wallard 1951 Winner 6.00 12.00
17 Rodger Ward 1955 6.00 12.00

1993 Fax Pax World of Sport

The 1993 Fax Pax World of Sport set was issued in Great Britain and contains 40 standard size cards. This multisport set spotlights notable sports figures from around the world, who are the best in their respective sports. An Olympic subset of seven cards (28-34) is included. The full-bleed fronts feature color action and posed photos with a red-edged white stripe intersecting the photo across the bottom. Within the white stripe is displayed the athlete's name and his country's flag. The horizontal, white backs carry the athlete's name and sport at the top followed by biographical information. Career summary and statistics are printed within a gray box, edged in red.

COMPLETE SET (40) 6.00 15.00

35 Nigel Mansell .30 .75
36 Richard Petty .75 2.00

1987 Formula One Italian

This set was produced in Italy in 1987 and features popular drivers of the Formula One circuit. The cards are unnumbered, oversized (2-3/4" by 4") and have rounded corners. A 1987 yearly calendar makes up the cardback, while cardfronts typically show two small driver photos along with an F1 car shot. The cards are listed below alphabetically according to the alphabetized pair of drivers featured.

COMPLETE SET (16) 8.00 20.00
1 Michele Alboreto .60 1.50
Stefan Johansson
2 Rene Arnoux .40 1.00
Jacques Laffite
3 Gerhard Berger .60 1.50
Teo Fabi
4 Thierry Boutsen .40 1.00
Marc Surer
5 Martin Brundle .60 1.50
Eddie Cheever
6 Ivan Capeli .40 1.00
Christian Danner
7 Elio DeAngelis .60 1.50
Riccardo Patrese
8 Andrea DeCesais .40 1.00
Alessandro Nannini
9 Johnny Dumfries 1.50 4.00
Ayrton Senna
10 Alan Jones .60 1.50
Patrick Tambay
11 Nigel Mansell .75 2.00
Nelson Piquet
12 Jonathan Palmer .40 1.00
13 Alain Prost .60 1.50
14 Alain Prost .60 1.50
Keke Rosberg
15 Checklist Card w .40 1.00
drivers
16 Cover Card w .40 1.00
cars

1992 Golden Era Grand Prix The Early Years

This 25-card set was produced by Rainbow Press of Loughton Essex England. The cards feature illustrations by British artist Robert R. Wisdom. The cards depict a colorful selection of the most thrilling and spectacular racing cars to ever grace the Grand Prix circuits of the World, driven by the famous and legendary drivers of the day.

COMPLETE SET (25) 4.00 10.00
1 Jimmy Murphy's Car .20 .50
2 Antonio Ascari's Car .20 .50
3 Bugatti Type 35B .20 .50
4 Robert Benoist's Car .20 .50
5 Auto Union A-Type .20 .50
6 Alfa Romeo Tipo B .20 .50
7 Von Brauchitsch's Car .20 .50
8 Raymond Mays' Car .20 .50
9 Mercedes W125 .20 .50
10 Giuseppe Farina's Car .20 .50
11 Tazio Nuvolari's Car .20 .50
12 Mercedes W163 .20 .50
13 Peter Whitehead's Car .20 .50
14 Giuseppe Farina's Car .20 .50
15 Juan Manuel Fangio's Car .20 .50
16 Alberto Ascari's Car .20 .50
17 Juan Manuel Fangio's Car .20 .50
18 Alberto Ascari's Car .20 .50
19 Stirling Moss' Car .40 1.00
20 Stirling Moss' Car .40 1.00
21 Stirling Moss' Car .40 1.00
22 Mike Hawthorn's Car .20 .50
23 Jack Brabham's Car .20 .50
24 Phil Hill's Car .20 .50
25 Jim Clark's Car .20 .50
NNO Cover Card .08 .25

1978-79 Grand Prix

The 1978-79 Grand Prix set was produced with an album intended to house the 240-card set. The album is written entirely in French. The card fronts feature a color photo of a top Grand Prix driver, while the backs include the card number and, on most, a short card title.

COMPLETE SET (240) 75.00 135.00
1 Mario Andretti 2.00 5.00
2 Bruno Giacomelli .30 .75
3 Jan Lammers .30 .75
4 Didier Pironi .30 .75
Jean Pierre Jaussaud
5 Al Unser 1.50 4.00
6 Markku Alen .30 .75
7 Tony Carello .30 .75
8 Mario Andretti 2.00 5.00
9 Mario Andretti's Car 1.00 2.00
10 Carlos Reutemann's Car .20 .50
11 Didier Pironi's Car .20 .50
12 James Hunt's Car .20 .50
13 Niki Lauda's Car .30 .75
14 Mario Andretti's Car 1.00 2.00
15 Gilles Villeneuve's Car .30 .75
16 Arturo Merzario's Car .20 .50
17 Jean Pierre Jarier's Car .20 .50
18 Emerson Fittipaldi 1.25 3.00
19 Carlos Reutemann's Car .20 .50
20 Emerson Fittipaldi's Car .60 1.50
21 Niki Lauda's Car .30 .75
22 Grand Prix Action .20 .50
23 Gilles Villeneuve's Car .30 .75
24 Ronnie Peterson's Car .20 .50
25 Alan Jones' Car .30 .75
26 Eddie Cheever's Car .30 .75
27 Jacques Laffite's Car .20 .50
28 Ronnie Peterson .30 .75
29 Patrick Depailler's Car .20 .50
30 Riccardo Patrese's Car .30 .75
31 Jean Pierre Jabouille's Car .20 .50
32 John Watson's Car .20 .50
33 Didier Pironi's Car .20 .50
34 Eddie Cheever's Car .30 .75
35 Carlos Reutemann's Car .20 .50
36 Rolf Stommelen's Car .20 .50
37 Rene Arnoux's Car .20 .50
38 Carlos Reutemann .30 .75
39 Carlos Reutemann's Car .20 .50
40 Mario Andretti's Car 1.00 2.00
41 Alan Jones' Car .30 .75
42 Patrick Depailler's Car .20 .50
43 Clay Regazzoni .40 1.00
Gilles Villeneuve Cars
44 Jody Scheckter's Car .20 .50
45 Hans Stuck's Car .20 .50
46 Lamberto Leoni's Car .20 .50
47 Jacques Laffite .20 .50
Riccardo Patrese Cars
48 Patrick Depailler .30 .75
49 Grand Prix Action .20 .50
50 Niki Lauda's Car .30 .75
51 Carlos Reutemann's Car .20 .50
52 Patrick Tambay's Car .20 .50
53 Didier Pironi .30 .75
Riccardo Patrese
54 John Watson's Car .20 .50
55 Jean Pierre Jabouille's Car .20 .50
56 Mario Andretti's Car 1.00 2.00
57 Wolf-Ford .20 .50
58 Mario Andretti 2.00 5.00
59 Mario Andretti's Car 1.00 2.00
60 Alan Jones' Car .30 .75
61 Carlos Reutemann's Car .20 .50
62 Gilles Villeneuve's Car .30 .75
63 Bruno Giacomelli's Car .20 .50
64 Didier Pironi .20 .50
Rene Arnoux
Rolf Stommelen's Cars
65 Rene Arnoux' Car .20 .50
66 Brett Lunger's Car .20 .50
67 Jochen Mass' Car .20 .50
68 Mario Andretti's Car 1.00 2.00
69 Jacques Laffite's Car .20 .50
70 Jody Scheckter's Car .20 .50
71 James Hunt's Car .20 .50
72 Jacques Laffite .30 .75
73 Ronnie Peterson's Car .20 .50
74 John Watson's Car .20 .50
75 Hector Rebaque's Car .20 .50
76 Emilio Villota's Car .20 .50
77 Rupert Keegan's Car .20 .50
78 Niki Lauda .60 1.50
79 Niki Lauda's Car .30 .75
80 Mario Andretti's Car 1.00 2.00
81 Riccardo Patrese's Car .30 .75
82 Patrick Tambay's Car .20 .50
83 Mario Andretti's Car 1.00 2.00
84 Ronnie Peterson's Car .20 .50
85 Geoff Brabham's Car .30 .75
86 Clay Regazzoni's Car .20 .50
87 Grand Prix Action .20 .50
88 Mario Andretti's Car 1.00 2.00
89 Ronnie Peterson's Car .20 .50
90 James Hunt's Car .20 .50
91 Riccardo Patrese's Car .30 .75
92 Niki Lauda's Car .30 .75
93 James Hunt's Car .20 .50
94 Jody Scheckter's Car .20 .50
95 Jacques Laffite's Car .20 .50
96 Alan Jones' Car .30 .75
97 Carlos Reutemann's Car .20 .50
98 Carlos Reutemann .30 .75
99 Carlos Reutemann's Car .20 .50
100 Niki Lauda's Car .30 .75
101 Mario Andretti's Car 1.00 2.00
102 Patrick Depailler's Car .20 .50
103 Alan Jones' Car .30 .75
104 Grand Prix Action .20 .50
105 Hans Stuck's Car .20 .50
106 Patrick Tambay's Car .20 .50
107 Bruno Giacomelli's Car .20 .50
108 Mario Andretti's Car 1.00 2.00
109 Jody Scheckter's Car .20 .50
110 Jody Scheckter .30 .75
111 Jacques Laffite's Car .20 .50
112 Harald Ertl .30 .75
113 Emerson Fittipaldi's Car .60 1.50
114 Didier Pironi .60 1.50
Emerson Fittipaldi
115 Keke Rosberg's Car .30 .75
116 John Watson's Car .20 .50
117 Gilles Villeneuve's Car .30 .75
118 Ronnie Peterson's Car .20 .50
119 Patrick Depailler .30 .75
Niki Lauda Cars
120 Vittorio Brambilla's Car .20 .50
121 Mario Andretti's Car 1.00 2.00
122 Niki Lauda's Car .30 .75
123 Gilles Villeneuve .40 1.00
Patrick Depailler
Hans Stuck Car
124 Nelson Piquet's Car .30 .75
125 Carlos Reutemann's Car .20 .50
126 Jean Pierre Jabouille's Car .20 .50
127 Derek Daly's Car .20 .50
128 Mario Andretti 2.00 5.00
129 John Watson's Car .20 .50
130 Jean Pierre Jabouille's Car .20 .50
131 Michael Bleekemolen's Car .20 .50
132 Gilles Villeneuve's Car .30 .75
133 Emerson Fittipaldi's Car .60 1.50
134 Patrick Tambay's Car .20 .50
135 James Hunt's Car .20 .50
136 Jochen Mass' Car .20 .50
137 Derek Daly's Car .20 .50
138 John Watson .30 .75
139 Niki Lauda's Car .30 .75
140 Mario Andretti's Car 1.00 2.00
141 Ronnie Peterson's Car .20 .50
142 Ronnie Peterson .30 .75
143 John Watson's Car .20 .50
144 Gilles Villeneuve's Car .30 .75
145 Patrjck Tambay's Car .20 .50
146 Vittorio Brambilla's Car .20 .50
147 Nelson Piquet's Car .30 .75
148 Carlos Reutemann's Car .20 .50
149 Carlos Reutemann .30 .75
150 Alan Jones' Car .30 .75
151 Jean Pierre Jabouille's Car .20 .50
152 Jean Pierre Jarier's Car .20 .50
153 James Hunt's Car .20 .50
154 Patrick Tambay's Car .20 .50
155 Clay Regazzoni .60 1.50
Emerson Fittipaldi
156 Rene Arnoux's Car .20 .50
157 Bobby Rahal's Car .40 1.00
158 Gilles Villeneuve's Car .30 .75
159 Gilles Villeneuve .40 1.00
160 Jody Scheckter's Car .20 .50
161 Jean Pierre Jarier's Car .20 .50
162 Riccardo Patrese's Car .30 .75
163 Grand Prix Action .20 .50
164 Grand Prix Action .20 .50
165 Derek Daly's Car .20 .50
166 Nelson Piquet's Car .30 .75
167 Keke Rosberg's Car .30 .75
168 Bruno Giacomelli's Car .20 .50
169 Marc Surer's Car .20 .50
170 March-BMW .20 .50
171 Derek Daly's Car .20 .50
172 Piero Necchi's Car .20 .50
173 Alex Dias Ribeiro's Car .20 .50
174 Keke Rosberg's Car .30 .75
175 Jan Lammers' Car .20 .50
176 Anders Olofsson's Car .20 .50
177 Patrick Gaillard's Car .20 .50
178 Nelson Piquet's Car .30 .75
179 Derek Warwick's Car .20 .50
180 Alain Prost's Car .40 1.00
181 Chico Serra's Car .20 .50
182 Umberto Grano's Car .20 .50
183 Armin Hahne's Car .20 .50
184 Clemens Schickentanz .20 .50
Hans Heyer Car
185 Carlo Facetti .20 .50
Martini Finotto's Car
186 Willi Bergmeistr .20 .50
Jorg Siegrst Car
187 Gordon Spice .20 .50
Teddy Pilette Car
188 Helmut Bauer's Car .20 .50
189 Hezemans .20 .50
Ludwig Cars
190 Bob Wollek .20 .50
Henri Pescarolo's Car
191 Eddie Cheever .40 1.00
Giorgio Francia Car
192 Tomaso Pantera's Car .20 .50
193 Hans Heyer's Car .20 .50
194 Harald Ertl's Car .20 .50
195 Rolf Stommelen's Car .20 .50
196 Didier Pironi .20 .50
Jean Pierre Jaussaud's Car
197 Didier Pironi .30 .75
198 Bob Wollek .20 .50
Jurgen Barth's Car
199 Patrick Depailler .20 .50
Jean Pierre Jabouille's Car
200 Renault Alpine A442A .20 .50
201 Porsche 936 .20 .50
202 Rolf Stommelen .20 .50
Manfred Schurti's Car
203 Redman's Car .20 .50
204 Jacques Laffite .20 .50
Vern Schuppan's Car
205 Grand Prix 78-79 .20 .50
206 512 Berlinetta Boxer .20 .50
207 Pironi Jaussaud's Car .20 .50
208 Al Unser 1.50 4.00
209 Al Unser's Car .75 2.00
210 Grand Prix 78-79 .20 .50
211 Tom Sneva's Car .40 1.00
212 Bobby Unser .60 1.50
Wally Dallenbach Sr.'s Car
213 Janet Guthrie's Car .60 1.50
214 Mario Andretti's Car 1.00 2.00
215 Martin Schanche's Car .20 .50
216 Andreas Bentza's Car .20 .50
217 Ake Anderson's Car .20 .50
218 Grand Prix 78-79 .20 .50
219 Jos Fassbender's Car .20 .50
220 Antero Laine's Car .20 .50
221 Franz Wurz's Car .20 .50
222 Jean Pierre Nicolas' Car .20 .50
223 Jean Ragnotti's Car .20 .50
224 Markku Alen's Car .20 .50
225 Hannu Nikkola's Car .20 .50
226 Anders Kullang's Car .20 .50
227 Jean Pierre Nicolas' Car .20 .50
228 Vic Preston's Car .20 .50
229 Datsun 160J .20 .50
230 Toyota Celica .20 .50
231 Pentti Airikkala's Car .20 .50
232 Bjorn Waldegaard's Car .20 .50
233 Tony Pond's Car .20 .50
234 Tony Carello's Car .20 .50
235 Gilbert Staepelaere's Car .20 .50
236 Franz Wittmann's Car .20 .50
237 Roger Clark's Car .20 .50
238 Michel Mouton's Car .20 .50
239 Bernard Darniche's Car .20 .50
240 Antonio Zanini's Car .20 .50

1992 Grid Formula One

Released in foil packs and complete factory set form, this 200-card issue features top Formula One drivers and machines. The cards were produced with gold foil layering on the cardfronts and heavy UV coating. The set is highlighted by a large number of Ayrton Senna cards.

COMPLETE SET (200) 3.00 7.00
COMPLETE FACT.SET (200) 3.00 7.00
1 Ayrton Senna's Car .08 .25
2 Gerhard Berger's Car .02 .10
3 Olivier Grouillard's Car .01 .05
4 Andrea deCesaris' Car .01 .05
5 Nigel Mansell's Car .05 .15
6 Riccardo Patrese's Car .01 .05
7 Eric van de Poele's Car .01 .05
8 Damon Hill's Car .05 .15
9 Giovanna Amati's Car .01 .05
10 Michele Alboreto's Car .01 .05
11 Aguri Suzuki's Car .01 .05
12 Mika Hakkinen's Car .01 .05
13 Johnny Herbert's Car .01 .05
14 Andrea Chiesa's Car .01 .05
15 Gabriele Tarquini's Car .01 .05
16 Karl Wendlinger's Car .01 .05
17 Paul Belmondo's Car .01 .05
18 Michael Schumacher's Car .05 .15
19 Martin Brundle's Car .01 .05
20 J.J. Lehto's Car .01 .05
21 Pierluigi Martini's Car .01 .05
22 Christian Fittipaldi's Car .01 .05
23 Gianni Morbidelli's Car .01 .05
24 Thierry Boutsen's Car .01 .05
25 Erik Comas' Car .01 .05
26 Jean Alesi's Car .02 .10
27 Ivan Capelli's Car .01 .05
28 Ukyo Katayama's Car .01 .05
29 Bertrand Gachot's Car .01 .05
30 Stefano Modena's Car .01 .05
31 Mauricio Gugelmin's Car .01 .05
32 Roberto Moreno's Car .01 .05
33 Perry McCarthy's Car .01 .05
34 Ayrton Senna .10 .30
35 Gerhard Berger .08 .25
36 Olivier Grouillard .02 .10
37 Andrea deCesaris .02 .10
38 Nigel Mansell .08 .25
39 Riccardo Patrese .05 .15
40 Eric van de Poele .02 .10
41 Damon Hill .08 .25
42 Giovanna Amati .02 .10
43 Michele Alboreto .02 .10
44 Aguri Suzuki .02 .10
45 Mika Hakkinen .02 .10
46 Johnny Herbert .02 .10
47 Andrea Chiesa .02 .10
48 Gabriele Tarquini .02 .10
49 Karl Wendlinger .02 .10
50 Paul Belmondo .02 .10
51 Michael Schumacher .08 .25
52 Martin Brundle .02 .10
53 J.J. Lehto .02 .10
54 Pierluigi Martini .02 .10
55 Christian Fittipaldi .02 .10
56 Gianni Morbidelli .02 .10
57 Thierry Boutsen .02 .10
58 Erik Comas .02 .10
59 Jean Alesi .05 .15
60 Ivan Capelli .02 .10
61 Bertrand Gachot .02 .10
62 Ukyo Katayama .02 .10
63 Stefano Modena .02 .10
64 Mauricio Gugelmin .02 .10
65 Roberto Moreno .02 .10
66 Perry McCarthy .02 .10
67 Ayrton Senna .10 .30
68 Gerhard Berger .08 .25
69 Olivier Grouillard .02 .10
70 Andrea deCesaris .02 .10
71 Nigel Mansell .08 .25
72 Riccardo Patrese .05 .15
73 Eric van de Poele .02 .10
74 Damon Hill .08 .25
75 Giovanna Amati .02 .10
76 Michele Alboreto .02 .10
77 Aguri Suzuki .02 .10
78 Mika Hakkinen .02 .10
79 Johnny Herbert .02 .10
80 Andrea Chiesa .02 .10
81 Gabriele Tarquini .02 .10
82 Karl Wendlinger .02 .10
83 Paul Belmondo .02 .10
84 Michael Schumacher .08 .25
85 Martin Brundle .02 .10
86 J.J. Lehto .02 .10
87 Pierluigi Martini .02 .10
88 Christian Fittipaldi .02 .10
89 Gianni Morbidelli .02 .10
90 Thierry Boutsen .02 .10
91 Erik Comas .02 .10
92 Jean Alesi .05 .15
93 Ivan Capelli .02 .10
94 Bertrand Gachot .02 .10
95 Ukyo Katayama .02 .10
96 Stefano Modena .02 .10
97 Mauricio Gugelmin .02 .10
98 Roberto Moreno .02 .10
99 Perry McCarthy .02 .10
100 Ayrton Senna .05 .15
Prost
Piquet
101 Ayrton Senna Win .08 .25
102 Ayrton Senna .05 .15
Berger
Lehto
103 Ayrton Senna .05 .15
Mansell
Alesi
104 Nelson Piquet .02 .10
Stefano Modena
Riccardo Patrese
105 Ayrton Senna .05 .15
Patese
Mansell
106 Ayrton Senna .05 .15
N.Mansell
Prost
107 Nigel Mansell .05 .15
Gerhard Berger
Alain Prost
108 Riccardo Patrese .05 .15
Nigel Mansell
Jean Alesi
109 Ayrton Senna .05 .15
Mansell
Patrese
110 Ayrton Senna Win .08 .25
111 Ayrton Senna .05 .15
N.Mansell
Prost
112 Riccardo Patrese Win .02 .10
113 Nigel Mansell .05 .15
Alain Prost
Riccardo Patrese
114 Ayrton Senna .05 .15
Berger
Patrese
115 Ayrton Senna Win .08 .25
116 South Africa Race Track .01 .05
117 Mexico Race Track .01 .05
118 Brazil Race Track .01 .05
119 Spain Race Track .01 .05
120 San Marino Race Track .01 .05
121 Monaco Race Track .01 .05
122 Canada Race Track .01 .05
123 France Race Track .01 .05
124 England Race Track .01 .05
125 Germany Race Track .01 .05
126 Hungary Race Track .01 .05
127 Belgium Race Track .01 .05
128 Italy Race Track .01 .05
129 Portugal Race Track .01 .05
130 Japan Race Track .01 .05
131 Australia Race Track .01 .05
132 Frank Williams .01 .05
133 Don Dennis .01 .05
134 Tom Walkinshaw .01 .05
135 Luca di Montezemolo .01 .05
136 Gerard Larrousse .01 .05
137 Eddie Jordan .01 .05
138 Giancarlo Minardi .01 .05
139 Charlie Moody .01 .05
140 Ken Tyrrell .01 .05
141 Peter Collins .01 .05
142 Jackie Oliver .01 .05
143 Guy Ligier .01 .05
144 Andrea Sasetti .01 .05
145 Dennis Nursey .01 .05
146 Gabriele Rumi .01 .05
147 Gianpaola Dallara .01 .05
148 Gilles Villeneuve's Car .02 .10
149 Gilles Villeneuve's Car .02 .10
150 Gilles Villeneuve's Car .02 .10
151 Gilles Villeneuve's Car .02 .10
152 Gilles Villeneuve's Car .02 .10
153 Gilles Villeneuve's Car .02 .10
154 Gilles Villeneuve's Car .02 .10
155 Gilles Villeneuve's Car .02 .10
156 Gilles Villeneuve's Car .02 .10
157 Gilles Villeneuve's Car .02 .10
158 Checklist Card .01 .05
159 Gilles Villeneuve .05 .15
160 Davy Jones .02 .10
161 Mark Blundell .02 .10
162 Al Unser Jr. .08 .25
163 David Coulthard .05 .15
164 Rubens Barrichello .02 .10
165 Alan McNish .02 .10
166 Checklist Card .01 .05
167 Paul Tracy .05 .15
168 Emanuelle Naspetti .02 .10
169 Alessandro Zanardi .02 .10
170 Eddie Irvine .02 .10
171 Antonio Tamburini .02 .10
172 Jacques Villeneuve .08 .25
173 Jordi Gene .02 .10
174 Michael Bartels .02 .10
175 Jimmy Vasser .02 .10
176 Eric Bachelart .02 .10
177 Robby Gordon .50 1.25
178 Alberto Ascari .02 .10
179 Alberto Ascari's Car .01 .05
180 Graham Hill .02 .10
181 Graham Hill's Car .01 .05
182 Emerson Fittipaldi .05 .15
183 Emerson Fittipaldi's Car .01 .05
184 Keke Rosberg .05 .15
185 1982 Ferrari .01 .05
186 Ayrton Senna .10 .30
187 Ayrton Senna's Car .08 .25
188 Ayrton Senna .10 .30
189 Ayrton Senna's Car .08 .25
190 Alain Prost .05 .15
191 Jordan's First Points .01 .05
192 Nigel Mansell's Car .05 .15
193 Bertrand Gachot's Car .01
194 Michael Schumacher .08
195 Nelson Piquet's Car .01
196 J.P.Balestre .02
197 Alain Prost .05
198 Nigel Mansell Crash .02
199 Saturo Nakajima .02
200 Michael Andretti's Car .05

1960 Hawes Wax Indy

Although often considered to be one of the first American auto racing card sets, the 50-card Hawes Wax issue was printed by Parkhurst in Canada for distribution in Hawes Wax products. This set features 39 cards portraying Indy 500 ra winners from 1911-1959; 11 cards featuring rac action scenes, and one card featuring the Purdu University Marching Band. Cardbacks are printe in both English and French. It's interesting to no that card #50 lists the winners of the Parkhurst Z Gum Hockey Contest originally offered on the backs of 1958-59 Parkhurst hockey cards. Oversized versions (approximately 3" by 4") of s cards exist featuring the fronts of 12 Hawes Wax cards (#9/26/29/31/33/35/37/38/39/40/43/44) placed back-to-back. Reportedly, the six cards were part of a game produced in Canada that als included additional cards of non-racing subjects These six cards are valued at approximately $20.00 each.

COMPLETE SET (50) 500.00 800.0
1 Ray Harroun 12.00 20.0
2 Joe Dawson 12.00 20.0
3 Jules Goux 12.00 20.0
4 Rene Thomas 12.00 20.0
5 Ralph dePalma 15.00 25.0
6 Dario Resta 12.00 20.0
7 Howard Wilcox 12.00 20.0
8 Gaston Chevrolet 15.00 25.0
9 Tommy Milton 12.00 20.0
10 Jimmy Murphy 12.00 20.0
11 Tommy Milton 12.00 20.0
12 L.L.Corum 12.00 20.0
Joe Boyer
13 Peter DePaolo 12.00 20.0
14 Frank Lockhart 12.00 20.0
15 George Souders 12.00 20.0
16 Louis Meyer 12.00 20.0
17 Ray Keech 12.00 20.00
18 Billy Arnold 12.00 20.0
19 Louis Schneider 12.00 20.0
20 Fred Frame 12.00 20.0
21 Louis Meyer 12.00 20.00
22 Bill Cummings 12.00 20.00
23 Kelly Petillo 12.00 20.00
24 Louis Meyer 12.00 20.00
25 Wilbur Shaw 12.00 20.00
26 Floyd Roberts 12.00 20.00
27 Wilbur Shaw 12.00 20.00
28 Purdue University Band 12.00 20.00
29 Mauri Rose 12.00 20.00
Floyd Davis
30 George Robson 12.00 20.00
31 Mauri Rose 12.00 20.00
32 Rodger Ward VL 15.00 25.00
33 Bill Holland 12.00 20.00
34 Johnnie Parsons 15.00 25.00
35 Lee Wallard 12.00 20.00
36 Troy Ruttman 12.00 20.00
37 Bill Vukovich 15.00 25.00
38 Start of Parade Lap 12.00 20.00
39 Bob Sweikert 12.00 20.00
40 Pat Flaherty 12.00 20.00
41 Sam Hanks 12.00 20.00
42 Jimmy Bryan 12.00 20.00
43 Rodger Ward 15.00 25.00
44 Tony Bettenhausen in Pits 15.00 25.00
45 Rodger Ward w 15.00 25.00
wife
46 The Borg-Warner Trophy 12.00 20.00
47 Main Gate of IMS 12.00 20.00
48 IMS Museum 12.00 20.00
49 Paul Russo in Pits 12.00 20.00
50 Parade Lap 12.00 20.00

1992 Hi-Tech Indy Prototypes

Hi-Tech produced this 6-card set to promote several upcoming releases. The cards represent samples from different sets intended to be released by Hi-Tech. The cover card mentions that 15,000 Prototype sets were produced. The sets were also sold matted under glass and framed. The matting carried the number (of 15,000) for

each set.
COMPLETE SET (6) 6.00 15.00
1 Mario Andretti 1.50 4.00
2 Al Unser Jr's Car / Scott Goodyear's Car
3 Michael Andretti 1.00 2.50
4 Paul Newman 2.00 5.00
5 Cover Card .40 1.00
6 Scott Goodyear 1.50 4.00

1992 Hi-Tech Mario Andretti

Hi-Tech produced this set in 1992, but actually released it in early 1993. The cards were distributed in factory set form in a tin box package. The set commemorates the long career of Mario Andretti and was limited to 100,000 51-card sets. A #52 card was also produced (5000 made) with 2500 signed copies randomly inserted in some factory sets. It is not considered part of the complete set price.

COMPLETE FACT.SET (51) 10.00 20.00
1 Mario Andretti .30 .75
2 Mario Andretti / Aldo Andretti .30 .75
3 Mario Andretti's Car .12 .30
4 Mario Andretti's Car .12 .30
5 Mario Andretti in Car .30 .75
6 Mario Andretti / Ed Mataka / Bill Mataka .30 .75
7 Mario Andretti in Car .30 .75
8 Mario Andretti in Car .30 .75
9 Mario Andretti in Car .30 .75
10 Mario Andretti in Car .30 .75
11 Mario Andretti in Car .30 .75
12 Mario Andretti .30 .75
13 Mario Andretti .30 .75
14 Mario Andretti in Car .30 .75
15 Mario Andretti / A.J.Foyt Cars .30 .75
16 Mario Andretti / Clint Brawner .30 .75
17 Mario Andretti / Chuck Rodee .30 .75
18 Mario Andretti in Car .30 .75
19 Mario Andretti .30 .75
20 Mario Andretti's Car .12 .30
21 Mario Andretti in Car .30 .75
22 Mario Andretti .30 .75
23 Mario Andretti w Car .30 .75
24 Mario Andretti in Car .30 .75
25 Mario Andretti's Car .12 .30
26 Mario Andretti .30 .75
27 Mario Andretti in Car .30 .75
28 Mario Andretti in Car .30 .75
29 Mario Andretti in Car .30 .75
30 Mario Andretti / Jackie Ickx .30 .75
31 Mario Andretti in Car .30 .75
32 Mario Andretti in Car .30 .75
33 Mario Andretti in Car .30 .75
34 Mario Andretti .30 .75
35 Mario Andretti in Car .30 .75
36 Mario Andretti .30 .75
37 Mario Andretti in Car .30 .75
38 Mario Andretti's Car .12 .30
39 Mario Andretti's Car .12 .30
40 Mario Andretti .30 .75
41 Mario Andretti in Car .30 .75
42 Mario Andretti's Car .12 .30
43 Mario Andretti's Car .12 .30
44 Mario Andretti / Michael Andretti .30 .75
45 Mario Andretti .30 .75
46 Mario Andretti / Al Unser Jr. / Tom Sneva .30 .75
47 Mario Andretti .30 .75
48 Mario Andretti .30 .75
49 Mario Andretti / Foyt / Mears Cars .30 .75
50 Mario Andretti's Car .12 .30
51 Checklist Card .07 .20
52 Mario Andretti Signature Card .30 .75
P1 Mario Andretti Prototype .60 1.50

1993 Hi-Tech Indy Prototypes

Hi-Tech produced these six-cards to preview the 1993 IndyCar set. The cards are numbered P1/6, P2/6, etc. and are often sold as a complete set.

COMPLETE SET (6) 8.00 16.00
P1 Danny Sullivan 1.50 3.00
P2 Scott Goodyear 1.50 3.00
P3 Eddie Cheever's Car .75 2.00
P4 Bobby Rahal's Car FOIL 1.50 3.00
P5 Eddie Cheever's Car FOIL .75 2.00
P6 Al Unser's Car FOIL 2.00 4.00

1993 Hi-Tech Indy

Hi-Tech produced this set featuring drivers of the 1992 Indianapolis 500. The cards were released in 10-card packs with 36-packs per box. Reportedly, production was limited to 4000 cases. Cards from the Checkered Flag Finishers set were randomly inserted into packs.

COMPLETE SET (81) 4.00 10.00
1 Roberto Guerrero .08 .25
2 Eddie Cheever .05 .15
3 Mario Andretti .30 .75
4 Arie Luyendyk .08 .25
5 Gary Bettenhausen .08 .25
6 Michael Andretti .15 .40
7 Scott Brayton .05 .15
8 Danny Sullivan .08 .25
9 Rick Mears .15 .40
10 Bobby Rahal .08 .25
11 Emerson Fittipaldi .15 .40
12 Al Unser Jr. .15 .40
13 Stan Fox .05 .15
14 John Andretti .15 .40
15 Eric Bachelart .05 .15
16 Philippe Gache .05 .15
17 Scott Pruett .05 .15
18 John Paul Jr. .05 .15
19 Paul Tracy .08 .25
20 Jeff Andretti .15 .40
21 Jim Crawford .05 .15
22 Al Unser .08 .25
23 A.J. Foyt .15 .40
24 Buddy Lazier .05 .15
25 Raul Boesel .05 .15
26 Brian Bonner .05 .15
27 Lyn St. James .08 .25
28 Jimmy Vasser .05 .15
29 Dominic Dobson .05 .15
30 Tom Sneva .08 .25
31 Gordon Johncock .08 .25
32 Ted Prappas .05 .15
33 Scott Goodyear .05 .15
34 Al Unser Jr. Indy Champ .15 .40
35 Roberto Guerrero Pole Win .08 .25
36 Al Unser Jr. .15 .40
37 Scott Goodyear .05 .15
38 Al Unser .08 .25
39 Eddie Cheever .05 .15
40 Danny Sullivan .08 .25
41 Bobby Rahal .08 .25
42 Raul Boesel .05 .15
43 John Andretti .15 .40
44 A.J. Foyt .15 .40
45 John Paul Jr. .05 .15
46 Lyn St. James .08 .25
47 Dominic Dobson .05 .15
48 Michael Andretti .15 .40
49 Buddy Lazier .05 .15
50 Arie Luyendyk .08 .25
51 Ted Prappas .05 .15
52 Gary Bettenhausen .08 .25
53 Jeff Andretti .15 .40
54 Brian Bonner .05 .15
55 Paul Tracy .08 .25
56 Jimmy Vasser .05 .15
57 Scott Brayton .05 .15
58 Mario Andretti .30 .75
59 Emerson Fittipaldi .15 .40
60 Jim Crawford .05 .15
61 Rick Mears .15 .40
62 Stan Fox .05 .15
63 Philippe Gache .05 .15
64 Gordon Johncock .08 .25
65 Scott Pruett .05 .15
66 Tom Sneva .08 .25
67 Eric Bachelart .05 .15
68 Roberto Guerrero .08 .25
69 1992 Pace Car .05 .15
70 Mario Andretti / Guerrero / Chee .20 .50
71 Mar.Andretti / Mic.Andretti Cars .08 .25
72 Al Unser Jr.'s Car .08 .25
73 Race Start .05 .15
74 Pit Crew Practice .05 .15
75 Tom Sneva / Jimmy Vasser Cars .05 .15
76 Nelson Piquet's Car .05 .15
77 Gordon Johncock's Car .05 .15
78 Protective Coverings (Pit Row) .05 .15
79 Eric Bachelart's Car .05 .15
80 Race Accidents .05 .15
81 Checklist Card .05 .15

1993 Hi-Tech Indy Checkered Flag Finishers

Randomly inserted in 1993 Hi-Tech Indy packs, these 12-cards feature top drivers printed on holographic foil card stock.

COMPLETE SET (12) 15.00 30.00
SP2 Scott Goodyear 1.00 2.00
SP4 Eddie Cheever 1.00 2.00
SP5 Danny Sullivan 1.50 3.00
SP6 Bobby Rahal 1.50 3.00
SP7 Raul Boesel 1.00 2.00
SP8 John Andretti 1.50 3.00
SP10 John Paul Jr. 1.00 2.00
SP11 Lyn St. James 1.00 2.00
SP12 Dominic Dobson 1.00 2.00

1994 Hi-Tech Indy Prototypes

Hi-Tech produced these three cards to preview the 1994 IndyCar set. The cards are numbered P1/3, P2/3 and P3/3 and are often sold as a complete set.

COMPLETE SET (3) 4.00 8.00
P1 Nigel Mansell's Car .75 2.00
P2 Mario Andretti's Car 1.00 2.50
P3 Mario Andretti 1.50 4.00

1994 Hi-Tech Indy

The 1993 Indianapolis 500 is the subject of this Hi-Tech production. The cards were distributed in complete set form with all insert cards. There were a reported 25,000 sets produced.

COMPLETE SET (51) 4.00 8.00
1 Cover Card / E.Fittipaldi .05 .15
2 Emerson Fittipaldi .15 .40
3 Arie Luyendyk's Car .05 .15
4 Nigel Mansell .15 .40
5 Raul Boesel's Car .05 .15
6 Mario Andretti .30 .75
7 Scott Brayton's Car .05 .15
8 Scott Goodyear .05 .15
9 Al Unser Jr. .15 .40
10 Teo Fabi's Car .05 .15
11 John Andretti .15 .40
12 Stefan Johansson .05 .15
13 Al Unser .15 .40
14 Jimmy Vasser .05 .15
15 Kevin Cogan .05 .15
16 Davy Jones .05 .15
17 Eddie Cheever in Pits .05 .15
18 Gary Bettenhausen .08 .25
19 Hiro Matsushita's Car .05 .15
20 Stephan Gregoire in Pits .05 .15
21 Tony Bettenhausen's Car .05 .15
22 Willy T. Ribbs .05 .15
23 Didier Theys' Car .05 .15
24 Dominic Dobson .05 .15
25 Jim Crawford .05 .15
26 Lyn St. James .15 .40
27 Geoff Brabham's Car .05 .15
28 Robby Gordon's Car .08 .25
29 Roberto Guerrero .05 .15
30 Jeff Andretti's Car .05 .15
31 Paul Tracy .08 .25
32 Stan Fox in Pits .05 .15
33 Nelson Piquet .05 .15
34 Danny Sullivan .08 .25
35 Mark Smith .05 .15
36 Bobby Rahal .15 .40
37 1993 Rookies .08 .25
38 A.J. Foyt Salute .08 .25
39 Arie Luyendyk Pole Win .05 .15
40 Luyendyk / Andret / Boesel .15 .40
41 The Staring Grid .05 .15
42 A.Luyendyk / Mario Andretti / R.Boesel Cars .05 .15
43 The Start .05 .15
44 Pit Action .05 .15
45 Nigel Mansell in Pits .05 .15
46 Jeff Andretti / Roberto Guerrero Crash .05 .15
47 Emerson Fittipaldi's Car .05 .15
48 Emerson Fittipaldi WIN .05 .15
49 Rick Mears / Brian Armenoff .05 .15
50 Brian Armenoff .05 .15
51 Checklist Card .05 .15

1994 Hi-Tech Indy Championship Drivers

Inserted one set per 1994 Hi-Tech Indy factory set, these cards feature top IndyCar drivers with extensive biographical information on the cardback.

COMPLETE SET (36) 7.50 15.00
CD1 Jeff Andretti .20 .50
CD2 John Andretti .30 .75
CD3 Mario Andretti .50 1.25
CD4 Michael Andretti .30 .75
CD5 Ross Bentley .20 .50
CD6 Gary Bettenhausen .20 .50
CD7 Raul Boesel .20 .50
CD8 Scott Brayton .20 .50
CD9 Robbie Buhl .20 .50
CD10 Eddie Cheever .20 .50
CD11 Jim Crawford .20 .50
CD12 Dominic Dobson .20 .50
CD13 Emerson Fittipaldi .30 .75
CD14 A.J. Foyt .40 1.00
CD15 Stan Fox .20 .50
CD16 Scott Goodyear .20 .50
CD17 Mike Groff .20 .50
CD18 Roberto Guerrero .20 .50
CD19 Stefan Johansson .20 .50
CD20 Gordon Johncock .20 .50
CD21 Buddy Lazier .20 .50
CD22 Arie Luyendyk .20 .50
CD23 Rick Mears .30 .75
CD24 Johnny Parsons Jr. .20 .50
CD25 Ted Prappas .20 .50
CD26 Scott Pruett .20 .50
CD27 Bobby Rahal .30 .75
CD28 Johnny Rutherford .30 .75
CD29 Lyn St. James .30 .75
CD30 Mark Smith .20 .50
CD31 Tom Sneva .20 .50
CD32 Danny Sullivan .30 .75
CD33 Didier Theys .20 .50
CD34 Paul Tracy .30 .75
CD35 Al Unser Jr. .20 .50
CD36 Jimmy Vasser .20 .50

1994 Hi-Tech Indy A.J. Foyt

A.J.Foyt is the focus of this Hi-Tech issue. The cards were inserted one set per 1994 Hi-Tech Indy factory set and highlight Foyt's first and last races, as well as his four wins at IMS.

COMPLETE SET (6) 2.50 5.00
COMMON CARD (AJ1-AJ6) .50 1.00

1994 Hi-Tech Indy Rick Mears

Rick Mears is the focus of this Hi-Tech issue. The cards were inserted one set per 1994 Hi-Tech Indy factory set and highlight Mears' first and last races, as well as his four wins at IMS.

COMPLETE SET (6) 2.50 5.00
COMMON CARD (RM1-RM6) .50 1.00

1995 Hi-Tech Indy Championship Drivers

This 11-card set features some of the top drivers on the IndyCar circuit. The sets were sold in complete set form at Indianapolis Motor Speedway. They were also made available to Hi-Tech Club members.

COMPLETE SET (11) 6.00 15.00
CD1 Al Unser Jr. .75 2.00
CD2 Eddie Cheever .30 .75
CD3 Emerson Fittipaldi .75 2.00
CD4 Scott Pruett .30 .75
CD5 Raul Boesel .30 .75
CD6 Paul Tracy .50 1.25
CD7 Jacques Villeneuve .50 1.25
CD8 Michael Andretti .75 2.00
CD9 Danny Sullivan .50 1.25
CD10 Paul Newman .75 2.00
CD11 Mario Andretti 1.25 3.00

1997 Hi-Tech IRL

This set commemorates the first season of the Indy Racing League. The set comes in a factory box that contains all 94-cards and a Dodge Viper Pace Car die-cast. There are six different sets within the factory set box. The 38-card base set features drivers from the IRL circuit. The 20-card Indy 500 set features the 80th Anniversary of the Indy 500. There was also a 10-card Disney 200 set, a nine card Phoenix set, a eight-card tribute to Scott Brayton and a eight-card set featuring the Dodge Viper.

COMP.FACT.SET (94) 10.00 25.00
COMP. IRL SET (38) 6.00 15.00
1 IRL Cover Card .07 .20
2 Scott Sharp .15 .40
3 Buzz Calkins .15 .40
4 Robbie Buhl .15 .40
5 Richie Hearn .15 .40
6 Roberto Guerrero .15 .40
7 Mike Groff .15 .40
8 Arie Luyendyk .30 .75
9 Tony Stewart XRC 4.00 10.00
10 Davey Hamilton .07 .20
11 Johnny O'Connell .07 .20
12 Michele Alboreto .07 .20
13 Lyn St.James .15 .40
14 Stephan Gregoire .07 .20
15 Buddy Lazier .15 .40
16 John Paul Jr. .07 .20
17 Eddie Cheever .07 .20
18 Johnny Parsons .07 .20
19 Scott Brayton .30 .75
20 David Kudrave .07 .20
21 Michel Jourdain .07 .20
22 Jim Guthrie .07 .20
23 Fermin Velez .07 .20
24 Eliseo Salazar .07 .20
25 Johnny Unser .15 .40
26 Stan Wattles .07 .20
27 Davy Jones .15 .40
28 Paul Durant .07 .20
29 Alessandro Zampedri .07 .20
30 Danny Ongais .07 .20
31 Hideshi Matsuda .07 .20
32 Scott Harrington .07 .20
33 Racin Gardner .07 .20
34 Mark Dismore .07 .20
35 Joe Gosek .07 .20
36 Brad Murphey .07 .20
37 Marco Greco .07 .20
NNO Checklist .07 .20

1997 Hi-Tech IRL Disney 200

These 10-cards were issued along with the rest of the 1997 Hi-Tech IRL release in factory set form. The set was produced to commemorate the inaugural Disney 200 IRL event.

COMPLETE SET (10) 2.50 6.00
D1 Disney Track .08 .25
D2 The Field .08 .25
D3 T.Stewart / B.Calkins' Cars 1.50 4.00
D4 Mike Groff's Car .15 .40
D5 Johnny Parson / Eddie Chever's Cars .40 1.00
D6 Stephan Gregoire / Buddy Lazier's Cars .40 1.00
D7 Michele Alboreto's Car .15 .40
D8 The Field .08 .25
D9 Buzz Calkins' Car .15 .40
D10 Buzz Calkins .30 .75

1997 Hi-Tech IRL Indy 500

This set features top drivers and cars that participated in the Indy 500. The set was issued one per 1997 Hi-Tech IRL factory set.

COMPLETE SET (20) 2.50 6.00
I1 Indy 500 Cover Card .07 .20
I2 Scott Brayton .20 .50
I3 Starting Grid .07 .20
I4 Zampedri / Jourdain / Calkins' Cars .10 .30
I5 The Field .07 .20
I6 Viper Pace Car .07 .20
I7 A.J. Foyt .50 1.25
I8 Scott Sharp's Car .20 .50
I9 Michele Alboreto's Car .10 .30
I10 Eliseo Salazar's Car .20 .50
I11 Viper Pace Car .07 .20
I12 Robbie Buhl's Car .20 .50
I13 Danny Ongais's Car .10 .30
I14 Buddy Lazier's Car .20 .50
I15 Davy Jones's Car .20 .50
I16 Richie Hearn's Car .20 .50
I17 Alessandro Zampedri's Car .10 .30
I18 Roberto Guerrero's Car .20 .50
I19 Buddy Lazier's Car .20 .50
I20 Buddy Lazier .30 .75

1997 Hi-Tech IRL Phoenix

This set features top driver's and participants in the IRL event run in Phoenix. One set was included in each 1997 Hi-Tech IRL factory set.

COMPLETE SET (10) 1.25 3.00
P1 Phoenix Track .07 .20
P2 Tony George .15 .40
P3 Scott Brayton's Car .15 .40
P4 Pace Car .07 .20
P5 The Field .07 .20
P6 Pace Car .07 .20
P7 R.Guerrero / T.Stewart Cars .60 1.50
P8 A.Luyendyk / S.Brayton's Cars .15 .40
P9 Arie Luyendyk .20 .50
P10 Cover Card .07 .20

1997 Hi-Tech IRL Scott Brayton

This set is a tribute to Scott Brayton. One set was included in each 1997 Hi-Tech IRL factory set.

COMPLETE SET (8) .75 2.00
COMMON CARD (BR1-BR8) .10 .30

1997 Hi-Tech IRL Viper Pace Car

This set features the Dodge Viper Pace car for the Indy 500. One 8-card set was included in each 1997 Hi-Tech IRL factory set.

COMPLETE SET (8) .20 .50
COMMON CARD (V1-V8) .02 .10

1988 Heraclio Fournier Formula One

This set of 34-cards are pieces of a card game produced in Spain. They contain a typical playing card back, are a small size (2-1/4" by 3-1/2) and feature Grand Prix drivers on the cardfront. All text is in Spanish and the cards are numbered similarly to other playing card decks.

COMPLETE SET (34) 4.00 10.00
1A Rosenberg's Car .07 .20
1B Riccardo Patrese's Car .20 .50
1C Rene Arnoux's Car .07 .20
1D Martin Brundle's Car .10 .30
2A Michele Alborelo's Car .10 .30
2B Alan Jones' Car .07 .20
2C Patrick Tambay's Car .07 .20
2D Thierry Boutsen's Car .10 .30
3A Stefan Johansson's Car .10 .30
3B Pierluigi Martini's Car .10 .30
3C Piercarlo Ghinzani's Car .07 .20
3D Gerhard Berger's Car .20 .50
4A Alain Prost's Car .20 .50
4B Ayrton Senna's Car .75 2.00
4C Thackwell's Car .07 .20
4D Jonathan Palmer's Car .07 .20
5A Emerson Fittipaldi's Car .20 .50
5B Rick Mears' Car .20 .50
5C Al Unser Jr.'s Car .30 .75
5D Mauricio Gugelmin's Car .10 .30
6A Kaiser's Car .07 .20
6B Thackwell's Car .07 .20
6C Philippe Streiff's Car .07 .20
6D Raphanel's Car .07 .20
7A Morin's Car .07 .20
7B Huysmann's Car .07 .20
7C Nicola Larini's Car .07 .20
7D Trolle's Car .07 .20
8A Stefano Modena's Car .07 .20
8B Yannick Dalmas' Car .07 .20
8C Artztet's Car .07 .20
8D Birne's Car .07 .20
NNO Cover Card / Rene Arnoux .07 .20

2009 Hot Wheels

This six card set was released as a sheet of cards inside the Summer 2009 Hot Wheels magazine. The cards were preforated on the sheet. Each card has a blue background and a red Hot Wheels logo of the upper left side of the card fronts. They were not numbered so we have arranged them in alphabetical order.

COMPLETE SET (6) 6.00 15.00
COMP.SHEET (6) 8.00 20.00
NNO Ed Carpenter 1.00 2.50
NNO Scott Dixon 1.00 2.50
NNO Dario Franchitti 1.50 4.00
NNO Tony Kanaan 1.50 4.00
NNO Danica Patrick 4.00 10.00
NNO Dan Wheldon 1.25 3.00

2002 Indianapolis 500

This set of 16-cards was released at the 2002 Indianapolis 500 as a perforated sheet. Each card features a color photo of an IRL driver surrounded by a brown border. The cardbacks are a simple white card stock with black lettering.

COMPLETE SET (16) 7.50 15.00
1 Alex Barron .30 .75
2 Billy Boat .30 .75
3 Robbie Buhl .30 .75
4 Eddie Cheever Jr. .40 1.00
5 Airton Dare .30 .75
6 Sarah Fisher 1.00 2.50
7 Felipe Giaffone .30 .75
8 Sam Hornish Jr. .60 1.50
9 Buddy Lazier .40 1.00
10 Arie Luyendyk .40 1.00
11 George Mack .30 .75
12 Robby McGehee .30 .75
13 Greg Ray .40 1.00
14 Scott Sharp .60 1.50
15 Al Unser Jr. .60 1.50
16 Jeff Ward .30 .75

1991 K-Mart

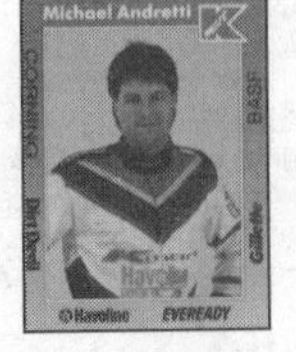

K-Mart produced and distributed this two card set in 1991 featuring the K-Mart/Texaco Havoline sponsored IndyCar Racing Team.

COMPLETE SET (2) 1.25 3.00
1 Mario Andretti .75 2.00
2 Michael Andretti .40 1.00

1992 K-Mart

This two card set was produced and distributed by K-Mart Stores in 1992. It features the K-Mart/Texaco Havoline sponsored IndyCar Racing Team.

COMPLETE SET (2) 1.25 3.00
1 Mario Andretti .75 2.00
2 Michael Andretti .50 1.25

1993 K-Mart

K-Mart produced and distributed this two card set in 1992 featuring the K-Mart/Texaco Havoline sponsored IndyCar Racing Team. The cards are distinguishable by the silver border.

COMPLETE SET (2) 1.25 3.00
1 Mario Andretti .75 2.00
2 Nigel Mansell .40 1.00

1994 K-Mart

Silver and black borders help distinguish the fourth K-Mart issue from the previous three releases. It again features the K-Mart/Texaco Havoline sponsored IndyCar Racing Team headlined by Mario Andretti.

COMPLETE SET (2) 1.25 3.00
1 Mario Andretti .75 2.00
2 Nigel Mansell .40 1.00

1991 Langenberg American IndyCar Series

Langenberg Racing produced this set entitled 1991 Hot Stuff. The set features then present and past drivers of the American IndyCar Series. The set features the only Unser to run at the IRL's 1996 Indy 500, Johnny. The set also includes Rodger Ward, the winner of the 1959 and 1962 Indy 500.

COMPLETE SET (18) 4.00 10.00
1 Cover Card .10 .30
2 Bill Tempero .20 .50
3 Robby Unser in Car .30 .75
4 Johnny Unser .30 .75
5 Jimmy Santos .20 .50
6 Rick Sutherland .20 .50
7 Jim Buick .20 .50
8 Eddie Miller .20 .50
9 Bob Tankersley .20 .50
10 Bill Hansen .20 .50
11 Rocco Desimone .20 .50
12 Don Johnson .20 .50
13 Ken Petrie .20 .50
14 Kevin Whitesides .20 .50
15 Ken Petrie .20 .50
Eddie Miller Cars
16 Todd Snyder .30 .75
Robby Unser Cars
17 Rodger Ward .30 .75
18 Checklist Card .10 .30

1991 Legends of Indy

The first of two Legends of Indy sets was produced in 1991 by Collegiate Collection of Kentucky to celebrate the 75th Indy 500. The cards were distributed in complete set form and feature past and present stars of the IndyCar circuit. An album to house the cards was also produced and originally sold for $8.95 plus $2.50 shipping. The final card in the set could have been redeemed for a special card of the 1991 race winner Rick Mears.

COMPLETE SET (100) 6.00 15.00
1 The Start .02 .10
2 Largest Starting Field .02 .10
3 Norman Batten .02 .10
4 Parnelli Jones' Car .05 .15
5 Paul Russo's Car .02 .10
6 Eddie Sachs .02 .10
A.J.Foyt Cars
7 Transporters .02 .10
8 Bill Holland .02 .10
M.Rose cars
9 Carl G.Fisher .02 .10
A.Newby
F.Wheeler
J.Allison
10 New Garage Area .02 .10
11 The Brick Surface .02 .10
12 Jim Clark's Car .02 .10
13 1939 Rear-Engine Car .02 .10
14 Ralph dePalma in Pits .02 .10
15 Mary Fendrich Hulman .02 .10
16 Pete DePaolo .05 .15
17 Johnnie Parsons' Car .02 .10
18 Lee Wallard .05 .15
19 Arie Luyendyk's Car .10 .30
20 Sam Hanks' Car .02 .10
21 Pre-500 Garage Area .02 .10
22 The 1911 Front Row .02 .10
23 First Pace Car .02 .10
24 Pit Stop .02 .10
25 Jules Goux w .05 .15
Car
26 Economical Maxwell .02 .10
27 Tony Hulman .02 .10
Luke Walton
28 Freddie Agabashian's Car .02 .10
29 Tommy Milton .05 .15
Louis Meyer
30 Wilbur Shaw .05 .15
31 Rick Mears' Car .10 .30
32 Eddie Rickenbacker .05 .15
Tony Hulman
33 Lou Moore's Car .02 .10
34 Dale Evans' Car .02 .10
35 Duke Nalon's Crash .05 .15
36 Tangled Start .02 .10
37 Wilbur Shaw's Crash .05 .15
38 Early Effort By Ford .02 .10
39 Rick Mears .10 .30
Gordon Johncock Cars
40 Sampson Special .02 .10
41 Chester Gardner's Car .02 .10
42 Jack Brabham's Car .02 .10
43 Parnelli Jones w .10 .30
Crew
44 Billy Devore's Car .02 .10
45 Joe Leonard's Car .05 .15
46 Bobby Unser w .20 .50
Car
47 Chester Miller w .05 .15
Car
48 Danny Sullivan's Car .10 .30
49 Speedway's First Event .02 .10
50 Motorcycles .02 .10
51 B.Rahal .10 .30
R.Mears
Kevin Cogan Cars
52 The Stutz Team .02 .10
53 Chet Miller's Car .02 .10
54 Garage Fire .02 .10
55 Bobby Johns' Car .02 .10
56 Brick to Asphalt .02 .10
57 Jim Clark's Car .05 .15
58 New Tower and Pit Lane .02 .10
59 Al Unser Jr. .20 .50
E.Fittipaldi Cars
60 Dave Lewis' Car .02 .10
61 Streamliners .02 .10
62 Tom Sneva w .10 .30
Crew
63 Studebakers .02 .10
64 Old Victory Lane .02 .10
65 Tony Hulman .40 1.00
A.J.Foyt
66 Janet Guthrie w .20 .50
Car
67 The 1923 Lineup .02 .10
68 Emerson Fittipaldi w .20 .50
Car
69 Balloons .02 .10
70 Bobby Unser's Car .10 .30
71 Al Unser's Car .20 .50
72 Troy Ruttman's Car .02 .10
73 Louis Schwitzer's Car .02 .10
74 R.Mears .20 .50
D.Sullivan
Al Unser Cars
75 Ralph dePalma w .05 .15
Car
76 Bill Vukovich .05 .15
Jimmy Bryan's Cars
77 Drivers' Meeting .02 .10
78 The Pagoda .02 .10
79 The Old Front Gate .02 .10
80 Tom Sneva's Car .10 .30
81 Aerial View, 1922 .02 .10
82 Aerial View Today .02 .10
83 Jimmy Murphy's Car .05 .15
84 Hall Of Fame Museum .02 .10
85 Jim Rathmann .05 .15
R.Ward Cars
86 Mario Andretti .50 1.25
Andy Granatelli
87 Ray Harroun's Car .02 .10
88 Johnny Rutherford's Car .10 .30
89 Paul Russo's Car .02 .10
90 Bleak Days .02 .10
91 A Winter's Scene .02 .10
92 Fact Card .02 .10
93 Fact Card .02 .10
94 Fact Card .02 .10
95 Fact Card .02 .10
96 Fact Card .02 .10
97 Fact Card .02 .10
98 Fact Card .02 .10
99 Fact Card .02 .10
100A Cover Card .02 .10
100B Rick Mears '91 Race Winner 10.00 25.00

1992 Legends of Indy

The last of two Legends of Indy sets was produced in 1992 by G.S.S. of Indiana to celebrate the Indy 500. The cards were distributed in 10-card packs and feature past and present stars of the IndyCar circuit. Factory sets numbered of 25,000 were wrapped in a blister type packaging. An album to house the cards was also produced and offered for sale, along with the 1991 card album, for $9.95 plus $2.50 shipping. The coupon for the album offer also contained an offer to purchase complete sets of the 1991 series at $14.95 plus $3.50 shipping.

COMPLETE SET (100) 4.00 10.00
1 Rick Mears .08 .25
2 Rick Mears' Car .05 .15
3 Michael Andretti's Car .08 .25
4 Arie Luyendyk's Car .05 .15
5 Al Unser Jr.'s Car .08 .25
6 John Andretti's Car .05 .15
7 Gordon Johncock's Car .02 .10
8 Mario Andretti's Car .08 .25
9 Stan Fox's Car .02 .10
10 Tony Bettenhausen in Pits .02 .10
11 Danny Sullivan's Car .02 .10
12 Emerson Fittipaldi's Car .05 .15
13 Scott Pruett's Car .02 .10
14 Dominic Dobson's Car .02 .10
15 Randy Lewis's Car .02 .10
16 Jeff Andretti's Car .02 .10
17 Hiro Matsushita's Car .02 .10
18 Scott Brayton's Car .02 .10
19 Bernard Jourdain's Car .02 .10
20 Bobby Rahal in Pits .05 .15
21 Geoff Brabham's Car .02 .10
22 Pancho Carter's Car .02 .10
23 Gary Bettenhausen's Car .02 .10
24 Tero Palmroth's Car .02 .10
25 Mike Groff's Car .02 .10
26 John Paul Jr.'s Car .02 .10
27 Jim Crawford's Car .02 .10
28 Scott Goodyear's Car .02 .10
29 A.J. Foyt Jr.'s Car .08 .25
30 Kevin Cogan's Car .02 .10
31 Roberto Guerrero's Car .05 .15
32 Eddie Cheever's Car .02 .10
33 Willy T. Ribbs's Car .02 .10
34 Buddy Lazier's Car .02 .10
35 Hiro Matsushita's Car .02 .10
36 Willy T. Ribbs .02 .10
37 Arie Luyendyk .05 .15
38 Danny Sullivan's Car .02 .10
39 1991 Pace Car .02 .10
40 John Andretti .05 .15
Pruett
Johncock Cars
41 Norman Schwartzkopf .02 .10
42 Rick Mears .05 .15
Michael Andretti Cars
43 Rick Mears .05 .15
Foyt
Mario Andretti Cars
44 Rick Mears' Car .05 .15
45 1991 Start .02 .10
46 A.J.Foyt's Car .05 .15
47 1980 Pace Car .02 .10
48 1981 Pace Car .02 .10
49 1982 Pace Car .02 .10
50 1983 Pace Car .02 .10
51 1984 Pace Car .02 .10
52 1985 Pace Car .02 .10
53 1986 Pace Car .02 .10
54 1987 Pace Car .02 .10
55 1988 Pace Car .02 .10
56 1989 Pace Car .02 .10
57 A.J.Foyt .20 .50
Tony George
58 Mario Andretti's Car .08 .25
59 Hall of Fame Museum .02 .10
60 Alberto Ascari's Car .02 .10
61 Janet Guthrie .05 .15
Dick Simon
62 Al Unser's Car .05 .15
63 1968 Pace Lap .02 .10
64 A.J.Foyt .08 .25
Johnny Rutherford Cars
65 Yellow Flag .02 .10
66 How They Line Up .02 .10
67 Pre-Race Laps .02 .10
68 1969 Start .02 .10
69 Mario Andretti's Car .08 .25
70 Joe Leonard .02 .10
Granatelli in Pits
71 P.Jones .02 .10
Don Branson
Jim Hurtubise Cars
72 Al Unser's Car .05 .15
73 T.Milton .02 .10
H.Stutz
Howdy Wilcox w
cars
74 Chet Miller's Car .02 .10
75 Peter Revson w .02 .10
Car
76 Danny Sullivan .05 .15
Mario Andretti Cars
77 Lloyd Ruby in Pits .02 .10
78 T.Sneva .02 .10
Al Unser
Al Unser Jr. Cars
79 Eddie Sachs .02 .10
80 Dan Gurney's Car .02 .10
81 Mark Donohue's Car .02 .10
82 Duane Carter Sr.'s Car .02 .10
83 Balloons .02 .10
84 T.Sneva .02 .10
D.Ongais
Mears Cars
85 Pit Stops .02 .10
86 Pat Flaherty .02 .10
87 Victory Circle .02 .10
88 M.Mosley .02 .10
Sneva
T.Bigelow
Brayton Cars
89 Bobby Rahal .08 .25
90 Gordon Johncock w .05 .15
Car
91 Roger McCluskey's Car .02 .10
92 Parnelli Jones .05 .15
Andy Granatelli in Pits
93 1911 Lineup .02 .10
94 Bill Cheesbourg's Car .02 .10
95 Bobby Rahal .05 .15
Kevin Cogan Cars
96 Tony Bettenhausen .02 .10
Paul Russo
97 Parnelli Jones' Car .02 .10
98 Old Main Entrance .02 .10
99 Sam Hanks .02 .10
Jimmy Bryan Car
100 Checklist Card .02 .10
P1 Mi.Andretti's Car Prototype .40 1.00

1992 Limited Appeal Formula One

Cars of ten of the top 1991 Formula One drivers are the featured subject of this set produced by Limited Appeal of England. The cardfronts include a color photo in an attractive white ghosted-out border. The backs include driver information from the 1991 season and carry a 1992 year copyright line. The unnumbered cards are listed below alphabetically and were released as a complete set (Nigel Mansell was featured on the set wrapper).

COMPLETE SET (10) 4.00 10.00
1 Mark Blundell .30 .75
2 Ivan Capelli .30 .75
3 Erik Comas .30 .75
4 Andrea deCesaris .30 .75
5 Mika Hakkinen .30 .75
6 Nigel Mansell .60 1.50
7 Stefano Modena .30 .75
8 Alain Prost .40 1.00
9 Michael Schumacher .75 2.00
10 Ayrton Senna 1.25 3.00

1962 Marhoefer Indy

Marhoefer Meats of Muncie Indiana distributed this Indy car set in 1962 through its various meat products. The cards feature top IndyCar drivers in black and white photos. As is common with most issues distributed with meat products, the cards were produced with a wax film covering and are often found with product stains. The unnumbered cards are oversized (approximately 4" by 5-1/4") and contain rounded corners.

COMPLETE SET (16) 250.00 500.00
1 Chuck Arnold 18.00 30.00
2 Don Branson 18.00 30.00
3 Bob Christie 18.00 30.00
4 Don Davis 18.00 30.00
5 A.J.Foyt 50.00 75.00
6 Elmer George 18.00 30.00
7 Cliff Griffith 18.00 30.00
8 Gene Hartley 18.00 30.00
9 Roger McCluskey 18.00 30.00
10 Dick Rathmann 18.00 30.00
11 Lloyd Ruby 18.00 30.00
12 Eddie Sachs 18.00 30.00
13 Len Sutton 18.00 30.00
14 Jack Turner 18.00 30.00
15 Rodger Ward 20.00 35.00
16 Wayne Weiler 18.00 30.00

1993 Maxx Williams Racing

This 100-card set was produced by Maxx and features present and past drivers of the Williams Formula One racing team. It was sold through Club Maxx for $14.95 per set.

COMPLETE SET (100) 7.50 20.00
1 Nigel Mansell .25 .60
2 Riccardo Patrese .10 .30
3 Alain Prost .10 .30
4 Damon Hill .10 .30
5 Mark Blundell .07 .20
6 Thierry Boutsen .07 .20
7 Jean-Louis Schlesser .07 .20
8 Martin Brundle .07 .20
9 Jonathan Palmer .07 .20
10 Jacques Laffite .07 .20
11 Keke Rosberg .07 .20
12 Nelson Piquet .10 .30
13 Derek Daly .07 .20
14 Carlos Reutemann .10 .30
15 Mario Andretti .75 2.00
16 Alan Jones .10 .30
17 Clay Regazzoni .07 .20
18 The Helmets .02 .10
19 Frank Williams .07 .20
20 Patrick Head .07 .20
21 Adrian Newey .07 .20
22 David Brown .07 .20
23 The Conference Centre .02 .10
24 The Trophies .02 .10
25 The Crash Test .02 .10
26 Clay Regazzoni's Car .02 .10
27 Alan Jones' Car .07 .20
28 Alan Jones' Car .07 .20
29 Alan Jones' Car .07 .20
30 Alan Jones' Car .07 .20
31 Alan Jones' Car .07 .20
32 Alan Jones' Car .07 .20
33 Alan Jones' Car .07 .20
34 Alan Jones' Car .07 .20
35 Jackie Stewart .25 .60
Alan Jones
36 Alan Jones' Car .07 .20
37 Alan Jones .10 .30
38 Alan Jones' Car .07 .20
39 Carlos Reutemann's Car .07 .20
40 Carlos Reutemann's Car .07 .20
41 Alan Jones' Car .07 .20
42 Keke Rosberg's Car .02 .10
43 Keke Rosberg's Car .02 .10
44 Keke Rosberg's Car .02 .10
45 Keke Rosberg's Car .02 .10
46 Keke Rosberg's Car .02 .10
47 Keke Rosberg's Car .02 .10
48 Nigel Mansell's Car .10 .30
49 Nigel Mansell .25 .60
50 Nigel Mansell .25 .60
51 Nelson Piquet's Car .07 .20
52 Nigel Mansell's Car .10 .30
53 Nigel Mansell's Car .10 .30
54 Nigel Mansell's Car .10 .30
55 Nigel Mansell's Car .10 .30
56 Nigel Mansell's Car .10 .30
57 Nigel Mansell's Car .10 .30
58 Nelson Piquet's Car .07 .20
59 Nigel Mansell's Car .10 .30
60 Nigel Mansell's Car .10 .30
61 Nigel Mansell's Car .10 .30
62 Nigel Mansell .25 .60
63 Nelson Piquet's Car .07 .20
64 Nelson Piquet's Car .07 .20
65 Nigel Mansell's Car .10 .30
66 Nelson Piquet's Car .07 .20
67 Nigel Mansell .25 .60
68 Nigel Mansell's Car .10 .30
69 Nelson Piquet's Car .07 .20
70 Nigel Mansell's Car .10 .30
71 Thierry Boutsen's Car .02 .10
72 Thierry Boutsen .10 .30
Riccardo Patrese
73 Riccardo Patrese's Car .07 .20
74 Thierry Boutsen's Car .02 .10
75 Riccardo Patrese's Car .07 .20
76 Nigel Mansell's Car .10 .30
77 Nigel Mansell's Car .10 .30
78 Nigel Mansell's Car .10 .30
79 Nigel Mansell's Car .10 .30
80 Riccardo Patrese's Car .07 .20
81 Nigel Mansell's Car .10 .30
82 Nigel Mansell's Car .10 .30
83 Nigel Mansell's Car .10 .30
84 Nigel Mansell's Car .10 .30
85 Nigel Mansell's Car .10 .30
86 Nigel Mansell's Car .10 .30
87 Riccardo Patrese's Car .07 .20
88 Nigel Mansell's Car .10 .30
89 Nigel Mansell's Car .10 .30
90 Nigel Mansell's Car .10 .30
91 Nigel Mansell's Car .10 .30
92 Nigel Mansell's Car .10 .30
93 Keke Rosberg's Car .02 .10
94 Alan Jones' Car .07 .20
95 Alan Jones' Car .07 .20
96 Nigel Mansell's Car .10 .30
97 Ford Cosworth DFV .02 .10
98 Honda V6 .02 .10
99 Judd V8 .02 .10
100 Renault V10 .02 .10

1971 Mobil The Story of Grand Prix Motor Racing

This 36-card set highlights some of the great drivers and their cars from 1906 to 1969. Famous names like Ralph de Palma and Jackie Stewart are depicted on the fronts of the cards via artist renderings. The set was sponsored by Mobil and issued in Europe.

COMPLETE SET (36) 12.50 25.00
1 Szisz Renault's Car .30 .75
2 Felice Nazzaro's Car .30 .75
3 C.Lautenschlager's Car .30 .75
4 Georges Boillot's Car .30 .75
5 C.Lautenschlager's Car .30 .75
6 Ralph de Palma's Car .75 1.50
7 Jimmy Murphy's Car .30 .75
8 P. Bordino's Car .30 .75
9 Henry Segrave's Car .30 .75
10 G.Campari's Car .30 .75
11 M.Costantini's Car .30 .75
12 R.Benoist's Car .30 .75
13 Rene Dreyfus' Car .30 .75
14 Sir Henry Birkin's Car .30 .75
15 Luigi Fagioli's Car .30 .75
16 Tazio Nuvolari's Car .30 .75
17 R.Carraciola's Car .30 .75
18 Tazio Nuvolari's Car .30 .75
19 B.Rosemeyer's Car .30 .75
20 Richard Seaman's Car .30 .75
21 Louis Chiron's Car .30 .75
22 Jean Pierre Wimille's Car .30 .75
23 Baron de Graffenried's Car .30 .75
24 Giuseppe Farina's Car .30 .75
25 Alberto Ascari's Car .30 .75
26 Mike Hawthorn's Car .30 .75
27 Juan Manuel Fangio's Car .50 1.00
28 Tony Brooks's Car .30 .75
29 Peter Collins' Car .30 .75
30 Juan Manuel Fangio's Car .50 1.00
31 Stirling Moss' Car .50 1.00
32 Mike Hawthorn's Car .30 .75
33 Jack Brabham's Car .30 .75
34 Graham Hill's Car .50 1.00
35 Jim Clark's Car .30 .75
36 Jackie Stewart's Car .75 1.50

1973 Nabisco Sugar Daddy Speedway Collection

Cards from the Speedway Collection set were inserted into Sugar Daddy and Sugar Mama candies in 1973. A wall poster was also produced that was used by collectors to mount their card sets using the adhesive on the cardbacks.The cards themselves are small (approximately 1" by 2-3/4") and feature art renderings of cars from various auto racing circuits along with a racing sponsor logo on the right side of the cardfront. The sponsor logos were to be cut out and mounted separately to the poster. A few of the cards pertain to a particular driver as noted below. There were also six 5" X 7" premiums also issued with the set. The premium cards were available in the bottom of the Sugar Daddy's boxes. They were printed on text-weight paper.

COMPLETE SET (25) 400.00 700.00
1 Jackie Stewart's Car 20.00 40.00
2 Peter Revson's Car 15.00 25.00
3 Mark Donohue's Car 15.00 25.00
4 Mario Andretti 20.00 40.00
Jackie Ickx Car
5 Porsche 917 IMC 15.00 25.00
6 Al Unser's Car 20.00 40.00
7 A.J.Foyt's Car 20.00 40.00
8 Rally 15.00 25.00
9 Off-Road 15.00 25.00
10 2-5 Challenge 15.00 25.00
11 IMC 15.00 25.00
12 Off-Road 15.00 25.00
13 Don Garlits' Car 20.00 40.00
14 Ed McCulloch's Car 20.00 40.00
15 Bill Jenkins' Car 15.00 25.00
16 Hill Climb 15.00 25.00
17 A-Production 15.00 25.00
18 John Morton's Car 15.00 25.00
19 H-Production 15.00 25.00
20 Blue Flame 15.00 25.00
21 Goldenrod 15.00 25.00
22 Gary Bettenhausen's Car 20.00 40.00
23 David Hobbs' Car 20.00 40.00
24 Formula B 15.00 25.00
25 Formula Vee 15.00 25.00

1974 New York News This Day in Sports

These cards are newspaper clippings of drawings by Hollreiser and are accompanied by textual description highlighting a player's unique sports feat. Cards are approximately 2" X 4 1/4". These are multisport cards and arranged in chronological order.

COMPLETE SET 50.00 120.00
16 Peter Revson 1.00 2.00
July 25, 1971

1931 Ogden's Motor Races

This 50-card series features artist renderings of cars and motorcycles at various racing events in 1931. The cards were produced for Imperial Tobacco Company of Great Britain and Ireland's Ogden cigarettes branch. The cards measure 1 3/8" X 2 5/8". The fronts of the cards depict cars or motorcycles in race action. "Ogden's Cigarettes" and the title and date of the event are on the front of every card. The card backs state at the top "Motor Races 1931" and "A series of 50". This dating gives the specific year all the racing events featured were run. The latest event featured is October 17, 1931, which in turn leads us to believe that the cards were probably not produced or issued until 1932. The cards backs also feature a brief story on the event featured on that card. The bottom of the card backs state "Issued by Ogden's." The series is broken into two groups, automobile races and motorcycle races. Cards 1-33 are the automobile races and cards 34-50 feature the motorcycle races.

COMPLETE SET (50) 200.00 400.00
1 Sir Malcom Campbell 3.00 8.00
Blue Bird, Daytona, Feb 5
2 Swedish Winter Grand Prix 3.00 8.00
(Feb. 23)
3 Argentine National Grand Prix 3.00 8.00
March
4 Tunis Grand Prix, March 29 3.00 8.00
5 Austrailian Grand Prix, March 3.00 8.00
6 The Italian, 1000 Miles Race 3.00 8.00
(April 11-12)
7 Monaco Grand Prix, April 20 3.00 8.00
8 The Double Twelve Race 3.00 8.00
Brooklands, May 8-9
10 Grand Prix, Casablanca 3.00 8.00
(May 17)
11 Italian Grand Prix, Monza 3.00 8.00
(May 24)
12 The 500 Miles Race 3.00 8.00
Indianapolis, May 30
13 Ernesto Maserati 3.00 8.00
Royal Prix de Roma, June 7
14 Grand Prix d'Endurance 3.00 8.00
LeMans, June 12-13
15 Grand Prix, Automobile 3.00 8.00
Club de France, June 21
16 Southport 100 Mile Race 3.00 8.00
(June 27)
17 Junior Car Club, High-Speed 3.00 8.00
Trial, July 4
18 Belgian 24-Hours Race 3.00 8.00
(July 4-5)
19 Irish Grand Prix, Saorstat Cup 3.00 8.00
(July 5)
20 Irish Grand Prix, Eireann Cup 3.00 8.00
(July 6)
21 Shelsley Walsh Hill Climb 3.00 8.00
(July 11)
22 Belgian Grand Prix, July 12 3.00 8.00
23 Sand Race, Skegness, July 18 3.00 8.00
24 The German Grand Prix 3.00 8.00
(July 19)
25 Relay Race, Brooklands 3.00 8.00
(July 25)
26 Circuit de Dieppe 3.00 8.00
27 Circuit de Dieppe 3.00 8.00
28 Mile Record, Brooklands 3.00 8.00
(August 8)
30 Mont Ventoux Hill Climb 3.00 8.00
(August 30)
31 Monza Grand Prix, Sept. 6 3.00 8.00
32 Circuit des Routes pavees 3.00 8.00
33 Sir Henry Birkin 3.00 8.00
at Brooklands, Oct. 17
34 The 100-Miles Sand Race 3.00 8.00
Southport, May 9
35 The Austrian Tourist Trophy 3.00 8.00
(May 10)
36 Junior Motorcycle Tourist 3.00 8.00
Trophy, June 15
37 Lightweight Motorcycle 3.00 8.00
Tourist Trophy, June 17
38 Senior Motorcycle 3.00 8.00
Tourist Trophy, June 19
40 F.I.C.M. Grand Prix 3.00 8.00
41 German Grand Prix 3.00 8.00
(500cc class, July 5)
42 Dutch Motorcycle 3.00 8.00
Tourist Trophy, July 11
43 Italian Tourist Trophy, July 12 3.00 8.00
44 Phoenix Park Road Races 3.00 8.00
(July 18)
45 Belgian Grand Prix, July 19 3.00 8.00
46 The Dieppe Grand Prix, July 3.00 8.00
47 Ulster Grand Prix, Sept. 5 3.00 8.00
48 Swedish Grand Prix, Sept. 6 3.00 8.00
49 Manx Junior Grand Prix 3.00 8.00
(Sept. 8)
50 Manx Senior Grand Prix 3.00 8.00
(Sept. 10)

1987-88 Panini Spanish Stickers

The 1987-88 Panini Spanish Supersport Sticker set consists of 161 stickers, each measuring approximately 2 1/8" by 3". The stickers were designed to be placed in an album measuring approximately 9 1/8" by 10 3/4". The sticker fronts display color photos of athletes from several countries and representing various sports. Among the sports represented are Basketball (1-42), Track and Field (43-84), Soccer (85-126), Motor Sports (127-140), Bicyling (141-147), and Tennis (148-161).

COMPLETE SET (161) 200.00 400.00
127 Luca Cadalora .20 .50
128 Stefan Dorflinger .20 .50
129 Wayne Gardner .20 .50
130 Ezio Gianola .20 .50
131 Fausto Gresini .20 .50
132 Manuel Herreros .20 .50
133 Eddie Lawson .20 .50
134 Randy Mamola .20 .50
135 Anton Mang .20 .50
136 Alfonso Pons .20 .50
137 Jorge Martinez .20 .50
138 Nelson Piquet .40 1.00
139 Alain Prost .40 1.00
140 Ayrton Senna 2.00 5.00

1943-48 Parade Sportive

These blank-backed photo sheets of sports figures from the Montreal area around 1945 measure approximately 5" by 8 1/4". They were issued to promote a couple of Montreal radio stations that used to broadcast interviews with some of the pictured athletes. The sheets feature white-bordered black-and-white player photos, some of them crudely retouched. The player's name appears in the bottom white margin and also as a facsimile autograph across the photo. The sheets are unnumbered and are checklisted below in alphabetical order within sport as follows: hockey (1-75), baseball (76-95) and various other sports (96-101). Additions to this checklist are appreciated. Many players are known to appear with two different poses. Since the values are the same for both poses, we have put a (2) next to the players name but have placed a value on only one of the photos.

COMPLETE SET 1250.00 2500.00
96 Gerard Cote 12.50 25.00
Racing

1935 J.A. Pattreiouex Sporting Events and Stars

28 Sir Malcolm Campbell 6.00 12.00
Auto Racing
61 Captain G. Eyston 6.00 12.00
Auto Racing
64 John Cobb 6.00 12.00
Auto Racing
67 Freddie Dixon 6.00 12.00
Auto Racing

1962 Petpro Limited Grand Prix Racing Cars

This 35-card set was issued by Petpro Limited of Crawley, Sussex England. The cards feature artist paintings of many of the top Grand Prix cards than raced between 1939 and 1961. The cards measure 2 1/2" X 1 1/8".

COMPLETE SET (35) 15.00 30.00
1 Tony Brook's Car .40 1.00
2 Achille Varzi's Car .40 1.00
3 W.F. Moss' Car .40 1.00
4 Tony Rolt's Car .40 1.00
5 B. Bira's Car .40 1.00
6 Reg Parnell's Car .40 1.00
7 Louis Rosier's Car .40 1.00
8 Guiseppe Farina's Car .40 1.00
9 Guiseppe Farina's Car .40 1.00
10 Arthur Dobson's Car .40 1.00
11 Joe Kelly's Car .40 1.00
12 Peter Whitehead's Car .40 1.00
13 Froilan Gonzales' Car .40 1.00
14 International Racing Flags .40 1.00
15 Lance Macklin's Car .40 1.00
16 Mike Hawthorn's Car .40 1.00
17 Juan Manuel Fangio's Car .60 1.50
18 Ken Wharton's Car .40 1.00
19 Tony Rolt's Car .40 1.00
20 Jack Brabham's Car .40 1.00
21 John Surtees' Car .40 1.00
22 Albert Ascari's Car .40 1.00
23 Jean Behra's Car .40 1.00
24 Karl Kling's Car .40 1.00
25 Stirling Moss' Car .75 2.00
26 Jean Behra's Car .40 1.00
27 Archie Scot Brown's Car .40 1.00
28 Froilan Gonzales' Car .40 1.00
29 Chuck Daigh's Car .40 1.00
30 Jack Brabham's Car .40 1.00
31 Jimmy Clark's Car .40 1.00
32 Phil Hill's Car .40 1.00
33 Joachim Bonnier's Car .40 1.00
34 Graham Hill's Car .60 1.50
35 Stirling Moss' Car .75 2.00

1991 Pro Tracs Formula One

Canadian based Pro Tracs produced this 1991 issue focusing on Formula One drivers and top F1 teams. The cards were distributed in 10-card packs with 36-packs per box. The set is sometimes called Vroom, the name contained on foil boxes.

COMPLETE SET (200) 4.00 10.00
1 Ayrton Senna .30 .75
2 Ayrton Senna's Car .10 .30
3 Gerhard Berger .07 .20
4 Gerhard Berger's Car .02 .10
5 Saturo Nakajima .02 .10
6 Saturo Nakajima's Car .01 .05
7 Stefano Modena .02 .10
8 Stefano Modena's Car .01 .05
9 Nigel Mansell .10 .30
10 Nigel Mansell's Car .07 .20
11 Riccardo Patrese .07 .20
12 Riccardo Patrese's Car .02 .10
13 Martin Brundle .02 .10
14 Martin Brundle's Car .01 .05
15 Martin Brundle's Car .01 .05
16 Mark Blundell .02 .10
17 Mark Blundell's Car .01 .05
18 Mark Blundell's Car .01 .05
19 Michele Alboreto .02 .10
20 Michele Alboreto's Car .01 .05
21 Michele Alboreto's Car .01 .05
22 Alex Caffi .02 .10
23 Alex Caffi's Car .01 .05
24 Stefan Johansson .07 .20
25 Stefan Johansson's Car .02 .10
26 Mika Hakkinen .02 .10
27 Mika Hakkinen's Car .01 .05
28 Julian Bailey .02 .10
29 Julian Bailey's Car .01 .05
30 Johnny Herbert .02 .10
31 Johnny Herbert's Car .01 .05
32 Olivier Grouillard .02 .10
33 Olivier Grouillard's Car .01 .05
34 Olivier Grouillard's Car .01 .05
35 Mauricio Gugelmin .02 .10
36 Mauricio Gugelmin's Car .01 .05
37 Ivan Capelli .02 .10
38 Ivan Capelli's Car .01 .05
39 Gabriele Tarquini .02 .10
40 Gabriele Tarquini's Car .01 .05
41 Stefan Johansson .07 .20
42 Stefan Johansson's Car .02 .10
43 Fabrizio Barbazza .02 .10
44 Fabrizio Barbazza's Car .01 .05
45 Roberto Moreno .02 .10
46 Roberto Moreno's Car .01 .05
47 Roberto Moreno's Car .01 .05
48 Nelson Piquet .07 .20
49 Nelson Piquet's Car .02 .10
50 Nelson Piquet's Car .02 .10
51 Emanuele Pirro .02 .10
52 Emanuele Pirro's Car .01 .05
53 J.J. Lehto .02 .10
54 J.J. Lehto's Car .01 .05
55 Pierluigi Martini .02 .10
56 Pierluigi Martini's Car .01 .05
57 Gianni Morbidelli .02 .10
58 Gianni Morbidelli's Car .01 .05
59 Thierry Boutsen .02 .10
60 Thierry Boutsen's Car .01 .05
61 Erik Comas .02 .10
62 Erik Comas' Car .01 .05
63 Alain Prost .07 .20
64 Alain Prost's Car .02 .10
65 Jean Alesi .02 .10
66 Jean Alesi's Car .01 .05
67 Eric Bernard .02 .10
68 Eric Bernard's Car .01 .05
69 Aguri Suzuki .02 .10
70 Aguri Suzuki's Car .01 .05
71 Pedro Matos Chaves .02 .10
72 Pedro Matos Chaves' Car .01 .05
73 Bertrand Gachot .02 .10
74 Bertrand Gachot's Car .01 .05
75 Andrea deCesaris .02 .10
76 Andrea deCesaris' Car .01 .05
77 Nicola Larini .02 .10
78 Nicola Larini's Car .01 .05
79 Eric Van de Poele .02 .10
80 Eric Van de Poele's Car .01 .05
81 USA Race Track .01 .05
82 Brazil Race Track .01 .05
83 San Marino Race Track .01 .05
84 Monaco Race Track .01 .05
85 Canada Race Track .01 .05
86 Mexico Race Track .01 .05
87 France Race Track .01 .05
88 Great Britain Track .01 .05
89 Germany Race Track .01 .05
90 Hungary Race Track .01 .05
91 Belgium Race Track .01 .05
92 Italy Race Track .01 .05
93 Portugal Race Track .01 .05
94 Spain Race Track .01 .05
95 Japan Race Track .01 .05
96 Australia Race Track .01 .05
97 Ayrton Senna's Car .10 .30
98 Ayrton Senna's Car .10 .30
99 Ayrton Senna's Car .10 .30
100 Ayrton Senna's Car .10 .30
101 Ayrton Senna's Car .10 .30
102 Ayrton Senna's Car .10 .30
103 Ayrton Senna's Car .10 .30
104 Ayrton Senna's Car .10 .30
105 Ayrton Senna's Car .10 .30
106 Ayrton Senna .30 .75
107 Ayrton Senna in Car .30 .75
108 Alain Prost .07 .20
109 Alain Prost's Car .02 .10
110 Alain Prost's Car .02 .10
111 Alain Prost's Car .02 .10
112 Alain Prost's Car .02 .10
113 Alain Prost's Car .02 .10
114 Alain Prost's Car .02 .10
115 Alain Prost's Car .02 .10
116 Alain Prost's Car .02 .10
117 Alain Prost's Car .02 .10
118 Alain Prost .07 .20
119 Alain Prost's Car .02 .10
120 Alain Prost .07 .20
121 Nigel Mansell's Car .07 .20
122 Nigel Mansell's Car .07 .20
123 Nigel Mansell's Car .07 .20
124 Nigel Mansell's Car .07 .20
125 Nigel Mansell's Car .07 .20
126 Nigel Mansell's Car .07 .20
127 Nigel Mansell's Car .07 .20
128 Nigel Mansell's Car .07 .20
129 Nigel Mansell's Car .07 .20
130 Nigel Mansell's Car .07 .20
131 Nigel Mansell .10 .30
132 Porsche Engine .01 .05
133 Yamaha Engine .01 .05
134 Lamborghini Engine .01 .05
135 Honda Engine .01 .05
136 Ferrari Engine .01 .05
137 Ford Engine .01 .05
138 Renault Engine .01 .05
139 Ilmor Engine .01 .05
140 Judd Engine .01 .05
141 Judd Engine .01 .05
142 Honda Engine .01 .05
143 Ford Engine .01 .05
144 Ayrton Senna's Car .10 .30
145 Alain Prost USA .07 .20
146 Nelson Piquet .07 .20
147 Ayrton Senna's Car .10 .30
148 Ayrton Senna .30 .75
Patrese
Berger
149 Riccardo Patrese's Car .02 .10
150 Gerhard Berger's Car .02 .10
151 Ayrton Senna .30 .75
152 Ayrton Senna's Car .10 .30
153 San Marino .01 .05
154 Ayrton Senna's Car .10 .30
155 Monaco .01 .05
156 Monaco .01 .05
157 Nelson Piquet's Car .02 .10
158 Nigel Mansell's Car .07 .20
159 Nelson Piquet's Car .02 .10
160 French Grand Prix .01 .05
161 Aguri Suzuki .02 .10
Eric Bernard
162 Riccardo Patrese .07 .20
Alain Prost
163 Great Britain Grand Prix .01 .05
164 Silverstone .01 .05
GB
165 Ayrton Senna .10 .30
N.Mansell Cars
166 Ayrton Senna .30 .75
167 Hockenheim .01 .05
GER
168 Start .01 .05
GER
169 Thierry Boutsen .02 .10
170 Thierry Boutsen's Car .01 .05
171 Martin Donnelly's Car .01 .05
172 Ayrton Senna .10 .30
Berger
173 Start HUN .01 .05
174 View BEL .01 .05
175 Ferrari ITA .01 .05
176 Start ITA .01 .05
177 Monza ITA .01 .05
178 Race Grid POR .01 .05
179 Nigel Mansell's Car .07 .20
180 Nigel Mansell .10 .30
181 Alain Prost .07 .20
182 Alain Prost's Car .02 .10
183 SPA .01 .05
184 Nelson Piquet .07 .20
185 Roberto Moreno .07 .20
Nelson Piquet
186 Johnny Herbert's Car .01 .05
187 Nelson Piquet .07 .20
188 Stag Hotel AUS .01 .05
189 Yannick Dalmas' Car .01 .05
190 Jody Scheckter .02 .10
191 Keke Rosberg's Car .01 .05
192 Niki Lauda .07 .20
193 Nigel Mansell .07 .20
C.Chapman
194 Patrick Tambay's Car .01 .05
195 John Watson .02 .10
196 Gilles Villeneuve's Car .07 .20
197 Gilles Villeneuve's Car .07 .20
198 Alain Prost's Car .02 .10
199 Checklist .01 .05
200 Checklist .01 .05

2007 Rittenhouse IRL

COMPLETE SET (54) 15.00 40.00
WAX BOX HOBBY 70.00 100.00
WAX BOX ARCHIVES 400.00 750.00
1 Danica Patrick RC 4.00 10.00
2 Danica Patrick's Car 1.50 4.00
3 Danica Patrick RC 4.00 10.00
4 Dan Wheldon RC 1.00 2.50
5 Dan Wheldon's Car .40 1.00
6 Dan Wheldon RC 1.00 2.50
7 Tony Kanaan RC 1.00 2.50
8 Tony Kanaan's Car .40 1.00
9 Tony Kanaan RC 1.00 2.50
10 Scott Dixon RC .25 .60
11 Scott Dixon's Car .10 .25
12 Scott Dixon RC .25 .60
13 Vitor Meira RC .25 .60
14 Vitor Meira's Car .10 .25
15 Vitor Meira RC .25 .60
16 Milka Duno RC 1.00 2.50
17 Milka Duno's Car .40 1.00
18 Milka Duno RC 1.00 2.50
19 Marco Andretti RC 1.00 2.50
20 Marco Andretti's Car .40 1.00
21 Marco Andretti RC 1.00 2.50
22 Dario Franchitti RC 1.00 2.50
23 Dario Franchitti's Car .40 1.00
24 Dario Franchitti RC 1.00 2.50
25 Tomas Scheckter RC .40 1.00
26 Tomas Scheckter's Car .15 .40
27 Tomas Scheckter RC .40 1.00
28 Scott Sharp .25 .60
29 Scott Sharp's Car .10 .25
30 Scott Sharp .25 .60
31 Kosuke Matsuura RC .25 .60
32 Kosuke Matsuura's Car .10 .25
33 Kosuke Matsuura RC .25 .60
34 Ed Carpenter RC .25 .60
35 Ed Carpenter's Car .10 .25
36 Ed Carpenter RC .25 .60
37 Buddy Rice RC .25 .60
38 Buddy Rice's Car .10 .25
39 Buddy Rice RC .25 .60
40 Jeff Simmons RC .25 .60
41 Jeff Simmons' Car .10 .25
42 Jeff Simmons RC .25 .60
43 Marty Roth RC .25 .60
44 Marty Roth's Car .10 .25
45 Marty Roth RC .25 .60
46 Sarah Fisher RC 1.50 4.00
47 Sarah Fisher's Car .60 1.50
48 Sarah Fisher RC 1.50 4.00
49 A.J. Foyt IV .40 1.00
50 A.J. Foyt IV Car .15 .40
51 A.J. Foyt IV .40 1.00
52 Darren Manning RC .50 1.25
53 Darren Manning's Car .20 .50
54 Darren Manning RC .50 1.25
P1 Danica Patrick Promo 4.00 10.00
NNO Dario Franchitti
Indy 500 Champ. 12.50 25.00

2007 Rittenhouse IRL Autographs

STATED ODDS 1:12
1 Marco Andretti 15.00 30.00
2 Ed Carpenter 10.00 20.00
3 Scott Dixon 10.00 20.00
4 Milka Duno 15.00 30.00
5 Sarah Fisher 15.00 40.00
6 Dario Franchitti 15.00 30.00
7 A.J. Foyt IV 15.00 40.00
8 Tony Kanaan 15.00 30.00
9 Darren Manning 10.00 20.00
10 Kosuke Matsuura 7.50 15.00
11 Vitor Meira 10.00 20.00
12 Danica Patrick 125.00 250.00
13 Buddy Rice 7.50 15.00
14 Tomas Scheckter 7.50 15.00
15 Scott Sharp 10.00 20.00
16 Jeff Simmons 10.00 20.00
17 Dan Wheldon 20.00 50.00

2007 Rittenhouse IRL Foyt 50th Anniversary

COMPLETE SET (9) 30.00 60.00
COMMON FOYT 4.00 8.00
STATED ODDS 1:24
1 A.J. Foyt 1958 4.00 8.00
2 A.J. Foyt '61 Indy 500 Champ 4.00 8.00
3 A.J. Foyt '61 Indy 500 Champ 4.00 8.00
4 A.J. Foyt '64 Indy 500 Champ 4.00 8.00
5 A.J. Foyt 1964 Indy 500 Champ 4.00 8.00
6 A.J. Foyt '67 Indy 500 Champ 4.00 8.00
7 A.J. Foyt '67 Indy 500 Champ 4.00 8.00
8 A.J. Foyt '77 Indy 500 Champ 4.00 8.00
9 A.J. Foyt '07 4.00 8.00

2007 Rittenhouse IRL Foyt 50th Anniversary Autograph

STATED ODDS 1:864
NNO A.J. Foyt 75.00 125.00

2007 Rittenhouse IRL Road to Victory Indy 500

COMPLETE SET (9) 10.00 20.00
STATED ODDS 1:8
V1 Dario Franchitti 1.25 3.00
V2 Dario Franchitti 1.25 3.00
V3 Dario Franchitti 1.25 3.00
V4 Dario Franchitti 1.25 3.00
V5 Dario Franchitti 1.25 3.00
V6 Dario Franchitti 1.25 3.00
V7 Dario Franchitti 1.25 3.00
V8 Dario Franchitti 1.25 3.00
V9 Dario Franchitti 1.25 3.00

2007 Rittenhouse IRL Shades of Victory

COMPLETE SET (9) 12.50 30.00
STATED ODDS 1:12
R1 Danica Patrick 8.00 20.00
R2 Dan Wheldon 2.00 5.00
R3 Dario Franchitti 2.00 5.00
R4 Tony Kanaan 2.00 5.00
R5 Vitor Meira .50 1.25
R6 Scott Dixon .50 1.25
R7 Buddy Rice .50 1.25
R8 Marco Andretti 2.00 5.00
R9 A.J. Foyt IV .75 2.00

1970 Shell Racing Cars of the World

COMPLETE SET (48) 25.00 50.00
1 1901 Panhard .75 2.00
2 1901 Renault .75 2.00
3 1906 Locomobile .75 2.00
4 1908 Mors .75 2.00
5 1910 Bugatti .75 2.00
6 1913 Peugeot .75 2.00
7 1914 Mercedes .75 2.00
8 1919 Ballot .75 2.00
9 1921 Sunbeam Talbot Darracq .75 2.00
10 1923 Voisin .75 2.00
11 1924 Duesenberg .75 2.00
12 1927 Delage .75 2.00
13 1927 Fiat Type 806 .75 2.00
14 1928 Amilcar .75 2.00
15 1930 Bugatti .75 2.00
16 1931 Alfa Romeo .75 2.00
17 1935 Gilmore Special .75 2.00
18 1938 Auto Union .75 2.00
19 1938 Mercedes Benz .75 2.00
20 1946 Sparks .75 2.00
21 1950 Wynn .75 2.00
22 1950 Alfa Romeo .75 2.00
23 1950 Lago Talbot .75 2.00
24 1951 HWM .75 2.00
25 1952 Connaught .75 2.00
26 1952 Ferrari .75 2.00
27 1954 Lancia .75 2.00
28 1955 Mercedes Benz .75 2.00
29 1956 Maserati 250F .75 2.00
30 1956 Lycoming Special .75 2.00
31 1957 Cooper 500 .75 2.00
32 1957 Maserati .75 2.00
33 1957 Lister Jaguar .75 2.00
34 1958 Vanwall .75 2.00
35 1959 Cooper .75 2.00
36 1959 BRM .75 2.00
37 1959 Aston Martin DBR 4/250 .75 2.00
38 1960 Ferrari .75 2.00
39 1960 Lotus .75 2.00
40 1960 Lotus Climax .75 2.00
41 1961 Ferguson .75 2.00
42 1961 Ferrari .75 2.00
43 1961 SAAB .75 2.00
44 1961 Peugeot .75 2.00
45 1961 Cooper .75 2.00
46 1961 Elfin .75 2.00
47 1962 BRM .75 2.00
48 1962 Lola .75 2.00

1995 SkyBox Indy 500

This 108-card set was the first Indy set produced by SkyBox. The oversized cards 2 1/2" X 4 1/2" feature the top names in Indy Car racing. There are two topical subsets within the set: Qualifying Position (19-51) and Finishing Position (73-105). There was also a special 1994 Indy Champion insert of Al Unser Jr. The card was randomly inserted at a rate of one per 44 packs. A special Jacques Villeneuve Indy 500 Winner mail away card was produced as well. Both cards are priced at the bottom of the set listing but not included in the set price.

COMPLETE SET (108) 8.00 15.00
1 Cover .10 .25
Checklist Card
2 IMS Speedway .10 .25
3 Borg-Warner Trophy .10 .25
4 IMS Speedway .10 .25
5 Paul Tracy's Car .10 .25
6 Robby Gordon's Car .10 .25
7 Michael Andretti's Car .20 .50
8 P.Tracy .15 .40
Al Unser
E.Fittipaldi's Car
9 Stefan Johansson .10 .25
10 Bryan Herta .20 .50
A.J.Foyt
11 Emerson Fittipaldi w .20 .50
Car
12 Mario Andretti w .20 .50
Car
13 Jacques Villeneuve RQ .20 .50
14 Al Unser Jr. .20 .50
Penske w
Crew
15 Al Unser Sr. Retires .20 .50
16 Johnny Rutherford .15 .40
17 Bobby Rahal in Car .15 .40
18 E.Fittipaldi .20 .50
R.Boesel
Unser Jr.
19 Al Unser Jr. in Car .20 .50
20 Raul Boesel .10 .25
21 Emerson Fittipaldi .20 .50
22 Jacques Villeneuve in Car .20 .50
23 Michael Andretti in Car .20 .50
24 Lyn St. James .10 .25
25 Nigel Mansell .15 .40
26 Arie Luyendyk .15 .40
27 Mario Andretti in Car .20 .50
28 John Andretti .15 .40
29 Eddie Cheever .10 .25
30 Dominic Dobson .10 .25
31 Stan Fox .10 .25
32 Hideshi Matsuda .10 .25
33 Dennis Vitolo .10 .25
34 Jimmy Vasser .10 .25
35 Scott Sharp .15 .40
36 Hiro Matsushita .10 .25
37 Robby Gordon .15 .40
38 Roberto Guerrero .15 .40
39 Brian Till .10 .25
40 Bryan Herta .10 .25
41 Scott Brayton .10 .25
42 Teo Fabi .15 .40
43 Paul Tracy .15 .40
44 Adrian Fernandez .10 .25
45 Stefan Johansson .10 .25
46 Bobby Rahal .15 .40
47 Mauricio Gugelmin .10 .25
48 John Paul Jr. .10 .25
49 Mike Groff .10 .25
50 Marco Greco .10 .25
51 Scott Goodyear .10 .25
52 Al Unser Jr. MVP .20 .50
53 Jim Nabors .10 .25
54 Robby Gordon .15 .40
R.Guerrero
Bryan Till
55 IMS Speedway .10 .25
56 IMS Speedway .10 .25
57 IMS Speedway .10 .25
58 Dennis Vitolo's Car .10 .25
59 Mario Andretti in Pits .20 .50
60 Mike Groff .10 .25
Dominic Dobson Crash
61 Adrian Fernandez's Car .10 .25
62 Jacques Villeneuve's Car .20 .50
63 Robby Gordon .10 .25
Raul Boesel Cars
64 Hideshi Matsuda's Car .10 .25
65 Dennis Vitolo .10 .25
Nigel Mansell Cars
66 Emerson Fittipaldi's Car .15 .40
67 Emerson Fittipaldi's Car .15 .40
68 Stan Fox's Car .10 .25
69 Al Unser Jr.'s Car .20 .50
70 Al Unser Jr. in Car .20 .50
71 Al Unser Jr. WIN .20 .50
72 Al Unser Jr. WIN .20 .50
73 Al Unser Jr. .20 .50
74 Jacques Villeneuve .20 .50
75 Bobby Rahal .15 .40
76 Jimmy Vasser .10 .25
77 Robby Gordon .15 .40
78 Michael Andretti in Car .20 .50
79 Teo Fabi .15 .40
80 Eddie Cheever .10 .25
81 Bryan Herta .10 .25
82 John Andretti .15 .40
83 Mauricio Gugelmin .10 .25
84 Brian Till .10 .25
85 Stan Fox .10 .25
86 Hiro Matsushita .10 .25
87 Stefan Johansson .10 .25
88 Scott Sharp .15 .40
89 Emerson Fittipaldi .20 .50
90 Arie Luyendyk .15 .40
91 Lyn St. James .10 .25
92 Scott Brayton .15 .40
93 Raul Boesel .10 .25
94 Nigel Mansell .15 .40
95 Paul Tracy .15 .40
96 Hideshi Matsuda .10 .25
97 John Paul Jr. .10 .25
98 Dennis Vitolo .10 .25
99 Marco Greco .10 .25
100 Adrian Fernandez .10 .25
101 Dominic Dobson .10 .25
102 Scott Goodyear .10 .25
103 Mike Groff .10 .25
104 Mario Andretti in Car .20 .50
105 Roberto Guerrero .15 .40
106 Al Unser Jr. w .20 .50
Car
107 Mario Andretti .20 .50
108 Al Unser Jr. .20 .50
P1 Al Unser Jr.'s Car Promo .75 2.00
P2 Jacques Villeneuve Promo .75 2.00
FIN1 Jacques Villeneuve WIN .75 2.00
NNO Al Unser Jr. Champion .75 2.00

1995 SkyBox Indy 500 Heir to Indy

This six-card insert set features some of the best of the youngest drivers on the Indy circuit. The cards were printed on silver foil board and were inserted at a rate of one per 29 packs.

COMPLETE SET (6) 15.00 30.00
1 Raul Boesel 2.00 5.00
2 Jimmy Vasser 2.00 5.00
3 Robby Gordon 2.50 6.00
4 Michael Andretti 2.50 6.00
5 Paul Tracy 2.50 6.00
6 Jacques Villeneuve 5.00 10.00

1995 SkyBox Indy 500 Past Champs

This 18-card insert set features some of the Indy 500 winners since 1962. The cards were printed on silver foil board and were inserted randomly at a rate of one per 10 packs.

COMPLETE SET (18) 15.00 40.00
1 Al Unser Jr. 1.50 4.00
2 Emerson Fittipaldi 1.50 4.00
3 Rick Mears 1.50 4.00
4 Arie Luyendyk .75 2.00
5 Al Unser 1.25 3.00
6 Bobby Rahal 1.25 3.00
7 Danny Sullivan .75 2.00
8 Tom Sneva .75 2.00
9 Gordon Johncock .75 2.00
10 Bobby Unser 1.25 3.00
11 Johnny Rutherford 1.25 3.00
12 Mark Donohue .75 2.00
13 Mario Andretti 1.50 4.00
14 A.J. Foyt 1.50 4.00
15 Graham Hill .75 2.00
16 Jim Clark .75 2.00
17 Parnelli Jones .75 2.00
18 Rodger Ward .75 2.00

1996 SkyBox Indy 500

The 1996 SkyBox Indy set was issued in a single 100 card series. The cards feature the drivers of the 1995 Indy 500. The cards were standard size for the first time in SkyBox racing cards history. There are four topical subsets within the set: Qualifying Position (10-42), Indy 500 Car Owners (50-54), Finishing Position (55-87), Anatomy of the Modern Indy Car (91-99).

COMPLETE SET (100) 6.00 15.00
1 Christian Fittipaldi .10 .25
2 Firestone's Return .05 .15
3 Honda's Comeback .05 .15
4 Dick Simon .10 .25
Lyn St.James
5 Scott Brayton .10 .25
6 Qualifying Highlights .05 .15
7 Scott Brayton w .10 .25
Crew
8 Al Unser, Jr. .40 1.00
9 Emerson Fittipaldi .15 .40
10 Scott Brayton's Car .05 .15
11 Arie Luyendyk's Car .05 .15
12 Scott Goodyear's Car .05 .15
13 Michael Andretti's Car .10 .25
14 Jacques Villeneuve's Car .15 .40
15 Mauricio Gugelmin's Car .05 .15
16 Robby Gordon's Car .10 .25
17 Scott Pruett's Car .05 .15
18 Jimmy Vasser's Car .05 .15
19 Hiro Matsushita's Car .05 .15
20 Stan Fox's Car .05 .15
21 Andre Ribeiro's Car .05 .15
22 Roberto Guerrero's Car .05 .15
23 Eddie Cheever's Car .05 .15
24 Teo Fabi's Car .05 .15
25 Paul Tracy's Car .10 .25
26 Alessandro Zampedri's Car .05 .15
27 Danny Sullivan's Car .05 .15
28 Gil de Ferran's Car .05 .15
29 Hideshi Matsuda's Car .05 .15
30 Bobby Rahal's Car .10 .25
31 Raul Boesel's Car .05 .15
32 Buddy Lazier's Car .05 .15
33 Eliseo Salazar's Car .05 .15
34 Adrian Fernandez's Car .05 .15
35 Eric Bachelart's Car .05 .15
36 Christian Fittipaldi's Car .05 .15
37 Lyn St. James's Car .10 .25
38 Carlos Guerrero's Car .05 .15
39 Scott Sharp's Car .05 .15
40 Stefan Johansson's Car .05 .15
41 Davy Jones's Car .05 .15
42 Bryan Herta's Car .05 .15
43 Robby Gordon in Pits .10 .25
44 Green Flag .05 .15
45 Stan Fox's Car .05 .15
46 Scott Goodyear .05 .15
Arie Luyendyk's Cars
47 Scott Goodyear's Car .05 .15
48 Checkered Flag .05 .15
49 Jacques Villeneuve .30 .75
50 Joe Montana 1.25 3.00
Chip Ganassi
51 Roger Penske .05 .15
52 Paul Newman .10 .25
Carl Haas
53 A.J. Foyt .15 .40
54 Walter Payton 1.00 2.50
Dale Coyne
55 Jacques Villeneuve .30 .75
56 Christian Fittipaldi .10 .25
57 Bobby Rahal .15 .40
58 Eliseo Salazar .10 .25
59 Robby Gordon .15 .40
60 Mauricio Gugelmin .10 .25
61 Arie Luyendyk .10 .25
62 Teo Fabi .10 .25
63 Danny Sullivan .10 .25
64 Hiro Matsushita .10 .25
65 Alessandro Zampedri .10 .25
66 Roberto Guerrero .10 .25
67 Bryan Herta .10 .25
68 Scott Goodyear .10 .25
69 Hideshi Matsuda .10 .25
70 Stefan Johansson .10 .25
71 Scott Brayton .10 .25
72 Andre Ribeiro .10 .25
73 Scott Pruett .10 .25
74 Raul Boesel .10 .25
75 Adrian Fernandez .10 .25
76 Jimmy Vasser .10 .25
77 Davy Jones .10 .25
78 Paul Tracy .15 .40
79 Michael Andretti .60 1.50
80 Scott Sharp .10 .25
81 Buddy Lazier .10 .25
82 Eric Bachelart .10 .25
83 Gil de Ferran .10 .25
84 Stan Fox .10 .25
85 Eddie Cheever .10 .25
86 Lyn St. James .15 .40
87 Carlos Guerrero .10 .25
88 Jacques Villeneuve w .30 .75
Crew
89 Mauricio Gugelmin .10 .25
90 Scott Goodyear .10 .25
91 Feel the 500 - Tires .05 .15
Gas
92 Feel the 500 - Suspension .05 .15
93 Feel the 500 - Cockpit .05 .15
94 Feel the 500 - Engine .05 .15
95 Feel the 500 - Rear End .05 .15
96 Feel the 500 - Hauler .05 .15
97 Feel the 500 - Ground Effects .05 .15
98 Feel the 500 - Noise Piece .05 .15
99 Feel the 500 - IMS .05 .15
100 Checklist .05 .15

1996 SkyBox Indy 500 Champions Collection

Randomly inserted in packs at a rate of one in five, this six-card insert set features six former Indy 500 Champions. The cards printed on silver foil board offers pictures of the past champions standing next to the Borg-Warner Trophy on the fronts of the cards and sitting in the actual winning car they drove on the backs.

COMPLETE SET (6) 6.00 15.00
1 Al Unser, Jr. 3.00 6.00
2 Emerson Fittipaldi 1.00 2.50
3 Bobby Rahal 1.00 2.50
4 Arie Luyendyk .75 2.00
5 Danny Sullivan .75 2.00
6 Jacques Villeneuve 2.50 5.00

1996 SkyBox Indy 500 Rookies of the Year

This nine-card insert set features the Indy 500 Rookies of the Year from 1987-94. This includes the Co-Rookies of the Year in 1989, Bernard Jourdain and Scott Pruett. The cards feature gold foil stamping and are die cut. Rookie of the Year cards could be found at a rate of one per three packs.

COMPLETE SET (9) 6.00 15.00
1 Fabrizio Barbazza .40 1.00
2 Billy Vukovich III .40 1.00
3 Bernard Jourdain .40 1.00
4 Scott Pruett .40 1.00
5 Eddie Cheever .40 1.00
6 Jeff Andretti .75 2.00
7 Lyn St. James .75 2.00
8 Nigel Mansell 1.50 4.00
9 Jacques Villeneuve 1.50 4.00

1978 Sports I.D. Patches

This set features full color pictures of some of the top drivers in Indy Car on cloth patches. The patches are not numbered, so they appear below alphabetically.

COMPLETE SET (12) 100.00 200.00
1 Mario Andretti 15.00 30.00
2 Gary Bettenhausen 10.00 20.00
3 Wally Dallenbach Sr. 10.00 20.00
4 A.J. Foyt 15.00 30.00
5 Gordon Johncock 10.00 20.00
6 Sheldon Kinser 10.00 20.00
7 Danny Ongais 10.00 20.00
8 Johnny Parsons 10.00 20.00
9 Johnny Rutherford 12.50 25.00
10 Tom Sneva 12.50 25.00
11 Al Unser 15.00 30.00
12 Bobby Unser 12.50 25.00

1954 Stark and Wetzel Indy Winners

Stark and Wetzel Meats produced and distributed these cards in 1954. The issue features past winners of the Indy 500 and their cars. Since the cards were distributed in packages of meat products, they were produced with a wax covering that is often found stained making Near Mint copies especially tough to find. The cards are blankbacked and have lightly perforated edges. The cards are unnumbered and listed below in order of winning year.

COMPLETE SET (37) 600.00 1000.00
1911 Ray Harroun 18.00 30.00
1912 Joe Dawson 18.00 30.00
1913 Jules Goux 18.00 30.00
1914 Rene Thomas 18.00 30.00
1915 Ralph DePalma 25.00 40.00
1916 Dario Resta 18.00 30.00
1919 Howard Wilcox 18.00 30.00
1920 Gaston Chevrolet 25.00 40.00
1921 Tommy Milton 18.00 30.00
1922 Jimmy Murphy 18.00 30.00
1923 Tommy Milton 18.00 30.00
1924 Joe Boyer 18.00 30.00
L.L.Corum
1925 Peter DePaolo 18.00 30.00
1926 Frank Lockhart 18.00 30.00
1927 George Souders 18.00 30.00
1928 Louis Meyer 18.00 30.00
1929 Ray Keech 18.00 30.00
1930 Billy Arnold 18.00 30.00
1931 Louis Schneider 18.00 30.00
1932 Fred Frame 18.00 30.00
1933 Louis Meyer 18.00 30.00
1934 Bill Cummings 18.00 30.00
1935 Kelly Petillo 18.00 30.00
1936 Louis Meyer 18.00 30.00
1937 Wilbur Shaw 25.00 40.00
1938 Floyd Roberts 18.00 30.00
1939 Wilbur Shaw 25.00 40.00
1940 Wilbur Shaw 25.00 40.00
1941 Floyd Davis 25.00 40.00
Mauri Rose
1946 George Robson 18.00 30.00
1947 Mauri Rose 25.00 40.00
1948 Mauri Rose 25.00 40.00
1949 Bill Holland 18.00 30.00
1950 Johnnie Parsons 25.00 40.00
1951 Lee Wallard 18.00 30.00
1952 Troy Ruttman 18.00 30.00
1953 Bill Vukovich 18.00 30.00

1966 Strombecker

These cards were presumably made in Europe by the Strombecker Corporation. There are 12 known unnumbered cards with each featuring a type of race car from various manufacturers. The cardfronts include a gold or yellow border, a color photo of the car and the flag of the manufacturer's home country. The backs are blue and include detailed stats on the featured car.

COMPLETE SET (12) 150.00 300.00
1 BRM Formula One 12.50 25.00
2 Cobra 12.50 25.00
3 Cooper Formula One 12.50 25.00
4 Ferrari Formula One 12.50 25.00
5 Ferrari GTO 12.50 25.00
6 Ford GT 12.50 25.00
7 Jaguar D-Type 12.50 25.00
8 Jaguar XK-E 12.50 25.00
9 Lotus 19 12.50 25.00
10 Lotus 38 12.50 25.00
11 Plymouth Barracuda 12.50 25.00
12 Porsche 904 12.50 25.00

1937 Thrilling Moments

Doughnut Company of America produced these cards and distributed them on the outside of doughnut boxes twelve per box. The cards were to be cut from the boxes and affixed to an album that housed the set. The set's full name is Thrilling Moments in the Lives of Famous Americans. Only seven athletes were included among 65-other famous non-sport American figures. Each blankbacked card measures roughly 1 7/8" by 2 7/8" when neatly trimmed. The set was produced in four different colored backgrounds: blue, green, orange, and yellow with each subject being printed in only one background color.

47 Barney Oldfield 40.00 80.00
(racing)

1911 Turkey Red Automobile Series

This 50-card set features most of the race cars from the early 1900's. The cards were made in New York City and released in the Turkish cigarette brand from the American Tobacco Company. The cards measure 2" X 2 5/8" and came one per pack or box. Many of the card backs talk about the 1910 Vanderbilt Cup and therefore it has been determined that the set was issued either in late 1910 or in 1911. There is a possibility that the set was released over a period of years from 1909-1911. The set was reprinted by Bowman in 1953 and called Antique Autos. The reprint cards have 3-D backs that required the wearing of 3-D glasses for reading.

COMPLETE SET (50) 400.00 800.00
COMMON CARDS 5.00 12.00

1937 Wilbur Shaw Indy 500 Game

COMPLETE SET (48) 350.00 600.00
1 Billy Arnold 8.00 20.00
(red back)
2 Norman Batten 8.00 20.00
(blue back)
3 Cliff Bergere 8.00 20.00
(blue back)
4 Joe Boyer 8.00 20.00
(red back)
5 Bob Carey 8.00 20.00
(red back)
6 Gaston Chevrolet 8.00 20.00
(red back)
7 Earl Cooper 8.00 20.00
(blue back)
8 Bill Cummings 8.00 20.00
(blue back)
9 Ralph DePalma 10.00 25.00
(blue back)
10 Peter DePaolo 10.00 25.00
(blue back)
11 Leon Duray 8.00 20.00
(red back)
12 Eddie Edenburn 8.00 20.00
(red back)
13 Dave Evans 8.00 20.00
(blue back)
14 Chet Gardner 8.00 20.00
(red back)
15 Tony Gulotta 8.00 20.00
(blue back)
16 Ray Harroun 8.00 20.00
(red back)
17 Harry Hartz 8.00 20.00
(red back)
18 Ralph Hepburn 8.00 20.00
(blue back)
19 Ted Horn 8.00 20.00
(blue back)
20 Ray Keech 8.00 20.00
(red back)
21 Deacon Litz 8.00 20.00
(blue back)
22 Frank Lockhart 8.00 20.00
23 Doc Mackenzie 8.00 20.00
(red back)
24 Rex Mays 8.00 20.00
(blue back)
25 Charles Merz 8.00 20.00
(red back)
26 Louie Meyer 8.00 20.00
(blue back)
27 Zeke Meyer 8.00 20.00
(blue back)
28 Pop Meyers VP 8.00 20.00
(blue back)
29 Chet Miller 8.00 20.00
(red back)
30 Tommy Milton 8.00 20.00
(blue back)
31 Jimmy Murphy 8.00 20.00
(red back)
32 Kelly Petillo 8.00 20.00
(red back)
33 Odis Porter Chief Timer 8.00 20.00
(blue back)
34 Dario Resta 8.00 20.00
35 Eddie Rickenbacker 12.00 30.00
(blue back)
36 Floyd Roberts 8.00 20.00
(blue back)
37 Mauri Rose 10.00 25.00
(blue back)
38 Louie Schneider 8.00 20.00
(blue back)
39 Red Shafer 8.00 20.00
(red back)
40 Wilbur Shaw 10.00 25.00
(red back)
41 Russel Snowberger 8.00 20.00
(red back)
42 Babe Stapp 8.00 20.00
(blue back)
43 Louie Switzer 8.00 20.00
44 Ernie Triplett 8.00 20.00
(red back)
45 Ira Vail 8.00 20.00
(blue back)
46 Howdy Wilcox 8.00 20.00
(red back)
47 Billy Winn 8.00 20.00
(blue back)
48 Cliff Woodbury 8.00 20.00
(blue back)

1924 Willard's Chocolates Sports Champions V122

28 Jimmy Murphy 20.00 40.00

1930 Wills Cigarettes

This eight-card European tobacco issue is part of a bigger 50 card set. The cards were produced by Imperial Tobacco Company of Great Britain and Ireland. The set features all types of transportation vehicles. The cards measure 1 3/8" X 2 5/8" and feature artwork of the vehicles for card fronts. The backs give a bio of the car pictured.

COMPLETE SET (8) 15.00 30.00
23 Malcom Campbell 2.00 5.00
24 Sir Henry Segrave 2.00 5.00
25 Captain Henry Birkin 2.00 5.00
26 Mrs. Victor Bruce 2.00 5.00
27 Boris Ivanonski 2.00 5.00
28 Kay Don 2.00 5.00
29 Rudolf Carcciola 2.00 5.00
30 Sv. Holbrook 2.00 5.00

1938 Wills' Cigarettes

This European tobacco issue is part of a bigger 50 card set. The set is titled Speed and features all types of transportation vehicles. The cards measure 1 3/8" X 2 5/8" and feature artwork of the vehicles for card fronts. The backs give a bio of the car pictured.

COMPLETE SET (8) 10.00 20.00
16 Captain G.E.T. Eyston 1.25 3.00
17 Malcom Campbell 1.25 3.00
18 Ab Jenkins 1.25 3.00
19 John Cobb 1.25 3.00
20 Major Goldie Gardner 1.25 3.00
21 Raymond Mays 1.25 3.00
22 Rudolf Caracciola 1.25 3.00
23 Bernt Rosemeyer 1.25 3.00

1991 Bull Ring

Bull Ring Race Cards produced this set in 1991 featuring popular drivers of short track competition. The cards include a color driver photo on the cardfront and a driver career summary on the back. Butch Lindley, Card number 1 is a memorial card.

COMPLETE SET (144) 6.00 12.00
1 Butch Lindley .02 .10
2 Jerry Goodwin .02 .10
3 Todd Massey .02 .10
4 Bobby Gill .02 .10
5 Rich Bickle .07 .20
6 Freddie Query .02 .10
7 Mike Garvey .02 .10
8 Jay Fogelman .02 .10
9 Andy Thurman .02 .10
10 Beano Francis .02 .10
11 David Smith .02 .10
12 Karen Schulz .02 .10
13 Jerry McCart .02 .10
14 Rick Crawford .02 .10
15 Mark Day .02 .10
16 Hal Goodson .02 .10
17 Jerry Allen VanHorn .02 .10
18 Joe Frasson .02 .10
19 Kevin Smith .02 .10
20 Sammy Pegram .02 .10
21 Donnie York .02 .10
22 Doug Noe .02 .10
23 Dickie Linville .02 .10
24 Granny Tatroe's Car .02 .10
25 Mike Cope .02 .10
26 Robby Faggart .02 .10
27 James Trammell .02 .10
28 Billy Bigley, Jr. .02 .10
29 Mitchell Barrett .02 .10
30 Scott Kilby .02 .10
31 Brian Pack .02 .10
32 Randy Porter .02 .10
33 Jimmy McClain .02 .10
34 Larry Beaver .02 .10
35 Robby Johnson .02 .10
36 David Russell .02 .10
37 Larry Raines .02 .10
38 Steve Walker .02 .10
39 Stephen Grimes .02 .10
40 Dale Fischlein .02 .10
41 Max Prestwood, Jr. .02 .10
42 Tres Wilson .02 .10
43 Jerry Williams .02 .10
44 Larry Caudill .07 .20
45 Phil Gann .02 .10
46 Danny Blevins .02 .10
47 Ronnie Payne .07 .20
48 Mike Miller .02 .10
49 Debbie Lunsford .02 .10
50 John Gerstner II .02 .10
51 Chrissy Oliver .02 .10
52 Scotty Lovelady .02 .10
53 Duke Southard .02 .10
54 Bob Pressley .02 .10
55 Debris Brown .02 .10
56 Robert Powell .02 .10
57 Jason Keller .75 2.00
58 John Kelly .02 .10
59 Robert Pressley .20 .50
60 Don Carlton .02 .10
61 Mike Pressley .07 .20
62 Smiley Rich .02 .10
63 Mark Miner .02 .10
64 John Earl Barton .02 .10
65 Rodger Gentry .02 .10
66 Wesley Mills .02 .10
67 Joey Sims .02 .10
68 Lloyd Slagle .02 .10
69 Sidney Minton .02 .10
70 Ronnie Davidson .02 .10
71 Donnie Bishop .02 .10
72 Johnny Cochran .02 .10
73 Scott Sutherland .02 .10
74 Jack Sprague .20 .50
75 Robert Huffman .02 .10
76 Tim Roberts .02 .10
77 Ted Hodgdon .02 .10
78 Gary Bradberry .07 .20
79 Steve Holzhausen .02 .10
80 Danny Shortt .02 .10
81 Lee Faulk .02 .10
82 Barry Beggarly .07 .20
83 Rodney Howard .02 .10
84 Kevin Evans .02 .10
85 Greg Hendrix .02 .10
86 Tim Gordon .02 .10
87 Danny Slack .02 .10
88 Chris Mullinax .02 .10
89 Brian Butler .02 .10
90 Randy Couch .02 .10
91 Dennis Setzer .07 .20
92 Dick Anderson .02 .10
93 Junior Niedecken .02 .10
94 Gary Nix .02 .10
95 Terry Davis .02 .10
96 Charlie Stokes .02 .10
97 Marty Ward .02 .10
98 Jody Ridley .02 .10
99 Chris Diamond .02 .10
100 Tom Usry .02 .10
101 Robin Hayes .02 .10
102 Johnny Reynolds .02 .10
103 Shelton McNair, Jr. .02 .10
104 Grump Wills .02 .10
105 Jeff Agnew .02 .10
106 Ronald Walls .02 .10
107 Eddie Hanks .02 .10
108 Mickey York .02 .10
109 Larry Ogle .02 .10
110 Jacky Workman .02 .10
111 Tuck Trentham .02 .10
112 Richard Landreth, Jr. .02 .10
113 David Rogers .02 .10
114 Mike Harmon .02 .10
115 Toby Porter .02 .10
116 Stacy Compton .40 1.00
117 Ricky Vaughn .02 .10
118 Tommy Grimes .02 .10
119 Mike McSwain .02 .10
120 Roy Chatham .02 .10
121 Johnny Rumley .02 .10
122 Doug Strickland .02 .10
123 Tommy Ruff .02 .10
124 Jeff Williams .02 .10
125 Mike Love .02 .10
126 A.J. Sanders .02 .10
127 Dallas Wilcox .02 .10
128 Dennis Crump .02 .10
129 Kevin Barrett .02 .10
130 Mike Toemmes .02 .10
131 Gene Pack .02 .10
132 Robbie Ferguson .02 .10
133 Buddy Vance .02 .10
134 Ralph Carnes .02 .10
135 Rick Lambert .02 .10
136 Bart Ingram .02 .10
137 Pete Orr .02 .10
138 Shawna Robinson .60 1.50
139 Mike Porter .02 .10
140 Scott Green .02 .10
141 Darrell Holman .02 .10
142 Jeff Finley .02 .10
143 Junior Franks .02 .10
144 Jabe Jones .02 .10

1992 Bull Ring

This 200-card set was the second complete set produced by Bull Ring Race Cards. The 1992 features popular drivers of short track competition. The cards include a color driver photo on the cardfront with a blue border and a driver career summary and biographical information on the back.

COMPLETE SET (200) 15.00 25.00
1 Checklist Card .02 .10
2 Jerry Goodwin .02 .10
3 Beano Francis .02 .10
4 Edward Jordan .02 .10
5 Rickie Bickle .15 .40
6 Stacy Compton .40 1.00
7 Mike Garvey .02 .10
8 Jay Fogelman .02 .10
9 C.J. Johnson .02 .10
10 Chad Chaffin .15 .40
11 David Rogers .02 .10
12 Karen Schulz .02 .10
13 Jerry McCart .02 .10
14 Rick Crawford .02 .10
15 Clay Brown .02 .10
16 Hal Goodson .02 .10
17 Jerry A. Van Horn .02 .10
18 Joe Frasson .02 .10
19 Scotty Lovelady .02 .10
20 Dallas Wilcox .02 .10
21 Sammy Pegram .02 .10
22 Doug Noe .02 .10
23 Brad Sorenson .02 .10
24 Mike Harmon .02 .10
25 Mike Cope .02 .10
26 Tuck Trentham .02 .10
27 Danny Fair .02 .10
28 Billy Bigley, Jr. .02 .10
29 Chris Mullinax .02 .10
30 Mike Love .02 .10
31 Gary Balough .02 .10
32 Randy Porter .02 .10
33 Jimmy McClain .02 .10
34 Scott Green .02 .10
35 Wesley Mills .02 .10
36 David Russell .02 .10
37 Larry Raines .02 .10
38 Pete Orr .02 .10
39 Robert Huffman .02 .10
40 Chrissy Oliver CL .02 .10
41 Max Prestwood, Jr. .02 .10
42 Tres Wilson .02 .10
43 Mike Borghi .02 .10
44 Larry Caudill .15 .40
45 Duke Southard .02 .10
46 Wade Buttrey .02 .10
47 Phil Warren .02 .10
48 Jack Sprague .15 .40
49 Debbie Lunsford .02 .10
50 Mike Buffkin .02 .10
51 Jeff Purvis .15 .40
52 Tammy Kirk .02 .10
53 Charlie Ragan, Jr. .02 .10
54 Bob Pressley .02 .10
55 Debris Brown .02 .10
56 Robert Powell .02 .10
57 Jason Keller .25 .60
58 Jeff Agnew .02 .10
59 Robert Pressley .15 .40
60 Ralph Carnes .02 .10
61 Tim Steele .15 .40
62 Buckshot Jones .60 1.50
63 Chuck Abell .02 .10
64 John Earl Barton .02 .10
65 Robert Hester .02 .10
66 Freddie Query .02 .10

Card	Low	High
67 Rodney Howard	.02	.10
68 Mark Day	.02	.10
69 Sidney Minton	.02	.10
70 Granny Tatroe	.02	.10
71 Donnie Bishop	.02	.10
72 Eddie Mercer	.02	.10
73 John Livinston, Jr.	.02	.10
74 Wayne Willard	.02	.10
75 Bobby Brack	.02	.10
76 Dennis Schoenfeld	.02	.10
77 Johnny Chapman	.02	.10
78 Gary Bradberry	.15	.40
79 Robby Faggart	.02	.10
80 Randy Porter CL	.02	.10
81 Mike Pressley	.02	.10
82 Barry Beggarly	.08	.25
83 Bubba Gale	.02	.10
84 Sean Graham	.02	.10
85 Joe Winchell	.02	.10
86 Bubba Adams	.02	.10
87 Ron Barfield	.15	.40
88 Mike McCrary, Jr.	.02	.10
89 Steve Walker	.02	.10
90 Stan Eads	.02	.10
91 Todd Massey	.02	.10
92 Dick Anderson	.02	.10
93 Junior Niedecken	.02	.10
94 Johnny Reynolds	.02	.10
95 Robert Elliott	.02	.10
96 Jack Cook	.02	.10
97 Marty Ward	.02	.10
98 Jody Ridley	.15	.40
99 Charlie Stokes	.02	.10
100 Chrissy Oliver	.02	.10
101 Eddie Perry	.02	.10
102 Claude Gwin, Jr.	.02	.10
103 Shelton McNair, Jr.	.02	.10
104 Charles Powell III	.02	.10
105 Jeff Agnew	.02	.10
106 P.B. Crowell III	.02	.10
107 Eddie Hanks	.02	.10
108 Tink Reedy	.02	.10
109 Larry Ogle	.02	.10
110 David Showers	.02	.10
111 David Rogers	.02	.10
112 Danny Sikes	.02	.10
113 Charlie Brown	.02	.10
114 Roy Hendrick	.02	.10
115 Randy Bynum	.02	.10
116 Mike Howell	.02	.10
117 Mark Miner	.02	.10
118 Danny Shortt	.02	.10
119 Kevin Smith	.02	.10
120 Larry Caudill CL	.08	.25
121 Johnny Rumley	.08	.25
122 Mickey York	.02	.10
123 Dickie Linville	.02	.10
124 A.W. Kirby, Jr.	.02	.10
125 Mike Love	.02	.10
126 Gary Nix	.02	.10
127 Jeff Burkett	.02	.10
128 Rick Lambert	.02	.10
129 Marc Kinley	.02	.10
130 Mardy Lindley	.02	.10
131 Mitchell Barrett	.02	.10
132 Robbie Ferguson	.02	.10
133 Rodney Combs, Jr.	.15	.40
134 Ned Combs	.02	.10
135 Terry Davis	.02	.10
136 Bobby Knox	.02	.10
137 Richard Hargrove	.02	.10
138 Curtis Markham	.08	.25
139 Stephen Grimes	.02	.10
140 Penn Crim, Jr.	.02	.10
141 Brian Butler	.02	.10
142 Terry Lee	.02	.10
143 David Bonnett	.15	.40
144 Lloyd Slagle	.02	.10
145 Greg Motes	.02	.10
146 Don Carlton	.02	.10
147 David Smith	.02	.10
148 Darrell Holman	.02	.10
149 Orvil Reedy	.02	.10
150 Craig Gower	.02	.10
151 Bill Posey	.02	.10
152 Phil Gann	.02	.10
153 Bugs Hairfield	.02	.10
154 Ronnie Thomas	.02	.10
155 Dennis Southerlin	.02	.10
156 Brian King	.02	.10
157 Ed Meredith	.02	.10
158 Andy Houston	.02	.10
159 Ronnie Roach	.02	.10
160 Checklist Card	.02	.10
161 Elton Sawyer	.15	.40
162 Danny Blevins	.02	.10
163 Greg Marlowe	.02	.10
164 Mike Reynolds	.02	.10
165 Tommy Spangler	.02	.10
166 Dennis Setzer	.15	.40
167 Jabe Jones	.02	.10
168 Jacky Workman	.02	.10
169 Jimmy Cope	.02	.10
170 Mike Dillon	.08	.25
171 Bobby Gill	.02	.10
172 Chris Diamond	.02	.10
173 Scott Kilby	.02	.10
174 Pete Hughes	.02	.10
175 Donnie York	.02	.10
176 Junior Franks	.02	.10
177 Ron Young	.02	.10
178 Tom Usry	.02	.10
179 Greg Hendrix	.02	.10
180 Toby Porter	.02	.10
181 Mike Hovis	.02	.10
182 Richard Landreth, Jr.	.02	.10
183 Kevin Barrett	.02	.10
184 Marty Houston	.02	.10
185 G.C. Campbell	.02	.10
186 Tony Ponder	.02	.10
187 Danny Slack	.02	.10
188 Michael McSwain	.02	.10
189 Kevin Evans	.02	.10
190 Tim Roberts	.02	.10
191 Greg Cecil	.02	.10
192 A.J. Sanders	.02	.10
193 Richard Starkey	.02	.10
194 Hal Perry	.02	.10
195 Dennis Crump	.02	.10
196 Rob Underwood	.02	.10
197 Donn Fenn	.02	.10
198 Mark Cox	.02	.10
199 Lee Tissot	.02	.10
200 Butch Lindley	.02	.10

2002 Choice Rising Stars

This set was produced in 2002 by Choice Marketing. Each card was printed on glossy card stock with a full color driver image on the front and a black and white cardback. The set features some of the top short track drivers in the country including the first card of Kyle Busch. A second version of the Kyle Busch card surfaced in 2015 with a much large font printed on the back. We have yet to be able to verify the autenticity of this version.

Card	Low	High
COMPLETE SET (28)	8.00	20.00
1 Chris Wimmer	.30	.75
2 Pat Kelly	.30	.75
3 Zach Niessner	.30	.75
4 Gary St.Amant	.30	.75
5 Joey Clanton	.30	.75
6 Jake Hodges	.30	.75
7 Rich Gardner	.30	.75
8 Scott Null	.30	.75
9 Greg Williams	.30	.75
10 J.C. Beattie	.30	.75
11 Jeff Emery	.30	.75
12 Robbie Pyle	.40	1.00
13 John Silverthorne	.30	.75
14 Ed Brown	.30	.75
15 Doug Mahlik	.30	.75
16 Brandon Miller	.30	.75
17 Wayne Anderson	.30	.75
18 Kyle Busch	1.25	3.00
19 Russ Tuttle	.30	.75
20 Chad Wood	.30	.75
21 Dan Fredrickson	.30	.75
22 Reed Sorenson	.60	1.50
23 Mike Garvey	.40	1.00
24 Rick Beebe	.30	.75
25 Todd Kluever	.50	1.25
26 Greg Stewart	.30	.75
27 Kevin Cywinski	.30	.75
28 Mike Cope	.30	.75

1992 Corter Selinsgrove and Clinton County Speedways

Corter Race Cards produced this set commemorating drivers of the Pennsylvania Selinsgrove and Clinton County Speedways. Sets were packaged in a plastic case and each was individually numbered of 1,200.

Card	Low	High
COMPLETE SET (36)	5.00	12.00
1 David Corter's Car	.10	.30
2 Steve Campbell's Car	.10	.30
3 Lenny Krautheim's Car	.10	.30
4 Dale Schweikart's Car	.10	.30
5 Barry Knouse's Car	.10	.30
6 Jim Nace	.20	.50
7 Dennis Hahn	.20	.50
8 Richard Jensen's Car	.10	.30
9 Bill Glenn's Car	.10	.30
10 George Fultz's Car	.10	.30
11 Todd Shaffer	.20	.50
12 Craig Lindsey's Car	.10	.30
13 Penrose Kester's Car	.10	.30
14 Eric Hons' Car	.10	.30
15 Luke Hoffner's Car	.10	.30
16 Jim Stine w Car	.20	.50
17 Alan Cole's Car	.10	.30
18 Fred Rahmer's Car	.10	.30
19 Ed Shafer's Car	.10	.30
20 Steve Byers' Car	.10	.30
21 Donald Schick, Jr.'s Car	.10	.30
22 Dustin Hoffman w Car	.20	.50
23 James Gearhart	.20	.50
24 Wesley Matthews w Car	.20	.50
25 John Hafer's Car	.10	.30
26 Glenn Fitzcharles' Car	.10	.30
27 Arthur Probst, Jr.	.20	.50
28 Scott Barrett's Car	.10	.30
29 Franklin Benfer's Car	.10	.30
30 Dwayne Wasson	.20	.50
31 Jerry Hollenbach w Car	.20	.50
32 Chuck Reinert, Jr.'s Car	.10	.30
33 David Matthews w Car	.20	.50
34 Robby Smith's Car	.10	.30
35 C.W. Smith's Car	.10	.30
36 Robin Johnson	.20	.50

1993 Corter Selinsgrove and Clinton County Speedways

This 36-card set is the second edition from Corter Race Cards. The sets feature drivers and their cars that raced at the Pennsylvania speedway. There were 1,000 sets produced. Each set comes in a snap it case and has a cover card with the number of 1,000 that each particular set is. An uncut sheet of the set was given to each of the drivers that appeared in the set.

Card	Low	High
COMPLETE SET (36)	4.00	10.00
1 Richie Jensen	.10	.30
2 Steve Campbell	.10	.30
3 Lenny Krautheim III	.10	.30
4 Dale Schweikart	.10	.30
5 Dwayne Wasson	.20	.50
6 Jim Nace	.20	.50
7 Dustin Hoffman	.20	.50
8 Chuck Reinert Jr.	.10	.30
9 Boyd Toner Sr.	.10	.30
10 George Fultz	.10	.30
11 Jim Stine	.20	.50
12 Craig Lindsey	.10	.30
13 David Brouse Sr.	.10	.30
14 Eric Hons	.10	.30
15 Luke Hoffner	.10	.30
16 Vern Wasson	.10	.30
17 Alan Cole	.10	.30
18 James Gearhart	.20	.50
19 Ed Shafer In Memory	.20	.50
20 Pen Kester's Car	.10	.30
21 Don Schick Jr.	.10	.30
22 Timothy Bowmaster	.10	.30
23 Larry Bair	.10	.30
24 Bob Bertasavage	.10	.30
25 John Hafer's Car	.10	.30
26 Glenn Fitzcharles	.20	.50
27 Wayne Peeling	.10	.30
28 Dave Lundgren	.10	.30
29 Bill Crawford	.10	.30
30 Grover Graham	.10	.30
31 Loren Armes	.10	.30
32 Edward Overdorf	.10	.30
33 Ron Kramer	.10	.30
34 Robby Smith	.10	.30
35 Joey Borich	.10	.30
36 Christa Koch Ms.Selinsgrove	.10	.30

1991 Dirt Trax

Volunteer Racing produced this set in two series. Each series was released in its own plastic factory set box. The cards were printed on thin stock and carry blue borders and yellow cardbacks.

Card	Low	High
COMPLETE SET (72)	6.00	12.00
COMPLETE SERIES 1 (36)	3.00	6.00
COMPLETE SERIES 2 (36)	3.00	6.00
1 Buck Simmons	.07	.20
2 Herman Goddard	.07	.20
3 H.E. Vinegard	.07	.20
4 Billy Moyer Jr.'s Car UER	.10	.30
5 Rodney Combs	.20	.50
6 Bob Pierce	.07	.20
7 Jack Boggs	.20	.50
8 Jack Pennington	.07	.20
9 Ronnie Johnson	.10	.30
10 Hot Rod LaMance	.07	.20
11 Scott Bloomquist	.20	.50
12 Donnie Moran	.10	.30
13 Eddie Carrier's Car	.07	.20
14 Ed Basey	.07	.20
15 Dale McDowell	.07	.20
16 Ed Gibbons	.07	.20
17 Mike Balzano	.10	.30
18 John Gill's Car	.07	.20
19 Jack Trammell	.10	.30
20 Skip Arp	.07	.20
21 David Bilbrey	.07	.20
22 James Cline	.07	.20
23 Wade Knowles	.10	.30
24 Joe Meadows' Car	.07	.20
25 Clay Hall's Car	.07	.20
26 Bob Cowen	.07	.20
27 Bob Wearing, Jr.	.10	.30
28 Rusty Goddard	.07	.20
29 Scott Sexton	.07	.20
30 Steve Francis	.20	.50
31 Billy Ogle, Jr.	.10	.30
32 Barry Hurt	.07	.20
33 Mark Vineyard	.07	.20
34 Bobby Thomas's Car	.07	.20
35 John Mason's Car	.07	.20
36 Cover Card CL	.07	.20
37 Buck Simmons	.07	.20
38 Jerry Inmon	.07	.20
39 Billy Moyer	.20	.50
40 Mike Head	.07	.20
41 Stan Massey	.07	.20
42 Mike Duvall	.10	.30
43 Jack Pennington	.07	.20
44 Jeff Purvis	.30	.75
45 Eddie Pace	.07	.20
46 Bill Ingram	.07	.20
47 Hot Rod LaMance	.07	.20
48 Ricky Weeks' Car	.07	.20
49 Lynn Geisler	.07	.20
50 Kevin Claycomb	.07	.20
51 Nathan Durboraw	.07	.20
52 Doug McCammon	.07	.20
53 Ed Basey	.07	.20
54 C.J. Rayburn	.07	.20
55 Bobby Thomas	.07	.20
56 Gary Stuhler	.07	.20
57 Davey Johnson	.10	.30
58 Clay Kelley	.07	.20
59 Chub Frank	.20	.50
60 Tom Rients	.07	.20
61 Todd Andrews	.07	.20
62 Paul Croft's Car	.07	.20
63 Wendall Wallace	.07	.20
64 Tom Helfrich w Car	.07	.20
65 John Jones	.07	.20
66 Tony Cardin w Car	.07	.20
67 Dion Deason's Car	.07	.20
68 Marty Calloway	.07	.20
69 Mark Gansmann	.07	.20
70 Jeff Treece	.07	.20
71 Darrell Lanigan	.07	.20
72 Cover Card CL	.07	.20

1992 Dirt Trax

Volunteer Racing Promotions produced this set featuring popular drivers of the Dirt Track Series. The blue bordered cards were sold in complete factory set form as well as through 10-card cello wrappers called wax pax. There were four Gold cards also produced (1000 of each) as a random insert in packs.

Card	Low	High
COMPLETE SET (100)	5.00	12.00
1 Cover Checklist Card	.05	.15
2 Freddy Smith	.15	.40
3 Jerry Inmon	.05	.15
4 Delmas Conley	.05	.15
5 Herman Goddard	.05	.15
6 Tom Nesbitt	.05	.15
7 Larry Moore	.05	.15
8 Billy Moyer	.15	.40
9 Mike Head	.05	.15
10 Bob Pierce	.05	.15
11 Rodney Combs	.15	.40
12 Jack Boggs	.08	.25
13 Mike Duvall	.08	.25
14 Ronnie Johnson	.08	.25
15 Rick Aukland	.08	.25
16 Steve Kosiski	.05	.15
17 Scott Bloomquist	.15	.40
18 Bill Ingram	.05	.15
19 Rod LaMance	.05	.15
20 Donnie Moran	.08	.25
21 Ed Basey	.05	.15
22 Pete Parker	.05	.15
23 Delbert Smith	.05	.15
24 Nathan Durboraw	.05	.15
25 Rex Richey	.05	.15
26 Bill Ogle Sr.	.05	.15
27 Mike Balzano	.08	.25
28 Tom Rients	.05	.15
29 John Gill	.08	.25
30 Skip Arp	.05	.15
31 David Bilbrey	.05	.15
32 Clay Kelley	.05	.15
33 Chub Frank	.15	.40
34 Todd Andrews	.05	.15
35 Wade Knowles	.08	.25
36 Bill Frye	.08	.25
37 Kevin Weaver	.08	.25
38 Joe Meadows	.05	.15
39 John Booper Bare	.05	.15
40 Ron Davies	.05	.15
41 Gary Hall	.05	.15
42 John Jones	.05	.15
43 Dick Barton	.05	.15
44 Andy Dill	.05	.15
45 Steve Francis	.15	.40
46 Davey Johnson	.08	.25
47 Billy Ogle Jr.	.08	.25
48 Troy Green	.05	.15
49 Gary Green	.05	.15
50 Jake Lowry	.05	.15
51 Checklist Card	.05	.15
52 Ronnie Johnson Jack Boggs Scott Bloomquist	.08	.25
53 Roger Bagwell	.05	.15
54 Randy Boggs	.05	.15
55 Denny Bonebrake	.05	.15
56 Marty Calloway	.05	.15
57 Tony Cardin	.05	.15
58 Perry County Speedway	.05	.15
59 Gene Chupp	.05	.15
60 Kevin Claycomb	.05	.15
61 Phil Coltrane	.05	.15
62 Tootle Estes	.05	.15
63 Red Farmer	.15	.40
64 Mark Gansmann	.05	.15
65 Lynn Geisler	.05	.15
66 Ed Gibbons	.05	.15
67 Matt Gilardi	.05	.15
68 Rusty Goddard	.05	.15
69 Tom Helfrich	.05	.15
70 Doug Ingalls	.05	.15
71 Joe Kosiski	.05	.15
72 Darrell Lanigan	.05	.15
73 Freddie Lee	.05	.15
74 Tiny Lund	.15	.40
75 John Mason	.05	.15
76 Stan Massey	.05	.15
77 Larry McDaniels	.05	.15
78 Dale McDowell	.05	.15
79 Ben Miley	.05	.15
80 Buddy Morris	.05	.15
81 David Moyer	.05	.15
82 Eddie Pace	.05	.15
83 Jack Pennington	.05	.15
84 C.J. Rayburn	.05	.15
85 Scott Sexton	.05	.15
86 Steve Shaver	.05	.15
87 Buck Simmons	.05	.15
88 Jeff Smith	.05	.15
89 Steve Smith	.08	.25
90 Steve Smith	.08	.25
91 Gary Stuhler	.05	.15
92 Charlie Swartz	.05	.15
93 Bobby Thomas	.05	.15
94 Jack Trammell	.08	.25
95 Carl Trimmer	.05	.15
96 Wendall Wallace	.05	.15
97 Bob Wearing Jr. Bob Wearing Sr.	.05	.15
98 Ricky Weeks	.05	.15
99 Johnny Williams	.05	.15
100 Ivan Russell	.05	.15

2003 Dirt Trax

Volunteer Racing Promotions produced this set featuring popular drivers of various Dirt Track Series. The borderless cards were sold in complete factory set form and printed on very thin glossy stock. The cards were not numbered but have been assigned card numbers below based upon the listings on the two checklist cards.

Card	Low	High
COMPLETE SET (50)	8.00	20.00
1 Todd Andrews	.20	.50
2 Skip Arp's Car	.20	.50
3 Rick Aukland's Car	.40	1.00
4 Shannon Babb's Car	.40	1.00
5 Mike Balzano	.40	1.00
6 Brian Birkhofer	.20	.50
7 Robbie Blair	.40	1.00
8 Randle Chupp	.20	.50
9 Delmas Conley's Car	.20	.50
10 R.J. Conley's Car	.20	.50
11 Rod Conley's Car	.20	.50
12 Ray Cook's Car	.20	.50
13 Mike Duvall's Car	.40	1.00
14 Rick Eckert	.40	1.00
15 Terry English's Car	.40	1.00
16 Dennis Erb Jr.'s Car	.40	1.00
17 Chris Francis	.40	1.00
18 Steve Francis	.60	1.50
19 Chub Frank	.60	1.50
20 Bill Frye's Car	.40	1.00
21 John Gill's Car	.40	1.00
22 Bart Hartman's Car	.20	.50
23 Mike Head's Car	.20	.50
24 Tim Hitt's Car	.20	.50
25 Checklist 1	.20	.50
26 Duayne Hommell's Car	.40	1.00
27 Davey Johnson	.40	1.00
28 Johnny Johnson's Car	.20	.50
29 Mike Johnson	.20	.50
30 Ronnie Johnson's Car	.40	1.00
31 Randy Korte's Car	.20	.50
32 Jimmy Mars	.20	.50
33 Dale McDowell	.20	.50
34 Matt Miller	.40	1.00
35 Donnie Moran	.40	1.00
36 Billy Moyer's Car	.60	1.50
37 Terrence Nowell's Car	.20	.50
38 Don O'Neal's Car	.20	.50
39 Earl Pearson Jr.	.20	.50
40 Terry Phillips's Car	.40	1.00
41 Bob Pierce's Car	.20	.50
42 Dan Schlieper	.20	.50
43 Steve Shaver	.20	.50
44 Clint Smith's Car	.20	.50
45 Freddy Smith's Car	.60	1.50
46 Jeff Smith's Car	.20	.50
47 Gary Stuhler	.20	.50
48 Wendall Wallace's Car	.20	.50
49 Chris Francis Steve Francis	.60	1.50
50 Checklist 2	.20	.50

1991 DK IMCA Dirt Track

This 53-card set features Dirt Track drivers from the IMCA series. The cards were issued in complete set form.

Card	Low	High
COMPLETE SET (53)	6.00	12.00
1 Checklist Card	.07	.20
2 Terry Gallaher	.07	.20
3 Steve Watts	.07	.20
4 Danny Breuer	.07	.20
5 Curt Daughters	.07	.20
6 Mike Carr	.07	.20
7 Kelly Shryock	.07	.20
8 Red Dralle	.07	.20
9 Scott Strothman	.07	.20
10 Jay Johnson	.07	.20
11 Rusty Patterson	.07	.20
12 Kevin Cale	.07	.20
13 Ron Jackson	.07	.20
14 Terry Ryan	.07	.20
15 Wade Russell	.07	.20
16 Steve Sutliff	.07	.20
17 Brian Birkhofer	.07	.20
18 Jerry Pilcher	.07	.20
19 Lynn Richard	.07	.20
20 Tony Stewart	2.00	5.00
21 Steve Hennies	.07	.20
22 Jeff Johnson	.07	.20
23 David Birkhofer	.07	.20
24 Mike Fitzpatrick	.07	.20
25 Rollie Frink	.07	.20
26 Bob Jennings	.07	.20
27 Mike Smith	.07	.20
28 Frank Springsteen	.07	.20
29 Don Wood	.07	.20
30 Kurt Stewart	.07	.20
31 Steve Fraise	.07	.20
32 Curt Martin	.07	.20
33 Ray Guss, Jr.	.07	.20
34 Gary Webb	.07	.20
35 Sonny Smyser	.07	.20
36 Les Verly	.07	.20
37 Harry Walker	.07	.20
38 Greg Kastli	.07	.20
39 Ron Boyse	.07	.20
40 Jeff Alkey	.07	.20
41 Rick Wendling	.07	.20
42 Dan Forsyth	.07	.20
43 Bryan Wanner	.07	.20
44 Jay Johnson	.07	.20
45 Doug Hopkins	.07	.20
46 Craig Jacobs	.07	.20
47 Bobby Greiner Jr.	.07	.20
48 Johnny Johnson	.07	.20
49 Darrel DeFrance	.07	.20
50 Marty Gall	.07	.20
51 Randy Krampe	.07	.20
52 Ted Pallister	.07	.20
53 Bob LeKander	.07	.20

1991 Hav-A-Tampa

Produced by Volunteer Racing, this 28-card set features drivers and cars of the Hav-A-Tampa series. The cards feature black borders with color photos and were distributed in complete set form. The cover/checklist card is not numbered, but was intended to be card #1.

Card	Low	High
COMPLETE SET (28)	3.00	6.00
1 Cover Card CL	.08	.25
2 Top 24 Drivers	.08	.25
3 Bill Ingram	.08	.25
4 Tony Reaid J.Mosteller/1991 Champion	.08	.25
5 Tony Reaid	.08	.25
6 Rex Richey	.08	.25
7 Rodney Combs Sr.	.15	.40
8 Phil Coltrane	.08	.25
9 Wade Knowles	.15	.40
10 Mike Head	.08	.25
11 Ed Basey	.08	.25
12 James Cline	.08	.25
13 Bobby Thomas	.08	.25
14 Granger Howell's Car UER	.08	.25
15 Ronnie Johnson's Car	.08	.25
16 Derrick Rainey	.08	.25
17 Wayne Echols' Car	.08	.25
18 Freddie Lee's Car	.08	.25
19 Wayne McCullough	.08	.25
20 Jeff Stansberry	.08	.25
21 Bill Ingram's Car	.08	.25
22 Steve Nicholson	.08	.25
23 John Jones	.08	.25
24 David Moyer's Car	.08	.25
25 Stan Massey	.08	.25
26 Skip Arp	.08	.25
27 Jody Summerville	.08	.25
28 Buddy Morris w Car	.08	.25

1992 Hav-A-Tampa

Volunteer Racing Promotions produced this set featuring drivers of the Hav-A-Tampa Series. The cards include the top 24 drivers of the series along with a checklist card and were sold in complete set form.

Card	Low	High
COMPLETE SET (28)	4.00	8.00
1 Cover Checklist Card	.10	.30
2 Top 24 Group	.10	.30
3 Jimmy Mosteller	.10	.30
4 Red Farmer Capitol Sports Radio	.10	.30
5 Buddy Morris	.10	.30
6 Ronnie Johnson's Car	.10	.30
7 Phil Coltrane's Car	.10	.30
8 Rex Richey's Car	.10	.30
9 Wade Knowles' Car	.20	.50
10 Rodney Combs' Car	.20	.50
11 Bobby Turner's Car	.10	.30
12 Dale McDowell's Car	.10	.30
13 Mike Head's Car	.10	.30
14 Stan Massey w car	.10	.30
15 Tony Reaid's Car	.10	.30
16 Freddie Lee's Car	.10	.30
17 Ricky Williams' Car	.10	.30
18 Jody Summerville's Car	.10	.30
19 David Chancy's Car	.10	.30
20 Greg Knight's Car	.10	.30
21 Bobby Thomas' Car	.10	.30
22 Rodney Martin's Car	.10	.30
23 Granger Howell's Car	.10	.30
24 Buckshot Miles' Car	.10	.30

25 Wayne Echols' Car .10 .30
26 Buster Goss' Car .10 .30
27 John Jones' Car .10 .30
28 Ed Basey's Car .10 .30

1995 Hav-A-Tampa

Speed Graphics produced this set featuring drivers of the Hav-A-Tampa Series. The cards include the top personalities of the series along with a checklist card and were sold in complete set form.

COMPLETE SET (42) 6.00 15.00
1 Cover Card .15 .40
2 Bill Frye .25 .60
3 Drivers Meeting .15 .40
4 Jeff Smith .15 .40
5 Ronnie Johnson .25 .60
6 Jack Boggs .30 .75
7 Dale McDowell .15 .40
8 Clint Smith .15 .40
9 Rodney Martin .15 .40
10 Dixie Speedway .15 .40
11 Freddy Smith .30 .75
12 Jeff Smith .15 .40
13 Larry Moore .15 .40
14 David Gibson .15 .40
15 Danny McClure .15 .40
16 Kenny Morrow .15 .40
17 C.S.Fitzgerald .15 .40
18 DeWayne Johnson .15 .40
19 Kenny Merchant .15 .40
20 Bill Ogle Jr. .25 .60
21 Johnny Virden .15 .40
22 Bobby Thomas .15 .40
23 Gar Dickson .15 .40
24 Mike Carter .15 .40
25 Wendall Wallace .15 .40
26 Rex Richey .15 .40
27 Tony Reaid .15 .40
28 Earl Pearson Jr. .15 .40
29 Rick Aukland .25 .60
30 Donnie Moran UER .25 .60
31 Billy Moyer .30 .75
32 Curtis Gattis .15 .40
33 Frank Ingram .15 .40
34 Marshall Green .15 .40
35 Mark Miner .15 .40
36 Ray Cook .15 .40
37 Stan Massey .15 .40
38 Rod LaMance .15 .40
39 Mike Duvall .25 .60
40 Bill Ingram .15 .40
41 Jimmy Mosteller FOUND .15 .40
42 HAT Officials CL .15 .40

1991 JAGS

JAGS Race Cards produced this set featuring top drivers of Dirt Late Model competition. This was the first of four sets and featured a light gray card border.

COMPLETE SET (50) 6.00 12.00
1 Scott Bloomquist .30 .75
2 Jack Boggs' Car .10 .30
3 Donnie Moran's Car .20 .50
4 Mike Duvall .20 .50
5 Gene Chupp's Car .07 .20
6 Gary Stuhler's Car .07 .20
7 Ronnie Johnson's Car .07 .20
8 John Gill .20 .50
9 James Cline's Car .07 .20
10 C.J. Rayburn's Car .07 .20
11 Jim Curry .10 .30
12 Mike Balzano's Car .20 .50
13 Rex Richey's Car .07 .20
14 Kris Patterson .10 .30
15 Tony Cardin .10 .30
16 Eddie Carrier .10 .30
17 Mike Head's Car .07 .20
18 John Provenzano .10 .30
19 Bill Frye's Car .07 .20
20 Steve Francis .30 .75
21 Randy Boggs' Car .07 .20
22 Roger Long .10 .30
23 Daryl Key .10 .30
24 Bob Pohlman .10 .30
25 Scott Bloomquist's Car .20 .50
26 Johnny Stokes' Car .07 .20
27 Steve Barnett .10 .30
28 Rex McCroskey .10 .30
29 Mitch Johnson .10 .30
30 Wade Knowles .20 .50
31 Darrell Mooneyham .10 .30
32 John Mason's Car .07 .20
33 Ken Essary's Car .07 .20
34 Wendall Wallace .10 .30
35 Leslie Essary .10 .30
36 Rodney Franklin .10 .30
37 Jerry Inmon .10 .30
38 Tom Rients .10 .30
39 Earl Pepper Newby .10 .30
40 Bob Wearing Jr. .10 .30
41 Dale McDowell .10 .30
42 John Booper Bare .10 .30
43 Buck Simmons' Car .07 .20
44 Steve Kosiski's Car .07 .20
45 John Jones' Car .07 .20
46 Hot Rod LaMance's Car .07 .20
47 Ricky Weeks' Car .07 .20
48 Billy Scott .10 .30
49 Ed Basey's Car .07 .20
50 Bob Pierce .10 .30

1992 JAGS

JAGS Race Cards produced this set featuring top drivers of Dirt Late Model competition. This was the second of four sets released by JAGS and featured a light blue card border. The set was distributed in two separate series.

COMPLETE SET (256) 15.00 30.00
COMPLETE SERIES 1 (128) 7.50 15.00
COMPLETE SERIES 2 (128) 7.50 15.00
1 Skip Arp .05 .15
2 Rick Aukland .08 .25
3 Doug Ault .05 .15
4 Mark Banal .05 .15
5 Dick Barton .05 .15
6 Shannon Bearden .05 .15
7 Mike Bechelli .05 .15
8 Jim Bernheisel .05 .15
9 Scott Bloomquist .15 .40
10 Jack Boggs .15 .40
11 Johnny Bone Jr. .05 .15
12 Mike Brown .05 .15
13 Tony Cardin .05 .15
14 Darrell Carpenter .05 .15
15 Denny Chamberlain .05 .15
16 Kevin Claycomb .05 .15
17 Mike Clonce .05 .15
18 Phil Coltrane .05 .15
19 Paul Croft .05 .15
20 Randy Dunn .05 .15
21 Hank Edwards .05 .15
22 Rick Egersdorf .05 .15
23 Terry English .08 .25
24 Dennis Erb .08 .25
25 Ken Essary .05 .15
26 Rocky Estes .05 .15
27 Danny Felker .05 .15
28 Ed Ferree .05 .15
29 Jeff Floyd .05 .15
30 Chub Frank .15 .40
31 Rollie Frink .05 .15
32 Bill Frye .08 .25
33 Lynn Geisler .05 .15
34 Ed Gibbons .05 .15
35 Herman Goddard .05 .15
36 Gary Green .05 .15
37 Marshall Green .05 .15
38 Kevin Gundaker .05 .15
39 Phil Hall .05 .15
40 Paul Harris .05 .15
41 Mike Head .05 .15
42 Tom Helfrich .05 .15
43 Jack Hewitt .08 .25
44 Brian Hickman .05 .15
45 Bob Hill .05 .15
46 Don Hobbs .05 .15
47 Bruce Hogue .05 .15
48 J.D. Howard .05 .15
49 Charlie Hughes .05 .15
50 Sam Hurd .05 .15
51 Doug Ingalls .05 .15
52 Bill Ingram .05 .15
53 Mike Jewell .05 .15
54 Johnny Johnson .05 .15
55 Ronnie Johnson .08 .25
56 Harvey Jones Jr. .05 .15
57 Gary Keeling .05 .15
58 Ed Kosiski .05 .15
59 Steve Kosiski .05 .15
60 Willy Kraft .05 .15
61 Ted Lackey .05 .15
62 Larry Lambeth .05 .15
63 Steve Landrum .05 .15
64 Darrell Lanigan .05 .15
65 Jerry Lark .05 .15
66 John Lawhorn .05 .15
67 Tommy Lawrell .05 .15
68 Rick Lebow .05 .15
69 Mike Luna .05 .15
70 Donald Marsh .05 .15
71 Bill Martin .05 .15
72 Stan Massey .05 .15
73 Doug McCammon .05 .15
74 Gary McPherson .05 .15
75 Audie McWilliams .05 .15
76 Joe Meadows .05 .15
77 Buckshot Miles .05 .15
78 Brett Miller .05 .15
79 Larry Moore .05 .15
80 Donnie Moran .08 .25
81 David Moyer .05 .15
82 Tom Nesbitt .05 .15
83 Bill Ogle .08 .25
84 Don O'Neal .05 .15
85 Eddie Pace .05 .15
86 Pete Parker .05 .15
87 Bob Pierce .05 .15
88 Ronnie Poche .05 .15
89 Al Purkey .05 .15
90 Jim Rarick .05 .15
91 Frank Reaber .05 .15
92 Tony Reaid .05 .15
93 Joe Rice .05 .15
94 Rex Richey .05 .15
95 Eddie Rickman .05 .15
96 Jerry Robertson .05 .15
97 Jeff Robinson .05 .15
98 Steve Russell .05 .15
99 Doug Sanders .05 .15
100 Charlie Schaffer .05 .15
101 Ken Schrader .05 .15
102 Frank Seder .05 .15
103 Randy Sellars .05 .15
104 Scott Sexton .05 .15
105 Paul Shafer .05 .15
106 Steve Shaver .05 .15
107 Clint Smith .05 .15
108 Delbert Smith .05 .15
109 Earl Smith .05 .15
110 Steve Smith .08 .25
111 Gibby Steinhaus .05 .15
112 Charlie Swartz .05 .15
113 Dick Taylor .05 .15
114 Bobby Thomas .05 .15
115 Jack Trammell .08 .25
116 John Utsman .05 .15
117 Troy VanderVeen .05 .15
118 H.E. Vineyard .05 .15
119 Wendall Wallace .05 .15
120 Bob Wearing Jr. .05 .15
121 Kevin Weaver .08 .25
122 Gary Webb .08 .25
123 Doug Wiggs .05 .15
124 Rick Williams .05 .15
125 Randy Woodling .05 .15
126 Jeff Aikey's Car .05 .15
127 Tony Albright's Car .05 .15
128 Chris Anderson's Car .05 .15
129 Todd Anderson's Car .05 .15
130 Todd Andrews' Car .05 .15
131 Brian Ater .08 .25
132 Steve Baker .08 .25
133 Mike Balzano's Car .08 .25
134 Jr. Banks .08 .25
135 John Booper Bare's Car .05 .15
136 Joe Barnett .08 .25
137 Steve Barnett .08 .25
138 Ed Basey's Car .05 .15
139 Dave Bilbrey's Car .05 .15
140 Randy Boggs' Car .05 .15
141 Don Bohlander's Car .05 .15
142 Denny Bonebrake's Car .05 .15
143 Mike Bowers' Car .05 .15
144 Jay Brinkley .08 .25
145 Randy Carte .08 .25
146 David Chancy .08 .25
147 Gene Chupp .08 .25
148 Jimmy Clifton's Car .05 .15
149 Tory Collins' Car .05 .15
150 Delmas Conley's Car .05 .15
151 Rick Corbin's Car .05 .15
152 Jim Curry's Car .05 .15
153 Jim Donofrio's Car .05 .15
154 Nelson Dowd's Car .05 .15
155 Bryan Dunaway .05 .15
156 Mike Duvall's Car .05 .15
157 Rick Eckert .08 .25
158 Leslie Essary .08 .25
159 Don Eyerly's Car .05 .15
160 Lee Fleetwood .08 .25
161 Randy Floyd .08 .25
162 Steve Francis' Car .08 .25
163 Rodney Franklin .08 .25
164 Andy Fries .08 .25
165 Andy Genzman's Car .05 .15
166 John Gill's Car .05 .15
167 Ray Godsey's Car .05 .15
168 Barry Goodman's Car .05 .15
169 Gary Gorby .08 .25
170 Troy Green's Car .05 .15
171 Phil Gregory's Car .05 .15
172 Don Gross' Car .05 .15
173 Johnny Schuler's Car .05 .15
174 Dave Hoffman's Car .05 .15
175 Dewayne Hughes' Car .05 .15
176 Mike Hurlbert's Car .05 .15
177 Ricky Idom's Car .05 .15
178 Ricky Ingalls .08 .25
179 Jerry Inmon .05 .15
180 Tony Izzo Jr. .08 .25
181 Mitch Johnson's Car .05 .15
182 John Jones' Car .05 .15
183 (Big) Jim Kelly's Car .05 .15
184 Daryl Key's Car .05 .15
185 Terry King's Car .05 .15
186 Wade Knowles's Car .05 .15
187 Joe Kosiski's Car .05 .15
188 Hot Rod LaMance's Car .05 .15
189 Freddie Lee's Car .05 .15
190 Junior Lemmings .08 .25
191 Joe Littlejohn's Car .05 .15
192 Roger Long's Car .05 .15
193 B.K. Luna .08 .25
194 Garry Mahoney .08 .25
195 Donnie Marcoullier Jr. .08 .25
196 Bill Mason's Car .05 .15
197 John Mason's Car .05 .15
198 Lance Matthees' Car .05 .15
199 Rex McCroskey's Car .05 .15
200 Dale McDowell's Car .05 .15
201 Ben Miley .05 .15
202 Matt Miller .08 .25
203 Matt Mitchell .08 .25
204 Darrell Mooneyham .08 .25
205 Bill Morgan .08 .25
206 Mike Mullvain .08 .25
207 Terry Muskrat's Car .05 .15
208 Earl Pepper Newby .08 .25
209 Bobby Joe Nicely's Car .05 .15
210 Mike Norris' Car .05 .15
211 Keith Nosbisch's Car .05 .15
212 Jimmy Nowlin .08 .25
213 Chuck Nutzmann's Car .05 .15
214 Mike Nutzmann's Car .05 .15
215 Lee Olibas's Car .05 .15
216 Jim O'Conner .08 .25
217 Marty O'Neal .08 .25
218 Skip Pannell's Car .05 .15
219 Kris Patterson's Car .05 .15
220 Terry Phillips .08 .25
221 Bob Pohlman Jr.'s Car .05 .15
222 John Provenzano .08 .25
223 C.J. Rayburn .05 .15
224 Jerry Rice .08 .25
225 Tom Rients .05 .15
226 Kevin Roderick's Car .05 .15
227 Todd Rust's Car .05 .15
228 Ed Sans Jr.'s Car .05 .15
229 Eric Sayre's Car .05 .15
230 Darwin Scarlett's Car .05 .15
231 Billy Scott .08 .25
232 Russ Sell's Car .05 .15
233 Steve Shute's Car .05 .15
234 Buck Simmons' Car .05 .15
235 Lavon Sloan's Car .05 .15
236 Buddy Smith's Car .05 .15
237 Sonny Smyser .08 .25
238 Tommy Snell's Car .05 .15
239 Mark Stevens .08 .25
240 Johnny Stokes .08 .25
241 Jim Tyron's Car .05 .15
242 Wren Turner .08 .25
243 Johnny Virdon's Car .05 .15
244 Mike Walker's Car .05 .15
245 Bob Wearing Jr.'s Car .05 .15
246 Ricky Weeks' Car .05 .15
247 Jimmie White .08 .25
248 Dill Whittymore .08 .25
249 Sam Williams' Car .05 .15
250 Charlie Williamson's Car .05 .15
NNO Cover Card .05 .15
Checklist 85-125
NNO Cover Card .05 .15
Checklist 43-84
NNO Cover Card .05 .15
Checklist 126-167
NNO Cover Card .05 .15
Checklist 1-42
NNO Cover Card .05 .15
Checklist 210-250
NNO Cover Card .05 .15
Checklist 168-209

1993 JAGS

JAGS Race Cards produced this set featuring top drivers of Dirt Late Model competition. This was the third of four sets released by JAGS and featured a light tan border.

COMPLETE SET (52) 4.00 10.00
1 Tony Albright .07 .20
2 Stan Amacher .07 .20
3 Scott Bloomquist .20 .50
4 Mike Boland .07 .20
5 Jimmy Burwell .07 .20
6 Marty Calloway .07 .20
7 Randle Chupp .07 .20
8 Kevin Coffey .07 .20
9 Gar Dickson .07 .20
10 Ed Dixon .07 .20
11 Patrick Duggan .07 .20
12 Randy Dunn .07 .20
13 Jimmy Edwards Jr. .07 .20
14 Paul Feistritzer .07 .20
15 Mike Freeman .07 .20
16 Fred F. Flatt .07 .20
17 John Gill .10 .30
18 Ray Guss Jr. .07 .20
19 Billy Hicks .07 .20
20 Kent Hicks .07 .20
21 Casey Huffman .07 .20
22 Sonny Huskey .07 .20
23 Bill Ingram .07 .20
24 Frank Ingram .07 .20
25 Willy Kraft .07 .20
26 Darrell Lanigan .07 .20
27 B.K. Luna .07 .20
28 Mike Luna .07 .20
29 Gary Mann .07 .20
30 Mark DIRT Martin .07 .20
31 Dale McDowell .07 .20
32 Monty Miller .07 .20
33 Tony W. Moody .07 .20
34 Donnie Moran .10 .30
35 Billy Moyer .20 .50
36 Ken Nosbisch .07 .20
37 Bill Palmer .07 .20
38 Pete Parker .07 .20
39 Steve D. Russell .07 .20
40 Doug Sanders .07 .20
41 Randy Sellars .07 .20
42 Terry Shannon .07 .20
43 Clint Smith .07 .20
44 Freddy Smith .20 .50
45 Jeff Smith .07 .20
46 Josh Tarter .07 .20
47 John A. Utsman .07 .20
48 Jeff Walker .07 .20
49 Kevin Weaver .10 .30
50 Randy Weaver .07 .20
51 Cover Card CL .07 .20
NNO Jennifer Dunn .07 .20
Miss JAGS

1994 JAGS

JAGS Race Cards produced this set featuring top drivers of Dirt Late Model competition. This was the last of four sets released by JAGS and featured a purple border.

COMPLETE SET (63) 4.00 10.00
1 Tony Albright .07 .20
2 Brian Ater .07 .20
3 Steve Barnett .07 .20
4 Wade Beaty .07 .20
5 Eddie Benfield .07 .20
6 Scott Bloomquist .20 .50
7 Jackie Boggs Jr. .07 .20
8 Rudy Boutwell .07 .20
9 Jay Brinkley .07 .20
10 Dave Burks .07 .20
11 Ronnie Caldwell .07 .20
12 Buster Cardwell .07 .20
13 Randall Carte .07 .20
14 Kevin Coffey .07 .20
15 Ray Cook .07 .20
16 Billy Drake .07 .20
17 Patrick Duggan .07 .20
18 Bryan Dunaway .07 .20
19 Rick Eckert .10 .30
20 Terry English .10 .30
21 Wayne Fielden .07 .20
22 Steve Francis .20 .50
23 Billy Hicks .07 .20
24 Rick Hixson .07 .20
25 Larry Isley .07 .20
26 Travis Johnson .07 .20
27 Gary Keeling .07 .20
28 Kenny LeCroy .07 .20
29 Jr. Lemmings .07 .20
30 Roger Long .07 .20
31 Keith Longmire .07 .20
32 Mike Luna .07 .20
33 Gary Mabe .07 .20
34 Tom Maddox .07 .20
35 Robby Mason .07 .20
36 Gary May .07 .20
37 Jimmy McCormick .07 .20
38 Dale McDowell .07 .20
39 Gary McPherson .07 .20
40 Byron L. Michael .07 .20
41 Donnie Moran .10 .30
42 Mike Mullvain .07 .20
43 Billy Ogle Jr. .10 .30
44 Carnell Parker .07 .20
45 Jamie Perry .07 .20
46 Bob Pierce .07 .20
47 Phillip Richardson .07 .20
48 Bobby Richey Jr. .07 .20
49 Rick Rogers .07 .20
50 Joe Ross Jr. .07 .20
51 Randy Sellars .07 .20
52 Scott Sexton .07 .20
53 J.R. Shickel .07 .20
54 Freddy Smith .20 .50
55 Jeff Smith .07 .20
56 Dick Taylor .07 .20
57 Paul Tims .07 .20
58 Mike Tinker .07 .20
59 Leroy Vann .07 .20
60 Kevin Weaver .10 .30
61 Neil P. Welch .07 .20
62 Rick Williams .07 .20
63 Cover Card CL .07 .20

1995 JSK Iceman

JSK Collectable Promotions produced this 27-card set featuring drivers of the Iceman Super Car Series. The cards are numbered according to the driver's car number and were distributed through souvenir stands at series' tracks. Set production was limited to 4000 sets that had an original cost of $12.50. Uncut sheets (52 made) were distributed for the set as well at a cost of $17.

COMPLETE SET (27) 5.00 12.00
1 Dennis Berry's Car .30 .75
4 Scott Baker's Car .20 .50
6 Tom Fedewa's Car .20 .50
7 Jason Mignogna's Car .20 .50
9 Matt Hutter's Car .20 .50
10 Stan Perry's Car .20 .50
13 Jerry Cook's Car .20 .50
15 Kenny Phillips' Car .20 .50
20 Ed Hage's Car .20 .50
21 Dan Morse's Car .20 .50
24 Dave Kuhlman's Car .20 .50
32 Dennis Strickland's Car .20 .50
48 Kenny Howard's Car .20 .50
56 Chase Howe w .20 .50
Car
65 Tim Ice's Car .40 1.00
69 Ron Allen's Car .20 .50
70 Fred Campbell's Car .30 .75
72 Scott Hantz's Car .20 .50
77 Kenny Sword's Car .20 .50
81 Gary Camelot's Car .20 .50
83 Bob Sibila's Car .20 .50
90 Tim Curry's Car .20 .50
97 Steve Sauve's Car .20 .50
99 John Sawatsky's Car .20 .50
0 Chuck Roumell's Car .30 .75
NNO Cover Card .20 .50
NNO Schedule Card .20 .50

1995 JSK Iceman Past Champions

JSK Collectable Promotions produced this 7-card set featuring past champs of the Iceman Super Car Series. Six cards focus on the champion drivers and cars, along with one cover card. The cards are numbered according to the driver's car number. Set production was limited to 4000 sets that had an original cost of $5. Uncut sheets (52 made) were distributed for the set as well at a cost of $7.

COMPLETE SET (7) 2.50 6.00
40 Bruce Vanderlaan's Car .40 1.00
51/52 Dennis Berry .40 1.00
Butch Miller Cars
61 Dennis Berry w .40 1.00
Car
65 Tim Ice w .75 2.00
Car
70 Fred Campbell's Car .40 1.00
0 Chuck Roumell's Car .40 1.00
NNO Cover Card .40 1.00

1995 JSK S.O.D. Sprints

JSK Collectable Promotions produced this 24-card set featuring drivers of the S.O.D. Sprints series. The cards are numbered according to the driver's car number and were distributed through souvenir stands at series' tracks. Set production was limited to 4000 sets that had an original cost of $10. Uncut sheets (52 made) were distributed for the set as well at a cost of $15.

COMPLETE SET (24) 4.00 10.00
1 Scott Seaton's Car .20 .50
2 Mike Katz's Car .20 .50
3S Brian Tyler's Car .20 .50
5 Steve VanNote's Car .20 .50
6 Jeff Bloom's Car .20 .50
10 Ron Koehler's Car .20 .50
16 Mike Mouch's Car .20 .50
20 Bill Tyler's Car .20 .50
21 Rocky Fisher's Car .20 .50
22R Jay Sherston's Car .20 .50
35 Ryan Katz's Car .20 .50
37 Hank Lower's Car .20 .50
42 Gary Fedewa's Car .30 .75
43 Dan Osburn's Car .20 .50
44J Bill Jacoby's Car .20 .50
47 Bob Clark's Car .20 .50
49 Lisa Ward's Car .20 .50
72 Pat York's Car .20 .50
77B Steve Burch's Car .20 .50
77T John Turner's Car .20 .50
83 Wayne Landon's Car .20 .50
NNO John Boy Hotchkiss .20 .50
NNO Cover Card .20 .50
NNO Schedule Card .20 .50

1990 K and W Dirt Track

K and W Race Cards produced a series of sets featuring drivers of DIRT Modifieds sold through local area tracks. A percentage of set sales proceeds went to the DIRT driver's injury fund. This 42-card set was the first edition in the series and was printed with color photos surrounded by a black border on the cardfront. Cardbacks were printed in black and white. Reportedly, 2,500 sets were produced and 500 of each card were made available to the drivers. The remaining 2,000 sets were then distributed. The unnumbered cards are listed below alphabetically.

COMPLETE SET (42) 3.00 8.00
1 Steve Ay .08 .25
2 Johnny Bennett Jr. .08 .25
3 Dave Bently .08 .25

4 Frances Blauvelt	.08	.25
5 Billy Brennen	.08	.25
6 Ed Brown Jr.	.08	.25
7 Hal Browning	.08	.25
8 Barry Buckhart	.08	.25
9 Tom Capie	.08	.25
10 Darryl Carman	.08	.25
11 Richard Cass	.08	.25
12 Chic Cossaboone	.08	.25
13 Brian Donley	.08	.25
14 Joe Edwards	.08	.25
15 Rick Elliott	.08	.25
16 Butch Glisson	.08	.25
17 Garry Gollub	.08	.25
18 Newt Hartman	.08	.25
19 Frank Hayes	.08	.25
20 Jim Horton Sr.	.15	.40
21 Jimmy Horton	.20	.50
22 James Jackson	.08	.25
23 Bucky Kell	.08	.25
24 Robbie Keller	.08	.25
25 Bear Kelly	.08	.25
26 Ron Keys	.08	.25
27 Roger Laureno	.08	.25
28 John Leach	.08	.25
29 Mick MacNeir	.08	.25
30 Jimmy Martin	.08	.25
31 Ernie Miles Jr.	.08	.25
32 Jamie Mills	.08	.25
33 Brad Nash	.08	.25
34 Fred Orchard Jr.	.08	.25
35 Bobby Parks	.08	.25
36 Richie Pratt	.08	.25
37 Scott Pursell	.08	.25
38 Erwin Schlenger	.08	.25
39 Glenn Smith	.08	.25
40 Paul Weaver	.08	.25
41 Wayne Weaver	.08	.25
42 Edward Zehner	.08	.25

1991 K and W Dirt Track

This set of 50-cards featuring top Northeast DIRT Track drivers was produced and distributed by Kand W Race Cards. The black bordered cards include 49-drivers and one cover/checklist card and were released in complete set form. A percentage of set sales proceeds went to the DIRT driver's injury fund. Reportedly, 2,500 sets were produced and 500 of each card were made available to the drivers. The remaining 2,000 were then distributed.

COMPLETE SET (50)	4.00	10.00
1 Brett Hearn	.08	.25
2 Billy Pauch	.08	.25
3 Doug Hoffman	.08	.25
4 Scott Irwin	.08	.25
5 Johnny Betts	.08	.25
6 Chip Slocum	.08	.25
7 Fred Brightbill	.08	.25
8 Glenn Smith	.08	.25
9 Rick Elliott	.08	.25
10 John Leach	.08	.25
11 Jamie Mills	.08	.25
12 Wayne Weaver	.08	.25
13 Ron Keys	.08	.25
14 Newt Hartman	.08	.25
15 Garry Gollub	.08	.25
16 Mark Kenyon	.08	.25
17 Jimmy Chester	.08	.25
18 Sam Martz	.08	.25
19 John Pinter	.08	.25
20 Bobby Wilkins	.08	.25
21 Hal Browning	.08	.25
22 Donnie Wetmore	.08	.25
23 Tom Capie	.08	.25
24 Bucky Kell	.08	.25
25 Chic Cossaboone	.08	.25
26 Randy Glenski	.08	.25
27 Roger Laureno	.08	.25
28 Dave Adams	.08	.25
29 Bobby Parks	.08	.25
30 Pete Visconti	.08	.25
31 Ronnie Tobias	.08	.25
32 Richie Pratt	.08	.25
33 Frank Cozze	.08	.25
34 Jack Johnson	.08	.25
35 Jimmy Horton	.20	.50
36 Toby Tobias Jr.	.08	.25
37 Scott Pursell	.08	.25
38 Kenny Tremont	.08	.25
39 Steve Paine	.08	.25
40 Billy Decker	.08	.25
41 Whitey Kidd Jr.	.08	.25
42 Tom Peck	.15	.40
43 Ernie Miles Jr.	.08	.25
44 Bill Tanner	.08	.25
45 Fred Orchard	.08	.25
46 Bob Lineman	.08	.25
47 Deron Rust	.08	.25
48 Gary Bruckler	.08	.25
49 Craig Von Dohren	.08	.25
50 Cover Checklist Card	.08	.25

1991 K and W URC Sprints

This set of 43-cards featuring top drivers of the United Racing Club Sprint Car series was produced and distributed by Kand W Race Cards. The blue bordered cards include 41-drivers, one cover/checklist card and a card of Miss URC. Reportedly 2,500 sets were produced and 500 of each card were made available to the drivers. The remaining 2,000 sets were then distributed.

COMPLETE SET (43)	5.00	12.00
1 Glenn Fitzcharles	.15	.40
2 Bruce Thompson	.15	.40
3 Jimmy Martin	.15	.40
4 Billy Ellis	.15	.40
5 Lou Cicconi Jr.	.20	.50
6 Stew Brown	.15	.40
7 Sam Gangemi	.15	.40
8 Mike Conway	.15	.40
9 Todd Rittenhouse	.15	.40
10 Mike Wells	.15	.40
11 Wayne Rice	.15	.40
12 Dave McGough	.15	.40
13 Dan Nerl	.15	.40
14 Tom Wanner	.15	.40
15 Bob Kellar	.15	.40
16 Tim Higgins	.15	.40
17 Bruce Bowen	.15	.40
18 Mares Stellfox	.15	.40
19 Kramer Williamson	.15	.40
20 Jerry Dinnen	.15	.40
21 Ray Winiecki Jr.	.15	.40
22 Tony Smolenyak	.15	.40
23 Billy Hughes	.15	.40
24 Bob Swavely	.15	.40
25 Fran Hogue	.15	.40
26 Gary Hieber	.15	.40
27 John Jenkins	.15	.40
28 Jim Baker	.15	.40
29 Jon Holmquist Jr.	.15	.40
30 Lance Dewease	.15	.40
31 Midge Miller	.15	.40
32 Dave McGough	.15	.40
33 Mike Haggenbottom	.15	.40
34 Bob Fisher Jr.	.15	.40
35 Jon Eldreth	.15	.40
36 Rich Bates	.15	.40
37 Don Souders Jr.	.15	.40
38 Larry Winchell	.15	.40
39 Greg Coverdale	.15	.40
40 Ralph Stettenbauer	.15	.40
41 Glenn Fitzcharles	.15	.40
42 Kolleen Reimel	.15	.40
43 Cover Checklist Card	.15	.40

1992 K and W Dirt Track

K and W Race Cards produced a series of sets featuring drivers of DIRT Modifieds sold through local area tracks. A percentage of set sales proceeds went to the DIRT driver's injury fund. This 65-card set was printed with color photos surrounded by an orange-red border on the cardfront. Cardbacks were printed in black and white. 2,500 of each card were produced and 500 of those cards were made available to the drivers. The remaining 2,000 sets were then distributed.

COMPLETE SET (65)	3.00	8.00
1 Billy Pauch	.05	.15
2 Doug Hoffman	.05	.15
3 Brett Hearn	.05	.15
4 Bob McCreadie	.05	.15
5 Jimmy Horton	.20	.50
6 Jack Johnson	.05	.15
7 Toby Tobias Jr.	.05	.15
8 Ronnie Tobias	.05	.15
9 Steve Paine	.05	.15
10 Kenny Tremont	.05	.15
11 Billy Decker	.05	.15
12 Rick Elliott	.05	.15
13 Bobby Wilkins	.05	.15
14 Tom Hager	.05	.15
15 Kevin Collins	.05	.15
16 David Lape	.05	.15
17 C.D. Coville	.05	.15
18 Duane Howard	.05	.15
19 Frank Cozze	.05	.15
20 Ron Keys	.05	.15
21 John Leach	.05	.15
22 Roger Laureno	.05	.15
23 Dave Adams	.05	.15
24 Chic Cossaboone	.05	.15
25 Jimmy Chester	.05	.15
26 Garry Gollub	.05	.15
27 Glenn Smith	.05	.15
28 Jamie Mills	.05	.15
29 Wayne Weaver	.05	.15
30 John Pinter	.05	.15
31 Randy Glenski	.05	.15
32 Buck Ward	.05	.15
33 Richie Pratt	.05	.15
34 H.J. Bunting, III	.05	.15
35 Deron Rust	.05	.15
36 Bobby Sapp	.05	.15
37 Greg Humlhanz	.05	.15
38 Ed Brown, Jr.	.05	.15
39 David Hill	.05	.15
40 John Bennett, Jr.	.05	.15
41 Landy Adams	.05	.15
42 Pete Visconti	.05	.15
43 Scott Pursell	.05	.15
44 Chip Slocum	.05	.15
45 Tom Capie	.05	.15
46 Whitey Kidd, Jr.	.05	.15
47 Ernie Miles, Jr.	.05	.15
48 Bill Tanner	.05	.15
49 Bobby Parks	.05	.15
50 Craig Von Dohren	.05	.15
51 Tom Mayberry	.05	.15
52 Dennis Bailey	.05	.15
53 Jeff Strunk	.05	.15
54 Rick Schaffer	.05	.15
55 Jack Follweiler	.05	.15
56 Tom Carberry	.05	.15
57 Fred Dmuchowski	.05	.15
58 Steve Bottcher	.05	.15
59 Joe Plazek	.05	.15
60 Smokey Warren	.05	.15
61 Ray Swinehart	.05	.15
62 Bucky Kell	.05	.15
63 Newt Hartman	.05	.15
64 Sam Martz	.05	.15
65 Checklist Card	.05	.15

1994 K and W Dirt Track

K and W Race Cards produced a series of sets featuring drivers of DIRT Modifieds sold through local area tracks. A percentage of set sales proceeds went to the local driver's injury fund. This 40-card set was printed with color photos surrounded by a blue border on the cardfront. Cardbacks were printed in black and white. Reportedly, 2,500 sets were produced and 500 of each card were made available to the drivers. The remaining 2,000 sets were then distributed.

COMPLETE SET (40)	4.00	10.00
1 Brett Hearn	.10	.30
2 Doug Hoffman	.10	.30
3 Bob McCreadie	.10	.30
4 Bobby Wilkins	.10	.30
5 Billy Pauch	.10	.30
6 Mitch Gibbs	.10	.30
7 Toby Tobias, Jr.	.10	.30
8 Kenny Tremont	.10	.30
9 Rick Elliott	.10	.30
10 Duane Howard	.10	.30
11 Jimmy Horton	.20	.50
12 Kevin Collins	.10	.30
13 Steve Paine	.10	.30
14 Pete Visconti	.10	.30
15 Jack Johnson	.10	.30
16 Craig Von Dohren	.10	.30
17 Billy Decker	.10	.30
18 Randy Glenski	.10	.30
19 Frank Cozze	.10	.30
20 Ray Swinehart	.10	.30
21 Roger Laureno	.10	.30
22 David Lape	.10	.30
23 Tom Mayberry	.10	.30
24 Ron Keys	.10	.30
25 Ronnie Tobias	.10	.30
26 Fred Dmuchowski	.10	.30
27 John Leach	.10	.30
28 Joe Plazek	.10	.30
29 Bucky Kell	.10	.30
30 Jamie Mills	.10	.30
31 Tom Hager	.10	.30
32 Dave Adams	.10	.30
33 Bobby Sapp	.10	.30
34 Jimmy Chester	.10	.30
35 Greg Humlhanz	.10	.30
36 Deron Rust	.10	.30
37 Chip Slocum	.10	.30
38 Rick Schaffer	.10	.30
39 Jeff Strunk	.10	.30
40 Cover Checklist Card	.10	.30

1995 K and W Dirt Track

K and W Race Cards produced a series of sets featuring drivers of DIRT Modifieds sold through local area tracks. A percentage of set sales proceeds went to the local driver's injury fund. This 42-card set was printed with color photos surrounded by a white border on the cardfront. Cardbacks were printed in black and white. Reportedly, 2,500 sets were produced and 500 of each card were made available to the drivers. The remaining 2,000 sets were then distributed.

COMPLETE SET (42)	5.00	12.00
1 Bob McCreadie	.10	.30
2 Dale Planck	.10	.30
3 Brett Hearn	.10	.30
4 Doug Hoffman	.10	.30
5 Rick Elliott	.10	.30
6 Mitch Gibbs	.10	.30
7 Alan Johnson	.10	.30
8 Jack Johnson	.10	.30
9 Danny Johnson	.20	.50
10 Bobby Wilkins	.10	.30
11 Joe Plazek	.10	.30
12 Billy Pauch	.10	.30
13 Jimmy Horton	.30	.75
14 Kenny Tremont	.10	.30
15 Craig Von Dohren	.10	.30
16 Frank Cozze	.10	.30
17 Garry Gollub	.10	.30
18 Meme DeSantis	.10	.30
19 Steve Paine	.10	.30
20 Billy Decker	.10	.30
21 Jimmy Chester	.10	.30
22 Wade Hendrickson	.10	.30
23 Billy Pauch	.10	.30
24 H.J. Bunting, III	.10	.30
25 David Lape	.10	.30
26 Dave Adams	.10	.30
27 Pete Visconti	.10	.30
28 Sammy Beavers	.10	.30
29 Ron Keys	.10	.30
30 Norman Short Jr.	.10	.30
31 Fred Dmuchowski	.10	.30
32 Randy Glenski	.10	.30
33 Tom Hager	.10	.30
34 Roger Laureno	.10	.30
35 John Leach	.10	.30
36 Greg Humlhanz	.10	.30
37 Jamie Mills	.10	.30
38 Mike Sena	.10	.30
39 Deron Rust	.10	.30
40 John Wyers	.10	.30
41 Wayne Weaver	.10	.30
42 Cover Checklist Card	.10	.30

1990 Langenberg Rockford Speedway/Hot Stuff

M.B. Langenberg produced this set in 1990 under the title Hot Stuff. The cards feature drivers of various circuits that raced at the Rockford (Illinois) Speedway. As with most Langenberg sets, the cards feature a checkered flag design and black and white cardbacks. The card numbering is unusual in that it begins with 1001 and ends with 1045. We've shortened the numbering in the listings as reflected below.

COMPLETE SET (45)	3.00	8.00
1 John Ganley	.07	.20
2 Jim Rieger	.07	.20
3 Mark Higby	.07	.20
4 Gary Anderson	.07	.20
5 Tom Cormack	.07	.20
6 Bob Torkelson	.07	.20
7 Walter Reitz	.07	.20
8 Bobby Wilberg	.07	.20
9 Curt Tillman	.07	.20
10 John Knaus	.07	.20
11 Bobby Davis	.07	.20
12 Steve Erickson	.07	.20
13 Dale Cox	.07	.20
14 Dave Cox	.07	.20
15 Gary Loos	.07	.20
16 Bob Parisot	.07	.20
17 Jim Reynolds	.07	.20
18 Dave Wagner	.07	.20
19 Terry Rahl	.07	.20
20 Dennis Miller	.07	.20
21 Larry Schuler	.07	.20
22 Bart Reinen	.07	.20
23 Jeff Watson	.07	.20
24 Bill McCoy	.07	.20
25 Nolan McBride	.07	.20
26 Dave Nelson	.07	.20
27 Brad Wagner	.07	.20
28 Dave Foltz	.07	.20
29 Mark Hartline	.07	.20
30 B.J.Sparkman	.07	.20
31 Jon Reynolds	.07	.20
32 Tom Gille	.07	.20
33 Bryan Young	.07	.20
34 Bobby LaPier	.07	.20
35 Todd Aldrich	.07	.20
36 Mike Lloyd	.07	.20
37 Don Russell	.07	.20
38 Dana Czach	.07	.20
39 Bruce Tucker	.07	.20
40 Tim Loos	.07	.20
41 Steve Gray	.07	.20
42 Dan Johnson Stock	.07	.20
43 Murt Dunn	.07	.20
44 Jerry Gille	.07	.20
45 Al Sheppard	.07	.20

1991 Langenberg Rockford Speedway

This 66-card set features various drivers who raced at the Rockford (Illinois) Speedway. The set was produced by M.B. Langenberg. It was the second consecutive year a Rockford Speedway set was issued.

COMPLETE SET (66)	4.00	10.00
1 Curt Tillman	.07	.20
2 Ricky Bilderback	.07	.20
3 Jerry Gille	.07	.20
4 Scott Dolliver	.07	.20
5 Tom Gille	.07	.20
6 Jim Reynolds	.07	.20
7 Kurt Danko	.07	.20
8 Don Russell	.07	.20
9 Bruce Devoy	.07	.20
10 Brian Johnson	.07	.20
11 Robert Parisot	.07	.20
12 Murt Dunn	.07	.20
13 Dennis Miller	.07	.20
14 Tom Graves	.07	.20
15 Daryl Luepkes	.07	.20
16 Ron Smykay	.07	.20
17 Bobby Hacker	.07	.20
18 Roy Crettol	.07	.20
19 Jeff Taber	.07	.20
20 Dave Lapier	.07	.20
21 Ricky Bilderback Dennis Miller John Knaus	.07	.20
22 Allan Merfeld	.07	.20
23 Dale Yardley	.07	.20
24 Mike Lloyd	.07	.20
25 Jeff Watson	.07	.20
26 John Knaus	.07	.20
27 Bill McCoy	.07	.20
28 Scott Lawver Tom Schneider Doug Fermanich	.07	.20
29 George Compo	.07	.20
30 Mike O'Leary	.07	.20
31 Gene Hill	.07	.20
32 Rodney Gilley	.07	.20
33 Brad Wagner	.07	.20
34 Bob Miller	.07	.20
35 Doug Fermanich	.07	.20
36 Darrell Williams	.07	.20
37 Scott Bryden	.07	.20
38 Mike Martindale	.07	.20
39 Mike Loos	.07	.20
40 Alan Sheppard	.07	.20
41 Mark Magee	.07	.20
42 Gary Head	.07	.20
43 Bobby Wilberg	.07	.20
44 B.J. Sparkman	.07	.20
45 Nolan McBride	.07	.20
46 Elmo Deery	.07	.20
47 Thomas Powell	.07	.20
48 Todd Aldrich	.07	.20
49 Jim Sanders	.07	.20
50 Dave Lee	.07	.20
51 Dale Cox	.07	.20
52 Patrick Rossmann	.07	.20
53 Derrick Spack	.07	.20
54 Lon Ritz	.07	.20
55 Jerry Ahlquist	.07	.20
56 Dave Wagner	.07	.20
57 Stan Burdick	.07	.20
58 Dana Czach	.07	.20
59 Larry O'Brien	.07	.20
60 Bobby Wilberg Gary Head Brad Wagner Kurt Danko	.10	.30
61 Rockford Speedway	.07	.20
62 Rockford Speedway	.07	.20
63 Rockford Speedway	.07	.20
64 Dave Wagner Bill McCoy B Devoy R.Sanders R.Parisot	.07	.20
65 Scott Tripp Brian Steward Tom Ragner Sr.	.07	.20
66 Checklist Card	.07	.20

1991 Langenberg Seekonk Speedway

M.B. Langenberg produced this set of 29 cards. The cards feature various drivers who have raced at Seekonk Speedway. This set was done in conjunction with the tracks 45th anniversary.

COMPLETE SET (29)	3.00	8.00
1 Vinny Annarummo	.10	.30
2 Ray Lee	.10	.30
3 Dick Houlihan	.10	.30
4 Rick Martin	.10	.30
5 Jimmy Wilkins	.10	.30
6 Joey Cerullo	.10	.30
7 Len Ellis	.10	.30
8 Jimmy Kuhn	.10	.30
9 John Tripp	.10	.30
10 David Berghman	.10	.30
11 Don Dionne	.10	.30
12 Carl Stevens	.10	.30
13 Wayne Dion	.10	.30
14 Tony Kias, Jr.	.10	.30
15 Fred Astle, Jr.	.10	.30
16 Jim McCallum	.10	.30
17 Bruce Taylor	.10	.30
18 Jeff Mecure	.10	.30
19 Manny Dias	.10	.30
20 Bob Stockel	.10	.30
21 Mike Santiano	.10	.30
22 Richard Hanatow	.10	.30
23 Bobby Tripp	.10	.30
24 Jim Proulx	.10	.30
25 D.Anthony Venditti	.10	.30
26 Jimmy Kuhn	.10	.30
27 Seekonk Speedway	.10	.30
28 Checklist 1-29	.10	.30
29 Cover Card	.10	.30

1992 Langenberg Rockford Speedway

This was the third consecutive year M.B. Langenberg produced a Rockford Speedway set. The cards feature various drivers who have run at the track.The 61-card set is listed in alphabetical order.

COMPLETE SET (61)	5.00	12.00
1 Jerry Ahlquist	.08	.25
2 Ricky Bilderback	.08	.25
3 Ricky Bilderback	.08	.25
4 George Bohn	.08	.25
5 Scotty Bryden	.08	.25
6 Stan Burdick	.08	.25
7 George Compo	.08	.25
8 Kurt Danko	.08	.25
9 Joe Darnell	.08	.25
10 Jack Deery	.08	.25
11 Steve DeMarb	.08	.25
12 Steve DeMarb	.08	.25
13 Scott Dolliver	.08	.25
14 Dave Ebrecht	.08	.25
15 Jerry Eckel	.08	.25
16 John Ganley	.08	.25
17 John Ganley	.08	.25
18 Jerry Gille	.08	.25
19 Tom Gille	.08	.25
20 Tom Gille	.08	.25
21 Rodney Gilley	.08	.25
22 Tom Graves	.08	.25
23 Bobby Hacker	.08	.25
24 Gary Head	.08	.25
25 Gary Head	.08	.25
26 Brian Johnson	.08	.25
27 Ron Johnson	.08	.25
28 John Knaus	.08	.25
29 John Knaus	.08	.25
30 Tom Kurth	.08	.25
31 Ritchie Lane	.08	.25
32 Marty Langenberg	.08	.25
33 Mike Lloyd	.08	.25
34 Daryl Luepkes	.08	.25
35 Mark Magee	.08	.25
36 Billy McCoy	.08	.25
37 Gary Meisman	.08	.25
38 Bob Miller	.08	.25
39 James Nuelle	.08	.25
40 Al Papini, III	.08	.25
41 Bob Parisot	.08	.25
42 Tom Powell	.08	.25
43 Jim Reynolds	.08	.25
44 John Robinson	.08	.25
45 Stephan Rubeck	.08	.25
46 Andi Rushiti	.08	.25
47 Kevin Smith	.08	.25
48 B.J. Sparkman	.08	.25
49 B.J. Sparkman	.08	.25
50 George Sparkman	.08	.25
51 Jeff Taber	.08	.25
52 Brad Wagner	.08	.25
53 Brad Wagner	.08	.25
54 David Wagner	.08	.25
55 Rob Wagner	.08	.25
56 Howie Ware	.08	.25
57 Jeff Watson	.08	.25
58 Jeff Watson	.08	.25
59 Bobby Wilberg	.08	.25
60 Bobby Wilberg	.08	.25
61 Darrell Williams	.08	.25

1992 Racing Legends Sprints

Racing Legends produced this set in 1992 to highlight the stars of Sprint Car racing. The 30-card set was released in factory set form with a certificate numbering it amongst the production run of 10,000 sets.

COMPLETE SET (30)	5.00	12.00
1 Steve Kinser w Car	.60	1.50
2 Sammy Swindell w Car	.40	1.00
3 Sammy Swindell	.40	1.00
4 Johnny Herrera's Car	.10	.30
5 Johnny Herrera	.20	.50
6 Steve Beitler's Car	.10	.30
7 Steve Beitler	.10	.30
8 Joe Gaerte's Car	.10	.30
9 Mark Kinser's Car	.10	.30
10 Mark Kinser	.20	.50
11 Dave Blaney's Car	1.00	2.50
12 Bobby Fletcher's Car	.10	.30
13 Stevie Smith's Car	.10	.30
14 Stevie Smith Jr.	.20	.50
15 Steve Stambaugh's Car	.10	.30
16 Kenny Jacobs' Car	.10	.30
17 Fred Rahmer's Car	.10	.30
18 Glenn Fitzcharles' Car	.10	.30
19 Jim Carr's Car	.10	.30
20 Joey Kuhn's Car	.10	.30
21 Bobby Weaver's Car	.10	.30
22 Paul Lotier's Car	.10	.30
23 Cris Eash's Car	.10	.30
24 Johnny Mackison Jr.'s Car	.10	.30
25 Bobby Allen's Car	.10	.30
26 Me Me DeSantis' Car	.10	.30
27 Randy Wolfe's Car	.10	.30
28 Bobby Davis Jr.'s Car	.10	.30
29 Donnie Krietz Jr.'s Car	.10	.30
30 Brent Kaeding's Car	.20	.50

1992 STARS Modifieds

Short Track Auto Racing Stars (STARS) released this 48-card set in 1992. The cards were sold in complete set form and feature photos of top drivers of the STARS modifieds series.

COMPLETE SET (48)	6.00	15.00
1 Blaine Aber	.10	.30
2 Dub Barnhouse	.10	.30
3 Mike Balzano w Car	.10	.30
4 Bob Adams, Jr.	.10	.30
5 Dick Barton	.10	.30
6 Booper Bare	.10	.30
7 Andy Bond	.10	.30
8 Jack Boggs	.20	.50
9 Larry Bond	.10	.30
10 Todd Andrews	.10	.30
11 Jim Gentry	.10	.30

12 Keith Berner .10 .30
13 Bob Cowen .10 .30
14 Jim Curry .10 .30
15 Darrell Lanigan w Car .10 .30
16 Rodney Franklin .10 .30
17 Nathan Durboraw w Car .10 .30
18 Ron Davies .10 .30
19 Denny Chamberlain .10 .30
20 Mark Banal .10 .30
21 Mike Duvall .20 .50
22 Chub Frank .10 .30
23 Paul Davis .10 .30
24 B.A. Malcuit .10 .30
25 Davey Johnson w Car .20 .50
26 Rocky Hodges .10 .30
27 Tim Hitt .10 .30
28 Lynn Geisler .10 .30
29 Don Gross .10 .30
30 Bob Wearing, Jr. w Car .10 .30
31 Gary Stuhler w Car .10 .30
32 Freddy Smith .30 .75
33 Buck Simmons .10 .30
34 Steve Shaver w Car .10 .30
35 Harold Redman .10 .30
36 Bob Pierce .10 .30
37 Mark Myers .10 .30
38 Donnie Moran .20 .50
39 Billy Moyer w Car .30 .75
40 John Mason .10 .30
41 Chuck Maloney .10 .30
42 Ed Gibbons .10 .30
43 Steve Francis .30 .75
44 Butch McGill w Car .10 .30
45 Rodney Combs .30 .75
46 Larry Moore w Car .10 .30
47 Joe Meadows' Car .10 .30
NNO Cover Card CL .10 .30

1994 STARS Modifieds

Short Track Auto Racing Stars (STARS) licensed this 54-card set released in 1994. The cards were sold in complete set form and feature action photos of top drivers of the STARS modifieds series.

COMPLETE SET (54) 4.80 12.00
1 Davey Johnson .15 .40
2 Todd Andrews .08 .25
3 Dan Armbruster .08 .25
4 Rick Aukland .08 .25
5 Mike Balzano .08 .25
6 John Booper Bare .08 .25
7 Steve Barnett .08 .25
8 Scott Bloomquist .15 .40
9 Larry Bond .08 .25
10 Denny Bonebrake .08 .25
11 Kevin Claycomb .08 .25
12 D.J. Cline .08 .25
13 Delmas Conley .08 .25
14 R.J. Conley .08 .25
15 Rod Conley .08 .25
16 Ron Davies .08 .25
17 Nathan Durboraw .08 .25
18 Mike Duvall .15 .40
19 Terry Eaglin .08 .25
20 Rick Eckert .15 .40
21 Vince Fanello .08 .25
22 Steve Francis .25 .60
23 Chub Frank .08 .25
24 Ed Gibbons .08 .25
25 Ed Griffin .08 .25
26 Don Gross .08 .25
27 Doug Hall .08 .25
28 Mike Harrison .08 .25
29 Scott Hartley .08 .25
30 Bart Hartman .08 .25
31 Billy Hicks .08 .25
32 Tim Hitt .08 .25
33 Bruce Hordusky .08 .25
34 Bubby James .08 .25
35 Tony Izzo Jr. .08 .25
36 Darrell Lanigan .08 .25
37 John Mason .08 .25
38 Donnie Moran .15 .40
39 Billy Moyer .25 .60
40 Don O'Neal .08 .25
41 Bob Pierce .08 .25
42 Dick Potts .08 .25
43 C.J. Rayburn .08 .25
44 Brian Ruhlman .08 .25
45 Steve Shaver .08 .25
46 Eddie Smith .08 .25
47 Freddy Smith .25 .60
48 Michael Smith .08 .25
49 Gary Stuhler .08 .25
50 Kevin Weaver .08 .25
51 Greg Williams .08 .25
52 Rick Workman .08 .25
53 Ricky Weeks .08 .25
NNO STARS Checklist .08 .25

1992 Traks Dirt

The 1992 Traks Dirt set features 15 numbered DIRT modified driver cards and one unnumbered cover/checklist card. The set was distributed by Traks through hobby channels.

COMPLETE SET (16) 1.60 4.00
1 Dave Lape .10 .30
2 Jack Johnson .10 .30
3 Alan Johnson .10 .30
4 Jeff Trombley .10 .30
5 Brett Hearn .10 .30
6 Steve Paine .10 .30
7 Jeff Heotzler .10 .30
8 Joe Plazek .10 .30
9 Dick Larkin .10 .30
10 Billy Decker .10 .30
11 Frank Cozze .10 .30
12 Bob McCreadie .10 .30
13 Kenny Tremont .10 .30
14 Doug Hoffman .10 .30
15 Danny Johnson .10 .30
NNO Checklist .10 .30

1992 Volunteer Racing East Alabama Speedway

This 20-card set feautres some of the top drivers that have run dirt cars at East Alabama Speedway. The set was produced by Volunteer racing and includes drivers like Buck Simmons, Jack Boggs and Scott Bloomquist. Also, included are a couple of cards of Busch Grand National regular Jeff Purvis.

COMPLETE SET (20) 2.50 6.00
1 Checklist Card .08 .25
2 Bobby Thomas .08 .25
3 Bud Lunsford .08 .25
4 Charlie Hughes .08 .25
5 Buck Simmons .15 .40
6 Billy Thomas .08 .25
7 Don Hester .08 .25
8 Tom Helfrich .08 .25
9 Larry Moore .08 .25
10 Jeff Purvis .30 .75
11 Jeff Purvis .30 .75
12 Buddy Boutwell .08 .25
13 Jeff Purvis .30 .75
14 Jack Boggs .08 .25
15 Billy Moyer .30 .75
16 Freddy Smith .30 .75
17 Bobby Thomas .08 .25
18 Scott Bloomquist .15 .40
19 Jimmy Thomas .15 .40
20 Parade Lap .08 .25

1992 Volunteer Racing Lernersville Speedway Series One

This 72-card set features some of the top sprint car drivers to have raced at Lernersville Speedway. This is the first of a two set series produced by Volunteer Racing. The set includes such notables as Brad Doty and an unnumbered promo card of Dale and Lou Blaney.

COMPLETE SET (72) 3.20 8.00
1 Checklist Card (1-36) .05 .15
2 Checklist Card (37-72) .05 .15
3 Jim Andrews .05 .15
4 Johnny Axe .05 .15
5 Bob Axe .05 .15
6 Johnny Beaber .05 .15
7 Johnny Beaber .05 .15
8 Lou Blaney .05 .15
9 Lou Blaney .05 .15
10 John Braymer .05 .15
11 John Britsky .05 .15
12 Paul Brown .05 .15
13 Mark Cassella .05 .15
14 Ron Davies .05 .15
15 Brad Doty .08 .25
16 Bill Emig .05 .15
17 Ernie Gardina .05 .15
18 Lou Gentile .05 .15
19 Lou Gentile .05 .15
20 Dale Hafer .05 .15
21 Dave Hess .05 .15
22 Dave Hoffman .05 .15
23 Dave Hoffman .05 .15
24 Chuck Kennedy .05 .15
25 Denny Keppel .05 .15
26 Bob Kirchner .05 .15
27 Mark Lezanic .05 .15
28 Rick Majors .05 .15
29 Jerry Matus .05 .15
30 Chuck McDowell .05 .15
31 Kevin McKinney .05 .15
32 Ben Miley .05 .15
33 Ben Miley .05 .15
34 Jim Minton .05 .15
35 Brian Muehlman .05 .15
36 Carl Murdick .05 .15
37 Bill Nobles .05 .15
38 Mike Norris .05 .15
39 Gary Pease .05 .15
40 Dave Pegher .05 .15
41 Barry Peters .05 .15
42 Tom Phillips .05 .15
43 Frank Raiti .05 .15
44 Craig Rankin .05 .15
45 L.B. Roenigk .05 .15
46 Terry Rosenberger .05 .15
47 Deek Scott .05 .15
48 Herb Scott .05 .15
49 Jack Sodeman .05 .15
50 Ralph Spithaler, Jr. .05 .15
51 Al Stivenson .05 .15
52 Rod Stockdale .05 .15
53 Rick Strong .05 .15
54 Tom Sturgis .05 .15
55 Mike Sutton .05 .15
56 Dick Swartzlander .05 .15
57 Mel Swartzlander .05 .15
58 Dave Thompson .05 .15
59 Tom Valasek .05 .15
60 Blackie Watt .05 .15
61 Blackie Watt .05 .15
62 Blackie Watt .05 .15
63 Bob Wearing .05 .15
64 Bob Wearing .05 .15
65 Bob Wearing .05 .15
66 Bob Wearing .05 .15
67 Don Wigton .05 .15
68 Ted Wise .05 .15
69 Russ Woolsey .05 .15
70 Helen Martin .05 .15
71 Don Martin .05 .15
NNO Dale Blaney .08 .25
Lou Blaney Promo

1992 Volunteer Racing Lernersville Speedway Series Two

This is the second set of the Lernersville Speedway cards produced by Volunteer Racing. The 72-card set features various sprint car drivers to have raced at Lernersville Speedway. The set includes a card of the 1995 World of Outlaw champion, Dave Blaney.

COMPLETE SET (72) 3.20 8.00
1 Checklist Card 1 .05 .15
2 Checklist Card 2 .05 .15
3 Earl Bauman .05 .15
4 Johnny Beaber .05 .15
5 Rodney Beltz .05 .15
6 Rodney Beltz .05 .15
7 Helene Bertges .05 .15
8 Dave Blaney .50 1.25
9 Lou Blaney .05 .15
10 Lou Blaney .05 .15
11 Lou Blaney .05 .15
12 Tony Burke .05 .15
13 Ben Bussard .05 .15
14 Tim Campbell .05 .15
15 Marty Edwards .05 .15
16 Bob Felmlee .05 .15
17 Rick Ferkel .05 .15
18 Bucky Fleming .05 .15
19 George Frederick .05 .15
20 Lynn Geisler .05 .15
21 Lou Gentile .05 .15
22 Lou Gentile .05 .15
23 Rod George .05 .15
24 Bob Graham .05 .15
25 Mark Harvanek .05 .15
26 Mark Hein .05 .15
27 Gary Henry .05 .15
28 Dave Hess .05 .15
29 Dave Hoffman .05 .15
30 Callen Hull .05 .15
31 Tom Jarrett .05 .15
32 Chuck Kennedy .05 .15
33 Bud Kunkel .05 .15
34 Ed Lynch, Sr. .05 .15
35 Jean Lynch .05 .15
36 Ed Lynch, Jr. .05 .15
37 Don Luffy .05 .15
38 Ed Lynch, Jr. .05 .15
39 Ed Lynch, Sr. .05 .15
40 Lynn Geisler .05 .15
41 Bob Wearing .05 .15
42 Ben Miley .05 .15
43 Art Malies .05 .15
44 Angelo Mariani .05 .15
45 Don Martin .05 .15
46 Jerry Matus .05 .15
47 Brian Muehlman .05 .15
48 Glenn Noland .05 .15
49 Gary Pease .05 .15
50 Dave Pegher .05 .15
51 Barry Peters .05 .15
52 Andy Phillips .05 .15
53 Tom Phillips .05 .15
54 Joe Pitkavish .05 .15
55 Ralph Quarterson .05 .15
56 Ralph Quarterson .05 .15
57 Ralph Quarterson .05 .15
58 Tommy Quarterson .05 .15
59 Craig Rankin .05 .15
60 Donny Roenigk .05 .15
61 Dave Rupp .05 .15
62 Barb Smith .05 .15
Ron Smith
63 Jack Sodeman .05 .15
64 Bill Steinbach .05 .15
65 William VanGuilder .05 .15
66 Chuck Ward .05 .15
67 Blackie Watt .05 .15
68 Blackie Watt .05 .15
69 Blackie Watt .05 .15
70 Bob Wearing .05 .15
71 Bobby Wearing .05 .15
NNO Bucky Ogle Promo .08 .25

1991 Winner's Choice Modifieds

Winner's Choice, Inc. produced this set in 1991 featuring popular Modified car drivers with 14-cards devoted to the late Richie Evans. The black-bordered cards look very similar to 1991 Winner's Choice New England cards and include a color driver or car photo surrounded by a checkered flag frame. The cards were packaged and sold in complete factory set form.

COMPLETE SET (104) 6.00 15.00
1 Cover Card .02 .10
2 Carl Pasteryak .05 .15
3 Carl Pasteryak's Car .02 .10
4 Tony Ferrante Jr. .05 .15
5 Tony Ferrante Jr.'s Car .02 .10
6 Tim Arre .05 .15
7 Tim Arre's Car .02 .10
8 Johnny Bush .05 .15
9 Johnny Bush's Car .02 .10
10 Jan Leaty .05 .15
11 Jan Leaty's Car .02 .10
12 Bob Park .05 .15
13 Bob Park's Car .02 .10
14 Richie Gallup .05 .15
15 Richie Gallup's Car .02 .10
16 Doug Heveron .05 .15
17 Doug Heveron's Car .02 .10
18 Jeff Fuller .10 .30
19 Jeff Fuller's Car .02 .10
20 Charlie Rudolph .05 .15
21 Charlie Rudolph's Car .02 .10
22 Satch Worley .05 .15
23 Satch Worley's Car .02 .10
24 George Brunnhoelzl .05 .15
25 George Brunnhoelzl's Car .02 .10
26 Randy Hedger .05 .15
27 Randy Hedger's Car .02 .10
28 S.J. Evonsion .05 .15
29 S.J. Evonsion's Car .02 .10
30 Mike Ewanitsko .05 .15
31 Mike Ewanitsko's Car .02 .10
32 Wayne Anderson .05 .15
33 Wayne Anderson's Car .02 .10
34 Steve Park 1.50 3.00
35 Checklist Card .02 .10
36 Steve Park's Car .50 1.25
37 Tom Bolles .05 .15
38 Tom Bolles' Car .02 .10
39 Ed Kennedy .05 .15
40 Ed Kennedy's Car .02 .10
41 Jerry Marquis .05 .15
42 Jerry Marquis' Car .02 .10
43 Rick Fuller .10 .30
44 Rick Fuller's Car .02 .10
45 Stan Greger .05 .15
46 Stan Greger's Car .02 .10
47 Dan Avery .05 .15
48 Dan Avery's Car .02 .10
49 Charlie Pasteryak .05 .15
50 Charlie Pasteryak's Car .02 .10
51 Bruce D'Alessandro .05 .15
52 Bruce D'Alessandro's Car .02 .10
53 Jamie Tomaino .05 .15
54 Jamie Tomaino's Car .02 .10
55 Bruce Haley .05 .15
56 Bruce Haley's Car .02 .10
57 Gary Drew .05 .15
58 Gary Drew's Car .02 .10
59 Mike Stefanik .30 .75
60 Mike Stefanik's Car .02 .10
61 Willie Elliott .05 .15
62 Willie Elliott's Car .02 .10
63 Kirby Monteith .05 .15
64 Kirby Monteith's Car .02 .10
65 George Kent .05 .15
66 George Kent's Car .02 .10
67 John Preston .05 .15
68 John Preston's Car .02 .10
69 Reggie Ruggiero .05 .15
70 Checklist Card .02 .10
71 Reggie Ruggiero's Car .02 .10
72 Pete Rondeau .05 .15
73 Pete Rondeau's Car .02 .10
74 Tom Baldwin .10 .30
75 Tom Baldwin's Car .02 .10
76 Greg Tomaino .05 .15
77 Greg Tomaino's Car .02 .10
78 Ted Christopher .05 .15
79 Ted Christopher's Car .02 .10
80 Bo Gunning .05 .15
81 Bo Gunning's Car .02 .10
82 Bob Potter .05 .15
83 Bob Potter's Car .02 .10
84 Tony Hirschman .05 .15
85 Tony Hirschman's Car .02 .10
86 Steve Chowansky .05 .15
87 Steve Chowansky's Car .02 .10
88 Mike Christopher .05 .15
89 Mike Christopher's Car .02 .10
90 Richie Evans .30 .75
91 Richie Evans' Car .10 .30
92 Richie Evans' Car .10 .30
93 Richie Evans w/Car .30 .75
94 Richie Evans' Car .10 .30
95 Richie Evans w/Car .30 .75
96 Richie Evans w/Car .30 .75
97 Richie Evans' Car .10 .30
98 Richie Evans .30 .75
99 Richie Evans' Car .10 .30
100 Richie Evans w/Car .30 .75
101 Richie Evans w/Car .30 .75
102 Richie Evans .30 .75
103 Richie Evans .30 .75
104 Checklist Card .02 .10
NNO Cover Card .02 .10

1987 World of Outlaws

This marked the first year of World of Outlaws factory sets produced by James International Art, Inc. The cards are skip numbered and include two different number one Steve Kinser cards. The set is most famous for including the first card of Jeff Gordon. While the card sets from 1987-90 look very similar, the 1987 set can be differentiated by the driver's name appearing in a blue box on the cardfront.

COMPLETE SET (52) 20.00 50.00
1A Steve Kinser XRC 2.00 5.00
1B Steve Kinser 2.00 5.00
2 Brad Doty .60 1.50
3 Bobby Davis Jr. .15 .40
4 Jac Haudenschild .75 2.00
5 Ron Shuman .15 .40
6 Mark Kinser 1.25 3.00
7 Danny Smith .15 .40
8 Johnny Herrera .15 .40
9 Cris Eash .15 .40
10 Craig Keel .15 .40
11 Rich Bubak .15 .40
12 Sammy Swindell .75 2.00
13 Lee Brewer Jr. .15 .40
14 Bobby Allen .15 .40
15 Jimmy Sills .15 .40
16 Tim Gee .15 .40
17 Dave Blaney 3.00 8.00
18 Greg Wooley .15 .40
19 Tommie Estes Jr. .15 .40
22 Kenny Jacobs .15 .40
23 Keith Kauffman .15 .40
24 Rocky Hodges .15 .40
25 Lealand McSpadden .15 .40
26 Darrell Hanestad .15 .40
27 Rick Ungar .15 .40
28 Rickey Hood .15 .40
29 Tony Armstrong .15 .40
30 Shane Carson .15 .40
31 Steve Siegel .15 .40
32 Terry Gray .15 .40
33 Andy Hillenburg .60 1.50
34 Joey Allen .15 .40
35 Steve Kent .15 .40
36 Brent Kaeding .40 1.00
37 Stevie Smith Jr. .60 1.50
38 Jack Hewitt .40 1.00
39 Terry McCarl .15 .40
41 Steve Butler .15 .40
42 Jeff Swindell .60 1.50
43 Chuck Gurney .15 .40
44 Ted Lee .15 .40
45 Richard Griffin .15 .40
47 Joe Gaerte .15 .40
48 Bobby Fletcher .15 .40
49 Jason McMillen .15 .40
50 Randy Smith .15 .40
51 Tim Green .15 .40
52 Jeff Gordon XRC 25.00 50.00
NNO Cover Card .15 .40
Checklist

1988 World of Outlaws

James International Art again produced a World of Outlaws set in 1988. The cards were released in factory set form only and are skip numbered. The set includes early cards of popular drivers Jeff Gordon and Steve Kinser. Two unnumbered driver cards were part of the set as well as an unnumbered checklist card. While the card sets from 1987-90 look very similar, the 1988 set can be differentiated by the driver's name appearing in a red box on the cardfront.

COMPLETE SET (48) 15.00 40.00
1 Steve Kinser 1.50 4.00
2 Sammy Swindell .60 1.50
3 Bobby Davis Jr. .10 .30
6 Andy Hillenburg .25 .60
7 Cris Eash .10 .30
8 Jac Haudenschild .60 1.50
10 Danny Smith .10 .30
11 Greg Wooley .10 .30
12 Bobby Allen .10 .30
13 Jeff Swindell .25 .60
14 Johnny Herrera .10 .30
16 Jimmy Sills .10 .30
17 Joey Allen .10 .30
18 Lee Brewer Jr. .10 .30
19 Craig Keel .10 .30
20 Tony Armstrong .10 .30
21 Kenny Jacobs .10 .30
22 Tommie Estes Jr. .10 .30
23 Jack Hewitt .25 .60
24 Tim Green .10 .30
25 Rich Bubak .10 .30
26 Joe Gaerte .10 .30
27 Robbie Stanley .10 .30
28 Terry McCarl .10 .30
29 Donnie Kreitz Jr. .10 .30
30 Steve Siegel .10 .30
31 Steve Kent .10 .30
32 Keith Kauffman .10 .30
33 Rick Ungar .10 .30
34 Rocky Hodges .10 .30
35 Tim Gee .10 .30
36 Steve Butler .10 .30
38 Randy Wolfe .10 .30
39 Ron Shuman .10 .30
40 Jim Carr .10 .30
41 Chuck Miller .10 .30
43 Danny Burton .10 .30
45 Gary Dunkle .10 .30
46 Rickey Hood .10 .30
48 Lealand McSpadden .10 .30
50 Chuck Gurney .10 .30
54 Jeff Gordon 12.00 30.00
NNO Checklist .10 .30
NNO Max Dumesny .10 .30
NNO Brent Kaeding .25 .60

1989 World of Outlaws

For the third year, James International Art produced a World of Outlaws set in 1989. The cards were released in factory set form only with a 32-card standard sized set and a 13-card postcard sized set together. Although packaged together, the two sets are often considered independent issues and, therefore, listed separately. The 32-card set is again skip-numbered and includes several unnumbered cards as well. The numbered cards are listed according to 1989 final points standings. While the card sets from 1987-90 look very similar, the 1989 set can be differentiated by the driver's name appearing in a yellow box on the cardfront.

COMPLETE SET (32) 10.00 20.00
1 Bobby Davis Jr. .10 .30
2 Jeff Swindell .40 1.00
3 Cris Eash .10 .30
4 Tim Green .10 .30
5 Joe Gaerte .10 .30
6 Jac Haudenschild .75 2.00
7 Andy Hillenburg .40 1.00
8 Keith Kauffman .10 .30
9 Doug Wolfgang .40 1.00
10 Steve Siegel .10 .30
11 Craig Keel .10 .30
13 Steve Beitler .10 .30
14 Jack Hewitt .25 .60
15 Bobby Allen .10 .30
16 Johnny Herrera .10 .30
17 Dave Blaney 3.00 6.00
19 Kenny Jacobs .10 .30
20 Danny Smith .10 .30
21 Brent Kaeding .10 .30
25 Joey Allen .10 .30
29 Danny Lasoski .25 .60
31 Rickey Hood .10 .30
33 Mark Kinser .60 1.50
34 Steve Kinser 1.50 4.00
35 Frankie Kerr .25 .60
38 Tommie Estes Jr. .10 .30
64 Ron Shuman .10 .30
65 Rich Vogler .10 .30
NNO Checklist .10 .30
NNO Wayne C. Helland .10 .30
NNO Lealand McSpadden .10 .30
NNO Jimmy Sills .10 .30

1989 World of Outlaws Postcards

This 13-card set was included as an insert into 1989 World of Outlaws factory sets. The cards are oversized (3-1/2" by 5") and numbered according to the featured car's number.

COMPLETE SET (13) 4.00 8.00
2 Andy Hillenburg's Car .60 1.50
2S Steve Siegel's Car .25 .60
4 Let's Do It .25 .60
7TW Joe Gaerte's Car .25 .60
8D Doug Wolfgang's Car .60 1.50
10 Bobby Davis Jr.'s Car .50 1.25
11X Jeff Swindell's Car .60 1.50
14 Tim Green's Car .25 .60
17E Cris Eash's Car .25 .60
48 Keith Kauffman's Car .25 .60
77 Pit Action .25 .60
NNO Jim Kingwell .25 .60
NNO Transporter Hauler .25 .60

1990 World of Outlaws

For the fourth year, James International Art produced a World of Outlaws set. The cards were released in factory set form only with a 36-card standard sized set and a 10-card postcard sized set together. Although packaged together; the two sets are often considered independent issues and, therefore, listed separately. The 36-card set is again skip-numbered and includes the first card of popular driver Sammy Swindell. Two unnumbered cards were produced as well. The numbered cards are listed according to 1990 final points standings. While the card sets from 1987-90 look very similar, the 1990 set can be differentiated by the driver's name appearing in an orange box on the cardfront.

COMPLETE SET (36) 7.50 20.00
1 Steve Kinser 1.50 4.00
2 Doug Wolfgang .40 1.00
3 Joe Gaerte .10 .30
4 Bobby Davis Jr. .10 .30
5 Stevie Smith Jr. .40 1.00
6 Cris Eash .10 .30
7 Dave Blaney 1.50 4.00

8 Keith Kauffman .10 .30
9 Steve Beitler .10 .30
10 Sammy Swindell .75 2.00
11 Johnny Herrera .10 .30
13 Bobby Allen .10 .30
14 Jac Haudenschild .75 2.00
16 Danny Lasoski .10 .30
17 Kenny Jacobs .10 .30
18 Jeff Swindell .25 .60
19 Andy Hillenburg .25 .60
20 Danny Smith .10 .30
21 Brent Kaeding .25 .60
22 Jim Carr .10 .30
23 Lee Brewer Jr. .10 .30
28 Jack Hewitt .25 .60
30 Tim Green .10 .30
31 Jimmy Sills .10 .30
34 Rickey Hood .10 .30
40 Mike Peters .10 .30
41 Joey Kuhn .10 .30
42 Steve Smith Sr. .10 .30
43 Craig Keel .10 .30
46 Ed Lynch Jr. .10 .30
49 Rick Ferkel .10 .30
50 Rick Ungar .10 .30
NNO J.W. Hunt .10 .30
NNO Checklist .10 .30

1990 World of Outlaws Postcards

This 13-card set was included as an insert into 1990 World of Outlaws factory sets. The cards are oversized (3-1/2" by 5") and are numbered according to the featured car's number.

COMPLETE SET (10) 4.00 8.00
1 Sammy Swindell 1.25 2.50
1A Bobby Allen .25 .60
7C Dave Blaney's Car 1.00 2.50
8 Doug Wolfgang's Car .60 1.50
10 Bobby Davis Jr.'s Car .25 .60
11 Stevie Kinser's Car 1.00 2.50
23S Frankie Kerr's Car .40 1.00
69 Brent Kaeding's Car .40 1.00
77 Stevie Smith Jr.'s Car .40 1.00
NNO Only the Best Go Four .25 .60

1991 World of Outlaws

James International Art produced the largest World of Outlaws set to date in 1991. The cards were released in 10-card foil pack form with a 114-card regular set and four Most Wanted insert cards. The cards were redesigned from previous issues and contain a yellow border. Production and packaging problems resulted in a reportedly shorter print run for the 1991 set. Cards numbered 112-114 are considered in shorter supply. A Steve Kinser Promo card was released as well and is not considered part of the regular set.

COMPLETE SET (114) 20.00 40.00
WAX BOX 15.00 30.00
1 Checklist .10 .30
2 Steve Kinser 1.50 3.00
3 Mark Kinser .60 1.50
4 Joe Gaerte .10 .30
5 Stevie Smith Jr. .40 1.00
6 Dave Blaney 1.00 2.50
7 Johnny Herrera .10 .30
8 Steve Beitler .10 .30
9 Jim Carr .10 .30
10 Checklist .10 .30
11 Sammy Swindell .75 2.00
12 Gary Cameron II .10 .30
13 Bobby Davis Jr. .10 .30
14 Bobby Allen .10 .30
15 Danny Lasoski .10 .30
16 Doug Wolfgang .40 1.00
17 Greg Hodnett .10 .30
18 Keith Kauffman .10 .30
19 Jac Haudenschild .75 2.00
20 Jeff Swindell .40 1.00
21 Craig Keel .10 .30
22 Gary Wright .10 .30
23 Dale Laakso .10 .30
24 Terry Gray .10 .30
25 Kenny Jacobs .10 .30
26 Aaron Berryhill .10 .30
27 Danny Smith .10 .30
28 Mike Peters .10 .30
29 Cris Eash .10 .30
30 Brent Kaeding .25 .60
31 Ronnie Day .10 .30
32 Donnie Kreitz Jr. .10 .30
33 Frankie Kerr .25 .60
34 Terry McCarl .10 .30
35 Jimmy Sills .10 .30
36 Steve Kent .10 .30
37 Tommie Estes Jr. .10 .30
38 Dan Hamilton .10 .30
39 Darrell Hanestad .10 .30
40 Paul McMahan .10 .30
41 Jason McMillen .10 .30
42 Toni Lutar .10 .30
43 Tim Green .10 .30
44 Greg DeCaires IV .10 .30
45 Ricky Stenhouse .10 .30
46 Bobby Fletcher .10 .30
47 Paul Lotier .10 .30
48 Shane Carson .10 .30
49 Steve Siegel .10 .30
50 Rich Bubak .10 .30
51 Bobby McMahan .10 .30
52 Chuck Miller .10 .30
53 Lealand McSpadden .10 .30
54 Dennis Rodriguez .10 .30
55 Rickie Gaunt .10 .30
56 Lee Brewer Jr. .10 .30
57 Rick Hirst .10 .30
58 Rickey Hood .10 .30
59 Jason Earls .10 .30
60 Ron Shuman .10 .30
61 Checklist .10 .30
62 Ted Johnson .10 .30
63 Dion Appleby .10 .30
64 Tom Basinger .10 .30
65 Dale Blaney .10 .30
66 Billy Boat .10 .30
67 Greg Brown .10 .30
68 Steve Butler .10 .30
69 Dan Dietrich .10 .30
70 Checklist .10 .30
71 Kevin Doty .10 .30
72 Kenny French .10 .30
73 Rick Haas .10 .30
74 Jack Hewitt .25 .60
75 Larry Hillerod .10 .30
76 Rocky Hodges .10 .30
77 Sparky Howard .10 .30
78 Chris Ikard .10 .30
79 Howard Kaeding .10 .30
80 Todd Kane .10 .30
81 Dave Kelly .10 .30
82 Kelly Kinser .10 .30
83 Joey Kuhn .10 .30
84 Nick Losasso .10 .30
85 Ed Lynch Jr. .10 .30
86 Rick Martin .10 .30
87 Fred Rahmer .10 .30
88 Nick Rescino .10 .30
89 Tommy Scott .10 .30
90 Todd Shaffer .10 .30
91 Terry Shepherd .10 .30
92 Steve Smith Sr. .10 .30
93 Steve Stambaugh .10 .30
94 Jason Statler .10 .30
95 Mitch Sue .10 .30
96 Bobby Weaver .10 .30
97 Max Dumesny .10 .30
98 Melinda Dumesny .10 .30
99 Skip Jackson .10 .30
100 Jamie Moyle .10 .30
101 Steve Kinser's Car .75 2.00
102 Mark Kinser's Car .10 .30
103 Joe Gaerte .10 .30
104 Dave Blaney's Car .75 2.00
105 Johnny Herrera's Car .10 .30
106 Steve Beitler's Car .10 .30
107 Sammy Swindell's Car .50 1.25
108 Bobby Davis Jr.'s Car .10 .30
109 Greg Hodnett's Car .10 .30
110 Gary Wright's Car .10 .30
111 Terry Gray's Car .10 .30
112 Aaron Berryhill's Car SP 1.50 3.00
113 Frankie Kerr's Car SP 1.50 3.00
114 Jimmy Sills' Car SP 1.25 2.50
P1 Steve Kinser Promo 2.00 5.00

1991 World of Outlaws Most Wanted

This six-card Most Wanted set was issued in both foil packs of 1991 World of Outlaws and in complete set form. The four driver cards were released through packs first and then re-issued as a complete set with the cover and checklist cards. The card design is very similar to other Most Wanted sets, but can be distinguished by the border color of black.

COMPLETE SET (6) 5.00 10.00
1 Stevie Smith Jr. .75 2.00
2 Danny Lasoski 1.50 3.00
3 Jimmy Sills .60 1.50
4 Bobby Davis Jr. .75 2.00
NNO Checklist .30 .75
NNO Cover Card .30 .75

1992 World of Outlaws Most Wanted

James International Art produced only 12-card Most Wanted set in 1992. The card design is very similar to other Most Wanted sets, but can be distinguished by the border color of Maroon. The cover card describes the set as Most Wanted series two.

COMPLETE SET (12) 5.00 10.00
2 Johnny Herrera .30 .75
3 Steve Beitler .30 .75
4 Jack Hewitt .30 .75
5 Sammy Swindell .75 2.00
6 Jim Carr .30 .75
7 Danny Smith .30 .75
8 Keith Kauffman .30 .75
9 Dale Blaney .30 .75
10 Andy Hillenburg .30 .75
NNO Cover Card .25 .60
NNO Checklist .25 .60

1993 World of Outlaws Most Wanted

James International Art produced only a 12-card Most Wanted set in 1993. The card design is very similar to other Most Wanted sets, but can be distinguished by the border color of blue. The cover card describes the set as Most Wanted series three.

COMPLETE SET (12) 5.00 10.00
1 Dave Blaney 1.00 2.50
2 Kenny Jacobs .50 1.25
3 Craig Keel .30 .75
4 Joe Gaerte .30 .75
5 Ed Lynch Jr. .30 .75
6 Tommie Estes Jr. .30 .75
7 Cris Eash .30 .75
8 Garry Lee Maier .30 .75
9 Gary Cameron II .30 .75
10 Kevin Huntley .30 .75
NNO Cover Card .25 .60
NNO Checklist .25 .60

1994 World of Outlaws

After a two year hiatus, James International once again produced a regular issue World of Outlaws set in 1994, as well as a Most Wanted set. The cards were re-designed and include 50 to the set released in a factory set box.

COMPLETE SET (50) 10.00 20.00
1 Checklist .10 .30
2 Steve Kinser 1.00 2.50
3 Dave Blaney .75 2.00
4 Stevie Smith Jr. .40 1.00
5 Kenny Jacobs .10 .30
6 Andy Hillenburg .25 .60
7 Jac Haudenschild .60 1.50
8 Greg Hodnett .25 .60
9 Johnny Herrera .10 .30
10 Richard Day .10 .30
11 Steve Beitler .10 .30
12 Craig Keel .10 .30
13 Jeff Swindell .25 .60
14 Mark Kinser .40 1.00
15 Aaron Berryhill .10 .30
16 Joe Gaerte .10 .30
17 Danny Lasoski .25 .60
18 Terry McCarl .10 .30
19 Bobby Davis Jr. .10 .30
20 Ed Lynch Jr. .10 .30
21 Bobby Allen .10 .30
22 Donnie Kreitz Jr. .10 .30
23 Keith Kauffman .10 .30
24 Danny Smith .10 .30
25 Gary Wright .10 .30
26 Johnny Mackison Jr. .10 .30
27 Jim Carr .10 .30
28 Randy Smith .10 .30
29 Garry Lee Maier .10 .30
30 Steve Kent .10 .30
31 Max Dumesny .10 .30
32 Jimmy Sills .10 .30
33 Gary Cameron II .10 .30
34 Kevin Huntley .10 .30
35 Rocky Hodges .10 .30
36 Brent Kaeding .25 .60
37 Frankie Kerr .25 .60
38 Tim Green .10 .30
39 Fred Rahmer .25 .60
40 Steve Smith Sr. .25 .60
41 Brad Noffsinger .10 .30
42 Randy Hannagan .10 .30
43 Garry Rush .10 .30
44 Jason McMillen .10 .30
45 Todd Kane .10 .30
46 Dale Blaney .10 .30
47 Rusty McClure .10 .30
48 Kevin Pylant .10 .30
49 Rod Henderson .10 .30
50 Ron Shuman .10 .30

1994 World of Outlaws Most Wanted

James International Art this 12-card Most Wanted set in 1994. The card design is very similar to other Most Wanted sets, but can be distinguished by the border color of brown. The cover card describes the set as Most Wanted series four and includes an offer to purchase complete sets or uncut sheets from previous year's sets.

COMPLETE SET (12) 5.00 10.00
1 Steve Kinser 1.25 2.50
2 Greg Hodnett .30 .75
3 Mark Kinser .75 1.50
4 Frankie Kerr .40 1.00
5 Aaron Berryhill .30 .75
6 Terry McCarl .30 .75
7 Jeff Swindell .40 1.00
8 Brent Kaeding .40 1.00
9 Lance Dewease .30 .75
10 Steve Kent .30 .75
NNO Cover Card .25 .60
NNO Checklist .25 .60

2003 McFarlane NASCAR Series 1

McFarlane's debut NASCAR was issued in late September/early November 2003. The set features six drives with several different variations. Key pieces include Dale Earnhardt Senior, Junior and Jeff Gordon. Cases were packaged with 12 figures in each case. Also included with the set, but not in the complete set price is a special limited edition #'d to 56,376 Dale Earnhardt Jr. piece that was given away at Talladega Raceway

NNO D.Earnhardt R Blk Hat 12.50 25.00
NNO D.Earnhardt R Blk Hat w/Glass 15.00 30.00
NNO D.Earnhardt H Red Hat 12.50 25.00
NNO Earnhardt Jr. R Red/Blk Suit w/Glass 12.50 25.00
NNO Earnhardt Jr. R Org Goss Suit 20.00 40.00
NNO Earnhardt Jr. H Red/Blk Suit 15.00 30.00
NNO Earnhardt Jr. H Red/Blk Suit w/Glass 12.50 25.00
NNO Earnhardt Jr. Talladega Trib w/Glass 20.00 40.00
NNO Earnhardt Jr. Talladega Trib w/o Glass 50.00 100.00
NNO J.Gordon R w/o Hat 10.00 20.00
NNO J.Gordon R w/Hat 10.00 20.00
NNO J.Gordon H w/o Hat 10.00 20.00
NNO J.Gordon H w/Hat and Glass 10.00 20.00
NNO R.Newman R Gatorade w/Hat 7.50 15.00
NNO R.Newman R Gatorade w/o Hat 7.50 15.00
NNO R.Newman H Champagne w/Hat 7.50 15.00
NNO R.Newman H Champagne w/o Hat 12.50 25.00
NNO T.Stewart R w/o Hat 7.50 15.00
NNO T.Stewart R w/Hat and Glass 10.00 20.00
NNO T.Stewart H Trophy w/Hat 10.00 20.00
NNO T.Stewart H Trophy w/o Hat 12.50 25.00
NNO R.Wallace R Rusty Suit Rusty Hat 10.00 20.00
NNO R.Wallace R Rusty Suit Elvis Hat 12.50 25.00
NNO R.Wallace H Miller Lite Suit 10.00 20.00
NNO R.Wallace H Miller Lite Suit w/Glass 10.00 20.00

2004 McFarlane NASCAR Series 2

COMMON PIECE 7.50 15.00
NNO Bobby Labonte H Shrek without Trophy 7.50 15.00
NNO Bobby Labonte R Interstate Batteries with Trophy 7.50 15.00
NNO Dale Earnhardt H Coke 10.00 20.00
NNO D.Earnhardt Coke w/glass VAR 12.50 25.00
NNO Dale Earnhardt Jr. H Oreo w/o Hat and Glasses 10.00 20.00
NNO Dale Earnhardt Jr. H Oreo with Hat and Glasses 10.00 20.00
NNO Dale Earnhardt Jr. R Red w/o Hat w/o Glasses 7.50 15.00
NNO Dale Earnhardt Jr. R Red with Hat 10.00 20.00
NNO Dale Earnhardt Jr. R Red with Hat and Glasses 15.00 30.00
NNO Dale Earnhardt R Delco 10.00 20.00
NNO D.Earnhardt Delco w/glass VAR 10.00 20.00
NNO Jeff Gordon H Pepsi with Hat 12.50 25.00
NNO Jeff Gordon H Pepsi without Hat 12.50 25.00
NNO Jeff Gordon R DuPont with Hat 10.00 20.00
NNO Jeff Gordon R DuPont with Hat and Glasses 10.00 20.00
NNO Jimmie Johnson FP R Lowes without Glasses Photo 7.50 15.00
NNO Jimmie Johnson H Lowes 7.50 15.00
NNO J.Johnson Lowes w/glass VAR 7.50 15.00
NNO Richard Petty FP R 12.50 25.00
NNO Richard Petty H Yankees 12.50 25.00

2004 McFarlane NASCAR Dale Earnhardt Deluxe Boxed Set

10 Dale Earnhardt 12.50 30.00

2004 McFarlane NASCAR Shrek 2 Boxed Sets

10 B.Labonte w/Shrek 12.50 25.00
20 T.Stewart w/Donkey 12.50 25.00

2005 McFarlane NASCAR Series 3

COMMON PIECE 7.50 15.00
NNO Dale Earnhardt Jr. H 7.50 15.00
NNO Dale Earnhardt Jr. R 10.00 20.00
NNO Dale Jarrett H A.Palmer 15.00 30.00
NNO Dale Jarrett R 7.50 15.00
NNO Dale Jarrett R Glasses 10.00 20.00
NNO Darrell Waltrip H Stooges 15.00 30.00
NNO Darrell Waltrip R 7.50 15.00
NNO Darrell Waltrip R Glasses 25.00 50.00
NNO Jamie McMurray H Retro 10.00 20.00
NNO Jamie McMurray R FP 7.50 15.00
NNO Jamie McMurray R Glasses 10.00 20.00
NNO John Force H XII Red 12.50 25.00
NNO J.Force Red w/Glass VAR 15.00 30.00
NNO John Force R 7.50 15.00
NNO John Force R Glasses 10.00 20.00
NNO Kevin Harvick H Realtree 10.00 20.00
NNO K.Harvick RT w/Glass VAR 10.00 20.00
NNO Kevin Harvick R 10.00 20.00
NNO Kevin Harvick R Glasses 10.00 20.00
NNO Tony Stewart H Kid Rock with Glasses 12.50 25.00
NNO Tony Stewart R 7.50 15.00
NNO Tony Stewart R Glasses 10.00 20.00

2005 McFarlane NASCAR Series 4

COMMON PIECE 10.00 20.00
20 Dale Earnhardt Jr. R Daytona 10.00 20.00
21 D.Earnhardt Jr. R Day Blk Hat 12.50 25.00
25 Dale Earnhardt Jr. H Daytona 10.00 20.00
40 Jeff Gordon R 10.00 20.00
41 Jeff Gordon R Glasses 12.50 25.00
45 Jeff Gordon H Pepsi 12.50 25.00
70 Jimmie Johnson R Glasses 10.00 20.00
72 Jimmie Johnson R w/o Glasses 10.00 20.00
75 Jimmie Johnson H 12.50 25.00
80 Kasey Kahne H 10.00 20.00
85 Kasey Kahne R FP 12.50 25.00
100 Ryan Newman R Hat 10.00 20.00
103 Ryan Newman R w/o Hat 10.00 20.00
105 Ryan Newman H Hat 12.50 25.00
107 Ryan Newman H w/o Hat 12.50 25.00
110 Elliott Sadler R Glasses 10.00 20.00
112 Elliott Sadler R w/o Glasses 10.00 20.00
115 Elliott Sadler H Blk&Wht 12.50 25.00
130 Rusty Wallace R 10.00 20.00
131 Rusty Wallace R Hat Glasses 10.00 25.00
135 Rusty Wallace H Miller Lite 12.50 25.00

2005 McFarlane NASCAR Series 5

COMMON PIECE 10.00 20.00
10 Davey Allison 10.00 20.00
30 John Force 15.00 30.00
40 Kevin Harvick Reese's 10.00 20.00
50 Kevin Harvick Goodwrench 12.50 25.00
70 Dale Jarrett 10.00 20.00
90 Tony Stewart 10.00 20.00
110 Martin Truex Jr. FP 10.00 20.00

2005 McFarlane NASCAR Series 6

COMMON PIECE 10.00 20.00
NNO Adam Petty FP 12.50 25.00
NNO Bill Elliott 10.00 20.00
NNO Dale Earnhardt Jr. Oreo Ritz 12.50 25.00
NNO D.Earnhardt Jr. No Glass VAR 12.50 25.00
NNO Jeff Gordon 10.00 20.00
NNO Jimmie Johnson 10.00 20.00
NNO J.Johnson No Glass VAR 12.50 25.00
NNO Neil Bonnett FP 10.00 20.00
NNO Rusty Wallace 10.00 20.00

2005 McFarlane NASCAR 12-Inch Figures Series 1

NNO Jeff Gordon 20.00 40.00
NNO Kasey Kahne 20.00 40.00

2005 McFarlane NASCAR 3-Inch Series 1

20 Jeff Gordon 5.00 10.00
40 Dale Jarrett 4.00 8.00
60 Jimmie Johnson 4.00 8.00
80 Bobby Labonte 4.00 8.00
100 Richard Petty 5.00 10.00
120 Tony Stewart 4.00 8.00
140 Rusty Wallace 4.00 8.00

1997 SLU Racing Winner's Circle

The first set of NASCAR figures included two versions of Earnhardt and Gordon, as well as five other popular drivers.

1 Ward Burton 4.00 10.00
2A Dale Earnhardt Black Glasses 8.00 20.00
2B Dale Earnhardt Gold Glasses 8.00 20.00
3 John Force 4.00 10.00
4A Jeff Gordon w o Pepsi 6.00 15.00
4B Jeff Gordon w Pepsi 4.00 10.00
5 Dale Jarrett 4.00 10.00
6 Bobby Labonte 4.00 10.00
7 Darrell Waltrip 4.00 10.00

1998 SLU Racing Winner's Circle

Produced for the second year by the Cincinnati based Kenner Company, and distributed in one assortment, this 15-piece set features popular drivers from the Racing circuit. Five of the drivers have two different pieces, one in their regular uniform and one in a special uniform. The pieces are not numbered and listed below in alphabetical order. Prices below are for mint, in package pieces.

1 Ward Burton 3.00 8.00
2A Dale Earnhardt '97 uni 6.00 15.00
2B Dale Earnhardt '98 uni 6.00 15.00
3A John Force 3.00 8.00
3B John Force Elvis 5.00 12.00
4A Jeff Gordon 5.00 12.00
4B Jeff Gordon JP 5.00 12.00
5 Kenny Irwin FP 4.00 10.00
6 Dale Jarrett 3.00 8.00
7A Bobby Labonte 3.00 8.00
7B Bobby Labonte Small Soldiers 4.00 10.00
8 Mike Skinner FP 3.00 8.00
9 Kenny Wallace FP 3.00 8.00
12A Rusty Wallace FP 4.00 10.00
12B Rusty Wallace FP Elvis 4.00 10.00

1999 SLU Racing Winner's Circle

Although eleven figurines are listed under this set, only five different drivers are featured, due to the multiple Earnhardt, Earnhardt Jr., and Gordon pieces.

10 Dale Earnhardt Coca Cola 6.00 15.00
11 Dale Earnhardt GM 6.00 15.00
12 Dale Earnhardt Jr. Coca Cola 6.00 15.00
13 Dale Earnhardt Jr. AC Delco 6.00 15.00
20 Jeff Gordon Dupont '98 4.00 10.00
21 Jeff Gordon Pepsi 4.00 10.00
22 Jeff Gordon Dupont '99 4.00 10.00
23 Jeff Gordon Superman Wal. 4.00 10.00
24 Jeff Gordon Chroma Boscov 6.00 15.00
30 Dale Jarrett 3.00 8.00
40 Bobby Labonte 3.00 8.00

1999 SLU Racing Winner's Circle 12-inch Figures

These popular 12-inch dolls featured three of the top racers of the time: Earnhardt, Gordon, and Wallace.

1 Dale Earnhardt 10.00 25.00
2 Jeff Gordon 10.00 25.00
3 Rusty Wallace 10.00 25.00

2000 SLU Racing Winner's Circle

A small set in 2000, Winner's Circle added the rookie piece of Tony Stewart to the Racing lineup.

10 Dale Earnhardt 10.00 25.00
20 Jeff Gordon 8.00 20.00
30 Jeff Burton 6.00 15.00
40 Tony Stewart FP 8.00 20.00

2000 SLU Racing Winner's Circle 12-inch Figures

Patterned after 1999's 12-inch dolls, this set featured new versions of Earnhardt and Gordon, as well as a new Earnhardt, Jr. figure.

10 Dale Earnhardt 15.00 40.00
20 Dale Earnhardt Jr. 12.00 30.00
30 Jeff Gordon 10.00 25.00

2004 SportCoins

3 Dale Earnhardt 3 b-RCR 35th Anniversary/1003 8.00 20.00
8 Dale Earnhardt Jr 8 b-DEI/4008 8.00 20.00
18 Bobby Labonte 2000 Champion b-Joe Gibbs Racing/518 5.00 12.00
20 Tony Stewart 2002 Champion b-Joe Gibbs Racing/520 6.00 15.00
24 Jeff Gordon Flames 24 b-HMS 20th Anniversary/2024 8.00 20.00
24 Jeff Gordon Flames 24 b-Brickyard 400 Winner/2024 8.00 20.00
29 Kevin Harvick Goodwrench 29 b-RCR 35th Anniversary/529 6.00 15.00
30 Johnny Sauter AOL 30 b-RCR 35th Anniversary/50 8.00 20.00
31 Robby Gordon Cingular 31 b-Gas On Flames/531 6.00 15.00
31 Robby Gordon Cingular 31 b-RCR 35th Anniversary/531 5.00 12.00
43 Richard Petty The King b-Accomplishments/500 8.00 20.00
48 Jimmie Johnson 48 b-HMS 20th Anniversary/548 6.00 15.00
NNO Petty Enterprises/500 6.00 15.00
NNO Coca Cola 600 20th Anniversary/825 5.00 12.00

2005 SportCoins

2 Rusty Wallace Miller Lite Last Call b-Penske/1002 6.00 15.00
3 Dale Earnhardt 3 b-DEI/1503 8.00 20.00
3 Dale Earnhardt 1998 Daytona b-3/2003 8.00 20.00
5 Kyle Busch Kellogg's b-HMS/505 5.00 12.00
6 Mark Martin 6 b-Roush/506 6.00 15.00
8 Dale Earnhardt Jr. 8 b-DEI/10,008 8.00 20.00
8 Dale Earnhardt 2004 Daytona b-8/2008 8.00 20.00
8 Martin Truex Jr. 8 b-Chance 2/508 6.00 15.00
9 Kasey Kahne 9 b-Evernham/1009 6.00 15.00
12 Ryan Newman 12 b-Penske/512 5.00 12.00
15 Michael Waltrip 15 b-DEI/515 5.00 12.00
16 Greg Biffle 16 b-Roush/516 5.00 12.00
17 Matt Kenseth DeWalt 17 b-Roush/517 6.00 15.00
18 Bobby Labonte Interstate Batteries 18 b-Joe Gibbs Racing/1518 5.00 12.00
19 Jeremy Mayfield 19 b-Evernham/519 5.00 12.00
20 Tony Stewart Home Depot 20 b-JGR/1520 6.00 15.00
21 Ricky Rudd 21 b-Wood Brothers/521 5.00 12.00
24 Jeff Gordon DuPont Flames 24 b-HMS/5024 8.00 20.00
24 Jeff Gordon 2005 Daytona Winner b-24 Flames/5024 8.00 20.00
24 Jeff Gordon Jeff Gordon Network b-24 Flames Fan Club Exclusive 5.00 12.00
25 Brian Vickers GMAC 25 b-HMS/525 5.00 12.00
29 Kevin Harvick Goodwrench b-RCR/1029 6.00 15.00
31 Jeff Burton Cingular 31 b-RCR/531 5.00 12.00
43 Richard Petty The King b-Accomplishments Gold/543 8.00 20.00
48 Jimmie Johnson Lowe's 48 b-HMS/1048 8.00 20.00
97 Kurt Busch Sharpie 97 b-Roush/597 5.00 12.00
99 Carl Edwards 99 b-Roush/599 8.00 20.00
01 Joe Nemechek Army b-MB2 5.00 12.00
07 Dave Blaney Jack Daniel's b-RCR/1007 8.00 20.00

2000-01 Action Racing Collectables Ceramic 1:12

3 Dale Earnhardt 200.00 400.00
Goodwrench
1997 Monte Carlo Crash/5004 2001
3 Dale Earnhardt 175.00 300.00
Goodwrench Taz 2000
24 Jeff Gordon 250.00 500.00
DuPont

2003 Action Road Racing 1:12

3 Dale Earnhardt 400.00 650.00
Dale Earnhardt Jr.
Andy Pilgrim
Kelly Collins
2001 C5-R Corvette RCCA/100

1990-03 Action Racing Collectables Pit Wagon Banks 1:16

These 1:16 scale replicas of Pit Wagons were produced by Action Racing Collectibles. ARC began producing them in 1994 and each is a coin bank.

2 Rusty Wallace 30.00 60.00
Ford Motorsports
2 Rusty Wallace 25.00 60.00
Miller Genuine Draft/2508 1995
2 Rusty Wallace 25.00 60.00
Miller Lite 1997
2 Rusty Wallace 25.00 60.00
Miller Lite
in plastic case/3500 1998
3 Dale Earnhardt 50.00 120.00
Goodwrench/3000 1995
3 Dale Earnhardt 50.00 100.00
Goodwrench
1994 Champ/5000 19955
3 Dale Earnhardt 50.00 120.00
Goodwrench RCCA/2500 1996
3 Dale Earnhardt 60.00 120.00
Goodwrench 7-Time Champion
3 Dale Earnhardt 75.00 175.00
Goodwrench Plus Bass Pro 1998
3 Dale Earnhardt 75.00 150.00
Goodwrench 1999
3 Dale Earnhardt 50.00 120.00
Goodwrench
25th Anniversary/2508 1999
3 Dale Earnhardt 80.00 175.00
Goodwrench Taz No Bull
3 Dale Earnhardt 100.00 200.00
Goodwrench Peter Max paint 2000
3 Dale Earnhardt 50.00 120.00
Wrangler/2508 1999
3 Dale Earnhardt 75.00 150.00
Wheaties/3756 1997
3 Dale Earnhardt Jr. 40.00 80.00
AC Delco Superman/4308 1999
11 Bill Elliott 30.00 80.00
Budweiser/2508 1994
16 Ted Musgrave 10.00 20.00
Family Channel 1994
18 Dale Jarrett 15.00 30.00
Interstate Batteries
24 Jeff Gordon 60.00 150.00
DuPont 1993 ROY 1994
24 Jeff Gordon 60.00 120.00
DuPont 1996 Monte Carlo/2500
24 Jeff Gordon 35.00 75.00
DuPont Superman/3504 1999
24 Jeff Gordon 50.00 120.00
Jurassic Park 3 1997
24 Jeff Gordon 25.00 50.00
Pepsi/2508 1999
28 Davey Allison 30.00 60.00
Havoline RCCA 1990
28 Davey Allison 30.00 80.00
Havoline Mac Tools RCCA 1993
28 Ernie Irvan 20.00 40.00
Havoline
28 Ernie Irvan 20.00 40.00
Mac Tools
28 Kenny Irwin 40.00 60.00
Havoline Joker
29 Kevin Harvick 30.00 60.00
Snap-On/7494 2002
30 Michael Waltrip 10.00 25.00
Pennzoil/2508 1994
41 Joe Nemechek 15.00 30.00
Meineke/2508 1994
42 Kyle Petty 15.00 30.00
Mello Yello
51 Neil Bonnett 20.00 50.00
Country Time/5216 1994
88 Dale Jarrett 35.00 60.00
Quality Care Batman
94 Bill Elliott 15.00 40.00
Mac Tonight 1997
94 Bill Elliott 20.00 35.00
McDonald's/2508 1995
NNO Dale Earnhardt 20.00 35.00
Legacy/3333 2003

1998 Action Racing Collectables 1:18

3 Dale Earnhardt 125.00 250.00
Goodwrench Plus Bass Pro
3 Dale Earnhardt 75.00 150.00
Goodwrench Plus Daytona/4008
3 Dale Earnhardt 200.00 300.00
Goodwrench Silver
1995 Monte Carlo/7000
3 Dale Earnhardt 100.00 200.00
Wheaties
1997 Monte Carlo/7008
24 Jeff Gordon 125.00 225.00
DuPont Chromalusion
28 Kenny Irwin 50.00 100.00
Joker
31 Dale Earnhardt Jr. 50.00 120.00
Sikkens Blue
1997 Monte Carlo/7596
31 Dale Earnhardt Jr. 50.00 120.00
Wrangler 1997 Monte Carlo/7596
88 Dale Jarrett 60.00 100.00
Batman

1999 Action Racing Collectables 1:18

These 1:18 scale cars were distributed by Action through their distributor network.

1 Dale Earnhardt Jr. 70.00 100.00
Coke
1 Steve Park 25.00 60.00
Pennzoil/2508
1 Steve Park 30.00 75.00
Pennzoil Shark
2 Ron Fellows 30.00 80.00
John Paul Jr.
hris Kneifel
Goodwrench C5-R Corvette
2 Rusty Wallace 30.00 80.00
Miller Lite/2508
2 Rusty Wallace 30.00 80.00
Miller Lite Harley/3504
3 Dale Earnhardt 75.00 150.00
Coke
3 Dale Earnhardt 75.00 150.00
Goodwrench/4008
3 Dale Earnhardt 100.00 200.00
Goodwrench Sign/3000
3 Dale Earnhardt 175.00 300.00
Goodwrench Sign
Last Lap/2508
3 Dale Earnhardt 75.00 150.00
Wrangler
3 Dale Earnhardt Jr. 75.00 150.00
AC Delco
3 Dale Earnhardt Jr. 75.00 150.00
AC Delco Superman
5 Terry Labonte 25.00 60.00
K-Sentials/2508
5 Terry Labonte 30.00 60.00
Kellogg's NASCAR Racers/2508
8 Dale Earnhardt Jr. 60.00 120.00
Budweiser 2000/2508
10 Ricky Rudd 30.00 60.00
Tide Kid's
18 Bobby Labonte 30.00 80.00
Interstate Batteries
NASCAR Racers/2508
20 Tony Stewart 60.00 120.00
Home Depot/5508
20 Tony Stewart 25.00 60.00
Home Depot Habitat/10,008
24 Jeff Gordon 60.00 125.00
DuPont
24 Jeff Gordon 75.00 150.00
DuPont Superman/3000
24 Jeff Gordon 75.00 150.00
DuPont NASCAR Racers
24 Jeff Gordon 50.00 100.00
Pepsi
24 Jeff Gordon 30.00 80.00
Pepsi Star Wars/3000
27 Casey Atwood 25.00 60.00
Castrol
31 Dale Earnhardt Jr. 50.00 100.00
Mom 'N' Pop's
1996 Monte Carlo/2508
31 Dale Earnhardt Jr. 70.00 120.00
Sikkens White 1997 Monte Carlo
36 Ernie Irvan 20.00 50.00
M&M's
36 Ernie Irvan 20.00 50.00
M&M's Countdown
36 Ernie Irvan 25.00 60.00
M&M's Millennium
40 Sterling Marlin 40.00 100.00
Coors Lite Brooks & Dunn
55 Kenny Wallace 25.00 60.00
Square D NASCAR Racers/2508
88 Dale Jarrett 30.00 60.00
Quality Care

2000 Action Racing Collectables 1:18

These 1:18 scale cars were distributed by Action through their distributor network.

3 Dale Earnhardt 150.00 250.00
Goodwrench
3 Dale Earnhardt 250.00 400.00
Goodwrench Peter Max/3000
3 Dale Earnhardt 150.00 250.00
Goodwrench Taz No Bull
3 Ron Fellows 100.00 150.00
Justan Bell
Cris Kneifel
Goodwrench C5-R Corvette
4 Franck Freon 100.00 150.00
Andy Pilgrim
Kelly Collins
Goodwrench C5-R Corvette
8 Dale Earnhardt Jr. 75.00 150.00
Bud/3504
8 Dale Earnhardt Jr. 80.00 125.00
Budweiser Olympic
18 Bobby Labonte 30.00 60.00
Interstate Batteries All Star Game
20 Tony Stewart 50.00 100.00
Home Depot
20 Tony Stewart 30.00 60.00
Home Depot ROY/2508
24 Jeff Gordon 50.00 100.00
DuPont/3504
24 Jeff Gordon 60.00 120.00
DuPont Millennium/3504
24 Jeff Gordon 75.00 125.00
DuPont Peanuts
24 Jeff Gordon 75.00 125.00
DuPont Winston
24 Jeff Gordon 50.00 100.00
Pepsi
25 Jerry Nadeau 25.00 50.00
Holigan Coast Guard/2004
28 Ricky Rudd 30.00 60.00
Havoline Marines/2000
36 Ken Schrader 30.00 60.00
M&M's Keep Back/2004
66 Darrell Waltrip 30.00 80.00
Big K Route 66 Flames
88 Dale Jarrett 30.00 60.00
Quality Care/2004
88 Dale Jarrett 35.00 70.00
Quality Care Air Force
94 Bill Elliott 30.00 60.00
McDonald's/2004
94 Bill Elliott 30.00 60.00
McDonald's 25th Anniversary

2001 Action Racing Collectables 1:18

2 Ron Fellows 45.00 100.00
Johnny O'Connell
Franck Freon
Chris Kneifel
C5-R Corvette/8748
2 Ron Fellows 70.00 150.00
Johnny O'Connell
Franck Freon
Chris Kneifel
C5-R Corvette raced version/1008
3 Dale Earnhardt 50.00 100.00
Goodwrench w
sonic decal/20,004
3 Dale Earnhardt 175.00 300.00
Goodwrench Oreo Daytona/3000
3 Dale Earnhardt 100.00 200.00
Dale Earnhardt Jr
Andy Pilgrim
Kelly Collins
C5-R Corvette/16,752
3 Dale Earnhardt 125.00 250.00
Dale Earnhardt Jr
Andy Pilgrim
Kelly Collins
C5-R Corvette raced version/1008
3 Dale Earnhardt 175.00 300.00
Dale Earnhardt Jr
Andy Pilgrim
Kelly Collins
C5-R Corvette 24Kt.Gold/2000
3 Dale Earnhardt 75.00 150.00
Dale Earnhardt Jr
Andy Pilgrim
Kelly Collins
C5-R Corvette Color Chrome/7500
3 Dale Earnhardt 100.00 200.00
Dale Earnhardt Jr
Andy Pilgrim
Kelly Collins
C5-R Corvette Color Chrome
Raced Version/7500
3 Dale Earnhardt 150.00 250.00
Dale Earnhardt Jr
Andy Pilgrim
Kelly Collins
C5-R Corvette Platinum/2508
9 Bill Elliott 35.00 75.00
Dodge Spiderman
18 Bobby Labonte 40.00 80.00
Interstate Batteries Cal Ripken
18 Bobby Labonte 30.00 60.00
Interstate Batteries Coke Bear/2508
20 Tony Stewart 40.00 80.00
Home Depot Coke Bear/2504
24 Jeff Gordon 75.00 150.00
DuPont Flames/2508
29 Kevin Harvick 50.00 120.00
Goodwrench/6000
29 Kevin Harvick 60.00 120.00
Goodwrench Taz/3504
88 Dale Jarrett 40.00 80.00
UPS Flames/3000

2002 Action Racing Collectables 1:18

3 Dale Earnhardt 75.00 135.00
Goodwrench Oreo/2508
3 Dale Earnhardt Jr. 70.00 120.00
Oreo Color Chrome/2508
3 Dale Earnhardt Jr. 60.00 100.00
Nilla Wafers/3504
3 Dale Earnhardt Jr. 50.00 100.00
Oreo/4008
8 Dale Earnhardt Jr. 60.00 100.00
Bud/3504
8 Dale Earnhardt Jr. 75.00 135.00
Bud Color Chrome/2508
8 Dale Earnhardt Jr. 45.00 80.00
Bud All-Star/4512
8 Dale Earnhardt Jr. 45.00 80.00
Looney Tunes/3384
24 Jeff Gordon 45.00 80.00
DuPont Flames/4008
24 Jeff Gordon 45.00 80.00
DuPont Bugs Bunny/2472
24 Jeff Gordon 45.00 80.00
DuPont 200th Ann./3504
29 Kevin Harvick 40.00 80.00
Goodwrench/4008
29 Kevin Harvick 40.00 80.00
Goodwrench ET/3000
29 Kevin Harvick 45.00 80.00
Goodwrench Taz/1008
40 Sterling Marlin 60.00 100.00
Coors Light/1800
48 Jimmie Johnson 40.00 80.00
Lowe's Sylvester&Tweety/2268
NNO Dale Earnhardt 60.00 100.00
Monte Carlo SS/11,952

2002 Action/RCCA 1:18

8 Dale Earnhardt Jr. 60.00 100.00
Bud MLB All-Star/504
8 Dale Earnhardt Jr. 60.00 100.00
Looney Tunes/504
24 Jeff Gordon 45.00 80.00
DuPont Bugs Bunny/504
48 Jimmie Johnson 40.00 80.00
Lowe's Sylvester &Tweety/504
NNO Dale Earnhardt 125.00 250.00
Monte Carlo SS/408
NNO Dale Earnhardt 125.00 250.00
Monte Carlo SS Color Chrome/1008

2003 Action Racing Collectables 1:18

3 Dale Earnhardt 50.00 100.00
Foundation/3876
8 Dale Earnhardt Jr. 60.00 100.00
Bud/3832
8 Dale Earnhardt Jr. 60.00 100.00
Bud All-Star Game/3324
8 Dale Earnhardt Jr. 50.00 90.00
Bud StainD/2748
8 Dale Earnhardt Jr. 60.00 100.00
Dirty Mo Posse/4002
8 Dale Earnhardt Jr. 60.00 100.00
E Concert/3024
8 Dale Earnhardt Jr. 50.00 100.00
Oreo Ritz/504
8 Tony Stewart 50.00 80.00
3 Doors Down/1836
20 Tony Stewart 50.00 80.00
Home Depot/2532
24 Jeff Gordon 50.00 80.00
DuPont Flames/2094
24 Jeff Gordon 50.00 80.00
Pepsi Billion $/1996
24 Jeff Gordon 50.00 80.00
DuPont Wright Brothers/1804
48 Jimmie Johnson 40.00 80.00
Lowe's Power of Pride/1866
NNO Jeff Gordon 75.00 150.00
Monte Carlo SS/4842

2003 Action/RCCA 1:18

8 Dale Earnhardt Jr. 50.00 80.00
Bud/600

2004 Action Road Racing 1:18

2 Dale Earnhardt Jr. 40.00 65.00
Tony Stewart
Andy Wallace
Citgo/7188
2 Dale Earnhardt Jr. 50.00 75.00
Tony Stewart
Andy Wallace
Citgo Brushed Metal/300
2 Dale Earnhardt Jr. 40.00 65.00
Tony Stewart
Andy Wallace
Citgo GM Dealers/516
2 Dale Earnhardt Jr. 50.00 75.00
Tony Stewart
Andy Wallace
Citgo Raced w
tire/6684
4 Jimmie Johnson 40.00 65.00
Butch Leitzinger
Elliott Forbes-Robinson
Boss/1812
4 J.Johnson 50.00 75.00
B.Leitzinger
E.Forbes-Robinson
Boss
Color Chrome/240
4 Jimmie Johnson 40.00 65.00
Butch Leitzinger
Elliott Forbes-Robinson
Boss QVC/504
4 Jimmie Johnson 40.00 65.00
Butch Leitzinger
Elliott Forbes-Robinson
Boss RCCA/144
8 Dale Earnhardt Jr. 60.00 120.00
Boris Said
Corvette C-5R/4014
8 Dale Earnhardt Jr. 60.00 120.00
Boris Said
Corvette C-5R
GM Dealers/324
8 Dale Earnhardt Jr. 60.00 120.00
Boris Said
Corvette C-5R RCCA/600
20 Tony Stewart 40.00 65.00
Andy Wallace
Citgo/936
20 Tony Stewart 50.00 75.00
Andy Wallace
Citgo Color Chrome/204
20 Tony Stewart 40.00 65.00
Andy Wallace
Citgo QVC/204
20 Tony Stewart 40.00 65.00
Andy Wallace
Citgo RCCA/204
09 Robby Gordon 40.00 65.00
Doug Goad
Stephan Gregorie
Milka Duno
Citgo/1170
09 Robby Gordon 50.00 75.00
Doug Goad
Stephan Gregorie
Milka Duno
Citgo Color Chrome/204

2004 Action Racing Collectables 1:18

2 Rusty Wallace 40.00 80.00
Miller Lite/1248
2 Rusty Wallace 50.00 100.00
Miller Lite Last Call/1224
8 Dale Earnhardt Jr. 50.00 100.00
Bud/1788
8 Dale Earnhardt Jr. 50.00 100.00
Bud Born On Feb. 15
NNO Dale Earnhardt 30.00 60.00
Monte Carlo SS/5060
NNO Dale Earnhardt Jr. 30.00 60.00
Monte Carlo SS/6840

2005 Action Racing Collectables 1:18

8 Dale Earnhardt Jr. 50.00 80.00
Bud/1194
8 Dale Earnhardt Jr. 50.00 80.00
Bud Born On Feb.12/624
8 Dale Earnhardt Jr. 50.00 80.00
Bud Born On Feb.17/630
8 Dale Earnhardt Jr. 50.00 80.00
Bud Born On Feb.20/1056

2005 Action/RCCA 1:18

8 Dale Earnhardt Jr. 60.00 100.00
Bud Color Chrome/288
8 Dale Earnhardt Jr. 60.00 100.00
Bud Born On Feb.12
Color Chrome/140
8 Dale Earnhardt Jr. 60.00 100.00
Bud Born On Feb.17
Color Chrome/88
8 Dale Earnhardt Jr. 60.00 100.00
Bud Born On Feb.20
Color Chrome/200

2006 Action Racing Collectables 1:18

8 Dale Earnhardt Jr. 75.00 125.00
Bud 3 Days of Dale Tribute/2437
8 Dale Earnhardt Jr. 75.00 125.00
Bud Father's Day/612
8 Dale Earnhardt Jr. 75.00 125.00
Bud Father's Day
GM Dealers/204
24 Jeff Gordon 60.00 100.00
DuPont Hot Hues
Foose Design
NNO Dale Earnhardt 60.00 100.00
Hall of Fame Dale Tribute/2508
NNO Dale Earnhardt 60.00 100.00
Hall of Fame Dale Tribute
GM Dealers/180

2006 Action/RCCA 1:18

8 Dale Earnhardt Jr. 100.00 150.00
Bud 3 Days of Dale Tribute
Color Chrome/333
8 Dale Earnhardt Jr. 75.00 150.00
Bud Father's Day
Chrome/408

2007 Action/Motorsports Authentics Driver's Select 1:18

SOME PRINT RUNS LISTED ON PACKAGE
SOME PRINT RUNS PROVIDED BY MA
8 Dale Earnhardt Jr. 60.00 100.00
Bud/2004

1994 Action Racing Collectables 1:24

These 1:24 scale replicas were produced by Action Racing Collectibles. Most pieces were packaged in a blue or red box and have the Action Racing Collectibles logo or the Racing Collectibles Inc. logo on the box.

1 Winston Show Car 20.00 40.00
2 Ricky Craven 30.00 80.00
DuPont
2 Mark Martin 30.00 60.00
Miller American
1984 ASA Bank
2 Rusty Wallace 100.00 175.00
Ford Motorsports Bank/3504
3 Dale Earnhardt 200.00 350.00
Goodwrench 1994
Lumina Bank/5016
3 Dale Earnhardt 250.00 350.00
Wrangler
1984 Monte Carlo Bank/5016
3 D.Earnhardt 250.00 400.00
Wrangler 1988 Monte Carlo
Aerocoupe Bank/5016
5 Terry Labonte 150.00 300.00
Kellogg's Bank/2508
7 Alan Kulwicki 75.00 150.00
Hooters
7 Alan Kulwicki 60.00 120.00
Zerex
8 Kenny Wallace 40.00 80.00
Red Dog Bank
11 Bill Elliott 75.00 150.00
Budweiser/2508
11 Bill Elliott 50.00 90.00
Budweiser Bank
11 Darrell Waltrip 50.00 100.00
Budweiser 1984 Monte Carlo Bank
11 Darrell Waltrip 50.00 125.00
Budweiser 1984 Thunderbird
11 Darrell Waltrip 40.00 80.00
Bud Red 1986 Monte
Carlo Bank
12 Neil Bonnett 40.00 100.00
Budweiser White
1984 Monte Carlo

12 Neil Bonnett Bud White 1984 Monte Carlo Bank 60.00 100.00
12 Neil Bonnett Bud Red 1986 Monte Carlo Bank/5000 40.00 75.00
15 Lake Speed Quality Care/2508 8.00 20.00
16 Ted Musgrave Family Channel Bank 100.00 200.00
16 Ted Musgrave Primestar 8.00 20.00
21 David Pearson Chattanooga Chew Bank/3500 40.00 80.00
28 Ernie Irvan Havoline 30.00 60.00
28 Dale Jarrett Havoline Bank 35.00 60.00
41 Joe Nemechek Meineke/2508 15.00 30.00
42 Kyle Petty Mello Yello/2508 60.00 100.00
51 Neil Bonnett Country Time Bank 70.00 120.00
75 Buddy Baker Valvoline Bank 40.00 80.00
94 Bill Elliott McDonald's 25.00 45.00
98 Derrike Cope Fingerhut/2508 8.00 20.00

1994 Action/RCCA 1:24

These 1:24 scale pieces were distributed through Action's Racing Collectibles Club of America.

1 Jeff Gordon Baby Ruth Revell/7500 100.00 200.00
2 Rusty Wallace Ford Motorsports 45.00 90.00
2 Rusty Wallace Miller Genuine Draft 1995 Thunderbird 45.00 90.00
3 Richard Childress Black Gold Bank 30.00 50.00
3 Dale Earnhardt Goodwrench In Memory of Neil/5016 200.00 350.00
3 Dale Earnhardt Goodwrench Bank/5016 150.00 250.00
3 Dale Earnhardt Wrangler 1981 Pontiac Bank/5016 200.00 300.00
3 Dale Earnhardt Wrangler 1985 Monte Carlo Bank/5016 200.00 300.00
3 Dale Earnhardt Wrangler 1987 Monte Carlo 400.00 500.00
3 Dale Earnhardt Wrangler 1987 Monte Carlo Bank/5016 250.00 400.00
9 Ted Musgrave Action Racing Collectables 20.00 40.00
16 Ted Musgrave Primestar Bank 30.00 60.00
18 Dale Jarrett Interstate Batteries/2608 125.00 200.00
23 Jimmy Spencer Smokin' Joe's 200.00 350.00
25 Ken Schrader Budweiser Bank 40.00 60.00
28 Ernie Irvan Havoline Bank retail 20.00 40.00
28 Ernie Irvan Havoline Bank gold foil sticker/13,500 25.00 50.00
30 Michael Waltrip Pennzoil 50.00 100.00
51 Neil Bonnett Country Time/5216 125.00 200.00

1995 Action Racing Collectables 1:24

1 Rick Mast Skoal in acrylic case 40.00 80.00
2 Dale Earnhardt Wrangler 1981 Pontiac/5016 250.00 400.00
2 Rusty Wallace Miller Genuine Draft/7500 75.00 150.00
2 Rusty Wallace Miller Genuine Draft Bank/15,000 60.00 120.00
2/43 Dale Earnhardt Richard Petty 7&7 Champions 2-Bank Set 125.00 250.00
3 Richard Childress Black Gold 1978 25.00 60.00
3 Richard Childress CRC Chemical Bank/5004 1980 Oldsmobile 25.00 50.00
3 Dale Earnhardt Goodwrench/6000 175.00 300.00
3 Dale Earnhardt Goodwrench Black Window Promo 60.00 150.00
3 Dale Earnhardt Goodwrench Bank Sports Image 60.00 120.00
3 Dale Earnhardt Goodwrench Bank 1994 Winston Cup Champion with headlights 75.00 150.00
3 Dale Earnhardt Goodwrench Bank without headlights 60.00 150.00
3 Dale Earnhardt Goodwrench Brickyard/10,000 150.00 300.00
3 Dale Earnhardt Goodwrench Silver Bank GM logo on hood black wheels 300.00 500.00
3 Dale Earnhardt Goodwrench Silver Bank GM logo on hood with red wheels 300.00 500.00
3 Dale Earnhardt Goodwrench Silver Bank GM Parts logo on hood with black wheels 250.00 400.00
3 Dale Earnhardt Goodwrench Silver Bank GM Parts logo on hood with red wheels 250.00 500.00
3 Dale Earnhardt Goodwrench Silver Desk Set 100.00 175.00
3 Dale Earnhardt Wrangler 1981 Pontiac/5016 200.00 400.00
3 Dale Earnhardt Wrangler 1985 Monte Carlo Aerocoupe/6000 250.00 400.00
3 Dale Earnhardt Wrangler 1987 Monte Carlo/6000 175.00 350.00
3 Jeff Green Goodwrench/5004 30.00 75.00
3/24 Dale Earnhardt Jeff Gordon Brickyard 2-car set/5000 125.00 250.00
4 Sterling Marlin Kodak/5004 15.00 40.00
6 Mark Martin Folgers 1991 Bank/5004 75.00 150.00
6 Mark Martin Valvoline/5496 40.00 80.00
6 Mark Martin Valvoline Brickyard/8520 50.00 120.00
6 Mark Martin VValvoline Brickyard Bank/5004 25.00 60.00
7 Geoff Bodine Exide 8.00 20.00
7 Alan Kulwicki Hooters Bank/2508 60.00 125.00
9 Ted Musgrave Action/2508 12.50 30.00
10 Ricky Rudd Tide Bank/5004 15.00 40.00
11 Brett Bodine Lowe's Bank/5004 15.00 35.00
11 Darrell Waltrip Mountain Dew/6000 60.00 120.00
15 Dale Earnhardt Wrangler 1983 Thunderbird/5004 300.00 450.00
21 Buddy Baker Valvoline Bank 1983 Thunderbird/5004 40.00 80.00
21 Neil Bonnett Hodgdon Bank/5004 30.00 60.00
22 Bobby Allison Miller High Life/5004 1983 Buick 60.00 120.00
22 Bobby Allison Miller High Life 1983 Buick Bank/5004 50.00 100.00
23 Jimmy Spencer Camel/5004 125.00 200.00
24 Jeff Gordon DuPont Bank/9504 100.00 200.00
24 Jeff Gordon DuPont 1995 Champion Bank/20,124 50.00 100.00
25 Ken Schrader Bud Bank/6204 20.00 50.00
27 Rusty Wallace Kodiak Bank/6210 1989 Grand Prix in plastic case 125.00 200.00
28 Ernie Irvan avoline Employee Bank/13,500 100.00 175.00
28 Ernie Irvan Havoline retail Bank/8000 20.00 35.00
28 Dale Jarrett Havoline Bank/7992 30.00 60.00
35 Alan Kulwicki Quincy's Steakhouse Bank/6000 60.00 120.00
42 Kyle Petty Coors Light/5004 35.00 60.00
88 Ernie Irvan Havoline Bank Promo 15.00 40.00
88 Darrell Waltrip Gatorade 1977 Olds Bank/2508 70.00 110.00
94 Bill Elliott McDonald's Bank/5004 25.00 50.00
94 Bill Elliott McDonald's Thunderbat Bank/5000 50.00 120.00
95 David Green Busch Beer Bank/4704 20.00 50.00

1995 Action/RCCA 1:24

1 Rick Mast Skoal in acrylic case/7500 40.00 70.00
1 Winston Show Car Bank/3504 25.00 50.00
2 Dale Earnhardt Wrangler 1981 Pontiac Bank/5016 150.00 250.00
2/43 Dale Earnhardt Richard Petty 7 and 7 Special 2-car set 150.00 250.00
3 Richard Childress CRC Chemical 1980 Olds/3500 50.00 100.00
3 Dale Earnhardt Goodwrench 1988 Monte Carlo Aerocoupe/5016 250.00 400.00
3 Dale Earnhardt Goodwrench with SkyBox card/5016 125.00 250.00
3 Dale Earnhardt Goodwrench Bank with headlights 50.00 120.00
3 Dale Earnhardt Goodwrench Bank without headlights 50.00 120.00
3 Dale Earnhardt Goodwrench Silver GM Parts ith black wheels 250.00 450.00
3 Dale Earnhardt Goodwrench Silver GM Parts red wheels 250.00 500.00
3 Dale Earnhardt Goodwrench Silver GM black wheels 350.00 600.00
3 Dale Earnhardt Goodwrench Silver GM with red wheels 400.00 750.00
3 Dale Earnhardt Wrangler 1984 Monte Carlo blue deck lid/5016 175.00 350.00
3 Dale Earnhardt Wrangler 1984 Monte Carlo ellow deck lid/5016 200.00 400.00
3 Jeff Green Goodwrench Bank/2508 25.00 50.00
4 Sterling Marlin Kodak Bank/2508 20.00 50.00
6 Mark Martin Folgers 1991/2508 150.00 250.00
6 Mark Martin Valvoline Bank/4500 30.00 50.00
6 Mark Martin Valvoline Brickyard Bank 40.00 70.00
7 Geoff Bodine Exide Bank/2508 15.00 40.00
7 Alan Kulwicki Hooters Bank/5004 75.00 150.00
7 Alan Kulwicki Zerex Bank/2508 90.00 150.00
9 Ted Musgrave RCCA/2508 15.00 40.00
10 Ricky Rudd Tide/2508 40.00 70.00
11 Brett Bodine Lowe's/2508 12.00 30.00
11 Darrell Waltrip Mountain Dew Bank 1981 Buick/5000 45.00 80.00
15 Dale Earnhardt Wrangler Bank 1983 T-bird/10,008 125.00 250.00
22 Bobby Allison Miller High Life/5004 1983 Buick 20.00 50.00
24 Jeff Gordon DuPont/5004 150.00 250.00
25 Ken Schrader Bud/5004 35.00 60.00
26 Hut Stricklin Quaker State/2508 15.00 40.00
27 Rusty Wallace Kodiak 1989 Grand Prix/5000 250.00 400.00
28 Dale Jarrett Havoline/5016 40.00 80.00
42 Kyle Petty Coors Light Bank/5004 35.00 60.00
42 Kyle Petty Coors Light Pumpkin/5004 in plastic case 150.00 300.00
88 Ernie Irvan Havoline Bank 15.00 40.00
88 Darrell Waltrip Gatorade Bank 1980 Monte Carlo/2508 50.00 100.00
94 Bill Elliott McDonald's/5004 25.00 50.00
94 Bill Elliott McDonald's Thunderbat 75.00 150.00
95 David Green Busch Beer/2508 20.00 50.00

1995-96 Action Racing Collectables SuperTrucks 1:24

3 Mike Skinner Goodwrench 1995 25.00 40.00
3 Mike Skinner Goodwrench 1996 20.00 40.00
7 Geoff Bodine Exide/6000 1995 15.00 40.00
16 Ron Hornaday Action 1995 20.00 40.00
16 Ron Hornaday NAPA 1996 20.00 40.00
24 Jack Sprague Quaker State Bank/3500 1996 12.50 30.00
28 Ernie Irvan NAPA/4008 30.00 45.00
71 Kenji Momota Marukatsu/4008 1995 20.00 40.00
84 Joe Ruttman Mac Tools/5004 15.00 40.00
84 Joe Ruttman Mac Tools Bank 30.00 45.00
98 Butch Miller Raybestos Bank/6000 1995 15.00 40.00

1995-96 Action/RCCA SuperTrucks 1:24

The top SuperTruck driver's trucks are featured in these die-cast pieces. Most pieces were distributed either through the Action Dealer Network or Action's Racing Collectibles Club of America. Some were made available through both outlets. There are two versions of most trucks, a bank and a regular version. The banks have a slot in the truck bed for the coin.

3 Mike Skinner Goodwrench Bank 1995 35.00 50.00
3 Mike Skinner Goodwrench Bank/1000 1996 40.00 60.00
6 Rick Carelli Total Petroleum 30.00 45.00
6 Rick Carelli Total Petroleum Bank 30.00 45.00
7 Geoff Bodine Exide Bank 20.00 45.00
16 Ron Hornaday Action Bank/6004 1995 15.00 40.00
16 Ron Hornaday NAPA 1996 20.00 40.00
16 Ron Hornaday NAPA Bank 1996 20.00 40.00
16 Ron Hornaday NAPA Gold 1996 35.00 60.00
16 Ron Hornaday NAPA Gold Bank 1996 35.00 60.00
16 Ron Hornaday Papa John's 1995 25.00 45.00
16 Ron Hornaday Papa John's Bank Platinum Series 1995 25.00 45.00
24 Scott Lagasse DuPont 1995 30.00 45.00
24 Scott Lagasse DuPont Bank 1995 30.00 45.00
24 Jack Sprague Quaker State/2500 20.00 40.00
28 Ernie Irvan NAPA Bank 30.00 50.00
52 Ken Schrader AC Delco/2508 1995 20.00 40.00
52 Ken Schrader AC Delco Bank Platinum Series/5004 1995 20.00 40.00
71 Kenji Momota Marukatsu Bank 30.00 45.00
80 Joe Ruttman JR's Garage 30.00 60.00
84 Joe Ruttman Mac Tools 25.00 40.00

1996 Action Racing Collectables 1:24

These 1:24 scale replicas were produced by Action Racing Collectibles. Most pieces were packaged in a blue box and have the Action Racing Collectibles logo or the Racing Collectibles Inc. logo on the box. The banks were issued in the same boxes with a blue "Bank" sticker attached to the sides. All 1996 banks have black windows.

2 Mark Martin Miller 1985 ASA 30.00 70.00
2 Mark Martin Miller 1985 ASA Bank/6000 35.00 75.00
2 Rusty Wallace Miller Splash 70.00 120.00
2 Rusty Wallace Miller Genuine Draft Silver 25th Anniversary 40.00 100.00
2 Rusty Wallace Miller Splash Bank 40.00 75.00
3 Dale Earnhardt AC-Delco 100.00 200.00
3 Dale Earnhardt AC-Delco Snap-On 75.00 200.00
3 Dale Earnhardt Goodwrench 1996 Monte Carlo 75.00 150.00
3 Dale Earnhardt Olympic Bank 100.00 200.00
3 Dale Earnhardt Olympic Food City Promo box 100.00 250.00
3 Dale Earnhardt Olympic Goodwrench Box 250.00 350.00
3 Dale Earnhardt Olympic Green Box 200.00 400.00
3 Dale Earnhardt Olympic Green Box No Trademark on Hood of Car 75.00 200.00
3 Dale Earnhardt Olympic Mom-n-Pop's box 100.00 225.00
3 Dale Earnhardt Olympic Sports Image blue box 75.00 200.00
5 Terry Labonte Kellogg's Iron Man Silver Bank/10,000 75.00 150.00
5 Terry Labonte Kellogg's Japan Bank 40.00 80.00
6 Mark Martin Valvoline Bank 30.00 60.00
7 Geoff Bodine QVC Bank 20.00 50.00
10 Ricky Rudd Tide 40.00 80.00
10 Ricky Rudd Tide Bank 35.00 60.00
14 Jeff Green Tide Racing For Kids 20.00 40.00
15 Dale Earnhardt Wrangler 1982 Thunderbird Bank/2508 125.00 250.00
18 Bobby Labonte Interstate Batteries 45.00 90.00
18 Bobby Labonte Interstate Batteries Pro Football Hall of Fame 75.00 150.00
21 Michael Waltrip Citgo 15.00 40.00
21 Michael Waltrip Citgo Star Trek Bank 25.00 50.00
22 Ward Burton MBNA Bank/5000 25.00 40.00
24 Jeff Gordon DuPont Bank/12,500 35.00 75.00
25 Tim Richmond Folgers 1987 Monte Carlo Bank/7500 50.00 100.00
25 Ken Schrader Bud Bank/6204 20.00 50.00
29 Steve Grissom Flintstones Bank 25.00 50.00
29 No Driver Association Scooby-Doo 20.00 50.00
29 Steve Grissom WCW Bank/5000 25.00 50.00
29 No Driver Association Scooby-Doo Bank/10,000 25.00 50.00
31 Mike Skinner Snap-On/5000 30.00 80.00
31 Mike Skinner Snap-On Promo 70.00 125.00
42 Robby Gordon Tonka Bank 25.00 50.00
42 Kyle Petty Coors Light/7500 30.00 60.00
42 Kyle Petty Coors Light Black Bank/7500 35.00 60.00
43 Bobby Hamilton STP '72 Blue 20.00 50.00
43 Bobby Hamilton STP '72 Blue Bank/2500 15.00 40.00
43 Bobby Hamilton STP '72 Blue&Red 20.00 50.00
43 Bobby Hamilton STP '72 Blue&Red Bank/2500 15.00 40.00
43 Bobby Hamilton STP '79 Blue&Red red sides blue roof 20.00 50.00
43 Bobby Hamilton STP '79 Blue&Red Bank/2500 red sides blue roof 15.00 40.00
43 Bobby Hamilton STP '84 Blue&Red blue sides w red stripes 20.00 50.00
43 Bobby Hamilton STP '84 Blue&Red Bank/2500 blue sides w red stripes 15.00 40.00
43 Bobby Hamilton STP Silver 25th Anniversary 25.00 60.00
43 Bobby Hamilton STP Silver 25th Anniversary Bank/2500 20.00 50.00
57 Jason Keller Halloween Havoc/5004 15.00 40.00
88 Ernie Irvan Havoline 30.00 70.00
88 Ernie Irvan Havoline Bank 25.00 60.00
88 Dale Jarrett Quality Care 30.00 60.00
98 Jeremy Mayfield RCA 20.00 50.00

1996 Action/RCCA 1:24

These 1:24 scale pieces were distributed through Action's Racing Collectibles Club of America. The pieces are 1:24 replicas of the cars that have raced in NASCAR. Each was issued in a black RCCA box or colorful box with the team's colors. The banks were issued in the same boxes with the addition of a "Bank" sticker to the box. All 1996 banks feature black windows.

1 Winston Show Car/7000 25.00 50.00
2 Rusty Wallace Miller Genuine Draft Bank 45.00 70.00
2 Rusty Wallace Miller Genuine Draft Silver 25th Anniversary Bank 30.00 80.00
2 Rusty Wallace Miller Genuine Draft 45.00 90.00
3 Dale Earnhardt AC-Delco Bank 40.00 100.00
3 Dale Earnhardt Goodwrench Bank 60.00 150.00
5 Terry Labonte Kellogg's Iron Man Silver 100.00 175.00
5 Terry Labonte Kellogg's Japan/5000 30.00 80.00
6 Mark Martin Valvoline Thunderbird 40.00 80.00
11 Darrell Waltrip Budweiser 1984 Monte Carlo Bank 35.00 75.00
12 Neil Bonnett Budweiser 1984 Monte Carlo Bank 40.00 75.00
14 Jeff Green Racing For Kids Bank 25.00 60.00
15 Dale Earnhardt Wrangler 1982 Thunderbird/10,000 150.00 300.00
15 Dale Earnhardt Wrangler 1982 Thunderbird Bank 100.00 175.00
17 Darrell Waltrip Parts America 30.00 60.00
17 Darrell Waltrip Parts America Bank/5000 25.00 50.00
17 Darrell Waltrip Tide 1988 Monte Carlo 50.00 100.00
18 Bobby Labonte Interstate Batteries Bank/5000 20.00 50.00
18 Bobby Labonte Interstate Batteries Pro Football HOF Bank/10,000 35.00 75.00
21 Neil Bonnett Hodgdon 1981 Buick/5004 25.00 60.00
21 Michael Waltrip Citgo Bank/5000 20.00 50.00
21 Michael Waltrip Citgo Star Trek 30.00 60.00
22 Bobby Allison Miller American/2500 1985 Monte Carlo 35.00 60.00
22 Ward Burton MBNA/5000 20.00 50.00
24 Jeff Gordon DuPont/12,500 40.00 80.00
25 Tim Richmond olgers 1987 Monte Carlo Bank/5000 50.00 100.00
25 Ken Schrader Bud/3500 20.00 50.00

28 Ernie Irvan 25.00 50.00
Havoline Bank
29 Steve Grissom 25.00 60.00
Flintstones/10,000
29 Steve Grissom 25.00 60.00
WCW/5000
30 Johnny Benson 25.00 60.00
Pennzoil Bank/5000
31 Mike Skinner 40.00 80.00
Lowe's Bank
31 Mike Skinner 40.00 100.00
Snap-On Bank/3500
33 Robert Pressley 25.00 60.00
Skoal/5000
42 Kyle Petty 35.00 65.00
Coors Light Bank/5000
42 Robby Gordon 30.00 60.00
Tonka/3500
42 Kyle Petty 40.00 65.00
Coors Light Black/5000
43 Bobby Hamilton 20.00 50.00
STP '72 Blue/3500
43 Bobby Hamilton 20.00 50.00
STP '72 Blue&Red/3500
43 Bobby Hamilton 20.00 50.00
STP '79 Blue&Red/3500
red sides
blue roof
43 Bobby Hamilton 20.00 50.00
STP '84 Blue&Red/3500
blue sides w
red stripes
43 Bobby Hamilton 25.00 60.00
STP Silver 25th Anniversary
57 Jason Keller 20.00 50.00
Halloween Havoc Bank/3500
88 Ernie Irvan 25.00 60.00
Havoline Bank
88 Dale Jarrett 35.00 60.00
Quality Care Bank
94 Bill Elliott 25.00 60.00
McDonald's Bank/5000
99 Jeff Burton 20.00 50.00
Exide Bank/3500

1997 Action Racing Collectables 1:24

These 1:24 scale replicas were produced by Action Racing Collectibles. Most pieces were packaged in a blue box and have the Action Racing Collectibles logo or the Racing Collectibles Inc. logo on the box. The banks were issued in the same boxes with the addition of a "Bank" sticker on the sides. Note that all banks in this series have black windows.

1 Hermie Sadler 15.00 40.00
DeWalt Bank/3500
1 Gargoyles 500 Promo 10.00 20.00
2 Rusty Wallace 30.00 60.00
Miller Lite/10,500
2 Rusty Wallace 25.00 50.00
Miller Japan/7500
2 Rusty Wallace 25.00 60.00
Miller Lite Texas Bank/7584
3 Dale Earnhardt 60.00 120.00
AC Delco Bank
3 Dale Earnhardt 60.00 150.00
Goodwrench Bank
3 Dale Earnhardt 40.00 80.00
Goodwrench Plus
3 Dale Earnhardt 40.00 80.00
Goodwrench Plus Bank
3 Dale Earnhardt 60.00 120.00
Goodwrench Brickyard/7500
3 Dale Earnhardt 125.00 225.00
Lowes Food Bank/7992
3 Dale Earnhardt 60.00 120.00
Wheaties Hood Open
black window netting
3 Dale Earnhardt 100.00 200.00
Wheaties HO black
netting Snap-On Tools
3 Dale Earnhardt 40.00 100.00
Wheaties mail-In
red window netting
3 Dale Earnhardt 75.00 150.00
Wheaties Snap-On Bank
3 Dale Earnhardt 100.00 200.00
Wheaties Sports Image
3 Dale Earnhardt 100.00 200.00
Wrangler Bank
1984 Monte Carlo Daytona paint
3 Steve Park 40.00 100.00
AC Delco Bank/6504
3 Ricky Rudd 35.00 80.00
Piedmont 1983
Monte Carlo Bank/3500
4 Sterling Marlin 15.00 40.00
Kodak Bank/6300
4 Sterling Marlin 15.00 40.00
Kodak Mac Tools Bank/1500
6 Mark Martin 30.00 60.00
Valvoline
6 Mark Martin 40.00 75.00
Valvoline Mac Tools
8 Hut Stricklin 8.00 20.00
Circuit City
9 Jeff Burton 20.00 50.00
Track Gear Bank/3500
10 Phil Parsons 8.00 20.00
Channellock/3500
10 Ricky Rudd 30.00 50.00
Tide Bank/6000
11 Brett Bodine 8.00 20.00
Close Call/8004
12 Kenny Wallace 8.00 20.00
Gray Bar/6504
14 Steve Park 50.00 125.00
Burger King/6000
16 Ted Musgrave 8.00 20.00
Primestar/5604
17 Darrell Waltrip 15.00 40.00
Parts America Bank
Blue&White
17 Darrell Waltrip 25.00 60.00
Parts America Bank
Chrome
17 Darrell Waltrip 15.00 40.00
Parts America Bank
Green w
green number
17 Darrell Waltrip 15.00 40.00
Parts America Bank
Green w
white no.
17 Darrell Waltrip 15.00 40.00
Parts America Bank
Orange
17 Darrell Waltrip 15.00 40.00
Parts America Bank
Red&White
17 Darrell Waltrip 15.00 40.00
Parts America Bank
Yellow&White
18 Bobby Labonte 25.00 60.00
Interstate Batteries
18 Bobby Labonte 75.00 150.00
Interstate Batteries Mac Tools
22 Bobby Allison 40.00 80.00
Miller American Bank/5304
1985 Monte Carlo
22 Ward Burton 20.00 40.00
MBNA/5292
22 Ward Burton 20.00 40.00
MBNA Gold Bank
23 Jimmy Spencer 40.00 100.00
Camel
24 Jeff Gordon 50.00 100.00
DuPont
24 Jeff Gordon 50.00 100.00
DuPont Mac Tools
24 Jeff Gordon 50.00 100.00
DuPont Brickyard/7500
black windows
24 Jeff Gordon 100.00 200.00
DuPont ChromaPremier Promo
24 Jeff Gordon 125.00 250.00
DuPont CromaPremier
Sports Image/7500
24 Jeff Gordon 75.00 150.00
DuPont ChromaPremier Bank/28,000
24 Jeff Gordon 40.00 75.00
DuPont Million Dollar Date Bank
24 Jeff Gordon 40.00 75.00
DuPont Million $ Date
Mac Tools Bank
24 Jeff Gordon 75.00 150.00
Jurassic Park 3
24 Jeff Gordon 50.00 100.00
Jurassic Park 3 Bank
25 Ricky Craven 20.00 40.00
Bud/3500
25 Ricky Craven 25.00 60.00
Bud Bank/8400
26 Rich Bickle 15.00 40.00
KFC Bank/3852
27 Kenny Irwin 30.00 60.00
Action/3500
27 Kenny Irwin 20.00 50.00
G.I. Joe Bank/5000
27 Kenny Irwin 25.00 60.00
Tonka/5700
27 Kenny Irwin 25.00 60.00
Tonka Mac Tools/1500
27 Rusty Wallace 75.00 135.00
Miller Genuine Draft
1990 Grand Prix Bank/6000
in plastic case
29 Jeff Green 25.00 60.00
Tom & Jerry
29 Elliott Sadler 25.00 50.00
Phillips 66 Bank/3500
30 Johnny Benson 8.00 30.00
Pennzoil
31 Mike Skinner 15.00 40.00
Lowe's
31 Mike Skinner 15.00 30.00
Lowe's Japan/5000
31 Mike Skinner 15.00 30.00
Lowe's Japan Bank/6500
32 Dale Jarrett 20.00 50.00
White Rain Bank/7956
33 Ken Schrader 35.00 55.00
Skoal Bank
36 Todd Bodine 20.00 40.00
Stanley Bank
36 Derrike Cope 15.00 40.00
Skittles Bank/6708
37 Mark Green 10.00 25.00
Timber Wolf/3500
37 Jeremy Mayfield 15.00 40.00
K-Mart RC-Cola Bank/6000
40 Robby Gordon 20.00 50.00
Coors Light Bank/7500
41 Steve Grissom 20.00 50.00
Kodiak Bank
42 Joe Nemechek 10.00 30.00
BellSouth/7716
46 Wally Dallenbach 8.00 20.00
First Union/6792
60 Mark Martin 35.00 60.00
Winn Dixie Bank
71 Dave Marcis 25.00 60.00
Realtree Bank
71 Dave Marcis 25.00 60.00
Realtree Making of Champions Bank
75 Rick Mast 8.00 20.00
Remington/6000
75 Rick Mast 15.00 30.00
Remington Camo
81 Kenny Wallace 15.00 40.00
Square D Bank
88 Dale Jarrett 25.00 50.00
Quality Care/5960
88 Dale Jarrett 25.00 60.00
Quality Care Mac Tools/4000
88 Dale Jarrett 35.00 60.00
Quality Care Brickyard/7500
94 Bill Elliott 45.00 80.00
McDonald's Bank
94 Bill Elliott 25.00 50.00
Mac Tonight/8700
96 David Green 15.00 40.00
Caterpillar Bank/6504
99 Jeff Burton 15.00 40.00
Exide
99 Jeff Burton 15.00 40.00
Exide Mac Tools/4000
00 Buckshot Jones 15.00 40.00
Aqua Fresh/3500

1997 Action/RCCA 1:24

These 1:24 scale pieces were distributed through Action's Racing Collectibles Club of America. The pieces are 1:24 replicas of the cars that have raced in NASCAR. All banks in this series have black windows.

2 Rusty Wallace 30.00 60.00
Miller Lite Bank
2 Rusty Wallace 30.00 60.00
Miller Japan Bank/5000
2 Rusty Wallace 60.00 100.00
Miller Lite Texas
3 Dale Earnhardt 60.00 120.00
AC Delco/1200
3 Dale Earnhardt 125.00 250.00
Goodwrench/3500
3 Dale Earnhardt 60.00 120.00
Goodwrench Plus
3 Dale Earnhardt 60.00 120.00
Goodwrench Plus Bank/10,000
3 Dale Earnhardt 150.00 250.00
Lowes Food/10,000
3 Dale Earnhardt 100.00 200.00
Wheaties Bank
3 Dale Earnhardt 150.00 250.00
Wrangler 1984 Monte
Carlo Daytona/10,000
3 Steve Park 100.00 175.00
AC Delco
3 Ricky Rudd 50.00 100.00
Piedmont 1983 Monte Carlo/3500
4 Sterling Marlin 15.00 40.00
Kodak/2500
6 Mark Martin 35.00 60.00
Valvoline Bank
9 Jeff Burton 20.00 50.00
Track Gear/3500
10 Phil Parsons 20.00 50.00
Channellock Bank/2500
10 R.Rudd 25.00 50.00
Tide/2500
11 Brett Bodine 15.00 40.00
Close Call Bank/2500
12 Kenny Wallace 15.00 40.00
Gray Bar Bank/2500
14 Steve Park 50.00 100.00
Burger King Bank/5000
16 Ted Musgrave 15.00 40.00
Primestar Bank/2500
17 Darrell Waltrip 15.00 40.00
Parts America
Blue&White/6000
17 Darrell Waltrip 30.00 80.00
Parts America Chrome/6000
17 Darrell Waltrip 15.00 40.00
Parts America Green
with green number/6000
17 Darrell Waltrip 15.00 40.00
Parts America Green
with white number/6000
17 Darrell Waltrip 15.00 40.00
Parts America Orange/6000
17 Darrell Waltrip 15.00 40.00
Parts America Red&White/6000
17 Darrell Waltrip 15.00 40.00
Parts America
Yellow&White/6000
18 Bobby Labonte 25.00 50.00
Interstate Batteries Bank/3500
22 Ward Burton 20.00 50.00
MBNA Gold/2500
23 Jimmy Spencer 75.00 150.00
Camel Bank
24 Jeff Gordon 40.00 100.00
DuPont Bank/3500
24 Jeff Gordon 75.00 150.00
DuPont ChromaPremier/15,000
24 Jeff Gordon 40.00 75.00
DuPont Million Dollar Date/15,000
24 Jeff Gordon 60.00 120.00
Jurassic Park 3
25 Ricky Craven 25.00 60.00
Budweiser/3500
26 Rich Bickle 15.00 40.00
KFC/3500
27 Kenny Irwin 30.00 60.00
Action/3500
27 Kenny Irwin 30.00 60.00
G.I. Joe
27 Kenny Irwin 25.00 50.00
Nerf Bank
27 Kenny Irwin 25.00 50.00
Tonka Bank/3500
27 Rusty Wallace 125.00 200.00
Miller Genuine Draft
1990 Grand Prix/5000
in plastic case
29 Jeff Green 15.00 40.00
Tom & Jerry Bank/3500
29 Elliott Sadler 25.00 60.00
Phillips 66
31 Mike Skinner 15.00 40.00
Lowe's Bank/3500
31 Mike Skinner 15.00 30.00
Lowe's Japan
32 Dale Jarrett 20.00 50.00
White Rain
33 Ken Schrader 50.00 90.00
Skoal
36 Todd Bodine 20.00 50.00
Stanley
36 Derrike Cope 15.00 40.00
Skittles/5000
37 Mark Green 20.00 50.00
Timber Wolf Bank
37 Jeremy Mayfield 30.00 80.00
K-Mart RC-Cola
40 Robby Gordon 25.00 60.00
Coors Light/2500
41 Steve Grissom 20.00 50.00
Kodiak/2500
42 Joe Nemechek 20.00 40.00
BellSouth Bank
46 Wally Dallenbach 20.00 40.00
First Union Bank
60 Mark Martin 40.00 80.00
Winn Dixie/5500
71 Dave Marcis 25.00 60.00
Realtree/2500
71 Dave Marcis 25.00 60.00
Realtree Making of Champions/2500
75 Rick Mast 15.00 40.00
Remington Bank/2500
75 Rick Mast 20.00 45.00
Remington Camo Bank
81 Kenny Wallace 15.00 40.00
Square D
88 Dale Jarrett 20.00 50.00
Quality Care Bank/5000
94 Bill Elliott 30.00 80.00
Mac Tonight Bank/7500
94 Bill Elliott 35.00 70.00
McDonald's
96 David Green 15.00 40.00
Caterpillar/3500
97 Chad Little 20.00 60.00
John Deere
97 Chad Little 15.00 40.00
John Deere Bank/2500
97 Chad Little 30.00 60.00
John Deere 160th Anniversary
97 Chad Little 25.00 55.00
John Deere
160th Anniversary Bank/2500
99 Jeff Burton 40.00 70.00
Exide Bank/2500
00 Buckshot Jones 15.00 40.00
Aqua Fresh Bank/2500

1997 Action/RCCA Elite 1:24

This series consists of upgraded versions of their standard production cars. It was started in 1997. The cars from this series contain serial number plates on the undercarriage at the end of the car.

2 Rusty Wallace 50.00 120.00
Miller Lite/5000
2 Rusty Wallace 30.00 80.00
Miller Japan/5000
2 Rusty Wallace 60.00 120.00
Miller Lite Texas/1500
3 Dale Earnhardt 75.00 150.00
AC Delco/12,500
3 Dale Earnhardt 250.00 400.00
Goodwrench/3500
3 Dale Earnhardt 100.00 200.00
Goodwrench Plus/12,500
3 Dale Earnhardt 250.00 400.00
Wheaties
Gold number plate/5000
3 Dale Earnhardt 150.00 300.00
Wheaties
Brass number plate/8618
3 Steve Park 125.00 200.00
AC Delco
4 Sterling Marlin 30.00 80.00
Kodak/1500
6 Mark Martin 60.00 120.00
Valvoline/2500
9 Jeff Burton 25.00 60.00
Track Gear/1500
10 Ricky Rudd 40.00 80.00
Tide/1500
14 Steve Park 75.00 150.00
Burger King/3500
17 Darrell Waltrip 40.00 100.00
Parts America/4008
17 Darrell Waltrip 75.00 150.00
Parts America Chrome/3500
18 Bobby Labonte 75.00 150.00
Interstate Batteries/1500
22 Ward Burton 40.00 100.00
MBNA Gold/1500
24 Jeff Gordon 125.00 250.00
DuPont/3500
24 Jeff Gordon 100.00 175.00
DuPont Million Dollar Date/10,000
24 Jeff Gordon 175.00 300.00
DuPont ChromaPremier/5000
24 Jeff Gordon 125.00 250.00
Jurassic Park 3/7500
25 Ricky Craven 40.00 80.00
Budweiser/1500
29 Jeff Green 30.00 60.00
Tom & Jerry/3500
29 No Driver Associated 60.00 120.00
Scooby-Doo
29 Robert Pressley 40.00 80.00
Scooby-Doo/1200
29 Elliot Sadler 30.00 60.00
Phillips 66/1200
31 Mike Skinner 50.00 100.00
Lowe's/5000
31 Mike Skinner 40.00 80.00
Lowe's Japan
32 Dale Jarrett 75.00 150.00
White Rain
36 Todd Bodine 90.00 150.00
Stanley/1500
36 Derrike Cope 25.00 60.00
Skittles/1200
37 Mark Green 60.00 150.00
Timber Wolf
37 Jeremy Mayfield 40.00 100.00
K-Mart RC-Cola
46 Wally Dallenbach 25.00 50.00
First Union/1500
60 Mark Martin 60.00 120.00
Winn Dixie/3500
75 Rick Mast 25.00 60.00
Remington/2500
88 Dale Jarrett 50.00 120.00
Quality Care/2000
94 Bill Elliott 75.00 150.00
McDonald's/1500
94 Bill Elliott 40.00 80.00
Mac Tonight/7500
96 David Green 25.00 50.00
Caterpillar/2500
97 Chad Little 40.00 100.00
John Deere
97 Chad Little 40.00 100.00
John Deere
160th Anniversary/2500
99 Jeff Burton 50.00 120.00
Exide/2500
00 Buckshot Jones 30.00 80.00
Aqua Fresh/1200

1998 Action Racing Collectables 1:24

These 1:24 scale replicas were produced by Action Racing Collectibles. Most pieces were packaged in a blue box and have the Action Racing Collectibles logo or the Racing Collectibles Inc. logo on the box.

1 Dale Earnhardt Jr. 25.00 60.00
Coke Bear
1 Dale Earnhardt Jr. 25.00 60.00
Coke Bear Bank
1 Jeff Gordon 50.00 100.00
Baby Ruth 1992 Thunderbird
1 Jeff Gordon 40.00 80.00
Baby Ruth 1992
Thunderbird Bank/7500
1 Steve Park 50.00 100.00
Pennzoil Black Roof/8500
1 Steve Park 50.00 100.00
Pennzoil Black Roof Bank
1 Steve Park 30.00 60.00
Pennzoil Yellow Roof
1 Steve Park 25.00 60.00
Pennzoil Yellow Roof
Bank/3000
1 Darrell Waltrip 35.00 75.00
Pennzoil
1 Darrell Waltrip 40.00 80.00
Pennzoil Bank
1/3 Dale Earnhardt 100.00 175.00
Dale Earnhardt Jr.
Coke Bear Snap-on 2-car set
packaged with wrench
2 Rusty Wallace 20.00 50.00
Adventures of Rusty
2 Rusty Wallace 20.00 50.00
Miller Lite
2 Rusty Wallace 20.00 50.00
Miller Lite Bank/2500
2 Rusty Wallace 25.00 50.00
Miller Lite Elvis
2 Rusty Wallace 20.00 50.00
Miller Lite Elvis Bank/15,996
2 Rusty Wallace 25.00 50.00
Miller Lite TCB Elvis
2 Rusty Wallace 20.00 50.00
Miller Lite TCB
Elvis Bank/2508
3 Dale Earnhardt 60.00 120.00
Coke
3 Dale Earnhardt 60.00 120.00
Coke Bank
3 Dale Earnhardt 50.00 100.00
Goodwrench Plus
3 Dale Earnhardt 50.00 100.00
Goodwrench Plus Bank
with Coke decal
3 Dale Earnhardt 75.00 150.00
Goodwrench Plus Bank
without Coke decal
3 Dale Earnhardt 60.00 120.00
Goodwrench Plus Bass Pro
3 Dale Earnhardt 50.00 100.00
Goodwrench Plus Bass Pro
Black Window Promo
3 Dale Earnhardt 50.00 100.00
Goodwrench Plus Bass Pro Bank
3 Dale Earnhardt 75.00 150.00
Goodwrench Plus Daytona
3 Dale Earnhardt 60.00 120.00
Goodwrench Plus
Daytona Bank/15,000
3 Dale Earnhardt 800.00 1200.00
Goodwrench Plus Gold/500
3 Dale Earnhardt 500.00 1000.00
Dale Earnhardt Jr.
Goodwrench AC Delco Split/624
3 Dale Earnhardt Jr. 75.00 150.00
AC Delco/15,000
3 Dale Earnhardt Jr. 75.00 150.00
AC Delco Bank/2500
3 Dale Earnhardt Jr. 50.00 100.00
AC Delco
1998 BGN Champ
3 Dale Earnhardt Jr. 50.00 100.00
AC Delco
1998 BGN Champ Bank
3 Race Rock Promo/2504 15.00 30.00
4 Bobby Hamilton 8.00 20.00
Kodak/5000
4 Bobby Hamilton 25.00 50.00
Kodak Bank
5 Terry Labonte 20.00 50.00
Blasted Fruit Loops/7500
5 Terry Labonte 25.00 60.00
Blasted Fruit Loops Bank
5 Terry Labonte 30.00 60.00
Kellogg's
5 Terry Labonte 35.00 75.00
Kellogg's Bank
5 Terry Labonte 30.00 80.00
Kellogg's Corny
5 Terry Labonte 30.00 70.00
Kellogg's Corny Bank/3500
5 Terry Labonte 40.00 80.00
Kellogg's Ironman
5 Terry Labonte 40.00 80.00
Kellogg's Ironman Bank
8 Dale Earnhardt 60.00 150.00
RPM 1975 Dodge/7500
8 Dale Earnhardt 50.00 100.00
RPM 1975 Dodge Bank/10,000
8 Hut Stricklin 8.00 20.00
Circuit City/5004
8 Hut Stricklin 15.00 30.00
Circuit City Bank
9 Jerry Nadeau 100.00 175.00
Power Puff/2508
9 Jerry Nadeau 30.00 70.00
Scooby Zombie Island
9 Lake Speed 20.00 50.00
Birthday Cake/6000
9 Lake Speed 25.00 50.00
Birthday Cake Bank
9 Lake Speed 20.00 50.00
Huckleberry Hound/7500
9 Lake Speed 30.00 70.00
Huckleberry Hound Bank
10 Ricky Rudd 35.00 60.00
Tide

Ricky Rudd Tide Bank 30.00 60.00
Ricky Rudd Tide Give Kids the World 30.00 80.00
Jeremy Mayfield Mobil 1/15,000 20.00 50.00
Jeremy Mayfield Mobil 1 Bank 20.00 50.00
Jimmy Spencer Zippo/2000 60.00 120.00
Jimmy Spencer Zippo Bank 125.00 200.00
Patty Moise Rhodes Xena/5004 35.00 80.00
Patty Moise Rhodes Xena Bank 30.00 80.00
Bobby Labonte Interstate Batteries/5000 30.00 80.00
Bobby Labonte Interstate Batteries Bank/2500 20.00 50.00
Bobby Labonte Interstate Batteries Hot Rod/10,992 50.00 100.00
Bobby Labonte Interstate Batteries Hot Rod Bank 40.00 80.00
Bobby Labonte Interstate Batteries Small Soldiers/2508 30.00 80.00
Bobby Labonte Interstate Batteries Small Soldiers Bank 30.00 80.00
Michael Waltrip Citgo/4008 15.00 30.00
Michael Waltrip Citgo Woody/2508 40.00 80.00
Ward Burton MBNA/5004 15.00 40.00
Jimmy Spencer No Bull 30.00 80.00
Jimmy Spencer No Bull Bank/2500 30.00 80.00
Jeff Gordon DuPont 40.00 80.00
Jeff Gordon DuPont Bank/7500 40.00 80.00
Jeff Gordon DuPont Brickyard Win/2508 75.00 125.00
Jeff Gordon DuPont Mac Tools 60.00 100.00
Jeff Gordon DuPont Chromalusion 60.00 120.00
Jeff Gordon DuPont Chromalusion Bank/15,000 50.00 100.00
Jeff Gordon DuPont Chromalusion Mac Tools 75.00 150.00
Jeff Gordon DuPont No Bull 50.00 80.00
Jeff Gordon DuPont No Bull Bank 40.00 80.00
3 Kenny Irwin Havoline/10,000 20.00 50.00
3 Kenny Irwin Havoline Joker 25.00 60.00
3 Kenny Irwin Havoline Joker Bank 25.00 60.00
0 Derrike Cope Gumout/3504 12.00 30.00
Dale Earnhardt Jr. Sikkens Blue 1997 Monte Carlo/5000 100.00 175.00
1 Dale Earnhardt Jr. Sikkens Blue Bank 1997 Monte Carlo/5004 60.00 150.00
1 Dale Earnhardt Jr. Wrangler 1997 Monte Carlo/10,008 100.00 200.00
1 Dale Earnhardt Jr. Wrangler Bank 1997 Monte Carlo/2508 60.00 150.00
1 Mike Skinner Lowe's/6000 20.00 50.00
1 Mike Skinner Lowe's Bank/2500 20.00 50.00
1 Mike Skinner Lowe's Special Olympics 25.00 60.00
1 Mike Skinner Lowe's Special Olympics Bank/2500 20.00 50.00
2 Dale Jarrett White Rain/6000 30.00 60.00
3 Tim Fedewa Kleenex/2000 25.00 60.00
3 Tim Fedewa Kleenex Bank 20.00 50.00
3 Ken Schrader Skoal/3504 40.00 80.00
4 Mike McLaughlin Goulds/2000 25.00 60.00
4 Mike McLaughlin Goulds Bank 25.00 60.00
5 Todd Bodine Tabasco Orange&White 15.00 40.00
5 Todd Bodine Tabasco Orange&White Bank 15.00 40.00
5 Todd Bodine Tabasco Red&Black 20.00 40.00
5 Todd Bodine Tabasco Red&Black Bank/2508 15.00 40.00
6 Ernie Irvan M&M's/10,008 50.00 100.00
6 Ernie Irvan M&M's Mac Tools Bank/4500 40.00 80.00
6 Ernie Irvan Skittles/10,008 20.00 50.00
6 Ernie Irvan Skittles Mac Tools Bank/4500 20.00 50.00
6 Ernie Irvan Wildberry Skittles/10,008 20.00 50.00
6 Ernie Irvan Wildberry Skittles Mac Tools Bank/4500 20.00 50.00
0 Sterling Marlin Coors Light 25.00 60.00
1 Steve Grissom Kodiak/3500 20.00 50.00
1 Steve Grissom Kodiak Bank/2500 20.00 50.00
2 Joe Nemechek 15.00 40.00
BellSouth/4008
42 Joe Nemechek BellSouth Bank 20.00 50.00
42 Marty Robbins 1974 Dodge Charger/6000 60.00 120.00
44 Tony Stewart Shell/5508 100.00 175.00
44 Tony Stewart Shell Bank/2508 50.00 100.00
44 Tony Stewart Shell Small Soldiers/10,992 50.00 100.00
44 Tony Stewart Shell Small Soldiers ank/2508 50.00 100.00
50 Ricky Craven Budweiser 20.00 50.00
50 Ricky Craven Bud Bank 30.00 80.00
50 Ricky Craven Bud Mac Tools Bank/3500 30.00 80.00
50 No Driver Association Bud Louie 25.00 60.00
50 No Driver Association Bud Louie Bank 25.00 60.00
72 Mike Dillon Detroit Gasket/4008 12.50 30.00
81 Kenny Wallace Square D/2508 15.00 40.00
81 Kenny Wallace Square D Lightning/4008 20.00 50.00
88 Dale Jarrett Quality Care 40.00 70.00
88 Dale Jarrett Quality Care Bank 30.00 70.00
88 Dale Jarrett Batman 60.00 100.00
88 Dale Jarrett Batman Bank 40.00 80.00
90 Dick Trickle Heilig-Meyers/3500 25.00 50.00
96 David Green Caterpillar/6996 8.00 20.00
98 Greg Sacks Thorn Apple Valley/4008 12.50 30.00
98 Rich Bickle Thorn Apple Valley Go Grill Crazy/2508 12.50 30.00
300 Darrell Waltrip Flock Special/3500 40.00 100.00
300 Darrell Waltrip Tim Flock Special Bank 30.00 80.00
00 Buckshot Jones Alka Seltzer 15.00 40.00
K2 Dale Earnhardt Dayvault's '56 Ford Dark Roof/10,000 50.00 100.00
K2 Dale Earnhardt Dayvault's '56 Ford Dark Roof Bank 40.00 80.00
K2 Dale Earnhardt Dayvault's '56 Ford Pink Roof 50.00 100.00

1998 Action Racing Collectables NAPA 1:24

This set was only available thru participating NAPA dealers.

7 Alan Kulwicki Hooters 1992 Thunderbird 45.00 90.00
7 Alan Kulwicki Hooters Gold 1992 T-bird 100.00 175.00
11 Ned Jarrett Richmond Ford 1965 Ford 50.00 90.00
11 Ned Jarrett Richmond Ford Gold 1965 Ford 100.00 175.00
11 Cale Yarborough 1976 Monte Carlo 30.00 75.00
11 Cale Yarborough Gold 1976 Monte Carlo 75.00 150.00
22 Red Byron Overseas Motors 1949 Hudson 30.00 60.00
22 Red Byron Overseas Motors Gold 1949 Hudson 100.00 175.00
28 Buddy Baker NAPA 1980 Olds 50.00 100.00
28 Buddy Baker NAPA Gold 1980 Olds 100.00 200.00
99 Curtis Turner 1956 Ford 30.00 60.00
99 Curtis Turner Gold 1956 Ford 60.00 120.00

1998 Action/RCCA Banks 1:24

These cars were produced by Action and distributed through the club (RCCA). Each car has a slot in the back window for a coin bank. All banks have clear windows.

1 Dale Earnhardt Jr. Coke Bear/12,500 60.00 120.00
1 Jeff Gordon Baby Ruth 1992 Thunderbird 60.00 120.00
1 Steve Park Pennzoil/2000 60.00 120.00
1 Darrell Waltrip Pennzoil 40.00 80.00
2 Rusty Wallace Adventures of Rusty/3500 25.00 60.00
2 Rusty Wallace Miller Lite/6000 20.00 50.00
2 Rusty Wallace Miller Lite Elvis/20,000 20.00 50.00
2 Rusty Wallace Miller Lite TCB Elvis 15.00 40.00
3 Dale Earnhardt Coke/15,000 75.00 150.00
3 Dale Earnhardt Goodwrench Plus/12,500 75.00 150.00
3 Dale Earnhardt Goodwrench Plus Bass Pro/12,500 60.00 120.00
3 Dale Earnhardt Goodwrench Plus Daytona Win 75.00 150.00
3 Dale Earnhardt Jr. AC Delco/2500 75.00 150.00
4 Bobby Hamilton Kodak/3500 15.00 40.00
5 Terry Labonte Blasted Fruit Loops/5000 20.00 50.00
5 Terry Labonte Kellogg's/5000 20.00 50.00
5 Terry Labonte Kellogg's Corny/3500 25.00 60.00
5 Terry Labonte Kellogg's Ironman 40.00 80.00
8 Dale Earnhardt RPM 1975 Dodge/12,500 50.00 120.00
8 Hut Stricklin Circuit City 20.00 50.00
9 Jerry Nadeau Scooby Zombie Island/2500 30.00 80.00
9 Lake Speed Birthday Cake 25.00 60.00
9 Lake Speed Huckleberry Hound 30.00 60.00
10 Ricky Rudd Tide/2500 30.00 70.00
12 Jeremy Mayfield Mobil 1/3500 25.00 50.00
12 Jimmy Spencer Zippo/600 50.00 100.00
14 Patty Moise Rhodes Xena/2500 25.00 50.00
18 Bobby Labonte Interstate Batteries/1500 30.00 75.00
18 Bobby Labonte Interstate Batteries Small Soldiers/7500 25.00 60.00
23 Jimmy Spencer No Bull/2500 25.00 60.00
24 Jeff Gordon DuPont/12,500 40.00 80.00
24 Jeff Gordon DuPont No Bull 30.00 60.00
24 Jeff Gordon DuPont Chromalusion/10,000 50.00 100.00
28 Kenny Irwin Havoline/5000 30.00 80.00
28 Kenny Irwin Havoline Joker/5000 30.00 80.00
31 Dale Earnhardt Jr. Sikkens Blue 1997 Monte Carlo/3500 75.00 200.00
31 Mike Skinner Lowe's/3500 15.00 40.00
31 Mike Skinner Lowe's Special Olympic/3500 20.00 50.00
32 Dale Jarrett White Rain/2000 30.00 60.00
33 Tim Fedewa Kleenex 25.00 60.00
34 Mike McLaughlin Goulds/600 25.00 60.00
35 Todd Bodine Tabasco Orange&White/1000 20.00 50.00
35 Todd Bodine Tabasco Red&Black/4000 20.00 50.00
36 Ernie Irvan M&M's 50.00 100.00
36 Ernie Irvan Skittles 40.00 80.00
36 Ernie Irvan Wildberry Skittles 30.00 60.00
41 Steve Grissom Kodiak/2500 30.00 60.00
42 Joe Nemechek BellSouth 25.00 60.00
42 Marty Robbins 1974 Dodge Charger/2500 60.00 120.00
44 Tony Stewart Shell/1500 60.00 120.00
44 Tony Stewart Shell Small Soldiers/5000 60.00 100.00
50 Ricky Craven Budweiser 30.00 80.00
50 No Driver Association Bud Louie/2000 40.00 80.00
81 Kenny Wallace Square D/1500 25.00 60.00
81 Kenny Wallace Square D Lightning/2500 25.00 60.00
88 Dale Jarrett Quality Care/5000 30.00 75.00
88 Dale Jarrett Quality Care Batman/7500 40.00 100.00
88 Dale Jarrett Quality Care No Bull/2500 30.00 75.00
90 Dick Trickle Heilig-Meyers/1500 25.00 60.00
96 David Green Caterpillar/1500 15.00 40.00
98 Greg Sacks Thorn Apple Valley 15.00 40.00
300 Darrell Waltrip Flock Special/2000 40.00 100.00
K2 Dale Earnhardt Dayvault's Pink Roof 1956 Ford 50.00 100.00

1998 Action/RCCA Elite 1:24

This series was consists of upgraded versions of their standard production cars. The cars from this series contain serial number plates on the undercarriage at the end of the car.

1 Dale Earnhardt Jr. Coke Bear/10,000 90.00 150.00
1 Steve Park Pennzoil Black Roof 60.00 120.00
1 Steve Park Pennzoil Yellow Roof/3200 50.00 100.00
1 Darrell Waltrip Pennzoil/1200 100.00 175.00
2 Rusty Wallace Adventures of Rusty/1320 60.00 120.00
2 Rusty Wallace Miller Lite/2500 50.00 100.00
2 Rusty Wallace Miller Lite Elvis/2500 50.00 100.00
2 Rusty Wallace Miller Lite TCB Elvis/1000 50.00 100.00
3 Dale Earnhardt Coke/12,500 150.00 250.00
3 Dale Earnhardt Goodwrench Plus/7500 125.00 250.00
3 Dale Earnhardt Goodwrench Plus Bass Pro/10,000 100.00 200.00
3 Dale Earnhardt Goodwrench Plus Daytona Win/9996 raced version with tire swatch 150.00 300.00
3 Dale Earnhardt Goodwrench Plus Gold/100 1200.00 1600.00
3 Dale Earnhardt Goodwrench 1995 Monte Carlo Silver/20,000 150.00 250.00
3 Dale Earnhardt Jr. AC Delco/1500 200.00 350.00
3 Dale Earnhardt Jr. AC Delco Gold Promo/100 800.00 1400.00
4 Bobby Hamilton Kodak 30.00 80.00
5 Terry Labonte Blasted Fruit Loops 50.00 120.00
5 Terry Labonte Kellogg's/3000 50.00 120.00
5 Terry Labonte Kellogg's Corny/1500 60.00 120.00
5 Terry Labonte Kellogg's Ironman/3500 50.00 100.00
8 Dale Earnhardt RPM 1975 Dodge/10,000 75.00 150.00
8 Hut Stricklin Circuit City 25.00 60.00
9 Jerry Nadeau Scooby Zombie Island 50.00 120.00
9 Lake Speed Birthday Cake 40.00 100.00
9 Lake Speed Huckleberry Hound 40.00 100.00
10 Ricky Rudd Tide 50.00 120.00
12 Jeremy Mayfield Mobil 1 40.00 80.00
12 Jimmy Spencer Zippo/400 125.00 200.00
14 Patty Moise Rhodes Xena 40.00 100.00
18 Bobby Labonte Interstate Batteries Hot Rod/1200 75.00 150.00
18 Bobby Labonte Interstate Batteries Small Soldiers/5000 75.00 150.00
22 Ward Burton MBNA/1200 30.00 80.00
23 Jimmy Spencer No Bull/1200 60.00 150.00
24 Jeff Gordon DuPont/3500 100.00 175.00
24 Jeff Gordon DuPont No Bull/1500 125.00 225.00
24 Jeff Gordon DuPont Chromalusion/7500 125.00 250.00
28 Kenny Irwin Havoline 60.00 120.00
28 Kenny Irwin Havoline Joker/3500 60.00 120.00
31 Dale Earnhardt Jr. Sikkens Blue/2500 1997 Monte Carlo 125.00 250.00
31 Mike Skinner Lowe's 30.00 80.00
31 Mike Skinner Lowe's Special Olympics/2500 25.00 60.00
33 Tim Fedewa Kleenex 100.00 175.00
34 Mike McLaughlin Goulds 75.00 150.00
35 Todd Bodine Tabasco Red&Black/1700 50.00 120.00
36 Ernie Irvan M&M's 125.00 200.00
36 Ernie Irvan Skittles 50.00 120.00
36 Ernie Irvan Wildberry Skittles/2000 40.00 100.00
41 Steve Grissom Kodiak/1200 40.00 80.00
42 Marty Robbins 1974 Dodge Charger/1500 100.00 175.00
44 Tony Stewart Shell/1200 150.00 300.00
44 Tony Stewart Shell Small Soldiers/3500 60.00 120.00
50 Ricky Craven Budweiser 50.00 100.00
50 No Driver Association Bud Louie/1000 60.00 120.00
81 Kenny Wallace Square D 50.00 100.00
81 Kenny Wallace Square D Lightning 50.00 100.00
88 Dale Jarrett Batman/5000 75.00 150.00
88 Dale Jarrett Quality Care Proto
88 Dale Jarrett Quality Care 60.00 120.00
88 Dale Jarrett Quality Care No Bull/1200 60.00 120.00
96 David Green Caterpillar/1200 25.00 60.00
98 Greg Sacks Thorn Apple Valley/1000 25.00 60.00
300 Darrell Waltrip Flock Special/1200 60.00 120.00
K2 Dale Earnhardt Dayvault's/10,000 75.00 150.00

1998-00 Action Racing Collectables Crystal 1:24

1 Dale Earnhardt Jr. Coke Bear/9000 1999 25.00 50.00
1 Jeff Gordon Baby Ruth 1992 Thunderbird/4008 1999 25.00 50.00
3 Dale Earnhardt Coke/9000 1998 50.00 100.00
3 Dale Earnhardt Goodwrench 1999 60.00 100.00
3 Dale Earnhardt Goodwrench Taz/2500 '00 60.00 100.00
3 Dale Earnhardt Wrangler/5000 1999 60.00 100.00
3 Dale Earnhardt Jr. AC Delco Superman/4008 1999 25.00 50.00
8 Dale Earnhardt Jr. Bud 1999 25.00 50.00
24 Jeff Gordon DuPont 1999 25.00 50.00
24 Jeff Gordon DuPont Superman/6000 1999 30.00 60.00
24 Jeff Gordon Pepsi/8000 1999 25.00 50.00

1998 Action Racing Collectables Fan Fueler 1:24

This series of 1:24 cars was produced for mass retailers and trackside sales by Action. Each piece is packaged in a clear window box with the name "Fan Fueler" printed clearly on the sides. No production run totals were given.

2 Rusty Wallace Ford Motorsports 10.00 25.00
3 Dale Earnhardt Goodwrench Plus 15.00 30.00
24 Jeff Gordon DuPont 12.50 25.00
88 Dale Jarrett Quality Care 10.00 25.00

1999 Action Performance 1:24

These cars were issued in an "AP" or Action Performance clear window or solid box. The red and black "AP" logo and a checkered flag design on both box varieties helps to identify this year along with the obvious notation of "1999" at the bottom of the box.

3 Dale Earnhardt Jr. AC Delco 12.50 25.00
8 Dale Earnhardt Jr. Budweiser 15.00 30.00
20 Tony Stewart Home Depot HO Black Windows 90.00 150.00
20 Tony Stewart Home Depot HO Black Windows Rookie Stripes 40.00 80.00
20 Tony Stewart Home Depot HO Clear Windows Rookie Stripes 30.00 60.00
20 Tony Stewart Home Depot not HO Clear Windows Rookie Stripes 12.50 30.00
20 Tony Stewart Home Depot Habitat HO 20.00 50.00
20 Tony Stewart Home Depot Habitat not HO 12.50 30.00
22 Ward Burton Caterpiller 15.00 25.00
24 Jeff Gordon DuPont 15.00 30.00
28 Kenny Irwin Havoline Flames 10.00 25.00
88 Dale Jarrett Quality Care 10.00 25.00

1999 Action Racing Collectables 1:24

This year Action mounted their Alcohol and Tobacco cars on a base that resembles a pit wall and labeled them "For adults only" so as not to confuse their collectables with toys.

ALCOHOL/TOBACCO CARS ON PIT WALL BASE

1 Jeff Gordon Carolina Ford 1991 Thunderbird 40.00 80.00
1 Jeff Gordon Carolina Ford 1991 Thunderbird Bank 50.00 80.00
1 Jeff Gordon Carolina '91 T-bird Mac Tools 30.00 80.00
1 Steve Park Pennzoil 30.00 60.00
1 Steve Park Pennzoil Bank 25.00 60.00
1 Steve Park Pennzoil Shark 30.00 60.00
2 Rusty Wallace Miller Lite/15,000 30.00 80.00
2 Rusty Wallace Miller Lite Bank/2508 40.00 80.00
2 Rusty Wallace Miller Lite Harley/2508 black windows 30.00 80.00
2 Rusty Wallace Miller Lite Harley clear windows 40.00 80.00
2 Rusty Wallace Miller Lite Harley Bank/5004 30.00 60.00
2 Rusty Wallace Miller Lite Last Lap/10,080 30.00 80.00
2 Rusty Wallace Miller Lite Last Lap Bank 30.00 80.00
2 Rusty Wallace Miller Lite Texas 40.00 80.00
3 Dale Earnhardt Goodwrench 75.00 150.00
3 Dale Earnhardt Goodwrench Bank/10,008 60.00 120.00
3 Dale Earnhardt Goodwrench 25th Anniversary/2500 75.00 150.00
3 Dale Earnhardt Goodwrench 25th Anniversary Bank 75.00 125.00
3 Dale Earnhardt Goodwrench Crash 1997 Monte Carlo 250.00 400.00
3 Dale Earnhardt Goodwrench Sign 60.00 120.00
3 Dale Earnhardt Goodwrench Sign Last Lap/15,504 150.00 250.00
3 Dale Earnhardt Goodwrench Sign Last Lap Bank/2508 100.00 200.00
3 Dale Earnhardt Wrangler/5004 75.00 150.00
3 Dale Earnhardt 60.00 120.00

Wrangler Bank/5004
3 Dale Earnhardt Jr. AC Delco 30.00 80.00
3 Dale Earnhardt Jr. AC Delco Bank/5004 50.00 100.00
3 Dale Earnhardt Jr. AC Delco Last Lap/12,000 60.00 120.00
3 Dale Earnhardt Jr. AC Delco Last Lap Bank 70.00 120.00
3 Dale Earnhardt Jr. AC Delco Superman 40.00 100.00
3 Dale Earnhardt Jr. AC Delco Superman Bank 40.00 100.00
4 Bobby Hamilton Advantix 15.00 40.00
4 Jeff Purvis Lance/4008 12.50 30.00
5 Terry Labonte Kellogg's 30.00 70.00
5 Terry Labonte Kellogg's Bank/2508 25.00 60.00
5 Terry Labonte Kellogg's Bank Mac Tools 20.00 50.00
5 Terry Labonte Kellogg's NASCAR Racers/7500 25.00 60.00
5 Terry Labonte K-Sentials 30.00 80.00
5 Terry Labonte K-Sentials Bank/2508 25.00 60.00
5 Terry Labonte Rice Krispies/10,080 25.00 60.00
5 Terry Labonte Rice Krispies Bank/2508 25.00 60.00
8 Dale Earnhardt Jr. Bud 60.00 120.00
8 Dale Earnhardt Jr. Bud Bank/3000 50.00 100.00
8 Dale Earnhardt Jr. Bud Atlanta/7008 60.00 120.00
8 Dale Earnhardt Jr. Bud Michigan/6708 60.00 120.00
8 Dale Earnhardt Jr. Bud New Hampshire/6708 60.00 120.00
8 Dale Earnhardt Jr. Bud Richmond/6708 60.00 120.00
9 Jerry Nadeau Dexter's Lab/7500 20.00 50.00
9 Jerry Nadeau Dexter's Lab Bank/2508 20.00 50.00
9 Jerry Nadeau Jetsons/5004 20.00 50.00
10 Ricky Rudd Tide/4008 35.00 75.00
10 Ricky Rudd Tide Mac Tools 30.00 75.00
10 Ricky Rudd Tide Kids 30.00 80.00
11 Dale Jarrett Green Bay Packers/6084 75.00 125.00
11 Dale Jarrett Rayovac 20.00 50.00
12 Jeremy Mayfield Mobil 1 25.00 60.00
12 Jeremy Mayfield Mobil 1 Kentucky Derby 20.00 50.00
12 Jeremy Mayfield Mobil 1 Kentucky Derby Bank/5004 15.00 40.00
15 Ken Schrader Oakwood Homes/3504 15.00 40.00
16 Ron Hornaday NAPA SuperTruck/2940 30.00 80.00
16 Ron Hornaday NAPA Superman SuperTruck/7920 20.00 50.00
17 Matt Kenseth DeWalt/4008 60.00 120.00
17 Matt Kenseth DeWalt Bank/2508 50.00 100.00
18 Bobby Labonte Interstate Batteries 40.00 75.00
18 Bobby Labonte Interstate Batt.Bank 35.00 70.00
18 Bobby Labonte Interstate Batteries NASCAR Racers/7500 35.00 70.00
18 Bobby Labonte MBNA/4608 30.00 80.00
19 Mike Skinner Yellow Freight/4008 25.00 60.00
20 Tony Stewart Home Depot/5004 125.00 250.00
20 Tony Stewart Home Depot black windows 60.00 120.00
20 Tony Stewart Home Depot Bank/2508 100.00 200.00
20 Tony Stewart Home Depot Gold QVC Race Fans/2508 100.00 200.00
20 Tony Stewart Home Depot Fan Club AUTO 125.00 250.00
20 Tony Stewart Home Depot Habitat 30.00 80.00
21 Elliott Sadler Citgo/4008 25.00 60.00
22 Ward Burton Caterpillar/3804 30.00 80.00
22 Ward Burton Caterpillar Mac Tools/5004 30.00 80.00
23 Jimmy Spencer No Bull 20.00 50.00
23 Jimmy Spencer No Bull Bank/2508 20.00 50.00
23 Jimmy Spencer Winston Lights 15.00 40.00
23 Jimmy Spencer Winston Lights Mac Tools 20.00 40.00
23 Jimmy Spencer Winston Lights Bank/2508 20.00 50.00
24 Jeff Gordon DuPont 25.00 60.00
24 Jeff Gordon DuPont Black Window/7500 20.00 50.00
24 Jeff Gordon DuPont Mac Tools 30.00 60.00
24 Jeff Gordon DuPont Bank/7500 25.00 60.00
24 Jeff Gordon DuPont Brickyard/2500 50.00 100.00
24 Jeff Gordon DuPont Gold 1998 3-Time Champ 100.00 200.00
24 Jeff Gordon DuPont NASCAR Racers/7800 75.00 150.00
24 Jeff Gordon DuPont Superman 50.00 100.00
24 Jeff Gordon DuPont Superman Mac Tools 50.00 100.00
24 Jeff Gordon DuPont Superman Bank 50.00 100.00
24 Jeff Gordon Pepsi 30.00 80.00
24 Jeff Gordon Pepsi Bank/7500 25.00 60.00
24 Jeff Gordon Pepsi Mac Tools 30.00 60.00
24 Jeff Gordon Pepsi Star Wars 60.00 120.00
24 Jeff Gordon Pepsi Star Wars Bank 50.00 100.00
24 Jeff Gordon Pepsi Star Wars Mac Tools 40.00 80.00
25 Wally Dallenbach Bud/5004 25.00 60.00
25 Wally Dallenbach Bud Bank/2508 20.00 50.00
25 Wally Dallenbach Bud Bank Mac Tools 20.00 50.00
27 Casey Atwood Castrol/6312 20.00 50.00
27 Casey Atwood Castrol Last Lap/5004 20.00 50.00
27 Casey Atwood Castrol Last Lap Bank 25.00 60.00
28 Kenny Irwin Havoline/5004 25.00 60.00
28 Kenny Irwin Havoline Bank 35.00 65.00
30 Derrike Cope Bryan/2508 12.00 30.00
30 Derrike Cope Jimmy Dean 12.00 30.00
30 Dale Earnhardt Army 1976 Malibu 75.00 150.00
30 Dale Earnhardt Army '76 Malibu Bank/2508 75.00 150.00
31 Dale Earnhardt Jr. Gargoyles 1997 Monte Carlo/8500 75.00 135.00
31 Dale Earnhardt Jr. Gargoyles 1997 Monte Carlo Bank/2508 60.00 110.00
31 Dale Earnhardt Jr. Mom 'N' Pop's 1996 Monte Carlo 40.00 100.00
31 Dale Earnhardt Jr. Mom 'N' Pop's 1996 Monte Carlo Bank/2508 40.00 100.00
31 Dale Earnhardt Jr. Sikkens White 997 Monte Carlo/5000 50.00 100.00
31 Dale Earnhardt Jr. Sikkens White 1997 Monte Carlo Bank/6000 40.00 80.00
31 Mike Skinner Lowe's/3504 15.00 40.00
32 Jeff Green Kleenex 75th 25.00 50.00
33 Ken Schrader Skoal/6000 40.00 75.00
33 Ken Schrader Skoal Red/6000 40.00 75.00
36 Ernie Irvan M&M's 30.00 60.00
36 Ernie Irvan M&M's Mac Tools 20.00 50.00
36 Ernie Irvan M&M's Countdown/9000 20.00 50.00
36 Ernie Irvan M&M's Millennium 20.00 50.00
36 Ernie Irvan M&M's Millennium Bank 15.00 40.00
36 Ernie Irvan Crispy M&M's 20.00 50.00
36 Ernie Irvan Crispy M&M's Bank/2508 25.00 60.00
36 Ernie Irvan Pedigree/9012 20.00 50.00
36 Tim Fedewa Stanley 15.00 40.00
36 Tim Fedewa Stanley Bank/2508 15.00 40.00
37 Kevin Grubb Timber Wolf/5004 20.00 50.00
40 Coca-Cola 600/4608 20.00 60.00
40 Kerry Earnhardt Channellock/6504 30.00 75.00
40 Kerry Earnhardt Channellock Mac Tools/5004 30.00 75.00
40 Sterling Marlin Coors Light/600 25.00 60.00
40 Sterling Marlin Coors Light Brooks & Dunn 30.00 80.00
40 Sterling Marlin Coors Light Brooks & Dunn Bank/2508 25.00 60.00
40 Sterling Marlin Coors Light John Wayne/11,364 25.00 60.00
40 Sterling Marlin Coors Light John Wayne Bank/2508 25.00 60.00
44 Justin Labonte Slim Jim 20.00 50.00
45 Rich Bickle 10-10-345 25.00 60.00
50 Mark Green Dr Pepper 15.00 40.00
55 Kenny Wallace Square D 25.00 60.00
55 Kenny Wallace Square D NASCAR Racers/7764 20.00 50.00
59 Mike Dillon Kingsford 15.00 40.00
66 Darrell Waltrip 25.00 60.00
Big K Route 66/8508
66 Darrell Waltrip Big K Route 66 Victory Tour/4008 25.00 60.00
71 Dave Marcis Realtree/5004 25.00 60.00
77 Dale Earnhardt Hy-Gain 1976 Malibu 75.00 150.00
77 Dale Earnhardt Hy-Gain 1976 Malibu Bank 75.00 150.00
88 Dale Jarrett Quality Care/14,508 30.00 60.00
88 Dale Jarrett Quality Care Bank/2508 30.00 60.00
88 Dale Jarrett Quality Care Mac Tools/5004 20.00 50.00
88 Dale Jarrett Quality Care White/8208 50.00 80.00
88 Dale Jarrett Quality Care White Bank 40.00 70.00
88 Dale Jarrett Quality Care Last Lap/12,000 40.00 75.00
88 Dale Jarrett Quality Care Last Lap Bank 40.00 80.00
88 Dale Jarrett Quality Care Gold QVC Race Fans/2508 50.00 100.00
99 Kevin Lepage Red Man 20.00 50.00
00 Buckshot Jones Crown Fiber/9012 15.00 40.00
00 Larry Pearson Cheez-it/3000 15.00 40.00

1999 Action/RCCA Banks 1:24

These cars were available only through the club, and were very limited. All banks have clear windows.

1 Jeff Gordon Carolina Ford 1991 Thunderbird 75.00 125.00
1 Steve Park Pennzoil 70.00 110.00
1 Steve Park Pennzoil Shark/2000 50.00 100.00
2 Rusty Wallace Miller Lite/3500 50.00 100.00
2 Rusty Wallace Miller Lite Harley-Davidson 50.00 100.00
2 Rusty Wallace Miller Lite Last Lap/3000 25.00 60.00
2 Rusty Wallace Miller Lite True to Texas/1500 50.00 100.00
3 Dale Earnhardt Goodwrench 100.00 200.00
3 Dale Earnhardt Goodwrench 25th Anniversary/8000 75.00 125.00
3 Dale Earnhardt Goodwrench Sign 75.00 150.00
3 Dale Earnhardt Goodwrench Sign Last Lap/10,000 75.00 150.00
3 Dale Earnhardt Wrangler/10,020 60.00 120.00
3 Dale Earnhardt Jr. AC Delco/4500 40.00 100.00
3 Dale Earnhardt Jr. AC Delco Superman/15,000 40.00 100.00
3 Dale Earnhardt Jr. AC Delco Last Lap/10,000 60.00 120.00
4 Bobby Hamilton Advantix 30.00 80.00
5 Terry Labonte Kellogg's/3500 25.00 60.00
5 Terry Labonte Kellogg's NASCAR Racers/3500 25.00 60.00
5 Terry Labonte K-Sentials 40.00 80.00
5 Terry Labonte Rice Krispies/3500 40.00 80.00
8 Dale Earnhardt Jr. Bud/5000 60.00 120.00
8 Dale Earnhardt Jr. Bud Atlanta/2500 60.00 120.00
8 Dale Earnhardt Jr. Bud Michigan/2500 60.00 120.00
8 Dale Earnhardt Jr. Bud New Hamp./2500 60.00 120.00
8 Dale Earnhardt Jr. Bud Richmond/2500 60.00 120.00
9 Jerry Nadeau Dexter's Laboratory 40.00 80.00
9 Jerry Nadeau Jetsons 40.00 80.00
10 Ricky Rudd Tide 30.00 80.00
10 Ricky Rudd Tide Peroxide/1500 30.00 80.00
11 Dale Jarrett Green Bay Packers/1500 50.00 100.00
12 Jeremy Mayfield Mobil 1/2500 25.00 60.00
12 Jeremy Mayfield Mobil 1 Kentucky Derby 30.00 80.00
15 Ken Schrader Oakwood Homes 30.00 80.00
16 Ron Hornaday NAPA Superman SuperTruck/3500 20.00 50.00
17 Matt Kenseth DeWalt/2500 50.00 100.00
18 Bobby Labonte Interstate Batteries 40.00 80.00
18 Bobby Labonte Interstate Batteries NASCAR Racers/3500 40.00 80.00
19 Mike Skinner Yellow Freight 40.00 80.00
20 Tony Stewart Home Depot/2500 100.00 200.00
20 Tony Stewart Home Depot Habitat/8000 30.00 80.00
21 Elliott Sadler Citgo/1000 30.00 80.00
22 Ward Burton Caterpillar Proto
23 Jimmy Spencer No Bull/2508 30.00 80.00
23 Jimmy Spencer Winston Lights/5000 30.00 80.00
24 Jeff Gordon DuPont/8500 40.00 100.00
24 Jeff Gordon DuPont NASCAR Racers/8500 75.00 150.00
24 Jeff Gordon DuPont Superman 50.00 100.00
24 Jeff Gordon Pepsi/5000 30.00 80.00
24 Jeff Gordon Pepsi Star Wars/10,000 50.00 100.00
25 Wally Dallenbach Budweiser 25.00 60.00
27 Casey Atwood Castrol 25.00 60.00
27 Casey Atwood Castrol Last Lap/3000 20.00 50.00
28 Kenny Irwin Havoline/2500 20.00 50.00
30 Derrike Cope Jimmy Dean 20.00 50.00
30 Dale Earnhardt Army 1976 Malibu Bank/4000 75.00 150.00
31 Dale Earnhardt Jr. Gargoyles 1997 Monte Carlo/7500 60.00 100.00
31 Dale Earnhardt Jr. Mom 'N' Pop's 1996 Monte Carlo/7500 50.00 100.00
31 Dale Earnhardt Jr. Sikkens White 1997 Monte Carlo/7500 40.00 80.00
31 Dale Earnhardt Jr. Wrangler 1997 Monte Carlo/4500 50.00 100.00
31 Mike Skinner Lowe's 25.00 60.00
33 Ken Schrader Skoal/2000 40.00 80.00
33 Ken Schrader Skoal Red/2000 40.00 80.00
36 Ernie Irvan M&M's 30.00 80.00
36 Ernie Irvan Crispy M&M's/1800 30.00 80.00
36 Ernie Irvan Pedigree 25.00 60.00
40 Coca-Cola 600 25.00 60.00
40 Kerry Earnhardt Channellock 40.00 80.00
40 Sterling Marlin Coors Light 40.00 80.00
40 Sterling Marlin Coors Light Brooks & Dunn 40.00 80.00
40 Sterling Marlin Coors Light John Wayne 40.00 80.00
44 Justin Labonte Slim Jim 20.00 50.00
45 Rich Bickle 10-10-345 25.00 60.00
50 Mark Green Dr Pepper/2000 25.00 60.00
55 Kenny Wallace Square D 20.00 50.00
55 Kenny Wallace Square D NASCAR Racers/3500 20.00 50.00
66 Darrell Waltrip Big K Route 66/1500 25.00 60.00
71 Dave Marcis Realtree 25.00 60.00
77 Robert Pressley Jasper/2500 20.00 50.00
88 Dale Jarrett Quality Care/2500 25.00 60.00
88 Dale Jarrett Quality Care No Bull 30.00 80.00
88 Dale Jarrett Quality Care Last Lap 30.00 60.00
88 Dale Jarrett Quality Care White/2500 40.00 80.00
99 Kevin Lepage Red Man/2000 20.00 50.00
00 Buckshot Jones Crown Fiber 25.00 60.00
02 Mark Martin J-Mar Trucking/2500 50.00 100.00

1999 Action/RCCA Elite 1:24

1 Jeff Gordon Baby Ruth 1992 Thunderbird/2500 150.00 250.00
1 Jeff Gordon Carolina 1991 Thunderbird/1500 100.00 175.00
1 Steve Park Pennzoil 90.00 150.00
1 Steve Park Pennzoil Shark 60.00 120.00
2 Rusty Wallace Miller Lite 90.00 150.00
2 Rusty Wallace Miller Lite Last Lap/1500 75.00 150.00
2 Rusty Wallace Miller Lite Harley/2500 100.00 175.00
3 Dale Earnhardt Goodwrench/5000 125.00 200.00
3 Dale Earnhardt Goodwrench 25th Anniversary/7500 100.00 200.00
3 Dale Earnhardt Goodwrench Sign/5000 100.00 200.00
3 Dale Earnhardt Goodwrench Sign Last Lap/8500 150.00 250.00
3 Dale Earnhardt Wrangler/7500 125.00 250.00
3 Dale Earnhardt Jr. AC Delco/8500 100.00 200.00
3 Dale Earnhardt Jr. AC Delco Last Lap/8500 75.00 150.00
3 Dale Earnhardt Jr. AC Delco Platinum/300 300.00 600.00
3 Dale Earnhardt Jr. AC Delco Superman/10,000 75.00 150.00
4 Bobby Hamilton Advantix/800 30.00 80.00
5 Terry Labonte Kellogg's/2500 25.00 60.00
5 Terry Labonte Kellogg's NASCAR Racers/2500 40.00 100.00
5 Terry Labonte K-Sentials 75.00 150.00
5 Terry Labonte Rice Krispies 75.00 150.00
6 Mark Martin Jim Magill Green 1983 Monte Carlo/2500 75.00 125.00
8 Dale Earnhardt Jr. Bud/5004 100.00 200.00
8 Dale Earnhardt Jr. Bud Atlanta/1000 100.00 200.00
8 Dale Earnhardt Jr. Bud Michigan/1000 100.00 200.00
8 Dale Earnhardt Jr. Bud New Hampshire/1000 100.00 200.00
8 Dale Earnhardt Jr. Bud Richmond/1000 100.00 200.00
9 Jerry Nadeau Dexter's Lab/1000 40.00 100.00
9 Jerry Nadeau Jetsons/600 40.00 100.00
10 Ricky Rudd Tide 50.00 120.00
10 Ricky Rudd Tide Kids 50.00 120.00
11 Dale Jarrett Green Bay Packers 80.00 150.00
12 Jeremy Mayfield Mobil 1/1500 40.00 100.00
12 Jeremy Mayfield Mobil 1 Kentucky Derby/3500 30.00 80.00
17 Matt Kenseth DeWalt/1000 125.00 200.00
18 Bobby Labonte Interstate Batteries/1000 75.00 150.00
18 Bobby Labonte Interstate Batteries NASCAR Racers/2500 60.00 120.00
18 Bobby Labonte MBNA/800 60.00 120.00
19 Mike Skinner Yellow Freight/1000 40.00 100.00
20 Tony Stewart Home Depot/1000 300.00 500.00
20 Tony Stewart Home Depot Habitat/5000 75.00 150.00
22 Ward Burton Caterpiller 125.00 225.00
23 Jimmy Spencer No Bull 50.00 120.00
23 Jimmy Spencer Winston Lights/3500 40.00 100.00
24 Jeff Gordon DuPont/5000 75.00 150.00
24 Jeff Gordon DuPont NASCAR Racers/5500 100.00 200.00
24 Jeff Gordon DuPont Superman/10,000 75.00 150.00
24 Jeff Gordon Pepsi/3500 60.00 120.00
24 Jeff Gordon Pepsi Star Wars/7500 60.00 150.00
25 Wally Dallenbach Budweiser 40.00 100.00
27 Casey Atwood Castrol/1000 40.00 100.00
27 Casey Atwood Castrol Last Lap/1500 40.00 100.00
28 Kenny Irwin Havoline/1000 50.00 120.00
30 Derrike Cope Jimmy Dean/800 30.00 80.00
30 Dale Earnhardt Army 1976 Malibu/2500 150.00 250.00
31 Dale Earnhardt Jr. Gargoyles 1997 Monte Carlo/3500 125.00 225.00
31 Dale Earnhardt Jr. Mom 'N' Pop's 1996 Monte Carlo/5000 60.00 120.00
31 Dale Earnhardt Jr. Sikkens White 1997 Monte Carlo/4000 75.00 150.00
31 Dale Earnhardt Jr. Wrangler 1997 Monte Carlo/3500 75.00 150.00
31 Mike Skinner Lowe's/1000 40.00 100.00
33 Ken Schrader Skoal 125.00 200.00
33 Ken Schrader Skoal Red 125.00 200.00
36 Ernie Irvan M&M's 75.00 150.00
36 Ernie Irvan M&M's Countdown/1500 50.00 100.00
36 Ernie Irvan M&M's Millennium 50.00 100.00
36 Ernie Irvan Crispy M&M's/1000 60.00 120.00
36 Ernie Irvan Pedigree 50.00 100.00
40 Coca-Cola 600 80.00 125.00
40 Kerry Earnhardt Channellock/800 75.00 150.00
40 Sterling Marlin Coors Light 50.00 100.00
40 Sterling Marlin Coors Light Brooks & Dunn/800 60.00 120.00
40 Sterling Marlin Coors Light John Wayne 60.00 120.00
45 Rich Bickle 10-10-345/800 30.00 80.00

Mark Green Dr Pepper/1000	40.00	100.00
Kenny Wallace Square D/1000	25.00	60.00
Kenny Wallace Square D NASCAR Racers/2500	25.00	60.00
Darrell Waltrip Big K Route 66/1000	40.00	100.00
Dave Marcis Realtree	75.00	150.00
Dale Earnhardt Hy-Gain 1976 Malibu/2500	150.00	250.00
Robet Pressley Jasper/1000	25.00	60.00
Dale Jarrett Quality Care/1000	100.00	175.00
Dale Jarrett Quality Care White/1000	125.00	200.00
Dale Jarrett Quality Care Last Lap/1000	75.00	150.00
Mark Martin J-Mar Trucking/1000	100.00	200.00

1999 Action/RCCA SelectNet Banks 1:24

Jeff Gordon Carolina Ford 1991	50.00	100.00
Dale Earnhardt Jr. AC Delco	25.00	60.00
Dale Earnhardt Wrangler	30.00	80.00
Dale Earnhardt Jr. Bud	50.00	120.00
Dale Jarrett Green Bay Packers/2500	75.00	125.00
Matt Kenseth DeWalt	40.00	80.00
Tony Stewart Home Depot	125.00	200.00
Tony Stewart Home Depot Habitat for Humanity/1600	60.00	100.00
Jeff Gordon Pepsi/804	25.00	60.00
Casey Atwood Castrol/800	25.00	50.00
Dale Earnhardt Jr. Sikkens White 1997 Monte Carlo	30.00	80.00
Dale Earnhardt Jr. Wrangler 1997 Monte Carlo/600	40.00	100.00
3 Ken Schrader Skoal/250	25.00	60.00
5 Ernie Irvan M&M's	20.00	50.00

1999 Action/RCCA SelectNet Elite 1:24

Goracing.com	40.00	80.00
Dale Earnhardt Jr. Bud/1500	75.00	150.00
Matt Kenseth DeWalt/1000	75.00	150.00
0 Tony Stewart Home Depot/1500	150.00	250.00
0 Tony Stewart Home Depot Habitat/1600	50.00	100.00
Jeff Gordon Pepsi/600	40.00	100.00
Casey Atwood Castrol/800	30.00	60.00
Dale Earnhardt Jr. Sikkens White 1997/1000	75.00	150.00
Dale Earnhardt Jr. Wrangler 1997/500	75.00	150.00
3 Ken Schrader Skoal	40.00	80.00
6 Ken Schrader M&M's	30.00	80.00

2000 Action Performance 1:24

hese cars were packaged in an "AP" Action Performance box. any were issued in both the clear window box or solid box riety. The solid boxes are black and red with the year 2000 early printed on them. The window boxes are also black and d with the year notation except for a few pieces that were sued in a colorful promo style window box.

Kevin Harvick AC Delco	15.00	30.00
Rusty Wallace Rusty	12.50	25.00
Dale Earnhardt Goodwrench	25.00	50.00
Ron Hornaday NAPA	10.00	20.00
Ron Hornaday NAPA 75th Anniversary in Promo style packaging	10.00	20.00
Dale Earnhardt Jr. Dale Earnhardt Jr.	15.00	30.00
8 Bobby Labonte Interstate Batteries	15.00	30.00
0 Tony Stewart Home Depot solid box	15.00	30.00
0 Tony Stewart Home Depot window box	15.00	30.00
1 Mike Dillon Quantis	10.00	20.00
24 Jeff Gordon DuPont	15.00	30.00
24 Jeff Gordon Pepsi	15.00	30.00
28 Ricky Rudd Havoline	15.00	25.00
31 Mike Skinner Lowe's	10.00	20.00
36 Ken Schrader M&M's	10.00	20.00
37 Kevin Grubb Timber Wolf	12.50	25.00
38 Dale Jarrett Quality Care	12.50	25.00

2000 Action Racing Collectables 1:24

hese 1:24 scale replicas were produced by Action Racing Collectibles. Most pieces were packaged in a blue box and have he Action Racing Collectibles logo or the Racing Collectibles nc. logo on the box.

1 Randy LaJoie Bob Evan's	15.00	30.00
1 Randy LaJoie Bob Evan's Bank/608	12.50	25.00
1 Randy LaJoie Bob Evan's Monsters/4800	12.50	25.00
1 Randy LaJoie Bob Evan's Monsters Bank	20.00	40.00
1 Steve Park Pennzoil/7008	25.00	60.00
1 Steve Park Pennzoil Bank/1008	20.00	50.00
1 Steve Park Pennzoil Shark Snap-on Promo Black Window Promo	15.00	30.00
2 Kevin Harvick AC Delco/5004	100.00	200.00
2 Mark Martin G&G Trucking '83 ASA Firebird/5940	15.00	40.00
2 Mark Martin Hartley's 1979 ASA Camaro/5508	25.00	60.00
2 Rusty Wallace Miller Lite/10,500	20.00	50.00
2 Rusty Wallace Miller Lite Bank/2508	20.00	50.00
2 Rusty Wallace Miller Lite 10th Ann./6000	25.00	50.00
2 Rusty Wallace Miller Lite Harley/19,704	60.00	120.00
2 Rusty Wallace Miller Lite Harley Bank/3276	30.00	60.00
3 Dale Earnhardt Goodwrench/34,992	75.00	150.00
3 Dale Earnhardt Goodwrench Bank/3504	100.00	250.00
3 Dale Earnhardt Goodwrench Brickyard	75.00	150.00
3 Dale Earnhardt Goodwrench Clear	150.00	250.00
3 Dale Earnhardt Goodwrench No Bull raced version	50.00	100.00
3 Dale Earnhardt Goodwrench No Bull Bank raced version/13,333	30.00	60.00
3 Dale Earnhardt Goodwrench Peter Max/101,916	75.00	150.00
3 Dale Earnhardt Goodwr.Peter Max BW car/100,247	60.00	120.00
3 Dale Earnhardt Goodwrench Peter Max Snap-on black window car/7500	60.00	120.00
3 Dale Earnhardt Goodwrench Peter Max Bank/5004	75.00	150.00
3 Dale Earnhardt Goodwrench Platinum 75th Win/25,008	75.00	150.00
3 Dale Earnhardt Goodwrench Talladega Win No Bull/10.003	60.00	120.00
3 Dale Earnhardt Goodwrench Taz No Bull/16,008	100.00	200.00
3 Dale Earnhardt Goodwrench Taz No Bull black window/16,008	60.00	120.00
3 Dale Earnhardt Goodwrench Taz No Bull Bank	60.00	120.00
3 Ron Hornaday NAPA/4008	20.00	50.00
3 Ron Hornaday NAPA 75th Anniversary/4008	20.00	50.00
3 Ron Hornaday NAPA 75th Ann.Bank	20.00	40.00
3 Ron Hornaday NAPA Monsters/8004	20.00	40.00
3 Ron Hornaday NAPA Monsters Bank	20.00	40.00
4 Bobby Hamilton Kodak/3504	15.00	40.00
4 Bobby Hamilton Kodak Navy/12,252	25.00	50.00
4 Bobby Hamilton Kodak Navy Bank/2508	25.00	50.00
4 Ernie Irvan Kodak 1991 Lumina	30.00	60.00
4 Ernie Irvan Kodak 1991 Lumina Mac Tools/3000	20.00	50.00
4 Mark Martin Jim Magill Orange 1983 Monte Carlo	20.00	50.00
4 Jeff Purvis Porter Cable/3504	15.00	40.00
5 Terry Labonte Froot Loops/14,148	20.00	50.00
5 Terry Labonte Froot Loops Mac Tools/3000	20.00	50.00
5 Terry Labonte Froot Loops Bank/2508	20.00	50.00
5 Terry Labonte Frost.Flakes Bank/1008	20.00	50.00
5 Terry Labonte Kellogg's	25.00	60.00
5 Terry Labonte Kellogg's Mac Tools/3000	25.00	60.00
5 Terry Labonte Kellogg's Bank	25.00	60.00
5 Terry Labonte Kellogg's Grinch	30.00	60.00
5 Terry Labonte Rice Krispies	20.00	50.00
5 Terry Labonte Rice Krispies Mac Tools/3000	20.00	50.00
6 Ernie Irvan Kroger 1987 Monte Carlo Aero Coupe/3504	35.00	60.00
6 Mark Martin Jim Magill Green 1983 Monte Carlo/7008	25.00	60.00
6 Mark Martin Jim Magill Green 1983 Monte Carlo Bank/6500	25.00	60.00
7 Michael Waltrip Nations Rent	15.00	40.00
7 Michael Waltrip Nations Rent Bank	15.00	40.00
8 Jeff Burton Baby Ruth 1990 Thunderbird/8004	25.00	60.00
8 Dale Earnhardt Jr. Bud/30,000	100.00	200.00
8 Dale Earnhardt Jr. Bud Bank/3504	90.00	150.00
8 Dale Earnhardt Jr. Bud Brickyard/2508	150.00	250.00
8 Dale Earnhardt Jr. Bud Olympic/37,440	50.00	100.00
8 Bobby Hillin Kleenex/2508	15.00	40.00
10 Johnny Benson Aaron's/4008	20.00	40.00
10 Jeff Green Nesquik	25.00	60.00
11 Jason Jarrett Rayovac/3504	15.00	30.00
11 Jason Jarrett Rayovac Bank/1008	15.00	30.00
11 Darrell Waltrip Hodgdon 1984 Camaro/3000	20.00	50.00
11 Darrell Waltrip Pepsi '83 Firebird/4008	15.00	40.00
11 Darrell Waltrip Mountain Dew 1984 Camaro/3000	20.00	50.00
11 Cale Yarborough Holly Farms 1976 Malibu/5640	30.00	60.00
12 Jeremy Mayfield Mobil 1/5004	15.00	40.00
12 Jeremy Mayfield Mobil 1 Bank	20.00	50.00
12 Jeremy Mayfield Mobil 1 World Series/7896	15.00	40.00
12 Jeremy Mayfield Mobil 1 World Series Bank/1008	20.00	50.00
12 Bobby Allison Coke 1974 Malibu/3504	30.00	60.00
12 Bobby Allison Coke 1974 Malibu Bank/1008	25.00	60.00
13 Robby Gordon Menards Monsters/5712	20.00	50.00
13 Robby Gordon Menards Monsters Bank/1380	20.00	40.00
14 Rusty Wallace Southland 1981 Camaro/3000	100.00	200.00
15 Mike Skinner Albertsons/2508	15.00	40.00
15 Mike Skinner Albertsons Bank	20.00	40.00
15 Tony Stewart Vision3 1996 Grand Prix/10,536	40.00	80.00
18 Bobby Labonte Interstate Batteries	25.00	60.00
18 Bobby Labonte Interstate Batteries Bank	20.00	50.00
18 Bobby Labonte Interstate Batteries Clear/4008	15.00	40.00
18 Bobby Labonte Interstate Batteries All Star Game/15,482	25.00	60.00
18 Bobby Labonte Interstate Batteries All Star Game Bank/2808	20.00	50.00
18 Bobby Labonte Interstate Batteries Frankenstein/11,664	40.00	80.00
18 Jason Leffler MBNA/3504	20.00	50.00
18 Jason Leffler MBNA Monsters	15.00	40.00
18 Jason Leffler MBNA Monsters Bank	20.00	40.00
19 Casey Atwood Motorola	30.00	80.00
19 Dodge Show Car/49,900	20.00	40.00
20 Tony Stewart Home Depot/29,508	30.00	60.00
20 Tony Stewart Home Depot Bank/2508	30.00	60.00
20 Tony Stewart Home Depot Brushed Metal Autographed Fan Club Promo/4000	100.00	200.00
20 Tony Stewart Home Depot Brickyard	40.00	100.00
20 Tony Stewart Home Depot Kids/23,676	30.00	60.00
20 Tony Stewart Home Depot Kids Mac Tools/3000	30.00	60.00
20 Tony Stewart Home Depot Kids Bank/2400	25.00	50.00
21 Mike Dillon Quantis/1008	20.00	40.00
21 Mike Dillon Rockwell/3504	15.00	40.00
21 Mike Dillon Rockwell Bank	20.00	50.00
21 Dale Jarrett Citgo 1991 Thunderbird/3216	75.00	150.00
21 Elliott Sadler Citgo/3504	15.00	40.00
21 Elliott Sadler Citgo 1950's/2004 red car w white numbers	15.00	40.00
21 Elliott Sadler Citgo 1970's Paint/2004 white car w red roof	15.00	40.00
21 Elliott Sadler Citgo Virgina Tech/3504	30.00	60.00
24 Jeff Gordon DuPont/29,220	20.00	50.00
24 Jeff Gordon DuPont Mac Tools/3000	20.00	50.00
24 Jeff Gordon DuPont Bank/3504	20.00	50.00
24 Jeff Gordon DuPont Brickyard/2508	50.00	100.00
24 Jeff Gordon DuPont Millennium	40.00	100.00
24 Jeff Gordon DuPont Millennium Bank/5004	40.00	100.00
24 Jeff Gordon DuPont Sign	75.00	150.00
24 Jeff Gordon DuPont Peanuts/48,480	40.00	100.00
24 Jeff Gordon DuPont Peanuts Mac Tools/3000	40.00	100.00
24 Jeff Gordon DuPont Winston	50.00	100.00
24 Jeff Gordon Pepsi/27,282	25.00	60.00
24 Jeff Gordon Pepsi Bank/5000	25.00	60.00
24 Ricky Hendrick GMAC/2004	20.00	40.00
24 Jack Sprague GMAC SuperTruck/2508	20.00	50.00
25 Jerry Nadeau Holigan	20.00	40.00
25 Jerry Nadeau Holigan Bank	20.00	40.00
25 Jerry Nadeau Holigan Coast Guard	20.00	40.00
25 Jerry Nadeau Holigan Coast Guard Bank/2508	20.00	40.00
25 Kenny Wallace Lance/3504	20.00	50.00
26 Jimmy Spencer Big K/4500	25.00	50.00
26 Jimmy Spencer Big K Bank/1008	15.00	40.00
27 Casey Atwood Castrol Busch	20.00	50.00
27 Casey Atwood Castrol Bank	25.00	60.00
27 Casey Atwood Castrol Monsters	20.00	50.00
27 Casey Atwood Castrol Monsters Bank/1008	20.00	50.00
28 Ricky Rudd Havoline/13,056	25.00	60.00
28 Ricky Rudd Havoline Mac Tools/3000	25.00	60.00
28 Ricky Rudd Havoline Bank/2736	25.00	60.00
28 Ricky Rudd Havoline Marines	25.00	60.00
28 Ricky Rudd Havoline Marines Bank/2508	25.00	50.00
28 Ricky Rudd Havoline Silver Promo in window box	12.50	25.00
30 Chad Little Little Trees/1992	20.00	50.00
31 Steve Park Whelen/1180	75.00	125.00
31 Mike Skinner Lowe's/7500	15.00	40.00
31 Mike Skinner Lowe's Bank	15.00	40.00
31 Mike Skinner Lowe's Army/9456	20.00	50.00
31 Mike Skinner Lowe's Army Bank/2508	15.00	40.00
32 Dale Jarrett Nestle 1990 Grand Prix/3000	50.00	80.00
33 Tony Raines Alka Seltzer Plus/2508	15.00	40.00
34 David Green AFG Glass	15.00	40.00
36 Ken Schrader M&M's	20.00	50.00
36 Ken Schrader M&M's Mac Tools/3000	20.00	50.00
36 Ken Schrader M&M's Bank	20.00	50.00
36 Ken Schrader M&M's Green/8004	25.00	60.00
36 Ken Schrader M&M's Green Bank	25.00	50.00
36 Ken Schrader M&M's Halloween/4680	30.00	60.00
36 Ken Schrader M&M's Halloween Mac Tools/3000	30.00	60.00
36 Ken Schrader M&M's Keep Back/14,400	25.00	60.00
36 Ken Schrader M&M's Keep Back Mac Tools/3000	25.00	60.00
36 Ken Schrader M&M's Keep Back Bank/2508	25,00	60.00
36 Ken Schrader M&M's July 4th	25.00	60.00
37 Kevin Grubb Timber Wolf/3504	20.00	40.00
40 Sterling Marlin Coors Light/3504	25.00	60.00
40 Sterling Marlin Coors Light Black/4008	25.00	60.00
40 Sterling Marlin Coors Light Black Bank	25.00	50.00
40 Sterling Marlin Coors Light Brooks & Dunn/7560	25.00	60.00
42 Kenny Irwin BellSouth/3504	30.00	70.00
44 Terry Labonte Piedmont 1984 Monte Carlo/2508	150.00	250.00
44 Justin Labonte Slim Jim/5004	20.00	50.00
44 Justin Labonte Slim Jim Bank/1008	20.00	50.00
48 Mike McLaughlin Goulds Pumps/2508	10.00	25.00
50 Tony Roper Dr. Pepper Busch	75.00	150.00
53 Hank Parker Jr. Team Marines/2508	25.00	60.00
55 Kenny Wallace Square D/3504	15.00	40.00
55 Kenny Wallace Square D Bank/2508	15.00	40.00
56 Ernie Irvan Earnhardt 1987 Monte Carlo Silver/18,300	25.00	50.00
56 Ernie Irvan Earnhardt 1987 Monte Carlo White/16,836	25.00	50.00
60 Geoffery Bodine Power Team/5004	15.00	40.00
60 Geoff Bodine Power Team Bank	20.00	40.00
66 Todd Bodine Blue Light Special	15.00	40.00
66 Darrell Waltrip Big K Route 66	25.00	50.00
66 Darrell Waltrip Big K Route 66 Bank/2508	15.00	40.00
66 Darrell Waltrip Big K Route 66 Flames/6996	25.00	60.00
66 Darrell Waltrip Big K Route 66 Flames Bank/2508	15.00	40.00
66 Rusty Wallace Alugard 1984 Camaro Black/3000	125.00	200.00
66 Rusty Wallace Alugard 1984 Camaro Red Yellow/3000	40.00	80.00
67 Jeff Gordon Outback Steakhouse 1990 Grand Prix/28,992	30.00	60.00
71 Dave Marcis Realtree/3504	30.00	60.00
75 Wally Dallenbach Powerpuff Girls	20.00	50.00
75 Wally Dallenbach Powerpuff Girls Bank	15.00	40.00
77 Robert Pressley Jasper/5004	15.00	40.00
77 Robert Pressley Jasper Federal Red/2508	15.00	40.00
77 Robert Pressley Jasper Federal Red Bank	20.00	50.00
87 Joe Nemechek CellularOne/3504	20.00	50.00
88 Dale Jarrett Quality Care	20.00	50.00
88 Dale Jarrett Quality Care Bank/2508	20.00	50.00
88 Dale Jarrett Quality Care Air Force	20.00	50.00
88 Dale Jarrett Qual.Care Air Force Bank/2508	20.00	50.00
88 Dale Jarrett Quality Care Last Ride/5008	20.00	50.00
88 Darrell Waltrip Gatorade 1976 Malibu/5784	25.00	60.00
92 Jimmie Johnson Alltel/3000	100.00	200.00
94 Bill Elliott McDonald's/10,500	20.00	50.00
94 Bill Elliott McDonald's Bank/2508	15.00	40.00
94 Bill Elliott McDonald's 25th Anniversary/15,000	20.00	50.00
94 Bill Elliott McDonald's 25th Anniversary Bank	15.00	40.00
94 Bill Elliott McDonald's McFlurry	20.00	50.00
97 Alan Kulwicki WLPX 1981 Firebird Yellow/3504	25.00	60.00
97 Alan Kulwicki WLPX '81 Firebird White Prototype/3504	25.00	60.00
97 Alan Kulwicki WLPX 1983 Firebird/3792	25.00	60.00
97 Alan Kulwicki 1983 Firebird Prototype	25.00	60.00
97 Alan Kulwicki West Bend Tire 1983 Firebird/4500	30.00	60.00
98 Elton Sawyer Lysol	20.00	50.00
01 Mark Martin Activision 1983 Monte Carlo/6500	30.00	60.00
00 Buckshot Jones Cheez-it/3504	20.00	40.00
2000 Jeff Gordon Action Fantasy/1800	150.00	300.00

2000 Action QVC For Race Fans Only 1:24

The cars in this set were only available on QVC and are finished in either Color Chrome, 24k. Gold, or Platinum.

2 Rusty Wallace Miller Lite Gold/2000	100.00	200.00
3 Dale Earnhardt Goodwrench Color Chrome/3504	200.00	350.00
3 Dale Earnhardt Goodwrench Gold/2000	200.00	400.00
3 Dale Earnhardt Goodwrench No Bull Gold/5000	100.00	200.00
3 Dale Earnhardt Goodwrench No Bull Platinum/2508	100.00	200.00
3 Dale Earnhardt Goodwrench Taz No Bull Gold/2000	200.00	350.00
3 Dale Earnhardt Goodwrench Taz No Bull Color Chrome/3504	150.00	300.00
3 Dale Earnhardt Goodwrench Peter Max Gold/2000	175.00	350.00
5 Terry Labonte Froot Loops Gold/2000	75.00	150.00
5 Terry Labonte Kellogg's Gold	80.00	175.00
5 Terry Labonte Kellogg's Grinch Gold/1000	100.00	175.00
8 Dale Earnhardt Jr. Bud Color Chrome/3504	100.00	200.00
8 Dale Earnhardt Jr. Bud Gold/2000	125.00	250.00
8 Dale Earnhardt Jr. Bud Olympic Color Chrome/20,000	75.00	150.00
8 Dale Earnhardt Jr. Bud Olympic Gold/2000	100.00	200.00
18 Bobby Labonte nterstate Batteries All-Star Game Color Chrome/1000	75.00	150.00
18 Bobby Labonte Interstate Batteries All-Star Gold/1000	75.00	150.00
18 Bobby Labonte Interstate Batteries Frankenstein Gold/2000	75.00	150.00
20 Tony Stewart Home Depot Gold/2000	75.00	150.00
20 Tony Stewart Home Depot Kids Gold/1000	90.00	150.00
20 Tony Stewart Home Depot Kids 2-car set/2000	60.00	120.00

24 Jeff Gordon DuPont Gold/2000 100.00 200.00
24 Jeff Gordon DuPont Peanuts Gold/2000 125.00 250.00
24 Jeff Gordon DuPont Winston Gold/2000 100.00 250.00
24 Jeff Gordon Pepsi Gold 100.00 200.00
36 Ken Schrader M&M's Gold 100.00 200.00
36 Ken Schrader M&M's Green Gold 70.00 150.00
67 Jeff Gordon Outback Steakhouse Gold 80.00 150.00
94 Bill Elliott McDonald's Gold 100.00 200.00
94 Bill Elliott McDonald's 25th Anniversary Platinum 100.00 200.00

2000 Action/RCCA Banks 1:24

These banks are available solely through the RCCA club and feature clear windows.

1 Mark Martin Activision 1983 Monte Carlo/6500 25.00 50.00
1 Steve Park Pennzoil/2500 20.00 50.00
2 Dale Earnhardt Curb '80 Olds/2004 100.00 175.00
2 Kevin Harvick AC Delco/2004 40.00 100.00
2 Rusty Wallace Miller Lite/2508 25.00 60.00
2 Rusty Wallace Miller Lite 10th Anniversary Color Chrome/2196 25.00 60.00
2 Rusty Wallace Miller Lite Harley Davidson/2004 50.00 100.00
3 Dale Earnhardt Goodwrench/7000 75.00 150.00
3 Dale Earnhardt Goodwrench No Bull/5052 75.00 150.00
3 Dale Earnhardt Goodwrench Peter Max/7500 75.00 150.00
3 Dale Earnhardt Goodwrench Taz No Bull/13,500 75.00 150.00
3 Dale Earnhardt Goodwrench Under he Lights/2304 200.00 400.00
3 Dale Earnhardt Wrangler 1987 Monte Carlo Aerocoupe/2004 125.00 250.00
3 Ron Hornaday NAPA/2508 20.00 50.00
4 Bobby Hamilton Kodak Navy/2004 20.00 50.00
4 Ernie Irvan Kodak 1991 Lumina/1500 20.00 50.00
4 Mark Martin Jim Magill Orange 1983 Monte Carlo/6500 15.00 40.00
5 Terry Labonte Kellogg's 15.00 40.00
6 Mark Martin Jim Magill Green 1983 Monte Carlo/6500 15.00 40.00
7 Michael Waltrip Nations Rent/1008 15.00 40.00
8 Jeff Burton Baby Ruth 1990 Thunderbird/1500 15.00 40.00
8 Dale Earnhardt Jr. Bud/7000 90.00 150.00
8 Dale Earnhardt Jr. Bud No Bull/5052 75.00 150.00
8 Dale Earnhardt Jr. Bud Olympic/7500 90.00 150.00
8 Bobby Hillin Kleenex/504 20.00 50.00
12 Jeremy Mayfield Mobil 1/1008 15.00 40.00
18 Bobby Labonte Interstate Batteries/1500 30.00 80.00
20 Tony Stewart Home Depot/3600 30.00 80.00
20 Tony Stewart Home Depot Kids/2808 25.00 60.00
24 Jeff Gordon DuPont/7500 30.00 60.00
24 Jeff Gordon DuPont Millennium/10,992 25.00 60.00
24 Jeff Gordon DuPont Peanuts 50.00 100.00
25 Jerry Nadeau Holigan/2004 15.00 40.00
25 Jerry Nadeau Holigan Coast Guard/2508 20.00 50.00
25 Kenny Wallace Lance 20.00 40.00
27 Casey Atwood Castrol 15.00 40.00
28 Ricky Rudd Havoline/3504 20.00 50.00
28 Ricky Rudd Havoline Marines/4500 20.00 50.00
30 Chad Little Little Trees/804 20.00 40.00
31 Mike Skinner Lowe's/1500 20.00 40.00
33 Tony Raines Alka Seltzer Plus/996 15.00 40.00
36 Ken Schrader M&M's/2508 15.00 40.00
40 Sterling Marlin Coors Light/2508 30.00 60.00
40 Sterling Marlin Coors Light Black/3504 20.00 50.00
44 Justin Labonte Slim Jim/2004 15.00 40.00
44 Terry Labonte Piedmont 1984 Monte Carlo/1009 150.00 250.00
53 Hank Parker Jr. Team Marines/1008 20.00 40.00
55 Kenny Wallace Square D 20.00 40.00
66 Darrell Waltrip Big K Route 66/1008 20.00 50.00
66 Darrell Waltrip Big K Route 66 Flames/1008 20.00 50.00
75 Wally Dallenbach Powerpuff Girls 20.00 50.00
77 Robert Pressley Jasper 20.00 40.00
88 Dale Jarrett Quality Care Air Force/4500 20.00 50.00
94 Bill Elliott McDonald's/3000 20.00 50.00
94 Bill Elliott McDonald's 25th Ann./4500 20.00 50.00
00 Buckshot Jones Cheez-it/804 15.00 40.00

2000 Action/RCCA Elite 1:24

These cars are available solely through the RCCA club and feature exacting detail.

1 Randy LaJoie Bob Evan's Monsters/492 30.00 80.00
1 Mark Martin Activision 1983 Monte Carlo/2500 60.00 120.00
1 Steve Park Pennzoil/1008 60.00 120.00
2 Dale Earnhardt Curb 1980 Olds/2700 200.00 400.00
2 Kevin Harvick AC Delco/1008 75.00 150.00
2 Rusty Wallace Miller Lite/1000 60.00 120.00
2 Rusty Wallace Miller Lite 10th Ann./816 50.00 100.00
2 Rusty Wallace Miller Lite Harley/1008 75.00 150.00
3 Dale Earnhardt Goodwrench/5000 100.00 200.00
3 Dale Earnhardt Goodwrench No Bull/3504 100.00 200.00
3 Dale Earnhardt Goodwrench Peter Max/7500 125.00 250.00
3 Dale Earnhardt Goodwrench Taz No Bull/9504 100.00 200.00
3 Dale Earnhardt Goodwrench Test/3500 100.00 200.00
3 Dale Earnhardt Goodwrench Under the Lights/1200 250.00 500.00
3 Dale Earnhardt Goodwrench 75th Win Platinum/3504 200.00 350.00
3 Dale Earnhardt Wrangler 1987 Monte Carlo Aerocoupe/2700 250.00 450.00
3 Ron Hornaday NAPA/1500 30.00 80.00
3 Ron Hornaday NAPA 75th Anniv./1008 30.00 80.00
3 Ron Hornaday NAPA Monsters/1200 30.00 80.00
4 Bobby Hamilton Kodak Max/804 25.00 60.00
4 Mark Martin Jim Magill Orange 1983 Monte Carlo/2500 40.00 100.00
5 Terry Labonte Kellogg's 100.00 150.00
5 Terry Labonte Froot Loops 100.00 175.00
5 Terry Labonte Kellogg's Grinch/804 70.00 120.00
8 Jeff Burton Baby Ruth 1990 Thunderbird/804 30.00 80.00
8 Dale Earnhardt Jr. Bud/5000 125.00 300.00
8 Dale Earnhardt Jr. Bud Test Gray/3500 100.00 200.00
8 Dale Earnhardt Jr. Bud No Bull/3504 125.00 250.00
8 Dale Earnhardt Jr. Bud Olympic/4992 100.00 300.00
10 Johnny Benson Aaron's/492 25.00 60.00
11 Jason Jarrett Rayovac/804 30.00 80.00
11 Cale Yarborough Holly Farms 1976 Malibu/600 80.00 150.00
12 Bobby Allison Coke 1974 Malibu/804 125.00 250.00
15 Tony Stewart Vision 3/1992 100.00 200.00
18 Dale Jarrett Freedlander 1987 Monte Carlo/492 125.00 200.00
18 Bobby Labonte Interstate Batteries/1000 60.00 120.00
18 Bobby Labonte Interstate Batteries All-Star Game/1008 40.00 100.00
18 Bobby Labonte Interstate Batteries Frankenstein/696 40.00 100.00
20 Tony Stewart Home Depot/5000 75.00 150.00
20 Tony Stewart Home Depot ROY/5000 60.00 120.00
20 Tony Stewart Home Depot Kids/1404 60.00 120.00
21 Dale Jarrett Citgo 1991 Thunderbird/804 50.00 90.00
21 Elliott Sadler Citgo/804 40.00 70.00
22 Bobby Allison Miller High Life 1983 Monte Carlo 60.00 120.00
24 Jeff Gordon DuPont/5000 75.00 150.00
24 Jeff Gordon DuPont Test/3000 125.00 200.00
24 Jeff Gordon DuPont Millennium/7500 60.00 120.00
24 Jeff Gordon DuPont Peanuts/3456 60.00 120.00
24 Jeff Gordon DuPont Winston/1008 150.00 300.00
24 Jeff Gordon Pepsi/3504 60.00 120.00
24 Ricky Hendrick GMAC/504 25.00 60.00
25 Jerry Nadeau Holigan/1008 25.00 60.00
26 Jimmy Spencer Big K/804 60.00 120.00
27 Casey Atwood Castrol/1500 50.00 100.00
27 Casey Atwood Castrol Monsters 60.00 120.00
28 Ricky Rudd Havoline/1500 75.00 150.00
28 Ricky Rudd Havoline Marines/2004 50.00 100.00
31 Mike Skinner Lowe's Army/1500 30.00 80.00
32 Dale Jarrett Nestle 1990 Grand Prix/492 100.00 200.00
36 Ken Schrader M&M's Keep Back 100.00 150.00
40 Sterling Marlin Coors Light/804 60.00 100.00
40 Sterling Marlin Coors Light Black/1008 40.00 100.00
44 Justin Labonte Slim Jim/1008 20.00 50.00
44 Terry Labonte Piedmont 1984 Monte Carlo/800 200.00 350.00
53 Hank Parker Jr. Team Marines/804 30.00 80.00
67 Jeff Gordon Outback Steakhouse 1990 Grand Prix/3000 50.00 100.00
88 Dale Jarrett Quality Care/1500 50.00 100.00
88 Dale Jarrett Quality Care Air Force/2004 60.00 120.00
88 Dale Jarrett Quality Care Last Ride/600 50.00 100.00
88 Dale Jarrett UPS Test/2508 60.00 120.00
88 Darrell Waltrip Gatorade 1976 Malibu/600 60.00 100.00
92 Jimmie Johnson Alltel/492 250.00 400.00
94 Bill Elliott McDonald's/1000 60.00 150.00
94 Bill Elliott McDonald's 25th Ann. 40.00 100.00
2000 DEI Pit Practice/1008 175.00 300.00

2001 Action Performance 1:24

These "AP" or Action Performance cars were primarily distributed to mass retail and to trackside retailers. Unless noted below, each was packaged in a 2-sided clear window red and brown box with a white "AP" logo on the sides.

3 Dale Earnhardt Goodwrench w sonic logo window box 12.50 25.00
3 Dale Earnhardt Goodwrench Promo without Sonic logo, solid box 45.00 80.00
8 Dale Earnhardt Jr. Dale Jr. 20.00 35.00
15 Michael Waltrip NAPA Daytona Win Promo 15.00 40.00
24 Jeff Gordon DuPont Flames 20.00 35.00
88 Dale Jarrett UPS 20.00 35.00

2001 Action Racing Collectables 1:24

1 Neil Bonnett B&H Motors 1964 Chevelle/7836 20.00 50.00
1 Steve Park Pennzoil 40.00 80.00
1 Steve Park Pennzoil Bank/1008 40.00 90.00
1 Steve Park Pennzoil Sylvester&Tweety/28,212 25.00 60.00
1 Steve Park Pennzoil Sylvester and Tweety Bank/1908 20.00 50.00
2 Kerry Earnhardt Kannapolis Intimidators/2004 35.00 60.00
2 Kerry Earnhardt Kannapolis Intimidators Bank/804 25.00 50.00
2 Kerry Earnhardt Kannapolis Intimidators Clear/6000 30.00 60.00
2 Kevin Harvick AC Delco/3300 60.00 120.00
2 Kevin Harvick AC Delco 2001 Busch Champion/30,000 30.00 60.00
2 Kevin Harvick AC Delco Bank/600 60.00 120.00
2 Kevin Harvick AC Delco 2001 Busch Champ GM Dealers/2496 30.00 60.00
2 Rusty Wallace Miller Lite/12,036 25.00 60.00
2 Rusty Wallace Miller Lite Bank/1500 25.00 60.00
2 Rusty Wallace Miller Lite Harley/19,884 40.00 80.00
2 Rusty Wallace Miller Lite Harley Clear/6792 20.00 50.00
2/29 Kevin Harvick AC Delco Goodwrench dual sponsor split paint/5004 40.00 100.00
3 Dale Earnhardt Goodwrench/33,504 125.00 250.00
3 Dale Earnhardt Goodwrench White Gold Promo/5000 125.00 250.00
3 Dale Earnhardt Goodwrench Bank/2508 125.00 250.00
3 Dale Earnhardt Goodwrench Oreo/55,008 125.00 250.00
3 Dale Earnhardt Goodwrench Oreo Bank/15,000 125.00 250.00
3 Dale Earnhardt Goodwrench Oreo Clear/6000 100.00 200.00
3 Dale Earnhardt Goodwrench Oreo GM Dealers White Gold/5000 125.00 250.00
3 Dale Earnhardt Goodwrench Clear/5004 125.00 250.00
3 Dale Earnhardt Goodwrench Talladega Win No Bull Bank/13,333 40.00 80.00
3 Dale Earnhardt Jr. Mom 'N' Pop's 1994 Camaro/10,008 125.00 225.00
5 Terry Labonte Kellogg's/7704 35.00 70.00
5 Terry Labonte Kellogg's Monster's Inc./6000 35.00 70.00
5 Terry Labonte Kellogg's Wile E. Road Runner/19,944 35.00 80.00
5 Terry Labonte Kellogg's Wile E. Road Runner Mac Tools/3000 35.00 80.00
5 Terry Labonte Kellogg's Wile E. and Road Runner Bank 30.00 80.00
7 Dale Earnhardt Jr. Church Brothers 1997 Monte Carlo/5028 125.00 200.00
8 Dale Earnhardt Docs Cycle Center 1964 Chevelle/86,924 40.00 100.00
8 Dale Earnhardt Docs 1964 Chevelle Bank 40.00 150.00
8 Dale Earnhardt Goodwrench 1987 Nova/10,008 100.00 250.00
8 Dale Earnhardt Jr. Bud/27,180 75.00 135.00
8 Dale Earnhardt Jr. Bud Bank/2088 60.00 120.00
8 Dale Earnhardt Jr. Bud Promo in plastic case/3750 50.00 100.00
8 Dale Earnhardt Jr. Bud w Remington on deck lid 75.00 135.00
8 Dale Earnhardt Jr. Bud Van Camp's Promo 40.00 80.00
8 Dale Earnhardt Jr. Bud Talladega Win No Bull w flag/64,676 50.00 100.00
8 Dale Earnhardt Jr. Bud MLB All-Star/54,408 125.00 250.00
8 Dale Earnhardt Jr. Bud All-Star Bank/2508 100.00 200.00
9 Bill Elliott Dodge/29,508 35.00 75.00
9 Bill Elliott Dodge Bank/4812 25.00 60.00
9 Bill Elliott Dodge Muhammad Ali/28,008 30.00 60.00
9 Bill Elliott Dodge Muhammad Ali Bank/1500 25.00 60.00
9 Bill Elliott Dodge Spider-Man/23,865 20.00 50.00
9 Bill Elliott Dodge Spider Man Bank/1836 20.00 50.00
9 Bill Elliott Dodge Spider Man Clear/4008 20.00 50.00
9 Bill Elliott Dodge Test black/5004 25.00 60.00
9 Bill Elliott Dahlonega 1976 Ford Torino/9000 50.00 100.00
10 Johnny Benson Valvoline James Dean/13,728 20.00 50.00
10 Johnny Benson Valvoline James Dean Bank 20.00 50.00
10 Jeff Green Nesquik/2376 15.00 40.00
10 Jeff Green Nesquik Bank/504 15.00 40.00
11 Darrell Waltrip Budweiser 1985 Monte Carlo/8508 100.00 175.00
12 Jeremy Mayfield Mobil 1/3732 15.00 40.00
12 Jeremy Mayfield Mobil 1 Bank/1008 15.00 40.00
14 Larry Foyt Harrah's/3504 20.00 50.00
15 Michael Waltrip NAPA/6228 25.00 60.00
15 Michael Waltrip NAPA Bank 25.00 60.00
15 Michael Waltrip NAPA Stars&Stripes/27,348 20.00 50.00
15 Michael Waltrip NAPA Stars&Stripes Bank/1008 20.00 50.00
18 Bobby Labonte Interstate Batteries 30.00 60.00
18 Bobby Labonte Interstate Batteries Bank 30.00 60.00
18 Bobby Labonte Interstate Batteries Color Chrome 2000 WC Champ/19,188 25.00 60.00
18 Bobby Labonte Interstate Batteries Cal Ripken/24,636 30.00 60.00
18 Bobby Labonte Interstate Batteries Coke Bear/25,320 25.00 60.00
18 Bobby Labonte Interstate Batteries Coke Bear Bank/2004 25.00 60.00
18 Bobby Labonte Interstate Batteries Coke Bear Mac Tools/3000 25.00 60.00
18 Bobby Labonte Interstate Batteries Coke Bear Clear 25.00 60.00
18 Bobby Labonte Interstate Batteries Jurassic Park 3/21,096 25.00 60.00
18 Bobby Labonte Interstate Batteries Jurassic Park 3 Bank/1788 25.00 60.00
18 Bobby Labonte Interstate Batteries Jurassic Park 3 Clear/6000 25.00 60.00
18 Jeff Purvis MBNA/2016 15.00 40.00
18 Bobby Labonte Interstate Batteries Jurassic Park 3 Mac Tools/3000 20.00 50.00
19 Casey Atwood Dodge/11,196 20.00 50.00
19 Casey Atwood Dodge Mountain Dew/16,104 20.00 50.00
19 Casey Atwood Dodge Mountain Dew Bank 20.00 50.00
19 Casey Atwood Dodge Spider-Man/18,924 20.00 50.00
19 Casey Atwood Dodge Spider-Man Mac Tools/3000 20.00 50.00
20 Tony Stewart Home Depot 30.00 80.00
20 Tony Stewart Home Depot Bank 25.00 60.00
20 Tony Stewart Home Depot Coke Bear/26,280 25.00 60.00
20 Tony Stewart Home Depot Coke Bear Bank/2004 25.00 60.00
20 Tony Stewart Home Depot Jurassic Park 3/22,128 30.00 80.00
20 Tony Stewart Home Depot Jurassic Park 3 Bank/1584 25.00 60.00
20 Tony Stewart Home Depot Jurassic Park 3 Clear/6000 25.00 60.00
22 Alan Kulwicki Miller 1984 Pontiac/4500 40.00 80.00
24 Jeff Gordon DuPont Flames/38,004 75.00 150.00
24 Jeff Gordon DuPont Flames Bank/1800 50.00 100.00
24 Jeff Gordon DuPont Flames Clear/6996 50.00 100.00
24 Jeff Gordon DuPont Flames Mac Tools Promo/3500 60.00 120.00
24 Jeff Gordon DuPont Flames Brickyard Win/3504 40.00 80.00
24 Jeff Gordon DuPont Flames Las Vegas Raced Clear Window Bank/2508 25.00 60.00
24 Jeff Gordon Gordon Foundation/36,528 20.00 50.00
24 Jeff Gordon DuPont Bugs Bunny/64,800 25.00 60.00
24 Jeff Gordon DuPont Bugs Bunny Bank/3300 25.00 60.00
24 Jeff Gordon DuPont Bugs Bunny Clear/6792 25.00 60.00
24 Jeff Gordon Pepsi/13,032 25.00 60.00
24 Jeff Gordon Pepsi Bank/1644 25.00 60.00
24 Jeff Gordon Pepsi Clear/3000 25.00 60.00
25 Jerry Nadeau UAW/3000 20.00 50.00
25 Jerry Nadeau UAW Bank/504 20.00 50.00
26 Jimmy Spencer K-Mart/2856 15.00 40.00
26 Jimmy Spencer K-Mart Bank 15.00 40.00
27 Jamie McMurray Williams Promo in window box 15.00 40.00
28 Alan Kulwicki Hardee's 1984 Pontiac/4752 40.00 80.00
28 Ricky Rudd Havoline/7308 25.00 60.00
28 Ricky Rudd Havoline Bank/1008 25.00 60.00
28 Ricky Rudd Havoline Bud Shoot Out 25.00 60.00
28 Ricky Rudd Havoline Bud Shoot Out Bank 25.00 60.00
28 Ricky Rudd Havoline Flag/9000 30.00 80.00
28 Ricky Rudd Havoline Need for Speed/10,296 25.00 60.00
28 Ricky Rudd Havoline Need for Speed Bank/1308 25.00 60.00
29 Kevin Harvick Goodwrench/102,432 60.00 120.00
29 Kevin Harvick Goodwrench Clear/8292 40.00 80.00
29 Kevin Harvick Goodwrench White Gold Promo/5000 50.00 100.00
29 Kevin Harvick Goodwrench Rookie of the Year/37,812 20.00 50.00
29 Kevin Harvick Goodwrench Van Camp's box Promo 25.00 60.00
29 Kevin Harvick Goodwrench Make-a-Wish/6816 25.00 60.00
29 Kevin Harvick Goodwrench AOL/46,500 25.00 60.00
29 Kevin Harvick Goodwrench AOL Bank/2004 25.00 60.00
29 Kevin Harvick Goodwrench AOL Col.Chrome 25.00 60.00
29 Kevin Harvick Goodwrench Oreo Show car/56,196 30.00 80.00
29 Kevin Harvick Goodwrench Taz/92,748 25.00 60.00
29 Kevin Harvick Goodwrench Taz Clear/7164 25.00 60.00
30 Jeff Green AOL Bank/504 25.00 50.00
30 Jeff Green AOL Daffy Duck/8496 20.00 50.00
30 Jeff Green AOL Daffy Duck Bank/1008 20.00 50.00
31 Mike Skinner Lowe's/4008 20.00 50.00
31 Mike Skinner Lowe's Bank 20.00 50.00
31 Mike Skinner Lowe's Yosemite Sam/4008 20.00 50.00
31 Mike Skinner Lowe's Yosemite Sam Bank 20.00 50.00
36 Hank Parker Jr. GNC Live Well/2280 20.00 50.00
36 Hank Parker Jr. GNC Live Well Bank 20.00 50.00
36 Hank Parker Jr. GNC Live Well Pearl/816 20.00 50.00
36 Ken Schrader M&M's 30.00 60.00
36 Ken Schrader M&M's Bank 30.00 60.00

36 Ken Schrader M&M's Halloween/9348 30.00 60.00
36 Ken Schrader M&M's July 4th/7788 30.00 60.00
36 Ken Schrader Pedigree/3252 20.00 50.00
36 Ken Schrader Pedigree Bank 20.00 50.00
36 Ken Schrader Snickers/5904 20.00 50.00
36 Ken Schrader Snickers Bank 20.00 50.00
40 Sterling Marlin Coors Light/12,852 30.00 80.00
40 Sterling Marlin Coors Light Kiss/27,108 30.00 80.00
40 Sterling Marlin Coors Light Kiss Bank/504 30.00 60.00
40 Sterling Marlin Proud to be American/16,000 30.00 80.00
55 Bobby Hamilton Square D Marvin the Martian/8196 20.00 50.00
55 Bobby Hamilton Square D Marvin the Martian Bank 20.00 50.00
66 Todd Bodine Big K 20.00 50.00
66 Todd Bodine Big K Blue Light/2964 20.00 50.00
66 Rusty Wallace Child's 1981 Camaro Red 25.00 50.00
72 Benny Parsons Kings Row 1976 Chevy Malibu/3000 60.00 120.00
88 Dale Jarrett UPS/28,524 25.00 60.00
88 Dale Jarrett UPS Mac Tools/4008 25.00 60.00
88 Dale Jarrett UPS Bank 25.00 60.00
88 Dale Jarrett UPS Chrome/1020 30.00 80.00
88 Dale Jarrett UPS Clear/6792 25.00 60.00
88 Dale Jarrett UPS Employee Promo 40.00 100.00
88 Dale Jarrett UPS Flag/12,000 40.00 100.00
88 Dale Jarrett UPS Split Clear/3500 25.00 60.00
88 Dale Jarrett UPS Flames/48,780 25.00 60.00
88 Dale Jarrett UPS Flames Clear/7000 25.00 60.00
92 Jimmie Johnson Excedrin/2016 125.00 250.00
95 Davey Allison Miller 1986 Nova/5808 75.00 150.00
2001 DEI Pit Practice Car/2508 40.00 100.00
2001 DEI Pit Practice Car Snap-on Carolina Run 50.00 100.00
01 NDA Brickyard 400 2001 15.00 40.00
02 Ryan Newman Alltel/2412 75.00 150.00
02 Ryan Newman Alltel Bank/600 50.00 100.00
NNO Monte Carlo 400 Looney Tunes/9504 15.00 40.00
NNO Monte Carlo 400 Looney Tunes Clear/5508 15.00 40.00
NNO Monte Carlo 400 Looney Tunes Color Chrome/504 40.00 100.00

2001 Action QVC For Race Fans Only 1:24

2 Kevin Harvick AC Delco Color Chrome/1000 75.00 150.00
2 Kevin Harvick AC Delco Gold/1000 100.00 175.00
2 Rusty Wallace Miller Lite Gold/1000 75.00 150.00
2 Rusty Wallace Miller Lite Harley Color Chrome/2508 60.00 120.00
2 Rusty Wallace Miller Lite Harley Gold/2000 90.00 150.00
2 Rusty Wallace Miller Lite Harley Platinum/624 100.00 200.00
3 Dale Earnhardt Goodwrench Gold/10,000 150.00 300.00
3 Dale Earnhardt Goodwrench Platinum/2508 200.00 400.00
3 Dale Earnhardt Goodwrench w Sonic decal 125.00 250.00
3 Dale Earnhardt Goodwrench Oreo Gold/2000 150.00 300.00
3 Dale Earnhardt Goodwrench Oreo Platinum/624 200.00 400.00
8 Dale Earnhardt Jr. Bud Color Chrome/2508 100.00 200.00
8 Dale Earnhardt Jr. Bud Gold/2500 125.00 250.00
8 Dale Earnhardt Jr. Bud Platinum/624 150.00 300.00
8 Dale Earnhardt Jr. Bud MLB All-Star Gold/2000 135.00 225.00
8 Dale Earnhardt Jr. Bud MLB All-Star Platinum/624 150.00 300.00
9 Bill Elliott Dodge Muhammad Ali Gold/1000 70.00 135.00
18 Bobby Labonte Interstate Batteries Coke Bear Col.Chrome/1000 50.00 120.00
18 Bobby Labonte Interstate Batteries Coke Bear Gold/1000 60.00 120.00
18 Bobby Labonte Interstate Batteries Coke Bear Platinum/624 75.00 150.00
18 Bobby Labonte Interstate Batteries Jurassic Park 3 Gold/1000 50.00 120.00
18 Bobby Labonte Interstate Batteries Jurassic Park 3 Platinum/624 75.00 150.00
20 Tony Stewart Home Depot Coke Bear Color Chrome/1008 75.00 150.00
20 Tony Stewart Home Depot Coke Bear Gold/1000 75.00 150.00
20 Tony Stewart Home Depot Coke Bear Platinum/624 125.00 200.00
20 Tony Stewart Home Depot Jurassic Park 3 Gold/1000 90.00 150.00
20 Tony Stewart Home Depot Jurassic Park 3 Platinum/624 100.00 200.00
24 Jeff Gordon DuPont Bugs Bunny Gold/2000 125.00 250.00
24 Jeff Gordon DuPont Bugs Bunny Platinum/624 100.00 200.00
24 Jeff Gordon DuPont Flames Color Chrome/2508 60.00 120.00
24 Jeff Gordon DuPont Flames Gold/2000 125.00 250.00
24 Jeff Gordon DuPont Flames Color Chrome HMS 100th Win/2508 60.00 120.00
24 Jeff Gordon DuPont Flames Platinum/624 125.00 225.00
24 Jeff Gordon Pepsi Color Chrome/2508 60.00 120.00
24 Jeff Gordon Pepsi Gold/2000 100.00 200.00
24 Jeff Gordon Pepsi Platinum/624 125.00 250.00
29 Kevin Harvick Goodwrench Gold/10,000 75.00 150.00
29 Kevin Harvick Goodwrench Platinum/624 100.00 200.00
29 Kevin Harvick Goodwrench AOL Gold/1000 60.00 150.00
29 Kevin Harvick Goodwrench AOL Platinum/624 75.00 150.00
29 Kevin Harvick Goodwrench Oreo Platinum/624 75.00 150.00
29 Kevin Harvick Goodwrench Taz Chrome/3504 60.00 120.00
29 Kevin Harvick Goodwrench Taz Gold 75.00 150.00
29 Kevin Harvick Goodwrench Taz Platinum/624 90.00 150.00
29 Kevin Harvick Goodwrench Oreo Platinum/624 125.00 200.00
88 Dale Jarrett UPS Gold/2000 70.00 120.00
88 Dale Jarrett UPS Platinum/624 100.00 175.00
88 Dale Jarrett UPS Flames Color Chrome/2508 50.00 120.00
88 Dale Jarrett UPS Flames Gold./2000 70.00 120.00
88 Dale Jarrett UPS Flames Platinum/624 100.00 175.00

2001 Action/RCCA Banks 1:24

2 Kevin Harvick AC Delco/1200 60.00 120.00
3 Dale Earnhardt Goodwrench/3996 125.00 250.00
3 Dale Earnhardt Goodwrench Oreo/4008 125.00 250.00
3 Dale Earnhardt Goodwrench 1988 Monte Carlo/2005 125.00 250.00
5 Terry Labonte Kellogg's Wile E. and Road Runner/720 40.00 80.00
8 Dale Earnhardt Goodwrench 1987 Nova Bank/2304 125.00 225.00
8 Dale Earnhardt Jr. Bud/1500 75.00 150.00
8 Dale Earnhardt Jr. Bud color chrome/3600 75.00 150.00
8 Dale Earnhardt Jr. Bud All-Star/5004 100.00 200.00
8 Dale Earnhardt Jr. Bud All-Star Raced/3504 90.00 150.00
9 Bill Elliott Dodge/2508 25.00 60.00
9 Bill Elliott Dodge Muhammad Ali/1008 25.00 60.00
15 Michael Waltrip NAPA/900 30.00 60.00
18 Bobby Labonte Interstate Batteries/1500 30.00 60.00
19 Casey Atwood Dodge 25.00 60.00
20 Tony Stewart Home Depot/3600 25.00 60.00
24 Jeff Gordon DuPont Flames/3456 40.00 75.00
24 Jeff Gordon DuPont Bugs Bunny/5004 30.00 60.00
24 Jeff Gordon Pepsi 30.00 60.00
25 Jerry Nadeau UAW/720 15.00 40.00
28 Ricky Rudd Havoline/1200 25.00 60.00
29 Kevin Harvick Goodwrench/3000 30.00 80.00
29 Kevin Harvick Goodwrench AOL/2504 25.00 60.00
29 Kevin Harvick Goodwrench Oreo Show car Bank/2004 40.00 80.00
29 Kevin Harvick Goodwrench Taz/3200 25.00 60.00
36 Ken Schrader M&M's Halloween/720 25.00 60.00
36 Ken Schrader Snickers 20.00 50.00
40 Sterling Marlin Coors Light/600 30.00 60.00
55 Bobby Hamilton Square D Marvin the Martian/600 20.00 50.00
66 Todd Bodine Big K Blue Light/360 15.00 40.00
88 Dale Jarrett UPS/2700 25.00 60.00
88 Dale Jarrett UPS Flames/1836 35.00 60.00
01 NDA Brickyard 400/804 15.00 40.00
02 Ryan Newman Alltel/492 75.00 150.00

2001 Action/RCCA Elite 1:24

1 Steve Park Pennzoil 60.00 120.00
1 Steve Park Pennzoil Sylvester&Tweety/1800 50.00 100.00
2 Kevin Harvick AC Delco/804 100.00 200.00
2 Kevin Harvick AC Delco Color Chrome/1200 100.00 175.00
2 Rusty Wallace Miller Lite/1008 60.00 120.00
2 Rusty Wallace Miller Lite Metal/3504 50.00 100.00
2 Rusty Wallace Miller Lite Harley/3996 75.00 150.00
3 Dale Earnhardt Goodwrench/2496 200.00 400.00
3 Dale Earnhardt Goodwrench Split Clear/3504 125.00 250.00
3 Dale Earnhardt Goodwr.Metal/7500 100.00 200.00
3 Dale Earnhardt Goodwrench Test/3504 175.00 300.00
3 Dale Earnhardt Goodwrench Oreo/5004 150.00 250.00
3 Dale Earnhardt Goodwrench 1988 Monte Carlo Aerocoupe/3205 250.00 400.00
5 Terry Labonte Kellogg's 50.00 120.00
5 Terry Labonte Kellogg's Wile E. Road Runner/1200 60.00 120.00
7 Dale Earnhardt Jr. Church Brothers 1997 Monte Carlo/1500 100.00 300.00
8 Dale Earnhardt Goodwrench 1987 Nova/2304 250.00 400.00
8 Dale Earnhardt Jr. Bud/2004 125.00 250.00
8 Dale Earnhardt Jr. Bud Color Chrome/2400 125.00 250.00
8 Dale Earnhardt Jr. Bud Dover Win w flag/2508 100.00 200.00
8 Dale Earnhardt Jr. Bud Talladega Win No Bull/2508 100.00 200.00
8 Dale Earnhardt Jr. Bud Test/3504 100.00 250.00
8 Dale Earnhardt Jr. Bud All-Star Game/5996 175.00 300.00
8 Dale Earnhardt Jr. Bud All-Star raced version/4008 125.00 250.00
9 Bill Elliott Dodge Spiderman/720 30.00 60.00
10 Johnny Benson Valvoline James Dean/1008 40.00 80.00
10 Jeff Green Nesquik/1008 30.00 60.00
11 Darrell Waltrip Budweiser 1985 Monte Carlo/720 100.00 200.00
12 Jeremy Mayfield Mobil 1/720 30.00 60.00
15 Michael Waltrip NAPA/1008 60.00 120.00
15 Michael Waltrip NAPA Daytona Raced/2800 issued with tire swatch 60.00 120.00
18 Bobby Labonte Interstate Batteries/1008 60.00 120.00
18 Bobby Labonte Interstate Batteries Test/3504 50.00 100.00
18 Bobby Labonte Interstate Batteries Coke Bear/1008 60.00 120.00
18 Bobby Labonte Interstate Batteries Cal Ripken Farwell/600 125.00 250.00
18 Bobby Labonte Interstate Batteries Jurassic Park 3/804 50.00 100.00
18 Jeff Purvis MBNA/492 40.00 80.00
20 Tony Stewart Home Depot/2004 75.00 150.00
20 Tony Stewart Home Depot Test/3504 60.00 120.00
20 Tony Stewart Home Depot Coke Bear/1392 60.00 120.00
20 Tony Stewart Home Depot Jurassic Park 3/1200 60.00 120.00
24 Jeff Gordon DuPont Flames/3600 150.00 300.00
24 Jeff Gordon DuPont Flames Metal/3504 125.00 225.00
24 Jeff Gordon DuPont Flames Split Clear/5004 100.00 200.00
24 Jeff Gordon DuPont Flames No Bull Las Vegas Raced/3504 75.00 150.00
24 Jeff Gordon DuPont Flames Platinum HMS 100th Win/1800 150.00 300.00
24 Jeff Gordon DuPont Test/2508 125.00 250.00
24 Jeff Gordon DuPont Bugs Bunny/7500 60.00 120.00
24 Jeff Gordon Gordon Foundation/3996 50.00 100.00
24 Jeff Gordon Pepsi/1800 75.00 150.00
24 Jeff Gordon Pepsi Color Chrome/3000 60.00 120.00
25 Jerry Nadeau UAW/720 40.00 80.00
26 Jimmy Spencer K-Mart/720 25.00 60.00
28 Ricky Rudd Havoline/804 60.00 120.00
28 Ricky Rudd Havoline Bud Shoot Out/1200 60.00 175.00
28 Ricky Rudd Havoline Need for Speed/720 75.00 150.00
29 Kevin Harvick Goodwrench/4996 75.00 150.00
29 Kevin Harvick Goodwrench Split Clear/5004 50.00 100.00
29 Kevin Harvick Goodwrench Make a Wish Foundation/2496 60.00 120.00
29 Kevin Harvick Goodwrench Oreo Show car/4200 60.00 120.00
29 Kevin Harvick Goodwrench Taz/5996 50.00 100.00
29 Kevin Harvick Goodwrench AOL/4008 50.00 100.00
30 Jeff Green AOL Daffy Duck/600 40.00 80.00
31 Mike Skinner Lowe's Yosemite Sam/720 40.00 80.00
36 Ken Schrader Snickers/1200 40.00 80.00
36 Ken Schrader M&M's/804 40.00 80.00
36 Ken Schrader M&M's Halloween/804 40.00 80.00
36 Ken Schrader M&M's July 4th/1008 40.00 80.00
36 Ken Schrader Pedigree/492 30.00 60.00
40 Sterling Marlin Coors Light Kiss/1008 75.00 150.00
55 Bobby Hamilton Square D Marvin the Martian/600 40.00 80.00
88 Dale Jarrett UPS/3204 60.00 120.00
88 Dale Jarrett UPS Chrome/2004 60.00 120.00
88 Dale Jarrett UPS Test/2508 60.00 120.00
88 Dale Jarrett UPS Flames/3000 60.00 120.00
92 Jimmie Johnson Excedrin/492 250.00 400.00
2001 DEI Pit Practice Car/2796 60.00 120.00
01 Brickyard 400/804 40.00 80.00
NNO Looney Tunes/1800 50.00 100.00

2002 Action Performance 1:24

These "AP" or Action Performance cars were primarily distributed to mass retail and to trackside retailers. Unless noted below, each was packaged in a 2-sided clear window red and black box with a red "A" and white "P" AP logo on the sides.

1 Steve Park Pennzoil 15.00 30.00
3 Dale Earnhardt Goodwrench 25.00 40.00
8 Dale Earnhardt Jr. Dale Jr. 20.00 35.00
18 Bobby Labonte Interstate Batteries 15.00 30.00
20 Tony Stewart Home Depot 15.00 30.00
24 Jeff Gordon DuPont Flames 20.00 35.00
29 Kevin Harvick Goodwrench 20.00 35.00
40 Sterling Marlin Sterling 15.00 30.00
88 Dale Jarrett UPS 15.00 30.00
88 Dale Jarrett UPS Employee/5004 25.00 50.00

2002 Action Racing Collectables 1:24

1 Dale Earnhardt True Value 1999 IROC 20.00 50.00
1 Dale Earnhardt True Value 2000 IROC Lt. Blue/39,960 35.00 60.00
1 Dale Earnhardt True Value 2001 IROC Green/28,512 35.00 60.00
1 Jeff Gordon Autolite 1989 T-bird/15,036 35.00 60.00
1 Jeff Gordon Autolite 1989 T-bird Bank/1608 35.00 60.00
1 Kevin Harvick True Value 2001 IROC/6996 25.00 50.00
1 Bobby Labonte True Value '01 IROC/4668 20.00 50.00
1 Steve Park Pennzoil/25,008 20.00 50.00
1 Steve Park Pennzoil Bank/888 20.00 50.00
2 Dale Earnhardt Wrangler 1979 Monte Carlo Rookie of the Year car/68,016 20.00 50.00
2 Dale Earnhardt Wrangler '79 MC Bank/4500 20.00 50.00
2 Dale Earnhardt Coke 1980 Pontiac/64,836 20.00 50.00
2 Dale Earnhardt Coke '80 Pontiac Bank/4044 20.00 50.00
2 Mark Martin Amsoil 1980 ASA/3240 60.00 100.00
2 Mark Martin Miller 1986 ASA/4656 30.00 60.00
2 Johnny Sauter AC Delco/6000 20.00 50.00
2 Johnny Sauter AC Delco Bank/504 20.00 50.00
2 Rusty Wallace Miller Lite/21,024 20.00 50.00
2 Rusty Wallace Miller Lite Bank/1200 20.00 50.00
2 Rusty Wallace Miller Lite Elvis Bank/1800 20.00 50.00
2 Rusty Wallace Miller Lite Elvis/23,696 20.00 50.00
2 Rusty Wallace Miller Lite Elvis Clear/4884 20.00 50.00
2 Rusty Wallace Miller Lite Harley Flames/18,072 40.00 80.00
2 Rusty Wallace Miller Lite Harley Flames Bank/672 30.00 80.00
2 Rusty Wallace Miller Lite Flames/8592 25.00 60.00
2 Rusty Wallace MGD 1991 Thunderbird/8940 30.00 60.00
2 Rusty Wallace MGD 1995 Thunderbird 30.00 60.00
3 Dale Earnhardt Jr. Nilla Wafers/91,512 25.00 60.00
3 Dale Earnhardt Jr. Nilla Wafers Bank/2508 25.00 60.00
3 Dale Earnhardt Jr. Nilla Wafers Clear/7008 15.00 40.00
3 Dale Earnhardt Jr. Oreo/112,996 20.00 50.00
3 Dale Earnhardt Jr. Oreo Bank/2508 20.00 50.00
3 Dale Earnhardt Jr. Oreo Clear/7008 15.00 40.00
3 Dale Earnhardt Jr. Oreo Snap-On Black Window Car/21,012 20.00 50.00
3 Dale Earnhardt Jr. Sun Drop 1994 Lumina/24,504 30.00 60.00
4 Mike Skinner Kodak Max Yosemite Sam/9612 15.00 40.00
4 Mike Skinner Kodak Max Yosemite Sam Bank/612 15.00 40.00
5 Terry Labonte Cheez-It/6000 15.00 40.00
5 Terry Labonte Kellogg's/11,676 15.00 40.00
5 Terry Labonte Kellogg's Bank/1008 15.00 40.00
5 Terry Labonte Kellogg's Road Runner and Wile E.Coyote/15,528 15.00 40.00
6 Mark Martin Stroh's Light '89 T-bird/5004 30.00 60.00
7 Casey Atwood Sirius/8652 20.00 50.00
7 Casey Atwood Sirius Bank 20.00 50.00
7 Casey Atwood Sirius Mac Tools/2172 20.00 50.00
7 Casey Atwood Sirius Muppets/6552 20.00 50.00
7 Casey Atwood Sirius Muppets Mac Tools/2172 20.00 50.00
7 Casey Atwood Sirius Muppets Bank/504 20.00 50.00
8 Dale Earnhardt Jr. Bud/70,068 40.00 80.00
8 Dale Earnhardt Jr. Bud Bank/2508 30.00 80.00
8 Dale Earnhardt Jr. Bud White Gold Promo/5004 60.00 120.00
8 Dale Earnhardt Jr. Bud Clear/7008 30.00 80.00
8 Dale Earnhardt Jr. Bud Champion Spark Plug Promo 20.00 50.00
8 Dale Earnhardt Jr. Bud Employee in acrylic case 100.00 175.00
8 Dale Earnhardt Jr. Bud All-Star/103,152 25.00 60.00
8 Dale Earnhardt Jr. Bud All-Star Bank/2652 25.00 60.00
8 Dale Earnhardt Jr. Bud All-Star Snap-On BW Car 20.00 50.00
8 Dale Earnhardt Jr. Bud All-Star Red Clear/5304 20.00 50.00
8 Dale Earnhardt Jr. Bud All-Star White Gold Promo/5004 60.00 120.00
8 Dale Earnhardt Jr. Looney Tunes/79,992 20.00 50.00
8 Dale Earnhardt Jr. Looney Tunes Bank/1980 20.00 50.00
9 Bill Elliott Dodge/18,468 20.00 50.00
9 Bill Elliott Dodge Clear/6792 20.00 50.00
9 Bill Elliott Dodge Mac Tools/2172 20.00 50.00
9 Bill Elliott Dodge Muppet/12,924 15.00 40.00
9 Bill Elliott Dodge Muppet Bank/708 15.00 40.00
9 Bill Elliott Dodge Viper/7008 20.00 50.00
10 Johnny Benson Valvoline/6948 15.00 40.00

Item	Low	High
10 Johnny Benson Valvoline Muppet/13,572	15.00	40.00
10 Johnny Benson Valvoline Muppet Bank/1008	15.00	40.00
11 Dale Earnhardt Jr. True Value 1999 IROC/33,876	20.00	50.00
11 Tony Stewart True Value 2001 IROC/8456	25.00	60.00
12 Kerry Earnhardt 10-10-220/9624	20.00	50.00
12 Kerry Earnhardt JaniKing Yosemite Sam/10,368	20.00	50.00
12 Kerry Earnhardt JaniKing Yosemite Sam GM Dealers/444	20.00	50.00
12 Kerry Earnhardt JaniKing Yosemite Sam Bank/612	20.00	50.00
12 Kerry Earnhardt Supercuts	20.00	50.00
12 Ryan Newman Alltel/10,404	35.00	70.00
12 Ryan Newman Mobil 1/11,292	30.00	60.00
15 Dale Earnhardt Wrangler 1979 Pontiac Ventura/58,716	20.00	50.00
15 Dale Earnhardt Wrangler 1979 Pontiac Ventura GM Dealers/3504	20.00	50.00
15 Dale Earnhardt Wrangler 1979 Pontiac Ventura Bank/2508	20.00	50.00
15 Michael Waltrip NAPA/17,280	25.00	50.00
15 Michael Waltrip NAPA Bank/1332	25.00	50.00
15 Michael Waltrip NAPA Clear/4548	15.00	40.00
15 Michael Waltrip NAPA Stars&Stripes/9650	25.00	50.00
15 Michael Waltrip NAPA Stars&Stripes Bank/1008	25.00	50.00
17 Darrell Waltrip Tide 1989 Monte Carlo/8340	25.00	50.00
17 Darrell Waltrip Tide SuperTruck/4008	30.00	60.00
18 Bobby Labonte 3M 100th Anniversary	75.00	125.00
18 Bobby Labonte Interstate Batteries/19,860	30.00	60.00
18 Bobby Labonte Interstate Batteries Bank/1008	30.00	60.00
18 Bobby Labonte Interstate Batteries Clear/5064	20.00	50.00
18 Bobby Labonte Interstate Batteries Mac Tools/2172	30.00	60.00
18 Bobby Labonte Interstate Batteries Muppet/17,076	20.00	50.00
18 Bobby Labonte Interstate Batteries Muppet Bank/960	20.00	50.00
18 Bobby Labonte Let's Roll/11,158	75.00	125.00
18 Bobby Labonte Let's Roll Bank/600	75.00	125.00
18 Bobby Labonte Let's Roll Mac Tools/1798	75.00	125.00
18 Mike McLaughlin MBNA/2004	20.00	50.00
19 Jeremy Mayfield Dodge/13,344	15.00	40.00
19 Jeremy Mayfield Dodge Bank/804	15.00	40.00
19 Jeremy Mayfield Dodge Mac Tools/2172	15.00	40.00
19 Jeremy Mayfield Dodge Muppet/12,612	12.00	30.00
19 Jeremy Mayfield Dodge Muppet Bank/708	12.00	30.00
19 Jeremy Mayfield Mountain Dew/11,508	15.00	40.00
19 Jeremy Mayfield Mountain Dew Bank/804	15.00	40.00
19 Jeremy Mayfield Mountain Dew Promo in can	10.00	20.00
20 Tony Stewart Home Depot/26,508	60.00	120.00
20 Tony Stewart Home Depot Bank/1624	50.00	100.00
20 Tony Stewart Home Depot Clear/4008	25.00	60.00
20 Tony Stewart Home Depot Mac Tools/2172	60.00	120.00
20 Tony Stewart Home Depot 2002 Champion Color Chrome/17,640	40.00	75.00
20 Tony Stewart Home Depot Maintenance Warehouse Promo/3504	100.00	200.00
20 Tony Stewart Home Depot Peanuts Black/22,928	25.00	60.00
20 Tony Stewart Home Depot Peanuts Black Bank/984	25.00	60.00
20 Tony Stewart Home Depot Peanuts Black Clear/2508	20.00	50.00
20 Tony Stewart Home Depot Peanuts Orange/20,866	25.00	60.00
20 Tony Stewart Home Depot Peanuts Orange Bank/1068	25.00	60.00
20 Tony Stewart Home Depot Peanuts Orange Clear/2508	20.00	50.00
20 Tony Stewart Home Depot Peanuts Orange Mac Tools/1860	25.00	60.00
21 Jeff Green Jason Sauter Rockwell Automation/2904	15.00	40.00
23 Davey Allison Sims Bros. 1981 Camaro/3504	30.00	60.00
24 Jeff Gordon DuPont 200th Anniversary/78,180	25.00	50.00
24 Jeff Gordon DuPont 200th Anniversary Bank/3000	25.00	50.00
24 Jeff Gordon DuPont 200th Anniversary Clear/7152	25.00	50.00
24 Jeff Gordon DuPont Bugs Bunny/44,958	30.00	60.00
24 Jeff Gordon DuPont Bugs Bunny Bank/1644	30.00	50.00
24 Jeff Gordon DuPont Flames/70,224	40.00	80.00
24 Jeff Gordon DuPont Flames Bank/2508	30.00	60.00
24 Jeff Gordon DuPont Flames Clear/7008	30.00	60.00
24 Jeff Gordon Elmo/26,844	20.00	50.00
24 Jeff Gordon Pepsi Daytona/37,836	25.00	60.00
24 Jeff Gordon Pepsi Daytona Bank/1800	25.00	60.00
24 Jeff Gordon Pepsi Talladega/19,020	25.00	60.00
24 Jeff Gordon Pepsi Talladega Bank/1800	25.00	60.00
24 Jeff Gordon Pepsi Talladega Color Chrome/2508	60.00	120.00
24 Jeff Gordon Pepsi Talladega Color Chrome Bank/1008	60.00	120.00
25 Jerry Nadeau UAW/4008	20.00	50.00
25 Jerry Nadeau UAW Mac Tools/2172	25.00	50.00
25 Jerry Nadeau UAW Bank/504	20.00	50.00
25 Joe Nemechek UAW Speedy Gonzalez/9144	20.00	50.00
25 Joe Nemechek UAW Speedy Gonzalez Bank/600	15.00	40.00
28 Davey Allison Havoline black&white 1987 Thunderbird/10,200	50.00	80.00
28 Davey Allison Havoline 1990 Thunderbird/6936	35.00	70.00
28 Ricky Rudd Havoline/17,436	30.00	60.00
28 Ricky Rudd Havoline Bank/1500	25.00	50.00
28 Ricky Rudd Havoline Clear/4512	15.00	40.00
28 Ricky Rudd Havoline Iron Man/10,920	30.00	60.00
28 Ricky Rudd Havoline Iron Man Mac Tools/2172	30.00	60.00
28 Ricky Rudd Havoline Muppet/15,744	20.00	50.00
28 Ricky Rudd Havoline Muppet Bank/984	20.00	50.00
28 Cale Yarborough Hardee's 1984 Monte Carlo/4728	35.00	60.00
29 Kevin Harvick Action ET/22,860	20.00	50.00
29 Kevin Harvick Action ET Color Chrome Bank/1284	20.00	50.00
29 Kevin Harvick Flag GM Dealers/3420	175.00	300.00
29 Kevin Harvick Goodwrench/103,716	15.00	40.00
29 Kevin Harvick Goodwrench Bank/3144	15.00	40.00
29 Kevin Harvick Goodwrench Clear/4812	15.00	40.00
29 Kevin Harvick Goodwrench GM Dealer/11,616	15.00	40.00
29 Kevin Harvick Goodwrench ET/64,860	20.00	50.00
29 Kevin Harvick Goodwrench ET GM Dealers/8508	20.00	50.00
29 Kevin Harvick Goodwrench ET Clear/6288	20.00	50.00
29 Kevin Harvick Goodwrench ET Color Chrome Bank/2700	20.00	50.00
29 Kevin Harvick Goodwrench Now Sell Tires/28,896	20.00	50.00
29 Kevin Harvick Goodwrench Now Sell Tires GM Dealers/2004	20.00	50.00
29 Kevin Harvick Goodwrench Taz/21,684	20.00	50.00
29 Kevin Harvick Goodwrench Taz Bank/1056	20.00	50.00
29 Kevin Harvick Goodwrench Taz GM Dealers/8508	20.00	50.00
29 Kevin Harvick Goodwrench Taz GM Dealers White Gold/2496	50.00	100.00
29 Kevin Harvick Reese's Fastbreak/3504	350.00	450.00
29 Kevin Harvick Sonic/21,768	20.00	50.00
29 Kevin Harvick Sonic Bank/1008	20.00	50.00
29 Kevin Harvick Sylvania/8016	20.00	50.00
29 Kevin Harvick Sylvania Bank/504	20.00	50.00
29 Kevin Harvick Sylvania GM Dealers/1008	20.00	50.00
29 Kevin Harvick Snap-On/23,712	20.00	50.00
30 Jeff Green AOL/9494	15.00	40.00
30 Jeff Green AOL Bank/504	25.00	50.00
30 Jeff Green AOL Daffy Duck/8796	15.00	40.00
30 Jeff Green AOL Daffy Duck Bank/696	15.00	40.00
30 Jeff Green AOL Scooby-Doo/9072	20.00	50.00
31 Robby Gordon Cingular/7008	20.00	50.00
31 Robby Gordon Cingular Bank/600	20.00	50.00
31 Robby Gordon Cingular Pepe le Pew/9060	20.00	50.00
31 Robby Gordon Cingular Pepe le Pew Bank/1644	15.00	40.00
31 Mark Martin Fat Boys BBQ 1987 Thunderbird/3444	30.00	60.00
33 Tony Stewart Monaco SuperTruck/8652	35.00	60.00
36 Ken Schrader M&M's/6744	25.00	50.00
36 Ken Schrader M&M's Halloween/6684	25.00	60.00
36 Ken Schrader M&M's Halloween Bank/600	25.00	60.00
36 Ken Schrader M&M's July 4th/6936	20.00	50.00
40 Sterling Marlin Coors Light/21,708	20.00	50.00
40 Sterling Marlin Coors Original/15,804	20.00	50.00
40 Sterling Marlin Coors Original Bank/804	20.00	50.00
41 Jimmy Spencer Energizer/6168	20.00	50.00
41 Jimmy Spencer Fujifilm/3480	20.00	50.00
41 Jimmy Spencer Target/7764	20.00	50.00
41 Jimmy Spencer Target Bank/900	20.00	50.00
41 Jimmy Spencer Target Muppet/10,956	15.00	40.00
41 Jimmy Spencer Target Muppet Bank/900	15.00	40.00
48 Jimmie Johnson Lowe's/19,704	60.00	120.00
48 Jimmie Johnson Lowe's Power of Pride/15,552	25.00	60.00
48 Jimmie Johnson Lowe's Power of Pride Bank	25.00	60.00
48 Jimmie Johnson Lowe's Sylvester.&Tweety/25,212	25.00	60.00
48 Jimmie Johnson Lowe's Sylvester and Tweety Bank/1140	25.00	60.00
48 Darrell Waltrip Crowell & Reed 1964 Chevelle/3840	25.00	50.00
48 Darrell Waltrip Crowell & Reed 1964 Chevelle Bank/408	25.00	50.00
55 Bobby Hamilton Square D Marvin/7128	20.00	50.00
55 Bobby Hamilton Square D Marvin Bank/636	20.00	50.00
71 Dave Marcis Realtree Retirement/4008	40.00	75.00
88 Dale Jarrett UPS/42,052	20.00	50.00
88 Dale Jarrett UPS Clear/6180	15.00	40.00
88 Dale Jarrett UPS Color Chrome Bank/2508	20.00	50.00
88 Dale Jarrett UPS Muppet/28,140	15.00	40.00
88 Dale Jarrett UPS Muppet Bank/1200	15.00	40.00
91 Hank Parker Jr. USG Promo	30.00	60.00
97 Alan Kulwicki Prototype Engines '83 Pontiac Firebird/260	15.00	40.00
98 Kasey Kahne Channellock/3024	50.00	100.00
2002 DEI Pit Practice/2508	40.00	100.00
NNO Dale Earnhardt Legacy/58,212	35.00	60.00
NNO Looney Tunes Rematch/15,528	12.00	30.00
NNO Looney Tunes Rematch GM Dealers/504	12.00	30.00
NNO Muppet Show 25th Anniversary/18,204	12.00	30.00
NNO Muppet Show 25th Anniversary Clear/3384	12.00	30.00

2002 Action QVC For Race Fans Only 1:24

Item	Low	High
2 Rusty Wallace Miller Lite Harley Flames Color Chrome/1008	60.00	120.00
3 Dale Earnhardt Jr. Nilla Wafers Color Chrome/7500	60.00	100.00
3 Dale Earnhardt Jr. Nilla Wafers Gold/2508	125.00	200.00
3 Dale Earnhardt Jr. Nilla Wafers Platinum/624	125.00	250.00
3 Dale Earnhardt Jr. Oreo Color Chrome/2508	60.00	100.00
3 Dale Earnhardt Jr. Oreo Gold/2508	125.00	200.00
3 Dale Earnhardt Jr. Oreo Platinum/624	125.00	250.00
8 Dale Earnhardt Jr. Bud Color Chrome/2508	60.00	120.00
8 Dale Earnhardt Jr. Bud Gold/2508	75.00	150.00
8 Dale Earnhardt Jr. Bud Platinum/624	125.00	225.00
8 Dale Earnhardt Jr. Bud All-Star Gold/2508	75.00	150.00
8 Dale Earnhardt Jr. Bud All-Star Platinum/624	125.00	225.00
8 Dale Earnhardt Jr. Looney Tunes Color Chrome/5004	60.00	100.00
8 Dale Earnhardt Jr. Looney Tunes Gold/2508	100.00	175.00
8 Dale Earnhardt Jr. Looney Tunes Platinum/624	125.00	225.00
12 Ryan Newman Alltel ROY Gold/1008	100.00	200.00
12 Ryan Newman Alltel ROY Platinum/624	135.00	225.00
20 Tony Stewart Home Depot Color Chrome/2508	90.00	150.00
20 Tony Stewart Home Depot Peanuts Black Color Chrome/2508	75.00	150.00
20 Tony Stewart Home Depot Peanuts Black Platinum/624	150.00	250.00
20 Tony Stewart Home Depot Peanuts Orange Color Chrome/2508	75.00	150.00
20 Tony Stewart Home Depot Peanuts Orange Platinum/624	150.00	250.00
24 Jeff Gordon DuPont 200th Ann. Gold/2508	100.00	175.00
24 Jeff Gordon DuPont 200th Anniversary Platinum/624	125.00	200.00
24 Jeff Gordon DuPont Bugs Color Chrome/5004	60.00	100.00
24 Jeff Gordon DuPont Bugs Gold/2508	75.00	150.00
24 Jeff Gordon DuPont Bugs Platinum/624	125.00	200.00
24 Jeff Gordon DuPont Flames Color Chrome/22,424	50.00	80.00
24 Jeff Gordon DuPont Flames Gold/2508	100.00	175.00
24 Jeff Gordon DuPont Flames Platinum/624	125.00	225.00
24 Jeff Gordon Pepsi Daytona Color Chrome/7500	60.00	100.00
24 Jeff Gordon Pepsi Daytona Gold/2508	90.00	150.00
24 Jeff Gordon Pepsi Daytona Platinum/624	125.00	200.00
24 Jeff Gordon Pepsi Talladega Color Chrome/2508	60.00	120.00
24 Jeff Gordon Pepsi Talladega Gold/2508	70.00	135.00
24 Jeff Gordon Pepsi Talladega Platinum/624	125.00	200.00
29 Kevin Harvick Goodwrench Gold/2508	75.00	150.00
29 Kevin Harvick Goodwrench Platinum/624	125.00	200.00
29 Kevin Harvick Goodwrench ET Gold/2508	75.00	150.00
29 Kevin Harvick Goodwrench ET Chrome/3504	40.00	100.00
29 Kevin Harvick Goodwrench ET Platinum/624	75.00	150.00
29 Kevin Harvick Goodwrench Taz Color Chome/2508	40.00	80.00
88 Dale Jarrett UPS Color Chrome/1000	40.00	100.00
88 Dale Jarrett UPS Muppets Color Chrome/2508	70.00	120.00

2002 Action/RCCA 1:24

Item	Low	High
1 Jeff Gordon Autolite 1989 Thunderbird Bank/1800	35.00	60.00
1 Steve Park Pennzoil Bank/720	30.00	60.00
2 Dale Earnhardt Coke '80 Pontiac Bank/5004	30.00	60.00
2 Johnny Sauter AC Delco Bank/600	30.00	60.00
2 Rusty Wallace MGD 1995 Thunderbird Bank/600	35.00	60.00
2 Rusty Wallace Miller Lite Color Chrome Bank/1008	30.00	60.00
2 Rusty Wallace Miller Lite Split Clear/2508	35.00	60.00
2 Rusty Wallace Miller Lite Elvis Bank/1200	20.00	50.00
2 Rusty Wallace Miller Lite Harley Flames Bank/1008	25.00	60.00
2K2 Childress Racing Pit Practice Bank/1008	35.00	70.00
3 Dale Earnhardt Goodwrench Bank '90 Lumina/4008	35.00	60.00
3 Dale Earnhardt Jr. Nilla Wafers Bank/5004	20.00	50.00
3 Dale Earnhardt Jr. Nilla Wafers Split Clear/3000	20.00	50.00
3 Dale Earnhardt Jr. Oreo Bank/5004	20.00	50.00
3 Dale Earnhardt Jr. Oreo Split Clear/3000	20.00	50.00
4 Mike Skinner Kodak Max Yosemite Sam Bank/600	20.00	50.00
5 Terry Labonte Cheez-It Bank/720	20.00	50.00
5 Terry Labonte Kellogg's Road Runner & Wile E.Coyote Bank/600	20.00	50.00
7 Casey Atwood Sirius Bank/408	25.00	50.00
7 Casey Atwood Sirius Muppet Bank/408	25.00	50.00
8 Dale Earnhardt Docs '64 Chevelle Bank/3504	30.00	60.00
8 Dale Earnhardt Jr. Bud Bank/3504	40.00	75.00
8 Dale Earnhardt Jr. Bud Split Clear/4500	40.00	80.00
8 Dale Earnhardt Jr. Bud Color Chrome Bank/3600	40.00	75.00
8 Dale Earnhardt Jr. Bud All-Star Bank/4800	40.00	75.00
8 Dale Earnhardt Jr. Bud All-Star Split Clear/2508	40.00	75.00
8 Dale Earnhardt Jr. Bud Talladega April 2002 Win Raced/1008	40.00	75.00
8 Dale Earnhardt Jr. Looney Tunes Bank/4008	40.00	75.00
8 Dale Earnhardt Jr. Looney Tunes Split Clear/2508	40.00	75.00
9 Bill Elliott Dodge Bank/600	25.00	60.00
9 Bill Elliott Dodge Muppet Bank/720	20.00	50.00
9 Bill Elliott Dodge Viper Bank/600	25.00	60.00
10 Johnny Benson Valvoline Bank/408	20.00	50.00
12 Kerry Earnhardt 10-10-220 Bank/1008	25.00	50.00
12 Kerry Earnhardt JaniKing Yosemite Sam Bank/720	25.00	50.00
12 Kerry Earnhardt Supercuts Bank/1008	30.00	60.00
12 Ryan Newman Alltel Bank/1008	45.00	80.00
12 Ryan Newman Alltel Rookie of the Year Color Chrome/10,248	40.00	75.00
12 Ryan Newman Mobil 1 Bank/804	45.00	80.00
15 Dale Earnhardt Wrangler 1979 Pontiac Ventura Bank/3000	40.00	70.00
15 Michael Waltrip NAPA Bank/600	20.00	50.00
15 Michael Waltrip NAPA Stars and Stripes Bank/504	20.00	50.00
17 Darrell Waltrip Tide SuperTruck/504	45.00	80.00
18 Bobby Labonte Interstate Batteries Bank/804	30.00	60.00
18 Bobby Labonte Interstate Batteries Muppet Bank/720	30.00	60.00
18 Bobby Labonte Let's Roll Bank/600	60.00	120.00
19 Jeremy Mayfield Dodge Clear/3816	20.00	50.00
19 Jeremy Mayfield Dodge Muppet Bank/600	20.00	50.00
19 Jeremy Mayfield Mountain Dew Bank/492	20.00	50.00
20 Tony Stewart Home Depot Bank/720	60.00	120.00
20 Tony Stewart Home Depot Split Clear/2508	25.00	60.00
20 Tony Stewart Home Depot 2002 Champion Color Chrome Bank/1008	40.00	70.00
20 Tony Stewart Home Depot Peanuts Black Bank/1008	40.00	70.00
20 Tony Stewart Home Depot Peanuts Black Split Clear/504	40.00	70.00
20 Tony Stewart Home Depot Peanuts Orange Bank/1008	40.00	70.00
20 Tony Stewart Home Depot Peanuts Orange Split Clear/504	40.00	70.00
24 Jeff Gordon DuPont 200th Anniversary Bank/4008	35.00	70.00
24 Jeff Gordon DuPont 200th Anniversary Split Clear/2508	35.00	60.00
24 Jeff Gordon DuPont 200th Anniversary Clear/7152	30.00	60.00
24 Jeff Gordon DuPont Bugs Bunny Bank/4008	40.00	75.00
24 Jeff Gordon DuPont Flames Bank/2800	40.00	70.00
24 Jeff Gordon Elmo Bank/2004	20.00	50.00
24 Jeff Gordon Pepsi Daytona Bank/3012	25.00	60.00
24 Jeff Gordon Pepsi Talladega Split Clear/2508	25.00	60.00
24 Jeff Gordon Pepsi Talladega Color Chrome Bank/1800	30.00	60.00
28 Davey Allison Havoline 1990 Thunderbird Bank/1008	30.00	60.00
28 Ricky Rudd Havoline Bank/804	30.00	60.00
28 Ricky Rudd Havoline Iron Man Bank/720	30.00	60.00
28 Cale Yarborough Hardee's 1984 Monte Carlo Bank/504	30.00	60.00
29 Kevin Harvick Action ET Bank/1200	20.00	50.00
29 Kevin Harvick Goodwrench Bank/5004	15.00	40.00
29 Kevin Harvick Goodwrench Split Clear/2508	15.00	40.00
29 Kevin Harvick Goodwrench ET Bank/2004	20.00	50.00
29 Kevin Harvick Goodwrench Now Sell Tires Bank/1500	20.00	50.00
29 Kevin Harvick Sonic Bank/1008	20.00	50.00

Kevin Harvick Sylvania Bank/1008 20.00 50.00
Jeff Green AOL Bank/492 25.00 50.00
Jeff Green AOL Daffy Duck Bank/600 30.00 60.00
Jeff Green AOL Scooby-Doo Bank/720 25.00 50.00
Robby Gordon Cingular Bank/720 30.00 60.00
Robby Gordon Cingular Pepe le Pew Bank/600 30.00 60.00
Mark Martin Fat Boys BBQ 1987 Thunderbird Bank/600 30.00 50.00
Ken Schrader M&M's Halloween Bank/600 30.00 60.00
Ken Schrader M&M's July 4th Bank/504 30.00 60.00
Sterling Marlin Coors Light Bank/804 20.00 50.00
Sterling Marlin Coors Original Bank/900 20.00 50.00
Jimmy Spencer Energizer Bank/408 30.00 60.00
Jimmy Spencer Target Bank/600 30.00 60.00
Jimmy Spencer Target Muppet Bank/600 15.00 40.00
3 Jimmie Johnson Lowe's Bank/600 60.00 120.00
3 Jimmie Johnson Lowe's Power of Pride Bank/900 35.00 60.00
3 Jimmie Johnson Lowe's Sylv.&Tweety Bank/1500 35.00 60.00
3 Darrell Waltrip Crowell&Reed 1964 Chevelle Bank/720 30.00 60.00
5 Bobby Hamilton Square D Marvin the Martian Bank/600 30.00 60.00
8 Dale Jarrett UPS Bank/2004 20.00 50.00
8 Dale Jarrett UPS Muppet Bank/1500 20.00 50.00
8 Kasey Kahne Channellock Bank/408 50.00 100.00
NNO Dale Earnhardt Legacy Bank/2004 25.00 60.00
NNO Looney Tunes Rematch Bank/804 15.00 40.00

2002 Action/RCCA Elite 1:24

Steve Park Pennzoil/600 50.00 100.00
Dale Earnhardt Coke '80 Pontiac/5004 50.00 100.00
Rusty Wallace MGD 1995 Thunderbird/900 75.00 135.00
Rusty Wallace Miller Lite Color Chrome/1608 60.00 120.00
Rusty Wallace Miller Lite Elvis/2004 60.00 120.00
Rusty Wallace Miller Lite Harley Flames/1800 100.00 200.00
Rusty Wallace Miller Lite Test Flames/1488-A 60.00 120.00
Rusty Wallace Miller Lite Flames/1200 50.00 100.00
K2 Childress Racing Pit Practice/1200 50.00 100.00
3 Dale Earnhardt Goodwrench Plus No Bull 76th Win/4500 100.00 175.00
3 Dale Earnhardt Jr. Nilla Wafers/6504 60.00 120.00
3 Dale Earnhardt Jr. Oreo/8988 60.00 120.00
3 Dale Earnhardt Jr. Oreo Raced Version/2004 60.00 120.00
3 Dale Earnhardt Jr. Oreo Test Gray/3504 60.00 120.00
4 Mike Skinner Kodak Max Yosemite Sam/600 50.00 100.00
5 Terry Labonte Cheez-It/540-A 50.00 100.00
5 Terry Labonte Kellogg's/600 50.00 100.00
5 Terry Labonte Kellogg's Road Runner & Wile E.Coyote/600 50.00 100.00
7 Casey Atwood Sirius/408 40.00 80.00
7 Casey Atwood Sirius Muppet/408 40.00 80.00
8 Dale Earnhardt Docs '64 Chevelle/3504 75.00 150.00
8 Dale Earnhardt Jr. Bud/1200 150.00 300.00
8 Dale Earnhardt Jr. Bud Color Chrome/4200 100.00 200.00
8 Dale Earnhardt Jr. Bud Talladega April 2002 Win Raced/1500 175.00 300.00
8 Dale Earnhardt Jr. Bud Test Red/5004 60.00 120.00
8 Dale Earnhardt Jr. Bud All-Star/6996 60.00 120.00

8 Dale Earnhardt Jr. Looney Tunes/6000 80.00 135.00
8 Dale Earnhardt Jr. Looney Tunes Raced Version Richmond/2004 70.00 120.00
9 Bill Elliott Dodge/600 60.00 120.00
9 Bill Elliott Dodge Muppet/804 60.00 120.00
9 Bill Elliott Dodge Raced Version Brickyard/600 60.00 120.00
9 Bill Elliott Dodge Viper/600 60.00 120.00
10 Johnny Benson Valvoline/600 50.00 100.00
10 Johnny Benson Valvoline Muppet/408 50.00 100.00
12 Kerry Earnhardt 10-10-220/1008 40.00 80.00
12 Kerry Earnhardt JaniKing Yosemite Sam/1008 40.00 80.00
12 Kerry Earnhardt Supercuts/1008 40.00 80.00
12 Ryan Newman Alltel/1392 100.00 200.00
12 Ryan Newman Alltel Rookie of the Year Color Chrome/1140 75.00 150.00
12 Ryan Newman Mobil 1/1008 75.00 150.00
15 Dale Earnhardt Wrangler 1979 Pontiac Ventura/4008 75.00 125.00
15 Michael Waltrip NAPA/600 50.00 100.00
15 Michael Waltrip NAPA Stars and Stripes/540A 50.00 100.00
17 Darrell Waltrip Tide '89 MC Daytona Win/600 125.00 250.00
18 Bobby Labonte Interstate Batteries/1008 50.00 100.00
18 Bobby Labonte Interstate Batteries Muppet/960 50.00 100.00
18 Bobby Labonte Let's Roll/900 125.00 250.00
19 Jeremy Mayfield Dodge/804 40.00 80.00
19 Jeremy Mayfield Dodge Muppet/600 40.00 80.00
19 Jeremy Mayfield Mountain Dew/600 40.00 80.00
20 Tony Stewart Home Depot/1404 150.00 300.00
20 Tony Stewart Home Depot 2002 Champion Color Chrome/2004 60.00 120.00
20 Tony Stewart Home Depot Metal/1800 75.00 150.00
20 Tony Stewart Home Depot Peanuts Black/1500 60.00 120.00
20 Tony Stewart Home Depot Peanuts Orange/1500 60.00 120.00
24 Jeff Gordon DuPont 200th Anniversary/5004 50.00 100.00
24 Jeff Gordon DuPont Flames/3204 100.00 175.00
24 Jeff Gordon DuPont Test black/4500 60.00 110.00
24 Jeff Gordon DuPont Bugs Bunny/6000 50.00 100.00
24 Jeff Gordon Elmo/3600 50.00 100.00
24 Jeff Gordon Pepsi Daytona/4500 50.00 100.00
24 Jeff Gordon Pepsi Talladega/2504 50.00 100.00
25 Joe Nemechek UAW Speedy Gonzalez/600 50.00 100.00
28 Ricky Rudd Havoline/1008 50.00 100.00
28 Ricky Rudd Havoline Iron Man/804 50.00 100.00
28 Ricky Rudd Havoline Muppet/804 50.00 100.00
29 Kevin Harvick Action ET/2004 40.00 80.00
29 Kevin Harvick Goodwrench/7500 30.00 60.00
29 Kevin Harvick Goodwrench ET/4212 40.00 80.00
29 Kevin Harvick Goodwrench Now Sell Tires/3000 40.00 80.00
29 Kevin Harvick Goodwrench Test Gray/3000 30.00 60.00
29 Kevin Harvick Goodwrench Taz/1800 40.00 80.00
29 Kevin Harvick Sonic/1008 40.00 80.00
29 Kevin Harvick Sylvania/1500 30.00 60.00
30 Jeff Green AOL/600 40.00 80.00
30 Jeff Green AOL Daffy Duck/600 40.00 80.00
30 Jeff Green AOL Scooby-Doo/720 40.00 80.00
31 Robby Gordon Cingular/720 50.00 100.00
31 Robby Gordon Cingular Pepe le Pew/600 50.00 100.00
31 Mark Martin Fat Boys BBQ 1987 Thunderbird/600 60.00 120.00
36 Ken Schrader M&M's Halloween/600 50.00 100.00
36 Ken Schrader M&M's July 4th/1008 50.00 100.00
40 Sterling Marlin Coors Light/1008 50.00 100.00
40 Sterling Marlin Coors Original/1200 50.00 100.00
40 Jamie McMurray Coors Light 1st Win raced version/600 50.00 100.00
41 Jimmy Spencer Energizer/408 40.00 80.00
41 Jimmy Spencer Target/600 40.00 80.00
41 Jimmy Spencer Target Muppet/600 40.00 80.00
48 Jimmie Johnson Lowe's/900 150.00 300.00
48 Jimmie Johnson Lowe's California Raced/1008 100.00 200.00
48 Jimmie Johnson Lowe's Power of Pride/1200 60.00 120.00
48 Jimmie Johnson Lowe's Sylv.&Tweety/2220 60.00 120.00
55 Bobby Hamilton Square D Marvin/600 50.00 100.00
88 Dale Jarrett UPS/2800 40.00 80.00
88 Dale Jarrett UPS Muppet/2004 40.00 80.00
88 Dale Jarrett UPS Metal/1500 40.00 80.00
98 Kasey Kahne Channellock/408 75.00 150.00
2002 DEI Racing Pit Practice/2002 70.00 120.00
02 Action Performance Gold/100 125.00 250.00
NNO Dale Earnhardt Legacy/3000 125.00 200.00
NNO Looney Tunes Rematch/1200 25.00 60.00
NNO Muppet Show 25th Anniversary/600-A 25.00 60.00

2003 Action Performance 1:24

2 Rusty Wallace Rusty 15.00 25.00
3 Dale Earnhardt Goodwrench Forever the Man window box 15.00 30.00
8 Dale Earnhardt Jr. Dale Jr. 15.00 25.00
8 Dale Earnhardt Jr. JR 15.00 25.00
15 Michael Waltrip NAPA Daytona Win Promo 18.00 30.00
15 Michael Waltrip NAPA Nilla Wafers Promo 12.50 25.00
15 Michael Waltrip NAPA Stars&Stripes Promo 10.00 25.00
18 Bobby Labonte Interstate Batteries 12.50 25.00
20 Tony Stewart Home Depot 15.00 25.00
24 Jeff Gordon DuPont Flames 15.00 25.00
29 Kevin Harvick Goodwrench 12.50 25.00
88 Dale Jarrett UPS 15.00 25.00

2003 Action Racing Collectables 1:24

1 Donnie Allison Hawaiian Tropic 1977 Oldsmobile/3228 50.00 100.00
1 Jeff Green Pennzoil Synthetic/4476 20.00 50.00
1 Mark Martin True Value 1998 IROC/5976 30.00 60.00
1 Jamie McMurray Yellow Freight/4104 20.00 50.00
1 Steve Park Pennzoil/6300 35.00 60.00
1 Steve Park Pennzoil GM Dealers/504 35.00 60.00
2 Kurt Busch True Value IROC Lt.Blue/3540 35.00 60.00
2 Kurt Busch True Value IROC Light Blue AU/5004 40.00 75.00
2 Ron Hornaday AC Delco/4152 20.00 50.00
2 Ron Hornaday AC Delco Black Window Bank/312 15.00 40.00
2 Ron Hornaday AC Delco Franky Perez/2076 20.00 50.00
2 Ron Hornaday AC Delco Franky Perez GM Dealers/288 20.00 50.00
2 Jason Leffler ASE Carquest SuperTruck Promo in window box 30.00 60.00
2 Jason Leffler Hulk SuperTruck/15,076 20.00 50.00
2 Mark Martin SAI Roofing 1987 Thunderbird/3660 35.00 60.00
2 Rusty Wallace Miller Lite/18,012 50.00 80.00
2 Rusty Wallace Miller Lite Black Window Bank/708 40.00 70.00
2 Rusty Wallace Miller Lite Victory Lap/7476 60.00 100.00
2 Rusty Wallace Miller Lite Victory Lap Clear Window Bank/420 60.00 100.00
2 Rusty Wallace Miller Lite 600th/9936 40.00 75.00
2 Rusty Wallace Miller Lite 600th Clear Window Bank/504 40.00 70.00
2 Rusty Wallace Miller Time Live Goo Goo Dolls/12,688 40.00 70.00
2 Rusty Wallace Miller Time Live Goo Goo Dolls Clear Window Bank/856 30.00 60.00
3 Dale Earnhardt Foundation/53,796 25.00 50.00
3 Dale Earnhardt Foundation Clear Window Bank/2004 25.00 50.00
3 Dale Earnhardt Goodwrench 1990 Lumina/35,664 40.00 70.00
3 Dale Earnhardt Goodwrench 1990 Lumina GM Dealers/1908 40.00 70.00
3 Dale Earnhardt Goodwrench Silver Select 1995 Monte Carlo Clear Window Bank/33,333 40.00 70.00
3 Dale Earnhardt Goodwrench No Bull 2000 Monte Carlo/25,244 45.00 75.00
3 Dale Earnhardt Goodwrench No Bull 2000 Monte Carlo Clear Window Bank/1596 30.00 60.00
3 Dale Earnhardt Goodwrench No Bull 2000 MC GM Dealers/3504 45.00 75.00
3 Dale Earnhardt Goodwrench 2001 Monte Carlo Clear Window Bank/15,360 45.00 75.00
3 Dale Earnhardt Goodwrench 2001 Monte Carlo Clear/6108 35.00 60.00
3 Dale Earnhardt Goodwrench 2001 Monte Carlo Clear GM Dealers/300 35.00 60.00
3 Dale Earnhardt Goodwrench Bass Pro Bank/16,944 40.00 70.00
3 Dale Earnhardt Victory Lap/29,628 40.00 70.00
3 Dale Earnhardt Victory Lap CW Bank/1260 40.00 70.00
3 Dale Earnhardt Victory Lap GM Dealers/3300 40.00 70.00
3 Dale Earnhardt Victory Lap Color Chrome/6012 50.00 80.00
3 Dale Earnhardt Victory Lap Color Chrome GM Dealers/744 50.00 80.00
3 Dale Earnhardt Wheaties 1997 Monte Carlo Clear Window Bank/9900 45.00 75.00
3 Dale Earnhardt Jr. Goodwrench 1997 Monte Carlo/24,396 40.00 70.00
3 Dale Earnhardt Jr. Goodwrench 1997 Monte Carlo GM Dealers/1416 40.00 75.00
3 Dale Earnhardt Jr. Prime Sirloin '95 Monte Carlo brushed metal /3504 40.00 70.00
5 Terry Labonte Kellogg's/4152 40.00 70.00
5 Terry Labonte Kellogg'sGot Milk/4320 40.00 70.00
5 Terry Labonte Kellogg's Victory Lap/5148 35.00 60.00
5 Terry Labonte Kellogg's Victory Lap Clear Window Bank/396 35.00 60.00
5 Terry Labonte Kellogg's Victory Lap GM Dealers/324 35.00 60.00
5 Brian Vickers GMAC Raced Win AU/1908 50.00 100.00
6 Jeff Gordon True Value 1998 IROC/900 45.00 75.00
6 Kevin Harvick kevinharvick.com SuperTruck 1st Win/3504 40.00 70.00
7 Greg Biffle Kleenex Wolfman/1572 20.00 50.00
7 Greg Biffle Kleenex Wolfman Clear Window Bank/240 20.00 50.00
7 Dale Jarrett True Value 2001 IROC AU/3864 40.00 80.00
7 Jimmie Johnson True Value IROC/2616 35.00 60.00
7 Jimmie Johnson True Value IROC AU/3144 60.00 100.00
7 Alan Kulwicki Hooters '93 T-bird/6010 35.00 60.00
7 Alan Kulwicki Victory Lap/5700 40.00 70.00
7 Alan Kulwicki Victory Lap Clear Window Bank/372 40.00 70.00
7 Alan Kulwicki Zerex 1987 T-Bird/4242 20.00 50.00
7 Alan Kulwicki Zerex 1987 T-Bird Clear Window Bank/972 20.00 50.00
7 Kyle Petty 7-11 1985 Thunderbird/2556 35.00 60.00
7 Jimmy Spencer Sirius/3600 20.00 50.00
7 Jimmy Spencer Sirius 3 Stooges/3444 20.00 50.00
8 Dale Earnhardt Jr. Bud/105,248 50.00 80.00
8 Dale Earnhardt Jr. Bud GM Dealer/8504 40.00 80.00
8 Dale Earnhardt Jr. Bud Black Window Bank/3300 40.00 75.00
8 Dale Earnhardt Jr. Bud No Bull 2000 Monte Carlo/28,764 45.00 75.00
8 Dale Earnhardt Jr. Bud No Bull 2000 Monte Carlo Clear Window Bank/1536 45.00 75.00
8 Dale Earnhardt Jr. Bud No Bull '00 Mon.Carlo GM Dealers/3504 45.00 75.00
8 Dale Earnhardt Jr. Bud Talladega '02/17,052 45.00 75.00
8 Dale Earnhardt Jr. Bud Talladega '02 CW Bank/1008 45.00 75.00
8 Dale Earnhardt Jr. Budweiser Talladega/45,024 45.00 75.00
8 Dale Earnhardt Jr. Bud All-Star Game/60,456 45.00 75.00
8 Dale Earnhardt Jr. Bud All-Star Clear Window Bank/1475 45.00 75.00
8 Dale Earnhardt Jr. Bud All-Star Red Clear/4320 30.00 60.00
8 Dale Earnhardt Jr. Bud All-Star Red Clear GM Dealer/240 30.00 60.00
8 Dale Earnhardt Jr. Bud StainD/60,204 45.00 75.00
8 Dale Earnhardt Jr. Bud StainD Clear Window Bank/1968 40.00 75.00
8 Dale Earnhardt Jr. Bud StainD GM Dealer/3504 40.00 75.00
8 Dale Earnhardt Jr. Dirty Mo Posse/59,796 40.00 70.00
8 Dale Earnhardt Jr. Dirty Mo Posse Black Window Bank/2292 40.00 70.00
8 Dale Earnhardt Jr. Dirty Mo Posse Clear/5304 40.00 70.00
8 Dale Earnhardt Jr. Dirty Mo Posse GM Dealers/3504 40.00 70.00
8 Dale Earnhardt Jr. E Concert/74,352 40.00 70.00
8 Dale Earnhardt Jr. E Concert Black Window Bank/2304 40.00 70.00
8 Dale Earnhardt Jr. E Concert GM Dealers/5004 40.00 70.00
8 Dale Earnhardt Jr. Oreo Ritz/77,208 40.00 75.00
8 Dale Earnhardt Jr. Oreo Ritz Bank/2268 30.00 60.00
8 Dale Earnhardt Jr. Oreo Ritz Clear/6588 35.00 60.00
8 Dale Earnhardt Jr. Oreo Ritz GM Dealers/5004 40.00 75.00
8 Dale Earnhardt Jr. Oreo Ritz White Gold/2496 75.00 125.00
8 Kerry Earnhardt Mom N' Pops 1996/5232 20.00 50.00
8 Mark Martin True Value IROC Green/6748 35.00 60.00
8 Steve Park Cheese Nips/5760 35.00 60.00
8 Steve Park Cheese Nips Black Window Bank/516 35.00 60.00
8 Steve Park Maxwell House/6540 40.00 70.00
8 Steve Park Maxwell House GM Dealers/240 40.00 70.00
8 Hank Parker Jr. Remmington Bass Pro Shops/3972 20.00 50.00
8 Hank Parker Jr. Remmington Bass Pro Shops GM Dealers/240 20.00 50.00
8 Hank Parker Jr. Remmington Bass Pro Shops Clear Window Bank/420 20.00 50.00
8 Hank Parker Jr. Remmington Dick's Sporting Goods/3372 20.00 50.00
8 Tony Stewart 3 Doors Down/26,916 40.00 70.00
8 Tony Stewart 3 Doors Down Clear Window Bank/1272 35.00 70.00
9 Bill Elliott Coors 1984 T-bird/5592 45.00 75.00
9 Bill Elliott Coors Winston Million 1985 Thunderbird/5508 45.00 75.00
9 Bill Elliott Coors Winston Million 1985 Thunderbird Clear Window Bank/432 45.00 75.00
9 Bill Elliott Coors '87 Thunderbird/6864 45.00 75.00
9 Bill Elliott Coors 1987 Thunderbird Black Window Bank/636 40.00 70.00
9 Bill Elliott Coors 1988 Thunderbird/6228 40.00 70.00
9 Bill Elliott Dodge/8856 35.00 60.00
9 Bill Elliott Dodge Black Window Bank/792 30.00 60.00
9 Bill Elliott Dodge Clear/2748 30.00 60.00
9 Bill Elliott Dodge Lion King/3612 35.00 60.00
9 Bill Elliott Dodge Lion King Clear Window Bank/324 35.00 60.00
9 Bill Elliott Dodge 10th Anniversary Brickyard/6528 35.00 60.00
9 Bill Elliott Dodge 10th Brickyard Clear Window Bank/540 35.00 60.00
9 Bill Elliott Dodge Victory Lap/6132 40.00 60.00
9 Bill Elliott Dodge Victory Lap Clear Window Bank/420 40.00 60.00
9 Bill Elliott Melling 1982 Thunderbird/5196 30.00 60.00
10 Johnny Benson Valvoline/3048 20.00 50.00
11 Kevin Harvick True Value IROC Yellow/7128 40.00 70.00
11 Dale Jarrett True Value IROC Blue/6648 45.00 70.00
11 Darrell Waltrip Victory Lap/6360 40.00 60.00
11 Darrell Waltrip Victory Lap Clear Window Bank/348 40.00 60.00
11 Cale Yarborough Victory Lap/4044 35.00 60.00
11 Cale Yarborough Victory Lap Clear Window Bank/336 35.00 60.00
12 Kerry Earnhardt Hot Tamales red/5232 20.00 50.00
15 Michael Waltrip NAPA/8304 40.00 70.00
15 Michael Waltrip NAPA Bank/480 40.00 70.00
15 Michael Waltrip NAPA GM Dealer/504 40.00 70.00
15 Michael Waltrip NAPA Hootie & the Blowfish/10,008 25.00 50.00

15 Michael Waltrip NAPA Hootie & The Blowfish Clear Window Bank/684 25.00 50.00

15 Michael Waltrip NAPA Hootie GM Dealers/504 25.00 50.00

15 Michael Waltrip NAPA Nilla Wafers/7164 25.00 50.00

15 Michael Waltrip NAPA Nilla Wafers Clear Window Bank/456 25.00 50.00

15 Michael Waltrip NAPA Stars & Stripes/8652 35.00 60.00

15 Michael Waltrip NAPA Stars&Stripes Clear Window Bank/492 35.00 60.00

17 Darrell Waltrip Aaron's Rent 3 Stooges SuperTruck/6108 35.00 60.00

17 Darrell Waltrip Boogity Boogity AU/4356 75.00 125.00

17 Darrell Waltrip Boogity Boogity GM Dealers AU/240 75.00 125.00

17 Darrell Waltrip Tide Give Kids the World SuperTruck/4512 35.00 60.00

18 Coy Gibbs MBNA/1392 20.00 50.00

18 Bobby Labonte Interstate Batteries/11,244 40.00 75.00

18 Bobby Labonte Interstate Batteries Black Window Bank/504 40.00 70.00

18 Bobby Labonte Interstate Batteries GM Dealers/288 40.00 75.00

18 Bobby Labonte Interstate Batteries Advair Green/5784 40.00 70.00

18 Bobby Labonte Interstate Batteries Advair Purple/7068 40.00 70.00

18 Bobby Labonte Interstate Batteries Advair Purple GM Dealers/300 40.00 70.00

18 Bobby Labonte Interstate Batteries Hulk/10,884 40.00 70.00

18 Bobby Labonte Interstate Batteries Clear Window Bank/720 40.00 70.00

18 Bobby Labonte Interstate Batteries Victory Lap/6876 40.00 70.00

18 Bobby Labonte Interstate Batteries Victory Lap Clear Window Bank/420 40.00 70.00

18 Bobby Labonte Interstate Batteries Victory Lap GM Dealers/336 40.00 70.00

18 Bobby Labonte Interstate Batteries Victory Lap Mac Tools/288 40.00 70.00

18 Bobby Labonte Interstate Batteries 3M Employee Promo/2700 50.00 75.00

19 Dale Earnhardt Beldon Asphalt 1977 Malibu/24,716 35.00 60.00

19 Dale Earnhardt Beldon Asphalt 1977 Malibu Clear Window Bank/1884 35.00 60.00

19 Jeremy Mayfield Dodge/4584 20.00 50.00

19 Jeremy Mayfield Dodge Black Window Bank/696 20.00 50.00

19 Jeremy Mayfield Dodge Lion King/2004 20.00 50.00

19 Jeremy Mayfield Dodge Lion King Clear Window Bank/288 20.00 50.00

19 Jeremy Mayfield Mountain Dew/3612 20.00 50.00

19 Jeremy Mayfield Mountain Dew CW Bank/324 20.00 50.00

20 Mike Bliss Rockwell Automation/2796 20.00 50.00

20 Mike Bliss Rockwell Automation Bell Tower/3504 20.00 50.00

20 Mike Bliss Rockwell Automation Frankenstein/1780 20.00 50.00

20 Mike Bliss Rockwell Automation Frankenstein Clear Window Bank/240 20.00 50.00

20 Tony Stewart Home Depot/29,700 40.00 75.00

20 Tony Stewart Home Depot Black Window Bank/1068 40.00 70.00

20 Tony Stewart Home Depot BW Bank Mac Tools/288 40.00 70.00

20 Tony Stewart Home Depot GM Dealers/1008 40.00 75.00

20 Tony Stewart Home Depot Declaration of Independence/23,940 35.00 60.00

20 Tony Stewart Home Depot Declaration of Independence Clear Window Bank/1008 30.00 60.00

20 Tony Stewart Home Depot Victory Lap/10,488 40.00 70.00

20 Tony Stewart Home Depot Victory Lap Clear Window Bank/492 40.00 70.00

20 Tony Stewart Home Depot Victory Lap GM Dealers/588 40.00 70.00

20 Tony Stewart Home Depot Victory Lap Mac Tools/288 40.00 70.00

21 Buddy Baker Valvoline 1983 Thunderbird/2796 20.00 50.00

21 Kevin Harvick Payday/12,888 40.00 65.00

21 Kevin Harvick Payday Black Window Bank/720 35.00 60.00

21 Johnny Sauter Payday/624 20.00 50.00

22 Bobby Allison Victory Lap/4140 35.00 60.00

22 Bobby Allison Victory Lap Clear Window Bank/324 35.00 60.00

22 Bobby Allison Victory Lap GM Dealers/312 35.00 60.00

23 Scott Wimmer Stacker 2 Dracula/1822 20.00 40.00

23 Scott Wimmer Stacker 2 Dracula Clear Window Bank/300 20.00 40.00

24 Jeff Gordon Cookie Monster Foundation/21,552 40.00 70.00

24 Jeff Gordon DuPont Flames/34,332 40.00 75.00

24 Jeff Gordon DuPont Flames GM Dealers 40.00 75.00

24 Jeff Gordon DuPont Victory Lap/14,592 45.00 75.00

24 Jeff Gordon DuPont Victory Lap Clear Window Bank/672 45.00 75.00

24 Jeff Gordon DuPont Wright Bros./26,520 40.00 70.00

24 Jeff Gordon DuPont Wright Bros Clear Window Bank/1440 30.00 60.00

24 Jeff Gordon DuPont Yosemite Sam/19,416 30.00 60.00

24 Jeff Gordon DuPont Yosemite Sam Bank/1092 25.00 50.00

24 Jeff Gordon Pepsi/22,752 40.00 70.00

24 Jeff Gordon Pepsi Dark Window Bank/864 40.00 70.00

24 Jeff Gordon Pepsi GM Dealers/1008 40.00 70.00

24 Jeff Gordon Pepsi Mac Tools/288 40.00 70.00

24 Jeff Gordon Pepsi Billion $/22,692 40.00 70.00

24 Jeff Gordon Pepsi Billion $ Clear Window Bank/1272 30.00 60.00

24 Jeff Gordon Pepsi Billion $ GM Dealers/648 40.00 70.00

24 Tim Richmond Pepsi 1985 Firebird/2664 35.00 60.00

25 Joe Nemechek UAW Delphi/2640 20.00 50.00

25 Joe Nemechek UAW Delphi DW Bank/384 20.00 50.00

25 Joe Nemechek UAW Delphi Bugs Bunny/5004 20.00 50.00

25 Joe Nemechek UAW Delphi Bugs Bunny Clear Window Bank/444 20.00 50.00

25 Joe Nemechek UAW Delphi Uncle Kracker/3000 20.00 50.00

25 Joe Nemechek UAW Delphi Uncle Kracker Clear Window Bank/420 20.00 50.00

27 Kenny Irwin Raybestos 1998 Thunderbird/2316 30.00 60.00

29 Kevin Harvick Goodwrench/19,416 40.00 70.00

29 Kevin Harvick Goodwrench Black Window Bank/804 25.00 50.00

29 Kevin Harvick Goodwrench GM Dealers/2496 40.00 70.00

29 Kevin Harvick Goodwrench Raced/8532 75.00 150.00

29 Kevin Harvick Goodwrench Raced GM Dealers/1644 75.00 150.00

29 Kevin Harvick Goodwrench Red GM Dealers/12,000 35.00 60.00

29 Kevin Harvick Goodwrench Sugar Ray/8520 35.00 60.00

29 Kevin Harvick Goodwrench Sugar Ray Clear Window Bank/624 35.00 60.00

29 Kevin Harvick Snap-On/20,004 40.00 70.00

29 Kevin Harvick Snap-On GM Dealers/1440 40.00 70.00

30 Jeff Green AOL/3180 20.00 50.00

30 Steve Park GM Card/1908 35.00 60.00

30 Steve Park AOL Kraft 100th Anniversary/4008 20.00 50.00

30 Steve Park AOL Daffy/3576 20.00 50.00

30 Steve Park AOL Daffy Clear Window Bank/408 20.00 50.00

30 Steve Park AOL Daffy GM Dealers/60 35.00 60.00

30 Steve Park AOL Third Eye Blind/4596 35.00 60.00

30 Steve Park AOL Third Eye Blind Clear Window Bank/456 35.00 60.00

30 Steve Park AOL Third Eye Blind GM Dealers/504 35.00 60.00

31 Robby Gordon Cingular black/4836 25.00 50.00

31 Robby Gordon Cingular black Black Window Bank/648 20.00 50.00

31 Robby Gordon Cingular black GM Dealers/120 25.00 50.00

31 Robby Gordon Cingular orange/6000 25.00 50.00

31 Robby Gordon Cingular oranget Black Window Bank/408 20.00 50.00

31 Robby Gordon Cingular Charlie's Angels 2/3956 25.00 50.00

31 Robby Gordon Cingular FDNY/6420 25.00 50.00

31 Robby Gordon Cingular FDNY Clear Window Bank/532 20.00 50.00

31 Robby Gordon Cingular FDNY GM Dealers/240 25.00 50.00

31 Robby Gordon Cingular TRAPT/6000 25.00 50.00

31 Robby Gordon Cingular TRAPT Clear Window Bank 20.00 50.00

32 Ricky Craven Tide/3996 20.00 50.00

32 Ricky Craven Tide Clear Window Bank/480 20.00 50.00

33 Tony Stewart Monaco Diamond Rio SuperTruck/9424 35.00 60.00

33 Tony Stewart Monaco Diamond Rio SuperTruck GM Dealers/360 35.00 60.00

33 Tony Stewart Monaco Diamond Rio SuperTruck Mac Tools/288 35.00 60.00

35 Alan Kulwicki Quincy's Steakhouse 1986 Thunderbird/3780 35.00 60.00

38 Elliott Sadler Combos/4932 20.00 50.00

38 Elliott Sadler M&M's/8712 25.00 50.00

38 Elliott Sadler M&M's Mac Tools/288 25.00 40.00

38 Elliott Sadler M&M's Groovy/9312 20.00 50.00

38 Elliott Sadler M&M's Groovy Clear Window Bank/792 20.00 50.00

38 Elliott Sadler M&M's Halloween/6504 25.00 50.00

38 Elliott Sadler M&M's Halloween Clear Window Bank/480 25.00 50.00

38 Elliott Sadler M&M's Pedigree/3984 20.00 50.00

40 Sterling Marlin Coors Light/10,152 35.00 60.00

40 Sterling Marlin Coors Light Black Window Bank/792 30.00 60.00

40 Sterling Marlin Coors Light Clear/2808 30.00 60.00

40 Sterling Marlin Coors Light Scary Movie 3 Twins/3384 35.00 60.00

40 Sterling Marlin Coors Light Scary Movie 3 Twins Clear Window Bank/264 30.00 60.00

40 Sterling Marlin Coors Light Target 2001 Dodge/3504 35.00 60.00

40 Sterling Marlin Coors Original 2001/4428 40.00 70.00

41 Casey Mears Fuji Film/2040 20.00 50.00

41 Casey Mears Fuji Film Clear Window Bank/384 20.00 50.00

41 Casey Mears Target/4536 20.00 50.00

41 Casey Mears Target House/1932 20.00 50.00

41 Casey Mears Target House Clear Window Bank/228 20.00 50.00

42 Jamie McMurray Havoline/11,100 35.00 60.00

42 Jamie McMurray Havoline Black Window Bank/792 20.00 50.00

42 Jamie McMurray Havoline ROY/4404 25.00 50.00

42 Jamie McMurray Havoline ROY Clear Window Bank/360 25.00 50.00

42 Jamie McMurray Havoline Terminator 3/10,260 20.00 50.00

42 Jamie McMurray Havoline Terminator 3 Clear Window Bank/812 20.00 50.00

42 Jamie McMurray Havoline White/7608 30.00 60.00

42 Jamie McMurray Havoline White Clear Window Bank/552 30.00 60.00

42 Jamie McMurray Havoline White Mac Tools/288 30.00 60.00

43 John Andretti Cheerios/4092 20.00 50.00

43 John Andretti Cheerios Berry Burst/3624 20.00 50.00

43 John Andretti Cheerios Berry Burst Clear Window Bank/408 20.00 50.00

43 Jeff Green Pop Secret/1380 20.00 50.00

43 Jeff Green Pop Secret Clear Window Bank/240 20.00 50.00

43 Richard Petty Victory Lap/7440 40.00 70.00

43 Richard Petty Victory Lap Clear Window Bank/468 40.00 70.00

43 Richard Petty Yankees 100th Anniversary/5700 40.00 70.00

43 Richard Petty Yankees 100th Anniversary AUTO/6100 60.00 100.00

43 Richard Petty STP 1975 Dodge Charger/8268 150.00 250.00

43 Richard Petty STP 1975 Charger Clear Window Bank/619 125.00 200.00

44 Christian Fittipaldi Yankees 100th Anniversary/4836 20.00 50.00

44 Christian Fittipaldi Yankees 100th Anniversary Clear Window Bank/588 20.00 50.00

45 Kyle Petty Georgia Pacific/4608 20.00 50.00

45 Kyle Petty Hands to Victory/2868 20.00 50.00

45 Kyle Petty Hands to Victory Clear Window Bank/252 20.00 50.00

45 Kyle Petty Georgia Pacific Garfield/4296 20.00 50.00

48 Jimmie Johnson Lowe's/30,070 35.00 60.00

48 Jimmie Johnson Lowe's Black Window Bank/936 35.00 60.00

48 Jimmie Johnson Lowe's GM Dealers/1008 35.00 60.00

48 Jimmie Johnson Lowe's Power of Pride/13,728 30.00 60.00

48 Jimmie Johnson Lowe's Power of Pride Clear Window Bank/648 25.00 60.00

48 Jimmie Johnson Lowe's SpongeBob/15,672 35.00 60.00

48 Jimmie Johnson Lowe's SpongeBob GM Dealer/504 35.00 60.00

48 Jimmie Johnson Lowe's SpongeBob Clear Window Bank/948 35.00 60.00

54 Todd Bodine National Guard/3252 30.00 60.00

66 Rusty Wallace Motion 1985 Thunderbird/4356 40.00 70.00

72 Benny Parsons Victory Lap/3768 35.00 60.00

72 Benny Parsons Victory Lap Clear Window Bank/324 35.00 60.00

72 Benny Parsons Victory Lap GM Dealers/252 35.00 60.00

77 Dave Blaney Jasper/4008 20.00 50.00

81 Jason Keller Kraft 100 Years/3372 20.00 50.00

81 Martin Truex Jr. Chance 2/3504 35.00 60.00

81 Martin Truex Jr. Chance 2 GM Dealers/180 35.00 60.00

83 Kerry Earnhardt Hot Tamales black/7692 20.00 50.00

87 Kyle Busch ditech.com AU/2400 75.00 125.00

87 Kyle Busch ditech.com GM Dealers AU/120 75.00 125.00

87 Kyle Busch ditech.com Mummy/3372 25.00 60.00

87 Kyle Busch ditech.com Mummy Clear Window Bank/516 25.00 60.00

88 Dale Jarrett UPS Brown Logo/11,184 35.00 60.00

88 Dale Jarrett UPS Brown Logo Black Window Bank/780 35.00 60.00

88 Dale Jarrett UPS Brown Yellow Logo/11,832 40.00 70.00

88 Dale Jarrett UPS Brown&Yellow Logo Black Window Bank/790 35.00 60.00

88 Dale Jarrett UPS Brown Yellow Logo Clear/1752 35.00 60.00

88 Dale Jarrett UPS Store/5028 40.00 70.00

88 Dale Jarrett UPS Store Clear Window Bank/396 40.00 70.00

88 Dale Jarrett UPS Store Mac Tools/288 40.00 70.00

88 Dale Jarrett UPS Victory Lap/6252 40.00 70.00

88 Dale Jarrett UPS Victory Lap Clear Window Bank/372 40.00 70.00

88 Darrell Waltrip Gatorade '79 Monte Carlo/4164 35.00 60.00

91 Casey Atwood Mountain Dew Live Wire/2604 20.00 50.00

91 Casey Atwood Mountain Dew Live Wire Clear Window Bank/288 20.00 50.00

91 Casey Atwood Mountain Dew Live Wire Mac Tools/288 20.00 50.00

91 Hank Parker Jr. USG Promo 50.00 100.00

99 Michael Waltrip Aaron's Rent/3504 25.00 50.00

99 Michael Waltrip Aaron's Rent Cat in the Hat/4968 25.00 50.00

99 Michael Waltrip Aaron's Rent Three Stooges/7584 25.00 50.00

99 Michael Waltrip Aaron's Rent Terminator 3/8004 20.00 50.00

99 Michael Waltrip Aaron's Rent T3 Clear Window Bank/692 20.00 50.00

99 Michael Waltrip Aaron's Rent T3 GM Dealers/360 20.00 50.00

01 Jerry Nadeau Army/4404 25.00 50.00

03 Cat in the Hat Event Car/1428 20.00 40.00

03 Cat in the Hat Event Car Clear Window Bank/216 20.00 40.00

03 Hulk Event Car/4632 20.00 40.00

03 Terminator 3 Event Car Color Chrome/3432 20.00 40.00

06 Mark Martin Carolina Ford Dealers 1986 Thunderbird/2736 40.00 70.00

06 Mark Martin Carolina Ford Dealers '86 Thunderbird Clear Window Bank/600 40.00 70.00

2003 DEI Pit Practice/2508 40.00 70.00

2003 Hendrick Motor Sports Pit Practice/2424 35.00 60.00

NNO Chevy Rock & Roll Event Car/3504 20.00 40.00

NNO Looney Tunes Event Car/4631 20.00 40.00

NNO Looney Tunes Event Car GM Dealers/564 20.00 40.00

NNO Victory Lap Event Car Color Chrome/5064 50.00 80.00

NNO Victory Lap Event Color Chrome Clear Window Bank/312 50.00 80.00

2003 Action QVC For Race Fans Only 1:24

2 Rusty Wallace Miller Lite Color Chrome/1008 100.00 150.00

2 Rusty Wallace Miller Lite Gold/1000 100.00 150.00

2 Rusty Wallace Miller Lite Platinum/624 125.00 200.00

2 Rusty Wallace Miller Lite 600th Consecutive Start Col.Chrome/1008 100.00 150.00

2 Rusty Wallace Miller Time Live Goo Goo Dolls Color Chrome/1000 100.00 150.00

3 Dale Earnhardt Foundation Gold/3333 125.00 200.00

3 Dale Earnhardt Foundation Platinum/1008 125.00 200.00

3 Dale Earnhardt Goodwrench 1990 Lumina Gold/2508 100.00 150.00

3 Dale Earnhardt Goodwrench 1990 Lumina Pearlized/2508 60.00 100.00

3 Dale Earnhardt Goodwrench 1990 Lumina Platinum/1008 150.00 225.00

8 Dale Earnhardt Jr. Bud Gold/2508 100.00 150.00

8 Dale Earnhardt Jr. Bud Platinum/624 150.00 250.00

8 Dale Earnhardt Jr. Bud All-Star Color Chrome/2508 90.00 135.00

8 Dale Earnhardt Jr. Bud All-Star Gold/2508 100.00 150.00

8 Dale Earnhardt Jr. Bud All-Star Platinum/624 150.00 225.00

8 Dale Earnhardt Jr. Bud StainD Brushed Metal/2508 60.00 100.00

8 Dale Earnhardt Jr. Bud StainD Color Chrome/3504 75.00 125.00

8 Dale Earnhardt Jr. Bud StainD Gold/1000 75.00 125.00

8 Dale Earnhardt Jr. Bud StainD Platinum/624 100.00 150.00

8 Dale Earnhardt Jr. DMP Gold/2508 100.00 150.00

8 Dale Earnhardt Jr. DMP Platinum/624 150.00 225.00

8 Dale Earnhardt Jr. E Concert Color Chrome/3508 60.00 120.00

8 Dale Earnhardt Jr. E Concert Gold/2508 75.00 125.00

8 Dale Earnhardt Jr. E Concert Platinum/624 150.00 225.00

8 Dale Earnhardt Jr. Oreo Ritz Gold/2508 100.00 150.00

8 Dale Earnhardt Jr. Oreo Ritz Platinum/624 150.00 225.00

8 Tony Stewart 3 Doors Down Color Chrome/2508 50.00 100.00

8 Tony Stewart 3 Doors Down Gold 75.00 125.00

8 Tony Stewart 3 Doors Down Platinum/1272 50.00 100.00

20 Tony Stewart Home Depot Declaration of Independence Color Chrome/1008 50.00 100.00

20 Tony Stewart Home Depot Declaration of Independence Platinum/624 100.00 175.00

24 Jeff Gordon DuPont Flames Gold/1000 100.00 150.00

24 Jeff Gordon DuPont Flames Platinum/624 125.00 200.00

24 Jeff Gordon DuPont Flames Yosemite Sam Color Chrome/1008 100.00 150.00

24 Jeff Gordon Pepsi Billion $ Color Chrome/2508 100.00 150.00

24 Jeff Gordon Pepsi Billion $ Gold/1000 100.00 150.00

24 Jeff Gordon Pepsi Billion $ Platinum/674 100.00 175.00

24 Jeff Gordon DuPont Wright Brothers Gold/1008 90.00 135.00

24 Jeff Gordon Wright Brothers Platinum/624 125.00 200.00

43 Richard Petty Yankees 100th Anniversary olor Chrome/1008 75.00 125.00

48 Jimmie Johnson Lowe's Power of Pride Gold/504 75.00 125.00

48 Jimmie Johnson Lowe's Power of Pride Platinum/624 125.00 200.00

48 Jimmie Johnson Lowe's SpongeBob Color Chrome/1008 75.00 125.00

48 Jimmie Johnson Lowe's SpongeBob Gold/504 75.00 125.00

NNO Dale Earnhardt Legacy Gold/3333 90.00 135.00

NNO Dale Earnhardt Legacy Platinum/1008 100.00 175.00

2003 Action/RCCA 1:24

1 Donnie Allison Hawaiian Tropic 1979 Oldsmobile/580 50.00 100.00
1 Jeff Green Pennzoil Synthetic/400 15.00 40.00
1 Jamie McMurray Yellow Freight/360 15.00 40.00
1 Steve Park Pennzoil Clear Window Bank/504 15.00 40.00
2 Ron Hornaday AC Delco Bank/408 15.00 40.00
2 Jason Leffler Hulk SuperTruck/580 15.00 40.00
2 Mark Martin SAI Roofing 1987 Thunderbird/504 30.00 60.00
2 Rusty Wallace Miller Lite Clear Window Bank/1200 30.00 60.00
2 Rusty Wallace Miller Lite Victory Lap/600 40.00 75.00
2 Rusty Wallace Miller Lite 600 Starts/600 40.00 70.00
2 Rusty Wallace Miller Time Live Goo Goo Dolls/1204 30.00 60.00
3 Dale Earnhardt Earnhardt Foundation/3100 50.00 75.00
3 Dale Earnhardt Goodwrench 1990 Lumina/4008 50.00 80.00
3 Dale Earnhardt Goodwrench No Bull 2000 Monte Carlo/2508 50.00 80.00
3 Dale Earnhardt Goodwrench '01 Monte Carlo/3333 50.00 80.00
3 Dale Earnhardt Goodwrench Bass Pro Shops/4500 40.00 70.00
3 Dale Earnhardt Goodwrench Silver 1995 Monte Carlo/4800 50.00 80.00
3 Dale Earnhardt Victory Lap/2400 45.00 75.00
3 Dale Earnhardt Jr. Mom 'n' Pops Prime Sirloin/4800 50.00 75.00
3 Dale Earnhardt Jr. Sundrop 1994 Lumina/4800 50.00 75.00
5 Terry Labonte Kellogg's Bank/444 15.00 40.00
5 Terry Labonte Got Milk Clear Window Bank/496 15.00 40.00
5 Terry Labonte Kellogg's Victory Lap/408 40.00 75.00
5 Brian Vickers GMAC Raced Win AU/300 60.00 120.00
7 Greg Biffle Kleenex Wolfman/300 15.00 40.00
7 Alan Kulwicki Hooters Bank 1993 Thunderbird/504 40.00 70.00
7 Alan Kulwicki Victory Lap/504 40.00 70.00
7 Jimmy Spencer Sirius/444 15.00 40.00
7 Jimmy Spencer Sirius Three Stooges/424 15.00 40.00
8 Dale Earnhardt Jr. Bud Bank/3300 40.00 70.00
8 Dale Earnhardt Jr. Bud No Bull 2000 Monte Carlo/2508 40.00 70.00
8 Dale Earnhardt Jr. Bud Talladega Raced/1300 40.00 70.00
8 Dale Earnhardt Jr. Bud Talladega October 2002 Win, Raced Clear Window Bank/1008 40.00 70.00
8 Dale Earnhardt Jr. Bud MLB All-Star Game/3300 40.00 70.00
8 Dale Earnhardt Jr. Bud StainD/3100 20.00 50.00
8 Dale Earnhardt Jr. Dirty Mo Posse Bank/3204 15.00 40.00
8 Dale Earnhardt Jr. Dirty Mo Posse Split Clear/1008 15.00 40.00
8 Dale Earnhardt Jr. E Concert Bank/3600 20.00 50.00
8 Dale Earnhardt Jr. E Concert Raced/600 40.00 70.00
8 Dale Earnhardt Jr. Oreo Ritz Clear Window Bank/3600 15.00 40.00
8 Dale Earnhardt Jr. Oreo Ritz Raced/520 30.00 60.00
8 Dale Earnhardt Jr. Oreo Ritz plit Clear/1008 15.00 40.00
8 Steve Park Cheese Nips Clear Window Bank/504 15.00 40.00
8 Steve Park Maxwell House Bank/504 15.00 40.00
8 Hank Parker Jr. Dick's Sporting Goods/520 15.00 40.00
8 Tony Stewart 3 Doors Down/1200 30.00 60.00
9 Bill Elliott Coors 1984 Thunderbird/804 45.00 75.00
9 Bill Elliott Coors Winston Million '85 t-bird/504 45.00 75.00
9 Bill Elliott Coors 1987 Thunderbird Bank/804 50.00 80.00
9 Bill Elliott Coors 1988 Thunderbird/804 45.00 75.00
9 Bill Elliott Dodge Clear Window Bank/444 30.00 60.00
9 Bill Elliott Dodge Lion King/444 20.00 50.00
9 Bill Elliott Dodge Split Clear/408 20.00 50.00
9 Bill Elliott Dodge Victory Lap/408 40.00 75.00
9 Bill Elliott Dodge 10th Brickyard/448 20.00 50.00
10 Johnny Benson Valvoline/300 15.00 40.00
11 Dale Jarrett True Value 2002 IROC Blue/360 35.00 60.00
11 Darrell Waltrip Victory Lap/804 35.00 60.00
11 Cale Yarborough Victory Lap/504 40.00 70.00
12 Kerry Earnhardt Hot Tamales red/504 15.00 40.00
15 Michael Waltrip NAPA Bank/504 15.00 40.00
15 Michael Waltrip NAPA Hootie & the Blowfish/496 15.00 40.00
15 Michael Waltrip NAPA Nilla Wafers Clear Window Bank/504 15.00 40.00
15 Michael Waltrip NAPA Stars&Stripes/504 15.00 40.00
18 Bobby Labonte Interstate Batteries Clear Window Bank/504 20.00 50.00
18 Bobby Labonte Interstate Batt. Advair Green/360 15.00 40.00
18 Bobby Labonte Interstate Batteries Advair Purple/444 15.00 40.00
18 Bobby Labonte Interstate Batteries Hulk Clear Window Bank/600 40.00 65.00
18 Bobby Labonte Interstate Batteries Victory Lap/600 45.00 75.00
19 Dale Earnhardt Belden Asphalt 1976 Malibu/3600 30.00 60.00
19 Jeremy Mayfield Dodge Bank/504 15.00 40.00
19 Jeremy Mayfield Dodge Lion King/400 15.00 40.00
19 Jeremy Mayfield Dodge Mountain Dew/300 20.00 50.00
20 Mike Bliss Rockwell Automation Bell Tower/144 15.00 40.00
20 Mike Bliss Rockwell Automation Frankenstein/300 15.00 40.00
20 Tony Stewart Home Depot Clear Window Bank/1500 30.00 60.00
20 Tony Stewart Home Depot Pocono Raced/504 30.00 60.00
20 Tony Stewart Home Depot Declaration of Independence/1600 30.00 60.00
20 Tony Stewart Home Depot Victory Lap/804 35.00 60.00
21 Kevin Harvick Payday Clear Window Bank/1008 20.00 50.00
21 Johnny Sauter Payday Clear Window Bank/300 15.00 40.00
22 Bobby Allison Victory Lap/504 40.00 65.00
23 Scott Wimmer Stacker 2 Dracula/300 15.00 40.00
24 Jeff Gordon Cookie Monster/1800 30.00 60.00
24 Jeff Gordon DuPont Flames Clear Window Bank/2124 40.00 70.00
24 Jeff Gordon DuPont Flames Martinsville Raced/604 45.00 75.00
24 Jeff Gordon DuPont Victory Lap/1500 45.00 75.00
24 Jeff Gordon DuPont Wright Brothers/2404 30.00 60.00
24 Jeff Gordon DuPont Yosemite Sam/1900 30.00 60.00
24 Jeff Gordon Pepsi Bank/1524 30.00 60.00
24 Jeff Gordon Pepsi Billion $/2224 30.00 60.00
25 Joe Nemechek UAW Delphi Clear Window Bank/408 15.00 40.00
25 Joe Nemechek UAW Delphi Uncle Kracker/300 15.00 40.00
29 Kevin Harvick Goodwrench Bank/1300 20.00 50.00
29 Kevin Harvick Goodwrench Raced/444 100.00 150.00
29 Kevin Harvick Goodwrench Sugar Ray/600 15.00 40.00
29 Kevin Harvick Snap-On Clear Window Bank/2004 20.00 50.00
30 Jeff Green AOL Clear Window Bank/600 15.00 40.00
30 Jeff Green AOL Kraft 100 Years/460 15.00 40.00
30 Steve Park AOL Third Eye Blind/300 15.00 40.00
31 Robby Gordon Cingular Bank/444 15.00 40.00
31 Robby Gordon Cingular Orange Reverse Paint Clear Window Bank/444 15.00 40.00
31 Robby Gordon Cingular Charlie's Angels 2/400 15.00 40.00
31 Robby Gordon Cingular FDNY Special Olympics/400 15.00 40.00
31 Robby Gordon Cingular TRAPT/300 15.00 40.00
32 Ricky Craven Tide/504 15.00 40.00
35 Alan Kulwicki Quincy's Steakhouse 1986 Thunderbird/504 20.00 50.00
38 Elliott Sadler Combos/604 15.00 40.00
38 Elliott Sadler M&M's Clear Window Bank/600 20.00 50.00
38 Elliott Sadler M&M's Groovy/504 20.00 50.00
38 Elliott Sadler Pedigree/300 15.00 40.00
40 Sterling Marlin Coors Light Bank/804 35.00 60.00
40 Sterling Marlin Coors Light Split Clear/2808 20.00 50.00
40 Sterling Marlin Coors Light Scary Movie 3/408 20.00 50.00
40 Sterling Marlin Coors Original 2001/408 30.00 60.00
40 Sterling Marlin Target '01 Dodge/400 15.00 40.00
41 Casey Mears Fuji/300 15.00 40.00
41 Casey Mears Target Clear Window Bank/400 15.00 40.00
42 Jamie McMurray Havoline Clear Window Bank/804 25.00 50.00
42 Jamie McMurray Havoline '03 Rookie of the Year/600 25.00 50.00
42 Jamie McMurray Havoline Terminator 3/700 15.00 40.00
42 Jamie McMurray Havoline White/600 30.00 60.00
43 John Andretti Cheerios Clear Window Bank/600 15.00 40.00
43 John Andretti Cheerios Berry Burst/580 15.00 40.00
43 Jeff Green Pop Secret/360 15.00 40.00
43 Richard Petty STP 1975 Charger/1000 150.00 250.00
43 Richard Petty Victory Lap/804 40.00 70.00
43 Richard Petty Yankees 100th Anniversary/500 25.00 50.00
43 Richard Petty Yankees 100th Anniversary AUTO/700 75.00 125.00
44 Christian Fittipaldi 100th Anniversary Yankees/600 15.00 40.00
45 Kyle Petty Georgia Pacific/400 15.00 40.00
45 Kyle Petty Georgia Pacific Hands to Victory/288 15.00 40.00
45 Kyle Petty Georgia Pacific Garfield/400 15.00 40.00
48 Jimmie Johnson Lowe's Bank/1500 30.00 60.00
48 Jimmie Johnson Lowe's Power of Pride/1444 30.00 60.00
48 Jimmie Johnson Lowe's SpongeBob/1300 30.00 60.00
54 Todd Bodine National Guard/300 30.00 60.00
72 Benny Parsons Victory Lap/504 30.00 60.00
77 Dave Blaney Jasper Clear Window Bank/400 15.00 40.00
81 Jason Keller Kraft 100 Years/460 15.00 40.00
81 Martin Truex Jr. Chance 2/400 15.00 40.00
83 Kerry Earnhardt Hot Tamales black/460 15.00 40.00
87 Kyle Busch Ditech.com AU/240 100.00 150.00
87 Kyle Busch Ditech.com Mummy/300 25.00 50.00
88 Dale Jarrett UPS Brown Logo Clear Window Bank/600 25.00 50.00
88 Dale Jarrett UPS Brown Yellow Logo Split Clear/504 25.00 50.00
88 Dale Jarrett UPS Store/504 30.00 60.00
88 Dale Jarrett UPS Victory Lap/408 40.00 70.00
88 Darrell Waltrip Gatorade Bank 1979 Monte Carlo/600 20.00 50.00
91 Casey Atwood Mountain Dew Live Wire/300 15.00 40.00
99 Michael Waltrip Aaron's Rent/444 15.00 40.00
99 Michael Waltrip Aaron's Rent Cat in the Hat/444 15.00 40.00
99 Michael Waltrip Aaron's Rent Terminator 3/504 15.00 40.00
01 Jerry Nadeau Army/600 20.00 50.00
03 Cat in the Hat Event Car/300 15.00 40.00
03 Hulk Event Car/408 15.00 40.00
06 Mark Martin Carolina Ford Dealers Bank '86 Thunderbird/600 35.00 60.00
NNO Victory Lap Color Chrome Event Car/360 50.00 75.00

2003 Action/RCCA Elite 1:24

1 Jamie McMurray Yellow Freight/360 50.00 100.00
1 Steve Park Pennzoil/504 60.00 100.00
1 Steve Park Pennzoil Synthetic/400 60.00 100.00
2 Ron Hornaday AC Delco/408 50.00 100.00
2 Mark Martin SAI Roofing 1987 Thunderbird/504 60.00 100.00
2 Rusty Wallace Miller Lite/2004 60.00 100.00
2 Rusty Wallace Miller Lite Color Chrome/408 75.00 125.00
2 Rusty Wallace Miller Lite Victory Lap/600 75.00 125.00
2 Rusty Wallace Miller Lite 600 Starts/900 75.00 125.00
2 Rusty Wallace Miller Time Live Goo Goo Dolls/804 60.00 100.00
3 Dale Earnhardt Earnhardt Foundation/4300 75.00 150.00
3 Dale Earnhardt Goodwrench No Bull 2000 Monte Carlo/4500 90.00 150.00
3 Dale Earnhardt Victory Lap/3000 90.00 135.00
5 Terry Labonte Got Milk/496 60.00 120.00
5 Terry Labonte Kellogg's Victory Lap/408 60.00 100.00
7 Greg Biffle Kleenex Wolfman/300 50.00 100.00
7 Kyle Petty 7-11 '85 t-bird/408 75.00 125.00
8 Dale Earnhardt Jr. Bud/5700 100.00 175.00
8 Dale Earnhardt Jr. Bud Color Chrome/2004 90.00 150.00
8 Dale Earnhardt Jr. Bud/4000 90.00 135.00
8 Dale Earnhardt Jr. Bud Talladega October '02 Win Raced/1500 125.00 200.00
8 Dale Earnhardt Jr. Bud Talladega 2003 Win Raced/2200 125.00 200.00
8 Dale Earnhardt Jr. Bud Test/4800 80.00 135.00
8 Dale Earnhardt Jr. Bud All-Star Game/5544 80.00 135.00
8 Dale Earnhardt Jr. Bud StainD/5500 90.00 150.00
8 Dale Earnhardt Jr. Busch Test/1600 90.00 135.00
8 Dale Earnhardt Jr. Dirty Mo Posse/5004 50.00 100.00
8 Dale Earnhardt Jr. Earnhardt Tribute Concert/6300 75.00 125.00
8 Dale Earnhardt Jr. E Concert Raced/1008 90.00 150.00
8 Dale Earnhardt Jr. Oreo Ritz/6000 50.00 100.00
8 Dale Earnhardt Jr. Oreo Ritz Raced/1000 50.00 100.00
8 Steve Park Cheese Nips/504 60.00 100.00
8 Steve Park Maxwell House/504 60.00 100.00
8 Hank Parker Jr. Dick's Sporting Goods/520 40.00 80.00
8 Hank Parker Jr. Remmington Bass Pro Shops/520 40.00 80.00
8 Tony Stewart 3 Doors Down/1800 75.00 125.00
9 Bill Elliott Coors Winston Million '85 t-bird/600 70.00 120.00
9 Bill Elliott Dodge/600 60.00 100.00
9 Bill Elliott Dodge Color Chrome/408 75.00 125.00
9 Bill Elliott Dodge Lion King/600 60.00 100.00
9 Bill Elliott Dodge Victory Lap/408 75.00 125.00
9 Bill Elliott Dodge 10th Brickyard/604 60.00 100.00
12 Kerry Earnhardt Hot Tamales red/504 60.00 100.00
15 Michael Waltrip NAPA/604 75.00 125.00
15 Michael Waltrip NAPA Raced/604 60.00 100.00
15 Michael Waltrip NAPA Hootie & The Blowfish/496 40.00 80.00
15 Michael Waltrip NAPA Nilla Wafers/804 40.00 80.00
15 Michael Waltrip NAPA Stars & Stripes/804 60.00 100.00
17 Darrell Waltrip Boogity Boogity AU/528 100.00 200.00
18 Bobby Labonte Interstate Batteries/720 75.00 125.00
18 Bobby Labonte Interstate Batteries Advair Purple/444 60.00 100.00
18 Bobby Labonte Interstate Batteries Hulk/900 60.00 100.00
18 Bobby Labonte Interstate Batteries Victory Lap/600 60.00 100.00
19 Dale Earnhardt Beldon Asphalt 1976 Malibu/3600 60.00 120.00
19 Jeremy Mayfield Dodge Mountain Dew/400 50.00 100.00
20 Mike Bliss Rockwell Automation Frankenstein/300 40.00 80.00
20 Tony Stewart Home Depot/1500 75.00 125.00
20 Tony Stewart Home Depot Color Chrome/1008 60.00 120.00
20 Tony Stewart Home Depot Pocono Raced/504 90.00 135.00
20 Tony Stewart Home Depot Test/1300 80.00 125.00
20 Tony Stewart Home Depot Declaration of Independence/2800 100.00 135.00
20 Tony Stewart Home Depot Victory Lap/1200 90.00 135.00
21 Kevin Harvick Payday/1500 50.00 100.00
23 Scott Wimmer Stacker 2 Dracula/300 40.00 80.00
24 Jeff Gordon Cookie Monster/3000 60.00 100.00
24 Jeff Gordon DuPont Flames/3624 100.00 150.00
24 Jeff Gordon DuPont Flames Color Chrome/804 125.00 250.00
24 Jeff Gordon DuPont Flames Martinsville Raced/1000 90.00 135.00
24 Jeff Gordon DuPont Victory Lap/2004 100.00 150.00
24 Jeff Gordon DuPont Wright Brothers/4024 75.00 125.00
24 Jeff Gordon DuPont Yosemite Sam/3000 75.00 125.00
24 Jeff Gordon Pepsi/2724 90.00 135.00
24 Jeff Gordon Pepsi Billion $/3724 60.00 100.00
27 Kenny Irwin Raybestos 1998 Thunderbird/600 60.00 100.00
29 Kevin Harvick Goodwrench/2500 75.00 125.00
29 Kevin Harvick Goodwrench Raced/444 175.00 300.00
29 Kevin Harvick Goodwrench Sugar Ray/1008 60.00 100.00
29 Kevin Harvick Snap-On/2004 60.00 100.00
30 Jeff Green AOL Kraft 100 Years/600 50.00 100.00
30 Steve Park AOL Kraft 100 Years/600 50.00 100.00
31 Robby Gordon Cingular black/444 50.00 100.00
31 Robby Gordon Cingular orange/444 50.00 100.00
31 Robby Gordon Cingular Charlie's Angels 2/400 50.00 100.00
31 Robby Gordon Cingular FDNY Special Olympics/400 50.00 100.00
35 Alan Kulwicki Quincy's Steakhouse 1986 Thunderbird/504 50.00 100.00
38 Elliott Sadler Combos/400 50.00 100.00
38 Elliott Sadler M&M's/900 50.00 100.00
38 Elliott Sadler M&M's Groovy/720 50.00 100.00
38 Elliott Sadler M&M's Halloween/504 50.00 100.00
40 Sterling Marlin Coors Light/1200 60.00 120.00
40 Sterling Marlin Coors Light Test/1008 50.00 100.00
40 Sterling Marlin Coors Light Scary Movie 3/408 50.00 100.00
40 Sterling Marlin Coors Original 2001/400 50.00 100.00
40 Sterling Marlin Target '01 Dodge/400 50.00 100.00
42 Jamie McMurray Havoline/804 60.00 100.00
42 Jamie McMurray Havoline '03 Rookie of the Year/600 50.00 100.00
42 Jamie McMurray Havoline Terminator 3/700 50.00 100.00
42 Jamie McMurray Havoline White/804 60.00 100.00
43 Richard Petty STP 1975 Charger/1300 175.00 300.00
43 Richard Petty Victory Lap/1200 60.00 100.00
43 Richard Petty Yankees 100th Anniversary/520 60.00 120.00
43 Richard Petty Yankees 100th Anniversary AUTO/700 100.00 150.00
45 Kyle Petty Georgia Pacific Hands to Victory/288 50.00 100.00
45 Kyle Petty Georgia Pacific Garfield/300 40.00 80.00
48 Jimmie Johnson Lowe's/2400 50.00 100.00
48 Jimmie Johnson Lowe's Color Chrome/804 75.00 125.00
48 Jimmie Johnson Lowe's/1600 75.00 125.00
48 Jimmie Johnson Lowe's Test/1900 50.00 100.00
48 Jimmie Johnson Lowe's Power of Pride/2200 50.00 100.00
48 Jimmie Johnson Lowe's SpongeBob/1648 50.00 100.00
54 Todd Bodine National Guard/300 50.00 100.00
87 Kyle Busch Ditech.com AU/240 125.00 200.00
87 Kyle Busch Ditech.com Mummy/300 60.00 120.00
88 Dale Jarrett UPS/1008 50.00 100.00
88 Dale Jarrett UPS Color Chrome/408 60.00 120.00
88 Dale Jarrett UPS Store/504 50.00 100.00
88 Dale Jarrett UPS Victory Lap/408 60.00 120.00
91 Casey Atwood Mountain Dew Live Wire/300 50.00 100.00
99 Michael Waltrip Aaron's Rent/444 50.00 100.00
99 Michael Waltrip Aaron's Rent Cat in the Hat/444 50.00 100.00
99 Michael Waltrip Aaron's Rent Three Stooges/460 50.00 100.00
99 Michael Waltrip Aaron's Rent T3/804 50.00 100.00
2003 DEI Pit Practice/1008 75.00 125.00
03 Hulk Event Car/600 50.00 100.00
06 Mark Martin Carolina Ford Dealers 1986 Thunderbird/600 60.00 120.00

Item	Low	High
NNO HMS Pit Practice Car/496	75.00	125.00
NNO Looney Tunes Event Car/408	60.00	120.00
NNO Victory Lap Event Car/360		
NNO Victory Lap Color Chrome Event Car/360	100.00	175.00

2004 Action Performance 1:24

Item	Low	High
2 Rusty Wallace Miller Lite Last Call	30.00	60.00
9 Kasey Kahne Dodge refresh	25.00	50.00
20 Tony Stewart Home Depot Shrek 2	20.00	40.00
24 Jeff Gordon DuPont Flames	20.00	40.00

2004 Action Racing Collectables 1:24

Item	Low	High
1 John Andretti Coke C2/1584	35.00	60.00
1 John Andretti Coke C2 Clear Window Bank/240	35.00	60.00
1 John Andretti Post Maxwell House/3792	35.00	60.00
1 John Andretti Legacy Snap-On/3468	40.00	60.00
2 Ron Hornaday AC Delco/1260	35.00	60.00
2 Ron Hornaday AC Delco Clear Window bank/204	35.00	60.00
2 Ron Hornaday AC Delco KISS/1716	40.00	60.00
2 Ron Hornaday AC Delco KISS Clear Window Bank/228	40.00	60.00
2 Ron Hornaday AC Delco RCR35th Anniversary/1332	35.00	60.00
2 Ron Hornaday AC Delco RCR35th Anniversary Clear Window Bank/264	35.00	60.00
2 Rusty Wallace Kodak/4836	40.00	70.00
2 Rusty Wallace Kodak Clear Window Bank/324	40.00	70.00
2 Rusty Wallace Miller Lite/12,420	40.00	70.00
2 Rusty Wallace Miller Lite Clear Window Bank/384	40.00	70.00
2 Rusty Wallace Miller Lite Mac Tools/288	40.00	70.00
2 Rusty Wallace Miller Lite Martinsville Raced w tire/4188	45.00	75.00
2 Rusty Wallace Miller Lite Nextel Incentive/2004	50.00	100.00
2 Rusty Wallace Miller Lite Father's Day/4188	40.00	70.00
2 Rusty Wallace Miller Lite Father's Day Clear Window Bank/384	40.00	70.00
2 Rusty Wallace Miller Lite Miller Can/2560	40.00	70.00
2 Rusty Wallace Miller Lite Last Call	75.00	150.00
2 Rusty Wallace Miller Lite Last Call Clear Window Bank/228	60.00	100.00
2 Rusty Wallace Miller Lite Last Call Color Chrome/2004	75.00	150.00
2 Rusty Wallace Miller Lite President of Beers/5412	40.00	70.00
2 Rusty Wallace Miller Lite President of Beers Clear Window Bank/384	40.00	70.00
2 Rusty Wallace Miller Lite Puddle of Mudd/4884	40.00	70.00
2 Rusty Wallace Miller Lite Puddle of Mudd Clear Window Bank/336	40.00	70.00
2 Rusty Wallace Miller Lite Penske 50th/5628	40.00	70.00
2 Rusty Wallace Miller Lite Penske 50th Clear Window Bank/348	40.00	70.00
5 Kyle Busch Lowe's/2328	45.00	75.00
5 Kyle Busch Lowe's Clear Window Bank/264	40.00	70.00
5 Kyle Busch Lowe's SpongeBob/3396	40.00	70.00
5 Kyle Busch Lowe's SpongeBob Clear Window Bank	40.00	70.00
5 Terry Labonte Delphi/2508	40.00	70.00
5 Terry Labonte Delphi Clear Window Bank/264	40.00	70.00
5 Terry Labonte Kellogg's/3816	40.00	70.00
5 Terry Labonte Kellogg's Clear Window Bank/288	40.00	70.00
5 Terry Labonte Kellogg's GM Dealers/276	40.00	70.00
5 Terry Labonte Kellogg's Mac Tools/288	40.00	70.00
5 Terry Labonte Kellogg's Father's Day/2640	40.00	70.00
5 Terry Labonte Kellogg's Father's Day Clear Window Bank	40.00	70.00
5 Terry Labonte Kellogg's HMS 20th Anniversary/2412	40.00	70.00
5 Terry Labonte Kellogg's HMS 20th Anniversary Clear Window Bank/300	40.00	70.00
5 Terry Labonte Kellogg's HMS 20th GM Dealers/168	40.00	70.00
5 Terry Labonte Kellogg's Incredibles/1236	40.00	70.00
5 Terry Labonte Kellogg's Incredibles Clear Window Bank/228	40.00	70.00
5 Terry Labonte Kellogg's Olympics/3048	40.00	70.00
5 Terry Labonte Kellogg's Olympics Clear Window Bank/336	40.00	70.00
6 Matt Crafton Goodwrench SuperTruck/1428	40.00	70.00
6 Matt Crafton Goodwrench KISS/1752	45.00	75.00
6 Matt Crafton Goodwrench KISS QVC/120		
6 Bill Elliott Lucas Oil Elvis/4248	45.00	75.00
6 Bill Elliott Lucas Oil Elvis Clear Window Bank/384	45.00	75.00
8 Dale Earnhardt Jr. Bud/72,072	40.00	70.00
8 Dale Earnhardt Jr. Bud Clear Window Bank/1260	40.00	70.00
8 Dale Earnhardt Jr. Bud GM Dealers/7548	40.00	70.00
8 Dale Earnhardt Jr. Bud Mac Tools/288	40.00	70.00
8 Dale Earnhardt Jr. Bud Bristol Raced/8808	50.00	80.00
8 Dale Earnhardt Jr. Bud Talladega Raced/7368	50.00	80.00
8 Dale Earnhardt Jr. Bud Talladega Raced QVC/1008	50.00	80.00
8 Dale Earnhardt Jr. Bud Born On Feb.7/16,392	75.00	125.00
8 Dale Earnhardt Jr. Bud Born On Feb.7 Clear Window Bank/888	75.00	125.00
8 Dale Earnhardt Jr. Bud Born On Feb.7 GM Dealers/1500	75.00	125.00
8 Dale Earnhardt Jr. Bud Born On Feb.12 Raced/28,884	60.00	100.00
8 Dale Earnhardt Jr. Bud Born On Feb.12 Raced GM Dealers/3504	60.00	100.00
8 Dale Earnhardt Jr. Bud Born On Feb.12 Raced QVC/2004	60.00	100.00
8 Dale Earnhardt Jr. Bud Born On Feb.15/5004	175.00	300.00
8 Dale Earnhardt Jr. Bud Born On Feb.15 Raced GM Dealers/4008	60.00	100.00
8 Dale Earnhardt Jr. Bud Born On Feb.15 Raced/68,808	60.00	100.00
8 Dale Earnhardt Jr. Bud Born On Feb.15 Raced w tire CW Bank/5004	60.00	100.00
8 Dale Earnhardt Jr. Bud Dave Matthews Band/20,700	40.00	70.00
8 Dale Earnhardt Jr. Bud Dave Matthews Band Clear Window Bank/600	40.00	70.00
8 Dale Earnhardt Jr. Bud Father's Day/41,880	60.00	100.00
8 Dale Earnhardt Jr. Bud Father's Day Clear Window Bank/1008	60.00	100.00
8 Dale Earnhardt Jr. Bud Father's Day GM Dealers/4008	60.00	100.00
8 Dale Earnhardt Jr. Bud World Series/21,324	40.00	70.00
8 Dale Earnhardt Jr. Bud World Series Clear Window Bank/900	40.00	70.00
8 Dale Earnhardt Jr. Bud World Series Liquid Metal/4008	75.00	125.00
8 Dale Earnhardt Jr. Oreo/34,828	40.00	70.00
8 Dale Earnhardt Jr. Oreo Clear Window Bank/1008	40.00	70.00
8 Dale Earnhardt Jr. Oreo GM Dealers/2496	40.00	70.00
8 Dale Earnhardt Jr. Oreo Mac Tools/288	40.00	65.00
8 Martin Truex Jr. Bass Pro Shops/6384	50.00	75.00
8 Martin Truex Jr. Bass Pro Shops Clear Window Bank/288	50.00	75.00
8 Martin Truex Jr. Bass Pro Shops GM Dealers/360	50.00	75.00
8 Martin Truex Jr. Bass Pro Shops Talladega Raced/2904	50.00	75.00
8 Martin Truex Jr. Bass Pro Shops Talladega Raced GM Dealers/144	50.00	75.00
8 Martin Truex Jr. Bass Pro Shops '04 Champion Color Chrome/5004	60.00	100.00
8 Martin Truex Jr. Chance 2 Ralph Earnhardt/5016	40.00	70.00
8 Martin Truex Jr. Chance 2 Ralph Earnhardt GM Dealers/396	40.00	70.00
8 Martin Truex Jr. Chance 2 Richie Evans/2940	40.00	70.00
8 Martin Truex Jr. Chance 2 Richie Evans GM Dealers/144	40.00	70.00
8 Martin Truex Jr. Chance 2 Tear Away/3216	40.00	70.00
8 Martin Truex Jr. Chance 2 Tear Away GM Dealers/144	40.00	70.00
8 Martin Truex Jr. KFC Dover Raced/1896	50.00	75.00
8 Martin Truex Jr. KFC Dover Raced GM Dealers/348	50.00	75.00
8 Martin Truex Jr. KFC Dover Raced QVC/288	50.00	75.00
8 Martin Truex Jr. Long John Silvers/3948	40.00	70.00
8 Martin Truex Jr. Long John Silvers CW Bank/264	40.00	70.00
8 Martin Truex Jr. Taco Bell Bristol Raced/6576	40.00	70.00
8 Martin Truex Jr. Taco Bell Bristol Raced GM Dealers/240	40.00	70.00
8 Martin Truex Jr. Wrangler/6000	45.00	75.00
8 Martin Truex Jr. Wrangler Clear Window Bank/396	45.00	75.00
8 Martin Truex Jr. Wrangler GM Dealers/456	45.00	75.00
8 Martin Truex Jr. Wrangler Retro Darlington Raced/5616	45.00	75.00
8 Martin Truex Jr. Wrangler Retro Darlington Raced QVC/288	45.00	75.00
9 Bill Elliott Milestones/1872	40.00	70.00
9 Bill Elliott Milestones Clear Window Bank/216	40.00	70.00
9 Kasey Kahne Dodge/3936	125.00	200.00
9 Kasey Kahne Dodge Clear Window Bank/264	100.00	175.00
9 Kasey Kahne Dodge refresh/12,564	50.00	80.00
9 Kasey Kahne Dodge refresh liquid chrome ROY AU/4596	100.00	150.00
9 Kasey Kahne Dodge refresh liquid chrome ROY AU QVC/804	100.00	150.00
9 Kasey Kahne Dodge refresh QVC/360	50.00	80.00
9 Kasey Kahne Dodge Mad Magazine/9024	50.00	80.00
9 Kasey Kahne Dodge Mad Magazine Clear Window Bank/456	50.00	80.00
9 Kasey Kahne Dodge Mopar/8592	50.00	80.00
9 Kasey Kahne Dodge Mopar Alcone/1008	50.00	80.00
9 Kasey Kahne Dodge Mopar Color Chrome/1248	60.00	120.00
9 Kasey Kahne Dodge Mopar QVC/504	50.00	80.00
9 Kasey Kahne Dodge Pit Cap/7752	50.00	80.00
9 Kasey Kahne Dodge Pit Cap Clear Window Bank/384	50.00	80.00
9 Kasey Kahne Dodge Pit Cap QVC/504	50.00	80.00
9 Kasey Kahne Dodge Popeye 75th Anniversary/3780	60.00	100.00
9 Kasey Kahne Dodge Popeye 75th Anniversary Clear Window Bank/324	50.00	80.00
9 Kasey Kahne Mountain Dew/6216	75.00	125.00
9 Kasey Kahne Mountain Dew Clear Window Bank/480	75.00	125.00
10 Scott Riggs Valvoline/2532	35.00	60.00
10 Scott Riggs Valvoline Clear Window Bank/288	35.00	60.00
10 Scott Riggs Valvoline Wizard of Oz/1668	35.00	60.00
10 Scott Riggs Valvoline Wizard of Oz Clear Window Bank/252	35.00	60.00
12 Ryan Newman Crown Royal IROC/5004	40.00	70.00
15 Michael Waltrip NAPA/13,596	40.00	70.00
15 Michael Waltrip NAPA Clear Window Bank/396	40.00	70.00
15 Michael Waltrip NAPA GM Dealers/2004	40.00	70.00
15 Michael Waltrip NAPA Mac Tools/288	40.00	70.00
15 Michael Waltrip NAPA Nextel Incentive/2304	45.00	70.00
15 Michael Waltrip NAPA Father's Day/5184	40.00	70.00
15 Michael Waltrip NAPA Father's Day Clear Window Bank/324	40.00	70.00
15 Michael Waltrip NAPA Stars&Stripes/4488	40.00	70.00
15 Michael Waltrip NAPA Stars&Stripes Clear Window Bank/252	40.00	70.00
15 Michael Waltrip NAPA Stars&Stripes GM Dealers/288	40.00	70.00
16 Jack Sprague SilveradoTrucks SuperTruck/2300	35.00	60.00
17 Matt Kenseth Crown Royal IROC/4500	40.00	70.00
17 Matt Kenseth Crown Royal IROC '04 Champion pearl/1368	40.00	70.00
17 Darrell Waltrip King of Bristol AU/2508	75.00	125.00
18 Bobby Labonte Interstate Batteries/12,612	40.00	60.00
18 Bobby Labonte Interstate Batteries Clear Window Bank/372	40.00	60.00
18 Bobby Labonte Interstate Batteries GM Dealers/1896	40.00	60.00
18 Bobby Labonte Interstate Batteries Mac Tools/288	40.00	60.00
18 Bobby Labonte Interstate Batteries Nextel Incentive/2304	50.00	100.00
18 Bobby Labonte Interstate Batteries D-Day/6060	40.00	70.00
18 Bobby Labonte Interstate Batteries D-Day CW Bank/360	40.00	70.00
18 Bobby Labonte Interstate Batteries D-Day GM Dealers/432	40.00	70.00
18 Bobby Labonte Interstate Batteries Father's Day/3528	40.00	60.00
18 Bobby Labonte Interstate Batteries Father's Day Clear Window Bank/360	40.00	60.00
18 Bobby Labonte Interstate Batteries Father's Day GM Dealers/180	40.00	60.00
18 Bobby Labonte Interstate Batteries Shrek 2/8292	40.00	60.00
18 Bobby Labonte Interstate Batteries Shrek 2 Clear Window Bank/336	40.00	60.00
18 Bobby Labonte Interstate Batteries Shrek 2 GM Dealers/548	40.00	60.00
18 Bobby Labonte Interstate Batteries Shrek 2 Mac Tools/288	40.00	60.00
18 Bobby Labonte Wellbutrin/2784	40.00	70.00
18 Bobby Labonte Wellbutrin Clear Window Bank/288	40.00	70.00
18 Bobby Labonte Wellbutrin GM Dealers/108	40.00	70.00
18 J.J. Yeley Vigoro/2400	35.00	60.00
19 Bobby Labonte Banquet/1608	40.00	60.00
19 Bobby Labonte Banquet Clear Window Bank/240	40.00	60.00
19 Bobby Labonte Banquet GM Dealers/24	40.00	60.00
19 Jeremy Mayfield Dodge/2808	35.00	60.00
19 Jeremy Mayfield Dodge Clear Window Bank/240	35.00	60.00
19 Jeremy Mayfield Dodge HEMI/2508	35.00	60.00
19 Jeremy Mayfield Dodge HEMI Clear Window Bank/216	35.00	60.00
19 Jeremy Mayfield Dodge Mad Magazine/1956	35.00	60.00
19 Jeremy Mayfield Dodge Mad Magazine Mac Tools/204	35.00	60.00
19 Jeremy Mayfield Dodge NHL All Star/2376	35.00	60.00
19 Jeremy Mayfield Dodge NHL All Star Clear Window Bank/276	35.00	60.00
19 Jeremy Mayfield Dodge Popeye 75th Anniversary/2304	40.00	70.00
19 Jeremy Mayfield Dodge Popeye 75th Anniversary Clear Window Bank/300	35.00	60.00
19 Jeremy Mayfield Mountain Dew/2220	40.00	70.00
20 Tony Stewart Coke C2/4728	45.00	75.00
20 Tony Stewart Coke C2 Clear Window Bank/336	40.00	70.00
20 Tony Stewart Coke C2 GM Dealers/456	40.00	70.00
20 Tony Stewart Coke C2 Mac Tools/468	40.00	70.00
20 Tony Stewart Coke C2 QVC/504	40.00	70.00
20 Tony Stewart Home Depot/17,460	40.00	70.00
20 Tony Stewart Home Depot Clear Window Bank/516	40.00	70.00
20 Tony Stewart Home Depot GM Dealers/2244	40.00	70.00
20 Tony Stewart Home Depot Mac Tools/288	40.00	70.00
20 Tony Stewart Home Depot Nextel Incentive/3704	60.00	100.00
20 Tony Stewart Home Depot Reverse Paint Black/9756	40.00	70.00
20 Tony Stewart Home Depot Reverse Paint Black Clear Window Bank/432	40.00	70.00
20 Tony Stewart Home Depot Reverse Paint Black Mac Tools/288	40.00	70.00
20 Tony Stewart Home Depot Father's Day/5916	40.00	70.00
20 Tony Stewart Home Depot Father's Day Clear Window Bank/420	40.00	70.00
20 Tony Stewart Home Depot Father's Day Hamilton/156	40.00	70.00
20 Tony Stewart Home Depot Father's Day QVC/504	40.00	70.00
20 Tony Stewart Home Depot Olympics/4008	40.00	70.00
20 Tony Stewart Home Depot Olympics Clear Window Bank/252	40.00	70.00
20 Tony Stewart Home Depot Olympics Mac Tools/468	40.00	70.00
20 Tony Stewart Home Depot Olympics QVC/288	40.00	70.00
20 Tony Stewart Home Depot Shrek 2/10,836	40.00	70.00
20 Tony Stewart Home Depot Shrek 2 Clear Window Bank/348	40.00	70.00
20 Tony Stewart Home Depot Shrek 2 GM Dealers/576	40.00	70.00
20 Tony Stewart Home Depot 25th Anniversary/8664	40.00	70.00
20 Tony Stewart Home Depot 25th Anniversary Clear Window Bank	40.00	70.00
20 Tony Stewart 25 Years of Hard Nosed Racing/3504	40.00	70.00
21 Clint Bowyer Reese's/1008	50.00	100.00
21 Clint Bowyer Reese's GM Dealers/144	50.00	100.00
21 Kevin Harvick Hershey's Kisses/8004	40.00	70.00
21 Kevin Harvick Hershey's Kisses Clear Window Bank/408	40.00	70.00
21 Kevin Harvick Hershey's Kisses GM Dealers/1224	40.00	70.00
21 Kevin Harvick Meijer Reese's White Chocolate/3744	40.00	70.00
21 Kevin Harvick Meijer Reese's White Chocolate CW Bank/228	40.00	70.00
21 Kevin Harvick Reese's/11,376	35.00	60.00
21 Kevin Harvick Reese's Clear Window Bank/384	35.00	60.00
21 Kevin Harvick Reese's GM Dealers/1224	35.00	60.00
21 Kevin Harvick Reese's Mac Tools/288	35.00	60.00
21 Kevin Harvick Reese's Las Vegas Raced/3000	35.00	60.00
21 Kevin Harvick Reese's RCR 35th Anniversary/4812	40.00	70.00
21 Kevin Harvick Reese's RCR 35th Anniversary Clear Window Bank/324	40.00	70.00
22 Jason Keller Miller High Life/2640	35.00	60.00
22 Jason Keller Miller High Life Clear Window Bank/264	35.00	60.00
23 Kenny Wallace Stacker 2/1560	40.00	60.00
23 Kenny Wallace Stacker 2 Clear Window Bank/240	30.00	60.00
24 Jeff Gordon Big Bird/9612	45.00	75.00
24 Jeff Gordon DuPont Flames/22,716	45.00	75.00
24 Jeff Gordon DuPont Flames Clear Window Bank/636	45.00	75.00
24 Jeff Gordon DuPont Flames GM Dealers/2796	45.00	75.00
24 Jeff Gordon DuPont Flames Mac Tools/288	50.00	80.00
24 Jeff Gordon DuPont Flames Nextel Incentive/4704	75.00	125.00
24 Jeff Gordon DuPont Flames Brickyard Raced/6612	50.00	80.00
24 Jeff Gordon DuPont Flames Brickyard Raced w tire/1596	60.00	100.00
24 Jeff Gordon DuPont Flames California Raced/3012	45.00	75.00
24 Jeff Gordon DuPont Flames HMS 20th Anniversary/8232	45.00	75.00
24 Jeff Gordon DuPont Flames HMS 20th Anniversary Clear Window Bank/528	45.00	75.00
24 Jeff Gordon DuPont Flames HMS 20th Anniversary GM Dealers/420	45.00	75.00
24 Jeff Gordon DuPont Flames HMS 20th Anniversary Mac Tools/468	45.00	75.00
24 Jeff Gordon DuPont Racing Stripes/4920	45.00	75.00
24 Jeff Gordon DuPont Racing Stripes GM Dealers/468	45.00	75.00
24 Jeff Gordon DuPont Rainbow/12,900	50.00	80.00
24 Jeff Gordon DuPont Rainbow Clear Window Bank/552	50.00	80.00
24 Jeff Gordon DuPont Rainbow GM Dealers/960	50.00	80.00
24 Jeff Gordon DuPont Wizard of Oz/14,088	45.00	75.00
24 Jeff Gordon DuPont Wizard of Oz Clear Window Bank/528	45.00	75.00
24 Jeff Gordon Pepsi Billion/9564	45.00	75.00
24 Jeff Gordon Pepsi Billion Clear Window Bank/1008	45.00	75.00
24 Jeff Gordon Pepsi Billion GM Dealers/312	50.00	75.00
24 Jeff Gordon	45.00	75.00

Pepsi Billion Daytona Raced/2892
24 Jeff Gordon Pepsi Billion Daytona Raced QVC/504 45.00 75.00
24 Jeff Gordon Pepsi Shards/11,028 50.00 75.00
24 Jeff Gordon Pepsi Shards Clear Window Bank/576 50.00 75.00
24 Jeff Gordon Pepsi Shards GM Dealers/504 50.00 75.00
24 Jeff Gordon Pepsi Shards Talladega Raced/4524 50.00 75.00
24 Jeff Gordon Pepsi Shards Talladega Raced Mac Tools/468 50.00 75.00
24 Jeff Gordon Santa/6132 45.00 75.00
24 Jeff Gordon Santa QVC 45.00 75.00
24 Jeff Gordon 400 Career Starts/3504 45.00 75.00
24 Jeff Gordon 400 Career Starts GM Dealers/408 45.00 75.00
25 Brian Vickers Ditech/5976 40.00 70.00
25 Brian Vickers Ditech Clear Window Bank/300 40.00 70.00
25 Brian Vickers Ditech GM Dealers/288 40.00 70.00
25 Brian Vickers Ditech Father's Day/2868 35.00 60.00
25 Brian Vickers Ditech Father's Day Clear Window Bank/312 35.00 60.00
25 Brian Vickers Ditech Father's Day GM Dealers/144 35.00 60.00
25 Brian Vickers Ditech HMS 20th Anniversary/2448 35.00 60.00
25 Brian Vickers Ditech HMS 20th Anniversary Clear Window Bank/276 35.00 60.00
25 Brian Vickers Ditech HMS 20th GM Dealers/144 35.00 60.00
29 Ricky Craven ESGR Navy/1788 40.00 60.00
29 Ricky Craven ESGR Navy Clear Window Bank/276 40.00 60.00
29 Ricky Craven ESGR Navy GM Dealers/156 40.00 60.00
29 Kerry Earnhardt ESGR Air Force/2052 40.00 60.00
29 Kerry Earnhardt ESGR Air Force Clear Window Bank/252 40.00 60.00
29 Kevin Harvick Coke C2/5472 45.00 75.00
29 Kevin Harvick Coke C2 Clear Window Bank/288 40.00 70.00
29 Kevin Harvick Coke C2 GM Dealers/288 45.00 75.00
29 Kevin Harvick Coke C2 Mac Tools/468 40.00 70.00
29 Kevin Harvick Crown Royal IROC/4776 40.00 70.00
29 Kevin Harvick ESGR Coast Guard/4824 40.00 70.00
29 Kevin Harvick ESGR Coast Guard Clear Window Bank/348 40.00 70.00
29 Kevin Harvick Goodwrench/13,884 40.00 70.00
29 Kevin Harvick Goodwrench Clear Window Bank/432 40.00 70.00
29 Kevin Harvick Goodwrench GM Dealers/2280 40.00 70.00
29 Kevin Harvick Goodwrench Mac Tools/288 40.00 70.00
29 Kevin Harvick Goodwrench Nextel Incentive/2904 60.00 120.00
29 Kevin Harvick Goodwrench KISS/8148 60.00 100.00
29 Kevin Harvick Goodwrench KISS Clear Window Bank/420 60.00 100.00
29 Kevin Harvick Goodwrench RCR 35th Anniversary/7596 40.00 70.00
29 Kevin Harvick Goodwrench RCR 35th Ann. Clear Window Bank/444 40.00 70.00
29 Kevin Harvick Goodwrench Realtree/7572 40.00 70.00
29 Kevin Harvick Goodwrench Realtree Clear Window Bank/432 40.00 70.00
29 Kevin Harvick Goodwrench Realtree GM Dealers/1092 40.00 70.00
29 Kevin Harvick Ice Breakers Liquid Ice/8748 40.00 70.00
29 Kevin Harvick Ice Breakers Liquid Ice Clear Window Bank/444 40.00 70.00
29 Kevin Harvick Powerade/3288 40.00 70.00
29 Kevin Harvick Powerade Clear Window Bank/336 40.00 70.00
29 Kevin Harvick Snap-On/8652 40.00 70.00
29 Kevin Harvick Snap-On Clear Window Bank/432 40.00 70.00
29 Kevin Harvick Snap-On GM Dealers/1080 40.00 70.00
29 Bobby Labonte ESGR Army/4824 40.00 60.00
29 Bobby Labonte ESGR Army Clear Window Bank/300 40.00 60.00
29 Bobby Labonte ESGR Army GM Dealers/300 40.00 60.00
29 Tony Stewart ESGR Marines/7308 40.00 70.00
29 Tony Stewart ESGR Marines Clear Window Bank/384 40.00 70.00
29 Tony Stewart ESGR Marines GM Dealers/372 40.00 70.00
29 Tony Stewart Kid Rock/14,076 40.00 70.00
29 Tony Stewart Kid Rock Clear Window Bank/636 40.00 70.00
29 Tony Stewart Kid Rock GM Dealers/1044 40.00 70.00
30 Jeff Burton AOL RCR 35th Ann./1848 40.00 60.00
30 Johnny Sauter AOL/2532 40.00 70.00
30 Johnny Sauter AOL Clear Window Bank/252 40.00 70.00
30 Johnny Sauter AOL IMAX/2592 40.00 70.00
30 Johnny Sauter AOL IMAX Clear Window Bank/228 40.00 70.00
30 Johnny Sauter AOL IMAX GM Dealers/156 40.00 70.00
30 Johnny Sauter AOL RCR 35th Anniversary/1848 40.00 60.00
30 Johnny Sauter AOL RCR 35th Anniversary Clear Window Bank 40.00 60.00
31 Robby Gordon Cingular/3804 35.00 60.00
31 Robby Gordon Cingular Clear Window Bank/276 35.00 60.00
31 Robby Gordon Cingular Black/2844 40.00 70.00
31 Robby Gordon Cingular Black Clear Window Bank/240 40.00 70.00
31 Robby Gordon Cingular RCR 35th Anniversary/2508 40.00 60.00
31 Robby Gordon Cingular RCR 35th Anniversary Clear Window Bank/276 40.00 60.00
32 Ricky Craven Tide/2988 35.00 60.00
32 Ricky Craven Tide Clear Window Bank/276 35.00 60.00
33 Kerry Earnhardt Bass Pro Shops/4548 40.00 70.00
33 Kerry Earnhardt Bass Pro Shops Clear Window Bank/288 40.00 70.00
33 Kerry Earnhardt Bass Pro Shops Father's Day/7836 40.00 70.00
33 Kerry Earnhardt Bass Pro Shops Father's Day Clear Window Bank/396 40.00 70.00
33 Kerry Earnhardt Bass Pro Shops NRA/2448 35.00 60.00
33 Kerry Earnhardt Bass Pro Shops NRA Clear Window Bank/252 35.00 60.00
38 Kasey Kahne Great Clips/6636 50.00 80.00
38 Kasey Kahne Great Clips Shark Tales/5004 40.00 65.00
38 Kasey Kahne Great Clips Shark Tales Clear Window Bank/336 40.00 65.00
38 Elliott Sadler M&M's/9000 35.00 60.00
38 Elliott Sadler M&M's Clear Window Bank/360 35.00 60.00
38 Elliott Sadler M&M's Mac Tools/288 35.00 60.00
38 Elliott Sadler M&M's Texas Raced w tire swatch/3504 45.00 75.00
38 Elliott Sadler M&M's Black&White/5880 60.00 100.00
38 Elliott Sadler M&M's Black&White Clear Window Bank/336 45.00 75.00
38 Elliott Sadler M&M's Black&White Raced with tire swatch/2484 60.00 100.00
38 Elliott Sadler M&M's Black&White Raced Clear Window Bank/408 40.00 70.00
38 Elliott Sadler M&M's Halloween/2556 35.00 60.00
38 Elliott Sadler M&M's Halloween Clear Window Bank/204 35.00 60.00
38 Elliott Sadler M&M's Halloween Mac Tools/204 35.00 60.00
38 Elliott Sadler M&M's Halloween QVC/288 35.00 60.00
38 Elliott Sadler M&M's July 4th/4644 35.00 60.00
38 Elliott Sadler Pedigree Wizard of Oz/3540 35.00 60.00
38 Elliott Sadler Pedigree Wizard of Oz Clear Window Bank/252 35.00 60.00
40 Sterling Marlin Aspen Edge/2472 40.00 70.00
40 Sterling Marlin Aspen Edge Clear Window Bank/264 40.00 70.00
40 Sterling Marlin Coors Light/4644 40.00 70.00
40 Sterling Marlin Coors Light Clear Window Bank/312 40.00 70.00
40 Sterling Marlin Coors Light Nextel Incentive/2004 50.00 75.00
40 Sterling Marlin Coors Light Father's Day/2808 40.00 70.00
40 Sterling Marlin Coors Light Father's Day Clear Window Bank/324 40.00 70.00
40 Sterling Marlin Coors Light Kentucy Derby/2988 40.00 70.00
40 Sterling Marlin Coors Light Kentucy Derby Clear Window Bank/216 35.00 60.00
40 Sterling Marlin Prilosec OTC/2100 35.00 60.00
40 Sterling Marlin Prilosec OTC Clear Window Bank/204 35.00 60.00
41 Jamie McMurray Discount Tire Phoenix Raced/4152 45.00 75.00
41 Casey Mears Target/2832 35.00 60.00
41 Casey Mears Target Clear Window Bank/240 35.00 60.00
41 Casey Mears Target Father's Day/1452 35.00 60.00
41 Casey Mears Target Father's Day Clear Window Bank 35.00 60.00
41 Casey Mears Target SpongeBob/2832 35.00 60.00
41 Casey Mears Target SpongeBob Clear Window Bank/240 35.00 60.00
42 Jamie McMurray Havoline/8976 40.00 60.00
42 Jamie McMurray Havoline Clear Window Bank/300 40.00 60.00
42 Jamie McMurray Havoline Mac Tools/288 40.00 60.00
42 Jamie McMurray Havoline Mac Tools/288 40.00 60.00
42 Jamie McMurray Havoline Nextel Incentive/2004 50.00 100.00
42 Jamie McMurray Havoline Father's Day/3408 40.00 60.00
42 Jamie McMurray Havoline Father's Day Clear Window Bank 40.00 60.00
42 Jamie McMurray Havoline Texaco/2700 40.00 60.00
42 Jamie McMurray Havoline Walk of Fame 40.00 60.00
43 Jeff Green Cheerios/1788 35.00 60.00
43 Jeff Green Cheerios Clear Window Bank/228 35.00 60.00
45 Kyle Petty Brawny/1920 40.00 60.00
45 Kyle Petty Brawny Clear Window Bank/228 40.00 60.00
45 Kyle Petty Geogia Pacific/2040 40.00 60.00
45 Kyle Petty Georgia Pacific Clear Window Bank/264 40.00 60.00
45 Kyle Petty Georgia Pacific Father's Day/2844 40.00 60.00
45 Kyle Petty Georgia Pacific Father's Day Clear Window Bank/216 40.00 60.00
46 Dennis Setzer Silverado Trucks SuperTruck/2300 40.00 60.00
47 Ward Burton Silverado Joe Nichols SuperTruck/1932 40.00 70.00
47 Tony Stewart Silverado Sara Evans SuperTruck/4308 40.00 70.00
47 Tony Stewart Sara Evans SuperTruck QVC/504 40.00 70.00
47 Michael Waltrip Silverado Sheryl Crow SuperTruck/4344 40.00 70.00
48 Jimmie Johnson Crown Royal IROC/3792 40.00 70.00
48 Jimmie Johnson Lowe's/9300 40.00 70.00
48 Jimmie Johnson Lowe's Clear Window Bank/384 35.00 60.00
48 Jimmie Johnson Lowe's GM Dealers/1896 40.00 70.00
48 Jimmie Johnson Lowe's Mac Tools/288 40.00 70.00
48 Jimmie Johnson Lowe's Nextel Incentive/2004 60.00 100.00
48 Jimmie Johnson Lowe's Atlanta Raced/13,788 w Bracelet 50.00 75.00
48 Jimmie Johnson Lowe's Atlanta Raced Clear Window Bank/432 50.00 75.00
48 Jimmie Johnson Lowe's Atlanta Raced GM Dealers/852 50.00 75.00
48 Jimmie Johnson Lowe's Atlanta Raced QVC/804 w Bracelet 50.00 75.00
48 Jimmie Johnson Lowe's Father's Day/3372 40.00 70.00
48 Jimmie Johnson Lowe's Father's Day Clear Window Bank/348 40.00 70.00
48 Jimmie Johnson Lowe's HMS20th Anniversary/10,008 40.00 70.00
48 Jimmie Johnson Lowe's HMS20th Anniversary Clear Window Bank/300 40.00 70.00
48 Jimmie Johnson Lowe's HMS20th GM Dealers/180 40.00 70.00
48 Jimmie Johnson Lowe's SpongeBob/2364 40.00 70.00
48 Jimmie Johnson Lowe's SpongeBob Clear Window Bank 40.00 70.00
48 Jimmie Johnson Lowe's Tool World/2508 40.00 70.00
48 Jimmie Johnson Lowe's Tool World Clear Window Bank/240 40.00 70.00
49 Ken Schrader Schwan's Foods/2928 40.00 60.00
55 Robby Gordon Fruit of the Loom/2172 40.00 60.00
55 Robby Gordon Fruit of the Loom CW Bank/216 40.00 60.00
66 Jamie McMurray Duraflame Darlington Raced/1356 40.00 65.00
66 Billy Parker Jr. Duraflame/1200 40.00 60.00
66 Rusty Wallace Duraflame/2340 40.00 70.00
66 Rusty Wallace Duraflame Clear Window Bank/204 40.00 70.00
74 Kerry Earnhardt Smith & Wesson/2364 40.00 60.00
74 Kerry Earnhardt Smith & Wesson Clear Window Bank/300 40.00 60.00
77 Brendan Gaughan Kodak/3312 45.00 70.00
77 Brendan Gaughan Kodak Clear Window Bank/240 35.00 60.00
77 Brendan Gaughan Kodak QVC/288 45.00 70.00
77 Brendan Gaughan Kodak Jasper Engines/2628 40.00 70.00
77 Brendan Gaughan Kodak Jasper Engines Clear Window Bank/288 40.00 70.00
77 Brendan Gaughan Kodak Jasper Engines QVC/288 40.00 70.00
77 Brendan Gaughan Kodak Punisher/2844 35.00 60.00
77 Brendan Gaughan Kodak Punisher Clear Window Bank/276 35.00 60.00
77 Brendan Gaughan Kodak Wizard of Oz/2496 35.00 60.00
77 Brendan Gaughan Kodak Wizard of Oz Clear Window Bank/264 35.00 60.00
80 J.J. Yeley Crown Royal IROC/2856 45.00 75.00
80 J.J. Yeley Crown Royal IROC Chrome/204 50.00 75.00
81 Dale Earnhardt Jr. KFC/24,828 40.00 65.00
81 Dale Earnhardt Jr. KFC Clear Window Bank/1068 40.00 65.00
81 Dale Earnhardt Jr. KFC GM Dealers/1944 40.00 65.00
81 Dale Earnhardt Jr. Menards Bristol Raced/8808 40.00 65.00
81 Dale Earnhardt Jr. Taco Bell/28,656 40.00 65.00
81 Dale Earnhardt Jr. Taco Bell Clear Window Bank/1092 40.00 65.00
81 Dale Earnhardt Jr. Taco Bell GM Dealers/1584 40.00 65.00
81 Tony Stewart Bass Pro Shops 40.00 70.00
81 Tony Stewart Bass Pro Shops Clear Window Bank/408 40.00 70.00
81 Martin Truex Jr. Chance 2/4092 40.00 70.00
81 Martin Truex Jr. Chance 2 GM Dealers/180 40.00 70.00
81 Martin Truex Jr. Chance 2 Robert Gee/2880 40.00 70.00
81 Martin Truex Jr. Chance 2 Robert Gee GM Dealers/144 40.00 70.00
84 Kyle Busch Carquest/3084 45.00 75.00
84 Kyle Busch Carquest CW Bank/276 45.00 70.00
84 Kyle Busch Carquest GM Dealers/144 45.00 75.00
88 Dale Jarrett UPS/7440 40.00 70.00
88 Dale Jarrett UPS Clear Window Bank/324 40.00 70.00
88 Dale Jarrett UPS Nextel Incentive/2004 50.00 100.00
88 Dale Jarrett UPS Arnold Palmer/6024 45.00 75.00
88 Dale Jarrett UPS Arnold Palmer Clear Window Bank/312 45.00 75.00
88 Dale Jarrett UPS Bud Shootout Raced w tire/4188 50.00 75.00
88 Dale Jarrett UPS Monsters/3000 45.00 75.00
88 Dale Jarrett UPS Monsters Clear Window Bank/240 45.00 75.00
88 Dale Jarrett UPS Monsters Mac Tools/204 45.00 75.00
91 Bill Elliott UAW Daimler Chrysler w tire swatch/5148 50.00 75.00
91 Bill Elliott Visteon/2400 40.00 70.00
91 Bill Elliott Visteon Clear Window Bank 40.00 70.00
91 Bill Elliott Visteon Mac Tools/204 40.00 70.00
91 Bill Elliott Visteon QVC/288 40.00 70.00
92 Kevin Harvick Goodwrench SuperTruck/3480 45.00 75.00
92 Kevin Harvick Snap On SuperTruck/4062 40.00 70.00
92 Tony Stewart McDonald's/3516 45.00 75.00
92 Tony Stewart McDonald's Clear Window Bank/288 45.00 75.00
92 Tony Stewart McDonald's QVC/444 45.00 75.00
97 Kurt Busch Crown Royal IROC/2940 40.00 70.00
97 Kurt Busch Crown Royal IROC Chrome/288 50.00 75.00
98 Bill Elliott Coke C2/2520 40.00 70.00
98 Bill Elliott Coke C2 Clear Window Bank/276 40.00 70.00
98 Bill Elliott McDonald's/2376 40.00 70.00
98 Bill Elliott McDonald's Clear Window Bank/216 40.00 70.00
99 Michael Waltrip Aaron's/2664 35.00 60.00
99 Michael Waltrip Aaron's Clear Window Bank/240 35.00 60.00
99 Michael Waltrip Aaron's Mac Tools/288 35.00 60.00
99 Michael Waltrip Aaron's LeAnn Rimes/2124 40.00 70.00
99 Michael Waltrip Aaron's LeAnn Rimes Clear Window Bank/192 40.00 70.00
99 Michael Waltrip Aaron's LeAnn Rimes GM Dealers/240 40.00 70.00
99 Michael Waltrip Aaron's Mad Magazine/2364 40.00 60.00
99 Michael Waltrip Aaron's Mad Magazine Clear Window Bank/240 40.00 60.00
99 Michael Waltrip Aaron's Mad Magazine Mac Tools/204 40.00 60.00
99 Michael Waltrip Aaron's Mad Magazine QVC/288 40.00 60.00
99 Michael Waltrip Aaron's Operation Marathon/1296 40.00 60.00
99 Michael Waltrip Best Western/2748 35.00 60.00
99 Michael Waltrip Best Western Clear Window Bank 35.00 60.00
99 Michael Waltrip Domino's Pizza/2100 35.00 60.00
0 Ward Burton NetZero/2244 40.00 70.00
0 Ward Burton NetZero Clear Window Bank/216 40.00 70.00
0 Ward Burton NetZero GM Dealers/144 40.00 70.00
0 Ward Burton NetZero Shark Tales/1956 40.00 70.00
0 Ward Burton NetZero Shark Tales Clear Window Bank/288 40.00 70.00
0 Ward Burton NetZero Shark Tales GM Dealers/60 40.00 70.00
00 Jason Leffler Haas/1200 40.00 60.00
00 Jason Leffler Haas Clear Window Bank/240 35.00 60.00
00 Kenny Wallace Aaron's Rent Mad Magazine/1860 40.00 60.00
0 Kenny Wallace Aaron's Rent Mad Magaine Clear Window Bank/216 40.00 60.00
01 Joe Nemechek Army/2064 40.00 70.00
01 Joe Nemechek Army Clear Window Bank/276 40.00 70.00
01 Joe Nemechek Army GI Joe/2496 35.00 60.00
01 Joe Nemechek Army GI Joe Clear Window Bank/240 35.00 60.00
01 Joe Nemechek Army Time Magazine/2376 40.00 70.00
01 Joe Nemechek Army Time Magazine Clear Window Bank/300 40.00 70.00
01 Joe Nemechek Army Time Magazine GM Dealers/144 40.00 70.00
04 Chase for the Nextel Cup brushed metal/1956 40.00 70.00
04 Nextel Inaugural Event Car/5112 40.00 70.00
04 Nextel Inaugural Event Car GM Dealers/288 40.00 70.00
04 Victory Junction Gang Event Car/2292 40.00 60.00
04 Victory Junction Event Car Clear Window Bank/240 30.00 60.00
04 Wizard of Oz Event Car/1836 30.00 60.00
04 Wizard of Oz Event GM Dealers/228 30.00 60.00
35th RCR 35th Anniversary/2520 40.00 60.00
35th RCR 35th Anniversary Clear Window Bank/276 40.00 60.00
35th RCR 35th Anniversary GM Dealers/348 40.00 60.00
NNO Chevy Rock & Roll Event Car/1656 35.00 60.00
NNO Chevy Rock & Roll Event Car GM Dealers/216 35.00 60.00
NNO HMS 20th Anniversary Event Car/1728 40.00 60.00
NNO Shrek 2 Event Car/1788 35.00 60.00

2004 Action Racing Collectables Historical Series 1:24

1 Dale Earnhardt True Value 1999 IROC Orange/6372 40.00 70.00
2 Dale Earnhardt Mello Yello 1979 Pontiac Ventura/11,664 50.00 80.00
2 Dale Earnhardt Mello Yello '79 Pontiac Ventura GM Dealers/984 50.00 80.00
3 Dale Earnhardt Goodwrench Olympic 1996 Monte Carlo Clear Window Bank/6696 50.00 80.00
3 Dale Earnhardt 40.00 75.00

Wrangler 1985 Camaro/21,000
3 Dale Earnhardt 40.00 75.00
Wrangler 1985 Camaro
GM Dealers/1092
3 Dale Earnhardt Jr. 50.00 75.00
Sun Drop 1994 Lumina
Color Chrome/11,136
3 Dale Earnhardt Jr. 50.00 80.00
Sun Drop '94 Lum.
Color Chrome Mac Tools/288
7 Dale Earnhardt Jr. 40.00 75.00
Church Brothers 1997 Monte Carlo
Clear Window Bank/7008
8 Dale Earnhardt Jr. 50.00 75.00
Bud Olympics 2000 Monte Carlo
CW Bank/6138
8 Dale Earnhardt Jr. 60.00 100.00
Bud 2003 Phoenix Raced/7116
8 Dale Earnhardt Jr. 60.00 100.00
Bud '03 Phoenix Raced
GM Dealers/324
9 Bill Elliott 45.00 75.00
Coors '85 t-bird/3660
9 Bill Elliott 45.00 75.00
Coors '85 t-bird
Clear Window Bank/348
9 Bill Elliott 45.00 75.00
Coors Light '91 t-bird/4032
9 Bill Elliott 45.00 75.00
Coors Light 1991 t-bird
Clear Window Bank/348
17 Darrell Waltrip 40.00 70.00
Tide 1987 400 Chevy Wins
Color Chrome/3132
24 Jeff Gordon 50.00 80.00
DuPont 1996 Monte Carlo
400 Chevy Wins Color Chrome/6192
28 Davey Allison 45.00 75.00
Texaco 1993 Thunderbird/2988
28 Davey Allison 45.00 75.00
Texaco 1993 Thunderbird
Clear Window Bank/360
29 Kevin Harvick 50.00 80.00
Goodwrench Service Plus
2001 Monte Carlo
black numbers/33,000
29 Kevin Harvick 50.00 80.00
Goodwrench Service Plus
2001 Monte Carlo
Clear Window Bank/240
38 Kelley Earnhardt 40.00 70.00
Mom & Pop's
1995 Camaro/3588
43 Richard Petty 50.00 80.00
STP 1980 400 Chevy Wins
Color Chrome/3924
43 Richard Petty 50.00 80.00
STP 200th Win
1984 Grand Prix/4992
43 Richard Petty 40.00 70.00
STP 200th Win
1984 Tribute/3768
48 Jimmie Johnson 60.00 100.00
Lowe's 2003 Monte Carlo
400 Chevy Wins Color Chrome/3204

2004 Action QVC For Race Fans Only 1:24

2 Rusty Wallace 75.00 150.00
Miller Lite Martinsville Raced
Color Chrome AU/504
2 Rusty Wallace 75.00 125.00
Miller Lite Last Call
Color Chrome/1500
3 Dale Earnhardt 60.00 100.00
Goodwrench Olympic
1996 Monte Carlo Color Chrome/5004
3 Dale Earnhardt 100.00 200.00
Goodwrench Crash
'97 Daytona Raced Color Chrome/5004
3 Dale Earnhardt 100.00 200.00
Goodwrench Crash
'97 Daytona Raced Gold/504
3 Dale Earnhardt 75.00 150.00
Goodwrench Peter Max
'00 Monte Carlo Color Chrome/504
8 Dale Earnhardt Jr. 125.00 200.00
Bud Brushed Metal/1008
8 Dale Earnhardt Jr. 60.00 100.00
Bud Color Chrome/5016
8 Dale Earnhardt Jr. 80.00 130.00
Bud Gold/1008
8 Dale Earnhardt Jr. 150.00 250.00
Bud Platinum/504
8 Dale Earnhardt Jr. 90.00 150.00
Bud Born On Feb.7
Color Chrome/5004
8 Dale Earnhardt Jr. 100.00 175.00
Bud Born On
Feb.7 Gold/504
8 Dale Earnhardt Jr. 200.00 350.00
Bud Born On
Feb.7 Platinum/300
8 Dale Earnhardt Jr. 75.00 125.00
Bud Born On Feb.15
Raced Color Chrome/7500
8 Dale Earnhardt Jr. 75.00 125.00
Bud Dave Matthews Band
Color Chrome/6000
8 Dale Earnhardt Jr. 60.00 100.00
Bud Father's Day
Brushed Metal/504
8 Dale Earnhardt Jr. 75.00 125.00
Bud World Series
Color Chrome/6000
8 Dale Earnhardt Jr. 75.00 125.00
Bud World Series
Gold/500
8 Dale Earnhardt Jr. 75.00 125.00
Oreo Brushed Metal/504
8 Dale Earnhardt Jr. 75.00 125.00
Oreo Color Chrome/5016
8 Dale Earnhardt Jr. 100.00 175.00
Oreo Gold/504
8 Dale Earnhardt Jr. 175.00 300.00
Oreo Platinum/300
8 Martin Truex Jr. 125.00 200.00
Wrangler
Color Chrome AU/408
9 Kasey Kahne 60.00 100.00
Dodge Refresh Color Chrome/504
9 Kasey Kahne 150.00 250.00
Dodge Refresh Gold/300
9 Kasey Kahne 150.00 250.00
Dodge Refresh
Platinum/300
9 Kasey Kahne 50.00 75.00
Dodge ROY Brushed Metal/504
9 Kasey Kahne 50.00 75.00
Dodge Mad Magazine
Color Chrome/408
9 Kasey Kahne 100.00 175.00
Dodge Popeye
Color Chrome/504
9 Kasey Kahne 60.00 100.00
Mopar Color Chrome/1008
9 Kasey Kahne 125.00 200.00
Mountain Dew Color Chrome/408
24 Jeff Gordon 60.00 100.00
DuPont Flames
Brushed Metal/1008
24 Jeff Gordon 90.00 150.00
DuPont Flames
Color Chrome/504
24 Jeff Gordon 100.00 175.00
DuPont Flames Platinum/300
24 Jeff Gordon 100.00 175.00
DuPont Flames
Wizard of Oz Platinum/300
24 Jeff Gordon 60.00 100.00
DuPont Rainbow
Color Chrome/504
81 Dale Earnhardt Jr. 60.00 100.00
Chance 2 KFC
Color Chrome/5004
81 Dale Earnhardt Jr. 60.00 100.00
Chance 2 Taco Bell
Color Chrome/5004

2004 Action/RCCA 1:24

1 John Andretti 25.00 50.00
Coke C2/288
1 John Andretti 40.00 70.00
Legacy Snap-On/288
1 John Andretti 25.00 50.00
Post Maxwell House/300
2 Ron Hornaday 40.00 60.00
AC Delco KISS/288
2 Rusty Wallace 30.00 60.00
Kodak/600
2 Rusty Wallace 40.00 70.00
Miller Lite/1200
2 Rusty Wallace 30.00 60.00
Miller Lite
Can Promotion/408
2 Rusty Wallace 30.00 60.00
Miller Lite
Father's Day/240
2 Rusty Wallace 50.00 100.00
Miller Lite
Last Call/600
2 Rusty Wallace 50.00 75.00
Miller Lite
Martinsville Raced w
tire/240
2 Rusty Wallace 40.00 70.00
Miller Lite
Penske 50th/504
2 Rusty Wallace 30.00 60.00
Miller Lite
President of Beers/600
2 Rusty Wallace 25.00 50.00
Miller Lite
Puddle of Mudd/504
5 Kyle Busch 50.00 75.00
Lowe's/288
5 Kyle Busch 30.00 60.00
Lowe's SpongeBob/360
5 Terry Labonte 30.00 60.00
Kellogg's/300
5 Terry Labonte 30.00 60.00
Kellogg's Father's Day/240
5 Terry Labonte 30.00 60.00
Kellogg's HMS 20th Anniversary/288
5 Terry Labonte 25.00 50.00
Kellogg's Incredibles/408
5 Terry Labonte 25.00 50.00
Kellogg's UAW Delphi/288
6 Bill Elliott 40.00 70.00
Lucas Oil Elvis/540
8 Dale Earnhardt Jr. 30.00 60.00
Bud/3600
8 Dale Earnhardt Jr. 50.00 75.00
Bud Born On
Feb.12 Raced/3000
8 Dale Earnhardt Jr. 60.00 100.00
Bud Born On
Feb.7/3000
8 Dale Earnhardt Jr. 60.00 100.00
Bud Born On
Feb.15 Raced/4800
8 Dale Earnhardt Jr. 30.00 60.00
Bud Dave Matthews Band/2388
8 Dale Earnhardt Jr. 50.00 75.00
Bud Father's Day/1200
8 Dale Earnhardt Jr. 30.00 60.00
Bud World Series/2508
8 Dale Earnhardt Jr. 30.00 60.00
Oreo/3000
8 Martin Truex Jr. 50.00 75.00
Bass Pro Shops/444
8 Martin Truex Jr. 60.00 100.00
Bass Pro Shops
'04 Champion Color Chrome/600
8 Martin Truex Jr. 40.00 70.00
Chance 2 Ralph Earnhardt/444
8 Martin Truex Jr. 30.00 60.00
Chance 2 Richie Evans/360
8 Martin Truex Jr. 30.00 60.00
Chance 2 Tear Away/444
8 Martin Truex Jr. 30.00 60.00
KFC Dover Raced/300
8 Martin Truex Jr. 30.00 60.00
Long John Silver's/360
8 Martin Truex Jr. 30.00 60.00
Taco Bell
Bristol Raced/540
8 Martin Truex Jr. 30.00 60.00
Wrangler/444
9 Bill Elliott 30.00 60.00
Milestones/408
9 Kasey Kahne 60.00 120.00
Dodge/288
9 Kasey Kahne 75.00 150.00
Dodge refresh ROY AU/504
9 Kasey Kahne 40.00 70.00
Dodge Mad Magazine/600
9 Kasey Kahne 40.00 70.00
Dodge Mopar/444
9 Kasey Kahne 40.00 70.00
Dodge Pit Cap/600
9 Kasey Kahne 40.00 70.00
Dodge Popeye/576
9 Kasey Kahne 60.00 100.00
Mountain Dew/540
10 Scott Riggs 25.00 50.00
Valvoline/360
10 Scott Riggs 25.00 50.00
Valvoline Wizard of Oz/288
12 Ryan Newman 30.00 60.00
Crown Royal IROC
Color Chrome/288
15 Michael Waltrip 25.00 50.00
NAPA/600
15 Michael Waltrip 25.00 50.00
NAPA Father's Day/240
15 Michael Waltrip 25.00 50.00
NAPA Stars & Stripes/288
17 Matt Kenseth 30.00 60.00
Crown Royal IROC Color Chrome/288
17 Matt Kenseth 30.00 60.00
Crown Royal IROC
'04 Champion Pearl/360
17 Darrell Waltrip 50.00 100.00
King of Bristol AU/360
18 Bobby Labonte 25.00 50.00
Interstate Batteries/504
18 Bobby Labonte 25.00 50.00
Interstate Batteries
Father's Day/240
18 Bobby Labonte 25.00 50.00
Interstate Batteries
D-Day/504
18 Bobby Labonte 25.00 50.00
Interstate Batteries Shrek 2/600
18 Bobby Labonte 25.00 50.00
Wellbutrin/360
18 J.J. Yeley 15.00 40.00
Vigoro/204
19 Bobby Labonte 25.00 50.00
Banquet/288
19 Jeremy Mayfield 25.00 50.00
Dodge HEMI/288
19 Jeremy Mayfield 25.00 50.00
Dodge Mad Magazine/288
19 Jeremy Mayfield 25.00 50.00
Dodge NHL All Star Game/288
19 Jeremy Mayfield 25.00 50.00
Dodge Popeye/360
20 Tony Stewart 25.00 50.00
Coke C2/600
20 Tony Stewart 30.00 60.00
Home Depot/1500
20 Tony Stewart 30.00 60.00
Home Depot Black Reverse/1008
20 Tony Stewart 30.00 60.00
Home Depot
Father's Day/204
20 Tony Stewart 25.00 50.00
Home Depot
Olympic/600
20 Tony Stewart 25.00 50.00
Home Depot Shrek 2/1008
20 Tony Stewart 25.00 50.00
Home Depot 25th Anniversary
21 Clint Bowyer 40.00 80.00
Reese's/144
21 Kevin Harvick 25.00 50.00
Hershey's Kisses/720
21 Kevin Harvick 25.00 50.00
Meijer Reese's White Chocolate/288
21 Kevin Harvick 25.00 50.00
Reese's/900
21 Kevin Harvick 25.00 50.00
Reese's RCR 35th Anniversary/444
22 Jason Keller 30.00 60.00
Miller High Life/288
23 Kenny Wallace 15.00 40.00
Stacker 2/288
24 Jeff Gordon 25.00 50.00
Big Bird/1500
24 Jeff Gordon 50.00 75.00
DuPont Flames/1800
24 Jeff Gordon 60.00 100.00
DuPont Flames
Brickyard Raced/524
24 Jeff Gordon 30.00 60.00
DuPont Flames
Wizard of Oz/1800
24 Jeff Gordon 50.00 75.00
DuPont Flames HMS 20th Anniversary/1500
24 Jeff Gordon 30.00 60.00
DuPont Racing Stripes/660
24 Jeff Gordon 50.00 75.00
DuPont Rainbow/1200
24 Jeff Gordon 30.00 60.00
Pepsi Billion/1200
24 Jeff Gordon 30.00 60.00
Pepsi Billion
Daytona Raced/444
24 Jeff Gordon 30.00 60.00
Pepsi Shards/720
24 Jeff Gordon 30.00 60.00
Pepsi Shards
Talladega Raced/300
25 Brian Vickers 25.00 50.00
ditech/288
25 Brian Vickers 25.00 50.00
ditech Father's Day/240
25 Brian Vickers 25.00 50.00
ditech HMS 20th Anniversary/288
29 Kevin Harvick 30.00 60.00
Coke C2/600
29 Kevin Harvick 30.00 60.00
Crown Royal IROC
Color Chrome/288
29 Kevin Harvick 25.00 50.00
ESGR Coast Guard/600
29 Kevin Harvick 30.00 60.00
Goodwrench/1008
29 Kevin Harvick 50.00 75.00
Goodwrench KISS/1008
29 Kevin Harvick 30.00 60.00
Goodwrench RCR
35th Anniversary/900
29 Kevin Harvick 30.00 60.00
Goodwrench Realtree/1200
29 Kevin Harvick 25.00 50.00
Ice Breakers/504
29 Kevin Harvick 25.00 50.00
Powerade/600
29 Kevin Harvick 25.00 50.00
Snap-On/804
29 Bobby Labonte 25.00 50.00
ESGR Army/600
29 Tony Stewart 25.00 50.00
ESGR Marines/1008
29 Tony Stewart 30.00 60.00
Kid Rock/1200
30 Johnny Sauter 25.00 50.00
AOL/288
30 Johnny Sauter 25.00 50.00
AOL IMAX/288
31 Robby Gordon 25.00 50.00
Cingular Black/300
31 Robby Gordon 25.00 50.00
Cingular RCR 35th Ann./288
32 Ricky Craven 25.00 50.00
Tide/300
33 Kerry Earnhardt 25.00 50.00
Bass Pro Shops/504
38 Kasey Kahne 30.00 60.00
Great Clips/360
38 Kasey Kahne 30.00 60.00
Great Clips Shark Tale/560
38 Elliott Sadler 40.00 70.00
M&M's/300
38 Elliott Sadler 40.00 70.00
M&M's Texas Raced/240
38 Elliott Sadler 40.00 70.00
M&M's Black&White/360
38 Elliott Sadler 60.00 100.00
M&M's Black&White
Raced w
tire/240
38 Elliott Sadler 30.00 60.00
M&M's Halloween/408
38 Elliott Sadler 30.00 60.00
M&M's July 4/288
38 Elliott Sadler 25.00 50.00
Pedigree
Wizard of Oz/360
40 Sterling Marlin 25.00 50.00
Aspen Edge/288
40 Sterling Marlin 30.00 60.00
Coors Light/300
40 Sterling Marlin 30.00 60.00
Coors Light Father's Day/240
40 Sterling Marlin 30.00 60.00
Coors Light
Kentucky Derby/204
40 Sterling Marlin 25.00 50.00
Prilosec/288
41 Casey Mears 25.00 50.00
Target/408
41 Casey Mears 25.00 50.00
Target SpongeBob/288
42 Jamie McMurray 30.00 60.00
Havoline Father's Day/240
42 Jamie McMurray 30.00 60.00
Havoline Texaco Rising Star/360
43 Jeff Green 25.00 50.00
Cheerios/288
45 Kyle Petty 25.00 50.00
Brawny/300
45 Kyle Petty 25.00 50.00
Georgia Pacific/300
45 Kyle Petty 25.00 50.00
Georgia Pacific Father's Day/240
48 Jimmie Johnson 30.00 60.00
Crown Royal IROC
Color Chrome/288
48 Jimmie Johnson 40.00 70.00
Lowe's/804
48 Jimmie Johnson 30.00 60.00
Lowe's Father's Day/240
48 Jimmie Johnson 40.00 70.00
Lowe's HMS 20th Anniversary/600
48 Jimmie Johnson 30.00 60.00
Lowe's SpongeBob/504
48 Jimmie Johnson 40.00 70.00
Lowe's Tool World/600
55 Robby Gordon 25.00 50.00
Fruit of the Loom/336
66 Billy Parker 25.00 50.00
Duraflame/300
66 Rusty Wallace 30.00 60.00
Duraflame/408
77 Brendan Gaughan 25.00 50.00
Kodak/288
77 Brendan Gaughan 25.00 50.00
Kodak Punisher/288
77 Brendan Gaughan 25.00 50.00
Kodak Wizard of Oz/288
77 Brendan Gaughan 25.00 50.00
Jasper/288
81 Dale Earnhardt Jr. 25.00 50.00
KFC/3000
81 Dale Earnhardt Jr. 25.00 50.00
Menards Bristol Raced/1008
81 Dale Earnhardt Jr. 25.00 50.00
Taco Bell/1800
81 Tony Stewart 30.00 60.00
Bass Pro Shops/600
81 Martin Truex Jr. 25.00 50.00
Chance 2
Robert Gee/360
84 Kyle Busch 40.00 70.00
CarQuest/360
88 Dale Jarrett 30.00 60.00
UPS/300
88 Dale Jarrett 50.00 75.00
UPS Raced w
tire/240
88 Dale Jarrett 25.00 50.00
UPS Monsters/540
91 Bill Elliott 50.00 75.00
UAW Daimler Chrysler
w
tire swatch/288
91 Bill Elliott 30.00 60.00
Visteon/360
92 Kevin Harvick 30.00 60.00
Goodwrench
SuperTruck/444
92 Tony Stewart 25.00 50.00
McDonald's/600
97 Kurt Busch 30.00 60.00
Crown Royal IROC
Color Chrome/288
98 Bill Elliott 30.00 60.00
Coke C2/360
98 Bill Elliott 25.00 50.00
McDonald's/360
99 Michael Waltrip 25.00 50.00
Aaron's Dream Machine
LeAnn Rimes/288
99 Michael Waltrip 25.00 50.00
Aaron's Dream Machine
Mad Magazine/288
99 Michael Waltrip 25.00 50.00
Aaron's Dream Machine
Operation Marathon/360
99 Michael Waltrip 25.00 50.00
Domino's Pizza/360
0 Ward Burton 25.00 50.00
NetZero Hi Speed/204
0 Ward Burton 25.00 50.00
NetZero Hi Speed
Shark Tale/444
0 Jason Leffler 25.00 50.00
HAAS/288
0 Kenny Wallace 25.00 50.00
Aaron's Mad Magazine/288
01 Joe Nemechek 30.00 60.00
Army/288
01 Joe Nemechek 30.00 60.00
Army GI Joe/288
01 Joe Nemechek 30.00 60.00
Army Time Magazine/360
04 Nextel Inaugural Event Car/444 25.00 50.00
04 Victory Junction Gang 25.00 50.00
Event Car/360
04 Wizard of Oz Event Car/396 25.00 50.00
35th RCR 35th Anniversary 25.00 50.00
Event Car/288
NNO Chevy Rock&Roll 25.00 50.00
Event Car/288
NNO HMS 20th Anniversary 25.00 50.00
Event Car/288
NNO Shrek 2 Event Car/300 25.00 50.00

2004 Action/RCCA Elite 1:24

1 John Andretti 50.00 100.00
Legacy Snap-On/288
1 John Andretti 40.00 80.00
Post Maxwell House/300
2 Rusty Wallace 50.00 100.00
Kodak/600
2 Rusty Wallace 250.00 350.00
Kodak White Gold/25
2 Rusty Wallace 60.00 120.00
Miller Lite/1500
2 Rusty Wallace 75.00 125.00
Miller Lite Color Chrome/408
2 Rusty Wallace 60.00 120.00
Miller Lite
Martinsville Raced/240
2 Rusty Wallace 60.00 120.00
Miller Lite
Can Promotion/504
2 Rusty Wallace 75.00 150.00
Miller Lite Last Call/804
2 Rusty Wallace 250.00 350.00
Miller Lite Last Call
Platinum/204
2 Rusty Wallace 350.00 500.00
Miller Lite Last Call
White Gold/25
2 Rusty Wallace 60.00 120.00
Miller Lite
Penske 50th/504
2 Rusty Wallace 50.00 100.00
Miller Lite
Puddle of Mudd/504
2 Rusty Wallace 50.00 100.00
Miller Lite
President of Beers/600
5 Kyle Busch 100.00 175.00
Lowe's/288
5 Kyle Busch 60.00 120.00
Lowe's SpongeBob/300
5 Kyle Busch 200.00 300.00
Lowe's SpongeBob
White Gold/25
5 Terry Labonte 50.00 100.00

Kellogg's/300
5 Terry Labonte Kellogg's HMS 20th Ann/288 50.00 100.00
5 Terry Labonte Kellogg's Incredibles/408 50.00 100.00
5 Terry Labonte Kellogg's Incredibles White Gold/25 300.00 450.00
5 Terry Labonte Kellogg's Olympic/360 50.00 100.00
5 Terry Labonte Kellogg's UAW Delphi/288 60.00 120.00
6 Bill Elliott Lucas Oil Elvis/540 50.00 100.00
6 Bill Elliott Lucas Oil Elvis White Gold/25 200.00 350.00
8 Dale Earnhardt Jr. Bud/5004 60.00 120.00
8 Dale Earnhardt Jr. Bud Color Chrome/2400 75.00 150.00
8 Dale Earnhardt Jr. Bud Platinum/408 200.00 350.00
8 Dale Earnhardt Jr. Bud Bristol Raced/1200 60.00 120.00
8 Dale Earnhardt Jr. Bud Talladega Raced/804 60.00 120.00
8 Dale Earnhardt Jr. Bud Born On Feb.7/4008 60.00 120.00
8 Dale Earnhardt Jr. Bud Born On Feb.7 Platinum/408 250.00 400.00
8 Dale Earnhardt Jr. Bud Born On Feb.12 Raced/2400 60.00 120.00
8 Dale Earnhardt Jr. Bud Born On Feb.15 Raced/6996 75.00 150.00
8 Dale Earnhardt Jr. Bud Born On Feb.15 Raced Platinum/408 250.00 400.00
8 Dale Earnhardt Jr. Bud Dave Matthews Band/3888 50.00 100.00
8 Dale Earnhardt Jr. Bud Dave Matthews Band Platinum/360 100.00 200.00
8 Dale Earnhardt Jr. Bud Dave Matthews Band White Gold/25 300.00 450.00
8 Dale Earnhardt Jr. Bud Father's Day/2200 75.00 150.00
8 Dale Earnhardt Jr. Bud Father's Day Platinum/300 150.00 300.00
8 Dale Earnhardt Jr. Bud World Series/2888 50.00 100.00
8 Dale Earnhardt Jr. Bud World Series Platinum/300 175.00 300.00
8 Dale Earnhardt Jr. Bud World Series White Gold/50 300.00 450.00
8 Dale Earnhardt Jr. Oreo/4800 50.00 100.00
8 Dale Earnhardt Jr. Oreo Platinum/300 175.00 300.00
8 Dale Earnhardt Jr. Test/4000 50.00 100.00
8 Martin Truex Jr. Bass Pro Shops/444 60.00 120.00
8 Martin Truex Jr. Bass Pro Shops '04 Champion Color Chrome/600 75.00 150.00
8 Martin Truex Jr. Chance 2 Ralph Earnhardt/444 50.00 100.00
8 Martin Truex Jr. Chance 2 Richie Evans/360 40.00 80.00
8 Martin Truex Jr. Chance 2 Tear Away/360 40.00 80.00
8 Martin Truex Jr. KFC Dover Raced/300 40.00 80.00
8 Martin Truex Jr. Long John Silver's/360 40.00 80.00
8 Martin Truex Jr. Taco Bell Bristol Raced/540 60.00 120.00
8 Martin Truex Jr. Wrangler/444 50.00 100.00
9 Bill Elliott Milestones/408 50.00 100.00
9 Bill Elliott Milestones White Gold/40 250.00 400.00
9 Kasey Kahne Dodge/288 350.00 500.00
9 Kasey Kahne Dodge Refresh Color Chrome/444 100.00 200.00
9 Kasey Kahne Dodge refresh ROY AU/600 175.00 300.00
9 Kasey Kahne Dodge refresh ROY liquid metal/100 150.00 300.00
9 Kasey Kahne Dodge Mad Magazine/804 75.00 150.00
9 Kasey Kahne Dodge Mad Magazine White Gold/50 300.00 450.00
9 Kasey Kahne Dodge Mopar/444 75.00 150.00
9 Kasey Kahne Dodge Pit Cap/600 75.00 150.00
9 Kasey Kahne Dodge Pit Cap White Gold/50 300.00 500.00
9 Kasey Kahne Dodge Popeye/576 75.00 150.00
9 Kasey Kahne Mountain Dew/540 100.00 200.00
10 Scott Riggs Valvoline Wizard of Oz/288 40.00 80.00
15 Michael Waltrip NAPA/800 40.00 80.00
15 Michael Waltrip NAPA Color Chrome/300 50.00 100.00
15 Michael Waltrip NAPA Test Daytona/504 40.00 80.00
15 Michael Waltrip NAPA Stars & Stripes/288 40.00 80.00
17 Darrell Waltrip King of Bristol AU/360 60.00 120.00
18 Bobby Labonte Interstate Batteries/720 50.00 100.00
18 Bobby Labonte Interstate Batteries Color Chrome/300 60.00 120.00
18 Bobby Labonte Interstate Batteries D-Day/504 40.00 80.00
18 Bobby Labonte Interstate Batteries Shrek 2/600 30.00 60.00
18 Bobby Labonte Wellbutrin/360 40.00 80.00
18 J.J. Yeley Vigoro/204 40.00 80.00
19 Bobby Labonte Banquet/288 50.00 100.00
19 Jeremy Mayfield Dodge HEMI/288 40.00 80.00
20 Tony Stewart Coke C2/600 50.00 100.00
20 Tony Stewart Home Depot/1800 60.00 120.00
20 Tony Stewart Home Depot Color Chrome/600 75.00 150.00
20 Tony Stewart Home Depot Black Reverse/1500 60.00 120.00
20 Tony Stewart Home Depot Olympic/900 60.00 120.00
20 Tony Stewart Home Depot Olympic White Gold/25 400.00 600.00
20 Tony Stewart Home Depot Shrek 2/1500 60.00 120.00
20 Tony Stewart Home Depot Test/1200 60.00 120.00
20 Tony Stewart Home Depot 25th Anniversary/1008 60.00 120.00
21 Kevin Harvick Hershey's Kisses/1008 50.00 100.00
21 Kevin Harvick Meijer Reese's White Chocolate/288 50.00 100.00
21 Kevin Harvick Reese's/1200 50.00 100.00
21 Kevin Harvick Reese's Las Vegas Raced/240 50.00 100.00
21 Kevin Harvick Reese's RCR 35th Anniversary/444 50.00 100.00
24 Jeff Gordon Big Bird/2004 50.00 100.00
24 Jeff Gordon DuPont Flames/2400 75.00 125.00
24 Jeff Gordon DuPont Flames Color Chrome/804 100.00 175.00
24 Jeff Gordon DuPont Flames Brickyard Raced/524 75.00 125.00
24 Jeff Gordon DuPont Flames HMS 20th Anniversary/1800 75.00 125.00
24 Jeff Gordon DuPont Flames HMS 20th Ann. Platinum/300 200.00 300.00
24 Jeff Gordon DuPont Flames Wizard of Oz/2700 50.00 100.00
24 Jeff Gordon DuPont Flames Wizard of Oz Platinum/360 125.00 250.00
24 Jeff Gordon DuPont Flames Wizard of Oz White Gold/25 400.00 600.00
24 Jeff Gordon DuPont HMS20 Years Test/1824 75.00 125.00
24 Jeff Gordon DuPont Racing Stripes/660 60.00 120.00
24 Jeff Gordon DuPont Rainbow/1800 75.00 150.00
24 Jeff Gordon Pepsi Billion/1500 60.00 120.00
24 Jeff Gordon Pepsi Billion Daytona Raced/444 60.00 120.00
24 Jeff Gordon Pepsi Shards/1008 60.00 120.00
24 Jeff Gordon Pepsi Shards Talladega Raced/480 60.00 120.00
24 Jeff Gordon Santa/900 50.00 100.00
24 Jeff Gordon 400 Career Starts/624 125.00 250.00
25 Brian Vickers ditech.com/444 40.00 80.00
25 Brian Vickers ditech HMS 20th Ann/288 40.00 80.00
29 Ricky Craven ESGR Navy/288 40.00 80.00
29 Kerry Earnhardt ESGR Air Force/504 40.00 80.00
29 Kevin Harvick Coke C2/600 40.00 80.00
29 Kevin Harvick ESGR Coast Guard/600 40.00 80.00
29 Kevin Harvick Goodwrench/1500 50.00 100.00
29 Kevin Harvick Goodwrench Color Chrome/600 60.00 120.00
29 Kevin Harvick Goodwrench KISS/1500 75.00 150.00
29 Kevin Harvick Goodwrench RCR 35th Anniversary/1200 50.00 100.00
29 Kevin Harvick Goodwrench Realtree/1500 50.00 100.00
29 Kevin Harvick Ice Breakers/804 50.00 100.00
29 Kevin Harvick Powerade/600 50.00 100.00
29 Kevin Harvick Snap-On/1200 50.00 100.00
29 Bobby Labonte ESGR Army/600 50.00 100.00
29 Tony Stewart ESGR Marines/1500 50.00 100.00
29 Tony Stewart Kid Rock/1500 50.00 100.00
30 Johnny Sauter 40.00 80.00
AOL IMAX/288
31 Robby Gordon Cingular/408 40.00 80.00
31 Robby Gordon Cingular Color Chrome/288 50.00 100.00
31 Robby Gordon Cingular Black/288 40.00 80.00
31 Robby Gordon Cingular RCR 35th Ann./288 40.00 80.00
33 Kerry Earnhardt Bass Pro Shops/504 40.00 80.00
33 Kerry Earnhardt Bass Pro Shops Father's Day/360 50.00 100.00
33 Kerry Earnhardt Bass Pro Shops NRA/288 40.00 80.00
38 Kasey Kahne Great Clips/360 50.00 100.00
38 Kasey Kahne Great Clips Shark Tale/560 40.00 80.00
38 Kasey Kahne Great Clips Shark Tale White Gold/25 200.00 350.00
38 Elliott Sadler M&M's/300 60.00 120.00
38 Elliott Sadler M&M's Texas Raced/240 60.00 120.00
38 Elliott Sadler M&M's Black&White/360 60.00 120.00
38 Elliott Sadler M&M's Black&White Raced w tire/240 75.00 150.00
38 Elliott Sadler M&M's Halloween/408 50.00 100.00
38 Elliott Sadler M&M's July 4/288 50.00 100.00
38 Elliott Sadler Pedigree Wizard of Oz/360 40.00 80.00
40 Sterling Marlin Aspen Edge/288 40.00 80.00
40 Sterling Marlin Coors Light Kentucky Derby/204 50.00 100.00
41 Casey Mears Target SpongeBob/240 40.00 80.00
42 Jamie McMurray Havoline/900 50.00 100.00
42 Jamie McMurray Havoline Texaco Rising Star/360 50.00 100.00
43 Jeff Green Cheerios 40.00 80.00
45 Kyle Petty Brawny/300 40.00 80.00
45 Kyle Petty Georgia Pacific/300 40.00 80.00
45 Kyle Petty Georgia Pacific Father's Day/240 40.00 80.00
48 Jimmie Johnson Lowe's/1200 60.00 120.00
48 Jimmie Johnson Lowe's Color Chrome/480 75.00 125.00
48 Jimmie Johnson Lowe's Atlanta Raced/848 100.00 150.00
48 Jimmie Johnson Lowe's Atlanta Raced White Gold/48 300.00 450.00
48 Jimmie Johnson Lowe's HMS 20th Anniversary/900 60.00 120.00
48 Jimmie Johnson Lowe's SpongeBob/504 50.00 100.00
48 Jimmie Johnson Lowe's SpongeBob White Gold/25 300.00 450.00
48 Jimmie Johnson Lowe's Tool World/900 50.00 100.00
48 Jimmie Johnson Lowe's Tool World White Gold/25 300.00 450.00
55 Robby Gordon Fruit of the Loom/336 40.00 80.00
66 Rusty Wallace Duraflame/600 40.00 80.00
74 Kerry Earnhardt Smith & Wesson/288 40.00 80.00
77 Brendan Gaughan Kodak/288 40.00 80.00
77 Brendan Gaughan Kodak Punisher/288 40.00 80.00
77 Brendan Gaughan Kodak Wizard of Oz/288 40.00 80.00
81 Dale Earnhardt Jr. KFC/4440 40.00 80.00
81 Dale Earnhardt Jr. Menards Bristol Raced/1500 40.00 80.00
81 Dale Earnhardt Jr. Menards Bristol Raced White Gold/48 200.00 350.00
81 Dale Earnhardt Jr. Taco Bell/3000 40.00 80.00
81 Dale Earnhardt Jr. Taco Bell Platinum/300 175.00 300.00
81 Tony Stewart Bass Pro Shops/900 40.00 80.00
81 Martin Truex Jr. Chance 2 Robert Gee/360 30.00 60.00
84 Kyle Busch CarQuest/360 40.00 80.00
88 Dale Jarrett UPS/300 50.00 100.00
88 Dale Jarrett UPS Color Chrome/300 60.00 120.00
88 Dale Jarrett UPS Raced w tire/240 60.00 120.00
88 Dale Jarrett UPS Arnold Palmer/492 75.00 125.00
88 Dale Jarrett UPS Monsters/540 40.00 80.00
88 Dale Jarrett UPS Monsters White Gold/25 200.00 350.00
91 Bill Elliott UAW Daimler Chrysler w tire swatch/288 75.00 125.00
91 Bill Elliott 40.00 80.00
Visteon/360
92 Tony Stewart McDonald's/600 40.00 80.00
98 Bill Elliott Coke C2/360 40.00 80.00
98 Bill Elliott McDonald's/360 40.00 80.00
99 Michael Waltrip Aaron's Dream Machine LeAnn Rimes/288 40.00 80.00
99 Michael Waltrip Best Western/228 40.00 80.00
0 Ward Burton NetZero Hi Speed/204 40.00 80.00
0 Ward Burton NetZero Hi Speed Shark Tale/444 40.00 80.00
01 Joe Nemechek Army GI Joe/288 50.00 100.00
01 Joe Nemechek Army Time Magazine/360 50.00 100.00
04 Nextel Inaugural Event Car/444 40.00 80.00

2004 Action/RCCA Historical Series 1:24

2 Dale Earnhardt Mello Yello '80 Ventura/1800 40.00 70.00
3 Dale Earnhardt AC Delco '96 Monte Carlo/1500 45.00 75.00
3 Dale Earnhardt Goodwrench Olympic '96 Monte Carlo/2700 45.00 75.00
3 Dale Earnhardt Goodwrench Peter Max '00 Monte Carlo/2400 60.00 100.00
3 Dale Earnhardt Wheaties 1997 Monte Carlo/2508 50.00 80.00
3 Dale Earnhardt Wrangler 1985 Camaro/2400 45.00 75.00
7 Dale Earnhardt Jr. Church Brothers 1997 Monte Carlo/2508 50.00 75.00
7 Kyle Petty 7-Eleven 1985 T-bird/408 40.00 60.00
8 Dale Earnhardt Jr. Bud Olympic '00 Monte Carlo/2508 50.00 75.00
8 Dale Earnhardt Jr. Bud 2003 Monte Carlo Phoenix Raced/504 50.00 75.00
9 Bill Elliott Coors 1985 T-bird/504 50.00 80.00
9 Bill Elliott Coors Light 1991 Thunderbird/504 45.00 75.00
17 Darrell Waltrip Tide 200th Chevy Win '87 Monte Carlo/600 40.00 60.00
24 Jeff Gordon DuPont 300th Chevy Win '96 Monte Carlo Chrome/900 45.00 75.00
28 Davey Allison Havoline 1993 Thunderbird/600 35.00 60.00
29 Kevin Harvick Goodwrench Service Plus '01 Monte Carlo black numbers/1008 50.00 80.00
43 Richard Petty STP 100th Chevy Win 1980 Monte Carlo Chrome/600 45.00 75.00
43 Richard Petty STP 200th Win 1984 Grand Prix/444 60.00 100.00
43 Richard Petty STP 200th Win '84 Grand Prix Brushed Metal/444 45.00 75.00
43 Richard Petty STP 200th Win '84 Grand Prix Brushed Metal Clear Window Bank/504 45.00 75.00
43 Richard Petty STP 20th Anniversary 200th Win/444 35.00 60.00
48 Jimmie Johnson Lowe's 400th Chevy Win 2003 Monte Carlo Chrome/600 45.00 75.00

2004 Action/RCCA Historical Series Elite 1:24

2 Dale Earnhardt Mello Yello '80 Ventura/2508 70.00 110.00
3 Dale Earnhardt AC Delco '96 Monte Carlo Platinum/408 100.00 175.00
3 Dale Earnhardt Goodwrench Crash '97 Daytona Raced/10,000 250.00 400.00
3 Dale Earnhardt Goodwrench Crash 1997 Daytona Raced Platinum/504 275.00 450.00
3 Dale Earnhardt Goodwrench Olympic 1996 Monte Carlo/3996 75.00 125.00
3 Dale Earnhardt Goodwrench Olympic 1996 Monte Carlo Platinum/408 200.00 300.00
3 Dale Earnhardt Goodwrench Peter Max '00 Monte Carlo Plat./408 125.00 200.00
7 Kyle Petty 7-Eleven 1985 T-bird/408 80.00 125.00
8 Dale Earnhardt Jr. Bud 2003 Monte Carlo Phoenix Raced/1008 90.00 150.00
8 Dale Earnhardt Jr. Bud Olympic 2000 Monte Carlo Platinum/408 125.00 250.00
9 Bill Elliott Coors 1985 T-bird/504 80.00 125.00
9 Bill Elliott Coors Light '91 Thunderbird/504 90.00 135.00
28 Davey Allison Havoline 1993 Thunderbird/600 90.00 135.00
29 Kevin Harvick Goodwrench Service Plus 2001 Monte Carlo black numbers/1500 90.00 150.00
29 Kevin Harvick Goodwrench Service Plus 2001 Monte Carlo black numbers Platinum/300 100.00 175.00
43 Richard Petty STP 20th Anniversary 200th Win AU/444 150.00 250.00

2004 Action/RCCA Metal Elite 1:24

15 Michael Waltrip NAPA/800 50.00 100.00
29 Kevin Harvick Goodwrench/1200 50.00 100.00

2005 Action Clearly Collectibles 1:24

SOME CARS NOT PRICED DUE TO SCARCITY
2 Rusty Wallace Atlanta Raced Spark Plug/8
2 Rusty Wallace Bristol Raced Spark Plug/8
2 Rusty Wallace Daytona Raced Spark Plug/8
2 Rusty Wallace Talladega Raced Spark Plug/8
2 Rusty Wallace Texas Raced Spark Plug/8
9 Kasey Kahne Richmond Raced Tire/650 60.00 120.00
24 Jeff Gordon Daytona Raced Tire/2000 75.00 150.00
48 Jimmie Johnson Daytona Raced Lugnut/100 60.00 120.00
48 Jimmie Johnson Las Vegas Raced Lugnut/100 60.00 120.00
48 Jimmie Johnson Las Vegas Raced Spark Plug/8
88 Dale Jarrett Raced Sheet Metal/200 60.00 120.00

2005 Action Performance 1:24

2 Rusty Wallace Miller Lite Hometown Saint Louis 35.00 60.00
2 Rusty Wallace Miller Lite Last Call 25.00 50.00
9 Kasey Kahne Dodge Hometown Enumclaw 35.00 60.00
9/43 Kasey Kahne Richard Petty Dodge '75 Charger STP '05 Charger/1896 50.00 100.00
9/43 Kasey Kahne Richard Petty Dodge STP QVC/504 50.00 100.00
20 Tony Stewart Home Depot Hometown Columbus 35.00 60.00
20 Tony Stewart Home Depot Madagascar Promo 20.00 40.00
20 DeAngelo Williams Memphis Tigers Promo The Race is On 125.00 175.00
24 Jeff Gordon Halston Z-14 Promo in window box 50.00 100.00
24 Jeff Gordon Milestones '94 Charlotte Win/6000 40.00 80.00
24 Jeff Gordon Milestones 3-Time Daytona Winner/6000 40.00 80.00
24 Jeff Gordon Milestones 4-Time Champion/6000 40.00 80.00
24 Jeff Gordon Milestones 4-Time Brickyard Winner/6000 40.00 80.00
27 Rusty Wallace Milestones '89 Champion/4008 40.00 80.00
29 Kevin Harvick Goodwrench 35.00 60.00

Hometown Bakersfield
31 Jeff Burton Cingular 25.00 40.00
31 Jeff Burton Cingular black AP box 20.00 35.00
38 Elliott Sadler M&M's Hometown Emporia 35.00 60.00
88 Dale Jarrett UPS Hometown Conover 35.00 60.00
88 Dale Jarrett UPS Herbie 20.00 40.00
07 Dave Blaney Jack Daniel's 25.00 50.00
07 Dave Blaney Jack Daniel's in plain black AP box 20.00 40.00

2005 Action President's Platinum Series 1:24

2 Rusty Wallace Miller Lite AU/1100 w Fred Wagenhals AU 125.00 225.00

2005 Action Racing Collectables 1:24

1 Martin Truex Jr. Bass Pro Shops/6120 45.00 70.00
1 Martin Truex Jr. Bass Pro Shops Clear Window Bank/228 45.00 70.00
1 Martin Truex Jr. Bass Pro Shops GM Dealers/768 45.00 70.00
1 Martin Truex Jr. Bass Pro Shops Matco/72 45.00 70.00
1 Martin Truex Jr. Bass Pro Shops QVC/400 45.00 70.00
1 Martin Truex Jr. Bass Pro Shops Black/3000 60.00 100.00
1 Martin Truex Jr. Bass Pro Shops Black GM Dealers/204 60.00 100.00
1 Martin Truex Jr. Bass Pro Shops Black QVC/288 60.00 100.00
1 Martin Truex Jr. Enterprise RAC/5808 100.00 250.00
2 Clint Bowyer AC Delco/2148 35.00 60.00
2 Clint Bowyer AC Delco Chris Cagle/816 35.00 60.00
2 Clint Bowyer AC Delco Chris Cagle GM Dealers/156 35.00 60.00
2 Jimmy Spencer Snap-On 85th Anniversary/732 40.00 65.00
2 Jimmy Spencer Snap-On 85th Anniversary Snap-On/3000 40.00 65.00
2 Rusty Wallace Kodak/5568 45.00 70.00
2 Rusty Wallace Kodak Clear Window Bank/228 45.00 70.00
2 Rusty Wallace Kodak Liquid Metal/708 60.00 100.00
2 Rusty Wallace Kodak Matco/48 45.00 70.00
2 Rusty Wallace Kodak QVC/504 45.00 70.00
2 Rusty Wallace Miller Genuine Draft/9012 45.00 70.00
2 Rusty Wallace Miller Genuine Draft Clear Window Bank/264 45.00 70.00
2 Rusty Wallace Miller Genuine Draft Matco/72 45.00 70.00
2 Rusty Wallace Miller Genuine Draft Pearl Chrome/720 60.00 100.00
2 Rusty Wallace Miller Genuine Draft QVC/1008 45.00 70.00
2 Rusty Wallace Miller Lite/7584 45.00 70.00
2 Rusty Wallace Miller Lite Clear Window Bank/276 45.00 70.00
2 Rusty Wallace Miller Lite Color Chrome/2004 75.00 125.00
2 Rusty Wallace Miller Lite Liquid Metal/2004 60.00 100.00
2 Rusty Wallace Miller Lite Mac Tools/108 45.00 70.00
2 Rusty Wallace Miller Lite Matco/180 45.00 70.00
2 Rusty Wallace Miller Lite QVC/1008 45.00 70.00
2 Rusty Wallace Miller Lite Flames Bristol/4008 45.00 70.00
2 Rusty Wallace Miller Lite Flames Bristol QVC/1008 45.00 70.00
2 Rusty Wallace Miller lite Last Call Daytona Shootout/4476 50.00 75.00
2 Rusty Wallace Miller Lite Last Call Daytona Shootout Clear Window Bank/204 50.00 75.00
2 Rusty Wallace Miller Lite Last Call Daytona Shootout Liquid Metal/2004 75.00 125.00
2 Rusty Wallace Miller Lite Last Call Daytona Shootout QVC/504 50.00 75.00
2 Rusty Wallace Miller Lite Last Call Test/2484 50.00 75.00
2 Rusty Wallace Miller Lite Last Call Test QVC/288 50.00 75.00
2 Rusty Wallace Miller Lite Last Race/3504 50.00 75.00
2 Rusty Wallace Miller Lite Last Race Mac Tools/120 50.00 75.00
2 Rusty Wallace Miller Lite Last Race Matco/98 50.00 75.00
2 Rusty Wallace Miller Lite Last Race QVC/2004 50.00 75.00
2 Rusty Wallace Miller Lite Sirius/2508 50.00 75.00
2 Rusty Wallace Miller Lite Sirius QVC/288 50.00 75.00
2 Rusty Wallace Miller Lite 500 Consecutive Starts/2508 50.00 75.00
2 Rusty Wallace Mobil/5676 45.00 70.00
2 Rusty Wallace Mobil Clear Window Bank/276 45.00 70.00
2 Rusty Wallace Mobil QVC/504 45.00 70.00
2 Rusty Wallace Snap-On 85th Anniversary/5508 45.00 70.00
2 Rusty Wallace Snap-On 85th Anniversary Clear Window Bank/252 45.00 70.00
2 Rusty Wallace Snap-On 85th Anniversary Pearl Chrome/720 60.00 100.00
2 Rusty Wallace 700 Starts/3816 60.00 100.00
2 Rusty Wallace 700 Starts Matco/48 60.00 100.00
2 Rusty Wallace 700 Starts QVC/504 60.00 100.00
5 Kyle Busch CarQuest/1284 50.00 75.00
5 Kyle Busch Kellogg's/2340 60.00 100.00
5 Kyle Busch Kellogg's Clear Window Bank/192 60.00 100.00
5 Kyle Busch Kellogg's GM Dealers/144 60.00 100.00
5 Kyle Busch Kellogg's Matco/36 60.00 100.00
5 Kyle Busch Kellogg's QVC/144 60.00 100.00
5 Kyle Busch Kellogg's California Raced/2508 60.00 100.00
5 Kyle Busch Kellogg's California Raced QVC/120 60.00 100.00
5 Kyle Busch Kellogg's Rookie of the Year Color Chrome/5004 75.00 125.00
5 Kyle Busch Kellogg's ROY Color Chrome GM Dealers/288 75.00 125.00
5 Kyle Busch Kellogg's Rookie of the Year Color Chrome QVC/504 75.00 125.00
5 Kyle Busch Kellogg's Star Wars/2484 50.00 75.00
5 Kyle Busch Kellogg's Star Wars Clear Window Bank/204 50.00 75.00
5 Blake Feese Lowe's AU/900 40.00 65.00
5 Adrian Fernandez Lowe's/1500 40.00 65.00
5 Adrian Fernandez Lowe's GM Dealers/60 40.00 65.00
5 Boston Reid Lowe's AU/824 40.00 65.00
6 Bill Elliott Charlie Brown Christmas/4008 50.00 75.00
6 Bill Elliott Charlie Brown Christmas QVC/288 50.00 75.00
6 Ron Hornaday Goodwrench SuperTruck/812 40.00 65.00
6 Mark Martin Crown Royal IROC/2232 75.00 125.00
6 Mark Martin Crown Royal IROC Brushed Metal/360 100.00 150.00
6 Mark Martin Crown Royal IROC GM Dealers/84 75.00 125.00
6 Mark Martin Crown Royal IROC QVC/504 75.00 125.00
7 Robby Gordon Jim Beam/4752 50.00 75.00
7 Robby Gordon Jim Beam Clear Window Bank/144 50.00 75.00
7 Robby Gordon Jim Beam GM Dealers/312 50.00 75.00
7 Robby Gordon Jim Beam Liquid Metal/720 60.00 100.00
7 Robby Gordon Jim Beam QVC/288 50.00 75.00
8 Dale Earnhardt Jr. Bud/33,960 40.00 70.00
8 Dale Earnhardt Jr. Bud Anheuser Busch/336 40.00 70.00
8 Dale Earnhardt Jr. Bud Clear Window Bank/612 40.00 70.00
8 Dale Earnhardt Jr. Bud GM Dealers/5004 40.00 70.00
8 Dale Earnhardt Jr. Bud Liquid Metal/3504 60.00 100.00
8 Dale Earnhardt Jr. Bud Mac Tools/300 40.00 70.00
8 Dale Earnhardt Jr. Bud Matco/492 40.00 70.00
8 Dale Earnhardt Jr. Bud QVC/7500 40.00 70.00
8 Dale Earnhardt Jr. Bud Born On Feb.12/5004 75.00 125.00
8 Dale Earnhardt Jr. Bud Born On Feb.12 Clear Window Bank/708 50.00 75.00
8 Dale Earnhardt Jr. Bud Born On Feb.12 GM Dealers/2640 75.00 125.00
8 Dale Earnhardt Jr. Bud Born On Feb.12 Matco/480 75.00 125.00
8 Dale Earnhardt Jr. Bud Born On Feb.12 QVC/504 75.00 125.00
8 Dale Earnhardt Jr. Bud Born On Feb.17/13,752 60.00 100.00
8 Dale Earnhardt Jr. Bud Born On Feb.17 Clear Window Bank/648 50.00 75.00
8 Dale Earnhardt Jr. Bud Born On Feb.17 GM Dealers/2280 60.00 100.00
8 Dale Earnhardt Jr. Bud Born On Feb.17 GM Dealers Chrome/1512 75.00 125.00
8 Dale Earnhardt Jr. Bud Born On Feb.17 Matco/480 60.00 100.00
8 Dale Earnhardt Jr. Bud Born On Feb.17 QVC/600 60.00 100.00
8 Dale Earnhardt Jr. Bud Born On Feb.20/22,668 60.00 100.00
8 Dale Earnhardt Jr. Bud Born On Feb.20 Clear Window Bank/900 50.00 75.00
8 Dale Earnhardt Jr. Bud Born On Feb.20 GM Dealers/3588 60.00 100.00
8 Dale Earnhardt Jr. Bud Born On Feb.20 Mac Tools/300 60.00 100.00
8 Dale Earnhardt Jr. Bud Born On Feb.20 Matco/480 60.00 100.00
8 Dale Earnhardt Jr. Bud Born On Feb.20 QVC/2004 60.00 100.00
8 Dale Earnhardt Jr. Bud MLB All Star Game/15,804 40.00 70.00
8 Dale Earnhardt Jr. Bud MLB All Star Game Anheuser Busch/156 40.00 70.00
8 Dale Earnhardt Jr. Bud MLB All Star Game Clear Window Bank/600 40.00 70.00
8 Dale Earnhardt Jr. Bud MLB All Star Game GM Dealers Chrome/1992 60.00 100.00
8 Dale Earnhardt Jr. Bud MLB All Star Game Mac Tools/300 40.00 70.00
8 Dale Earnhardt Jr. Bud MLB All Star Game Matco/96 40.00 70.00
8 Dale Earnhardt Jr. Bud MLB All Star Game QVC/2004 40.00 70.00
8 Dale Earnhardt Jr. Bud MLB All Star Game Chicago Raced/2880 50.00 75.00
8 Dale Earnhardt Jr. Bud MLB All Star Game Chicago Raced QVC/2004 50.00 75.00
8 Dale Earnhardt Jr. Bud Test w Tony Eury AU/5016 60.00 100.00
8 Dale Earnhardt Jr. Bud 3 Doors Down/15,468 40.00 70.00
8 Dale Earnhardt Jr. Bud 3 Doors Down Clear Window Bank/636 40.00 70.00
8 Dale Earnhardt Jr. Bud 3 Doors Down Anhauser Busch/996 40.00 70.00
8 Dale Earnhardt Jr. Bud 3 Doors Down GM Dealers/2160 40.00 70.00
8 D.Earnhardt Jr. Bud 3 Doors Down Mac Tools/348 40.00 70.00
8 Dale Earnhardt Jr. Bud 3 Doors Down Matco/108 40.00 70.00
8 Dale Earnhardt Jr. Bud 3 Doors Down QVC/2004 40.00 70.00
8 Martin Truex Jr. Bass Pro/5004 40.00 65.00
8 Martin Truex Jr. Bass Pro Clear Window Bank/204 40.00 65.00
8 Martin Truex Jr. Bass Pro GM Dealers/552 40.00 65.00
8 Martin Truex Jr. Bass Pro QVC/504 40.00 65.00
8 Martin Truex Jr. Bass Pro Indy Raced/1812 50.00 75.00
8 Martin Truex Jr. Bass Pro Indy Raced QVC/288 50.00 75.00
8 Martin Truex Jr. Bass Pro Mexico City Raced/2028 40.00 65.00
8 Martin Truex Jr. Bass Pro Mexico City Raced GM Dealers/360 40.00 65.00
8 Martin Truex Jr. Bass Pro Talladega Raced/2652 40.00 65.00
8 Martin Truex Jr. Bass Pro Talladega Raced GM Dealers/444 40.00 65.00
8 Martin Truex Jr. Bass Pro Talladega Raced QVC/288 40.00 65.00
8 Martin Truex Jr. Crown Royal IROC/2172 40.00 65.00
8 Martin Truex Jr. Crown Royal IROC QVC/288 40.00 65.00
8 Martin Truex Jr. Chance 2 Test/1848 40.00 65.00
8 Martin Truex Jr. Chance 2 Test GM Dealers/252 40.00 65.00
8 Martin Truex Jr. Chance 2 Test QVC/288 40.00 65.00
9 Kasey Kahne Dodge/13,284 50.00 75.00
9 Kasey Kahne Dodge Clear Window Bank/396 50.00 75.00
9 Kasey Kahne Dodge Liquid Metal/2508 60.00 100.00
9 Kasey Kahne Dodge Mac Tools/300 50.00 75.00
9 Kasey Kahne Dodge Matco/108 50.00 75.00
9 Kasey Kahne Dodge QVC/1500 50.00 75.00
9 Kasey Kahne Dodge Richmond Raced/9420 50.00 75.00
9 Kasey Kahne Dodge Richmond Raced Liquid Metal/1056 60.00 100.00
9 Kasey Kahne Dodge Richmond Raced QVC/1008 50.00 75.00
9 Kasey Kahne Dodge Longest Yard/4344 50.00 75.00
9 Kasey Kahne Dodge Longest Yard QVC/288 50.00 75.00
9 Kasey Kahne Dodge Mega Cab/2520 50.00 75.00
9 Kasey Kahne Dodge Mega Cab QVC/288 50.00 75.00
9 Kasey Kahne Dodge Pit Cap White/7476 50.00 75.00
9 Kasey Kahne Dodge Pit Cap White Clear Window Bank/336 50.00 75.00
9 Kasey Kahne Dodge Pit Cap White QVC/504 50.00 75.00
9 Kasey Kahne Dodge Retro Bud Shootout/6000 50.00 75.00
9 Kasey Kahne Dodge Retro Bud Shootout Clear Window Bank/300 50.00 75.00
9 Kasey Kahne Dodge Retro Bud Shootout Liquid Metal/1008 60.00 100.00
9 Kasey Kahne Dodge Retro Bud Shootout QVC/1008 50.00 75.00
9 Kasey Kahne Dodge Test/1452 50.00 75.00
9 Kasey Kahne Mopar/4500 60.00 100.00
9 Kasey Kahne Mopar QVC/288 60.00 100.00
9 Kasey Kahne Mountain Dew/8016 50.00 75.00
9 Kasey Kahne Mountain Dew Clear Window Bank/348 50.00 75.00
9 Kasey Kahne Mountain Dew QVC/600 50.00 75.00
10 Scott Riggs Valvoline/696 40.00 65.00
10 Scott Riggs Valvoline QVC/120 40.00 65.00
10 Scott Riggs Valvoline Herbie Fully Loaded/1140 40.00 65.00
10 Scott Riggs Valvoline Herbie Clear Window Bank/144 40.00 65.00
10 Scott Riggs Valvoline Nickelback/1152 40.00 65.00
10 Scott Riggs Valvoline Nickelback GM Dealers/60 40.00 65.00
10 Scott Riggs Valvoline Nickelback QVC/120 40.00 65.00
11 Steve Kinser Crown Royal IROC/1464 40.00 65.00
11 Jason Leffler FedEx/3960 40.00 65.00
11 Jason Leffler FedEx QVC/120 40.00 65.00
11 Jason Leffler FedEx Freight/5352 40.00 65.00
11 Jason Leffler FedEx Ground/2208 40.00 65.00
11 Jason Leffler FedEx Ground GM Dealers/48 40.00 65.00
11 Jason Leffler FedEx Kinkos/2448 40.00 65.00
12 Darrell Waltrip Tundra One & Done/3504 50.00 75.00
12 Darrell Waltrip Tundra One & Done BD&A/1752 50.00 75.00
15 Kyle Busch ditech.com SuperTruck Charlotte Raced w tire/1956 40.00 70.00
15 Kyle Busch ditech.com SuperTruck Charlotte Raced w tire QVC/144 40.00 70.00
15 Michael Waltrip Napa/4512 40.00 65.00
15 Michael Waltrip Napa Clear Window Bank/192 40.00 65.00
15 Michael Waltrip Napa Matco/72 40.00 65.00
15 Michael Waltrip Napa QVC/360 40.00 65.00
15 Michael Waltrip Napa Stars & Stripes/1440 40.00 65.00
15 Michael Waltrip Napa Stars & Stripes GM Dealers/84 40.00 65.00
17 Matt Kenseth Crown Royal IROC/1272 40.00 65.00
18 Bobby Labonte Boniva/996 60.00 100.00
18 Bobby Labonte FedEx/2508 60.00 100.00
18 Bobby Labonte FedEx GM Dealers/180 60.00 100.00
18 Bobby Labonte FedEx Mac Tools/120 60.00 100.00
18 Bobby Labonte Interstate Batteries/4872 40.00 65.00
18 Bobby Labonte Interstate Batteries Clear Window Bank/204 40.00 65.00
18 Bobby Labonte Interstate Batteries GM Dealers/360 40.00 65.00
18 Bobby Labonte Interstate Batteries Matco/84 40.00 65.00
18 Bobby Labonte Interstate Batteries QVC/288 40.00 65.00
18 Bobby Labonte Interstate Batteries Madagascar/3864 40.00 65.00
18 Bobby Labonte Interstate Batteries Madagascar Clear Window Bank/144 40.00 65.00
18 Bobby Labonte Interstate Batteries Madagascar GM Dealers/144 40.00 65.00
18 Bobby Labonte Interstate Batteries Madagascar Matco/84 40.00 65.00
18 Bobby Labonte Interstate Batteries Madagascar QVC/408 40.00 65.00
18 J.J. Yeley Vigoro AU/2832 50.00 75.00
18 J.J. Yeley Vigoro Clear Window Bank AU/120 50.00 75.00
18 J.J. Yeley Vigoro Matco AU/36 50.00 75.00
19 Jeremy Mayfield Dodge/2304 35.00 60.00
19 Jeremy Mayfield Dodge Clear Window Bank/156 35.00 60.00
19 Jeremy Mayfield Dodge Matco/60 35.00 60.00
19 Jeremy Mayfield Dodge QVC/144 35.00 60.00
19 Jeremy Mayfield Dodge Bad News Bears/1884 35.00 60.00
19 Jeremy Mayfield Dodge Black Reverse/2880 35.00 60.00
19 Jeremy Mayfield Dodge Retro Bud Shootout/1356 35.00 60.00
19 Jeremy Mayfield Dodge Retro Bud Shootout Clear Window Bank/240 35.00 60.00
19 Jeremy Mayfield Dodge Retro Bud Shootout QVC/144 35.00 60.00
19 Jeremy Mayfield Mountain Dew Pitch Black/5004 40.00 65.00
19 Jeremy Mayfield Mountain Dew Pitch Black QVC/120 40.00 65.00
20 Danny Lasoski Crown Royal IROC/1344 40.00 65.00
20 Tony Stewart Home Depot/9000 75.00 125.00
20 Tony Stewart Home Depot Clear Window Bank/264 60.00 100.00
20 Tony Stewart Home Depot GM Dealers/1008 75.00 125.00
20 Tony Stewart Home Depot Matco/300 75.00 125.00
20 Tony Stewart Home Depot QVC/720 75.00 125.00
20 Tony Stewart Home Depot Brickyard Raced/3012 100.00 175.00
20 Tony Stewart Home Depot Champion Color Chrome/8492 75.00 125.00
20 T.Stewart Home Depot Champion Color Chrome Mac Tools/504 75.00 125.00
20 Tony Stewart Home Depot Champion Color Chrome QVC/2508 75.00 125.00
20 Tony Stewart Home Depot Brickyard Raced GM Dealers/288 75.00 125.00
20 Tony Stewart Home Depot Brickyard Raced QVC/504 75.00 125.00
20 Tony Stewart Home Depot Daytona Raced/2700 75.00 125.00
20 Tony Stewart Home Depot Daytona Raced QVC/288 75.00 125.00
20 Tony Stewart Home Depot KaBOOM/3000 50.00 75.00
20 Tony Stewart Home Depot KaBOOM GM Dealers/168 50.00 75.00
20 Tony Stewart Home Depot KaBOOM QVC/288 50.00 75.00
20 Tony Stewart Home Depot Madagascar/4752 50.00 75.00
20 Tony Stewart Home Depot Madagascar Clear Window Bank/216 50.00 75.00
20 Tony Stewart Home Depot Madagascar GM Dealers/204 50.00 75.00
20 Tony Stewart Home Depot Madagascar Liquid Metal/600 60.00 100.00
20 Tony Stewart Home Depot Madagascar Mac Tools/300 50.00 75.00
20 Tony Stewart Home Depot Madagascar Matco/144 50.00 75.00
20 Tony Stewart Home Depot Madagascar QVC/504 50.00 75.00
20 Tony Stewart Home Depot Test 75.00 125.00

Greg Zipadelli AU/2508
1 Kevin Harvick Hershey's Take 5/4872 35.00 60.00
1 Kevin Harvick Hershey's Take 5 GM Dealers/468 35.00 60.00
1 Kevin Harvick Hershey's Take 5 QVC/288 35.00 60.00
1 Kevin Harvick Pelon Pelo Rico/2400 35.00 60.00
1 Kevin Harvick Pelon Pelo Rico Clear Window Bank/168 35.00 60.00
1 Kevin Harvick Pelon Pelo Rico GM Dealers/228 35.00 60.00
1 Kevin Harvick Reese's/6144 40.00 65.00
1 Kevin Harvick Reese's GM Dealers/600 40.00 65.00
1 Kevin Harvick Reese's QVC/288 40.00 65.00
1 Kevin Harvick Reese's Honey Roasted/2340 40.00 65.00
1 Kevin Harvick Reese's Honey Roasted Liquid Metal/1164 50.00 75.00
1 Kevin Harvick Twizzlers/1680 35.00 60.00
1 Kevin Harvick Twizzlers GM Dealers/168 35.00 60.00
1 Brandon Miller Reese's/804 40.00 65.00
24 Jeff Gordon DuPont Flames/12,744 50.00 75.00
24 Jeff Gordon DuPont Flames Clear Window Bank/408 50.00 75.00
24 Jeff Gordon DuPont Flames GM Dealers/2700 50.00 75.00
24 Jeff Gordon DuPont Flames Matco/204 50.00 75.00
24 Jeff Gordon DuPont Flames QVC/1500 50.00 75.00
24 Jeff Gordon DuPont Flames Daytona Raced/8856 50.00 75.00
24 Jeff Gordon DuPont Flames Daytona Raced GM Dealers/638 50.00 75.00
24 Jeff Gordon DuPont Flames Daytona Raced QVC/624 50.00 75.00
24 Jeff Gordon DuPont Flames Martinsville Raced/3528 50.00 75.00
24 Jeff Gordon DuPont Flames Martinsville Raced GM Dealers/180 50.00 75.00
24 Jeff Gordon DuPont Flames Martinsville Raced QVC/288 50.00 75.00
24 Jeff Gordon DuPont Flames Performance Alliance Reverse/10,020 50.00 75.00
24 Jeff Gordon DuPont Flames Performance Alliance Reverse Clear Window Bank/402 50.00 75.00
24 Jeff Gordon DuPont Flames Performance Alliance Reverse GM Dealers/768 50.00 75.00
24 Jeff Gordon DuPont Flames Performance Alliance Reverse Liquid Metal/1008 75.00 125.00
24 Jeff Gordon DuPont Flames Performance Alliance Reverse QVC/1500 50.00 75.00
24 Jeff Gordon DuPont Test Robbie Loomis AU/2508 50.00 75.00
24 Jeff Gordon Mighty Mouse/7356 50.00 75.00
24 Jeff Gordon Mighty Mouse Clear Window Bank/432 50.00 75.00
24 Jeff Gordon Mighty Mouse GM Dealers/648 50.00 75.00
24 Jeff Gordon Mighty Mouse Liquid Metal/1008 60.00 100.00
24 Jeff Gordon Mighty Mouse QVC/1800 50.00 75.00
24 Jeff Gordon Pepsi Daytona/8160 50.00 75.00
24 Jeff Gordon Pepsi Daytona Clear Window Bank/360 50.00 75.00
24 Jeff Gordon Pepsi Daytona GM Dealers/720 50.00 75.00
24 Jeff Gordon Pepsi Daytona Mac Tools/300 50.00 75.00
24 Jeff Gordon Pepsi Daytona QVC/504 50.00 75.00
24 Jeff Gordon Pepsi Star Wars/10,896 50.00 75.00
24 Jeff Gordon Pepsi Star Wars Clear Window Bank/468 50.00 75.00
24 Jeff Gordon Pepsi Star Wars GM Dealers/720 50.00 75.00
24 Jeff Gordon Pepsi Star Wars Mac Tools/300 50.00 75.00
24 Jeff Gordon Pepsi Star Wars Matco/84 50.00 75.00
24 Jeff Gordon Pepsi Star Wars QVC/2508 50.00 75.00
24 Jeff Gordon Pepsi Star Wars Talladega Raced/6756 50.00 75.00
24 Jeff Gordon Pepsi Star Wars Talladega Raced GM Dealers/608 50.00 75.00
24 Jeff Gordon Pepsi Star Wars Talladega Raced QVC/1008 50.00 75.00
24 Jeff Gordon Santa Holiday/3504 50.00 75.00
25 Brian Vickers GMAC/1488 40.00 65.00
25 B.Vickers GMAC QVC/288 40.00 65.00
25 Brian Vickers GMAC Green Day/1272 40.00 65.00
25 Brian Vickers GMAC Green Day GM Dealers/72 40.00 65.00
29 Kevin Harvick Goodwrench/6564 40.00 65.00
29 Kevin Harvick Goodwrench Clear Window Bank/216 40.00 65.00
29 Kevin Harvick Goodwrench GM Dealers/1200 40.00 65.00
29 Kevin Harvick Goodwrench Matco/120 40.00 65.00
29 Kevin Harvick Goodwrench QVC/504 40.00 65.00
29 Kevin Harvick Goodwrench Bristol Raced/2400 40.00 65.00
29 Kevin Harvick Goodwrench Bristol Raced GM Dealers/276 40.00 65.00
29 Kevin Harvick Goodwrench Atlanta/6000 40.00 65.00
29 Kevin Harvick Goodwrench Atlanta Clear Window Bank/240 40.00 65.00
29 Kevin Harvick Goodwrench Atlanta GM Dealers/492 40.00 65.00
29 Kevin Harvick Goodwrench Atlanta GM Dealers Chrome/2508 60.00 100.00
29 Kevin Harvick Goodwrench Brickyard/4032 40.00 65.00
29 Kevin Harvick Goodwrench Brickyard Clear Window Bank/204 40.00 65.00
29 Kevin Harvick Goodwrench Brickyard GM Dealers/720 40.00 65.00
29 Kevin Harvick Goodwrench Brickyard GM Dealers Chrome/1500 60.00 100.00
29 Kevin Harvick Goodwrench Brickyard QVC/504 40.00 65.00
29 Kevin Harvick Goodwrench Daytona/5304 40.00 65.00
29 Kevin Harvick Goodwrench Daytona Clear Window Bank/216 40.00 65.00
29 Kevin Harvick Goodwrench Daytona GM Dealers/2004 40.00 65.00
29 Kevin Harvick Goodwrench Daytona GM Dealers Chrome/2508 60.00 100.00
29 Kevin Harvick Goodwrench Daytona QVC/504 40.00 65.00
29 Kevin Harvick Goodwrench Gretchen Wilson/3480 40.00 65.00
29 Kevin Harvick Goodwrench Gretchen Wilson GM Dealers/1200 40.00 65.00
29 Kevin Harvick Goodwrench Gretchen Wilson QVC/120 40.00 65.00
29 Kevin Harvick Goodwrench Quicksilver/5004 40.00 65.00
29 Kevin Harvick Goodwrench Quicksilver CW Bank/168 40.00 65.00
29 Kevin Harvick Goodwrench Quicksilver GM Dealers Chrome/1500 60.00 100.00
29 Kevin Harvick Goodwrench Quicksilver QVC/288 40.00 65.00
29 Kevin Harvick Goodwrench Test Todd Berrier AU/2508 50.00 75.00
29 Kevin Harvick Reese's Big Cup/1632 40.00 65.00
29 Kevin Harvick Reese's Big Cup GM Dealers/336 40.00 65.00
29 Kevin Harvick Snap-On/2508 45.00 70.00
29 Kevin Harvick Snap-On Snap On/3000 45.00 70.00
31 Jeff Burton Cingular/2438 50.00 75.00
31 Jeff Burton Cingular Clear Window Bank/144 50.00 75.00
31 Jeff Burton Cingular Cingular/30,000 50.00 75.00
31 Jeff Burton Cingular Beneficial/1164 50.00 75.00
31 Jeff Burton Cingular GM Dealers/144 50.00 75.00
31 Jeff Burton Cingular Matco/36 50.00 75.00
31 Jeff Burton Cingular QVC/144 50.00 75.00
31 Jeff Burton Cingular Big & Rich/1452 40.00 65.00
31 Jeff Burton Cingular Big & Rich QVC/120 40.00 65.00
33 Tony Raines The Outdoor Channel/250 100.00 200.00
33 Tony Raines Yardman/250 35.00 60.00
33 Tony Stewart James Dean 50th Anniversary/5244 40.00 65.00
33 Tony Stewart James Dean 50th Anniversary GM Dealers/432 40.00 65.00
33 Tony Stewart James Dean 50th Anniversary QVC/504 40.00 65.00
33 Tony Stewart Mr.Clean AutoDry/2364 40.00 65.00
33 Tony Stewart Mr.Clean AutoDry Clear Window Bank/144 40.00 65.00
33 Tony Stewart Mr.Clean AutoDry Daytona Raced/4284 40.00 65.00
33 Tony Stewart Mr.Clean AutoDry Daytona Raced GM Dealers/240 40.00 65.00
33 Tony Stewart Mr.Clean AutoDry Daytona Raced QVC/288 40.00 65.00
33 Tony Stewart Old Spice/2760 40.00 65.00
33 Tony Stewart Old Spice Clear Window Bank/180 40.00 65.00
33 Tony Stewart Old Spice GM Dealers/144 40.00 65.00
38 Kasey Kahne Great Clips/2820 35.00 60.00
38 Kasey Kahne Great Clips Clear Window Bank/144 35.00 60.00
38 Kasey Kahne Great Clips QVC/144 35.00 60.00
38 Kasey Kahne Great Clips Spy v. Spy Kids/3504 35.00 60.00
38 Kasey Kahne Great Clips Spy v. Spy Kids QVC/120 35.00 60.00
38 Elliott Sadler Combos/1524 35.00 60.00
38 Elliott Sadler M&M's/5856 40.00 65.00
38 Elliott Sadler M&M's Matco/72 40.00 65.00
38 Elliott Sadler M&M's QVC/504 40.00 65.00
38 Elliott Sadler M&M's Halloween/4008 40.00 65.00
38 Elliott Sadler M&M's Halloween QVC/288 40.00 65.00
38 Elliott Sadler M&M's July 4th/3204 40.00 65.00
38 Elliott Sadler M&M's July 4th Clear Window Bank/144 40.00 65.00
38 Elliott Sadler M&M's July 4th QVC/144 40.00 65.00
38 Elliott Sadler M&M's Star Wars/4332 40.00 65.00
38 Elliott Sadler M&M's Star Wars Clear Window Bank/204 40.00 65.00
38 Elliott Sadler M&M's Star Wars Matco/48 40.00 65.00
38 Elliott Sadler M&M's Star Wars QVC/408 40.00 65.00
38 Elliott Sadler M&M's Test/792 40.00 65.00
38 Elliott Sadler M&M's Test QVC/144 40.00 65.00
38 Elliott Sadler Pedigree/1488 35.00 60.00
38 Elliott Sadler Pedigree Matco/12 35.00 60.00
38 Elliott Sadler Pedigree QVC/144 35.00 60.00
38 Elliott Sadler 30th Birthday Fantasy/2640 35.00 60.00
38 Elliott Sadler 30th Birthday Fantasy Matco/12 35.00 60.00
39 Bill Elliott Coors Retro Bud Shootout/3528 50.00 75.00
39 Bill Elliott Coors Retro Bud Shootout Liquid Metal/1500 75.00 125.00
39 Bill Elliott Coors Retro Bud Shootout QVC/120 50.00 75.00
39 Reed Sorenson Discount Tire/1908 50.00 75.00
39 David Stremme Committ/3216 50.00 75.00
40 Sterling Marlin Coors Light/3036 40.00 65.00
40 Sterling Marlin Coors Light Clear Window Bank/168 40.00 65.00
40 Sterling Marlin Coors Light Matco/72 40.00 65.00
40 Sterling Marlin Coors Light QVC/288 40.00 65.00
41 Casey Mears Nicorette/2676 40.00 65.00
41 Casey Mears Target/2064 40.00 65.00
41 Casey Mears Target Clear Window Bank/144 40.00 65.00
41 Casey Mears Target Matco/24 40.00 65.00
41 Casey Mears Target QVC/144 40.00 65.00
41 Casey Mears Target Pink/2240 50.00 75.00
41 Reed Sorenson Discount Tire/3228 50.00 75.00
41 Reed Sorenson Discount Tire Clear Window Bank/168 50.00 75.00
41 Reed Sorenson Discount Tire Coats Nashville Raced/3036 50.00 75.00
41 Reed Sorenson Home 123/2508 40.00 65.00
42 Jamie McMurray Havoline/4392 35.00 60.00
42 Jamie McMurray Havoline Clear Window Bank/180 35.00 60.00
42 Jamie McMurray Havoline Matco/48 35.00 60.00
42 Jamie McMurray Havoline QVC/288 35.00 60.00
42 Jamie McMurray Havoline Autism Society/1440 35.00 60.00
42 Jamie McMurray Havoline Autism Society Clear Window Bank/144 35.00 60.00
42 Jamie McMurray Havoline Autism Society Matco/48 35.00 60.00
42 Jamie McMurray Havoline Autism Society QVC/120 35.00 60.00
42 Jamie McMurray Havoline Shine On Charlotte/2052 35.00 60.00
42 Jamie McMurray Havoline Shine On Charlotte Matco/24 35.00 60.00
42 Jamie McMurray Havoline Shine On Charlotte QVC/144 35.00 60.00
42 Jamie McMurray Havoline Shine On Sonoma/1848 35.00 60.00
42 Jamie McMurray Havoline Shine On Sonoma QVC/120 35.00 60.00
42 Jamie McMurray Havoline Shine On Talladega/1896 35.00 60.00
42 Jamie McMurray Havoline Shine On Talladega QVC/120 35.00 60.00
42 Jamie McMurray Havoline Shine On Texas/2592 35.00 60.00
42 Jamie McMurray Havoline Shine On Texas Matco/48 35.00 60.00
42 Jamie McMurray Havoline Shine On Texas QVC/120 35.00 60.00
43 Jeff Green Cheerios Narnia/2160 40.00 65.00
44 Terry Labonte Kellogg's/2172 40.00 65.00
44 Terry Labonte Kellogg's Clear Window Bank/204 40.00 65.00
44 Terry Labonte Kellogg's GM Dealers/108 40.00 65.00
44 Terry Labonte Kellogg's QVC/288 40.00 65.00
44 Terry Labonte Pizza Hut/1188 40.00 65.00
45 Kyle Petty Georgia Pacific/612 40.00 65.00
45 Kyle Petty Georgia Pacific Clear Window Bank/144 40.00 65.00
45 Kyle Petty Georgia Pacific QVC/120 40.00 65.00
45 Kyle Petty Georgia Pacific Mother's Day/1884 40.00 65.00
45 Kyle Petty Georgia Pacific Mother's Day Clear Window Bank/204 40.00 65.00
45 Kyle Petty Georgia Pacific Mother's Day Matco/12 40.00 65.00
45 Kyle Petty Georgia Pacific Mother's Day QVC/288 40.00 65.00
45 Kyle Petty Georgia Pacific Narnia/2160 40.00 60.00
47 Bobby Labonte Silverado Trick Pony SuperTruck Martinsville Raced w tire/1416 60.00 100.00
48 Jimmie Johnson Lowe's/3660 40.00 65.00
48 Jimmie Johnson Lowe's GM Dealers/780 40.00 65.00
48 Jimmie Johnson Lowe's Matco/84 40.00 65.00
48 Jimmie Johnson Lowe's QVC/504 40.00 65.00
48 Jimmie Johnson Lowe's Las Vegas Raced/2772 40.00 65.00
48 Jimmie Johnson Lowe's Las Vegas Raced QVC/144 40.00 65.00
48 Jimmie Johnson Lowe's Kobalt/1848 45.00 70.00
48 Jimmie Johnson Lowe's Kobalt GM Dealers/180 45.00 70.00
48 Jimmie Johnson Lowe's Test Chad Knaus AU/2508 50.00 75.00
48 Jimmie Johnson Lowe's '06 Preview/6000 50.00 100.00
48 Jimmie Johnson Lowe's '06 Preview GM Dealers/360 50.00 100.00
48 Jimmie Johnson Lowe's '06 Preview QVC/288 50.00 100.00
64 Jeremy Mayfield Miller High Life Light/1116 35.00 60.00
64 Jamie McMurray Top Flite Golf/1512 35.00 60.00
64 Jamie McMurray Top Flite Golf Clear Window Bank/204 35.00 60.00
64 Rusty Wallace Bell Helicopter/6192 40.00 65.00
64 Rusty Wallace Bell Helicopter Clear Window Bank/204 40.00 65.00
64 Rusty Wallace Bell Helicopter QVC/504 40.00 65.00
64 Rusty Wallace Miller High Life Saint Louis Family Tribute/5280 40.00 65.00
64 Rusty Wallace Miller High Life Saint Louis Family Tribute Clear Window Bank/228 40.00 65.00
64 Rusty Wallace Miller High Life St. Louis Family Tribute QVC/600 40.00 65.00
64 Rusty Wallace Top Flite/2652 40.00 65.00
64 Rusty Wallace Top Flite QVC/288 40.00 65.00
77 Travis Kvapil Kodak/2832 40.00 65.00
77 Travis Kvapil Mobil Clean/936 40.00 65.00
79 Jeremy Mayfield Auto Value/576 35.00 60.00
79 Jeremy Mayfield 35.00 60.00
Auto Value Clear Window Bank/204
79 Kasey Kahne Auto Value/2532 35.00 60.00
79 Kasey Kahne Auto Value Clear Window Bank/168 35.00 60.00
79 Kasey Kahne Trus Joist/2004 40.00 80.00
81 Dale Earnhardt Jr. Chance 2 Test/2616 40.00 65.00
81 Dale Earnhardt Jr. Chance 2 Test GM Dealers/288 40.00 65.00
81 Dale Earnhardt Jr. Chance 2 Test QVC/288 40.00 65.00
81 Dale Earnhardt Jr. Menards/7668 40.00 65.00
81 Dale Earnhardt Jr. Menards GM Dealers/1008 40.00 65.00
81 Dale Earnhardt Jr. Menards Matco/72 40.00 65.00
81 Dale Earnhardt Jr. Menards QVC/1508 40.00 65.00
81 Dale Earnhardt Jr. Oreo Ritz/15,516 40.00 65.00
81 Dale Earnhardt Jr. Oreo Ritz Clear Window Bank/564 40.00 65.00
81 Dale Earnhardt Jr. Oreo Ritz GM Dealers/2016 40.00 65.00
81 Dale Earnhardt Jr. Oreo Ritz QVC/3000 40.00 65.00
88 Dale Jarrett UPS/2664 50.00 75.00
88 Dale Jarrett UPS Matco/96 50.00 75.00
88 Dale Jarrett UPS QVC/360 50.00 75.00
88 Dale Jarrett UPS Talladega Raced w tire/1500 60.00 100.00
88 Dale Jarrett UPS Herbie Fully Loaded/3624 40.00 65.00
88 Dale Jarrett UPS Herbie Clear Window Bank/192 40.00 65.00
88 Dale Jarrett UPS Herbie Matco/24 40.00 65.00
88 Dale Jarrett UPS Herbie QVC/504 40.00 65.00
88 Dale Jarrett UPS Mother's Day/2664 40.00 65.00
88 Dale Jarrett UPS Mother's Day Clear Window Bank/168 40.00 65.00
88 Dale Jarrett UPS Mother's Day Mac Tools/108 40.00 65.00
88 Dale Jarrett UPS Mother's Day Matco/24 40.00 65.00
88 Dale Jarrett UPS Mother's Day QVC/288 40.00 65.00
88 Dale Jarrett UPS Star Wars/4908 40.00 65.00
88 Dale Jarrett UPS Star Wars Clear Window Bank/192 40.00 65.00
88 Dale Jarrett UPS Star Wars Matco/48 40.00 65.00
88 Dale Jarrett UPS Store Toys for Tots/4008 50.00 75.00
88 Dale Jarrett UPS Test/612 40.00 65.00
88 Dale Jarrett UPS Test QVC/144 40.00 65.00
88 Steve Wallace Last Call Action Scheck ARCA AU/2364 60.00 100.00
90 Dale Jarrett Citifinancial 35.00 60.00
90 Stephen Leicht Action 40.00 65.00
90 Elliott Sadler Citifinancial/864 35.00 60.00
91 Bill Elliott Auto Value/1224 50.00 75.00
91 Bill Elliott Auto Value Clear Window Bank/168 50.00 75.00
91 Bill Elliott McDonald's 50th Anniversary/2340 45.00 70.00
91 Bill Elliott McDonald's 50th Anniversary Clear Window Bank/168 45.00 70.00
91 Bill Elliott McDonald's 50th Anniversary QVC/288 45.00 70.00
91 Bill Elliott Stanley Tools/1764 45.00 70.00
91 Bill Elliott Stanley Tools Clear Window Bank/216 45.00 70.00
91 Bill Elliott Stanley Tools QVC/144 45.00 70.00
92 Kevin Harvick Goodwrench SuperTruck/1452 40.00 65.00
92 Kevin Harvick Yard-Man SuperTruck/1440 35.00 60.00
92 Kevin Harvick Yard-Man SuperTruck GM Dealers/96 35.00 60.00
92 Kevin Harvick Yard-Man SuperTruck Liquid Metal/300 60.00 100.00
97 Kurt Busch Crown Royal IROC/1152 25.00 50.00
99 Michael Waltrip Aaron's/1200 40.00 65.00
99 Michael Waltrip Aaron's 50th Anniversary/3660 40.00 65.00
99 Michael Waltrip Aaron's 50th Anniversary GM Dealers/24 40.00 65.00
99 Michael Waltrip Aaron's 50th Anniversary Matco/24 40.00 65.00
99 Michael Waltrip Domino's Pizza/2508 40.00 65.00
99 Michael Waltrip Domino's Pizza 40.00 65.00

Item	Low	High
GM Dealers/36		
00 Kenny Wallace Aaron's 50th Anniversary/1764	40.00	65.00
00 Kenny Wallace Aaron's 50th Anniversary Matco/12	40.00	65.00
01 Joe Nemechek Army Camo Call to Duty/2220	60.00	100.00
01 Joe Nemechek Army Camo Call to Duty GM Dealers/96	60.00	100.00
05 Star Wars Event	25.00	50.00
05 Star Wars Event GM Dealers/144	25.00	50.00
05 Star Wars Event Matco/24	25.00	50.00
07 Dave Blaney Jack Daniel's/10,464	50.00	75.00
07 Dave Blaney Jack Daniel's Color Chrome/1440	60.00	100.00
07 Dave Blaney Jack Daniel's GM Dealers/960	50.00	75.00
07 Dave Blaney Jack Daniel's Country Cocktails/5904	40.00	70.00
07 Dave Blaney Jack Daniel's Country Cocktails GM Dealers/444	40.00	70.00
07 Dave Blaney Jack Daniel's Country Cocktails QVC/504	40.00	70.00
07 Dave Blaney Jack Daniel's Drive-By Truckers/3468	40.00	70.00
07 Dave Blaney Jack Daniel's Drive-By Truckers GM Dealers/156	40.00	70.00
07 Dave Blaney Jack Daniel's Drive-By Truckers QVC/504	40.00	70.00
07 Dave Blaney Jack Daniel's Happy Birthday/4740	40.00	70.00
07 Dave Blaney Jack Daniel's Happy Birthday Black Pearl/720	50.00	75.00
07 Dave Blaney Jack Daniel's Happy Birthday GM Dealers/528	40.00	70.00
07 Dave Blaney Jack Daniel's Happy Birthday QVC/504	40.00	70.00
07 Dave Blaney Jack Daniel's Snap-On 85th Anniversary/5004		
NNO Chevy Rock&Roll Event/1692	25.00	50.00
NNO Chevy Rock&Roll Event GM Dealers/144	25.00	50.00

2005 Action Racing Collectables Historical Series 1:24

Item	Low	High
2 Rusty Wallace Aluguard '85 Grand Prix/2376	40.00	65.00
2 Rusty Wallace Aluguard '85 Grand Prix GM Dealers/144	40.00	65.00
2 Rusty Wallace Aluguard '85 Grand Prix QVC/288	40.00	65.00
3 Dale Earnhardt Goodwrench '91 Lumina/5004	60.00	100.00
3 Dale Earnhardt Goodwrench '91 Lumina QVC/1008	60.00	100.00
11 Darrell Waltrip Pepsi '83 Monte Carlo/1332	40.00	65.00
12 Dale Earnhardt Budweiser IROC '87 Camaro/3276	60.00	100.00
12 Dale Earnhardt Budweiser IROC '87 Camaro GM Dealers/360	60.00	100.00
12 Dale Earnhardt Budweiser IROC '87 Camaro GM Dealers Chrome/564	60.00	100.00
12 D.Earnhardt Budweiser IROC '87 Camaro Liquid Metal/6684	60.00	100.00
14 Dale Earnhardt Budweiser IROC Lime Green '88 Camaro/5844	50.00	75.00
24 Jeff Gordon DuPont '93 Lumina ROY/5004	60.00	100.00
43 Richard Petty STP '79 Olds/2952	50.00	75.00
43 Richard Petty STP '92 Grand Prix AU/1716	125.00	175.00
43 Richard Petty STP '92 Grand Prix AU QVC/504	125.00	175.00

2005 Action QVC For Race Fans Only 1:24

Item	Low	High
2 Rusty Wallace Kodak Color Chrome/2004	50.00	75.00
2 Rusty Wallace Miller Genuine Draft Brushed Metal/504	50.00	75.00
2 Rusty Wallace Miller Genuine Draft Color Chrome/2004	75.00	125.00
2 Rusty Wallace Miller Genuine Draft Color Chrome Chrome 2-car set/504	100.00	200.00
2 Rusty Wallace Miller Genuine Draft Gold/300	100.00	150.00
2 Rusty Wallace Miller Genuine Draft Platinum/144	100.00	150.00
2 Rusty Wallace Miller Lite Color Chrome/1008	75.00	125.00
2 Rusty Wallace Miller Lite Gold/300	100.00	150.00
2 Rusty Wallace Mobil Color Chrome/960	75.00	125.00
2 Rusty Wallace Snap On Miller Lite Brushed Metal/288	60.00	100.00
2 Rusty Wallace Snap On Miller Lite Gold/204	100.00	175.00
2 Rusty Wallace Snap On Miller Lite Platinum/108	150.00	250.00
2 Rusty Wallace 700 Starts Color Chrome	60.00	100.00
3 Dale Earnhardt Goodwrench Plus '98 MC Daytona Win Color Chrome/5004	75.00	150.00
8 Dale Earnhardt Jr. Bud Brushed Metal/504	50.00	75.00
8 Dale Earnhardt Jr. Bud Color Chrome/3504	60.00	100.00
8 Dale Earnhardt Jr. Bud Platinum/300	175.00	300.00
8 Dale Earnhardt Jr. Bud Born On Feb.20 Brushed Metal/504	50.00	75.00
8 Dale Earnhardt Jr. Bud Born On Feb.20 Color Chrome/3504	60.00	100.00
8 Dale Earnhardt Jr. Bud MLB All Star Brushed Metal/288	50.00	75.00
8 Dale Earnhardt Jr. Bud MLB All Star Gold/204	75.00	125.00
8 Dale Earnhardt Jr. Bud 3 Doors Down Brushed Metal/288	50.00	75.00
8 Dale Earnhardt Jr. Bud 3 Doors Down Color Chrome/2004	100.00	150.00
8 Dale Earnhardt Jr. Milestones '04 Daytona 500 Color Chrome/5004	60.00	100.00
9 Kasey Kahne Dodge Brushed Metal/504	60.00	100.00
9 Kasey Kahne Dodge Gold/300	100.00	175.00
9 Kasey Kahne Dodge Pit Cap Reverse Brushed Metal AU/900	100.00	175.00
9 Kasey Kahne Dodge Pit Cap Reverse Gold/300	75.00	125.00
9 Kasey Kahne Dodge Pit Cap Reverse Platinum/144	100.00	175.00
9 Kasey Kahne Dodge Retro Bud Shootout Color Chrome/1008	75.00	125.00
9 Kasey Kahne Dodge Retro Bud Shootout Gold/288	100.00	150.00
9 Kasey Kahne Dodge Retro Bud Shootout Platinum/144	100.00	175.00
9 Kasey Kahne Mountain Dew Brushed Metal AU/504	100.00	175.00
9 Kasey Kahne Mountain Dew Color Chrome/1008	60.00	100.00
9/43 Kasey Kahne Richard Petty Dodge '75 Charger STP Color Chrome/1008	100.00	150.00
12 Dale Earnhardt Budweiser IROC '87 Camaro Color Chrome/504	75.00	125.00
20 Tony Stewart Home Depot Brickyard Raced Color Chrome/1008	100.00	175.00
20 Tony Stewart Home Depot Madagascar Color Chrome/300	60.00	100.00
24 Jeff Gordon DuPont Flames Brushed Metal/504	50.00	75.00
24 Jeff Gordon DuPont Flames Performance Alliance Reverse Color Chrome/3504	100.00	150.00
24 Jeff Gordon Mighty Mouse Color Chrome/3504	60.00	100.00
24 Jeff Gordon Pepsi Daytona Color Chrome/3456	75.00	125.00
24 Jeff Gordon Pepsi Star Wars Color Chrome/3504	75.00	125.00
24 Jeff Gordon Pepsi Star Wars Gold/300	100.00	175.00
24 Jeff Gordon Pepsi Star Wars Platinum/144	175.00	300.00
24 Jeff Gordon Pepsi Star Wars Talladega Raced Brushed Copper/288	100.00	200.00
24 Jeff Gordon Pepsi Star Wars Talladega Raced Silver/624	100.00	200.00
29 Kevin Harvick Goodwrench Color Chrome/360	75.00	125.00
29 Kevin Harvick Goodwrench Quicksilver Color Chrome/360	75.00	125.00
33 Tony Stewart James Dean 50th Anniversary Color Chrome/300	50.00	75.00
38 Elliott Sadler M&M's Color Chrome/360	50.00	75.00
81 Dale Earnhardt Jr. Oreo Color Chrome/3508	75.00	125.00
81 Dale Earnhardt Jr. Oreo Ritz Platinum/300	100.00	200.00

2005 Action/RCCA 1:24

Item	Low	High
1 Martin Truex Jr. Bass Pro Shops/408	40.00	65.00
2 Clint Bowyer AC Delco/288	35.00	60.00
2 Jimmy Spencer Snap-On 85th Anniversary Color Chrome/288	50.00	75.00
2 Rusty Wallace Kodak/408	35.00	60.00
2 Rusty Wallace Milestones Last Call/502	50.00	75.00
2 Rusty Wallace Milestones 700th Start/602	60.00	100.00
2 Rusty Wallace Milestones 9X Bristol Winner/502		
2 Rusty Wallace Miller Lite/480	50.00	75.00
2 Rusty Wallace Miller Lite Color Chrome/288	60.00	100.00
2 Rusty Wallace Miller Lite Last Call Daytona Shootout/600	50.00	75.00
2 Rusty Wallace Miller Lite Last Call Test/360	50.00	75.00
2 Rusty Wallace Mobil/444	50.00	75.00
2 Rusty Wallace Snap-On Miller Lite/540	40.00	65.00
3 Dale Earnhardt Jr. Milestones '98-'99 BGN Champ/1500	50.00	75.00
5 Kyle Busch CarQuest/288	50.00	75.00
5 Kyle Busch Kellogg's/444	50.00	75.00
5 Kyle Busch Kellogg's Color Chrome/144	60.00	100.00
5 Kyle Busch Kellogg's Liquid Metal/144	75.00	125.00
5 Kyle Busch Kellogg's California Raced/240		
5 Kyle Busch Kellogg's Star Wars/408	50.00	75.00
6 Mark Martin Crown Royal IROC Brushed Metal/360	50.00	75.00
7 Robby Gordon Jim Beam/408	50.00	75.00
8 Dale Earnhardt Jr. Bud/1500	35.00	60.00
8 Dale Earnhardt Jr. Bud Color Chrome/804	50.00	75.00
8 Dale Earnhardt Jr. Bud Born On Feb.20/2400	50.00	75.00
8 Dale Earnhardt Jr. Bud MLB All-Star/1800	50.00	75.00
8 Dale Earnhardt Jr. Bud MLB All-Star Chicago Raced/444	40.00	70.00
8 Dale Earnhardt Jr. Bud Test/804	40.00	70.00
8 Dale Earnhardt Jr. Milestones '00 All-Star Win/999		
8 Dale Earnhardt Jr. Milestones '01 Daytona Win/1200	60.00	100.00
8 Dale Earnhardt Jr. Milestones '04 Daytona Win/1800	60.00	100.00
8 Martin Truex Jr. Bass Pro/408	40.00	65.00
8 Martin Truex Jr. Bass Pro Mexico City Raced/424	40.00	65.00
8 Martin Truex Jr. Bass Pro Talladega Raced/144	40.00	65.00
8 Martin Truex Jr. Chance 2 Test/288	40.00	65.00
9 Kasey Kahne Dodge/600	50.00	75.00
9 Kasey Kahne Dodge Color Chrome/408	75.00	125.00
9 Kasey Kahne Dodge Liquid Metal/408	75.00	125.00
9 Kasey Kahne Dodge Richmond Raced/499	50.00	75.00
9 Kasey Kahne Dodge Longest Yard/504	50.00	75.00
9 Kasey Kahne Dodge Pit Cap White/504	50.00	75.00
9 Kasey Kahne Dodge Retro Bud Shootout/600	50.00	75.00
9 Kasey Kahne Dodge Test/408	50.00	80.00
9 Kasey Kahne Mountain Dew/444	50.00	75.00
10 Scott Riggs Valvoline/240	35.00	60.00
11 Jason Leffler Fed Ex/288	40.00	65.00
15 Kyle Busch ditech.com SuperTruck Charlotte Raced w tire/360	40.00	70.00
15 Michael Waltrip Napa/288	35.00	60.00
18 Bobby Labonte Interstate Batteries/288	40.00	65.00
18 Bobby Labonte Interstate Batteries Color Chrome/204	50.00	75.00
18 Bobby Labonte Interstate Batteries Test/360	40.00	65.00
18 J.J. Yeley Vigoro AU/240	40.00	65.00
19 Jeremy Mayfield Dodge/288	35.00	60.00
20 Tony Stewart Home Depot/600	75.00	125.00
20 Tony Stewart Home Depot Color Chrome/288	60.00	100.00
20 Tony Stewart Home Depot Brickyard Raced/288	100.00	175.00
20 Tony Stewart Home Depot Daytona Raced/204	75.00	125.00
20 Tony Stewart Home Depot Hometown Columbus Brushed Bronze/204	50.00	75.00
20 Tony Stewart Home Depot Madagascar/504	40.00	65.00
20 Tony Stewart Home Depot Test/600	40.00	65.00
20 Tony Stewart Milestones First Win/600	50.00	75.00
20 Tony Stewart Milestones ROY/600	50.00	75.00
20 Tony Stewart Milestones '05 Brickyard Win/550	50.00	75.00
20 Tony Stewart Milestones 2X Champion/450	50.00	75.00
21 Kevin Harvick Hershey's Take 5/504	40.00	65.00
21 Kevin Harvick Pelon Pelo Rico/360	40.00	65.00
21 Kevin Harvick Reese's/288	40.00	65.00
21 Kevin Harvick Twizzlers/144	40.00	65.00
21 Brandon Miller Reese's/204	25.00	50.00
24 Jeff Gordon DuPont Flames/1008	50.00	75.00
24 Jeff Gordon DuPont Flames Color Chrome/408	60.00	100.00
24 Jeff Gordon DuPont Flames Daytona Raced/824	50.00	75.00
24 Jeff Gordon DuPont Flames Martinsville Raced/424	50.00	75.00
24 Jeff Gordon DuPont Test/804	50.00	75.00
24 Jeff Gordon Mighty Mouse/900	50.00	75.00
24 Jeff Gordon Milestones First Win/1008	50.00	75.00
24 Jeff Gordon Milestones 4X Brickyard Winner/900		
24 Jeff Gordon Milestones 4X Champion/1800	50.00	75.00
24 Jeff Gordon Milestones 4X Daytona Winner/1800		
24 Jeff Gordon Pepsi Star Wars/1200	50.00	75.00
27 Rusty Wallace Milestones '89 Champ/802	50.00	75.00
29 Kevin Harvick Goodwrench/600	40.00	65.00
29 Kevin Harvick Goodwrench Color Chrome/288	50.00	75.00
29 Kevin Harvick Goodwrench Bristol Raced/204	40.00	65.00
29 Kevin Harvick Goodwrench Daytona/804	35.00	60.00
29 Kevin Harvick Goodwrench Test/408	40.00	65.00
33 Tony Stewart James Dean 50th Anniversary/504	40.00	65.00
33 Tony Stewart Mr.Clean AutoDry Daytona Raced/288	40.00	65.00
33 Tony Stewart Old Spice/252	40.00	65.00
38 Elliott Sadler Combos/204	35.00	60.00
38 Elliott Sadler M&M's/408	40.00	65.00
38 Elliott Sadler M&M's Color Chrome/204	50.00	75.00
38 Elliott Sadler M&M's Star Wars/408	40.00	65.00
38 Elliott Sadler M&M's Test/360	40.00	65.00
38 Elliott Sadler Pedigree/288	35.00	60.00
38 Elliott Sadler 30th Birthday Fantasy/300	40.00	65.00
41 Reed Sorenson Discount Tire/288	75.00	125.00
41 Reed Sorenson Discount Tire Nashville Raced/144	75.00	125.00
42 Jamie McMurray Havoline Shine On Charlotte/240	35.00	60.00
44 Terry Labonte Kellogg's/408	50.00	75.00
47 Kevin Harvick KISS Army/1200	50.00	75.00
47 Bobby Labonte Silverado Trick Pony Martinsville Raced w tire/288	50.00	75.00
48 Jimmie Johnson Lowe's/444	40.00	65.00
48 Jimmie Johnson Lowe's Color Chrome/240	60.00	100.00
48 Jimmie Johnson Lowe's Las Vegas Raced/144	50.00	75.00
48 Jimmie Johnson Lowe's Kobalt Truck Boxes/240	50.00	75.00
48 Jimmie Johnson Lowe's Test/408	40.00	65.00
64 Rusty Wallace Bell Helicopter/408	40.00	65.00
77 Travis Kvapil Kodak/288	35.00	60.00
79 Kasey Kahne Auto Value/360	35.00	60.00
79 Kasey Kahne Trus Joist/204	50.00	75.00
81 Dale Earnhardt Jr. Chance 2 Test/408	40.00	65.00
81 Dale Earnhardt Jr. Oreo Ritz/1800	40.00	65.00
88 Dale Jarrett UPS/444	40.00	65.00
88 Dale Jarrett UPS Color Chrome/204	50.00	75.00
88 Dale Jarrett UPS Mother's Day/288	40.00	65.00
88 Dale Jarrett UPS Star Wars/444	40.00	65.00
88 Dale Jarrett UPS Test/360	40.00	65.00
05 Star Wars Event/408	40.00	60.00
07 Dave Blaney Jack Daniel's/408	50.00	75.00

2005 Action/RCCA Elite 1:24

Item	Low	High
1 Martin Truex Jr. Bass Pro Shops/504	50.00	100.00
1 Martin Truex Jr. Bass Pro Black/288	75.00	125.00
2 Rusty Wallace Kodak/408	75.00	125.00
2 Rusty Wallace Kodak White Gold/25	250.00	400.00
2 Rusty Wallace Milestones Last Call/502	75.00	125.00
2 Rusty Wallace Milestones 700th Start/602	100.00	150.00
2 Rusty Wallace Milestones 9X Bristol Winner/502	100.00	150.00
2 Rusty Wallace Miller Genuine Draft/720	75.00	125.00
2 Rusty Wallace Miller Genuine Draft White Gold/30	250.00	400.00
2 Rusty Wallace Miller Lite/720	75.00	125.00
2 Rusty Wallace Miller Lite Color Chrome/480	90.00	135.00
2 Rusty Wallace Miller Lite White Gold/30	300.00	500.00
2 Rusty Wallace Miller Lite Bristol/600	100.00	150.00
2 Rusty Wallace Miller Lite Bristol White Gold/25	300.00	500.00
2 Rusty Wallace Miller Lite Hometown Saint Louis Brushed Bronze/288	100.00	150.00
2 Rusty Wallace Miller Lite Last Call Daytona Shootout/600	125.00	250.00
2 Rusty Wallace Miller Lite Last Call Daytona Shootout White Gold/25	250.00	400.00
2 Rusty Wallace Miller Lite Last Call Test/444	100.00	150.00
2 Rusty Wallace Mobil/540	90.00	135.00
2 Rusty Wallace Mobil White Gold/25	250.00	400.00
2 Rusty Wallace Snap-On Miller Lite/540	100.00	150.00
2 Rusty Wallace Snap-On Miller Lite White Gold/25	250.00	400.00
3 Dale Earnhardt Jr. Milestones '98-'99 Busch Champion/1500	100.00	150.00
5 Kyle Busch CarQuest/288	100.00	150.00
5 Kyle Busch CarQuest White Gold/25	250.00	400.00
5 Kyle Busch Kellogg's/444	125.00	200.00
5 Kyle Busch Kellogg's Color Chrome/144	100.00	150.00
5 Kyle Busch Kellogg's White Gold/25	300.00	500.00
5 Kyle Busch Kellogg's California Raced/240	150.00	250.00
5 Kyle Busch Kellogg's Star Wars/408	75.00	125.00
5 Kyle Busch Kellogg's Star Wars White Gold/25	275.00	400.00
7 Robby Gordon Jim Beam/408	75.00	125.00
7 Robby Gordon Jim Beam White Gold/25	275.00	400.00
8 Dale Earnhardt Jr. Bud/2400	75.00	125.00
8 Dale Earnhardt Jr. Bud Color Chrome/1200	75.00	125.00
8 D.Earnhardt Jr. Bud White Gold/50	450.00	650.00
8 Dale Earnhardt Jr. Bud Born On Feb.12/600	50.00	100.00
8 Dale Earnhardt Jr. Bud Born On Feb.12 Platinum/140	200.00	350.00
8 Dale Earnhardt Jr. Bud Born On Feb.12 White Gold/33	350.00	600.00
8 Dale Earnhardt Jr. Bud Born On Feb.17 Platinum/88	150.00	300.00
8 Dale Earnhardt Jr. Bud Born On Feb.17 White Gold/25	400.00	600.00
8 Dale Earnhardt Jr. Bud Born On Feb.20/3300	60.00	120.00
8 Dale Earnhardt Jr. Bud Born On Feb.20 Platinum/200	150.00	300.00
8 Dale Earnhardt Jr. Bud Born On Feb.20 White Gold/50	350.00	600.00
8 Dale Earnhardt Jr. Bud MLB All-Star/2400	75.00	125.00
8 Dale Earnhardt Jr. Bud MLB All-Star Platinum/144	125.00	250.00
8 Dale Earnhardt Jr. Bud MLB All-Star White Gold/44	350.00	600.00
8 Dale Earnhardt Jr. Bud Test/2005	75.00	125.00
8 Dale Earnhardt Jr. Bud 3 Doors Down/2100	60.00	120.00
8 Dale Earnhardt Jr. Bud 3 Doors Down Platinum/144	150.00	250.00
8 Dale Earnhardt Jr. Bud 3 Doors Down White Gold/50	350.00	600.00
8 Dale Earnhardt Jr. Milestones '00 All-Star Win/999	60.00	120.00
8 Dale Earnhardt Jr. Milestones '01 Daytona Win/1000	60.00	120.00
8 Dale Earnhardt Jr. Milestones '04 Daytona Win/1800	60.00	120.00
8 Martin Truex Jr. Bass Pro/600	60.00	120.00
8 Martin Truex Jr. Bass Pro White Gold/25	250.00	400.00
8 Martin Truex Jr. Bass Pro Mexico City Raced/200	60.00	120.00
8 Martin Truex Jr. Bass Pro Talladega Raced/144	60.00	120.00
8 Martin Truex Jr. Chance 2 Test/408	50.00	100.00
9 Kasey Kahne Dodge/900	100.00	150.00
9 Kasey Kahne Dodge Color Chrome/600	100.00	150.00
9 Kasey Kahne Dodge Color Chrome AU/132	125.00	200.00
9 Kasey Kahne Dodge Platinum/144	150.00	250.00
9 Kasey Kahne Dodge White Gold/30	350.00	600.00
9 Kasey Kahne Dodge Richmond Raced/899	100.00	150.00
9 Kasey Kahne	125.00	200.00

odge Richmond Raced AU/144
asey Kahne 200.00 350.00
odge Richmond Raced
latinum/99
asey Kahne 75.00 125.00
odge Hometown Enumclaw
rushed Bronze/288
asey Kahne 75.00 125.00
odge Longest Yard/600
sey Kahne 250.00 400.00
odge Longest Yard
Vhite Gold/25
sey Kahne 90.00 135.00
odge Pit Cap White/600
sey Kahne 250.00 500.00
odge Pit Cap White
Vhite Gold/30
sey Kahne 100.00 150.00
odge Retro Bud Shootout/900
sey Kahne 150.00 250.00
odge Retro Bud Shootout
latinum/144
sey Kahne 250.00 400.00
odge Retro Bud Shootout
Vhite Gold/50
asey Kahne 100.00 150.00
lopar/480
asey Kahne 250.00 400.00
lopar White Gold/25
asey Kahne 100.00 150.00
lountain Dew/804
sey Kahne 125.00 200.00
lountain Dew AU/138
asey Kahne 300.00 500.00
lountain Dew
Vhite Gold/30
Michael Waltrip 60.00 100.00
lapa/408
Michael Waltrip 75.00 125.00
lapa Color Chrome/204
Michael Waltrip 150.00 300.00
lapa White Gold/25
Michael Waltrip 60.00 100.00
lapa Stars & Stripes/288
Bobby Labonte 100.00 175.00
edEx Freight/240
Bobby Labonte 60.00 100.00
nterstate Batteries/408
Bobby Labonte 75.00 125.00
nterstate Batteries
Color Chrome/204
Bobby Labonte 200.00 400.00
nterstate Batteries
White Gold/25
Bobby Labonte 60.00 100.00
nterstate Batteries Madagascar/408
Bobby Labonte 60.00 100.00
nterstate Batteries Test/408
Jeremy Mayfield 40.00 80.00
Dodge/288
Jeremy Mayfield 40.00 80.00
Mountain Dew Pitch Black/360
Jeremy Mayfield 200.00 350.00
Mountain Dew Pitch Black
White Gold/25
Jeremy Mayfield 40.00 80.00
Dodge Retro Bud Shootout/288
Jeremy Mayfield 200.00 350.00
Dodge Retro Bud Shootout
White Gold/25
Tony Stewart 125.00 250.00
Home Depot/804
Tony Stewart 125.00 200.00
Home Depot
Color Chrome/360
Tony Stewart 500.00 650.00
Home Depot
White Gold/30
Tony Stewart 75.00 150.00
Home Depot Hometown Columbus
Brushed Bronze/204
Tony Stewart 60.00 120.00
Home Depot KaBOOM/504
Tony Stewart 350.00 500.00
Home Depot KaBOOM
White Gold/25
Tony Stewart 60.00 120.00
Home Depot Lithium Ion/408
Tony Stewart 200.00 350.00
Home Depot Lithium Ion
Platinum/8
Tony Stewart 200.00 350.00
Home Depot Lithium Ion
White Gold/25
Tony Stewart 60.00 120.00
Home Depot Madagascar/600
Tony Stewart 60.00 120.00
Home Depot Test/600
Tony Stewart 60.00 120.00
Milestones First Win/600
Tony Stewart 60.00 120.00
Milestones ROY/600
Tony Stewart 75.00 150.00
Milestones '05 Brickyard Win/550
Tony Stewart 75.00 150.00
Milestones 2X Champion/450
Kevin Harvick 60.00 100.00
Hershey's Take 5/504
Kevin Harvick 60.00 100.00
Pelon Pelo Rico/360
Kevin Harvick 60.00 100.00
Reese's/288
Jeff Gordon 100.00 150.00
DuPont Flames/1500
Jeff Gordon 100.00 150.00
DuPont Flames
Color Chrome/600
Jeff Gordon 125.00 250.00
DuPont Flames Platinum/144
Jeff Gordon 600.00 800.00
DuPont Flames
White Gold/50
Jeff Gordon 100.00 150.00
DuPont Flames Daytona Raced/1524
Jeff Gordon 500.00 750.00
DuPont Flames Daytona Raced
White Gold/40
Jeff Gordon 100.00 150.00
DuPont Flames

Martinsville Raced/524
24 Jeff Gordon 100.00 150.00
DuPont Flames Reverse
Performance Alliance/1500
24 Jeff Gordon 500.00 750.00
DuPont Flames Performance Alliance Reverse
White Gold/30
24 Jeff Gordon 75.00 125.00
DuPont Test/1200
24 Jeff Gordon 100.00 175.00
Foundation Holiday/600
24 Jeff Gordon 100.00 150.00
Mighty Mouse/1500
24 Jeff Gordon 125.00 250.00
Mighty Mouse Platinum/144
24 Jeff Gordon 400.00 650.00
Mighty Mouse White Gold/30
24 Jeff Gordon 100.00 150.00
Milestones First Win/1008
24 Jeff Gordon 100.00 150.00
Milestones 4X Brickyard Winner/900
24 Jeff Gordon 100.00 150.00
Milestones 4X Champion/1200
24 Jeff Gordon 100.00 150.00
Milestones 4X Daytona Winner/1800
24 Jeff Gordon 100.00 150.00
Pepsi Daytona/1224
24 Jeff Gordon 175.00 300.00
Pepsi Daytona Platinum/144
24 Jeff Gordon 500.00 750.00
Pepsi Daytona White Gold/34
24 Jeff Gordon 100.00 150.00
Pepsi Star Wars/2004
24 Jeff Gordon 600.00 800.00
Pepsi Star Wars
White Gold/44
24 Jeff Gordon 100.00 150.00
Pepsi Star Wars
Talladega Raced/624
25 Brian Vickers 60.00 100.00
GMAC Green Day/204
25 Brian Vickers 75.00 150.00
GMAC Green Day AU/144
27 Rusty Wallace 100.00 150.00
Milestones '89 Champion/802
29 Kevin Harvick 75.00 125.00
Goodwrench/804
29 Kevin Harvick 100.00 150.00
Goodwrench AU/144
29 Kevin Harvick 75.00 125.00
Goodwrench Color Chrome/360
29 Kevin Harvick 250.00 400.00
Goodwrench
White Gold/30
29 Kevin Harvick 60.00 120.00
Goodwrench Bristol Raced/204
29 Kevin Harvick 60.00 120.00
Goodwrench Atlanta/600
29 Kevin Harvick 100.00 150.00
Goodwrench Atlanta AU/144
29 Kevin Harvick 175.00 350.00
Goodwrench Atlanta
White Gold/29
29 Kevin Harvick 60.00 120.00
Goodwrench Brickyard/504
29 Kevin Harvick 175.00 350.00
Goodwrench Brickyard
White Gold/30
29 Kevin Harvick 60.00 120.00
Goodwrench Daytona/900
29 Kevin Harvick 100.00 150.00
Goodwrench Daytona AU/144
29 Kevin Harvick 175.00 350.00
Goodwrench Daytona
White Gold/48
29 Kevin Harvick 60.00 20.00
Goodwrench Gretchen Wilson/444
29 Kevin Harvick 60.00 120.00
Goodwrench Hometown
Brushed Bronze/144
29 Kevin Harvick 60.00 120.00
Goodwrench Quicksilver
29 Kevin Harvick 200.00 350.00
Goodwrench Quicksilver
White Gold/25
29 Kevin Harvick 50.00 100.00
Goodwrench Test/600
29 Kevin Harvick 50.00 100.00
Reese's Big Cup/204
31 Jeff Burton 60.00 100.00
Cingular/288
31 Jeff Burton 75.00 150.00
Cingular AU/150
31 Jeff Burton 300.00 450.00
Cingular White Gold/25
31 Jeff Burton 60.00 100.00
Cingular Big & Rich/204
31 Jeff Burton 75.00 150.00
Cingular Big & Rich AU/121
33 Tony Stewart 75.00 125.00
James Dean 50th Anniversary/600
33 Tony Stewart 400.00 600.00
James Dean 50th Anniversary
White Gold/30
33 Tony Stewart 75.00 125.00
Mr.Clean AutoDry
Daytona Raced/288
33 Tony Stewart 60.00 100.00
Old Spice/252
38 Kasey Kahne 40.00 80.00
Great Clips/240
38 Elliott Sadler 75.00 125.00
M&M's/408
38 Elliott Sadler 75.00 125.00
M&M's Color Chrome/204
38 Elliott Sadler 200.00 350.00
M&M White Gold/25
38 Elliott Sadler 200.00 350.00
M&M's Halloween
White Gold/25
38 Elliott Sadler 60.00 100.00
M&M's July 4/288
38 Elliott Sadler 75.00 125.00
M&M's Star Wars/480
38 Elliott Sadler 75.00 150.00
M&M's Star Wars AU/141
38 Elliott Sadler 75.00 125.00
M&M's Test/408
38 Elliott Sadler 75.00 125.00

30th Birthday Fantasy/204
39 Bill Elliott 50.00 100.00
Coors Daytona Shootout/300
39 Bill Elliott 250.00 400.00
Coors Daytona Shootout
White Gold/25
39 Reed Sorenson 75.00 150.00
Discount Tire/144
40 Sterling Marlin 200.00 350.00
Coors Light White Gold/25
41 Reed Sorenson 75.00 150.00
Coats Discount Tire
Nashville Raced/144
41 Reed Sorenson 200.00 350.00
Home 123 White Gold/25
42 Jamie McMurray 75.00 125.00
Havoline/288
42 Jamie McMurray 250.00 400.00
Havoline White Gold/25
42 Jamie McMurray 75.00 125.00
Havoline
Autism Society of America/360
42 Jamie McMurray 60.00 100.00
Havoline Shine On Texas/240
44 Terry Labonte 75.00 125.00
Kellogg's/408
44 Terry Labonte 250.00 400.00
Kellogg's White Gold/25
48 Jimmie Johnson 100.00 150.00
Lowe's/504
48 Jimmie Johnson 90.00 135.00
Lowe's
Color Chrome/288
48 Jimmie Johnson 500.00 750.00
Lowe's White Gold/25
48 Jimmie Johnson 75.00 150.00
Lowe's Las Vegas Raced/204
48 Jimmie Johnson 75.00 125.00
Lowe's Test/504
48 Jimmie Johnson 350.00 500.00
Lowe's '06 Preview
White Gold/25
64 Rusty Wallace 60.00 100.00
Bell Helicopter/408
64 Rusty Wallace 275.00 400.00
Bell Helicopter White Gold/25
64 Rusty Wallace 60.00 100.00
Miller High Life Saint Louis
amily Tribute/600
64 Rusty Wallace 300.00 450.00
Miller High Life
Saint Louis Family Tribute
White Gold/25
79 Kasey Kahne 75.00 150.00
Auto Value/360
79 Kasey Kahne 75.00 150.00
Trus Joist/204
81 Dale Earnhardt Jr. 60.00 100.00
Chance 2 Test/1008
81 Dale Earnhardt Jr. 60.00 100.00
Menards/1200
81 Dale Earnhardt Jr. 300.00 450.00
Menards White Gold/25
81 Dale Earnhardt Jr. 75.00 125.00
Oreo Ritz/2400
81 Dale Earnhardt Jr. 150.00 250.00
Oreo Ritz Platinum/240
81 Dale Earnhardt Jr. 250.00 400.00
Oreo Ritz
White Gold/48
88 Dale Jarrett 60.00 100.00
UPS/504
88 Dale Jarrett 75.00 125.00
UPS Color Chrome/240
88 Dale Jarrett 100.00 175.00
UPS Color Chrome AU/59
88 Dale Jarrett 275.00 400.00
UPS White Gold/25
88 Dale Jarrett 60.00 100.00
UPS Herbie Fully Loaded/600
88 Dale Jarrett 75.00 125.00
UPS Herbie AU/144
88 Dale Jarrett 200.00 350.00
UPS Herbie Fully Loaded
White Gold/28
88 Dale Jarrett 90.00 135.00
UPS Hometown Conover
Brushed Bronze/144
88 Dale Jarrett 60.00 100.00
UPS Mother's Day/288
88 Dale Jarrett 60.00 100.00
UPS Star Wars/600
88 Dale Jarrett 300.00 450.00
UPS Star Wars
White Gold/25
88 Dale Jarrett 250.00 400.00
UPS Store Toys for Tots
White Gold/25
88 Dale Jarrett 75.00 125.00
UPS Test/408
91 Bill Elliott 200.00 350.00
McDonald's White Gold/25
91 Bill Elliott 75.00 125.00
Stanley Tools/288
07 Dave Blaney 100.00 175.00
Jack Daniel's/444
07 Dave Blaney 350.00 500.00
Jack Daniel's White Gold/25
07 Dave Blaney 100.00 150.00
Jack Daniel's Country Cocktails/504
07 Dave Blaney 200.00 350.00
Jack Daniel's Country Cocktails
White Gold/33
07 Dave Blaney 200.00 350.00
Jack Daniel's Happy Birthday Jack
White Gold/25

2005 Action/RCCA Historical Series 1:24

3 Dale Earnhardt 50.00 75.00
Coke '98 Monte Carlo/903
3 Dale Earnhardt 50.00 75.00
Goodwrench Service Plus
Daytona Win '98 Monte Carlo/903
3 Dale Earnhardt 50.00 75.00
Goodwrench Service Plus
Talladega Win '00 Monte Carlo/903
3 Dale Earnhardt 50.00 75.00
Wrangler '99 Monte Carlo/903
11 Darrell Waltrip 40.00 65.00
Pepsi '83 Monte Carlo/444
12 Dale Earnhardt 50.00 75.00
Bud '87 Camaro/804
14 Dale Earnhardt 60.00 100.00
Budweiser IROC Lime Green
'88 Camaro Color Chrome/504
43 Richard Petty 50.00 75.00
STP '79 Olds/480

2005 Action/RCCA Historical Series Elite 1:24

3 Dale Earnhardt 90.00 135.00
Coke '98 Monte Carlo
Color Chrome/603
3 Dale Earnhardt 175.00 300.00
Coke '98 Monte Carlo Platinum/203
3 Dale Earnhardt 400.00 650.00
Coke '98 Monte Carlo
White Gold/33
3 Dale Earnhardt 90.00 135.00
Goodwrench Service Plus
'98 Daytona Raced Color Chrome/603
3 Dale Earnhardt 175.00 300.00
Goodwrench Service Plus
Daytona Raced '98 Monte Carlo Platinum/203
3 Dale Earnhardt 400.00 650.00
Goodwrench Service Plus
'98 Daytona Raced White Gold/33
3 Dale Earnhardt 90.00 135.00
Goodwrench Service Plus
'00 Talladega Raced Color Chrome/603
3 Dale Earnhardt 175.00 300.00
Goodwrench Service Plus
Talladega Raced '00 Monte Carlo Platinum/203
3 Dale Earnhardt 400.00 650.00
Goodwrench Service Plus
'00 Talladega Raced White Gold/33
3 Dale Earnhardt 90.00 135.00
Wrangler '99 Monte Carlo
Color Chrome/603
3 Dale Earnhardt 175.00 300.00
Wrangler '99 Monte Carlo Platinum/203
3 Dale Earnhardt 400.00 650.00
Wrangler '99 Monte Carlo
White Gold/33
11 Darrell Waltrip 75.00 125.00
Pepsi '83 Monte Carlo/288
24 Jeff Gordon 125.00 200.00
DuPont '93 Lumina/1224
43 Richard Petty 60.00 100.00
STP '79 Olds/480
43 Richard Petty 250.00 400.00
STP '79 Olds White Gold/25
43 Richard Petty 100.00 150.00
STP '92 Grand Prix/408

2005 Action/RCCA Metal Elite 1:24

9 Kasey Kahne 75.00 125.00
Dodge/600
18 Bobby Labonte 60.00 100.00
Interstate Batteries/408
38 Elliott Sadler 60.00 100.00
M&M's/408
38 Elliott Sadler 75.00 150.00
M&M's AU/144

2006 Action Performance 1:24

22 Kenny Wallace 15.00 30.00
Auto Zone Promo
in window box
29 Jeff Burton 20.00 40.00
Holiday Inn Promo
in split window box
66 Jeff Green 20.00 40.00
Best Buy Promo in window box
88 Dale Jarrett 20.00 40.00
UPS in AP box

2006 Action Racing Collectables 1:24

* DENOTES TOTAL PRODUCTION RUNS
LISTED ON BASIC ARC PIECE
1 Martin Truex Jr. 50.00 75.00
Bass Pro Shops/6000
1 Martin Truex Jr. 50.00 75.00
Bass Pro Shops
Clear Window Bank/204
1 Martin Truex Jr. 50.00 75.00
Bass Pro Shops GM Dealers/1008
1 Martin Truex Jr. 50.00 75.00
Bass Pro Shops Mac Tools/300
1 Martin Truex Jr. 50.00 75.00
Bass Pro Shops Matco/72
1 Martin Truex Jr. 50.00 75.00
Bass Pro Shops QVC/288
1 Martin Truex Jr. 60.00 100.00
Bass Pro Shops
3 Days of Dale
Tribute/3504
1 Martin Truex Jr. 60.00 100.00
Bass Pro Shops
3 Days of Dale
Tribute GM Dealers/1488
1 Martin Truex Jr. 50.00 75.00
Bass Pro Shops Test/3504
1 Martin Truex Jr. 50.00 75.00
Bass Pro Shops Test
GM Dealers/504
2 Clint Bowyer 40.00 65.00
AC Delco/2052
2 Clint Bowyer 40.00 65.00
AC Delco Clear Window Bank/144
2 Clint Bowyer 40.00 65.00
AC Delco GM Dealers/504
2 Rusty Wallace 50.00 75.00
Legendary/4220
5 Kyle Busch 50.00 75.00

Carquest/2508
5 Kyle Busch 50.00 75.00
Carquest
GM Dealers/72
5 Kyle Busch 50.00 75.00
Delphi/1356
5 Kyle Busch 50.00 75.00
Delphi GM Dealers/96
5 Kyle Busch 50.00 75.00
Kellogg's/3864
5 Kyle Busch 50.00 75.00
Kellogg's GM Dealers/360
5 Kyle Busch 50.00 75.00
Kellogg's QVC/120
5 Kyle Busch 50.00 75.00
Kellogg's Cars/3000
5 Kyle Busch 50.00 75.00
Kellogg's Ice Age/2556
5 Kyle Busch 50.00 75.00
Kellogg's Ice Age
Clear Window Bank
5 Kyle Busch 50.00 75.00
Kellogg's Ice Age
GM Dealers/288
5 Kyle Busch 50.00 75.00
Lowe's
6 Mark Martin 50.00 75.00
AAA Holiday/1584*
6 Mark Martin 50.00 75.00
AAA Holiday QVC*
6 Mark Martin 50.00 75.00
Crown Royal IROC/2316
6 Mark Martin 50.00 75.00
Crown Royal IROC
GM Dealers/192
8 Dale Earnhardt Jr. 60.00 100.00
Bud/30,000
8 Dale Earnhardt Jr. 60.00 100.00
Bud AB/600
8 Dale Earnhardt Jr. 60.00 100.00
Bud Clear Window Bank/504
8 Dale Earnhardt Jr. 60.00 100.00
Bud GM Dealers/2508
8 Dale Earnhardt Jr. 60.00 100.00
Bud Mac Tools/504
8 Dale Earnhardt Jr. 60.00 100.00
Bud Matco/228
8 Dale Earnhardt Jr. 60.00 100.00
Bud QVC/6500
8 Dale Earnhardt Jr. 75.00 125.00
Bud Richmond Raced/8556
8 Dale Earnhardt Jr. 75.00 125.00
Bud Richmond Raced
GM Dealers/2652
8 Dale Earnhardt Jr. 75.00 125.00
Bud 3 Days of Dale Tribute/44,169*
8 Dale Earnhardt Jr. 75.00 125.00
Bud 3 Days of Dale Tribute
Anheuser Busch*
8 Dale Earnhardt Jr. 75.00 125.00
Bud Dale Tribute
GM Dealers/7392
8 Dale Earnhardt Jr. 75.00 125.00
Bud 3 Days of Dale Tribute
Hamilton*
8 Dale Earnhardt Jr. 75.00 125.00
Bud 3 Days of Dale Tribute
Mac Tools*
8 Dale Earnhardt Jr. 75.00 125.00
Bud 3 Days of Dale Tribute
QVC*
8 Dale Earnhardt Jr. 75.00 125.00
Bud 3 Days of Dale Tribute
Snap On*
8 Dale Earnhardt Jr. 75.00 125.00
Bud Father's Day/30,456*
8 Dale Earnhardt Jr. 75.00 125.00
Bud Father's Day
Anheuser Busch*
8 Dale Earnhardt Jr. 75.00 125.00
Bud Father's Day
Clear Window Bank/492
8 Dale Earnhardt Jr. 75.00 125.00
Bud Father's Day
GM Dealers/3792
8 Dale Earnhardt Jr. 75.00 125.00
Bud Father's Day
Hamilton*
8 Dale Earnhardt Jr. 75.00 125.00
Bud Father's Day
Mac Tools*
8 Dale Earnhardt Jr. 75.00 125.00
Bud Father's Day
QVC*
8 Dale Earnhardt Jr. 75.00 125.00
Bud Father's Day
Snap-On*
8 Dale Earnhardt Jr. 50.00 75.00
Bud Test/5196*
8 Dale Earnhardt Jr. 50.00 75.00
Bud Test GM Dealers/720
8 Dale Earnhardt Jr. 50.00 75.00
Bud Test Mac Tools*
8 Dale Earnhardt Jr. 50.00 75.00
Bud Test Matco*
8 Dale Earnhardt Jr. 50.00 75.00
Bud Test QVC*
8 Dale Earnhardt Jr. 50.00 75.00
Oreo/6000
8 Dale Earnhardt Jr. 50.00 75.00
Oreo Clear Window Bank/480
8 Dale Earnhardt Jr. 60.00 100.00
Oreo GM Dealers
Brushed Metal/504
8 Dale Earnhardt Jr. 50.00 75.00
Oreo Mac Tools/360
8 Dale Earnhardt Jr. 50.00 75.00
Oreo QVC/1008
8 Dale Earnhardt Jr. 50.00 75.00
250 Starts/7812*
8 Dale Earnhardt Jr. 50.00 75.00
250 Starts GM Dealers/1980
8 Dale Earnhardt Jr. 50.00 75.00
250 Starts Hamilton*
8 Tony Stewart 50.00 75.00
Goody's/1644
8 Martin Truex Jr. 50.00 75.00
Bass Pro Shops '05 BGN Champ
Color Chrome/4680*

8 Martin Truex Jr. Bass Pro Shops '05 BGN Champ Color Chrome GM Dealers/504 50.00 75.00
8 Martin Truex Jr. Bass Pro Shops '05 BGN Champ Color Chrome QVC* 50.00 75.00
8 Martin Truex Jr. Bass Pro Shops 3 Days of Dale Tribute Talladega Raced/3900 60.00 100.00
8 Martin Truex Jr. Bass Pro Shops 3 Days of Dale Tribute Talladega Raced GM Dealers/1104 60.00 100.00
8 Martin Truex Jr. Crown Royal IROC/1404 50.00 75.00
8 Martin Truex Jr. Crown Royal IROC GM Dealers/204 50.00 75.00
9 Kasey Kahne Click Michigan Raced/2388 50.00 75.00
9 Kasey Kahne Dodge/10,000 60.00 100.00
9 Kasey Kahne Dodge Clear Window Bank/360 60.00 100.00
9 Kasey Kahne Dodge Mac Tools/504 60.00 100.00
9 Kasey Kahne Dodge Matco/72 60.00 100.00
9 Kasey Kahne Dodge QVC/504 60.00 100.00
9 Kasey Kahne Dodge Holiday/1296* 50.00 75.00
9 Kasey Kahne Dodge Holiday QVC* 50.00 75.00
9 Kasey Kahne Dodge SRT/1728 50.00 75.00
9 Kasey Kahne Dodge Test/3504 50.00 75.00
9 Kasey Kahne Dodge UAW Daimler Chrysler 400/1500 50.00 75.00
9 Kasey Kahne Dodge UAW Daimler Chrysler 400 Clear Window Bank/144 50.00 75.00
9 Kasey Kahne Mopar/1980 50.00 75.00
9 Kasey Kahne McDonald's/1644 50.00 75.00
9 Kasey Kahne McDonald's Clear Window Bank/132 50.00 75.00
9 Kasey Kahne Ragu/2580 50.00 75.00
9 Kasey Kahne Vitamin Water/2232 50.00 75.00
9 Boris Said Ingersoll Rand Clear Window Bank/144 50.00 75.00
10 Scott Riggs Advance Auto Bumper to Bumper 40.00 70.00
10 Scott Riggs Stanley Tools/2220 50.00 75.00
10 Scott Riggs Valvoline/3504 50.00 75.00
10 Scott Riggs Valvoline Cars/2508 50.00 75.00
11 Denny Hamlin Fed Ex Express/7728 75.00 125.00
11 Denny Hamlin Fed Ex Express Daytona Shootout Raced/2208 75.00 125.00
11 Denny Hamlin Fed Ex Express Daytona Shootout Raced GM Dealers/552 75.00 125.00
11 Denny Hamlin Fed Ex Express 2006 Rookie of the Year LE 75.00 125.00
11 Denny Hamlin Fed Ex Express 2006 Rookie of the Year GM Dealers/504 75.00 125.00
11 Denny Hamlin Fed Ex Freight/5208 60.00 100.00
11 Denny Hamlin Fed Ex Ground/3000 60.00 100.00
11 Denny Hamlin Fed Ex Ground Clear Window Bank/240 60.00 100.00
11 Denny Hamlin Fed Ex Ground GM Dealers/300 60.00 100.00
11 Denny Hamlin Fed Ex Ground Pocono Raced/2952 60.00 100.00
11 Denny Hamlin Fed Ex Ground Pocono Raced GM Dealers/636 60.00 100.00
11 Denny Hamlin Fed Ex Home Delivery/2209* 60.00 100.00
11 Denny Hamlin Fed Ex Home Delivery Clear Window Bank/300 60.00 100.00
11 Denny Hamlin Fed Ex Home Delivery GM Dealers/648 60.00 100.00
11 Denny Hamlin Fed Ex Home Delivery QVC* 60.00 100.00
11 Denny Hamlin Fed Ex Kinko's Clear Window Bank/144 60.00 100.00
11 Denny Hamlin Fed Ex Kinko's GM Dealers/300 60.00 100.00
11 Steve Kinser Crown Royal IROC/804 50.00 75.00
11 Steve Kinser Crown Royal IROC GM Dealers/72 50.00 75.00
11 Paul Menard Menard's 3 Days of Dale Tribute/3333 60.00 100.00
11 Paul Menard Menard's 3 Days of Dale Tribute GM Dealers/1272 60.00 100.00
11 Paul Menard Menard's Johns Manville/2090 50.00 75.00
12 Ryan Newman Crown Royal IROC/1056 50.00 75.00
12 Ryan Newman Crown Royal IROC GM Dealers/132 50.00 75.00
14 Sterling Marlin Waste Management/2280 50.00 75.00
15 Paul Menard Quaker State/1284 50.00 75.00
17 Matt Kenseth Crown Royal IROC/1128 50.00 75.00
17 Matt Kenseth Crown Royal IROC GM Dealers/132 50.00 75.00
18 J.J. Yeley Husqvarna/1992 50.00 75.00
18 J.J. Yeley Husqvarna GM Dealers/108 50.00 75.00
18 J.J. Yeley Interstate Batteries/3000 no rookie stripes 50.00 75.00
18 J.J. Yeley Interstate Batteries GM Dealers/144 no rookie stripes 50.00 75.00
19 Jeremy Mayfield Dodge/5004 40.00 70.00
19 Jeremy Mayfield Dodge Mac Tools/300 40.00 70.00
19 Jeremy Mayfield Dodge QVC/60 40.00 70.00
19 Elliott Sadler Dodge Holiday/576* 50.00 75.00
19 Elliott Sadler Dodge Holiday QVC* 50.00 75.00
20 Denny Hamlin Rockwell Automation/2508 50.00 75.00
20 Tony Stewart Crown Royal IROC/3024 50.00 75.00
20 Tony Stewart Crown Royal IROC GM Dealers/204 50.00 75.00
20 Tony Stewart Home Depot/9000 60.00 100.00
20 Tony Stewart Home Depot GM Dealers/1200 60.00 100.00
20 Tony Stewart Home Depot Mac Tools/504 60.00 100.00
20 Tony Stewart Home Depot Matco/156 60.00 100.00
20 Tony Stewart Home Depot QVC/504 60.00 100.00
20 Tony Stewart Home Depot Martinsville Raced/2520* 60.00 100.00
20 Tony Stewart Home Depot Martinsville Raced GM Dealers/360 60.00 100.00
20 Tony Stewart Home Depot Martinsville Raced QVC* 60.00 100.00
20 Tony Stewart Home Depot Holiday/1551* 50.00 75.00
20 Tony Stewart Home Depot Holiday GM Dealers/432 50.00 75.00
20 Tony Stewart Home Depot Holiday QVC* 50.00 75.00
20 Tony Stewart Home Depot Lithium-Ion/2508 50.00 75.00
20 Tony Stewart Home Depot Lithium-Ion GM Dealers/504 50.00 75.00
20 Tony Stewart Home Depot Test/3588* 50.00 75.00
20 Tony Stewart Home Depot Test GM Dealers/288 50.00 75.00
20 Tony Stewart Home Depot Test Matco* 50.00 75.00
20 Tony Stewart Powerade/3852* 50.00 75.00
20 Tony Stewart Powerade Clear Window Bank/204 50.00 75.00
20 Tony Stewart Powerade GM Dealers/696 50.00 75.00
20 Tony Stewart Powerade Mac Tools* 50.00 75.00
20 Tony Stewart Powerade QVC* 50.00 75.00
21 Jeff Burton Coast Guard/804 50.00 75.00
21 Jeff Burton Coast Guard GM Dealers/288 50.00 75.00
21 Kevin Harvick Coast Guard/2004 75.00 125.00
21 Kevin Harvick Coast Guard Clear Window Bank/144 75.00 125.00
21 Kevin Harvick Coast Guard 2006 Busch Series Champion LE 75.00 125.00
21 Kevin Harvick Coast Guard 2006 Busch Champion GM Dealers/384 75.00 125.00
21 Kevin Harvick Coast Guard Reserve Richmond Raced/1056 75.00 125.00
21 Kevin Harvick Coast Guard Reserve Richmond Raced GM Dealers/72 75.00 125.00
24 Jeff Gordon DuPont Flames/10,008 60.00 100.00
24 Jeff Gordon DuPont Flames GM Dealers/1008 60.00 100.00
24 Jeff Gordon DuPont Flames Mac Tools/504 60.00 100.00
24 Jeff Gordon DuPont Flames Matco/216 60.00 100.00
24 Jeff Gordon DuPont Flames QVC/504 60.00 100.00
24 Jeff Gordon DuPont Flames Chicagoland Raced/2475 100.00 175.00
24 Jeff Gordon DuPont Flames Chicagoland Raced Platinum/75 650.00 1000.00
24 Jeff Gordon DuPont Flames Chicagoland Raced Platinum/125 275.00 400.00
24 Jeff Gordon DuPont Flames Performance Alliance/6528* 50.00 75.00
24 Jeff Gordon DuPont Flames Performance Alliance Clear Window Bank/240 50.00 75.00
24 Jeff Gordon DuPont Flames Performance Alliance GM Dealers/696 50.00 75.00
24 Jeff Gordon DuPont Flames Performance Alliance QVC* 50.00 75.00
24 Jeff Gordon DuPont Flames Sonoma Raced/678 400.00 600.00
24 Jeff Gordon DuPont Flames Test/4584* 60.00 100.00
24 Jeff Gordon DuPont Flames Test Matco* 60.00 100.00
24 Jeff Gordon DuPont Flames Test QVC* 60.00 100.00
24 Jeff Gordon DuPont Hot Hues Foose Design/18,240 60.00 100.00
24 Jeff Gordon DuPont Hot Hues Foose Design Mac Tools/504 60.00 100.00
24 Jeff Gordon DuPont Hot Hues Foose Design Matco/84 60.00 100.00
24 Jeff Gordon DuPont Hot Hues Foose Design QVC/1500 60.00 100.00
24 Jeff Gordon Holiday Jeff Gordon Foundation/3252* 50.00 75.00
24 Jeff Gordon Holiday JG Foundation GM Dealers/2478 50.00 75.00
24 Jeff Gordon Holiday Jeff Gordon Foundation QVC* 50.00 75.00
24 Jeff Gordon Mighty Mouse/6072* 50.00 75.00
24 Jeff Gordon Mighty Mouse Clear Window Bank/360 50.00 75.00
24 Jeff Gordon Mighty Mouse GM Dealers/708 50.00 75.00
24 Jeff Gordon Mighty Mouse Matco* 50.00 75.00
24 Jeff Gordon Nicorette/7512* 60.00 100.00
24 Jeff Gordon Nicorette Clear Window Bank/360 60.00 100.00
24 Jeff Gordon Nicorette QVC* 60.00 100.00
24 Jeff Gordon Pepsi/8868* 60.00 100.00
24 Jeff Gordon Pepsi Clear Window Bank/240 60.00 100.00
24 Jeff Gordon Pepsi GM Dealers/900 60.00 100.00
24 Jeff Gordon Pepsi Mac Tools* 60.00 100.00
24 Jeff Gordon Pepsi Matco* 60.00 100.00
24 Jeff Gordon Pepsi QVC* 60.00 100.00
24 Jeff Gordon Superman/9823* 60.00 100.00
24 Jeff Gordon Superman GM Dealers/1356 60.00 100.00
24 Jeff Gordon Superman GM Dealers Brushed Metal/504 75.00 125.00
24 Jeff Gordon Superman Mac Tools* 60.00 100.00
24 Jeff Gordon Superman Matco* 60.00 100.00
24 Jeff Gordon Superman QVC* 60.00 100.00
24 Jeff Gordon World Series of Poker Jeff Gordon Foundation/9828 60.00 100.00
24 Jeff Gordon World Series of Poker Jeff Gordon Foundation Clear Window Bank/240 60.00 100.00
24 Jeff Gordon World Series of Poker Jeff Gordon Foundation GM Dealers/804 60.00 100.00
25 Brian Vickers GMAC/3744 50.00 75.00
25 Brian Vickers GMAC QVC/60 50.00 75.00
26 Ricky Bobby Laughing Clown Malt Liquor/2508 35.00 60.00
26 Ricky Bobby Wonder Bread/2508 35.00 60.00
29 Jeff Burton Holiday Inn/1356 50.00 75.00
29 Jeff Burton Holiday Inn AU 60.00 100.00
29 Kevin Harvick Goodwrench/5004 50.00 75.00
29 Kevin Harvick Goodwrench Clear Window Bank/204 50.00 75.00
29 Kevin Harvick Goodwrench GM Dealers/1200 50.00 75.00
29 Kevin Harvick Goodwrench Mac Tools/504 50.00 75.00
29 Kevin Harvick Goodwrench Matco/72 50.00 75.00
29 Kevin Harvick Goodwrench QVC/144 50.00 75.00
29 Kevin Harvick Goodwrench Holiday/1044* 50.00 75.00
29 Kevin Harvick Goodwrench Holiday GM Dealers/437 50.00 75.00
29 Kevin Harvick Goodwrench Holiday QVC* 50.00 75.00
29 Kevin Harvick Hershey's/2940* 50.00 75.00
29 Kevin Harvick Hershey's Clear Window Bank/204 50.00 75.00
29 Kevin Harvick Hershey's GM Dealers/600 50.00 75.00
29 Kevin Harvick Hershey's Mac Tools* 50.00 75.00
29 Kevin Harvick Hershey's QVC* 50.00 75.00
29 Kevin Harvick Hershey's Kissables/4008 50.00 75.00
29 Kevin Harvick Hershey's Kissables Clear Window Bank/204 50.00 75.00
29 Kevin Harvick Reese's/5244 50.00 75.00
29 Kevin Harvick Reese's Clear Window Bank/204 50.00 75.00
29 Kevin Harvick Reese's Caramel/2508 50.00 75.00
29 Kevin Harvick Reese's Caramel GM Dealers/288 50.00 75.00
31 Jeff Burton Cingular/3504 50.00 75.00
31 Jeff Burton Cingular Clear Window Bank 50.00 75.00
31 Jeff Burton Cingular QVC/48 50.00 75.00
31 Jeff Burton Cingular Dover Raced/836 50.00 75.00
33 Tony Stewart Old Spice/3504 50.00 75.00
33 Tony Stewart Old Spice GM Dealers/204 50.00 75.00
38 David Gilliland M&M's Halloween/1896 60.00 100.00
38 Elliott Sadler M&M's/5244 50.00 75.00
38 Elliott Sadler M&M's Clear Window Bank/252 50.00 75.00
38 Elliott Sadler M&M's Mac Tools/504 50.00 75.00
38 Elliott Sadler M&M's Matco/48 50.00 75.00
38 Elliott Sadler M&M's QVC/96 50.00 75.00
38 Elliott Sadler M&M's Pirates of the Caribbean/7560* 50.00 75.00
38 Elliott Sadler M&M's Pirates of the Caribbean Clear Window Bank/300 50.00 75.00
38 Elliott Sadler M&M's Pirates of the Caribbean Mac Tools* 50.00 75.00
38 Elliott Sadler M&M's Pirates of the Caribbean Matco* 50.00 75.00
38 Elliott Sadler Pedigree/2508 50.00 75.00
38 Elliott Sadler Snickers/2868* 50.00 75.00
38 Elliott Sadler Snickers Clear Window Bank/144 50.00 75.00
38 Elliott Sadler Snickers Mac Tools* 50.00 75.00
40 David Stremme Coors Light/4008 60.00 100.00
40 David Stremme Lone Star Steakhouse/3504 50.00 75.00
41 Reed Sorenson Discount Tire/3012 60.00 100.00
41 Reed Sorenson Discount Tire Clear Window Bank/204 50.00 75.00
41 Reed Sorenson Target/5004 60.00 100.00
41 Reed Sorenson Target Clear Window Bank/240 50.00 75.00
42 Casey Mears Havoline/2754* 50.00 75.00
42 Casey Mears Havoline QVC* 50.00 75.00
43 Bobby Labonte Gogurt/1296 50.00 75.00
43 Bobby Labonte STP/2616 50.00 75.00
44 Terry Labonte Kellogg's 50.00 75.00
44 Terry Labonte Kellogg's Clear Window Bank/144 50.00 75.00
44 Terry Labonte Kellogg's Farewell Tribute/1008 175.00 300.00
45 Kyle Petty Wells Fargo/1356 75.00 125.00
47 Cal Naughton Jr. Old Spice/1500 35.00 60.00
48 Jimmie Johnson Lowe's/5484 75.00 125.00
48 Jimmie Johnson Lowe's Mac Tools/504 75.00 125.00
48 Jimmie Johnson Lowe's Matco/120 75.00 125.00
48 Jimmie Johnson Lowe's QVC/96 75.00 125.00
48 J.Johnson Lowe's Daytona Raced Employee/280 150.00 250.00
48 Jimmie Johnson Lowe's Daytona Raced w tire/1872 150.00 300.00
48 Jimmie Johnson Lowe's Daytona Raced w tire GM Dealers/336 150.00 300.00
48 Jimmie Johnson Lowe's Flames Test/3552* 60.00 100.00
48 Jimmie Johnson Lowe's Flames Test GM Dealers/216 60.00 100.00
48 Jimmie Johnson Lowe's Flames Test Matco* 60.00 100.00
48 Jimmie Johnson Lowe's Holiday/840 50.00 75.00
48 Jimmie Johnson Lowe's Holiday GM Dealers/288 50.00 75.00
48 Jimmie Johnson Lowe's Jimmie Johnson Foundation/1500* 60.00 100.00
48 Jimmie Johnson Lowe's Jimmie Johnson Foundation GM Dealers/1500 60.00 100.00
48 Jimmie Johnson Lowe's Sea World/8556* 50.00 75.00
48 Jimmie Johnson Lowe's Sea World GM Dealers/552 50.00 75.00
48 Jimmie Johnson Lowe's Sea World Matco* 50.00 75.00
48 Jimmie Johnson Lowe's Sea World QVC* 50.00 75.00
48 Jimmie Johnson Lowe's 60th Anniversary/3036 60.00 100.00
48 Jimmie Johnson Lowe's 60th Anniversary GM Dealers/564 60.00 100.00
48 Jimmie Johnson Lowe's 2006 Nextel Champion LE 75.00 125.00
48 Jimmie Johnson Lowe's 2006 Nextel Champion GM Dealers/696 75.00 125.00
55 Jean Girard Perrier/1500 35.00 60.00
57 Brian Vickers Mountain Dew/2832 35.00 60.00
57 Brian Vickers Mountain Dew Clear Window Bank/144 35.00 60.00
57 Brian Vickers Mountain Dew GM Dealers/144 35.00 60.00
57 Brian Vickers Ore-Ida/2544 35.00 60.00
57 Brian Vickers Ore-Ida GM Dealers/72 35.00 60.00
62 Ricky Bobby ME/1500 35.00 60.00
85 Dennis Setzer Flex Fuel SuperTruck/1212 50.00 75.00
88 Dale Jarrett UPS/5244 50.00 75.00
88 Dale Jarrett UPS Mac Tools/300 50.00 75.00
88 Dale Jarrett UPS Matco/48 50.00 75.00
88 Dale Jarrett UPS QVC/504 50.00 75.00
88 Dale Jarrett UPS Freight/3104 50.00 75.00
88 Mark McFarland Navy/2004 40.00 65.00
88 Mark McFarland Navy Clear Window Bank/180 40.00 65.00
90 Elliott Sadler Citifinancial/2004 50.00 75.00
96 Terry Labonte HDTV DLP/2004 50.00 75.00
96 Terry Labonte HDTV DLP Clear Window Bank/144 50.00 75.00
96 Tony Raines HDTV DLP/1008 50.00 75.00
96 Tony Raines HDTV DLP Troy Aikman HOF/1500 50.00 75.00
96 Tony Raines HDTV DLP Hall of Fame GM Dealers/144 50.00 75.00
98 Erin Crocker Cheerios/2988* 50.00 75.00
98 Erin Crocker Cheerios QVC* 50.00 75.00
99 Carl Edwards Office Depot Holiday/1075* 50.00 75.00
99 Carl Edwards Office Depot Holiday QVC* 50.00 75.00
01 Joe Nemechek Army/2076 50.00 75.00
06 Sam Bass Holiday/987* 50.00 75.00
06 Sam Bass Holiday GM Dealers/288 40.00 65.00
06 Sam Bass Holiday QVC* 40.00 65.00
07 Clint Bowyer Jack Daniel's/4488 60.00 100.00
07 Clint Bowyer Jack Daniel's GM Dealers/760 60.00 100.00
07 Clint Bowyer Jack Daniel's QVC/288 60.00 100.00
07 Clint Bowyer Jack Daniel's Country Cocktails/3504 50.00 75.00
07 Clint Bowyer Jack Daniel's Country Cocktails GM Dealers/504 50.00 75.00
07 Clint Bowyer Jack Daniel's Directv/2328 50.00 75.00
07 Clint Bowyer Jack Daniel's Directv GM Dealers/456 50.00 75.00
07 Clint Bowyer Jack Daniel's Happy Birthday Jack/876 50.00 75.00
07 Clint Bowyer Jack Daniel's Happy B-Day GM Dealers/372 50.00 75.00
07 Clint Bowyer Jack Daniel's Sopranos/2580 60.00 100.00
07 Clint Bowyer Jack Daniel's Texas/600 50.00 75.00
07 Clint Bowyer Jack Daniel's Texas GM Dealers/504 50.00 75.00
NNO Dale Earnhardt Hall of Fame/33,333 50.00 75.00
NNO Dale Earnhardt Hall of Fame GM Dealers/2004 50.00 75.00

2006 Action Racing Collectables Historical Series 1:24

3 Dale Earnhardt Bud IROC '89 Camaro/8500* 50.00 75.00
3 Dale Earnhardt Bud IROC '89 Camaro GM Dealers/792 50.00 75.00
3 Dale Earnhardt Bud IROC '89 Camaro QVC* 50.00 75.00
5 Darrell Waltrip Bud IROC '84 Camaro/2916* 40.00 70.00
5 Darrell Waltrip Bud IROC '84 Camaro GM Dealers/228 40.00 70.00
5 Darrell Waltrip 40.00 70.00

ud IROC '84 Camaro QVC*
arrell Waltrip 50.00 75.00
lountain Dew '81 Buick
quid Chrome/1500

:006 Action QVC For Race Fans Only 1:24

rk Martin 50.00 75.00
rown Royal IROC
olor Chrome/504
e Earnhardt Jr. 75.00 125.00
ud Color Chrome/3504
e Earnhardt Jr. 100.00 150.00
ud Gold/504
e Earnhardt Jr. 75.00 125.00
ud Richmond Raced
olor Chrome/2508
e Earnhardt Jr. 125.00 200.00
ud Richmond Raced
lver/504
e Earnhardt Jr. 125.00 200.00
ud 3 Days of Dale Tribute
latinum/411
e Earnhardt Jr. 100.00 150.00
ud 3 Days of Dale Tribute
lver/504
e Earnhardt Jr. 100.00 150.00
ud Father's Day
latinum/288
e Earnhardt Jr. 60.00 100.00
reo Color Chrome/3504
sey Kahne 60.00 100.00
odge Color Chrome/504
sey Kahne 60.00 100.00
odge Mesma Chrome/288
enny Hamlin 100.00 175.00
ed Ex Ground Pocono Raced
olor Chrome AU/504
ony Stewart 60.00 100.00
ome Depot
olor Chrome/504
ony Stewart 75.00 125.00
ome Depot
latinum/108
eff Gordon 75.00 125.00
uPont Flames
lesma Chrome/408
eff Gordon 100.00 150.00
uPont Hot Hues
oose Design Gold/108
eff Gordon 60.00 100.00
lighty Mouse
opper/288
eff Gordon 60.00 100.00
uperman Copper/408
eff Gordon 100.00 150.00
uperman Gold/144
eff Gordon 125.00 200.00
uperman Platinum/144
eff Gordon 100.00 150.00
uperman Silver/288
immie Johnson 60.00 100.00
owe's SeaWorld
olor Chrome/504
Dale Earnhardt 60.00 100.00
all of Fame
lesma Chrome/1008

2006 Action/RCCA 1:24

artin Truex Jr. 60.00 100.00
Bass Pro Shops
Color Chrome/180
artin Truex Jr. 60.00 100.00
Bass Pro 3 Days of Dale Tribute/250
artin Truex Jr. 50.00 75.00
Bass Pro Test/250
yle Busch 50.00 75.00
Kellogg's/120
yle Busch 50.00 75.00
Kellogg's Ice Age/288
yle Busch 50.00 75.00
Lowe's/120
ark Martin 50.00 75.00
Crown Royal White Pearl/288
lark Martin 100.00 175.00
Scotts SuperTruck AU/408
ale Earnhardt Jr. 50.00 75.00
Bud/1008
ale Earnhardt Jr. 75.00 125.00
Bud Color Chrome/288
ale Earnhardt Jr. 60.00 100.00
Bud Richmond Raced/888
ale Earnhardt Jr. 60.00 100.00
Bud 3 Days of Dale Tribute/3333
ale Earnhardt Jr. 60.00 100.00
Bud Father's Day/2333
ale Earnhardt Jr. 50.00 75.00
Bud Test/700
ale Earnhardt Jr. 50.00 75.00
250th Start/1008
asey Kahne 50.00 75.00
Click Michigan Raced/350
asey Kahne 50.00 75.00
Dodge/408
asey Kahne 50.00 75.00
Dodge SRT/200
asey Kahne 50.00 75.00
Dodge UAW Daimler Chrysler 400/250
asey Kahne 50.00 75.00
Mopar/200
asey Kahne 50.00 75.00
McDonald's/250
asey Kahne 50.00 75.00
Vitamin Water/100
Denny Hamlin 75.00 125.00
Fed Ex Express/311
11 Denny Hamlin 75.00 125.00
Fed Ex Express
Daytona Shootout Raced/311
11 Denny Hamlin 75.00 125.00
Fed Ex Freight/211
11 Denny Hamlin 75.00 125.00
Fed Ex Ground/311
11 Denny Hamlin 75.00 125.00
Fed Ex Ground
Pocono Raced/299
11 Denny Hamlin 75.00 125.00
Fed Ex Home Delivery/211
11 Denny Hamlin 75.00 125.00
Fed Ex Kinko's/211
11 Paul Menard 50.00 75.00
Menard's
Johns Manville/144
11 Paul Menard 50.00 75.00
Turtle Wax/144
11 Paul Menard 60.00 100.00
Turtle Wax 3 Days of Dale Tribute/203
20 Tony Stewart 40.00 65.00
Crown Royal White Pearl/288
20 Tony Stewart 50.00 75.00
Home Depot/600
20 Tony Stewart 75.00 125.00
Home Depot Color Chrome/160
20 Tony Stewart 50.00 75.00
Home Depot Martinsville Raced/150
21 Jeff Burton 50.00 75.00
Coast Guard/120
21 Kevin Harvick 60.00 100.00
Coast Guard/120
21 Kevin Harvick 75.00 125.00
Coast Guard Reserve
Richmond Raced/150
24 Jeff Gordon 60.00 100.00
DuPont Flames Color Chrome/288
24 Jeff Gordon 60.00 100.00
DuPont Hot Hues
Foose Designs/1400
24 Jeff Gordon 60.00 100.00
Superman/1500
24 Jeff Gordon 60.00 100.00
World Series of Poker
JG Foundation/600
26 Ricky Bobby 40.00 65.00
Laughing Clown/200
26 Ricky Bobby 40.00 65.00
Wonderbread/200
29 Kevin Harvick 50.00 75.00
Goodwrench/288
29 Kevin Harvick 60.00 100.00
Goodwrench Color Chrome/120
29 Kevin Harvick 40.00 65.00
Hershey's/360
29 Kevin Harvick 50.00 75.00
Reese's/240
31 Jeff Burton 50.00 75.00
Cingular/204
38 David Gilliland 60.00 100.00
M&M's Halloween/200
38 Elliott Sadler 50.00 75.00
M&M's/288
38 Elliott Sadler 50.00 75.00
M&M's Pirates of the Caribbean/300
43 Bobby Labonte 50.00 75.00
Gogurt/200
44 Terry Labonte 150.00 250.00
Kellogg's Tribute/244
45 Kyle Petty 60.00 100.00
Wells Fargo/144
48 Jimmie Johnson 60.00 100.00
Lowe's/288
48 Jimmie Johnson 60.00 100.00
Lowe's Color Chrome/144
48 Jimmie Johnson 75.00 125.00
Lowe's Daytona Raced w
tire/248
48 Jimmie Johnson 50.00 75.00
Lowe's Sea World/448
88 Dale Jarrett 50.00 75.00
UPS/288
96 Terry Labonte 50.00 75.00
DLP/144
96 Tony Raines 60.00 100.00
DLP HOF
Color Chrome/100
98 Erin Crocker 50.00 75.00
Cheerios/120
07 Clint Bowyer 50.00 75.00
Directv/277
07 Clint Bowyer 60.00 100.00
Jack Daniel's/222

2006 Action/RCCA Elite 1:24

SOME DC NOT PRICED
DUE TO SCARCITY
1 Martin Truex Jr. 60.00 120.00
Bass Pro Shops/408
1 Martin Truex Jr. 75.00 125.00
Bass Pro Shops Color Chrome/200
1 Martin Truex Jr.
Bass Pro Shops
Platinum/8
1 Martin Truex Jr. 250.00 400.00
Bass Pro Shops White Gold/25
1 Martin Truex Jr.
Bass Pro Shops Dale Tribute
Platinum/5
1 Martin Truex Jr. 75.00 125.00
Bass Pro Shops Test/300
1 Martin Truex Jr.
Bass Pro Shops Test
Platinum/6
2 Clint Bowyer 60.00 120.00
AC Delco/144
2 Clint Bowyer
AC Delco Platinum/2
2 Kurt Busch
Miller Lite Platinum/5
2 Rusty Wallace 75.00 125.00
Legendary/444
2 Rusty Wallace
Legendary Platinum/8
2 Rusty Wallace 250.00 400.00
Legendary White Gold/25
5 Kyle Busch 60.00 120.00
Carquest/120
5 Kyle Busch
Carquest Platinum/2
5 Kyle Busch 75.00 125.00
Kellogg's/288
5 Kyle Busch 100.00 150.00
Kellogg's AU/50
5 Kyle Busch 75.00 125.00
Kellogg's Color Chrome/108
5 Kyle Busch 450.00 600.00
Kellogg's Platinum/5
5 Kyle Busch 200.00 350.00
Kellogg's White Gold/25
5 Kyle Busch 75.00 125.00
Kellogg's Cars/200
5 Kyle Busch 100.00 175.00
Kellogg's Cars AU/144
5 Kyle Busch
Kellogg's Cars
Platinum/7
5 Kyle Busch 250.00 400.00
Kellogg's Cars
White Gold/25
5 Kyle Busch 60.00 120.00
Kellogg's Ice Age 2/288
5 Kyle Busch
Kellogg's Ice Age 2
Platinum/5
6 Mark Martin 100.00 150.00
AAA Holiday/250
6 Mark Martin
AAA Holiday
Platinum/5
8 Dale Earnhardt Jr. 90.00 150.00
Bud/1500
8 Dale Earnhardt Jr. 100.00 175.00
Bud Color Chrome/444
8 Dale Earnhardt Jr. 600.00 800.00
Bud Platinum/30
8 Dale Earnhardt Jr. 600.00 800.00
Bud White Gold/30
8 Dale Earnhardt Jr. 125.00 200.00
Bud Richmond Raced/1388
8 Dale Earnhardt Jr.
Bud Richmond Raced
Platinum/27
8 Dale Earnhardt Jr. 175.00 300.00
Bud 3 Days of Dale Tribute/3333
8 Dale Earnhardt Jr. 400.00 600.00
Bud Dale Tribute Platinum/66
8 Dale Earnhardt Jr. 600.00 900.00
Bud 3 Days of Dale Tribute
White Gold/33
8 Dale Earnhardt Jr. 100.00 175.00
Bud Father's Day/3333
8 Dale Earnhardt Jr. 350.00 500.00
Bud Father's Day
Platinum/50
8 Dale Earnhardt Jr. 500.00 750.00
Bud Father's Day
White Gold/33
8 Dale Earnhardt Jr. 90.00 150.00
Bud Test/1000
8 Dale Earnhardt Jr.
Bud Test
Platinum/20
8 Dale Earnhardt Jr.
Goody's Platinum/3
8 Dale Earnhardt Jr. 75.00 125.00
Menards
Daytona Raced/1500
8 Dale Earnhardt Jr.
Menards
Daytona Raced Platinum/30
8 Dale Earnhardt Jr. 75.00 125.00
Oreo/1200
8 Dale Earnhardt Jr.
Oreo Platinum/24
8 Dale Earnhardt Jr. 250.00 400.00
Oreo White Gold/30
8 Dale Earnhardt Jr. 75.00 150.00
250th Start/1500
8 Dale Earnhardt Jr.
250th Start
Platinum/30
8 Dale Earnhardt Jr. 350.00 500.00
250th Start
White Gold/33
8 Martin Truex Jr. 100.00 150.00
Bass Pro 3 Days of Dale Tribute
Talladega Raced/250
8 Martin Truex Jr.
Bass Pro Shops Dale Tribute
Talladega Raced Platinum/5
8 Martin Truex Jr. 75.00 125.00
Ritz/300
8 Martin Truex Jr.
Ritz Platinum/6
8 Martin Truex Jr. 250.00 400.00
Ritz White Gold/25
9 Kasey Kahne 75.00 125.00
Click Michigan Raced/350
9 Kasey Kahne
Click Michigan Raced
Platinum/7
9 Kasey Kahne 75.00 125.00
Dodge/600
9 Kasey Kahne 100.00 175.00
Dodge AU/216
9 Kasey Kahne 90.00 150.00
Dodge Color Chrome/144
9 Kasey Kahne 650.00 900.00
Dodge Platinum/12
9 Kasey Kahne 400.00 600.00
Dodge White Gold/25
9 Kasey Kahne
Dodge Texas Raced
Platinum/4
9 Kasey Kahne 75.00 125.00
Dodge Flames/350
9 Kasey Kahne
Dodge Flames Platinum/7
9 Kasey Kahne 60.00 120.00
Dodge Holiday/250
9 Kasey Kahne
Dodge Holiday Platinum/5
9 Kasey Kahne 75.00 125.00
Dodge SRT/250
9 Kasey Kahne
Dodge SRT Platinum/6
9 Kasey Kahne 250.00 400.00
Dodge SRT
White Gold/25
9 Kasey Kahne 75.00 125.00
Dodge Test/400
9 Kasey Kahne
Dodge Test Platinum/8
9 Kasey Kahne 75.00 125.00
Dodge UAW Daimler Chrysler 400/300
9 Kasey Kahne
Dodge UAW Daimler Chrysler 400
Platinum/6
9 Kasey Kahne 250.00 400.00
Dodge UAW Daimler Chrysler 400
White Gold/25
9 Kasey Kahne 75.00 125.00
Mopar/250
9 Kasey Kahne
Mopar Platinum/5
9 Kasey Kahne 300.00 450.00
Mopar White Gold/25
9 Kasey Kahne 75.00 125.00
McDonald's/250
9 Kasey Kahne 100.00 175.00
McDonald's AU/72
9 Kasey Kahne
McDonald's Platinum/5
9 Kasey Kahne 250.00 400.00
McDonald's White Gold/25
9 Kasey Kahne 75.00 125.00
Ragu/204
9 Kasey Kahne
Ragu Platinum/4
9 Kasey Kahne 75.00 125.00
Vitamin Water/150
9 Kasey Kahne
Vitamin Water
Platinum/3
10 Scott Riggs
Valvoline Platinum/2
10 Scott Riggs 125.00 250.00
Valvoline White Gold/25
10 Scott Riggs
Valvoline Cars Platinum/2
11 Denny Hamlin 125.00 200.00
FedEx Express/411
11 Denny Hamlin
Fed Ex Express
Platinum/8
11 Denny Hamlin
Fed Ex Express
White Gold/25
11 Denny Hamlin 125.00 200.00
FedEx Express
Daytona Shootout Raced/311
11 Denny Hamlin
Fed Ex Express
Daytona Shootout Raced Platinum/4
11 Denny Hamlin 100.00 175.00
FedEx Freight/299
11 Denny Hamlin
Fed Ex Freight
Platinum/5
11 Denny Hamlin 100.00 175.00
FedEx Ground/411
11 Denny Hamlin 400.00 600.00
Fed Ex Ground
Platinum/8
11 Denny Hamlin 400.00 600.00
FedEx Ground
White Gold/25
11 Denny Hamlin 100.00 175.00
Fed Ex Ground
Pocono Raced/299
11 Denny Hamlin
Fed Ex Ground
Pocono Raced Platinum/5
11 Denny Hamlin 100.00 150.00
Fed Ex Home Delivery/411
11 Denny Hamlin
Fed Ex Home Delivery
Platinum/8
11 Denny Hamlin 400.00 600.00
Fed Ex Home Delivery
White Gold/25
11 Denny Hamlin 100.00 175.00
FedEx Kinko's/299
11 Denny Hamlin
Fed Ex Kinko's
Platinum/5
11 Denny Hamlin 100.00 175.00
Fed Ex Kinko's
Pocono Raced/299
11 Denny Hamlin
Fed Ex Kinko's
Pocono Raced Platinum/5
11 Denny Hamlin 100.00 150.00
Fed Ex PGA Cup/299
11 Denny Hamlin
Fed Ex PGA Cup
Platinum/5
11 Denny Hamlin 400.00 600.00
Fed Ex PGA Cup
White Gold/25
11 Paul Menard 60.00 120.00
Menard's Johns Manville/144
11 Paul Menard
Menard's Johns Manville
Platinum/2
11 Paul Menard
Turtle Wax Platinum/2
11 Paul Menard 90.00 150.00
Turtle Wax 3 Days of Dale Tribute/203
11 Paul Menard
Turtle Wax Dale Tribute
Platinum/4
12 Ryan Newman
Alltel Platinum/4
14 Sterling Marlin 75.00 125.00
Waste Management/144
14 Sterling Marlin
Waste Management
Platinum/2
15 Paul Menard 60.00 120.00
Quaker State/120
15 Paul Menard
Quaker State Platinum/2
16 Greg Biffle
National Guard
Platinum/4
17 Matt Kenseth
DeWalt Platinum/5
17 Matt Kenseth
DeWalt White Gold/25
18 J.J. Yeley 90.00 150.00
Interstate Batteries/200
18 J.J. Yeley
Interstate Batteries
Platinum/4
18 J.J. Yeley 250.00 400.00
Interstate Batteries
White Gold/25
19 Jeremy Mayfield 50.00 100.00
Dodge/288
19 Jeremy Mayfield
Dodge Platinum/5
19 Jeremy Mayfield 200.00 350.00
Dodge White Gold/25
19 Jeremy Mayfield
Dodge SRT
Platinum/5
19 Jeremy Mayfield
Dodge SRT
White Gold/25
19 Elliott Sadler
Dodge Holiday
Platinum/4
19 Elliott Sadler 175.00 350.00
Dodge Holiday
White Gold/25
20 Denny Hamlin 75.00 125.00
Rockwell Automation/144
20 Denny Hamlin
Rockwall Automation
Platinum/2
20 Tony Stewart 90.00 150.00
Home Depot/800
20 Tony Stewart 90.00 150.00
Home Depot Color Chrome/220
20 Tony Stewart
Home Depot
Platinum/16
20 Tony Stewart 400.00 600.00
Home Depot
White Gold/30
20 Tony Stewart 100.00 175.00
Home Depot Daytona Raced/250
20 Tony Stewart
Home Depot Daytona Raced
Platinum/5
20 Tony Stewart 75.00 125.00
Home Depot
Martinsville Raced/200
20 Tony Stewart
Home Depot
Martinsville Raced Platinum/4
20 Tony Stewart 100.00 150.00
Home Depot Holiday/250
20 Tony Stewart
Home Depot Holiday
Platinum/5
20 Tony Stewart 400.00 600.00
Home Depot Holiday
White Gold/25
20 Tony Stewart 75.00 125.00
Home Depot Test/600
20 Tony Stewart
Home Depot Test
Platinum/5
20 Tony Stewart 75.00 125.00
Powerade/400
20 Tony Stewart
Powerade Platinum/8
20 Tony Stewart 400.00 600.00
Powerade White Gold/25
20 Tony Stewart 100.00 175.00
Six Flags/400
20 Tony Stewart
Six Flags Platinum/8
20 Tony Stewart 400.00 600.00
Six Flags
White Gold/25
21 Kevin Harvick 125.00 200.00
Coast Guard/120
21 Kevin Harvick
Coast Guard Platinum/2
21 Kevin Harvick 125.00 200.00
Coast Guard Reserve
Richmond Raced/200
21 Kevin Harvick
Coast Guard Reserve
Richmond Raced Platinum/4
24 Jeff Gordon 75.00 125.00
DuPont Flames/1008
24 Jeff Gordon 100.00 175.00
DuPont Flames Color Chrome/288
24 Jeff Gordon 700.00 1000.00
DuPont Flames Platinum/20
24 Jeff Gordon 500.00 750.00
DuPont Flames White Gold/30
24 Jeff Gordon
DuPont Flames
Chicagoland Raced Platinum/7
24 Jeff Gordon 75.00 125.00
DuPont Flames
Performance Alliance/416
24 Jeff Gordon
DuPont Flames
Performance Alliance Platinum/12
24 Jeff Gordon 250.00 400.00
DuPont Flames Test/724
24 Jeff Gordon 700.00 1000.00
DuPont Flames Test Platinum/14
24 Jeff Gordon 90.00 150.00
DuPont Hot Hues
Chip Foose/1900
24 Jeff Gordon 125.00 200.00
DuPont Hot Hues
Chip Foose Designs AU/200
24 Jeff Gordon 600.00 900.00
DuPont Hot Hues
Chip Foose Designs Platinum/38
24 Jeff Gordon 350.00 500.00
DuPont Hot Hues
Chip Foose Designs White Gold/40
24 Jeff Gordon 100.00 150.00
Holiday JG Foundation

Color Chrome/494
24 Jeff Gordon Holiday JG Foundation Platinum/10
24 Jeff Gordon Holiday JG Foundation White Gold/25 500.00 750.00
24 Jeff Gordon Mighty Mouse Jeff Gordon Foundation/900 75.00 125.00
24 Jeff Gordon Mighty Mouse Jeff Gordon Foundation Platinum/18
24 Jeff Gordon Mighty Mouse Jeff Gordon Foundation White Gold/30 500.00 750.00
24 Jeff Gordon Nicorette/999 75.00 125.00
24 Jeff Gordon Nicorette Platinum/19 400.00 600.00
24 Jeff Gordon Nicorette White Gold/30 500.00 750.00
24 Jeff Gordon Pepsi/900 90.00 150.00
24 Jeff Gordon Pepsi Platinum/18
24 Jeff Gordon Pepsi White Gold/40 400.00 650.00
24 Jeff Gordon Superman/1800 90.00 150.00
24 Jeff Gordon Superman Platinum/36 500.00 750.00
24 Jeff Gordon Superman White Gold/40 400.00 600.00
24 Jeff Gordon World Series of Poker Jeff Gordon Foundation/600 75.00 125.00
24 Jeff Gordon WSOP JG Foundation Platinum/18
24 Jeff Gordon WSOP JG Foundation White Gold/33 500.00 750.00
25 Brian Vickers GMAC Platinum/2
26 Jamie McMurray Crown Royal Platinum/4
29 Kevin Harvick Goodwrench/408 75.00 125.00
29 Kevin Harvick Goodwrench Color Chrome/144 90.00 150.00
29 Kevin Harvick Goodwrench Platinum/8
29 Kevin Harvick Goodwrench White Gold/25 250.00 400.00
29 Kevin Harvick Goodwrench Barenaked Ladies Richmond Raced Platinum/5
29 Kevin Harvick Goodwrench Holiday/250 75.00 125.00
29 Kevin Harvick Goodwrench Holiday Platinum/5
29 Kevin Harvick Goodwrench Holiday White Gold/25 200.00 350.00
29 Kevin Harvick Hershey's/429 60.00 120.00
29 Kevin Harvick Hershey's Platinum/8
29 Kevin Harvick Hershey's White Gold/25 250.00 400.00
29 Kevin Harvick Hershey's Kissables/240 60.00 120.00
29 Kevin Harvick Hershey's Kissables Platinum/4
29 Kevin Harvick Hershey's Kissables White Gold/25 200.00 350.00
29 Kevin Harvick Reese's/240 60.00 120.00
29 Kevin Harvick Reese's Platinum/4
29 Kevin Harvick Reese's White Gold/25 250.00 400.00
29 Kevin Harvick Reese's Caramel/240 60.00 120.00
29 Kevin Harvick Reese's Caramel Platinum/4
29 Kevin Harvick Reese's Caramel White Gold/25
31 Jeff Burton Cingular/204 75.00 125.00
31 Jeff Burton Cingular AU/50 100.00 175.00
31 Jeff Burton Cingular Platinum/4 600.00 800.00
31 Jeff Burton Cingular White Gold/25 200.00 350.00
31 Jeff Burton Cingular Dover Raced Platinum/2
33 Kevin Harvick Dollar General Platinum/2
33 Tony Stewart Dollar General Platinum/2
33 Tony Stewart Old Spice/288 75.00 125.00
33 Tony Stewart Old Spice Platinum/5
33 Tony Stewart Old Spice White Gold/25
38 David Gilliland M&M's Halloween/200 100.00 150.00
38 David Gilliland M&M's Halloween Platinum/4
38 David Gilliland M&M's Halloween White Gold/25 250.00 400.00
38 Elliott Sadler M&M's/408 60.00 120.00
38 Elliott Sadler M&M's Color Chrome/120 60.00 120.00
38 Elliott Sadler M&M's Platinum/8
38 Elliott Sadler 250.00 400.00
M&M's White Gold/25
38 Elliott Sadler M&M's Mega Platinum/3
38 Elliott Sadler M&M's Pirates of the Caribbean White Gold/25 200.00 350.00
38 Elliott Sadler Snickers/250 60.00 120.00
38 Elliott Sadler Snickers Platinum/5
38 Elliott Sadler Snickers White Gold/25 200.00 350.00
39 Kurt Busch Penske Texas Raced Platinum/2
40 David Stremme Coors Light/120 90.00 150.00
40 David Stremme Coors Light Platinum/2
40 David Stremme Coors Light White Gold/25 200.00 350.00
40 David Stremme Lonestar Steakhouse/120 75.00 125.00
40 David Stremme Lone Star Steakhouse Platinum/2
40 David Stremme Lone Star Steakhouse White Gold/25
41 Reed Sorenson Discount Tire/144 60.00 120.00
41 Reed Sorenson Discount Tire Platinum/2
41 Reed Sorenson Target/240 90.00 150.00
41 Reed Sorenson Target Platinum/4
41 Reed Sorenson Target White Gold/25 250.00 400.00
42 Casey Mears Havoline Platinum/3
42 Casey Mears Havoline White Gold/25 200.00 350.00
43 Bobby Labonte Cheerios/200 75.00 125.00
43 Bobby Labonte Cheerios Platinum/4
43 Bobby Labonte Cheerios White Gold/25 250.00 400.00
43 Bobby Labonte Gogurt/200 90.00 150.00
43 Bobby Labonte Gogurt Platinum/4
43 Bobby Labonte Gogurt White Gold/25 250.00 400.00
43 Bobby Labonte STP/300 75.00 125.00
43 Bobby Labonte STP Platinum/6
43 Bobby Labonte STP White Gold/25 250.00 400.00
44 Terry Labonte Kellogg's/200 90.00 150.00
44 Terry Labonte Kellogg's Platinum/4
44 Terry Labonte Kellogg's White Gold/25 200.00 350.00
44 Terry Labonte Kellogg's Tribute/344 175.00 350.00
44 Terry Labonte Kellogg's Tribute Platinum/6
48 Jimmie Johnson Lowe's/408 100.00 200.00
48 Jimmie Johnson Lowe's Brickyard Raced/240 100.00 200.00
48 Jimmie Johnson Lowe's Color Chrome/144 100.00 200.00
48 Jimmie Johnson Lowe's Platinum/8
48 Jimmie Johnson Lowe's White Gold/25 400.00 600.00
48 Jimmie Johnson Lowe's Daytona Raced AU/200 350.00 500.00
48 Jimmie Johnson Lowe's Daytona Raced w tire/248 200.00 350.00
48 Jimmie Johnson Lowe's Daytona Raced Platinum/4
48 Jimmie Johnson Lowe's Flames Test/200 75.00 150.00
48 Jimmie Johnson Lowe's Flames Test Platinum/4
48 Jimmie Johnson Lowe's Holiday/250 60.00 120.00
48 Jimmie Johnson Lowe's Holiday Platinum/5
48 Jimmie Johnson Lowe's Holiday White Gold/25 300.00 450.00
48 Jimmie Johnson Lowe's Jimmie Johnson Foundation/120 75.00 150.00
48 Jimmie Johnson Lowe's JJ Foundation Platinum/2
48 Jimmie Johnson Lowe's SeaWorld/548 60.00 120.00
48 Jimmie Johnson Lowe's SeaWorld AU/100 125.00 200.00
48 Jimmie Johnson Lowe's SeaWorld Platinum/10
48 Jimmie Johnson Lowe's SeaWorld White Gold/25 300.00 500.00
48 Jimmie Johnson Lowe's 60th Anniversary/300 60.00 120.00
48 Jimmie Johnson Lowe's 60th Anniversary Platinum/6
48 Jimmie Johnson Lowe's 60th Anniversary White Gold/25 350.00 600.00
57 Brian Vickers Mountain Dew Platinum/2
57 Brian Vickers Ore-Ida Platinum/2
64 Steve Wallace Top Flite/120 60.00 100.00
64 Steve Wallace Top Flite Platinum/2
88 Dale Jarrett UPS Color Chrome/120 90.00 150.00
88 Dale Jarrett UPS Platinum/8
88 Dale Jarrett UPS White Gold/25 350.00 500.00
88 Dale Jarrett UPS Freight/200 100.00 175.00
88 Dale Jarrett UPS Freight Platinum/4
88 Mark McFarland Navy/144 75.00 125.00
88 Mark McFarland Navy Platinum/2
90 Stephen Leicht Citifinancial/60 75.00 125.00
90 Stephen Leicht Citifinancial Platinum/1
90 Matt McCall Citifinancial/60 75.00 125.00
90 Matt McCall Citifinancial Platinum/1
90 Elliott Sadler Citifinancial Platinum/2
96 Terry Labonte DLP Platinum/2
96 Terry Labonte DLP White Gold/25 200.00 350.00
98 Erin Crocker Cheerios/120 75.00 125.00
98 Erin Crocker Cheerios Platinum/2
99 Carl Edwards Office Depot Platinum/4
99 Carl Edwards Office Depot Holiday/200 100.00 150.00
99 Carl Edwards Office Depot Holiday Platinum/4
99 Carl Edwards Office Depot Holiday White Gold/25 250.00 400.00
0 Bill Elliott Burger King Platinum/6
01 Joe Nemechek Army Platinum/2
06 Holiday Event Car Platinum/3
06 Holiday Event Car White Gold/25 175.00 300.00
07 Clint Bowyer Directv/277 90.00 150.00
07 Clint Bowyer Directv Platinum/5
07 Clint Bowyer Directv White Gold/25 300.00 450.00
07 Clint Bowyer Jack Daniel's/333 90.00 150.00
07 Clint Bowyer Jack Daniel's Platinum/6
07 Clint Bowyer Jack Daniel's White Gold/25 300.00 450.00
07 Clint Bowyer Jack Daniel's Country Cocktails/250 90.00 150.00
07 Clint Bowyer Jack Daniel's Country Cocktails Platinum/5
07 Clint Bowyer Jack Daniel's Country Cocktails White Gold/25 300.00 450.00
07 Clint Bowyer Jack Daniel's Happy Birthday/203 90.00 150.00
07 Clint Bowyer Jack Daniel's Happy B-Day Platinum/5
07 Clint Bowyer Jack Daniel's Happy Birthday White Gold/25 300.00 450.00
07 Clint Bowyer Jack Daniel's Sopranos/277 90.00 150.00
07 Clint Bowyer Jack Daniel's Sopranos Platinum/5
07 Clint Bowyer Jack Daniel's Sopranos White Gold/25 300.00 450.00
07 Clint Bowyer Jack Daniel's Texas/250 90.00 150.00
07 Clint Bowyer Jack Daniel's Texas Platinum/5
07 Clint Bowyer Jack Daniel's Texas White Gold/25 300.00 450.00
NNO Dale Earnhardt HOF/2333 40.00 80.00
NNO Dale Earnhardt HOF Platinum/46
NNO Dale Earnhardt HOF White Gold/33 200.00 350.00

2006 Action/RCCA Elite Historical 1:24

3 Dale Earnhardt GM Goodwrench '91 Lumina/1333 100.00 150.00
3 Dale Earnhardt GM Goodwrench '91 Lumina White Gold/33

2006 Action/RCCA Historical 1:24

3 Dale Earnhardt Budweiser '89 IROC/1333 50.00 75.00

2007 Action/Motorsports Authentics Dale The Movie 1:24

2 Dale Earnhardt Mike Curb '80 Olds 1st Championship/7003 75.00 125.00
2 Dale Earnhardt Wrangler '81 Pontiac 75.00 125.00
1st Wrangler Win/7003
3 Dale Earnhardt Wrangler '86 Monte Carlo Muddy Windshield/7003 75.00 125.00
3 Dale Earnhardt Wrangler '87 Monte Carlo ass in the Grass/7003 75.00 125.00
3 Dale Earnhardt Goodwrench '88 Monte Carlo 1st Goodwrench Win/7003 75.00 125.00
3 Dale Earnhardt Goodwrench '90 Lumina Engine Change/7003 75.00 125.00
3 Dale Earnhardt Goodwrench '94 Lumina Four Tire Stop/7003 75.00 125.00
3 Dale Earnhardt Goodwrench '94 Lumina Number 7/7003 75.00 125.00
3 Dale Earnhardt Goodwrench Silver '95 Monte Carlro Silver Select/7003 75.00 125.00
3 Dale Earnhardt Goodwrench '95 Monte Carlo Bricks/7003 75.00 125.00
3 Dale Earnhardt Goodwrench '96 Monte Carlo Starting in Front/7003 75.00 125.00
3 Dale Earnhardt Goodwrench Plus '98 Monte Carlo The 500/7003 75.00 125.00

2007 Action/Motorsports Authentics Driver's Select 1:24

SOME PRINT RUNS LISTED ON PACKAGE
*SOME PRINT RUNS PROVIDED BY MA
1 Martin Truex Jr. Bass Pro Shops/4800* 40.00 70.00
1 Martin Truex Jr. Bass Pro Shops COT/1570* 40.00 70.00
1 Martin Truex Jr. Bass Pro Shops COT Dover Raced/2248* 40.00 70.00
1 Martin Truex Jr. Bass Pro Shops National Wild Turkey Foundation/1704* 40.00 70.00
1 Martin Truex Jr. Bass Pro Shops 35th Anniversary/1404* 40.00 70.00
1 Martin Truex Jr. Bass Pro Shops '57 Chevy/1536* 40.00 70.00
2 Clint Bowyer BB&T/2176* 40.00 70.00
2 Kurt Busch Miller Lite/4008* 40.00 70.00
2 Kurt Busch Miller Lite COT/1104* 50.00 75.00
2 Kurt Busch Miller Lite Wolrd Beer Challenge/1176* 40.00 70.00
4 Ward Burton Air Force American Heroes/1056 40.00 70.00
5 Kyle Busch Carquest/1800* 35.00 60.00
5 Kyle Busch Carquest COT Bristol Raced/1368* 40.00 70.00
5 Kyle Busch Kellogg's/1800* 35.00 60.00
5 Kyle Busch Kellogg's COT/1163* 40.00 70.00
6 David Ragan AAA/6624* 40.00 70.00
6 David Ragan AAA COT/708* 50.00 75.00
6 David Ragan AAA Insurance/804* 40.00 70.00
6 David Ragan AAA Show Your Card/852* 40.00 70.00
6 David Ragan AAA Travel/804* 40.00 70.00
6 David Ragan Discount Tire/1200* 35.00 60.00
7 Mike Wallace Geico/1000* 40.00 70.00
8 Dale Earnhardt Jr. Bud/26,904* 75.00 125.00
8 Dale Earnhardt Jr. Bud COT/33,934* 75.00 125.00
8 Dale Earnhardt Jr. Bud Camo American Heroes/41,520 50.00 100.00
8 Dale Earnhardt Jr. Bud Elvis COT/35,816* 60.00 75.00
8 Dale Earnhardt Jr. Bud Stars & Stripes31,272* 50.00 100.00
8 Dale Earnhardt Jr. Bud '57 Chevy/19,504* 40.00 70.00
8 Dale Earnhardt Jr. JM Menards/2232* 30.00 60.00
8 Dale Earnhardt Jr. Sharpie/13,182* 30.00 60.00
8 Dale Earnhardt Jr. Veritas/1896* 40.00 70.00
8 Martin Truex Jr. Ritz Oreo 35.00 60.00
9 Kasey Kahne Dodge Dealers/9504* 40.00 70.00
9 Kasey Kahne Dodge Dealers COT/2616* 50.00 75.00
9 Kasey Kahne Dodge Dealers Holiday Sam Bass/894* 40.00 70.00
9 Kasey Kahne 35.00 60.00
Doublemint/1704*
9 Kasey Kahne Hellmann's/2208* 35.00 60.
9 Kasey Kahne McDonald's/1296* 40.00 70.
9 Kasey Kahne Mopar/1608* 40.00 70.
9 Kasey Kahne Vitamin Water/1674* 40.00 70.
10 Scott Riggs Stanley Tools/1008* 35.00 60.
10 Scott Riggs Stanley Tools COT/708* 40.00 70.
10 Scott Riggs Valvoline/1404* 35.00 60.
10 Scott Riggs Valvoline COT/708* 40.00 70.
11 Denny Hamlin Fed Ex Express/9000* 40.00 70.
11 Denny Hamlin Fed Ex Express COT/1408* 50.00 75.
11 Denny Hamlin Fed Ex Express Sam Bass Holiday/1020* 50.00 75.
11 Denny Hamlin Fed Ex Freight/7008* 40.00 70.
11 Denny Hamlin Fed Ex Freight COT/1152* 50.00 75.
11 Denny Hamlin Fed Ex Freight Marines American Heroes/3240 40.00 70.
11 Denny Hamlin Fed Ex Ground/3756* 40.00 70.0
11 Denny Hamlin Fed Ex Ground COT/1260* 50.00 75.0
11 Denny Hamlin Fed Ex Ground COT New Hampshire Raced/888 50.00 75.0
11 Denny Hamlin Fed Ex Kinko's/3216* 40.00 70.0
11 Denny Hamlin Fed Ex Kinko's COT/1372* 50.00 75.0
12 Kurt Busch Penske/1000* 40.00 70.0
12 Sam Hornish Jr. Mobil 1/1200* 50.00 75.0
12 Ryan Newman Alltel/3700* 40.00 70.0
12 Ryan Newman Alltel COT/2488* 40.00 70.0
12 Ryan Newman Alltel My Circle/800* 40.00 70.0
12 Ryan Newman Kodak/1852* 40.00 70.0
12 Ryan Newman Mobil 1/1400* 40.00 70.0
14 Sterling Marlin Waste Management/1236* 40.00 70.0
15 Paul Menard JM Menards/2208* 40.00 70.0
15 Paul Menard JM Menards COT/514* 40.00 70.0
15 Paul Menard JM Menards '57 Chevy/348 40.00 70.0
16 Greg Biffle Aflac COT/1086* 40.00 70.0
16 Greg Biffle Ameriquest/3000* 30.00 60.0
16 Greg Biffle Ameriquest COT/700* 40.00 70.0
16 Greg Biffle Dish Network COT/700* 40.00 70.0
16 Greg Biffle Jackson Hewitt/700* 30.00 60.0
16 Greg Biffle 3M/2100* 40.00 70.0
16 Greg Biffle 3M Blue Tape/600* 100.00 175.0
16 Greg Biffle 3M Coast Guard American Heroes/2568 50.00 75.0
16 Greg Biffle 3M Finishmast/60* 60.00 100.0
17 Matt Kenseth Aflac/1452* 40.00 70.0
17 Matt Kenseth Arby's/2240* 50.00 75.0
17 Matt Kenseth Carhartt/1900* 40.00 70.0
17 Matt Kenseth Carhartt California Raced/1200* 50.00 75.0
17 Matt Kenseth Carhartt for Women/700* 40.00 70.0
17 Matt Kenseth Carhartt COT/900* 50.00 75.0
17 Matt Kenseth DeWalt/3708* 50.00 75.0
17 Matt Kenseth DeWalt Homestead-Miami Raced/864* 50.00 75.0
17 Matt Kenseth DeWalt COT/2182* 50.00 75.0
17 Matt Kenseth DeWalt Holiday Sam Bass/780* 40.00 70.0
17 Matt Kenseth Dish Network/1116* 40.00 70.0
17 Matt Kenseth iLevel Wayerhouser/948* 40.00 70.0
17 Matt Kenseth R&L Carriers/1900* 40.00 70.0
17 Matt Kenseth R&L Carriers COT/756* 50.00 75.0
17 Matt Kenseth USG Sheetrock/3434* 40.00 70.0
18 J.J. Yeley Interstate Batteries/2508* 50.00 75.0
18 J.J. Yeley Interstate Batteries COT/708* 40.00 70.0
18 J.J. Yeley Interstate Batteries '57 Chevy/456* 40.00 70.0
19 Elliott Sadler Dodge Dealers/4508* 40.00 70.0
19 Elliott Sadler Dodge Dealers COT/1104* 50.00 75.0
19 Elliott Sadler Dodge Dealers Holiday 40.00 70.0

m Bass/387*
iott Sadler 50.00 75.00
emen's COT/1212*
ey Logano 200.00 350.00
Racing Oil/720*
ny Stewart 40.00 70.00
me Depot/8508*
ny Stewart 50.00 75.00
me Depot
ckyard Raced/3744*
ny Stewart 50.00 75.00
me Depot
icagoland Raced/1248*
ny Stewart 50.00 75.00
me Depot
d Shootout Daytona Raced/2007*
ny Stewart 50.00 75.00
me Depot
in 150s Daytona Raced/2028*
ny Stewart 50.00 75.00
me Depot
atkins Glen Raced/1116*
ny Stewart 50.00 75.00
me Depot COT/7392*
ny Stewart 40.00 70.00
me Depot Holiday
m Bass/1572*
ny Stewart 50.00 75.00
me Depot '57 Chevy/300*
vin Harvick 40.00 70.00
to Zone/2208*
vin Harvick 50.00 75.00
to Zone Daytona Raced/1908*
n Wood 50.00 75.00
Force
nerican Heroes/1548*
K.Harvick 75.00 125.00
to Zone Daytona Raced
ell Pennzoil Daytona Raced 2-car set
ve Blaney 40.00 70.00
T/1978*
ve Blaney 40.00 70.00
T COT/708*
ve Blaney 40.00 70.00
T D6T/1408*
ve Blaney 40.00 70.00
T M-Series/960*
ve Blaney 40.00 70.00
Tused.com/792*
ff Gordon 50.00 75.00
Pont Department of Defense
nerican Heroes/7008
ff Gordon 50.00 75.00
Pont Flames/13,500*
ff Gordon 50.00 75.00
Pont Flames
in 150s Daytona Raced/2256*
ff Gordon 60.00 100.00
Pont Flames
cono Raced/1576*
ff Gordon 50.00 75.00
Pont Flames
lladega Raced/7777*
ff Gordon 175.00 300.00
Pont Flames
omax Pro Employee/711
ff Gordon 60.00 100.00
Pont Flames Car of Tomorrow/19,228*
ff Gordon 60.00 100.00
Pont Flames COT
arlington Raced/2892*
ff Gordon 50.00 75.00
Pont Flames COT
oenix Raced/7676*
ff Gordon 175.00 300.00
Pont Flames COT
oneer Employee/711
ff Gordon 50.00 75.00
Pont Flames '57 Chevy/6180*
ff Gordon 40.00 70.00
oliday Sam Bass
ff Gordon Foundation/3288*
ff Gordon 50.00 75.00
icorette/5704*
ff Gordon 50.00 75.00
icorette COT/4662*
ff Gordon 50.00 75.00
epsi/5704*
ff Gordon 50.00 75.00
epsi COT/5788*
ff Gordon 60.00 100.00
epsi COT
lladega Raced/3192*
ff Gordon 50.00 75.00
nderdog JG Foundation/5180*
asey Mears 50.00 75.00
ational Guard/2758*
asey Mears 40.00 70.00
ational Guard COT/2016*
asey Mears 40.00 70.00
ational Guard Camo
merican Heroes/912*
asey Mears 40.00 70.00
ational Guard Camo
merican Heroes Charlotte Raced/1190*
mie McMurray 40.00 70.00
lac/1008*
amie McMurray 50.00 75.00
rown Royal/2256*
amie McMurray 50.00 75.00
rown Royal COT/1152*
amie McMurray 40.00 70.00
ish Network/700*
amie McMurray 40.00 70.00
win Tools/1200*
ff Burton 40.00 70.00
oliday Inn/816*
evin Harvick 40.00 70.00
ennzoil Platinum All Star
harlotte Raced/3255*
evin Harvick 50.00 75.00
ennzoil Platinum COT/2700*
evin Harvick 50.00 75.00
eese's/3000*
evin Harvick 450.00 700.00
eese's Elvis/723*
evin Harvick 50.00 75.00
hell Pennzoil/13,924*
evin Harvick 60.00 100.00

Shell Pennzoil
Daytona Raced/7029*
29 Kevin Harvick 50.00 75.00
Shell Pennzoil
Daytona Raced Liquid Chrome/729
29 Kevin Harvick 50.00 75.00
Shell Pennzoil COT/10,008*
29 Kevin Harvick 40.00 70.00
Shell Pennzoil Holiday
Sam Bass/1129*
29 Scott Wimmer 40.00 70.00
Holiday Inn/144*
31 Jeff Burton 40.00 70.00
AT&T COT/2135*
31 Jeff Burton 50.00 75.00
Cingular/3264*
31 Jeff Burton 40.00 70.00
Lenox/708*
31 Jeff Burton 40.00 70.00
Prilosec/2264*
31 Jeff Burton 50.00 75.00
Prilosec Texas Raced/840
33 Kevin Harvick 40.00 70.00
Road Loans/1120*
33 Tony Stewart 40.00 70.00
Old Spice/1320*
38 David Gilliland 50.00 75.00
M&M's/4404*
38 David Gilliland 50.00 75.00
M&M's COT/1428*
38 David Gilliland 40.00 70.00
M&M's Holiday
Sam Bass/396*
38 David Gilliland 30.00 60.00
M&M's July 4/1020*
38 David Gilliland 40.00 70.00
M&M's Pink
Susan G. Komen/1318*
38 David Gilliland 50.00 75.00
M&M's Shrek/2424*
39 Sam Hornish Jr. 40.00 70.00
Mobil 1/639*
40 David Stremme 50.00 75.00
Coors Light/1500*
40 David Stremme 50.00 75.00
Coors Light COT/708*
40 David Stremme 25.00 50.00
Lone Star Steakhouse/1104*
41 Bryan Clauson 40.00 70.00
Memorex/708*
41 Reed Sorenson 40.00 70.00
Fuji Film/708*
41 Reed Sorenson 40.00 70.00
Juicy Fruit/778*
41 Reed Sorenson 40.00 70.00
Target/2004*
41 Reed Sorenson 50.00 75.00
Target COT/708*
42 Dario Franchitti 50.00 75.00
Target/708*
42 Juan Pablo Montoya 40.00 70.00
Big Red/3464*
42 Juan Pablo Montoya 60.00 100.00
Texaco Havoline/6504*
42 Juan Pablo Montoya 50.00 75.00
Texaco Havoline
Mexico City Raced/1366*
42 Juan Pablo Montoya 60.00 100.00
Texaco Havoline COT1752*
42 Juan Pablo Montoya 50.00 75.00
Texaco Havoline COT
Infineon Raced/828*
42 Juan Pablo Montoya 40.00 70.00
Texaco Havoline Holiday
Sam Bass/381*
43 Bobby Labonte 50.00 75.00
Cheerios/4204*
43 Bobby Labonte 50.00 75.00
Cheerios COT/960*
43 Bobby Labonte 40.00 70.00
Cheerios Pink
Susan G. Komen/1056*
43 Bobby Labonte 40.00 70.00
Cheerios Spiderman/2032*
43 Bobby Labonte 40.00 70.00
Cheerios 500 Starts COT/840*
43 Bobby Labonte 40.00 70.00
General Mills COT/1140*
44 Dale Jarrett 40.00 70.00
UPS/9504*
44 Dale Jarrett 40.00 70.00
UPS COT/2208*
44 Dale Jarrett 50.00 75.00
UPS Kentucky Derby/3540*
44 Dale Jarrett 40.00 70.00
UPS Toys for Tots/876*
44 Dale Jarrett 40.00 70.00
UPS 100th Anniversary COT/1794*
45 Kyle Petty 40.00 70.00
Marathon Oil/1404*
45 Kyle Petty 40.00 70.00
Marathon Oil COT/708*
45 Kyle Petty 40.00 70.00
Wells Fargo1896*
45 Kyle Petty 40.00 70.00
Wells Fargo COT/2200*
48 Jimmie Johnson 50.00 75.00
Lowe's/7500*
48 Jimmie Johnson 50.00 75.00
Lowe's Las Vegas Raced/1380*
48 Jimmie Johnson 50.00 75.00
Lowe's
Fall Martinsville Raced/792*
48 Jimmie Johnson 60.00 100.00
Lowe's Car of Tomorrow/6012*
48 Jimmie Johnson 40.00 70.00
Lowe's COT
Martinsville Raced/1320*
48 Jimmie Johnson 50.00 75.00
Lowe's COT
Richmond Raced/1320*
48 Jimmie Johnson 40.00 70.00
Lowe's Holiday
Sam Bass/1166*
48 Jimmie Johnson 50.00 75.00
Lowe's Jimmie Johnson Foundation/708*
48 Jimmie Johnson 50.00 75.00
Lowe's Kobalt/1572*
48 Jimmie Johnson 60.00 100.00

Lowe's Kobalt
Atlanta Raced/1537*
48 Jimmie Johnson 50.00 75.00
Lowe's Kobalt
Fall Atlanta Raced/853*
48 Jimmie Johnson 50.00 75.00
Lowe's Kobalt
Texas Raced/792*
48 Jimmie Johnson 50.00 75.00
Lowe's Power of Pride
American Heroes/4164
48 Jimmie Johnson 50.00 75.00
Lowe's '57 Chevy/1906*
55 Michael Waltrip 40.00 70.00
NAPA/10,404*
55 Michael Waltrip 40.00 70.00
NAPA COT/1416*
60 Carl Edwards 40.00 70.00
Aflac/1116*
60 Carl Edwards 40.00 70.00
Scotts/1608*
60 Carl Edwards 40.00 70.00
Scotts '07 BGN Champion/1084*
60 Carl Edwards 40.00 70.00
World Financial/708*
66 Steve Wallace 40.00 70.00
Home Life/700*
83 Brian Vickers 50.00 75.00
Red Bull/2460*
83 Brian Vickers 40.00 70.00
Red Bull COT/804*
84 A.J. Allmendinger 50.00 75.00
Red Bull/1308*
84 A.J. Allmendinger 40.00 70.00
Red Bull COT/700*
88 Shane Huffman 40.00 70.00
Navy/1400*
88 Shane Huffman 50.00 75.00
Navy American Heroes/840
88 Shane Huffman 60.00 100.00
Navy SEALS/1092*
88 Ricky Rudd 40.00 70.00
Combos COT/708*
88 Ricky Rudd 40.00 70.00
Pedigree COT/852*
88 Ricky Rudd 35.00 60.00
Snickers/2832*
88 Ricky Rudd 50.00 75.00
Snickers COT/1017*
88 Ricky Rudd 40.00 70.00
Snickers Dark/708*
90 Stephen Leicht 40.00 70.00
Citifinancial/1000*
96 Tony Raines 40.00 70.00
DLP/1200*
96 Tony Raines 40.00 70.00
DLP COT/700*
96 Tony Raines 50.00 75.00
DLP Shrek
Car of Tomorrow/1440*
96 Tony Raines 40.00 70.00
DLP '57 Chevy/312*
99 Carl Edwards 100.00 200.00
Boston Red Sox COT/1764*
99 Carl Edwards 50.00 75.00
Office Depot/3756*
99 Carl Edwards 40.00 70.00
Office Depot COT/1056*
99 Carl Edwards 40.00 70.00
Office Depot Holiday
Sam Bass/520*
99 David Reutimann 50.00 75.00
Aaron's/3488*
00 David Reutimann 50.00 75.00
Burger King/2200*
00 David Reutimann 40.00 70.00
Burger King COT/708*
00 David Reutimann 40.00 70.00
Domino's Pizza/2508*
00 David Reutimann 50.00 75.00
Domino's Pizza COT/700*
00 Josh Wise 40.00 70.00
Aaron's SuperTruck/1704*
01 Mark Martin 40.00 70.00
Principal Financial Group/1224*
01 Mark Martin 40.00 70.00
U.S. Army/11,340*
01 Mark Martin 50.00 75.00
U.S. Army COT/2508*
01 Mark Martin 40.00 70.00
U.S. Army American Heroes/3204
01 Mark Martin 40.00 70.00
U.S. Army Holiday
Sam Bass/912*
01 Mark Martin 40.00 70.00
U.S. Army '57 Chevy/1248*
01 Regan Smith 60.00 100.00
U.S. Army/1004*
06 Mark Martin 40.00 70.00
Dish Network/756*
07 Clint Bowyer 40.00 70.00
Directv/708*
07 Clint Bowyer 50.00 75.00
Jack Daniel's/5412*
07 Clint Bowyer 50.00 75.00
Jack Daniel's COT/3448*
07 Clint Bowyer 50.00 75.00
Jack Daniel's COT
New Hamshire Raced/1224*

2007 Action/Motorsports Authentics Driver's Select GM Dealers 1:24

1 Martin Truex Jr. 50.00 75.00
Bass Pro Shops/600
1 Martin Truex Jr. 50.00 75.00
Bass Pro Shops
Car of Tomorrow/360
2 Clint Bowyer 50.00 75.00
BB&T/72
5 Kyle Busch 50.00 75.00
Carquest/144
5 Kyle Busch 50.00 75.00
Carquest COT
Bristol Raced/1368
5 Kyle Busch 50.00 75.00
Kellogg's/288
5 Kyle Busch 50.00 75.00
Kellogg's Car of Tomorrow/240
5 Mark Martin 50.00 75.00
Autoguard/1152
8 Dale Earnhardt Jr. 75.00 125.00
Bud/3792
8 Dale Earnhardt Jr. 75.00 125.00
Bud Car of Tomorrow/3630
8 Dale Earnhardt Jr. 50.00 75.00
Bud Stars & Stripes/31,272
8 Dale Earnhardt Jr. 50.00 75.00
JM Menards/600
8 Dale Earnhardt Jr. 50.00 75.00
Sharpie/1500
8 Dale Earnhardt Jr. 50.00 75.00
Vertis Communications/636
11 Denny Hamlin 50.00 75.00
Fed Ex Express/360
11 Denny Hamlin 50.00 75.00
Fed Ex Express
Car of Tomorrow/360
11 Denny Hamlin 50.00 75.00
Fed Ex Freight/432
11 Denny Hamlin 50.00 75.00
Fed Ex Freight
Car of Tomorrow/288
11 Denny Hamlin 50.00 75.00
Fed Ex Ground/432
11 Denny Hamlin 50.00 75.00
Fed Ex Ground
Car of Tomorrow/288
11 Denny Hamlin 50.00 75.00
Fed Ex Kinko's/432
11 Denny Hamlin 50.00 75.00
Fed Ex Kinko's
Car of Tomorrow/288
14 Sterling Marlin 50.00 75.00
Waste Management/144
15 Paul Menard 50.00 75.00
Menards/288
15 Paul Menard 50.00 75.00
Menards Car of Tomorrow/288
18 J.J. Yeley 50.00 75.00
Interstate Batteries/144
18 J.J. Yeley 50.00 75.00
Interstate Batteries
Car of Tomorrow/96
20 Tony Stewart 60.00 100.00
Home Depot/1152
20 Tony Stewart 60.00 100.00
Home Depot
Car of Tomorrow/1128
21 Kevin Harvick 50.00 75.00
Auto Zone/396
24 Jeff Gordon 50.00 75.00
DuPont Flames/2400
24 Jeff Gordon 50.00 75.00
DuPont Flames
Talladega Raced
24 Jeff Gordon 60.00 100.00
DuPont Flames
Car of Tomorrow/1200
24 Jeff Gordon 60.00 100.00
DuPont Flames COT
Phoenix Raced/7676
24 Jeff Gordon 50.00 75.00
Nicorette/876
24 Jeff Gordon 60.00 100.00
Nicorette
Car of Tomorrow/876
24 Jeff Gordon 50.00 75.00
Pepsi/876
25 Casey Mears 50.00 75.00
National Guard/576
25 Casey Mears 50.00 75.00
National Guard
Car of Tomorrow/288
29 Jeff Burton 50.00 75.00
Holiday Inn/144
29 Kevin Harvick 50.00 75.00
Pennzoil Platinum COT/2700
29 Kevin Harvick 60.00 100.00
Reese's Car of Tomorrow/720
29 Kevin Harvick 50.00 75.00
Shell Pennzoil/2004
29 Kevin Harvick 50.00 75.00
Shell Pennzoil
Car of Tomorrow/1500
31 Jeff Burton 50.00 75.00
AT&T COT
31 Jeff Burton 50.00 75.00
Cingular/360
31 Jeff Burton 50.00 75.00
Lenox Tools/156
31 Jeff Burton 50.00 75.00
Prilosec/360
31 Jeff Burton 50.00 75.00
Prilosec Texas Raced/840
33 Kevin Harvick 50.00 75.00
Road Loans/288
33 Tony Stewart 50.00 75.00
Old Spice/288
48 Jimmie Johnson 60.00 100.00
Lowe's/480
48 Jimmie Johnson 60.00 100.00
Lowe's
Car of Tomorrow/840
48 Jimmie Johnson 50.00 75.00
Lowe's Kobalt/432
48 Jimmie Johnson 50.00 75.00
Lowe's JJ Foundation/804
88 Shane Huffman 50.00 75.00
Navy/288
88 Shane Huffman 50.00 75.00
Navy SEALS/84
96 Tony Raines 50.00 75.00
DLP/144
96 Tony Raines 50.00 75.00
DLP Car of Tomorrow/96
01 Mark Martin 60.00 100.00
U.S. Army/1008
01 Mark Martin 60.00 100.00
U.S. Army Car of Tomorrow/996
01 Mark Martin 60.00 100.00
U.S. Army
American Heroes/3204
01 Regan Smith 50.00 75.00
U.S. Army/96
07 Clint Bowyer 50.00 75.00
Directv/180
07 Clint Bowyer 60.00 100.00
Jack Daniel's/1200
07 Clint Bowyer 60.00 100.00
Jack Daniel's Car of Tomorrow/696

2007 Action/Motorsports Authentics Owner's Elite 1:24

*ACTUAL PRINT RUNS PROVIDED BY MA
1 Martin Truex Jr. 60.00 120.00
Bass Pro Shops/708*
1 Martin Truex Jr. 75.00 150.00
Bass Pro Shops COT/504
1 Martin Truex Jr. 75.00 150.00
Bass Pro Shops COT
Dover Raced/504
2 Kurt Busch 50.00 100.00
Miller Lite/1500*
2 Kurt Busch 75.00 150.00
Miller Lite AU/504
2 Kurt Busch 75.00 150.00
Miller Lite COT/504*
4 Ward Burton 60.00 120.00
Air Force American Heroes/504*
5 Kyle Busch 60.00 120.00
Kellogg's/504
5 Kyle Busch 75.00 150.00
Kellogg's COT/504
6 David Ragan 60.00 120.00
AAA/504*
8 Dale Earnhardt Jr. 75.00 150.00
Bud/2007
8 Dale Earnhardt Jr. 600.00 800.00
Bud Platinum/25
8 Dale Earnhardt Jr. 275.00 400.00
Bud White Gold/100
8 Dale Earnhardt Jr. 125.00 250.00
Bud Car of Tomorrow/2007
8 Dale Earnhardt Jr. 500.00 750.00
Bud COT Platinum/25
8 Dale Earnhardt Jr. 300.00 500.00
Bud COT White Gold/50*
8 Dale Earnhardt Jr. 100.00 175.00
Bud Camo American Heroes/2007
8 Dale Earnhardt Jr. 100.00 175.00
Bud Camo American Heroes
Color Chrome/2007
8 Dale Earnhardt Jr. 400.00 600.00
Bud Camo American Heroes
Platinum/25
8 Dale Earnhardt Jr. 250.00 400.00
Bud Camo American Heroes
White Gold/50*
8 Dale Earnhardt Jr. 100.00 200.00
Bud Elvis COT/2007
8 Dale Earnhardt Jr. 400.00 600.00
Bud Elvis COT
Platinum/25
8 Dale Earnhardt Jr. 250.00 450.00
Bud Elvis COT White Gold/50*
8 Dale Earnhardt Jr. 75.00 150.00
Bud Stars & Stripes/2007
8 Dale Earnhardt Jr. 75.00 150.00
Bud Stars & Stripes
Color Chrome/2007
8 Dale Earnhardt Jr. 350.00 600.00
Bud Stars & Stripes
Platinum/25
8 Dale Earnhardt Jr. 200.00 350.00
Bud Stars & Stripes
White Gold/50*
8 Dale Earnhardt Jr. 60.00 120.00
Bud Test/2007
8 Dale Earnhardt Jr. 60.00 120.00
Bud '57 Chevy/1008
8 Dale Earnhardt Jr. 600.00 800.00
Bud '57 Chevy
Platinum/25
8 Dale Earnhardt Jr. 350.00 500.00
Bud '57 Chevy
White Gold/50
8 Dale Earnhardt Jr. 50.00 100.00
JM Menards/1008*
8 Dale Earnhardt Jr. 50.00 100.00
Sharpie/2007
8 Dale Earnhardt Jr. 400.00 600.00
Sharpie Platinum/25
8 Dale Earnhardt Jr. 200.00 350.00
Sharpie White Gold/100
9 Kasey Kahne 75.00 125.00
Dodge Dealers/1212*
9 Kasey Kahne 300.00 500.00
Dodge Dealers Platinum/25
9 Kasey Kahne 250.00 500.00
Dodge Dealers White Gold/100
9 Kasey Kahne 100.00 150.00
Dodge Dealers COT/708*
9 Kasey Kahne 60.00 120.00
Dodge Dealers Test/708*
9 Kasey Kahne 60.00 120.00
Doublemint/504*
9 Kasey Kahne 200.00 400.00
Doublemint Platinum/25
9 Kasey Kahne 250.00 400.00
Doublemint White Gold/50*
10 Scott Riggs 60.00 120.00
Valvoline/504*
11 Denny Hamlin 50.00 100.00
Fed Ex Express/1200*
11 Denny Hamlin 200.00 400.00
Fed Ex Express
Platinum/25
11 Denny Hamlin 150.00 300.00
Fed Ex Express
White Gold/100
11 Denny Hamlin 60.00 120.00
Fed Ex Express COT/708
11 Denny Hamlin 60.00 120.00
Fed Ex Express
2006 Rookie of the Year/1011
11 Denny Hamlin 100.00 200.00
Fed Ex Express
2006 Rookie of the Year
Color Chrome/100
11 Denny Hamlin 125.00 200.00
Fed Ex Express
'06 ROY w
tire/111
11 Denny Hamlin 150.00 300.00
Fed Ex Express
'06 ROY White Gold/100
11 Denny Hamlin 50.00 100.00

Item	Low	High
Fed Ex Freight/504*		
11 Denny Hamlin Fed Ex Freight Marines Heroes/1200*	50.00	100.00
11 Denny Hamlin Fed Ex Freight Marines American Heroes Platinum/25	275.00	400.00
11 Denny Hamlin Fed Ex Freight Marines American Heroes White Gold/50*	250.00	400.00
11 Denny Hamlin Fed Ex Ground/504*	50.00	100.00
11 Denny Hamlin Fed Ex Kinko's/504*	50.00	100.00
11 Denny Hamlin Fed Ex Kinko's Platinum/25	275.00	400.00
11 Denny Hamlin Fed Ex Kinko's White Gold/50*	175.00	350.00
11 Denny Hamlin Fed Ex Test/1200*	50.00	100.00
12 Ryan Newman Alltel/708*	75.00	125.00
12 Ryan Newman Alltel COT/504*	75.00	125.00
14 Sterling Marlin Waste Management/504*	50.00	100.00
15 Paul Menard JM Menards/504*	50.00	100.00
16 Greg Biffle Ameriquest/708*	50.00	100.00
16 Greg Biffle 3M Coast Guard/504*	50.00	100.00
17 Matt Kenseth DeWalt/708*	60.00	120.00
17 Matt Kenseth DeWalt COT/504	75.00	150.00
18 J.J. Yeley Interstate Batteries/504*	50.00	100.00
19 Elliott Sadler Dodge Dealers/504*	50.00	100.00
19 Elliott Sadler Dodge Dealers COT/504*	50.00	100.00
20 Tony Stewart Home Depot/1212*	60.00	120.00
20 Tony Stewart Home Depot Platinum/25	400.00	600.00
20 Tony Stewart Home Depot White Gold/100	250.00	400.00
20 Tony Stewart Home Depot Brickyard Raced/504*	60.00	120.00
20 Tony Stewart Home Depot Daytona Shootout Raced/2007	75.00	150.00
20 Tony Stewart Home Depot COT/1212	75.00	150.00
20 Tony Stewart Home Depot COT Platinum/25	400.00	600.00
20 Tony Stewart Home Depot COT White Gold/50*	250.00	400.00
20 Tony Stewart Home Depot Holiday Sam Bass/504*	50.00	100.00
20 Tony Stewart Home Depot Holiday Sam Bass Platinum/25	400.00	600.00
20 Tony Stewart Home Depot Holiday Sam Bass White Gold/50*	250.00	400.00
20 Tony Stewart Home Depot Test/1200*	60.00	120.00
21 Kevin Harvick Coast Guard '06 NBS Champion Liquid Color/541	100.00	175.00
21 Jon Wood Air Force American Heroes/708*	50.00	100.00
22 Dave Blaney CAT/504*	50.00	100.00
24 Jeff Gordon DuPont Department of Defense American Heroes/1200*	75.00	125.00
24 Jeff Gordon DuPont Holiday Sam Bass/504*	50.00	100.00
24 Jeff Gordon DuPont Holiday Sam Bass Platinum/25	250.00	500.00
24 Jeff Gordon DuPont Holiday Sam Bass White Gold/50*	175.00	350.00
24 Jeff Gordon DuPont Flames/2007	60.00	120.00
24 Jeff Gordon DuPont Flames Platinum/25	750.00	1000.00
24 Jeff Gordon DuPont Flames White Gold/50*	275.00	400.00
24 Jeff Gordon DuPont Flames COT/2007	75.00	150.00
24 Jeff Gordon DuPont Flames COT Platinum/25	600.00	800.00
24 Jeff Gordon DuPont Flames COT Platinum/25		
24 Jeff Gordon DuPont Flames COT Phoenix Raced/1492*	75.00	150.00
24 Jeff Gordon DuPont Flames COT Phoenix Raced Platinum/25	450.00	650.00
24 Jeff Gordon DuPont Flames COT Phoenix Raced White Gold/50*	250.00	500.00
24 Jeff Gordon DuPont Flames Test/2007	60.00	120.00
24 Jeff Gordon DuPont Flames '57 Chevy/504	75.00	150.00
24 Jeff Gordon Milestones 77th Win/1200	60.00	120.00
24 Jeff Gordon Nicorette/2007	50.00	100.00
24 Jeff Gordon Nicorette Platinum/25	450.00	600.00
24 Jeff Gordon Nicorette White Gold/50*	175.00	350.00
24 Jeff Gordon Nicorette COT/1142*	60.00	120.00
24 Jeff Gordon Nicorette COT Platinum/25	125.00	250.00
24 Jeff Gordon Pepsi/1504*	60.00	120.00
24 Jeff Gordon Pepsi COT Talladega Raced/504*	75.00	150.00
24 Jeff Gordon Underdog JG Foundation/708*	60.00	120.00
25 Casey Mears National Guard AU/504*	75.00	125.00
25 Casey Mears National Guard Camo American Heroes/504*	60.00	120.00
26 Jamie McMurray Crown Royal/504*	75.00	125.00
26 Jamie McMurray Crown Royal COT/504*	75.00	125.00
29 Kevin Harvick Pennzoil Platinum All Star Win/708*	60.00	120.00
29 Kevin Harvick Pennzoil Platinum COT/504*	75.00	125.00
29 Kevin Harvick Shell Pennzoil/1008*	100.00	150.00
29 Kevin Harvick Shell Pennzoil Platinum/25	350.00	500.00
29 Kevin Harvick Shell Pennzoil White Gold/100	175.00	350.00
29 Kevin Harvick Shell Pennzoil Daytona Raced/1200*	100.00	150.00
29 Kevin Harvick Shell Pennzoil Daytona Raced Platinum/25	300.00	500.00
29 Kevin Harvick Shell Pennzoil Daytona Raced White Gold/50*	175.00	350.00
29 Kevin Harvick Shell Pennzoil COT/1008	100.00	150.00
29 Kevin Harvick Shell Pennzoil COT Platinum/25	350.00	500.00
29 Kevin Harvick Shell Pennzoil COT White Gold/50*	175.00	350.00
29 Kevin Harvick Shell Pennzoil Holiday Sam Bass/504	75.00	125.00
29 Kevin Harvick Shell Pennzoil Test/1008*	75.00	125.00
31 Jeff Burton AT&T COT/504*	60.00	120.00
31 Jeff Burton Cingular/504*	75.00	150.00
31 Jeff Burton Prilosec Texas Raced/504	60.00	120.00
31 Jeff Burton Prilosec Texas Raced Platinum/25	200.00	350.00
31 Jeff Burton Prilosec Texas Raced White Gold/50*	150.00	300.00
38 David Gilliland M&M's/1008*	60.00	120.00
38 David Gilliland M&M's COT/504	60.00	120.00
38 David Gilliland M&M's July 4/504	60.00	120.00
38 David Gilliland M&M's Pink Susan G. Komen Foundation/504	60.00	120.00
38 David Gilliland M&M's Pink Platinum/25	250.00	400.00
38 David Gilliland M&M's Pink White Gold/100	175.00	350.00
38 David Gilliland M&M's Shrek/504	60.00	120.00
40 David Stremme Coors Light/504*	60.00	120.00
41 Reed Sorenson Target/504*	60.00	120.00
42 Juan Pablo Montoya Big Red/1008	60.00	120.00
42 Juan Pablo Montoya Big Red Platinum/25	300.00	500.00
42 Juan Pablo Montoya Big Red White Gold/50*	175.00	300.00
42 Juan Pablo Montoya Texaco Havoline/1008*	75.00	150.00
42 Juan Pablo Montoya Texaco Havoline Platinum/25	300.00	500.00
42 Juan Pablo Montoya Texaco Havoline White Gold/100	175.00	350.00
42 Juan Pablo Montoya Texaco Havoline Sonoma Raced/504*	100.00	150.00
42 Juan Pablo Montoya Texaco Havoline COT/504*	100.00	200.00
42 Juan Pablo Montoya Texaco Havoline Test/708*	60.00	120.00
43 Bobby Labonte Cheerios/504*	60.00	120.00
43 Bobby Labonte Cheerios COT/504	75.00	150.00
43 Bobby Labonte Cheerios COT Platinum/25	300.00	450.00
43 Bobby Labonte Cheerios COT White Gold/50	150.00	300.00
44 Dale Jarrett UPS/1008*	60.00	120.00
44 Dale Jarrett UPS Platinum/25	300.00	450.00
44 Dale Jarrett UPS White Gold/50*	175.00	350.00
44 Dale Jarrett UPS COT/504	75.00	150.00
44 Dale Jarrett UPS 100th Anniversary COT/708*	75.00	125.00
48 Jimmie Johnson Lowe's/1200*	100.00	175.00
48 Jimmie Johnson Lowe's Platinum/25	400.00	600.00
48 Jimmie Johnson Lowe's White Gold/50*	200.00	400.00
48 Jimmie Johnson Lowe's COT/1008	100.00	175.00
48 Jimmie Johnson Lowe's Holiday Sam Bass/504*	60.00	120.00
48 Jimmie Johnson Lowe's Kobalt/708	100.00	150.00
48 Jimmie Johnson Lowe's Power of Pride American Heroes/708*	75.00	125.00
48 Jimmie Johnson Lowe's Test/708	60.00	120.00
48 Jimmie Johnson Lowe's '57 Chevy/504	60.00	120.00
55 Michael Waltrip NAPA/1008*	75.00	125.00
55 Michael Waltrip NAPA COT/504*	75.00	125.00
84 A.J. Allmendinger Red Bull/504*	75.00	125.00
88 Shane Huffman Navy American Heroes/708	60.00	120.00
88 Shane Huffman Navy American Heroes Platinum/25	250.00	450.00
88 Shane Huffman Navy American Heroes White Gold/96*	150.00	300.00
88 Shane Huffman Navy Test/708*	60.00	120.00
88 Shane Huffman Navy SEALS/504*	60.00	120.00
88 Ricky Rudd Pedigree COT/504*	75.00	125.00
88 Ricky Rudd Pedigree COT Platinum/25	250.00	400.00
88 Ricky Rudd Pedigree COT White Gold/50*	150.00	300.00
88 Ricky Rudd Snickers/708*	75.00	125.00
88 Ricky Rudd Snickers Platinum/25	250.00	400.00
88 Ricky Rudd Snickers White Gold/100	175.00	300.00
88 Ricky Rudd Snickers COT/504*	75.00	125.00
96 Tony Raines DLP/504*	60.00	120.00
99 Carl Edwards Office Depot/1008*	60.00	120.00
99 Carl Edwards Office Depot Platinum/25	200.00	400.00
99 Carl Edwards Office Depot White Gold/50*	125.00	250.00
99 Carl Edwards Office Depot COT/504*	75.00	150.00
00 David Reutimann Burger King/504*	60.00	120.00
00 David Reutimann Burger King COT/504*	75.00	125.00
00 David Reutimann Domino's/504*	60.00	120.00
00 David Reutimann Domino's COT/504*	100.00	150.00
01 Mark Martin U.S. Army/1200*	60.00	120.00
01 Mark Martin U.S. Army Platinum/25	200.00	400.00
01 Mark Martin U.S. Army White Gold/100	150.00	300.00
01 Mark Martin U.S. Army American Heroes/708*	50.00	100.00
01 Mark Martin U.S. Army Car of Tomorrow/708*	75.00	150.00
07 Clint Bowyer Jack Daniel's/504*	75.00	125.00
07 Clint Bowyer Jack Daniel's Platinum/25	275.00	400.00
07 Clint Bowyer Jack Daniel's White Gold/50*	175.00	350.00
07 Clint Bowyer Jack Daniel's COT/504	100.00	150.00
07 Clint Bowyer Jack Daniel's COT Platinum/25	275.00	400.00
07 Clint Bowyer Jack Daniel's COT White Gold/50*	175.00	350.00
08 Daytona 500 50th Anniversary COT Red/504*	50.00	100.00
08 Daytona 500 50th Anniversary COT White/504*	50.00	100.00
08 Daytona 500 50th Anniversary COT Platinum/25	125.00	250.00
08 Daytona 500 50th Anniversary COT White Gold/50*	100.00	200.00

2007 Action/Motorsports Authentics Owner's Elite Trackside 1:24

PACKAGE STATES MAXIMUM OF 2007
*ACTUAL PRINTS RUNS PROVIDED BY MA

Item	Low	High
1 Martin Truex Jr. Bass Pro Shops/408*	60.00	100.00
2 Kurt Busch Miller Lite/708*	60.00	100.00
5 Kyle Busch Carquest/204*	40.00	80.00
5 Kyle Busch Kellogg's/204*	60.00	100.00
6 David Ragan AAA/1500*	100.00	150.00
6 David Ragan Discount Tire/144*	100.00	150.00
7 Mike Wallace Geico/144*	75.00	125.00
8 Dale Earnhardt Jr. Bud/2007*	125.00	175.00
8 Dale Earnhardt Jr. Bud Camo American Heroes/708*	100.00	150.00
8 Dale Earnhardt Jr. Sharpie/576*	60.00	100.00
9 Kasey Kahne Dodge Dealers/408*	100.00	150.00
9 Kasey Kahne Doublemint/504*	60.00	100.00
10 Scott Riggs Stanley Tools/334*	40.00	80.00
10 Scott Riggs Valvoline/204*	60.00	100.00
11 Denny Hamlin Fed Ex Express/504*	75.00	125.00
11 Denny Hamlin Fed Ex Express '06 ROY Color Chrome/96*	60.00	100.00
11 Denny Hamlin Fed Ex Freight/504*	75.00	125.00
11 Denny Hamlin Fed Ex Freight Marines American Heroes/100*	60.00	100.00
11 Denny Hamlin Fed Ex Ground/400*	75.00	125.00
11 Denny Hamlin Fed Ex Kinko's/404*	60.00	100.00
12 Kurt Busch Penske/144*	60.00	100.00
12 Ryan Newman Mobil 1/204*	60.00	100.00
12 Ryan Newman Alltel/800*	75.00	125.00
12 Ryan Newman Kodak/144*	75.00	125.00
15 Paul Menard JM Menards/204*	75.00	125.00
16 Greg Biffle Ameriquest/408*	75.00	125.00
16 Greg Biffle 3M Coast Guard American Heroes/100*	60.00	100.00
17 Matt Kenseth Carhartt/408*	75.00	125.00
17 Matt Kenseth DeWalt/908*	100.00	150.00
18 J.J. Yeley Interstate Batteries/504*	75.00	125.00
19 Elliott Sadler Dodge Dealers/1716*	60.00	120.00
20 Tony Stewart Home Depot/1704*	75.00	125.00
21 Kevin Harvick Coast Guard '06 BGN Champ Color Chrome/96*	60.00	100.00
21 Jon Wood Air Force American Heroes/100*	40.00	80.00
22 Dave Blaney CAT/204*	75.00	125.00
24 Jeff Gordon DuPont Dept. of Defense American Heroes/100*	75.00	125.00
24 Jeff Gordon DuPont Flames/1008*	100.00	150.00
24 Jeff Gordon Nicorette/504*	75.00	125.00
24 Jeff Gordon Pepsi/1008*	75.00	125.00
25 Casey Mears National Guard/904*	75.00	125.00
26 Jamie McMurray Crown Royal/300*	75.00	125.00
26 Jamie McMurray Irwin Tools/204*	60.00	100.00
29 Kevin Harvick Shell Pennzoil/1500*	125.00	175.00
29 Kevin Harvick Shell Pennzoil Daytona Raced/729*	60.00	100.00
31 Jeff Burton Cingular/300*	100.00	150.00
38 David Gilliland M&M's/1008*	100.00	150.00
39 Sam Hornish Jr. Mobil 1/144*	60.00	100.00
40 David Stremme Coors Light/204*	40.00	80.00
40 David Stremme Lonestar Steakhouse/204*	40.00	80.00
41 Reed Sorenson Target/204*	75.00	125.00
42 Juan Pablo Montoya Big Red/432*	60.00	100.00
42 Juan Pablo Montoya Texaco Havoline/708*	75.00	125.00
43 Bobby Labonte Cheerios/204*	75.00	125.00
44 Dale Jarrett UPS/1000*	75.00	125.00
45 Kyle Petty Wells Fargo/204*	50.00	100.00
48 Jimmie Johnson Lowe's/1008*	100.00	150.00
48 Jimmie Johnson Lowe's Power of Pride American Heroes/96*	100.00	150.00
48 Jimmie Johnson Lowe's '57 Chevy/100*	40.00	80.00
55 Michael Waltrip NAPA/1000*	75.00	125.00
83 Brian Vickers Red Bull/304*	60.00	100.00
84 A.J. Allmendinger Red Bull/304*	60.00	100.00
88 Shane Huffman Navy/144*	50.00	100.00
88 Ricky Rudd Snickers/504*	50.00	100.00
90 Stephen Leicht CitiFinancial/144*	50.00	100.00
96 Tony Raines DLP/204*	40.00	80.00
99 Carl Edwards Office Depot/708*	75.00	125.00
99 David Reutimann Aaron's/144*	60.00	100
00 David Reutimann Burger King/300*	40.00	80
00 David Reutimann Domino's Pizza/300*	75.00	125
01 Mark Martin U.S.Army/504*	50.00	100
01 Mark Martin U.S.Army American Heroes/100*	50.00	100
07 Clint Bowyer Jack Daniels/1068*	60.00	100

2007 Action/Motorsports Authentics Pit S 1:24

Item	Low	High
25 Casey Mears National Guard	15.00	25

2007 Action/Motorsports Authentics QVC Race Fans Only 1:24

Item	Low	High
1 Martin Truex Jr. Bass Pro Shops '57 Chevy Color Chrome/1500	100.00	175
2 Kurt Busch Miller Lite Chrome/288	125.00	200
2 Kurt Busch Miller Lite Color Chrome/96	100.00	175
5 Kyle Busch Carquest Chrome/96	125.00	200
5 Kyle Busch Carquest Color Chrome/96	100.00	175
5 Kyle Busch Kellogg's Chrome/96	125.00	200
5 Kyle Busch Kellogg's Color Chrome/96	100.00	175
8 Dale Earnhardt Jr. Bud Chrome/2004	125.00	200
8 Dale Earnhardt Jr. Bud Color Chrome/2508	100.00	175
8 Dale Earnhardt Jr. Bud Gold/288	100.00	175
8 Dale Earnhardt Jr. Bud Gold Chrome/3888	75.00	125
8 Dale Earnhardt Jr. Bud Mesma Chrome/2508	75.00	125
8 Dale Earnhardt Jr. Bud Platinum/144	125.00	200
8 Dale Earnhardt Jr. Bud COT Chrome/504	125.00	200
8 Dale Earnhardt Jr. Bud COT Color Chrome/2508	100.00	175
8 Dale Earnhardt Jr. Bud COT Gold/288	100.00	175
8 Dale Earnhardt Jr. Bud COT Gold Chrome/3888	75.00	125
8 Dale Earnhardt Jr. Bud COT Mesma Chrome/2508	75.00	125
8 Dale Earnhardt Jr. Bud COT Platinum/204	125.00	200
8 Dale Earnhardt Jr. Bud Camo Heroes Chrome/504	125.00	200
8 Dale Earnhardt Jr. Bud Camo American Heroes Color Chrome/3888	60.00	100
8 Dale Earnhardt Jr. Bud Camo American Heroes Gold/288	75.00	125
8 Dale Earnhardt Jr. Bud Camo Heroes Mesma Chrome/2508	100.00	150
8 Dale Earnhardt Jr. Bud Camo Heroes Platinum/144	150.00	250
8 Dale Earnhardt Jr. Bud Elvis COT Chrome/3888	100.00	150
8 Dale Earnhardt Jr. Bud Elvis COT Gold/188	125.00	200
8 Dale Earnhardt Jr. Bud Elvis COT Gold Chrome/3888	60.00	100
8 Dale Earnhardt Jr. Bud Elvis COT Mesma Chrome/888	100.00	175
8 Dale Earnhardt Jr. Bud Elvis COT Mesma Chrome/888	60.00	100
8 Dale Earnhardt Jr. Bud Elvis COT Platinum/108	125.00	200
8 Dale Earnhardt Jr. Bud Stars & Stripes Chrome/504	100.00	150
8 Dale Earnhardt Jr. Bud Stars & Stripes Color Chrome/2508	75.00	125
8 Dale Earnhardt Jr. Bud Stars & Stripes Gold Chrome/3888	60.00	100
8 Dale Earnhardt Jr. Bud Stars & Stripes Mesma Chrome/2508	60.00	100
8 Dale Earnhardt Jr. Bud Stars & Stripes Platinum/108	125.00	200
8 Dale Earnhardt Jr. Bud '57 Chevy Chrome/504	75.00	125
8 Dale Earnhardt Jr. Bud '57 Chevy Color Chrome/3888	60.00	100
8 Dale Earnhardt Jr. Bud '57 Chevy Gold/188	75.00	125
8 Dale Earnhardt Jr. Bud '57 Chevy Mesma Chrome/888	60.00	100

arnhardt Jr. 57 Chevy um/108 125.00 200.00
arnhardt Jr. pie Chrome/288 75.00 125.00
arnhardt Jr. pie Color Chrome/2508 75.00 125.00
arnhardt Jr. pie Gold/108 75.00 150.00
arnhardt Jr. pie Mesma Chrome/2508 75.00 125.00
arnhardt Jr. pie Platinum/108 100.00 175.00
Kahne e Dealers me/288 100.00 150.00
Kahne e Dealers Chrome/288 100.00 150.00
Kahne e Dealers Copper/288 75.00 125.00
Kahne e Dealers na Chrome/288 60.00 100.00
y Hamlin Ex Express Chrome/108 100.00 150.00
y Hamlin Ex Express per/108 60.00 100.00
Newman Chrome/204 60.00 100.00
Biffle iquest Chrome/96 125.00 200.00
Kenseth Carriers Chrome/96 150.00 300.00
t Sadler ge Dealers r Chrome/96 100.00 150.00
Stewart e Depot Brickyard Raced r Chrome/288 100.00 175.00
Stewart e Depot Brickyard Raced per/288 100.00 150.00
Stewart e Depot Daytona Shootout Raced r Chrome/288 100.00 175.00
Stewart e Depot Daytona Shootout Raced per/288 100.00 150.00
Stewart e Depot COT r Chrome/504 100.00 175.00
Stewart e Depot COT /108 100.00 150.00
Stewart e Depot COT per/504 60.00 100.00
Stewart e Depot COT na Chrome/288 100.00 150.00
Stewart e Depot COT num/108 125.00 200.00
Gordon ont Department of Defense me/504 100.00 175.00
Gordon ont Dept.of Defense or Chrome/1008 75.00 150.00
Gordon ont Department of Defense per/504 60.00 100.00
Gordon ont Department of Defense /108 125.00 200.00
Gordon ont Department of Defense ma Chrome/504 75.00 125.00
Gordon ont Department of Defense rican Heroes Platinum/108 175.00 350.00
Gordon ont Flames adega Raced Color Chrome/1500 75.00 150.00
Gordon ont Flames adega Raced Copper/504 60.00 100.00
Gordon ont Flames adega Raced Mesma Chrome/324 75.00 125.00
Gordon ont Flames COT me/288 100.00 175.00
Gordon ont Flames COT or Chrome/1008 75.00 125.00
Gordon ont Flames COT per/504 60.00 100.00
Gordon Pont Flames COT /144 75.00 125.00
Gordon Pont Flames COT ma Chrome/324 60.00 100.00
Gordon Pont Flames COT inum/108 125.00 200.00
Gordon Pont Flames '57 Chevy ome/288 100.00 175.00
Gordon Pont Flames COT enix Raced Color Chrome/1500 75.00 125.00
Gordon Pont Flames COT enix Raced Copper/504 75.00 125.00
Gordon Pont Flames Holiday n Bass Color Chrome/1500 75.00 125.00
Gordon Pont Flames '57 Chevy or Chrome/1500 75.00 125.00

24 Jeff Gordon DuPont Flames '57 Chevy Copper/504 60.00 100.00
24 Jeff Gordon DuPont Flames '57 Chevy Gold/108 75.00 125.00
24 Jeff Gordon DuPont Flames '57 Chevy Gold Chrome/1008 60.00 100.00
24 Jeff Gordon DuPont Flames '57 Chevy Mesma Chrome/324 60.00 100.00
24 Jeff Gordon DuPont Flames '57 Chevy Platinum/144 125.00 200.00
24 Jeff Gordon Nicorette Color Chrome/1008 75.00 125.00
24 Jeff Gordon Nicorette Mesma Chrome/504 60.00 100.00
24 Jeff Gordon Nicorette COT Color Chrome/1500 75.00 125.00
24 Jeff Gordon Nicorette COT Copper/504 60.00 100.00
24 Jeff Gordon Nicorette COT Mesma Chrome/504 100.00 150.00
24 Jeff Gordon Pepsi Color Chrome/1008 75.00 125.00
24 Jeff Gordon Pepsi Mesma Chrome/504 75.00 125.00
25 Casey Mears National Guard Camo American Heroes/504 50.00 75.00
29 Kevin Harvick Reese's/1008 50.00 75.00
29 Kevin Harvick Reese's Color Chrome/504 60.00 100.00
29 Kevin Harvick Shell Pennzoil Chrome/504 75.00 150.00
29 Kevin Harvick Shell Pennzoil Color Chrome/1500 75.00 125.00
29 Kevin Harvick Shell Pennzoil Copper/504 60.00 100.00
29 Kevin Harvick Shell Pennzoil Gold/108 75.00 150.00
29 Kevin Harvick Shell Pennzoil Mesma Chrome/504 60.00 100.00
29 Kevin Harvick Shell Pennzoil Platinum/108 100.00 175.00
29 Kevin Harvick Shell Pennzoil Daytona Raced Color Chrome/1500 75.00 125.00
29 Kevin Harvick Shell Pennzoil Daytona Raced Copper/504 60.00 100.00
29 Kevin Harvick Shell Pennzoil COT 50.00 75.00
29 Kevin Harvick Shell Pennzoil COT Color Chrome/1500 75.00 125.00
29 Kevin Harvick Shell Pennzoil Car of Tomorrow Copper/504 60.00 100.00
29 Kevin Harvick Shell Pennzoil COT Gold/108 125.00 200.00
29 Kevin Harvick Shell Pennzoil COT Mesma Chrome/288 60.00 100.00
29 Kevin Harvick Shell Pennzoil Car of Tomorrow Platinum/108 150.00 250.00
44 Dale Jarrett UPS Chrome/288 75.00 125.00
44 Dale Jarrett UPS Copper/108 60.00 100.00
44 Dale Jarrett UPS Mesma Chrome/504 60.00 100.00
48 Jimmie Johnson Lowe's Color Chrome/288 75.00 125.00
48 Jimmie Johnson Lowe's Gold/108 100.00 175.00
48 Jimmie Johnson Lowe's Copper/288 60.00 100.00
48 Jimmie Johnson Lowe's Mesma Chrome/288 60.00 100.00
48 Jimmie Johnson Lowe's Platinum/108 125.00 200.00
48 Jimmie Johnson Lowe's COT Color Chrome/288 100.00 175.00
48 Jimmie Johnson Lowe's COT Copper/288 100.00 175.00
48 Jimmie Johnson Lowe's COT Copper/288
48 Jimmie Johnson Lowe's '06 Champ Mesma Chrome/504 100.00 150.00
99 Carl Edwards Office Depot Chrome/204 75.00 125.00
01 Mark Martin U.S. Army Chrome/504 100.00 150.00
01 Mark Martin U.S. Army Color Chrome/504 75.00 125.00
01 Mark Martin U.S. Army Color Chrome AU/504 125.00 200.00
01 Mark Martin U.S. Army Copper AU/288 125.00 200.00
01 Mark Martin U.S. Army Gold/288 100.00 175.00
01 Mark Martin U.S. Army Mesma Chrome AU/504 125.00 200.00
01 Mark Martin U.S. Army American Heroes Color Chrome/504 75.00 125.00
01 Mark Martin U.S. Army American Heroes Copper/504 60.00 100.00
01 Mark Martin U.S. Army American Heroes Gold/288 125.00 200.00
01 Mark Martin U.S. Army American Heroes Mesma Chrome/288 60.00 100.00
07 Clint Bowyer Jack Daniel's Color Chrome/108 75.00 125.00
07 Clint Bowyer Jack Daniel's Copper/108 60.00 100.00

2007 Action/Motorsports Authentics/RCCA Owner's Club Select 1:24

8 Dale Earnhardt Jr. Bud/3000* 100.00 175.00
8 Dale Earnhardt Jr. Bud Camo American Heroes/2007* 50.00 75.00
8 Dale Earnhardt Jr. Bud Stars & Stripes/3000* 50.00 75.00
8 Dale Earnhardt Jr. Bud '57 Chevy/1008* 50.00 75.00
9 Kasey Kahne Dodge Dealers/1500* 50.00 75.00
9 Kasey Kahne Dodge Dealers Holiday Sam Bass/96* 40.00 65.00
11 Denny Hamlin Fed Ex Express/708* 50.00 75.00
11 Denny Hamlin Fed Ex Express Holiday Sam Bass/144* 40.00 65.00
11 Denny Hamlin Fed Ex Freight/708* 40.00 65.00
11 Denny Hamlin Fed Ex Freight Marines American Heroes/708* 50.00 75.00
11 Denny Hamlin Fed Ex Ground/708* 40.00 65.00
11 Denny Hamlin Fed Ex Kinko's/708* 40.00 65.00
17 Matt Kenseth DeWalt/1200* 50.00 75.00
17 Matt Kenseth DeWalt Holiday Sam Bass/96* 40.00 65.00
19 Elliott Sadler Dodge Dealers Holiday Sam Bass/96* 40.00 65.00
20 Tony Stewart Home Depot/2100* 50.00 75.00
24 Jeff Gordon DuPont Flames/1500* 50.00 75.00
24 Jeff Gordon DuPont Flames '57 Chevy/288 50.00 75.00
24 Jeff Gordon Nicorette/1500* 40.00 65.00
24 Jeff Gordon Pepsi/1500* 40.00 65.00
29 Kevin Harvick Shell Pennzoil/1500* 50.00 75.00
38 David Gilliland M&M's/708* 40.00 65.00
38 David Gilliland M&M's Holiday Sam Bass/96* 40.00 65.00
42 Juan Pablo Montoya Big Red/708* 40.00 65.00
42 Juan Pablo Montoya Texaco Havoline/708* 60.00 100.00
42 Juan Pablo Montoya Texaco Havoline Holiday Sam Bass/96* 40.00 65.00
43 Bobby Labonte Cheerios/708* 40.00 65.00
44 Dale Jarrett UPS/504* 40.00 65.00
48 Jimmie Johnson Lowe's/1500* 60.00 100.00
48 Jimmie Johnson Lowe's '57 Chevy/288* 50.00 75.00
55 Michael Waltrip NAPA/708* 40.00 65.00
88 Shane Huffman Navy/708* 40.00 65.00
88 Ricky Rudd Snickers/708* 40.00 65.00
99 Carl Edwards Office Depot/1200* 40.00 65.00
99 Carl Edwards Office Depot Holiday Sam Bass/96* 40.00 65.00
01 Mark Martin U.S. Army/1200* 50.00 75.00
01 Mark Martin U.S. Army Holiday Sam Bass/96* 50.00 75.00
07 Clint Bowyer Jack Daniels/1200 40.00 65.00

2008 Action Racing Collectables Advanced Production 1:24

3 Dale Earnhardt Goodwrench '98 Daytona COT/333 300.00 500.00
3 Dale Earnhardt Johnny Cash/333 100.00 175.00
3 Dale Earnhardt John Wayne/333 100.00 175.00
3 Dale Earnhardt John Wayne TMS/333 125.00 200.00
18 Kyle Busch M&M's Summer/318 100.00 150.00
24 Jeff Gordon DuPont Salute the Troops/124 125.00 250.00
29 Kevin Harvick Pennzoil Platinum/144 100.00 150.00
43 Bobby Labonte Petty 50th Anniversary/143 75.00 125.00
44 Dale Jarrett UPS All-Star/144 150.00 250.00
83 Dale Earnhardt Jr. Navy JR Motorsports/383 75.00 125.00
88 Dale Earnhardt Jr. Mountian Dew Retro/888 150.00 250.00
88 Dale Earnhardt Jr. National Guard Citizen Soldier/888 125.00 250.00
88 Dale Earnhardt Jr. National Guard Digital Camo/888 150.00 250.00
88 Dale Earnhardt Jr. National Guard Salute the Troops/888 100.00 200.00
88 Brad Keselowski Navy Salute the Troops/88 75.00 150.00
07 Clint Bowyer Jack Daniel's Salute the Troops/107 100.00 200.00

2008 Action Racing Collectables Black Label 1:24

3 Dale Earnhardt Goodwrench '00 Monte Carlo/2503 75.00 150.00
9 Kasey Kahne Bud/1509 50.00 75.00
24 Jeff Gordon DuPont/2424 60.00 100.00
29 Kevin Harvick Shell/1029 50.00 75.00
48 Jimmie Johnson Lowe's/1048 75.00 125.00
88 Dale Earnhardt Jr. AMP/5088 60.00 100.00
99 Carl Edwards Aflac/999 60.00 100.00
07 Clint Bowyer Jack Daniel's/777 60.00 100.00

2008 Action Pit Stop 1:24

1 Martin Truex Jr. Bass Pro 12.50 25.00
3 Dale Earnhardt Johnny Cash Promo 15.00 30.00
3 Dale Earnhardt John Wayne Promo 15.00 30.00
6 David Ragan AAA 12.50 25.00
6 David Ragan AAA Insurance 12.50 25.00
6 David Ragan AAA Travel 12.50 25.00
8 Mark Martin U.S. Army 15.00 30.00
9 Kasey Kahne Bud 15.00 30.00
10 Patrick Carpentier Auto Value Bumper to Bumper Promo 15.00 30.00
10 Patrick Carpentier Auto Value Promo 15.00 30.00
11 Denny Hamlin Fed Ex Express Promo 15.00 30.00
12 Ryan Newman Alltel Daytona Raced Promo 15.00 30.00
16 Greg Biffle 3M Promo 15.00 30.00
17 Matt Kenseth Carhartt Promo 15.00 30.00
17 Matt Kenseth DeWalt 12.50 25.00
17 Matt Kenseth DeWalt Promo 15.00 30.00
18 Kyle Busch M&M's 15.00 30.00
18 Farm Bureau Promo 20.00 40.00
19 Elliott Sadler Best Buy Promo 15.00 30.00
20 Tony Stewart Home Depot 12.50 25.00
20 Tony Stewart Home Depot Promo 15.00 30.00
24 Jeff Gordon DuPont 15.00 30.00
29 Kevin Harvick Shell 12.50 30.00
37 D.Bean Glock Promo 15.00 30.00
40 Dario Franchitti Fastenal Promo 15.00 30.00
42 Juan Pablo Montoya Texaco Havoline 12.50 30.00
43 Bobby Labonte General Mills Promo 15.00 30.00
44 David Reutimann UPS Promo 15.00 30.00
45 Kyle Petty Wells Fargo 12.50 25.00
48 Jimmie Johnson Lowe's 15.00 30.00
88 Dale Earnhardt Jr. AMP 12.50 25.00
88 Dale Earnhardt Jr. AMP AU Promo 100.00 150.00
88 Dale Earnhardt Jr. AMP Promo 20.00 40.00
88 Dale Earnhardt Jr. AMP Ride Along 20.00 40.00
88 Dale Earnhardt Jr. Mountain Dew Retro Promo 20.00 40.00
88 Dale Earnhardt Jr. National Guard 12.50 25.00
88 Dale Earnhardt Jr. National Guard AU Promo 100.00 150.00
88 Dale Earnhardt Jr. National Guard Citizen Soldier Promo 20.00 40.00
88 Dale Earnhardt Jr. National Guard Digital Camo Promo 20.00 40.00
88 Dale Earnhardt Jr. National Guard Promo 20.00 40.00
99 Carl Edwards Office Depot 12.50 25.00
99 David Reutimann XM Radio Promo 15.00 30.00
07 Clint Bowyer Directv Hot Pass Promo 15.00 30.00
NNO NASCAR Hall of Fame 60th Anniversary Promo 12.50 30.00

2008 Action Pit Stop Trucks 1:24

6 C.Braun Con-Way/2500 15.00 30.00

2008 Action Racing Collectables Platinum 1:24

1 Martin Truex Jr. Bass Pro Shops/4956 50.00 75.00
1 Martin Truex Jr. Bass Pro Shops Realtree/447 50.00 75.00
2 Clint Bowyer BB&T/480 50.00 75.00
2 Kurt Busch Miller Lite/3408 50.00 75.00
3 Austin Dillon Garage Equiptment/1012 40.00 70.00
3 Dale Earnhardt GM Plus '98 Daytona COT/24729 60.00 100.00
3 Dale Earnhardt Johnny Cash/10109 50.00 75.00
3 Dale Earnhardt John Wayne/6996 50.00 75.00
5 Landon Cassill National Guard/889 50.00 75.00
5 Dale Earnhardt Jr. All Star Test/3169 50.00 75.00
5 Dale Earnhardt Jr. All Star Test/9204 50.00 75.00
5 Dale Earnhardt Jr. Delphi/5378 50.00 75.00
5 Dale Earnhardt Jr. GoDaddy/6770 50.00 75.00
5 Dale Earnhardt Jr. National Guard/4934 50.00 75.00
5 Mark Martin Delphi/1250 40.00 65.00
5 Mark Martin Delphi Las Vegas Raced/710 40.00 65.00
5 Mark Martin GoDaddy/1358 40.00 65.00
5 Casey Mears Carquest1224 40.00 65.00
5 Casey Mears Kellogg's/3564 40.00 65.00
6 David Ragan AAA Insurance/1320 40.00 65.00
6 David Ragan Discount Tire/700 40.00 65.00
8 Aric Almirola U.S. Army/317 50.00 75.00
8 Mark Martin Principal Financial/1138 40.00 65.00
8 Mark Martin Steak-Umm/1498 40.00 65.00
8 Mark Martin U.S. Army/8004 50.00 75.00
8 Mark Martin U.S. Army AU/1000 75.00 125.00
8 Mark Martin U.S. Army Salute the Troops/1337 50.00 75.00
8 Mark Martin U.S. Army Salute the Troops Liquid Color/508 50.00 75.00
8 Martin Truex Jr. Freightliner/2194 50.00 75.00
9 Kasey Kahne Bud/24,600 50.00 75.00
9 Kasey Kahne Bud All-Star Raced/779 50.00 75.00
9 Kasey Kahne Bud Charlotte Raced/871 50.00 75.00
9 Kasey Kahne Bud Charlotte Raced AU/288 75.00 125.00
9 Kasey Kahne Bud Clydesdales/1683 50.00 75.00
9 Kasey Kahne Bud Sam Bass Holiday/588 50.00 75.00
10 Patrick Carpentier Valvoline/1429 50.00 75.00
11 Denny Hamlin Fed Ex Express/5148 50.00 75.00
11 Denny Hamlin Fed Ex Express Gatorade Duel 150 Raced/1476 50.00 75.00
11 Denny Hamlin Fed Ex Express Gatorade Duel 150 Raced AU/288 75.00 125.00
11 Denny Hamlin Fed Ex Freight/2117 50.00 75.00
11 Denny Hamlin Fed Ex Ground/2160 50.00 75.00
11 Denny Hamlin Fed Ex Kinko's/1860 50.00 75.00
11 Denny Hamlin Fed Ex March of Dimes/1296 50.00 75.00
11 Denny Hamlin Fed Ex March of Dimes AU/360 75.00 125.00
11 Darrell Waltrip Mountian Dew '81 Buick Green Chrome/4038 60.00 100.00
11 Darrell Waltrip Mountian Dew '81 Buick Green Chrome AU/288 100.00 150.00
11 Darrell Waltrip Pepsi Challenge '83 Monte Carlo/888 60.00 100.00
12 Ryan Newman Alltel/3276 50.00 75.00
12 Ryan Newman Alltel Daytona Raced/2750 50.00 75.00
12 Ryan Newman Alltel Daytona Raced AU/288 75.00 125.00
12 Ryan Newman Alltel Daytona Raced Gold/550 50.00 75.00
12 Ryan Newman Avis/801 40.00 65.00
12 Ryan Newman Kodak/938 40.00 65.00
12 Ryan Newman Kodak Mummy/1080 40.00 65.00

15 Paul Menard 40.00 65.00
Menards/816
16 Greg Biffle 40.00 65.00
Citifinancial
16 Greg Biffle 40.00 65.00
Dish Network New Hampshire Raced
16 Greg Biffle 40.00 65.00
3M/2928
16 Greg Biffle 40.00 65.00
3M Dover Raced
17 Matt Kenseth 50.00 75.00
Carhartt/3144
17 Matt Kenseth 50.00 75.00
DeWalt/6672
17 Matt Kenseth 50.00 75.00
DeWalt Nano/1477
17 Matt Kenseth 50.00 75.00
Ritz/949
17 Matt Kenseth 50.00 75.00
R&L Carriers/1788
17 Matt Kenseth 50.00 75.00
USG Sheetrock/2004
18 Kyle Busch 50.00 75.00
Combo's/1416
18 Kyle Busch 50.00 75.00
Interstate Batteries
18 Kyle Busch 50.00 75.00
Combos Dover Raced/783
18 Kyle Busch 60.00 100.00
Combos Dover Raced AU/288
18 Kyle Busch 75.00 125.00
M&M's/5448
18 Kyle Busch 100.00 150.00
M&M's Liquid Color/4306
18 Kyle Busch 50.00 75.00
M&M's Talladega Raced/1438
18 Kyle Busch 100.00 150.00
M&M's Talladega Raced AU/288
18 Kyle Busch 50.00 75.00
M&M's Halloween/2668
18 Kyle Busch 60.00 100.00
M&M's Indiana Jones/1980
18 Kyle Busch 60.00 100.00
M&M's Pink/3052
18 Kyle Busch 50.00 75.00
M&M's Rowdy Fantasy/949
18 Kyle Busch 50.00 75.00
M&M's Sam Bass Holiday/1260
18 Kyle Busch 50.00 75.00
M&M's Summer of Fun/3758
18 Kyle Busch 50.00 75.00
Pedigree/1956
18 Kyle Busch 50.00 75.00
Snickers/1704
18 Kyle Busch 50.00 75.00
Snickers Atlanta Raced/4138
18 Kyle Busch 75.00 125.00
Snicker's Atlanta Raced AU/288
19 Elliott Sadler 40.00 65.00
Best Buy/1824
18 NDA 75.00 125.00
Farm Bureau/2508
19 Elliott Sadler 40.00 65.00
McDonald's/818
19 Elliott Sadler 40.00 65.00
Siemens/853
19 Elliott Sadler 40.00 65.00
Stanley Tools/901
20 Kyle Busch 50.00 75.00
Doosan Mexico City Raced/1423
20 Joey Logano 40.00 65.00
Gamestop/3082
20 Joey Logano 50.00 75.00
Gamestop Kentucky Raced/3180
20 Tony Stewart 50.00 75.00
Home Depot/26,880
20 Tony Stewart 50.00 75.00
Home Depot Sam Bass Holiday/840
20 Tony Stewart 50.00 75.00
Home Depot 10th Anniversary/3744
20 Tony Stewart 50.00 75.00
Old Spice Talladega Raced/1270
20 Tony Stewart 50.00 75.00
Smoke/3934
20 Tony Stewart 50.00 75.00
Subway/3382
24 Jeff Gordon 50.00 75.00
DuPont Flames/37,032
24 Jeff Gordon 50.00 75.00
DuPont Salute the Troops/2990
24 Jeff Gordon 50.00 75.00
DuPont Salute the Troops Liquid Color/1024
24 Jeff Gordon 50.00 75.00
JG Foundation Holiday/1906
24 Jeff Gordon 50.00 75.00
JG Foundation Test/3242
24 Jeff Gordon 50.00 75.00
Nicorette/21,468
24 Jeff Gordon 50.00 75.00
Pepsi/22,008
24 Jeff Gordon 50.00 75.00
Pepsi Stuff/3388
24 Jeff Gordon 100.00 150.00
Pepsi Stuff AU/216
24 Jeff Gordon 50.00 75.00
Speed Racer/5052
25 Brad Keselowski 50.00 75.00
GoDaddy
25 Joey Logano 40.00 65.00
Joe Gibbs Racing Oil Raced/2712
26 Jamie McMurray 50.00 75.00
Crown Royal/2532
26 Jamie McMurray 50.00 75.00
Irwin Tools/1416
29 Jeff Burton 50.00 75.00
Holiday Inn/610
29 Kevin Harvick 50.00 75.00
Pennzoil Platinum/2086
29 Kevin Harvick 50.00 75.00
Reese's/3777
29 Kevin Harvick 50.00 75.00
Shell Pennzoil/11,736
29 Kevin Harvick 50.00 75.00
Shell Pennzoil Realtree Camo/987
29 Kevin Harvick 50.00 75.00
Shell Sam Bass Holiday/1369
29 Scott Wimmer 50.00 75.00
Holiday Inn/406
31 Jeff Burton 50.00 75.00
AT&T/8396
31 Jeff Burton 50.00 75.00
AT&T Bristol Raced/730
31 Jeff Burton 50.00 75.00
Lennox/1353
31 Jeff Burton 40.00 65.00
Prilosec/756
33 Kevin Harvick 50.00 75.00
Camping World/837
33 Kevin Harvick 50.00 75.00
Road Loans/1109
40 Dario Franchitti 40.00 65.00
Fastenal/891
40 Dario Franchitti 40.00 65.00
Tums/1007
41 Reed Sorenson 40.00 65.00
Polaroid/1202
41 Reed Sorenson 40.00 65.00
Target/876
41 Reed Sorenson 40.00 65.00
Tums/588
41 Reed Sorenson 50.00 75.00
Tums AU/150
42 Juan Pablo Montoya 50.00 75.00
Big Red/1092
42 Juan Pablo Montoya 50.00 75.00
Juicy Fruit/1181
42 Juan Pablo Montoya 50.00 75.00
Powerade/571
42 Juan Pablo Montoya 50.00 75.00
Texaco Havoline/3612
42 Juan Pablo Montoya 75.00 125.00
Texaco Havoline AU/204
42 Juan Pablo Montoya 50.00 75.00
Texaco Havoline '07 ROY w
tire/708
42 Richard Petty 50.00 75.00
Petty 1st Car/1242
43 Bobby Labonte 50.00 75.00
Cheerios/3300
43 Bobby Labonte 50.00 75.00
Cheerios Pink/1220
43 Bobby Labonte 40.00 65.00
General Mills/1366
43 Bobby Labonte 40.00 65.00
Petty 50th Anniversary/1170
43 Richard Petty 50.00 75.00
Petty 1st Win COT/1143
43 Richard Petty 125.00 200.00
Petty 1st Win COT Gold Chrome/43
43 Richard Petty 100.00 175.00
Petty 1st Win COT Polished Nickel/243
43 Richard Petty 50.00 75.00
Petty 100th Win COT/1143
43 Richard Petty 100.00 175.00
Petty 100th Win COT Color Chrome/443
43 Richard Petty 125.00 200.00
Petty 100th Win COT Gold Chrome/43
43 Richard Petty 50.00 75.00
Petty 200th Win COT/1543
44 Dale Jarrett 50.00 75.00
UPS/5496
44 Dale Jarrett 50.00 75.00
UPS All Star/2984
44 David Reutimann 50.00 75.00
UPS/3800
44 David Reutimann 50.00 75.00
UPS Kentucky Derby/1092
44 David Reutimann 50.00 75.00
UPS Toys for Tots/708
45 Terry Labonte 50.00 75.00
Petty 50th Anniversary/728
45 Terry Labonte 50.00 75.00
PVA.org/356
45 Kyle Petty 40.00 65.00
Marathon Oil/780
45 Kyle Petty 40.00 65.00
PVA.org/708
45 Kyle Petty 40.00 65.00
Wells Fargo/1284
48 Jimmie Johnson 100.00 175.00
Lowe's/15,292
48 Jimmie Johnson 100.00 150.00
Lowe's JJ Foundation/808
48 Jimmie Johnson 100.00 150.00
Lowe's Kobalt/2237
48 Jimmie Johnson 50.00 75.00
Lowe's Sam Bass Holiday/673
48 Jimmie Johnson 250.00 400.00
Lowe's 250 Starts/100
55 Michael Waltrip 50.00 75.00
Napa/5388
60 Carl Edwards 50.00 75.00
Planters/961
60 Carl Edwards 50.00 75.00
Save A Lot/866
60 Carl Edwards 50.00 75.00
Scotts/1030
60 Carl Edwards 50.00 75.00
Vitamin Water/1393
60 Carl Edwards 75.00 125.00
Vitamin Water AU/400
77 Sam Hornish Jr. 40.00 65.00
Mobil 1/1284
77 Sam Hornish Jr. 40.00 65.00
Penske/1002
83 Dale Earnhardt Jr. 50.00 75.00
Navy JR Division/8383
83 Brian Vickers 50.00 75.00
Red Bull/1476
84 A.J. Allmendinger 50.00 75.00
Red Bull/1344
88 Dale Earnhardt Jr. 50.00 75.00
AMP/108,088
88 Dale Earnhardt Jr. 50.00 75.00
AMP Mac Tools/1200
88 Dale Earnhardt Jr. 50.00 75.00
AMP QVC/27252
88 Dale Earnhardt Jr. 50.00 75.00
AMP Gatorade Duel 150 Raced/8888
88 Dale Earnhardt Jr. 50.00 75.00
AMP Michigan Raced/5606
88 Dale Earnhardt Jr. 50.00 75.00
AMP Sam Bass Holiday/5563
88 Dale Earnhardt Jr. 50.00 75.00
AMP Test/3433
88 Dale Earnhardt Jr. 50.00 75.00
Mountian Dew Retro/42888
88 Dale Earnhardt Jr. 50.00 75.00
National Guard/80,488
88 Dale Earnhardt Jr. 50.00 75.00
National Guard Mac Tools/1200
88 Dale Earnhardt Jr. 50.00 75.00
National Guard QVC/22,752
88 Dale Earnhardt Jr. 50.00 75.00
National Guard Bud Shootout Raced/8888
88 Dale Earnhardt Jr. 50.00 75.00
National Guard Citizen Soldier/38088
88 Dale Earnhardt Jr. 50.00 75.00
National Guard Digital Camo/30126
88 Dale Earnhardt Jr. 50.00 75.00
National Guard Salute the Troops/8582
88 Dale Earnhardt Jr. 60.00 100.00
National Guard Salute the Troops Liquid Color/1888
88 Brad Keselowski 50.00 75.00
Navy/1057
88 Brad Keselowski 50.00 75.00
Navy First Win/1454
88 Brad Keselowski 50.00 75.00
Navy Blue Angels/1088
88 Brad Keselowski 60.00 100.00
Navy Blue Angels AU/288
88 Brad Keselowski 50.00 75.00
Navy Salute the Troops/1717
99 Carl Edwards 50.00 75.00
Aflac/6352
99 Carl Edwards 50.00 75.00
Aflac Texas Raced/708
99 Carl Edwards 100.00 150.00
Aflac Texas Raced AU/288
99 Carl Edwards 50.00 75.00
Aflac Sam Bass Holiday/528
99 Carl Edwards 50.00 75.00
Claritin/1296
99 Carl Edwards 50.00 75.00
Dish Network California Raced/564
99 Carl Edwards 50.00 75.00
Office Depot/7248
07 Clint Bowyer 50.00 75.00
Jack Daniel's/10,740
07 Clint Bowyer 50.00 75.00
BB&T Richmond Raced/1443
07 Clint Bowyer 50.00 75.00
Directv/712
07 Clint Bowyer 50.00 75.00
Jack Daniel's Realtree/459
07 Clint Bowyer 50.00 75.00
Jack Daniel's Salute the Troops/1112
07 Clint Bowyer 50.00 75.00
Jack Daniel's Salute the Troops Liquid Color/407
08 ARC Relaunch Car/150 40.00 65.00
08 Daytona 500 50th Anniversary Red/1056 40.00 65.00
08 Daytona 500 50th Anniversary White/1104 40.00 65.00
08 NASCAR 60th Anniversary/804 40.00 65.00
08 Salute the Troops Program Car/1554 40.00 65.00
08 Sam Bass Holiday Program Car/531 40.00 65.00
08 Sprint Cup/850 40.00 65.00
NNO Dale Earnhardt Jr. 50.00 75.00
Whisky River/10526
NNO Daytona 500 Pace Car Corvette Z06/5144 40.00 65.00

2008 Action Racing Collectables Platinum Daytona 1:24

3 Dale Earnhardt 60.00 100.00
GM Plus
'98 Monte Carlo/7104
4 Sterling Marlin 45.00 70.00
Kodak '94 Lumina/324
8 Dale Earnhardt Jr. 50.00 75.00
Bud Born On Feb. 15
'04 Monte Carlo/6180
9 Bill Elliott 50.00 75.00
Coors '85 T-bird/900
15 Michael Waltrip 40.00 65.00
Napa '01 Monte Carlo/480
17 Darrell Waltrip 50.00 75.00
Tide '83 Monte Carlo/1188
18 Dale Jarrett 45.00 70.00
Interstate Batteries '93 Lumina/780
24 Jeff Gordon 50.00 75.00
DuPont '97 Monte Carlo/2832
28 Davey Allison 60.00 100.00
Havoline '92 T-bird/1236
29 Kevin Harvick 45.00 70.00
Shell '07 Monte Carlo/912
43 Richard Petty 50.00 75.00
'64 Plymouth Belvedere/1964
43 Richard Petty 75.00 125.00
'64 Plymouth Liquid Color AU
43 Richard Petty 50.00 75.00
STP '81 Buick/1632
48 Jimmie Johnson 45.00 70.00
Lowe's '06 Monte Carlo/1068
72 Benny Parsons 60.00 100.00
Kings Row '75 Malibu/804

2008 Action Racing Collectables Platinum GM Dealers 1:24

1 Martin Truex Jr. 50.00 75.00
Bass Pro Shops/636
1 Martin Truex Jr. 50.00 75.00
Bass Pro Shops Brushed Metal/180
2 Clint Bowyer 50.00 75.00
BB&T/144
2 Clint Bowyer 50.00 75.00
BB&T Brushed Metal/144
3 Austin Dillon 50.00 80.00
Garage Equiptment/300
3 Austin Dillon 50.00 80.00
Garage Equiptment Brushed Metal/144
3 Dale Earnhardt 60.00 100.00
GM Plus '98 Daytona COT/3333
3 Dale Earnhardt 75.00 125.00
GM Plus '98 Daytona COT Brushed Metal/533
3 Dale Earnhardt 50.00 75.00
Johnny Cash/796
3 Dale Earnhardt 60.00 100.00
Johnny Cash Brushed Metal/288
3 Dale Earnhardt 50.00 75.00
John Wayne/576
3 Dale Earnhardt 60.00 100.00
John Wayne Brushed Metal/144
5 Casey Mears 50.00 75.00
Carquest/204
5 Casey Mears 50.00 75.00
Carquest Brushed Metal/120
5 Casey Mears 50.00 75.00
Kellogg's/204
5 Casey Mears 50.00 75.00
Kellogg's Brushed Metal/144
5 Dale Earnhardt Jr. 60.00 100.00
All Star Test/1200
5 Dale Earnhardt Jr. 60.00 100.00
All Star Test Brushed Metal/1200
8 Aric Almirola 50.00 75.00
U.S. Army/144
8 Aric Almirola 50.00 75.00
U.S. Army Brushed Metal/144
8 Mark Martin 50.00 75.00
U.S. Army/888
8 Mark Martin 50.00 75.00
U.S. Army Brushed Metal/180
15 Paul Menard 50.00 75.00
Menards/252
15 Paul Menard 50.00 75.00
Menards Brushed Metal/144
24 Jeff Gordon 50.00 75.00
DuPont/1500
24 Jeff Gordon 60.00 100.00
DuPont Brushed Metal/360
24 Jeff Gordon 50.00 75.00
Nicorette/1200
24 Jeff Gordon 60.00 100.00
Nicorette Brushed Metal/300
24 Jeff Gordon 50.00 75.00
Pepsi/792
24 Jeff Gordon 60.00 100.00
Pepsi Brushed Metal/300
24 Jeff Gordon 50.00 75.00
Pepsi Stuff/288
24 Jeff Gordon 60.00 100.00
Pepsi Stuff Brushed Metal/144
24 Jeff Gordon 50.00 75.00
Speed Racer/360
24 Jeff Gordon 60.00 100.00
Speed Racer Brushed Metal/144
29 Kevin Harvick 50.00 75.00
Pennzoil Platinum/288
29 Kevin Harvick 50.00 75.00
Pennzoil Platinum Brushed Metal/144
29 Kevin Harvick 50.00 75.00
Reese's/384
29 Kevin Harvick 50.00 75.00
Reese's Brushed Metal/144
29 Kevin Harvick 50.00 75.00
Shell/1200
29 Kevin Harvick 50.00 75.00
Shell Brushed Metal/300
31 Jeff Burton 50.00 75.00
AT&T/432
31 Jeff Burton 50.00 75.00
AT&T Brushed Metal/288
31 Jeff Burton 50.00 75.00
Lenox/144
31 Jeff Burton 50.00 75.00
Lenox Brushed Metal/144
48 Jimmie Johnson 60.00 100.00
Lowe's/852
48 Jimmie Johnson 75.00 125.00
Lowe's Brushed Metal/300
83 Dale Earnhardt Jr. 50.00 75.00
Navy JR Division/288
83 Dale Earnhardt Jr. 50.00 75.00
Navy Brushed Metal/144
88 Dale Earnhardt Jr. 50.00 75.00
AMP/8800
88 Dale Earnhardt Jr. 60.00 100.00
AMP Brushed Metal/2008
88 Dale Earnhardt Jr. 60.00 100.00
AMP Gatorade Duel 150 Raced/808
88 Dale Earnhardt Jr. 75.00 125.00
AMP Gatorade Duel 150 Raced Brushed Metal/188
88 Dale Earnhardt Jr. 60.00 100.00
AMP Michigan Raced/600
88 Dale Earnhardt Jr. 60.00 100.00
Mountian Dew Retro/2000
88 Dale Earnhardt Jr. 75.00 125.00
Mountian Dew Retro Brushed Metal/1000
88 Dale Earnhardt Jr. 60.00 100.00
National Guard/8800
88 Dale Earnhardt Jr. 75.00 125.00
National Guard Brushed Metal/2008
88 Dale Earnhardt Jr. 60.00 100.00
National Guard Bud Shootout Raced/808
88 Dale Earnhardt Jr. 75.00 125.00
National Guard Bud Shootout Raced Brushed Metal/188
88 Dale Earnhardt Jr. 60.00 100.00
National Guard Citizen Soldier/1500
88 Dale Earnhardt Jr. 75.00 125.00
National Guard Citizen Soldier Brushed Metal/480
88 Dale Earnhardt Jr. 60.00 100.00
National Guard Digital Camo/1500
88 Dale Earnhardt Jr. 75.00 125.00
National Guard Digital Camo Brushed Metal/432
07 Clint Bowyer 50.00 75.00
Jack Daniel's/432
07 Clint Bowyer 50.00 75.00
Jack Daniel's Brushed Metal/288

2008 Action Racing Collectables Platinum Trucks 1:24

2 Ryan Newman 75.00 125.00
American Commercial
Raced AU/888
2 Jack Sprague 50.00 75.00
American Commercial/1500

2008 Action Racing Collectables Silver 1:24

6 David Ragan 60.00 100.00
Discount Tire Promo/2500
9 Kasey Kahne 60.00 100.00
Bud Promo/999
9 Kasey Kahne 75.00 125.00
Bud Color Chrome Promo/999
9 Chase Miller 60.00 100.00
Verizon Promo/849
16 Greg Biffle 150.00 250.00
Red Cross
16 Greg Biffle 175.00 300.00
Sherwin Williams Promo/1500
16 Greg Biffle 75.00 125.00
3M Liquid Color/144
18 Kyle Busch 50.00 75.00
M&M's Atlanta Raced Promo/6000
18 Kyle Busch 60.00 100.00
Pedigree Petsmart Promo/1500
18 Farm Bureau Promo/2508 75.00 12
31 Jeff Burton 60.00 10
AT&T Olympics Promo/700
37 USPS Promo/1500 50.00 7
38 Jason Leffler 50.00 7
Great Clips Promo/1500
42 Juan Pablo Montoya 50.00 7
Powerade Promo/200
43 Bobby Labonte 50.00 7
Cheerios Promo/1860
43 Bobby Labonte 50.00 7
General Mills Promo/100
55 Michael Waltrip 50.00 7
Napa Canada Promo/876
88 Dale Earnhardt Jr. 100.00 20
National Guard Platinum Promo/50
08 Allstate Promo/1500 50.00 7
08 Car Fax Promo/1500 50.00 7
08 Coke Zero 400 500 Club Promo/500 50.00 7
08 Coke Zero 400 Promo/1000 50.00 7
08 Richmond Torque Club Promo/750 50.00 7
08 Sprint Cup Promo/2788 50.00 7
NNO Goodyear Tire Turkey Promo/13000 50.00 7
NNO Joe Gibbs Racing Test Promo/700 75.00 12

2008 Action/QVC For Race Fans Only 1:

1 Martin Truex Jr. 60.00 10
Bass Pro Shops Color Chrome/288
1 Martin Truex Jr.
Bass Pro Shops Gold/24
1 Martin Truex Jr.
Bass Pro Shops Platinum/24
2 Kurt Busch 60.00 10
Miller Lite Color Chrome/144
2 Kurt Busch
Miller Lite Gold/24
3 Dale Earnhardt 75.00 15
GM Plus '98 Monte Carlo Daytona Gold Chrome/500
3 Dale Earnhardt 50.00 7
GM Plus '98 Daytona COT/283
3 Dale Earnhardt 60.00 10
GM Plus '98 Daytona COT Color Chrome/3573
3 Dale Earnhardt 100.00 17
GM Plus '98 Daytona COT Gold/393
3 Dale Earnhardt 100.00 20
GM Plus '98 Daytona COT Gold Chrome/483
3 Dale Earnhardt 100.00 20
GM Plus '98 Daytona COT Gun Metal/873
3 Dale Earnhardt 60.00 10
Johnny Cash Color Chrome/4128
3 Dale Earnhardt 75.00 12
Johnny Cash Gold/300
3 Dale Earnhardt 75.00 12
Johnny Cash Polished Nickel/396
3 Dale Earnhardt 75.00 12
John Wayne Gold/144
3 Dale Earnhardt 60.00 10
John Wayne Polished Nickel/2116
4 Sterling Marlin 60.00 10
Kodak '94 Lumina Daytona Gold Chrome/144
5 Dale Earnhardt Jr. 60.00 10
All Star Test Color Chrome/2800
5 Dale Earnhardt Jr. 100.00 20
All Star Test Copper/504
5 D.Earnhardt Jr. 100.00 20
All Star Test Gold/108
5 Dale Earnhardt Jr. 100.00 20
All Star Test Gun Metal/504
5 Dale Earnhardt Jr. 60.00 10
GoDaddy Color Chrome/9000
5 Dale Earnhardt Jr. 75.00 15
GoDaddy Copper/504
5 Dale Earnhardt Jr. 75.00 15
GoDaddy Gold Chrome/708
5 Dale Earnhardt Jr. 75.00 15
GoDaddy Gun Metal/2508
8 Mark Martin 60.00 10
U.S. Army Color Chrome/144
8 Mark Martin
U.S. Army Gold/24
9 Kasey Kahne 60.00 10
Bud Color Chrome/288
9 Kasey Kahne
Bud Gold/24
9 Kasey Kahne 100.00 20
Bud Gold Chrome/288
9 Bill Elliott 100.00 20
Coors '85 T-bird Daytona Gold Chrome/504
9 Kasey Kahne
Bud Platinum/24
11 Denny Hamlin 60.00 10
Fed Ex Express Color Chrome/144
11 Denny Hamlin
Fed Ex Express Gold/24
11 Denny Hamlin
Fed Ex Express Platinum/24
15 Michael Waltrip 100.00 20
Napa '01 Monte Carlo Daytona Gold Chrome/144
17 Matt Kenseth 60.00 10
Carhartt Color Chrome/96
17 Matt Kenseth 60.00 10
R&L Carriers Color Chrome/96
18 Kyle Busch
Combo's Dover Raced Gold/24
18 Kyle Busch 100.00 15
M&M's Color Chrome/96
18 Kyle Busch
M&M's Gold/24
18 Kyle Busch
M&M's Platinum/24
18 Kyle Busch
M&M's Talladega Raced Gold/24
18 Kyle Busch 75.00 15
M&M's Halloween Color Chrome/238
18 Kyle Busch
M&M's Halloween Gold/24
18 Kyle Busch 75.00 15
M&M's Pink Color Chrome/433
18 Kyle Busch
M&M's Pink Gold/24
18 Kyle Busch
Snicker's Atlanta Raced Gold/24
18 Kyle Busch
Snicker's Atlanta Raced Gold
18 Kyle Busch 75.00 15
M&M's Summer Color Chrome/360
18 Kyle Busch

M&M's Summer Gold/24
20 Tony Stewart 60.00 100.00
Home Depot Color Chrome/288
20 Tony Stewart 75.00 150.00
Home Depot Copper/288
20 Tony Stewart 175.00 350.00
Home Depot Gold/48
20 Tony Stewart 100.00 200.00
Home Depot Gold Chrome/504
20 Tony Stewart 75.00 150.00
Home Depot Mesma Chrome/288
20 Tony Stewart 175.00 350.00
Home Depot Platinum/48
24 Jeff Gordon 100.00 200.00
DuPont Chrome/324
24 Jeff Gordon 60.00 100.00
DuPont Color Chrome/1500
24 Jeff Gordon 75.00 150.00
DuPont Copper/504
24 Jeff Gordon 125.00 250.00
DuPont Gold/108
24 Jeff Gordon 100.00 200.00
DuPont Gold Chrome/504
24 Jeff Gordon 125.00 250.00
DuPont Mesma Chrome/324
24 Jeff Gordon 150.00 300.00
DuPont Platinum/108
24 Jeff Gordon 125.00 250.00
Nicorette Chrome/324
24 Jeff Gordon 60.00 100.00
Nicorette Color Chrome/1500
24 Jeff Gordon 75.00 150.00
Nicorette Copper/504
24 Jeff Gordon 100.00 200.00
Nicorette Gold Chrome/504
24 Jeff Gordon 100.00 200.00
Nicorette Mesma Chrome/324
24 Jeff Gordon 100.00 200.00
Pepsi Chrome/324
24 Jeff Gordon 60.00 100.00
Pepsi Color Chrome/1500
24 Jeff Gordon 75.00 150.00
Pepsi Copper/504
24 Jeff Gordon 100.00 200.00
Pepsi Gold Chrome/504
24 Jeff Gordon 100.00 200.00
Pepsi Mesma Chrome/324
24 Jeff Gordon 125.00 250.00
Speed Racer Chrome/125
24 Jeff Gordon 60.00 100.00
Speed Racer Color Chrome/600
24 Jeff Gordon 100.00 200.00
DuPont '97 Monte Carlo Daytona Gold Chrome/1008
28 Davey Allison 125.00 250.00
Havoline '92 T-bird Daytona Gold Chrome/504
29 Kevin Harvick 60.00 100.00
Shell Color Chrome/288
29 Kevin Harvick 75.00 125.00
Shell Copper/288
29 Kevin Harvick
Shell Gold/24
29 Kevin Harvick 100.00 175.00
Shell Gold Chrome/288
29 Kevin Harvick 100.00 150.00
Shell Mesma Chrome/288
29 Kevin Harvick
Shell Platinum/24
29 Kevin Harvick 100.00 200.00
Shell '07 Monte Carlo Daytona Gold Chrome/288
31 Jeff Burton 60.00 100.00
AT&T Color Chrome/96
31 Jeff Burton
AT&T Gold/24
42 Juan Pablo Montoya 60.00 100.00
Texaco Havoline Color Chrome/96
42 Juan Pablo Montoya
Texaco Havoline Gold/24
42 Juan Pablo Montoya
Texaco Havoline Platinum/24
42 Richard Petty 100.00 200.00
Petty 1st Car Polished Nickel/242
43 Richard Petty 100.00 200.00
STP '81 Buick Gold Chrome/777
42 Richard Petty 150.00 300.00
Petty 1st Car Gold/42
43 Richard Petty 60.00 100.00
Petty 200th Win Color Chrome/543
43 Richard Petty 150.00 300.00
Petty 200th Win Gold/43
43 Richard Petty 100.00 200.00
'64 Belvedere Gold Chrome/777
48 Jimmie Johnson 100.00 200.00
Lowe's Color Chrome/288
48 Jimmie Johnson 125.00 250.00
Lowe's Copper/288
48 Jimmie Johnson
Lowe's Gold/24
48 Jimmie Johnson 125.00 250.00
Lowe's Gold Chrome/288
48 Jimmie Johnson
Lowe's Platinum/24
48 Jimmie Johnson 150.00 300.00
Lowe's '06 Monte Carlo Daytona Gold Chrome/288
88 Dale Earnhardt Jr. 75.00 150.00
AMP Color Chrome/2673
88 Dale Earnhardt Jr. 60.00 100.00
AMP Color
Mesma Chrome/25888
88 Dale Earnhardt Jr. 75.00 125.00
AMP Copper/2508
88 Dale Earnhardt Jr. 125.00 250.00
AMP Gold/288
88 Dale Earnhardt Jr. 75.00 150.00
AMP Gold Chrome/5000
88 Dale Earnhardt Jr. 75.00 150.00
AMP Gun Metal/2508
88 Dale Earnhardt Jr. 150.00 300.00
AMP Platinum/144
88 Dale Earnhardt Jr. 75.00 150.00
Mountian Dew Retro Color Chrome/1088
88 Dale Earnhardt Jr. 60.00 100.00
Mountian Dew Retro Color
Mesma Chrome/7325
88 Dale Earnhardt Jr. 60.00 120.00
Mountian Dew Retro Copper/1088
88 Dale Earnhardt Jr. 125.00 250.00
Mountian Dew Retro Gold/188
88 Dale Earnhardt Jr. 100.00 200.00
Mountian Dew Retro Gold Chrome/708
88 Dale Earnhardt Jr. 75.00 150.00
Mountian Dew Retro Gun Metal/2508
88 Dale Earnhardt Jr. 60.00 100.00
National Guard Color
Mesma Chrome/25888
88 Dale Earnhardt Jr. 75.00 125.00
National Guard Copper/2508
88 Dale Earnhardt Jr. 125.00 250.00
National Guard Gold/288
88 Dale Earnhardt Jr. 75.00 150.00
National Guard Gold Chrome/5000
88 Dale Earnhardt Jr. 75.00 150.00
National Guard Gun Metal/2508
88 Dale Earnhardt Jr. 150.00 300.00
National Guard Platinum/144
88 Dale Earnhardt Jr. 75.00 150.00
National Guard Citizen Soldier Color Chrome/2088
88 Dale Earnhardt Jr. 75.00 150.00
National Guard Citizen Soldier Copper/588
88 Dale Earnhardt Jr. 125.00 250.00
National Guard Citizen Soldier Gold/188
88 Dale Earnhardt Jr. 100.00 200.00
National Guard Citizen Soldier Gold Chrome/888
88 Dale Earnhardt Jr. 75.00 150.00
National Guard Citizen Soldier Gun Metal/1088
88 Dale Earnhardt Jr. 75.00 150.00
national Guard Digital Camo Color Chrome/1850
88 Dale Earnhardt Jr. 75.00 150.00
National Guard Digital Camo Copper/488
88 Dale Earnhardt Jr. 100.00 200.00
national Guard Digital Camo Gold/188
88 Dale Earnhardt Jr. 100.00 200.00
National Guard Digital Camo Gold Chrome/488
88 Dale Earnhardt Jr. 75.00 150.00
National Guard Digital Camo Gun Metal/1088
88 Dale Earnhardt Jr. 100.00 200.00
National Guard Digital Camo Polished Nickel/488
99 Carl Edwards 60.00 100.00
Office Depot Color Chrome/96
99 Carl Edwards
Office Depot Gold/24
99 Carl Edwards
Office Depot Platinum/24
07 Clint Bowyer 60.00 100.00
Jack Daniel's Color Chrome/96
07 Clint Bowyer
Jack Daniel's Platinum/24
NNO Dale Earnhardt Jr. 60.00 100.00
Whisky River Color Chrome/2088
NNO Dale Earnhardt Jr. 100.00 200.00
Whisky River Copper/188
NNO Dale Earnhardt Jr. 100.00 200.00
Whisky River Gold/188
NNO Dale Earnhardt Jr. 75.00 150.00
Whisky River Gun Metal/388
NNO Ashley Force 75.00 150.00
Castrol GTX Color Chrome/120
NNO Ashley Force 100.00 200.00
Castrol GTX Pink ROY Color Chrome/250
NNO John Force 60.00 100.00
Castrol GTX Color Chrome/60
NNO John Force 60.00 100.00
Castrol Retro Color Chrome/120
NNO Robert Hight 60.00 100.00
AAA Color Chrome/60
NNO Robert Hight 60.00 100.00
AAA Dodgers 50th Anniversary Color Chrome
NNO Mike Neff 60.00 100.00
Old Spice Color Chrome/60

2008 Action/RCCA Club 1:24

1 Martin Truex Jr. 50.00 75.00
Bass Pro Shops/156
2 Kurt Busch 50.00 75.00
Miller Lite/150
3 Dale Earnhardt 75.00 125.00
Goodwrench '98 Daytona COT/700
3 Dale Earnhardt 50.00 75.00
Goodwrench Realtree
3 Dale Earnhardt 50.00 75.00
Johnny Cash/350
3 Dale Earnhardt 50.00 75.00
John Wayne/300
5 Dale Earnhardt Jr. 50.00 75.00
Delphi/300
5 Dale Earnhardt Jr. 50.00 75.00
GoDaddy/300
5 Dale Earnhardt Jr. 50.00 75.00
National Guard/300
5 Casey Mears 50.00 75.00
Kellogg's/150
6 David Ragan 50.00 75.00
AAA/150
8 Aric Almirola 50.00 75.00
U.S. Army/120
8 Mark Martin 50.00 75.00
U.S. Army/204
8 Mark Martin 50.00 75.00
U.S. Army
Salute the Troops/150
9 Kasey Kahne 50.00 75.00
Bud/504
9 Kasey Kahne 50.00 75.00
Bud Sam Bass Holiday/144
10 Patrick Carpentier 50.00 75.00
Valvoline/150
11 Denny Hamlin 50.00 75.00
Fed Ex Express/252
11 Denny Hamlin 50.00 75.00
Fed Ex Freight/150
11 Denny Hamlin 50.00 75.00
Fed Ex Ground/150
11 Darrell Waltrip 60.00 100.00
Mountian Dew '81 Buick/504
12 Ryan Newman 50.00 75.00
Alltel/150
15 Paul Menard 50.00 75.00
Menards/300
15 Paul Menard 50.00 75.00
Menards Realtree/150
16 Greg Biffle 50.00 75.00
3M/150
17 Matt Kenseth 50.00 75.00
Carhartt/150
17 Matt Kenseth 50.00 75.00
DeWalt/150
18 Kyle Busch 100.00 150.00
M&M's/250
18 Kyle Busch 50.00 75.00
M&M's Sam Bass Holiday/144
19 Elliott Sadler 50.00 75.00
Best Buy/150
20 Tony Stewart 50.00 75.00
Home Depot/408
20 Tony Stewart 50.00 75.00
Home Depot Sam Bass Holiday/144
20 Tony Stewart 50.00 75.00
Home Depot
10th Anniversary/300
20 Tony Stewart 50.00 75.00
Smoke/300
20 Tony Stewart 50.00 75.00
Subway/200
24 Jeff Gordon 50.00 75.00
DuPont Flames/700
24 Jeff Gordon 50.00 75.00
DuPont Flames
Salute the Troops/500
24 Jeff Gordon 50.00 75.00
JG Foundation Holiday/240
24 Jeff Gordon 50.00 75.00
Nicorette/500
24 Jeff Gordon 50.00 75.00
Pepsi/500
24 Jeff Gordon 50.00 75.00
Pepsi Stuff/500
24 Jeff Gordon 50.00 75.00
Speed Racer/500
26 Jamie McMurray 50.00 75.00
Crown Royal/150
26 Jamie McMurray 50.00 75.00
Irwin Tools/150
29 Kevin Harvick 50.00 75.00
Pennzoil Platinum/150
29 Kevin Harvick 50.00 75.00
Shell/300
31 Jeff Burton 50.00 75.00
AT&T/156
41 Reed Sorenson 50.00 75.00
Target/156
29 Kevin Harvick 50.00 75.00
Shell Realtree/144
42 Juan Pablo Montoya 50.00 75.00
Texaco/252
43 Bobby Labonte 50.00 75.00
Cheerios/150
43 Richard Petty 50.00 75.00
Petty 200th Win COT/300
44 Dale Jarrett 50.00 75.00
UPS/300
44 Dale Jarrett 50.00 75.00
UPS All Star/150
44 David Reutimann 50.00 75.00
UPS Kentucky Derby/150
44 David Reutimann 50.00 75.00
UPS Toys for Tots/150
48 Jimmie Johnson 75.00 125.00
Lowe's/300
48 Jimmie Johnson 50.00 75.00
Lowe's JJ Foundation/144
55 Michael Waltrip 50.00 75.00
Napa/120
60 Carl Edwards 50.00 75.00
Aflac Sam Bass Holiday/99
83 Dale Earnhardt Jr. 50.00 75.00
Navy JR Division/300
88 Dale Earnhardt Jr. 50.00 75.00
AMP/2100
88 Dale Earnhardt Jr. 50.00 75.00
AMP Sam Bass Holiday/300
88 Dale Earnhardt Jr. 50.00 75.00
Mountian Dew Retro/1200
88 Dale Earnhardt Jr. 50.00 75.00
National Guard Bud Shootout Raced/450
88 Dale Earnhardt Jr. 50.00 75.00
National Guard/1000
88 Dale Earnhardt Jr. 50.00 75.00
National Guard
Citizen Soldier/1200
88 Dale Earnhardt Jr. 50.00 75.00
National Guard
Salute the Troops/500
07 Clint Bowyer 50.00 75.00
Jack Daniel's/150
07 Clint Bowyer 50.00 75.00
Jack Daniel's
Salute the Troops/250
08 Daytona 500 Program/2208 50.00 75.00
08 Daytona 500 Program Color Chrome/600 60.00 100.00

2008 Action/RCCA Club Daytona 1:24

4 Sterling Marlin 50.00 75.00
Kodak '94 Lumina Liquid Color/120
9 Bill Elliott 50.00 75.00
Coors '85 T-bird Liquid Color/360
15 Michael Waltrip 50.00 75.00
Napa '01 Monte Carlo Liquid Color/120
17 Darrell Waltrip 50.00 75.00
Tide '89 Monte Carlo Liquid Color/504
43 Richard Petty 50.00 75.00
'64 Belvedere Liquid Color/1964
43 Richard Petty 60.00 100.00
STP '81 Buick Liquid Color/1981
72 Benny Parsons 60.00 100.00
King's Row '75 Malibu Liquid Color/300

2008 Action/RCCA Elite 1:24

1 Martin Truex Jr. 75.00 125.00
Bass Pro Shops Realtree/300
1 Martin Truex Jr. 75.00 125.00
Bass Pro Shops/300
1 Martin Truex Jr. 175.00 300.00
Bass Pro Shops
Platinum/25
1 Martin Truex Jr. 175.00 300.00
Bass Pro Shops
White Gold/50
2 Kurt Busch 75.00 125.00
Miller Lite/300
2 Kurt Busch 175.00 300.00
Miller Lite Platinum/25
2 Kurt Busch 175.00 300.00
Miller Lite White Gold/50
3 Dale Earnhardt 100.00 175.00
Goodwrench '98 Daytona COT/1000
3 Dale Earnhardt 300.00 500.00
Goodwrench '98 Daytona COT Platinum/53
3 Dale Earnhardt 250.00 400.00
Goodwrench '98 Daytona COT White Gold/103
3 Dale Earnhardt 75.00 125.00
John Wayne/708
3 Dale Earnhardt 75.00 125.00
Johnny Cash/1200
5 Dale Earnhardt Jr. 100.00 150.00
City Chevrolet Test/1200
5 Dale Earnhardt Jr. 75.00 125.00
Delphi/1000
5 Dale Earnhardt Jr. 75.00 125.00
GoDaddy/1000
5 Dale Earnhardt Jr. 100.00 150.00
National Guard/1200
5 Mark Martin 75.00 125.00
Delphi/400
5 Casey Mears 75.00 125.00
Kellogg's/300
5 Casey Mears 175.00 300.00
Kellogg's Platinum/25
5 Casey Mears 175.00 300.00
Kellogg's White Gold/50
8 Mark Martin 75.00 125.00
U.S. Army/408
8 Mark Martin 200.00 350.00
U.S. Army Platinum/25
8 Mark Martin 200.00 350.00
U.S. Army White Gold/50
8 Mark Martin 100.00 150.00
U.S. Army
Salute the Troops/300
8 Mark Martin 200.00 350.00
U.S. Army
Salute the Troops Platinum/25
8 Mark Martin 200.00 350.00
U.S. Army
Salute the Troops White Gold/50
8 Mark Martin 75.00 125.00
Principal Financial/300
9 Kasey Kahne 100.00 150.00
Bud/1500
9 Kasey Kahne 75.00 125.00
Bud All Star Raced/300
9 Kasey Kahne 250.00 400.00
Bud Platinum/25
9 Kasey Kahne 250.00 400.00
Bud White Gold/50
11 Denny Hamlin 75.00 125.00
Fed Ex Express/408
11 Denny Hamlin 200.00 350.00
Fed Ex Express Platinum/25
11 Denny Hamlin 200.00 350.00
Fed Ex Express White Gold/50
11 Denny Hamlin 75.00 125.00
Fed Ex Ground/300
11 Denny Hamlin 75.00 125.00
Fed Ex Kinko's/300
11 Denny Hamlin 200.00 350.00
Fed Ex Kinko's Platinum/25
11 Denny Hamlin 200.00 350.00
Fed Ex Kinko's White Gold/50
11 Darrell Waltrip 200.00 350.00
Mountian Dew '81 Buick Platinum/25
12 Ryan Newman 100.00 150.00
Alltel/300
12 Ryan Newman 200.00 350.00
Alltel Platinum/25
12 Ryan Newman 200.00 350.00
Alltel White Gold/50
12 Ryan Newman 75.00 125.00
Alltel Mummy 3/400
12 Ryan Newman 175.00 300.00
Alltel Mummy 3
Platinum/25
12 Ryan Newman 175.00 300.00
Alltel Mummy 3
White Gold/50
12 Ryan Newman 100.00 200.00
Alltel Daytona Raced/300
16 Greg Biffle 75.00 125.00
3M/300
16 Greg Biffle 175.00 300.00
3M Platinum/25
16 Greg Biffle 175.00 300.00
3M White Gold/50
17 Matt Kenseth 75.00 125.00
DeWalt/300
18 Kyle Busch 250.00 500.00
M&M's Platinum/25
18 Kyle Busch 350.00 600.00
M&M's White Gold/50
18 Kyle Busch 75.00 125.00
M&M's Red White Blue/504
18 Kyle Busch 275.00 400.00
M&M's Red White Blue/ Platinum/25
18 Kyle Busch 275.00 400.00
M&M's Red White Blue
White Gold/50
18 Kyle Busch 125.00 200.00
M&M's/408
18 Kyle Busch 100.00 150.00
M&M's Halloween/300
18 Kyle Busch 100.00 175.00
M&M's Pink/504
18 Kyle Busch 300.00 500.00
M&M's Pink Platinum/25
18 Kyle Busch 275.00 400.00
M&M's Pink White Gold/50
18 Kyle Busch 100.00 150.00
M&M's Sam Bass Holiday/300
18 Kyle Busch 100.00 175.00
M&M's Summer/504
18 Kyle Busch 300.00 500.00
M&M's Summer Platinum/25
18 Kyle Busch 275.00 400.00
M&M's Summer White Gold/50
18 Kyle Busch 100.00 175.00
Snicker's Atlanta Raced/708
18 Kyle Busch 300.00 500.00
Snicker's Atlanta Raced Platinum/25
18 Kyle Busch 275.00 400.00
Snicker's Atlanta Raced White Gold/50
19 Elliott Sadler 75.00 125.00
Best Buy/300
19 Elliott Sadler 75.00 125.00
McDonald's/300
20 Tony Stewart 100.00 150.00
Home Depot/1200
20 Tony Stewart 250.00 400.00
Home Depot Platinum/25
20 Tony Stewart 250.00 400.00
Home Depot White Gold/50
20 Tony Stewart 75.00 125.00
Home Depot Sam Bass Holiday/300
20 Tony Stewart 200.00 400.00
Home Depot Sam Bass Holiday Platinum/25
20 Tony Stewart 150.00 300.00
Home Depot Sam Bass Holiday White Gold/50
20 Tony Stewart 75.00 125.00
Subway Talladega Raced
20 Tony Stewart 100.00 150.00
Smoke/504
20 Tony Stewart 100.00 150.00
Home Depot
10th Anniversary/1000
20 Tony Stewart 250.00 400.00
Home Depot
10th Anniversary Platinum/25
20 Tony Stewart 250.00 400.00
Home Depot
10th Anniversary White Gold/50
20 Tony Stewart 75.00 125.00
Subway/504
20 Tony Stewart 200.00 350.00
Subway Platinum/25
20 Tony Stewart 200.00 350.00
Subway White Gold/50
24 Jeff Gordon 100.00 150.00
DuPont Flames Salute the Troops/1000
24 Jeff Gordon 100.00 150.00
DuPont Flames/1200
24 Jeff Gordon 350.00 600.00
DuPont Flames
Platinum/25
24 Jeff Gordon 350.00 500.00
DuPont Flames
White Gold/50
24 Jeff Gordon 75.00 125.00
Speed Racer/1000
24 Jeff Gordon 250.00 400.00
Speed Racer
Platinum/25
24 Jeff Gordon 250.00 400.00
Speed Racer
White Gold/50
24 Jeff Gordon 75.00 125.00
Nicorette/700
24 Jeff Gordon 250.00 400.00
Nicorette Platinum/25
24 Jeff Gordon 250.00 400.00
Nicorette White Gold/50
24 Jeff Gordon 75.00 125.00
Pepsi Stuff/1000
24 Jeff Gordon 250.00 400.00
Pepsi Stuff Platinum/25
24 Jeff Gordon 250.00 400.00
Pepsi Stuff White Gold/50
24 Jeff Gordon 75.00 125.00
Pepsi/700
24 Jeff Gordon 250.00 400.00
Pepsi Platinum/25
24 Jeff Gordon 250.00 400.00
Pepsi White Gold/50
24 Jeff Gordon 100.00 150.00
DuPont Test/504
24 Jeff Gordon 75.00 125.00
JG Foundation Holiday/400
24 Jeff Gordon 200.00 400.00
JG Foundation Holiday Platinum/25
24 Jeff Gordon 150.00 300.00
JG Foundation Holiday White Gold/50
24 Jeff Gordon 125.00 250.00
Pepsi Stuff AU/288
26 Jamie McMurray 75.00 125.00
Crown Royal/300
26 Jamie McMurray 175.00 300.00
Crown Royal Platinum/25
26 Jamie McMurray 175.00 300.00
Crown Royal White Gold/50
29 Kevin Harvick 75.00 125.00
Reese's/708
29 Kevin Harvick 75.00 125.00
Shell/708
29 Kevin Harvick 200.00 350.00
Shell Platinum/25
29 Kevin Harvick 200.00 350.00
Shell White Gold/50
29 Kevin Harvick 75.00 125.00
Penzoil Platinum/300
29 Kevin Harvick 175.00 300.00
Penzoil Platinum
Platinum/25
29 Kevin Harvick 175.00 300.00
Penzoil Platinum
White Gold/50
29 Kevin Harvick 75.00 125.00
Shell Realtree/300
29 Kevin Harvick 200.00 350.00
Shell Realtree Platinum/25
29 Kevin Harvick 125.00 250.00
Shell Realtree White Gold/50
31 Jeff Burton 75.00 125.00
AT&T/300
42 Juan Pablo Montoya 75.00 125.00
Texaco/504
42 Juan Pablo Montoya 200.00 350.00
Texaco Platinum/25
42 Juan Pablo Montoya 200.00 350.00
Texaco White Gold/50
43 Bobby Labonte 75.00 125.00
Cheerios/300
43 Bobby Labonte 175.00 300.00
Cheerios Platinum/25
43 Bobby Labonte 175.00 300.00
Cheerios White Gold/50
43 Bobby Labonte 75.00 125.00
Cheerios Pink/300
43 Richard Petty 75.00 125.00
Petty 100th Win COT/400
43 Richard Petty 75.00 125.00
Petty 1st Car COT/400
43 Richard Petty 75.00 125.00
Petty 1st Win COT/400
43 Richard Petty 75.00 125.00
Petty 200th Win COT/708
43 Richard Petty 250.00 400.00
Petty 200th Win COT Platinum/25
43 Richard Petty 175.00 300.00

Petty 200th Win COT White Gold/50
44 Dale Jarrett UPS/600 75.00 150.00
44 David Reutimann UPS/300 75.00 125.00
44 David Reutimann UPS Toys for Tots/300 75.00 125.00
44 David Reutimann UPS Kentucky Derby/300 75.00 125.00
44 David Reutimann UPS Kentucky Derby Platinum/25 175.00 300.00
44 David Reutimann UPS Kentucky Derby White Gold/50 175.00 300.00
44 Dale Jarrett UPS All Star/444 75.00 125.00
44 Dale Jarrett UPS All Star Platinum/25 250.00 400.00
44 Dale Jarrett UPS All Star White Gold/50 250.00 400.00
44 Dale Jarrett UPS White Gold/50 250.00 400.00
44 Dale Jarrett UPS Platinum/25 250.00 400.00
45 Kyle Petty Wells Fargo/300 75.00 125.00
48 Jimmie Johnson Lowe's/500 125.00 200.00
48 Jimmie Johnson Lowe's Platinum/25 300.00 450.00
48 Jimmie Johnson Lowe's White Gold/50 250.00 400.00
48 Jimmie Johnson Lowe's JJ Foundation/300 100.00 200.00
48 Jimmie Johnson Lowe's JJ Foundation Platinum/25 250.00 500.00
48 Jimmie Johnson Lowe's JJ Foundation White Gold/50 175.00 350.00
48 Jimmie Johnson Lowe's '07 Champion/300 100.00 200.00
48 Jimmie Johnson Lowe's '07 Champion Platinum/25 250.00 500.00
48 Jimmie Johnson Lowe's '07 Champion White Gold/50 175.00 350.00
55 Michael Waltrip Napa/300 75.00 125.00
55 Michael Waltrip Napa Platinum/25 175.00 350.00
55 Michael Waltrip Napa White Gold/50 175.00 350.00
77 Sam Hornish Jr. Mobil/300 75.00 125.00
83 Dale Earnhardt Jr. Navy JR Division/1000 75.00 125.00
88 Dale Earnhardt Jr. Mountian Dew Retro/3000 100.00 150.00
88 Dale Earnhardt Jr. AMP/5000 100.00 150.00
88 Dale Earnhardt Jr. AMP Gatorade Duel 150 Raced/1088 100.00 150.00
88 Dale Earnhardt Jr. AMP Sam Bass Holiday/708 75.00 125.00
88 Dale Earnhardt Jr. AMP Sam Bass Holiday Platinum/25 250.00 500.00
88 Dale Earnhardt Jr. AMP Sam Bass Holiday White Gold/50 200.00 400.00
88 Dale Earnhardt Jr. National Guard Bud Shootout Raced/1888 100.00 150.00
88 Dale Earnhardt Jr. National Guard Citizen Soldier/3000 100.00 150.00
88 Dale Earnhardt Jr. National Guard Citizen Soldier Platinum/25 300.00 500.00
88 Dale Earnhardt Jr. National Guard Citizen Soldier White Gold/50 300.00 500.00
88 Dale Earnhardt Jr. AMP Platinum/25 350.00 600.00
88 Dale Earnhardt Jr. AMP White Gold/50 350.00 600.00
88 Dale Earnhardt Jr. Mountain Dew Retro Platinum/25 300.00 500.00
88 Dale Earnhardt Jr. Mountian Dew Retro White Gold/50 300.00 500.00
88 Dale Earnhardt Jr. National Guard Salute the Troops/1000 100.00 150.00
88 Dale Earnhardt Jr. National Guard/3000 100.00 150.00
88 Dale Earnhardt Jr. National Guard Platinum/25 350.00 600.00
88 Dale Earnhardt Jr. National Guard White Gold/50 300.00 500.00
88 Dale Earnhardt Jr. National Guard Test/708 100.00 150.00
88 Dale Earnhardt Jr. AMP Test/504 100.00 150.00
88 Brad Keselowski Navy Salute the Troops/300 75.00 125.00
88 Brad Keselowski Navy Salute the Troops Platinum/25 175.00 300.00
88 Brad Keselowski Navy Salute the Troops White Gold/50 175.00 300.00
99 Carl Edwards Office Depot/300 100.00 150.00
99 Carl Edwards Office Depot Platinum/25 300.00 450.00
99 Carl Edwards Office Depot White Gold/50 250.00 400.00
99 Carl Edwards Aflac Texas Raced/300 75.00 125.00
02 Brad Keselowski Navy Salute the Troops/300 125.00 250.00
07 Clint Bowyer Jack Daniel's/300 75.00 125.00
07 Clint Bowyer Jack Daniel's Platinum/25 175.00 300.00
07 Clint Bowyer Jack Daniel's White Gold/50 175.00 300.00
07 Clint Bowyer Jack Daniel's Salute the Troops 175.00 300.00
White Gold/50
07 Clint Bowyer Jack Daniel's Salute the Troops Platinum/25 175.00 300.00
07 Clint Bowyer Jack Daniel's Salute the Troops/500 100.00 150.00
07 Clint Bowyer Jack Daniel's Realtree/300 75.00 125.00
08 Daytona 500 50th Anniversary White/504 100.00 150.00
08 Daytona 500 50th Anniversary Red/504 100.00 150.00
NNO Dale Earnhardt Jr. Whisky River Irish/300 75.00 125.00
NNO Dale Earnhardt Jr. Whisky River/420 75.00 125.00
NNO Realtree Program Car 60.00 100.00
NNO Salute the Troops Program Car/300 60.00 100.00

2008 Action/RCCA Elite Daytona 1:24

3 Dale Earnhardt GM Plus '98 Daytona Liquid Color/3000 100.00 175.00
18 Dale Jarrett Interstate Batteries '93 Lumina Liquid Color/504 75.00 125.00
24 Jeff Gordon DuPont '97 Monte Carlo Liquid Color/1997 100.00 150.00
28 Davey Allison Havoline '92 T-bird Liquid Color/504 100.00 175.00
29 Kevin Harvick Shell '07 Monte Carlo Liquid Color/720 75.00 125.00

2009 Action Racing Collectables Platinum 1:24

1 Martin Truex Jr. Bass Pro Shops 50.00 75.00
1 Martin Truex Jr. Bass Pro Shops AU 75.00 125.00
2 Kurt Busch Miller Lite 50.00 75.00
3 Dale Earnhardt Elvis 60.00 100.00
3 Dale Earnhardt Goodwrench Real Tree 50.00 75.00
5 Dale Earnhardt Jr. Degree V12 50.00 75.00
5 Dale Earnhardt Jr. Fastenal 50.00 75.00
5 Dale Earnhardt Jr. Go Daddy 50.00 75.00
5 Dale Earnhardt Jr. Hellmann's 50.00 75.00
5 Dale Earnhardt Jr. Klondike 50.00 75.00
5 Mark Martin Carquest 75.00 125.00
5 Mark Martin Carquest Real Tree/1008 50.00 75.00
5 Mark Martin Kellogg's 75.00 125.00
5 Mark Martin Kellogg's AU 100.00 175.00
5 Mark Martin Kellogg's/ Brushed Metal 60.00 100.00
5 Mark Martin Lipton 50.00 75.00
5 Mark Martin Lipton AU 75.00 125.00
5 Mark Martin Pop Tarts 60.00 100.00
5 Mark Martin Pop Tarts AU 75.00 125.00
5 Tony Stewart Delphi 50.00 75.00
6 David Ragan UPS 50.00 75.00
6 David Ragan UPS Freight 50.00 75.00
6 David Ragan UPS Freight AU 75.00 125.00
07 Casey Mears Jack Daniel's/ Brushed Metal 60.00 100.00
9 Kasey Kahne Bud 50.00 75.00
9 Kasey Kahne Bud/ Anheuser Busch 50.00 75.00
11 Denny Hamlin Fed Ex Express 50.00 75.00
11 Denny Hamlin Fed Ex Freight 50.00 75.00
11 Denny Hamlin Fed Ex Ground 50.00 75.00
11 Denny Hamlin Fed Ex Kinko's Office 50.00 75.00
14 Tony Stewart Burger King AU 125.00 200.00
14 Tony Stewart Burger King/2102 100.00 175.00
14 Tony Stewart OD Holiday/ Sam Bass 50.00 75.00
14 Tony Stewart Office Depot/ Back To School 75.00 125.00
14 Tony Stewart Old Spice Real Tree/1960 50.00 75.00
14 Tony Stewart Old Spice Swagger 60.00 100.00
14 Tony Stewart Old Spice 50.00 75.00
14 Tony Stewart Old Spice/ Brushed Metal 75.00 125.00
14 Tony Stewart Office Depot 50.00 75.00
14 Tony Stewart Office Depot/ Brushed Metal 75.00 125.00
16 Greg Biffle 3M 50.00 75.00
16 Greg Biffle 3M/ Brushed Metal 60.00 100.00
17 Matt Kenseth Carhartt 50.00 75.00
17 Matt Kenseth DeWalt 50.00 75.00
17 Matt Kenseth R&L Carriers 50.00 75.00
17 Matt Kenseth USG Sheetrock 50.00 75.00
18 Kyle Busch Combos 50.00 75.00
18 Kyle Busch Interstate Batteries 50.00 75.00
18 Kyle Busch Interstate Batteries Retro 50.00 75.00
18 Kyle Busch M&M's 50.00 75.00
18 Kyle Busch M&M's Halloween 50.00 75.00
18 Kyle Busch M&M's Holiday/ Sam Bass 50.00 75.00
18 Kyle Busch M&M's Las Vegas Raced/298 150.00 250.00
18 Kyle Busch M&M's Pink 50.00 75.00
18 Kyle Busch M&M's/ Brushed Metal 60.00 100.00
18 Kyle Busch NOS Energy/1344 150.00 250.00
18 Kyle Busch Pedigree 50.00 75.00
18 Kyle Busch Pizza Ranch 50.00 75.00
18 Kyle Busch Snickers 50.00 75.00
19 Elliott Sadler Best Buy 50.00 75.00
19 Elliott Sadler Stanley Tools 50.00 75.00
20 Joey Logano Home Depot 60.00 100.00
20 Joey Logano Home Depot/ Brushed Metal 75.00 125.00
24 Jeff Gordon DuPont 60.00 100.00
24 Jeff Gordon DuPont Test 50.00 75.00
24 Jeff Gordon DuPont/ Brushed Metal 60.00 100.00
24 Jeff Gordon DuPont/ Real Tree 50.00 75.00
24 Jeff Gordon HMS 25th Anniversary 60.00 100.00
24 Jeff Gordon National Guard 60.00 100.00
24 Jeff Gordon National Guard AU 125.00 200.00
24 Jeff Gordon National Guard/ Brushed Metal 60.00 100.00
24 Jeff Gordon Nicorette Ice/1324 50.00 75.00
24 Jeff Gordon Pepsi 50.00 75.00
24 Jeff Gordon Pepsi Retro 60.00 100.00
24 Jeff Gordon Pepsi Retro AU 125.00 200.00
24 Jeff Gordon Pepsi/ Brushed Metal 60.00 100.00
24 Jeff Gordon Speed Racer 50.00 75.00
25 Brad Keselowski Godaddy 50.00 75.00
26 Jamie McMurray Crown Royal 50.00 75.00
26 Jamie McMurray Crown Royal/ Brushed Metal 60.00 100.00
26 Jamie McMurray Irwin Tools 50.00 75.00
29 Kevin Harvick Reese's 50.00 75.00
29 Kevin Harvick Reese's/ Brushed Metal 60.00 100.00
29 Kevin Harvick Shell Pennzoil 50.00 75.00
29 Kevin Harvick Shell/ Brushed Metal 60.00 100.00
31 Jeff Burton CAT 50.00 75.00
31 Jeff Burton CAT Financial 50.00 75.00
31 Jeff Burton CAT Real Tree 50.00 75.00
31 Jeff Burton CAT/ Brushed Metal 60.00 100.00
33 Clint Bowyer Cheerios 50.00 75.00
33 Clint Bowyer Cheerios/ Brushed Metal 60.00 100.00
33 Clint Bowyer General Mills 50.00 75.00
33 Kevin Harvick Jimmy John's 50.00 75.00
39 Ryan Newman U.S. Army/2046 75.00 125.00
42 Juan Pablo Montoya Target 50.00 75.00
43 Reed Sorenson Air Force 50.00 75.00
44 A.J. Allmendinger Valvoline 50.00 75.00
44 A.J. Allmendinger Valvoline Retro/756 50.00 75.00
48 Jimmie Johnson HMS 25th Anniversary 60.00 120.00
48 Jimmie Johnson Lowe's 100.00 200.00
48 Jimmie Johnson Lowe's JJ Foundation 75.00 125.00
48 Jimmie Johnson Lowe's Kobalt 75.00 150.00
48 Jimmie Johnson Lowe's Kobalt/ Brickyard Raced/832 75.00 125.00
48 Jimmie Johnson Lowe's/ Brushed Metal 60.00 120.00
55 Michael Waltrip Napa 50.00 75.00
55 Michael Waltrip Napa Pink/1966 50.00 75.00
55 Michael Waltrip Napa/ Brushed Metal 60.00 100.00
77 Sam Hornish Jr. AAA 50.00 75.00
77 Sam Hornish Jr. Mobil 1 50.00 75.00
82 Scott Speed Red Bull 50.00 75.00
83 Brian Vickers Red Bull 50.00 75.00
88 Dale Earnhardt Jr. AMP 50.00 75.00
88 Dale Earnhardt Jr. AMP Get On 50.00 75.00
88 Dale Earnhardt Jr. AMP Real Tree 50.00 75.00
88 Dale Earnhardt Jr. AMP Sugar Free 50.00 75.00
88 Dale Earnhardt Jr. AMP/ Brushed Metal 60.00 100.00
88 Dale Earnhardt Jr. HMS 25th Anniversary 60.00 100.00
88 Dale Earnhardt Jr. Mountain Dew 60.00 100.00
88 Dale Earnhardt Jr. Mountain Dew/ Brushed Metal 60.00 100.00
88 Dale Earnhardt Jr. National Guard 50.00 75.00
88 Dale Earnhardt Jr. National Guard Camo 50.00 75.00
88 Dale Earnhardt Jr. National Guard/ Brushed Metal 60.00 100.00
88 Dale Earnhardt Jr. National Guard/ Drive the Guard 50.00 75.00
88 Brad Keselowski Godaddy NW 50.00 75.00
88 Brad Keselowski Hellmann's 50.00 75.00
88 Brad Keselowski Klondike 50.00 75.00
90 Tony Stewart Hendrick cars.com/ Daytona Raced/936 60.00 100.00
96 Bobby Labonte Ask.com 50.00 75.00
99 Carl Edwards Aflac 50.00 75.00
99 Carl Edwards Aflac Cancer Center/970 50.00 75.00
99 Carl Edwards Aflac Holiday/ Sam Bass 50.00 75.00
99 Carl Edwards Aflac Real Tree 50.00 75.00
99 Carl Edwards Aflac/ Brushed Metal 60.00 100.00
99 Carl Edwards Scotts 50.00 75.00
99 Carl Edwards Subway 50.00 75.00
01 Danny O'Quinn Sundrop 50.00 75.00
07 Casey Mears Jack Daniel's 50.00 75.00

2009 Action Racing Collectables Platinum Black Label 1:24

5 Mark Martin Kellogg's/1005 50.00 75.00
14 Tony Stewart Old Spice/1014 50.00 75.00
24 Jeff Gordon National Guard/1024 50.00 75.00
88 Dale Earnhardt Jr. AMP Get On/1088 50.00 75.00
99 Carl Edwards Aflac/999 50.00 75.00

2009 Action Racing Collectables Platinum GM Dealers 1:24

1 Martin Truex Jr. Bass Pro Shops 50.00 75.00
5 Dale Earnhardt Jr. Hellmann's 50.00 75.00
5 Mark Martin Carquest 75.00 125.00
5 Mark Martin Kellogg's 75.00 125.00
14 Tony Stewart Burger King 75.00 125.00
14 Tony Stewart Office Depot 50.00 75.00
14 Tony Stewart Old Spice 50.00 75.00
14 Tony Stewart Office Depot/ Back To School/133 75.00 125.00
24 Jeff Gordon DuPont 60.00 100.00
24 Jeff Gordon National Guard 60.00 100.00
24 Jeff Gordon Pepsi 50.00 75.00
24 Jeff Gordon Speed Racer 50.00 75.00
29 Kevin Harvick Pennzoil 50.00 75.00
29 Kevin Harvick Reese's 50.00 75.00
29 Kevin Harvick Shell 50.00 75.00
31 Jeff Burton CAT 50.00 75.00
33 Clint Bowyer Cheerios 50.00 75.00
39 Ryan Newman U.S. Army 50.00 75.00
48 Jimmie Johnson Lowe's 100.00 200.00
48 Jimmie Johnson Lowe's Test 75.00 150.00
88 Dale Earnhardt Jr. AMP 50.00 75.00
88 Dale Earnhardt Jr. AMP Test 50.00 75.00
88 Dale Earnhardt Jr. Mountain Dew 50.00 75.00
88 Dale Earnhardt Jr. National Guard 50.00 75.00
88 Dale Earnhardt Jr. National Guard Camo/190 50.00 75.00
07 Casey Mears Jack Daniel's 50.00 75.00

2009 Action/QVC For Race Fans Only 1:24

1 Martin Truex Jr. Bass Pro Shops/ Gold 100.00 150.00
11 Denny Hamlin Fed Ex Express/ Color Chrome 60.00 100.00
11 Denny Hamlin Fed Ex Express/ Gold 100.00 150.00
11 Denny Hamlin Fed Ex Express/ Gun Metal 60.00 100.00
11 Denny Hamlin Fed Ex Express/ Polished Nickel 75.00 125.00
14 Tony Stewart Burger King/ Color Chrome 125.00 200.00
14 Tony Stewart Office Depot/ Color Chrome 60.00 100.00
14 Tony Stewart Office Depot/ Copper 60.00 100.00
14 Tony Stewart Office Depot/ Gold 100.00 150.00
14 Tony Stewart Office Depot/ Gold Chrome 100.00 150.00
14 Tony Stewart Office Depot/ Gun Metal 60.00 100.00
14 Tony Stewart Office Depot/ Polished Nickel 75.00 125.00
14 Tony Stewart Old Spice/ Color Chrome 60.00 100.00
14 Tony Stewart Old Spice/ Copper 60.00 100.00
14 Tony Stewart Old Spice/ Gold 100.00 150.00
14 Tony Stewart Old Spice/ Gold Chrome 100.00 150.00
14 Tony Stewart Old Spice/ Gun Metal 60.00 100.00
14 Tony Stewart Old Spice/ Polished Nickel 75.00 125.00
18 Kyle Busch Combos/ Color Chrome 60.00 100.00
18 Kyle Busch Combos/ Gold 100.00 150.00
18 Kyle Busch Interstate Batteries/ Color Chrome 60.00 100.00
18 Kyle Busch M&M's/ Color Chrome 60.00 100.00
18 Kyle Busch M&M's/ Gold 100.00 150.00
18 Kyle Busch M&M's/ Gun Metal 60.00 100.00
18 Kyle Busch M&M's/ Polished Nickel 75.00 125.00
18 Kyle Busch Snickers/ Color Chrome 60.00 100.00
18 Kyle Busch Snickers/ Gold 100.00 150.00
20 Joey Logano Home Depot/ Color Chrome 75.00 125.00
20 Joey Logano Home Depot/ Gold 100.00 150.00
20 Joey Logano Home Depot/ Gun Metal 75.00 125.00
20 Joey Logano Home Depot/ Polished Nickel 100.00 175.00
24 Jeff Gordon DuPont Test/ Color Chrome 60.00 100.00
24 Jeff Gordon DuPont/ Color Chrome 60.00 100.00
24 Jeff Gordon DuPont/ Copper 75.00 125.00
24 Jeff Gordon DuPont/ Gold 100.00 150.00
24 Jeff Gordon DuPont/ Gold Chrome 100.00 175.00
24 Jeff Gordon DuPont/ Gun Metal 60.00 100.00
24 Jeff Gordon DuPont/ Polished Nickel 75.00 125.00
24 Jeff Gordon National Guard/ Color Chrome 60.00 100.00
24 Jeff Gordon National Guard/ Gold 100.00 150.00
24 Jeff Gordon National Guard/ Gun Metal 60.00 100.00
24 Jeff Gordon Pepsi Retro/ Color Chrome 60.00 100.00
24 Jeff Gordon Pepsi Retro/ Gold 100.00 150.00
24 Jeff Gordon Pepsi Retro/ Gun Metal 60.00 100.00
24 Jeff Gordon Speed Racer/ Color Chrome 60.00 100.00
24 Jeff Gordon Speed Racer/ Gold 100.00 150.00
24 Jeff Gordon Speed Racer/ Gun Metal 60.00 100.00
29 Kevin Harvick Shell/ Color Chrome 60.00 100.00
29 Kevin Harvick Shell/ Gold 100.00 150.00
29 Kevin Harvick Shell/ Gun Metal 60.00 100.00
29 Kevin Harvick Shell/ Polished Nickel 75.00 125.00
39 Ryan Newman U.S. Army/ Color Chrome 60.00 100.00
39 Ryan Newman U.S. Army/ Gold 100.00 150.00
39 Ryan Newman U.S. Army/ Gun Metal 60.00 100.00
39 Ryan Newman U.S. Army/ Polished Nickel 75.00 125.00
48 Jimmie Johnson Lowe's Test/ Color Chrome 75.00 125.00
48 Jimmie Johnson Lowe's/ Color Chrome 100.00 150.00
48 Jimmie Johnson Lowe's/ Gold 100.00 175.00
48 Jimmie Johnson Lowe's/ Gun Metal 75.00 150.00
48 Jimmie Johnson Lowe's/ Polished Nickel 100.00 175.00
88 Dale Earnhardt Jr. AMP Test/ Color Chrome 60.00 100.00
88 Dale Earnhardt Jr. AMP/ Color Chrome 60.00 100.00
88 Dale Earnhardt Jr. AMP/ Copper 60.00 100.00
88 Dale Earnhardt Jr. AMP/ Gold 100.00 150.00
88 Dale Earnhardt Jr. AMP/ Gold Chrome 100.00 150.00
88 Dale Earnhardt Jr. AMP/ Gun Metal 60.00 100.00
88 Dale Earnhardt Jr. AMP/ Polished Nickel 75.00 125.00
88 Dale Earnhardt Jr. JR Foundation/ Copper 60.00 100.00
88 Dale Earnhardt Jr. JR Foundation/ Gold Chrome 100.00 175.00
88 Dale Earnhardt Jr. JR Foundation/ Gun Metal 60.00 100.00

Item	Low	High
88 Dale Earnhardt Jr. Mountain Dew/ Color Chrome	60.00	100.00
88 Dale Earnhardt Jr. Mountain Dew/ Copper	60.00	100.00
88 Dale Earnhardt Jr. Mountain Dew/ Gold	100.00	150.00
88 Dale Earnhardt Jr. Mountain Dew/ Gold Chrome AU	125.00	200.00
88 Dale Earnhardt Jr. Mountain Dew/ Gun Metal	60.00	100.00
88 Dale Earnhardt Jr. Mountain Dew/ Mesma Chrome	100.00	175.00
88 Dale Earnhardt Jr. National Guard/ Color Chrome	60.00	100.00
88 Dale Earnhardt Jr. National Guard/ Copper	60.00	100.00
88 Dale Earnhardt Jr. National Guard/ Gold	100.00	150.00
88 Dale Earnhardt Jr. National Guard/ Gold Chrome	100.00	175.00
88 Dale Earnhardt Jr. National Guard/ Gun Metal	60.00	100.00
88 Dale Earnhardt Jr. National Guard/ Polished Nickel	75.00	125.00
99 Carl Edwards Aflac/ Color Chrome	60.00	100.00
99 Carl Edwards Aflac/ Gold	100.00	150.00
99 Carl Edwards Aflac/ Gun Metal	60.00	100.00
99 Carl Edwards Aflac/ Polished Nickel	75.00	125.00
99 Carl Edwards Subway AU	100.00	175.00
NNO Dale Earnhardt Jr. Whisky River/ Color Chrome	60.00	100.00
NNO Dale Earnhardt Jr. Whisky River/ Gold	100.00	150.00

2009 Action/RCCA Club 1:24

Item	Low	High
5 Mark Martin Kellogg's	75.00	125.00
9 Kasey Kahne Bud	50.00	75.00
14 Tony Stewart Burger King	75.00	125.00
14 Tony Stewart Office Depot	50.00	75.00
14 Tony Stewart Old Spice	50.00	75.00
18 Kyle Busch M&M's	50.00	75.00
18 Kyle Busch Snickers	50.00	75.00
20 Joey Logano Home Depot	75.00	125.00
24 Jeff Gordon DuPont	60.00	100.00
24 Jeff Gordon DuPont Test	50.00	75.00
24 Jeff Gordon National Guard	60.00	100.00
24 Jeff Gordon Pepsi	50.00	75.00
24 Jeff Gordon Pepsi Retro	60.00	100.00
24 Jeff Gordon Speed Racer	50.00	75.00
26 Jamie McMurray Crown Royal	50.00	75.00
26 Jamie McMurray Crown Royal AU	75.00	125.00
39 Ryan Newman Haas	50.00	75.00
39 Ryan Newman U.S. Army	50.00	75.00
48 Jimmie Johnson Lowe's	100.00	200.00
48 Jimmie Johnson Lowe's Test	75.00	150.00
88 Dale Earnhardt Jr. AMP	50.00	75.00
88 Dale Earnhardt Jr. AMP Test	50.00	75.00
88 Dale Earnhardt Jr. JR Foundation	50.00	75.00
88 Dale Earnhardt Jr. Mountain Dew	50.00	75.00
88 Dale Earnhardt Jr. National Guard	50.00	75.00
99 Carl Edwards Aflac	50.00	75.00

2009 Action/RCCA Elite 1:24

Item	Low	High
2 Kurt Busch Miller Lite/144	100.00	150.00
5 Mark Martin Carquest/150	125.00	200.00
5 Mark Martin Kellogg's	125.00	200.00
5 Mark Martin Kellogg's/ Brushed Metal	125.00	200.00
5 Mark Martin Kellogg's/ White Gold	250.00	400.00
5 Dale Earnhardt Jr. Hellmann's	100.00	150.00
6 David Ragan UPS/144	100.00	150.00
07 Casey Mears Jack Daniel's	100.00	150.00
07 Casey Mears Jack Daniel's/ Brushed Metal	125.00	200.00
9 Kasey Kahne Bud/500	100.00	175.00
9 Kasey Kahne Bud AU	125.00	250.00
9 Kasey Kahne Bud/ Brushed Metal	125.00	200.00
9 Kasey Kahne Bud/ Brushed Metal AU	125.00	250.00
9 Kasey Kahne Bud/ White Gold	300.00	500.00
11 Denny Hamlin Fed Ex Express	100.00	150.00
11 Denny Hamlin Fed Ex Express/ Brushed Metal	125.00	200.00
11 Denny Hamlin Fed Ex Express/ White Gold	250.00	400.00
14 Tony Stewart Burger King/ Brushed Metal	200.00	300.00
14 Tony Stewart Burger King/ White Gold	500.00	700.00
14 Tony Stewart Office Depot/ Brushed Metal	400.00	600.00
14 Tony Stewart Office Depot/ White Gold	450.00	600.00
14 Tony Stewart Old Spice/ Bronze	125.00	200.00
14 Tony Stewart Old Spice/ Brushed Metal	125.00	200.00
14 Tony Stewart Old Spice/ Gold	125.00	200.00
14 Tony Stewart Old Spice/ Platinum	500.00	750.00
14 Tony Stewart Old Spice/ White Gold	450.00	600.00
14 Tony Stewart Old Spice/1000	125.00	200.00
14 Tony Stewart Office Depot/1000	125.00	200.00
14 Tony Stewart Burger King/303	200.00	300.00
16 Greg Biffle 3M	100.00	150.00
16 Greg Biffle 3M AU	125.00	200.00
17 Matt Kenseth Carhartt	100.00	150.00
17 Matt Kenseth DeWalt/ Brushed Metal	125.00	200.00
17 Matt Kenseth DeWalt/ White Gold	250.00	450.00
17 Matt Kenseth DeWalt/150	100.00	150.00
18 Kyle Busch Interstate Batteries/150	100.00	175.00
18 Kyle Busch Snicker's/300	100.00	175.00
18 Kyle Busch Combos	100.00	150.00
18 Kyle Busch Combos AU	125.00	200.00
18 Kyle Busch Combos/ Brushed Metal	125.00	200.00
18 Kyle Busch Combos/ White Gold	400.00	600.00
18 Kyle Busch Interstate Batteries/ Brushed Metal	125.00	200.00
18 Kyle Busch Interstate Batteries/ White Gold	400.00	600.00
18 Kyle Busch M&M's	100.00	175.00
18 Kyle Busch M&M's AU	150.00	250.00
18 Kyle Busch M&M's Halloween	100.00	175.00
18 Kyle Busch M&M's Halloween/ White Gold	400.00	600.00
18 Kyle Busch M&M's Pink	100.00	175.00
18 Kyle Busch M&M's/ Brushed Metal	125.00	200.00
18 Kyle Busch M&M's/ White Gold	400.00	600.00
18 Kyle Busch Snickers AU	150.00	250.00
18 Kyle Busch Snickers/ Brushed Metal	125.00	200.00
18 Kyle Busch Snickers/ White Gold	400.00	600.00
19 Elliott Sadler Stanley Tools	100.00	150.00
20 Joey Logano Home Depot/ Bronze	200.00	300.00
20 Joey Logano Home Depot/ Brushed Metal	200.00	300.00
20 Joey Logano Home Depot/ Gold	200.00	300.00
20 Joey Logano Home Depot/ Platinum	500.00	750.00
20 Joey Logano Home Depot/ White Gold	400.00	600.00
20 Joey Logano Home Depot/1000	125.00	200.00
24 Jeff Gordon HMS 25th/500	100.00	150.00
24 Jeff Gordon DuPont/1500	100.00	175.00
24 Jeff Gordon Nicorette Ice/300	100.00	175.00
24 Jeff Gordon National Guard AU/240	200.00	300.00
24 Jeff Gordon DuPont Test	100.00	175.00
24 Jeff Gordon DuPont/ Bronze	125.00	200.00
24 Jeff Gordon DuPont/ Brushed Metal	125.00	200.00
24 Jeff Gordon DuPont/ Gold	150.00	250.00
24 Jeff Gordon DuPont/ Platinum	600.00	800.00
24 Jeff Gordon DuPont/ White Gold	500.00	750.00
24 Jeff Gordon National Guard	100.00	175.00
24 Jeff Gordon National Guard/ Brushed Metal	125.00	200.00
24 Jeff Gordon National Guard/ White Gold	500.00	750.00
24 Jeff Gordon Pepsi	100.00	150.00
24 Jeff Gordon Pepsi Retro	100.00	175.00
24 Jeff Gordon Pepsi Retro/ Bronze AU	250.00	350.00
24 Jeff Gordon Pepsi Retro/ Brushed Metal	150.00	250.00
24 Jeff Gordon Pepsi Retro/ Gold AU	250.00	350.00
24 Jeff Gordon Pepsi Retro/ Platinum AU	700.00	1000.00
24 Jeff Gordon Pepsi Retro/ White Gold	500.00	750.00
24 Jeff Gordon Pepsi/ Brushed Metal	125.00	200.00
24 Jeff Gordon Pepsi/ White Gold	400.00	600.00
24 Jeff Gordon Speed Racer	100.00	150.00
24 Jeff Gordon Speed Racer/ Brushed Metal	125.00	200.00
24 Jeff Gordon Speed Racer/ White Gold	400.00	600.00
24 Jeff Gordon Nicorette Ice/300	100.00	150.00
29 Kevin Harvick Shell	100.00	150.00
29 Kevin Harvick Shell/ Brushed Metal	125.00	200.00
29 Kevin Harvick Shell/ White Gold	350.00	500.00
31 Jeff Burton CAT	100.00	150.00
31 Jeff Burton CAT/ Brushed Metal	125.00	200.00
31 Jeff Burton CAT/ White Gold	250.00	400.00
33 Clint Bowyer Cheerios	100.00	150.00
33 Clint Bowyer Cheerios/ Brushed Metal	125.00	200.00
33 Clint Bowyer Cheerios/ White Gold	250.00	400.00
39 Ryan Newman U.S. Army	100.00	150.00
39 Ryan Newman U.S. Army/ Brushed Metal	200.00	300.00
39 Ryan Newman U.S. Army/ White Gold	400.00	600.00
48 Jimmie Johnson Lowe's Kobalt	125.00	250.00
48 Jimmie Johnson Lowe's Kobalt/ Brushed Metal	125.00	250.00
48 Jimmie Johnson Lowe's Kobalt/ White Gold	400.00	600.00
48 Jimmie Johnson Lowe's Test	150.00	300.00
48 Jimmie Johnson Lowe's/ Brushed Metal	125.00	250.00
48 Jimmie Johnson Lowe's/ White Gold	400.00	600.00
48 Jimmie Johnson Lowe's/300	175.00	350.00
55 Michael Waltrip Napa	100.00	150.00
82 Scott Speed Red Bull	100.00	175.00
83 Brian Vickers Red Bull	100.00	150.00
88 Brad Keselowski Godaddy NW	100.00	150.00
88 Dale Earnhardt Jr. AMP	100.00	175.00
88 Dale Earnhardt Jr. AMP Test	100.00	150.00
88 Dale Earnhardt Jr. AMP/ Bronze	150.00	250.00
88 Dale Earnhardt Jr. AMP/ Brushed Metal	150.00	250.00
88 Dale Earnhardt Jr. AMP/ Gold	150.00	250.00
88 Dale Earnhardt Jr. AMP/ Platinum	600.00	800.00
88 Dale Earnhardt Jr. AMP/ White Gold	500.00	750.00
88 Dale Earnhardt Jr. JR Foundation	100.00	150.00
88 Dale Earnhardt Jr. JR Foundation/ Brushed Metal	125.00	200.00
88 Dale Earnhardt Jr. JR Foundation/ White Gold	400.00	600.00
88 Dale Earnhardt Jr. Mountain Dew	100.00	175.00
88 Dale Earnhardt Jr. Mountain Dew/ Brushed Metal	150.00	250.00
88 Dale Earnhardt Jr. Mountain Dew/ White Gold	500.00	750.00
88 Dale Earnhardt Jr. National Guard	100.00	175.00
88 Dale Earnhardt Jr. National Guard/ Brushed Metal	150.00	250.00
88 Dale Earnhardt Jr. National Guard/ White Gold	500.00	750.00
88 Dale Earnhardt Jr. HMS 25th/700		
88 Dale Earnhardt Jr. HMS 25th/700	100.00	150.00
99 Carl Edwards Aflac/250	100.00	175.00
99 Carl Edwards Aflac		
99 Carl Edwards Aflac/ Brushed Metal	125.00	200.00
99 Carl Edwards Aflac/ White Gold	300.00	500.00
99 Carl Edwards Subway	100.00	150.00
99 Carl Edwards Subway/ Bronze	125.00	200.00
99 Carl Edwards Subway/ Gold	125.00	200.00
99 Carl Edwards Subway/ Platinum	400.00	600.00
07 Casey Mears Jack Daniel's/ White Gold	200.00	350.00

2010 Action Pit Stop 1:24

This set consists of 1:24 scale die-casts with plastic chassis and the hoods and trunks do not open. The original SRP for these cars were between $20 and $25. They were not serial numbered, but the print run information listed was provided by Action.

Item	Low	High
5 Mark Martin Go Daddy/2292*	20.00	30.00
10 Digger Gopher Cam Annie/999*	15.00	25.00
10 Digger Gopher Cam Friends/1141*	15.00	25.00
10 Digger Gopher Cam/1929*	15.00	25.00
10 NASCAR Hall of Fame	20.00	30.00
14 Tony Stewart Office Depot/1988*	20.00	30.00
99 Carl Edwards Aflac Silver/1976*	20.00	30.00

2010 Action Racing Collectables Gold 1:24

This set of die-casts consists of promotional-type die-casts that predominately feature Hood Open only cars. Some of these may not have opening hoods, but they have the packaging like the Action Racing Collectables Platinum line of cars. Most of these also have plastic chassis. The print runs noted in the checklist below are what is stated on the silver label on the box, unless it has an asterisk, then it is the actual production numbers provided by Action.

Item	Low	High
2 Kurt Busch Miller Lite/2500*	40.00	65.00
5 Mark Martin Carquest Honor Our Soldiers/3423*	50.00	75.00
5 Mark Martin Go Daddy/5130*	40.00	65.00
6 Colin Braun Con-Way Trucking/3012*	50.00	75.00
6 David Ragan UPS/2443*	40.00	65.00
9 Kasey Kahne Bud/2506*	50.00	75.00
10 Bill France NHOF/2499*	40.00	65.00
10 Bill France Jr. NHOF/2499*	40.00	65.00
10 Junior Johnson NHOF/2500*	40.00	65.00
10 No Driver Association NHOF Class of '10/3293*	40.00	65.00
14 Tony Stewart Burger King/2499*	40.00	65.00
14 Tony Stewart Office Depot/5583*	40.00	65.00
14 Tony Stewart Office Depot BTS/4024*	50.00	75.00
14 Tony Stewart Old Spice/5090*	40.00	65.00
14 Tony Stewart Old Spice Matterhorn/4077*	40.00	65.00
14 Tony Stewart Smoke/3118*	40.00	65.00
16 Greg Biffle 3M Super 33/2922*	60.00	100.00
18 Kyle Busch M&M's/6401*	40.00	65.00
20 Joey Logano Home Depot/2553*	40.00	65.00
20 Joey Logano Home Depot/11010*	40.00	65.00
24 Jeff Gordon Dupont/3998*	40.00	65.00
24 Jeff Gordon Dupont Honor Our Soldiers/3817*	40.00	65.00
33 Kevin Harvick Kevin Harvick Inc/1006*	75.00	125.00
33 Kevin Harvick Ollies Bargain Outlet/1966*	75.00	125.00
33 Ron Hornaday Longhorn SuperTruck/567*	60.00	100.00
48 Jimmie Johnson Lowe's/3202*	50.00	75.00
48 Jimmie Johnson Lowe's Honor Our Soldiers/3301*	50.00	75.00
88 Dale Earnhardt Jr. AMP/3672*	40.00	65.00
88 Dale Earnhardt Jr. AMP Energy Juice/2518*	40.00	65.00
88 Dale Earnhardt Jr. AMP Sugar Free/1066*	40.00	65.00
88 Dale Earnhardt Jr. JR Foundation/1342*	40.00	65.00
88 Dale Earnhardt Jr. National Guard/2798*	40.00	65.00
88 Dale Earnhardt Jr. National Guard Honor Our Soldiers/1882*	40.00	65.00
88 Dale Earnhardt Jr. National Guard Honor Our Soldiers/4708*	40.00	65.00
88 Dale Earnhardt Jr. National Guard Camo 8 Soldiers 8 Missions/1018*	40.00	65.00
99 Carl Edwards Aflac/2525*	40.00	65.00
00 David Reutimann Aaron's/1000*	40.00	65.00
00 David Reutimann Aaron's Alabama BCS Champions/8014*	50.00	75.00

2010 Action Racing Collectables Platinum 1:24

The print runs noted in the checklist below are what is stated on the silver label on the box, unless it has an asterisk, then it is the actual production numbers provided by Action.

Item	Low	High
1 Jamie McMurray Bass Pro Shops/968*	50.00	75.00
1 Jamie McMurray Bass Pro Shops/ Brickyard Raced/958*	50.00	75.00
1 Jamie McMurray Bass Pro Shops/ Brickyard Raced AU/106*	60.00	100.00
1 Jamie McMurray Bass Pro Shops/ Daytona Raced/1977*	60.00	100.00
1 Jamie McMurray Bass Pro Shops/ Daytona Raced AU/206*	75.00	125.00
1 Jamie McMurray Bass Pro Shops Earnhardt HOF Tribute/1585*	60.00	100.00
1 Jamie McMurray McDonald's/596*	50.00	75.00
2 Kurt Busch Miller Lite/2607	50.00	75.00
2 Kurt Busch Miller Lite/ Brushed Metal/117*	75.00	125.00
2 Kurt Busch Miller Lite/ Atlanta Raced/847*	50.00	75.00
2 Kurt Busch Miller Lite Vortex/930*	50.00	75.00
2 Kurt Busch Miller Lite Vortex/ All Star Raced/1031*	60.00	100.00
2 Kevin Harvick Tide SuperTruck/846*	60.00	100.00
3 Austin Dillon Mom-N-Pops/726*	60.00	100.00
3 Dale Earnhardt NHOF/3482*	60.00	100.00
3 Dale Earnhardt Wheaties '97 MC/3331*	60.00	100.00
3 Dale Earnhardt Jr. Wrangler/18,573	75.00	125.00
3 Dale Earnhardt Jr. Wrangler/ Color Chrome/333	125.00	250.00
3 Dale Earnhardt Jr. Wrangler/ Daytona Raced/18333*	75.00	125.00
3 Dale Earnhardt Jr. Wrangler/ Daytona Raced/ Color Chrome/333*	125.00	250.00
3 Dale Earnhardt Jr. Wrangler/ Flashcoat Silver/1722*	75.00	125.00
3 Dale Earnhardt Jr. Wrangler/ Liquid Color/303*	100.00	175.00
4 Tony Stewart Oreo Ritz/1663*	50.00	75.00
4 Tony Stewart Oreo Ritz/ Liquid Color/235*	75.00	125.00
4 Tony Stewart Oreo Ritz/ NW Daytona Raced/989*	50.00	75.00
5 Mark Martin Carquest/3115*	50.00	75.00
5 Mark Martin Carquest Honor Our Soldiers/1801*	60.00	100.00
5 Mark Martin Carquest Honor Our Soldiers/ Flashcoat Silver/295*	75.00	125.00
5 Mark Martin Delphi/1652*	50.00	75.00
5 Mark Martin Go Daddy	50.00	75.00
5 Mark Martin Go Daddy/ Brushed Metal/413*	75.00	125.00
5 Mark Martin GoDaddy Flashcoat Silver/827	75.00	125.00
5 Mark Martin Hendrickcars.com/1254*	50.00	75.00
6 David Ragan UPS/3694	50.00	75.00
6 David Ragan UPS Bushed Metal/215	60.00	120.00
6 David Ragan UPS Flashcoat Silver/412	60.00	120.00
6 David Ragan UPS Freight/1491*	50.00	75.00
6 David Ragan UPS United Way/594*	50.00	75.00
7 Steve Arpin Wow Foods/603*	50.00	75.00
7 Steve Arpin Wow Foods AU/60*	60.00	100.00
7 Danica Patrick Go Daddy/8043	60.00	100.00
7 Danica Patrick Go Daddy/ Brushed Metal/126*	100.00	150.00
7 Danica Patrick Go Daddy/ Flashcoat Silver/1523	100.00	150.00
7 Danica Patrick Go Daddy ARCA	60.00	100.00
7 Danica Patrick Tissot/2014*	60.00	100.00
7 Danica Patrick Tissot/ Flashcoat Silver/357*	100.00	150.00
9 Kasey Kahne Bud/3316	50.00	75.00
9 Kasey Kahne Bud Brushed Metal/319	75.00	125.00
9 Kasey Kahne Bud Olympics/2040	50.00	75.00
9 Kasey Kahne Bud Retro/2039*	50.00	75.00
10 Bill France Jr NASCAR HOF/468	50.00	75.00
10 Bill France Sr. NASCAR HOF/520	50.00	75.00
10 Dale Earnhardt NASCAR HOF/3458	60.00	100.00
10 Junior Johnson NASCAR HOF	50.00	75.00
10 Richard Petty NASCAR HOF	50.00	75.00
10 No Driver Association NHOF Class of '10/1565*	50.00	75.00
11 Denny Hamlin Fed Ex Express/1261	60.00	100.00
11 Denny Hamlin Fedex Freight/728*	50.00	75.00
11 Denny Hamlin Fedex Ground/738*	50.00	75.00
11 Denny Hamlin Fedex Office/727*	50.00	75.00
12 Brad Keselowski Dodge/647*	50.00	75.00
12 Brad Keselowski Dodge/ Color Chrome/71*	100.00	150.00
12 Brad Keselowski Penske/2348	50.00	75.00
14 Tony Stewart Burger King/4497	50.00	75.00
14 Tony Stewart Burger King/ Brushed Metal/211*	75.00	150.00
14 Tony Stewart Burger King Color Chrome/144	100.00	150.00
14 Tony Stewart Burger King/ Gold/48*	125.00	200.00
14 Tony Stewart Burger King Gun Metal/24	125.00	250.00
14 Tony Stewart Burger King/ Polished Nickel/24*	125.00	200.00
14 Tony Stewart Office Depot/6492	50.00	75.00
14 Tony Stewart Office Depot Brushed Metal/412	75.00	150.00
14 Tony Stewart Office Depot Color Chrome/144	100.00	150.00
14 Tony Stewart Office Depot Flashcoat Silver/1200	75.00	125.00
14 Tony Stewart Office Depot/ Gold/48*	125.00	200.00
14 Tony Stewart Office Depot Gun Metal/24	100.00	200.00
14 Tony Stewart Office Depot/ Polished Nickel/23*	125.00	200.00
14 Tony Stewart Office Depot BTS/2020*	50.00	75.00
14 Tony Stewart Office Depot Fantasy/726*	50.00	75.00
14 Tony Stewart Office Depot Go Green/1958*	50.00	75.00
14 Tony Stewart	125.00	200.00

Office Depot Go Green/ Gold Chrome/75*
14 Tony Stewart Old Spice/5571 50.00 75.00
14 Tony Stewart Old Spice Brushed Metal/412 75.00 150.00
14 Tony Stewart Old Spice Color Chrome/144 100.00 150.00
14 Tony Stewart Old Spice Flashcoat Silver/1277 75.00 125.00
14 Tony Stewart Old Spice/ Gold/48* 125.00 200.00
14 Tony Stewart Old Spice/ Gun Metal/23* 75.00 125.00
14 Tony Stewart Old Spice/ Polished Nickel/23* 125.00 200.00
14 Tony Stewart Old Spice Matterhorn/2457* 50.00 75.00
14 Tony Stewart Old Spice Matterhorn/ Flashcoat Silver/448* 75.00 125.00
14 Tony Stewart Smoke/3169* 50.00 75.00
14 Tony Stewart Smoke/ Brushed Metal/225* 60.00 120.00
16 Greg Biffle Post-It/878* 40.00 65.00
16 Greg Biffle 3M/1339 40.00 65.00
16 Greg Biffle 3M Brushed Metal/115 60.00 120.00
16 Greg Biffle 3M Pit Bulls/708* 40.00 65.00
17 Matt Kenseth Crown Royal/4143* 50.00 75.00
17 Matt Kenseth Crown Royal/ Brushed Metal/304* 75.00 125.00
17 Matt Kenseth Crown Royal/ Flashcoat Silver/758* 75.00 125.00
17 Matt Kenseth Crown Royal Black/1822* 50.00 75.00
17 Matt Kenseth Crown Royal Patriotic Camo/1499* 60.00 100.00
17 Matt Kenseth Jeremiah Weed/1217* 40.00 65.00
17 Matt Kenseth Valvoline/1086* 40.00 65.00
18 Kyle Busch Combos/1242* 40.00 65.00
18 Kyle Busch Doublemint/1366* 40.00 65.00
18 Kyle Busch Doublemint/ Brushed Metal/341* 75.00 125.00
18 Kyle Busch Doublemint/ Flashcoat Silver/376* 75.00 125.00
18 Kyle Busch Interstate Batteries/980 50.00 75.00
18 Kyle Busch Interstate Batteries/ Brushed Metal/133* 75.00 125.00
18 Kyle Busch M&M's/6257 50.00 75.00
18 Kyle Busch M&M's Brushed Metal/315 75.00 125.00
18 Kyle Busch M&M's Flashcoat Silver/768 75.00 125.00
18 Kyle Busch M&M's Pretzel/1320* 50.00 75.00
18 Kyle Busch M&M's Pretzel AU/117* 100.00 150.00
18 Kyle Busch M&M's Vote/762* 50.00 75.00
18 Kyle Busch M&M's Vote AU/71* 100.00 150.00
18 Kyle Busch NOS/ '09 NW Champion/841* 60.00 100.00
18 Kyle Busch Pedigree/545* 40.00 65.00
18 Kyle Busch Snickers/839* 40.00 65.00
18 Kyle Busch Z-Line Pink/1448* 50.00 75.00
18 Kyle Busch Z-Line Pink AU/100* 100.00 150.00
18 Kyle Busch Z-Line Pink/ Color Chrome AU/56* 100.00 175.00
18 Kyle Busch Z-Line/ '09 NW Champion/1338* 60.00 100.00
19 Elliott Sadler Stanley Tools/896 50.00 75.00
20 Joey Logano Home Depot/2475 50.00 75.00
20 Joey Logano Home Depot/ Brushed Metal/103* 75.00 125.00
20 Joey Logano Home Depot Color Chrome/48 100.00 150.00
20 Joey Logano Home Depot Flashcoat Silver/398 75.00 125.00
20 Joey Logano Home Depot/ Gold/24* 125.00 200.00
20 Joey Logano Home Depot/ Gun Metal/24* 100.00 150.00
20 Joey Logano Home Depot/ Polished Nickel/24 100.00 200.00
20 Joey Logano Home Depot '09 ROTY/824* 60.00 100.00
22 Scott Steckly Canadian Tire Jumpstart/700 100.00 150.00
24 Jeff Gordon DuPont/6884 50.00 75.00
24 Jeff Gordon DuPont Brushed Metal/416 100.00 150.00
24 Jeff Gordon Dupont/ Color Chrome/286* 100.00 200.00
24 Jeff Gordon DuPont Flashcoat Silver/1323 100.00 150.00
24 Jeff Gordon Dupont/ Gold/48* 150.00 250.00
24 Jeff Gordon Dupont/ Gun Metal/46* 125.00 200.00
24 Jeff Gordon DuPont/ Polished Nickel/48 125.00 250.00
24 Jeff Gordon Dupont Horor Our Soldiers/2574* 60.00 100.00
24 Jeff Gordon Dupont Horor Our Soldiers/ Flashcoat Silver/409* 75.00 125.00
24 Jeff Gordon Dupont Law Enforcement/2186* 50.00 75.00
24 Jeff Gordon Dupont Law Enforcement AU/250* 150.00 250.00
24 Jeff Gordon 60.00 100.00
National Guard/2849
24 Jeff Gordon National Guard Brushed Metal/324 75.00 150.00
24 Jeff Gordon National Guard Flashcoat Silver/516 75.00 125.00
24 Jeff Gordon National Guard Military Intelligence/1720* 50.00 75.00
24 Jeff Gordon National Guard Special Forces/2507* 50.00 75.00
24 Jeff Gordon National Guard Special Forces/ Color Chrome/289* 100.00 200.00
24 Jeff Gordon Pepsi Max/2956* 50.00 75.00
24 Jeff Gordon Pepsi Max/ Flashcoat Silver/744* 75.00 125.00
29 Kevin Harvick Reese's/937* 50.00 75.00
29 Kevin Harvick Shell 50.00 75.00
29 Kevin Harvick Shell/ Brushed Metal/109* 75.00 125.00
29 Kevin Harvick Shell/ Flashcoat Silver/410* 75.00 125.00
29 Kevin Harvick Shell/ Daytona Shootout Raced/829* 60.00 100.00
31 Jeff Burton CAT/1442* 40.00 65.00
31 Jeff Burton CAT/ Brushed Metal/122* 60.00 120.00
31 Jeff Burton CAT/ Flashcoat Silver/249* 60.00 120.00
31 Jeff Burton CAT Financial/499* 40.00 65.00
33 Clint Bowyer BB&T/774* 40.00 65.00
33 Clint Bowyer BB&T/ Flashcoat Silver/164* 60.00 120.00
33 Clint Bowyer Cheerios/1348 40.00 65.00
33 Clint Bowyer Cheerios/ Brushed Metal/115* 60.00 120.00
33 Clint Bowyer Cheerios/ Flashcoat Silver/255* 60.00 120.00
33 Clint Bowyer Hartford/723* 40.00 65.00
33 Kevin Harvick Jimmy Johns/504 50.00 75.00
33 Kevin Harvick Miracle Whip/706* 50.00 75.00
33 Kevin Harvick Rheem/504 50.00 75.00
33 Kevin Harvick Rheem COT AU/507* 125.00 200.00
39 Ryan Newman Haas Automation/1010* 50.00 75.00
39 Ryan Newman Tornados/1371* 50.00 75.00
39 Ryan Newman Tornados AU/252* 75.00 125.00
39 Ryan Newman Tornados/ Phoenix Raced/785* 50.00 75.00
39 Ryan Newman Tornados/ Phoenix Raced/ Gun Metal/42* 75.00 125.00
39 Ryan Newman U.S. Army/3693 50.00 75.00
39 Ryan Newman U.S. Army Brushed Metal/312 75.00 125.00
39 Ryan Newman U.S. Army/ Color Chrome/23* 100.00 150.00
39 Ryan Newman U.S. Army/ Gold/23* 125.00 200.00
39 Ryan Newman U.S. Army/ Gun Metal/23* 100.00 175.00
39 Ryan Newman U.S. Army/ Polished Nickel/23* 125.00 200.00
42 Juan Pablo Montoya Target/1448* 40.00 65.00
43 A.J. Allmendinger Best Buy/1092* 40.00 65.00
43 A.J. Allmendinger Geek Squad/808* 40.00 65.00
43 A.J. Allmendinger Hall Of Fame Petty Tribute/898* 40.00 65.00
43 A.J. Allmendinger Insignia/702* 40.00 65.00
43 Richard Petty NHOF/2019* 40.00 65.00
48 Jimmie Johnson Lowe's 60.00 120.00
48 Jimmie Johnson Lowe's Brushed Metal/314 100.00 200.00
48 Jimmie Johnson Lowe's/ Color Chrome/62* 125.00 250.00
48 Jimmie Johnson Lowe's Flashcoat Silver/766 100.00 200.00
48 Jimmie Johnson Lowe's/ Gold/23* 150.00 250.00
48 Jimmie Johnson Lowe's/ Gun Metal/47* 125.00 200.00
48 Jimmie Johnson Lowe's/ Polished Nickel/24 125.00 250.00
48 Jimmie Johnson Lowe's/ Bristol Raced/709* 60.00 100.00
48 Jimmie Johnson Lowe's/ Bristol Raced/ Gold Chrome/138* 150.00 250.00
48 Jimmie Johnson Lowe's/ Daytona Duel Raced/627* 60.00 100.00
48 Jimmie Johnson Lowe's/ Sonoma Raced/737* 60.00 100.00
48 Jimmie Johnson Lowe's/ Honoring Our Soldiers/1,666 60.00 100.00
48 Jimmie Johnson Lowe's Honor Our Soldiers/ Flashcoat Silver/321* 100.00 200.00
48 Jimmie Johnson Lowe's Johns Manville/1508* 60.00 100.00
48 Jimmie Johnson Jimmie Johnson Foundation/1087* 60.00 100.00
48 Jimmie Johnson Kobalt Tools/1810 60.00 100.00
48 Jimmie Johnson Kobalt Tools Brushed Metal/248 100.00 175.00
48 Jimmie Johnson Kobalt Tools Flashcoat Silver/301 100.00 175.00
48 Jimmie Johnson Kobalt Tools/ California Raced/685* 60.00 100.00
48 Jimmie Johnson Kobalt Tools/ Las Vegas Raced/689* 60.00 100.00
51 Michael Waltrip 40.00 65.00
NAPA/632*
55 Michael Waltrip Aaron's 55th Anniversary/337* 40.00 65.00
56 Martin Truex Jr. NAPA/2498 40.00 65.00
56 Martin Truex Jr. NAPA/ Brushed Metal/213* 60.00 120.00
56 Martin Truex Jr. NAPA/ Flashcoat Silver/246* 60.00 120.00
60 Carl Edwards Copart/1464* 40.00 65.00
60 Carl Edwards Fastenal/692* 40.00 65.00
60 Carl Edwards Save A Lot Pink/687* 40.00 65.00
77 Sam Hornish Jr. Mobil 1/876* 40.00 65.00
83 Brian Vickers Red Bull/989* 50.00 75.00
88 Dale Earnhardt Jr. AMP/6590 50.00 75.00
88 Dale Earnhardt Jr. AMP Brushed Metal/300 100.00 150.00
88 Dale Earnhardt Jr. AMP/ Color Chrome/287* 100.00 200.00
88 Dale Earnhardt Jr. AMP Flashcoat Silver/1274 100.00 150.00
88 Dale Earnhardt Jr. AMP/ Gold Chrome AU/163* 175.00 300.00
88 Dale Earnhardt Jr. AMP/ Gold/24* 150.00 250.00
88 Dale Earnhardt Jr. AMP/ Gun Metal/224* 100.00 175.00
88 Dale Earnhardt Jr. AMP/ Polished Nickel/48* 150.00 250.00
88 Dale Earnhardt Jr. AMP Energy Juice/2643* 50.00 75.00
88 Dale Earnhardt Jr. AMP Energy Juice/ Gun Metal/206* 75.00 125.00
88 Dale Earnhardt Jr. AMP Sugar Free/2492* 50.00 75.00
88 Dale Earnhardt Jr. Hellmann's/1198* 50.00 75.00
88 Dale Earnhardt Jr. JR Foundation/2584* 50.00 75.00
88 Dale Earnhardt Jr. JR Foundation AU/88* 125.00 200.00
88 Dale Earnhardt Jr. National Guard/4810 50.00 75.00
88 Dale Earnhardt Jr. National Guard Brushed Metal/215 100.00 150.00
88 Dale Earnhardt Jr. National Guard/ Color Chrome/287* 100.00 200.00
88 Dale Earnhardt Jr. National Guard Flashcoat Silver/931 100.00 150.00
88 Dale Earnhardt Jr. National Guard/ Gold/24* 150.00 250.00
88 Dale Earnhardt Jr. National Guard/ Gun Metal/211* 100.00 175.00
88 Dale Earnhardt Jr. National Guard/ Polished Nickel/49* 150.00 250.00
88 Dale Earnhardt Jr. National Guard Drive the Guard/1862* 50.00 75.00
88 Dale Earnhardt Jr. National Guard Honor Our Soldiers/3277* 60.00 100.00
88 Dale Earnhardt Jr. National Guard Honor Our Soldiers/ Flashcoat Silver/511* 100.00 150.00
88 Dale Earnhardt Jr. National Guard Camo 8 Soldiers 8 Missions/2787* 60.00 100.00
88 Dale Earnhardt Jr. National Guard Camo 8 Soldiers 8 Missions AU/87* 125.00 200.00
88 Dale Earnhardt Jr. Realtree/2490* 50.00 75.00
88 Ron Fellows AER/367* 40.00 65.00
88 Ron Fellows Canadian Tire/1936* 40.00 65.00
88 Greg Sacks GT Vodka/600* 40.00 65.00
88 Greg Sacks GT Vodka AU/100* 60.00 100.00
88 Elliott Sadler Realtree/299* 50.00 75.00
99 Carl Edwards Aflac/3969 50.00 75.00
99 Carl Edwards Aflac Brushed Metal/215 75.00 125.00
99 Carl Edwards Aflac/ Color Chrome/83* 100.00 150.00
99 Carl Edwards Aflac Flashcoat Silver/788 75.00 125.00
99 Carl Edwards Aflac/ Gold/23* 125.00 200.00
99 Carl Edwards Aflac/ Gun Metal/53* 75.00 125.00
99 Carl Edwards Aflac/ Polished Nickel/48* 125.00 200.00
99 Carl Edwards Aflac Silver/1440 50.00 75.00
99 Carl Edwards Aflac U Don't Know Quack/900* 50.00 75.00
99 Carl Edwards Cheez-It/935* 50.00 75.00
99 Carl Edwards Kellogg's/1015* 50.00 75.00
99 Carl Edwards Scott's/739* 50.00 75.00
99 Carl Edwards Scott's Ez Seed/718* 50.00 75.00
99 Carl Edwards Scott's Turf Builder/806* 50.00 75.00
99 Carl Edwards Subway/904* 50.00 75.00
00 David Reutimann Aaron's/1105* 50.00 75.00
00 David Reutimann Aaron's/ Flashcoat Silver/253* 60.00 120.00
00 David Reutimann Aaron's Armed Forces/332* 50.00 75.00
00 David Reutimann Best Western/514* 50.00 75.00
00 David Reutimann Tums/517* 50.00 75.00

2010 Action Racing Collectables Platinum GM Dealers 1:24

This set of die-casts is identical to the ARC Platinum line, with GM Dealers notation on the packaging, and these are typically only available for initial purchase through General Motors Pro Shops before they find the secondary market. The print runs noted in the checklist below are what is stated on the silver label on the box, unless it has an asterisk, then it is the actual production numbers provided by Action.

3 Dale Earnhardt Wheaties '97 MC/132* 60.00 100.00
3 Dale Earnhardt Jr. Wrangler/602* 60.00 100.00
5 Mark Martin Carquest/100* 50.00 75.00
5 Mark Martin Go Daddy/145 50.00 75.00
7 Danica Patrick Go Daddy ARCA/206* 60.00 120.00
14 Tony Stewart Burger King/144 50.00 75.00
14 Tony Stewart Office Depot144 50.00 75.00
14 Tony Stewart Old Spice/144 50.00 75.00
14 Tony Stewart Old Spice Matterhorn/100* 50.00 75.00
24 Jeff Gordon DuPont/144 50.00 75.00
24 Jeff Gordon National Guard/144 50.00 75.00
24 Jeff Gordon National Guard Special Forces/99* 50.00 75.00
24 Jeff Gordon Pepsi Max/82* 50.00 75.00
33 Clint Bowyer Cheerios/99* 50.00 75.00
39 Ryan Newman U.S. Army/144 50.00 75.00
48 Jimmie Johnson Lowe's/144 60.00 100.00
88 Dale Earnhardt Jr. AMP/148* 50.00 75.00
88 Dale Earnhardt Jr. AMP Energy Juice/149* 50.00 75.00
88 Dale Earnhardt Jr. AMP Sugar Free/147* 50.00 75.00
88 Dale Earnhardt Jr. JR Foundation/127* 50.00 75.00
88 Dale Earnhardt Jr. National Guard/143* 50.00 75.00
88 Dale Earnhardt Jr. National Guard Camo 8 Soldiers 8 Missions/137* 60.00 100.00

2010 Action Racing Collectables Silver 1:24

This set of die-casts consists of promotional-type die-casts that typically look and feel like the standard Action Racing Collectables Platinum line of cars. Most of these also have Hood Open and Trunk Open features along with die-cast chassis. These cars are also equipted with a DIN number like the ARC cars as well. Most of these ewere used as a promotional die-cast, whether at a hospitality tent trackside or as an employee incentive, these can be found on the secondary market and they usually will carry somewhat of a premium as they are typically seen as having a limited supply. The print runs noted in the checklist below are what is stated on the silver label on the box, unless it has an asterisk, then it is the actual production numbers provided by Action.

2 Kevin Harvick Stubb's BBQ SuperTruck AU/707* 60.00 120.00
6 Colin Braun Con-Way Trucking/2522* 50.00 75.00
10 No Driver Association Atlanta Fall Program Car/1000* 40.00 60.00
10 No Driver Association Carfax/4044* 40.00 60.00
10 No Driver Association Daytona Club 500/300* 40.00 60.00
10 No Driver Association Daytona Club Coke/700* 40.00 60.00
10 No Driver Association Daytona Club/400* 40.00 60.00
10 No Driver Association Daytona Club/1150* 40.00 60.00
10 No Driver Association Michigan Acceleration/1000* 40.00 60.00
10 No Driver Association Michigan Program Car/500* 40.00 60.00
10 No Driver Association Sprint/700* 40.00 60.00
11 Denny Hamlin Fed Ex Express/1503* 40.00 65.00
16 Greg Biffle Sherwin Williams/3050* 60.00 100.00
16 Greg Biffle 3M/1000* 40.00 60.00
16 Greg Biffle 3M Red Cross/4500* 60.00 100.00
16 Greg Biffle 3M Scotch Blue Tape/1098* 60.00 100.00
16 Greg Biffle 3M Super 33/824* 60.00 100.00
18 Kyle Busch Doublemint/1500* 50.00 75.00
18 Brad Coleman Sandvik Coromat/1003* 60.00 100.00
24 Jeff Gordon Dupont Carscoll/108* 60.00 100.00
24 Jeff Gordon Dupont Law Enforcement/500* 50.00 75.00
24 Jeff Gordon National Guard/1000* 50.00 75.00
29 Kevin Harvick Pennzoil Ultra AU/709* 75.00 150.00
39 Ryan Newman Tornados/1391* 50.00 75.00
39 Ryan Newman Tornados AU/120* 60.00 120.00
55 Michael Waltrip Aaron's 55th Anniversary/181* 50.00 75.00
77 Sam Hornish Jr. AAA/1000* 60.00 100.00
78 Rick Boysal Medical Staffing/15* 75.00 150.00
78 Rick Boysal No Sponsor/35* 60.00 100.00
88 Dale Earnhardt Jr. 40.00 60.00
National Guard/50004*
88 Ron Fellows AER/1020* 60.00 100.00
00 David Reutimann Aaron's/156* 40.00 65.00
00 David Reutimann Aaron's/ Flashcoat Silver/48* 60.00 100.00
00 David Reutimann Aaron's Alabama BCS Champions/2012* 60.00 100.00
00 David Reutimann Aaron's Armed Forces/246* 50.00 75.00
NNO No Driver Association NRA/48* 40.00 65.00
NNO No Driver Association NRA/910* 40.00 65.00

2010 Action/RCCA 1:24

3 Dale Earnhardt Jr. Wrangler/ Color Chrome/332* 125.00 250.00
3 Dale Earnhardt Jr. Wrangler/ Daytona Raced/ Brushed Metal/333* 75.00 125.00
18 Kyle Busch M&M's Vote/35* 50.00 75.00

2010 Action/RCCA Elite 1:24

1 Jamie McMurray Bass Pro Shops/ Brickyard Raced AU/233* 100.00 175.00
1 Jamie McMurray Bass Pro Shops/ Brickyard Raced/ Color Chrome AU/33* 100.00 175.00
1 Jamie McMurray Bass Pro Shops/ Brickyard Raced/ Polished Nickel AU/33* 200.00 300.00
1 Jamie McMurray Bass Pro Shops/ Daytona Raced/203* 125.00 200.00
1 Jamie McMurray Bass Pro Shops Earnhardt HOF Tribute/132* 100.00 150.00
1 Jamie McMurray Bass Pro Shops Earnhardt HOF Tribute/ Gold/33* 200.00 300.00
2 Kurt Busch Miller Lite/101* 100.00 150.00
2 Kurt Busch Miller Lite/ Copper/24* 150.00 250.00
2 Kurt Busch Miller Lite/ White Gold/25*
2 Kurt Busch Miller Lite/ Atlanta Raced/149* 100.00 150.00
2 Kurt Busch Miller Lite Vortex/ Bronze/12*
2 Kurt Busch Miller Lite Vortex AU/200* 100.00 200.00
2 Kurt Busch Miller Lite Vortex/ Gold/12*
2 Kurt Busch Miller Lite Vortex/ Platinum/12*
2 Kurt Busch Miller Lite Vortex/ All Star Raced/200* 100.00 150.00
3 Dale Earnhardt Wheaties '97 MC/332* 100.00 175.00
3 Dale Earnhardt Wheaties '97 MC/ Bronze/23*
3 Dale Earnhardt Wheaties '97 MC/ Color Chrome/33* 150.00 250.00
3 Dale Earnhardt Wheaties '97 MC/ Copper/23*
3 Dale Earnhardt Wheaties '97 MC/ Gold/33* 200.00 350.00
3 Dale Earnhardt Wheaties '97 MC/ Platinum/33* 200.00 350.00
3 Dale Earnhardt Wheaties '97 MC/ White Gold/33* 300.00 450.00
3 Dale Earnhardt Jr. Wrangler/703 125.00 200.00
3 Dale Earnhardt Jr. Wrangler/ Bronze/33* 200.00 350.00
3 Dale Earnhardt Jr. Wrangler/ Copper/33 200.00 350.00
3 Dale Earnhardt Jr. Wrangler/ Gold/33* 200.00 350.00
3 Dale Earnhardt Jr. Wrangler/ Platinum/33* 200.00 350.00
3 Dale Earnhardt Jr. Wrangler/ White Gold/33 300.00 450.00
3 Dale Earnhardt Jr. Wrangler/ Daytona Raced/1003* 100.00 175.00
5 Mark Martin Carquest/157* 75.00 125.00
5 Mark Martin Carquest AU/48* 100.00 200.00
5 Mark Martin Carquest/ Copper/25* 100.00 200.00
5 Mark Martin Carquest/ White Gold/25* 150.00 300.00
5 Mark Martin Carquest Honor Our Soldiers/142* 100.00 150.00
5 Mark Martin Carquest Honor Our Soldiers AU/60* 125.00 200.00
5 Mark Martin Carquest Honor Our Soldiers/ Copper/37* 125.00 200.00
5 Mark Martin Carquest Honor Our Soldiers/ Copper AU/17*
5 Mark Martin Carquest Honor Our Soldiers/ White Gold/26* 200.00 400.00
5 Mark Martin Delphi/95* 75.00 125.00
5 Mark Martin Delphi AU/108* 100.00 200.00
5 Mark Martin Go Daddy/305 100.00 150.00
5 Mark Martin Go Daddy/ Bronze/24* 200.00 350.00
5 Mark Martin Go Daddy/ Copper/50 200.00 350.00
5 Mark Martin Go Daddy/ Gold/24* 200.00 350.00
5 Mark Martin Go Daddy/ Platinum/24* 250.00 400.00
5 Mark Martin Go Daddy/ White Gold/25* 250.00 400.00
7 Danica Patrick Go Daddy/257 125.00 200.00
7 Danica Patrick Go Daddy/ Brushed Metal/127 125.00 250.00
7 Danica Patrick Go Daddy/ Copper/26* 150.00 250.00
7 Danica Patrick Go Daddy/ Platinum/36 275.00 400.00
7 Danica Patrick Go Daddy/ White Gold/25 250.00 400.00
7 Danica Patrick 100.00 175.00

Daddy ARCA/257
ca Patrick 125.00 250.00
Daddy ARCA/ Copper/25
ca Patrick 200.00 350.00
Daddy ARCA/ White Gold/25
ca Patrick 100.00 175.00
sot/307*
ca Patrick 150.00 250.00
sot/ Bronze/36*
ca Patrick 150.00 250.00
sot/ Copper/50*
ca Patrick 150.00 250.00
sot/ Gold/36*
ca Patrick 150.00 250.00
sot/ Platinum/48*
ca Patrick 200.00 350.00
sot/ White Gold/25*
ey Kahne 100.00 175.00
d AU/109*
ey Kahne 175.00 300.00
d AU/109
ey Kahne 150.00 250.00
d/ Copper/26*
ey Kahne 250.00 400.00
d/ White Gold/25*
ey Kahne 125.00 200.00
d Olympics/209
ey Kahne 150.00 250.00
d Olympics/ Copper/25*
ey Kahne 200.00 350.00
d Olympics/ White Gold/27*
ey Kahne 100.00 175.00
d Olympics/ Daytona Duel Raced/151*
ey Kahne 100.00 150.00
d Retro/125
ey Kahne 125.00 200.00
d Retro/ Color Chrome AU/91*
ey Kahne 200.00 350.00
d Retro/ White Gold/25*
Driver Association 100.00 200.00
CA Member/75*
ad Keselowski 75.00 125.00
nske/114*
ad Keselowski
nske/ Bronze/13*
ad Keselowski 125.00 200.00
nske/ Copper/27*
ad Keselowski
nske/ Gold/12*
ad Keselowski
nske/ Platinum/12*
ad Keselowski 150.00 250.00
nske/ White Gold/26*
ny Stewart 100.00 150.00
urger King/414
ny Stewart 125.00 200.00
urger King AU/110*
ny Stewart
urger King/ Bronze/16*
ny Stewart
urger King/ Bronze AU/20*
ony Stewart 300.00 400.00
urger King/ Copper/50
ony Stewart
urger King/ Gold/19*
ony Stewart
urger King/ Gold AU/17*
ony Stewart 300.00 400.00
urger King/ Platinum/32*
ony Stewart
urger King/ Platinum AU/16*
ony Stewart 350.00 500.00
urger King/ White Gold/25
ony Stewart 100.00 150.00
ffice Depot/314
ony Stewart 125.00 200.00
ffice Depot AU/120*
ony Stewart 300.00 400.00
ffice Depot/ Bronze/30*
ony Stewart
ffice Depot/ Bronze AU/6*
ony Stewart 300.00 400.00
ffice Depot/ Copper/50*
ony Stewart 300.00 400.00
Office Depot/ Gold/33*
ony Stewart
Office Depot/ Gold AU/3*
Tony Stewart 250.00 350.00
Office Depot/ Platinum/50*
Tony Stewart 300.00 500.00
Office Depot/ White Gold/26*
Tony Stewart 100.00 150.00
Office Depot BTS/215*
Tony Stewart 200.00 300.00
Office Depot BTS/ Copper/50*
Tony Stewart 300.00 450.00
Office Depot BTS/ White Gold/25*
Tony Stewart 100.00 150.00
Office Depot Go Green/213*
Tony Stewart 200.00 300.00
Office Depot Go Green/ Copper/25*
Tony Stewart 300.00 450.00
Office Depot Go Green/ White Gold/25*
Tony Stewart 100.00 150.00
Old Spice/242*
Tony Stewart 125.00 200.00
Old Spice AU/72*
Tony Stewart 200.00 300.00
Old Spice/ Copper/50*
Tony Stewart
Old Spice/ Copper AU/1*
Tony Stewart 300.00 450.00
Old Spice/ White Gold/25*
Tony Stewart 100.00 150.00
Old Spice Matterhorn/294*
Tony Stewart 125.00 200.00
Old Spice Matterhorn AU/24*
Tony Stewart 200.00 300.00
Old Spice Matterhorn/ Copper/25*
Tony Stewart 300.00 450.00
Old Spice Matterhorn/ White Gold/25*
Tony Stewart 100.00 150.00
Smoke/258*
Tony Stewart 125.00 200.00
Smoke AU/60*
Tony Stewart 150.00 250.00
Smoke/ Copper/45*
Tony Stewart

Smoke/ Copper AU/9*
14 Tony Stewart 200.00 350.00
Smoke/ White Gold/25*
17 Matt Kenseth 100.00 150.00
Crown Royal/213*
17 Matt Kenseth
Crown Royal/ Bronze/17*
17 Matt Kenseth 125.00 250.00
Crown Royal/ Copper/43*
17 Matt Kenseth
Crown Royal/ Gold/17*
17 Matt Kenseth
Crown Royal/ Platinum/17*
17 Matt Kenseth 200.00 350.00
Crown Royal/ White Gold/26*
17 Matt Kenseth 75.00 125.00
Crown Royal Black/110*
17 Matt Kenseth 125.00 250.00
Crown Royal Black/ Copper/25*
17 Matt Kenseth 200.00 350.00
Crown Royal Black/ White Gold/25*
17 Matt Kenseth 100.00 175.00
Crown Royal Patriotic Camo/143*
17 Matt Kenseth 75.00 125.00
Valvoline/111*
17 Matt Kenseth
Valvoline/ Copper/17*
17 Matt Kenseth
Valvoline/ White Gold/17*
18 Kyle Busch 75.00 125.00
Doublemint/120*
18 Kyle Busch 100.00 200.00
Doublemint AU/96*
18 Kyle Busch 125.00 250.00
Doublemint/ Copper/26*
18 Kyle Busch 200.00 350.00
Doublemint/ White Gold/26*
18 Kyle Busch 100.00 150.00
Interstate Batteries/44*
18 Kyle Busch 125.00 200.00
Interstate Batteries AU/72*
18 Kyle Busch 125.00 250.00
Interstate Batteries/ Copper/25*
18 Kyle Busch 200.00 350.00
Interstate Batteries/ White Gold/25*
18 Kyle Busch 100.00 175.00
M&M's/112*
18 Kyle Busch
M&M's AU/5*
18 Kyle Busch
M&M's/ Bronze/18*
18 Kyle Busch 150.00 300.00
M&M's/ Copper/25*
18 Kyle Busch
M&M's/ Gold/19*
18 Kyle Busch
M&M's/ Platinum/18*
18 Kyle Busch 250.00 400.00
M&M's/ White Gold/25*
18 Kyle Busch 125.00 200.00
NOS/ '09 NW Champion/ Color Chrome/235*
18 Kyle Busch 150.00 250.00
NOS/ '09 NW Champion/ Color Chrome AU/24*
18 Kyle Busch 125.00 250.00
NOS/ '09 NW Champion/ Copper/26*
18 Kyle Busch 200.00 350.00
NOS/ '09 NW Champion/ White Gold/25*
18 Kyle Busch 100.00 175.00
Z-Line/ '09 NW Champion/214*
18 Kyle Busch
Z-Line/ '09 NW Champion AU/11*
20 Joey Logano 100.00 175.00
Home Depot/120
20 Joey Logano 125.00 200.00
Home Depot AU/36*
20 Joey Logano 150.00 300.00
Home Depot/ Copper/25*
20 Joey Logano 300.00 450.00
Home Depot/ White Gold/25
20 Joey Logano 125.00 200.00
Home Depot ROTY/194*
20 Joey Logano 150.00 250.00
Home Depot ROTY AU/24*
24 Jeff Gordon 100.00 150.00
Dupont/524*
24 Jeff Gordon 150.00 250.00
Dupont/ Copper/52*
24 Jeff Gordon 400.00 600.00
DuPont/ White Gold/25
24 Jeff Gordon 100.00 175.00
Dupont Honor Our Soldiers/330*
24 Jeff Gordon 150.00 250.00
Dupont Honor Our Soldiers/ Bronze/39*
24 Jeff Gordon 150.00 250.00
Dupont Honor Our Soldiers/ Copper/53*
24 Jeff Gordon 250.00 400.00
Dupont Honor Our Soldiers/ Gold/38*
24 Jeff Gordon 250.00 400.00
Dupont Honor Our Soldiers/ Platinum/48*
24 Jeff Gordon 300.00 500.00
Dupont Honor Our Soldiers/ White Gold/25*
24 Jeff Gordon 100.00 150.00
Dupont Law Enforcement/294*
24 Jeff Gordon 150.00 250.00
Dupont Law Enforcement/ Copper/50*
24 Jeff Gordon 300.00 500.00
Dupont Law Enforcement/ White Gold/25*
24 Jeff Gordon 100.00 150.00
National Guard/424
24 Jeff Gordon 150.00 250.00
National Guard/ Bronze/36*
24 Jeff Gordon 150.00 250.00
National Guard/ Copper/50*
24 Jeff Gordon 250.00 400.00
National Guard/ Gold/38*
24 Jeff Gordon 250.00 400.00
National Guard/ Platinum/48*
24 Jeff Gordon 300.00 500.00
National Guard/ White Gold/25*
24 Jeff Gordon 100.00 200.00
National Guard Military Intelligence/300*
24 Jeff Gordon 150.00 250.00
National Guard Military Intelligence/ Copper/50*
24 Jeff Gordon 300.00 450.00
National Guard Military Intelligence/ White Gold/25*
24 Jeff Gordon 100.00 150.00
National Guard Special Forces/224
24 Jeff Gordon 175.00 250.00

National Guard Special Forces AU/100
24 Jeff Gordon 150.00 250.00
National Guard Special Forces/ Copper/50*
24 Jeff Gordon 300.00 450.00
National Guard Special Forces/ White Gold/25*
24 Jeff Gordon 100.00 150.00
Pepsi Max/321*
24 Jeff Gordon 150.00 250.00
Pepsi Max/ Copper/47*
24 Jeff Gordon 250.00 400.00
Pepsi Max/ White Gold/25*
29 Kevin Harvick 150.00 250.00
Pennzoil Ultra AU/128*
29 Kevin Harvick 200.00 350.00
Pennzoil Ultra/ White Gold/29*
29 Kevin Harvick 100.00 150.00
Shell/ Daytona Shootout Raced/300*
31 Jeff Burton 75.00 125.00
CAT/99*
31 Jeff Burton 100.00 200.00
CAT/ Copper/26*
31 Jeff Burton 175.00 300.00
CAT/ White Gold/27*
39 Ryan Newman 75.00 125.00
Tornados/127*
39 Ryan Newman 150.00 300.00
Tornados/ White Gold/25*
39 Ryan Newman 75.00 125.00
Tornados/ Phoenix Raced/149*
39 Ryan Newman 150.00 250.00
U.S. Army/100
39 Ryan Newman 175.00 300.00
U.S. Army/ Copper/26*
39 Ryan Newman 200.00 400.00
U.S. Army/ White Gold/25*
42 Juan Pablo Montoya 75.00 125.00
Target/84*
42 Juan Pablo Montoya 100.00 200.00
Target AU/59*
42 Juan Pablo Montoya
Target/ Copper/19*
42 Juan Pablo Montoya
Target/ Copper AU/6*
42 Juan Pablo Montoya 175.00 300.00
Target/ White Gold/25*
48 Jimmie Johnson 100.00 200.00
Jimmie Johnson Foundation/108*
48 Jimmie Johnson 125.00 250.00
Jimmie Johnson Foundation/ Color Chrome/48*
48 Jimmie Johnson 150.00 250.00
Lowe's Kobalt/148
48 Jimmie Johnson 150.00 250.00
Kobalt Tools/ Copper/53*
48 Jimmie Johnson 300.00 500.00
Kobalt Tools/ White Gold/25*
48 Jimmie Johnson 150.00 250.00
Kobalt Tools/ California Raced/192*
48 Jimmie Johnson 175.00 300.00
Lowe's/248
48 Jimmie Johnson 250.00 400.00
Lowe's/ Bronze/24*
48 Jimmie Johnson 250.00 400.00
Lowe's/ Copper/51*
48 Jimmie Johnson 300.00 500.00
Lowe's/ Gold/25*
48 Jimmie Johnson 350.00 600.00
Lowe's/ Platinum/24*
48 Jimmie Johnson 350.00 600.00
Lowe's/ White Gold/25*
48 Jimmie Johnson 150.00 250.00
Lowe's/ Bristol Raced/143*
48 Jimmie Johnson 150.00 250.00
Lowe's/ Daytona Duel Raced/142*
48 Jimmie Johnson 150.00 250.00
Lowe's/ Sonoma Raced/200*
48 Jimmie Johnson 175.00 300.00
Lowe's Honor Our Soldiers/242*
48 Jimmie Johnson 200.00 300.00
Lowe's Honor Our Soldiers/ Copper/54*
48 Jimmie Johnson 400.00 600.00
Lowe's Honor Our Soldiers/ White Gold/26*
56 Martin Truex Jr. 100.00 150.00
NAPA/62*
56 Martin Truex Jr. 100.00 200.00
NAPA AU/35*
56 Martin Truex Jr.
NAPA/ Copper/7*
56 Martin Truex Jr.
NAPA/ Copper AU/17*
56 Martin Truex Jr.
NAPA/ White Gold/15*
56 Martin Truex Jr.
NAPA/ White Gold AU/11*
88 Dale Earnhardt Jr. 100.00 150.00
AMP/488
88 Dale Earnhardt Jr. 200.00 300.00
AMP/ Copper/50*
88 Dale Earnhardt Jr. 350.00 500.00
AMP/ White Gold/25*
88 Dale Earnhardt Jr. 100.00 150.00
AMP Energy Juice/495*
88 Dale Earnhardt Jr. 175.00 300.00
AMP Energy Juice/ Copper/52*
88 Dale Earnhardt Jr. 250.00 450.00
AMP Energy Juice/ White Gold/25*
88 Dale Earnhardt Jr. 100.00 150.00
AMP Sugar Free/299*
88 Dale Earnhardt Jr. 75.00 125.00
JR Foundation/289*
88 Dale Earnhardt Jr. 100.00 200.00
JR Foundation/ Copper/50*
88 Dale Earnhardt Jr. 200.00 350.00
JR Foundation/ White Gold/25*
88 Dale Earnhardt Jr. 100.00 150.00
National Guard/488
88 Dale Earnhardt Jr. 200.00 300.00
National Guard/ Bronze/36*
88 Dale Earnhardt Jr. 200.00 300.00
National Guard/ Copper/53*
88 Dale Earnhardt Jr. 250.00 400.00
National Guard/ Gold/36*
88 Dale Earnhardt Jr. 300.00 450.00
National Guard/ Platinum/50*
88 Dale Earnhardt Jr. 300.00 500.00
National Guard/ White Gold/25
88 Dale Earnhardt Jr. 100.00 150.00
National Guard Drive the Guard/288*
88 Dale Earnhardt Jr. 100.00 200.00

National Guard Drive the Guard/ Copper/25*
88 Dale Earnhardt Jr. 300.00 450.00
National Guard Drive the Guard/ White Gold/25*
88 Dale Earnhardt Jr. 100.00 175.00
National Guard Honor Our Soldiers/391*
88 Dale Earnhardt Jr. 100.00 200.00
National Guard Honor Our Soldiers/ Bronze/36*
88 Dale Earnhardt Jr. 100.00 200.00
National Guard Honor Our Soldiers/ Copper/52*
88 Dale Earnhardt Jr. 150.00 300.00
National Guard Honor Our Soldiers/ Gold/37*
88 Dale Earnhardt Jr. 150.00 300.00
National Guard Honor Our Soldiers/ Platinum/48*
88 Dale Earnhardt Jr. 200.00 400.00
National Guard Honor Our Soldiers/ White Gold/47*
88 Dale Earnhardt Jr. 100.00 175.00
National Guard Camo 8 Soldiers 8 Missions/287*
88 Dale Earnhardt Jr. 200.00 300.00
National Guard Camo 8 Soldiers 8 Missions/ Copper/25*
88 Dale Earnhardt Jr. 250.00 400.00
National Guard Camo 8 Soldiers 8 Missions/ White Gold/25*
99 Carl Edwards 75.00 125.00
Aflac/194*
99 Carl Edwards
Aflac/ Bronze/12*
99 Carl Edwards 125.00 200.00
Aflac/ Copper/25*
99 Carl Edwards
Aflac/ Gold/12*
99 Carl Edwards
Aflac/ Platinum/13*
99 Carl Edwards 200.00 350.00
Aflac/ White Gold/25*
99 Carl Edwards 100.00 150.00
Aflac Silver/99
99 Carl Edwards 125.00 200.00
Aflac Silver/ Copper/26*
99 Carl Edwards 200.00 350.00
Aflac Silver/ White Gold/25*
99 Carl Edwards 75.00 125.00
Scott's Turf Builder/120*
99 Carl Edwards 150.00 300.00
Scott's Turf Builder/ White Gold/25*
NNO No Driver Association 75.00 125.00
NHOF Class of '10/200*

2011 Action/Lionel RCCA Elite 1:24

2 Brad Keselowski 75.00 125.00
Miller Lite/250
2 Brad Keselowski 100.00 175.00
Miller Lite Ghost/36
4 Kasey Kahne 75.00 125.00
Red Bull/300
4 Tony Stewart 75.00 125.00
Oreo Ritz
Daytona Raced/300
5 Dale Earnhardt Jr. 250.00 400.00
Hellmann's Platinum/25
5 Jimmie Johnson 175.00 300.00
Lowe's All Star AU/150
5 Mark Martin 100.00 175.00
GoDaddy Ghost/24
5 Mark Martin 75.00 125.00
Quaker State/225
5 Mark Martin 250.00 400.00
Quaker State Platinum/24
7 Danica Patrick 125.00 200.00
GoDaddy
Color Chrome/48
7 Danica Patrick 150.00 225.00
GoDaddy
Gold/36
7 Danica Patrick 250.00 400.00
GoDaddy
White Gold/24
7 Danica Patrick 125.00 200.00
Get Your.net Remember 9/11 AU/407
9 Marcos Ambrose 100.00 150.00
Stanley/90
9 Marcos Ambrose 125.00 200.00
Stanley Ghost/24
11 Denny Hamlin 75.00 125.00
Fed Ex Express/70
11 Denny Hamlin 100.00 175.00
Fed Ex Express
Ghost/24
11 Denny Hamlin 125.00 200.00
Fed Ex Express
Gold/24
11 Denny Hamlin 75.00 125.00
Fed Ex Ground/78
11 Denny Hamlin 100.00 150.00
Fed Ex Ground
Color Chrome/24
11 Denny Hamlin 125.00 200.00
Fed Ex Office
Platinum/24
11 NASCAR HOF Class of 2011/150 60.00 120.00
14 Tony Stewart 75.00 125.00
Burger King/275
14 Tony Stewart 75.00 125.00
Mobil 1/400
14 Tony Stewart 150.00 250.00
Mobil 1 Copper/36
14 Tony Stewart 100.00 175.00
Mobil 1 Ghost/48
14 Tony Stewart 300.00 500.00
Mobil 1 Platinum/36
14 Tony Stewart 150.00 225.00
Mobil 1 White Gold/24
14 Tony Stewart 125.00 200.00
Office Depot
Color Chrome/48
14 Tony Stewart 100.00 175.00
Office Depot Ghost/48
14 Tony Stewart 300.00 500.00
Office Depot Platinum/36
14 Tony Stewart 300.00 500.00
Office Depot White Gold/24
16 Greg Biffle 75.00 125.00
3M/80
16 Greg Biffle 100.00 175.00
3M Ghost/24
17 Matt Kenseth 125.00 200.00
Crown Royal
Color Chrome/36
17 Matt Kenseth 75.00 125.00
Crown Royal Black

Texas Raced/125
17 Matt Kenseth 75.00 125.00
Valvoline/117
18 Kyle Busch 125.00 200.00
Interstate Batteries
Color Chrome/24
18 Kyle Busch 250.00 400.00
Interstate Batteries
White Gold/24
18 Kyle Busch 100.00 175.00
M&M's Ghost/24
18 Kyle Busch 75.00 125.00
M&M's Bristol Raced/125
18 Kyle Busch 250.00 400.00
M&M's Bristol Raced
White Gold/25
18 Kyle Busch 75.00 125.00
M&M's Pretzel
Richmond Raced/125
18 Kyle Busch 75.00 125.00
Pedigree/120
18 Kyle Busch 125.00 200.00
Pedigree
Color Chrome/30
18 Kyle Busch 100.00 175.00
Snickers Ghost/24
18 Kyle Busch 250.00 400.00
Snickers Peanut Butter
White Gold/24
20 Joey Logano 75.00 125.00
Home Depot/100
20 Joey Logano 125.00 200.00
Home Depot
Color Chrome/24
20 Joey Logano 100.00 175.00
Home Depot
Ghost/24
21 Trevor Bayne 100.00 175.00
Motorcraft
Daytona Raced/1221
21 Trevor Bayne 175.00 300.00
Motorcraft Daytona Raced
Color Chrome AU
David Pearson AU
Glen Wood AU
Len Wood AU/250
21 Trevor Bayne 150.00 250.00
Motorcraft
Daytona Raced Copper/36
21 Kurt Busch 75.00 125.00
AAA/150
22 Kurt Busch 125.00 200.00
AAA Color Chrome/24
22 Kurt Busch 75.00 125.00
Pennzoil/250
22 Kurt Busch 125.00 200.00
Pennzoil Color Chrome/36
22 Kurt Busch 100.00 175.00
Pennzoil Ghost/36
22 Kurt Busch 75.00 125.00
Pennzoil Bud Shootout Raced/130
22 Kurt Busch 125.00 200.00
Pennzoil Bud Shootout Raced
Color Chrome/24
24 Jeff Gordon 75.00 125.00
Drive To End Hunger/500
24 Jeff Gordon 125.00 200.00
Drive To End Hunger
Color Chrome/48
24 Jeff Gordon 150.00 250.00
Drive To End Hunger
Copper/36
24 Jeff Gordon 125.00 200.00
Drive To End Hunger
Ghost/48
24 Jeff Gordon 300.00 500.00
Drive To End Hunger
Platinum/36
24 Jeff Gordon 350.00 600.00
Drive To End Hunger
White Gold/48
24 Jeff Gordon 75.00 125.00
Drive To End Hunger
Phoenix Raced/624
24 Jeff Gordon 125.00 200.00
Drive To End Hunger
Phoenix Raced Color Chrome/48
24 Jeff Gordon 75.00 125.00
DuPont/300
24 Jeff Gordon 125.00 200.00
DuPont Ghost/48
24 Jeff Gordon 350.00 600.00
DuPont White Gold/36
24 Jeff Gordon 125.00 200.00
JG Children's Foundation
Color Chrome/48
24 Jeff Gordon 75.00 125.00
Pepsi Max/225
24 Jeff Gordon 150.00 250.00
Pepsi Max Copper/24
24 Jeff Gordon 125.00 200.00
Pepsi Max Ghost/48
24 Jeff Gordon 250.00 400.00
Pepsi Max Platinum/24
29 Kevin Harvick 100.00 175.00
Bud/440
29 Kevin Harvick 150.00 225.00
Bud Ghost/36
29 Kevin Harvick 350.00 600.00
Bud White Gold/36
29 Kevin Harvick 100.00 175.00
Bud
Martinsville Raced/375
29 Kevin Harvick 350.00 600.00
Bud
Martinsville Raced White Gold/25
29 Kevin Harvick 100.00 150.00
Bud
Armed Forces/400
29 Kevin Harvick 150.00 250.00
Bud
Armed Forces Color Chrome/24
29 Kevin Harvick 125.00 200.00
Bud
Armed Forces Ghost/36
29 Kevin Harvick 350.00 600.00
Bud
Armed Forces
White Gold/24

29 Kevin Harvick Bud July 4/300 100.00 150.00
29 Kevin Harvick Jimmy John's/300 75.00 125.00
29 Kevin Harvick Jimmy John's Color Chrome/36 125.00 200.00
29 Kevin Harvick Jimmy John's Ghost/36 100.00 175.00
29 Kevin Harvick Jimmy John's Fontana Raced White Gold/25 250.00 400.00
29 Kevin Harvick Rheem/250 75.00 125.00
31 Jeff Burton Cat Ghost/24 100.00 175.00
33 Clint Bowyer Cheerios Ghost/24 100.00 175.00
39 Ryan Newman U.S.Army Color Chrome/36 150.00 225.00
39 Ryan Newman U.S.Army Ghost/24 100.00 175.00
48 Jimmie Johnson Kobalt Tools Ghost/48 125.00 200.00
48 Jimmie Johnson Kobalt Tools White Gold/48 350.00 600.00
48 Jimmie Johnson Lowe's/300 100.00 150.00
48 Jimmie Johnson Lowe's Copper/36 175.00 300.00
48 Jimmie Johnson Lowe's Ghost/48 150.00 225.00
48 Jimmie Johnson Lowe's Gold/36 150.00 250.00
48 Jimmie Johnson Lowe's JJ Foundation Color Chrome/48 150.00 225.00
48 Jimmie Johnson Lowe's Power of Pride White Gold/36 350.00 600.00
56 Martin Truex Jr. NAPA Ghost/24 100.00 175.00
88 Dale Earnhardt Jr. AMP/300 75.00 125.00
88 Dale Earnhardt Jr. AMP Gold Bristol/350 100.00 150.00
88 Dale Earnhardt Jr. AMP Sugar Free/400 100.00 150.00
88 Dale Earnhardt Jr. JR Foundation VH1/450 75.00 125.00
88 Dale Earnhardt Jr. JR Foundation VH1 Color Chrome/48 125.00 200.00
88 Dale Earnhardt Jr. JR Foundation VH1 White Gold/48 300.00 500.00
88 Dale Earnhardt Jr. National Guard Ghost/48 150.00 225.00
88 Dale Earnhardt Jr. National Guard Heritage Color Chrome/48 150.00 225.00
99 Carl Edwards Aflac Color Chrome/36 125.00 200.00
99 Carl Edwards Subway Ghost/24 100.00 175.00

1998-01 Action Racing Collectables 1:32

These 1:32 scale cars debuted in 1998. These cars were sold through GM and Ford dealerships as well as through various TV outlets.

2 Rusty Wallace Miller Lite 1998 15.00 40.00
3 Dale Earnhardt Goodwrench Sign Last Lap/3504 30.00 60.00
3 Dale Earnhardt Goodwrench 25th Anniversary 30.00 60.00
3 Dale Earnhardt Goodwrench Plus Bass Pro/5000 30.00 80.00
3 Dale Earnhardt Goodwrench Plus Daytona Win/20,000 1998 30.00 60.00
3 Dale Earnhardt Goodwrench Silver 1995 Monte Carlo/5000 40.00 80.00
3 Dale Earnhardt Goodwrench Taz No Bull 60.00 120.00
3 Dale Earnhardt Jr. AC Delco/12,000 1998 30.00 70.00
3 Dale Earnhardt Jr. AC Delco Last Lap 1999 20.00 50.00
5 Terry Labonte Corny Blasted Froot Loops 2-car set in tin/4500 1998 20.00 40.00
5 Terry Labonte Kellogg's Ironman/5000 1998 15.00 40.00
5 Terry Labonte Kellogg's Ironman II
5/18 Terry Labonte Bobby Labonte Kelloggs Interstate Batteries 2-car set 1998 25.00 60.00
8 Dale Earnhardt Jr. Bud/12,000 1999 25.00 50.00
12 Jeremy Mayfield Mobil 1/3500 '98 12.50 30.00
12 Jeremy Mayfield Mobil 1 Kentucky Derby/3504 1999 15.00 40.00
18/44 Bobby Labonte Tony Stewart Small Soldiers 2-cars/4500 1998 20.00 40.00
24 Jeff Gordon DuPont Chromalusion/3500 1998 25.00 50.00
24 Jeff Gordon DuPont Superman/3504 1999 25.00 50.00
24 Jeff Gordon Pepsi/12,000 w helmet 20.00 50.00
28 Kenny Irwin Havoline '98 15.00 40.00
28 Kenny Irwin Havoline Joker 1998 15.00 40.00
31 Dale Earnhardt Jr. Gargoyles 1997 Monte Carlo 20.00 50.00
88 Dale Jarrett Batman 1998 20.00 50.00
88 Dale Jarrett Quality Care 1998 12.50 30.00
88 Dale Jarrett UPS Flames Van/4008 40.00 75.00

1998 Action/RCCA Gold 1:32

These 1:32 scale cars were distributed by Action through RCCA.

1 Steve Park Pennzoil/1500 25.00 60.00
2 Rusty Wallace Miller Lite 25.00 60.00
3 Dale Earnhardt Goodwrench Bass Pro 75.00 150.00
3 Dale Earnhardt Jr. AC Delco/5000 50.00 100.00
5 Terry Labonte Kellogg's 25.00 60.00
12 Jeremy Mayfield Mobil 1/1000 25.00 60.00
18 Bobby Labonte Interstate Batteries 40.00 100.00
23 Jimmy Spencer No Bull 25.00 60.00
24 Jeff Gordon DuPont/3500 50.00 100.00
28 Kenny Irwin Havoline 25.00 60.00
36 Ernie Irvan M&M's 25.00 60.00
88 Dale Jarrett Quality Care/700 25.00 60.00

1999-00 Action/RCCA 1:32

3 Dale Earnhardt Wrangler/3500 30.00 60.00
19 Dodge Red Show Ceramic Pit Scene/2592 2000 20.00 40.00
20 Tony Stewart Home Depot/7500 20.00 50.00
27 Casey Atwood Castrol/3500 12.50 30.00

2002 Action/RCCA 1:32

1 Dale Earnhardt Jr. Coke '98 Monte Carlo in vending machine tin/2004 30.00 60.00
2/29 Kevin Harvick AC Delco Goodwrench 2-car set/3000 30.00 60.00
3 Dale Earnhardt Coke 1998 Monte Carlo in vending machine tin/2004 30.00 60.00
3 Dale Earnhardt Goodwrench/3600 2001 Monte Carlo 35.00 60.00
3 Dale Earnhardt Goodwrench Gold/720 2001 Monte Carlo 60.00 120.00
3 Dale Earnhardt Goodwrench Oreo 2001 Monte Carlo/3000 35.00 60.00
3 Dale Earnhardt Goodwrench Oreo Gold 2001 Monte Carlo/600 35.00 60.00
3 Dale Earnhardt Goodwrench Peter Max 2000 Monte Carlo/3600 35.00 60.00
3 Dale Earnhardt Goodwrench Gold Peter Max 2000 Monte Carlo/960 50.00 100.00
3 Dale Earnhardt Jr. Nilla Wafers Oreo -car set/2016 35.00 60.00
8 Dale Earnhardt Jr. Bud/3000 with Fan Scan card 30.00 50.00
8 Dale Earnhardt Jr. Bud Gold/652 50.00 100.00
8 Dale Earnhardt Jr. Bud 2001 All-Star/1416 35.00 60.00
8 Dale Earnhardt Jr. Bud 2001 All-Star Gold/600 40.00 80.00
8 Dale Earnhardt Jr. Bud '02 All-Star/1416 35.00 60.00
8 Dale Earnhardt Jr. Bud '02 All-Star Gold/600 40.00 80.00
8 Dale Earnhardt Jr. Looney Tunes/1416 25.00 50.00
8 Dale Earnhardt Jr. Looney Tunes Gold/600 40.00 80.00
24 Jeff Gordon DuPont Flames 2001 WC Champ/3600 25.00 50.00
24 Jeff Gordon DuPont Bugs/1416 25.00 40.00
24 Jeff Gordon DuPont Bugs Gold/600 40.00 80.00
24 Jeff Gordon Pepsi Daytona/2280 25.00 40.00
24 Jeff Gordon Pepsi Daytona Gold/720 45.00 80.00
29 Kevin Harvick Goodwrench with Fan Scan card/2280 20.00 40.00
29 Kevin Harvick Goodwrench Gold/532 30.00 60.00
29 Kevin Harvick Goodwrench '01 AC Delco '01 set/3000 35.00 60.00
48 Jimmie Johnson Lowe's/1536 30.00 60.00
48 Jimmie Johnson Lowe's Gold/480 50.00 100.00
NNO Dale Earnhardt Jr. Legacy/2004 40.00 80.00

2003 Action/RCCA 1:32

3 Dale Earnhardt Earnhardt Foundation/1012 25.00 50.00
3 Dale Earnhardt Goodwrench Bass Pro Shops 20.00 40.00
3 Dale Earnhardt Goodwrench Silver Select 1995 Monte Carlo/1800 25.00 50.00
8 Dale Earnhardt Jr. Bud/1572 25.00 50.00
8 Dale Earnhardt Jr. Bud 24K/444 35.00 60.00
8 Dale Earnhardt Jr. Bud MLB All-Star Game 24K/316 35.00 60.00
8 Dale Earnhardt Jr. Bud MLB All-Star Game/844 25.00 50.00
8 Dale Earnhardt Jr. Bud StainD/844 25.00 50.00
8 Dale Earnhardt Jr. Oreo Ritz/2004 30.00 50.00
8 Dale Earnhardt Jr. Oreo Ritz Gold/588 35.00 60.00
8 Dale Earnhardt Jr. Dirty Mo Posse/1572 25.00 50.00
8 Dale Earnhardt Jr. Dirty Mo Posse 24K/444 35.00 60.00
8 Dale Earnhardt Jr. E Concert/1572 30.00 50.00
8 Dale Earnhardt Jr. E Concert 24K/444 35.00 60.00
8 Tony Stewart 3 Doors Down/844 25.00 50.00
20 Tony Stewart Home Depot/1572 25.00 50.00
20 Tony Stewart Home Depot Gold/444 30.00 60.00
20 Tony Stewart Home Depot Peanuts Orange Peanuts Black 3-car set/2004 50.00 90.00
24 Jeff Gordon DuPont Flames/1572 25.00 50.00
24 Jeff Gordon DuPont Flames 24K/444 35.00 60.00
24 Jeff Gordon DuPont Wright Brothers/844 25.00 50.00
24 Jeff Gordon DuPont Wright Bros. 24K/316 35.00 60.00
24 Jeff Gordon Pepsi in Vending Machine/2004 35.00 60.00
24 Jeff Gordon Pepsi Billion $/844 25.00 50.00
24 Jeff Gordon Pepsi Billion $ 24K/316 35.00 60.00
88 Dale Jarrett Race For a Cure 30.00 60.00

2003 Action/RCCA Elite 1:32

3 Dale Earnhardt Earnhardt Foundation/1012 30.00 50.00
3 Dale Earnhardt Goodwrench No Bull 2000 Monte Carlo/1008 30.00 50.00
3 Dale Earnhardt Goodwrench Bass Pro Shops/1800 25.00 50.00
3 Dale Earnhardt Goodwrench Silver Select 1995 Monte Carlo/1800 35.00 50.00
8 Dale Earnhardt Jr. Bud/1500 30.00 50.00
8 Dale Earnhardt Jr. Bud No Bull 2000 Monte Carlo/1008 30.00 50.00
8 Dale Earnhardt Jr. Bud MLB All-Star Game/844 30.00 50.00
8 Dale Earnhardt Jr. Bud StainD/844 30.00 50.00
8 Tony Stewart 3 Doors Down/844 30.00 50.00
20 Tony Stewart Home Depot/1008 30.00 50.00
24 Jeff Gordon DuPont Flames/1008 30.00 50.00
24 Jeff Gordon DuPont Wright Brothers/804 30.00 50.00
24 Jeff Gordon Pepsi Billion $/844 30.00 50.00

2004 Action Racing Collectables 1:32

8 Dale Earnhardt Jr. Bud/2508 20.00 40.00
8 Dale Earnhardt Jr. Bud Born On Feb.7/1764 20.00 40.00
8 Dale Earnhardt Jr. Oreo/1584 15.00 30.00
20 Tony Stewart Home Depot/1488 20.00 40.00
24 Jeff Gordon DuPont Flames/1512 20.00 40.00
29 Tony Stewart Kid Rock/1308 15.00 30.00

2004 Action Racing Collectables Historical Series 1:32

3 Dale Earnhardt Wheaties 1997 Monte Carlo/2200 30.00 50.00
3 Dale Earnhardt Wheaties '97 Monte Carlo Mac Tools/288 30.00 50.00
3 Dale Earnhardt Jr. AC Delco Last Lap of the Century Color Chrome/1452 35.00 60.00
7 Dale Earnhardt Jr. Church Bros 1997 Monte Carlo/2316 30.00 50.00
8 Dale Earnhardt Jr. Bud Olympics '00 Monte Carlo/1304 30.00 50.00
8 Dale Earnhardt Jr. Bud Olympics '00 Monte Carlo QVC/216 30.00 50.00

2004 Action/RCCA 1:32

8 Dale Earnhardt Jr. Bud/600 15.00 30.00
8 Dale Earnhardt Jr. Bud Born On Feb.7/408 20.00 40.00
8 Dale Earnhardt Jr. Bud Born On Feb.15/960 20.00 40.00
8 Dale Earnhardt Jr. Oreo/600 15.00 30.00
20 Tony Stewart Home Depot/600 20.00 40.00
24 Jeff Gordon DuPont Flames/600 20.00 40.00
29 Tony Stewart Kid Rock/408 15.00 30.00

2004 Action/RCCA Elite 1:32

8 Dale Earnhardt Jr. Bud/600 25.00 50.00
8 Dale Earnhardt Jr. Bud Born On Feb.7/408 25.00 50.00
8 Dale Earnhardt Jr. Bud Born On Feb.15/960 25.00 50.00
8 Dale Earnhardt Jr. Oreo/600 25.00 50.00
20 Tony Stewart Home Depot/844 25.00 50.00
24 Jeff Gordon DuPont Flames/600 25.00 50.00
29 Tony Stewart Kid Rock/408 25.00 50.00

2004 Action/RCCA Historical Series 1:32

3 Dale Earnhardt Wheaties '97 Monte Carlo/804 25.00 50.00
3 Dale Earnhardt Jr. AC Delco Last Lap 1999 Monte Carlo/480 25.00 50.00
7 Dale Earnhardt Jr. Church Brothers 1997 Monte Carlo/600 25.00 50.00
8 Dale Earnhardt Jr. Bud Olympic 2000 Monte Carlo/408 25.00 50.00

2004 Action/RCCA Historical Series Elite 1:32

3 Dale Earnhardt Wheaties 1997 Monte Carlo/804 35.00 60.00
3 Dale Earnhardt Jr. AC Delco Last Lap 1999 Monte Carlo/480 35.00 60.00
7 Dale Earnhardt Jr. Church Brothers 1997 Monte Carlo/600 35.00 60.00
8 Dale Earnhardt Jr. Bud Olympic 2000 Monte Carlo/408 40.00 60.00

2004 Action RCR 1:32

These 1:32 scale cars were produced and released May through December of 2004. They were available via distributors and through Action/RCCA. Each car was individually serial numbered on the rear window deck using the ink jet method. All cars have RCR molded into the chassis. All packaging is in a generic RCR skybox with a special sleeve. The first 2500 serial numbered copies are only available through Action/RCCA the remaining copies are Action Racing Collectables pieces.

3 Dale Earnhardt AC Delco Japan 1997 Monte Carlo/4296 25.00 50.00
3 Dale Earnhardt AC Delco Japan '97 Monte Carlo GM Dealers/624 25.00 50.00
3 Dale Earnhardt Coca Cola Japan 1998 Monte Carlo/3672 25.00 50.00
3 Dale Earnhardt Coca Cola Japan '98 Monte Carlo GM Dealers/528 25.00 50.00
3 Dale Earnhardt Goodwrench 1996 Monte Carlo/4296 25.00 50.00
3 Dale Earnhardt Goodwrench 1996 Monte Carlo GM Dealers/504 25.00 50.00
3 Dale Earnhardt Goodwrench Olympics 1996 Monte Carlo/4344 25.00 50.00
3 Dale Earnhardt Goodwrench Olympics 1996 Monte Carlo GM Dealers/408 25.00 50.00
3 Dale Earnhardt Goodwrench Crash 1997 Monte Carlo/15,516 35.00 60.00
3 Dale Earnhardt Goodwrench Crash '97 MC GM Dealers/936 35.00 60.00
3 Dale Earnhardt Goodwrench Service Plus Daytona Win 1998 Monte Carlo/3168 25.00
3 Dale Earnhardt Goodwrench Plus Daytona Win '98 MC GM Dealers/264 25.00
3 Dale Earnhardt Goodwrench Sign 1999 Monte Carlo/4008 25.00
3 Dale Earnhardt Goodwrench Sign 1999 Monte Carlo GM Dealers/648 25.00
3 Dale Earnhardt Goodwrench Talladega 2000 Monte Carlo/3432 30.00
3 Dale Earnhardt Goodwrench Peter Max 2000 Monte Carlo/5784 30.00
3 Dale Earnhardt Goodwrench Peter Max 2000 Monte Carlo GM Dealers/888 30.00
3 Dale Earnhardt Goodwrench Taz '00 Monte Carlo 30.00
3 Dale Earnhardt Wrangler 1999 Monte Carlo/4380 25.00
3 Dale Earnhardt Wrangler 1999 Monte Carlo GM Dealers/648 25.00

2004 Action/RCCA RCR 1:32

These 1:32 scale cars were produced and released May December of 2004. They were available via distribut through Action/RCCA. Each car was individually numbered on the rear window deck using the ink jet r All cars have RCR molded into the chassis. All packagin generic RCR skybox with a special sleeve. The first 250 numbered copies are only available through Action/RC remaining copies are Action Racing Collectables pieces.

3 Dale Earnhardt Coca Cola Japan 1998 Monte Carlo/1500 35.00 6
3 Dale Earnhardt Goodwrench 1996 Monte Carlo/1500 35.00 6
3 Dale Earnhardt Goodwrench Olympics 1996 Monte Carlo/1500 35.00 6
3 Dale Earnhardt Goodwrench Crash '97 Monte Carlo Daytona Raced/1500 40.00 7
3 Dale Earnhardt Goodwrench Peter Max 2000 Monte Carlo/1500 35.00 6
3 Dale Earnhardt Wrangler 1999 Monte Carlo/1500 35.00 6

2005 Action RCR 1:32

3 Dale Earnhardt Bass Pro '98 Monte Carlo/2604 25.00 5
3 Dale Earnhardt Goodwrench 25th Anniversary '99 Monte Carlo/1728 25.00 5
3 Dale Earnhardt Goodwrench Under the Lights '00 Monte Carlo/3504 25.00 5
3 Dale Earnhardt Goodwrench Under the Lights '00 Monte Carlo GM Dealers/312 25.00 5
3 Dale Earnhardt Goodwrench Under the Lights '00 Monte Carlo QVC/1200 25.00 5
3 Dale Earnhardt Oreo '01 Monte Carlo/1740 25.00 5
3 Dale Earnhardt Oreo '01 Monte Carlo GM Dealers/312 25.00 5
3 Dale Earnhardt Oreo '01 Monte Carlo QVC/1500 25.00 5
3 Dale Earnhardt Wheaties '97 Monte Carlo/1776 25.00 5

2005 Action/RCCA RCR 1:32

3 Dale Earnhardt Goodwrench Under the Lights '00 Monte Carlo/1008 25.00 5

2000-01 Action Road Racing 1:43

3 Dale Earnhardt Dale Earnhardt Jr Andy Pilgrim Kelly Collins C5-R Corvette/12,024 2001 40.00 100
3 Dale Earnhardt Dale Earnhardt Jr Andy Pilgrim Kelly Collins C5-R Corvette raced version/2424 2001 30.00 75.
3 Ron Fellows Justan Bell Chris Kneifel Goodwrench C5-R/2352 2000 15.00 40.

2004 Action Road Racing 1:43

8 Dale Earnhardt Jr. Boris Said Corvette C-5R/3198 20.00 40.

2003 Action Racing Collectables 1:43

88 Dale Jarrett UPS Store promo in window box 7.50 20.

2005 Action Racing Collectables 1:43

aul Menard Ienards Promo in window box	15.00	30.00
ale Earnhardt Jr. Ienards Promo in window box	15.00	30.00
ale Jarrett PS Store Toys for Tots romo in wind.box	10.00	20.00

2010 Action Racing Collectables 1:43

rk Martin o Daddy/1500*	12.50	25.00
nica Patrick o Daddy/2675*	20.00	40.00
igger opher Cam Friends/1499*	7.50	15.00
ony Stewart urger King/1500*	12.50	25.00
ony Stewart ffice Depot/1498*	12.50	25.00
ony Stewart ld Spice/1522*	12.50	25.00
yle Busch M&M's/3514*	12.50	25.00
eff Gordon upont/2124*	12.50	25.00
immie Johnson owe's/1536*	12.50	25.00
ale Earnhardt Jr. MP/1698*	12.50	25.00
arl Edwards flac/1488*	12.50	25.00

1991-92 Action/RCCA Revell 1:64

s set marks the first issue of current NASCAR drivers ased by Racing Collectables, Inc. which soon was chased by Action to become Action/RCCA. The cars nselves were produced by Revell but distributed by RCI, efore they are often referred to as Revell pieces. Each was ed in a white clear window cardboard box. The name cing Collectibles, Inc." is printed on the front along with the number and model and sometimes the sponsor noted at the tom below the window. Either a 1991 or 1992 date is uded on the copyright line on the box bottoms.

eff Gordon Baby Ruth Revell	25.00	60.00
usty Wallace Pontiac Excitement Revell	4.00	8.00
ale Earnhardt Goodwrench	20.00	40.00
icky Rudd Tide Promo	6.00	12.00
ark Martin Valvoline	6.00	12.00
ac Tools/7500	10.00	20.00
Derrike Cope Purolator	4.00	10.00
Ricky Rudd Motorcraft red	5.00	12.00
Darrell Waltrip Western Auto	6.00	15.00
Dale Jarrett Interstate Batteries	4.00	8.00
Rob Moroso Swisher Sweets Promo '89 Rookie of the Year ed car	6.00	15.00
Rob Moroso Swisher Sweets Promo 1989 Rookie of the Year red car w yellow stripe	6.00	15.00
/25 Rob Moroso Swisher Sweets 2-car Promo set in box/13,628	15.00	30.00
Morgan Shepherd Citgo	2.00	5.00
Sterling Marlin Maxwell House	3.00	6.00
Bill Venturini Rain-X	2.00	5.00
6 Brett Bodine Quaker State	1.50	5.00
3 Davey Allison Havoline black	10.00	25.00
) Michael Waltrip Pennzoil	2.00	5.00
Harry Gant Skoal with Mug Promo	15.00	30.00
6 Kenny Wallace Cox Lumber	2.00	5.00
6 Kenny Wallace Dirt Devil	2.00	5.00
2 Kyle Petty Mello Yello	2.00	5.00
3 Richard Petty STP	10.00	25.00
4 Larry Caudill Army	2.00	5.00
3 Chuck Bown Nescafe Promo blister/15,000	5.00	12.00
6 Jimmy Hensley TropArtic Phillips 66	2.00	5.00
8 Bobby Hamilton Country Time	2.00	5.00
7 Joe Nemechek Texas Pete	3.00	8.00
9 Jim Sauter Evinrude	2.00	5.00
0 Mike Wallace Heilig-Meyers Promo	5.00	10.00
1 Clifford Allison Mac Tools Promo/20,160	15.00	30.00
3 Mike Wallace Racing Collectables Inc.	2.00	5.00
9 Ricky Craven DuPont	2.00	5.00

1991-92 Action/RCCA Legends, Oldsmobiles and T-Birds 1:64

hese 1:64 die cast cars were issued between 1990 and 1992 nd feature past legends of NASCAR as well as replicas of 1991 ldsmobiles and Thunderbirds that were driven between 1983-986. We've included all of these cars into one listing for ease n cataloging. All were produced by a variety of manufacturers or RCCA and can be found inside one of three different cardboard window box designs with some being released in more than one type of box at different times: white Racing Collectables Club of America Inc. Legend Series, black Racing Collectables Inc. Collector's Series, or black Racing Collectables Inc. Legend Series 1 of 16 box. The last box also had the year and car model listed on the front of the box along with an announced print run of 15,000. The #25 Tim Richmond Fan Club Promo piece was issued on a Legends Series blister along with a Tim Richmond trading card. It was produced for RCCA by Racing Champions before RCCA was acquired by Action.

1 Paul Goldsmith Packer Pontiac 1962	8.00	20.00
3 David Pearson Gerry Earl Pontiac 1962	10.00	20.00
4 Rex White Sherwood Chevy '63	6.00	15.00
6 Cotton Owens Hines Pontiac 1962	6.00	15.00
7 Kyle Petty 7-Eleven	15.00	40.00
8 Elmo Langley 1957 Chevy Convertible	6.00	15.00
8 Joe Weatherly Gillman Pontiac 1962	15.00	40.00
9 Bill Elliott Melling	15.00	30.00
13 Johnny Rutherford 1963 Chevy	6.00	15.00
15 Dale Earnhardt Wrangler	40.00	80.00
15 Ricky Rudd Motorcraft red&white	10.00	20.00
16 Tom Pistone S&K 1957	6.00	15.00
21 Buddy Baker Valvoline with V logo on deck lid	5.00	10.00
21 Buddy Baker Valvoline with Valvoline on deck lid	10.00	20.00
21 Tiny Lund English Motors 1963	8.00	20.00
21 Marvin Panch English Motors 1963	6.00	15.00
21 Marvin Panch Augusta Motors '65	8.00	20.00
21 David Pearson Pearson Racing white&black	20.00	40.00
21 David Pearson Pearson Racing white&brown	15.00	30.00
22 Bobby Allison Gold Wheels	20.00	40.00
22 Ed Berrier Greased Lightning	3.00	6.00
22 Bobby Allison Silver Wheels	15.00	30.00
22 Fireball Roberts Stephens Pontiac 1962	10.00	20.00
22 Firebell Roberts Young Ford dark purple 1963	8.00	20.00
22 Fireball Roberts Young Ford light purple 1963	8.00	20.00
24 Larry Frank 1957 Chevy	6.00	15.00
25 Rob Moroso Swisher Sweets	6.00	15.00
25 Tim Richmond Fan Club Promo blister black bordered card (1990 car made by Racing Champions)	10.00	20.00
25 Tim Richmond Fan Club Promo blister tan bordered serial #'d card	10.00	20.00
26 Curtis Turner Ed Martin Ford 1963	6.00	15.00
27 A.J. Foyt Sheraton Thompson Ford 1965	8.00	20.00
27 Junior Johnson Hansford Pontiac 1962	10.00	20.00
28 Davey Allison Havoline black&white	15.00	30.00
28 Dan Gurney LaFayette Ford 1963	6.00	15.00
28 Fred Lorenzen LaFayette Ford 1963	6.00	15.00
28 Fred Lorenzen LaFayette Ford 1965 Fastback	6.00	15.00
28 Cale Yarborough Hardee's	15.00	30.00
29 Nelson Stacy Ron's Ford 1963	6.00	15.00
31 Ralph Earnhardt Jimmy Rivers Body Shop Ford	25.00	60.00
32 Bristol Food City 500 promo blister/15,000 1963 Ford	5.00	10.00
34 Wendell Scott 1963 Orange Ford	8.00	20.00
34 Wendell Scott 1965 Blue Ford	8.00	20.00
35 Alan Kulwicki Quincy's Steakhouse	25.00	60.00
35 Dick May Hanover Printing	5.00	10.00
39 Lee Roy Yarborough H&B Auto Parts 1962	10.00	25.00
41 Curtis Turner Harvest Motors '65 Fastback	8.00	20.00
44 Bobby Labonte Penrose	20.00	50.00
44 Sterling Marlin Piedmont	10.00	20.00
44 Bob Welborn Frizzle Pontiac 1962	10.00	20.00
46 Johnny Allen Hansford Pontiac 1962	6.00	15.00
47 Buck Baker Miller Pontiac 1962	8.00	20.00
49 Bob Welborn Nalley Chevrolet 1957 Chevy Convertible	6.00	15.00
54 Ralph Earnhardt Adamson Motors Ford	15.00	40.00
54 Jimmy Pardue Scenic Motors 1963	6.00	15.00
57 Dick May McClure Motors 1963	6.00	15.00
57 Jody Ridley Nationwise	5.00	10.00
64 Rodney Combs Sunny King small numbers on roof	5.00	10.00
64 Rodney Combs Jr. Sunny King large numbers on roof	5.00	10.00
66 Johnny Allen Commonwealth Ford 1963	6.00	15.00
67 Buddy Arrington Arrington Racing	5.00	10.00
70 J.D. McDuffie Lockhart	5.00	10.00
71 Dave Marcis Shoney's	20.00	50.00
71 Lee Roy Yarborough Harison&Gulley '63	6.00	15.00
73 Phil Barkdoll XR-1	4.00	8.00
77 Joe Lee Johnson 1957 Chevy	6.00	15.00
87 Curtis Turner Blanket Order 1963	6.00	15.00
88 Buddy Baker Red Baron Pizza	15.00	30.00
90 Junie Donlavey Chameleon	5.00	10.00
90 Ken Schrader Red Baron Pizza	15.00	40.00
90 Ken Schrader Sunny King	10.00	20.00
92 Daytona Circle Track Show promo blister/15,000 1992	5.00	10.00
94 Banjo Mathews Warrior Motel 1962	6.00	15.00
121 Dan Gurney Harvest Motors 1965	6.00	15.00
0 Dan Gurney LaFayette Ford 1963	6.00	15.00
0 Tiny Lund Pulliam Motor Co. 1963	6.00	15.00
03 G.C. Spencer Cottrell Bakery '63	6.00	15.00
03 Red Wickersham Bailey's Used Cars '65	6.00	15.00
06 Larry Frank Schwister Ford 1963	6.00	15.00
06 Larry Frank Schwister 1963 Ford/10,000 Southern 500 30-year Anniversary promo blister	5.00	10.00

1993 Action Racing Collectables 1:64

3/24 Dale Earnhardt Jeff Gordon Dual package Kellogg's Promo	40.00	80.00
5/24 Terry Labonte Jeff Gordon Dual package Kellogg's Promo	25.00	50.00
6 Tommy Houston Roses promo/10,000	4.00	8.00
7 Alan Kulwicki Army Promo blister/10,000 black window car	20.00	50.00
7 Alan Kulwicki Hooters 1992 Ford Thunderbird	25.00	50.00
7 Alan Kulwicki Hooters AK Racing blister/10,000	15.00	30.00

1993 Action Racing Collectables AC Racing 1:64

Each car in this set of 1:64 die cast were issued in a blue promo AC Racing blister pack. Total print run figure of 10,000 was also printed on the front.

2 Rusty Wallace Pontiac Excitement	4.00	10.00
3 Dale Earnhardt Goodwrench	12.50	25.00
4 Ernie Irvan Kodak	4.00	8.00
17 Darrell Waltrip Western Auto	6.00	15.00
24 Jeff Gordon DuPont	15.00	40.00
25 Ken Schrader GMAC	4.00	8.00
40 Kenny Wallace Dirt Devil	4.00	8.00
41 Phil Parsons AC Racing	4.00	8.00
42 Kyle Petty Mello Yello	4.00	8.00

1993 Action Racing Collectables Delco Remy 1:64

Action issued each car in this set in a black and yellow Delco Remy promo blister. The total print run figure of 10,000 was also printed on the front.

2 Rusty Wallace Pontiac Excitement	6.00	10.00
4 Ernie Irvan Kodak	5.00	8.00
17 Darrell Waltrip Western Auto	10.00	20.00

1993 Action Racing Collectables Valvoline Team 1:64

Each car in this set of 1:64 die cast were issued in a light blue checkerboard promo blister pack. The total print run figure of 10,000 was also printed on the front.

6 Mark Martin Valvoline	5.00	8.00
16 Wally Dallenbach Jr. Roush Racing	25.00	50.00
24 Jeff Gordon DuPont	20.00	35.00
25 Ken Schrader GMAC	3.00	8.00
46 Al Unser Jr. Valvoline	15.00	40.00

1993 Action/RCCA 1:64

These 1:64 scale cars were made by Action and distributed through the RCCA club. Most were distributed in a small cardboard window box printed in yellow, orange, and black with the name "Stock Car H.O. Collector Series" on it with gold foil printing on the plastic window that includes the year model and make of the car and the production run.

2 Mark Martin Miller Acrylic	7.50	15.00
2 Rusty Wallace Miller Genuine Draft Club Only	9.00	18.00
3 Richard Childress CRC Chemical 1980 Olds	6.00	12.00
6 Mark Martin Folgers Promo blister	15.00	40.00
6 Mark Martin Stroh's Light 2 car combo/15,000	30.00	50.00
6 Mark Martin Valvoline/15,000	6.00	15.00
9 Bill Elliott Melling Club Only	10.00	20.00
11 Darrell Waltrip Budweiser 1984 Monte Carlo notchback/10,080	8.00	20.00
12 Neil Bonnett Budweiser 1984 Monte Carlo notchback/16,128	7.50	15.00
12 Hut Stricklin Raybestos	2.00	5.00
17 Darrell Waltrip Superflo ASA Camaro	6.00	15.00
21 Morgan Shepherd Cheerwine Morema	5.00	12.00
24 Jeff Gordon DuPont/15,000	15.00	40.00
24 Jeff Gordon DuPont in gray box	10.00	25.00
25 Ricky Craven 1991 BGN Champion Promo	7.50	15.00
27 Rusty Wallace Kodiak 1989 Pontiac in plastic case	18.00	30.00
28 Davey Allison Havoline/28,000	12.50	25.00
28 Davey Allison Mac Tools Promo	12.50	25.00
35 Shawna Robinson Polaroid Captiva Promo blister/10,000	12.50	30.00
42 Kyle Petty Mello Yello/15,000	5.00	12.00
88 Darrell Waltrip Gatorade 1980 Monte Carlo/10,080	7.50	15.00
90 Bobby Hillin Jr. Heilig-Meyers Promo	6.00	12.00
93 Action Platinum Series Promo blister/15,000	5.00	10.00
93 RCCA Christmas Car	10.00	20.00
93 RCCA Lumina Primer/10,000	5.00	10.00
93 RCCA Pontiac Primer/10,000	5.00	10.00
93 RCCA Thunderbird Primer/10,000	5.00	10.00
94 Casey Elliott RCCA/10,000	5.00	12.00
94 Casey Elliott RCCA in a gray Grand National Series box	5.00	12.00

1994 Action Racing Collectables 1:64

These 1:64 scale cars feature some of the top cars in NASCAR racing. Action used the "Platinum Series" clamshell packaging for the first time in 1994 on this series of cars. Most pieces also include an Action trading card.

2 Ricky Craven DuPont	10.00	20.00
2 Rusty Wallace Ford Motorsports	5.00	10.00
3 Dale Earnhardt Goodwrench/16,128	15.00	40.00
3 Dale Earnhardt Goodwrench 1988 Monte Carlo Aerocoupe	30.00	60.00
3 Dale Earnhardt Wrangler 1984 Monte Carlo	25.00	60.00
3 Dale Earnhardt 16-car set	125.00	250.00
4 Sterling Marlin Kodak	5.00	12.00
5 Terry Labonte Kellogg's/10,000	4.00	10.00
11 Bill Elliott Budweiser	12.50	25.00
11 Darrell Waltrip Budweiser 1987 Monte Carlo	20.00	40.00
12 Neil Bonnett Budweiser 1987 Monte Carlo	12.00	20.00
15 Lake Speed Quality Care/10,080	3.00	8.00
16 Ted Musgrave Family Channel	3.00	8.00
24 Jeff Gordon uPont	25.00	40.00
26 Sammy Swindell Bull Hannah	3.00	8.00
28 Ernie Irvan Havoline	6.00	12.00
41 Joe Nemechek Meineke/10,080	3.00	8.00
42 Kyle Petty Mello Yello/10,080	3.00	8.00
51 Neil Bonnett Country Time	7.50	20.00
93 Lumina Prototype	4.00	8.00
93 Pontiac Prototype	4.00	8.00
93 Thunderbird Prototype	4.00	8.00
98 Derrike Cope Fingerhut	3.00	8.00
07 George Crenshaw Campbell's Promo/10,000	20.00	35.00

1994 Action/RCCA 1:64

These 1:64 scale cars were made by Action and distributed through the RCCA club. Each was distributed in a small cardboard window box printed in yellow, orange, and black with the name "Stock Car H.O. Collector Series" on it (the same as the 1993 box) or a red checkerboard pattern RCCA box with the year printed on it. All box varieties have gold foil printing on the plastic window that includes the driver's name, the year model and make of the car, and the production run.

3 Dale Earnhardt Goodwrench/16,128	25.00	50.00
3 Dale Earnhardt Goodwrench 1994 Club Only	25.00	50.00
3 Dale Earnhardt Wrangler 1985 Monte Carlo Notchback	30.00	60.00
3 Dale Earnhardt Wrangler 1987 Monte Carlo Fastback	30.00	60.00
3 Dale Earnhardt Jr. Mom 'N' Pop's/10,080	50.00	80.00
5 Terry Labonte Kellogg's	15.00	30.00
8 Kerry Earnhardt Mom-n-Pop's/10,080	10.00	20.00
11 Bill Elliott Budweiser/10,080	7.50	15.00
15 Lake Speed Quality Care/10,080	7.50	15.00
16 Ted Musgrave Family Channel/10,000	7.50	15.00
17 Darrell Waltrip Western Auto	6.00	12.00
18 Dale Jarrett Interstate Batteries/10,000	12.50	25.00
21 David Pearson Chattanooga Chew 1985 Monte Carlo/16,128	5.00	12.00
24 Jeff Gordon DuPont	18.00	30.00
27 Tim Richmond Old Milwaukee/16,128 1985 Pontiac Grand Prix	6.00	15.00
28 Davey Allison Havoline black&gold	10.00	20.00
28 Davey Allison Havoline black&orange	10.00	20.00
30 Michael Waltrip Pennzoil/10,000	6.00	12.00
38 Kelley Earnhardt Mom-n-Pop's/10,080	7.50	15.00
41 Joe Nemechek Meineke	2.00	5.00
42 Kyle Petty Mello Yello	6.00	12.00
51 Neil Bonnett Country Time	30.00	50.00
51 Neil Bonnett Country Time Promo blister	6.00	15.00
98 Derrike Cope Fingerhut	5.00	12.00

1995 Action Racing Collectables 1:64

These 1:64 scale cars feature the top cars in NASCAR racing and were issued in a cardboard window box "Platinum Series" packaging including a cardboard backer used for retail display racks. Most of the 1995 Platinum Series cars were issued with an oversized SkyBox card. In most cases, the SkyBox card was specifically made for those Platinum Series pieces and was not distributed in any other method. Action also produced their own cards for inclusion with some die-cast pieces.

2 Dale Earnhardt Wrangler 1981 Pontiac/24,912	20.00	50.00
2 Rusty Wallace Miller Geniune Draft in acrylic display case	8.00	20.00
2/43 Dale Earnhardt Goodwrench Richard Petty STP 7&7 Championship 2-car blister	25.00	50.00
3 Richard Childress Black Gold 1979	5.00	10.00
3 Dale Earnhardt Goodwrench	20.00	40.00

3 Dale Earnhardt Goodwrench Brickyard/30,000 20.00 50.00
3 Dale Earnhardt Goodwrench Silver Platinum Series 35.00 75.00
3 Dale Earnhardt Goodwrench Silver Winston Select blister 35.00 75.00
3 Dale Earnhardt Goodwrench Silver Race World blister 15.00 40.00
3 Jeff Green Goodwrench 5.00 10.00
3/24 Dale Earnhardt Jeff Gordon Brickyard Special 2-car set/25,000 25.00 60.00
4 Sterling Marlin Kodak/24,912 5.00 12.00
6 Mark Martin Folgers/24,912 20.00 40.00
6 Mark Martin Valvoline 5.00 10.00
6 Mark Martin Valvoline Brickyard Platinum Series 6.00 12.00
6 Mark Martin Valvoline Brickyard blister 5.00 12.00
7 Geoff Bodine Exide/26,928 3.00 8.00
7 Alan Kulwicki Zerex ASA Camaro/24,912 8.00 20.00
8 Dale Earnhardt ASA Camaro 1985 20.00 40.00
11 Brett Bodine Lowe's/24,912 3.00 8.00
11 Darrell Waltrip Mountain Dew 1982 Buick/20,000 7.50 20.00
11 Darrell Waltrip Pepsi Camaro ASA/16,128 5.00 10.00
17 Darrell Waltrip Tide ASA Camaro 12.50 25.00
17 Darrell Waltrip Western Auto/24,912 6.00 15.00
21 Neil Bonnett Hodgdon/16,128 1982 Thunderbird 7.50 15.00
22 Bobby Allison Miller High Life/24,912 1983 Buick in acrylic case 8.00 20.00
23 Jimmy Spencer Smokin' Joe's in acrylic case 20.00 40.00
24 Jeff Gordon uPont 10.00 25.00
24 Jeff Gordon DuPont 1995 Champion in blister package 10.00 25.00
25 Ken Schrader Budweiser/24,912 5.00 12.00
27 Tim Richmond Old Milwaukee/16,128 5.00 12.00
28 Dale Jarrett Havoline/29,808 8.00 20.00
42 Kyle Petty Coors Light in acrylic case 6.00 15.00
52 Ken Schrader AC Delco/24,912 4.00 10.00
52 Ken Schrader AC Delco Busch Promo 5.00 10.00
88 Ernie Irvan Havoline 4.00 10.00
88 Darrell Waltrip Gatorade 1980 Olds/16,128 6.00 15.00
94 Bill Elliott McDonald's 4.00 10.00
94 Bill Elliott Thunderbat 18.00 30.00
95 David Green Busch Beer 3.00 8.00

1995 Action/RCCA 1:64

These "club" cars were issued by Action for the 1995 RCCA collector's club. Each is packaged in a small cardboard window box clearly marked with the Racing Collector's Club of America notation. Some boxes were serial numbered and all cars feature opening hoods. A few were issued in acrylic, or plastic, display cases as noted below.

1 Winston Cup show car in acrylic case 8.00 20.00
2 Mark Martin Miller American 1985 ASA/10,000 10.00 20.00
2 Rusty Wallace Miller Genuine Draft in acrylic case 7.50 15.00
3 Richard Childress CRC Chemical/10,080 1980 Oldsmobile 6.00 15.00
3 Dale Earnhardt Goodwrench 1994 Lumina/16,128 15.00 40.00
3 Dale Earnhardt Goodwrench Silver 50.00 100.00
3 Dale Earnhardt Wrangler 1981 Pontiac/16,128 25.00 50.00
4 Sterling Marlin Kodak/10,080 4.00 10.00
6 Mark Martin Valvoline/10,080 6.00 15.00
6 Mark Martin Valvoline Brickyard 5.00 12.00
7 Geoff Bodine Exide/10,080 4.00 10.00
7 Alan Kulwicki Hooters/10,000 15.00 30.00
7 Alan Kulwicki Zerex/10,080 12.50 30.00
9 Ted Musgrave RCCA/10,080 4.00 10.00
10 Ricky Rudd Tide/10,080 5.00 12.00
11 Brett Bodine Lowe's/10,080 4.00 10.00
17 Darrell Waltrip Superflo Camaro ASA/10,080 6.00 15.00
17 Darrell Waltrip Western Auto/10,080 6.00 15.00
23 Jimmy Spencer Smokin' Joe's/10,080 in acrylic case 25.00 50.00
24 Jeff Gordon DuPont 1994 Lumina/16,128 10.00 20.00
25 Ken Schrader Budweiser 7.50 15.00
26 Steve Kinser Quaker State 6.00 15.00
27 Rusty Wallace Kodiak 1989 Grand Prix in plastic case/20,000 20.00 35.00
28 Dale Jarrett Havoline 6.00 15.00
42 Kyle Petty Coors Light/15,000 in acrylic case 5.00 12.00
42 Kyle Petty Coors Light Pumpkin in acrylic case/15,000 30.00 60.00
88 Ernie Irvan Havoline/15,000 5.00 10.00
88 Darrell Waltrip Gatorade/10,080 6.00 15.00
94 Bill Elliott McDonald's/16,128 6.00 15.00
94 Bill Elliott McDonald's Thunderbat 8.00 20.00
95 David Green Busch Beer 6.00 15.00

1995-96 Action Racing Collectables SuperTrucks 1:64

These pieces are 1:64 scale replicas of the SuperTrucks that race in the NASCAR SuperTruck Series. Each was issued in a blister pack.

3 Mike Skinner Goodwrench 1995 5.00 12.00
3 Mike Skinner Goodwrench 1996 5.00 10.00
6 Rick Carelli Total Petroleum 1995 4.00 8.00
7 Geoff Bodine Exide 3.00 8.00
7 Geoff Bodine Exide 20.00 45.00
16 Ron Hornaday Action '95 5.00 10.00
16 Ron Hornaday NAPA '96 5.00 10.00
16 Ron Hornaday Papa John's Pizza 1995 6.00 15.00
24 Scott Lagasse DuPont/24,912 1995 6.00 15.00
24 Jack Sprague Quaker State 1996 5.00 12.00
28 Ernie Irvan NAPA/18,000 6.00 12.00
52 Ken Schrader AC Delco 3.00 8.00
71 Kenji Momota Action/18,000 3.00 6.00
84 Joe Ruttman Mac Tools/18,000 3.00 6.00
98 Butch Miller Raybestos/24,912 3.00 6.00

1996 Action Racing Collectables 1:64

Most of these 1:64 scale cards were issued as part of the Platinum Series. Cars with alcohol and/or tobacco sponsorship were packaged in clear plastic cases.

2 Mark Martin Miller American 1985 ASA/20,000 5.00 12.00
2 Rusty Wallace Miller Genuine Draft 6.00 15.00
2 Rusty Wallace Miller Genuine Draft Silver 25th Anniversary 6.00 15.00
3 Dale Earnhardt AC-Delco Japan 12.50 30.00
3 Dale Earnhardt Goodwrench 12.50 30.00
3 Dale Earnhardt Goodwrench Race Day Blister 10.00 25.00
3 Dale Earnhardt Goodwrench Pit Stop blister 6.00 15.00
3 Dale Earnhardt Olympic Hood Open clear windows blister 12.50 30.00
3 Dale Earnhardt Olympic black windows blister 10.00 25.00
3 Dale Earnhardt Olympic HO clear windows blue box 20.00 50.00
5 Terry Labonte Kellogg's Iron Man Silver 6.00 15.00
5 Terry Labonte Kellogg's Japan 6.00 15.00
6 Mark Martin Valvoline 4.00 10.00
6 Mark Martin Valvoline Race Day blister 4.00 8.00
7 Geoff Bodine Exide 2.50 6.00
10 Ricky Rudd Tide 3.00 8.00
14 Jeff Green Racing For Kids 5.00 10.00
18 Bobby Labonte Interstate Batteries 3.00 8.00
18 Bobby Labonte Interstate Batteries Pro Football Hall of Fame 7.50 20.00
21 Michael Waltrip Citgo 3.00 8.00
21 Michael Waltrip Citgo Star Trek 6.00 15.00
22 Bobby Allison Miller American/10,080 1985 Monte Carlo 6.00 12.00
22 Ward Burton MBNA 3.00 8.00
24 Jeff Gordon uPont Monte Carlo 7.50 15.00
24 Jeff Gordon DuPont Race Day blister 5.00 10.00
25 Tim Richmond Folgers 1987 Monte Carlo 6.00 15.00
28 Davey Allison Vinyl Tech 1987 5.00 12.00
28 Ernie Irvan Havoline 5.00 10.00
29 Steve Grissom Flintstones 4.00 10.00
29 Steve Grissom WCW 4.00 10.00
29 No Driver Association Scooby-Doo 5.00 10.00
30 Johnny Benson Pennzoil 4.00 10.00
42 Kyle Petty Coors Light 6.00 12.00
42 Kyle Petty Coors Light Black 10.00 20.00
43 Bobby Hamilton STP '72 Blue 4.00 10.00
43 Bobby Hamilton STP '72 Blue&Red 4.00 10.00
43 Bobby Hamilton STP '79 Blue&Red red sides blue roof 4.00 10.00
43 Bobby Hamilton STP '84 Blue&Red blue sides w red stripes 4.00 10.00
43 Bobby Hamilton STP Silver 25th Anniversary 6.00 15.00
57 Jason Keller Halloween Havoc 3.00 8.00
88 Ernie Irvan Havoline 5.00 12.00
88 Dale Jarrett Quality Care 5.00 10.00
94 Bill Elliott McDonald's 4.00 10.00
96 David Green Caterpillar 3.00 8.00

1996 Action/RCCA 1:64

These 1:64 scale cars were made by Action and distributed through their club -- RCCA. Most of the cars were produced as hood open models and packaged in boxes in contrast to their basic issue Action counterparts which are typically issued in blister packs.

2 Rusty Wallace Miller Genuine Draft 7.50 15.00
2 Rusty Wallace Miller Genuine Draft Silver 25th Anniversary in plastic case 10.00 20.00
3 Dale Earnhardt AC Delco 10.00 25.00
3 Dale Earnhardt Goodwrench/20,000 12.50 30.00
4 Sterling Marlin Kodak 6.00 15.00
5 Terry Labonte Kellogg's Iron Man Silver/10,000 10.00 25.00
5 Terry Labonte Kellogg's Japan 7.50 20.00
6 Mark Martin Valvoline/10,000 5.00 12.00
7 Geoff Bodine Exide 5.00 12.00
14 Jeff Green Racing For Kids/10,000 5.00 12.00
15 Dale Earnhardt Wrangler 1982 Thunderbird/20,000 10.00 25.00
17 Darrell Waltrip Tide 1988 Monte Carlo/10,080 5.00 12.00
18 Bobby Labonte Interstate Batteries/10,000 6.00 15.00
18 Bobby Labonte Interstate Batteries Pro Football Hall of Fame/10,000 10.00 25.00
21 Michael Waltrip Citgo Star Trek/10,000 6.00 15.00
24 Jeff Gordon DuPont/15,000 10.00 20.00
25 Tim Richmond Folgers 1987 Monte Carlo/10,000 10.00 20.00
28 Ernie Irvan Havoline/10,000 6.00 15.00
29 Steve Grissom Flintstones 7.50 15.00
29 No Driver Association Scooby-Doo 7.50 15.00
30 Johnny Benson Pennzoil/10,000 5.00 12.00
42 Kyle Petty Coors Light 5.00 12.00
42 Kyle Petty Coors Light Black in plastic case/10,000 10.00 20.00
43 Bobby Hamilton STP Silver/10,000 6.00 15.00
57 Jason Keller Halloween Havoc/8000 5.00 12.00
88 Dale Jarrett Quality Care 6.00 15.00
94 Bill Elliott McDonald's/10,000 6.00 15.00

1997 Action Racing Collectables 1:64

Most of these 1:64 scale cards were issued as part of the Platinum Series. Cars with alcohol and/or tobacco sponsorship are packaged in acrylic cases.

2 Rusty Wallace Miller Lite 6.00 12.00
2 Rusty Wallace Miller Japan/12,000 6.00 15.00
2 Rusty Wallace Miller Lite Texas 7.50 15.00
3 Dale Earnhardt AC Delco 12.50 25.00
3 Dale Earnhardt AC Delco Black Window blister 10.00 25.00
3 Dale Earnhardt Goodwrench 10.00 25.00
3 Dale Earnhardt Goodwrench Brickyard/14,256 12.50 25.00
3 Dale Earnhardt Goodwrench Plus in blister 12.50 30.00
3 Dale Earnhardt Goodwrench Plus in box 20.00 40.00
3 Dale Earnhardt Wheaties 20.00 40.00
3 Dale Earnhardt Wheaties Black Window blister 12.50 25.00
3 Dale Earnhardt Wheaties Hood Open Sports Image 25.00 60.00
3 Dale Earnhardt Wheaties Mail-In 12.50 25.00
3 Steve Park AC Delco/12,024 10.00 20.00
3 Ricky Rudd Piedmont 1983 Monte Carlo/10,080 10.00 20.00
4 Sterling Marlin Kodak 5.00 12.00
6 Mark Martin Valvoline 5.00 10.00
9 Jeff Burton Track Gear 4.00 8.00
10 Ricky Rudd Tide/9000 5.00 10.00
10 Ricky Rudd Tide Mac Tools/1000 5.00 10.00
11 Brett Bodine Close Call/10,944 2.50 6.00
12 Kenny Wallace Gray Bar 3.00 8.00
14 Steve Park Burger King 12.00 20.00
16 Ted Musgrave Primestar/12,080 3.00 6.00
17 Darrell Waltrip Parts America Blue&White 4.00 10.00
17 Darrell Waltrip Parts America Chrome Box 6.00 15.00
17 Darrell Waltrip Parts America Green with green number 4.00 10.00
17 Darrell Waltrip Parts America Green with white number 4.00 10.00
17 Darrell Waltrip Parts America Orange 4.00 10.00
17 Darrell Waltrip Parts America Red&White 4.00 10.00
17 Darrell Waltrip Parts America Yellow&White 4.00 10.00
18 Bobby Labonte Interstate Batteries 5.00 12.00
22 Ward Burton MBNA 4.00 10.00
22 Ward Burton MBNA Gold/11,016 5.00 12.00
23 Jimmy Spencer Camel 12.50 25.00
24 Jeff Gordon DuPont 8.00 20.00
24 Jeff Gordon DuPont Bickyard/14,256 8.00 20.00
24 Jeff Gordon DuPont Million Dollar Date 8.00 20.00
24 Jeff Gordon DuPont Million Dollar Date black windows 8.00 20.00
24 Jeff Gordon DuPont Million Dollar Date Mac Tools black window 8.00 20.00
24 Jeff Gordon DuPont ChromaPremier/25,000 15.00 40.00
24 Jeff Gordon Jurassic Park 3 10.00 25.00
24 Jeff Gordon Jurassic Park 3 black window blister 8.00 20.00
24 Jeff Gordon Jurassic Park 3 Hood Open Sports Image 15.00 40.00
24 Jeff Gordon 3-Car Promo blister DuPont car DuPont Million Dollar Jurassic Park 3 10.00 20.00
25 Ricky Craven Budweiser 4.00 10.00
26 Rich Bickle KFC 4.00 10.00
27 Kenny Irwin G.I. Joe 7.50 15.00
27 Kenny Irwin Tonka/10,080 6.00 15.00
27 Rusty Wallace Miller Genuine Draft 1990 Grand Prix/10,080 35.00 60.00
29 Jeff Green Tom & Jerry/12,888 5.00 12.00
29 Elliott Sadler Phillips 66 4.00 10.00
31 Mike Skinner Lowe's 4.00 10.00
31 Mike Skinner Lowe's Blister Pack 4.00 10.00
31 Mike Skinner Lowe's Japan 4.00 10.00
32 Dale Jarrett White Rain/10,080 5.00 12
36 Todd Bodine Stanley 4.00 10
36 Derrike Cope Skittles 3.00 8
37 Mark Green Timber Wolf 5.00 12
37 Jeremy Mayfield K-Mart RC-Cola 4.00 10
40 Robby Gordon Coors Light/12,024 5.00 12
41 Steve Grissom Kodiak/7500 5.00 12
46 Wally Dallenbach First Union/10,080 3.00 8
60 Mark Martin Winn Dixie 5.00 12
71 Dave Marcis Realtree 6.00 15
75 Rick Mast Remington/10,080 4.00 10.
75 Rick Mast Remington Camo 4.00 10.
77 Bobby Hillin Jr. Jasper 4.00 10.
81 Kenny Wallace Square D/16,488 4.00 10.
88 Dale Jarrett Quality Care 4.00 10.
88 Dale Jarrett Quality Care Brickyard/14,256 4.00 10.
94 Bill Elliott McDonald's 5.00 12.
94 Bill Elliott Mac Tonight 4.00 10.
96 David Green Caterpillar 3.00 10.
99 Jeff Burton Exide 4.00 10.
00 Buckshot Jones Aqua Fresh 3.00 8.

1997 Action/RCCA 1:64

These 1:64 scale cars were made by Action and distrib through their collector's club (RCCA). All cars have ope hoods and were packaged in small clear window boxes.

1 Gargoyles 300 Promo/5000 3.00 6.0
2 Rusty Wallace Miller Lite 8.00 16.0
2 Rusty Wallace Miller Japan 9.00 18.0
2 Rusty Wallace Miller Lite Texas 9.00 18.0
3 Dale Earnhardt AC Delco/20,000 20.00 40.0
3 Dale Earnhardt Goodwrench/5000 30.00 50.0
3 Dale Earnhardt Goodwrench Plus/25,000 10.00 25.0
3 Dale Earnhardt Lowes Foods 30.00 60.0
3 Dale Earnhardt Wheaties 30.00 60.0
3 Steve Park AC Delco 15.00 30.0
4 Sterling Marlin Kodak/5000 5.00 12.0
6 Mark Martin Valvoline/5000 6.00 15.0
9 Jeff Burton Track Gear/3500 7.50 15.0
10 Ricky Rudd Tide 8.00 16.0
11 Brett Bodine Close Call/5000 4.00 10.0
12 Kenny Wallace Gray Bar/3500 5.00 12.0
14 Steve Park Burger King 15.00 30.00
16 Ted Musgrave Primestar/5000 4.00 10.00
17 Darrell Waltrip Parts America Blue&White/5000 5.00 12.00
17 Darrell Waltrip Parts America Chrome/5000 10.00 20.00
17 Darrell Waltrip Parts America Green with green number/5000 5.00 12.00
17 Darrell Waltrip Parts America Green with white number/5000 5.00 12.00
17 Darrell Waltrip Parts America Orange/5000 5.00 12.00
17 Darrell Waltrip Parts America Red&White/5000 5.00 12.00
17 Darrell Waltrip Parts America Yellow&White/5000 5.00 12.00
18 Bobby Labonte Interstate Batteries/5000 10.00 20.00
22 Ward Burton MBNA 8.00 16.00
22 Ward Burton MBNA Gold 8.00 16.00
23 Jimmy Spencer Camel/5000 25.00 40.00
24 Jeff Gordon DuPont/5000 18.00 30.00
24 Jeff Gordon DuPont Million Dollar Date/25,000 12.50 25.00
24 Jeff Gordon DuPont ChromaPremier 25.00 50.00
24 Jeff Gordon Jurassic Park 3 18.00 30.00
24 Jeff Gordon Jurassic Park 3 w card set 30.00 50.00
25 Ricky Craven Budweiser 6.00 15.00
26 Rich Bickle KFC/5000 6.00 15.00
27 Kenny Irwin G.I. Joe/7500 8.00 20.00
27 Kenny Irwin 8.00 20.00

Tonka
Jeff Green 6.00 15.00
Tom & Jerry/5000
Elliott Sadler 5.00 12.00
Phillips 66/3500
Mike Skinner 6.00 15.00
Lowe's
Mike Skinner 6.00 15.00
Lowe's Japan
Dale Jarrett 5.00 12.00
White Rain/3500
Todd Bodine 5.00 10.00
Stanley/5000
Derrike Cope 5.00 12.00
Skittles
Mark Green 5.00 12.00
Timber Wolf/5000
Jeremy Mayfield 5.00 12.00
K-Mart RC-Cola/5000
Steve Grissom 5.00 12.00
Kodiak/5000
Wally Dallenbach 5.00 12.00
First Union/3500
Mark Martin 8.00 16.00
Winn Dixie
Dave Marcis 10.00 25.00
Realtree
Rick Mast 5.00 12.00
Remington/5000
Rick Mast 6.00 12.00
Remington Camo
Bobby Hillin Jr. 5.00 12.00
Jasper/5000
Kenny Wallace 5.00 12.00
Square D/5000
Dale Jarrett 10.00 20.00
Quality Care/5000
Mike Skinner 12.50 25.00
Llumar SuperTruck Promo
Bill Elliott 8.00 16.00
McDonald's/5000
Bill Elliott 10.00 20.00
Mac Tonight
David Green 5.00 12.00
Caterpillar
Chad Little 5.00 12.00
John Deere
Chad Little 8.00 16.00
John Deere
160th Anniversary/10,080
Jeff Burton 5.00 12.00
Exide/5000
) Buckshot Jones 5.00 12.00
Aqua Fresh/3500

1998 Action Racing Collectables 1:64

Most of these 1:64 scale cards were issued as part of the Platinum Series. Cars with alcohol and/or tobacco sponsorship are packaged in acrylic cases.

Dale Earnhardt Jr. 6.00 15.00
Coke Bear
Steve Park 6.00 15.00
Pennzoil Black Roof/15,000
Steve Park 6.00 15.00
Pennzoil Yellow Roof
Steve Park 10.00 20.00
Darrell Waltrip
Pennzoil
2-car set in tin
Darrell Waltrip 6.00 15.00
Pennzoil
2 Rusty Wallace 6.00 15.00
Adventures of Rusty
2 Rusty Wallace 6.00 15.00
Miller Lite
2 Rusty Wallace 6.00 15.00
Miller Lite Elvis
2 Rusty Wallace 6.00 15.00
Miller Lite TCB Elvis
2/12 Rusty Wallace 8.00 20.00
Jeremy Mayfield
2-car set
on pit wall base
3 Dale Earnhardt 12.50 30.00
Coke/10,000
3 Dale Earnhardt 12.50 30.00
Goodwrench Plus
3 Dale Earnhardt 15.00 30.00
Goodwrench Plus Blister Pack
3 Dale Earnhardt 10.00 25.00
Goodwrench Plus Daytona Win
3 Dale Earnhardt 20.00 40.00
Goodwrench Plus Bass Pro
3 Dale Earnhardt Jr. 15.00 25.00
AC Delco
3 Dale Earnhardt Jr. 12.00 20.00
AC Delco
1998 BGN Champ blister
4 Bobby Hamilton 3.00 8.00
Kodak
5 Terry Labonte 5.00 12.00
Kellogg's/9000
5 Terry Labonte 5.00 12.00
Blasted Fruit Loops
5 Terry Labonte 5.00 12.00
Kellogg's Corny/15,000
5 Terry Labonte 5.00 12.00
Kellogg's Ironman
8 Dale Earnhardt 10.00 25.00
10,000 RPM 1975 Dodge
8 Hut Stricklin 3.00 8.00
Circuit City/10,080
9 Jerry Nadeau 15.00 30.00
Power Puff/7560
9 Jerry Nadeau 6.00 12.00
Scooby Zombie Island
9 Lake Speed 5.00 12.00
Birthday Cake/12,000
9 Lake Speed 5.00 12.00
Huckleberry Hound/15,000
10 Ricky Rudd 5.00 10.00
Tide/9000
10 Ricky Rudd 5.00 12.00
Tide Mac Tools/1000
10 Ricky Rudd 5.00 10.00
Give Kids the World
12 Jeremy Mayfield 4.00 10.00
Mobil 1
14 Patty Moise 5.00 12.00
Rhodes Xena/12,024
18 Bobby Labonte 5.00 12.00
Interstate Batteries
18 Bobby Labonte 5.00 12.00
Interstate Batteries Hot Rod
18 Bobby Labonte 5.00 12.00
Interstate Batteries Small Soldiers
22 Ward Burton 4.00 10.00
MBNA/10,080
23 Jimmy Spencer 7.50 15.00
No Bull
24 Jeff Gordon 7.50 15.00
DuPont
24 Jeff Gordon 7.50 15.00
DuPont Brickyard Winner/10,024
24 Jeff Gordon 10.00 25.00
DuPont Chromalusion
24 Jeff Gordon 7.50 15.00
DuPont No Bull
28 Kenny Irwin 4.00 8.00
Havoline
28 Kenny Irwin 7.50 15.00
Havoline Joker
30 Derrike Cope 3.00 8.00
Gumout/10,080
31 Dale Earnhardt Jr. 15.00 25.00
Sikkens Blue
1997 Monte Carlo
31 Mike Skinner 4.00 10.00
Lowe's
31 Mike Skinner 4.00 10.00
Lowe's Special Olympic
32 Dale Jarrett 4.00 8.00
White Rain
32 Dale Jarrett 6.00 15.00
White Rain Promo
in die cut blister
35 Todd Bodine 6.00 12.00
Tabasco Orange
35 Todd Bodine 6.00 12.00
Tabasco Red
36 Ernie Irvan 9.00 18.00
M&M's
36 Ernie Irvan 6.00 12.00
Skittles/10,080
36 Ernie Irvan 7.50 15.00
Wildberry Skittles
40 Sterling Marlin 6.00 15.00
Coors Light/7560
41 Steve Grissom 7.50 15.00
Kodiak
44 Tony Stewart 12.50 25.00
Shell/10,080
44 Tony Stewart 12.50 25.00
Shell Small Soldiers/16,992
50 Ricky Craven 5.00 10.00
Budweiser
50 NDA 6.00 12.00
Bud Louie
72 Mike Dillon 5.00 10.00
Detroit Gasket
75 Rick Mast 3.00 8.00
Remington/12,024
75 Rick Mast 4.00 8.00
Remington Mac Tools/1000
81 Kenny Wallace 4.00 8.00
Square D
81 Kenny Wallace 4.00 8.00
Square D Lightning
88 Dale Jarrett 6.00 12.00
Quality Care
88 Dale Jarrett 8.00 20.00
Batman
90 Dick Trickle 4.00 10.00
Heilig-Meyers/12,024
96 David Green 3.00 8.00
Caterpillar/10,080
300 Darrell Waltrip 6.00 12.00
Flock Special
00 Buckshot Jones 4.00 10.00
Alka Seltzer/11,016
K2 Dale Earnhardt 12.50 30.00
Dayvault's Dark Roof
1956 Ford
K2 Dale Earnhardt 12.50 30.00
Dayvault's Pink Roof
1956 Ford

1998 Action/RCCA 1:64

These were the 1:64 scale cars that were made by Action and distributed through the club (RCCA). All cars have open hoods. These cars are packaged in boxes in contrast to their ARC counterparts.

1 Dale Earnhardt Jr. 15.00 30.00
Coke Bear
1 Jeff Gordon 20.00 35.00
Baby Ruth 1992 Thunderbird
1 Steve Park 18.00 30.00
Pennzoil Black Roof
1 Darrell Waltrip 9.00 18.00
Pennzoil
2 Rusty Wallace 10.00 20.00
Adventures of Rusty
2 Rusty Wallace 6.00 15.00
Miller Lite/7500
2 Rusty Wallace 10.00 20.00
Miller Lite Elvis
2 Rusty Wallace 10.00 20.00
Miller Lite TCB Elivs
3 Dale Earnhardt 25.00 50.00
Coke
3 Dale Earnhardt 15.00 40.00
Goodwrench Plus
3 Dale Earnhardt 40.00 80.00
Goodwrench Plus Bass Pro
3 Dale Earnhardt 12.50 25.00
Goodwrench Plus
Fan Club box
3 Dale Earnhardt Jr. 20.00 40.00
AC Delco/3500
3 Race Rock Promo/10,080 6.00 12.00
4 Bobby Hamilton 6.00 15.00
Kodak/5000
5 Terry Labonte 6.00 15.00
Blasted Fruit Loops/7500
5 Terry Labonte 6.00 15.00
Kellogg's/5000
5 Terry Labonte 7.50 15.00
Kellogg's Corny
5 Terry Labonte 7.50 15.00
Kellogg's Ironman/10,000
8 Dale Earnhardt 12.50 30.00
RPM 1975 Dodge/12,500
8 Hut Stricklin 6.00 15.00
Circuit City/2500
9 Jerry Nadeau 7.50 15.00
Scooby Zombie Island/3550
9 Lake Speed 6.00 15.00
Birthday Cake
9 Lake Speed 6.00 15.00
Huckleberry Hound/5000
10 Ricky Rudd 6.00 15.00
Tide/3500
12 Jeremy Mayfield 6.00 15.00
Mobil 1/5000
14 Patty Moise 6.00 15.00
Rhodes Xena/3500
18 Bobby Labonte 7.50 15.00
Interstate Batteries
18 Bobby Labonte 15.00 30.00
Interstate Batteries Hot Rod
18 Bobby Labonte 7.50 15.00
Interstate Batteries
Small Soldiers/10,000
24 Jeff Gordon 10.00 20.00
DuPont
24 Jeff Gordon 20.00 40.00
DuPont Chromalusion/15,000
24 Jeff Gordon 15.00 25.00
DuPont No Bull
28 Kenny Irwin 6.00 15.00
Havoline/7500
28 Kenny Irwin 6.00 15.00
Havoline Joker/7500
31 Dale Earnhardt Jr. 20.00 40.00
Sikkens Blue
1997 Monte Carlo
31 Mike Skinner 6.00 15.00
Lowe's/5000
31 Mike Skinner 7.50 15.00
Lowe's Special Olympics
32 Dale Jarrett 7.50 15.00
White Rain/2500
35 Todd Bodine 6.00 15.00
Tabasco Orange&White
35 Todd Bodine 6.00 15.00
Tabasco Red&Black/7500
36 Ernie Irvan 7.50 15.00
Skittles
36 Ernie Irvan 7.50 15.00
Wildberry Skittles/5000
41 Steve Grissom 7.50 15.00
Kodiak/3500
44 Tony Stewart 15.00 30.00
Shell/3500
44 Tony Stewart 12.50 25.00
Shell Small Soldiers/7500
50 Ricky Craven 6.00 15.00
Bud/3500
81 Kenny Wallace 6.00 15.00
Square D/3500
81 Kenny Wallace 7.50 15.00
Square D Lightning
88 Dale Jarrett 7.50 15.00
Quality Care/5000
88 Dale Jarrett 7.50 15.00
Batman
90 Dick Trickle 6.00 15.00
Heilig-Meyers
98 Greg Sacks 6.00 15.00
Thorn Apple Valley/2500
300 Darrell Waltrip 8.00 18.00
Tim Flock Special
K2 Dale Earnhardt 12.50 30.00
Dayvault's Pink Roof
1956 Ford
NNO NASCAR 50th Anniversary 5.00 12.00
SuperTruck/7500

1999 Action Performance 1:64

These cars were issued in an "AP" Action Performance blister packs. Each package includes the year on the front along with a checkered flag background design and a black and red AP logo.

3 Dale Earnhardt 10.00 20.00
Goodwrench
3 Dale Earnhardt Jr. 5.00 12.00
AC Delco in AP box
3 Dale Earnhardt Jr. 5.00 10.00
AC Delco Promo Blister
20 Tony Stewart 10.00 20.00
Home Depot HO in box
24 Jeff Gordon 5.00 10.00
DuPont
28 Andy Kirby 3.00 8.00
Williams Promo
36 Ken Schrader 3.00 6.00
M&M's Promo
88 Dale Jarrett 4.00 8.00
Quality Care

1999 Action Racing Collectables 1:64

These 1:64 scale cards were issued as part of the Platinum Series. The Alcohol/Tobacco cars were released on a pit wall base.

1 Jeff Gordon 7.50 15.00
Carolina 1991 Thunderbird
1 Jeff Gordon 6.00 12.00
Baby Ruth 1992 Thunderbird
1 Steve Park 5.00 12.00
Pennzoil/9000
1 Steve Park 5.00 12.00
Pennzoil Shark/9000
2 Rusty Wallace 6.00 15.00
Miller Lite
2 Rusty Wallace 5.00 12.00
Miller Lite Harley
2 Rusty Wallace 6.00 15.00
Miller Lite Last Lap
2 Rusty Wallace 6.00 12.00
Miller Lite Texas
3 Dale Earnhardt 12.50 30.00
Goodwrench
3 Dale Earnhardt 12.50 30.00
Goodwrench 25th Anniversary
3 Dale Earnhardt 15.00 40.00
Goodwrench Sign
3 Dale Earnhardt 12.50 30.00
Goodwrench Last Lap
3 Dale Earnhardt 15.00 40.00
Wrangler
3 Dale Earnhardt Jr. 6.00 15.00
AC Delco
3 Dale Earnhardt Jr. 6.00 15.00
AC Delco Promo/10,080
3 Dale Earnhardt Jr. 7.50 20.00
AC Delco Last Lap
3 Dale Earnhardt Jr. 7.50 20.00
AC Delco Superman
4 Bobby Hamilton 4.00 10.00
Advantix
5 Terry Labonte 6.00 15.00
Kellogg's/10,080
5 Terry Labonte 6.00 15.00
Kellogg's Mac Tools/1008
5 Terry Labonte 6.00 15.00
K-Sentials
5 Terry Labonte 7.50 20.00
Kellogg's NASCAR Racers
5 Terry Labonte 5.00 12.00
Rice Krispies
8 Dale Earnhardt Jr. 12.50 25.00
Bud
8 Dale Earnhardt Jr. 10.00 20.00
Bud Atlanta/10,080
8 Dale Earnhardt Jr. 10.00 20.00
Bud Michigan/10,080
8 Dale Earnhardt Jr. 10.00 20.00
Bud New Hampshire/10,080
8 Dale Earnhardt Jr. 10.00 20.00
Bud Richmond/10,080
9 Jerry Nadeau 5.00 12.00
Dexter's Lab/12,024
9 Jerry Nadeau 5.00 12.00
Jetsons/12,024
10 Ricky Rudd 4.00 10.00
Tide Kids blister package
11 Dale Jarrett 5.00 12.00
Rayovac
11 Dale Jarrett 5.00 12.00
Green Bay
12 Jeremy Mayfield 4.00 10.00
Mobil 1
12 Jeremy Mayfield 4.00 10.00
Mobil 1 Kentucky Derby
12 Jeremy Mayfield 5.00 12.00
Mobil 1 Kentucky Derby
2-car Promo blister
15 Ken Schrader 4.00 10.00
Oakwood Homes/7056
16 Ron Hornaday 6.00 12.00
NAPA Superman
SuperTruck
17 Matt Kenseth 7.50 15.00
DeWalt 1997 Monte Carlo/7056
18 Bobby Labonte 6.00 15.00
Interstate Batteries
18 Bobby Labonte 7.50 20.00
Interstate Batteries NASCAR Racers
18 Bobby Labonte 6.00 15.00
MBNA/7488
20 Tony Stewart 25.00 50.00
Home Depot/10,080
20 Tony Stewart 5.00 12.00
Home Depot Promo blister
20 Tony Stewart 10.00 25.00
Home Depot Habitat
20 Tony Stewart 6.00 15.00
Home Depot
Habitat
2-car promo set
21 Elliott Sadler 4.00 10.00
Citgo
22 Ward Burton 6.00 15.00
Caterpillar/8280
23 Jimmy Spencer 6.00 15.00
No Bull
23 Jimmy Spencer 6.00 15.00
No Bull Mac Tools
23 Jimmy Spencer 6.00 15.00
Winston Lights
24 Jeff Gordon 6.00 15.00
DuPont
24 Jeff Gordon 15.00 30.00
DuPont NASCAR Racers
24 Jeff Gordon 6.00 15.00
DuPont Superman
24 Jeff Gordon 8.00 20.00
Pepsi/10,000
24 Jeff Gordon 8.00 20.00
Pepsi Star Wars
25 W.Dallenbach 4.00 10.00
Budweiser
27 Casey Atwood 6.00 15.00
Castrol/8064
27 Casey Atwood 6.00 15.00
Castrol Last Lap/12,024
28 Kenny Irwin 5.00 10.00
Havoline/10,080
28 Kenny Irwin 5.00 10.00
Havoline Mac Tools/1008
28/88 Kenny Irwin 15.00 30.00
Dale Jarrett
Batman & Joker
30 Dale Earnhardt 15.00 30.00
Army '76 Malibu
31 Dale Earnhardt Jr. 8.00 18.00
Gargoyles
1997 Monte Carlo/10,080
31 Dale Earnhardt Jr. 10.00 20.00
Sikkens White
1997 Monte Carlo
31 Dale Earnhardt Jr. 18.00 30.00
Wrangler 1997 Monte Carlo
31 Mike Skinner 4.00 10.00
Lowe's
33 Ken Schrader 6.00 15.00
Skoal
36 Ernie Irvan 6.00 15.00
M&M's/13,032
36 Ernie Irvan 10.00 20.00
M&M's Millennium
Red on package
36 Ernie Irvan 10.00 20.00
M&M's Millennium
Yellow on package
36 Ernie Irvan 6.00 15.00
M&M's Millennium
Countdown/14,040
36 Ernie Irvan 5.00 12.00
Crispy M&M's
36 Ernie Irvan 6.00 15.00
Pedigree/7056
36 Tim Fedewa 4.00 10.00
Stanley
40 Coca-Cola 600 3.00 8.00
40 Kerry Earnhardt 6.00 15.00
Channellock
40 Sterling Marlin 5.00 12.00
Coors Light
40 Sterling Marlin 5.00 12.00
Coors Light
Brooks & Dunn
40 Sterling Marlin 5.00 12.00
Coors Light John Wayne
55 Kenny Wallace 4.00 10.00
Square D
55 Kenny Wallace 6.00 15.00
Square D NASCAR Racers
66 Darrell Waltrip 5.00 12.00
Big K Route 66
ictory Tour/10,080
71 Dave Marcis 8.00 20.00
Realtree
77 Dale Earnhardt 12.50 25.00
HyGain 1976 Malibu
88 Dale Jarrett 5.00 12.00
Quality Care/14,876
88 Dale Jarrett 8.00 20.00
Quality Care White/14,976
88 Dale Jarrett 25.00 50.00
Quality Care and
Quality Care White 2 Car Tin
88 Dale Jarrett 7.50 15.00
Quality Care Last Lap
99 Cracker Barrel 500 6.00 12.00
Promo in clear box
00 Buckshot Jones 4.00 10.00
Crown Fiber/9000
NNO Superman 9-car set in tin 60.00 110.00

1999 Action/RCCA 1:64

These car were available only through the club, and were very limited. All cars have opening hoods.

1 Jeff Gordon 12.00 20.00
Carolina 1991 Thunderbird
1 Steve Park 8.00 18.00
Pennzoil/5000
1 Steve Park 10.00 20.00
Pennzoil Shark/3500
2 Rusty Wallace 7.50 20.00
Miller Lite/5000
2 Rusty Wallace 7.50 20.00
Miller Lite
Last Lap/3000
2 Rusty Wallace 6.00 15.00
Miller Lite Harley/7500
2 Rusty Wallace 6.00 15.00
Wallace Fan Club
3 Dale Earnhardt 15.00 40.00
Goodwrench/10,000
3 Dale Earnhardt 15.00 40.00
Goodwrench
25th Anniversary/10,000
3 Dale Earnhardt 15.00 40.00
Goodwrench Sign/10,000
3 Dale Earnhardt 12.50 30.00
Goodwrench Sign
Last Lap/15,000
3 Dale Earnhardt 20.00 50.00
Wrangler/15,192
3 Dale Earnhardt Jr. 12.50 25.00
AC Delco/10,000
3 Dale Earnhardt Jr. 7.50 20.00
AC Delco Last Lap
3 Dale Earnhardt Jr. 10.00 20.00
AC Delco Superman
4 Bobby Hamilton 7.50 15.00
Advantix

5 Terry Labonte Kellogg's/4500 7.50 15.00
5 Terry Labonte K-Sentials 7.50 15.00
5 NASCAR Cafe Promo/10,000 10.00 20.00
8 Dale Earnhardt Jr. Bud 12.50 30.00
8 Dale Earnhardt Jr. Bud Atlanta/3500 10.00 20.00
8 Dale Earnhardt Jr. Bud Michigan/3500 10.00 20.00
8 Dale Earnhardt Jr. Bud New Hampshire/3500 10.00 20.00
8 Dale Earnhardt Jr. Bud Richmond/3500 10.00 20.00
9 Jerry Nadeau Dexter's Lab/3500 7.50 15.00
9 Jerry Nadeau Jetsons/3500 7.50 15.00
10 Ricky Rudd Tide/2500 10.00 20.00
11 Dale Jarrett Green Bay Packers/2500 25.00 50.00
12 Jeremy Mayfield Mobil 1/3500 7.50 15.00
12 Jeremy Mayfield Mobil 1 Kentucky Derby 7.50 15.00
17 Matt Kenseth DeWalt 1997 Monte Carlo/3000 12.00 20.00
18 Bobby Labonte Interstate Batteries 8.00 18.00
20 Tony Stewart Home Depot/3500 35.00 60.00
20 Tony Stewart Home Depot Habitat 15.00 30.00
21 Elliott Sadler Citgo/2500 7.50 15.00
23 Jimmy Spencer No Bull/5000 6.00 15.00
23 Jimmy Spencer Winston Lights/5000 6.00 15.00
24 Jeff Gordon DuPont/15,000 7.50 20.00
24 Jeff Gordon DuPont NASCAR Racers/10,000 20.00 40.00
24 Jeff Gordon DuPont Superman 7.50 20.00
24 Jeff Gordon Pepsi/10,000 7.50 20.00
24 Jeff Gordon Pepsi Star Wars/15,000 10.00 25.00
25 Wally Dallenbach Bud/2508 6.00 15.00
25 Dura Lube Promo 5.00 10.00
27 Casey Atwood Castrol/2500 7.50 20.00
27 Casey Atwood Castrol Last Lap/3000 7.50 20.00
28 Kenny Irwin Havoline/3500 6.00 15.00
30 Dale Earnhardt Army 1976 Malibu/5000 25.00 50.00
31 Dale Earnhardt Jr. Gargoyles 1997 Monte Carlo/12,000 12.50 25.00
31 Dale Earnhardt Jr. Sikkens White 1997 Monte Carlo/10,000 15.00 25.00
31 Dale Earnhardt Jr. Wrangler 1997 Monte Carlo/7500 15.00 25.00
31 Mike Skinner Lowe's/2500 6.00 15.00
33 Ken Schrader Skoal/3500 12.50 25.00
36 Ernie Irvan M&M's 6.00 15.00
36 Ernie Irvan M&M's Countdown/6500 6.00 15.00
36 Ernie Irvan Crispy M&M's/3500 7.50 20.00
40 Kerry Earnhardt Channellock/5000 7.50 20.00
40 Sterling Marlin Coors Light/2500 6.00 15.00
55 Kenny Wallace Square D/2500 6.00 15.00
55 Kenny Wallace Square D NASCAR Racers/4500 6.00 15.00
71 Dave Marcis Realtree 7.50 20.00
77 Dale Earnhardt Hy-Gain 1976 Malibu 15.00 30.00
88 Dale Jarrett Quality Care White 12.50 25.00
00 Buckshot Jones Crown Fiber 6.00 15.00

2000 Action Performance 1:64

These 1:64 cars were issued in a black and red AP "Action Performance" blister with cardboard backer. The year of issue is clearly printed on the backer board. The cars were distributed primarily by mass retailers.

1 Steve Park Pennzoil 3.00 8.00
2 Rusty Wallace Rusty Red Cell Batteries Promo 5.00 12.00
3 Dale Earnhardt Goodwrench 6.00 15.00
3 Dale Earnhardt Goodwrench Red Call Batteries Promo 10.00 20.00
4 Jeff Purvis 30.00 50.00
Porter-Cable
5 Terry Labonte Kellogg's 3.00 8.00
5 Terry Labonte Kellogg's Red Cell Batteries Promo 4.00 8.00
18 Bobby Labonte Interstate Batteries 3.00 8.00
20 Tony Stewart Home Depot 4.00 8.00
24 Jeff Gordon DuPont 4.00 8.00
25 Jerry Nadeau Holigan 3.00 6.00
28 Ricky Rudd Havoline 3.00 6.00
28 Ricky Rudd Havoline Red Cell Batteries Promo 4.00 8.00
36 Ken Schrader M&M's 3.00 6.00
75 Wally Dallenbach Red Cell Batteries Promo 4.00 8.00
88 Dale Jarrett Quality Care 3.00 6.00

2000 Action Racing Collectables 1:64

These 1:64 scale cards were issued as part of the Platinum Series. The Alcohol/Tobacco sponsored cars were released on a pit wall base and packaged in a clear window box similar to the RCCA releases. The rest were packaged in a plastic clam-shell blister.

1 Coca-Cola in a can 6.00 15.00
1 Randy LaJoie Bob Evan's/7560 4.00 8.00
1 Randy LaJoie Bob Evan's Monsters 4.00 8.00
1 Steve Park Pennzoil/10,080 5.00 12.00
2 Rusty Wallace Miller Lite/15,048 5.00 12.00
3 Dale Earnhardt Goodwrench/30,024 12.50 25.00
3 Dale Earnhardt Goodwrench No Bull raced/76,003 10.00 25.00
3 Dale Earnhardt Goodwrench Taz No Bull 15.00 30.00
3 Ron Hornaday NAPA/7560 4.00 10.00
3 Ron Hornaday NAPA 75th Anniv./7560 4.00 10.00
3 Ron Hornaday NAPA Monsters/7560 4.00 10.00
4 Bobby Hamilton Kodak 4.00 8.00
4 Bobby Hamilton Kodak Navy/10,080 4.00 10.00
5 Terry Labonte Froot Loops/16,272 5.00 10.00
5 Terry Labonte Kellogg's 5.00 12.00
7 Michael Waltrip Nations Rent 4.00 8.00
8 Jeff Burton Baby Ruth '90 T-bird/9720 4.00 8.00
8 Dale Earnhardt Jr. Bud 12.50 25.00
10 Jeff Green Nesquik 4.00 8.00
11 Jason Jarrett Rayovac/7560 4.00 8.00
11 Jason Jarrett Rayovac Promo blister 5.00 10.00
12 Jeremy Mayfield Mobil 1/9000 4.00 8.00
12 Jeremy Mayfield Mobil 1 World Series/8712 4.00 8.00
13 Robby Gordon Menards Monsters/7056 5.00 10.00
15 Tony Stewart Vision3 1996 Grand Prix/9720 5.00 10.00
15 Michael Waltrip Nations Rent/7560 4.00 8.00
18 Bobby Labonte Interstate Batteries 5.00 10.00
18 Bobby Labonte Interstate Batteries Frankenstein/9360 5.00 10.00
18/20 Bobby Labonte Interstate Batteries Tony Stewart Home Depot Chef Boyardee blister 2-car promo set 12.50 25.00
19 Dodge Show Car 4.00 10.00
20 Tony Stewart Home Depot 5.00 12.00
20 Tony Stewart Home Depot Brickyard/7500 5.00 15.00
20 Tony Stewart Home Depot Kids 6.00 15.00
24 Jeff Gordon DuPont/34,272 5.00 12.00
24 Jeff Gordon DuPont Millennium 7.50 15.00
24 Jeff Gordon Pepsi/22,752 6.00 12.00
25 Jerry Nadeau Holigan/7560 4.00 10.00
25 Jerry Nadeau Holigan Coast Guard/10,008 4.00 10.00
25 Kenny Wallace Lance 4.00 8.00
26 Jimmy Spencer Big K 4.00 10.00
27 Casey Atwood Castrol 4.00 10.00
28 Ricky Rudd Havoline 5.00 12.00
28 Ricky Rudd Havoline Marines/20,016 5.00 12.00
31 Dale Earnhardt Jr. Mom 'N' Pop's 1996 Monte Carlo 7.50 15.00
31 Mike Skinner Lowe's 4.00 10.00
31 Mike Skinner Lowe's Army 4.00 10.00
34 David Green AFG Busch Promo 3.00 8.00
36 Ken Schrader M&M's/10,896 5.00 10.00
36 Ken Schrader M&M's Green 6.00 12.00
36 Ken Schrader M&M's Keep Back 5.00 10.00
36 Ken Schrader M&M's Promo blister 5.00 10.00
40 Sterling Marlin Coors/7560 6.00 15.00
40 Sterling Marlin Coors Brooks & Dunn/7560 5.00 12.00
40 Sterling Marlin Coors Light/7560 5.00 12.00
40 Sterling Marlin Coors Light Black 5.00 12.00
42 Kenny Irwin BellSouth/7560 5.00 12.00
53 Hank Parker Jr. Team Marines/6552 4.00 10.00
55 Kenny Wallace Square D 4.00 10.00
55 Kenny Wallace Square D NASCAR Racers/4500 4.00 10.00
60 Geoffrey Bodine Power Team 4.00 10.00
66 Darrell Waltrip Big K Route 66/9000 4.00 8.00
66 Darrell Waltrip Big K Route 66 Flames/12,744 4.00 8.00
67 Jeff Gordon Outback Steakhouse 1990 Grand Prix 6.00 12.00
71 Dave Marcis Realtree 5.00 10.00
75 Wally Dallenbach Powerpuff Girls/9000 4.00 8.00
77 Robert Pressley Jasper 4.00 10.00
88 Dale Jarrett Quality Care/20,016 6.00 12.00
88 Dale Jarrett Quality Care Air Force 6.00 12.00
94 Bill Elliott McDonald's/18,216 5.00 12.00
94 Bill Elliott McDonald's 25th Ann./20,016 5.00 12.00
00 Buckshot Jones Cheez-it 4.00 10.00
2000 NAPA Atlanta Promo in PVC box 2.00 5.00
2000 Sam Bass Promo in PVC box 4.00 10.00
NNO Armed Forces 5-car set in Promo blister/4. Bobby Hamilton Navy/25. Jerry Nadeau Coast Guard/28. Ricky Rudd Marines/31. Mike Skinner Army/88. Dale Jarrett Air Force 15.00 30.00
NNO Armed Forces 5-car set Gold 40.00 100.00

2000 Action/RCCA 1:64

These cars are available solely through the club. Alcohol and Tobacco sponsored cars were mounted on a clear base.

1 Randy LaJoie Bob Evan's/2016 4.00 10.00
1 Randy LaJoie Bob Evan's Monsters/1500 4.00 10.00
1 Steve Park Pennzoil/3523 5.00 10.00
2 Rusty Wallace Miller Lite 12.00 20.00
3 Dale Earnhardt Goodwrench/10,008 12.50 25.00
3 Dale Earnhardt Goodwrench Peter Max/5544 35.00 60.00
3 Dale Earnhardt Goodwrench Taz No Bull/17,000 20.00 50.00
3 Ron Hornaday NAPA/3528 4.00 10.00
3 Ron Hornaday NAPA Monsters/2736 5.00 10.00
3/8 Dale Earnhardt Dale Earnhardt Jr. No Bull 2-cars in tin/6504 45.00 80.00
4 Bobby Hamilton Kodak/3528 5.00 12.00
6 Mark Martin Jim Magill Green 1983 Monte Carlo/7560 5.00 10.00
7 Michael Waltrip Nations Rent/2016 5.00 10.00
8 Jeff Burton Baby Ruth '90 T-bird/2520 5.00 10.00
8 Dale Earnhardt Jr. Bud/10,000 15.00 30.00
8 Dale Earnhardt Jr. Bud Olympic/5040 20.00 40.00
11 Jason Jarrett Rayovac/1512 4.00 10.00
13 Robby Gordon Menards Monsters/1500 5.00 10.00
18 Bobby Labonte Interstate Batteries/2520 7.50 15.00
18 Bobby Labonte Interstate Batteries All Star Game/2880 10.00 20.00
18 Bobby Labonte Interstate Batteries NASCAR Racers/4500 7.50 15.00
20 Tony Stewart Home Depot/10,000 6.00 15.00
20 Tony Stewart Home Depot Kids 10.00 20.00
24 Jeff Gordon DuPont/10,008 10.00 20.00
24 Jeff Gordon DuPont Millennium/8496 12.50 25.00
24 Jeff Gordon DuPont Peanuts in lunch box/3800 50.00 100.00
24 Jeff Gordon DuPont Winston/1500 12.50 25.00
25 Jerry Nadeau Holigan/3528 5.00 12.00
25 Kenny Wallace Lance/2520 5.00 10.00
26 Jimmy Spencer Big K/1500 5.00 10.00
27 Casey Atwood Castrol/3500 6.00 15.00
28 Ricky Rudd Havoline/2520 6.00 15.00
31 Dale Earnhardt Jr. Mom 'N' Pop's 1996 Monte Carlo/10,000 12.50 25.00
31 Mike Skinner Lowe's/2520 5.00 10.00
36 Ken Schrader M&M's/3528 5.00 10.00
36 Ken Schrader M&M's July 4th/2520 5.00 12.00
40 Sterling Marlin Coors 12.50 25.00
40 Sterling Marlin Coors Light/2016 6.00 15.00
40 Sterling Marlin Coors Light Black/3528 6.00 15.00
42 Kenny Irwin BellSouth 12.00 20.00
53 Hank Parker Jr. Team Marines/1512 4.00 10.00
55 Kenny Wallace Square D/2016 4.00 10.00
60 Geoff Bodine Power Team/2520 5.00 10.00
66 Darrell Waltrip Big K Route 66/2520 5.00 10.00
66 Darrell Waltrip Big K Route 66 Flames/2520 5.00 10.00
67 Jeff Gordon Outback Steakhouse 1990 Grand Prix 6.00 15.00
71 Dave Marcis Realtree/1584 5.00 10.00
75 Wally Dallenbach Powerpuff Girls 5.00 10.00
88 Dale Jarrett Quality Care 6.00 15.00
92 Aaron's 312 Promo 10.00 20.00
94 Bill Elliott McDonald's/3042 6.00 15.00
94 Bill Elliott McDonald's 25th Ann./3528 6.00 15.00
00 Buckshot Jones Cheez-it Promo/1512 5.00 12.00
00 Atlanta Cracker Barrel 500 Promo/22,500 5.00 12.00

2000 Action/RCCA Total View 1:64

This set marks the debut of Total View, Actions top of the line 1:64. This car features a removable die-cast body that can be lifted from an authentically constructed roll cage and chassis, and snaps back on.

2 Rusty Wallace Miller Lite Harley-Davidson 12.50 25.00
3 Dale Earnhardt Goodwrench No Bull 40.00 80.00
3 Dale Earnhardt Goodwrench Peter Max/5760 50.00 100.00
4 Bobby Hamilton Kodak Navy 6.00 15.00
8 Dale Earnhardt Jr. Bud No Bull 18.00 30.00
8 Dale Earnhardt Jr. Bud Olympic/4032 20.00 40.00
24 Jeff Gordon DuPont Millennium 15.00 35.00
24 Jeff Gordon DuPont Peanuts/3024 12.50 25.00
24 Jeff Gordon Pepsi 15.00 25.00
25 Jerry Nadeau Holigan Coast Guard 6.00 15.00
28 Ricky Rudd Havoline/2544 6.00 15.00
28 Ricky Rudd Havoline Marines/2016 6.00 15.00
31 Mike Skinner Lowe's Army 6.00 15.00
88 Dale Jarrett Quality Care Air Force 12.00 25.00

2000 Action Total Concept 1:64

1 Randy LaJoie Bob Evan's Monsters/5832 6.00 15.00
2 Rusty Wallace Miller Lite Harley/20,808 10.00 20.00
3 Dale Earnhardt Goodwrench Peter Max paint/69,480 20.00 50.00
3 Ron Hornaday NAPA Monsters 6.00 15.00
4 Bobby Hamilton Kodak Navy 5.00 12.00
5 Terry Labonte Kellogg's Grinch 7.50 15.00
8 Dale Earnhardt Jr. Bud Olympic/26,568 10.00 20.00
13 Robby Gordon Menards Monsters 6.00 15.00
18 Bobby Labonte Interstate Batteries All Star Game/15,336 10.00 20.
18 Bobby Labonte Interstate Batteries Monsters 10.00 20.
19 Dodge Show Car 6.00 15.
20 Tony Stewart Home Depot Kids/11,367 10.00 20.
24 Jeff Gordon DuPont Peanuts/21,456 8.00 20.
24 Jeff Gordon DuPont Winston/41,400 8.00 20.
25 Jerry Nadeau Holigan Coast Guard 6.00 15.
27 Casey Atwood Castrol Monsters 6.00 15.
28 Ricky Rudd Havoline/5040 6.00 15.
28 Ricky Rudd Havoline Marines/8712 6.00 15.0
31 Mike Skinner Lowe's Army/7128 5.00 12.0
36 Ken Schrader M&M's Halloween/7560 6.00 15.0
88 Dale Jarrett Quality Care Air Force 6.00 15.0
94 Bill Elliott McDonald's 6.00 15.0
94 Bill Elliott McDonald's McFlurry/7920 6.00 15.0

2001 Action Performance 1:64

These cars are packaged in an Action "AP" blister. T cardboard backer is red and black with a blueprint type draw of a car in the background. The 2001 pieces look very simila the 2002 releases, but can be identified by the copyright y found on the backs. Most of the 2001 cars also include "Action Sports Image" logo on the front below the car.

3 Dale Earnhardt Goodwrench BP 5.00 12.0
3 Dale Earnhardt Goodwrench w Sonic decal 15.00 30.0
3 Dale Earnhardt Goodwrench Promo in clear plastic box 12.50 25.0
24 Jeff Gordon DuPont Flames 4.00 8.0
29 Kevin Harvick Goodwrench 4.00 8.0
88 Dale Jarrett UPS 4.00 8.0

2001 Action Racing Collectables 1:64

This series was issued in a clamshell type packaging with ma pieces including the typical silver Action sticker with the c model information and production run total. Both Total Conce and regular issue pieces are included in the listing below. T Total Concept cars are hood open with a removable body.

1 Steve Park Pennzoil in Can/8688 15.00 25.00
1 Steve Park Pennzoil Sylvester&Tweety/24,912 10.00 20.00
2 Kerry Earnhardt Kannapolis Intimidators/20,016 7.50 15.00
2 Rusty Wallace Miller Lite in Can 15.00 25.00
2 Rusty Wallace Miller Lite Harley/14,592 7.50 15.00
2 Rusty Wallace Miller Light Harley in Can 15.00 25.00
2/29 Kevin Harvick AC Delco Goodwrench 2-cars in tin/35,040 15.00 30.00
3 Dale Earnhardt Goodwrench/20,880 15.00 30.00
3 Dale Earnhardt Goodwrench Oreo/55,040 15.00 30.00
3 Dale Earnhardt Goodwrench Oreo Tin/34,161 20.00 40.00
3 Dale Earnhardt Goodwrench Talladega No Bull Win 12.50 25.00
5 Terry Labonte Kellogg's/7560 10.00 20.00
5 Terry Labonte Kellogg's Wile E. Coyote and Road Runner/10,080 12.50 25.00
8 Dale Earnhardt Jr. Bud in can/30,768 30.00 60.00
8 Dale Earnhardt Jr. Bud MLB All-Star/30,060 25.00 40.00
9 Bill Elliott Dodge/21,024 6.00 12.00
9 Bill Elliott Dodge Muhammad Ali/24,984 5.00 12.00
9 Bill Elliott 10.00 20.00

Dodge Spider-Man Lunch Box
Bill Elliott 6.00 12.00
Dodge Spider-Man Promo in blister
10 Johnny Benson 6.00 12.00
Valvoline James Dean/10,080
11 Darrell Waltrip 6.00 15.00
Bud '85MC in a can/21,000
15 Michael Waltrip 10.00 20.00
NAPA
15 Michael Waltrip 10.00 20.00
NAPA Stars&Stripes/22,104
18 Bobby Labonte 10.00 20.00
Interstate Batteries/10,500
18 Bobby Labonte 10.00 25.00
Interstate Batteries in a Coke Bottle/21,524
18 Bobby Labonte 10.00 20.00
Interstate Batteries Jurassic Park 3/16,128
18/20 Bobb Labonte 7.50 15.00
Tony Stewart Coke Bear 2-car promo blister
19 Casey Atwood 6.00 12.00
Dodge
19 Casey Atwood 12.00 25.00
Dodge Mountain Dew in a can/16,128
19 Casey Atwood 7.50 15.00
Dodge Spider-Man/14,112
20 Tony Stewart 10.00 20.00
Home Depot/14,472
20 Tony Stewart 12.50 25.00
Home Depot Coke Bear in Coke bottle/20,516
20 Tony Stewart 10.00 20.00
Home Depot Jurassic Park 3/19,128
24 Jeff Gordon 15.00 30.00
DuPont Bugs Bunny/50,496
24 Jeff Gordon 15.00 30.00
DuPont Flames
24 Jeff Gordon 10.00 20.00
DuPont Flames 2001 Championship in tin/37,560
24 Jeff Gordon 12.50 25.00
Pepsi in Can
28 Ricky Rudd 10.00 25.00
Havoline in oil bottle/9024
28 Ricky Rudd 12.00 20.00
Havoline Bud Shoot Out/8712
28 Ricky Rudd 4.00 10.00
Havoline Need for Speed Regular Promo
28 Ricky Rudd 4.00 10.00
Havoline Need for Speed Custom Promo
28 Ricky Rudd 4.00 10.00
Havoline Need for Speed Special Promo
29 Kevin Harvick 10.00 25.00
Goodwrench/44,568
29 Kevin Harvick 10.00 20.00
Goodwrench AOL/30,456
29 Kevin Harvick 10.00 20.00
Goodwrench Taz/52,704
29 Kevin Harvick 25.00 50.00
Goodwrench Taz QVC 4-car set in tin/2000
30 Jeff Green 7.50 15.00
AOL Daffy Duck/8568
31 Mike Skinner 6.00 12.00
Lowe's Yosemite Sam/12,888
36 Ken Schrader 6.00 12.00
M&M's/9576
36 Ken Schrader 6.00 12.00
M&M's Halloween/12,096
36 Ken Schrader 6.00 12.00
M&M's July 4th/7776
36 Ken Schrader 6.00 12.00
Snickers/8784
40 Sterling Marlin 12.50 25.00
Coors Light in a can/15,408
40 Sterling Marlin 7.50 15.00
Coors Light Kiss/24,672
55 Bobby Hamilton 6.00 15.00
Square D Marvin Martian
88 Dale Jarrett 12.00 20.00
UPS/23,112
88 Dale Jarrett 10.00 20.00
UPS Flames/37,224
NNO Hendrick 100th Win 8-car set in tin/7560 30.00 80.00

2001 Action/RCCA 1:64

2 Kerry Earnhardt 12.50 25.00
Kannapolis Intimidators/1584
2 Rusty Wallace 15.00 30.00
Miller Lite/1584
2 Rusty Wallace 10.00 20.00
Miller Lite Harley/3600
3 Dale Earnhardt 40.00 80.00
Goodwrench/3024
3 Dale Earnhardt 50.00 100.00
Goodwrench Platinum 7-car set/5004
3 Dale Earnhardt 40.00 60.00
Goodwrench Oreo/3168
5 Terry Labonte 15.00 30.00
Kellogg's/1584
5 Terry Labonte 12.50 25.00
Kellogg's Wile E. Road Runner
8 Dale Earnhardt Jr. 25.00 50.00
Bud/2016
8 Dale Earnhardt Jr. 25.00 50.00
Bud MLB All-Star/5040
9 Bill Elliott 15.00 30.00
Dodge/3600
9 Bill Elliott 15.00 30.00
Dodge Muhammad Ali/1776
9 Bill Elliott 15.00 30.00
Dodge Spider-Man/2160
10 Johnny Benson 10.00 20.00
Valvoline James Dean
15 Michael Waltrip 15.00 30.00
NAPA/1584
15 Michael Waltrip 12.50 25.00
NAPA Stars&Stripes/1104
18 Bobby Labonte 15.00 30.00
Interstate Batteries/1584
18 Bobby Labonte 10.00 20.00
Interstate Batteries Coke Bear/1800
18 Bobby Labonte 10.00 20.00
Interstate Batteries Jurassic Park 3/1484
19 Casey Atwood 10.00 25.00
Dodge/1584
19 Casey Atwood 15.00 30.00
Dodge Mountain Dew Color Chrome/1800
19 Casey Atwood 12.50 25.00
Dodge Spider-Man/1584
20 Tony Stewart 12.50 25.00
Home Depot/2594
20 Tony Stewart 10.00 20.00
Home Depot Coke Bear/1800
20 Tony Stewart 20.00 40.00
Home Depot Jurassic Park 3/1584
24 Jeff Gordon 25.00 40.00
DuPont/3312
24 Jeff Gordon 20.00 40.00
DuPont Bugs Bunny in lunch box/5004
24 Jeff Gordon 25.00 40.00
Pepsi/1584
28 Ricky Rudd 15.00 30.00
Havoline
28 Ricky Rudd 10.00 25.00
Havoline Bud Shoot Out/1584
29 Kevin Harvick 12.50 25.00
Goodwrench/4272
29 Kevin Harvick 10.00 20.00
Goodwrench AOL/3888
29 Kevin Harvick 18.00 30.00
Goodwrench Taz in lunch box/4008
29 Kevin Harvick 6.00 15.00
Goodwrench Nilla Wafers Promo
31 Mike Skinner 10.00 20.00
Lowe's Yosemite Sam/1584
36 Ken Schrader 10.00 20.00
M&M's July 4th/1584
36 Ken Schrader 6.00 15.00
Snickers
40 Sterling Marlin 12.50 25.00
Coors Light/1584
40 Sterling Marlin 12.50 25.00
Coors Light Kiss/1584
88 Dale Jarrett 12.50 25.00
UPS

2001 Action/RCCA Elite 1:64

New detail for this year includes opening hood and trunk, better engine and chassis detail. Alcohol cars are on a clear base.

1 Steve Park 15.00 30.00
Pennzoil Sylvester&Tweety/1584
2 Kerry Earnhardt 15.00 30.00
Kannapolis Intimidators/1584
2 Rusty Wallace 25.00 50.00
Miller Lite/1104
2 Rusty Wallace 30.00 60.00
Miller Lite Harley-Davidson
3 Dale Earnhardt 50.00 100.00
Goodwrench/2976
3 Dale Earnhardt 75.00 150.00
Goodwrench Metal/7500
3 Dale Earnhardt 50.00 100.00
Goodwrench Oreo/3168
5 Terry Labonte 20.00 40.00
Kellogg's
8 Dale Earnhardt Jr. 30.00 80.00
Bud/2016
8 Dale Earnhardt Jr. 50.00 100.00
Bud All-Star/2976
15 Michael Waltrip 15.00 30.00
NAPA Stars&Stripes/1104
18 Bobby Labonte 15.00 40.00
Interstate Batteries
18 Bobby Labonte 15.00 30.00
Interstate Batteries Coke Bear/1296
18 Bobby Labonte 15.00 30.00
Interstate Batteries Jurassic Park 3/1104
20 Tony Stewart 15.00 40.00
Home Depot/1824
20 Tony Stewart 15.00 40.00
Home Depot Coke Bear/1296
20 Tony Stewart 15.00 40.00
Home Depot Jurassic Park 3/1104
24 Jeff Gordon 30.00 60.00
DuPont Flames/2688
24 Jeff Gordon 20.00 40.00
DuPont Bugs Bunny/3960
24 Jeff Gordon 30.00 60.00
Pepsi/1104
28 Ricky Rudd 15.00 30.00
Havoline
29 Kevin Harvick 40.00 75.00
Goodwrench/2160
29 Kevin Harvick 15.00 30.00
Goodwrench AOL/3000
29 Kevin Harvick 15.00 30.00
Goodwrench Taz/3024
36 Ken Schrader 12.50 30.00
M&M's/1584
88 Dale Jarrett 25.00 50.00
UPS
88 Dale Jarrett 15.00 30.00
UPS Flames/1800
NNO Looney Tunes/1800 20.00 40.00

2002 Action Performance 1:64

These cars are packaged in an Action "AP" blister. The cardboard backer is red and black with a larger blueprint type drawing of a car in the background versusu the 2001 release. The 2002 releases can be identified by the copyright year found on the backs and the lack of the "Action Sports Image" logo on the front.

2 Rusty Wallace 3.00 6.00
Rusty
3 Dale Earnhardt 4.00 8.00
Goodwrench
8 Dale Earnhardt Jr 4.00 8.00
Dale Jr.
18 Bobby Labonte 3.00 6.00
Interstate Batteries
20 Tony Stewart 3.00 6.00
Home Depot
24 Jeff Gordon 4.00 8.00
DuPont Flames
28 Ricky Rudd 3.00 6.00
Havoline
29 Kevin Harvick 3.00 6.00
Goodwrench
40 Sterling Marlin 3.00 6.00
Sterling
88 Dale Jarrett 3.00 6.00
UPS

2002 Action Racing Collectables 1:64

1 Dale Earnhardt Jr. 15.00 30.00
Coke '98 Monte Carlo in vending machine tin/25,883
1 Jeff Gordon 6.00 12.00
Autolite '89 T-bird/13,464
1 Steve Park 10.00 20.00
Pennzoil in oil filter/16,716
2 Dale Earnhardt 6.00 15.00
Coke '80 Pontiac in a Coke can/61,680
2 Dale Earnhardt 6.00 15.00
Wrangler '79 Monte Carlo/30,744
2 Rusty Wallace 10.00 20.00
MGD 1991 Thunderbird in a can/16,272
2 Rusty Wallace 10.00 20.00
Miller Lite in a bottle/39,288
2 Rusty Wallace 10.00 20.00
Miller Lite Elvis/24,864 in a tin box
2 Rusty Wallace 10.00 20.00
Miller Lite Harley Flames/16,680
2 Rusty Wallace 10.00 20.00
Miller Lite Flames/9000
3 Dale Earnhardt 15.00 30.00
Coke '98 Monte Carlo in vending machine tin/25,883
3 Dale Earnhardt Jr. 10.00 20.00
Nilla Wafers/57,600
3 Dale Earnhardt Jr. 20.00 35.00
Nilla Wafers Oreo Color Chrome set/8333
3 Dale Earnhardt Jr. 10.00 20.00
Oreo/66,096
3 Dale Earnhardt Jr. 10.00 20.00
Oreo Promo in box
3/3 Dale Earnhardt 35.00 60.00
Dale Earnhardt Jr. Oreo White Gold 2-car set in tin/7560
4 Mike Skinner 5.00 12.00
Kodak Max Yosemite Sam/8568
5 Terry Labonte 7.50 15.00
Cheez-It/7056
5 Terry Labonte 5.00 12.00
Kellogg's in cereal box/15,360
5 Terry Labonte 5.00 12.00
Kellogg's Road Runner nd Wile E.Coyote/10,872
7 Casey Atwood 5.00 12.00
Sirius/8640
7 Casey Atwood 5.00 12.00
Sirius Muppets/8064
8 Dale Earnhardt Jr. 12.50 25.00
Bud in bottle/80,016
8 Dale Earnhardt Jr. 10.00 20.00
Bud MLB All-Star/51,984
8 Dale Earnhardt Jr. 20.00 35.00
Bud All-Star 2001 and 2002 2-car Color Chrome set/8888
8 Dale Earnhardt Jr. 10.00 20.00
Looney Tunes/41,688
9 Bill Elliott 6.00 15.00
Dodge in tin/15,120
9 Bill Elliott 7.50 15.00
Dodge Muppet/14,040
10 Johnny Benson 6.00 12.00
Vavoline in oil can/7656
10 Johnny Benson 5.00 12.00
Valvoline Muppet/11,664
12 Kerry Earnhardt 5.00 12.00
JaniKing Yosemite Sam/10,008
12 Kerry Earnhardt 6.00 12.00
Supercuts
12 Kerry Earnhardt 5.00 10.00
Supercuts Promo in clear box
12 Ryan Newman 6.00 15.00
Alltel/11,664
12 Ryan Newman 7.50 15.00
Alltel ROY/6640
12 Ryan Newman 6.00 15.00
Mobil 1/9936
15 Dale Earnhardt 6.00 15.00
Wrangler 1979 Pontiac Ventura/30,744
15 Michael Waltrip 7.50 15.00
NAPA/16,920
15 Michael Waltrip 7.50 15.00
NAPA Stars&Stripes/10,388
18 Bobby Labonte 7.50 15.00
Interstate Batteries/18,864
18 Bobby Labonte 7.50 15.00
Interstate Batteries Muppet/14,544
18 Bobby Labonte 12.50 25.00
Let's Roll/8856
18 Bobby Labonte 15.00 30.00
Let's Roll in tin/4464
19 Jeremy Mayfield 6.00 12.00
Dodge/11,448
19 Jeremy Mayfield 5.00 12.00
Dodge Muppet/11,952
19 Jeremy Mayfield 12.50 25.00
Mountain Dew in vending machine/12,660
20 Tony Stewart 10.00 20.00
Home Depot/23,040
20 Tony Stewart 6.00 15.00
Home Depot 2002 Winston Cup Champion/17,640
20 Tony Stewart 5.00 12.00
Home Depot Promo Old Spice window box
20 Tony Stewart 10.00 20.00
Home Depot Promo Maintenance Warehouse blister
20 Tony Stewart 10.00 20.00
Home Depot Peanuts Black/15,048
20 Tony Stewart 10.00 20.00
Home Depot Peanuts Orange/15,048
20 Tony Stewart 7.50 15.00
Home Depot Peanuts 2-car set promo blister
20 Tony Stewart 18.00 30.00
Old Spice Promo in box
21 Jy Sauter 10.00 20.00
Jeff Green Rockwell Promo blister
24 Jeff Gordon 6.00 15.00
DuPont in paint can/62,016
24 Jeff Gordon 45.00 80.00
DuPont 4-cars/2000
24 Jeff Gordon 10.00 20.00
DuPont 200th Anniversary/52,056
24 Jeff Gordon 10.00 20.00
DuPont Bugs Bunny/24,312
24 Jeff Gordon 10.00 20.00
Elmo/17,424
24 Jeff Gordon 12.50 25.00
Pepsi Daytona in vending machine/35,952
24 Jeff Gordon 12.50 25.00
Pepsi Talladega in a can/23,712
25 Joe Nemechek 5.00 12.00
UAW Speedy Gonzalez/8640
28 Ricky Rudd 6.00 12.00
Havoline/16,272
28 Ricky Rudd 7.50 15.00
Havoline Iron Man/9000
28 Ricky Rudd 5.00 12.00
Havoline Muppet/14,832
29 Kevin Harvick 7.50 15.00
Action ET/18,000
29 Kevin Harvick 7.50 15.00
Goodwrench/68,112
29 Kevin Harvick 7.50 15.00
Goodwrench ET/40,032
29 Kevin Harvick 7.50 15.00
Goodwrench Now Sell Tires/15,408
29 Kevin Harvick 7.50 20.00
Goodwrench Taz/12,024
29 Kevin Harvick 6.00 15.00
Sylvania/9000
30 Jeff Green 7.50 15.00
AOL/12,096
30 Jeff Green 7.50 15.00
AOL Daffy Duck/9720
30 Jeff Green 7.50 15.00
AOL Scooby-Doo/10,296
31 Robby Gordon 7.50 15.00
Cingular/7992
31 Robby Gordon 5.00 12.00
Cingular Pepe le Pew/10,224
36 Ken Schrader 7.50 15.00
M&M's/10,008
36 Ken Schrader 5.00 12.00
M&M's Halloween/8640
36 Ken Schrader 5.00 12.00
M&M's July 4th/5976
40 Sterling Marlin 12.50 25.00
Coors Light in a bottle/32,784
40 Sterling Marlin 12.50 25.00
Coors Original in a can/18,288
41 Jimmy Spencer 5.00 12.00
Energizer/7560
41 Jimmy Spencer 7.50 15.00
Target/10,080
41 Jimmy Spencer 10.00 20.00
Target Muppet/12,240
48 Jimmie Johnson 12.50 25.00
Lowe's/13,608
48 Jimmie Johnson 10.00 20.00
Lowe's Sylvester and Tweety/19,689
55 Bobby Hamilton 5.00 12.00
Square D Marvin/8064
88 Dale Jarrett 6.00 15.00
UPS/38,088
88 Dale Jarrett 5.00 12.00
UPS Muppet/22,824
88 Dale Jarrett 7.50 20.00
UPS Van Color Chrome/22,752
02 Tropicana 400 Promo blister 3.00 8.00
NNO Dale Earnhardt 7.50 15.00
Legacy/29,088
NNO Looney Tunes Rematch/13,464 6.00 15.00
NNO Muppet Show 25th Anniversary/19,152 5.00 12.00

2002 Action/RCCA 1:64

1 Dale Earnhardt Jr. 12.50 25.00
Coke 1998 Monte Carlo in vending machine/3000
1 Steve Park 7.50 15.00
Pennzoil/1584
2 Dale Earnhardt 10.00 20.00
Coke '80 Pontiac/6480
2 Rusty Wallace 15.00 25.00
Miller Lite/1584
2 Rusty Wallace 10.00 25.00
Miller Lite Elvis/1800
2 Rusty Wallace 15.00 30.00
Miller Lite Harley Flames/1800
2 Rusty Wallace 12.50 25.00
Miller Lite Flames/1596
2/3 Dale Earnhardt 90.00 150.00
7-car set Gold/10,000
1980 Mike Curb car
1986 Wrangler car
1987 Wrangler car
1990 Goodwrench car
1991 Goodwrench car
1993 Goodwrench car/ 1994 Goodwrench car
2K2 Childress Racing 7.50 15.00
Pit Practice/2448
3 Dale Earnhardt 12.50 25.00
Goodwrench Plus No Bull 76th Win/6048
3 Dale Earnhardt Jr. 12.50 25.00
Nilla Wafers/6000
3 Dale Earnhardt Jr. 4.00 10.00
Nilla Wafers Promo
3 Dale Earnhardt Jr. 12.50 25.00
Oreo/6000
3 Dale Earnhardt Jr. 4.00 10.00
Oreo Promo
4 Mike Skinner 7.50 15.00
Kodak Max Yosemite Sam/1584
5 Terry Labonte 10.00 20.00
Cheez-It/1584
5 Terry Labonte 10.00 20.00
Kellogg's/1584
5 Terry Labonte 10.00 20.00
Kellogg's Road Runner & Wile E.Coyote/1584
7 Casey Atwood 10.00 20.00
Sirius/1584
8 Dale Earnhardt Jr. 12.50 25.00
Bud Color Chrome/5040
8 Dale Earnhardt Jr. 12.50 25.00
Bud All-Star/6000
8 Dale Earnhardt Jr. 12.50 25.00
Looney Tunes/6000
9 Bill Elliott 10.00 20.00
Dodge/1584
9 Bill Elliott 10.00 20.00
Dodge Muppet/1800
10 Johnny Benson 10.00 20.00
Valvoline/1584
12 Kerry Earnhardt 10.00 20.00
10-10-220/1584
12 Kerry Earnhardt 10.00 20.00
JaniKing Yosemite Sam/1584
12 Kerry Earnhardt 10.00 20.00
Supercuts/1584
12 Ryan Newman 15.00 30.00
Alltel/1584
12 Ryan Newman 15.00 30.00
Mobil 1/1584
15 Dale Earnhardt 10.00 20.00
Wrangler 1979 Pontiac Ventura/4200
15 Michael Waltrip 10.00 20.00
NAPA/1584
15 Michael Waltrip 7.50 15.00
NAPA Stars and Stripes/1584
18 Bobby Labonte 10.00 20.00
Interstate Batteries/1584
18 Bobby Labonte 10.00 20.00
Interstate Batteries Muppet/1584
18 Bobby Labonte 15.00 25.00
Let's Roll/1584
19 Jeremy Mayfield 10.00 20.00
Dodge/1584
19 Jeremy Mayfield 10.00 20.00
Mountain Dew/1584
20 Tony Stewart 15.00 30.00
Home Depot/1584
20 Tony Stewart 12.00 20.00
Home Depot 2002 Champion Color Chrome/1212
20 Tony Stewart 12.50 25.00
Home Depot Peanuts Black/1800
20 Tony Stewart 12.50 25.00
Home Depot Peanuts Orange/1800
24 Jeff Gordon 12.50 25.00
DuPont 200th Anniversary/3312
24 Jeff Gordon 10.00 20.00
DuPont Bugs Bunny/4032
24 Jeff Gordon 12.50 25.00
DuPont Flames/2856
24 Jeff Gordon 15.00 25.00
Elmo/4032
24 Jeff Gordon 12.00 20.00
Pepsi Daytona/3600
24 Jeff Gordon 12.00 20.00
Pepsi Talladega Color Chrome/1584
25 Joe Nemechek 7.50 15.00
UAW Speedy Gonzalez/1584
28 Ricky Rudd 10.00 20.00
Havoline/1584
28 Ricky Rudd 10.00 20.00
Havoline Iron Man/1584
28 Ricky Rudd 10.00 20.00
Havoline Muppet/1584
29 Kevin Harvick 10.00 20.00
Action ET/2304

Item	Low	High
29 Kevin Harvick Goodwrench/4500	10.00	20.00
29 Kevin Harvick Goodwrench ET/4008	10.00	20.00
29 Kevin Harvick Goodwrench Now Sell Tires/2304	10.00	20.00
29 Kevin Harvick Goodwrench Taz/1584	10.00	20.00
29 Kevin Harvick Sonic/1584	10.00	20.00
29 Kevin Harvick Sylvania/1800	12.50	25.00
30 Jeff Green AOL/1584	7.50	15.00
30 Jeff Green AOL Daffy Duck/1584	6.00	12.00
30 Jeff Green AOL Scooby-Doo/1584	10.00	20.00
31 Robby Gordon Cingular/1584	7.50	15.00
31 Robby Gordon Cingular Pepe le Pew/1584	6.00	12.00
36 Ken Schrader M&M's Halloween/1584	10.00	20.00
36 Ken Schrader M&M's July 4th/1584	10.00	20.00
40 Sterling Marlin Coors Light/1800	10.00	20.00
40 Sterling Marlin Coors Original/1800	10.00	20.00
41 Jimmy Spencer Energizer/1584	7.50	15.00
41 Jimmy Spencer Target/1584	7.50	15.00
48 Jimmie Johnson Lowe's/1584	10.00	20.00
48 Jimmie Johnson Lowe's Power of Pride/5928	10.00	20.00
48 Jimmie Johnson Lowe's Sylv.&Tweety/2016	10.00	20.00
55 Bobby Hamilton Square D Marvin/1584	10.00	20.00
88 Dale Jarrett UPS/2880	10.00	20.00
88 Dale Jarrett UPS Muppet/2196	10.00	20.00
91 Hank Parker Jr. USG Promo	15.00	30.00
NNO Dale Earnhardt Legacy/3036	10.00	20.00
NNO Looney Tunes Rematch/1584	7.50	15.00
NNO Muppet Show 25th Ann./2016	7.50	15.00

2002 Action/RCCA Elite 1:64

Item	Low	High
1 Steve Park Pennzoil/1200	12.50	25.00
2 Rusty Wallace Miller Lite/1584	18.00	30.00
2 Rusty Wallace Miller Lite Elvis/1800	18.00	30.00
2 Rusty Wallace Miller Lite Harley lames/1800	20.00	35.00
2 Rusty Wallace Miller Lite Flames/1212	18.00	30.00
2K2 Childress Racing Pit Practice/2160	15.00	25.00
3 Dale Earnhardt Jr. Nilla Wafers/4000	18.00	30.00
3 Dale Earnhardt Jr. Oreo/4000	18.00	30.00
5 Terry Labonte Kellogg's/1200	12.50	25.00
8 Dale Earnhardt Jr. Bud Color Chrome/3600	20.00	35.00
8 Dale Earnhardt Jr. Bud All-Star/4612	15.00	30.00
8 Dale Earnhardt Jr. Looney Tunes/4008	15.00	30.00
12 Kerry Earnhardt 10-10-220/1200	10.00	20.00
12 Kerry Earnhardt JaniKing Yosemite Sam/1200	10.00	20.00
12 Kerry Earnhardt Supercuts/1584	12.50	25.00
12 Ryan Newman Alltel/1584	15.00	30.00
12 Ryan Newman Mobil 1/1584	15.00	30.00
15 Michael Waltrip NAPA Stars and Stripes/1152A	12.50	25.00
18 Bobby Labonte Interstate Batteries/1200	12.50	25.00
18 Bobby Labonte Interstate Batteries Muppet/1200	15.00	25.00
20 Tony Stewart Home Depot/1200	20.00	40.00
20 Tony Stewart Home Depot 2002 Champion Color Chrome/1212	15.00	30.00
20 Tony Stewart Home Depot Peanuts Black/1584	18.00	30.00
20 Tony Stewart Home Depot Peanuts Orange/1584	18.00	30.00
24 Jeff Gordon DuPont 200th Anniversary/3000	15.00	30.00
24 Jeff Gordon DuPont Flames/2160	15.00	30.00
24 Jeff Gordon DuPont Bugs Bunny/4008	15.00	30.00
24 Jeff Gordon Elmo/2016	15.00	30.00
24 Jeff Gordon Pepsi Daytona/3000	15.00	30.00
24 Jeff Gordon Pepsi Talladega/1200	15.00	30.00
28 Ricky Rudd Havoline/1200	12.50	25.00
28 Ricky Rudd Havoline Iron Man/1200	12.50	25.00
28 Ricky Rudd Havoline Muppet/1200	12.50	25.00
29 Kevin Harvick Action ET/2016	15.00	25.00
29 Kevin Harvick Goodwrench/4000	12.50	25.00
29 Kevin Harvick Goodwrench Now Sell Tires/2004	12.50	25.00
29 Kevin Harvick Goodwrench ET/3400	15.00	25.00
29 Kevin Harvick Goodwrench Taz/1200	15.00	25.00
29 Kevin Harvick Sonic/1536-A	15.00	30.00
29 Kevin Harvick Sylvania/1200	15.00	30.00
30 Jeff Green AOL Scooby-Doo/1200	15.00	25.00
31 Robby Gordon Cingular/1584	10.00	20.00
48 Jimmie Johnson Lowe's/1584	20.00	40.00
48 Jimmie Johnson Lowe's Power of Pride/1584	12.50	30.00
48 Jimmie Johnson Lowe's Sylvester and Tweety/1584	15.00	30.00
88 Dale Jarrett UPS/1584	12.50	25.00
88 Dale Jarrett UPS Muppet/1800	12.50	25.00
NNO Dale Earnhardt Legacy/2028	18.00	30.00
NNO Looney Tunes Rematch/1200	10.00	20.00

2003 Action Performance 1:64

Item	Low	High
2 Rusty Wallace Rusty	3.00	6.00
3 Dale Earnhardt Goodwrench Forever the Man blister	4.00	8.00
8 Dale Earnhardt Jr. Dale Jr.	4.00	8.00
8 Dale Earnhardt Jr. JR	4.00	8.00
18 Bobby Labonte Interstate Batteries	3.00	6.00
20 Tony Stewart Home Depot	4.00	8.00
24 Jeff Gordon DuPont Flames	4.00	8.00
29 Kevin Harvick Goodwrench	4.00	8.00
88 Dale Jarrett UPS	3.00	6.00

2003 Action Racing Collectables 1:64

Item	Low	High
1 Dale Earnhardt True Value '99 IROC Blue/12,096	7.50	15.00
1 Dale Earnhardt True Value '00 IROC Lt.Blue/11,736	7.50	15.00
1 Dale Earnhardt True Value '01 IROC Green/11,736	7.50	15.00
1 Steve Park Pennzoil/6912	5.00	12.00
2 Rusty Wallace Miller Lite/15,360	10.00	20.00
2 Rusty Wallace Miller Lite Victory Lap/5976	7.50	15.00
2 Rusty Wallace Miller Lite 600th/9936	10.00	20.00
2 Rusty Wallace Miller Time Live Goo Goo Dolls/9360	6.00	15.00
3 Dale Earnhardt Foundation/30,888	7.50	15.00
3 Dale Earnhardt Goodwrench No Bull 2000 Monte Carlo/15,264	10.00	20.00
3 Dale Earnhardt Victory Lap/14,040	7.50	15.00
5 Terry Labonte Kellogg's/5808	6.00	15.00
5 Terry Labonte Kellogg's Victory Lap/8532	6.00	15.00
7 Alan Kulwicki Victory Lap/8676	5.00	12.00
8 Dale Earnhardt Jr. Bud/36,288	10.00	20.00
8 Dale Earnhardt Jr. Bud Talladega 4-car raced wins set /5940	25.00	50.00
8 Dale Earnhardt Jr. Bud All-Star Game/12,984	10.00	20.00
8 Dale Earnhardt Jr. Bud No Bull 2000 Monte Carlo/15,264	10.00	20.00
8 Dale Earnhardt Jr. Bud StainD/20,520	7.50	15.00
8 Dale Earnhardt Jr. Dirty Mo Posse/38,936	6.00	15.00
8 Dale Earnhardt Jr. Earnhardt Tribute Concert/35,568	7.50	15.00
8 Dale Earnhardt Jr. Oreo Ritz/46,944	7.50	15.00
8 Steve Park Cheese Nips/5400	5.00	12.00
8 Steve Park Maxwell House/6120	5.00	12.00
8 Tony Stewart 3 Doors Down/14,976	7.50	15.00
9 Bill Elliott Coors Winston Million 1985 Thunderbird in can/6088	10.00	20.00
9 Bill Elliott Coors 1987 Thunderbird/6912	7.50	15.00
9 Bill Elliott Coors 1988 Thunderbird in can	10.00	20.00
9 Bill Elliott Dodge/9432	7.50	15.00
9 Bill Elliott Dodge Lion King/3456	7.50	15.00
9 Bill Elliott Dodge Victory Lap/5472	7.50	15.00
9 Bill Elliott Dodge 10th Anniversary Brickyard/5292	7.50	15.00
11 Dale Earnhardt Jr. True Value 1999 IROC Orange/10,728	7.50	15.00
11 Darrell Waltrip Victory Lap/8856	7.50	15.00
11 Cale Yarborough Victory Lap/4320	5.00	12.00
15 Michael Waltrip NAPA/9072	5.00	12.00
15 Michael Waltrip NAPA Hootie & the Blowfish/7200	5.00	12.00
15 Michael Waltrip NAPA Nilla Wafers	5.00	12.00
15 Michael Waltrip NAPA Stars & Stripes/7992	5.00	12.00
18 Bobby Labonte Interstate Batteries/10,728	7.50	15.00
18 Bobby Labonte Interstate Batteries Hulk/5256	7.50	15.00
18 Bobby Labonte Interstate Batteries Victory Lap/9324	7.50	15.00
19 Dale Earnhardt Beldon Asphalt 1977 Malibu/11,376	7.50	15.00
19 Jeremy Mayfield Dodge/5760	5.00	12.00
20 Mike Bliss Rockwell Automation Promo in blister package	12.50	25.00
20 Tony Stewart Home Depot/21,384	7.50	15.00
20 Tony Stewart Home Depot Declaration of Independence/16,344	7.50	15.00
21 Kevin Harvick Payday/6912	7.50	15.00
21 Johnny Sauter Payday/1440	5.00	12.00
22 Bobby Allison Victory Lap/4608	5.00	12.00
24 Jeff Gordon Cookie Monster Foundation/14,976	7.50	15.00
24 Jeff Gordon DuPont Flames/24,696	7.50	15.00
24 Jeff Gordon DuPont Flames Victory Lap/13,212	8.00	20.00
24 Jeff Gordon DuPont Wright Bros./17,856	7.50	15.00
24 Jeff Gordon DuPont Yosemite Sam/11,544	7.50	15.00
24 Jeff Gordon Pepsi	7.50	15.00
24 Jeff Gordon Pepsi Billion $/13,752	7.50	15.00
28/42 Davey Allison Texaco Jamie McMurray Havoline 2-car set/6480	15.00	30.00
29 Kevin Harvick Goodwrench/13,968	7.50	15.00
29 Kevin Harvick Goodwrench Sugar Ray/6192	7.50	15.00
29 Kevin Harvick Snap-On/12,528	7.50	15.00
30 Jeff Green AOL	5.00	12.00
30 No Driver Association AOL Promo in PVC box	10.00	20.00
31 Robby Gordon Cingular black/6984	5.00	12.00
31 Robby Gordon Cingular orange/5976	5.00	12.00
33 Tony Stewart Monaco Diamond Rio SuperTruck	7.50	15.00
38 Elliott Sadler M&M's/9576	5.00	12.00
38 Elliott Sadler M&M's Groovy/8424	5.00	12.00
38 Elliott Sadler M&M's Halloween/6696	5.00	12.00
41 Casey Mears Target/5832	5.00	12.00
42 Jamie McMurray Havoline/9648	10.00	20.00
42 Jamie McMurray Havoline ROY/6480	6.00	15.00
42 Jamie McMurray Havoline Rookie Of the Year color chrome in oil can/2352	12.50	25.00
42 Jamie McMurray Havoline Terminator 3/8784	5.00	12.00
43 Richard Petty STP 1975 Dodge Charger/6294	7.50	15.00
43 Richard Petty Yankees 100th Anniversary/6408	7.50	15.00
43 Richard Petty Victory Lap/10,620	7.50	15.00
44 Christian Fittipaldi Yankees 100th Ann/4248	5.00	12.00
45 Kyle Petty Georgia Pacific/6264	5.00	12.00
45 Kyle Petty Hands to Victory/3240	5.00	12.00
46 Frank Kimmel Advance Auto Parts Promo in blister pack	5.00	12.00
48 Jimmie Johnson Lowe's/19,008	7.50	15.00
48 Jimmie Johnson Lowe's Power of Pride	7.50	15.00
48 Jimmie Johnson Lowe's SpongeBob/11,532	10.00	20.00
72 Benny Parsons Victory Lap/4320	5.00	12.00
81 Jason Keller Kraft 100 Years Promo in window box	20.00	40.00
83 Kerry Earnhardt Hot Tamales black/10,584	5.00	12.00
88 Dale Jarrett UPS/10,584	7.50	15.00
88 Dale Jarrett UPS Store/4320	7.50	15.00
88 Dale Jarrett UPS Victory Lap/8820	7.50	15.00
99 Michael Waltrip Aaron's Rent Cat in the Hat/3888	5.00	12.00
99 Michael Waltrip Aaron's Rent Terminator 3/6912	5.00	12.00
99 Michael Waltrip Aaron's Rent 3 Stooges/6408	5.00	12.00
01 Jerry Nadeau Army/5616	5.00	12.00
03 Hulk Event Car/5256	7.50	15.00
03 Tropicana 400 Promo in bottle	15.00	25.00
NNO Victory Lap Event Color Chrome/4608	12.50	25.00
NNO Winston Cup Champions 14-car set in oak case Allison Earnhardt Elliott Gordon Jarrett Kulwicki/ Labonte/ Labonte/ Parsons/ Petty/ Stewart/ Wallace/ Waltrip/ Yarborough/3492	125.00	200.00

2003 Action/RCCA 1:64

Item	Low	High
1 Steve Park Pennzoil/1020	7.50	15.00
2 Rusty Wallace Miller Lite/1500	10.00	20.00
2 Rusty Wallace Miller Lite 600 Starts/1012	8.00	20.00
2 Rusty Wallace Miller Time Live Goo Goo Dolls/1444	8.00	20.00
3 Dale Earnhardt Earnhardt Foundation/3604	10.00	20.00
3 Dale Earnhardt Victory Lap/1500	12.50	25.00
5 Terry Labonte Kellogg's/1020	7.50	15.00
8 Dale Earnhardt Jr. Bud/3748	15.00	30.00
8 Dale Earnhardt Jr. Bud All-Star Game/3316	12.50	25.00
8 Dale Earnhardt Jr. Bud All-Star Game in baseball tin/2340	20.00	35.00
8 Dale Earnhardt Jr. Bud StainD/4036	10.00	20.00
8 Dale Earnhardt Jr. Dirty Mo Posse/4670	10.00	20.00
8 Dale Earnhardt Jr. E Concert/3300	15.00	30.00
8 Dale Earnhardt Jr. Oreo Ritz/6060	10.00	20.00
8 Steve Park Cheese Nips/1020	7.50	15.00
8 Steve Park Cheese Nips Promo	7.50	15.00
8 Steve Park Maxwell House/1020	7.50	15.00
8 Hank Parker Jr. Bass Pro Promo	12.50	25.00
8 Tony Stewart 3 Doors Down/2016	8.00	20.00
9 Bill Elliott Coors '87 Thunderbird/1164	8.00	20.00
9 Bill Elliott Dodge/1012	8.00	20.00
9 Bill Elliott Dodge Lion King/1012	8.00	20.00
9 Bill Elliott Dodge 10th Brickyard/1012	8.00	20.00
15 Michael Waltrip NAPA/1020	7.50	15.00
15 Michael Waltrip NAPA Hootie & the Blowfish/1012	7.50	15.00
15 Michael Waltrip NAPA Nilla Wafers/1020	7.50	15.00
15 Michael Waltrip NAPA Stars&Stripes/1020	7.50	15.00
18 Bobby Labonte Interstate Batteries/1212	8.00	20.00
18 Bobby Labonte Interstate Batteries Hulk/1020	8.00	20.00
19 Dale Earnhardt Beldon Asphalt 1976 Malibu/3460	10.00	20.00
19 Jeremy Mayfield Dodge/1452	7.50	15.00
20 Tony Stewart Home Depot/2308	8.00	20.00
20 Tony Stewart Home Depot Declaration of Independence/2020	8.00	20.00
21 Kevin Harvick Payday/1300	8.00	20.00
21 Johnny Sauter Payday/504	7.50	15.00
24 Jeff Gordon Cookie Monster/2596	10.00	20.00
24 Jeff Gordon DuPont Flames/2172	12.50	25.00
24 Jeff Gordon DuPont Victory Lap/1008	12.50	25.00
24 Jeff Gordon DuPont Wright Brothers/3328	10.00	20.00
24 Jeff Gordon DuPont Yosemite Sam/2448	10.00	20.00
24 Jeff Gordon Pepsi/2460	10.00	20.00
24 Jeff Gordon Pepsi Billion $/3040	10.00	20.00
28/42 Davey Allison Jamie McMurray Havoline White/1080	25.00	50.00
29 Kevin Harvick Goodwrench/2028	8.00	20.00
29 Kevin Harvick Goodwrench Sugar Ray/1300	8.00	20.00
29 Kevin Harvick Snap-On/1588	8.00	20.00
30 Jeff Green AOL/1492	7.50	15.00
30 Steve Park GM Card Promo	15.00	30.00
31 Robby Gordon Cingular black/1596	7.50	15.00
31 Robby Gordon Cingular orange/1020	7.50	15.00
38 Elliott Sadler M&M's/1300	7.50	15.00
38 Elliott Sadler M&M's Groovy/1012	8.00	20.00
38 Elliott Sadler M&M's Halloween/1012	7.50	15.00
40 Sterling Marlin Coors Light in a keg/12,144	15.00	30.00
42 Jamie McMurray Havoline/1596	7.50	15.00
42 Jamie McMurray Havoline Terminator 3/1300	7.50	15.00
43 Richard Petty STP 1975 Charger/1444	8.00	20.00
43 Richard Petty Victory Lap/1008	8.00	20.00
43 Richard Petty Yankees 100th Anniversary/1012	8.00	20.00
44 Christian Fittipaldi 100th Ann.Yankees/1020	7.50	15.00
45 Kyle Petty Georgia Pacific/1020	7.50	15.00
48 Jimmie Johnson Lowe's/2460	8.00	20.00
48 Jimmie Johnson Lowe's Power of Pride/2460	8.00	20.00
48 Jimmie Johnson Lowe's SpongeBob/1588	8.00	20.00
88 Dale Jarrett UPS/1184	8.00	20.00
88 Dale Jarrett UPS Store/1008	8.00	20.00
99 Michael Waltrip Aaron's Rent Cat in the Hat/1020	7.50	15.00
99 Michael Waltrip Aaron's Rent Three Stooges/1020	7.50	15.00
99 Michael Waltrip Aaron's Rent Terminator 3/1020	7.50	15.00
01 Jerry Nadeau Army/1300	7.50	15.00
03 Hulk Event Car/1212	7.50	15.00
NNO Victory Lap Color Chrome/1008	12.50	25.00

2003 Action/RCCA Elite 1:64

Item	Low	High
1 Steve Park Pennzoil/1020	10.00	20.00
2 Rusty Wallace Miller Lite/1500	15.00	30.00
2 Rusty Wallace Miller Lite 600 Starts/1012	15.00	30.00
2 Rusty Wallace Miller Time Live Goo Goo Dolls/1204	15.00	30.00
3 Dale Earnhardt Earnhardt Foundation/2500	12.50	30.00
8 Dale Earnhardt Jr. Bud/3660	20.00	35.00
8 Dale Earnhardt Jr. Bud MLB All-Star Game/3300	20.00	35.00
8 Dale Earnhardt Jr. Bud StainD/2980	20.00	35.00
8 Dale Earnhardt Jr. Dirty Mo Posse/2988	20.00	35.00
8 Dale Earnhardt Jr. E Concert/3300	20.00	35.00
8 Dale Earnhardt Jr. Oreo Ritz/4380	15.00	30.00
8 Steve Park Cheese Nips/1020	10.00	20.00
8 Steve Park Maxwell House/1020	10.00	20.00
8 Tony Stewart 3 Doors Down/2028	15.00	30.00
9 Bill Elliott Dodge/1012	10.00	20.00
9 Bill Elliott Dodge Lion King/1012	15.00	30.00
9 Bill Elliott Dodge 10th Brickyard/1012	10.00	20.00
15 Michael Waltrip NAPA/1020	10.00	20.00
15 Michael Waltrip NAPA Hootie & the Blowfish/1012	10.00	20.00
15 Michael Waltrip NAPA Nilla Wafers/1020	10.00	20.00
15 Michael Waltrip NAPA Stars&Stripes/1020	10.00	20.00
18 Bobby Labonte Interstate Batteries/1212	10.00	20.00
18 Bobby Labonte Interstate Batteries Hulk/1200	12.50	25.00
20 Tony Stewart Home Depot/2220	15.00	30.00
20 Tony Stewart Home Depot Declaration of Independence/2020	15.00	30.00
21 Kevin Harvick Payday/1156	12.50	25.00
24 Jeff Gordon Cookie Monster/1588	15.00	30.00
24 Jeff Gordon DuPont Flames/2124	20.00	40.00
24 Jeff Gordon DuPont Wright Brothers/2128	15.00	30.00
24 Jeff Gordon DuPont Yosemite Sam/1924	20.00	40.00
24 Jeff Gordon Pepsi/1824	15.00	30.00
24 Jeff Gordon Pepsi Billion $/2128	15.00	30.00
29 Kevin Harvick Goodwrench/1588	12.50	25.00
29 Kevin Harvick Goodwrench Sugar Ray/1012	20.00	35.00
29 Kevin Harvick Snap-On/1300	12.50	25.00
31 Robby Gordon Cingular/1012	10.00	20.00
38 Elliott Sadler M&M's Groovy/1012	12.50	25.00
38 Elliott Sadler M&M's Halloween/1012	10.00	20.00

Sterling Marlin 12.50 25.00
Coors Light/1012
Jamie McMurray 12.50 25.00
Havoline/1212
Jamie McMurray 12.50 25.00
Havoline Terminator 3/1212
Jamie McMurray 12.50 25.00
Havoline White/1012
Richard Petty 15.00 30.00
Yankees 100th Anniversary/1012
Jimmie Johnson 15.00 30.00
Lowe's/1500
Jimmie Johnson 15.00 30.00
Lowe's Power of Pride/1548
Jimmie Johnson 15.00 30.00
Lowe's SpongeBob/1300
Dale Jarrett 12.50 25.00
UPS/1020
Michael Waltrip 10.00 20.00
Aaron's Rent Terminator 3/1020

2004 Action Performance 1:64

Dale Earnhardt Jr. 25.00 40.00
Nextel Cup 6-car set
Bud
Bud Born On Feb. 8
Bud Born On Feb. 15 raced
Bud Father's Day
Bud Dave Matthews Band
Bud World Series
Martin TruexJr. 25.00 40.00
Busch Series 6-car set
Bass Pro Shops
KFC
Long John Silvers
Oreo Ritz
Taco Bell
Wrangler
9 Kasey Kahne 25.00 40.00
Nextel Cup 6-car set
Dodge
Dodge Refresh
Dodge Mad Magazine
Dodge Pit Cap
Dodge Popeye
Mountain Dew
18 Bobby Labonte 3.00 6.00
Interstate Batteries
20 Tony Stewart 5.00 10.00
Home Depot Olympic
20 Tony Stewart 5.00 10.00
Home Depot Shrek 2
20 Tony Stewart 25.00 40.00
Nextel Cup 6-car set
Coke C2
Home Depot
Home Depot Black
Home Depot Olympic
Home Depot Shrek 2
Home Depot 25th Anniversary
24 Jeff Gordon 25.00 40.00
Nextel Cup 6-car set
Dupont Flames
DuPont Flames HMS 20th Anniversary
DuPont Flames Wizard of Oz
DuPont Rainbow
Pepsi Billion $
Pepsi Shards
29 Kevin Harvick 25.00 40.00
Nextel Cup 6-car set
Coke C2
Goodwrench
Goodwrench KISS
Ice Breakers
Realtree
Snap-On
32 Ricky Craven 2.00 5.00
Tide
66 Billy Parker Jr. 60.00 100.00
Duraflame Promo

2004 Action Racing Collectables 1:64

2 Rusty Wallace 7.50 15.00
Kodak/4128
2 Rusty Wallace 7.50 15.00
Miller Lite/8496
2 Rusty Wallace 12.50 25.00
Miller Lite in keg
2 Rusty Wallace 10.00 20.00
Miller Lite Last Call/3936
2 Rusty Wallace 7.50 15.00
Miller Lite
Puddle of Mudd/4464
3 Dale Earnhardt 40.00 80.00
Goodwrench Olympics
Goodwrench
AC Delco Japan
Goodwrench Crash
Coke Japan
Goodwrench Talladega
Goodwrench Sign/ Wrangler/ Goodwrench Peter Max/
9-car set/5004 w
case
3/8/8 Dale Earnhardt Jr. 20.00 40.00
3-car set in tin/7128
2002 Oreo 2003 Oreo Ritz 2004 Oreo
5 Terry Labonte 6.00 12.00
Kellogg's/9168
6 Bill Elliott 7.50 15.00
Lucas Oil Elvis/4224
8 Dale Earnhardt Jr. 10.00 20.00
Bud/30,480
on a base
8 Dale Earnhardt Jr. 10.00 20.00
Bud Born On Feb.7/13,296
8 Dale Earnhardt Jr. 10.00 20.00
Bud Born On Feb.12
Raced/15,000
8 Dale Earnhardt Jr. 10.00 20.00
Bud Born On
Feb.15 Raced/22,004
8 Dale Earnhardt Jr. 7.50 15.00
Bud Dave Matthews Band
8 Dale Earnhardt Jr. 10.00 20.00
Bud World Series
8 Dale Earnhardt Jr. 7.50 15.00
Oreo/18,288
8 Martin Truex Jr. 7.50 15.00
Bass Pro Shops/8496
8 Martin Truex Jr. 7.50 15.00
Wrangler/5040
8/33 Dale Earnhardt Jr. 15.00 30.00
Bud Father's Day
Kerry Earnhardt
Bass Pro Shop Father's Day
2-car set/12,288
8/81 Dale Earnhardt Jr. 25.00 40.00
Bristol Raced 2-car set
Bud Bristol Raced
Menards Bristol Raced
9 Kasey Kahne 15.00 25.00
Dodge/4128
9 Kasey Kahne 10.00 20.00
Dodge refresh/9120
9 Kasey Kahne 10.00 20.00
Dodge refresh Rookie of the Year
Color Chrome
9 Kasey Kahne 7.50 15.00
Dodge Mopar
9 Kasey Kahne 25.00 40.00
Mountain Dew in vending tin/5124
15 Michael Waltrip 6.00 12.00
NAPA/8976
15 Michael Waltrip 6.00 12.00
NAPA Stars&Stripes/3792
18 Bobby Labonte 6.00 12.00
Interstate Batteries/8640
18 Bobby Labonte 6.00 12.00
Interstate Batteries D-Day/5568
18 Bobby Labonte 6.00 12.00
Interstate Batteries
Shrek 2/5712
20 Tony Stewart 7.50 15.00
Home Depot/13,584
20 Tony Stewart 10.00 20.00
Home Depot in tool box/3540
20 Tony Stewart 7.50 15.00
Home Depot Reverse Paint
Black/6576
20 Tony Stewart 7.50 15.00
Home Depot
Shrek 2/7728
20 Tony Stewart 7.50 15.00
Home Depot 25th Anniversary/6336
21 Kevin Harvick 6.00 12.00
Hershey's Kisses/6884
21 Kevin Harvick 6.00 12.00
Reese's/7248
24 Jeff Gordon 7.50 15.00
Big Bird/7440
24 Jeff Gordon 7.50 15.00
DuPont Flames/22,848
24 Jeff Gordon 10.00 20.00
DuPont Flames
Brickyard Raced/5040
24 Jeff Gordon 10.00 20.00
DuPont Flame
HMS 20th Anniversary/5952
24 Jeff Gordon 10.00 20.00
DuPont Rainbow/8400
24 Jeff Gordon 7.50 15.00
DuPont Wizard of Oz/9024
24 Jeff Gordon 7.50 15.00
Pepsi Billion/7776
24 Jeff Gordon 7.50 15.00
Pepsi Shards/8064
24 Jeff Gordon 7.50 15.00
Santa/5040
25 Brian Vickers 6.00 12.00
ditech/5040
29 Kevin Harvick 6.00 12.00
Goodwrench/10,752
29 Kevin Harvick 7.50 15.00
Goodwrench KISS/5280
29 Kevin Harvick 6.00 12.00
Goodwrench RCR 35th Anniversary/5568
29 Kevin Harvick 6.00 12.00
Goodwrench Realtree/5568
29 Kevin Harvick 6.00 12.00
Ice Breakers Liquid Ice/5328
29 Kevin Harvick 6.00 12.00
Snap-On/5616
29 Tony Stewart 6.00 12.00
Kid Rock/7488
31 Robby Gordon 6.00 12.00
Cingular/4080
33 Kerry Earnhardt 6.00 12.00
Bass Pro Shops/5376
38 Kasey Kahne 7.50 15.00
Great Clips Shark Tales/4464
38 Elliott Sadler 6.00 12.00
M&M's/6576
38 Elliott Sadler 7.50 15.00
M&M's Black&White/5184
38 Elliott Sadler 6.00 12.00
M&M's Halloween
38 Elliott Sadler 6.00 12.00
Pedigree Wizard of Oz/4560
40 Sterling Marlin 6.00 12.00
Coors Light/4944
40 Sterling Marlin 15.00 30.00
Coors Light Keg tin/2952
on a base
42 Jamie McMurray 6.00 12.00
Havoline/10,272
45 Kyle Petty 6.00 12.00
Georgia Pacific/6264
48 Jimmie Johnson 7.50 15.00
Lowe's/12,960
48 Jimmie Johnson 7.50 15.00
Lowe's HMS 20th Anniversary/3408
48 Jimmie Johnson 7.50 15.00
Lowe's Power of Pride/11,616
48 Jimmie Johnson 6.00 12.00
Lowe's SpongeBob/3984
77 Brendan Gaughan 7.50 15.00
Kodak/4512
77 Brendan Gaughan 6.00 12.00
Kodak Wizard of Oz/3504
81 Dale Earnhardt Jr. 7.50 15.00
KFC/12,288
81 Dale Earnhardt Jr. 7.50 15.00
Taco Bell/11,664
81 Tony Stewart 6.00 12.00
Bass Pro/5088
88 Dale Jarrett 7.50 15.00
UPS/6144
88 Dale Jarrett 7.50 15.00
UPS Arnold Palmer/8400
88 Dale Jarrett 12.50 25.00
UPS Arnold Palmer/8400
with golf ball
01 Joe Nemechek 6.00 12.00
Army GI Joe/3168

2004 Action Racing Collectables Historical Series 1:64

2 Dale Earnhardt 10.00 20.00
Mello Yello
1979 Pontiac Ventura/6960
9 Bill Elliott 7.50 15.00
Coors Light 1991 t-bird/3984
29 Kevin Harvick 8.00 20.00
Goodwrench Service Plus
2001 Monte Carlo black numbers/10,944

2004 Action/RCCA 1:64

1 John Andretti 7.50 15.00
Post Maxwell House Promo
2 Rusty Wallace 7.50 15.00
Kodak/576
2 Rusty Wallace 7.50 15.00
Miller Lite/1588
2 Rusty Wallace 12.50 25.00
Miller Lite Last Call/576
3/8/8 Dale Earnhardt Jr. 20.00 35.00
2002 Oreo 2003 Oreo Ritz 2004 Oreo Ritz
3-car set in tin
5 Terry Labonte 7.50 15.00
Kellogg's/720
8 Dale Earnhardt Jr. 12.50 25.00
Bud/3024
8 Dale Earnhardt Jr. 12.50 25.00
Bud Born On
Feb.7/3024
8 D.Earnhardt Jr. 20.00 35.00
Bud Born On
Feb.12&15 Raced 2-car set/4008
8 Dale Earnhardt Jr. 10.00 20.00
Bud Dave Matthews Band/2880
8 Dale Earnhardt Jr. 12.50 25.00
Bud World Series/2448
8 Dale Earnhardt Jr. 10.00 20.00
Oreo/4032
8 Martin Truex Jr. 7.50 15.00
Bass Pro Shops/720
8/33 Dale Earnhardt Jr. 20.00 35.00
Bud Father's Day
Kerry Earnhardt
Bass Pro Shops Father's Day/1500
2-car set
8/81 Dale Earnhardt Jr. 25.00 40.00
Bristol Raced 2-car set/960
Bud Bristol Raced
Menards Bristol Raced
9 Kasey Kahne 25.00 40.00
Dodge/576
9 Kasey Kahne 20.00 35.00
Dodge Mopar/576
9 Kasey Kahne 25.00 40.00
Mountain Dew in vending tin/600
15 Michael Waltrip 7.50 15.00
NAPA/1008
15 Michael Waltrip 7.50 15.00
NAPA Stars & Stripes/720
18 Bobby Labonte 7.50 15.00
Interstate Batteries
D-Day/576
18 Bobby Labonte 7.50 15.00
Interstate Batteries Shrek 2/1008
18 Bobby Labonte 7.50 15.00
Wellbutrin
20 Tony Stewart 10.00 20.00
Coke C2/576
20 Tony Stewart 15.00 30.00
Home Depot
in tool box/1500
20 Tony Stewart 10.00 20.00
Home Depot Black Reverse/1152
20 Tony Stewart 10.00 20.00
Home Depot Shrek 2/1008
20 Tony Stewart 10.00 20.00
Home Depot 25th Anniversary/1008
21 Kevin Harvick 10.00 20.00
Reese's/1008
24 Jeff Gordon 12.50 25.00
DuPont Flames
HMS 20th Anniversary/1440
24 Jeff Gordon 10.00 20.00
Pepsi Billion/1008
24 Jeff Gordon 12.50 25.00
Pepsi Shards/1296
24 Jeff Gordon 12.50 25.00
Santa/576
25 Brian Vickers 7.50 15.00
ditech.com/504
29 Kevin Harvick 10.00 20.00
Goodwrench
KISS/1584
29 Kevin Harvick 10.00 20.00
Goodwrench
RCR 35th Ann/1008
29 Kevin Harvick 10.00 20.00
Ice Breakers/720
29 Kevin Harvick 10.00 20.00
Snap-On/1008
29 Tony Stewart 10.00 20.00
Kid Rock/1200
31 Robby Gordon 7.50 15.00
Cingular/720
33 Kerry Earnhardt 7.50 15.00
Bass Pro Shops/576
38 Kasey Kahne 10.00 20.00
Great Clips Shark Tale/576
38 Elliott Sadler 7.50 15.00
M&M's/720
38 Elliott Sadler 7.50 15.00
M&M's Black&White/1008
40 Sterling Marlin 7.50 15.00
Coors Light/504
42 Jamie McMurray 7.50 15.00
Havoline/1008
48 Jimmie Johnson 10.00 20.00
Lowe's/1008
48 Jimmie Johnson 10.00 20.00
Lowe's HMS 20th Anniversary/720
48 Jimmie Johnson 10.00 20.00
Lowe's SpongeBob/576
81 Dale Earnhardt Jr. 10.00 20.00
KFC/3600
81 Dale Earnhardt Jr. 12.50 25.00
Menards Bristol Raced/720
81 Dale Earnhardt Jr. 10.00 20.00
Taco Bell/1800
81 Tony Stewart 10.00 20.00
Bass Pro Shops/720
88 Dale Jarrett 7.50 15.00
UPS/504
88 Dale Jarrett 15.00 30.00
UPS Arnold Palmer
with golf ball/720
99 Michael Waltrip 7.50 15.00
Aaron's Dream Machine Promo

2004 Action/RCCA Elite 1:64

2 Rusty Wallace 12.50 25.00
Kodak/576
2 Rusty Wallace 15.00 30.00
Miller Lite/1500
2 Rusty Wallace 20.00 35.00
Miller Lite Last Call/528
2 Rusty Wallace 15.00 30.00
Miller Lite
Puddle of Mudd/528
6 Bill Elliott 12.50 25.00
Lucas Oil Elvis/480
8 Dale Earnhardt Jr. 20.00 40.00
Bud/2400
8 Dale Earnhardt Jr. 20.00 40.00
Bud Born On
Feb.7/2016
8 Dale Earnhardt Jr. 20.00 40.00
Bud Dave Matthews Band/1968
8 Dale Earnhardt Jr. 20.00 40.00
Bud World Series/1824
8 Dale Earnhardt Jr. 20.00 40.00
Oreo/2880
9 Kasey Kahne 25.00 50.00
Dodge/576
9 Kasey Kahne 25.00 40.00
Dodge Refresh Color Chrome/528
9 Kasey Kahne 15.00 30.00
Dodge refresh ROY/480
9 Kasey Kahne 20.00 40.00
Dodge Mopar/480
9 Kasey Kahne 25.00 50.00
Mountain Dew/528
15 Michael Waltrip 12.50 25.00
NAPA/720
18 Bobby Labonte 12.50 25.00
Interstate Batteries/1008
18 Bobby Labonte 12.50 25.00
Interstate Batteries D-Day/528
18 Bobby Labonte 12.50 25.00
Interstate Batteries
Shrek 2/720
20 Tony Stewart 15.00 30.00
Home Depot/1440
20 Tony Stewart 15.00 30.00
Home Depot
Black Reverse/1008
20 Tony Stewart 15.00 30.00
Home Depot Shrek 2/1008
20 Tony Stewart 15.00 30.00
Home Depot 25th Anniversary/720
21 Kevin Harvick 12.50 25.00
Hershey's Kisses/720
21 Kevin Harvick 12.50 25.00
Reese's/720
24 Jeff Gordon 15.00 30.00
Big Bird/1200
24 Jeff Gordon 20.00 35.00
DuPont Flames/1440
24 Jeff Gordon 15.00 30.00
DuPont Flames
Wizard of Oz/1200
24 Jeff Gordon 20.00 35.00
DuPont Rainbow/1008
24 Jeff Gordon 12.50 25.00
Pepsi Billion/1008
24 Jeff Gordon 15.00 30.00
Pepsi Shards/1008
24 Jeff Gordon 15.00 30.00
Santa/480
29 Kevin Harvick 15.00 30.00
Goodwrench/1008
29 Kevin Harvick 15.00 30.00
Goodwrench KISS/1008
29 Kevin Harvick 15.00 30.00
Goodwrench RCR 35th Anniversary/576
29 Kevin Harvick 12.50 25.00
Goodwrench Realtree/1008
29 Kevin Harvick 12.50 25.00
Ice Breakers/528
29 Kevin Harvick 12.50 25.00
Snap-On/720
29 Tony Stewart 12.50 25.00
Kid Rock/1008
31 Robby Gordon 12.50 25.00
Cingular Black/1584
33 Kerry Earnhardt 12.50 25.00
Bass Pro Shops/528
38 Elliott Sadler 15.00 30.00
M&M's/504
42 Jamie McMurray 15.00 30.00
Havoline/1008
48 Jimmie Johnson 15.00 30.00
Lowe's/720
48 Jimmie Johnson 15.00 30.00
Lowe's HMS 20th Anniversary/624
48 Jimmie Johnson 12.50 25.00
Lowe's SpongeBob/480
81 Dale Earnhardt Jr. 15.00 30.00
KFC/2400
81 Dale Earnhardt Jr. 15.00 30.00
Taco Bell/1200
81 Tony Stewart 12.50 25.00
Bass Pro Shops/528
88 Dale Jarrett 15.00 30.00
UPS/504
88 Dale Jarrett 15.00 30.00
UPS Arnold Palmer/528

2004 Action/RCCA Historical Series 1:64

29 Kevin Harvick 10.00 20.00
Goodwrench Service Plus
2001 MC black numbers/1296
43 Richard Petty 15.00 30.00
STP '72 Charger Promo
43 Richard Petty 15.00 30.00
STP '04 Fantasy Promo
43 Richard Petty 10.00 20.00
STP '84 Grand Prix Promo
NNO Jeff Gordon 30.00 60.00
DuPont '96 Monte Carlo
Jimmie Johnson
Lowe's 2003 Monte Carlo
Richard Petty
STP 1980 Monte Carlo
Darrell Waltrip
Tide 1987 Monte Carlo/ Chevy Wins 4-car tin set

2004 Action/RCCA Historical Series Elite 1:64

29 Kevin Harvick 12.50 25.00
Goodwrench Service Plus
2001 MC black numbers/720

2005 Action Performance 1:64

2/64 Rusty Wallace 25.00 40.00
Nextel Cup 6-car set series 1
64.Bell Helicopter
2.Kodak
2.Miller Lite
2.Miller Lite Last Call
2.Mobil Clean 7500
2.Snap-On 85th Anniversary
2/64 Rusty Wallace 25.00 40.00
Nextel Cup 6-car set series 2
64.Miller High Life
64.Top Flite
2.Miller Lite Last Race
2.Miller Lite Bristol
2.Miller Lite Sirius
2.Miller Genuine Draft
3 Dale Earnhardt 4.00 8.00
Goodwrench '00 MC
8 Dale Earnhardt Jr. 4.00 8.00
JR
9 Kasey Kahne 4.00 8.00
Dodge
9 Kasey Kahne 25.00 40.00
Nextel Cup 6-car set
Dodge
Dodge Pit Cap White
Mountain Dew
Dodge Mega Cab
Dodge Mopar
Dodge Retro
15 Michael Waltrip 4.00 8.00
Napa
18 Bobby Labonte 4.00 8.00
Interstate Batteries
19 Jeremy Mayfield 25.00 40.00
Nextel Cup 6-car set
Dodge
Dodge Black Reverse
Dodge Retro Daytona Shootout
Mountain Dew Pitch Black
79.AutoValue
20 Tony Stewart 4.00 8.00
Home Depot
20 Tony Stewart 25.00 40.00
Nextel Cup 6-car set
20.Home Depot
20.Home Depot Test
20.Home Depot Madagascar
20.Home Depot Daytona
20.Home Depot KaBOOM
20.Home Depot Brickyard
38 Elliott Sadler 4.00 8.00
M&M's
88 Dale Jarrett 4.00 8.00
UPS

2005 Action Promos 1:64

11 Jason Leffler 12.50 25.00
FedEx Express
11 Jason Leffler 12.50 25.00
FedEx Freight
11 Jason Leffler 12.50 25.00
FedEx Ground
11 Jason Leffler 12.50 25.00

FedEx Kinko's
31 Jeff Burton 10.00 20.00
Cingular in window box
43 Richard Petty 12.50 25.00
STP '72 Charger
in window box
43 Richard Petty 12.50 25.00
STP '84 Grand Prix
in window box
43 Richard Petty 10.00 20.00
STP Fantasy
in window box
96 DLP Hall of Fame Racing Promo 40.00 60.00
in bag

2005 Action Racing Collectables 1:64

1 Martin Truex Jr. 6.00 12.00
Bass Pro Shops
2 Rusty Wallace 15.00 25.00
Miller Genuine Draft
in can/4068
2 Rusty Wallace 6.00 12.00
Miller Lite
2 Rusty Wallace 15.00 25.00
Miller Lite in a can
2 Rusty Wallace 6.00 12.00
Miller Lite Last Call
Daytona Shootout
6 Bill Elliott 10.00 20.00
Charlie Brown Christmas
6/22/64 Wallace Family Tribute 3-car tin/3000 15.00 30.00
4.Mike Wallace
Ragu
23.Kenny Wallace
Whelen
64.Rusty Wallace
Miller High Life
8 Dale Earnhardt Jr. 7.50 15.00
Bud
8 Dale Earnhardt Jr. 7.50 15.00
Bud MLB All Star Game
8 Dale Earnhardt Jr. 7.50 15.00
Bud 3 Doors Down
8 Dale Earnhardt Jr. 25.00 40.00
Bud Born On Feb.12th
Bud Born On Feb.17
Bud Born On Feb.20
3-car set in tin/8000
8 Martin Truex Jr. 6.00 12.00
Bass Pro
9 Kasey Kahne 6.00 12.00
Dodge
9 Kasey Kahne 6.00 12.00
Dodge Pit Cap White
9 Kasey Kahne 6.00 12.00
Dodge Retro
Bud Shootout
9 Kasey Kahne 6.00 12.00
Mopar
9 Kasey Kahne 6.00 12.00
Mountain Dew
9 Kasey Kahne 12.50 25.00
Mountain Dew in can
15 Michael Waltrip 6.00 12.00
Napa
18 Bobby Labonte 6.00 12.00
Interstate Batteries
18 Bobby Labonte 6.00 12.00
Interstate Batteries Madagascar
19 Jeremy Mayfield 5.00 10.00
Dodge
20 Tony Stewart 6.00 12.00
Home Depot
20 Tony Stewart 6.00 12.00
Home Depot KaBOOM
20 Tony Stewart 6.00 12.00
Home Depot Madagascar
21 Kevin Harvick 6.00 12.00
Hershey's Take 5
21 Kevin Harvick 6.00 12.00
Pelon Pelo Rico
21 Kevin Harvick 6.00 12.00
Reese's
24 Jeff Gordon 7.50 15.00
DuPont Flames
24 Jeff Gordon 7.50 15.00
DuPont Flames Performance Alliance
Reverse
24 Jeff Gordon 7.50 15.00
Mighty Mouse
24 Jeff Gordon 7.50 15.00
Pepsi Daytona
24 Jeff Gordon 7.50 15.00
Pepsi Star Wars
24 Jeff Gordon 7.50 15.00
Santa Holiday
29 Kevin Harvick 6.00 12.00
Goodwrench
29 Kevin Harvick 6.00 12.00
Goodwrench Atlanta
29 Kevin Harvick 6.00 12.00
Goodwrench Brickyard
29 Kevin Harvick 6.00 12.00
Goodwrench Daytona
29 Kevin Harvick 6.00 12.00
Goodwrench Quicksilver
33 Tony Stewart 6.00 12.00
James Dean 50th Anniversary
38 Kasey Kahne 6.00 12.00
Great Clips
38 Elliott Sadler 6.00 12.00
M&M's
38 Elliott Sadler 6.00 12.00
M&M's Halloween
38 Elliott Sadler 6.00 12.00
M&M's July 4th
40 Sterling Marlin 6.00 12.00
Coors Light
41 Casey Mears 6.00 12.00
Target
42 Jamie McMurray 6.00 12.00
Havoline
44 Terry Labonte 6.00 12.00
Kellogg's
48 Jimmie Johnson 6.00 12.00
Lowe's
48 Jimmie Johnson 7.50 15.00
Lowe's '06 Preview
77 Travis Kvapil 6.00 12.00
Kodak
79 Kasey Kahne 6.00 12.00
Auto Value
81 Dale Earnhardt Jr. 6.00 12.00
Menards
81 Dale Earnhardt Jr. 6.00 12.00
Oreo Ritz
88 Dale Jarrett 6.00 12.00
UPS
88 Dale Jarrett 6.00 12.00
UPS Herbie Fully Loaded
88 Dale Jarrett 6.00 12.00
UPS Store Toys for Tots
91 Bill Elliott 6.00 12.00
Auto Value
91 Bill Elliott 6.00 12.00
McDonald's 50th Anniversary
99 Michael Waltrip 6.00 12.00
Aaron's
99/00 Michael Waltrip 12.50 25.00
Kenny Wallace
Aaron's 50th Anniversary
2-car set in tin

2005 Action Racing Collectables Historical Series 1:64

3 Dale Earnhardt 7.50 15.00
Goodwrench Daytona Crash
'97 Monte Carlo
9 Bill Elliott 7.50 15.00
Mel Gear '81 T-bird
1st Pole

2005 Action/RCCA 1:64

1 Martin Truex Jr. 10.00 20.00
Bass Pro Shops/576
2 Rusty Wallace 10.00 20.00
Miller Genuine Draft/576
2 Rusty Wallace 10.00 20.00
Miller Lite/576
2 Rusty Wallace 10.00 20.00
Miller Lite Last Call
Daytona Shootout/576
8 Dale Earnhardt Jr. 10.00 20.00
Bud/1584
8 Dale Earnhardt Jr. 10.00 20.00
Bud MLB All-Star/2016
8 Dale Earnhardt Jr. 10.00 20.00
Bud 3 Doors Down/1584
8 MartinTruex Jr. 10.00 20.00
Bass Pro/576
9 Kasey Kahne 10.00 20.00
Dodge/720
9 Kasey Kahne 10.00 20.00
Dodge Pit Cap White/576
9 Kasey Kahne 10.00 20.00
Dodge Retro Bud Shootout/720
9 Kasey Kahne 10.00 20.00
Mountain Dew/720
9 Kasey Kahne 12.50 25.00
Mountain Dew
in can/504
18 Bobby Labonte 10.00 20.00
Interstate Batteries/576
20 Tony Stewart 10.00 20.00
Home Depot/864
20 Tony Stewart 10.00 20.00
Home Depot KaBOOM/480
20 Tony Stewart 7.50 15.00
Home Depot Madagascar/576
24 Jeff Gordon 10.00 20.00
DuPont Flames/1008
24 Jeff Gordon 10.00 20.00
Foundation Holiday/432
24 Jeff Gordon 10.00 20.00
Mighty Mouse/1296
24 Jeff Gordon 10.00 20.00
Pepsi Star Wars/1584
29 Kevin Harvick 7.50 15.00
Goodwrench/864
29 Kevin Harvick 7.50 15.00
Goodwrench Atlanta/720
29 Kevin Harvick 7.50 15.00
Goodwrench Daytona/864
33 Tony Stewart 7.50 15.00
James Dean 50th Anniversary
38 Elliott Sadler 7.50 15.00
M&M's/576
38 Elliott Sadler 7.50 15.00
M&M's July 4/432
48 Jimmie Johnson 10.00 20.00
Lowe's/576
48 Jimmie Johnson 10.00 20.00
Lowe's '06 Preview/288
81 Dale Earnhardt Jr. 10.00 20.00
Oreo Ritz/2016
88 Dale Jarrett 10.00 20.00
UPS/576
88 Dale Jarrett 10.00 20.00
UPS Herbie Fully Loaded/720
88 Dale Jarrett 10.00 20.00
UPS Store
Toys for Tots/408
91 Bill Elliott 10.00 20.00
McDonald's/432

2005 Action/RCCA Elite 1:64

2 Rusty Wallace 12.50 25.00
Miller Lite/480
2 Rusty Wallace 12.50 25.00
Miller Lite Last Call
Daytona Shootout/480
8 Dale Earnhardt Jr. 15.00 30.00
Bud/1200
8 Dale Earnhardt Jr. 15.00 30.00
Bud MLB All-Star/1440
9 Kasey Kahne 15.00 30.00
Dodge/576
9 Kasey Kahne 12.50 25.00
Dodge Pit Cap White/480
9 Kasey Kahne 12.50 25.00
Dodge Retro Bud Shootout/528
9 Kasey Kahne 15.00 30.00
Mountain Dew/528
20 Tony Stewart 12.50 25.00
Home Depot/576
20 Tony Stewart 12.50 25.00
Home Depot Madagascar/480
24 Jeff Gordon 15.00 30.00
DuPont Flames/864
24 Jeff Gordon 25.00 50.00
Foundation Holiday/288
24 Jeff Gordon 15.00 30.00
Mighty Mouse/816
24 Jeff Gordon 15.00 30.00
Pepsi Star Wars/1200
33 Tony Stewart 12.50 25.00
James Dean 50th Anniversary/528
44 Terry Labonte 15.00 30.00
Kellogg's/480
48 Jimmie Johnson 15.00 30.00
Lowe's/480
48 Jimmie Johnson 25.00 50.00
Lowe's '06 Preview/240
81 Dale Earnhardt Jr. 12.50 25.00
Oreo Ritz/1584
88 Dale Jarrett 20.00 40.00
UPS Store
Toys for Tots/480

2006 Action Performance 1:64

1 Martin Truex Jr. 5.00 10.00
Bass Pro Shops
9 Kasey Kahne 5.00 10.00
Dodge
20 Tony Stewart 5.00 10.00
Home Depot
24 Jeff Gordon 5.00 10.00
DuPont Flames
26/47/55 Talladega Nights 5-car set 15.00 30.00
26.Ricky Bobby
Laughing Clown Malt Liquor
26.Ricky Bobby
ME
26.Ricky Bobby
Wonderbread
47.Cal Naughton Jr./ Old Spice/ 55.Jean Girard/ Perrier
48 Jimmie Johnson 5.00 10.00
Lowe's

2006 Action Promos 1:64

11 Denny Hamlin 10.00 20.00
Fed Ex Express in blister
11 Denny Hamlin 10.00 20.00
Fed Ex Freight in blister
11 Denny Hamlin 10.00 20.00
Fed Ex Ground in blister
11 Denny Hamlin 10.00 20.00
Fed Ex Kinko's in blister
22 Kenny Wallace 5.00 10.00
Auto Zone in blister
38 Elliott Sadler 10.00 20.00
M&M's & Snicker's 2-car blister pack
64 Jamie McMurray 7.50 15.00
USG Sheetrock in window box
66 Jeff Green 10.00 20.00
Best Buy in blister

2006 Action Racing Collectables 1:64

1 Martin Truex Jr. 6.00 12.00
Bass Pro Shops
1 Martin Truex Jr. 7.50 15.00
Bass Pro Shops
3 Days of Dale Tribute
5 Kyle Busch 6.00 12.00
Kellogg's
5 Kyle Busch 6.00 12.00
Kellogg's Cars
5 Kyle Busch 6.00 12.00
Kellogg's Ice Age
6 Mark Martin 7.50 15.00
AAA Holiday
8 Dale Earnhardt Jr. 7.50 15.00
Bud
8 Dale Earnhardt Jr. 7.50 15.00
Bud Richmond Raced
8 Dale Earnhardt Jr. 10.00 20.00
Bud 3 Days of Dale Tribute
8 Dale Earnhardt Jr. 10.00 20.00
Bud Father's Day
8 Dale Earnhardt Jr. 7.50 15.00
Oreo
8 Dale Earnhardt Jr. 7.50 15.00
250 Starts
8 Martin Truex Jr. 7.50 15.00
Bass Pro 3 Days of Dale Tribute
Talladega Raced
9 Kasey Kahne 7.50 15.00
Dodge
10 Scott Riggs 6.00 12.00
Stanley Tools
10 Scott Riggs 6.00 12.00
Valvoline
10 Scott Riggs 6.00 12.00
Valvoline Cars
11 Denny Hamlin 10.00 20.00
Fed Ex Express
11 Denny Hamlin 10.00 20.00
Fed Ex Freight
11 Denny Hamlin 10.00 20.00
Fed Ex Ground
11 Denny Hamlin 10.00 20.00
Fed Ex Kinko's
11 Paul Menard 7.50 15.00
Turtle Wax 3 Days of Dale Tribute
19 Jeremy Mayfield 5.00 10.00
Dodge
20 Denny Hamlin 6.00 12.00
Rockwell Automation
20 Tony Stewart 7.50 15.00
Home Depot
24 Jeff Gordon 7.50 15.00
DuPont Flames
24 Jeff Gordon 7.50 15.00
DuPont Flames
Performance Alliance
24 Jeff Gordon 7.50 15.00
DuPont Hot Hues
Foose Design
24 Jeff Gordon 6.00 12.00
Holiday Jeff Gordon Foundation
24 Jeff Gordon 6.00 12.00
Mighty Mouse
Jeff Gordon Foundation
24 Jeff Gordon 7.50 15.00
Nicorette
24 Jeff Gordon 7.50 15.00
Pepsi
24 Jeff Gordon 7.50 15.00
Superman
24 Jeff Gordon 7.50 15.00
World Series of Poker
Jeff Gordon Foundation
25 Brian Vickers 6.00 12.00
GMAC
29 Kevin Harvick 6.00 12.00
Goodwrench
29 Kevin Harvick 6.00 12.00
Hershey's
29 Kevin Harvick 6.00 12.00
Hershey's Kissables
29 Kevin Harvick 6.00 12.00
Reese's
31 Jeff Burton 6.00 12.00
Cingular
38 David Gilliland 7.50 15.00
M&M's Halloween
38 Elliott Sadler 6.00 12.00
M&M's
38 Elliott Sadler 6.00 12.00
M&M's Pirates of the Caribbean
38 Elliott Sadler 6.00 12.00
Snickers
40 David Stremme 7.50 15.00
Coors Light
41 Reed Sorenson 7.50 15.00
Target
43 Bobby Labonte 6.00 12.00
Cheerios
43 Bobby Labonte 6.00 12.00
STP
44 Terry Labonte 6.00 12.00
Kellogg's
48 Jimmie Johnson 7.50 15.00
Lowe's
48 Jimmie Johnson 60.00 100.00
Lowe's Dover Win w
Monster/3948
48 Jimmie Johnson 6.00 12.00
Lowe's SeaWorld
48 Jimmie Johnson 7.50 15.00
Lowe's 60th Anniversary
88 Dale Jarrett 6.00 12.00
UPS
90 Elliott Sadler 6.00 12.00
Citifinancial
06 Sam Bass Holiday 5.00 10.00
NNO Dale Earnhardt 7.50 15.00
Hall of Fame

2006 Action/RCCA 1:64

5 Kyle Busch 10.00 20.00
Kellogg's Cars/288
5 Kyle Busch 10.00 20.00
Kellogg's Ice Age/288
8 Dale Earnhardt Jr. 12.50 25.00
Bud/936
8 Dale Earnhardt Jr. 15.00 30.00
Bud 3 Days of Dale Tribute/2133
8 Dale Earnhardt Jr. 12.50 25.00
Bud Father's Day/2008
8 Dale Earnhardt Jr. 10.00 20.00
250th Start/1008
11 Denny Hamlin 12.50 25.00
Fed Ex Express/384
11 Denny Hamlin 12.50 25.00
Fed Ex Freight/288
11 Denny Hamlin 12.50 25.00
Fed Ex Ground/360
11 Denny Hamlin 12.50 25.00
Fed Ex Kinko's/288
20 Denny Hamlin 10.00 20.00
Rockwall Automation/288
20 Tony Stewart 10.00 20.00
Home Depot/600
24 Jeff Gordon 12.50 25.00
DuPont Flames/720
24 Jeff Gordon 10.00 20.00
DuPont Hot Hues Foose/1008
24 Jeff Gordon 10.00 20.00
DuPont Flames
Performance Alliance/600
24 Jeff Gordon 10.00 20.00
Holiday Jeff Gordon Foundation/432
24 Jeff Gordon 10.00 20.00
Mighty Mouse
Jeff Gordon Foundation/576
24 Jeff Gordon 10.00 20.00
Nicorette/720
24 Jeff Gordon 10.00 20.00
Pepsi/864
24 Jeff Gordon 10.00 20.00
Superman/1296
24 Jeff Gordon 12.50 25.00
World Series of Poker
Jeff Gordon Foundation/720
29 Kevin Harvick 10.00 20.00
Goodwrench/432
29 Kevin Harvick 10.00 20.00
Hershey's/360
29 Kevin Harvick 10.00 20.00
Hershey's Kissables/432
29 Kevin Harvick 10.00 20.00
Reese's/288
38 David Gilliland 12.50 25.00
M&M's Halloween/288
38 Elliott Sadler 10.00 20.00
M&M's Pirates of the Caribbean/240
41 Reed Sorenson 12.50 25.00
Target/288
43 Bobby Labonte 10.00 20.00
STP/288
48 Jimmie Johnson 10.00 20.00
Lowe's/528
48 Jimmie Johnson 10.00 20.00
Lowe's Sea World/408
48 Jimmie Johnson 10.00 20.00
Lowe's 60th Anniversary/432
NNO Dale Earnhardt 10.00 20.00
Dale Tribute Hall Of Fame/1584

2006 Action/RCCA Elite 1:64

8 Dale Earnhardt Jr. 20.00 40.00
Bud 3 Days of Dale Tribute/1533
8 Dale Earnhardt Jr. 20.00 40.00
Bud Father's Day/1508
8 Dale Earnhardt Jr. 15.00 30.00
250th Start/720
9 Kasey Kahne 15.00 30.00
Dodge/288
11 Denny Hamlin 25.00 50.00
Fed Ex Express/144
20 Denny Hamlin 15.00 30.00
Rockwell Automation/288
20 Tony Stewart 15.00 30.00
Home Depot/384
24 Jeff Gordon 20.00 40.00
DuPont Flames/432
24 Jeff Gordon 15.00 30.00
DuPont Flames
Performance Alliance/240
24 Jeff Gordon 20.00 40.00
DuPont Hot Hues
Foose Designs/720
24 Jeff Gordon 15.00 30.00
Holiday JG Foundation/288
24 Jeff Gordon 15.00 30.00
Nicorette/480
24 Jeff Gordon 20.00 40.00
Pepsi/528
24 Jeff Gordon 20.00 40.00
Superman/720
24 Jeff Gordon 20.00 40.00
WSOP
JG Foundation/480
29 Kevin Harvick 15.00 30.00
Goodwrench/240
29 Kevin Harvick 12.50 25.00
Hershey's/240
29 Kevin Harvick 12.50 25.00
Reese's/144
31 Jeff Burton 12.50 25.00
Cingular/144
38 David Gilliland 20.00 40.00
M&M's Halloween/144
38 Elliott Sadler 12.50 25.00
M&M's
Pirates of the Caribbean/240
43 Bobby Labonte 12.50 25.00
STP/204
48 Jimmie Johnson 20.00 40.00
Lowe's/288
48 Jimmie Johnson 20.00 40.00
Lowe's SeaWorld/240
48 Jimmie Johnson 20.00 40.00
Lowe's 60th Anniversary/240
NNO Dale Earnhardt 20.00 40.00
HOF/933

2007 Action/Motorsports Authentics Driver's Select 1:64

2 Kurt Busch 5.00 10.00
Miller Lite
2 Kurt Busch 6.00 12.00
Miller Lite COT
5 Kyle Busch 5.00 10.00
Kellogg's
5 Kyle Busch 6.00 12.00
Kellogg's COT
6 David Ragan 7.50 15.00
AAA
6 David Ragan 7.50 15.00
AAA COT
6 David Ragan 6.00 12.00
AAA Insurance
6 David Ragan 6.00 12.00
AAA Show Your Card
6 David Ragan 6.00 12.00
AAA Travel
6 David Ragan 6.00 12.00
Discount Tire
8 Dale Earnhardt Jr. 7.50 15.00
Bud
8 Dale Earnhardt Jr. 6.00 12.00
Bud Stars & Stripes
9 Kasey Kahne 5.00 10.00
Dodge Dealers
9 Kasey Kahne 6.00 12.00
Dodge Dealers COT
9 Kasey Kahne 5.00 10.00
Hellmann's
9 Kasey Kahne 5.00 10.00
McDonald's
10 Scott Riggs 4.00 8.00
Stanley Tools
10 Scott Riggs 4.00 8.00
Valvoline
11 Denny Hamlin 5.00 10.00
Fed Ex Express
11 Denny Hamlin 6.00 12.00
Fed Ex Express COT
11 Denny Hamlin 5.00 10.00
Fed Ex Freight
11 Denny Hamlin 6.00 12.00
Fed Ex Freight COT
11 Denny Hamlin 6.00 12.00
Fed Ex Freight Marines
American Heroes
11 Denny Hamlin 5.00 10.00
Fed Ex Ground
11 Denny Hamlin 6.00 12.00
Fed Ex Ground COT
11 Denny Hamlin 5.00 10.00
Fed Ex Kinko's
11 Denny Hamlin 6.00 12.00
Fed Ex Kinko's COT
12 Kurt Busch 6.00 12.00
Penske
12 Sam Hornish Jr. 6.00 12.00
Mobil 1
12 Ryan Newman 5.00 10.00
Alltel

12 Ryan Newman 5.00 10.00
Alltel My Circle
16 Greg Biffle 4.00 8.00
Ameriquest
16 Greg Biffle 4.00 8.00
Jackson Hewitt
16 Greg Biffle 5.00 10.00
3M Coast Guard
American Heroes
17 Matt Kenseth 6.00 12.00
Carhartt COT
17 Matt Kenseth 6.00 12.00
iLevel Wayerhouser
18 J.J. Yeley 6.00 12.00
Interstate Batteries
19 Elliott Sadler 5.00 10.00
Dodge Dealers
19 Elliott Sadler 6.00 12.00
Siemen's COT
20 Tony Stewart 6.00 12.00
Home Depot
20 Tony Stewart 6.00 12.00
Home Depot COT
21 Kevin Harvick 6.00 12.00
Auto Zone
21 Jon Wood 6.00 12.00
Air Force American Heroes
22 Dave Blaney 6.00 12.00
CAT COT
24 Jeff Gordon 7.50 15.00
DuPont Department of Defense
American Heroes
24 Jeff Gordon 7.50 15.00
DuPont Flames
24 Jeff Gordon 7.50 15.00
DuPont Flames COT
24 Jeff Gordon 6.00 12.00
DuPont Flames '57 Chevy
24 Jeff Gordon 6.00 12.00
Pepsi
24 Jeff Gordon 6.00 12.00
Nicorette COT
25 Casey Mears 5.00 10.00
National Guard
26 Jamie McMurray 5.00 10.00
Dish Network
29 Kevin Harvick 6.00 12.00
Pennzoil Platinum COT
29 Kevin Harvick 5.00 10.00
Shell Pennzoil
29 Kevin Harvick 6.00 12.00
Shell Pennzoil COT
31 Jeff Burton 6.00 12.00
Cingular
33 Tony Stewart 6.00 12.00
Old Spice
38 David Gilliland 6.00 12.00
M&M's
38 David Gilliland 4.00 8.00
M&M's July 4
40 David Stremme 3.00 6.00
Lone Star Steakhouse
41 Reed Sorenson 6.00 12.00
Target
42 Juan Pablo Montoya 5.00 10.00
Big Red
42 Juan Pablo Montoya 6.00 12.00
Texaco Havoline
42 Juan Pablo Montoya 6.00 12.00
Texaco Havoline COT
43 Bobby Labonte 6.00 12.00
Cheerios
48 Jimmie Johnson 6.00 12.00
Lowe's
48 Jimmie Johnson 6.00 12.00
Lowe's COT
48 Jimmie Johnson 6.00 12.00
Lowe's Power of Pride
American Heroes
48 Jimmie Johnson 5.00 10.00
Lowe's '57 Chevy
48 Jimmie Johnson 6.00 12.00
Lowe's '06 Nextel Champ
88 Shane Huffman 6.00 12.00
Navy American Heroes
88 Ricky Rudd 3.00 6.00
Snickers
88 Ricky Rudd 3.00 6.00
Snickers COT
88 Ricky Rudd 3.00 6.00
Snickers Dark
96 Tony Raines 6.00 12.00
DLP
99 Carl Edwards 6.00 12.00
Office Depot
01 Mark Martin 6.00 12.00
U.S. Army
01 Mark Martin 6.00 12.00
U.S. Army American Heroes

2007 Action/Motorsports Authentics Owner's Elite 1:64

1 Martin Truex Jr. 15.00 30.00
Bass Pro Shops/1008*
4 Ward Burton 15.00 30.00
Air Force American Heroes/504*
8 Dale Earnhardt Jr. 20.00 40.00
Bud/2007*
8 Dale Earnhardt Jr. 20.00 40.00
Bud Camo
American Heroes/1500*
8 Dale Earnhardt Jr. 20.00 40.00
Bud Stars & Stripes/2007
8 Dale Earnhardt Jr. 15.00 30.00
Sharpie/2007
9 Kasey Kahne 20.00 40.00
Dodge Dealers/2007*
11 Denny Hamlin 15.00 30.00
Fed Ex Express/2007*
11 Denny Hamlin 15.00 30.00
Fed Ex Freight Marines
American Heroes/1507*
11 Denny Hamlin 15.00 30.00
Fed Ex Kinko's/1008*
16 Greg Biffle 15.00 30.00
3M Coast Guard/504*
17 Matt Kenseth 15.00 30.00
DeWalt/2007*
20 Tony Stewart 20.00 40.00
Home Depot/2007*
21 Jon Wood 15.00 30.00
Air Force American Heroes/504*
24 Jeff Gordon 20.00 40.00
DuPont Department of Defense
American Heroes/504*
24 Jeff Gordon 20.00 40.00
DuPont Flames/2007*
24 Jeff Gordon 15.00 30.00
Nicorette/1008*
24 Jeff Gordon 15.00 30.00
Pepsi/2007*
29 Kevin Harvick 20.00 40.00
Shell Pennzoil/2007*
38 David Gilliland 15.00 30.00
M&M's/1008*
42 Juan Pablo Montoya 20.00 40.00
Texaco Havoline/1008*
43 Bobby Labonte 15.00 30.00
Cheerios/1008*
44 Dale Jarrett 15.00 30.00
UPS/2007*
48 Jimmie Johnson 15.00 30.00
Lowe's/2007*
48 Jimmie Johnson 15.00 30.00
Lowe's Power of Pride
American Heroes/504*
55 Michael Waltrip 15.00 30.00
NAPA/1008*
88 Shane Huffman 15.00 30.00
Navy American Heroes/1008*
88 Ricky Rudd 15.00 30.00
Snickers/1008*
99 Carl Edwards 15.00 30.00
Office Depot/2007*
00 David Reutimann 15.00 30.00
Domino's/1008*
01 Mark Martin 15.00 30.00
U.S. Army/1008*
01 Mark Martin 15.00 30.00
U.S. Army American Heroes/1008*

2007 Action/Motorsports Authentics Pit Stop 1:64

1 Martin Truex Jr. 3.00 6.00
Bass Pro Shops
1 Martin Truex Jr. 4.00 8.00
Bass Pro Shops COT
2 Kurt Busch 3.00 6.00
Kurt
2 Kurt Busch 4.00 8.00
Kurt COT
5 Kyle Busch 5.00 10.00
Kellogg's
6 David Ragan 4.00 8.00
AAA
6 David Ragan 4.00 8.00
AAA COT
6 David Ragan 4.00 8.00
AAA Insurance
6 David Ragan 4.00 8.00
AAA Show Your Card
6 David Ragan 4.00 8.00
AAA Travel
6 David Ragan 4.00 8.00
Discount Tire
7 Mike Wallace 5.00 10.00
Geico
8 Dale Earnhardt Jr. 3.00 6.00
DEI
8 Dale Earnhardt Jr. 4.00 8.00
DEI Camo
American Heroes
8 Dale Earnhardt Jr. 5.00 10.00
DEI Elvis Car of Tomorrow
8 Dale Earnhardt Jr. 5.00 10.00
DEI Stars & Stripes
8 Dale Earnhardt Jr. 3.00 6.00
DEI '57 Chevy
8 Dale Earnhardt Jr. 3.00 6.00
JM Menards
8 Dale Earnhardt Jr. 3.00 6.00
Sharpie
9 Kasey Kahne 4.00 8.00
Dodge Dealers
9 Kasey Kahne 4.00 8.00
Doublemint
10 Scott Riggs 3.00 6.00
Stanley Tools
10 Scott Riggs 3.00 6.00
Valvoline
11 Denny Hamlin 3.00 6.00
Fed Ex Express
11 Denny Hamlin 5.00 10.00
Fed Ex Express Car of Tomorrow
11 Denny Hamlin 3.00 6.00
Fed Ex Freight
11 Denny Hamlin 5.00 10.00
Fed Ex Freight Car of Tomorrow
11 Denny Hamlin 3.00 6.00
Fed Ex Freight Marines
American Heroes
11 Denny Hamlin 3.00 6.00
Fed Ex Ground
11 Denny Hamlin 5.00 10.00
Fed Ex Ground Car of Tomorrow
11 Denny Hamlin 3.00 6.00
Fed Ex Kinko's
11 Denny Hamlin 5.00 10.00
Fed Ex Kinko's Car of Tomorrow
12 Ryan Newman 5.00 10.00
Alltel
12 Ryan Newman 5.00 10.00
Kodak
12 Ryan Newman 5.00 10.00
Mobil 1
14 Sterling Marlin 3.00 6.00
Waste Management
15 Paul Menard 4.00 8.00
JM Menards
16 Greg Biffle 3.00 6.00
Ameriquest
16 Greg Biffle 3.00 6.00
Jackson Hewitt
16 Greg Biffle 4.00 8.00
3M
16 Greg Biffle 4.00 8.00
3M Coast Guard
American Heroes
17 Matt Kenseth 4.00 8.00
Arby's
17 Matt Kenseth 5.00 10.00
DeWalt
17 Matt Kenseth 5.00 10.00
DeWalt Car of Tomorrow
17 Matt Kenseth 4.00 8.00
Dish Network
17 Matt Kenseth 4.00 8.00
R&L Carriers COT
17 Matt Kenseth 4.00 8.00
USG Sheetrock
18 J.J. Yeley 5.00 10.00
Interstate Batteries
19 Elliott Sadler 4.00 8.00
Dodge Dealers
19 Elliott Sadler 5.00 10.00
Siemen's COT
20 Tony Stewart 4.00 8.00
Home Depot
20 Tony Stewart 5.00 10.00
Home Depot COT
21 Kevin Harvick 3.00 6.00
Auto Zone
21 Jon Wood 4.00 8.00
Air Force American Heroes
22 Dave Blaney 4.00 8.00
CAT
22 Dave Blaney 4.00 8.00
CAT D6T
22 Dave Blaney 4.00 8.00
CAT M-Series
24 Jeff Gordon 5.00 10.00
DuPont Department of Defense
American Heroes
24 Jeff Gordon 5.00 10.00
DuPont Flames
24 Jeff Gordon 6.00 12.00
DuPont Flames Car of Tomorrow
24 Jeff Gordon 4.00 8.00
Nicorette
24 Jeff Gordon 5.00 10.00
Nicorette Car of Tomorrow
24 Jeff Gordon 5.00 10.00
Pepsi
24 Jeff Gordon 5.00 10.00
Underdog JG Foundation
25 Casey Mears 4.00 8.00
National Guard
26 Jamie McMurray 4.00 8.00
Irwin Tools
29 Kevin Harvick 5.00 10.00
Reese's
29 Kevin Harvick 5.00 10.00
Shell Pennzoil
29 Kevin Harvick 6.00 12.00
Shell Pennzoil Car of Tomorrow
29 Kevin Harvick 5.00 10.00
Pennzoil Platinum COT
31 Jeff Burton 5.00 10.00
Cingular
38 David Gilliland 5.00 10.00
M&M's
38 David Gilliland 5.00 10.00
M&M's Car of Tomorrow
38 David Gilliland 3.00 6.00
M&M's July 4
38 David Gilliland 3.00 6.00
M&M's Pink
38 David Gilliland 3.00 6.00
M&M's Shrek
41 Reed Sorenson 4.00 8.00
Juicy Fruit
41 Reed Sorenson 4.00 8.00
Target
42 Juan Pablo Montoya 4.00 8.00
Big Red
42 Juan Pablo Montoya 5.00 10.00
Texaco Havoline
42 Juan Pablo Montoya 5.00 10.00
Texaco Havoline COT
43 Bobby Labonte 5.00 10.00
Cheerios
44 Dale Jarrett 5.00 10.00
UPS
44 Dale Jarrett 5.00 10.00
UPS Kentucky Derby
45 Kyle Petty 5.00 10.00
Wells Fargo
48 Jimmie Johnson 5.00 10.00
Lowe's
48 Jimmie Johnson 6.00 12.00
Lowe's Car of Tomorrow
48 Jimmie Johnson 5.00 10.00
Lowe's Kobalt
48 Jimmie Johnson 5.00 10.00
Lowe's Power of Pride
American Heroes
48 Jimmie Johnson 5.00 10.00
Lowe's Sam Bass Holiday
55 Michael Waltrip 5.00 10.00
NAPA
60 Carl Edwards 4.00 8.00
Scotts
83 Brian Vickers 4.00 8.00
Red Bull
88 Shane Huffman 5.00 10.00
Navy
88 Shane Huffman 5.00 10.00
Navy American Heroes
88 Shane Huffman 4.00 8.00
Navy SEALS
88 Ricky Rudd 3.00 6.00
Pedigree COT
88 Ricky Rudd 3.00 6.00
Snickers
88 Ricky Rudd 3.00 6.00
Snickers COT
88 Ricky Rudd 3.00 6.00
Snickers Dark
90 Stephen Leicht 5.00 10.00
Citifinancial
96 Tony Raines 5.00 10.00
DLP
96 Tony Raines 4.00 8.00
DLP Shrek
Car of Tomorrow
99 Carl Edwards 5.00 10.00
Office Depot
99 Carl Edwards 5.00 10.00
Scotts
99 David Reutimann 5.00 10.00
Aaron's
00 David Reutimann 5.00 10.00
Burger King
00 David Reutimann 5.00 10.00
Domino's Pizza
01 Mark Martin 3.00 6.00
U.S. Army
01 Mark Martin 4.00 8.00
U.S. Army Car of Tomorrow
01 Mark Martin 3.00 6.00
U.S. Army American Heroes
07 Daytona 500 Event Car 3.00 6.00

2007 Action/Motorsports Authentics Pit Stop Blister 1:64

8 Dale Earnhardt Jr. 4.00 8.00
DEI
9 Kasey Kahne 3.00 6.00
Dodge Dealers
19 Elliott Sadler 3.00 6.00
Dodge Dealers
20 Tony Stewart 3.00 6.00
Home Depot
24 Jeff Gordon 4.00 8.00
DuPont Flames
29 Kevin Harvick 4.00 8.00
Shell Pennzoil
48 Jimmie Johnson 3.00 6.00
Lowe's

2008 Action Pit Stop 1:64

1 Martin Truex Jr. 4.00 8.00
Bass Pro Shops
2 Kurt Busch 4.00 8.00
Kurt
3 Dale Earnhardt 6.00 12.00
GM Plus '98 Daytona COT
3 Dale Earnhardt 5.00 10.00
Johnny Cash
3 Dale Earnhardt 5.00 10.00
John Wayne
4 JVC Nationwide 4.00 8.00
5 Landon Cassill 5.00 10.00
National Guard
5 Dale Earnhardt Jr. 5.00 10.00
All Star Test
5 Dale Earnhardt Jr. 5.00 10.00
Delphi
5 Dale Earnhardt Jr. 5.00 10.00
GoDaddy
5 Dale Earnhardt Jr. 5.00 10.00
National Guard
5 Casey Mears 4.00 8.00
Kellogg's
6 David Ragan 4.00 8.00
AAA
6 David Ragan 4.00 8.00
AAA Insurance
6 David Ragan 4.00 8.00
AAA Show Your Card
6 David Ragan 4.00 8.00
AAA Travel
8 Mark Martin 4.00 8.00
U.S. Army
8 Mark Martin 5.00 10.00
U.S. Army Salute the Troops
9 Kasey Kahne 4.00 8.00
KK
10 Patrick Carpentier 4.00 8.00
Valvoline
11 Denny Hamlin 4.00 8.00
Fed Ex Express
11 Denny Hamlin 4.00 8.00
Fed Ex Freight
11 Denny Hamlin 4.00 8.00
Fed Ex Ground
11 Denny Hamlin 4.00 8.00
Fed Ex Kinko's
11 Darrell Waltrip 7.50 15.00
Mountian Dew '81 Buick in can
12 Ryan Newman 5.00 10.00
Alltel
12 Ryan Newman 4.00 8.00
Kodak
12 Ryan Newman 4.00 8.00
Kodak Mummy 3
16 Greg Biffle 4.00 8.00
Citifinancial
16 Greg Biffle 6.00 12.00
Sherwin Williams Promo
16 Greg Biffle 4.00 8.00
3M
16 Greg Biffle 6.00 12.00
3M MSC Promo
17 Matt Kenseth 4.00 8.00
Carhartt
17 Matt Kenseth 6.00 12.00
Carhartt Promo
17 Matt Kenseth 4.00 8.00
DeWalt
17 Matt Kenseth 4.00 8.00
DeWalt Nano
17 Matt Kenseth 4.00 8.00
R&L Carriers
17 Matt Kenseth 5.00 10.00
USG Sheetrock Promo
18 Kyle Busch 5.00 10.00
Combo's
18 Kyle Busch 7.50 15.00
Combo's CVS Promo
18 Kyle Busch 7.50 15.00
Combo's Promo
18 Kyle Busch 6.00 12.00
M&M's
18 Kyle Busch 5.00 10.00
M&M's Halloween
18 Kyle Busch 6.00 12.00
M&M's Indiana Jones
18 Kyle Busch 6.00 12.00
M&M's Pink
18 Kyle Busch 5.00 10.00
M&M's Sam Bass Holiday
18 Kyle Busch 5.00 10.00
M&M's Summer
18 Kyle Busch 10.00 20.00
M&M's
Snickers 2-car set
18 Kyle Busch 5.00 10.00
Pedigree
18 Kyle Busch 5.00 10.00
Snicker's
18 Farm Bureau Promo 10.00 20.00
19 Elliott Sadler 4.00 8.00
Best Buy
19 Elliott Sadler 4.00 8.00
McDonald's
19 Elliott Sadler 4.00 8.00
Siemens
19 Elliott Sadler 4.00 8.00
Stanley Tools
20 Joey Logano 6.00 12.00
Gamestop
20 Tony Stewart 5.00 10.00
Home Depot
20 Tony Stewart 5.00 10.00
Home Depot 10th Anniversary
20 Tony Stewart 4.00 8.00
Subway
20 Tony Stewart 6.00 12.00
Subway Promo
24 Jeff Gordon 5.00 10.00
DuPont Flames
24 Jeff Gordon 5.00 10.00
DuPont Salute the Troops
24 Jeff Gordon 5.00 10.00
JG Foundation Holiday
24 Jeff Gordon 5.00 10.00
Nicorette
24 Jeff Gordon 4.00 10.00
Pepsi
24 Jeff Gordon 5.00 10.00
Pepsi Stuff
24 Jeff Gordon 5.00 10.00
Speed Racer
25 Bobby Hamilton Jr. 6.00 12.00
Eckrich Promo
26 Jamie McMurray 4.00 8.00
Irwin Tools
29 Kevin Harvick 4.00 8.00
Pennzoil Platinum
29 Kevin Harvick 4.00 8.00
Reese's
29 Kevin Harvick 4.00 8.00
Shell
29 Kevin Harvick 4.00 8.00
Shell Realtree
31 Jeff Burton 4.00 8.00
AT&T
37 D.Bean 5.00 10.00
Glock Promo
37 USPS Promo 5.00 10.00
38 Jason Leffler 5.00 10.00
Great Clips Promo
40 Dario Franchitti 5.00 10.00
Fastenal
40 Dario Franchitti 6.00 12.00
Hartford Promo
42 Juan Pablo Montoya 4.00 8.00
Big Red
42 Juan Pablo Montoya 4.00 8.00
Texaco Havoline
43 Bobby Labonte 4.00 8.00
Cheerios
43 Bobby Labonte 4.00 8.00
General Mills
43 Bobby Labonte 5.00 10.00
Petty 50th Anniversary
44 Dale Jarrett 4.00 8.00
UPS
44 Dale Jarrett 6.00 12.00
UPS Promo
44 Dale Jarrett 5.00 10.00
UPS All Star
44 David Reutimann 4.00 8.00
UPS
44 David Reutimann 6.00 12.00
UPS Promo
44 David Reutimann 4.00 8.00
UPS Kentucky Derby
45 Kyle Petty 4.00 8.00
Marathon Oil
45 Kyle Petty 4.00 8.00
Wells Fargo
48 Jimmie Johnson 6.00 12.00
Lowe's
48 Jimmie Johnson 10.00 20.00
Lowe's 250th Start
55 Michael Waltrip 4.00 8.00
Napa
55 Michael Waltrip 6.00 12.00
Napa Promo
60 Carl Edwards 7.50 15.00
Save A Lot Promo
60 Carl Edwards 4.00 8.00
Scotts
60 Carl Edwards 4.00 8.00
Vitamin Water
77 Ron Hornaday 6.00 12.00
VFW Promo
77 Sam Hornish Jr. 4.00 8.00
Mobil
77 Sam Hornish Jr. 4.00 8.00
Penske
83 Dale Earnhardt Jr. 5.00 10.00
Navy JR Division
83 Brian Vickers 4.00 8.00
Red Bull
84 A.J. Allmendinger 4.00 8.00
Red Bull
88 Dale Earnhardt Jr. 5.00 10.00
AMP
88 Dale Earnhardt Jr. 10.00 20.00
AMP
National Guard 2-car set
88 Dale Earnhardt Jr. 5.00 10.00
AMP Sam Bass Holiday
88 Dale Earnhardt Jr. 5.00 10.00
Mountain Dew Retro
88 Dale Earnhardt Jr. 5.00 10.00
National Guard
88 Dale Earnhardt Jr. 5.00 10.00
National Guard Citizen Soldier
88 Dale Earnhardt Jr. 5.00 10.00

National Guard Digital Camo
88 Dale Earnhardt Jr. 5.00 10.00
National Guard Salute the Troops
88 Brad Keselowski 5.00 10.00
Navy
88 Brad Keselowski 5.00 10.00
Navy Salute the Troops
99 Carl Edwards 4.00 8.00
Aflac
99 Carl Edwards 4.00 8.00
Office Depot
99 Carl Edwards 6.00 12.00
Office Depot Promo
NNO Jasper Engines 4.00 8.00
NNO NASCAR Hall of Fame Promo 4.00 8.00
08 Atlanta Fall Program Car 4.00 8.00
08 Atlanta Spring Program Car 4.00 8.00
08 Bristol Fall Program Car 4.00 8.00
08 Bristol Spring Program Car 4.00 8.00
08 California Fall Program Car 4.00 8.00
08 Car Fax Promo 4.00 8.00
08 Charlotte Fall Program Car 4.00 8.00
08 Charlotte Spring Program Car 4.00 8.00
08 Chicagoland Program Car 4.00 8.00
08 Darlington Spring Program Car 4.00 8.00
08 Daytona 500 Program Car 4.00 8.00
08 Daytona Program Car 4.00 8.00
08 Fontana Spring Program Car 4.00 8.00
08 Infineon Program Car 4.00 8.00
08 Kansas Program Car 4.00 8.00
08 Kentucky Craftsman Program Truck 4.00 8.00
08 Kentucky Nationwide Program Car 4.00 8.00
08 Las Vegas Program Car 4.00 8.00
08 Martinsville Fall Program Car 4.00 8.00
08 Martinsville Spring Program Car 4.00 8.00
08 Miami-Homestead Program Car 4.00 8.00
08 Michigan Fall Program Car 4.00 8.00
08 Michigan Spring Program Car 4.00 8.00
08 Motor Racing Outreach Promo 4.00 8.00
08 New Hampshire Fall Program Car 4.00 8.00
08 New Hampshire Spring Program Car 4.00 8.00
08 Phoenix Fall Program Car 4.00 8.00
08 Phoenix Spring Program Car 4.00 8.00
08 Pocono Fall Program Car 4.00 8.00
08 Pocono Spring Program Car 4.00 8.00
08 Richmond Fall Program Car 4.00 8.00
08 Richmond Spring Program Car 4.00 8.00
08 Talladega Fall Program Car 4.00 8.00
08 Talladega Spring Program Car 4.00 8.00
08 Texas Fall Program Car 4.00 8.00
08 Texas Spring Program Car 4.00 8.00
08 Watkins Glen Program Car 4.00 8.00

2008 Action Pit Stop Trucks 1:64

6 C.Braun 6.00 12.00
Con-Way/5000

2008 Action Racing Collectables Platinum 1:64

1 Martin Truex Jr. 7.50 15.00
Bass Pro Shops/5856
2 Kurt Busch 6.00 12.00
Miller Lite/3744
3 Dale Earnhardt 10.00 20.00
GM Plus '98 Daytona COT/9301
3 Dale Earnhardt 10.00 20.00
Johnny Cash/2500
5 Dale Earnhardt Jr. 7.50 15.00
GoDaddy/5415
8 Mark Martin 7.50 15.00
U.S. Army/3408
9 Kasey Kahne 7.50 15.00
Bud/11808
11 Denny Hamlin 7.50 15.00
Fed Ex Express/3120
17 Matt Kenseth 7.50 15.00
DeWalt/3024
18 Kyle Busch 10.00 20.00
M&M's/6192
18 Kyle Busch 12.50 25.00
M&M's Liquid Color/5808
20 Tony Stewart 7.50 15.00
Home Depot/14160
20 Tony Stewart 10.00 20.00
Home Depot Liquid Color/2500
20 Tony Stewart 10.00 20.00
Smoke/2692
24 Jeff Gordon 10.00 20.00
DuPont Flames/13,824
24 Jeff Gordon 7.50 15.00
Nicorette/5136
24 Jeff Gordon 7.50 15.00
Pepsi/5232
24 Jeff Gordon 12.50 25.00
Pepsi in can
29 Kevin Harvick 7.50 15.00
Shell/8880
42 Juan Pablo Montoya 6.00 12.00
Juicy Fruit/3876
43 Bobby Labonte 7.50 15.00
Cheerios/3024
48 Jimmie Johnson 12.50 25.00
Lowe's/8208
77 Sam Hornish Jr. 6.00 12.00
Mobil/5004
88 Dale Earnhardt Jr. 10.00 20.00
AMP/44972
88 Dale Earnhardt Jr. 12.50 25.00
AMP Liquid Color/25008
88 Dale Earnhardt Jr. 12.50 25.00
Mountain Dew Retro in can/10088
88 Dale Earnhardt Jr. 10.00 20.00
National Guard/30720
88 Dale Earnhardt Jr. 10.00 20.00
National Guard Citizen Soldier/9206
88 Dale Earnhardt Jr. 10.00 20.00
National Guard Digital Camo/5558
88 Dale Earnhardt Jr. 12.50 25.00
National Guard Liquid Color/10032
99 Carl Edwards 10.00 20.00
Office Depot/3504

2008 Action/RCCA Elite 1:64

3 Dale Earnhardt 25.00 50.00
GM Plus '98 Daytona COT/1000
5 Dale Earnhardt Jr. 20.00 40.00
Delphi/1000
5 Dale Earnhardt Jr. 20.00 40.00
GoDaddy/1000
5 Dale Earnhardt Jr. 20.00 40.00
National Guard/1000
24 Jeff Gordon 20.00 40.00
DuPont/1000
24 Jeff Gordon 20.00 40.00
DuPont Salute the Troops/1000
24 Jeff Gordon 15.00 30.00
JG Foundation Holiday
24 Jeff Gordon 20.00 40.00
Nicoretle/1000
24 Jeff Gordon 20.00 40.00
Pepsi Stuff/1000
24 Jeff Gordon 15.00 30.00
Speed Racer/1000
29 Kevin Harvick 15.00 30.00
Shell/1008
83 Dale Earnhardt Jr. 15.00 30.00
Navy JR Division/1000
88 Dale Earnhardt Jr. 20.00 40.00
AMP/1500
88 Dale Earnhardt Jr. 15.00 30.00
AMP Sam Bass Holiday/1000
88 Dale Earnhardt Jr. 20.00 40.00
Mountian Dew Retro/1500
88 Dale Earnhardt Jr. 20.00 40.00
National Guard/1000
88 Dale Earnhardt Jr. 20.00 40.00
National Guard Citizen Soldier/1500
88 Dale Earnhardt Jr. 20.00 40.00
National Guard Salute the Troops/1000

2009 Action Pit Stop 1:64

00 David Reutimann 20.00 40.00
Aaron's
1 Martin Truex Jr. 4.00 8.00
Bass Pro Shops
02 David Gilliland 7.50 15.00
Farm Bureau
2 Kurt Busch 3.00 6.00
Kurt
3 Dale Earnhardt 5.00 10.00
Elvis
5 Dale Earnhardt Jr. 7.50 15.00
Hellmann's
5 Mark Martin 5.00 10.00
Carquest
5 Mark Martin 4.00 8.00
Carquest Holiday/ Sam Bass
5 Mark Martin 5.00 10.00
Kellogg's
6 David Ragan 3.00 6.00
UPS
9 Kasey Kahne 3.00 6.00
KK
09 Digger Holiday 3.00 6.00
Sam Bass
09 Holiday Sam Bass 3.00 6.00
11 Denny Hamlin 3.00 6.00
Fed Ex Express
11 Denny Hamlin 3.00 6.00
Fed Ex Freight
11 Denny Hamlin 3.00 6.00
Fed Ex Ground
11 Denny Hamlin 3.00 6.00
Fed Ex Kinko's Office
14 Tony Stewart 4.00 8.00
Office Depot
14 Tony Stewart 4.00 8.00
Old Spice
14 Tony Stewart 15.00 30.00
Burger King
14 Tony Stewart 5.00 10.00
Office Depot Holiday/ Sam Bass
14 Tony Stewart 10.00 20.00
Office Depot/ Back To School
14 Tony Stewart 5.00 10.00
Old Spice Swagger
14 Tony Stewart 5.00 10.00
Smoke Fantasy
16 Greg Biffle 3.00 6.00
Citifinancial
16 Greg Biffle 3.00 6.00
3M
17 Matt Kenseth 3.00 6.00
Carhartt
17 Matt Kenseth 3.00 6.00
DeWalt
18 Kyle Busch 4.00 8.00
M&M's
18 Kyle Busch 3.00 6.00
Snickers
18 Kyle Busch 3.00 6.00
Combo's
18 Kyle Busch 3.00 6.00
M&M's Halloween
18 Kyle Busch 4.00 8.00
M&M's Holiday/ Sam Bass
18 Kyle Busch 4.00 8.00
M&M's Pink
18 Kyle Busch 5.00 10.00
M&M's/ Indiana Jones
19 Elliott Sadler 3.00 6.00
Stanley Tools
19 Elliott Sadler 3.00 6.00
Best Buy
20 Joey Logano 5.00 10.00
Home Depot
24 Jeff Gordon 5.00 10.00
DuPont
24 Jeff Gordon 5.00 10.00
DuPont Holiday/ Sam Bass
24 Jeff Gordon 5.00 10.00
NG Youth Challenge
24 Jeff Gordon 4.00 8.00
Pepsi
24 Jeff Gordon 4.00 8.00
Pepsi Retro
24 Jeff Gordon 4.00 8.00
Speed Racer/ JG Foundation
26 Jamie McMurray 3.00 6.00
Irwin Tools
28 Kenny Wallace 20.00 40.00
Border Patrol
29 Kevin Harvick 3.00 6.00
Reese's
29 Kevin Harvick 3.00 6.00
Shell Pennzoil
31 Jeff Burton 3.00 6.00
CAT
33 Clint Bowyer 3.00 6.00
Cheerios
33 Kevin Harvick 5.00 10.00
VFW
39 Ryan Newman 20.00 40.00
U.S. Army
42 Juan Pablo Montoya 15.00 30.00
Target
48 Jimmie Johnson 4.00 8.00
Lowe's Holiday/ Sam Bass
48 Jimmie Johnson 4.00 8.00
Lowe's Kobalt
48 Jimmie Johnson 4.00 8.00
Lowe's
55 Michael Waltrip 3.00 6.00
Napa
77 Sam Hornish Jr. 3.00 6.00
Mobil 1
82 Scott Speed 6.00 12.00
Red Bull
83 Brian Vickers 7.50 15.00
Red Bull
88 Dale Earnhardt Jr. 4.00 8.00
AMP Get On
88 Dale Earnhardt Jr. 4.00 8.00
JR Foundation/ All Star White
88 Dale Earnhardt Jr. 4.00 8.00
Mountian Dew
88 Dale Earnhardt Jr. 4.00 8.00
NG Digital Camo
88 Dale Earnhardt Jr. 4.00 8.00
NG Drive the Guard
88 Dale Earnhardt Jr. 4.00 8.00
NG Holiday/ Sam Bass
88 Dale Earnhardt Jr. 4.00 8.00
AMP
88 Dale Earnhardt Jr. 4.00 8.00
AMP
99 Carl Edwards 4.00 8.00
Aflac
99 Carl Edwards 4.00 8.00
Aflac Holiday/ Sam Bass
99 Carl Edwards 4.00 8.00
Aflac Silver
99 Carl Edwards 4.00 8.00
Subway

2009 Action Racing Collectables Platinum 1:64

3 Dale Earnhardt 7.50 15.00
Elvis
5 Mark Martin 7.50 15.00
Kellogg's
9 Kasey Kahne 6.00 12.00
Bud
14 Tony Stewart 6.00 12.00
Office Depot
14 Tony Stewart 6.00 12.00
Old Spice
18 Kyle Busch 6.00 12.00
M&M's
20 Joey Logano 7.50 15.00
Home Depot
24 Jeff Gordon 7.50 15.00
DuPont
24 Jeff Gordon 7.50 15.00
NG Youth Challenge
29 Kevin Harvick 6.00 12.00
Shell Pennzoil
33 Clint Bowyer 10.00 20.00
The Hartford
48 Jimmie Johnson 6.00 12.00
Lowe's
88 Dale Earnhardt Jr. 6.00 12.00
AMP
88 Dale Earnhardt Jr. 6.00 12.00
National Guard
99 Carl Edwards 6.00 12.00
Aflac

2010 Action Racing Collectables Gold 1:64

This set consists of 1:24 scale die-casts with plastic chassis and the hoods and trunks do not open. The original SRP for these cars was $4.

2 Kurt Busch 3.00 6.00
KURT
9 Kasey Kahne 3.00 6.00
KK
10 Digger 2.50 5.00
Gopher Cam Annie
10 Digger 2.50 5.00
Gopher Cam

2010 Action Pit Stop Promos 1:64

This set consists of 1:64 scale die-casts with plastic chassis and the hoods and trunks do not open. These were used as track and sponsor promotional cars, typically given away with purchase. They were not serial numbered, but the print run information listed was provided by Action.

6 Colin Braun 5.00 10.00
Con-Way Trucking
6 Ricky Stenhouse Jr. 5.00 10.00
Blackwell Angus
7 No Driver Association 2.00 4.00
Pine Branch Coal
10 Nick Igdalsky 5.00 10.00
Modspace Motorsports
10 No Driver Association 2.00 4.00
Atlanta Fall Program Car
10 No Driver Association 2.00 4.00
Atlanta Spring Program Car
10 No Driver Association 2.00 4.00
Bristol Fall Program Car
10 No Driver Association 2.00 4.00
Bristol Spring Program Car
10 No Driver Association 2.00 4.00
California Fall Program Car
10 No Driver Association 2.00 4.00
California Spring Program Car
10 No Driver Association 2.00 4.00
Carfax
10 No Driver Association 2.00 4.00
Charlotte Fall Program Car
10 No Driver Association 2.00 4.00
Charlotte Spring Program Car
10 No Driver Association 2.00 4.00
Chicago Program Car
10 No Driver Association 2.00 4.00
Darlington Spring Program Car
10 No Driver Association 2.00 4.00
Daytona Fall Program Car
10 No Driver Association 2.00 4.00
Daytona Spring Program Car
10 No Driver Association 2.00 4.00
Dover Spring Program Car
10 No Driver Association 2.00 4.00
Infineon Program Car
10 No Driver Association 2.00 4.00
Iowa Program Car
10 No Driver Association 2.00 4.00
Iowa Program Truck
10 No Driver Association 2.00 4.00
Kansas Program Car
10 No Driver Association 2.00 4.00
Kentucky Program Car
10 No Driver Association 2.00 4.00
Keyes Automotive
10 No Driver Association 2.00 4.00
Las Vegas Program Car
10 No Driver Association 2.00 4.00
Martinsville Fall Program Car
10 No Driver Association 2.00 4.00
Martinsville Spring Program Car
10 No Driver Association 2.00 4.00
Miami-Homestead Program Car
10 No Driver Association 2.00 4.00
Michigan Fall Program Car
10 No Driver Association 2.00 4.00
Michigan Spring Program Car
10 No Driver Association 2.00 4.00
New Hampshire Fall Program Car
10 No Driver Association 2.00 4.00
New Hampshire Spring Program Car
10 No Driver Association 2.00 4.00
Phoenix Fall Program Car
10 No Driver Association 2.00 4.00
Phoenix Spring Program Car
10 No Driver Association 2.00 4.00
Pocono Fall Program Car
10 No Driver Association 2.00 4.00
Pocono Spring Program Car
10 No Driver Association 2.00 4.00
Richmond Fall Program Car
10 No Driver Association 2.00 4.00
Richmond Spring Program Car
10 No Driver Association 2.00 4.00
Road America
10 No Driver Association 2.00 4.00
Service Master
10 No Driver Association 2.00 4.00
Sprint
10 No Driver Association 2.00 4.00
Talladega Fall Program Car
10 No Driver Association 2.00 4.00
Talladega Spring Program Car
10 No Driver Association 2.00 4.00
Texas Fall Program Car
10 No Driver Association 2.00 4.00
Texas Spring Program Car
10 No Driver Association 2.00 4.00
Watkins Glen Program Car
11 No Driver Association 2.00 4.00
Tom Wood Automotive
14 Tony Stewart 4.00 8.00
Old Spice
14 Tony Stewart 4.00 8.00
Old Spice Matterhorn
16 Greg Biffle 4.00 8.00
Sherwin Williams
16 Greg Biffle 5.00 10.00
3M Scotch Blue Tape
18 Kyle Busch 4.00 8.00
Combos
18 Kyle Busch 6.00 12.00
Fleet Locate
18 Kyle Busch 10.00 20.00
M&M's
Doublemint/ 2-car set
18 Brad Coleman 5.00 10.00
Sandvik Coromat
20 Matt DiBenedetto 5.00 10.00
Pizza Ranch
24 Jeff Gordon 4.00 8.00
Dupont
24 Jeff Gordon 4.00 8.00
Dupont Law Enforcement
33 Clint Bowyer 5.00 10.00
Hartford
33 Kevin Harvick 6.00 12.00
Armour
43 No Driver Association 4.00 8.00
Petty Driving Experience
55 Michael Waltrip 4.00 8.00
Aaron's 55th Anniversary
56 Martin Truex Jr. 4.00 8.00
NAPA
60 Carl Edwards 4.00 8.00
Save A Lot Pink
78 No Driver Association 2.00 4.00
Furniture Row
88 Kelly Bires 5.00 10.00
Hellmann's
88 Dale Earnhardt Jr. 3.00 8.00
AMP
88 Dale Earnhardt Jr. 3.00 8.00
National Guard
00 David Reutimann 4.00 8.00
Aaron's
00 David Reutimann 4.00 8.00
Aaron's Armed Forces
00 David Reutimann 4.00 8.00
Best Western
NNO A.J. Allmendinger 4.00 8.00
Best Buy
NNO No Driver Association 2.00 4.00
ISC
NNO No Driver Association 6.00 12.00
Oregon State

2010 Action Racing Collectables Platinum 1:64

1 Jamie McMurray 7.50 15.00
Bass Pro Shops/2640*
1 Jamie McMurray 10.00 20.00
Bass Pro Shops Earnhardt HOF Tribute/2576*
1 Jamie McMurray 7.50 15.00
McDonald's/2500*
3 Dale Earnhardt 7.50 15.00
NHOF/6147*
3 Dale Earnhardt 12.50 25.00
Wheaties '97 MC/2503*
3 Dale Earnhardt Jr. 12.50 25.00
Wrangler/9565*
5 Mark Martin 7.50 15.00
Carquest/6363*
5 Mark Martin 7.50 15.00
Delphi/2328*
5 Mark Martin 7.50 15.00
Go Daddy/12062*
5 Mark Martin 7.50 15.00
Hendrickcars.com/2489*
6 David Ragan 7.50 15.00
UPS/10934*
6 David Ragan 7.50 15.00
UPS Freight/2530*
7 Danica Patrick 10.00 20.00
Tissot/3275*
10 No Driver Association 7.50 15.00
NHOF/3119*
11 Denny Hamlin 7.50 15.00
Fedex Express/3948*
11 Denny Hamlin 7.50 15.00
Fedex Freight/3101*
11 Denny Hamlin 7.50 15.00
Fedex Ground/3107*
11 Denny Hamlin 7.50 15.00
Fedex Office/2893*
12 Brad Keselowski 7.50 15.00
Penske/4789*
14 Tony Stewart 7.50 15.00
Burger King/7167*
14 Tony Stewart 10.00 20.00
Office Depot/17904*
14 Tony Stewart 7.50 15.00
Office Depot Go Green/2541*
14 Tony Stewart 10.00 20.00
Old Spice/12288*
16 Greg Biffle 7.50 15.00
3M/7538*
17 Matt Kenseth 7.50 15.00
Valvoline/2813*
18 Kyle Busch 7.50 15.00
Doublemint/5915*
18 Kyle Busch 7.50 15.00
Interstate Batteries/2490*
18 Kyle Busch 10.00 20.00
M&M's/21201*
18 Kyle Busch 10.00 20.00
M&M's Pretzel/3335*
18 Kyle Busch 7.50 15.00
Pedigree/2499*
18 Kyle Busch 7.50 15.00
Snickers/3568*
18 Kyle Busch 7.50 15.00
Z-Line Pink/4429*
19 Elliott Sadler 7.50 15.00
Stanley Tools/7929*
24 Jeff Gordon 10.00 20.00
Dupont/14530*
24 Jeff Gordon 10.00 20.00
Dupont Law Enforcement/2369*
24 Jeff Gordon 10.00 20.00
National Guard/4296*
24 Jeff Gordon 10.00 20.00
National Guard Special Forces/2934*
24 Jeff Gordon 7.50 15.00
Pepsi Max/3125*
29 Kevin Harvick 7.50 15.00
Reese's/2587*
29 Kevin Harvick 7.50 15.00
Shell/5293*
31 Jeff Burton 7.50 15.00
Caterpillar/6720*
33 Clint Bowyer 7.50 15.00
BB&T/4175*
33 Clint Bowyer 7.50 15.00
Cheerios/7345*
39 Ryan Newman 7.50 15.00
Haas Automation/2500*
39 Ryan Newman 7.50 15.00
Tornados/4488*
39 Ryan Newman 10.00 20.00
U.S. Army/8533*
42 Juan Pablo Montoya 7.50 15.00
Target/5313*
43 A.J. Allmendinger 7.50 15.00
Best Buy/3180*
43 Richard Petty 7.50 15.00
NHOF/3983*
48 Jimmie Johnson 12.50 25.00
Kobalt Tools/5009*
48 Jimmie Johnson 12.50 25.00
Lowe's/11489*
48 Jimmie Johnson 12.50 25.00
Lowe's Johns Manville/2219*
55 Michael Waltrip 7.50 15.00
Aaron's 55th Anniversary/1054*
56 Martin Truex Jr. 7.50 15.00
NAPA/5614*
60 Carl Edwards 7.50 15.00
Copart/5694*
77 Sam Hornish Jr. 7.50 15.00
Mobil 1/6559*
83 Brian Vickers 7.50 15.00
Red Bull/5010*
88 Dale Earnhardt Jr. 10.00 20.00
AMP/14932*
88 Dale Earnhardt Jr. 10.00 20.00
AMP Energy Juice/4690*
88 Dale Earnhardt Jr. 10.00 20.00
AMP Sugar Free/3555*
88 Dale Earnhardt Jr. 7.50 15.00
Hellmann's/2535*
88 Dale Earnhardt Jr. 7.50 15.00
JR Foundation/3417*
88 Dale Earnhardt Jr. 10.00 20.00
National Guard/10083*

Item	Low	High
88 Dale Earnhardt Jr. National Guard Camo 8 Soldiers 8 Missions/2878*	10.00	20.00
99 Carl Edwards Aflac/12558*	7.50	15.00
99 Carl Edwards Aflac Silver/3753*	7.50	15.00
99 Carl Edwards Aflac U Don't Know Quack/3047*	7.50	15.00
99 Carl Edwards Cheez-It/2489*	7.50	15.00
99 Carl Edwards Kellogg's/2947*	7.50	15.00
99 Carl Edwards Scott's/2480*	7.50	15.00
99 Carl Edwards Scott's Turf Builder/2474*	7.50	15.00
99 Carl Edwards Subway/3734*	7.50	15.00
00 David Reutimann Aaron's/4100*	7.50	15.00
00 David Reutimann Aaron's Armed Forces/1046*	10.00	20.00

1997-99 Brookfield 1:24

Item	Low	High
3 Dale Earnhardt AC Delco/15,000 1997	25.00	60.00

1999 Brookfield 1:24

Item	Low	High
3 Dale Earnhardt Goodwrench Wrangler/7500 2-car set	60.00	120.00
3 Dale Earnhardt Wrangler Silver Incentive/624	50.00	100.00
3 Dale Earnhardt Jr. AC Delco Superman Silver/624 1999	125.00	200.00

1994-03 Brookfield Sets 1:24

Item	Low	High
1/3 Dale Earnhardt Dale Earnhardt Jr. Coke Coke Bear 2-car set/5000 1998	50.00	100.00
3 Dale Earnhardt Foundation Black Brushed Metal 2-car set/55,000	75.00	125.00
3 Dale Earnhardt Goodwrench Coke 2-car set/10,000 1996	50.00	100.00
3/24 Dale Earnhardt Jeff Gordon Brickyard 400 2-car set/5000 1995	125.00	225.00
8 Dale Earnhardt Jr. Bud First Win QVC 2-car set/2000 2000	125.00	200.00
8 Dale Earnhardt Jr. Bud All-Star QVC 2-car set/5004 2001	75.00	150.00
8 Dale Earnhardt Jr. Bud All-Star QVC 2001 and 2002 2-car set/20,004 2002	125.00	225.00
24 Jeff Gordon DuPont Brickyard 2-car set with Pace Car 1994	50.00	100.00
24 Jeff Gordon DuPont Charlotte QVC regular and brushed metal 2-car set/2000 2000	75.00	150.00
24 Jeff Gordon DuPont Peanuts QVC regular and chrome 2-car set/20,000 2000	60.00	120.00
29 Kevin Harvick Goodwrench QVC 2001 2-car set/2000 white car and brushed metal	60.00	100.00
36 Ken Schrader M&M's QVC 2-car set/2000 2000	40.00	80.00
88 Dale Jarrett Quality Care QVC 2-car set/2000 2000	75.00	135.00

2004 Brookfield 1:24

Item	Low	High
8 Martin Truex Jr. Wrangler Retro Raced/240	25.00	40.00

2005 Brookfield 1:24

Item	Low	High
1 Martin Truex Jr. Bass Pro Shops/204	20.00	40.00
2 Rusty Wallace Miller Lite/444	25.00	50.00
5 Kyle Busch Kellogg's/204	20.00	40.00
8 Dale Earnhardt Jr. Bud/804	25.00	50.00
8 Dale Earnhardt Jr. Bud Born On Feb.12/408	25.00	50.00
8 Dale Earnhardt Jr. Bud Born On Feb.17/300	25.00	50.00
8 Dale Earnhardt Jr. Bud Born On Feb.20/900	25.00	50.00
8 Martin Truex Jr. Bass Pro Shops/204	20.00	40.00
9 Kasey Kahne Dodge Pit Cap White/240	25.00	40.00
9 Kasey Kahne Mountain Dew/288	25.00	50.00
15 Michael Waltrip Napa/204	20.00	40.00
20 Tony Stewart Home Depot/360	20.00	40.00
20 Tony Stewart Home Depot Madagascar/204	20.00	40.00
24 Jeff Gordon DuPont Flames/600	25.00	50.00
24 Jeff Gordon Mighty Mouse/408	25.00	50.00
24 Jeff Gordon Pepsi Star Wars/600	25.00	50.00
29 Kevin Harvick Goodwrench/360	20.00	40.00
29 Kevin Harvick Goodwrench Atlanta/300	20.00	40.00
31 Jeff Burton Cingular/288	20.00	40.00
44 Terry Labonte Kellogg's/204	20.00	40.00
48 Jimmie Johnson Lowe's/300	20.00	40.00
81 Dale Earnhardt Jr. Oreo Ritz/804	25.00	40.00
05 Star Wars Event/900	20.00	40.00
07 Dave Blaney Jack Daniel's/444	30.00	50.00

2006 Brookfield 1:24

Item	Low	High
8 Dale Earnhardt Jr. Bud/300	50.00	75.00
8 Dale Earnhardt Jr. Bud 3 Days of Dale Tribute/833	60.00	100.00
8 Dale Earnhardt Jr. Bud 3 Days of Dale Tribute Color Chrome Chrome 2-car set/2004	75.00	125.00
8 Dale Earnhardt Jr. Bud Father's Day/508	60.00	100.00
8 Dale Earnhardt Jr. Oreo/300	50.00	75.00
24 Jeff Gordon DuPont Hot Hues Foose Designs/300	60.00	100.00
24 Jeff Gordon Nicorette/222	50.00	75.00
24 Jeff Gordon Superman/300	50.00	75.00
24 Jeff Gordon WSOP JG Foundation/200	60.00	100.00
48 Jimmie Johnson Lowe's/144	50.00	75.00
NNO Dale Earnhardt HOF/333	30.00	60.00

1995 Brookfield Sets 1:64

Item	Low	High
3 Dale Earnhardt Goodwrench Olympic 3-car set/10,000 1995	40.00	80.00

2007 Checkered Flag Sports Champions 1:24

Item	Low	High
4 Ward Burton State Water Heaters	40.00	65.00
7 Robby Gordon Jim Beam/3120	50.00	75.00
7 Robby Gordon Jim Beam Car of Tomorrow/3000	50.00	75.00
7 Robby Gordon Jim Beam Black/3000	50.00	75.00
7 Robby Gordon Jim Beam Black Car of Tomorrow/3000	50.00	75.00
14 Sterling Marlin Waste Management/3504	40.00	65.00
22 Dave Blaney CAT	40.00	65.00
83 Shane Huffman Make A Wish/2508	40.00	65.00
01 Mark Martin U.S. Army/10,000	50.00	75.00
01 Mark Martin U.S. Army Car of Tomorrow/10,000	60.00	100.00
07 Dodge Program/2400	40.00	60.00
07 Dodge Program Test/2400	40.00	60.00
07 Dodge Program Test Car of Tomorrow/2400	40.00	60.00
07 JR Motorsports Grand Opening/3883	40.00	60.00
07 Toyota Program/2400	40.00	60.00
07 Toyota Program Car of Tomorrow/2400	40.00	60.00
07 Toyota Program Test/2400	40.00	60.00
07 Toyota Program Test Car of Tomorrow/2400	40.00	60.00

2007 Checkered Flag Sports Champions Black Liquid Chrome 1:24

Item	Low	High
4 Ward Burton State Water Heaters	50.00	75.00
7 Robby Gordon Jim Beam/390	75.00	125.00
7 Robby Gordon Jim Beam Car of Tomorrow/375	75.00	125.00
7 Robby Gordon Jim Beam Black/375	75.00	125.00
7 Robby Gordon Jim Beam Black Car of Tomorrow/375	75.00	125.00
14 Sterling Marlin Waste Management/438	50.00	75.00
22 Dave Blaney CAT	50.00	75.00
88 Shane Huffman Make A Wish	50.00	75.00
01 Mark Martin U.S. Army/1250	75.00	125.00
01 Mark Martin U.S. Army COT	100.00	150.00
07 JR Motorsports/833	50.00	75.00
07 JR Motorsports AU/833	100.00	150.00
07 JR Motorsports 24K/283	75.00	125.00

2007 Checkered Flag Sports Contender 1:24

Item	Low	High
4 Ward Burton State Water Heaters	10.00	20.00
7 Robby Gordon Jim Beam	15.00	25.00
7 Robby Gordon Jim Beam Car of Tomorrow	15.00	30.00
7 Robby Gordon Jim Beam Black	15.00	25.00
7 Robby Gordon Jim Beam Black Car of Tomorrow	15.00	30.00
7 Robby Gordon Mapei Menards Car of Tomorrow	15.00	25.00
7 Robby Gordon Monster Car of Tomorrow	15.00	25.00
7 Robby Gordon Motorola	15.00	25.00
14 Sterling Marlin Waste Management	10.00	20.00
21 Ken Schrader Motorcraft	15.00	30.00
21 Jon Wood Air Force no rookie stripes	20.00	40.00
22 Dave Blaney CAT Car of Tomorrow	15.00	25.00
55 Robby Gordon Verizon	15.00	25.00
66 Jeff Green Best Buy	15.00	25.00
66 Jeff Green Comcast	15.00	25.00
66 Jeff Green Garmin	15.00	25.00
01 Mark Martin U.S. Army	15.00	30.00
01 Mark Martin U.S. Army Car of Tomorrow	20.00	40.00
07 Dodge Program	15.00	25.00
07 Dodge Program Test	15.00	25.00
07 Ford Program	15.00	25.00
07 Ford Program Car of Tomorrow	15.00	25.00
07 NASCAR on FOX Car of Tomorrow	15.00	25.00
07 Toyota Program	15.00	25.00
07 Toyota Program Car of Tomorrow	15.00	25.00
07 Toyota Program Test	15.00	25.00
07 Toyota Program Test Car of Tomorrow	15.00	25.00

2008 Checkered Flag Sports Champion 1:24

Item	Low	High
1 Martin Truex Jr. Bass Pro Shops	40.00	65.00
7 Robby Gordon Jim Beam	40.00	65.00
8 Mark Martin U.S. Army	40.00	65.00
8 Mark Martin Steak-Umm	40.00	65.00
22 Dave Blaney Cat	40.00	65.00
96 Tony Raines DLP	40.00	65.00
08 Toyota Camry	40.00	65.00
08 Dodge Charger	40.00	65.00

2008 Checkered Flag Sports Contender 1:24

Item	Low	High
1 Martin Truex Jr. Bass Pro Shops	25.00	50.00
7 Robby Gordon Jim Beam	25.00	50.00
8 Mark Martin U.S. Army	25.00	50.00
15 Paul Menard Menards	25.00	50.00
22 Dave Blaney Cat	25.00	50.00
96 Tony Raines DLP	25.00	50.00

2007 Checkered Flag Sports Contender 1:64

Item	Low	High
4 Ward Burton State Water Heaters	3.00	6.00
14 Sterling Marlin Waste Management	3.00	6.00
14 Sterling Marlin Waste Management Car of Tomorrow	4.00	8.00
21 Ken Schrader Motorcraft	3.00	6.00
21 Jon Wood Air Force no rookie stripes	4.00	8.00
22 Dave Blaney CAT	3.00	6.00
66 Jeff Green Best Buy	3.00	6.00
96 Tony Raines DLP Car of Tomorrow	4.00	8.00
01 Mark Martin U.S. Army	4.00	8.00
01 Mark Martin U.S. Army Car of Tomorrow	5.00	10.00
07 Dodge Program	2.50	5.00
07 Dodge Program Car of Tomorrow	3.00	6.00
07 Ford Program	2.50	5.00
07 Ford Program Car of Tomorrow	3.00	6.00
07 NASCAR on FOX COT	3.00	6.00
07 Toyota Program	2.50	5.00
07 Toyota Program Car of Tomorrow	3.00	6.00
07 Toyota Program Test	2.50	5.00
07 Toyota Program Test Car of Tomorrow	3.00	6.00

2008 Checkered Flag Sports Contender 1:64

Item	Low	High
1 Martin Truex Jr. Bass Pro Shops	3.00	6.00
8 Mark Martin U.S. Army	3.00	6.00
22 Dave Blaney Cat	3.00	6.00
96 Tony Raines DLP	3.00	6.00

1992 Ertl 1:18

Item	Low	High
3 Dale Earnhardt Goodwrench/40,000	60.00	150.00
4 Ernie Irvan Kodak	20.00	40.00
6 Mark Martin Valvoline	25.00	50.00
10 Derrike Cope Purolator	20.00	40.00
15 Geoff Bodine Motorcraft	60.00	125.00
17 Darrell Waltrip Western Auto Parts America	25.00	50.00
18 Dale Jarrett Interstate Batteries	25.00	40.00
30 Michael Waltrip Pennzoil	12.50	25.00
42 Kyle Petty Mello Yello	20.00	40.00
43 Richard Petty STP	20.00	50.00
59 Robert Pressley Alliance/2502	60.00	150.00

1993 Ertl 1:18

Cars in this series were packaged in clear window boxes that typically included the year of issue on the box bottom. Many of the 1:18 scale cars are commonly referred to as American Muscle since that name is often found on the packaging. Some of the newer pieces were issued in 2-car or 3-car sets. Ertl no longer produces a line of 1:18 scale racing cars to be distributed by themselves but does produce 1:18 cars for other companies.

Item	Low	High
11 Bill Elliott Budweiser	20.00	40.00
12 Jimmy Spencer Meineke Bank/2500 White Rose Collectibles	40.00	100.00
20 Bobby Hamilton Fina Lube Bank/5000	20.00	50.00
21 Bobby Bowsher Quality Farm	20.00	50.00
28 Davey Allison Havoline	30.00	60.00
42 Andy Hillenburg Budget Gourmet Promo Bank	40.00	75.00
87 Joe Nemechek Dentyne Bank/2500 White Rose Collectibles	60.00	150.00

1994 Ertl 1:18

Item	Low	High
6 Mark Martin Valvoline/30,000	20.00	50.00
7 Alan Kulwicki Army Buck Fever/5000	60.00	120.00
7 Alan Kulwicki Hooters Buck Fever/5000	100.00	175.00
7 Alan Kulwicki Zerex Buck Fever/5000	60.00	120.00
14 John Andretti Kanawaha	20.00	40.00
16 Chad Chaffin 31W Insulation	30.00	50.00
21 Morgan Shepherd Cheerwine	35.00	60.00
24 Jeff Gordon DuPont raced version/5000	40.00	80.00
24 Jeff Gordon DuPont Bank White Rose Collectibles with serial # on bottom of 5000	150.00	300.00
24 Jeff Gordon DuPont Bank White Rose Collectibles without serial number on bottom	50.00	120.00
33 Brad Loney Winnebago Promo	20.00	50.00
59 Andy Belmont Dr. Die Cast Bank/3500	20.00	50.00
59 Dennis Setzer Alliance/5000	40.00	75.00
59 Dennis Setzer Alliance 2-car set	125.00	225.00
60 Mark Martin Winn Dixie GMP/3500	45.00	80.00
84 Benny Senneker Lane Automotive/2500	20.00	50.00

1995 Ertl 1:18

Item	Low	High
1 Davey Allison Lancaster/4000	35.00	60.00
1 Jeff Gordon Baby Ruth 1992 T-bird Buck Fever/5000	50.00	100.00
1 Rick Mast Skoal black&green	30.00	60.00
1 Rick Mast Skoal black&white Hoosier Tires	30.00	60.00
1 Rick Mast Skoal black&white Goodyear Tires	20.00	50.00
2 Rusty Wallace Miller Genuine Draft/5000	40.00	80.00
3 Dale Earnhardt Goodwrench 7-Time Champion/10,000	60.00	150.00
3 Dale Earnhardt Goodwrench Silver Buck Fever/15,000	60.00	150.00
3 Jeff Green Goodwrench Buck Fever/3500	25.00	45.00
3 Mike Skinner Goodwrench SuperTruck	25.00	45.00
4 Sterling Marlin Kodak Funsaver	25.00	60.00
4 Jeff Purvis Kodak Funsaver	20.00	50.00
4 Dennis Sensiba Lane Automotive/2500	20.00	50.00
6 Mark Martin Valvoline/15,000	20.00	50.00
7 Geoff Bodine Exide GMP	30.00	60.00
7 Harry Gant Manheim/2502	20.00	50.00
8 Jeff Burton Raybestos	20.00	40.00
10 Ricky Rudd Tide GMP	30.00	60.00
11 Brett Bodine Lowe's White Rose/2500	20.00	50.00
21 Morgan Shepherd Citgo/3500	20.00	40.00
23 Davey Allison Miller American Bank/5000	25.00	60.00
23 Davey Allison Miller High Life Bank/5000	25.00	60.00
23 Jimmy Spencer Smokin' Joe's	90.00	150.00
24 Jeff Gordon DuPont Buck Fever/5000	40.00	80.00
24 Jeff Gordon DuPont GMP/3500	40.00	80.00
26 Steve Kinser Quaker State/3864	40.00	80.00
27 Tim Richmond Old Milwaukee	25.00	50.00
27 Rusty Wallace Kodiak 1989 Grand Prix/3500	100.00	175.00
28 Ernie Irvan Havoline/7500	25.00	60.00
28 Dale Jarrett Havoline/4000	25.00	60.00
32 Dale Jarrett Mac Tools/5000	30.00	60.00
33 Harry Gant Manheim/2502	20.00	50.00
33 Harry Gant Skoal/5004	35.00	60.00
33 Harry Gant Skoal Bandit/5004	35.00	60.00
33 Robert Pressley Skoal	25.00	60.00
41 Ricky Craven Kodiak GMP/2800	25.00	60.00
43 Rodney Combs Jr. French's	50.00	90.00
43 Richard Petty STP 7-Time Champion/10,000	40.00	75.00
43 Robert Pressley French's/1250	50.00	90.00
44 David Green Slim Jim/2500	20.00	50.00
52 Butch Miller Liberty Ford/5000	20.00	50.00
52 Ken Schrader AC Delco	30.00	50.00
52 Ken Schrader AC Delco Bank GMP	20.00	50.00
52 Ken Schrader AC Delco SuperTruck	30.00	50.00
54 Robert Pressley Manheim/2502	20.00	50.00
59 Chad Chaffin Dr. Die Cast	30.00	45.00
59 Dennis Setzer Alliance/2500	30.00	60.00
71 Dave Marcis Olive Garden/2502	20.00	50.00
90 Ernie Irvan Bulls Eye	25.00	60.00
94 Bill Elliott McDonald's	20.00	45.00
94 Bill Elliott McDonald's Thunderbat	30.00	50.00
95 Andy Belmont Old Milwaukee	25.00	45.00
98 Jeremy Mayfield Fingerhut/3500	20.00	40.00
99 Dick Trickle Articat/5000	30.00	50.00

1996 Ertl 1:18

Item	Low	High
1 Rick Mast Hooters	30.00	50.00
2 Rusty Wallace Miller Silver/10,000	25.00	60.00
3 Dale Earnhardt Goodwrench '95 Monte Carlo Buck Fever/15,000	40.00	100.00
4 Sterling Marlin Kodak 1995 Monte Carlo Buck Fever/3500	20.00	50.00
5 Terry Labonte Kellogg's	20.00	50.00
5 Terry Labonte Kellogg's Silver	25.00	60.00
6 Mark Martin Valvoline/10,000	30.00	50.00
7 Gary St.Amant Wynn's ASA	30.00	60.00
8 Bobby Dotter Lubteck ASA	30.00	60.00
8 Kenny Wallace Red Dog/3000	20.00	50.00
8 Kenny Wallace Red Dog Bank	30.00	60.00
9 Lake Speed SPAM	25.00	50.00
16 Ted Musgrave Family Channel Primestar	20.00	40.00
17 Bill Sedgwick Die Hard SuperTruck	25.00	50.00
21 Doug George Ortho SuperTruck	20.00	40.00
23 Chad Little	25.00	60.00

John Deere in plastic case
23 Chad Little 150.00 300.00
John Deere Autographed
25 Ken Schrader 20.00 40.00
Budweiser
27 Rusty Wallace 45.00 80.00
Miller Genuine Draft
28 Davey Allison 40.00 70.00
Havoline Black&Gold
28 Davey Allison 40.00 70.00
Havoline Black&White
33 Brad Loney 35.00 60.00
Winnebago
42 Kyle Petty 30.00 60.00
Coors Light GMP
42 Kyle Petty 30.00 60.00
Coors Light White Rose
43 Rodney Combs Jr. 40.00 75.00
Hulk Hogan Bank
43 Bobby Hamilton 15.00 40.00
1972 STP Blue paint
43 Bobby Hamilton 15.00 40.00
1972 STP Blue
Red paint
43 Bobby Hamilton 15.00 40.00
1979 STP paint
43 Bobby Hamilton 15.00 40.00
1984 STP paint
43 Bobby Hamilton 20.00 50.00
STP Silver
75 Todd Bodine 15.00 40.00
Factory Stores Buck Fever
87 Joe Nemechek 20.00 50.00
Burger King GMP
88 Dale Jarrett 25.00 45.00
Quality Care
90 Mike Wallace 20.00 40.00
Heilig-Meyers/2500
94 Bill Elliott 25.00 45.00
McDonald's
95 David Green 30.00 60.00
Busch/1500
95 David Green 30.00 60.00
Busch Bank/1500
95 David Green 25.00 60.00
Caterpillar GMP
95 David Green 25.00 60.00
Caterpillar White Rose Bank
98 Kenny Irwin 25.00 50.00
Raybestos

1997 Ertl 1:18

4 Sterling Marlin 20.00 50.00
Kodak
5 Terry Labonte 100.00 175.00
Honey Crunch GMP
6 Mark Martin 20.00 50.00
Valvoline/10,000
7 Geoff Bodine 20.00 45.00
QVC
16 Ted Musgrave 20.00 40.00
Family Channel Primestar
24 Jack Sprague 20.00 40.00
Quaker State SuperTruck
30 Johnny Benson Jr. 20.00 40.00
Pennzoil
36 Derrike Cope 15.00 40.00
Skittles
37 Jeremy Mayfield 25.00 60.00
K-Mart GMP
94 Ron Barfield 25.00 60.00
New Holland
94 Bill Elliott 30.00 60.00
McDonald's
96 David Green 25.00 60.00
Caterpillar/5000
97 Chad Little 40.00 100.00
John Deere Autographed Box

1997 Ertl Prestige Series 1:18

5 Terry Labonte 40.00 100.00
Honey Crunch/2898
5 Terry Labonte 40.00 100.00
Kellogg's Tony/2898
25 Ricky Craven 25.00 60.00
Budweiser/2502
37 Jeremy Mayfield 25.00 60.00
K-Mart RC-Cola/2502
94 Bill Elliott 30.00 80.00
Mac Tonight/2898

1998 Ertl 1:18

26 Johnny Benson 15.00 40.00
Cheerios
40 Sterling Marlin 20.00 50.00
Coors
43 John Andretti 20.00 50.00
STP

1999 Ertl 1:18

22 Fireball Roberts 15.00 40.00
Aiken-Mitchell Motors
1957 Chevy Hardtop
22 Fireball Roberts 15.00 40.00
Atlanta Tune-Up
1957 Chevy Convertible
97 Chad Little 25.00 50.00
John Deere Promo

2000 Ertl Proshop 1:18

6 Mark Martin 50.00 100.00
Valvoline
12 Jeremy Mayfield 25.00 60.00
Mobil 1
14 Mike Bliss 25.00 60.00
Conseco
17 Matt Kenseth 50.00 100.00
DeWalt
22 Ward Burton 35.00 75.00
Caterpillar Dealers
22 Ward Burton 35.00 75.00
Caterpillar Bud Shoot Out
93 Dave Blaney 25.00 60.00
Amoco
94 Bill Elliott 35.00 75.00
McDonald's
99 Jeff Burton 30.00 80.00
Exide

2003 Ertl 75 Years of Pontiac 1:18

STATED PRODUCTION RUN 2500
22 Fireball Roberts 40.00 75.00
Stephens 1962 Catalina
NNO Arnie Beswick 40.00 75.00
Seltzer 1962 Catalina
NNO Packer Pontiac 40.00 75.00

2000 Ertl Proshop 1:24

5 Terry Labonte 15.00 30.00
Kellogg's
6 Mark Martin 15.00 30.00
Valvoline
17 Matt Kenseth 20.00 40.00
DeWalt
22 Ward Burton 12.50 25.00
Caterpillar Dealers
22 Ward Burton 15.00 30.00
Caterpillar Bud Shoot Out
22 Ward Burton 30.00 60.00
Wildlife Foundation
75 Wally Dallenbach 12.50 25.00
Powerpuff Girls
93 Dave Blaney 10.00 25.00
Amoco
97 Chad Little 12.50 25.00
John Deere

1982-84 Ertl 1:25

This series of cars was released in the early to mid-1980s. Each is packaged in an Ertl window display box with either a "Superstock Race Car" or "Stock Car" notation at the top of the package. A small photo of the featured driver was also included on the right side of the package.

11 Darrell Waltrip 125.00 200.00
Mountain Dew Caprice
Superstock package
11 Darrell Waltrip 125.00 200.00
Pepsi Challenger
Stock Car Package
43 Richard Petty 100.00 200.00
STP Stock Car Package
43 Richard Petty 100.00 200.00
STP Superstock Package
88 Darrell Waltrip 125.00 200.00
Gatorade Caprice
Superstock package

1982 Ertl Motorized Pullback 1:43

These cars was released in the early 1980s. Each was packaged in an Ertl window display box with "Motorized Pullback Race Car" printed at the top of the package. A small photo of the featured driver was also included on the right side of the package. The back features a short write-up on the driver.

11 Darrell Waltrip 25.00 50.00
Mountain Dew
33 Harry Gant 20.00 40.00
Skoal
43 Richard Petty 40.00 80.00
STP

1981 Ertl Superstock 1:64

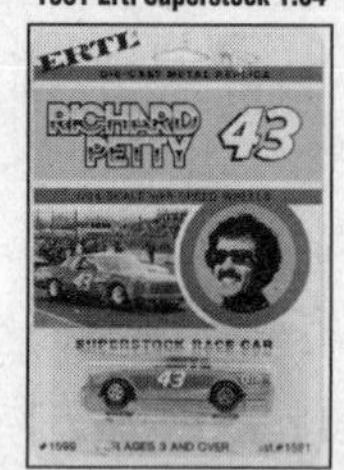

This series of die-cast was issued in the early 1980s by Ertl and is one of the earliest 1:64 NASCAR racing die-cast series. Each car was included on a blister pack that featured a photo of the driver's car on the left and a photo of the driver on the right within a circle design. The driver's name and car number were included above the photos along with the Ertl logo and the die-cast piece was attached below the photos.

11 Darrell Waltrip 10.00 20.00
Mountain Dew 1980 Chevy
(issue #1598)
11 Darrell Waltrip 10.00 20.00
Mountain Dew Buick
(issue #1946)
27 Cale Yarborough 10.00 20.00
Valvoline
(issue #1943)
43 Richard Petty 12.50 25.00
STP 1980 Chevy blue above
and below red stripe on sides
(issue #1599)
43 Richard Petty 12.50 25.00
STP Buick red above
and blue below on sides
(issue #1942)
88 Bobby Allison 10.00 20.00
Gatorade Buick
(issue #1944)
88 Darrell Waltrip 10.00 20.00
Gatorade 1980 Chevy
(issue #1598)

1984 Ertl Pow-R Pull 1:64

Ertl issued this series of 1:64 die-cast cars in the mid-1980s. Each car was packaged on a large green blister with a photo of the featured driver. A mechanism was also included to be used to provide power to the car so that it could propel itself across the ground.

7 Kyle Petty 40.00 80.00
Seven-Eleven
15 Dale Earnhardt 175.00 300.00
Wrangler
28 Cale Yarborough 40.00 80.00
Hardee's
43 Richard Petty 60.00 120.00
STP

1986-93 Ertl 1:64

These cars were distributed by Ertl in the late 1980s and early 1990s. Each was packaged in either a white checkered flag designed blister pack or a promo design blister with sponsor logos and artwork. The year of issue is included on the back of the packaging. Some drivers are not specifically identified on the car or the packaging. However, we've included the names below of the driver's on those cars for the year of issue.

4 NDA 5.00 12.00
Kodak 1990
(Rick Wilson's Car)
15 Brett Bodine 5.00 12.00
Crisco 1988
15 No Driver Association 5.00 12.00
Crisco Promo 1990
(Brett Bodine's Car)
15 Dale Earnhardt 200.00 350.00
Wrangler Promo
17 Sterling Marlin 7.50 15.00
Hesco 1983 Monte
Carlo/15,000 1993
21 NDA 5.00 12.00
Citgo 1990
(Dale Jarrett's Car)
21 Kyle Petty 6.00 15.00
Citgo 1988
21 Kyle Petty 6.00 15.00
Citgo Promo 1987
25 NDA 5.00 12.00
Folgers 1990
(Tim Richmond's Car)
25 Tim Richmond 7.50 20.00
Folgers Promo 1986
ith T.G. Shephard on package
30 NDA 5.00 12.00
Country Time
Maxwell House 1990
(Michael Waltrip's Car)
43 NDA 7.50 20.00
STP 1990
(Richard Petty's Car)
49 Buddy Baker 5.00 12.00
Six Pack Camaro Promo
49 Buddy Baker 5.00 12.00
Six Pack Thunderbird Promo
55 Phil Parsons 5.00 12.00
Crown Promo 1989
59 Robert Pressley 4.00 10.00
Alliance Promo 1991
59 Robert Pressley 4.00 10.00
Alliance Promo/10,000 1992
Pressley's picture on blister
88 Buddy Baker 15.00 30.00
Crisco Promo 1986
00 Sam Ard 4.00 10.00
Thomas Bros.Country Ham 1991
1984 BGN Championship car

1992-93 Ertl 1930s Stock Cars 1:64

9 Curtis Crider 5.00 12.00
Fathers of Racing/10,000
11 Fireball Roberts 5.00 12.00
Roquemore Motor Supply
Start Your Engines Promo/10,000 1993
70 Cotton Owens 5.00 12.00
Founding Fathers Promo/10,000 1992
94 Louise Smith 5.00 12.00
First Ladies of Racing/10,000

2000 Ertl Proshop 1:64

This series was issued in a large black box that includes a picture of the featured driver and his car. Each box also includes the year of issue and the production run of 10,000.

5 Terry Labonte 5.00 12.00
Kellogg's
6 Mark Martin 6.00 12.00
Valvoline
12 Jermey Mayfield 4.00 10.00
Mobil 1
17 Matt Kenseth 6.00 15.00
DeWalt
22 Ward Burton 4.00 10.00
Caterpillar Dealers
22 Ward Burton 5.00 12.00
Caterpillar Bud Shoot Out
97 Chad Little 4.00 10.00
John Deere
99 Jeff Burton 4.00 10.00
Exide

1992 Funstuf Pit Row 1:43

These 1:43 scale cars were distributed through retail outlets and packaged in standard blister packs. The series features an early Jeff Gordon Baby Ruth BGN car.

1 Jeff Gordon 15.00 30.00
Baby Ruth
6 Mark Martin 2.50 5.00
Valvoline
11 Bill Elliott 2.50 5.00
Amoco
12 Hut Stricklin 2.50 5.00
Raybestos
16 Wally Dallenbach Jr. 3.00 6.00
Roush Racing
18 Dale Jarrett 2.50 5.00
Interstate Batteries
21 Morgan Shepherd 2.50 5.00
Citgo
22 Sterling Marlin 2.50 6.00
Maxwell House
33 Harry Gant 2.50 5.00
Leo Jackson Motors
41 Greg Sacks 3.00 6.00
Kellogg's
49 Stanley Smith 2.50 5.00
Ameritron Batteries
66 Jimmy Hensley 2.50 5.00
TropArtic
66 Chad Little 2.00 5.00
TropArtic
75 Joe Ruttman 2.50 5.00
Dinner Bell
83 Jeff McClure 3.00 6.00
Collector's World
98 Jimmy Spencer 2.50 5.00
Moly Black Gold

1992 Funstuf Pit Row 1:64

This series of 1:64 cars was produced by Pit Row and distributed through retail outlets. The series features an early Jeff Gordon Baby Ruth BGN car. A variation of the #94 Terry Labonte car exists as well as variations on some cars with or without a "Winston" decal on the fender.

1 Jeff Gordon 12.00 20.00
Baby Ruth
11 Bill Elliott 1.00 3.00
Amoco on the Deck Lid
11 Bill Elliott 1.00 3.00
Amoco on the Hood
11 No Driver Association 1.00 3.00
Baby Ruth
12 Ken Schulz 2.00 5.00
Piggly Wiggly
15 Morgan Shepherd 1.00 3.00
Motorcraft
15 Morgan Shepherd 3.00 7.00
Motorcraft with
Winston Decal on Fender
15 No Driver Association 1.00 3.00
Motorcraft
18 Dale Jarrett 1.00 3.00
Interstate Batteries
18 No Driver Association 1.00 3.00
Interstate Batteries
20 Michael Waltrip 2.00 5.00
Orkin
21 Dale Jarrett 1.00 3.00
Citgo
21 Dale Jarrett 3.00 7.00
Citgo
with Winston Decal on Fender
21 Morgan Shepherd 1.00 3.00
Citgo
23 Eddie Bierschwale 2.00 5.00
AutoFinders
27 Ward Burton 2.00 5.00
Gaultney
27 Jeff McClure 2.00 5.00
Race For Life
41 Greg Sacks 2.00 5.00
Kellogg's
43 Richard Petty 1.00 3.00
STP
43 Richard Petty 3.00 7.00
STP
with Winston Decal on Fender
49 Stanley Smith 2.00 5.00
Ameritron Batteries
66 Jimmy Hensley 1.00 3.00
TropArtic
66 Chad Little 1.25 3.00
TropArtic
66 Lake Speed 1.00 3.00
TropArtic
75 No Driver Association 1.00 3.00
Dinner Bell
75 Joe Ruttman 1.00 3.00
Dinner Bell
83 Jeff McClure 2.00 5.00
Collector's World
94 Terry Labonte 1.00 3.00
Sunoco
94 Terry Labonte 2.00 5.00
Sunoco with Busch decal
NNO 6-Car Set/11. Baby Ruth/22. S.Marlin 6.00 15.00
Maxwell Huse/43. R.Petty
STP/71. D.Marcis
Big Apple/94. T.Labonte
Sunoco
Pit Row Pace Car

1992 Funstuf Trackside 1:64

8 Jeff Burton 1.50 4.00
TIC Financial
9 Chad Little 1.50 4.00
Melling
11 Bill Elliott 1.50 4.00
Amoco
16 Wally Dallenbach 1.50 4.00
Roush Racing
20 Mike Wallace 1.50 4.00
First Ade
27 Hut Stricklin 1.50 4.00
McDonald's
36 Kenny Wallace 1.50 4.00
Dirt Devil
41 Greg Sacks 1.50 4.00
Kellogg's
55 Ted Musgrave 1.50 4.00
Jasper
83 Lake Speed 1.50 4.00
Purex

2002-04 General Mills Petty Promos 1:64

These 1:64 scale cars were released in 2002 and 2003 in various General Mills products. Each includes black windows and was packaged in either a clear promo style bag or shrinked wrapped on a thin backer board with the copyright "2002 General Mills" on the back. The year the car model ran is also printed on the fronts of the 4-shrinked wrapped die-cast. Those four were initially released in early 2003.

43 John Andretti 2.00 5.00
2003 Cheerios on card
43 John Andretti 2.00 5.00
2002 Chex Party Mix on card
43 John Andretti 2.00 5.00
2001 Honey Nut Cheerios
on card
43 John Andretti 2.00 5.00
Pop Secret on card
43 John Andretti 2.00 5.00
2002 Honey Nut Cheerios
in bag
43 John Andretti 2.00 5.00
2000 Wheaties on card
43 Berry Burst Cheerios in bag 2003 10.00 20.00
43 Betty Crocker in bag 2.50 6.00
43 Box Tops Education in bag 2004 6.00 15.00
43 Cheerios in bag 2003 2.00 5.00
43 Fruit Roll-Ups in bag 2004 4.00 10.00
43 Hamburger Helper in bag 2003 3.00 8.00
43 LeSueur Peas in bag 2004 6.00 15.00
43 Old El Paso in bag 2003 2.50 6.00
43 Pillsbury Grands in bag 2003 2.50 6.00
43 Pop Secret in bag 2003 2.00 5.00
43 Star Wars Attack of the Clones in bag 2002 6.00 15.00
43 Star Wars Phantom Menace in bag 2002 6.00 15.00
43 Star Wars Trilogy in bag 2002 6.00 15.00
43/44/45 John Andretti 10.00 20.00
Cheerios
Petty Enterprises
Kyle Petty
Sprint
3-car gold set in bag
44 Brawny in bag 2004 2.00 5.00
44 Bugles in bag 2004 3.00 8.00
45 Kyle Petty 2.00 5.00
Sprint in bag 2003

2004 General Mills Hot Wheels Petty Promos 1:64

These 10-die-cast cars were issued inside specially marked boxes of General Mills cereals in 2004. The cars consist of models of actual Richard Petty stock cars over the course of his career as well as a few "fantasy" cars featuring new cereal paint schemes on vintage stock cars. Each car was manufactured by Hot Wheels and issued in an oversized clear plastic wrapper.

43 Cheerios 1974 Charger 2.50 6.00
43 Cheerios 2004 Dodge Intrepid 2.50 6.00
43 Chex 1970 Barracuda 2.50 6.00
43 Honey Nut Cherrios 1970 Roadrunner 2.50 6.00
43 Lucky Charms 1971 Plymouth GTX 2.50 6.00
43 Lucky Charms 2004 Dodge Intrepid 2.50 6.00
43 Pop Secret 1964 Plymouth 2.50 6.00
43 Pop Secret 1970 Barracuda 2.50 6.00
43 Pop Secret 1974 Charger 2.50 6.00
43 Pop Secret 1984 Grand Prix 2.50 6.00
43 Wheaties 1967 GTO 2.50 6.00
43 Richard Petty 3.00 8.00
STP 1964 Plymouth
43 Richard Petty 3.00 8.00
STP 1974 Charger

2003 GreenLight 1:24

10 Brickyard 400 10th Anniversary 12.50 25.00
Event Car/2003

2003 GreenLight 1:64

03 Brickyard 400 Event Car Orange 4.00 8.00
with Silver Hood/4080
03 Brickyard 400 Event Car Silver 6.00 12.00
with Oragne Hood/4080

2002 Hot Wheels Thunder Series Motorcycles 1:18

5 Terry Labonte 5.00 10.00
Kellogg's
6 Mark Martin 5.00 10.00
Pfizer
10 Johnny Benson 5.00 10.00
Valvoline
10 Scott Riggs 5.00 10.00
Nesquik
12 Ryan Newman 5.00 10.00
Alltel
14 Larry Foyt 5.00 10.00
Harrah's
17 Matt Kenseth 5.00 10.00
DeWalt
22 Ward Burton 5.00 10.00
Caterpillar
25 Randy Tolsma 5.00 10.00
Marines Red
Black
36 Ken Schrader 5.00 10.00
M&M's
40 Sterling Marlin 5.00 10.00

Silver
43 John Andretti Cheerios 5.00 10.00
45 Kyle Petty Sprint 5.00 10.00
99 Jeff Burton Citgo 5.00 10.00

2004 Hot Wheels Racing Justice League Thunder Rides 1:18

6 Mark Martin Batman 7.50 15.00
16 Greg Biffle Flash 6.00 12.00
17 Matt Kenseth Martian Manhunter 6.00 12.00
21 Ricky Rudd Wonder Woman 6.00 12.00
97 Kurt Busch Superman 6.00 12.00
99 Jeff Burton Green Lantern 6.00 12.00

1998 Hot Wheels Legends 1:24

44 Kyle Petty Blues Brothers 25.00 50.00
44 Kyle Petty Hot Wheels 25.00 50.00

1998 Hot Wheels Racing 1:24

This series of 1:24 scale cars was released in 1998. Each was packaged in a Hot Wheels Racing black window box. Note that a similar box was also used in 1999, but that series was entitled "Hot Wheels Pro Racing."

6 Mark Martin Valvoline 10.00 25.00
12 Jeremy Mayfield Mobil 1 8.00 20.00
26 Johnny Benson Cheerios 8.00 20.00
35 Todd Bodine Tabasco 8.00 20.00
36 Ernie Irvan Skittles 8.00 20.00
42 Joe Nemechek Bell South 8.00 20.00
44 Kyle Petty Blues Brothers 10.00 25.00
44 Kyle Petty Hot Wheels 10.00 25.00
58 Ricky Craven Turbine Solutions 20.00 40.00
97 Chad Little John Deere 8.00 20.00

1998 Hot Wheels Racing 2-Car Sets 1:24/1:64

6 Mark Martin Eagle One w Valvoline 1:64 10.00 25.00
43 John Andretti STP 8.00 20.00
44 Kyle Petty Hot Wheels 10.00 25.00

1998 Hot Wheels Racing Electronic Fast Facts 1:24

This series was prodcued with each car acting as an electonic trivia game complete with questions and answers about the specific driver featured. Each was packaged in a black "Hot Wheels Racing Electonic Fast Facts" window box.

12 Jeremy Mayfield Mobil One 10.00 20.00
44 Kyle Petty Hot Wheels 10.00 20.00

1999 Hot Wheels Crew's Choice 1:24

These 1:24 scale cars feature bodies that are detachable from the chassis. Each was packaged in a solid black Hot Wheels Crew's Choice box.

10 Ricky Rudd Tide 8.00 20.00
12 Jeremy Mayfield Mobil 1 8.00 20.00
14 Sterling Marlin Tennessee 20.00 35.00
17 Matt Kenseth DeWalt 20.00 40.00
22 Ward Burton Caterpillar 8.00 20.00
26 Jimmy Spencer Big K 8.00 20.00
36 Ernie Irvan M&M's 15.00 30.00
40 Sterling Marlin Coors 15.00 40.00
43 John Andretti STP 8.00 20.00
44 Kyle Petty Hot Wheels 12.50 30.00
45 Adam Petty Spree 30.00 60.00
55 Kenny Wallace Square D Aerosmith 8.00 20.00
94 Bill Elliott McDonald's 10.00 25.00
94 Bill Elliott Toy Story 2 75.00 125.00
99 Jeff Burton Exide 8.00 20.00

1999 Hot Wheels Deluxe 1:24

This series of cars was isued through retail outlets in a red and blue window box. The box features the title "Deluxe" in the lower right hand corner. Please note that the same box was also used in 2000 with the addition of the words "Race Day" to the Deluxe title.

5 Terry Labonte Kellogg's 10.00 25.00
6 Mark Martin Valvoline Black Chrome 10.00 25.00
17 Matt Kenseth DeWalt 10.00 25.00
22 Ward Burton Caterpillar Black Chrome 8.00 20.00
32 Scott Pruett Tide 8.00 20.00
36 John Andretti Cheerios 8.00 20.00
42 Joe Nemechek BellSouth 8.00 20.00
45 Adam Petty Sprint 15.00 40.00
94 Bill Elliott McDonald's Drive Thru 8.00 20.00

1999 Hot Wheels Fresh Paint 1:24

These 1:24 scale die-casts were issued in Hot Wheels Fresh Paint window box. Each box includes the notation "Speedway Special Edition" on the front along with the stated production run of 7998.

5 Terry Labonte K-Sentials 5.00 10.00
6 Mark Martin Zerex 5.00 10.00
7 Michael Waltrip Sealy 4.00 8.00
99 Jeff Burton Citgo 4.00 8.00

1999 Hot Wheels Pro Racing 1:24

These 1:24 scale cars were available primarily through retail outlets. Each was packaged in a solid black Hot Wheels Pro Racing window box. Note that a similar box was used in 1998, but that series was called "Hot Wheels Racing."

5 Terry Labonte Kellogg's 15.00 30.00
6 Mark Martin Valvoline 15.00 30.00
10 Ricky Rudd Tide 8.00 20.00
12 Jeremy Mayfield Mobil 1 8.00 20.00
14 Sterling Marlin Tennessee 35.00 60.00
26 Johnny Benson Betty Crocker 8.00 20.00
26 Johnny Benson Cheerios 8.00 20.00
35 Todd Bodine Tabasco Red 8.00 20.00
36 Ernie Irvan M&M's 15.00 30.00
42 Joe Nemechek BellSouth 8.00 20.00
43 Richard Petty STP '81 Buick 15.00 40.00
44 Kyle Petty Blues Brothers 12.50 30.00
44 Kyle Petty Hot Wheels 12.50 30.00
44 Kyle Petty Players Inc. 12.50 30.00
94 Bill Elliott McDonald's Drive Thru 8.00 20.00
97 Chad Little John Deere 8.00 20.00

1999 Hot Wheels Racing NASCAR Rocks 1:24

Each of these 1:24 scale cars were issued in a black Hot Wheels window box. A small plastic guitar was also packaged with each car. The cars were produced with a production run of 15,000.

5 Terry Labonte Kellogg's 10.00 25.00
6 Mark Martin Valvoline 12.50 25.00
9 Jerry Nadeau Dexter's Lab 10.00 25.00
10 Ricky Rudd Tide 10.00 25.00
12 Jeremy Mayfield Mobil 1 10.00 25.00
22 Ward Burton Caterpillar 10.00 25.00
26 Johnny Benson Cheerios 10.00 25.00
44 Kyle Petty Hot Wheels 10.00 25.00
66 Darrell Waltrip Big K 10.00 25.00
94 Bill Elliott McDonald's Drive Thru 10.00 25.00
97 Chad Little John Deere 10.00 25.00
99 Jeff Burton Exide 10.00 25.00

1999 Hot Wheels Racing Select 1:24

These 1:24 scale die-cast cars were issued by Hot Wheels in a black window box. The "Select" name appears in red in the lower right hand corner of the box. The stated production run was 10,000. A few pieces were also issued in a Toy Story 2 promo window box. The Toy Story logo appears in the lower right hand corner with the Select name on the top of the box.

STATED PRODUCTION RUN 10,000
4 Bobby Hamilton Kodak Advantix 8.00 20.00
5 Terry Labonte Kellogg's 10.00 25.00
6 Mark Martin Valvoline 10.00 25.00
26 Johnny Benson Cheerios 8.00 20.00
26 Johnny Benson Cheerios Toy Story 2 8.00 20.00
36 Ken Schrader M&M's 8.00 20.00
43 John Andretti STP 8.00 20.00
44 Kyle Petty Hot Wheels 8.00 20.00
44 Kyle Petty Hot Wheels Toy Story 2 8.00 20.00
94 Bill Elliott McDonald's Drive Thru 8.00 20.00
97 Chad Little John Deere 8.00 20.00
99 Jeff Burton Exide 8.00 20.00

1999 Hot Wheels Select Clear 1:24

These 1:24 scale plastic body cars were issued by Hot Wheels primarily to the hobby. Each was packaged in a blue and black window box with the driver's photo and the "Select Clear" name in the lower right hand corner of the box. Each was produced with a clear plastic body.

6 Mark Martin Valvoline 8.00 20.00
21 Elliott Sadler Citgo 8.00 20.00
43 John Andretti STP 8.00 20.00
44 Kyle Petty Hot Wheels 8.00 20.00
60 Geoff Bodine Power Team 8.00 20.00
66 Darrell Waltrip Big K 8.00 20.00
94 Bill Elliott McDonald's Drive Thru 8.00 20.00
99 Jeff Burton Exide 8.00 20.00

1999 Hot Wheels Trading Paint 1:24

These 1:24 scale cars feature painting detail that creates a race damaged look. Each car was packaged in a black Hot Wheels window box.

7 Michael Waltrip Phillips 8.00 20.00
12 Jeremy Mayfield Mobil 1 8.00 20.00
22 Ward Burton Caterpillar 8.00 20.00
43 John Andretti STP 8.00 20.00
44 Kyle Petty Hot Wheels 8.00 20.00
66 Darrell Waltrip Big K 8.00 20.00
94 Bill Elliott McDonald's 10.00 20.00
99 Jeff Burton Exide 8.00 20.00

2000 Hot Wheels Crew's Choice 1:24

The Hot Wheels Crew's Choice brand was produced as the company's highest quality 1:24 die-cast. Each car was built with more than 25-detailed parts and a removable body. They were packaged in a solid box (in the colors of the driver's car) with the "Crew's Choice" name and year of issue clearly defined. Each car also included a certificate of authenticty that noted a production run of 4998 of each piece.

4 Bobby Hamilton Kodak 8.00 20.00
6 Mark Martin Valvoline 10.00 25.00
7 Michael Waltrip Nations Rent 8.00 20.00
12 Jeremy Mayfield Mobil 1 8.00 20.00
14 Mike Bliss Conseco 8.00 20.00
17 Matt Kenseth DeWalt 15.00 30.00
22 Ward Burton Caterpillar 8.00 20.00
26 Jimmy Spencer Big K 8.00 20.00
32 Scott Pruett Tide 8.00 20.00
33 Joe Nemechek Oakwood Homes 8.00 20.00
40 Sterling Marlin Coors Light 15.00 30.00
42 Kenny Irwin BellSouth 15.00 30.00
43 John Andretti STP 1972 paint scheme 8.00 20.00
43 John Andretti STP 8.00 20.00
43 John Andretti Cheerios 8.00 20.00
43 John Andretti STP Texas 8.00 20.00
43 John Andretti Wheaties 10.00 25.00
44 Kyle Petty Hot Wheels 10.00 25.00
45 Adam Petty Sprint PCS 15.00 40.00
55 Kenny Wallace Square D 8.00 20.00
60 Geoff Bodine Power Team 8.00 20.00
66 Darrell Waltrip Big K Route 66 8.00 20.00
77 Robert Pressley Jasper 8.00 20.00
94 Bill Elliott McDonald's 10.00 25.00
97 Chad Little John Deere 8.00 20.00
97 Anthony Lazzaro McDonald's 8.00 20.00
99 Jeff Burton Exide 8.00 20.00

2000 Hot Wheels Race Day Deluxe 1:24

These cars were available through retail outlets, in a black and blue box with a window to let you see the driver side and top of the car. The box features the title "Race Day Deluxe" in the lower right hand corner. Please note that the same box was also used in 1999 without the words "Race Day" in the Deluxe title.

4 Bobby Hamilton Kodak 8.00 20.00
5 Terry Labonte Kellogg's 10.00 25.00
6 Mark Martin Valvoline 10.00 25.00
7 Michael Waltrip NationsRent 8.00 20.00
12 Jeremy Mayfield Mobil 1 8.00 20.00
14 Mike Bliss Conseco 8.00 20.00
17 Matt Kenseth DeWalt 15.00 30.00
21 Elliott Sadler Citgo 8.00 20.00
22 Ward Burton Caterpillar 8.00 20.00
25 Jerry Nadeau Holigan 8.00 20.00
26 Jimmy Spencer Big K 8.00 20.00
32 Scott Pruett Tide 8.00 20.00
33 Joe Nemechek Oakwood Homes 8.00 20.00
42 Kenny Irwin BellSouth 15.00 40.00
43 John Andretti Cheerios 8.00 20.00
43 John Andretti STP 8.00 20.00
43 John Andretti Wheaties 8.00 20.00
44 Kyle Petty Hot Wheels 10.00 25.00
45 Adam Petty Sprint 15.00 40.00
55 Kenny Wallace Aerosmith 8.00 20.00
60 Geoffery Bodine Power Team 8.00 20.00
94 Bill Elliott McDonald's Drive Thru 10.00 25.00
97 Anthony Lazzaro McDonald's 8.00 20.00
97 Chad Little John Deere 8.00 20.00
99 Jeff Burton Exide 8.00 20.00

2000 Hot Wheels Select 1:24

These 1:24 scale die-cast cars were issued by Hot Wheels primarily to the hobby. Each was packaged in a blue and black window box with the driver's photo and the "Select 2000" name in the lower right hand corner of the box. The stated production run was 9998 of each car.

12 Jeremy Mayfield Mobil 1 8.00 20.00
17 Matt Kenseth DeWalt 10.00 25.00
22 Ward Burton Caterpillar 8.00 20.00
43 John Andretti STP 8.00 20.00
44 Kyle Petty Hot Wheels 8.00 20.00

2001 Hot Wheels Racing 1:24

5 Terry Labonte Kellogg's Tony 10.00 25.00
6 Mark Martin Pfizer 10.00 25.00
10 Johnny Benson Valvoline 8.00 20.00
10 Jeff Green Nesquik 8.00 20.00
12 Jeremy Mayfield Mobil 1 8.00 20.00
17 Matt Kenseth DeWalt Yellow&Black 12.00 30.00
17 Matt Kenseth DeWalt Black 12.00 30.00
21 Elliott Sadler Motorcraft 8.00 20.00
22 Ward Burton Caterpillar 8.00 20.00
25 Jerry Nadeau UAW Delphi 8.00 20.00
32 Scott Pruett Tide 8.00 20.00
32 Scott Pruett Tide Alabama 12.50 30.00
32 Ricky Craven Tide Downy Promo 6.00 15.00
33 Joe Nemechek Oakwood Homes 8.00 20.00
36 Ken Schrader M&M's 10.00 25.00
43 John Andretti Cheerios 8.00 20.00
44 Buckshot Jones Four Generations of Petty 8.00 20.00
44 Buckshot Jones Georgia Pacific 8.00 20.00
45 Kyle Petty Sprint PCS 8.00 20.00
45 Kyle Petty Sprint Charity Ride 8.00 20.00
60 Greg Biffle Grainger 8.00 20.00
96 Andy Houston McDonald's 8.00 20.00
99 Jeff Burton Citgo 8.00 20.00
02 Ryan Newman Alltel 12.50 25.00

2002 Hot Wheels Racing 1:24

5 Terry Labonte Kellogg's 10.00 20.00
5 Terry Labonte Monster's Inc. 12.50 25.00
6 Mark Martin Pfizer 10.00 20.00
10 Johnny Benson Eagle One 10.00 20.00
10 Scott Riggs Nesquik 10.00 20.00
12 Ryan Newman Alltel 12.50 25.00
14 Larry Foyt Harrah's 10.00 20.00
17 Matt Kenseth DeWalt 10.00 20.00
22 Ward Burton Caterpillar 10.00 20.00
25 Randy Tolsma Marines red black 10.00 20.00
25 Randy Tolsma Marines red white blue 12.50 25.00
36 Ken Schrader M&M's 10.00 20.00
43 John Andretti Cheerios 10.00 20.00
43 John Andretti Hamburger Helper 10.00 20.00
43 John Andretti Honey Nut Cheerios 10.00 20.00
43 John Andretti Pop Secret 10.00 20.00
45 Kyle Petty Sprint 10.00 20.00
97 Kurt Busch Rubbermaid 10.00 20.00
99 Jeff Burton Citgo 10.00 20.00

2003 Hot Wheels Racing 1:24

6 Mark Martin Pfizer 12.50 25.00
10 Scott Riggs Nesquik 12.50 25.00
12 Ryan Newman Alltel 15.00 25.00
12 Ryan Newman Mobil 1 12.50 25.00
12 Ryan Newman Mobil 1 First Win/1212 15.00 30.00
16 Greg Biffle Grainger 12.50 25.00
17 Matt Kenseth DeWalt 15.00 25.00
21 Ricky Rudd Motorcraft 12.50 25.00
25 Bobby Hamilton Jr. Marines 15.00 25.00
36 Ken Schrader M&M's Haloween 12.50 25.00
43 John Andretti Cheerios 12.50 25.00
43 John Andretti Pop Secret 12.50 25.00
45 Kyle Petty Georgia Pacific Brawny 12.50 25.00
97 Kurt Busch Rubbermaid 15.00 25.00
97 Kurt Busch Rubbermaid Little Tikes 15.00 25.00
99 Jeff Burton Citgo 12.50 25.00
99 Jeff Burton Citgo Bass Masters 12.50 25.00
01 Jerry Nadeau Army 12.50 25.00

2003 Hot Wheels Racing Matt Kenseth Championship 1:24

17 Matt Kenseth DeWalt 12.50 25.00
17 Matt Kenseth DeWalt/10,000 18.00 30.00

2003 Hot Wheels Racing Stock Car Cruisers 1:24

6 Mark Martin Pfizer 12.50 25.00
12 Ryan Newman Alltel 12.50 25.00
17 Matt Kenseth DeWalt 12.50 25.00
97 Kurt Busch Rubbermaid 12.50 25.00

2004 Hot Wheels Racing Alternative Paint Scheme 1:24

6 Mark Martin Oscar Mayer 10.00 20.00
21 Ricky Rudd Air Force 10.00 20.00
45 Kyle Petty Brawny 10.00 20.00

2004 Hot Wheels Racing Artist Collection 1:24

6 Mark Martin Pfizer 15.00 30.00
12 Ryan Newman Alltel 12.50 25.00
16 Greg Biffle Grainger 12.50 25.00
17 Matt Kenseth DeWalt 15.00 30.00
21 Ricky Rudd Motorcraft 12.50 25.00
97 Kurt Busch Rubbermaid 12.50 25.00
99 Jeff Burton Citgo 12.50 25.00

2004 Hot Wheels Racing Chase for the Cup 1:24

6 Mark Martin Viagra/6000 15.00 30.00
12 Ryan Newman Alltel/6000 12.50 25.00
17 Matt Kenseth DeWalt/6000 15.00 30.00
97 Kurt Busch Irwin Tools/6000 12.50 25.00

2004 Hot Wheels Racing Justice League 1:24

6 Mark Martin Batman 15.00 30.00
9 Mark Martin Batman 15.00 30.00
16 Greg Biffle Flash 10.00 20.00
21 Ricky Rudd Wonder Woman 10.00 20.00

60 Greg Biffle Flash 10.00 20.00
97 Kurt Busch Superman 15.00 25.00
99 Jeff Burton Green Lantern 10.00 20.00
04 Justic League Super Heroes 10.00 20.00
04 Justic League Villains 10.00 20.00

2004 Hot Wheels Racing Race Day 1:24

6 Mark Martin Viagra 15.00 25.00
12 Ryan Newman Alltel 10.00 20.00
17 Matt Kenseth DeWalt 15.00 25.00
21 Ricky Rudd Motorcraft 10.00 20.00
45 Kyle Petty Georgia Pacific 10.00 20.00
97 Kurt Busch Sharpie 10.00 20.00

2004 Hot Wheels Racing Stockerz 1:24

6 Mark Martin Oscar Mayer 12.50 25.00
6 Mark Martin Pfizer 12.50 25.00
12 Ryan Newman Alltel 12.50 25.00
17 Matt Kenseth DeWalt 18.00 30.00
21 Ricky Rudd Motorcraft 12.50 25.00
24 Jeff Gordon DuPont Flames 18.00 30.00
29 Kevin Harvick Goodwrench 12.50 25.00
97 Kurt Busch Rubbermaid 10.00 20.00
97 Kurt Busch Sharpie 10.00 20.00

2004 Hot Wheels Racing Test Track 1:24

6 Mark Martin Pfizer 12.50 25.00
12 Ryan Newman Alltel 10.00 20.00
16 Greg Biffle Grainger 10.00 20.00
17 Matt Kenseth DeWalt 12.50 25.00
43 Richard Petty STP 12.50 25.00
97 Kurt Busch Sharpie 10.00 20.00

2005 Hot Wheels Alternative Paint Scheme 1:24

17 Matt Kenseth Trex 10.00 20.00
21 Ricky Rudd Air Force 10.00 20.00
97 Kurt Busch Irwin Tools 10.00 20.00
99 Carl Edwards Office Depot 15.00 30.00

2005 Hot Wheels Batman Begins 1:24

6 Mark Martin Batman 15.00 30.00

2005 Hot Wheels Race Day 1:24

16 Greg Biffle National Guard 10.00 20.00
21 Ricky Rudd Motorcraft 10.00 20.00
97 Kurt Busch Sharpie 10.00 20.00
99 Carl Edwards AAA 15.00 30.00

1998 Hot Wheels Racing 1:43

These 1:43 scale cars were produced by Hot Wheels and marks their introduction in the NASCAR market. These cars were distributed through hobby, retail and trackside outlets.

5 Terry Labonte Kellogg's 6.00 15.00
6 Mark Martin Valvoline 6.00 15.00
7 Michael Waltrip Phillips 5.00 12.00
10 Ricky Rudd Tide 5.00 12.00
12 Jeremy Mayfield Mobil 1 5.00 12.00
35 Todd Bodine Tabasco 5.00 12.00
43 John Andretti STP 5.00 12.00
44 Kyle Petty Hot Wheels 5.00 12.00
99 Jeff Burton Exide 5.00 12.00

1999 Hot Wheels Crew's Choice 1:43

These 1:43 scale cars feature bodies that are detachable from the chassis.

6 Mark Martin Valvoline 10.00 20.00
36 Ernie Irvan M&M's 8.00 20.00
44 Kyle Petty Hot Wheels 8.00 20.00
66 Darrell Waltrip Big K 8.00 20.00
94 Bill Elliott McDonald's 8.00 20.00

1999 Hot Wheels Deluxe Black Chrome 1:43

4 Bobby Hamilton Kodak Max 4.00 10.00
5 Terry Labonte Kellogg's 5.00 10.00
6 Mark Martin Valvoline 5.00 10.00
12 Jeremy Mayfield Mobil 1 4.00 10.00
21 Elliott Sadler Citgo 4.00 10.00
22 Ward Burton Caterpillar 4.00 10.00
43 John Andretti STP 4.00 10.00
44 Kyle Petty Hot Wheels 4.00 10.00
60 Geoff Bodine Power Team 4.00 10.00
97 Chad Little John Deere 4.00 10.00
99 Jeff Burton Exide 4.00 10.00

1999 Hot Wheels Pro Racing 1:43

These 1:43 scale cars were available through retail outlets.

5 Terry Labonte Kellogg's 6.00 15.00
6 Mark Martin Valvoline 6.00 15.00
6 Mark Martin Synpower 6.00 15.00
10 Ricky Rudd Tide 5.00 12.00
12 Jeremy Mayfield Mobil 1 5.00 12.00
22 Ward Burton Caterpillar 5.00 12.00
26 Johnny Benson Cheerios 5.00 12.00
36 Ernie Irvan M&M's 5.00 12.00
36 Ernie Irvan Skittles 5.00 12.00
43 John Andretti STP 5.00 12.00
44 Kyle Petty Hot Wheels 5.00 12.00
94 Bill Elliott McDonald's 6.00 15.00
97 Chad Little John Deere 5.00 12.00

1999 Hot Wheels Radical Rides 1:43

This series features a highly exaggerated modified stock car with an oversized driver figure on top. The scale is roughly 1:43 and each was packaged in a Hot Wheels blister with the title "Radical Rides" printed in blue and yellow in the upper right hand corner.

6 Mark Martin Valvoline 6.00 12.00
17 Matt Kenseth DeWalt 6.00 12.00
43 John Andretti Cheerios 5.00 10.00
43 Richard Petty STP 6.00 12.00
44 Kyle Petty Hot Wheels 5.00 10.00
45 Adam Petty Sprint 10.00 20.00
66 Darrell Waltrip K-Mart Route 66 5.00 10.00
97 Chad Little John Deere 5.00 10.00
99 Jeff Burton Exide 5.00 10.00

1999 Hot Wheels Select 1:43

These 1:43 scale die-cast cars were issued by Hot Wheels in a black window box. The "Select" name appears in red in the lower right hand corner of the box. The stated production run was 10,000.

12 Jeremy Mayfield Mobil 1 4.00 10.00
22 Ward Burton Caterpillar 4.00 10.00
36 Ken Schrader M&M's 6.00 12.00
44 Kyle Petty Hot Wheels 4.00 10.00
99 Jeff Burton Exide 4.00 10.00

1999 Hot Wheels Select Clear 1:43

These 1:43 scale plastic body cars were issued by Hot Wheels primarily to the hobby. Each was packaged in a blue and black window box with the driver's photo and the "Select Clear" name in the lower right hand corner of the box. Each was produced with a clear plastic body.

6 Mark Martin Valvoline 6.00 12.00
12 Jeremy Mayfield Mobil 1 4.00 10.00
21 Elliott Sadler Citgo 4.00 10.00
43 John Andretti STP 4.00 10.00
55 Kenny Wallace Square D 4.00 10.00
66 Darrell Waltrip Big K 4.00 10.00
94 Bill Elliott McDonald's 5.00 12.00
94 Bill Elliott McDonald's Drive Thru 5.00 10.00
98 No Driver Association Woody Woodpecker 4.00 10.00
99 Jeff Burton Exide 4.00 10.00

1999 Hot Wheels Track Edition 1:43

The track edition set comes with a 1:64 scale car.

12 Jeremy Mayfield Mobil 1 6.00 15.00
16 Kevin Lepage Primestar 6.00 15.00
36 Ernie Irvan M&M's 6.00 15.00
94 Bill Elliott Drive Thru 6.00 15.00
97 Chad Little John Deere 6.00 15.00

2000 Hot Wheels Deluxe 1:43

4 Bobby Hamilton Kodak 4.00 10.00
22 Ward Burton Caterpillar 4.00 10.00
33 Joe Nemechek Oakwood Homes 4.00 10.00
43 John Andretti STP 4.00 10.00
44 Kyle Petty Hot Wheels 4.00 10.00

2000 Hot Wheels Select 1:43

These 1:43 scale die-cast cars were issued by Hot Wheels primarily to the hobby. Each was packaged in a blue and black window box with the driver's photo and the "Select" name in the lower right hand corner of the box.

43 John Andretti STP 4.00 10.00
44 Kyle Petty Hot Wheels 4.00 10.00
94 Bill Elliott McDonald's Drive Thru 4.00 10.00

2001 Hot Wheels Racing Radical Rods 1:43

6 Mark Martin Valvoline 5.00 12.00
12 Jeremy Mayfield Mobil 1 4.00 10.00
17 Matt Kenseth DeWalt 6.00 12.00
22 Ward Burton Caterpillar 4.00 10.00
32 Scott Pruett Tide 4.00 10.00
33 Joe Nemechek Oakwood Homes 4.00 10.00
43 John Andretti Cheerios 4.00 10.00
43 Richard Petty STP 4.00 10.00
45 Kyle Petty Hot Wheels 4.00 10.00
45 Kyle Petty Sprint 4.00 10.00
99 Jeff Burton Citgo 4.00 10.00

1992 Hot Wheels Pro Circuit 1:64

These 1:64 cars were issued in 1992 was part of the Hot Wheels Pro Circuit series. Each car was packaged in a "Pro Circuit" blister along with a silver bordered foil trading card.

2 Rusty Wallace Pontiac 3.00 6.00
6 Mark Martin Valvoline 3.00 6.00
21 Morgan Shepherd Citgo 2.00 5.00
26 Brett Bodine Quaker State 2.00 5.00
42 Kyle Petty Mello Yello 2.00 5.00
43 Richard Petty STP 3.00 6.00

1995-96 Hot Wheels 1:64

Each of these 1:64 cars were issued in a Hot Wheels window display box. The boxes also included a backer board and a copyright date on the bottoms.

44 Kyle Petty Hot Wheels in blue box 1996 3.00 6.00
94 Bill Elliott McDonald's Thunderbat 1995 4.00 10.00

1997 Hot Wheels First Edition 1:64

This series was produced by Hot Wheels in blister packs that featured the title "First Edition 1997." Each 1:64 car was packaged with a Hot Wheels trading card.

4 Sterling Marlin Kodak 3.00 8.00
5 Terry Labonte Kellogg's 3.00 6.00
6 Mark Martin Valvoline 3.00 6.00
7 Geoff Bodine QVC 2.00 4.00
8 Hut Stricklin Circuit City 2.00 4.00
10 Ricky Rudd Tide 2.00 4.00
16 Ted Musgrave Primestar 2.00 4.00
21 Michael Waltrip Citgo 2.00 4.00
28 Ernie Irvan Havoline 3.00 6.00
30 Johnny Benson Pennzoil 2.00 4.00
43 Bobby Hamilton STP 2.00 4.00
44 Kyle Petty Hot Wheels (with signature on card) 3.00 6.00
44 Kyle Petty Hot Wheels (no signature on card) 4.00 10.00
94 Bill Elliott McDonald's 2.00 4.00
98 John Andretti RCA 3.00 6.00
99 Jeff Burton Exide 2.00 4.00

1997 Hot Wheels Short Track 1:64

4 Sterling Marlin Kodak 1.50 4.00
5 Terry Labonte Kellogg's 3.00 6.00
5 Terry Labonte Kellogg's Tony 4.00 8.00
6 Mark Martin Valvoline 3.00 6.00
7 Geoff Bodine QVC 1.50 4.00
8 Hut Stricklin Circuit City 1.50 4.00
10 Ricky Rudd Spring Fresh 1.50 4.00
10 Ricky Rudd Tide 1.50 4.00
16 Ted Musgrave Primestar 1.50 4.00
21 Michael Waltrip Citgo 1.50 4.00
21 Michael Waltrip Citgo Red top 1.50 4.00
28 Ernie Irvan Havoline 1.50 4.00
30 Johnny Benson Pennzoil 1.50 4.00
37 Jeremy Mayfield K-Mart 1.50 4.00
43 Bobby Hamilton STP 1.50 4.00
44 Kyle Petty Hot Wheels 3.00 6.00
91 Mike Wallace Spam 1.50 4.00
94 Bill Elliott McDonald's 2.00 4.00
94 Bill Elliott Mac Tonight 3.00 6.00
96 David Green Caterpillar 1.50 4.00
99 Jeff Burton Exide 1.50 4.00

1997 Hot Wheels Pro Racing Superspeedway 1:64

This series of 1:64 cars marks Hot Wheels second mass-market venture into NASCAR. These cars are the upgraded versions of those cars available in the Pro Racing series.

4 Sterling Marlin Kodak 2.00 4.00
5 Terry Labonte Kellogg's 3.00 6.00
6 Mark Martin Valvoline 3.00 6.00
7 Geoff Bodine QVC 2.00 4.00
8 Hut Stricklin Circuit City 2.00 4.00
10 Ricky Rudd Tide 2.00 4.00
16 Ted Musgrave Primestar 2.00 4.00
21 Michael Waltrip Citgo 2.00 4.00
28 Ernie Irvan Havoline 2.00 4.00
30 Johnny Benson Pennzoil 2.00 4.00
37 Jeremy Mayfield K-Mart 2.00 4.00
43 Bobby Hamilton STP 2.00 4.00
44 Kyle Petty Hot Wheels 3.00 6.00
91 Mike Wallace Spam 2.00 4.00
94 Bill Elliott McDonald's 2.00 4.00
96 David Green Caterpillar 2.00 4.00
98 John Andretti RCA 2.00 4.00
99 Jeff Burton Exide 2.00 4.00

1997 Hot Wheels Track Edition 1:64

4 Sterling Marlin Kodak 5.00 12.00
28 Ernie Irvan Havoline 5.00 10.00
28 Ernie Irvan Hot Wheels SuperTruck 25.00 40.00
43 Bobby Hamilton STP with yellow nose 25.00 40.00
43 Bobby Hamilton STP with blue nose 5.00 10.00
44 Kyle Petty Hot Wheels Blue Box 10.00 25.00
44 Kyle Petty Hot Wheels White Box 150.00 250.00

1997 Hot Wheels Pro Racing 1:64

This series of 1:64 cars marks Hot Wheels first mass-market venture into NASCAR. These cars are packaged with cardboard backing shaped like a number one.

4 Sterling Marlin Kodak 1.50 4.00
5 Terry Labonte Kellogg's 1.50 4.00
6 Mark Martin Valvoline 1.50 4.00
7 Geoff Bodine QVC 1.50 4.00
8 Hut Stricklin Circuit City 1.50 4.00
10 Ricky Rudd Tide 1.50 4.00
16 Ted Musgrave Primestar 1.50 4.00
21 Michael Waltrip Citgo 1.50 4.00
28 Ernie Irvan Havoline 1.50 4.00
30 Johnny Benson Pennzoil 1.50 4.00
37 Jeremy Mayfield K-Mart 1.50 4.00
43 Bobby Hamilton STP 1.50 4.00
44 Kyle Petty Hot Wheels 1.50 4.00
91 Mike Wallace Spam 1.50 4.00
94 Bill Elliott McDonald's 1.50 4.00
96 David Green Caterpillar 1.50 4.00
98 John Andretti RCA 1.50 4.00
99 Jeff Burton Exide 1.50 4.00

1998 Hot Wheels First Edition 1:64

This series was released by Hot Wheels in early 1998. Each car was packaged in a Hot Wheels blister with a "1st Edition" logo in the upper right hand corner.

4 Bobby Hamilton Kodak 2.00 5.00
5 Terry Labonte Kellogg's 2.50 6.00
6 Mark Martin Eagle One 2.50 6.00
6 Mark Martin Eagle One Promo with bottle of car wax 5.00 12.00
6 Mark Martin Synpower 2.50 6.00
6 Mark Martin Valvoline 2.50 6.00
8 Hut Stricklin Circuit City 2.00 5.00
10 Ricky Rudd Tide 2.00 5.00
11 Brett Bodine Paychex 2.00 5.00
12 Jeremy Mayfield Mobil One 2.00 5.00
13 Jerry Nadeau First Plus 2.00 5.00
21 Michael Waltrip Citgo 2.00 5.00
26 Johnny Benson Cheerios 2.00 5.00
30 Derrike Cope Gumout 2.00 5.00
35 Todd Bodine Tabasco Green 2.00 5.00
35 Todd Bodine Tabasco Red 2.00 5.00
35 Todd Bodine Tabasco Orange 2.00 5.00
36 Ernie Irvan Skittles 2.00 5.00
40 Sterling Marlin Marlin 2.50 6.00
42 Joe Nemechek BellSouth blue 2.00 5.00
42 Joe Nemechek BellSouth Yellow Pages 2.00 5.00
43 John Andretti STP 2.00 5.00
44 Kyle Petty Blues Brothers 2.00 5.00

44 Kyle Petty Hot Wheels 2.00 5.00
44 Kyle Petty Hot Wheels Players Inc. 2.00 5.00
46 Wally Dallenbach First Union 2.00 5.00
46 Wally Dallenbach Tampa Bay Devil Rays 2.00 5.00
50 Ricky Craven Hendrick 2.00 5.00
89 Bill Elliott McRib 2.50 6.00
90 Dick Trickle Heilig-Meyers 2.00 5.00
94 Bill Elliott McDonald's 2.50 6.00
96 David Green Caterpillar 2.00 5.00
97 Chad Little John Deere 2.00 5.00
99 Jeff Burton Exide 2.00 5.00

1998 Hot Wheels Preview Edition 1:64

These cars came out before the start of the 1998 season and are painted to reflect the '97 paint jobs. The cars were sold in blister packs with a "Preview Edition" logo in the upper right hand corner.

4 Bobby Hamilton Kodak 4.00 8.00
5 Terry Labonte Kellogg's 4.00 8.00
6 Mark Martin Eagle One 5.00 10.00
6 Mark Martin Syntec 5.00 10.00
6 Mark Martin Valvoline 4.00 8.00
8 Hut Stricklin Circuit City 4.00 8.00
10 Ricky Rudd Tide 5.00 10.00
12 Jeremy Mayfield Mobil 1 4.00 8.00
13 Jerry Nadeau First Plus 4.00 8.00
16 Ted Musgrave Primestar 4.00 8.00
21 Michael Waltrip Citgo 4.00 8.00
26 Johnny Benson Cheerios 4.00 8.00
30 Derrike Cope Gumout 4.00 8.00
35 Todd Bodine Tabasco 4.00 8.00
35 Todd Bodine Tabasco Green 4.00 8.00
35 Todd Bodine Tabasco Red 4.00 8.00
36 Ernie Irvan Skittles 4.00 8.00
40 Sterling Marlin Sabco 4.00 8.00
42 Joe Nemechek BellSouth 4.00 8.00
42 Joe Nemechek BellSouth Black 4.00 8.00
43 John Andretti STP 4.00 8.00
43 John Andretti STP Players Inc. 4.00 8.00
44 Kyle Petty Blues Brothers 2000 4.00 10.00
44 Kyle Petty Hot Wheels 4.00 10.00
44 Kyle Petty Players Inc. 4.00 10.00
50 Ricky Craven Hendrick 4.00 8.00
89 Dennis Setzer McRib 6.00 12.00
90 Dick Trickle Heilig-Meyers 4.00 8.00
94 Bill Elliott McDonalds 4.00 8.00
96 David Green Caterpiller 4.00 8.00
97 Chad Little John Deere 4.00 8.00
99 Jeff Burton Exide 4.00 8.00

1998 Hot Wheels Pro Racing 1:64

This was Hot Wheels basic issue NASCAR brand for 1998. Each car was issued in a blue and red blister package in the shape of the #1.

4 Bobby Hamilton Kodak 1.50 4.00
5 Terry Labonte Kellogg's 2.00 5.00
6 Mark Martin Valvoline 2.00 5.00
10 Ricky Rudd Tide 1.50 4.00
12 Jeremy Mayfield Mobil 1 1.50 4.00
16 Kevin Lepage Primestar 1.50 4.00
26 Johnny Benson Cheerios 1.50 4.00
35 Todd Bodine Tabasco 1.50 4.00
36 Ernie Irvan Skittles 1.50 4.00
43 John Andretti STP 1.50 4.00
43/44/45 John Andretti Kyle Petty Adam Petty Generations Target 12.50 25.00
44 Kyle Petty Hot Wheels 1.50 4.00
94 Bill Elliott McDonald's 2.00 5.00
96 Steve Grissom Caterpillar 1.50 4.00
97 Chad Little John Deere 1.50 4.00

1998 Hot Wheels Pro Racing Pit Crew 1:64

These 1:64 scale cars were produced by Hot Wheels and were packaged in blister packs with their corresponding pit wagon. They were distributed through hobby, retail and trackside outlets. The blister reads "1998 Pit Crew" in the upper right hand corner and the driver's name appears on the cardboard base. A Gold version of some drivers was made. These were packaged in a similar blister with the words "Limited Edition Series" on the front. The driver's name is not included on the base for the Gold version.

4 Sterling Marlin Kodak 4.00 10.00
5 Terry Labonte Kellogg's 4.00 10.00
6 Mark Martin Valvoline 4.00 10.00
8 Hut Stricklin 4.00 8.00
10 Ricky Rudd Tide 4.00 8.00
12 Jeremy Mayfield Mobil 1 4.00 8.00
13 Jerry Nadeau First Plus 4.00 8.00
16 Ted Musgrave Primestar 4.00 8.00
21 Michael Waltrip Citgo 4.00 8.00
28 Ernie Irvan Havoline 4.00 8.00
30 Derrike Cope Gumout 4.00 8.00
33 Tim Fedewa Kleenex 4.00 8.00
35 Todd Bodine Tabasco 4.00 8.00
36 Matt Hutter Stanley 4.00 8.00
36 Ernie Irvan Skittles 4.00 8.00
40 Sterling Marlin Sabco 4.00 8.00
43 Bobby Hamilton STP 4.00 8.00
44 Kyle Petty Hot Wheels 4.00 8.00
74 Randy LaJoie Fina 4.00 8.00
94 Bill Elliott McDonald's 4.00 8.00
96 David Green Caterpillar 4.00 8.00
97 Chad Little John Deere 4.00 8.00
99 Jeff Burton Exide 4.00 8.00

1998 Hot Wheels Pro Racing Pit Crew Gold 1:64

4 Sterling Marlin Kodak 5.00 12.00
5 Terry Labonte Kellogg's 5.00 12.00
6 Mark Martin Valvoline 5.00 12.00
8 Hut Stricklin 5.00 10.00
10 Ricky Rudd Tide Gold 5.00 10.00
12 Jeremy Mayfield Mobil 1 5.00 10.00
13 Jerry Nadeau First Plus 5.00 10.00
16 Ted Musgrave Primestar 5.00 10.00
21 Michael Waltrip Citgo 5.00 10.00
28 Ernie Irvan Havoline 5.00 10.00
33 Tim Fedewa Kleenex 5.00 10.00
35 Todd Bodine Tabasco 5.00 10.00
36 Matt Hutter Stanley 5.00 10.00
36 Ernie Irvan Skittles 5.00 10.00
40 Sterling Marlin Sabco 5.00 10.00
43 Bobby Hamilton STP 5.00 10.00
44 Kyle Petty Hot Wheels 5.00 10.00
74 Randy LaJoie Fina 5.00 10.00
94 Bill Elliott McDonald's 5.00 10.00
96 David Green Caterpillar 5.00 10.00
97 Chad Little John Deere 5.00 10.00
99 Jeff Burton Exide 5.00 10.00

1998 Hot Wheels Test Track 1:64

These 1:64 scale cars were produced by Hot Wheels. They are packaged in blister packs and have primer coating as most test cars do. These cars were distributed through hobby and retail.

4 Bobby Hamilton Kodak 2.50 5.00
5 Terry Labonte Kellogg's 2.50 5.00
6 Mark Martin Valvoline 2.50 5.00
10 Ricky Rudd Tide 2.50 5.00
21 Michael Waltrip Citgo 2.50 5.00
28 Ernie Irvan Havoline 2.50 5.00
43 John Andretti STP 2.50 5.00
44 Kyle Petty Hot Wheels 2.50 5.00
99 Jeff Burton Exide 2.50 5.00

1998 Hot Wheels Track Edition 1:64

These 1:64 scale cars are in a black box and were only available thru hobby or trackside sale.

4 Bobby Hamilton Kodak 6.00 15.00
5 Terry Labonte Kellogg's 8.00 20.00
6 Mark Martin Valvoline 8.00 20.00
6 Mark Martin Eagle One 10.00 25.00
6 Mark Martin Synpower 8.00 20.00
8 Hut Stricklin Circuit City 6.00 15.00
10 Ricky Rudd Tide 6.00 15.00
12 Jeremy Mayfield Mobil 1 6.00 15.00
13 Jerry Nadeau First Plus 6.00 15.00
21 Michael Waltrip Citgo 6.00 15.00
26 Johnny Benson Cheerios 6.00 15.00
30 Derrike Cope Gumout 6.00 15.00
35 Todd Bodine Tabasco Orange 6.00 15.00
35 Todd Bodine Tabasco Green 6.00 15.00
35 Todd Bodine Tabasco Red 6.00 15.00
36 Ernie Irvan Skittles 6.00 15.00
40 Sterling Marlin Sabco 6.00 15.00
42 Joe Nemechek BellSouth 6.00 15.00
42 Joe Nemechek BellSouth Black 6.00 15.00
43 John Andretti STP 6.00 15.00
43 John Andretti Players Inc. 6.00 15.00
44 Kyle Petty Hot Wheels 6.00 15.00
44 Kyle Petty Blues Brothers 2000 6.00 15.00
44 Kyle Petty Players Inc. 6.00 15.00
50 Ricky Craven Hendrick 6.00 15.00
50 No Driver Association Boy Scouts 6.00 15.00
89 Dennis Setzer McRib 10.00 25.00
90 Dick Trickle Heilig-Meyers 6.00 15.00
94 Bill Elliott McDonald's 8.00 20.00
96 David Green Caterpiller 6.00 15.00
97 Chad Little John Deere 6.00 15.00
99 Jeff Burton Exide 6.00 15.00

1998 Hot Wheels Pro Racing Trading Paint 1:64

These 1:64 scale cars show the wear and tear a NASCAR is subjected to during a 500 mile race including road grime, paint scrapes, and wheel rub marks.

6 Mark Martin Valvoline 6.00 15.00
12 Jeremy Mayfield Mobil 1 3.00 8.00
13 Jerry Nadeau First Plus 5.00 12.00
16 Ted Musgrave Primestar 3.00 8.00
21 Michael Waltrip Citgo 3.00 8.00
35 Todd Bodine Tabasco 6.00 15.00
40 Sterling Marlin Sabco 3.00 8.00
42 Joe Nemechek BellSouth 3.00 8.00
43 John Andretti STP 5.00 12.00
44 Kyle Petty Hot Wheels 5.00 12.00
46 Wally Dallenbach First Union 3.00 8.00
96 David Green Caterpillar 3.00 8.00
99 Jeff Burton Exide 4.00 10.00

1999 Hot Wheels Racing Daytona 500 1:64

4 Bobby Hamilton Adantix 2.00 5.00
6 Mark Martin Valvoline 2.50 6.00
7 Michael Waltrip Phillips 2.00 5.00
10 Ricky Rudd Tide 2.00 5.00
11 Brett Bodine Paychex 2.00 5.00
12 Jeremy Mayfield Mobil 1 2.00 5.00
16 Kevin Lepage Primestar 2.00 5.00
21 Michael Waltrip Citgo 2.00 5.00
22 Ward Burton Caterpillar 2.00 5.00
26 Johnny Benson Cheerios 2.00 5.00
30 Derrike Cope Bryan 2.00 5.00
30 Derrike Cope State Fair 2.00 5.00
36 Ernie Irvan M&M's 2.00 5.00
40 Sterling Marlin Marlin Racing 2.00 5.00
42 Joe Nemechek BellSouth 2.00 5.00
43 John Andretti STP 2.00 5.00
44 Kyle Petty Hot Wheels 2.00 5.00
66 Darrell Waltrip K-Mart 2.00 5.00
94 Bill Elliott McDonald's 2.50 6.00
97 Chad Little John Deere 2.00 5.00
99 Jeff Burton Exide 2.00 5.00

1999 Hot Wheels Racing Deluxe 1:64

This series was issued in a Hot Wheels Racing blister with the word "Deluxe" printed in red at the lower right hand corner. A Hot Wheels trading card was packaged with each car.

44 Kyle Petty Hot Wheels 3.00 6.00
45 Adam Petty Sprint 5.00 12.00

1999 Hot Wheels Racing NASCAR Rocks 1:64

Each of these 1:64 scale cars was packaged with a miniature guitar painted in the color scheme of the driver's car. Both were packaged in a NASCAR Rocks America blister package.

6 Mark Martin Valvoline 5.00 10.00
11 Brett Bodine Paychex 4.00 8.00
12 Jeremy Mayfield Mobil 1 4.00 8.00
43 John Andretti STP 4.00 8.00
44 Kyle Petty Hot Wheels 4.00 8.00
66 Darrell Waltrip Big K 4.00 8.00

1999 Hot Wheels Pro Racing 1:64

These black box cars were available at the track or through hobby dealers.

4 Bobby Hamilton Kodak 2.00 4.00
5 Terry Labonte Kellogg's 2.00 4.00
6 Mark Martin Valvoline 2.00 4.00
7 Geoffery Bodine Philips 2.00 4.00
7 Geoff Bodine Klaussner 2.00 4.00
9 Jerry Nadeau Jetsons 2.00 4.00
10 Ricky Rudd Tide 2.00 4.00
11 Brett Bodine Paychex 2.00 4.00
12 Jeremy Mayfield Mobil 1 2.00 4.00
16 Kevin Lepage Primestar 2.00 4.00
22 Ward Burton Caterpillar 2.00 4.00
25 Wally Dallenbach Dallenbach 2.00 4.00
26 Johnny Benson Betty Crocker 2.00 4.00
28 Davey Allison Havoline 3.00 8.00
36 Ernie Irvan M&M's 2.00 4.00
40 Sterling Marlin Sabco 2.00 4.00
42 Joe Nemechek BellSouth 2.00 4.00
43 Richard Petty STP '64 3.00 8.00
43 Richard Petty STP '67 3.00 8.00
43 Richard Petty STP '72 3.00 8.00
43 John Andretti STP 2.00 4.00
43/44/45 John Andretti Jimmy Hensley Kyle Petty Adam Petty 50th Anniversary 4-car set 10.00 25.00
43/44/45 John Andretti Kyle Petty Adam Petty Generations Father's Day 1999 10.00 25.00
44 Kyle Petty Hot Wheels 2.00 4.00
66 Darrell Waltrip Big K 2.00 4.00
94 Bill Elliott Drive Thru 2.00 4.00
97 Chad Little John Deere 2.00 4.00
99 Jeff Burton Exide 2.00 4.00

1999 Hot Wheels Racing Pit Crew 1:64

These 1:64 scale cars were packaged with a replica pit wagon tool box. There were two different blister packages used. One blister included the title Hot Wheels Racing with "Pit Crew" within a green box in the upper right hand corner. The other included the title Hot Wheels Pro Racing with "Pit Crew 1999" within a gold seal in the upper right corner similar to the 1998 set. The name of the team, not the driver's name, appears on the cardboard base. The stated production run was 20,000. A Gold version was also created for a select number of pieces, with both the pit wagon and car being detailed in gold paint.

4 Bobby Hamilton Kodak Advantix 4.00 8.00
5 Terry Labonte Kellogg's 4.00 8.00
5 Terry Labonte Kellogg's Gold 4.00 8.00
6 Mark Martin Valvoline 5.00 10.00
6 Mark Martin Valvoline Gold 5.00 10.00
7 Michael Waltrip Phillips 4.00 8.00
9 Jerry Nadeau Dexter's Laboratory 4.00 8.00
9 Jerry Nadeau Jetsons with Dexter's Lab pit wagon 4.00 8.00
10 Ricky Rudd Tide 4.00 8.00
10 Ricky Rudd Tide Gold 4.00 8.00
11 Brett Bodine Paychex 4.00 8.00
12 Jeremy Mayfield Mobil 1 4.00 8.00
12 Jeremy Mayfield Mobil 1 Gold 4.00 8.00
17 Matt Kenseth DeWalt 5.00 12.00
21 Michael Waltrip Citgo 4.00 8.00
25 Wally Dallenbach Hendrick 4.00 8.00
26 Johnny Benson Cheerios 4.00 8.00
30 Derrike Cope Jimmy Dean 4.00 8.00
30 Derrike Cope State Fair 4.00 8.00

34 Mike McLaughlin Goulds Pumps 4.00 8.00
36 Tim Fedewa Stanley 4.00 8.00
36 Ernie Irvan M&M's 4.00 8.00
40 Sterling Marlin Sabco 4.00 8.00
43 John Andretti STP 4.00 8.00
43 John Andretti STP Gold 4.00 8.00
44 Kyle Petty Hot Wheels 4.00 8.00
44 Kyle Petty Hot Wheels Gold 4.00 8.00
44 Kyle Petty Players Inc. 4.00 8.00
58 Ricky Craven Turbine 10.00 20.00
60 Mark Martin Winn Dixie 5.00 10.00
66 Todd Bodine Phillips 66 4.00 8.00
66 Darrell Waltrip Big K 4.00 8.00
94 Bill Elliott McDonald's 4.00 8.00
94 Bill Elliott Drive Thru Gold 4.00 8.00
97 Chad Little John Deere 4.00 8.00
97 Chad Little John Deere Gold 4.00 8.00
99 Jeff Burton Exide 4.00 8.00
99 Jeff Burton Exide Gold 4.00 8.00

1999 Hot Wheels Racing Pit Cruisers 1:64

These 1:64 scale die-casts were NASCAR versions of miniature golf carts. Each was limited to 15,000 pieces.

6 Mark Martin Valvoilne 5.00 12.00
10 Rudd Rudd Tide 4.00 10.00
43 John Andretti STP 4.00 10.00
44 Kyle Petty Hot Wheels 4.00 10.00

1999 Hot Wheels Racing Promos 1:64

6 Mark Martin 1995 Valvoline (packaged with Valvoline fuel treatment) 6.00 15.00
6 Mark Martin 1997 Valvoline (packaged with Valvoline fuel treatment) 6.00 15.00
6 Mark Martin 1999 Valvoline (packaged with Valvoline fuel treatment) 6.00 15.00
26/44 Johnny Benson Kyle Petty Cheerios Hot Wheels Promo 3.00 8.00
64 VISA Promo 3.00 8.00

1999 Hot Wheels Racing Speed and Thunder 1:64

Each 1:64 scale car in this series was packaged in a Hot Wheels Speed and Thunder blister. The stated production run was 25,000 of each piece.

6 Mark Martin Valvoline 2.50 6.00
9 Jerry Nadeau Dexter's Lab 2.00 5.00
11 Brett Bodine Paychex 2.00 5.00
30 Michael Waltrip State Fair 2.00 5.00
36 Ernie Irvan M&M's 2.00 5.00
42 Joe Nemechek BellSouth 2.00 5.00
44 Kyle Petty Hot Wheels 2.00 5.00

1999 Hot Wheels Racing Track Edition 1:64

These 1:64 scale black box cars were available at the track or through a hobby dealer.

4 Bobby Hamilton Kodak 6.00 15.00
5 Terry Labonte Kellogg's 8.00 20.00
6 Mark Martin Valvoline 8.00 20.00
7 Michael Waltrip Klaussner Philips 6.00 15.00
10 Ricky Rudd Tide 6.00 15.00
11 Brett Bodine Paychex 6.00 15.00
12 Jeremy Mayfield Mobil 1 6.00 15.00
14 Sterling Marlin Tennessee 12.00 25.00
21 Elliott Sadler Citgo 6.00 15.00
22 Ward Burton Caterpillar 6.00 15.00
25 Wally Dallenbach Dallenbach 6.00 15.00
26 Johnny Benson Cheerios 6.00 15.00
28 Davey Allison Havoline 10.00 20.00
36 Ernie Irvan M&M's 6.00 15.00
40 Sterling Marlin Sabco 6.00 15.00
42 Joe Nemechek BellSouth 6.00 15.00
43 Richard Petty STP '64 10.00 20.00
43 Richard Petty STP '67 10.00 20.00
43 Richard Petty STP '72 10.00 20.00
43 John Andretti STP 6.00 15.00
44 Kyle Petty Hot Wheels 6.00 15.00
66 Darrell Waltrip Big K 6.00 15.00
94 Bill Elliott Drive Thru 6.00 15.00
97 Chad Little John Deere 6.00 15.00

1999 Hot Wheels Racing Test Track 1:64

This is the first in a series of Treasure Hunt Cars limited to 15,000

10 Ricky Rudd Tide 6.00 15.00
12 Jeremy Mayfield Mobil 1 6.00 15.00
44 Kyle Petty Hot Wheels 6.00 15.00
99 Jeff Burton Exide 6.00 15.00

1999 Hot Wheels Racing Trading Paint 1:64

This is the second in a series of Treasure Hunt Cars with each limited in production to 15,000.

5 Terry Labonte Kellogg's 8.00 20.00
6 Mark Martin Valvoline 8.00 20.00
44 Kyle Petty Hot Wheels 6.00 15.00
97 Chad Little John Deere 6.00 15.00

2000 Hot Wheels Deluxe 1:64

These cars are available through retail outlets.

4 Bobby Hamilton Kodak 2.00 4.00
5 Terry Labonte Kellogg's 3.00 6.00
6 Mark Martin Valvoline 3.00 6.00
7 Michael Waltrip NationsRent 3.00 6.00
10 Jeff Green Nesquik Promo 4.00 8.00
12 Jeremy Mayfield Mobil 1 2.00 4.00
14 Mike Bliss Conseco 2.00 4.00
17 Matt Kenseth DeWalt 3.00 6.00
21 Elliott Sadler Citgo 2.00 4.00
22 Ward Burton Caterpillar 2.00 4.00
25 Jerry Nadeau Holigan 2.00 4.00
26 Jimmy Spencer Big K 2.00 4.00
26/44/94 Johnny Benson Kyle Petty Bill Elliott Toy Story 2 12.50 25.00
32 Scott Pruett Tide 5.00 10.00
33 Joe Nemechek Oakwood Homes 2.00 4.00
40 Sterling Marlin Marlin 2.00 5.00
42 Kenny Irwin BellSouth 2.00 5.00
43 John Andretti Cheerios 2.00 4.00
43 John Andretti STP 2.00 4.00
43 John Andretti STP Historic Paint 4.00 8.00
43 John Andretti Wheaties 2.50 5.00
44 Kyle Petty Hot Wheels 2.00 4.00
44 Kyle Petty Hot Wheels Chrome 3.00 6.00
45 Adam Petty Sprint PCS 10.00 25.00
55 Kenny Wallace Aerosmith 5.00 10.00
55 Kenny Wallace Square D 2.00 4.00
60 Geoffrey Bodine Power Team 2.00 4.00
66 Darrell Waltrip Big K 2.00 4.00
75 Wally Dallenbach Cartoon Network 2.00 4.00
77 Robert Pressley Jasper 2.00 4.00
94 Bill Elliott McDonald's Drive Thru 3.00 6.00
97 Chad Little John Deere 2.00 4.00
97 Anthony Lazzaro McDonald's 2.00 4.00
99 Jeff Burton Exide 2.00 4.00

2000 Hot Wheels Deluxe Draggin' Wagon 1:64

5 Terry Labonte Kellogg's 2.00 5.00
33 Joe Nemechek Oakwood Homes 2.00 5.00
43 John Andretti Cheerios 2.00 5.00
75 Wally Dallenbach Cartoon Network 2.00 5.00

2000 Hot Wheels Deluxe Go Kart 1:64

4 Bobby Hamilton Kodak 4.00 10.00
6 Mark Martin Valvoline 5.00 12.00
98 Rick Mast Woody 4.00 10.00
99 Jeff Burton Exide 4.00 10.00

2000 Hot Wheels Deluxe Helicopter 1:64

22 Ward Burton Caterpillar 3.00 6.00
32 Scott Pruett Tide 3.00 6.00
33 Joe Nemechek Oakwood Homes 3.00 6.00
99 Jeff Burton Exide 3.00 6.00

2000 Hot Wheels Deluxe Hot Rod 1:64

21 Elliott Sadler Citgo 4.00 10.00
32 Scott Pruett Tide 4.00 10.00
66 Darrell Waltrip Big K 4.00 10.00
94 Bill Elliott McDonald's 4.00 10.00

2000 Hot Wheels Deluxe Hydroplane 1:64

4 Bobby Hamilton Kodak 2.00 5.00
7 Michael Waltrip Nations Rent 2.00 5.00
12 Jeremy Mayfield Mobil 1 2.00 5.00
44 Kyle Petty Hot Wheels 2.00 5.00

2000 Hot Wheels Deluxe Pit Crew 1:64

Each of these 1:64 scale cars was packaged with a replica pit wagon. Both pieces were packaged together in a blister that included the name "Pit Crew" in the upper right in red and the word "Deluxe" in the lower right.

4 Bobby Hamilton Kodak 3.00 6.00
5 Terry Labonte Kellogg's 4.00 8.00
6 Mark Martin Valvoline 4.00 8.00
12 Jeremy Mayfield Mobil 1 3.00 6.00
14 Mike Bliss Conseco 3.00 6.00
17 Matt Kenseth DeWalt 5.00 10.00
22 Ward Burton Caterpillar 3.00 6.00
33 Joe Nemechek Oakwood Homes 3.00 6.00
40 Sterling Marlin Sabco 3.00 6.00
43 John Andretti STP 3.00 6.00
44 Kyle Petty Hot Wheels 3.00 6.00
55 Kenny Wallace Square D 3.00 6.00
60 Geoffrey Bodine Power Team 3.00 6.00
66 Darrell Waltrip Big K 3.00 6.00
75 Wally Dallenbach Power Puff Girls 3.00 6.00
94 Bill Elliott McDonald's 4.00 8.00
97 Chad Little John Deere 3.00 6.00
98 Rick Mast Woody 3.00 6.00

2000 Hot Wheels Deluxe Pit Crew Daytona 500 1:64

Each 1:64 scale car in this series was issued with a Daytona 500 commemorative pit wagon. The packaging is identical to the basic issue 2000 Deluxe Pit Crew series, but the pit wagon has been switched from the driver's team version to the Daytona version.

4 Bobby Hamilton Kodak 3.00 6.00
5 Terry Labonte Kellogg's 4.00 8.00
12 Jeremy Mayfield Mobil 1 3.00 6.00
22 Ward Burton Caterpillar 3.00 6.00
43 John Andretti STP 3.00 6.00
44 Kyle Petty Hot Wheels 3.00 6.00
55 Kenny Wallace Square D 3.00 6.00
60 Geoffrey Bodine Power Team 3.00 6.00
98 Rick Mast Woody 3.00 6.00

2000 Hot Wheels Deluxe RV 1:64

14 Mike Bliss Conseco 2.00 5.00
44 Kyle Petty Hot Wheels 2.00 5.00
77 Robert Pressley Jasper 2.00 5.00
97 Anthony Lazzaro McDonald's 2.00 5.00

2000 Hot Wheels Deluxe School Bus 1:64

22 Ward Burton Caterpillar 4.00 10.00
43 John Andretti STP 4.00 10.00
44 Kyle Petty Hot Wheels 4.00 10.00
94 Bill Elliott McDonald's 4.00 10.00

2000 Hot Wheels Deluxe Scorchin Scooter 1:64

These are from the Hot Wheels mainline release, and are limited.

4 Bobby Hamilton Kodak 4.00 10.00
5 Terry Labonte Kellogg's 5.00 12.00
6 Mark Martin Valvoline 5.00 12.00
12 Jeremy Mayfield Mobil 1 4.00 10.00
21 Elliott Sadler Citgo 4.00 10.00
22 Ward Burton Caterpillar 4.00 10.00
43 John Andretti STP 4.00 10.00
44 Kyle Petty Hot Wheels 4.00 10.00
45 Adam Petty Sprint 10.00 25.00
55 Kenny Wallace Square D 4.00 10.00
60 Geoffrey Bodine Power Team 4.00 10.00
66 Darrell Waltrip Big K 4.00 10.00
94 Bill Elliott McDonald's 5.00 12.00
97 Chad Little John Deere 4.00 10.00
98 Rick Mast Woody Woodpecker 4.00 10.00
99 Jeff Burton Exide 4.00 10.00
NNO Complete Factory Set 50.00 100.00

2000 Hot Wheels Deluxe Suburban 1:64

5 Terry Labonte Kellogg's 4.00 8.00
40 Sterling Marlin Sabco 4.00 8.00
55 Kenny Wallace Square D 4.00 8.00
60 Geoffrey Bodine Power Team 3.00 8.00

2000 Hot Wheels Deluxe Treasure Hunt 1:64

44 California 10.00 25.00
44 Darlington 10.00 25.00
44 Daytona 15.00 30.00
44 Daytona Night Race 15.00 30.00
44 Miami 10.00 25.00
44 Michigan 10.00 25.00
44 Phoenix 15.00 30.00
44 Talladega Spring Race 15.00 30.00
44 Talladega Fall Race 15.00 30.00
44 Watkins Glen 10.00 25.00

2000 Hot Wheels Racing 1:64

4 Bobby Hamilton Kodak 2.00 5.00
5 Terry Labonte Kellogg's 2.00 5.00
6 Mark Martin Valvoline 2.50 6.00
32 Scott Pruett Tide 2.00 5.00
43 John Andretti STP 2.00 5.00
44 Kyle Petty Hot Wheels 2.00 5.00
45 Adam Petty Sprint 4.00 10.00
97 Chad Little John Deere 2.00 5.00
98 Rick Mast Woody Woodpecker 2.00 5.00
99 Jeff Burton Exide Batteries 2.00 5.00

2000 Hot Wheels Racing Crew's Choice 1:64

The cars in this series feature bodies that are removable from the chassis. Each was packaged within a styrofoam shell within a solid Hot Wheels Racing Crew's Choice box. A small certificate of authenticity was also issued that featured a stated production run total of 9998 for each die-cast piece.

4 Bobby Hamilton Kodak 5.00 12.00
6 Mark Martin Valvoline 10.00 20.00
17 Matt Kenseth DeWalt 10.00 20.00
22 Ward Burton Caterpillar 5.00 12.00
32 Scott Pruett Tide 5.00 12.00
33 Joe Nemechek Oakwood Homes 5.00 12.00
40 Sterling Marlin Sterling 6.00 15.00
43 John Andretti STP 5.00 12.00
43 John Andretti Cheerios 5.00 12.00
43 John Andretti STP 1972 paint 6.00 15.00
44 Kyle Petty Hot Wheels 5.00 12.00
45 Adam Petty Sprint PCS 20.00 50.00
55 Kenny Wallace Square D 5.00 12.00
60 Geoffrey Bodine Power Team 5.00 12.00
66 Darrell Waltrip Big K 5.00 12.00
97 Anthony Lazzaro McDonald's 5.00 12.00
99 Jeff Burton Exide 5.00 12.00

2000 Hot Wheels Racing Promos 1:64

32 Scott Pruett Tide Promo 2.00 5.00
32 Scott Pruett Tide Kids Promo 3.00 6.00

2000 Hot Wheels Racing Radical Rides 1:64

6 Mark Martin Valvoline 5.00 12.00
7 Michael Waltrip Nations Rent 4.00 10.00
12 Jeremy Mayfield Mobil 1 4.00 10.00
17 Matt Kenseth DeWalt 4.00 10.00
43 Richard Petty STP 4.00 10.00
43 John Andretti STP 4.00 10.00
44 Kyle Petty Hot Wheels 4.00 10.00
45 Adam Petty Sprint 10.00 20.00
66 Darrell Waltrip Big K 4.00 10.00
97 Chad Little John Deere 4.00 10.00
99 Jeff Burton Exide 4.00 10.00

2000 Hot Wheels Racing Track Edition 1:64

This series of 1:64 cars was issued in a Hot Wheels Track Edition 2000 clear window box. The blue and black box featured a backer board that could be used to hang the car on a retail sales rack.

4 Bobby Hamilton Kodak 4.00 8.00
6 Mark Martin Valvoline 5.00 10.00
7 Michael Waltrip Nations Rent 4.00 8.00
12 Jeremy Mayfield Mobil 1 4.00 8.00
14 Mike Bliss Conseco 4.00 8.00
17 Matt Kenseth DeWalt 5.00 10.00
22 Ward Burton Caterpillar 4.00 8.00
32 Scott Pruett Tide 6.00 12.00
33 Joe Nemechek Oakwood Homes 4.00 8.00
42 Kenny Irwin BellSouth 4.00 10.00
43 John Andretti STP 4.00 8.00
43 John Andretti Cheerios 4.00 8.00
43 John Andretti STP Texas 5.00 10.00
43 John Andretti STP 1972 paint 5.00 10.00
44 Kyle Petty Hot Wheels 4.00 8.00
45 Adam Petty Sprint 15.00 30.00
55 Kenny Wallace Square D
60 Geoffrey Bodine Power Team 4.00 8.00
66 Jimmy Spencer

Big K-Mart		
66 Darrell Waltrip Big K	4.00	8.00
77 Robert Pressley Jasper	4.00	8.00
94 Bill Elliott McDonald's Drive Thru	5.00	10.00
97 Chad Little John Deere	4.00	8.00
97 Anthony Lazzaro McDonald's	4.00	8.00
99 Jeff Burton Exide	4.00	8.00

2000 Hot Wheels Select 1:64

This is the first year of the high end Select series in 1:64 scale. It was sold in a blister pack featuring a display stand which resembles a track wall complete with fence and tire marks. The stated production run was 24,998.

4 Bobby Hamilton Kodak	3.00	8.00
6 Mark Martin Valvoline	4.00	10.00
12 Jeremy Mayfield Mobil 1	3.00	8.00
14 Mike Bliss Conseco	3.00	8.00
17 Matt Kenseth DeWalt	4.00	10.00
21 Elliott Sadler Citgo	3.00	8.00
22 Ward Burton Caterpillar	3.00	8.00
26 Jimmy Spencer Big K	3.00	8.00
32 Scott Pruett Tide	3.00	8.00
33 Joe Nemechek Oakwood Homes	3.00	8.00
40 Sterling Marlin Sterling	3.00	8.00
42 Kenny Irwin BellSouth	5.00	12.00
43 John Andretti Cheerios	3.00	8.00
43 John Andretti STP	3.00	8.00
43 John Andretti Wheaties	3.00	8.00
44 Kyle Petty Hot Wheels	3.00	8.00
45 Adam Petty Sprint PCS	8.00	20.00
55 Kenny Wallace Square D	3.00	8.00
60 Geoffery Bodine Power Team	3.00	8.00
66 Darrell Waltrip Big K	3.00	8.00
77 Robert Pressley Jasper	3.00	8.00
94 Bill Elliott McDonald's Drive Thru	4.00	10.00
96 Anthony Lazzaro McDonald's	3.00	8.00
97 Chad Little John Deere	3.00	8.00
99 Jeff Burton Exide	3.00	8.00

2000 Hot Wheels Valvoline 10 Years Promos 1:64

Cars in this series were issued to commemorate Valvoline's 10th Year of sponsoring Winston Cup Racing. Each car was packaged on an oversized blister that included a photo of the car.

6 Mark Martin Valvoline 1995	3.00	6.00
6 Mark Martin Valvoline 1997	3.00	6.00
6 Mark Martin Valvoline 1999	3.00	6.00

2001 Hot Wheels Racing Anglia 1:64

5 Terry Labonte Kellogg's Tony	5.00	10.00
6 Mark Martin Pfizer		
36 Ken Schrader M&M's	6.00	12.00
44 Buckshot Jones Georgia Pacific		

2001 Hot Wheels Racing Blimp 1:64

12 Jeremy Mayfield Mobil 1 1/4	6.00	12.00
17 Matt Kenseth DeWalt 2/4	6.00	12.00
32 Scott Pruett Tide 3/4	5.00	10.00
99 Jeff Burton Citgo 4/4	7.50	15.00

2001 Hot Wheels Racing Roush Commemorative 1:64

This set of 5-cars was issued to commemorate the Roush Racing team and its 50th Winston Cup win. Each car is packaged in a hard plastic clear box inside a cardboard overwrap along with a small metal medallion.

6 Mark Martin Pfizer	6.00	15.00
17 Matt Kenseth DeWalt	6.00	15.00
60 Greg Biffle Grainger	5.00	12.00
97 Kurt Busch Sharpie	6.00	15.00
99 Jeff Burton Citgo	5.00	12.00

2001 Hot Wheels Racing Deora 1:64

12 Jeremy Mayfield Mobil 1 3/4	4.00	8.00
17 Matt Kenseth DeWalt 2/4	5.00	10.00
43 John Andretti STP 4/4	5.00	10.00
99 Jeff Burton Citgo 1/4	4.00	8.00

2001 Hot Wheels Racing Pit Board 1:64

This release from Hot Wheels has two piece wheels, a plastic chassis, and comes with a plastic pit board.

5 Terry Labonte Kellogg's Tony	3.00	6.00
6 Mark Martin Pfizer	3.00	6.00
10 Johnny Benson Valvoline	2.00	4.00
10 Jeff Green Nesquik	2.00	4.00
12 Jeremy Mayfield Mobil 1	2.00	4.00
17 Matt Kenseth DeWalt	3.00	6.00
21 Elliott Sadler Motorcraft	2.00	4.00
22 Ward Burton Caterpillar	2.00	4.00
25 Jerry Nadeau UAW	2.00	4.00
26 Jimmy Spencer K-Mart	2.00	4.00
32 Scott Pruett Tide	2.00	4.00
32 Ricky Craven Tide	2.00	4.00
33 Joe Nemechek Oakwood Homes	2.00	4.00
36 Ken Schrader M&M's	2.00	4.00
36 Ken Schrader M&M'S Halloween	2.00	5.00
36 Ken Schrader M&M'S July 4th	3.00	6.00
40 Sterling Marlin Sterling Marlin	2.00	5.00
43 John Andretti Cheerios	2.00	4.00
44 Buckshot Jones Four Generations of Petty	4.00	8.00
44 Buckshot Jones Georgia Pacific	4.00	8.00
45 Kyle Petty Sprint PCS	3.00	6.00
45 Kyle Petty Sprint Charity Ride	4.00	8.00
60 Greg Biffle Grainger	2.50	6.00
96 Andy Houston McDonald's	2.00	4.00
99 Jeff Burton Citgo	4.00	8.00
99 Jeff Burton Exide	3.00	6.00
02 Ryan Newman Alltel	7.50	15.00

2001 Hot Wheels Racing Promos 1:64

32 Scott Pruett Tide Downy	2.50	6.00
32 Scott Pruett Tide Downy with French language sticker	3.00	8.00
01 Daytona Speed of Light	6.00	12.00
01 VISA in blister	10.00	20.00

2001 Hot Wheels Racing Select 1:64

The Hot Wheels Select brand was produced as a higher end 1:64 die-cast complete with opening hoods and more detailed engine and underbody work. They were packaged in a blister pack on a mirrored base designed to display the underbody of the car. The year of issue was printed on the front of the packaging in the lower right hand corner.

5 Terry Labonte Kellogg's	5.00	10.00
6 Mark Martin Pfizer	5.00	10.00
10 Johnny Benson Valvoline	4.00	8.00
11 Darrell Waltrip Mountain Dew	4.00	8.00
12 Jeremy Mayfield Mobil 1	4.00	8.00
17 Matt Kenseth DeWalt	5.00	10.00
17 Matt Kenseth DeWalt Black	5.00	10.00
21 Elliott Sadler Motorcraft	4.00	8.00
22 Ward Burton Caterpillar	4.00	8.00
25 Jerry Nadeau UAW	4.00	8.00
32 Scott Pruett Tide	4.00	8.00
33 Joe Nemechek Oakwood Homes	4.00	8.00
36 Ken Schrader M&M's	4.00	8.00
40 Sterling Marlin Sterling	4.00	8.00
40 Pete Hamilton 7-up 1970 Plymouth	6.00	15.00
42 Lee Petty 1957 Olds	6.00	15.00
43 John Andretti Cheerios	4.00	8.00
43 Richard Petty 1957 Olds	7.50	15.00
43 Richard Petty 1963 Plymouth	12.00	25.00
43 Richard Petty 1967 Plymouth	12.00	25.00
43 Richard Petty 1970 Plymouth Superbird	8.00	20.00
44 Buckshot Jones 4- Generations of Petty	5.00	12.00
45 Kyle Petty Sprint PCS	6.00	12.00
99 Jeff Burton Citgo	4.00	8.00

2001 Hot Wheels Racing Tail Draggers 1:64

These are labeled as 2001 Hot Wheels series but are painted in the 2000 season colors.

5 Terry Labonte Kellogg's	4.00	10.00
6 Mark Martin Valvoline	6.00	15.00
7 Micheal Waltrip Nations Rent	4.00	10.00
12 Jeremy Mayfield Mobil 1	4.00	10.00
17 Matt Kenseth DeWalt	7.50	15.00
22 Ward Burton Caterpillar	4.00	10.00
33 Joe Nemechek Oakwood Homes	4.00	8.00
43 John Andretti STP	4.00	8.00
44 Kyle Petty Hot Wheels	5.00	12.00
45 Adam Petty Sprint PCS	10.00	25.00
55 Kenny Wallace Square D	4.00	8.00
99 Jeff Burton Exide	4.00	8.00

2001 Hot Wheels Racing Tail Gunner 1:64

10 Johnny Benson Valvoline	4.00	8.00
33 Joe Nemechek Oakwood Homes	4.00	8.00
45 Kyle Petty Sprint	4.00	8.00
96 Andy Houston McDonald's	4.00	8.00

2001 Hot Wheels Racing The Demon 1:64

6 Mark Martin Pfizer	4.00	8.00
21 Elliott Sadler Motorcraft	3.00	6.00
22 Ward Burton Caterpillar	3.00	6.00
40 Sterling Marlin Sterling Marlin	3.00	6.00

2001 Hot Wheels Racing Treasure Hunt 1:64

Each of these die-casts were issued in a Hot Wheels Treasure Hunt blister. The model is wrecker truck with each being painted in the colors of a NASCAR track.

NNO California	12.50	25.00
NNO Darlington	10.00	25.00
NNO Daytona 500	10.00	25.00
NNO Daytona Night Race	10.00	25.00
NNO Homestead Miami	10.00	25.00
NNO Kansas	12.50	25.00
NNO Phoenix	10.00	25.00
NNO Talladega 500	12.50	25.00
NNO Talladega Superspeedway	12.50	25.00
NNO Watkins Glen	10.00	25.00
NNO Complete J.C.Penney Set/1500	90.00	150.00

2001 Hot Wheels Racing Twin Mill 1:64

10 Johnny Benson Valvoline 2/4	3.00	6.00
22 Ward Burton Caterpillar 1/4	3.00	6.00
32 Scott Pruett Tide 4/4	3.00	6.00
99 Jeff Burton Citgo 3/4	3.00	6.00

2001 Hot Wheels Racing Way 2 Fast 1:64

12 Jeremy Mayfield Mobil 1	3.00	6.00
36 Ken Schrader M&M's	3.00	6.00
45 Kyle Petty Sprint	3.00	6.00
96 Andy Houston McDonald's	3.00	6.00

2002 Hot Wheels Racing Sticker 1:64

5 Terry Labonte Kellogg's	3.00	6.00
5 Terry Labonte Monster's Inc.	3.00	6.00
6 Mark Martin Pfizer	3.00	6.00
10 Scott Riggs Nesquik	3.00	6.00
12 Ryan Newman Alltel	3.00	8.00
14 Larry Foyt Harrah's	3.00	6.00
17 Matt Kenseth DeWalt	4.00	10.00
21 Elliott Sadler Motorcraft	3.00	6.00
22 Ward Burton Caterpillar	3.00	6.00
25 Randy Tolsma Marines red black	3.00	6.00
25 Randy Tolsma Marines red white blue	3.00	6.00
32 Ricky Rudd Tide	3.00	6.00
36 Ken Schrader M&M's	3.00	6.00
36 Ken Schrader M&M's Promo w o Sticker	5.00	10.00
36 Ken Schrader M&M's Halloween	3.00	6.00
36 Ken Schrader M&M's Vote Aqua #1	8.00	20.00
36 Ken Schrader M&M's Vote Purple #2	8.00	20.00
36 Ken Schrader M&M's Vote Pink #3	15.00	40.00
36 Ken Schrader M&M's Vote Campaign #4	4.00	10.00
40 Sterling Marlin Sterling	3.00	6.00
43 John Andretti Cheerios	3.00	6.00
43 John Andretti Honey Nut Cheerios	3.00	6.00
43 John Andretti Pop Secret	3.00	6.00
43 Carlos Contreras Hot Wheels SuperTruck	3.00	6.00
44 Buckshot Jones Georgia-Pacific	3.00	6.00
45 Kyle Petty Sprint	3.00	6.00
60 Greg Biffle Grainger	3.00	6.00
97 Kurt Busch Rubbermaid	4.00	10.00
99 Jeff Burton Citgo	3.00	6.00

2002 Hot Wheels Racing '33 Roadster 1:64

99 Jeff Burton Citgo 1	3.00	6.00

2002 Hot Wheels Racing '57 Chevy 1:64

5 Terry Labonte Kellogg's	3.00	6.00
25 Jerry Nadeau UAW	3.00	6.00
55 Bobby Hamilton Square D 3	3.00	6.00

2002 Hot Wheels Racing '57 T-Bird 1:64

6 Mark Martin Pfizer 1	3.00	8.00
10 Scott Riggs Nesquik 4	2.50	6.00
12 Ryan Newman Alltel 3	4.00	10.00
99 Jeff Burton Citgo 2	3.00	8.00

2002 Hot Wheels Racing Hooligan 1:64

45 Kyle Petty Sprint	2.00	5.00

2002 Hot Wheels Racing Limozeen 1:64

10 Johnny Benson Vavoline 1	3.00	8.00
36 Ken Schrader M&M's 2	6.00	15.00
45 Kyle Petty Sprint 3	3.00	8.00

2002 Hot Wheels Racing Phaeton 1:64

5 Terry Labonte Kellogg's 7	3.00	6.00
6 Mark Martin Pfizer 2	3.00	8.00
10 Scott Riggs Nesquik 8	3.00	6.00
25 Jerry Nadeau UAW 10	3.00	6.00
36 Ken Schrader M&M's 6	3.00	8.00
40 Sterling Marlin Sterling 9	3.00	6.00
43 John Andretti Cheerios 4	3.00	6.00
45 Kyle Petty Sprint 3	3.00	6.00
99 Jeff Burton Citgo 1	3.00	6.00
02 Ryan Newman Alltel 5	3.00	8.00

2002 Hot Wheels Racing Promos 1:64

6 Mark Martin Kraft blister	12.50	25.00
10 Scott Riggs Nesquik blister	7.50	15.00
36 Ken Schrader M&M's blister	6.00	12.00
44 Brawny blister	10.00	20.00
92 Todd Bodine Excedrin in box	6.00	15.00

2002 Hot Wheels Racing Record Times 1:64

Record Times was a series created by Hot Wheels that combined a 1:64 scale die-cast car with a stop watch produced in the racing team's colors. Each car and stop watch combination was packaged together in an oversized blister pack.

5 Terry Labonte Kellogg's	4.00	10.00
6 Mark Martin Pfizer	4.00	10.00
10 Johnny Benson Valvoline	4.00	10.00
17 Matt Kenseth DeWalt	5.00	12.00
25 Jerry Nadeau UAW	4.00	10.00
36 Ken Schrader M&M's	4.00	10.00
43 John Andretti Cheerios	4.00	10.00
44 Buckshot Jones Georgia Pacific	4.00	10.00
45 Kyle Petty Sprint	4.00	10.00
99 Jeff Burton Citgo	4.00	10.00

2002 Hot Wheels Racing Treasure Hunt 1:64

NNO California	10.00	25.00
NNO Darlington	10.00	25.00
NNO Daytona	10.00	25.00
NNO Daytona Night	10.00	25.00
NNO Kansas	10.00	25.00
NNO Miami	10.00	25.00
NNO Phoenix	10.00	25.00
NNO Talladega Red and Blue	10.00	25.00
NNO Talladega Superspeedway	10.00	25.00
NNO Watkins Glen	10.00	25.00
NNO 10-Car Set/1500	125.00	250.00

2002 Hot Wheels Daytona Set-Up 1:64

This series was produced by Hot Wheels and packaged in a large blister. Each included a 1:64 car along with a portion of plastic race track. The 12-cars and track pieces could be assembled to represent a section of track from Daytona International Speedway.

5 Terry Labonte Kellogg's	4.00	8.00
6 Mark Martin Pfizer	4.00	10.00
10 Johnny Benson Valvoline	4.00	8.00
17 Matt Kenseth DeWalt	4.00	10.00
21 Elliott Sadler Motorcraft	4.00	8.00
25 Jerry Nadeau UAW	4.00	8.00
36 Ken Schrader M&M's	4.00	10.00
40 Sterling Marlin Sterling	4.00	10.00
43 John Andretti Cheerios	4.00	8.00
45 Kyle Petty Sprint	4.00	8.00
99 Jeff Burton Citgo	4.00	8.00
02 Ryan Newman Alltel	6.00	12.00

2003 Hot Wheels Racing Color Change 1:64

5 Terry Labonte Kellogg's	4.00	8.00
12 Ryan Newman Alltel	5.00	10.00
12 Ryan Newman Sony Wega	5.00	10.00
17 Matt Kenseth DeWalt	5.00	10.00
18 Bobby Labonte Interstate Batteries	4.00	8.00
20 Tony Stewart Home Depot	5.00	12.00
24 Jeff Gordon DuPont Flames	5.00	12.00
24 Jeff Gordon Pepsi	5.00	12.00
29 Kevin Harvick Goodwrench	5.00	10.00
29 Kevin Harvick Snap-On	5.00	10.00
45 Kyle Petty Georgia Pacific	4.00	8.00
48 Jimmie Johnson Lowe's	5.00	10.00
48 Jimmie Johnson Lowe's Power of Pride	5.00	10.00

2003 Hot Wheels Racing Luxury Rides 1:64

4 Mike Skinner Kodak 7.50 15.00
6 Mark Martin Pfizer 7.50 15.00
10 Johnny Benson Valvoline 7.50 15.00
10 Scott Riggs Nesquik 7.50 15.00
12 Ryan Newman Alltel 8.00 20.00
17 Matt Kenseth DeWalt 7.50 15.00
21 Ricky Rudd Motorcraft 8.00 20.00
36 Ken Schrader M&M's 8.00 20.00
43 John Andretti Cheerios 7.50 15.00
43 Richard Petty STP 8.00 20.00
45 Kyle Petty Sprint 7.50 15.00
97 Kurt Busch Rubbermaid 7.50 15.00
99 Jeff Burton Citgo 7.50 15.00

2003 Hot Wheels Racing Matt Kenseth Championship 1:64

17 Matt Kenseth DeWalt 4.00 8.00
17 Matt Kenseth DeWalt Color Change 5.00 10.00

2003 Hot Wheels Racing Power Launchers 1:64

5 Terry Labonte Kellogg's 5.00 10.00
17 Matt Kenseth DeWalt 5.00 10.00
24 Jeff Gordon DuPont Flames 6.00 12.00
48 Jimmie Johnson Lowe's 5.00 10.00

2003 Hot Wheels Racing Promos 1:64

1 Land o' Frost blue nose blister 3.00 8.00
1 Land o' Frost red nose blister 3.00 8.00
17 Matt Kenseth DeWalt Oscar Mayer Wienermobile 20.00 40.00

2003 Hot Wheels Racing Race Day 1:64

6 Mark Martin Pfizer 4.00 8.00
10 Johnny Benson Valvoline 4.00 8.00
10 Scott Riggs Nesquik 4.00 8.00
12 Ryan Newman Alltel 4.00 10.00
16 Greg Biffle Grainger 4.00 8.00
17 Matt Kenseth DeWalt 4.00 10.00
21 Ricky Rudd Motorcraft 4.00 8.00
25 Bobby Hamilton Jr. Marines 4.00 8.00
25 Joe Nemechek UAW-Delphi 4.00 8.00
43 John Andretti Cheerios 4.00 8.00
45 Kyle Petty Georgia Pacific Brawny 4.00 8.00
97 Kurt Busch Rubbermaid 4.00 8.00
01 Jerry Nadeau Army 4.00 8.00

2003 Hot Wheels Racing Recreational Vehicles ATV 1:64

5 Terry Labonte Kellogg's 5.00 10.00
6 Mark Martin Pfizer 5.00 10.00
17 Matt Kenseth DeWalt 5.00 10.00
45 Kyle Petty Georgia Pacific Brawny 5.00 10.00
97 Kurt Busch Rubbermaid 5.00 10.00

2003 Hot Wheels Racing Recreational Vehicles Bass Boat 1:64

6 Mark Martin Pfizer 5.00 10.00
12 Ryan Newman Alltel 5.00 10.00
17 Matt Kenseth DeWalt 5.00 10.00
45 Kyle Petty Georgia Pacific Brawny 4.00 8.00
45 Kyle Petty Sprint 4.00 8.00
97 Kurt Busch Rubbermaid 5.00 10.00
99 Jeff Burton Citgo 4.00 8.00

2003 Hot Wheels Racing Recreational Vehicles Motorcycle 1:64

6 Mark Martin Pfizer 5.00 10.00
12 Ryan Newman Alltel 4.00 10.00
16 Greg Biffle Grainger 5.00 10.00
17 Matt Kenseth DeWalt 4.00 10.00
45 Kyle Petty Georgia Pacific Brawny 5.00 10.00
97 Kurt Busch Rubbermaid 4.00 10.00

2003 Hot Wheels Racing Recreational Vehicles Truck 1:64

5 Terry Labonte Kellogg's 4.00 8.00
6 Mark Martin Pfizer 4.00 8.00
12 Ryan Newman Alltel 4.00 10.00
97 Kurt Busch Rubbermaid 4.00 8.00
99 Jeff Burton Citgo 4.00 8.00

2003 Hot Wheels Racing Special Paint 1:64

This series is entitled "Special Paint Scheme" as noted in the upper right hand corner of the blister. Each car is accompanied by a Hot Wheels standard sized trading card of the driver. The Mattel copyright line year on the back is 2000. However, they were initally released in late 2002 and all of 2003 therefore are considered the first of the 2003 Hot Wheels Racing releases.

6 Mark Martin Pfizer White 5.00 10.00
12 Ryan Newman Mobil 1 3.00 8.00
12 Ryan Newman Mobil 1 First Win/1212 7.50 15.00
12 Ryan Newman Sony Wega 4.00 8.00
21 Ricky Rudd Air Force 4.00 8.00
25 Bobby Hamilton Jr. Marines 4.00 8.00
36 Ken Schrader M&M's Halloween 5.00 10.00
43 John Andretti Pop Secret 4.00 8.00
97 Kurt Busch Rubbermaid Little Tikes 4.00 8.00
97 Kurt Busch Sharpie 4.00 8.00
99 Jeff Burton Bass Masters 4.00 8.00

2003 Hot Wheels Racing Treasure Hunt 1:64

5 Terry Labonte Kellogg's 6 6.00 12.00
6 Mark Martin Pfizer 2 10.00 25.00
12 Ryan Newman Alltel 1 5.00 10.00
16 Greg Biffle Grainger 7 10.00 20.00
21 Ricky Rudd Motorcraft 10 10.00 20.00
43 Richard Petty STP 9 20.00 40.00
45 Kyle Petty GP Brawny 8 15.00 30.00
97 Kurt Busch Sharpie 4 6.00 12.00
99 Jeff Burton Citgo 3 6.00 12.00

2003 Hot Wheels Racing Wrenchin' and Racin' 1:64

4 Mike Skinner Kodak 8.00 20.00
6 Mark Martin Pfizer 8.00 20.00
10 Johnny Benson Valvoline 8.00 20.00
12 Ryan Newman Alltel 10.00 20.00
16 Greg Biffle Grainger 8.00 20.00
17 Matt Kenseth DeWalt 10.00 20.00
21 Ricky Rudd Motorcraft 8.00 20.00
25 Bobby Hamilton Jr. Marines 12.50 25.00
43 John Andretti Cheerios 8.00 20.00
45 Kyle Petty Sprint 12.50 25.00
97 Kurt Busch Rubbermaid 10.00 20.00
99 Jeff Burton Citgo 8.00 20.00

2004 Hot Wheels Racing Alternative Paint Scheme 1:64

6 Mark Martin Oscar Mayer 5.00 10.00
21 Ricky Rudd Air Force 4.00 8.00
21 Ricky Rudd Rent-A-Center 4.00 8.00
45 Kyle Petty Brawny 4.00 8.00

2004 Hot Wheels Racing Artist Collection 1:64

6 Mark Martin Pfizer 5.00 10.00
12 Ryan Newman Alltel 4.00 8.00
16 Greg Biffle Grainger 4.00 8.00
17 Matt Kenseth DeWalt 5.00 10.00
21 Ricky Rudd Motorcraft 4.00 8.00

2004 Hot Wheels Racing Chase for the Cup 1:64

6 Mark Martin Viagra 7.50 15.00
17 Matt Kenseth DeWalt 7.50 15.00
97 Kurt Busch Irwin Tools 5.00 10.00
97 Kurt Busch Sharpie 5.00 10.00

2004 Hot Wheels Racing Color Change 1:64

6 Mark Martin Oscar Mayer 5.00 10.00
12 Ryan Newman Alltel 5.00 10.00
17 Matt Kenseth DeWalt 5.00 10.00
45 Kyle Petty Brawny 4.00 8.00
45 Kyle Petty Georgia Pacific 4.00 8.00
97 Kurt Busch Rubbermaid 4.00 8.00
97 Kurt Busch Sharpie 4.00 8.00

2004 Hot Wheels Racing Goodyear Showcase 1:64

6 Mark Martin Batman/15,000 10.00 20.00
6 Mark Martin Viagra/15,000 12.50 25.00
6 Mark Martin Viagra White/15,000 10.00 20.00
12 Ryan Newman Mobil 1/15,000 7.50 15.00
16 Greg Biffle National Guard/15,000 7.50 15.00
17 Matt Kenseth DeWalt/15,000 10.00 20.00
21 Ricky Rudd Motorcraft/15,000 7.50 15.00
21 Ricky Rudd Motorcraft Parts & Service/15,000 7.50 15.00
97 Kurt Busch Irwin Tools/15,000 7.50 15.00
97 Kurt Busch Sharpie/15,000 7.50 15.00
97 Kurt Busch Superman/15,000 7.50 15.00

2004 Hot Wheels Racing Justice League 1:64

6 Mark Martin Batman 10.00 20.00
9 Mark Martin Batman 10.00 20.00
12 Ryan Newman Justice League 10.00 20.00
16 Greg Biffle Flash 7.50 15.00
17 Matt Kenseth Martian Manhunter 10.00 20.00
21 Ricky Rudd Wonder Woman 7.50 15.00
60 Greg Biffle Flash 7.50 15.00
97 Kurt Busch Superman 7.50 15.00
99 Jeff Burton Green Lantern 7.50 15.00
04 Justice League Super Heroes 6.00 12.00
04 Justice League Villains 6.00 12.00

2004 Hot Wheels Racing Justice League w/Figure 1:64

6 Mark Martin Batman 12.50 25.00
16 Greg Biffle Flash 10.00 20.00
17 Matt Kenseth Martian Manhunter 12.50 25.00
21 Ricky Rudd Wonder Woman 12.50 25.00
97 Kurt Busch Superman 12.50 25.00
99 Jeff Burton Green Lantern 10.00 20.00

2004 Hot Wheels Racing Pit Cruisers 1:64

6 Mark Martin Batman 30.00 60.00
17 Matt Kenseth DeWalt 5.00 10.00

2004 Hot Wheels Racing Promos 1:64

99 Jeff Burton Hot Wheels Back in Black/10,000 15.00 30.00

2004 Hot Wheels Racing Race Day 1:64

6 Mark Martin Viagra 5.00 12.00
12 Ryan Newman Alltel 4.00 8.00
17 Matt Kenseth DeWalt 4.00 8.00
21 Ricky Rudd Motorcraft 4.00 8.00
32 Ricky Craven Tide 4.00 8.00
43 Jeff Green Cheerios 4.00 8.00
45 Kyle Petty Georgia Pacific 4.00 8.00

2004 Hot Wheels Racing Stockerz 1:64

6 Mark Martin Oscar Mayer 4.00 8.00
6 Mark Martin Pfizer 4.00 8.00
12 Ryan Newman Alltel 4.00 8.00
17 Matt Kenseth DeWalt 4.00 8.00
21 Ricky Rudd Motorcraft 4.00 8.00
24 Jeff Gordon DuPont Flames 5.00 10.00
29 Kevin Harvick Goodwrench 4.00 8.00
45 Kyle Petty Brawny 4.00 8.00
97 Kurt Busch Rubbermaid 4.00 8.00
97 Kurt Busch Sharpie 4.00 8.00

2004 Hot Wheels Racing Test Track 1:64

6 Mark Martin Pfizer 4.00 8.00
12 Ryan Newman Alltel 5.00 10.00
16 Greg Biffle Grainger 4.00 8.00
17 Matt Kenseth DeWalt 6.00 12.00
21 Ricky Rudd Motorcraft 4.00 8.00
43 Richard Petty STP 5.00 10.00
45 Kyle Petty Petty Racing 4.00 8.00
97 Kurt Busch Sharpie 4.00 8.00

2004 Hot Wheels Racing Treasure Hunt 1:64

99 Jeff Burton Hot Wheels/10,000 12.50 25.00

2005 Hot Wheels Alternative Paint Scheme 1:64

6 Mark Martin Kraft 4.00 8.00
12 Ryan Newman Mobil 1 4.00 8.00
16 Greg Biffle Post-It 4.00 8.00
17 Matt Kenseth Trex 4.00 8.00
21 Ricky Rudd Air Force 4.00 8.00
97 Kurt Busch Irwin Tools 4.00 8.00
99 Carl Edwards Office Depot 7.50 15.00

2005 Hot Wheels Batman Begins 1:64

6 Mark Martin Batman 6.00 12.00

2005 Hot Wheels Race Day 1:64

6 Mark Martin Pfizer 4.00 8.00
16 Greg Biffle National Guard 4.00 8.00
17 Matt Kenseth DeWalt 4.00 8.00
21 Ricky Rudd Motorcraft 3.00 6.00
43 Jeff Green Cheerios 3.00 6.00
43 Richard Petty '67 Plymouth 4.00 8.00

2006 Hot Wheels Promos 1:64

10 Scott Riggs Valvoline Cars in blister 5.00 10.00

1998 Johnny Lightning Stock Car Legends 1:64

These 1:64 scale cars take a look back at some of the most successful drivers in NASCAR history along with their top rides. Each car was produced as a hood open model.

5 Neil Bonnett Jim Stacy 1977 Dodge 6.00 12.00
6 Buddy Baker Dodge Daytona 1969 6.00 12.00
6 Pete Hamilton American Brakeblok 1971 Plymouth GTX 6.00 12.00
11 Mario Andretti Bunnell Motor 1967 Ford Fairlane 6.00 12.00
11 Darrell Waltrip Pepsi 1983 Monte Carlo 6.00 12.00
11 Cale Yarborough First American City Travelers Checks 1978 Oldsmobile 442 6.00 12.00
17 David Pearson East Tennessee Motors 1969 Ford Torino 6.00 12.00
17 David Pearson 1967 Ford Fairlane 6.00 12.00
21 Donnie Allison Purolator 1971 Mercury Cylone 6.00 12.00
21 Buddy Baker Vavoline 1984 Thunderbird 6.00 12.00
27 Benny Parsons Melling 1980 Monte Carlo 6.00 12.00
28 Cale Yarborough Hardee's 1984 Monte Carlo 6.00 12.00
32 Dick Brooks Bestline 1970 6.00 12.00
40 Pete Hamilton 7-up 1970 Plymouth 6.00 12.00
42 Marty Robbins 1973 Dodge Charger 6.00 12.00
50 Geoff Bodine Spectrum 1982 Grand Prix 6.00 12.00
51 A.J. Foyt Valvoline 1979 Olds 10.00 20.00
71 Bobby Isaac K&K Insurance 1970 Dodge Daytona 6.00 12.00
88 Rusty Wallace Gatorade 1984 Grand Prix 6.00 12.00
88 Darrell Waltrip Gatorade 1979 Monte Carlo 6.00 12.00
98 Lee Roy Yarborough 1969 Ford Torino 6.00 12.00
99 Fred Lorenzen STP 1971 Plymouth 6.00 12.00

1997 Lindberg ARCA 1:64

Die-cast in this series feature drivers from the ARCA racing circuit. Each is packaged on a blister that reads "Super Car Collectible" and includes a trading card. The blister also features the Lindberg logo, the American Racing Series logo, and the year of issue on the front.

16 Tim Steele Craft House 2.00 5.00

1990-92 Matchbox White Rose Super Stars 1:64

These were the first series of NASCAR replica cars distributed by White Rose. The cars were produced by Matchbox and were issued in either a blister package, a small window box or a promo style polybag.

1 Jeff Gordon Baby Ruth Orange Lettering '92 BX 10.00 20.00
1 Jeff Gordon Baby Ruth Red Lettering '92 BX 6.00 12.00
2 Rusty Wallace Pontiac Excitement '92 BL 2.00 5.00
3 Dale Earnhardt GM '90 BX 35.00 75.00
3 Dale Earnhardt GM Parts '91 BX 25.00 50.00
3 Dale Earnhardt Goodwrench '92 BL 10.00 25.00

3 Dale Earnhardt 10.00 20.00
Mom-n-Pop's '92 polly bag
4 Ernie Irvan 2.00 5.00
Kodak '92 BL
7 Harry Gant 4.00 8.00
Mac Tools '92 BX
7 Jimmy Hensley 4.00 8.00
White Rose Collectibles '92 BX
7 Alan Kulwicki 15.00 30.00
Hooters '92 BL
7 Alan Kulwicki 10.00 20.00
Hooters Naturally Fresh '92 BL
8 Jeff Burton 1.50 4.00
TIC Financial '92 BX
8 Dick Trickle 1.50 4.00
Snicker's '92 BL
9 No Driver Association 1.50 4.00
Melling 1992 BL
10 Derrike Cope 1.50 4.00
Purolator '92 BL
10 Ernie Irvan 10.00 20.00
Mac Tools '91 BX
11 Bill Elliott 1.50 4.00
Amoco '92 BL
12 Hut Stricklin 1.50 4.00
Raybestos '92 BL
15 No Driver Association 1.50 4.00
Motorcraft '92 BL
15 Morgan Shepherd 1.50 4.00
Motorcraft '92 BL
18 Dale Jarrett 2.00 5.00
Interstate Batteries '92 BL
22 Sterling Marlin 2.00 5.00
Maxwell House '92 BL
26 Brett Bodine 1.50 4.00
uaker State '92 BL
28 Davey Allison 7.50 15.00
Havoline '92 BL
28 Davey Allison 7.50 15.00
Havoline Mac Tools '92 BL
29 No Driver Association 2.50 5.00
Matchbox Racing
White Rose Collectibles '92 BX
29 Phil Parsons 10.00 20.00
Parsons Racing '92 BX
30 Michael Waltrip 1.50 4.00
Pennzoil '92 BL
41 James Smith 1.50 4.00
White House Apple Juice '92 BL
42 Kyle Petty 1.50 4.00
Mello Yello '92 BL
43 Richard Petty 1.50 4.00
STP '92 BL
44 Bobby Labonte 4.00 8.00
Penrose '92 BX
44 Bobby Labonte 4.00 8.00
Slim Jim '92 BX
48 James Hylton 1.50 4.00
Valtrol '92 BL
49 Ed Ferree 1.50 4.00
Fergaed Racing '92 BX
55 Ted Musgrave 1.50 4.00
Jasper Engines
66 Chad Little 1.50 4.00
Phillips 66 red car '92 BL
66 No Driver Association 1.50 4.00
Phillips 66 black car '92 BL
68 Bobby Hamilton 1.50 4.00
Country Time '92 BL
87 Joe Nemechek 1.50 4.00
Texas Pete '92 BX
89 Jim Sauter 1.50 4.00
Evinrude '92 BL
92 No Driver Association 25.00 35.00
White Rose Collectibles '92 BL
92 Hut Stricklin 1.50 4.00
Stanley Tools '92 BX
14 Terry Labonte 2.00 5.00
MW Windows BX
21 Morgan Shepherd 1.50 4.00
Citgo BL
22 Bobby Labonte 3.00 6.00
Maxwell House BL
24 Jeff Gordon 6.00 10.00
DuPont BL
25 Hermie Sadler 1.50 4.00
VA is for Lovers BX
28 Davey Allison 10.00 18.00
Havoline BL
29 Phil Parsons 1.50 4.00
Matchbox BL
31 Bobby Hillin Jr. 1.50 4.00
Team Ireland BL
32 Jimmy Horton 1.50 4.00
Active Racing BL
32 Dale Jarrett 2.00 5.00
Pic-N-Pay BX
40 Kenny Wallace 1.50 4.00
Dirt Devil BL
41 Phil Parsons 1.50 4.00
Manheim BL
48 Sterling Marlin 2.00 5.00
Cappio BX
69 Jeff Sparker 6.00 12.00
WFE Challenge BL
71 Dave Marcis 1.50 4.00
nick's Catering BL
83 Lake Speed 1.50 4.00
Purex
87 Joe Nemechek 1.50 4.00
Dentyne
93 No Driver Association 20.00 35.00
White Rose Collectibles BL
93 No Driver Association 4.00 8.00
American Zoom poly bag
94 Terry Labonte 3.00 6.00
Sunoco BL
98 Derrike Cope 1.50 4.00
Bojangles BL
98 Jimmy Spencer 1.50 4.00
Moly Black Gold BL
99 Ricky Craven 1.50 4.00
DuPont BX

1993 Matchbox White Rose Super Stars 1:64

This series features six Jimmy Hensley cars honoring many of the sponsors of the number 7 car. Each piece either comes in a blister package or a small window box. The year is on the end of each of the box packages.

1 Rodney Combs Jr. 10.00 18.00
Luxaire Promo blister/5000
1 Rodney Combs Jr. 9.00 16.00
{Goody's BX
6 Mark Martin 3.00 5.00
Valvoline BX
7 Jimmy Hensley 5.00 9.00
Bobsled BX
7 Jimmy Hensley 5.00 9.00
Bojangles BL
7 Jimmy Hensley 5.00 9.00
Cellular One BX
7 Jimmy Hensley 5.00 9.00
Family Channel BX
7 Jimmy Hensley 5.00 9.00
Hanes BX
7 Jimmy Hensley 5.00 9.00
Matchbox BX
8 Jeff Burton 1.50 4.00
TIC Financal BX
8 Jeff Burton 1.50 4.00
Baby Ruth BX
8 Sterling Marlin 2.00 5.00
Raybestos BL
8 Bobby Dotter 1.50 4.00
Dewalt BX
9 Mike Wallace 1.50 4.00
FDP Brakes BX
12 Jimmy Spencer 1.50 4.00
Meineke BL

1994 Matchbox White Rose Super Stars 1:64

This is considered the second Super Stars Series distributed by White Rose Collectibles. Each standard car was issued in a small window box. There were special cars released that featured "Future Cup Stars" and drivers who won "Super Star Awards." The Super Star Awards cars came in a jewelry type box with the car being painted in gold.

2 Ricky Craven 1.50 4.00
DuPont BX
2 Rusty Wallace 1.50 4.00
Ford Motorsports BX
3 Dale Earnhardt 25.00 50.00
Gold Lumina
Super Star Awards
4 Sterling Marlin 1.50 4.00
Kodak BX
4 Sterling Marlin 1.50 4.00
Kodak FunSaver BX
5 Terry Labonte 2.00 4.00
Kellogg's BX
6 Mark Martin 2.00 4.00
Valvoline BX
7 Geoff Bodine 3.00 8.00
Exide BX
7 Harry Gant 1.50 4.00
Manheim BX
8 Jeff Burton 1.50 4.00
Raybestos BX
12 Derrike Cope 1.50 4.00
Straight Arrow BX
15 Lake Speed 1.50 4.00
Quality Care BX
16 Ted Musgrave 1.50 4.00
Family Channel BX
17 Darrell Waltrip 1.50 4.00
Western Auto BX
19 Loy Allen Jr. 1.50 4.00
Hooters BX
23 Hut Stricklin 10.00 20.00
Smokin' Joe's BX
24 Jeff Gordon 5.00 10.00
DuPont BX
26 Brett Bodine 1.50 4.00
Quaker State BX
29 Phil Parsons 6.00 15.00
Baltimore Colts BL Promo/5000
29 Phil Parsons 1.50 4.00
Matchbox White Rose Collectibles BX
30 Michael Waltrip 1.50 4.00
Pennzoil BX
32 Dale Jarrett 2.00 4.00
Pic-N-Pay BX
33 Harry Gant 12.50 25.00
Gold Lumina
Super Star Awards in box
34 Mike McLaughlin 1.50 4.00
Fiddle Faddle BL
37 Loy Allen Jr. 3.00 8.00
Naturally Fresh
Future Cup Stars '94 BX
40 Bobby Hamilton 1.50 4.00
Kendall BX
41 Joe Nemechek 1.50 4.00
Meineke BX
43 Rodney Combs Jr. 3.00 8.00
Black Flag BX
43 Rodney Combs Jr. 12.50 25.00
French's Black Flag BL
43 Rodney Combs Jr. 3.00 8.00
French's BX
46 Shawna Robinson 12.50 25.00
Polaroid BL
52 Ken Schrader 1.50 4.00
AC Delco BX
55 Jimmy Hensley 7.50 15.00
Petron Plus BL Promo/5000
60 Mark Martin 5.00 10.00
Winn Dixie BX
66 Mike Wallace 3.00 8.00
Duron Paint
Future Cup Stars '94 BX
75 Todd Bodine 1.50 4.00
Factory Stores of America BX
87 Joe Nemechek 3.00 8.00
Cintas
Future Cup Stars '94 BX
92 Burn Foundation promo blister 2.00 4.00
92 Larry Pearson 1.50 4.00
Stanley Tools BX
94 No Driver Association 12.50 25.00
Matchbox White Rose Collectibles BL
94 No Driver Association 4.00 8.00
Series 2 preview BX
98 Derrike Cope 1.50 4.00
Fingerhut BX
0 Jeff Burton 5.00 10.00
TIC Financial
Future Cup Stars '94 BX

1995 Matchbox White Rose Super Stars 1:64

This is the continuation of the second Super Stars Series. The Super Star Awards cars again come in a special box and are gold.

1 Mike Chase 3.00 5.00
Sears Diehard SuperTruck
1 Hermie Sadler 3.00 5.00
DeWalt
2 Ricky Craven 3.00 5.00
DuPont
3 Dale Earnhardt 20.00 40.00
Gold 7-Time Champion
Super Star Awards
3 Dale Earnhardt 10.00 20.00
Goodwrench
3 Mike Skinner 3.00 5.00
Goodwrench SuperTruck
5 Terry Labonte 3.00 5.00
Kellogg's
6 Rick Carelli 3.00 5.00
Total SuperTruck
6 Mark Martin 3.00 5.00
Valvoline
7 Geoff Bodine 3.00 5.00
Exide
8 Jeff Burton 3.00 5.00
Raybestos
8 Jeff Burton 10.00 20.00
Raybestos
Super Star Awards
8 Bobby Dotter 3.00 5.00
Hyde Tools
11 Brett Bodine 3.00 5.00
Lowe's
12 Derrike Cope 3.00 5.00
Straight Arrow
18 Bobby Labonte 3.00 5.00
Interstate Batteries
24 Jeff Gordon 4.00 8.00
DuPont
24 Scott Lagasse 3.00 5.00
DuPont SuperTruck
24 Mickey York 4.00 10.00
Cobra Promo/7000
25 Ken Schrader 7.50 15.00
Budweiser in acrylic Case
26 Steve Kinser 3.00 5.00
Quaker State
28 Dale Jarrett 3.00 5.00
avoline
40 Patty Moise 3.00 5.00
ial Purex
42 Kyle Petty 7.50 15.00
Coors Light in acrylic Case
57 Jason Keller 3.00 5.00
Budget Gourmet
71 Kevin Lepage 3.00 5.00
Vermont Teddy Bear
72 Tracy Leslie 3.00 5.00
Detroit Gasket
74 Johnny Benson Jr. 3.00 5.00
Lipton Tea
87 Joe Nemechek 7.50 15.00
BellSouth Mobility Promo/7000
87 Joe Nemechek 3.00 5.00
Burger King
90 Mike Wallace 3.00 5.00
Heilig-Meyers
94 Bill Elliott 10.00 20.00
Gold Thunderbird
SuperStars Awards
94 Bill Elliott 3.00 5.00
McDonald's
94 Bill Elliott 7.50 15.00
McDonald's Thunderbat Promo
95 John Tanner 3.00 5.00
Caterpillar
99 Phil Parsons 3.00 5.00
Luxaire

1996 Matchbox White Rose Super Stars 1:64

This series of 1:64 replicas were packaged in a small clear window box featuring the name "Racing SuperStars." They were manufactured by Matchbox and licensed and distributed by White Rose Collectibles. A production run of 10,000 was noted on the outside of the box as well. The listings below also include four special issue SuperStar Awards cars that were produced in gold chrome and feature winners of the Winston Cup Series, the SuperTruck Series, the Winston Cup Rookie of the Year and the Busch Grand National Series winner. Those four were housed in an oversized solid box.

2 Mike Bliss 3.00 5.00
ASE SuperTruck
3 Mike Skinner 10.00 18.00
Gold SuperStars Awards SuperTruck
4 Sterling Marlin 3.00 5.00
Kodak
5 Terry Labonte 3.00 5.00
Kellogg's
6 Mark Martin 3.00 5.00
Valvoline
9 Lake Speed 3.00 5.00
SPAM
10 Phil Parsons 3.00 5.00
Channellock SuperTruck
10 Ricky Rudd 3.00 5.00
Tide
12 Derrike Cope 6.00 15.00
Badcock Promo/5000
15 Wally Dallenbach 6.00 15.00
Hayes Modems Promo/5000
16 Ted Musgrave 3.00 5.00
Family Channel
21 Tobey Butler 3.00 5.00
Ortho SuperTruck
21 Michael Waltrip 3.00 5.00
Citgo
22 Ward Burton 3.00 5.00
MBNA
24 Jeff Gordon 4.00 8.00
DuPont
24 Jeff Gordon 15.00 25.00
DuPont Gold SuperStars Awards
24 Jack Sprague 3.00 5.00
Quaker State SuperTruck
25 White Rose Santa Promo/2500 3.00 8.00
34 Mike McLaughlin 3.00 5.00
Royal Oak
37 John Andretti 3.00 5.00
K-Mart
40 Tim Fedewa 3.00 5.00
Kleenex
41 Ricky Craven 3.00 5.00
Kodiak
41 Ricky Craven 10.00 18.00
Rookie of the Year
Gold SuperStars Awards
43 Rodney Combs 3.00 5.00
Lance
74 Johnny Benson Jr. 10.00 18.00
Lipton Tea
Gold SuperStar Awards
77 Bobby Hillin Jr. 3.00 5.00
Jasper
87 Joe Nemechek 5.00 10.00
BellSouth Promo
87 Joe Nemechek 3.00 5.00
Burger King
87 Joe Nemechek 3.00 8.00
Burger King Promo/5000
88 Dale Jarrett 3.00 5.00
Quality Care
94 Ron Barfield 3.00 5.00
New Holland
94 Bill Elliott 4.00 10.00
McDonald's Monopoly Promo/5000
94 Bill Elliott 3.00 5.00
McDonald's
95 David Green 3.00 5.00
Caterpiller
99 Jeff Burton 3.00 5.00
Exide
0 Rick Eckert 4.00 8.00
Ray-Vest SuperTruck Promo

1997 Matchbox White Rose Super Stars 1:64

This series of 1:64 replicas were issued in a Matchbox by White Rose window box. In addition the release also features two Super Star Awards cars and three other cars packaged in glass bottles. The most unique car from this series is that of Rick Mast which is packaged in a glass replica of a shotgun shell.

2 Rusty Wallace 50.00 75.00
Miller Lite
packaged in a bottle
5 Terry Labonte 3.00 6.00
Kellogg's
5 Terry Labonte 15.00 25.00
Kellogg's SSA Gold
25 Ricky Craven 40.00 60.00
Budweiser
packaged in a bottle
36 Derrike Cope 2.50 5.00
Skittles
40 Robby Gordon 40.00 60.00
Coors Light
packaged in a bottle
74 Randy LaJoie 2.50 5.00
Fina
74 Randy LaJoie 10.00 20.00
Fina SSA Gold
75 Rick Mast 35.00 50.00
Remington
packaged in a shotgun shell
75 Rick Mast 30.00 50.00
Remington Camo
in a shotgun shell
75 Rick Mast 30.00 50.00
Stren in a shotgun shell
88 Kevin Lepage 2.50 5.00
Hype
94 Bill Elliott 2.50 5.00
McDonald's
94 Bill Elliott 4.00 10.00
Mac Tonight Promo blister
96 David Green 2.50 5.00
Caterpillar

1996 Miscellaneous Promos 1:24

5 Terry Labonte 12.50 25.00
Kellogg's Korny Bank 1998
produced by Nevins&Garner
5 Terry Labonte 15.00 25.00
Kellogg's Tony Food City
produced by Nevins&Garner
32 Dale Jarrett 60.00 120.00
Band-Aid DAJ Racing/5000
44 Bobby Labonte 30.00 50.00
Shell 1996 EPI

1991-03 Miscellaneous Promos 1:43

5 Terry Labonte 12.50 25.00
Kellogg's Bi-lo 2003
5 Terry Labonte 10.00 25.00
Kellogg's Giant 2003
5 Terry Labonte 6.00 15.00
Kellogg's Tops 2003
8 Bobby Hillin 6.00 15.00
Snickers Promo 1991
issued w
candy bars
8 Dick Trickle 6.00 15.00
Snickers Promo 1992
issued w
candy bars

1991-04 Miscellaneous Promos 1:64

These 1:64 die-cast pieces were issued as promotional itmes for various businesses and other entities. Most were issued in blister packs or in separate poly bags. There is no definative die-cast manufacturer noted on the cars or boxes.

1 Jeff Gordon 12.50 25.00
Baby Ruth First BGN Win
Motorsports Properties
blister/20,000 1993
5 Terry Labonte 5.00 12.00
Apple Jacks black windows
in bag '=1999
5 Terry Labonte 4.00 10.00
Honey Frosted Mini-Wheats
in bag 2002
5 Terry Labonte 4.00 10.00
Kellogg's Promo 1995
black windows
produced by Nevin International
5 Terry Labonte 4.00 10.00
Kellogg's Promo 1996
black windows
produced by Nevin International
5 Terry Labonte 2.00 5.00
Kellogg's Promo 2000
black windows Garner and Nevin
5 Terry Labonte 5.00 12.00
Mini-Wheats Red
in bag 2001
6 Mark Martin 20.00 35.00
Stroh Light Trackside Souvenirs
9 Bill Elliott 20.00 35.00
Melling Trackside Souvenirs
18 Bobby Labonte 5.00 12.00
Banquet in bag 2002
18 Bobby Labonte 3.00 8.00
Interstate Batteries
EPI Motorsports blister 1996
22 Rob Moroso 3.00 8.00
Moroso Racing blister 1991
22 Rob Moroso 3.00 8.00
Prestone blister 1991
27 Ward Burton 10.00 20.00
Gwaltney Promo in blister/20,000 1992
44 Bobby Labonte 3.00 8.00
Shell EPI Motorsports blister 1996
54 Rich Bickle 15.00 25.00
Kleenex in bag
54 Kevin Grubb 7.50 15.00
Toys 'R' Us blister 2002
64 Elmo Langley 4.00 10.00
Start Your Engines promo 1992
91 Rich Bickle 10.00 20.00
Aqua Velva in
J.B. Williams clamshell 2000
92 Jimmie Johnson 30.00 50.00
Alltel blister/20,000 2000
92 Jimmie Johnson 30.00 60.00
Alltel window box/10,000 2000
93 Dave Blaney 1.50 3.00
Amoco in bag 2001
94 Bill Elliott 5.00 12.00
McDonald's Mac Tonight
2-car Promo blister 1997
97 Energizer Bunny Promo in bag 1997 5.00 10.00
02 Jim Inglebright 3.00 8.00
Jelly Belly SuperTruck 2000
packaged with jelly beans on blister

2006 Motorsports Authentics Steel 1:16

8 Dale Earnhardt Jr. 125.00 250.00
Bud/1100
8 Dale Earnhardt Jr. 175.00 300.00
Bud Dale Tribute/2133
8 Dale Earnhardt Jr. 175.00 300.00
Bud Father's Day/1800

1991-92 Pole Position 1:64

These 1:64 die-cast pieces were issued in a Pole Position blister pack. The bottom half of the package was printed in a red and orange checkered flag design and the top of the package is black and dark purple. The cars were released over a 2-year period from 1991-1992.

1 Jeff Gordon 7.50 15.00
Baby Ruth
4 Ernie Irvan 3.00 6.00
Kodak
7 Harry Gant 3.00 6.00
Mac Tools
11 Bill Elliott 3.00 6.00
Amoco
21 Morgan Shepherd 3.00 6.00
Citgo
21 Morgan Shepherd 3.00 6.00
Motorcraft
22 Sterling Marlin 3.00 8.00
Maxwell House
33 Harry Gant 3.00 6.00
Leo Jackson
36 Kenny Wallace 3.00 6.00
Dirt Devil
43 Richard Petty 4.00 10.00
STP
52 Jimmy Means 3.00 6.00

Taco Bell
66 Jimmy Hensley Trop Artic 3.00 6.00
68 Bobby Hamilton Country Time 3.00 6.00
71 Dave Marcis Big Apple 3.00 6.00
73 Phil Barkdoll X-1R 3.00 6.00
75 Butch Miller Food Country 3.00 6.00
75 Joe Ruttman Dinner Bell 3.00 6.00
94 Terry Labonte Sunoco 3.00 8.00
98 Jimmy Spencer Food City 3.00 6.00
98 Jimmy Spencer Moly Black Gold 3.00 6.00

1993 Pole Position 1:64

14 Donnie Neuenberger Promo Blister 4.00 8.00

1996 Press Pass Sets 1:24/64

Card manufacturer Press Pass ventured into die-cast with these three pieces. Each piece is a boxed set containing a 1:24 bank or Hauler, a 1:64 car and one Burning Rubber card produced by Press Pass. Each piece was also serial numbered on the outside of the box.

2 Rusty Wallace Miller 25th Anniversary/1996 1:24 Revell Bank, 1:64 Revell car and Press Pass Burning Rubber I card 40.00 100.00
5 Terry Labonte Kellogg's Silver/1996 1:24 Action black window bank, 1:64 car, and Burning Rubber II card 50.00 120.00
18 Bobby Labonte Interstate Batteries/1008 1:64 Revell car, 1:64 GMP hauler, and Press Pass Burning Rubber card 50.00 120.00

1997 Race Image 1:43

6 Mark Martin Valvoline 5.00 12.00
9 Jeff Burton Track Gear 4.00 10.00
21 Michael Waltrip Citgo 4.00 10.00
99 Jeff Burton Exide 4.00 10.00

1998 Race Image 1:43

This series of 1:43 scale cars was distributed by Dimension 4 and entitled "Race Image." Each car was packaged in a window display box.

4 Bobby Hamilton Kodak Gold 4.00 10.00
6 Mark Martin Eagle One 5.00 12.00
6 Mark Martin Valvoline 5.00 12.00
6 Mark Martin Valvoline SynPower 5.00 12.00
8 Hut Stricklin Circuit City 4.00 10.00
16 Ted Musgrave Primestar 4.00 10.00
18 Bobby Labonte Interstate Batteries 5.00 12.00
21 Michael Waltrip Citgo 4.00 10.00
26 Johnny Benson Cheerios 4.00 10.00
35 Todd Bodine Tabasco Orange&White 5.00 12.00
35 Todd Bodine Tabasco Red&Black 5.00 12.00
40 Sterling Marlin Coors Light 5.00 12.00
41 Steve Grissom Grissom Racing 4.00 10.00
41 Steve Grissom Kodiak Chrome 12.50 30.00
42 Joe Nemechek BellSouth 4.00 10.00
42 Joe Nemechek Yellow Pages 4.00 10.00
43 John Andretti STP 4.00 10.00
50 Mark Green Diet Dr.Pepper 4.00 10.00
55 Brad Leighton Coed Naked 4.00 10.00
90 Dick Trickle Heilig-Meyers 4.00 10.00
97 Chad Little John Deere 5.00 12.00
98 Rich Bickle Thorn Apple Valley 4.00 10.00

1998 Race Image Service Kit 1:43

These 1:43 scale cars were issued in a black Race Image blister pack and distributed by Dimension 4. Each car included a group of race day supplies, such as extra tires, a gas can, and jack.

6 Mark Martin Eagle One 5.00 12.00
6 Mark Martin Zerex 5.00 12.00
17 Matt Kenseth DeWalt 7.50 15.00
21 Michael Waltrip Citgo 4.00 10.00

41 Steve Grissom Grissom Racing 4.00 10.00
57 Andy Santerre Monroe 4.00 10.00
90 Dick Trickle Heilig-Meyers 4.00 10.00
98 Rich Bickle Thorn Apple Valey 4.00 10.00

1992-97 Raceway Replicas 1:24

This manufacturer of high end 1:24 scale die cast replicas has produced this series of cars. The cars are sold directly to the public usually through ads in racing publications.

4 Sterling Marlin Kodak 1996 100.00 150.00
6 Mark Martin Valvoline 1994 100.00 175.00
11 Bill Elliott Budweiser 1992 100.00 175.00
27 Hut Stricklin McDonald's 1993 90.00 130.00
28 Davey Allison Havoline 1993 100.00 175.00
96 David Green Caterpillar 1997 80.00 130.00

1995 Racing Champions Premier 1:18

4 Sterling Marlin Kodak 15.00 40.00
17 Darrell Waltrip Western Auto 15.00 30.00
18 Bobby Labonte Interstate Batteries 25.00 50.00
24 Jeff Gordon DuPont 25.00 50.00
25 Ken Schrader Budweiser 15.00 30.00
74 Johnny Benson Lipton Tea 15.00 30.00
87 Joe Nemechek Burger King 15.00 40.00

1995-96 Racing Champions SuperTrucks 1:18

This is a 1:18 scale series of SuperTrucks. The Mike Skinner piece is available both in a hood open version and the regular hood sealed version.

2 Mike Bliss ASE 12.50 30.00
3 Mike Skinner Goodwrench 1995 25.00 45.00
3 Mike Skinner Goodwrench 1995 Craftsman Truck Series Champion 20.00 40.00
6 Rick Carelli Total 12.50 30.00
7 Geoff Bodine QVC 12.50 30.00
9 Joe Bessey New Hampshire Speedway 12.50 30.00
14 Butch Gilliland Stroppe 12.50 30.00
17 Bill Sedgwick Die Hard 12.50 30.00
17 Darrell Waltrip Western Auto 12.50 30.00
20 Walker Evans Dana 12.50 30.00
21 Doug George Ortho 12.50 30.00
24 Jack Sprague Quaker State 12.50 30.00
29 Bob Keselowski Winnebago 12.50 30.00
30 Jimmy Hensley Mopar 12.50 30.00
35 Bill Venturini Rain X 12.50 30.00
43 Rich Bickle Cummins 12.50 30.00
52 Ken Schrader AC Delco 1995 25.00 40.00
75 Bobby Gill Spears 12.50 30.00
83 Steve Portenga Coffee Critic 12.50 30.00
98 Butch Miller Raybestos 12.50 30.00

1996 Racing Champions Premier 1:18

This series of cars was the first entry into the 1:18 scale size by manufacturer Racing Champions. The cars were sold through retail outlets and through hobby shops packaged in a red Racing Champions window box.

1 Rick Mast Hooters 20.00 40.00
2 Ricky Craven DuPont 25.00 50.00
2 Rusty Wallace MGD 20.00 40.00
5 Terry Labonte Bayer 25.00 50.00
7 Geoff Bodine QVC 15.00 40.00
9 Joe Bessey Delco Remy 15.00 30.00
15 Wally Dallenbach Hayes Modems 20.00 40.00
16 Ted Musgrave Primestar 10.00 25.00
22 Ward Burton MBNA 15.00 30.00
24 Jeff Gordon DuPont 20.00 50.00
24 Jeff Gordon DuPont Signature Series 25.00 50.00
24 Jeff Gordon DuPont 1995 WC Champ 25.00 50.00
25 Ken Schrader Budweiser 20.00 50.00
25 Ken Schrader Bud Olympic/1826 20.00 40.00
25 Ken Schrader Budweiser Olympic Chrome 150.00 300.00
29 Steve Grissom Scooby Doo 15.00 30.00
30 Johnny Benson Pennzoil 15.00 30.00
31 Mike Skinner Realtree 30.00 60.00
34 Mike McLaughlin Royal Oak 15.00 30.00
43 Bobby Hamilton STP Anniversary/2496 1972 Red Blue 15.00 30.00
43 Bobby Hamilton STP Anniversary/2496 1972 Blue 15.00 30.00
43 Bobby Hamilton STP Anniversary/2496 1979 Red Blue 15.00 30.00
43 Bobby Hamilton STP Anniversary/2496 1984 Red Blue 15.00 30.00
43 Bobby Hamilton STP Anniversary 1996 Silver 20.00 35.00
47 Jeff Fuller Sunoco 15.00 30.00
51 Chuck Bown Lucks 15.00 30.00
52 Ken Schrader AC Delco 15.00 30.00
57 Jim Bown Matco 20.00 40.00
57 Jason Keller Halloween Havoc 15.00 30.00
57 Jason Keller Slim Jim 15.00 30.00
88 Dale Jarrett Quality Care 15.00 30.00
94 Bill Elliott McDonald's Monopoly 15.00 30.00
97 Chad Little Sterling Cowboy 12.00 30.00

1997 Racing Champions Premier 1:18

This series of 1:18 scale cars was distributed primarily through hobby outlets. Each basic issue car carried a production run of 800-830. A Gold version of most cars was also produced with each Gold being produced in quantities of 166-200.

2 Rusty Wallace Miller Lite 30.00 60.00
2 Rusty Wallace Miller Lite Gold 100.00 200.00
5 Terry Labonte Kellogg's Tony/800 25.00 50.00
5 Terry Labonte Kellogg's Tony Gold/200 75.00 150.00
6 Mark Martin Valvoline 30.00 60.00
6 Mark Martin Valvoline Gold 100.00 200.00
10 Ricky Rudd Tide/830 20.00 50.00
10 Ricky Rudd Tide Gold/166 75.00 150.00
17 Darrell Waltrip Parts America Chrome 35.00 60.00
18 Bobby Labonte Interstate Batteries 25.00 50.00
18 Bobby Labonte Interstate Batteries Gold 75.00 150.00
36 Derrike Cope Skittles/830 20.00 50.00
36 Derrike Cope Skittles Gold/166 60.00 120.00
75 Rick Mast Remington/830 25.00 50.00
75 Rick Mast Remington Gold/166 75.00 150.00
94 Bill Elliott McDonald's/830 25.00 50.00
94 Bill Elliott McDonald's Gold/166 75.00 150.00
94 Bill Elliott Mac Tonight/800 25.00 50.00
94 Bill Elliott Mac Tonight Gold/200 75.00 150.00
96 David Green Caterpillar Promo 15.00 40.00

1997 Racing Champions SuperTrucks 1:18

This is the series edition of 1:18 SuperTrucks released by Racing Champions.

2 Mike Bliss Team ASE 12.50 30.00
15 Mike Cope Penrose 12.50 30.00
18 Mike Dokken Dana 12.50 30.00
24 Jack Sprague Quaker State 12.50 30.00
44 Boris Said Federated Auto 12.50 30.00
66 Bryan Refner Carlin 12.50 30.00
75 Dan Press Spears 12.50 30.00
80 Joe Ruttman LCI 12.50 30.00
87 Joe Nemechek BellSouth 12.50 30.00
07 Tammy Jo Kirk Loveable 12.50 30.00

1998 Racing Champions Gold Hood Open 1:18

This is a special series produced by Racing Champions to celebrate NASCAR's 50th anniversary. Each car is a limited edition of 1,998. Each car is also plated in gold chrome and contains a serial number on its chassis.

4 Bobby Hamilton Kodak 25.00 60.00
5 Terry Labonte Kellogg's 60.00 100.00
8 Hut Stricklin Circuit City 25.00 60.00
30 Derrike Cope Gumout 25.00 60.00
33 Ken Schrader Petree 25.00 60.00
35 Todd Bodine Tabasco 25.00 60.00
36 Ernie Irvan Skittles 40.00 80.00

1998 Racing Champions Premier 1:18

92 Derrike Cope Kraft Promo/5000 40.00 75.00

1998 Racing Champions Stock Rods 1:18

93 Dave Blaney Amoco Ultimate Promo 1968 Dodge Charger 20.00 40.00

2000 Racing Champions 1:18

22 Ward Burton Caterpillar 20.00 40.00

2002 Racing Champions Stock Rods 1:18

5 Terry Labonte Kellogg's/999 30.00 60.00
5 Terry Labonte Kellogg's Chrome/199 40.00 80.00
10 Johnny Benson Valvoline/999 25.00 50.00
10 Johnny Benson Valvoline Chrome/199 40.00 80.00
22 Ward Burton Caterpillar/999 25.00 50.00
22 Ward Burton Caterpillar Chrome/199 40.00 80.00
36 Ken Schrader M&M's/999 35.00 70.00
36 Ken Schrader M&M's Chrome/199 60.00 100.00
48 Jimmie Johnson Lowe's/999 40.00 75.00
48 Jimmie Johnson Lowe's 1970 Chevelle Chrome/199 60.00 120.00

2003 Racing Champions Stock Rods 1:18

5 Terry Labonte Kellogg's Corvette 25.00 40.00
5 Terry Labonte Kellogg's Mach V 25.00 60.00
10 Johnny Benson Valvoline 1996 Firebird 25.00 40.00
22 Ward Burton Cat 1970 Challenger 25.00 40.00
22 Ward Burton Cat 1971 GTX 25.00 40.00
22 Ward Burton Cat 1969 Charger 25.00 40.00
32 Ricky Craven Tide 1969 GTO 25.00 40.00
48 Jimmie Johnson Lowe's 1955 Chevy 25.00 40.00
48 Jimmie Johnson Lowe's 1966 Nova 25.00 40.00
48 Jimmie Johnson Lowe's '69 Camaro 25.00 40.00
01 Jerry Nadeau Army 1966 GTO 25.00 40.00

2004 Racing Champions Stock Rods 1:18

5 Terry Labonte Kellogg's '70 Chevelle 25.00 40.00
22 Scott Wimmer Caterpillar '71 Dodge Demon 25.00 50.00
25 Brian Vickers Ditech.com '67 Chevelle 25.00 40.00
25 Brian Vickers Ditech.com '69 Nova 25.00 40.00
48 Jimmie Johnson Lowe's '64 Impala SS 25.00 40.00

1991-92 Racing Champions 1:24

This series of 1:24 cars features some of the most expensive and toughest to find die cast pieces. The pieces were packaged in a black box and were distributed through retail outlets and hobby shops. The Kenny Wallace Dirt Devil car and the Cox Lumber car are the two toughest to come by.

1 Jeff Gordon Baby Ruth 1992 250.00 500.00
1 Rick Mast Majik Market 15.00 30.00
2 Rusty Wallace AC Delco 30.00 60.00
2 Rusty Wallace Pontiac Excitement 20.00 40.00
3 Dale Earnhardt Goodwrench with fender stickers 1992 75.00 150.00
3 Dale Earnhardt Goodwrench with tampo decals 1992 60.00 150.00
4 Ernie Irvan Kodak 10.00 20.00
5 Ricky Rudd Tide 20.00 40.00
6 Mark Martin Valvoline 25.00 50.00
7 Harry Gant Morema 30.00 50.00
7 No Driver Association Easy Off 30.00 50.00
7 No Driver Association French's 35.00 60.00
7 No Driver Association Gulf Lite 35.00 60.00
7 Jimmy Hensley Bojangles 30.00 50.00
7 Tommy Kendall Family Channel 20.00 60.00
7 Alan Kulwicki Hooters 1992 50.00 120.00
9 Joe Bessey AC Delco 400.00 600.00
9 Bill Elliott Melling 40.00 80.00
10 Derrike Cope Purolator 8.00 20.00
11 Bill Elliott Amoco 10.00 25.00
15 Geoff Bodine Motorcraft 8.00 20.00
15 Morgan Shepherd Motorcraft 8.00 20.00
16 Wally Dallenbach Jr. Roush Racing 1992 40.00 80.00
17 Darrell Waltrip Western Auto with fender stickers 10.00 25.00
17 Darrell Waltrip Western Auto with tampo decals 12.50 30.00
18 Dale Jarrett Interstate Batteries 30.00 70.00
18 Gregory Trammell Melling 8.00 20.00
21 Dale Jarrett Citgo 1991 50.00 90.00
21 Morgan Shepherd Citgo 10.00 20.00
22 Sterling Marlin Maxwell House 1991 35.00 60.00
25 Ken Schrader No Sponsor with Large K on roof 15.00 30.00
25 Ken Schrader No Sponsor 8.00 20.00
25 Bill Venturini Rain X 300.00 500.00
28 Davey Allison Havoline 1992 50.00 125.00
30 Michael Waltrip Pennzoil 8.00 20.00
33 Harry Gant No Sponsor Oldsmobile 20.00 40.00
33 Harry Gant No Sponsor Chevrolet 15.00 30.00
36 Kenny Wallace Cox Lumber 100.00 200.00
36 Kenny Wallace Dirt Devil 150.00 300.00
42 Bobby Hillin Jr. Mello Yello 1991 20.00 40.00
42 Kyle Petty Mello Yello 15.00 30.00
42/43 Kyle Petty Mello Yello Richard Petty STP 2-cars 1:24 60.00 100.00
43 Richard Petty STP 1991 30.00 50.00
43 Richard Petty STP with Blue Wheels 1992 15.00 25.00
49 Stanley Smith Ameritron Batteries 125.00 250.00
51 No Driver Association Racing Champions 90.00 160.00
55 Ted Musgrave Jasper 500.00 800.00
59 Andy Belmont FDP Brakes 250.00 500.00
60 Mark Martin Winn Dixie with Red Numbers 100.00 175.00
60 Mark Martin Winn Dixie with White Numbers 60.00 100.00
63 Chuck Bown Nescafe 350.00 600.00
66 Jimmy Hensley TropArtic 10.00 22.00
66 Chad Little TropArtic 8.00 20.00
66 No Driver Association TropArtic Red Car 12.50 25.00
66 Cale Yarborough TropArtic 15.00 40.00
68 Bobby Hamilton Country Time 20.00 40.00
70 J.D. McDuffie Son's Auto 8.00 20.00
71 Dave Marcis Big Apple Market 25.00 60.00
75 Butch Miller Food Country 250.00 400.00
83 Lake Speed Purex 125.00 175.00
87 Joe Nemechek Texas Pete 250.00 400.00
94 Terry Labonte Sunoco 50.00 120.00
94 Terry Labonte Sunoco Arrow on decal points to tire 75.00 150.00

1992 Racing Champions IROC 1:24

11 True Value IROC Black
19 Rusty Wallace True Value IROC Purple 60.00 100.00

1992 Racing Champions Pit Stop 1:24

Each if these "Pit Stop Show Case" scenes were packaged in a hard plastic case inside a Racing Champions black window box or promo box printed in sponsor colors. Each car was mounted on a black base with plastic crew members surrounding the car as if it were in a pit stall during a race.

3 Dale Earnhardt Goodwrench 50.00 100.00
5 Ricky Rudd Tide 20.00 40.00
7 Alan Kulwicki Hooters 45.00 80.00
9 Bill Elliott Melling blue 20.00 40.00
17 Darrell Waltrip Western Auto Promo 10.00 25.00
42 Kyle Petty Mello Yello 20.00 40.00
43 Richard Petty STP 20.00 40.00

1992-94 Racing Champions Super Collector's Set 1:24/43/64

Each boxed set consists of a grouping of 1:24, 1:43, and/or 1:64 scale die-cast cars. A 1:64 and/or 1:87 die-cast Transporter was also included in some sets to round out the package. Each set was packaged together in a black clear window box.

Entry		
3 Dale Earnhardt Goodwrench 2-cars 1:24, 1:64 and 2-Transporters 1:64, 1:87	30.00	60.00
3 Dale Earnhardt Goodwrench 3-cars 1:24, 1:43, 1:64 and a 1:64 Transporter	35.00	60.00
5 Ricky Rudd Tide 2-cars 1:24 and 1:64 and 2-Transporters 1:64, 1:87	12.50	30.00
7 Alan Kulwicki Hooters 3-cars 1:24, 1:43, 1:64 and a 1:64 Transporter	40.00	80.00
28 Davey Allison Havoline 2-cars 1:24, 1:64 and 2-Transporters	15.00	40.00
28 Davey Allison Havoline 3-cars 1:24, 1:43, 1:64 and a 1:64 Transporter	25.00	50.00
30 Michael Waltrip Pennzoil 3-cars 1:24/64/87 and 2-Transporters	20.00	40.00
33 Harry Gant Leo Jackson 3-cars: 1:24/43/64 & Transporter 1994	15.00	40.00
43 Richard Petty STP Fan Tour 2-cars 1:24, 1:43 & Transporter 1992	10.00	25.00
43 Richard Petty STP 3-cars 1:24, 1:43, 1:64 and a 1:64 Transporter 1992	20.00	50.00
66 Cale Yarborough Phillips 66 3-cars 1:24/64/87 and 2-Transporters	20.00	40.00
70 J.D. McDuffie Son's Auto Supply 3-cars 1:24, 1:43, 1:64 and 1:64 transporter	20.00	40.00

1992-94 Racing Champions Banks 1:24

These 1:24 scale cars were prodcued as banks with a slot in the back window to slip your money into. The cars, as with most die cast banks, have blacked in windows. Most were issued in a small solid red box with a black #51 car pictured on the outside. A sticker can often be found on the bottom of the box with a brief description of the car found inside along with the production run total.

Entry		
0 Dick McCabe Fisher Snow Plows	18.00	30.00
1 Ford Manufacturers/5000 1992	10.00	20.00
1 Rick Mast Precision Products	12.50	25.00
2 Ward Burton Hardee's/5000 1992	20.00	35.00
2 Ricky Craven DuPont	15.00	25.00
2 Rusty Wallace Ford Motorsports	20.00	35.00
2 Rusty Wallace Pontiac Excitement/2500	100.00	200.00
3 Dale Earnhardt Goodwrench 1993 Mom-n-Pop's rear fender	50.00	120.00
3 Dale Earnhardt Goodwrench Western Steer on fender/10,000 1993	75.00	150.00
3 Dale Earnhardt Goodwrench/10,000 with numbered box 1992	75.00	150.00
3 Dale Earnhardt Goodwrench no serial #'d box 1992	40.00	100.00
3 Dale Earnhardt Goodwrench with Snap On	75.00	150.00
3 Dale Earnhardt Goodwrench Sports Image Mom-n-Pop's on rear fender 1994	50.00	120.00
4 Ernie Irvan Kodak	20.00	35.00
4 Sterling Marlin Kodak	18.00	30.00
4 Sterling Marlin Kodak Fun Saver	18.00	30.00
5 Terry Labonte Kellogg's	25.00	50.00
5 Ricky Rudd Tide/7500 1992	25.00	50.00
6 Mark Martin Valvoline	18.00	30.00
6 Mark Martin Valvoline Reese's	18.00	30.00
7 Geoff Bodine Exide	10.00	25.00
7 Harry Gant Black Flag/2500 1994	30.00	45.00
7 Harry Gant Easy Off/2500 1993	25.00	45.00
7 Harry Gant French's/1994	30.00	45.00
7 Harry Gant Gulf Lite	30.00	45.00
7 Harry Gant Manheim	30.00	45.00
7 Harry Gant Morema	30.00	45.00
7 Harry Gant Woolite/2500 1993	25.00	45.00
7 Jimmy Hensley Bojangles	15.00	25.00
7 Tommy Kendall Family Channel	18.00	30.00
7 Alan Kulwicki Army 1994	30.00	80.00
7 Alan Kulwicki Hooters/10,000 1992	100.00	200.00
7 Alan Kulwicki Zerex/5000 1993	50.00	100.00
8 Sterling Marlin Raybestos	12.50	25.00
8 Kenny Wallace TIC Financial	12.50	25.00
10 Ricky Rudd Tide	20.00	35.00
10 Jimmy Spencer Kleenex/2825 1992	50.00	100.00
11 Bill Elliott Amoco	25.00	40.00
11 Bill Elliott Bud/7500 1993	30.00	50.00
11 Bill Elliott Bud Busch/5000 1993	25.00	50.00
11 Bill Elliott Budweiser Hardy Boys car	25.00	40.00
12 Clifford Allison Sports Image	25.00	40.00
12 Jimmy Spencer Meineke	35.00	60.00
14 John Andretti Kanawaha	18.00	30.00
14 Terry Labonte MW Windows/2500 1994	60.00	100.00
15 Geoff Bodine Motorcraft	10.00	25.00
15 Lake Speed Quality Care	12.50	25.00
16 Chad Chaffin Dr. Die Cast	15.00	25.00
16 Ted Musgrave Family Channel	15.00	25.00
17 Darrell Waltrip Tide Orange paint scheme	30.00	50.00
17 Darrell Waltrip Tide Primer gray car	20.00	40.00
17 Darrell Waltrip Western Auto	90.00	150.00
18 Dale Jarrett Interstate Batteries/10,000 1993	40.00	75.00
20 Randy LaJoie Fina/2500 1994	15.00	30.00
20 Joe Ruttman Fina	20.00	35.00
20 Joe Ruttman Fina 520 made	25.00	40.00
21 Morgan Shepherd Cheerwine	18.00	30.00
21 Morgan Shepherd Citgo	12.50	25.00
22 Bobby Labonte Maxwell House/7500 1993	50.00	100.00
23 Chad Little Bayer	8.00	20.00
24 Jeff Gordon DuPont/10,000 1993	75.00	150.00
24 Jeff Gordon DuPont Brickyard Win/5024 1994	60.00	120.00
24 Jeff Gordon DuPont Coca-Cola 600 Win 1994	100.00	200.00
24 Jeff Gordon DuPont Snickers on deck lid 1994	40.00	80.00
25 Hermie Sadler Virginia is for Lovers	12.50	25.00
26 Brett Bodine Quaker State	10.00	25.00
27 Hut Stricklin McDonald's	18.00	30.00
28 Davey Allison Havoline black and white/28,000 1992	30.00	50.00
28 Davey Allison Havoline black&white and gold/5000 1993	40.00	80.00
28 Davey Allison Havoline black 1993	50.00	120.00
28 Ernie Irvan Havoline	25.00	40.00
28 Ernie Irvan Mac Tools/7541 1993	25.00	40.00
28 Davey Allison Havoline Mac Tools/5000 1992	50.00	120.00
30 Michael Waltrip Pennzoil	12.50	25.00
31 Steve Grissom Channellock	12.50	25.00
31 Tom Peck Channellock	12.50	25.00
33 Harry Gant Farewell Tour	20.00	35.00
33 Harry Gant Leo Jackson	15.00	25.00
33 Harry Gant Manheim Auctions	50.00	75.00
33 Harry Gant Manheim Auctions Autographed	75.00	125.00
33 Bobby Labonte Dentyne/2500 1994	40.00	80.00
34 Mike McLaughlin Fiddle Faddle	12.50	25.00
35 Shawna Robinson Polaroid Captiva	30.00	80.00
38 Elton Sawyer Ford Credit	15.00	25.00
41 Ernie Irvan Mac Tools	25.00	40.00
42 Kyle Petty Mello Yello/5000 1993	25.00	40.00
43 Rodney Combs French's Black Flag 1994	40.00	80.00
43 Wally Dallenbach Jr. STP	12.50	25.00
43 Richard Petty STP	30.00	50.00
44 David Green Slim Jim/2500 1994	15.00	30.00
44 Bobby Hillin Jr. Buss Fuses	15.00	25.00
44 Rick Wilson STP	15.00	25.00
46 Shawna Robinson Polaroid	25.00	60.00
51 Racing Champions/3000 1992	50.00	100.00
52 Ken Schrader AC Delco	15.00	25.00
52 Ken Schrader Morema	20.00	35.00
54 Robert Pressley Manheim Auctions	20.00	35.00
55 Ted Musgrave US Air/2500 1993	30.00	50.00
59 Andy Belmont Metal Arrester	15.00	30.00
59 Robert Pressley Alliance	45.00	70.00
59 Dennis Setzer Alliance	30.00	45.00
60 Mark Martin Winn Dixie of 5000 1993	45.00	75.00
60 Mark Martin Winn Dixie of 10,000	20.00	35.00
63 Jim Bown Lysol	12.50	25.00
70 J.D. McDuffie Son's Auto/2500 1994	12.50	25.00
71 Dave Marcis Earnhardt Chevrolet/2500 1993	35.00	60.00
75 Todd Bodine Factory Stores	12.50	25.00
77 Greg Sacks US Air	20.00	35.00
83 Sherry Blakely Ramses	18.00	30.00
87 Joe Nemechek Dentyne	15.00	25.00
92 Larry Pearson Stanley Tools	12.50	25.00
93 Racing Champions Collector's Club/1440 1993	50.00	100.00
93 Rockingham/2500 1993	20.00	35.00
94 Brickyard 400 Special	20.00	35.00
97 Joe Bessey Auto Palace	18.00	30.00
97 Joe Bessey Johnson AC Delco	18.00	30.00
98 Derrike Cope Bojangles Black car	20.00	35.00
98 Derrike Cope Bojangles Yellow car	20.00	35.00
98 Jody Ridley Ford Motorsports	25.00	40.00

1993 Racing Champions 1:24

These 1:24 scale cars come in a Red box and feature some of the top names in racing.

Entry		
2 Davey Allison True Value IROC/5000	60.00	150.00
2 Rusty Wallace Pontiac Excitement	15.00	25.00
3 Dale Earnhardt Goodwrench Goodyear in White	60.00	120.00
3 Dale Earnhardt Goodwrench Goodyear in Yellow	40.00	100.00
3 Dale Earnhardt Goodwrench Mom-n-Pop's on fender	60.00	150.00
4 Ernie Irvan Kodak Gold Film	8.00	20.00
4 Ernie Irvan Kodak Gold Film Promo sticker decals	50.00	100.00
4 Ernie Irvan Kodak Gold Plus	8.00	20.00
4 Ernie Irvan Kodak Gold Plus Promo sticker decals	50.00	100.00
5 Ricky Rudd Tide Exxon	8.00	20.00
5 Ricky Rudd Tide Valvoline	8.00	20.00
6 Mark Martin Valvoline	15.00	30.00
7 Alan Kulwicki Hooters	50.00	100.00
7/42 Alan Kulwick Hooters Kyle Petty Mello Yello 2-Car set	90.00	150.00
8 Sterling Marlin Raybestos	8.00	20.00
8 Sterling Marlin Raybestos Douglas Batteries	12.00	22.00
10 Bill Elliott True Value IROC/5000	40.00	75.00
11 Bill Elliott Amoco	12.00	20.00
12 Jimmy Spencer Meineke	8.00	20.00
14 Terry Labonte Kellogg's	60.00	120.00
15 Geoff Bodine Motorcraft	8.00	20.00
17 Darrell Waltrip Western Auto	8.00	20.00
18 Dale Jarrett Interstate Batteries	20.00	40.00
21 Morgan Shepherd Citgo red pillar post	8.00	20.00
21 Morgan Shepherd Citgo Tri-color Pillar Post	8.00	20.00
22 Bobby Labonte Maxwell House	75.00	150.00
24 Jeff Gordon DuPont	60.00	150.00
25 Ken Schrader No Sponsor	20.00	40.00
26 Brett Bodine Quaker State	8.00	20.00
27 Hut Stricklin McDonald's	8.00	20.00
28 Davey Allison Havoline Black and Gold paint scheme	40.00	80.00
28 Davey Allison Havoline Black Orange	25.00	60.00
28 Davey Allison Havoline Black and White paint scheme	60.00	120.00
30 Michael Waltrip Pennzoil	15.00	35.00
42 Kyle Petty Mello Yello	15.00	30.00
44 Rick Wilson STP	15.00	30.00
49 Stanley Smith Ameritron Batteries	75.00	125.00
59 Andy Belmont FDP Brakes	60.00	100.00
60 Mark Martin Winn Dixie	20.00	50.00
75 No Driver Association Auto Value	15.00	25.00
75 No Driver Association Factory Stores	8.00	20.00
87 Joe Nemechek Dentyne	20.00	40.00
96 Auto Value Promo	10.00	25.00
98 Derrike Cope Bojangles	12.50	25.00

1993 Racing Champions Pit Stop 1:24

Each if these "Pit Stop Show Case" scenes were packaged in a hard plastic case inside a Racing Champions red window box. Each car was mounted on a black base with plastic crew members surrounding the car as if it were in a pit stall during a race.

Entry		
7 A.Kulwicki Hooters	45.00	80.00
24 Jeff Gordon DuPont	45.00	80.00
27 Hut Stricklin McDonald's	15.00	30.00

1994 Racing Champions 1:24

These 1:24 scale cars were issued primarily in red clear window display boxes but a few could be found in race team colors. The year of issue can be found on the back of the box and most were distributed through hobby and retail outlets.

Entry		
1 Rick Mast Percision Products	7.50	15.00
2 Ricky Craven DuPont	20.00	40.00
2 Rusty Wallace Ford Motorsports Black Ford Oval	10.00	20.00
2 Rusty Wallace Ford Motorsports Blue Ford Oval	10.00	20.00
3 Dale Earnhardt Goodwrench	100.00	200.00
4 Sterling Marlin Kodak	8.00	20.00
5 Terry Labonte Kellogg's	40.00	80.00
6 Mark Martin Valvoline Reese's	20.00	40.00
7 Geoff Bodine Exide	7.50	15.00
7 Harry Gant Manheim	15.00	25.00
7 Alan Kulwicki Zerex	40.00	80.00
8 Jeff Burton Raybestos with Goodyear tires	20.00	40.00
8 Jeff Burton Raybestos with Hoosier tires	15.00	40.00
8 Kenny Wallace TIC Financial	7.50	15.00
12 Clifford Allison Sports Image	30.00	60.00
14 John Andretti Kanawaha	20.00	40.00
14 Terry Labonte MW Windows	60.00	125.00
15 Lake Speed Quality Care	7.50	15.00
16 Chad Chaffin Dr. Die Cast	7.50	15.00
16 Ted Musgrave Family Channel	7.50	15.00
17 Darrell Waltrip Western Auto	7.50	15.00
18 Dale Jarrett Interstate Batteries	35.00	60.00
19 Loy Allen Hooters	12.50	25.00
20 Bobby Hillin Jr. Fina	7.50	15.00
20 Randy LaJoie Fina	7.50	15.00
21 Morgan Shepherd Citgo	7.50	15.00
22 Bobby Labonte Maxwell House	60.00	100.00
23 Chad Little Bayer	7.50	15.00
23 Hut Stricklin Smokin' Joe's in plastic case	50.00	120.00
24 Jeff Gordon DuPont with plain red deck lid	75.00	125.00
24 Jeff Gordon DuPont Snickers on deck lid	75.00	125.00
24 Jeff Gordon DuPont Coca-Cola 600 Win in plastic case/2000	90.00	150.00
24 Jeff Gordon DuPont Brickyard Special in purple box/10,024	40.00	80.00
25 Ken Schrader GMAC	25.00	40.00
26 Brett Bodine Quaker State	7.50	15.00
27 Jimmy Spencer McDonald's	30.00	75.00
28 Ernie Irvan Havoline	12.00	22.00
30 Michael Waltrip Pennzoil	12.50	25.00
31 Steve Grissom Channellock	7.50	15.00
31 Tom Peck Channellock	7.50	15.00
33 Harry Gant No Sponsor	7.50	15.00
33 Harry Gant Leo Jackson Motorsports	7.50	15.00
33 Harry Gant Manheim Auctions	20.00	40.00
33 Bobby Labonte Dentyne	90.00	150.00
34 Mike McLaughlin Fiddle Faddle	7.50	15.00
35 Shawna Robinson Polaroid Captiva	20.00	35.00
38 Elton Sawyer Ford Credit	7.50	15.00
40 Bobby Hamilton Kendall	7.50	15.00
42 Kyle Petty Mello Yello	10.00	20.00
44 David Green Slim Jim	7.50	15.00
44 Bobby Hillin Jr. Buss Fuses	7.50	15.00
46 Shawna Robinson Polaroid	20.00	35.00
52 Ken Schrader AC Delco	7.50	15.00
54 Robert Pressley Manheim	7.50	15.00
59 Andy Belmont Metal Arrester	7.50	15.00
59 Dennis Setzer Alliance	18.00	30.00
60 Mark Martin Winn Dixie	20.00	40.00
63 Jim Bown Lysol	7.50	15.00
70 J.D. McDuffie Son's Auto	7.50	15.00
75 Todd Bodine Factory Stores of America	7.50	15.00
79 Dave Rezendes Lipton Tea	7.50	15.00
83 Sherry Blakely Ramses	15.00	40.00
92 Larry Pearson Stanley Tools	7.50	15.00
94 No Driver Association Auto Value	15.00	25.00
94 No Driver Association Brickyard 400 Purple Box	15.00	30.00
97 Joe Bessey Johnson	7.50	15.00
98 Derrike Cope ingerhut	7.50	15.00
0 Dick McCabe Fisher Snow Plows	12.00	20.00

1995 Racing Champions Preview 1:24

This is the first time Racing Champions did a preview series for its 1:24 scale series. The cars were a preview of some of the cars that raced in the 1995 season.

Entry		
2 Rusty Wallace Ford Motorsports	10.00	18.00
6 Mark Martin Valvoline	10.00	18.00
7 Geoff Bodine Exide with Goodyear tires	6.00	15.00
7 Geoff Bodine Exide with Hoosier tires	6.00	15.00
10 Ricky Rudd Tide	12.50	25.00
57 Jason Keller Budget Gourmet	9.00	18.00
63 Curtis Markham Lysol	9.00	18.00
94 Bill Elliott McDonald's	10.00	18.00
98 Jeremy Mayfield Fingerhut	25.00	50.00

1995 Racing Champions 1:24

This series of 1:24 cars features both Winston Cup cars and Busch Grand National cars. Featured in the series is Bill Elliott's Thunderbat car. The car was a promotion done in conjunction with the movie Batman Forever.

Entry		
2 Ricky Craven DuPont	15.00	30.00
2 Rusty Wallace Ford Motorsports	10.00	20.00
4 Sterling Marlin Kodak	10.00	25.00
4 Jeff Purvis Kodak Fun Saver	7.50	15.00
5 Terry Labonte Kellogg's	15.00	30.00
6 Tommy Houston Red Devil	7.50	15.00
6 Mark Martin Valvoline	10.00	20.00
7 Geoff Bodine Exide	7.50	15.00
7 Stevie Reeves Clabber Girl	7.50	15.00
8 Jeff Burton Raybestos	20.00	40.00
8 Kenny Wallace Red Dog Promo	40.00	80.00
8 Bobby Dotter Hyde Tools	7.50	15.00
10 Ricky Rudd Tide	7.50	15.00
12 Derrike Cope Mane N' Tail	7.50	15.00
15 Dick Trickle Quality Care	7.50	15.00
16 Ted Musgrave Family Channel	7.50	15.00
17 Darrell Waltrip Western Auto	10.00	20.00
18 Bobby Labonte Interstate Batteries	30.00	60.00
21 Morgan Shepherd Citgo	7.50	15.00

23 Chad Little Bayer	7.50	15.00
24 Jeff Gordon DuPont	40.00	80.00
24 Jeff Gordon DuPont Signature Series	45.00	90.00
24 Jeff Gordon DuPont Signature Series Hood Open	60.00	150.00
25 Johnny Rumley Big Johnson	12.50	25.00
25 Ken Schrader Budweiser	10.00	20.00
26 Steve Kinser Quaker State	15.00	30.00
27 Loy Allen Hooters	15.00	30.00
28 Dale Jarrett Havoline	35.00	60.00
29 Steve Grissom Meineke	7.50	15.00
34 Mike McLaughlin French's	18.00	30.00
37 John Andretti K-Mart	15.00	30.00
38 Elton Sawyer Red Carpet Lease	7.50	15.00
40 Patty Moise Dial Purex	15.00	30.00
41 Ricky Craven Larry Hedrick Mtrsprts.	7.50	15.00
44 David Green Slim Jim	7.50	15.00
44 Jeff Purvis Jackaroo	7.50	15.00
51 Jim Bown Luck's	7.50	15.00
60 Mark Martin Winn Dixie	12.50	25.00
71 Kevin Lepage Vermont Teddy Bear	15.00	30.00
71 Dave Marcis Olive Garden	30.00	75.00
75 Todd Bodine Factory Stores of America	7.50	15.00
81 Kenny Wallace TIC Financial	7.50	15.00
87 Joe Nemechek Burger King	7.50	15.00
88 Ernie Irvan Havoline	15.00	25.00
90 Mike Wallace Heilig-Meyers	7.50	15.00
94 Bill Elliott McDonald's	10.00	20.00
94 Bill Elliott McDonald's Thunderbat Promo	25.00	50.00
95 Auto Value Promo	7.50	15.00

1995 Racing Champions Banks 1:24

This series of 1:24 cars offers the collector the option to use them as bank. Each car has a slot in the rear window or in some cases the deck lid.

2 Rusty Wallace Ford Motorsports	15.00	25.00
4 Sterling Marlin Kodak	15.00	30.00
5 Terry Labonte Kellogg's	15.00	25.00
6 Mark Martin Valvoline	15.00	25.00
7 Geoff Bodine Exide	12.00	25.00
8 Jeff Burton Raybestos	15.00	25.00
8 Kenny Wallace Red Dog Hood Open Promo	25.00	40.00
12 Derrike Cope Straight Arrow	15.00	25.00
16 Ted Musgrave Family Channel	16.00	25.00
24 Jeff Gordon DuPont/10,000	30.00	60.00
24 Jeff Gordon DuPont Signature Series Hood Open	40.00	80.00
24 Jeff Gordon DuPont Signature Series 1995 Champion Hood Open	40.00	80.00
25 Ken Schrader Budweiser	16.00	25.00
25 Ken Schrader Budweiser Hood Open	15.00	30.00
27 Loy Allen Hooters	16.00	25.00
28 Dale Jarrett Havoline Hood Open	30.00	50.00
32 Dale Jarrett Mac Tools/4000	30.00	50.00
37 John Andretti K-Mart Hood Open Promo	20.00	35.00
44 David Green Slim Jim	10.00	25.00
59 Dennis Setzer Alliance	15.00	30.00
60 Mark Martin Winn Dixie/10,000	20.00	35.00
74 Johnny Benson Lipton Tea Hood Open	25.00	40.00
88 Ernie Irvan Texaco Hood Open	25.00	40.00
94 Bill Elliott McDonald's	15.00	30.00
94 Bill Elliott McDonald's Thunderbat	25.00	50.00

1995 Racing Champions Pit Stop 1:24

24 Jeff Gordon DuPont Signature Series	30.00	60.00
74 Johnny Benson Lipton 1995 BGN Champion	15.00	40.00

1995 Racing Champions SuperTrucks 1:24

This 1:24 scale series is representitive of the many different trucks that raced in the inaugural SuperTruck series. Each was pacakged in a red and white clear window display box with the year of issue printed on the top.

1 P.J. Jones Sears Diehard Chevrolet	7.50	15.00
1 P.J. Jones Vessells Ford	7.50	15.00
2 David Ashley Southern California Ford	7.50	15.00
3 Mike Skinner Goodwrench	10.00	25.00
6 Mike Bliss Ultra Wheels	7.50	15.00
6 Butch Gilliland Ultra Wheels	7.50	15.00
6 Rick Carelli Total Petroleum	7.50	15.00
7 Geoff Bodine Exide	7.50	15.00
7 Geoff Bodine Exide Salsa	7.50	15.00
7 Dave Rezendes Exide	7.50	15.00
8 Mike Bliss Ultra Wheels	7.50	15.00
10 Stan Fox Made for You	7.50	15.00
12 Randy MacCachren Venable	7.50	15.00
18 Johnny Benson Hella Lights	7.50	15.00
21 Tobey Butler Ortho with Green Nose piece	7.50	15.00
21 Tobey Butler Ortho with Yellow Nose piece	7.50	15.00
23 T.J. Clark ASE with Blue scheme	7.50	15.00
23 T.J. Clark ASE with White scheme	7.50	15.00
24 Jeff Gordon DuPont	20.00	40.00
24 Jeff Gordon DuPont Signature Series	15.00	30.00
24 Scott Lagasse DuPont	10.00	20.00
24 Scott Lagasse DuPont Bank	12.00	25.00
37 Bob Strait Target Expediting	7.50	15.00
38 Sammy Swindell Channellock	7.50	15.00
51 Kerry Teague Rosenblum Racing	7.50	15.00
52 Ken Schrader AC Delco	7.50	15.00
54 Steve McEachern McEachern Racing	7.50	15.00
61 Todd Bodine Roush Racing	7.50	15.00
75 Bill Sedgwick Spears Motorsports	7.50	15.00
83 Steve Portenga Coffee Critic	7.50	15.00
95 No Driver Association Brickyard 400 Special	10.00	20.00
95 No Driver Association Brickyard 400 Special Bank	15.00	25.00
98 Butch Miller Raybestos	7.50	15.00

1996 Racing Champions Preview 1:24

This series of 1:24 die cast replicas featured a preview of some of the new paint jobs to run in the 1996 season. The Terry Labonte Bayer car is one of the first for this new car.

2 Ricky Craven DuPont	7.50	15.00
4 Sterling Marlin Kodak	8.00	20.00
5 Terry Labonte Kellogg's	8.00	20.00
5 Terry Labonte Bayer	8.00	20.00
6 Mark Martin Valvoline	8.00	20.00
7 Stevie Reeves Clabber Girl	7.50	15.00
9 Joe Bessey Delco Remy	7.50	15.00
9 Lake Speed SPAM	7.50	15.00
10 Ricky Rudd Tide	7.50	15.00
11 Brett Bodine Lowe's	7.50	15.00
12 Derrike Cope Mane N' Tail	7.50	15.00
14 Patty Moise Dial Purex	7.50	15.00
16 Ted Musgrave Family Channel	7.50	15.00
17 Darrell Waltrip Western Auto	7.50	15.00
18 Bobby Labonte Interstate Batteries	10.00	25.00
22 Ward Burton MBNA	7.50	15.00
24 Jeff Gordon DuPont	15.00	40.00
30 Johnny Benson Pennzoil	7.50	15.00
40 Tim Fedewa Kleenex	7.50	15.00
41 Ricky Craven Kodiak	10.00	25.00
47 Jeff Fuller Sunoco	7.50	15.00
51 Chuck Bown Lucks	7.50	15.00
52 Ken Schrader AC Delco	7.50	15.00
57 Jason Keller Slim Jim	7.50	15.00
74 Johnny Benson Lipton Tea	7.50	15.00
87 Joe Nemechek Burger King	10.00	25.00
90 Mike Wallace Heilig-Meyers	7.50	15.00
94 Bill Elliott McDonald's	8.00	20.00

1996 Racing Champions 1:24

The 1:24 scale cars that appear in this series are replicas of many of the cars that ran during the 1996 season. The Rusty Wallace Miller Genuine Draft car is one of the few times that Racing Champions has offered a collectible die cast that included a beer logo.

1 Rick Mast Hooter's	15.00	30.00
2 Ricky Craven DuPont	7.50	15.00
2 Rusty Wallace Miller Genuine Draft	18.00	30.00
2 Rusty Wallace Miller Splash Promo	12.50	25.00
2 Rusty Wallace Penske Racing	25.00	40.00
3 Mike Skinner Goodwrench	12.50	25.00
4 Sterling Marlin Kodak Back to Back Special	12.50	25.00
5 Terry Labonte Kellogg's	10.00	20.00
5 Terry Labonte Kellogg's Silver car	25.00	40.00
6 Tommy Houston Suburban Propane	7.50	15.00
6 Mark Martin Valvoline	12.50	25.00
6 Mark Martin Valvoline DuraBlend	50.00	90.00
7 Geoff Bodine QVC	7.50	15.00
8 Hut Stricklin Circuit City	7.50	15.00
9 Joe Bessey Delco Remy	7.50	15.00
9 Lake Speed SPAM	7.50	15.00
10 Ricky Rudd Tide	7.50	15.00
11 Brett Bodine Lowe's	7.50	15.00
11 Brett Bodine Lowe's 50th Anniversary Paint Scheme	15.00	40.00
14 Patty Moise Purex	7.50	15.00
15 Wally Dallenbach Hayes Modems	30.00	50.00
16 Ted Musgrave Primestar	7.50	15.00
17 Darrell Waltrip Parts America	7.50	15.00
18 Bobby Labonte Interstate Batteries	20.00	40.00
19 Loy Allen Healthsource	7.50	15.00
21 Michael Waltrip Citgo	7.50	15.00
22 Ward Burton MBNA	7.50	15.00
23 Chad Little John Deere	15.00	30.00
23 Chad Little John Deere in a John Deere Box	15.00	40.00
24 Jeff Gordon DuPont	30.00	60.00
24 Jeff Gordon DuPont 1995 Champion	30.00	60.00
24 Jeff Gordon DuPont Bristol Win in plastic case/2424	50.00	100.00
24 Jeff Gordon DuPont Darlington in plastic case/2424	50.00	100.00
24 Jeff Gordon DuPont The Kid in plastic case/2424	50.00	100.00
24 Jeff Gordon DuPont Pocono Win in plastic case/2424	50.00	100.00
25 Ken Schrader Budweiser	25.00	40.00
25 Ken Schrader Bud Olympic Chrome/400	125.00	250.00
25 Ken Schrader Hendrick Motorsports	7.50	15.00
28 Ernie Irvan Havoline	7.50	15.00
29 Steve Grissom Cartoon Network	7.50	15.00
29 Steve Grissom WCW	10.00	25.00
29 No Driver Association Scooby-Doo in Scooby Box	7.50	15.00
29 No Driver Association WCW Sting	7.50	15.00
30 Johnny Benson Pennzoil	7.50	15.00
31 Mike Skinner Realtree	30.00	80.00
34 Mike McLaughlin Royal Oak	7.50	15.00
37 John Andretti K-Mart	7.50	15.00
38 Dennis Setzer Lipton	7.50	15.00
40 Tim Fedewa Kleenex	7.50	15.00
40 Jim Sauter First Union	7.50	15.00
41 Ricky Craven Larry Hedrick Racing	7.50	15.00
41 Ricky Craven Kodiak in Acrylic case	25.00	50.00
41 Ricky Craven Manheim	7.50	15.00
43 Bobby Hamilton STP Anniversary 1972 Red Blue	10.00	20.00
43 Bobby Hamilton STP Anniversary 1972 Blue	10.00	20.00
43 Bobby Hamilton STP Anniversary 1979 Red Blue	10.00	20.00
43 Bobby Hamilton STP Anniversary 1984 Red Blue	10.00	20.00
43 Bobby Hamilton STP Anniversary 1996 Silver	12.50	25.00
43 Bobby Hamilton STP 5-trailer set	75.00	150.00
44 Bobby Labonte Shell	25.00	50.00
52 Ken Schrader AC Delco	7.50	15.00
57 Jason Keller Halloween Havoc	7.50	15.00
60 Mark Martin Winn Dixie	15.00	30.00
63 Curtis Markham Lysol	7.50	15.00
74 Johnny Benson Lipton Tea 1995 BGN Champion	7.50	15.00
75 Morgan Shepherd Remington	15.00	30.00
77 Bobby Hillin Jr. Jasper Engines	7.50	15.00
81 Kenny Wallace Square D	7.50	15.00
87 Joe Nemechek Burger King	30.00	60.00
88 Dale Jarrett Quality Care	7.50	15.00
90 Mike Wallace Duron	7.50	15.00
94 Ron Barfield New Holland	7.50	15.00
94 Bill Elliott McDonald's	8.00	18.00
94 Bill Elliott McDonald's Monopoly	10.00	20.00
96 Auto Value Promo	7.50	15.00
96 David Green Busch Chrome	100.00	250.00
96 David Green Busch Hobby	15.00	35.00
97 Chad Little Sterling Cowboy	7.50	15.00
99 Glenn Allen Luxaire	7.50	15.00
99 Jeff Burton Exide	7.50	15.00

1996 Racing Champions Banks 1:24

This series of 1:24 cars offers the collector the option to use them as bank. Each car has a slot in the rear window or in some cases the deck lid. These banks have blacked in windows.

6 Mark Martin Valvoline	16.00	25.00
23 Chad Little John Deere	20.00	40.00
29 Steve Grissom Cartoon Network	15.00	30.00
32 Dale Jarrett Band-Aid	30.00	60.00
47 Jeff Fuller Sunoco	16.00	25.00
51 Chuck Bown Lucks	10.00	25.00
94 Bill Elliott McDonald's	16.00	25.00
94 Bill Elliott McDonald's Monopoly	15.00	30.00

1996 Racing Champions Premier Banks 1:24

These 1:24 scale banks were distributed with the chrome banks through hobby outlets.

2 Rusty Wallace Penske	20.00	40.00
2 Rusty Wallace Penske Chrome/166	75.00	150.00
4 Sterling Marlin Kodak	20.00	50.00
4 Sterling Marlin Kodak Chrome/166	60.00	120.00
5 Terry Labonte Kellogg's	20.00	40.00
5 Terry Labonte Kellogg's Silver Chrome/166	200.00	400.00
6 Mark Martin Valvoline	20.00	40.00
6 Mark Martin Valvoline Chrome/166	175.00	350.00
10 Ricky Rudd Tide	20.00	40.00
10 Ricky Rudd Tide Chrome/166	60.00	120.00
11 Brett Bodine Lowe's 50th Anniversary	12.00	35.00
17 Darrell Waltrip Parts America	20.00	40.00
17 Darrell Waltrip Parts America Chrome/166	60.00	120.00
18 Bobby Labonte Interstate Batteries/1826	20.00	40.00
18 Bobby Labonte Interstate Batteries Chrome/166	60.00	120.00
24 Jeff Gordon DuPont/1830	25.00	50.00
24 Jeff Gordon DuPont Chrome/166	1000.00	1400.00
25 Ken Schrader Bud Olympic	25.00	50.00
25 Ken Schrader Bud Chrome/166	75.00	150.00
29 Steve Grissom Cartoon Network	20.00	40.00
29 Steve Grissom Cartoon Network Chrome/166	60.00	120.00
29 No Driver Association Scooby-Doo	20.00	40.00
29 No Driver Association Scooby-Doo Chrome/166	60.00	120.00
37 John Andretti K-Mart	20.00	40.00
37 John Andretti K-Mart Chrome/166	60.00	120.00
88 Dale Jarrett Quality Care	20.00	40.00
88 Dale Jarrett Quality Care Chrome/166	75.00	150.00
94 Bill Elliott McDonald's	20.00	40.00
94 Bill Elliott McDonald's Chrome/166	75.00	150.00
96 David Green Busch	15.00	40.00
96 David Green Busch Chrome/166	60.00	120.00

1996 Racing Champions Premier Hood Open 1:24

1 Rick Mast Hooter's	18.00	30.00
2 Ricky Craven DuPont	15.00	25.00
2 Rusty Wallace Miller Genuine Draft	25.00	40.00
5 Terry Labonte Bayer	30.00	60.00
5 Terry Labonte Kellogg's	25.00	35.00
5 Terry Labonte Kellogg's Silver Ironman	20.00	40.00
6 Mark Martin Valvoline	25.00	35.00
9 Joe Bessey Delco Remy	15.00	25.00
11 Brett Bodine Lowe's	10.00	25.00
11 Brett Bodine Lowe's 50th Anniversary Paint Scheme	8.00	20.00
15 Wally Dallenbach Hayes Modems	20.00	35.00
21 Michael Waltrip Citgo	15.00	30.00
23 Chad Little John Deere	15.00	40.00
24 Jeff Gordon DuPont 1995 Champion	30.00	60.00
28 Ernie Irvan Havoline	15.00	30.00
29 Steve Grissom Cartoon Network	12.50	25.00
29 Steve Grissom WCW	12.50	30.00
30 Johnny Benson Pennzoil	25.00	45.00
31 Mike Skinner Realtree	60.00	90.00
47 Jeff Fuller Sunoco	15.00	25.00
51 Jim Bown Lucks	15.00	25.00
52 Ken Schrader AC Delco	15.00	25.00
57 Jason Keller Slim Jim	15.00	30.00
60 Mark Martin Winn Dixie	25.00	35.00
74 Johnny Benson Lipton Tea 1995 BGN Champion	15.00	30.00
75 Morgan Shepherd Remington	20.00	35.00
88 Dale Jarrett Quality Care	15.00	30.00
94 Bill Elliott McDonald's	15.00	30.00
94 Bill Elliott McDonald's Monopoly	15.00	30.00
96 David Green Busch/1859	10.00	25.00

1996 Racing Champions Hood Open Banks 1:2

These 1:24 scale banks have open hood and were distribute through hobby and retail outlets.

2 Rusty Wallace Miller Genuine Draft	20.00	35.00
5 Terry Labonte Kellogg's Silver	20.00	35.00
21 Michael Waltrip Citgo	20.00	35.00
23 Chad Little John Deere	20.00	50.00
25 Ken Schrader Budweiser	20.00	35.00
57 Steve Seligman Matco Tools/5000	20.00	40.00
60 Mark Martin Winn Dixie Promo/10,000	25.00	40.00
75 Morgan Shepherd Remington	20.00	35.00
88 Dale Jarrett Quality Care	20.00	35.00
94 Bill Elliott McDonald's Monopoly	20.00	35.00

1996 Racing Champions SuperTrucks 1:24

Racing Champions continued their line of 1:24 SuperTrucks i 1996. This series features many of the circuit's first-tim drivers.

2 Mike Bliss ASE	10.00	20.00
2 Mike Bliss Super Wheels	10.00	20.00
3 Mike Skinner Goodwrench Premier	12.50	25.00
3 Mike Skinner Goodwrench Snap-On Promo/10,000	10.00	25.00
6 Rick Carelli Chesrown	10.00	20.00
7 Geoff Bodine QVC	10.00	20.00
14 Butch Gilliland Stropps	10.00	20.00
17 Bill Sedgwick Die Hard	10.00	20.00
19 Lance Norick Macklenburg-Duncan	10.00	20.00
20 Walker Evans Dana	10.00	20.00

21 Doug George Ortho 10.00 20.00
24 Jack Sprague Quaker State 10.00 20.00
29 Bob Keselowski Winnebago 10.00 20.00
30 Jimmy Hensley Mopar 10.00 20.00
34 Bob Brevak Concor 10.00 20.00
43 Rich Bickle Cummins 10.00 20.00
44 Bryan Refner 1-800-Collect 10.00 20.00
52 Ken Schrader AC Delco 10.00 20.00
57 Robbie Pyle Aisyn 10.00 20.00
75 Bobby Gill Spears 10.00 20.00
78 Mike Chase Petron Plus 10.00 20.00
83 Steve Portenga Coffee Critic 10.00 20.00
96 DeVilbiss Superfinish 200 Promo 15.00 30.00
98 Butch Miller Raybestos 10.00 20.00

1997 Racing Champions Preview 1:24

This series of 1:24 die cast replicas featured a preview at some of the new paint jobs to run in the 1997 season. The Rick Mast Remington car and the Robert Pressley Scooby Doo car features two of the numerous driver changes for the 97 Winston Cup season.

4 Sterling Marlin Kodak 8.00 18.00
5 Terry Labonte Kellogg's 8.00 18.00
6 Mark Martin Valvoline 8.00 18.00
10 Ricky Rudd Tide 7.50 15.00
18 Bobby Labonte Interstate Batteries 8.00 18.00
21 Michael Waltrip Citgo 7.50 15.00
24 Jeff Gordon DuPont 10.00 20.00
28 Ernie Irvan Havoline 7.50 15.00
29 Robert Pressley Scooby-Doo 7.50 15.00
30 Johnny Benson Pennzoil 7.50 15.00
75 Rick Mast Remington 7.50 15.00
94 Bill Elliott McDonald's 8.00 18.00

1997 Racing Champions 1:24

The 1:24 scale cars that appear in this series are replicas of many of the cars that ran in the 1996 season. The series is highlighted by the Terry Labonte Kellogg's car commemorating his 1996 Winston Cup Championship. This car is available in two variations: standard and hood open. The Lake Speed University of Nebraska car is believed to be in short supply because of the dissolved team sponsorship. It is also believed to be available in a red tampo and black tampo version.

1 Hermie Sadler DeWalt 7.50 15.00
1 Morgan Shepherd Delco Remy Crusin' America 7.50 15.00
1 Morgan Shepherd R&L Carriers 7.50 15.00
2 Ricky Craven Raybestos 7.50 15.00
2 Rusty Wallace Penske 7.50 15.00
4 Sterling Marlin Kodak 8.00 20.00
5 Terry Labonte Bayer 15.00 25.00
5 Terry Labonte Kellogg's 8.00 20.00
5 Terry Labonte Kellogg's 1996 Champion Premier/9996 15.00 25.00
5 Terry Labonte Kellogg's 1996 Champion Hood Open 25.00 40.00
5 Terry Labonte Kellogg's 1996 Champion Bank 30.00 45.00
5 Terry Labonte Kellogg's '96 Champion Chrome Bank/166 250.00 400.00
5 Terry Labonte Kellogg's Tony 15.00 30.00
6 Tommy Houston Suburban Propane 7.50 15.00
6 Mark Martin Valvoline 8.00 20.00
7 Geoff Bodine QVC 7.50 15.00
7 Geoff Bodine QVC Gold Rush 10.00 25.00
8 Hut Stricklin Circuit City 7.50 15.00
9 Lake Speed University of Nebraska 40.00 80.00
9 Joe Bessey Power Team 7.50 15.00
9 Jeff Burton Track Gear 7.50 15.00
10 Phil Parsons Channellock 7.50 15.00
10 Ricky Rudd Tide 7.50 15.00
10 Ricky Rudd Tide Brickyard Win/2800 in solid box 30.00 50.00
11 Brett Bodine Close Call 7.50 15.00
11 Jimmy Foster Speedvision 7.50 15.00
16 Ted Musgrave Primestar 7.50 15.00
17 Darrell Waltrip Parts America 8.00 18.00
17 Darrell Waltrip Parts America Chrome 12.50 25.00
17 Darrell Waltrip Parts America Chrome Promo 15.00 25.00
18 Bobby Labonte Interstate Batt. 7.50 15.00
19 Gary Bradberry CSR 7.50 15.00
21 Michael Waltrip Citgo 7.50 15.00
24 Jeff Gordon DuPont 12.50 25.00
25 Ricky Craven Bud Lizard 15.00 30.00
25 Ricky Craven Bud Lizard 3-car set 50.00 75.00
25 Ricky Craven Hendrick 7.50 15.00
28 Ernie Irvan Havoline 7.50 15.00
28 Ernie Irvan Havoline 10th Anniversary Promo in solid box 15.00 30.00
28 Ernie Irvan Havoline 10th Anniversary Promo in window box 15.00 30.00
28 Ernie Irvan Havoline 10th Anniv.Chrome 125.00 250.00
28 Ernie Irvan Havoline 10th Anniversary Bank 25.00 40.00
28 Ernie Irvan Havoline 10th Anniversary Texaco Marketing Consultant Promo Bank/144 50.00 100.00
29 Jeff Green Tom and Jerry 7.50 15.00
29 Robert Pressley Cartoon Network 7.50 15.00
29 Elliott Sadler Phillips 66 12.50 25.00
30 Johnny Benson Pennzoil 7.50 15.00
32 Dale Jarrett White Rain 8.00 20.00
32 Dale Jarrett Gillette 8.00 20.00
33 Ken Schrader Petree Racing 7.50 15.00
34 Mike McLaughlin Royal Oak 7.50 15.00
36 Todd Bodine Stanley Tools 7.50 15.00
36 Derrike Cope Skittles 7.50 15.00
37 Jeremy Mayfield K-Mart 7.50 15.00
38 Elton Sawyer Barbasol 7.50 15.00
40 Robby Gordon Sabco Racing 7.50 15.00
41 Steve Grissom Larry Hedrick Racing 7.50 15.00
42 Joe Nemechek Bell South 7.50 15.00
46 Wally Dallenbach First Union 7.50 15.00
47 Jeff Fuller Sunoco 7.50 15.00
49 Kyle Petty nWo 15.00 30.00
57 Jason Keller Slim Jim 7.50 15.00
60 Mark Martin Winn Dixie Promo 15.00 35.00
72 Mike Dillon Detroit Gasket 7.50 15.00
74 Randy LaJoie Fina 7.50 15.00
74 Randy LaJoie Fina 1996 Busch Champion 15.00 30.00
75 Rick Mast Remington 7.50 15.00
75 Rick Mast Remington Camo 7.50 15.00
75 Rick Mast Remington Stren 7.50 15.00
87 Joe Nemechek Bell South 7.50 15.00
88 Kevin Lepage Hype 7.50 15.00
90 Dick Trickle Heilig-Meyers 7.50 15.00
91 Mike Wallace Spam 7.50 15.00
94 Bill Elliott McDonald's 8.00 18.00
94 Ron Barfield New Holland 7.50 15.00
94 Bill Elliott Mac Tonight 8.00 18.00
94 Bill Elliott Mac Tonight Bank 35.00 50.00
94 Bill Elliott Mac Tonight 3-car set 50.00 80.00
96 David Green Caterpillar 7.50 15.00
96 David Green Caterpillar Bank 20.00 40.00
96 David Green Caterpillar Promo 8.00 20.00
97 Donnie Allison Auto Value Promo 6.00 15.00
97 Chad Little John Deere 7.50 15.00
97 Chad Little John Deere Promo 12.50 30.00
97 No Driver Association Brickyard 500 12.00 20.00
99 Glenn Allen Luxaire 7.50 15.00
99 Jeff Burton Exide 7.50 15.00
00 Buckshot Jones Aqua Fresh Promo/1250 7.50 15.00

1997 Racing Champions Premier Banks 1:24

These 1:24 scale banks were distributed through hobby outlets.

2 Rusty Wallace Miller Lite/1992 20.00 40.00
2 Rusty Wallace Miller Lite Gold/166 100.00 200.00
6 Mark Martin Valvoline 20.00 40.00
6 Mark Martin Valvoline Gold/166 100.00 200.00
10 Ricky Rudd Tide/1992 20.00 40.00
10 Ricky Rudd Tide Gold/166 50.00 120.00
18 Bobby Labonte Interstate Batteries/4992 20.00 40.00
18 Bobby Labonte Interstate Batteries Gold/166 75.00 150.00
36 Derrike Cope Skittles 15.00 40.00
36 Derrike Cope Skittles Gold/166 40.00 100.00
40 Robby Gordon Coors Light 15.00 40.00
40 Robby Gordon Coors Light Gold/166 30.00 80.00
75 Rick Mast Remington 20.00 40.00
75 Rick Mast Remington Gold/166 40.00 100.00
94 Bill Elliott McDonald's 20.00 40.00
94 Bill Elliott McDonald's Gold/166 50.00 120.00

1997 Racing Champions Hood Open Banks 1:24

These 1:24 scale banks were distributed through retail outlets. Each car features an opening hood and was individually serial numbered.

2 Rusty Wallace Miller Lite Matco 35.00 60.00
2 Rusty Wallace Miller Lite Matco Chrome 75.00 150.00
5 Terry Labonte Kellogg's/4992 20.00 35.00
6 Mark Martin Valvoline/4992 20.00 35.00
10 Ricky Rudd Tide/4992 15.00 30.00
28 Ernie Irvan Havoline/4992 20.00 35.00
29 Robert Pressley Scooby-Doo/4992 15.00 30.00
36 Derrike Cope Skittles/4992 15.00 30.00
60 Mark Martin Winn Dixie Promo/5000 25.00 40.00
75 Rick Mast Remington/4992 15.00 30.00
94 Bill Elliott McDonald's/4992 20.00 35.00
96 David Green Caterpillar/4992 15.00 30.00
97 Chad Little John Deere/4992 15.00 30.00

1997 Racing Champions Stock Rods 1:24

These 1:24 scale cars are replicas of vintage stock rods with NASCAR paint schemes. Cars are listed by issue number instead of car number.

1 Darrell Waltrip Parts America 8.00 20.00
2 Sterling Marlin Kodak 8.00 20.00
3 Steve Grissom Larry Hedrick Racing 8.00 20.00
4 Ken Schrader Petree 8.00 20.00
5 Dennis Setzer Lance 8.00 20.00
6 Ricky Craven Hendrick 8.00 20.00
7 Ricky Rudd Tide 8.00 20.00
8 Rusty Wallace Penske 8.00 20.00
9 Rick Mast Remington 8.00 20.00
10 Terry Labonte Spooky Loops 25.00 40.00
11 Bill Elliott Mac Tonight 10.00 25.00
12 Bobby Hamilton Kodak 8.00 20.00
13 Terry Labonte Spooky Loops 10.00 25.00
14 Terry Labonte Kellogg's 10.00 25.00

1997 Racing Champions SuperTrucks 1:24

Racing Champions continued their line of 1:24 SuperTrucks in 1997. This series features many of the circuit's first-time drivers and Winston Cup regulars.

1 Michael Waltrip MW Windows 10.00 20.00
2 Mike Bliss Team ASE 6.00 15.00
4 Bill Elliott Team ASE 7.50 15.00
6 Rick Carelli ReMax 6.00 15.00
7 Tammy Kirk Loveable 6.00 15.00
15 Mike Cope Penrose 6.00 15.00
15 Mike Colabucci VISA 6.00 15.00
18 Johnny Benson Pennzoil 6.00 15.00
18 Mark Dokken Dana 6.00 15.00
19 Tony Raines Pennzoil 6.00 15.00
24 Jack Sprague Quaker State 6.00 15.00
29 Bob Keselowski Mopar 6.00 15.00
35 Dave Rezendes Ortho 6.00 15.00
49 Rodney Combs Lance 6.00 15.00
52 Tobey Butler Purolator 6.00 15.00
66 Bryan Refner Carlin 6.00 15.00
75 Dan Press Spears 6.00 15.00
80 Joe Ruttman LCI 6.00 15.00
86 Stacy Compton Valvoline 6.00 15.00
87 Joe Nemechek Bell South 6.00 15.00
92 Mark Kinser Rotary 6.00 15.00
98 Kenny Irwin Raybestos 10.00 25.00
99 Chuck Bown Exide 6.00 15.00
99 Jeff Burton Exide 6.00 15.00
99 Mark Martin Exide 100.00 175.00

1998 Racing Champions 1:24

The 1:24 scale cars that appear in this series are replicas of many of the cars that ran in the 1998 season. The Mark Martin Kosei car is one of the cars that highlights this series.

1 Little Debbie Promo/5000 20.00 40.00
4 Bobby Hamilton Kodak 7.50 15.00
5 Terry Labonte Blasted Fruit Loops 10.00 20.00
5 Terry Labonte Kellogg's 10.00 20.00
5 Terry Labonte Kellogg's Corny 10.00 20.00
5 Terry Labonte Kellogg's Corny Bank Promo 10.00 20.00
6 Joe Bessey Power Team 7.50 15.00
6 Mark Martin Eagle One 15.00 30.00
6 Mark Martin Kosei Promo/2500 125.00 200.00
6 Mark Martin Synpower 15.00 30.00
6 Mark Martin Valvoline 10.00 25.00
6 Mark Martin 3-car set/5000 Eagle One Synpower Valvoline 30.00 60.00
7 Geoff Bodine Phillips 10.00 25.00
8 Bobby Hillin Jr. Clean Shower Mac Attack Promo/10,000 12.50 25.00
8 Hut Stricklin Circuit City 7.50 15.00
9 Jeff Burton Track Gear 7.50 15.00
9 Lake Speed Birthday Cake 7.50 15.00
9 Lake Speed Huckleberry Hound 7.50 15.00
10 Ricky Rudd Tide 7.50 15.00
10 Ricky Rudd Tide Give Kids The World 7.50 15.00
11 Brett Bodine Paychex 7.50 15.00
13 Ted Christopher Whelen Promo 25.00 40.00
13 Jerry Nadeau First Plus 12.50 25.00
16 Ted Musgrave Primestar 7.50 15.00
17 Matt Kenseth Lycos 35.00 60.00
17 Darrell Waltrip Builders' Square 20.00 50.00
19 Tom Hubert Bradford White Water Heaters Promo 35.00 60.00
19 Tony Raines Yellow Freight Promo 15.00 40.00
20 Blaise Alexander Rescue Engine 12.50 30.00
20 Jimmy Spencer All Pro Stores Promo 25.00 50.00
21 Michael Waltrip Citgo 7.50 15.00
23 Jimmy Spencer No Bull in plastic case 40.00 100.00
26 Johnny Benson Betty Crocker 15.00 30.00
26 Johnny Benson Cheerios 10.00 20.00
28 Kenny Irwin Havoline 20.00 35.00
28 Kenny Irwin Havoline Bank Promo 10.00 25.00
29 Hermie Sadler DeWalt 7.50 15.00
30 Derrike Cope Gumout 7.50 15.00
30 Mike Cope Slim Jim 7.50 15.00
33 Tim Fedewa Kleenex Promo 7.50 15.00
33 Ken Schrader Petree 7.50 15.00
35 Todd Bodine Tabasco 10.00 20.00
36 Ernie Irvan M&M's 10.00 25.00
36 Ernie Irvan Skittles 8.00 18.00
36 Ernie Irvan Wildberry Skittles 7.50 15.00
40 Andy Belmont AOL Promo 30.00 50.00
40 Sterling Marlin Sabco 7.50 15.00
41 Steve Grissom Larry Hedrick Racing 7.50 15.00
42 Joe Nemechek BellSouth 7.50 15.00
43 John Andretti STP Firefighters Promo 2-car set w gold car/4343 15.00 40.00
46 Wally Dallenbach First Union 7.50 15.00
46 Deka Batteries Promo 15.00 30.00
50 NDA Budweiser Promo 12.50 25.00
50 Ricky Craven Hendrick 7.50 15.00
50 NASCAR 50th Anniversary 7.50 15.00
50 NDA Dr. Pepper 7.50 15.00
59 Robert Pressley Kingsford 7.50 15.00
60 Mark Martin Winn Dixie Most BGN Wins Promo/5000 40.00 75.00
64 Dick Trickle Schneider 25.00 50.00
66 Elliott Sadler Phillips 66 7.50 15.00
72 Mike Dillon Detroit Gasket 7.50 15.00
75 Rick Mast Remington 7.50 15.00
78 Gary Bradberry Pilot 7.50 15.00
84 North American Insurance Promo/2004 30.00 50.00
87 Joe Nemechek Bell South 7.50 15.00
88 Kevin Schwantz Ryder 7.50 15.00
90 Dick Trickle Heilig-Meyers 7.50 15.00
91 Dick Trickle Invinca-Shield Promo 10.00 20.00
94 Bill Elliott Big Mac/5000 40.00 100.00
94 Bill Elliott Happy Meal 7.50 15.00
94 Bill Elliott Mac Tonight 7.50 15.00
94 Bill Elliott McDonald's 7.50 15.00
94 Bill Elliott McDonald's with NASCAR 50th Anniv.logo on hood 7.50 15.00
96 David Green Caterpiller 7.50 15.00
96 David Green Caterpillar Promo 10.00 25.00
98 Rich Bickle Thorn Apple Valley 7.50 15.00
98 Marathon Oil Promo/5000 10.00 25.00
98 Greg Sacks Thorn Apple Valley 7.50 15.00
99 Glenn Allen Luxaire 7.50 15.00
99 Jeff Burton Exide 7.50 15.00
300 Darrell Waltrip Tim Flock Special 7.50 15.00
00 Buckshot Jones Bayer 7.50 15.00

1998 Racing Champions Authentics 1:24

These 1:24 scale cars mark the first in a series by Racing Champions. These cars and banks were distributed through hobby and trackside outlets. Each car is packaged in a special black snap case.

6 Mark Martin Eagle One/7100 25.00 60.00
6 Mark Martin Eagle One Bank 25.00 60.00
6 Mark Martin Synpower/7000 25.00 60.00
6 Mark Martin Synpower Mac Tools/4000 25.00 60.00
6 Mark Martin Synpower Bank/2500 25.00 60.00
6 Mark Martin Valvoline/7000 25.00 60.00
6 Mark Martin Valvoline Bank 25.00 60.00
16 Kevin Lepage Primestar/3100 15.00 40.00
16 Kevin Lepage Primestar Bank/1400 15.00 40.00
26 Johnny Benson Betty Crocker/4500 20.00 50.00
26 Johnny Benson Betty Crocker Bank/1700 15.00 40.00
26 Johnny Benson Cheerios/4500 15.00 40.00
26 Johnny Benson Cheerios Bank/1700 15.00 40.00
26 Johnny Benson Trix/4600 20.00 50.00
26 Johnny Benson Trix Bank 25.00 60.00
97 Chad Little John Deere/4000 25.00 60.00
97 Chad Little John Deere Bank/1700 20.00 50.00
99 Jeff Burton Bruce Lee 25.00 60.00
99 Jeff Burton 60.00 120.00

Bruce Lee Bank/500
99 Jeff Burton Exide/4300 25.00 60.00
99 Jeff Burton Exide Bank 40.00 80.00

1998 Racing Champions Driver's Choice Banks 1:24

These 1:24 scale banks were distributed through trackside and hobby outlets.

5 Terry Labonte Kellogg's 30.00 50.00
6 Mark Martin Valvoline 30.00 50.00
10 Ricky Rudd Tide 30.00 45.00
94 Bill Elliott McDonald's 30.00 50.00

1998 Racing Champions Gold 1:24

This is a special series produced by Racing Champions to celebrate NASCAR's 50th anniversary. Each car or bank was plated in gold chrome and the numbered versions contained the serial number on its chassis. Some cars were also issued in red window boxes or white solid boxes which were not not serial numbered. Unless noted below, the cars were packaged in a gold Racing Champions window box that included the production run notation of 2500 cars produced.

2 Ron Barfield New Holland 10.00 25.00
4 Bobby Hamilton Kodak 10.00 25.00
5 Terry Labonte Blasted Fruit Loops 12.00 30.00
5 Terry Labonte Kellogg's 12.00 30.00
5 Terry Labonte Kellogg's Corny 12.00 30.00
6 Joe Bessey Power Team 10.00 25.00
6 Mark Martin Eagle One 12.00 30.00
6 Mark Martin Syntec 12.00 30.00
6 Mark Martin Valvoline 12.00 30.00
6 Mark Martin Valvoline Bank 15.00 40.00
8 Hut Stricklin Circuit City 10.00 25.00
9 Jeff Burton Track Gear 10.00 25.00
9 Jerry Nadeau Zombie Island 10.00 25.00
9 Lake Speed Huckleberry Hound 10.00 25.00
9 Lake Speed Birthday Cake 10.00 25.00
9 Lake Speed Huckleberry Hound Bank 10.00 25.00
10 Phil Parsons Duralube 10.00 25.00
10 Ricky Rudd Tide 10.00 25.00
10 Ricky Rudd Tide Bank 10.00 25.00
11 Brett Bodine Paychex 10.00 25.00
11 Brett Bodine Paychex 10.00 25.00
13 Jerry Nadeau First Plus 10.00 25.00
14 Patty Moise Rhodes 10.00 25.00
16 Ted Musgrave Primestar 10.00 25.00
17 Matt Kenseth Lycos 60.00 100.00
17 Darrell Waltrip HQ Builders' Square 10.00 25.00
19 Tony Raines Yellow Freight 10.00 25.00
20 Blaise Alexander Rescue Engine 10.00 25.00
21 Michael Waltrip Citgo 10.00 25.00
21 Michael Waltrip Citgo Bank 10.00 25.00
23 Lance Hooper WCW 10.00 25.00
23 Jimmy Spencer No Bull 90.00 150.00
26 Johnny Benson Cheerios 10.00 25.00
26 Johnny Benson Cheerios Bank 10.00 25.00
28 Kenny Irwin Havoline Mac Tools 50.00 100.00
29 Hermie Sadler DeWalt 10.00 25.00
30 Derrike Cope Gumout 10.00 25.00
30 Mike Cope Slim Jim 10.00 25.00
33 Tim Fedewa Kleenex 10.00 25.00
33 Ken Schrader Petree 10.00 25.00
34 Mike McLaughlin Goulds 10.00 25.00
35 Todd Bodine Tabasco 10.00 25.00
36 Matt Hutter Stanley 10.00 25.00
36 Ernie Irvan M&M's 12.00 30.00
36 Ernie Irvan Skittles 10.00 25.00
36 Ernie Irvan Wildberry Skittles 12.00 30.00
40 Rick Fuller Channellock 10.00 25.00
40 Kevin Lepage Channellock 10.00 25.00
40 Sterling Marlin Sabco 12.00 30.00
41 Steve Grissom Larry Hedrick Racing 10.00 25.00
42 Joe Nemechek BellSouth 10.00 25.00
46 Wally Dallenbach First Union 10.00 25.00
47 Andy Santerie Monroe 10.00 25.00
50 Ricky Craven Hendrick 10.00 25.00
50 No Driver Association 50th Anniversary 10.00 25.00
59 Robert Pressley Kingsford 10.00 25.00
60 Mark Martin Winn Dixie 12.00 30.00
64 Dick Trickle Schneider 10.00 25.00
66 Eliott Sadler Phillips 66 10.00 25.00
72 Mike Dillon Detroit Gasket 10.00 25.00
74 Randy LaJoie Fina 10.00 25.00
75 Rick Mast Remington 10.00 25.00
77 Robert Pressley Jasper 10.00 25.00
78 Gary Bradberry Pilot 10.00 25.00
87 Joe Nemechek BellSouth 10.00 25.00
88 Kevin Schwantz Ryder 10.00 25.00
90 Dick Trickle Helig-Meyers 10.00 25.00
94 Bill Elliott Big Mac/4998 12.00 30.00
94 Bill Elliott Happy Meal 12.00 30.00
94 Bill Elliott Mac Tonight with Super 8 logo on side 10.00 25.00
94 Bill Elliott McDonald's/5000 12.00 30.00
94 Bill Elliott McDonald's Bank 12.00 30.00
94 Bill Elliott McDonald's with NASCAR 50th Anniv.logo on hood 12.00 30.00
96 David Green Caterpiller 10.00 25.00
97 Chad Little John Deere P 50.00 100.00
98 Rich Bickle Go Grill Crazy 10.00 25.00
98 Greg Sacks Thorn Apple Valley 10.00 25.00
99 Glen Allen Luxaire 10.00 25.00
99 Jeff Burton Exide 10.00 25.00
99 Jeff Burton Exide Bank 10.00 25.00
300 Darrell Waltrip Flock Special 12.00 30.00
400 No Driver Association Brickyard 400 10.00 25.00
00 Buckshot Jones Alka Seltzer 10.00 25.00
00 Buckshot Jones Aqua Fresh 10.00 25.00
00 Buckshot Jones Bayer 10.00 25.00

1998 Racing Champions Gold Hood Open 1:24

This is a special series produced by Racing Champions to celebrate NASCAR's 50th anniversary. The cars all have opening hoods and were issued in red window boxes unless noted below. Each car or bank was plated in gold chrome.

4 Bobby Hamilton Kodak 12.00 30.00
5 Terry Labonte Blasted Fruit Loops 15.00 40.00
5 Terry Labonte Blasted Froot Loops Bank 15.00 40.00
5 Terry Labonte Kellogg's 15.00 40.00
5 Terry Labonte Kellogg's Corny 15.00 40.00
5 Terry Labonte Kellogg's Corny Bank/1998 in gold box 15.00 40.00
6 Joe Bessey Power Team 12.00 30.00
6 Mark Martin Eagle One Bank 15.00 40.00
6 Mark Martin Synpower 15.00 40.00
6 Mark Martin Synpower Bank 15.00 40.00
6 Mark Martin Valvoline 15.00 40.00
6 Mark Martin Valvoline Bank 15.00 40.00
8 Hut Stricklin Circuit City 12.00 30.00
9 Lake Speed Huckleberry Hound 12.00 30.00
10 Ricky Rudd Tide 12.00 30.00
10 Ricky Rudd Tide Bank 12.00 30.00
11 Brett Bodine Paychex 12.00 30.00
16 Ted Musgrave Primestar 12.00 30.00
17 Darrell Waltrip Builders' Square 15.00 40.00
19 Tony Raines Yellow Freight 12.00 30.00
21 Michael Waltrip Goodwill Games 12.00 30.00
30 Derrike Cope Gumout 12.00 30.00
33 Ken Schrader Petree 12.00 30.00
35 Todd Bodine Tabasco 12.00 30.00
36 Ernie Irvan M&M's Bank 12.00 30.00
36 Ernie Irvan Skittles 12.00 30.00
36 Ernie Irvan Skittles Bank 12.00 30.00
36 Ernie Irvan Wildberry Skittles 12.00 30.00
36 Ernie Irvan Wildberry Skittles Bank 12.00 30.00
40 Sterling Marlin Sabco 15.00 40.00
50 Ricky Craven Hendrick 12.00 30.00
50 50th Anniversary Chevy/5000 12.00 30.00
50 50th Anniversary Ford/5000 12.00 30.00
50 50th Anniversary Pontiac/5000 12.00 30.00
77 Robert Pressley Jasper 12.00 30.00
78 Gary Bradberry Pilot 12.00 30.00
90 Dick Trickle Heilig-Meyers 12.00 30.00
94 Bill Elliott Big Mac white box 10.00 25.00
94 Bill Elliott Happy Meal gold box/1998 15.00 40.00
94 Bill Elliott Happy Meal Bank 15.00 40.00
94 Bill Elliott Mac Tonight red box with New Holland logo on side 10.00 25.00
94 Bill Elliott Mac Tonight white box with Super 8 logo on side 10.00 25.00
94 Bill Elliott Mac Tonight white box with New Holland logo on side 10.00 25.00
94 Bill Elliott McDonald's red box 15.00 40.00
94 Bill Elliott McDonald's white box New Holland logo on side 10.00 25.00
94 Bill Elliott McDonald's with NASCAR 50th Anniv.logo on hood 15.00 40.00
98 Greg Sacks Thorn Apple Valley 12.00 30.00
99 Jeff Burton Exide 12.00 30.00
99 Jeff Burton Exide Bank 12.00 30.00
400 No Driver Association Brickyard 400 12.00 30.00

1998 Racing Champions Gold NASCAR Fans Hood Open 1:24

Each car in this special series was produced by Racing Champions and packaged in a gold "NASCAR Fans" window box. The cars all have opening hoods and were plated in gold chrome. The stated production run was 1998 of each car.

5 Terry Labonte Kellogg's Corny green roof 15.00 40.00
5 Terry Labonte Kellogg's Corny white hood 15.00 40.00
6 Mark Martin Valvoline Synpower 15.00 40.00
40 Sterling Marlin Sabco 15.00 40.00
98 Greg Sacks Thorn Apple Valley 12.00 30.00

1998 Racing Champions 24K Gold 1:24

This is a special series produced by Racing Champions to celebrate NASCAR's 50th anniversary. Each was packaged in a black and gold window box with the notation "Reflections in Gold 24K Gold" on the front. Each car was limited to a production run of 4998 and was produced in an all-gold plated finish. Each also included a serial number on its chassis.

4 Bobby Hamilton Kodak 12.50 25.00
5 Terry Labonte Kellogg's Corny 25.00 50.00
6 Joe Bessey Power Team 12.50 25.00
6 Mark Martin Eagle One 25.00 60.00
6 Mark Martin Valvoline 25.00 60.00
8 Hut Stricklin Circuit City 12.50 25.00
9 Lake Speed Huckleberry Hound 12.50 25.00
10 Phil Parsons Duralube 12.50 25.00
10 Ricky Rudd Tide 12.50 25.00
11 Brett Bodine Paychex 12.50 25.00
13 Jerry Nadeau First Plus 25.00 50.00
16 Ted Musgrave Primestar 12.50 25.00
20 Blaise Alexander Rescue Engine 15.00 40.00
21 Michael Waltrip Citgo 12.50 25.00
23 Lance Hooper WCW 12.50 25.00
26 Johnny Benson Cheerios 12.50 25.00
29 Hermie Sadler DeWalt 12.50 25.00
30 Derrike Cope Gumout 12.50 25.00
33 Tim Fedewa Kleenex 12.50 25.00
33 Ken Schrader Petree 12.50 25.00
34 Mike McLaughlin Goulds 12.50 25.00
35 Todd Bodine Tabasco 12.50 25.00
36 Ernie Irvan Skittles 15.00 40.00
40 Sterling Marlin Sabco 15.00 30.00
41 Steve Grissom Larry Hedrick Racing 12.50 25.00
42 Joe Nemechek Bell South 12.50 25.00
46 Wally Dallenbach First Union 12.50 25.00
47 Andy Santerie Monroe 12.50 25.00
50 Ricky Craven Budweiser 15.00 40.00
59 Robert Pressley Kingsford 12.50 25.00
60 Mark Martin Winn Dixie 25.00 50.00
63 Tracy Leslie Lysol 12.50 25.00
64 Dick Trickle Schneider 12.50 25.00
72 Mike Dillon Detroit Gasket 12.50 25.00
74 Randy LaJoie Fina 12.50 25.00
75 Rick Mast Remington 12.50 25.00
90 Dick Trickle Heilig-Meyers 12.50 25.00
94 Bill Elliott McDonald's 25.00 50.00
97 Chad Little John Deere in black case 20.00 50.00
99 Jeff Burton Exide 15.00 40.00
00 Buckshot Jones Aqua Fresh 12.50 25.00

1998 Racing Champions Race Day 1:24

16 Ted Musgrave Primestar 1.50 4.00
41 Steve Grissom Kodiak 1.50 4.00
00 Buckshot Jones Aqua Fresh 1.50 4.00

1998 Racing Champions Signature Series 1:24

This is a special series produced by Racing Champions to celebrate NASCAR's 50th anniversary. It parallels the regular 1998 1:24 scale series. Each car is a packaged in a decorative box with the driver's facsimile autograph on the front.

5 Terry Labonte Kellogg's 10.00 20.00
6 Mark Martin Valvoline 10.00 20.00
9 Jeff Burton Track Gear 8.00 20.00
9 Lake Speed Huckleberry Hound 8.00 20.00
10 Phil Parsons Duralube 8.00 20.00
10 Ricky Rudd Tide 8.00 20.00
11 Brett Bodine Paychex 8.00 20.00
13 Jerry Nadeau First Plus 8.00 20.00
16 Ted Musgrave Primestar 8.00 20.00
26 Johnny Benson Cheerios 8.00 20.00
30 Derrike Cope Gumout 8.00 20.00
33 Ken Schrader Petree 8.00 20.00
35 Todd Bodine Tabasco 8.00 20.00
36 Ernie Irvan Skittles 8.00 20.00
50 Ricky Craven Hendrick 8.00 20.00
75 Rick Mast Remington 8.00 20.00
94 Bill Elliott McDonald's 10.00 20.00
98 Greg Sacks Thorn Apple Valley 8.00 20.00

1998 Racing Champions Stock Rods 1:24

These 1:24 scale cars are replicas of vintage stock rods with NASCAR paint schemes. Cars are listed by issue number instead of car number.

15 Jeff Green Cartoon Network 6.00 15.00
16 Kevin Schwantz Ryder 6.00 15.00
17 Glen Allen Luxaire 6.00 15.00
18 Jeff Burton Exide 6.00 15.00
19 Michael Waltrip Citgo 6.00 15.00
20 Robert Pressley Kingsford 6.00 15.00
21 Kevin Schwantz Ryder 6.00 15.00
22 Ken Schrader Petree 6.00 15.00
23 Dick Trickle Heilig-Meyers 6.00 15.00
24 Joe Bessey Power Team 6.00 15.00
25 Glen Allen Luxaire 6.00 15.00
26 Jerry Nadeau First Plus 6.00 15.00
27 Hut Stricklin Circuit City 6.00 15.00
28 Terry Labonte Kellogg's 8.00 20.00
29 Wally Dallenbach First Union 6.00 15.00
30 Joe Nemechek BellSouth 6.00 15.00
31 Robert Pressley Kingsford 6.00 15.00
32 Hut Stricklin Circuit City 6.00 15.00
33 Elliot Sadler Phillips 66 6.00 15.00
34 Hermie Sadler DeWalt 6.00 15.00
35 Steve Grissom Hedrick Racing Gold 8.00 20.00
36 Lake Speed Huckleberry Hound 6.00 15.00
37 Bill Elliott McDonald's Gold 15.00 40.00
38 Michael Waltrip Citgo 6.00 15.00
39 Jeff Burton Track Gear 6.00 15.00
40 Mark Martin Valvoline 8.00 20.00
41 Bill Elliott McDonald's 8.00 20.00
42 Jeff Burton Exide Gold 10.00 25.00
43 Jerry Nadeau First Plus Gold 8.00 20.00
44 Jeff Burton Exide 6.00 15.00
45 Rick Fuller Channellock 6.00 15.00
46 Ted Musgrave Primestar 6.00 15.00
47 Ricky Craven Hendrick 6.00 15.00
48 Terry Labonte Kellogg's Gold 15.00 40.00
49 Hut Stricklin Circuit City Gold 8.00 20.00
50 NDA NASCAR 50th Anniversary 6.00 15.00
51 Wally Dallenbach First Union 6.00 15.00
52 Terry Labonte Kellogg's Corny 8.00 20.00
53 Elliot Sadler Phillips 66 6.00 15.00
54 Bill Elliott McDonald's Gold 15.00 40.00
55 Steve Grissom Hedrick Racing Gold 8.00 20.00
56 Terry Labonte Kellogg's 8.00 20.00
57 Bobby Hamilton Kodak 6.00 15.00
58 Bill Elliott McDonald's Gold 15.00 40.00
59 Mark Martin Valvoline 8.00 20.00
60 Hut Stricklin Circuit City Gold 8.00 20.00
61 Ricky Rudd Tide 6.00 15.00
62 Johnny Benson Cheerios 6.00 15.00
63 Ricky Craven Hendrick Gold 10.00 25.00
64 Michael Waltrip Citgo 6.00 15.00
65 Hermie Sadler DeWalt 6.00 15.00
66 Ken Schrader Petree 6.00 15.00
67 Bill Elliott McDonald's Gold 15.00 40.00
68 Joe Nemechek Bell South Gold 8.00 20.00
69 Bill Elliott McDonald's 8.00 20.00
70 Steve Grissom Larry Hedrick Racing 6.00 15.00
71 Mark Martin Valvoline 8.00 20.00
72 Ken Schrader Petree 6.00 15.00
73 Michael Waltrip Citgo Gold 8.00 20.00

1998 Racing Champions Stock Rods 24K Gold 1:24

These 1:24 scale cars are replicas of vintage stock rods with NASCAR paint schemes and gold plating. Cars are listed by issue number instead of car number.

1 Bill Elliott McDonald's 20.00 40.00
2 Todd Bodine Tabasco 10.00 25.00
3 Terry Labonte Kellogg's 20.00 40.00
4 Bobby Hamilton Kodak 10.00 25.00
5 Mark Martin Valvoline 20.00 40.00
6 Jeff Burton Exide 15.00 30.00
7 Ernie Irvan Skittles 15.00 35.00
8 Ted Musgrave Primestar 10.00 25.00
9 Terry Labonte Kellogg's 20.00 40.00
10 Ken Schrader Petree 10.00 25.00
11 Dick Trickle Schneider 10.00 25.00
12 Michael Waltrip Citgo 10.00 25.00

1998 Racing Champions SuperTrucks 1:24

Racing Champions continued their line of 1:24 SuperTrucks in 1998. This series features many of the circuit's first-time drivers and Winston Cup regulars.

2 Mike Bliss Team ASE 8.00 20.00
6 Rick Carelli Remax 8.00 20.00
18 No Driver Association Dana 8.00 20.00
19 Tony Raines Pennzoil 8.00 20.00
29 Bob Keselowski Mopar 8.00 20.00
31 Tony Roper Concor Tools 8.00 20.00
35 Ron Barfield Ortho 8.00 20.00
44 Boris Said Federated 8.00 20.00
50 Greg Biffle Grainger 100.00 175.00
52 Mike Wallace Pure One 8.00 20.00

66 Bryan Refner Carlin 8.00 20.00
84 Wayne Anderson Porter Cable 8.00 20.00
86 Stacy Compton RC Cola 8.00 20.00
87 Joe Nemechek BellSouth 8.00 20.00
90 Lance Norick National Hockey League 8.00 20.00
94 Bill Elliott Team ASE 8.00 20.00

1998 Racing Champions SuperTrucks Gold 1:24

This is a special series produced by Racing Champions to celebrate NASCAR's 50th anniversary. It parallels the regular 1998 1:24 scale series. Each truck is a limited edition of 2,500. Each truck is also plated in gold chrome and contains a serial number on its chassis.

2 Mike Bliss Team ASE 10.00 25.00
6 Rick Carelli Remax 10.00 25.00
29 Bob Keselowski Mopar 10.00 25.00
50 Greg Biffle Grainger 60.00 100.00
66 Bryan Refner Carlin 10.00 25.00
86 Stacy Compton RC Cola 10.00 25.00

1999 Racing Champions 1:24

The 1:24 scale cars that appear in this series are replicas of many of the cars that ran in the 1999 season.

1 Iowa Hawkeyes Promo 15.00 30.00
1 Mac Tools Promo 10.00 20.00
4 Don Thomas Jr. Home Hardware Promo 35.00 60.00
4 Bobby Hamilton Kodak 7.50 15.00
4 Bobby Hamilton Kodak Advantix 7.50 15.00
5 HK Fabarm Promo 30.00 50.00
5 Terry Labonte Kellogg's 7.50 15.00
5 Terry Labonte Kellogg's Chrome/2499 20.00 50.00
5 Dick Trickle Schneider Promo 10.00 25.00
6 Mark Martin Valvoline 7.50 15.00
6 Mark Martin Valvoline Chrome/2499 25.00 60.00
6 Mark Martin Zerex 15.00 35.00
6 Mark Martin Zerex Chrome/2499 25.00 60.00
7 Michael Waltrip Philips 15.00 35.00
9 Jerry Nadeau Dexter's Laboratory 7.50 15.00
9 Jerry Nadeau WCW nWo 7.50 15.00
9 Jerry Nadeau Goldberg 12.50 25.00
10 Racing Champions Silver 10.00 25.00
10 Ricky Rudd Tide 7.50 15.00
10 Ricky Rudd Tide Peroxide 7.50 15.00
11 Brett Bodine Paychex 7.50 15.00
12 Jeremy Mayfield Mobil 1 7.50 15.00
12 Jimmy Spencer Zippo 15.00 30.00
12 Jeremy Mayfield Mobil 1 Chrome/2499 20.00 40.00
14 Rick Crawford Circle Bar Super Truck 7.50 15.00
15 Ken Schrader Oakwood Homes Promo box shaped like mobile home 15.00 30.00
16 Kevin Lepage Primestar 7.50 15.00
17 Matt Kenseth DeWalt 15.00 30.00
17 Matt Kenseth Luxaire Promo 35.00 70.00
18 Butch Miller Dana SuperTruck Promo 12.50 25.00
20 Tony Stewart Arvin Racing Promo/5000 15.00 40.00
21 Elliott Sadler Citgo 7.50 15.00
21 Elliott Sadler Citgo Chrome/2499 20.00 40.00
23 Jimmy Spencer TCE 7.50 15.00
23 Jimmy Spencer TCE Chrome/2499 20.00 50.00
24 Jack Sprague GMAC Super Truck 7.50 15.00
25 Wally Dallenbach Hendrick 7.50 15.00
26 Johnny Benson Cheerios 7.50 15.00
30 Derrike Cope Bryan Foods 7.50 15.00
30 Derrike Cope Rudy's Farm 35.00 50.00
32 Jeff Green Kleenex 7.50 15.00
33 Ken Schrader Petree 7.50 15.00
34 Mike McLaughlin Goulds Pumps 7.50 15.00
36 Ernie Irvan Crispy M&M's 12.50 25.00
36 Ernie Irvan M&M's 12.50 25.00
36 Ernie Irvan M&M's Chrome/2499 20.00 50.00
36 Ernie Irvan M&M's Promo 15.00 30.00
36 Ernie Irvan Pedigree Promo 15.00 30.00
38 Glen Allen Barbasol 7.50 15.00
40 Sterling Marlin John Wayne 15.00 40.00
40 Sterling Marlin Brooks & Dunn Promo 10.00 25.00
42 Joe Nemechek BellSouth 7.50 15.00
42 Joe Nemechek BellSouth Promo 15.00 30.00
43 John Andretti STP 7.50 15.00
44 Justin Labonte Slim Jim 7.50 15.00
44 Tery Labonte Justin Labonte Slim Jim Penrose 2-car Promo set 12.50 25.00
45 Adam Petty Spree 30.00 60.00
45 Polaris Promo 15.00 30.00
50 Greg Biffle Grainger SuperTruck Promo 75.00 135.00
50 Mark Green Dr.Pepper 7.50 15.00
55 No Driver Association Florida Gators Promo 18.00 30.00
55 Kenny Wallace Square D 7.50 15.00
59 Mike Dillon Kingsford 7.50 15.00
60 Mark Martin Winn Dixie 15.00 35.00
60 Mark Martin Winn Dixie Beef People Promo 18.00 30.00
63 NDA Exxon SuperFlo 25.00 40.00
66 Todd Bodine Phillips 66 Promo 10.00 25.00
66 Darrell Waltrip Big K 7.50 15.00
75 Ted Musgrave Polaris ATVs Promo 12.50 25.00
75 Ted Musgrave Remington 7.50 15.00
77 Robert Pressley Jasper 7.50 15.00
86 Stacy Compton RC Cola SuperTruck 7.50 15.00
90 Hills Bros. Nesquik Promo 20.00 35.00
94 Bill Elliott Drive Thru 8.00 20.00
94 Bill Elliott McDonald's Name Game Promo 15.00 30.00
97 Chad Little John Deere 7.50 15.00
98 Kevin Harvick Porter-Cable SuperTruck Promo 200.00 300.00
99 Auto Value Promo 15.00 30.00
99 Jeff Burton Exide 7.50 15.00
99 Jeff Burton Exide Bruce Lee 7.50 15.00
99 Snap-On Southern Thunder Promo/10,000 12.50 25.00
00 Cheez-It Promo (driven by Larry Pearson) 30.00 50.00
00 Connectiv Promo 12.50 25.00
NNO Jeg's SuperTruck Promo 15.00 30.00

1999 Racing Champions 2-Car Sets 1:24

These 1:24 scale die-cast cars were packaged together in a large Racing Champions window box. Each regular version car was issued with a silver or gold chrome version.

4 Bobby Hamilton Kodak Advantix 10.00 20.00
36 Ernie Irvan M&M's 10.00 20.00
94 Bill Elliott McDonald's/5000 10.00 20.00
99 Jeff Burton Bruce Lee/4000 10.00 25.00

1999 Racing Champions 2-Car Sets 1:24/1:64

6 Mark Martin Valvoline/9999 10.00 20.00
6 Mark Martin Zerex Chrome 3-piece set with 1:24 car, 1:64 car and 1:64 Valvoline transporter 20.00 40.00
7 Michael Waltrip Phillips Promo 10.00 20.00
40 Sterling Marlin John Wayne 20.00 40.00
50 Mark Green Dr.Pepper Chrome 3-piece set with 1:24 car, 1:64 car and 1:64 transporter 20.00 40.00
77 Robert Pressley Jasper/9999 7.50 20.00

1999 Racing Champions 3-Car Sets 1:24

5/6/94 Terry Labonte Kellogg's Mark Martin Valvoline Bill Elliott McDonald's 25.00 50.00

1999 Racing Champions Authentics 1:24

6 Mark Martin Eagle One/8500 40.00 75.00
6 Mark Martin Valvoline/8500 40.00 75.00
6 Mark Martin Zerex/8500 40.00 75.00
9 Jeff Burton Track Gear/2000 20.00 50.00
9 Jerry Nadeau Jetsons/5000 12.50 30.00
10 Ricky Rudd Tide/2500 25.00 50.00
10 Ricky Rudd Tide Peroxide/5000 20.00 50.00
16 Kevin Lepage TV Guide/2000 25.00 50.00
23 Jimmy Spencer Winston/5000 in black case 25.00 50.00
26 Johnny Benson Cheerios/2000 20.00 50.00
55 No Driver Association Florida Gators Promo/1008 30.00 50.00
60 Mark Martin Winn Dixie/2000 25.00 50.00
94 Bill Elliott McDonald's Drive Thru/7500 25.00 50.00
94 Bill Elliott McDonald's Win $1 Million/5000 30.00 80.00
97 Chad Little John Deere/3500 25.00 50.00
97 Chad Little John Deere FFA/7500 25.00 50.00
99 Jeff Burton Exide/5000 25.00 50.00

1999 Racing Champions Gold 1:24

This is a special series produced by Racing Champions to celebrate their 10th anniversary. Each car was produced in a limited edition of 4,999 and featured a gold chrome finish as well as a serial number on its chassis. A few cars were also produced in an upgraded Hood Open model that carried a production run of 1999.

4 Bobby Hamilton Kodak 12.50 25.00
5 Terry Labonte Kellogg's 20.00 40.00
6 Mark Martin Valvoline 20.00 40.00
9 Jerry Nadeau Dexter's Laboratory 12.50 25.00
10 Ricky Rudd Tide 12.50 25.00
11 Brett Bodine Paychex 12.50 25.00
15 Ken Schrader Oakwood Homes 12.50 25.00
25 Wally Dallenbach Hendrick 12.50 25.00
26 Johnny Benson Cheerios 12.50 25.00
33 Ken Schrader Petree 12.50 25.00
36 Ernie Irvan M&M's 15.00 30.00
45 Adam Petty Spree Hood Open/1999 40.00 75.00
55 Kenny Wallace Square D 12.50 25.00
60 Mark Martin Winn Dixie 20.00 40.00
66 Darrell Waltrip Big K 12.50 25.00
77 Robert Pressley Jasper 12.50 25.00
94 Bill Elliott McDonald's Drive Thru 15.00 40.00
99 Jeff Burton Exide 12.50 25.00
99 Jeff Burton Exide Bruce Lee 12.50 25.00
00 Larry Pearson Cheez-It 12.50 25.00

1999 Racing Champions Petty Collection 1:24

These 1:24 cars were issued to commemorate the racing history of the Petty Family. Each was packaged in an STP blue clear window box with the Petty Racing 50th Anniversary logo.

42 Lee Petty 1949 Plymouth 50.00 90.00
42 Richard Petty 1957 Oldsmobile 150.00 225.00
43 Richard Petty 1964 Plymouth 90.00 150.00
43 Richard Petty 1970 Superbird 40.00 80.00
43 Richard Petty 1981 Buick 30.00 70.00
43 John Andretti 1999 Pontiac 25.00 40.00

1999 Racing Champions Platinum 1:24

This is a special series produced by Racing Champions to celebrate their 10th anniversary. It parallels the regular 1999 1:24 scale series. Each car is a limited edition of 4,999. Each car is also plated in platinum chrome and contains a serial number on its chassis.

4 Bobby Hamilton Kodak 20.00 40.00
5 Terry Labonte Kellogg's 30.00 75.00
6 Mark Martin Valvoline 30.00 75.00
9 Jerry Nadeau Dexter's Laboratory 20.00 40.00
9 Jeff Burton Track Gear 20.00 40.00
10 Ricky Rudd Tide 20.00 40.00
11 Brett Bodine Paychex 20.00 40.00
16 Kevin Lepage Primestar 20.00 40.00
25 Wally Dallenbach Hendrick 20.00 40.00
26 Johnny Benson Cheerios 20.00 40.00
33 Ken Schrader Petree 20.00 40.00
36 Ernie Irvan M&M's 20.00 40.00
42 Joe Nemechek BellSouth 20.00 40.00
55 Kenny Wallace Square D 20.00 40.00
77 Robert Pressley Jasper 20.00 40.00
94 Bill Elliott Drive Thru 30.00 75.00
97 Chad Little John Deere 20.00 40.00
99 Jeff Burton Exide 20.00 40.00

1999 Racing Champions Premier 1:24

Each of these 1:24 scale die-cast pieces were issued in a solid (not window) Racing Champions Premier box.

6 Mark Martin Eagle One Mac Tools/5000 25.00 50.00
6 Mark Martin Valvoline/3000 20.00 50.00
6 Mark Martin Valvoline Bank/500 30.00 60.00
6 Mark Martin Zerex Mac Tools/5000 15.00 40.00
9 Jeff Burton Track Gear Bank/500 20.00 50.00
60 Mark Martin Winn Dixie/3000 20.00 50.00
60 Mark Martin Winn Dixie Bank/500 30.00 60.00
97 Chad Little John Deere 10.00 25.00
97 Chad Little John Deere Bank/500 25.00 50.00
99 Jeff Burton Exide/3000 12.50 30.00
99 Jeff Burton Exide Bank/500 20.00 50.00

1999 Racing Champions Signature Series 1:24

This is a special series produced by Racing Champions to celebrate their 10th anniversary. It parallels the regular 1999 1:24 scale series. Each car is a packaged in a decorative box with the driver's facsimile autograph on the front.

4 Bobby Hamilton Kodak 8.00 20.00
4 Bobby Hamilton Kodak Chrome 20.00 40.00
5 Terry Labonte Kellogg's 10.00 20.00
5 Terry Labonte Kellogg's Chrome 35.00 60.00
6 Joe Bessey Power Team 8.00 20.00
6 Mark Martin Valvoline 10.00 20.00
6 Mark Martin Valvoline Chrome 35.00 60.00
9 Jerry Nadeau Dexter's Laboratory 8.00 20.00
9 Jerry Nadeau Dexter's Laboratory Chrome 30.00 60.00
10 Ricky Rudd Tide 8.00 20.00
11 Brett Bodine Paychex 8.00 20.00
12 Jeremy Mayfield Mobil 1 8.00 20.00
12 Jeremy Mayfield Mobil 1 Chrome 20.00 40.00
16 Kevin Lepage Primestar 8.00 20.00
16 Kevin Lepage Primestar Chrome 20.00 40.00
25 Wally Dallenbach Hendrick 8.00 20.00
25 Wally Dallenbach Hendrick Chrome 20.00 40.00
26 Johnny Benson Cheerios 8.00 20.00
32 Jeff Green Kleenex 8.00 20.00
34 Mike McLaughlin Goulds Pump 8.00 20.00
36 Ernie Irvan M&M's 10.00 20.00
36 Ernie Irvan M&M's Chrome 30.00 60.00
40 Sterling Marlin John Wayne 10.00 25.00
77 Robert Pressley Jasper 8.00 20.00
77 Robert Pressley Jasper Chrome 20.00 40.00
94 Bill Elliott McDonald's Drive Thru 10.00 20.00
94 Bill Elliott McDonald's Drive Thru Chrome 35.00 60.00
99 Jeff Burton Exide 8.00 20.00

1999 Racing Champions Stock Rods 1:24

These 1:24 scale cars are replicas of various types vintage stock hot rods with NASCAR paint schemes. Since some paint schemes were issued more than once (in different car models), we've listed them below by issue number instead of car number.

74 Jeff Burton Exide 6.00 15.00
75 Kevin Lepage Primestar 6.00 15.00
76 Terry Labonte Kellogg's Iron Man 8.00 20.00
77 Bobby Hamilton Kodak 6.00 15.00
78 Terry Labonte Blasted Fruit Loops 8.00 20.00
79 Rick Mast Remington 6.00 15.00
80 Kevin Lepage Primestar Gold 8.00 20.00
81 Bobby Hamilton Kodak Gold 8.00 20.00
82 Bobby Hamilton Kodak 6.00 15.00
83 Terry Labonte Kellogg's Iron Man 8.00 20.00
84 Mark Martin Valvoline 8.00 20.00
85 Jeff Burton Exide 6.00 15.00
86 Bobby Hamilton Kodak 6.00 15.00
87 Brett Bodine Paychex 6.00 15.00
88 Wally Dallenbach Hendrick 6.00 15.00
89 Wally Dallenbach Hendrick Gold 8.00 20.00
90 Ernie Irvan M&M's 8.00 20.00
91 Ernie Irvan M&M's Gold 12.00 30.00
92 Bobby Hamilton Kodak Gold 8.00 20.00
93 Brett Bodine Paychex Gold 6.00 15.00
94 Bill Elliott Drive Thru Gold 15.00 40.00
95 Bill Elliott Drive Thru 8.00 20.00
96 Jerry Nadeau Dexter's Laboratory 6.00 15.00
97 Sterling Marlin John Wayne 8.00 20.00
99 Robert Pressley Jasper 6.00 15.00
100 Robert Pressley Jasper Gold 8.00 20.00
101 Ken Schrader Andy Petree Racing 6.00 15.00
102 Serling Marlin John Wayne 8.00 20.00
103 Jeff Burton Bruce Lee 6.00 15.00
104 Terry Labonte Kellogg's 8.00 20.00
105 Ricky Rudd Tide 6.00 15.00
106 Derrike Cope Bryan Foods 6.00 15.00
107 Ken Schrader APR Blue 6.00 15.00
108 Jimmy Spencer TCE 6.00 15.00

1999 Racing Champions Trackside 1:24

These 1:24 cars were primarily available at the race track. Each was packaged in a "Trackside" labeled window box with each including the production run total of 2499.

9 Jerry Nadeau Atlanta Braves 20.00 40.00
9 Jerry Nadeau Dexter's Lab 12.50 30.00
9 Jerry Nadeau Dexter's Lab Platinum 15.00 40.00
9 Jerry Nadeau WCW nWo 12.50 30.00
23 Jimmy Spencer No Bull 15.00 40.00
43 John Andretti STP 12.50 30.00
45 Adam Petty Spree 40.00 80.00
94 Bill Elliott McDonald's Drive Thru Platinum 15.00 40.00
99 Chevrolet Racing Platinum 10.00 25.00
99 Crew Chief Club 10.00 20.00
99 Ford Racing Platinum 10.00 25.00

1999 Racing Champions Under the Lights 1:24

4 Johnny Benson Kodak Max 8.00 20.00
5 Terry Labonte Kellogg's K-Sentials/5000 8.00 20.00
6 Mark Martin Valvoline 10.00 25.00
6 Mark Martin Zerex/7500 12.50 25.00
10 Ricky Rudd Tide 8.00 20.00
12 Jeremy Mayfield Mobil 1 8.00 20.00
21 Elliott Sadler Citgo 8.00 20.00
22 Ward Burton Caterpillar 8.00 20.00
43 John Andretti STP 10.00 25.00
60 Mark Martin Winn Dixie 10.00 25.00
66 Darrell Waltrip Big K 8.00 20.00
94 Bill Elliott McDonald's Drive Thru/5000 10.00 25.00
99 Jeff Burton Exide 8.00 20.00

1999 Racing Champions 24K Gold 1:24

This is a special series produced by Racing Champions to celebrate their 10th anniversary. It parallels the regular 1998 1:24 scale series. Each car is a limited edition of 4,999. Each car is also plated in gold chrome and contains a serial number on its chassis.

4 Bobby Hamilton Kodak 20.00 40.00
5 Terry Labonte Kellogg's 30.00 75.00
6 Joe Bessey Power Team 20.00 40.00
6 Mark Martin Valvoline 30.00 75.00
9 Jerry Nadeau Dexter's Laboratory 30.00 50.00
9 Jeff Burton Track Gear 20.00 40.00
10 Ricky Rudd Tide 20.00 40.00
11 Brett Bodine Paychex 20.00 40.00
16 Kevin Lepage 20.00 40.00

Primestar
26 Johnny Benson Cheerios 20.00 40.00
42 Joe Nemechek BellSouth 20.00 40.00
77 Robert Pressley Jasper 20.00 40.00
97 Chad Little John Deere 20.00 40.00
99 Jeff Burton Exide 20.00 40.00

2000 Racing Champions Preview 1:24

5 Terry Labonte Kellogg's 10.00 20.00
6 Mrak Martin Valvoline 10.00 20.00
7 Michael Waltrip Nation's Rent 7.50 15.00
12 Jeremy Mayfield Mobil 1 7.50 15.00
17 Matt Kenseth DeWalt 10.00 20.00
22 Ward Burton Caterpillar 7.50 15.00
22 Ward Burton Caterpillar Bud Shoot Out 8.00 20.00
33 Joe Nemechek Oakwood Homes 7.50 15.00
66 Darrell Waltrip Big K Flames 7.50 15.00
75 Wally Dallenbach Cartoon Network 7.50 15.00
77 Robert Pressley Jasper 7.50 15.00
99 Jeff Burton Exide 7.50 15.00
99 Jeff Burton Exide Chrome/999 12.50 25.00

2000 Racing Champions Premier Preview 1:24

6 Mark Martin Valvoline 10.00 25.00
17 Matt Kenseth DeWalt 10.00 25.00
99 Jeff Burton Exide 10.00 25.00

2000 Racing Champions 1:24

1 MSD Ignition Syst.Promo/2508 20.00 40.00
1 Peter Gibbons Candian Tire Promo 15.00 40.00
4 Bobby Hamilton Dana SuperTruck Promo 20.00 35.00
5 Terry Labonte Kellogg's 10.00 25.00
5 Terry Labonte Kellogg's Chrome/999 20.00 50.00
6 Mark Martin Valvoline 10.00 25.00
6 Mark Martin Valvoline Chrome/999 25.00 50.00
7 Michael Waltrip Nation's Rent 7.50 15.00
7 Michael Waltrip Nations Rent Chrome/999 15.00 40.00
9 Stacy Compton Kodiak Promo 10.00 20.00
9 Jeff Burton NorthernLight.com 7.50 15.00
12 Jeremy Mayfield Mobil 1 7.50 15.00
14 Mike Bliss Conseco 7.50 15.00
14 Rick Crawford Milwaukee Tools SuperTruck Promo 10.00 20.00
17 Matt Kenseth DeWalt 10.00 20.00
20 Arvin Racing Promo 15.00 25.00
22 Ward Burton Caterpillar 7.50 15.00
22 Ward Burton Caterpillar Promo 10.00 25.00
22 Ward Burton Caterpillar Bud Shoot Out 10.00 20.00
22 Ward Burton Cat Dealers Promo 10.00 25.00
22 Ward Burton Caterpillar Bosch Promo 10.00 25.00
25 Jerry Nadeau Holigan 7.50 15.00
33 Joe Nemechek Oakwood Bud Shoot Out 7.50 15.00
39 Schaeffer's Racing Oil Promo 25.00 40.00
40 Sterling Marlin Sabco 7.50 15.00
42 Kenny Irwin BellSouth 10.00 25.00
44 Doc Brewer Pabst Blue Ribbon Promo 25.00 50.00
48 Mike McGlaughlin Goulds Pumps Promo 60.00 100.00
50 Greg Biffle Grainger SuperTruck Promo 100.00 175.00
50 Tony Roper Dr. Pepper Promo 30.00 60.00
59 Mark Gibson Cornwell Tools Promo 30.00 50.00
64 Mark Dilley NTN Promo 30.00 50.00
66 Darrell Waltrip Big K 7.50 15.00
66 Darrell Waltrip Big K Flames 7.50 15.00
66 Darrell Waltrip Big K 500 Promo in solid box 25.00 50.00
75 Wally Dallenbach Rotozip Promo 25.00 40.00
75 Wally Dallenbach Scooby Doo 7.50 15.00
77 Robert Pressley Federal Mogul Red romo 10.00 20.00
77 Robert Pressley Jasper 7.50 15.00
77 Robert Pressley Jasper Blue Promo 10.00 25.00
77 Robert Pressley Jasper Teal Promo 10.00 25.00
90 Ed Berrier Hills Bros.Promo set with two 1:64 cars 35.00 60.00
91 Rich Bickle Aqua Velva Promo/2508 10.00 25.00
91 Rich Bickle Popeyes Promo 12.50 25.00
93 Dave Blaney Amoco 10.00 25.00
93 Dave Blaney Amoco Ultimate Promo 15.00 30.00
97 Chad Little John Deere 7.50 15.00
99 Jeff Burton Exide 7.50 15.00
99 Jeff Burton Exide Chrome/999 20.00 50.00
99 Kurt Busch Exide SuperTruck Promo 100.00 200.00
99 Michael Waltrip Aaron's Promo 20.00 35.00
2000 Kroger Fred Meyer Promo/4700 15.00 30.00
00 Auto Value Gold Chrome Promo 15.00 30.00
00 Ryan McGlynn Howes Lubricator 80th Anniversary SuperTruck Promo 25.00 40.00
00 Snap-On Racing Promo/5000 7.50 20.00

2000 Racing Champions Authentics 1:24

6 Mark Martin Eagle One/4000 25.00 50.00
6 Mark Martin Valvoline 25.00 50.00
7 Michael Waltrip Nations Rent Matco Tools/3100 40.00 80.00
22 Ward Burton Caterpillar 15.00 40.00
22 Ward Burton Cat Dealers/2000 30.00 50.00
22 Ward Burton Caterpillar No Bull 25.00 50.00
40 Sterling Marlin Coors Light Matco Tools 50.00 100.00
42 Kenny Irwin BellSouth Matco Tools 60.00 100.00
75 Wally Dallenbach Power Puff Girls/1000 20.00 45.00
82 Sterling Marlin Channellock Matco Tools 30.00 60.00
87 Joe Nemechek Cellularone Matco Tools 30.00 60.00
93 Dave Blaney Amoco 15.00 40.00

2000 Racing Champions Model Kits 1:24

Cars in this series were issued in a large Racing Champions window box with the title "Die Cast Model Kit" on the front and top along with the NASCAR2000 logo. The kit is essentially a metal die-cast model that was to be assembled by the collector. The car came complete with a small screwdriver and model glue.

5 Terry Labonte Kellogg's 8.00 20.00
6 Mark Martin Valvoline 8.00 20.00
22 Ward Burton Caterpillar 6.00 15.00
99 Jeff Burton Exide 6.00 15.00

2000 Racing Champions Premier 1:24

4 Bobby Hamilton Kodak 10.00 20.00
5 Terry Labonte Froot Loops CherryBerry 12.50 25.00
5 Terry Labonte Kellogg's Tony 12.50 25.00
6 Mark Martin Valvoline 12.50 25.00
6 Mark Martin Valvoline No Bull 12.50 25.00
12 Jeremy Mayfield Mobil 1 10.00 20.00
17 Matt Kenseth DeWalt 15.00 30.00
17 Matt Kenseth DeWalt 24 Volt 15.00 30.00
22 Ward Burton Caterpillar 10.00 20.00
22 Ward Burton Caterpillar No Bull 12.50 25.00
42 Kenny Irwin BellSouth 10.00 20.00
42 Kenny Irwin BellSouth Chrome/999 15.00 30.00
60 Mark Martin Winn Dixie Farewell Tour Promo in solid box 75.00 125.00
60 Mark Martin Winn Dixie Flag in window box 75.00 125.00
99 Jeff Burton Exide 12.50 25.00
99 Jeff Burton Exide Chrome/999 20.00 40.00

2000 Racing Champions Stock Rods 1:24

1 Mark Martin Valvoline 1937 Ford 7.50 15.00
2 Jeff Burton Exide 1932 Ford 7.50 15.00
3 Bobby Hamilton Kodak 1967 Chevelle 6.00 12.00

2000 Racing Champions Time Trial 2000 1:24

New for 2000, Racing Champions introduced a series that focuses on the testing and development of NASCAR stock cars rather than the final race-ready car - Time Trial stock car replicas. Sporting just a coat of gray primer and the team number.

6 Mark Martin Valvoline 12.00 20.00
17 Matt Kenseth DeWalt 50.00 100.00
97 Chad Little John Deere 10.00 20.00
99 Jeff Burton Exide 12.00 20.00

2000 Racing Champions Under the Lights 1:24

5 Terry Labonte Kellogg's K-Sentials/5000 12.50 25.00
6 Mark Martin Zerex 12.50 30.00
22 Ward Burton Caterpillar/2288 15.00 40.00
99 Jeff Burton Exide 2-car set/2500 regular issue car and chrome hood car 12.50 25.00
2K Ford Chrome/10,000 10.00 20.00
Y2K Chevy Chrome/10,000 10.00 20.00

2000 Racing Champions War Paint 1:24

5 Terry Labonte Kellogg's 10.00 20.00
5 Terry Labonte Kellogg's Hood Open 10.00 20.00
6 Mark Martin Valvoline 12.50 25.00
6 Mark Martin Valvoline Hood Open 12.50 25.00
22 Ward Burton Caterpillar 10.00 20.00
22 Ward Burton Caterpillar Hood Open 10.00 20.00
99 Jeff Burton Exide 10.00 20.00
99 Jeff Burton Exide Hood Open 10.00 20.00

2001 Racing Champions Preview 1:24

5 Terry Labonte Kellogg's Tony 10.00 20.00
5 Terry Labonte Kellogg's Tony Chrome 25.00 50.00
10 Johnny Benson Valvoline 8.00 20.00
12 Jeremy Mayfield Mobil 1 10.00 20.00
12 Jeremy Mayfield Mobil 1 Layin' Rubber 15.00 40.00
14 Ron Hornaday Conseco 8.00 20.00
22 Ward Burton Caterpillar 8.00 20.00
22 Ward Burton Caterpillar Autographed 40.00 80.00
22 Ward Burton Caterpillar Chrome 20.00 50.00
22 Ward Burton Caterpillar Layin' Rubber 20.00 50.00
36 Ken Schrader M&M's 8.00 20.00
36 Ken Schrader M&M's Chrome 25.00 50.00
55 Bobby Hamilton Square D 8.00 20.00
55 Bobby Hamilton Square D Chrome/1500 20.00 40.00
92 Stacy Compton Compton 8.00 20.00
92 Stacy Compton Compton Chrome 20.00 40.00
93 Dave Blaney Amoco 8.00 20.00
93 Dave Blaney Amoco Chrome 15.00 40.00
NNO Dodge Test Car 10.00 25.00

2001 Racing Champions Premier Preview 1:24

5 Terry Labonte Frosed Flakes 2000 12.50 25.00
5 Terry Labonte Kellogg's Tony 20.00 35.00
10 Johnny Benson Valvoline 12.50 25.00
12 Jeremy Mayfield Mobil 1 12.50 25.00
12 Jeremy Mayfield Mobil 1 Layin' Rubber 20.00 50.00

2001 Racing Champions 1:24

1 Justice Bros. Promo 25.00 40.00
1 Ted Musgrave Mopar SuperTruck Promo 15.00 40.00
1 Racing Experience Promo 30.00 50.00
2 Scott Riggs ASE SuperTruck 25.00 50.00
4 Graybar Lutron Promo/3600 20.00 35.00
5 Terry Labonte Kellogg's Tony 12.00 30.00
5 Terry Labonte Kellogg's Tony Chrome/1500 25.00 50.00
5 Terry Labonte Kellogg's 15.00 40.00
5 Terry Labonte Kellogg's Autographed
5 Terry Labonte Monsters Inc.Promo 15.00 30.00
7 Randy LaJoie Kleenex Promo 10.00 20.00
8 Willie T. Ribbs Dodge SuperTruck 12.50 25.00
10 Johnny Benson Valvoline 8.00 20.00
12 Jeremy Mayfield Mobil 1 8.00 20.00
12 Jeremy Mayfield Mobil Autographed
12 Jeremy Mayfield Mobil Layin' Rubber 20.00 40.00
12 Jeremy Mayfield Mobil Race Rubber 20.00 45.00
12 Jeremy Mayfield Sony-Mobil 1 12.00 30.00
12 Jeremy Mayfield Sony Chrome/1500 15.00 30.00
13 Hermie Sadler Virginia Lottery Promo 15.00 30.00
14 Rick Crawford Milwaukee Tools SuperTruck Promo 5.00 10.00
14 Ron Hornaday Conseco 8.00 20.00
16 Brendan Gaughan NAPA Promo 30.00 50.00
16 Wisconsin Cheese Promo 15.00 30.00
18 Dave Heitzhaus Pro Hardware Promo in blister 8.00 20.00
21 Elliott Sadler Motorcraft 12.00 30.00
21 Elliott Sadler Motorcraft Layin' Rubber 20.00 40.00
22 Ward Burton Caterpillar 8.00 20.00
22 Ward Burton Caterpillar Autographed
22 Ward Burton Caterpillar Chrome/1500 25.00 50.00
22 Ward Burton Caterpillar 24kt.Gold Promo 25.00 50.00
22 Ward Burton Caterpillar Layin' Rubber 15.00 40.00
22 Ward Burton Caterpillar Race Rubber 25.00 50.00
22 Ward Burton Cat Black Time Trial 12.50 25.00
22 Ward Burton Cat Black Time Trial Chrome/1500 25.00 50.00
22 Ward Burton Caterpillar War Chrome/1500 25.00 50.00
22 Ward Burton Caterpillar Promo 15.00 25.00
22 Ward Burton Cat Tractor 20.00 50.00
22 Ward Burton Cat Tractor Layin' Rubber/500 40.00 75.00
25 Jerry Nadeau UAW 8.00 20.00
25 Jerry Nadeau UAW Chrome/1500 20.00 40.00
25 Jerry Nadeau UAW Promo Mac Tools box/3000 25.00 40.00
26 Bobby Hamilton Jr. Dr.Pepper Promo 15.00 30.00
26 Jimmy Spencer K-Mart 8.00 20.00
26 Jimmy Spencer K-Mart Grinch 15.00 30.00
28 Brad Baker Whitetails Unlimited 18.00 30.00
36 Hank Parker Jr. GNC Live Well 45.00 80.00
36 Ken Schrader M&M's 8.00 20.00
36 Ken Schrader M&M's Layin' Rubber 25.00 50.00
36 Ken Schrader M&M's Promo Mac Tools box/3000 25.00 40.00
36 Ken Schrader M&M's July 4th 8.00 20.00
36 Ken Schrader M&M's July 4th Race Rubber 25.00 50.00
36 Ken Schrader Snickers 25.00 50.00
36 Ken Schrader Snickers Chrome/1500 20.00 40.00
38 Christian Elder Deka Batteries Promo 18.00 30.00
38 Christian Elder Great Clips Promo 18.00 30.00
40 Sterling Marlin Coors Light 24K Gold Promo 25.00 50.00
40 Sterling Marlin Marlin 12.00 30.00
43 Jay Sauter Morton's Salt Promo 30.00 50.00
43 Jay Sauter Quality Farm Promo 35.00 60.00
55 Bobby Hamilton Square D 8.00 20.00
55 Bobby Hamilton Square D Chrome/1500 15.00 30.00
55 Bobby Hamilton Square D Lightning Layin' Rubber/500 15.00 40.00
55 Bobby Hamilton Square D Encompass 30.00 50.00
57 Jason Keller Albertsons Promo 8.00 20.00
60 Travis Kvapil Cat Rental SuperTruck Promo 15.00 30.00
66 Todd Bodine Phillips 66 8.00 20.00
66 Todd Bodine Phillips 66 Chrome/1500 15.00 30.00
92 Stacy Compton Compton 12.00 30.00
92 Stacy Compton Kodiak Promo/2500 10.00 20.00
92 Stacy Compton Compton Chrome/1500 15.00 30.00
93 Dave Blaney Amoco 8.00 20.00
93 Dave Blaney Amoco Chrome/1500 15.00 30.00
93 Dave Blaney Amoco Layin' Rubber 20.00 40.00
93 Dave Blaney Amoco 24kt. Gold Promo 15.00 40.00
93 Dave Blaney Amoco BP 8.00 20.00
93 Dave Blaney Amoco BP Race Rubber 15.00 40.00
93 Dave Blaney Amoco Siemens Promo 6.00 15.00
93 Dave Blaney Mac Tools/4000 12.00 30.00
98 Elton Sawyer Auburn U. Promo 25.00 40.00
98 Elton Sawyer Georgia U. Promo/1250 25.00 40.00
98 Elton Sawyer Miami U. Promo/1250 25.00 40.00
98 Elton Sawyer Michigan University Promo/1250 25.00 40.00
98 Elton Sawyer North Carolina University Promo/1250 25.00 40.00
98 Elton Sawyer Tennessee University Promo/1250 25.00 40.00
01 All-Pro Auto Value Promo 15.00 30.00
01 Chik-fil-a Peach Bowl Promo 7.50 15.00
01 Jason Leffler Cingular 12.00 30.00
01 Jason Leffler Cingular Layin' Rubber/500 20.00 40.00
01 Jason Leffler Cingular Special Olympics Promo 15.00 30.00
01 Jason Leffler Cingular Promo 15.00 40.00
01 Michigan International Speedway 15.00 30.00
01 Mountain Dew Tropicana 400 Promo 25.00 40.00
01 Ratheon Six Sigma Promo 20.00 40.00
01 Shop 'n Save Promo 10.00 20.00
NNO NDA Dodge Test Team 12.00 30.00

2001 Racing Champions Premier 1:24

5 Terry Labonte Frosted Flakes 2000 15.00 40.00
5 Terry Labonte Kellogg's 15.00 40.00
5 Terry Labonte Kellogg's Chrome 30.00 60.00
10 Johnny Benson Valvoline 12.00 30.00
10 Johnny Benson Valvoline Layin Rubber 15.00 40.00
12 Jeremy Mayfield Mobil 1 12.00 30.00
12 Jeremy Mayfield Mobil Autographed
12 Jeremy Mayfield Mobil Chrome 25.00 50.00
12 Jeremy Mayfield Mobil Firesuit 25.00 50.00
12 Jeremy Mayfield Mobil Layin Rubber 25.00 50.00
12 Jeremy Mayfield Mobil Race Rubber 25.00 50.00
12 Jeremy Mayfield Mobil Real Steel 40.00 80.00
21 Elliott Sadler Motorcraft 12.00 30.00
21 Elliott Sadler Motorcraft Chrome/1500 15.00 40.00
21 Elliott Sadler Motorcraft Layin Rubber 25.00 50.00
22 Ward Burton Caterpillar 12.00 30.00
22 Ward Burton Caterpillar Autographed
22 Ward Burton Caterpillar Race Rubber 30.00 60.00
22 Ward Burton Caterpillar Real Steel 40.00 80.00
25 Jerry Nadeau UAW 12.00 30.00
25 Jerry Nadeau UAW Chrome/1500 20.00 40.00
25 Jerry Nadeau UAW Layin Rubber 20.00 50.00
26 Jimmy Spencer K-Mart 12.00 30.00
26 Jimmy Spencer K-Mart Layin Rubber 15.00 40.00
36 Ken Schrader M&M's 12.00 30.00
36 Ken Schrader M&M's Chrome 20.00 40.00
36 Ken Schrader M&M's Firesuit 25.00 50.00
36 Ken Schrader M&M's Real Steel 40.00 80.00
93 Dave Blaney Amoco 12.00 30.00
93 Dave Blaney Amoco Firesuit 20.00 50.00
98 Elton Sawyer Huskers 20.00 35.00

2001 Racing Champions Authentics 1:24

5 Terry Labonte Kellogg'sTony Mac Tools Promo/3000 20.00 50.00
10 Johnny Benson Valvoline Firesuit/1200 20.00 40.00
10 Johnny Benson Valvoline Sheetmetal/1200 20.00 40.00
11 Smuckers Promo/8000 25.00 50.00
22 Ward Burton Caterpillar Firesuit/1500 30.00 60.00
22 Ward Burton Cat Tractors 100.00 175.00
22 Ward Burton Cat Tractors Chrome/250 125.00 200.00
36 Ken Schrader M&M's Firesuit/1200 20.00 40.00
36 Ken Schrader M&M's Race Rubber/1200 20.00 40.00
36 Ken Schrader M&M's Sheetmetal/1200 20.00 40.00
40 Sterling Marlin Coors Firesuit 75.00 135.00
40 Sterling Marlin Coors Chrome/250 70.00 120.00
40 Sterling Marlin Coors Light Firesuit/1200 50.00 100.00
93 Dave Blaney Amoco Firesuit/1200 15.00 40.00
93 Dave Blaney Amoco Sheetmetal/1200 15.00 40.00
01 Dave Blaney Amoco Ultimate Promo without Firesuit 7.50 20.00
01 Dave Blaney Amoco Ultimate Promo Firesuit/1200 15.00 30.00

2002 Racing Champions 1:24

1 Jimmy Spencer Yellow Freight 10.00 20.00
1 Jimmy Spencer Yellow Freight Tire 20.00 50.00
2 Jason Leffler CarQuest SuperTruck Promo w/1:64 car 15.00 30.00
4 Mike Skinner Kodak 10.00 20.00
5 Terry Labonte Cheez-it 12.50 25.00
5 Terry Labonte Cheez-it Car Cover/500 30.00 60.00
5 Terry Labonte Cheez-it Firesuit 60.00 100.00
5 Terry Labonte Got Milk 15.00 25.00
5 Terry Labonte Got Milk AUTO 40.00 80.00
5 Terry Labonte Kellogg's 10.00 25.00
5 Terry Labonte Kellogg's Cover/500 30.00 60.00
5 Terry Labonte Kellogg's Firesuit 50.00 100.00
10 Johnny Benson Eagle One 10.00 25.00
10 Johnny Benson Eagle One AUTO 30.00 80.00
10 Johnny Benson Eagle One Firesuit 40.00 80.00
10 Johnny Benson Valvoline 10.00 25.00
10 Johnny Benson Valvoline Steel 50.00 100.00
10 Johnny Benson Zerex 10.00 20.00
10 Johnny Benson Zerex Firesuit/25 50.00 100.00
10 Johnny Benson Zerex Tire 25.00 50.00
10 Johnny Benson 100 Years of Kentucky BK 25.00 40.00
10 Johnny Benson 100 Years of Kentucky Basketball Promo/835 35.00 60.00
10 Johnny Benson 100 Years of Kentucky Basketball Color Chrome Promo/167 60.00 100.00
10 Scott Riggs Nestea Promo 15.00 30.00
10 Scott Riggs Nestle Toll House Halloween Promo 15.00 30.00
10 Scott Riggs Nesquik 10.00 25.00
11 Brett Bodine Hooters 15.00 30.00
12 Carey Heath Aubuchon Hardware Promo 12.50 25.00
14 Stacy Compton Conseco 10.00 25.00
15 Robin Buck NAPA Promo 20.00 35.00
19 Tim Sauter Motorsports Park 131 18.00 30.00
21 Elliott Sadler Motorcraft 20.00 40.00
22 Ward Burton Caterpillar Daytona Win 12.50 25.00
22 Ward Burton Caterpillar Daytona Win AUTO 40.00 80.00
22 Ward Burton Caterpillar Daytona Win Chrome/1500 20.00 40.00
22 Ward Burton Cat Dealers '02 packaging 20.00 35.00
22 Ward Burton Cat Dealers '03 packaging 12.50 25.00
22 Ward Burton Cat Dealers Chrome/1500 2003 packaging 25.00 40.00
22 Ward Burton Wildlife Foundation Promo 50.00 80.00
23 Hut Stricklin Hills Bros. 15.00 30.00
24 Jack Sprague NETZERO 10.00 20.00
25 Jerry Nadeau UAW 10.00 20.00
26 Lyndon Amick Dr.Pepper Spider-Man 15.00 30.00
26 Ron Hornaday Dr.Pepper Promo Error Bobby Hamilton Jr. name on car 20.00 35.00
26 Ron Hornaday Red Fusion Promo 20.00 35.00
26 Ron Hornaday Red Fusion Color Chrome Promo 30.00 50.00
26 Joe Nemechek K-Mart 10.00 20.00
27 Scott Wimmer Siemens Promo/625 25.00 50.00
27 Scott Wimmer Siemens Brushed Metal Promo/125 30.00 60.00
28 Brad Baker Whitetails Unlimited 15.00 30.00
30 Christian Fittipaldi Mike's Hard Lemonade Promo/625 25.00 40.00
30 Christian Fittipaldi Mike's Hard Lemonade Brushed Metal Promo/125 30.00 50.00
32 Ricky Craven Tide 10.00 20.00
32 Ricky Craven Tide Chrome/1500 15.00 40.00
32 Ricky Craven Tide Promo 12.50 25.00
32 Ricky Craven Tide First Win Raced 10.00 25.00
32 Ricky Craven Tide Kids 10.00 25.00
32 Ricky Craven Tide Kids AUTO
33 John Komarinski Rolling Rock Promo/1333 30.00 60.00
33 Kenny Wallace 1-800-CALL-ATT Promo 30.00 50.00
33 Mike Wallace Preen Promo 30.00 60.00
36 Hank Parker Jr GNC 10.00 25.00
36 Ken Schrader Combos Promo 60.00 120.00
36 Ken Schrader M&M's 12.50 25.00
36 Ken Schrader M&M's AUTO 30.00 60.00
36 Ken Schrader M&M's Chrome/1500 15.00 40.00
36 Ken Schrader M&M's Car Cover/500 30.00 60.00
36 Ken Schrader M&M's Firesuit 50.00 100.00
36 Ken Schrader M&M's Steel 50.00 100.00
36 Ken Schrader M&M's Halloween 2003 packaging 12.50 25.00
36 Ken Schrader M&M's July 4th 12.50 25.00
36 Ken Schrader Pedigree 12.50 25.00
36 Ken Schrader Pedigree Firesuit
40 Brian Vickers EMP Promo 75.00 150.00
43 Jay Sauter Morton Salt Promo 25.00 40.00
44 Pabst Blue Ribbon Promo 20.00 35.00
46 Ashton Lewis Civil Air Patrol Promo 20.00 40.00
47 Shane Hmiel Mike's Hard Cranberry Promo/625 25.00 40.00
47 Shane Hmiel Mike's Hard Cranberry Brushed Metal Promo/125 30.00 50.00
47 Shane Hmiel Mike's Hard Lemonade Promo/625 25.00 40.00
47 Shane Hmiel Mike's Hard Lemonade Brushed Metal Promo/125 30.00 50.00
47 Shane Hmiel Mike's Hard Iced Tea Promo/625 25.00 40.00
47 Shane Hmiel Mike's Hard Iced Tea Brushed Metal Promo/125 30.00 50.00
48 Jimmie Johnson Lowe's 15.00 30.00
48 Jimmie Johnson Lowe's Chrome/1500 50.00 80.00
48 Jimmie Johnson Lowe's Car Cover/500 40.00 80.00
48 Jimmie Johnson Lowe's Steel/25 100.00 175.00
48 Jimmie Johnson Lowe's with Press Pass card 10.00 20.00
48 Jimmie Johnson Lowe's Power of Pride 15.00 30.00
48 Jimmie Johnson Lowe's Power of Pride Car Cover/500
48 Jimmie Johnson Lowe's Power of Pride Chrome/1500 25.00 60.00
48 Jimmie Johnson Lowe's Power of Pride with Press Pass card 10.00 20.00
49 Shawna Robinson BAM Promo 25.00 50.00
54 Kevin Grubb Toys 'R' Us Promo 12.50 25.00
55 Bobby Hamilton Schneider 10.00 20.00
55 Bobby Hamilton Schneider Chrome/1500 15.00 30.00
55 Bobby Hamilton Schneider Car Cover/500 20.00 40.00
55 Bobby Hamilton Schneider Tire/250 25.00 60.00
57 Jason Keller Albertsons Flag 10.00 20.00
57 Jason Keller Albertson's Promo 12.00 20.00
66 Casey Mears Phillips 66 25.00 40.00
66 Robin Buck UAP NAPA Promo box in French&English 18.00 30.00
77 Dave Blaney Jasper 10.00 20.00
77 Dave Blaney Jasper Car Cover/500 20.00 40.00
77 Dave Blaney Jasper Promo 15.00 30.00
93 Travis Benjamin Irving Promo 18.00 30.00
98 Kenny Wallace Stacker 2 in 2003 packaging 15.00 30.00
99 Michael Waltrip Aaron's Rent 10.00 20.00
01 K-Resin Promo 18.00 30.00
02 All Pro Auto Value Flames Promo 18.00 30.00
02 Cabela's 250 Promo 18.00 30.00
02 Foodland Super Market Promo 15.00 30.00
02 Nebraska Blackshirts Promo 25.00 40.00
02 Snap-On Promo 25.00 40.00
02 Timken Store Promo 35.00 60.00

2002 Racing Champions Premier 1:24

1 Snap-On Team Memphis Promo in a box 18.00 30.00
5 Terry Labonte Kellogg's 15.00 30.00
5 Terry Labonte Kellogg's Firesuit
5 Terry Labonte Kellogg's Steel
10 Johnny Benson Eagle One 15.00 30.00
10 Johnny Benson Eagle One AUTO 30.00 80.00
10 Johnny Benson Valvoline Maxlife 15.00 30.00
10 Johnny Benson Zerex 15.00 30.00
10 Johnny Benson Zerex AUTO
10 Johnny Benson Zerex Car Cover/500 25.00 50.00
10 Johnny Benson Zerex Firesuit/25 50.00 100.00
22 Ward Burton Caterpillar Daytona Win 15.00 30.00
22 Ward Burton Caterpillar Daytona Win AU/100 50.00 100.00
22 Ward Burton Caterpillar Daytona Win Chrome/1500 20.00 40.00
22 Ward Burton Cat Dealers in 2003 packaging 15.00 30.00
22 Ward Burton Cat Dealers Chrome/1500 in 2003 packaging 20.00 40.00
32 Ricky Craven Tide 15.00 30.00
32 Ricky Craven Tide Car Cover/500 25.00 50.00
32 Ricky Craven Tide Chrome/1500 20.00 40.00
32 Ricky Craven Tide Kids 15.00 30.00
40 Sterling Marlin Flag 15.00 30.00
48 Jimmie Johnson Lowe's 20.00 40.00
48 Jimmie Johnson Lowe's Car Cover/500 50.00 100.00
48 Jimmie Johnson Lowe's First Win 15.00 40.00
48 Jimmie Johnson Lowe's First Win Car Cover/500 25.00 60.00
48 Jimmie Johnson Lowe's Power of Pride 15.00 40.00
48 Jimmie Johnson Lowe's Power of Pride#[Chrome/1500 30.00 80.00
48 Jimmie Johnson Lowe's Press Pass/2500 15.00 30.00
55 Bobby Hamilton Schneider 15.00 30.00
77 Dave Blaney Jasper 15.00 30.00

2002 Racing Champions American Muscle Body Shop 1:24

32 Scott Pruett Tide SuperTruck 7.50 15.00
64 Chuck Erdman 1964 Plymouth Belvedere 7.50 15.00

2002 Racing Champions Premier Preview 1:24

5 Terry Labonte Kellogg's 12.50 30.00
5 Terry Labonte Kellogg's Chrome/1500 20.00 50.00
5 Terry Labonte Kellogg's Tire
10 Johnny Benson Valvoline 12.50 30.00
10 Johnny Benson Valvoline Firesuit 40.00 80.00
10 Johnny Benson Valvoline Firesuit Tire
10 Johnny Benson Valvoline Tire 25.00 50.00
22 Ward Burton Caterpillar 12.50 30.00
22 Ward Burton Caterpillar Car Cover/500 20.00 40.00
22 Ward Burton Caterpillar Firesuit 40.00 80.00
22 Ward Burton Caterpillar Steel
25 Jerry Nadeau UAW 12.50 30.00
25 Jerry Nadeau UAW Car Cover/500 15.00 40.00
25 Jerry Nadeau UAW Chrome 20.00 40.00
36 Ken Schrader M&M's 12.50 30.00
40 Sterling Marlin Marlin Flag 15.00 35.00

2002 Racing Champions Preview 1:24

5 Terry Labonte Kellogg's 12.50 25.00
5 Terry Labonte Kellogg's Chrome/1500 15.00 40.00
10 Johnny Benson Valvoline 12.50 25.00
10 Johnny Benson Valvoline Chrome/1500 15.00 40.00
10 Johnny Benson Valvoline Firesuit 40.00 80.00
10 Johnny Benson Valvoline Tire 25.00 50.00
22 Ward Burton Caterpillar 12.50 25.00
22 Ward Burton Caterpillar Car Cover/500 20.00 50.00
22 Ward Burton Caterpillar Firesuit 40.00 80.00
22 Ward Burton Caterpillar Steel
25 Jerry Nadeau UAW 12.50 25.00
25 Jerry Nadeau UAW Tire
26 Jimmy Spencer K-Mart Shrek 15.00 30.00
32 Ricky Craven Tide 12.50 25.00
32 Ricky Craven Tide Car Cover/500 20.00 40.00
36 Ken Schrader M&M's 12.50 25.00
40 Sterling Marlin Marlin Flag 12.50 30.00
57 Jason Keller Albertsons Flag Promo 7.50 15.00

2002 Racing Champions Authentics 1:24

1 Jimmy Spencer Yellow Freight 25.00 50.00
1 Jimmy Spencer Yellow Freight Chrome/139 30.00 80.00
4 Mike Skinner Kodak/999 25.00 50.00
4 Mike Skinner Kodak Chrome/199 30.00 80.00
5 Terry Labonte Got Milk/999 30.00 60.00
5 Terry Labonte Got Milk Chrome/199 30.00 80.00
7 Randy LaJoie Kleenex 30.00 60.00
10 Johnny Benson Eagle One/999 25.00 50.00
10 Johnny Benson Eagle One Chrome/199 50.00 100.00
10 Johnny Benson Valvoline/999 25.00 50.00
10 Johnny Benson Valvoline Chrome/199 50.00 120.00
11 Brett Bodine Hooters/699 30.00 60.00
11 Brett Bodine Hooters Chrome/199 50.00 100.00
11 Brett Bodine Wells Fargo Promo/2000 45.00 80.00
21 Elliott Sadler Air Force/999 25.00 50.00
21 Elliott Sadler Air Force Chrome/199 30.00 80.00
21 Elliott Sadler Motorcraft/999 20.00 40.00
21 Elliott Sadler Motorcraft Chrome/199 25.00 60.00
22 Ward Burton Caterpillar/999 25.00 60.00
22 Ward Burton Caterpillar Chrome/199 60.00 120.00
22 Ward Burton Caterpillar Daytona Win 40.00 80.00
22 Ward Burton Caterpillar Flag 30.00 60.00
22 Ward Burton Cat Dealers/999 60.00 100.00
22 Ward Burton Cat Dealers Chrome/199 75.00 125.00
23 Hut Stricklin Hills Bros./999 25.00 50.00
23 Hut Stricklin Hills Bros.Chrome/199 40.00 80.00
24 Jack Sprague NETZERO/699 20.00 50.00
24 Jack Sprague NETZERO Chrome/139 30.00 80.00
25 Joe Nemechek UAW/999 25.00 50.00
25 Joe Nemechek UAW Chrome 50.00 100.00
26 Lyndon Amick Dr.Pepper Spider-Man/699 25.00 50.00
26 Lyndon Amick Dr.Pepper Spider-Man Chrome/149 40.00 80.00
30 Chistian Fittipaldi Mike's Hard Lemonade/585 50.00 80.00
30 Christian Fittipaldi Mike's Hard Lemonade Chrome/117 60.00 100.00
32 Ricky Craven Tide/999 25.00 50.00
32 Ricky Craven Tide Chrome/199 40.00 80.00
32 Ricky Craven Tide Kids/999 25.00 50.00
32 Ricky Craven Tide Kids Chrome/199 40.00 80.00
36 Ken Schrader M&M's/999 25.00 60.00
36 Ken Schrader M&M's Chrome/199 50.00 100.00
36 Ken Schrader M&M's July 4th/999 25.00 60.00
36 Ken Schrader M&M's July 4th Chrome/199 50.00 100.00
36 Hank Parker Jr. GNC/699 25.00 50.00
36 Hank Parker Jr. GNC Chrome/139 40.00 80.00
37 Jeff Purvis Timberwolf/699 25.00 50.00
37 Jeff Purvis Timberwolf Chrome/149 30.00 60.00
40 Sterling Marlin Proud to be American 40.00 80.00
43 Richard Petty Garfield/999 30.00 60.00
48 Jimmie Johnson Lowe's/999 75.00 150.00
48 Jimmie Johnson Lowe's Chrome/199 150.00 300.00
48 Jimmie Johnson Lowe's First Win/2555 40.00 80.00
48 Jimmie Johnson Lowe's First Win Chrome/511 75.00 150.00
48 Jimmie Johnson Lowe's Sylvester and Tweety/4167 30.00 60.00
48 Jimmie Johnson Lowe's Sylvester and Tweety Chrome/833 50.00 100.00
48 Jimmie Johnson Lowe's 2001 Power of Pride/999 60.00 120.00
48 Jimmie Johnson Lowe's Power of Pride/999 60.00 120.00
48 Jimmie Johnson Lowe's Power of Pride Chrome/199 100.00 200.00
48 Jimmie Johnson Lowe's Power of Pride Employee/10,000 50.00 120.00
49 Shawna Robinson BAM/699 35.00 60.00
49 Shawna Robinson BAM Chrome/139 60.00 100.00
52 Donnie Neuenberger Maryland University Promo 30.00 60.00
66 Casey Mears Kansas Jayhawks Promo 40.00 75.00

2002 Racing Champions Ironman 1:24

5 Terry Labonte Kellogg's/504 30.00 50.00
10 Johnny Benson Valvoline/504 25.00 50.00
22 Ward Burton Caterpillar/504 25.00 50.00
32 Ricky Craven Tide/504 30.00 50.00
48 Jimmie Johnson Lowe's/504 60.00 100.00

2002 Racing Champions Under the Lights 1:24

Racing Champions issued this series of 1:24 die-cast cars packaged along with the counterpart 1:64 car. Each was produced in a chrome finish to give the car the appearance of a night race event.

48 Jimmie Johnson Lowe's 30.00 50.00

2002 Racing Champions War Paint 1:24

Racing Champions issued this series of 1:24 die-cast cars packaged along with the counterpart 1:64 car. Each was produced with tire marks on the sides to give the car a post-race appearance.

48 Jimmie Johnson Lowe's 25.00 50.00

2003 Racing Champions 1:24

1 Jamie McMurray Yellow Freight 10.00 20.00
1 Ted Musgrave Mopar SuperTruck Promo measures slightly larger than 1:24 scale 40.00 80.00
4 Mike Skinner Kodak 10.00 20.00
4 Mike Skinner Kodak Rain Delay/500 20.00 40.00
4 Square D SuperTruck Promo 15.00 30.00
5 Terry Labonte Kellogg's 10.00 20.00
5 Terry Labonte Finding Nemo 10.00 25.00
5 Terry Labonte Finding Nemo AU/100 50.00 100.00
5 Terry Labonte Power of Cheese 10.00 20.00
5 Terry Labonte Power of Cheese AU/100 50.00 100.00
5 Brian Vickers GMAC 15.00 25.00
7 Alan Kulwicki Hooters 20th Anniv. Chrome Promo 35.00 60.00
7 Randy LaJoie Kleenex Promo 18.00 30.00
7 Jimmy Spencer Sirius 15.00 30.00
8 Bill Lester Dodge SuperTruck Promo measures slightly larger than 1:24 scale 15.00 40.00
10 Johnny Benson Valvoline 10.00 20.00
10 Johnny Benson Valvoline Firesuit/50 30.00 50.00
10 Johnny Benson Valvoline Steel/50 40.00 80.00
11 Brett Bodine Hooters 10.00 20.00
11 Brett Bodine Hooters 20th Anniversary 10.00 25.00
11 Brett Bodine US Micro Brick Promo 30.00 50.00
12 Shane Riffel USS Hornet SuperTruck Promo 20.00 40.00
14 Rick Crawford Strategic Air Command Promo 18.00 30.00
18 Chad Chaffin Dickies SuperTruck Promo measures slightly larger than 1:24 scale 15.00 30.00
22 Ward Burton Caterpillar 10.00 20.00
22 Ward Burton Caterpillar Chrome/1500 18.00 30.00
22 Ward Burton Caterpillar Firesuit/50 40.00 80.00
22 Ward Burton Caterpillar Rain Delay/500 18.00 30.00
22 Ward Burton Caterpillar Steel/50 40.00 80.00
22 Ward Burton Caterpillar Time Trial/5000 15.00 25.00
22 Ward Burton 15.00 25.00

Cat Acert

22 Ward Burton Cat Acert Promo 20.00 35.00

23 Scott Wimmer Stacker 2 Fast & Furious 10.00 25.00

25 Joe Nemechek UAW Delphi 12.50 25.00

25 Joe Nemechek UAW Delphi AU/100 25.00 50.00

25 Joe Nemechek UAW Delphi Chrome/1500 12.50 30.00

25 Joe Nemechek UAW Delphi Rain Delay/500 15.00 30.00

26 Todd Bodine Discover 12.50 25.00

26 Kevin Grubb Dr.Pepper 20.00 35.00

31 Tina Gordon Scotch Transparent Duct Tape Promo 15.00 30.00

31 Tina Gordon 3M Post-it Promo 15.00 30.00

32 Ricky Craven Tide 10.00 20.00

32 Ricky Craven Tide Rain Delay/500 20.00 40.00

32 Ricky Craven Tide TCF Bank Promo 25.00 40.00

33 John Komarinski Rock Light Promo/1033 20.00 40.00

33 Tony Raines Outdoor Channel Promo 25.00 50.00

37 Derrike Cope Friendly's Promo 30.00 50.00

37 David Green Timberwolf Promo Adult Collectible box 15.00 40.00

37 David Green Timberwolf Promo Age 8+ box 20.00 50.00

48 Shane Hmiel Thomas Automotive 25.00 50.00

48 Jimmie Johnson Lowe's 15.00 25.00

48 Jimmie Johnson Lowe's Chrome/1500 with Press Pass card 20.00 35.00

48 Jimmie Johnson Lowe's Firesuit/50 60.00 120.00

48 Jimmie Johnson Lowe's Rain Delay/500 25.00 50.00

48 Jimmie Johnson Lowe's Steel/50 75.00 150.00

48 Jimmie Johnson Lowe's Power of Pride with Ultra Series card 15.00 25.00

48 Jimmie Johnson Lowe's Power of Pride Chrome/1500 15.00 30.00

48 Jimmie Johnson Lowe's Power of Pride Firesuit/50 60.00 120.00

48 Jimmie Johnson Lowe's Power of Pride Rain Delay 20.00 40.00

48 Jimmie Johnson Lowe's Power of Pride Steel/50 60.00 120.00

48 Jimmie Johnson Lowe's SpongeBob 15.00 25.00

48 Jimmie Johnson Lowe's SpongeBob Chrome/1500 25.00 40.00

49 Ken Schrader 1-800-CALL-ATT Promo 25.00 60.00

50 Scooby-Doo SD Racing 15.00 30.00

54 Todd Bodine National Guard Promo 20.00 40.00

57 Jason Keller Albertson's 10.00 20.00

62 Brendan Gaughan American Racing SuperTruck Promo in solid box measures slightly larger than 1:24 scale 30.00 50.00

77 Dave Blaney First Tennessee Promo 30.00 50.00

77 Dave Blaney Jasper Fast&Furious 10.00 25.00

90 Lance Norick Express Personnel Promo 20.00 40.00

01 Jerry Nadeau Army 12.50 25.00

01 Jerry Nadeau Army Chrome/1500 15.00 40.00

01 Jerry Nadeau Army Camo 12.50 25.00

01 Jerry Nadeau Army Camo Chrome/1500 15.00 40.00

03 Ward Burton CertainTeed Promo 25.00 50.00

03 Dana Fantasy Racing Promo 30.00 50.00

03 Parts Master Promo/7500 15.00 30.00

03 Jay Sauter Timken SuperTruck Promo 15.00 30.00

G3 Goodyear G3Xpress Promo 15.00 30.00

2003 Racing Champions Premier 1:24

11 Brett Bodine Hooters 20.00 35.00

11 Brett Bodine Hooters 20th Anniversary 20.00 35.00

22 Ward Burton Caterpillar 15.00 30.00

22 Ward Burton Caterpillar Chrome/1500 25.00 40.00

22 Ward Burton Caterpillar Rain Delay/500 20.00 40.00

57 Jason Keller Albertsons 18.00 30.00

2003 Racing Champions Premier Preview 1:24

22 Ward Burton Caterpillar 18.00 30.00

22 Ward Burton Caterpillar Firesuit/50 40.00 80.00

22 Ward Burton Caterpillar Rain Delay/500 20.00 40.00

22 Ward Burton Cat Rental 18.00 30.00

22 Ward Burton Cat Rental Chrome/1500 25.00 40.00

22 Ward Burton Cat Rental Firesuit/50 45.00 80.00

22 Ward Burton Cat Rental Firesuit Steel/50 50.00 100.00

22 Ward Burton Cat Rental Rain Delay/500 12.50 25.00

26 Todd Bodine Discover 18.00 30.00

48 Jimmie Johnson Lowe's 2002 Season to Remember 18.00 30.00

2003 Racing Champions Preview 1:24

5 Terry Labonte Kellogg's 10.00 20.00

22 Ward Burton Caterpillar 12.50 25.00

22 Ward Burton Caterpillar Firesuit/50 50.00 100.00

22 Ward Burton Caterpillar Rain Delay/500 18.00 30.00

22 Ward Burton Caterpillar Steel/50 40.00 100.00

22 Ward Burton Cat Rental 12.50 25.00

22 Ward Burton Cat Rental Chrome/1500 20.00 40.00

22 Ward Burton Cat Rental Firesuit/50 40.00 100.00

22 Ward Burton Cat Rental Rain Delay/500 18.00 30.00

26 Todd Bodine Discover 10.00 25.00

32 Ricky Craven Tide 10.00 20.00

48 Jimmie Johnson Lowe's 2002 Season to Remember 10.00 25.00

2003 Racing Champions Authentics 1:24

1 Jamie McMurray Yellow Freight/700 30.00 60.00

1 Jamie McMurray Yellow Freight Chrome/140 75.00 135.00

11 Brett Bodine Hooters/1585 40.00 70.00

11 Brett Bodine Hooters Chrome/317 50.00 90.00

11 Brett Bodine Hooters 20th Anniv./700 40.00 70.00

11 Brett Bodine Hooters 20th Anniv. Chrome/140 60.00 100.00

22 Ward Burton Caterpillar/3690 25.00 50.00

22 Ward Burton Caterpillar Chrome/738 45.00 80.00

22 Ward Burton Cat Acert/1685 30.00 60.00

22 Ward Burton Cat Acert Chrome/337 50.00 90.00

22 Ward Burton Cat Rental/3140 25.00 50.00

22 Ward Burton Cat Rental Chrome/628 40.00 75.00

48 Jimmie Johnson Lowe's/4540 30.00 60.00

48 Jimmie Johnson Lowe's Chrome/908 50.00 100.00

48 Jimmie Johnson Lowe's Power of Pride/3470 30.00 60.00

48 Jimmie Johnson Lowe's Power of Pride Chrome/694 50.00 100.00

48 Jimmie Johnson Lowe's SpongeBob/2020 35.00 60.00

48 Jimmie Johnson Lowe's Spongebob Chrome/404 60.00 100.00

2004 Racing Champions 1:24

1 Johnny Benson Yellow Freight Promo 20.00 35.00

11 Darrell Waltrip Toyota TRD SuperTruck Promo 25.00 40.00

17 David Reutimann NTN Bearings SuperTruck Promo 35.00 60.00

27 Johnny Sauter Kleenex Promo 25.00 40.00

35 Brad Leighton Irving Oil Promo 15.00 30.00

38 Kasey Kahne Great Clips Promo 25.00 40.00

38 Elliott Sadler Combos Promo 12.50 25.00

38 Elliott Sadler M&M's Promo 15.00 30.00

38 Brandon Whitt Werner Ladders SuperTruck Promo 40.00 80.00

42 Mike Skinner Toyota TRD SuperTruck Promo 15.00 30.00

43 Aaron Fike Ollie's Bargain Outlet 12.50 25.00

49 Ken Schrader Red Baron Promo 30.00 60.00

49 Ken Schrader Schwan's Promo 30.00 60.00

67 Jason Jarrett Gladiator Bennigan's Promo 40.00 70.00

74 Tony Raines The Outdoor Channel Promo 15.00 30.00

2004 Racing Champions Authentics 1:24

5 Terry Labonte Kellogg's 30.00 50.00

22 Scott Wimmer Cat/2400 25.00 50.00

22 Scott Wimmer Cat Chrome/480 60.00 100.00

25 Brian Vickers Ditech 30.00 50.00

25 Brian Vickers Ditech.com Matco Promo 20.00 40.00

43 Richard Petty Blue 1957 Oldsmobile/800 100.00 175.00

43 Richard Petty Blue 1957 Oldsmobile Chrome/200 150.00 225.00

48 Jimmie Johnson Lowe's/2400 30.00 50.00

48 Jimmie Johnson Lowe's Chrome 50.00 80.00

48 Jimmie Johnson Lowe's HMS 20th Anniversary/2500 30.00 50.00

48 Jimmie Johnson Lowe's HMS 20th Anniversary Chrome/500 40.00 70.00

48 Jimmie Johnson Lowe's SpongeBob/2500 25.00 50.00

48 Jimmie Johnson Lowe's SpongeBob Chrome/500 35.00 60.00

48 Jimmie Johnson Lowe's Tool World 30.00 50.00

48 Jimmie Johnson Lowe's Tool World Chrome/500 40.00 70.00

0 Ward Burton NetZero 30.00 50.00

0 Ward Burton NetZero Chrome/168 35.00 60.00

2004 Racing Champions Ultra Previews 1:24

10 Scott Riggs Valvoline 10.00 25.00

48 Jimmie Johnson Lowe's 10.00 25.00

48 Jimmie Johnson Lowe's Chrome/1500 20.00 40.00

2004 Racing Champions Ultra 1:24

5 Kyle Busch Lowe's 15.00 30.00

5 Kyle Busch Lowe's SpongeBob 10.00 20.00

5 Terry Labonte Delphi 10.00 20.00

5 Terry Labonte Kellogg's 10.00 20.00

5 Terry Labonte Kellogg's Chrome/1500 20.00 40.00

5 Terry Labonte Kellogg's HMS 20th Ann. in '05 packaging 10.00 20.00

5 Terry Labonte Kellogg's Incredibles in '05 packaging 10.00 20.00

10 Scott Riggs Harlem Globetrotters 10.00 20.00

10 Scott Riggs Valvoline 10.00 20.00

10 Scott Riggs Valvoline Firesuit/50 25.00 50.00

10 Scott Riggs Valvoline Steel/50 30.00 60.00

22 Scott Wimmer Caterpillar 10.00 20.00

22 Scott Wimmer Caterpillar Chrome 20.00 40.00

22 Scott Wimmer Cat Dealer 10.00 20.00

22 Scott Wimmer Cat Rental 10.00 20.00

25 Brian Vickers ditech.com 10.00 20.00

48 Jimmie Johnson Lowe's 10.00 20.00

48 Jimmie Johnson Lowe's HMS 20th Ann. in '05 packaging 12.50 25.00

48 Jimmie Johnson Lowe's HMS 20th Anniversary Chrome/500 20.00 40.00

48 Jimmie Johnson Lowe's SpongeBob 10.00 20.00

48 Jimmie Johnson Lowe's Tool World 10.00 20.00

48 Jimmie Johnson Lowe's Tool World in '05 packaging 10.00 20.00

0 Ward Burton NetZero 15.00 30.00

0 Ward Burton NetZero Chrome/1500 25.00 50.00

0 Ward Burton NetZero Rain Delay/500 20.00 40.00

01 Joe Nemechek Army 10.00 20.00

2005 Racing Champions 1:24

1 Johnny Sauter Yellow Promo 20.00 35.00

5 Mike Skinner Toyota TRD SuperTruck Promo 25.00 40.00

10 Terry Cook Powerstroke Diesel SuperTruck Promo 25.00 40.00

12 Robert Huffman Toyota TRD SuperTruck Promo 25.00 40.00

17 David Reutimann Toyota TRD SuperTruck Promo 25.00 40.00

27 David Green Kleenex Promo 15.00 30.00

34 Randy Lajoie Dollar General Promo 15.00 30.00

66 Greg Biffle Royal Office Products Promo 20.00 40.00

66 Matt Martin Gatorade SuperTruck Promo 25.00 50.00

2005 Racing Champions Authentics 1:24

40 Pete Hamilton '70 Superbird/1002 35.00 60.00

40 Pete Hamilton '70 Superbird Black Chrome/72 50.00 100.00

40 Pete Hamilton '70 Superbird Silver Chrome/72 50.00 100.00

41 Lee Petty '64 Belvedere/630 60.00 120.00

42 Lee Petty '57 Hardtop/630 75.00 125.00

42 Lee Petty '57 Hardtop Chrome/126 100.00 175.00

43 Richard Petty '64 Plymouth Belvedere/800 50.00 75.00

43 Richard Petty '64 Plymouth Belvedere Black Chrome/200 100.00 150.00

43 Richard Petty '70 Superbird/1002 60.00 100.00

43 Richard Petty '70 Superbird Black Chrome/72 100.00 150.00

43 Richard Petty '70 Superbird Silver Chrome/72 100.00 150.00

43 Richard Petty '70 Superbird Marc Times/1002 60.00 100.00

43 Richard Petty '70 Superbird Marc Times Black Chrome/72 100.00 150.00

43 Richard Petty '70 Superbird Marc Times Silver Chrome/72 100.00 150.00

43 Richard Petty '70 Superbird Southern Chrysler/1002 60.00 100.00

43 Richard Petty '70 Superbird Southern Chrysler Black Chrome/72 100.00 150.00

43 Richard Petty '70 Superbird Southern Chrysler Silver Chrome/72 100.00 150.00

48 Jimmie Johnson Lowe's/2400 40.00 65.00

48 Jimmie Johnson Lowe's Chrome/480 50.00 80.00

2005 Racing Champions Ultra Previews 1:24

22 Scott Wimmer Cat Chrome 15.00 30.00

2005 Racing Champions Ultra 1:24

5 Kyle Busch Kellogg's 10.00 20.00

5 Blake Feese Boston Reid Lowe's 12.50 25.00

10 Scott Riggs Valvoline 10.00 20.00

14 John Andretti JA 10.00 20.00

25 Brian Vickers GMAC 10.00 20.00

36 Boris Said Centex Financial 12.50 25.00

44 Terry Labonte Kellogg's 10.00 20.00

44 Terry Labonte Kellogg's Chrome 15.00 30.00

48 Jimmie Johnson Lowe's 10.00 20.00

48 Jimmie Johnson Lowe's Chrome 15.00 30.00

57 Brian Vickers Ore Ida 10.00 20.00

57 Brian Vickers Ore Ida Chrome 15.00 30.00

66 Greg Biffle Duraflame 10.00 20.00

0 Mike Bliss NetZero Best Buy 10.00 20.00

01 Joe Nemechek Army Chrome 12.50 25.00

2006 Racing Champions 1:24

9 Ted Musgrave Toyota Team ASE SuperTruck Promo 100.00 150.00

23 Johnny Benson Toyota Certified SuperTruck Promo 75.00 150.00

23 Johnny Benson Toyota Exide SuperTruck Promo 150.00 225.00

30 Todd Bodine Germain Toyota SuperTruck Promo 40.00 70.00

51 Mike Garvey Marathon Oil Promo in window box 12.50 25.00

66 Greg Biffle Cub Cadet Promo 20.00 40.00

2006 Racing Champions Authentics 1:24

43 Richard Petty '64 Belvedere 1st Championship 1st Daytona/5004 series 2 on box 50.00 75.00

1991 Racing Champions 1:43

This was the first 1:43 scale size series from Racing Champions. Each piece was issued in a black clear-window style box with a dated copyright line on the back.

2 Rusty Wallace Pontiac Excitement 5.00 12.00

4 Ernie Irvan Kodak 3.00 6.00

6 Mark Martin Valvoline 5.00 12.00

9 Bill Elliott Melling 5.00 12.00

11 Geoff Bodine No Sponsor 3.00 6.00

15 Morgan Shepherd Motorcraft 3.00 6.00

18 Gregory Trammell Melling 3.00 6.00

21 Dale Jarrett Citgo 5.00 12.00

22 Sterling Marlin Maxwell House 3.00 8.00

25 Ken Schrader No Sponsor 3.00 6.00

36 Kenny Wallace Cox Lumber 3.00 6.00

42 Kyle Petty Mello Yello 3.00 6.00

43 Richard Petty STP 3.00 6.00

66 Cale Yarborough TropArtic 3.00 6.00

70 J.D. McDuffie Son's Auto 4.00 10.00

72 Ken Bouchard ADAP 3.00 6.00

89 Jim Sauter Evinrude/ 3.00 6.00

1991 Racing Champions 2-Car Sets 1:43

9/9 Bill Elliott Melling/25,000 7.50 20.00

9/15 Bill Elliott Melling Blue Morgan Shepherd Motorcraft 6.00 15.00

9/90 Bill Elliott Melling Wally Dallenbach Ford Motorsport 6.00 15.00

11/22 Geoff Bodine Sterling Marlin Maxwell House 6.00 15.00

11/98 Bil Elliott Bud Jody Ridley Ford Motorsport 6.00 15.00

15/26 Geoff Bodine Motorcraft Brett Bodine Quaker State 6.00 15.00

18/21 Greg Trammell Melling Dale Jarrett Citgo 6.00 15.00

25/43 Ken Schrader Richard Petty STP 7.50 20.00

25/89 Ken Schrader Jim Sauter 6.00 15.00

84/84 Bill Elliott Ford Motorsport/25,000 7.50 20.00

1992 Racing Champions 1:43

This series of 1:43 scale cars was issued in black boxes or on blister packages. They were distributed through both hobby stores and retail outlets.

1 Jeff Gordon Baby Ruth 45.00 75.00

1 Rick Mast Majik Market 3.00 6.00

3 Dale Earnhardt Goodwrench 40.00 80.00

5 Ricky Rudd Tide 3.00 6.00

7 Alan Kulwicki Hooters 20.00 40.00

11 Bill Elliott Amoco 5.00 10.00

17 Darrell Waltrip Western Auto 3.00 6.00

17 Darrell Waltrip Western Auto Promo 4.00 8.00

18 Dale Jarrett Interstate Batteries 5.00 10.00

28 Davey Allison Havoline 10.00 20.00

30 Michael Waltrip Pennzoil 3.00 6.00

33 Harry Gant NS 15.00 30.00

43 Richard Petty STP 1970 Superbird 15.00 30.00

66 Chad Little TropArtic 3.00 6.00

72 Ken Bouchard Auto Palace 3.00 6.00

1992 Racing Champions Pit Stop 1:43

Each if these 1:43 scale "Pit Stop Show Case" scenes were packaged in a hard plastic case inside a Racing Champions black window box. Each car was mounted on a black base with plastic crew members surrounding the car as if it were in a pit stall during a race.

3 Dale Earnhardt Goodwrench 25.00 50.00

4 Ernie Irvan Kodak 12.50 30.00

7 Alan Kulwicki Hooters 25.00 50.00

11 Bill Elliott Bud 20.00 40.00

98 Jody Ridley Ford 10.00 25.00

1992 Racing Champions Racing Relatives 1:43

Cars from this series were issued in black window box. Each box included 2-1:43 scale cars of "Racing Relatives" or family members who both raced in the NASCAR circuit.

2/36 Rusty Wallace Pontiac Excitement Kenny Wallace Cox Lumber 7.50 20.00

15/26 Geoff Bodine Motorcraft Brett Bodine Quaker State 6.00 15.00

12/43 Kle Petty 7.50 20.00
Mello Yello
Richard Petty
STP

1993 Racing Champions 1:43

2 Rusty Wallace 4.00 8.00
Pontiac Excitement
3 Dale Earnhardt 25.00 60.00
Goodwrench
4 Ernie Irvan 3.00 6.00
Kodak
5 Ricky Rudd 3.00 6.00
Tide
6 Mark Martin 4.00 8.00
Valvoline
7 Alan Kulwicki 12.50 25.00
Hooters blister
7 Alan Kulwicki 12.00 25.00
Hooters in Box
8 Sterling Marlin 12.00 20.00
Raybestos
11 Bill Elliott 4.00 8.00
Amoco
14 Terry Labonte 4.00 8.00
Kellogg's
15 Geoff Bodine 3.00 6.00
Motorcraft
17 Darrell Waltrip 3.00 6.00
Western Auto
21 Morgan Shepherd 3.00 6.00
Citgo
24 Jeff Gordon 20.00 40.00
DuPont
25 Bill Venturini 6.00 12.00
Rain X
26 Brett Bodine 3.00 6.00
Quaker State
27 Hut Stricklin 3.00 6.00
McDonald's
28 Davey Allison 6.00 12.00
Havoline
33 Harry Gant 3.00 6.00
No Sponsor
42 Kyle Petty 3.00 6.00
Mello Yello
44 Rick Wilson 3.00 6.00
STP
51 No Driver Association 6.00 12.00
Chevrolet with Primer paint
51 No Driver Association 6.00 12.00
Ford with Primer paint
51 No Driver Association 6.00 12.00
Pontiac with Primer paint
59 Andy Belmont 6.00 12.00
FDP Brakes
60 Mark Martin 5.00 10.00
Winn Dixie

1993 Racing Champions 1964 Ford Legends 1:43

Each 1:43 scale car in this series was issued in a clear plastic (PVC) box with gold foil lettering. The title "Racing Champions 1964 Ford" is printed on the top of the box along with "Limited Edition of 5000."

4 Dick Hutcherson 15.00 30.00
Ford
21 Marvin Panch 20.00 35.00
Augusta Motors
26 Curtis Turner 12.50 25.00
Ed Martin Ford
27 Junior Johnson 12.50 25.00
Ford
28 Fred Lorenzen 20.00 35.00
LaFayette Ford
29 Nelson Stacy 20.00 35.00
Ron's Ford
31 Ralph Earnhardt 15.00 30.00
Ford
32 Tiny Lund 12.50 25.00
Ford
49 G.C. Spencer 15.00 30.00
Ford
51 Racing Champions Primer 12.50 25.00
59 Tom Pistone 12.50 25.00
Ford
70 J.D. McDuffie 12.50 25.00
Ford
73 Buddy Arrington 15.00 30.00
Ford
76 Larry Frank 12.50 25.00
Ford
99 Bobby Isaac 12.50 25.00
Ford
06 Cale Yarborough 12.50 25.00
Ford

1993 Racing Champions Pit Stop 1:43

Each if these "Pit Stop Show Case" scenes were packaged in a hard plastic case inside a Racing Champions yellow window box. Each car was mounted on a black base with plastic crew members surrounding the car as if it were in a pit stall during a race.

3 Dale Earnhardt 25.00 50.00
Goodwrench
5 Ricky Rudd 12.50 25.00
Tide
7 Alan Kulwicki 20.00 40.00
Hooters
16 Ted Musgrave 12.50 25.00
Family Channel
24 Jeff Gordon 25.00 50.00
DuPont
27 Hut Stricklin 12.50 25.00
McDonald's

1993 Racing Champions Premier 1:43

This is the first year that Racing Champions did a Premier series for its 1:43 scale size.

2 Ward Burton 6.00 15.00
Hardee's
3 Dale Earnhardt 40.00 80.00
Goodwrench/10,000
5 Ricky Rudd 6.00 15.00
Tide
6 Mark Martin 10.00 20.00
Valvoline/10,000
7 Alan Kulwicki 30.00 60.00
Hooters/10,000
8 Sterling Marlin 6.00 15.00
Raybestos
11 Bill Elliott 7.50 15.00
Amoco
11 Bill Elliott 12.00 22.00
Budweiser/10,000
17 Darrell Waltrip 6.00 15.00
Western Auto/10,000
24 Jeff Gordon 40.00 80.00
DuPont/10,000
27 Hut Stricklin 6.00 15.00
McDonald's
28 Davey Allison 20.00 35.00
Havoline Black&Orange/10,000
28 Davey Allison 15.00 30.00
Havoline Black&White/10,000
28 Ernie Irvan 15.00 30.00
Havoline
33 Harry Gant 6.00 15.00
No Sponsor
42 Kyle Petty 6.00 15.00
Mello Yello
59 Robert Pressley 25.00 45.00
Alliance
60 Mark Martin 15.00 25.00
Winn Dixie/5000
87 Joe Nemechek 20.00 60.00
Dentyne
97 Joe Bessey 6.00 15.00
AC Delco
98 Derrike Cope 40.00 75.00
Bojangles by RCCC

1994 Racing Champions 1:43

This was one of the last years that Racing Champions did a regular issue 1:43 scale series. Each car was packaged in a red clear window box with the year of issue printed on the top. A checklist of drivers appears on the bottom of the box, but not all drivers were issued for this series.

1 Rick Mast 2.00 5.00
Precision Products
4 Sterling Marlin 2.00 5.00
Kodak
5 Terry Labonte 3.00 6.00
Kellogg's
10 Ricky Rudd 2.00 5.00
Tide
19 Loy Allen 2.00 5.00
Hooters
24 Jeff Gordon 20.00 40.00
DuPont
24 Jeff Gordon 25.00 50.00
DuPont Coca-Cola 600 Win
in plastic case
26 Brett Bodine 2.00 5.00
Quaker State
33 Harry Gant 8.00 16.00
Farewell Tour
33 Harry Gant 2.00 5.00
Leo Jackson
42 Kyle Petty 2.00 5.00
Mello Yello
60 Mark Martin 4.00 10.00
Winn Dixie

1994 Racing Champions Pit Stop 1:43

Each if these "Pit Stop Show Case" scenes were packaged in a hard plastic case inside a Racing Champions yellow window box. Each car was mounted on a black base with plastic crew members surrounding the car as if it were in a pit stall during a race.

28 Ernie Irvan 12.50 25.00
Havoline
28 Ernie Irvan 12.50 25.00
Mac Tools

1994 Racing Champions Premier 1:43

This was the second year that Racing Champions did a 1:43 Premier series. Highlighting the series are two Alan Kulwicki cars (Zerex and Army).

1 Rick Mast 7.50 15.00
Precision Products
2 Rusty Wallace 10.00 18.00
Ford Motorsports
3 Dale Earnhardt 50.00 100.00
Goodwrench
4 Sterling Marlin 8.00 20.00
Kodak
5 Terry Labonte 10.00 20.00
Kellogg's
6 Mark Martin 10.00 18.00
Valvoline
7 Harry Gant 15.00 25.00
Manheim
7 Jimmy Hensley 7.50 15.00
Bojangles
7 Tommy Kendall 7.50 15.00
Family Channel
7 Alan Kulwicki 15.00 30.00
Army
7 Alan Kulwicki 15.00 30.00
Zerex
12 Clifford Allison 12.00 20.00
Sports Image
15 Lake Speed 7.50 15.00
Quality Care
16 Ted Musgrave 7.50 15.00
Family Channel
21 Morgan Shepherd 7.50 15.00
Cheerwine
22 Bobby Labonte 15.00 30.00
Maxwell House/5000
24 Jeff Gordon 30.00 60.00
DuPont Snickers
25 Ken Schrader 7.50 15.00
GMAC
26 Brett Bodine 7.50 15.00
Quaker State
28 Ernie Irvan 12.00 20.00
Havoline
28 Ernie Irvan 15.00 25.00
Mac Tools/7500
30 Michael Waltrip 7.50 15.00
Pennzoil
33 Harry Gant 7.50 15.00
Farewell Tour
33 Harry Gant 7.50 15.00
Leo Jackson Motorsports
59 Dennis Setzer 7.50 15.00
Alliance
60 Mark Martin 12.00 20.00
Winn Dixie
77 Greg Sacks 7.50 15.00
US Air

1995 Racing Champions Premier 1:43

In 1995, Racing Champions only produced 1:43 size cars for special circumstances. The Jeff Gordon was a salute to the inaugural Brickyard Winner and the Mark Martin was done as a promo. The Martin piece was available through Winn Dixie stores.

24 Jeff Gordon 25.00 60.00
Brickyard Win in plastic case
60 Mark Martin 10.00 20.00
Winn Dixie

1997 Racing Champions 1:43

10 Ricky Rudd 4.00 10.00
Tide Mountain Spring Promo

1998 Racing Champions 1:43

10 Ricky Rudd 5.00 10.00
Tide Kids Promo

1999 Racing Champions Petty Collection 1:43

43 Richard Petty 6.00 12.00
1970 Superbird
43 R.Petty/'70 Superbird 3-car set 12.50 25.00

1999 Racing Champions Under the Lights 1:43

These 1:43 scale cars feature special anodized paint to give that under the lights appearance.

5 Terry Labonte 5.00 10.00
Kellogg's
12 Jeremy Mayfield 4.00 8.00
Mobil 1
94 Bill Elliott 8.00 20.00
Drive Thru

1989 Racing Champions Flat Bottom 1:64

This was the first series of NASCAR die cast cars produced by Racing Champions. The series is commonly referred to as flat bottoms because the blister package the car came in was flat across the bottom. In all subsequent years there was a bubble across the bottom to help the package freely stand up.

3 Dale Earnhardt 75.00 150.00
Goodwrench
9 Bill Elliott 50.00 100.00
Motorcraft Melling Ford
16 Larry Pearson 30.00 60.00
No Sponsor
28 Davey Allison 70.00 120.00
Havoline
30 Michael Waltrip 30.00 60.00
Country Time
94 Sterling Marlin 30.00 60.00
Sunoco

1990 Racing Champions 1:64

This was the first full series of 1:64 scale cars produced by Racing Champions. Many of the cars came with rubber tires as opposed to plastic. Cars with rubber tires usually carry a $5.00 to $10.00 premium. The cars used many different body styles.

1 Terry Labonte 30.00 60.00
Majik Market Oldsmobile
3 Dale Earnhardt 75.00 150.00
Goodwrench
3 Dale Earnhardt 20.00 50.00
GM Performance Parts
9 Bill Elliott 60.00 100.00
Orange and Blue Stripe
No Melling on the car
9 Bill Elliott 35.00 60.00
Orange and Blue Stripe
with Melling on the car
9 Bill Elliott 30.00 50.00
Red and Blue Stripe
with Melling on the car
10 Derrike Cope 50.00 100.00
Lumina
14 A.J. Foyt 75.00 125.00
Buick
14 A.J. Foyt 60.00 120.00
Lumina
14 A.J. Foyt 30.00 60.00
Old Pontiac body style
14 A.J. Foyt 25.00 50.00
Oldsmobile
14 A.J. Foyt 20.00 40.00
Pontiac
15 Morgan Shepherd 20.00 40.00
Red and White color scheme
15 Morgan Shepherd 15.00 30.00
Red and Cream color scheme
16 Larry Pearson 75.00 125.00
Buick with White Bumper
16 Larry Pearson 18.00 35.00
Buick with brown bumper
river name in script
16 Larry Pearson 15.00 30.00
Buick with Brown Bumper
driver name in print
16 Larry Pearson 40.00 75.00
Lumina with Brown Bumper
16 Larry Pearson 40.00 75.00
Old Pontiac with Brown Bumper
16 Larry Pearson 40.00 75.00
Oldsmobile with Brown Bumper
16 Larry Pearson 12.50 25.00
Pontiac with Brown Bumper
18 Greg Sacks 18.00 30.00
Slim Fast
20 Rob Moroso 15.00 30.00
Red Stripe
21 Neil Bonnett 20.00 50.00
Citgo
25 Tim Richmond 4.00 10.00
Fan Club Promo
in bag and PVC Box
26 Kenny Bernstein 20.00 40.00
Buick
26 Kenny Bernstein 25.00 50.00
Lumina
26 Kenny Bernstein 25.00 50.00
Old Pontiac body style
26 Kenny Bernstein 20.00 40.00
Oldsmobile
27 Rusty Wallace 40.00 80.00
Old Pontiac Miller Genuine Draft
27 Rusty Wallace 60.00 100.00
Oldsmobile
27 Rusty Wallace 30.00 60.00
Pontiac Miller Genuine Draft
27 Rusty Wallace 30.00 60.00
Pontiac Miller
27 Rusty Wallace 40.00 80.00
Pontiac with Silver Decals
27 Rusty Wallace 8.00 20.00
1989 Champion
Promo/30,000
28 Davey Allison 30.00 80.00
Black and White paint scheme
28 Davey Allison 25.00 50.00
Black and Gold paint scheme
30 Michael Waltrip 35.00 70.00
Country Time
30 Michael Waltrip 4.00 10.00
Country Time Promo
30 Michael Waltrip 12.50 30.00
Maxwell House
30 Michael Waltrip 4.00 10.00
Maxwell House Promo
33 Harry Gant 20.00 40.00
Pontiac
42 Kyle Petty 50.00 100.00
Buick with Blue and White paint
42 Kyle Petty 50.00 100.00
Lumina with Blue and White paint
42 Kyle Petty 30.00 60.00
Old Pontiac with Blue and White paint
42 Kyle Petty 50.00 100.00
Oldsmobile with Blue and White paint
42 Kyle Petty 15.00 30.00
Peak with Sabco on deck lid
42 Kyle Petty 15.00 30.00
Peak without Sabco on deck lid
Blue and Pink paint scheme
43 Richard Petty 20.00 40.00
Pontiac
94 Sterling Marlin 50.00 120.00
Buick
94 Sterling Marlin 40.00 80.00
Lumina
94 Sterling Marlin 50.00 90.00
Old Pontiac
94 Sterling Marlin 20.00 40.00
Oldsmobile
NNO 12-car set in case 40.00 80.00
Earnhardt
Goodwrench
Elliott
Melling Red
Foyt
Shepherd
Motorcraft
Pearson
Bonnett
Citgo
Bernstein
Quaker State
Wallace
MGD
Allison
Havoline
Waltrip
Maxwell House
Petty
Peak
Marlin
Sunoco

1990-91 Racing Champions Roaring Racers 1:64

2 Rusty Wallace 4.00 10.00
No sponsor BW 1991
3 Dale Earnhardt 12.50 25.00
Goodwrench SW '90
9 Bill Elliott 4.00 10.00
Melling Blue BW 1991
9 Bill Elliott 4.00 10.00
Melling Red SW 1990
9 Bill Elliott 4.00 10.00
Melling Red BW 1991
9 Bill Elliott 4.00 10.00
Melling Red SW 1991
10 Derrike Cope 3.00 8.00
Purolator BW 1991
10 Derrike Cope 3.00 8.00
Purolator SW 1991
11 Geoff Bodine 3.00 8.00
Bodine Racing BW 1991
11 Geoff Bodine 3.00 8.00
Bodine Racing SW 1991
14 Bobby Allison 3.00 8.00
No Sponsor SW 1991
14 A.J. Foyt 3.00 8.00
Foyt Racing 1991
14 A.J.Foyt 3.00 8.00
Foyt Racing SW 1991
15 Morgan Shepherd 3.00 8.00
Motorcraft 1990
15 Morgan Shepherd 3.00 8.00
Motorcraft SW 1991
18 Greg Trammell 3.00 8.00
Melling SW 1991
21 Dale Jarrett 4.00 10.00
Citgo BW 1991
21 Dale Jarrett 4.00 10.00
Citgo SW 1991
22 Sterling Marlin 4.00 10.00
Maxwell House BW 1991
25 Ken Schrader 3.00 8.00
Schrader Racing 1991
26 Kenny Bernstein 3.00 8.00
Quaker State SW 1991
28 Davey Allison 6.00 15.00
Havoline SW 1990
28 Davey Allison 6.00 15.00
Havoline SW 1991
30 Michael Waltrip 3.00 8.00
Pennzoil 1990
33 Harry Gant 3.00 8.00
Gant Racing SW 1991
36 Kenny Wallace 3.00 8.00
Cox Lumber BW 1991
42 Kyle Petty 3.00 8.00
Mello Yello BW 1991
42 Kyle Petty 3.00 8.00
Peak SW 1990
42 Kyle Petty 3.00 8.00
Peak SW 1991
43 Richard Petty 5.00 12.00
STP BW 1991
43 Richard Petty 5.00 12.00
STP SW 1991
52 Jimmy Means 3.00 8.00
No sponsor 1991
66 Cale Yarborough 4.00 10.00
Phillips 66 BW 1991
66 Cale Yarborough 4.00 10.00
Phillips 66 SW 1991
68 Bobby Hamilton 3.00 8.00
Country Time SW 1991
71 Dave Marcis 3.00 8.00
Big Apple 1991
72 Ken Bouchard 3.00 8.00
ADAP BW 1991
72 Tracy Leslie 3.00 8.00
Detroit Gasket BW 1991

1990-92 Racing Champions 3-Pack 1:64

These Racing Champions 1:64 cars were packaged 3-per large blister and were issued over a period of years. Some included a theme, such as the Daytona 500, while others included 10-bonus cards in each pack.

1/68/96 Rick Mast 7.50 15.00
Bobby Hamilton
Tom Peck
1992 with 10-extra cards
3/15/43 Dale Earnhardt 25.00 50.00
Goodwrench
Morgan Shepherd
Motorcraft
Richard Petty
STP
1990 with 10-extra cards
10/15/43 Derrike Cope 10.00 20.00
Puralator
Morgan Shepherd
Motorcraft
Richard Petty
STP
1990 with 10-extra cards
15/21/28 1992 Daytona 500 Top 3 7.50 20.00
Davey Allison
Morgan Shepherd
Geoff Bodine
16/20/26 Larry Pearson 6.00 15.00

uick
Rob Moroso
Crown Xtra
Kenny Bernstein
Quaker State
1990 with 10-extra cards
26/52/66 Brett Bodine 6.00 15.00
Quaker State
Jimmy Means
Cale Yarborough
Phillips 66
1991 with 10-extra cards
28/30/94 Davey Allison 10.00 20.00
Michael Waltrip
Sterling Marlin
1990 with 10-extra cards

1991 Racing Champions 1:64

This series of 1:64 scale Racing Champion cars has many different package variations, although all were issued in the typical cardboard and plastic blister pack. The front of the backer board featured a red #51 car, while the backs were printed with up to three different variations. One has Dale Earnhardt on the back of the package (abbreviated EB in the listing). Another has Richard Petty on the back of the package (abbreviated PB). Finally a third variation comes with NASCAR Properties on the stand the car sits on. Additionally, some cars were produced in different body styles as well.

1 Terry Labonte 15.00 30.00
Oldsmobile EB
1 Terry Labonte 20.00 40.00
Oldsmobile NP
1 Terry Labonte 15.00 30.00
Oldsmobile PB
1 Rick Mast 3.00 6.00
Buick PB
1 Rick Mast 2.00 5.00
Oldsmobile PB
2 Rusty Wallace 7.50 15.00
Pontiac EB
2 Rusty Wallace 5.00 10.00
Pontiac PB
2 Rusty Wallace 5.00 12.00
Mobil 1 Promo
3 Dale Earnhardt 30.00 80.00
Lumina EB
3 Dale Earnhardt 75.00 150.00
Lumina NP
3 Dale Earnhardt 25.00 60.00
Lumina PB
4 Ernie Irvan 2.00 5.00
Kodak PB
5 Jay Fogleman 6.00 12.00
Lumina PB
9 Bill Elliott 2.00 5.00
Ford PB
9 Bill Elliott 12.50 25.00
Ford EB
Car is 1/2 blue
9 Bill Elliott 9.00 18.00
Ford EB
Car is 3/4 blue
9 Bill Elliott 15.00 30.00
Old Ford body style EB
Orange and White paint scheme
9 Bill Elliott 18.00 35.00
Old Ford body style NP
Orange and White paint scheme
10 Derrike Cope 3.00 6.00
Purolator EB
with 2 rows of checkers
10 Derrike Cope 12.50 25.00
Purolator EB
with 3 rows of checkers
10 Derrike Cope 2.00 5.00
Purolator PB
with 2 rows of checkers
10 Derrike Cope 7.50 15.00
Purolator PB
with 3 rows of checkers
11 Geoff Bodine 2.00 5.00
Ford EB
11 Geoff Bodine 2.00 5.00
Ford PB
12 Bobby Allison 2.00 5.00
Buick PB
12 Hut Stricklin 2.00 5.00
Buick PB
12 Hut Stricklin 2.00 5.00
Lumina PB
14 A.J. Foyt 25.00 50.00
Buick PB
14 A.J. Foyt 15.00 30.00
Oldsmobile EB
14 A.J. Foyt 25.00 60.00
Oldsmobile NP
14 A.J. Foyt 8.00 16.00
Oldsmobile PB
15 Morgan Shepherd 5.00 10.00
Ford with Red paint scheme EB
15 Morgan Shepherd 7.50 15.00
Ford EB
with Red and White paint scheme
15 Morgan Shepherd 2.00 5.00
Ford PB
15 Morgan Shepherd 5.00 10.00
Old Ford EB
15 Morgan Shepherd 30.00 60.00
Old Ford NP
16 Larry Pearson 3.00 6.00
Buick EB
16 Larry Pearson 30.00 60.00
Buick NP
16 Larry Pearson 2.00 5.00
Buick PB
16 Larry Pearson 12.50 25.00
Lumina PB
18 Gregory Trammell 2.00 5.00
Melling PB
20 Rob Moroso 15.00 30.00
Crown Oldsmobile EB
20 Rob Moroso 25.00 50.00
Crown Oldsmobile
with STP decal NP
21 Neil Bonnett 15.00 30.00
Old Ford EB
21 Neil Bonnett 50.00 90.00
Old Ford NP
21 Dale Jarrett 10.00 20.00
Ford EB
21 Dale Jarrett 4.00 8.00
Ford PB
22 Sterling Marlin 2.00 5.00
Ford with Black wheels PB
22 Sterling Marlin 15.00 40.00
Ford with Silver Wheels PB
25 Ken Schrader 2.00 5.00
Lumina PB
26 Kenny Bernstein 3.00 6.00
Buick EB
26 Kenny Bernstein 30.00 60.00
Buick Quaker State NP
26 Kenny Bernstein 2.00 5.00
Buick PB
26 Kenny Bernstein 5.00 10.00
Oldsmobile PB
26 Brett Bodine 2.00 5.00
Buick Quaker State PB
26 Brett Bodine 1.50 4.00
Lumina PB
27 Rusty Wallace 30.00 60.00
Pontiac Miller Genuine Draft EB
27 Rusty Wallace 50.00 90.00
Pontiac Miller Genuine Draft NP
27 Rusty Wallace 25.00 50.00
Pontiac no MGD EB
27 Rusty Wallace 20.00 40.00
Pontiac Miller EB
28 Davey Allison 25.00 50.00
Ford EB
28 Davey Allison 18.00 35.00
Ford PB
28 Davey Allison 20.00 40.00
Old Ford EB
28 Davey Allison 50.00 90.00
Old Ford NP
28 Davey Allison 15.00 30.00
Old Ford PB
30 Michael Waltrip 12.50 25.00
Pontiac Country Time EB
30 Michael Waltrip 6.00 12.00
Pontiac Pennzoil EB
with STP decal
30 Michael Waltrip 6.00 12.00
Pontiac Pennzoil EB
without STP decal
30 Michael Waltrip 30.00 60.00
Pontiac NP
30 Michael Waltrip 2.00 5.00
Pontiac PB
33 Harry Gant 10.00 20.00
Buick PB
33 Harry Gant 7.50 15.00
Oldsmobile EB
33 Harry Gant 6.00 12.00
Oldsmobile PB
33 Harry Gant 7.50 15.00
Pontiac EB
33 Harry Gant 30.00 60.00
Pontiac NP
34 Todd Bodine 2.00 5.00
Welco
36 Kenny Wallace 2.00 5.00
Cox Lumber
41 No Driver Association 2.50 6.00
Kellogg's Promo in bag
42 Kyle Petty 4.00 8.00
Mello Yello PB
42 Kyle Petty 7.50 15.00
Peak EB
42 Kyle Petty 18.00 35.00
Peak NB
42 Kyle Petty 10.00 20.00
Peak PB
43 Richard Petty 7.50 15.00
STP EB
43 Richard Petty 30.00 60.00
STP NP
43 Richard Petty 4.00 8.00
STP PB
52 Jimmy Means 2.00 5.00
Pontiac PB
59 Robert Pressley 2.00 5.00
Alliance
66 Cale Yarborough 4.00 8.00
Pontiac PB
68 Bobby Hamilton 2.00 5.00
Oldsmobile PB
68 NDA 4.00 8.00
Country Time Promo
68 Bobby Hamilton 10.00 20.00
Buick PB
70 J.D. McDuffie 2.00 5.00
Son's Auto
71 Dave Marcis 8.00 20.00
Lumina PB
72 Ken Bouchard 10.00 20.00
ADAP PB
72 Tracy Leslie 2.00 5.00
Detroit Gaskets PB
84 Mike Alexander 2.00 5.00
Nashville Ford
84 NDA 30.00 50.00
Miler High Life
in plastic box
84 Dick Trickle 45.00 80.00
Miler High Life
in plastic box
89 Jim Sauter 2.00 5.00
Pontiac PB
89 Jim Sauter 5.00 10.00
Pontiac Day Glow PB
91 Phoenix International 3.00 6.00
November 3 Promo
91 Racing Champions Club Promo 5.00 12.00
94 Terry Labonte 6.00 12.00
Buick PB
94 Terry Labonte 4.00 8.00
Oldsmobile PB
94 Sterling Marlin 5.00 10.00
Oldsmobile EB
94 Sterling Marlin 12.50 25.00
Oldsmobile NP
96 Tom Peck 18.00 35.00
Lumina PB
96 Tom Peck 2.00 5.00
Oldsmobile PB
S1 Robert Griggs 4.00 10.00
Winston Cup Scene
NNO Collectors Edition 12-car set 15.00 40.00
Ernie Irvan
Jay Fogleman
Bill Elliott
Bobby Allison
Sterling Marlin
Todd Bodine
Kenny Wallace
Cale Yarborough
Bobby Hamilton
Dave Marcis
Tracy Leslie
Tom Peck
NNO Collectors Edition 12-car set 15.00 40.00
R.Mast
Majik Market
B.Elliott
Melling Blue
D.Cope
Purolator
G.Trammell
S.Marlin
Maxwell House
K.Schrader
H.Gant
R.Petty
STP
J.Means
C.Yaborough
Phillips 66
D.Marcis
T.Labonte
Sunoco
NNO Daytona 5-car Military set 10.00 25.00
We Support Our Troops/7. Alan Kulwicki
Army/18. Dale Jarrett
Navy/24. Air Force/71. Dave Marcis
Coast Guard/88. Marines
NNO Sears 13-car set 15.00 40.00
Mast
Majik Market
Wallace
Elliott
Melling
Stricklin
Raybestos
Foyt
Marlin
Maxwell House
Wallace
Cox Lumber
Petty
Mello Yello
Petty
STP
Yarborough
Phillips 66
Hamilton
Country Time
Sauter
Evinrude

1991 Racing Champions with Figure 1:64

Each 1:64 car in this series was packaged with a plastic collectible figurine of the featured driver. A die-cast piece, card and driver statue were all issued in a large "Racing Superstars" blister pack.

9 Bill Elliott 5.00 12.00
Melling
10 Derrike Cope 4.00 10.00
Purolator
22 Sterling Marlin 5.00 12.00
Maxwell House
25 Ken Schrader 4.00 10.00
43 Richard Petty 6.00 15.00
STP
68 Bobby Hamilton 4.00 10.00
Country Time

1991-92 Racing Champions Legends 1:64

This series of NASCAR legends was issued in 1991 and 1992. Each car was packaged in one of two different blisters: "Racing Superstars" packaged with a white bordered trading card, or simply "Racing Champions" packaged with a "Collector's Series" black bordered card.

1 Bud Moore 4.00 10.00
1969 Dodge Daytona
3 Don White 4.00 10.00
1969 Dodge Daytona
4 John Sears 4.00 10.00
1964 Ford
4 John Sears 4.00 10.00
1969 Ford Torino
5 Buddy Arrington 4.00 10.00
1969 Dodge Daytona
5 Pete Hamilton 4.00 10.00
1969 Ford Torino
7 Ramo Stott 4.00 10.00
1970 Plymouth Superbird
10 Buddy Baker 4.00 10.00
1964 Ford
11 Ned Jarrett 4.00 10.00
1964 Ford
14 Bill Ellis 4.00 10.00
1970 Plymouth Superbird
17 David Pearson 4.00 10.00
1969 Ford Torino
18 Joe Frasson 4.00 10.00
1969 Dodge Daytona
21 Marvin Panch 4.00 10.00
1964 Ford
21 Cale Yarborough 4.00 10.00
1969 Ford Torino
22 Dick Brooks 4.00 10.00
1969 Dodge Daytona
22 Fireball Roberts 4.00 10.00
1964 Ford
27 Donnie Allison 4.00 10.00
1969 Ford Torino
28 Fred Lorenzen 4.00 10.00
1964 Ford Fastback
29 Bobby Allison 4.00 10.00
1969 Ford Torino
29 Bud Moore 4.00 10.00
1969 Ford Torino
30 Dave Marcis 4.00 10.00
1969 Dodge Daytona
31 Ralph Earnhardt 15.00 30.00
1964 Ford
32 Dick Brooks 4.00 10.00
1970 Plymouth Superbird
1969 Rookie of the Year
34 Wendell Scott 4.00 10.00
1964 Ford
40 Pete Hamilton 5.00 12.00
Plymouth only on fender
1970 Superbird
Racing Superstars blister
40 Pete Hamilton 4.00 10.00
Plymouth by Petty on fender
1970 Superbird
Racing Superstars blister
42 Marty Robbins 25.00 40.00
43 Richard Petty 5.00 12.00
1969 Ford Torino
43 Richard Petty 5.00 12.00
1970 Plymouth Superbird
Racing Superstars blister
48 James Hylton 4.00 10.00
1969 Dodge Daytona
55 Tiny Lund 4.00 10.00
1969 Dodge Daytona
61 Hoss Ellington 4.00 10.00
1969 Ford Torino
64 Elmo Langley 4.00 10.00
1964 Ford
70 J.D. McDuffie 4.00 10.00
1964 Ford
70 J.D. McDuffie 4.00 10.00
1969 Ford Torino
71 Bobby Isaac 4.00 10.00
1969 Dodge Daytona
73 Buddy Arrington 4.00 10.00
1964 Ford
88 Benny Parsons 4.00 10.00
1969 Ford Torino
99 Charlie Glotzbach 4.00 10.00
1969 Dodge Daytona
06 Neil Castles 4.00 10.00
1969 Dodge Daytona
06 Cale Yarborough 4.00 10.00
1964 Ford

1992 Racing Champions 1:64

Every regular issue piece in this series was produced with both a photo of Richard Petty on the back of the blister card and a checklist on the back. The blister pack fronts feature a checkered flag design on the bottom half and artwork for a red car #51 on the top half of the package. A trading card was also packaged with each car. The promo pieces were issued with sponsor logos and artwork on the fronts of the blisters. This was Jeff Gordon's first appearance in a Racing Champions die cast series.

1 Ford Motorsport Promo/10,000 3.00 8.00
1 Jeff Gordon 25.00 60.00
Baby Ruth
1 Jeff Gordon 8.00 20.00
Baby Ruth Promo
black windows
1 Rick Mast 1.50 4.00
Majik Market
2 Rusty Wallace 6.00 12.00
Pontiac Excitement
3 Dale Earnhardt 30.00 60.00
Goodwrench 5-Time
Champion card
4 Ernie Irvan 4.00 8.00
Kodak
4U Boyd Adams 4.00 10.00
Nashville Raceway Promo
5 Jay Fogleman 1.50 4.00
Inn Keeper
5 Ricky Rudd 1.50 4.00
Tide
5 Ricky Rudd 5.00 10.00
Tide Promo black windows
6 Mark Martin 12.00 20.00
Valvoline
6 Mark Martin 15.00 30.00
Valvoline 2-car set
7 Harry Gant 10.00 20.00
Mac Tools
7 Alan Kulwicki 15.00 40.00
Hooters
8 Jeff Burton 2.50 6.00
TIC Financial Promo/15,000
8 Bobby Dotter 1.50 4.00
Team R
9 Joe Bessey 6.00 12.00
AC Delco
9 Bill Elliott 20.00 40.00
Coors Light Promo in bag
9 Bill Elliott 5.00 12.00
Melling
9 Bill Elliott 5.00 10.00
Melling Motorcraft 500
Promo black windows
9 Chad Little 4.00 10.00
Melling Performance
9/14 Joe Bessey 3.00 8.00
Mike Stefanik
Auto Palace Promo 2-car set
10 No Driver Association 4.00 10.00
Bull Frog Promo/20,000
(Derrike Cope's Car)
10 Derrike Cope 2.00 5.00
Purolator Adam's Mark
10 Derrike Cope 2.00 5.00
Purolator with name in Blue
10 Derrike Cope 6.00 15.00
Purolator with name in White
10 Sterling Marlin 5.00 12.00
Maxwell House
11 Geoff Bodine 1.50 4.00
No Sponsor
11 Bill Elliott 6.00 12.00
Amoco
11 Bill Elliott 6.00 12.00
Amoco Jan.2, 1992
12 Bobby Allison 1.50 4.00
No Sponsor
12 Karen Schulz 6.00 15.00
Piggly Wiggly Promo/10,000
12 Hut Stricklin 1.50 4.00
Raybestos
14 A.J. Foyt 10.00 20.00
No Sponsor
15 Geoff Bodine 1.50 4.00
Motorcraft
15 Chad Chaffin 6.00 12.00
N&S Parts Promo/15,000
15 Chad Chaffin 10.00 20.00
Shoney's Promo/15,000
16 Wally Dallenbach Jr. 7.50 15.00
Roush Racing
17 Darrell Waltrip 1.50 4.00
Western Auto
17 Darrell Waltrip 4.00 10.00
Western Auto Promo
18 Dale Jarrett 4.00 8.00
Interstate Batteries
18 Gregory Trammell 1.50 4.00
Melling
19 Chad Little 1.50 4.00
Tyson
20 Mike Wallace 4.00 8.00
First Aide
21 Dale Jarrett 4.00 8.00
Citgo
21 Morgan Shepherd 1.50 4.00
Citgo
22 Sterling Marlin 1.25 3.00
Maxwell House
25 Ken Schrader 2.00 5.00
Hendrick Motorsports
25 Bill Venturini 2.00 5.00
Amoco Rain X
26 Brett Bodine 1.50 4.00
Quaker State
27 Hut Stricklin 4.00 10.00
McDonald's Promo
28 Davey Allison 7.50 15.00
Havoline
28 Davey Allison 7.50 15.00
Havoline 7-Up Promo
28 Bobby Hillin Jr. 7.50 15.00
Havoline
30 Michael Waltrip 1.50 4.00
Pennzoil
31 Steve Grissom 20.00 50.00
Big Mama Promo
31 Steve Grissom 4.00 10.00
Roddenbery's Promo
31 Bobby Hillin Jr. 2.00 5.00
Team Ireland
33 Harry Gant 1.50 4.00
No Sponsor
34 Todd Bodine 2.00 5.00
Welco Quick Stop
36 Kenny Wallace 2.00 5.00
Cox Lumber
36 Kenny Wallace 3.00 6.00
Dirt Devil
42 Bobby Hillin Jr. 9.00 18.00
Mello Yello
42 Kyle Petty 4.00 8.00
Mello Yello
43 Richard Petty 6.00 12.00
STP with Black wheels
43 Richard Petty 6.00 12.00
STP with Blue wheels
44 Bill Caudill 1.50 4.00
Army
49 Stanley Smith 5.00 10.00
Ameritron
55 Ted Musgrave 5.00 10.00
Jasper Engines
56 Jerry Glanville 3.00 6.00
Atlanta Falcons Promo
59 Andy Belmont 3.00 6.00
FDP Brakes
59 Robert Pressley 5.00 12.00
Alliance Promo
60 Mark Martin 4.00 8.00
Winn Dixie
63 Chuck Bown 1.50 4.00
Nescafe
66 Jimmy Hensley 1.50 4.00
TropArtic
66 Chad Little 1.50 4.00
TropArtic
66 Cale Yarborough 3.00 6.00
TropArtic Ford

6 Cale Yarborough 1.50 4.00
TropArtic Pontiac
8 Bobby Hamilton 1.50 4.00
Country Time
0 J.D. McDuffie 1.50 4.00
Son's Auto
1 Dave Marcis 3.00 8.00
Big Apple Market
2 Ken Bouchard 4.00 8.00
ADAP
2 Tracy Leslie 1.50 4.00
Detroit Gasket
5 Butch Miller 1.50 4.00
Food Country
3 Lake Speed 3.00 6.00
Purex
3 Lake Speed 5.00 10.00
Purex Promo/20,000
7 Joe Nemechek 1.50 4.00
Texas Pete
9 Jim Sauter 1.50 4.00
Evinrude
2 NDA 1.50 4.00
Hungry Jack Promo in bag
2 Racing Champions Club Promo 4.00 10.00
2 Sam Bass Promo 3.00 8.00
4 Terry Labonte 6.00 12.00
Sunoco with blue bumper
4 Terry Labonte 10.00 20.00
Sunoco with yellow bumper
6 Tom Peck 1.50 4.00
Thomas Brothers
8 Jody Ridley 3.00 8.00
Ford Motorsport Promo/10,000
NO Collectors Edition 4-car set/15. Geoff Bodine 6.00
5.00
Motorcraft/30. Michael Waltrip
Pennzoil/68. Bobby Hamilton
Country Time/70. J.D. McDuffie
Son's Auto
NO Collectors Edition 6-car set/5. Ricky Rudd 10.00 25.00
Tide/8. Bobby Dotter/15. Geoff Bodine
Motorcraft/28. Davey Allison
Havoline/70. J.D. McDuffie
Son's Automotive/94. Terry Labonte
Sunoco
NO Collectors 12-car set 15.00 40.00
Mast
Majik Markets
Cope
Purolator
Stricklin
Raybestos
Marlin
Maxwell House
Gant
Bodine
Wellco
Petty
Mello Yello
Hamilton
Country Time
Racing Champions
Peck
Thomas
Ridley
McCabe
Fisher Snowplows
NO Collectors 12-car set 15.00 40.00
Wallace
Pontiac Excite.
Irvan
Kodak Film
Rudd
Tide
Martin
ValvolineElliott
Waltrip
Western Auto
Shepherd
Citgo
Allison
Havoline
Waltrip
Pennzoil
Petty
STP
McDuffie
Son's Auto
RC
NO Sears 12-car set 15.00 40.00
Wallace
Pontiac Excite.
Irvan
Kodak
Rudd
Tide
Martin
Valvoline
Bodine
Waltrip
WesternAuto
Shepherd
Citgo
Allison
Havoline
Waltrip
Pennzoil
Petty
STP
McDuffie
Son's Auto
Racing Champions

1992 Racing Champions AC Racing Promos 1:64

Rusty Wallace 4.00 8.00
Pontiac Excitement
Dale Earnhardt 6.00 15.00
Goodwrench
Ernie Irvan 3.00 6.00
Kodak
Ricky Rudd 3.00 6.00
Tide
2 Hut Stricklin 3.00 6.00
Raybestos

17 Darrell Waltrip 3.00 6.00
Western Auto
25 Ken Schrader 3.00 6.00
Hendrick
42 Kyle Petty 3.00 6.00
Mello Yello

1992 Racing Champions Milkhouse Cheese Promos 1:64

This series of die-cast cars was produced by Racing Champions for promotional use and distributed by Milkhouse Cheese. Each car was packaged on a yellow and checkered flag designed blister with the Milkhouse Cheese logo on the package. A Racing Champions card was also included in the blister pack. The stated production run of each piece was 14,400.

2 Rusty Wallace 6.00 15.00
Miller Genuine Draft
6 Mark Martin 10.00 20.00
Valvoline
7 Alan Kulwicki 7.50 20.00
Hooters
11 Bill Elliott 6.00 15.00
Milkhouse Cheese
17 Darrell Waltrip 6.00 15.00
Western Auto

1992 Racing Champions NFL 1:64

18 Dale Jarrett 6.00 12.00
Interstate Batteries Atlanta Falcons
18 Dale Jarrett 6.00 12.00
Interstate Batteries
Cincinnati Bengals
18 Dale Jarrett 6.00 12.00
Interstate Batteries
Cleveland Browns
18 Dale Jarrett 6.00 12.00
Interstate Batteries
Los Angeles Raiders
18 Dale Jarrett 6.00 12.00
Interstate Batteries
Los Angeles Rams
18 Dale Jarrett 6.00 12.00
Interstate Batteries
Miami Dolphins
18 Dale Jarrett 6.00 12.00
Interstate Batteries
New York Giants
18 Dale Jarrett 6.00 12.00
Interstate Batteries
New York Jets
18 Dale Jarrett 6.00 12.00
Interstate Batteries
Seattle Seahawks
18 Dale Jarrett 6.00 12.00
Interstate Batteries
St. Louis Cardinals

1992 Racing Champions Petty Fan Appreciation Tour 1:64

Racing Champions issued this series to commemorate Richard Petty's 1992 farewell tour. Each car was packaged in a Racing Champions blister along with a card commemorating one track event for 1992. Only the trading cards are different in each package.

43 Richard Petty 5.00 12.00
Atlanta Motor Speedway
March 15
43 Richard Petty 5.00 12.00
Atlanta Hooters 500
November 15
43 Richard Petty 5.00 12.00
Bristol April 3
43 Richard Petty 5.00 12.00
Bristol August 29
43 Richard Petty 5.00 12.00
Charlotte One Hot
Night May 16
43 Richard Petty 5.00 12.00
Charlotte May 24
43 Richard Petty 5.00 12.00
Charlotte October 11
43 Richard Petty 5.00 12.00
Darlington March 29
43 Richard Petty 5.00 12.00
Darlington September 6
43 Richard Petty 5.00 12.00
Daytona 500 Feb.16
43 Richard Petty 5.00 12.00
Daytona July 4
43 Richard Petty 5.00 12.00
Dover Downs May 31
43 Richard Petty 5.00 12.00
Dover Downs Sept.20
43 Richard Petty 5.00 12.00
Martinsville April 26
43 Richard Petty 5.00 12.00
Martinsville Sept.27
43 Richard Petty 5.00 12.00
Michigan June 21
43 Richard Petty 5.00 12.00
Michigan Aug.16
43 Richard Petty 5.00 12.00
North Wilkesboro April 12
43 Richard Petty 5.00 12.00
North Wilkesboro Oct.4
43 Richard Petty 5.00 12.00
Phoenix Nov.1
43 Richard Petty 5.00 12.00
Pocono Raceway June 14
43 Richard Petty 5.00 12.00
Pocono July 19
43 Richard Petty 5.00 12.00
Richmond March 8
43 Richard Petty 5.00 12.00
Richmond September 12
43 Richard Petty 5.00 12.00
Rockingham March 1
43 Richard Petty 5.00 12.00
Rockingham October 25
43 Richard Petty 5.00 12.00
Sears Point June 7
43 Richard Petty 5.00 12.00
Talladega May 3
43 Richard Petty 5.00 12.00
Talladega July 26
43 Richard Petty 5.00 12.00
Watkins Glen August 9

1992 Racing Champions Premier 1:64

This 5-piece series was the first time Racing Champions did a Premier Series. Each piece comes in a black shadow box with the quantity produced on the front of the box.

3 Dale Earnhardt 20.00 50.00
Goodwrench/40,000
11 Bill Elliott 7.50 15.00
Amoco/20,000
17 Darrell Waltrip 6.00 14.00
Western Auto/20,000
28 Davey Allison 18.00 30.00
Havoline/20,000
43 Richard Petty 10.00 20.00
STP/20,000
51 Black Lumina Club Promo/5000 8.00 20.00
in clear box
92 White Lumina Promo/5000 8.00 20.00
in clear box

1992 Racing Champions Track Promos 1:64

92 Atlanta March 15 1.50 4.00
92 Bristol August 29 1.50 4.00
92 Charlotte October 11 1.50 4.00
92 Darlington March 29 1.50 4.00
92 Darlington September 6 1.50 4.00
92 Dayona 500 February 16 1.50 4.00
92 Daytona Pepsi 400 July 4 1.50 4.00
92 Dover May 31 1.50 4.00
92 Martinsville 45th Anniversary 1.50 4.00
92 Michigan International June 21 1.50 4.00
92 North Wilkesboro April 12 1.50 4.00
92 Pocono June 14 1.50 4.00
92 Pocono July 19 1.50 4.00
92 Richmond March 8 1.50 4.00
92 Richmond September 12 1.50 4.00
92 Rockingham March 1 1.50 4.00
92 Rockingham October 25 1.50 4.00
92 Sears Point June 7 1.50 4.00
92 Talladega May 3 1.50 4.00
92 Talladega July 26 1.50 4.00
92 Watkins Glen August 9 1.50 4.00

1992 Racing Champions with Figure 1:64

Each 1:64 car in this series was packaged with a plastic collectible figurine of the featured driver. Both the die-cast and driver statue were issued with a card in a large "Racing Champions" blister pack.

2 Rusty Wallace 6.00 15.00
Pontiac Excitement
4 Ernie Irvan 5.00 12.00
Kodak
12 Hut Stricklin 4.00 10.00
Raybestos
33 Harry Gant 4.00 10.00
42 Kyle Petty 5.00 12.00
Mello Yello

1993 Racing Champions 1:64

This series of 1:64 scale cars features the top names in racing. The cars came in a blister pack and were sold through both hobby and retail outlets.

0 Dick McCabe 1.50 4.00
Fisher Snow Plows
1/1 Jeff Gordon 12.50 25.00
Mark Martin
Carolina Ford
2-car promo set
2 Ward Burton 3.00 8.00
Hardee's Promo
2 Rusty Wallace 2.00 5.00
Pontiac Excitement
3 Dale Earnhardt 30.00 80.00
Goodwrench
3 Dale Earnhardt 25.00 60.00
Goodwrench
Mom-n-Pop's blister Promo
3 Dale Earnhardt 10.00 20.00
Goodwrench 1988
Monte Carlo Promo blister
3 Dale Earnhardt 10.00 20.00
Goodwrench 1989
Monte Carlo Promo blister
4 Ernie Irvan 2.00 5.00
Kodak
5 Terry Labonte 4.00 8.00
Kellogg's Promo black windows
5 Ricky Rudd 1.50 4.00
Tide
6 Mark Martin 5.00 10.00
Valvoline
7 Harry Gant 5.00 12.00
Black Flag Promo/15,000
7 Harry Gant 5.00 12.00
Easy-Off Promo/15,000
7 Harry Gant 5.00 12.00
French's Promo/15,000
7 Harry Gant 5.00 12.00
Gulf Lite Promo/15,000
7 Harry Gant 5.00 12.00
Woolite Promo/15,000
7 Alan Kulwicki 6.00 15.00
Hooters 1992 Champ card
8 Sterling Marlin 1.50 4.00
Raybestos
11 Bill Elliott 2.00 5.00
Amoco
12 Jimmy Spencer 1.50 4.00
Meineke
14 Terry Labonte 12.50 25.00
Kellogg's
15 Geoff Bodine 1.50 4.00
Motorcraft
17 Darrell Waltrip 1.50 4.00
Western Auto
18 Dale Jarrett 5.00 10.00
Interstate Batteries
20 Joe Ruttman 3.00 8.00
Fina Promo
21 Morgan Shepherd 1.50 4.00
Citgo
21 Morgan Shepherd 2.50 6.00
Citgo Promo
22 Bobby Labonte 25.00 50.00
Maxwell House
24 Jeff Gordon 40.00 80.00
uPont
25 Ken Schrader 5.00 10.00
Kodiak
25 Bill Venturini 1.50 4.00
Rain X
26 Brett Bodine 1.50 4.00
Quaker State
27 Hut Stricklin 1.50 4.00
McDonald's
28 Davey Allison 5.00 12.00
Havoline
28 Davey Allison 6.00 15.00
Havoline
with Black and White paint scheme
28 Ernie Irvan 5.00 10.00
Havoline
31 Steve Grissom 3.00 8.00
Channellock Promo
33 Harry Gant 1.50 4.00
No Sponsor Lumina
33 Harry Gant 1.50 4.00
No Sponsor Oldsmobile
42 Kyle Petty 1.50 4.00
Mello Yello
44 Rick Wilson 1.50 4.00
STP
59 Andy Belmont 4.00 8.00
FDP Brakes
59 Robert Pressley 4.00 8.00
Alliance
60 Mark Martin 4.00 8.00
Winn Dixie
71 Dave Marcis 4.00 10.00
STG
75 Butch Mock 1.50 4.00
Factory Stores of America
87 Joe Nemechek 1.50 4.00
Dentyne
98 Derrike Cope 1.50 4.00
Bojangles

1993 Racing Champions Craftsman Motorsports Promos 1:64

8 Sterling Marlin 2.50 6.00
Raybestos
11 Bill Elliott 2.50 6.00
Amoco
14 Terry Labonte 2.50 6.00
Kellogg's
15 Geoff Bodine 2.50 6.00
Motorcraft
17 Darrell Waltrip 2.50 6.00
Western Auto
33 Harry Gant 2.50 6.00
No Sponsor

1993 Racing Champions Mercury Cyclones 1:64

12 Bobby Allison 4.00 10.00
1969 Mercury Cyclone
16 Tiny Lund 4.00 10.00
1969 Mercury Cyclone red
21 Donnie Allison 4.00 10.00
1969 Mercury Cyclone white
21 A.J. Foyt 4.00 10.00
1969 Mercury Cyclone
21 Cale Yarborough 4.00 10.00
1969 Mercury Cyclone
24 Cecil Gordon 4.00 10.00
1969 Mercury Cyclone
26 Lee Roy Yarborough 4.00 10.00
1969 Mercury Cyclone
27 Donnie Allison 4.00 10.00
1969 Mercury Cyclone red
52 A.J. Foyt 4.00 10.00
1969 Mercury Cyclone
55 Tiny Lund 4.00 10.00
1969 Mercury Cyclone blue
64 Elmo Langley 4.00 10.00
1969 Mercury Cyclone

1993 Racing Champions Premier 1:64

This was the second year of the 1:64 scale Premier series. The series is highlighted by the Alan Kulwicki Hooters car and the three different Champion Forever Davey Allison pieces.

1 Rodney Combs 3.00 8.00
Jebco Clocks
2 Ward Burton 6.00 15.00
Hardee's/10,000
2 Rusty Wallace 5.00 12.00
Pontiac Excitement/40,000
3 Dale Earnhardt 30.00 80.00
Goodwrench/20,000
3 Dale Earnhardt 30.00 80.00
Goodwrench/20,000
DEI on package
4 Ernie Irvan 3.00 8.00
Kodak/60,000
4 Jeff Purvis 7.50 15.00
Kodak
5 Ricky Rudd 3.00 8.00
Tide/40,000
6 Mark Martin 4.00 10.00
Valvoline
6 Mark Martin 7.00 15.00
Valvoline
Four in a Row Promo
6 Mike Stefanik 5.00 10.00
Valvoline Auto Palace
7 Jimmy Hensley 15.00 30.00
Alan Kulwicki Racing
7 Alan Kulwicki 20.00 50.00
Hooters/60,000
1992 Champion card
7 Alan Kulwicki 15.00 30.00
Zerex/10,000
8 Sterling Marlin 3.00 8.00
Raybestos
11 Bill Elliott 8.00 20.00
Budweiser Promo
12 Jimmy Spencer 3.00 8.00
Meineke/40,000
14 Terry Labonte 12.50 25.00
Kellogg's
15 Geoff Bodine 3.00 8.00
Motorcraft/40,000
18 Dale Jarrett 5.00 10.00
Interstate Batteries/20,000
21 Morgan Shepherd 3.00 8.00
Citgo/40,000
24 Jeff Gordon 20.00 50.00
DuPont/40,000
26 Brett Bodine 3.00 8.00
Quaker State/40,000
27 Hut Stricklin 3.00 8.00
McDonald's/40,000
27 Hut Stricklin 3.00 8.00
Mr. Pibb
28 Davey Allison 10.00 20.00
Havoline Black paint scheme
28 Davey Allison 7.50 15.00
Havoline Black and Gold
Champion Forever/28,000
28 Davey Allison 10.00 20.00
Havoline Black and Orange
Champion Forever/28,000
28 Davey Allison 10.00 20.00
Havoline Black and White
Champion Forever/28,000
28 Ernie Irvan 10.00 20.00
Havoline
31 Neil Bonnett 25.00 50.00
Mom-n-Pop's/10,000
33 Harry Gant 3.00 8.00
No Sponsor
41 Ernie Irvan 6.00 15.00
Mac Tools/16,041
42 Kyle Petty 3.00 8.00
Mello Yello/40,000
44 Jimmy Hensley 3.00 8.00
STP
59 Robert Pressley 8.00 20.00
Alliance
59 Dennis Setzer 7.50 15.00
Alliance
60 Mark Martin 10.00 20.00
Winn Dixie
87 Joe Nemechek 3.00 8.00
Dentyne/20,000
93 DCD Anniversary/5000 3.00 8.00
97 Joe Bessey 3.00 8.00
Auto Palace
98 Derrike Cope 3.00 8.00
Bojangles with Black paint scheme
98 Derrike Cope 3.00 8.00
Bojangles with Yellow paint scheme
02 Frank Kimmel 20.00 40.00
Harley Davidson

1993 Racing Champions PVC Box 1:64

Most die-casts in this series were produced for a special race occasion. Each piece comes packaged in a clear PVC box featuring the driver's name, what the occasion was, and the quantity produced all printed in gold foil.

2 Rusty Wallace 5.00 10.00
Pontiac Excitement
Feb.28th Win/5000
2 Rusty Wallace 5.00 10.00
Pontiac Excitement
April 4th Win/5000
2 Rusty Wallace 5.00 10.00
Pontiac Excitement
April 18th Win/5000
2 Rusty Wallace 5.00 10.00
Pontiac Excitement
April 25th Win/5000
2 Rusty Wallace 5.00 10.00
Pontiac Excitement
July 11th Win
2 Rusty Wallace 5.00 10.00
Pontiac Excitement
September 11th Win
2 Rusty Wallace 5.00 10.00
Pontiac Excitement
September 19th Win
2 Rusty Wallace 5.00 10.00
Pontiac Excitement
October 3rd Win
2 Rusty Wallace 5.00 10.00
Pontiac Excitement
October 24th Win
2 Rusty Wallace 5.00 10.00
Pontiac Excitement
November 14th Win
3 Dale Earnhardt 25.00 60.00
1993 WC Champ/5000
3 Dale Earnhardt 30.00 60.00
1993 WC Champ
with Red Flags in box
3 Dale Earnhardt 25.00 60.00
Back in Black/5000
3 Dale Earnhardt 25.00 60.00
Busch Clash Win/5000
3 Dale Earnhardt 25.00 60.00
Coca-Cola 600 Win/7500
3 Dale Earnhardt 25.00 60.00
Pepsi 400 Win
3 Dale Earnhardt 25.00 60.00
June 6th Win/5000
3 Dale Earnhardt 25.00 60.00
One Hot Night Win/7500
3 Dale Earnhardt 25.00 60.00
Die Hard 500 Win/5000
4 Ernie Irvan 4.00 10.00
Kodak Talladega Win
5 Max Dumesny 4.00 10.00
Valvoline
5 Ricky Rudd 4.00 10.00
Tide June 20th Win/1000
6 Mark Martin 5.00 10.00
Valvoline Aug.8 Win/5000
6 Mark Martin 5.00 10.00
Valvoline Aug.15 Win/5000
7 Harry Gant 4.00 10.00
Morema/5000
7 Jimmy Hensley 4.00 10.00
Hanes
7 Jimmy Hensley 4.00 10.00
Purolator
8 Sterling Marlin 15.00 30.00
Raybestos Winston Open/2500
12 David Bonnett 4.00 10.00
Plasti-Kote
16 Wally Dallenbach 15.00 25.00
Keystone Promo
18 Dale Jarrett 5.00 10.00
Interstate Batteries
Daytona Win/10,000
20 Pocono 20th Anniversary/7500 4.00 10.00
21 Morgan Shepherd 4.00 10.00
Cheerwine
24 Jeff Gordon 20.00 50.00
DuPont/5000
24 Jeff Gordon 30.00 60.00
DuPont Fan Club
24 Jeff Gordon 20.00 50.00
DuPont Daytona/5000
24 Jeff Gordon 20.00 50.00
DuPont Twin 125 Win/5000
27 Hut Stricklin 4.00 10.00
McDonald's All-American
27 Hut Stricklin 10.00 20.00
McDonald's Daytona
27 Hut Stricklin 25.00 50.00
McDonald's 250 produced
27 Hut Stricklin 4.00 10.00
McDonald's Taylorsville
April 19, 1993
28 Alan Kulwicki 25.00 50.00
Hardee's
28 Davey Allison 10.00 20.00
Havoline race win/5000
28 Ernie Irvan 10.00 20.00
Havoline
28 Ernie Irvan 10.00 20.00
Havoline Charlotte
40 Kenny Wallace 8.00 20.00
Dirt Devil/5000
42 Kyle Petty 10.00 20.00
Mello Yello Daytona Pole/5000
44 David Green 8.00 20.00
Slim Jim
44 Rick Wilson 4.00 10.00
STP/5000
46 Al Unser Jr. 12.50 25.00
Valvoline/5000
51 Lumina Racing Champions 20.00 40.00
51 Pontiac Racing Champions 20.00 40.00
51 Thunderbird Racing Champions 20.00 40.00
51 Racing Champions Mascot 20.00 40.00
52 Ken Schrader 4.00 10.00
Morema/5000
55 Ted Musgrave 4.00 10.00
Jasper/5000
56 Ernie Irvan 25.00 60.00
Earnhardt Chevrolet
1987 Monte Carlo/5000
59 Robert Pressley 10.00 20.00
Alliance Fan Club
59 Robert Pressley 10.00 20.00
Alliance Pressley
59 Robert Pressley 18.00 35.00
Alliance September 1993
60 Mark Martin 7.50 15.00
Winn Dixie
68 Bobby Hamilton 40.00 80.00
Country Time/1000
February 14, 1993
82 Derrike Cope 12.50 25.00
Zook Racing/2000
89 Jeff McClure 4.00 10.00
Bero Motors
93 Bristol April 4 5.00 12.00
93 Bristol August 28/5000 4.00 10.00
93 Bud 500/5000 5.00 12.00
93 Racing Champions Club 5.00 12.00
93 Slick 50 300 5.00 12.00
98 Derrike Cope 4.00 10.00
Bojangles'/5000

1994 Racing Champions 1:64

These 1:64 scale pieces were mainly packaged in a red blister pack and distributed through hobby shops and retail outlets. The year of issue is printed on the blister for the regular issue pieces. Most promo die-casts were issued in blisters printed in the sponsor's colors.

1 Rick Mast 1.50 4.00
Precision Products
1/24 Jeff Gordon 20.00 40.00
Frosted Mini-Wheats Promo
Baby Ruth & DuPont cars
with Sprint car in blister
2 Ricky Craven 3.00 6.00
DuPont
2 Rusty Wallace 4.00 8.00
Ford Motorsports
2 Rusty Wallace 4.00 8.00
Ford Motorsports with no Blue
4 Sterling Marlin 1.50 4.00
Kodak
5 Terry Labonte 3.00 6.00
Kellogg's
5 Terry Labonte 4.00 10.00
Kellogg's Promo black windows
5/10/17 Ricky Rudd 4.00 10.00
Darrell Waltrip
Tide 3-car Promo set
6 Mark Martin 2.00 5.00
Valvoline
7 Geoff Bodine 1.50 4.00
Exide
7 Harry Gant 4.00 8.00
Manheim
8 Jeff Burton 4.00 8.00
Raybestos
8 Kenny Wallace 1.50 4.00
TIC Financial
10 Ricky Rudd 1.50 4.00
Tide
10 Ricky Rudd 4.00 10.00
Tide Promo black windows
12 Clifford Allison 5.00 10.00
Sports Image
14 John Andretti 1.50 4.00
Kanawaha
15 Lake Speed 1.50 4.00
Quality Care
16 Ted Musgrave 1.50 4.00
Family Channel
17 Darrell Waltrip 1.50 4.00
Western Auto
18 Dale Jarrett 6.00 15.00
Interstate Batteries
19 Loy Allen 4.00 8.00
Hooters
20 Randy LaJoie 1.50 4.00
Fina
21 Morgan Shepherd 1.50 4.00
Citgo
22 Bobby Labonte 10.00 20.00
Maxwell House
23 Hut Stricklin 5.00 10.00
Smokin' Joe's in plastic case
24 Jeff Gordon 25.00 50.00
DuPont
24 Jeff Gordon 20.00 40.00
DuPont Coca-Cola 600 Win
in plastic case
24 Jeff Gordon 20.00 40.00
DuPont Brickyard
25 Hermie Sadler 1.50 4.00
Virginia is for Lovers
25 Ken Schrader 1.50 4.00
GMAC
26 Brett Bodine 1.50 4.00
Quaker State
27 Jimmy Spencer 1.50 4.00
McDonald's
27 Jimmy Spencer 4.00 8.00
McDonald's Promo
black windows
28 Ernie Irvan 2.00 5.00
Havoline
28 Ernie Irvan 4.00 10.00
Havoline Promo
30 Michael Waltrip 1.50 4.00
Pennzoil
31 Ward Burton 10.00 20.00
Hardees Promo
31 Tom Peck 1.50 4.00
Channellock
33 Harry Gant 20.00 40.00
No Sponsor
33 Bobby Labonte 40.00 80.00
Dentyne
38 Elton Sawyer 1.50 4.00
Ford Credit
40 Bobby Hamilton 1.50 4.00
Kendall
42 Kyle Petty 1.50 4.00
Mello Yello
44 Bobby Hillin Jr. 1.50 4.00
Buss Fuses
46 Shawna Robinson 5.00 10.00
Polaroid
52 Ken Schrader 3.00 6.00
AC Delco
54 Robert Pressley 1.50 4.00
Manheim
60 Mark Martin 5.00 12.00
Winn Dixie
63 Jim Bown 1.50 4.00
Lysol
63 NDA 10.00 20.00
Lysol Promo
75 Todd Bodine 1.50 4.00
Factory Stores of America
79 Dave Rezendes 4.00 10.00
Lipton Tea
83 Sherry Blakely 1.50 4.00
Ramses
92 Larry Pearson 1.50 4.00
Stanley Tools
94 Brickyard 400 Promo 1.50 4.00
94 McDonald's All-Star Promo 1.50 4.00
3/24/2 car numbers on deck lid
94 Sunoco Ultra 94 Promo 3.00 8.00
black windows
97 Joe Bessey 1.50 4.00
Johnson
98 Derrike Cope 1.50 4.00
Fingerhut
00 Johnny Rumley 4.00 8.00
Big Dog Coal

1994 Racing Champions Hobby Yellow Box 1:64

This series was distributed through hobby channels. Each piece came in a yellow box.

1 Rick Mast 1.50 4.00
Precision Products
2 Ricky Craven 1.50 4.00
DuPont
2 Rusty Wallace 2.00 5.00
Ford Motorsports
4 Sterling Marlin 1.50 4.00
Kodak
4 Sterling Marlin 1.50 4.00
Kodak Funsaver
5 Terry Labonte 3.00 6.00
Kellogg's
6 Mark Martin 4.00 8.00
Valvoline
7 Geoff Bodine 1.50 4.00
Exide
8 Jeff Burton 1.50 4.00
Raybestos
14 Terry Labonte 8.00 20.00
MW Windows
15 Lake Speed 1.50 4.00
Quality Care
16 Ted Musgrave 1.50 4.00
Family Channel
17 Darrell Waltrip 1.50 4.00
Western Auto
18 Dale Jarrett 6.00 15.00
Interstate Batteries
19 Loy Allen 1.50 4.00
Hooters
22 Brett Bodine 4.00 10.00
Maxwell House
23 Chad Little 5.00 12.00
Bayer
24 Jeff Gordon 20.00 40.00
DuPont
25 Hermie Sadler 1.50 4.00
Virginia is for Lovers
26 Brett Bodine 1.50 4.00
Quaker State
27 Jimmy Spencer 1.50 4.00
McDonald's
30 Michael Waltrip 1.50 4.00
Pennzoil
31 Tom Peck 1.50 4.00
Channellock
33 Harry Gant 1.50 4.00
No Sponsor
34 Mike McLaughlin 1.50 4.00
Fiddle Faddle
38 Elton Sawyer 1.50 4.00
Ford Credit
40 Bobby Hamilton 1.50 4.00
Kendall
42 Kyle Petty 1.50 4.00
Mello Yello
46 Shawna Robinson 4.00 10.00
Polaroid
63 Jim Bown 1.50 4.00
Lysol
75 Todd Bodine 1.50 4.00
Factory Stores of America
92 Larry Pearson 1.50 4.00
Stanley Tools
94 No Driver Association 1.50 4.00
Brickyard 400
98 Derrike Cope 1.50 4.00
Fingerhut

1994 Racing Champions Country Time Legends Promos 1:64

This series of die-cast cars was produced by Racing Champions and distributed through a promotional offer from Kraft General Foods and Country Time Drink Mix in 1994. Note that each car features a retired legendary NASCAR driver in a vintage car with a 1991 copyright date on the bottom. Each was also issued in a "Legends of Racing" black and checkered box with the Country Time logo and driver checklist present.

11 Ned Jarrett 6.00 15.00
Bowani 1963 Ford
21 Cale Yarborough 6.00 15.00
1969 Ford
22 Fireball Roberts 5.00 12.00
Young Ford 1963 Ford
28 Fred Lorenzen 5.00 12.00
LaFayette Ford 1963 Ford
29 Bobby Allison 6.00 15.00
1969 Ford
51 Neil Bonnett 6.00 15.00
Country Time

1994 Racing Champions Premier 1:64

This series of 1:64 Premier series was issued by Racing Champions through retail outlets and hobby dealers. The pieces come in a black shadow box and have the quantity produced stamped in gold on the front of the box.

1 Davey Allison 10.00 20.00
Lancaster
2 Ricky Craven 3.00 6.00
DuPont
2 Rusty Wallace 6.00 12.00
Miller Genuine Draft/20,000
2 Rusty Wallace 10.00 20.00
Mac Tools
3 Dale Earnhardt 25.00 60.00
Goodwrench 6-time
champ/10,000
4 Sterling Marlin 3.00 8.00
Kodak
4 Sterling Marlin 5.00 12.00
Kodak Funsaver
5 Terry Labonte 15.00 30.00
Kellogg's/20,000
6 Mark Martin 3.00 6.00
Valvoline
6 Mark Martin 7.00 14.00
Valvoline
four in a row special
7 Geoff Bodine 3.00 6.00
Exide
7 Harry Gant 7.50 15.00
Manheim
7 Alan Kulwicki 15.00 30.00
Army
7 Alan Kulwicki 7.50 15.00
Zerex Promo blister/20,000
8 Jeff Burton 3.00 6.00
Raybestos/20,000
8 Kenny Wallace 3.00 6.00
TIC Financial
12 Clifford Allison 10.00 20.00
Sports Image/10,000
15 Lake Speed 3.00 6.00
Quality Care
16 Chad Chaffin 6.00 12.00
31W Insulation
16 Ted Musgrave 3.00 6.00
Family Channel
18 Dale Jarrett 5.00 10.00
Interstate Batteries
19 Loy Allen 3.00 6.00
Hooters
20 Randy LaJoie 3.00 6.00
Fina
21 Johnny Benson 7.50 15.00
Berger
24 Jeff Gordon 12.50 30.00
DuPont/20,000
24 Jeff Gordon 12.50 30.00
DuPont 1993 Rookie
of the Year/20,000
25 Hermie Sadler 6.00 12.00
Virgina is for Lovers
25 Ken Schrader 3.00 6.00
Kodiak

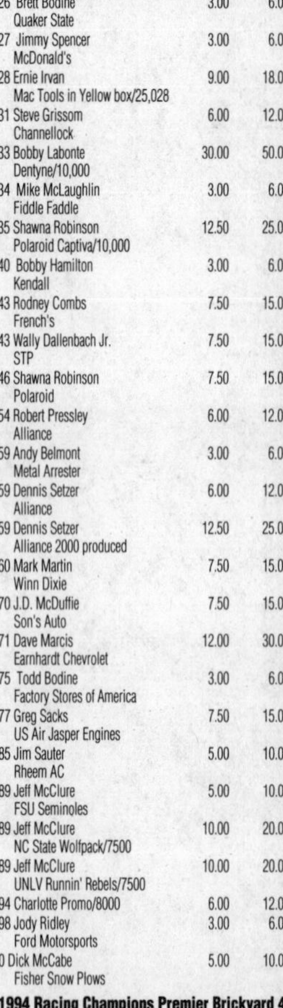

26 Brett Bodine 3.00 6.00
Quaker State
27 Jimmy Spencer 3.00 6.00
McDonald's
28 Ernie Irvan 9.00 18.00
Mac Tools in Yellow box/25,028
31 Steve Grissom 6.00 12.00
Channellock
33 Bobby Labonte 30.00 50.00
Dentyne/10,000
34 Mike McLaughlin 3.00 6.00
Fiddle Faddle
35 Shawna Robinson 12.50 25.00
Polaroid Captiva/10,000
40 Bobby Hamilton 3.00 6.00
Kendall
43 Rodney Combs 7.50 15.00
French's
43 Wally Dallenbach Jr. 7.50 15.00
STP
46 Shawna Robinson 7.50 15.00
Polaroid
54 Robert Pressley 6.00 12.00
Alliance
59 Andy Belmont 3.00 6.00
Metal Arrester
59 Dennis Setzer 6.00 12.00
Alliance
59 Dennis Setzer 12.50 25.00
Alliance 2000 produced
60 Mark Martin 7.50 15.00
Winn Dixie
70 J.D. McDuffie 7.50 15.00
Son's Auto
71 Dave Marcis 12.00 30.00
Earnhardt Chevrolet
75 Todd Bodine 3.00 6.00
Factory Stores of America
77 Greg Sacks 7.50 15.00
US Air Jasper Engines
85 Jim Sauter 5.00 10.00
Rheem AC
89 Jeff McClure 5.00 10.00
FSU Seminoles
89 Jeff McClure 10.00 20.00
NC State Wolfpack/7500
89 Jeff McClure 10.00 20.00
UNLV Runnin' Rebels/7500
94 Charlotte Promo/8000 6.00 12.00
98 Jody Ridley 3.00 6.00
Ford Motorsports
0 Dick McCabe 5.00 10.00
Fisher Snow Plows

1994 Racing Champions Premier Brickyard 400 1:64

This series was issued in conjunction with the first Brickyard 400 race. The boxes are the usual shadow box style, but are easily distinguishable due to their purple color. Each piece included a gold bordered Brickyard 400 photo card that included a facsimile driver's signature. The outside of the box featured the production run total of 20,000.

3 Dale Earnhardt 20.00 50.00
Goodwrench
6 Mark Martin 5.00 12.00
Valvoline
18 Dale Jarrett 7.50 15.00
Interstate Batteries
21 Morgan Shepherd 3.00 8.00
Citgo
24 Jeff Gordon 40.00 75.00
DuPont
26 Brett Bodine 3.00 8.00
Quaker State
27 Jimmy Spencer 3.00 8.00
McDonald's
30 Michael Waltrip 3.00 8.00
Pennzoil
42 Kyle Petty 3.00 8.00
Mello Yello

1994 Racing Champions PVC Box 1:64

24 Jeff Gordon
DuPont Fan Club/3000
24 Jeff Gordon 10.00 20.00
DuPont ROY/5000

1994 Racing Champions Short Track Champions 1:64

2 Mark Martin 4.00 10.00
RECO
5 Ernie Irvan 3.00 8.00
Terminal Trucking
23 Davey Allison 4.00 10.00
No sponsor
33 Harry Gant 3.00 8.00
Dillon
52 Butch Miller 3.00 8.00
Lane
66 Rusty Wallace 4.00 10.00
Alugard
99 Dick Trickle 3.00 8.00
Prototype

1994 Racing Champions To the Maxx 1:64

s was the first series issued by Racing Champions that uded a Maxx Premier Plus card.

usty Wallace	4.00	8.00
Ford Motorsports		
Sterling Marlin	4.00	10.00
Kodak		
erry Labonte	5.00	10.00
Kellogg's		
lark Martin	4.00	8.00
Valvoline		
Ted Musgrave	4.00	7.00
Family Channel		
Jeff Gordon	15.00	25.00
DuPont		
Ernie Irvan	4.00	8.00
Havoline		
Kyle Petty	4.00	7.00
Mello Yello		

1995 Racing Champions Preview 1:64

s series of 1:64 replica cars was a Preview to many of the s that raced in the 1995 season. The packaging is a dboard and plastic blister with a black #51 car printed on the cker board. A Racing Champions Preview card was also ckaged with each car. The Geoff Bodine Exide car can be nd with either Hoosier or Goodyear tires.

Rick Mast	1.50	4.00
Precision Products		
icky Craven	1.50	4.00
DuPont		
Rusty Wallace	2.00	5.00
Ford Motorsports		
Sterling Marlin	2.00	5.00
Kodak		
Mark Martin	2.00	4.00
Valvoline		
Geoff Bodine	1.50	4.00
Exide with Goodyear tires		
Geoff Bodine	1.50	4.00
Exide with Hoosier tires		
Ricky Rudd	1.50	4.00
Tide		
Terry Labonte	6.00	12.00
MW Windows		
Ted Musgrave	1.50	4.00
Family Channel		
Morgan Shepherd	1.50	4.00
Citgo		
Chad Little	1.50	4.00
Bayer		
Jeff Gordon	7.50	15.00
DuPont		
Kirk Shelmerdine	3.00	6.00
Big Johnson		
Steve Kinser	1.50	4.00
Quaker State		
Dale Jarrett	2.50	5.00
Havoline		
Michael Waltrip	1.50	4.00
Pennzoil		
Elton Sawyer	1.50	4.00
Ford Credit		
Bobby Hamilton	1.50	4.00
Kendall		
Patty Moise	1.50	4.00
Dial Purex		
Ken Schrader	1.50	4.00
AC Delco		
Jason Keller	1.50	4.00
Budget Gourmet		
Curtis Markham	1.50	4.00
Lysol		
Todd Bodine	1.50	4.00
Factory Stores of America		
Larry Pearson	1.50	4.00
Stanley Tools		
Bill Elliott	2.00	4.00
McDonald's		
Jeremy Mayfield	1.50	4.00
Fingerhut		

1995 Racing Champions 1:64

This is the regular issued of the 1:64 scale 1995 Racing Champions series. The Bobby Labonte car comes with and without roof flaps. This was one of the first cars to incorporate the new NASCAR safety feature into a die cast.

1 Rick Mast	1.50	4.00
Precision		
2 Ricky Craven	1.50	4.00
DuPont		
2 Rusty Wallace	2.00	5.00
Ford Motorsports		
4 Sterling Marlin	1.50	4.00
Kodak		
4 Jeff Purvis	1.50	4.00
Kodak Funsaver		
5 Terry Labonte	2.50	5.00
Kellogg's		
6 Tommy Houston	1.50	4.00
Red Devil		
6 Mark Martin	2.00	5.00
Valvoline		
7 Geoff Bodine	1.50	4.00
Exide		
7 Stevie Reeves	1.50	4.00
Clabber Girl		
8 Jeff Burton	1.50	4.00
Raybestos		
8 Jeff Burton	1.50	4.00
Raybestos with Blue numbers		
8 Bobby Dotter	1.50	4.00
Hyde Tools		
8 Kenny Wallace	4.00	8.00
Red Dog		
10 Ricky Rudd	1.50	4.00
Tide		
10 Ricky Rudd	4.00	10.00
Tide Promo black windows		
12 Derrike Cope	1.50	4.00
Straight Arrow		
14 Terry Labonte	15.00	30.00
MW Windows		
15 Jack Nadeau	1.50	4.00
Buss Fuses		
15 Jerry Nadeau	3.00	8.00
Buss Fuses Promo		
packaged with fuses		
15 Dick Trickle	1.50	4.00
Ford Quality		
16 Stub Fadden	4.00	10.00
NAPA Promo in bag		
16 Ted Musgrave	1.50	4.00
Family Channel		
17 Darrell Waltrip	1.50	4.00
Western Auto		
18 Bobby Labonte	4.00	8.00
Interstate Batteries		
with roof flaps		
18 Bobby Labonte	3.00	6.00
Interstate Batteries		
without roof flaps		
21 Morgan Shepherd	1.50	4.00
Citgo		
22 Randy LaJoie	1.50	4.00
MBNA		
23 Chad Little	1.50	4.00
Bayer		
24 Jeff Gordon	15.00	30.00
DuPont		
24 Jeff Gordon	15.00	30.00
DuPont Coca-Cola		
24 Jeff Gordon	20.00	35.00
DuPont Fan Club/2000		
in PVC box		
25 Johnny Rumley	2.50	5.00
Big Johnson		
25 Ken Schrader	1.50	4.00
Hendrick		
25 Kirk Shelmerdine	1.50	4.00
Big Johnson		
26 Steve Kinser	1.50	4.00
Quaker State		
27 Loy Allen	1.50	4.00
Hooters		
28 Dale Jarrett	2.00	5.00
Havoline		
29 Steve Grissom	1.50	4.00
Meineke		
30 Michael Waltrip	1.50	4.00
Pennzoil		
34 Mike McLaughlin	1.50	4.00
French's		
37 John Andretti	1.50	4.00
K-Mart		
40 Patty Moise	1.50	4.00
Dial Purex		
41 Ricky Craven	1.50	4.00
Larry Hedrick Racing		
44 David Green	1.50	4.00
Slim Jim		
44 Jeff Purvis	1.50	4.00
Jackaroo		
47 Jeff Fuller	1.50	4.00
Sunoco		
51 Jim Bown	1.50	4.00
Luck's		
52 Ken Schrader	1.50	4.00
AC Delco		
57 Jason Keller	1.50	4.00
Budget Gourmet		
60 Mark Martin	2.00	5.00
Winn Dixie		
60 Mark Martin	5.00	12.00
Winn Dixie Promo		
71 Kevin Lepage	4.00	10.00
Vermont Teddy Bear		
71 Dave Marcis	5.00	15.00
Olive Garden		
75 Todd Bodine	1.50	4.00
Factory Stores of America		
81 Kenny Wallace	1.50	4.00
TIC Financial		
82 Derrike Cope	1.50	4.00
FDP Brakes		
84 Bob Senneker	12.00	20.00
Jacksonville		
Bratwurst Promo/10,000		
87 Joe Nemechek	1.50	4.00
Burger King		
90 Mike Wallace	1.50	4.00
Heilig-Meyers		
92 Larry Pearson	1.50	4.00
Stanley Tools		
94 Bill Elliott	4.00	8.00
McDonald's		
94 Bill Elliott	4.00	8.00
McDonald's Upper Deck Promo		
94 Bill Elliott	5.00	10.00
McDonald's Thunderbat Promo		
99 Phil Parsons	1.50	4.00
Luxaire		

1995 Racing Champions Matched Serial Numbers 1:64

This series features cards and die cast whose serial numbers match. The cars come in a black blister pack with a card. The card has a gold border and features the driver of the car.

2 Rusty Wallace	4.00	7.00
Ford		
5 Terry Labonte	5.00	10.00
Kellogg's		
6 Mark Martin	5.00	10.00
Valvoline		
7 Geoff Bodine	2.50	6.00
Exide		
18 Bobby Labonte	5.00	10.00
Interstate Batteries		
24 Jeff Gordon	12.50	25.00
DuPont		

1995 Racing Champions Premier 1:64

This is the 1995 series of the 1:64 Premier pieces. The cars are again packaged in a black shadow box and feature a gold foil number on the front of the box that states how many pieces were made. The cars were distributed through both hobby and retail.

2 Rusty Wallace	3.50	8.00
Ford Motorsports		
4 Sterling Marlin	3.00	8.00
Kodak		
6 Mark Martin	3.50	8.00
Valvoline		
8 Jeff Burton	3.00	6.00
Raybestos		
8 Kenny Wallace	60.00	120.00
Red Dog Promo		
18 Bobby Labonte	3.00	6.00
Interstate Batteries		
24 Jeff Gordon	20.00	35.00
DuPont/20,000		
24 Jeff Gordon	15.00	30.00
DuPont Signature Series		
24 Jeff Gordon	15.00	30.00
DuPont Signature Series		
combo with SuperTruck		
25 Ken Schrader	3.00	6.00
Budweiser		
26 Steve Kinser	3.00	6.00
Quaker State		
27 Loy Allen	3.00	6.00
Hooters		
28 Dale Jarrett	3.00	8.00
Havoline		
40 Bobby Hamilton	3.00	6.00
Kendall		
40 Patty Moise	3.00	6.00
Dial Purex		
59 Dennis Setzer	3.00	6.00
Alliance		
60 Mark Martin	5.00	10.00
Winn Dixie		
75 Todd Bodine	3.00	6.00
Factory Stores of America		
81 Kenny Wallace	3.00	6.00
TIC Financial		
94 Bill Elliott	10.00	20.00
McDonald's		

1995 Racing Champions PVC Box 1:64

95 Charlotte October 8/36,000	5.00	12.00
95 Richmond Sept.9	5.00	12.00
SuperTruck/18,000		

1995 Racing Champions To the Maxx 1:64

These pieces represent the second through fifth series of Racing Champions To the Maxx line. Each package includes a Maxx Premier Plus card that is only available with the die cast piece and was not inserted in any packs of the Premier Plus product.

2 Rusty Wallace	5.00	10.00
Ford Motorsports		
4 Sterling Marlin	3.00	8.00
Kodak		
4 Jeff Purvis	3.00	8.00
Kodak		
6 Tommy Houston	3.00	8.00
Dirt Devil		
6 Mark Martin	5.00	10.00
Valvoline		
7 Geoff Bodine	3.00	8.00
Exide		
7 Stevie Reeves	3.00	8.00
Clabber Girl		
8 Jeff Burton	3.00	8.00
Raybestos		
10 Ricky Rudd	3.00	8.00
Tide		
12 Derrike Cope	3.00	8.00
Mane N Tail		
14 Terry Labonte	3.00	8.00
MW Windows		
15 Dick Trickle	3.00	8.00
Quality Care		
17 Darrell Waltrip	3.00	8.00
Western Auto		
18 Bobby Labonte	3.00	8.00
Interstate Batteries		
21 Morgan Shepherd	3.00	8.00
Citgo		
22 Randy LaJoie	3.00	8.00
MBNA		
23 Chad Little	3.00	8.00
Bayer		
24 Jeff Gordon	5.00	10.00
DuPont		
26 Steve Kinser	3.00	8.00
Quaker State		
28 Dale Jarrett	5.00	10.00
Havoline		
29 Steve Grissom	3.00	8.00
Meineke		
34 Mike McLaughlin	3.00	8.00
French's		
38 Elton Sawyer	3.00	8.00
Ford Credit		
44 David Green	3.00	8.00
Slim Jim		
44 Jeff Purvis	3.00	8.00
Jackaroo		
52 Ken Schrader	3.00	8.00
AC Delco		
57 Jason Keller	3.00	8.00
Budget Gourmet		
75 Todd Bodine	3.00	8.00
Factory Stores of America		
81 Kenny Wallace	3.00	8.00
TIC Financial		
90 Mike Wallace	3.00	8.00
Heilig-Meyers		
92 Larry Pearson	3.00	8.00
Stanley Tools		
94 Bill Elliott	3.00	8.00
McDonald's		

1995 Racing Champions SuperTrucks 1:64

This series of 1:64 SuperTrucks includes a good sampling of many of the trucks that competed in the first NASCAR SuperTruck series. Each was packaged in a white and red blister that included a Racing Champions collector card.

1 P.J. Jones	3.00	6.00
Sears Diehard		
1 P.J. Jones	5.00	10.00
Vessells Ford		
1 Richmond Night Race Special	10.00	20.00
1 Tucson April 8 Race	12.50	25.00
2 David Ashley	3.00	6.00
Southern California Ford		
3 Mike Skinner	3.00	6.00
Goodwrench		
6 Mike Bliss	3.00	6.00
Ultra Wheels		
6 Butch Gilliland	3.00	6.00
Ultra Wheels		
6 Rick Carelli	3.00	6.00
Total Petroleum		
7 Geoff Bodine	3.00	6.00
Exide		
7 Geoff Bodine	3.00	6.00
Exide Salsa		
7 Dave Rezendes	3.00	6.00
Exide		
8 Mike Bliss	3.00	6.00
Ultra Wheels		
8 Craig Huartson	3.00	6.00
AC Delco		
10 Stan Fox	3.00	6.00
Made for You		
12 Randy MacCachren	3.00	6.00
Venable		
18 Johnny Benson	3.00	6.00
Hella Lights		
21 Tobey Butler	3.00	6.00
Ortho with Green Nose		
21 Tobey Butler	3.00	6.00
Ortho with Yellow Nose		
23 T.J. Clark	3.00	6.00
ASE with Blue paint scheme		
23 T.J. Clark	3.00	6.00
ASE with White paint scheme		
24 No Driver Association	3.00	6.00
DuPont Gordon Signature Series		
24 No Driver Association	4.00	8.00
DuPont with Gordon on the card		
37 Bob Strait	3.00	6.00
Target Expediting		
38 Sammy Swindell	3.00	6.00
Channellock		
with White Goodyear on tires		
38 Sammy Swindell	3.00	6.00
Channellock		
with Yellow Goodyear on tires		
51 Kerry Teague	3.00	6.00
Rosenblum Racing		
52 Ken Schrader	3.00	6.00
AC Delco		
54 Steve McEachern	3.00	6.00
McEachern Racing		
61 Todd Bodine	3.00	6.00
Roush Racing		
75 Bill Sedgwick	3.00	6.00
Spears Motorsports		
83 Steve Portenga	3.00	6.00
Coffee Critic		
95 Brickyard 400 special	3.00	6.00
95 Brickyard 400 Premier/20,000	4.00	10.00
98 Butch Miller	3.00	6.00
Raybestos		

1995 Racing Champions SuperTrucks Matched Serial Numbers 1:64

This series features trucks and cards with matching serial numbers. The truck has a serial number stamp on the bottom of it. The card has a black serial number stamped on the front of it. The truck sits on a stand that also has a serial number that matches.

1 Mike Chase	4.00	7.00
Sears Diehard		
3 Mike Skinner	4.00	7.00
Goodwrench		
6 Rick Carelli	4.00	7.00
Total Petroleum		
24 Scott Lagasse	4.00	7.00
DuPont		
75 Bill Sedgwick	4.00	7.00
Spears Motorsports		
98 Butch Miller	4.00	7.00
Raybestos		

1995 Racing Champions SuperTrucks To the Maxx 1:64

This is the first series of SuperTruck To the Maxx pieces. Each piece is packaged in a red blister pack and comes with a Crown Chrome acetate card.

1 P.J. Jones	3.00	6.00
Sears Diehard		
3 Mike Skinner	4.00	8.00
Goodwrench		
6 Rick Carelli	3.00	6.00
Total Petroleum		
7 Geoff Bodine	3.00	6.00
Exide		
21 Tobey Butler	3.00	6.00
Ortho		
24 Jeff Gordon	5.00	10.00
DuPont		
38 Sammy Swindell	3.00	6.00
Channellock		
98 Butch Miller	3.00	6.00
Raybestos		

1996 Racing Champions Preview 1:64

This series features some of the new paint schemes and driver changes for the 1996 season. The cars again come in a red blister with the word preview appearing below the year in the upper right hand corner.

2 Ricky Craven	1.50	4.00
DuPont		
4 Sterling Marlin	2.00	5.00
Kodak		
5 Terry Labonte	2.00	4.00
Kellogg's		
6 Mark Martin	2.00	4.00
Valvoline		
7 Stevie Reeves	1.50	4.00
Clabber Girl		
9 Joe Bessey	1.50	4.00
Delco Remy		
9 Lake Speed	1.50	4.00
SPAM		
10 Ricky Rudd	1.50	4.00
Tide		
11 Brett Bodine	1.50	4.00
Lowe's		
12 Derrike Cope	1.50	4.00
Mane N' Tail		
14 Patty Moise	1.50	4.00
Dial Purex		
16 Ted Musgrave	1.50	4.00
Family Channel		
17 Darrell Waltrip	1.50	4.00
Western Auto		
18 Bobby Labonte	1.50	4.00
Interstate Batteries		
22 Ward Burton	1.50	4.00
MBNA		
24 Jeff Gordon	6.00	15.00
DuPont		
30 Johnny Benson	1.50	4.00
Pennzoil		
40 Tim Fedewa	1.50	4.00
Kleenex		
41 Ricky Craven	1.50	4.00
Kodiak		
47 Jeff Fuller	1.50	4.00
Sunoco		
52 Ken Schrader	1.50	4.00
AC Delco		
57 Jason Keller	1.50	4.00
Slim Jim		
74 Johnny Benson	1.50	4.00

Lipton Tea
87 Joe Nemechek 1.50 4.00
Burger King
90 Mike Wallace 1.50 4.00
Heilig-Meyers
94 Bill Elliott 2.00 4.00
McDonald's

1996 Racing Champions 1:64

This set features some unique pieces that Racing Champions had never issued before. Some pieces came with a metal and plastic medallion in the blister package with the car. The Rusty Wallace was also available in both the Penske Racing and the MGD car.

1 Rick Mast 12.00 20.00
Hooters
1 Rick Mast 30.00 50.00
Hooter's Chrome/1996
2 Ricky Craven 2.00 4.00
DuPont
2 Rusty Wallace 8.00 15.00
Miller Genuine Draft
2 Rusty Wallace 50.00 100.00
Miller Genuine Draft Chrome/1996
2 Rusty Wallace 2.00 4.00
Penske Racing
4 Sterling Marlin 1.50 4.00
Kodak
4 Sterling Marlin 35.00 75.00
Kodak Chrome/1996
5 Terry Labonte 2.00 4.00
Kellogg's
5 Terry Labonte 40.00 100.00
Kellogg's Chrome/1996
5 Terry Labonte 4.00 10.00
Kellogg's Honey Crunch
Promo black windows
5 Terry Labonte 6.00 15.00
Kellogg's with Iron Man card
5 Terry Labonte 4.00 10.00
Kellogg's Iron Man
Promo in large box
5 Terry Labonte 4.00 8.00
Kellogg's Silver car
6 Tommy Houston 2.00 4.00
Suburban Propane
6 Mark Martin 2.00 4.00
Valvoline
6 Mark Martin 50.00 100.00
Valvoline Chrome/1996
6 Mark Martin 10.00 20.00
Valvoline Dura Blend
6 Mark Martin 7.00 12.00
Roush Box Promo
7 Geoff Bodine 2.00 4.00
QVC
8 Hut Stricklin 2.00 4.00
Circuit City
10 Phil Parsons 2.00 4.00
Channellock
10 Ricky Rudd 2.00 4.00
Tide
10 Ricky Rudd 25.00 50.00
Tide Chrome/1996
10 Ricky Rudd 4.00 10.00
Tide Promo black windows
11 Brett Bodine 2.00 4.00
Lowe's
11 Brett Bodine 6.00 15.00
Lowe's 50th Anniversary
12 Derrike Cope 7.50 15.00
Badcock
12 Michael Waltrip 3.00 6.00
MW Windows
14 Patty Moise 2.00 4.00
Dial Purex
16 Ted Musgrave 2.00 4.00
Family Channel
17 Darrell Waltrip 2.00 4.00
Parts America
17 Darrell Waltrip 25.00 50.00
Parts America Chrome/1996
17 Darrell Waltrip 4.00 8.00
Parts America Promo
18 Bobby Labonte 2.00 4.00
Interstate Batteries
18 Bobby Labonte 30.00 60.00
Interstate Batteries Chrome/1996
19 Loy Allen 7.50 15.00
Healthsource
21 Michael Waltrip 2.00 4.00
Citgo
21 Michael Waltrip 4.00 8.00
Citgo Promo
22 Ward Burton 7.50 15.00
MBNA
23 Chad Little 2.50 6.00
ohn Deere
23 Chad Little 5.00 12.00
John Deere Promo
24 Jeff Gordon 15.00 30.00
DuPont
24 Jeff Gordon 125.00 200.00
DuPont Chrome/1996
24 Jeff Gordon 20.00 40.00
DuPont Fan Club
in PVC box/1500
24 Jeff Gordon 7.50 15.00
DuPont Union 76 Promo
28 Ernie Irvan 2.00 4.00
Havoline
28 Ernie Irvan 30.00 80.00
Havoline Chrome/1996
28 Ernie Irvan 3.00 8.00
Havoline Promo
29 Steve Grissom 5.00 10.00
Cartoon Network
29 Steve Grissom 5.00 12.00
WCW
29 No Driver Association 4.00 8.00
Scooby-Doo
29 No Driver Association 6.00 12.00
WCW Sting
30 Johnny Benson 2.00 4.00
Pennzoil
31 Mike Skinner 15.00 30.00
Realtree
32 Dale Jarrett 4.00 10.00
Band-Aid Promo
34 Mike McLaughlin 6.00 12.00
Royal Oak
37 John Andretti 2.00 4.00
K-Mart
37 John Andretti 4.00 8.00
K-Mart Promo
38 Dennis Setzer 2.00 4.00
Lipton Tea
40 Tim Fedewa 2.00 4.00
Kleenex
40 Jim Sauter 3.00 6.00
First Union
41 Ricky Craven 2.00 4.00
Larry Hedrick Racing
41 Ricky Craven 2.00 4.00
Manheim
41 Ricky Craven 18.00 30.00
Team Hedrick Promo
43 Rodney Combs 2.00 4.00
Lance
43 Bobby Hamilton 60.00 100.00
5-trailer set 25th Anniversary
43 Bobby Hamilton 15.00 30.00
5-car set 25th Anniversary
43 Bobby Hamilton 20.00 50.00
STP 25th Anniversary set
Hood Open 5-STP cars and bonus
#5 Terry Labonte
Kellogg's Silver
43 Bobby Hamilton 3.00 8.00
STP Anniversary
1972 Red
Blue
43 Bobby Hamilton 3.00 8.00
STP Anniversary 1972 Blue
43 Bobby Hamilton 3.00 8.00
STP Anniversary
1979 Red
Blue
43 Bobby Hamilton 3.00 8.00
STP Anniversary
1984 Blue
Red
43 Bobby Hamilton 7.50 15.00
STP Anniversary 1996 Silver
43 Bobby Hamilton 9.00 18.00
STP Anniversary 1996 Silver
in Red and Blue Box
43 Bobby Hamilton 5.00 12.00
STP Anniversary
Promo/5000
44 Bobby Labonte 5.00 10.00
Shell
47 Jeff Fuller 2.00 4.00
Sunoco
47 Jeff Fuller 4.00 10.00
Sunoco Diamond Car Promo
51 Jim Bown 2.00 4.00
Lucks
51 Mike Stefanik 20.00 35.00
Burnham Boilers Promo
57 Jim Bown 5.00 10.00
Matco Tools
57 Jason Keller 2.00 4.00
Halloween Havoc
57 Jason Keller 2.00 4.00
Slim Jim
58 Mike Cope 2.00 4.00
Penrose
60 Mark Martin 4.00 8.00
Winn Dixie Promo
61 Mike Olsen 4.00 10.00
Little Trees Promo in bag
63 Curtis Markham 2.00 4.00
Lysol
74 Randy LaJoie 2.00 4.00
Fina
75 Morgan Shepherd 4.00 8.00
Remington
81 Kenny Wallace 7.50 15.00
TIC Financial
87 Joe Nemechek 6.00 12.00
BellSouth
87 Joe Nemechek 12.50 25.00
Burger King
88 Dale Jarrett 5.00 10.00
Quality Care
88 Dale Jarrett 30.00 80.00
Quality Care Chrome/1996
90 Mike Wallace 2.00 4.00
Duron
92 David Pearson 2.00 4.00
Stanley Tools
94 Ron Barfield 2.00 4.00
New Holland
94 Bill Elliott 2.00 4.00
McDonald's
94 Bill Elliott 25.00 60.00
McDonald's Chrome/1996
94 Bill Elliott 2.00 4.00
McDonald's Monopoly
94 Bill Elliott 40.00 70.00
10-Time Most Popular
Driver Silver
94 Harry Gant 3.00 6.00
McDonald's
96 David Green 4.00 10.00
Busch
96 Stevie Reeves 2.00 4.00
Clabber Girl
97 Chad Little 5.00 12.00
Sterling Cowboy
99 Glenn Allen 2.00 4.00
Luxaire
99 Jeff Burton 2.00 4.00
Exide
NNO Kellogg's 6-car 1990-96 Promo 10.00 20.00
#97 Chuck Bown (1990)
#41 (1991-92)
#14 Terry Labonte (1993)
#5 Terry Labonte (1994)
#5 Terry Labonte (1995)
#5 Terry Labonte Silver (1996)
NNO 12-Cars 25.00 50.00
Wallace
Marlin
Labonte
Kell.Yellow
Labonte
Kell.Gray
Martin
Rudd
Waltrip
Wndws
Musgrave
Waltrip
Gordon
DPnt
Irvan
Havo
Grissom
WCW
Benson
Andretti
Keller
Shepherd
Jarrett
Elliott
McD's
Elliott
McD's Mnply

1996 Racing Champions Classics 1:64

1 Bud Moore 2.00 5.00
1969 Dodge Daytona
1 Dick Hutcherson 2.00 5.00
1964 Ford
3 Don White 2.00 5.00
1969 Dodge Daytona
3 Fred Lorenzen 2.00 5.00
1969 Dodge Daytona
4 John Sears 2.00 5.00
1964 Ford
5 Pete Hamilton 2.00 5.00
1969 Ford Talladega
6 Buddy Baker 2.00 5.00
1969 Dodge Daytona
10 Buddy Baker 2.00 5.00
1964 Ford
11 Ned Jarrett 2.00 5.00
Bowani Inc. 1964 Ford
12 Bobby Allison 2.50 6.00
1969 Mercury Cyclone
16 Tiny Lund 2.00 5.00
1969 Mercury Cyclone
17 David Pearson 2.50 6.00
1969 Ford Talladega
17 David Pearson 2.50 6.00
1969 Mercury Cyclone
21 Donnie Allison 2.00 5.00
1969 Mercury Cyclone
21 Marvin Panch 2.00 5.00
1964 Ford
21 Jack Bowsher 2.00 5.00
1969 Ford Torino
22 Bobby Allison 2.50 6.00
1969 Dodge Daytona
22 Fireball Roberts 2.00 5.00
Young Ford 1964 Ford
22 Dick Brooks 2.00 5.00
1969 Dodge Daytona
24 Cecil Gordon 2.00 5.00
1969 Mercury Cyclone
27 Donnie Allison 2.00 5.00
1969 Ford Talladega
27 Banjo Mathews 2.00 5.00
1964 Ford
28 Fred Lorenzen 2.00 5.00
1969 Dodge Daytona
29 Bud Moore 2.00 5.00
1969 Ford Talladega
29 Bobby Allison 2.50 6.00
1969 Ford Talladega
31 Jim Vandiver 2.00 5.00
1969 Dodge Daytona
32 Dick Brooks 2.00 5.00
1970 Plym.Superbird
34 Wendell Scott 2.00 5.00
1969 Ford Talladega
48 James Hylton 2.00 5.00
1969 Ford Talladega
48 James Hylton 2.00 5.00
1969 Mercury Cyclone
55 Tiny Lund 2.00 5.00
1969 Dodge Daytona
57 Dick May 2.00 5.00
1964 Ford
57 Dick May 2.00 5.00
1969 Ford Talladega
64 Elmo Langley 2.00 5.00
1964 Ford
64 Elmo Langley 2.00 5.00
1969 Ford Talladega
64 Elmo Langley 2.00 5.00
1969 Mercury Cyclone
71 Bobby Isaac 2.00 5.00
K&K Insurance
1969 Dodge Daytona
73 Buddy Arrington 2.00 5.00
1964 Ford
76 Larry Frank 2.00 5.00
1964 Ford
88 Benny Parsons 2.00 5.00
1969 Ford Talladega
98 Lee Roy Yarborough 2.00 5.00
1969 Ford Talladega
99 Charlie Glotzbach 2.00 5.00
1969 Dodge Daytona
99 Bobby Isaac 2.00 5.00
1964 Ford
06 Neil Castles 2.00 5.00
1969 Dodge Daytona

1996 Racing Champions Hobby 1:64

These pieces were released through Hobby outlets only. Each car was issued in a 1996 Edition window box.

4 Sterling Marlin 3.00 8.00
Kodak
6 Mark Martin 3.00 6.00
Valvoline
18 Bobby Labonte 3.00 6.00
Interstate Batteries
24 Jeff Gordon 3.00 6.00
DuPont
47 Jeff Fuller 3.00 6.00
Sunoco
81 Kenny Wallace 3.00 6.00
Square D

1996 Racing Champions Premier with Medallion 1:64

These pieces are the same as the standard Racing Champions 1:64 1996 pieces with the exception of the packaging. Each car is packaged with a medallion instead of a card.

1 Rick Mast 6.00 12.00
Hooters Hood Open
1 Hermie Sadler 3.00 8.00
DeWalt
2 Ricky Craven 3.00 8.00
DuPont
2 Ricky Craven 5.00 10.00
DuPont Hood Open
2 Rusty Wallace 6.00 12.00
Miller Genuine Draft Hood Open
In Miller Package
3 Mike Skinner 3.00 8.00
Goodwrench
4 Sterling Marlin 4.00 10.00
Kodak
5 Terry Labonte 5.00 10.00
Bayer Hood Open
5 Terry Labonte 5.00 10.00
Kellogg's Silver car Hood Open
6 Mark Martin 5.00 10.00
Valvoline Dura Blend Hood Open
7 Geoff Bodine 3.00 8.00
QVC
10 Ricky Rudd 5.00 10.00
Tide Hood Open
11 Brett Bodine 3.00 8.00
Lowe's
15 Wally Dallenbach 10.00 20.00
Hayes Modems
16 Ted Musgrave 3.00 8.00
Family Channel
18 Bobby Labonte 3.00 8.00
Interstate Batteries
18 Bobby Labonte 5.00 10.00
Interstate Batteries Hood Open
22 Ward Burton 3.00 8.00
MBNA
23 Chad Little 4.00 10.00
John Deere Hood Open
23 Chad Little 6.00 15.00
John Deere Hood Open Promo
24 Jeff Gordon 6.00 12.00
DuPont
24 Jeff Gordon 7.50 15.00
DuPont Hood Open
24 Jeff Gordon 6.00 12.00
DuPont 1995 Champion
25 Ken Schrader 6.00 15.00
Budweiser
25 Ken Schrader 50.00 90.00
Budweiser Silver
25 Ken Schrader 3.00 8.00
Hendrick
28 Ernie Irvan 5.00 10.00

Havoline Hood Open
29 Steve Grissom 3.00 8.00
Cartoon Network
29 Steve Grissom 6.00 12.00
Cartoon Network Hood Open
29 Steve Grissom 25.00 50.00
Cartoon Network 5-car set
29 No Driver Association 3.00 8.00
Scooby-Doo
29 No Driver Association 3.00 8.00
Shaggy
30 Johnny Benson 3.00 8.00
Pennzoil
31 Mike Skinner 20.00 35.00
Realtree
34 Mike McLaughlin 3.00 8.00
Royal Oak
37 John Andretti 3.00 8.00
K-Mart
41 Ricky Craven 3.00 8.00
arry Hedrick Racing
43 Bobby Hamilton 6.00 12.00
STP Hood Open
43 Bobby Hamilton 6.00 12.00
STP Silver Hood Open
43 Bobby Hamilton 30.00 55.00
STP 5-car set
44 Bobby Labonte 10.00 20.00
Shell
52 Ken Schrader 3.00 8.00
AC Delco
52 Ken Schrader 5.00 10.00
AC Delco Hood Open
57 Chuck Bown 3.00 8.00
Matco
71 Dave Marcis 10.00 25.00
Prodigy
74 Johnny Benson 3.00 8.00
Lipton Tea
87 Joe Nemechek 6.00 15.00
Burger King
88 Dale Jarrett 3.00 8.00
Quality Care
92 Larry Pearson 3.00 8.00
Stanley Tools
94 Bill Elliott 5.00 10.00
McDonald's Hood Open
94 Bill Elliott 5.00 10.00
McDonald's Monopoly Hood Open
94 Bill Elliott 4.00 8.00
McDonald's Monopoly
Hood Open Promo
96 David Green 3.00 8.00
Busch
97 Chad Little 3.00 8.00
Sterling Cowboy

1996 Racing Champions PVC Box 1:64

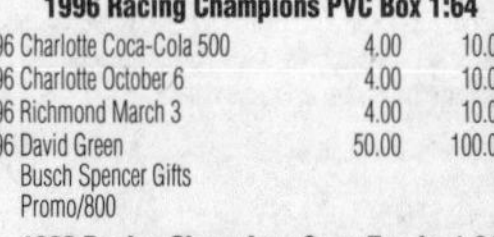

96 Charlotte Coca-Cola 500 4.00 10.00
96 Charlotte October 6 4.00 10.00
96 Richmond March 3 4.00 10.00
96 David Green 50.00 100.00
Busch Spencer Gifts
Promo/800

1996 Racing Champions SuperTrucks 1:64

Racing Champions continued their line of 1:64 SuperTrucks 1996. Each truck was packaged in a small red and black wind box with an extra backer board so the piece could be hung or peg board retail display.

2 Mike Bliss 2.00 4.00
Team ASE
3 Mike Skinner 2.00 4.00
Goodwrench
5 Darrell Waltrip 2.00 4.00
Die Hard
6 Rick Carelli 2.00 4.00
Chesrown
6 Rick Carelli 2.00 4.00
Total
9 Joe Bessey 2.00 4.00
New Hampshire Speedway
14 Butch Gilliland 2.00 4.00
Stroppe
17 Bill Sedgwick 2.00 4.00
Die Hard
17 Darrell Waltrip 2.00 4.00
Western Auto
19 Lance Norick 2.00 4.00
Macklenburg-Duncan
20 Walker Evans 2.00 4.00
Dana
21 Doug George 2.00 4.00
Ortho
24 Jack Sprague 2.00 4.00
Quaker State
29 Bob Keselowski 2.00 4.00
Winnebago
30 Jimmy Hensley 2.00 4.00
Mopar
52 Ken Schrader 2.00 4.00
AC Delco
57 Robbie Pyne 2.00 4.00
Aisyn
75 Bobby Gill 2.00 4.00
Spears

Mike Chase Petron Plus	2.00	4.00
Joe Ruttman .R.Garage	2.00	4.00
Steve Portenga Coffee Critic	2.00	4.00
Butch Miller Raybestos	2.00	4.00

1997 Racing Champions Preview 1:64

series of 1:64 die cast replicas featured a preview of some e new paint jobs to run in the 1997 season. The Rick Mast ington car and the Robert Pressley Scooby Doo car feature of the numerous driver changes for the 97 Winston Cup son.

terling Marlin Kodak	2.00	5.00
erry Labonte Kellogg's	2.00	4.00
lark Martin Valvoline	2.00	4.00
Bobby Labonte Interstate Batteries	1.50	4.00
Michael Waltrip Citgo	1.50	4.00
Jeff Gordon DuPont	2.50	5.00
Ernie Irvan Havoline	1.50	4.00
Robert Pressley Scooby-Doo	1.50	4.00
Johnny Benson Pennzoil	1.50	4.00
Rick Mast Remington	1.50	4.00
Bill Elliott McDonald's	2.00	4.00
Jeff Burton Exide	1.50	4.00

97 Racing Champions Premier Preview with Medallion 1:64

is the first time Racing Champions has issued a Preview of Premier. Each car comes with a medallion like the standard mier cars.

Sterling Marlin Kodak	3.00	8.00
erry Labonte Kellogg's	4.00	8.00
Mark Martin Valvoline	3.00	6.00
Bobby Labonte Interstate Batteries	3.00	6.00
Jeff Gordon DuPont	4.00	10.00
Robert Pressley Scooby-Doo	3.00	6.00
Bill Elliott McDonald's	3.00	6.00

1997 Racing Champions 1:64

1:64 scale cars that appear in this series are replicas of ny of the cars that ran in the 1997 season. The series is hlighted by the Terry Labonte Kellogg's car commemorating 1996 Winston Cup Championship. This car is available in variations: standard and hood open.

ndy Hillenburg Gravy Train Promo	12.50	25.00
Hermie Sadler DeWalt	2.00	4.00
Morgan Shepherd R&L Carriers	2.00	4.00
Morgan Shepherd R&L Carriers Promo	10.00	20.00
Ricky Craven Raybestos	2.00	4.00
Rusty Wallace Miller Lite Matco Promo/20,000	5.00	10.00
Rusty Wallace Penske Racing	2.00	4.00
Sterling Marlin Kodak	2.00	5.00
5 Terry Labonte Bayer	2.00	4.00
5 Terry Labonte Kellogg's 1996 Champion	3.00	8.00
5 Terry Labonte Kellogg's 1996 Champion Chrome/1997	75.00	125.00
5 Terry Labonte Kellogg's 2-car Promo Set	6.00	15.00
5 Terry Labonte Kellogg's 3-car Promo 1996 Champion blister	6.00	15.00
5 Terry Labonte Kellogg's Tony	3.00	6.00
5 Terry Labonte Kellogg's Tony Promo lack windows	4.00	10.00
6 Joe Bessey Power Team	2.00	4.00
6 Mark Martin Valvoline	2.00	4.00
6 Mark Martin Valvoline Kosei Promo/5000	40.00	75.00
7 Geoff Bodine QVC	2.00	4.00
7 Geoff Bodine QVC Chrome/1997	15.00	40.00
7 Geoff Bodine QVC Gold Rush	3.00	8.00
8 Hut Stricklin ircuit City	2.00	4.00
9 Joe Bessey Power Team	2.00	4.00
9 Jeff Burton Track Gear	2.00	4.00
10 Phil Parsons Channellock	2.00	4.00
10 Ricky Rudd Tide	2.00	4.00
10 Ricky Rudd Tide Promo	4.00	10.00
11 Jimmy Foster Speedvision	2.00	4.00
11 Brett Bodine Close Call	2.00	4.00
15 C.Long Austin Crackers Promo	60.00	100.00
16 Ted Musgrave Primestar	2.00	4.00
16 Ted Musgrave Primestar Chrome/1997	20.00	40.00
17 Tim Bender Kraft Singles promo in bag	10.00	20.00
17 Darrell Waltrip Parts America	2.00	4.00
17 Darrell Waltrip Parts America Chrome	3.00	8.00
18 Bobby Labonte Interstate Batteries	2.00	4.00
19 Gary Bradberry CSR	2.00	4.00
21 Michael Waltrip Citgo	2.00	4.00
21 Michael Waltrip Citgo Chrome/1997	20.00	40.00
24 Jeff Gordon DuPont	4.00	8.00
25 Ricky Craven Bud Lizard	6.00	12.00
25 Ricky Craven Bud Lizard Chrome/1997	20.00	40.00
25 Ricky Craven Hendrick	2.00	4.00
28 Ernie Irvan Havoline	2.00	4.00
28 Ernie Irvan Havoline 10th Anniversary	2.00	4.00
29 Robert Pressley Cartoon Network	2.00	4.00
29 Jeff Green Tom and Jerry	2.00	4.00
29 Elliott Sadler Phillips 66	2.00	4.00
30 Johnny Benson Pennzoil	2.00	4.00
30 Johnny Benson Pennzoil Chrome/1997	15.00	40.00
32 Dale Jarrett White Rain	2.00	4.00
33 Ken Schrader Petree Racing	2.00	4.00
34 Mike McLaughlin Royal Oak	2.00	4.00
36 Todd Bodine Stanley Tools	2.00	4.00
36 Derrike Cope Skittles	2.00	4.00
36 Derrike Cope Skittles Chrome/1997	15.00	40.00
36 Derrike Cope Skittles Promo in box	2.00	5.00
37 Jeremy Mayfield K-Mart	2.00	4.00
38 Elton Sawyer Barbasol	2.00	4.00
40 Tim Fedewa Kleenex	2.00	4.00
40 Robby Gordon Sabco Racing	2.00	4.00
40 Robby Gordon Sabco Chrome/1997	20.00	40.00
41 Steve Grissom Larry Hedrick Racing	2.00	4.00
42 Joe Nemechek BellSouth	2.00	4.00
42 Joe Nemechek BellSouth Chrome/1997	20.00	40.00
43 Rodney Combs Lance	2.00	4.00
43 Dennis Setzer Lance	2.00	4.00
46 Wally Dallenbach First Union	2.00	4.00
46 Wally Dallenbach First Union Chrome/1997	20.00	40.00
47 Jeff Fuller Sunoco	2.00	4.00
49 Kyle Petty NWO	4.00	8.00
57 Jason Keller Slim Jim	2.00	4.00
59 Lou Rettenmeier Mobil Promo	18.00	30.00
60 Mark Martin Winn Dixie	4.00	8.00
72 Mike Dillon Detriot Gasket	2.00	4.00
74 Randy LaJoie Fina	2.00	4.00
74 Randy LaJoie Fina Promo	4.00	8.00
75 Rick Mast Remington	2.00	4.00
75 Rick Mast Remington Camo	2.00	4.00
75 Rick Mast Remington Stren	2.00	4.00
75 Rick Mast Remington Chrome/1997	20.00	40.00
76 NASCAR Thunder TNN Promo/4000	6.00	15.00
85 Shane Hall Luck's Beans Promo	12.50	25.00
88 Kevin Lepage Hype	2.00	4.00
90 Dick Trickle Heilig-Meyers	2.00	4.00
91 Mike Wallace Spam	2.00	4.00
94 Ron Barfield New Holland	2.00	4.00
94 Bill Elliott McDonald's	2.00	4.00
94 Bill Elliott Mac Tonight	2.00	4.00
94 Bill Elliott Mac Tonight Chrome/1997	25.00	50.00
96 David Green Caterpillar	2.00	4.00
96 David Green Caterpillar Chrome/1997	15.00	40.00
96 David Green Caterpillar Promo	3.00	8.00
97 No Driver Association Brickyard 400	3.00	6.00
97 No Driver Association www.racingchamps.com	10.00	18.00
97 Chad Little John Deere	2.00	4.00
97 Chad Little John Deere Chrome/1997	15.00	40.00
97 Chad Little John Deere Promo	3.00	8.00
98 No Driver Association EA Sports	2.00	4.00
99 Glenn Allen Luxaire	2.00	4.00
99 Jeff Burton Exide	2.00	4.00
99 Jeff Burton Exide Chrome/1997	25.00	50.00
00 Buckshot Jones qua Fresh	2.00	4.00
NNO 12-Car set S.Marlin Kodak T.Labonte Kellogg's Tony Martin Valvoline Bodine QVC Rudd Tide Musgrave Primestar B.Labonte Inter.Batteries Irvan Havoline Cartoon Network Benson Pennzoil Elliott Mac Tonight D.Green Cat	15.00	40.00

1997 Racing Champions Pinnacle Series 1:64

This marks the second time Racing Champions have teamed up with a card manufacturer to product a line of die cast car with trading cards. Each car is boxed in similar packaging as the standard cars, but Pinnacle cards are featured in place of Racing Champions generic cards.

4 Sterling Marlin Kodak	4.00	10.00
5 Terry Labonte Kellogg's	5.00	10.00
6 Mark Martin Valvoline	4.00	8.00
7 Geoff Bodine QVC	3.00	8.00
8 Hut Stricklin Circuit City	3.00	8.00
10 Ricky Rudd Tide	3.00	8.00
16 Ted Musgrave Primestar	3.00	8.00
18 Bobby Labonte Interstate Batteries	3.00	8.00
21 Michael Waltrip Citgo	3.00	8.00
28 Ernie Irvan Havoline	3.00	8.00
29 Robert Pressley Cartoon Network	3.00	8.00
30 Johnny Benson Pennzoil	3.00	8.00
36 Derrike Cope Skittles	3.00	8.00
37 Jeremy Mayfield K-Mart	3.00	8.00
75 Rick Mast Remington	3.00	8.00
87 Joe Nemechek BellSouth	3.00	8.00
94 Bill Elliott McDonald's	4.00	8.00
96 David Green Caterpillar	3.00	8.00
97 Chad Little John Deere	3.00	8.00
99 Jeff Burton Exide	3.00	8.00

1997 Racing Champions Premier Gold 1:64

These 1:64 scale cars were distributed primarily through hobby outlets in a Racing Champions" Premier Gold" solid black box. The total production run was 4800 of each car with 4600 of those being produced with a standard paint scheme and 200 in gold chrome paint.

2 Rusty Wallace Miller Lite	4.00	8.00
6 Mark Martin Valvoline	4.00	8.00
10 Ricky Rudd Tide	4.00	8.00
18 Bobby Labonte Interstate Batteries	4.00	8.00
36 Derrike Cope Skittles	3.00	8.00
40 Robby Gordon Coors Light	4.00	8.00
75 Rick Mast Remington	4.00	8.00
94 Bill Elliott McDonald's	4.00	8.00

1997 Racing Champions Premier Gold Chrome 1:64

These 1:64 scale cars were distributed through hobby outlets in a Racing Champions" Premier Gold" solid black box. The total production run was 4800 of each car with 200 of those being produced with a gold chrome finish.

2 Rusty Wallace Miller Lite	50.00	100.00
6 Mark Martin Valvoline	50.00	100.00
10 Ricky Rudd Tide	40.00	80.00
18 Bobby Labonte Interstate Batteries	40.00	80.00
36 Derrike Cope Skittles	30.00	80.00
40 Robby Gordon Coors Light	40.00	80.00
75 Rick Mast Remington	40.00	80.00
94 Bill Elliott McDonald's	50.00	100.00

1997 Racing Champions Premier with Medallion 1:64

These pieces are the same as the standard Racing Champions 1:64 1997 pieces with the exception of the packaging. Each car is packaged with a medallion instead of a card. A few cars were produced in a limited silver parallel version as well.

1 Morgan Shepherd Crusin' America	3.00	8.00
2 Rusty Wallace Penske	4.00	8.00
5 Terry Labonte Kellogg's Tony	5.00	10.00
5 Terry Labonte Kellogg's Tony Chrome/997	25.00	60.00
6 Mark Martin Valvoline	4.00	8.00
7 Geoff Bodine QVC	3.00	8.00
7 Geoff Bodine QVC Chrome/997	20.00	50.00
8 Hut Stricklin Circuit City	3.00	8.00
9 Lake Speed University of Nebraska	15.00	30.00
10 Ricky Rudd Tide	3.00	8.00
10 Ricky Rudd Tide Chrome/997	20.00	50.00
11 Brett Bodine Close Call	3.00	8.00
16 Ted Musgrave Primestar	3.00	8.00
16 Ted Musgrave Primestar Chrome/997	20.00	50.00
17 Darrell Waltrip Parts America	3.00	8.00
17 Darrell Waltrip Parts America Chrome/997	5.00	10.00
18 Bobby Labonte Interstate Batteries	3.00	8.00
18 Bobby Labonte Intertstate Batteries Silver/997	20.00	50.00
21 Michael Waltrip Citgo	3.00	8.00
28 Ernie Irvan Havoline	3.00	8.00
28 Ernie Irvan Havoline Chrome/997	20.00	50.00
28 Ernie Irvan Havoline 10th Anniversary	5.00	10.00
29 Robert Pressley Scooby-Doo	3.00	8.00
29 No Driver Assocation Tom and Jerry	3.00	8.00
30 Johnny Benson Pennzoil	3.00	8.00
36 Derrike Cope Skittles	3.00	8.00
37 Jeremy Mayfield K-Mart	3.00	8.00
75 Rick Mast Remington	3.00	8.00
75 Rick Mast Remington Camo	3.00	8.00
75 Rick Mast Remington Stren	3.00	8.00
94 Bill Elliott Mac Tonight	4.00	8.00
96 David Green Caterpillar	3.00	8.00
96 David Green Caterpillar Promo	5.00	12.00
97 Chad Little John Deere	3.00	8.00
97 Chad Little John Deere Promo	5.00	12.00
99 Jeff Burton Exide	3.00	8.00

1997 Racing Champions Roaring Racers 1:64

4 Sterling Marlin Kodak	5.00	12.00
5 Terry Labonte Kellogg's	5.00	12.00
5 Terry Labonte Kellogg's Tony	5.00	12.00
6 Mark Martin Valvoline	5.00	12.00
16 Ted Musgrave Primestar	4.00	10.00
18 Bobby Labonte Interstate Batteries	5.00	12.00
21 Michael Waltrip Citgo	4.00	10.00
28 Ernie Irvan Havoline	4.00	10.00
29 Robert Pressley Cartoon Network	4.00	10.00
36 Derrike Cope kittles	4.00	10.00
94 Bill Elliott Mac Tonight	5.00	12.00
97 Chad Little John Deere	4.00	10.00

1997 Racing Champions Stock Rods 1:64

These 1:64 scale cars are replicas of vintage stock rods with NASCAR paint schemes. Cars are listed by issue number instead of car number.

1 Terry Labonte Kellogg's	6.00	15.00
2 Bill Elliott McDonald's	5.00	12.00
3 Mark Martin Valvoline	5.00	12.00
4 Robert Pressley Scooby-Doo	3.00	8.00
5 Ted Musgrave Primestar	3.00	8.00
6 Jeff Burton Exide	3.00	8.00
7 Bobby Labonte Interstate Batteries	3.00	8.00
8 Ricky Craven Hendrick	3.00	8.00
9 Darrell Waltrip Parts America	3.00	8.00
10 Rusty Wallace Miller Lite	60.00	120.00
11 Derrike Cope Skittles	3.00	8.00
12 Ricky Rudd Tide	3.00	8.00
13 Rick Mast Remington	3.00	8.00
14 Ricky Craven Hendrick	3.00	8.00
15 Jeff Green Tom & Jerry	3.00	8.00
16 Bill Elliott Mac Tonight	3.00	8.00
17 Mark Martin Valvoline	3.00	8.00
18 Rusty Wallace Penske	3.00	8.00
19 Ted Musgrave Primestar	3.00	8.00
20 Jeff Burton Exide	3.00	8.00
21 Darrell Waltrip Parts America	3.00	8.00
22 Ricky Rudd Tide	3.00	8.00
23 Rick Mast Remington	3.00	8.00
24 Steve Grissom Larry Hedrick Racing	3.00	8.00
25 Bill Elliott Mac Tonight	3.00	8.00
26 Glen Allen Luxaire	3.00	8.00
27 Dennis Setzer Lance	3.00	8.00
28 Bill Elliott McDonald's	3.00	8.00
29 Ricky Craven	3.00	8.00

Hendrick		
30 Sterling Marlin Sabco	3.00	8.00
31 Jeff Green Cartoon Network	3.00	8.00
32 Joe Nemechek Bell South	3.00	8.00
33 Ernie Irvan Havoline	3.00	8.00
34 Ricky Rudd Tide	3.00	8.00
35 Rusty Wallace Penske	3.00	8.00
36 Ernie Irvan Havoline	3.00	8.00
37 Mark Martin Valvoline	3.00	8.00
38 Terry Labonte Spooky Loops	5.00	10.00
39 Terry Labonte Spooky Loops	5.00	10.00
40 Derrike Cope Skittles	3.00	8.00
41 Steve Grissom Larry Hedrick Racing	3.00	8.00
42 Terry Labonte Spooky Loops Chrome	30.00	50.00
43 Terry Labonte Spooky Loops	7.50	15.00
44 Jeff Burton Exide	3.00	8.00
45 Bill Elliott McDonald's	3.00	8.00
46 Ted Musgrave Primestar	3.00	8.00
47 Mark Martin Valvoline	3.00	8.00
48 Ricky Rudd Tide	3.00	8.00
49 Glen Allen Luxaire	3.00	8.00
50 Terry Labonte Spooky Loops	3.00	8.00
51 Joe Bessey Power Team	3.00	8.00
52 Terry Labonte Kellogg's	3.00	8.00
53 Wally Dallenbach First Union	3.00	8.00
54 Ricky Craven Hendrick	3.00	8.00
55 Ricky Craven Hendrick	3.00	8.00

1997 Racing Champions SuperTrucks 1:64

Racing Champions continued their line of 1:64 SuperTrucks in 1997. This series features many of the circuit's first-time drivers and Winston Cup regulars.

1 Michael Waltrip MW Windows	2.00	4.00
2 Mike Bliss Team ASE	2.00	4.00
4 Bill Elliott Team ASE	2.00	4.00
6 Rick Carelli Remax	2.00	4.00
7 Tammy Kirk Loveable	2.00	4.00
13 Mike Colabucci VISA	2.00	4.00
15 Mike Colabucci VISA	2.00	4.00
15 Mike Cope Penrose	2.00	4.00
18 Johnny Benson Pennzoil	2.00	4.00
18 Mike Dokken Dana	2.00	4.00
19 Tony Raines Pennzoil	2.00	4.00
20 Butch Miller The Orleans	2.00	4.00
23 T.J. Clark CRG Motorsports	2.00	4.00
24 Jack Sprague Quaker State	2.00	4.00
29 Bob Keselowski Mopar	2.00	4.00
35 Dave Rezendes Ortho	2.00	4.00
44 Boris Said Federated Auto	2.00	4.00
49 Rodney Combs Lance	2.00	4.00
52 Tobey Butler Purolater	2.00	4.00
66 Bryan Refner Carlin	2.00	4.00
75 Dan Press Spears	2.00	4.00
80 Joe Ruttman LCI	2.00	4.00
86 Stacy Compton Valvoline	2.00	4.00
87 Joe Nemechek Bell South	2.00	4.00
92 Mark Kinser Rotary	2.00	4.00
94 Ron Barfield Super 8	2.00	4.00
99 Chuck Bown Exide	2.00	4.00
99 Jeff Burton Exide	2.00	4.00
99 Mark Martin Exide	12.50	25.00

1998 Racing Champions 1:64

The 1:64 scale cars that appear in this series are replicas of many of the cars that ran in the 1997 season, but also include some cars slated to appear in 1998. They were packaged in red blister packs that display the NASCAR 50th anniversary logo. A yellow bordered card was also inserted into each regular issue piece. Chrome versions were produced of some cars with Winston Cup driver's die-casts being numbered of 5050 and Busch Series cars of 1000 produced. Most promo pieces were issued without the card and in a blister pack that more closely follows the paint scheme of the featured driver's car or die-cast sponsor.

4 Bobby Hamilton Kodak	2.00	4.00
4 Jeff Purvis Lance	2.00	4.00
5 Terry Labonte Kellogg's	2.00	5.00
5 Terry Labonte Kellogg's Chrome/5050	20.00	50.00
5 Terry Labonte Kellogg's Corny	2.00	5.00
5 Terry Labonte Kellogg's Corny Chrome/5050	20.00	50.00
6 Joe Bessey Power Team	2.00	4.00
6 Mark Martin Eagle One	2.00	4.00
6 Mark Martin Eagle One Chrome/5050	20.00	50.00
6 Mark Martin Kosei Promo/5000	30.00	50.00
6 Mark Martin Valvoline	2.00	4.00
6 Mark Martin Valvoline Chrome/5050	20.00	50.00
8 Hut Stricklin Circuit City 4th of July	2.00	4.00
8 Hut Stricklin Circuit City Chrome/5050	15.00	40.00
9 Jeff Burton Track Gear	2.00	4.00
9 Jeff Burton Track Gear Chrome/1000	15.00	40.00
9 Lake Speed Birthday Cake	2.00	4.00
10 Ricky Rudd Tide	2.00	4.00
10 Ricky Rudd Tide Chrome/5050	15.00	40.00
10 Ricky Rudd Tide Promo	4.00	10.00
10 Ricky Rudd Tide 5th Anniversary Promo	4.00	10.00
10 Ricky Rudd Tide Kids Promo	4.00	10.00
11 Brett Bodine Paychex	2.00	4.00
12 Jeremy Mayfield Mobil 1	2.00	4.00
13 Jerry Nadeau First Plus	2.00	4.00
16 Ted Musgrave Primestar	2.00	4.00
16 Ted Musgrave Primestar Chrome	15.00	40.00
17 Matt Kenseth Lycos	10.00	20.00
17 Darrell Waltrip Builder's Square	3.00	6.00
19 Tony Raines Yellow Freight	2.00	4.00
19 Tony Raines Yellow Freight Promo	4.00	8.00
20 Blaise Alexander Rescue Engine	4.00	8.00
20 Blaise Alexander Rescue Engine Chrome/1000	15.00	40.00
21 Michael Waltrip Citgo	2.00	4.00
21 Michael Waltrip Goodwill Games	2.00	4.00
23 Lance Hooper WCW	2.00	4.00
23 Lance Hooper WCW Chrome/1000	15.00	40.00
23 Jimmy Spencer No Bull Promo box on blister	8.00	20.00
23 Jimmy Spencer No Bull Gold Promo box on blister	10.00	25.00
23 Jimmy Spencer No Bull Stock Rod Promo box on blister	8.00	20.00
23 Jimmy Spencer No Bull Stock Rod Gold John Deere Promo on blister	10.00	25.00
25 David Morgan Austin Crackers	15.00	30.00
26 Johnny Benson Betty Crocker	25.00	50.00
26 Johnny Benson Cheerios	2.00	4.00
26 Johnny Benson Cheerios Chrome/5050	15.00	40.00
26 Johnny Benson Lucky Charms	4.00	8.00
28 Tony's Pizza Promo	5.00	10.00
29 Hermie Sadler DeWalt	2.00	4.00
30 Derrike Cope Gumout	2.00	4.00
30 Mike Cope Slim Jim	2.00	4.00
33 Tim Fedewa Kleenex Chrome	15.00	40.00
33 Tim Fedewa Kleenex	2.00	4.00
33 Ken Schrader Petree	2.00	4.00
33 Ken Schrader Skoal Promo in box/1992	18.00	30.00
34 Mike McLaughlin Goulds Chrome/1000	15.00	40.00
35 Todd Bodine Tabasco Orange	2.00	4.00
35 Todd Bodine Tabasco Chrome/5050	15.00	40.00
36 Matt Hutter Stanley	2.00	4.00
36 Matt Hutter Stanley Chrome	15.00	40.00
36 Ernie Irvan Skittles	2.00	4.00
36 Ernie Irvan Skittles Chrome/5050	15.00	40.00
38 Elton Sawyer Barbasol Chrome/1000	20.00	40.00
40 Kevin Lepage Chanellock	2.00	4.00
40 Kevin Lepage Channellock Chrome/1000	15.00	40.00
40 Sterling Marlin Coors Light Promo box on blister	5.00	12.00
40 Sterling Marlin Coors Light Chrome Promo box on blister	6.00	15.00
40 Sterling Marlin Coors Light Gold Promo box on blister	15.00	40.00
40 Sterling Marlin Coors Light Stock Rod/5000 Promo in box on blister	6.00	15.00
40 Sterling Marlin Sabco	2.00	4.00
41 Steve Grissom Larry Hedrick Racing	2.00	4.00
42 Joe Nemechek BellSouth	2.00	4.00
43 Shane Hall Tecumseh Promo in bag	15.00	25.00
46 Wally Dallenbach First Union	2.00	4.00
50 Ricky Craven Hendrick	2.00	4.00
50 Ricky Craven Bud Promo box on blister/5000	6.00	12.00
50 Ricky Craven Bud Stock Rod/5000 romo box on blister	6.00	12.00
50 Ricky Craven Bud Stock Rod Gold/5000 romo box on blister	8.00	20.00
50 NASCAR 50th Anniversary Gold Chrome in clear plastic box	5.00	10.00
50 TBS Promo in PVC Box	10.00	20.00
54 Kathryn Teasdale IGA	18.00	30.00
59 Robert Pressley Kingsford	2.00	4.00
60 Mark Martin Winn Dixie	2.00	4.00
60 Mark Martin Winn Dixie Chrome/1000	20.00	50.00
60 Mark Martin Winn Dixie Promo	3.00	8.00
64 Dick Trickle Schneider	2.00	4.00
64 Dick Trickle Schneider Chrome	15.00	40.00
66 Elliot Sadler Phillips 66	2.00	4.00
74 Randy LaJoie Fina	2.00	4.00
74 Randy LaJoie Fina Chrome	15.00	40.00
75 Rick Mast Remington	2.00	4.00
78 Gary Bradberry Pilot	2.00	4.00
85 Shane Hall Big A Auto Parts Promo	50.00	100.00
94 Bill Elliott Big Mac Promo in Happy Meal Box	15.00	30.00
94 Bill Elliott McDonald's	2.00	4.00
94 Bill Elliott McDonald's Chrome/5050	20.00	50.00
94 Bill Elliott McDonald's Gold 2-car promo set/2500	7.50	20.00
96 David Green Caterpiller	2.00	4.00
97 Chad Little John Deere Promo	3.00	8.00
99 Glen Allen Luxaire	2.00	4.00
99 Jeff Burton Exide	2.00	4.00
99 Jeff Burton Exide Chrome/5050	15.00	40.00
300 Darrell Waltrip Flock Special	3.00	6.00
0 Steven Christian BellSouth Promo	15.00	40.00
00 Buckshot Jones Alka Seltzer	2.00	4.00
00 Buckshot Jones Alka Seltzer Chrome/1000	15.00	40.00
00 Buckshot Jones Aqua Fresh	2.00	4.00
NNO Collector's Set 1/5000 12-car set	10.00	20.00
NNO Collector's Set 2/5000 12-car set	10.00	20.00
T.Labonte Kellogg's T.Labonte Froot Loops Nadeau Cartoon Nadeau Scooby Benson Trix Irvan M&M's Irvan Skittles Elliott Happy Meal Elliott McDonald's Elliott Mac Tonight D.Waltrip Flock Gold		
NNO Chrome 12-car set/3000	40.00	80.00
NNO Roush Racing 5-Pack	6.00	15.00
97. Chad Little John Deere 6. Mark Martin Valvoline 16. Kevin LePage Primestar 99. Jeff Burton Exide 26. Johnny Benson Cheerios		
NNO Roush Racing AUTO Gold/1000	40.00	80.00
5-cars: 6/16/26/97/99 Mark Martin, Kevin Lepage Johnny Benson, Chad Little and Jeff Burton with Certificate signed by all 5-drivers and Jack Roush		

1998 Racing Champions 50 Years of NASCAR 1:64

1 1949	1.50	4.00
2 1950	1.50	4.00
3 1951	1.50	4.00
4 1952	1.50	4.00
5 1953	1.50	4.00
6 1954	1.50	4.00
7 1955	1.50	4.00
8 1956	1.50	4.00
9 1957	1.50	4.00
10 1958	1.50	4.00
11 1959	1.50	4.00
12 1960	1.50	4.00
13 1961	1.50	4.00
14 1962	1.50	4.00
15 1963	1.50	4.00
16 1964	1.50	4.00
17 1965	1.50	4.00
18 1966	1.50	4.00
19 1967	1.50	4.00
20 1970	1.50	4.00
21 1971	1.50	4.00
22 1972	1.50	4.00
23 1973	1.50	4.00
24 1974	1.50	4.00
25 1975	1.50	4.00
26 1976	1.50	4.00
27 1977	1.50	4.00
28 1978	1.50	4.00
29 1979	1.50	4.00
30 1980	1.50	4.00
31 1981	1.50	4.00
32 1982	1.50	4.00
33 1983	1.50	4.00
34 1984	1.50	4.00
35 1985	1.50	4.00
36 1986	1.50	4.00
37 1987	1.50	4.00
38 1988	1.50	4.00
39 1989	1.50	4.00
40 1990	1.50	4.00
41 1991	1.50	4.00
42 1992	1.50	4.00
43 1993	1.50	4.00
44 1994	1.50	4.00
45 1995	1.50	4.00
46 1996	1.50	4.00
47 1997	1.50	4.00
48 1998	1.50	4.00

1998 Racing Champions Fan Appreciation 5 Pack 1:64

This set was issued 5-cars at a time in Racing Champions Pack blister and box combinations. Each package was enti "Fan Appreciation" at the bottom and issued to commemo the 50th Anniversary of NASCAR. A special 50th Annivers NASCAR Gold Chrome die-cast was one of the five cars in e package. Some cars were only issued in these special 5-pa An issue number was assigned to each package near the u right hand corner. We've cataloged the pieces below by reported issue number.

1 4. Bobby Hamilton Kodak Max 5. Terry Labonte Kellogg's 50. NASCAR Rivalries Gold Chrome 50. No Driver Assoc. Dr.Pepper 26. Johnny Benson Trix Lucky Charms	6.00	15.0
2 6. Mark Martin Valvoline 13. Jerry Nadeau First Plus 50. NASCAR Gold Chrome 9. Lake Speed Cartoon Network 94. Bill Elliott McDonald's Gold Chrome	6.00	15.0
3 10. Ricky Rudd Tide 96. David Green Caterpillar 50. NASCAR Fans Gold Chrome 14. Patty Moise Rhodes 11. Brett Bodine Paycheck	6.00	15.0
4 23. Lance Hooper WCW 5. Terry Labonte Blasted Froot Loops 50. NASCAR Country Gold Chrome 19. Tony Raines Yellow Freight 36. Ernie Irvan Skittles	6.00	15.0
5 33. Ken Schrader APR 26. Johnny Benson Cheerios 50. NASCAR Rivalries Chrome 63. Tracy Leslie Lysol 10. Ricky Rudd Tide Kids	6.00	15.0
6 35. NDA Tabasco Orange & White 26. Johnny Benson Trix Lucky Charms 50. NASCAR Fans Chrome 21. Michael Waltrip Citgo 21. Michael Waltrip Citgo Goodwill Games	6.00	15.0
7 94. Bill Elliott McDonald's 36. Ernie Irvan Skittles WildBerry 50. NASCAR Country Chrome 10. Phil Parsons Dura Lube 26. Johnny Benson Betty Crocker	6.00	15.0
8 16. Kevin Lepage Primestar 30. Derrike Cope Gumout 50. NASCAR Legends Chrome 94. Bill Elliott Mac Tonight 99. Jeff Burton Exide	6.00	15.0

1998 Racing Champions Gold with Medallio 1:64

This is a special series produced by Racing Champions celebrate NASCAR's 50th anniversary. It parallels the reg 1998 1:64 scale series. Each car is a limited edition of 5, Each car is also plated in gold chrome and contains a s number on its chassis. This series is packaged with medal sponsor emblems in blister packs.

2 Ron Barfield New Holland	6.00	15.0
4 Bobby Hamilton Kodak	6.00	15.0
4 Jeff Purvis Lance	6.00	15.0
5 Terry Labonte Blasted Fruit Loops	12.00	30.0
5 Terry Labonte Kellogg's	12.00	30.0
5 Terry Labonte Kellogg's Corny	12.00	30.0
6 Joe Bessey Power Team	6.00	15.0
6 Mark Martin Eagle One	12.00	30.0
6 Mark Martin Syntec	12.00	30.0
6 Mark Martin Valvoline	12.00	30.0
8 Hut Stricklin	6.00	15.0

ircuit City		
f Burton	6.00	15.00
rack Gear		
ry Nadeau	6.00	15.00
ombie Island		
ke Speed	6.00	15.00
irthday Cake		
ke Speed	6.00	15.00
uckleberry Hound		
hil Parsons	6.00	15.00
uralube		
icky Rudd	6.00	15.00
ide		
rett Bodine	6.00	15.00
aychex		
erry Nadeau	8.00	20.00
irst Plus		
atty Moise	6.00	15.00
hodes		
ed Musgrave	6.00	15.00
rimestar		
Matt Kenseth	12.50	30.00
ycos.com		
ony Raines	6.00	15.00
ellow Freight		
laise Alexander	15.00	30.00
escue Engine		
lichael Waltrip	6.00	15.00
itgo		
ance Hooper	6.00	15.00
VCW		
ohnny Benson	6.00	15.00
heerios		
ermie Sadler	6.00	15.00
eWalt		
errike Cope	6.00	15.00
umout		
Mike Cope	6.00	15.00
lim Jim		
im Fedewa	6.00	15.00
leenex		
en Schrader	6.00	15.00
etree		
Mike McLaughlin	6.00	15.00
oulds		
odd Bodine	6.00	15.00
abasco		
Matt Hutter	6.00	15.00
tanley		
rnie Irvan	10.00	25.00
M&M's		
rnie Irvan	6.00	15.00
kittles		
rnie Irvan	8.00	20.00
Wildberry Skittles		
lton Sawyer	6.00	15.00
arbasol		
ick Fuller	6.00	15.00
hannellock		
evin Lepage	6.00	15.00
hannellock		
terling Marlin	6.00	15.00
abco		
teve Grissom	6.00	15.00
arry Hedrick Racing		
oe Nemechek	6.00	15.00
BellSouth		
Wally Dallenbach	6.00	15.00
First Union		
icky Craven	6.00	15.00
Hendrick		
NDA	6.00	15.00
Dr.Pepper		
Robert Pressley	6.00	15.00
Kingsford		
Mark Martin	12.00	30.00
Winn Dixie		
Tracy Leslie	6.00	15.00
Lysol		
Dick Trickle	6.00	15.00
Schneider		
Elliot Sadler	6.00	15.00
Phillips 66		
Mike Dillon	6.00	15.00
Detroit Gasket		
Randy LaJoie	6.00	15.00
Fina		
Rick Mast	6.00	15.00
Remington		
Gary Bradberry	6.00	15.00
Pilot		
Joe Nemechek	6.00	15.00
BellSouth		
Kevin Schwantz	6.00	15.00
Ryder		
Dick Trickle	6.00	15.00
Heilig-Meyers		
Bill Elliott	10.00	30.00
Happy Meal		
Bill Elliott	10.00	30.00
McDonald's		
David Green	6.00	15.00
Caterpillar		
Chad Little	12.50	30.00
John Deere Promo/20,000		
Greg Sacks	6.00	15.00
Thorn Apple Valley		
Glen Allen	6.00	15.00
Luxaire		
Jeff Burton	6.00	15.00
Exide		
Darrell Waltrip	10.00	25.00
Flock Special		
Buckshot Jones	6.00	15.00
Alka Seltzer		
Buckshot Jones	6.00	15.00
Aqua Fresh		

98 Racing Champions NASCAR Legends 1:64

ick Hutcherson	2.00	5.00
1964 Ford		
ud Moore	2.00	5.00
1969 Dodge Daytona		
ohn Sears	2.00	5.00
1964 Ford		
ohn Sears	2.00	5.00
1969 Ford Talladega		
uddy Arrington	2.00	5.00
1969 Dodge Daytona		
5 Pete Hamilton	2.00	5.00
1969 Ford Talladega		
6 Buddy Baker	2.00	5.00
1969 Dodge Daytona		
7 Ramo Stott	2.50	6.00
1970 Plymouth Superbird		
10 Buddy Baker	2.00	5.00
1964 Ford		
11 Ned Jarrett	2.00	5.00
1964 Ford		
11 Ned Jarrett	2.00	5.00
1969 Ford Talladega		
12 Bobby Allison	2.50	6.00
1969 Mercury Cyclone		
13 Smokey Yunick	2.00	5.00
1964 Ford		
16 Tiny Lund	2.00	5.00
1969 Mercury Cyclone		
17 Fred Lorenzen	2.00	5.00
1969 Dodge Daytona		
17 Fred Lorenzen	2.50	6.00
1969 Ford Talladega		
17 David Pearson	2.50	6.00
1969 Mercury Cyclone		
18 Joe Frasson	2.00	5.00
1969 Dodge Daytona		
21 Donnie Allison	2.00	5.00
1969 Mercury Cyclone		
21 Jack Bowsher	2.00	5.00
1969 Ford Talladega		
21 Jack Bowsher	2.00	5.00
1969 Dodge Daytona		
21 Marvin Panch	2.00	5.00
1964 Ford		
21 Marvin Panch	2.00	5.00
1969 Ford Talladega		
22 Bobby Allison	2.50	6.00
1969 Dodge Daytona		
22 Fierball Roberts	2.00	5.00
1964 Ford		
24 Cecil Gordon	2.00	5.00
1969 Mercury Cyclone		
26 Curtis Turner	2.00	5.00
1964 Ford		
27 Donnie Allison	2.00	5.00
1969 Ford Talladega		
27 Donnie Allison	2.00	5.00
1969 Mercury Cyclone		
27 Banjo Mathews	2.00	5.00
1964 Ford		
28 Fred Lorenzen	2.00	5.00
1964 Ford		
29 Bobby Allison	2.50	6.00
1969 Ford Talladega		
29 Bud Moore	2.00	5.00
1969 Ford Talladega		
31 Jim Vandiver	2.00	5.00
1969 Dodge Daytona		
32 Dick Brooks	2.00	5.00
1970 Plymouth Superbird		
48 James Hylton	2.00	5.00
1969 Dodge Daytona		
48 James Hylton	2.00	5.00
1969 Mercury Cyclone		
49 G.C. Spencer	2.00	5.00
1964 Ford		
55 Tiny Lund	2.00	5.00
1969 Dodge Daytona		
57 Dick May	2.00	5.00
1964 Ford		
59 Tom Pistone	2.00	5.00
1964 Ford		
61 Hoss Ellington	2.00	5.00
1969 Ford Talladega		
64 Elmo Langley	2.00	5.00
1969 Ford Talladega		
64 Elmo Langley	2.00	5.00
1969 Mercury Cyclone		
67 Dick May	2.00	5.00
1969 Ford Talladega		
71 Bobby Isaac	2.00	5.00
1969 Dodge Daytona		
72 Benny Parsons	2.00	5.00
1969 Mercury Cyclone		
73 Buddy Arrington	2.00	5.00
1964 Ford		
76 Larry Frank	2.00	5.00
1964 Ford		
99 Bobby Isaac	2.00	5.00
1964 Ford		
99 Charlie Glotzbach	2.00	5.00
1969 Dodge Daytona		
06 Neil Castles	2.00	5.00
1969 Dodge Daytona		

1998 Racing Champions Pinnacle Series 1:64

This marks the second year Racing Champions teamed up with Pinnacle to produce a line of die cast cars with trading cards. Each car is boxed in similar packaging as the standard cars, but Pinnacle cards are featured in place of Racing Champions generic cards.

4 Bobby Hamilton	3.00	6.00
Kodak		
5 Terry Labonte	3.00	6.00
Kellogg's		
6 Mark Martin	3.00	6.00
Valvoline		
8 Hut Stricklin	3.00	6.00
Circuit City		
9 Jeff Burton	3.00	6.00
Track Gear		
10 Ricky Rudd	3.00	6.00
Tide		
21 Michael Waltrip	3.00	6.00
Citgo		
33 Tim Fedewa	3.00	6.00
Kleenex		
33 Ken Schrader	3.00	6.00
Petree Racing		
35 Todd Bodine	3.00	6.00
Tabasco		
36 Ernie Irvan	3.00	6.00
Skittles		
40 Sterling Marlin	3.00	6.00
Sabco Racing		
42 Joe Nemechek	3.00	6.00
Bell South		
46 Wally Dallenbach	3.00	6.00
First Union		
50 Ricky Craven	3.00	6.00
Hendrick		
74 Randy LaJoie	3.00	6.00
Fina		
75 Rick Mast	3.00	6.00
Remington		
90 Dick Trickle	3.00	6.00
Heilig Meyers		
94 Bill Elliott	3.00	6.00
McDonald's		
96 David Green	3.00	6.00
Caterpiller		

1998 Racing Champions Press Pass Series 1:64

This series is a continuation of the Pinnacle series that was stopped when Press Pass was purchased by Racing Champions. Each car is packaged in a typical blister pack along with one Press Pass/Racing Champions card. The backer board to the blister pack was printed in gold with a large NASCAR 50th Anniversary logo. The cars are hood open with each being serial numbered of 19,998 produced.

4 Bobby Hamilton	3.00	6.00
Kodak		
5 Terry Labonte	3.00	6.00
Kellogg's		
6 Mark Martin	3.00	6.00
Eagle One		
6 Mark Martin	3.00	6.00
Valvoline		
9 Jeff Burton	3.00	6.00
Track Gear		
10 Ricky Rudd	3.00	6.00
Tide		
11 Brett Bodine	3.00	6.00
Paychex		
13 Jerry Nadeau	3.00	6.00
First Plus		
16 Ted Musgrave	3.00	6.00
Primestar		
17 Darrell Waltrip	3.00	6.00
Builders' Square		
21 Michael Waltrip	3.00	6.00
Goodwill Games		
26 Johnny Benson	3.00	6.00
Cheerios		
30 Derrike Cope	3.00	6.00
Gumout		
33 Tim Fedewa	3.00	6.00
Kleenex		
33 Ken Schrader	3.00	6.00
Petree		
35 Todd Bodine	3.00	6.00
Tabasco		
36 Ernie Irvan	3.00	6.00
M&M's		
40 Sterling Marlin	3.00	6.00
Sabco		
41 Steve Grissom	3.00	6.00
Larry Hedrick Racing		
42 Joe Nemechek	3.00	6.00
Bell South		
50 Ricky Craven	3.00	6.00
Hendrick		
59 Robert Pressley	3.00	6.00
Kingsford		
60 Mark Martin	3.00	6.00
Winn Dixie		
66 Elliott Sadler	3.00	6.00
Phillips 66		
75 Rick Mast	3.00	6.00
Remington		
90 Dick Trickle	3.00	6.00
Heilig-Meyers		
94 Bill Elliott	3.00	6.00
McDonald's		
94 Bill Elliott	3.00	6.00
Happy Meal		
96 David Green	3.00	6.00
Caterpillar		
97 Chad Little	3.00	6.00
John Deere		
98 Greg Sacks	3.00	6.00
Thorn Apple Valley		
99 Jeff Burton	3.00	6.00
Exide		
0 Buckshot Jones	3.00	6.00
Aqua Fresh		

1998 Racing Champions Race Day 1:64

10 Ricky Rudd	2.50	6.00
Tide		
21 Michael Waltrip	2.50	6.00
Citgo		
46 Wally Dallenbach	2.00	5.00
First Union		
90 Dick Trickle	2.00	5.00
Heilig Meyers		
99 Glenn Allen	2.00	5.00
Luxaire		
00 Buckshot Jones	2.00	5.00
Aquafresh		

1998 Racing Champions 24K Gold 1:64

This is a special series produced by Racing Champions to celebrate NASCAR's 50th anniversary. Each car is packaged in a "Reflections in Gold 24K Gold" blister with a limited edition of 9,998. Each car was plated in gold chrome and contains a serial number on its chassis.

4 Bobby Hamilton	6.00	15.00
Kodak		
4 Jeff Purvis	6.00	15.00
Lance		
5 Terry Labonte	12.00	30.00
Kellogg's		
6 Joe Bessey	6.00	15.00
Power Team		
6 Mark Martin	12.00	30.00
Valvoline		
8 Hut Stricklin	6.00	15.00
Circuit City		
9 Jeff Burton	6.00	15.00
Track Gear		
9 Lake Speed	6.00	15.00
Huckleberry Hound		
10 Phil Parsons	6.00	15.00
Duralube		
10 Ricky Rudd	6.00	15.00
Tide		
11 Brett Bodine	6.00	15.00
Paychex		
13 Jerry Nadeau	6.00	15.00
First Plus		
16 Ted Musgrave	6.00	15.00
Primestar		
20 Blaise Alexander	12.50	25.00
Rescue		
21 Michael Waltrip	6.00	15.00
Citgo		
26 Johnny Benson	6.00	15.00
Cheerios		
29 Hermie Sadler	6.00	15.00
DeWalt		
30 Derrike Cope	6.00	15.00
Gumout		
30 Mike Cope	6.00	15.00
Slim Jim		
33 Tim Fedewa	6.00	15.00
Kleenex		
33 Ken Schrader	6.00	15.00
Petree		
34 Mike McLaughlin	6.00	15.00
Goulds		
35 Todd Bodine	6.00	15.00
Tabasco		
36 Ernie Irvan	6.00	15.00
Skittles		
38 Elton Sawyer	6.00	15.00
Barbasol		
40 Sterling Marlin	6.00	15.00
Sabco		
41 Steve Grissom	6.00	15.00
Larry Hedrick Racing		
42 Joe Nemechek	6.00	15.00
Bell South		
43 Richard Petty	20.00	40.00
STP 4-car set w		
transporter		
1964 Plymouth		
1964 Ford		
1970 Plymouth Superbird		
1981 Buick		
46 Wally Dallenbach	6.00	15.00
First Union		
47 Andy Santerre	6.00	15.00
Monroe		
50 Ricky Craven	6.00	15.00
Hendrick		
59 Robert Pressley	6.00	15.00
Kingsford		
60 Mark Martin	12.00	30.00
Winn Dixie		
63 Tracy Leslie	6.00	15.00
Lysol		
75 Rick Mast	6.00	15.00
Remington		
77 Robert Pressley	6.00	15.00
Jasper		
90 Dick Trickle	6.00	15.00
Heilig-Meyers		
94 Bill Elliott	12.00	30.00
McDonald's		
98 Rich Bickle	6.00	15.00
Go Grill Crazy		
98 Greg Sacks	6.00	15.00
Thorn Apple Valley		
99 Glen Allen	6.00	15.00
Luxaire		
99 Jeff Burton	6.00	15.00
Exide		
00 Buckshot Jones	6.00	15.00
Aqua Fresh		

1998 Racing Champions Signature Series 1:64

This is a special series produced by Racing Champions to celebrate NASCAR's 50th anniversary. It parallels the regular 1998 1:64 scale series. Each car is packaged in a decorative box with the driver's facsimile autograph on the front.

4 Bobby Hamilton	2.00	5.00
Kodak		
5 Terry Labonte	3.00	6.00
Kellogg's		
6 Mark Martin	3.00	6.00
Valvoline		
8 Hut Stricklin	2.00	5.00
Circuit City		
9 Jeff Burton	2.00	5.00
Track Gear		
9 Lake Speed	2.00	5.00
Huckleberry Hound		
10 Ricky Rudd	2.00	5.00
Tide		
11 Brett Bodine	2.00	5.00
Paychex		
13 Jerry Nadeau	2.00	5.00
First Plus		
16 Ted Musgrave	2.00	5.00
Family Channel Primestar		
21 Michael Waltrip	2.00	5.00
Citgo		
26 Johnny Benson	2.00	5.00
Cheerios		
30 Mike Cope	2.00	5.00
Slim Jim		
33 Ken Schrader	2.00	5.00
Petree		
35 Todd Bodine	2.00	5.00
Tabasco		
36 Ernie Irvan	2.00	5.00
Skittles		
38 Elton Sawyer	2.00	5.00
Barbasol		
40 Sterling Marlin	2.00	6.00
Saboc		
42 Joe Nemechek	2.00	5.00
Bell South		
46 Wally Dallenbach	2.00	5.00
First Union		
50 Ricky Craven	2.00	5.00
Hendrick		
59 Robert Pressley	2.00	5.00
Kingsford		
75 Rick Mast	2.00	5.00
Remington		
90 Dick Trickle	2.00	5.00
Helig-Meyers		
94 Bill Elliott	3.00	6.00
Happy Meal		
94 Bill Elliott	3.00	6.00
McDonald's		
97 Chad Little	2.00	5.00
John Deere		
98 Greg Sacks	2.00	5.00
Thorn Apple Valley		
99 Jeff Burton	2.00	5.00
Exide		
00 Buckshot Jones	2.00	5.00
Aqua Fresh		

1998 Racing Champions Stock Rods 1:64

These 1:64 scale cars are replicas of vintage stock rods with NASCAR paint schemes. Cars are listed by issue number instead of car number.

56 Terry Labonte	4.00	8.00
Spooky Loops		
57 Terry Labonte	4.00	8.00
Kellogg's		
58 Glen Allen	3.00	6.00
Luxaire		
59 Bobby Hamilton	3.00	6.00
Kodak		
60 Dick Trickle	3.00	6.00
Heilig-Meyers		
61 Robert Pressley	3.00	6.00
Kingsford		
62 Ted Musgrave	3.00	6.00
Primestar		
63 Hut Stricklin	3.00	6.00
Circuit City		
64 Kevin Schwantz	3.00	6.00
Ryder		
65 Michael Waltrip	3.00	6.00
Citgo		
66 Buckshot Jones	3.00	6.00
Alka Seltzer		
67 Ken Schrader	3.00	6.00
Petree		
68 Bobby Hamilton	3.00	6.00
Kodak		
69 Hut Stricklin	3.00	6.00
Circuit City		
70 Terry Labonte	4.00	8.00
Kellogg's		
71 Rick Mast	3.00	6.00
Remington		
72 Joe Nemechek	3.00	6.00
Bell South		
73 Ricky Rudd	3.00	6.00
Tide		
74 Bill Elliott	4.00	8.00
McDonald's		
75 Ernie Irvan	3.00	6.00
M&M's		
76 Terry Labonte	4.00	8.00
Kellogg's		
77 Michael Waltrip	3.00	6.00
Citgo		
78 Ricky Rudd	4.00	8.00
Tide Gold		
79 Bill Elliott	12.00	20.00
McDonald's Gold		
80 Bobby Hamilton	4.00	8.00
Kodak Gold		
81 Hut Stricklin	4.00	8.00
Circuit City Gold		
82 Mark Martin	4.00	8.00
Valvoline		
83 Ted Musgrave	3.00	6.00
Primestar		
84 Jeff Burton	3.00	6.00
Exide		
85 Mark Martin	4.00	8.00
Winn Dixie		

Item	Low	High
86 Jeff Burton Exide Gold	6.00	12.00
87 Bill Elliott McDonald's Gold	12.00	20.00
88 Todd Bodine Tabasco	3.00	6.00
89 Lake Speed Huckleberry Hound	3.00	6.00
90 Jeff Burton Exide	3.00	6.00
91 Bill Elliott McDonald's	4.00	8.00
92 Mark Martin Winn Dixie	4.00	8.00
93 Mark Martin Valvoline	4.00	8.00
94 Lake Speed Cartoon Network	3.00	6.00
95 Terry Labonte Kellogg's Corny	4.00	8.00
96 Terry Labonte Kellogg's Corny Gold	12.00	20.00
97 Jeff Burton Exide Gold	6.00	15.00
98 Rick Mast Remington	3.00	6.00
99 Terry Labonte Kellogg's	4.00	8.00
100 Joe Nemechek Bell South	3.00	6.00
101 Robert Pressley Kingsford	3.00	6.00
102 Bill Elliott McDonald's	4.00	8.00
103 Mark Martin Winn Dixie	4.00	8.00
104 Jeff Burton Exide Gold	6.00	15.00
105 Bobby Hamilton Kodak Gold	4.00	8.00
106 Terry Labonte Kellogg's	4.00	8.00
107 Bill Elliott McDonald's	4.00	8.00
108 Mark Martin Valvoline	4.00	8.00
109 Jeff Burton Track Gear	3.00	6.00
110 Ted Musgrave Primestar	3.00	6.00
111 Lake Speed Huckleberry Hound	3.00	6.00
112 Terry Labonte Kellogg's Corny Gold	12.00	20.00
113 Ricky Rudd Tide Gold	4.00	8.00
114 Bobby Hamilton Kodak	3.00	6.00
115 Ken Schrader Petree	3.00	6.00
116 Dick Trickle Heilig-Meyers	3.00	6.00
117 Todd Bodine Tabasco	3.00	6.00
118 Terry Labonte Kellogg's	4.00	8.00
119 Terry Labonte Kellogg's	4.00	8.00
120 Joe Nemechek Bell South	3.00	6.00
121 Kevin Schwantz Ryder	3.00	6.00
122 Robert Pressley Kingsford	3.00	6.00
123 Bill Elliott McDonald's	4.00	8.00
124 Mark Martin Valvoline	4.00	8.00
125 Michael Waltrip Citgo	3.00	6.00
126 Dick Trickle Heilig-Meyers	3.00	6.00
127 Ted Musgrave Primestar	3.00	6.00
128 Michael Waltrip Citgo	3.00	6.00
129 Bobby Hamilton Kodak	3.00	6.00
130 Bill Elliott McDonald's	4.00	8.00
131 Terry Labonte Kellogg's	4.00	8.00
132 Rick Mast Remington Gold	4.00	8.00
133 Robert Pressley Kingsford	3.00	6.00
134 Michael Waltrip Citgo	3.00	6.00
135 Ken Schrader Petree Gold	4.00	8.00
136 Mark Martin Valvoline	4.00	8.00
137 Jeff Burton Track Gear	3.00	6.00
138 Bill Elliott McDonald's	4.00	8.00
139 Terry Labonte Kellogg's Corny	4.00	8.00
140 Rick Mast Remington	3.00	6.00
141 Terry Labonte Blasted Fruit Loops	4.00	8.00
142 Michael Waltrip Citgo Gold	4.00	8.00
143 Terry Labonte Kellogg's Gold	12.00	20.00

1998 Racing Champions Stock Rods Reflections of Gold 1:64

These 1:64 scale cars are replicas of vintage stock rods with NASCAR paint schemes and gold plating. Cars are listed by issue number instead of car number.

Item	Low	High
1 Terry Labonte Kellogg's	12.00	30.00
2 Jerry Nadeau First Plus	6.00	15.00
3 Bobby Hamilton Kodak	6.00	15.00
4 Todd Bodine Tabasco	6.00	15.00
5 Mark Martin Valvoline	12.00	30.00
6 Bill Elliott McDonald's	12.00	30.00
7 Ted Musgrave Primestar	6.00	15.00
8 Jeff Burton Exide	8.00	20.00

1998 Racing Champions Toys 'R Us Gold 1:64

This is a special series produced by Racing Champions to celebrate NASCAR's 50th anniversary. Each car is a limited edition of 19,998. Each car is also plated in gold chrome. These cars were distributed in Toys 'R Us stores.

Item	Low	High
5 Terry Labonte Blasted Fruit Loops	5.00	12.00
5 Terry Labonte Kellogg's Corny	5.00	12.00
6 Joe Bessey Power Team	3.00	8.00
6 Mark Martin Eagle One	5.00	12.00
6 Mark Martin Valvoline	5.00	12.00
9 Jerry Nadeau Zombie Island	2.50	6.00
9 Lake Speed Birthday Cake	2.50	6.00
10 Phil Parsons Duralube	2.50	6.00
10 Ricky Rudd Give Kids The World	2.50	6.00
11 Brett Bodine Paychex	2.50	6.00
13 Jerry Nadeau First Plus	2.50	6.00
17 Matt Kenseth Lycos	15.00	25.00
17 Darrell Waltrip Builders' Square	2.50	6.00
19 Tony Raines Yellow Freight	2.50	6.00
20 Blaise Alexander Rescue Engine	2.50	6.00
21 Michael Waltrip Goodwill Games	2.50	6.00
23 Lance Hooper WCW	2.50	6.00
26 Johnny Benson Betty Crocker	2.50	6.00
26 Johnny Benson Cheerios	2.50	6.00
33 Tim Fedewa Kleenex	2.50	6.00
33 Ken Schrader Petree	2.50	6.00
35 Todd Bodine Tabasco	2.50	6.00
36 Ernie Irvan Wildberry Skittles	3.00	8.00
42 Joe Nemechek Bell South	2.50	6.00
50 NDA Dr. Pepper	2.50	6.00
60 Mark Martin Winn Dixie	4.00	10.00
63 Tracy Leslie Lysol	2.50	6.00
64 Dick Trickle Schneider	2.50	6.00
74 Randy LaJoie Fina	2.50	6.00
77 Robert Pressley Jasper	2.50	6.00
87 Joe Nemechek Bell South	2.50	6.00
94 Bill Elliott Happy Meal	5.00	12.00
98 Greg Sacks Thorn Apple Valley	2.50	6.00
99 Jeff Burton Exide	2.50	6.00
300 Darrell Waltrip Flock Special	3.00	8.00

1998 Racing Champions SuperTrucks 1:64

Racing Champions continued their line of 1:64 SuperTrucks in 1998. This series features many of the circuit's first-time drivers and Winston Cup regulars.

Item	Low	High
2 Mike Bliss Team ASE	2.00	4.00
6 Rick Carelli Remax	2.00	4.00
18 No Driver Association Dana	2.00	4.00
19 Tony Raines Pennzoil	2.00	4.00
29 Bob Keselowski Mopar	2.00	4.00
31 Tony Roper Concor Tools	2.00	4.00
35 Ron Barfield Ortho	2.00	4.00
44 Boris Said Federated	2.00	4.00
52 Mike Wallace Pure One	2.00	4.00
66 Bryan Refner Carlin	2.00	4.00
75 Kevin Harvick Spears	50.00	100.00
84 Wayne Anderson Porter Cable	2.00	4.00
86 Stacy Compton RC Cola	2.00	4.00
87 Joe Nemechek BellSouth	2.00	4.00
90 Lance Norick National Hockey League	2.00	4.00
94 Bill Elliott Team ASE	2.00	4.00

1998 Racing Champions SuperTrucks Gold 1:64

This is a special series produced by Racing Champions to celebrate NASCAR's 50th anniversary. It parallels the regular 1998 1:24 scale series. Each truck is a limited edition of 5,000. Each truck is also plated in gold chrome and contains a serial number on its chassis.

Item	Low	High
2 Mike Bliss Team ASE	10.00	20.00
6 Rick Carelli Remax	10.00	20.00
29 Bob Keselowski Mopar	10.00	20.00
66 Bryan Refner Carlin	10.00	20.00
84 Wayne Anderson Porter Cable	10.00	20.00
86 Stacy Compton RC Cola	10.00	20.00

1999 Racing Champions 1:64

The 1:64 scale cars that appear in this series are replicas of many of the cars that ran in the 1998 season, but also cars slated to appear in the 1999 season. They were packaged in blister packs that display the "Racing Champions The Originals" 10th anniversary logo along with an oversized die cut card. A Chrome parallel version (production of 9999) was also created for some cars.

Item	Low	High
1 Tecumseh Promo in PVC box	7.50	15.00
4 Brad Baker Logan's Roadhouse Promo	20.00	40.00
4 Bobby Hamilton Kodak	2.00	4.00
4 Bobby Hamilton Kodak Advantix	2.00	4.00
5 Terry Labonte Kellogg's	2.00	4.00
5 Terry Labonte Kellogg's Chrome/9999	8.00	15.00
5 Terry Labonte Kellogg's Promo black windows	4.00	10.00
5 Terry Labonte Rice Krispies Treats Promo black windows	4.00	10.00
6 Mark Martin Valvoline	2.00	4.00
6 Mark Martin Valvoline Chrome/9999	8.00	15.00
6 Mark Martin Zerex	6.00	10.00
6 Mark Martin Zerex Chrome/9999	10.00	20.00
7 Michael Waltrip Philips	2.00	4.00
9 Jerry Nadeau Goldberg	4.00	8.00
9 Jerry Nadeau Dexter's Laboratory	2.00	4.00
9 Jerry Nadeau Dexter's Lab Chrome/9999	6.00	12.00
10 Ricky Rudd Tide	2.00	4.00
10 Ricky Rudd Tide Peroxide	2.00	4.00
10 Ricky Rudd Tide Promo	4.00	10.00
11 Brett Bodine Paychex	2.00	4.00
12 Jeremy Mayfield Mobil 1	2.00	4.00
12 Jeremy Mayfield Mobil 1 Chrome/9999	6.00	12.00
14 Rick Crawford Circle Bar SuperTruck	2.00	4.00
14 Donnie Neuenberger Cofab Steel Promo	10.00	25.00
15 Ken Schrader Oakwood Homes	2.00	4.00
15 Ken Schrader Oakwood Homes Chrome/9999	6.00	12.00
16 Kevin Lepage Primestar	2.00	4.00
16 Kevin Lepage Primestar Chrome/9999	6.00	12.00
16 Kevin Lepage TV Guide	2.00	4.00
17 Matt Kenseth DeWalt	5.00	12.00
17 Matt Kenseth DeWalt Chrome/9999	10.00	25.00
17 Matt Kenseth DeWalt Kraft Promo	5.00	12.00
17 Matt Kenseth Visine Kraft Promo/10,000	6.00	15.00
21 Elliott Sadler Citgo	2.00	4.00
21 Elliott Sadler Citgo Chrome/9999	6.00	12.00
23 Jimmy Spencer TCE	2.00	4.00
23 Jimmy Spencer TCE Chrome/9999	6.00	12.00
23 Jimmy Spencer TCE Lights	2.00	4.00
24 Jack Sprague GMAC SuperTruck	2.00	4.00
25 Wally Dallenbach Budweiser	2.00	4.00
25 Wally Dallenbach Hendrick Chrome/9999	6.00	12.00
26 Johnny Benson Cheerios	2.00	4.00
30 Derrike Cope Bryan	2.00	4.00
30 Derrike Cope Bryan Chrome/9999	6.00	12.00
32 Jeff Green Kleenex	2.00	4.00
32 Jeff Green Kleenex Chrome/9999	6.00	12.00
33 Ken Schrader Petree	2.00	4.00
34 Mike McLaughlin Goulds Pumps	2.00	4.00
35 Lyndon Amick Powertel Scana Promo	35.00	60.00
36 Ernie Irvan M&M's	2.00	4.00
36 Ernie Irvan M&M's Chrome/9999	10.00	20.00
37 Bob Huffman White House Promo	20.00	35.00
38 Glen Allen Barbersol	2.00	4.00
40 Andy Belmont AOL Promo in window box	5.00	12.00
40 Sterling Marlin Brooks & Dunn	2.00	5.00
40 Sterling Marlin John Wayne	2.00	5.00
42 Joe Nemechek BellSouth	2.00	4.00
43 John Andretti STP	2.00	4.00
43 John Andretti STP Chrome/9999	8.00	15.00
43 Shane Hall Tecumseh CT Promo	20.00	40.00
43 NDA Richard Petty Driving Experience Promo	5.00	10.00
43 Richard Petty STP 7-car Championship set with transporter	40.00	80.00
45 Adam Petty Spree	10.00	25.00
50 Mark Green Dr. Pepper	2.00	4.00
55 Kenny Wallace Square D	2.00	4.00
59 Mike Dillon Kingsford	2.00	4.00
59 Mike Dillon Kingsford Chrome/9999	6.00	12.00
60 Mark Martin Winn Dixie	2.00	5.00
60 Mark Martin Winn Dixie Chrome/9999	10.00	20.00
66 Darrell Waltrip Big K	2.00	4.00
75 Ted Musgrave Remington	2.00	4.00
77 Robert Pressley Jasper	2.00	4.00
86 Stacy Compton RC Cola SuperTruck	2.00	4.00
93 Dave Blaney Amoco Promo box	5.00	10.00
94 Bill Elliott McDonald's	2.00	4.00
94 Bill Elliott Drive Thru Chrome/9999	8.00	15.00
94 Bill Elliott QPC	3.00	8.00
97 Chad Little John Deere	2.00	4.00
97 Chad Little John Deere Promo with Medallion	3.00	8.00
98 Kevin Harvick Porter-Cable SuperTruck Promo	40.00	75.00
99 Jeff Burton Exide	2.00	4.00
99 Jeff Burton Exide Bruce Lee	2.00	4.00
00 Buckshot Jones Crown Fiber	2.00	4.00
00 Larry Pearson Cheez-It	2.00	4.00
00 Larry Pearson Cheez-it Chrome/9999	6.00	12.00
02 Ward Burton Siemens Promo	6.00	15.00
NNO Roush Racing AUTO Gold set/3000 5-cars: 6/16/26/97/99 Mark Martin, Kevin Lepage Johnny Benson, Chad Little and Jeff Burton with Certificate signed by all 5-drivers and Jack Roush	25.00	50.00
NNO Roush Racing AUTO Platinum set/2000 5-cars: 6/16/26/97/99 Mark Martin, Kevin Lepage Johnny Benson, Chad Little and Jeff Burton with Certificate signed by all 5-drivers and Jack Roush	40.00	80.00

1999 Racing Champions 2-Car Sets 1:64

Item	Low	High
5 Terry Labonte Kellogg's with Gold car/2499	15.00	30.00
6 Mark Martin Eagle One with Chrome car/1999	15.00	30.00
6 Mark Martin Valvoline with Chrome car/5000	15.00	30.00
6 Mark Martin Zerex with Chrome car/2999	15.00	30.00
36 Ernie Irvan M&M's with Chrome car/2998	15.00	30.00
36 Ernie Irvan Skittles with Gold car/5000	15.00	30.00
43 Richard Petty STP 1966 Pontiac with Gold car/4343	15.00	30.00
94 Bill Elliott McDonald's with Chrome car/2499	15.00	30.00
94 Bill Elliott McDonald's with Gold car/2499	15.00	30.00
99 Jeff Burton Exide with Gold car/5000	15.00	30.00

1999 Racing Champions 12-Car Sets 1:64

Item	Low	High
1 12-Car Set 1 BHamilton Kodak Adventure Purvis Lance Labonte Kellogg's Rudd Tide Mayfield Mobil 1 Cope Bryan Gold Jarrett Bayer Schrader Kenny Marlin Sabco Petty Spree Dillon Kingsford Jones Crown Fiber	12.50	30.00
2 12-Car Set 2 Hamilton Kodak Gold Martin Valvoline Parsons Alltel Lepage Primestar Kenseth DeWalt Spencer TCE Cope Jimmy Dean Nemechek BellSouth Waltrip Big K Sadler MGM Brakes Burton Bruce Lee Pearson Cheez-it	12.50	30.00
3 12-Car Set 3 Nadeau Cartoon Schrader Oakwood Sadler Citgo Dallenbach Hendrick Cope StateFr Jarrett AlkaSeltzer Schrader SchraderGold McLaughlin GouldPumps Irvan M&Ms Marlin JohnWayne Pressley Jasper Burton Exide	12.50	30.00
4 12-Car Set 4 Trickle Schneider Bodine Paychex Cope Rudys Farm Green Kleenex Schrader Red Andretti STP Wallace Square D Bodine Power Team Pressley Jasper Yellow Elliott McDonald's Little John Deere Sawyer Lysol	12.50	30.00
NNO Chase Car Collection -car set/2000 Labonte Kelloggs Martin Valvine Martin	25.00	50.00

u
n
ld

e
tar
er

bach
ck

s
ti

CAR Intro. 15.00 40.00
e 12-car set/25000
on

te
gs

u

e

u

eere

Lee
AR
ard Petty Dodge Motorsports/11-historical Petty cars 60.00 100.00
ld Dodge truck

Racing Champions Buss Fuses Promos 1:64

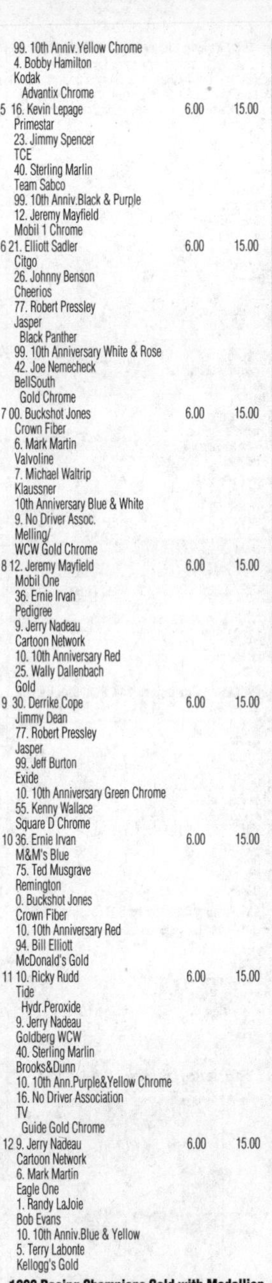

in this series was packaged with two small boxes of a clam-shell type package. Buss Fuses sponsored the rs produced by Racing Champions.

sgrave 10.00 25.00
SuperTruck
abonte 5.00 12.00
gg's
lartin 5.00 12.00
ine
Rudd 4.00 10.00

liott 4.00 10.00
nald's Drive Thru
urton 4.00 10.00

Racing Champions Fan Appreciation 5-Pack 1:64

was issued 5-cars at a time in Racing Champions 5-ter and box combinations. Each package was entitled reciation" at the bottom and issued to commemorate Anniversary of Racing Champions. A special 10th ary die-cast was one of the five cars in each package package also including an issue number at the top. s were only issued in these special 5-packs. The total of 19,999 was included on each package as well. aloged the pieces below by the reported issue number.

by Hamilton 6.00 15.00
k
rk Martin
line
en Schrader
's
0th Anniv.Maroon Chrome
ff Burton
Lee Gold Chrome
y Labonte 6.00 15.00
gg's
Driver Assoc.
ng WCW
had Little
Deere
0th Anniv.Blue Chrome
terling Marlin
Wayne
cky Rudd 6.00 15.00

en Schrader

ohn Andretti

Anniversary Red & Black
ill Elliott
onald's Drive Thru
ett Bodine 6.00 15.00
heck
errike Cope

en Schrader
Blue & White

99. 10th Anniv.Yellow Chrome
4. Bobby Hamilton
Kodak
Advantix Chrome
5 16. Kevin Lepage 6.00 15.00
Primestar
23. Jimmy Spencer
TCE
40. Sterling Marlin
Team Sabco
99. 10th Anniv.Black & Purple
12. Jeremy Mayfield
Mobil 1 Chrome
6 21. Elliott Sadler 6.00 15.00
Citgo
26. Johnny Benson
Cheerios
77. Robert Pressley
Jasper
Black Panther
99. 10th Anniversary White & Rose
42. Joe Nemecheck
BellSouth
Gold Chrome
7 00. Buckshot Jones 6.00 15.00
Crown Fiber
6. Mark Martin
Valvoline
7. Michael Waltrip
Klaussner
10th Anniversary Blue & White
9. No Driver Assoc.
Melling/
WCW Gold Chrome
8 12. Jeremy Mayfield 6.00 15.00
Mobil One
36. Ernie Irvan
Pedigree
9. Jerry Nadeau
Cartoon Network
10. 10th Anniversary Red
25. Wally Dallenbach
Gold
9 30. Derrike Cope 6.00 15.00
Jimmy Dean
77. Robert Pressley
Jasper
99. Jeff Burton
Exide
10. 10th Anniversary Green Chrome
55. Kenny Wallace
Square D Chrome
10 36. Ernie Irvan 6.00 15.00
M&M's Blue
75. Ted Musgrave
Remington
0. Buckshot Jones
Crown Fiber
10. 10th Anniversary Red
94. Bill Elliott
McDonald's Gold
11 10. Ricky Rudd 6.00 15.00
Tide
Hydr.Peroxide
9. Jerry Nadeau
Goldberg WCW
40. Sterling Marlin
Brooks&Dunn
10. 10th Ann.Purple&Yellow Chrome
16. No Driver Association
TV
Guide Gold Chrome
12 9. Jerry Nadeau 6.00 15.00
Cartoon Network
6. Mark Martin
Eagle One
1. Randy LaJoie
Bob Evans
10. 10th Anniv.Blue & Yellow
5. Terry Labonte
Kellogg's Gold

1999 Racing Champions Gold with Medallion 1:64

This is a special series produced by Racing Champions to celebrate their 10th anniversary. Each car is also plated in gold chrome.

4 Bobby Hamilton 6.00 12.00
Kodak
4 Bobby Hamilton 6.00 12.00
Kodak Advantix
5 Terry Labonte 12.00 30.00
Kellogg's
6 Mark Martin 12.00 30.00
Valvoline
6 Joe Bessey 6.00 12.00
Power Team
9 Jerry Nadeau 6.00 12.00
Dexter's Laboratory
10 Ricky Rudd 6.00 12.00
Tide
10 Phil Parsons 6.00 12.00
Alltel
11 Brett Bodine 6.00 12.00
Paychex
12 Jeremy Mayfield 6.00 12.00
Mobil 1
15 Ken Schrader 6.00 12.00
Oakwood Homes
16 Kevin Lepage 6.00 12.00
Primestar
23 Jimmy Spencer 6.00 12.00
TCE
25 Wally Dallenbach 6.00 12.00
Hendrick
26 Johnny Benson 6.00 12.00
Cheerios
30 Derrike Cope 6.00 12.00
Jimmy Dean
32 Jeff Green 6.00 12.00
Kleenex
33 Ken Schrader 6.00 12.00
Petree
36 Ernie Irvan 6.00 15.00
M&M's

55 Kenny Wallace 6.00 12.00
Square D
60 Mark Martin 12.00 30.00
Winn Dixie
66 Darrell Waltrip 8.00 20.00
Big K
77 Robert Pressley 6.00 12.00
Jasper
78 Garry Bradberry 6.00 12.00
Pilot
94 Bill Elliott 10.00 25.00
Drive Thru
97 Chad Little 6.00 12.00
John Deere
99 Jeff Burton 6.00 12.00
Exide

1999 Racing Champions NASCAR Rules 1:64

Packaged with a display stand and collector card that explains some of the technical rules that govern NASCAR, these 1:64 scale replicas have an opening hood with detailed engine, opening trunk with fuel cell, and a replica NASCAR template. The stated production run was 9999.

6 Mark Martin 10.00 20.00
Eagle One
6 Mark Martin 10.00 20.00
Valvoline
6 Mark Martin 10.00 20.00
Zerex
9 Jerry Nadeau 5.00 12.00
WCW nWo
9 Jeff Burton 5.00 12.00
Track Gear
10 Ricky Rudd 5.00 12.00
Tide
12 Jeremy Mayfield 5.00 12.00
Mobil 1
16 Kevin LePage 5.00 12.00
Primestar
21 Elliott Sadler 5.00 12.00
Citgo
23 Jimmy Spencer 5.00 12.00
TCE
26 Johnny Benson 5.00 12.00
Cheerios
43 John Andretti 5.00 12.00
STP
60 Mark Martin 10.00 20.00
Winn Dixie
66 Darrell Waltrip 5.00 12.00
Big K
94 Bill Elliott 6.00 15.00
Drive Thru
97 Chad Little 5.00 12.00
John Deere
99 Jeff Burton 6.00 15.00
Exide
99 Jeff Burton 6.00 15.00
Bruce Lee

1999 Racing Champions Petty Collection 1:64

Racing Champions issued one car for each of 50-years of Petty Racing in 1999. Each car was packaged in a commemorative blister with the year that car represents noted on the base of each car along with a stated production run of 19,043. This series remains one of the most collected of all 1:64 scale Racing Champions releases. Note that we've cataloged the cars by year of issue and that the first 3-year's of Lee Petty car models do not match the exact year in which that car was raced. There was also a 50-car factory complete set issued by Racing Champions. Each card in the factory set was inserted into a plastic bag and placed into one of two 25-car trays inside a larger box.

50 Lee Petty 30.00 60.00
1949 Plymouth
51 Lee Petty 40.00 75.00
1949 Plymouth
52 Lee Petty 35.00 60.00
1950 Plymouth
53 Lee Petty 7.50 20.00
1953 Dodge Coronet
54 Lee Petty 7.50 20.00
1954 Dodge Coronet
55 Lee Petty 7.50 20.00
1955 Chrysler 300-B
56 Lee Petty 12.50 30.00
1956 Dodge Coronet
57 Lee Petty 30.00 60.00
1957 Oldsmobile
58 Richard Petty 40.00 75.00
1958 Oldsmobile
1958 on package

59 Richard Petty 20.00 35.00
1959 Plymouth Plaza
60 Richard Petty 7.50 20.00
1960 Plymouth Fury
61 Richard Petty 7.50 20.00
1961 Plymouth Fury
62 Richard Petty 7.50 20.00
1962 Plymouth Savoy
63 Richard Petty 7.50 20.00
1963 Plymouth Savoy
64 Richard Petty 7.50 20.00
1964 Plymouth Belvedere
65 Richard Petty 7.50 20.00
1965 Plymouth Barracuda
66 Richard Petty 7.50 20.00
1966 Plymouth Belvedere
67 Richard Petty 7.50 20.00
1967 Plymouth Belvedere GTX
68 Richard Petty 7.50 20.00
1968 Plymouth Roadrunner
69 Richard Petty 7.50 20.00
1969 Ford Torino
70 Richard Petty 7.50 20.00
1970 Plymouth Superbird
71 Richard Petty 5.00 12.00
Pepsi 1971 Plymouth Roadrunner
72 Richard Petty 6.00 15.00
STP 1972 Plymouth Roadrunner
73 Richard Petty 6.00 15.00
STP 1973 Dodge Charger
74 Richard Petty 6.00 15.00
STP 1974 Dodge Charger
75 Richard Petty 6.00 15.00
STP 1975 Dodge Charger
76 Richard Petty 6.00 15.00
STP 1976 Dodge Charger
77 Richard Petty 6.00 15.00
STP 1977 Dodge Charger
78 Richard Petty 5.00 12.00
STP 1977 Monte Carlo
1978 on package
79 Richard Petty 5.00 12.00
STP 1977 Monte Carlo
1979 on package
80 Richard Petty 5.00 12.00
STP 1977 Monte Carlo
1980 on package
81 Richard Petty 12.50 25.00
STP 1981 Buick Regal
82 Richard Petty 6.00 15.00
STP 1982 Pontiac Grand Prix
83 Richard Petty 5.00 12.00
STP 1982 Pontiac Grand Prix
1983 on package
84 Richard Petty 5.00 12.00
STP '82 Pontiac Grand Prix
1984 on package
85 Richard Petty 5.00 12.00
STP 1985 Pontiac Grand Prix
86 Richard Petty 5.00 12.00
STP 1985 Pontiac Grand Prix
1986 on package
87 Richard Petty 5.00 12.00
STP 1987 Pontiac Grand Prix
88 Richard Petty 5.00 12.00
STP 1988 Pontiac Grand Prix
89 Richard Petty 5.00 12.00
STP 1989 Pontiac Grand Prix
90 Richard Petty 5.00 12.00
STP 1990 Pontiac Grand Prix
91 Richard Petty 10.00 20.00
STP 1991 Pontiac Grand Prix
92 Richard Petty 8.00 20.00
STP 1992 Pontiac Grand Prix
93 Rick Wilson 5.00 12.00
STP 1993 Pontiac Grand Prix
94 John Andretti 5.00 12.00
STP 1994 Pontiac Grand Prix
95 Bobby Hamilton 5.00 12.00
STP 1995 Grand Prix
96 Bobby Hamilton 5.00 12.00
STP 1996 Grand Prix
97 Bobby Hamilton 5.00 12.00
STP 1997 Grand Prix
98 John Andretti 5.00 12.00
STP 1998 Grand Prix
99 John Andretti 5.00 12.00
STP 1999 Grand Prix
NNO Complete 50-Car Factory Set 150.00 250.00

1999 Racing Champions Platinum 1:64

This is a special series produced by Racing Champions to celebrate their 10th anniversary. It parallels the regular 1999 1:24 scale series. Each car is a limited edition of 9,999. Each car is also plated in platinum chrome and contains a serial number on its chassis.

4 Bobby Hamilton 6.00 12.00
Kodak
4 Bobby Hamilton 6.00 12.00
Kodak Max
5 Terry Labonte 10.00 20.00
Kellogg's
6 Joe Bessey 6.00 12.00
Power Team
6 Mark Martin 12.00 20.00
Valvoline
9 Jerry Nadeau 6.00 12.00
Dexter's Laboratory
9 Jeff Burton 6.00 12.00
Track Gear
10 Ricky Rudd 6.00 12.00
Tide
10 Ricky Rudd 6.00 12.00
Tide Happy Holiday
11 Brett Bodine 6.00 12.00
Paychex
16 Kevin Lepage 6.00 12.00
Primestar
25 Wally Dallenbach 6.00 12.00
Hendrick
26 Johnny Benson 6.00 12.00
Cheerios

32 Jeff Green 6.00 12.00
Kleenex
33 Ken Schrader 6.00 12.00
Petree
36 Ernie Irvan 6.00 15.00
M&M's
42 Joe Nemechek 6.00 12.00
BellSouth
55 Kenny Wallace 6.00 12.00
Square D
77 Robert Pressley 6.00 12.00
Jasper
94 Bill Elliott 6.00 15.00
Drive Thru
97 Chad Little 6.00 12.00
John Deere
99 Jeff Burton 6.00 12.00
Exide

1999 Racing Champions Platinum Stock Rods 1:64

1P Bobby Hamilton 5.00 10.00
Valvoline
2P Terry Labonte 5.00 10.00
Kellogg's
3P Mark Martin 5.00 10.00
Valvoline
4P Ricky Rudd 5.00 10.00
Tide
5P Bill Elliott 5.00 10.00
Drive Thru
6P Ernie Irvan 5.00 10.00
M&M's

1999 Racing Champions Precious Metals Team Colors 1:64

6 Mark Martin 5.00 12.00
Valvoline/9500
12 Jeremy Mayfield 4.00 10.00
Mobil
94 Bill Elliott 4.00 10.00
McDonald's/7500

1999 Racing Champions Press Pass Series 1:64

These 1:64 scale cars come packaged with a Press Pass card and feature opening hoods and two piece tires.

4 Bobby Hamilton 3.00 6.00
Kodak
4 Bobby Hamilton 3.00 6.00
Advantix
5 Terry Labonte 3.00 6.00
Kellogg's
6 Mark Martin 3.00 6.00
Valvoline
6 Joe Bessey 3.00 6.00
Power Team
7 Michael Waltrip 3.00 6.00
Philips
9 Jerry Nadeau 3.00 6.00
Dexter's Laboratory
9 Jeff Burton 3.00 6.00
Track Gear
10 Ricky Rudd 3.00 6.00
Tide
11 Brett Bodine 3.00 6.00
Paychex
15 Ken Schrader 3.00 6.00
Oakwood Homes
16 Kevin Lepage 3.00 6.00
Primestar
21 Elliott Sadler 3.00 6.00
Citgo
25 Wally Dallenbach 3.00 6.00
Hendrick
26 Johnny Benson 3.00 6.00
Cheerios
30 Derrike Cope 3.00 6.00
Bryan Foods
32 Jeff Green 3.00 6.00
Kleenex
33 Elton Sawyer 3.00 6.00
Lysol
33 Ken Schrader 3.00 6.00
Petree
33 Ken Schrader 3.00 6.00
APR Blue
34 Mike McLaughlin 3.00 6.00
Goulds Pumps
36 Ernie Irvan 3.00 6.00
M&M's
40 Sterling Marlin 4.00 8.00
John Wayne
42 Joe Nemechek 3.00 6.00
BellSouth
55 Kenny Wallace 3.00 6.00
Square D
60 Geoffery Bodine 3.00 6.00
Power Team
66 Darrell Waltrip 3.00 6.00
Big K
66 Todd Bodine 3.00 6.00
Phillips 66
72 Hermie Sadler 3.00 6.00
MGM Brakes

77 Robert Pressley 3.00 6.00
Jasper
78 Gary Bradberry 3.00 6.00
Pilot
94 Bill Elliott 3.00 6.00
Drive Thru
97 Chad Little 3.00 6.00
John Deere
98 Elton Sawyer 3.00 6.00
Lysol
99 Jeff Burton 3.00 6.00
Exide
00 Buckshot Jones 3.00 6.00
Crown Fiber

1999 Racing Champions Radio Controled Die Cast 1:64

These cars are touted as the smallest RC cars available. They came with a pit box remote and a pit stop recharging base. These remote control cars were capable of forward and reverse only.

5 Terry Labonte 15.00 30.00
Kellogg's
6 Mark Martin 15.00 30.00
Valvoline
12 Jeremy Mayfield 15.00 30.00
Mobil 1
36 Ernie Irvan 20.00 40.00
M&M's
43 John Andretti 20.00 40.00
STP
94 Bill Elliott 15.00 30.00
Drive Thru

1999 Racing Champions Signature Series 1:64

This is a special series produced by Racing Champions to celebrate their 10th anniversary. Each car was packaged in a decorative box and wrapped inside a blister pack. Some cars were also issued in a Chrome version with each carrying a production run of 4999.

4 Bobby Hamilton 2.00 5.00
Kodak
4 Bobby Hamilton 7.50 15.00
Kodak Chrome/4999
4 Jeff Purvis 2.00 5.00
Lance Snacks
5 Terry Labonte 2.50 6.00
Kellogg's
6 Joe Bessey 2.00 5.00
Power Team
6 Mark Martin 2.50 6.00
Valvoline
6 Mark Martin 15.00 30.00
Valvoline Chrome/4999
6 Mark Martin 15.00 30.00
Zerex Chrome/4999
7 Michael Waltrip 2.00 5.00
Philips
9 Jerry Nadeau 2.00 5.00
Dexter's Laboratory
9 Jerry Nadeau 10.00 20.00
Dexter's Lab Chrome/4999
10 Ricky Rudd 2.00 5.00
Tide
11 Brett Bodine 2.00 5.00
Paychex
12 Jeremy Mayfield 2.00 5.00
Mobil 1
12 Jeremy Mayfield 7.50 15.00
Mobil 1 Chrome/4999
16 Kevin Lepage 2.00 5.00
Primestar
16 Kevin Lepage 7.50 15.00
Primestar Chrome/4999
17 Matt Kenseth 3.00 8.00
DeWalt
23 Jimmy Spencer 2.00 5.00
TCE
23 Jimmy Spencer 7.50 15.00
TCE Chrome/4999
25 Wally Dallenbach 2.00 5.00
Hendrick
25 Wally Dallenbach 7.50 15.00
Hendrick Chrome/4999
26 Johnny Benson 2.00 5.00
Cheerios
32 Jeff Green 2.00 5.00
Kleenex
34 Mike McLaughlin 2.00 5.00
Goulds Pump
36 Ernie Irvan 2.50 6.00
M&M's
36 Ernie Irvan 7.50 15.00
M&M's Chrome/4999
40 Sterling Marlin 2.00 5.00
John Wayne
60 Mark Martin 2.50 6.00
Winn Dixie
77 Robert Pressley 2.00 5.00
Jasper
77 Robert Pressley 7.50 15.00
Jasper Chrome/4999
94 Bill Elliott 2.50 6.00
Drive Thru
94 Bill Elliott 15.00 30.00
Drive Thru Chrome/4999
99 Jeff Burton 2.00 5.00
Exide
00 Buckshot Jones 2.00 5.00
Crown Fiber

1999 Racing Champions Stock Rods 1:64

These 1:64 scale cars are replicas of vintage stock rods with NASCAR paint schemes. Cars are listed by issue number instead of car number.

144 Terry Labonte 4.00 8.00
Kellogg's Iron Man
145 Rick Mast 3.00 6.00
Remington
146 Terry Labonte 4.00 8.00
Kellogg's
147 Ricky Rudd 3.00 6.00
Tide
148 Kevin Lepage 3.00 6.00
Primestar
149 Terry Labonte 4.00 8.00
Kellogg's Corny
150 Terry Labonte 4.00 8.00
ron Man Gold
151 Ricky Rudd 4.00 8.00
Tide Gold
152 Bobby Hamilton 3.00 6.00
Kodak
153 Terry Labonte 4.00 8.00
Kellogg's Iron Man
154 Mark Martin 4.00 8.00
Valvoline
155 Ricky Rudd 3.00 6.00
Tide
156 Kevin Lepage 3.00 6.00
Primestar
157 Jeff Burton 3.00 6.00
Exide
158 Jeff Burton 6.00 15.00
Exide Gold
159 Bobby Hamilton 3.00 6.00
Kodak
160 Wally Dallenbach 3.00 6.00
Hendrick
161 Wally Dallenbach 4.00 8.00
Hendrick Gold
162 Ernie Irvan 4.00 8.00
M&M's
163 Ernie Irvan 8.00 12.00
M&M's Gold
164 Bobby Hamilton 3.00 6.00
Kodak
165 Brett Bodine 3.00 6.00
Paychex
166 Brett Bodine 3.00 6.00
Paychex
167 Ken Schrader 3.00 6.00
etree
168 Ken Schrader 4.00 8.00
Petree Gold
169 Bill Elliott 4.00 8.00
Drive Thru
170 Bill Elliott 10.00 15.00
Drive Thru Gold
171 Jerry Nadeau 4.00 8.00
Dexter's Laboratory
172 Brett Bodine 3.00 6.00
Paychex
173 Brett Bodine 3.00 6.00
Paychex Gold
174 Wally Dallenbach 3.00 6.00
Hendrick
175 Ernie Irvan 3.00 6.00
M&M's
176 Kenny Wallace 3.00 6.00
Square D
177 Kenny Wallace 4.00 8.00
Square D Gold
178 Robert Pressley 3.00 6.00
Jasper
179 Sterling Marlin 5.00 10.00
John Wayne
180 Sterling Marlin 10.00 25.00
John Wayne Gold
181 Bobby Hamilton 3.00 6.00
Kodak
182 Ricky Rudd 4.00 8.00
Tide
183 Jimmy Spencer 3.00 6.00
TCE
184 Jerry Nadeau 3.00 6.00
Dexter's Laboratory
185 Robert Pressly 3.00 6.00
Jasper
186 Mark Martin 4.00 8.00
Valvoline
187 Derrike Cope 4.00 8.00
Bryan
188 Ken Schrader 3.00 6.00
APR Blue
189 Sterling Marlin 3.00 6.00
Sabco
190 Darrell Waltrip 4.00 8.00
Big K
191 Jeff Burton 4.00 8.00
Exide
192 Darrell Waltrip 10.00 15.00
Big K Gold
193 Ken Schrader 3.00 6.00
APR Maroon
194 Wally Dallenbach 3.00 6.00
Hendrick
195 Ernie Irvan 4.00 8.00
M&M's
196 Sterling Marlin 5.00 10.00
John Wayne
197 Darrell Waltrip 4.00 8.00
Big K

1999 Racing Champions Toys R Us Chrome Chase 1:64

These Chrome plated cars were packaged in special Toys "R" Us blister pack and were only available at Toys "R" Us.

4 Bobby Hamilton 2.00 5.00
Kodak
5 Terry Labonte 4.00 8.00
Kellogg's
6 Mark Martin 4.00 8.00
Valvoline
9 Jerry Nadeau 2.00 5.00
Dexter's Laboratory
10 Ricky Rudd 2.00 5.00
Tide
11 Brett Bodine 2.00 5.00
Paychex
23 Jimmy Spencer 2.00 5.00
TCE
25 Wally Dallenbach 2.00 5.00
Hendrick
33 Ken Schrader 2.00 5.00
Petree
36 Ernie Irvan 4.00 8.00
M&M's
55 Kenny Wallace 2.00 5.00
Square D
94 Bill Elliott 4.00 8.00
Drive Thru
99 Jeff Burton 2.50 6.00
Exide

1999 Racing Champions Trackside 1:64

These 1:64 cars came in a special "Trackside" clamshell type package. They were distributed primarily at race events at the track. The production run for each was 4999 pieces.

9 Jerry Nadeau 7.50 20.00
Atlanta Braves
9 Jerry Nadeau 10.00 20.00
Dexter's Laboratory
9 Jerry Nadeau 10.00 20.00
WCW nWo
23 Jimmy Spencer 12.50 25.00
No Bull
43 John Andretti 10.00 20.00
STP
45 Adam Petty 10.00 25.00
Spree
94 Bill Elliott 12.50 25.00
McDonald's Drive Thru
99 Crew Chief Club 7.50 15.00

1999 Racing Champions Trackside Platinum 1:64

The Platinum Trackside cars were packaged in a clamshell with the name "Trackside Platinum" clearly printed on the packaging. Each carried an announced print run of 2499.

9 Jerry Nadeau 12.50 25.00
Dexter's Lab
9 Jerry Nadeau 12.50 25.00
WCW nWo
23 Jimmy Spencer 15.00 30.00
No Bull

1999 Racing Champions Under the Lights 1:64

These 1:64 scale cars feature special color chrome paint to give that "Under the Lights" appearance. Most were issued in a clear clamshell packaging along with a trading card featuring foil highlights. Some were also issued as 2-car sets instead of just one.

4 Bobby Hamilton 4.00 8.00
Kodak
5 Terry Labonte 8.00 12.00
Kellogg's
6 Mark Martin 8.00 12.00
Valvoline
6 Mark Martin 12.00 20.00
Valvoline 2-car set
6 Mark Martin 4.00 10.00
Valvoline Ames/5000
6 Mark Martin 12.00 20.00
Valvoline Eagle One 2-car set
6 Mark Martin 12.00 20.00
Valvoline Zerex 2-car set
10 Ricky Rudd 4.00 8.00
Tide
12 Jeremy Mayfield 4.00 8.00
Mobil 1
21 Elliott Sadler 4.00 8.00
Citgo
43 John Andretti 4.00 8.00
STP
94 Bill Elliott 8.00 12.00
McDonald's Drive Thru
94 Bill Elliott 12.00 20.00
McDonald's Drive Thru
2-car set
99 Jeff Burton 8.00 12.00
Exide
99 Jeff Burton 12.00 20.00
Exide 2-car set

1999 Racing Champions 24K Gold 1:64

This is a special series produced by Racing Champions to celebrate their 10th anniversary. It parallels the regular 1998 1:64 scale series. Each car is a limited edition of 9,999. Each car is also plated in gold chrome and contains a serial number on its chassis.

4 Bobby Hamilton 7.50 15.00
Kodak Advantix
5 Terry Labonte 10.00 25.00
Kellogg's
6 Joe Bessey 7.50 15.00
Power Team
6 Mark Martin 15.00 30.00
Valvoline
9 Jerry Nadeau 7.50 15.00
Dexter's Laboratory
9 Jeff Burton 7.50 15.00
Track Gear
10 Ricky Rudd 7.50 15.00
Tide
10 Ricky Rudd 7.50 15.00
Tide Happy Holiday
11 Brett Bodine 5.00 12.00
Paychex
16 Kevin Lepage 7.50 15.00
Primestar
25 Wally Dallenbach 7.50 15.00
Hendrick
26 Johnny Benson 7.50 15.00
Cheerios
33 Ken Schrader 7.50 15.00
Petree
36 Ernie Irvan 10.00 20.00
M&M's
42 Joe Nemechek 7.50 15.00
BellSouth
77 Robert Pressley 7.50 15.00
Jasper
97 Chad Little 6.00 15.00
John Deere
99 Jeff Burton 7.50 15.00
Exide

1999 Racing Champions 24K Gold Stock Rods 1:64

1G Bobby Hamilton 4.00 8.00
Kodak
2G Terry Labonte 6.00 15.00
Kellogg's
3G Mark Martin 6.00 15.00
Valvoline
4G Ricky Rudd 6.00 15.00
Tide
5G Bill Elliott 6.00 15.00
Drive Thru
6G Ernie Irvan 6.00 15.00
M&M's

1999 Racing Champions 3-D Originals 1:64

This set features a hood open car with a 3-D card.

5 Terry Labonte 6.00 15.00
Kellogg's
6 Mark Martin 6.00 15.00
Valvoline
12 Jeremy Mayfield 4.00 8.00
Mobil 1
94 Bill Elliott 6.00 15.00
Drive Thru

2000 Racing Champions Preview 1:64

6 Mark Martin 3.00 6.00
Valvoline
7 Michael Waltrip 3.00 6.00
Nation's Rent
17 Matt Kenseth 4.00 8.00
DeWalt
22 Ward Burton 3.00 6.00
Caterpillar
22 Ward Burton 3.00 6.00
Cat Dealers
33 Joe Nemechek 3.00 6.00
Oakwood Homes
36 Ernie Irvan 3.00 6.00
M&M's '99
66 Darrell Waltrip 3.00 6.00
Big K Flames
75 Wally Dallenbach 3.00 6.00
Power Puff Girls
99 Jeff Burton 3.00 6.00
Exide
Y2K NDA 3.00 6.00
Ford Taurus

2000 Racing Champions Premier Preview 1:64

This series was issued in a red and black checkered blister pack design with a the NASCAR 2000 logo. A Racing Champions collector's card was also packaged with the car as well as a rain delay car cover. Each car features an opening hood an[d] piece wheels.

5 Terry Labonte 5.00 1
Kellogg's
6 Mark Martin 5.00 1
Valvoline
14 Mike Bliss 5.00 1
Conseco
17 Matt Kenseth 5.00 1
DeWalt
22 Ward Burton 5.00 1
Caterpillar
66 Darrell Waltrip 4.00
Big K
66 Darrell Waltrip 5.00 1
Big K Flames
99 Jeff Burton 5.00 1
Exide

2000 Racing Champions 1:64

1 Dennis Setzer 7.50 1
Mopar SuperTruck
Promo in PVC Box
4 Bobby Hamilton 2.00
Kodak
5 Terry Labonte 2.50
Kellogg's
5 Wix Filters 3-car Promo set in box 20.00 4
stock car, dragster and supertruck
5 Terry Labonte 2.50
Froot Loops CherryBerry
5 Terry Labonte 10.00 2
Froot Loops CherryBerry
Chrome/999
6 Mark Martin 2.50
Eagle One
6 Mark Martin 2.50
Valvoline
6 Mark Martin 15.00 3
Valvoline Chrome/999
6 Mark Martin 2.50
Valvoline No Bull
6 Mark Martin 2.00
Valvoline Promo in bag
6 Mark Martin 2.50
Valvoline Stars&Stripes
6 Mark Martin 2.50
Zerex
7 Michael Waltrip 2.00
Nation's Rent
8 Bobby Hillin 6.00 1
Kleenex Promo
9 Jeff Burton 2.00
Exide Promo in clear box
9 Jeff Burton 20.00 3
Northern Light Promo
9 Stacy Compton 7.50 1
Compton Promo in PVC Box
12 Jeremy Mayfield 2.00
Mobil 1
13 Robby Gordon 10.00 2
Turtle Wax Promo in bag
14 Mike Bliss 2.00
Conseco
14 Rick Crawford 5.00 1
Milwaukee Electric
SuperTruck Promo
16 Kevin Lepage 2.50
familyclick.com
17 Matt Kenseth 4.00
DeWalt
17 Matt Kenseth 4.00
DeWalt 24 Volt
18 Joe Ruttman 7.50 1
Dana SuperTruck
Promo in PVC box
20 Scott Wimmer 25.00 4
AT&T Promo
22 Ward Burton 2.00
Caterpillar
22 Ward Burton 15.00 3
Caterpillar Chrome/999
22 Ward Burton 2.00
Caterpillar Promo
in large window box
25 Jerry Nadeau 2.00
Holigan
25 Randy Tolsma 6.00 1
SuperGard SuperTruck
Promo in PVC box
26 Jimmy Spencer 2.00
Big K
40 Sterling Marlin 2.00
Coors Light Brooks & Dunn
40 Sterling Marlin 2.00
Sabco
42 Kenny Irwin 2.00
BellSouth
43 Steve Grissom 7.50 1
Dodge SuperTruck
Promo in PVC box
43 Pro-Cuts Promo in window box 15.00 2
50 Tony Roper 8.00 2
Dr.Pepper 2-car promo set in box
57 Jason Keller 4.00
Excedrin Promo box
57 Jason Keller 3.00
Excedrin Migraine Promo box
60 Mark Martin 2.50
Winn Dixie
60 Mark Martin 15.00 3
Winn Dixie Chrome/999
60 Mark Martin 10.00 2
Winn Dixie Farewell Promo
75 Wally Dallenbach 15.00 2
Rotozip Promo
75 Wally Dallenbach 2.50
Scooby Doo
75 Wally Dallenbach 2.50
WCW
77 Robert Pressley 8.00 1
Jasper Promo
77 Robert Pressley 10.00 2

er Federal Mogul
ar Promo set
y Compton 6.00 15.00
Cola SuperTruck
no in PVC box
Nemechek 5.00 12.00
ularOne Promo
errier 8.00 20.00
Bros Promo
Bickle 6.00 12.00
eyes Promo
indow box
e Blaney 1.50 4.00
oco Promo in box
ve Blaney 2.50 6.00
oco Sprint Car
no in box
ve Blaney 2.50 6.00
aco Pontiac
no in box
e Blaney 5.00 12.00
nens Promo
d Little 1.50 4.00
n Deere
n Sawyer 6.00 10.00
ol Promo
Burton 15.00 30.00
e Chrome/999
hael Waltrip 2.50 6.00
on's Promo
rry Labonte 15.00 30.00
Club Promo
kshot Jones 1.50 4.00
eez-It
y Sutton 12.00 30.00
axone Promo
oxed 12-car set/2500 20.00 40.00
nilton
lak
onte
ogg's
tin
voline
trip
on
yfield
bil
s
seco
seth
Walt
ton
erpillar
ton
Dealers
nechek
wood
lenbach
toon
ton
de
oxed 12-car set/2500 20.00 50.00
ne Trials
nilton
lak
ss
nseco
ssley
per
le
ere
seth
Walt
dler
go
n
lSouth
ney
oco
onte
logg's
rtin
voline
rton

rton
de

2000 Racing Champions 5-Pack 1:64

5-packs were issued in the usual blister and box ...nation just like the Fan Appreciation sets. However, the ...ging was printed with a brown and white photograph of a ...cene. Some sets included the NASCAR 2000 logo while ... feature the older NASCAR logo. Some cars were only ... in these 5-packs. We've cataloged each set in order ...g with the top car down to the bottom. No issue numbers ...sed for 2000.

5. Terry Labonte 7.50 20.00
oot Loops
Sterling Marlin
ooks&Dunn
Mark Martin
voline
Sterling Marlin
am Sabco
Mark Martin
gle One
6. Mark Martin 7.50 20.00
gle One
Mark Martin
voline
. Jeff Burton
uce Lee
. Ernie Irvan
&M's
. Jeff Burton
Bull
6. Mark Martin 6.00 15.00
voline
. Joe Nemechek
kwood Homes
. Dave Blaney
timate
. Robert Pressley
sper
. Wally Dallenbach
rtoon Network

NNO 6. Mark Marttin 6.00 15.00
Valvoline/33. Joe Nemecheck.Oakwood Homes/99. Jeff Burton
Citgo/2K Ford/55. Kenny Wallace
Square D
NNO 6. Mark Martin 7.50 20.00
Valvoline
99. Jeff Burton
Citgo
75. Wally Dallenbach
WCW
7. Michael Waltrip
Nation's Rent
40. Sterling Marlin
Brooks&Dunn
NNO 9. Jerry Nadeau 6.00 15.00
Dexter's Lab
9. No Driver
Cartoon Network Pink
9. Jerry Nadeau
Jetsons
9. Jerry Nadeau
Goldberg
WCW
2K. Red,White & Blue Ford
NNO 21. Elliott Sadler 10.00 20.00
Citgo 5-car set
Five different paint schemes
NNO 22. Ward Burton 6.00 15.00
Caterpillar
17 Matt Kenseth
DeWalt
5 Terry Labonte
Kellogg's
12 Jeremy Mayfield
Mobil 1
40. Sterling Marlin
John Wayne
NNO 42. Kenny Irwin 10.00 25.00
BellSouth
21. Elliott Sadler
Citgo
9. Stacy Compton
Compton
34. No Driver Association
50. Tony Roper
Dr.Pepper
NNO 57. Jason Keller 6.00 15.00
Excedrin
60. Geoff Bodine
Power Team
36. No Driver Assoc.
Stanley
60. Mark Martin
Winn Dixie Flames
22. Ward Burton
Caterpillar
NNO NASCAR SuperTrucks 6.00 15.00
86. Stacy Compton
Royal Crown
43. Jimmy Hensley
Dodge
24. Jack Sprague
GMAC
50. Greg Biffle
Grainger
2. No Driver Association
ASE
NNO 99. Jeff Burton 6.00 15.00
Citgo
14. Mike Bliss
Conseco
66. Darrell Waltrip
K-mart Route 66
97. Chad Little
John Deere
4. Bobby Hamilton
Kodak

2000 Racing Champions Buss Fuses Promos 1:64

For the second year Buss Fuses sponsored a set of die-cast cars issued in clam-shell packages with two small boxes of fuses. Racing Champions produced the cars and the cardboard backing was printed in yellow for the basic promos and printed in white for NAPA promos.

5 Terry Labonte 4.00 8.00
Kellogg's
6 Mark Martin 5.00 10.00
Valvoline NAPA
8 Bill Lester 4.00 10.00
Dodge SuperTruck
10 Johnny Benson 3.00 6.00
Valvoline
12 Jeremy Mayfield 3.00 6.00
Mobil 1
18 Dana SuperTruck 4.00 10.00
18 Robert Pressley 4.00 10.00
Dodge SuperTruck
22 Ward Burton 3.00 6.00
Caterpillar
22 Ward Burton 4.00 10.00
Cat Rental
36 Ken Schrader 4.00 8.00
M&M's
43 Steve Grissom 4.00 10.00
Dodge SuperTruck
86 RC Cola SuperTruck 4.00 10.00
90 Lance Norick 4.00 10.00
Express SuperTruck
99 Jeff Burton 4.00 10.00
Exide NAPA

2000 Racing Champions High Octane 1:64

The High Octane series was packaged in a red and black blister with a Racing Champions card. Each car is painted in the race team colors, but is a replica of a typical street car not a NASCAR Winston Cup car.

5 Terry Labonte 2.00 5.00
Kellogg's
12 Jeremy Mayfield 2.00 5.00
Mobil 1
17 Matt Kenseth 4.00 8.00
DeWalt
25 Jerry Nadeau 2.00 5.00
Holligan Homes
99 Jeff Burton 2.00 5.00
Exide

2000 Racing Champions Model Kits 1:64

This set was issued in a large box with a clear blister package inside. The car had to be assembled by the collector and the package comes complete with all parts and even the needed screwdriver.

5 Terry Labonte 6.00 12.00
Kellogg's
6 Mark Martin 6.00 12.00
Valvoline
22 Ward Burton 6.00 12.00
Caterpillar
99 Jeff Burton 6.00 12.00
Exide

2000 Racing Champions Nascar Rules 1:64

Introduced in 1999, NASCAR Rules returned in 2000 with the new Ford, Pontiac, and Chevy body styles featuring exacting car detail and complete team graphics. Packaged in a large all-plastic clamshell, each piece included a display stand and a collector card that explains some of the technical rules that govern NASCAR. These 1:64 scale replicas have an opening hood with detailed engine, opening trunk with fuel cell, and a replica NASCAR template.

5 Terry Labonte 6.00 12.00
Kellogg's Preview
6 Mark Martin 6.00 12.00
Valvoline
6 Mark Martin 20.00 40.00
Valvoline Chrome/999
6 Mark Martin 6.00 12.00
Valvoline Preview
7 Michael Waltrip 5.00 10.00
Nation's Rent
14 Mike Bliss 5.00 10.00
Conseco
17 Matt Kenseth 10.00 20.00
DeWalt
22 Ward Burton 5.00 10.00
Caterpillar Preview
22 Ward Burton 10.00 25.00
Caterpillar Chrome/999
22 Ward Burton 6.00 12.00
Cat Dealers
22 Ward Burton 12.50 30.00
Cat Dealers Chrome/999
33 Joe Nemechek 5.00 10.00
Oakwood Homes
55 Kenny Wallace 5.00 10.00
Square D
93 Dave Blaney 4.00 10.00
Amoco
97 Chad Little 4.00 10.00
John Deere
99 Jeff Burton 5.00 10.00
Exide

2000 Racing Champions Pit Crew 1:64

The Pit Crew series is a look at what it is like on NASCAR's pit row. Each blister pack features a 1:64 scale car with replica pit wagon and small pit crew figures. All are mounted to a pit row base that electronically simulates the sounds heard in the pits during a pit stop.

4 Bobby Hamilton 6.00 15.00
Kodak
5 Terry Labonte 8.00 20.00
Kellogg's
6 Mark Martin 8.00 20.00
Valvoline
6 Mark Martin 10.00 20.00
Valvoline Chrome/999
7 Michael Waltrip 6.00 15.00
Naions Rent
12 Jeremy Mayfield 6.00 15.00
Mobil 1
17 Matt Kenseth 8.00 20.00
DeWalt
17 Matt Kenseth 10.00 20.00
DeWalt 24 Volt
17 Matt Kenseth 15.00 25.00
DeWalt 24 Volt Chrome/999
55 Kenny Wallace 6.00 15.00
Square D
97 Chad Little 6.00 15.00
John Deere
99 Jeff Burton 8.00 20.00
Exide
99 Jeff Burton 10.00 20.00
Exide Chrome/999

2000 Racing Champions Premier 1:64

4 Bobby Hamilton 3.00 6.00
Kodak
5 Terry Labonte 4.00 8.00
Froot Loops CherryBerry
5 Terry Labonte 4.00 8.00
Kellogg's
6 Mark Martin 4.00 8.00
Valvoline
6 Mark Martin 4.00 8.00
Valvoline No Bull
6 Mark Martin 4.00 8.00
Zerex
7 Michael Waltrip 3.00 6.00
Nation's Rent
12 Jeremy Mayfield 3.00 6.00
Mobil 1
14 Mike Bliss 3.00 6.00
Conseco
16 Kevin Lepage 3.00 6.00
FamilyClick.com
17 Matt Kenseth 4.00 10.00
DeWalt
17 Matt Kenseth 5.00 10.00
DeWalt 24 Volt
22 Ward Burton 3.00 6.00
Caterpillar
22 Ward Burton 3.00 6.00
Caterpillar No Bull
22 Ward Burton 4.00 8.00
Caterpillar Bud Shoot Out
22 Ward Burton 12.50 25.00
Caterpillar Dealers
Bud Shoot Out Chrome
40 Sterling Marlin 3.00 6.00
Sabco
42 Kenny Irwin 3.00 6.00
BellSouth
93 Dave Blaney 2.50 6.00
Amoco
97 Chad Little 2.50 6.00
John Deere
99 Jeff Burton 4.00 8.00
Exide
99 Jeff Burton 4.00 8.00
Exide No Bull

2000 Racing Champions Stock Rods 1:64

1 Mark Martin 3.00 8.00
Valvoline 1968 Mustang
2 Jeff Burton 3.00 8.00
Exide 1969 Cougar
3 Matt Kenseth 3.00 8.00
DeWalt 1956 Ford
4 Mark Martin 3.00 8.00
Valvoline 1940 Ford
5 Jeff Burton 3.00 8.00
Exide 1967 Mustang
6 Terry Labonte 3.00 8.00
Kellogg's 1950 Oldsmobile
7 Ward Burton 3.00 8.00
Caterpillar Bud Shoot Out
1967 Firebird
8 Ward Burton 3.00 8.00
Caterpillar 1966 Pontiac GTO
14 Chad Little 5.00 12.00
John Deere Promo
1941 Lincoln

2000 Racing Champions Time Trial 1:64

New for 2000, Racing Champions introduced a series that focuses on the testing and development of NASCAR stock cars rather than the final race-ready cars. These Time Trial stock car replicas sport just a coat of gray primer and the team number and sponsor. They also feature opening hoods and two piece tires. Each was packaged in a blister along with a die cut card.

5 Terry Labonte 5.00 10.00
Kellogg's

6 Mark Martin 5.00 10.00
Valvoline
17 Matt Kenseth 6.00 12.00
DeWalt
22 Ward Burton 4.00 8.00
Caterpillar
99 Jeff Burton 5.00 10.00
Exide

2000 Racing Champions Under the Lights 1:64

Each of these "Under the Lights" die-cast pieces were issued in a Racing Champions solid box as 2-car sets - one car in regular paint and the other in chrome. A small car cover was also included with each set.

2K Ford Silver Chrome 5.00 12.00
Chevy Red Chrome
5 Terry Labonte 6.00 15.00
Kellogg's
6 Mark Martin 6.00 15.00
Valvoline/2288
99 Jeff Burton 6.00 15.00
Exide/2596

2000 Racing Champions War Paint 1:64

5 Terry Labonte 10.00 25.00
Kellogg's 2-car set
6 Mark Martin 4.00 8.00
Valvoline
6 Mark Martin 10.00 25.00
Valvoline 2-car set
7 Michael Waltrip 4.00 8.00
Nations Rent
22 Ward Burton 8.00 20.00
Caterpillar 2-car set
22 Ward Burton 4.00 8.00
Caterpillar
42 Kenny Irwin 4.00 8.00
BellSouth
93 Dave Blaney 3.00 8.00
Amoco
99 Jeff Burton 4.00 8.00
Exide
99 Jeff Burton 8.00 20.00
Exide 2-car set

2001 Racing Champions Preview 1:64

5 Terry Labonte 5.00 10.00
Kellogg's
5 Terry Labonte 10.00 20.00
Kellogg's Chrome
5 Terry Labonte 5.00 10.00
Frosted Flakes 2000
10 Johnny Benson 5.00 10.00
Valvoline
10 Johnny Benson 10.00 20.00
Valvoline Chrome
12 Jeremy Mayfield 5.00 10.00
Mobil 1
12 Jeremy Mayfield 10.00 20.00
Mobil 1 Chrome
12 Jeremy Mayfield 25.00 50.00
Mobil 1 Autographed
12 Jeremy Mayfield 10.00 25.00
Mobil 1 Layin' Rubber
12 Jeremy Mayfield 15.00 30.00
Mobil 1 Race Rubber
14 Ron Hornaday 5.00 10.00
Conseco
22 Ward Burton 5.00 10.00
Caterpillar
22 Ward Burton 10.00 20.00
Caterpillar Chrome
22 Ward Burton 25.00 50.00
Caterpillar Autographed
22 Ward Burton 10.00 25.00
Caterpillar Layin' Rubber
36 Ken Schrader 4.00 8.00
M&M's
36 Ken Schrader 10.00 25.00
M&M's Layin' Rubber
55 Bobby Hamilton 4.00 8.00
Square D
55 Bobby Hamilton 20.00 50.00
Square D Autographed
55 Bobby Hamilton 10.00 20.00
Square D Layin' Rubber
55 Bobby Hamilton 4.00 8.00
Square D Lightning
92 Stacy Compton 4.00 8.00
Compton
92 Stacy Compton 10.00 20.00
Compton Chrome
93 Dave Blaney 3.00 8.00
Amoco
93 Dave Blaney 8.00 20.00
Amoco Chrome
NNO Dodge Test Car 5.00 10.00

2001 Racing Champions Premier Preview 1:64

5 Terry Labonte 6.00 12.00
Kellogg's
5 Terry Labonte 12.50 25.00
Kellogg's Chrome
5 Terry Labonte 6.00 12.00
Kellogg's Tony
5 Terry Labonte 15.00 40.00
Kellogg's Tony
Layin' Rubber
6 Mark Martin 6.00 12.00

Zerex 2000
10 Johnny Benson Valvoline 6.00 12.00
12 Jeremy Mayfield Mobil 1 6.00 12.00
12 Jeremy Mayfield Mobil 1 Autograph 25.00 50.00
12 Jeremy Mayfield Mobil 1 Chrome 12.50 25.00
12 Jeremy Mayfield Mobil 1 Race Rubber 20.00 40.00
12 Jeremy Mayfield Mobil 1 Real Steel 40.00 80.00
12 Jeremy Mayfield Mobil 1 Layin' Rubber 12.50 30.00
17 Matt Kenseth DeWalt 2000 6.00 12.00

2001 Racing Champions 1:64

1 Ted Musgrave Mopar SuperTruck in Tomar PVC box 7.50 15.00
2 Scott Riggs ASE SuperTruck in Tomar Motorsports PVC box 15.00 30.00
5 Terry Labonte Frosted Flakes 2000 3.00 8.00
5 Terry Labonte Frosted Flakes Promo black windows 3.00 8.00
5 Terry Labonte Kellogg's 3.00 8.00
5 Terry Labonte Kellogg's Autographed 40.00 80.00
5 Terry Labonte Kellogg's Chrome/1500 7.50 15.00
5 Terry Labonte Monsters Inc.Promo 4.00 10.00
7 Randy LaJoie Kleenex Busch 3.00 6.00
7 Randy LaJoie Kleenex Promo 4.00 8.00
8 Willy T. Ribbs Dodge SuperTruck in Tomar PVC box 15.00 30.00
10 Johnny Benson Valvoline 3.00 8.00
10 Johnny Benson Valvoline AUTO 25.00 60.00
10 Johnny Benson Valvoline Chrome/1500 6.00 12.00
10 Johnny Benson Valvoline Race Rubber 7.50 15.00
10 Johnny Benson Valvoline Mrs.Smith's Promo 5.00 10.00
11 Brett Bodine Ralph's 4.00 10.00
12 Jeremy Mayfield Mobil 1 2.50 6.00
12 Jeremy Mayfield Mobil Autographed 40.00 80.00
12 Jeremy Mayfield Mobil Chrome/1500 6.00 12.50
12 Jeremy Mayfield Mobil Layin' Rubber 7.50 15.00
12 Jeremy Mayfield Mobil Race Rubber 10.00 20.00
12 Jeremy Mayfield Mobil 1 Sony 4.00 10.00
13 Hermie Sadler Virginia Lottery Promo 15.00 30.00
14 Ron Hornaday Conseco 2.50 6.00
14 Ron Hornaday Conseco Layin' Rubber/500 6.00 12.00
18 Dave Heitzhaus Pro Hardware Promo 6.00 12.00
21 Elliott Sadler Motorcraft 3.00 8.00
21 Elliott Sadler Motorcraft Layin' Rubber 7.50 15.00
22 Ward Burton Caterpillar 3.00 8.00
22 Ward Burton Caterpillar Autographed
22 Ward Burton Caterpillar Chrome/1500 7.50 15.00
22 Ward Burton Caterpillar Layin' Rubber 10.00 20.00
22 Ward Burton Caterpillar Race Rubber 10.00 20.00
22 Ward Burton Caterpillar Promo 5.00 12.00
22 Ward Burton Caterpillar War-Chrome/1500 7.50 15.00
22 Ward Burton aterpillar The Winston 3.00 8.00
22 Ward Burton Caterpillar Winston Autographed
22 Ward Burton Cat WB Fan Club Promo in PVC Box 5.00 10.00
25 Jerry Nadeau UAW 3.00 8.00
25 Jerry Nadeau UAW Chrome/1500 6.00 12.00
25 Jerry Nadeau UAW Race Rubber 7.50 15.00
26 Jimmy Spencer K-Mart 2.50 6.00
26 Jimmy Spencer K-Mart Layin' Rubber 6.00 15.00
26 Jimmy Spencer K-Mart Race Rubber 7.50 20.00
26 Jimmy Spencer K-Mart Grinch 10.00 20.00
28 Brad Baker Whitetails Unlimited Promo 7.50 15.00
34 David Green AFG Glass 2.50 6.00
36 Hank Parker Jr. GNC 3.00 8.00
36 Hank Parker Jr. GNC Promo in box 3.00 8.00
36 Ken Schrader M&M's 3.00 8.00
36 Ken Schrader M&M's AUTO 40.00 80.00
36 Ken Schrader M&M's Layin' Rubber 7.50 15.00
36 Ken Schrader M&M's July 4th 4.00 10.00
36 Ken Schrader M&M's July 4th Race Rubber 10.00 20.00
36 Ken Schrader Snickers 4.00 10.00
36 Ken Schrader Snickers Chrome/1500 5.00 10.00
36 Ken Schrader Snickers Cruncher Promo 5.00 10.00
38 Christian Elder Great Clips Promo 6.00 15.00
40 Sterling Marlin Sterling 2.50 6.00
40 Sterling Marlin Sterling Chrome/1500 7.50 20.00
43 Jay Sauter Morton Salt Promo 18.00 30.00
43 Jay Sauter Quality Farm Promo 5.00 12.00
48 Kenny Wallace Goulds Pumps Promo 20.00 50.00
51 Donnie Neuenberger IHOP SuperTruck Promo 7.50 15.00
55 Bobby Hamilton Square D 2.50 6.00
55 Bobby Hamilton Square D Chrome/1500 5.00 10.00
55 Bobby Hamilton Square D AUTO 25.00 60.00
55 Bobby Hamilton Square D Lightning 2.50 6.00
55 Bobby Hamilton Square D Lightning Autographed 25.00 60.00
55 Bobby Hamilton Square D Lightning Layin' Rubber 6.00 15.00
55 Brad Leighton Burnham Boilers Promo 5.00 10.00
57 Jason Keller Albertsons 2.50 6.00
57 Jason Keller Albertsons Promo 3.00 6.00
59 Rich Bickle Kingsford Trail's Best Promo 5.00 12.00
60 Travis Kvapil Cat Rental SuperTruck Promo in window box 6.00 15.00
63 Shane Hall Lance's Promo in box 4.00 8.00
66 Todd Bodine K-Mart 2.50 6.00
66 Todd Bodine K-Mart Chrome/1500 5.00 10.00
66 Tim Fedewa Phillips 66 2.50 6.00
77 Robert Pressley Jasper Promo box 4.00 10.00
87 Joe Nemechek Cellular 2.50 6.00
90 Lance Norick AB Chioce SuperTruck Promo 20.00 35.00
90 Hut Stricklin Hills Bros.Promo 20.00 35.00
92 Stacy Compton Compton 2.50 6.00
92 Stacy Compton Compton Autographed
92 Stacy Compton Compton Chrome/1500 5.00 10.00
92 Stacy Compton Compton Race Rubber 7.50 20.00
92 Stacy Compton Kodiak Promo 6.00 15.00
92 Jimmie Johnson xcedrin Cooling Pads Promo BX 12.50 25.00
92 Jimmie Johnson Excedrin PM Promo in box 4.00 10.00
93 Dave Blaney Amoco 2.50 6.00
93 Dave Blaney Amoco Chrome/1500 5.00 12.00
93 Dave Blaney Amoco Layin' Rubber 7.50 15.00
93 Dave Blaney Amoco Race Rubber 7.50 20.00
93 Dave Blaney Amoco Avenger Promo in box 3.00 6.00
93 Dave Blaney Amoco Charger Promo in box 3.00 6.00
93 Dave Blaney Amoco Pick-up Promo in box 3.00 6.00
93 Dave Blaney Amoco Viper Promo in box 3.00 6.00
93 Dave Blaney Amoco Siemens Promo 5.00 10.00
98 Elton Sawyer Auburn U. Promo 7.50 15.00
98 Elton Sawyer U.Connecticut Promo 7.50 15.00
98 Elton Sawyer East Carolina U. Promo 7.50 15.00
98 Elton Sawyer Georgia U. Promo 7.50 15.00
98 Elton Sawyer Illinois U. Promo 7.50 15.00
98 Elton Sawyer Kansas St.U. Promo 7.50 15.00
98 Elton Sawyer Michigan Promo 7.50 15.00
98 Elton Sawyer Miami U. Promo 7.50 15.00
98 Elton Sawyer Nebraska U. Promo 7.50 15.00
98 Elton Sawyer N.Carolina Promo 7.50 15.00
98 Elton Sawyer N.Carolina St. Promo 7.50 15.00
98 Elton Sawyer Purdue U. Promo 7.50 15.00
98 Elton Sawyer Tennessee U. Promo 7.50 15.00
98 Elton Sawyer Wisconsin U. Promo 7.50 15.00
98 Elton Sawyer Starter 7.50 15.00
01 Bell South Peach Bowl Promo/5000 12.50 30.00
01 Jason Leffler Cingular 4.00 10.00
01 Jason Leffler Cingular Layin' Rubber/500 10.00 20.00
01 Jason Leffler Cingular Special Olympics Promo 4.00 10.00
NNO Dodge Inaug.Season/1200 0-car set 50.00 80.00
lliott Dodge
twood Dodge
urton Caterpillar
arlin Coors
ndretti Cheerios
ones Georgia Pac./ Petty
Sprint/ Blaney
Amoco/ Compton
Kodiak/ Leffler
Cingular
NNO Dodge Test Car Black 3.00 8.00
NNO Dodge Test Car Gray 3.00 8.00

2001 Racing Champions Premier 1:64

5 Terry Labonte Frosted Flakes 2000 4.00 10.00
5 Terry Labonte Kellogg's 4.00 10.00
5 Terry Labonte Kellogg's Autographed
5 Terry Labonte Kellogg's Chrome/1500 12.00 25.00
5 Terry Labonte Kellogg's Layin' Rubber 10.00 25.00
6 Mark Martin Zerex 2000 4.00 10.00
10 Johnny Benson Valvoline 4.00 10.00
10 Johnny Benson Valvoline Layin' Rubber 10.00 20.00
10 Johnny Benson Valvoline Race Rubber 10.00 20.00
12 Jeremy Mayfield Mobil 1 4.00 10.00
12 Jeremy Mayfield Mobil 1 Autographed 40.00 80.00
12 Jeremy Mayfield Mobil 1 Chrome/1500 7.50 15.00
12 Jeremy Mayfield Mobil 1 Layin' Rubber 10.00 20.00
12 Jeremy Mayfield Mobil 1 Race Rubber 15.00 30.00
12 Jeremy Mayfield Mobil Real Steel 40.00 80.00
17 Matt Kenseth DeWalt Black 4.00 10.00
21 Elliott Sadler Motorcraft 4.00 10.00
22 Ward Burton Caterpillar 4.00 10.00
22 Ward Burton Caterpillar Autographed
22 Ward Burton Caterpillar Race Rubber 12.00 25.00
22 Ward Burton Caterpillar Real Steel 40.00 80.00
22 Ward Burton Caterpillar The Winston 5.00 12.00
25 Jerry Nadeau Uaw 4.00 10.00
25 Jerry Nadeau UAW Chrome/1500 8.00 20.00
25 Jerry Nadeau UAW Layin' Rubber 10.00 25.00
26 Jimmy Spencer K-Mart 4.00 10.00
26 Jimmy Spencer K-Mart Layin' Rubber 7.50 20.00
36 Ken Schrader M&M's 5.00 12.00
36 Ken Schrader M&M's Chrome/1500 8.00 20.00
36 Ken Schrader Snickers 5.00 12.00
36 Ken Schrader Snickers Chrome/1500 7.50 15.00
55 Bobby Hamilton Square D 4.00 10.00
55 Bobby Hamilton Square D Layin' Rubber 7.50 20.00
93 Dave Blaney Amoco 3.00 10.00
93 Dave Blaney Amoco Firesuit
93 Dave Blaney Amoco BP 5.00 12.00
93 Dave Blaney Amoco BP Chrome/1500 6.00 15.00
93 Dave Blaney Amoco BP Race Rubber 12.50 25.00
NNO Dodge Test Car Red 5.00 12.00

2001 Racing Champions 5-Pack 1:64

These cars were issued five at a time together in one large blister package wrapped inside a box. A selection of 5-random 1:64 cars was included in each package which was printed in red and black. We've listed each below beginning with the top car in the package down to the bottom car. No issue numbers were used for 2001. Some cars were only released in these 5-packs.

NNO 10. Johnny Benson Valvoline 6.00 15.00
22. Ward Burton Caterpillar
93. Dave Blaney Amoco
NNO Black Dodge Show car
26. Bobby Hamilton Dr.Pepper
NNO 22. Ward Burton Caterpillar 7.50 20.00
17. Matt Kenseth DeWalt
5. Terry Labonte Kellogg's
12. Jeremy Mayfield Mobil 1
40. Sterling Marlin John Wayne
NNO 36. Ken Schrader Snickers 6.00 15.00
55. Bobby Hamilton Square D
25. Jerry Nadeau UAW
11. Ralph's
7. Cottonelle
NNO 55. Bobby Hamilton Square D 6.00 15.00
66. Todd Bodine Big K Route 66
36. Ken Schrader July 4th
12. Jeremy Mayfield Mobil 1 Sony Wega
25. Jerry Nadeau UAW
NNO 92. Jimmie Johnson Excedrin 15.00 40.00
77. Dave Blaney Jasper
22. Ward Burton Caterpillar
25. Jerry Nadeau UAW
5. Terry Labonte Kellogg's Tony

2001 Racing Champions Model Kits 1:64

5 Terry Labonte Kellogg's 5.00 10.00
10 Johnny Benson Valvoline 5.00 10.00
12 Jeremy Mayfield Mobil 1 4.00 8.00
22 Ward Burton Caterpillar 5.00 10.00
25 Jerry Nadeau Uaw 4.00 8.00
36 Ken Schrader M&M's 4.00 8.00
40 Sterling Marlin Sterling 4.00 8.00
55 Bobby Hamilton Square D 4.00 8.00
99 Jeff Burton Exide 4.00 8.00

2002 Racing Champions 1:64

These cars were issued in a red and black blister package along with a Racing Champions card. It is a continuation of the Chase the Race theme with many cars being issued in chase versions of chrome paint or ones packaged with race used material. The autographed (AUTO below) pieces feature the driver's signature on the card but not the die cast car.

1 Ted Musgrave Mopar Chrysler Financial SuperTruck Promo in bag 5.00 12.00
1 Jimmy Spencer Yellow Freight 2.50 5.00
1 Jimmy Spencer Yellow Freight Tire 10.00 20.00
4 Mike Skinner Kodak Max 3.00 6.00
4 Mike Skinner Kodak Max AUTO 30.00 60.00
5 Ricky Hendrick GMAC 4.00 8.00
5 Terry Labonte Cheez-it 3.00 6.00
5 Terry Labonte Cheez-it AUTO 30.00 80.00
5 Terry Labonte Cheez-it Firesuit/25 60.00 120.00
5 Terry Labonte Cheez-it Promo in plastic bag 5.00 12.00
5 Terry Labonte Got Milk 4.00 10.00
5 Terry Labonte Kellogg's 3.00
5 Terry Labonte Kellogg's Firesuit 60.00 12
5 Terry Labonte Kellogg's Steel 75.00 15
5 Shane Riffel Race Cow Promo 7.50 1
7 Randy LaJoie Kleenex Promo 5.00 1
10 Johnny Benson Eagle One 3.00
10 Johnny Benson Eagle One AUTO
10 Johnny Benson Eagle One Firesuit 40.00 8
10 Johnny Benson Valvoline 2.00
10 Johnny Benson Valvoline Car Cover/500 12.50 2
10 Johnny Benson Valvoline Steel 30.00 6
10 Johnny Benson Valvoline Maxlife 3.00
10 Johnny Benson Zerex 2.50
10 Johnny Benson Zerex AUTO 50.00 10
10 Johnny Benson Zerex Firesuit/25 60.00 12
10 Johnny Benson 100 Yrs.Kentucky BK in 2003 packaging 6.00 1
10 Scott Riggs Nesquik 3.00
10 Scott Riggs Nestle Toll House Halloween in '03 packaging 3.00
11 Brett Bodine Hooters 8.00 2
11 Josh Richeson Smucker's Promo in box 10.00 2
11 Brett Bodine Wells Fargo Promo in box 12.50 3
14 Stacy Compton Conseco 3.00
21 Elliott Sadler Motorcraft 5.00 1
22 Ward Burton Caterpillar 2.00
22 Ward Burton Caterpillar Chrome/1500 6.00 1
22 Ward Burton Caterpillar Flag 4.00
22 Ward Burton Caterpillar Daytona Win 4.00
22 Ward Burton Caterpillar Daytona Win AU/100 30.00 6
22 Ward Burton Caterpillar Daytona Win Chrome/1500 8.00 2
22 Ward Burton Cat Dealers '03 packaging 3.00
22 Ward Burton Cat Dealers Chrome/1500 in 2003 packaging 12.50 2
22 Ward Burton Caterpillar Daytona Win Promo w Track Section 12.50 2
23 Hut Stricklin Hills Bros. 4.00 1
23 Hut Stricklin Hills Bros.Car Cover/500 25.00 5
23 Scott Wimmer Siemens 4.00 1
24 Jack Sprague NETZERO 2.50
25 Jerry Nadeau UAW 2.50
25 Jerry Nadeau UAW AUTO 40.00 8
25 Jerry Nadeau UAW Steel/25 40.00 8
26 Lyndon Amick Dr.Pepper Spider-Man 4.00 1
26 Ron Hornaday Dr.Pepper Promo Error Bobby Hamilton Jr. name on car 15.00 3
26 Joe Nemechek K-Mart 2.00
27 Jamie McMurray Williams 5.00 1
32 Ricky Craven Tide 2.00
32 Ricky Craven Tide AUTO 25.00 6
32 Ricky Craven Tide Car Cover/500 12.50 3
32 Ricky Craven Tide Chrome/1500 10.00 2
32 Ricky Craven Tide Promo 2.50
32 Ricky Craven Tide Clean Breeze 3.00
32 Ricky Craven Tide Kids Promo 6.00 1
33 Mike Wallace AutoLiv 4.00 1
33 Mike Wallace Preen Promo 15.00 3
36 Hank Parker Jr. GNC 2.50
36 Ken Schrader Combos 3.00
36 Ken Schrader Combos AUTO 50.00 8
36 Ken Schrader Combos Firesuit/25 60.00 12
36 Ken Schrader M&M's 3.00

6 Ken Schrader M&M's AUTO		
6 Ken Schrader M&M's Chrome/1500	7.50	20.00
36 Ken Schrader M&M's Car Cover/500	20.00	40.00
36 Ken Schrader M&M's Firesuit	50.00	100.00
36 Ken Schrader M&M's Steel	50.00	100.00
36 Ken Schrader M&M's Promo box	4.00	10.00
36 Ken Schrader M&M's Halloween in 2003 packaging	3.00	8.00
36 Ken Schrader M&M's July 4th	4.00	10.00
36 Ken Schrader M&M's July 4th Promo	4.00	8.00
36 Ken Schrader Pedigree	3.00	8.00
36 Ken Schrader Pedigree Firesuit/25	60.00	120.00
37 Jeff Purvis Purvis	3.00	8.00
40 Sterling Marlin Stars and Stripes Flag	3.00	6.00
43 Richard Petty Garfield	5.00	12.00
46 Frank Kimmel Advance Auto Parts Promo	7.50	15.00
46 Ashton Lewis Civil Air Patrol Promo	8.00	20.00
48 Jimmie Johnson Lowe's	5.00	12.00
48 Jimmie Johnson Lowe's Cover/500	25.00	50.00
48 Jimmie Johnson Lowe's Steel/25		
48 Jimmie Johnson Lowe's First Win	4.00	10.00
48 Jimmie Johnson Lowe's First Win Car Cover/500	20.00	40.00
48 Jimmie Johnson Lowe's Promo w o card	12.50	25.00
48 Jimmie Johnson Lowe's Power of Pride	5.00	12.00
48 Jimmie Johnson Lowe's Power of Pride AUTO		
48 Jimmie Johnson Lowe's Power of Pride Chrome/1500	20.00	35.00
48 Kenny Wallace Stacker 2	4.00	10.00
49 Shawna Robinson BAM	6.00	15.00
55 Bobby Hamilton Schneider White	2.00	5.00
55 Bobby Hamilton Schneider White Chrome/1500	10.00	20.00
55 Bobby Hamilton Schneider White Tire	20.00	40.00
55 Bobby Hamilton Square D	4.00	10.00
55 Bobby Hamilton Square D AUTO	15.00	40.00
55 Bobby Hamilton Square D Flag	2.50	6.00
55 Bobby Hamilton Square D Flag Autographed	25.00	50.00
57 Jason Keller Albertsons	2.50	6.00
57 Jason Keller Albertsons Flag	2.00	5.00
57 Jason Keller Albertsons Flag Promo	2.50	6.00
59 Stacy Compton Johnsonville Promo	7.50	15.00
59 Stacy Compton Kingsford Promo	7.50	15.00
60 Andy Houston Cat Rental SuperTruck Promo in box	10.00	20.00
66 Todd Bodine K-Mart	2.50	6.00
66 Casey Mears Kansas Jayhawks Promo/2500	10.00	20.00
66 Casey Mears Phillips 66	3.00	8.00
77 Dave Blaney Jasper	2.00	5.00
77 Donnie Neuenberger Maryland University Promo in window box	10.00	20.00
77 Dave Blaney Jasper Promo	6.00	12.00
77 Robert Pressley Jasper Flag	2.50	6.00
87 Joe Nemechek Cellular One	2.00	5.00
90 Lance Norick Express SuperTruck Promo	10.00	20.00
93 Bill Hoff Mike's Famous Harley Promo	10.00	20.00
98 Kenny Wallace Stacker 2 in 2003 packaging	5.00	10.00
99 Michael Waltrip Aaron's	2.00	5.00
300 Tim Flock Hagood Bros. Mercury Outboards	5.00	12.00
02 Bristol Motor Speedway Promo in clear box	10.00	20.00
02 Cabela's 250 Promo	5.00	12.00
02 Cabela's Kansas City Promo	6.00	12.00
02 Cabela's Outfitters Promo	6.00	12.00
02 Ricky Craven Milk Chug Promo in clear box	15.00	40.00
02 Kroger 300 SuperTruck Promo	7.50	15.00
02 Kelly Sutton Copaxone Promo box	6.00	15.00

2002 Racing Champions 5-Pack 1:64

1 33. Mike Wallace Autoliv 36. Ken Schrader Combos 23. Scott Wimmer Seimens 22. Ward Burton Caterpillar 5. Terry Labonte Cheez-it	7.50	15.00
2 36. Ken Schrader Combos 22. Ward Burton Caterpillar 55. Bobby Hamilton Scheider 4. Mike Skinner Kodak 5. Terry Labonte Cheez-it	7.50	15.00

2002 Racing Champions Premier 1:64

1 Jimmy Spencer Yellow Freight	4.00	8.00
1 Jimmy Spencer Yellow Freight Steel	40.00	80.00
1 Jimmy Spencer Yellow Freight Tire	20.00	50.00
4 Mike Skinner Kodak	4.00	8.00
5 Terry Labonte Cheez-it	4.00	10.00
5 Terry Labonte Cheez-it AUTO	40.00	100.00
5 Terry Labonte Cheez-it Firesuit	40.00	80.00
5 Terry Labonte Got Milk	6.00	12.00
5 Terry Labonte Kellogg's	4.00	10.00
5 Terry Labonte Kellogg's Firesuit		
5 Terry Labonte Kellogg's Steel		
5 Jack Sprague NetZero	5.00	10.00
10 Johnny Benson Eagle One	4.00	8.00
10 Johnny Benson Eagle One AUTO	40.00	80.00
10 Johnny Benson Eagle One Chrome/1500	10.00	20.00
10 Johnny Benson Eagle One Firesuit	60.00	100.00
10 Johnny Benson Valvoline	4.00	8.00
10 Johnny Benson Valvoline Car Cover/500	20.00	40.00
10 Johnny Benson Zerex	4.00	8.00
10 Johnny Benson Zerex AUTO		
10 Johnny Benson Zerex Cover		
10 Johnny Benson Zerex Firesuit		
10 Johnny Benson 100 Yrs.Kentucky BK in 2003 packaging	6.00	15.00
10 Scott Riggs Nesquik	4.00	8.00
14 Stacy Compton Conseco	4.00	8.00
22 Ward Burton Caterpillar	4.00	8.00
22 Ward Burton Caterpillar Chrome/1500	10.00	20.00
22 Ward Burton Caterpillar Flag	6.00	12.00
22 Ward Burton Caterpillar Promo	5.00	12.00
22 Ward Burton Caterpillar Daytona Win	5.00	10.00
22 Ward Burton Caterpillar Daytona Win AUTO/100	30.00	80.00
22 Ward Burton Caterpillar Daytona Chrome/1500	10.00	20.00
22 Ward Burton Cat Dealers in 2003 packaging	5.00	10.00
23 Hut Stricklin Hills Bros.	7.50	15.00
23 Hut Stricklin Hills Bros. Car Cover/500	15.00	40.00
24 Jack Sprague NETZERO	4.00	8.00
25 Jerry Nadeau UAW	4.00	8.00
25 Jerry Nadeau UAW Steel/25	40.00	80.00
26 Joe Nemechek K-Mart	4.00	8.00
32 Ricky Craven Tide	4.00	8.00
32 Ricky Craven Tide Chrome	10.00	20.00
36 Hank Parker Jr. GNC	4.00	8.00
36 Ken Schrader M&M's	4.00	8.00
36 Ken Schrader M&M's Car Cover/500	20.00	40.00
36 Ken Schrader M&M's Steel	40.00	80.00
36 Ken Schrader M&M's Halloween in '03 packaging	3.00	8.00
36 Ken Schrader M&M's July 4th	5.00	10.00
36 Ken Schrader Pedigree	4.00	10.00
36 Ken Schrader Pedigree AUTO	40.00	80.00
36 Ken Schrader Pedigree Firesuit	40.00	80.00
40 Sterling Marlin Marlin Flag	5.00	10.00
48 Jimmie Johnson Lowe's	6.00	15.00
48 Jimmie Johnson Lowe's Chrome/1500	20.00	50.00
48 Jimmie Johnson Lowe's Car Cover/500	25.00	60.00
48 Jimmie Johnson Lowe's First Win	5.00	12.00
48 Jimmie Johnson Lowe's First Win Car Cover/500	25.00	50.00
48 Jimmie Johnson Lowe's Power of Pride	6.00	15.00
48 Jimmie Johnson Lowe's Power of Pride Chrome/1500	25.00	50.00
48 Jimmie Johnson Lowe's 3-car set	12.50	25.00
55 Bobby Hamilton Schneider White	4.00	8.00
55 Bobby Hamilton Schneider Black	4.00	8.00
55 Bobby Hamilton Schneider Black AUTO		
66 Todd Bodine K-Mart	5.00	12.00
77 Dave Blaney Jasper	4.00	8.00
77 Dave Blaney Jasper Tire	25.00	50.00
98 Kenny Wallace Stacker 2 in 2003 packaging	6.00	12.00
99 Michael Waltrip Aaron's	4.00	8.00

2002 Racing Champions Premier Preview 1:64

This series was issued in a newly designed "wind tunnel" blister pack that actually allows the collector to rotate the car without opening the package. A Racing Champions card was included and some cars were produced with various "chase" versions in keeping with the Chase the Race theme. Each car features an opening hood.

5 Terry Labonte Kellogg's	5.00	10.00
5 Terry Labonte Kellogg's Cover/500	15.00	40.00
5 Terry Labonte Kellogg's Tire	25.00	50.00
10 Johnny Benson Valvoline	4.00	8.00
10 Johnny Benson Valvoline Chrome/1500	7.50	15.00
10 Johnny Benson Valvoline Firesuit		
22 Ward Burton Caterpillar	4.00	8.00
22 Ward Burton Caterpillar Cover/500	12.50	30.00
22 Ward Burton Caterpillar Firesuit		
22 Ward Burton Caterpillar Steel		
25 Jerry Nadeau UAW	4.00	8.00
25 Jerry Nadeau UAW Tire	12.50	30.00
32 Ricky Craven Tide	4.00	8.00
36 Ken Schrader M&M's	5.00	10.00

2002 Racing Champions Preview 1:64

These cars were issued in a red and black blister pack with the name "Chase the Race" and the year clearly printed on the front of the packaging. A Racing Champions card was also packaged with each 1:64 car. None feature opening hoods.

4 Mike Skinner Kodak	2.00	5.00
5 Terry Labonte Kellogg's	2.50	5.00
5 Terry Labonte Kellogg's Chrome/1500	7.50	20.00
5 Terry Labonte Kellogg's Car Cover/500	15.00	30.00
5 Terry Labonte Kellogg's Tire	15.00	40.00
10 Johnny Benson Valvoline	2.00	4.00
10 Johnny Benson Valvoline Firesuit	20.00	50.00
22 Ward Burton Caterpillar	2.00	5.00
22 Ward Burton Caterpillar Car Cover/500	15.00	30.00
22 Ward Burton Caterpillar Firesuit	40.00	80.00
22 Ward Burton Caterpillar Steel		
25 Jerry Nadeau UAW	2.00	5.00
25 Jerry Nadeau UAW Chrome/1500	7.50	15.00
25 Jerry Nadeau UAW Tire	12.50	30.00
26 Jimmy Spencer Shrek	5.00	10.00
32 Ricky Craven Tide	2.00	5.00
36 Ken Schrader M&M's	2.50	5.00

2002 Racing Champions Stock Rods 1:64

CARS ARE LISTED BY RELEASE NUMBER

4 Jim Dunn Mooneyes	3.00	6.00
8 Johnny Benson Valvoline 1969 Firebird	3.00	6.00
9 Ward Burton Caterpillar 1971 Barracuda	3.00	6.00
10 Mike Skinner Kodak	3.00	6.00
11 Johnny Benson Valvoline 1969 GTO	3.00	8.00
12 Ken Schrader M&M's 1937 Rapide	3.00	8.00
13 Terry Labonte Kellogg's 1969 Corvette	3.00	8.00

2002 Racing Champions Stock Rods Preview 1:64

CARS ARE LISTED BY RELEASE NUMBER

1 Terry Labonte Kellogg's Monsters Inc. (Monster Truck)	4.00	10.00
2 Ward Burton Caterpillar	3.00	6.00
3 Johnny Benson Valvoline (1978 Firebird)	3.00	6.00
5 John Force Castrol (1997 Mustang)	3.00	8.00
6 Ward Burton Caterpillar 1968 Plymouth	3.00	6.00
7 Ricky Craven Tide	3.00	6.00

2003 Racing Champions 1:64

This series features 1:64 scale die-cast cars packaged with a mini (roughly 2 /14" by 3") sized Racing Champions trading card. Each card features the year and an issue number on the front. All pieces were issued with the "2003 Edition" notation on the left side of the blister while some pieces were also issued on blister variations without the "2003 Edition" designation.

1 Andy Belmont Verizon Promo	12.50	25.00
1 Jamie McMurray Yellow Freight	3.00	8.00
1 Ted Musgrave Mopar SuperTruck Promo measures slightly larger than 1:64 scale	7.50	20.00
4 Square D SuperTruck Promo in window box	10.00	25.00
4 Mike Skinner Kodak	3.00	6.00
4 Mike Skinner Kodak Rain Delay/500	7.50	20.00
4 Mike Wallace Geico Promo	12.50	25.00
5 Terry Labonte Cheez-It Promo in bag	3.00	8.00
5 Terry Labonte Kellogg's	4.00	10.00
5 Terry Labonte Kellogg's Firesuit/50	50.00	100.00
5 Terry Labonte Kellogg's Steel/50	50.00	100.00
5 Terry Labonte Power of Cheese Promo in box	10.00	20.00
6 Andy Santerre Castle Promo	10.00	25.00
7 Randy LaJoie Kleenex Promo	7.50	20.00
7 Randy LaJoie Kleenex Cub Foods Promo	10.00	20.00
7 Randy LaJoie Kleenex Food City Promo	7.50	20.00
7 Randy LaJoie Kleenex Meijer Promo	15.00	40.00
7 Jimmy Spencer Sirius	5.00	10.00
8 Bill Lester Dodge SuperTruck Promo measures slightly larger than 1:64 scale	7.50	20.00
10 Johnny Benson Valvoline w year on blister	3.00	6.00
10 Johnny Benson Valvoline without year on blister	3.00	6.00
10 Johnny Benson Valvoline Firesuit/50	40.00	80.00
10 Johnny Benson Valvoline Time Trial/5000	5.00	10.00
10 Scott Riggs Nesquik	4.00	8.00
10 Scott Riggs Nesquik Cub Foods Promo	6.00	15.00
11 Brett Bodine Hooters	3.00	8.00
16 Austin Cameron NAPA Promo in box	6.00	12.00
16/20 Austin Cameron NAPA Jim Inglebright Jelly Belly 2-car Promo	15.00	30.00
18 Chad Chaffin Dickies SuperTruck Promo measures slightly larger than 1:24 scale	7.50	20.00
20 Jim Inglebright Jelly Belly Promo in window box	7.50	15.00
22 Ward Burton Caterpillar with year on blister	3.00	8.00
22 Ward Burton Caterpillar without year on blister	3.00	8.00
22 Ward Burton Caterpillar Chrome/1500	7.50	15.00
22 Ward Burton Caterpillar Steel/50	40.00	80.00
22 Ward Burton Cat Acert	4.00	10.00
22 Ward Burton Cat Acert Promo	10.00	25.00
23 Scott Wimmer Stacker 2	4.00	8.00
23 Scott Wimmer Stacker 2 Fast&Furious Promo	3.00	8.00
25 Joe Nemechek UAW Delphi	4.00	8.00
30 Jimmy Vasser Aventis Promo blister	30.00	50.00
30 Jimmy Vasser Aventis Promo in window box	12.50	30.00
32 Ricky Craven Tide with year on blister	3.00	8.00
32 Ricky Craven Tide without year on blister	3.00	8.00
32 Ricky Craven Tide w o year on blister Rain Delay/500	7.50	20.00
32 Ricky Craven Tide Downy Promo	4.00	10.00
32 Ricky Craven Tide Kids Promo	6.00	12.00
33 Paul Menard Turtle Wax Promo in window box	12.50	30.00
38 Elliott Sadler Combos Promo in window box	25.00	40.00
38 Elliott Sadler M&M's Groovy Summer Promo in window box	10.00	20.00
48 Jimmie Johnson Lowe's	3.00	8.00
48 Jimmie Johnson Lowe's '02 Season to Remember	4.00	8.00
48 Jimmie Johnson Lowe's Chrome/500	10.00	20.00
48 Jimmie Johnson Lowe's Firesuit/50	40.00	100.00
48 Jimmie Johnson Lowe's Rain Delay/1500	10.00	25.00
48 Jimmie Johnson Lowes Steel/50	40.00	80.00
48 Jimmie Johnson Lowe's SpongeBob Promo in Signature Colors box	25.00	60.00
49 Ken Schrader 1-800-CALL-ATT Promo	12.50	30.00
54 Todd Bodine National Guard	6.00	15.00
54 Todd Bodine National Guard Promo	5.00	12.00
55 Mike Stefanik Burnham Boilers Promo	7.50	15.00
57 Jason Keller Albertsons with year on blister	3.00	8.00
57 Jason Keller Albertsons without year on blister	3.00	8.00
77 Dave Blaney Jasper	3.00	8.00
77 Dave Blaney Jasper Fast&Furious Promo	3.00	8.00
77 Dave Blaney Jasper Fast&Furious Promo AUTO/100	25.00	50.00
77 University of Maryland Promo in box	7.50	20.00
90 Lance Norick Express Personnel Promo	15.00	30.00
01 Jerry Nadeau Army	4.00	10.00
01 Jerry Nadeau Army Chrome/1500	6.00	15.00
01 Jerry Nadeau Army Time Trial/5000	5.00	12.00
01 Jery Nadeau Tony Schumacher Dragster Army Camo Promo 2-car blister	6.00	15.00
01 Jerry Nadeau USG promo in box	7.50	15.00
03 Ward Burton Certainteed Promo	10.00	20.00

03 Sharpie Bristol Food City 400 Promo in PVC box 10.00 20.00
03 Tanimura&Antle Promo in window box 10.00 20.00

2003 Racing Champions 5-Pack 1:64

NNO 5. Brian Vickers GMAC / 48. Jimmie Johnson Lowe's POP / 01. Jerry Nadeau Army / 22. Ward Burton Cat / 10. Johnny Benson Valvoline 10.00 20.00
NNO 22. Ward Burton CAT Acert/54. Todd Bodine National Guard/7. Jimmy Spencer Sirius/5. Terry Labonte Kellogg's/48. Jimmie Johnson Lowe's 7.50 15.00
NNO 48. Jimmie Johnson Lowe's / 10. Johnny Benson Eagle One / 11. Brett Bodine Hooters Anniv. / 01. Jerry Nadeau USG / 5. Terry Labonte Finding Nemo 7.50 15.00
NNO 48. Jimmy Johnson Lowe's Power of Pride/23. Scott Wimmer Stacker 2 Fast&Furious/30. Jimmy Vasser Aventis/33. Paul Menard Turtle Wax/45. Kyle Petty GP Garfied 7.50 15.00

2003 Racing Champions Preview 1:64

Racing Champions created a smaller more narrow blister pack for 2003. This series features the title "2003 Preview" on the left side of the blister. Each die-cast car was packaged with a mini (roughly 2 /14" by 3") sized Press Pass card.

22 Ward Burton Caterpillar 3.00 8.00
22 Ward Burton Caterpillar Firesuit/50 45.00 80.00
22 Ward Burton Caterpillar Rain Delay/500 7.50 20.00
22 Ward Burton Cat Rental 3.00 8.00
22 Ward Burton Cat Rental Chrome/1500 6.00 15.00
22 Ward Burton Cat Rental Firesuit/50 45.00 80.00
22 Ward Burton Cat Rental Rain Delay/500 7.50 20.00
22 Ward Burton Caterpillar Steel/50 40.00 80.00
22 Ward Burton Cat Time Trial/5000 4.00 10.00
22 Ward Burton Cat Time Trial Rain Delay/500 10.00 20.00
22 Ward Burton Caterpillar War Paint/5000 4.00 10.00
26 Todd Bodine Discover 3.00 8.00
48 Jimmie Johnson Lowe's 2002 A Season to Remember 3.00 8.00

2003 Racing Champions Premier 1:64

4 Mike Skinner Kodak 4.00 8.00
4 Mike Skinner Kodak Rain Delay/500 12.50 25.00
5 Terry Labonte Kellogg's 4.00 8.00
5 Terry Labonte Kellogg's Firesuit/50 25.00 50.00
7 Jimmy Spencer Sirius 4.00 8.00
10 Johnny Benson Valvoline 4.00 8.00
10 Johnny Benson Valvoline Firesuit/50 40.00 80.00
10 Johnny Benson Valvoline Firesuit Steel/50 50.00 100.00
10 Johnny Benson Valvoline Steel/50 45.00 80.00
11 Brett Bodine Hooters 4.00 8.00
11 Brett Bodine Hooters Chrome/1500 12.50 25.00
22 Ward Burton Caterpillar 3.00 6.00
22 Ward Burton Cat Acert 4.00 8.00
25 Joe Nemechek UAW Delphi 4.00 8.00
32 Ricky Craven Tide 4.00 8.00
32 Ricky Craven Tide Rain Delay/500 8.00 20.00
48 Jimmie Johnson Lowe's 5.00 12.00
48 Jimmie Johnson Lowe's Chrome/1500 12.50 25.00
48 Jimmie Johnson Lowe's Firesuit Steel/50 60.00 120.00
57 Jason Keller Albertson's 4.00 8.00
01 Jerry Nadeau Army 6.00 15.00
01 Jerry Nadeau Army Chrome/1500 15.00 30.00

2003 Racing Champions Premier Preview 1:64

22 Ward Burton Caterpillar 4.00 10.00
22 Ward Burton Caterpillar Chrome/1500 8.00 20.00
22 Ward Burton Caterpillar Firesuit/50 60.00 120.00
22 Ward Burton Caterpillar Rain Delay/500 12.50 25.00
22 Ward Burton Cat Time Trial/5000 5.00 12.00
22 Ward Burton Cat Time Trial Rain Delay/500 12.50 25.00
22 Ward Burton Caterpillar War Paint/5000 5.00 12.00
22 Ward Burton Cat Rental 4.00 10.00
22 Ward Burton Caterpillar Rental Chrome/1500 8.00 20.00
22 Ward Burton Cat Rental Firesuit/50 40.00 80.00
22 Ward Burton Cat Rental Firesuit and Sheet Metal/50 60.00 120.00
22 Ward Burton Cat Rental Rain Delay/500 25.00 50.00
26 Todd Bodine Discover 4.00 10.00
48 Jimmie Johnson Lowe's 2002 Season to Remember 5.00 12.00

2003 Racing Champions Slammers 1:64

5 Terry Labonte Kellogg's 6.00 12.00
10 Johnny Benson Valvoline 6.00 12.00
22 Ward Burton Caterpillar 6.00 12.00
32 Ricky Craven Tide 6.00 12.00
45 Kyle Petty GP Garfield 6.00 12.00
48 Jimmie Johnson Lowe's 6.00 12.00
48 Jimmie Johnson Lowe's Power of Pride 6.00 12.00
48 Jimmie Johnson Lowe's SpongeBob Squarepants 6.00 12.00
01 Jerry Nadeau Army 6.00 12.00

2003 Racing Champions Stock Rods Preview 1:64

Racing Champions created a smaller more narrow blister pack for 2003. This series features the title "2003 Preview" on the left side of the blister. Each vintage car replica die-cast was packaged with a mini (roughly 2 /14" by 3") sized Racing Champions trading card.

5 Terry Labonte Kellogg's '55 Chevy (card reads "1970 Chevelle in error) 3.00 8.00
22 Ward Burton Caterpillar 1941 Willys 3.00 8.00
32 Ricky Craven Tide '69 GTO 3.00 8.00
48 Jimmie Johnson Lowe's 1970 Chevelle 4.00 10.00

2003 Racing Champions Stock Rods 1:64

This series is a continuation of the 2003 Preview release. Each vintage car replica die-cast was packaged with a mini (roughly 2 /14" by 3") sized Racing Champions trading card which features just the car number and Stock Rods logo. Each card also contains an issue number. All pieces were issued with the "2003 Edition" notation on the left side of the blister. Some pieces were also issued on blister variations without the "2003 Edition" designation.

22 Ward Burton Cat Rental 1941 Willys with year on package 3.00 8.00
22 Ward Burton Cat Rental 1941 Willys no year on package 3.00 8.00
01 Jerry Nadeau Army 1968 Camaro 4.00 8.00

2003 Racing Champions Ultra 1:64

4 Mike Skinner Kodak Easyshare 5.00 10.00
4 Mike Skinner Kodak Easyshare AU/100 25.00 50.00
5 Terry Labonte Cheez-It 4.00 8.00
5 Terry Labonte Cheez-It AU/100 30.00 80.00
5 Terry Labonte Finding Nemo 5.00 10.00
5 Terry Labonte Power of Cheese 4.00 8.00
5 Terry Labonte Power of Cheese AU/100 40.00 80.00
5 Brian Vickers GMAC 6.00 12.00
10 Johnny Benson Eagle One 4.00 8.00
10 Johnny Benson Eagle One Chrome/1500 7.50 20.00
10 Johnny Benson Valvoline 3.00 6.00
10 Johnny Benson Valvoline Chrome/1500 10.00 20.00
10 Johnny Benson Valvoline Firesuit/50 40.00 80.00
10 Johnny Benson Valvoline Rain Delay/500 6.00 15.00
10 Johnny Benson Valvoline Steel/50 50.00 100.00
11 Brett Bodine Hooters 20th Anniversary 5.00 10.00
22 Ward Burton Caterpillar 3.00 6.00
22 Ward Burton Caterpillar Firesuit/50 50.00 100.00
25 Joe Nemechek UAW Delphi 4.00 8.00
25 Joe Nemechek UAW Delphi Rain Delay/500 10.00 20.00
45 Kyle Petty GP Garfield 6.00 12.00
45 Ken Schrader 1-800-CALLATT 6.00 12.00
48 J.Johnson Lowe's 4.00 8.00
48 Jimmie Johnson Lowe's Steel/50 40.00 80.00
48 Jimmie Johnson Lowe's Power of Pride 4.00 8.00
48 Jimmie Johnson Lowe's Power of Pride Chrome/1500 10.00 20.00
48 Jimmie Johnson Lowe's SpongeBob Promo 5.00 12.00
48 Jimmie Johnson Lowe's SpongeBob Chrome Promo/1500 10.00 20.00
60 Brian Vickers HAAS 6.00 12.00
87 Kyle Busch Ditech.com 4.00 8.00
87 Joe Nemechek Cellular One 3.00 6.00
0 Jack Sprague NetZero 7.50 20.00
01 Jerry Nadeau Army 4.00 8.00
01 Jerry Nadeau Army Rain Delay/500 15.00 30.00
01 Jerry Nadeau Army Camo 4.00 10.00
01 Jerry Nadeau USG Sheet Rock 4.00 8.00

2004 Racing Champions 1:64

1 Johnny Benson Yellow Freight Promo 10.00 20.00
2 Kelly Sutton Team Copaxone Promo 15.00 30.00
4 Bobby Hamilton Square D SuperTruck Promo in wind.box 10.00 20.00
5 Terry Labonte Incredibles Promo in bag 25.00 50.00
27 Johnny Sauter Kleenex Promo 6.00 12.00
27 Johnny Sauter Kleenex Aldi Promo 6.00 12.00
27 Johnny Sauter Kleenex Cub Foods Promo 12.50 25.00
27 Johnny Sauter Kleenex Dollar General Promo 20.00 35.00
27 Johnny Sauter Kleenex Food World Promo 25.00 40.00
35 Brad Leighton Irving Oil Promo In wind.box 10.00 20.00
38 Elliott Sadler M&M's Yellow Promo 15.00 30.00
38 Elliott Sadler M&M's Black&White Promo 12.50 25.00
43 Aaron Fike Ollie's Bargain Outlet 30.00 60.00
44 Justin Labonte Coast Guard Promo 10.00 20.00
49 Ken Schrader Red Baron Promo in wind.box 35.00 60.00
49 Ken Schrader Schwan's Promo in wind.box 30.00 50.00
01 Joe Nemechek USG Promo in window box 12.50 25.00

2004 Racing Champions Bare Metal Previews 1:64

10 Scott Riggs Valvoline 4.00 8.00
22 Scott Wimmer Caterpillar 4.00 8.00
48 Jimmie Johnson Lowe's 3.00 6.00

2004 Racing Champions 5-Pack 1:64

NNO 01. Joe Nemechek USG/5. Terry Labonte Kellogg's/10. Scott Riggs Harlem Globetrotters/25. Brian Vickers ditech.com/59. Stacy Compton Kingsford 10.00 20.00
NNO 01. Joe Nemechek Army / 5. Terry Labonte Kellogg's Incredibles / 22. Scott Wimmer Cat Acert / 38. Kasey Kahne Great Clips / 84. Kyle Busch Carquest in '05 packaging 12.50 25.00
NNO 01. Joe Nemechek Army / 22. Scott Wimmer Cat / 44. Justin Labonte Coast Guard / 48. Jimmie Johnson Lowe's Tool World / 49. Ken Schrader Schwan's in '05 packaging 12.50 25.00
NNO 10. Scott Riggs Valvoline/22. Scott Wimmer Caterpillar/25. Brian Vickers ditech.com/27. Johnny Sauter Kleenex/48. Jimmie Johnson Lowe's 10.00 20.00
NNO 10. Scott Riggs Valvoline/22. Scott Wimmer Caterpillar/48. Jimmie Johnson Lowe's/60. Brian Vickers Hendrick's Team/87. Kyle Busch Ditech.com 10.00 20.00

2004 Racing Champions Real Steel 1:64

5 Terry Labonte Kellogg's 5.00 12.00
10 Scott Riggs Valvoline 5.00 12.00
22 Scott Wimmer Cat 5.00 12.00
25 Brian Vickers Ditech.com 5.00 12.00
48 Jimmie Johnson Lowe's 5.00 12.00
0 Ward Burton NetZero 5.00 12.00
01 Joe Nemechek Army 5.00 12.00

2004 Racing Champions Ultra Previews 1:64

10 Scott Riggs Valvoline 3.00 8.00
22 Scott Wimmer Cat 3.00 8.00
48 Jimmie Johnson Lowe's 3.00 6.00
48 Jimmie Johnson Lowe's Chrome 12.50 25.00

2004 Racing Champions Ultra 1:64

5 Kyle Busch Lowe's 5.00 12.00
5 Kyle Busch Lowe's SpongeBob 5.00 10.00
5 Terry Labonte Delphi 4.00 8.00
5 Terry Labonte Kellogg's 4.00 8.00
5 Terry Labonte Kellogg's Chrome 10.00 20.00
5 Terry Labonte Kellogg's HMS 20th Ann. in 05 packaging 4.00 8.00
5 Terry Labonte Kellogg's Incredibles in '05 packaging 4.00 8.00
10 Scott Riggs Harlem Globetrotters 5.00 10.00
10 Scott Riggs Valvoline 3.00 8.00
22 Scott Wimmer Cat 4.00 8.00
22 Scott Wimmer Cat Chrome 7.50 15.00
22 Scott Wimmer Cat Dealer 4.00 8.00
22 Scott Wimmer Cat Rental 4.00 8.00
23 Kenny Wallace Stacker 2 4.00 8.00
25 Brian Vickers ditech.com 5.00 10.00
25 Brian Vickers Ditech.com HMS 20 Ann. in '05 packaging 4.00 8.00
27 Johnny Sauter Kleenex 4.00 8.00
47 Robert Pressley Clorox 5.00 12.00
48 Jimmie Johnson Lowe's 3.00 8.00
48 Jimmie Johnson Lowe's HMS 20th Anniversary 4.00 8.00
48 Jimmie Johnson Lowe's HMS 20th Ann. in '05 packaging 4.00 8.00
48 Jimmie Johnson Lowe's SpongeBob 4.00 8.00
48 Jimmie Johnson Lowe's Tool World 4.00 8.00
48 Jimmie Johnson Lowe's Tool World in '05 packaging 4.00 8.00
84 Kyle Busch Carquest in '05 packaging 4.00 8.00
0 Ward Burton NetZero 5.00 10.00
0 Ward Burton NetZero Chrome 8.00 20.00
01 Joe Nemechek Army 5.00 10.00
01 Joe Nemechek USG 5.00 10.00
04 Nextel Cup Chevy 4.00 8.00
04 Nextel Cup Dodge 4.00 8.00

2004 Racing Champions Window Cling 1:64

5 Terry Labonte Kellogg's 4.00 8.00
10 Scott Riggs Valvoline 4.00 8.00
22 Scott Wimmer Cat 4.00 8.00
25 Brian Vickers Ditech 4.00 8.00
48 Jimmie Johnson Lowe's 4.00 8.00
01 Joe Nemechek Army 4.00 8.00

2005 Racing Champions 1:64

1 Johnny Sauter Yellow Fleet Pride Promo 6.00 12.00
9 Shigeaki Hattori Toyota TRD SuperTruck Promo 15.00 30.00
10 Scott Riggs Valvoline Promo in window box 6.00 12.00
22 Bill Lester Rally's Checker's SuperTruck Promo 30.00 60.00
25 Brad Leighton Irving Oil Promo in window box 7.50 15.00
25 Ashton Lewis Team Marines Promo 20.00 35.00
27 David Green Kleenex Promo 7.50 15.00
27 David Green Kleenex Bi-Lo Promo 7.50 15.00
27 David Green Kleenex Cub Foods Promo 7.50 15.00
32 Bobby Hamilton Jr. Tide Promo 5.00 10.00
34 Randy Lajoie Dollar General Promo 6.00 12.00
35 Jason Keller McDonald's Promo 10.00 20.00
36 Boris Said USG Durock Promo in window box 12.50 25.00
66 Greg Biffle Royal Office Products Promo 15.00 30.00

2005 Racing Champions Ultra Previews 1:64

22 Scott Wimmer Cat 4.00 8.00
22 Scott Wimmer Cat Chrome 6.00 12.00

2005 Racing Champions Ultra 1:64

5 Kyle Busch Delphi 4.00 8.00
5 Kyle Busch Kellogg's 5.00 10.00
5 Blake Feese Boston Reid Lowe's 6.00 12.00
7 Robby Gordon Fruit of the Loom 5.00 10.00
7 Robby Gordon Harrah's 5.00 10.00
10 Scott Riggs Valvoline 4.00 8.00
14 John Andretti JA 4.00 8.00
22 Kenny Wallace Stacker 2 4.00 8.00
22 Scott Wimmer CAT 4.00 8.00
22 Scott Wimmer CAT Chrome 6.00 12.00
25 Brian Vickers GMAC 4.00 8.00
36 Boris Said Centex Financial 5.00 10.00
40 Sterling Marlin Cottman 4.00 8.00
44 Terry Labonte GMAC 4.00 8.00
44 Terry Labonte GMAC Chrome 5.00 10.00
44 Terry Labonte Kellogg's 4.00 8.00
44 Terry Labonte Kellogg's Chrome 7.50 15.00
44 Terry Labonte Kellogg's Ironman 5.00 10.00
48 Jimmie Johnson Lowe's 4.00 8.00
48 Jimmie Johnson Lowe's Chrome 7.50 15.00
48 Jimmie Johnson Lowe's Firesuit/50 25.00 50.00
48 Jimmie Johnson Lowe's Kobalt 4.00 8.00
49 Ken Schrader Schwan's 6.00 12.00
57 Brian Vickers Ore Ida 4.00 8.00
66 Greg Biffle Duraflame 4.00 8.00
87 Joe Nemechek Cellular One 4.00 8.00
0 Mike Bliss NetZero Best Buy 4.00 8.00
01 Joe Nemechek Army 4.00 8.00
01 Joe Nemechek Army Chrome 6.00 12.00

2006 Racing Champions Promos 1:64

17 David Reutimann Tundra SuperTruck in blister 5.00 10.00
32 Travis Kvapil Tide in blister 4.00 8.00
58 Donnie Neuenberger Cayman Islands in window box 5.00 10.00
66 Jeff Green Certain Teed in blister 4.00 8.00

1991 Racing Champions 5-Pack 1:144

These 1:144 scale cars were issued in a Racing Champions "Mini Stock Cars" blister package.

NNO 3. Dale Earnhardt Goodwrench/27. Rusty Wallace//28. Davey Allison Havoline/30. Bobby Hamilton Max.House/43. Richard Petty STP 10.00 20.00

NNO 9. Bill Elliott 7.50 15.00
Melling/27. Rusty Wallace/30. Bobby Hamilton
Max.House/33. Harry Gant/94. Sterling Marlin
Sunoco

1996 Racing Champions 1:144

These 1:144 scale mini cars were issued in a red and black Racing Champions blister package. The blister reads "1996 Edition, First Production" on the front. Each was also packaged with a yellow bordered trading card.

2 Rusty Wallace 5.00 12.00
MGD
4 Sterling Marlin 4.00 10.00
Kodak
6 Mark Martin 5.00 12.00
Valvoline
17 Darrell Waltrip 4.00 10.00
Parts America
18 Bobby Labonte 4.00 10.00
Interstate Batteries
21 Michael Waltrip 4.00 10.00
Citgo
24 Jeff Gordon 5.00 12.00
DuPont
28 Ernie Irvan 4.00 10.00
Havoline
29 No Driver Association 4.00 10.00
Scooby-Doo
87 Joe Nemechek 4.00 10.00
BellSouth
88 Dale Jarrett 5.00 12.00
Quality Care
94 Bill Elliott 4.00 10.00
McDonald's

1997 Racing Champions Preview 1:144

4 Sterling Marlin 2.50 6.00
Kodak
5 Terry Labonte 2.00 5.00
Kellogg's
6 Mark Martin 2.50 6.00
Valvoline
9 Joe Bessey 2.00 5.00
Power Team
18 Bobby Labonte 2.50 6.00
Interstate Batteries
21 Michael Waltrip 2.00 5.00
Citgo
24 Jeff Gordon 3.00 8.00
DuPont
28 Ernie Irvan 2.00 5.00
Havoline
29 Robert Pressley 2.00 5.00
Cartoon Network
30 Johnny Benson 2.00 5.00
Pennzoil
75 Rick Mast 2.00 5.00
Remington
94 Bill Elliott 2.50 6.00
McDonald's
99 Jeff Burton 2.00 5.00
Exide

1997 Racing Champions 1:144

These 1:144 scale mini Transporters were issued in a red and black Racing Champions blister package. The blister reads "1997 Edition" on the front. Each was also packaged with a yellow bordered trading card.

1 Hermie Sadler 2.00 5.00
DeWalt
2 Rusty Wallace 2.50 6.00
Penske
2 Ricky Craven 2.00 5.00
Raybestos
4 Sterling Marlin 2.50 6.00
Kodak
5 Terry Labonte 2.50 6.00
Bayer
5 Terry Labonte 2.50 6.00
Kellogg's
5 Terry Labonte 2.50 6.00
Kellogg's Tony
5 Terry Labonte 2.50 6.00
Kellogg's 1996 Champ
6 Mark Martin 2.50 6.00
Valvoline
7 Geoff Bodine 2.00 5.00
QVC
8 Hut Stricklin 2.00 5.00
Circuit City
9 Joe Bessey 2.00 5.00
Power Team
10 Phil Parsons 2.00 5.00
Channellock
11 Jimmy Foster 2.00 5.00
SpeedVision
11 Brett Bodine 2.00 5.00
Close Call
16 Ted Musgrave 2.00 5.00
Family Channel
17 Darrell Waltrip 2.00 5.00
Parts America
17 Darrell Waltrip 2.00 5.00
Parts America Chrome
18 Bobby Labonte 2.50 6.00
Interstate Batteries
19 Gary Bradberry 2.00 5.00
Child Support
21 Michael Waltrip 2.00 5.00
Citgo
24 Jeff Gordon 3.00 8.00
DuPont
25 Ricky Craven 2.00 5.00
Hendrick
28 Ernie Irvan 2.00 5.00
Havoline black&orange
28 Ernie Irvan 2.00 5.00
Havoline black&white
29 Elliott Sadler 2.00 5.00
Phillips 66
29 Robert Pressley 2.00 5.00
Cartoon Network
29 Jeff Green 2.00 5.00
Tom&Jerry
30 Johnny Benson 2.00 5.00
Pennzoil
32 Dale Jarrett 2.00 5.00
White Rain
33 Ken Schrader 2.00 5.00
Petree Racing
36 Todd Bodine 2.00 5.00
Stanley
36 Derrike Cope 2.00 5.00
Skittles
37 Jeremy Mayfield 2.00 5.00
K-Mart
38 Elton Sawyer 2.00 5.00
Barbasol
40 Robby Gordon 2.00 5.00
Sabco
42 Joe Nemechek 2.00 5.00
BellSouth
43 Dennis Setzer 2.00 5.00
Lance
46 Wally Dallenbach 2.00 5.00
First Union
47 Jeff Fuller 2.00 5.00
Sunoco
49 Kyle Petty 2.00 5.00
NWO
57 Jason Keller 2.00 5.00
Slim Jim
60 Mark Martin 2.50 6.00
Winn Dixie
74 Randy LaJoie 2.00 5.00
Fina
75 Rick Mast 2.00 5.00
Remington
75 Rick Mast 2.00 5.00
Remington Camo
75 Rick Mast 2.00 5.00
Remington Stren
87 Joe Nemechek 2.00 5.00
BellSouth
88 Kevin Lepage 2.00 5.00
Hype
90 Dick Trickle 2.00 5.00
Heilig-Meyers
91 Mike Wallace 2.00 5.00
Spam
94 Ron Barfield 2.00 5.00
New Holland
94 Bill Elliott 2.50 6.00
McDonald's
94 Bill Elliott 2.50 6.00
Mac Tonight
96 David Green 2.00 5.00
Caterpillar
97 Chad Little 2.00 5.00
John Deere
99 Glenn Allen 2.00 5.00
Luxaire
99 Jeff Burton 2.00 5.00
Exide
00 Buckshot Jones 2.00 5.00
Aquafresh

1997 Racing Champions 5-Pack 1:144

NNO 24. Jeff Gordon 4.00 10.00
DuPont/32. Dale Jarrett
White Rain/40. Sterling Marlin/94. Bill Elliott
McDonld's/97. Chad Little
John Deere

1997 Racing Champions 5-Pack Preview 1:144

These 1:144 scale cars were issued in a Racing Champions 1997 Preview blister. The cars came with a card for each driver and a black display stand for the set.

NNO 4. Sterling Marlin 4.00 10.00
Kodak/5. Terry Labonte
Kellogg's/9. Joe Bessey
Power Team/24. Jeff Gordon
DuPont/29. Robert Pressley
Cartoon Network
NNO 5. Terry Labonte 4.00 10.00
Kellogg's/6. Mark Martin
Valvoline/21. Michael Waltrip
Citgo/24. Jeff Gordon
DuPont/28. Ernie Irvan
Havoline
NNO 5. Terry Labonte 4.00 10.00
Kellogg's/24. Jeff Gordon
DuPont/30. Johnny Benson
Pennzoil/94. Bill Elliott
McDonald's/99. Jeff Burton
Exide
NNO 10. Phil Parsons 4.00 10.00
Channellock/36. Todd Bodine
Stanley Tools/42. Joe Nemechek
BellSouth/46. Wally Dallenbach
First Union/94. Bill Elliott
Mac Tonight

1997 Racing Champions SuperTrucks 5-Pack 1:144

NNO 99. Mark Martin
Exide/99. Jeff Burton
Exide/1. Michael Waltrip
MW Windows/15. Ernie Irvan
VISA/18. Johnny Benson
Valvoline

1997 Racing Champions SuperTrucks 1:144

These 1:144 scale mini dragsters were issued in a red and black Racing Champions NASCAR Craftsman Truck blister package. The blister reads "1997 Edition" on the front. Each was also packaged with a yellow bordered trading card.

1 Michael Waltrip 2.00 5.00
MW Windows
2 Mike Bliss 2.00 5.00
ASE
4 Bill Elliott 2.50 6.00
Wagner
6 Rick Carelli 2.00 5.00
Remax
15 Mike Colabucci 2.00 5.00
VISA
15 Mike Cope 2.00 5.00
Pennrose
18 Mike Dokken 2.00 5.00
Dana
18 Johnny Benson 2.00 5.00
Pennzoil
19 Tony Raines 2.00 5.00
Pennzoil
23 T.J. Clark 2.00 5.00
CRG Motorsports
24 Jack Sprague 2.00 5.00
Quaker State
29 Bob Keselowski 2.00 5.00
Mopar
35 Dave Rezendes 2.00 5.00
Ortho
44 Boris Said 2.00 5.00
Federated
52 Tobey Butler 2.00 5.00
Pure One
66 Bryan Refner 2.00 5.00
Carlin
75 Dan Press 2.00 5.00
Spears
80 Joe Ruttman 2.00 5.00
LCI
86 Stacy Compton 2.00 5.00
Valvoline
87 Joe Nemechek 2.00 5.00
BellSouth
92 Mark Kinser 2.00 5.00
Rotary
94 Ron Barfield 2.00 5.00
Super 8
98 Kenny Irwin 3.00 8.00
Raybestos
99 Jeff Burton 2.00 5.00
Exide
99 Mark Martin 2.50 6.00
Exide
01 Billy Ogle 2.00 5.00
DCD
07 Tammy Kirk 2.00 5.00
Lovable

1998 Racing Champions 1:144

These 1:144 scale mini Transporters were issued in a red Racing Champions blister package that reads "1998 Edition." Each was also packaged with a trading card.

5 Terry Labonte 2.50 5.00
Kellogg's
6 Joe Bessey 2.00 5.00
Power Team
6 Mark Martin 2.50 6.00
Valvoline
8 Hut Stricklin 2.00 5.00
Circuit City
9 Lake Speed 2.00 5.00
Birthday Cake
9 Lake Speed 2.00 5.00
Huckleberry Hound
12 Jeremy Mayfield 2.00 5.00
K-Mart
13 Jerry Nadeau 2.00 5.00
First Plus
21 Michael Waltrip 2.00 5.00
Citgo
26 Johnny Benson 2.00 5.00
Cheerios
29 Hermie Sadler 2.00 5.00
DeWalt
30 Derrike Cope 2.00 5.00
Gumout
35 Todd Bodine 2.00 5.00
Tabasco Black
35 Todd Bodine 2.00 5.00
Tabasco Orange
36 Ernie Irvan 2.00 5.00
M&M's
40 Sterling Marlin 2.50 6.00
Sabco
41 Steve Grissom 2.00 5.00
Larry Hedrick Racing
42 Joe Nemechek 2.00 5.00
BellSouth
59 Robert Pressley 2.00 5.00
Kingsford
64 Dick Trickle 2.00 5.00
Schneider
66 Elliott Sadler 2.00 5.00
Phillips 66
75 Rick Mast 2.00 5.00
Remington
94 Bill Elliott 2.50 6.00
McDonald's
96 David Green 2.00 5.00
Caterpillar
97 Chad Little 2.00 5.00
John Deere Promo
99 Glenn Allen 2.00 5.00
Luxaire
99 Jeff Burton 2.00 5.00
Exide
00 Buckshot Jones 2.00 5.00
Alka Seltzer
00 Buckshot Jones 2.00 5.00
Aqua Fresh

1998 Racing Champions 5-Pack 1:144

NNO 5. Terry Labonte 3.00 8.00
Kellogg's/8. Hut Stricklin
Circuit City/35. Todd Bodine
Tabasco/50. Ricky Craven
Hendrick/59. Robert Pressley
Kingsford
NNO 5. Terry Labonte 3.00 8.00
Kellogg's/30. Mike Cope
Slim Jim/35. Todd Bodine
Tabasco/36. Ernie Irvan
Skittles/50. NASCAR 50th Anniversary
NNO 5. Terry Labonte 3.00 8.00
Kellogg's/30.Mike Cope
Slim Jim/36. Ernie Irvan
Skittles/50. Ricky Craven
Hendrick
50. NASCAR 50th Anniversary
NNO 5. Terry Labonte 3.00 8.00
Kellogg's/35. Todd Bodine
Tabasco/40. Sterling Marlin/99. Glenn Allen
Luxaire/00. Buckshot Jones
Bayer

1998 Racing Champions Stock Rods 1:144

23 Hut Stricklin 2.50 6.00
Circuit City
38 Wally Dallenbach 2.50 6.00
First Union
42 Buckshot Jones 2.50 6.00
Aqua Fresh
43 Michael Waltrip 2.50 6.00
Pennzoil
44 Wally Dallenbach 2.50 6.00
First Union

1998 Racing Champions Stock Rods 5-Pack 1:144

NNO 50. Ricky Craven 3.00 8.00
Hendrick/59. Robert Pressley
Kingsford/90. Dick Trickle
Heilig Meyers/99. Jeff Burton
Exide/99. Glenn Allen
Luxaire

1997 Revell Club 1:18

These 1:18 scale cars were from the same production run as the Collection cars. Each car distributed by the club has a serial number on the chassis. The boxes were uniquely colored to match the colors on the car.

1 Coca-Cola 600 50.00 100.00
5 Terry Labonte 90.00 150.00
Spooky Loops
5 Terry Labonte 100.00 175.00
Kellogg's Tony
23 Jimmy Spencer 100.00 175.00
Camel/504
33 Ken Schrader 90.00 150.00
Skoal
46 Wally Dallenbach 50.00 120.00
Woody Woodpecker
88 Dale Jarrett 80.00 120.00
Quality Care
97 Chad Little 60.00 150.00
John Deere/504

1997 Revell Collection 1:18

This series marks Revell's first attempt to produce a 1:18 scale car. It was distributed to hobby dealers as part of Revell's Collection line.

1 Coca-Cola 600/3624 25.00 60.00
2 Rusty Wallace 40.00 100.00
Miller Lite/11,766
3 Dale Earnhardt 60.00 120.00
Wheaties/10,008
4 Sterling Marlin 40.00 80.00
Kodak
5 Terry Labonte 50.00 100.00
Kellogg's
5 Terry Labonte 40.00 100.00
Spooky Loops/6006
5 Terry Labonte 40.00 100.00
Kellogg's Tony/6012
6 Mark Martin 50.00 80.00
Valvoline
10 Ricky Rudd 40.00 80.00
Tide/3120
18 Bobby Labonte 40.00 80.00
Interstate Batteries
18 Bobby Labonte 40.00 80.00
Interstate Batteries
Texas/3120
21 Michael Waltrip 25.00 60.00
Citgo Top Dog/3120
23 Jimmy Spencer 60.00 120.00
Camel/5004
24 Jeff Gordon 60.00 120.00
Jurassic Park 3/5004
25 Ricky Craven 40.00 100.00
Bud Lizard
28 Ernie Irvan 40.00 100.00
Havoline 10th Anniversary
white and black
29 Jeff Green 30.00 80.00
Scooby-Doo
29 Jeff Green 30.00 80.00
Tom & Jerry
29 Steve Grissom 30.00 80.00
Flintstones
33 Ken Schrader 30.00 80.00
Skoal/3624
35 Todd Bodine 40.00 80.00
Tabasco
37 Jeremy Mayfield 40.00 80.00
K-Mart RC-Cola
40 Robby Gordon 40.00 75.00
Coors Light/5004
41 Steve Grissom 40.00 80.00
Kodiak
43 Bobby Hamilton 40.00 80.00
STP Goody's
46 Wally Dallenbach 40.00 80.00
Woody Woodpecker
60 Mark Martin 50.00 90.00
Winn Dixie
88 Dale Jarrett 40.00 80.00
Ford Credit
94 Bill Elliott 40.00 80.00
McDonald's
94 Bill Elliott 40.00 80.00
Mac Tonight
97 Chad Little 40.00 90.00
John Deere AUTO/2616
97 Texas Motor Speedway/5004 35.00 70.00

1998 Revell Club 1:18

These 1:18 scale cars were from the same production run as the Collection cars. Each car distributed by the club has a serial number on the chassis. The boxes were uniquely colored to match the colors on the car.

1 Dale Earnhardt Jr. 50.00 100.00
Coke Bear/2004
1 Steve Park 40.00 100.00
Pennzoil Black Roof
1 Steve Park 30.00 80.00
Pennzoil Yellow Roof/504
2 Rusty Wallace 60.00 120.00
Adventures of Rusty
2 Rusty Wallace 60.00 120.00
Miller Lite Elvis/1002
3 Dale Earnhardt 75.00 150.00
Coke/2004
3 Dale Earnhardt 150.00 250.00
Goodwrench Plus
3 Dale Earnhardt 200.00 300.00
Goodwrench Plus Bass Pro/504
3 Dale Earnhardt 200.00 250.00
Goodwrench Plus
Daytona Win/504
3 Dale Earnhardt Jr. 75.00 150.00
AC Delco
5 Terry Labonte 60.00 120.00
Blasted Fruit Loops/504
5 Terry Labonte 60.00 120.00
Kellogg's Corny
9 Lake Speed 40.00 100.00
Birthday Cake
9 Lake Speed 40.00 100.00
Huckleberry Hound/504
18 Bobby Labonte 50.00 100.00
Interstate Batteries Hot Rod/504
18 Bobby Labonte 50.00 100.00
Interstate Batteries
Small Soldiers/1002
23 Jimmy Spencer 125.00 200.00
No Bull/504
24 Jeff Gordon 60.00 150.00
DuPont/1008
24 Jeff Gordon 100.00 200.00
DuPont Chromalusion
28 Kenny Irwin 60.00 120.00
Havoline/504
28 Kenny Irwin 60.00 120.00
Havoline Joker/504
31 Mike Skinner 40.00 100.00
Lowe's
35 Todd Bodine 50.00 100.00
Tabasco
36 Ernie Irvan 60.00 120.00
M&M's/504
36 Ernie Irvan 60.00 120.00
Wildberry Skittles
44 Tony Stewart 90.00 150.00
Shell/504
44 Tony Stewart 90.00 150.00
Shell Small Soldiers/1002
50 Ricky Craven 50.00 100.00
Bud/504
81 Kenny Wallace 30.00 80.00
Square D Lightning/504
88 Dale Jarrett 75.00 150.00
Batman/1002
88 Dale Jarrett 50.00 120.00
Quality Care/504

1998 Revell Collection 1:18

This series marks Revell's second year producing a 1:18 scale car. It was distributed to hobby dealers are part of Revell's Collection line.

1 Dale Earnhardt Jr. 40.00 100.00
Coke Bear/4002
1 Steve Park 40.00 100.00
Pennzoil Black Roof/3120
1 Steve Park 30.00 80.00
Pennzoil Yellow Roof/2508
2 Rusty Wallace 30.00 80.00
Adventures of Rusty/5004
2 Rusty Wallace 30.00 80.00
Miller Lite/5004
2 Rusty Wallace 25.00 60.00
Miller Lite Elvis/5004
2 Rusty Wallace 30.00 80.00
Miller Lite TCB Elvis
3 Dale Earnhardt 60.00 120.00
Coke/4008
3 Dale Earnhardt 60.00 120.00
Goodwrench Plus Bass Pro/8010

3 Dale Earnhardt Goodwrench Plus Daytona Win/5004 60.00 120.00
3 Dale Earnhardt Goodwrench Plus Brickyard Win 150.00 250.00
3 Dale Earnhardt Jr. AC Delco/3120 50.00 120.00
5 Terry Labonte Blasted Fruit Loops 30.00 80.00
5 Terry Labonte Kellogg's Corny/3120 30.00 80.00
5 Terry Labonte Kellogg's Ironman 30.00 60.00
9 Lake Speed Birthday Cake 40.00 80.00
9 Lake Speed Huckleberry Hound/3624 40.00 80.00
18 Bobby Labonte Interstate Batteries Hot Rod/3120 30.00 80.00
18 Bobby Labonte Interstate Batteries Small Soldiers 30.00 80.00
23 Jimmy Spencer No Bull 50.00 100.00
24 Jeff Gordon DuPont/5004 40.00 100.00
24 Jeff Gordon DuPont Brickyard Win 50.00 100.00
24 Jeff Gordon DuPont Chromalusion/5004 60.00 120.00
28 Kenny Irwin Havoline/3120 30.00 80.00
31 Dale Earnhardt Jr. Sikkens Blue 1997 Monte Carlo 40.00 80.00
31 Dale Earnhardt Jr. Wrangler 1997 Monte Carlo/3120 60.00 150.00
31 Mike Skinner Lowe's/3120 25.00 60.00
35 Todd Bodine Tabasco 40.00 80.00
36 Ernie Irvan M&M's/3120 40.00 80.00
36 Ernie Irvan Wildberry Skittles 30.00 80.00
44 Tony Stewart Shell/3120 40.00 80.00
44 Tony Stewart Shell Small Soldiers/3120 30.00 60.00
46 Jeff Green First Union Devil Rays/3120 25.00 60.00
50 Ricky Craven Budweiser 30.00 60.00
50 No Driver Association Bud Louie 30.00 80.00
81 Kenny Wallace (Square D Lightning/3120 25.00 60.00
88 Dale Jarrett Batman/3120 40.00 80.00
88 Dale Jarrett Quality Care/3120 30.00 80.00

1999 Revell Club 1:18

These 1:18 scale cars were produced in very small numbers and were only available through the club.

3 Dale Earnhardt Goodwrench 150.00 250.00
20 Tony Stewart Home Depot Habitat/2508 30.00 80.00
23 Jimmy Spencer No Bull 60.00 120.00
24 Jeff Gordon DuPont/1008 40.00 100.00
24 Jeff Gordon DuPont Superman 50.00 120.00
24 Jeff Gordon Pepsi/1008 40.00 100.00
31 Dale Earnhardt Jr. Gargoyles 1997 Monte Carlo 100.00 175.00
36 Ernie Irvan M&M's Millennium 30.00 80.00

1999 Revell Collection 1:18

This series marks Revell's third year producing a 1:18 scale car. It was distributed to hobby dealers as part of Revell's Collection line.

2 Rusty Wallace Miller Lite 25.00 60.00
2 Rusty Wallace Miller Lite Harley/2508 30.00 80.00
3 Dale Earnhardt Goodwrench 100.00 200.00
3 Dale Earnhardt Goodwrench 25th Anniversary/2508 50.00 120.00
3 Dale Earnhardt Wrangler/6000 50.00 120.00
3 Dale Earnhardt Jr. AC Delco Superman/4800 40.00 100.00
8 Dale Earnhardt Jr. Bud/5004 50.00 120.00
12 Jeremy Mayfield Mobil 1 Kentucky Derby 30.00 80.00
18 Bobby Labonte Interstate Batteries/2508 30.00 80.00
20 Tony Stewart Home Depot 100.00 175.00
23 Jimmy Spencer No Bull/2508 25.00 60.00
23 Jimmy Spencer Winston Lights/2508 25.00 60.00
24 Jeff Gordon DuPont/2508 40.00 100.00
24 Jeff Gordon DuPont NASCAR Racers/2508 40.00 100.00
24 Jeff Gordon DuPont Superman/7500 30.00 80.00
24 Jeff Gordon Pepsi 40.00 100.00
24 Jeff Gordon Pepsi Star Wars 40.00 100.00
28 Kenny Irwin Havoline/2508 25.00 60.00
31 Dale Earnhardt Jr. Gargoyles 1997 Monte Carlo/2508 40.00 80.00
31 Dale Earnhardt Jr. Sikkens White 1997 Monte Carlo/2508 40.00 80.00
36 Ernie Irvan M&M's TBS/2508 25.00 60.00
40 Coca-Cola 600 30.00 60.00
40 Sterling Marlin Coors Light Brooks & Dunn 30.00 80.00
40 Sterling Marlin Coors Light John Wayne/2508 30.00 80.00

2000 Revell Club 1:18

3 Dale Earnhardt Goodwrench Taz No Bull/2508 75.00 150.00
8 Dale Earnhardt Jr. Bud/2508 40.00 100.00
20 Tony Stewart Home Depot/2508 30.00 80.00
20 Tony Stewart Home Depot ROY/2508 30.00 80.00
24 Jeff Gordon DuPont Millennium/2508 30.00 80.00

2000 Revell Collection 1:18

3 Dale Earnhardt Goodwrench Peter Max/2508 175.00 300.00
3 Dale Earnhardt Goodwrench Taz No Bull/2508 75.00 150.00
8 Dale Earnhardt Jr. Bud 90.00 150.00
18 Bobby Labonte Interstate Batteries 75.00 125.00
20 Tony Stewart Home Depot/2508 90.00 150.00
20 Tony Stewart Home Depot Rookie of the Year 75.00 150.00
24 Jeff Gordon DuPont Peanuts 40.00 100.00
94 Bill Elliott McDonald's Drive Thru/2508 30.00 80.00

2001 Revell Collection 1:18

3 Dale Earnhardt Goodwrench with Sonic decal 150.00 250.00

1991-95 Revell 1:24

This set features many NASCAR's top drivers. Many of the pieces were issued through retail outlets but some were distributed through each driver's souvenir trailer.

1 Jeff Gordon Baby Ruth produced for RCI 250.00 500.00
3 Dale Earnhardt Goodwrench Kellogg's Promo 100.00 175.00
3 Dale Earnhardt Goodwrench Black Wheels Sports Image 1993 100.00 200.00
3 Dale Earnhardt Goodwrench Silver Wheels Sports Image 1991 75.00 125.00
3 Dale Earnhardt Goodwrench Sports Image 1995 60.00 120.00
3 Dale Earnhardt Goodwrench 6-Time Champion 100.00 250.00
4 Rick Wilson Kodak produced for GMP 15.00 30.00
6 Mark Martin Valvoline 20.00 40.00
7 Harry Gant Mac Tools Morema/5000 1993 35.00 60.00
7 Harry Gant Morema 25.00 40.00
7 No Driver Association Mac Tools RCCA/7500 1992 10.00 20.00
8 Dick Trickle Snickers 20.00 40.00
8 1/2 No Driver Association Racing For Kids 8.00 20.00
10 Derrike Cope Purolator Flag 1991 8.00 20.00
15 Geoff Bodine Ford Motorsports 15.00 35.00
17 Darrell Waltrip Western Auto 20.00 40.00
18 Dale Jarrett Interstate Batteries 35.00 60.00
21 Morgan Shepherd Cheerwine 15.00 30.00
21 Morgan Shepherd Citgo 12.00 20.00
22 Sterling Marlin Maxwell House 15.00 40.00
26 Brett Bodine Quaker State 8.00 20.00
28 Davey Allison Havoline 1992 50.00 100.00
28 Davey Allison Mac Tools 60.00 120.00
28 Ernie Irvan Mac Tools 50.00 100.00
28 Ernie Irvan Mac Tools Promo 12.50 25.00
30 Michael Waltrip Pennzoil 1991 15.00 30.00
32 Dale Jarrett Mac Tools 40.00 80.00
33 Harry Gant Farewell Tour 25.00 50.00
42 Kyle Petty Mello Yello 20.00 40.00
52 Ken Schrader Morema/5000 1993 20.00 30.00
57 No Driver Association Heinz 57 15.00 30.00
59 Robert Pressley Alliance produced RCI 30.00 55.00
60 Mark Martin Winn Dixie produced for GMP 1995 30.00 60.00
66 No Driver Association Phillips 66 TropArtic 10.00 20.00
66 Dick Trickle Phillips 66 TropArtic 25.00 50.00
68 Bobby Hamilton Country Time 25.00 50.00
75 Joe Ruttman Dinner Bell 10.00 20.00
83 Lake Speed Purex produced for GMP 1994 15.00 30.00
90 Bobby Hillin Jr. Heilig-Meyers 15.00 30.00
94 Binney&Smith Crayola Promo 1994 15.00 30.00
94 Terry Labonte Sunoco 1992 75.00 125.00

1994 Revell Hobby 1:24

These pieces were distributed through hobby outlets. Each piece came in a black or yellow clear window box with a few additional colors that matched the driver's car. No piece was numbered and there were no announced production runs.

4 Sterling Marlin Kodak 20.00 50.00
5 Terry Labonte Kellogg's 40.00 80.00
7 Geoff Bodine Exide 12.50 30.00
15 Lake Speed Quality Care 15.00 30.00
24 Jeff Gordon DuPont 50.00 100.00
31 Ward Burton Hardee's 40.00 80.00
41 Joe Nemechek Meineke 20.00 40.00
43 Wally Dallenbach Jr. STP 20.00 40.00

1995 Revell Retail 1:24

These die-cast pieces were part of the continued growth of Revell's presence in the NASCAR market. The 1995 pieces were updated with driver and sponsor changes. The boxes were black with a stripe of color to match the predominant color on the car.

4 Sterling Marlin Kodak 10.00 25.00
6 Mark Martin Valvoline 20.00 40.00
7 Geoff Bodine Exide Promo 10.00 20.00
15 Dick Trickle Ford Quality Care 15.00 30.00
16 Ted Musgrave Family Channel 8.00 20.00
18 Bobby Labonte Interstate Batteries 40.00 80.00
21 Morgan Shepherd Citgo 10.00 20.00
23 Chad Little Bayer 10.00 25.00
24 Jeff Gordon DuPont 40.00 80.00
24 Jeff Gordon DuPont Coke deck lid 15.00 30.00
24 Jeff Gordon DuPont Dealer Promo Coke logo on deck lid issued in plain white box 30.00 60.00
24 Jeff Gordon DuPont Dealer Promo DuPont logo on deck lid issued in plain white box 30.00 60.00
25 Ken Schrader Budweiser 12.00 20.00
26 Steve Kinser Quaker State 10.00 20.00
31 Ward Burton Hardee's Promo/5000 30.00 60.00
32 Dale Jarrett Mac Tools Promo/5000 40.00 80.00
44 David Green Slim Jim 8.00 20.00
71 Kevin Lepage Vermont Teddy Bear 20.00 40.00
71 Dave Marcis Olive Garden Promo/5000 40.00 75.00
75 Todd Bodine Factory Stores of America 10.00 20.00
87 Joe Nemechek Burger King 20.00 40.00
95 DANA Perfect Circle Promo/5000 12.50 25.00

1996 Revell Retail 1:24

This series was distributed in retail outlets. These cars were packaged in colored boxes that matched the color schemes of the cars.

2 Rusty Wallace Miller Silver 12.50 25.00
2 Rusty Wallace Penske Motorsports 12.00 20.00
3 Dale Earnhardt Goodwrench 40.00 100.00
3 Dale Earnhardt Olympic car 30.00 80.00
4 Sterling Marlin Kodak 12.00 20.00
5 Terry Labonte Kellogg's 15.00 40.00
6 Mark Martin Valvoline 20.00 50.00
7 Geoff Bodine QVC in solid box 12.00 30.00
10 Ricky Rudd Tide 15.00 30.00
11 Brett Bodine Lowe's 8.00 20.00
16 Ron Hornaday Smith Wesson 25.00 50.00
16 Ted Musgrave Family Channel Primestar 8.00 20.00
17 Darrell Waltrip Parts America 15.00 30.00
18 Bobby Labonte Interstate Batteries 20.00 50.00
21 Michael Waltrip Citgo 10.00 20.00
24 Jeff Gordon DuPont 25.00 60.00
28 Ernie Irvan Havoline 20.00 40.00
37 John Andretti K-Mart Little Caesars 10.00 20.00
75 Morgan Shepherd Remington 10.00 20.00
75 Morgan Shepherd Remington Camouflage 12.50 25.00
75 Morgan Shepherd Stren 10.00 22.00
77 Bobby Hillin Jr. Jasper Engines 15.00 25.00
87 Joe Nemechek Burger King 20.00 50.00
88 Dale Jarrett Quality Care 20.00 40.00
96 Lawson Products Promo 18.00 30.00
99 Jeff Burton Exide 20.00 40.00

1996 Revell Collection 1:24

This series was produced for and distributed in hobby outlets. These cars have significant upgrades in comparison to the standard Revell Retail 1:24 pieces. Each car is packaged mounted to a black plastic base. The Terry Labonte Honey Crunch car saw a large portion of the production run sold to the general public before they were distributed to hobby distributors.

2 Rusty Wallace Miller Genuine Draft Silver 25th Anniversary 25.00 45.00
2 Rusty Wallace Penske 20.00 35.00
3 Dale Earnhardt Olympic 40.00 100.00
4 Sterling Marlin Kodak 20.00 40.00
5 Terry Labonte Honey Crunch/5004 150.00 300.00
5 Terry Labonte Honey Crunch Promo Sports Impressions 125.00 200.00
5 Terry Labonte Kellogg's/4020 25.00 60.00
5 Terry Labonte Kellogg's Iron Man Silver/10,008 30.00 80.00
6 Mark Martin Valvoline 20.00 35.00
8 Kenny Wallace Red Dog 25.00 50.00
10 Ricky Rudd Tide 25.00 40.00
11 Brett Bodine Lowe's 50th Anniversary 12.00 30.00
16 Ted Musgrave Family Channel Primestar 20.00 35.00
17 Darrell Waltrip Parts America 20.00 35.00
18 Bobby Labonte Interstate Batteries/2700 20.00 35.00
22 Rusty Wallace Miller Genuine Draft Suzuka Thunder SuperTruck/3120 40.00 60.00
22 Rusty Wallace Miller Genuine Draft Silver 25th Anniversary SuperTruck/2504 100.00 200.00
22 Rusty Wallace Miller Splash SuperTruck/2508 125.00 200.00
23 Chad Little John Deere 30.00 60.00
23 Chad Little John Deere Autographed signed box 40.00 80.00
23 Chad Little John Deere Bank set w/1:64 car 25.00 60.00
23 Chad Little John Deere Bank set with 1:64 car/2508 Autographed box 40.00 80.00
24 Jeff Gordon DuPont/8292 30.00 50.00
24 Jack Sprague Quaker State 20.00 35.00
25 Ken Schrader Bud/5004 20.00 35.00
25 Ken Schrader Budweiser Olympic car 20.00 35.00
28 Ernie Irvan Havoline 20.00 35.00
30 Johnny Benson Pennzoil/7008 15.00 35.00
37 Jeremy Mayfield K-Mart Little Caesars/5004 20.00 35.00
52 Jack Sprague Pedigree 20.00 35.00
75 Morgan Shepherd Remington 20.00 35.00
75 Morgan Shepherd Remington Camo/5004 30.00 50.00
75 Morgan Shepherd Stren/3120 20.00 35.00
76 David Green Smith and Wesson 15.00 35.00
77 Bobby Hillin Jr. Jasper Engines/3120 20.00 35.00
87 Joe Nemechek Burger King/3120 20.00 40.00
88 Dale Jarrett Quality Care/5004 30.00 50.00
96 Revell Collection SuperTruck Promo 15.00 30.00
99 Jeff Burton Exide 20.00 35.00

1997 Revell Club 1:24

These pieces were also a part of the continued growth of Revell's presence in the die cast market. In the last quarter of 1997, Revell formed a collector's club to which they distributed cars in this series. The actual cars themselves were from the same production run as the Collection cars and banks. Each car distributed by the club has a serial number on the chassis. The boxes were uniquely colored to match the colors on the car and feature the name "Revell Collection Club." Each piece is housed inside a clear plastic or acrylic box.

1 Coca-Cola 600/1596 30.00 60.00
1 Revell Club/10,002 15.00 40.00
2 Rusty Wallace Miller Lite 40.00 80.00
4 Sterling Marlin Kodak/1596 20.00 50.00
5 Terry Labonte Kellogg's/1596 30.00 80.00
5 Terry Labonte Kellogg's Tony/1596 50.00 100.00
5 Terry Labonte Kellogg's Tony Bank set w/1:64 car 60.00 150.00
5 Terry Labonte Spooky Loops 125.00 200.00
5 Terry Labonte Spooky Loops Bank 100.00 200.00
6 Mark Martin Valvoline/1596 40.00 100.00
10 Ricky Rudd Tide/1596 25.00 60.00
18 Bobby Labonte Interstate Batteries/1596 20.00 50.00
18 Bobby Labonte Interstate Batteries Texas/1596 50.00 100.00
21 Michael Waltrip Citgo Pearson white&red/1596 20.00 50.00
21 Michael Waltrip Citgo Top Dog/1596 25.00 60.00
23 Jimmy Spencer Camel/1596 60.00 150.00
23 Jimmy Spencer Winston/2300 150.00 300.00
25 Ricky Craven Budweiser/1596 25.00 60.00
28 Ernie Irvan Havoline black 70.00 120.00
28 Ernie Irvan Havoline 10th Anniversary white and black 90.00 150.00
28 Ernie Irvan Havoline 10th Anniversary white and black Bank set w/1:64 car 60.00 150.00
33 Ken Schrader Skoal/1596 25.00 60.00
35 Todd Bodine Tabasco/1596 20.00 50.00
36 Derrike Cope Skittles/1596 20.00 50.00
37 Jeremy Mayfield K-Mart RC-Cola/1596 40.00 80.00
40 Robby Gordon Coors Light/1596 30.00 60.00
41 Steve Grissom Kodak/1596 20.00 50.00
43 Bobby Hamilton STP Goody's/1596 25.00 60.00
43 Jimmy Hensley Cummins SuperTruck/1596 20.00 50.00
46 Wally Dallenbach Woody Woodpecker 25.00 60.00
75 Rick Mast Remington 40.00 80.00
94 Bill Elliott McDonald's/1596 25.00 60.00
96 David Green Caterpillar/1596 20.00 50.00
97 California 500/1596 15.00 40.00
97 Chad Little John Deere/1596 40.00 100.00
97 Chad Little John Deere 160th Anniversary/1596 50.00 100.00
97 Texas Motor Speedway/1596 20.00 50.00

1997 Revell Collection 1:24

This series is the continuation of the 1996 Revell Collection. It signals Revell's continued expansion into the die cast market by its larger number of cars and banks. Each is packaged in a clear acrylic Revell Collection box which is wrapped inside a colorful outer cardboard box.

1 Coca-Cola 600 12.00 30.00
2 Rusty Wallace Miller Japan/5496 25.00 60.00
2 Rusty Wallace Miller Lite/25,000 20.00 50.00
2 Rusty Wallace Miller Lite Texas 30.00 60.00
4 Sterling Marlin Kodak/3120 25.00 60.00
5 Terry Labonte Kellogg's/5004 25.00 60.00
5 Terry Labonte Kellogg's distributed by Mac Tools 50.00 80.00
5 Terry Labonte Kellogg's 1996 Champion/5004 50.00 90.00
5 Terry Labonte Kellogg's Texas Motor Speedway 70.00 120.00
5 Terry Labonte Spooky Loops 30.00 80.00
5 Terry Labonte Spooky Loops Bank set with 1:64 car/1506 25.00 60.00
5 Terry Labonte Kellogg's Tony/6600 50.00 100.00
5 Terry Labonte Kellogg's Tony Bank set w/1:64 car/1506 40.00 100.00
6 Mark Martin Valvoline 35.00 50.00
7 Geoff Bodine QVC/5004 15.00 40.00
8 Hut Stricklin Circuit City 15.00 40.00
10 Ricky Rudd Tide/3120 25.00 45.00
11 Brett Bodine Close Call/3120 12.00 30.00
15 Mike Colabucci VISA SuperTruck 25.00 45.00
16 Ted Musgrave Primestar 15.00 40.00
17 Rich Bickle Die Hard SuperTruck/3120 15.00 40.00
17 Darrell Waltrip Parts America 30.00 45.00

bby Labonte erstate Batteries/5004	30.00	50.00
bby Labonte erstate Batteries xas/8598	60.00	100.00
bby Labonte erstate Batteries xas Motor Speedway Bank	90.00	150.00
ny Raines nnzoil SuperTruck/3120	25.00	45.00
chael Waltrip go Orange/4122	15.00	40.00
chael Waltrip go Pearson white&red	20.00	40.00
chael Waltrip go Top Dog/5004	15.00	40.00
nmy Spencer mel/5004	50.00	100.00
nmy Spencer nston/3323	100.00	200.00
cky Craven dweiser	20.00	50.00
cky Craven dweiser Lizard	20.00	50.00
nie Irvan voline black	20.00	50.00
nie Irvan voline Bank black	50.00	80.00
nie Irvan voline 10th Anniversary ite and black/5004	25.00	60.00
nie Irvan voline 10th Anniversary ite and black nk set w/1:64 car	20.00	50.00
ff Green ooby-Doo	25.00	40.00
ff Green ooby-Doo Bank	50.00	80.00
eve Grissom intstones	15.00	40.00
bert Pressley ooby-Doo	25.00	50.00
bert Pressley om & Jerry	25.00	40.00
hnny Benson ennzoil/6630	25.00	45.00
le Jarrett hite Rain	25.00	40.00
en Schrader koal/5004	20.00	50.00
odd Bodine abasco/5004	20.00	40.00
odd Bodine abasco Bank et w/1:64 car/1002	15.00	40.00
odd Bodine anley/3120	15.00	40.00
errike Cope kittles/6636	15.00	40.00
avid Green leff Green ed Man SuperTruck	15.00	40.00
lark Green Timber Wolf/3120	15.00	40.00
eremy Mayfield -Mart Kids/5004	15.00	40.00
eremy Mayfield -Mart Lady Luck	25.00	45.00
eremy Mayfield -Mart RC-Cola	15.00	40.00
obby Gordon Coors Light/5004	25.00	40.00
Steve Grissom Kodiak/5004	15.00	40.00
Joe Nemechek BellSouth	15.00	40.00
Bobby Hamilton STP Goody's/5004	15.00	40.00
Jimmy Hensley Cummins SuperTruck	15.00	40.00
Wally Dallenbach First Union Bank	35.00	70.00
Wally Dallenbach Woody Woodpecker/5004	20.00	40.00
Wally Dallenbach Woody Woodpecker Bank	50.00	80.00
Michael Waltrip Sealy	15.00	40.00
Mark Martin Winn Dixie	35.00	50.00
Rick Mast Remington/4716	15.00	40.00
Dale Jarrett Quality Care	15.00	40.00
Dick Trickle Heilig-Meyers/3120	15.00	40.00
Mike Wallace Spam/6600	15.00	40.00
Mike Wallace Spam Bank	25.00	60.00
Ron Barfield New Holland/3120	15.00	40.00
Bill Elliott McDonald's	20.00	40.00
Bill Elliott Mac Tonight	15.00	40.00
David Green Caterpillar/5004	15.00	40.00
California 500/25,000	12.50	30.00
California 500 Bank set w/1:64 car	12.50	30.00
Chad Little John Deere Autographed box	30.00	80.00
Chad Little John Deere Bank Autographed box	30.00	70.00
Chad Little John Deere 160th Anniversary/5004	35.00	70.00
Chad Little John Deere 160th Anniversary Bank autographed box	50.00	80.00
Texas Motor Speedway/6000	20.00	40.00
John Andretti RCA/3120	20.00	40.00
99 Chuck Bown Exide SuperTruck/3120	15.00	40.00
99 Jeff Burton Exide/2502	20.00	40.00
99 Jeff Burton Exide Texas	25.00	60.00

1997 Revell Select 1:24

These cars were produced to appease those collectors who wanted an upgraded production die cast without the upgrade price. The cars themselves appear to have similar production qualities as the Collection cars, but were priced much lower intially and were packaged in black window boxes. Although the box does not include the "Select" name, this series in black boxes is considered the first of the new Select line by Revell.

2 Rusty Wallace Miller Lite	25.00	40.00
4 Sterling Marlin Kodak	20.00	40.00
5 Terry Labonte Kellogg's	20.00	35.00
5 Terry Labonte Kellogg's Texas	20.00	35.00
5 Terry Labonte Spooky Loops	30.00	60.00
5 Terry Labonte Tony the Tiger	20.00	40.00
6 Mark Martin Valvoline	20.00	35.00
10 Ricky Rudd Tide	20.00	35.00
17 Darrell Waltrip Parts America	20.00	35.00
18 Bobby Labonte Interstate Batteries	15.00	30.00
18 Bobby Labonte Interstate Batteries Texas	40.00	70.00
21 Michael Waltrip Citgo Top Dog paint scheme	20.00	35.00
23 Jimmy Spencer Camel	25.00	50.00
23 Jimmy Spencer No Bull	15.00	40.00
25 Ricky Craven Budweiser Lizard	20.00	40.00
28 Ernie Irvan Havoline black	20.00	35.00
28 Ernie Irvan Havoline 10th Anniversary white and black	25.00	40.00
29 Jeff Green Tom & Jerry	15.00	30.00
29 Steve Grissom Flintstones	15.00	30.00
29 Robert Pressley Scooby-Doo	15.00	30.00
29 Robert Pressley Tom & Jerry	15.00	30.00
33 Ken Schrader Skoal	25.00	40.00
36 Derrike Cope Skittles	15.00	35.00
37 Jeremy Mayfield K-Mart Kids Against Drugs	20.00	35.00
40 Robby Gordon Coors Light	20.00	35.00
41 Steve Grissom Kodiak	15.00	30.00
42 Joe Nemechek Bell South	15.00	30.00
43 Bobby Hamilton STP Goody's	15.00	30.00
46 Wally Dallenbach First Union Bank	30.00	50.00
46 Wally Dallenbach Woody Woodpecker	15.00	30.00
75 Rick Mast Remington	20.00	35.00
91 Mike Wallace Spam	15.00	30.00
94 Bill Elliott McDonald's	20.00	35.00
94 Bill Elliott Mac Tonight	20.00	35.00
97 Chad Little John Deere 160th Anniversary paint scheme	30.00	35.00
97 Texas Motor Speedway	15.00	30.00
98 John Andretti RCA	15.00	30.00
99 Jeff Burton Exide	20.00	35.00

1997 Revell Retail 1:24

This series, Revell Racing, was produced for and distributed to the mass-market. Each piece was packaged in a colorful clear window box with the sponsor logos and designs on the box. No production run numbers were given for the retail version.

1 Coca-Cola 600	10.00	20.00
1 Mac Tools packaged in collectible tin	45.00	75.00
2 Rusty Wallace Penske	12.50	25.00
4 Sterling Marlin Kodak	15.00	40.00
5 Terry Labonte Kellogg's Texas Motor Speedway	12.50	25.00
5 Terry Labonte Spooky Loops	12.50	30.00
5 Terry Labonte Tony The Tiger packaged in Food City box	15.00	30.00
6 Mark Martin Valvoline	12.50	25.00
10 Ricky Rudd Tide	15.00	30.00
16 Ted Musgrave Primestar	15.00	30.00
17 Darrell Waltrip Parts America blue&white	10.00	20.00
17 Darrell Waltrip Parts America Chrome Box	15.00	30.00
17 Darrell Waltrip Parts America Green with green number	10.00	20.00
17 Darrell Waltrip Parts America Green with white number	10.00	20.00
17 Darrell Waltrip Parts America Red&White	10.00	20.00
17 Darrell Waltrip Parts America Yellow&White	10.00	20.00
21 Michael Waltrip Citgo Top Dog paint scheme	12.50	25.00
21 Michael Waltrip Citgo Pearson white&red	10.00	25.00
23 Jimmy Spencer Camel	25.00	40.00
28 Ernie Irvan Havoline Black	12.50	25.00
28 Ernie Irvan Havoline 10th Anniversary white and black	12.50	25.00
29 Jeff Green Tom & Jerry on hood	10.00	20.00
29 Robert Pressley Scooby-Doo	10.00	20.00
29 Robert Pressley Flintstones	10.00	20.00
37 Jeremy Mayfield K-Mart RC-Cola	12.50	25.00
37 Jeremy Mayfield K-Mart Kids Against Drugs	10.00	25.00
46 Wally Dallenbach Woody Woodpecker	10.00	20.00
75 Rick Mast Remington	10.00	20.00
88 Dale Jarrett Quality Care	12.50	25.00
91 Mike Wallace Spam	10.00	25.00
97 California 500	10.00	20.00
97 Texas Motor Speedway	10.00	20.00
99 Jeff Burton Exide	12.50	25.00

1998 Revell Club 1:24

These 1:24 scale cars were from the same production run as the Collection cars. Each car distributed by the club has a serial number on the chassis. The boxes were uniquely colored to match the colors on the car.

1 Dale Earnhardt Jr. Coke Bear/3330	40.00	100.00
1 Steve Park Pennzoil Black Roof/1002	40.00	100.00
1 Steve Park Pennzoil Yellow Roof	40.00	100.00
2 Rusty Wallace Miller Lite/1002	50.00	120.00
2 Rusty Wallace Adventures of Rusty/1002	60.00	150.00
2 Rusty Wallace Miller Lite Elvis1596	50.00	120.00
3 Dale Earnhardt Coke/3333	60.00	150.00
3 Dale Earnhardt Goodwrench Plus/1596	75.00	150.00
3 Dale Earnhardt Goodwrench Plus Bass Pro/1002	60.00	120.00
3 Dale Earnhardt Goodwrench Plus Daytona Win/1596	75.00	150.00
3 Dale Earnhardt Jr. AC Delco	75.00	150.00
4 Bobby Hamilton Kodak Max/1596	20.00	50.00
4 Bobby Hamilton Kodak Gold/1596	20.00	50.00
5 Terry Labonte Blasted Fruit Loops/2004	40.00	100.00
5 Terry Labonte Kellogg's/1596	30.00	80.00
5 Terry Labonte Kellogg's Corny	40.00	100.00
5 Terry Labonte Kellogg's Ironman/2004	50.00	120.00
12 Jeremy Mayfield Mobil 1	30.00	80.00
18 Bobby Labonte Interstate Batteries Hot Rod	40.00	100.00
18 Bobby Labonte Interstate Batteries Small Soldiers/2004	30.00	80.00
21 Michael Waltrip Citgo/1002	25.00	60.00
23 Jimmy Spencer No Bull	125.00	200.00
24 Jeff Gordon DuPont/1596	40.00	100.00
24 Jeff Gordon DuPont Chromalusion/2424	60.00	120.00
25 John Andretti Bud/1002	30.00	80.00
28 Kenny Irwin Havoline	40.00	100.00
28 Kenny Irwin Havoline Joker/1002	40.00	100.00
31 Mike Skinner Lowe's	30.00	80.00
31 Mike Skinner Lowe's Special Olympics	30.00	80.00
33 Ken Schrader Skoal	40.00	100.00
33 Ken Schrader Skoal Bud Shootout	40.00	100.00
35 Todd Bodine Tabasco	25.00	60.00
36 Ernie Irvan M&M's/1002	30.00	80.00
36 Ernie Irvan Wildberry Skittles	40.00	100.00
40 Sterling Marlin Coors Light/804	40.00	100.00
41 Steve Grissom Kodiak/1002	20.00	50.00
42 Joe Nemechek BellSouth	20.00	50.00
44 Tony Stewart Shell/1002	75.00	150.00
44 Tony Stewart Shell Small Soldiers	70.00	120.00
46 Wally Dallenbach First Union	25.00	60.00
46 Jeff Green First Union Devil Rays	25.00	60.00
50 Ricky Craven Budweiser	50.00	120.00
50 No Driver Association Bud Louie	40.00	100.00
74 Randy LaJoie Fina	25.00	60.00
75 Rick Mast Remington	20.00	50.00
81 Kenny Wallace Square D Lightning	20.00	50.00
88 Dale Jarrett Batman	40.00	100.00
88 Dale Jarrett Quality Care	40.00	100.00
90 Dick Trickle Heilig-Meyers	25.00	60.00
96 David Green Caterpillar/1002	20.00	50.00
98 Greg Sacks Thorn Apple Valley	20.00	50.00

1998 Revell Collection 1:24

This series was produced for and distributed in hobby outlets.

1 Dale Earnhardt Jr. Coke Bear Bank	50.00	100.00
1 Dale Earnhardt Jr. Coke Bear/18,000	35.00	75.00
1 Steve Park Pennzoil Black Roof/5598	25.00	60.00
1 Steve Park Pennzoil Yellow Roof/5598	25.00	60.00
2 Rusty Wallace Adventures of Rusty	25.00	60.00
2 Rusty Wallace Miller Lite/5598	20.00	50.00
2 Rusty Wallace Miller Lite Elvis	25.00	60.00
2 Rusty Wallace Miller Lite TCB Elvis	25.00	60.00
2 Rusty Wallace Miller Lite TCB Elvis Bank/1002	50.00	100.00
3 Dale Earnhardt Coke/18,000	40.00	80.00
3 Dale Earnhardt Coke Bank set with 1:64 car/2502	60.00	120.00
3 Dale Earnhardt Goodwrench Plus Daytona Win/7512	40.00	100.00
3 Dale Earnhardt Goodwrench Plus Bass Pro/14,994	40.00	100.00
3 Dale Earnhardt Goodwrench Plus Brickyard Win/10,008	50.00	100.00
3 Dale Earnhardt Jr. AC Delco Dealer Issued/3500	75.00	125.00
3 Dale Earnhardt Jr. AC Delco Trackside Issued	75.00	125.00
4 Bobby Hamilton Kodak Gold	25.00	40.00
5 Terry Labonte Blasted Fruit Loops/5598	25.00	60.00
5 Terry Labonte Kellogg's/5598	20.00	50.00
5 Terry Labonte Kellogg's Bank set with 1:64 car/1002	30.00	80.00
5 Terry Labonte Kellogg's Corny/5598	30.00	80.00
5 Terry Labonte Kellogg's Corny Bank set with 1:64 car/1002	30.00	80.00
5 Terry Labonte Kellogg's Ironman	20.00	50.00
5 Terry Labonte Kellogg's Ironman Bank set with 1:64 car	25.00	60.00
8 Hut Stricklin Circuit City/3120	15.00	40.00
9 Lake Speed Birthday Cake	20.00	40.00
9 Lake Speed Huckleberry Hound	20.00	40.00
9 Lake Speed Huckleberry Hound Bank	40.00	80.00
12 Jeremy Mayfield Mobil 1/5598	15.00	40.00
18 Bobby Labonte Interstate Batteries/5598	20.00	50.00
18 Bobby Labonte Interstate Batteries Hot Rod/5598	20.00	50.00
18 Bobby Labonte Interstate Batteries Small Soldiers/5598	25.00	60.00
21 Michael Waltrip Citgo	15.00	40.00
23 Jimmy Spencer No Bull/5598	20.00	40.00
24 Jeff Gordon DuPont/6000	30.00	70.00
24 Jeff Gordon DuPont Brickyard Win/10,008	25.00	60.00
24 Jeff Gordon DuPont Chromalusion/14,400	40.00	100.00
25 John Andretti Bud/3120	20.00	40.00
28 Kenny Irwin Havoline/5598	20.00	50.00
28 Kenny Irwin Havoline Joker/6000	25.00	60.00
31 Dale Earnhardt Jr. Wrangler 1997 Monte Carlo/5004	75.00	150.00
31 Dale Earnhardt Jr. Wrangler Bank 1997 Monte Carlo/2504	75.00	150.00
31 Mike Skinner Lowe's/5598	20.00	40.00
31 Mike Skinner Lowe's Special Olympics	20.00	50.00
33 Ken Schrader Skoal/6600	25.00	50.00
33 Ken Schrader Skoal Bud Shootout/5598	15.00	40.00
35 Todd Bodine Tabasco	20.00	40.00
36 Ernie Irvan M&M's/5598	20.00	50.00
36 Ernie Irvan Wildberry Skittles/5598	15.00	40.00
40 Sterling Marlin Coors Light/3120	20.00	50.00
41 Steve Grissom Kodiak/5598	20.00	40.00
42 Joe Nemechek BellSouth/3120	15.00	40.00
44 Tony Stewart Shell	35.00	70.00
44 Tony Stewart Shell Small Soldiers	25.00	50.00
46 Wally Dallenbach First Union/3120	15.00	40.00
46 Jeff Green First Union Devil Rays/5598	15.00	40.00
50 Ricky Craven Bud/6600	30.00	60.00
50 No Driver Association Bud Louie/6000	25.00	50.00
74 Randy LaJoie Fina/3120	15.00	40.00
75 Rick Mast Remington/3120	15.00	40.00
81 Kenny Wallace Square D Lightning	20.00	50.00
88 Dale Jarrett Batman/6000	40.00	80.00
88 Dale Jarrett Batman Bank	40.00	100.00
88 Dale Jarrett Quality Care	30.00	60.00
90 Dick Trickle Heilig-Meyers/3120	15.00	40.00
96 David Green Caterpillar/5598	15.00	40.00
98 Greg Sacks Thorn Apple Valley/3120	15.00	40.00

1998 Revell Select 1:24

The Revell Select series returned in 1998 with an upgraded production die-cast car without the upgrade price. The cars themselves appear to have similar production qualities as the Collection cars and some are mounted to a Revell Collection base. However, were issued at a lower initial price point and are packaged in Revell Select window boxes in the color of the sponsor's paint scheme.

1 Steve Park Pennzoil Black Roof	25.00	45.00
2 Rusty Wallace Adventures of Rusty	20.00	35.00
2 Rusty Wallace Miller Lite	20.00	35.00
2 Rusty Wallace Miller Lite Elvis	20.00	35.00
3 Dale Earnhardt Goodwrench Plus	40.00	80.00
3 Dale Earnhardt Goodwrench Plus Bass Pro	40.00	80.00
3 Dale Earnhardt Jr. AC Delco	20.00	50.00
4 Bobby Hamilton Kodak	15.00	30.00
5 Terry Labonte Blasted Fruit Loops	15.00	30.00
5 Terry Labonte Kellogg's	15.00	30.00
5 Terry Labonte Kellogg's Corny	15.00	30.00
8 Hut Stricklin Circuit City	12.50	30.00
9 Lake Speed Birthday Cake	15.00	30.00
9 Lake Speed Huckleberry Hound	15.00	30.00
18 Bobby Labonte Interstate Batteries	15.00	30.00
18 Bobby Labonte Interstate Batteries Hot Rod	15.00	30.00
21 Michael Waltrip Citgo	15.00	30.00
23 Jimmy Spencer No Bull	12.50	30.00
24 Jeff Gordon DuPont	25.00	40.00
28 Kenny Irwin Havoline	15.00	30.00
31 Mike Skinner Lowe's	15.00	30.00
33 Ken Schrader Skoal Bud Shootout	15.00	30.00
35 Todd Bodine Tabasco	15.00	30.00
36 Ernie Irvan M&M's	12.50	30.00
36 Ernie Irvan Wildberry Skittles	12.50	30.00
44 Tony Stewart Shell	15.00	30.00
50 Ricky Craven Budweiser	15.00	30.00
50 NDA Bud Louie	15.00	30.00
77 Robert Pressley Jasper	15.00	30.00
81 Kenny Wallace Square D Lightning	15.00	30.00
88 Dale Jarrett Quality Care	20.00	35.00

1999 Revell Club 1:24

These 1:24 scale cars were produced in very small numbers and were only available through the club.

2 Rusty Wallace Miller Lite/504 50.00 100.00
2 Rusty Wallace Miller Lite Harley/1002 30.00 80.00
3 Dale Earnhardt Goodwrench/2004 50.00 120.00
3 Dale Earnhardt Goodwrench 25th/1002 50.00 100.00
3 Dale Earnhardt GM Goodwrench Sign 100.00 200.00
3 Dale Earnhardt Wrangler/3333 60.00 150.00
3 Dale Earnhardt Jr. AC Delco/2004 40.00 100.00
3 Dale Earnhardt Jr. AC Delco Superman/1500 60.00 150.00
4 Bobby Hamilton Advantix 40.00 100.00
5 Terry Labonte K-Sentials/1002 25.00 60.00
5 Terry Labonte Rice Krispy 40.00 100.00
8 Dale Earnhardt Jr. Bud/1002 90.00 150.00
9 Jerry Nadeau Dextor's Lab/1002 25.00 60.00
9 Jerry Nadeau Jetsons 30.00 80.00
10 Ricky Rudd Tide 40.00 100.00
11 Dale Jarrett Green Bay Packers/1002 75.00 150.00
12 Jeremy Mayfield Mobil 1 25.00 60.00
12 Jeremy Mayfield Kentucky Derby 25.00 60.00
17 Matt Kenseth DeWalt/3508 40.00 80.00
18 Bobby Labonte Interstate Batteries 50.00 120.00
20 Tony Stewart Home Depot/1002 150.00 250.00
20 Tony Stewart Home Depot Habitat for Humanity 40.00 100.00
23 Jimmy Spencer No Bull/1002 30.00 80.00
23 Jimmy Spencer Winston Lights/2004 30.00 80.00
24 Jeff Gordon DuPont/2424 30.00 80.00
24 Jeff Gordon DuPont Daytona 90.00 150.00
24 Jeff Gordon DuPont Superman/3500 50.00 120.00
24 Jeff Gordon Pepsi/2004 40.00 100.00
24 Jeff Gordon Pepsi Star Wars 40.00 100.00
27 Casey Atwood Castrol 30.00 80.00
28 Kenny Irwin Havoline 50.00 100.00
31 Dale Earnhardt Jr. Gargoyles 1997 Monte Carlo/2004 50.00 100.00
31 Dale Earnhardt Jr. Mom 'N' Pop's 1996 Monte Carlo/2004 50.00 100.00
31 Dale Earnhardt Jr. Sikkens Blue 1997 Monte Carlo/1002 60.00 100.00
31 Dale Earnhardt Jr. Sikkens White 1997 Monte Carlo/2004 50.00 100.00
33 Ken Schrader Skoal Blue/1002 60.00 150.00
36 Ernie Irvan M&M's/1002 30.00 80.00
36 Ernie Irvan M&M's Countdown/1002 25.00 60.00
36 Ernie Irvan Crispy M&M's/1002 40.00 100.00
36 Ernie Irvan Pedigree/504 30.00 80.00
40 Kerry Earnhardt Channelock/1002 25.00 60.00
40 Sterling Marlin Coors Light Brooks & Dunn 30.00 80.00
40 Sterling Marlin Coors Light John Wayne 30.00 80.00
55 Kenny Wallace Square D 25.00 60.00
66 Darrell Waltrip Big K Route 66/1002 25.00 60.00
88 Dale Jarrett Quality Care 40.00 100.00
88 Dale Jarrett Quality Care White/1002 40.00 80.00

1999 Revell Collection 1:24

This series was produced for and distributed in hobby outlets.

1 Steve Park Pennzoil 40.00 70.00
1 Steve Park Pennzoil Shark/2508 25.00 60.00
2 Rusty Wallace Miller Lite/5004 20.00 50.00
2 Rusty Wallace Miller Lite Harley/5004 30.00 60.00
2 Rusty Wallace 40.00 75.00
Miller Lite Harley Matco Tools promo
3 Dale Earnhardt Goodwrench/7992 60.00 150.00
3 Dale Earnhardt Goodwrench 25th 90.00 150.00
3 Dale Earnhardt Goodwrench Sign 50.00 120.00
3 Dale Earnhardt Wrangler/14,400 40.00 100.00
3 Dale Earnhardt Jr. AC Delco/10,530 25.00 60.00
3 Dale Earnhardt Jr. AC Delco Superman/10,530 30.00 60.00
3 Dale Earnhardt Jr. AC Del.Superman Bank set w/1:64 car/2004 30.00 80.00
4 Bobby Hamilton Advantix 20.00 50.00
5 Terry Labonte Kellogg's/4008 20.00 50.00
5 Terry Labonte K-Sentials/4008 20.00 50.00
5 Terry Labonte Rice Krispies/3120 20.00 50.00
8 Dale Earnhardt Jr. Bud/12,024 45.00 80.00
8 Dale Earnhardt Jr. Bud Bank set w/1:64 car/2508 50.00 100.00
9 Jerry Nadeau Dexter's Laboratory/3120 20.00 50.00
9 Jerry Nadeau Jetsons/4128 20.00 50.00
9 Jerry Nadeau Dexter's Lab Bank 40.00 100.00
10 Ricky Rudd Tide/3120 20.00 50.00
10 Ricky Rudd Tide Kids Bank set w/1:64 car/3504 20.00 50.00
11 Dale Jarrett Rayovac/2508 25.00 60.00
11 Dale Jarrett Green Bay Packers 40.00 70.00
12 Jeremy Mayfield Mobil 1 20.00 50.00
12 Jeremy Mayfield Mobil 1 Bank set w/1:64 car 20.00 50.00
12 Jeremy Mayfield Mobil 1 Kentucky Derby/5004 20.00 50.00
18 Bobby Labonte Interstate Batteries/4000 25.00 60.00
20 Tony Stewart Home Depot/3120 100.00 175.00
20 Tony Stewart Home Depot Habitat for Humanity 50.00 100.00
20 Tony Stewart Home Depot Habitat Bank set w/1:64 car/4008 40.00 100.00
22 Ward Burton Caterpillar/2508 25.00 60.00
23 Jimmy Spencer No Bull/4212 20.00 50.00
23 Jimmy Spencer Winston Lights 20.00 50.00
24 Jeff Gordon DuPont/7512 25.00 60.00
24 Jeff Gordon DuPont Daytona/4008 60.00 120.00
24 Jeff Gordon DuPont Superman/16,872 40.00 100.00
24 Jeff Gordon Pepsi/10,008 25.00 60.00
24 Jeff Gordon Pepsi/3504 set with 1:64 car 25.00 60.00
24 Jeff Gordon Pepsi Star Wars/5004 30.00 80.00
25 Wally Dallenbach Budweiser 20.00 50.00
27 Casey Atwood Castrol/4008 20.00 50.00
27 Casey Atwood Castrol Last Lap Mac Tools/5004 15.00 40.00
28 Kenny Irwin Havoline/4000 20.00 50.00
30 Derrike Cope Jimmy Dean/3120 15.00 40.00
31 Dale Earnhardt Jr. Gargoyles 1997 Monte Carlo/5004 50.00 100.00
31 Dale Earnhardt Jr. Mom 'N' Pop's 1996 Monte Carlo/3120 40.00 100.00
31 Dale Earnhardt Jr. Sikkens Blue 1997 Monte Carlo/8500 30.00 70.00
31 Dale Earnhardt Jr. Sikkens White 1997 Monte Carlo 30.00 70.00
31 Mike Skinner Lowe's 20.00 50.00
33 Ken Schrader Skoal Blue/3120 50.00 75.00
36 Ernie Irvan M&M's/3120 20.00 50.00
36 Ernie Irvan M&M's Countdown/5004 20.00 50.00
36 Ernie Irvan Crispy M&M's/3120 20.00 50.00
36 Ernie Irvan Pedigree 20.00 50.00
40 Kerry Earnhardt Channelock 20.00 50.00
40 Sterling Marlin Coors Light Brooks & Dunn 30.00 80.00
40 Sterling Marlin Coors Light John Wayne 30.00 80.00
55 Kenny Wallace Square D/3120 15.00 40.00
66 Darrell Waltrip Big K Route 66/2508 20.00 50.00
88 Dale Jarrett Quality Care 30.00 70.00
88 Dale Jarrett QC White 30.00 70.00
88 Dale Jarrett Quality Care Last Lap Mac Tools/5004 25.00 60.00
99 Kevin Lepage Red Man 15.00 40.00
00 Buckshot Jones Crown Fiber/3120 15.00 40.00
00 Larry Pearson Cheez-it/3120 15.00 40.00

1999 Revell Select 1:24

The Revell Select series was issued again in 1999 with an upgraded production die-cast car without the upgrade price. The cars themselves appear to have similar production qualities as the Collection cars and some are mounted to a Revell Collection base. However, were issued at a lower initial price point and are packaged in black window boxes.

2 Rusty Wallace Miller Lite Last Lap 12.50 25.00
3 Dale Earnhardt Goodwrench 25th Anniv. 20.00 40.00
3 Dale Earnhardt Goodwrench Sign 20.00 40.00
24 Jeff Gordon Pepsi 12.50 30.00
24 Jeff Gordon Pepsi Star Wars 12.50 30.00
36 Ernie Irvan M&M's Millennium 10.00 25.00
88 Dale Jarrett Quality Care Last Lap 10.00 25.00

2000 Revell Club 1:24

3 Dale Earnhardt Goodwrench/2004 40.00 100.00
3 Dale Earnhardt Goodwrench Peter Max/2004 75.00 150.00
3 Dale Earnhardt Goodwrench Taz/3333 50.00 120.00
4 Bobby Hamilton Kodak Navy/1002 15.00 40.00
8 Dale Earnhardt Jr. Bud/2004 70.00 120.00
18 Bobby Labonte Interstate Batteries/1002 30.00 80.00
18 Bobby Labonte Interstate Batteries All Star Game 75.00 150.00
20 Tony Stewart Home Depot/2004 40.00 100.00
20 Tony Stewart Home Depot Rookie of the Year/2508 30.00 80.00
24 Jeff Gordon DuPont Millennium 75.00 150.00
24 Jeff Gordon DuPont Peanuts 75.00 125.00
24 Jeff Gordon Pepsi/2508 40.00 100.00
25 Jerry Nadeau Holigan Coast Guard/1002 15.00 40.00
27 Casey Atwood Castrol 15.00 40.00
28 Ricky Rudd Havoline/1002 15.00 40.00
28 Ricky Rudd Havoline Marines/1002 15.00 40.00
31 Mike Skinner Lowe's Army/1002 25.00 60.00
36 Ken Schrader M&M's July 4th/1002 25.00 60.00
37 Kevin Grubb Timber Wolf/1002 20.00 50.00
66 Darrell Waltrip Big K Route 66 Flames/1002 15.00 40.00
88 Dale Jarrett Quality Care/1500 25.00 60.00
88 Dale Jarrett Quality Care Air Force 25.00 60.00
94 Bill Elliott McDonald's Drive Thru/1002 15.00 40.00
94 Bill Elliott McDonald's 25th/1002 15.00 40.00

2000 Revell Collection 1:24

These cars are mounted on a display base with a clear plastic cover.

2 Rusty Wallace Miller Lite/3120 15.00 40.00
2 Rusty Wallace Miller Lite Harley 25.00 60.00
3 Dale Earnhardt Goodwrench/5004 50.00 120.00
3 Dale Earnhardt Goodwrench Peter Max/5508 150.00 300.00
3 Dale Earnhardt Goodwrench Peter Max Bank set with 1:64 car/1008 125.00 200.00
3 Dale Earnhardt Goodwrench Taz Bank set with 1:64 car/14,400 60.00 120.00
3 Dale Earnhardt Goodwrench Test/1500 75.00 150.00
3 Ron Hornaday NAPA Monsters/2508 20.00 50.00
4 Bobby Hamilton Kodak Navy/3120 20.00 50.00
4 Bobby Hamilton Kodak Navy Bank set with 1:64 car 20.00 50.00
5 Terry Labonte Kellogg's 20.00 50.00
8 Dale Earnhardt Jr. Bud/5004 50.00 100.00
8 Dale Earnhardt Jr. Bud Bank set with 1:64 car 60.00 120.00
8 Dale Earnhardt Jr. Bud Olympic/3120 50.00 100.00
8 Dale Earnhardt Jr. Bud Test/1500 90.00 175.00
12 Jeremy Mayfield Mobil 1 20.00 50.00
12 Jeremy Mayfield Mobil 1 World Series/2004 20.00 50.00
15 Derrick Gilchrist Hot Tamales/2508 15.00 40.00
18 Bobby Labonte Interstate Batteries 40.00 90.00
18 Bobby Labonte Interstate Batteries All Star Game w baseball/3120 25.00 60.00
18 Bobby Labonte Interstate Batteries Frankenstein/2508 25.00 60.00
19 Dodge Show Car/2508 25.00 50.00
20 Tony Stewart Home Depot/5504 25.00 60.00
20 Tony Stewart Home Depot Kids/2004 25.00 60.00
20 Tony Stewart Home Depot 1999 Rookie of the Year/7500 40.00 70.00
20 Tony Stewart Home Depot 1999 Rookie of the Year Bank set w/1:64 car 35.00 70.00
21 Elliott Sadler Citgo MDA/3120 20.00 50.00
21 Elliott Sadler Citgo MDA Jerry Lewis Telethon Promo 12.50 25.00
21 Elliott Sadler Citgo '60's Red and White/3120 20.00 50.00
24 Jeff Gordon DuPont/10,080 30.00 80.00
24 Jeff Gordon DuPont Millennium 50.00 100.00
24 Jeff Gordon DuPont Millennium Bank set with 1:64 car 80.00 120.00
24 Jeff Gordon DuPont Peanuts 50.00 100.00
24 Jeff Gordon DuPont Test/1500 75.00 150.00
24 Jeff Gordon DuPont Winston/3120 40.00 100.00
24 Jeff Gordon DuPont Winston Bank set with 1:64 car/2508 40.00 100.00
24 Jeff Gordon Pepsi 30.00 80.00
24 Jeff Gordon Pepsi Bank set with 1:64 car 20.00 50.00
25 Jerry Nadeau Holigan Coast Guard/3120 20.00 50.00
25 Jerry Nadeau Holigan Coast Guard Bank set with 1:64 car 20.00 50.00
26 Jimmy Spencer Big K 40.00 80.00
27 Casey Atwood Castrol 20.00 50.00
28 Ricky Rudd Havoline/5004 20.00 50.00
28 Ricky Rudd Havoline Marines/3120 20.00 50.00
28 Ricky Rudd Havoline Marines Bank set with 1:64 car/1008 20.00 50.00
31 Mike Skinner Lowe's Army/3120 20.00 50.00
31 Mike Skinner Lowe's Army Bank set with 1:64 car/1008 20.00 50.00
36 Ken Schrader M&M's Green/3120 20.00 50.00
36 Ken Schrader M&M's Green Bank set with 1:64 car/504 20.00 50.00
36 Ken Schrader M&M's Halloween/2508 25.00 60.00
36 Ken Schrader M&M's July 4th/3120 20.00 50.00
36 Ken Schrader M&M's Keep Back/5004 20.00 50.00
36 Ken Schrader M&M's Keep Back Bank set with 1:64 car 20.00 50.00
36 Ken Schrader Pedigree 20.00 50.00
37 Kevin Grubb Timber Wolf/3120 20.00 50.00
66 Darrell Waltrip Big K-Mart Flames 20.00 50.00
71 Dave Marcis Realtree Camo/2508 20.00 50.00
75 Wally Dallenbach Powerpuff Girls/2508 20.00 50.00
77 Robert Pressley Jasper Cat 20.00 50.00
88 Dale Jarrett Quality Care 20.00 50.00
88 Dale Jarrett Quality Care Air Force/3120 20.00 50.00
88 Dale Jarrett Quality Care Air Force Bank set with 1:64 car 20.00 50.00
94 Bill Elliott McDonald's Drive Thru/3120 20.00 50.00
94 Bill Elliott McDonald's Drive Thru Bank set with 1:64 car 20.00 50.00
94 Bill Elliott McDonald's 25th Anniversary/8120 20.00 50.00
94 Bill Elliott McDonald's 25th Ann.Bank set with 1:64 car 25.00 60.00

2000 Revell Select 1:24

3 D.Earnhardt Goodwrench Taz 30.00 50.00
5 Terry Labonte Kellogg's Grinch 12.50 25.00
36 K.Schrader M&M's Halloween 12.50 25.00

2001 Revell Club 1:24

3 Dale Earnhardt Goodwrench with Sonic decal/10,000 80.00 175.00
3 Dale Earnhardt Goodwrench Oreo/9996 100.00 200.00
8 Dale Earnhardt Jr. Bud/2508 80.00 175.00
24 Jeff Gordon Pepsi/1200 60.00 120.00
29 Kevin Harvick Goodwrench/1500 60.00 120.00
88 Dale Jarrett UPS 50.00 100.00

2001 Revell Collection 1:24

1 Steve Park Pennzoil 20.00 5
1 Steve Park Pennzoil Rockingham Win/12,996 20.00 5
1 Steve Park Pennzoil Looney Toons with figure 20.00 5
2 Rusty Wallace Miller Lite California Win 25.00 6
3 Dale Earnhardt Goodwrench No Bull 75.00 15
3 Dale Earnhardt Goodwrench Oreo 150.00 30
3 Dale Earnhardt Goodwrench Test 250.00 40
3 Dale Earnhardt Goodwrench with Sonic decal/10,000 50.00 12
5 Terry Labonte Kellogg's 30.00 6
5 Terry Labonte Kellogg's Bank 60.00 12
5 Terry Labonte Kellogg's Looney Toons with figure 20.00 5
8 Dale Earnhardt Jr. Bud/22,764 50.00 10
8 Dale Earnhardt Jr. Bud All-Star 100.00 17
8 Dale Earnhardt Jr. Bud All-Star Game Raced version Daytona Win/40,008 75.00 15
8 Dale Earnhardt Jr. Bud No Bull Win 60.00 12
8 Dale Earnhardt Jr. Bud Test gray/2508 50.00 12
15 Michael Waltrip NAPA Daytona Win/21,016 25.00 6
18 Bobby Labonte Interstate Batteries Jurassic Park 3 25.00 6
20 Tony Stewart Home Depot Jurassic Park 3/3120 30.00 6
24 Jeff Gordon uPont Bugs with figure 50.00 10
24 Jeff Gordon DuPont No Bull Las Vegas Raced/25,020 40.00 10
24 Jeff Gordon DuPont Test black/2508 50.00 12
24 Jeff Gordon Pepsi/15,016 25.00 6
27 Jamie McMurray Williams/3054 30.00 6
29 Kevin Harvick Goodwrench Atlanta Win/17,000 25.00 6
29 Kevin Harvick Goodwrench Chicago Win 25.00 6
29 Kevin Harvick Goodwrench Taz with figure/10,044 25.00 6
29 Kevin Harvick Goodwrench Taz Bank/3504 75.00 15
30 Jeff Green AOL Daffy Duck with figure/3000 25.00 6
31 Mike Skinner Lowe's Yosemite Sam with Figure 30.00 8
55 Bobby Hamilton Square D Looney Toons w/figure 30.00 6
88 Dale Jarrett UPS/1500 25.00 6
88 Dale Jarrett UPS Color Chrome/1500 25.00 6
88 Dale Jarrett UPS Darlington Win/14,372 25.00 6
88 Dale Jarrett UPS Test/2508 75.00 15
K2 Kerry Earnhardt Kannapolis Intimidators/9000 20.00 5

2001 Revell Select 1:24

3 Dale Earnhardt Goodwrench 20.00 4
3 Dale Earnhardt Goodwrench Oreo 20.00 4
8 Dale Earnhardt Jr. Bud All-Star 90.00 15
24 Jeff Gordon DuPont Flames 15.00 3

2002 Revell Collection 1:24

2 Rusty Wallace Miller Lite Test w flames/5502 25.00 60.
3 Dale Earnhardt Jr. Oreo Daytona Win w CD ROM/48,236 20.00 50.
3 Dale Earnhardt Jr. Oreo Test Gray/7776 25.00 60
8 Dale Earnhardt Jr. Bud/14,952 25.00 60
8 Dale Earnhardt Jr. Bud Dover Win with Wilson Volleyball/38,792 40.00 80.
8 Dale Earnhardt Jr. Bud Talladega Win raced version/18,908 30.00 60.
8 Dale Earnhardt Jr. Bud Test Red/7620 30.00 60.
8 Dale Earnhardt Jr. Looney Tunes raced version 30.00 60.
9 Bill Elliott Dodge Brickyard Win raced version 20.00 50.
19 Jeremy Mayfield Dodge Test/3504 35.00 80.
20 Tony Stewart Home Depot Atlanta Win w hula dancer/8358 30.00 60.
24 Jeff Gordon DuPont Color Chrome 2001 Champion/42,024 40.00 80.
24 Jeff Gordon 25.00 60.

Pont Test/8058
vin Harvick 20.00 50.00
oodwrench Test/7584
erling Marlin 25.00 50.00
iors Light Darlington
n raced version/5082
amie McMurray 25.00 50.00
oors Light raced
arlotte Win/4032
nmie Johnson 25.00 50.00
we's raced
alifornia Win/10,844
rry Earnhardt 25.00 60.00
cing.usa.com
opicana 400 25.00 50.00

2002 Revell Select 1:24

Earnhardt Jr. 15.00 30.00
lla Wafer
Earnhardt Jr. 15.00 30.00
ud All-Star
Harvick 12.50 25.00
oodwrench
Harvick 12.50 25.00
oodwrench ET
Harvick 12.50 25.00
oodwrench Taz

2003 Revell Collection 1:24

le Earnhardt Jr. 35.00 60.00
ud Test/5622
le Earnhardt Jr. 35.00 60.00
ud Test Red/5622
ale Earnhardt Jr. 35.00 60.00
Concert Talladega Raced/4872
le Earnhardt Jr. 35.00 50.00
reo Ritz Raced/3888
ale Earnhardt Jr. 30.00 50.00
est White/4902
Michael Waltrip 35.00 50.00
NAPA Raced/4824
Tony Stewart 35.00 50.00
Home Depot Pocono Win
Raced/1888
Tony Stewart 30.00 50.00
Home Depot Test Gray
Jeff Gordon 35.00 60.00
DuPont Flames
Martinsville Raced/3168
Sterling Marlin 25.00 50.00
Coors Light Test/2856
Jimmie Johnson 30.00 50.00
Lowe's Test Black

2003 Revell Select 1:24

ale Earnhardt 25.00 40.00
Oreo '01 Monte Carlo
ale Earnhardt Jr. 20.00 35.00
Dirty Mo Posse
ony Stewart 20.00 35.00
3 Doors Down

2004 Revell Collection 1:24

ale Earnhardt Jr. 35.00 60.00
Bud Test Brown/3570
Michael Waltrip 35.00 60.00
NAPA Test/1278
with Stopwatch
Tony Stewart 35.00 60.00
Home Depot Test/3504
Jeff Gordon 40.00 70.00
DuPont Test/1848

2004 Revell Select 1:24

Dale Earnhardt Jr. 25.00 50.00
Bud Born On
Feb.15

2005 Revell Collection 1:24

Dale Earnhardt Jr. 40.00 65.00
Bud Born On Feb.20/1500
Dale Earnhardt Jr. 45.00 75.00
Bud Test/1752
8 Bobby Labonte 40.00 65.00
Interstate Batteries Test/732
0 Tony Stewart 40.00 70.00
Home Depot Test/972
4 Jeff Gordon 45.00 75.00
DuPont Test/1284
9 Kevin Harvick 40.00 65.00
Goodwrench Test/816
8 Jimmie Johnson 40.00 70.00
Lowe's Test/744
1 Bill Elliott 40.00 65.00
Auto Value

1997 Revell Collection 1:43

This series marks Revell's first attempt to produce a 1:43 scale car. It was distributed to hobby dealers as part of the Revell Collection line. Each piece was packaged in a hard plastic display case with a cardboard box overwrap. Most featured a stated production run number on the top of the outer box.

1 Coca-Cola 600/7512 10.00 25.00
2 Rusty Wallace 15.00 30.00
Miller Lite
5 Terry Labonte 15.00 30.00
Kellogg's/5772
5 Terry Labonte 12.50 30.00
Kellogg's Tony/10,016
5 Terry Labonte 12.50 30.00
Spooky Loops/10,520
6 Mark Martin 18.00 30.00
Valvoline
21 Michael Waltrip 10.00 25.00
Citgo
21 Michael Waltrip 10.00 25.00
Citgo Top Dog paint scheme
23 Jimmy Spencer 25.00 40.00
Camel/7512
25 Ricky Craven 18.00 30.00
Budweiser
28 Ernie Irvan 18.00 30.00
Havoline black
28 Ernie Irvan 20.00 35.00
Havoline 10th Anniversary
white and black/5004
29 Steve Grissom 10.00 25.00
Flintstones/5004
29 Jeff Green 10.00 25.00
Tom & Jerry
29 Robert Pressley 10.00 25.00
Flintstones
29 Robert Pressley 10.00 25.00
Scooby-Doo
30 Johnny Benson 10.00 25.00
Pennzoil
33 Ken Schrader 12.00 30.00
Skoal/7512
36 Derrike Cope 10.00 25.00
Skittles
37 Jeremy Mayfield 10.00 25.00
K-Mart Kids Against Drugs
41 Steve Grissom 10.00 25.00
Kodiak/7508
43 Bobby Hamilton 10.00 25.00
STP Goody's/5004
46 Wally Dallenbach 10.00 25.00
Woody Woodpecker/8012
88 Dale Jarrett 12.50 30.00
Quality Care/10,584
94 Bill Elliott 20.00 35.00
Mac Tonight/7512
94 Bill Elliott 10.00 25.00
McDonald's/5772
96 David Green 10.00 25.00
Caterpillar
97 Chad Little 12.50 30.00
John Deere
97 Chad Little 12.50 30.00
John Deere
160th Anniversary AUTO/4008
99 Jeff Burton 10.00 25.00
Exide/7512

1998 Revell Collection 1:43

This series marks Revell's second attempt to produce a 1:43 scale car. It was distributed to hobby dealers as part of Revell's Collection line.

1 Dale Earnhardt Jr. 15.00 30.00
Coke Bear/7512
1 Steve Park 8.00 20.00
Pennzoil Black Roof
1 Steve Park 8.00 20.00
Pennzoil Yellow Roof
2 Rusty Wallace 10.00 25.00
Adventures of Rusty/5004
2 Rusty Wallace 10.00 25.00
Miller Lite Elvis/7512
2 Rusty Wallace 10.00 25.00
Miller Lite TCB Elvis/5004
3 Dale Earnhardt 15.00 40.00
Coke
3 Dale Earnhardt 20.00 50.00
Goodwrench Plus
Daytona Win/5004
3 Dale Earnhardt 30.00 80.00
Goodwrench Plus Bass Pro
5 Terry Labonte 10.00 25.00
Blasted Fruit Loops/5004
5 Terry Labonte 10.00 25.00
Kellogg's
5 Terry Labonte 10.00 25.00
Kellogg's Corny
5 Terry Labonte 10.00 25.00
Kellogg's Ironman/4008
12 Jeremy Mayfield 8.00 20.00
Mobil 1/5004
18 Bobby Labonte 10.00 25.00
Interstate Batteries
18 Bobby Labonte 10.00 25.00
Interstate Batteries
Hot Rod/5004
18 Bobby Labonte 10.00 25.00
Interstate Batteries
Small Soldiers/5004
23 Jimmy Spencer 15.00 40.00
No Bull
24 Jeff Gordon 20.00 40.00
DuPont/5004
24 Jeff Gordon 20.00 40.00
DuPont Brickyard Win/5024
24 Jeff Gordon 25.00 50.00
DuPont Chromalusion
28 Kenny Irwin 12.50 30.00
Havoline/5004
28 Kenny Irwin 12.50 30.00
Havoline Joker
31 Dale Earnhardt Jr. 20.00 50.00
Wrangler 1997 Monte Carlo
31 Mike Skinner 8.00 20.00
Lowe's
31 Mike Skinner 8.00 20.00
Lowe's Special Olympics
33 Ken Schrader 15.00 30.00
Skoal Bud Shootout
36 Ernie Irvan 10.00 25.00
M&M's
36 Ernie Irvan 10.00 25.00
Wildberry Skittles/5004
41 Steve Grissom 8.00 20.00
Kodiak/5004
44 Tony Stewart 15.00 30.00
Shell Small Soldiers/5004
50 Ricky Craven 8.00 20.00
Bud/5004
50 No Driver Association 8.00 20.00
Bud Louie/5004
81 Kenny Wallace 8.00 20.00
Square D
81 Kenny Wallace 8.00 20.00
Square D Lightning/5004
88 Dale Jarrett 10.00 25.00
Quality Care/5004
88 Dale Jarrett 12.50 30.00
Batman/4008

1999 Revell Collection 1:43

This series was produced for and distributed in hobby outlets.

2 Rusty Wallace 12.50 30.00
Miller Lite Harley/3000
3 Dale Earnhardt 25.00 50.00
Goodwrench
3 Dale Earnhardt 20.00 40.00
Wrangler/5004
3 Dale Earnhardt Jr. 15.00 30.00
AC Delco/4008
3 Dale Earnhardt Jr. 12.50 30.00
AC Delco Superman/5508
8 Dale Earnhardt Jr. 15.00 30.00
Bud
12 Jeremy Mayfield 12.50 30.00
Mobil 1 Kentucky Derby/4008
20 Tony Stewart 15.00 30.00
Home Depot Habitat/3000
23 Jimmy Spencer 12.50 25.00
No Bull/3508
23 Jimmy Spencer 12.50 25.00
Winston Lights/3508
24 Jeff Gordon 15.00 30.00
DuPont/4008
24 Jeff Gordon 20.00 35.00
DuPont Superman
24 Jeff Gordon 18.00 30.00
Pepsi
24 Jeff Gordon 12.50 30.00
Pepsi Star Wars/5508
40 Coca-Cola 600 10.00 20.00

2000 Revell Collection 1:43

These cars come in a plastic display with the car mounted to the base.

3 Dale Earnhardt 25.00 50.00
Goodwrench Taz/4000
3 Dale Earnhardt 30.00 60.00
Goodwrench Peter Max/3000
20 Tony Stewart 12.50 25.00
Home Depot/3000
20 Tony Stewart 12.50 20.00
Home Depot
Rookie of the Year/3000
24 Jeff Gordon 12.50 25.00
DuPont Millennium
28 Ricky Rudd 10.00 20.00
Havoline/3504
94 Bill Elliott 10.00 20.00
McDonald's Drive Thru/3000

2001 Revell Collection 1:43

3 Dale Earnhardt 12.50 30.00
Goodwrench Oreo/48,084
3 Dale Earnhardt 30.00 60.00
Goodwrench Oreo Daytona

1993-95 Revell Promos 1:64

5 Ricky Rudd 5.00 12.00
Tide box 1993
9 Lake Speed 7.50 20.00
Spam blister 1995
32 Dale Jarrett 15.00 30.00
Mac Tools blister 1995
43 Richard Petty 7.50 20.00
STP blue
Wisk promo blister
43 Richard Petty 7.50 20.00
STP red&blue '72 Charger
Wisk promo blister
43 Richard Petty 7.50 20.00
STP red&blue Pontiac
Wisk promo blister
52 Ken Schrader 12.50 25.00
Eastman Chemical 1994
62 Sons of Confederate Veterans 10.00 20.00
1994 box//10,080
71 Dave Marcis 10.00 20.00
Olive Garden 1995

1996 Revell Retail 1:64

This series was distributed in retail outlets. These cars were packaged in Revell blister packs.

2 Rusty Wallace 4.00 8.00
Miller Genuine Draft
Silver 25th Anniversary
2 Rusty Wallace 5.00 10.00
Miller Genuine Draft
Silver 25th Anniversary
Race Day blister
2 Rusty Wallace 4.00 8.00
Penske Racing
3 Dale Earnhardt 7.50 20.00
Goodwrench
3 Dale Earnhardt 6.00 15.00
Olympic blister
3 Dale Earnhardt 6.00 15.00
Olympic Small Box
4 Sterling Marlin 3.00 6.00
Kodak
5 Terry Labonte 3.00 6.00
Kellogg's
6 Mark Martin 3.00 6.00
Valvoline
9 Lake Speed 3.00 6.00
SPAM
10 Ricky Rudd 3.00 6.00
Tide
11 Brett Bodine 3.00 6.00
Lowe's
16 Ron Hornaday 3.00 6.00
Smith and Wesson
16 Ted Musgrave 3.00 6.00
Family Channel Primestar
17 Darrell Waltrip 3.00 6.00
Parts America
18 Bobby Labonte 3.00 6.00
Interstate Batteries
21 Michael Waltrip 3.00 6.00
Citgo
21 Michael Waltrip 5.00 10.00
Citgo with Eagle on deck lid
24 Jeff Gordon 4.00 8.00
DuPont
24 Jack Sprague 3.00 6.00
Quaker State
28 Ernie Irvan 3.00 6.00
Havoline
37 Jeremy Mayfield 3.00 6.00
K-Mart Little Caesars
43 Bobby Hamilton 10.00 20.00
STP Anniversary
Promo in blister
71 Dave Marcis 6.00 15.00
Olive Garden Promo
75 Morgan Shepherd 3.00 6.00
Remington
75 Morgan Shepherd 3.00 6.00
Remington Camouflage
77 Bobby Hillin Jr. 3.00 6.00
Jasper Engines
87 Joe Nemechek 3.00 6.00
Bell South
87 Joe Nemechek 3.00 6.00
Burger King
99 Jeff Burton 3.00 6.00
Exide

1996 Revell Collection 1:64

This series was produced for and distributed through hobby outlets. These cars have significant upgrades in comparison to the standard 1996 Revell 1:64 pieces. Each car is packaged in a box which has the same color scheme as the car. Many include the production run number on the outside of the box.

2 Rusty Wallace 6.00 15.00
Miller Genuine Draft/14,400
2 Rusty Wallace 7.50 20.00
Miller Genuine Draft
Silver 25th Anniversary/14,400
3 Dale Earnhardt 15.00 30.00
Olympic
4 Sterling Marlin 4.00 10.00
Kodak
5 Terry Labonte 30.00 50.00
Honey Crunch/10,080
5 Terry Labonte 10.00 25.00
Kellogg's/10,080
6 Mark Martin 4.00 10.00
Valvoline/6912
6 Mark Martin 5.00 10.00
Valvoline Dura Blend
10 Ricky Rudd 4.00 8.00
Tide/10,080
11 Brett Bodine 4.00 8.00
Lowe's Gold
16 Ted Musgrave 4.00 8.00
Family Channel Primestar
17 Darrell Waltrip 4.00 8.00
Parts America
18 Bobby Labonte 5.00 10.00
Interstate Batteries
23 Chad Little 4.00 10.00
John Deere/10,080
25 Ken Schrader 4.00 10.00
Bud/10,080
25 Ken Schrader 4.00 10.00
Bud Olympic/10,080
28 Ernie Irvan 4.00 8.00
Havoline
30 Johnny Benson 4.00 8.00
Pennzoil
37 Jeremy Mayfield 4.00 8.00
K-Mart Little Caesars
75 Morgan Shepherd 4.00 8.00
Remington
75 Morgan Shepherd 4.00 8.00
Remington Camouflage
75 Morgan Shepherd 4.00 8.00
Stren
76 David Green 4.00 8.00
Smith and Wesson SuperTruck
87 Joe Nemechek 4.00 8.00
Burger King
88 Dale Jarrett 4.00 8.00
Quality Care/10,574
99 Jeff Burton 4.00 8.00
Exide

1997 Revell Collection 1:64

This series is the continuation of the 1996 series. It signals Revell's expansion into the die cast market by its sheer number of cars in the series.

1 Coca-Cola 600 5.00 10.00
2 Rusty Wallace 6.00 12.00
Miller Lite/30,000
2 Rusty Wallace 6.00 12.00
Miller Lite Texas/10,080
5 Terry Labonte 6.00 12.00
Kellogg's
5 Terry Labonte 8.00 20.00
Kellogg's 1996 Champion/10,080
5 Terry Labonte 7.50 15.00
Kellogg's Tony/10,080
5 Terry Labonte 6.00 15.00
Spooky Loops/10,080
5/18 Bobby and Terry Labonte 20.00 35.00
Interstate Batteries and Kellogg's
2-car Tin Set
6/60 Mark Martin 20.00 35.00
Valvoline
Winn Dixie
2 car set
16 Ted Musgrave 5.00 10.00
Primestar
23 Jimmy Spencer 10.00 20.00
Camel/10,080
23/97 Chad Little 20.00 30.00
John Deere 2 car set
Autographed tin
28 Ernie Irvan 7.50 15.00
Havoline 10th Anniversary
white and black/10,008
28 Ernie Irvan 20.00 30.00
Havoline 2-car tin
30 Johnny Benson 5.00 10.00
Pennzoil
33 Ken Schrader 6.00 15.00
Skoal
36 Derrike Cope 4.00 10.00
Skittles
37 Jeremy Mayfield 5.00 10.00
K-Mart RC Cola
40 Robby Gordon 5.00 10.00
Coors Light
41 Steve Grissom 6.00 15.00
Kodiak/10,080
43 Bobby Hamilton 7.50 15.00
STP Goody's
91 Mike Wallace 5.00 10.00
Spam
97 Chad Little 5.00 12.00
John Deere
97 Chad Little 15.00 30.00
John Deere 2-car tin
97 California 500 4.00 10.00

1997 Revell Select Hobby 1:64

This series, Revell Select, was produced to appease those collectors who wanted an upgraded production die cast without the upgrade price. They were distributed primarily to hobby outlets. The cars themselves appear to have similar production qualities as the Collection cars, but were intially lower in price. Each was packaged in the typical Revell hard plastic clear box with an outer cardboard black window box with gold trim. There is a basic red, white, blue and yellow Revell logo on the box as well.

1 Coca-Cola 600 4.00 8.00
2 Rusty Wallace 5.00 10.00
Miller Lite
4 Sterling Marlin 4.00 10.00
Kodak
5 Terry Labonte 4.00 8.00
Kellogg's
5 Terry Labonte 5.00 10.00
Spooky Loops
5 Terry Labonte 5.00 10.00
Tony the Tiger
6 Mark Martin 4.00 8.00
Valvoline
7 Geoff Bodine 4.00 8.00
QVC
17 Darrell Waltrip 4.00 8.00
Parts America blue&white
17 Darrell Waltrip 5.00 12.00
Parts America Chrome
17 Darrell Waltrip 4.00 8.00
Parts America Green
with green number
17 Darrell Waltrip 4.00 8.00
Parts America Green
with white number
17 Darrell Waltrip 4.00 8.00
Parts America Orange
17 Darrell Waltrip 4.00 8.00
Parts America Red&White
17 Darrell Waltrip 4.00 8.00
Parts America Yellow&White
18 Mike Dokken 4.00 8.00
Dana SuperTruck
18 Bobby Labonte 4.00 8.00
Interstate Batteries
18 Bobby Labonte 4.00 8.00
Interstate Batteries Texas
21 Michael Waltrip 4.00 8.00
Citgo Top Dog paint scheme
25 Ricky Craven 5.00 10.00
Bud Lizard
28 Ernie Irvan 4.00 8.00
Havoline black
28 Ernie Irvan 4.00 8.00
Havoline 10th Anniversary
white and black
29 Jeff Green 4.00 8.00
Tom & Jerry
29 Steve Grissom 4.00 8.00
Flintstones
29 Bob Keselowski 4.00 8.00
Mopar
29 Robert Pressley 4.00 8.00
Scooby-Doo
32 Dale Jarrett 4.00 8.00
White Rain
33 Ken Schrader 4.00 8.00
Skoal
35 Todd Bodine 4.00 8.00
Tabasco
36 Derrike Cope 4.00 8.00
Skittles
37 Jeremy Mayfield 4.00 8.00
K-Mart Kids Against Drugs
40 Robby Gordon 4.00 8.00
Coors Silver Bullet
41 Steve Grissom 4.00 8.00
Kodiak
42 Joe Nemechek 4.00 8.00
Bell South
43 Bobby Hamilton 4.00 8.00
STP Goody's
43 Jimmy Hensley 4.00 8.00
Cummins SuperTruck

75 Rick Mast Remington 4.00 8.00
94 Bill Elliott McDonald's 4.00 8.00
94 Bill Elliott Mac Tonight 4.00 8.00
97 California 500 4.00 8.00
97 Chad Little John Deere 160th Anniversary 4.00 8.00
97 Texas Motor Speedway 4.00 8.00

1997 Revell Retail 1:64

This series was produced for and distributed primarily to mass-market retailers. Each piece is packaged in a blister pack with many printed to match the team colors or sponsor theme.

1 Coca-Cola 600 3.00 6.00
2 Rusty Wallace Penske 3.00 6.00
5 Terry Labonte Kellogg's Texas 3.00 6.00
5 Terry Labonte Spooky Loops 3.00 6.00
6 Mark Martin Valvoline 3.00 6.00
16 Ted Musgrave Primestar 3.00 6.00
18 Bobby Labonte Interstate Batteries Texas 3.00 6.00
18 Bobby Labonte Interstate Batteries 3.00 6.00
21 Michael Waltrip Citgo Top Dog paint scheme 3.00 6.00
28 Ernie Irvan Havoline Black 3.00 6.00
29 Robert Pressley Cartoon Network 3.00 6.00
29 Robert Pressley Tom & Jerry 3.00 6.00
30 Johnny Benson Pennzoil 3.00 6.00
35 Todd Bodine Tabasco Promo box 4.00 10.00
37 Jeremy Mayfield K-Mart Kids Against Drugs 3.00 6.00
37 Jeremy Mayfield K-Mart RC Cola 3.00 6.00
42 Joe Nemechek BellSouth 3.00 6.00
91 Mike Wallace Spam 3.00 6.00
97 California 500 3.00 6.00
97 Texas Motor Speedway 3.00 6.00

1998 Revell Collection 1:64

These cars come in a driver detailed box. Cars are mounted to a base and have a clear plastic cover.

1 Dale Earnhardt Jr. Coke Bear/27,000 10.00 20.00
1 Steve Park Pennzoil Black Roof/10,080 6.00 15.00
1 Steve Park Pennzoil Yellow Roof/12,024 6.00 15.00
2 Rusty Wallace Adventures of Rusty 6.00 12.00
2 Rusty Wallace Miller Lite 6.00 12.00
2 Rusty Wallace Miller Lite Elvis 6.00 12.00
2 Rusty Wallace Miller Lite TCB Elvis 6.00 12.00
3 Dale Earnhardt Coke/27,000 15.00 30.00
3 Dale Earnhardt Goodwrench Plus Daytona Win/14,400 10.00 25.00
3 Dale Earnhardt Goodwrench Plus Bass Pro 20.00 40.00
3 Dale Earnhardt Goodwrench Plus Brickyard Win/20,016 12.50 25.00
3 Dale Earnhardt Jr. AC Delco 15.00 30.00
4 Bobby Hamilton Kodak Max/10,080 4.00 10.00
5 Terry Labonte Blasted Fruit Loops/10,080 6.00 15.00
5 Terry Labonte Kellogg's/10,080 5.00 12.00
5 Terry Labonte Kellogg's Corny/10,080 6.00 15.00
5 Terry Labonte Kellogg's Ironman/10,080 6.00 15.00
9 Lake Speed Birthday Cake 4.00 10.00
9 Lake Speed Huckleberry Hound 4.00 10.00
12 Jeremy Mayfield Mobil 1/10,080 5.00 12.00
18 Bobby Labonte Interstate Batteries 7.50 15.00
18 Bobby Labonte Interstate Batteries Hot Rod 6.00 15.00
18 Bobby Labonte Interstate Batteries Small Soldiers 6.00 15.00
21 Michael Waltrip Citgo 5.00 12.00
23 Jimmy Spencer No Bull 7.50 15.00
24 Jeff Gordon DuPont/10,080 6.00 15.00
24 Jeff Gordon DuPont Brickyard Win 6.00 15.00
24 Jeff Gordon DuPont Chromalusion/24,984 15.00 40.00
25 John Andretti Budweiser 5.00 12.00
28 Kenny Irwin Havoline 6.00 12.00
28 Kenny Irwin Havoline Joker 6.00 12.00
31 Mike Skinner Lowe's/10,080 3.00 8.00
31 Mike Skinner Lowe's Special Olympics 4.00 10.00
33 Ken Schrader Skoal 5.00 12.00
33 Ken Schrader Skoal Bud Shootout 6.00 12.00
36 Ernie Irvan M&M's 6.00 15.00
36 Ernie Irvan Wildberry Skittles 6.00 12.00
40 Sterling Marlin Coors Light 5.00 12.00
41 Steve Grissom Kodiak/10,080 3.00 8.00
42 Joe Nemechek Bell South/10,080 3.00 8.00
44 Tony Stewart Shell/10,080 6.00 12.00
44 Tony Stewart Shell Small Soldiers/10,080 7.50 15.00
46 Wally Dallenbach irst Union/10,080 3.00 8.00
46 Jeff Green First union Devil Rays/10,080 3.00 8.00
50 Ricky Craven Bud/10,080 3.00 8.00
50 No Driver Association Bud Louie/10,080 6.00 12.00
75 Rick Mast Remington/10,080 3.00 8.00
81 Kenny Wallace Square D Lightning/10,080 3.00 8.00
88 Dale Jarrett Batman 6.00 15.00
88 Dale Jarrett Quality Care/10,080 6.00 15.00

1998 Revell Select Hobby 1:64

This series, Revell Select, was produced to appease those collectors who wanted an upgraded production die cast without the upgrade price. The cars themselves appear to have similar production qualities as the Collection cars, but were initially offered at a lower price point and were packaged in black window boxes.

1 Steve Park Pennzoil Black Roof 5.00 10.00
2 Rusty Wallace Miller Lite 4.00 8.00
3 Dale Earnhardt Goodwrench Plus 5.00 12.00
3 Dale Earnhardt Goodwrench Plus Bass Pro 6.00 12.00
3 Dale Earnhardt Jr. AC Delco 7.50 20.00
4 Bobby Hamilton Kodak Max 3.00 8.00
5 Terry Labonte Kellogg's 3.00 8.00
5 Terry Labonte Kellogg's Corny 4.00 10.00
8 Hut Stricklin Circuit City 3.00 8.00
9 Lake Speed Huckleberry Hound 3.00 8.00
18 Bobby Labonte Interstate Batteries 4.00 8.00
18 Bobby Labonte Interstate Batteries Hot Rod 4.00 8.00
21 Michael Waltrip Citgo 3.00 8.00
23 Jimmy Spencer No Bull 6.00 12.00
24 Jeff Gordon DuPont 5.00 10.00
31 Mike Skinner Lowe's 3.00 8.00
33 Ken Schrader Skoal 4.00 10.00
35 Todd Bodine Tabasco Green Black Promo blister 3.00 8.00
35 Todd Bodine Tabasco Orange White Promo blister 3.00 8.00
35 Todd Bodine Tabasco Red Black Promo blister 3.00 8.00
36 Ernie Irvan M&M's 4.00 10.00
44 Tony Stewart Shell 6.00 12.00
44 Tony Stewart Shell Small Soldiers 6.00 12.00
50 No Driver Association Bud Louie 3.00 8.00
77 Robert Pressley Jasper 3.00 8.00
81 Kenny Wallace Square D Lightning 3.00 8.00

1999 Revell Collection 1:64

This series was produced for and distributed through hobby outlets. Each piece was issued in a Revell Collection clear plastic box.

1 Steve Park Pennzoil/7992 6.00 15.00
2 Rusty Wallace Miller Lite 7.50 15.00
2 Rusty Wallace Miller Lite Harley 5.00 12.00
3 Dale Earnhardt Goodwrench/14,400 12.50 30.00
3 Dale Earnhardt Goodwrench 25th 15.00 30.00
3 Dale Earnhardt Goodwrench Sign 15.00 30.00
3 Dale Earnhardt Wrangler/18,000 12.50 30.00
3 Dale Earnhardt Jr. AC Delco/13,104 6.00 15.00
3 Dale Earnhardt Jr. AC Delco Superman/20,016 7.50 20.00
4 Bobby Hamilton Advantix 4.00 10.00
5 Terry Labonte Kellogg's 5.00 12.00
5 Terry Labonte K-Sentials 5.00 12.00
5 Terry Labonte Rice Krispies 5.00 12.00
8 Dale Earnhardt Jr. Bud 10.00 18.00
9 Jerry Nadeau Dexter's Lab/10,080 4.00 10.00
9 Jerry Nadeau Jetsons 4.00 10.00
11 Dale Jarrett Green Bay Packers/7992 12.50 25.00
12 Jeremy Mayfield Mobil 1 4.00 10.00
12 Jeremy Mayfield Mobil 1 Kentucky Derby/10,080 4.00 10.00
18 Bobby Labonte Interstate Batteries 7.50 15.00
20 Tony Stewart Home Depot/7992 25.00 40.00
20 Tony Stewart Home Depot Habitat for Humanity/10,080 12.50 30.00
21 Elliott Sadler Citgo 4.00 10.00
23 Jimmy Spencer No Bull 6.00 15.00
23 Jimmy Spencer Winston Lights 6.00 15.00
24 Jeff Gordon DuPont 7.50 15.00
24 Jeff Gordon DuPont Superman/23,472 8.00 18.00
24 Jeff Gordon DuPont Daytona 500 10.00 20.00
24 Jeff Gordon Pepsi 7.50 15.00
24 Jeff Gordon Pepsi Star Wars 8.00 18.00
27 Casey Atwood Castrol 4.00 10.00
28 Kenny Irwin Havoline/10,080 5.00 12.00
31 Dale Earnhardt Jr. Gargoyles 1997 Monte Carlo 10.00 20.00
31 Dale Earnhardt Jr. Mom 'N' Pop's 1996 Monte Carlo 6.00 15.00
31 Dale Earnhardt Jr. Sikkens Blue 1997 Monte Carlo/10,080 7.50 15.00
31 Dale Earnhardt Jr. Sikkens White 1997 Monte Carlo 7.50 15.00
31 Mike Skinner Lowe's 4.00 10.00
36 Ernie Irvan M&M's/10,080 7.50 15.00
36 Ernie Irvan M&M's Countdown/10,080 4.00 10.00
36 Ernie Irvan M&M's Millennium/10,080 4.00 10.00
36 Ernie Irvan Crispy M&M's 4.00 10.00
36 Ernie Irvan Pedigree/10,080 4.00 10.00
40 Sterling Marlin Coors Light John Wayne/10,080 7.50 20.00
40 Sterling Marlin Coors Light Brooks & Dunn/10,080 7.50 20.00
40 Kerry Earnhardt Channellock/10,080 4.00 10.00
88 Dale Jarrett Quality Care/10,080 5.00 12.00

2000 Revell Collection 1:64

These 1:64 scale cars were issued in a plastic box with a cardboard box overwrap. The outer box featured a hologram Revell sticker that featured the production run. Each car was mounted to a black plastic base. All cars have opening hoods.

2 Rusty Wallace Miller Lite 6.00 15.00
2 Rusty Wallace Miller Lite Harley/7992 5.00 12.00
3 Dale Earnhardt Goodwrench/12,024 20.00 40.00
3 Dale Earnhardt Goodwrench Peter Max/1008 20.00 40.00
3 Dale Earnhardt Goodwrench Taz No Bull/30,384 15.00 40.00
4 Bobby Hamilton Kodak Navy/10,088 5.00 12.00
8 Dale Earnhardt Jr. Bud/7992 10.00 20.00
8 Dale Earnhardt Jr. Bud Olympic/9000 12.50 25.00
12 Jeremy Mayfield Mobil 1 World Series/5040 5.00 12.00
18 Bobby Labonte Interstate Batteries/7992 6.00 15.00
20 Tony Stewart Home Depot/13,176 10.00 20.00
20 Tony Stewart Home Depot Rookie of the Year/12,080 10.00 20.00
20 Tony Stewart Home Depot Kids 10.00 20.00
21 Elliott Sadler Citgo MDA Promo blister 4.00 10.00
24 Jeff Gordon DuPont/10,080 5.00 12.00
24 Jeff Gordon DuPont Millennium 10.00 20.00
24 Jeff Gordon DuPont Peanuts 10.00 20.00
24 Jeff Gordon DuPont Winston 5.00 12.00
24 Jeff Gordon Pepsi 6.00 15.00
25 Jerry Nadeau Holigan Coast Guard 5.00 12.00
27 Casey Awood Castrol 5.00 12.00
28 Ricky Rudd Havoline 6.00 15.00
28 Ricky Rudd Havoline Marines/11,088 5.00 12.00
31 Mike Skinner Lowe's Army/11,088 5.00 12.00
36 Ken Schrader M&M's 5.00 12.00
36 Ken Schrader M&M's Green/8496 5.00 12.00
36 Ken Schrader M&M's July 4th/8496 5.00 12.00
36 Ken Schrader M&M's Keep Back/9000 6.00 15.00
88 Dale Jarrett Quality Care 5.00 12.00
88 Dale Jarrett Quality Care Air Force/11,088 5.00 12.00
94 Bill Elliott McDonald's Drive Thru 5.00 12.00
94 Bill Elliott McDonald's 25th/9000 5.00 12.00

2001 Revell Collection 1:64

3 Dale Earnhardt Goodwrench Oreo Tin 20.00 50.00
8 Dale Earnhardt Jr. Bud 12.50 25.00
8 Dale Earnhardt Jr. Bud All-Star Raced/20,016 20.00 40.00
8/15 Dale Earnhardt Jr. Michael Waltrip Bud MLB All-Star Game NAPA Stars and Stripes 2-car set in tin/12,000 20.00 40.00
18 Bobby Labonte Interstate Batteries 2000 Winston Cup Champ 2-car set in tin/6432 15.00 30.00
18/20 Bobby Labonte Tony Stewart Jurassic Park 3 in tin/7992 12.50 25.00
24 Jeff Gordon DuPont Flames/24,984 7.50 20.00
24 Jeff Gordon Pepsi/17,280 7.50 20.00
88 Dale Jarrett UPS 6.00 15.00

2002 Revell Collection 1:64

3 Dale Earnhardt Jr. Nilla Wafers in cookie box/28,608 7.50 20.00
3 Dale Earnhardt Jr. Oreo in Cookie tin/20,016 12.50 25.00
3/8/8 Ralph Earnhardt 1969 Camaro Dale Earnhardt 2000 Goodwrench MC Dale Earnhardt Jr. 2000 Budweiser MC 3-car tin/27,597 25.00 50.00
8 Dale Earnhardt Jr. Bud/15,336 10.00 20.00
8 Dale Earnhardt Jr. Bud Talladega Win 10.00 20.00

2002 Revell Collection Train Sets 1:64

3 Dale Earnhardt 9-car train set/19,504 Goodwrench Silver Wheaties Goodwrench Bass Pro Goodwrench Daytona Coca-Cola Wrangler/ Goodwrench Taz/ Goodwrench Peter Max/ Goodwrench Oreo 125.00 200.00
8 Dale Earnhardt Jr. Looney Tunes 3-car train set/600 30.00 50.00

2003 Revell Collection Train Sets 1:64

3 Dale Earnhardt Earnhardt Foundation/7560 20.00 35.00
8 Dale Earnhardt Jr. Dirty Mo Posse/5328 15.00 30.00
8 Dale Earnhardt Jr. E Concert/5688 18.00 30.00
8 Dale Earnhardt Jr. Oreo Ritz/5160 15.00 30.00
NNO Dale Earnhardt Earnhardt Legacy/5292 18.00 30.00

2004 Revell Collection Train Sets 1:64

7 Dale Earnhardt Jr. Church Brothers 1997 Monte Carlo/2556 25.00 50.00
8 Dale Earnhardt Jr. Oreo/2862 25.00 50.00

1992 Road Champs 1:43

Road Champs released this series of 1:43 die-cast cars with each packaged in a window box that included a cardboard backer. The driver's photo and car image also appeared on the package.

2 Rusty Wallace Pontiac 5.00 12.00
4 Ernie Irvan Kodak 4.00 10.00
6 Mark Martin Valvoline 5.00 12.00
21 Morgan Shepherd Citgo 4.00 10.00
43 Richard Petty STP 4.00 10.00

1992 Road Champs Pull Back Action

4 Ernie Irvan Kodak 4.00
21 Morgan Shepherd Citgo 4.00
43 Richard Petty STP 5.00

1992 Road Champs Sounds of Power

Each die-cast car in this release was produced by Road and packaged in a window box that included a ca backer. The driver's photo and car image also appeare package. The die-cast car itself could play real racing when one of the wheels were pushed.

2 Rusty Wallace Pontiac 3.00
4 Ernie Irvan Kodak 3.00
43 Richard Petty STP 5.00

1992 Road Champs 1:64

1 Jeff Gordon Baby Ruth 5.00
2 Rusty Wallace Pontiac 4.00
4 Ernie Irvan Kodak 3.00
6 Mark Martin Valvoline 4.00
21 Morgan Shepherd Citgo 3.00
43 Richard Petty STP 4.00
87 Joe Nemechek Texas Pete Promo in bag/15,000 distributed by The Source International with a card set in a white box 6.00 1

2004 Team Caliber Pit Stop 1:18

6 Mark Martin Viagra 20.00 3
12 Ryan Newman Alltel 20.00 3
17 Matt Kenseth DeWalt 20.00 3
97 Kurt Busch Sharpie 15.00 3

2004 Team Caliber/Motorworks Model H 1:18

5 Terry Labonte Kellogg's 15.00 2
16 Greg Biffle National Guard 15.00 2
17 Matt Kenseth DeWalt '03 Champ. w hat 25.00 4
25 Brian Vickers ditech.com 15.00 2
01 Joe Nemechek Army 15.00 2

1999 Team Caliber 1:24

This marks Team Calibers inaugural year in the Die market.

1 Randy LaJoie Bob Evan's/3120 25.00 60
4 Bobby Hamilton Kodak/3120 20.00 50
5 Terry Labonte Kellogg's Corny 40.00 80
5 Terry Labonte Kellogg's K-Sentials/5004 40.00 80
5 Terry Labonte Rice Krispies/5004 40.00 80
5 Dick Trickle Schneider/3120 25.00 60
6 Mark Martin Valvoline/5004 40.00 80
6 Mark Martin 60.00 120

Eagle One
Michael Waltrip Phillips 25.00 60.00
0 Ricky Rudd Tide/3120 25.00 60.00
0 Ricky Rudd Tide Peroxide/3120 20.00 50.00
2 Jeremy Mayfield Mobil 1/5004 40.00 80.00
2 Jeremy Mayfield Mobil 25th Anniversary 80.00 150.00
2 Jeremy Mayfield Mobil 1 Chrome 150.00 250.00
2 Jimmy Spencer Zippo/3120 30.00 80.00
2 Jimmy Spencer Chips Ahoy/3120 30.00 80.00
5 Ken Schrader Oakwood Homes/3120 25.00 60.00
7 Matt Kenseth DeWalt/5004 75.00 150.00
17 Matt Kenseth DeWalt Roush/3120 100.00 175.00
23 Jimmy Spencer Winston No Bull 40.00 80.00
23 Jimmy Spencer Winston Lights Gold 50.00 100.00
25 Wally Dallenbach Budweiser/3120 25.00 60.00
25 Wally Dallenbach Bud World Series/3120 40.00 80.00
30 Derike Cope Jimmy Dean/3120 20.00 50.00
30 Derrike Cope State Fair/3120 25.00 60.00
40 Sterling Marlin Coors Light/3120 30.00 80.00
40 Sterling Marlin Coors John Wayne/3120 50.00 120.00
42 Joe Nemechek BellSouth/5004 30.00 60.00
43 John Andretti STP/5004 30.00 80.00
44 Terry Labonte Slim Jim/3120 20.00 50.00
44 Kyle Petty Hot Wheels/2340 40.00 80.00
45 Adam Petty Sprint/3120 50.00 100.00
55 Kenny Wallace Square D/3120 25.00 60.00
60 Geoffery Bodine Power Team/3120 25.00 60.00
75 Ted Musgrave Polaris/3120 25.00 60.00
98 Rick Mast Woody Woodpecker/3120 30.00 60.00
99 Jeff Burton Exide 45.00 90.00
99 Jeff Burton Exide No Bull 45.00 90.00

1999 Team Caliber Banks 1:24

This marks Team Caliber's inaugural year in the die-cast market. Each 1:24 scale bank was packaged in a black Team Caliber solid box along with a certificate of authenticity. The production run for each bank was 1008.

1 Randy LaJoie Bob Evan's/1008 30.00 80.00
5 Terry Labonte Kellogg's K-Sentials 30.00 80.00
5 Terry Labonte Rice Krispies 30.00 80.00
10 Ricky Rudd Tide 40.00 100.00
12 Jeremy Mayfield Mobil 1 30.00 80.00
12 Jeremy Mayfield Mobil 1 25th Anniversary 30.00 80.00
23 Jimmy Spencer No Bull 40.00 100.00
23 Jimmy Spencer Winston Lights 40.00 100.00
25 Wally Dallenbach Budweiser 30.00 80.00
40 Sterling Marlin Coors Light 30.00 80.00
40 Sterling Marlin Coors Light John Wayne 40.00 100.00
43 John Andretti STP 40.00 100.00
44 Terry Labonte Slim Jim 30.00 80.00
45 Adam Petty Sprint 60.00 120.00
55 Kenny Wallace Square D 30.00 80.00

2000 Team Caliber Owners Series 1:24

4 Bobby Hamilton Kodak/2340 25.00 60.00
5 Terry Labonte Kellogg's/2340 30.00 80.00
5 Terry Labonte CherryBerry/3120 30.00 80.00
5 Terry Labonte Kellogg's Grinch 30.00 80.00
5 Terry Labonte Kellogg's Frosted Flakes 30.00 80.00
6 Mark Martin Valvoline/5004 60.00 100.00
6 Mark Martin Valvoline Eagle One/5004 40.00 125.00
6 Mark Martin Valvoline Max Life/5004 40.00 100.00
6 Mark Martin Valvoline Flag/5004 40.00 100.00
6 Mark Martin Valvoline Zerex/5004 40.00 100.00
7 Michael Waltrip Nations Rent/2340 30.00 80.00
8 Shawna Robinson Kids RAD/2340 50.00 100.00
9 Jeff Burton Northern Light/2340 50.00 100.00
10 Johnny Benson Lycos/2340 40.00 80.00
10 Jeff Green Nesquik 35.00 70.00
11 Brett Bodine Ralph's/2340 30.00 60.00
12 Jeremy Mayfield Mobil 1/3120 30.00 80.00
13 Robby Gordon Burger King Flintsones/3120 25.00 60.00
14 Rick Mast Conseco/2340 20.00 50.00
16 Kevin Lepage Clemson 2340 30.00 60.00
16 Kevin Lepage Familyclick.com/2340 20.00 50.00
16 Kevin Lepage Mac Tools/2340 20.00 50.00
17 Matt Kenseth DeWalt/5004 60.00 120.00
17 Matt Kenseth DeWalt 24 Volt/5004 70.00 110.00
17 Matt Kenseth DeWalt Emazing.com/5004 60.00 100.00
17 Matt Kenseth Visine/2340 40.00 80.00
21 Elliott Sadler Citgo/2340 20.00 50.00
21 Elliott Sadler Citgo VT/2340 35.00 70.00
24 Ricky Hendrick GMAC/2340 20.00 50.00
25 Jerry Nadeau Holigan/2340 20.00 50.00
26 Jimmy Spencer Big K/2340 25.00 60.00
27 Ryan Newman Alltel/3500 50.00 100.00
40 Sterling Marlin Coors Light/2340 25.00 60.00
40 Sterling Marlin Coors Light John Wayne/3120 25.00 60.00
40 Sterling Marlin Coors Light Brooks & Dunn/3120 25.00 60.00
42 Kenny Irwin BellSouth/3120 25.00 60.00
42 Kenny Irwin BellSouth Busch/3120 25.00 60.00
43 John Andretti Cheerios/2340 35.00 70.00
43 John Andretti STP/2340 35.00 70.00
44 Justin Labonte Slim Jim/2340 20.00 50.00
44 Kyle Petty Hot Wheels 35.00 70.00
45 Adam Petty Sprint PCS/3120 100.00 200.00
55 Kenny Wallace Square D/2340 40.00 80.00
57 Jason Keller Excedrin/2340 20.00 50.00
60 Geoffery Bodine Power Team/2340 25.00 60.00
60 Mark Martin Winn Dixie/3120 75.00 125.00
60 Mark Martin Winn Dixie Flames/3120 40.00 150.00
60 Mark Martin Winn Dixie Flag/3120 80.00 135.00
63 Mark Green SuperFlo/2340 20.00 50.00
66 Darrell Waltrip Big K/2340 25.00 60.00
66 Darrell Waltrip Big K Flames/2340 50.00 100.00
77 Robert Pressley Jasper Panther/2340 40.00 80.00
97 Chad Little John Deere 2340 35.00 70.00
99 Jeff Burton Citgo Mac Tools/3000 30.00 60.00
99 Jeff Burton Citgo Steel/3120 40.00 100.00
99 Jeff Burton Exide/3120 40.00 80.00
01 Tim Steele Friends of the NRA/2340 25.00 60.00

2000 Team Caliber Owners Series Gold 1:24

6 Mark Martin Valvoline/1200 75.00 150.00
6 Mark Martin Valvoline Eagle One/1200 75.00 150.00
17 Matt Kenseth DeWalt/1200 90.00 150.00
99 Jeff Burton Exide/1200 60.00 125.00

2000 Team Caliber Preferred 1:24

4 Bobby Hamilton Kodak/5508 15.00 40.00
5 Terry Labonte Cherry Berry/5508 20.00 50.00
5 Terry Labonte Froot Loops/5508 20.00 50.00
5 Terry Labonte Kelloggs/5508 20.00 50.00
6 Mark Martin Valvoline/20,004 25.00 60.00
6 Mark Martin Valvoline Eagle One/20,004 20.00 50.00
6 Mark Martin Valvoline Flag/20,004 25.00 50.00
6 Mark Martin Valvoline Max Life/20,004 30.00 60.00
6 Mark Martin Zerex/5004 20.00 50.00
7 Michael Waltrip Nations Rent/5508 25.00 60.00
8 Shawna Robinson Kids RAD/5508 25.00 50.00
9 Jeff Burton Northern Light 25.00 50.00
10 Johnny Benson Lycos/5508 15.00 40.00
11 Brett Bodine Ralph's/5508 15.00 50.00
12 Jeremy Mayfield Mobil 1/10,008 15.00 40.00
14 Rick Mast Conseco/5508 15.00 40.00
16 Kevin Lepage Clemson/5508 20.00 50.00
16 Kevin Lepage familyclick.com/7560 15.00 40.00
16 Kevin Lepage Mac Tools/5508 15.00 40.00
17 Matt Kenseth DeWalt/20,004 50.00 100.00
17 Matt Kenseth DeWalt 24 Volt/20,004 60.00 100.00
17 Matt Kenseth Visine/5508 40.00 80.00
21 Elliott Sadler Citgo/5508 15.00 40.00
21 Elliott Sadler Citgo Virginia Tech/5508 25.00 50.00
24 Ricky Hendrick GMAC/1836 15.00 40.00
25 Jerry Nadeau Holigan/5508 15.00 40.00
26 Jimmy Spencer ig K/5508 15.00 40.00
40 Sterling Marlin Coors Light/5508 20.00 50.00
40 Sterling Marlin Coors Light Brooks & Dunn/5508 20.00 50.00
42 Kenny Irwin BellSouth/5508 25.00 60.00
44 Justin Labonte Slim Jim/5508 15.00 40.00
45 Adam Petty Sprint PCS/5508 75.00 150.00
55 Kenny Wallace Square D/5508 15.00 40.00
57 Jason Keller Excedrin/5508 15.00 40.00
60 Geoff Bodine Power Team/5508 15.00 40.00
60 Mark Martin Winn Dixie/20,008 30.00 80.00
60 Mark Martin Winn Dixie Flames/5508 70.00 120.00
60 Mark Martin Winn Dixie Flag/5508 70.00 110.00
63 Mark Green Super Flo/2340 15.00 40.00
66 Darrell Waltrip Route 66/5508 20.00 50.00
66 Darrell Waltrip Route 66 Flames/5508 20.00 50.00
77 Robert Pressley Jasper Cat/2340 15.00 40.00
97 Chad Little John Deere/10,008 25.00 60.00
99 Jeff Burton Exide/10,008 20.00 50.00
01 Tim Steele Friends of NRA/5580 15.00 40.00

2000 Team Caliber Preferred Banks 1:24

5 Terry Labonte Froot Loops/504 20.00 50.00
5 Terry Labonte Kellogg's/504 25.00 50.00
6 Mark Martin Eagle One/756 20.00 80.00
6 Mark Martin Valvoline/756 30.00 80.00
6 Mark Martin Valvoline Max Life/756 20.00 60.00
6 Mark Martin Zerex/504 25.00 50.00
9 Jeff Burton Northern Light/504 20.00 50.00
10 Johnny Benson Lycos/504 15.00 50.00
11 Brett Bodine Ralphs 15.00 50.00
12 Jeremy Mayfield Mobil 1/504 25.00 60.00
14 Rick Mast Conseco/504 15.00 50.00
16 Kevin Lepage Clemson/504 25.00 50.00
16 Kevin Lepage Familyclick.com/504 15.00 50.00
16 Kevin Lepage Mac Tools/504 15.00 50.00
17 Matt Kenseth DeWalt/756 50.00 100.00
17 Matt Kenseth DeWalt 24 Volt/756 50.00 100.00
17 Matt Kenseth Visine/504 50.00 100.00
21 Elliott Sadler Citgo/504 15.00 50.00
21 Elliott Sadler Citgo Virginia Tech/756 15.00 50.00
24 Ricky Hendrick GMAC/504 30.00 60.00
25 Jerry Nadeau Holigan/504 15.00 50.00
26 Jimmy Spencer Big K-Mart/504 15.00 50.00
40 Sterling Marlin Coors Light/504 30.00 60.00
40 Sterling Marlin Coors Light Brooks & Dunn/504 30.00 60.00
42 Kenny Irwin BellSouth/504 40.00 80.00
43 John Andretti Cheerios/504 15.00 50.00
44 Justin Labonte Slim Jim/504 25.00 60.00
44 Kyle Petty Hot Wheels/504 30.00 60.00
45 Adam Petty Sprint PCS/732 75.00 150.00
57 Jason Keller Excedrin/504 15.00 50.00
60 Mark Martin Winn Dixie/504 60.00 100.00
60 Mark Martin Winn Dixie Flag/504 60.00 100.00
66 Darrell Waltrip Route 66/504 25.00 50.00
66 Darrell Waltrip Route 66 Flames/504 25.00 50.00
97 Chad Little John Deere/504 25.00 80.00
99 Jeff Burton Exide/504 25.00 80.00

2000 Team Caliber White Knuckle Racing 1:24

These cars are massed produced and come in exclusive packaging. The 1:24 scale cars have an opening hood and are packaged in a clear window box.

6 Mark Martin Valvoline 8.00 20.00
6 Mark Martin Eagle One 8.00 20.00
17 Matt Kenseth DeWalt 8.00 20.00
17 Matt Kenseth Visine HO 12.50 25.00
97 Chad Little John Deere 8.00 20.00
99 Jeff Burton Exide 8.00 20.00

2001 Team Caliber Owners Series 1:24

1 Jimmy Spencer Flight 93/1200 125.00 250.00
5 Terry Labonte Kellogg's/2844 20.00 50.00
5 Terry Labonte Kellogg's Mini Wheats/2340 20.00 50.00
5 Terry Labonte Kellogg's Monsters Inc./1638 20.00 50.00
6 Mark Martin JR's Garage/3120 50.00 100.00
6 Mark Martin JR's Garage Promo/200 90.00 175.00
6 Mark Martin Pfizer/7494 30.00 80.00
6 Mark Martin Stroh's Light 1989 Thunderbird/7998 40.00 80.00
6 Mark Martin Viagra/7494 25.00 60.00
6 Mark Martin Viagra Metal Flake/4824 40.00 80.00
9 Jeff Burton Gain/1500 20.00 50.00
10 Johnny Benson Eagle One/1596 15.00 40.00
10 Johnny Benson Valvoline/3120 15.00 40.00
10 Johnny Benson Valvoline Employees/1800 15.00 40.00
10 Jeff Green Nesquik/1200 15.00 40.00
12 Jeremy Mayfield Mobil 1 Sony Wega/1008 15.00 40.00
17 Matt Kenseth DeWalt/5004 40.00 80.00
17 Matt Kenseth DeWalt AT&T/2058 30.00 80.00
17 Matt Kenseth DeWalt Flag/804 400.00 600.00
17 Matt Kenseth DeWalt Rookie of the Year Yellow Hood/2840 100.00 175.00
17 Matt Kenseth DeWalt Saw/1200 50.00 100.00
17 Matt Kenseth Visine-A/2532 30.00 60.00
21 Elliott Sadler Air Force/2400 20.00 50.00
21 Elliott Sadler Motorcraft/2340 20.00 50.00
22 Ward Burton Caterpillar/4050 20.00 50.00
22 Ward Burton Caterpillar Flag 40.00 80.00
24 Ricky Hendrick GMAC/1008 15.00 40.00
25 Jerry Nadeau UAW Delphi/1800 15.00 40.00
32 Ricky Craven Tide/1230 20.00 50.00
33 Joe Nemechek Oakwood Homes Charlie Daniels/1200 15.00 40.00
40 Sterling Marlin Coors Light/2400 30.00 60.00
40 Sterling Marlin Coors Light Brooks & Dunn/2406 35.00 60.00
40 Sterling Marlin Coors Light John Wayne/2400 30.00 60.00
40 Sterling Marlin Flag/2586 50.00 90.00
43 John Andretti Cheerios/3396 15.00 40.00
43 John Andretti Cheerios Mac Tools/3000 15.00 40.00
43 Dodge by Petty/3120 15.00 40.00
44 Buckshot Jones Four Generations Petty/1896 15.00 40.00
44 Buckshot Jones Georgia-Pacific 15.00 40.00
44 Buckshot Jones Georgia Pacific Mac Tools/3000 15.00 40.00
45 Kyle Petty Sprint PCS/4050 30.00 60.00
45 Kyle Petty Sprint PCS Mac Tools/3000 30.00 60.00
45 Kyle Petty Sprint PCS Charity Ride/2100 30.00 60.00
60 Greg Biffle Grainger/1960 30.00 60.00
77 Robert Pressley Forever in our Hearts Flag/978 40.00 80.00
96 Andy Houston McDonalds/1200 15.00 40.00
97 Kurt Busch Sharpie/2310 100.00 150.00
97 Kurt Busch Rubbermaid Flag/904 175.00 300.00
97 Kurt Busch 100 Years Ford/1800 50.00 100.00
99 Jeff Burton Citgo/2250 20.00 50.00
99 Jeff Burton Citgo MDA/2250 20.00 50.00
99 Jeff Burton Citgo Stars&Stripes/1068 75.00 125.00
100 Hendrick Motor Sports 100 Wins with 8-pewter driver figures/504 40.00 80.00
01 Kansas Protection One/1380 15.00 40.00
01 NDA Friends of the NRA 15.00 40.00
02 Ryan Newman Alltel/1200 125.00 250.00

2001 Team Caliber Owners Series Banks 1:24

5 Terry Labonte Kellogg's/504 20.00 50.00
5 Terry Labonte Kellogg's Mini Wheats/504 35.00 70.00
5 Terry Labonte Monster's Inc/168 30.00 60.00
6 Mark Martin JR's Garage/754 50.00 90.00
6 Mark Martin Pfizer/1008 40.00 80.00
6 Mark Martin Viagra/1008 40.00 80.00
9 Jeff Burton Gain/504 20.00 50.00
10 Johnny Benson Eagle One/258 25.00 60.00
10 Johnny Benson Valvoline/504 30.00 60.00
10 Jeff Green Nesquik/258 20.00 50.00
12 Jeremy Mayfield Mobil 1/504 20.00 50.00
17 Matt Kenseth DeWalt/1008 45.00 80.00
17 Matt Kenseth DeWalt AT&T/426 25.00 60.00
17 Matt Kenseth DeWalt Saw/504 35.00 60.00
17 Matt Kenseth DeWalt Rookie of the Year/756 50.00 100.00
17 Matt Kenseth Visine-A/504 30.00 60.00
21 Elliott Sadler Motorcraft/756 25.00 60.00
22 Ward Burton Caterpillar 30.00 60.00
24 Ricky Hendrick GMAC/300 20.00 50.00
25 Jerry Nadeau UAW-Delphi/504 20.00 50.00
32 Ricky Craven Tide/258 35.00 70.00
33 Joe Nemechek Oakwood Homes Charlie Daniels Band/258 20.00 50.00
43 John Andretti Cheerios/756 30.00 60.00
44 Buckshot Jones Georgia-Pacific/756 20.00 50.00
44 Buckshot Jones Four Generations of Petty/756 25.00 60.00
45 Kyle Petty Sprint PCS 40.00 80.00
45 Kyle Petty Sprint PCS Charity Ride/504 20.00 50.00
60 Greg Biffle Grainger/756 50.00 90.00
97 Kurt Busch Sharpie/504 60.00 120.00
97 Kurt Busch 100 Years of Ford/258 50.00 100.00
99 Jeff Burton Citgo/426 25.00 60.00
02 Ryan Newman Alltel/258 150.00 225.00

2001 Team Caliber Owners Series Gold 1:24

5 Terry Labonte Monster's Inc/180 60.00 100.00
5 Terry Labonte Kellogg's 40.00 80.00
5 Terry Labonte Kellogg's Mini Wheats/504 25.00 60.00
6 Mark Martin JR's Garage 45.00 80.00
6 Mark Martin Pfizer/1008 40.00 80.00
6 Mark Martin Stroh's Light 1989 Thunderbird Mac Tools/5004 40.00 80.00
6 Mark Martin Viagra/1008 75.00 150.00
9 Jeff Burton Gain/504 30.00 60.00
10 Johnny Benson Valvoline Employees/258 25.00 50.00
10 Johnny Benson Eagle One/258 30.00 60.00
10 Jeff Green Nesquik/258 25.00 50.00
12 Jeremy Mayfield Mobil 1 30.00 60.00
12 Jeremy Mayfield Sony Wega/258 30.00 60.00
17 Matt Kenseth DeWalt/1008 75.00 150.00
17 Matt Kenseth Visine-A/504 50.00 100.00
21 Elliott Sadler Air Force/258 35.00 75.00
21 Elliott Sadler Motorcraft/504 30.00 60.00
22 Ward Burton Caterpillar/756 30.00 60.00
24 Ricky Hendrick GMAC/300 30.00 60.00
25 Jerry Nadeau UAW-Delphi/504 30.00 60.00
32 Ricky Craven Tide/258 25.00 50.00
33 Joe Nemechek Oakwood Homes Charlie Daniels Band/258 30.00 60.00
40 Sterling Marlin Coors Light/504 45.00 80.00
43 John Andretti Cheerios/756 30.00 70.00
44 Buckshot Jones Georgia-Pacific 25.00 60.00
44 Buckshot Jones

Four Generations Petty/756
45 Kyle Petty Sprint PCS/756 30.00 60.00
45 Kyle Petty Sprint PCS Charity Ride/504 30.00 60.00
60 Greg Biffle Grainger/756 50.00 100.00
96 Andy Houston McDonalds/258 20.00 50.00
97 Kurt Busch Sharpie/504 100.00 175.00
97 Kurt Busch 100 Years of Ford/258 75.00 150.00
99 Jeff Burton Citgo/1008 25.00 60.00
02 Ryan Newman Alltel/258 250.00 400.00

2001 Team Caliber Owners Series Steel 1:24

5 Terry Labonte Kellogg's/504 30.00 80.00
5 Terry Labonte Kellogg's Mini Wheats/504 25.00 50.00
5 Terry Labonte Kellogg's Monster's Inc/138 60.00 100.00
6 Mark Martin JR's Garage 45.00 80.00
6 Mark Martin Pfizer/1008 40.00 80.00
6 Mark Martin Viagra/1008 50.00 100.00
9 Jeff Burton Gain/504 30.00 60.00
10 Johnny Benson Eagle One/258 30.00 60.00
12 Jeremy Mayfield Sony Wega/258 25.00 50.00
17 Matt Kenseth DeWalt/1008 75.00 150.00
17 Matt Kenseth Visine-A/504 50.00 100.00
21 Elliott Sadler Motorcraft/504 25.00 50.00
22 Ward Burton Caterpillar/756 35.00 75.00
24 Ricky Hendrick GMAC/300 25.00 50.00
25 Jerry Nadeau UAW-Delphi/504 30.00 60.00
32 Ricky Craven Tide/258 30.00 60.00
33 Joe Nemechek Oakwood Homes Charlie Daniels/258 25.00 50.00
43 John Andretti Cheerios/756 25.00 50.00
44 Buckshot Jones Four Generations Petty/756 30.00 60.00
44 Buckshot Jones Georgia-Pacific/756 25.00 50.00
45 Kyle Petty Sprint PCS 50.00 75.00
45 Kyle Petty Sprint PCS Charity Ride/504 30.00 60.00
60 Greg Biffle Grainger/756 50.00 100.00
96 Andy Houston McDonalds/258 25.00 60.00
97 Kurt Busch Sharpie/504 75.00 150.00
97 Kurt Busch 100 Years of Ford/258 60.00 120.00
99 Jeff Burton Citgo/1008 35.00 75.00
99 Jeff Burton Citgo MDA/426 30.00 60.00
02 Ryan Newman Alltel/258 200.00 350.00

2001 Team Caliber Pit Stop 1:24

6 Mark Martin Pfizer 15.00 30.00
6 Mark Martin Viagra/3120 20.00 40.00
17 Matt Kenseth DeWalt/3120 10.00 20.00
17 Matt Kenseth DeWalt Saw/3120 10.00 20.00
22 Ward Burton Caterpillar/2400 10.00 20.00
40 Sterling Marlin Coors Light John Wayne 20.00 40.00
99 Jeff Burton Citgo 10.00 20.00

2001 Team Caliber Preferred 1:24

5 Terry Labonte Kellogg's 20.00 50.00
5 Terry Labonte Kellogg's Mini Wheats/2106 20.00 50.00
5 Terry Labonte Kellogg's Monster's Inc/4608 20.00 50.00
6 Mark Martin Pfizer/10080 20.00 50.00
6 Mark Martin Viagra/4996 20.00 50.00
6 Mark Martin Viagra Dark Chrome Mac Tools/5004 40.00 80.00
6 Mark Martin Viagra Metal Flake/10,080 20.00 50.00
9 Jeff Burton Gain/1008 25.00 50.00
10 Johnny Benson Eagle One/3624 20.00 40.00
10 Johnny Benson Valvoline/4920 20.00 40.00
10 Johnny Benson Valvoline Employees/5220 15.00 40.00
12 Jeremy Mayfield Sony Wega/900 25.00 50.00
17 Matt Kenseth DeWalt/2760 20.00 40.00
17 Matt Kenseth DeWalt AT&T/1896 20.00 40.00
17 Matt Kenseth DeWalt Saw/1896 20.00 40.00
17 Matt Kenseth Visine-A/5136 20.00 40.00
17 Matt Kenseth Visine-A Mac Tools/3000 15.00 30.00
21 Elliott Sadler Motorcraft/1500 25.00 50.00
22 Ward Burton Caterpillar/10080 20.00 40.00
24 Ricky Hendrick GMAC/900 20.00 40.00
25 Jerry Nadeau UAW-Delphi/1200 20.00 40.00
26 Jimmy Spencer The Mummy/4920 20.00 40.00
32 Ricky Craven Tide/3624 25.00 50.00
33 Joe Nemechek Oakwood Homes Charlie Daniels Band/900 25.00 50.00
36 Ken Schrader Stars&Stripes/10,700 125.00 250.00
40 Sterling Marlin Coors Light/1104 30.00 50.00
40 Sterling Marlin Coors Light Brook&Dunn/2802 25.00 60.00
40 Sterling Marlin Coors Light John Wayne/2940 20.00 40.00
43 John Andretti Cheerios/1980 20.00 40.00
44 Buckshot Jones Four Generations Petty/1800 20.00 40.00
44 Buckshot Jones Georgia-Pacific/4320 20.00 40.00
45 Kyle Petty Sprint PCS/5640 20.00 40.00
45 Kyle Petty Sprint PCS Charity Ride/1224 25.00 50.00
60 Greg Biffle Grainger/5004 20.00 40.00
60 Greg Biffle Grainger Mac Tools/3000 30.00 50.00
96 Andy Houston McDonald's/900 20.00 40.00
97 Kurt Busch Sharpie/5220 50.00 100.00
97 Kurt Busch 100 Years of Ford/4020 45.00 80.00
99 Jeff Burton Citgo MDA/5004 20.00 40.00
99 Jeff Burton Citgo MDA Mac Tools/3000 20.00 40.00
02 Ryan Newman Alltel/3876 70.00 120.00
02 Ryan Newman Alltel Promo/756 30.00 60.00
02 Ryan Newman Alltel AUTO with figurine/1800 100.00 200.00

2001 Team Caliber Promos 1:24

10 Scott Riggs Nesquik/2400 12.50 25.00
26 Jimmy Spencer Mummy Returns 12.50 25.00
32 Dan Pardus Outdoor Channel 15.00 30.00
71 Kevin Lepage Mini Corn Dogs 15.00 30.00
71 Kevin Lepage State Fair Corn Dogs 12.50 25.00

2002 Team Caliber Owners Series 1:24

1 Jimmy Spencer Yellow Freight/1200 40.00 70.00
5 Ricky Hendrick GMAC/1200 30.00 60.00
5 Terry Labonte Cheez-It/2340 30.00 60.00
5 Terry Labonte Got Milk/2400 30.00 60.00
5 Terry Labonte Kellogg's/2400 30.00 60.00
6 Mark Martin Kraft/10008 40.00 80.00
6 Mark Martin Pfizer/5004 45.00 80.00
6 Mark Martin Viagra/10008 45.00 80.00
6 Mark Martin Viagra No Bull/6504 50.00 100.00
9 Jeff Burton Gain/1200 40.00 75.00
10 Johnny Benson Valvoline/3120 35.00 70.00
10 Johnny Benson Zerex/1200 40.00 75.00
12 Ryan Newman Alltel/5004 75.00 125.00
12 Ryan Newman Alltel Blue Chrome Rookie of the Year/2400 70.00 120.00
12 Ryan Newman Alltel Sony WEGA/3120 70.00 120.00
12 Ryan Newman Mobil 1/3120 70.00 120.00
17 Matt Kenseth DeWalt/3120 50.00 100.00
17 Matt Kenseth AT&T/2400 50.00 100.00
17 Matt Kenseth DeWalt Flames/3120 50.00 100.00
17 Matt Kenseth DeWalt Million $ Challenge/2400 50.00 100.00
21 Elliott Sadler Air Force/2400 40.00 70.00
21 Elliott Sadler Motorcraft/1800 30.00 60.00
24 Jack Sprague NetZero/1200 30.00 60.00
25 Bobby Hamilton Jr. Marines/1200 40.00 70.00
25 Jerry Nadeau UAW-Delphi/2400 25.00 60.00
27 Jamie McMurray USPS Heroes of 9-11/1500 75.00 150.00
32 Ricky Craven Tide/1200 40.00 70.00
36 Ken Schrader M&Ms/2400 40.00 80.00
36 Ken Schrader M&Ms Halloween/2400 40.00 80.00
36 Ken Schrader M&Ms July 4th/2400 40.00 80.00
36 Ken Schrader M&Ms Vote/3120 40.00 80.00
36 Ken Schrader M&Ms Vote Purple/2438 50.00 90.00
43 John Andretti Cheerios/2400 35.00 80.00
43 John Andretti StarWars/2400 40.00 80.00
43 Richard Petty Garfield/3120 40.00 75.00
45 Kyle Petty Sprint PCS/2400 40.00 80.00
45 Kyle Petty Sprint Charity Ride/1800 50.00 80.00
48 Jimmie Johnson Lowe's/3120 50.00 100.00
48 Jimmie Johnson Lowe's Power of Pride/5004 40.00 80.00
60 Greg Biffle Grainger Red Chrome BGN Champ/1200 75.00 125.00
60 Greg Biffle Grainger/3120 50.00 90.00
60 Jack Sprague HAAS/1200 30.00 60.00
97 Kurt Busch Rubbermaid/2400 40.00 75.00
97 Kurt Busch Rubbermaid Commercial/2400 40.00 70.00
97 Kurt Busch Rubbermaid Little Tikes/1800 45.00 80.00
97 Kurt Busch Sharpie 500/3120 45.00 80.00
97 Kurt Busch Sharpie Million $/2400 40.00 70.00
99 Jeff Burton Citgo/3120 30.00 60.00
99 Jeff Burton Citgo Bass Masters/1800 40.00 75.00
99 Jeff Burton Citgo Peel Out, Reel In & Win/2400 40.00 75.00
02 Daytona 500/1560 25.00 50.00
NNO NDA NBC/1008 50.00 80.00
NNO NDA TNT/1008 50.00 80.00

2002 Team Caliber Owners Series Banks 1:24

1 Jimmy Spencer Yellow Freight/60 40.00 70.00
2 NDA Daytona/1560 25.00 50.00
5 Ricky Hendrick GMAC/180 30.00 60.00
5 Terry Labonte Cheez-It/108 30.00 60.00
5 Terry Labonte Got Milk/180 30.00 60.00
5 Terry Labonte Kellogg's/264 30.00 60.00
6 Mark Martin Kraft/642 30.00 60.00
6 Mark Martin Pfizer/372 30.00 60.00
6 Mark Martin Viagra/576 35.00 60.00
6 Mark Martin Viagra No Bull/372 35.00 60.00
9 Jeff Burton Gain/180 40.00 75.00
10 Johnny Benson Valvoline/180 30.00 60.00
12 Ryan Newman Alltel/324 75.00 125.00
12 Ryan Newman Alltel Sony WEGA/198 70.00 120.00
12 Ryan Newman Mobil 1/192 70.00 120.00
17 Matt Kenseth DeWalt/270 60.00 100.00
17 Matt Kenseth DeWalt Flames/204 60.00 100.00
17 Matt Kenseth DeWalt Million $ Challenge/198 50.00 90.00
21 Elliott Sadler Air Force/180 30.00 60.00
21 Elliott Sadler Motorcraft/222 25.00 50.00
24 Jack Sprague NetZero/60 30.00 60.00
25 J.Nadeau UAW-Delphi/294 40.00 70.00
36 Ken Schrader M&Ms/180 30.00 70.00
36 Ken Schrader M&Ms July 4th/180 40.00 70.00
36 Ken Schrader M&Ms Vote/180 40.00 70.00
36 Ken Schrader M&Ms Vote Purple/180 40.00 80.00
43 John Andretti Cheerios/1134 25.00 50.00
43 Richard Petty Garfield/180 30.00 60.00
43 John Andretti StarWars/180 40.00 75.00
45 Kyle Petty Sprint PCS/180 30.00 60.00
48 Jimmie Johnson Lowe's/504 40.00 80.00
48 Jimmie Johnson Lowe's Power of Pride/390 40.00 80.00
60 Greg Biffle Grainger/228 40.00 75.00
60 Jack Sprague HAAS/180 30.00 60.00
97 Kurt Busch Rubbermaid/252 30.00 60.00
97 Kurt Busch Rubbermaid Commercial/180 30.00 60.00
97 Kurt Busch Rubbermaid Little Tikes/180 40.00 70.00
97 Kurt Busch Sharpie 500/180 40.00 70.00
97 Kurt Busch Sharpie Million $ Challenge/180 30.00 60.00
99 Jeff Burton Citgo/288 40.00 75.00
99 Jeff Burton Citgo Bass Masters/180 40.00 75.00
99 Jeff Burton Citgo Peel Reel Win/180 50.00 80.00

2002 Team Caliber Owners Series Dark Chrome 1:24

1 Jimmy Spencer Yellow Freight/96 40.00 70.00
5 Ricky Hendrick GMAC/180 45.00 75.00
5 Terry Labonte Cheez-It/180 40.00 75.00
5 Terry Labonte Got Milk/504 40.00 75.00
5 Terry Labonte Kellogg's/264 40.00 75.00
6 Mark Martin Kraft/1296 40.00 75.00
6 Mark Martin Pfizer/426 50.00 90.00
6 Mark Martin Viagra/1026 60.00 100.00
6 Mark Martin Viagra No Bull/942 60.00 100.00
9 Jeff Burton Gain/504 50.00 90.00
10 Johnny Benson Valvoline/216 40.00 75.00
10 Johnny Benson Zerex/252 40.00 75.00
12 Ryan Newman Alltel/558 125.00 225.00
12 Ryan Newman Alltel Sony WEGA/1008 70.00 120.00
12 Ryan Newman Alltel The Winston/1212 90.00 150.00
12 Ryan Newman Mobil 1/378 60.00 100.00
17 Matt Kenseth DeWalt/354 125.00 250.00
17 Matt Kenseth AT&T/504 75.00 125.00
17 Matt Kenseth DeWalt Flames/930 70.00 120.00
17 Matt Kenseth DeWalt Million Dollar Challenge/588 50.00 100.00
21 Elliott Sadler Air Force/336 50.00 100.00
21 Elliott Sadler Motorcraft/180 40.00 70.00
24 Jack Sprague NetZero/174 40.00 70.00
25 Bobby Hamilton Jr. Marines/180 50.00 90.00
25 Jerry Nadeau UAW-Delphi/180 30.00 60.00
32 Ricky Craven Tide/180 40.00 70.00
36 Ken Schrader M&Ms/432 50.00 90.00
36 Ken Schrader M&Ms Halloween/540 50.00 90.00
36 Ken Schrader M&Ms July 4th/504 50.00 90.00
36 Ken Schrader M&Ms Vote/288 60.00 100.00
36 Ken Schrader M&Ms Vote Purple/900 60.00 100.00
43 John Andretti Cheerios/180 40.00 70.00
43 John Andretti StarWars/342 50.00 90.00
43 Richard Petty Garfield/396 50.00 90.00
45 Kyle Petty Sprint PCS/180 40.00 70.00
45 Kyle Petty Sprint Charity Ride/336 45.00 80.00
48 Jimmie Johnson Lowe's/1002 60.00 120.00
48 Jimmie Johnson Lowe's Power of Pride/1002 50.00 100.00
60 Greg Biffle Grainger/354 60.00 100.00
60 Jack Sprague HAAS/180 30.00 60.00
97 Kurt Busch Rubbermaid/288 40.00 80.00
97 Kurt Busch Rubbermaid Commercial/330 40.00 80.00
97 Kurt Busch Rubbermaid Little Tikes 40.00 80.00
97 Kurt Busch Sharpie Million $ Challenge/540 40.00 80.00
97 Kurt Busch Sharpie 500/600 40.00 80.00
99 Jeff Burton Citgo/384 30.00 60.00
99 Jeff Burton Citgo Bass Masters/426 40.00 80.00
99 Jeff Burton Citgo Peel Out, Reel In & Win/504 40.00 75.00
02 Santa Claus Holiday/3504 50.00 100.00

2002 Team Caliber Owners Series Vintage 1:24

6 Mark Martin Folgers 1989 Thunderbird/7770 100.00 175.00
6 Mark Martin Stroh's Light 1991 ThunderBird 45.00 80.00
6 Mark Martin Stroh's Light '91 T-Bird Dark Chrome/5004 40.00 80.00
21 Neil Bonnett Citgo 1989 Thunderbird/3120 40.00 100.00

2002 Team Caliber Pit Stop 1:24

These cars were released in 2002 and packaged in a gray black cardboard box with a clear window to view the car ins The cars are hood open models.

1 Jimmy Spencer Yellow Freight 12.50 25.00
5 Terry Labonte Got Milk/2400 12.50 25.00
5 Terry Labonte Kellogg's/2400 12.50 25.00
6 Mark Martin Kraft/5532 15.00 30.00
6 Mark Martin Pfizer/3810 12.50 25.00
6 Mark Martin Viagra/7494 20.00 35.00
10 Johnny Benson Zerex/900 15.00 30.00
12 Ryan Newman Alltel/2724 15.00 30.00
12 Ryan Newman Alltel Sony WEGA/2400 20.00 35.00
17 Matt Kenseth DeWalt/5520 15.00 30.00
17 Matt Kenseth AT&T/1800 15.00 30.00
17 Matt Kenseth DeWalt Million $ Challenge/3120 15.00 30.00
25 Jerry Nadeau UAW-Delphi/2400 12.50 25.00
32 Ricky Craven Tide Promo/2400 12.50 25.00
36 Ken Schrader M&Ms/2400 12.50 25.00
36 Ken Schrader M&Ms Halloween/2400 12.50 25.00
36 Ken Schrader M&Ms July 4th/2400 15.00 30.00
36 Ken Schrader M&Ms Vote/3120 12.50 25.00
36 Ken Schrader M&M's Vote Purple/3120 15.00 30.00
43 Richard Petty Garfield/2400 15.00 30.00
43 John Andretti StarWars/3456 15.00 30.00
45 Kyle Petty Sprint PCS/708 12.50 25.00
45 Kyle Petty Sprint Charity Ride/2400 15.00 30.00
48 Jimmie Johnson Lowe's 20.00 35.00
48 Jimmie Johnson Lowe's Power of Pride 20.00 35.00
55 Bobby Hamilton Square D Promo 15.00 30.00
60 Greg Biffle Grainger/2400 12.50 25.00
97 Kurt Busch Rubbermaid/2532 15.00 30.00
97 Kurt Busch Rubbermaid Commercial/2400 15.00 30.00
97 Kurt Busch Sharpie Million $ Challenge/2400 15.00 30.00
97 Kurt Busch Sharpie 500/2400 15.00 30.00
99 Jeff Burton Citgo/3120 12.50 25.00
99 Jeff Burton Citgo Peel Out, Reel In & Win/2400 12.50 25.00
02 Daytona 2002 12.50 25.00

2002 Team Caliber Preferred 1:24

1 Jimmy Spencer Yellow Freight/480 25.00 50.00
5 Ricky Hendrick GMAC/672 20.00 50.00
5 Terry Labonte Cheez-It/924 25.00 50.00
5 Terry Labonte Got Milk/1428 25.00 50.00
5 Terry Labonte Kellogg's/2028 20.00 50.00
6 Mark Martin Kraft/6196 30.00 60.00
6 Mark Martin Kraft Mac Tools/2400 30.00 60.00
6 Mark Martin Pfizer/2550 30.00 60.00
6 Mark Martin Viagra/8196 30.00 60.00
6 Mark Martin Viagra Mac Tools/2400 30.00 60.00
6 Mark Martin Viagra No Bull/1480 30.00 60.00
9 Jeff Burton Gain/4020 25.00 50.00
10 Johnny Benson Valvoline/2448 20.00 50.00
10 Johnny Benson Zerex/3876 25.00 50.00
12 Ryan Newman Alltel/2820 30.00 60.00
12 Ryan Newman Alltel Sony WEGA/5004 40.00 75.00
12 Ryan Newman Mobil 1/1536 35.00 60.00
17 Matt Kenseth DeWalt/2448 40.00 80.00
17 Matt Kenseth DeWalt Mac Tools/2400 40.00 80.00
17 Matt Kenseth AT&T/4128 30.00 60.00
17 Matt Kenseth DeWalt Flames/1200 40.00 80.00
17 Matt Kenseth DeWalt Million $ Challenge/1392 40.00 80.00
21 Neil Bonnett Citgo 1989 Thunderbird Mac Tools/1500 75.00 125.00
21 Elliott Sadler Air Force/4260 30.00 60.00
21 Elliott Sadler 20.00 50.00

Motorcraft/1176
Jack Sprague NetZero/612 25.00 50.00
Bobby Hamilton Jr. Marines/900 30.00 50.00
Jerry Nadeau UAW-Delphi/1608 20.00 50.00
Ricky Craven Tide/600 30.00 60.00
Ken Schrader M&Ms/2676 35.00 60.00
Ken Schrader M&Ms Halloween/4344 25.00 50.00
Ken Schrader M&Ms July 4th/1380 35.00 60.00
Ken Schrader M&M's Vote Purple/4008 35.00 60.00
Ken Schrader M&Ms Vote/5544 35.00 60.00
John Andretti Cheerios/180 20.00 50.00
Richard Petty Garfield/4428 35.00 60.00
John Andretti StarWars/4572 35.00 60.00
Adam Petty 2000 Sprint PCS Mac Tools/1506 75.00 125.00
5 Kyle Petty Sprint PCS/1152 20.00 50.00
5 Kyle Petty Sprint Charity Ride/900 25.00 50.00
8 Jimmie Johnson Lowe's/10,080 45.00 80.00
8 Jimmie Johnson Lowe's Power of Pride 45.00 80.00
0 Greg Biffle Grainger/2340 25.00 50.00
0 Jack Sprague HAAS/900 30.00 60.00
7 Kurt Busch Rubbermaid/2340 30.00 60.00
7 Kurt Busch Rubbermaid Commercial/4116 30.00 60.00
7 Kurt Busch Rubbermaid Little Tikes/4320 40.00 70.00
7 Kurt Busch Sharpie 500/2400 35.00 60.00
7 Kurt Busch Sharpie Million $ Challenge/4668 30.00 60.00
9 Jeff Burton Citgo/2340 20.00 50.00
9 Jeff Burton Citgo Bass Masters/4020 25.00 50.00
9 Jeff Burton Citgo Peel Out, Reel In and Win/4128 25.00 50.00

2002 Team Caliber Promos 1:24

2 Winston No Bull 5 10.00 20.00
27 Jamie McMurray USPS Heroes 15.00 25.00
60 Greg Biffle Grainger/1960 25.00 50.00
2 AT&T Daytona 500 15.00 30.00

2003 Team Caliber First Choice 1:24

5 Terry Labonte Kellogg's/250 50.00 100.00
6 Mark Martin Viagra/756 50.00 100.00
12 Ryan Newman Alltel/756 50.00 100.00
16 Greg Biffle Grainger/250 100.00 175.00
17 Matt Kenseth DeWalt/756 150.00 225.00
17 Matt Kenseth DeWalt '03 Champion Employee Promo/2000 250.00 400.00
17 Matt Kenseth DeWalt Victory Lap/717 125.00 250.00
17 Matt Kenseth Smirnoff Champ/717 150.00 225.00
21 Ricky Rudd Motorcraft/756 40.00 80.00
45 Kyle Petty Georgia Pacific/250 30.00 60.00
48 Jimmie Johnson Lowe's/756 60.00 120.00
97 Kurt Busch Rubbermaid/504 30.00 60.00

2003 Team Caliber Owners Series 1:24

5 Terry Labonte Kellogg's/1200 45.00 75.00
5 Terry Labonte Kellogg's Cheez-It/1500 45.00 75.00
5 Terry Labonte Finding Nemo/1800 50.00 80.00
5 Terry Labonte Got Milk/1500 45.00 75.00
5 Terry Labonte Power of Cheese/1800 45.00 75.00
6 Mark Martin Kraft/1200 45.00 75.00
6 Mark Martin Pfizer/1200 45.00 75.00
6 Mark Martin Viagra/10,080 45.00 80.00
6 Mark Martin Viagra Blue Chrome/10,080 50.00 80.00
6 Mark Martin Viagra Blue Daytona/1800 50.00 80.00
6 Mark Martin Viagra White/1800 45.00 80.00
6 Mark Martin Viagra 500 Starts/1800 175.00 300.00
9 Greg Biffle Oreo/1200 45.00 75.00
10 Johnny Benson Eagle One/1500 40.00 70.00
10 Johnny Benson Valvoline/2400 40.00 70.00
12 Ryan Newman Alltel/7560 50.00 80.00
12 Ryan Newman Alltel 50th Win/1200 100.00 200.00
12 Ryan Newman Mobil 1/2400 50.00 80.00
12 Ryan Newman Sony Wega/2400 50.00 80.00
16 Greg Biffle Grainger/5004 45.00 80.00
17 Matt Kenseth Alka-Seltzer Plus/1008 50.00 80.00
17 Matt Kenseth Alka-Seltzer Morning Relief/1008 50.00 80.00
17 Matt Kenseth Bayer/1008 50.00 80.00
17 Matt Kenseth Bayer Aleve/1008 50.00 80.00
17 Matt Kenseth DeWalt/7560 90.00 175.00
17 Matt Kenseth DeWalt 2003 Champion/6504 60.00 100.00
17 Matt Kenseth DeWalt Million $ Challenge/2400 50.00 80.00
17 Matt Kenseth DeWalt Pearl Gold 2003 Champ/1008 100.00 200.00
17 Matt Kenseth Smirnoff Ice 2003 Champion/7500 60.00 100.00
17 Matt Kenseth DeWalt Victory Lap/5004 60.00 120.00
21 Ricky Rudd Air Force/2400 40.00 70.00
21 Ricky Rudd AF Cross Into Blue/2400 45.00 75.00
21 Ricky Rudd Ford 100 Years/1200 45.00 75.00
21 Ricky Rudd Motorcraft/7560 50.00 80.00
21 Ricky Rudd Motorcraft 700 Starts/1800 45.00 75.00
23 Kenny Wallace Stacker 2/1200 40.00 70.00
25 Bobby Hamilton Jr. Marines/1800 40.00 70.00
25 Bobby Hamilton Jr. Marines Flag/1212 75.00 150.00
25 Joe Nemechek UAW Delphi/1200 40.00 70.00
32 Ricky Craven Tide/1200 40.00 70.00
43 John Andretti Cheerios/1200 40.00 65.00
43 John Andretti Cheerios Berry Burst/1008 40.00 70.00
43 John Andretti Pillsbury/1500 40.00 65.00
45 Kyle Petty Brawny/1800 45.00 75.00
45 Kyle Petty Georgia Pacific/1600 45.00 75.00
45 Kyle Petty Georgia Pacific Charity Ride/1800 45.00 75.00
45 Kyle Petty GP Garfield/2400 40.00 70.00
48 Jimmie Johnson Lowe's/7560 45.00 75.00
48 Jimmie Johnson Lowe's Blue Chrome/2400 60.00 100.00
48 Jimmie Johnson Lowe's Power of Pride/2400 45.00 75.00
60 Brian Vickers HAAS/1200 40.00 65.00
66 Chad Blount Miller High Life/1200 50.00 80.00
87 Kyle Busch Ditech.com/1800 40.00 70.00
97 Kurt Busch Rubbermaid/5004 50.00 80.00
97 Kurt Busch Blue Ice 50.00 80.00
97 Kurt Busch Rubbermaid Commercial Products/2400 50.00 80.00
97 Kurt Busch Irwin Tools/2400 45.00 75.00
97 Kurt Busch Sharpie/2400 50.00 80.00
99 Jeff Burton Citgo/7560 40.00 70.00
99 Jeff Burton Velveeta/1200 40.00 70.00
99 Kenny Wallace Cardinals/1200 40.00 70.00
01 Jerry Nadeau Army/1200 40.00 70.00
01 Jerry Nadeau Army Camouflage/1800 40.00 70.00
01 Jerry Nadeau USG Sheet Rock/1500 40.00 70.00

2003 Team Caliber Owners Series Banks 1:24

5 Terry Labonte Kellogg's/180 45.00 75.00
5 Terry Labonte Kellogg's Power of Cheese/180 40.00 75.00
6 Mark Martin Kraft/300 60.00 100.00
6 Mark Martin Pfizer/180 50.00 90.00
6 Mark Martin Viagra/2400 50.00 90.00
6 Mark Martin Viagra Blue Daytona/180 50.00 80.00
6 Mark Martin Viagra White/180 50.00 90.00
6 Mark Martin Viagra 500 Starts/180 100.00 150.00
9 Greg Biffle Oreo/180 40.00 75.00
10 Johnny Benson Valvoline/180 45.00 75.00
12 Ryan Newman Alltel/300 70.00 120.00
12 Ryan Newman Alltel 50th Win/180 100.00 175.00
12 Ryan Newman Mobil 1/180 75.00 125.00
12 Ryan Newman Sony Wega/180 75.00 125.00
16 Greg Biffle Grainger/300 50.00 90.00
17 Matt Kenseth DeWalt/300 90.00 150.00
17 Matt Kenseth DeWalt Million $ Challenge/180 50.00 100.00
21 Ricky Rudd Air Force/180 40.00 75.00
21 Ricky Rudd AF Cross Into Blue/180 40.00 75.00
21 Ricky Rudd Ford 100 Years/180 40.00 75.00
21 Ricky Rudd Motorcraft/300 40.00 75.00
21 Ricky Rudd Motorcraft 700 Starts/180 40.00 75.00
23 Kenny Wallace Stacker 2/180 45.00 75.00
25 Bobby Hamilton Jr. Marines/180 40.00 75.00
25 Joe Nemechek UAW Delphi/180 45.00 75.00
32 Ricky Craven Tide/180 45.00 75.00
43 John Andretti Cheerios/120 45.00 75.00
43 John Andretti Cheerios Berry Burst/180 45.00 75.00
45 Kyle Petty Georgia Pacific/180 40.00 80.00
45 Kyle Petty Georgia Pacific Charity Ride/180 40.00 75.00
45 Kyle Petty GP Garfield/180 40.00 75.00
48 Jimmie Johnson Lowe's/180 50.00 90.00
87 Kyle Busch Ditech.com/180 40.00 70.00
97 Kurt Busch Blue Ice/180 50.00 90.00
97 Kurt Busch Rubbermaid/300 50.00 90.00
97 Kurt Busch Rubbermaid Commercial Products/180 50.00 80.00
97 Kurt Busch Irwin Tools/180 50.00 80.00
97 Kurt Busch Sharpie/180 50.00 80.00
99 Jeff Burton Citgo/300 50.00 90.00
99 Jeff Burton Velveeta/180 50.00 80.00
01 Jerry Nadeau Army/180 45.00 75.00
01 Jerry Nadeau Army Camoflauge/180 45.00 75.00
03 Daytona 500/180 45.00 75.00

2003 Team Caliber Owners Series Dark Chrome 1:24

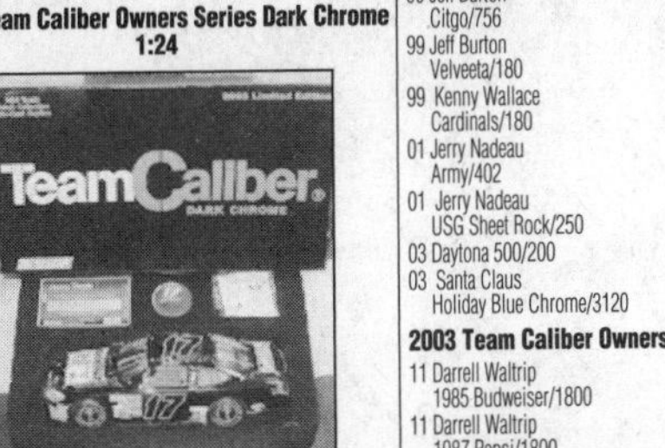

5 Terry Labonte Kellogg's/250 50.00 90.00
5 Terry Labonte Kellogg's Cheez-It/180 50.00 80.00
5 Terry Labonte Finding Nemo/252 60.00 100.00
5 Terry Labonte Kellogg's Got Milk/180 50.00 90.00
5 Terry Labonte Power of Cheese/180 50.00 90.00
6 Mark Martin Kraft/300 60.00 100.00
6 Mark Martin Pfizer/402 60.00 100.00
6 Mark Martin Viagra/1002 60.00 100.00
6 Mark Martin Viagra Blue Daytona/324 50.00 100.00
6 Mark Martin Viagra 500 Starts/300 100.00 175.00
6 Mark Martin Viagra White/360 60.00 100.00
9 Greg Biffle Oreo/180 50.00 80.00
10 Johnny Benson Eagle One/180 50.00 80.00
10 Johnny Benson Valvoline/180 50.00 80.00
12 Ryan Newman Alltel/1008 75.00 125.00
12 Ryan Newman Alltel 50th Win/180 125.00 250.00
12 Ryan Newman Mobil 1/324 100.00 175.00
12 Ryan Newman Alltel 2003 Driver of the Year Silver Chrome/1200 60.00 100.00
12 Ryan Newman Sony Wega/220 125.00 250.00
16 Greg Biffle Grainger/756 60.00 100.00
17 Matt Kenseth Bayer/234 60.00 100.00
17 Matt Kenseth DeWalt/840 90.00 150.00
17 Matt Kenseth DeWalt Million $ Challenge/402 60.00 120.00
17 Matt Kenseth Smirnoff Ice 2003 Champion Pearl Chrome/1008 75.00 125.00
17 Matt Kenseth Victory Lap/600 100.00 175.00
21 Ricky Rudd Air Force/360 50.00 90.00
21 Ricky Rudd AF Cross Into Blue/240 50.00 90.00
21 Ricky Rudd Ford 100 Years/282 50.00 90.00
21 Ricky Rudd Motorcraft/1008 50.00 90.00
21 Ricky Rudd Motorcraft 700 Starts/180 50.00 90.00
23 Kenny Wallace Stacker 2/240 50.00 80.00
25 Bobby Hamilton Jr. Marines/180 50.00 80.00
25 Bobby Hamilton Jr. Marines Flag Blue Chrome/180 100.00 200.00
25 Joe Nemechek UAW Delphi/180 50.00 80.00
32 Ricky Craven Tide/180 50.00 80.00
43 John Andretti Cheerios/180 45.00 75.00
43 John Andretti Cheerios Berry Burst/324 60.00 100.00
43 John Andretti Pillsbury/180 45.00 75.00
45 Kyle Petty Brawny/300 50.00 90.00
45 Kyle Petty Georgia Pacific/225 50.00 90.00
45 Kyle Petty Georgia Pacific Charity Ride/180 50.00 90.00
45 Kyle Petty GP Garfield/180 50.00 90.00
48 Jimmie Johnson Lowe's/684 60.00 100.00
48 Jimmie Johnson Lowe's Power of Pride Winston/180 60.00 120.00
60 Brian Vickers HAAS/204 40.00 80.00
66 Chad Blount Miller High Life/180 60.00 90.00
87 Kyle Busch Ditech.com/180 50.00 75.00
97 Kurt Busch Blue Ice/360 50.00 100.00
97 Kurt Busch Rubbermaid/504 50.00 100.00
97 Kurt Busch Rubbermaid Commercial Products/300 50.00 100.00
97 Kurt Busch Irwin Tools/240 50.00 100.00
97 Kurt Busch Sharpie/360 50.00 100.00
99 Jeff Burton Citgo/756 45.00 80.00
99 Jeff Burton Velveeta/180 50.00 90.00
99 Kenny Wallace Cardinals/180 45.00 80.00
01 Jerry Nadeau Army/402 50.00 80.00
01 Jerry Nadeau USG Sheet Rock/250 45.00 75.00
03 Daytona 500/200 50.00 90.00
03 Santa Claus Holiday Blue Chrome/3120 50.00 80.00

2003 Team Caliber Owners Series Vintage 1:24

11 Darrell Waltrip 1985 Budweiser/1800 50.00 80.00
11 Darrell Waltrip 1987 Pepsi/1800 50.00 80.00
17 Darrell Waltrip 1995 Parts America/1200 45.00 80.00
17 Darrell Waltrip 1992 Western Auto/1200 45.00 80.00
28 Davey Allison 1990 Texaco Thunderbird/2400 40.00 70.00
28 Davey Allison 1990 Texaco Dark Chrome Mac Tools/1506 60.00 100.00

2003 Team Caliber Pit Stop 1:24

1 Jamie McMurray Yellow Freight 10.00 20.00
5 Terry Labonte Kellogg's 10.00 20.00
5 Terry Labonte Finding Nemo 10.00 20.00
5 Terry Labonte Got Milk 10.00 20.00
5 Terry Labonte Power of Cheese 10.00 20.00
5 Brian Vickers Carquest 12.50 25.00
5 Brian Vickers GMAC 15.00 30.00
6 Mark Martin Kraft/2400 12.50 25.00
6 Mark Martin Pfizer 12.50 25.00
6 Mark Martin Viagra 12.50 25.00
6 Mark Martin Viagra Blue Daytona 12.50 25.00
6 Mark Martin Viagra White 12.50 25.00
6 Mark Martin Viagra 500 Starts 15.00 30.00
10 Johnny Benson Valvoline 10.00 20.00
12 Ryan Newman Alltel/3120 12.50 25.00
12 Ryan Newman Mobil 1 12.50 25.00
12 Ryan Newman Sony Wega 12.50 25.00
16 Greg Biffle Grainger/3120 12.50 25.00
16 Greg Biffle Grainger 1st Win 12.50 25.00
17 Matt Kenseth Bayer 12.50 25.00
17 Matt Kenseth DeWalt/1200 12.50 25.00
17 Matt Kenseth DeWalt 2003 Champion 15.00 25.00
17 Matt Kenseth DeWalt Million $ Challenge 12.50 25.00
17 Matt Kenseth Victory Lap 12.50 25.00
21 Ricky Rudd Air Force 10.00 20.00
21 Ricky Rudd AF Cross Into Blue 10.00 20.00
21 Ricky Rudd Ford 100 Years 10.00 20.00
21 Ricky Rudd Motorcraft/3120 10.00 20.00
21 Ricky Rudd Motorcraft 700 Starts 10.00 20.00
23 Kenny Wallace Stacker 2 10.00 20.00
23 Kenny Wallace Stacker 2 YJ Stinger 10.00 20.00
25 Bobby Hamilton Jr. Marines 10.00 20.00
25 Joe Nemechek UAW Delphi 10.00 20.00
32 Ricky Craven Tide 10.00 20.00
43 John Andretti Cheerios 10.00 20.00
43 John Andretti Cheerios Berry Burst 10.00 20.00
45 Kyle Petty Brawny 10.00 20.00
45 Kyle Petty Georgia Pacific 10.00 20.00
45 Kyle Petty Georgia Pacific Charity Ride 10.00 20.00
45 Kyle Petty GP Garfield 10.00 20.00
45 Kyle Petty Victory Junction Hands 10.00 20.00
48 Jimmie Johnson Lowe's 12.50 30.00
48 Jimmie Johnson Lowe's Power of Pride 12.50 25.00
60 Brian Vickers HAAS 10.00 20.00
66 Chad Blount Miller High Life 15.00 30.00
77 Dave Blaney Jasper Panther 10.00 20.00
87 Kyle Busch Ditech.com 12.50 25.00
97 Kurt Busch Rubbermaid Blue Ice 10.00 20.00
97 Kurt Busch Rubbermaid/3120 10.00 20.00
97 Kurt Busch Rubbermaid Commercial Products 10.00 20.00
97 Kurt Busch Irwin Tools 10.00 20.00
97 Kurt Busch Sharpie 10.00 20.00
99 Jeff Burton Citgo 10.00 20.00
99 Jeff Burton Velveeta 10.00 20.00
99 Kenny Wallace Cardinals 10.00 20.00
01 Jerry Nadeau Army 10.00 20.00
01 Jerry Nadeau Army Camouflage 10.00 20.00
01 Jerry Nadeau USG Sheet Rock 10.00 20.00
03 Daytona 500 12.50 25.00

2003 Team Caliber Preferred 1:24

5 Terry Labonte Kellogg's/900 30.00 60.00
5 Terry Labonte Kellogg's Cheez-It 35.00 60.00
5 Terry Labonte Finding Nemo/5004 40.00 70.00
5 Terry Labonte Got Milk/1500 35.00 60.00
5 Terry Labonte Power of Cheese/4020 35.00 60.00
6 Mark Martin Kraft/10,080 35.00 60.00
6 Mark Martin Pfizer/900 35.00 60.00
6 Mark Martin Viagra/5004 25.00 60.00
6 Mark Martin Viagra Blue Daytona/10,080 35.00 60.00
6 Mark Martin Viagra White/2004 35.00 60.00
6 Mark Martin 60.00 100.00

Viagra 500 Starts
9 Greg Biffle 35.00 60.00
Oreo/4020
10 Johnny Benson 35.00 60.00
Eagle One/4020
10 Johnny Benson 35.00 60.00
Valvoline/4020
12 Ryan Newman 35.00 60.00
Alltel/20,008
12 Ryan Newman 75.00 150.00
Alltel 50th Win/4090
12 Ryan Newman 35.00 60.00
Mobil 1/1200
12 Ryan Newman 35.00 60.00
Sony Wega/4320
16 Greg Biffle 30.00 60.00
Grainger/10,008
17 Matt Kenseth 40.00 70.00
Bayer/4020
17 Matt Kenseth 40.00 70.00
DeWalt/2400
17 Matt Kenseth 45.00 70.00
DeWalt 2003 Champion/10,080
17 Matt Kenseth 100.00 175.00
DeWalt 2003 Champ Gold/504
17 Matt Kenseth 40.00 70.00
DeWalt
Million $ Challenge/4128
17 Matt Kenseth 40.00 70.00
Smirnoff Ice 2003 Champion
17 Matt Kenseth 45.00 70.00
DeWalt Victory Lap/10,080
17 Matt Kenseth 150.00 250.00
DeWalt Victory Lap Gold/205
21 Ricky Rudd 30.00 60.00
Air Force/1200
21 Ricky Rudd 35.00 60.00
AF Cross Into Blue/4320
21 Ricky Rudd 35.00 60.00
Ford 100 Years/900
21 Ricky Rudd 35.00 60.00
Motorcraft/3120
21 Ricky Rudd 35.00 60.00
Motorcraft 700 Starts/4020
23 Kenny Wallace 35.00 60.00
Stacker 2/600
25 Bobby Hamilton Jr. 35.00 60.00
Marines/4020
25 Joe Nemechek 30.00 60.00
UAW Delphi/4116
32 Ricky Craven 35.00 60.00
Tide/900
43 John Andretti 35.00 60.00
Cheerios/900
43 John Andretti 25.00 60.00
Cheerios Berry Burst/1008
43 John Andretti 30.00 60.00
Pillsbury/4020
45 Kyle Petty 35.00 60.00
Brawny/4020
45 Kyle Petty 35.00 60.00
Georgia Pacific/900
45 Kyle Petty 40.00 70.00
Georgia Pacific Charity Ride/1008
45 Kyle Petty 40.00 70.00
GP Garfield
48 Jimmie Johnson 30.00 60.00
Lowe's/1200
48 Jimmie Johnson 30.00 60.00
Lowe's Power of Pride/4320
60 Brian Vickers 40.00 70.00
HAAS
87 Kyle Busch 30.00 60.00
Ditech.com/4020
97 Kurt Busch 30.00 60.00
Rubbermaid/10,080
97 Kurt Busch 35.00 60.00
Blue Ice/2004
97 Kurt Busch 30.00 60.00
Rubbermaid Commercial Products/4128
97 Kurt Busch 35.00 60.00
Irwin Tools/6708
97 Kurt Busch 35.00 60.00
Sharpie/4320
99 Jeff Burton 30.00 60.00
Citgo/10,152
99 Jeff Burton 25.00 60.00
Velveeta/4020
99 Kenny Wallace 35.00 60.00
Cardinals/4320
01 Jerry Nadeau 40.00 65.00
Army/4128
01 Jerry Nadeau 35.00 60.00
Army Camouflage/4020
01 Jerry Nadeau 35.00 60.00
USG Sheet Rock/5004
03 Daytona 500/1500 25.00 50.00

2003 Team Caliber Promos 1:24

4 Mike Wallace 20.00 40.00
Geico Promo
5 Brian Vickers 18.00 30.00
Carquest Promo
17 Matt Kenseth 300.00 450.00
Bayer Blue/400
17 Matt Kenseth 20.00 35.00
Bayer Yellow
21 Ricky Rudd 25.00 40.00
Rent-A-Center

2003 Team Caliber/Motorworks 1:24

17 Matt Kenseth 18.00 30.00
DeWalt Victory Lap
25 Brian Vickers 15.00 25.00
ditech.com

2003 Team Caliber/Motorworks Model Kits 1:24

6 Mark Martin 12.50 25.00
Viagra
12 Ryan Newman 12.50 25.00
Alltel
16 Greg Biffle 12.50 25.00
Grainger
17 Matt Kenseth 12.50 25.00
DeWalt
21 Ricky Rudd 12.50 25.00
Motorcraft
97 Kurt Busch 12.50 25.00
Irwin Tools
97 Kurt Busch 12.50 25.00
Rubbermaid

2004 Team Caliber First Choice 1:24

5 Terry Labonte 50.00 100.00
Spiderman/250
6 Mark Martin 90.00 150.00
Batman/250
6 Mark Martin 90.00 150.00
Viagra White night race/504
12 Ryan Newman 90.00 150.00
Justice League/250
12 Ryan Newman 75.00 125.00
Mobil 1 30th Anniversary/250
16 Greg Biffle 60.00 120.00
National Guard/250
17 Matt Kenseth 90.00 150.00
DeWalt/504
17 Matt Kenseth 60.00 120.00
Martian Manhunter/250
17 Matt Kenseth 60.00 120.00
Smirnoff/504
97 Kurt Busch 50.00 100.00
Irwin Tools/250
97 Kurt Busch 50.00 100.00
Sharpie/250
97 Kurt Busch 125.00 250.00
Sharpie '04 Champion
Employee w
Trophy
97 Kurt Busch 60.00 120.00
Superman/250
99 Carl Edwards 175.00 300.00
World Financial Group/250
01 Joe Nemechek 50.00 100.00
Army/250
04 Disney Event Mickey Mouse/250 40.00 80.00

2004 Team Caliber Owners Series 1:24

5 Kyle Busch 40.00 70.00
Lowe's
5 Terry Labonte 40.00 70.00
Delphi
5 Terry Labonte 40.00 70.00
Kellogg's/2400
5 Terry Labonte 40.00 70.00
Kellogg's Olympics/2340
5 Terry Labonte 40.00 70.00
Spiderman/1200
6 Mark Martin 60.00 100.00
Batman/7560
6 Mark Martin 40.00 70.00
Oscar Mayer/3120
6 Mark Martin 40.00 80.00
Pfizer/3120
6 Mark Martin 40.00 80.00
Viagra/5004
6 Mark Martin 40.00 80.00
Viagra White night race/3120
9 Jeff Burton 40.00 70.00
Pennzoil/1200
9 Matt Kenseth 40.00 70.00
Pennzoil/1200
9 Mark Martin 40.00 70.00
Pennzoil/1200
9 Mark Martin 60.00 100.00
Batman/3120
10 Scott Riggs 40.00 70.00
Valvoline/1800
12 Ryan Newman 50.00 80.00
Alltel/5004
12 Ryan Newman 50.00 80.00
Justice League/7560
12 Ryan Newman 50.00 80.00
Mobil 1/5004
12 Ryan Newman 50.00 80.00
Mobil 1 30th Anniversary/5004
12 Ryan Newman 50.00 80.00
Sony Wega/3120
16 Greg Biffle 40.00 70.00
Coke C2/2400
16 Greg Biffle 25.00 50.00
Flash/3120
16 Greg Biffle 40.00 70.00
National Guard/3200
17 Matt Kenseth 60.00 100.00
Carhartt/5004
17 Matt Kenseth 60.00 100.00
DeWalt/6240
17 Matt Kenseth 60.00 100.00
Martian Manhunter/5004
17 Matt Kenseth 40.00 70.00
Smirnoff/7560
21 Ricky Rudd 40.00 70.00
Air Force/3120
21 Ricky Rudd 40.00 70.00
Coke C2/2400
21 Ricky Rudd 40.00 70.00
Motorcraft/3120
21 Ricky Rudd 40.00 70.00
Rent A Center/2400
21 Ricky Rudd 40.00 70.00
Wonder Woman/3120
22 Scott Wimmer 40.00 70.00
Caterpillar/1200
25 Bobby Hamilton Jr. 40.00 70.00
Marines Flames/2400
25 Brian Vickers 40.00 70.00
Ditech.com/1200
43 Jeff Green 40.00 70.00
Cheerios/2400
45 Kyle Petty 40.00 70.00
Brawny/2400
45 Kyle Petty 40.00 70.00
Georgia Pacific/2400
48 Jimmie Johnson 50.00 80.00
Lowe's/2400
60 Greg Biffle 40.00 70.00
Charter/2400
60 Greg Biffle 25.00 50.00
Flash/2400
84 Kyle Busch 40.00 70.00
Car Quest/2400
97 Kurt Busch 30.00 60.00
Coke C2/2400
97 Kurt Busch 30.00 60.00
Irwin Tools/2400
97 Kurt Busch 40.00 70.00
Irwin Tools
'04 Champion/2400
97 Kurt Busch 40.00 70.00
Sharpie/2400
97 Kurt Busch 40.00 70.00
Sharpie '04 Champion/2400
97 Kurt Busch 30.00 60.00
Sharpie 40th Anniversary/3120
97 Kurt Busch 40.00 70.00
Superman/5004
99 Jeff Burton 40.00 70.00
Coke C2/2400
99 Jeff Burton 40.00 70.00
Green Lantern/3120
99 Jeff Burton 40.00 70.00
SKF/2400
01 Jerry Nadeau 40.00 70.00
Army
NNO Disney Event Car Donald Duck/3120 40.00 70.00
NNO Disney Event Car Goofy/3120 40.00 70.00
NNO Disney Event Car Mickey Mouse/3120 40.00 70.00
NNO Disney Event Car Minnie Mouse/3120 40.00 70.00
NNO Disney Event Car PegLeg/3120 40.00 70.00
NNO Justice League Event Car/3120 40.00 70.00
NNO Justice League Villain Event Car/3120 40.00 70.00

2004 Team Caliber Owners Series Pearl Chrome 1:24

5 Kyle Busch 50.00 75.00
Lowe's/180
5 Kyle Busch 50.00 75.00
Lowe's SpongeBob/250
5 Terry Labonte 60.00 100.00
Kellogg's/504
5 Terry Labonte 50.00 80.00
Delphi/504
5 Terry Labonte 50.00 80.00
Kellogg's Olympics/240
5 Terry Labonte 60.00 100.00
Spiderman/756
6 Mark Martin 75.00 125.00
Batman/1008
6 Mark Martin 60.00 100.00
Oscar Mayer/300
6 Mark Martin 60.00 100.00
Pfizer/402
6 Mark Martin 60.00 100.00
Viagra/504
6 Mark Martin 60.00 100.00
Viagra White night race/504
9 Matt Kenseth 60.00 100.00
Pennzoil/300
9 Mark Martin 60.00 100.00
Pennzoil/252
9 Mark Martin 75.00 125.00
Batman/504
10 Scott Riggs 60.00 100.00
Valvoline/180
12 Ryan Newman 90.00 150.00
Alltel/504
12 Ryan Newman 75.00 125.00
Justice League/1008
12 Ryan Newman 75.00 125.00
Mobil 1/600
12 Ryan Newman 75.00 125.00
Mobil 1 30th Ann./504
12 Ryan Newman 60.00 100.00
Sony Wega/756
16 Greg Biffle 50.00 80.00
Coke C2 Red Chrome/250
16 Greg Biffle 40.00 80.00
Flash/504
16 Greg Biffle 40.00 80.00
National Guard/300
17 Matt Kenseth 60.00 100.00
Carhartt/756
17 Matt Kenseth 60.00 100.00
DeWalt/600
17 Matt Kenseth 125.00 200.00
DeWalt All Star Yellow Chrome AU/1717
17 Matt Kenseth 50.00 80.00
Martian Manhunter
17 Matt Kenseth 60.00 100.00
Smirnoff/1008
21 Ricky Rudd 50.00 80.00
Air Force/600
21 Ricky Rudd 50.00 80.00
Coke C2 Red Chrome/250
21 Ricky Rudd 50.00 80.00
Motorcraft/276
21 Ricky Rudd 50.00 80.00
Rent A Center/180
21 Ricky Rudd 50.00 80.00
Wonder Woman
22 Scott Wimmer 50.00 80.00
Caterpillar/300
25 Bobby Hamilton Jr. 60.00 100.00
Marines Flames
25 Brian Vickers 75.00 125.00
Ditech.com/300
45 Kyle Petty 60.00 100.00
Brawny/180
45 Kyle Petty 60.00 100.00
Georgia Pacific/180
48 Jimmie Johnson 75.00 125.00
Lowe's/222
48 Jimmie Johnson 60.00 100.00
Lowe's SpongeBob/354
60 Greg Biffle 60.00 100.00
Charter/180
60 Greg Biffle 50.00 80.00
Flash
84 Kyle Busch 50.00 75.00
Car Quest/222
97 Kurt Busch 30.00 60.00
Irwin Tools/300
97 Kurt Busch 40.00 80.00
Sharpie/504
97 Kurt Busch 30.00 80.00
Sharpie 40th Anniversary/504
97 Kurt Busch 40.00 80.00
Superman/756
99 Jeff Burton 50.00 80.00
Coke C2 Red Chrome
99 Jeff Burton 60.00 100.00
Green Lantern/504
99 Jeff Burton 45.00 75.00
SKF/180
01 Joe Nemechek 50.00 80.00
Army/300
04 Justice League Event Car/504 45.00 75.00
04 Justice League Villain Event Car/504 45.00 75.00
NNO Disney Event Car Donald Duck/504 50.00 80.00
NNO Disney Event Car Goofy/504 50.00 80.00
NNO Disney Event Car Mickey Mouse/504 50.00 80.00
NNO Disney Event Car Minnie Mouse/504 50.00 80.00
NNO Disney Event Car PegLeg/504 50.00 80.00

2004 Team Caliber Owners Series Vintage 1:24

28 Davey Allison 50.00 80.00
Texaco '87 t-bird/1500

2004 Team Caliber Pit Stop 1:24

5 Kyle Busch 15.00 25.00
Lowe's
5 Kyle Busch 10.00 20.00
Lowe's SpongeBob
5 Terry Labonte 10.00 20.00
Delphi
5 Terry Labonte 10.00 20.00
Kellogg's
5 Terry Labonte 10.00 20.00
Kellogg's Olympics
5 Terry Labonte 10.00 20.00
Spiderman
6 Mark Martin 15.00 25.00
Batman
6 Mark Martin 10.00 20.00
Oscar Mayer
6 Mark Martin 12.50 25.00
Pfizer
6 Mark Martin 12.50 25.00
Viagra
6 Mark Martin 12.50 25.00
Viagra White
9 Jeff Burton 10.00 20.00
Cottman
9 Jeff Burton 10.00 20.00
Pennzoil
9 Matt Kenseth 10.00 20.00
Pennzoil
9 Mark Martin 10.00 20.00
Pennzoil
9 Mark Martin 15.00 25.00
Batman
10 Scott Riggs 10.00 20.00
Harlem Globetrotters
10 Scott Riggs 10.00 20.00
Valvoline
12 Ryan Newman 12.50 25.00
Alltel
12 Ryan Newman 15.00 25.00
Justice League
12 Ryan Newman 12.50 25.00
Mobil 1
12 Ryan Newman 12.50 25.00
Mobil 1 30th Anniversary
12 Ryan Newman 12.50 25.00
Sony Wega
14 Casey Atwood 10.00 20.00
Navy
16 Greg Biffle 10.00 20.00
Coke C2
16 Greg Biffle 10.00 20.00
Flash
16 Greg Biffle 10.00 20.00
Jackson-Hewitt
16 Greg Biffle 12.50 25.00
National Guard
16 Greg Biffle 12.50 25.00
Subway
16 Greg Biffle 10.00 20.00
Travelodge
17 Matt Kenseth 12.50 25.00
Bayer
17 Matt Kenseth 12.50 25.00
Carhartt
17 Matt Kenseth 12.50 25.00
DeWalt
17 Matt Kenseth 10.00 20.00
Express Personnel
17 Matt Kenseth 12.50 25.00
Martian Manhunter
21 Ricky Rudd 10.00 20.00
Air Force
21 Ricky Rudd 10.00 20.00
Coke C2
21 Ricky Rudd 10.00 20.00
Motorcraft
21 Ricky Rudd 10.00 20.00
Rent A Center
21 Ricky Rudd 10.00 20.00
Wonder Woman
22 Scott Wimmer 10.00 20.00
Caterpillar
25 Brian Vickers 10.00 20.00
Ditech.com
25 Bobby Hamilton Jr. 10.00 20.00
Marines Flames
43 Jeff Green 10.00 20.00
Cheerios
43 Jeff Green 10.00 20.00
Lucky Charms
45 Kyle Petty 10.00 20.00
Brawny
45 Kyle Petty 10.00 20.00
Georgia Pacific
48 Jimmie Johnson 12.50 25.00
Lowe's
48 Jimmie Johnson 10.00 20.00
Lowe's SpongeBob
60 Greg Biffle 10.00 20.00
Charter
60 Greg Biffle 10.00 20.00
Flash
84 Kyle Busch 12.50 25.00
Car Quest
97 Kurt Busch 10.00 20.00
Coke C2
97 Kurt Busch 10.00 20.00
Irwin Tools
97 Kurt Busch 10.00 20.00
Sharpie 40th Anniversary
97 Kurt Busch 12.50 25.00
Superman
99 Jeff Burton 10.00 20.00
Coke C2
99 Jeff Burton 10.00 20.00
Green Lantern
99 Jeff Burton 10.00 20.00
Pennzoil
99 Jeff Burton 10.00 20.00
SKF
99 Jeff Burton 10.00 20.00
TNT NBA All Star Game
01 Jerry Nadeau 10.00 20.00
Army
04 Justice League Event Car 10.00 20.00
04 Justice League Villain Event Car 10.00 20.00
NNO Disney Event Car Donald Duck 10.00 20.00
NNO Disney Event Car Goofy 10.00 20.00
NNO Disney Event Car Mickey Mouse 10.00 20.00
NNO Disney Event Car Minnie Mouse 10.00 20.00
NNO Disney Event Car PegLeg 10.00 20.00

2004 Team Caliber Preferred 1:24

5 Kyle Busch 45.00 75.00
Lowe's/10,080
5 Kyle Busch 40.00 70.00
Lowe's SpongeBob/3120
5 Terry Labonte 40.00 70.00
Delphi/10,080
5 Terry Labonte 40.00 70.00
Kellogg's/10,080
5 Terry Labonte 40.00 70.00
Kellogg's Olympics/10,080
5 Terry Labonte 40.00 70.00
Spiderman/5004
6 Mark Martin 45.00 75.00
Batman/7560
6 Mark Martin 75.00 125.00
Batman Gold/504
6 Mark Martin 75.00 125.00
Batman Yellow Chrome/504
6 Mark Martin 40.00 70.00
Oscar Mayer/10,008
6 Mark Martin 45.00 75.00
Pfizer/10,008
6 Mark Martin 45.00 75.00
Viagra
6 Mark Martin 50.00 80.00
Viagra Chase/1600
6 Mark Martin 40.00 70.00
Viagra White/10,008
9 Jeff Burton 35.00 60.00
Pennzoil/5004
9 Matt Kenseth 40.00 70.00
Pennzoil/5004
9 Mark Martin 45.00 75.00
Batman/5004
9 Mark Martin 75.00 125.00
Batman Gold/504
9 Mark Martin 40.00 70.00
Pennzoil/5004
10 Scott Riggs 35.00 60.00
Valvoline/10,008
12 Ryan Newman 45.00 75.00
Alltel/20,080
12 Ryan Newman 50.00 80.00
Alltel Chase/1100
12 Ryan Newman 45.00 75.00
Justice League
12 Ryan Newman 75.00 125.00
Justice League Gold/504
12 Ryan Newman 100.00 150.00
Justice League Red Chrome/504
12 Ryan Newman 45.00 75.00
Mobil 1/10,080
12 Ryan Newman 45.00 75.00
Mobil 1 30th Anniversary/10,080
12 Ryan Newman 45.00 75.00
Sony Wega/5004
16 Greg Biffle 40.00 70.00
Coke C2/10,080
16 Greg Biffle 40.00 70.00
Flash/3120
16 Greg Biffle 40.00 70.00
National Guard/10,080
17 Matt Kenseth 35.00 60.00
Bayer/4020
17 Matt Kenseth 40.00 70.00
Carhartt/7560
17 Matt Kenseth 35.00 60.00
DeWalt/20,080
17 Matt Kenseth 45.00 75.00
DeWalt Chase/1300
17 Matt Kenseth 40.00 70.00
Martian Manhunter/7560
17 Matt Kenseth 75.00 125.00
Martian Manhunter Gold/250
17 Matt Kenseth 75.00 125.00
Martian Manhunter
Green Chrome/504
17 Matt Kenseth 40.00 70.00
Smirnoff/20,080
17 Matt Kenseth 50.00 80.00
Smirnoff Chase/750
21 Ricky Rudd 40.00 70.00
Air Force/10,080
21 Ricky Rudd 40.00 60.00
Coke C2/10,080
21 Ricky Rudd 35.00 60.00
Motorcraft/10,080
21 Ricky Rudd 40.00 70.00
Rent-A-Center/10,008
21 Ricky Rudd 40.00 70.00
Wonder Woman/5004
22 Scott Wimmer 35.00 60.00
Caterpillar
25 Bobby Hamilton Jr. 40.00 70.00
Marines Flames/10,080
25 Brian Vickers 40.00 70.00
Ditech.com/10,008
36 Boris Said 40.00 70.00
Centrix/1250

3 Jeff Green 35.00 60.00
Cheerios/10,080
4 Justin Labonte 35.00 60.00
Cosat Guard/288
4 Justin Labonte 35.00 60.00
Cosat Guard Promo box/2000
45 Kyle Petty 40.00 70.00
Brawny/10,080
45 Kyle Petty 40.00 70.00
Georgia Pacific/10,080
48 Jimmie Johnson 40.00 70.00
Lowe's/10,080
48 Jimmie Johnson 50.00 80.00
Lowe's Chase/500
48 Jimmie Johnson 40.00 60.00
Lowe's SpongeBob/3120
60 Greg Biffle 40.00 70.00
Charter/10,080
60 Greg Biffle 40.00 70.00
Flash/3120
34 Kyle Busch 40.00 70.00
Car Quest/10,080
97 Kurt Busch 35.00 60.00
Coke C2/10,080
97 Kurt Busch 35.00 60.00
Irwin Tools
97 Kurt Busch 40.00 100.00
Irwin Tools Chase/900
97 Kurt Busch 40.00 80.00
Irwin Tools
'04 Champion/2400
97 Kurt Busch 35.00 60.00
Sharpie/10,080
97 Kurt Busch 40.00 80.00
Sharpie Chase/1000
97 Kurt Busch 40.00 80.00
Sharpie '04 Champion/10,080
97 Kurt Busch 35.00 60.00
Sharpie 40th Anniversary/5004
97 Kurt Busch 40.00 70.00
Superman/7560
97 Kurt Busch 75.00 125.00
Superman Gold Chrome/250
99 Jeff Burton 35.00 60.00
Coke C2/10,080
99 Jeff Burton 40.00 70.00
Green Lantern/5004
99 Jeff Burton 35.00 60.00
SKF/5004
01 Jerry Nemechek 35.00 60.00
Army
04 Justice League Event Car/5004 35.00 60.00
04 Justice League Villain Event Car/5004 35.00 60.00
NNO Disney Event Car Donald Duck/10,008 40.00 70.00
NNO Disney Event Car Goofy/10,008 40.00 70.00
NNO Disney Event Car Mickey Mouse/20,080 40.00 70.00
NNO Disney Event Car Minnie Mouse/10,008 40.00 70.00
NNO Disney Event Car PegLeg/10,008 40.00 70.00

2004 Team Caliber/Motorworks 1:24

5 Terry Labonte 10.00 20.00
Kellogg's
14 Casey Atwood 10.00 20.00
Navy
22 Scott Wimmer 10.00 20.00
CAT
25 Bobby Hamilton Jr. 10.00 20.00
Marines Flames
25 Brian Vickers 12.50 25.00
ditech.com
01 Joe Nemechek 10.00 20.00
Army
NNO Disney Event Car Donald Duck 10.00 20.00
NNO Disney Event Car Minnie Mouse 10.00 20.00

2004 Team Caliber/Motorworks Model Kits 1:24

5 Terry Labonte 10.00 20.00
Kellogg's

2005 Team Caliber Owners Series 1:24

PRINT RUNS LISTED BELOW ARE FIRST RUN ONLY
FINAL PRODUCTION NUMBERS MAY END UP DIFFERENT
PRINT RUNS LISTED WITH * ARE SECOND RUN

5 Kyle Busch 60.00 100.00
Kellogg's/900
6 Mark Martin 75.00 125.00
Batman/756
6 Mark Martin 75.00 125.00
Kraft/600
6 Mark Martin 100.00 150.00
Viagra/1200
6 Mark Martin 100.00 150.00
Viagra/600*
6 Mark Martin 75.00 125.00
Viagra Blue
Retro Stroh's Light/900
6 Mark Martin 75.00 125.00
Viagra Orange AU/1800
6 Mark Martin 100.00 175.00
Viagra Red
Retro Folgers/900
6 Mark Martin 75.00 150.00
Viagra Red, White & Blue
Retro Valvoline/900
6 Mark Martin 75.00 150.00
Viagra Red, White & Blue Retro Valvoline
All Star AU/737
6 Mark Martin 75.00 125.00
Viagra Salute to You/1500
10 Scott Riggs 50.00 75.00
Valvoline/600
12 Ryan Newman 60.00 100.00
Alltel/1200
12 Ryan Newman 60.00 100.00
Mobil 1/600
12 Ryan Newman 60.00 100.00
Mobil 1 Gold/600
16 Greg Biffle 60.00 100.00
National Guard/600
17 Matt Kenseth 60.00 100.00
Carhartt/600
17 Matt Kenseth 60.00 100.00
DeWalt/1200
17 Matt Kenseth 60.00 100.00
Trex/600
17 Matt Kenseth 60.00 100.00
USG/600
21 Ricky Rudd 60.00 100.00
Motorcraft/600
22 Scott Wimmer 50.00 75.00
Cat/600
25 Brian Vickers 60.00 100.00
GMAC/1200
44 Terry Labonte 60.00 100.00
Kellogg's/600
48 Jimmie Johnson 60.00 100.00
Lowe's/600
60 Carl Edwards 75.00 150.00
Charter AU/600
97 Kurt Busch 60.00 100.00
Crown Royal/756
97 Kurt Busch 60.00 100.00
Crown Royal/600*
97 Kurt Busch 50.00 100.00
Irwin Tools/600
97 Kurt Busch 50.00 100.00
Sharpie/804
97 Kurt Busch 50.00 100.00
Sharpie Autographs for Education/600
97 Kurt Busch 60.00 100.00
Smirnoff/600
99 Carl Edwards 75.00 125.00
AAA/600
99 Carl Edwards 75.00 125.00
Office Depot/600
99 Carl Edwards 125.00 250.00
Scotts 1st Win AU/999
99 Carl Edwards 75.00 125.00
Stonebridge Life
Pocono Raced/600
01 Joe Nemechek 50.00 75.00
Army/600

2005 Team Caliber Pit Stop 1:24

5 Kyle Busch 12.50 25.00
CarQuest
5 Kyle Busch 15.00 25.00
Kellogg's
5 Kyle Busch 12.50 25.00
Kellogg's Johnny Bravo
6 Mark Martin 15.00 25.00
Batman
6 Mark Martin 10.00 20.00
Kraft
6 Mark Martin 15.00 25.00
Viagra
6 Mark Martin 15.00 25.00
Viagra Blue
Retro Stroh's Light
6 Mark Martin 10.00 20.00
Viagra Orange
6 Mark Martin 15.00 25.00
Viagra Red Retro Folgers
6 Mark Martin 15.00 25.00
Viagra Red, White & Blue
Retro Valvoline
9 Matt Kenseth 10.00 20.00
Pennzoil
9 Mark Martin 10.00 20.00
Pennzoil
10 Scott Riggs 15.00 30.00
Checker's Promo
10 Scott Riggs 10.00 20.00
Valvoline
12 Ryan Newman 12.50 25.00
Alltel
12 Ryan Newman 12.50 25.00
Mobil 1
12 Ryan Newman 12.50 25.00
Mobil 1 Gold
16 Greg Biffle 10.00 20.00
National Guard
16 Greg Biffle 12.50 25.00
Post-It
16 Greg Biffle 12.50 25.00
Subway
17 Matt Kenseth 10.00 20.00
Carhartt
17 Matt Kenseth 10.00 20.00
DeWalt
17 Matt Kenseth 10.00 20.00
Trex
17 Matt Kenseth 12.50 25.00
USG
17 Matt Kenseth 12.50 25.00
Waste Management
21 Ricky Rudd 10.00 20.00
Motorcraft
22 Scott Wimmer 12.50 25.00
Cat
25 Brian Vickers 12.50 25.00
GMAC
25 Brian Vickers 12.50 25.00
GMAC Scooby Doo
36 Boris Said 12.50 25.00
Centrix
43 Jeff Green 12.50 25.00
Cheerios
43 Jeff Green 12.50 25.00
Wheaties
44 Justin Labonte 12.50 25.00
Coast Guard
44 Terry Labonte 12.50 25.00
Kellogg's
45 Kyle Petty 12.50 25.00
Georgia Pacific
45 Kyle Petty 12.50 25.00
Quilted Northern
48 Jimmie Johnson 15.00 25.00
Lowe's
60 Carl Edwards 12.50 25.00
Charter
66 Greg Biffle 12.50 25.00
USPS promo in window box
76 Jerrick Johnson 30.00 60.00
American Legion Promo
97 Kurt Busch 10.00 20.00
Irwin Tools
97 Kurt Busch 10.00 20.00
Sharpie
97 Kurt Busch 10.00 20.00
Sharpie Autographs For Education
99 Carl Edwards 15.00 25.00
AAA
99 Carl Edwards 15.00 25.00
Round Up
99 Carl Edwards 15.00 25.00
Office Depot
99 Carl Edwards 15.00 25.00
Office Depot Promo
in window box
99 Carl Edwards 20.00 35.00
Office Depot
Back To School Promo
in window box
99 Carl Edwards 12.50 25.00
Stonebridge Life
Pocono Raced
01 Joe Nemechek 12.50 25.00
Army
05 Batman Begins Event 10.00 20.00
05 Daytona Disney Big Bad Wolf 10.00 20.00
05 Daytona Disney Daisy 10.00 20.00
05 Daytona Disney Donald Duck 10.00 20.00
05 Daytona Disney Goofy 10.00 20.00
05 Daytona Disney Mickey Mouse 10.00 20.00
05 Daytona Disney Minnie Mouse 10.00 20.00

2005 Team Caliber Preferred 1:24

5 Kyle Busch 60.00 100.00
Kellogg's/1200
5 Kyle Busch 60.00 100.00
Kellogg's California Win/1800
5 Kyle Busch 50.00 75.00
Kellogg's Johnny Bravo/1500
6 Mark Martin 50.00 75.00
Batman
6 Mark Martin 50.00 75.00
Kraft/2400
6 Mark Martin 50.00 75.00
Viagra/5004
6 Mark Martin 50.00 75.00
Viagra Blue
Retro Stroh's Light/3120
6 Mark Martin 75.00 125.00
Viagra Orange AU/5004
6 Mark Martin 50.00 75.00
Viagra Red
Retro Folgers/2400
6 Mark Martin 100.00 200.00
Viagra Red Retro Folgers
Color Chrome
Chrome AU/600
2-car set
6 Mark Martin 50.00 75.00
Viagra Red, White & Blue
Retro Valvoline/7560
6 Mark Martin 50.00 75.00
Viagra Red, White & Blue All Star Win/7560
6 Mark Martin 50.00 75.00
Viagra Salute to You
7 Robby Gordon 50.00 75.00
Fruit of the Loom/1800
7 Robby Gordon 50.00 75.00
Harrah's
7 Robby Gordon 50.00 75.00
Jim Beam
7 Robby Gordon 50.00 75.00
Jim Beam Black
7 Robby Gordon 50.00 75.00
Menard's
9 Matt Kenseth 50.00 75.00
Pennzoil/600
9 Mark Martin 50.00 75.00
Pennzoil/1200
10 Scott Riggs 40.00 65.00
Valvoline/1800
12 Ryan Newman 50.00 75.00
Alltel/7560
12 Ryan Newman 60.00 100.00
Alltel Gold/624
12 Ryan Newman 50.00 75.00
Mobil 1/2400
12 Ryan Newman 50.00 75.00
Mobil 1 Gold/2400
12 Ryan Newman 50.00 75.00
Sony HDTV/1200
16 Greg Biffle 40.00 65.00
Charter Michigan Win/1800
16 Greg Biffle 40.00 65.00
National Guard/1800
16 Greg Biffle 40.00 65.00
Post-It/3120
17 Matt Kenseth 45.00 70.00
Carhartt/1800
17 Matt Kenseth 50.00 75.00
DeWalt/5004
17 Matt Kenseth 45.00 70.00
Trex/1800
17 Matt Kenseth 45.00 70.00
USG/1200
17 Matt Kenseth 50.00 75.00
Waste Management/3120
21 Ricky Rudd 40.00 65.00
Motorcraft/3120
22 Scott Wimmer 40.00 65.00
Cat/5004
25 Brian Vickers 40.00 65.00
GMAC/3120
25 Brian Vickers 40.00 65.00
GMAC Scooby Doo/1200
39 Ryan Newman 100.00 150.00
Alltel/1800
44 Justin Labonte 40.00 65.00
Coast Guard/3204
44 Terry Labonte 40.00 65.00
GMAC/1200
44 Terry Labonte 50.00 75.00
Kellogg's/1200
44 Terry Labonte 40.00 65.00
Kellogg's Iron Man
44 Terry Labonte 40.00 65.00
Pizza Hut
48 Jimmie Johnson 50.00 75.00
Lowe's/3120
60 Carl Edwards 50.00 75.00
Charter/1500
66 Greg Biffle 40.00 65.00
USPS/1800
97 Kurt Busch 50.00 75.00
Crown Royal/3120
97 Kurt Busch 75.00 125.00
Crown Royal
Color Chrome AU/1008
97 Kurt Busch 50.00 75.00
Irwin Tools/3120
97 Kurt Busch 50.00 75.00
Sharpie/3120
97 Kurt Busch 50.00 75.00
Sharpie Autographs for Education/2400
97 Kurt Busch 50.00 75.00
Smirnoff/3120
99 Carl Edwards 50.00 75.00
AAA/2400
99 Carl Edwards 60.00 100.00
Office Depot/5004
99 Carl Edwards 50.00 75.00
Ortho/600
99 Carl Edwards 50.00 75.00
Round Up/1800
99 Carl Edwards 60.00 100.00
Scotts 1st Win/10,008
99 Carl Edwards 125.00 175.00
Scotts 1st Win AU
99 Carl Edwards 125.00 200.00
Scotts 1st Win
Color Chrome AU/1008
99 Carl Edwards 50.00 75.00
Stonebridge Life
Pocono Win/3120
99 Carl Edwards 100.00 150.00
World Financial
Color Chrome AU/600
01 Joe Nemechek 40.00 65.00
Army/1800
05 Daytona Disney 40.00 60.00
Minnie Mouse/5004

2005 Team Caliber Preferred Nickel 1:24

5 Kyle Busch 75.00 125.00
Kellogg's/504
5 Kyle Busch 50.00 75.00
Kellogg's Johnny Bravo/180
6 Mark Martin 50.00 75.00
Batman/402
6 Mark Martin 50.00 75.00
Kraft/300
6 Mark Martin 60.00 100.00
Viagra/756
6 Mark Martin 75.00 125.00
Viagra Orange AU/756
7 Robby Gordon 40.00 60.00
Fruit of the Loom/180
7 Robby Gordon 40.00 60.00
Harrah's
7 Robby Gordon 50.00 75.00
Jim Beam
7 Robby Gordon 40.00 60.00
Menard's
9 Mark Martin 50.00 75.00
Pennzoil/504
10 Scott Riggs 40.00 60.00
Valvoline/180
12 Ryan Newman 50.00 75.00
Alltel/504
12 Ryan Newman 60.00 100.00
Mobil 1/180
16 Greg Biffle 60.00 100.00
National Guard/180
17 Matt Kenseth 50.00 75.00
Carhartt/300
17 Matt Kenseth 60.00 100.00
DeWalt/1008
17 Matt Kenseth 50.00 75.00
Trex/180
17 Matt Kenseth 50.00 75.00
USG/180
17 Matt Kenseth 50.00 75.00
Waste Management/180
21 Ricky Rudd 50.00 75.00
Motorcraft/180
22 Scott Wimmer 40.00 60.00
Cat/180
25 Brian Vickers 40.00 60.00
GMAC/300
44 Terry Labonte 40.00 60.00
GMAC/180
44 Terry Labonte 40.00 60.00
Kellogg's/180
44 Terry Labonte 50.00 75.00
Pizza Hut
48 Jimmie Johnson 75.00 150.00
Lowe's/180
60 Carl Edwards 50.00 75.00
Charter/180
97 Kurt Busch 50.00 75.00
Crown Royal/756
97 Kurt Busch 45.00 70.00
Irwin Tools/504
97 Kurt Busch 45.00 70.00
Sharpie/504
97 Kurt Busch 45.00 70.00
Sharpie Autographs For Education/180
97 Kurt Busch 45.00 70.00
Smirnoff/300
99 Carl Edwards 50.00 75.00
AAA/180
99 Carl Edwards 75.00 125.00
Office Depot/504
99 Carl Edwards 50.00 75.00
Ortho/180
99 Carl Edwards 60.00 100.00
Scotts 1st Win/504
99 Carl Edwards 50.00 75.00
Stonebridge Life
Pocono Win/180
01 Joe Nemechek 40.00 60.00
Army/180
05 Daytona Disney Big Bad Wolf/504 25.00 50.00
05 Daytona Disney Daisy Duck/504 25.00 50.00
05 Daytona Disney Donald Duck/504 25.00 50.00
05 Daytona Disney Goofy/504 25.00 50.00
05 Daytona Disney Mickey Mouse/1008 25.00 50.00
05 Daytona Disney Minnie Mouse/576 25.00 50.00

2005 Team Caliber Preferred sets 1:24 and 1:64

05 Daytona Disney Big Bad Wolf/504 35.00 60.00
05 Daytona Disney Daisy/504 35.00 60.00
05 Daytona Disney Donald Duck/750 35.00 60.00
05 Daytona Disney Goofy/1200 35.00 60.00
05 Daytona Disney 35.00 60.00
Mickey Mouse/2700
05 Daytona Disney 35.00 60.00
Minnie Mouse/1500

2005 Team Caliber/Motorworks Model Kits 1:24

6 Mark Martin 12.50 25.00
Viagra
17 Matt Kenseth 10.00 20.00
DeWalt
97 Kurt Busch 10.00 20.00
Sharpie

2006 Team Caliber Owner's Series 1:24

2 Kurt Busch 60.00 100.00
Miller Lite/2400
6 Mark Martin 75.00 125.00
AAA/5004
6 Mark Martin 75.00 125.00
AAA Insurance/2808
6 Mark Martin 100.00 150.00
AAA Last Ride/1080
6 Mark Martin 75.00 125.00
Ameriquest Soaring Dreams/1800
6 Mark Martin 100.00 150.00
Ford The Road Home AU/2400
12 Ryan Newman 75.00 125.00
Alltel/2400
12 Ryan Newman 60.00 100.00
Mobil/1500
16 Greg Biffle 60.00 100.00
National Guard/2400
17 Matt Kenseth 60.00 100.00
DeWalt/2400
26 Jamie McMurray 60.00 100.00
Crown Royal Day
Purple/1800
26 Jamie McMurray 60.00 100.00
Crown Royal Night
White
55 Michael Waltrip 60.00 100.00
Napa/2400
99 Carl Edwards 60.00 100.00
Office Depot/2400
00 Bill Elliott 75.00 125.00
Burger King/1800

2006 Team Caliber Pit Stop 1:24

2 Kurt Busch 12.50 25.00
Miller Lite
6 Mark Martin 15.00 30.00
AAA
6 Mark Martin 15.00 25.00
AAA Insurance
6 Mark Martin 12.50 25.00
Ameriquest
6 Mark Martin 12.50 25.00
Pennzoil
6 Mark Martin 15.00 30.00
Scott's SuperTruck
7 Robby Gordon 12.50 25.00
Harrah's
7 Robby Gordon 12.50 25.00
Menard's
12 Ryan Newman 12.50 25.00
Alltel
12 Ryan Newman 12.50 25.00
Alltel Black Brickyard
12 Ryan Newman 12.50 25.00
Mobil 1

12 Ryan Newman Sony HDTV 12.50 25.00
14 Sterling Marlin Waste Management 15.00 25.00
16 Greg Biffle Ameriquest 12.50 25.00
16 Greg Biffle Jackson Hewitt 12.50 25.00
16 Greg Biffle National Guard 12.50 25.00
16 Greg Biffle Subway 12.50 25.00
17 Matt Kenseth Ameriquest 12.50 25.00
17 Matt Kenseth Ameriquest Soaring Dreams 12.50 25.00
17 Matt Kenseth Carhartt 12.50 25.00
17 Matt Kenseth DeWalt 12.50 25.00
17 Matt Kenseth Pennzoil 12.50 25.00
17 Matt Kenseth Post 12.50 25.00
17 Matt Kenseth R&L Carriers 12.50 25.00
21 Ken Schrader Air Force 12.50 25.00
21 Ken Schrader Little Debbie Promo 20.00 40.00
21 Ken Schrader Motorcraft 12.50 25.00
22 Dave Blaney CAT 12.50 25.00
23 Bill Lester Waste Management 15.00 30.00
26 Jamie McMurray Irwin Tools 12.50 25.00
26 Jamie McMurray Lenox 12.50 25.00
26 Jamie McMurray Sharpie 12.50 25.00
39 Kurt Busch Penske 12.50 25.00
43 Bobby Labonte Cheerios 12.50 25.00
55 Michael Waltrip Domino's 12.50 25.00
55 Michael Waltrip Napa 12.50 25.00
55 Michael Waltrip Napa Stars & Stripes 12.50 25.00
60 Carl Edwards Ameriquest 12.50 25.00
99 Carl Edwards Office Depot 12.50 25.00
99 Michael Waltrip Aaron's 12.50 25.00
99 Michael Waltrip Aaron's UT Longhorns 12.50 25.00
99 Michael Waltrip Best Western 12.50 25.00
00 Bill Elliott Burger King 15.00 25.00
00 Johnny Sauter Fleet Pride Promo 15.00 30.00
01 Joe Nemechek Army 12.50 25.00
06 Todd Kluever 3M 15.00 30.00
06 Daytona Disney Buzz Lightyear 10.00 20.00
06 Daytona Disney Kermit 10.00 20.00
06 Daytona Disney Mickey Mouse 10.00 20.00
06 Daytona Disney Princess 10.00 20.00
06 Daytona Disney Tigger 10.00 20.00

2006 Team Caliber Preferred 1:24

2 Kurt Busch Miller Lite 50.00 75.00
6 Mark Martin AAA/20,004 50.00 75.00
6 Mark Martin AAA Insurance/5004 50.00 75.00
6 Mark Martin Ameriquest/2400 50.00 75.00
6 Mark Martin Ameriquest Soaring Dreams/3500 50.00 75.00
6 Mark Martin Folger's '89 t-bird Red Chrome AU/1056 100.00 175.00
6 Mark Martin Pennzoil/3000 50.00 75.00
7 Robby Gordon Harrah's/1800 50.00 75.00
7 Robby Gordon Jim Beam/2100 50.00 75.00
7 Robby Gordon Jim Beam Black/1800 50.00 75.00
12 Ryan Newman Alltel 50.00 75.00
12 Ryan Newman Alltel Black Brickyard/1800 40.00 65.00
12 Ryan Newman Mobil 1 50.00 75.00
12 Ryan Newman My Circle/1200 60.00 100.00
12 Ryan Newman Sony HDTV/1800 50.00 75.00
14 Sterling Marlin Waste Management 50.00 75.00
16 Greg Biffle Ameriquest 50.00 75.00
16 Greg Biffle Ameriquest Soaring Dreams/3000 50.00 75.00
16 Greg Biffle Jackson Hewitt/2700 50.00 75.00
16 Greg Biffle National Guard 50.00 75.00
16 Greg Biffle Subway/2508 50.00 75.00
17 Matt Kenseth Ameriquest/1800 50.00 75.00
17 Matt Kenseth Ameriquest Soaring Dreams/3000 50.00 75.00
17 Matt Kenseth Carhartt/2016 50.00 75.00
17 Matt Kenseth DeWalt/5004 50.00 75.00
17 Matt Kenseth Pennzoil/2700 50.00 75.00
17 Matt Kenseth Post/1800 50.00 75.00
17 Matt Kenseth R&L Carriers/1800 50.00 75.00
17 Matt Kenseth USG Promo/3210 60.00 100.00
21 Ken Schrader Air Force/1800 50.00 75.00
21 Ken Schrader Motorcraft/1800 50.00 75.00
22 Dave Blaney CAT 50.00 75.00
23 Bill Lester Waste Management 50.00 75.00
26 Jamie McMurray Crown Royal Day Purple/5004 50.00 75.00
26 Jamie McMurray Crown Royal Day Purple Clear Window Bank AU/300 100.00 150.00
26 Jamie McMurray Crown Royal Night White/3120 50.00 75.00
26 Jamie McMurray Irwin Tools/3120 50.00 75.00
26 Jamie McMurray Lenox/3000 50.00 75.00
26 Jamie McMurray Sharpie 50.00 75.00
39 Kurt Busch Penske/2400 50.00 75.00
43 Bobby Labonte Cheerios/2400 50.00 75.00
43 Richard Petty '69 Torino AU/5035 100.00 175.00
43 Richard Petty '69 Torino 100th Win Wix Filters/500 75.00 150.00
55 Michael Waltrip Domino's/3000 50.00 75.00
55 Michael Waltrip Napa/5004 50.00 75.00
55 Michael Waltrip Napa Stars & Stripes/2700 50.00 75.00
60 Carl Edwards Ameriquest/2400 50.00 75.00
60 Carl Edwards Ameriquest Soaring Dreams/3300 50.00 75.00
60 Carl Edwards iLevel Weyerhaeuser/2700 50.00 75.00
99 Carl Edwards Office Depot/7500 50.00 75.00
99 Carl Edwards Office Depot Back To School/1800 50.00 75.00
99 Darrell Waltrip Aaron's 50.00 75.00
99 Michael Waltrip Aaron's/6504 50.00 75.00
99 Michael Waltrip Best Western/1800 50.00 75.00
00 Bill Elliott Burger King/2400 60.00 100.00
06 Todd Kluever 3M 50.00 75.00
06 Daytona Disney Buzz Lightyear/756 25.00 50.00
06 Daytona Disney Kermit 25.00 50.00
06 Daytona Disney Mickey Mouse/1800 25.00 50.00
06 Daytona Disney Princess/1200 25.00 50.00
06 Daytona Disney Tigger/1200 25.00 50.00

2006 Team Caliber Preferred Copper 1:24

6 Mark Martin AAA 60.00 100.00
6 Mark Martin AAA Insurance 50.00 75.00
6 Mark Martin Ameriquest/360 50.00 75.00
6 Mark Martin Pennziol/540 50.00 75.00
12 Ryan Newman Alltel/756 50.00 75.00
12 Ryan Newman Mobil 1 50.00 75.00
12 Ryan Newman Sony HDTV/180 50.00 75.00
14 Sterling Marlin Waste Management/360 50.00 75.00
16 Greg Biffle National Guard 50.00 75.00
16 Greg Biffle Subway/360 50.00 75.00
17 Matt Kenseth Pennzoil/360 50.00 75.00
17 Matt Kenseth Post 50.00 75.00
17 Matt Kenseth R&L Carriers 50.00 75.00
22 Dave Blaney CAT 50.00 75.00
23 Bill Lester Waste Management 50.00 75.00
26 Jamie McMurray Crown Royal Day Purple 50.00 75.00
26 Jamie McMurray Crown Royal Night White 50.00 75.00
26 Jamie McMurray Irwin Tools/432 50.00 75.00
26 Jamie McMurray Lenox 50.00 75.00
26 Jamie McMurray Sharpie/504 50.00 75.00
26 Jamie McMurray Smirnoff Ice/504 50.00 75.00
43 Bobby Labonte Cheerios/432 50.00 75.00
43 Richard Petty '69 Torino AU/180 75.00 125.00
55 Michael Waltrip Napa 50.00 75.00
55 Michael Waltrip Napa Stars & Stripes/180 50.00 75.00
60 Carl Edwards iLevel Weyerhaeuser/360 50.00 75.00
99 Carl Edwards Office Depot 50.00 75.00
99 Darrell Waltrip Aaron's 50.00 75.00
99 Michael Waltrip Aaron's 50.00 75.00
99 Michael Waltrip Best Western/180 50.00 75.00

2006 Team Caliber Preferred Trackside 1:24

1 Martin Truex Jr. Bass Pro/144 125.00 250.00
5 Kyle Busch Kellogg's/48 125.00 250.00
11 Paul Menard Menard's/48 75.00 150.00
64 Steve Wallace Top Flite/48 75.00 150.00

2003 Team Caliber Pit Stop 1:43

NNO Centennial of Speed 3-car set 1 40.00 75.00
300A. Tim Flock/1956 Chrysler
10. Bill France Sr./1935 Ford
300. Lee Petty/1956 Chrysler
NNO Centennial of Speed 3-car set 2 40.00 75.00
6. Marshall Teague/1952 Hudson
10. Bill France/1935 Ford
301.Buck Baker Outboard Chrysler

2003 Team Caliber Preferred 1:43

16A Buck Baker Florida Hurricanes 1940 Ford/3120 20.00 40.00

1999 Team Caliber 1:64

This marks Team Caliber's inaugural year in the Die-Cast market.

5 Terry Labonte Kellogg's Corny/7560 6.00 15.00
5 Terry Labonte Kellogg's K-Sentials/10,080 6.00 15.00
5 Terry Labonte Rice Krispies/10,080 8.00 20.00
6 Mark Martin Valvoline/7560 8.00 20.00
6 Mark Martin Eagle One 8.00 20.00
7 Michael Waltrip Phillips 6.00 15.00
10 Ricky Rudd Tide/8208 8.00 20.00
12 Jeremy Mayfield Mobil 1 8.00 20.00
12 Jeremy Mayfield Mobil 25th Anniversary 8.00 20.00
12 Jeremy Mayfield Mobil 1 Promo without Speedpass on trunk lid 10.00 20.00
12 Jeremy Mayfield Mobil 25th Anniversary Promo 12.50 25.00
12 Jimmy Spencer Chips Ahoy 20.00 35.00
17 Matt Kenseth DeWalt 12.50 25.00
23 Jimmy Spencer No Bull 8.00 20.00
23 Jimmy Spencer Winston Lights 15.00 30.00
40 Sterling Marlin Coors Light John Wayne/7560 12.00 25.00
40 Sterling Marlin Coors Light Brooks & Dunn 12.00 30.00
43 John Andretti STP 10.00 25.00
45 Adam Petty Sprint/7560 20.00 40.00
55 Kenny Wallace Square D/7560 6.00 15.00
75 Ted Musgrave Polaris/8208 6.00 15.00
97 Chad Little John Deere 6.00 15.00
99 Jeff Burton Exide 6.00 15.00

2000 Team Caliber Owners Series 1:64

The set of die-cast pieces was issued in its own clear hard plastic box with a colorful cardboard box overwrap. The year of issue and the name "Team Caliber Owner's Series" are clearly printed on the cardboard box along with the announced production run. Each piece features an opening hood and was issued with a credit card type certificate of authenticity.

5 Terry Labonte Kellogg's/7560 8.00 20.00
5 Terry Labonte CherryBerry 8.00 20.00
6 Mark Martin Eagle One/10,080 10.00 25.00
6 Mark Martin Valvoline/10,080 10.00 25.00
6 Mark Martin Valvoline Max Life 8.00 20.00
6 Mark Martin Valvoline Stars & Stripes/7560 10.00 25.00
6 Mark Martin Zerex/7560 8.00 20.00
7 Michael Waltrip Nations Rent 8.00 20.00
9 Jeff Burton Northern Light/7560 8.00 20.00
12 Jeremy Mayfield Mobil 1 8.00 20.00
14 Rick Mast Conseco 8.00 20.00
16 Kevin Lepage familyclick.com 8.00 20.00
17 Matt Kenseth DeWalt/10,080 12.50 25.00
17 Matt Kenseth DeWalt 24 Volt/10,080 12.50 25.00
17 Matt Kenseth DeWalt Emazing.com/7560 10.00 20.00
17 Matt Kenseth Visine/7560 8.00 20.00
21 Elliott Sadler Citgo/7560 8.00 20.00
25 Jerry Nadeau Holigan 8.00 20.00
26 Jimmy Spencer Big K 8.00 20.00
40 Sterling Marlin Coors Light Brooks & Dunn/7560 6.00 15.00
42 Kenny Irwin BellSouth/7560 8.00 20.00
45 Adam Petty Sprint PCS Busch 40.00 100.00
60 Geoffery Bodine Power Team/7560 6.00 15.00
60 Mark Martin Winn Dixie/7560 10.00 25.00
60 Mark Martin Winn Dixie Flames/7560 10.00 25.00
60 Mark Martin Winn Dixie Stars & Stripes/7560 8.00 20.00
66 Darrell Waltrip Big K Route 66/7560 8.00 20.00
77 Robert Pressley Jasper Cat 10.00 25.00
97 Chad Little John Deere/7560 8.00 20.00
99 Jeff Burton Exide/7560 8.00 20.00

2000 Team Caliber Promos 1:64

21 Elliott Sadler Citgo in bag 3.00 8.00
63 Mark Green SuperFlo 2.00 5.00

2000 Team Caliber White Knuckle Racing 1:64

These cars are packaged in a cardboard and plastic blister pack along with the name "White Knuckle Racing" and year of issue at the top. The 1:64 blister pack promo pieces were printed with a photo of the driver and the car on the back board but do not mention "White Knuckle Racing." The cars in this series do not have opening hoods.

6 Mark Martin Eagle One Promo 3.00 8.00
6 Mark Martin Valvoline 3.00 8.00
12 Jeremy Mayfield Mobil 1 4.00 8.00
17 Matt Kenseth DeWalt 5.00 10.00
17 Matt Kenseth Visine Promo 10.00 20.00
21 Elliott Sadler Citgo Promo 10.00 20.00
97 Chad Little John Deere 3.00 8.00
99 Jeff Burton Exide 3.00 8.00
99 Jeff Burton Exide Promo 5.00 12.00

2001 Team Caliber Owners Series 1:64

These 1:64 pieces were issued in a hard clear plastic case inside a cardboard box. The box was printed in gray with a picture of a typical race grandstands. The prodcution run total and the year are given on the outside of the box as well.

6 Mark Martin Pfizer/7560 8.00 20.00
6 Mark Martin Viagra/7560 10.00 25.00
6 Mark Martin Viagra Metal Flake/6264 8.00 20.00
17 Matt Kenseth DeWalt/7560 12.50 25.00
17 Matt Kenseth DeWalt ROY 10.00 20.00
40 Sterling Marlin Coors Light 10.00 25.00
97 Kurt Busch Sharpie/5544 10.00 25.00
99 Jeff Burton Citgo 8.00 20.00

2001 Team Caliber Pit Stop 1:64

The 2001 Pit Stop series cars were packaged with a cardboard and clear plastic blister pack. The set name and year are clearly printed on the cardboard backing. The regular issue die cast have a night racing photo of the grandstands in the background, while the Ryan Newman promo piece was issued in a box with the team's colors and a photo of the car.

5 Terry Labonte Kellogg's 5.00 10.00
6 Mark Martin Pfizer 5.00 10.00
10 Johnny Benson Valvoline 5.00 10.00
12 Jeremy Mayfield Mobil 1 3.00 6.00
17 Matt Kenseth DeWalt Yellow 5.00 10.00
17 Matt Kenseth DeWalt Yellow and Black/21168 5.00 10.00
17 Matt Kenseth DeWalt Saw/3120 5.00 10.00
21 Elliott Sadler Motorcraft 3.00 6.00
22 Ward Burton Caterpillar 4.00 10.00
25 Jerry Nadeau UAW-Delphi 4.00 8.00
43 John Andretti Cheerios 3.00 6.00
44 Buckshot Jones Georgia-Pacific 2.50 6.00
45 Kyle Petty Sprint PCS 4.00 8.00
60 Greg Biffle Grainger 3.00 8.00
96 Andy Houston McDonalds 3.00 6.00
97 Kurt Busch Sharpie 7.50 15.00
99 Jeff Burton Citgo 5.00 10.00

2001 Team Caliber Promos 1:64

10 Jeff Green Nestea 7.50 20.00
12 Jeremy Mayfield Mobil 1 25th Anniversary 2.00 5.00
17 Matt Kenseth AT&T in PVC box 35.00 60.00
33 No Driver Association Aleve 2.00 4.00
33 No Driver Association Alka-Seltzer 2.00 4.00
33 No Driver Association Bayer 2.00 4.00
33 Tony Raines Aleve 2.00 4.00
50 Jon Wood Auto Concierge 12.50 25.00
71 Kevin Lepage Mini Corn Dogs 5.00 12.00
71 Kevin Lepage State Fair Dogs 5.00 12.00
01 Tropicana 400 blister 3.00 8.00
02 Ryan Newman Alltel 5.00 12.00

2002 Team Caliber Owners Series 1:64

6 Mark Martin Kraft/7560 10.00 20.00
6 Mark Martin Pfizer/5004 10.00 20.00
6 Mark Martin Viagra/10080 10.00 20.00
12 Ryan Newman Alltel/8136 10.00 20.00
12 Ryan Newman Alltel Blue Chrome Rookie of the Year/7560 15.00 30.00
17 Matt Kenseth DeWalt/5004 10.00 20.00
36 Ken Schrader M&Ms/5004 7.50 15.00
36 Ken Schrader M&Ms Vote/5004 7.50 15.00
43 John Andretti StarWars/5004 10.00 20.00
48 Jimmie Johnson Lowes/5004 12.50 25.00
48 Jimmie Johnson Lowe's Power of Pride/5004 12.50 25.00
60 Greg Biffle Grainger/5004 12.50 25.00
97 Kurt Busch Rubbermaid/5004 12.50 25.00
97 Kurt Busch Rubbermaid Commercial/5004 10.00 20.00
97 Kurt Busch Sharpie Million $ Challenge/5004 10.00 20.00
99 Jeff Burton Citgo/5004 7.50 15.00
99 Jeff Burton Citgo Peel Out, Reel In & Win/5004 7.50 15.00

2002 Team Caliber Pit Stop 1:64

The Pit Stop release was issued in a clear plastic clamshell type packaging. Each piece has the year of issue and set name printed on the colorful cardboard insert. We've included the announced production runs below when known. The packaging itself does not include production run information.

1 Jimmy Spencer Yellow Freight 5.00 10.00
5 Terry Labonte Got Milk/7560 4.00 10.00
5 Terry Labonte Kellogg's/7560 4.00 8.00
6 Mark Martin Kraft/10,368 5.00 10.00
6 Mark Martin Pfizer/8076 5.00 10.00
6 Mark Martin Viagra/25,604 5.00 10.00
12 Ryan Newman Alltel/17,592 5.00 10.00
12 Ryan Newman Alltel Sony WEGA/7992 5.00 10.00
12 Ryan Newman Mobil 1/7560 5.00 10.00
17 Matt Kenseth AT&T 5.00 10.00
17 Matt Kenseth DeWalt/7560 4.00 8.00
17 Matt Kenseth DeWalt Million $ Challenge/7560 4.00 8.00
21 Elliott Sadler 5.00 10.00

Air Force/5004
25 Jerry Nadeau UAW-Delphi/7560 3.00 6.00
36 Ken Schrader M&Ms/7560 4.00 8.00
36 Ken Schrader M&Ms Halloween/7560 5.00 10.00
36 Ken Schrader M&Ms July 4th 5.00 10.00
36 Ken Schrader M&Ms Vote/7560 5.00 10.00
36 Ken Schrader M&Ms Vote Purple/900 6.00 12.00
43 Richard Petty Garfield/7560 5.00 12.00
43 John Andretti StarWars/10,080 5.00 10.00
45 Kyle Petty Sprint PCS/7560 4.00 8.00
45 Kyle Petty Sprint Charity Ride/7560 5.00 10.00
48 Jimmie Johnson Lowe's/1002 6.00 12.00
48 Jimmie Johnson Lowe's Power of Pride 6.00 12.00
60 Greg Biffle Grainger/7560 3.00 6.00
97 Kurt Busch Rubbermaid/14,120 4.00 8.00
97 Kurt Busch Rubbermaid Commercial/7560 4.00 8.00
97 Kurt Busch Rubbermaid Little Tikes 5.00 10.00
97 Kurt Busch Sharpie Million $ Challenge/7560 4.00 8.00
97 Kurt Busch Sharpie 500/7572 6.00 12.00
99 Jeff Burton Citgo/10,080 3.00 6.00
99 Jeff Burton Citgo Bass Masters/7560 4.00 8.00
99 Jeff Burton Citgo Peel Out, Reel In and Win/4128 4.00 8.00
02 Santa Claus Holiday/3504 5.00 10.00
02 Daytona 2002/10,584 5.00 10.00

2002 Team Caliber Promos 1:64

9 Jeff Burton Gain 7.50 20.00
12 Ryan Newman Alltel Sony WEGA in Sears window box 5.00 10.00
21 Elliott Sadler Air Force Charlotte Race Air Force Recruiters in box 10.00 20.00
33 Tony Raines Alka Seltzer issued in a box 7.50 15.00
97 Kurt Busch Sharpie 2.00 5.00
99 Jeff Burton Citgo 2.00 5.00
02 Lowe's UAW GM 500 issued in clear box 15.00 30.00
02 Ryan Newman Alltel with cellular phone face plate 7.50 15.00

2003 Team Caliber Model Kits 1:64

5 Terry Labonte Finding Nemo 7.50 15.00
6 Mark Martin Viagra 7.50 15.00
6 Mark Martin Viagra White 7.50 15.00
12 Ryan Newman Alltel 7.50 15.00
17 Matt Kenseth DeWalt 7.50 15.00
17 Matt Kenseth DeWalt Million $ Challenge/2400 7.50 15.00
21 Ricky Rudd Motorcraft 7.50 15.00
87 Kyle Busch Ditech.com 7.50 15.00
97 Kurt Busch Blue Ice 7.50 15.00
01 Jerry Nadeau Army 7.50 15.00

2003 Team Caliber Owners Series 1:64

6 Mark Martin Kraft/5004 8.00 20.00
6 Mark Martin Pfizer/5004 8.00 20.00
6 Mark Martin Viagra/10,080 10.00 20.00
6 Mark Martin Viagra Blue Chrome/10,080 12.50 25.00
6 Mark Martin Viagra White 10.00 20.00
10 Johnny Benson Valvoline 10.00 20.00
12 Ryan Newman Alltel/10,080 10.00 20.00
12 Ryan Newman Mobil 1 10.00 20.00
16 Greg Biffle Grainger/5004 10.00 20.00
17 Matt Kenseth DeWalt/5004 12.50 25.00
21 Ricky Rudd Air Force 7.50 15.00
21 Ricky Rudd Motorcraft/10,080 7.50 15.00
23 Kenny Wallace Stacker 2 7.50 15.00
25 Joe Nemechek UAW Delphi 7.50 15.00
43 John Andretti Cheerios 7.50 15.00
45 Kyle Petty Georgia Pacific 7.50 15.00
48 Jimmie Johnson Lowe's 8.00 20.00
48 Jimmie Johnson Lowe's Blue Chrome/7560 15.00 30.00
97 Kurt Busch Rubbermaid/5004 10.00 20.00
99 Jeff Burton Citgo/5004 7.50 15.00
01 Jerry Nadeau Army 10.00 20.00

2003 Team Caliber Pit Stop 1:64

1 Jamie McMurray Yellow Freight 4.00 8.00
5 Terry Labonte Kellogg's 4.00 8.00
5 Terry Labonte Kellogg's Cheez-It 4.00 8.00
5 Terry Labonte Finding Nemo 5.00 10.00
5 Terry Labonte Got Milk 4.00 8.00
5 Terry Labonte Power of Cheese 4.00 8.00
5 Brian Vickers Carquest 5.00 10.00
5 Brian Vickers GMAC 5.00 10.00
6 Mark Martin Kraft 4.00 8.00
6 Mark Martin Pfizer 4.00 8.00
6 Mark Martin Viagra 4.00 8.00
6 Mark Martin Viagra Blue Daytona 5.00 10.00
6 Mark Martin Viagra White 4.00 8.00
6 Mark Martin Viagra 500 Starts 5.00 10.00
9 Greg Biffle Oreo 5.00 10.00
10 Johnny Benson Eagle One 4.00 8.00
10 Johnny Benson Valvoline 4.00 8.00
12 Ryan Newman Alltel 4.00 8.00
12 Ryan Newman Mobil 1 4.00 8.00
12 Ryan Newman Sony Wega 4.00 8.00
16 Greg Biffle Grainger 4.00 8.00
16 Greg Biffle Grainger 1st Win 5.00 10.00
17 Matt Kenseth DeWalt 5.00 10.00
17 Matt Kenseth DeWalt 2003 Champion 5.00 10.00
17 Matt Kenseth DeWalt Million $ Challenge 4.00 8.00
17 Matt Kenseth Victory Lap 5.00 10.00
21 Ricky Rudd Air Force 4.00 8.00
21 Ricky Rudd AF Cross Into Blue 4.00 8.00
21 Centennial of Speed 3-car set Ricky Rudd Air Force Ricky Rudd Ford 100 Years 10.Bill France Sr./1935 Ford 18.00 30.00
21 R.Rudd Ford 100 Years 4.00 8.00
21 Ricky Rudd Motorcraft/15,060 4.00 8.00
21 Ricky Rudd Motorcraft 700 Starts 4.00 8.00
23 Kenny Wallace Stacker 2 4.00 8.00
25 Bobby Hamilton Jr. Marines 4.00 8.00
25 Joe Nemechek UAW Delphi 4.00 8.00
32 Ricky Craven Tide 4.00 8.00
32/97 Ricky Craven Tide Kurt Busch Rubbermaid Darlington finish 2-car set 12.50 25.00
38 K.Kahne Great Clips 7.50 15.00
43 John Andretti Cheerios 4.00 8.00
43 John Andretti Cheerios Berry Burst 4.00 8.00
43 John Andretti Pillsbury 4.00 8.00
45 Kyle Petty Brawny 4.00 8.00
45 Kyle Petty Georgia Pacific 4.00 8.00
45 Kyle Petty Georgia Pacific Charity 4.00 8.00
45 Kyle Petty Victory Junction Hands 4.00 8.00
48 Jimmie Johnson Lowe's 4.00 8.00
48 Jimmie Johnson Lowe's Power of Pride 4.00 8.00
60 Brian Vickers HAAS 5.00 10.00
77 Dave Blaney Jasper Panther 4.00 8.00
87 Kyle Busch Ditech.com 4.00 8.00
97 Kurt Busch Blue Ice 4.00 8.00
97 Kurt Busch Rubbermaid 4.00 8.00
97 Kurt Busch Rubbermaid Commercial Products 4.00 8.00
97 Kurt Busch Irwin Tools 4.00 8.00
97 Kurt Busch Sharpie 4.00 8.00
99 Jeff Burton Citgo 4.00 8.00
99 Jeff Burton Velveeta 4.00 8.00
99 Kenny Wallace Cardinals 4.00 8.00
0 University of Oregon Ducks 7.50 15.00
01 Jerry Nadeau Army 5.00 10.00
01 Jerry Nadeau Army Camouflage 5.00 10.00
01 Jerry Nadeau USG Sheet Rock 4.00 8.00
03 Daytona 500 4.00 8.00
03 Santa Claus Holiday Blue Chrome 5.00 10.00

2003 Team Caliber Promos 1:64

12 Ryan Newman Alltel 6.00 12.00
17 Matt Kenseth Aleve 6.00 15.00
17 Matt Kenseth Alka-Seltzer Morning 6.00 15.00
17 Matt Kenseth Alka-Seltzer Plus 6.00 15.00
17 Matt Kenseth Bayer 6.00 15.00
17 Matt Kenseth 4-car set Alka-Seltzer Morning, Alka-Seltzer Plus, Aleve and Bayer cars 20.00 40.00
21 Ricky Rudd Rent-A-Center 10.00 20.00
300 Centennial of Speed Chrysler 5.00 10.00
03 Centennial of Speed 1936 Ford Coupe 5.00 10.00
03 Centennial of Speed Hudson Hornet 5.00 10.00

2003 Team Caliber/Motorworks 1:64

5 Terry Labonte Finding Nemo 3.00 8.00
12 Ryan Newman Alltel 4.00 10.00
17 Matt Kenseth DeWalt Victory Lap 4.00 10.00
87 Kyle Busch ditech.com 3.00 8.00
03 Christmas Blue Snowman 3.00 6.00
03 Christmas Green Red Santa 3.00 6.00
03 Christmas Red Reindeer 3.00 6.00
03 Christmas Red Elf 3.00 6.00
03 Christmas Yellow Reindeer 3.00 6.00

2004 Team Caliber Owners Series 1:64

17 Matt Kenseth DeWalt/5004 10.00 20.00
97 Kurt Busch Irwin Tools 10.00 20.00

2004 Team Caliber Pit Stop 1:64

5 Kyle Busch Lowe's 4.00 8.00
5 Kyle Busch Lowe's SpongeBob 4.00 8.00
5 Terry Labonte Delphi 4.00 8.00
5 Terry Labonte Kellogg's 4.00 8.00
5 Terry Labonte Kellogg's Olympics 4.00 8.00
5 Terry Labonte Spiderman 4.00 8.00
6 Mark Martin Batman 4.00 8.00
6 Mark Martin Oscar Mayer 4.00 8.00
6 Mark Martin Pfizer 4.00 8.00
6 Mark Martin Viagra 4.00 8.00
6 Mark Martin Viagra White 4.00 8.00
9 Jeff Burton Cottman 3.00 6.00
9 Jeff Burton Pennzoil 3.00 6.00
9 Matt Kenseth Pennzoil 3.00 6.00
9 Mark Martin Pennzoil 3.00 6.00
9 Mark Martin Batman 4.00 8.00
10 Scott Riggs Harlem Globetrotters 4.00 8.00
10 Scott Riggs Valvoline 4.00 8.00
12 Ryan Newman Alltel 5.00 10.00
12 Ryan Newman Justice League 4.00 8.00
12 Ryan Newman Mobil 1 5.00 10.00
12 Ryan Newman Mobil 1 30th Anniversary 5.00 10.00
12 Ryan Newman Sony Wega 5.00 10.00
14 Casey Atwood Navy 3.00 6.00
16 Greg Biffle Coke C2 4.00 8.00
16 Greg Biffle Flash 4.00 8.00
16 Greg Biffle Jackson-Hewitt 3.00 6.00
16 Greg Biffle National Guard 4.00 8.00
16 Greg Biffle Subway 4.00 8.00
16 Greg Biffle Travelodge 3.00 6.00
17 Matt Kenseth Bayer 4.00 8.00
17 Matt Kenseth Carhartt 4.00 8.00
17 Matt Kenseth DeWalt 4.00 8.00
17 Matt Kenseth Express Personnel 4.00 8.00
17 Matt Kenseth Martian Manhunter 4.00 8.00
21 Ricky Rudd Air Force 4.00 8.00
21 Ricky Rudd Coke C2 4.00 8.00
21 Ricky Rudd Motorcraft 4.00 8.00
21 Ricky Rudd Rent A Center 4.00 8.00
21 Ricky Rudd Wonder Woman 4.00 8.00
22 Scott Wimmer Caterpillar 3.00 6.00
25 Bobby Hamilton Jr. Marines Flames 4.00 8.00
25 Brian Vickers Ditech.com 4.00 8.00
43 Jeff Green Cheerios 3.00 6.00
43 Jeff Green Lucky Charms 3.00 6.00
45 Kyle Petty Brawny 3.00 6.00
45 Kyle Petty Georgia Pacific 3.00 6.00
48 Jimmie Johnson Lowe's 4.00 8.00
48 Jimmie Johnson Lowe's SpongeBob 3.00 6.00
60 Greg Biffle Charter 4.00 8.00
60 Greg Biffle Flash 4.00 8.00
84 Kyle Busch Car Quest 4.00 8.00
97 Kurt Busch Coke C2 4.00 8.00
97 Kurt Busch Irwin Tools 4.00 8.00
97 Kurt Busch Irwin Tools '04 Champion 4.00 8.00
97 Kurt Busch Sharpie 4.00 8.00
97 Kurt Busch Sharpie '04 Champion 4.00 8.00
97 Kurt Busch Sharpie 40th Anniversary 4.00 8.00
97 Kurt Busch Superman 4.00 8.00
99 Jeff Burton Coke C2 3.00 6.00
99 Jeff Burton Green Lantern 4.00 8.00
99 Jeff Burton Pennzoil 3.00 6.00
99 Jeff Burton SKF 3.00 6.00
99 Jeff Burton TNT NBA All Star Game 3.00 6.00
01 Jerry Nadeau Army 3.00 6.00
04 Holiday Event Car 3.00 6.00
04 Justice League Event Car 4.00 8.00
04 Justice League Villain Event Car 4.00 8.00
NNO Disney Event Car Donald Duck 3.00 6.00
NNO Disney Event Car Goofy 3.00 6.00
NNO Disney Event Car Mickey Mouse 3.00 6.00
NNO Disney Event Car Minnie Mouse 3.00 6.00
NNO Disney Event Car PegLeg 3.00 6.00

2004 Team Caliber Promos 1:64

5 Kyle Busch Lowe's SpongeBob 6.00 12.00
16 Greg Biffle Jackson Hewitt 10.00 20.00
17 Matt Kenseth Carhartt in window box 10.00 20.00
32 David Stremme TrimSpa 20.00 40.00
32 David Stremme TrimSpa Promo in window box 60.00 100.00
48 Jimmie Johnson Lowe's SpongeBob 6.00 12.00

2004 Team Caliber/Motorworks 1:64

5 Terry Labonte Kellogg's 3.00 6.00
10 Scott Riggs Valvoline 3.00 6.00
14 Casey Atwood Navy 3.00 6.00
22 Scott Wimmer CAT 3.00 6.00
25 Brian Vickers Ditect.com 3.00 6.00
01 Joe Nemechek Army 3.00 6.00
NNO Disney Event Car Donald Duck 3.00 6.00
NNO Disney Event Car Goofy 3.00 6.00
NNO Disney Event Car Mickey Mouse 3.00 6.00
NNO Disney Event Car Minnie Mouse 3.00 6.00

2005 Team Caliber Pit Stop 1:64

5 Kyle Busch Kellogg's 4.00 8.00
6 Mark Martin Batman 5.00 10.00
6 Mark Martin Kraft 4.00 8.00
6 Mark Martin Viagra 4.00 8.00
6 Mark Martin Viagra Blue Retro Stroh's Light 5.00 10.00
6 Mark Martin Viagra Orange 5.00 10.00
6 Mark Martin Viagra Red Retro Folgers 5.00 10.00
6 Mark Martin Red, White & Blue Viagra Retro Valvoline 5.00 10.00
6 Mark Martin Viagra Salute to You 5.00 10.00
9 Matt Kenseth Pennzoil 3.00 6.00
9 Mark Martin Pennzoil 3.00 6.00
10 Scott Riggs Valvoline 3.00 6.00
12 Ryan Newman Alltel 4.00 8.00
12 Ryan Newman Mobil 1 4.00 8.00
12 Ryan Newman Mobil 1 Gold 4.00 8.00
12 Ryan Newman Sony HDTV 4.00 8.00
16 Greg Biffle National Guard 3.00 6.00
16 Greg Biffle Post-It 3.00 6.00
16 Greg Biffle Subway 3.00 6.00
17 Matt Kenseth Carhartt 4.00 8.00
17 Matt Kenseth DeWalt 4.00 8.00
17 Matt Kenseth Trex 4.00 8.00
17 Matt Kenseth USG 4.00 8.00
17 Matt Kenseth Waste Management 4.00 8.00
21 Ricky Rudd Air Force 3.00 6.00
21 Ricky Rudd Motorcraft 3.00 6.00
22 Scott Wimmer Cat 3.00 6.00
22 Scott Wimmer CAT Dealers 3.00 6.00
25 Brian Vickers GMAC 3.00 6.00
36 Boris Said Centrix Financial 5.00 10.00
43 Jeff Green Cheerios 3.00 6.00
44 Terry Labonte Kellogg's 3.00 6.00
45 Kyle Petty Georgia Pacific 3.00 6.00
48 Jimmie Johnson Lowe's 4.00 8.00
60 Carl Edwards Charter 5.00 10.00
97 Kurt Busch Irwin Tools 3.00 6.00
97 Kurt Busch Sharpie 3.00 6.00
97 Kurt Busch Sharpie Autographs for Education 3.00 6.00
99 Carl Edwards AAA 6.00 12.00
99 Carl Edwards Office Depot 6.00 12.00
99 Carl Edwards Scotts 1st Win 10.00 20.00
01 Joe Nemechek Army 3.00 6.00
05 Batman Begins Event 4.00 8.00
05 Daytona 500 Event Car 4.00 8.00
05 Christmas Event Car 4.00 8.00
NNO Daytona Disney Big Bad Wolf 3.00 6.00
NNO Daytona Disney Daisy 3.00 6.00
NNO Daytona Disney Donald Duck 3.00 6.00
NNO Daytona Disney Goofy 3.00 6.00
NNO Daytona Disney Mickey Mouse 3.00 6.00
NNO Daytona Disney Minnie Mouse 3.00 6.00

2005 Team Caliber Promos 1:64

16 Greg Biffle National Guard in window box 15.00 30.00
17 Matt Kenseth USG in window box 7.50 15.00
17 Matt Kenseth Waste Management in window box 15.00 30.00
66 Greg Biffle USPS in window box 20.00 40.00
77 Travis Kvapil Jasper Engines in window box 12.50 25.00

2006 Team Caliber Pit Stop 1:64

2 Kurt Busch 5.00 10.00
Kurt
2 Kurt Busch 6.00 12.00
Miller Lite in window box
6 Mark Martin 7.50 15.00
AAA
6 Mark Martin 6.00 12.00
AAA Insurance
6 Mark Martin 6.00 12.00
Ameriquest
6 Mark Martin 6.00 12.00
Pennzoil
7 Robby Gordon 6.00 12.00
Menard's
10 Scott Riggs 6.00 12.00
Valvoline
12 Ryan Newman 6.00 12.00
Alltel
12 Ryan Newman 6.00 12.00
Alltel Black Brickyard
12 Ryan Newman 6.00 12.00
Mobil 1
12 Ryan Newman 6.00 12.00
Sony HDTV
14 Sterling Marlin 6.00 12.00
Waste Management
16 Greg Biffle 6.00 12.00
Ameriquest
16 Greg Biffle 6.00 12.00
Jackson Hewitt
16 Greg Biffle 6.00 12.00
iLevel Weyerhaeuser
16 Greg Biffle 6.00 12.00
National Guard
17 Matt Kenseth 6.00 12.00
Ameriquest
17 Matt Kenseth 6.00 12.00
Ameriquest Soaring Dreams
17 Matt Kenseth 6.00 12.00
Carhartt
17 Matt Kenseth 6.00 12.00
DeWalt
17 Matt Kenseth 6.00 12.00
Pennzoil
17 Matt Kenseth 6.00 12.00
Post
17 Matt Kenseth 6.00 12.00
R&L Carriers
21 Ken Schrader 6.00 12.00
Air Force
21 Ken Schrader 6.00 12.00
Motorcraft
22 Dave Blaney 6.00 12.00
CAT
22 Dave Blaney 6.00 12.00
CAT Engines
22 Dave Blaney 6.00 12.00
CAT Financial
22 Dave Blaney 6.00 12.00
CAT Rental
23 Bill Lester 7.50 15.00
Waste Management
26 Jamie McMurray 6.00 12.00
Irwin Tools
26 Jamie McMurray 6.00 12.00
Lenox
26 Jamie McMurray 6.00 12.00
Sharpie
39 Kurt Busch 6.00 12.00
Penske
43 Bobby Labonte 6.00 12.00
Cheerios
55 Michael Waltrip 6.00 12.00
Domino's
55 Michael Waltrip 6.00 12.00
Napa
55 Michael Waltrip 6.00 12.00
Napa Stars & Stripes
60 Carl Edwards 6.00 12.00
Ameriquest
60 Carl Edwards 6.00 12.00
Ameriquest Soaring Dreams
60 Carl Edwards 6.00 12.00
iLevel Weyerhaeuser
99 Carl Edwards 7.50 15.00
Office Depot
99 Darrell Waltrip 6.00 12.00
Aaron's
99 Michael Waltrip 6.00 12.00
Aaron's
99 Michael Waltrip 6.00 12.00
Best Western
00 Bill Elliott 7.50 15.00
Burger King
01 Joe Nemechek 6.00 12.00
Army
06 Todd Kluever 7.50 15.00
3M
06 Disney Event Car Buzz Lightyear 6.00 12.00
06 Disney Event Car Kermit 6.00 12.00
06 Disney Event Car Mickey Mouse 6.00 12.00
06 Disney Event Car Princess 6.00 12.00
06 Disney Event Car Tigger 6.00 12.00

2006 Team Caliber Promos 1:64

9 Kasey Kahne 10.00 20.00
Ragu in window box
9 Kasey Kahne 7.50 15.00
Ultimate Chargers in window box
14 Sterling Marlin 10.00 20.00
Waste Management
in window box
17 Matt Kenseth 7.50 15.00
USG Sheetrock
in window box
21 Ken Schrader 20.00 40.00
Little Debbie
Air Force
Motorcraft
3-car set in window box
27 David Green 6.00 12.00
Kleenex in window box
32 Jason Leffler 6.00 12.00
ABF U-Pack
in window box
66 Greg Biffle 7.50 15.00
Cub Cadet in window box
00 Johnny Sauter 6.00 12.00
Yellow Freight in window box
06 Atlanta Bass Pro Shops 500 5.00 10.00
in window box
06 Atlanta Nicorette 300 5.00 10.00
in window box
06 Bristol Sharpie 500 5.00 10.00
in window box
06 California Speedway Auto Club 500 5.00 10.00
in window box
06 California Sony HD 500 5.00 10.00
in window box
06 Chicagoland USG Sheetrock 400 5.00 10.00
in window box
06 Daytona 500 in window box 5.00 10.00
06 Daytona Pepsi 400 in window box 5.00 10.00
06 Infineon Save Mart 350 5.00 10.00
in window box
06 Kansas Banquet 400 5.00 10.00
in window box
06 Kentucky Speedway Meijer 300 5.00 10.00
in window box
06 Las Vegas UAW Daimler-Chrysler 400 5.00 10.00
in window box
06 Lowe's Motor Speedway Bank of America 500 5.00
10.00
in window box
06 Lowe's Motor Speedway Coca-Cola 600 5.00 10.00
in window box
06 Martinsville Directv 500 5.00 10.00
in window box
06 Miami-Homestead Ford 400 5.00 10.00
in window box
06 Michigan GFS Marketplace 400 5.00 10.00
in window box
06 Michigan 3M Performance 400 5.00 10.00
in window box
06 Phoenix Checker Auto Parts 500 5.00 10.00
in window box
06 Phoenix Subway Fresh 500 5.00 10.00
in window box
06 Richmond Chevy Rock & Roll 400 5.00 10.00
in window box
06 Richmond Crown Royal 400 5.00 10.00
in window box
06 Talladega Aaron's 499 5.00 10.00
in window box
06 Talladega UAW Ford 500 5.00 10.00
in window box
06 Texas Dickies 500 5.00 10.00
in window box
06 Texas Samsung Radio Shack 500 5.00 10.00
in window box
06 Watkins Glen AMD at The Glen 5.00 10.00
in window box

2002 Team Caliber Pull Backs 1:87

These 1:87 scale cars were issued on Team Caliber blister packages. Each car features black windows and was produced to be motorized when pulled back across a smooth surface. The car paint schemes are far less detailed then on the larger scale models.

6 Mark Martin 3.00 8.00
Pfizer
16 Greg Biffle 3.00 6.00
Grainger
17 Matt Kenseth 3.00 8.00
DeWalt
21 Ricky Rudd 3.00 6.00
Motorcraft
99 Jeff Burton 3.00 6.00
Citgo

2003 Team Caliber/Motorworks 4-Packs 1:87

NNO 01.Jerry Nadeau 7.50 15.00
Army
10.Johnny Benson
Valvoline
03.Red Santa
03.Blue Snowman
NNO 01.Jerry Nadeau 7.50 15.00
Army
43.John Andertti
Berry Burst
03.Yellow Reindeer
03.Red Elf
NNO 5.Terry Labonte 7.50 15.00
Kellogg's
12.Ryan Newman
Alltel
03.Red Santa
03.Yellow Reindeer
NNO 5.Terry Labonte 7.50 15.00
Kellogg's
45.Kyle Petty
Brawny
03.Red Elf
03.Blue Snowman
NNO 10.Johnny Benson 7.50 15.00
Valvoline
12.Ryan Newman
Alltel
03.Blue Snowman
03.Yellow Reindeer
NNO 10.Johnny Benson 7.50 15.00
Valvoline
45.Kyle Petty
Brawny
03.Red Elf
03.Yellow Reindeer

2008 Toolbox Treasures 1:24

88 Ralph Earnhardt 75.00 125.00
'57 Olds Convertible/ Richard Petty AU
188 Ralph Earnhardt 75.00 125.00
'57 Olds Hardtop/ Richard Petty AU

2002 Winner's Circle 1:18

3 Dale Earnhardt 25.00 50.00
Goodwrench
3 Dale Earnhardt 25.00 50.00
Goodwrench Oreo
3 Dale Earnhardt 35.00 60.00
Goodwrench Peter Max
3 Dale Earnhardt 25.00 50.00
Goodwrench Plus
No Bull
8 Dale Earnhardt Jr. 25.00 50.00
Dale Jr.
24 Jeff Gordon 25.00 50.00
DuPont Flames
29 Kevin Harvick 20.00 40.00
Goodwrench
88 Dale Jarrett 25.00 40.00
UPS

2003 Winner's Circle 1:18

3 Dale Earnhardt 25.00 40.00
Foundation
3 Dale Earnhardt 25.00 40.00
Goodwrench No Bull '00
3 Dale Earnhardt 30.00 50.00
Goodwrench Peter Max '00
3 Dale Earnhardt 25.00 40.00
Goodwrench Service Plus '00
3 Dale Earnhardt 25.00 40.00
Goodwrench Oreo '01
8 Dale Earnhardt Jr. 25.00 40.00
Dale Jr.
8 Dale Earnhardt Jr. 25.00 40.00
Earnhardt Tribute Concert
in '02 package
8 Dale Earnhardt Jr. 25.00 40.00
MLB All Star '03
8 Dale Earnhardt Jr. 20.00 35.00
Looney Tunes 2002
9 Bill Elliott 25.00 50.00
Dodge
24 Jeff Gordon 25.00 40.00
DuPont Flames
24 Jeff Gordon 25.00 40.00
Pepsi Talladega '01
24 Jeff Gordon 25.00 40.00
Pepsi Billion $
29 Kevin Harvick 25.00 40.00
Goodwrench
38 Elliott Sadler 25.00 40.00
M&M's
48 Jimmie Johnson 25.00 40.00
Lowe's Sylvester & Tweety

2004 Winner's Circle 1:18

3 Dale Earnhardt 20.00 35.00
Goodwrench Service Plus
2001 Monte Carlo
8 Dale Earnhardt Jr 20.00 35.00
JR
8 Dale Earnhardt Jr. 20.00 35.00
Oreo
9 Kasey Kahne 35.00 60.00
Dodge
9 Kasey Kahne 25.00 40.00
Dodge refresh
20 Tony Stewart 15.00 30.00
Coke C2
20 Tony Stewart 20.00 35.00
Home Depot
20 Tony Stewart 15.00 30.00
Home Depot Black
Reverse Paint
20 Tony Stewart 15.00 30.00
Home Depot Declaration of
Independence '03
21 Kevin Harvick 15.00 30.00
Hershey's Kisses
24 Jeff Gordon 25.00 40.00
DuPont Flames
24 Jeff Gordon 20.00 35.00
DuPont Rainbow
24 Jeff Gordon 20.00 35.00
Pepsi Shards
29 Kevin Harvick 15.00 30.00
Coke C2
29 Kevin Harvick 15.00 30.00
Goodwrench
38 Elliott Sadler 15.00 30.00
M&M's
81 Tony Stewart 20.00 35.00
Bass Pro Shops
99 Michael Waltrip 15.00 30.00
Aaron's Cat in the Hat

2005 Winner's Circle 1:18

3 Dale Earnhardt 25.00 40.00
Goodwrench '00
20 Tony Stewart 25.00 40.00
Home Depot

2007 Winner's Circle 1:18

8 Dale Earnhardt Jr. 25.00 40.00
DEI
9 Kasey Kahne 20.00 35.00
Dodge Dealers
11 Denny Hamlin 20.00 35.00
Fed Ex Express
20 Tony Stewart 20.00 35.00
Home Depot
24 Jeff Gordon 25.00 40.00
DuPont Flames
48 Jimmie Johnson 25.00 40.00
Lowe's
99 Carl Edwards 20.00 35.00
Office Depot
01 Mark Martin 20.00 35.00
U.S. Army

1996 Winner's Circle 1:24

This first series of die-cast cars by Winner's Circle were issued in a blue and red cardboard double window box that included the "Winner's Circle" name and year of issue. A small picture of the driver was also included on the box in the lower right hand corner.

3 Dale Earnhardt 15.00 40.00
Goodwrench
24 Jeff Gordon 12.50 25.00
DuPont

1997 Winner's Circle 1:24

This series marks the teaming of Action Performance and Hasbro. This line of cars was produced for and distributed in the mass-market. It is highlighted by the Jeff Gordon Lifetime Series and the Dale Earnhardt lifetime Series.

3 Dale Earnhardt 25.00 60.00
AC Delco 1996 Monte Carlo
3 Dale Earnhardt 40.00 100.00
Goodwrench
3 Dale Earnhardt 20.00 50.00
Goodwrench Plus
3 Dale Earnhardt 45.00 100.00
Wheaties gray interior
3 Dale Earnhardt 40.00 80.00
Wheaties orange interior
3 Jay Sauter 10.00 25.00
Goodwrench SuperTruck
16 Ron Hornaday 8.00 20.00
NAPA SuperTruck
17 Darrell Waltrip 8.00 20.00
Parts America
18 Bobby Labonte 10.00 25.00
Interstate Batteries
22 Ward Burton 8.00 20.00
MBNA Gold
24 Jeff Gordon 20.00 50.00
DuPont
24 Jeff Gordon 20.00 50.00
DuPont Million Dollar Date
24 Jeff Gordon 25.00 60.00
DuPont ChromaPremier
24 Jeff Gordon 25.00 60.00
Lost World
27 Kenny Irwin 10.00 25.00
Tonka
31 Mike Skinner 10.00 25.00
Lowe's
81 Kenny Wallace 10.00 25.00
Square D
88 Dale Jarrett 10.00 25.00
Quality Care
Ford Credit on fender
88 Dale Jarrett 10.00 25.00
Quality Care Red Carpet
Lease on fender

1998 Winner's Circle 1:24

1 Dale Earnhardt Jr. 15.00 30.00
Coke
1 Steve Park 12.50 30.00
Pennzoil
2 Rusty Wallace 10.00 20.00
Rusty
2 Rusty Wallace 15.00 30.00
Rusty Elvis
3 Dale Earnhardt 35.00 75.00
Coke
3 Dale Earnhardt 30.00 60.00
Goodwrench Plus
3 Dale Earnhardt 30.00 80.00
Goodwrench Bass Pro
3 Dale Earnhardt 35.00 80.00
Goodwrench Daytona
3 Dale Earnhardt 30.00 80.00
Goodwrench Silver
3 Dale Earnhardt Jr. 30.00 75.00
AC Delco
12 Jeremy Mayfield 8.00 20.00
Mobil 1
18 Bobby Labonte 10.00 25.00
Interstate Batteries
18 Bobby Labonte 10.00 25.00
Interstate Batteries
Small Soldiers
22 Ward Burton 8.00 20.00
MBNA
24 Jeff Gordon 20.00 50.00
DuPont
24 Jeff Gordon 25.00 60.00
DuPont Million Dollar win
24 Jeff Gordon 20.00 50.00
DuPont Walmart
28 Kenny Irwin 10.00 25.00
Havoline
28 Kenny Irwin 15.00 40.00
Havoline Joker
31 Mike Skinner 10.00 25.00
Lowe's
44 Tony Stewart 15.00 30.00
Shell
44 Tony Stewart 15.00 30.00
Shell Small Soldiers
88 Dale Jarrett 10.00 25.00
Quality Care
88 Dale Jarrett 10.00 25.00
Quality Care Batman

1998 Winner's Circle with Figure 1:24

1 Dale Earnhardt Jr 10.00 25.00
Coke
3 Dale Earnhardt 12.50 30.00
Coke
3 Dale Earnhardt Jr 12.50 25.00
AC Delco
24 Jeff Gordon 10.00 25.00
DuPont No Bull
24 Jeff Gordon 10.00 25.00
Pepsi

1999 Winner's Circle 1:24

This line is the result of an alliance between Action and Hasbro to bring exclusive license such as Gordon and Earnhardt to the mass market.

1 Steve Park 12.50 30.00
Pennzoil
2 Rusty Wallace 10.00 25.00
Rusty
3 Dale Earnhardt 30.00 80.00
Goodwrench
3 Dale Earnhardt 30.00 80.00
Goodwrench 25th Anniversary
Silver Trunk
3 Dale Earnhardt 30.00 75.00
Wrangler
3 Dale Earnhardt Jr. 20.00 50.00
AC Delco
3 Dale Earnhardt Jr. 30.00 75.00
AC Delco Superman
8 Dale Earnhardt Jr. 20.00 40.00
Dale Jr.
12 Jeremy Mayfield 10.00 25.00
Mobil 1 Kentucky Derby
18 Bobby Labonte 12.00 30.00
Interstate Batteries
20 Tony Stewart 20.00 50.00
Home Depot
22 Ward Burton 12.00 30.00
Caterpillar
24 Jeff Gordon 20.00 50.00
DuPont Daytona 500
24 Jeff Gordon 20.00 50.00
DuPont No Bull
24 Jeff Gordon 20.00 50.00
DuPont Superman
24 Jeff Gordon 15.00 40.00
Pepsi
24 Jeff Gordon 15.00 40.00
Pepsi with figure
24 Jeff Gordon 15.00 40.00
Star Wars
28 Kenny Irwin 15.00 40.00
Havoline
31 Mike Skinner 8.00 20.00
Lowe's
88 Dale Jarrett 8.00 20.00
Quality Care

2000 Winner's Circle Preview 1:24

Winner's Circle takes on a new look for 2000.

3 Dale Earnhardt 30.00 75.00
GM Goodwrench Sign
3 Dale Earnhardt 40.00 100.00
Goodwrench Taz No Bull
18 Bobby Labonte 10.00 25.00
Interstate Batteries
20 Tony Stewart 10.00 25.00
Home Depot
24 Jeff Gordon 15.00 30.00
DuPont

2000 Winner's Circle 1:24

3 Dale Earnhardt 40.00 80.00
Goodwrench
3 Dale Earnhardt 60.00 100.00
Goodwrench Peter Max
3 Dale Earnhardt 30.00 80.00
Goodwrench Sign
3 Dale Earnhardt 40.00 80.00
Goodwrench Taz No Bull
9 Bill Elliott 12.50 25.00
Dodge Limited Edition
18 Bobby Labonte 12.50 25.00
Interstate Batteries
20 Tony Stewart 15.00 40.00
Home Depot
Rookie of the Year
24 Jeff Gordon 15.00 40.00
DuPont
24 Jeff Gordon 30.00 60.00
DuPont Peanuts 2000
24 Jeff Gordon 20.00 50.00
DuPont Millennium
24 Jeff Gordon 15.00 40.00
Pepsi
27 Casey Atwood 12.50 30.00
Castrol
28 Ricky Rudd 12.00 30.00
Havoline
36 Ken Schrader 15.00 30.00
M&M's
88 Dale Jarrett 12.00 30.00
Quality Care
88 Dale Jarrett 12.50 25.00
Quality Care Air Force
88 Dale Jarrett 12.00 30.00
Quality 1999 Winston Cup Champion

2001 Winner's Circle 1:24

1 Steve Park 15.00 30.00
Pennzoil Tweety
2 Rusty Wallace 12.50 25.00
Rusty Harley
3 Dale Earnhardt 30.00 60.00
Goodwrench
3 Dale Earnhardt 40.00 75.00
Goodwrench Oreo
8 Dale Earnhardt Jr. 20.00 40.00
Dale Jr.
9 Bill Elliott 25.00 50.00
Dodge
9 Bill Elliott 15.00 40.00
Dodge Spiderman
15 Michael Waltrip 12.50 25.00
NAPA
18 Bobby Labonte 15.00 30.00
Interstate Batteries
18 Bobby Labonte 12.50 25.00
Interstate Batteries
Jurassic Park 3
19 Casey Atwood 10.00 25.00
Mountain Dew
19 Casey Atwood 15.00 40.00
Dodge
20 Tony Stewart 20.00 40.00
Home Depot Kids 2000
24 Jeff Gordon 20.00 40.00
DuPont Flames
Quaker State Decal on rear fender
28 Ricky Rudd 12.50 25.00
Havoline
29 Kevin Harvick 12.50 30.00
Goodwrench Taz

29 Kevin Harvick Goodwrench White 12.50 25.00

88 Dale Jarrett UPS 20.00 35.00

88 Dale Jarrett UPS Flames 12.50 25.00

NNO Dodge Test Car 15.00 30.00

2001 Winner's Circle Lifetime Series 1:24

3 Dale Earnhardt AC Delco 20.00 40.00

3 Dale Earnhardt Goodwrench Olympic 20.00 40.00

8 Dale Earnhardt Jr. Dale Jr. 20.00 40.00

31 Dale Earnhardt Jr. Mom 'N' Pop's 20.00 40.00

44 Tony Stewart Shell 20.00 40.00

2002 Winner's Circle 1:24

1 Steve Park Pennzoil 12.50 25.00

2 Rusty Wallace Rusty 15.00 30.00

3 Dale Earnhardt Goodwrench Oreo 15.00 30.00

3 Dale Earnhardt Jr. Nilla Wafers 15.00 30.00

3 Dale Earnhardt Jr. Oreo 15.00 30.00

4 Mike Skinner Kodak Max Yosemite Sam 12.50 25.00

5 Terry Labonte Kellogg's Road Runner&Coyote 15.00 30.00

7 Casey Atwood Sirius Muppets 12.50 25.00

8 Dale Earnhardt Jr. 2002 All-Star Game 15.00 30.00

8 Dale Earnhardt Jr. Looney Tunes 20.00 40.00

9 Bill Elliott Dodge Muppets 15.00 30.00

12 Kerry Earnhardt Jani-King Yosemite Sam 12.50 25.00

12 Kerry Earnhardt Super Cuts 12.50 25.00

18 Bobby Labonte Interstate Batteries 12.50 25.00

18 Bobby Labonte Interstate Batteries Coke 12.50 25.00

18 Bobby Labonte Interstate Batteries Jurassic Park 3 12.50 25.00

18 Bobby Labonte Interstate Batteries Muppets 12.50 25.00

19 Jeremy Mayfield Dodge Muppets 12.50 25.00

20 Tony Stewart Home Depot Coke 15.00 25.00

20 Tony Stewart Home Depot Peanuts Black 20.00 35.00

24 Jeff Gordon DuPont Flames Lowe's Decal on rear fender 15.00 30.00

24 Jeff Gordon DuPont 200th Anniversary 15.00 30.00

24 Jeff Gordon DuPont Bugs 2001 15.00 25.00

24 Jeff Gordon DuPont Bugs Rematch 15.00 25.00

24 Jeff Gordon Pepsi Daytona 15.00 30.00

25 Joe Nemechek UAW Speedy Gonzalez 12.50 25.00

28 Ricky Rudd Havoline 12.50 25.00

28 Ricky Rudd Havoline Iron Man 12.50 25.00

28 Ricky Rudd Havoline Muppets 12.50 25.00

29 Kevin Harvick Action ET 15.00 25.00

29 Kevin Harvick Goodwrench 15.00 25.00

29 Kevin Harvick Goodwrench ET 12.50 25.00

29 Kevin Harvick Goodwrench Taz 12.50 25.00

29 Kevin Harvick Reese's Fast Break 12.50 25.00

30 Jeff Green AOL Daffy Duck 12.50 25.00

31 Robby Gordon Cingular 12.50 25.00

31 Robby Gordon Cingular Pepe le Pew 12.50 25.00

37 Jeremy Mayfield Kmart RC Cola 12.50 25.00

40 Sterling Marlin Sterling Marlin 15.00 30.00

41 Jimmy Spencer Target 12.50 25.00

41 Jimmy Spencer Target Muppets 12.50 25.00

55 Bobby Hamilton Square D Marvin the Martian 12.50 25.00

88 Dale Jarrett UPS 12.50 25.00

88 Dale Jarrett UPS Muppets 12.50 25.00

2002 Winner's Circle Die-Cast Kits 1:24

2 Rusty Wallace Rusty 20.00 35.00

3 Dale Earnhardt Jr. Nilla Wafer 25.00 40.00

8 Dale Earnhardt Jr. Dale Jr. 25.00 40.00

8 Dale Earnhardt Jr. Looney Tunes 25.00 40.00

9 Bill Elliott Dodge 20.00 35.00

24 Jeff Gordon DuPont Bugs Rematch 25.00 40.00

24 Jeff Gordon DuPont Flames 25.00 40.00

29 Kevin Harvick Goodwrench 20.00 35.00

40 Sterling Marlin Sterling 20.00 35.00

41 Jimmy Spencer Target 18.00 30.00

88 Dale Jarrett UPS 20.00 35.00

2003 Winner's Circle 1:24

2 Rusty Wallace Rusty 12.50 25.00

3 Dale Earnhardt Foundation 20.00 35.00

3 Dale Earnhardt 2000 Goodwrench No Bull 18.00 30.00

3 Dale Earnhardt 2000 Goodwrench Peter Max 30.00 50.00

8 Dale Earnhardt Jr. JR 18.00 30.00

8 Dale Earnhardt Jr. JR thin base 18.00 30.00

8 Dale Earnhardt Jr. Earnhardt Tribute Concert 20.00 35.00

8 Dale Earnhardt Jr. Looney Tunes 2002 18.00 30.00

8 Dale Earnhardt Jr. MLB All Star 2003 paint 18.00 30.00

8 Dale Earnhardt Jr. Oreo Ritz 18.00 30.00

9 Bill Elliott Dodge 15.00 25.00

20 Tony Stewart Home Depot 18.00 30.00

20 Tony Stewart Home Depot thin base 18.00 30.00

20 Tony Stewart Home Depot Peanuts Black 18.00 30.00

20 Tony Stewart Home Depot Peanuts Orange 2002 Champion Sticker 20.00 40.00

24 Jeff Gordon DuPont Flames 20.00 40.00

24 Jeff Gordon DuPont Bugs Rematch '02 18.00 30.00

24 Jeff Gordon 2002 Elmo 20.00 35.00

24 Jeff Gordon 2001 Pepsi Stars&Stripes 18.00 30.00

24 Jeff Gordon Pepsi Billion $ 18.00 30.00

29 Kevin Harvick Goodwrench Taz 15.00 25.00

31 Robby Gordon Cingular 15.00 25.00

38 Elliott Sadler M&M's 15.00 25.00

38 Elliott Sadler M&M's Groovy 15.00 25.00

40 Sterling Marlin Sterling 15.00 25.00

45 Kyle Petty Hands to Victory 15.00 30.00

48 Jimmie Johnson Lowe's Distributor Exclusive Sticker 12.50 25.00

48 Jimmie Johnson Lowe's Sylvester.&Tweety 18.00 30.00

88 Dale Jarrett UPS 12.50 25.00

NNO Dale Earnhardt Legacy 25.00 40.00

2003 Winner's Circle Die-Cast Kits 1:24

3 Dale Earnhardt Jr. Oreo 2002 15.00 30.00

9 Bill Elliott Dodge 12.50 25.00

24 Jeff Gordon Dupont Bugs Rematch 2002 15.00 30.00

2003 Winner's Circle Victory Lap 1:24

2 Rusty Wallace Miller Lite Victory Lap 15.00 30.00

3 Dale Earnhardt Goodwrench Victory Lap 20.00 40.00

20 Tony Stewart Home Depot Victory Lap 15.00 30.00

24 Jeff Gordon DuPont Victory Lap 20.00 40.00

43 Richard Petty STP Victory Lap 18.00 30.00

88 Dale Jarrett UPS Victory Lap 15.00 30.00

2004 Winner's Circle 1:24

2 Rusty Wallace Kodak 15.00 25.00

2 Rusty Wallace Rusty 15.00 25.00

3 Dale Earnhardt Coke '98 Monte Carlo 18.00 30.00

3 Dale Earnhardt Goodwrench Olympic 1996 Monte Carlo 18.00 30.00

8 Dale Earnhardt Jr. JR 18.00 30.00

8 Dale Earnhardt Jr. Oreo 18.00 30.00

9 Kasey Kahne Dodge Refresh 25.00 50.00

9 Kasey Kahne Dodge Popeye 25.00 40.00

15 Michael Waltrip NAPA 15.00 25.00

18 Bobby Labonte Interstate Batteries 15.00 25.00

18 Bobby Labonte Interstate Batteries D-Day 15.00 25.00

18 Bobby Labonte Interstate Batteries Shrek 2 15.00 25.00

19 Jeremy Mayfield Dodge NHL All Star 15.00 25.00

19 Jeremy Mayfield Dodge Popeye 15.00 25.00

20 Tony Stewart Coke C2 15.00 25.00

20 Tony Stewart Home Depot 15.00 25.00

20 Tony Stewart Home Depot Black 15.00 25.00

20 Tony Stewart Home Depot Shrek 2 15.00 25.00

20 Tony Stewart Home Depot 25th Anniversary 15.00 25.00

21 Kevin Harvick Hershey's Kisses 15.00 25.00

21 Kevin Harvick Reese's 15.00 25.00

24 Jeff Gordon DuPont Flames 18.00 30.00

24 Jeff Gordon DuPont Flames HMS 20th Anniversary 20.00 35.00

24 Jeff Gordon DuPont Rainbow 20.00 35.00

24 Jeff Gordon DuPont Wizard of Oz 20.00 35.00

24 Jeff Gordon Pepsi 20.00 35.00

24 Jeff Gordon Pepsi Billion 20.00 35.00

29 Kevin Harvick Coke C2 15.00 25.00

29 Kevin Harvick Goodwrench 15.00 25.00

29 Kevin Harvick Goodwrench KISS 18.00 30.00

29 Kevin Harvick Goodwrench Realtree 15.00 25.00

29 Kevin Harvick Goodwrench RCR 35th Anniversary 18.00 30.00

29 Kevin Harvick Powerade 15.00 25.00

29 Bobby Labonte ESGR Army 15.00 25.00

38 Kasey Kahne Great Clips 20.00 35.00

38 Kasey Kahne Great Clips Shark Tale 18.00 30.00

38 Elliott Sadler M&M's 15.00 25.00

38 Elliott Sadler M&M's black&white 20.00 35.00

38 Elliott Sadler M&M's July 4 15.00 25.00

38 Elliott Sadler Pedigree Wizard of Oz 15.00 25.00

42 Jamie McMurray Havoline 15.00 25.00

77 Brendan Gaughan Kodak Punisher 15.00 25.00

81 Tony Stewart Bass Pro Shops 15.00 25.00

81 Dale Earnhardt Jr. KFC 15.00 25.00

81 Dale Earnhardt Jr. Taco Bell 15.00 25.00

88 Dale Jarrett UPS 18.00 30.00

92 Tony Stewart McDonald's 15.00 25.00

98 Bill Elliott Coke C2 15.00 25.00

01 Joe Nemechek Army Time Man of the Year 18.00 30.00

2004 Winner's Circle Die-Cast Kits 1:24

8 Dale Earnhardt Jr JR 20.00 35.00

9 Kasey Kahne Dodge Popeye 20.00 35.00

20 Tony Stewart Home Depot 20.00 35.00

24 Jeff Gordon DuPont Rainbow 20.00 35.00

38 Elliott Sadler M&M's 15.00 30.00

38 Elliott Sadler M&M's July 4 15.00 30.00

2005 Winner's Circle 1:24

2 Clint Bowyer Timberland 15.00 30.00

2 Clint Bowyer AC Delco 15.00 30.00

2 Rusty Wallace Rusty 15.00 25.00

3 Dale Earnhardt Foundation '03 15.00 25.00

8 Dale Earnhardt Jr. DEI 15.00 30.00

8 Dale Earnhardt Jr. JR 15.00 30.00

8 Martin Truex Jr. Bass Pro 15.00 25.00

9 Bill Elliott Milestones 15.00 30.00

9 Kasey Kahne Dodge Longest Yard 15.00 30.00

9 Kasey Kahne Dodge Retro Daytona Shootout 15.00 30.00

9 Kasey Kahne Dodge 15.00 30.00

9 Kasey Kahne Dodge 2004 Rookie of the Year 20.00 35.00

9 Kasey Kahne Dodge Mopar '04 20.00 35.00

9 Kasey Kahne Mountain Dew 15.00 30.00

15 Michael Waltrip Napa Stars 15.00 25.00

19 Jeremy Mayfield Dodge 12.50 25.00

19 Jeremy Mayfield Dodge Retro Daytona Shootout 15.00 25.00

20 Tony Stewart Home Depot 20.00 35.00

21 Kevin Harvick Reese's 15.00 25.00

24 Jeff Gordon DuPont Flames 15.00 30.00

29 Kevin Harvick Goodwrench 15.00 25.00

29 Kevin Harvick Goodwrench Atlanta 15.00 25.00

29 Kevin Harvick Goodwrench Daytona 15.00 25.00

29 Kevin Harvick Goodwrench Brickyard 15.00 25.00

29 Kevin Harvick Goodwrench Gretchen Wilson 15.00 25.00

29 Kevin Harvick Goodwrench Quicksilver 15.00 25.00

33 Tony Stewart James Dean 50th Anniversary 15.00 30.00

33 Tony Stewart Mr. Clean AutoDry 15.00 30.00

33 Tony Stewart Old Spice 15.00 30.00

38 Kasey Kahne Great Clips 15.00 30.00

38 Elliott Sadler Pedigree 15.00 25.00

38 Elliott Sadler M&M's 15.00 25.00

41 Reed Sorenson Discount Tire Coats '05 Nashville Raced 15.00 30.00

42 Jamie McMurray Havoline 15.00 25.00

42 Jamie McMurray Havoline Shine On '05 Charlotte 15.00 25.00

42 Jamie McMurray Havoline Shine On '05 Sonoma 15.00 25.00

42 Jamie McMurray Havoline Shine On '05 Talladega 15.00 25.00

81 Dale Earnhardt Jr. Oreo Ritz 15.00 30.00

88 Dale Jarrett UPS 15.00 25.00

99 Michael Waltrip Domino's Pizza 15.00 25.00

NNO Dale Earnhardt Legacy '02 10.00 20.00

2006 Winner's Circle 1:24

1 Martin Truex Jr. Bass Pro 3 Days of Dale Tribute split window box 15.00 30.00

5 Kyle Busch Kellogg's 15.00 25.00

6 Mark Martin AAA 20.00 35.00

8 Dale Earnhardt Jr. Bud 3 Days of Dale Tribute split window box 20.00 40.00

8 Dale Earnhardt Jr. 250 Starts 15.00 25.00

8 Martin Truex Jr. Bass Pro 15.00 25.00

8 Martin Truex Jr. Bass Pro 3 Days of Dale Tribute Talladega Raced split window box 15.00 30.00

9 Kasey Kahne Dodge 15.00 25.00

9 Kasey Kahne Dodge Raced 15.00 25.00

9 Kasey Kahne Dodge SRT 15.00 25.00

11 Paul Menard Menard's 3 Days of Dale Tribute split window box 15.00 30.00

12 Ryan Newman Alltel 15.00 25.00

16 Greg Biffle National Guard 15.00 25.00

17 Matt Kenseth DeWalt 15.00 25.00

19 Jeremy Mayfield Dodge 15.00 25.00

19 Jeremy Mayfield Mountain Dew Pitch Black 12.50 25.00

20 Tony Stewart Home Depot 15.00 25.00

24 Jeff Gordon DuPont Flames 15.00 25.00

24 Jeff Gordon DuPont Hot Hues Foose Design 15.00 25.00

24 Jeff Gordon Holiday JG Foundation 15.00 25.00

26 Jamie McMurray Sharpie 15.00 25.00

29 Kevin Harvick Goodwrench 15.00 25.00

31 Jeff Burton Cingular 15.00 25.00

33 Tony Stewart Old Spice 15.00 25.00

38 Elliott Sadler M&M's 15.00 25.00

48 Jimmie Johnson Lowe's 15.00 25.00

48 Jimmie Johnson Lowe's Sea World 15.00 25.00

64 Rusty Wallace Bell Helicopter '05 15.00 25.00

88 Dale Jarrett UPS 15.00 25.00

99 Carl Edwards Office Depot 15.00 25.00

01 Joe Nemechek Army Camo Call to Duty 15.00 25.00

NNO Dale Earnhardt Hall of Fame Dale Tribute split window box 15.00 30.00

2007 Winner's Circle 1:24

1 Martin Truex Jr. Bass Pro Shops 15.00 25.00

2 Kurt Busch Kurt 15.00 25.00

8 Dale Earnhardt Jr. DEI 15.00 30.00

9 Kasey Kahne Dodge Dealers 15.00 25.00

11 Denny Hamlin Fed Ex Express 15.00 25.00

12 Ryan Newman Alltel 15.00 25.00

16 Greg Biffle Ameriquest 15.00 25.00

17 Matt Kenseth DeWalt 15.00 25.00

20 Tony Stewart Home Depot 15.00 30.00

20 Tony Stewart Home Depot Daytona Shootout Raced 15.00 30.00

24 Jeff Gordon DuPont Flames 15.00 30.00

24 Jeff Gordon Nicorette 15.00 30.00

24 Jeff Gordon Pepsi 15.00 30.00

26 Jamie McMurray Irwin Tools 15.00 25.00

29 Kevin Harvick Shell Pennzoil Daytona Raced 20.00 40.00

29 Kevin Harvick Shell Pennzoil 20.00 40.00

38 David Gilliland M&M's 15.00 25.00

42 Juan Pablo Montoya Texaco Havoline 15.00 30.00

44 Dale Jarrett UPS 15.00 25.00

48 Jimmie Johnson Lowe's 15.00 25.00

55 Michael Waltrip NAPA 15.00 25.00

88 Ricky Rudd Snickers 15.00 25.00

99 Carl Edwards Office Depot 15.00 25.00

2007 NEXTEL Schedule Car 12.50 25.00

00 David Reutimann Burger King 15.00 25.00

01 Mark Martin U.S. Army 20.00 40.00

07 Clint Bowyer Directv 15.00 25.00

2007 Winner's Circle American Heroes 1:24

8 Dale Earnhardt Jr. Bud Camo American Heroes logo 20.00 40.00

8 Dale Earnhardt Jr. DEI Camo American Hero logo 15.00 30.00

11 Denny Hamlin Fed Ex Freight Marines American Heroes 15.00 30.00

24 Jeff Gordon DuPont Department of Defense American Hero logo 15.00 30.00

48 Jimmie Johnson Lowe's Power of Pride American Heroes 15.00 30.00

01 Mark Martin Army American Hero logo 15.00 30.00

2007 Winner's Circle Limited Edition 1:24

8 Dale Earnhardt Jr. Bud 20.00 40.00

8 Dale Earnhardt Jr. Bud Stars & Stripes 20.00 40.00

8 Dale Earnhardt Jr. Bud Test 20.00 35.00

8 Dale Earnhardt Jr. DEI Stars & Stripes 15.00 30.00

8 Dale Earnhardt Jr. Sharpie 15.00 30.00

2008 Winner's Circle 1:24

1 Martin Truex Jr. Bass Pro Shops 15.00 30.00

2 Kurt Busch Kurt 15.00 30.00

5 Casey Mears Carquest 15.00 25.00

5 Casey Mears Kellogg's 15.00 25.00

8 Mark Martin U.S. Army 15.00 30.00

9 Kasey Kahne KK 15.00 30.00

11 Denny Hamlin Fed Ex Express 15.00 30.00

12 Ryan Newman Alltel 15.00 25.00

17 Matt Kenseth DeWalt 15.00 30.00

18 Kyle Busch M&M's 30.00 50.00

20 Tony Stewart Home Depot	15.00	30.00
24 Jeff Gordon DuPont Flames	20.00	35.00
24 Jeff Gordon Nicorette	20.00	35.00
24 Jeff Gordon Pepsi	20.00	35.00
29 Kevin Harvick Shell	15.00	30.00
31 Jeff Burton AT&T	15.00	25.00
42 Juan Pablo Montoya Big Red	15.00	25.00
42 Juan Pablo Montoya Texaco Havoline	15.00	30.00
44 Dale Jarrett UPS	15.00	30.00
48 Jimmie Johnson Lowe's	20.00	40.00
55 Michael Waltrip Napa	15.00	25.00
88 Dale Earnhardt Jr. AMP	20.00	35.00
88 Dale Earnhardt Jr. National Guard	20.00	35.00
99 Carl Edwards Office Depot	20.00	40.00

2008 Winner's Circle Daytona 500 1:24

1 Martin Truex Jr. Bass Pro Shops	25.00	40.00
9 Kasey Kahne Bud	35.00	60.00
9 Kasey Kahne KK	25.00	40.00
17 Matt Kenseth DeWalt	25.00	40.00
20 Tony Stewart Home Depot	25.00	40.00
24 Jeff Gordon DuPont Flames	25.00	40.00
29 Kevin Harvick Shell Pennzoil	25.00	40.00
42 Juan Pablo Montoya Texaco	25.00	40.00
48 Jimmie Johnson Lowe's	25.00	40.00
88 Dale Earnhardt Jr. AMP	25.00	40.00
88 Dale Earnhardt Jr. National Guard	25.00	40.00
99 Carl Edwards Office Depot	25.00	40.00

2008 Winner's Circle Limited Edition 1:24

88 Dale Earnhardt Jr. AMP	25.00	40.00

2009 Winner's Circle 1:24

11 Denny Hamlin Fed Ex Express	12.50	25.00
14 Tony Stewart Office Depot/ Back to School	20.00	40.00
14 Tony Stewart Old Spice Swagger	15.00	30.00
14 Tony Stewart Smoke Fantasy	20.00	40.00
14 Tony Stewart Office Depot	15.00	30.00
14 Tony Stewart Old Spice	15.00	30.00
18 Kyle Busch M&M's	12.50	25.00
18 Kyle Busch Snicker's	12.50	25.00
24 Jeff Gordon National Guard	15.00	30.00
24 Jeff Gordon DuPont	15.00	30.00
88 Dale Earnhardt Jr. AMP Get On	12.50	25.00
88 Dale Earnhardt Jr. Mountain Dew	12.50	25.00
88 Dale Earnhardt Jr. National Guard	12.50	25.00
88 Dale Earnhardt Jr. NG Drive the Guard	12.50	25.00
99 Carl Edwards Aflac	15.00	25.00

2009 Winner's Circle Daytona 1:24

9 Kasey Kahne Bud	15.00	25.00
14 Tony Stewart Office Depot	15.00	30.00
14 Tony Stewart Old Spice	15.00	30.00
18 Kyle Busch M&M's	15.00	25.00
24 Jeff Gordon DuPont	15.00	30.00
48 Jimmie Johnson Lowe's	15.00	25.00
88 Dale Earnhardt Jr. AMP	15.00	25.00
88 Dale Earnhardt Jr. National Guard	15.00	25.00

2009 Winner's Circle HMS 1:24

24 Jeff Gordon DuPont	20.00	40.00
48 Jimmie Johnson Lowe's	20.00	40.00
88 Dale Earnhardt Jr. AMP	20.00	40.00
88 Dale Earnhardt Jr. National Guard	20.00	40.00

2010 Winner's Circle 1:24

14 Tony Stewart Office Depot	15.00	25.00
14 Tony Stewart Old Spice	15.00	25.00
18 Kyle Busch M&M's	15.00	25.00
24 Jeff Gordon DuPont	15.00	30.00
88 Dale Earnhardt Jr. AMP	15.00	25.00
99 Carl Edwards Aflac		
99 Carl Edwards Aflac Silver	15.00	25.00

2010 Winner's Circle Hall of Fame 1:24

10 Dale Earnhardt NASCAR HOF	20.00	40.00
10 Richard Petty NASCAR HOF	20.00	40.00

1998 Winner's Circle 1:43

This series marks the teaming of Action Performance and Hasbro. This line of cars was produced for and distributed in the mass-market.

1 Dale Earnhardt Jr. Coke	8.00	20.00
2 Rusty Wallace Rusty	6.00	15.00
2 Rusty Wallace Rusty Elvis	6.00	15.00
3 Dale Earnhardt Coke	20.00	40.00
3 Dale Earnhardt Goodwrench Bass Pro	20.00	40.00
3 Dale Earnhardt Goodwrench Plus	20.00	40.00
3 Dale Earnhardt Jr. AC Delco	8.00	20.00
12 Jeremy Mayfield Mobil 1	6.00	15.00
24 Jeff Gordon DuPont	6.00	15.00
24 Jeff Gordon DuPont Million Dollar Win	6.00	15.00
24 Jeff Gordon DuPont Winston Cup Champion Walmart special	8.00	20.00
28 Kenny Irwin Havoline	6.00	15.00
31 Dale Earnhardt Jr. Sikkens Blue	6.00	15.00
33 Ken Schrader Schrader	5.00	12.00
88 Dale Jarrett Quality Care	6.00	15.00
88 Dale Jarrett Quality Care Batman	5.00	12.00

1998 Winner's Circle For Kids 1:43

Each car in this series is close to the scale of 1:43 but not exact. The die-cast piece was issued with a rip cord that could be used to propel the car across the ground. Both the cord and car were packaged in a Winner's Circle blister.

3 Dale Earnhardt Goodwrench	10.00	20.00
24 Jeff Gordon DuPont	7.50	15.00

1998 Winner's Circle Victory Celebration 1:43

3 Dale Earnhardt Brickyard 400 8/5/95	20.00	40.00
3 Dale Earnhardt Daytona 500 2/15/98	10.00	20.00
3 Dale Earnhardt Jr. Busch Champion	8.00	20.00
24 Jeff Gordon Charlotte Win	8.00	20.00
24 Jeff Gordon DuPont Million Dollar win 8/31/97	8.00	20.00

1999 Winner's Circle 1:43

This line is the result of an alliance between Action and Hasbro to bring exclusive licenses such as Gordon and Earnhardt to the mass market.

1 Steve Park Pennzoil	6.00	15.00
2 Rusty Wallace Rusty	5.00	12.00
3 Dale Earnhardt Goodwrench 25th Anniv. logo on package	12.50	25.00
3 Dale Earnhardt Goodwrench 25th Anniv. Dale on package	12.50	30.00
3 Dale Earnhardt Jr. AC Delco	8.00	20.00
3 Dale Earnhardt Jr. AC Delco Superman	12.00	30.00
12 Jeremy Mayfield Mobil 1	6.00	15.00
12 Jeremy Mayfield Mobil 1 Kentucky Derby	6.00	15.00
18 Bobby Labonte Interstate Batteries	8.00	20.00
20 Tony Stewart Home Depot	12.00	30.00
22 Ward Burton Caterpillar	8.00	20.00
24 Jeff Gordon DuPont	10.00	25.00
24 Jeff Gordon DuPont Daytona 500	10.00	25.00
24 Jeff Gordon DuPont Superman	12.00	30.00
24 Jeff Gordon Pepsi	8.00	20.00
24 Jeff Gordon Pepsi Star Wars	10.00	25.00
28 Kenny Irwin Havoline	8.00	20.00
31 Mike Skinner Lowe's	6.00	15.00
88 Dale Jarrett Quality Care 1999 Winston Cup Champ.	6.00	15.00
88 Dale Jarrett Quality Care No Bull 5 Win	12.00	20.00

1999 Winner's Circle Select 1:43

This set features cars Dale Earnhardt drove in various Winston Select races.

3 Dale Earnhardt Goowrench Silver '95	20.00	40.00
3 Dale Earnhardt Goodwrench Olympic '96	25.00	50.00
3 Dale Earnhardt Goodwrench Bass Pro '98	15.00	30.00
3 Dale Earnhardt Goodwrench Wrangler '99	15.00	30.00

1999 Winner's Circle Speedweeks 1:43

These cars are preview cars for the 1999 Daytona 500.

3 Dale Earnhardt Goodwrench	15.00	30.00
3 Dale Earnhardt Jr. AC Delco	6.00	12.00
18 Bobby Labonte Interstate Batteries	6.00	12.00
24 Jeff Gordon DuPont	6.00	12.00

1999 Winner's Circle Victory Celebration 1:43

3 Dale Earnhardt Jr. Coca-Cola 300 4/4/98	10.00	25.00
3 Dale Earnhardt Jr. Richmond 6/5/98	10.00	25.00
12 Jeremy Mayfield Pocono 500 6/21/98	8.00	20.00
24 Jeff Gordon Daytona 500	10.00	25.00
24 Jeff Gordon Daytona 500 2/16/97	10.00	25.00
88 Dale Jarrett Quality Care No Bull 5-win 11/11/98	8.00	20.00

2000 Winner's Circle Preview 1:43

Winner's Circle takes on a new look for 2000.

3 Dale Earnhardt Jr. AC Delco Superman '99	8.00	20.00
8 Dale Earnhardt Jr. Dale Jr.	8.00	20.00
18 Bobby Labonte Interstate Batteries	6.00	15.00
20 Tony Stewart Home Depot	6.00	15.00
24 Jeff Gordon DuPont	6.00	15.00

2000 Winner's Circle 1:43

3 Dale Earnhardt Goodwrench	15.00	30.00
18 Bobby Labonte Interstate Batteries	6.00	15.00
24 Jeff Gordon Pepsi	6.00	15.00
36 Ernie Irvan M&M's	6.00	15.00

2000 Winner's Circle Double Platinum 1:43

3 Dale Earnhardt Richard Childress Goodwrench	35.00	75.00
8 Dale Earnhardt Jr. Dale Earnhardt Dale Jr.	40.00	80.00
18 Bobby Labonte Joe Gibbs Interstate Batteries	10.00	20.00
19 Casey Atwood Ray Evernham Dodge	6.00	15.00
36 Ken Schrader M&M's	10.00	20.00

2000 Winner's Circle Garage Scene 1:43

3 Dale Earnhardt Goodwrench	25.00	50.00
20 Tony Stewart Home Depot	8.00	20.00
24 Jeff Gordon DuPont	8.00	20.00

2000 Winner's Circle Sam Bass 1:43

Each car in this series was mounted to a black plastic base that included the driver's name, the title of the art work, and the NASCAR and Sam Bass signature logos. They were packaged in a blister that also included a large (roughly 3 1/2" by 5") card created from a Sam Bass illustration.

3 Dale Earnhardt Goodwrench	20.00	50.00
3 Dale Earnhardt Goodwrench 7-time Champ	25.00	40.00
3 Dale Earnhardt Goodwrench 2001 Oreo	15.00	40.00
3 Dale Earnhardt Goodwrench Peter Max	25.00	50.00
3 Dale Earnhardt Goodwrench Taz No Bull	30.00	60.00
3 Dale Earnhardt Wrangler 1987 Monte Carlo	25.00	40.00
8 Dale Earnhardt Jr. Dale Jr.	15.00	40.00
20 Tony Stewart Home Depot	6.00	15.00
24 Jeff Gordon DuPont	6.00	15.00
88 Dale Jarrett Quality Care	5.00	12.00

2000 Winner's Circle VIP Pass 1:43

3 Dale Earnhardt Goodwrench Plus	12.50	25.00
20 Tony Stewart Home Depot	10.00	20.00

2001 Winner's Circle Double Platinum 1:43

These cars were produced by Action Performance for their Winner's Circle line. Each was packaged in a clear blister pack along with a double-fold holofoil card.

1 Steve Park Pennzoil Tweety	7.50	15.00
2 Rusty Wallace Robin Pemberton Rusty	7.50	15.00
3 Dale Earnhardt Richard Childress Goodwrench	10.00	20.00
8 Dale Earnhardt Jr. Dale with Dale Earnhardt Sr. on card	10.00	20.00
9 Bill Elliott Ray Evernham Dodge	10.00	20.00
24 Jeff Gordon DuPont	10.00	20.00
24 Jeff Gordon DuPont Bugs	10.00	20.00
29 Kevin Harvick Goodwrench Taz	7.50	20.00
88 Dale Jarrett UPS Flames	10.00	20.00

2002 Winner's Circle Double Platinum 1:43

3 Dale Earnhardt Jr. Nilla Wafer	10.00	20.00
3 Dale Earnhardt Jr. Oreo	10.00	20.00
8 Dale Earnhardt Jr. Dale Jr.	10.00	20.00
8 Dale Earnhardt Jr. Looney Tunes	10.00	20.00
8 Dale Earnhardt Jr 2002 MLB All-Star Game	10.00	20.00
20 Tony Stewart Home Depot	10.00	20.00
24 Jeff Gordon DuPont Bugs 2001	10.00	20.00
24 Jeff Gordon DuPont Flames	10.00	20.00
24 Jeff Gordon DuPont Bugs Rematch 2002	10.00	20.00
24 Jeff Gordon DuPont 200th Anniversary	10.00	20.00
29 Kevin Harvick Reese's Fast Break	10.00	20.00
29 Kevin Harvick Goodwrench	10.00	20.00
29 Kevin Harvick Goodwrench Taz	10.00	20.00

2002 Winner's Circle Race Hood 1:43

This series was produced by Winner's Circle and packaged in the typical blue blister with the title "Race Hood" printed in the upper right hand corner. Each car was a 1:43 scale die-cast with the hood being roughly 1:12 scale. The year of issue is noted on the back within the copyright information.

2 Rusty Wallace Rusty	10.00	20.00
3 Dale Earnhardt Jr. Nilla Wafers	12.50	25.00
3 Dale Earnhardt Jr. Oreo	12.50	25.00
4 Mike Skinner Kodak Yosemite Sam	10.00	20.00
7 Casey Atwood Sirius Muppets	10.00	20.00
8 Dale Earnhardt Jr. 2002 All-Star Game	12.50	25.00
8 Dale Earnhardt Jr. Looney Tunes	12.50	25.00
9 Bill Elliott Dodge Muppets	10.00	20.00
12 Kerry Earnhardt Jani-King Yosemite Sam	10.00	20.00
15 Michael Waltrip NAPA	10.00	20.00
18 Bobby Labonte Interstate Batteries Muppets	10.00	20.00
19 Jeremy Mayfield Dodge Muppets	10.00	20.00
24 Jeff Gordon DuPont Bugs 2002	12.50	25.00
24 Jeff Gordon DuPont Flames	12.50	25.00
24 Jeff Gordon DuPont 200th Anniversary	12.50	25.00
29 Kevin Harvick Reese's Fast Break	10.00	20.00
29 Kevin Harvick Goodwrench	10.00	20.00
29 Kevin Harvick Goodwrench Taz	10.00	20.00
55 Bobby Hamilton Square D Marvin Martian	10.00	20.00
88 Dale Jarrett UPS Muppets	10.00	20.00

2003 Winner's Circle Double Platinum 1:43

8 Dale Earnhardt Jr. Looney Tunes	10.00	20.00
20 Tony Stewart Home Depot Peanuts Black	10.00	20.00
20 Tony Stewart Home Depot Peanuts Orange	10.00	20.00
21 Kevin Harvick Payday	7.50	15.00
25 Joe Nemechek UAW Speedy Gonzalez	7.50	15.00
29 Kevin Harvick Goodwrench Taz	8.00	20.00
30 Jeff Green AOL Daffy	7.50	15.00
48 Jimmie Johnson Lowe's Sylvester	8.00	20.00

2003 Winner's Circle Race Hood 1:43

8 Dale Earnhardt Jr. Earnhardt Tribute Concert	10.00	20.00
8 Dale Earnhardt Jr. Looney Tunes 2002	10.00	20.00
8 Dale Earnhardt Jr. Oreo Ritz	10.00	20.00
9 Bill Elliott Dodge	7.50	15.00
20 Tony Stewart Home Depot Declaration of Independence	7.50	15.00
20 Tony Stewart Home Depot Peanuts Black	7.50	15.00
20 Tony Stewart Home Depot Peanuts Orange	7.50	15.00
24 Jeff Gordon DuPont Flames Yosemite Sam	7.50	15.00
24 Jeff Gordon Pepsi	7.50	15.00
25 Joe Nemechek UAW-Delphi Speedy Gonzalez	7.50	15.00
29 Kevin Harvick Goodwrench Taz	7.50	15.00
30 Jeff Green AOL Daffy	7.50	15.00
38 Elliott Sadler M&M's	7.50	15.00
48 Jimmie Johnson Lowe's Sylvester&Tweety	7.50	15.00
88 Dale Jarrett UPS brown logo	7.50	15.00
NNO Dale Earnhardt Legacy	10.00	20.00

2004 Winner's Circle Race Hood 1:43

8 Dale Earnhardt Jr. JR	10.00	20.00
9 Bill Elliott Dodge Lion King	10.00	20.00

2010 Winner's Circle 1:43

14 Tony Stewart Old Spice Swagger	10.00	20.00
24 Jeff Gordon National Guard	10.00	20.00
88 Dale Earnhardt Jr. AMP Black	10.00	20.00

1996 Winner's Circle 1:64

2 Mike Bliss ASE SuperTruck	4.00	8.00
3 Dale Earnhardt Goodwrench	15.00	30.00
16 Ron Hornaday NAPA SuperTruck	4.00	8.00
24 Jeff Gordon DuPont	6.00	15.00
31 Mike Skinner Lowe's	4.00	8.00
88 Dale Jarrett Quality Care	5.00	12.00

1997 Winner's Circle 1:64

This series marks the teaming of Action Performance and Hasbro. This line of cars was produced for and distributed to mass-market retailers. Some 1996 pieces were re-released in early 1997 with only the addition of a sticker that read "1997 Stock Car Series" over the 1996 year on the front of the package. On those, the copyright line still reads 1996 on the back.

2 Mike Bliss Team ASE SuperTruck	2.00	6.00
3 Dale Earnhardt Goodwrench	15.00	30.00
3 Jay Sauter Goodwrench SuperTruck	2.00	6.00
16 Ron Hornaday NAPA	3.00	8.00
18 Bobby Labonte Interstate Batteries	2.00	6.00
22 Ward Burton MBNA	2.00	6.00
22 Ward Burton MBNA Gold	2.00	6.00
24 Jeff Gordon DuPont	5.00	10.00
24 Jeff Gordon DuPont Million $ Date	5.00	10.00
27 Kenny Irwin	4.00	8.00

G.I. Joe
27 Kenny Irwin 4.00 8.00
Tonka
31 Mike Skinner 2.00 6.00
Lowe's
81 Kenny Wallace 2.00 6.00
Square D
88 Dale Jarrett 2.00 6.00
Quality Care

1996-97 Winner's Circle Lifetime Dale Earnhardt 1:64

2 Dale Earnhardt 12.50 30.00
Curb 1980 Olds 4/12
LTS Logo on package
2 Dale Earnhardt 12.50 30.00
Curb 1980 Olds 4/12
no LTS Logo on backer
2 Dale Earnhardt 10.00 25.00
Wrangler 1981 Pontiac 8/12
3 Dale Earnhardt 10.00 25.00
Wrangler 1984 Monte Carlo 9/12
3 Dale Earnhardt 10.00 25.00
Wrangler 1986 Monte Carlo 10/12
3 Dale Earnhardt 15.00 30.00
Goodwrench 1988 Camaro 7/12
LTS logo on package
3 Dale Earnhardt 15.00 30.00
Goodwrench 1988 Camaro 7/12
no LTS logo on backer
3 Dale Earnhardt 10.00 20.00
Lowes 1989 Pontiac 11/12
3 Dale Earnhardt 10.00 25.00
Goodwrench 1990 Lumina 12/12
3 Dale Earnhardt 10.00 25.00
Goodwrench Silver
1995 Monte Carlo 3/12
1996 package
3 Dale Earnhardt 10.00 25.00
Goodwrench Silver
1995 Monte Carlo 3/12
1997 Package
3 D.Earnhardt 10.00 25.00
GW Silver '95 MC 3/12
LTS logo on package
with red number and lettering
3 Dale Earnhardt 10.00 25.00
Goodwrench Silver
1995 Monte Carlo 3/12
LTS logo on package
with orange number and lettering
3 Dale Earnhardt 25.00 60.00
AC Delco 1996 Monte Carlo 2/12
3 Dale Earnhardt 10.00 25.00
Goodwrench 1997 Monte
Carlo 1/12
1997 package
3 Dale Earnhardt 10.00 25.00
Goodwrench 1997
Monte Carlo 1/12
LTS logo on package
3 Dale Earnhardt 15.00 30.00
Wheaties 1997 Monte
Carlo 5/12
no LTS Logo on package
3 Dale Earnhardt 15.00 30.00
Wheaties 1997 Monte
Carlo 5/12 with LTS Logo
on package and gray interior
3 Dale Earnhardt 15.00 30.00
Wheaties 1997 Monte
Carlo 5/12 with LTS Logo
on package and orange interior
3 Dale Earnhardt 50.00 100.00
Wheaties 1997 Monte
Carlo 5/12 with LTS Logo
on package and gray interior
with Wheaties trading card
8 Dale Earnhardt 12.50 30.00
RPM 1975 Dodge
Charger Bonus
98 Dale Earnhardt 15.00 40.00
1978 Monte Carlo 6/12
LTS logo on package
98 Dale Earnhardt 15.00 40.00
1978 Monte Carlo 6/12
no LTS logo on package

1996-97 Winner's Circle Lifetime Jeff Gordon 1:64

1 Jeff Gordon 5.00 12.00
Baby Ruth 1992 Thunderbird 4/6
1 Jeff Gordon 6.00 15.00
Carolina 1991 Thunderbird 5/6
24 Jeff Gordon 8.00 20.00
DuPont 1993 Lumina 6/6
with car card
24 Jeff Gordon 8.00 20.00
DuPont 1993 Lumina 6/6
with Gordon card and
LTS logo on package
24 Jeff Gordon 8.00 20.00
DuPont 1993 Lumina 6/6
with Gordon card and
no LTS logo on package
24 Jeff Gordon 8.00 20.00
DuPont 1997 MC 1/6
1996 Package
24 Jeff Gordon 8.00 20.00
DuPont 1997 Monte Carlo 1/6
1997 Package
24 Jeff Gordon 8.00 20.00
DuPont 1997 Monte Carlo 1/6
LTS logo on package
24 Jeff Gordon 6.00 12.50
DuPont 1997 Million Dollar Date
LTS Bonus
24 Jeff Gordon 10.00 25.00
DuPont ChromaPremiere
1997 Monte Carlo 2/6
1996 Package
24 Jeff Gordon 10.00 25.00
DuPont ChromaPremiere
1997 Monte Carlo 2/6
1997 Package
24 Jeff Gordon 10.00 20.00
Lost World
1997 Monte Carlo 3/6
LTS logo on package
24 Jeff Gordon 10.00 20.00
Lost World
1997 Monte Carlo 3/6
no LTS logo on package
40 Jeff Gordon 12.00 30.00
1987 Sprint bonus
LTS logo on left edge
40 Jeff Gordon 12.00 30.00
1987 Sprint bonus
LTS logo in upper right

1997 Winner's Circle Lifetime Darrell Waltrip 1:64

17 Darrell Waltrip 6.00 12.00
Parts America 1975-1980 Paint 1/6
17 Darrell Waltrip 6.00 12.00
Parts America 1981-1982 Paint 4/6
17 Darrell Waltrip 6.00 12.00
Parts America 1983 Paint 6/6
17 Darrell Waltrip 6.00 12.00
Parts America 1984-1986 Paint 5/6
17 Darrell Waltrip 6.00 12.00
Parts America 1990-1997 Paint 3/6
17 Darrell Waltrip 6.00 12.00
Parts America Chroma 1997 Paint 2/6

1998 Winner's Circle 1:64

These blister packs include one 1:64 die-cast car and a red bordered card of the featured driver. The NASCAR 50th Anniversary logo is also featured on the packaging.

1 Dale Earnhardt Jr. 7.50 15.00
Coke
1 Steve Park 4.00 10.00
Pennzoil
2 Rusty Wallace 6.00 15.00
Adventures of Rusty
2 Rusty Wallace 6.00 15.00
Elvis
2 Rusty Wallace 5.00 12.00
Rusty
3 Dale Earnhardt 12.50 25.00
Coke
3 Dale Earnhardt 25.00 50.00
Goodwrench
3 Dale Earnhardt 25.00 50.00
Goodwrench
with 25th Anniversary sticker
3 Dale Earnhardt 15.00 30.00
Goodwrench Plus
1998 Preview blister
3 Dale Earnhardt 25.00 50.00
Goodwrench Plus
Daytona 500 blister
3 Dale Earnhardt 20.00 40.00
Goodwrench Plus
Toy's R Us blister
3 Dale Earnhardt Jr. 10.00 25.00
AC Delco
3 Dale Earnhardt Jr. 10.00 25.00
AC Delco Busch Champion
3/3 Dale Earnhardt 25.00 50.00
Goodwrench 25th
Wrangler 2-car set
12 Jeremy Mayfield 4.00 10.00
Mobil 1
16 Ron Hornaday 4.00 10.00
NAPA SuperTruck
18 Bobby Labonte 6.00 15.00
Interstate Batteries
18 Bobby Labonte 12.50 25.00
Interstate Batteries Hot Rod
18 Bobby Labonte 8.00 20.00
Interstate Batteries
Small Soldiers
22 Ward Burton 4.00 10.00
MBNA
24 Jeff Gordon 12.50 30.00
DuPont Champion 11/16/97
with figure
24 Jeff Gordon 8.00 20.00
uPont 1998 Preview blister
24 Jeff Gordon 8.00 20.00
DuPont 1998
Winston Cup Champion
24 Jeff Gordon 8.00 20.00
DuPont Daytona 500 blister
24 Jeff Gordon 8.00 20.00
DuPont Million Dollar win card
24 Jeff Gordon 6.00 15.00
DuPont Walmart blister
28 Kenny Irwin 5.00 12.00
Havoline
28 Kenny Irwin 5.00 12.00
Havoline 1998 Rookie of the Year
28 Kenny Irwin 6.00 15.00
Havoline Joker
28 Kenny Irwin 5.00 12.00
Havoline Speedweek
Special card
31 Dale Earnhardt Jr. 6.00 15.00
Sikkens Blue
31 Mike Skinner 4.00 10.00
Lowe's Japan Win
31 Mike Skinner 4.00 10.00
Lowe's Rookie of the Year
32 Dale Jarrett 6.00 15.00
White Rain
33 Ken Schrader 4.00 10.00
Schrader
40 Coca-Cola Racing 4.00 10.00
44 Tony Stewart 8.00 20.00
Shell
44 Tony Stewart 8.00 20.00
Shell Small Soldiers
81 Kenny Wallace 4.00 10.00
Square D
88 Dale Jarrett 6.00 15.00
Quality Care
88 Dale Jarrett 6.00 15.00
Quality Care Batman
88 Dale Jarrett 6.00 15.00
Quality Care Million Dollar Win
88 Dale Jarrett 6.00 15.00
Quality Care
Speedweek Special card

1998 Winner's Circle Lifetime Dale Earnhardt 1:64

K2 Dale Earnhardt 15.00 30.00
Pink 1956 Ford 6/11
3 Dale Earnhardt 20.00 40.00
Goodwrench 1991 Champ 1/11
Stock Car Series card
3 Dale Earnhardt 20.00 40.00
Goodwrench 1991 Champ 1/11
High Performance Collectibles card
3 Dale Earnhardt 10.00 20.00
Goodwrench 1998 Monte Carlo 2/11
3 Dale Earnhardt 12.50 25.00
Goodwrench 1994 Champ 4/11
3 Dale Earnhardt 20.00 40.00
Wrangler 1985 Monte Carlo 5/11
3 Dale Earnhardt 12.50 25.00
Goodwrench 1998 Bass Pro 7/11
3 Dale Earnhardt 20.00 40.00
Goodwrench 1993 Champ. 8/11
3 Dale Earnhardt 20.00 40.00
Wrangler 1987 Champion 9/11
3 Dale Earnhardt 10.00 20.00
Goodwrench 1996 Olympic 10/11
3 Dale Earnhardt 15.00 30.00
Goodwrench 1988 Monte
Carlo fastback 11/11
15 Dale Earnhardt 12.50 25.00
Wrangler 1982 Thunderbird 3/11

1998 Winner's Circle Lifetime Jeff Gordon 1:64

16 Jeff Gordon 15.00 30.00
1985 Sprint car
24 Jeff Gordon 8.00 20.00
DuPont 1994 First Win
24 Jeff Gordon 5.00 12.00
DuPont 1998 Monte Carlo
Stock Car Series card
24 Jeff Gordon 5.00 12.00
DuPont 1998 Monte Carlo
High Performance Collectibles card

1999 Winner's Circle Lifetime Alan Kulwicki 1:64

7 Alan Kulwicki 4.00 10.00
Hooters 1992 Thunderbird 1/3
7 Alan Kulwicki 5.00 10.00
Army 1991 Thunderbird 3/3
7 Alan Kulwicki 4.00 10.00
Zerex 1990 Thunderbird 2/3

1998 Winner's Circle Pit Row 1:64

Cars in this set are displayed on pit road being serviced by the crew. Some were issued with variations in the position of the car and/or the crew members as noted below. Others were issued in blister packaging that did or did not include a Fanscan logo.

1 Dale Earnhardt Jr. 7.50 15.00
Coke
1 Steve Park 7.50 15.00
Pennzoil left side raised
2 Rusty Wallace 7.50 15.00
Rusty offical behind car
2 Rusty Wallace 7.50 15.00
Rusty no offical
2 Rusty Wallace 7.50 15.00
Elvis Fanscan package
3 Dale Earnhardt 15.00 30.00
Coke
3 Dale Earnhardt 20.00 35.00
Goodwrench 25th Anniversary
3 Dale Earnhardt 25.00 50.00
Goodwrench Bass Pro
3 Dale Earnhardt 12.50 30.00
Goodwrench Plus
jumping over wall
3 Dale Earnhardt 12.50 30.00
Goodwrench Plus
changing tires
with gray interior
3 Dale Earnhardt 12.50 30.00
Goodwrench Plus
changing tires
with red interior
3 Dale Earnhardt 6.00 15.00
Goodwrench Plus Daytona
Pit Road Celebration
3 Dale Earnhardt 6.00 15.00
Goodwrench Plus Daytona
Victory Donuts
3 Dale Earnhardt Jr. 7.50 15.00
AC Delco tires off
3 Dale Earnhardt Jr. 7.50 15.00
AC Delco Fanscan package
12 Jeremy Mayfield 7.50 15.00
Mobil 1 tires on ground
18 Bobby Labonte 7.50 15.00
Interstate Batteries
left side raised
18 Bobby Labonte 7.50 15.00
Interstate Batteries
Small Soldiers
22 Ward Burton 7.50 15.00
MBNA
24 Jeff Gordon 7.50 15.00
DuPont Fanscan package
left side raised
24 Jeff Gordon 7.50 15.00
DuPont Fanscan package
four tires on ground
24 Jeff Gordon 7.50 15.00
DuPont approaching to
change right rear tire
24 Jeff Gordon 7.50 15.00
DuPont right rear tire
already changed
24 Jeff Gordon 7.50 15.00
Pepsi
28 Kenny Irwin 7.50 15.00
Havoline in pit stall
28 Kenny Irwin 7.50 15.00
Havoline Joker
31 Mike Skinner 7.50 15.00
Lowe's in pit stall
33 Ken Schrader 7.50 15.00
Schrader
81 Kenny Wallace 6.00 15.00
Square D
88 Dale Jarrett 7.50 15.00
Quality Care
right side raised
88 Dale Jarrett 10.00 25.00
Quality Care Batman

1998 Winner's Circle Tech Series 1:64

3 Dale Earnhardt 12.50 30.00
Goodwrench
12 Jeremy Mayfield 4.00 8.00
Mobil 1
24 Jeff Gordon 7.50 20.00
DuPont
28 Kenny Irwin 4.00 8.00
Havoline
88 Dale Jarrett 4.00 8.00
Quality Care

1998-99 Winner's Circle Championship with Figure 1:64

2 Dale Earnhardt 7.50 15.00
1980 Championship
3 Dale Earnhardt 7.50 15.00
Goodwrench 1993 Champion
3 Dale Earnhardt 7.50 15.00
Goodwrench 1994 Champion
3 Dale Earnhardt 7.50 15.00
Goodwrench Plus
1998 Daytona 500
3 Dale Earnhardt 7.50 15.00
Wrangler 1986 Championship
3 Dale Earnhardt 7.50 15.00
Wrangler 1987 Championship
3 Dale Earnhardt Jr. 6.00 12.00
AC Delco
1998 BGN Champion
7 Alan Kulwicki 5.00 10.00
Hooters 1999
24 Jeff Gordon 5.00 10.00
DuPont 1995 Championship
24 Jeff Gordon 5.00 10.00
DuPont 1997 Championship
24 Jeff Gordon 5.00 10.00
DuPont 1998 Championship
24 Jeff Gordon 5.00 10.00
DuPont 1999 Daytona 500

1998-99 Winner's Circle Cool Customs 1:64

Cool Customs includes a 1:64 scale vintage stock car painted in the color scheme of the featured driver's current stock car. Each piece was packaged in a blister pack along with a trading card of the driver unless noted below. The cars were produced by Hasbro.

1/3 Dale Earnhardt Jr. 12.50 25.00
Dale Earnhardt
Coke 2-car set
no card included
2 Rusty Wallace 5.00 12.00
Rusty 1965 Ford Galaxie
2 Rusty Wallace 6.00 15.00
Rusty
Adventures of Rusty
2-car set
3 Dale Earnhardt 12.50 25.00
Goodwrench 1957 Chevy hardtop
3 Dale Earnhardt 12.50 25.00
Goodwrench 1957 Chevy Convertible
3 Dale Earnhardt 15.00 30.00
Goodwrench Silver 1957 Chevy hardtop
3 Dale Earnhardt Jr. 6.00 15.00
AC Delco 1957 Chevy hardtop
12 Jeremy Mayfield 4.00 10.00
Mobil 1 1956 Fairlane
24 Jeff Gordon 6.00 15.00
DuPont 1957 Chevy Convertible
24 Jeff Gordon 6.00 15.00
DuPont 1963 Chevy Impala
24 Jeff Gordon 6.00 15.00
Pepsi 1957 Chevy 1999
24 Jeff Gordon 6.00 15.00
Pepsi Superman
1957 Chevy 1999
28 Kenny Irwin 5.00 12.00
Havoline 1956 Ford Crown Victoria
88 Dale Jarrett 5.00 12.00
Quality Care
1956 Ford Crown Victoria
88 Dale Jarrett 5.00 12.00
Quality Care
1965 Ford Galaxie

1998-99 Winner's Circle Fantasy Pack 1:64

This set includes a plane, a boat, and a car all in same paint.

3 Dale Earnhardt 10.00 25.00
Goodwrench Plus 1998
3 Dale Earnhardt 10.00 25.00
Goodwrench 1999
3 Dale Earnhardt 10.00 25.00
Wrangler
3 Dale Earnhardt Jr. 6.00 15.00
AC Delco
24 Jeff Gordon 6.00 15.00
DuPont
24 Jeff Gordon 6.00 15.00
DuPont 1999
24 Jeff Gordon 6.00 15.00
DuPont Superman 1999
24 Jeff Gordon 6.00 15.00
Pepsi

1999 Winner's Circle 1:64

This line is the result of an alliance between Action and Hasbro to bring exclusive licenses such as Gordon and Earnhardt to the mass market.

1 Steve Park 2.50 6.00
Pennzoil
2 Rusty Wallace 2.50 6.00
Rusty
2 Rusty Wallace 8.00 20.00
Rusty True to Texas
3 Dale Earnhardt 12.50 25.00
Goodwrench Plus
3 Dale Earnhardt Jr. 4.00 10.00
AC Delco
3 Dale Earnhardt Jr. 5.00 12.00
AC Delco Superman
8 Dale Earnhardt Jr. 6.00 15.00
Dale
12 Jeremy Mayfield 2.50 6.00
Mobil 1
12 Jeremy Mayfield 2.50 6.00
Mobil 1 Kentucky Derby
16 Ron Hornaday 2.50 6.00
NAPA '98 Champ
18 Bobby Labonte 3.00 8.00
Interstate Batteries
19 Mike Skinner 5.00 12.00
Yellow Freight
20 Tony Stewart 10.00 25.00
Home Depot
20 Tony Stewart 8.00 20.00
Home Depot with rookie stripe
22 Ward Burton 2.50 6.00
Caterpillar
24 Jeff Gordon 5.00 12.00
DuPont
24 Jeff Gordon 6.00 15.00
DuPont LTS package
24 Jeff Gordon 6.00 15.00
Pepsi Star Wars
28 Kenny Irwin 3.00 8.00
Havoline
31 Dale Earnhardt Jr. 5.00 12.00
Gargoyles
31 Dale Earnhardt Jr. 5.00 12.00
Wrangler
31 Mike Skinner 6.00 15.00
Kolbalt
31 Mike Skinner 2.50 6.00
Lowe's
33 Ken Schrader 2.50 6.00
APR
55 Kenny Wallace 2.50 6.00
Square D
88 Dale Jarrett 2.50 6.00
Quality Care
88 Dale Jarrett 2.50 6.00
Quality Care No Bull 5 win
88 Dale Jarrett 2.50 6.00
Quality Care White

1999 Winner's Circle 24K Gold 1:64

These cars are gold plated on a gold plated base.

3 Dale Earnhardt 25.00 50.00
Goodwrench
3 Dale Earnhardt Jr. 12.00 20.00
AC Delco
24 Jeff Gordon 12.00 20.00
DuPont
24 Jeff Gordon 12.00 20.00
Pepsi

1999 Winner's Circle Lifetime Dale Earnhardt 1:64

2 Dale Earnhardt 7.50 15.00
1979 Rookie of the Year 1/13
2 Dale Earnhardt 10.00 20.00
Wrangler 1980 7/13
3 Dale Earnhardt 10.00 20.00
Wrangler 1984 11/13
3 Dale Earnhardt 10.00 20.00
Wrangler 1987 5/13
3 Dale Earnhardt 7.50 15.00
Goodwrench 1989 Lumina 6/13
3 Dale Earnhardt 7.50 15.00
Goodwrench 1995 Brickyard Win 2/13
3 Dale Earnhardt 7.50 15.00
Goodwrench 1996 Monte Carlo 10/13
3 Dale Earnhardt 7.50 15.00
Goodwrench Wrangler 1999 8/13
8 Dale Earnhardt 7.50 15.00

Goodwrench 1988 Daytona 4/13
30 Dale Earnhardt Army 1976 Malibu 12/13 10.00 20.00
77 Dale Earnhardt Hi-Gain 1976 13/13 10.00 20.00

1999 Winner's Circle Lifetime Jeff Gordon 1:64

4 Jeff Gordon Pepsi 1990 Midget 8/8 7.50 15.00
24 Jeff Gordon DuPont 1992 Lumina 7/8 5.00 12.50
24 Jeff Gordon DuPont 1995 Cup Champ 4/8 5.00 12.50
24 Jeff Gordon DuPont 1999 Monte Carlo 1/8 5.00 12.50
24 Jeff Gordon DuPont 1999 Test 6/8 10.00 20.00
24 Jeff Gordon DuPont Superman 5/8 6.00 15.00
24 Jeff Gordon Pepsi 1999 Monte Carlo 2/8 6.00 12.00
67 Jeff Gordon Outback 1990 Grand Prix 3/8 10.00 20.00

1999 Winner's Circle Pit Row 1:64

1 Steve Park Pennzoil tires off 7.50 15.00
3 Dale Earnhardt Goodwrench 10.00 20.00
3 Dale Earnhardt Goodwrench 25th Anniv. 10.00 20.00
3 D.Earnhardt Goodwrench '95 Brickyard 10.00 20.00
3 Dale Earnhardt Wrangler 15.00 30.00
3 Dale Earnhardt Wrangler tires off 15.00 30.00
3 Dale Earnhardt Jr. AC Delco left side raised 7.50 15.00
3 Dale Earnhardt Jr. AC Delco Superman 7.50 15.00
12 Jeremy Mayfield Mobil 1 tires off 7.50 15.00
18 Bobby Labonte Interstate Batteries right side raised 6.00 15.00
20 Tony Stewart Home Depot 15.00 30.00
22 Ward Burton Caterpillar 6.00 15.00
24 Jeff Gordon Dupont tires off 7.50 15.00
24 Jeff Gordon Dupont tires off Kellogg's package 7.50 15.00
24 Jeff Gordon Superman pulling in 8.00 20.00
24 Jeff Gordon Superman pulling out 8.00 20.00
27 Casey Atwood Castrol 12.50 25.00
28 Kenny Irwin Havoline pulling out 7.50 15.00
31 Mike Skinner Lowe's Union 76 package 7.50 15.00
88 Dale Jarrett Quality Care tires on ground 7.50 15.00

1999 Winner's Circle Silver Series 1:64

2 Dale Earnhardt 1980 Champ 1/7 15.00 45.00
3 Dale Earnhardt 1986 Champ 2/7 15.00 45.00
3 Dale Earnhardt 1987 Champ 3/7 15.00 45.00
3 Dale Earnhardt 1990 Champ 4/7 15.00 45.00
3 Dale Earnhardt 1991 Champ 5/7 15.00 45.00
3 Dale Earnhardt 1993 Champ 6/7 15.00 45.00
3 Dale Earnhardt 1994 Champ 7/7 15.00 45.00

1999 Winner's Circle Speedweeks 1:64

These 7-cars were released at Speedweeks as a preview to the 1999 Daytona 500. Each is packaged in a blister with the Daytona 500 and Speedweeks 1999 logos on the front. A gold bordered card was also packaged with each car.

2 Rusty Wallace Rusty 4.00 8.00
3 Dale Earnhardt Goodwrench 15.00 30.00
12 Jeremy Mayfield Mobil 1 4.00 8.00
18 Bobby Labonte Interstate Batteries 4.00 8.00
24 Jeff Gordon DuPont 5.00 10.00
28 Kenny Irwin Havoline 4.00 8.00
88 Dale Jarrett Quality Care 4.00 8.00

1999 Winner's Circle Stats and Standings 1:64

This set was issued with a 1:64 car and a large "Stats and Standings" driver guide book. Both pieces were packaged in a large blister pack.

2 Rusty Wallace Rusty 4.00 10.00
3 Dale Earnhardt Goodwrench 6.00 15.00
24 Jeff Gordon DuPont 5.00 12.00
88 Dale Jarrett Quality Care 4.00 10.00

1999 Winner's Circle Tech Series 1:64

These 1:64 scale cars feature bodies that are removable from the chassis.

2 Rusty Wallace Penske 4.00 8.00
3 Dale Earnhardt Jr. AC Delco 7.50 15.00
18 Bobby Labonte Interstate Batteries 7.50 20.00
24 Jeff Gordon DuPont Superman 7.50 20.00
31 Mike Skinner Lowe's 3.00 8.00

1999 Winner's Circle Track Support Crew 1:64

This set features Support vehicles in the drivers colors.

3 Dale Earnhardt Goodwrench 15.00 30.00
3 Dale Earnhardt Jr. AC Delco 10.00 20.00
24 Jeff Gordon DuPont 12.50 25.00
24 Jeff Gordon Pepsi 10.00 20.00

1999 Winner's Circle Victory Lane 1:64

3 Dale Earnhardt Goodwrench Daytona Win 2/15/98 25.00 50.00
24 Jeff Gordon DuPont Daytona 2/14/99 8.00 16.00

2000 Winner's Circle Sneak Previews 1:64

Winner's Circle took on a new look for 2000 by packaging the car at an angle on the blister pack. Each car and card combo package also included the NASCAR 2000 logo and the "Sneak Preview Series" set name.

2 Rusty Wallace Rusty 3.00 8.00
3 Dale Earnhardt GM Goodwrench Sign 12.50 25.00
18 Bobby Labonte Interstate Batteries 3.00 8.00
20 Tony Stewart Home Depot First Win 4.00 8.00
24 Jeff Gordon DuPont 5.00 10.00
27 Casey Atwood Castrol New Stars of NASCAR 3.00 8.00
31 Mike Skinner Lowe's 3.00 8.00
36 Ken Schrader M&M's with M&M's card 3.00 8.00
88 Dale Jarrett Quality Care 3.00 8.00

2000 Winner's Circle 1:64

3 Dale Earnhardt GM Goodwrench Sign 12.50 25.00
3 Dale Earnhardt Goodwrench 15.00 30.00
5 Terry Labonte Kellogg's NASCAR Racers 10.00 20.00
8 Dale Earnhardt Jr. New Stars Black Roof 5.00 12.00
8 Dale Earnhardt Jr. New Stars Red Roof 5.00 12.00
18 Bobby Labonte Interstate Batteries 4.00 10.00
18 Bobby Labonte Interstate Batteries NASCAR Racers 7.50 15.00
20 Tony Stewart Home Depot First Win 4.00 10.00
20 Tony Stewart Home Depot Three Win Rookie 4.00 10.00
24 Jeff Gordon DuPont NASCAR Racers 10.00 20.00
27 Casey Atwood Castrol 4.00 10.00
27 Casey Atwood Castrol New Stars 4.00 10.00
28 Ricky Rudd Havoline 4.00 10.00
31 Mike Skinner Lowe's 4.00 10.00
36 Ernie Irvan M&M's 4.00 10.00
55 Kenny Wallace Square D NASCAR Racers 5.00 12.00
88 Dale Jarrett Quality Care 1999 Winston Cup Champion 4.00 10.00

2000 Winner's Circle Cool Customs 1:64

24 Jeff Gordon Pepsi 1957 Convertible 4.00 8.00
24 Jeff Gordon Superman 1957 Chevy Hard Top 4.00 8.00

2000 Winner's Circle Deluxe Race Hood 1:64

These 1:64 scale cars were packaged with a larger replica hood painted in the sponsor's colors. Both were issued in a blue blister pack with many also featuring the NASCAR 2000 and Hasbro logos. Some packages read "Deluxe Collection" only as a set name while others include the name "Deluxe Race Hood Series."

3 Dale Earnhardt Goodwrench 25.00 40.00
3 Dale Earnhardt Goodwrench Sign 20.00 40.00
3 Dale Earnhardt Goodwrench Peter Max 40.00 80.00
3 Dale Earnhardt Taz No Bull 12.50 30.00
8 Dale Earnhardt Jr. Dale Jr. black roof no remington 15.00 30.00
8 Dale Earnhardt Jr. Dale Jr. black roof Remington on deck lid 30.00 60.00
8 Dale Earnhardt Jr. Dale Jr. red roof no Remington 20.00 35.00
8 Dale Earnhardt Jr. Dale Jr. red roof Remington on deck lid 50.00 100.00
18 Bobby Labonte Interstate Batteries 4.00 10.00
20 Tony Stewart Home Depot 6.00 15.00
20 Tony Stewart Home Depot Habitat 6.00 15.00
20 Tony Stewart Home Depot Kids 15.00 30.00
24 Jeff Gordon DuPont Corian deck lid 10.00 20.00
24 Jeff Gordon DuPont Tyvek deck lid 10.00 20.00
24 Jeff Gordon DuPont Silver 15.00 25.00
24 Jeff Gordon Pepsi 5.00 12.00
27 Casey Atwood Castrol 4.00 10.00
28 Ricky Rudd Havoline 4.00 10.00
31 Mike Skinner Lowe's 12.50 25.00
36 Ken Schrader M&M's 10.00 20.00
88 Dale Jarrett Quality Care 4.00 10.00
94 Bill Elliott McDonald's 12.50 25.00

2000 Winner's Circle Deluxe Driver Sticker 1:64

These die-cast pieces entitled "Deluxe Driver Sticker Series" were packaged in a blue blister with a red stars and stripes design around the car. Each package also included an oversized driver sponsor sticker with the Hasbro logo at the bottom of the package. Some were issued in a blister package that read "Deluxe Collection" only at the top right hand corner.

4 Bobby Hamilton Kodak Navy 3.00 6.00
24 Jeff Gordon DuPont 5.00 10.00
24 Jeff Gordon DuPont Peanuts 6.00 15.00
25 Jerry Nadeau Holigan Homes Coast Guard 3.00 6.00
28 Ricky Rudd Havoline Marines 3.00 6.00
31 Mike Skinner Lowe's Army 3.00 6.00
88 Dale Jarrett Quality Care Air Force 3.00 6.00

2000-01 Winner's Circle Driver Hood 1:64

3 Dale Earnhardt Goodwrench 2000 car is horizontal in package 12.50 30.00
3 Dale Earnhardt Goodwrench 2001 car is slanted inside package 12.50 30.00
8 Dale Earnhardt Jr. Dale Jr. 10.00 20.00
9 Bill Elliott Dodge 6.00 15.00
18 Bobby Labonte Interstate Batteries 6.00 12.00
20 Tony Stewart Home Depot 12.50 25.00
NNO Dodge Test Gray 5.00 10.00

2000 Winner's Circle Deluxe Winston Cup Scene 1:64

These 1:64 scale cars were packaged with a miniature replica Winston Cup Scene magazine featuring a headline for that driver. Both were issued in a blue blister pack with many also featuring the NASCAR 2000 logo and all including the Hasbro manufacturer logo. Some packages read "Deluxe Collection" only as a set name while others include the name "Deluxe Winston Cup Scene Series."

2 Rusty Wallace Rusty 50th Win 3.00 8.00
3 Dale Earnhardt Goodwrench Richmond Win 15.00 30.00
8 Dale Earnhardt Jr. Dale Texas Win 5.00 12.00
88 Dale Jarrett Quality Care 1999 Winston Cup Champion 4.00 10.00

2000 Winner's Circle Lifetime Dale Earnhardt 1:64

3 Dale Earnhardt Goodwrench 1992 Chevy Lumina 5/6 15.00 30.00
3 Dale Earnhardt Goodwrench 1999 Chevy Monte Carlo Notchback 2/6 15.00 30.00
3 Dale Earnhardt Goodwrench 1999 Brickyard 1/6 15.00 30.00
3 Dale Earnhardt Goodwrench 2000 Chevy Monte Carlo 3/6 15.00 30.00
15 Dale Earnhardt Wrangler 1983 Thunderbird 4/6 15.00 30.00

2000 Winner's Circle Lifetime Jeff Gordon 1:64

4 Jeff Gordon Beast 1990 Sprint Car 2/6 15.00 30.00
24 Jeff Gordon DuPont 1992 Lumina 4/6 4.00 10.00
24 Jeff Gordon DuPont 1993 Lumina 5/6 5.00 10.00
24 Jeff Gordon DuPont 1996 Monte Carlo 6/6 4.00 10.00
24 Jeff Gordon DuPont 2000 Monte Carlo 3/6 4.00 10.00
24 Jeff Gordon Pepsi 2000 Monte Carlo 1/6 4.00 10.00

2000 Winner's Circle New Stars 1:64

8 Dale Earnhardt Jr. Dale Jr. 5.00 10.00
20 Tony Stewart Home Depot 4.00 10.00
27 Casey Atwood Castrol 3.00 8.00

2001 Winner's Circle Classic Hood 1:64

3 Dale Earnhardt Goodwrench Silver Select 1995 10.00 20.00
24 Jeff Gordon ChromaPremier 10.00 20.00

2001 Winner's Circle Driver Sticker 1:64

These die-cast pieces entitled "Driver Sticker Collection" were packaged in a blue blister with a red stars and stripes design around the car. Each package also included an oversized driver sponsor sticker with the Hasbro logo at the bottom of the package.The oval sticker was produced slightly slanted in 2001 versus the traditional oval shaped sticker for 2002.

3 Dale Earnhardt Goodwrench 12.50 25.00
8 Dale Earnhardt Jr. Dale Jr. July 4th 5.00 10.00
8 Dale Earnhardt Jr. 2001 MLB All-Star Game 5.00 12.00
9 Bill Elliott Dodge 4.00 8.00
19 Casey Atwood Dodge 4.00 10.00
20 Tony Stewart Home Depot 5.00 10.00
24 Jeff Gordon DuPont Flames 6.00 15.00
24 Jeff Gordon DuPont Peanuts 6.00 15.00
28 Ricky Rudd Havoline 4.00 10.00
36 Ken Schrader M&M's 3.00 8.00
88 Dale Jarrett UPS 4.00 10.00

2001 Winner's Circle Gallery 1:64

This series of 1:64 die-cast pieces was issued in the typical blue with red stars Winner's Circle blister packaging. Each car was accompanied by a large framed work of art featuring the subject of the car or team sponsorship. The set title "Gallery Series" is clearly labeled in the upper right hand corner of the blister pack.

1 Steve Park Pennzoil Sylvester & Tweety 7.50 15.00
5 Terry Labonte Kellogg's Road Runner and Wile E. Coyote 7.50 15.00
24 Jeff Gordon DuPont Bugs Bunny 7.50 15.00
29 Kevin Harvick Goodwrench Taz 7.50 15.00
30 Jeff Green AOL Daffy Duck 7.50 15.00
31 Mike Skinner Lowe's Yosemite Sam 7.50 15.00
55 Bobby Hamilton Square D Marvin the Martian 7.50 15.00

2001 Winner's Circle License Plate Series 1:64

3 Dale Earnhardt Goodwrench 15.00 40.00
8 Dale Earnhardt Jr. Dale Jr. 6.00 15.00
9 Bill Elliott Dodge 5.00 12.00
18 Bobby Labonte Interstate Batteries 5.00 12.00
20 Tony Stewart Home Depot 6.00 12.00
28 Ricky Rudd Havoline 4.00 10.00
36 Ken Schrader M&M's 4.00 10.00

2001-02 Winner's Circle Lifetime Dale Earnhardt 1:64

Winner's Circle used its typical blue blister pack with the 1:64 scale Lifetime Series. The series takes a look at the various rides of five top drivers on the Winston Cup circuit with each piece including a series number. A card commemorating the historical ride or an event in the life of the featured driver was also included with each piece. The series started in 2001 and was continued with some pieces being released in 2002.

2 Dale Earnhardt Hodgdon 1979 5/8 5.00 12.00
3 Dale Earnhardt Goodwrench 1993 6/8 5.00 12.00
3 Dale Earnhardt Goodwrench 1992 3/8 5.00 12.00
3 Dale Earnhardt Goodwrench 1994 1/8 5.00 12.00
3 Dale Earnhardt AC Delco 1997 4/8 5.00 12.00
3 Dale Earnhardt Goodwrench 2001 8/8 5.00 12.00
8 D.Earnhardt Goodwrench '86 7/8 5.00 12.00

2001-02 Winner's Circle Lifetime Dale Jr. 1:64

3 Dale Earnhardt Jr. Goodwrench 1996 4/5 5.00 12.00
8 Dale Earnhardt Jr. Dale Jr. 1999 1/5 10.00 20.00
8 Dale Earnhardt Jr. Dale 2001 5/5 5.00 12.00
31 Dale Earnhardt Jr. Mom 'N' Pops 1996 3/5 5.00 12.00
31 Dale Earnhardt Jr. Sikkens White 1997 2/5 5.00 12.00

2001-02 Winner's Circle Lifetime Jeff Gordon 1:64

6 Jeff Gordon Sprint Car 1989 4/6 5.00 12.00
24 Jeff Gordon DuPont Brickyard 1994 3/6 5.00 12.00
24 Jeff Gordon DuPont Chromalusion 1998 6/6 5.00 12.00
24 Jeff Gordon DuPont 50th Win 1/6 5.00 12.00
24 Jeff Gordon DuPont 2000 2/6 5.00 12.00
24 Jeff Gordon DuPont Flames 2001 5/6 5.00 12.00

2001-02 Winner's Circle Lifetime Dale Jarrett 1:64

28 Dale Jarrett Havoline 1995 1/4 4.00 10.00
88 Dale Jarrett Quality Care 1996 3/4 4.00 10.00

2001-02 Winner's Circle Lifetime Tony Stewart 1:64

9 Tony Stewart Beast '95 1/5 10.00 25.00
15 Tony Stewart Vision 3 '96 3/5 5.00 12.00
20 Tony Stewart Home Depot 2001 4/5 5.00 12.00
44 Tony Stewart Shell 1998 2/5 5.00 12.00

2001-02 Winner's Circle Race Hood 1:64

These 1:64 cars were packaged with a plastic replica race hood. The packaging is a blister pack printed in blue with a white box in the upper right containing the set name of "Race Hood Series."

1 Steve Park Pennzoil 5.00 12.00
2 Kevin Harvick AC Delco 6.00 15.00
2 Rusty Wallace Rusty 10.00 20.00
2 Rusty Wallace Rusty Harley 10.00 20.00
3 Dale Earnhardt Goodwrench 7.50 20.00
3 Dale Earnhardt Goodwrench Oreo 15.00 40.00
3 Dale Earnhardt Goodwrench Silver 12.50 25.00
3 Dale Earnhardt Jr. Oreo 6.00 15.00
8 Dale Earnhardt Jr. Dale Jr. 6.00 12.00
9 Bill Elliott Dodge 5.00 12.00
15 Michael Waltrip NAPA 5.00 12.00
18 Bobby Labonte Interstate Batteries 5.00 12.00
18 Bobby Labonte Interstate Batteries Coke Bear 5.00 12.00
19 Casey Atwood Dodge 5.00 12.00
20 Tony Stewart Home Depot 6.00 12.00
20 Tony Stewart Home Depot Coke Bear 5.00 12.00
24 Jeff Gordon DuPont ChromaPremier 6.00 12.00
24 Jeff Gordon DuPont Flames 6.00 15.00
24 Jeff Gordon DuPont 200th Anniversary 6.00 12.00
24 Jeff Gordon Pepsi 2002 5.00 12.00
29 Kevin Harvick AOL 5.00 12.00
29 Kevin Harvick Goodwrench White 5.00 12.00
88 Dale Jarrett UPS 5.00 12.00
88 Dale Jarrett UPS Flames 2002 5.00 12.00
NNO Dodge Test Team 4.00 10.00

2001 Winner's Circle Sam Bass Gallery 1:64

This Sam Bass version of the Gallery Series includes a series of 1:64 die-cast pieces accompanied by a large framed work of art by noted racing artist Sam Bass. Each was issued in the typical blue with red stars Winner's Circle blister packaging with the set title "Sam Bass Gallery Series" clearly labeled on the front of the blister pack.

3 Dale Earnhardt AC Delco with Dale Jr. on artwork 10.00 20.00
3 Dale Earnhardt Goodwrench 7.50 15.00
3 Dale Earnhardt Goodwrench Bass Pro 7.50 15.00
3 Dale Earnhardt Goodwrench Plus 7.50 15.00
3 Dale Earnhardt Wrangler 7.50 15.00
7 Alan Kulwicki Hooters 6.00 15.00

2001 Winner's Circle Team Authentics 1:64

2 Rusty Wallace Rusty Firesuit 25.00 60.00
2 Rusty Wallace Rusty Sheetmetal 25.00 60.00
3 Dale Earnhardt Goodwrench Firesuit 100.00 200.00
3 Dale Earnhardt Goodwrench Taz Sheetmetal 75.00 150.00
8 Dale Earnhardt Jr. 50.00 100.00

Dale Jr. Firesuit
8 Dale Earnhardt Jr. 50.00 100.00
Dale Jr. Sheetmetal
18 Bobby Labonte 30.00 60.00
Interstate Batteries Firesuit
18 Bobby Labonte 30.00 60.00
Interstate Batteries Sheetmetal
20 Tony Stewart 50.00 120.00
Home Depot Firesuit
20 Tony Stewart 50.00 120.00
Home Depot Sheetmetal
24 Jeff Gordon 50.00 120.00
DuPont Firesuit
24 Jeff Gordon 50.00 120.00
DuPont Sheetmetal
28 Ricky Rudd 25.00 50.00
Havoline Firesuit
28 Ricky Rudd 25.00 50.00
Havoline Sheetmetal
31 Mike Skinner 15.00 30.00
Lowe's Firesuit
31 Mike Skinner 15.00 40.00
Lowe's Sheetmetal

2001 Winner's Circle Winston Cup Scene 1:64

18 Bobby Labonte 4.00 8.00
Interstate Batteries No Recount

2002 Winner's Circle Autographed Hood 1:64

The Autographed Hood Series is a 1:64 car packaged with a plastic replica hood featuring a facsimile driver autograph. Each is sealed in a blue and red blister pack.

3 Dale Earnhardt Jr. 5.00 12.00
Oreo
3 Dale Earnhardt Jr. 5.00 12.00
Nilla Wafers
9 Bill Elliott 6.00 15.00
Dodge Muppets
12 Kerry Earnhardt 6.00 15.00
Super Cuts
24 Jeff Gordon 5.00 12.00
DuPont 200th Anniversary
24 Jeff Gordon 6.00 15.00
Pepsi Daytona
29 Kevin Harvick 5.00 12.00
Action ET
29 Kevin Harvick 6.00 15.00
Goodwrench ET
29 Kevin Harvick 5.00 12.00
Reese's Fast Break

2002 Winner's Circle Die-Cast Kits 1:64

These 1:64 pieces were issued in a large blue window box with the date printed on the back within a copyright line. Each piece is a die-cast model kit that was to be assembled by the collector. The cars came complete with a small screwdriver to help assemble the model.

2 Rusty Wallace 6.00 12.00
Rusty
8 Dale Earnhardt Jr. 6.00 12.00
Dale Jr.
8 Dale Earnhardt Jr. 6.00 12.00
Looney Tunes
24 Jeff Gordon 6.00 12.00
DuPont Flames
24 Jeff Gordon 6.00 12.00
DuPont Bugs Rematch
29 Kevin Harvick 6.00 10.00
Goodwrench
40 Sterling Marlin 5.00 10.00
Sterling
41 Jimmy Spencer 6.00 10.00
Target
88 Dale Jarrett 6.00 10.00
UPS
88 Dale Jarrett 6.00 10.00
UPS Flames

2002 Winner's Circle Driver Sticker 1:64

The 2002 Drivers Sticker Series was packaged in the same blue and red blister pack design as 2001. Some 2001 pieces were re-issued in 2002 with only a slight difference in the packaging. However most of the stickers for 2002 are a slanted rectangular card with a photo of the driver, his car, or the sponsor logo on them. The year of issue can be found on the copyright line on the back of the blister.

2 Kerry Earnhardt 6.00 12.00
K Intimidator
2 Kevin Harvick 6.00 12.00
AC Delco '01 BGN Champ
8 Dale Earnhardt Jr. 6.00 12.00
Looney Tunes
8 Dale Earnhardt Jr. 6.00 12.00
2001 MLB All-Star Game
8 Dale Earnhardt Jr. 6.00 12.00
2002 MLB All Star Game
20 Tony Stewart 5.00 12.00
Home Depot Jurassic
24 Jeff Gordon 6.00 12.00
DuPont Bugs Rematch 2002
24 Jeff Gordon 5.00 10.00
DuPont Flames
24 Jeff Gordon 5.00 10.00
DuPont Flames
2001 WC Champ
29 Kevin Harvick 5.00 10.00
Goodwrench Taz
29 Kevin Harvick 6.00 12.00
Goodwrench White
2001 Rookie of the Year
48 Jimmie Johnson 6.00 12.00
Lowe's Sylvester

2002 Winner's Circle Fast Pack 1:64

15/1/8 Micheal Waltrip 7.50 15.00
NAPA
Steve Park
Pennzoil
Dale Earnhardt Jr.
Dale Jr.
19/9/7 Jeremy Mayfield 7.50 15.00
Dodge
Bill Elliott
Dodge
Casey Atwood
Sirius
29/30/31 Kevin Harvick 7.50 15.00
Goodwrench Silver
Jeff Green
AOL
Robby Gordon
Cingular

2002 Winner's Circle Gallery 1:64

The 2002 Gallery Series is nearly identical to the 2001 release but can be distinguished by the copyright line on the back of the package. Each die-cast piece was issued in the typical blue with red stars Winner's Circle blister packaging and included a large framed work of art featuring the subject of the car or team sponsorship. The set title "Gallery Series" is clearly labeled in the upper right hand corner of the blister pack.

20 Tony Stewart 7.50 15.00
Home Depot Coke Bear
24 Jeff Gordon 7.50 15.00
DuPont Flames
2001 WC Champ
29 Kevin Harvick 7.50 15.00
Goodwrench

2002 Winner's Circle Gift Pack 1:64

2 Rusty Wallace 10.00 20.00
Rusty
Rusty Harley
Mobil 25th Anniversary
8 Dale Earnhardt Jr. 15.00 30.00
Dale
Oreo
Nilla Wafers
20 Tony Stewart 10.00 25.00
Home Depot
Coke
Home Depot w
black trim
24 Jeff Gordon 15.00 30.00
Pepsi
DuPont Flames
DuPont 200th Anniversary
29 Kevin Harvick 10.00 25.00
Goodwrench White
Taz
Goodwrench Silver
88 Dale Jarrett 10.00 20.00
UPS '01
UPS '02
UPS Flames

2002 Winner's Circle Gift Pack With Photo 1:64

8 Dale Earnhardt Jr. 20.00 35.00
2001 All-Star Game
2002 All-Star Game
Dale Jr.
18 Bobby Labonte 18.00 30.00
Interstate Batteries
Interstate Batteries Muppets
Interstate Batteries Coke
20 Tony Stewart 18.00 30.00
Black Peanuts
Orange Peanuts
Home Depot
24 Jeff Gordon 20.00 35.00
DuPont Bugs
DuPont 200th Anniversary
DuPont Flames

2002 Winner's Circle Pit Pass Preview 1:64

These 1:64 cars were packaged with a plastic card that resembles a race day pit pass. The card includes a photo of the featured driver and the packaging is the usual Winner's Circle blue blister.

2 Rusty Wallace 5.00 10.00
Rusty
8 Dale Earnhardt Jr. 6.00 12.00
Dale Jr.
9 Bill Elliott 5.00 10.00
Dodge
15 Michael Waltrip 5.00 10.00
NAPA
18 Bobby Labonte 5.00 10.00
Interstate Batteries
19 Casey Atwood 5.00 10.00
Dodge
19 Jeremy Mayfield 5.00 10.00
Dodge
20 Tony Stewart 5.00 10.00
Home Depot
24 Jeff Gordon 5.00 10.00
DuPont Flames
28 Ricky Rudd 5.00 10.00
Havoline
29 Kevin Harvick 5.00 10.00
Goodwrench Silver
30 Jeff Green 5.00 10.00
AOL
31 Robby Gordon 5.00 10.00
Cingular
88 Dale Jarrett 5.00 10.00
UPS

2003 Winner's Circle Autographed Hood 1:64

This series is a continuation of the Winner's Circle Race Hoods. However each car and oversized hood was packaged in the new 2003 blister pack with the black printed portion at the top. Please note that no mention of "Race Hood" appears on the package unlike previous years. The early pieces were released in late 2002, but are considered part of the 2003 set.

1 Dale Earnhardt Jr. 6.00 15.00
Coke Japan 1998
2 Rusty Wallace 4.00 8.00
Rusty
3 Dale Earnhardt 6.00 15.00
Coke Japan 1998
8 Dale Earnhardt Jr. 6.00 15.00
Dirty Mo Posse
8 Dale Earnhardt Jr. 6.00 15.00
Earnhardt Tribute Concert
8 Dale Earnhardt Jr. 5.00 12.00
Oreo Ritz
Dale Earnhardt Jr. Hood
8 Dale Earnhardt Jr. 5.00 12.00
Oreo Ritz Dale Jr. Hood
18 Bobby Labonte 4.00 8.00
Interstate Batteries
20 Tony Stewart 5.00 12.00
Home Depot
Declaration of Independence
20 Tony Stewart 4.00 8.00
Home Depot
Peanuts Orange
21 Kevin Harvick 6.00 12.00
Payday
24 Jeff Gordon 5.00 12.00
DuPont Flames
24 Jeff Gordon 5.00 12.00
DuPont Flames in small package
24 Jeff Gordon 6.00 15.00
Pepsi Billion $
24 Jeff Gordon 5.00 12.00
Pepsi Daytona
38 Elliott Sadler 4.00 8.00
M&M's Groovy
40 Sterling Marlin 4.00 8.00
Sterling

2003 Winner's Circle Decade of Champions 1:64

3 Dale Earnhardt 5.00 12.00
Goodwrench 1993
3 Dale Earnhardt 5.00 12.00
Goodwrench 1994
5 Terry Labonte 5.00 10.00
Kellogg's 1996
18 Bobby Labonte 5.00 10.00
Interstate Batteries 2000
20 Tony Stewart 6.00 15.00
Home Depot 2002
24 Jeff Gordon 5.00 10.00
DuPont 1995
24 Jeff Gordon 5.00 10.00
DuPont 1997
24 Jeff Gordon 5.00 10.00
DuPont 1998
24 Jeff Gordon 5.00 10.00
DuPont Flames 2001
88 Dale Jarrett 5.00 10.00
Quality Care 1999

2003 Winner's Circle Die-Cast Kits 1:64

3 Dale Earnhardt 8.00 20.00
Goodwrench No Bull 2000
8 Dale Earnhardt Jr. 8.00 20.00
Looney Tunes 2002
9 Bill Elliott 7.50 15.00
Dodge
20 Tony Stewart 6.00 15.00
Home Depot 2002
24 Jeff Gordon 6.00 15.00
Dupont Bugs Rematch 2002
24 Jeff Gordon 6.00 15.00
DuPont Flames

2003 Winner's Circle Driver Sticker 1:64

The 2003 Driver Stcker series was initially released in late 2002. Those pieces feature a 2002 copyright date on the backs but were issued in the newly designed 2003 style Winner's Circle blister packaging. Note that a specific product or "set" name is not included but each die-cast piece was packaged with a driver sticker.

1 Dale Earnhardt 7.50 15.00
True Value 2000 IROC
1 Dale Earnhardt 7.50 15.00
True Value 2001 IROC
1 Bobby Labonte 6.00 12.00
True Value 2001 IROC
1 Mark Martin 6.00 12.00
True Value 1998 IROC
1 Steve Park 5.00 10.00
Pennzoil
2 Rusty Wallace 6.00 12.00
Rusty Flames
3 Dale Earnhardt 6.00 12.00
Foundation
3 Dale Earnhardt 6.00 12.00
Foundation short package
3 Dale Earnhardt 6.00 12.00
Goodwrench Plus Sign 1999
3 Dale Earnhardt 6.00 12.00
Goodwrench No Bull
76th Win 2000
3 Dale Earnhardt 6.00 15.00
Goodwrench Peter Max 2000
4 Mike Skinner 4.00 8.00
Kodak Yosemite Sam
5 Terry Labonte 5.00 10.00
Kellogg's Coyote and
Road Runner
6 Jeff Gordon 7.50 15.00
True Value 1998 IROC
8 Dale Earnhardt 7.50 15.00
RPM 1975
8 Dale Earnhardt Jr. 7.50 15.00
JR
8 Dale Earnhardt Jr. 7.50 15.00
JR short package
8 Dale Earnhardt Jr. 7.50 15.00
Dale Jr.
8 Dale Earnhardt Jr. 6.00 12.00
DMP
8 Dale Earnhardt Jr. 6.00 12.00
Looney Tunes
9 Bill Elliott 5.00 10.00
Dodge
11 Dale Earnhardt Jr. 8.00 20.00
True Value 1999 IROC
11 Tony Stewart 6.00 15.00
True Value 2001 IROC
11 Tony Stewart 6.00 15.00
True Value '01 IROC
'02 Champ. Sticker
12 Kerry Earnhardt 4.00 8.00
JaniKing Yosemite Sam
15 Michael Waltrip 5.00 10.00
NAPA
19 Jeremy Mayfield 5.00 10.00
Dodge
20 Tony Stewart 6.00 12.00
Home Depot
20 Tony Stewart 6.00 12.00
Home Depot short package
20 Tony Stewart 5.00 10.00
Home Depot
Peanuts black
20 Tony Stewart 5.00 10.00
Home Depot
Peanuts Orange
24 Jeff Gordon 5.00 12.00
Cookie Monster
24 Jeff Gordon 5.00 10.00
Dupont Bugs Rematch 2002
24 Jeff Gordon 8.00 20.00
Elmo 2002
24 Jeff Gordon 5.00 12.00
Pepsi Talladega
25 Joe Nemechek 4.00 8.00
UAW-Delphi Speedy Gonzalez
29 Kevin Harvick 6.00 12.00
Goodwrench Taz
30 Dale Earnhardt 6.00 12.00
Army 1976
30 Jeff Green 4.00 8.00
AOL Daffy Duck
31 Robby Gordon 4.00 8.00
Cingular Pepe Le Pew
48 Jimmie Johnson 5.00 10.00
Lowe's Distributor Exclusive
48 Jimmie Johnson 5.00 10.00
Lowe's Sylvester&Tweety
55 Bobby Hamilton 5.00 10.00
Square D Marvin Martian
77 Dale Earnhardt 7.50 15.00
Hy-Gain 1976
88 Dale Jarrett 5.00 10.00
UPS
88 Dale Jarrett 5.00 10.00
UPS Flames
K2 Dale Earnhardt 6.00 12.00
Dayvault's 1956 Ford
NNO Dale Earnhardt 7.50 15.00
Legacy
NNO Dale Earnhardt 7.50 15.00
Legacy short package

2003 Winner's Circle Fast Pack 1:64

1/8/15 Steve Park 7.50 15.00
Pennzoil
Dale Earnhardt Jr.
Dale Jr.
Michael Waltrip
NAPA
7/9/19 Casey Atwood 6.00 12.00
Sirius
Bill Elliott
Dodge
Jeremy Mayfield
odge
29/30/31 Kevin Harvick 6.00 12.00
Goodwrench
Jeff Green
AOL
Robby Gordon
Cingular

2003 Winner's Circle Pit Pass Preview 1:64

Winner's Circle released these die-cast blisters in late 2002 and early 2003. Each includes the newly designed 2003 packaging with the black strip across the top and no specific product release name included. A gold foil sticker was attached in the upper right hand corner that notes "2003 Preview," otherwise the release might be considered a 2002 issue since that is the copyright line date on the backs.

1 Steve Park 4.00 8.00
Pennzoil
1 Steve Park 4.00 8.00
Pennzoil '03 Preview sticker
2 Rusty Wallace 4.00 8.00
Rusty
2 Rusty Wallace 4.00 8.00
Rusty '03 Preview sticker
7 Casey Atwood 4.00 8.00
Sirius
8 Dale Earnhardt Jr. 6.00 12.00
JR
8 Dale Earnhardt Jr. 6.00 12.00
JR '03 Preview sticker
9 Bill Elliott 4.00 8.00
Dodge
15 Michael Waltrip 4.00 8.00
NAPA
15 Michael Waltrip 4.00 8.00
NAPA '03 Preview sticker
19 Jeremy Mayfield 4.00 8.00
Dodge
29 Kevin Harvick 6.00 12.00
Goodwrench
31 Robby Gordon 4.00 8.00
Cingular
88 Dale Jarrett 4.00 8.00
UPS

2003 Winner's Circle Pit Scene 1:64

This series was produced by Winner's Circle in 2002. However each piece was packaged in the slightly re-designed 2003 packaging style with the black striped area at the top of the package. A 1:64 scale car is included mounted on a pit road scene base complete with plastic crew members, pit wall, gas cans and cart, and a pit wagon.

2 Rusty Wallace 10.00 20.00
Rusty Level
3 Dale Earnhardt 12.50 25.00
Goodwrench Coming In
20 Tony Stewart 10.00 20.00
Home Depot Pulling out
24 Jeff Gordon 10.00 20.00
Pepsi Coming In
24 Jeff Gordon 10.00 20.00
DuPont Tires Off

2003 Winner's Circle Race Hood 1:64

2 Rusty Wallace 5.00 12.00
Rusty
8 Dale Earnhardt Jr. 5.00 12.00
MLB All Star 2003
20 Tony Stewart 5.00 12.00
Home Depot 2002 Champion
20 Tony Stewart 5.00 12.00
Home Depot
Declaration of Independence
20 Tony Stewart 6.00 12.00
Home Depot
Peanuts Orange
24 Jeff Gordon 6.00 12.00
DuPont Flames
38 Elliott Sadler 6.00 12.00
M&M's
40 Sterling Marlin 5.00 10.00
Sterling
45 Kyle Petty 6.00 12.00
Hands to Victory

2003 Winner's Circle Victory Lap 1:64

2 Rusty Wallace 5.00 10.00
Miller Lite Victory Lap
3 Dale Earnhardt 6.00 15.00
Goodwrench Victory Lap
20 Tony Stewart 5.00 10.00
Home Depot Victory Lap
24 Jeff Gordon 5.00 12.00
DuPont Victory Lap
43 Richard Petty 5.00 10.00
STP Victory Lap
88 Dale Jarrett 5.00 10.00
UPS Victory Lap

2004 Winner's Circle 1:64

2 Rusty Wallace 7.50 15.00
Miller Lite
2 Rusty Wallace 7.50 15.00
Miller Lite Last Call
2 Rusty Wallace 7.50 15.00
Miller Lite
President of Beers
2 Rusty Wallace 6.00 12.00
Miller Lite
Puddle of Mudd
8 Dale Earnhardt Jr. 10.00 20.00
Bud
8 Dale Earnhardt Jr. 10.00 20.00
Bud Born On Feb.7
8 Dale Earnhardt Jr. 10.00 20.00
Bud Born On Feb.15 Raced
40 Sterling Marlin 6.00 12.00
Coors Light
40 Sterling Marlin 5.00 10.00
Coors Light Kentucky Derby

2004 Winner's Circle Autographed Hood 1:64

2 Rusty Wallace 5.00 12.00
Kodak
3 Dale Earnhardt 6.00 15.00
Coke
3 Dale Earnhardt 6.00 15.00
Goodwrench Olympic 1996 Monte Carlo
8 Dale Earnhardt Jr. 5.00 12.00
Dave Matthews Band
8 Dale Earnhardt Jr. 6.00 15.00
JR
8 Dale Earnhardt Jr. 6.00 15.00
JR short package
8 Dale Earnhardt Jr. 5.00 12.00
Oreo
8 Dale Earnhardt Jr. 5.00 12.00
StainD
9 Bill Elliott 4.00 10.00
Dodge Lion King
9 Kasey Kahne 10.00 20.00
Dodge
9 Kasey Kahne 10.00 20.00
Dodge Mad Magazine
9 Kasey Kahne 10.00 20.00
Dodge Popeye
9 Kasey Kahne 12.50 25.00
Mountain Dew short package
10 Scott Riggs 4.00 10.00
Valvoline Wizard of Oz
18 Bobby Labonte 5.00 12.00
Interstate Batteries
short package
18 Bobby Labonte 5.00 12.00
Interstate Batteries
D-Day short package
18 Bobby Labonte 4.00 10.00
Interstate Batteries Shrek 2
18 Bobby Labonte 4.00 10.00
Interstate Batteries
Shrek 2 small package
19 Jeremy Mayfield 4.00 10.00
Dodge Mad Magazine
19 Jeremy Mayfield 4.00 10.00
Dodge NHL All Star
19 Jeremy Mayfield 6.00 12.00
Dodge Popeye
20 Tony Stewart 5.00 12.00
Home Depot
20 Tony Stewart 5.00 12.00
Home Depot Black
Reverse Paint
20 Tony Stewart 5.00 12.00
Home Depot Shrek 2
20 Tony Stewart 5.00 12.00
Home Depot Shrek 2
small package
20 Tony Stewart 5.00 12.00
Home Depot 25th Anniversary
21 Kevin Harvick 4.00 10.00
Hershey's Kisses
21 Kevin Harvick 4.00 10.00
Reese's
21 Kevin Harvick 5.00 12.00

Reese's 35th Anniversary RCR
24 Jeff Gordon 6.00 15.00
DuPont Flames
HMS 20th Anniversary
24 Jeff Gordon 5.00 12.00
DuPont Flames
Wizard of Oz
24 Jeff Gordon 5.00 12.00
DuPont Flames '03 Yose.Sam
24 Jeff Gordon 5.00 12.00
DuPont Rainbow
24 Jeff Gordon 5.00 12.00
Pepsi
24 Jeff Gordon 4.00 10.00
Pepsi Billion
24 Jeff Gordon 4.00 10.00
Pepsi Billion short package
29 Kevin Harvick 4.00 10.00
Coke C2
29 Kevin Harvick 10.00 20.00
ESGR Coast Guard short package
29 Kevin Harvick 5.00 12.00
Goodwrench
29 Kevin Harvick 6.00 15.00
Goodwrench KISS
29 Kevin Harvick 4.00 10.00
Goodwrench Realtree
29 Kevin Harvick 6.00 15.00
Goodwrench RCR 35th Anniversary
29 Kevin Harvick 4.00 10.00
Powerade
29 Bobby Labonte 4.00 10.00
ESGR Army
38 Kasey Kahne 6.00 15.00
Great Clips
38 Kasey Kahne 6.00 15.00
Great Clips Shark Tales
38 Elliott Sadler 4.00 10.00
M&M's
38 Elliott Sadler 4.00 10.00
M&M's short package
38 Elliott Sadler 5.00 12.00
M&M's black&white
38 Elliott Sadler 5.00 12.00
M&M's July 4
38 Elliott Sadler 4.00 10.00
Pedigree Wizard of Oz
40 Sterling Marlin 5.00 12.00
Sterling
41 Casey Mears 4.00 10.00
Target
42 Jamie McMurray 5.00 12.00
Havoline
77 Brendan Gaughan 4.00 10.00
Kodak Punisher
77 Brendan Gaughan 4.00 10.00
Kodak Wizard of Oz
81 Dale Earnhardt Jr. 5.00 12.00
KFC
81 Dale Earnhardt Jr. 5.00 12.00
KFC short package
81 Dale Earnhardt Jr. 5.00 12.00
Taco Bell
81 Tony Stewart 5.00 12.00
Bass Pro Shops
88 Dale Jarrett 7.50 15.00
UPS Arnold Palmer
92 Tony Stewart 5.00 12.00
McDonald's
99 Michael Waltrip 4.00 10.00
Aaron's Cat in the Hat
01 Joe Nemechek 5.00 12.00
Army G.I. Joe
01 Joe Nemechek 5.00 12.00
Army Time Magazine

2004 Winner's Circle Driver Sticker 1:64

8 Dale Earnhardt Jr. 6.00 12.00
JR sparkle
9 Kasey Kahne 12.50 25.00
Dodge sparkle
9 Kasey Kahne 7.50 15.00
Dodge Refresh sparkle
20 Tony Stewart 5.00 10.00
Home Depot sparkle
short package
24 Jeff Gordon 6.00 12.00
DuPont Flames sparkle
short package
24 Jeff Gordon 7.50 15.00
DuPont Flames
Fontana Raced sparkle
24 J.Gordon 7.50 15.00
Pepsi Shards
Talladega Raced sparkle
29 Kevin Harvick 7.50 15.00
Goodwrench '01 black number
29 Tony Stewart 5.00 10.00
Kid Rock
short package
38 Elliott Sadler 5.00 10.00
M&M's Texas Raced sparkle
38 Elliott Sadler 5.00 10.00
M&M's July 4 sparkle

2004 Winner's Circle Driver Sticker RCR Museum Series 1 1:64

3 Dale Earnhardt 6.00 12.00
AC Delco
1996 Monte Carlo
3 Dale Earnhardt 6.00 12.00
Coke Japan
1998 Monte Carlo
3 Dale Earnhardt 6.00 12.00
Goodwrench 1996 Monte Carlo
3 Dale Earnhardt 6.00 12.00
Goodwrench Olympic
'96 Monte Carlo
3 Dale Earnhardt 10.00 20.00
Goodwrench '97 Monte Carlo
Crash Daytona Raced
3 Dale Earnhardt 6.00 12.00
Goodwrench Sign '99 Monte Carlo
3 Dale Earnhardt 6.00 12.00
Goodwrench 2000 Monte Carlo Talladega
3 Dale Earnhardt 6.00 12.00
Goodwrench Peter Max
'00 Monte Carlo
3 Dale Earnhardt 6.00 12.00
Wrangler 1999 Monte Carlo

2004 Winner's Circle Pit Pass Preview 1:64

2 Rusty Wallace 4.00 8.00
Rusty
8 Dale Earnhardt Jr. 5.00 10.00
JR
15 Michael Waltrip 4.00 8.00
NAPA
18 Bobby Labonte 4.00 8.00
Interstate Batteries
20 Tony Stewart 4.00 8.00
Home Depot
24 Jeff Gordon 5.00 10.00
DuPont Flames
29 Kevin Harvick 4.00 8.00
Goodwrench
42 Jamie McMurray 4.00 8.00
Havoline
88 Dale Jarrett 4.00 8.00
UPS

2004 Winner's Circle Race Hood 1:64

8 Dale Earnhardt Jr. 6.00 12.00
JR
9 Bill Elliott 5.00 10.00
Lion King
99 Michael Waltrip 4.00 8.00
Cat in the Hat
04 Wizard of Oz Event Car 5.00 10.00

2005 Winner's Circle 1:64

2 Rusty Wallace 7.50 15.00
Miller Genuine Draft
2 Rusty Wallace 6.00 12.00
Miller Lite
2 Rusty Wallace 5.00 10.00
Miller Lite Last Call
2 Rusty Wallace 5.00 10.00
Miller Lite Last Call
Daytona Shootout
8 Dale Earnhardt Jr. 7.50 15.00
Bud Test
8 Dale Earnhardt Jr. 6.00 12.00
Bud World Series '04
39 Bill Elliott 6.00 12.00
Coors Retro

2005 Winner's Circle Autographed Hood 1:64

2 Clint Bowyer 7.50 15.00
AC Delco Chris Cagle
2 Clint Bowyer 7.50 15.00
Timberland
2 Rusty Wallace 7.50 15.00
Mobil Clean 7500
5 Kyle Busch 7.50 15.00
Kellogg's Johnny Bravo
6 Bill Elliott 10.00 20.00
Hellman's Charlie Brown
8 Dale Earnhardt Jr. 10.00 20.00
DEI
8 Martin Truex Jr. 7.50 15.00
Chance 2 Test '04 Champion
9 Bill Elliott 7.50 15.00
Dodge
9 Kasey Kahne 10.00 20.00
Dodge Ram Mega Cab
9 Kasey Kahne 7.50 15.00
Dodge
9 Kasey Kahne 10.00 20.00
Dodge '04 Rookie of the Year
9 Kasey Kahne 10.00 20.00
Dodge Longest Yard
9 Kasey Kahne 10.00 20.00
Dodge Mopar '04
9 Kasey Kahne 7.50 15.00
Dodge Mopar
9 Kasey Kahne 10.00 20.00
Dodge Pit Cap White
9 Kasey Kahne 10.00 20.00
Mountain Dew
10 Scott Riggs 7.50 15.00
Valvoline Herbie
10 Scott Riggs 6.00 12.00
Valvoline Nickelback
15 Michael Waltrip 7.50 15.00
Napa Stars & Stripes
18 Bobby Labonte 7.50 15.00
Boniva
18 Bobby Labonte 7.50 15.00
Interstate Batteries
18 Bobby Labonte 7.50 15.00
Interstate Batteries Madagascar
19 Jeremy Mayfield 7.50 15.00
Dodge
19 Jeremy Mayfield 5.00 10.00
Dodge Retro Daytona Shootout
19 Jeremy Mayfield 6.00 12.00
Mountain Dew Pitch Black
20 Tony Stewart 7.50 15.00
Home Depot
20 Tony Stewart 7.50 15.00
Home Depot Madagascar
21 Kevin Harvick 7.50 15.00
Hershey's Take 5
21 Kevin Harvick 7.50 15.00
Pelon Pelo Rico
25 Brian Vickers 6.00 12.00
GMAC Green Day
25 Brian Vickers 7.50 15.00
GMAC Scooby Doo
29 Kevin Harvick 7.50 15.00
Goodwrench
29 Kevin Harvick 7.50 15.00
Goodwrench Brickyard
29 Kevin Harvick 7.50 15.00
Goodwrench
Gretchen Wilson
29 Kevin Harvick 6.00 12.00
Reese's Big Cup
31 Jeff Burton 6.00 12.00
Cingular Big & Rich
33 Tony Stewart 7.50 15.00
James Dean 50th Anniversary
33 Tony Stewart 7.50 15.00
Mr.Clean AutoDry
38 Kasey Kahne 7.50 15.00
Great Clips
38 Elliott Sadler 7.50 15.00
M&M's
38 Elliott Sadler 7.50 15.00
M&M's Halloween
38 Elliott Sadler 7.50 15.00
M&M's July 4
38 Elliott Sadler 7.50 15.00
M&M's July 4
Green M&M
38 Elliott Sadler 6.00 12.00
Pedigree
41 Reed Sorenson 10.00 20.00
Discount Tire
41 Reed Sorenson 10.00 20.00
Home 123
42 Jamie McMurray 10.00 20.00
Havoline
42 Jamie McMurray 7.50 15.00
Havoline Shine On Charlotte
42 Jamie McMurray 7.50 15.00
Havoline Shine On Sonoma
42 Jamie McMurray 7.50 15.00
Havoline Shine On Talladega
64 Jamie McMurray 7.50 15.00
Top Flite
77 Travis Kvapil 6.00 12.00
Mobil
81 Dale Earnhardt Jr. 7.50 15.00
Chance 2 Test '98,'99 Champion
88 Dale Jarrett 7.50 15.00
UPS
88 Dale Jarrett 7.50 15.00
UPS Toys for Tots
91 Bill Elliott 10.00 20.00
Stanley Tools
99 Michael Waltrip 10.00 20.00
Aaron's
99 Michael Waltrip 10.00 20.00
Domino's Pizza

2005 Winner's Circle Driver Photo Hood 1:64

2 Clint Bowyer 10.00 20.00
AC Delco
2 Rusty Wallace 10.00 20.00
Rusty
5 Kyle Busch 10.00 20.00
Kellogg's
8 Dale Earnhardt Jr. 10.00 20.00
DEI
9 Kasey Kahne 10.00 20.00
Dodge Retro Daytona Shootout
19 Jeremy Mayfield 6.00 12.00
Dodge Retro Daytona Shootout
20 Tony Stewart 10.00 20.00
Home Depot
24 Jeff Gordon 10.00 20.00
DuPont Flames
24 Jeff Gordon 10.00 20.00
DuPont Flames Reverse
Performance Alliance
25 Brian Vickers 7.50 15.00
GMAC
31 Jeff Burton 7.50 15.00
Cingular
41 Reed Sorenson 10.00 20.00
Discount Tire Coats
Nashville Raced
64 Rusty Wallace 7.50 15.00
Bell Helicopter

2005 Winner's Circle Driver Sticker 1:64

9 Kasey Kahne 10.00 20.00
Dodge Richmond Raced
18 Bobby Labonte 6.00 12.00
Interstate Batteries
24 Jeff Gordon 7.50 15.00
DuPont Flames Performance
Alliance Reverse
24 Jeff Gordon 7.50 15.00
DuPont Flames Daytona Raced
38 Elliott Sadler 6.00 12.00
M&M's
43 Richard Petty 7.50 15.00
STP '75 Charger
43 Richard Petty 6.00 12.00
STP '84 Grand Prix

2005 Winner's Circle Driver Sticker RCR Museum Series 2 1:64

3 Dale Earnhardt 10.00 20.00
Goodwrench Silver
'95 Monte Carlo
3 Dale Earnhardt 6.00 12.00
Goodwrench 25th Anniversary
3 Dale Earnhardt 6.00 12.00
Goodwrench Plus '98 MC Daytona Win
3 Dale Earnhardt 6.00 12.00
Goodwrench Taz '00 Monte Carlo
3 Dale Earnhardt 12.50 25.00
Wheaties '97 Monte Carlo

2005 Winner's Circle Event Series 1:64

2 Rusty Wallace 7.50 15.00
Miller Lite
'04 Martinsville Win
8 Dale Earnhardt Jr. 7.50 15.00
Bud '04 Atlanta Win
8 Dale Earnhardt Jr. 7.50 15.00
Bud '04 Richmond Win
8 Dale Earnhardt Jr. 7.50 15.00
Bud Born On
Feb.15 '04 Daytona Win
Feb.7 car
24 Jeff Gordon 7.50 15.00
DuPont Flames
'04 California Win
24 Jeff Gordon 7.50 15.00
Pepsi Shards
'04 Talladega Win
38 Elliott Sadler 7.50 15.00
M&M's '04 Texas Win

2005 Winner's Circle Schedule Hood 1:64

8 Dale Earnhardt Jr. 6.00 12.00
JR
15 Michael Waltrip 6.00 12.00
Napa
18 Bobby Labonte 5.00 10.00
Interstate Batteries
20 Tony Stewart 5.00 10.00
Home Depot
21 Kevin Harvick 5.00 10.00
Hershey's Take 5
21 Kevin Harvick 5.00 10.00
Reese's
24 Jeff Gordon 6.00 12.00
DuPont Flames
38 Elliott Sadler 5.00 10.00
M&M's
81 Dale Earnhardt Jr. 6.00 12.00
Oreo Ritz
88 Dale Jarrett 6.00 12.00
UPS

2005 Winner's Circle Test Hood 1:64

9 Kasey Kahne 15.00 30.00
Dodge
18 Bobby Labonte 6.00 12.00
Interstate Batteries
20 Tony Stewart 6.00 12.00
Home Depot
24 Jeff Gordon 20.00 40.00
DuPont
29 Kevin Harvick 7.50 15.00
Goodwrench
38 Elliott Sadler 10.00 20.00
M&M's
88 Dale Jarrett 12.50 25.00
UPS

2006 Winner's Circle 1:64

1/8/11 Dale Tribute 5-car set 20.00 35.00
1.Martin Truex Jr.
Bass Pro
8.Dale Earnhardt Jr.
Bud
8.Martin Truex Jr.
Bass Pro Talladega Raced
11.Paul Menard/ Menard's / NNO.Dale Earnhardt/ Hall of Fame
2 Rusty Wallace 4.00 8.00
Miller Lite Bristol '05
2 Rusty Wallace 4.00 8.00
Miller Lite 700 Starts '05
8 Dale Earnhardt Jr. 5.00 10.00
Bud
8 Dale Earnhardt Jr. 5.00 10.00
Bud MLB All Star '05
8 Dale Earnhardt Jr. 5.00 10.00
Bud Test
8 Dale Earnhardt Jr. 5.00 10.00
Bud 3 Doors Down '05

2006 Winner's Circle Autographed Hood 1:64

1 Martin Truex Jr. 5.00 10.00
Bass Pro Shops
1 Martin Truex Jr. 5.00 10.00
Bass Pro 3 Days of Dale Tribute
split window box
1 Martin Truex Jr. 5.00 10.00
Bass Pro Shops Test
2 Rusty Wallace 6.00 12.00
Rusty Bristol Flames
6 Mark Martin 10.00 20.00
AAA
8 Dale Earnhardt Jr. 7.50 15.00
Bud 3 Days of Dale Tribute
split window box
8 Dale Earnhardt Jr. 7.50 15.00
DEI
8 Dale Earnhardt Jr. 7.50 15.00
Oreo
8 Martin Truex Jr. 6.00 12.00
Bass Pro 3 Days of Dale Tribute
Talladega Raced split window box
9 Kasey Kahne 7.50 15.00
Dodge Test
11 Denny Hamlin 10.00 20.00
Fed Ex Express
11 Paul Menard 5.00 10.00
Menard's Dale Tribute
12 Ryan Newman 6.00 12.00
Alltel
16 Greg Biffle 5.00 10.00
National Guard
17 Matt Kenseth 6.00 12.00
DeWalt
19 Jeremy Mayfield 5.00 10.00
Dodge
20 Tony Stewart 7.50 15.00
Home Depot Test
24 Jeff Gordon 7.50 15.00
DuPont Flames
24 Jeff Gordon 7.50 15.00
DuPont Flames Test
24 Jeff Gordon 10.00 20.00
DuPont Hot Hues
Sam Foose
24 Jeff Gordon 7.50 15.00
Nicorette
26 Ricky Bobby 6.00 12.00
Laughing Clown Malt Liquor
26 Jamie McMurray 6.00 12.00
Sharpie
43 Jeff Green 6.00 12.00
Cheerios Narnia
45 Kyle Petty 6.00 12.00
GP Narnia
47 Cal Naughton Jr. 5.00 10.00
Old Spice
48 Jimmie Johnson 7.50 15.00
Lowe's
48 Jimmie Johnson 7.50 15.00
Lowe's Flames Test
55 Jean Girard 5.00 10.00
Perrier
99 Carl Edwards 7.50 15.00
Office Depot
01 Joe Nemechek 6.00 12.00
Army Camo Call to Duty
NNO Dale Earnhardt 6.00 12.00
Hall of Fame Dale Tribute
split window box

2006 Winner's Circle Award Winners 1:64

11 Denny Hamlin 10.00 20.00
Fed Ex Express
Rookie of the Year
21 Kevin Harvick 15.00 30.00
Coast Guard
2006 Busch Series Champion
48 Jimmie Johnson 12.50 25.00
Lowe's 2006 Nextel Cup Champion

2006 Winner's Circle Pit Sign 1:64

8 Dale Earnhardt Jr. 5.00 10.00
DEI
9 Kasey Kahne 4.00 8.00
Dodge
20 Tony Stewart 4.00 8.00
Home Depot
24 Jeff Gordon 5.00 10.00
DuPont Flames
48 Jimmie Johnson 4.00 8.00
Lowe's

2006 Winner's Circle Schedule Hood 1:64

5 Kyle Busch 6.00 12.00
Kellogg's
9 Kasey Kahne 7.50 15.00
Dodge
18 Bobby Labonte 6.00 12.00
Interstate Batteries
19 Jeremy Mayfield 5.00 10.00
Dodge
20 Tony Stewart 7.50 15.00
Home Depot
24 Jeff Gordon 7.50 15.00
DuPont Flames
33 Tony Stewart 7.50 15.00
Old Spice
38 Elliott Sadler 6.00 12.00
M&M's
48 Jimmie Johnson 7.50 15.00
Lowe's
88 Dale Jarrett 6.00 12.00
UPS

2006 Winner's Circle Sticker 1:64

8 Dale Earnhardt Jr. 7.50 15.00
DEI
9 Kasey Kahne 6.00 12.00
Dodge
20 Tony Stewart 6.00 12.00
Home Depot
24 Jeff Gordon 7.50 15.00
DuPont Flames
29 Kevin Harvick 6.00 12.00
Goodwrench
48 Jimmie Johnson 6.00 12.00
Lowe's

2007 Winner's Circle American Heroes Hood 1:64

4 Ward Burton 5.00 10.00
Air Force American Heroes
8 Dale Earnhardt Jr. 7.50 15.00
Bud Camo American Heroes
8 Dale Earnhardt Jr. 6.00 12.00
DEI Camo AH
11 Denny Hamlin 6.00 12.00
Fed Ex Freight Marines American Heroes
16 Greg Biffle 5.00 10.00
3M Coast Guard American Heroes
21 Jon Wood 5.00 10.00
Air Force American Heroes
24 Jeff Gordon 6.00 12.00
DuPont Department of Defense
American Heroes
48 Jimmie Johnson 6.00 12.00
Lowe's Power of Pride
American Heroes
88 Shane Huffman 5.00 10.00
Navy
01 Mark Martin 6.00 12.00
U.S. Army American Heroes

2007 Winner's Circle Dale the Movie Hoods 1:64

2 Dale Earnhardt 6.00 12.00
Curb '80 Olds
2 Dale Earnhardt 6.00 12.00
Wrangler '81 Pontiac
3 Dale Earnhardt 6.00 12.00
Wrangler '86 Monte Carlo
3 Dale Earnhardt 6.00 12.00
Wrangler '87 Monte Carlo
3 Dale Earnhardt 5.00 10.00
Goodwrench '88 Monte Carlo
3 Dale Earnhardt 5.00 10.00
Goodwrench '90 Lumina
3 Dale Earnhardt 5.00 10.00
Goodwrench '94 Monte Carlo
3 Dale Earnhardt 5.00 10.00
Goodwrench '94 Monte Carlo Clinch
3 Dale Earnhardt 5.00 10.00
Goodwrench Silver Select
'95 Monte Carlo

3 Dale Earnhardt Goodwrench '95 Monte Carlo 5.00 10.00
3 Dale Earnhardt Goodwrench '96 Monte Carlo 5.00 10.00
3 Dale Earnhardt Goodwrench Plus '98 Monte Carlo 5.00 10.00

2007 Winner's Circle Helmets 1:64

1 Martin Truex Jr. Bass Pro Shops 4.00 8.00
8 Dale Earnhardt Jr. DEI 5.00 10.00
9 Kasey Kahne Dodge Dealers 4.00 8.00
10 Scott Riggs Valvoline 4.00 8.00
11 Denny Hamlin Fed Ex Express 4.00 8.00
20 Tony Stewart Home Depot 4.00 8.00
24 Jeff Gordon DuPont Flames 5.00 10.00
48 Jimmie Johnson Lowe's 4.00 8.00
88 Ricky Rudd Snickers 4.00 8.00

2007 Winner's Circle Hoods 1:64

8 Dale Earnhardt Jr. DEI 5.00 10.00
9 Kasey Kahne Dodge Dealers Test 4.00 8.00
19 Elliott Sadler Dodge Dealers 4.00 8.00
20 Tony Stewart Home Depot Test 5.00 10.00
24 Jeff Gordon DuPont Flames 5.00 10.00
24 Jeff Gordon Pepsi 5.00 10.00
38 David Gilliland M&M's Shrek 4.00 8.00
48 Jimmie Johnson Lowe's 4.00 8.00

2007 Winner's Circle License Plate 1:64

8 Dale Earnhardt Jr. DEI 5.00 10.00
9 Kasey Kahne Dodge Dealers 4.00 8.00
10 Scott Riggs Valvoline 4.00 8.00
11 Denny Hamlin Fed Ex Express 4.00 8.00
12 Ryan Newman Alltel 4.00 8.00
15 Paul Menard JM Menards 4.00 8.00
17 Matt Kenseth DeWalt 4.00 8.00
20 Tony Stewart Home Depot 4.00 8.00
24 Jeff Gordon DuPont Flames 5.00 10.00
29 Kevin Harvick Reese's 4.00 8.00
48 Jimmie Johnson Lowe's 4.00 8.00
96 Tony Raines DLP 4.00 8.00
99 Carl Edwards Office Depot 4.00 8.00

2007 Winner's Circle Limited Edition 1:64

2 Kurt Busch Miller Lite 5.00 10.00
8 Dale Earnhardt Jr. Bud 6.00 12.00
8 Dale Earnhardt Jr. Bud Test 6.00 12.00
8 Dale Earnhardt Jr. Sharpie 6.00 12.00

2007 Winner's Circle Limited Edition Hoods 1:64

8 Dale Earnhardt Jr. Bud Stars & Stripes 7.50 15.00
8 Dale Earnhardt Jr. DEI Stars & Stripes 6.00 12.00

2007 Winner's Circle Medallion 1:64

8 Dale Earnhardt Jr. DEI 5.00 10.00
9 Kasey Kahne Dodge Dealers 4.00 8.00
19 Elliott Sadler Dodge Dealers 4.00 8.00
20 Tony Stewart Home Depot 5.00 10.00
24 Jeff Gordon DuPont Flames 5.00 10.00
25 Casey Mears National Guard 4.00 8.00
26 Jamie McMurray Irwin Tools 4.00 8.00
29 Kevin Harvick Shell Pennzoil 5.00 10.00
38 David Gilliland M&M's 4.00 8.00
48 Jimmie Johnson Lowe's 4.00 8.00
01 Mark Martin U.S. Army 5.00 10.00

2007 Winner's Circle Photo Hoods 1:64

5 Kyle Busch Kellogg's 4.00 8.00
31 Jeff Burton Prilosec 4.00 8.00
38 David Gilliland M&M's Pink 5.00 10.00
88 Shane Huffman Navy SEALS 4.00 8.00

2007 Winner's Circle Photo Hood Spiderman LE 1:64

43 Bobby Labonte Cheerios Spiderman 5.00 10.00

2007 Winner's Circle Pit Pass 1:64

8 Dale Earnhardt Jr. DEI 5.00 10.00
9 Kasey Kahne Dodge 4.00 8.00
11 Denny Hamlin Fed Ex Express 4.00 8.00
16 Greg Biffle Ameriquest 4.00 8.00
19 Elliott Sadler Dodge Dealers 4.00 8.00
20 Tony Stewart Home Depot 4.00 8.00
22 Dave Blaney CAT 4.00 8.00
24 Jeff Gordon DuPont Flames 5.00 10.00
24 Jeff Gordon Nicorette 5.00 10.00
48 Jimmie Johnson Lowe's 4.00 8.00
01 Mark Martin U.S. Army 5.00 10.00

2007 Winner's Circle Pit Sign 1:64

6 David Ragan AAA 6.00 12.00
8 Dale Earnhardt Jr. DEI 5.00 10.00
9 Kasey Kahne Dodge Dealers 4.00 8.00
17 Matt Kenseth DeWalt 4.00 8.00
20 Tony Stewart Home Depot 4.00 8.00
24 Jeff Gordon DuPont Flames Test 6.00 12.00
24 Jeff Gordon Pepsi 5.00 10.00
29 Kevin Harvick Shell Pennzoil Test 6.00 12.00
42 Juan Pablo Montoya Texaco Havoline Test 5.00 10.00
44 Dale Jarrett UPS 4.00 8.00
48 Jimmie Johnson Lowe's Test 6.00 12.00

2007 Winner's Circle Sam Bass Hoods 1:64

9 Kasey Kahne Dodge Dealers Holiday 4.00 8.00
11 Denny Hamlin Fed Ex Express Holiday 4.00 8.00
17 Matt Kenseth DeWalt Holiday 4.00 8.00
20 Tony Stewart Home Depot Holiday 4.00 8.00
24 Jeff Gordon DuPont Flames Holiday 5.00 10.00
29 Kevin Harvick Shell Pennzoil Holiday 4.00 8.00
38 David Gilliland M&M's Holiday 4.00 8.00
42 Juan Pablo Montoya Texaco Havoline Holiday 5.00 10.00
48 Jimmie Johnson Lowe's Holiday 5.00 10.00
99 Carl Edwards Office Depot Holiday 4.00 8.00
01 Mark Martin U.S. Army Holiday 4.00 8.00

2007 Winner's Circle Schedule Hood 1:64

2 Kurt Busch Kurt 5.00 10.00
5 Kyle Busch Kellogg's 5.00 10.00
8 Dale Earnhardt Jr. DEI 6.00 12.00
9 Kasey Kahne Dodge Dealers 5.00 10.00
11 Denny Hamlin Fed Ex Express 5.00 10.00
12 Ryan Newman Alltel 5.00 10.00
16 Greg Biffle Ameriquest 5.00 10.00
17 Matt Kenseth DeWalt 5.00 10.00
20 Tony Stewart Home Depot 6.00 12.00
24 Jeff Gordon DuPont Flames 6.00 12.00
25 Casey Mears National Guard 5.00 10.00
26 Jamie McMurray Irwin Tools 5.00 10.00
31 Jeff Burton Cingular 5.00 10.00
42 Juan Pablo Montoya Texaco Havoline 6.00 12.00
48 Jimmie Johnson Lowe's 5.00 10.00
55 Michael Waltrip NAPA 5.00 10.00
99 Carl Edwards Office Depot 5.00 10.00
2007 NEXTEL Event Car 5.00 10.00

2007 Winner's Circle Victory Lane Hoods 1:64

1 Martin Truex Jr. Bass Pro Shops COT Dover Raced 6.00 12.00
2 Kurt Busch Miller Lite Michigan Raced 7.50 15.00
2 Kurt Busch Miller Lite Pocono Raced 7.50 15.00
5 Kyle Busch Carquest COT Bristol Raced 6.00 12.00
11 Denny Hamlin Fed Ex Express COT New Hampshire Raced 6.00 12.00
16 Greg Biffle Aflac Kansas Raced 7.50 15.00
17 Matt Kenseth Carhartt California Raced 10.00 20.00
17 Matt Kenseth DeWalt Homestead-Miami Raced 10.00 20.00
20 Tony Stewart Home Depot Brickyard Raced 7.50 15.00
20 Tony Stewart Home Depot Chicagoland Raced 7.50 15.00
20 Tony Stewart Home Depot Daytona Shootout Raced 7.50 15.00
20 Tony Stewart Home Depot COT Watkins Glen Raced 10.00 15.00
24 Jeff Gordon DuPont Flames Charlotte Raced 7.50 15.00
24 Jeff Gordon DuPont Flames Pocono Raced 7.50 15.00
24 Jeff Gordon DuPont Flames Talladega Raced 7.50 15.00
24 Jeff Gordon DuPont Flames COT Darlington Raced 10.00 20.00
24 Jeff Gordon DuPont Flames COT Phoenix Raced 10.00 20.00
24 Jeff Gordon DuPont Flames COT Talladega Raced 10.00 20.00
25 Casey Mears National Guard Camo Charlotte Raced 6.00 12.00
26 Jamie McMurray Irwin Tools Daytona Raced 6.00 12.00
29 Kevin Harvick Pennzoil Platinum Charlotte Raced 6.00 12.00
29 Kevin Harvick Shell Pennzoil Daytona Raced 10.00 20.00
31 Jeff Burton Prilosec Texas Raced 6.00 12.00
42 Juan Pablo Montoya Texaco Havoline Infineon Raced 10.00 20.00
48 Jimmie Johnson Lowe's Fall Atlanta Raced 10.00 20.00
48 Jimmie Johnson Lowe's California Raced 10.00 20.00
48 Jimmie Johnson 10.00 20.00
Lowe's Las Vegas Raced
48 Jimmie Johnson Lowe's Texas Raced 10.00 20.00
48 Jimmie Johnson Lowe's COT Martinsville Raced 12.50 25.00
48 Jimmie Johnson Lowe's COT Fall Martinsville Raced 12.50 25.00
48 Jimmie Johnson Lowe's COT Fall Phoenix Raced 12.50 25.00
48 Jimmie Johnson Lowe's COT Richmond Raced 12.50 25.00
48 Jimmie Johnson Lowe's COT Fall Richmond Raced 12.50 25.00
48 Jimmie Johnson Lowe's Kobalt Atlanta Raced 10.00 20.00
99 Carl Edwards Office Depot Michigan Raced 6.00 12.00
99 Carl Edwards Office Depot COT Bristol Raced 6.00 12.00
99 Carl Edwards Office Depot COT Dover Raced 6.00 12.00

2008 Winner's Circle Autographed Hoods 1:64

1 Martin Truex Jr. Bass Pro 5.00 10.00
2 Kurt Busch Kurt 5.00 10.00
17 Matt Kenseth DeWalt 5.00 10.00
18 Kyle Busch M&M'S 7.50 15.00
20 Tony Stewart Home Depot 6.00 12.00
24 Jeff Gordon DuPont Flames 6.00 12.00
26 Jamie McMurray Irwin 5.00 10.00
42 Juan Pablo Montoya Texaco 5.00 10.00
43 Bobby Labonte Cheerios 5.00 10.00
88 Dale Earnhardt Jr. AMP 6.00 12.00
88 Dale Earnhardt Jr. National Guard 6.00 12.00

2008 Winner's Circle Daytona 500 1:64

1 Martin Truex Jr. Bass Pro Shops 7.50 15.00
9 Kasey Kahne KK 10.00 20.00
17 Matt Kenseth DeWalt 10.00 20.00
20 Tony Stewart Home Depot 12.50 25.00
24 Jeff Gordon DuPont Flames 12.50 25.00
48 Jimmie Johnson Lowe's 10.00 20.00
88 Dale Earnhardt Jr. AMP 12.50 25.00
88 Dale Earnhardt Jr. National Guard 12.50 25.00

2008 Winner's Circle Daytona 500 Hoods 1:64

1 Martin Truex Jr. Bass Pro Shops 5.00 10.00
9 Kasey Kahne Bud 10.00 20.00
9 Kasey Kahne KK 6.00 12.00
17 Matt Kenseth DeWalt 6.00 12.00
20 Tony Stewart Home Depot 7.50 15.00
24 Jeff Gordon DuPont Flames 7.50 15.00
29 Kevin Harvick Shell Pennzoil 6.00 12.00
42 Juan Pablo Montoya Texaco Havoline 6.00 12.00
48 Jimmie Johnson Lowe's 7.50 15.00
88 Dale Earnhardt Jr. AMP 7.50 15.00
88 Dale Earnhardt Jr. National Guard 7.50 15.00
99 Carl Edwards Office Depot 6.00 12.00

2008 Winner's Circle Daytona 500 2-car sets 1:64

20/88 Tony Stewart Home Depot Daytona 500 Event Car 10.00 20.00
24/08 Jeff Gordon DuPont Flames Daytona 500 Event Car 12.50 25.00
29/08 Kevin Harvick Shell Pennzoil Daytona 500 Event Car 10.00 20.00
48/08 Jimmie Johnson Lowe's Daytona 500 Event Car 10.00 20.00
88/08 Dale Earnhardt Jr. AMP Daytona 500 Event Car 12.50 25.00
88/08 Dale Earnhardt Jr. National Guard Daytona 500 Event Car 12.50 25.00

2008 Winner's Circle Hoods 1:64

88 Dale Earnhardt Jr. AMP 10.00 20.00

2008 Winner's Circle Number Magnet 1:64

1 Martin Truex Jr. Bass Pro 5.00 10.00
5 Casey Mears Car Quest 5.00 10.00
5 Casey Mears Kellogg's 5.00 10.00
6 David Ragan AAA Insurance 5.00 10.00
8 Mark Martin U.S. Army 5.00 10.00
9 Kasey Kahne KK 5.00 10.00
11 Denny Hamlin FedEx Express 5.00 10.00
12 Ryan Newman Alltel 5.00 10.00
16 Greg Biffle 3M 5.00 10.00
17 Matt Kenseth DeWalt 5.00 10.00
18 Kyle Busch M&M's 7.50 15.00
20 Tony Stewart Home Depot 6.00 12.00
24 Jeff Gordon DuPont Flames 6.00 12.00
29 Kevin Harvick Shell 5.00 10.00
42 Juan Pablo Montoya Big Red 5.00 10.00
48 Jimmie Johnson Lowe's 7.50 15.00
55 Michael Waltrip NAPA 5.00 10.00
88 Dale Earnhardt Jr. Amp 6.00 12.00
88 Dale Earnhardt Jr. National Guard 6.00 12.00
99 Carl Edwards Office Depot 5.00 10.00

2008 Winner's Circle Pit Board 1:64

88 Dale Earnhardt Jr. AMP 5.00 10.00

2008 Winner's Circle Sam Bass 1:64

9 Kasey Kahne KK 6.00 12.00
19 Elliott Sadler Best Buy 6.00 12.00
20 Tony Stewart Home Depot 7.50 15.00
24 Jeff Gordon Foundation Test 7.50 15.00
31 Jeff Burton AT&T 6.00 12.00
44 David Reutimann UPS 6.00 12.00
48 Jimmie Johnson Lowe's 7.50 15.00
60 NASCAR 60th Anniversary 7.50 15.00
88 Dale Earnhardt Jr. Amp 7.50 15.00
88 Dale Earnhardt Jr. National Guard 7.50 15.00
88 Brad Keselowski Navy 6.00 12.00

2008 Winner's Circle Schedule Hoods 1:64

1 Martin Truex Jr. Bass Pro Shops 4.00 8.00
2 Kurt Busch Kurt 4.00 8.00
9 Kasey Kahne KK 4.00 8.00
17 Matt Kenseth DeWalt 4.00 8.00
18 Kyle Busch M&M's 4.00 8.00
20 Tony Stewart Home Depot 5.00 10.00
24 Jeff Gordon DuPont Flames 5.00 10.00
29 Kevin Harvick Shell Pennzoil 4.00 8.00
42 Juan Pablo Montoya Texaco Havoline 4.00 8.00
48 Jimmie Johnson Lowe's 5.00 10.00
88 Dale Earnhardt Jr. AMP 5.00 10.00
88 Dale Earnhardt Jr. National Guard 5.00 10.00
99 Carl Edwards Office Depot 4.00 8.00

2008 Winner's Circle Stickers 1:64

1 Martin Truex Jr. Bass Pro 5.00 10.00
5 Dale Earnhardt Jr. All Star Test Car 7.50 15.00
5 Casey Mears Car Quest 5.00 10.00
5 Casey Mears Kellogg's 5.00 10.00
8 Mark Martin U.S. Army 5.00 10.00
9 Kasey Kahne KK 5.00 10.00
11 Denny Hamlin FedEx Express 5.00 10.00
12 Ryan Newman Alltel 5.00 10.00
17 Matt Kenseth Carhartt 5.00 10.00
18 Kyle Busch M&M'S 7.50 15.00
20 Tony Stewart Home Depot 6.00 12.00
24 Jeff Gordon Pepsi 6.00 12.00
29 Kevin Harvick Shell 5.00 10.00
42 Juan Pablo Montoya Texaco 5.00 10.00
43 Bobby Labonte Cheerios 5.00 10.00
48 Jimmie Johnson 6.00 12.00

Lowe's 2007 Champ
55 Michael Waltrip 5.00 10.00
NAPA
88 Dale Earnhardt Jr. 6.00 12.00
National Guard
99 Carl Edwards 5.00 10.00
Office Depot

2008 Winner's Circle 2-Car Set w/Hood 1:64

20 Tony Stewart 10.00 20.00
Home Depot/ Home Depot Color Chrome
24 Jeff Gordon 12.50 25.00
DuPont Flames/ Nicorette
88 Dale Earnhardt Jr. 12.50 25.00
AMP/ National Guard

2008 Winner's Circle 2-Car Set w/Pit Board 1:64

9 Kasey Kahne 10.00 20.00
Bud/ Bud Color Chrome

2009 Winner's Circle Daytona Hood 1:64

5 Mark Martin 4.00 8.00
Kellogg's
9 Kasey Kahne 6.00 12.00
Bud
14 Tony Stewart 5.00 10.00
Office Depot
14 Tony Stewart 5.00 10.00
Old Spice
18 Kyle Busch 4.00 8.00
M&M's
24 Jeff Gordon 5.00 10.00
DuPont
48 Jimmie Johnson 4.00 8.00
Lowe's
88 Dale Earnhardt Jr. 4.00 8.00
AMP
88 Dale Earnhardt Jr. 4.00 8.00
National Guard
99 Carl Edwards 4.00 8.00
Aflac

2009 Winner's Circle HMS Hood 1:64

24 Jeff Gordon 6.00 12.00
DuPont
48 Jimmie Johnson 6.00 12.00
Lowe's
88 Dale Earnhardt Jr. 6.00 12.00
AMP
88 Dale Earnhardt Jr. 6.00 12.00
National Guard

2009 Winner's Circle Schedule Hood 1:64

9 Kasey Kahne 4.00 8.00
KK
11 Denny Hamlin 4.00 8.00
Fed Ex Express
14 Tony Stewart 5.00 10.00
Old Spice
18 Kyle Busch 4.00 8.00
M&M's
20 Joey Logano 6.00 12.00
Home Depot
24 Jeff Gordon 5.00 10.00
DuPont
48 Jimmie Johnson 4.00 8.00
Lowe's
88 Dale Earnhardt Jr. 4.00 8.00
AMP
88 Dale Earnhardt Jr. 6.00 12.00
AMP HMS Anniversary
99 Carl Edwards 5.00 10.00
Aflac

2010 Winner's Circle Hall of Fame 1:64

10 Dale Earnhardt 5.00 10.00
NASCAR HOF
10 Junior Johnson 5.00 10.00
NASCAR HOF
10 Richard Petty 5.00 10.00
NASCAR HOF

2010 Winner's Circle Hoods 1:64

3 Dale Earnhardt 5.00 10.00
Goodwrench Realtree
6 David Ragan 4.00 8.00
UPS
10 Digger 4.00 8.00
14 Tony Stewart 5.00 10.00
Burger King
14 Tony Stewart 4.00 8.00
Old Spice
14 Tony Stewart 4.00 8.00
Old Spice Realtree
14 Tony Stewart 4.00 8.00
Old Spice Swagger
16 Greg Biffle 4.00 8.00
3M
18 Kyle Busch 4.00 8.00
M&M's
24 Jeff Gordon 5.00 10.00
DuPont
24 Jeff Gordon 5.00 10.00
DuPont Realtree
48 Jimmie Johnson 5.00 10.00
Lowe's
88 Dale Earnhardt Jr. 4.00 8.00
AMP
88 Dale Earnhardt Jr. 4.00 8.00
AMP Black
88 Dale Earnhardt Jr. 5.00 10.00
AMP Realtree
88 Dale Earnhardt Jr. 5.00 10.00
National Guard
99 Carl Edwards 4.00 8.00
Aflac Silver

2010 Winner's Circle NASCAR on Fox 1:64

10 Annie 4.00 8.00
10 Digger 4.00 8.00
10 Digger Cam 4.00 8.00

2010 Winner's Circle Pit Caps 1:64

5 Mark Martin 5.00 10.00
GoDaddy
14 Tony Stewart 5.00 10.00
Burger King
16 Greg Biffle 4.00 8.00
3M
18 Kyle Busch 5.00 10.00
Snicker's
20 Joey Logano 4.00 8.00
Home Depot
24 Jeff Gordon 5.00 10.00
DuPont
48 Jimmie Johnson 5.00 10.00
Lowe's
88 Dale Earnhardt Jr. 4.00 8.00
AMP
88 Dale Earnhardt Jr. 5.00 10.00
National Guard

2010 Winner's Circle Schedule Hoods 1:64

11 Denny Hamlin 4.00 8.00
Fed Ex Express
14 Tony Stewart 4.00 8.00
Office Depot
14 Tony Stewart 4.00 8.00
Old Spice
24 Jeff Gordon 5.00 10.00
DuPont
88 Dale Earnhardt Jr. 4.00 8.00
AMP
99 Carl Edwards 4.00 8.00
Aflac

2006 Winner's Circle 1:87

6 Mark Martin 3.00 6.00
AAA
8 Dale Earnhardt Jr. 3.00 6.00
DEI
8 Dale Earnhardt Jr.
250 Starts
9 Kasey Kahne 3.00 6.00
Dodge
9 Kasey Kahne
Dodge SRT
12 Ryan Newman 3.00 6.00
Alltel
16 Greg Biffle 2.50 5.00
National Guard
17 Matt Kenseth 2.50 5.00
DeWalt
19 Jeremy Mayfield 2.50 5.00
Dodge
20 Tony Stewart
Home Depot
24 Jeff Gordon 3.00 6.00
DuPont Flames
24 Jeff Gordon
DuPont Hot Hues Foose Design
26 Jamie McMurray 2.50 5.00
Sharpie
38 Elliott Sadler 2.50 5.00
M&M's
48 Jimmie Johnson 3.00 6.00
Lowe's
48 Jimmie Johnson
Lowe's Sea World
99 Carl Edwards 3.00 6.00
Office Depot

2007 Winner's Circle 1:87

1 Martin Truex Jr. 2.50 5.00
Bass Pro Shops
2 Kurt Busch 2.50 5.00
Kurt
5 Kyle Busch 2.50 5.00
Kellogg's
6 David Ragan 3.00 6.00
AAA
8 Dale Earnhardt Jr. 4.00 8.00
DEI
8 Dale Earnhardt Jr. 4.00 8.00
DEI Stars & Stripes
9 Kasey Kahne 3.00 6.00
Dodge Dealers
11 Denny Hamlin 2.50 5.00
Fed Ex Express
12 Ryan Newman 2.50 5.00
Alltel
16 Greg Biffle 2.50 5.00
Ameriquest
19 Elliott Sadler 2.50 5.00
Dodge Dealers
20 Tony Stewart 3.00 6.00
Home Depot
24 Jeff Gordon 4.00 8.00
DuPont Flames
24 Jeff Gordon 3.00 6.00
Nicorette
24 Jeff Gordon 3.00 6.00
Pepsi
25 Casey Mears 2.50 5.00
National Guard
26 Jamie McMurray 2.50 5.00
Irwin Tools
29 Kevin Harvick 3.00 6.00
Shell Pennzoil
38 David Gilliland 2.50 5.00
M&M's
38 David Gilliland 2.50 5.00
M&M's Shrek
42 Juan Pablo Montoya 4.00 8.00
Texaco Havoline
44 Dale Jarrett 2.50 5.00
UPS
48 Jimmie Johnson 3.00 6.00
Lowe's
55 Michael Waltrip 2.50 5.00
NAPA
88 Ricky Rudd 2.50 5.00
Snickers
99 Carl Edwards 2.50 5.00
Office Depot
00 David Reutimann 2.50 5.00
Burger King
01 Mark Martin 3.00 6.00
U.S. Army

2007 Winner's Circle American Heroes 1:87

4 Ward Burton 2.50 5.00
Air Force American Heroes
8 Dale Earnhardt Jr. 4.00 8.00
Bud Camo American Heroes
11 Denny Hamlin 3.00 6.00
Fed Ex Freight Marines American Heroes
16 Greg Biffle 3.00 6.00
3M Coast Guard
American Heroes
21 Jon Wood 2.50 5.00
Air Force American Heroes
24 Jeff Gordon 4.00 8.00
DuPont Department of Defense
American Heroes
48 Jimmie Johnson 3.00 6.00
Lowe's Power of Pride American Heroes
88 Shane Huffman 2.50 5.00
Navy American Heroes
01 Mark Martin 3.00 6.00
U.S. Army American Heroes
NNO 4. Ward Burton 6.00 12.00
Air Force American Heroes
24. Jeff Gordon
DuPont Department of Defense
American Heroes
48. Jimmie Johnson
Lowe's Power of Pride American Heroes
3-car set
NNO 8. Dale Earnhardt Jr. 6.00 12.00
Bud Camo American Heroes
16. Greg Biffle
3M Coast Guard American Heroes
Shane Huffman
Navy American Heroes
3-car set
NNO 11. Denny Hamlin 5.00 10.00
Fed Ex Freight Marines American Heroes
21. Jon Wood
Air Force American Heroes
01. Mark Martin
U.S. Army American Heroes
3-car set
NNO American Heroes 9-car set 20.00 35.00
4.Burton
AF
8.Dale Jr.
Camo/
11.Hamlin
Marines
16.Biffle/3M National Guard
21.Wood
AF
24.Gordon
D.O.D.
48.Johnson
P.O.P./ 88.Huffman
Navy/ 01.Martin
Army

2007 Winner's Circle Limited Edition 1:87

8 Dale Earnhardt Jr. 5.00 10.00
Bud Stars & Stripes

2008 Winner's Circle 1:87

1 Martin Truex Jr. 2.50 5.00
Bass Pro Shops
8 Mark Martin 2.50 5.00
U.S. Army
9 Kasey Kahne 2.50 5.00
KK
11 Denny Hamlin 2.50 5.00
Fed Ex Express
17 Matt Kenseth 2.50 5.00
DeWalt
18 Kyle Busch 4.00 8.00
M&M's
20 Tony Stewart 3.00 6.00
Home Depot
24 Jeff Gordon 3.00 6.00
DuPont Flames
24 Jeff Gordon 3.00 6.00
Nicorette
29 Kevin Harvick 2.50 5.00
Shell Pennzoil
42 Juan Pablo Montoya 2.50 5.00
Big Red
42 Juan Pablo Montoya 2.50 5.00
Texaco
44 Dale Jarrett 2.50 5.00
UPS
48 Jimmie Johnson 4.00 8.00
Lowe's
55 Michael Waltrip 2.50 5.00
Napa
88 Dale Earnhardt Jr. 3.00 6.00
AMP
88 Dale Earnhardt Jr. 3.00 6.00
National Guard
99 Carl Edwards 2.50 5.00
Office Depot

2008 Winner's Circle Daytona 500 1:87

1 Martin Truex Jr. 2.50 5.00
Bass Pro Shops
17 Matt Kenseth 2.50 5.00
DeWalt
20 Tony Stewart 3.00 6.00
Home Depot
24 Jeff Gordon 3.00 6.00
DuPont Flames
29 Kevin Harvick 2.50 5.00
Shell Pennzoil
48 Jimmie Johnson 3.00 6.00
Lowe's
88 Dale Earnhardt Jr. 3.00 6.00
AMP
88 Dale Earnhardt Jr. 3.00 6.00
National Guard
99 Carl Edwards 2.50 5.00
Office Depot

2009 Winner's Circle 1:87

14 Tony Stewart 2.50 5.00
Old Spice
18 Kyle Busch 2.00 4.00
M&M's
88 Dale Earnhardt Jr. 2.00 4.00
AMP
88 Dale Earnhardt Jr. 2.50 5.00
AMP HMS Anniversary
88 Dale Earnhardt Jr. 2.00 4.00
National Guard

2009 Winner's Circle Daytona 1:87

5 Mark Martin 2.00 4.00
Kellogg's
14 Tony Stewart 2.50 5.00
Old Spice
17 Matt Kenseth 2.00 4.00
DeWalt
18 Kyle Busch 2.00 4.00
M&M's
24 Jeff Gordon 2.50 5.00
DuPont
48 Jimmie Johnson 2.00 4.00
Lowe's
88 Dale Earnhardt Jr. 2.00 4.00
AMP
88 Dale Earnhardt Jr. 2.00 4.00
National Guard

2009 Winner's Circle HMS 1:87

5 Mark Martin 2.50 5.00
Kellogg's
24 Jeff Gordon 3.00 6.00
DuPont
48 Jimmie Johnson 3.00 6.00
Lowe's
88 Dale Earnhardt Jr. 3.00 6.00
AMP
88 Dale Earnhardt Jr. 3.00 6.00
National Guard

1999 Winner's Circle Micro Machines 1:144

1/3 Steve Park 6.00 15.00
Pennzoil
Dale Earnhardt
Goodwrench
(Dueling Drivers)
2/24 Rusty Wallace 6.00 15.00
Rusty
Jeff Gordon
Pepsi
(Dueling Drivers)
2/18/24 Rusty Wallace 6.00 15.00
Rusty
Bobby Labonte
Interstate Batteries
Jeff Gordon
Pepsi
(Yellow Flag Series)
3 Dale Earnhardt 6.00 15.00
Goodwrench
Car and Transporter
(Race Hauler Series)
3 Dale Earnhardt 10.00 20.00
Goodwrench 3 Cars,
Transporter, helicopter & pit wagon
(Racing World series)
3 Dale Earnhardt Jr. 6.00 15.00
AC Delco
Car and Transporter
(Race Hauler Series)
3/3 Dale Earnhardt 10.00 20.00
Goodwrench
Dale Earnhardt Jr.
AC Delco
(Thunder Blaster)
24 Jeff Gordon 6.00 15.00
DuPont 3 Cars, Transporter,
tow truck & pit wagon
(Racing World series)
24 Jeff Gordon 7.50 15.00
Pepsi Car and Transporter
(Race Hauler Series)
24/28/88 eff Gordon 6.00 15.00
DuPont
Kenny Irwin
Havoline
Dale Jarrett
Quality Care
(Green Flag Series)
NNO 7-car Draft Pack/2. Rusty Wallace 7.50 15.00
Rusty/18. Bobby Labonte
Inter.Batteries/20. Tony Stewart
Home Depot/24. Jeff Gordon
DuPont/28. Kenny Irwin
Havoline/31. Mike Skinner
Lowe's/88.Dale Jarrett
Quality Care

2000 Winner's Circle Micro Machines 1:144

18/24 Bobby Labonte 6.00 15.00
Interstate Batteries
Jeff Gordon
DuPont
(Dueling Drivers)
31/88 Mike Skinner 5.00 12.00
Lowe's
Dale Jarrett
Quality Care
(Dueling Drivers)

1994 Action/RCCA Dually Trucks 1:24

The majority of these 1:24 scale die cast replicas are banks. Some were issued with a Chaparral type show trailer while others were simply released as single trucks. A dually truck is a pick-up truck with four rear wheels, two on each side. They were distributed through both Action's dealer network and the Racing Collectibles Club of America.

3 Dale Earnhardt 40.00 100.00
Goodwrench PLS
Bank/5016
5 Terry Labonte 30.00 60.00
Kellogg's Bank PLS/2508
11 Bill Elliott 30.00 80.00
Budweiser Bank/2500
16 Ted Musgrave 25.00 40.00
Family Channel
PLS Bank/2508
18 Dale Jarrett 25.00 40.00
Interstate Batteries
PLS Bank/4248
21 Morgan Shepherd 25.00 40.00
Cheerwine Bank
22 Bobby Labonte 40.00 80.00
Maxwell House
PLS Bank/2508
24 Jeff Gordon 80.00 120.00
DuPont Coke Bank
28 Davey Allison 60.00 120.00
Havoline Bank RCCA/2800
59 Dennis Setzer 25.00 40.00
Alliance Bank PLS/2500
98 Derrike Cope 20.00 40.00
Fingerhut Bank PLS/2508

1995 Action/RCCA Dually Trucks 1:24

2 Rusty Wallace 40.00 75.00
Miller Genuine Draft
Bank in plastic case
3 Dale Earnhardt 40.00 100.00
Goodwrench PLS
Bank/5016
3 Dale Earnhardt 75.00 200.00
Goodwrench Bank
7-Time Champion
24 Jeff Gordon 30.00 80.00
DuPont PLS Bank/2508
24 Jeff Gordon 20.00 50.00
DuPont RCCA/2008
28 Dale Jarrett 25.00 60.00
Havoline PLS Bank/4248
51 Neil Bonnett 25.00 60.00
Country Time PLS
Bank/5216

1996 Action/RCCA Dually Trucks 1:24

2 Rusty Wallace 20.00 50.00
Miller Splash Bank/5000
2 Rusty Wallace 40.00 75.00
Miller Genuine Draft
Silver 25th Anniversary
Bank/2500
3 Dale Earnhardt 60.00 150.00
Goodwrench RCCA
Bank/3504
5 Terry Labonte 25.00 60.00
Kellogg's RCCA Bank/2500
6 Mark Martin 35.00 70.00
Valvoline PLS Bank/4512
18 Bobby Labonte 40.00 75.00
Interstate Batteries
RCCA Bank/2500
24 Jeff Gordon 30.00 60.00
DuPont RCCA Bank/5000
28 Ernie Irvan 20.00 50.00
Havoline RCCA Bank/3500
42 Kyle Petty 20.00 50.00
Coors Light RCCA Bank/2500
88 Dale Jarrett 20.00 50.00
Quality Care PLS Bank/3500
94 Bill Elliott 20.00 50.00
McDonald's PLS Bank/4500

1997 Action/RCCA Dually Trucks 1:24

2 Rusty Wallace 30.00 75.00
Miller Lite Bank/2500
3 Dale Earnhardt 60.00 120.00
Wheaties Bank/5000
17 Darrell Waltrip 25.00 60.00
Parts America Chrome
RCCA Bank/2500
94 Bill Elliott 50.00 80.00
Mac Tonight Bank

1998-00 Action/RCCA Dually Trucks 1:24

24 Jeff Gordon 30.00 60.00
DuPont PLS
Bank/3000 1998
24 Jeff Gordon 40.00 80.00
DuPont Millennium
Silver Bank/3000 2000

1994 Action/RCCA Dually Trucks with Trailer 1:64

This series of 1:64 scale dually Trucks was issued with a Chaparral show trailer. The entire package of the dually and show trailer is a replica of what most teams use to carry their show cars from event to event. Most were issued by the RCCA club with many featuring a production run total on the box.

3 Dale Earnhardt 50.00 120.00
Goodwrench PLS/2748
3/8/3 Earnhardt Kids 175.00 300.00
Mom-n-Pop's/3750
with 3-cars
3. Dale Earnhardt Jr.
8. Kerry Earnhardt
38. Kelley Earnhardt
7 Geoff Bodine 20.00 50.00
Exide
11 Bill Elliott 30.00 60.00
Budweiser
18 Dale Jarrett 25.00 50.00
Interstate Batteries
21 Morgan Shepherd 25.00 50.00
Cheerwine
23 Jimmy Spencer 60.00 100.00
Smokin' Joe's
in plastic case/2508
24 Jeff Gordon 60.00 100.00
DuPont
28 Ernie Irvan 25.00 50.00
Mac Tools
28 Dale Jarrett 25.00 60.00
Havoline
42 Kyle Petty 30.00 60.00
Coors Light

1995 Action/RCCA Dually Trucks with Trailer 1:64

2 Rusty Wallace 30.00 60.00
Miller Genuine Draft
3 Dale Earnhardt 50.00 120.00
Goodwrench PLS/3492
7 Geoff Bodine 15.00 40.00
Exide/4008
24 Jeff Gordon 30.00 80.00
DuPont RCCA/2508
42 Kyle Petty 15.00 40.00
Coors Light PLS
in plastic case/4008
94 Bill Elliott 25.00 50.00
McDonald's PLS/2508

1996 Action/RCCA Dually Trucks with Trailer 1:64

1 Jeff Gordon Baby Ruth w car/2500	75.00	150.00
2 Rusty Wallace Miller in plastic case/2500	30.00	60.00
3 Dale Earnhardt Goodwrench RCCA/2500	50.00	120.00
3 Dale Earnhardt Goodwrench Silver	50.00	120.00
24 Jeff Gordon DuPont/2500	40.00	80.00

1997 Action/RCCA Dually Trucks with Trailer 1:64

2 Rusty Wallace Miller Lite/3000	35.00	60.00
3 Dale Earnhardt Wheaties/5000	75.00	150.00
17 Darrell Waltrip Parts America Chrome/4000	25.00	60.00
94 Bill Elliott Mac Tonight/3500	25.00	60.00

1998 Action/RCCA Dually Trucks with Trailer 1:64

3 Dale Earnhardt Goodwrench Bass Pro/5004	50.00	120.00
5 Terry Labonte Kellogg's Corny/3500	25.00	60.00
24 Jeff Gordon DuPont PLS/3500	40.00	80.00
24 Jeff Gordon DuPont Chromalusion/4500	40.00	100.00
88 Dale Jarrett Batman PLS/3500	50.00	100.00

1999 Action/RCCA Dually Trucks with Trailer 1:64

3 Dale Earnhardt Goodwrench 25th Anniversary/3000	60.00	150.00
3 Dale Earnhardt Goodwrench Sign/2508	50.00	100.00
3 Dale Earnhardt Wrangler/3504	50.00	120.00
3 Dale Earnhardt Jr. AC Delco Superman/3504	30.00	60.00
12 Jeremy Mayfield Mobil 1 Kentucky Derby	20.00	40.00

2000 Action/RCCA Dually Trucks with Trailer 1:64

2 Rusty Wallace Miller Lite in plastic case	40.00	100.00
3 Dale Earnhardt Goodwrench Taz/2508	60.00	120.00
3 Dale Earnhardt Goodwrench Peter Max/2508	90.00	175.00

2001 Action/RCCA Dually Trucks with Trailer 1:64

1 Steve Park Pennzoil Sylvester and Tweety/2508	20.00	50.00
5 Terry Labonte Kellogg's Coyote Road Runner/2508	20.00	50.00
5 Terry Labonte Kellogg's Coyote and Road Runner RCCA/738	30.00	60.00
8 Dale Earnhardt Jr. Bud All-Star/2640	60.00	100.00
24 Jeff Gordon DuPont Bugs/3000	40.00	75.00
29 Kevin Harvick Goodwrench Taz/2508	25.00	50.00

2003 Action/RCCA Dually Trucks with Trailer 1:64

29 Kevin Harvick Snap-On/8904	40.00	70.00

1994-97 Action/RCCA Dually Trucks 1:64

This series of 1:64 scale dually Truck replicas were issued as individual trucks without trailers. Most were issued by the RCCA club or in a basic issue Platinum Series (PLS) box with many featuring a production run total on the box.

2 Rusty Wallace Miller/10,000 1996	12.50	25.00
3 Dale Earnhardt Goodwrench PLS in blister pack 1994	20.00	50.00
3 Dale Earnhardt Goodwrench PLS/15,000 1995	20.00	50.00
3 Dale Earnhardt Goodwrench/15,000 1996	25.00	60.00
3 Dale Earnhardt Wheaties 1997	30.00	60.00
18 Dale Jarrett Interstate Batteries RCCA/7875 1994	12.50	30.00
24 Jeff Gordon DuPont PLS/15,000 1995	12.50	30.00
24 Jeff Gordon DuPont RCCA/2000 1995	12.50	30.00
24 Jeff Gordon DuPont/5000 1996	15.00	30.00
28 Dale Jarrett Havoline 1994	12.50	25.00
30 Michael Waltrip Pennzoil RCCA/7572 1994	10.00	20.00

1992 Action/RCCA Transporters 1:64

3 Dale Earnhardt Goodwrench DEI	150.00	250.00
28 Davey Allison Havoline	50.00	80.00
43 Richard Petty STP RCCA	45.00	75.00
44 Bobby Labonte Penrose Sausage RCCA/5000	40.00	75.00
59 Robert Pressley Alliance	45.00	75.00
66 Cale Yarborough Trop Artic RCCA/7500	25.00	50.00

1993 Action/RCCA Transporters 1:64

2 Rusty Wallace Delco Remy PLS/1000	50.00	80.00
3 Dale Earnhardt Goodwrench RCCA in box with 2-cars	75.00	150.00
3 Dale Earnhardt Goodwrench RCCA in wooden box with 2-cars/500	100.00	200.00
3 Dale Earnhardt Goodwrench RCCA with 1:64 car in black case/10,000	100.00	200.00
4 Ernie Irvan Delco Remy Platinum Series	45.00	75.00
6 Mark Martin Valvoline RCCA with car/2500	40.00	80.00
7 Harry Gant Morema	50.00	80.00
9 Bill Elliott Melling RCCA with 1:64 car	60.00	90.00
11 Bill Elliott Budweiser	60.00	90.00
17 Darrell Waltrip Delco Remy Platinum Series	35.00	75.00
17 Darrell Waltrip Western Auto RCCA/1392	25.00	60.00
24 Jeff Gordon DuPont GMP in case/2800	70.00	130.00
25 Rob Moroso Swisher RCCA	30.00	60.00
25 Ken Schrader Kodiak	50.00	80.00
28 Davey Allison Havoline RCCA/7500	60.00	120.00
28 Davey Allison Havoline Mac Tools RCCA/5004	50.00	100.00
35 Shawna Robinson Polaroid	40.00	100.00
59 Robert Pressley Alliance Fan Club	60.00	90.00

1994 Action/RCCA Transporters 1:64

This series of 1:64 scale transporters were distributed through both the club and Action's dealer network. Action was also contracted to produce many of the haulers distributed by Peachstate and GMP. Those pieces are listed within the Peachstate set.

2 Rusty Wallace Miller	40.00	90.00
3 Dale Earnhardt Goodwrench RCCA/2508	60.00	120.00
3 Dale Earnhardt 7-Time Champ 1994 Awards Banquet Promo in plastic case	100.00	200.00
3 Dale Earnhardt 1985 Wrangler blue RCCA/5016	50.00	120.00
3 Dale Earnhardt 1987 Wrangler yellow RCCA/5016	50.00	120.00
11 Bill Elliott Budwesier	60.00	90.00
21 David Pearson Chattanooga Chew	30.00	75.00
21 Morgan Shepherd Cheerwine/5000	25.00	60.00
23 Jimmy Spencer Smokin' Joe's	75.00	125.00
24 Jeff Gordon DuPont RCCA/5016	40.00	80.00
27 Tim Richmond Old Milwaukee/2500	20.00	50.00
28 Dale Jarrett Havoline	30.00	60.00
41 Joe Nemechek Meineke Platinum Series	30.00	60.00
42 Kyle Petty Coors Light	50.00	90.00
51 Neil Bonnett Country Time PLS/5216	30.00	60.00
51 Neil Bonnett Country Time RCCA	60.00	100.00
79 Dave Rezendes KPR Racing	35.00	60.00

1995 Action/RCCA Transporters 1:64

Action issued both Platinum Series and RCCA transporters again in 1995. Each club piece was issued in a large black RCCA box with the tractor and trailer packaged inside a styrofoam shell. Most of the regular (PLS) transporter releases were issued in a blue Platinum Series box that included an oversized SkyBox card.

1 Rick Mast Skoal/5004	15.00	30.00
2 Rusty Wallace Miller Genuine Draft Platinum Series	30.00	80.00
2 Rusty Wallace Miller Geniune Draft RCCA/3000	25.00	50.00
3 Dale Earnhardt Goodwrench RCCA/5004	50.00	100.00
3 Dale Earnhardt Goodwrench Service RCCA/5000	50.00	100.00
3/43 Dale Earnhardt Richard Petty 7 and 7 Champion special RCCA/3000	30.00	80.00
6 Mark Martin Valvoline	40.00	80.00
7 Alan Kulwicki Zerex/2508	50.00	100.00
11 Brett Bodine Lowe's/2508	15.00	40.00
23 Jimmy Spencer Smokin' Joe's RCCA in plastic case/2508	40.00	75.00
24 Jeff Gordon DuPont/4008	25.00	50.00
25 Ken Schrader Bud RCCA/2508	25.00	60.00
26 Brett Bodine Lowe's RCCA/2508	15.00	40.00
28 Dale Jarrett Havoline RCCA/4500	15.00	40.00
42 Kyle Petty Coors Light PLS/4008	15.00	40.00
42 Kyle Petty Coors Light RCCA/3000	15.00	40.00
94 Bill Elliott McDonald's/2508	15.00	40.00
94 Bill Elliott McDonald's RCCA/3504	20.00	50.00

1996-97 Action/RCCA Transporters 1:64

3 Dale Earnhardt Goodwrench 1996	50.00	100.00
29 Steve Grissom Cartoon Network RCCA/2500 1996	15.00	40.00
42 Joe Nemechek BellSouth Matco Tools/1765 '97	15.00	40.00

2001 Action Racing Collectables Transporters 1:64

3 Dale Earnhardt Goodwrench/6004	30.00	80.00
3 Dale Earnhardt Oreo/2508	75.00	135.00
18 Bobby Labonte Interstate Batteries Jurassic Park 3	25.00	50.00
18/20 Bobby Labonte Tony Stewart Coke Bears/4008	30.00	60.00
20 Tony Stewart Home Depot Jurassic Park 3/2052	30.00	60.00
20 Tony Stewart Home Depot Jurassic Park 3 RCCA/456	35.00	70.00
24 Jeff Gordon DuPont Bugs/2508	40.00	80.00
24 Jeff Gordon DuPont Flames/2520	75.00	135.00
29 Kevin Harvick Goodwrench/7500	25.00	50.00
88 Dale Jarrett UPS/2004	30.00	80.00

2001 Action/RCCA Transporters 1:64

18 Bobby Labonte Interstate Batteries Color Chrome Jurassic Park 3 RCCA/456	35.00	70.00
24 Jeff Gordon DuPont Bugs Color Chrome RCCA	70.00	125.00
24 Jeff Gordon DuPont Flames Color Chrome RCCA/204	175.00	300.00
88 Dale Jarrett UPS Color Chrome RCCA/504	70.00	120.00

2002 Action Racing Collectables Transporters 1:64

2 Rusty Wallace Miller Lite/2676	40.00	70.00
3 Dale Earnhardt Forever the Man/28,672	20.00	50.00
3 Dale Earnhardt Goodwrench Legacy with signatures/50,094	20.00	50.00
3 Dale Earnhardt Jr. Oreo/5016	35.00	70.00
8 Dale Earnhardt Jr. Bud/9876	25.00	60.00
20 Tony Stewart Home Depot/3000	30.00	60.00
24 Jeff Gordon DuPont 4-Time Champ/7404	25.00	50.00
24 Jeff Gordon Pepsi Daytona/3132	25.00	50.00
29 Kevin Harvick Goodwrench/6000	25.00	50.00
29 Kevin Harvick Goodwrench ET/4608	25.00	60.00
NNO Looney Tunes Rematch/3888	25.00	50.00
NNO Muppets/2808	25.00	50.00

2002 Action/RCCA Transporters 1:64

2 Rusty Wallace Miller Lite/336	40.00	75.00
3 Dale Earnhardt Forever the Man/5004	30.00	60.00
3 Dale Earnhardt Jr. Nilla Wafers/2508	40.00	75.00
3 Dale Earnhardt Jr. Oreo Color Chrome/504	45.00	80.00
8 Dale Earnhardt Jr. Bud/2508	30.00	60.00
8 Dale Earnhardt Jr. Bud Color Chrome/504	45.00	80.00
20 Tony Stewart Home Depot/504	40.00	75.00
24 Jeff Gordon DuPont 200th Anniversary/1500	45.00	80.00
24 Jeff Gordon Pepsi Daytona	35.00	70.00
NNO Looney Tunes Rematch/996	20.00	50.00

2003 Action Racing Collectables Transporters 1:64

2 Rusty Wallace Miller Lite/2448	25.00	60.00
2 Rusty Wallace Miller Lite Route/2628	25.00	60.00
8 Dale Earnhardt Jr. Bud/9876	35.00	70.00
8 Dale Earnhardt Jr. DMP Chance 2/5560	25.00	60.00
20 Tony Stewart Home Depot/2848	25.00	60.00
29 Kevin Harvick Snap-On/12,504	35.00	60.00
40 Sterling Marlin Coors Light/2532	25.00	60.00
48 Jimmie Johnson Lowe's/2952	30.00	60.00
88 Dale Jarrett UPS	40.00	75.00
88 Dale Jarrett UPS Promo in window box	20.00	35.00
NNO Realtree Racing/2712 Dale Earnhardt pictured Dave Marcis pictured	30.00	60.00
NNO Victory Lap Event/2508	35.00	70.00

2003 Action/RCCA Transporters 1:64

2 Rusty Wallace Miller Lite Route Color Chrome/1008	30.00	60.00
8 Dale Earnhardt Jr. Bud/2508	40.00	70.00

2004 Action Racing Collectables Transporters 1:64

8 D.Earnhardt Jr. Bud/2352	35.00	60.00
88 Dale Jarrett UPS	35.00	60.00
NNO Dale Earnhardt Foundation Feed the Children/1764	35.00	60.00

2005 Action Racing Collectables Transporters 1:64

2 Rusty Wallace Miller Lite 1980's Tribute/1500	40.00	65.00
2 Rusty Wallace Miller Lite 1980's Tribute QVC/504	40.00	65.00
2 Rusty Wallace Miller Lite 1990's Tribute/1500	40.00	65.00
2 Rusty Wallace Miller Lite 1990's Tribute QVC/504	40.00	65.00
2 Rusty Wallace Miller Lite 2000's Tribute/1500	40.00	65.00
2 Rusty Wallace Miller Lite 2000's Tribute QVC/504	40.00	65.00
9 Kasey Kahne Dodge/1716	40.00	65.00
9 Kasey Kahne Dodge QVC/288	40.00	65.00
41 Reed Sorenson Discount Tire	40.00	65.00

2008 Action Pit Stop Transporter Banks 1:64

3 Dale Earnhardt Goodwrench Atlanta Tribute/2508	15.00	30.00
3 Dale Earnhardt Goodwrench Bristol Tribute/3000	15.00	30.00
3 Dale Earnhardt Goodwrench Darlington Tribute/2004	15.00	30.00
3 Dale Earnhardt Goodwrench Indianapolis Tribute/2004	15.00	30.00
3 Dale Earnhardt Goodwrench Talladega Tribute/3504	15.00	30.00
9 Kasey Kahne Bud/2004	10.00	20.00
11 Denny Hamlin Fed Ex Express/2004	10.00	20.00
16 Greg Biffle 3M/1608	10.00	20.00
17 Matt Kenseth DeWalt/2004	10.00	20.00
20 Tony Stewart Home Depot/2004	10.00	20.00
24 Jeff Gordon DuPont/2492	12.50	25.00
29 Kevin Harvick Shell/2004	10.00	20.00
88 Dale Earnhardt Jr. AMP/3751	12.50	25.00
88 Dale Earnhardt Jr. National Guard/3816	12.50	25.00
88 Dale Earnhardt Jr. National Guard Promo/2004	15.00	30.00
88 Dale Earnhardt Jr. National Guard Digital Camo	12.50	25.00
99 Carl Edwards Office Depot/2004	10.00	20.00

2008 Action/RCCA Transporters 1:64

1 Martin Truex Jr. Bass Pro Shops/708	35.00	60.00
9 Kasey Kahne Bud/708	35.00	60.00
17 Matt Kenseth DeWalt/700	35.00	60.00
18 Kyle Busch M&M's/708	40.00	70.00
43 Bobby Labonte Cheerios/708	35.00	60.00

1994-96 Action/RCCA Transporters 1:96

This series of 1:96 scale transporters features some of the best drivers in Winston Cup over the last 20 years. This is the smallest size piece that Action makes.

2 Rusty Wallace MGD/3000 1995	15.00	40.00
3 Dale Earnhardt Goodwrench/3000 '94	75.00	150.00
3 Dale Earnhardt Goodwrench/5000 '95	30.00	60.00
3 Dale Earnhardt Goodwrench/3000 1996	30.00	60.00
3 Dale Earnhardt 1985 Wrangler Blue/2508 1994	60.00	150.00
3 Dale Earnhardt 1987 Wrangler Yellow	75.00	125.00
23 Jimmy Spencer Smokin' Joe's RCCA in plastic case/2508 1995	50.00	80.00
24 Jeff Gordon DuPont PLS/4008 '95	25.00	60.00
25 Ken Schrader Bud/4008 1994	15.00	40.00
27 Tim Richmond Old Milwaukee RCCA/2500 1994	20.00	40.00
28 Dale Jarrett Havoline PLS/4008	15.00	40.00
42 Kyle Petty Coors Light Platinum Series/4008 1995	15.00	40.00
94 Bill Elliott McDonald's RCCA/3508	15.00	40.00

1993-95 Brookfield Dually with Car and Show Trailer 1:25

3 Dale Earnhardt Goodwrench/40,000 1993	75.00	150.00
3 Dale Earnhardt Goodwrench without car/5000 '94	60.00	120.00
3 Dale Earnhardt Goodwrench Plus/5000 1995	60.00	120.00
3/43 Dale Earnhardt Goodwrench 7&7/5000 Richard Petty STP 7&7 1995	75.00	150.00
5 Terry Labonte Kellogg's/5000 1994	40.00	80.00
24 Jeff Gordon DuPont without car/10,000 1995	75.00	150.00
25 Ken Schrader Bud without car/5000 1995	40.00	80.00
25 Ken Schrader Bud Silver without car/400 1995	60.00	120.00
30 Michael Waltrip Pennzoil without car/5000 1995	40.00	80.00
30 Michael Waltrip Pennzoil w o car Silver/250 1995	60.00	120.00
NNO Brickyard 400 without car 1994	40.00	80.00
NNO Brickyard 400 without car 1995	40.00	80.00

1997 Brookfield Dually with Car and Show Trailer 1:25

3 Dale Earnhardt Wheaties/10,000 1997	100.00	200.00
24 Jeff Gordon DuPont Lost World without car/7500 1997	75.00	150.00
24 Jeff Gordon DuPont Lost World Silver without car/400 1997	125.00	225.00

1998 Brookfield Dually with Car and Show Trailer 1:25

1 Dale Earnhardt Jr. Coke Bear/2500	75.00	150.00
3 Dale Earnhardt Coke/2500	100.00	200.00
3 Dale Earnhardt Goodwrench Plus Bass Pro/5000	150.00	250.00
24 Jeff Gordon DuPont 2-Time Champ/5000	100.00	200.00
24 Jeff Gordon DuPont ChromaPremier/5000	75.00	150.00

1999 Brookfield Dually with Car and Show Trailer 1:25

3 Dale Earnhardt Goodwrench Plus Silver/2584	100.00	200.00
3 Dale Earnhardt Wrangler/3992	175.00	300.00
3 Dale Earnhardt Jr. AC Delco/4224	75.00	150.00
3 Dale Earnhardt Jr. AC Delco Superman/4244	75.00	150.00
8 Dale Earnhardt Jr. Bud/2616	90.00	180.00
9 Jerry Nadeau	40.00	80.00

Jetsons/1500

20 Tony Stewart Home Depot/3716 100.00 175.00
20 Tony Stewart Home Depot Silver/799 175.00 300.00
20 Tony Stewart Home Depot Habitat for Humanity/2832 100.00 175.00
20 Tony Stewart Home Depot Habitat Silver/650 200.00 300.00
24 Jeff Gordon Superman/3168 125.00 225.00
36 Ernie Irvan M&M's/1320 60.00 120.00
36 Ernie Irvan M&M's Countdown to Millennium/1316 60.00 120.00
36 Ernie Irvan M&M's Countdown to Millenium Silver/314 75.00 150.00
36 Ernie Irvan M&M's Millennium/1316 60.00 120.00
36 Ernie Irvan M&M's Millennium Silver/313 75.00 150.00
94 Bill Elliott McDonald's Silver/1196 60.00 120.00

2000 Brookfield Dually with Car and Show Trailer 1:25

3 Dale Earnhardt Goodwrench Taz/2164 175.00 300.00
3 Dale Earnhardt Goodwrench Taz Silver/516 350.00 500.00
3 Dale Earnhardt Goodwrench Peter Max/2508 200.00 350.00
8 Dale Earnhardt Jr. Bud/2048 90.00 180.00
8 Dale Earnhardt Jr. Bud Olympics/1648 100.00 200.00
8 Dale Earnhardt Jr. Bud Olympic Silver Incentive/380 125.00 250.00
20 Tony Stewart Home Depot Kids Workshop/1212 60.00 120.00
24 Jeff Gordon DuPont Peanuts/2140 100.00 200.00
25 Jerry Nadeau Coast Guard/736 40.00 80.00
28 Ricky Rudd Havoline Marines/1880 40.00 80.00
28 Ricky Rudd Havoline Marines Silver/628 50.00 100.00
88 Dale Jarrett Quality Care/2008 50.00 100.00
88 Dale Jarrett Quality Care Silver/500 60.00 120.00
88 Dale Jarrett Quality Care Air Force/1880 50.00 100.00
88 Dale Jarrett Quality Care Air Force Silver/628 60.00 120.00
94 Bill Elliott McDonald's Drive Thru 25th Anniversary/1196 40.00 80.00
94 Bill Elliott McDonald's Drive Thru 25th Anniv.Silver/304 60.00 120.00

2001 Brookfield Dually with Car and Show Trailer 1:25

3 Dale Earnhardt Goodwrench Plus/10,000 60.00 150.00
3 Dale Earnhardt Goodwrench Silver/5004 50.00 100.00
3 Dale Earnhardt Oreo 2-Axle/6504 75.00 150.00
3 Dale Earnhardt Oreo 2-Axle Silver/1004 125.00 200.00
3 Dale Earnhardt Oreo 3-Axle/12,198 75.00 150.00
3 Dale Earnhardt Oreo 3-Axle Silver/2892 125.00 250.00
9 Bill Elliott Dodge Muhammad Ali without car/2028 50.00 100.00
9 Bill Elliott Dodge Muhammad Ali Silver without car/496 60.00 120.00
9 Bill Elliott Casey Atwood Dodge Spiderman 4-piece set/2328 90.00 150.00
9 Bill Elliott Casey Atwood Dodge Spiderman Silver 4-piece set/504 125.00 250.00
18 Bobby Labonte Interstate Batteries Jurassic Park 3 without car/2004 40.00 100.00
18 Bobby Labonte Interstate Batteries Jurassic Park 3 Silver without car/504 50.00 100.00
20 Tony Stewart Home Depot Jurassic Park 3 without car/2004 60.00 120.00
24 Jeff Gordon DuPont Flames/1788 100.00 200.00
88 Dale Jarrett UPS/1308
88 Dale Jarrett UPS Silver/1200 100.00 175.00

2002 Brookfield Dually with Car and Show Trailer 1:25

3 Dale Earnhardt Jr. Nilla Wafers/3000 50.00 120.00
3 Dale Earnhardt Jr. Nilla Wafers Silver/660 90.00 180.00
3 Dale Earnhardt Jr. Oreo/3608 75.00 150.00
3 Dale Earnhardt Jr. Oreo Silver/872 90.00 180.00
8 Dale Earnhardt Jr. 75.00 150.00
Bud without car/4480
8 Dale Earnhardt Jr. Bud Silver without car/1052 90.00 180.00
8 Dale Earnhardt Jr. Bud Color Chrome 90.00 180.00
24 Jeff Gordon DuPont Flames without car/3492 50.00 100.00
24 Jeff Gordon DuPont Flames Silver without car/784 60.00 150.00
24 Jeff Gordon Pepsi Daytona without car/2172 50.00 100.00
24 Jeff Gordon Pepsi Silver without car/536 75.00 150.00
29 Kevin Harvick Goodwrench/4924 50.00 100.00
29 Kevin Harvick Goodwrench Silver/1192 50.00 120.00

2003 Brookfield Dually and Show Trailer 1:25

8 Dale Earnhardt Jr. Bud All-Star Game 3-axle/2682 60.00 120.00
8 Dale Earnhardt Jr. Dirty Mo Posse 3-axle/2046 50.00 100.00
8 Dale Earnhardt Jr. DMP Silver 3-axle/929 60.00 120.00
8 Dale Earnhardt Jr. Oreo Ritz/2804 40.00 80.00
8 Dale Earnhardt Jr. Oreo Ritz Silver/572 60.00 120.00
24 Jeff Gordon Pepsi Billion $/2368 50.00 100.00
24 Jeff Gordon Pepsi Billion $ Silver/333 60.00 120.00

2005 Brookfield Dually and Show Trailer 1:24

24 Jeff Gordon DuPont Flames/1668 40.00 60.00
24 Jeff Gordon DuPont Flames GM Dealers/36 40.00 60.00
24 Jeff Gordon DuPont Flames QVC/400 40.00 60.00

1992-93 Brookfield Suburbans, Blazers, and Tahoes 1:25

Brookfield Collectors Guild began this series in 1992. The 1:25 scale SUVs include primarily Suburbans (with most being banks) and a few Blazers and Tahoes. Each is decorated in team or special event colors and was distributed either through direct sales or hobby outlets. Each was packaged in a clear window cardboard box and most included the year of issue and production run printed on the box.

3 Dale Earnhardt Goodwrench Bank/5000 1992 40.00 80.00
24 Jeff Gordon DuPont Rookie of the Year Bank/25,000 25.00 60.00
NNO Indianapolis 500 1993 10.00 25.00

1994 Brookfield Suburbans, Blazers, and Tahoes 1:25

30 Michael Waltrip Pennzoil/10,000 15.00 40.00
42 Kyle Petty Mello Yello Sabco Brickyard/5000 10.00 25.00
42 Kyle Petty Mello Yello Thanks Fans Brickyard/10,000 10.00 25.00
NNO Brickyard 400 Bank White paint/25,000 10.00 25.00
NNO Brickyard 400 Bank Yellow paint scheme 100.00 175.00
NNO Don Prudhomme Snake Final Strike Tour 25.00 50.00

1995 Brookfield Suburbans, Blazers, and Tahoes 1:25

3 Dale Earnhardt Brickyard/5000 25.00 50.00
3 Dale Earnhardt Goodwrench Tahoe Bank/10,000 25.00 50.00
3 Dale Earnhardt Goodwrench Silver Tahoe Bank/10,000 30.00 80.00
3 Dale Earnhardt Goodwrench Bank 7-Time Champ/30,000 30.00 80.00
3 Dale Earnhardt Goodwrench Bank 7-Time Champ Silver/1500 50.00 100.00
3/43 Dale Earnhardt Richard Petty 7-Time Champion 2-Suburban set/25,000 25.00 60.00
3/43 Dale Earnhardt Richard Petty 7-Time Champion Bank split paint scheme/30,000 20.00 40.00
3/43 Dale Earnhardt Richard Petty 7-Time Champion Bank split paint scheme tampos are reversed/30,000 20.00 40.00
5 Terry Labonte Kellogg's/10,000 15.00 40.00
24 Jeff Gordon DuPont Blue Bank/10,000 30.00 60.00
24 Jeff Gordon DuPont Silver Bank/10,000 30.00 60.00
24 Jeff Gordon DuPont White Bank/15,000 25.00 50.00
42 Kyle Petty Mello Yello Bank/10,000 15.00 40.00
NNO Brickyard 400 Silver Bank/5000 25.00 50.00
NNO Brickyard 400 White Bank/15,000 25.00 50.00
NNO John Force Castrol GTX 40.00 80.00

1996 Brookfield Suburbans, Blazers, and Tahoes 1:25

3 Dale Earnhardt Olympic Tahoe/10,000 40.00 80.00
3 Dale Earnhardt Olympic Tahoe Silver/832 50.00 120.00
5 Terry Labonte Kellogg's Silver 100.00 175.00
24 Jeff Gordon DuPont Blazer 20.00 50.00
24 Jeff Gordon DuPont Blazer Silver/150 75.00 150.00
24 Jeff Gordon DuPont Tahoe Bank/5000 20.00 50.00
25 Ken Schrader Bud Red 20.00 50.00
25 Ken Schrader Bud White 25.00 50.00
30 Johnny Benson Pennzoil 25.00 50.00

1997 Brookfield Suburbans, Blazers, and Tahoes 1:25

3 Dale Earnhardt Goodwrench Plus/5000 25.00 60.00
24 Jeff Gordon DuPont Gold 3-time Champ/5000 30.00 60.00
NNO California Inaugural 10.00 25.00

1998 Brookfield Suburbans, Blazers, and Tahoes 1:25

3 Dale Earnhardt Goodwrench Bass Pro Tahoe/5000 30.00 60.00
24 Jeff Gordon DuPont Chromalusion Tahoe/5000 20.00 50.00
24 Jeff Gordon DuPont Chromalusion Silver Tahoe/250 30.00 60.00

1999 Brookfield Suburbans, Blazers, and Tahoes 1:25

3 Dale Earnhardt AC-Delco Bank/5000 20.00 50.00
3 Dale Earnhardt Goodwrench 25th Anniversary Blazer/2508 25.00 60.00
3 Dale Earnhardt Goodwrench 25th Anniv. Tahoe/2508 25.00 60.00
3 Dale Earnhardt Wrangler/2508 20.00 50.00
8 Dale Earnhardt Jr. Bud/2508 30.00 60.00
24 Jeff Gordon DuPont Superman/2508 40.00 80.00
24 Jeff Gordon Pepsi Blazer/5004 25.00 60.00

2001 Brookfield Suburbans, Blazers, and Tahoes 1:25

8 Dale Earnhardt Jr. Bud/2464 30.00 60.00
8 Dale Earnhardt Jr. Bud Silver/620 40.00 80.00
8 Dale Earnhardt Jr. Bud All Star/2876 35.00 60.00
8 Dale Earnhardt Jr. Bud All Star Silver/658 40.00 80.00
29 Kevin Harvick Goodwrench Taz/4008 25.00 50.00

2002 Brookfield Suburbans, Blazers, and Tahoes 1:25

3 Dale Earnhardt Jr. Oreo Bank/2508 30.00 60.00
29 Kevin Harvick Goodwrench/4428 20.00 50.00
29 Kevin Harvick Goodwrench Incentive/386 25.00 50.00

2003 Brookfield Suburbans, Blazers, and Tahoes 1:25

3 Dale Earnhardt Goodwrench Bass Pro Suburban/3711 25.00 50.00
3 Dale Earnhardt Goodwrench Silver Select Suburban/2646 25.00 50.00

1995 Brookfield Trackside 1:25

These 3-piece sets are complete with a 1:24 scale car and a flatbed trailer. In some cases a Suburban or other truck type was substituted for the standard dually pick-up.

3 Dale Earnhardt AC Delco Silver/800 60.00 120.00
3 Dale Earnhardt Goodwrench/10,000 50.00 120.00
3 Dale Earnhardt Goodwrench Silver/10,000 50.00 120.00
24 Jeff Gordon DuPont/10,000 60.00 120.00

1996 Brookfield Trackside 1:25

3 Dale Earnhardt AC Delco/10,000 50.00 120.00
3 Dale Earnhardt Goodwrench Olympic/10,000 75.00 150.00
5 Terry Labonte Kellogg's Bank/5000 30.00 80.00
25 Wally Dallenbach Budweiser 30.00 60.00

1997 Brookfield Trackside 1:25

3 Dale Earnhardt Goodwrench Plus Suburban/5000 50.00 100.00
3 Dale Earnhardt Wheaties/10,000 75.00 150.00
3 Dale Earnhardt Wheaties Suburban/10,000 75.00 150.00

1998 Brookfield Trackside 1:25

1 Dale Earnhardt Jr. Coke Bear Suburban/4086 75.00 150.00
3 Dale Earnhardt Coke/2500 75.00 150.00
3 Dale Earnhardt Coke Suburban/3792 100.00 200.00
3 Dale Earnhardt Goodwrench Plus Bass Pro/10,000 60.00 150.00
3 Dale Earnhardt Jr. AC Delco 60.00 120.00
3 Dale Earnhardt Jr. AC Delco Silver/420 75.00 150.00
24 Jeff Gordon DuPont Chromapremier/10,000 60.00 120.00

1999 Brookfield Trackside 1:25

1 Dale Earnhardt Jr. Coke Suburban/1500 40.00 100.00
3 Dale Earnhardt Goodwrench Silver/5004 50.00 120.00
3 Dale Earnhardt Goodwrench 25th Anniversary Suburban/2748 100.00 175.00
3 Dale Earnhardt Goodwrench Plus/2508 50.00 120.00
3 Dale Earnhardt Wrangler/2508 50.00 100.00
3 Dale Earnhardt Wrangler Suburban/10,002 50.00 100.00
3 Dale Earnhardt Jr. AC Delco Suburban/2928 40.00 100.00
5 Terry Labonte K-Sentials Suburban/2202 40.00 80.00
8 Dale Earnhardt Jr. Bud/3072 75.00 150.00
12 Jeremy Mayfield Mobil 1 Kentucky Derby/1800 30.00 80.00
24 Jeff Gordon DuPont/2508 70.00 120.00
24 Jeff Gordon DuPont 24K Gold/3504 100.00 175.00
24 Jeff Gordon Pepsi/3504 60.00 120.00
24 Jeff Gordon Pepsi Suburban/2406 50.00 100.00
24 Jeff Gordon Superman/2508 100.00 200.00
31 Dale Earnhardt Jr. Gargoyles/2508 75.00 150.00
31 Dale Earnhardt Jr. Sikkens White/3000 50.00 100.00
36 Ernie Irvin M&M's/2508 70.00 120.00
40 Sterling Marlin Coors Light Brooks&Dunn/1086 50.00 100.00
88 Dale Jarrett Quality Care White/1932 75.00 150.00

2000 Brookfield Trackside 1:25

3 Dale Earnhardt Goodwrench Taz/2508 75.00 150.00
8 Dale Earnhardt Jr. Bud/3072 75.00 150.00

2001 Brookfield Trackside 1:25

2 Rusty Wallace Milelr Lite/1788 50.00 100.00
2 Rusty Wallace Miller Lite Silver/720 70.00 120.00
3 Dale Earnhardt Goodwrench/3504 50.00 120.00
3 Dale Earnhardt Goodwrench Silver/960 75.00 150.00
3 Dale Earnhardt Goodwrench Plus/5004 75.00 150.00
8 Dale Earnhardt Jr. Bud/2508 60.00 120.00
24 Jeff Gordon DuPont Flames/1788 50.00 100.00
24 Jeff Gordon DuPont Flames Silver/960 60.00 120.00
24 Jeff Gordon DuPont Flames 2001 Champ with Suburban and 24K Gold car/2508 125.00 200.00
29 Kevin Harvick Goodwrench Taz/2508 40.00 100.00

2002 Brookfield Trackside 1:25

3 Dale Earnhardt Jr. Oreo/2508 60.00 100.00
3 Dale Earnhardt Jr. Nilla Wafers/2508 60.00 100.00
8 Dale Earnhardt Jr. Bud Color Chrome/800 100.00 175.00
24 Jeff Gordon DuPont Flames/2172 50.00 100.00
24 Jeff Gordon DuPont Flames Color Chrome/960 60.00 150.00
29 Kevin Harvick Goodwrench olor Chrome/1708 50.00 100.00

2004 Brookfield Trackside 1:25

29 Kevin Harvick Snap On RCR 35th Ann./2508 100.00 175.00

2000 Brookfield Dually with Car and Show Trailer 1:64

3 Dale Earnhardt Goodwrench Taz/2508 50.00 100.00

2004 Brookfield Trackside 1:64

These were released in Skybox packaging.

8 Dale Earnhardt Jr. Bud/7624 on a base 15.00 30.00
8 Dale Earnhardt Jr. Bud Born On February 15/6384 15.00 30.00
8 Dale Earnhardt Jr. Oreo Ritz/4704 12.50 25.00
8 Martin Truex Jr. Bass Pro Shops/2400 15.00 30.00
9 Kasey Kahne Dodge refresh/4224 15.00 30.00
20 Tony Stewart Home Depot/4944 12.50 25.00
20 Tony Stewart Home Depot Black Reverse Paint/3000 12.50 25.00
29 Kevin Harvick Goodwrench/3924 12.50 25.00

2005 Brookfield Trackside 1:64

2 Rusty Wallace Miller Lite/2136 15.00 30.00
8 Dale Earnhardt Jr. Bud Born On Feb.20/4008 15.00 30.00
9 Kasey Kahne Dodge Retro Bud Shootout/2760 15.00 30.00

1993-95 Corgi Race Image Transporters 1:64

Each Transporter in this series was produced by Corgi ar distributed by Race Image. Each was packaged in a blue an black window box.

6 Mark Martin Valvoline 1993 15.00 40.00
22 Bobby Labonte Maxwell House 15.00 30.00
26 Brett Bodine Quaker State 15.00 30.00
28 Davey Allison Havoline 1993 15.00 40.00

1992 Ertl Founding Fathers Transporters 1:43

Each of these vintage transporters were issued in a red ar black checkered box with a picture of the featured driver's car o the outside. The trailer itself also included a picture of the car.

9 Curtis Crider 1948 Chevy 35.00 60.00
55 Tiny Lund 1950 Chevy 35.00 60.00
M3 Fireball Roberts 1937 Ford 35.00 60.00

1990 Ertl Transporters 1:64

These Transporters were issued by Ertl and packaged in a whi checkered flag designed blister with a large NASCAR log across the top.

4 NDA Kodak (Rick Wilson's Car) 6.00 15.00
21 NDA Citgo Wood Brothers (Dale Jarrett's Car) 12.50 25.00
30 NDA Country Time (Michael Waltrip's Car) 12.50 25.00
43 Richard Petty STP 10.00 25.00

1992-94 Ertl White Rose Transporters Promos 1:64

This series features many of the BGN drivers from the earl '90's and other special NASCAR promo pieces that wer contracted. The pieces were made by Ertl and distribute through White Rose Collectibles.

1 Jeff Burton Baby Ruth 1993 30.00 50.00
1 Jeff Gordon Baby Ruth 50.00 90.00
2 Ricky Craven DuPont 30.00 50.00
7 Alan Kulwicki 1992 Winston Cup Champion 100.00 160.00
11 Bill Elliott Budweiser in Wooden case 75.00 125.00
23 Hut Stricklin Smokin' Joe's in pastic case 35.00 60.00
29 Phil Parsons White Rose 25.00 45.00
33 Harry Gant Manheim 30.00 50.00
36 Kenny Wallace Dirt Devil 25.00 45.00
41 Stanley Smith White House Apple Juice 25.00 45.00
43 Richard Petty Petty 35th Anniversary Tour 100.00 175.00
52 Ken Schrader AC Delco 25.00 45.00
75 Jack Sprague Staff America 25.00 45.00
87 Joe Nemechek Dentyne 25.00 45.00
87 Joe Nemechek 1992 BGN Champion 45.00 75.00

1992-94 Ertl White Rose Transporters Past an Present 1:64

This series produced by Ertl and distributed by White Ros features many of the greats from Past and Present. The 1:6 scale replicas features greats like Davey Allison, Dale Earnharc and Richard Petty.

3 Dale Earnhardt Goodwrench 1993 50.00 120.00
3 Dale Earnhardt 1986 Wrangler 1992 60.00 150.00
7 Geoff Bodine Exide 30.00 60.00

Alan Kulwicki Hooters 1992 30.00 80.00
Alan Kulwicki Zerex 1994 30.00 80.00
Kyle Petty 7-Eleven 1993 25.00 50.00
1 Darrell Waltrip Mountain Dew 30.00 60.00
2 Jimmy Spencer Meineke 20.00 40.00
4 Terry Labonte Kellogg's 30.00 50.00
5 Lake Speed Quality Care 20.00 40.00
5 Ted Musgrave Family Channel 20.00 40.00
7 Darrell Waltrip Western Auto 1994 20.00 40.00
8 Dale Jarrett Interstate Batteries 1992 20.00 50.00
1 Neil Bonnett Warner Hodgdon 1992 35.00 70.00
1 Morgan Shepherd Citgo 25.00 45.00
4 Jeff Gordon DuPont 1993 40.00 100.00
7 Junior Johnson Mountain Dew 30.00 50.00
8 Davey Allison Havoline black&white 50.00 120.00
8 Cale Yarborough Hardee's 20.00 50.00
1 Phil Parsons Manheim 25.00 45.00
2/43 Kyle Petty Richard Petty STP Combo 1992 40.00 100.00
4 Sterling Marlin Piedmont 30.00 50.00
8 Derrike Cope Bojangles 20.00 40.00
NO Past and Present Promo 25.00 50.00

1997-99 Hartoy American Racing Scene Transporters 1:64

ach Transporter in this series was manufactured by Hartoy and ssued in an "American Racing Scene Series II" box. It was a ontinuation of the Winross American Racing Scene Series ransporters.

Sterling Marlin Kodak 1997 45.00 80.00
6 Ted Musgrave Family Channel 35.00 70.00

1998 Hot Wheels Transporters 1:64

hese 1:64 scale transporters were primarily distributed through tail outlets with each being packaged in a black Hot Wheels acing window box. The 1998 box features the NASCAR 50th nniversary logo.

Mark Martin Valvoline 7.50 15.00
2 Jeremy Mayfield Mobil 1 7.50 15.00
5 Todd Bodine Tabasco 7.50 15.00

1999 Hot Wheels Transporters 1:64

hese 1:64 scale transporters were primarily distributed through etail outlets with each being packaged in a black Hot Wheels acing window box. The box is similar to the 1998 release ithout the 50th Anniversary logo.

Mark Martin Valvoline 7.50 20.00
0 Ricky Rudd Tide 7.50 15.00
2 Jeremy Mayfield Mobil 1 7.50 15.00
6 Ken Schrader M&M's 10.00 20.00
3 John Andretti STP 7.50 15.00
4 Kyle Petty Hot Wheels 7.50 15.00
6 Darrell Waltrip Big K 7.50 15.00
7 Chad Little John Deere 7.50 15.00

2000 Hot Wheels Deluxe Transporters 1:64

3 John Andretti STP 10.00 20.00
4 Kyle Petty Hot Wheels 10.00 20.00
5 Adam Petty Sprint PCS 25.00 60.00
5 Kenny Wallace Square D 7.50 15.00
4 Bill Elliott McDonald's 7.50 20.00

2001 Hot Wheels Racing Transporters 1:64

hese Transporters were issued by Hot Wheels in an orange nd blue box with a display window. Each piece is identified pecifically as 2001 on the front of the package and entitled ither Team Transporter or Transporter Tribute.

Mark Martin Pfizer 10.00 20.00
0 Johnny Benson Valvoline 10.00 20.00
0 Jeff Green Nesquik 10.00 20.00
1 Davey Allison Davey Tribute 12.50 25.00
1 Darrell Waltrip Darrell Waltrip Tribute 12.50 25.00
2 Jeremy Mayfield Mobil 1 10.00 20.00
7 Matt Kenseth DeWalt 12.50 25.00
6 Ken Schrader M&M's 10.00 20.00
2 Kyle Petty STP Tribute 12.00 20.00
3 Richard Petty STP Tribute 12.00 20.00
5 Kyle Petty Sprint 10.00 20.00
5 Bobby Hamilton Square D 10.00 20.00

96 Andy Houston McDonald's 10.00 20.00
99 Jeff Burton Citgo 10.00 20.00

2002 Hot Wheels Transporters 1:64

These Transporters were issued by Hot Wheels in the same orange and blue boxes with a display window that were used in 2001. However, each piece is identified specifically as 2002 on the package itself and entitled either Team Transporter or Transporter Tribute.

5 Terry Labonte Kellogg's 10.00 20.00
10 Johnny Benson Valvoline 10.00 20.00
10 Scott Riggs Nesquik 10.00 20.00
11 Cale Yarborough Tribute 10.00 20.00
12 Ryan Newman Alltel 12.50 25.00
14 Larry Foyt Harrah's 10.00 20.00
17 Matt Kenseth DeWalt 12.50 25.00
21 Buddy Baker Valvoline Tribute 10.00 20.00
21 Elliott Sadler Motorcraft 10.00 20.00
22 Ward Burton Caterpillar 10.00 20.00
25 Jerry Nadeau UAW 10.00 20.00
25 Randy Tolsma Marines Red Black 10.00 20.00
32 Ricky Craven Tide 10.00 20.00
36 Ken Schrader M&M's 10.00 20.00
43 John Andretti Cheerios 10.00 20.00
45 Kyle Petty Sprint 10.00 20.00
60 Greg Biffle Grainger 12.50 25.00
NNO Hendrick 100-Victories Tribute Rick Hendrick, Jeff Gordon, Ken Schrader, Geoff Bodine, and Jerry Nadeau 12.00 20.00
NNO Petty Family Tribute Lee Petty, Richard Petty, Kyle Petty, and Adam Petty 12.50 25.00

2003 Hot Wheels Transporters 1:64

The 2003 Transporters are a re-package of a few die-cast pieces from 2002 and 2001 with a few new paint schemes included. The same orange and blue window box design from 2001 and 2002 was used except that a specific year of issue was omitted from the front of the box for 2003. The Kenseth Championship

6 Mark Martin Pfizer 12.00 20.00
10 Scott Riggs Nesquik 12.00 20.00
12 Ryan Newman Alltel 12.50 25.00
17 Matt Kenseth DeWalt 15.00 25.00
21 Ricky Rudd Motorcraft 15.00 25.00
25 Bobby Hamilton Jr. Marines 12.50 25.00
32 Ricky Craven Tide 12.00 20.00
36 Ken Schrader M&M's 12.00 20.00
43 John Andretti Cheerios 12.00 20.00
45 Kyle Petty Georgia Pacific 12.50 25.00
97 Kurt Busch Rubbermaid 12.50 25.00
99 Jeff Burton Citgo 12.00 20.00
M2 Fireball Roberts Tribute 12.00 20.00
NNO Ned Jarrett Tribute 12.00 20.00

2003 Hot Wheels Racing Matt Kenseth Championship Transporters 1:64

17 Matt Kenseth DeWalt 15.00 30.00

2004 Hot Wheels Team Transporters 1:64

12 Ryan Newman Alltel 12.50 25.00
16 Greg Biffle National Guard 12.50 25.00
04 Justice League Event 15.00 25.00
04 Justice League Villains 15.00 25.00

2004 Hot Wheels Victory Lane Transporters 1:64

12 Ryan Newman Alltel 15.00 25.00
12B Ryan Newman Alltel 15.00 25.00
16 Greg Biffle Grainger 15.00 25.00
17 Matt Kenseth DeWalt 15.00 25.00
97 Kurt Busch Rubbermaid 15.00 25.00
97B Kurt Busch Rubbermaid 15.00 25.00

2005 Hot Wheels Batman Begins Transporters 1:64

6 Mark Martin Batman 20.00 35.00

1990-93 Matchbox White Rose Team Convoys 1:64

Each set of die-cast in this series consists of one Team Convoy flatbed truck and 2-1:64 scale cars or 1-car and 1-truck or van. They were produced by Matchbox for White Rose and packaged in a cardboard window box. The year of issue was printed on the backs of the early pieces and on the fronts of the newer releases.

3 Dale Earnhardt Goodwrench with Van 1991 20.00 40.00
3 Dale Earnhardt Goodwrench 1991 Champ w Van '92 20.00 35.00
3 Dale Earnhardt Goodwrench 1993 15.00 30.00
4 Ernie Irvan Kodak w van 1991 10.00 20.00
7 Harry Gant Manheim Auctions 1994 10.00 20.00
7 Alan Kulwicki Hooters 1993 10.00 20.00
10 Derrike Cope Purolator w van 1991 10.00 20.00
11 Bill Elliott Amoco with truck 1992 10.00 20.00
15 Lake Speed Quality Care with truck 1993 10.00 20.00
24 Jeff Gordon DuPont Rookie of the Year 1993 20.00 35.00
25 Ken Schrader Hendrick w van 1993 10.00 20.00
28 Davey Allison Havoline 1993 12.50 25.00
30 Michael Waltrip Pennzoil w Van 1991 10.00 20.00
42 Kyle Petty Mello Yello w van 1992 7.50 20.00
43 Richard Petty STP w van 1992 10.00 25.00
68 Bobby Hamilton Country Time Daytona 500 1993 10.00 20.00

1993-94 Matchbox White Rose Transporters Promos 1:64

3 Dale Earnhardt Goodwrench 6-Time Champ in plastic case/5000 '93 100.00 200.00
3 Dale Earnhardt Goodwrench 7-Time Champ in plastic case/4000 '94 100.00 200.00

1997 Matchbox White Rose Transporters 1:64

This series of replica transporters represents the first year White Rose switched to the 1:64 scale size. The transporters were produced by Matchbox and distributed by White Rose Collectibles with each in its own acrylic case. The stated production run was 5000.

2 Rusty Wallace Miller Lite 45.00 70.00
5 Terry Labonte Kellogg's 30.00 60.00
25 Ricky Craven Budweiser 35.00 60.00
33 Ken Schrader Skoal 30.00 60.00
94 Bill Elliott McDonald's 35.00 60.00
94 Bill Elliott Mac Tonight 35.00 60.00

1994 Matchbox White Rose Transporters Super Star Series 1:80

This series of 1:80 scale replicas represents the first year White Rose switched to the 1:80 scale size. The transporters were produced by Matchbox and distributed by White Rose Collectibles.

2 Ricky Craven DuPont 5.00 10.00
3 Dale Earnhardt Goodwrench Snap-on 10.00 20.00
4 Sterling Marlin Kodak 5.00 12.00
5 Terry Labonte Kellogg's 5.00 10.00
7 Geoff Bodine Exide 5.00 10.00
7 Harry Gant Manheim Auctions 5.00 10.00
15 Lake Speed Quality Care 5.00 10.00
16 Ted Musgrave Family Channel 5.00 10.00
17 Darrell Waltrip Western Auto 5.00 10.00
19 Loy Allen Hooters 5.00 10.00
24 Jeff Gordon DuPont 10.00 20.00
29 Phil Parsons White Rose 5.00 10.00
32 Dale Jarrett Pic-N-Pay Shoes 5.00 10.00
40 Bobby Hamilton Kendall 5.00 10.00
41 Stanley Smith White House Apple Juice 5.00 10.00
41 Stanley Smith White House Apple Juice Gold box 12.00 18.00
43 Harry Gant Black Flag French's 5.00 10.00
46 Shawna Robinson Polaroid 5.00 10.00
52 Ken Schrader AC Delco 5.00 10.00
75 Todd Bodine Factory Stores of America 5.00 10.00
94 No Driver Association White Rose Promo 5.00 10.00
98 Derrike Cope Fingerhut 5.00 10.00

1995 Matchbox White Rose Transporters Super Star Series 1:80

This series of 1:80 scale transporters features drivers from the Winston Cup, Busch and SuperTruck circuits. The series includes special Ken Schrader Budweiser and Kyle Petty Coors Light pieces issued in a acrylic cases.

1 P.J. Jones Diehard 5.00 10.00
1 Hermie Sadler DeWalt 5.00 10.00
2 Ricky Craven DuPont 5.00 10.00
3 Dale Earnhardt Goodwrench 10.00 20.00
3 Dale Earnhardt Snap On 10.00 20.00
3 Mike Skinner Goodwrench 5.00 10.00
4 Sterling Marlin Kodak 5.00 10.00
6 Rick Carelli Total Petroleum 5.00 10.00
6 Mark Martin Valvoline 5.00 10.00
8 Jeff Burton Raybestos 5.00 10.00
11 Brett Bodine Lowe's 5.00 10.00
12 Derrike Cope Straight Arrow 5.00 10.00
23 Jimmy Spencer Smokin' Joe's 7.50 15.00
24 Jeff Gordon DuPont 7.50 15.00
24 Scott Lagasse DuPont 5.00 10.00
25 Ken Schrader Budweiser in acrylic case 12.50 25.00
26 Steve Kinser Quaker State 5.00 10.00
28 Dale Jarrett Havoline 5.00 10.00
40 Patty Moise Dial Purex 5.00 10.00
42 Kyle Petty Coors Light in acrylic case 12.50 25.00
57 Jason Keller Budget Gourmet 5.00 10.00
60 Mark Martin Winn Dixie 6.00 12.00
71 Kevin Lepage Vermont Teddy Bear 5.00 10.00
72 Tracy Leslie Detroit Gasket 5.00 10.00
74 Johnny Benson Lipton Tea 5.00 10.00
87 Joe Nemechek Burger King 5.00 10.00
90 Mike Wallace Heilig-Meyers 5.00 10.00
94 Bill Elliott McDonald's 8.00 12.00
95 John Tanner Caterpillar 5.00 10.00
99 Phil Parsons Luxaire 5.00 10.00
08 Bobby Dotter Hyde Tools 5.00 10.00

1996 Matchbox White Rose Transporters Super Star Series 1:80

These 1:80 scale transporters featured many of the new driver and color changes for 1996. The pieces are distributed through White Rose Collectibles and are produced by Matchbox.

2 Mike Bliss ASE 6.00 12.00
9 Lake Speed SPAM 6.00 12.00
10 Phil Parsons Channellock 6.00 12.00
21 Michael Waltrip Citgo 6.00 12.00
22 Ward Burton MBNA 6.00 12.00
24 Jack Sprague Quaker State 6.00 12.00
24 Jeff Gordon DuPont 7.50 15.00
34 Mike McLaughlin Royal Oak 6.00 12.00
37 John Andretti K-Mart Little Caesars 6.00 12.00
40 Tim Fedewa Kleenex 6.00 12.00
41 Ricky Craven Kodiak in acrylic case 12.00 20.00
43 Rodney Combs Lance 6.00 12.00
77 Bobby Hillin Jr. Jasper Engines 6.00 12.00
88 Dale Jarrett Quality Care 6.00 12.00
94 Bill Elliott McDonald's 6.00 12.00
95 David Green Caterpillar 6.00 12.00

1997 Matchbox White Rose Transporters Super Star Series 1:80

These 1:80 scale transporters featured many of the new driver and color changes for 1997. The pieces are distributed through White Rose Collectibles and are produced by Matchbox. Most transporters were packaged with a car.

8 Hut Stricklin Circuit City/3000 5.00 12.00
36 Derrike Cope Skittles 5.00 12.00
37 Mark Green Timber Wolf 5.00 12.00
74 Randy LaJoie Fina 5.00 12.00
96 David Green Caterpillar 5.00 12.00

1989 Matchbox White Rose Transporters Super Star Series 1:87

3 Dale Earnhardt Goodwrench 100.00 200.00
21 Neil Bonnett Citgo 100.00 160.00
28 Cale Yarborough Hardee's 90.00 150.00
43 Richard Petty STP 250.00 350.00

1990 Matchbox White Rose Transporters Super Star Series 1:87

This series of pieces represents some of the most valuable 1:87 scale die cast transporters available. The series features many greats from Winston Cup racing.

3 Dale Earnhardt Goodwrench 40.00 100.00
6 Mark Martin Folgers 90.00 150.00
9 Bill Elliott Melling 60.00 90.00
20 Rob Moroso Crown 40.00 75.00
43 Richard Petty STP 75.00 125.00
66 Dick Trickle TropArtic 35.00 60.00
94 Sterling Marlin Sunoco name on cab 125.00 225.00
94 Sterling Marlin Sunoco no name on cab 125.00 225.00
NNO Goodyear Racing 12.50 25.00

1991 Matchbox White Rose Transporters Super Star Series 1:87

This series of 1:87 scale transporters features the top names in Winston Cup racing from '91. The pieces are packaged in a red and black box and the year of the release is on the end of each box. The pieces were distributed by White Rose Collectibles.

3 Dale Earnhardt Goodwrench 15.00 40.00
4 Ernie Irvan Kodak 10.00 18.00
6 Mark Martin Folgers with Ford cab 10.00 20.00
6 Mark Martin Folgers with Mack cab 15.00 30.00
9 Bill Elliott Melling with Ford cab 10.00 20.00
9 Bill Elliott Melling with Mack cab 20.00 40.00
10 Derrike Cope Purolator Pink car 8.00 20.00
10 Derrike Cope Purolator Red car 15.00 30.00
10 Ernie Irvan Mac Tools 12.50 25.00
17 Darrell Waltrip Western Auto 10.00 20.00
22 Sterling Marlin Maxwell House 7.50 15.00
25 Ken Schrader No sponsor 7.50 15.00
28 Davey Allison Havoline black&gold 15.00 40.00
42 Kyle Petty Mello Yello 7.50 15.00
43 Richard Petty STP 20th Anniversary 15.00 30.00
66 Lake Speed TropArtic 7.50 15.00
68 Bobby Hamilton Country Time 7.50 15.00

1992 Matchbox White Rose Transporters Super Star Series 1:87

These pieces are a continuation in the Super Star Series produced by Matchbox and distributed by White Rose Collectibles. Each piece is packaged in a red and checkered flag designed box and has the year of release stamped on the end of the box.

1 Jeff Gordon Baby Ruth 20.00 50.00
2 Rusty Wallace Penske 6.00 12.00
3 Dale Earnhardt Goodwrench 12.50 25.00
7 Harry Gant Mac Tools 12.50 25.00
7 Alan Kulwicki Hooters 15.00 40.00
8 Dick Trickle Snickers 5.00 10.00
9 Bill Elliott Melling 7.50 15.00
12 Hut Stricklin aybestos 5.00 10.00
15 Morgan Shepherd Motorcraft 5.00 10.00
18 Dale Jarrett Interstate Batteries 6.00 12.00
26 Brett Bodine Quaker State 5.00 10.00
28 Davey Allison Havoline black&orange 12.50 30.00
30 Michael Waltrip Pennzoil 5.00 10.00
31 Bobby Hillin Jr. Team Ireland 5.00 10.00
43 Richard Petty STP 7.50 15.00
44 Bobby Labonte Slim Jim 6.00 12.00
49 Ed Ferree Fergaed Racing 5.00 10.00
55 Ted Musgrave Jasper Engines 5.00 10.00
59 Robert Pressley Alliance 10.00 20.00
72 Ken Bouchard ADAP 5.00 10.00
89 Jim Sauter Evinrude 5.00 10.00
92 Hut Stricklin Stanley Tools 5.00 10.00

1993 Matchbox White Rose Transporters Super Star Series 1:87

This is the last series of 1:87 scale size transporters done by Matchbox White Rose Collectibles. The pieces were distributed through White Rose Collectibles.

6 Mark Martin Valvoline	6.00	12.00
8 Jeff Burton TIC Financial	5.00	10.00
8 Jeff Burton Baby Ruth	5.00	10.00
8 Sterling Marlin Raybestos	5.00	10.00
12 Jimmy Spencer Meineke	5.00	10.00
14 Terry Labonte MW Windows	6.00	12.00
21 Morgan Shepherd Citgo	5.00	10.00
22 Bobby Labonte Maxwell House	6.00	12.00
24 Jeff Gordon DuPont	7.50	15.00
25 Hermie Sadler Virginia is for Lovers	5.00	10.00
28 Davey Allison Havoline Mac Tools	12.50	25.00
29 Phil Parsons Matchbox White Rose Collectibles	5.00	10.00
32 Jimmy Horton Active Racing	5.00	10.00
34 Todd Bodine Fiddle Faddle	5.00	10.00
40 Kenny Wallace Dirt Devil	7.50	15.00
41 Phil Parsons Manheim Auctions	5.00	10.00
48 Sterling Marlin Cappio	5.00	10.00
59 Robert Pressley Alliance	12.50	25.00
75 Jack Sprague Staff America	5.00	10.00
83 Lake Speed Purex	5.00	10.00
87 Joe Nemechek Dentyne	5.00	10.00
94 Terry Labonte Sunoco	6.00	12.00
98 Derrike Cope Bojangles	5.00	10.00
98 Jimmy Spencer Moly Black Gold	5.00	10.00
99 Ricky Craven DuPont	5.00	10.00
08 Bobby Dotter DeWalt	5.00	10.00

2007 Action/Motorsports Authentics/RCCA Transporters Bank 1:24

9 Kasey Kahne Dodge Dealers/708*	25.00	50.00
11 Denny Hamlin Fed Ex Express/708*	25.00	50.00
20 Tony Stewart Home Depot Home Depot/708*	25.00	50.00
24 Jeff Gordon DuPont Flames/708*	30.00	60.00
29 Kevin Harvick Shell Pennzoil/708*	25.00	50.00
44 Dale Jarrett UPS/708*	25.00	50.00
48 Jimmie Johnson Lowe's/708*	25.00	50.00
00 David Reutimann Domino's/708*	25.00	50.00
01 Mark Martin U.S. Army/708*	25.00	50.00

1996-01 Peachstate/GMP Transporters 1:64

These transporters were produced by GMP and distributed by Peachstate.

1 Jeff Gordon Baby Ruth RCCA/5000	100.00	150.00
1 Jeff Gordon Baby Ruth/2800	45.00	75.00
3 Dale Earnhardt Goodwrench/2500 1996	75.00	150.00
4 Ernie Irvan Kodak RCCA/3500 1993	40.00	75.00
5 Terry Labonte Kellogg's RCCA	40.00	75.00
6 Mark Martin Valvoline 1996	40.00	60.00
7 Harry Gant Mac Tools with Buick Logo/7500	50.00	80.00
7 Harry Gant Mac Tools w o Buick Logo/2500	60.00	100.00
8 Sterling Marlin Raybestos RCCA/3500	30.00	60.00
10 Ricky Rudd Tide/2004 1996	25.00	60.00
11 Steve Kinser Quaker State 1996/2800	30.00	60.00
12 Jeremy Mayfield Mobil 1 2001	35.00	60.00
16 Ted Musgrave Family Channel RCCA	40.00	75.00
18 Bobby Labonte Interstate Batteries 1996	40.00	60.00
20 Tony Stewart Home Depot/2400 1999 Rookie of the Year 2000	45.00	75.00
22 Bobby Labonte Maxwell House RCCA/2500	50.00	100.00
26 Johnny Benson Cheerios 2001	35.00	60.00
35 Todd Bodine Tabasco	35.00	60.00
36 Kenny Wallace Dirt Devil RCCA/5000	30.00	60.00
42 Kyle Petty Mello Yello RCCA/3500	25.00	60.00
60 Mark Martin Winn Dixie RCCA/3500	40.00	80.00
75 Rick Mast Remington	30.00	50.00
87 Joe Nemechek Burger King/2500 1996	25.00	60.00
87 Joe Nemechek Dentyne RCCA	35.00	60.00
92 Larry Pearson Stanley RCCA	30.00	55.00
94 Bill Elliott McDonald's/2004 1996	30.00	60.00
97 Chad Little John Deere/2004 1997	40.00	70.00
99 Jeff Burton Citgo SuperGard/1308 '01	35.00	60.00
99 Jeff Burton Exide/1440	35.00	60.00

2002 Peachstate/GMP Transporters 1:64

17 Matt Kenseth DeWalt/1200	30.00	60.00
20 Tony Stewart Home Depot/1500	30.00	60.00
21 Elliott Sadler Motorcraft/1400	30.00	60.00

2003 Peachstate/GMP Transporters 1:64

12 Ryan Newman Alltel/1200	30.00	60.00

1993 Racing Champions Transporters 1:43

3 Dale Earnhardt Goodwrench	20.00	40.00
7 Alan Kulwicki Hooters	30.00	50.00
8 Sterling Marlin Raybestos	12.50	25.00
24 Jeff Gordon DuPont	20.00	40.00
27 Hut Stricklin McDonald's	10.00	25.00
28 Davey Allison Havoline	12.50	25.00

1994 Racing Champions Transporters 1:43

10 Ricky Rudd Tide	10.00	25.00
19 Loy Allen Hooters	8.00	20.00

1991 Racing Champions Transporters 1:64

This small series was the first group of transporters done by Racing Champions. They were packaged in a black box and distributed through retail and hobby outlets.

2 Rusty Wallace Penske Racing	18.00	30.00
9 Bill Elliott Melling with Red paint scheme	60.00	100.00
11 Geoff Bodine	10.00	20.00
28 Davey Allison Havoline	30.00	50.00

1992 Racing Champions Transporters 1:64

This series of 1:64 scale transporters features many of the top names from both Winston Cup and Busch in 1992. The pieces were packaged in a black box and were distributed through hobby and retail outlets.

1 Jeff Gordon Baby Ruth	50.00	75.00
1 Rick Mast Majik Market	10.00	20.00
2 Rusty Wallace Penske	10.00	20.00
3 Dale Earnhardt Goodwrench	20.00	40.00
4 Ernie Irvan Kodak	8.00	16.00
5 Jay Fogleman Inn Keeper	6.00	12.00
5 Ricky Rudd Tide	7.50	15.00
6 Mark Martin Valvoline	8.00	16.00
7 Alan Kulwicki Hooters	30.00	60.00
9 Bill Elliott Melling with Blue paint scheme	12.50	25.00
9 Chad Little Melling	10.00	25.00
9 Joe Bessey Auto Palace	6.00	12.00
10 Derrike Cope Purolator	6.00	12.00
11 Bill Elliott Amoco	8.00	16.00
12 Bobby Allison Allison Motorsports	7.50	15.00
12 Hut Stricklin Raybestos	6.00	12.00
14 A.J. Foyt	10.00	20.00
15 Geoff Bodine Motorcraft	6.00	12.00
16 Wally Dallenbach Jr. Roush Racing	10.00	20.00
17 Darrell Waltrip Western Auto	6.00	12.00
17 Darrell Waltrip Western Auto Promo	7.50	15.00
18 Dale Jarrett Interstate Batteries	6.00	12.00
20 Joe Ruttman Fina	12.50	25.00
21 Morgan Shepherd Citgo	6.00	12.00
22 Sterling Marlin Maxwell House	6.00	12.00
25 Ken Schrader No Sponsor	7.50	15.00
25 Bill Venturini Rain X	25.00	50.00
26 Brett Bodine Quaker State	6.00	12.00
28 Davey Allison Havoline	15.00	30.00
30 Michael Waltrip Pennzoil	6.00	12.00
33 Harry Gant Food Lion	10.00	20.00
36 Kenny Wallace Dirt Devil	12.50	25.00
42 Kyle Petty Mello Yello	6.00	12.00
43 Richard Petty STP	7.50	15.00
43 Richard Petty STP Fan Appreciation Tour	10.00	20.00
49 Stanley Smith Ameritron Batteries	15.00	30.00
59 Andy Belmont FDP Brakes	15.00	30.00
59 Robert Pressley Alliance	25.00	50.00
60 Mark Martin Winn Dixie	15.00	30.00
66 Cale Yarborough TropArtic	6.00	12.00
68 Bobby Hamilton Country Time	6.00	12.00
70 J.D. McDuffie Son's Auto	15.00	30.00
71 Dave Marcis Big Apple Market	10.00	20.00
72 Ken Bouchard ADAP	6.00	12.00
90 Wally Dallenbach Jr. Ford Motorsports	15.00	30.00
97 Terry Labonte Sunoco	15.00	30.00

1993 Racing Champions Transporters 1:64

This series of 1:64 transporters was issued in red boxes along with a 1:64 scale car. The pieces feature the top names in racing. The Ricky Rudd piece in the series comes with two different paint schemes. Promo pieces were made of Dale Earnhardt, Darrell Waltrip and Hut Stricklin.

1 Jeff Gordon Baby Ruth	40.00	75.00
1 Rick Mast Majik Market	7.50	15.00
2 Rusty Wallace Penske	8.00	20.00
3 Dale Earnhardt Goodwrench	30.00	60.00
3 Dale Earnhardt Goodwrench Bank/10,000	35.00	60.00
3 Dale Earnhardt Goodwrench Promo	50.00	100.00
3 Dale Earnhardt Winston Win	40.00	75.00
4 Ernie Irvan Kodak	7.50	15.00
4 Ernie Irvan Kodak Bank	8.00	20.00
5 Ricky Rudd Tide with Orange paint scheme	7.50	15.00
5 Ricky Rudd Tide with White paint scheme	8.00	20.00
6 Mark Martin Valvoline	8.00	20.00
7 Alan Kulwicki Hooters	20.00	40.00
7 Alan Kulwicki Hooters Bank	20.00	40.00
8 Sterling Marlin Raybestos	6.00	12.00
11 Bill Elliott Amoco	8.00	20.00
11 Bill Elliott Amoco Bank/5000	8.00	20.00
12 Jimmy Spencer Meineke	6.00	12.00
14 Terry Labonte Kellogg's	15.00	30.00
15 Geoff Bodine Motorcraft	6.00	12.00
17 Darrell Waltrip Western Auto	6.00	12.00
17 Darrell Waltrip Western Auto Promo	7.50	15.00
18 Dale Jarrett Interstate Batteries	6.00	12.00
21 Morgan Shepherd Citgo	6.00	12.00
22 Bobby Labonte Maxwell House	25.00	50.00
24 Jeff Gordon DuPont	25.00	50.00
24 Jeff Gordon DuPont Bank/10,000	25.00	50.00
26 Brett Bodine Quaker State	6.00	12.00
27 Hut Stricklin McDonald's	6.00	12.00
27 Hut Stricklin McDonald's Bank/7500	12.50	25.00
27 Hut Stricklin McDonald's Promo	8.00	16.00
28 Davey Allison Havoline	12.50	25.00
28 Davey Allison Havoline Bank	20.00	40.00
30 Michael Waltrip Pennzoil	6.00	12.00
33 Harry Gant Food Lion	6.00	12.00
42 Kyle Petty Mello Yello	6.00	12.00
44 Rick Wilson STP	6.00	12.00
59 Andy Belmont FDP Brakes	12.50	25.00
60 Mark Martin Winn Dixie	10.00	20.00
75 Todd Bodine Factory Stores of America	6.00	12.00
87 Joe Nemechek Dentyne	6.00	12.00
98 Derrike Cope Bojangles	6.00	12.00
NNO Dodge IROC	10.00	20.00

1993 Racing Champions Premier Transporters 1:64

This was the first year Racing Champions did 1:64 scale Premier series pieces. The pieces come in a black shadow box. Each box has a gold stamped quantity of production on the front.

2 Rusty Wallace Ford Motorsports	20.00	35.00
3 Dale Earnhardt Goodwrench/7500	40.00	100.00
4 Ernie Irvan Kodak	20.00	35.00
5 Ricky Rudd Tide	20.00	35.00
7 Alan Kulwicki Hooters/7500	40.00	80.00
8 Sterling Marlin Raybestos	18.00	30.00
11 Bill Elliott Budweiser/5000	20.00	35.00
24 Jeff Gordon DuPont/7500	30.00	50.00
26 Brett Bodine Quaker State Bank/2500	18.00	30.00
27 Hut Stricklin McDonald's	18.00	30.00
28 Davey Allison Havoline/5028	25.00	50.00
28 Ernie Irvan Mac Tools	25.00	45.00
33 Harry Gant Chevrolet/3000	18.00	30.00
33 Harry Gant Chevrolet Food Lion Bank/2500	18.00	30.00
42 Kyle Petty Mello Yello	18.00	30.00
51 No Driver Association Primer Ford cab	18.00	30.00
51 No Driver Association Primer paint scheme Kenworth	15.00	25.00
94 No Driver Association Brickyard 400 special	30.00	50.00
NNO Dodge IROC Bank/5000	15.00	30.00

1994 Racing Champions Transporters Hobby 1:64

This series of Transporters was issued directly to hobby shops. Each was packaged in a Racing Champions yellow box.

2 Rusty Wallace Penske	10.00	20.00
4 Sterling Marlin Kodak	7.50	20.00
5 Terry Labonte Kellogg's	10.00	20.00
18 Dale Jarrett Interstate Batteries	10.00	20.00
30 Michael Waltrip Pennzoil	6.00	15.00
33 Harry Gant Leo Jackson	6.00	15.00
42 Kyle Petty Mello Yello	6.00	15.00

1994 Racing Champions Transporters Retail 1:64

This series features NASCAR racing transporters issued through retail outlets and packaged in a red clear window box. Some were also issued in a yellow box hobby version and solid red box bank versions. All packages include the hauler as well as a 1:64 die cast car. The year of issue is featured on the front of the box and a driver checklist on the back. Some drivers on the list were not produced for this set.

1 Rick Mast Majik Market	6.00	15.00
1 Rick Mast Precision Products	6.00	15.00
2 Ricky Craven DuPont	6.00	15.00
2 Rusty Wallace Penske	8.00	20.00
3 Dale Earnhardt Goodwrench Promo	40.00	80.00
4 Sterling Marlin Kodak	6.00	15.00
4 Sterling Marlin Kodak Bank/1500	8.00	20.00
5 Terry Labonte Kellogg's	8.00	20.00
6 Mark Martin Valvoline	8.00	20.00
7 Geoff Bodine Exide Batteries	6.00	15.00
7 Harry Gant Manheim Auctions	6.00	15.00
8 Jeff Burton Raybestos	6.00	15.00
10 Ricky Rudd Tide	6.00	15.00
11 Bill Elliott Amoco	6.00	15.00
15 Lake Speed Quality Care	6.00	15.00
16 Ted Musgrave Family Channel	6.00	15.00
17 Darrell Waltrip Western Auto	6.00	15.00
18 Dale Jarrett Interstate Batteries	6.00	15.00
19 Loy Allen Hooters	6.00	15.00
22 Bobby Labonte Maxwell House	6.00	15.00
24 Jeff Gordon DuPont	10.00	20.00
24 Jeff Gordon DuPont Bank	25.00	50.00
26 Brett Bodine Quaker State	6.00	15.00
27 Jimmy Spencer McDonald's	6.00	15.00
28 Ernie Irvan Havoline	6.00	15.00
30 Michael Waltrip Pennzoil	6.00	15.00
33 Harry Gant Leo Jackson	6.00	15.00
33 Bobby Labonte	30.00	50.00
Dentyne		
40 Bobby Hamilton Kendall	6.00	15.00
41 Joe Nemechek Meineke	6.00	15.00
42 Kyle Petty Mello Yello	6.00	15.00
52 Ken Schrader AC Delco	6.00	15.00
54 Robert Pressley Manheim Auctions	6.00	15.00
60 Mark Martin Winn Dixie	8.00	20.00
75 Todd Bodine Factory Stores of America	6.00	15.00
98 Derrike Cope Fingerhut	6.00	15.00

1994 Racing Champions Premier Transporters 1:64

This is a small series of 1:64 scale Premier transporters. It does however feature four of the best and most popular drivers in racing. The Jeff Gordon piece was a special made for the Winston Select.

3 Dale Earnhardt Goodwrench	75.00	150.00
4 Sterling Marlin Kodak FunSaver/3000	18.00	40.00
24 Jeff Gordon DuPont Winston Select special	20.00	35.00
33 Harry Gant Farewell Tour	20.00	35.00

1995 Racing Champions Preview Transporters 1:64

This series of 1:64 scale transporters was the first time Racing Champions produced preview pieces for transporters. The series features drivers from both the Winston Cup and Busch circuits.

2 Rusty Wallace Penske	8.00	20.00
7 Geoff Bodine Exide	7.50	15.00
10 Ricky Rudd Tide	7.50	15.00
14 Terry Labonte MW Windows	7.50	15.00
16 Ted Musgrave Family Channel	7.50	15.00
24 Jeff Gordon DuPont	10.00	20.00
27 Loy Allen Hooters	7.50	15.00
38 Elton Sawyer Red Carpet	7.50	15.00
40 Bobby Hamilton Kendall	7.50	15.00
57 Jason Keller Budget Gourmet	7.50	15.00

1995 Racing Champions Transporters 1:64

Many of the top names in Winston Cup and Busch are featured in this series. The pieces were distributed through both hobby and retail outlets. A special series of Jeff Gordon Signature Series die cast was issued in '95 and included a 1:64 transporter.

2 Rusty Wallace Penske	7.50	15.00
5 Terry Labonte Kellogg's	7.50	15.00
6 Tommy Houston Red Devil	6.00	12.00
6 Mark Martin Valvoline	7.50	15.00
7 Geoff Bodine Exide	6.00	12.00
8 Jeff Burton Raybestos	6.00	12.00
8 Kenny Wallace Red Dog	6.00	12.00
10 Ricky Rudd Tide	6.00	12.00
12 Derrike Cope Straight Arrow	6.00	12.00
18 Bobby Labonte Interstate Batteries	6.00	12.00
23 Chad Little Bayer	6.00	12.00
24 Jeff Gordon DuPont	10.00	18.00
24 Jeff Gordon DuPont Signature Series 995 WC Champion	20.00	35.00
26 Steve Kinser Quaker State	6.00	12.00
27 Loy Allen Hooter's	6.00	12.00
28 Dale Jarrett Ernie Irvan Havoline both signatures on trailer	6.00	12.00
34 Mike McLaughlin French's	6.00	12.00
40 Patty Moise Dial	6.00	12.00
44 David Green Slim Jim	6.00	12.00
47 Jeff Fuller Sunoco	6.00	12.00
60 Mark Martin Winn Dixie	7.50	15.00
90 Mike Wallace Heilig-Meyers	6.00	12.00
94 Bill Elliott McDonald's	7.50	15.00
94 Bill Elliott McDonald's Thunderbat	10.00	20.00
95 Brickyard 400 Bank/2500	6.00	12.00
99 Phil Parsons Luxaire	6.00	12.00

1995 Racing Champions Premier Transporters 1:64

This series of 1:64 scale transporters was higlighted by two beer special transporters. The Rusty Wallace Miller Genuine Draft transporter and the Kyle Petty Coors Light transporters both came in acrylic cases.

Item		
2 Rusty Wallace Miller Genuine Draft in acrylic case	30.00	45.00
2 Rusty Wallace Penske Bank	30.00	40.00
8 Jeff Burton Raybestos/1000	10.00	20.00
12 Derrike Cope Straight Arrow	10.00	20.00
26 Steve Kinser Quaker State	12.00	20.00
26 Steve Kinser Quaker State Bank	25.00	40.00
27 Loy Allen Hooters	10.00	20.00
32 Dale Jarrett Mac Tools/3000	25.00	40.00
40 Bobby Hamilton Kendall	10.00	20.00
40 Patty Moise Dial	10.00	20.00
42 Kyle Petty Coors Light in acrylic case	30.00	50.00
90 Mike Wallace Heilig-Meyers	10.00	20.00
94 Bill Elliott McDonald's	10.00	20.00
95 Brickyard 400/10,000	10.00	20.00

1996 Racing Champions Preview Transporters 1:64

This series of transporters was issued in a red box and has the word preview below the year of release. The pieces feature both Winston Cup and Busch series drivers.

Item		
4 Sterling Marlin Kodak	6.00	15.00
5 Terry Labonte Kellogg's	7.00	14.00
6 Mark Martin Valvoline	7.00	14.00
11 Brett Bodine Lowe's	6.00	12.00
12 Derrike Cope Mane N' Tail	6.00	12.00
16 Ted Musgrave Family Channel	6.00	12.00
17 Darrell Waltrip Western Auto	7.00	14.00
47 Jeff Fuller Sunoco	6.00	12.00
57 Jason Keller Slim Jim	6.00	12.00
90 Mike Wallace Heilig-Meyers	6.00	12.00

1996 Racing Champions Transporters 1:64

These pieces were issued in three different variations. Transporters were issued with no cars, one car, and with two cars. Transporters with one or two cars carry a slight premium over those issued without cars. The Chad Little transporters were issued in standard Racing Champion packaging and in John Deere promotional boxes. The Ken Scharder transporters were issued as part of a special Budweiser program. The Ricky Craven transporter was produced for and distributed by his fan club. The Mark Martin Winn Dixie transporter was distributed in Winn Dixie stores primarily in the Southeast.

Item		
1 Rick Mast Hooter's	10.00	20.00
1 Hermie Sadler DeWalt	10.00	20.00
2 Rusty Wallace Miller Genuine Draft	15.00	30.00
2 Rusty Wallace Penske	10.00	20.00
2 Rusty Wallace Penske with one car or two cars	12.50	25.00
3 Mike Skinner Goodwrench 1995 Champ with truck(s)	10.00	20.00
4 Sterling Marlin Kodak with one or two cars	12.50	25.00
5 Terry Labonte Kellogg's with one car or two cars	15.00	30.00
7 Geoff Bodine QVC	10.00	20.00
8 Hut Stricklin Circuit City	10.00	20.00
10 Ricky Rudd Tide with one car or two cars	12.50	25.00
11 Brett Bodine Lowe's	10.00	20.00
11 Brett Bodine Lowe's with one car or two cars	12.50	25.00
14 Patty Moise Dial Purex with one car or two cars	12.50	25.00
15 Wally Dallenbach Hayes	10.00	20.00
17 Darrell Waltrip Parts America	10.00	20.00
21 Michael Waltrip Citgo with one car or two cars	12.50	25.00
22 Ward Burton MBNA	10.00	20.00
23 Chad Little John Deere	10.00	20.00
23 Chad Little John Deere with one car or two cars	12.50	25.00
23 Chad Little John Deere Promo	10.00	25.00
23 Chad Little John Deere with one car Promo	15.00	35.00
24 Jeff Gordon DuPont with one car or two cars	15.00	30.00
25 Ken Schrader Budweiser	20.00	40.00
25 Ken Schrader Budweiser Chrome	150.00	300.00
28 Ernie Irvan Havoline	10.00	20.00
28 Ernie Irvan Havoline with one car or two cars	12.50	25.00
29 Steve Grissom Cartoon Network	10.00	20.00
29 Steve Grissom Cartoon Network with one car or two cars	12.50	25.00
29 Steve Grissom WCW	10.00	20.00
29 Steve Grissom WCW with one car or two cars	12.50	25.00
29 No Driver Association Scooby-Doo woth one car or two	10.00	20.00
30 Johnny Benson Pennzoil	10.00	20.00
32 Dale Jarrett Band-Aid with one car or two cars	25.00	40.00
37 John Andretti K-Mart Promo	15.00	25.00
41 Ricky Craven Kodiak Fan Club	20.00	40.00
43 Rodney Combs Lance	10.00	20.00
43 Bobby Hamilton STP	10.00	20.00
43 Bobby Hamilton STP with one car or two cars	12.50	25.00
44 Bobby Labonte Shell	15.00	25.00
47 Jeff Fuller Sunoco	10.00	20.00
60 Mark Martin Winn Dixie	15.00	25.00
60 Mark Martin Winn Dixie with one car or two cars	20.00	35.00
74 Johnny Benson Lipton Tea with one car or two cars	10.00	20.00
74 Randy LaJoie Fina	10.00	20.00
87 Joe Nemechek Bell South	10.00	20.00
87 Joe Nemechek Burger King	10.00	20.00
88 Dale Jarrett Quality Care	30.00	50.00
88 Dale Jarrett Quality Care with one car or two cars	30.00	50.00
94 Bill Elliott McDonald's	10.00	20.00
94 Bill Elliott McDonald's with one car or two cars	12.50	25.00
94 Bill Elliott McDonald's Monopoly	10.00	20.00
94 Bill Elliott McDonald's Monopoly with one or two cars	12.50	25.00

1996 Racing Champions Premier Transporters 1:64

These pieces were issued with a premier car and distributed through both hobby and retail outlets.

Item		
2 Rusty Wallace Penske	15.00	30.00
6 Mark Martin Valvoline	15.00	30.00
11 Brett Bodine Lowe's	12.50	25.00
24 Jeff Gordon DuPont	15.00	30.00
29 Steve Grissom Cartoon Network	12.50	25.00
29 Steve Grissom WCW	12.50	25.00
43 Bobby Hamilton STP Silver	12.50	25.00
88 Dale Jarrett Quality Care	15.00	30.00
94 Bill Elliott McDonald's	15.00	30.00

1997 Racing Champions Preview Transporters 1:64

Many of the top drivers from the Winston Cup circuit are featured in this series. The pieces were distributed through both hobby and retail outlets.

Item		
4 Sterling Marlin Kodak	12.00	25.00
5 Terry Labonte Kellogg's	12.00	20.00
6 Mark Martin Valvoline	12.00	20.00
7 Geoff Bodine QVC	10.00	20.00
8 Hut Stricklin Circuit City	10.00	20.00
24 Jeff Gordon DuPont	12.50	25.00
29 Robert Pressley Scooby-Doo	10.00	20.00
75 Rick Mast Remington	10.00	20.00

1997 Racing Champions Transporters 1:64

Like 1996, Racing Champions has distributed standard transporters in three different variations. These transporters come with one car, two cars, or no car. This series features drivers from both the Winston Cup and Busch circuits.

Item		
1 Hermie Sadler DeWalt	10.00	20.00
1 Hermie Sadler DeWalt with one car or two cars	12.50	25.00
2 Ricky Craven Raybestos	10.00	20.00
2 Rusty Wallace Penske	10.00	20.00
4 Sterling Marlin Kodak	10.00	20.00
4 Sterling Marlin Kodak with one car or two	12.50	25.00
5 Terry Labonte Kellogg's	10.00	20.00
5 Terry Labonte Kellogg's 1996 Winston Cup Champion	12.50	25.00
6 Mark Martin Valvoline	10.00	20.00
6 Mark Martin Valvoline with one car or two cars	12.50	25.00
7 Geoff Bodine QVC	10.00	20.00
8 Hut Stricklin Circuit City	10.00	20.00
9 Jeff Burton Track Gear	10.00	20.00
10 Phil Parsons Channellock	10.00	20.00
10 Ricky Rudd Tide	10.00	20.00
10 Ricky Rudd Tide with one car or two cars	12.50	25.00
11 Brett Bodine Close Call	10.00	20.00
11 Brett Bodine Close Call with one car or two cars	12.50	25.00
11 Jimmy Foster Speedvision	10.00	20.00
11 Jimmy Foster Speedvision with one car or two cars	12.50	25.00
16 Ted Musgrave Primestar	10.00	20.00
17 Darrell Waltrip Parts America	10.00	20.00
17 Darrell Waltrip Parts America with one or two cars	12.50	25.00
19 Gary Bradberry CSR	10.00	20.00
19 Gary Bradberry CSR with one car or two cars	12.50	25.00
21 Michael Waltrip Citgo	10.00	20.00
24 Jeff Gordon DuPont	12.50	25.00
25 Ricky Craven Bud Lizard with one car	20.00	35.00
28 Ernie Irvan Havoline 10th Anniversary paint scheme	10.00	20.00
28 Ernie Irvan Havoline with one or two cars 10th Anniversary paint scheme	12.50	25.00
29 No Driver Association Tom & Jerry	10.00	20.00
29 Jeff Green Tom and Jerry with one or two cars	12.50	25.00
29 Robert Pressley Cartoon Network	10.00	20.00
30 Johnny Benson Pennzoil	10.00	20.00
32 Dale Jarrett Gillette	10.00	20.00
32 Dale Jarrett Gillette with one or two cars	12.50	25.00
32 Dale Jarrett White Rain	10.00	20.00
33 Tim Fedewa Kleenex	10.00	20.00
34 Mike McLaughlin Royal Oak	10.00	20.00
34 Mike McLaughlin Royal Oak with one car or two cars	12.50	25.00
36 Todd Bodine Stanley	10.00	20.00
36 Derrike Cope Skittles	10.00	20.00
38 Elton Sawyer Barbasol	10.00	20.00
38 Elton Sawyer Barbasol with one or two cars	12.50	25.00
40 Robby Gordon Sabco Racing	10.00	20.00
43 Dennis Setzer Lance	10.00	20.00
43 Rodney Combs Lance	10.00	20.00
46 Wally Dallenbach First Union	10.00	20.00
57 Jason Keller Slim Jim	10.00	20.00
60 Mark Martin Winn Dixie	10.00	20.00
60 Mark Martin Winn Dixie Promo	18.00	30.00
63 Tracy Leslie Lysol	10.00	20.00
72 Mike Dillon Detroit Gasket	10.00	20.00
74 Randy LaJoie Fina	10.00	20.00
74 Randy LaJoie Fina with one or two cars	12.50	25.00
75 Rick Mast Remington	10.00	20.00
75 Rick Mast Remington with one or two cars	12.50	25.00
88 Kevin Lepage Hype	10.00	20.00
88 Kevin Lepage Hype with one or two cars	12.50	25.00
90 Dick Trickle Heilig-Meyers	10.00	20.00
94 Ron Barfield New Holland	10.00	20.00
94 Ron Barfield New Holland with one or two cars	12.50	25.00
94 Bill Elliott McDonald's	10.00	20.00
96 David Green Caterpillar	10.00	20.00
96 David Green Caterpillar Promo	10.00	25.00
97 No Driver Association Brickyard 400	10.00	20.00
97 Chad Little John Deere	8.00	20.00
97 Chad Little John Deere Promo with one car	10.00	20.00
99 Jeff Burton Exide	10.00	20.00
00 Buckshot Jones Aqua Fresh	10.00	20.00
00 Buckshot Jones Aqua Fresh with one or two cars	12.50	25.00

1997 Racing Champions Premier Transporters 1:64

This is the second year that Racing Champions has produced premier transporters that are packaged with a premier car. This series is highlighted by the special 1996 Winston Cup Champion Terry Labonte Kellogg's transporter.

Item		
5 Terry Labonte Kellogg's	20.00	35.00
29 Robert Pressley Cartoon Network	15.00	30.00
60 Mark Martin Winn Dixie	20.00	35.00

1998 Racing Champions Transporters 1:64

The 1:64 scale transpoters that appear in this series are replicas of many of the cars that ran in the 1997 season, but also many replicas are of the cars slated to appear in the 1998 season. The transporters in this series are packaged in special boxes that display the NASCAR 50th anniversary logo.

Item		
4 Bobby Hamilton Kodak	8.00	20.00
4 Bobby Hamilton Kodak with Car	10.00	25.00
4 Jeff Purvis Lance	8.00	20.00
4 Jeff Purvis Lance with car	10.00	25.00
5 Terry Labonte Kellogg's	10.00	25.00
5 Terry Labonte Kellogg's with car	12.00	30.00
5 Terry Labonte Kellogg's Corny	10.00	25.00
5 Terry Labonte Kellogg's Corny with car	12.00	30.00
6 Joe Bessey Power Team	8.00	20.00
6 Joe Bessey Power Team with car	10.00	25.00
6 Mark Martin Eagle One	10.00	20.00
6 Mark Martin Eagle One with car	10.00	25.00
8 Hut Stricklin Circuit City	8.00	20.00
8 Hut Stricklin Circuit City with car	10.00	25.00
9 Lake Speed Birthday Cake	8.00	20.00
9 Lake Speed Birthday Cake with car	10.00	25.00
9 Lake Speed Huckleberry Hound	8.00	20.00
9 Lake Speed Huckleberry Hound with car	10.00	25.00
10 Ricky Rudd Tide	10.00	20.00
10 Ricky Rudd Tide with car	10.00	25.00
11 Brett Bodine Paychex	8.00	20.00
13 Jerry Nadeau First Plus	8.00	20.00
13 Jerry Nadeau First Plus with car	10.00	25.00
21 Michael Waltrip Citgo	8.00	20.00
21 Michael Waltrip Citgo with car	10.00	25.00
21 Michael Waltrip Goodwill Games	8.00	20.00
21 Michael Waltrip Goodwill Games with car	10.00	25.00
30 Mike Cope Slim Jim	8.00	20.00
33 Ken Schrader Petree	8.00	20.00
35 Todd Bodine Tabasco	8.00	20.00
35 Todd Bodine Tabasco with car	10.00	25.00
36 Ernie Irvan M&M's	15.00	30.00
36 Ernie Irvan M&M's with car	15.00	35.00
36 Ernie Irvan Skittles	10.00	20.00
36 Ernie Irvan Skittles with car	10.00	25.00
40 Kevin Lepage Channellock	8.00	20.00
40 Sterling Marlin Sabco	10.00	20.00
40 Sterling Marlin Sabco with car	10.00	25.00
42 Joe Nemechek BellSouth	8.00	20.00
46 Wally Dallenbach First Union	8.00	20.00
50 Ricky Craven Hendrick	8.00	20.00
50 Ricky Craven Hendrick with car	10.00	25.00
59 Robert Pressley Kingsford	8.00	20.00
59 Robert Pressley Kingsford with car	10.00	25.00
60 Mark Martin Winn Dixie	10.00	20.00
60 Mark Martin Winn Dixie with car	10.00	25.00
60 Mark Martin Winn Dixie Promo with car	20.00	40.00
66 Elliott Sadler Phillips 66	8.00	20.00
66 Elliott Sadler Phillips 66 with car	10.00	25.00
75 Rick Mast Remington	8.00	20.00
94 Bill Elliott Happy Meal with car	10.00	25.00
94 Bill Elliott McDonald's Service Merchandise Promo with Gold car	10.00	25.00
96 David Green Caterpillar Promo with car	10.00	25.00
97 Chad Little John Deere	8.00	20.00
99 Jeff Burton Exide	8.00	20.00
99 Jeff Burton Exide with car	10.00	25.00
00 Buckshot Jones Aqua Fresh	8.00	20.00
00 Buckshot Jones Aqua Fresh with car	10.00	25.00

1998 Racing Champions Transporters Gold 1:64

This was a special series produced by Racing Champions to celebrate NASCAR's 50th anniversary. Each car was packaged in a gold window box and was produced in a limited edition of 1500. Each transporter and 1:64 car was plated in gold chrome and featured a serial number on its chassis.

Item		
4 Bobby Hamilton Kodak	12.50	30.00
4 Jeff Purvis Lance	12.50	30.00
5 Terry Labonte Kellogg's	20.00	50.00
5 Terry Labonte Kellogg's Corny	15.00	40.00
6 Joe Bessey Power Team	12.50	30.00
6 Mark Martin Eagle One	20.00	50.00
6 Mark Martin Valvoline	20.00	50.00
8 Hut Stricklin Circuit City	12.50	30.00
9 Jerry Nadeau Zombie Island	12.50	30.00
9 Lake Speed Birthday Cake	12.50	30.00
9 Lake Speed Huckleberry Hound	12.50	30.00
10 Ricky Rudd Tide	12.50	30.00
11 Brett Bodine Paychex	12.50	30.00
13 Jerry Nadeau First Plus	12.50	30.00
16 Ted Musgrave Primestar	12.50	30.00
19 Tony Raines Yellow Freight	12.50	30.00
21 Michael Waltrip Citgo	12.50	30.00
23 Jimmy Spencer Winston/1998 in solid box	15.00	40.00
29 Hermie Sadler Phillips 66 DeWalt	12.50	30.00
30 Mike Cope Slim Jim	12.50	30.00
33 Tim Fedewa Kleenex	12.50	30.00
33 Ken Schrader Petree	12.50	30.00
35 Todd Bodine Tabasco	12.50	30.00
36 Ernie Irvan Skittles	15.00	40.00
36 Ernie Irvan M&M's	20.00	50.00
40 Rick Fuller Channellock	12.50	30.00
40 Sterling Marlin Sabco	30.00	50.00
42 Joe Nemechek BellSouth	12.50	30.00
46 Wally Dallenbach First Union	12.50	30.00
50 Ricky Craven Bud/1998 in solid box	12.50	30.00
50 Ricky Craven Hendrick	12.50	30.00
59 Robert Pressley Kingsford	12.50	30.00
66 Elliott Sadler Phillips 66	12.50	30.00
74 Randy LaJoie Fina	12.50	30.00
75 Rick Mast Remington	12.50	30.00
78 Gary Bradberry Pilot	12.50	30.00
88 Kevin Schwantz Ryder	12.50	30.00
90 Dick Trickle Heilig-Meyers	12.50	30.00
94 Bill Elliott Happy Meal	20.00	50.00
94 Bill Elliott McDonald's	20.00	50.00
94 Bill Elliott Mac Tonight	20.00	50.00
94 Bill Elliott McDonald's w/5-cars	20.00	40.00
97 Chad Little John Deere Promo	20.00	50.00
00 Buckshot Jones Aqua Fresh	25.00	50.00

1998 Racing Champions Transporters Signature Series 1:64

This is a special series produced by Racing Champions to celebrate NASCAR's 50th anniversary. It parallels the regular 1998 series. Each car is packaged in a decorative box with the driver's facsimile autograph on the front.

Item		
4 Bobby Hamilton Kodak	6.00	15.00
5 Terry Labonte Kellogg's	10.00	20.00
6 Mark Martin Valvoline	10.00	20.00
8 Hut Stricklin Circuit City	6.00	15.00
9 Lake Speed Huckleberry Hound	6.00	15.00
10 Ricky Rudd Tide	10.00	20.00
11 Brett Bodine Paychex	6.00	15.00
13 Jerry Nadeau First Plus	6.00	15.00
21 Michael Waltrip Citgo	6.00	15.00
33 Ken Schrader Petree	6.00	15.00
35 Todd Bodine Tabasco	6.00	15.00
42 Joe Nemechek Bell South	6.00	15.00

59 Robert Pressley Kingsford 6.00 15.00
94 Bill Elliott Happy Meal 10.00 20.00

1999 Racing Champions Transporters 1:64

The 1:64 scale transporters that appear in this series are replicas of many of the cars that ran in the 1998 season, but also some slated to appear in 1999. The die-cast in this series were packaged in special boxes that display the Racing Champions "The Originals" 10th anniversary logo.

4 Bobby Hamilton Kodak 8.00 20.00
5 Terry Labonte Kellogg's 10.00 20.00
6 Joe Bessey Power Team 8.00 20.00
6 Mark Martin Valvoline 10.00 20.00
6 Mark Martin Valvoline Chrome/1499 15.00 30.00
9 Jerry Nadeau Dexter's Laboratory 8.00 20.00
10 Ricky Rudd Tide 8.00 20.00
11 Brett Bodine Paychex 8.00 20.00
11 Brett Bodine Paychex Chrome 12.50 25.00
15 Ken Schrader Oakwood Homes 8.00 20.00
16 Kevin Lepage Primestar 8.00 20.00
17 Matt Kenseth DeWalt 25.00 40.00
18 Butch Miller Dana SuperTruck Promo 30.00 50.00
23 Jimmy Spencer TCE Lights 8.00 20.00
25 Wally Dallenbach Hendrick 8.00 20.00
26 Johnny Benson Cheerios 8.00 20.00
30 Derrike Cope Bahari Racing set w/4-cars 15.00 30.00
36 Ken Schrader M&M's 10.00 20.00
36 Ken Schrader M&M's with 3-cars 12.50 25.00
38 Glen Allen Barbasol 8.00 20.00
43 Richard Petty STP w/7 championship cars 20.00 40.00
50 Mark Green Dr. Pepper 8.00 20.00
55 Kenny Wallace Square D 8.00 20.00
94 Bill Elliott Drive Thru 10.00 20.00
97 Chad Little John Deere 8.00 20.00
99 Jeff Burton Exide 8.00 20.00

1999 Racing Champions Transporters 24K Gold 1:64

These transporter and car sets were issued in a gold checkered flag designed "Reflections in Gold" window box. Each transporter and 1:64 scale car were produced with a complete gold chrome finish. The stated production run was 1499 for each piece.

4 Bobby Hamilton Kodak 15.00 40.00
5 Terry Labonte Kellogg's 30.00 60.00
6 Mark Martin Valvoline 30.00 60.00
6 Joe Bessey Power Team 15.00 40.00
10 Ricky Rudd Tide 20.00 40.00
11 Brett Bodine Paychex 15.00 40.00
16 Kevin Lepage Primestar 15.00 40.00
25 Wally Dallenbach Hendrick 15.00 40.00
32 Jeff Green Kleenex 15.00 40.00
36 Ernie Irvan M&M's 20.00 40.00
55 Kenny Wallace Square D 15.00 40.00
77 Robert Pressley Jasper 15.00 40.00
94 Bill Elliott Drive Thru 25.00 50.00
97 Chad Little John Deere 20.00 50.00
99 Jeff Burton Exide 15.00 40.00

1999 Racing Champions Transporters Gold 1:64

These transporter and car sets were issued in a gold checkered flag designed window box. Each transporter tractor and 1:64 scale car were produced using gold chrome paint. The stated production run was 2499 for each piece.

4 Bobby Hamilton Kodak 12.50 30.00
5 Terry Labonte Kellogg's 20.00 50.00
6 Mark Martin Valvoline 20.00 50.00
9 Jerry Nadeau Cartoon Network 12.50 30.00
10 Ricky Rudd Tide 12.50 30.00
11 Brett Bodine Paychex 12.50 30.00
15 Ken Schrader Oakwood Homes 12.50 30.00
16 Kevin Lepage Primestar 12.50 30.00
17 Matt Kenseth DeWalt 40.00 80.00
23 Jimmy Spencer TCE 12.50 30.00
25 Wally Dallenbach Hendrick 12.50 30.00
26 Johnny Benson Cheerios 12.50 30.00
33 Ken Schrader Petree 12.50 30.00
42 Joe Nemechek BellSouth 12.50 30.00
43 John Andretti STP 12.50 30.00
55 Kenny Wallace Square D 12.50 30.00
66 Darrell Waltrip Big K 12.50 30.00
77 Robert Pressley Jasper 12.50 30.00
78 Gary Bradberry Pilot 12.50 30.00
94 Bill Elliott Drive Thru 25.00 50.00
97 Chad Little John Deere 15.00 40.00
99 Jeff Burton Exide 20.00 40.00

1999 Racing Champions Transporters Platinum 1:64

These transporter and car sets were issued in a silver checkered flag "Reflections in Platinum" window box. Each transporter and 1:64 scale car were produced in a solid platinum chrome finish. The stated production run was 1499 for each piece.

4 Bobby Hamilton Kodak 20.00 40.00
5 Terry Labonte Kellogg's 30.00 60.00
6 Mark Martin Valvoline 30.00 60.00
6 Joe Bessey Power Team 12.50 30.00
9 Jerry Nadeau Dexter's Lab 12.50 30.00
10 Ricky Rudd Tide 20.00 40.00
11 Brett Bodine Paychex 12.50 30.00
15 Ken Schrader Oakwood Homes 12.50 30.00
16 Kevin Lepage Primestar 12.50 30.00
25 Wally Dallenbach Hendrick 12.50 30.00
32 Jeff Green Kleenex 12.50 30.00
40 Sterling Marlin Sabco 15.00 40.00
50 Mark Green Dr.Pepper 15.00 40.00
55 Kenny Wallace Square D 12.50 30.00
77 Robert Pressley Jasper 12.50 30.00
97 Chad Little John Deere 20.00 50.00
99 Jeff Burton Exide 20.00 50.00

1999 Racing Champions Transporters Signature Series 1:64

This is a special series produced by Racing Champions to celebrate their 10th anniversary. It parallels the regular 1999 series. Each car is a packaged in a decorative box with the driver's facsimile autograph on the front.

4 Bobby Hamilton Kodak 8.00 20.00
5 Terry Labonte Kellogg's 10.00 20.00
6 Mark Martin Valvoline 10.00 20.00
6 Joe Bessey Power Team 8.00 20.00
9 Jerry Nadeau Dexter's Laboratory 8.00 20.00
10 Ricky Rudd Tide 10.00 20.00
16 Kevin Lepage Primestar 8.00 20.00
25 Wally Dallenbach Hendrick 8.00 20.00
26 Johnny Benson Cheerios 8.00 20.00
30 Derrike Cope Bryan Foods 8.00 20.00
40 Sterling Marlin John Wayne 10.00 25.00
55 Kenny Wallace Square D 8.00 20.00
77 Robert Pressley Jasper 8.00 20.00
94 Bill Elliott Drive Thru 10.00 20.00
99 Jeff Burton Exide 8.00 20.00

1999 Racing Champions Transporters Under the Lights 1:64

4 Bobby Hamilton Kodak 12.50 20.00
5 Terry Labonte Kellogg's 15.00 25.00
6 Mark Martin Valvoline 15.00 25.00
94 Bill Elliott Drive Thru 15.00 25.00
99 Jeff Burton Exide 15.00 25.00

2000 Racing Champions Preview Transporters 1:64

These Transporters were issued in a red and black clear window display box with the NASCAR 2000 logo clearly printed on the front. Each came with a 1:64 scale car as well.

6 Mark Martin Valvoline 8.00 20.00
33 Joe Nemecheck Oakwood Homes 7.50 15.00
36 Ernie Irvan M&M's '99 8.00 20.00
66 Darrell Waltrip Big K 7.50 15.00
97 Chad Little John Deere 6.00 15.00
99 Jeff Burton Exide 7.50 15.00

2000 Racing Champions Premier Preview Transporters 1:64

6 Mark Martin Valvoline 8.00 20.00
99 Jeff Burton Exide 10.00 20.00
99 Jeff Burton Exide Chrome/999 15.00 30.00

2000 Racing Champions Transporters 1:64

4 Bobby Hamilton Kodak 6.00 12.00
5 Terry Labonte Kellogg's 7.50 15.00
6 Mark Martin Valvoline 7.50 15.00
6 Mark Martin Valvoline Chrome/999 25.00 50.00
7 Michael Waltrip Nation's Rent 6.00 12.00
12 Jeremy Mayfield Mobil 1 6.00 12.00
14 Mike Bliss Conseco 6.00 12.00
17 Matt Kenseth DeWalt 20.00 35.00
17 Matt Kenseth Visine Promo 20.00 40.00
22 Ward Burton Cat Dealers 6.00 12.00
22 Ward Burton Caterpillar Chrome/999 25.00 50.00
33 Joe Nemechek Oakwood Bud Shoot Out 6.00 12.00
36 Ernie Irvan M&M's 10.00 20.00
40 Sterling Marlin Team Sabco 6.00 15.00
66 Darrell Waltrip Big K 6.00 12.00
66 Todd Bodine Phillips 66 6.00 12.00
77 Robert Pressley Jasper 6.00 12.00
77 Robert Pressley Jasper Chrome/999 10.00 20.00
87 Joe Nemechek Cellular One 6.00 12.00
93 Dave Blaney Amoco 6.00 12.00
93 Dave Blaney Amoco Chrome/999 10.00 25.00
97 Chad Little John Deere 6.00 12.00
99 Jeff Burton Exide 6.00 12.00
99 Jeff Burton Exide Chrome/999 20.00 40.00

2000 Racing Champions Premier Transporters 1:64

4 Bobby Hamilton Kodak 10.00 20.00
6 Mark Martin Valvoline 15.00 30.00
17 Matt Kenseth DeWalt 20.00 35.00
66 Todd Bodine Phillips 66 10.00 20.00
99 Jeff Burton Exide 12.50 25.00
99 Jeff Burton Exide Chrome/999 20.00 40.00
Y2K NDA Ford Taurus 2000 8.00 20.00

2000 Racing Champions Transporters Time Trial 1:64

4 Bobby Hamilton Kodak 10.00 20.00
6 Mark Martin Valvoline 12.50 25.00
22 Ward Burton Caterpillar 12.50 25.00

2000 Racing Champions Transporters War Paint 1:64

6 Mark Martin Valvoline 10.00 20.00
99 Jeff Burton Exide 10.00 20.00

2001 Racing Champions Preview Transporters 1:64

10 Johnny Benson Valvoline 10.00 18.00
10 Johnny Benson Valvoline Chrome 20.00 30.00
12 Jeremy Mayfield Mobil 1 10.00 18.00
12 Jeremy Mayfield Mobil 1 Chrome 20.00 40.00
12 Jeremy Mayfield Mobil 1 Layin' Rubber 15.00 40.00
12 Jeremy Mayfield Mobil 1 Race Rubber 20.00 40.00
22 Ward Burton Caterpillar 10.00 18.00
22 Ward Burton Caterpillar Autographed 30.00 60.00
22 Ward Burton Caterpillar Chrome 15.00 40.00
22 Ward Burton Caterpillar Layin' Rubber/500 15.00 40.00
22 Ward Burton Caterpillar Race Rubber 20.00 40.00
55 Bobby Hamilton Square D 7.50 15.00
55 Bobby Hamilton Square D AUTO 25.00 50.00
55 Bobby Hamilton Square D Chrome 20.00 40.00
55 Bobby Hamilton Square D Race Rubber 15.00 40.00
92 Stacy Compton Melling 7.50 15.00
92 Stacy Compton Melling Autographed 30.00 60.00
NNO Dodge Test Car 7.50 15.00

2001 Racing Champions Transporters 1:64

5 Terry Labonte Kellogg's 12.50 25.00
5 Terry Labonte Kellogg's Chrome/1500 15.00 40.00
5 Terry Labonte Kellogg's Layin' Rubber/500 15.00 40.00
5 Terry Labonte Monster's Inc. 15.00 30.00
10 Johnny Benson Valvoline 10.00 20.00
10 Johnny Benson Valvoline Chrome/1500 15.00 30.00
12 Jeremy Mayfield Mobil 1 Chrome/1500 15.00 30.00
12 Jeremy Mayfield Mobil 1 Layin' Rubber 15.00 40.00
22 Ward Burton Caterpillar 10.00 20.00
22 Ward Burton Caterpillar Layin' Rubber 15.00 40.00
25 Jerry Nadeau UAW 10.00 20.00
25 Jerry Nadeau UAW Chrome/1500 15.00 30.00
25 Jerry Nadeau UAW Layin' Rubber/500 15.00 40.00
25 Jerry Nadeau UAW Race Rubber 20.00 40.00
36 Hank Parker Jr. GNC 10.00 20.00
36 Ken Schrader M&M's 10.00 20.00
36 Ken Schrader M&M's Layin' Rubber 15.00 40.00
36 Ken Schrader M&M's Race Rubber 20.00 40.00
55 Bobby Hamilton Square D 10.00 20.00
55 Bobby Hamilton Square D AUTO 25.00 50.00
55 Bobby Hamilton Square D Race Rubber 15.00 30.00
66 Todd Bodine K-Mart 10.00 20.00
93 Dave Blaney Amoco 10.00 20.00
93 Dave Blaney Amoco Layin' Rubber/500 15.00 40.00
93 Dave Blaney Amoco Race Rubber 15.00 40.00

2001 Racing Champions American Muscle Body Shop Transporters 1:64

This 1:64 Transporter and car set was produced by Racing Champions for their American Muscle Body Shop series. Each set was issued in a box and blister combination package and both the transporter and car had to be assembled by the collector similar to the line of Racing Champions Model Kits.

4 Mike Skinner Kodak 6.00 15.00
10 Johnny Benson Valvoline with Maxlife car 6.00 15.00
22 Ward Burton Caterpillar 6.00 15.00
25 Jerry Nadeau UAW 6.00 15.00
36 Ken Schrader M&M's with Stars&Stripes car 6.00 15.00
40 Sterling Marlin Sterling 6.00 15.00
55 Bobby Hamilton Square D 6.00 15.00
92 Stacy Compton Melling 6.00 15.00
93 Dave Blaney Amoco Ultimate 6.00 15.00

2002 Racing Champions Preview Transporters 1:64

4 Mike Skinner Kodak 10.00 18.00
5 Terry Labonte Kellogg's 10.00 18.00
10 Johnny Benson Valvoline 10.00 18.00
22 Ward Burton Caterpillar 10.00 18.00
25 Jerry Nadeau UAW 10.00 18.00
26 Jimmy Spencer K-Mart with Shrek car 10.00 18.00
36 Ken Schrader M&M's 10.00 18.00

2002 Racing Champions Transporters 1:64

1 Jimmy Spencer Yellow Freight 10.00 18.00
5 Terry Labonte Kellogg's with Got Milk 1:64 car 10.00 20.00
10 Johnny Benson Valvoline with Eagle One car 10.00 20.00
11 Brett Bodine Hooter's 15.00 30.00
22 Ward Burton Caterpillar Promo 12.50 25.00
22 Ward Burton Caterpillar Daytona Win 12.00 20.00
22 Ward Burton Cat Dealers '03 packaging 15.00 25.00
32 Ricky Craven Tide 10.00 20.00
32 Ricky Craven Tide with Give Kids 1:64 car 10.00 20.00
36 Ken Schrader M&M's w Halloween car in 2003 packaging 15.00 25.00
36 Ken Schrader M&M's with July 4th 1:64 car 12.50 25.00
48 Jimmie Johnson Lowe's 10.00 25.00
48 Jimmie Johnson Lowe's w Power of Pride car 15.00 30.00
48 Jimmie Johnson Lowe's with 3-cars 20.00 35.00
55 Bobby Hamilton Schneider 10.00 18.00

2003 Racing Champions Preview Transporters 1:64

Racing Champions created a more narrow clamshell package for its 2003 transporters. This series features the title "2003 Preview" in the lower right corner of the package. Each transporter included a die-cast car and was packaged with a mini (roughly 2 /14" by 3") sized Racing Champions or Press Pass card.

22 Ward Burton Caterpillar 10.00 20.00
22 Ward Burton Cat Rental 10.00 20.00
48 Jimmie Johnson Lowe's 2002 Season to Remember 12.50 25.00

2003 Racing Champions Transporters 1:64

1 Jamie McMurray Yellow Freight 12.50 25.00
5 Terry Labonte Kellogg's 12.50 25.00
10 Johnny Benson Valvoline 10.00 20.00
25 Joe Nemechek UAW Delphi 10.00 20.00
32 Ricky Craven Tide 10.00 20.00
48 Jimmie Johnson Lowe's 2002 Season to Remember 10.00 25.00
48 Jimmie Johnson Lowe's 2003 10.00 20.00
77 Dave Blaney Jasper 12.50 25.00
01 Jerry Nadeau Army 12.50 30.00

2004 Racing Champions Ultra Transporters 1:64

5 Terry Labonte Kellogg's 10.00 20.00
22 Scott Wimmer Caterpillar 10.00 20.00
25 Brian Vickers Ditech.com 10.00 20.00
48 Jimmie Johnson Lowe's 10.00 20.00
0 Ward Burton NetZero 15.00 30.00
01 Joe Nemechek Army 10.00 20.00

1993-94 Racing Champions Transporters Retail 1:87

This is one of the first series Racing Champions made of 1:87 scale transporters. They were issued primarily to retail outlets with each being packaged in a Racing Champions blister.

2 Rusty Wallace Penske 4.00 8.00
3 Dale Earnhardt Goodwrench 6.00 12.00
4 Ernie Irvan Kodak 3.00 6.00
5 Ricky Rudd Tide 3.00 6.00
6 Mark Martin Valvoline 3.00 6.00
7 Harry Gant Manheim Auctions 5.00 10.00
7 Harry Gant Morema 3.00 6.00
7 Alan Kulwicki Hooters 10.00 20.00
8 Sterling Marlin Raybestos 4.00 8.00
9 Chad Little IOF Hotline 3.00 6.00
11 Bill Elliott Amoco 3.00 6.00
12 Jimmy Spencer Meineke 3.00 6.00
14 Terry Labonte Kellogg's 3.00 8.00
15 Geoff Bodine Motorcraft 3.00 6.00
17 Darrell Waltrip Western Auto 3.00 6.00
18 Dale Jarrett Interstate Batteries 3.00 6.00
21 Morgan Shepherd Citgo 3.00 6.00
22 Bobby Labonte Maxwell House 4.00 8.00
24 Jeff Gordon DuPont 1993 7.50 15.00
25 Ken Schrader No sponsor 3.00 6.00
26 Brett Bodine Quaker State 3.00 6.00
27 Hut Stricklin McDonald's 3.00 6.00
28 Davey Allison Havoline 6.00 12.00
28 Davey Allison Havoline with Black and White paint scheme 7.50 15.00
30 Michael Waltrip Pennzoil 3.00 6.00
33 Harry Gant Food Lion 4.00 8.00
33 Harry Gant Morema 6.00 12.00
35 Bill Venturini Amoco 10.00 20.00
42 Kyle Petty Mello Yello 3.00 6.00
44 Rick Wilson STP 3.00 6.00
52 Ken Schrader AC Delco 3.00 6.00
52 Ken Schrader Morema 5.00 10.00
66 Cale Yarborough TropArtic 6.00 12.00

87 Joe Nemechek Dentyne 3.00 6.00
98 Derrike Cope Bojangles 3.00 6.00

1993 Racing Champions Premier Transporters 1:87

This is the first year that Racing Champions did a 1:87 scale Premier transporter. The set features the most popular drivers from Winston Cup racing. Each piece comes in a black shadow box and has the number produced stamped on the front of that box.

2 Ward Burton Hardee's/7500 10.00 20.00
2 Rusty Wallace Penske 15.00 30.00
3 Dale Earnhardt Goodwrench/15,000 15.00 30.00
3 Dale Earnhardt Goodwrench DEI/5000 20.00 50.00
4 Ernie Irvan Kodak/5000 10.00 20.00
5 Ricky Rudd Tide/15,000 10.00 20.00
6 Mark Martin Valvoline 10.00 20.00
7 Alan Kulwicki Hooters 40.00 75.00
8 Sterling Marlin Raybestos/2500 10.00 20.00
11 Bill Elliott Amoco/15,000 10.00 20.00
11 Bill Elliott Budweiser 18.00 35.00
12 Jimmy Spencer Meineke/10,000 10.00 20.00
14 Terry Labonte Kellogg's 10.00 20.00
15 Geoff Bodine Motorcraft/5000 10.00 20.00
18 Dale Jarrett Interstate Batteries 10.00 20.00
21 Morgan Shepherd Citgo/10,000 10.00 20.00
22 Bobby Labonte Maxwell House 10.00 25.00
24 Jeff Gordon DuPont/15,000 15.00 25.00
27 Hut Stricklin McDonald's/15,000 10.00 20.00
28 Davey Allison Havoline Black paint scheme 18.00 35.00
28 Davey Allison Havoline with Black and White paint scheme 18.00 35.00
28 Ernie Irvan Havoline/5000 15.00 25.00
33 Harry Gant Food Lion 10.00 20.00
42 Kyle Petty Mello Yello/3000 10.00 20.00
44 David Green Slim Jim/5000 10.00 20.00
44 Rick Wilson STP/5000 10.00 20.00
51 No Driver Association Chevy Prototype/7500 10.00 20.00
51 No Driver Association Ford Prototype/7500 10.00 20.00
51 No Driver Association Kenworth Prototype/7500 10.00 20.00
59 Robert Pressley Alliance/5000 10.00 20.00
60 Mark Martin Winn Dixie/5000 20.00 40.00
87 Joe Nemechek Dentyne 10.00 20.00
NNO NDA Dodge IROC/7500 10.00 20.00

1994 Racing Champions Transporters Hobby 1:87

This series of Transporters was issued directly to hobby shops. Each was packaged in a Racing Champions yellow box.

1 Rick Mast Precision Products 6.00 10.00
2 Rusty Wallace Penske 6.00 10.00
4 Sterling Marlin Kodak 6.00 15.00
5 Terry Labonte Kellogg's 6.00 10.00
6 Mark Martin Valvoline 6.00 10.00
8 Jeff Burton Raybestos 6.00 10.00
18 Dale Jarrett Interstate Batteries 6.00 10.00
24 Jeff Gordon DuPont 10.00 20.00
26 Brett Bodine Quaker State 6.00 10.00
30 Michael Waltrip Pennzoil 6.00 10.00
33 Harry Gant Leo Jackson 6.00 10.00
42 Kyle Petty Mello Yello 6.00 10.00
75 Todd Bodine Factory Stores of America 6.00 10.00

1994 Racing Champions Premier Transporters 1:87

Racing Champions continued their line of 1:87 Premier transporters in 1994. The pieces were again packaged in a black shadow box and carry the number produced on the front of that box.

2 Ward Burton Hardee's 10.00 20.00
2 Rusty Wallace Penske Mac Tools/7500 25.00 40.00
3 Dale Earnhardt Goodwrench 15.00 25.00
4 Sterling Marlin Kodak 12.00 25.00
4 Sterling Marlin Kodak FunSaver 12.00 25.00
5 Terry Labonte Kellogg's 10.00 20.00
7 Geoff Bodine Exide 10.00 20.00
7 Harry Gant Manheim Auctions 15.00 25.00
8 Kenny Wallace TIC Financial 10.00 20.00
15 Lake Speed Quality Care 10.00 20.00
16 Ted Musgrave Family Channel 10.00 20.00
17 Darrell Waltrip Western Auto 10.00 20.00
19 Loy Allen Hooters 10.00 20.00
21 Morgan Shepherd Cheerwine/7500 10.00 20.00
28 Ernie Irvan Havoline 15.00 25.00
28 Ernie Irvan Mac Tools Promo/15,028 12.50 25.00
32 Dale Jarrett Shoe World/2500 25.00 40.00
40 Bobby Hamilton Kendall 10.00 20.00
52 Ken Schrader AC Delco 10.00 20.00
60 Mark Martin Winn Dixie/7500 15.00 25.00
94 Brickyard 400 special 15.00 30.00
98 Derrike Cope Fingerhut 10.00 20.00

1995 Racing Champions Transporters 1:87

These 1:87 scale pieces were produced by Racing Champions. They were distributed through both hobby and retail outlets. This series is highlighted by the Rusty Wallace transporter which was released in an acrylic case.

2 Rusty Wallace Miller Genuine Draft in acrylic case 10.00 20.00
7 Geoff Bodine Exide 3.00 6.00
24 Jeff Gordon DuPont 7.50 15.00
26 Steve Kinser Quaker State 3.00 6.00
27 Loy Allen Hooters 3.00 6.00
28 Dale Jarrett Ernie Irvan Havoline both signatures on trailer 3.00 6.00
99 Phil Parsons Luxaire 3.00 6.00

1995 Racing Champions Premier Transporters 1:87

8 Jeff Burton Raybestos 10.00 20.00
12 Derrike Cope Straight Arrow 10.00 20.00
25 Ken Schrader Budweiser 10.00 20.00
26 Steve Kinser Quaker State 10.00 20.00
40 Patty Moise Dial Purex 10.00 20.00
90 Mike Wallace Heilig-Meyers 10.00 20.00
94 Bill Elliott McDonald's/5000 12.50 25.00
95 Brickyard 500/20,000 10.00 20.00

1996 Racing Champions Transporters 1:87

This series was produced by Racing Champions. It is highlighted by the Kyle Petty transporter which was released in an acrylic case.

1 Rick Mast Hooter's 3.00 6.00
1 Hermie Sadler DeWalt 3.00 6.00
2 Rusty Wallace Penske 3.00 6.00
4 Sterling Marlin Kodak 3.00 6.00
5 Terry Labonte Kellogg's 3.00 6.00
6 Mark Martin Valvoline 3.00 6.00
7 Geoff Bodine QVC 3.00 6.00
8 Hut Stricklin Circuit City 3.00 6.00
10 Ricky Rudd Tide 3.00 6.00
11 Brett Bodine Lowe's 3.00 6.00
12 Michael Waltrip MW Windows 3.00 6.00
15 Wally Dallenbach Hayes 3.00 6.00
16 Ted Musgrave Family Channel 3.00 6.00
17 Darrell Waltrip Parts America 3.00 6.00
18 Bobby Labonte Interstate Batteries 3.00 6.00
21 Michael Waltrip Citgo 3.00 6.00
22 Ward Burton MBNA 3.00 6.00
23 Chad Little John Deere 3.00 6.00
24 Jeff Gordon DuPont Premier 15.00 25.00
29 No Driver Association Scooby-Doo 3.00 6.00
30 Johnny Benson Pennzoil 3.00 6.00
34 Mike McLaughlin Royal Oak 3.00 6.00
37 John Andretti K-Mart 3.00 6.00
40 Tim Fedewa Kleenex 3.00 6.00
40 Patty Moise Dial Purex 3.00 6.00
42 Kyle Petty Coors Light in acrylic case 10.00 20.00
43 Rodney Combs Lance 3.00 6.00
44 David Green Slim Jim 3.00 6.00
44 Bobby Labonte Shell 4.00 8.00
47 Jeff Fuller Sunoco 3.00 6.00
74 Randy LaJoie Fina 3.00 6.00
81 Kenny Wallace TIC Financial 3.00 6.00
87 Joe Nemechek Bell South 3.00 6.00
87 Joe Nemechek Burger King 3.00 6.00
90 Mike Wallace Heilig-Meyers 3.00 6.00
99 Glenn Allen Jr. Luxaire 3.00 6.00

1997 Racing Champions Preview Transporters 1:87

The set features the most popular drivers from Winston Cup racing.

5 Terry Labonte Kellogg's 4.00 8.00
6 Mark Martin Valvoline 3.00 6.00
7 Geoff Bodine QVC 2.50 6.00
8 Hut Stricklin Circuit City 2.50 6.00
24 Jeff Gordon DuPont 4.00 8.00
29 Robert Pressley Cartoon Network 2.50 6.00

1997 Racing Champions Transporters 1:87

These 1:87 pieces were produced by Racing Champions. They were distributed through both hobby and retail outlets. This series features drivers from the Winston Cup and Busch circuits.

1 Hermie Sadler DeWalt 3.00 6.00
2 Ricky Craven Raybestos 3.00 6.00
2 Rusty Wallace Penske 3.00 6.00
4 Sterling Marlin Kodak 3.00 6.00
5 Terry Labonte Kellogg's 3.00 6.00
6 Mark Martin Valvoline 3.00 6.00
7 Geoff Bodine QVC 3.00 6.00
8 Hut Stricklin Circuit City 3.00 6.00
9 Jeff Burton Track Gear 3.00 6.00
10 Phil Parsons Channellock 3.00 6.00
10 Ricky Rudd Tide 3.00 6.00
11 Brett Bodine Close Call 3.00 6.00
11 Jimmy Foster Speedvision 3.00 6.00
16 Ted Musgrave Primestar 3.00 6.00
17 Darrell Waltrip Parts America 3.00 6.00
18 Bobby Labonte Interstate Batteries 3.00 6.00
19 Gary Bradberry CSR 3.00 6.00
21 Michael Waltrip Citgo 3.00 6.00
24 Jeff Gordon DuPont 4.00 8.00
28 Ernie Irvan Havoline 10th Anniversary paint scheme 3.00 6.00
29 Jeff Green Tom & Jerry 3.00 6.00
29 Robert Pressley Cartoon Network 3.00 6.00
30 Johnny Benson Pennzoil 3.00 6.00
32 Dale Jarrett Gillette 3.00 6.00
32 Dale Jarrett White Rain 3.00 6.00
34 Mike McLaughlin Royal Oak 3.00 6.00
36 Todd Bodine Stanley Tools 3.00 6.00
36 Derrike Cope Skittles 3.00 6.00
37 Jeremy Mayfield K-Mart 3.00 6.00
38 Elton Sawyer Barbasol 3.00 6.00
40 Robby Gordon Sabco Racing 3.00 6.00
43 Rodney Combs Lance 3.00 6.00
46 Wally Dallenbach First Union 3.00 6.00
57 Jason Keller Slim Jim 3.00 6.00
60 Mark Martin Winn Dixie 3.00 6.00
75 Rick Mast Remington 3.00 6.00
90 Dick Trickle Heilig-Meyers 3.00 6.00
94 Ron Barfield New Holland 3.00 6.00
94 Bill Elliott McDonald's 3.00 6.00
96 David Green Caterpillar 3.00 6.00
97 Chad Little John Deere 3.00 6.00
99 Jeff Burton Exide 3.00 6.00

1998 Racing Champions Transporters 1:87

These 1:87 pieces were produced by Racing Champions. They were distributed through both hobby and retail outlets. This series features drivers from the Winston Cup and Busch circuits.

4 Bobby Hamilton Kodak 3.00 6.00
4 Jeff Purvis Lance 3.00 6.00
5 Terry Labonte Kellogg's 3.00 6.00
6 Joe Bessey Power Team 3.00 6.00
6 Mark Martin Valvoline 3.00 6.00
8 Hut Stricklin Circuit City 3.00 6.00
9 Lake Speed Birthday Cake 3.00 6.00
9 Lake Speed Huckleberry Hound 3.00 6.00
10 Ricky Rudd Tide 3.00 6.00
11 Brett Bodine Paychex 3.00 6.00
13 Jerry Nadeau First Plus 3.00 6.00
21 Michael Waltrip Citgo 3.00 6.00
21 Michael Waltrip Goodwill Games 3.00 6.00
33 Ken Schrader Petree 3.00 6.00
35 Todd Bodine Tabasco 3.00 6.00
36 Ernie Irvan M&M's 3.00 6.00
36 Ernie Irvan Skittles 3.00 6.00
40 Sterling Marlin Sabco 3.00 6.00
42 Joe Nemechek BellSouth 3.00 6.00
46 Wally Dallenbach First Union 3.00 6.00
50 Ricky Craven Hendrick 3.00 6.00
59 Robert Pressley Kingsford 3.00 6.00
66 Elliott Sadler Phillips 66 3.00 6.00
75 Rick Mast Remington 3.00 6.00
00 Buckshot Jones Aqua Fresh 3.00 6.00

2002 Racing Champions Preview Transporters 1:87

These 1:87 haulers and cars were packaged in a red and black Racing Champions blister. The copyright date on the back is 2001, but they are considered an early 2002 release.

4 Mike Skinner Kodak 3.00 6.00
5 Terry Labonte Kellogg's 3.00 6.00
10 Johnny Benson Valvoline 3.00 6.00
22 Ward Burton Caterpillar 3.00 6.00
25 Jerry Nadeau UAW 3.00 6.00

2002 Racing Champions Transporters 1:87

5 Terry Labonte Kellogg's 3.00 6.00
10 Johnny Benson Valvoline 3.00 6.00
22 Ward Burton Caterpillar 3.00 6.00
25 Jerry Nadeau UAW 3.00 6.00
48 Jimmie Johnson Lowe's 5.00 10.00
55 Bobby Hamilton Scneider 3.00 6.00

1991-92 Racing Champions Transporters 1:144

This series of Transporters was issued by Racing Champions in the early 1990s. Several different blister packaging styles were used. The first of which features a black and checkered flag design with title "Racing Champions Haulers" and a notation of "Collectors Series 1 Racing Team" at the top. The second is entitled "Racing Champions Racing Team" and makes no mention of a series number. Unless noted each piece below was issued in this second packaging type. This second type can also be found with or without a mini car included.

1 Rick Mast Majik Market 3.00 8.00
4 Ernie Irvan Kodak 3.00 8.00
5 Jay Fogleman Innkeeper 3.00 8.00
6 Mark Martin Valvoline 4.00 10.00
8 Sterling Marlin Raybestos 4.00 10.00
9 Bill Elliott Melling Blue 4.00 10.00
9 Bill Elliott Melling Red 4.00 10.00
10 Derrike Cope Purolator with mini car 3.00 8.00
11 Bill Elliott Amoco 4.00 10.00
12 Bobby Allison No sponsor with mini car 4.00 10.00
12 Hut Stricklin Raybestos 3.00 8.00
14 A.J. Foyt No Sponsor 4.00 10.00
15 Geoff Bodine Motorcraft 3.00 8.00
15 Lake Speed Quality Care 3.00 8.00
17 Darrell Waltrip Western Auto 3.00 8.00
18 Dale Jarrett Interstate Batteries 4.00 10.00
21 Morgan Shepherd Citgo 3.00 8.00
22 Sterling Marlin Maxwell House 3.00 8.00
25 Ken Schrader No Sponsor 3.00 8.00
28 Davey Allison Havoline black&gold 6.00 15.00
30 Michael Waltrip Pennzoil with mini car 3.00 8.00
42 Kyle Petty Mello Yello 3.00 8.00
42 Kyle Petty Peak series 1 package 4.00 10.00
42 Kyle Petty Peak Racing Team package 3.00 8.00
42 Kyle Petty Peak Racing Team package with mini car 3.00 8.00
43 Richard Petty STP 5.00 12.00
66 Cale Yarborough Phillips 66 with mini car 3.00 8.00
68 Bobby Hamilton Country Time 3.00 8.00
71 Dave Marcis Big Apple 3.00 8.00
72 Ken Bouchard ADAP 3.00 8.00
94 Terry Labonte Sunoco 4.00 10.00

1994 Racing Champions Transporters 1:144

This series of Transporters was issued by Racing Champions in 1994. The blister packaging reads "Racing Team Transporter" on the front and is the same packaging used for 1995, except that there is no year designation on the 1994 release. Unless noted below each was also packaged with a mini car.

2 Rusty Wallace Penske 3.00 8.00
2 Ricky Craven DuPont 3.00 6.00
7 Geoff Bodine Exide 3.00 6.00
10 Ricky Rudd Tide 3.00 6.00
28 Ernie Irvan Havoline 3.00 8.00
41 Joe Nemechek Meineke 3.00 6.00

1995 Racing Champions Transporters 1:144

This series of Transporters was issued by Racing Champions in 1995. The blister packaging reads "Racing Team Transporter" on the front of most. A few pieces were released in a slightly different blister design without a "set name" with the scale being incorrectly identified as 1:87. Regardless, the year of issue is clearly printed on the front of both blister types. Unless noted below each was also packaged with a mini car.

7 Geoff Bodine Exide 3.00 6.00
24 Jeff Gordon DuPont 5.00 12.00
26 Steve Kinser Quaker State 3.00 6.00
28 Dale Jarrett Havoline 5.00 12.00
30 Michael Waltrip Pennzoil 3.00 6.00
37 John Andretti K-Mart 3.00 6.00
52 Ken Schrader AC Delco 4.00 8.00
94 Bill Elliott McDonald's 4.00 8.00

1996 Racing Champions Transporters 1:144

This series of Transporters was issued by Racing Champions in a red blister pack in 1996. The blister packaging reads "1996 Edition" on the front. Unless noted below each was also packaged with a mini car.

2 Rusty Wallace Penske 4.00 8.00
14 Patty Moise Dial Purex 3.00 6.00
16 Ted Musgrave Family Channel 3.00 6.00
24 Jeff Gordon DuPont 5.00 12.00

1997 Racing Champions Preview Transporters 1:144

These 1:144 scale mini Transporters were issued in a red and black Racing Champions blister package. The blister reads "1997 Preview Edition" on the front. Each was also packaged with a yellow bordered trading card and a 1:144 scale mini car.

5 Terry Labonte Kellogg's 3.00 8.00
7 Geoff Bodine QVC 3.00 6.00
8 Hut Stricklin Circuit City 3.00 6.00
29 Robert Pressley Cartoon Network 3.00 6.00

1997 Racing Champions Transporters 1:144

These 1:144 scale mini Transporters were issued in a red and black Racing Champions blister package. The blister reads "1997 Edition" on the front. Each was also packaged with a yellow bordered trading card and a 1:144 scale mini car.

00 Buckshot Jones Aquafresh 3.00 6.00
1 Hermie Sadler DeWalt 3.00 6.00
2 Ricky Craven DuPont 3.00 6.00
2 Rusty Wallace Penske 3.00 8.00
4 Sterling Marlin Kodak 3.00 8.00
5 Terry Labonte Bayer 3.00 8.00
5 Terry Labonte Kellogg's 3.00 8.00
5 Terry Labonte Kellogg's Tony 3.00 8.00
6 Mark Martin Valvoline 3.00 8.00
7 Geoff Bodine 3.00 6.00

QVC
9 Joe Bessey 3.00 6.00
Power Team
10 Phil Parsons 3.00 6.00
Channellock
11 Brett Bodine 3.00 6.00
Close Call
11 Jimmy Foster 3.00 6.00
Speedvision
16 Ted Musgrave 3.00 6.00
Family Channel
17 Darrell Waltrip 3.00 6.00
Western Auto
17 Darrell Waltrip 3.00 8.00
Western Auto Chrome
18 Bobby Labonte 3.00 8.00
Interstate Batteries
19 Gary Bradberry 3.00 6.00
Child Support
21 Michael Waltrip 3.00 6.00
Citgo
24 Jeff Gordon 6.00 12.00
DuPont
28 Ernie Irvan 3.00 8.00
Havoline w
black&orange car
28 Ernie Irvan 3.00 8.00
Havoline w
black&white car
29 Jeff Green 3.00 6.00
Tom&Jerry
29 Robert Pressley 3.00 6.00
Cartoon Network
30 Johnny Benson 3.00 6.00
Pennzoil
32 Dale Jarrett 3.00 8.00
White Rain
34 Mike McLaughlin 3.00 6.00
Royal Oak
36 Todd Bodine 3.00 6.00
Stanley Tools
36 Derrike Cope 3.00 6.00
Skittles
37 Jeremy Mayfield 3.00 6.00
K-Mart
40 Robby Gordon 3.00 6.00
Sabco
42 Joe Nemechek 3.00 6.00
BellSouth
43 Rodney Combs 3.00 6.00
Lance
46 Wally Dallenbach 3.00 6.00
First Union
57 Jason Keller 3.00 6.00
Slim Jim
60 Mark Martin 4.00 10.00
Winn Dixie
63 Tracy Leslie 3.00 6.00
Lysol
72 Mike Dillon 3.00 6.00
Detroit Gasket
74 Randy LaJoie 3.00 6.00
Fina
75 Rick Mast 3.00 6.00
Remington
88 Kevin Lepage 3.00 6.00
Hype
90 Dick Trickle 3.00 6.00
Heilig-Meyers
91 Mike Wallace 3.00 6.00
Spam
94 Ron Barfield 3.00 6.00
New Holland
94 Bill Elliott 3.00 8.00
McDonald's
94 Bill Elliott 3.00 8.00
Mac Tonight
96 David Green 3.00 6.00
Caterpillar
97 Chad Little 3.00 6.00
John Deere

1998 Racing Champions Transporters 1:144

These mini Transporters were issued in a red Racing Champions blister package that reads "1998 Edition" on the front. Each transporter was also packaged with a trading card and a 1:144 scale mini car.

4 Bobby Hamilton 3.00 6.00
Kodak
4 Jeff Purvis 3.00 6.00
Lance
5 Terry Labonte 3.00 8.00
Kellogg's
9 Lake Speed 3.00 6.00
Cartoon Network Red
9 Lake Speed 3.00 6.00
Cartoon Network White
13 Jerry Nadeau 3.00 6.00
First Plus
35 Todd Bodine 3.00 6.00
Tabasco
36 Ernie Irvan 3.00 6.00
M&M's
36 Ernie Irvan 3.00 6.00
Skittles
50 Ricky Craven 3.00 6.00
Hendrick
00 Buckshot Jones 3.00 6.00
Aqua Fresh

1997 Revell Transporters 1:64

97 Chad Little 40.00 75.00
John Deere AUTO/756
GMP produced
issued with 1:64 car

1998 Revell Select Hobby Transporters 1:64

These die-cast pieces are packaged in a Revell Select box with one 1:64 hauler and one 1:64 Revell Select car. There is an inner blister wrap that protects the die-cast inside the box.

3 Dale Earnhardt 20.00 35.00
Goodwrench
24 Jeff Gordon 15.00 30.00
DuPont
77 Robert Pressley 15.00 30.00
Jasper

1992 Road Champs Transporters 1:64

These 1:64 scale transporters were issued with two 1:64 scale cars in a large oversized Road Champs window box.

4 Ernie Irvan 7.50 20.00
Kodak
6 Mark Martin 10.00 25.00
Valvoline
43 Richard Petty 10.00 25.00
STP

1992 Road Champs Transporters 1:87

Each of these 1:87 Transporters was issued in a Road Champs blister that features both a small photo of the driver and his car.

1 Jeff Gordon 10.00 25.00
Baby Ruth
2 Rusty Wallace 6.00 15.00
Pontiac
4 Ernie Irvan 5.00 12.00
Kodak
6 Mark Martin 6.00 15.00
Valvoline
21 Morgan Shepherd 5.00 12.00
Citgo
43 Richard Petty 6.00 15.00
STP

1996-98 Scaleworks Transporters 1:24

5 Terry Labonte 75.00 150.00
Kellogg's 1998
5 Terry Labonte 75.00 150.00
Kellogg's Corny/1000
6 Mark Martin 90.00 150.00
Valvoline/2000 1997
28 Ernie Irvan 75.00 150.00
Havoline/2000 1996
36 Ernie Irvan 90.00 150.00
M&M's
36 Ernie Irvan 75.00 150.00
Skittles
43 Richard Petty 125.00 225.00
STP 25th Anniversary/1025 1997
88 Dale Jarrett 90.00 150.00
Quality Care/2000 1996
94 Bill Elliott 80.00 150.00
McDonald's/1000 1996
94 Bill Elliott 80.00 150.00
Mac Tonight/1000 1998

2003 Team Caliber Owners Series Transporters 1:64

6 Mark Martin 35.00 70.00
Viagra/1800
12 Ryan Newman 35.00 70.00
Alltel/1200
16 Greg Biffle 25.00 50.00
Grainger/1200
17 Matt Kenseth 40.00 80.00
DeWalt/1200
21 Ricky Rudd 25.00 50.00
Motorcraft/1200
23 Kenny Wallace 20.00 40.00
Stacker 2
48 Jimmie Johnson 30.00 60.00
Lowe's/800
97 Kurt Busch 20.00 40.00
Rubbermaid/1200
01 Jerry Nadeau 30.00 60.00
Army/600

2003 Team Caliber Pit Stop Transporters 1:64

5 Terry Labonte 12.50 25.00
Kellogg's
6 Mark Martin 15.00 30.00
Viagra
10 Johnny Benson 12.50 25.00
Valvoline
12 Ryan Newman 15.00 30.00
Alltel
16 Greg Biffle 12.50 25.00
Grainger
17 Matt Kenseth 15.00 30.00
DeWalt
23 Kenny Wallace 12.50 25.00
Stacker 2
43 John Andretti 12.50 25.00
Cheerios
45 Kyle Petty 12.50 25.00
Georgia Pacific
48 Jimmie Johnson 12.50 25.00
Lowe's
97 Kurt Busch 12.50 25.00
Rubbermaid
99 Jeff Burton 12.50 25.00
Citgo
01 Jerry Nadeau 15.00 30.00
Army

2004 Team Caliber Owners Series Transporters 1:64

17 Matt Kenseth 40.00 60.00
DeWalt/600

2004 Team Caliber Pit Stop Transporters 1:64

6 Mark Martin 18.00 30.00
Viagra
12 Ryan Newman 18.00 30.00
Alltel
17 Matt Kenseth 18.00 30.00
DeWalt
22 Scott Wimmer 18.00 30.00
Caterpillar
97 Kurt Busch 18.00 30.00
Sharpie
NNO Disney Event Car Mickey Mouse 12.50 25.00

1998 Winner's Circle Race 'N' Play Transporters 1:64

This series of Transporters was issued by Winner's Circle and packaged in the standard blue Winner's Circle window box. Each transporter when opened folded out into a larger pit scene racing set.

3 Dale Earnhardt 15.00 30.00
Goodwrench
24 Jeff Gordon 15.00 25.00
DuPont

2000 Winner's Circle Transporters 1:64

Transporters in this release were issued in a blue Winner's Circle box that featured a photo of the driver on the bottom right corner of the front of the box. Some pieces may have been released in 2001 as well, but have been included as a 2000 piece for ease in cataloging.

2 Rusty Wallace 10.00 20.00
Rusty
3 Dale Earnhardt 15.00 30.00
Goodwrench
Earnhardt photo with hat
no 2000 NASCAR logo
3 Dale Earnhardt 15.00 30.00
Goodwrench
Earnhardt photo with hat
with 2000 NASCAR logo
3 Dale Earnhardt 15.00 30.00
Goodwrench
Earnhardt photo w
o hat
8 Dale Earnhardt Jr. 20.00 40.00
Dale Jr.
18 Bobby Labonte 10.00 20.00
Interstate Batteries
light green trailer
18 Bobby Labonte 10.00 20.00
Interstate Batteries
dark green trailer
20 Tony Stewart 12.50 25.00
Home Depot
with small Home Depot
logo on side of trailer
20 Tony Stewart 12.50 25.00
Home Depot
without small Home Depot
logo on side of trailer
24 Jeff Gordon 15.00 30.00
DuPont without NASCAR
2000 logo on box
24 Jeff Gordon 15.00 30.00
DuPont with NASCAR
2000 logo on box
88 Dale Jarrett 12.50 25.00
Quality Care
NNO Everham Motorsports 15.00 30.00
Dodge Test Team

2001 Winner's Circle Transporters 1:64

Each Transporter in this release came in a blue Winner's Circle box that included a photo of a group of transporters on the bottom right corner. Please note that the 2001 box looks nearly identical to the 2002 year box. However, the 2001 does not included the words "Trailer Rig" on the front lower center of the box.

1 Steve Park 12.50 25.00
Pennzoil
3 Dale Earnhardt 20.00 40.00
Goodwrench
8 Dale Earnhardt Jr. 20.00 40.00
Dale Jr.
9 Bill Elliott 15.00 30.00
Dodge
24 Jeff Gordon 25.00 50.00
DuPont Flames
29 Kevin Harvick 12.50 25.00
Goodwrench White
29 Kevin Harvick 12.50 30.00
Goodwrench Taz
88 Dale Jarrett 25.00 50.00
UPS
88 Dale Jarrett 40.00 70.00
UPS Flames Truck

2002 Winner's Circle Transporters 1:64

These Transporters were issued in a blue Winner's Circle box that included an orange oval with the words "Trailer Rig" across the front. It also included a photo of a group of transporters on the bottom right corner just like the 2001 box.

2 Rusty Wallace 12.50 25.00
Rusty
3 Dale Earnhardt Jr. 15.00 30.00
Nilla Wafers
3 Dale Earnhardt Jr. 15.00 30.00
Oreo
7 Casey Atwood 12.50 25.00
Sirius Muppets
8 Dale Earnhardt Jr. 15.00 30.00
Dale Jr.
8 Dale Earnhardt Jr. 25.00 40.00
2001 MLB All-Star Game
8 Dale Earnhardt Jr. 15.00 30.00
2002 MLB All-Star Game
9 Bill Elliott 12.50 25.00
Dodge Muppets
12 Kerry Earnhardt 12.50 25.00
Jani-King Yoseemitie Sam
15 Michael Waltrip 12.50 25.00
NAPA
15 Michael Waltrip 12.50 25.00
NAPA Star&Stripes
18 Bobby Labonte 12.50 25.00
Interstate Batteries
18 Bobby Labonte 12.50 25.00
Interstate Batteries Jurassic
18 Bobby Labonte 12.50 25.00
Interstate Batteries Muppets
19 Jeremy Mayfield 12.50 25.00
Dodge Muppets
19 Jeremy Mayfield 12.50 25.00
Mountain Dew
20 Tony Stewart 12.50 25.00
Home Depot
20 Tony Stewart 12.50 25.00
Jurassic Park III
20 Tony Stewart 12.50 25.00
Home Depot Coca Cola
24 Jeff Gordon 12.50 25.00
DuPont Bugs Bunny
24 Jeff Gordon 12.50 30.00
DuPont Flames
24 Jeff Gordon 12.50 25.00
DuPont 200th Anniversary
24 Jeff Gordon 15.00 30.00
Pepsi Daytona
28 Ricky Rudd 12.50 25.00
Havoline Muppets
29 Kevin Harvick 12.50 25.00
Goodwrench Taz
31 Robby Gordon 12.50 25.00
Cingular Pepe le Pew
40 Sterling Marlin 15.00 30.00
Sterling
48 Jimmie Johnson 15.00 30.00
Lowe's Sylvester
88 Dale Jarrett 12.50 25.00
UPS Muppets

2003 Winner's Circle Transporters 1:64

These Transporters were issued in a blue Winner's Circle window box that closely resembles the 2001 and 2002 boxes. The difference can be found in the oval "Trailer Rig" logo across the front. The background of that logo for 2003 features a blue checkered flag pattern instead of solid orange for 2002. It also included a photo of a group of transporters on the bottom right corner just like the 2001 and 2002 boxes. Many of these transporters are simply a re-issue of a previous piece in the new box.

3 Dale Earnhardt 15.00 30.00
Forever the Man
4 Mike Skinner 12.50 25.00
Kodak Yosemite Sam
5 Terry Labonte 12.50 25.00
Kellogg's Road Runner
and Wile E.Coyote
8 Dale Earnhardt Jr. 15.00 30.00
2002 MLB All-Star Game
8 Dale Earnhardt Jr. 15.00 30.00
2003 All-Star
8 Dale Earnhardt Jr. 15.00 30.00
DMP Chance 2
8 Dale Earnhardt Jr. 18.00 30.00
E Tribute Concert
8 Dale Earnhardt Jr. 15.00 30.00
Looney Tunes
8 Dale Earnhardt Jr. 15.00 30.00
Oreo Ritz
8 Tony Stewart 18.00 30.00
Chance 2 3 Doors Down
12 Kerry Earnhardt 12.50 25.00
JaniKing Yosemite Sam
19 Jeremy Mayfield 12.50 25.00
Mountain Dew
20 Tony Stewart 15.00 30.00
Home Depot Peanuts Black 2002
20 Tony Stewart 15.00 30.00
Home Depot Peanuts Orange 2002
24 Jeff Gordon 15.00 30.00
DuPont 4-Time Champ
24 Jeff Gordon 12.50 25.00
DuPont Bugs 2001
24 Jeff Gordon 12.50 25.00
DuPont Bugs Rematch
24 Jeff Gordon 20.00 40.00
Elmo 2002
24 Jeff Gordon 15.00 30.00
Pepsi Billion $
25 Joe Nemechek 12.50 25.00
2002 UAW Delphi
Speedy Gonzales
29 Kevin Harvick 12.50 25.00
Goodwrench
29 Kevin Harvick 12.50 25.00
Goodwrench Taz
30 Jeff Green 12.50 25.00
AOL Daffy Duck
31 Robby Gordon 12.50 25.00
Cingular Pepe le Pew
38 Elliott Sadler 12.50 25.00
M&M's Groovy
48 Jimmie Johnson 12.50 25.00
Lowe's Sylvester
and Tweety
55 Bobby Hamilton 12.50 25.00
Square D Marvin the Martian '02

2004 Winner's Circle Transporters 1:64

8 Dale Earnhardt Jr. 20.00 35.00
JR
8 Dale Earnhardt Jr. 15.00 30.00
JR Souvenir
8 Dale Earnhardt Jr. 15.00 30.00
MLB All Star '03
8 Dale Earnhardt Jr. 15.00 30.00
Oreo
8 Dale Earnhardt Jr. 15.00 30.00
StainD
9 Kasey Kahne 15.00 30.00
Dodge Souvenir
9 Kasey Kahne 20.00 35.00
Dodge Mad Magazine
18 Bobby Labonte 15.00 25.00
Interstate Batteries
20 Tony Stewart 15.00 30.00
Home Depot
20 Tony Stewart 15.00 25.00
Home Depot Shrek 2
20 Tony Stewart 15.00 25.00
Home Depot Souvenir
21 Kevin Harvick 15.00 30.00
Hershey's Kisses
24 Jeff Gordon 20.00 35.00
DuPont Flames
24 Jeff Gordon 15.00 30.00
DuPont Flames
HMS 20th Anniversary
24 Jeff Gordon 15.00 30.00
DuPont Flames
Wizard of Oz
24 Jeff Gordon 15.00 30.00
DuPont Rainbow
24 Jeff Gordon 15.00 30.00
Pepsi Billion
24 Jeff Gordon 15.00 30.00
Pepsi Shards
29 Kevin Harvick 15.00 25.00
Goodwrench
38 Elliott Sadler 15.00 30.00
M&M's
38 Elliott Sadler 15.00 30.00
M&M's July 4
38 Elliott Sadler 15.00 30.00
Pedigree Wizard of Oz
77 Brendan Gaughan 15.00 30.00
Kodak Wizard of Oz
88 Dale Jarrett 15.00 30.00
UPS
99 Michael Waltrip 15.00 30.00
Aaron's Cat in the Hat

2005 Winner's Circle Transporters 1:64

6 Bill Elliott 15.00 30.00
Hellman's Charlie Brown
8 Dale Earnhardt Jr. 15.00 30.00
JR
9 Bill Elliott 15.00 25.00
Milestones
9 Kasey Kahne 15.00 25.00
Dodge Longest Yard
9 Kasey Kahne 15.00 30.00
Mopar
9 Kasey Kahne 15.00 30.00
Dodge
9 Kasey Kahne 15.00 30.00
Mountain Dew
9 Kasey Kahne 15.00 30.00
Dodge Pit Cap White
19 Jeremy Mayfield 12.50 25.00
Dodge
19 Jeremy Mayfield 15.00 25.00
Mountain Dew Pitch Black
20 Tony Stewart 15.00 30.00
Home Depot
21 Kevin Harvick 15.00 25.00
Reese's
21 Kevin Harvick 15.00 30.00
Take 5
24 Jeff Gordon 15.00 30.00
DuPont Flames
24 Jeff Gordon 15.00 30.00
Pepsi Daytona
29 Kevin Harvick 15.00 25.00
Goodwrench
33 Tony Stewart 15.00 25.00
Mr. Clean AutoDry
38 Kasey Kahne 15.00 30.00
Great Clips
38 Elliott Sadler 15.00 25.00
M&M's
38 Elliott Sadler 15.00 25.00
M&M's Halloween
38 Elliott Sadler 15.00 25.00
M&M's July 4
38 Elliott Sadler 15.00 25.00
M&M's
42 Jamie McMurray 15.00 25.00
Havoline
81 Dale Earnhardt Jr. 15.00 30.00
Oreo Ritz
88 Dale Jarrett 15.00 25.00
UPS
01 Joe Nemechek 15.00 25.00
Army
NNO James Dean 50th Anniversary Event 15.00 25.00

2006 Winner's Circle Transporters 1:64

19 Jeremy Mayfield 12.50 25.00
Dodge
20 Tony Stewart 15.00 30.00
Home Depot
29 Kevin Harvick 15.00 25.00
Hershey's
88 Dale Jarrett 15.00 25.00
UPS
NNO Dale Earnhardt 15.00 25.00
Hall of Fame Dale Tribute
split window box

2007 Winner's Circle Transporters 1:64

1 Martin Truex Jr. 10.00 20.00
Bass Pro Shops
2 Kurt Busch 10.00 20.00
Kurt
8 Dale Earnhardt Jr. 12.50 25.00
DEI
8 Dale Earnhardt Jr. 12.50 25.00
DEI Camo
American Heroes
8 Dale Earnhardt Jr. 12.50 25.00
DEI Stars & Stripes
9 Kasey Kahne 10.00 20.00
Dodge Dealers
9 Kasey Kahne 10.00 20.00
McDonald's
11 Denny Hamlin 10.00 20.00
Fed Ex Express
11 Denny Hamlin 10.00 20.00
Fed Ex Freight Marines
American Heroes
12 Ryan Newman 10.00 20.00
Alltel
17 Matt Kenseth 12.50 25.00
DeWalt
19 Elliott Sadler 15.00 30.00
Dodge Dealers
Fantastic 4
20 Tony Stewart 10.00 20.00
Home Depot
24 Jeff Gordon 10.00 20.00
DuPont Department of Defense
American Heroes
24 Jeff Gordon 12.50 25.00
DuPont Flames
24 Jeff Gordon 10.00 20.00
Pepsi
29 Kevin Harvick 10.00 20.00
Shell Pennzoil
38 David Gilliland 10.00 20.00
M&M's
43 Bobby Labonte 10.00 20.00
Spiderman
43 Bobby Labonte 10.00 20.00
STP
44 Dale Jarrett 12.50 25.00
UPS
48 Jimmie Johnson 10.00 20.00
Lowe's
48 Jimmie Johnson 10.00 20.00
Lowe's Power of Pride
American Heroes
55 Michael Waltrip 10.00 20.00
NAPA
00 David Reutimann 10.00 20.00
Burger King
01 Mark Martin 10.00 20.00
U.S. Army American Heroes

2008 Winner's Circle Daytona 500 Transporters 1:64

29 Kevin Harvick Shell Pennzoil 12.50 25.00
42 Juan Pablo Montoya Texaco Havoline 12.50 25.00
48 Jimmie Johnson Lowe's 15.00 30.00
88 Dale Earnhardt Jr. AMP 15.00 30.00

2008 Winner's Circle Dually w/Car on Trackside Trailer 1:64

Martin Truex Jr. Bass Pro Shops 10.00 20.00
9 Kasey Kahne KK 10.00 20.00
24 Jeff Gordon DuPont Flames 12.50 25.00
29 Kevin Harvick Shell 10.00 20.00
42 Juan Pablo Montoya Texaco 10.00 20.00
42 Juan Pablo Montoya Big Red 10.00 20.00
48 Jimmie Johnson Lowe's 12.50 25.00
88 Dale Earnhardt Jr. AMP 15.00 30.00
88 Dale Earnhardt Jr. National Guard 15.00 30.00

2008 Winner's Circle Transporters 1:64

9 Kasey Kahne KK 15.00 25.00
2 Ryan Newman Daytona 500 Win 15.00 25.00
8 Kyle Busch M&M's 25.00 40.00
20 Tony Stewart Home Depot 20.00 35.00
24 Jeff Gordon DuPont Flames 20.00 35.00
24 Jeff Gordon Pepsi 20.00 35.00
29 Kevin Harvick Shell 15.00 25.00
42 Juan Pablo Montoya Texaco 15.00 25.00
48 Jimmie Johnson Lowe's 20.00 35.00
88 Dale Earnhardt Jr. 3 Doors Down 20.00 35.00
88 Dale Earnhardt Jr. AMP 20.00 35.00
88 Dale Earnhardt Jr. Go Daddy 20.00 35.00
88 Dale Earnhardt Jr. National Guard 20.00 35.00

1987-90 Winross Transporters 1:64

Winross entered the transporter market in 1987. The pieces originally had a cost higher than the mass marketed pieces and were produced in short quantities. This makes these pieces some of the most valuable transporters available on the market.

NNO Bill Elliott Coors '90 100.00 200.00
NNO Bobby Gerhart ARCA '88 175.00 300.00
NNO Sterling Marlin Sunoco '90 60.00 100.00
NNO Stanley Smith Hamilton Trucking '88 90.00 150.00
NNO Rick Wilson Kodak Ford 1987 200.00 350.00
NNO Rick Wilson Kodak Mack 1987 300.00 500.00

1991 Winross Transporters 1:64

Winross continued their series of 1:64 transporters in 1991. They issued three different Bill Elliott transporters that year along with their first Richard Petty piece.

NNO Ken Bouchard ADAP 40.00 75.00
NNO Bill Elliott Coors Light 75.00 125.00
NNO Bill Elliott Fan Club 50.00 100.00
NNO Bill Elliott Museum with Blue Paint scheme 30.00 80.00
NNO Tommy Ellis Polaroid 100.00 175.00
NNO Terry Labonte Sunoco 90.00 160.00
NNO Richard Petty STP 100.00 175.00
NNO Ken Schrader Kodiak 50.00 90.00

1992 Winross Transporters 1:64

Winross produced several special issue transporters in their 1992 series. Dale Earnhardt was the focus of two of these specials having one produced for White Rose Collectibles and another one produced and packaged in a wooden box.

NNO Junie Donlavey Truxmore 50.00 90.00
NNO Bill Elliott Fan Club 50.00 90.00
NNO Bill Elliott Museum with red paint scheme 50.00 90.00
NNO Dale Earnhardt Goodwrench produced for White Rose Collectibles 90.00 150.00
NNO Dale Earnhardt Goodwrench in Wooden box 175.00 300.00
NNO Bobby Hamilton Country Time 30.00 60.00
NNO Tommy Ellis Polaroid 50.00 90.00
NNO Terry Labonte Sunoco 30.00 60.00
NNO Tiny Lund 20.00 40.00
NNO Jeff McClure Superior Performance 50.00 90.00
NNO J.D. McDuffie Pontiac Rumple 40.00 75.00
NNO Phil Parsons 50.00 90.00
NNO Kyle Petty Mello Yello 20.00 50.00
NNO Robert Pressley Alliance 90.00 150.00
NNO Richard Petty STP Fan Appreciation Tour 25.00 60.00
NNO Fireball (Glenn) Roberts 40.00 75.00
NNO Darrell Waltrip Western Auto Black,White&Red 30.00 80.00
NNO Darrell Waltrip Western Auto with Red paint scheme 75.00 125.00

1993 Winross Transporters 1:64

This series of Winross transporters is highlighted by a die cast for the late Alan Kulwicki. The series also includes the third year in a row that Winross produced a piece for the Bill Elliott Fan Club.

NNO Joe Bessey AC Delco 25.00 50.00
NNO Bill Elliott Fan Club 40.00 75.00
NNO Doyle Ford NASCAR Flags 20.00 40.00
NNO Jeff Gordon DuPont 30.00 80.00
NNO Steve Grissom Channellock 25.00 50.00
NNO Dale Jarrett Interstate Batteries 30.00 60.00
NNO Alan Kulwicki Hooters 40.00 80.00
NNO Sterling Marlin Maxwell House 30.00 60.00
NNO Mark Martin Valvoline 25.00 60.00
NNO Robert Pressley Alliance 50.00 90.00
NNO Mike Stefanik Auto Palace 25.00 50.00
NNO No Driver Association McClure Racing Kodak 75.00 125.00

1994 Winross Transporters 1:64

This series features a variation on the Davey Allison piece. The sponsors name was misspelled on the original pieces produced.

NNO Davey Allison Havoline misspelled Error 75.00 125.00
NNO Davey Allison Havoline Corrected 50.00 100.00
NNO Bill Elliott Budweiser 35.00 70.00
NNO Harry Gant Farewell Tour 50.00 90.00
NNO Goodyear Racing 25.00 50.00
NNO Terry Labonte Kellogg's 35.00 70.00
NNO Mac Tools Racing/4800 25.00 50.00
NNO Sterling Marlin Kodak 25.00 60.00
NNO Michael Waltrip Pennzoil 30.00 60.00

1995 Winross Transporters 1:64

This was the first series of transporters released under Winross' new price structure. The series features Bill Elliott's new McDonald's colors and Dale Jarrett sporting the colors of Mac Tools, his Busch ride at the time.

NNO Geoff Bodine Exide 25.00 60.00
NNO Bill Elliott McDonald's 35.00 70.00
NNO Dale Jarrett Mac Tools/2600 35.00 60.00
NNO Kevin Lepage Vermont Teddy Bear 35.00 60.00
NNO Dick Trickle Quality Care 35.00 60.00
NNO Mike Wallace Heilig-Meyers 35.00 60.00

1996 Winross Transporters 1:64

NNO Ward Burton MBNA 30.00 45.00
NNO Bill Elliott Mac Tonight 40.00 75.00
NNO David Green Caterpillar 20.00 45.00
NNO Ernie Irvan Havoline 45.00 60.00
NNO Sterling Marlin Kodak 35.00 60.00
NNO Michael Waltrip Citgo 35.00 50.00

1995 Action/RCCA Dragsters 1:24

This series of dragsters started with the Mac Tools releases at the beginning of 1995. The first pieces all featured a Mac Tools logo and are the most difficult of all the dragsters to find. The 1997 and 1998 RCCA upgrade pieces contain serial numbers on the chassis of each car. Most were issued in the typical Action Racing Collectibles box for that era of release, with many also featuring a production run number on the box itself.

NNO Joe Amato Valvoline/5640 30.00 80.00
NNO Joe Amato Valvoline Mac Tools 50.00 120.00
NNO Shelly Anderson Western Auto/5520 25.00 60.00
NNO Pat Austin Castrol Syntex 30.00 60.00
NNO Kenny Bernstein Budweiser King/6492 30.00 80.00
NNO Kenny Bernstein Budweiser King Mac Tools 50.00 120.00
NNO Larry Dixon Miller Genuine Draft/6000 125.00 250.00
NNO Mike Dunn La Victoria Mac Tools 250.00 400.00
NNO Gatornationals Mac Tools 60.00 150.00
NNO Darrell Gwynn Extra Gold Kendall 75.00 150.00
NNO Darrell Gwynn Extra Gold Quaker State/7000 40.00 80.00
NNO Darrell Gwynn Mopar Mac Tools 50.00 100.00
NNO Frank Hawley Coors Light 40.00 80.00
NNO Jim Head Smokin' Joe's/5004 (in plastic case) 200.00 400.00
NNO Eddie Hill 1988 Pennzoil Super Shops/3500 90.00 150.00
NNO Eddie Hill Pennzoil/6000 40.00 80.00
NNO Tommy Johnson Jr. Mopar 30.00 60.00
NNO Connie Kalitta American 25.00 50.00
NNO Shirley Muldowney Action/5004 50.00 100.00
NNO Gary Ormsby 1989 Castrol GTX RCCA/5712 30.00 80.00
NNO Don Prudhomme Skoal Bandit 100.00 200.00
NNO Don Prudhomme Skoal Bandit RCCA/5004 100.00 200.00
NNO Don Prudhomme Snake Final Strike 125.00 200.00
NNO Don Prudhomme Snake Final Strike Mac Tools 150.00 250.00
NNO Bill Reichert Bars Leak 25.00 60.00

1996 Action/RCCA Dragsters 1:24

NNO Joe Amato Keystone 30.00 60.00
NNO Shelly Anderson Parts America RCCA/6000 30.00 80.00
NNO Mike Austin Red Wing Shoes/3500 25.00 60.00
NNO Kenny Bernstein Budweiser/2544 25.00 60.00
NNO Kenny Bernstein Budweiser Mac Tools Champion 40.00 100.00
NNO Larry Dixon Miller Splash/7500 30.00 80.00
NNO Larry Dixon Miller Splash Silver/10,000 30.00 80.00
NNO Mike Dunn Mopar/9000 25.00 60.00
NNO Don Garlits 1992 Kendall Supershops RCCA/3000 100.00 175.00
NNO Gatornationals Mac Tools 15.00 40.00
NNO Darrell Gwynn 1988 Budweiser RCCA 25.00 60.00
NNO Blaine Johnson Travers Blue Yellow/7500 60.00 120.00
NNO Scott Kalitta American/7500 25.00 50.00
NNO Scott Kalitta American Mac Tools 40.00 80.00
NNO Chris Karamesines The Greek 25.00 50.00
NNO Cory McClenathan 1992 MacAttack 40.00 80.00
NNO Cory McClenathan McDonald's 25.00 60.00
NNO Cory McClenathan McDonald's Olympic/9000 25.00 60.00
NNO Tom McEwen Mobil RCCA/5500 25.00 60.00
NNO Shirley Muldowney Action RCCA 40.00 100.00
NNO Al Segrini Spies Hecker/5000 25.00 60.00
NNO Bob Vandergriff Jerzees 25.00 60.00
NNO Winston Eagle Red/7500 15.00 40.00
NNO Winston Select/5000 15.00 40.00

1997 Action/RCCA Dragsters 1:24

NNO Joe Amato Action White/1500 25.00 60.00
NNO Joe Amato Keystone 25.00 60.00
NNO Joe Amato Keystone Mac Tools 40.00 80.00
NNO Kenny Bernstein Budweiser/9008 25.00 60.00
NNO Kenny Bernstein Budweiser Mac Tools 50.00 100.00
NNO Kenny Bernstein Budweiser RCCA/3500 40.00 100.00
NNO Larry Dixon Miller Lite/10,000 30.00 60.00
NNO Gatornationals Mac Tools/8500 20.00 50.00
NNO Darrell Gwynn 1991 Coors Light/5004 40.00 80.00
NNO Jim Head Close Call 25.00 50.00
NNO Jim Head Close Call RCCA 30.00 60.00
NNO Doug Herbert Snap-On 25.00 60.00
NNO Eddie Hill Pennzoil/5700 40.00 80.00
NNO Blaine Johnson Travers Red and White/5000 50.00 100.00
NNO Scott Kalitta American RCCA/7500 25.00 60.00
NNO Cory McClenathan McDonald's 30.00 60.00
NNO Matco Supernationals 20.00 50.00
NNO Shirley Muldowney Action/5004 25.00 60.00
NNO Shirley Muldowney Action Mac Tools 50.00 100.00
NNO Shirley Muldowney Action RCCA 30.00 80.00
NNO Shirley Muldowney 1991 Otter Pops/5000 25.00 60.00
NNO Cristen Powell Royal Purple/4704 25.00 60.00
NNO Cristen Powell Royal Purple RCCA/2500 30.00 60.00
NNO Race Rock Cafe/1500 30.00 80.00
NNO Bruce Sarver CarQuest 20.00 50.00
NNO Gary Scelzi Winston 50.00 100.00
NNO Gary Scelzi Winston Matco Tools 50.00 100.00
NNO Gary Scelzi Winston RCCA/3000 50.00 100.00
NNO Bob Vandergriff Jerzees 25.00 60.00
NNO Bob Vandergriff Jerzees Mac Tools 30.00 80.00

1998 Action/RCCA Dragsters 1:24

NNO Joe Amato Tenneco/4008 25.00 60.00
NNO Joe Amato Tenneco Mac Tools/4500 30.00 60.00
NNO Joe Amato Tenneco RCCA 40.00 80.00
NNO Kenny Bernstein 1992 Budweiser 300 MPH/5000 50.00 100.00
NNO Kenny Bernstein 1992 Budweiser 300 MPH Mac Tools/4500 50.00 100.00
NNO Kenny Bernstein Budweiser/5000 40.00 80.00
NNO Kenny Bernstein Budweiser Mac Tools/4500 40.00 80.00
NNO Kenny Bernstein Budweiser RCCA/1200 50.00 100.00
NNO Kenny Bernstein Bud Lizard/5000 40.00 100.00
NNO Kenny Bernstein Bud Lizard Mac Tools 50.00 120.00
NNO Larry Dixon Miller Lite/4008 60.00 120.00
NNO Gatornationals Mac Tools/8000 15.00 40.00
NNO Eddie Hill Pennzoil/3500 30.00 60.00
NNO Cory McClenathan McDonald's 30.00 60.00
NNO Cory McClenathan McDonald's RCCA 40.00 75.00
NNO Cristen Powell Reebok White/3500 25.00 60.00
NNO Cristen Powell Reebok Orange 25.00 60.00
NNO Cristen Powell Reebok Orange RCCA 30.00 80.00
NNO Gary Scelzi Winston 40.00 80.00
NNO Gary Scelzi Winston RCCA/1500 40.00 100.00

1999 Action/RCCA Dragsters 1:24

NNO Joe Amato Dynomax Superman/7008 40.00 80.00
NNO Joe Amato Tenneco/3500 25.00 60.00
NNO Kenny Bernstein Bud 20th Ann/5508 30.00 80.00
NNO Larry Dixon Miller Lite Harley/5724 40.00 75.00
NNO Mike Dunn Mac Tools/5004 20.00 50.00
NNO Gatornationals Mac Tools/7500 20.00 50.00
NNO Gary Scelzi Winston/5004 25.00 60.00
NNO Gary Scelzi Winston Matco Tools/3000 30.00 60.00

2000 Action/RCCA Dragsters 1:24

NNO Joe Amato Dynomax/3708 30.00 80.00
NNO Joe Amato Dynomax Monsters/3816 40.00 80.00
NNO Kenny Bernstein Bud King/5004 25.00 60.00
NNO Kenny Bernstein Budweiser King Mac Tools/3000 25.00 60.00
NNO Kenny Bernstein Bud Olympic/7452 30.00 80.00
NNO Kenny Bernstein Budweiser Olympic Mac Tools/3000 30.00 80.00
NNO Larry Dixon Miller Lite Mac Tools/3300 30.00 80.00
NNO Mike Dunn Yankees Mac Tools/2498 40.00 100.00
NNO Mike Dunn Yankees DG Racing/1008 50.00 100.00
NNO Gatornationals Mac Tools/7000 20.00 50.00
NNO Doug Kalitta MGM Grand Mac Tools/3000 20.00 50.00
NNO Cory McClenathan MBNA 20.00 50.00
NNO Shirley Muldowney goracing.com RCCA/1500 20.00 50.00
NNO Tony Schumacher Exide/3504 25.00 50.00

2001 Action/RCCA Dragsters 1:24

NNO Kenny Bernstein Budweiser/2772 50.00 80.00
NNO Larry Dixon Miller Lite Color/2396 30.00 60.00
NNO Larry Dixon Miller Lite Color Chrome/1300 40.00 80.00
NNO Mike Dunn Yankees/4428 40.00 80.00
NNO Mike Dunn Yankees Mac Tools/3000 40.00 80.00
NNO Mike Dunn Yankees Blue Chrome RCCA/504 60.00 120.00
NNO Gatornationals Mac Tools Gold/6000 20.00 50.00
NNO Doug Kalitta KISS Mac Tools/6000 40.00 80.00
NNO Mac Tools Thunder Valley/5004 25.00 50.00
NNO Mac Tools U.S Nationals/5004 30.00 60.00
NNO Shirley Muldowney Cha Cha Mac Tools/5004 25.00 60.00
NNO Shirley Muldowney goosehead.com/2100 20.00 50.00
NNO Shirley Muldowney goosehead.com Color Chrome/900 40.00 80.00
NNO Darrell Russell Valvoline James Dean/3720 25.00 60.00
NNO Gary Scelzi Winston/4236 35.00 70.00
NNO Tony Schumacher Army Color Chrome/900 40.00 80.00

2002 Action/RCCA Dragsters 1:24

NNO Kenny Bernstein Budweiser Forever Red/9516 50.00 100.00
NNO Kenny Bernstein Budweiser Forever Red Mac Tools/1008 60.00 120.00
NNO Andrew Cowin Yankees/5796 30.00 60.00
NNO Andrew Cowin New York Yankees Muppets/4596 25.00 60.00
NNO Larry Dixon Miller Lite/3672 40.00 75.00
NNO Larry Dixon Miller Lite Mac Tools/1608 40.00 75.00
NNO Larry Dixon Miller Lite Elvis/5132 40.00 75.00
NNO Larry Dixon Miller Lite Elvis Mac Tools 40.00 80.00
NNO Larry Dixon Miller Lite Snake/1440 75.00 135.00
NNO Larry Dixon Miller Lite Snake Mac Tools/1296 90.00 150.00
NNO Don Garlits Matco Tools/5004 60.00 100.00
NNO Gatornationals Mac Tools/3504 25.00 60.00
NNO Doug Kalitta Mac Tools/3504 30.00 60.00
NNO Doug Kalitta Mac Tools KISS/3432 50.00 90.00
NNO Cory McClenathan Mac Tools U.S. Nationals/2500 30.00 60.00
NNO Shirley Muldowney Mac Tools Blue Angels/4104 30.00 70.00
NNO Shirley Muldowney Mac Tools Heart/6708 40.00 75.00
NNO Shirley Muldowney Mac Tools Muppet/7128 25.00 60.00
NNO Shirley Muldowney Mac Tools Peanuts/3676 25.00 60.00
NNO Darrell Russell Bilstein Engine Flush/3000 20.00 50.00
NNO Tony Schumacher Army/2346 30.00 60.00

2003 Action/RCCA Dragsters 1:24

NNO Brandon Bernstein Budweiser/3804 35.00 70.00
NNO Larry Dixon Miller Lite/2712 35.00 70.00
NNO Don Garlits Summit 35th Anniversary/3504 50.00 90.00
NNO Gatornationals Mac Tools/1200 45.00 70.00
NNO Doug Herbert Snap-On Hulk/14,224 35.00 70.00
NNO Doug Kalitta Kid Rock/3388 35.00 70.00
NNO Doug Kalitta Mac Tools/2532 35.00 70.00
NNO Doug Kalitta Mac Tools KISS/1002 40.00 75.00
NNO Doug Kalitta Wright Bros./2728 35.00 70.00
NNO Mac Tools U.S Nationals/1200 40.00 75.00
NNO Cory McClenathan Yankees 100th Anniversary/2538 30.00 60.00
NNO Cory McClenathan Yankees 100th Anniversary Mac Tools/288 40.00 75.00
NNO Shirley Muldowney Mac Tools Grease/2400 30.00 60.00
NNO Shirley Muldowney Mac Tools Grease Mac Tools/2000 30.00 60.00
NNO Shirley Muldowney Mac Tools Last Pass/4628 30.00 70.00
NNO Shirley Muldowney Mac Tools Terminator 3/4408 35.00 60.00
NNO Shirley Muldowney Pink Flames/2100 35.00 60.00
NNO Shirley Muldowney Pink Flames Mac Tools/2000 35.00 60.00
NNO Tony Schumacher Army/2304 35.00 60.00

2004 Action/RCCA Dragsters 1:24

NNO Brandon Bernstein Budweiser/2484 45.00 70.00
NNO Brandon Bernstein Budweiser Born On April 4/3984 45.00 70.00
NNO Larry Dixon Miller Lite/1512 40.00 60.00
NNO Larry Dixon Miller Lite Can Promotion/1728 40.00 60.00
NNO Larry Dixon 40.00 60.00

Miller Lite
Miller for President of Beers/1944
NNO Larry Dixon 40.00 60.00
Miller Lite President of Beers
Mac Tools/408
NNO Gatornationals Mac Tools 45.00 70.00
NNO Doug Herbert 40.00 60.00
Dougzilla Brainerd/540
NNO Doug Herbert 40.00 60.00
Dougzilla Chicago/696
NNO Doug Herbert 40.00 60.00
Dougzilla Denver/684
NNO D.Herbert 40.00 60.00
Dougzilla Gainesville
NNO Doug Herbert 40.00 60.00
Dougzilla Indianapolis/1536
NNO Doug Herbert 40.00 60.00
Dougzilla Pomona/1728
NNO Doug Herbert 40.00 60.00
Dougzilla Reading/504
NNO Doug Herbert 40.00 60.00
Dougzilla Saint Louis/684
NNO Doug Herbert 40.00 60.00
Dougzilla Sonoma/528
NNO Doug Herbert 45.00 75.00
Snap-On/3552
NNO Tony Schumacher 45.00 70.00
U.S. Army Time MOTY/2004

2005 Action/RCCA Dragsters 1:24

NNO Brandon Bernstein 60.00 100.00
Bud AU/1716
NNO Bradon Bernstein 60.00 100.00
Bud AU GM Dealers/278
NNO Larry Dixon 40.00 65.00
Miller Lite/1632
NNO Doug Kalitta 40.00 65.00
Mac Tools
James Dean 50th Anniversary/684
NNO Tony Schumacher 40.00 65.00
Army/1478

2006 Action/RCCA Dragsters 1:24

NNO Doug Kalitta 50.00 75.00
Mac Tools/1080*
NNO Doug Kalitta 50.00 75.00
Mac Tools GM Dealers*

2008 Action/RCCA Dragsters 1:24

NNO Brandon Bernstein 50.00 75.00
Budweiser/876
NNO Brandon Bernstein 50.00 75.00
Budweiser Anheuser Busch/702
NNO Brandon Bernstein 60.00 100.00
Budweiser Liquid Color/120
NNO Doug Herbert 50.00 75.00
Snap-On Tools/1026
NNO Doug Herbert 50.00 75.00
Snap-On Liquid Color/120
NNO Doug Herbert 50.00 75.00
Snap-On Tools Snap-On/1500
NNO Tony Schumacher 60.00 100.00
U.S. Army Liquid Color/300
NNO Tony Schumacher 50.00 75.00
U.S. Army Salute the Troops/648

2010 Action/RCCA Dragsters 1:24

NNO Brandon Bernstein 50.00 75.00
Copart/709*
NNO Anton Brown 50.00 75.00
Matco Tools/576*
NNO Anton Brown 75.00 125.00
Matco Tools
Color Chrome/66*
NNO Cory McClenathan 50.00 75.00
Fram/707*
NNO Cory McClenathan 75.00 125.00
Fram
Color Chrome/36*
NNO Tony Schumacher 60.00 100.00
U.S. Army/912*
NNO Tony Schumacher 100.00 150.00
U.S. Army
Color Chrome/48*

1994 Action/RCCA Drag Racing Legends 1:64

NNO Arnie Beswick 5.00 10.00
Mr. B's
NNO Bill Golden 5.00 10.00
Top Stock Eliminator

1996 Action/RCCA Dragsters 1:64

This series started in 1996 and is highlight by two Blaine Johnson issues. Each piece was packaged in a clear blister pack (Action Racing) or cardboard window box (RCCA). Most pieces featured a production run total on the package itself.

NNO Blaine Johnson 7.50 15.00
Travers
Blue and Yellow/22,128
NNO Blaine Johnson 10.00 20.00
Travers Blue
Yellow
RCCA/3500
NNO Cristen Powell 5.00 10.00
Reebok White/5976

1997 Action/RCCA Dragsters 1:64

NNO Joe Amato 5.00 12.00
Keystone/9000
NNO Joe Amato 5.00 12.00
Keystone RCCA/3500
NNO Kenny Bernstein 15.00 25.00
1992 Budweiser
300 MPH RCCA
NNO Kenny Bernstein 6.00 15.00
Bud King
NNO Larry Dixon 10.00 25.00
Miller Lite/9000
in acrylic case
NNO Gatornationals Mac Tools/10,000 5.00 12.00
NNO Jim Head 6.00 12.00
Close Call/10,080
NNO Eddie Hill 6.00 12.00
Pennzoil/9432
NNO Blaine Johnson 6.00 12.00
Travers Red and White
NNO Blaine Johnson 15.00 25.00
Travers Red and White RCCA
NNO Cory McClenathan 5.00 12.00
McDonald's
NNO Cory McClenathan 6.00 15.00
McDonald's RCCA
NNO Shirley Muldowney 6.00 12.00
Action
NNO Shirley Muldowney 6.00 12.00
1991 Otter Pops/10,080
NNO Cristen Powell 5.00 12.00
Royal Purple
NNO Gary Scelzi 6.00 12.00
Winston/12,000
NNO Gary Scelzi 6.00 12.00
Winston RCCA/2500

1998 Action/RCCA Dragsters 1:64

NNO Joe Amato 5.00 12.00
Tenneco/9000
NNO Kenny Bernstein 6.00 15.00
Budweiser/7272
NNO Kenny Bernstein 7.50 15.00
Budweiser RCCA/9772
NNO Kenny Bernstein 5.00 12.00
Bud Lizard
NNO Kenny Bernstein 6.00 15.00
Bud Lizard RCCA
NNO Larry Dixon 7.50 15.00
Miller Lite/7056
in acrylic case
NNO Gatornationals Mac Tools 4.00 10.00
NNO Cory McClenathan 5.00 12.00
McDonald's/7056
NNO Cory McClenathan 7.50 15.00
McDonald's RCCA/2500
NNO Cristen Powell 6.00 12.00
Reebok White/5976
NNO Cristen Powell 6.00 15.00
Reebok White RCCA
NNO Gary Scelzi 5.00 12.00
Winston
NNO Gary Scelzi 6.00 15.00
Winston RCCA

1999 Action/RCCA Dragsters 1:64

NNO Joe Amato 5.00 12.00
Dynomax Superman/7008
NNO Kenny Bernstein 7.50 15.00
Bud 20th Ann/9000
NNO Larry Dixon 15.00 25.00
Miller Lite Harley/7056
in acrylic case
NNO Mike Dunn 5.00 12.00
Mopar/6048
NNO Gary Scelzi 5.00 12.00
Winston/7560

2000 Action/RCCA Dragsters 1:64

NNO Kenny Bernstein 6.00 12.00
Bud Olympic

2002 Action/RCCA Funny Car 1:16

NNO John Force 50.00 90.00
Castrol GTX 11-Time
Champ/4248
NNO John Force 60.00 100.00
Castrol GTX 100th Win/4132
NNO John Force 60.00 100.00
Castrol GTX Norwalk
Experience/4200

2003 Action/RCCA Funny Car 1:16

NNO John Force 250.00 400.00
Castrol GTX High Mileage
Halloween/300
NNO John Force 50.00 90.00
Castrol GTX High Mileage
Space Shuttle/4350
NNO John Force 50.00 90.00
Castrol GTX High Mileage
Three Stooges/3642
NNO Tony Pedregon 50.00 90.00
Castrol Syntec/1000

2004 Action/RCCA Funny Car 1:16

NNO John Force 100.00 200.00
Castrol/770
NNO John Force 60.00 100.00
Castrol High Mileage/1178
NNO John Force 100.00 200.00
Castrol Mustang 40th Anniversary/714
NNO John Force 200.00 400.00
Castrol GTX Start-Up
Freedom's Flight/300

2005 Action/RCCA Funny Car 1:16

NNO John Force 75.00 125.00
GTX Start Up
James Dean 50th Anniversary/786
NNO John Force 100.00 150.00
Castrol GTX 13X Champ/1266

1996 Action/RCCA Funny Car 1:24

This series of Funny Cars is highlighted by the first John Force issues. The 1997 RCCA upgrade pieces contain serial numbers on the chassis of each car. Most were issued in the typical Action Racing Collectibles Platinum Series box with many also featuring a production run number on the box itself.

NNO Pat Austin 20.00 50.00
Red Wing Shoes/7500
NNO Whit Bazemore 60.00 100.00
Smokin' Joe's RCCA/7500
NNO Kenny Bernstein 60.00 120.00
1988 Bud King RCCA/10,000
NNO Gary Densham 20.00 50.00
NEC/5004
NNO Jim Epler 20.00 50.00
1994 Rug Doctor/7500
NNO John Force 50.00 100.00
1993 Castrol GTX RCCA/7500
NNO John Force 50.00 120.00
1994 Castrol GTX
Flames RCCA/15,000
NNO John Force 40.00 100.00
Castrol GTX
NNO John Force 150.00 250.00
Castrol GTX Black
NNO John Force 90.00 150.00
Castrol GTX Mac Tools
NNO John Force 100.00 150.00
Castrol GTX Mac Tools Champion
NNO Gatornationals Mac Tools 15.00 40.00
NNO Al Hofmann 20.00 50.00
Parts America/7500
NNO Kenji Okazaki 25.00 60.00
Mooneyes
NNO Cruz Pedregon 30.00 80.00
McDonald's
NNO Cruz Pedregon 30.00 80.00
McDonald's
RCCA/5000
NNO Winston Select RCCA/3500 30.00 60.00

1997 Action/RCCA Funny Car 1:24

NNO Randy Anderson 30.00 60.00
Parts America RCCA
NNO Whit Bazemore 20.00 50.00
1995 Fast Orange/6000
NNO Whit Bazemore 20.00 50.00
1995 Mobil 1/5508
NNO Whit Bazemore 20.00 50.00
1995 Mobil 1 RCCA/3500
NNO Whit Bazemore 40.00 80.00
Winston/5748
NNO Whit Bazemore 50.00 100.00
Winston RCCA/3500
NNO Raymond Beadle 25.00 60.00
1979 Blue Max/3500
NNO Kenny Bernstein 40.00 80.00
1979 Budweiser
NNO Kenny Bernstein 25.00 60.00
'79 Chelsea King/6000
NNO Kenny Bernstein 60.00 100.00
1979 Chelsea King RCCA/3500
NNO Kenny Bernstein 60.00 100.00
1989 Budweiser Mac Tools
NNO Ron Capps 40.00 100.00
Copenhagen/5468
NNO Ron Capps 40.00 100.00
Copenhagen Mac Tools/4000
NNO Mike Dunn 30.00 60.00
1992 Pisano
NNO Chuck Etchells 30.00 60.00
Kendall
NNO John Force 40.00 80.00
1977 Brute Force blue
NNO John Force 40.00 80.00
1978 Brute Force
orange/9000
NNO John Force 40.00 80.00
1978 Brute Force
orange RCCA/5000
NNO John Force 125.00 200.00
Castrol GTX 6X Champ
NNO John Force 60.00 100.00
Castrol GTX Mac Tools Mustang
NNO John Force 50.00 120.00
Castrol GTX RCCA/3500
Mustang
NNO John Force 30.00 80.00
Castrol GTX/15,000
Pontiac
NNO John Force 50.00 100.00
Castrol GTX RCCA Pontiac/3500
NNO John Force 40.00 80.00
Castrol GTX Driver of the Year
NNO John Force 60.00 100.00
Castrol GTX Driver of
the Year Mac Tools
NNO John Force 60.00 100.00
Castrol GTX Driver of the Year RCCA
NNO John Force 30.00 80.00
Castrol GTX Mustang
NNO Gatornationals 20.00 50.00
Mac Tools/10,000
NNO Tom Hoover 25.00 60.00
1975 Showtime/5000
NNO Tom Hoover 25.00 60.00
Pioneer/6000
NNO Bruce Larson 20.00 50.00
1989 Sentry/6000
NNO Bruce Larson 30.00 80.00
USA-1 1975 Monza
RCCA/3500
NNO Ed McCulloch 40.00 100.00
1988 Miller RCCA
NNO Ed McCulloch 20.00 50.00
1991 Otter Pops RCCA/3500
NNO Matco Supernationals 40.00 80.00
NNO Kenji Okazaki 30.00 60.00
Mooneyes
NNO Cruz Pedregon 25.00 60.00
McDonald's/5000
NNO Cruz Pedregon 35.00 70.00
McDonald's RCCA
NNO Tony Pedregon 25.00 60.00
Castrol GTX/5004
NNO Tony Pedregon 30.00 80.00
Castrol GTX RCCA
NNO Don Prudhomme 40.00 80.00
Army 1975 Monza
RCCA/3500
NNO Don Prudhomme 50.00 100.00
1978 Army/4008
NNO Don Prudhomme 75.00 125.00
1978 Army RCCA/800
NNO Dean Skuza 30.00 80.00
Matco

1998 Action/RCCA Funny Car 1:24

NNO Whit Bazemore 75.00 150.00
1996 Smokin' Joe's Mustang/4008
NNO Whit Bazemore 125.00 225.00
1996 Smokin' Joe's
Pontiac RCCA/1000
NNO Whit Bazemore 40.00 80.00
Winston Camaro/2508
NNO Whit Bazemore 40.00 80.00
Winston Mustang/5004
NNO Whit Bazemore 75.00 150.00
Winston Mac Tools
NNO Whit Bazemore 70.00 120.00
Winston No Bull
RCCA/2508
NNO Ron Capps 40.00 100.00
Copenhagen Mac Tools/4500
NNO John Force 40.00 80.00
Castrol GTX/9504
NNO John Force 50.00 100.00
Castrol GTX Mac Tools
NNO John Force 60.00 120.00
astrol GTX RCCA/2500
NNO John Force 75.00 150.00
Castrol GTX 7-Time Champ
NNO John Force 75.00 150.00
Castrol GTX 7X Champ
Mac Tools
NNO John Force 90.00 150.00
Castrol GTX 7X Champ
RCCA/2000
NNO John Force 30.00 80.00
Castrol GTX Elvis/15,000
NNO John Force 40.00 80.00
Castrol GTX Elvis
Mac Tools/5000
NNO John Force 50.00 100.00
Castrol GTX Elvis RCCA
NNO Gatornationals Mac Tools 20.00 50.00
NNO Al Hofmann 40.00 75.00
Goodwrench
NNO Tom Hoover 30.00 60.00
Pioneer
NNO Mac Tools 60th Anniversary 20.00 50.00
NNO Matco Supernationals/3000 25.00 60.00
NNO Cruz Pedregon 40.00 80.00
Interstate Batteries
NNO Cruz Pedregon 40.00 80.00
Interstate Batteries
Hot Rod RCCA/1000
NNO Cruz Pedregon 40.00 80.00
Interstate Batteries
Small Soldiers
NNO Cruz Pedregon 50.00 100.00
Interstate Batteries
Small Soldiers Mac Tools
NNO Cruz Pedregon 45.00 90.00
Interstate Batteries
Small Soldiers RCCA
NNO Tony Pedregon 35.00 70.00
Castrol Selena/7500
NNO Don Prudhomme 30.00 80.00
1983 Pepsi Challenge/4008
NNO Don Prudhomme 35.00 70.00
1983 Pepsi Challenge
Mac Tools
NNO Dean Skuza 30.00 80.00
Matco/3000
NNO Dean Skuza 40.00 80.00
Matco Texas
NNO Jerry Toliver 50.00 100.00
Mad
NNO Jerry Toliver 50.00 100.00
Mad RCCA/1200
NNO Jerry Toliver 50.00 100.00
Spy vs. Spy/3504
NNO Jerry Toliver 50.00 100.00
Spy vs. Spy RCCA/1100

1999 Action/RCCA Funny Car 1:24

NNO Phil Burkhart 30.00 60.00
Nitro Fish Mac Tools/5004
NNO Scotty Cannon 40.00 80.00
Oakley Yellow/7500
NNO Ron Capps 125.00 250.00
Copenhagen
NNO Ron Capps 75.00 150.00
Copenhagen Gold/4008
NNO John Force 50.00 100.00
Castrol GTX
NNO John Force 50.00 100.00
Castrol GTX Mac Tools/5004
NNO John Force 30.00 80.00
Castrol GTX 8-Time Champ
NNO John Force 75.00 150.00
Castrol GTX Superman/15,944
NNO John Force 75.00 150.00
Castrol GTX Superman
Mac Tools
NNO Gatornationals Mac Tools 20.00 50.00
NNO Cruz Pedregon 30.00 60.00
goracing.com/3504
NNO Frank Pedregon 25.00 60.00
Penthouse/4008
NNO Don Prudhomme 125.00 200.00
1989 Skoal Red/2508
NNO Jerry Toliver 40.00 80.00
WWF Smack Down
Mac Tools/4500

2000 Action/RCCA Funny Car 1:24

NNO Scotty Cannon 40.00 80.00
Oakley Silver/5004
NNO Scotty Cannon 40.00 80.00
Oakley Red/5004
NNO Ron Capps 25.00 60.00
U.S.Tobacco/4692
NNO Dale Creasy Jr. 30.00 60.00
Mad Ugly/3504
NNO Dale Creasy Jr. 30.00 60.00
Mad Vote/4402
NNO Jim Epler 30.00 60.00
WWF Kane/8424
NNO Jim Epler 30.00 60.00
WWF Undertaker/7500
NNO John Force 30.00 80.00
Castrol GTX/8292
NNO John Force 30.00 80.00
Castrol GTX
9-Time Champ/20,016
NNO John Force 150.00 250.00
Castrol GTX 9X Champ
QVC Gold/2000
NNO John Force 75.00 150.00
Cast.GTX Grinch/10,008
NNO John Force 50.00 100.00
Castrol GTX
Monsters/14,184
NNO Gatornationals Mac Tools/7000 20.00 50.00
NNO Al Hofmann 30.00 80.00
Mooneyes Yellow
NNO Al Hofmann 40.00 80.00
Mooneyes Yellow
Mac Tools/3000
NNO Al Hofmann 30.00 60.00
Mooneyes 50th/4008
NNO Al Hofmann 30.00 60.00
Mooneyes 50th
Mac Tools/3000
NNO Cruz Pedregon 25.00 60.00
Mac Tools Chili
Pepper/4008
NNO Tony Pedregon 25.00 60.00
Castrol Syntec/3504
NNO Tony Pedregon 30.00 60.00
Castrol Syntec Mac Tools/7000
NNO Tony Pedregon 30.00 80.00
Castrol Syntec
Monsters/5448
NNO Jerry Toliver 25.00 60.00
WWF The Rock/14,400
NNO Jerry Toliver 40.00 80.00
Stone Cold/7296

2001 Action/RCCA Funny Car 1:24

NNO Ron Capps 25.00 60.00
Skoal Blue Mac Tools/3000
NNO Ron Capps 25.00 60.00
Skoal Green Mac Tools/3000
NNO Gary Densham 25.00 60.00
Mac Tools/3646
NNO Chuck Etchells 25.00 60.00
Sunoco/3504
NNO John Force 25.00 60.00
Castrol GTX/10,968
NNO John Force 30.00 60.00
Castrol GTX
Color Chrome/6504
NNO John Force 20.00 50.00
Castrol GTX
10-Time Champ/20,016
NNO John Force 25.00 60.00
Castrol GTX 10X Champ
Mac Tools/3000
NNO John Force 30.00 80.00
Castrol GTX 10X
Champ RCCA/5004
NNO Gatornationals Mac Tools 20.00 50.00
Gold/3000
NNO Mac Tools Thunder Valley/5004 25.00 50.00
NNO Mac Tools U.S Nationals/5004 25.00 50.00
NNO Matco Supernationals/3500 30.00 60.00
NNO Cruz Pedregon 25.00 60.00
Flamin' Frank/2508
NNO Frank Pedregon 30.00 60.00
3A Racing/3504
NNO Frank Pedregon 30.00 60.00
CSK/3504
NNO Frank Pedregon 25.00 60.00
CSK Jurassic Park 3/6000
NNO Frank Pedregon 30.00 60.00
Fram/3504
NNO Frank Pedregon 30.00 60.00
Havoline/3504
NNO Tony Pedregon 25.00 60.00
Castrol Syntec/3888
NNO Tony Pedregon 30.00 60.00
Castrol Syntec
Mac Tools/1608
NNO Tony Pedregon 40.00 80.00
Castrol Syntec RCCA
NNO Tony Pedregon 50.00 100.00
Castrol Syntec KISS/4008
NNO Tony Pedregon 50.00 100.00
Castrol Syntec KISS
Mac Tools/3000
NNO Cristen Powell 25.00 60.00
Nitro Fish
NNO Dean Skuza 40.00 80.00
Mopar Spider-Man/4008
NNO Jerry Toliver 30.00 60.00
WWF Smackdown
Mac Tools/3000
NNO Jerry Toliver 20.00 50.00
XFL/5508
NNO Jerry Toliver 30.00 60.00
XFL Mac Tools/3000
NNO Del Worsham 50.00 100.00
Autolite/3504
NNO Del Worsham 40.00 80.00
Checker/3504
NNO Del Worsham 30.00 60.00
Checker
Jurassic Park 3/6000
NNO Del Worsham 60.00 120.00
Mountain Dew/3504

2002 Action/RCCA Funny Car 1:24

NNO Whit Bazemore Matco Tools Muppets/6288 25.00 60.00
NNO Ron Capps Skoal/3504 40.00 80.00
NNO Ron Capps Skoal Mac Tools/1704 50.00 80.00
NNO Gary Densham AAA of Southern California/4938 25.00 60.00
NNO Gary Densham AAA Mac Tools/1608 25.00 60.00
NNO John Force Castrol GTX/12,780 25.00 60.00
NNO John Force Castrol GTX Mac Tools/1800 30.00 80.00
NNO John Force Castrol GTX Clear/6396 20.00 50.00
NNO John Force Castrol GTX Color Chrome/1008 75.00 150.00
NNO John Force Castrol GTX 100th Win/4132 40.00 80.00
NNO John Force Castrol GTX 11-Time Champ/10,800 35.00 70.00
NNO John Force Castrol GTX 11-Time Champ Mac Tools/1800 45.00 80.00
NNO John Force Castrol GTX 11-Time Champ RCCA/480 75.00 125.00
NNO John Force Castrol GTX 11-Time Champ Mac Tools Platinum/504 300.00 500.00
NNO John Force Castrol GTX Elvis Chrome/2508 35.00 70.00
NNO John Force Castrol GTX Elvis Clear/5376 25.00 60.00
NNO John Force Castrol GTX Elvis Silver/18,036 25.00 60.00
NNO John Force Castrol GTX Norwalk Experience/5004 75.00 135.00
NNO John Force Castrol GTX Tasca unsigned 250.00 350.00
NNO John Force Castrol GTX Tasca Bob Tasca Signed/204 200.00 325.00
NNO John Force Castrol GTX Tasca Mac Tools/1299 150.00 250.00
NNO Gatornationals Mac Tools/3504 45.00 70.00
NNO Tommy Johnson Jr. Skoal/3504 50.00 100.00
NNO Tommy Johnson Jr. Skoal Mac Tools/1704 50.00 100.00
NNO Tommy Johnson Jr. Wildberry Skoal/2000 90.00 150.00
NNO Todd Paton Nitro Fish/2046 30.00 60.00
NNO Todd Paton Nitro Fish Mac Tools/1296 30.00 60.00
NNO Tony Pedregon Castrol Syntec/2754 30.00 60.00
NNO Tony Pedregon Castrol Syntec Mac Tools/1608 30.00 60.00
NNO Tony Pedregon Castrol Syntec KISS/3036 50.00 90.00
NNO Tony Pedregon Castrol Syntec Muppet/5124 30.00 60.00
NNO Tony Pedregon Castrol Syntec Muppet Mac Tools/1608 30.00 60.00
NNO Tim Wilkerson Mac Tools US Nationals/2508 30.00 60.00

2003 Action/RCCA Funny Car 1:24

NNO Gary Densham AAA/1776 35.00 60.00
NNO John Force Castrol GTX High Mileage/9756 35.00 60.00
NNO John Force Castrol GTX High Mileage Mac Tools/1464 40.00 75.00
NNO John Force Castrol GTX High Mileage 12X Champ Boxcars/9518 35.00 60.00
NNO John Force Castrol GTX High Mileage Halloween/2004 100.00 175.00
NNO John Force Castrol GTX High Mileage Three Stooges/9308 35.00 60.00
NNO John Force Castrol GTX King of the Hill/7800 35.00 60.00
NNO John Force Castrol King of Hill Mac Tools/1754 40.00 70.00
NNO John Force Castrol King of Hill Clear/2625 25.00 50.00
NNO Gatornationals Mac Tools/1200 45.00 70.00
NNO Mac Tools U.S Nationals 45.00 80.00
NNO Cruz Pedregon Advance Auto Parts/2028 35.00 60.00
NNO Cruz Pedregon Advance Auto Hulk/2354 35.00 60.00
NNO Tony Pedregon Castrol Syntec/2754 35.00 60.00
NNO Tony Pedregon Castrol Syntec Mac Tools/456 40.00 70.00
NNO Tony Pedregon Castrol Syntec KISS Green/3906 40.00 75.00
NNO Tony Pedregon Castrol Syntec X-Men/2754 35.00 60.00
NNO Dean Skuza Cornwell Tools Meatloaf/3378 35.00 70.00

2004 Action/RCCA Funny Car 1:24

NNO Gary Densham AAA of So.Cal/1500 40.00 60.00
NNO Gary Densham AAA of Southern California Popeye/1506 40.00 60.00
NNO John Force Castrol GTX High Mileage/4458 45.00 75.00
NNO John Force Castrol GTX Start Up/2418 45.00 75.00
NNO John Force Castrol GTX Start Up Mac Tools/408 45.00 75.00
NNO John Force Castrol GTX Start Up Freedom's Flight/1500 125.00 250.00
NNO John Force Castrol GTX Start-Up Mustang 40th Ann/2616 50.00 80.00
NNO John Force Castrol GTX Start-Up Mustang 40th Anniversary Color Chrome/444 150.00 250.00
NNO Gatornationals Mac Tools 45.00 70.00
NNO Eric Medlen Castrol Syntec/1992 100.00 200.00
NNO Cruz Pedregon Advanced Auto Supply Santana/996 50.00 80.00
NNO Tony Pedregon Quaker State/2340 45.00 70.00
NNO Tony Pedregon Quaker State Santana/1104 45.00 70.00
NNO Tony Pedregon Quaker State Shrek 2/2268 45.00 70.00
NNO Tony Pedregon Quaker State Shrek 2 RCCA/408 45.00 70.00
NNO Gary Scelzi Oakley HEMI/2082 60.00 100.00

2005 Action/RCCA Funny Car 1:24

NNO Whit Bazemore Matco Tools Vegas Centennial Liquid Metal/708 50.00 75.00
NNO Ron Capps Brut/1104 50.00 75.00
NNO Ron Capps Brut Hero Card/260 50.00 75.00
NNO John Force Castrol GTX Start Up Norwalk Bill Bader/2508 50.00 75.00
NNO John Force Castrol GTX Start Up Mustang/3324 50.00 75.00
NNO John Force Castrol GTX Start Up Mustang Color Chrome/444 75.00 150.00
NNO John Force Castrol GTX Start Up Mustang Liquid Color/108 100.00 175.00
NNO John Force Castrol GTX Start Up James Dean 50th Anniversary/2610 50.00 75.00
NNO John Force Castrol GTX Start Up James Dean 50th Anniversary Color Chrome/444 75.00 150.00
NNO John Force Castrol GTX Start Up James Dean 50th Ann Liquid Color/108 125.00 200.00
NNO John Force Castrol GTX 13X Champion/3600 50.00 75.00
NNO John Force Castrol GTX 13X Champ Hero Card/168 50.00 75.00
NNO John Force Castrol GTX 13X Champ Black Pearl/240 100.00 175.00
NNO John Force Castrol GTX 13X Champ Color Chrome/444 150.00 250.00
NNO John Force Milestones 30 Years of Racing/2364 50.00 75.00
NNO John Force Milestones 30 Years of Racing Color Chrome/360 75.00 150.00
NNO John Force Milestones 30 Years of Racing Mac Tools/300 50.00 75.00
NNO John Force Milestones 30 Years of Racing Maingate/150 50.00 75.00
NNO John Force Milestones 30 Years of Racing RCCA/444 50.00 75.00
NNO Eric Medlen Castrol Syntec/1650 75.00 150.00
NNO Eric Medlen Castrol Syntec Mac Tools/96 100.00 200.00
NNO Eric Medlen Castrol Syntec RCCA/240 100.00 200.00
NNO Eric Medlen Castrol Syntec RCCA Liquid Color/78 125.00 250.00
NNO Eric Medlen Castrol Syntec '04 Pomona Raced/792 100.00 175.00
NNO Eric Medlen Castrol Syntec '04 Pomona Raced Liquid Color/200 150.00 300.00
NNO Cruz Pedregon Advanced Auto/1096 40.00 65.00
NNO Gary Scelzi Oakley Mopar '05 Champion Chrome/444 60.00 100.00

2006 Action/RCCA Funny Car 1:24

NNO Whit Bazemore Matco Tools/1920 50.00 75.00
NNO Whit Bazemore Matco Tools Matco 50.00 75.00
NNO Ron Capps Brut/402 50.00 75.00
NNO Ron Capps Brut Matco 50.00 75.00
NNO John Force Castrol GTX/1668* 50.00 75.00
NNO John Force Castrol GTX Mac Tools* 50.00 75.00
NNO John Force Castrol GTX Matco* 50.00 75.00
NNO John Force Castrol GTX Carbon Fiber/2004 50.00 75.00
NNO John Force Castrol GTX Norwalk Raceway Soldier Tribute Color Chrome/2004 175.00 300.00
NNO John Force Castrol GTX Norwalk Soldier Tribute Liquid Color/2004 175.00 300.00
NNO John Force Castrol GTX Test/1500 50.00 75.00
NNO Robert Hight AAA So. Cal/780 50.00 75.00
NNO Robert Hight AAA Color Chrome/100 75.00 125.00
NNO Robert Hight AAA So. Cal. Mac Tools 50.00 75.00
NNO Robert Hight AAA White Gold/25 250.00 400.00
NNO Scott Kalitta Air Color Chrome/240 75.00 125.00
NNO Eric Medlen Castrol Syntec/672 75.00 150.00
NNO Eric Medlen Castrol Syntec Color Chrome/150 125.00 250.00
NNO Eric Medlen Castrol Syntec Mac Tools/692 75.00 150.00
NNO Eric Medlen Castrol Syntec White Gold/25 400.00 600.00
NNO Eric Medlen Castrol Syntec Fast & Furious Tokyo Drift/474 75.00 150.00
NNO Eric Medlen Castrol Syntec Fast & Furious Tokyo Drift Color Chrome/200 100.00 200.00
NNO Eric Medlen Castrol Syntec Fast & Furious Tokyo Drift White Gold/25 350.00 500.00
NNO Eric Medlen Ford Test/1200 75.00 150.00
NNO Eric Medlen Ford Test Color Chrome/240 100.00 175.00
NNO Cruz Pedregon Advance Auto Parts Color Chrome/300 75.00 125.00
NNO Tony Pedregon Quaker State Color Chrome/150 75.00 125.00

2006 Action/RCCA Funny Car Historical 1:24

6 John Force Castrol GTX '90 Champion/3072* 50.00 75.00
6 John Force Castrol GTX '90 Champion Mac Tools * 50.00 75.00
6 John Force Castrol GTX '90 Champion Matco * 50.00 75.00
6 John Force Castrol GTX '90 Champion Chrome/390 75.00 125.00
6 John Force Castrol GTX '90 Champion White Gold/25 600.00 800.00
NNO John Force Castrol GTX '91 Champion/3072* 50.00 75.00
NNO John Force Castrol GTX '91 Champion Mac Tools * 50.00 75.00
NNO John Force Castrol GTX '91 Champion Matco * 50.00 75.00
NNO John Force Castrol GTX '91 Champion Chrome/391 75.00 125.00
NNO John Force Castrol GTX '91 Champion White Gold/25 600.00 800.00
NNO John Force Castrol GTX '95 Champion/3072* 50.00 75.00
NNO John Force Castrol GTX '95 Champion Mac Tools * 50.00 75.00
NNO John Force Castrol GTX '95 Champion Matco * 50.00 75.00
NNO John Force Castrol GTX '95 Champion Chrome/395 75.00 125.00

2008 Action/RCCA Funny Cars 1:24

NNO Ashley Force Castrol GTX/6402 60.00 100.00
NNO Ashley Force Castrol GTX Liquid Color/504 60.00 100.00
NNO Ashley Force Castrol GTX Pink ROY/2500 125.00 200.00
NNO Ashley Force Castrol GTX Pink ROY Liquid Color/1008 100.00 175.00
NNO John Force Castrol Carbon Fiber Liquid Color 50.00 75.00
NNO John Force Castrol Liquid Color/500 60.00 100.00
NNO John Force Castrol GTX/3316 50.00 75.00
NNO John Force Castrol GTX Retro/4092 50.00 75.00
NNO John Force Castrol Retro Liquid Color/500 60.00 100.00
NNO John Force Norwalk Raceway/1500 75.00 125.00
NNO John Force Norwalk Raceway Color Chrome/300 75.00 125.00
NNO John Force Norwalk Raceway White Gold/20 250.00 400.00
NNO Robert Hight AAA/1158 50.00 75.00
NNO Robert Hight AAA Dodgers 50th Anniversary Liquid Color 60.00 100.00
NNO Tommy Johnson Monster/738 50.00 75.00
NNO Tommy Johnson Monster Liquid Color/120 50.00 75.00
NNO Mike Neff Old Spice/942 60.00 100.00
NNO Cruz Pedregon Advance Auto Parts/1212 50.00 75.00
NNO Cruz Pedregon Advance Auto Parts Liquid Color/120 50.00 75.00
NNO Tony Pedregon Quaker State Q Power Liquid Color/120 50.00 75.00

2009 Action/RCCA Funny Cars 1:24

NNO Ashley Force Castrol GTX McDonald's/ Liquid Color/200 100.00 175.00
NNO Ashley Force Castrol GTX/1185 125.00 200.00
NNO John Force Castrol Edge/ Liquid Color/362 100.00 175.00
NNO John Force Castrol GTX/ Color Chrome/320 100.00 175.00
NNO John Force Castrol GTX/1180 50.00 75.00
NNO John Force Castrol Night Stalker Norwalk/1600 100.00 175.00
NNO Mike Neff Ford Drive One/390 50.00 75.00
NNO Ron Capps NAPA/2002 50.00 75.00
NNO Robert Hight AAA/604 60.00 100.00
NNO Tony Pedregon Quaker State/ Color Chrome/75 75.00 125.00
NNO Tim Wilkerson LRS/744 50.00 75.00

2010 Action/RCCA Funny Cars 1:24

NNO Jack Beckman MTS/662* 50.00 75.00
NNO Jack Beckman MTS Color Chrome/61* 60.00 100.00
NNO Ron Capps NAPA/513* 50.00 75.00
NNO Ron Capps NAPA/ Liquid Color/123* 60.00 100.00
NNO Ashley Force Castrol/1705* 75.00 125.00
NNO Ashley Force Castrol/ Color Chrome/264* 100.00 175.00
NNO Ashley Force Castrol/ Copper/25* 200.00 300.00
NNO Ashley Force Castrol/ White Gold/25* 250.00 400.00
NNO Ashley Force Hood Castrol Queen of Hearts/1017* 100.00 150.00
NNO Ashley Force Hood Castrol Queen of Hearts/ Bronze/36* 150.00 250.00
NNO Ashley Force Hood Castrol Queen of Hearts/ Color Chrome/503* 125.00 200.00
NNO Ashley Force Hood Castrol Queen of Hearts/ Copper/25* 200.00 350.00
NNO Ashley Force Hood Castrol Queen of Hearts/ Gold/36* 200.00 350.00
NNO Ashley Force Hood Castrol Queen of Hearts/ Platinum/48* 200.00 350.00
NNO Ashley Force Hood Castrol Queen of Hearts/ White Gold/25* 250.00 400.00
NNO John Force Castrol/25* 100.00 200.00
NNO John Force Castrol American Warbird/1216* 100.00 175.00
NNO John Force Castrol American Warbird/ Color Chrome/128* 125.00 200.00
NNO John Force Castrol American Warbird/ White Gold/10*
NNO John Force Castrol 25th Anniversary/2592* 75.00 125.00
NNO John Force Castrol 25th Anniversary/ Color Chrome/365* 100.00 200.00
NNO John Force Castrol 25th Anniversary/ Copper/25* 125.00 250.00
NNO John Force Castrol 25th Anniversary/ Liquid Color/303* 100.00 200.00
NNO John Force Castrol 25th Anniversary/ White Gold/25* 200.00 350.00
NNO Robert Hight AAA/969* 50.00 75.00
NNO Robert Hight AAA/ Color Chrome/162* 60.00 100.00
NNO Robert Hight AAA/ '09 Champion/506* 60.00 100.00
NNO Robert Hight AAA/ '09 Champion/ Color Chrome/103* 75.00 125.00
NNO Tony Pedregon Nitro Fish/450* 50.00 75.00
NNO Tony Pedregon Nitro Fish Color Chrome/150* 60.00 100.00

1997-99 Action/RCCA Funny Car 1:32

NNO John Force Castrol GTX 6-Time Champ/5000 1997 25.00 50.00
NNO John Force Castrol GTX DOY '97 15.00 40.00
NNO John Force Castrol GTX '98 15.00 40.00
NNO John Force Castrol GTX Superman/3500 '99 30.00 60.00
NNO John Force Castrol GTX 8X Champ/3500 '99 15.00 40.00
NNO John Force Tony Pedregon Elvis Selena 2-car set '98 25.00 50.00
NNO Cruz Pedregon Inter.Batt.Hot Rod/2000 '99 15.00 30.00
NNO Frank Pedregon Penthouse/2500 '99 15.00 30.00
NNO Tony Pedregon Castrol Syntec RCCA/1500 '99 15.00 30.00
NNO Gary Scelzi Winston Mac Tools set with dragster 1998 35.00 80.00

1996 Action/RCCA Funny Car 1:64

This series of Funny Cars is highlighted by the John Force issues and the Whit Bazemore Smokin' Joe's piece.

NNO Pat Austin Red Wing Shoes/7500 5.00 12.00
NNO Gary Densham NEC 1996/13,580 5.00 12.00
NNO Jim Epler Rug Doctor 5.00 12.00
NNO John Force Castrol GTX 7.50 15.00
NNO John Force Castrol GTX black 15.00 25.00
NNO John Force Castrol GTX black Mac Tools 15.00 25.00
NNO John Force Castrol GTX black 6-time Champ Promo 3.00 8.00
NNO John Force Castrol GTX black 6-time Champ/20,000 10.00 20.00
NNO John Force Castrol GTX black 6-time Champ Fan Club 7.50 15.00
NNO Al Hofmann Parts America 6.00 15.00
NNO Kenji Okazaki Mooneyes 5.00 12.00

1997 Action/RCCA Funny Car 1:64

NNO Randy Anderson Parts America/9000 4.00 10.00
NNO Randy Anderson Parts America RCCA/3500 5.00 12.00
NNO Whit Bazemore 1995 Fast Orange 5.00 12.00
NNO Whit Bazemore 1995 Mobil 1 5.00 12.00
NNO Whit Bazemore 1995 Mobil 1 RCCA/9000 6.00 15.00
NNO Whit Bazemore Winston/9000 7.50 15.00
NNO Whit Bazemore Winston RCCA 15.00 30.00
NNO Raymond Beadle 1979 Blue Max/12,000 5.00 12.00
NNO Kenny Bernstein 1988 Budweiser RCCA/5000 12.50 25.00
NNO Kenny Bernstein 1979 Budweiser/10,728 10.00 20.00
NNO Kenny Bernstein 1979 Bud RCCA/2500 10.00 20.00
NNO Kenny Bernstein 1979 Chelsea King 7.50 15.00
NNO Kenny Bernstein 1979 Chelsea King RCCA/2000 7.50 15.00
NNO Mike Dunn 1992 Pisano 4.00 10.00
NNO Chuck Etchells Kendall 4.00 10.00
NNO John Force 1977 Brute Force blue/16,056 7.50 15.00
NNO John Force 1977 Brute Force blue RCCA/3500 8.00 20.00
NNO John Force 1978 Brute Force orange 6.00 15.00
NNO John Force 1993 Castrol GTX Jolly Rancher 6.00 15.00
NNO John Force 1994 Castrol GTX RCCA/5000 6.00 15.00
NNO John Force Castrol GTX Driver of the Year 6.00 15.00
NNO John Force Castrol GTX Driver of Year RCCA/10,000 6.00 15.00
NNO John Force Castrol GTX Mustang 6.00 15.00

NNO John Force 6.00 15.00
Castrol GTX Pontiac
NNO John Force 7.50 15.00
1994 Castrol GTX Flames
RCCA/5000
NNO Gatornationals Mac Tools/10,000 6.00 15.00
NNO Tom Hoover 5.00 12.00
Pioneer RCCA/10,080
NNO Bruce Larson 5.00 12.00
Sentry
NNO Bruce Larson 5.00 12.00
USA-1 1975 Monza
NNO Bruce Larson 6.00 12.00
USA-1 1975 Monza RCCA
NNO Ed McCulloch 6.00 15.00
Miller Acrylic
NNO Ed McCulloch 5.00 12.00
1991 Otter Pops
NNO Cruz Pedregon 5.00 12.00
McDonald's/10,080
NNO Cruz Pedregon 5.00 12.00
McDonald's RCCA/3500
NNO Tony Pedregon 5.00 12.00
Castrol GTX
NNO Don Prudhomme 6.00 15.00
Army 1975 Monza RCCA/3500
NNO Don Prudhomme 6.00 15.00
1978 Army

1998 Action/RCCA Funny Car 1:64

NNO Whit Bazemore 6.00 15.00
Winston/11,500
NNO Whit Bazemore 10.00 20.00
Winston RCCA/2500
NNO Ron Capps 6.00 15.00
Copenhagen
NNO John Force 7.50 15.00
Castrol GTX
NNO John Force 10.00 20.00
Castrol GTX RCCA
NNO John Force 6.00 15.00
Castrol GTX 7-Time Champ
NNO John Force 6.00 15.00
Castrol GTX Elvis
NNO John Force 7.50 15.00
Castrol GTX Elvis Mac Tools
NNO John Force 7.50 15.00
Castrol GTX Elvis RCCA
NNO Gatornationals Mac Tools/10,080 5.00 12.00
NNO Al Hofmann 6.00 15.00
Goodwrench
NNO Tom Hoover 5.00 12.00
Pioneer
NNO Cruz Pedregon 6.00 12.00
Interstate Batteries
NNO Cruz Pedregon 5.00 12.00
Interstate Batteries
Small Soldiers/12,000
NNO Cruz Pedregon 6.00 15.00
Interstate Batteries
Small Soldiers RCCA/3500
NNO Tony Pedregon 5.00 12.00
Castrol Selena
NNO Tony Pedregon 6.00 15.00
Castrol Selena
RCCA/5000
NNO Tony Pedregon 5.00 12.00
Castrol Syntec/8004
NNO Tony Pedregon 6.00 15.00
Castrol Syntec RCCA/2500
NNO Don Prudhomme 5.00 12.00
1983 Pepsi Challenge/7056
NNO Jerry Toliver 5.00 12.00
Mad/7056
NNO Jerry Toliver 6.00 15.00
Mad RCCA/2500
NNO Jerry Toliver 5.00 12.00
Spy vs. Spy/7056
NNO Jerry Toliver 6.00 15.00
Spy vs. Spy RCCA/2500

1999 Action/RCCA Funny Car 1:64

NNO John Force 6.00 15.00
Castrol GTX 8-Time Champ
NNO John Force 6.00 15.00
Castrol GTX Superman
NNO Cruz Pedregon 5.00 12.00
goracing.com/7500

2000 Action/RCCA Funny Car 1:64

NNO Dale Creasy Jr. 5.00 12.00
Mad Ugly
NNO Jim Epler 5.00 12.00
WWF Undertaker/7992
NNO John Force 7.50 15.00
Castrol GTX/7560
NNO John Force 6.00 15.00
Castrol GTX Monsters
NNO John Force 10.00 20.00
Castrol GTX 9-Time
Champ/19,008
NNO Tony Pedregon 6.00 15.00
Castrol Syntec
Monsters/4392
NNO Jerry Toliver 5.00 12.00
The Rock/9000
NNO Jerry Toliver 5.00 12.00
Stone Cold/7992

2001 Action/RCCA Funny Car 1:64

NNO John Force 7.50 15.00
Castrol GTX/12,000
NNO John Force 10.00 20.00
Castrol GTX RCCA/1104
NNO John Force 10.00 20.00
Castrol GTX in oil can
NNO John Force 7.50 15.00
Castrol GTX
10-Time Champ
NNO John Force 10.00 20.00
Castrol GTX 10-Time
Champ RCCA/504
NNO Tony Pedregon 20.00 40.00
Castrol Syntec KISS

2002 Action/RCCA Funny Car 1:64

NNO John Force 10.00 20.00
Castrol GTX/8856
NNO John Force 10.00 20.00
Castrol GTX 11-Time
Champ/7752
NNO John Force 40.00 80.00
Castrol GTX 4-car set/7500
NNO John Force 7.50 20.00
Castrol GTX Elvis
Silver in tin/17,280

2003 Action/RCCA Funny Car 1:64

NNO John Force 10.00 20.00
Castrol GTX High Mileage/6124
NNO John Force 10.00 20.00
Castrol GTX
King of the Hill/5796

2004 Action/RCCA Funny Car 1:64

NNO John Force 10.00 20.00
Castrol GTX High Mileage
w
tire/5136

2010 Action/RCCA Funny Cars 1:64

NNO Ashley Force 12.50 25.00
Castrol/8167*
NNO John Force 10.00 20.00
Castrol/8047*
NNO Robert Hight 7.50 15.00
AAA/2956*

1996 Action/RCCA Pro Stock 1:24

NNO Jerry Eckman 25.00 60.00
Pennzoil/5004
NNO Jerry Eckman 40.00 100.00
Pennzoil RCCA/1500

1997 Action/RCCA Pro Stock 1:24

This series of cars marks the entry of Action into the Pro Stock division of the NHRA. The series is highlighted by the RCCA pieces in which each chassis is serial numbered. The RCCA pieces also contain more detail than their Action counterparts.

NNO Darrell Alderman 30.00 60.00
Mopar white roof
NNO Darrell Alderman 40.00 80.00
Mopar black roof Mac Tools
NNO Darrell Alderman 30.00 60.00
Mopar black roof
RCCA/3500
NNO Darrell Alderman 40.00 80.00
Mopar white roof
RCCA/3500
NNO Bruce Allen 20.00 50.00
Slick 50
NNO Bruce Allen 40.00 80.00
Slick 50 RCCA
NNO Gatornationals Mac Tools/8000 20.00 50.00
NNO Scott Geoffrion 20.00 50.00
Mopar black roof/5504
NNO Scott Geoffrion 40.00 80.00
Mopar black roof
Mac Tools
NNO Scott Geoffrion 25.00 60.00
Mopar black roof RCCA
NNO Scott Geoffrion 20.00 50.00
Mopar white roof/9504
NNO Scott Geoffrion 25.00 60.00
Mopar white roof RCCA
NNO Bob Glidden 30.00 60.00
1996 Quality Care/6000
NNO Bob Glidden 40.00 80.00
1996 Quality Care RCCA
NNO Roy Hill 25.00 60.00
Castrol Hill's Racing School/6000
NNO Roy Hill 40.00 80.00
Castrol Hill's Racing School RCCA
NNO Allen Johnson 20.00 50.00
Amoco/6000
NNO Allen Johnson 40.00 80.00
Amoco RCCA/1500
NNO Kurt Johnson 20.00 50.00
AC Delco/7008
NNO Kurt Johnson 30.00 60.00
AC Delco GM Dealer/3000
NNO Warren Johnson 35.00 70.00
1995 Performance Parts/3508
NNO Warren Johnson 40.00 80.00
1995 Performance
Parts RCCA
NNO Warren Johnson 25.00 60.00
Performance Parts/7008
NNO Warren Johnson 40.00 80.00
Performance Parts RCCA/3508
NNO Warren Johnson 30.00 60.00
Goodwrench Plus/9024
NNO Warren Johnson 40.00 80.00
Goodwrench Plus RCCA
NNO Tom Martino 30.00 60.00
Six Flags
NNO Larry Morgan 25.00 60.00
Raybestos
NNO Larry Morgan 30.00 80.00
Raybestos RCCA
NNO Mark Pawuk 15.00 40.00
Summit Racing/6000
NNO Mark Pawuk 25.00 60.00
Summit Racing RCCA/1200
NNO Rickie Smith 20.00 50.00
Carrier
NNO Rickie Smith 40.00 80.00
Carrier RCCA
NNO Jim Yates 25.00 60.00
McDonald's
NNO Jim Yates 40.00 80.00
McDonald's RCCA

1998 Action/RCCA Pro Stock 1:24

NNO Darrell Alderman 35.00 70.00
Mopar
NNO Mike Edwards 20.00 50.00
JK Racing
NNO Gatornationals Mac Tools/8000 15.00 40.00
NNO Warren Johnson 30.00 60.00
GM Performance
1995 Olds RCCA/1500
NNO Scott Geoffion 30.00 60.00
Mopar
NNO Tom Martino 30.00 60.00
Six Flags

1999 Action/RCCA Pro Stock 1:24

NNO Jeg Coughlin 15.00 40.00
Jeg's Mac Tools/4000
NNO Jeg Coughlin 15.00 40.00
Jeg's ROY Mac Tools/4000
NNO Troy Coughlin 15.00 40.00
Jeg's Mac Tools/4000
NNO Gatornationals Mac Tools/7000 20.00 50.00
NNO Kurt Johnson 20.00 50.00
AC Delco/3000
NNO Warren Johnson 90.00 150.00
Goodwrench/3000
NNO Warren Johnson 60.00 100.00
Goodwrench Superman
NNO Pat Musi 20.00 50.00
NEC/2500
NNO Mark Pawuk 25.00 50.00
Summit Racing

2000 Action/RCCA Pro Stock 1:24

NNO Kurt Johnson 25.00 50.00
AC Delco/1500
NNO Warren Johnson 45.00 80.00
Goodwrench Plus/3684
NNO Gatornationals Mac Tools/6000 20.00 50.00

2001 Action/RCCA Pro Stock 1:24

NNO Gatornationals Mac Tools 20.00 50.00
Gold/3000
NNO Mac Tools U.S Nationals/5004 25.00 50.00
NNO Matco Supernationals/5000 20.00 50.00

2002 Action/RCCA Pro Stock 1:24

NNO Jeg Coughlin 25.00 60.00
Jeg's/4456
NNO M Edwards 25.00 50.00
Mac Tools
US Nationals/2508
NNO Gatornationals Mac Tools/3504 25.00 50.00
NNO Kurt Johnson 30.00 60.00
AC Delco/3612
NNO Kurt Johnson 40.00 80.00
AC Delco KISS/3760
NNO Mac Tools Thunder Valley/3504 20.00 50.00

2003 Action/RCCA Pro Stock 1:24

NNO Jeg Coughlin 30.00 60.00
Jeg's Mail Order/2988
NNO Troy Coughlin 30.00 60.00
Jeg's Mail Order/1896
NNO Gatornationals Mac Tools/1200 45.00 70.00
NNO Kurt Johnson 35.00 60.00
AC Delco KISS/3124
NNO Kurt Johnson
AC Delco KISS RCCA/340
NNO Mac Tools U.S Nationals/1200 45.00 70.00

2004 Action/RCCA Pro Stock 1:24

NNO Jeg Coughlin Jr. 45.00 70.00
Jeg's Mail Order/2008
NNO Jeg Coughlin Jr. 45.00 70.00
Jeg's Mail Order
Spy vs. Spy/888
NNO Troy Coughlin 45.00 70.00
Jeg's Mail Order/1656
NNO Gatornationals Mac Tools/1400 40.00 70.00
NNO Kurt Johnson 45.00 70.00
AC Delco/2712

1997 Action/RCCA Pro Stock 1:64

This series of cars marked the entry of Action into the Pro Stock division of the NHRA. The Action Racing pieces were issued in blister packages while the RCCA pieces were packaged in typical RCCA boxes. Most cars were serial numbered on the package itself. The RCCA pieces feature a serial numbered chassis as well.

NNO Darrell Alderman 5.00 12.00
Mopar black roof/16,244
NNO Darrell Alderman 6.00 15.00
Mopar black roof RCCA
NNO Darrell Alderman 5.00 12.00
Mopar white roof/9000
NNO Darrell Alderman 6.00 15.00
Mopar white roof RCCA
NNO Bruce Allen 5.00 12.00
Slick 50/10,080
NNO Bruce Allen 6.00 15.00
Slick 50 RCCA
NNO Jerry Eckman 5.00 12.00
Pennzoil/10,080
NNO Gatornationals Mac Tools 4.00 10.00
NNO Scott Geoffrion 5.00 12.00
Mopar black roof/9000
NNO Scott Geoffrion 6.00 15.00
Mopar black roof RCCA
NNO Scott Geoffrion 5.00 12.00
Mopar white roof/10,000
NNO Scott Geoffrion 6.00 15.00
Mopar white roof
RCCA/3500
NNO Bob Glidden 5.00 12.00
1996 Quality Care
NNO Bob Glidden 10.00 20.00
1996 Quality Care
RCCA/1500
NNO Allen Johnson 5.00 12.00
Amoco/9000
NNO Kurt Johnson 5.00 12.00
AC Delco/12,000
NNO Kurt Johnson 10.00 18.00
AC Delco RCCA/1500
NNO Warren Johnson 6.00 12.00
Performance Parts/12,024
NNO Warren Johnson 7.50 15.00
Performance Parts RCCA
NNO Warren Johnson 6.00 12.00
Goodwrench Plus/15,000
NNO Warren Johnson 10.00 20.00
Goodwrench
Plus RCCA/3500
NNO George Marnell
Marnell Red&White
NNO Larry Morgan 6.00 12.00
Raybestos
NNO Don Nicholson 6.00 12.00
Nalley&Nicholson
1963 Chevy/10,080
NNO Mark Pawuk 5.00 12.00
Summit Racing
NNO Rickie Smith 5.00 12.00
Carrier
NNO Rickie Smith 6.00 15.00
Carrier RCCA
NNO Dave Strickler 6.00 12.00
Old Reliable
1963 Chevy/10,080
NNO Jim Yates 5.00 12.00
McDonald's/10,000
NNO Jim Yates 6.00 15.00
McDonald's RCCA/3500

1998 Action/RCCA Pro Stock 1:64

NNO Gatornationals Mac Tools 4.00 10.00
NNO Warren Johnson 6.00 15.00
1995 Performance Parts
RCCA/3500

1999 Action/RCCA Pro Stock 1:64

NNO Warren Johnson 10.00 20.00
Goodwrench Superman

1995-02 Action/RCCA NHRA Transporters 1:64

This series of die-cast pieces features the trucks and transporters that haul the cars from race to race. The first piece released in this series was the Gator Nationals promotional piece.

NNO Joe Amato 50.00 90.00
Valvoline Mac Tools
NNO Mike Dunn 25.00 50.00
Yankees/2934 '01
NNO John Force 40.00 70.00
Castrol GTX Bus
NNO John Force 125.00 200.00
Castrol GTX Mac Tools 1996
NNO John Force 60.00 100.00
Castrol GTX
Mac Tools/4000 1997
NNO John Force 30.00 60.00
Castrol GTX/3012 '02
NNO John Force
Cast.GTX RCCA/120 '02
NNO John Force 30.00 80.00
Castrol GTX
Color Chrome/504 '02
NNO Gatornationals Mac Tools '95 250.00 350.00
NNO Gatornationals Mac Tools '96 25.00 60.00
NNO Gatornationals Mac Tools 25.00 60.00
'97/5000
NNO Gatornationals Mac Tools 20.00 50.00
'98/7500
NNO Gatornationals Mac Tools 20.00 50.00
'99/5000
NNO Gatornationals Mac Tools 20.00 40.00
'00/4000
NNO Gatornationals Mac Tools 20.00 40.00
'02/2508
NNO Bob Glidden 60.00 100.00
Quality Care Mac Tools
NNO Mac Tools U.S Nationals '01/5016 20.00 50.00
NNO Matco Supernationals '97 50.00 100.00

1999 Action/RCCA Pro Stock Bikes 1:9

These bikes were only available thru the club.

NNO Ron Ayers 75.00 150.00
Mac Tools/5000
NNO Antron Brown 75.00 150.00
Troy Vincent's/5000
NNO Gatornationals Mac Tools/7000 60.00 100.00
NNO Matt Hines 175.00 300.00
Superman/4440
NNO Matt Hines 75.00 150.00
Vance&Hines/5000
NNO Angelle Seeling 125.00 250.00
Winston/6000

2000 Action/RCCA Pro Stock Bikes 1:9

NNO Brian Ayers 30.00 60.00
Mac Tools/5004
NNO Ron Ayers 30.00 80.00
Mac Tools/3504
NNO Ron Ayers 30.00 80.00
Mac Tools Club/3000
NNO Gatornationals Mac Tools/5208 30.00 80.00
NNO Matt Hines 30.00 60.00
Eagle One
NNO Matt Hines 45.00 80.00
Eagle One
Mac Tools/3000
NNO Steve Johnson 25.00 60.00
Snap-on/4866
NNO John Myers 50.00 100.00
1996 Snap-on Torco/3066
NNO Tony Mullen 30.00 80.00
mall.com/3156
NNO Angelle Seeling 50.00 100.00
Close Call/3906

2001 Action/RCCA Pro Stock Bikes 1:9

NNO Ron Ayers 30.00 80.00
Mac Tools/2508
NNO Antron Brown 30.00 80.00
Jurassic Park III/5010
NNO Antron Brown 40.00 80.00
Mac Tools/2508
NNO Scotty Cannon 60.00 100.00
Oakley
NNO Gatornationals Mac Tools/6000 25.00 50.00
NNO Matt Hines 40.00 80.00
Eagle One James Dean/2676
NNO Steve Johnson 40.00 80.00
Snap-on/2850
NNO Mac Tools U.S.Nationals/5004 40.00 80.00
NNO Dave Schultz 50.00 100.00
Sunoco/4200
NNO Dave Schultz 60.00 100.00
Sunoco Dealer/1200
NNO Angelle Seeling 60.00 100.00
Winston/6196
NNO Angelle Seeling 60.00 100.00
Winston Dealer/3208
NNO Angelle Seeling 60.00 100.00
Winston Silver/3504
NNO Angelle Seeling 60.00 120.00
Winston Silver
RCCA/504

2002 Action/RCCA Pro Stock Bikes 1:9

NNO Antron Brown 90.00 150.00
Mac Tools/2000
NNO Gatornationals Mac Tools/2508 25.00 60.00
NNO Craig Treble 40.00 80.00
Matco Tools
Muppet/4014

2003 Action/RCCA Pro Stock Bikes 1:9

NNO Gatornationals Mac Tools/1200 75.00 125.00
NNO Mac Tools Thunder Valley/1200 90.00 150.00
NNO Mac Tools U.S.Nationals 75.00 150.00

2005 Action/RCCA Pro Stock Bikes 1:9

NNO Craig Treble 50.00 75.00
Matco Tools Las Vegas
100th Anniversary/228
NNO Craig Treble 50.00 75.00
Matco Tools Las Vegas
100th Anniversary Matco/750

2000 Action/RCCA Pro Stock Bikes 1:24

NNO Dave Schultz 15.00 30.00
Sunoco/4200
NNO Dave Schultz 25.00 50.00
Sunoco Mac Tools/3000

2000 Action/RCCA Pro Stock Bikes 1:43

NNO Matt Hines 15.00 30.00
Eagle One/5400

2000 Action QVC For Race Fans Only Funny Car 1:24

NNO John Force 125.00 200.00
Castrol GTX 9X Champ.
Gold/2000

2009 Auto World Funny Cars 1:24

NNO Jack Beckman 40.00 70.00
Valvoline
NNO Jack Beckman 40.00 70.00
Valvoline MTS
NNO Jerry Toliver 40.00 70.00
Canidae
NNO Tony Pedregon 50.00 75.00
Nitro Fish
NNO Tony Pedregon 50.00 75.00
Quaker State

1999 Brookfield NHRA Dually with Trailer 1:24

NNO John Force 100.00 175.00
Castrol GTX
Superman Mac Tools

2002 Brookfield NHRA Dually with Trailer 1:24

NNO John Force 50.00 100.00
Castrol GTX/1768
NNO John Force 75.00 135.00
Castrol GTX Silver/456

2004 Classic Garage/Ertl Vintage Pro Stock 1:18

NNO Dick Brannan 60.00 100.00
1964 Ford Thunderbolt/4000

2002 Ertl American Muscle Arnie Beswick 1:18

NNO Arnie Beswick 20.00 40.00
1962 Catalina
NNO Arnie Beswick 20.00 40.00
1968 GTO
NNO Arnie Beswick 20.00 40.00
1969 GTO
NNO Arnie Beswick 20.00 40.00
1973 Trans Am

1999 Ertl Proshop Funny Car 1:24

NNO Cory Lee 20.00 40.00
Pioneer/2499
NNO Frank Manzo 20.00 40.00
Kendall/2499
NNO Bob Newberry 15.00 40.00
Valvoline

1992-95 Ertl/Race Image NHRA Transporters 1:64

NNO Joe Amato 15.00 40.00
Valvoline 1992
NNO Pat Austin 15.00 40.00
Castrol GTX '93
NNO Mike Dunn 15.00 40.00
La Victoria '94
NNO Chuck Etchells 15.00 40.00
Wiz '93
NNO John Force 15.00 40.00
Castrol GTX 1993
NNO Bob Glidden 12.50 30.00
Quality Care '94
NNO Darrell Gwynn 15.00 40.00
Wiltel '92
NNO Al Hanna 15.00 40.00
Eastern Rider '92
NNO Eddie Hill 12.50 30.00
Pennzoil '93
NNO Warren Johnson 15.00 40.00
AC Delco '92
NNO Cruz Pedregon 15.00 40.00
McDonald's '93
NNO Rick Smith 15.00 40.00
Slick 50 '94

2002-03 GMP Vintage Dragsters 1:18

NNO Don Garlits 75.00 135.00
Swamp Rat 1/5004
NNO Don Garlits 75.00 125.00
Swamp Rat 1B/5904
NNO Don Garlits 75.00 125.00
Swamp Rat III
NNO Don Garlits 75.00 125.00
Swamp Rat VI
NNO Connie Kalitta 75.00 125.00
Bounty Hunter
NNO Don Prudhomme 60.00 120.00
Greer&Black

2002-03 GMP Vintage Dragsters 1:43

Item	Low	High
NNO Don Garlits Swamp Rat 1	18.00	30.00
NNO Don Garlits Swamp Rat 1B	18.00	30.00
NNO Don Garlits Swamp Rat III	18.00	30.00
NNO Don Garlits Swamp Rat VI	18.00	30.00
NNO Don Prudhomme Greer&Black	18.00	30.00

2002-03 GMP Vintage Pro Stock 1:18

Item	Low	High
NNO Mark Donohue Roger Penske Chevrolet 1967 Camaro	50.00	90.00
NNO Dick Harrell Fred Gibb Chevrolet 1968 Nova	50.00	90.00
NNO Bill Jenkins Grumpy's Toy/4400 1968 Chevy Nova	75.00	125.00

2002-03 GMP Vintage Pro Stock 1:43

Item	Low	High
NNO Dick Harrell Fred Gibb Chevrolet 1968 Nova	18.00	30.00
NNO Bill Jenkins Grumpy's Toy V 1968 Nova/2502	20.00	35.00

2004 Hot Wheels Dragsters Promos 1:64

Item	Low	High
NNO Ashley Force Mattel Toy Store Irvine Convention	20.00	40.00

1996 Johnny Lightning Top Fuel Legends Dragsters 1:64

Item	Low	High
NNO Jeb Allen Praying Mantis	2.00	5.00
NNO Jim Annin Annin Racing	2.00	5.00
NNO Sarge Arciero Jade Grenade	2.00	5.00
NNO Ron Attebury Jungle Jim	2.00	5.00
NNO Tim Beebe Beebe&Mullican	2.00	5.00
NNO Steve Carbone Carbone Racing	2.00	5.00
NNO Steve Carbone Creitz&Donavan	2.00	5.00
NNO Steve Carbone Soapy Sales	2.00	5.00
NNO Don Garlits Swamp Rat	2.00	5.00
NNO Don Garlits Swamp Rat 10	2.00	5.00
NNO Don Garlits Swamp Rat 22	2.00	5.00
NNO Don Garlits Swamp Rat 24	2.00	5.00
NNO Don Garlits Wynn's Charger	2.00	5.00
NNO Leroy Goldstein Ramchargers	2.00	5.00
NNO Tommy Ivo Nationwise	2.00	5.00
NNO Tommy Ivo Valvoline	2.00	5.00
NNO Don Moody Walton Cerny&Moody	2.00	5.00
NNO Tony Nancy Nancy Racing	2.00	5.00
NNO Bennie Osborn Osborn Racing	2.00	5.00
NNO Rick Ramsey Keeling&Clayton	2.00	5.00
NNO Jerry Ruth Ruth Racing	2.00	5.00
NNO Mike Snively Hawaiian	2.00	5.00
NNO Warren&Coburn Rain for Rent	2.00	5.00
NNO John Weibe Weibe Racing	2.00	5.00

1998 Johnny Lightning Super Magmas Funny Cars 1:24

Item	Low	High
NNO Jim Liberman Jungle Jim Vega	60.00	120.00
NNO Barry Setzer Chevy Vega	25.00	50.00
NNO Gene Snow Snowman Charger	40.00	75.00

1997 Johnny Lightning Dragsters USA Funny Cars and Pro Stock 1:64

This series was issued in 1997 by Johnny Lightning in "Dragsters USA" blister packages. Each die-cast piece featured a famous funny car ride from the 1990s and was packaged with a collectible coin that featured a picture of the car and an issue number. Each driver was issued more than once with a different color paint scheme and different issue number as noted below. We've included the issue number after each car description below. The stated production run was 15,000 of each piece.

Item	Low	High
NNO Whit Bazemore 1994 Fast Orange White&Blue 1	4.00	8.00
NNO Whit Bazemore 1994 Fast Orange White&Yellow 13	4.00	8.00
NNO Jim Epler 1994 Rug Doctor Red 15	4.00	8.00
NNO Jim Epler 1994 Rug Doctor Black 24	4.00	8.00
NNO Chuck Etchells 1995 Kendall Black 14	4.00	8.00
NNO Chuck Etchells 1995 Kendall Red 21	4.00	8.00
NNO Al Hofmann 1995 Western Auto Green&Black 25	4.00	8.00
NNO Al Hofmann 1995 Western Auto Orange&Black	4.00	8.00
NNO Tom Hoover 1994 Pioneer Green 11	4.00	8.00
NNO Tom Hoover 1994 Pioneer Blue 19	4.00	8.00
NNO Bruce Larson 1990 Sentry Red 4	4.00	8.00
NNO Bruce Larson 1990 Sentry Green 12	4.00	8.00
NNO Bruce Larson 1990 Sentry Red 23	4.00	8.00
NNO Ed McCulloch 1991 Otter Pops Purple 27	4.00	8.00
NNO Kenji Okazaki 1995 Mooneyes Orange	4.00	8.00
NNO Kenji Okazaki 1995 Mooneyes Orange	4.00	8.00
NNO K.C. Spurlock 1995 King of the Burnouts Blue 5	4.00	8.00
NNO K.C. Spurlock 1995 King of the Burnouts Purple 18	4.00	8.00
NNO K.C. Spurlock 1995 King of the Burnouts Purple 26	4.00	8.00

1999 Johnny Lightning Racing Dreams Funny Cars 1:64

Item	Low	High
NNO Frosted Frakes Promo	1.50	4.00

1999 Johnny Lightning Racing Machines 1:64

This series of 1:64 die-casts was issued by Johnny Lightning in their Racing Machines blister packs. Each package included a trading card along with the car. As noted below, drivers from a number of different non-NASCAR racing series are included in this set.

Item	Low	High
1 Olivier Beretta Oreca Viper GTS GT2 Racing Series	3.00	6.00
1 Paul Gentilozzi HomeLink Trans-Am Series	3.00	6.00
2 Greg Ray Glidden Menard Indy Racing League	3.00	6.00
8 Tom Coleman TWC Trans-Am Series	3.00	6.00
13 Tom Hoover Pioneer NHRA	3.00	6.00
14 Kenny Brack Power Team IRL	3.00	6.00
64 Johnny Miller Automation Trans-Am Series	3.00	6.00
296 Bunny Burkett Dodge Daytona NHRA	3.00	6.00

2000 Johnny Lightning Racing Machines 1:64

This series of 1:64 die-casts was issued by Johnny Lightning in their "Racing Machines" blister packs. Each package included a trading card along with the car. As noted below, drivers from a number of different non-NASCAR racing series are included in this set.

Item	Low	High
NNO Tim Wilkinson 1996 NAPA NHRA	3.00	8.00
NNO Frank Pedregon 1998 Johnny Lightning NHRA	3.00	8.00
NNO Ray Higley 1996 Red Line Oil	3.00	8.00

2003 Lane/Ertl Vintage Pro Stock 1:18

Item	Low	High
NNO Herb Fox Fred Gibb Chevrolet 1967 Camaro/2000	50.00	90.00
NNO Bill Hielscher Mr.Bardahl Camaro/2500	50.00	90.00
NNO Bill Jenkins Grumpy's Toy 1967 Camaro/5094	100.00	175.00
NNO Bill Knafel Tin Indian 1967 Firebird	50.00	100.00
NNO Dave Strickler Old Reliable 1968 Camaro/3996	50.00	90.00

2003 Ertl Chevy Legends Pro Stock 1:18

Item	Low	High
NNO Bill Jenkins Grumpy's Toy 1966 Nova	45.00	75.00
NNO Dave Strickler Old Reliable 1969 Camaro/2004	45.00	75.00

2003 Ertl Ford Racing Pro Stock 1:18

Item	Low	High
NNO Butch Leal 1964 Ford Thunderbolt/2004 black painted wheels	60.00	90.00
NNO Butch Leal 1964 Ford Thunderbolt chrome wheels	60.00	90.00
NNO Don Nicholson Dyno Don 1970 Mustang	60.00	90.00

2003 Ertl Mopar 50 Years of Hemi Pro Stock 1:18

Item	Low	High
NNO Don Carlton Motown Missile 1971 Dodge Challenger	45.00	75.00
NNO Don Carlton Motown Missile 1972 Plymouth Barracuda/2500	45.00	75.00
NNO Dick Landy 1968 Dodge Challenger	45.00	75.00
NNO Dick Landy 1971 Dodge Challenger	45.00	75.00
NNO Butch Leal California Flash 1971 Plymouth Duster	45.00	75.00
NNO Ronnie Sox Sox&Martin 1971 Plymouth Barracuda	45.00	75.00
NNO Arlen Vanke 1971 Plymouth Duster	45.00	75.00

2003 Milestone Development Dragsters 1:16

Item	Low	High
NNO Kenny Bernstein Budweiser/1500	135.00	200.00
NNO Clay Millican Werner/1250	135.00	200.00
NNO Tony Schumacher Army	135.00	200.00
NNO Tony Schumacher Army Camo/1750	135.00	200.00

2004 Milestone Development Dragsters 1:16

Item	Low	High
NNO Larry Dixon Miller Lite/1250	135.00	200.00

2002 Milestone Development Funny Car 1:16

Item	Low	High
NNO Whit Bazemore Matco Tools/1250	125.00	200.00
NNO Whit Bazemore Matco Tools Speed Racer/1250	125.00	200.00
NNO Scotty Cannon Oakley Idea/1500	125.00	200.00
NNO Scotty Cannon Oakley Time Bomb/3500	125.00	200.00

2003 Milestone Development Funny Car 1:16

Item	Low	High
NNO Whit Bazemore Matco Tools/1250	135.00	200.00
NNO Whit Bazemore Matco Tools Speed Racer/1250	150.00	225.00
NNO Whit Bazemore Mopar/1500	125.00	200.00
NNO Scotty Cannon Oakley Elite Forces/1250	135.00	200.00
NNO Scotty Cannon Oakley Sleep Tight/1250	135.00	200.00
NNO Gary Scelzi Dodge Grab Life/2600	135.00	200.00
NNO Gary Scelzi Oakley Time Bomb/1250	200.00	325.00

2004 Milestone Development Funny Car 1:16

Item	Low	High
NNO Whit Bazemore Matco Tools Rat Fink/1250	100.00	150.00
NNO Whit Bazemore Matco Tools 25th Anniversary	100.00	150.00
NNO Tony Pedregon Quaker State	100.00	150.00
NNO Gary Scelzi HEMI	100.00	150.00

2003 Milestone Development Pro Stock Bikes 1:9

Item	Low	High
NNO Doug Vancil Vance&Hines	100.00	180.00

2003 PMC Dragsters 1:24

Item	Low	High
NNO Brandon Bernstein Budweiser/1008	40.00	75.00
NNO Kenny Bernstein Budweiser Encore Color Chrome/564	60.00	100.00

2003 PMC Funny Car 1:24

Item	Low	High
NNO Bob Bode ProMotorsports.com/504	40.00	70.00
NNO Dean Skuza Black Label/504	40.00	70.00
NNO Tim Wilkerson Levi, Ray & Shoup/504	40.00	70.00
NNO Del Worsham Checker/1008	40.00	70.00

2004 PMC Funny Car 1:24

Item	Low	High
NNO Gary Scelzi Oakley HEMI/1008	50.00	75.00

2003 PMC Pro Stock 1:24

Item	Low	High
NNO Bruce Allen Reher-Morrison/1008	45.00	80.00
NNO Greg Anderson Vegas General/1008	45.00	80.00
NNO Warren Johnson GM Performance Parts/1008	75.00	125.00

2000 Racing Champions Authentics NHRA 1:24

Item	Low	High
NNO Joe Amato Valvoline	40.00	80.00
NNO Whit Bazemore Matco Tools Kendall/3100	25.00	60.00
NNO Kenny Bernstein Bud King	25.00	60.00
NNO Ron Capps U.S. Tobacco	30.00	60.00
NNO Dale Creasy MAD Magazine	25.00	60.00
NNO Gary Densham NEC	20.00	50.00
NNO Larry Dixon Miller Lite	40.00	80.00
NNO Al Hofmann Redline Mooneyes	25.00	60.00
NNO Doug Kalitta MGM Grand	30.00	60.00
NNO Don Lampus Express.com	40.00	80.00
NNO Cory Lee ProMotorsports Rat Fink/5000	30.00	70.00
NNO Frank Manzo Kendall Oil	30.00	60.00
NNO Matco Spring Supernationals/3100	30.00	60.00
NNO Cory McClenathan MBNA	20.00	50.00
NNO Frank Pedregon CSK Texaco	40.00	80.00
NNO Tony Schumacher Exide	40.00	80.00
NNO Dean Skuza Matco Tools/3100	25.00	60.00
NNO Dean Skuza Matco Tools Platinum	40.00	80.00
NNO Del Worsham CSK Texaco	30.00	60.00

2001 Racing Champions Authentics NHRA 1:24

Item	Low	High
NNO Joe Amato Dynomax/2500	15.00	40.00
NNO Whit Bazemore Matco Tools Black/3500	30.00	60.00
NNO Whit Bazemore Matco Tools Fire Red/3500	30.00	60.00
NNO Whit Bazemore Matco Tools Iron Eagle/3500	35.00	60.00
NNO Kenny Bernstein Bud/2500	30.00	60.00
NNO Kenny Bernstein Bud King Mac Tools/3000	20.00	50.00
NNO Ron Capps Skoal Mac Tools/3000	30.00	60.00
NNO Jeg Coughlin Jr. Jeg's/3000	20.00	40.00
NNO Larry Dixon Miller Lite Mac Tools/3000	15.00	40.00
NNO Jim Dunn Mooneyes Gold Chrome/416	50.00	90.00
NNO Mike Dunn Yankees Gold Mac Tools/1500	60.00	100.00
NNO Chuck Etchells Sunoco Matco Tools/3500	30.00	60.00
NNO Chuck Etchells Kendall Matco Tools/3500	30.00	60.00
NNO Jim Epler Bass Pro/3500	20.00	50.00
NNO Jim Epler Cabela's/3000	40.00	75.00
NNO Jim Epler Motley Crue/3000	50.00	90.00
NNO Jim Epler NAPA/3500	35.00	60.00
NNO Jim Epler Rug Doctor	25.00	60.00
NNO Jim Epler Toys'R'Us/3500	30.00	60.00
NNO Don Garlits Matco Tools/3011	20.00	50.00
NNO Don Garlits Matco Tools Stars&Stripes	60.00	100.00
NNO Al Hofmann Mooneyes Mac Tools/3000	15.00	40.00
NNO Tommy Johnson Skoal Mac Tools/3000	20.00	50.00
NNO Doug Kalitta Mac Tools/6000	20.00	50.00
NNO Doug Kalitta Mac Tools Gold/1500	35.00	60.00
NNO Matco Tools SuperNationals Englishtown/3500	25.00	50.00
NNO Mark Pawuk Summit/3500	20.00	50.00
NNO Frank Pedregon Checker	20.00	50.00
NNO Cristen Powell Nitro Fish/2500	20.00	40.00
NNO Cristen Powell Nitro Fish Gold/416	30.00	60.00
NNO Darrell Russell Matco Tools/3000	25.00	50.00
NNO Gary Scelzi Winston Matco Tools/3500	30.00	60.00
NNO Tony Schumacher Army/5000	15.00	40.00
NNO Tony Schumacher Army Gold/416	30.00	60.00
NNO Dean Skuza Mopar/2500	15.00	40.00
NNO Dean Skuza Mopar Gold/416	30.00	60.00

2002 Racing Champions Authentics NHRA 1:24

Item	Low	High
NNO Darrell Alderman Mopar	45.00	80.00
NNO Whit Bazemore Speed Racer Matco Tools/2400	60.00	100.00
NNO Kenny Bernstein Budweiser King Color Chrome	50.00	100.00
NNO Kenny Bernstein Bud Gold/199	75.00	150.00
NNO Jeg Coughlin Jr. Jeg's/999	25.00	50.00
NNO Jeg Coughlin Jeg's Gold/199	40.00	80.00
NNO Larry Dixon Miller Lite/999	30.00	60.00
NNO Vern Gaines Miller Lite/250	50.00	90.00
NNO Vern Gaines Miller Lite Chrome/250	50.00	100.00
NNO Johnny Gray Checker/1656	25.00	50.00
NNO Al Hofmann K&N Filters/999	35.00	70.00
NNO Al Hofmann K&N Filters Gold/199	75.00	150.00
NNO Clay Millican Werner Matco Tools/2000	30.00	50.00
NNO Clay Millican Werner Matco Tools Gold/199	40.00	80.00
NNO Mark Pawuk Summit/999	25.00	50.00
NNO Mark Pawuk Summit Gold/199	40.00	80.00
NNO Darrell Russell Bilstein/999	25.00	50.00
NNO Darrell Russell Joe Amato Racing	20.00	40.00
NNO Bruce Sarver White Cap/2000	60.00	120.00
NNO Tony Schumacher Army/999	30.00	60.00
NNO Tony Schumacher Army Gold/199	75.00	150.00
NNO Tony Schumacher Matco Tools/2750	25.00	50.00
NNO Dean Skuza Team Mopar/1000	35.00	60.00
NNO Del Worsham Checker/1656	30.00	50.00

2003 Racing Champions Authentics NHRA 1:24

Item	Low	High
NNO Greg Anderson Vegas General Mac Tools/1250	40.00	75.00
NNO Whit Bazemore Matco Animal House/2500	50.00	90.00
NNO Whit Bazemore Matco Distributor/2000	40.00	75.00
NNO Whit Bazemore Matco Fast&Furious/2150	40.00	75.00
NNO Whit Bazemore Matco Iron Eagle/2000	40.00	75.00
NNO Whit Bazemore Mopar Matco Tools/2000	45.00	80.00
NNO Scott Kalitta Mac Tools Jesse James/2500	45.00	80.00
NNO George Marnell Fast&Furious/2000	35.00	60.00
NNO Clay Millican Werner Matco Tools 104+ Octane		
NNO Darrell Russell Bilstein Matco Tools/2000	30.00	60.00
NNO Darrell Russell Matco Fast&Furious/2000	30.00	60.00
NNO Gary Scelzi Dodge Matco Tools/2150	60.00	100.00
NNO Gary Scelzi Dodge Matco Tools Chrome/250	70.00	120.00
NNO Tony Schumacher Army Matco Tools/2000	30.00	60.00
NNO Tony Schumacher Army Camo Matco Tools/2000	45.00	80.00

2004 Racing Champions Authentics NHRA 1:24

Item	Low	High
NNO Bob Gilbertson Jungle Jim/500	45.00	80.00
NNO Bob Gilbertson Jungle Jim Chrome/500	45.00	80.00
NNO Warren Johnson GM Performance Parts/1002	50.00	80.00
NNO Warren Johnson GM Performance Parts Chrome/252	125.00	200.00
NNO Dean Skuza Black Label Society/512	40.00	75.00

2003 Racing Champions Authentics Pro Stock Bikes 1:9

Item	Low	High
NNO Antron Brown Army/670	50.00	90.00
NNO Andrew Hines Vance&Hines Harley/2500	50.00	90.00
NNO Angelle Savoie Army/1066	50.00	90.00
NNO G.T. Tonglet Vance&Hines Harley	50.00	90.00
NNO Craig Treble Matco Fast&Furious/2000	60.00	100.00
NNO Craig Treble Matco Iron Eagle/2000	60.00	100.00

2005 Racing Champions Authentics Pro Stock Bikes 1:9

Item	Low	High
NNO Antron Brown Army/2004	35.00	60.00
NNO Angelle Sampey Army/2004	35.00	60.00
NNO GT Tonglett Harley Eagle/2202	35.00	60.00

1995 Racing Champions Dragsters 1:24

This was Racing Champions first 1:24 Dragster issue. Former Winston NHRA Top Fuel Champions Joe Amato and Eddie Hill are a couple of the featured drivers.

Item	Low	High
NNO Joe Amato Valvoline	20.00	40.00
NNO Shelly Anderson Western Auto	25.00	40.00
NNO Eddie Hill Pennzoil	25.00	40.00
NNO Doug Herbert Snap On	25.00	40.00
NNO Tommy Johnson Jr. Mopar	25.00	40.00
NNO Cory McClenathan McDonald's	25.00	40.00

1996 Racing Champions Dragsters 1:24

This was the second year that Racing Champions released 1:24 scale Dragsters. The most expensive and desired piece in the series is that of Blaine Johnson.

Item	Low	High
NNO Joe Amato Valvoline	15.00	30.00
NNO Shelly Anderson Parts America	15.00	30.00
NNO Bill Blair Fugowie! Lost Tribe	15.00	30.00
NNO Ron Capps RPR	15.00	30.00
NNO Chuck Etchells Kendall	15.00	30.00
NNO Rick Fuller Montana Express	15.00	30.00
NNO Gatornationals Mac Tools	15.00	30.00
NNO Spike Gorr Greer Motorsports	15.00	30.00
NNO Rhonda Hartman Hartman Enterprises	15.00	30.00
NNO Doug Herbert Snap On	15.00	30.00
NNO Eddie Hill Pennzoil	15.00	30.00
NNO Blaine Johnson Travers	20.00	40.00
NNO Lawren Jones Matco	20.00	40.00
NNO Connie Kalitta American	20.00	30.00
NNO Scott Kalitta American	15.00	30.00
NNO Cory McClenathan McDonald's	15.00	30.00
NNO Cory McClenathan McDonald's Olympic	15.00	30.00
NNO Rance McDaniel La Bac Systems	15.00	30.00
NNO Jack Ostrander	15.00	30.00

Vista Food		
NNO Bruce Sarver Carquest	15.00	30.00
NNO Bob Vandergriff Jerzees	15.00	30.00
NNO Winter Nationals	15.00	30.00

1997 Racing Champions Dragsters 1:24

This was the third year that Racing Champions released 1:24 scale Dragsters. The most expensive and desired piece in the series is that of Blaine Johnson.

NNO Joe Amato Keystone	15.00	30.00
NNO Shelly Anderson Parts America	25.00	50.00
NNO Tony Bartone Bartone Bros.	15.00	30.00
NNO Jim Epler Rug Doctor	15.00	30.00
NNO Doug Foxworth Havoc	15.00	30.00
NNO Spike Gorr Greer Motorsports	15.00	30.00
NNO Doug Grubnic Geronimo	12.00	30.00
NNO Rhonda Hartman Hartman Racing	15.00	30.00
NNO Jim Head Close Call	15.00	30.00
NNO Doug Herbert Snap On	20.00	40.00
NNO Eddie Hill Pennzoil	15.00	30.00
NNO Eddie Hill Pennzoil Matco	20.00	40.00
NNO Blaine Johnson Travers	40.00	80.00
NNO Connie Kalitta American	15.00	30.00
NNO Scott Kalitta American	15.00	30.00
NNO Cory McClenathan McDonald's	15.00	30.00
NNO Randy Parks Fluke	35.00	50.00
NNO Cristen Powell CP Racing	15.00	40.00
NNO Cristen Powell Royal Purple	20.00	45.00
NNO Bruce Sarver Carquest	15.00	30.00
NNO Tony Schumacher Peek Brothers	15.00	30.00
NNO John Shoemaker American Eagle	15.00	30.00
NNO Paul Smith Smith Racing School	15.00	30.00
NNO Bobby Taylor Turner Racing	15.00	30.00
NNO Marshall Topping Montana Express	15.00	30.00
NNO Bob Vandergriff Jerzees	15.00	30.00

1998 Racing Champions Dragsters 1:24

This was the fourth year that Racing Champions released 1:24 scale Dragsters.

NNO Jim Head Close Call	12.00	30.00
NNO Doug Herbert Snap On	12.00	30.00
NNO Larry Meirsch Powermate	12.00	30.00
NNO Cristen Powell Reebok	12.00	30.00
NNO Paul Romaine CarQuest	12.00	30.00
NNO Bob Vandergriff erzees	12.00	30.00

1999 Racing Champions Dragsters 1:24

NNO Gary Scelzi Winston Matco Tools	20.00	35.00

2001 Racing Champions Dragsters 1:24

NNO Joe Amato Dynomax	12.50	25.00
NNO Kenny Bernstein King Kenny	15.00	30.00
NNO Kenny Bernstein King Kenny AUTO	50.00	100.00
NNO Kenny Bernstein King Kenny Gold	20.00	50.00
NNO Larry Dixon The Snake	12.50	25.00
NNO Larry Dixon The Snake Gold	20.00	40.00
NNO Rhonda Hartman-Smith FRAM	10.00	25.00
NNO Doug Kalitta MGM Grand	12.50	25.00
NNO Doug Kalitta MGM Grand AUTO	30.00	60.00
NNO Mac Tools Thunder Valley/5000	12.50	25.00
NNO Gary Scelzi Matco Tools	12.50	25.00
NNO Gary Scelzi Matco Tools Gold/1000	12.50	30.00

2002 Racing Champions Dragsters 1:24

NNO Kenny Bernstein Bernstein	12.00	20.00
NNO Kenny Bernstein Bernstein Gold/1000	15.00	30.00
NNO Mike Dunn N.Y.Yankees	12.00	20.00
NNO Mike Dunn N.Y.Yankees Gold/1000	15.00	25.00
NNO Don Garlits Matco Tools	12.00	20.00
NNO Rhonda Hartman-Smith FRAM	12.00	20.00
NNO Rhonda Hartman-Smith FRAM Gold/1000	15.00	25.00
NNO Tony Schumacher Army with Army Card	12.00	20.00
NNO Tony Schumacher Army with Schumacher card	12.00	20.00

2005 Racing Champions Authentics Dragsters 1:24

NNO Morgan Lucas Lucas Oil/1200	40.00	65.00
NNO Cory McLenathan Fram/1254	40.00	65.00
NNO Clay Millican Werner/1002	40.00	65.00
NNO Tony Schumacher Army Camo Call to Duty/1002	40.00	65.00
NNO Melanie Troxell Skull Gear/1002	40.00	65.00

2006 Racing Champions Authentics Dragsters 1:24

NNO Cory McClenathan Jeg's Mail Order/1248	50.00	75.00

1989 Racing Champions Dragsters 1:64

NNO Joe Amato TRW	5.00	12.00
NNO Frank Bradley	5.00	12.00
NNO Don Garlits	6.00	12.00
NNO Darrell Gwynn	5.00	12.00
NNO Eddie Hill Super Shops	5.00	12.00
NNO Lori Johns Jolly Rancher	4.00	10.00
NNO Shirley Muldowney Otter Pops Blue	5.00	12.00
NNO Shirley Muldowney Pink	5.00	12.00
NNO Gary Ormsby Castrol GTX	4.00	10.00
NNO Don Prudhomme	5.00	12.00

1996 Racing Champions Dragsters 1:64

This was the first isssue of a Racing Champions 1:64 scale Dragster. The series is lead by the Blaine Johnson Travers piece. There was also a four pack available. There are many different combinations of Dragsters that could be found in those four packs.

NNO Joe Amato Keystone	4.00	10.00
NNO Shelly Anderson Parts America	4.00	10.00
NNO Bill Blair Fugowie! Lost Tribe	4.00	10.00
NNO Ron Capps RPR	4.00	10.00
NNO Rick Fuller Montana Express	4.00	10.00
NNO Spike Gorr Greer Motorsports	4.00	10.00
NNO Rhonda Hartman Hartman Enterprises	4.00	10.00
NNO Doug Herbert Snap On	4.00	10.00
NNO Eddie Hill Pennzoil	4.00	10.00
NNO Blaine Johnson Travers	7.50	15.00
NNO Lawren Jones Matco	6.00	12.00
NNO Connie Kalitta American	4.00	10.00
NNO Scott Kalitta American	4.00	10.00
NNO Cory McClenathan McDonald's	4.00	10.00
NNO Cory McClenathan McDonald's Olympic	4.00	10.00
NNO Rance McDaniel La Bac Systems	4.00	10.00
NNO Jack Ostrander Vista Food	4.00	10.00
NNO Bruce Sarver CarQuest	4.00	10.00
NNO Mac Tools U.S.Nationals	4.00	10.00
NNO Bob Vandergriff Jerzees	4.00	10.00
NNO 4 Car Drag Set (any of them)	18.00	25.00

1997 Racing Champions Dragsters 1:64

Racing Champions returned their 1:64 Dragster line in 1997. The series features former Winston NHRA Champions Joe Amato and Scott Kalitta.

NNO Joe Amato Keystone	4.00	10.00
NNO Shelly Anderson Parts America	4.00	10.00
NNO Jim Epler Rug Doctor	4.00	10.00
NNO Spike Gorr Greer Motorsports	4.00	10.00
NNO Doug Grubnic Geronimo	3.00	10.00
NNO Rhonda Hartman Hartman Racing	4.00	10.00
NNO Jim Head Close Call	4.00	10.00
NNO Doug Herbert Snap On	4.00	10.00
NNO Eddie Hill Pennzoil Matco	6.00	12.00
NNO Connie Kalita American	4.00	10.00
NNO Scott Kalitta American	4.00	10.00
NNO Randy Parks Fluke	4.00	10.00
NNO Cristen Powell Powell Racing	4.00	10.00
NNO Bruce Sarver Carquest	4.00	10.00
NNO Tony Schumacher Peek Brothers	4.00	10.00
NNO John Shoemaker American Eagle	4.00	10.00
NNO Paul Smith Roy Smith Racing School	4.00	10.00
NNO Bobby Taylor Turner Racing	4.00	10.00
NNO Marshall Topping Montana Express	4.00	10.00
NNO Bob Vandergriff Jerzees	4.00	10.00

2001 Racing Champions Preview Dragsters 1:64

NNO Gary Scelzi Matco Tools	3.00	6.00
NNO Tony Schumacher Army	3.00	6.00

2001 Racing Champions Dragsters 1:64

NNO Joe Amato Dynomax	3.00	6.00
NNO Kenny Bernstein King Kenny	3.00	8.00
NNO Kenny Bernstein King Kenny Gold	6.00	15.00
NNO Rhonda Hartman-Smith FRAM	2.00	5.00
NNO Doug Kalitta MGM Grand	3.00	6.00
NNO Clay Millican Werner Promo	6.00	15.00
NNO Tony Schumacher Exide	2.00	5.00
NNO Tony Schumacher Exide Gold	6.00	12.00

2002 Racing Champions Preview Dragsters 1:64

Each car in this series was packaged in a typical red and black Racing Champions Previews blister along with a card. Many of the cards feature the team and sponsor logos and not the driver himself. The packaging carries a 2001 copyright date on the back, but is considered a 2002 release. The various NHRA sanctioned racing series are represented. Some cars were also issued with either Chrome or Autographed card numbered "chase" versions.

NNO Kenny Bernstein Bernstein	3.00	6.00
NNO Kenny Bernstein Bernstein Chrome/1000	6.00	15.00
NNO Mike Dunn N.Y.Yankees	3.00	6.00
NNO Don Garlits Matco Tools	4.00	10.00
NNO Tony Schumacher Army w Army Card	3.00	6.00

2002 Racing Champions Dragsters 1:64

Similar to the Preview series, each car in this series was packaged in a typical red and black Racing Champions blister along with a card. The packaging carries a 2002 copyright date on the back and the various NHRA sanctioned racing series are represented. Some cars were also issued with either Chrome or Autographed card numbered "chase" versions.

NNO Mike Dunn N.Y.Yankees	3.00	6.00
NNO Tony Schumacher Army with Schumacher card	3.00	6.00

2006 Racing Champions Dragsters 1:64

NNO Tony Schumacher U.S. Army	5.00	10.00

1997 Racing Champions Dragsters 1:144

These 1:144 scale mini dragsters were issued in a red and black Racing Champions blister package. The blister reads "1997 Edition" on the front. Each was also packaged with a yellow bordered trading card.

NNO Joe Amato Keystone	2.00	5.00
NNO Doug Herbert Snap On	2.00	5.00
NNO Blaine Johnson Travers	2.00	5.00
NNO Scott Kalitta American	2.00	5.00
NNO Bob Vandergriff Jerzees	2.00	5.00

1995-96 Racing Champions Funny Car 1:24

This is the first 1:24 scale Funny Car series to hit the market. Racing Champions distributed the pieces through both hobby and retail outlets. The cars come in a red and black box.

NNO Randy Anderson Parts America 1996	12.50	30.00
NNO Whit Bazemore Mobil 1	15.00	30.00
NNO Gary Bolger Creasy 1996	12.50	30.00
NNO Jerry Caminito Blue Thunder	15.00	30.00
NNO Gary Clapshaw Fuelish Pleasure 1996	10.00	25.00
NNO Gary Densham NEC 1996	10.00	25.00
NNO Jim Epler Rug Doctor 1996	10.00	25.00
NNO Gatornationals Mac Tools	15.00	30.00
NNO Al Hofmann Parts America	15.00	30.00
NNO Tom Hoover Pioneer	15.00	30.00
NNO Kenji Okazaki Mooneyes	15.00	30.00
NNO Cruz Pedregon McDonald's 1996	12.50	30.00
NNO Tony Pedregon Geronimo	15.00	30.00
NNO Wyatt Radke Nitro Bandit 1996	15.00	30.00
NNO Tim Simpson Simpson Racing	15.00	30.00
NNO Dean Skuza Matco Promo 1996	20.00	40.00
NNO Mac Tools U.S.Nationals 1996	10.00	25.00
NNO Tim Wilkerson NAPA	15.00	30.00
NNO Winter Nationals	15.00	30.00
NNO Del Worsham Worsham Fink 1996	10.00	25.00

1997 Racing Champions Funny Car 1:24

This was the third year for Racing Champions to release the 1:24 scale Funny Car series. A couple of regulars on the Alcohol Funny Car circuit Randy Anderson and Tony Bartone are in the set. 1997 saw Randy Anderson move up to Top Fuel.

NNO Randy Anderson Parts America	15.00	30.00
NNO Tony Bartone Bartone Racing	15.00	30.00
NNO Tony Bartone Quaker State	15.00	30.00
NNO Bunny Burkett Mopar	15.00	30.00
NNO Gary Bolger Creasy	15.00	30.00
NNO Jim Dunn Moon Eyes	15.00	30.00
NNO Chuck Etchells Kendall	15.00	30.00
NNO Rhonda Hartman Geronimo	15.00	30.00
NNO Ray Higley Red Line Oil	15.00	30.00
NNO Tom Hoover Pioneer	15.00	30.00
NNO Frank Manzo Kendall	15.00	30.00
NNO Vern Moats Mopar	15.00	30.00
NNO Todd Payton Optima Batteries	15.00	30.00
NNO Cruz Pedregon McDonald's	15.00	30.00
NNO Jimmy Penland Penland Racing	15.00	30.00
NNO John Powell Etterman Racing	15.00	30.00
NNO Von Smith Atomic City Tools	15.00	30.00
NNO Dean Skuza Matco 1994	20.00	40.00
NNO Dean Skuza Matco 1994 Gold	125.00	250.00
NNO Dean Skuza Matco 1997	20.00	40.00
NNO Tim Wilkerson NAPA	15.00	30.00
NNO Del Worsham CSK	15.00	30.00

1999-00 Racing Champions Funny Car 1:24

NNO Matco Supernationals 1999	10.00	20.00
NNO Nitro Fish Promo 2000	10.00	20.00

1998 Racing Champions Funny Car 1:24

This was the fourth year for Racing Champions to release the 1:24 scale Funny Car series.

NNO Randy Anderson Parts America	12.00	30.00
NNO Bunny Burkett Burkett-Mopar	12.00	30.00
NNO Jim Epler East Care	12.00	30.00
NNO Brent Fanning Udder Nonsense	15.00	40.00
NNO Al Hofmann Hoffman Racing	15.00	30.00
NNO Tom Hoover Pioneer	12.00	30.00
NNO Frank Manzo Kendall	12.00	30.00
NNO Cruz Pedregon Interstate Batteries	15.00	30.00

2001 Racing Champions Funny Car 1:24

NNO Whit Bazemore Matco Tools	12.50	25.00
NNO Dale Creasy Jr. Mad Ugly	15.00	30.00
NNO Dale Creasy Jr. Nitromaniac	10.00	25.00
NNO Jim Epler Bass Pro Promo	12.50	30.00
NNO Jim Epler Matco Tools	10.00	25.00
NNO Jim Epler Matco Tools Gold/1000	12.50	30.00
NNO Al Hofmann Mooneyes	12.50	25.00
NNO Al Hofmann Mooneyes Gold/1000	20.00	40.00
NNO Mac Tools Thunder Valley/5000	12.50	25.00
NNO Matco Supernationals/3500	12.50	25.00
NNO Dean Skuza Matco Tools	12.50	25.00
NNO Dean Skuza Matco Tools Gold/1000	15.00	30.00

2005 Racing Champions Authentics Funny Car 1:24

NNO Tony Bartone Lucas Oil Got CMKX/1254	40.00	65.00
NNO Tony Bartone Lucas Oil Got CMKX Johnny Lightning/1266	40.00	65.00
NNO Phil Burkart Jr. CSK/1002	40.00	65.00
NNO Tim Wilkerson LRS/1002	40.00	65.00
NNO Del Worsham CSK/1500	40.00	65.00

2006 Racing Champions Funny Cars 1:24

NNO Del Worsham Checker Schuck's Kragen	10.00	20.00

1989 Racing Champions Funny Car 1:64

NNO Pat Austin Castrol GTX	4.00	10.00
NNO Raymond Beadle Blue Max	4.00	10.00
NNO Kenny Bernstein King Kenny	5.00	12.00
NNO Kenny Bernstein Quaker State	5.00	12.00
NNO Tom Hoover Showtime	4.00	10.00
NNO Bruce Larson Sentry	4.00	10.00
NNO Ed McCulloch The Ace	4.00	10.00
NNO Mark Oswald Motorcraft	4.00	10.00
NNO Don Prudhomme	5.00	10.00

1994-95 Racing Champions Funny Car 1:64

NNO Al Hofmann Western Auto Promo 1995	4.00	8.00
NNO Kenny Koretsky Sunoco Promo 1994	4.00	8.00

1996 Racing Champions Funny Car 1:64

This was the first year that Racing Champions did a 1:64 scal Funny Car. The only Winston Nitro Funny Car champion in 90' beside John Force, Cruz Pedregon (1992) is in the series.

NNO Randy Anderson Parts America	4.00	10.00
NNO Gary Bolger Creasy	4.00	10.00
NNO Gary Clapshaw Fuelish Pleasure	4.00	10.00
NNO Gary Densham NEC	4.00	10.00
NNO Chuck Etchells Kendall	4.00	10.00
NNO Al Hofmann Parts America	5.00	10.00
NNO Tom Hoover Pioneer	4.00	10.00
NNO Vern Moates Mopar	4.00	10.00
NNO Kenji Okazaki Mooneyes	4.00	10.00
NNO Cruz Pedregon McDonald's	5.00	10.00
NNO Jimmy Penland Penland Racing	4.00	10.00
NNO Wyatt Radke Nitro Bandit	4.00	10.00
NNO Dean Skuza Matco	4.00	10.00
NNO Tim Wilkerson NAPA	4.00	10.00
NNO Dle Worsham Worsham Fink	4.00	10.00
NNO 4 piece Funny Car set There are numerous combinations	18.00	25.00

1997 Racing Champions Funny Car 1:64

Long time Funny Car driver Bunny Burkett is one of the drivers to highlight this series. The cars feature drivers from both the Alcohol and Nitro Funny Car circuits.

NNO Randy Anderson Parts America	4.00	10.00
NNO Anthony Bartone Bartone Racing	4.00	10.00
NNO Anthony Bartone Quaker State	4.00	10.00
NNO Gary Bolger Creasy	4.00	10.00
NNO Bunny Burkett Burkett Racing	4.00	10.00
NNO Jim Dunn Moon Eyes	4.00	10.00
NNO Chuck Etchells Kendall	4.00	10.00
NNO Rhonda Hartman Geronimo	4.00	10.00
NNO Ray Higley Red Line Oil	6.00	15.00
NNO Tom Hoover Pioneer	4.00	10.00
NNO Frank Manzo Kendall	4.00	10.00
NNO Vern Moats Mopar	4.00	10.00
NNO Bob Newberry Keystone	10.00	20.00
NNO Cruz Pedregon McDonald's	4.00	10.00
NNO Jimmy Penland Penland Racing	6.00	15.00
NNO John Powell Etterman Racing	4.00	10.00
NNO Von Smith Atomic City Tools	4.00	10.00
NNO Dean Skuza	6.00	12.00

Matco 1994
NNO Dean Skuza 25.00 50.00
Matco 1994 Gold
NNO Dean Skuza 20.00 40.00
Matco Four Pack
NNO Tim Wilkerson 4.00 10.00
NAPA
NNO Del Worsham 4.00 10.00
CSK

2000 Racing Champions Funny Car 1:64

NNO Nitro Fish Promo in box 3.00 6.00

2001 Racing Champions Funny Car 1:64

NNO Whit Bazemore 2.00 5.00
Matco Tools
NNO Dale Creasy Jr. 3.00 6.00
Mad
NNO Jim Epler 3.00 6.00
Bass Pro Promo
NNO Jim Epler 2.00 5.00
Matco Tools Flames
NNO Al Hofmann 3.00 6.00
Mooneyes
NNO Al Hofmann
Mooneyes AUTO
NNO Al Hofmann 5.00 12.00
Mooneyes Chrome
NNO Nitro Fish 3.00 6.00
NNO Bruce Sarver 2.00 5.00
e-moola.com
NNO Bruce Sarver 5.00 12.00
e-moola.com Chrome/1000
NNO Del Worsham 2.00 5.00
Checker

2002 Racing Champions Preview Funny Car 1:64

NNO Whit Bazemore 3.00 6.00
Matco Tools
NNO Jim Dunn 3.00 6.00
Mooneyes
NNO Jim Dunn 6.00 15.00
Mooneyes Chrome/1000
NNO Warren Johnson 3.00 6.00
Goodwrench

2002 Racing Champions Funny Car 1:64

NNO Del Worsham 3.00 6.00
Checker

2006 Racing Champions Funny Cars 1:64

NNO Whit Bazemore 5.00 10.00
Matco Tools

1997 Racing Champions Funny Car 1:144

NNO Gary Bolger 2.00 5.00
Creasy
NNO Jim Epler 2.00 5.00
Winnebago
NNO Rhonda Hartman 2.00 5.00
Geronimo
NNO Tom Hoover 2.00 5.00
Pioneer
NNO Cruz Pedregon 2.00 5.00
McDonald's
NNO Jimmy Penland 2.00 5.00
Penland Racing

1997 Racing Champions Pro Stock 1:24

Racing Champions expanded its drag racing line to Pro Stockers with this release. The series features former Pro Stock Champions Warren Johnson and Jim Yates.

NNO Troy Coughlin 15.00 30.00
Jeg's
NNO Jerry Eckman 15.00 30.00
Checker
NNO Mike Edwards 15.00 30.00
Winnebago
NNO Ray Franks 15.00 30.00
Franks-Haas
NNO Vern Gaines 15.00 30.00
Western Racing
NNO Tommy Hammonds 15.00 30.00
Hammonds Racing
NNO Chuck Harris 15.00 30.00
Go Racing.com
NNO Kurt Johnson 20.00 40.00
AC Delco
NNO Warren Johnson 15.00 30.00
GM Performance
NNO George Marnell 15.00 30.00
Marnell Black
NNO Tony Martino 15.00 30.00
Martino Racing
NNO Larry Morgan 15.00 30.00
Raybestos
NNO Mark Osborne 15.00 30.00
MaMa Rosa
NNO Mark Pawuk 15.00 30.00
Summit Racing
NNO Steve Schmidt 15.00 30.00
Dynagear
NNO Mike Thomas 15.00 30.00
Gumout
NNO Jim Yates 15.00 30.00
McDonald's

1998 Racing Champions Pro Stock 1:24

This was the second year for Racing Champions to release the 1:24 scale Pro Stock series.

NNO Craig Eaton 12.50 25.00
ATSCO Autographed/2502
NNO George Marnell 12.00 30.00
Tenneco
NNO Tom Martino 12.00 30.00
Six Flags
NNO Mark Pawuk 12.00 30.00
Summit Racing
NNO Mike Thomas 12.00 30.00
Gumout
NNO Jim Yates 12.00 30.00
Peak-Split Fire

2005 Racing Champions Authentics Pro Stock 1:24

NNO Jeg Coughlin Jr. 40.00 65.00
Jeg's Mail Order
Cancer Research/1002
NNO Mike Edwards 40.00 65.00
Young Life Racing/1002
NNO Vieri Gaines 40.00 65.00
Kendall Dodge/1002
NNO Kurt Johnson 40.00 65.00
AC Delco/1254
NNO Kenny Koretsky 40.00 65.00
Nitro Fish/1002
NNO Jason Line 40.00 65.00
KB Framers/1002

2006 Racing Champions Pro Stock 1:24

NNO Kurt Johnson 10.00 20.00
AC Delco

1989 Racing Champions Pro Stock 1:64

NNO Darrell Alderman 4.00 10.00
NNO Bruce Allen 4.00 10.00
NNO Don Beverley 4.00 10.00
Crown
NNO Jerry Eckman 4.00 10.00
Pennzoil
NNO Warren Johnson 5.00 10.00
AC Delco
NNO Joe Lepone Jr. 4.00 10.00
NNO Larry Morgan 4.00 10.00
Castrol
NNO David Nickens 4.00 10.00
Castrol
NNO Rick Smith 4.00 10.00
STP

1997 Racing Champions Pro Stock 1:64

This was the first year Racing Champions released 1:64 scale series Pro Stock cars. The series is highlighted by the appearance of Warren Johnson and Jim Yates.

NNO Troy Coughlin 5.00 10.00
Jeg's
NNO Jerry Eckman 5.00 10.00
CSK
NNO Marty Edwards 5.00 10.00
Winnebago
NNO Ray Franks 5.00 10.00
Franks-Haas
NNO Vern Gaines 5.00 10.00
Western Racing
NNO Tommy Hammonds 5.00 10.00
Hammonds Racing
NNO Chuck Harris 5.00 10.00
Go Racing.com
NNO Kurt Johnson 5.00 10.00
AC Delco
NNO Warren Johnson 5.00 10.00
Performance Parts
NNO George Marnell 5.00 10.00
Marnell Black
NNO George Marnell 4.00 10.00
Marnell Red&White
NNO Tony Martino 5.00 10.00
Martino Racing
NNO Larry Morgan 5.00 10.00
Raybestos
NNO John Nobile 5.00 10.00
Nobile Trucking
NNO Mark Osborne 5.00 10.00
MaMa Rosa
NNO Mark Pawuk 5.00 10.00
Summit Racing
NNO S.Schmidt 5.00 10.00
Dynagear
NNO Mike Thomas 5.00 10.00
Gumout
NNO Pete Williams 5.00 10.00
Williams Racing
NNO Jim Yates 5.00 10.00
McDonald's

2002 Racing Champions Pro Stock 1:64

NNO Allen Johnson 3.00 6.00
Amoco Ultimate Promo in box

2006 Racing Champions Pro Stock 1:64

NNO Warren Johnson 5.00 10.00
GM Performance Parts
School's Out

1997 Racing Champions Pro Stock 1:144

NNO George Marnell 2.00 5.00
Marnell Red&White
NNO Jim Yates 2.00 5.00
McDonald's
NNO Mike Edwards 2.00 5.00
Winnebago
NNO Mark Osborne 2.00 5.00
MaMa Rosa
NNO Mark Pawuk 2.00 5.00
Summit Racing
NNO Mike Thomas 2.00 5.00
Gumout
NNO Vern Gaines 2.00 5.00
Western Racing
NNO Steve Schmidt 2.00 5.00
Dynagear
NNO Troy Coughlin 2.00 5.00
Jeg's
NNO Warren Johnson 2.00 5.00
Performance Parts

2002 Racing Champions Drivers of All Time NHRA 1:18

NNO John Force 20.00 40.00
1970 Mustang/1042
NNO John Force 35.00 60.00
1970 Mustang Chrome/208
NNO Don Garlits 50.00 90.00
1969 Charger/1042
NNO Don Garlits 40.00 75.00
1969 Charger Chrome/208
NNO Don Prudhomme 25.00 50.00
1969 Camaro/1042
NNO Don Prudhomme 40.00 75.00
1969 Camaro Chrome/208

2001 Racing Champions Force Field 1:64

NNO John Force 2.50 5.00
1953 Corvette
NNO John Force 2.50 5.00
1958 Edsel
NNO John Force 2.50 5.00
1957 Plymouth Fury
NNO John Force 2.50 5.00
1964 Mustang
NNO John Force 2.50 5.00
1968 Firebird
NNO John Force 2.50 5.00
1968 Plymouth
NNO John Force 2.50 5.00
1969 GTO
NNO John Force 2.50 5.00
1969 Olds
NNO John Force 2.50 5.00
1971 Cuda

2001 Racing Champions Wheels of Fame NHRA 1:64

NNO Joe Amato 3.00 6.00
1933 Willys
NNO Joe Amato 3.00 6.00
1939 Chevy Coupe
NNO Joe Amato 3.00 6.00
1957 Chevy Bel Air
NNO Kenny Bernstein 3.00 6.00
1966 Camaro
NNO Kenny Bernstein 3.00 6.00
1970 Buick GSX 2
NNO Kenny Bernstein 3.00 6.00
1971 Barracuda 12
NNO Kenny Bernstein 3.00 6.00
1996 Camaro
NNO Eddie Hill 3.00 6.00
1934 Ford Coupe
NNO Eddie Hill 3.00 6.00
1969 Olds
NNO Tom McEwen 3.00 6.00
1956 Chevy Nomade
NNO Tom McEwen 3.00 6.00
1967 Chevelle
NNO Don Prudhomme 3.00 6.00
1934 Ford Highboy
NNO Don Prudhomme 3.00 6.00
1969 Camaro

2001 Racing Champions NHRA Transporters 1:64

NNO Doug Kalitta 12.50 25.00
Mac Tools/3500
NNO Mac Tools Thunder Valley/5000 10.00 25.00

1998 Revell Dragsters 1:24

This series is the debut of the production of NHRA pieces by Revell.

NNO Joe Amato 20.00 50.00
Tenneco
NNO Eddie Hill 30.00 60.00
Pennzoil Matco/3000

1998-99 Revell Pro Stock 1:24

This series is the debut of the production of NHRA pieces by Revell.

NNO Kurt Johnson 25.00 60.00
AC Delco/2502 1998
NNO Warren Johnson 25.00 60.00
1997 GM Performance
Parts/2502
NNO Warren Johnson 40.00 80.00
Goodwrench
Superman/3000 1999
NNO Mac Tools 50th Anniversary '98 15.00 40.00

1998-00 Revell Club Dragsters 1:24

NNO Joe Amato 40.00 80.00
Superman/2502 1999
NNO Kenny Bernstein 50.00 100.00
Bud Lizard/1500 1999
NNO Kenny Bernstein 30.00 80.00
Bud King/2000 2000
NNO Doug Kalitta 20.00 50.00
MGM Grand/1500 2000
NNO Cory McClenathan 20.00 50.00
MBNA/1500 1998
NNO Gary Scelzi 40.00 80.00
Winston/1500 1999

2001 Revell Funny Car 1:24

NNO Tony Pedregon 25.00 60.00
Castrol Test/3504
NNO John Force 100.00 175.00
Aero Force Test/2508

2003 RSC Collectibles Vintage Pro Stock 1:24

NNN Bill Jenkins 50.00 90.00
Grumpy's Toys 1968 Camaro

1999-03 Supercar/Ertl Vintage Pro Stock 1:18

NNO Wally Booth 40.00 70.00
Rat Pack 1971 Camaro
NNO Don Grotheer 40.00 70.00
1970 Plymouth Barracuda/2000
NNO Bill Jenkins 175.00 300.00
Grumpy's Toy
1969 Camaro/2500 1999
NNO Bill Jenkins 70.00 110.00
Grumpy's Toy
1970 Camaro
NNO Don Nicholson 40.00 70.00
Cobra Jet 1968 Mustang
NNO Gas Ronda 50.00 90.00
Russ Davis Ford/2500
1964 Thunderbolt with 1:64 car
NNO Shirley Shahan 50.00 80.00
Drag-On-Lady 1969 AMX
NNO Ronnie Sox 60.00 100.00
Sox&Martin 1969
Plymouth GTX/5000 2000
NNO Ronnie Sox 60.00 100.00
Sox&Martin '70 Barracuda/3500

2002 Team Caliber Dragsters 1:24

NNO Brandon Bernstein 45.00 70.00
Budweiser/1200
NNO Kenny Bernstein 40.00 70.00
Budweiser King/1200
NNO Larry Dixon 35.00 70.00
Miller Lite/1200

2003 Team Caliber Owner's Series Dragsters 1:24

NNO Brandon Bernstein 45.00 80.00
Budweiser/1200
NNO Kenny Bernstein 60.00 100.00
Budweiser Mac Tools
Color Chrome

2004 Team Caliber Owner's Series Dragsters 1:24

NNO Scott Kalitta 60.00 100.00
Mac Tools Jesse James WCC
Mac Tools/200
NNO Tony Schumacher 40.00 60.00
Army Camo/1200

2001 Thirteen-Twenty Fuelers Dragsters 1:24

NNO Jim Dunn 35.00 60.00
Rainbow/3500
NNO Don Garlits 90.00 150.00
Swamp Rat XII/5000
NNO Dick Kalivoda 35.00 60.00
The Joker/3500
NNO John Mulligan 40.00 75.00
Fighting Irish/3500
NNO Tony Nancy 35.00 60.00
Superior Sizzler/5000
NNO Bruce Wheeler 40.00 75.00
Wheeler Dealer/5000

2002 Thirteen-Twenty Fuelers Dragsters 1:24

NNO Kenny Bernstein 35.00 60.00
Forever Red
Budweiser/5000
NNO Gary Cochran 35.00 60.00
Mr.C/3500
NNO Tommy Ivo 35.00 60.00
Valvoline Deist/5000
NNO Chris Karamesines 35.00 60.00
Captain of the Greek Fleet/3500
NNO Tom McEwen 35.00 60.00
Mongoose/5000
NNO Rick Ramsey 35.00 60.00
Keeling&Clayton
California Charger/5000
NNO Pete Robinson 40.00 75.00
Tinker Toy V/5000

2003 Thirteen-Twenty Fuelers Dragsters 1:24

NNO Steve Carbone
Black
NNO Larry Dixon Sr. 35.00 60.00
Rattler/2500
NNO Don Garlits 35.00 60.00
Swamp Rat X/5000
NNO Connie Kalitta 35.00 60.00
Bounty Hunter/3500
NNO Don Prudhomme 35.00 60.00
Wynn's Winder/3500
NNO Kenny Safford 35.00 60.00
Gotelli Speed Shop/2500

2004 Thirteen-Twenty Fuelers/Diggers Dragsters 1:24

NNO Steve Carbone 35.00 60.00
Crietz&Donovan/2500
NNO Don Garlits 40.00 70.00
Swamp Rat VI/5000
NNO Roland Leong 45.00 75.00
Hawaiian/5000
NNO Bennie Osborn 35.00 60.00
The Wizard/2000
NNO Tom McEwen 35.00 60.00
Yeakel Plymouth
NNO Don Prudhomme 35.00 60.00
Greer, Black&Prud/5000

2002 Thirteen-Twenty Floppers Funny Cars 1:24

NNO Don Cook 50.00 80.00
Damn Yankee/3500
NNO Jim Dunn 50.00 80.00
Dunn&Reath/5000
NNO Don Schumacher 50.00 80.00
Stardust/5000

2003 Thirteen-Twenty Floppers Funny Cars 1:24

NNO Leroy Goldstein 45.00 80.00
Candies&Hughes/2000
NNO Ed McCulloch 45.00 80.00
Wipple&McCulloch/2500
NNO Ron O'Donnell 45.00 80.00
Big Noise/2000
NNO Don Prudhomme 45.00 80.00
40th Anniversary/3500
NNO Don Prudhomme 45.00 80.00
Army/5000
NNO Don Schumacher 45.00 80.00
Wonder Wagon/2500

2004 Thirteen-Twenty Floppers Funny Cars 1:24

NNO Braskett&Burgin 40.00 60.00
NNO Jim Green 45.00 70.00
Green Elephant/1500
NNO Jim Liberman 40.00 60.00
Jungle Jim
NNO Mike Mitchell 45.00 80.00
Hippie
NNO Pisano&Matsubara/1500 50.00 75.00

1997 Winner's Circle Dragsters 1:24

This series marks the teaming of Action Performance and Hasbro. This line of cars was produced for and distributed in the mass-market.

NNO Kenny Bernstein 10.00 25.00
King of Speed
NNO Kenny Bernstein 10.00 25.00
Quaker State
NNO Larry Dixon 10.00 25.00
Don Prudhomme
NNO Mike Dunn 10.00 25.00
Mopar
NNO Shirley Muldowney 10.00 25.00
Action
NNO Don Prudhomme 10.00 25.00
MBNA

1996 Winner's Circle Dragsters 1:64

NNO Shirley Muldowney 5.00 10.00
Action

1997 Winner's Circle Dragsters 1:64

This series marks the teaming of Action Performance and Hasbro. This line of cars was produced for and distributed in the mass-market.

NNO Kenny Bernstein 7.50 15.00
King of Speed
NNO Larry Dixon 3.00 8.00
Don Prudhomme Black
NNO Larry Dixon 6.00 12.00
Don Prudhomme White
NNO M.Dunn 3.00 8.00
Mopar
NNO Eddie Hill 7.50 15.00
Pennzoil
NNO Shirley Muldowney 6.00 12.00
Action

1997 Winner's Circle Funny Car 1:24

This series marks the teaming of Action Performance and Hasbro. This line of cars was produced for and distributed in the mass-market. It is highlighted by the John Force Lifetime Series.

NNO Pat Austin Red Wing Shoes	10.00	25.00
NNO Chuck Etchells Kendell	12.50	25.00
NNO John Force Castrol GTX	15.00	30.00
NNO John Force Castrol GTX Black Flames	15.00	30.00
NNO Tom Hoover Pioneer	12.50	25.00

1998 Winner's Circle Funny Car 1:24

NNO John Force Castrol GTX	15.00	30.00
NNO John Force Castrol GTX Elvis	15.00	30.00

2000 Winner's Circle Funny Car 1:24

NNO John Force Castrol GTX Superman	20.00	35.00

2001 Winner's Circle Funny Car 1:24

NNO Tony Pedregon Castrol Syntec	10.00	25.00

2002 Winner's Circle Funny Car 1:24

NNO John Force Castrol GTX	10.00	25.00
NNO John Force Castrol GTX Elvis	10.00	25.00
NNO John Force Castrol GTX 11-Time Champ	15.00	30.00
NNO John Force Castrol GTX Tasca Red	15.00	30.00
NNO Tony Pedregon Castrol Muppets	15.00	30.00

2003 Winner's Circle Funny Car 1:24

NNO John Force Castrol GTX 11X Champ	15.00	30.00
NNO John Force Castrol King of Hill	12.50	25.00
NNO Tony Pedregon Castrol KISS	15.00	30.00

1997 Winner's Circle Funny Car 1:64

This series marks the teaming of Action Performance and Hasbro. This line of cars was produced for and distributed in the mass-market. It is highlighted by the John Force Lifetime Series.

NNO Pat Austin Red Wing	3.00	8.00
NNO Chuck Etchells Kendell	4.00	10.00
NNO John Force Castrol GTX	4.00	10.00
NNO John Force Castrol GTX Black	4.00	10.00
NNO Tom Hoover Pioneer	4.00	10.00

1998 Winner's Circle Funny Car 1:64

NNO John Force Castrol GTX Gold 7-Time Champ	4.00	10.00
NNO John Force Castrol GTX Elvis	4.00	10.00
NNO John Force Castrol GTX Superman	5.00	12.00
NNO Cruz Pedregon Interstate Batteries Small Soldiers	3.00	8.00

2002 Winner's Circle Driver Sticker Funny Car 1:64

NNO John Force Castrol GTX 11-Time Champ	5.00	10.00
NNO Tony Pedregon Castrol Muppets	5.00	10.00

2003 Winner's Circle Driver Sticker Funny Car 1:64

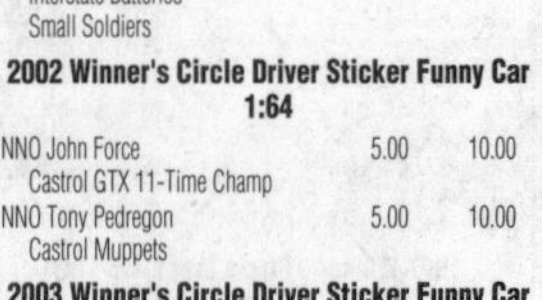

NNO John Force Castrol GTX King of the Hill	4.00	8.00

1998 Winner's Circle Lifetime Series John Force 1:64

1 John Force Castrol GTX 1997	3.00	6.00
2 John Force Castrol GTX Flames 1996	3.00	6.00
3 John Force Castrol GTX 1993	3.00	6.00
4 John Force Brute Force blue 1977	3.00	6.00
5 John Force Castrol GTX 1994 Champ	3.00	6.00
6 John Force Brute Force orange 1978	3.00	6.00
7 John Force Castrol GTX Black 1997	3.00	6.00
8 John Force Castrol GTX 1998	3.00	6.00

2002 Winner's Circle NHRA Transporters 1:64

NNO John Force Castrol GTX 11-Time Champ	12.50	25.00
NNO Tony Pedregon Castrol Muppets	12.50	25.00

1999 Action Indy Cars 1:18

4 Juan Montoya Target Renard/5000	75.00	125.00
6 Michael Andretti K-Mart Swift/5000	60.00	120.00
7 Max Papis Miller Lite Renard/3500	30.00	60.00
7 Max Papis Miller Harley-Davidson Renard/4008	60.00	120.00
8 Brian Herta Shell Renard/3500	35.00	70.00
10 Richie Hearn Budweiser/3500	45.00	80.00
12 Jimmy Vasser Target Renard/3500	40.00	80.00
12 Jimmy Vasser Target Superman/5784	125.00	250.00
17 Mauricio Gugelmin Pac West Renard/3500	20.00	50.00
33 Patrick Carpentier Forsythe Renard/3500	50.00	100.00
40 Adrian Fernandez Tecate	90.00	150.00
97 Cristiano Da Matta Pioneer Renard	60.00	100.00
99 Greg Moore Forsythe Renard/3500	125.00	200.00

2000 Action Indy Cars 1:18

1 Greg Ray Conseco Menards/2304	25.00	60.00
3 Al Unser Jr. Tickets.com G-Force/3504	30.00	60.00
3 Al Unser Jr. Tickets.com AP Box	20.00	35.00
3 Al Unser Jr. Tickets.com Dracula/1416	40.00	80.00
4 Scott Goodyear Pennzoil Dallara/2304	35.00	80.00
8 Kenny Brack Shell Renard/2502	30.00	60.00
9 Juan Montoya Target/2304	75.00	125.00
27 Dario Franchitti Team Green Reynard/3500	40.00	80.00
40 Adrian Frenandez Quaker State Tecate	60.00	100.00
97 Cristiano DaMatta Pioneer MCI/3504	50.00	100.00

2001 Action Indy Cars 1:18

1 NDA Indy 500 Event Car G-Force	40.00	80.00
8 Kenny Brack Shell Renard/3800	35.00	70.00
33 Tony Stewart Target Indy 500/7704	50.00	100.00
51 Eddie Cheever Excite@Home Infiniti/990	40.00	70.00
91 Buddy Lazier TaeBo/666	40.00	80.00

2002 Action Indy Cars 1:18

4 Sam Hornish Jr. Pennzoil/2004 in AP Box	60.00	90.00
5 Rick Treadway Meijer/3000 in an AP box	20.00	40.00
02 Indianapolis 500/108	40.00	75.00

2003 Action Indy Cars 1:18

3 Paul Tracy Forsythe Norick/1284 in window box	50.00	80.00
3 Paul Tracy It's Your World/1560	75.00	125.00
4 Sam Hornish Pennzoil/958	40.00	75.00
4 Sam Hornish Jr. Pennzoil T3/1196	40.00	75.00
5 Adrian Fernandez Tecate/144	90.00	150.00
5 Adrian Fernandez Tecate AP window box	40.00	75.00
7 Michael Andretti 7-11/2326	40.00	75.00
8 Scott Sharp Delphi/1328	40.00	70.00
10 Thomas Scheckter Target/1232	40.00	70.00
11 Tony Kanaan 7-11 Hulk/1272	40.00	75.00
31 Al Unser Jr. Corteco/1410	40.00	70.00
32 Patrick Carpentier It's Your World	60.00	100.00
51 Eddie Cheever Red Bull/1196	40.00	70.00

2004 Action Indy Cars 1:18

2 Sebastien Bourdais McDonald's/1008	75.00	125.00
3 Paul Tracy Forsythe Last Lap 2003 Champion/1596	90.00	150.00

1999 Action Indy Cars 1:43

1 Max Papis Miller Lite Renard/5000	12.50	25.00
4 Juan Montoya Target Renard/6000	20.00	40.00
6 Michael Andretti K-Mart Havoline/6000	15.00	30.00
12 Jimmy Vasser Target Renard	15.00	25.00
33 Patrick Carpentier Forsythe Renard/5000	12.50	25.00
40 Adrian Fernandez Tecate	20.00	40.00
99 Greg Moore Forsythe Renard/5000	40.00	80.00

2000 Action Indy Cars 1:43

26 Paul Tracy Kool Green/3816	15.00	40.00
NNO Team Ganassi Target 4 for 4 Champs Four car set in tin/2800 Jimmy Vasser Alex Zanardi Juan Montoya	30.00	50.00

2000 Action Indy Cars 1:64

3 Al Unser Jr. Tickets.com Dracula	3.00	8.00
4 Juan Montoya Target Renard Indy 500 Win	3.00	8.00

1998-04 Carousel 1 Vintage Indy 1:18

Carousel 1 produces this line of former Indy 500 racers. Each was manufactured in great detail and produced in limited quantities. The series began in 1998 with the A.J. Foyt 1961 Bowes Seal Fast car.

1 A.J. Foyt Bowes Seal Fast 1961	200.00	350.00
1 A.J. Foyt Sheraton Thompson 1964	75.00	135.00
2 Johnny Rutherford Gatorade 1975	75.00	125.00
2 Bill Vukovich Jr. Sugaripe Prunes 1973	60.00	120.00
3 Johnny Rutherford McLaren 1974	60.00	120.00
3 Rodger Ward Leader Card 1962	75.00	125.00
4 Jim Rathmann Ken-Paul 1960	75.00	125.00
4 Bill Vukovich Hopkins 1955	70.00	110.00
6 Bob Sweikert John Zink 1955	70.00	110.00
6 Bobby Unser Olsonite Eagle 1972	75.00	125.00
8 Pat Flaherty John Zink 1956	70.00	110.00
10 Tony Bettenhausen Chapman 1955	75.00	125.00
11 Pancho Carter Firestone 1974	60.00	120.00
12 Don Freeland Bob Estes Special 1955	70.00	110.00
12 Eddie Sachs Dean Van Lines 1961	70.00	110.00
14 A.J. Foyt Sheraton Thompson 1967	80.00	135.00
14 Bill Vukovich Fuel Injection 1953	70.00	110.00
16 Johnnie Parsons Trio Brass	70.00	110.00
19 Rodger Ward Filter Queen 1956	75.00	125.00
20 Gordon Johncock STP 1973	75.00	125.00
26 Norm Hall Nothing Special 1964	70.00	110.00
36 Dan Gurney Eagle-Gurney 1967	75.00	125.00
44 Jim Rathmann Simoniz Vista 1962	70.00	110.00
48 Jerry Grant Mystery 1972	75.00	125.00
48 Bobby Unser Jergensen 1975	75.00	125.00
56 Jim Hurtubise Travelon Trailer 1960	60.00	110.00
66 Mark Donohue Sunoco '73	75.00	125.00
73 David Hobbs Carling 1974	75.00	125.00
73 Mike Nazaruk McNamara 1954	75.00	125.00
82 Jim Clark Lotus 1965	75.00	135.00
86 Johnny Rutherford Bardahl 1964	75.00	125.00
98 Parnelli Jones Agajanian 1962	60.00	110.00
98 Lloyd Ruby Agajanian 1960	60.00	110.00

2002 Carousel 1 Hobby Horse Vintage Indy 1:43

1 A.J. Foyt Bowes Seal Fast 1961	40.00	75.00
3 Rodger Ward Leader Card 1962	20.00	35.00
4 Jim Rathmann Ken-Paul 1960	20.00	35.00
32 Ray Harroun Marmom Wasp 1911	20.00	35.00

1996 EPI Indy 1:24

28 Bryan Herta Shell/20,000	7.50	20.00

1998 Ertl Indy CART 1:18

4 Alex Zanardi Target	25.00	50.00
5 Gil DeFerran Valvoline	15.00	30.00
7 Bobby Rahal Miller Lite	15.00	40.00
12 Jimmy Vasser Target	20.00	40.00

1999 Ertl Indy CART 1:18

2 Target Coca-Cola	20.00	50.00
6 Michael Andretti Newman-Haas	25.00	50.00
11 Christian Fittipaldi K-Mart Coca-Cola	20.00	50.00

1985 Ertl Motorized Pullback Indy Cars 1:43

1 Rick Mears Gould	30.00	60.00
11 Bobby Unser Gould Norton Spirit	12.50	25.00
12 Bill Alsup A.B. Dick Pacemaker	10.00	20.00
12 Mario Andretti Essex	20.00	40.00

1998 Ertl Indy CART 1:43

3 Robbie Buhl Glidden	10.00	20.00
5 Arie Luyendyk Nortel	150.00	250.00

2004 GreenLight IRL 1:18

2 Mark Taylor Johns Mansville/1500	30.00	50.00
3 Helio Castroneves Penske Mobil 1/2502	35.00	50.00
4 Thomas Scheckter Pennzoil/2502	30.00	50.00
5 Adrian Fernandez Quaker State Tecate	30.00	50.00
6 Sam Hornish Jr. Penske Mobil 1/3504	35.00	50.00
8 Scott Sharp Delphi/2502	35.00	50.00
11 Tony Kanaan 7-11 Big Gulp/2004	35.00	50.00
14 A.J. Foyt IV Conseco/1002	35.00	50.00
26 Dan Wheldon Klein Tools/2004	30.00	50.00
27 Dario Franchitti Arca Ex/1500	30.00	50.00
39 Sarah Fisher Bryant/2502	35.00	50.00
70 Robby Gordon Meijer/1080	35.00	50.00
04 Indy 500 Event Car	30.00	50.00

2005 GreenLight IRL 1:18

16 Danica Patrick Argent white number/1500	100.00	200.00
16 Danica Patrick Argent yellow number/10,000	50.00	100.00

2007 GreenLight IRL Garage Series 1:18

3 Helio Castroneves Team Penske/1200	25.00	60.00
4 Vitor Meira Delphi	25.00	60.00
6 Sam Hornish Jr. Team Penske/1800	25.00	60.00
7 Danica Patrick Motorola/7500	40.00	80.00
8 Scott Sharp Patron Tequilla/996	25.00	60.00
9 Scott Dixon Target/750	25.00	60.00
10 Dan Wheldon Target/1002	25.00	60.00
11 Tony Kanaan 7-Eleven/2400	25.00	60.00
14 Darren Manning ABC Supply/3500	25.00	60.00
17 Jeff Simmons Ethanol/1800	25.00	60.00
26 Marco Andretti New York Stock Exchange/3000	25.00	60.00
26 Michael Andretti New York Stock Exchange/1500	25.00	60.00
27 Dario Franchitti Canadian Club/996	25.00	60.00

2002 GreenLight Indy Cars 1:64

2 Jaques Lazier Team Menard/1600	6.00	10.00
3 Helio Castroneves Penske Chrome 2002 Indy 500 Champ/5000	6.00	10.00
4 Sam Hornish Jr. Pennzoil 2002 IRL Champ/1600	6.00	10.00
7 Al Unser Jr. Corteco/2000	6.00	10.00
9 Jeff Ward Target/1200	6.00	10.00
23 Sarah Fisher SmartBlade/2400	6.00	12.00
03 Indy Racing Trophy/1600	7.50	15.00

2003 GreenLight Indy Cars 1:64

4 Sam Hornish Pennzoil/5000	7.50	15.00
7 Michael Andretti 7-11/3000	7.50	15.00
9 Scott Dixon Target Fuji/1200	7.50	20.00
10 Thomas Scheckter Target Fuji/3000	7.50	15.00
14 A.J. Foyt IV Conseco/3500	7.50	15.00
21 Filipe Giaffone MoNunn/3000	7.50	15.00
23 Sarah Fisher Purex/5000	7.50	20.00
24 Robbie Buhl Purex Dial/3000	7.50	15.00
31 Al Unser Jr. Corteco/3500	7.50	15.00
51 Eddie Cheever Jr. Red Bull/3500	7.50	15.00
03 Indianapolis 500/2003	7.50	15.00
03 IRL Art in Motion in box	6.00	12.00
03 IRL Art in Motion in box 500 Festival hood/750	7.50	15.00
NNO Indy Japan 300 Promo/3700	7.50	15.00
NNO Sam Schmidt Sprint PCS Paralysis Foundation Promo/5000	7.50	15.00

2004 GreenLight IRL 1:64

1 Scott Dixon Target Ganassi/4032	6.00	12.00
2 Mark Taylor Johns Manville/3204	6.00	12.00
3 Helio Castroneves Penske Mobil 1/5040	6.00	12.00
4 Thomas Scheckter Pennzoil/4032	6.00	12.00
6 Sam Hornish Jr. Penske Mobil 1/7536	6.00	12.00
8 Scott Sharp Delphi/3800	6.00	12.00
11 Tony Kanaan 7-11 Big Gulp/4512	6.00	12.00
14 A.J. Foyt IV Conseco/7008	6.00	12.00
26 Dan Wheldon Klein Tools/3024	6.00	12.00
27 Dario Franchitti Arca Ex/3024	6.00	12.00
39 Sarah Fisher Bryant/4512	6.00	12.00
04 Indy 500 Corvette Pace Car/2000	5.00	10.00
04 Indy 500 Event Car/2004	5.00	10.00

2005 GreenLight IRL 1:64

3 Helio Castroneves Penske Mobil	7.50	15.00
4 Tomas Schecker Pennzoil	7.50	15.00
6 Sam Hornish Jr. Penske Mobil	7.50	15.00
7 Brian Herta XM Satellite Radio	7.50	15.00
9 Scott Dixon Target	7.50	15.00
10 Darren Manning Target	7.50	15.00
11 Tony Kanaan 7-Eleven	10.00	20.00
15 Buddy Rice Argent	7.50	15.00
16 Danica Patrick Argent white number	15.00	30.00
16 Danica Patrick Argent yellow number	12.50	25.00
26 Dan Wheldon Klein Tools	10.00	20.00
27 Dario Franchitti Arca Ex	7.50	15.00

2006 GreenLight IRL 1:64

1 Michael Andretti Vonage	7.50	15.00

2007 GreenLight IRL Garage Series 1:64

lio Castroneves 6.00 12.00
eam Penske/4176
or Meira 6.00 12.00
elphi
m Hornish Jr. 6.00 12.00
eam Penske/4656
nica Patrick 7.50 15.00
Motorola/22,000
ott Dixon 6.00 12.00
arget/2544
an Wheldon 6.00 12.00
arget/4368
ony Kanaan 6.00 12.00
-Eleven/4176
arren Manning 6.00 12.00
BC Supply/6480
eff Simmons 6.00 12.00
thanol/10,032
Marco Andretti 6.00 12.00
New York Stock Exchange/12,000
ario Franchitti 6.00 12.00
anadian Club/1584

2003 GreenLight Indy Transporters 1:64

m Hornish Jr. 10.00 20.00
Pennzoil/1500
ddie Cheever Jr. 10.00 20.00
Red Bull/1500
) IndyCar Series/1500 10.00 20.00

1993 Hot Wheels Pro Circuit Indy 1:64

ichael Andretti 2.50 6.00
Texaco
ario Andretti 2.50 6.00
Texaco
Unser Jr. 2.00 5.00
Valvoline
ck Mears 2.00 5.00
Penske

1998 Hot Wheels First Edition Indy 1:64

ex Zanardi 4.00 10.00
Target
l DeFerran 3.00 8.00
Walker
ichael Andretti 3.00 8.00
Havoline
Patrick Carpentier 4.00 10.00
Alumax
Max Papis 3.00 8.00
MCI

1998 Hot Wheels Pro Racing 1 Indy 1:64

s was Hot Wheels basic issue CART IndyCar brand for 1998. n car was issued in a blue and red blister package in the pe of the #1.

il DeFerran 2.00 4.00
Walker
yan Herta 2.00 4.00
Team Rahal
Richie Hearn 2.00 4.00
Della Penna
Andre Ribeiro 2.00 4.00
Tasman

1970 Johnny Lightning Indy 500 1:64

) Al Unser
) A.J. Foyt

996 Johnny Lightning Indy 500 Champs and Pace Cars 1:64

h of these Indy Car Champion's die-cast was packaged with ie-cast replica of that year's Indy 500 pace car. There were different packaging types used for each of the two-car packs. of the packaging types featured a series number (from 1-5) he lower right hand corner. The sixth included no series nber. The top half of the blister pack for series 1-5 featured a erent race scene as follows: series 1-aerial view of track, 2-road action, 3-view down straight away, 4-car in a pit stall, 1 5-cars crossing the finish line. The final unnumbered kage included a large art image of an Indy car.

Mario Andretti 2.00 5.00
1969 Winner
l Unser 2.00 5.00
1970 Winner
l Unser 2.00 5.00
1978 Winner
ohnny Rutherford 2.00 5.00
1974 Winner
Al Unser Jr. 2.00 5.00
1992 Winner
Rick Mears 2.00 5.00
1979 Winner
A.J. Foyt 2.00 5.00
1977 Winner
Bobby Unser 2.00 5.00
1975 Winner

1999 Johnny Lightning Indy 1:64

Johnny Lightning issued these Indy Car die-cast in 1999 in traditional blister packaging. Most were part of their regular series of "Indy Racing League" as noted on the blisters in red lettering. Each of those also included a production run number of 7500. The others in this checklist are various promos issued through their club or at racing events throughout the season.

1 Al Unser 10.00 20.00
1971 Indy Winner
Club Promo/1000
2 Glidden/7500 2.00 5.00
4 Scott Goodyear 2.50 6.00
Pennzoil/7500
5 Arie Luyendyk 2.00 5.00
Sprint Meijer/7500
8 Scott Sharp 2.50 6.00
Delphi/7500
11 Billy Boat 2.00 5.00
Conseco/7500
14 Kenny Brack 3.00 6.00
Pep Boys
14 Kenny Brack 4.00 8.00
Power Team Indy 500 Win
28 Mark Dismore 3.00 6.00
MCIWorldcom/7500
99 Indy 500 Promo/12,000 2.50 6.00

2000 Johnny Lightning Indy 1:64

This series of Johnny Lightning die-cast pieces were issued in "IRL" blister packs as noted by the IRL logo in the center of the packaging. A few others listed below were issued in promo style blister packages.

4 S.Goodyear 2.50 6.00
Pennzoil
11 Greg Ray 2.50 6.00
Conseco
24 Robbie Buhl 2.50 6.00
Purex
28 Mark Dismore 2.50 6.00
Delphi/5000
91 Buddy Lazier 2.50 6.00
Tae Bo
0 Indy 500 Promo/15,000 2.50 6.00

2001 Johnny Lightning Indy 1:64

This series of Johnny Lightning die-cast pieces were issued in "IRL" blister packs as noted by the IRL logo in the center of the packaging. The packaging is virtually identical to the 2000 release except for the addition of a large silver sticker featuring the driver's name and the production total. The 2001 IRL season schedule is included on the back of the blisters.

15 Sarah Fisher 10.00 25.00
IRL/5000
31 Casey Mears 3.00 8.00
Sportsline.com/3000

1998 Maisto Indy Racing 1:18

1 Tony Stewart 70.00 120.00
Glidden
40 Jack Miller 15.00 40.00
Crest
91 Buddy Lazier 15.00 40.00
Delta Faucet
98 American Red Cross 20.00 40.00

1999 Maisto Indy Racing 1:18

5 Arie Luyendyk 30.00 60.00
Meijer/5000
22 Tony Stewart 75.00 150.00
Home Depot

1999 Maisto Indy Racing 1:24

1 Tony Stewart
Glidden

1999 Maisto Indy Racing 1:64

1 Tony Stewart 6.00 15.00
Glidden/20,000
3 Robbie Buhl 2.00 5.00
Johns Manville
4 Scott Goodyear 2.00 5.00
Pennzoil
5 Arie Luyendyk 2.00 5.00
Sprint Meijer
11 Billy Boat 2.00 5.00
Conseco
40 Jack Miller 2.00 5.00
Crest
91 Buddy Lazier 2.00 5.00
Delta Faucet

1991 Matchbox Indy 500 Coins/Die-Cast 1:55

This series was released in 1991 by Matchbox. Each yellow, red and black blister package included one Indy 500 collector coin featuring a car and/or driver of a race winning Indy 500 event or other event such as fastest lap. The coin was packaged with a random die-cast Indy car or other Indy related piece such as a fuel truck. Many of the plastic Indy cars were produced to resemble actual cars driven during the event while others are generic in nature. There are many different combinations of die-cast and coins packaged together at random so we've cataloged each blister package below only by the identification of the coin and in order of the year of the Indy event featured on the coin. Note also that the backs of the blisters sometimes feature a copyright year of 1990, but all were issued for the 75th running of the Indy 500 in 1991 as noted on the logo included on the blister.

1911 Ray Harroun 2.50 6.00
1956 Graham Hill 2.50 6.00
1965 Jim Clark 2.50 6.00
1966 Graham Hill 2.50 6.00
1977 A.J. Foyt 2.50 6.00
1987 Al Unser 2.50 6.00
1989 Rick Mears 2.50 6.00
1990 Emerson Fittipaldi 2.50 6.00

1992 Matchbox Indy 500 Coins/Die-Cast 1:55

This series was released in 1992 by Matchbox. Each yellow, red and black blister package included one die-cast Indy 500 collector coin featuring a car and/or driver of a race winning Indy 500 event or other event such as fastest lap. The coin was packaged with a random plastic Indy car or other Indy related piece such as a fuel truck. Many of the cars were produced to resemble actual Indy cars driven during the event while others are generic in nature. There are many different combinations of die-cast and coins packaged together at random so we've cataloged each blister package below only by the identification of the coin and in order of the year of the Indy event featured on the coin. Note also that the backs of the blisters sometimes feature a copyright year of 1990 or 1991, but all were issued for the 76th running of the Indy 500 in 1992 as noted on the logo included on the blister.

1911 Ray Harroun 2.50 6.00
1937 Wilbur Shaw 2.50 6.00
1956 Graham Hill 2.50 6.00
1965 Jim Clark 2.50 6.00
1977 A.J. Foyt 2.50 6.00
1977 Tom Sneva Fast Lap 2.50 6.00
1987 Al Unser 2.50 6.00
1990 Arie Luyendyk Fast Lap 2.50 6.00
1991 Rick Mears 5.00 10.00

1993 Matchbox Indy 500 Closest Finish 1:55

This series of die-cast cars was produced by Matchbox and issued on a blister card carrying the title "Indy 500 Closest Finish Ever." Each blister contained two Indy car die-casts positioned as if they were crossing the finish line at the race. Note that the copyright line on the back reads "1992" but is considered a 1993 issued since it was predominantly issued that year.

3/15 A.Unser Jr. 6.00 15.00
Valvoline
Scott Goodyear
MacKenzie

1993 Matchbox Indy 500 Coins/Die-Cast 1:55

This series was released in 1993 by Matchbox. Each yellow, red and blue blister package included one plastic Indy 500 collector coin featuring a car and/or driver of a race winning Indy 500 event or other event such as fastest lap. The coin was packaged with either a die-cast Indy car, a fuel truck, or a wrecker. There were six different die-cast cars produced to resemble actual Indy cars driven during the event, one generic Indy car die-cast (black, green and pink paint scheme), and the fuel truck and wrecker which were all randomly packaged with one of the coins. We've cataloged and priced each blister package below only by the identification of the coin and in order of the year of the Indy event featured on the coin since this is how they are normally sold. Slight premiums are often paid on combinations that include one of the more popular coins and a popular paint scheme of die-cast. Note also that the backs of the blisters feature a copyright year of 1992, but all were issued during 1993. This series is a continuation of the 1991 and 1992 sets and can be identified by the simple Indianapolis Motor Speedway logo on the front instead of the logos which indicate the year of issue used in 1991 and 1992. Also, the die-cast piece rests on top of a red cardboard display within the blister package.

1936 Louis Meyer 2.50 6.00
1980 Johnny Rutherford 2.50 6.00
1985 Danny Sullivan 2.50 6.00
1989 Emerson Fittipaldi 2.50 6.00
1992 Al Unser Jr. 2.50 6.00

1991 Matchbox Indy 500 Transporters 1:87

This series of was produced by Matchbox and issued in a yellow window box carrying the title "Indy 500" along with the logo for the 75th Indy 500. Each package contained an Indy car die-cast with a flat bed transporter or a tractor trailer rig with or without die-cast cars.

2 Rick Mears 5.00 12.00
Pennzoil Trailer Rig
2 Rick Mears 6.00 15.00
Pennzoil Flat Bed w
car
3 Al Unser Jr. 6.00 15.00
Valvoline Kraco
5 Emerson Fittipaldi 6.00 15.00
Valvoline Flat Bed
22 Scott Brayton 6.00 15.00
Amway
NNO Team Matchbox Rig 5.00 12.00
NNO 75th Indy 500 black&pink 10.00 20.00
Tractor Trailer Rig with 2-cars
NNO Team Valvoline Rig 5.00 12.00

1992 Matchbox Indy 500 Transporters 1:87

This series of was produced by Matchbox and issued in a yellow window box carrying the title "Indy 500" along with the logo for the 76th Indy 500. Each package contained a tractor trailer rig without a car or a flat bed truck with a car.

6 Michael Andretti 6.00 15.00
Havoline Flat Bed
NNO Pennzoil Rig 5.00 12.00
NNO K-Mart Havoline Rig 5.00 12.00
NNO Panasonic Rig 5.00 12.00

1993 Matchbox Indy 500 Transporters 1:87

This series of was produced by Matchbox and issued in a yellow window box carrying the title "Indy 500" along with a generic Indianapolis Motor Speedway logo instead of the year specific logos found in the 1991 and 1992 releases. Similar to 1991 and 1992, each package contained a tractor trailer rig without a car or a flat bed truck with a car. Additionally, a 1:55 scale Indy 500 event trailer was also released along with 2-Indy cars.

3 Al Unser Jr. 6.00 15.00
Valvoline Flat Bed
11 Raul Boesel 6.00 15.00
Panasonic Flat Bed
15 Scott Goodyear 6.00 15.00
Mackenzie Flat Bed
NNO Indy 500 1:55 scale Rig with 2-cars 10.00 20.00
NNO Team Mackenzie Rig 5.00 12.00
NNO Team Valvoline Rig 5.00 12.00

1993 MiniChamps Indy Road Course 1:18

3 Al Unser Jr. 150.00 250.00
Valvoline
4 Emerson Fittipaldi 75.00 125.00
Marlboro
5 Nigel Mansell 75.00 125.00
Kmart
6 Michael Andretti 60.00 100.00
K-Mart
9 Raul Boesel 40.00 75.00
Duracell
12 Paul Tracy 150.00 250.00
Marlboro/3333
12 Paul Tracy 60.00 100.00
Penske

1993 MiniChamps Indy Speedway 1:18

3 Al Unser Jr. 90.00 150.00
Valvoline
4 Emerson Fittipaldi 75.00 125.00
Marlboro
4 Emerson Fittipaldi 35.00 60.00
Penske
5 Nigel Mansell 40.00 75.00
Kmart
6 Michael Andretti 60.00 100.00
K-Mart
9 Raul Boesel 40.00 75.00
Duracell
12 Paul Tracy 125.00 200.00
Marlboro
12 Paul Tracy 60.00 100.00
Penske

1994 MiniChamps Indy Road Course 1:18

6 Michael Andretti 40.00 75.00
K-Mart
19 Alessandro Zampedri 40.00 60.00
Mi-Jack
23 Buddy Lazier 40.00 60.00
Owens
24 Willy T. Ribbs 40.00 75.00
Service Merchandise
31 Al Unser Jr. 125.00 200.00
Marlboro
31 Al Unser Jr. 90.00 150.00
Penske
55 John Andretti 40.00 60.00
Gillette

1994 MiniChamps Indy Speedway 1:18

2 Emerson Fittipaldi 125.00 200.00
Marlboro
2 Emerson Fittipaldi 40.00 75.00
Penske
3 Paul Tracy 125.00 200.00
Marlboro
19 Alessandro Zampedri 35.00 60.00
Mi-Jack
31 Al Unser Jr. 150.00 250.00
Marlboro
31 Al Unser Jr. 60.00 100.00
Penske

1995 MiniChamps Indy 1:18

3 Pual Tracy 100.00 175.00
Budweiser Kmart
5 Robby Gordon 40.00 75.00
Valvoline
6 Michael Andretti 75.00 125.00
K-Mart Texaco
9 Bobby Rahal 75.00 150.00
Miller Genuine Draft/3333
27 Jacques Villeneuve 250.00 400.00
Klein Tools Players/3333

1996 MiniChamps Indy IRL 1:18

4 Richie Hearn 35.00 50.00
Food For Less
12 Buzz Calkins 35.00 50.00
Bradley
36 Juan Fangio 30.00 50.00
Toyota-Castrol
91 Buddy Lazier 35.00 50.00
Delta
98 P.J. Jones 35.00 50.00
Toyota-Castrol

1997 MiniChamps Indy 1:18

31 Al Unser Jr. 40.00 75.00
Penske

1999 MiniChamps Indy 1:18

26 Paul Tracy 75.00 135.00
Klein Tools Green

1993 MiniChamps Indy 1:43

Each piece comes in both a road course and speedway version. This was the first year for Paul's Model Art to do 1:43 scale Indy cars.

3 Al Unser Jr. 15.00 30.00
Valvoline
4 Emerson Fittipaldi 12.50 25.00
Penske
5 Nigel Mansell 12.00 20.00
K-Mart
6 Mario Andretti 15.00 25.00
K-Mart
9 Raul Boesel 12.00 20.00
Duracell
12 Paul Tracy 12.00 20.00
Penske

1994 MiniChamps Indy Road Course 1:43

12 Jacques Villeneuve 200.00 350.00
Players/4444
19 Alessandro Zampedri 10.00 25.00
Mi-Jack
28 Arie Luyendyk 12.50 25.00
Regency IBM/4444
31 Al Unser Jr. 18.00 30.00
Penske

1994 MiniChamps Indy Speedway 1:43

2 Emerson Fittipaldi 20.00 35.00
Penske/5555
3 Paul Tracy 15.00 25.00
Penske/3333
5 Nigel Mansell 30.00 50.00
Kmart
6 Mario Andretti 15.00 25.00
K-Mart
7 Adrian Fernandez 15.00 25.00
Tecate/4444
8 Michael Andretti 25.00 40.00
Target
16 Stefan Johansson 12.00 20.00
Alumax
19 Alessandro Zampedri 12.00 20.00
Mi-Jack
22 Hiro Matsushita 12.00 20.00
Panasonic
31 Al Unser Jr. 18.00 30.00
Penske

1995 MiniChamps Indy Road Course 1:43

15 Christian Fittipaldi 15.00 25.00
Walker Racing/4444

27 Jacques Villeneuve Klein Tools/4444 40.00 75.00
31 Andre Ribeiro LCI 15.00 25.00

1995 MiniChamps Indy Speedway 1:43

27 Jacques Villeneuve Klein Tools/4444 40.00 75.00

1996 MiniChamps Indy IRL 1:43

Only three drivers and four Indy cars were released from Paul's Model Art in 1995. Each car features a Road Course set up.

4 Richie Hearn Food 4 Less 10.00 22.00
12 Buzz Calkins Bradley 10.00 22.00
20 Tony Stewart Menards Glidden/4444 25.00 40.00
20 Tony Stewart Quaker State/4444 15.00 30.00

1996 MiniChamps Indy Road Course 1:43

1 Nigel Mansell K-Mart 12.00 20.00
4 Bobby Rahal Miller Genuine Draft 12.00 20.00
6 Mario Andretti K-Mart 15.00 25.00
9 Robby Gordon Valvoline 15.00 25.00
17 Mauricio Gugelmin Hollywood 10.00 20.00
19 Alessandro Zampedri Mi-Jack 12.00 20.00
23 Buddy Lazier Randy Owens 12.00 20.00
24 Willy T. Ribbs Walker Racing 12.00 20.00
28 Arie Luyendyk Eurosports 12.00 20.00
31 Al Unser Jr. Penske 15.00 30.00
55 John Andretti Gillette 12.00 20.00

1993 Onyx Indy 1:24

This was the first year die-cast manufacturer Onyx began producing 1:24 scale indy cars. There were four cars featured.

2 Scott Goodyear Mackenzie Financial 20.00 35.00
3 Al Unser Jr. Valvoline 15.00 40.00
5 Nigel Mansell K-Mart 20.00 35.00
6 Mario Andretti K-Mart 20.00 35.00

1994 Onyx Indy 1:24

The late Scott Brayton highlights the two 1:24 Indy cars released by Onyx in 1994.

9 Raul Boesel Duracell 20.00 40.00
23 Scott Brayton Amway 25.00 50.00

1995 Onyx Indy 1:24

60 Scott Brayton Quaker State Menards Indy 500 Pole Win 60.00 100.00

1996 Onyx Indy 1:24

6 Arie Luyendyk Target 20.00 35.00
20 Tony Stewart Quaker State Menards Indy 500 Pole Win 75.00 150.00
NNO Scott Pruett Firestone 18.00 30.00

1990 Onyx Indy 1:43

This was the first year Onyx began producing 1:43 scale Indy cars. The series is highlighted by Rick Mears and variations of the Emerson Fittipaldi and Danny Sullivan cars.

1 Emerson Fittipaldi Marlboro w black wheels 50.00 80.00
1 Emerson Fittipaldi Marlboro w silver wheels 20.00 40.00
2 Rick Mears Pennzoil 50.00 100.00
3 Michael Andretti K-Mart 20.00 35.00
4 Teo Fabi Quaker State 15.00 25.00
5 Al Unser Jr. Valvoline 35.00 70.00
6 Mario Andretti K-Mart 25.00 40.00
7 Danny Sullivan Marlboro with decals 30.00 60.00
7 Danny Sullivan Marlboro w o decals 20.00 40.00
9 Tom Sneva RCA 12.50 25.00
11 Kevin Cogan Tuneup Masters 12.50 25.00
12 Randy Lewis AMP Oracle 12.50 25.00
14 A.J. Foyt Copenhagen 25.00 50.00
15 Jim Crawford Glidden 15.00 25.00
18 Bobby Rahal Kraco 18.00 30.00
19 Raul Boesel Budweiser 18.00 30.00
20 Roberto Guerrero Miller Genuine Draft 15.00 25.00
22 Scott Brayton Amway 25.00 40.00
25 Eddie Cheever Target 15.00 25.00
28 Scott Goodyear Mackenzie Financial 15.00 25.00
29 Pancho Carter Hardee's 12.50 25.00
30 Arie Luyendyk Domino's 30.00 50.00
40 Al Unser Sr. Miller 15.00 30.00
41 John Andretti Foster's Quaker State 15.00 25.00
70 Didier Theys Tuneup Masters RCA 12.50 25.00
86 Dominic Dobson Texaco 12.50 25.00

1991 Onyx Indy 1:43

Three members of the Andretti family had cars in this series, Mario, Michael and John. The Kevin Cogan/Glidden car is one of the most difficult of all the Onyx Indy die-cast to find.

2 Al Unser Jr. Valvoline 15.00 40.00
4 John Andretti Pennzoil 15.00 25.00
6 Mario Andretti K-Mart 15.00 25.00
9 Kevin Cogan Glidden 60.00 100.00
10 Michael Andretti K-Mart 25.00 40.00
51 Gary Bettenhausen Glidden 15.00 25.00

1992 Onyx Indy 1:43

This set is highlighted by the A.J.Foyt Copenhagen car. The series also has two beer sponsors Bud and Miller.

10 Scott Pruett Budweiser 12.00 20.00
12 Bobby Rahal Miller Genuine Draft 12.00 20.00
14 A.J. Foyt Copenhagen 25.00 50.00
15 Scott Goodyear Mackenzie Financial 10.00 20.00
23 Scott Brayton Amway 15.00 30.00
27 Al Unser Sr. Conseco 15.00 30.00
36 Roberto Guerrero Quaker State 10.00 20.00

1993 Onyx Indy 1:43

This series marks the first appearance by Nigel Mansell in an Indy car die-cast.

5 Nigel Mansell K-Mart 12.50 25.00
6 Arie Luyendyk Target 12.50 25.00
7 Danny Sullivan Molson 12.00 20.00
9 Raul Boesel Duracell 10.00 20.00
19 Robbie Buhl Mi-Jack 20.00 35.00
27 Geoff Brabham Glidden 20.00 40.00
29 Olivier Grouillard Eurosport 10.00 20.00
32 Eric Bachelart Marmon Wasp II 40.00 75.00
36 Roberto Guerrero Quaker State 10.00 20.00
39 Ross Bentley Rain-X 10.00 20.00

1994 Onyx Indy 1:43

This was the last year that Onyx made an entire line of 1:43 Indy cars.

1 Nigel Mansell K-Mart 10.00 20.00
3 Paul Tracy Penske 15.00 30.00
5 Raul Boesel Duracell 10.00 20.00
6 Mario Andretti K-Mart 10.00 20.00
7 Adrian Fernandez Tecate 10.00 20.00
8 Michael Andretti Target 12.50 25.00
9 Robby Gordon Valvoline 10.00 20.00
11 Teo Fabi Pennzoil 10.00 20.00
18 Jimmy Vasser Conseco 10.00 20.00
21 Roberto Guerrero Interstate Batteries 10.00 20.00
27 Eddie Cheever Quaker State 10.00 20.00
88 Mauricio Gugelmin Hollywood 10.00 20.00

1995 Onyx Indy 1:43

3 Paul Tracy Budweiser 12.50 25.00
60 Scott Brayton Quaker State Promo 15.00 40.00

1996 Onyx Indy 1:43

5 Arie Luyendyk Bryant 12.50 25.00
5 Arie Luyendyk Wavephore 12.50 25.00

1997 Onyx Indy 1:43

17 Mauricio Gugelmin Hollywood Pac West 10.00 20.00

1994-95 Racing Champions Indy Banks 1:24

6 Mario Andretti K-Mart Texaco Bank 1994 12.50 30.00
6 Mario Andretti K-Mart Texaco Bank 1995 12.50 30.00
9 Robby Gordon Valvoline 12.50 30.00

1994-95 Racing Champions Indy Series 1 1:24

Racing Champions issued their 1995 Indy cars in two series. The red, white and blue boxes the pieces come in the state which serie they are from.

1 Nigel Mansell Texaco 1994 12.50 25.00
2 Emerson Fittipaldi Penske Racing 10.00 20.00
3 Paul Tracy Penske 10.00 20.00
4 Bobby Rahal Rahal-Hogan 10.00 20.00
5 Raul Boesel Duracell 10.00 20.00
5 Nigel Mansell Texaco 10.00 20.00
6 Mario Andretti Texaco 10.00 20.00
7 Adrian Fernandez Tecate 10.00 20.00
8 Michael Andretti Target 1994 10.00 20.00
8 Gil de Farran Pennzoil 10.00 20.00
9 Robby Gordon Valvoline 10.00 20.00
10 Mike Groff Motorola 10.00 20.00
11 Teo Fabi Pennzoil 10.00 20.00
18 Jimmy Vasser Conseco 10.00 20.00
22 Hiro Matsushita Panasonic 10.00 20.00
24 Willy T. Ribbs Service Merchandise 10.00 20.00
28 Stefan Johansson Eurosports 10.00 20.00
31 Al Unser Jr. Penske Racing 15.00 30.00
90 Lynn St. James JC Penny's 12.00 22.00

1995 Racing Champions Indy Series 2 1:24

This is the second series of Indy cars from Racing Champions in 1995. The boxes state what series the cars are from.

1 Al Unser Jr. Penske 10.00 30.00
2 Emerson Fittipaldi Penske 10.00 20.00
3 Paul Tracy K-Mart 10.00 20.00
4 Bryan Herta Target 10.00 20.00
5 Robby Gordon Valvoline 12.50 25.00
6 Michael Andretti Valvoline 10.00 20.00
7 Alex Salazar Crystal 10.00 20.00
8 Gil de Ferran Pennzoil 10.00 20.00
9 Bobby Rahal Honda 10.00 20.00
10 Adrian Fernandez Tecate 10.00 20.00
11 Raul Boesel Duracell 10.00 20.00
12 Jimmy Vasser Target 10.00 20.00
15 Christian Fittipaldi Telesena 10.00 20.00
17 Danny Sullivan VISA 10.00 20.00
18 Stefan Johansson Alumax 10.00 20.00
20 Scott Pruett Firestone 10.00 20.00
22 Roberto Guerrero 10.00 20.00
25 Hiro Matsushita Panasonic 10.00 20.00
31 Alberto Ribeiro LCI 10.00 20.00
34 Alex Sampadri 10.00 20.00
79 Indy 500 Promo/20,000 7.50 20.00
99 David Hall Subway 10.00 20.00

1996 Racing Champions Indy Cart 1:24

This 1:24 scale Indy car series was highlighted by the appearance of Michael Andretti and Robby Gordon. There is also an ex-Formula 1 driver Marc Blundell in the series.

4 Alex Zanardi Target 12.50 25.00
5 Robby Gordon Valvoline 12.50 25.00
6 Michael Andretti Texaco 10.00 20.00
8 Gil de Ferran Pennzoil 10.00 20.00
12 Jimmy Vasser Target 10.00 20.00
15 Scott Goodyear Firestone 10.00 20.00
16 Stefan Johansson Alumax 10.00 20.00
17 Mauricio Gugelmin Hollywood Pac West 10.00 20.00
19 Hiro Matsushita Panasonic 10.00 20.00
20 Scott Pruett Firestone 10.00 20.00
21 Mark Blundell VISA 10.00 20.00
22 Michel Jourdain Herdez 10.00 20.00
31 Alberto Ribeiro LCI 10.00 20.00
49 Parker Johnstone Motorola 10.00 20.00
NNO Disney 200 Promo 10.00 20.00

1996 Racing Champions Indy Racing League 1:24

This was Racing Champions first year to make Indy Racing League cars.

5 Arie Luyendyk Bryant 12.00 22.00
12 Buzz Calkins Bradley 12.00 22.00
20 Tony Stewart Quaker State 30.00 60.00
45 Lyn St. James San Antonio 12.00 22.00
70 Davy Jones AC Delco 12.00 22.00
91 Buddy Lazier Delta Faucets 12.50 25.00

1997 Racing Champions Indy Racing League 1:24

Tony Stewart and Buddy Lazier are among the two most popular drivers in the Indy Racing League featured in this series.

1 Scott Sharp Conseco 12.00 22.00
4 Davy Jones Monsoon 12.00 22.00
10 Mike Groff Byrd's Cafeteria 12.00 22.00
20 Tony Stewart Glidden Menards 50.00 100.00
21 Roberto Guerrero Pennzoil 12.00 22.00
91 Buddy Lazier Delco 12.00 22.00

1998 Racing Champions Indy Cart 1:24

16 Helio Castroneves Alumax Promo 10.00 20.00

1994 Racing Champions Indy Premier 1:43

15 Jim Crawford Mac Tools/7500 12.00 20.00

1995 Racing Champions Indy Premier 1:43

This series of 1:43 scale Indy Cars come in a red, white and blue Premier series box. The pieces do have a serial number on the back but unlike most Premier issues the number of quantity produced is not stated anywhere on the box.

1 Nigel Mansell Texaco 7.00 12.00
2 Emerson Fittipaldi Penske Racing 7.00 12.00
3 Paul Tracy Penske 7.00 12.00
4 Bobby Rahal Rahal-Hogan 7.00 12.00
5 Raul Boesel Duracell 7.00 12.00
5 Nigel Mansell Texaco 7.00 12.00
6 Mario Andretti Texaco 7.00 12.00
7 Adrian Fernandez Tecate 7.00 12.00
8 Michael Andretti K-Mart 7.00 12.00
9 Robby Gordon Valvoline 7.50 15.00
11 Teo Fabi Pennzoil 7.00 12.00
18 Jimmy Vasser Conseco 7.00 12.00
31 Al Unser Jr. Penske Racing 7.50 15.00

1996 Racing Champions Indy Premier 1:43

91 Buddy Lazier Delta Hemelgarn Indy 500 Win/5091 15.00 25.00

1989-94 Racing Champions Indy Series 1 1:64

1 Emerson Fittipaldi black helmet 1990 2.50 6.00
1 Al Unser Jr. Valvoline 5.00 12.00
2 Rick Mears Pennzoil 1989 3.00 8.00
3 Mario Andretti Havoline 2.00 5.00
3 Rick Mears Mobil 1 Promo 1991 2.00 5.00
4 John Andretti Pennzoil 2.00 4.00
4 Rick Mears Pennzoil 2.00 5.00
4 Rick Mears Pennzoil yellow helmet '89 2.00 5.00
4 Bobby Rahal Rahal-Hogan 2.00 5.00
5 Mario Andretti Havoline with Black Helmet 1989 2.00 5.00
5 Mario Andretti Havoline with White Helmet 1989 2.00 5.00
5 Mario Andretti No Sponsor White Helmet 1989 2.00 5.00
5 Al Unser Jr. Valvoline 1989 6.00 12.00
6 Michael Andretti Havoline black helmet 1989 3.00 8.00
6 Michael Andretti Havoline white helmet 1989 3.00 8.00
8 John Andretti Pennzoil 2.00 4.00
8 Scott Pruett Red Roof Inn 1989 2.00 4.00
10 Derek Daly Black helmet with no driver name 1989 2.00 4.00
10 Derek Daly Black helmet with driver signature 1989 2.00 4.00
10 Derek Daly Red helmet 1989 2.00 4.00
14 A.J. Foyt 1991 4.00 8.00
16 Tony Bettenhausen Amax 2.00 4.00
18 Bobby Rahal Kraco 1991 3.00 6.00
21 Geoff Brabham Mac Tools 2.00 4.00
25 Al Unser Sr. Black helmet 1989 6.00 12.00
25 Al Unser Sr. Mobil 1 White helmet 1989 6.00 12.00
25 Al Unser Sr. White helmet 1989 6.00 12.00
86 Barry Dodson Havoline 2.00 4.00

1990 Racing Champions Indy 3-Car Sets 1:64

NNO Geoff Brabham A.J. Foyt Scott Pruett 12.50 25.00
NNO Dominic Dobson Rick Mears Al Unser 10.00 20.00
NNO Emerson Fittipaldi A.J. Foyt Bobby Rahal 10.00 20.

1994 Racing Champions Indy Premier 1:6

1 Nigell Mansel Texaco 3.00 6.
2 Emerson Fittipaldi Penske Racing 3.00 6.
4 Bobby Rahal Rahal-Hogan 3.00 6.
5 Nigell Mansel Texaco 4.00 8.
7 A Fernandez Tecate 3.00 6.
8 Michael Andretti Target 3.00 8.
10 M Groff Motorola 3.00 6.
11 Teo Fabi Pennzoil 3.00 6.
18 Jimmy Vasser Conseco 3.00 6.
22 Hito Matsushita Panasonic 3.00 6.
78 Indy 500 Promo/5000 3.00 8.

1995-96 Racing Champions Indy Series 2 Premier 1:64

This was the series two release of Racing Champions Pre Edition Indy 1:64 scale cars. The cars were released in late and early 1996 in typical Racing Champions style blister pa Each was also packaged with a Racing Champions stand sized card that includes the "series 2" set name.

1 Al Unser Jr. Penske 2.00 5.
2 Emerson Fittipaldi Penske 2.00 5.
3 Paul Tracy Penske 2.50 5.
4 Bryan Herta Target 2.00 4.
4 Alex Zanardi Target 2.00 5.
5 Robby Gordon Valvoline 4.00 10.
6 Michael Andretti K-Mart 2.00 5.
7 Eliseo Salazar Crystal 2.00 4.
8 Gil de Ferran Pennzoil 2.00 4.
9 Emerson Fittipaldi Mobil 1 2.00 5.
9 Bobby Rahal Honda 2.00 4.
10 Adrian Fernandez Tecate 2.00 4.
11 Raul Boesel Duracell 2.00 4.
12 Jimmy Vasser Target 2.00 4.
15 Christian Fittipaldi Telesena 2.00 4.
17 Danny Sullivan VISA 2.50 5.
18 Stefan Johansson Alumax 2.00 4.
20 Scott Pruett Firestone 2.00 4.
22 Roberto Guerrero 2.00 4.
25 Hiro Matsushita Panasonic 2.00 4.
31 Al Unser Jr. Penske 3.00 8.
31 Alberto Ribeiro LCI 2.00 4.
34 Alessandro Zampedri 2.00 4.
99 David Hall Subway 2.00 4.

1996 Racing Champions Indy Cart 1:64

This series was the regular release in 1996 of 1:64 scale cars. The series includes Michael Andretti and Jeff Krosnoff.

2 Al Unser Jr. Penske 3.00 6.0
3 Paul Tracy Penske 2.00 5.0
4 Alex Zanardi Target 2.50 6.0
4 Richie Hearn Ralph's Foods 2.00 5.0
5 Robby Gordon Valvoline 4.00 10.0
6 Michael Andretti Texaco 2.50 6.0
8 Gil de Ferran Pennzoil 2.00 5.0
9 Emerson Fittipaldi Hogan-Penske 2.00 5.0
10 Eddie Lawson Delco 2.00 5.0
12 Jimmy Vasser Target 2.00 5.0
15 Scott Goodyear Firestone 2.00 5.0
16 Stefan Johansson Alumax 2.00 5.0
17 Mauricio Gugelmin Hollywood 2.00 5.0
19 Hiro Matsushita Panazonic 2.00 5.0
20 Scott Pruett 2.00 5.0

Firestone
Mark Blundell 2.00 5.00
VISA
2 Michel Jourdain 2.00 5.00
Herdez
5 Jeff Krosnoff 2.00 5.00
Arciero Wines
3 Bryan Herta 2.00 5.00
Shell Promo
Alberto Ribeiro 2.00 5.00
LCI
9 Parker Johnstone 2.00 5.00
Motorola

1995 Racing Champions Premier Matched Serial Numbers Indy 1:64

Al Unser Jr. 2.00 5.00
Penske
Robby Gordon 3.00 8.00
Valvoline
Michael Andretti 2.50 6.00
Havoline
1 Raul Boesel 2.00 5.00
Duracell
2 Jimmy Vasser 2.00 5.00
Target
0 Scott Pruett 2.00 5.00
Firestone

1996 Racing Champions Indy Racing League 1:64

his series includes popular drivers Tony Stewart and Lyn St. ames. The cars came in a red white and blue blister package nd were sold through mass market retailers.

Scott Brayton 2.00 5.00
Glidden
Eddie Cheever 2.00 5.00
Quaker State
Richie Hearn 2.00 5.00
Food 4 Less
Arie Luyendyk 2.00 5.00
Bryant
Eliseo Salazar 2.00 5.00
Crystal
1 Scott Sharp 2.00 5.00
Conseco
2 Buzz Calkins 2.00 5.00
Bradley
20 Tony Stewart 5.00 12.00
Quaker State
21 Roberto Guerrero 2.00 5.00
Pennzoil
30 Mike Groff 2.00 5.00
Valvoline
70 Davy Jones 2.00 5.00
AC Delco
90 Lyn St. James 2.00 5.00
Lifetime Channel
91 Buddy Lazier 2.00 5.00
Delta Faucets

1997 Racing Champions Indy Cart 1:64

Jimmy Vasser 2.00 5.00
Target
4 Anthony Lazzaro 4.00 10.00
Per4mer Promo
(Atlantic Championship Series)
4 Alex Zanardi 2.00 5.00
Target
6 Micheal Andretti 2.00 5.00
K-Mart
11 Christian Fittipaldi 2.00 5.00
K-Mart
17 Mauricio Gugelmin 2.00 5.00
Hollywood Pacwest
18 Mark Blundell 2.00 5.00
Motorola
24 Hiro Matsushita 2.00 5.00
Panasonic
25 Max Papis 2.00 5.00
MCI Promo
36 Juan Manuel Fangio 2.00 5.00
Castrol

1997 Racing Champions Indy Racing League 1:64

This was the first series of 1:64 Indy Racing League cars issued by Racing Champions. The 1996 Indy 500 winner Buddy Lazier and NASCAR Champion Tony Stewart are key parts of the set.

1 Scott Sharp 2.00 5.00
Conseco
4 Mike Groff 2.50 6.00
Byrd's Cafeteria
4 Davy Jones 2.50 6.00
Monsoon
5 Arie Luyendyk 3.00 6.00
Bryant
10 Jack Miller 2.50 6.00
Crest
20 Tony Stewart 6.00 15.00
Glidden
21 Roberto Guerrero 2.50 6.00
Pennzoil
91 Buddy Lazier 3.00 6.00
Delco

1998 Racing Champions Indy Cart 1:64

1 Alex Zanardi 4.00 10.00
Target 1998 Champion

1999 Racing Champions Indy Racing League 1:64

22 Tony Stewart 6.00 15.00
Home Depot Promo/12,000

2002 Racing Champions IRL 1:64

39 Michael Andretti 5.00 10.00
Motorola Promo
in wind. Box

1994 Racing Champions Indy Transporters 1:64

NNO Scott Goodyear 10.00 20.00
Budweiser/7500

1997 UT Models Indy 1:18

Each car in this series was issued in a UT Models blue window box. The car itself was mounted to a cardboard base.

1 Alex Zanardi
Target

1997 UT Models Indy 1:43

Each car in this series was issued in a UT Models hard plastic case. The car itself was mounted on a blue cardboard base.

4 Alex Zanardi 20.00 35.00
Target

1998 UT Models Indy 1:43

Each car in this series was issued in a UT Models hard plastic case. The car itself was mounted to a white cardboard base.

1 Alex Zanardi 18.00 30.00
Target
7 Bobby Rahal 12.50 30.00
Miller Lite
8 Bryan Herta 15.00 30.00
Shell
9 J.J. Lehto 12.50 30.00
Hogan
12 Jimmy Vasser 12.50 30.00
Target
18 Mark Blundell 12.50 30.00
Motorola
27 Dario Franchitti 20.00 35.00
KOOL Green
40 Adrian Fernandez 18.00 30.00
Tecate

1998 Hot Wheels Racing F1 1:18

3 Michael Schumacher 30.00 60.00
Shell

1999 Hot Wheels Racing F1 1:18

Cars in this series were issued in a colorful Hot Wheels Racing window box. Each piece was mounted on a base that resembled a section of track.

3 Michael Schumacher 30.00 60.00
Shell
7 Damon Hill 30.00 60.00
Buzzin Hornets
8 Heinz-Harold Frentzen 30.00 60.00
Buzzin Hornets
16 Rubens Barrichello 40.00 80.00
HSBC
NNO Eddie Irvine 30.00 60.00
Shell
NNO Alex Zanardi 30.00 60.00
Williams

2000 Hot Wheels Racing F1 1:18

This series of 1:18 scale cars was produced by Hot Wheels. Each car was mounted to a black plastic base and packaged in a "2000 Hot Wheels Racing" black window box.

1 Mika Hakkinen 30.00 60.00
Mobil 1
2 David Coulthard 30.00 60.00
Mobil 1
3 Michael Schumacher 30.00 60.00
Shell Launch
4 Jarno Trulli 30.00 60.00
Buzzin Hornets
5 Heinz-Harold Frentzen 30.00 60.00
Buzzin Hornets
7 Eddie Irvine 30.00 60.00
HSBC
8 Johnny Herbert 25.00 50.00
HSBC
9 Ralf Schumacher 30.00 60.00
Compaq Allianz
9 Ralf Schumacher 30.00 60.00
Compaq Allianz Launch
10 Jenson Button 30.00 60.00
Compaq Allianz Launch
NNO Rubens Barrichello 30.00 60.00
Shell

2001 Hot Wheels Racing F1 1:18

1 Rubens Barrichello 25.00 60.00
Shell Launch Edition
1 Michael Schumacher 40.00 75.00
Shell Race Edition
1 Michael Schumacher 40.00 75.00
Shell King of Rain/14,999
3 Mika Hakkinen 35.00 60.00
Mobil 1 Launch Edition
3 Michael Schumacher 40.00 75.00
Shell 2000 World Champ
in plastic case
4 David Coulthard 25.00 60.00
Siemens Mobil 1
4 Jarno Trulli 30.00 60.00
Buzzin Hornets
5 Heinz-Harold Frentzen 35.00 60.00
Buzzin Hornets
Launch Edition
5 Juan Montoya 35.00 60.00
Compaq Allianz
Race Edition
5 Ralf Schumacher 35.00 60.00
Compaq Allianz
Launch Edition
18 Eddie Irvine 25.00 60.00
HSBC Launch Edition
18 Eddie Irvine 30.00 50.00
HSBC Race Edition

2002 Hot Wheels Racing F1 1:18

1 Michael Schumacher 35.00 60.00
Shell 2001 World Champ/25,000
in plastic case
1 Michael Schumacher 35.00 60.00
Shell/20,000
1 Michael Schumacher 40.00 75.00
Shell 5-Time
Champ/25,000
1 Michael Schumacher 40.00 75.00
Shell 52 Wins
2 Rubens Barrichello 30.00 50.00
Shell
4 Kimi Raikkonen 30.00 50.00
Kimi Mobil 1
5 Ralf Schumacher 30.00 50.00
HP Allianz
6 Juan Montoya 30.00 50.00
HP Allianz
10 Takuma Sato 30.00 50.00
DHL/1000
16 Eddie Irvine 25.00 50.00
HSBC

2003 Hot Wheels Racing F1 1:18

1 Michael Schumacher 100.00 175.00
Ferrari 9-11 Tribute/500
1 Michael Schumacher 40.00 75.00
Canadian Grand Prix/20,000
1 Michael Schumacher 60.00 100.00
Shell
1 Michael Schumacher 40.00 75.00
Shell Champ
3 Juan Montoya 35.00 50.00
Castrol HP
4 Ralf Schumacher 35.00 50.00
Castrol HP
6 Kimi Raikkonen 35.00 60.00
Kimi Mobil 1
6 Kimi Raikkonen 40.00 75.00
Kimi First Win/5000
7 Jarno Trulli 35.00 50.00
Elf
7 Jarno Trulli 50.00 80.00
Elf Mild Seven
8 Fernando Alonso 35.00 50.00
Elf
11 Giancarlo Fisichella 35.00 50.00
Be on Edge
11 Giancarlo Fisichella 35.00 60.00
Be on Edge First Win/5000
14 Mark Webber 35.00 50.00
HSBC
0 Rubens Barrichello 35.00 50.00
Shell

2004 Hot Wheels Racing F1 1:18

1 Michael Schumacher 40.00 65.00
Ferrari Sakhir Bahrain Raced/15,000
1 Michael Schumacher 200.00 300.00
Ferrari 75 Wins
w
figure and firesuit
2 Juan Montoya 40.00 65.00
Allianz
3 Nick Heidfeld 40.00 65.00
Jordon Ford
4 Ralf Schumacher 40.00 65.00
Allianz
7 Jarno Trulli 40.00 65.00
Elf
8 Fernando Alonso 40.00 65.00
Elf
14 Mark Webber 40.00 65.00
Jaguar

2000 Hot Wheels Racing F1 1:24

1 Mika Hakkinen 12.50 25.00
Mobil 1 Launch

2002 Hot Wheels Racing F1 1:24

1 Michael Schumacher 15.00 30.00
Shell
6 Juan Montoya 12.50 25.00
HP

1999 Hot Wheels Racing F1 1:43

3 Michael Schumacher 10.00 20.00
Shell
16 Rubens Barrichello 10.00 20.00
Stewart
NNO Johnny Herbert 10.00 20.00
Stewart
NNO Ralf Schumacher 10.00 20.00
Williams
NNO Alex Zanardi 10.00 20.00
Williams

2000 Hot Wheels Racing F1 1:43

2 David Coulthard 10.00 20.00
Mobil 1
3 Mika Hakkinen 10.00 20.00
Mobil 1
5 Heinz-Harold Frentzen 7.50 20.00
Buzzin Hornets
8 Johnny Herbert 10.00 20.00
HSBC
0 Jenson Button 7.50 20.00
Compaq Allianz
NNO Eddie Irvine 7.50 20.00
NNO Ralf Schumacher 10.00 20.00
Williams
NNO Jarno Trulli 10.00 20.00
Jordan Hart

2001 Hot Wheels Racing F1 1:43

1 Michael Schumacher 7.50 20.00
Shell
2 Rubens Barrichello 6.00 15.00
Shell
3 Mika Hakkinen 7.50 20.00
Mobil 1
4 David Coulthard 6.00 15.00
Mobil 1
5 Heinz-Harold Frentzen 7.50 20.00
Buzzin Hornets

2002 Hot Wheels Racing F1 1:43

This series of 1:43 scale plastic cars was produced by Hot Wheels. Each car was mounted to a black plastic base and packaged in a "Hot Wheels Racing" black window box.

1 Michael Schumacher 20.00 35.00
Shell
2 Rubens Barrichello 20.00 35.00
Shell
18 Rubens Barrichello 12.50 25.00
HSBC Ford/9998

2003 Hot Wheels Racing F1 1:43

1 Michael Schumacher 30.00 50.00
Shell 3-car set
NNO Rubens Barrichello 10.00 20.00
Ferrari

1999 Hot Wheels Racing F1 1:64

1/2 avid Coulthard 6.00 15.00
Mika Hakkinen
Mobil 1 2-car set

2001 Hot Wheels Racing F1 1:64

3 Mika Hakkinen 3.00 6.00
Mobil 1
18 Eddie Irvine 3.00 6.00
HSBC

2002 Hot Wheels Racing F1 1:64

3 David Coulthard 3.00 6.00
Mobil 1
16 Eddie Irvine 3.00 6.00
HSBC

2003 Hot Wheels Racing F1 1:64

1 Michael Schumacher 5.00 10.00
Shell
3 Juan Montoya 4.00 8.00
Castrol HP
5 David Coulthard 4.00 8.00
David Mobil 1
7 Jarno Trulli 4.00 8.00
Elf
11 Giancarlo Fisichella 4.00 8.00
Be on Edge
14 Mark Webber 4.00 8.00
HSBC

1988-92 MiniChamps F1 1:18

2 Gerhard Berger 50.00 80.00
Marlboro '91
2 Alan Prost 50.00 80.00
Marlboro '89
2 Gerhard Berger 50.00 80.00
Marlboro '92
11 Alan Prost 50.00 80.00
Marlboro WC '88
12 Ayrton Senna 50.00 100.00
Shell '88
19 Michael Schumacher 150.00 250.00
Camel '92
28 Gerhard Berger 30.00 60.00
Marlboro '90
NNO Saturo Nakajima 40.00 80.00
Lotus '87

1993 MiniChamps F1 1:18

0 Damon Hill 50.00 80.00
Canon
2 Alain Prost 50.00 80.00
Canon
5 Michael Schumacher 175.00 300.00
Camel Nordica
6 Riccardo Patrese 40.00 80.00
Camel
7 Mario Andretti 60.00 100.00
Marlboro
8 Ayrton Senna 60.00 100.00
Marlboro
27 Jean Alesi 60.00 100.00
Ferrari
28 Gerhard Berger 50.00 80.00
Ferrari
29 K.Wendlinger 40.00 80.00
Broker
Sauber
30 Heinz-Harold Frentzen 40.00 80.00
Broker Sauber
30 J.J.Lehto 40.00 80.00
Broker
Sauber

1994 MiniChamps F1 1:18

0 Damon Hill 40.00 75.00
othmans Presentation
0 Damon Hill 40.00 75.00
othmans
2 Ayrton Senna 50.00 100.00
othmans
2 Ayrton Senna 50.00 100.00
othmans Presentation
5 Michael Schumacher 125.00 200.00
ild Seven B194
5 Michael Schumacher 125.00 200.00
ild Seven German GP
5 Michael Schumacher 125.00 200.00
ild Seven BB(Bitburger)
5 Michael Schumacher 125.00 200.00
ild Seven B193B
6 J.J.Lehto 40.00 75.00
ild Seven
6 Jos Verstappen 40.00 75.00
ild Seven
6 Jos Verstappen 40.00 75.00
ild Seven German GP
7 Mika Hakkinen 40.00 75.00
arlboro
8 Martin Brundle 40.00 75.00
arlboro
27 Jean Alesi 60.00 100.00
errari
27 Nicola Larini 40.00 75.00
errari
28 Gerhard Berger 40.00 75.00
errari
29 Andrea deCesaris 40.00 75.00
Broker
Sauber
29 K.Wendlinger 40.00 75.00
issot
Sauber
30 Heinz-Harold Frentzen 40.00 75.00
Tissot Sauber

1995 MiniChamps F1 1:18

1 Alesi 150.00 250.00
Schumacher
MS Alesi 1st Win
1 Michael Schumacher 125.00 200.00
MS Europe GP
1 Michael Schumacher 250.00 400.00
MS French GP
1 Michael Schumacher 125.00 200.00
MS German GP
1 Michael Schumacher 125.00 200.00
MS Showcar
2 Jonny Herbert 35.00 50.00
Mild Seven British GP
2 Jonny Herbert 35.00 50.00
Mild Seven Showcar
5 Damon Hill 40.00 75.00
Rothmans
5 Damon Hill 40.00 75.00
Rothmans Test Car
6 David Coulthard 40.00 100.00
Rothmans
6 David Coulthard 40.00 100.00
Rothmans Test Car
7 Martin Brundle 35.00 50.00
Marlboro
7 Nigel Mansell 35.00 60.00
Marlboro
8 Mika Hakkinen 35.00 75.00
Marlboro
14 Rubens Barrichello 35.00 50.00
Peugeot
Jordan
15 Eddie Irvine 35.00 50.00
Peugeot
Jordan
25 Aguri Suzuki 35.00 50.00
Gitanes
Ligier
26 O.Panis 35.00 50.00
Gitanes
Ligier
27 Jean Alesi 60.00 100.00
Ferrari
28 Gerhard Berger 35.00 50.00
Ferrari
29 Karl Wendlinger 35.00 50.00
Red Bull
Sauber
30 Heinz-Harold Frentzen 35.00 50.00
Red Bull Sauber

1996 MiniChamps F1 1:18

1 Michael Schumacher 150.00 250.00
Benetton 1995 Champ
1 Michael Schumacher 125.00 200.00
Ferrari
1 Michael Schumacher 125.00 200.00
Ferrari Italian GP
1 Michael Schumacher 125.00 200.00
Ferrari Launch
1 Michael Schumacher 175.00 300.00
Ferrari Spanish GP/9662
2 Eddie Irvine 35.00 50.00
Shell Ferrari
2 Eddie Irvine 40.00 60.00
Shell Ferrari Launch
3 Jean Alesi 40.00 75.00
Mild Seven
4 Gerhard Berger 35.00 50.00
Mild Seven
5 Damon Hill 35.00 60.00
Rothmans
6 Jacques Villenueve 60.00 100.00
Rothmans
7 Mika Hakkinen 35.00 75.00
Marlboro
8 David Coulthard 30.00 80.00
Marlboro
11 Rubens Barrichello 35.00 50.00
Benson & Hedges
11 Rubens Barrichello 35.00 60.00
BH Launch
12 Martin Brundle 35.00 50.00
Benson & Hedges
12 Martin Brundle 35.00 60.00
BH Launch
14 Jonny Herbert 35.00 50.00
Petronas
15 Heinz-Harold Frentzen 35.00 50.00
Petronas

1997 MiniChamps F1 1:18

5 Michael Schumacher 100.00 175.00
Shell Ferrari
22 Rubens Barrichello 35.00 60.00
HSBC
23 J Magnussen 40.00 75.00
HSBC

1998 MiniChamps F1 1:18

1 Jacques Villeneuve 35.00 70.00
Williams
3 Jacques Villeneuve 75.00 125.00
Castrol 1997 Champ/4444
4 Eddie Irvine 45.00 80.00
Shell
5 Giancarlo Fisichella 40.00 80.00
Korean Air Benetton
9 Damon Hill 35.00 70.00

Buzzin Hornets
NNO Michael Schumacher 100.00 175.00
Ferrari Black Testcar/6500

1999 MiniChamps F1 1:18

1 Mika Hakkinen 30.00 75.00
Mobil 1 Mika
1 Alain Prost 30.00 60.00
PlayStation Peugeot
2 David Coulthard 30.00 60.00
Mobil 1
5 Ralf Schumacher 35.00 70.00
Williams
5 Ralf Schumacher 35.00 70.00
Williams Showcar/3333
10 Alexander Wurz 20.00 50.00
Benetton
12 Jacques Villeneuve 30.00 60.00
Supertec
15 Toranoskne Takagi 30.00 60.00
TWR
17 Pedro Diniz 30.00 60.00
Red Bull Petronas
18 Olivier Panis 25.00 60.00
Playstation Showcar/2222
23 Ricardo Zonta 30.00 60.00
Supertec

2000 MiniChamps F1 1:18

9 Ralf Schumacher 30.00 60.00
Allianz Compaq Williams
10 Jenson Button 30.00 60.00
Allianz Compaq Williams
11 Giancarlo Fisichella 30.00 60.00
Benetton
12 Alexander Wurz 30.00 60.00
Benetton
23 Ricardo Zonta 30.00 60.00
BAR Honda
NNO U.S. Grand Prix Gold 25.00 50.00

2001 MiniChamps F1 1:18

3 Mika Hakkinen 35.00 70.00
Siemens Mobil 1
5 Ralf Schumacher 25.00 50.00
Allianz Compaq
5 Ralf Schumacher 25.00 50.00
Allianz Compaq first win
6 Juan Montoya 35.00 70.00
Castrol Compaq Showcar
10 Jacques Villeneuve 35.00 70.00
Showcar/3000
17 Kimi Raikkonen 75.00 125.00
Petronas Showcar/800
00 Jenson Button 25.00 50.00
Marconi Korean Air

2002 MiniChamps F1 1:18

3 David Coulthard 40.00 75.00
Mobil 1
4 Kimi Raikkonen 40.00 75.00
Mobil 1
5 Ralf Schumacher 30.00 60.00
Castrol Compaq Launch
5 Ralf Schumacher 40.00 75.00
Castrol Compaq Race
6 Juan Montoya 30.00 60.00
Castrol Compaq Race
7 Nick Heidfeld 40.00 75.00
Petronas
8 Felipe Massa 25.00 50.00
Petronas Race
8 Felipe Massa 25.00 50.00
Petronas Showcar/1002
20 Heinz-Harold Frentzen 30.00 60.00
Orange
24 Mika Salo 30.00 60.00
Panasonic
24 Mika Salo 30.00 60.00
Panasonic Showcar/1200
25 Alan McNish 30.00 60.00
Panasonic Race
25 Alan McNish 30.00 60.00
Panasonic Showcar/750
02 Canadian Grand Prix/2002 30.00 50.00
NNO Panasonic Showcar/5002 35.00 60.00
in solid box

2003 MiniChamps F1 1:18

10 Jacques Villeneuve 35.00 60.00
BAR Honda/1206
14 Mark Webber 40.00 70.00
Jaguar Cosworth HSBC DuPont

2004 MiniChamps F1 1:18

9 Jenson Button 40.00 70.00
Bar Honda
9 Jenson Button 50.00 75.00
Bar Honda Lucky Strike/1002
10 Takuma Sato 40.00 70.00
Bar Honda
10 Takuma Sato 50.00 75.00
Bar Honda Lucky Strike/1002
14 Mark Webber 40.00 70.00
Jaguar HSBC DuPont
14 Mark Webber 50.00 75.00
Jaguar Showcar
HSBC DuPont

2004 MiniChamps Ayrton Senna Collection 1:18

2 Ayrton Senna 75.00 125.00
Williams Renault '94

2005 MiniChamps F1 1:18

11 Jacques Villenuve 50.00 80.00
Sauber Petronas/1602

1992 MiniChamps F1 1:43

This was the first year for Paul's Model Art to produce 1:43 scale Formula 1 die-cast. Three teams were represented.

5 Nigel Mansell 30.00 60.00
Canon Williams
6 Riccardo Patrese 30.00 60.00
Canon Williams
19 Michael Schumacher 125.00 200.00
Benetton
20 Marc Brundle 15.00 25.00
Benetton
27 Jean Alesi 18.00 30.00
Ferrari
28 Ivan Capelli 18.00 30.00
Ferrari

1993 MiniChamps F1 1:43

Damon Hill and Ayrton Senna make their first Paul's Model Art 1:43 scale appearance in this series.

0 Damon Hill 18.00 30.00
Canon Williams
2 Alain Prost 15.00 25.00
Canon Williams
5 Michael Schumacher 125.00 200.00
Benetton
6 Riccardo Patrese 15.00 25.00
Benetton
7 Michael Andretti 35.00 60.00
McLaren
7 Mika Hakkinen 25.00 50.00
McLaren
8 Ayrton Senna 25.00 40.00
McLaren
27 Jean Alesi 15.00 25.00
Ferrari
28 Gerhard Berger 15.00 25.00
Ferrari
29 Karl Wendlinger 15.00 25.00
Broker
Sauber
30 Heinz-Harold Frentzen 15.00 25.00
Liquid Moly
Sauber
30 J.J.Lehto 15.00 25.00
Liqui Moly Sauber

1994 MiniChamps F1 1:43

This was the first year that Paul's Model Art did special edition 1:43 cars. Michael Schumacher's F1 Championship car and Nigel Mansell's French Grand Prix car are among the most popular.

0 Damon Hill 15.00 25.00
Rothmans Williams FW15
0 Damon Hill 15.00 25.00
Rothmans Williams FW16
0 Damon Hill 15.00 25.00
Rothmans Williams FW16
British Grand Prix
2 Nigel Mansell 15.00 25.00
Rothmans FW16
French Grand Prix/11,111
2 David Coulthard 20.00 50.00
(Rothmans Williams/3333
2 Ayrton Senna 25.00 50.00
Rothmans
3 Ukyo Katayama 15.00 35.00
Calbee Tyrell
4 Mark Blundell 15.00 25.00
Calbee Tyrell
5 Michael Schumacher 90.00 150.00
Benetton
5 Michael Schumacher 90.00 150.00
Benetton German Grand Prix
5 Michael Schumacher 90.00 150.00
Benetton Formula 1 Champion
6 Johnny Herbert 15.00 25.00
Bitburger
6 J.J. Lehto 15.00 25.00
Mild Seven
6 Jos Verstappen 15.00 25.00
Mild Seven
6 Jos Verstappen 15.00 25.00
Mild Seven German Grand Prix
7 Mika Hakkinen 15.00 40.00
McLaren
8 Martin Brundle 15.00 25.00
McLaren
27 Jean Alesi 15.00 25.00
Ferrari
27 Nicola Larini 15.00 25.00
Ferrari
28 Gerhard Berger 15.00 25.00
Ferrari
29 Andrea deCesaris 15.00 25.00
Broker
200th Grand Prix
29 Andrea deCesaris 15.00 25.00
Broker
German Grand Prix
29 Karl Wendlinger 15.00 25.00
Broker Sauber
30 Heinz-Harold Frentzen 15.00 25.00
Broker Sauber
31 David Brabham 15.00 25.00
MTV Ford
32 Roland Ratzenberger 25.00 50.00
MTV Ford

1995 MiniChamps F1 1:43

Ayrton Senna is noticeably absent from this set. The show car of Damon Hill and the Test car of David Coulthard are the special editions in this series.

1 Michael Schumacher 125.00 200.00
Jean Alesi
Alesi 1st Win/11,695
1 Michael Schumacher 75.00 125.00
Mild Seven B195
2 Johnny Herbert 15.00 25.00
Mild Seven B195
3 Ukyo Katayama 15.00 25.00
Calbee Tyrell
4 Mika Salo 15.00 25.00
Calbee Tyrell
5 Damon Hill 15.00 25.00
Rothmans FW16 Showcar/4444
5 Damon Hill 15.00 25.00
Rothmans Williams FW17
6 David Coulthard 20.00 50.00
Rothmans FW17
6 David Coulthard 12.00 30.00
Rothmans FW 16 Test car
7 Mark Blundell 15.00 25.00
McLaren
7 Nigel Mansell 15.00 25.00
McLaren
8 Mika Hakkinen 15.00 40.00
McLaren
11 Mimmo Schiattarella 15.00 25.00
MTV Simtek Ford NI
12 Jos Verstappen 15.00 25.00
MTV Simtek Ford
14 Rubens Barrichello 15.00 25.00
Peugeot Jordan
15 Eddie Irvine 15.00 25.00
Peugeot Jordan
25 Martin Brundle 15.00 25.00
Gitanes Ligier
25 Aguri Suzuki 15.00 25.00
Gitanes Ligier
26 Olivier Panis 15.00 25.00
Gitanes Ligier
27 Jean Alesi 15.00 25.00
Ferrari
28 Gerhard Berger 15.00 25.00
Ferrari
29 Jean-Christophe Bouillion 15.00 25.00
Red Bull Sauber
29 Karl Wendlinger 15.00 25.00
Red Bull Sauber
30 Heinz-Harold Frentzen 15.00 25.00
Red Bull Sauber

1996 MiniChamps F1 1:43

Michael Schumacher has four different versions in this series. His first win in a Ferrari is commemorated as one of the special pieces.

1 Michael Schumacher 75.00 125.00
Ferrari
1 Michael Schumacher 150.00 250.00
Ferrari 1st Win/962
1 Michael Schumacher 75.00 125.00
Ferrari High Nose
1 Michael Schumacher 75.00 125.00
Ferrari Launch car
2 Eddie Irvine 25.00 40.00
Ferrari
2 Eddie Irvine 25.00 40.00
Ferrari Launch car
3 Jean Alesi 15.00 25.00
Benetton Mild Seven
4 Gerhard Berger 15.00 25.00
Benetton Mild Seven
5 Heinz-Harold Frentzen 15.00 25.00
Rothmans Test car
5 Damon Hill 15.00 25.00
Rothmans Williams FW18
6 Jacques Villeneuve 18.00 30.00
Rothmans
6 Jacques Villeneuve 18.00 30.00
Rothmans Test car
7 Mika Hakkinen 15.00 40.00
McLaren
8 David Coulthard 12.00 30.00
McLaren
9 Olivier Panis 15.00 25.00
Parmalat Ligier
9 Olivier Panis 40.00 80.00
Parmalat Ligier
Monaco Grand Prix Win/6000
10 Pedro Diniz 15.00 25.00
Parmalat Ligier
11 Rubens Barrichello 15.00 25.00
Peugeot Launch car
11 Rubens Barrichello 15.00 25.00
Peugeot
12 Martin Brundle 15.00 25.00
Peugeot Launch car
12 Martin Brundle 15.00 25.00
Peugeot
14 Johnny Herbert 15.00 25.00
Petronas Sauber
15 Heinz-Harold Frentzen 15.00 25.00
Petronas Sauber
18 Ukyo Katayama 15.00 25.00
Korean Air Tyrrell
19 Mika Salo 15.00 25.00
Korean Air Tyrrell

1997 MiniChamps F1 1:43

1 Damon Hill 50.00 100.00
Zepler Danka
6 Eddie Irvine 25.00 40.00
Shell
NNO Michael Schumacher 12.50 25.00
Shell/9999

1998 MiniChamps F1 1:43

1 Jacques Villeneuve 12.50 25.00
Veltins
3 Jacques Villeneuve 35.00 60.00
Castrol 1997 Champ/6666
4 Eddie Irvine 35.00 60.00
Shell/3333
8 Mika Hakkinen 12.50 25.00
Mobil 1
11 Olivier Panis 12.50 25.00
Playstation

1999 MiniChamps F1 1:43

11 Jean Alesi 18.00 30.00
Red Bull
NNO Olivier Panis 20.00 35.00
Playstation
NNO Jacques Villeneuve 20.00 35.00
Supertec Test

1999-02 MiniChamps Ayrton Senna Collection 1:43

CARS ARE LISTED BY MODEL NUMBER
STATED PRODUCTION RUN 600

1 Ayrton Senna 40.00 75.00
1988 Honda Turbo
2 Ayrton Senna 40.00 75.00
1989 Honda V10
3 Ayrton Senna 35.00 60.00
1990 Honda V10
4 Ayrton Senna 35.00 60.00
1993 Penske Chevrolet
5 Ayrton Senna 35.00 60.00
1991 Honda V12
6 Ayrton Senna 35.00 60.00
1992 Honda V12
7 Ayrton Senna 35.00 60.00
1994 Renault V12
8 Ayrton Senna 30.00 50.00
1993 Ford V8
9 Ayrton Senna 30.00 50.00
1985 Renault Turbo
10 Ayrton Senna 30.00 50.00
1984 Hart Turbo
11 Ayrton Senna 30.00 50.00
1984 Mercedes Benz
12 Ayrton Senna 30.00 50.00
1986 Renault Turbo
13 Ayrton Senna 30.00 50.00
1984 Hart Turbo
14 Ayrton Senna 15.00 40.00
1980&1993 Kart Models
15 Ayrton Senna 30.00 50.00
1987 Honda Turbo
16 Ayrton Senna 30.00 50.00
1983 Williams Ford
17 Ayrton Senna 30.00 50.00
1984 Porsche 956

2000 MiniChamps F1 1:43

11 Giancarlo Fisichella 18.00 30.00
Benetton
12 Alexander Wurz 18.00 30.00
Benetton
0 Jenson Button 15.00 30.00
Marconi Korean Air
First Test Drive/2999

2001 MiniChamps F1 1:43

3 Mika Hakkinen 20.00 35.00
Siemens Mobil 1
3 Kimi Raikkonen 25.00 40.00
Petronas
3 Kimi Raikkonen 35.00 60.00
Petronas Malaysian GP/2222
4 David Coulthard 20.00 35.00
Siemens Mobil 1
5 Ralf Schumacher 20.00 35.00
Castrol Compaq
5 Ralf Schumacher 20.00 35.00
Castrol Compaq
Keep Your Distance/5701
5 Ralf Schumacher 20.00 35.00
Castrol Compaq
First Grand Prix Win/7001
6 Juan Montoya 20.00 35.00
Castrol Compaq
6 Juan Montoya 20.00 35.00
Castrol Compaq
First Grand Prix Win
6 Juan Montoya 20.00 35.00
Castrol Compaq
Malaysian Grand Prix/3024
8 Jenson Button 10.00 25.00
Marconi Korean Air
Showcar/4500
17 Kimi Raikkonen 25.00 40.00
Petronas
17 Kimi Raikkonen 25.00 50.00
Petronas 1st Point
17 Kimi Raikkonen 35.00 60.00
Petronas Showcar/1400
0 Jenson Button 15.00 30.00
Marconi Korean Air
0 Jenson Button 15.00 30.00
Marconi Korean Air
US Grand Prix/2811
01 U.S. Grand Prix 10.00 20.00

2002 MiniChamps F1 1:43

4 Kimi Raikkonen 25.00 40.00
Mobil 1
5 Ralf Schumacher 20.00 35.00
Castrol Compaq
5 Ralf Schumacher 20.00 35.00
Castrol HP
5/6 R.Schumacher 50.00 80.00
Juan Montoya
Castrol Compaq
Malaysian Grand Prix
Finish 2-car set
6 Juan Montoya 20.00 35.00
Castrol Compaq
6 Juan Montoya 20.00 35.00
Castrol HP
6 Juan Montoya 20.00 35.00
Castrol Compaq Showcar
7 Nick Heidfeld 20.00 35.00
Petronas US GP/3024
8 Heinz-Harold Frentzen 20.00 35.00
Petronas US Grand Prix/3744
15 Jenson Button 15.00 30.00
Barcelona Test/3144
15 Jenson Button 15.00 30.00
Blue World Renault
15 Jenson Button 15.00 30.00
Launch Renault/2201
21 Anthony Davidson 20.00 35.00
KL Hungarian GP/1872
23 Mark Webber 20.00 35.00
KL
23 Mark Webber 20.00 35.00
KL Australian GP/3096
24 Mika Salo 20.00 35.00
Panasonic Raced
24 Mika Salo 20.00 35.00
Panasonic Showcar
25 Alan McNish 20.00 35.00
Panasonic Raced
25 Alan McNish 20.00 35.00
Panasonic Showcar
NNO Canadian Grand Prix/2002 25.00 40.00
NNO Panasonic Toyota Showcar/2002 25.00 40.00

2003 MiniChamps F1 1:43

3 Juan Montoya 20.00 35.00
Castrol HP
3 Juan Montoya 20.00 35.00
Castrol HP Showcar/2404
4 Ralf Schumacher 20.00 35.00
Castrol HP
4 Ralf Schumacher 20.00 35.00
Castrol HP Showcar/2160
5 David Coulthard 20.00 35.00
Siemens Mobil 1
6 Kimi Raikkonen 30.00 50.00
Siemens Mobil 1
9 Jenson Button 20.00 35.00
Bar Honda
14 Mark Webber 20.00 35.00
HSBC
16 Jacques Villeneuve 20.00 35.00
Honda Showcar/2448
17 Jenson Button 20.00 35.00
Honda Showcar/2016
18 Jos Verstappen 20.00 35.00
European Showcar/2160
19 John Wilson 20.00 35.00
European Trust/2808
19 John Wilson 20.00 35.00
European Showcar/1224
20 Olivier Panis 20.00 35.00
Panasonic/2303
21 Cristiano DaMatta 20.00 35.00
Panasonic
21 Cristiano DaMatta 20.00 35.00
Panasonic Showcar/2303
NNO Heinz-Harold Frentzen 20.00 35.00
Petronas/2448
NNO Nick Heidfeld 20.00 35.00
Petronas/2304
NNO Panasonic Showcar/2503 25.00 40.00
NNO USA Grand Prix 25.00 40.00

2003 MiniChamps F1 Michelin Promos 1:43

4 Ralf Schumacher 60.00 100.00
Castrol HP
5 David Coulthard 60.00 100.00
Siemens Mobil 1/504

2003 MiniChamps F1 Vintage 1:43

1 Eric Van de Poele 25.00 40.00
1992 Brabham Judd
2 Keke Rosberg 25.00 40.00
1986 McClaren Tag Turbo
3 Ronnie Peterson 25.00 40.00
1977 Tyrrell Ford
4 Patrick Depailler 25.00 40.00
1976 Tyrrell Ford
5 Emerson Fittipaldi 25.00 40.00
1974 McLaren Ford
7 Denis Hulme 25.00 40.00
1973 McLaren Ford
8 Damon Hill 25.00 40.00
1992 Brabham Judd
8 Peter Revson 25.00 40.00
1973 McLaren Ford
15 Eddie Irvine 25.00 40.00
1993 Barclay Jordan Hart/2808
22 Piers Courage 25.00 40.00
1970 DeTomaso Ford
34 Hans Stuck 25.00 40.00
1976 March Ford/3744

2004 MiniChamps F1 1:43

9 Jenson Button 20.00 40.00
Bar Honda
9 Jenson Button 20.00 40.00
Bar Honda 1st Pole San Marino/8784
9 Jenson Button 30.00 60.00
Bar Honda Lucky Strike 1st Pole
San Marino/8784
14 Mark Webber 20.00 40.00
Jaguar HSBC DuPont

2005 MiniChamps F1 1:43

10 Takuma Sato 75.00 125.00
Bar Honda Michelin
10 Takuma Sato 25.00 40.00
Bar Honda '04 Japanese GP/15,408
11 Jacques Villenuve 25.00 40.00
Sauber Petronas/2016

1995 Onyx F1 1:18

This was the first year for Onyx to produce 1:18 scale Formula cars. The two teams represented were the Williams team and th Ferrari team. The Williams cars were issued with an umbrel with variations on the sponsor featured.

5 Damon Hill 30.00 50.00
Rothmans with Renault Umbrella
5 Damon Hill 30.00 50.00
Rothmans with Rothmans Umbrella
6 David Coulthard 40.00 100.00
Rothmans with Renault Umbrella
6 David Coulthard 40.00 100.00
Rothmans with Rothmans Umbrella
27 Jean Alesi 30.00 50.00
Ferrari
28 Gerhard Berger 30.00 50.00
Ferrari

1996 Onyx F1 1:18

Onyx cut back in its 1996 1:18 line to only include the William team. The Jacques Villeneuve is one of his first Formula 1 die cast pieces.

5 Damon Hill 30.00 50.00
Rothmans
6 Jacques Villeneuve 30.00 50.00
Rothmans

1992 Onyx F1 1:24

This was the first year for Onyx to make 1:24 scale Formula cars. Williams, Ligier and Ferrari were the three teams represented in the set.

5 Nigel Mansell 16.00 28.00
Canon
6 Riccardo Patrese 15.00 25.00
Canon
25 Thierry Boutsen 15.00 25.00
Gitanes
26 Erik Comas 15.00 25.00
Gitanes
27 Jean Alesi 15.00 25.00
Ferrari
28 Ivan Capelli 15.00 25.00
Ferrari

1993 Onyx F1 1:24

This series of Formula 1 cars was cut down to just two teams Williams-Renault and Benetton-Ford.

0 Damon Hill 15.00 25.00
Canon
2 Alain Prost 15.00 25.00
Canon
5 Michael Schumacher 25.00 50.00
Benetton
6 Riccardo Patrese 15.00 25.00
Benetton

1994 Onyx F1 1:24

s of 1:24 scale Formula 1 cars includes test cars for on-Ford team. The cars are done in the Mild Seven me. For the second year in a row only the Williams- d Benetton-Ford teams were represented.

Hill 15.00 25.00
ans
ioulthard 20.00 50.00
ans
Mansell 16.00 28.00
ans
Senna 20.00 35.00
ans
Schumacher 25.00 50.00
on Bitburger
Schumacher 25.00 50.00
on Mild Seven
Schumacher 25.00 50.00
on Mild Seven Test car
stappen 15.00 25.00
on Mild Seven Test car
stappen 15.00 25.00
on Mild Seven
nto 15.00 25.00
on Mild Seven Test car
nto 15.00 25.00
on Mild Seven

1988 Onyx F1 1:43

he first year Onyx starting making 1:43 scale Formula . The key pieces in the set are Ayrton Senna and Alain oth of the pieces carry the popular Marlboro hip.

Piquet 30.00 50.00
Piquet 25.00 40.00
ulds
Nakajima 25.00 40.00
Nakajima 20.00 35.00
ulds
Prost 70.00 120.00
oro
Senna 50.00 100.00
oro
andro Nannini 25.00 40.00
on
y Boutsen 25.00 40.00
on
ele Alboreto 25.00 40.00
rd Berger 25.00 40.00

1989 Onyx F1 1:43

erent Formula 1 teams were represented in this series. popular cars for the second year in a row are the enna and Alain Prost with the Marlboro sponsorship. on Piquet and Saturo Nakajima cars carried another sponsor, Camel.

Senna 70.00 100.00
oro
Prost 45.00 75.00
oro
Boutsen 15.00 30.00
do Patrese 15.00 30.00
on Piquet 25.00 45.00
o Nakajima 15.00 30.00
icio Gugelmin 12.50 30.00
n House
Capelli 18.00 30.00
n House
sandro Nannini 25.00 40.00
ton
uele Pirro 15.00 30.00
ton 7Up
Caffi 15.00 30.00
oro Scuderi Italia
a deCesaris 15.00 30.00
oro Scuderi Italia
uigi Martini 15.00 30.00
Perez-Sala 12.50 30.00
Mansell 25.00 40.00
ard Berger 18.00 30.00
ele Alboreto 18.00 30.00
BP Larrousse
ppe Alliott 18.00 30.00
BP Larrousse

1990 Onyx F1 1:43

fferent Formula 1 teams were represented in this series. on Senna is the most difficult to find but unlike years the car doesn't carry the Marlboro sponsorship.

Prost 25.00 50.00
Mansell 15.00 25.00
Nakajima 12.00 20.00
Alesi 12.00 20.00
y Boutsen 18.00 30.00
do Patrese 12.00 20.00
k Warwick 15.00 25.00
in Donnelly 15.00 25.00
ricio Gugelmin 12.00 20.00
n House
Capelli 12.00 20.00
n House
erto Moreno 12.00 20.00
sandro Nannini 18.00 30.00
on Piquet 12.00 20.00
uigi Martini 12.00 20.00

SCM
24 Barilla Vittirio 12.00 20.00
SCM
27 Ayrton Senna 25.00 35.00
Honda Shell
28 Gerhard Berger 12.00 20.00
Honda Shell
29 Eric Bernard 12.00 20.00
Toshiba ESPO
30 Aguri Suzuki 12.00 20.00
Toshiba ESPO

1991 Onyx F1 1:43

The Michael Schumacher and Nelson Piquet cars in this series actually have multiple logos of a Camel on the car and not the printed word Camel. The Ayrton Senna and Gerhard Berger pieces are painted in the Marlboro colors but do not carry that actual sponsorship. It is also Michael Schumacher's first appearance in the Onyx 1:43 scale F1 cars.

1 Ayrton Senna 20.00 40.00
McLaren Honda
2 Gerhard Berger/ 15.00 25.00
3 Saturo Nakajima 10.00 20.00
Braun Epson
4 Stefano Modena 10.00 20.00
Braun Epson
5 Nigel Mansell 20.00 30.00
Canon
6 Riccardo Patrese 15.00 25.00
Canon
11 Mika Hakkinen 18.00 30.00
Yellow Hat
12 Johnny Herbert 12.00 20.00
Yellow Hat
19 Michael Schumacher 30.00 50.00
Camel Mobil1
20 Nelson Piquet 12.00 20.00
Camel Mobil1
27 Gianni Morbidelli 12.00 20.00
Ferrari
27 Alain Prost 12.00 20.00
Ferrari
28 Jean Alesi 15.00 25.00
Ferrari
29 Eric Bernard 10.00 20.00
Toshiba Larrousse
30 Aguri Suzuki 10.00 20.00
Toshiba Larrousse
32 Bertrand Gachot 15.00 25.00
7Up
32 Roberto Moreno 15.00 25.00
Pepsi
32 Alex Zanardi 12.00 20.00
Pepsi
33 Andrea deCesaris 12.00 20.00
7Up

1992 Onyx F1 1:43

Noticeably absent from this series is Ayrton Senna. The series represents eight different Formula 1 teams.

3 Olivier Grouillard 12.00 20.00
Calbee Tyrell
4 Andrea deCesaris 12.00 20.00
Calbee Tyrell
5 Nigel Mansell 15.00 25.00
Canon
6 Riccardo Patrese 12.00 20.00
Canon
9 Michele Alboreto 12.00 20.00
Footwork
10 Aguri Suzuki 12.00 20.00
Footwork
11 Mika Hakkinen 25.00 40.00
Hitachi
12 Johnny Herbert 12.00 20.00
Hitachi
19 Michael Schumacher 25.00 50.00
Benetton
20 Martin Brundle 12.00 20.00
Benetton
25 Thierry Boutsen 12.00 20.00
ELF Renault
26 Erik Comas 12.00 20.00
ELF Renault
27 Jean Alesi 12.00 20.00
Ferrari
28 Ivan Capelli 12.00 20.00
Ferrari
32 Stefano Modena 18.00 30.00
Sasol
33 Mauricio Gugelmin 12.00 20.00
Sasol

1993 Onyx F1 1:43

Michael Andretti stayed in Formula 1 just long enough to get a die-cast made by Onyx in 1993. He left Fl early in 1993 to return to the Indy Car circuit. The car is in the Marlboro team colors but doesn't carry the sponsor's name.

0 Damon Hill 15.00 25.00
Canon
2 Alain Prost 12.00 20.00
Canon
3 Ukyo Katayama 12.00 20.00
Calbee Tyrell
4 Andrea deCesaris 12.00 20.00
Calbee Tyrell
5 Nigel Mansell 35.00 50.00
K-Mart Benetton Back to Back
Two car set
5 Michael Schumacher 25.00 50.00
Benetton Camel Paint scheme
5 Michael Schumacher 25.00 50.00
Benetton Mild Seven paint scheme
5 Michael Schumacher 25.00 50.00
Kastle
5 Michael Schumacher 25.00 50.00
Killer Loop
5 Michael Schumacher 25.00 50.00
Nordica
5 Michael Schumacher 25.00 50.00
Prince
5 Michael Schumacher 25.00 50.00
Rollerblade
6 J.J. Lehto 12.00 20.00
Benetton
6 Riccardo Patrese 12.00 20.00
Benetton
6 Riccardo Patrese 12.00 20.00
Prince
6 Riccardo Patrese 12.00 20.00
Rollerblade
7 Michael Andretti 15.00 25.00
Shell
8 Ayrton Senna 18.00 30.00
Shell
11 Pedro Lamy 12.00 20.00
Castrol
11 Alex Zanardi 12.00 20.00
Castrol
12 Johnny Herbert 12.00 20.00
Castrol
14 Rubens Barrichello 12.00 20.00
Sasol
15 Thierry Boutsen 12.00 20.00
Sasol
27 Jean Alesi 12.00 20.00
Ferrari
28 Gerhard Berger 12.00 20.00
Ferrari
29 Karl Wendlinger 12.00 20.00
Liqui Moly
30 J.J. Lehto 12.00 20.00
Liqui Moly

1994 Onyx F1 1:43

This series marks the first appearance of special race cars. There are three different Australian Grand Prix cars with seven different teams represented in this series.

0 Damon Hill 15.00 25.00
Rothmans
0 Damon Hill 15.00 25.00
Rothmans Australian Grand Prix
0 Damon Hill 15.00 25.00
Rothmans Test car
2 David Coulthard 20.00 50.00
Rothmans
2 Nigel Mansell 15.00 25.00
Rothmans
2 Ayrton Senna 25.00 40.00
Rothmans
2 Ayrton Senna 20.00 35.00
Rothmans Test car
3 Ukyo Katayama 12.00 20.00
Calbee
4 Mark Blundell 12.00 20.00
Calbee
5 Damon Hill 15.00 25.00
Rothmans
5 Michael Schumacher 25.00 50.00
Benetton Mild Seven
5 Michael Schumacher 25.00 50.00
Benetton Mild Seven
Australian Grand Prix
6 David Coulthard 20.00 50.00
Rothmans
6 Johnny Herbert 12.00 20.00
Benetton Bitburger Mild Seven
Australian Grand Prix
6 J.J. Lehto 12.00 20.00
Benetton Mild Seven
6 Jos Verstappen 12.00 20.00
Benetton Mild Seven
11 Pedro Lamy 12.00 20.00
Loctite
12 Johnny Herbert 12.00 20.00
Loctite
14 Rubens Barrichello 12.00 20.00
Sasol
15 Andrea deCesaris 12.00 20.00
Sasol
15 Eddie Irvine 12.00 20.00
Sasol
25 Eric Bernard 12.00 20.00
ELF Renault
25 Martin Brundle 12.00 20.00
Hugo Pratt Art
26 Olivier Panis 12.00 20.00
ELF Renault
27 Nicola Larini 12.00 20.00
Ferrari
27 Jean Alesi 12.00 20.00
Ferrari 412 T1
27 Jean Alesi 12.00 20.00
Ferrari 412 T1b
28 Gerhard Berger 12.00 20.00
Ferrari
28 Gerhard Berger 12.00 20.00
Ferrari 412 T1b
29 Andrea deCesaris 12.00 20.00
Broker 200th Grand Prix
29 Andrea deCesaris 12.00 20.00
Tissot
29 Karl Wendlinger 12.00 20.00
Broker
Sauber
30 Heinz-Harold Frentzen 12.00 20.00
Broker
30 Heinz-Harold Frentzen 12.00 20.00
Tissot
33 Paul Belmondo 12.00 20.00
Ursus
34 Gachot Bernard 12.00 20.00
Ursus

1995 Onyx F1 1:43

Both Damon Hill and David Coulthard were represented with a regular and a Portugal Grand Prix car in this series. It was the last year that the Ferrari team was part of the set.

3 Ukyo Katayama 12.00 20.00
Nokia
3 Gabriele Tarquini 12.00 20.00
Nokia
4 Mika Salo 12.00 20.00
Nokia
5 Damon Hill 15.00 25.00
Rothmans Portugal Grand Prix
5 Damon Hill 15.00 25.00
Rothmans
6 David Coulthard 15.00 40.00
Rothmans
6 David Coulthard 20.00 50.00
Rothmans Protugal Grand Prix
9 Gianni Morbidelli 12.00 20.00
Hype
9 Max Papis 12.00 20.00
Hype
10 Taki Inoue 12.00 20.00
Hype
16 Jean-Denis Deletraz 12.00 20.00
Ursus
16 Giovanni Lavaggi 12.00 20.00
Ursus
16 Bertrand Gachot 12.00 20.00
Ursus
17 Andrea Montermini 12.00 20.00
Ursus
23 Pierluigi Martini 12.00 20.00
Lucchini
24 Luca Badoer 12.00 20.00
Lucchini
27 Jean Alesi 12.00 20.00
Ferrari
28 Gerhard Berger 12.00 20.00
Ferrari

1996 Onyx F1 1:43

Onyx retained only the Williams license and a few of the back marker teams for the 1996 series. Five teams were represented in this set.

5 Damon Hill 15.00 25.00
Rothmans French Grand Prix
5 Jacques Villeneuve 12.00 20.00
Rothmans French Grand Prix
16 Ricardo Rosset 12.00 20.00
Power Horse
17 Ricardo Rosset 12.00 20.00
Phillips
17 Jos Verstappen 12.00 20.00
Phillips
17 Jos Verstappen 12.00 20.00
Power Horse
18 Ukyo Katayama 12.00 20.00
Korean Air
19 Mika Salo 12.00 20.00
Korean Air
20 Pedro Lamy 12.00 20.00
Doimo
21 Giancarlo Fisichella 12.00 20.00
Doimo
21 Tarso Marques 12.00 20.00
Doimo
22 Luca Badoer 12.00 20.00
Forti Yellow Paint scheme
22 Luca Badoer 12.00 20.00
Shannon Green and White paint
23 Andre Montermini 12.00 20.00
Forti Yellow Paint scheme
23 Andre Montermini 12.00 20.00
Shannon Green and White paint

1997 Onyx F1 1:43

4 H.Frentzen 10.00 20.00
Castrol
16 Johnny Herbert 10.00 20.00
Red Bull

1998 Onyx F3 1:43

2 Mario Haberfeld 10.00 20.00
Copimax
5 Peter Dumbreck 10.00 20.00
Tom's
6 David Saelens 10.00 20.00
Fina

2005 Quartzo F1 1:18

4 Jim Clark 60.00 100.00
Lotus '68 Grand Prix
South Africa
5 Nigel Mansell 75.00 125.00
Elf Renault Canon
'92 Grand Prix South Africa/5000
24 Emerson Fittipaldi 75.00 125.00
Lotus
'70 Grand Prix USA/2500

1992-93 Tamiya F1 Collector's Club 1:20

5 Nigel Mansell 120.00 175.00
Canon 1992
5 Michael Schumacher 100.00 200.00
Benetton 1993
12 Mika Hakkinen 100.00 175.00
Castrol 1992
12 Johnny Herbert 100.00 160.00
Castrol 1993
12 Ayrton Senna 100.00 175.00
McLaren 1991 Champ
28 Jean Alesi 75.00 150.00
Ferrari 1993

1994 Action/RCCA Dirt Cars 1:24

5 Rodney Combs 25.00 40.00
Bull & Hannah
21 Billy Moyer 25.00 40.00
00 Freddy Smith 20.00 40.00
Bazooka/5004

1995 Action/RCCA Dirt Cars 1:24

1 Rodney Combs 20.00 40.00
Benson/5004
B4 Jack Boggs 30.00 60.00
Hawkeye Trucking/4500
5 Ronnie Johnson 25.00 40.00
Action
15 Steve Francis 20.00 40.00
Russell Baker/5520
18 Scott Bloomquist/5004 35.00 60.00
25 Ken Schrader 30.00 60.00
Budweiser/5004
41 Buck Simmons 25.00 40.00
One Stop/5568
75 John Gill 25.00 40.00
Mastersplit/5004

1996 Action/RCCA Dirt Cars 1:24

11 Bart Hartman 30.00 45.00
Pro Stocks
18 Scott Bloomquist 35.00 60.00
Action RCCA/4000
24 Rick Eckert 30.00 50.00
Raye-Vest/4008
28 Davey Allison 40.00 75.00
Havoline RCCA
99 Donnie Moran 30.00 45.00
Big Johnson/4008
00 Freddy Smith 30.00 45.00
Christenberry/5000
B12 Kevin Weaver 30.00 45.00
Rayburn Pizza Hut

1997 Action/RCCA Dirt Cars 1:24

E1 Mike Balzano 25.00 45.00
J.D. Cals/3504
3 Randy Sellars 25.00 40.00
5 Rodney Combs 25.00 40.00
Lance/2500
6M Wendall Wallace 25.00 40.00
Rebco
21 Billy Moyer 30.00 45.00
Bazooka/4008
28 Jimmy Mars 30.00 45.00
Parker Store/4000
30 Steve Shaver 25.00 40.00
Simonton/3500
66 Bob Frey 20.00 40.00
GRT
75 Terry Phillips/3348 25.00 40.00
89 Steve Barnett 25.00 40.00
Rayburn

1998 Action/RCCA Dirt Cars 1:24

5 Ronnie Johnson 30.00 45.00
12 Rick Auckland 60.00 100.00
EZ-Crusher/2508
21 Billy Moyer 60.00 100.00
Bazooka/3500
75 Bart Hartman 60.00 100.00
Pennzoil/2508
99 Donnie Moran/2508 25.00 50.00
0 Scott Bloomquist/4008 100.00 175.00

1999 Action/RCCA Dirt Cars 1:24

1 Jimmy Mars 50.00 80.00
Parker Stores/3168
5 Ronnie Johnson 50.00 80.00
AFCO/2508
21 Billy Moyer 40.00 75.00
Petroff Towing/3300
98 Tony Stewart 175.00 300.00
1998 J.D. Byrider/3000
00 Freddy Smith 35.00 60.00
Christenberry/3504

2000 Action/RCCA Dirt Cars 1:24

12 Ray Guss Jr. 40.00 75.00
PB Body Shop/2712
17M Dale McDowell 40.00 80.00
Dover Cylinder
Heads/2856
20 Tony Stewart 40.00 100.00
J.D.Byrider/9000
99 Donnie Moran 40.00 75.00
McCullough/2508

2001 Action/RCCA Dirt Cars 1:24

0 Scott Bloomquist 40.00 75.00
No Weak Links
15 Steve Francis 30.00 50.00
Valvoline/3504
18 Scott Bloomquist 40.00 75.00
Lane Automotive/4944
24 Rick Eckert 40.00 75.00
Raye-Vest/3504
53 Ray Cook 30.00 60.00
Youngblood/3504
56 Gary Webb 30.00 60.00
Moring Disposal/3612

2002 Action/RCCA Dirt Cars 1:24

1 Steve Francis 30.00 50.00
Valvoline Mopar/3504
21 Billy Moyer 30.00 50.00
Petroff Towing/4008
99 Ken Schrader 35.00 60.00
Federated/4560
201 Billy Ogle 30.00 50.00
Calhoun's/2892

2003 Action/RCCA Dirt Cars 1:24

99 Donnie Moran 30.00 50.00
QPI Tools/3168
99 Donnie Moran 175.00 300.00
QPI Tools Silver/192

2008 Action Late Model 1:24

24 Jeff Gordon 50.00 75.00
EA Sports/4524
48 Jimmie Johnson 50.00 75.00
Lowe's JJ Foundation/1428

1994 Action/RCCA Dirt Cars 1:64

These 1:64 dirt cars were produced and distributed by Action Performance. The cars were available through both the dealer network and Action's Racing Collectibles Club of America.

F1 Mike Duvall 5.00 10.00
1 C.J. Rayburn 5.00 10.00
1J Davey Johnson 5.00 12.00
5 Rodney Combs 5.00 10.00
Bull & Hannah
15 Jeff Purvis 10.00 20.00
18 Scott Bloomquist 15.00 40.00
21 Jack Hewitt 30.00 45.00
blister package
21 Jack Hewitt 6.00 12.00
box package
21 Billy Moyer 60.00 90.00
28 Davey Allison 10.00 18.00
Havoline RCCA/15,000
32 Bob Pierce 10.00 20.00
Tall Cool One
52 Ken Schrader 6.00 10.00
AC Delco
52 Ken Schrader 6.00 10.00
Bud
75 Bart Hartman 6.00 12.00

Pennzoil
00 Freddy Smith 6.00 15.00
Bazooka with Orange paint scheme

1995 Action/RCCA Dirt Cars 1:64

Each of these Late Model Dirt 1:64 cars were issued in an Action Platinum Series window box. The year "1995" is clearly labeled on the outside of the box.

1 Rodney Combs 5.00 12.00
Benson/20,880
1 Charlie Swartz 6.00 15.00
Malcuit Racing/16,128
B4 Jack Boggs 5.00 10.00
Hawkeye Trucking/18,000
5 Ronnie Johnson 5.00 10.00
Action/16,128
15 Steve Francis 5.00 10.00
in window box/21,888
18 Scott Bloomquist 10.00 20.00
Action Ford Motorsports
Promo/16,128
18 Scott Bloomquist 5.00 12.00
Action/30,000
25 Ken Schrader 6.00 15.00
Budweiser
41 Buck Simmons 5.00 10.00
One Stop/24,912
75 John Gill 5.00 10.00
Mastersplit/18,000
00 Freddy Smith 5.00 10.00
Bazooka Blue

1996 Action/RCCA Dirt Cars 1:64

This series of 1:64 cars were issued in an Action Platinum Series clam-shell style blister pack. An Action card of the featured driver was also included.

5 Ronnie Johnson 6.00 12.00
Hawkeye Trucking
11 Bart Hartman 5.00 10.00
Pro-Shocks
18 Scott Bloomquist 10.00 20.00
RCCA box/10,080
21 Billy Moyer 5.00 10.00
Bullet Baker
24 Rick Eckert 5.00 10.00
Raye-Vest
99 Donnie Moran 6.00 12.00
Big Johnson
00 Freddy Smith 5.00 10.00
Christenberry
B12 Kevin Weaver 5.00 10.00
Rayburn Pizza Hut

1997 Action/RCCA Dirt Cars 1:64

E1 Mike Balzano 5.00 10.00
J.D. Cals/10,080
5 Rodney Combs 60.00 90.00
Lance
6M Wendall Wallace 5.00 10.00
Rebco/10,080
21 Billy Moyer 10.00 20.00
Bazooka/10,080
28 Jimmy Mars 5.00 10.00
Parker Store
30 Steve Shaver 5.00 10.00
Simonton/10,080
56 Gary Webb/9000 6.00 12.00
66 Bob Frey 6.00 10.00
GRT/10,080
89 Steve Barnett 5.00 10.00
Rayburn/10,080

1998 Action/RCCA Dirt Cars 1:64

0 Scott Bloomquist 15.00 30.00
Miller Bros.Coal/9000
12 Rick Auckland 5.00 10.00
EZ-Crusher
21 Billy Moyer 10.00 20.00
Bazooka
75 Bart Hartman 6.00 12.00
BHR/7560

1999-00 Action/RCCA Dirt Cars 1:64

20 Tony Stewart 20.00 40.00
J.D.Byrider/9072 2000
98 Tony Stewart 35.00 60.00
1998 J.D. Byrider/7992
released in 1999

2008 Action Late Model 1:64

24 Jeff Gordon 7.50 15.00
EA Sports/2976
48 Jimmie Johnson 7.50 15.00
Lowe's JJ Foundation/1488

2003 ADC Dirt Late Model Cars 1:24

1 ADC Promo 40.00 75.00
1 Eddie Carrier Jr.
Hawkeye Trucking
1 Chub Frank 40.00 70.00
Corry Laser/2504
1 O'Reilly Mars Promo 40.00 70.00
1 Earl Pearson 40.00 70.00
Lucas Oil/1008
5 Rodney Combs 40.00 70.00
ADC Superman/2504
9 Dan Schlieper 50.00 80.00
MBC/1008
11 Batesville Topless Promo/250 60.00 120.00
15B Brian Birkhofer/1008 50.00 75.00
17M Dale McDowell/2504 40.00 70.00
21 Billy Moyer 40.00 70.00
Hawkeye/2504
31 Skip Arp/500 50.00 75.00
32 Bob Pierce 50.00 75.00
Clawson's/1008
37 Chuck LaSalle 40.00 70.00
NAPA
38 Jerry Pridal 40.00 70.00
D&K RV Sales
44 Clint Smith 50.00 75.00
CSR
71 Don O'Neal 40.00 70.00
Petroff/2504
88 Wendell Wallace 40.00 70.00
Craft/1008
89 Steve Barnett 40.00 70.00
J.D. Byrider/1008
89 Marshall Green 50.00 75.00
Hatfield
90 Gary Stuhler 40.00 70.00
Nininger/1008
96 Terry English 50.00 75.00
AAA Fence/500
99 Donnie Moran 50.00 75.00
McCullough Club/2504
00 Freddy Smith 40.00 70.00
White Oaks/2504
B12 Kevin Weaver/500 50.00 75.00
E1 Mike Balzano 40.00 70.00
Baker/1008

2003 ADC Dirt Modified Cars 1:24

3 Batesville Topless Promo/50 60.00 120.00
4G Gary Clark 40.00 70.00
4X Kevin Larkins 40.00 70.00
JET/1008
7 Ron Jones/1008 40.00 70.00
11C Chris Prussman 50.00 90.00
12 Jason Hughes 40.00 70.00
Hughes Racing/1008
20 Jimmy Owens 40.00 70.00
Hovis Racing/2504
69 John Logue 40.00 70.00
Pat Clemons/2504
74 Mark Noble 40.00 70.00
Yeager/2504
96 Johnny Saathoff 40.00 70.00
JET/2504
A1 George Handley
Handleys Auto Salvage

2004 ADC Dirt Late Model Cars 1:24

1 Frank Chubb 35.00 60.00
25th Anniversary/1008
1 Charlie Schwartz 35.00 60.00
1008
3 Kelly Shryock 35.00 60.00
Shyrock Racing/1008
9 Bill Elliott 50.00 80.00
5004
15 Steve Francis 35.00 60.00
3500
19 Davey Johnson 35.00 60.00
1008
24 Rick Eckert 35.00 60.00
Rayevest/1500
41 Buck Simmons 35.00 60.00
1008
44 Chris Madden 35.00 60.00
1008
50 Ed Dixon 35.00 60.00
1008
50B Larry McDaniels
53 Ray Cook 35.00 60.00
1008
66 Bill Frye 35.00 60.00
1008
71C R.J. Conley 35.00 60.00
1008
75 Bart Hartman 35.00 60.00
1008
75 John Gill 35.00 60.00
Helena/1008
75 Terry Phillips 35.00 60.00
1008
99 Ken Schrader 40.00 70.00
1008
114 Randall Chupp 35.00 60.00
1008
W11 Rob Blair 35.00 60.00
1008

2004 ADC Dirt Modified Cars 1:24

3L Jeff Leka 35.00 60.00
1008
17S M.Spaulding 35.00 60.00
Puggley's/1008
21S Denny Schwartz 35.00 60.00
1008
75 John Thompson 35.00 60.00
1008
97M Dave Murray 35.00 60.00
1008
99 Ken Schrader 35.00 60.00
1008
701 Henry Wilt 35.00 60.00
1008

2005 ADC Dirt Late Model Cars 1:24

00 Randy Korte 40.00 65.00
500

2003 ADC Dirt Late Model Cars 1:64

1 Chub Frank 10.00 20.00
Corry Laser/5004
5 Rodney Combs 10.00 20.00
ADC Superman/5004
17M Dale McDowell/5004 10.00 20.00
21 Billy Moyer 10.00 20.00
Petroff/5004
24 Rick Eckert 10.00 20.00
Rayevest/5004
32 Bob Pierce 10.00 20.00
Clawson's/5004
71 Don O'Neal 10.00 20.00
Petroff/5004
88 Wendall Wallace 10.00 20.00
Craft
99 Donnie Moran 15.00 25.00
McCullough Club/5004
99 Donnie Moran 10.00 20.00
QPI/5004
00 Freddy Smith 10.00 20.00
White Oaks/5004
E Steve Francis 10.00 20.00
Mopar

2003 ADC Dirt Modified Cars 1:64

20 Jimmy Owens 10.00 20.00
69 John Logue 10.00 20.00
Pat Clemons
74 Mark Noble 10.00 20.00
Yeager
96 Johnny Saathoff 10.00 20.00
JET

2004 ADC Dirt Late Model Cars 1:64

1 Frank Chubb 7.50 15.00
25th Anniversary/3500
3 Kelly Shryock 7.50 15.00
Shyrock Racing
9 Bill Elliott 10.00 20.00
5000
15 Steve Francis 7.50 15.00
4000
15B Brian Birkhofer 7.50 15.00
3500
20 Darrell Lanigan 7.50 15.00
3500
21 Billy Moyer 7.50 15.00
2504
75 John Gill 7.50 15.00
5004
75 Bart Hartman 7.50 15.00
3500
92 Dick Potts 7.50 15.00
3500
99 Ken Schrader 7.50 15.00
3500
E1 Mike Balzano 7.50 15.00
3500

2004 ADC Dirt Modified Cars 1:64

12B Johnny Bone Jr. 7.50 15.00
3500

1993 Ertl/Nutmeg Modified Legends 1:64

Ertl produced a series of 1:64 scale Modified Legends cars for Nutmeg Collectibles. Each piece in the 1993 release was issued in a small blue window display box that featured the Ertl notation on the top and the Nutmeg name on the front side. The driver's name, car number, and issue number (included below) of the series was also included. Each car was produced in quantities of 5000 and feature the Coupe body style unless noted below.

0 Bud Olsen #22 6.00 12.00
1 Charlie Jarzombek 6.00 12.00
Coupe #12
2 Frank Schneider 6.00 12.00
Frankie's Salvage #10
2X Ed Flemke #5 6.00 12.00
4 Ted Harfield 6.00 12.00
Adams Heating #23
4 Lou Lazzaro 8.00 20.00
Fonda Express #24
11 Ray Hendrick #21 6.00 12.00
12 Ken Bouchard 6.00 12.00
Sherwood Vega #20
12A Jack Johnson 6.00 12.00
Johnson's Garage #6
15 Bugsy Stevens #3 6.00 15.00
17 Ron Bouchard 6.00 12.00
Pinto #13
24 Will Cagle 8.00 20.00
Coupe #4
24 Will Cagle 6.00 12.00
Pinto #16
29 Ernie Gahan #11 6.00 12.00
33 Bill Wimble #26 10.00 25.00
38 Jerry Cook 8.00 20.00
B&M Speed #2
39 Al Tasnady 15.00 25.00
Piscopo's Auto #25
43 Bill Greco 6.00 12.00
Greco Auto Parts Pinto #15
61 Richie Evans 15.00 25.00
B&M Speed Yellow #1
61 Richie Evans 10.00 20.00
B&M Speed Orange #7
93 Gold Christmas Coupe/2000 7.50 15.00
93 Green Christmas Coupe/5000 3.00 6.00
93 Red Christmas Coupe/3000 5.00 10.00
93 Brian Ross #9 6.00 12.00
711 Bob Polverari 6.00 12.00
Perry Auto Vega #17
01 Ray Miller 6.00 12.00
Chamberlian Vega #18
V8 Bill Slater 6.00 12.00
Conn Valley #8
X3 Jim Hendrickson 6.00 12.00
Vega #19
X90 Fred Harbach 6.00 12.00
Flying Dutchman Pinto #14

1994 Ertl/Nutmeg Modified Legends 1:64

5 Stafford Speedway Show Promo 3.00 8.00

1996 Ertl/Nutmeg Modified Legends 1:64

Ertl produced this series of 1:64 scale Legends cars for Nutmeg Collectibles. Each was issued in a small window display box that featured a blue marbelized design. The driver's name, car number, and/or issue number of the series was included on the box. Each car was produced in quantities of 5000 and feature the Coupe body style unless noted below.

3 Fred DeSarro 6.00 12.00
Boehler's #31
7 Dutch Hoag 15.00 30.00
Genesee Beer #28
8 Jim Shampine 6.00 12.00
Village Collision #32
9J Don MacTavish #30 6.00 12.00
58 Merv Treichler #29 6.00 12.00
74 Rog Treichler 6.00 12.00
Jenny Power Vega #33
00 Buzzie Ruetimann 12.50 25.00
Dover Brake #27

1998 Ertl/Nutmeg Modified Legends 1:64

Ertl produced this series for Nutmeg Collectibles. Each was issued in a small window display box that featured the Ertl notation on the top and the Nutmeg name on the front side. The driver's name, car number, and issue number (noted below) of the series was also included. Each car was produced in quantities of 5000 and feature the Coupe body style unless noted below.

1 Charlie Jarzombek 6.00 12.00
Vega #37
3 Pete Corey #42 6.00 12.00
4 Leo Cleary #39 6.00 12.00
6 Richie Evans 6.00 12.00
N.Y. #40
8 Jim Shampine 6.00 12.00
Village Collision Pinto #43
13 Joe Kelly #46 6.00 12.00
17 Dick Tobias 6.00 12.00
Tobias Speed #45
18 Dutch Hoag #38 6.00 12.00
43 Billy Greco 6.00 12.00
Tasmanian Devil #36
44 Jim Tasnady #44 6.00 15.00
61 Richie Evans 6.00 12.00
B.R.DeWitt Pinto #35
77 Jackie Evans #34 6.00 12.00
99 Bobby Malzahn #47 6.00 12.00
XL1 Tommie Elliott #41 6.00 12.00

1990 Matchbox Modifieds Series 1 1:64

1 Tony Hirschman 6.00 12.00
Clark Concrete
15 Mike Stefanik 6.00 12.00
Koszela Speed Shop Red
44 Reggie Ruggiero 6.00 12.00
Magnum Oil Yellow
U2 Jamie Tomaino 6.00 12.00
Danny's Market

1991 Matchbox Modifieds Series 2 1:64

12 Mike McLaughlin 6.00 12.00
Sherri Cup
15 Mike Stefanik 6.00 12.00
Auto Palace ADAP
36 Mike Ewanitsko 6.00 12.00
Mutual Engraving
41 Jay Hedgecock 6.00 12.00
C&C

1992 Matchbox Modifieds Series 3 1:64

3 Doug Heveron 5.00 10.00
4 Satch Worley 5.00 10.00
Mystic River Marina
21 George Kent 5.00 10.00
U2 Jamie Tomaino 5.00 10.00

1992 Matchbox Modifieds Series 4 1:64

7NW Tom Baldwin 4.00 8.00
25 Jan Leaty 4.00 8.00
44 Rick Fuller 4.00 8.00
69 Reggie Ruggiero 4.00 8.00

1993 Matchbox Modifieds Series 5 1:64

STATED PRODUCTION RUN 5000 SETS
2X Jerry Marquis 4.00 8.00
5 Charlie Pasteryak 4.00 8.00
11 Ed Flemke 4.00 8.00
77 Rick Fuller 4.00 8.00

1994 Matchbox Modifieds Series 6 1:64

STATED PRODUCTION RUN 5000 SETS
15 Wayne Anderson 4.00 8.00
27 Jan Leaty 4.00 8.00
31 Tony Ferrante 4.00 8.00
56 Tim Arre 4.00 8.00

1994 Matchbox Modifieds Series 7 1:64

STATED PRODUCTION RUN 5000 SETS
0 Ed Kennedy 4.00 8.00
17 Jamie Tomaino 4.00 8.00
21 Mike McLaughlin 4.00 8.00
39 Bruce D'Alessandro 4.00 8.00

1992 Matchbox Modified Legends Series 1 1:64

STATED PRODUCTION RUN 10,000 SETS
3 Ron Bouchard 6.00 12.00
4 Carl Stevens 6.00 12.00
6 Maynard Troyer 6.00 12.00
38 Jerry Cook 6.00 12.00

1993 Matchbox Modified Legends Series 2 1:64

12 Brett Bodine 6.00 12.00
Sherri Cup
24 Jimmy Spencer 6.00 12.00
61 Richie Evans 6.00 12.00
B.R.DeWitt Orange
99 Geoff Bodine 6.00 12.00

1994 Matchbox Modified Legends Series 3 1:64

STATED PRODUCTION RUN 5000 SETS
1 Charlie Jarzombek 6.00 12.00
8 Mike McLaughlin 6.00 12.00
37 Mike Stefanik 6.00 12.00
73 B Roth 6.00 12.00

1992 Matchbox White Rose DIRT Super Stars 1:64

1 Doug Hoffman 7.50 15.00
Phelps Cement
6 Danny Johnson 7.50 15.00
Freightliner Trucks
7X Steve Paine 7.50 15.00
Turbo Blue
9 Bob McCreadie 7.50 15.00
Syracuse Frame
72 Brett Hearn 10.00
Kenyon
91 Billy Decker 10.00
Wheels Auto Supply

1993 Matchbox White Rose DIRT Super 1:64

1 Joe Plazek 6.00
Steak Out Restaurant
12 Jack Johnson 6.00
B.R.DeWitt
14J Alan Johnson 6.00
R.P. LaFrois
21J Jeff Trombley 6.00
Hutter Altair Audio
35 Toby Tobias 6.00
Tobias Speed
44 Frank Cozze 6.00
Carquest
74 Rick Elliott 6.00
Smith Bros. Concrete
115 Kenny Tremont 6.00
Fane Doherty Bros.

2003 Nutmeg Modified Legends 1:

2 Frankie Schneider 30.00
Frankie's Sausage 2
7 Dutch Hoag 30.00
Genesee 4
00 Buzzie Ruetimann 30.00
Dover Brake 1

1998-01 Action/RCCA Sprint 1:18

These 1:18 scale cars are part of the Action Racing Co Xtreme Series.

1BK Johnny Herrera 30.00
Burger King/2004 1999
7 Kevin Huntley 20.00
Peterbilt/4008 1998
11 Steve Kinser 50.00
Quaker State/2500 1998
11 Steve Kinser 40.00
Quaker State/2508 1999
11 Steve Kinser 125.00
Quaker State
Superman/8004 1999
11 Steve Kinser 30.00
Quaker State/3000 2000
12 Greg Hodnett 25.00
Wirtgen/1500 2000
12 Greg Hodnett 40.00
Apple Chevrolet/2508 1999
17 Joey Saldana 25.00
Mox Motorsport/2508 1999
19 Stevie Smith 50.00
Ingersoll-Rand 1998
20 Johnny Herrera 30.00
NetWorks/2004 2000
22 Jac Haudenschild 50.00
Pennzoil 1998
23S Frankie Kerr 20.00
Shoff/4008 1998
83 Danny Lasoski 50.00
Beef Packers/2508 1998

1994 Action/RCCA Sprint 1:24

11 Steve Kinser 50.00
Valvoline/3516
21 Fred Rahmer 50.00
Budweiser/2508
22 Jac Haudenschild 50.00
Pennzoil/1728
28D Brad Doty 45.00
Bower's/2508
38 Ken Schrader 45.00
Crawford/2508
55 Tim Richmond 30.00
Elder Cadillac/3516
63 Jack Hewitt 40.00
Murphy's IGA/3500

1995 Action/RCCA Sprint 1:24

1 Sammy Swindell 75.00
Hooters/2712
1 Sammy Swindell 30.00
Old Milwaukee/5004
1 Sammy Swindell 35.00
TMC/4800
5 Johnny Herrera 20.00
Jackpot Junction/3516
7TW Jeff Swindell 30.00
Gold Eagle/5004
10 Dave Blaney 125.00
ivarin/2508
18 Brad Doty 30.00
Coors Light Silver Bullet
Red and Silver RCCA/5004
18 Brad Doty 30.00
Coors Light Silver Bullet
Blue and Silver/2508
18 Brad Doty 30.00
Coors Light blue&silver
Platinum Series/5004
19 Tony Stewart 75.00
Triple Crown/3500
20 Jeff Gordon 125.00
Hap's RCCA/7500
33 Danny Drinan 35.00
IWX/2500

1996 Action/RCCA Sprint 1:24

1 Billy Pauch 12.50
Zemco/4500
1 Sammy Swindell 30.00
Channellock/5004

Hillenburg /4500	20.00	50.00
e Blaney rin/4500	40.00	80.00
e Kinser ker State/5000	50.00	100.00
y Stewart 5 Triple Crown/5004	75.00	135.00
ce Blevins o/4008	20.00	40.00
Haudenschild nzoil	35.00	60.00
Gordon ' Stanton RCCA/4008	150.00	300.00
nny Herrera nge King's Royal/4008	25.00	50.00
tevie Smith water/6000	15.00	40.00
y Saldana oar/4704	20.00	50.00

1997 Action/RCCA Sprint 1:24

ny Swindell annellock Silver/4008	35.00	60.00
'eley on blue/2508	25.00	50.00
'eley on red/2508	25.00	50.00
rk Kinser tgen/4008	30.00	50.00
eff Swindell d Eagle Flames/4008	15.00	40.00
e Blaney arin/4560	25.00	50.00
ve Kinser aker State/6000	30.00	60.00
ve Kinser aker State Mac Tools	100.00	150.00
eg Hodnett na Shell/4500	15.00	40.00
nny Schatz atz Crossroads/4008	12.50	30.00
vie Smith Jr. c Tools/3804	15.00	40.00
nt Kaeding neer Concrete	15.00	40.00
d Rahmer nheim Auctions/4224	20.00	50.00

1998 Action/RCCA Sprint 1:24

vie Smith Jr. ersoll-Rand/4008	25.00	50.00
onny Kreitz itzer Excavating	30.00	50.00

1999 Action/RCCA Sprint 1:24

Gordon 90 Diet Pepsi/7500	125.00	225.00
y Stewart 95 Beast/3500	75.00	135.00
an Newman arheads Lewis Racing/2508	100.00	175.00
nny Lasoski ef Packers Matco Tools	45.00	80.00

2000 Action/RCCA Sprint 1:24

y Pankratz -Rite/2004	35.00	60.00
ny Stewart rkey Night/4800	60.00	120.00
rah McCune E A-1/2508	20.00	40.00
ne Carter abash National digo Chevrolet City/2004	20.00	40.00

2001 Action/RCCA Sprint 1:24

nmy Swindell annellock/4104	20.00	40.00
ny Irwin 94 Wynn's/2808	25.00	50.00
ny Irwin 94 Wynn's Silver/504	40.00	80.00
lark Kinser opar Spider-Man/4212	30.00	60.00
eve Kinser pa/5004	25.00	50.00
eve Kinser aker State/5004	20.00	40.00
evie Smith gersoll-Rand	15.00	40.00
ny Stewart rformance/8004	25.00	50.00
nny Lasoski D.Byrider/4536	30.00	60.00
nny Lasoski D.Byrider rassic Park 3/5340	25.00	50.00
sey Kahne ngless Midget/2004	75.00	150.00

2002 Action/RCCA Sprint 1:24

eve Kinser aker State/3600	25.00	50.00
Stevie Smith Jr. varin/2856	25.00	50.00
onny Schatz rker/2220	20.00	50.00
nny Lasoski D.Byrider/3504	30.00	60.00
nny Lasoski D.Byrider Muppet/3648	25.00	50.00
nny Lasoski D.Byrider Muppet CCA/180	30.00	60.00
83 Danny Lasoski Beef Packers/2508	40.00	80.00

2003 Action/RCCA Sprint 1:24

1 Sammy Swindell Ore-Cal Beef Packers/2184	30.00	60.00
9 J.J.Yeley Beast '03 Champion/1908	35.00	60.00
11 Steve Kinser Quaker State 2002 Champ. Color Chrome/3684	35.00	60.00
11 Steve Kinser Quaker State 2002 Champ. Color Chrome RCCA/360		
11 Steve Kinser Quaker State Hulk/4468	35.00	60.00
20 Danny Lasoski J.D. Byrider/3496	30.00	60.00
20 Danny Lasoski J.D. Byrider Cat in the Hat/2392	35.00	60.00

2004 Action/RCCA Sprint 1:24

9 Kasey Kahne Dodge Curb Records/5004	60.00	100.00
11 Steve Kinser Quaker State 500th Win Raced/3168	40.00	60.00
11 Steve Kinser Quaker State Popeye/2438	40.00	60.00
15 Donny Schatz Parker Stores/2004	35.00	60.00
20 Danny Lasoski J.D. Byrider/2928	35.00	60.00
20 Danny Lasoski J.D. Byrider Mad Magazine/1908	35.00	60.00
20 Danny Lasoski J.D. Byrider Michael Ross Memorial Foundation/3000	35.00	60.00
20 Danny Lasoski J.D. Byrider Shrek 2/2496	35.00	60.00
20 Tony Stewart American Compressed Steel Michael Ross Foundation/4776	40.00	60.00

2005 Action/RCCA Sprint 1:24

9 Kasey Kahne Valvoline/4116	40.00	65.00
9 Kasey Kahne Valvoline Color Chrome/504	50.00	75.00
9 Kasey Kahne Valvoline QVC/480	40.00	65.00
11 Steve Kinser Quaker State James Dean 50th Anniversary/2304	40.00	65.00
11 Steve Kinser Quaker State '05 Champion/2100	40.00	65.00
11 Steve Kinser Quaker State '05 Champion Brushed Metal/408		
11 Steve Kinser Quaker State '05 Champion Color Chrome/2100	50.00	75.00
11 J.J. Yeley Old Spice/1800	40.00	65.00
11 J.J. Yeley Old Spice Color Chrome/300	50.00	75.00
19 Tyler Walker Dodge Curb Records AU/2508	50.00	75.00
20 Danny Lasoski Bass Pro/1872	40.00	65.00
20 Danny Lasoski Bass Pro Shops GM Dealers/36	40.00	65.00
20 Danny Lasoski Bass Pro Madagascar/1428	40.00	65.00
20 Danny Lasoski Bass Pro Michael Ross Foundation/1272	50.00	75.00
20 Danny Lasoski Mopar/2220	50.00	75.00
20 Tony Stewart Artic Cat Michael Ross Foundation/2148	50.00	75.00
20 Tony Stewart Bass Pro Shops/3276	125.00	200.00
20 Tony Stewart Bass Pro Shops Color Chrome/504	125.00	200.00
20 Tony Stewart Bass Pro Shops GM Dealers/60	125.00	200.00
20 Tony Stewart Bass Pro Shops QVC/120	125.00	200.00
20 Tony Stewart Bass Pro Shops Madagascar/4752	50.00	75.00
20 Tony Stewart Bass Pro Shops Madagascar Mac Tools/300	50.00	75.00
20 Tony Stewart Bass Pro Shops Madagascar Matco/144	50.00	75.00
20 Tony Stewart Bass Pro Shops Madagascar QVC/504	50.00	75.00
83 Kasey Kahne Beef Packers '03 QVC/120	50.00	80.00

2006 Action/RCCA Sprint 1:24

9 Kasey Kahne Sage Fruit/852	60.00	100.00
20 Tony Stewart Old Spice Color Chrome/300	125.00	200.00

1998-99 Action/RCCA Sprint 1:50

1 Sammy Swindell Channellock/9000 1998	6.00	15.00
5M Mark Kinser Wirtgen	6.00	12.00
5M Mark Kinser Mopar/6120 1999	7.50	20.00
7 Kevin Huntley Peterbilt/9000 1998	6.00	12.00
11 Steve Kinser Quaker State/5040 1998	15.00	40.00
11 Steve Kinser Quaker State Superman/17,496 1999	15.00	40.00
23 Frankie Kerr Shoff Motrosports	6.00	12.00
47 Johnny Herrera Strange	6.00	12.00
69K Donnie Kreitz Kreitzer Excavating	6.00	12.00

1995 Action/RCCA Sprint 1:64

1 Sammy Swindell TMC/10,080	5.00	12.00
7TW Jeff Swindell Gold Eagle	5.00	10.00

1996 Action/RCCA Sprint 1:64

1 Billy Pauch Zemco/10,080	5.00	10.00
22 Jac Haudenschild Pennzoil	5.00	10.00
40 Jeff Gordon 1987 Stanton/10,080	20.00	35.00

1997 Action/RCCA Sprint 1:64

1 Sammy Swindell Channellock/10,080	5.00	12.00
1 Sammy Swindell Channellock Silver/10,080	5.00	12.00
2 Andy Hillenburg STP/10,080	6.00	12.00
5 Steve Kinser Maxim	5.00	10.00
10 Dale Blaney Vivarin/10,080	4.00	10.00
11 Steve Kinser Quaker State/12,024	6.00	10.00
15 Donny Schatz Blue Beacon/10,000	3.00	8.00
19 Stevie Smith/8352	5.00	10.00
77 Fred Rahmer Manheim Auctions/10,080	5.00	10.00

1998 Action/RCCA Sprint 1:64

19 Stevie Smith Jr. Ingersoll-Rand	5.00	10.00
69K Donny Kreitz Kreitzer Excavating	5.00	10.00

1995 Ertl/Nutmeg Sprint Cars 1:55

Ertl produced this series of 1:55 scale sprint cars for Nutmeg. Each was issued in a clear window display box that featured a cardboard tab to attach the box to a retail rack display.

1 Sammy Swindell/7500	4.00	8.00
5 Mark Kinser/7500	4.00	10.00
23S Frankie Kerr Shoff/5000	4.00	8.00
77 Stevie Smith/7500	4.00	8.00

1992-94 Ertl Sprint Transporters 1:64

1 Billy Pauch Zemco	30.00	60.00
1 Sammy Swindell TMC Racing	50.00	100.00
1A Bobby Allen Allen Racing	45.00	80.00
1W Keith Kauffman LEW Racing	30.00	60.00
7TW Joe Gaerte Gaerte Engines	50.00	100.00
17 Chris Esch E&G Classics	40.00	80.00
19 Steve Smith Sr. Leiby's Mobile Homes	40.00	80.00
25 Dan Dietrich Cooper Motors	30.00	60.00
28 Brad Doty Bowers Coal 1993	45.00	80.00
69 Donnie Kreitz Jr.	50.00	100.00
99 Fred Rahmer Busch	50.00	100.00
NNO Fletcher's Racing	30.00	60.00

2002 GMP Vintage Sprint Cars 1:12

1 A.J.Foyt Bowes Seal/1500	175.00	350.00
1 Bobby Unser Bardahl	150.00	300.00
2 Mario Andretti Castrol Viceroy/900	175.00	350.00
2 Al Unser Johnny Lightning	300.00	500.00
4 Don Branson Wynn's/896	175.00	350.00

1996-01 GMP Sprint Cars 1:18

The first spring car piece released by GMP was the Steve Kinser. Upon release it was quickly one of the most popular pieces on the market. The Jeff Gordon and Jac Haudenschild pieces have also done well.

1 GMP Platinum/1200 '99	45.00	80.00
1 Steve Kinser Aristocrat/3504 1998	40.00	80.00
1 Billy Pauch Zemco/3504 1997	30.00	80.00
1 Jimmy Sills Sills/2808 1997	40.00	80.00
1 Sammy Swindell Channellock 1997	80.00	140.00
1 Sammy Swindell Channellock 25th Anniversary/3504 1997	150.00	250.00
1 Sammy Swindell Channellock/3792 1998	50.00	100.00
1 Sammy Swindell Old Milwaukee/3072 1998	60.00	120.00
1 Sammy Swindell TMC/3576 1997	70.00	120.00
1A Bobby Allen Shark/2400 1999	50.00	100.00
1N Sammy Swindell Nance/2508 2001	50.00	100.00
2 Andy Hillenburg Luxaire/1500 2001	50.00	90.00
2 Andy Hillenburg STP/3504 1997	30.00	80.00
2 Rich Volger Seibert Olds/1200	45.00	80.00
4X Jan Opperman Speedway Motors/3504 1998	75.00	135.00
5 Danny Lasoski Ethanol Jackpot Junction/3504 1997	65.00	90.00
5M Mark Kinser Wirtgen/3504 1997	50.00	100.00
5M Mark Kinser Mopar/2496 2000	70.00	110.00
6 Jeff Gordon Molds Unlimited/3672 1997	200.00	400.00
7TW Jeff Swindell Gold Eagle/3504	50.00	100.00
10 Dave Blaney Vivarin/3504 1997	50.00	100.00
10 Bobby Davis Jr. Casey Luma/1500 2000	45.00	80.00
10 Tyler Walker Ratbag/1404	60.00	100.00
11 Steve Kinser Aristocrat/3504	45.00	80.00
11 Steve Kinser Quaker State 1997	200.00	350.00
11H Greg Hodnett Vivarin/3192 1998	50.00	80.00
15 Donny Schatz Petro Blue Beacon/2504 1997	60.00	120.00
18 Brad Doty Coors Light/3504 1997	150.00	250.00
20 Tony Stewart Boles/3204 1994	100.00	200.00
20 Tony Stewart Boles 1995 Sprint Champ/3504 2000	150.00	250.00
22 Jac Haudenschild Pennzoil/3504 1997	70.00	120.00
22 Jac Haudenschild Pennzoil Black/2208 1998	75.00	125.00
22 Jac Haudenschild Radioactive Wild Child 1999	50.00	100.00
22 Jac Haudenschild Radioactive Krypton 1999	125.00	250.00
22 Jac Haudenschild Wild Child TNT/2068 2000	75.00	135.00
23 Kasey Kahne Speed Racer/2004 2001	75.00	125.00
29 Doug Wolfgang Weikert's Livestock 1999	90.00	150.00
40 Amoco Knoxville 40th Anniversary/1200 2000	50.00	90.00
40 Northern Auto Racing Club 40th Anniversary udweiser/2292 1999	40.00	80.00
47 Johnny Herrera Strange/3000 Casey's General Store 1997	60.00	110.00
63 Jack Hewitt Hampshire Racing/2400 '99	50.00	90.00
69 Brent Kaeding Pioneer Concrete/2904 1997	40.00	100.00
75 Brad Doty Stanton/2004 2000	40.00	80.00
93 Dale Blaney Amoco/1788 2000	50.00	120.00
96 Eldora Speedway 1997	90.00	150.00
97 Knoxville Raceway/3276 1997	50.00	100.00
98 Devil's Bowl Speedway Texas 1998	60.00	120.00
104 Jeff Swindell 104+ Octane/3204 1998	50.00	120.00
NNO Devil's Bowl 25th Anniv/2508	50.00	90.00

2002 GMP Sprint Cars 1:18

2 Brad Furr Sanmina green/2004	30.00	80.00
2 Brad Furr Sanmina red/2004	30.00	80.00
11 Steve Kinser Quaker State Black Chrome/2508	50.00	90.00
45 Cory Kruseman Willis Machine/1260	45.00	80.00
50 Richard Griffin Arizona Race Mart/1260	45.00	80.00

2003 GMP Sprint Cars 1:18

1 Ron Shuman Tamale Wagon/1000	50.00	80.00
3 Dave Darland Arctic Cat/1400	50.00	80.00
7 Craig Dollansky VMAC/1200	50.00	80.00
28D Brad Doty Bowers Coal/1200	50.00	80.00

2004 GMP Sprint Cars 1:18

2 Brad Furr Sanmina/2004	30.00	60.00

1998-03 GMP Vintage Sprint Cars 1:18

1 A.J. Foyt Bowes Seal/3504	200.00	300.00
1 A.J.Foyt Bowes Seal Black Chrome/2508 2002	50.00	90.00
1 A.J.Foyt Sheraton Thompson/3000	40.00	80.00
1 Parnelli Jones Fike Plumbing/3504	100.00	175.00
1 Ralph Pratt Jum White	40.00	80.00
1 Sprint Car Hall of Fame Black/950 2002	125.00	225.00
1 Sprint Car Hall of Fame Red/1999 '99	100.00	175.00
1 Sprint Car Hall of Fame White/1998 '98	125.00	225.00
1 Shorty Templeman Bardahl/2004	40.00	80.00
1 Al Unser Johnny Lightning/3504	70.00	120.00
1 Rodger Ward Kaiser Aluminum/3900 1999	50.00	80.00
2 A.J.Foyt Dart Kart/3996	60.00	100.00
2 Mario Andretti STP/4200	60.00	120.00
2 Jud Larson Watson Special/4104 2001	40.00	80.00
2 Roger McCluskey Konstant Hot/3624 1999	90.00	150.00
3 Don Branson Wynn's/3552 1998	100.00	175.00
3 Bobby Unser Key Special/3660 2000	60.00	100.00
5 Lloyd Axel Foster's Auto Supply/2196	40.00	80.00
5 Bobby Marshman Econo-Car/3192	40.00	80.00
6 A.J. Foyt Sheraton Thompson/4260 2000	80.00	135.00
6 Eddie Sachs Dean Van Lines/2592 2002	40.00	80.00
9 Johnny Rutherford 3504 1998	100.00	175.00
12 Rodger Ward Edelbrock V8/3900	50.00	100.00
22 Henry Banks Hopkins Special	40.00	80.00
27 Rodger Ward Edelbrock	45.00	80.00
44 Duke Nalon Bowes Seal/2508	40.00	80.00
56 Jim Hurtubise Sterling Plumbing/3552 1998	125.00	200.00
56 Jim Hurtubise Sterling Plumbing/2598 2002	40.00	80.00
83 Mario Andretti Gapco Special/4200	75.00	125.00
98 Parnelli Jones Willard Battery/2880	45.00	90.00
98 Bill Vukovich Rev 500	75.00	125.00
154 Freddie Agabashian Burgermeister	40.00	80.00

2000-02 GMP Sprint Car Sets 1:18/1:50

5 Jac Haudenschild Wirtgen 2002	50.00	90.00
11 Steve Kinser Quaker State/3000 2000	50.00	100.00
11 Steve Kinser Quaker State/2508 2002	60.00	120.00
15 Donny Schatz Parker Store/1500 2002	40.00	80.00
83 Sammy Swindell Ore-Cal Beef Packers/2508 2002	60.00	100.00
93 Kevin Gobrecht Amoco/2388 2000	50.00	100.00

1996-02 GMP Sprint Cars 1:25

With the release of the Dale Blaney piece in early 1997, GMP started a whole new scale size for Sprint Cars.

1 Lincoln Speedway/200 2002	30.00	60.00
1 Fred Rahmer O'Brien Stars&Stripes/2196	50.00	100.00
1 Sammy Swindell Channellock Raced/2004 2001	30.00	60.00
1F Dean Jacobs Frigidare/4404 1997	20.00	50.00
1W Danny Lasoski ConnWest/3480 1997	15.00	40.00
2 Andy Hillenburg Luxaire/2004 2001	50.00	90.00
2 Lincoln Speedway 50 Years/200	60.00	100.00
2A Bobby Adamson Johnny Lightning/3972 1997	40.00	70.00
2M Brent Kaeding Pioneer Concrete DuPont/2998	25.00	50.00
7TW Jeff Swindell Gold Eagle/3972 1997	35.00	60.00
8H Joe Gaerte Holbrook Motorsports/2196	25.00	50.00
10 Dale Blaney MBNA raced/1500 2001	20.00	40.00
11 Steve Kinser Quaker State/4404	30.00	80.00
11 Steve Kinser Quaker State/9804 1997	30.00	60.00
11 Steve Kinser Quaker St.Raced/2496 2001	50.00	100.00
15 Donny Schatz Parker Store/2004	25.00	50.00
19 Stevie Smith Jr. Ingersoll-Rand/3792	25.00	50.00
22 Jac Haudenschild Pennzoil/3972	25.00	60.00
23S Frankie Kerr Shoff Motrosports	25.00	50.00
35 Tyler Walker Air Sep/2504	25.00	50.00
69 Brent Kaeding Pioneer Concrete 1997	30.00	60.00
75 Joey Saldana Mopar/4404 1997	25.00	60.00
77 Fred Rahmer Manheim Auctions/2496 1997	20.00	50.00
83 Danny Lasoski Beef Packers/2196 1998	25.00	60.00
94 Dale Blaney	25.00	60.00

Hughes Axel/4404 1996
97 Eldora Speedway/2508 1997 30.00 80.00
U2 Keith Kauffman United/2196 25.00 50.00

2002 GMP Vintage Sprint Cars 1:43

1 Grimm Grant Piston Ring 15.00 25.00
15 Faulkner 15.00 25.00
27 Rodger Ward Edelbrock V8 15.00 25.00
45 Bill Vukovich 15.00 25.00
65 Oaks 15.00 25.00

2001-02 GMP Vintage Sprint Car Sets 1:43

NNO A.J.Foyt Bowes Seal/3504 2001 50.00 90.00
NNO Parnelli Jones Fike Plumbing Willard Batteries/2004 2002 40.00 75.00
NNO Roger McCluskey Konstant Hot/1500 2002 40.00 75.00

1998-01 GMP Sprint Cars 1:50

1 Sammy Swindell Channellock/3476 12.50 25.00
1A Bobby Allen Shark/4032 1999 10.00 20.00
2 Andy Hillenburg Luxaire/2448 2001 10.00 20.00
5 Jac Haudenschild Wirtgen/1728 12.50 25.00
10 Bobby Davis Jr. Casey Luma 15.00 25.00
11 Steve Kinser Quaker State/14,976 1998 10.00 20.00
11 Steve Kinser Quaker State/2592 2001 10.00 20.00
11H Greg Hodnett Vivarin 1998 7.50 15.00
15 Donny Schatz Petro Blue Beacon 7.50 15.00
19 Stevie Smith Jr. Ingersoll-Rand 1999 15.00 30.00
22 Jac Haudenschild Pennzoil black 10.00 20.00
22 Jac Haudenschild Radioactive Wild Child 12.50 25.00
23 Kasey Kahne Speed Racer/3600 2001 15.00 30.00
29 Doug Wolfgang Weikerts Livestock/5004 1999 7.50 15.00
35 Tyler Walker Air Sep 1999 7.50 15.00
40 Amoco Knoxville 40th Anniversary 10.00 20.00
63 Jack Hewitt Hampshire Motorsports/5004 7.50 15.00
77 Fred Rahmer Hamilton 7.50 15.00
83 Danny Lasoski Beef Packers 1999 10.00 20.00
93 Kevin Gobrecht Amoco/2016 2000 7.50 15.00

2002 GMP Sprint Cars 1:50

2 Brad Furr Sanmina/2160 7.50 15.00
10 Dale Blaney MBNA/2160 10.00 20.00
15 Donny Schatz Parker Store/1728 7.50 15.00
45 Cory Kruseman Willis Machine/1584 7.50 15.00
50 Richard Griffin Arizona Race Mart/1584 7.50 15.00
50 Lincoln Speedway/700 20.00 40.00

1991 Matchbox Sprint Cars 1:55

Matchbox issued this series of 1:55 scale sprint cars in red window display boxes. Each box included the year on the front as well as the "Series 1" notation. The packaging also featured a cardboard tab to attach the box to a retail rack display.

1 Sammy Swindell TMC 7.50 15.00
1A Bobby Allen Blue 4.00 10.00
5M Mark Kinser Williams 7.50 15.00
8D Doug Wolfgang White 4.00 10.00
11 Steve Kinser White 10.00 20.00
33X Steve Siegel Yellow 4.00 10.00

1992 Matchbox Sprint Cars 1:55

This series was produced in 1992 by Matchbox. Each 1:55 scale sprint car was packaged in a blue window display box. Each box included the year on the front as well as the "Series 2" notation. The packaging also featured a cardboard tab to attach the box to a retail rack display.

4 Bobby Davis Jr. Gambler 2.00 5.00
7C Dave Blaney Vivarin 2.50 6.00
7TW Joe Gaerte ed 2.00 5.00
17E Cris Eash E&S Classics 2.00 5.00
49 Doug Wolfgang Olsen 2.00 5.00
69K Donnie Kreitz Jr. Light Blue 2.00 5.00

1993 Matchbox Sprint Cars 1:55

This series of 1:55 scale sprint cars was issued by Matchbox in small window red display boxes. Each box included the year on the front as well as the "Series 3" or "Series 4" notation. The packaging also featured a cardboard tab to attach the box to a retail rack display.

1 Sammy Swindell TMC 2.00 5.00
1W Keith Kauffman 2.50 6.00
5M Mark Kinser Orange 2.00 5.00
10 Jac Haudenschild 3.00 8.00
11 Steve Kinser Valvoline 4.00 10.00
14 Tim Green 2.50 6.00
69 Brent Kaeding Black 2.00 5.00
69 Howard Kaeding White 2.00 5.00

1993-94 Racing Champions Sprint Cars 1:24

This series of 1:24 Racing Champions sprint cars is a good cross section of all the different drivers that raced World of Outlaws sprints at the time. Each piece is housed in a large black shadow box type box with a yellow interior. The year of issue is printed on the back of the box along with a driver checklist. Not all drivers on the list were produced for this set.

0 Rick Ferkel Kears 10.00 20.00
0 Randy Smith Mesquaki Bingo 12.50 25.00
1 Garry Brazier O'Brien 8.00 22.00
1 Sammy Swindell Bull and Hannah 30.00 50.00
1 Sammy Swindell TMC 45.00 70.00
1A Bobby Allen Kriners 30.00 60.00
2 Frankie Herr Family Ford 10.00 20.00
2 Frankie Herr Rifes RV 10.00 20.00
2 Andy Hillenburg STP with Dark Blue paint scheme 12.50 25.00
2 Andy Hillenburg STP with Light Blue paint scheme 15.00 40.00
2 Andy Hillenburg STP Signature Series 20.00 40.00
2 Garry Rush Castrol 10.00 20.00
2L Ed Lynch 12.50 25.00
U2 Rocky Hodges United Express 10.00 20.00
4A Greg Hodnett Mid So Forklift 10.00 20.00
4 Bobby Davis Jr. Pro Shocks 10.00 20.00
5 Max Dumesny Valvoline 60.00 90.00
5 Dennis Lasoski 30.00 50.00
7 Richard Griffin Sanders 8.00 20.00
7 Jimmy Sills Berry B Racing 8.00 20.00
7TW Jeff Swindell Gold Eagle 10.00 20.00
8TW Greg Hodnett Kele 8.00 20.00
9TW Joe Gaerte Gaerte Engines 8.00 20.00
10 Dave Blaney Vivarin 15.00 30.00
11 Steve Kinser Valvoline 20.00 50.00
11 Ron Shuman CH Enginering 8.00 20.00
12 Fred Rahmer Apple Chevrolet 15.00 30.00
12X Danny Smith Beaver Drill 12.50 25.00
14 Tim Green Swift Met Finish 12.50 25.00
14P Kevin Pylant Taco Bravo 10.00 20.00
18 Brad Doty Shaver Racing 15.00 30.00
21 Steve Beitler Brownfield 12.50 25.00
21 Lance Blevins Citgo 8.00 20.00
22 Jac Haudenschild Pennzoil with Red numbers 12.50 25.00
22 Jac Haudenschild Pennzoil with Yellow numbers 10.00 20.00
23S Frankie Kerr Shoff Motorsports 12.50 25.00
24 Jerry Stone Aeroweld Racing 8.00 20.00
27 Terry McCarl Westside Radiator 8.00 20.00
29 Keith Kauffman Weckert's Livestock 8.00 20.00
45 Doug Wolfgang Snap On 15.00 30.00
45X Johnny Herrera Herrera Motorsports 15.00 25.00
47 Danny Lasoski Casey's 15.00 25.00
49 Doug Wolfgang Bob Olsen 15.00 40.00
55 Max Dumesny 12.50 25.00
Halletts Mats
65 Jim Carr Maxim 12.50 25.00
66 Mike Peters TropArtic 12.50 25.00
69 Brent Kaeding JW Hunt 10.00 20.00
69 Brent Kaeding High-Five Pizza 8.00 20.00
69K Donnie Kreitz Jr. Vollmer Patterns 12.50 25.00
71M Kenny Jacobs Beltline 15.00 25.00
71M Kenny Jacobs Eco Water 8.00 20.00
77 J.Shepard Mac Tools 18.00 30.00
77 Stevie Smith Jr. Hamilton 10.00 20.00
77 Stevie Smith Jr. Mac Tools 20.00 35.00
97B Aaron Berryhill Berryhill Racing 10.00 20.00
00 Jason Statler Rios 8.00 20.00
07 Smokey Snellbaker Rifes RV 12.50 25.00

1995 Racing Champions Sprint Cars 1:24

This was the second year that Racing Champions produced a 1:24 sprint car series. The series again included many of the big names from the World of Outlaw circuit. Each was packaged in a black window box with "Series 2" clearly marked on the outside.

0 Danny Smith 7.50 15.00
0 Randy Smith Bingo Casino 7.50 15.00
1 Billy Pauch Zemco 8.00 20.00
1 Sammy Swindell Bull and Hannah 12.50 25.00
1 Sammy Swindell Hooters Series 2 12.50 25.00
2 Andy Hillenburg STP 10.00 20.00
2 Andy Hillenburg STP Oil 10.00 20.00
2J J.J. Yeley Bull&Hannah 12.50 25.00
4S Tommy Scott Scott Performance 7.50 15.00
5 Terry McCarl CS Enterprises 10.00 20.00
5M Mark Kinser Wirtgen 30.00 50.00
7TW Jeff Swindell Gold Eagle 10.00 20.00
8TW Greg Hodnett Kele with red numbers 8.00 20.00
8TW Greg Hodnett Kele with yellow numbers 15.00 25.00
9W Joe Gaerte Two Winners 10.00 20.00
9TW Gary Wright Action Rent 7.50 15.00
10 Dave Blaney Vivarin 12.50 25.00
11 Steve Kinser Valvoline 10.00 20.00
11 Ron Shuman CH Enginering 12.50 25.00
12 Fred Rahmer pple Chevrolet 10.00 20.00
14P Kevin Pylant Unicopy 10.00 20.00
16 Jeff Gordon JG Motorsports/5000 125.00 225.00
17E Cris Eash Miller Brothers 7.50 15.00
21 Steve Beitler Brownfield 7.50 15.00
21 Lance Blevins Citgo 7.50 15.00
21K Lou Kennedy CT Fleet 7.50 15.00
21K Lou Kennedy hamrock Carpet 7.50 15.00
22 Jac Haudenschild Pennzoil 10.00 20.00
23S Frankie Kerr 10.00 20.00
31 Sid Blandford Avenger 7.50 15.00
47 Danny Lasoski Housby Trucking 8.00 20.00
65 Jim Carr Maxim 7.50 15.00
66 Mike Peters TropArtic 7.50 15.00
69 Brent Kaeding Motorola 7.50 15.00
71M Kenny Jacobs EcoWater 7.50 15.00
71M Stevie Smith Jr. EcoWater 10.00 20.00
77 Joe Gaerte Cornwell 15.00 30.00
97B Aaron Berryhill 7.50 15.00

1996 Racing Champions Sprint Cars 1:24

For the thrid consecutive year Racing Champions produced 1:24 scale Sprint cars. The cars were primarily distributed through mass market retailiers. 1996 World of Outlaw Champion Mark Kinser is one of the highlights of the series.

1X Randy Hannagan Carrera 12.50 25.00
5 Danny Lasoski Jackpot Junction 8.00 20.00
5M Mark Kinser Wirtgen 8.00 20.00
7M Jim Carr American Fire Exting. 15.00 30.00
7TW Jeff Swindell Gold Eagle 10.00 20.00
9W Gary Wright 7.50 15.00
10 Dave Blaney Vivarin 7.50 20.00
11 Steve Kinser Quaker State 20.00 40.00
22 Jac Haudenschild 8.00 20.00
Pennzoil
47 Johnny Herrera 8.00 20.00
69 Brent Kaeding Motorola 7.50 15.00
71M Stevie Smith EcoWater 8.00 20.00
83 Joey Saldana Southwest Hide 7.50 15.00
461 Lance Dewease Dyer Masonary 7.50 15.00

1997 Racing Champions Sprint Cars 1:24

This was the fourth year of production of 1:24 scale Sprint cars by Racing Champions.

1 Billy Pauch Zemco 12.00 20.00
1F Dean Jacobs Frigidaire 12.50 25.00
1J Marlon Jones Energy Release 12.00 20.00
1X Randy Hannagan TRW 12.50 25.00
2 Andy Hillenburg STP 15.00 30.00
2 Ron Shuman Havoline 12.00 20.00
2M Brent Kaeding Pioneer 12.00 20.00
3G Joe Gaerte Gaerte Engines 12.00 20.00
7TW Jeff Swindell Gold Eagle 12.50 25.00
8 Terry McCarl Holbrook 12.00 20.00
8R Stevie Reeves D&B Racing 12.00 20.00
9W Gary Wright Action 12.00 20.00
11H Greg Hodnett Selma Shell 12.00 20.00
12 Keith Kauffman Apple Chevrolet 12.50 25.00
15 Donny Schatz Blue Beacon 12.00 20.00
17E Cris Eash Miller Brothers 12.00 20.00
21L Lance Blevins Citgo 12.00 20.00
22 Jac Haudenschild Pennzoil 12.00 20.00
23S Frankie Kerr Shoff Motorsports 12.00 20.00
28 Brian Paulus P&P Racing 12.00 20.00
29 Brent Kaeding BK Racing 12.00 20.00
29 Tommie Estes Jr. F&J Construction 12.00 20.00
47 Johnny Herrera Casey's 12.00 20.00
69K Donnie Kreitz Stockdale 10.00 20.00
83 Paul McMahan Beef Packers 12.00 20.00
88 Todd Shaffer Turnbaugh 12.00 20.00
92 Kenny Jacobs Imperial 12.00 20.00
94 Dale Blaney Hughes 8.00 20.00
461 Lance Dewease Dyer Masonary 12.00 20.00

1998 Racing Champions Sprint Cars 1:24

This series of 1:24 Sprint cars by Racing Champions was primarily issued through mass market retailers.

0 Jason Statler Rios Construction 12.00 20.00
1J Marlon Jones Energy Release 12.00 20.00
1W Craig Dollansky Conn West 12.00 20.00
2M Brent Kaeding Pioneer 12.00 20.00
3G Joe Gaerte Gaerte 12.00 20.00
7 Kevin Huntley Peterbilt 12.00 20.00
9S Shane Stewart RC Cola 12.00 20.00
11H Greg Hodnet Selma Shell 12.00 20.00
11H Greg Hodnett Vivarin 12.00 20.00
12S Shane Carson Helms Motorsports 12.00 20.00
15 Donny Schatz Blue Beacon 12.00 20.00
23S Frankie Kerr Shoff Motorsports 12.00 20.00
28 B.Paulus P&P Racing Not In 12.00 20.00
29 Brent Kaeding BK Motorsports 12.00 20.00
35 Tyler Walker Air Sep 12.00 20.00
47 Johnny Herrera Strange 12.00 20.00
55 Skip Jackson Jensen Construction 12.00 20.00
69K Donnie Kreitz Stockdale 12.00 20.00
83 Bob Auld Matco Tools Promo/5000 25.00 40.00
88 Tania Schafer Turnbaugh Oil 12.00 20.00
461 Lance Dewease Dyer 12.00 20.00
01 Paul McMahan Mt.Impact 12.00 20.00
U2 Keith Kauffman United Express 12.00 20.00

2003 Racing Champions Midwest Sprint Cars 1:24

1W Rob Tvedte Subway Shell/750 25.00 40.00
6R Roger Rager Donahue Harley/750 25.00 40.00
57X Jake Peters Folkens/750 25.00 4
75 Gordy Vogelaar Bob's Fleet/750 25.00 4

2004 Racing Champions Knoxville Sprint 1:24

2 Skip Jackson Mid Land Equipment/956 20.00 3
5J Jeff Mitrisin Cahill Racing/956 20.00 3
6 Brian Brown Casey's/956 20.00 3
6 Brian Brown Casey's Mopar/960 20.00 3
14 Randy Martin Diamond Pet Foods/956 20.00 3
17G Ricky Logan Lucas Oil/956 20.00 3
20 Bob Trostle B&B Performance/956 20.00 3
20 Doug Wolfgang Bob Trostle Racing/960 20.00 3
22 Billy Alley Ray Lipsey/956 20.00 3
24 Terry McCarl Big Game Hunting/956 20.00 3
71M Doug Wolfgang Beltline Body Shop/960 20.00 3

1993 Racing Champions Sprint Cars 1:6

This was the first release of World of Outlaws sprint c Racing Champions. Each car was packaged in a black-bo blister with one driver card. The print on the packaging and features an artist's rendering of a racing scene. Eac was packaged in one or more blister varieties: "Trac featuring only the #51 car at the top, or regular R Champions packaging with the #1, #11, and #22 cars #51, #93, and #00 cars at the top.

1 Sammy Swindell TMC 1/11/22 package 5.00 1
2 Andy Hillenburg STP black 1/11/22 package 3.00 6
2 Andy Hillenburg STP black Trackside 3.00 6
2 Andy Hillenburg STP dark blue 51/93/00 package 3.00 6
2 Andy Hillenburg STP light blue 3.00 6
2 Frankie Kerr Rifes RV 51/92/00 package 3.00 6
4 Bobby Davis Pro Shocks 1/11/22 package 3.00 6
4 Bobby Davis Pro Shocks 51/93/00 package 3.00 8
4 Bobby Davis Pro Shocks Trackside package 3.00 6
5 Danny Lasoski CS Enterprises 3.00 8
7 Richard Griffin Sanders 51/93/00 package 3.00 6
10 Dave Blaney Tums 51/93/00 package 12.50 2
10 Dave Blaney Vivarin 51/93/00 package 15.00 2
11 Steve Kinser Valvoline 1/11/22 package 4.00 1
11 Steve Kinser Valvoline Trackside package 5.00 1
11 Ron Shuman CH Engineering 51/93/00 package 7.50 1
14 Tim Green Swift Met Finish 51/93/00 package 3.00 6
14P Kevin Pylant VP Racing Fuels 51/93/00 package 3.00 6
18 Brad Doty Shaver 51/93/00 package 3.00 6
21 Steve Beitler Brownfield 4.00 10
22 Jac Haudenschild Pennzoil 51/93/00 package 3.00 8
22 Jac Haudenschild Pennzoil Trackside package 3.00 8
24 Jerry Stone Aeroweld 3.00 6
24 Jerry Stone Aeroweld Trackside package 3.00 6
27 Terry McCarl Westside 1/11/22 package 4.00 10
27 Terry McCarl Westside Trackside 3.00 8
29 Johnny Herrera G&W Trucking 1/11/22 package 3.00 8
29 Johnny Herrera GW Trucking 51/93/00 package 3.00 6
29 Johnny Herrera G&W Trucking Trackside package 3.00 8
29 Keith Kaufman Weikert's Livestock 51/93/00 package 3.00 6
45 Doug Wolfgang Snap On white Speedway Piece 4.00 10
49 Doug Wolfgang Olsen black 3.00 8
51 Racing Champions Prototype gray car in clear box/10,000 2.50 6
55 Max Dumesny Jensen Construction 3.00 6
65 Jim Carr Maxim 1/11/22 package 3.00 6
66 Mike Peters TropArtic 1/11/22 package 3.00 6
66 Mike Peters TropArtic Trackside 3.00 6
69K Donnie Kreitz Vollmer Patterns 3.00 6
77 Stevie Smith Jr. Hamilton 1/11/22 package 4.00 8
77 Stevie Smith Jr. Hamilton 51/93/00 package 4.00 8
97B Aaron Berryhill 3.00 6

Berryhill Racing
1/11/22 package
0 Jason Statler 3.00 6.00
Statler Racing
7 Smokey Snellbaker 3.00 6.00
Rifes RV's
51/93/00 package

1994 Racing Champions Sprint Cars 1:64

he blister packages for the 1994 and 1995 1:64 releases eature the #51, 93, and 00 sprint cars at the top. All of the 1995 ars include the words "series 2" at the top while a few of the ate year 1994 cars do also.

Garry Brazier 7.50 15.00
O'Brien
Sammy Swindell 10.00 20.00
Bull&Hannah White
Sammy Swindell 6.00 12.00
TMC black
51/93/00 package
2 Andy Hillenburg 4.00 8.00
STP dark blue
Series 2 package
2 Garry Rush 7.50 15.00
Castrol
2L Ed Lynch Jr. 7.50 15.00
Black
4 Bobby Davis 3.00 6.00
Pro Shocks 51/93/00 package
4A Greg Hodnett 3.00 6.00
Kele 51/93/00 package
7 Richard Griffin 4.00 8.00
Sanders 51/93/00 package
7 Jimmy Sills 3.00 6.00
Berry Brothers
51/93/00 package
7C Joe Gaerte 3.00 6.00
Gaerte Engines
7TW Jeff Swindell 3.00 8.00
Gold Eagle
8TW Greg Hodnett 3.00 6.00
Kele
11 Steve Kinser 3.00 8.00
Valvoline 51/93/00 package
12 Fred Rahmer 4.00 10.00
Apple Series 2 package
12X Danny Smith 3.00 6.00
Beaver 51/93/00 package
21 Lance Blevins 3.00 6.00
Citgo 51/93/00 package
22 Jac Haudenschild 5.00 10.00
Pennzoil with Red numbers
Series 2 package
23 Frankie Kerr 3.00 6.00
Shoff Motrosports
51/93/00 package
24 Jerry Stone 3.00 6.00
Aeroweld Racing
45X Johnny Herrera 3.00 6.00
Herrera Motorsports
47 Danny Lasoski 3.00 8.00
Casey's
49 Doug Wolfgang 3.00 6.00
Olsen 51/93/00 package
65 Jim Carr 3.00 6.00
Maxim 51/93/00 package
69 Brent Kaeding 3.00 6.00
Motorola Series 2 package
69K Donnie Kreitz 3.00 6.00
Vollmer Pattern
71M Kenny Jacobs 3.00 6.00
Ecowater 51/93/00 package
71M Kenny Jacobs 3.00 6.00
Ecowater Series 2
77 Joe Gaerte 3.00 6.00
Hamilton Series 2
97B Aaron Berryhill 3.00 6.00
Berryhill Racing
51/93/00 package
0 Rick Ferkel 4.00 10.00
Kears
U2 Rocky Hodges 3.00 6.00
United Express
51/93/00 package

1994 Racing Champions Sprint Transporters 1:64

7TW Jeff Swindell 12.50 25.00
Gold Eagle
8TW Greg Hodnett 10.00 20.00
Kele
22 Jac Haudenschild 12.50 25.00
Pennzoil
23 Frankie Kerr 15.00 30.00
Shoff Motorsports
45X Johnny Herrera 12.50 25.00
Herrera Motorsports
77 Jeff Shepard 10.00 20.00
Mac Tools

1995 Racing Champions Sprint Cars 1:64

The blister packages for the 1994 and 1995 1:64 releases feature the #51, 93, and 00 sprint cars at the top. The 1995 issue includes the words "series 2" at the top as well.

1 Garry Brazier 12.00 20.00
O'Brien
1 Sammy Swindell 18.00 30.00
Hooters Series 2 package
1W Keith Kauffman 15.00 25.00
Wahlie
2J J.J. Yeley 10.00 20.00
Bul&Hannah
4S Tommy Scott 3.00 6.00
Scott Performance
5 Terry McCarl 3.00 6.00
Jackpot Junction
7TW Jeff Swindell 4.00 10.00
Gold Eagle
8TW Greg Hodnett 4.00 8.00
Kele
8TW Greg Hodnett 4.00 8.00
Kele yellow numbers
9 Gary Wright 3.00 6.00
TKW
11 Steve Kinser 4.00 10.00
Valvoline Series 2 package
11 Ron Shuman 3.00 8.00
CH Engineering
12S Shane Carson 3.00 6.00
Helms
14P Kevin Pylant 3.00 6.00
Unicopy
16 Jeff Gordon 10.00 20.00
JG Motorsports Promo/10,000
21K Lou Kennedy 3.00 6.00
Superior Custom
Series 2 package
23 Frankie Kerr 3.00 6.00
Shoff Motrosports
31 Sid Blandford 3.00 6.00
Avenger Series 2 package
47 Danny Lasoski 5.00 10.00
Casey's
65 Jim Carr 3.00 6.00
Maxim Red&Blue
66 Mike Peters 3.00 6.00
TropArtic
97B Aaron Berryhill 3.00 6.00
Berryhill Racing

1996 Racing Champions Sprint Cars 1:64

This series of 1:64 scale Sprint cars features some of the most talented drivers in the World of Outlaws series. 14-time Champion Steve Kinser and Winston Cup star Jeff Gordon are a couple of the highlights in the series.

1 Sammy Swindell 10.00 20.00
Channellock
1W Jeff Shepard 7.50 15.00
Conn West
1X Randy Hannagan 3.00 6.00
Carrera
2 Andy Hillenburg 3.00 8.00
STP
4S Tommy Scott 6.00 15.00
Scott Performance/5000
5 Danny Lasoski 5.00 10.00
Jackpot Junction
5M Mark Kinser 3.00 6.00
Wirtgen
7M Jim Carr 15.00 25.00
American Fire Extinguisher
7TW Jeff Swindell 2.00 5.00
Gold Eagle
9 Gary Wright 3.00 6.00
TRW
10 Dave Blaney 6.00 12.00
Vivarin
11 Steve Kinser 7.50 15.00
Quaker State
11H Greg Hodnett 3.00 6.00
Selma Shell
16 Jeff Gordon 75.00 125.00
JG Motorsports
21 Lance Blevins 3.00 6.00
Citgo
22 Jac Haudenschild 3.00 8.00
Pennzoil New number 22
22 Jac Haudenschild 3.00 8.00
Pennzoil Old number 22
28D Brad Doty 10.00 18.00
Bower's Coal numbered of 5,000
28D Brad Doty 3.00 6.00
Bower's Coal unnumbered version
47 Johnny Herrera 3.00 6.00
Housby Trucks
51 Terry McCarl 4.00 10.00
McCroskey Chevrolet
69 Brent Kaeding 3.00 6.00
Motorola
69 Brent Kaeding 4.00 8.00
Pioneer Concrete
71M Stevie Smith 3.00 8.00
EcoWater No red stripe
71M Stevie Smith 3.00 8.00
EcoWater with Red stripe
83 Joey Saldana 3.00 6.00
Beef Packers
88 Todd Shaffer 3.00 6.00
Leiby's Mobile Home
94 Dale Blaney 3.00 6.00
Hughes Motorsports

461 Lance Dewease 6.00 12.00
Dyer Masonry

1997 Racing Champions Sprint Cars 1:64

This series of 1:64 Sprint cars by Racing Champions was primarily issued through mass market retailers. Two slightly different blister packages were used: one with a Pennzoil logo in the upper right hand corner and the other with "1997 Edition" printed in the upper right corner.

1 Billy Pauch 3.00 6.00
Zemco Pennzoil
1F Dean Jacobs 3.00 6.00
Frigidaire Pennzoil
1J Marlon Jones 3.00 6.00
Energy Release
1X Randy Hannagan 3.00 6.00
TRW 1997 Edition
2 Andy Hillenburg 3.00 8.00
STP
2 Ron Shuman 3.00 6.00
Havoline
2M Brent Kaeding 3.00 6.00
Pioneer 1997 Edition
3G Joe Gaerte 3.00 6.00
Gaerte Engines
4S Tommy Scott 4.00 8.00
On Broadway/5000
7TW Jeff Swindell 5.00 10.00
Gold Eagle
8 Terry McCarl 3.00 6.00
Holbrook
8R Stevie Reeves 3.00 6.00
D&B Racing
9W Gary Wright 3.00 6.00
Action
11H Greg Hodnett 3.00 6.00
Selma Shell 1997 Edition
12 Keith Kauffman 5.00 10.00
Apple Chevrolet 1997 Edition
15 Donny Schatz 6.00 12.00
Blue Beacon
17E Cris Eash 3.00 6.00
Miller Brothers
21L Lance Blevins 3.00 6.00
Citgo 1997 Edition
22 Jac Haudenschild 3.00 6.00
Pennzoil
23S Frankie Kerr 3.00 6.00
Shoff Motorsports
28 Brian Paulus 4.00 8.00
P&P Racing Pennzoil
29 Tommie Estes Jr. 3.00 6.00
F&J Construction Pennzoil
29 Brent Kaeding 3.00 6.00
BK Racing Pennzoil
36 Joe Gaerte 3.00 6.00
Gaerte Engines
47 Johnny Herrera 3.00 6.00
Casey's Pennzoil
69K Donnie Kreitz 3.00 6.00
Stockdale Pennzoil
83 Paul McMahan 3.00 6.00
Beef Packers maroon
1997 Edition
83 Paul McMahan 3.00 6.00
Beef Packers
maroon&white
88 Todd Shaffer 3.00 6.00
Turnbaugh 1997 Edition
92 Kenny Jacobs 3.00 6.00
Imperial 1997 Edition
94 Dale Blaney 3.00 6.00
Hughes Pennzoil
461 Lance Dewease 3.00 6.00
Dyer Masonry
U2 Keith Kauffman 7.50 15.00
United Express

1998 Racing Champions Sprint Cars 1:64

This series of 1:64 Sprint cars by Racing Champions was primarily issued through mass market retailers.

1 Billy Pauch 3.00 6.00
Zemco
1J Marlon Jones 3.00 6.00
Energy Release Pennzoil blister
1W Craig Dollansky 3.00 6.00
Conn West
1X Randy Hannagan 6.00 12.00
TIR
2M Brent Kaeding 7.50 15.00
Al's Roofing
2M Brent Kaeding 3.00 6.00
Pioneer
3G Joe Gaerte 3.00 6.00
Gaerte
4J Jeff Shepard 15.00 30.00
York Excavating
7 Kevin Huntley 3.00 6.00
Peterbilt Pennzoil blister
9S Shane Stewart 3.00 6.00
RC Cola
9S Shane Stewart 4.00 8.00
RC Cola Pennzoil blister
11H Greg Hodnet 3.00 6.00
Selma Shell
11H Greg Hodnett 3.00 6.00
Vivarin
12S Shane Carson 3.00 6.00
Helms Motorsports
15 Donny Schatz 3.00 6.00
Blue Beacon
18 Dion Hindi 15.00 30.00
Albuquerque

23S Frankie Kerr 3.00 6.00
Shoff Motorsports
24 Terry McCarl 4.00 10.00
McCroskey
28 Brian Paulus 3.00 8.00
Paulus Power
Pennzoil blister
28 Brian Paulus 3.00 8.00
P&P Racing Pennzoil blister
29 Tommie Estes Jr. 3.00 6.00
F&J Construction
29 Brent Kaeding 3.00 6.00
BK Motorsports
29 Brent Kaeding 4.00 8.00
BK Motorsports
Pennzoil blister
35 Tyler Walker 5.00 12.00
Air Sep
47 Johnny Herrera 3.00 8.00
Strange
55 Skip Jackson 3.00 6.00
Jensen Construction
69K Donny Kreitz Jr. 3.00 6.00
Stockdale
88 Tania Schafer 6.00 12.00
Turnbaugh Oil
94 Kenny Jacobs 3.00 8.00
Hughes Pennzoil blister
104 Sammy Swindell 20.00 35.00
104+ Octane
461 Lance Dewease 3.00 6.00
Dyer Pennzoil blister
00 Jason Statler 3.00 6.00
Rios Construction
maroon and white
01 Paul McMahan 6.00 12.00
Mt.Impact
U2 Keith Kauffman 3.00 6.00
United Express

2000 Racing Champions Sprint Cars 1:64

93 Dale Blaney 3.00 8.00
Amoco Promo box

2003 Racing Champions Midwest Sprint Cars 1:64

JACKSON SPEEDWAY "HALL OF FAME" COMMEMORATIVE SPRINTCAR 50TH YEAR 1954-2003 WOODKE RACING #1W SPRINTCAR

1W Loren Woodke 7.50 15.00
Woodke Racing
9 Matt Spies 7.50 15.00
Steve Evans Equipment
16 Marv DeWall 7.50 15.00
Randy's Towing/4000
98A Jack McCorkell 7.50 15.00
Woodke Racing

2004 Racing Champions Knoxville Sprint Cars 1:64

2 Skip Jackson 7.50 15.00
Mid Land Equipment/5000
5J Jeff Mitrisin 7.50 15.00
Cahill Racing/5000
6 Brian Brown 7.50 15.00
Casey's/2000
6 Casey's General Stores/3000 7.50 15.00
14 Randy Martin 7.50 15.00
Diamond Pet Foods/5000
17G Ricky Logan 7.50 15.00
Lucas Oil/5000
20 Doug Wolfgang 7.50 15.00
Beltline Body Shop/5000
22 Billy Alley 7.50 15.00
Ray Lipsey/5000
24 Terry McCarl 7.50 15.00
Big Game Hunting/5000

1993 Racing Champions Sprint Transporters 1:87

23 Frankie Kerr 5.00 10.00
Shoff Motorsports
45X Johnny Herrera 5.00 10.00
Herrera Motorsports
47 Danny Lasoski 5.00 10.00
Casey's
71M Kenny Jacobs 5.00 10.00
Ecowater

2005 Action/Funline Muscle Machines 1:18

3 Dale Earnhardt 25.00 40.00
Goodwrench '69 Chevelle/728
9 Kasey Kahne 30.00 50.00
Dodge '68 Dart/692
9 Kasey Kahne 30.00 50.00
Dodge '68 Dart RCCA/120
9 Kasey Kahne 30.00 50.00
Dodge '68 Dart QVC/400
9 Kasey Kahne 25.00 40.00
Dodge Pit Cap White '68 Dart/504
9 Kasey Kahne 25.00 40.00
Dodge Pit Cap White
'68 Dart RCCA/80
9 Kasey Kahne 25.00 40.00
Dodge Pit Cap White
'68 Dart QVC/504
9 Kasey Kahne 25.00 40.00
Dodge Pit Cap White '69 Charger/540
9 Kasey Kahne 25.00 40.00
Dodge Pit Cap White
'69 Charger RCCA/144
9 Kasey Kahne 25.00 40.00
Dodge Pit Cap White
'69 Charger QVC/504
9 Kasey Kahne 25.00 40.00
Mopar '68 Dart/516
9 Kasey Kahne 25.00 40.00
Mopar '68 Dart RCCA/60

9 Kasey Kahne 25.00 40.00
Mopar '68 Dart QVC/504
9 Kasey Kahne 25.00 40.00
Mopar '69 Charger/616
9 Kasey Kahne 25.00 40.00
Mopar '69 Charger RCCA/120
9 Kasey Kahne 25.00 40.00
Mopar '69 Charger QVC/504
20 Tony Stewart 25.00 40.00
Home Depot '69 Camaro/512
43 Richard Petty 30.00 50.00
STP '69 Charger/316
43 Richard Petty 30.00 50.00
STP '69 Charger RCCA/300
43 Richard Petty 30.00 50.00
STP '69 Charger QVC/180
48 Jimmie Johnson 25.00 40.00
Lowe's '69 Camaro/368
NNO John Force 25.00 40.00
Castrol GTX '66 Shelby/716

2008 Action/RCCA Muscle Machines 1:18

3 Dale Earnhardt 30.00 60.00
Goodwrench '57 Chevy/700
88 Dale Earnhardt Jr. 30.00 60.00
National Guard '62 Corvette/350
NNO John Force 30.00 60.00
Castrol Boss 302/350
NNO John Force 30.00 60.00
Castrol Retro Boss 302/350

2004 Action/Funline Muscle Machines 1:64

8 Dale Earnhardt Jr. 7.50 15.00
Earnhardt Jr. '69 Chevelle
20 Tony Stewart 7.50 15.00
Home Depot '69 Chevelle
24 Jeff Gordon 7.50 15.00
DuPont Flames '69 Chevelle

2004 Action/Funline Monster Truck 1:43

8 Dale Earnhardt Jr. 10.00 20.00
DMP
8 Dale Earnhardt Jr. 10.00 20.00
JR
18 Bobby Labonte 10.00 20.00
Interstate Batteries
20 Tony Stewart 10.00 20.00
Home Depot
20 Tony Stewart 10.00 20.00
Smoke
24 Jeff Gordon 10.00 20.00
DuPont Flames
29 Kevin Harvick 10.00 20.00
Kid Rock
29 Kevin Harvick 10.00 20.00
KISS
01 Joe Nemechek 10.00 20.00
Army GI Joe
NNO John Force 10.00 20.00
Castrol GTX Start-Up

2010 Action Racing Collectables Platinum Monster Cars 1:64

These are from the ARC Platinum line, but mix a 1:64 scale die-cast and add monster truck wheels and you get these collectibles. They are packaged the same as the ARC Platinum 1:64 scale cars.

5 Mark Martin 7.50 15.00
Go Daddy.com/2511*
10 Digger 6.00 12.00
Gopher Cam/2404*
14 Tony Stewart 7.50 15.00
Office Depot/2843*
14 Tony Stewart 7.50 15.00
Old Spice/2539*
18 Kyle Busch 7.50 15.00
M&M's/2456*
24 Jeff Gordon 10.00 20.00
Dupont/5828*
39 Ryan Newman 7.50 15.00
U.S. Army/2497*
48 Jimmie Johnson 10.00 20.00
Lowe's/2376*
88 Dale Earnhardt Jr. 10.00 20.00
AMP/5529*
88 Dale Earnhardt Jr. 10.00 20.00
National Guard/2397*
99 Carl Edwards 7.50 15.00
Aflac/2640*

2005 Brookfield Dually and Tailgate Set 1:24

24 Jeff Gordon 20.00 40.00
DuPont Flames/1440
24 Jeff Gordon 20.00 40.00
DuPont Flames QVC/504

2005 GreenLight Pace Cars 1:24

NNO Indianapolis 500 Corvette 15.00 30.00
NNO Daytona 500 Corvette 15.00 30.00

2005 GreenLight Pace Cars 1:64

NNO Daytona 500 Corvette 4.00 8.00
NNO Indianapolis 500 Corvette 4.00 8.00

2003 Action Racing Collectables MLB 1:24

NNO New York Yankees/1061 30.00 60.00

2004 Action Performance MLB 1:24

NNO Boston Red Sox/1512 35.00 60.00
NNO Boston Red Sox Promo/288 25.00 50.00

2005 Ertl Collectibles World Series Champions MLB 1:18

NNO Boston Red Sox '04 Corvette 40.00 70.00
NNO New York Mets '69 Mustang 35.00 60.00
NNO Pittsburgh Pirates '71 Mustang
NNO St. Louis Cardinals '64 Mustang 35.00 60.00

2005 Ertl Collectibles Cruzin' Series MLB 1:25

NNO Boston Red Sox '40 Ford Coupe 20.00 40.00
NNO Boston Red Sox '50 Olds Rocket 88 20.00 40.00
NNO Chicago Cubs '40 Ford Coupe 15.00 30.00
NNO New York Mets '40 Ford Coupe 12.50 25.00
NNO New York Yankees '40 Ford Coupe 20.00 40.00
NNO New York Yankees '50 Olds Rocket 88 20.00 40.00
NNO New York Yankees '57 Chevy Hardtop 20.00 40.00

2005 Ertl Collectibles Delivery Series MLB 1:25

NNO Boston Red Sox '36 Ford Panel Van 20.00 40.00
NNO Chicago Cubs '59 El Camino 15.00 30.00
NNO Los Angeles Dodgers '59 El Camino 15.00 30.00

NNO New York Yankees '57 Chevy Suburban 20.00 40.00
NNO St. Louis Cardinals '36 Ford Panel Van 15.00 30.00
NNO Washington Nationals '57 Chevy Suburban 12.50 25.00

2006 Ertl Collectibles Delivery Series Sports Truck MLB 1:25

NNO Boston Red Sox Silverado 20.00 40.00
NNO Chicago Cubs Silverado 15.00 30.00
NNO Cleveland Indians Durango 12.50 25.00
NNO New York Yankees Durango 20.00 40.00
NNO Philadelphia Phillies Durango 12.50 25.00
NNO St. Louis Cardinals Silverado 15.00 30.00
NNO Washington Nationals Silverado 12.50 25.00

2005 Ertl Collectibles Classic Rides MLB 1:64

NNO Boston Red Sox '64 Mustang 5.00 10.00
NNO Chicago Cubs '64 Mustang 4.00 8.00
NNO New York Mets '64 Mustang 4.00 8.00
NNO New York Yankees '64 Mustang 5.00 10.00
NNO St. Louis Cardinals '64 Mustang 4.00 8.00
NNO Washington Nationals '64 Mustang 4.00 8.00

2006 Ertl Collectibles Delivery Series Sports Truck MLB 1:64

NNO Atlanta Braves 6.00 12.00
NNO Baltimore Orioles 5.00 10.00
NNO Boston Red Sox 10.00 20.00
NNO Chicago Cubs 7.50 15.00
NNO Chicago White Sox 6.00 12.00
NNO Cleveland Indians 6.00 12.00
NNO New York Mets 6.00 12.00
NNO New York Yankees 10.00 20.00
NNO Philadelphia Phillies 6.00 12.00
NNO St. Louis Cardinals 7.50 15.00

2005 Ertl Collectibles Chopper Series MLB 1:10

NNO Boston Red Sox OCC 20.00 40.00
NNO Chicago Cubs OCC 15.00 30.00
NNO New York Yankees OCC 1 20.00 40.00
NNO New York Yankees OCC 2 20.00 40.00
NNO Los Angeles Dodgers OCC 15.00 30.00

2005 Ertl Collectibles Chopper Series MLB 1:18

NNO Boston Red Sox OCC 10.00 20.00
NNO Chicago Cubs OCC 7.50 15.00
NNO Houston Astros OCC
NNO New York Mets OCC 6.00 12.00
NNO New York Yankees OCC 10.00 20.00

2005 Ertl Collectibles Snowmobile Series MLB 1:18

NNO Boston Red Sox 15.00 30.00
NNO Colorado Rockies 10.00 20.00
NNO New York Yankess 15.00 30.00
NNO Chicago Cubs 12.50 25.00

2006 Ertl Collectibles Transporters Throwback Series MLB 1:64

NNO Boston Red Sox 12.50 25.00
NNO Chicago Cubs 10.00 20.00
NNO New York Yankees 12.50 25.00
NNO Pittsburgh Pirates 7.50 15.00

2005 Ertl Collectibles Transporters MLB 1:87

NNO Arizona Diamondbacks 5.00 10.00
NNO Atlanta Braves 6.00 12.00
NNO Baltimore Orioles 5.00 10.00
NNO Boston Red Sox 10.00 20.00
NNO Chicago White Sox 6.00 12.00
NNO Chicago Cubs 7.50 15.00
NNO Cincinnati Reds 5.00 10.00
NNO Cleveland Indians 5.00 10.00
NNO Colorado Rockies 5.00 10.00
NNO Detroit Tigers 5.00 10.00
NNO Florida Marlins 5.00 10.00
NNO Houston Astros 6.00 12.00
NNO Kansas City Royals 5.00 10.00
NNO Los Angeles Angels 5.00 10.00
NNO Los Angeles Dodgers 7.50 15.00
NNO Milwaukee Brewers 5.00 10.00
NNO Minnesota Twins 5.00 10.00
NNO New York Mets 6.00 12.00
NNO New York Yankees 10.00 20.00
NNO Oakland A's 5.00 10.00
NNO Philadelphia Phillies 5.00 10.00
NNO Pittsburgh Pirates 5.00 10.00
NNO San Diego Padres 5.00 10.00
NNO San Fransisco Giants 6.00 12.00
NNO Seattle Mariners 5.00 10.00
NNO St. Louis Cardinals 7.50 15.00
NNO Tampa Bay Devil Rays 5.00 10.00
NNO Toronto Blue Jays 5.00 10.00
NNO Texas Rangers 5.00 10.00
NNO Washington Nationals 6.00 12.00

2002 Fleer Collectibles BMW X-5 MLB 1:24

NNO Atlanta Braves/1000 10.00 20.00
NNO Baltimore Orioles/2000 10.00 20.00
NNO Boston Red Sox/1000 15.00 30.00
NNO Chicago Cubs/1000 12.50 25.00
NNO Cleveland Indians/1000 10.00 20.00
NNO New York Mets/1500 10.00 20.00
NNO New York Yankees/4000 15.00 30.00
NNO Philadelphia Phillies/1500 10.00 20.00
NNO Seattle Mariners/1000 10.00 20.00
NNO St. Louis Cardinals/1000 12.50 25.00

2002 Fleer Collectibles Greats of the Game MLB 1:24

8 New York Yankees Yogi Berra '57 Chevy 20.00 40.00
21 Pittsburgh Pirates Roberto Clemente '69 GTO 20.00 40.00
41 New York Mets Tom Seaver '69 GTO 15.00 30.00

2003 Fleer Collectibles All Stars of Today MLB 1:24

2 New York Yankees w Derek Jeter Porsche Boxter/2000 20.00 40.00
3 Texas Rangers w Alex Rodriguez Mercedes 500 SL/2000 20.00 40.00
5 Boston Red Sox w Nomar Garciaparra Jaguar XK180/2000 15.00 30.00
21 Chicago Cubs w Sammy Sosa Lamborghini Diablo/2000 15.00 30.00
25 New York Yankees w Jason Giambi Jaguar XK180/2000 12.50 25.00
25 San Francisco Giants w Barry Bonds Mercedes 500 SL/2000 20.00 40.00
31 New York Mets w Mike Piazza Porsche Boxter 15.00 30.00
51 Seattle Mariners w Ichiro Lamborghini Diablo 20.00 40.00

2003 Fleer Collectibles 1959 Corvettes MLB 1:24

NNO Atlanta Braves/1000 15.00 30.00
NNO Baltimore Orioles/1000 15.00 30.00
NNO Boston Red Sox/1000 20.00 40.00
NNO New York Mets/1000 15.00 30.00
NNO New York Yankees/1000 20.00 40.00
NNO San Francisco Giants/1000 15.00 30.00

2003 Fleer Collectibles Monster Trucks MLB 1:32

NNO Atlanta Braves/680 7.50 15.00
NNO Baltimore Orioles/500 7.50 15.00
NNO Boston Red Sox/700 7.50 15.00
NNO Cleveland Indians/700 7.50 15.00
NNO New York Mets/1000 7.50 15.00
NNO New York Yankees/3000 7.50 15.00

2002 Fleer Collectibles Prowler w/Ultra Card MLB 1:64

NNO Seattle Mariners w Ichiro Suzuki 10.00 20.00
NNO New York Mets w Mike Piazza 5.00 10.00
NNO New York Yankees w Derek Jeter 7.50 15.00

2002 Fleer Collectibles Team Bus MLB 1:64

NNO Seattle Mariners 5.00 10.00
NNO New York Mets 5.00 10.00
NNO Baltimore Orioles 5.00 10.00
NNO New York Yankees 7.50 15.00

2003 Fleer Collectibles Bullpen Cars 1:64

NNO Atlanta Braves 4.00 8.00
NNO Baltimore Orioles 4.00 8.00
NNO Boston Red Sox 5.00 10.00
NNO Cleveland Indians 4.00 8.00
NNO New York Mets 4.00 8.00
NNO New York Yankees 5.00 10.00

2003 Fleer Collectibles Monster Trucks MLB 1:64

NNO Atlanta Braves 4.00 8.00
NNO Anaheim Angels 4.00 8.00
NNO Baltimore Orioles 4.00 8.00
NNO Boston Red Sox 5.00 10.00
NNO Chicago Cubs 5.00 10.00
NNO Cleveland Indians 4.00 8.00
NNO Los Angeles Dodgers 5.00 10.00
NNO New York Mets 4.00 8.00
NNO New York Yankees 5.00 10.00
NNO Oakland A's 4.00 8.00
NNO San Francisco Giants 4.00 8.00
NNO St. Louis Cardinals 5.00 10.00

2003 Fleer Collectibles Mustang w/Ultra Card MLB 1:64

NNO New York Mets w Tom Glavine 4.00 8.00
NNO New York Mets w Mike Piazza 4.00 8.00
NNO New York Yankees w Jason Giambi 4.00 8.00
NNO New York Yankees w Derek Jeter 6.00 12.00

2003 Fleer Collectibles Transporters MLB 1:80

NNO Atlanta Braves 7.50 15.00
NNO Anaheim Angels '02 Champions 10.00 20.00
NNO Baltimore Orioles 7.50 15.00
NNO New York Mets 7.50 15.00
NNO New York Yankees 10.00 20.00
NNO San Francisco Giants 7.50 15.00

2005-06 Ertl Collectibles Choppers Series NBA 1:10

NNO Cleveland Cavaliers 15.00 30.00
NNO Los Angeles Lakers 15.00 30.00
NNO Miami Heat 15.00 30.00
NNO New York Knicks 12.50 25.00

2005-06 Ertl Collectibles Choppers Series NBA 1:18

NNO Boston Celtics 7.50 15.00
NNO Chicago Bulls 7.50 15.00
NNO Detroit Pistons 7.50 15.00
NNO Los Angeles Lakers 10.00 20.00
NNO Miami Heat 7.50 15.00
NNO Philadelphia 76ers 7.50 15.00

2005-06 Ertl Collectibles Cruzin' Series NBA 1:24

NNO Boston Celtics 12.50 25.00
NNO Chicago Bulls 12.50 25.00
NNO Los Angeles Lakers 15.00 30.00
NNO Philadelphia 76ers 12.50 25.00

2005-06 Ertl Collectibles Slammed F150 NBA 1:64

NNO Boston Celtics
NNO Chicago Bulls 4.00 8.00
NNO Cleveland Cavaliers 5.00 10.00
NNO Dallas Mavericks 5.00 10.00
NNO Denver Nuggets 4.00 8.00
NNO Detroit Pistons 4.00 8.00
NNO Houston Rockets 4.00 8.00
NNO Los Angeles Lakers 6.00 12.00
NNO Miami Heat 5.00 10.00
NNO Minnesota Timberwolves 4.00 8.00
NNO New Jersey Nets 4.00 8.00
NNO New York Knicks 4.00 8.00
NNO Philadelphia 76ers 4.00 8.00
NNO Phoenix Suns 4.00 8.00
NNO San Antonio Spurs 5.00 10.00
NNO Seattle Supersonics 4.00 8.00

2003-04 Fleer H2 w/Ultra card NBA 1:64

NNO Cleveland Cavaliers w LeBron James 15.00 30.00
NNO Denver Nuggets w Carmelo Anthony 10.00 20.00
NNO Toronto Raptors w Chris Bosh 6.00 12.00

2004-05 Fleer H2 NBA 1:43

NNO Boston Celtics 7.50 15.00
NNO Chicago Bulls 7.50 15.00
NNO Cleveland Cavaliers 7.50 15.00
NNO Dallas Mavericks 7.50 15.00
NNO Detroit Pistons 7.50 15.00
NNO Houston Rockets 7.50 15.00
NNO Los Angeles Lakers 10.00 20.00
NNO New Jersey Nets 7.50 15.00
NNO New York Knicks 7.50 15.00
NNO Philadelphia 76ers 7.50 15.00
NNO Sacramento Kings 7.50 15.00
NNO San Antonio Spurs 7.50 15.00

2004-05 Fleer H2 w/Ultra card NBA 1:64

NNO Boston Celtics w Paul Pierce 6.00 12.00
NNO Charlotte Bobcats w Emeka Okafor 7.50 15.00
NNO Chicago Bulls w Ben Gordon 7.50 15.00
NNO Cleveland Cavaliers w LeBron James 7.50 15.00
NNO Dallas Mavericks w Devon Harris 6.00 12.00
NNO Dallas Mavericks w Dirk Nowitzki 7.50 15.00
NNO Denver Nuggets w Carmelo Anthony 7.50 15.00
NNO Detroit Pistons w Ben Wallace 6.00 12.00
NNO Houston Rockets w Yao Ming 7.50 15.00
NNO Los Angeles Clippers w Shaun Livingston 6.00 12.00
NNO Los Angeles Lakers w Kobe Bryant 7.50 15.00
NNO Miami Heat w Dwyane Wade 7.50 15.00
NNO Miami Heat w Shaquille O'Neal 7.50 15.00
NNO Minnesota Timberwolves w Kevin Garnett 7.50 15.00
NNO New York Knicks w Stephon Marbury 6.00 12.00
NNO Orlando Magic w Dwight Howard 7.50 15.00
NNO Philadelphia 76ers w Allen Iverson 6.00 12.00
NNO Portland Trailblazers w Sebastian Telfair 6.00 12.00
NNO Sacramento Kings w Peja Stojakovic 6.00 12.00
NNO Utah Jazz w Carlos Arroyo 6.00 12.00

2004-05 Fleer Collectibles Transporters NBA 1:80

NNO Boston Celtics 7.50 15.00
NNO Cleveland Cavaliers 7.50 15.00
NNO Dallas Mavericks 7.50 15.00
NNO Denver Nuggets 7.50 15.00
NNO Detroit Pistons 7.50 15.00
NNO Houston Rockets 7.50 15.00
NNO Los Angeles Lakers 7.50 15.00
NNO Minnesota Timberwolves 10.00 20.00
NNO New Jersey Nets 7.50 15.00
NNO New York Knicks 7.50 15.00
NNO Philadelphia 76ers 7.50 15.00
NNO Sacramento Kings 7.50 15.00
NNO Toronto Raptors 7.50 15.00

2005-06 Upper Deck Cadillac Escalade w/UD card NBA 1:64

NNO Boston Celtics w Paul Pierce 5.00 10.00
NNO Chicago Bulls w Kurt Hinrich 6.00 12.00
NNO Cleveland Cavaliers w LeBron James 7.50 15.00
NNO Denver Nuggets w Carmelo Anthony 6.00 12.00
NNO Detroit Pistons w Ben Wallace 5.00 10.00
NNO Houston Rockets w Tracy McGrady 5.00 10.00
NNO Los Angeles Lakers w Kobe Bryant 7.50 15.00
NNO Miami Heat w Dwyane Wade 7.50 15.00
NNO Miami Heat w Shaquille O'Neal 7.50 15.00
NNO Minnesota Timberwolves w Kevin Garnett 6.00 12.00
NNO New York Knicks w Stephon Marbury 5.00 10.00
NNO San Antonio Spurs w Manu Ginobili 5.00 10.00

2003 Action Performance NFL 1:24

NNO Carolina Panthers 12.50 25.00
NNO Dallas Cowboys 20.00 40.00
NNO Green Bay Packers 20.00 40.00
NNO Oakland Raiders 20.00 40.00
NNO Philadelphia Eagles 15.00 30.00
NNO Pittsburgh Steelers 20.00 40.00
NNO San Francisco 49ers 20.00 40.00
NNO Tampa Bay Buccaneers 12.50 25.00
NNO Washington Redskins 15.00 30.00
NNO Super Bowl XXXVII 12.50 25.00

2003 Action Racing Collectables NFL 1:24

NNO Dallas Cowboys/1500 30.00 60.00
NNO Green Bay Packers/1500 30.00 60.00
NNO Pittsburgh Steelers/1397 30.00 60.00
NNO San Francisco 49ers/2327 30.00 60.00
NNO Washington Redskins/1307 25.00 50.00

2004 Action Performance NFL 1:24

NNO Chicago Bears 15.00 30.00
NNO Dallas Cowboys 20.00 40.00
NNO Denver Broncos 15.00 30.00
NNO Green Bay Packers 20.00 40.00
NNO Houston Texans 12.50 25.00
NNO Kansas City Chiefs 15.00 30.00
NNO Miami Dolphins 20.00 40.00
NNO Minnesota Vikings 15.00 30.00
NNO New England Patriots 12.50 25.00
NNO New York Giants 15.00 30.00
NNO New York Jets 12.50 25.00
NNO Oakland Raiders 20.00 40.00
NNO Philadelphia Eagles 15.00 30.00
NNO Pittsburgh Steelers 20.00 40.00
NNO San Francisco 49ers 20.00 40.00
NNO St. Louis Rams 12.50 25.00
NNO Tampa Bay Buccaneers 12.50 25.00
NNO Tennessee Titans 12.50 25.00
NNO Washington Redskins 15.00 30.00

2004 Action Racing Collectables NFL 1:24

NNO Chicago Bears/1464 30.00 60.00
NNO Dallas Cowboys/2004 40.00 80.00
NNO Denver Broncos/2004 30.00 60.00
NNO Green Bay Packers/3360 40.00 80.00
NNO Houston Texans/2000 25.00 50.00
NNO Kansas City Chiefs/1344 30.00 60.00
NNO Miami Dolphins/1440 40.00 80.00
NNO Minnesota Vikings/1536 30.00 60.00
NNO New York Giants/1584 30.00 60.00
NNO New York Jets/1644 25.00 50.00
NNO Oakland Raiders/1584 40.00 80.00
NNO Philadelphia Eagles/1392 30.00 60.00
NNO Pittsburgh Steelers/1248 40.00 80.00
NNO San Francisco 49ers/2004 40.00 80.00
NNO St. Louis Rams/1548 25.00 50.00
NNO Tampa Bay Buccaneers/1632 25.00 50.00
NNO Tennessee Titans/1380 25.00 50.00
NNO Washington Redskins/1272 30.00 60.00

2005 Ertl Collectibles Chopper Series NFL 1:10

NNO Dallas Cowboys 30.00 60.00
NNO Kansas City Chiefs 25.00 50.00
NNO New England Patriots 20.00 40.00
NNO New York Giants 25.00 50.00
NNO New York Jets 20.00 40.00
NNO Oakland Raiders 30.00 60.00
NNO Philadelphia Eagles 25.00 50.00

2005 Ertl Collectibles Chopper Series NFL 1:18

NNO Baltimore Ravens 7.50 15.00
NNO Green Bay Packers 12.50 25.00
NNO Kansas City Chiefs 10.00 20.00
NNO New York Jets 7.50 15.00
NNO Oakland Raiders 12.50 25.00
NNO Philadelphia Eagles 10.00 20.00
NNO Washington Redskins 10.00 20.00

2005 Ertl Collectibles Snowmobile Series NFL 1:18

NNO Buffalo Bills 12.50 25.00
NNO Chicago Bears 15.00 30.00
NNO Denver Broncos 15.00 30.00
NNO Detroit Lions 12.50 25.00
NNO Green Bay Packers 20.00 40.00
NNO Indianapolis Colts 12.50 25.00
NNO Minnesota Vikings 15.00 30.00
NNO New England Patriots 12.50 25.00

2005 Ertl Collectibles Super Bowl Series NFL 1:18

NNO New York Jets '68 30.00 60.00
NNO Miami Dolphins '72 Challenger 40.00 80.00
NNO Oakland Raiders '76 Gran Torino 40.00 80.00
NNO Dallas Cowboys '77 Firebird 40.00 80.00
NNO Chicago Bears '85 Corvette 40.00 80.00
NNO Green Bay Packers '96 Trans Am 40.00 80.00
NNO Pittsburgh Steelers '78 Warlock 40.00 80.00

2007 Ertl Collectibles Chopper Series NFL 1:18

NNO Green Bay Packers 12.50 25.00
NNO Indianapolis Colts 10.00 20.00
NNO New York Giants 10.00 20.00
NNO Oakland Raiders 10.00 20.00

2005 Ertl Collectibles Cruzin' Series NFL 1:25

NNO Atlanta Falcons '50 Olds Rocket 15.00 30.00
NNO Dallas Cowboys '40 Ford Coupe 20.00 40.00
NNO Dallas Cowboys '50 Olds Rocket 20.00 40.00
NNO Denver Broncos '57 Chevy 15.00 30.00
NNO Minnesota Vikings '57 Chevy 15.00 30.00
NNO New England Patriots '50 Olds Rocket 15.00 30.00
NNO New York Giants '50 Olds Rocket 15.00 30.00
NNO Oakland Raiders '40 Ford Coupe 20.00 40.00
NNO Oakland Raiders '57 Chevy 20.00 40.00
NNO Philadelphia Eagles '40 Ford Coupe 15.00 30.00
NNO Philadelphia Eagles '50 Olds Rocket 15.00 30.00
NNO Washington Redskins '40 Ford Coupe 15.00 30.00

2005 Ertl Collectibles Delivery Series NFL 1:2

NNO Dallas Cowboys '57 Suburban 20.00 40.00
NNO Indianapolis Colts '36 Ford Van 15.00 30.00
NNO Kansas City Chiefs '57 Suburban 15.00 30.00
NNO Kansas City Chiefs '59 El Camino 15.00 30.00
NNO New York Jets '57 Suburban 15.00 30.00
NNO Oakland Raiders '59 El Camino 20.00 40.00
NNO Philadelphia Eagles '57 Suburban 15.00 30.00
NNO Washington Redskins '36 Ford Van 15.00 30.00

2006 Ertl Collectibles Cruzin' Series NFL 1:2

NNO Carolina Panthers Cadillac Escalade
NNO Chicago Bears Toyota Supra
NNO Dallas Cowboys Toyota Supra
NNO Indianapolis Colts Cadillac Escalade
NNO New England Patriots Cadillac Escalade
NNO Philadelphia Eagles Toyota Supra
NNO Pittsburgh Steelers Toyota Supra
NNO Seattle Seahawks Cadillac Escalade
NNO Tampa Bay Buccaneers Cadillac Escalade
NNO Washington Redskins Toyota Supra

2006 Ertl Collectibles Delivery Series NFL 1:2

NNO Green Bay Packers Durango
NNO Kansas City Chiefs Silverado
NNO Miami Dolphins Silverado
NNO Minnesota Vikings Silverado
NNO New York Giants Durango
NNO Oakland Raiders Durango
NNO Pittsburgh Steelers Durango
NNO San Diego Chargers Silverado

2003 Fleer Collectibles Monster Trucks NFL 1:32

NNO Arizona Cardinals 15.00 30.00
NNO Atlanta Falcons 15.00 30.00
NNO Baltimore Ravens 15.00 30.00
NNO Buffalo Bills 15.00 30.00
NNO Carolina Panthers 15.00 30.00
NNO Chicago Bears 15.00 30.00
NNO Cincinnati Bengals 15.00 30.00
NNO Cleveland Browns 15.00 30.00
NNO Dallas Cowboys 20.00 40.00
NNO Denver Broncos 15.00 30.00
NNO Detroit Lions 15.00 30.00
NNO Green Bay Packers 20.00 40.00
NNO Indianapolis Colts 15.00 30.00
NNO Jacksonville Jaguars 15.00 30.00
NNO Kansas City Chiefs 15.00 30.00
NNO Miami Dolphins 15.00 30.00
NNO Minnesota Vikings 15.00 30.00
NNO New England Patriots 15.00 30.00
NNO New York Giants 15.00 30.00
NNO New York Jets 15.00 30.00
NNO Oakland Raiders 15.00 30.00
NNO Philadelphia Eagles 15.00 30.00
NNO Pittsburgh Steelers 20.00 40.00
NNO San Diego Chargers 15.00 30.00
NNO San Francisco 49ers 15.00 30.00
NNO Seattle Seahawks 15.00 30.00
NNO St. Louis Rams 15.00 30.00
NNO Tampa Bay Buccaneers 15.00 30.00
NNO Tennessee Titans 15.00 30.00
NNO Washington Redskins 15.00 30.00

2004 Fleer Collectibles Monster Trucks NFL 1:32

NNO Arizona Cardinals 15.00 30.00
NNO Atlanta Falcons 15.00 30.00
NNO Baltimore Ravens 15.00 30.00
NNO Buffalo Bills 15.00 30.00
NNO Carolina Panthers 15.00 30.00
NNO Chicago Bears 15.00 30.00
NNO Cincinnati Bengals 15.00 30.00
NNO Cleveland Browns 15.00 30.00
NNO Dallas Cowboys 20.00 40.00
NNO Denver Broncos 15.00 30.00
NNO Detroit Lions 15.00 30.00
NNO Green Bay Packers 20.00 40.00
NNO Indianapolis Colts 15.00 30.00
NNO Jacksonville Jaguars 15.00 30.00
NNO Kansas City Chiefs 15.00 30.00
NNO Miami Dolphins 15.00 30.00
NNO Minnesota Vikings 15.00 30.00
NNO New England Patriots 15.00 30.00
NNO New York Giants 15.00 30.00
NNO New York Jets 15.00 30.00
NNO Oakland Raiders 15.00 30.00
NNO Philadelphia Eagles 15.00 30.00
NNO San Francisco 49ers 15.00 30.00
NNO Seattle Seahawks 15.00 30.00
NNO St. Louis Rams 15.00 30.00
NNO Tampa Bay Buccaneers 15.00 30.00
NNO Tennessee Titans 15.00 30.00
NNO Washington Redskins 15.00 30.00

2003 Action Performance NFL 1:64

NNO Chicago Bears 7.50 15.00
NNO Dallas Cowboys 10.00 20.00
NNO Dallas Cowboys Promo 12.50 25.00
NNO Denver Broncos 7.50 15.00
NNO Green Bay Packers 10.00 20.00
NNO Miami Dolphins 10.00 20.00
NNO New York Giants 6.00 12.00
NNO Oakland Raiders 10.00 20.00
NNO Oakland Raiders Promo 12.50 25.00
NNO Philadelphia Eagles 7.50 15.00
NNO Pittsburgh Steelers 10.00 20.00
NNO San Francisco 49ers 10.00 20.00
NNO Washington Redskins 7.50 15.00

2005 Ertl Collectibles Classic Rides NFL 1:64

NNO Atlanta Falcons '40 Ford Coupe 6.00 12.00
NNO Chicago Bears '40 Ford Coupe 7.50 15.00
NNO Dallas Cowboys '64 Mustang 10.00 20.00
NNO Dallas Cowboys '70 Chevelle 10.00 20.00

Card	Low	High
NO Detroit Lions '64 Mustang	6.00	12.00
NO Green Bay Packers '40 Ford Coupe	10.00	20.00
NO Green Bay Packers '59 Cadillac	10.00	20.00
NO Kansas City Chiefs '64 Mustang	7.50	15.00
NO Minnesota Vikings '70 Chevelle	7.50	15.00
NO New York Giants '59 Cadillac	7.50	15.00
NO New York Jets '70 Chevelle	6.00	12.00
NO Oakland Raiders '64 Mustang	10.00	20.00
NO Philadelphia Eagles '59 Cadillac	7.50	15.00
NO Philadelphia Eagles '64 Mustang	7.50	15.00
NO St. Louis Rams '70 Chevelle	6.00	12.00
NO Washington Redskins '40 Ford Coupe	7.50	15.00

2001 Fleer Collectibles PT Cruiser w/Ultra Card NFL 1:64

Card	Low	High
NO Arizona Cardinals Jake Plummer	6.00	12.00
NO Baltimore Ravens Jamal Lewis	6.00	12.00
NO Buffalo Bills Eric Moulds	6.00	12.00
NO Carolina Panthers Chris Weinke	6.00	12.00
NO Cincinnati Bengals Peter Warrick	6.00	12.00
NO Cleveland Browns Tim Couch	6.00	12.00
NO Dallas Cowboys Emmitt Smith	10.00	20.00
NO Denver Broncos Terrell Davis	6.00	12.00
NO Detroit Lions Charlie Batch	6.00	12.00
NO Green Bay Packers w Brett Favre	10.00	20.00
NO Indianapolis Colts Edgerrin James	10.00	20.00
NO Indianapolis Colts Peyton Manning	10.00	20.00
NO Jacksonville Jaguars Fred Taylor	6.00	12.00
NO Kansas City Chiefs Tony Gonzalez	6.00	12.00
NO Miami Dolphins Zach Thomas	6.00	12.00
NO Minnesota Vikings Daunte Culpepper	7.50	15.00
NO Minnesota Vikings Randy Moss	7.50	15.00
NO New England Patriots Drew Bledsoe	6.00	12.00
NO New Orleans Saints Ricky Williams	6.00	12.00
NNO New York Giants Ron Dayne	6.00	12.00
NNO New York Jets Santana Moss	6.00	12.00
NNO Oakland Raiders Tim Brown	6.00	12.00
NNO Oakland Raiders Rich Gannon	6.00	12.00
NNO Philadelphia Eagles Donovan McNabb	7.50	15.00
NNO San Francisco 49ers Jeff Garcia	6.00	12.00
NNO Seattle Seahawks Koren Robinson	6.00	12.00
NNO St. Louis Rams Marshall Faulk	6.00	12.00
NNO St. Louis Rams Kurt Warner	6.00	12.00
NNO Tampa Bay Buccaneers Keyshawn Johnson	6.00	12.00
NNO Washington Redskins Stephen Davis	6.00	12.00
NNO Washington Redskins Rod Gardner	6.00	12.00

2001 Fleer Collectibles Transporters NFL 1:80

Card	Low	High
NNO Arizona Cardinals	10.00	20.00
NNO Atlanta Falcons	10.00	20.00
NNO Baltimore Ravens	10.00	20.00
NNO Buffalo Bills	10.00	20.00
NNO Carolina Panthers	10.00	20.00
NNO Chicago Bears	10.00	20.00
NNO Cincinnati Bengals	10.00	20.00
NNO Cleveland Browns	10.00	20.00
NNO Dallas Cowboys	12.50	25.00
NNO Denver Broncos	10.00	20.00
NNO Detroit Lions	10.00	20.00
NNO Green Bay Packers	15.00	30.00
NNO Indianapolis Colts	10.00	20.00
NNO Jacksonville Jaguars	10.00	20.00
NNO Kansas City Chiefs	10.00	20.00
NNO Miami Dolphins	10.00	20.00
NNO Minnesota Vikings	10.00	20.00
NNO New England Patriots	12.50	25.00
NNO New Orleans Saints	10.00	20.00
NNO New York Giants	10.00	20.00
NNO New York Jets	10.00	20.00
NNO Oakland Raiders	10.00	20.00
NNO Philadelphia Eagles	10.00	20.00
NNO Pittsburgh Steelers	12.50	25.00
NNO San Diego Chargers	10.00	20.00
NNO San Francisco 49ers	10.00	20.00
NNO Seattle Seahawks	10.00	20.00
NNO St. Louis Rams	10.00	20.00
NNO Tampa Bay Buccaneers	10.00	20.00
NNO Tennessee Titans	10.00	20.00
NNO Washington Redskins	10.00	20.00

2002 Fleer Collectibles Transporters NFL 1:80

Card	Low	High
NNO Arizona Cardinals	7.50	15.00
NNO Atlanta Falcons	7.50	15.00
NNO Baltimore Ravens	7.50	15.00
NNO Buffalo Bills	7.50	15.00
NNO Chicago Bears	7.50	15.00
NNO Cincinnati Bengals	7.50	15.00
NNO Cleveland Browns	7.50	15.00
NNO Dallas Cowboys	10.00	20.00
NNO Denver Broncos	7.50	15.00
NNO Detroit Lions	7.50	15.00
NNO Green Bay Packers	12.50	25.00
NNO Houston Texans	7.50	15.00
NNO Indianapolis Colts	7.50	15.00
NNO Jacksonville Jaguars	7.50	15.00
NNO Kansas City Chiefs	7.50	15.00
NNO Miami Dolphins	7.50	15.00
NNO Minnesota Vikings	7.50	15.00
NNO New England Patriots	7.50	15.00
NNO New York Jets	7.50	15.00
NNO Pittsburgh Steelers	10.00	20.00
NNO San Francisco 49ers	7.50	15.00
NNO Seattle Seahawks	7.50	15.00
NNO St. Louis Rams	7.50	15.00
NNO Tampa Bay Buccaneers	7.50	15.00
NNO Tennessee Titans	7.50	15.00
NNO Washington Redskins	7.50	15.00

2003 Fleer Collectibles Transporters NFL 1:80

Card	Low	High
NNO Arizona Cardinals	10.00	20.00
NNO Atlanta Falcons	10.00	20.00
NNO Baltimore Ravens	10.00	20.00
NNO Buffalo Bills	10.00	20.00
NNO Carolina Panthers	10.00	20.00
NNO Chicago Bears	10.00	20.00
NNO Cincinnati Bengals	10.00	20.00
NNO Cleveland Browns	10.00	20.00
NNO Dallas Cowboys	15.00	30.00
NNO Denver Broncos	10.00	20.00
NNO Detroit Lions	10.00	20.00
NNO Green Bay Packers	15.00	30.00
NNO Houston Texans	10.00	20.00
NNO Indianapolis Colts	10.00	20.00
NNO Jacksonville Jaguars	10.00	20.00
NNO Kansas City Chiefs	10.00	20.00
NNO Miami Dolphins	10.00	20.00
NNO Minnesota Vikings	10.00	20.00
NNO New England Patriots	10.00	20.00
NNO New Orleans Saints	10.00	20.00
NNO New York Giants	10.00	20.00
NNO New York Jets	10.00	20.00
NNO Oakland Raiders	10.00	20.00
NNO Pittsburgh Steelers	15.00	30.00
NNO San Diego Chargers	10.00	20.00
NNO San Francisco 49ers	10.00	20.00
NNO Seattle Seahawks	10.00	20.00
NNO St. Louis Rams	10.00	20.00
NNO Tampa Bay Buccaneers	10.00	20.00
NNO Tennessee Titans	10.00	20.00
NNO Washington Redskins	10.00	20.00

2004 Fleer Collectibles Transporters NFL 1:80

Card	Low	High
NNO Arizona Cardinals	10.00	20.00
NNO Atlanta Falcons	10.00	20.00
NNO Baltimore Ravens	10.00	20.00
NNO Buffalo Bills	10.00	20.00
NNO Carolina Panthers	10.00	20.00
NNO Chicago Bears	10.00	20.00
NNO Cincinnati Bengals	10.00	20.00
NNO Cleveland Browns	10.00	20.00
NNO Dallas Cowboys	15.00	30.00
NNO Denver Broncos	10.00	20.00
NNO Detroit Lions	10.00	20.00
NNO Green Bay Packers	15.00	30.00
NNO Houston Texans	10.00	20.00
NNO Indianapolis Colts	10.00	20.00
NNO Jacksonville Jaguars	10.00	20.00
NNO Kansas City Chiefs	10.00	20.00
NNO Miami Dolphins	10.00	20.00
NNO Minnesota Vikings	10.00	20.00
NNO New England Patriots	10.00	20.00
NNO New England Patriots Super Bowl Champs	10.00	20.00
NNO New Orleans Saints	10.00	20.00
NNO New York Giants	10.00	20.00
NNO New York Jets	10.00	20.00
NNO Oakland Raiders	10.00	20.00
NNO Philadelphia Eagles	10.00	20.00
NNO Pittsburgh Steelers	15.00	30.00
NNO San Diego Chargers	10.00	20.00
NNO San Francisco 49ers	10.00	20.00
NNO Seattle Seahawks	10.00	20.00
NNO St. Louis Rams	10.00	20.00
NNO Tampa Bay Buccaneers	10.00	20.00
NNO Tennessee Titans	10.00	20.00
NNO Washington Redskins	10.00	20.00

2005 Fleer Collectibles Transporters NFL 1:80

Card	Low	High
NNO Arizona Cardinals	10.00	20.00
NNO Atlanta Falcons	10.00	20.00
NNO Baltimore Ravens	10.00	20.00
NNO Buffalo Bills	10.00	20.00
NNO Carolina Panthers	10.00	20.00
NNO Chicago Bears	10.00	20.00
NNO Cincinnati Bengals	10.00	20.00
NNO Cleveland Browns	10.00	20.00
NNO Dallas Cowboys	15.00	30.00
NNO Denver Broncos	10.00	20.00
NNO Detroit Lions	10.00	20.00
NNO Green Bay Packers	15.00	30.00
NNO Houston Texans	10.00	20.00
NNO Indianapolis Colts	10.00	20.00
NNO Jacksonville Jaguars	10.00	20.00
NNO Kansas City Chiefs	10.00	20.00
NNO Miami Dolphins	10.00	20.00
NNO Minnesota Vikings	10.00	20.00
NNO New England Patriots	10.00	20.00
NNO New Orleans Saints	10.00	20.00
NNO New York Giants	10.00	20.00
NNO New York Jets	10.00	20.00
NNO Oakland Raiders	10.00	20.00
NNO Philadelphia Eagles	10.00	20.00
NNO Pittsburgh Steelers	15.00	30.00
NNO San Diego Chargers	10.00	20.00
NNO San Francisco 49ers	10.00	20.00
NNO Seattle Seahawks	10.00	20.00
NNO St. Louis Rams	10.00	20.00
NNO Tampa Bay Buccaneers	10.00	20.00
NNO Tennessee Titans	10.00	20.00
NNO Washington Redskins	10.0020.00	

1993 White Rose Transporters NFL 1:80

Card	Low	High
NNO Arizona Cardinals	10.00	20.00
NNO Atlanta Falcons	15.00	30.00
NNO Buffalo Bills	20.00	40.00
NNO Chicago Bears	20.00	40.00
NNO Cincinnati Bengals	10.00	20.00
NNO Cleveland Browns	15.00	30.00
NNO Dallas Cowboys	50.00	100.00
NNO Denver Broncos	20.00	40.00
NNO Detroit Lions	15.00	30.00
NNO Green Bay Packers	30.00	60.00
NNO Houston Oilers	20.00	40.00
NNO Indianapolis Colts	15.00	30.00
NNO Kansas City Chiefs	15.00	30.00
NNO Los Angeles Raiders	60.00	120.00
NNO Los Angeles Rams	15.00	30.00
NNO New England Patriots	20.00	40.00
NNO New Orleans Saints	15.00	30.00
NNO New York Giants	15.00	30.00
NNO New York Jets	15.00	30.00
NNO Philadelphia Eagles	15.00	30.00
NNO San Diego Chargers	15.00	30.00
NNO San Francisco 49ers	15.00	30.00
NNO Seattle Seahawks	15.00	30.00
NNO Tampa Bay Buccaneers	15.00	30.00
NNO Washington Redskins	15.00	30.00

1994 White Rose Transporters NFL 1:80

Card	Low	High
NNO Arizona Cardinals	10.00	20.00
NNO Atlanta Falcons	15.00	30.00
NNO Buffalo Bills	20.00	40.00
NNO Chicago Bears	20.00	40.00
NNO Cleveland Browns	15.00	30.00
NNO Dallas Cowboys	25.00	50.00
NNO Denver Broncos	50.00	100.00
NNO Detroit Lions	25.00	50.00
NNO Green Bay Packers	200.00	300.00
NNO Houston Oilers	30.00	60.00
NNO Indianapolis Colts	25.00	50.00
NNO Kansas City Chiefs	20.00	40.00
NNO Miami Dolphins	75.00	150.00
NNO Minnesota Vikings	50.00	100.00
NNO Los Angeles Raiders	50.00	100.00
NNO New England Patriots	30.00	60.00
NNO New Orleans Saints	20.00	40.00
NNO New York Giants	30.00	60.00
NNO New York Jets	40.00	80.00
NNO Philadelphia Eagles	50.00	100.00
NNO San Diego Chargers	15.00	30.00
NNO Seattle Seahawks	20.00	40.00
NNO St. Louis Rams	20.00	40.00
NNO Tampa Bay Buccaneers	20.00	40.00
NNO Washington Redskins	40.00	80.00

1995 White Rose Transporters NFL 1:80

Card	Low	High
NNO Arizona Cardinals	10.00	20.00
NNO Atlanta Falcons	15.00	30.00
NNO Baltimore Ravens	20.00	40.00
NNO Buffalo Bills	20.00	40.00
NNO Carolina Panthers	30.00	60.00
NNO Chicago Bears	20.00	40.00
NNO Cincinnati Bengals	10.00	20.00
NNO Cleveland Browns	15.00	30.00
NNO Dallas Cowboys	125.00	200.00
NNO Denver Broncos	40.00	80.00
NNO Detroit Lions	15.00	30.00
NNO Green Bay Packers	100.00	175.00
NNO Houston Oilers	20.00	40.00
NNO Indianapolis Colts	20.00	40.00
NNO Jacksonville Jaguars	25.00	50.00
NNO Kansas City Chiefs	40.00	80.00
NNO Miami Dolphins	60.00	120.00
NNO Minnesota Vikings	40.00	80.00
NNO New England Patriots	75.00	150.00
NNO New Orleans Saints	10.00	20.00
NNO New York Giants	30.00	60.00
NNO New York Jets	50.00	100.00
NNO Oakland Raiders	60.00	120.00
NNO Philadelphia Eagles	15.00	30.00
NNO Pittsburgh Steelers	60.00	120.00
NNO San Diego Chargers	15.00	30.00
NNO Seattle Seahawks	30.00	60.00
NNO St. Louis Rams	40.00	80.00
NNO Tampa Bay Buccaneers	30.00	60.00
NNO Washington Redskins	50.00	100.00

1996 White Rose Transporters NFL 1:80

Card	Low	High
NNO Miami Dolphins	15.00	30.00

1997 White Rose Transporters NFL 1:80

Card	Low	High
NNO Arizona Cardinals	15.00	30.00
NNO Atlanta Falcons	15.00	30.00
NNO Cincinnati Bengals	15.00	30.00
NNO Denver Broncos	15.00	30.00
NNO Detroit Lions	15.00	30.00
NNO Green Bay Packers	20.00	40.00
NNO Jacksonville Jaguars	15.00	30.00
NNO New England Patriots	15.00	30.00
NNO New Orleans Saints	15.00	30.00
NNO Philadelphia Eagles	15.00	30.00
NNO San Diego Chargers	15.00	30.00
NNO San Francisco 49ers	15.00	30.00
NNO Seattle Seahawks	15.00	30.00
NNO Tampa Bay Buccaneers	15.00	30.00
NNO Tennessee Oilers	15.00	30.00
NNO Washington Redskins	15.00	30.00

1998 White Rose Transporters NFL 1:80

Card	Low	High
NNO Arizona Cardinals	15.00	30.00
NNO Baltimore Ravens	15.00	30.00
NNO Buffalo Bills	15.00	30.00
NNO Carolina Panthers	15.00	30.00
NNO Detroit Lions	15.00	30.00
NNO Green Bay Packers	20.00	40.00
NNO Indianapolis Colts	15.00	30.00
NNO Jacksonville Jaguars	15.00	30.00
NNO Kansas City Chiefs	15.00	30.00
NNO Miami Dolphins	15.00	30.00
NNO New England Patriots	15.00	30.00
NNO New Orleans Saints	15.00	30.00
NNO New York Giants	15.00	30.00
NNO New York Jets	15.00	30.00
NNO Philadelphia Eagles	15.00	30.00
NNO Pittsburgh Steelers	20.00	40.00
NNO San Diego Chargers	15.00	30.00
NNO Seattle Seahawks	15.00	30.00
NNO St. Louis Rams	15.00	30.00
NNO Washington Redskins	15.00	30.00

1999 White Rose Transporters NFL 1:80

Card	Low	High
NNO Arizona Cardinals	10.00	20.00
NNO Buffalo Bills	15.00	30.00
NNO Carolina Panthers	15.00	30.00
NNO Chicago Bears	15.00	30.00
NNO Cincinnati Bengals	15.00	30.00
NNO Cleveland Browns	15.00	30.00
NNO Dallas Cowboys	20.00	40.00
NNO Denver Broncos	15.00	30.00
NNO Detroit Lions	15.00	30.00
NNO Green Bay Packers	20.00	40.00
NNO Indianapolis Colts	15.00	30.00
NNO Jacksonville Jaguars	15.00	30.00
NNO Kansas City Chiefs	15.00	30.00
NNO Miami Dolphins	15.00	30.00
NNO Minnesota Vikings	15.00	30.00
NNO New England Patriots	15.00	30.00
NNO New Orleans Saints	15.00	30.00
NNO New York Giants	15.00	30.00
NNO New York Jets	15.00	30.00
NNO Oakland Raiders	15.00	30.00
NNO Philadelphia Eagles	15.00	30.00
NNO Pittsburgh Steelers	20.00	40.00
NNO San Diego Chargers	15.00	30.00
NNO San Francisco 49ers	15.00	30.00
NNO Seattle Seahawks	15.00	30.00
NNO St. Louis Rams	15.00	30.00
NNO Tampa Bay Buccaneers	15.00	30.00
NNO Tennessee Titans	15.00	30.00
NNO Washington Redskins	15.00	30.00

2000 White Rose Transporters NFL 1:80

Card	Low	High
NNO Arizona Cardinals	10.00	20.00
NNO Buffalo Bills	15.00	30.00
NNO Chicago Bears	15.00	30.00
NNO Cincinnati Bengals	15.00	30.00
NNO Cleveland Browns	15.00	30.00
NNO Dallas Cowboys	20.00	40.00
NNO Denver Broncos	15.00	30.00
NNO Detroit Lions	15.00	30.00
NNO Green Bay Packers	20.00	40.00
NNO Indianapolis Colts	15.00	30.00
NNO Jacksonville Jaguars	15.00	30.00
NNO Kansas City Chiefs	15.00	30.00
NNO Miami Dolphins	15.00	30.00
NNO Minnesota Vikings	15.00	30.00
NNO New Orleans Saints	15.00	30.00
NNO New York Giants	15.00	30.00
NNO New York Jets	15.00	30.00
NNO San Diego Chargers	15.00	30.00
NNO San Francisco 49ers	15.00	30.00
NNO St. Louis Rams	15.00	30.00
NNO Tampa Bay Buccaneers	15.00	30.00
NNO Tennessee Titans	15.00	30.00
NNO Washington Redskins	15.00	30.00

2007 Ertl Collectibles Transporters NFL 1:87

Card	Low	High
NNO Chicago Bears	10.00	20.00
NNO Cinncinnati Bengals	10.00	20.00
NNO Denver Broncos	10.00	20.00
NNO Indianapolis Colts	10.00	20.00
NNO Minnesota Vikings	10.00	20.00
NNO New York Jets	10.00	20.00
NNO Pittsburgh Steelers	12.50	25.00
NNO Washington Redskins	10.00	20.00

2004 Action Performance Blisters Zamboni NHL 1:50

Card	Low	High
NNO Chicago Blackhawks/348	10.00	20.00
NNO Dallas Stars/300	10.00	20.00
NNO St. Louis Blues/300	10.00	20.00

2004 Action Performance Zamboni NHL 1:50

Card	Low	High
NNO Boston Bruins	6.00	12.00
NNO Chicago Blackhawks	6.00	12.00
NNO Dallas Stars	6.00	12.00
NNO Detroit Red Wings	6.00	12.00
NNO Minnesota Wild	5.00	10.00
NNO New Jersey Devils '03 Champs	7.50	15.00
NNO New York Rangers	6.00	12.00
NNO Pittsburgh Penguins	6.00	12.00
NNO St. Louis Blues	6.00	12.00

2005 Ertl Collectibles Choppers Series NHL 1:18

Card	Low	High
NNO Boston Bruins	7.50	15.00
NNO Calgary Flames	7.50	15.00
NNO Chicago Blackhawks	6.00	12.00
NNO Detroit Red Wings	10.00	20.00
NNO Edmonton Oilers	6.00	12.00
NNO Montreal Canadiens	7.50	15.00
NNO New York Rangers	6.00	12.00
NNO Ottawa Senators	6.00	12.00
NNO Philadelphia Flyers	6.00	12.00
NNO Toronto Maple Leafs	10.00	20.00
NNO Vancouver Canucks	7.50	15.00

2007 Ertl Collectibles Chopper Series NHL 1:18

Card	Low	High
NNO Calgary Flames	10.00	20.00
NNO Edmonton Oilers	10.00	20.00
NNO Montreal Canadiens	12.50	25.00
NNO New York Rangers	12.50	25.00
NNO Ottawa Senators	10.00	20.00
NNO Philadelphia Flyers	10.00	20.00
NNO Toronto Maple Leafs	12.50	25.00
NNO Vancouver Canucks	10.00	20.00

2005 Ertl Collectibles Snowmobile Series NHL 1:32

AVAILABLE IN CANADA ONLY

Card	Low	High
NNO Calgary Flames	7.50	15.00
NNO Detroit Red Wings	10.00	20.00
NNO Edmonton Oilers	6.00	12.00
NNO Montreal Canadiens	7.50	15.00
NNO Ottawa Senators	6.00	12.00
NNO Toronto Maple Leafs	10.00	20.00
NNO Vancouver Canucks	7.50	15.00

2005 Ertl Collectibles Zamboni NHL 1:50

Card	Low	High
NNO Anaheim Mighty Ducks	5.00	10.00
NNO Atlanta Thrashers	4.00	8.00
NNO Boston Bruins	5.00	10.00
NNO Buffalo Sabres	4.00	8.00
NNO Calgary Flames	5.00	10.00
NNO Carolina Hurricanes	4.00	8.00
NNO Chicago Blackhawks	5.00	10.00
NNO Colorado Avalanche	6.00	12.00
NNO Columbus Blue Jackets	4.00	8.00
NNO Dallas Stars	5.00	10.00
NNO Detroit Red Wings	6.00	12.00
NNO Edmonton Oilers	4.00	8.00
NNO Florida Panthers	4.00	8.00
NNO Los Angeles Kings	5.00	10.00
NNO Minnesota Wild	4.00	8.00
NNO Montreal Canadiens	5.00	10.00
NNO Nashville Predators	4.00	8.00
NNO New Jersey Devils	5.00	10.00
NNO New York Islanders	5.00	10.00
NNO New York Rangers	5.00	10.00
NNO Ottawa Senators	4.00	8.00
NNO Philadelphia Flyers	4.00	8.00
NNO Phoenix Coyotes	4.00	8.00
NNO Pittsburgh Penguins	5.00	10.00
NNO San Jose Sharks	4.00	8.00
NNO St Louis Blues	5.00	10.00
NNO Tampa Bay Lightning	5.00	10.00
NNO Toronto Maple Leafs	6.00	12.00
NNO Vancouver Canucks	5.00	10.00
NNO Washington Capitals	4.00	8.00

2007 Ertl Collectibles Zamboni NHL 1:50

Card	Low	High
NNO Anaheim Ducks	3.00	6.00
NNO Atlanta Thrashers	3.00	6.00
NNO Boston Bruins	5.00	10.00
NNO Buffalo Sabres	4.00	8.00
NNO Colorado Avalanche	5.00	10.00
NNO Columbus Bluejackets	3.00	6.00
NNO Dallas Stars	4.00	8.00
NNO Detroit Red Wings	5.00	10.00
NNO Los Angeles Kings	4.00	8.00
NNO Minnesota Wild	3.00	6.00
NNO Nashville Predators	3.00	6.00
NNO New York Rangers	5.00	10.00
NNO Pittsburgh Penguins	5.00	10.00
NNO St. Louis Blues	4.00	8.00
NNO Toronto Maple Leafs	5.00	10.00
NNO Washington Capitals	4.00	8.00

2005 Ertl Collectibles Classic Rides NHL 1:64

Card	Low	High
NNO Calgary Flames	5.00	10.00
NNO Detroit Red Wings	6.00	12.00
NNO Edmonton Oilers	5.00	10.00
NNO Montreal Canadiens	5.00	10.00
NNO Ottawa Senators	4.00	8.00
NNO Toronto Maple Leafs	6.00	12.00
NNO Vancouver Canucks	5.00	10.00

2002 Fleer Collectibles Zamboni NHL 1:50

Card	Low	High
NNO Detroit Red Wings Stanley Cup	10.00	20.00

2003 Fleer Collectibles Zamboni NHL 1:50

Card	Low	High
NNO All-Star Game Florida/2500	12.50	25.00
NNO Anaheim Mighty Ducks	3.00	6.00
NNO Atlanta Thrashers	3.00	6.00
NNO Boston Bruins	3.00	6.00
NNO Buffalo Sabres	3.00	6.00
NNO Calgary Flames	3.00	6.00
NNO Carolina Hurricanes	3.00	6.00
NNO Chicago Blackhawks	3.00	6.00
NNO Colorado Avalanche	4.00	8.00
NNO Columbus Blue Jackets	3.00	6.00
NNO Dallas Stars	3.00	6.00
NNO Detroit Red Wings	4.00	8.00
NNO Edmonton Oilers	3.00	6.00
NNO Florida Panthers	3.00	6.00
NNO Los Angeles Kings	3.00	6.00
NNO Minnesota Wild	3.00	6.00
NNO Montreal Canadiens	3.00	6.00
NNO Nashville Predators	3.00	6.00
NNO New Jersey Devils	3.00	6.00
NNO New Jersey Devils Stanley Cup	5.00	10.00
NNO New York Islanders	3.00	6.00
NNO New York Rangers	3.00	6.00
NNO Ottawa Senators	3.00	6.00
NNO Philadelphia Flyers	3.00	6.00
NNO Phoenix Coyotes	3.00	6.00
NNO Pittsburgh Penguins	3.00	6.00
NNO San Jose Sharks	3.00	6.00
NNO St. Louis Blues	3.00	6.00
NNO Tampa Bay Lightning	3.00	6.00
NNO Toronto Maple Leafs	3.00	6.00
NNO Vancouver Canucks	3.00	6.00
NNO Washington Capitals	3.00	6.00

2004 Fleer Collectibles Zamboni NHL 1:50

Card	Low	High
NNO All-Star Game Minnesota	10.00	20.00
NNO Atlanta Thrashers	3.00	6.00
NNO Boston Bruins	3.00	6.00
NNO Carolina Hurricanes	3.00	6.00
NNO Columbus Blue Jackets	3.00	6.00
NNO Detroit Red Wings	4.00	8.00
NNO Los Angeles Kings	3.00	6.00
NNO Montreal Canadiens	3.00	6.00
NNO Nashville Predators	3.00	6.00
NNO New Jersey Devils	3.00	6.00
NNO New York Islanders	3.00	6.00
NNO New York Rangers	3.00	6.00
NNO Philadelphia Flyers	3.00	6.00
NNO Pittsburgh Penguins	3.00	6.00
NNO Washington Capitals	3.00	6.00

2002 Fleer Collectibles Transporter NHL 1:80

Card	Low	High
NNO Detroit Red Wings Stanley Cup	12.50	25.00

2006 Upper Deck Zamboni w/card NHL 1:50

Card	Low	High
NNO Calgary Flames w Jarome Iginla	5.00	10.00
NNO Detroit Red Wings w Steve Yzerman	6.00	12.00
NNO Edmonton Oilers w Chris Pronger	5.00	10.00
NNO Montreal Canadiens w Jose Theodore	5.00	10.00
NNO New Jersey Devils w Martin Brodeur	5.00	10.00
NNO New York Islanders w Alexei Yashin	5.00	10.00
NNO New York Rangers w Jaromir Jagr	5.00	10.00
NNO Ottawa Senators w Dany Heatley	5.00	10.00
NNO Philadelphia Flyers w Peter Forsberg	5.00	10.00
NNO Pittsburgh Penguins w Sidney Crosby	7.50	15.00
NNO Toronto Maple Leafs w Eric Lindros	6.00	12.00
NNO Vancouver Canucks w Markus Naslund	5.00	10.00

Alphabetical Card Checklist

A.J. Allmendinger

2007 Press Pass Premium #83
2007 Press Pass Premium Red /5 #R83
2007 Press Pass Signings #3
2007 Press Pass Signings Blue /25 #1
2007 Press Pass Signings Gold /50 #1
2007 Press Pass Stealth #29
2007 Press Pass Stealth Chrome #29
2007 Press Pass Stealth Chrome Exclusives /99 #X29
2007 Press Pass Stealth Chrome Platinum /25 #P29
2007 Press Pass Stealth Maximum Access #MA1
2007 Press Pass Stealth Maximum Access Autographs /25 #MA1
2007 Press Pass Stealth Previews /5 #EB29
2007 Traks #32
2007 Traks Gold #G32
2007 Traks Holofoil /50 #H32
2007 Traks Previews /5 #EB32
2007 Traks Red /10 #R32
2007 VIP #84
2007 VIP Get A Grip Drivers /70 #GGD26
2007 VIP Get A Grip Teams /70 #GGT26
2007 VIP Previews /1 #EB84
2007 VIP Rookie Stripes /100 #RS1
2007 VIP Rookie Stripes Autographs /25 #RSAJ
2007 Wheels American Thunder /345 #84A
2007 Wheels American Thunder /50 #84B
2007 Wheels American Thunder Autographed Hat Instant Winner /1 #AH1
2007 Wheels American Thunder Cool Threads /299 #CT1
2007 Wheels American Thunder Single Hat /99 #SH1
2008 Press Pass Autographs #1
2008 Press Pass Autographs Press Plates Black /1 #1
2008 Press Pass Autographs Press Plates Cyan /1 #1
2008 Press Pass Autographs Press Plates Magenta /1 #1
2008 Press Pass Autographs Press Plates Yellow /1 #1
2008 Press Pass Eclipse Teammates Autographs /35 #AV
2008 Press Pass Legends #67
2008 Press Pass Legends Blue /599 #67
2008 Press Pass Legends Bronze /299 #67
2008 Press Pass Legends Gold /99 #67
2008 Press Pass Legends Holo /25 #67
2008 Press Pass Legends Printing Plates Black /1 #67
2008 Press Pass Legends Printing Plates Cyan /1 #67
2008 Press Pass Legends Printing Plates Magenta /1 #67
2008 Press Pass Legends Printing Plates Yellow /1 #67
2008 Press Pass Legends Solo /1 #67
2008 Press Pass Premium #33
2008 Press Pass Premium Previews /5 #EB33
2008 Press Pass Premium Red /15 #33
2008 Press Pass Signings #3
2008 Press Pass Signings Blue /25 #2
2008 Press Pass Signings Gold /50 #1
2008 Press Pass Signings Press Plates Black /1 #3
2008 Press Pass Signings Press Plates Black /1 #AA
2008 Press Pass Signings Press Plates Cyan /1 #3
2008 Press Pass Signings Press Plates Magenta /1 #3
2008 Press Pass Signings Press Plates Magenta #AA
2008 Press Pass Signings Press Plates Yellow /1 #3
2008 Press Pass Signings Silver /100 #1
2008 Press Pass Stealth #71
2008 Press Pass Stealth Chrome #71
2008 Press Pass Stealth Chrome Exclusives /25 #71
2008 Press Pass Stealth Chrome Exclusives Gold /99 #71
2008 Press Pass Stealth Maximum Access #MA1
2008 Press Pass Stealth Maximum Access Autographs /25 #MA1
2008 VIP #1
2008 VIP #58
2008 VIP Previews /5 #EB1
2008 Wheels American Thunder #2
2008 Wheels American Thunder Autographed Hat Winner /1 #WHAA
2008 Wheels American Thunder Delegates #D1
2008 Wheels American Thunder Double Hat /99 #DH1
2008 Wheels American Thunder Previews /5 #2
2008 Wheels American Thunder Trackside Treasury Autographs #AA
2008 Wheels American Thunder Trackside Treasury Autographs Gold /25 #AA
2008 Wheels American Thunder Trackside Treasury Autographs Printing Plates Black /1 #AA
2008 Wheels American Thunder Trackside Treasury Autographs Printing Plates Cyan /1 #AA
2008 Wheels American Thunder Trackside Treasury Autographs Printing Plates Magenta /1 #AA
2008 Wheels American Thunder Trackside Treasury Autographs Printing Plates Yellow /1 #AA
2008 Wheels Autographs #1
2008 Wheels Autographs Press Plates Black /1 #1
2008 Wheels Autographs Press Plates Cyan /1 #1
2008 Wheels Autographs Press Plates Magenta /1 #1
2008 Wheels Autographs Press Plates Yellow /1 #1
2008 Wheels High Gear Driven #DR27
2009 Press Pass #120
2009 Press Pass Autographs Gold #2
2009 Press Pass Autographs Printing Plates Black /1 #1
2009 Press Pass Autographs Printing Plates Cyan /1 #1
2009 Press Pass Autographs Printing Plates Magenta /1 #1
2009 Press Pass Autographs Printing Plates Yellow /1 #1
2009 Press Pass Autographs Silver #1
2009 Press Pass Blue #120
2009 Press Pass Gold #120
2009 Press Pass Gold Holofoil /100 #120
2009 Press Pass Pieces Race Used Memorabilia #AA
2009 Press Pass Pocket Portraits Wal-Mart #PPW14
2009 Press Pass Premium #27
2009 Press Pass Premium #64
2009 Press Pass Premium Previews /5 #EB27
2009 Press Pass Premium Signatures #1
2009 Press Pass Premium Signatures Gold /25 #1
2009 Press Pass Previews /5 #EB120
2009 Press Pass Red #120
2009 Press Pass Santa Hats /50 #SH1
2009 Press Pass Showcase /499 #17
2009 Press Pass Showcase /499 #34
2009 Press Pass Showcase 2nd Gear /125 #17
2009 Press Pass Showcase 2nd Gear /125 #34
2009 Press Pass Showcase 3rd Gear /50 #17
2009 Press Pass Showcase 3rd Gear /50 #34
2009 Press Pass Showcase 4th Gear /15 #17
2009 Press Pass Showcase 4th Gear /15 #34
2009 Press Pass Showcase Classic Collections Ink /45 #8
2009 Press Pass Showcase Classic Collections Ink Gold /25 #8
2009 Press Pass Showcase Classic Collections Ink Green /5 #8
2009 Press Pass Showcase Classic Collections Ink Melting /1 #8
2009 Press Pass Showcase Printing Plates Black /1 #17
2009 Press Pass Showcase Printing Plates Black /1 #34
2009 Press Pass Showcase Printing Plates Cyan /1 #17
2009 Press Pass Showcase Printing Plates Cyan /1 #34
2009 Press Pass Showcase Printing Plates Magenta /1 #17
2009 Press Pass Showcase Printing Plates Magenta /1 #34
2009 Press Pass Showcase Printing Plates Yellow /1 #17
2009 Press Pass Showcase Printing Plates Yellow /1 #34
2009 Press Pass Signings Gold #2
2009 Press Pass Stealth #1
2009 Press Pass Stealth #87
2009 Press Pass Stealth Chrome #1
2009 Press Pass Stealth Chrome #87
2009 Press Pass Stealth Chrome Brushed Metal /25 #1
2009 Press Pass Stealth Chrome Brushed Metal /25 #87
2009 Press Pass Stealth Chrome Gold /99 #1
2009 Press Pass Stealth Chrome Gold /99 #87
2009 Press Pass Stealth Previews /5 #EB1
2009 VIP #1
2009 VIP Guest List #GG3
2009 VIP Previews /5 #1
2009 VIP Purple /25 #1
2009 Wheels Autographs #80
2009 Wheels Autographs Press Plates Black /1 #AA
2009 Wheels Autographs Press Plates Cyan /1 #AA
2009 Wheels Autographs Press Plates Magenta /1 #AA
2009 Wheels Autographs Press Plates Yellow /1 #AA
2009 Wheels Main Event #29
2009 Wheels Main Event #41
2009 Wheels Main Event Fast Pass Purple /25 #29
2009 Wheels Main Event Fast Pass Purple /25 #41
2009 Wheels Main Event Foil #29
2009 Wheels Main Event Hat Dance Double /99 #HDAJ
2009 Wheels Main Event Hat Dance Patch /10 #HDAJ
2009 Wheels Main Event Marks Clubs #2
2009 Wheels Main Event Marks Diamonds /10 #2
2009 Wheels Main Event Marks Hearts /5 #2
2009 Wheels Main Event Marks Printing Plates Black /1 #2
2009 Wheels Main Event Marks Printing Plates Cyan /1 #2
2009 Wheels Main Event Marks Printing Plates Magenta /1 #2
2009 Wheels Main Event Marks Printing Plates Yellow /1 #2
2009 Wheels Main Event Marks Spades /1 #2
2009 Wheels Main Event Playing Cards Blue #7S
2009 Wheels Main Event Playing Cards Red #7S
2009 Wheels Main Event Previews /5 #29
2010 Element #22
2010 Element Blue /35 #22
2010 Element Green #22
2010 Element Previews /5 #EB22
2010 Element Purple /25 #22
2010 Element Red Target #22
2010 Press Pass #25
2010 Press Pass Autographs #2
2010 Press Pass Autographs Printing Plates Black /1 #2
2010 Press Pass Autographs Printing Plates Cyan /1 #2
2010 Press Pass Autographs Printing Plates Yellow /1 #2
2010 Press Pass Blue #25
2010 Press Pass By The Numbers #BN43
2010 Press Pass Eclipse #85
2010 Press Pass Eclipse Blue #85
2010 Press Pass Eclipse Gold #85
2010 Press Pass Gold #25
2010 Press Pass Holofoil /100 #25
2010 Press Pass Premium #23
2010 Press Pass Premium Purple /25 #23
2010 Press Pass Premium Signatures #PSAA
2010 Press Pass Premium Signatures Red Ink /24 #PSAA
2010 Press Pass Previews /5 #25
2010 Press Pass Purple /25 #25
2010 Press Pass Showcase /499 #23
2010 Press Pass Showcase Classic Collections Ink /15 #CCIOWN
2010 Press Pass Showcase Classic Collections Ink Gold /10 #CCIOWN
2010 Press Pass Showcase Classic Collections Ink Green /5 #CCIOWN
2010 Press Pass Showcase Classic Collections Ink Melting /1 #CCIOWN
2010 Press Pass Showcase Classic Collections Sheet Metal /75 #CCIRPM
2010 Press Pass Showcase Classic Collections Sheet Metal Gold /25 #CCIRPM
2010 Press Pass Showcase Gold /125 #23
2010 Press Pass Showcase Green /50 #23
2010 Press Pass Showcase Melting /15 #23
2010 Press Pass Showcase Platinum Holo /1 #23
2010 Press Pass Signings Blue /10 #2
2010 Press Pass Signings Gold /25 #2
2010 Press Pass Signings Red /15 #2
2010 Press Pass Signings Silver /99 #2
2010 Press Pass Stealth #1
2010 Press Pass Stealth #85
2010 Press Pass Stealth Black and White #1
2010 Press Pass Stealth Black and White #85
2010 Press Pass Stealth Mach 10 #MT6
2010 Press Pass Stealth Previews /5 #1
2010 Press Pass Stealth Purple /25 #1
2010 Wheels Autographs #2
2010 Wheels Autographs Printing Plates Black /1 #2
2010 Wheels Autographs Printing Plates Cyan /1 #2
2010 Wheels Autographs Printing Plates Magenta /1 #2
2010 Wheels Autographs Printing Plates Yellow /1 #2
2010 Wheels Autographs Target /10 #1
2010 Wheels Main Event #1
2010 Wheels Main Event Blue #1
2010 Wheels Main Event Fight Card #FC1
2010 Wheels Main Event Fight Card Checkered Flag #FC1
2010 Wheels Main Event Fight Card Full Color Retail #FC1
2010 Wheels Main Event Fight Card Gold /25 #FC1
2010 Wheels Main Event Marks Autographs /74 #2
2010 Wheels Main Event Marks Autographs Black /1 #2
2010 Wheels Main Event Marks Autographs Blue /52 #2
2010 Wheels Main Event Marks Autographs Red /25 #2
2010 Wheels Main Event Purple /25 #1
2011 Element #1
2011 Element Autographs /60 #2
2011 Element Autographs Blue /5 #2
2011 Element Autographs Gold /10 #2
2011 Element Autographs Printing Plates Black /1 #2
2011 Element Autographs Printing Plates Cyan /1 #2
2011 Element Autographs Printing Plates Magenta /1 #2
2011 Element Autographs Printing Plates Yellow /1 #2
2011 Element Autographs Silver /25 #2
2011 Element Black /35 #1
2011 Element Flagship Performers 2010 Green Flag Passes Blue-Yellow /50 #FPPAA
2011 Element Green #1
2011 Element Previews /5 #1
2011 Element Purple /25 #1
2011 Element Red #1
2011 Press Pass #1
2011 Press Pass #56
2011 Press Pass #171
2011 Press Pass Autographs Blue /10 #2
2011 Press Pass Autographs Bronze /99 #2
2011 Press Pass Autographs Gold /25 #2
2011 Press Pass Autographs Printing Plates Black /1 #2
2011 Press Pass Autographs Printing Plates Cyan /1 #2
2011 Press Pass Autographs Printing Plates Magenta /1 #2
2011 Press Pass Autographs Printing Plates Yellow /1 #2
2011 Press Pass Autographs Silver /50 #2
2011 Press Pass Blue Holofoil /10 #1
2011 Press Pass Blue Holofoil /10 #56
2011 Press Pass Blue Holofoil /10 #171
2011 Press Pass Blue Retail #1
2011 Press Pass Blue Retail #56
2011 Press Pass Blue Retail #171
2011 Press Pass Eclipse #1
2011 Press Pass Eclipse Blue #1
2011 Press Pass Eclipse Gold /55 #1
2011 Press Pass Eclipse Previews /5 #EB1
2011 Press Pass Eclipse Purple /25 #1
2011 Press Pass FanFare #1
2011 Press Pass FanFare Autographs Blue /5 #2
2011 Press Pass FanFare Autographs Bronze /50 #2
2011 Press Pass FanFare Autographs Gold /25 #2
2011 Press Pass FanFare Autographs Printing Plates Black /1 #2
2011 Press Pass FanFare Autographs Printing Plates Cyan /1 #2
2011 Press Pass FanFare Autographs Printing Plates Magenta /1 #2
2011 Press Pass FanFare Autographs Printing Plates Yellow /1 #2
2011 Press Pass FanFare Autographs Silver /15 #2
2011 Press Pass FanFare Blue Die Cuts #1
2011 Press Pass FanFare Emerald /25 #1
2011 Press Pass FanFare Holofoil Die Cuts #1
2011 Press Pass FanFare Magnificent Materials /199 #MMAA
2011 Press Pass FanFare Magnificent Materials Holofoil /50 #MMAA
2011 Press Pass FanFare Ruby Die Cuts /15 #1
2011 Press Pass FanFare Sapphire /10 #1
2011 Press Pass FanFare Silver /25 #1
2011 Press Pass Geared Up Holofoil /50 #GUAA
2011 Press Pass Gold /50 #1
2011 Press Pass Gold /50 #56
2011 Press Pass Gold /50 #171
2011 Press Pass Premium #1
2011 Press Pass Premium Purple /25 #1
2011 Press Pass Premium Signatures /200 #PSAJ
2011 Press Pass Previews /5 #EB1
2011 Press Pass Purple /25 #1
2011 Press Pass Showcase /499 #25
2011 Press Pass Showcase Classic Collections Ink /25 #CCMRPM
2011 Press Pass Showcase Classic Collections Ink Gold /5 #CCMRPM
2011 Press Pass Showcase Classic Collections Ink Melting /1 #CCMRPM
2011 Press Pass Showcase Classic Collections Sheet Metal /99 #CCMRPM
2011 Press Pass Showcase Gold /125 #25
2011 Press Pass Showcase Green /25 #25
2011 Press Pass Showcase Melting /1 #25
2011 Press Pass Signings Black and White /10 #PPSAA1
2011 Press Pass Signings Brushed Metal /60 #PPSAA1
2011 Press Pass Signings Holofoil /25 #PPSAA1
2011 Press Pass Stealth #37
2011 Press Pass Stealth #96
2011 Press Pass Stealth Black and White /25 #37
2011 Press Pass Stealth Black and White /25 #96
2011 Press Pass Stealth Holofoil /99 #37
2011 Press Pass Stealth Holofoil /99 #96
2011 Press Pass Stealth Metal of Honor Medal of Honor /50 #BAAJ
2011 Press Pass Stealth Metal of Honor Purple Heart /25 #MHAJ
2011 Press Pass Stealth Metal of Honor Silver Star /99 #BAAJ
2011 Press Pass Stealth Purple /25 #37
2011 Wheels Main Event #1
2011 Wheels Main Event Black and White #1
2011 Wheels Main Event Blue /75 #1
2011 Wheels Main Event Green /1 #1
2011 Wheels Main Event Marks Autographs Blue /10 #MEAA
2011 Wheels Main Event Marks Autographs Gold /25 #MEAA
2011 Wheels Main Event Marks Autographs Silver /50 #MEAA
2011 Wheels Main Event Red /20 #1
2012 Press Pass #1
2012 Press Pass Autographs Blue /10 #PPAAA1
2012 Press Pass Autographs Printing Plates Black /1 #PPAAA1
2012 Press Pass Autographs Printing Plates Cyan /1 #PPAAA1
2012 Press Pass Autographs Printing Plates Magenta /1 #PPAAA1
2012 Press Pass Autographs Printing Plates Yellow /1 #PPAAA1
2012 Press Pass Autographs Red /25 #PPAAA1
2012 Press Pass Autographs Silver /145 #PPAAA1
2012 Press Pass Blue #1
2012 Press Pass Blue Holofoil /35 #1
2012 Press Pass Gold #1
2012 Press Pass Ignite #1
2012 Press Pass Ignite #68
2012 Press Pass Ignite Materials Autographs Gun Metal /20 #IMAJ
2012 Press Pass Ignite Materials Autographs Red /5 #IMAJ
2012 Press Pass Ignite Materials Autographs Silver /125 #IMAJ
2012 Press Pass Ignite Materials Gun Metal /99 #IMAJ
2012 Press Pass Ignite Materials Red /10 #IMAJ
2012 Press Pass Ignite Materials Silver #IMAJ
2012 Press Pass Ignite Proofs Black and White /50 #1
2012 Press Pass Ignite Proofs Black and White /50 #68
2012 Press Pass Ignite Proofs Cyan #1
2012 Press Pass Ignite Proofs Cyan #68
2012 Press Pass Ignite Proofs Magenta #1
2012 Press Pass Ignite Proofs Magenta #68
2012 Press Pass Ignite Proofs Yellow /10 #1
2012 Press Pass Ignite Proofs Yellow /10 #68
2012 Press Pass Power Picks Blue /50 #26
2012 Press Pass Power Picks Blue /50 #71
2012 Press Pass Power Picks Gold /50 #26
2012 Press Pass Power Picks Gold /50 #71
2012 Press Pass Power Picks Holofoil /10 #26
2012 Press Pass Power Picks Holofoil /10 #71
2012 Press Pass Purple /35 #1
2012 Press Pass Redline #1
2012 Press Pass Redline Black /99 #1
2012 Press Pass Redline Cyan /50 #1
2012 Press Pass Redline Magenta /15 #1
2012 Press Pass Redline Signatures Blue /5 #RSAJ1
2012 Press Pass Redline Signatures Blue /5 #RSAJ2
2012 Press Pass Redline Signatures Gold /25 #RSAJ1
2012 Press Pass Redline Signatures Gold /15 #RSAJ2
2012 Press Pass Redline Signatures Holofoil /10 #RSAJ1
2012 Press Pass Redline Signatures Holofoil /10 #RSAJ2
2012 Press Pass Redline Signatures Melting /1 #RSAJ1
2012 Press Pass Redline Signatures Melting /1 #RSAJ2
2012 Press Pass Redline Signatures Red /45 #RSAJ1
2012 Press Pass Redline Signatures Red /25 #RSAJ2
2012 Press Pass Redline Yellow /1 #1
2012 Press Pass Showcase /499 #58
2012 Press Pass Showcase Classic Collections Memorabilia /99 #CCMPEN
2012 Press Pass Showcase Classic Collections Memorabilia Gold /50 #CCMPEN
2012 Press Pass Showcase Classic Collections Memorabilia Melting /5 #CCMPEN
2012 Press Pass Showcase Gold /125 #58
2012 Press Pass Showcase Green /5 #58
2012 Press Pass Showcase Melting /1 #58
2012 Press Pass Showcase Purple /1 #58
2012 Press Pass Showcase Red /25 #58
2012 Press Pass Signature Series Race Used /12 #PPAAA
2012 Press Pass Snapshots #SS1
2012 Press Pass Snapshots #SS67
2012 Press Pass Target Snapshots #SSTG1
2012 Total Memorabilia Dual Swatch Gold /75 #TMAA
2012 Total Memorabilia Dual Swatch Holofoil /25 #TMAA
2012 Total Memorabilia Dual Swatch Melting /5 #TMAA
2012 Total Memorabilia Dual Swatch Silver /99 #TMAA
2012 Total Memorabilia Single Swatch Gold /99 #TMAA
2012 Total Memorabilia Single Swatch Holofoil /50 #TMAA
2012 Total Memorabilia Single Swatch Melting /10 #TMAA
2012 Total Memorabilia Single Swatch Silver /299 #TMAA
2012 Total Memorabilia Triple Swatch Gold /50 #TMAA
2012 Total Memorabilia Triple Swatch Holofoil /25 #TMAA
2012 Total Memorabilia Triple Swatch Melting /1 #TMAA
2012 Total Memorabilia Triple Swatch Silver /99 #TMAA
2014 Press Pass American Thunder #1
2014 Press Pass American Thunder Autographs Blue /10 #ATAAJA
2014 Press Pass American Thunder Autographs Red /5 #ATAAJA
2014 Press Pass American Thunder Autographs White /25 #ATAAJA
2014 Press Pass American Thunder Black and White /50 #1
2014 Press Pass American Thunder Cyan #1
2014 Press Pass American Thunder Magenta #1
2014 Press Pass American Thunder Yellow /5 #1
2014 Press Pass Redline #1
2014 Press Pass Redline Black /75 #1
2014 Press Pass Redline Blue Foil #1
2014 Press Pass Redline Cyan /50 #1
2014 Press Pass Redline Green National Convention /5 #1
2014 Press Pass Redline Magenta /10 #1
2014 Press Pass Redline Relics Blue /25 #RRAJA
2014 Press Pass Redline Relics Gold /50 #RRAJA
2014 Press Pass Redline Relics Melting /1 #RRAJA
2014 Press Pass Redline Relics Red /75 #RRAJA
2014 Press Pass Redline Signatures Blue /25 #RSAJA
2014 Press Pass Redline Signatures Gold /50 #RSAJA
2014 Press Pass Redline Signatures Melting /10 #RSAJA
2014 Press Pass Redline Signatures Red /60 #RSAJA
2014 Press Pass Redline Yellow /1 #1
2015 Press Pass #1
2015 Press Pass #100
2015 Press Pass Burning Rubber Blue /50 #BRAJA
2015 Press Pass Burning Rubber Gold #BRAJA
2015 Press Pass Burning Rubber Green /10 #BRAJA
2015 Press Pass Burning Rubber Melting /1 #BRAJA
2015 Press Pass Cup Chase #1
2015 Press Pass Cup Chase #100
2015 Press Pass Cup Chase Blue /25 #1
2015 Press Pass Cup Chase Blue /25 #100
2015 Press Pass Cup Chase Gold /75 #1
2015 Press Pass Cup Chase Gold /75 #100
2015 Press Pass Cup Chase Green /10 #1
2015 Press Pass Cup Chase Green /10 #100
2015 Press Pass Cup Chase Melting /1 #1
2015 Press Pass Cup Chase Melting /1 #100
2015 Press Pass Purple #1
2015 Press Pass Purple #100
2015 Press Pass Red #1
2015 Press Pass Red #100
2015 Press Pass Signings Blue /99 #PPSAJ
2015 Press Pass Signings Gold #PPSAJ
2015 Press Pass Signings Green /25 #PPSAJ
2015 Press Pass Signings Melting /10 #PPSAJ
2015 Press Pass Signings Red /50 #PPSAJ
2016 Certified #15
2016 Certified Mirror Black /1 #15
2016 Certified Mirror Blue /50 #15
2016 Certified Mirror Gold /25 #15
2016 Certified Mirror Green /5 #15
2016 Certified Mirror Orange /99 #15
2016 Certified Mirror Purple /10 #15
2016 Certified Mirror Red /75 #15
2016 Certified Mirror Silver /99 #15
2016 Panini Prizm #39
2016 Panini Prizm Prizms #39
2016 Panini Prizm Prizms Black /3 #39
2016 Panini Prizm Prizms Blue Flag /99 #39
2016 Panini Prizm Prizms Camo /47 #39
2016 Panini Prizm Prizms Checkered Flag /1 #39
2016 Panini Prizm Prizms Gold /10 #39
2016 Panini Prizm Prizms Green Flag /149 #39
2016 Panini Prizm Prizms Rainbow /24 #39
2016 Panini Prizm Prizms Red Flag /75 #39
2016 Panini Prizm Prizms Red White and Blue #39
2016 Panini Prizm Prizms White Flag /5 #39
2016 Panini Torque #21
2016 Panini Torque Artist Proof /50 #21
2016 Panini Torque Blackout /1 #21
2016 Panini Torque Blue /125 #21
2016 Panini Torque Clear Vision #20
2016 Panini Torque Clear Vision Blue /99 #20
2016 Panini Torque Clear Vision Gold /149 #20
2016 Panini Torque Clear Vision Green /25 #20
2016 Panini Torque Clear Vision Purple /10 #20
2016 Panini Torque Clear Vision Red /49 #20
2016 Panini Torque Gold #21
2016 Panini Torque Holo Gold /5 #21
2016 Panini Torque Holo Silver /10 #21
2016 Panini Torque Horsepower Heroes #22
2016 Panini Torque Horsepower Heroes Gold /199 #22
2016 Panini Torque Horsepower Heroes Holo Silver /99 #22
2016 Panini Torque Printing Plates Black /1 #21
2016 Panini Torque Printing Plates Cyan /1 #21
2016 Panini Torque Printing Plates Magenta /1 #21
2016 Panini Torque Printing Plates Yellow /1 #21
2016 Panini Torque Purple /25 #21
2016 Panini Torque Red /99 #21
2016 Panini Torque Rubber Relics /399 #1
2016 Panini Torque Rubber Relics Blue /99 #1
2016 Panini Torque Rubber Relics Green /25 #1
2016 Panini Torque Rubber Relics Purple /10 #1
2016 Panini Torque Rubber Relics Red /49 #1
2016 Panini Torque Test Proof Black /1 #21
2016 Panini Torque Test Proof Cyan /1 #21
2016 Panini Torque Test Proof Magenta /1 #21
2016 Panini Torque Test Proof Yellow /1 #21
2016 Panini Torque Winning Vision #21
2016 Panini Torque Winning Vision Blue /99 #21
2016 Panini Torque Winning Vision Gold /149 #21
2016 Panini Torque Winning Vision Green /25 #21
2016 Panini Torque Winning Vision Purple /10 #21
2016 Panini Torque Winning Vision Red /49 #21
2017 Donruss #26
2017 Donruss #59
2017 Donruss #161
2017 Donruss #107
2017 Donruss Artist Proof /25 #26
2017 Donruss Artist Proof /25 #59
2017 Donruss Artist Proof /25 #161
2017 Donruss Artist Proof /25 #107
2017 Donruss Blue Foil /299 #26
2017 Donruss Blue Foil /299 #59
2017 Donruss Blue Foil /299 #161
2017 Donruss Blue Foil /299 #107
2017 Donruss Gold Foil /499 #26
2017 Donruss Gold Foil /499 #161
2017 Donruss Gold Foil /499 #59
2017 Donruss Gold Foil /499 #107
2017 Donruss Gold Press Proof /99 #26
2017 Donruss Gold Press Proof /99 #59
2017 Donruss Gold Press Proof /99 #161
2017 Donruss Gold Press Proof /99 #107
2017 Donruss Green Foil /199 #26
2017 Donruss Green Foil /199 #59
2017 Donruss Green Foil /199 #161
2017 Donruss Green Foil /199 #107
2017 Donruss Press Proof /49 #26
2017 Donruss Press Proof /49 #59
2017 Donruss Press Proof /49 #161
2017 Donruss Press Proof /49 #107
2017 Donruss Printing Plates Black /1 #26
2017 Donruss Printing Plates Black /1 #59
2017 Donruss Printing Plates Black /1 #161
2017 Donruss Printing Plates Black /1 #107
2017 Donruss Printing Plates Cyan /1 #26
2017 Donruss Printing Plates Cyan /1 #59
2017 Donruss Printing Plates Cyan /1 #161
2017 Donruss Printing Plates Cyan /1 #107
2017 Donruss Printing Plates Magenta /1 #26
2017 Donruss Printing Plates Magenta /1 #161
2017 Donruss Printing Plates Magenta /1 #59
2017 Donruss Printing Plates Magenta /1 #107
2017 Donruss Printing Plates Yellow /1 #26
2017 Donruss Printing Plates Yellow /1 #161
2017 Donruss Printing Plates Yellow /1 #59
2017 Donruss Printing Plates Yellow /1 #107
2017 Panini Father's Day Racing Memorabilia /100 #2
2017 Panini Father's Day Racing Memorabilia Cracked Ice /25 #2
2017 Panini Father's Day Racing Memorabilia Hyperplaid /1 #2
2017 Panini Father's Day Racing Memorabilia Shimmer /10 #2
2017 Panini National Treasures Associate Sponsor Patch Signatures 1 /1 #27
2017 Panini National Treasures Associate Sponsor Patch Signatures 10 /1 #27
2017 Panini National Treasures Associate Sponsor Patch Signatures 11 /1 #27
2017 Panini National Treasures Associate Sponsor Patch Signatures 12 /1 #27
2017 Panini National Treasures Associate Sponsor Patch Signatures 13 /1 #27
2017 Panini National Treasures Associate Sponsor Patch Signatures 14 /1 #27
2017 Panini National Treasures Associate Sponsor Patch Signatures 15 /1 #27
2017 Panini National Treasures Associate Sponsor Patch Signatures 16 /1 #27
2017 Panini National Treasures Associate Sponsor Patch Signatures 2 /1 #27
2017 Panini National Treasures Associate Sponsor Patch Signatures 3 /1 #27
2017 Panini National Treasures Associate Sponsor Patch Signatures 4 /1 #27
2017 Panini National Treasures Associate Sponsor Patch Signatures 5 /1 #27
2017 Panini National Treasures Associate Sponsor Patch Signatures 6 /1 #27
2017 Panini National Treasures Associate Sponsor Patch Signatures 7 /1 #27
2017 Panini National Treasures Associate Sponsor Patch Signatures 8 /1 #27
2017 Panini National Treasures Associate Sponsor Patch Signatures 9 /1 #27
2017 Panini National Treasures Car Manufacturer Patch Signatures /1 #27
2017 Panini National Treasures Dual Firesuit Materials Black /1 #3
2017 Panini National Treasures Dual Firesuit Materials Green /5 #3
2017 Panini National Treasures Dual Firesuit Materials Holo Gold /10 #3
2017 Panini National Treasures Dual Firesuit Materials Laundry Tag /1 #3
2017 Panini National Treasures Dual Firesuit Materials Printing Plates Black /1 #3
2017 Panini National Treasures Dual Firesuit Materials Printing Plates Cyan /1 #3
2017 Panini National Treasures Dual Firesuit Materials Printing Plates Magenta /1 #3
2017 Panini National Treasures Dual Firesuit Materials Printing Plates Yellow /1 #3
2017 Panini National Treasures Dual Firesuit Signatures /25 #3
2017 Panini National Treasures Dual Firesuit Signatures Black /1 #3
2017 Panini National Treasures Dual Firesuit Signatures Gold /15 #3
2017 Panini National Treasures Dual Firesuit Signatures Green /5 #3
2017 Panini National Treasures Dual Firesuit Signatures Holo Gold /10 #3
2017 Panini National Treasures Dual Firesuit Signatures Holo Silver /20 #3
2017 Panini National Treasures Dual Firesuit Signatures Laundry Tag /1 #3
2017 Panini National Treasures Dual Firesuit Signatures Printing Plates Black /1 #3
2017 Panini National Treasures Dual Firesuit Signatures Printing Plates Cyan /1 #3
2017 Panini National Treasures Dual Firesuit Signatures Printing Plates Magenta /1 #3
2017 Panini National Treasures Dual Firesuit Signatures Printing Plates Yellow /1 #3
2017 Panini National Treasures Dual Sheet Metal Signatures /25 #1
2017 Panini National Treasures Dual Sheet Metal Signatures Black /1 #1
2017 Panini National Treasures Dual Sheet Metal Signatures Gold /15 #1
2017 Panini National Treasures Dual Sheet Metal Signatures Green /5 #1
2017 Panini National Treasures Dual Sheet Metal Signatures Holo Gold /10 #1
2017 Panini National Treasures Dual Sheet Metal Signatures Holo Silver /20 #1
2017 Panini National Treasures Dual Sheet Metal Signatures Printing Plates Black /1 #1
2017 Panini National Treasures Dual Sheet Metal Signatures Printing Plates Cyan /1 #1
2017 Panini National Treasures Dual Sheet Metal Signatures Printing Plates Magenta /1 #1
2017 Panini National Treasures Dual Sheet Metal Signatures Printing Plates Yellow /1 #1
2017 Panini National Treasures Firesuit Manufacturer Patch Signatures /1 #27
2017 Panini National Treasures Goodyear Patch Signatures /2 #27
2017 Panini National Treasures Hats Off /13 #1
2017 Panini National Treasures Hats Off Gold /2 #1
2017 Panini National Treasures Hats Off Holo Gold /5 #1
2017 Panini National Treasures Hats Off Holo Silver /1 #1
2017 Panini National Treasures Hats Off Laundry Tag /6 #1
2017 Panini National Treasures Hats Off New Era /1 #1
2017 Panini National Treasures Hats Off Printing Plates Black /1 #1
2017 Panini National Treasures Hats Off Printing Plates Cyan /1 #1
2017 Panini National Treasures Hats Off Printing Plates Magenta /1 #1
2017 Panini National Treasures Hats Off Printing Plates Yellow /1 #1
2017 Panini National Treasures Hats Off Sponsor /5 #1
2017 Panini National Treasures Jumbo Firesuit Materials Black /1 #8
2017 Panini National Treasures Jumbo Firesuit Materials Green /5 #8
2017 Panini National Treasures Jumbo Firesuit Materials Laundry Tag /1 #8
2017 Panini National Treasures Jumbo Firesuit Materials Printing Plates Black /1 #8
2017 Panini National Treasures Jumbo Firesuit Materials Printing Plates Cyan /1 #8
2017 Panini National Treasures Jumbo Firesuit Materials Printing Plates Magenta /1 #8
2017 Panini National Treasures Jumbo Firesuit Materials Printing Plates Yellow /1 #8
2017 Panini National Treasures Jumbo Firesuit Signatures /25 #1
2017 Panini National Treasures Jumbo Firesuit Signatures Black /1 #1
2017 Panini National Treasures Jumbo Firesuit Signatures Gold /15 #1
2017 Panini National Treasures Jumbo Firesuit Signatures Green /5 #1
2017 Panini National Treasures Jumbo Firesuit Signatures Holo Gold /10 #1
2017 Panini National Treasures Jumbo Firesuit Signatures Holo Silver /20 #1
2017 Panini National Treasures Jumbo Firesuit Signatures Laundry Tag /1 #1
2017 Panini National Treasures Jumbo Firesuit Signatures Printing Plates Black /1 #1
2017 Panini National Treasures Jumbo Firesuit Signatures Printing Plates Cyan /1 #1
2017 Panini National Treasures Jumbo Firesuit Signatures Printing Plates Magenta /1 #1
2017 Panini National Treasures Jumbo Firesuit Signatures Printing Plates Yellow /1 #1
2017 Panini National Treasures Jumbo Tire Signatures /40 #1
2017 Panini National Treasures Jumbo Tire Signatures Black /1 #1
2017 Panini National Treasures Jumbo Tire Signatures Gold /15 #1
2017 Panini National Treasures Jumbo Tire Signatures Green /5 #1
2017 Panini National Treasures Jumbo Tire Signatures Holo Gold /10 #1
2017 Panini National Treasures Jumbo Tire Signatures Holo Silver /25 #1
2017 Panini National Treasures Jumbo Tire Signatures Printing Plates Black /1 #1
2017 Panini National Treasures Jumbo Tire Signatures Printing Plates Cyan /1 #1
2017 Panini National Treasures Jumbo Tire Signatures Printing Plates Magenta /1 #1
2017 Panini National Treasures Jumbo Tire Signatures Printing Plates Yellow /1 #1
2017 Panini National Treasures Nameplate Patch Signatures /2 #27
2017 Panini National Treasures NASCAR Patch Signatures /1 #27
2017 Panini National Treasures Quad Materials /25 #12
2017 Panini National Treasures Quad Materials Black /1 #12
2017 Panini National Treasures Quad Materials Gold /15 #12
2017 Panini National Treasures Quad Materials Green /5 #12
2017 Panini National Treasures Quad Materials Holo Gold /10 #12
2017 Panini National Treasures Quad Materials Holo Silver /20 #12
2017 Panini National Treasures Quad Materials Laundry Tag /1 #12
2017 Panini National Treasures Quad Materials Printing Plates Black /1 #12
2017 Panini National Treasures Quad Materials Printing Plates Cyan /1 #12
2017 Panini National Treasures Quad Materials Printing Plates Magenta /1 #12
2017 Panini National Treasures Quad Materials Printing Plates Yellow /1 #12
2017 Panini National Treasures Series Sponsor Patch Signatures /1 #27
2017 Panini National Treasures Sunoco Patch Signatures /1 #27
2017 Panini National Treasures Three Wide /25 #11
2017 Panini National Treasures Three Wide Black /1 #11
2017 Panini National Treasures Three Wide Gold /15 #11
2017 Panini National Treasures Three Wide Green /5 #11
2017 Panini National Treasures Three Wide Holo Gold /10 #11
2017 Panini National Treasures Three Wide Holo Silver /20 #11
2017 Panini National Treasures Three Wide Laundry Tag /1 #11
2017 Panini National Treasures Three Wide Printing Plates Black /1 #11
2017 Panini National Treasures Three Wide Printing Plates Cyan /1 #11
2017 Panini National Treasures Three Wide Printing Plates Magenta /1 #11

anini National Treasures Three Wide Printing Plates Yellow /1 #11
anini National Treasures Three Wide Signatures /25 #6
anini National Treasures Three Wide Signatures Black /1 #6
anini National Treasures Three Wide Signatures Gold /15 #6
anini National Treasures Three Wide Signatures Green /5 #6
anini National Treasures Three Wide Signatures Holo Gold /10 #6
anini National Treasures Three Wide Signatures Holo Silver /20 #6
anini National Treasures Three Wide Signatures Laundry Tag /1 #6
anini National Treasures Three Wide Signatures Printing Plates Black /1 #6
anini National Treasures Three Wide Signatures Printing Plates Cyan /1 #6
anini National Treasures Three Wide Signatures Printing Plates Magenta /1 #6
anini National Treasures Three Wide Signatures Printing Plates Yellow /1 #6
anini Torque #19
anini Torque #64
anini Torque Artist Proof /75 #19
anini Torque Artist Proof /75 #64
anini Torque Blackout /1 #19
anini Torque Blackout /1 #64
anini Torque Blue /150 #19
anini Torque Blue /150 #64
anini Torque Clear Vision #21
anini Torque Clear Vision Blue /99 #21
anini Torque Clear Vision Gold /149 #21
anini Torque Clear Vision Green /25 #21
anini Torque Clear Vision Purple /10 #21
anini Torque Clear Vision Red /49 #21
anini Torque Gold #19
anini Torque Gold #64
anini Torque Holo Gold /10 #19
anini Torque Holo Gold /10 #64
anini Torque Holo Silver /25 #19
anini Torque Holo Silver /25 #64
Panini Torque Pairings Materials Blue /49 #12
Panini Torque Pairings Materials Purple /10 #12
Panini Torque Pairings Materials Red /35 #12
Panini Torque Printing Plates Black /1 #19
Panini Torque Printing Plates Black /1 #64
Panini Torque Printing Plates Cyan /1 #19
Panini Torque Printing Plates Cyan /1 #64
Panini Torque Printing Plates Magenta /1 #19
Panini Torque Printing Plates Magenta /1 #64
Panini Torque Printing Plates Yellow /1 #19
Panini Torque Printing Plates Yellow /1 #64
Panini Torque Purple /50 #19
Panini Torque Purple /50 #64
Panini Torque Red /100 #19
Panini Torque Red /100 #64
Panini Torque Running Order #18
Panini Torque Running Order Blue /99 #18
Panini Torque Running Order Checkerboard /10 #18
Panini Torque Running Order Green /25 #18
7 Panini Torque Running Order Red /49 #18
7 Panini Torque Silhouettes Firesuit Signatures /217 #18
7 Panini Torque Silhouettes Firesuit Signatures Blue /99 #18
7 Panini Torque Silhouettes Firesuit Signatures Green /25 #18
7 Panini Torque Silhouettes Firesuit Signatures Purple /10 #18
7 Panini Torque Silhouettes Firesuit Signatures Red /49 #18
7 Panini Torque Test Proof Black /1 #19
7 Panini Torque Test Proof Black /1 #64
7 Panini Torque Test Proof Cyan /1 #19
7 Panini Torque Test Proof Cyan /1 #64
7 Panini Torque Test Proof Magenta /1 #19
7 Panini Torque Test Proof Magenta /1 #64
7 Panini Torque Test Proof Yellow /1 #19
7 Panini Torque Test Proof Yellow /1 #64
7 Select #22
7 Select #115
7 Select Prizms Black /3 #22
7 Select Prizms Black /3 #115
7 Select Prizms Blue /199 #22
17 Select Prizms Checkered Flag /1 #22
17 Select Prizms Checkered Flag /1 #115
17 Select Prizms Gold /10 #22
17 Select Prizms Gold /10 #115
17 Select Prizms Purple Pulsar #22
17 Select Prizms Red /99 #22
17 Select Prizms Red White and Blue Pulsar /299 #22
17 Select Prizms Silver #22
17 Select Prizms Tie Dye /24 #22
17 Select Prizms Tie Dye /24 #115
17 Select Prizms White /50 #22
17 Select Prizms White /50 #115
17 Select Select Stars #19
17 Select Select Stars Prizms Black /3 #19
17 Select Select Stars Prizms Checkered Flag /1 #19
17 Select Select Stars Prizms Gold /10 #19
17 Select Select Stars Prizms Tie Dye /24 #19
17 Select Select Stars Prizms White /50 #19
17 Select Select Swatches #45
17 Select Select Swatches Prizms Blue /199 #45
17 Select Select Swatches Prizms Checkered Flag /1 #45
17 Select Select Swatches Prizms Gold /10 #45
17 Select Select Swatches Prizms Red /99 #45
017 Select Signature Swatches Dual #1
017 Select Signature Swatches Dual Prizms Checkered Flag /1 #1
017 Select Signature Swatches Dual Prizms Gold /10 #1
017 Select Signature Swatches Dual Prizms Tie Dye /24 #1
017 Select Signature Swatches Dual Prizms White /50 #1
2017 Select Signatures #38
2017 Select Signatures Prizms Blue /49 #38
2017 Select Signatures Prizms Checkered Flag /1 #38
2017 Select Signatures Prizms Gold /10 #38
2017 Select Signatures Prizms Red /25 #38
2017 Select Speed Merchants #25
2017 Select Speed Merchants Prizms Black /3 #25
2017 Select Speed Merchants Prizms Checkered Flag /1 #25
2017 Select Speed Merchants Prizms Gold /10 #25
2017 Select Speed Merchants Prizms Tie Dye /24 #25
2017 Select Speed Merchants Prizms White /50 #25
2017 Select Up Close and Personal #3
2017 Select Up Close and Personal Prizms Black /3 #3
2017 Select Up Close and Personal Prizms Checkered Flag /1 #3
2017 Select Up Close and Personal Prizms Gold /10 #3
2017 Select Up Close and Personal Prizms Tie Dye /24 #3
2017 Select Up Close and Personal Prizms White /50 #3
2018 Certified #49
2018 Certified Black /1 #49
2018 Certified Blue /99 #49
2018 Certified Gold /49 #49
2018 Certified Green /10 #49
2018 Certified Mirror Black /1 #49
2018 Certified Mirror Gold /25 #49
2018 Certified Mirror Green /5 #49
2018 Certified Mirror Purple /10 #49
2018 Certified Orange /249 #49
2018 Certified Purple /25 #49
2018 Certified Red /199 #49
2018 Certified Skills /199 #17
2018 Certified Skills Black /1 #17
2018 Certified Skills Blue /99 #17
2018 Certified Skills Gold /49 #17
2018 Certified Skills Green /10 #17
2018 Certified Skills Mirror Black /1 #17
2018 Certified Skills Mirror Gold /25 #17
2018 Certified Skills Mirror Green /5 #17
2018 Certified Skills Mirror Purple /10 #17
2018 Certified Skills Purple /25 #17
2018 Certified Skills Red /149 #17
2018 Certified Stars /199 #10
2018 Certified Stars Black /1 #10
2018 Certified Stars Blue /99 #10
2018 Certified Stars Gold /49 #10
2018 Certified Stars Green /10 #10
2018 Certified Stars Mirror Black /1 #10
2018 Certified Stars Mirror Gold /25 #10
2018 Certified Stars Mirror Green /5 #10
2018 Certified Stars Mirror Purple /10 #10
2018 Certified Stars Purple /25 #10
2018 Certified Stars Red /149 #10
2018 Donruss #21
2018 Donruss #48A
2018 Donruss #98
2018 Donruss #138
2018 Donruss #48B
2018 Donruss Artist Proofs /25 #21
2018 Donruss Artist Proofs /25 #48A
2018 Donruss Artist Proofs /25 #98
2018 Donruss Artist Proofs /25 #138
2018 Donruss Artist Proofs /25 #48B
2018 Donruss Gold Foil /499 #21
2018 Donruss Gold Foil /499 #48A
2018 Donruss Gold Foil /499 #98
2018 Donruss Gold Foil /499 #138
2018 Donruss Gold Foil /499 #48B
2018 Donruss Gold Press Proofs /99 #21
2018 Donruss Gold Press Proofs /99 #48A
2018 Donruss Gold Press Proofs /99 #98
2018 Donruss Gold Press Proofs /99 #138
2018 Donruss Gold Press Proofs /99 #48B
2018 Donruss Green Foil /199 #21
2018 Donruss Green Foil /199 #48A
2018 Donruss Green Foil /199 #98
2018 Donruss Green Foil /199 #138
2018 Donruss Green Foil /199 #48B
2018 Donruss Press Proofs /49 #21
2018 Donruss Press Proofs /49 #48
2018 Donruss Press Proofs /49 #98
2018 Donruss Press Proofs /49 #138
2018 Donruss Press Proofs /49 #48B
2018 Donruss Printing Plates Black /1 #21
2018 Donruss Printing Plates Black /1 #48
2018 Donruss Printing Plates Black /1 #98
2018 Donruss Printing Plates Black /1 #138
2018 Donruss Printing Plates Black /1 #48B
2018 Donruss Printing Plates Cyan /1 #21
2018 Donruss Printing Plates Cyan /1 #48
2018 Donruss Printing Plates Cyan /1 #98
2018 Donruss Printing Plates Cyan /1 #138
2018 Donruss Printing Plates Cyan /1 #48B
2018 Donruss Printing Plates Magenta /1 #21
2018 Donruss Printing Plates Magenta /1 #48
2018 Donruss Printing Plates Magenta /1 #98
2018 Donruss Printing Plates Magenta /1 #138
2018 Donruss Printing Plates Magenta /1 #48B
2018 Donruss Printing Plates Yellow /1 #21
2018 Donruss Printing Plates Yellow /1 #48
2018 Donruss Printing Plates Yellow /1 #98
2018 Donruss Printing Plates Yellow /1 #138
2018 Donruss Printing Plates Yellow /1 #48B
2018 Donruss Racing Relics #1
2018 Donruss Racing Relics Black /10 #1
2018 Donruss Racing Relics Holo Gold /99 #1
2018 Donruss Red Foil /299 #21
2018 Donruss Red Foil /299 #48A
2018 Donruss Red Foil /299 #98
2018 Donruss Red Foil /299 #138
2018 Donruss Red Foil /299 #48B
2018 Donruss Rubber Relics #1
2018 Donruss Rubber Relics Black /10 #1
2018 Donruss Rubber Relics Holo Gold /99 #1
2018 Donruss Studio Signatures Black /1 #1
2018 Donruss Studio Signatures Holo Gold /2 #1
2018 Panini Victory Lane #24
2018 Panini Victory Lane Black /1 #24
2018 Panini Victory Lane Blue /25 #24
2018 Panini Victory Lane Engineered to Perfection Materials Black /25 #1
2018 Panini Victory Lane Engineered to Perfection Materials Green /99 #1
2018 Panini Victory Lane Gold /99 #24
2018 Panini Victory Lane Green /5 #24
2018 Panini Victory Lane Pedal to the Metal #1
2018 Panini Victory Lane Pedal to the Metal #69
2018 Panini Victory Lane Pedal to the Metal Black /1 #1
2018 Panini Victory Lane Pedal to the Metal Black /1 #69
2018 Panini Victory Lane Pedal to the Metal Blue /25 #1
2018 Panini Victory Lane Pedal to the Metal Blue /25 #69
2018 Panini Victory Lane Pedal to the Metal Green /5 #1
2018 Panini Victory Lane Pedal to the Metal Green /5 #69
2018 Panini Victory Lane Printing Plates Black /1 #24
2018 Panini Victory Lane Printing Plates Cyan /1 #24
2018 Panini Victory Lane Printing Plates Magenta /1 #24
2018 Panini Victory Lane Printing Plates Yellow /1 #24
2018 Panini Victory Lane Race Ready Materials Black /25 #1
2018 Panini Victory Lane Red /49 #24
2018 Panini Victory Lane Silver #24
2018 Panini Victory Lane Starting Grid #21
2018 Panini Victory Lane Starting Grid Black /1 #21
2018 Panini Victory Lane Starting Grid Blue /25 #21
2018 Panini Victory Lane Starting Grid Gold /99 #21
2018 Panini Victory Lane Starting Grid Green /5 #21
2018 Panini Victory Lane Starting Grid Printing Plates Black /1 #21
2018 Panini Victory Lane Starting Grid Printing Plates Cyan /1 #21
2018 Panini Victory Lane Starting Grid Printing Plates Magenta /1 #21
2018 Panini Victory Lane Starting Grid Printing Plates Yellow /1 #21
2018 Panini Victory Lane Starting Grid Red /49 #21
2018 Panini Victory Lane Victory Lane Prime Patches Associate Sponsor 1 /1 #1
2018 Panini Victory Lane Victory Lane Prime Patches Associate Sponsor 10 /1 #1
2018 Panini Victory Lane Victory Lane Prime Patches Associate Sponsor 2 /1 #1
2018 Panini Victory Lane Victory Lane Prime Patches Associate Sponsor 3 /1 #1
2018 Panini Victory Lane Victory Lane Prime Patches Associate Sponsor 4 /1 #1
2018 Panini Victory Lane Victory Lane Prime Patches Associate Sponsor 5 /1 #1
2018 Panini Victory Lane Victory Lane Prime Patches Associate Sponsor 6 /1 #1
2018 Panini Victory Lane Victory Lane Prime Patches Associate Sponsor 7 /1 #1
2018 Panini Victory Lane Victory Lane Prime Patches Associate Sponsor 8 /1 #1
2018 Panini Victory Lane Victory Lane Prime Patches Associate Sponsor 9 /1 #1
2018 Panini Victory Lane Victory Lane Prime Patches Car Manufacturer /1 #1
2018 Panini Victory Lane Victory Lane Prime Patches Firesuit Manufacturer /1 #1
2018 Panini Victory Lane Victory Lane Prime Patches Goodyear /2 #1
2018 Panini Victory Lane Victory Lane Prime Patches Nameplate /2 #1
2018 Panini Victory Lane Victory Lane Prime Patches NASCAR /1 #1
2018 Panini Victory Lane Victory Lane Prime Patches Series Sponsor /1 #1
2018 Panini Victory Lane Victory Lane Prime Patches Sunoco /1 #1

Aric Almirola

2007 Press Pass Signings #4
2007 Press Pass Signings Gold /50 #2
2007 Press Pass Signings Silver /100 #1
2007 Press Pass Top Prospects Gloves /200 #AAG
2007 Press Pass Top Prospects Sheet Metal /350 #AASM
2007 Press Pass Top Prospects Sheet Metal-Tire /75 #AAST
2007 Press Pass Top Prospects Shoes /200 #AAS
2007 Press Pass Top Prospects Tire Autographs /25 #AAA
2007 Press Pass Top Prospects Tires Gold /99 #AAT
2007 Press Pass Top Prospects Tires Silver /250 #AAT
2007 Traks #37
2007 Traks Gold #G37
2007 Traks Holofoil /50 #H37
2007 Traks Previews /5 #EB37
2007 Traks Red /10 #R37
2007 Wheels American Thunder Thunder Strokes #1
2007 Wheels American Thunder Thunder Strokes Press Plates Black /1 #1
2007 Wheels American Thunder Thunder Strokes Press Plates Cyan /1 #1
2007 Wheels American Thunder Thunder Strokes Press Plates Magenta /1 #1
2007 Wheels American Thunder Thunder Strokes Press Plates Yellow /1 #1
2008 Press Pass Autographs #2
2008 Press Pass Autographs Press Plates Black /1 #2
2008 Press Pass Autographs Press Plates Cyan /1 #2
2008 Press Pass Autographs Press Plates Magenta /1 #2
2008 Press Pass Autographs Press Plates Yellow /1 #2
2008 Press Pass Signings #4
2008 Press Pass Signings Gold /50 #2
2008 Press Pass Signings Press Plates Black #AA
2008 Press Pass Signings Press Plates Magenta #AA
2008 Press Pass Signings Press Plates Yellow #AA
2008 Press Pass Signings Silver /100 #2
2008 Press Pass Speedway #1
2008 Press Pass Speedway #63
2008 Press Pass Speedway Corporate Cuts Drivers /80 #CDAA
2008 Press Pass Speedway Corporate Cuts Drivers Patches /26 #CDAA
2008 Press Pass Speedway Corporate Cuts Team /165 #CTAA
2008 Press Pass Speedway Gold #G1
2008 Press Pass Speedway Gold #G63
2008 Press Pass Speedway Holofoil /50 #H1
2008 Press Pass Speedway Holofoil /50 #H63
2008 Press Pass Speedway Previews /5 #EB1
2008 Press Pass Speedway Red /10 #R1
2008 Press Pass Speedway Red /10 #R63
2008 Press Pass Stealth #65
2008 Press Pass Stealth Chrome #65
2008 Press Pass Stealth Chrome Exclusives /25 #65
2008 Press Pass Stealth Chrome Exclusives Gold /99 #65
2008 VIP #2
2008 VIP All Access #AA1
2008 VIP Previews /5 #EB2
2008 Wheels American Thunder /306 #86
2008 Wheels American Thunder Cool Threads /285 #CT10
2008 Wheels American Thunder Delegates #D2
2008 Wheels American Thunder Future Leaders Nicknames Autographs /53 #86
2008 Wheels American Thunder Trackside Treasury Autographs #AA
2008 Wheels American Thunder Trackside Treasury Autographs Gold /25 #AA
2008 Wheels American Thunder Trackside Treasury Autographs Printing Plates Black /1 #AA
2008 Wheels American Thunder Trackside Treasury Autographs Printing Plates Cyan /1 #AA
2008 Wheels American Thunder Trackside Treasury Autographs Printing Plates Magenta /1 #AA
2008 Wheels American Thunder Trackside Treasury Autographs Printing Plates Yellow /1 #AA
2009 Element #1
2009 Element Lab Report #LR1
2009 Element Previews /5 #1
2009 Element Radioactive /100 #1
2009 Press Pass #35
2009 Press Pass Autographs Gold #3
2009 Press Pass Autographs Printing Plates Black /1 #2
2009 Press Pass Autographs Printing Plates Cyan /1 #2
2009 Press Pass Autographs Printing Plates Magenta /1 #2
2009 Press Pass Autographs Printing Plates Yellow /1 #2
2009 Press Pass Autographs Silver #2
2009 Press Pass Blue #35
2009 Press Pass Eclipse #6
2009 Press Pass Eclipse #81
2009 Press Pass Eclipse Black and White #6
2009 Press Pass Eclipse Black and White #81
2009 Press Pass Eclipse Blue #6
2009 Press Pass Eclipse Blue #81
2009 Press Pass Gold #35
2009 Press Pass Gold Holofoil /100 #35
2009 Press Pass Premium #9
2009 Press Pass Premium Previews /5 #EB9
2009 Press Pass Premium Signatures #2
2009 Press Pass Premium Signatures Gold /25 #2
2009 Press Pass Previews /5 #EB35
2009 Press Pass Red #35
2009 Press Pass Signings Gold #3
2009 Press Pass Sponsor Swatches /200 #SSAA
2009 Press Pass Sponsor Swatches Select /10 #SSAA
2009 Press Pass Stealth #2
2009 Press Pass Stealth Chrome #2
2009 Press Pass Stealth Chrome Brushed Metal /25 #2
2009 Press Pass Stealth Chrome Gold /99 #2
2009 Press Pass Stealth Previews /5 #EB2
2009 Wheels Autographs #2
2009 Wheels Autographs Press Plates Black /1 #AA
2009 Wheels Autographs Press Plates Cyan /1 #AA
2009 Wheels Autographs Press Plates Magenta /1 #AA
2009 Wheels Autographs Press Plates Yellow /1 #AA
2009 Wheels Main Event Hat Dance Double /99 #HDAA
2009 Wheels Main Event Hat Dance Patch /10 #HDAA
2009 Wheels Main Event Marks Clubs #3
2009 Wheels Main Event Marks Diamonds /50 #3
2009 Wheels Main Event Marks Hearts /10 #3
2009 Wheels Main Event Marks Printing Plates Black /1 #3
2009 Wheels Main Event Marks Printing Plates Cyan /1 #3
2009 Wheels Main Event Marks Printing Plates Magenta /1 #3
2009 Wheels Main Event Marks Printing Plates Yellow /1 #3
2009 Wheels Main Event Marks Spades /1 #3
2010 Wheels Autographs #3
2010 Wheels Autographs Printing Plates Black /1 #3
2010 Wheels Autographs Printing Plates Cyan /1 #3
2010 Wheels Autographs Printing Plates Magenta /1 #3
2010 Wheels Autographs Printing Plates Yellow /1 #3
2010 Wheels Autographs Target /10 #2
2011 Press Pass FanFare #41
2011 Press Pass FanFare Autographs Blue /5 #3
2011 Press Pass FanFare Autographs Bronze /115 #3
2011 Press Pass FanFare Autographs Gold /99 #3
2011 Press Pass FanFare Autographs Printing Plates Black /1 #3
2011 Press Pass FanFare Autographs Printing Plates Cyan /1 #3
2011 Press Pass FanFare Autographs Printing Plates Magenta /1 #3
2011 Press Pass FanFare Autographs Printing Plates Yellow /1 #3
2011 Press Pass FanFare Autographs Silver /50 #3
2011 Press Pass FanFare Blue Die Cuts #41
2011 Press Pass FanFare Dual Autographs /10 #NNO
2011 Press Pass FanFare Emerald /25 #41
2011 Press Pass FanFare Holofoil Die Cuts #41
2011 Press Pass FanFare Magnificent Materials /199 #MMAA
2011 Press Pass FanFare Magnificent Materials Dual Swatches /50 #MMDAA
2011 Press Pass FanFare Magnificent Materials Dual Swatches Holofoil /10 #MMDAA
2011 Press Pass FanFare Magnificent Materials Holofoil /50 #MMAA
2011 Press Pass FanFare Magnificent Materials Signatures /99 #MMSEAA
2011 Press Pass FanFare Magnificent Materials Signatures Holofoil /25 #MMSEAA
2011 Press Pass FanFare Ruby Die Cuts /15 #41
2011 Press Pass FanFare Sapphire /10 #41
2011 Press Pass FanFare Silver /25 #41
2011 Press Pass Signings Black and White /10 #PPSAA2
2011 Press Pass Signings Brushed Metal /50 #PPSAA2
2011 Press Pass Signings Holofoil /25 #PPSAA2
2011 Press Pass Signings Printing Plates Cyan /1 #PPSAA2
2011 Press Pass Signings Printing Plates Magenta /1 #PPSAA2
2011 Press Pass Signings Printing Plates Yellow /1 #PPSAA2
2011 Press Pass Stealth #56
2011 Press Pass Stealth Black and White /25 #56
2011 Press Pass Stealth Holofoil /99 #56
2011 Press Pass Stealth Purple /25 #56
2011 Wheels Main Event #38
2011 Wheels Main Event Black and White #38
2011 Wheels Main Event Blue /75 #38
2011 Wheels Main Event Green /1 #38
2011 Wheels Main Event Marks Autographs Blue /10 #MEAA
2011 Wheels Main Event Marks Autographs Gold /25 #MEAA
2011 Wheels Main Event Marks Autographs Silver /65 #MEAA
2011 Wheels Main Event Red /20 #38
2012 Press Pass #38
2012 Press Pass Blue #38
2012 Press Pass Blue Holofoil /35 #38
2012 Press Pass Fanfare #1
2012 Press Pass Fanfare Autographs Blue /5 #AA
2012 Press Pass Fanfare Autographs Gold /25 #AA
2012 Press Pass Fanfare Autographs Red /10 #AA
2012 Press Pass Fanfare Autographs Silver /75 #AA
2012 Press Pass Fanfare Blue Foil Die Cuts #1
2012 Press Pass Fanfare Diamond /5 #1
2012 Press Pass Fanfare Holofoil Die Cuts #1
2012 Press Pass Fanfare Magnificent Materials /299 #MMAA
2012 Press Pass Fanfare Magnificent Materials Dual Swatches /50 #MMAA
2012 Press Pass Fanfare Magnificent Materials Dual Swatches Melting /10 #MMAA
2012 Press Pass Fanfare Magnificent Materials Gold /125 #MMAA
2012 Press Pass Fanfare Magnificent Materials Signatures /99 #AA
2012 Press Pass Fanfare Magnificent Materials Signatures Blue /25 #AA
2012 Press Pass Fanfare Sapphire /20 #1
2012 Press Pass Fanfare Silver /25 #1
2012 Press Pass Gold #38
2012 Press Pass Ignite #2
2012 Press Pass Ignite #63
2012 Press Pass Ignite Materials Autographs Gun Metal /20 #IMAA
2012 Press Pass Ignite Materials Autographs Red /5 #IMAA
2012 Press Pass Ignite Materials Autographs Silver /125 #IMAA
2012 Press Pass Ignite Materials Gun Metal /99 #IMAA
2012 Press Pass Ignite Materials Red /10 #IMAA
2012 Press Pass Ignite Materials Silver #IMAA
2012 Press Pass Ignite Proofs Black and White /50 #2
2012 Press Pass Ignite Proofs Black and White /50 #63
2012 Press Pass Ignite Proofs Cyan #2
2012 Press Pass Ignite Proofs Cyan #63
2012 Press Pass Ignite Proofs Magenta #2
2012 Press Pass Ignite Proofs Magenta #63
2012 Press Pass Ignite Proofs Yellow /10 #2
2012 Press Pass Ignite Proofs Yellow /10 #63
2012 Press Pass Power Picks Blue /50 #27
2012 Press Pass Power Picks Blue /50 #72
2012 Press Pass Power Picks Gold /50 #27
2012 Press Pass Power Picks Gold /50 #72
2012 Press Pass Power Picks Holofoil /10 #27
2012 Press Pass Power Picks Holofoil /10 #72
2012 Press Pass Purple /35 #38
2012 Press Pass Redline #2
2012 Press Pass Redline Black /99 #2
2012 Press Pass Redline Cyan /50 #2
2012 Press Pass Redline Magenta /15 #2
2012 Press Pass Redline Signatures Blue /5 #RSAA
2012 Press Pass Redline Signatures Gold /25 #RSAA
2012 Press Pass Redline Signatures Holofoil /10 #RSAA
2012 Press Pass Redline Signatures Melting /1 #RSAA
2012 Press Pass Redline Signatures Red /49 #RSAA
2012 Press Pass Redline Yellow /1 #2
2012 Press Pass Showcase /499 #59
2012 Press Pass Showcase Classic Collections Ink /10 #CCMRPM
2012 Press Pass Showcase Classic Collections Ink Gold /5 #CCMRPM
2012 Press Pass Showcase Classic Collections Ink Melting /1 #CCMRPM
2012 Press Pass Showcase Classic Collections Memorabilia /50 #CCMRPM
2012 Press Pass Showcase Classic Collections Memorabilia Gold /25 #CCMRPM
2012 Press Pass Showcase Classic Collections Memorabilia Melting /5 #CCMRPM
2012 Press Pass Showcase Gold /125 #59
2012 Press Pass Showcase Green /5 #59
2012 Press Pass Showcase Melting /1 #59
2012 Press Pass Showcase Purple /1 #59
2012 Press Pass Showcase Red /25 #59
2012 Press Pass Snapshots #SS40
2013 Press Pass #1
2013 Press Pass #80
2013 Press Pass Color Proofs Black #1
2013 Press Pass Color Proofs Black #80
2013 Press Pass Color Proofs Cyan /35 #1
2013 Press Pass Color Proofs Cyan /35 #80
2013 Press Pass Color Proofs Magenta #1
2013 Press Pass Color Proofs Magenta #80
2013 Press Pass Color Proofs Yellow /5 #1
2013 Press Pass Color Proofs Yellow /5 #80
2013 Press Pass Fanfare #1
2013 Press Pass Fanfare Autographs Blue /5 #AA
2013 Press Pass Fanfare Autographs Gold /25 #AA
2013 Press Pass Fanfare Autographs Green /6 #AA
2013 Press Pass Fanfare Autographs Red /10 #AA
2013 Press Pass Fanfare Autographs Silver /25 #AA
2013 Press Pass Fanfare Diamond Die Cuts /5 #1
2013 Press Pass Fanfare Green /3 #1
2013 Press Pass Fanfare Holofoil Die Cuts #1
2013 Press Pass Fanfare Magnificent Jumbo Materials Signatures /10 #AL
2013 Press Pass Fanfare Magnificent Materials Dual Swatches /50 #AA
2013 Press Pass Fanfare Magnificent Materials Dual Swatches Melting /10 #AA
2013 Press Pass Fanfare Magnificent Materials Gold /50 #AA
2013 Press Pass Fanfare Magnificent Materials Jumbo Swatches /25 #AA
2013 Press Pass Fanfare Magnificent Materials Signatures /99 #AL
2013 Press Pass Fanfare Magnificent Materials Signatures Blue /10 #AL
2013 Press Pass Fanfare Magnificent Materials Silver /199 #AA
2013 Press Pass Fanfare Red Foil Die Cuts #1
2013 Press Pass Fanfare Sapphire /20 #1
2013 Press Pass Fanfare Silver /25 #1
2013 Press Pass Ignite #1
2013 Press Pass Ignite Great American Treads Autographs Blue Holofoil /20 #GATAA
2013 Press Pass Ignite Great American Treads Autographs Red /1 #GATAA
2013 Press Pass Ignite Hot Threads Blue Holofoil /99 #HTAA
2013 Press Pass Ignite Hot Threads Patch Red /10 #HTAA
2013 Press Pass Ignite Hot Threads Silver #HTAA
2013 Press Pass Ignite Ink Black /75 #IIAA
2013 Press Pass Ignite Ink Blue /25 #IIAA
2013 Press Pass Ignite Ink Red /5 #IIAA
2013 Press Pass Ignite Proofs Black and White /50 #1
2013 Press Pass Ignite Proofs Cyan #1
2013 Press Pass Ignite Proofs Magenta #1
2013 Press Pass Ignite Proofs Yellow /5 #1
2013 Press Pass Power Picks Blue /99 #26
2013 Press Pass Power Picks Gold /50 #26
2013 Press Pass Power Picks Holofoil /10 #26
2013 Press Pass Redline #1
2013 Press Pass Redline #2
2013 Press Pass Redline Black /99 #1
2013 Press Pass Redline Black /99 #2
2013 Press Pass Redline Cyan /50 #1
2013 Press Pass Redline Cyan /50 #2
2013 Press Pass Redline Magenta /15 #1
2013 Press Pass Redline Magenta /15 #2
2013 Press Pass Redline Muscle Car Sheet Metal Blue /5 #MCMAA
2013 Press Pass Redline Muscle Car Sheet Metal Gold /10 #MCMAA
2013 Press Pass Redline Muscle Car Sheet Metal Melting /1 #MCMAA
2013 Press Pass Redline Muscle Car Sheet Metal Red /50 #MCMAA
2013 Press Pass Redline Muscle Car Sheet Metal Silver /25 #MCMAA
2013 Press Pass Redline Relic Autographs Blue /5 #RRSEAA
2013 Press Pass Redline Relic Autographs Gold /10 #RRSEAA
2013 Press Pass Redline Relic Autographs Melting /1 #RRSEAA
2013 Press Pass Redline Relic Autographs Red /99 #RRSEAA
2013 Press Pass Redline Relic Autographs Silver /43 #RRSEAA
2013 Press Pass Redline Signatures Blue /25 #RSAA1
2013 Press Pass Redline Signatures Blue /10 #RSAA2
2013 Press Pass Redline Signatures Gold /5 #RSAA1
2013 Press Pass Redline Signatures Gold /5 #RSAA2
2013 Press Pass Redline Signatures Holo /10 #RSAA1
2013 Press Pass Redline Signatures Holo /5 #RSAA2
2013 Press Pass Redline Signatures Melting /1 #RSAA1
2013 Press Pass Redline Signatures Melting /1 #RSAA2
2013 Press Pass Redline Signatures Red /43 #RSAA1
2013 Press Pass Redline Signatures Red /10 #RSAA2
2013 Press Pass Redline Yellow /1 #1
2013 Press Pass Redline Yellow /1 #2
2013 Press Pass Showcase Classic Collections Memorabilia Gold /25 #CCMRPM
2013 Press Pass Showcase Classic Collections Memorabilia Melting /5 #CCMRPM
2013 Press Pass Showcase Classic Collections Memorabilia Silver /75 #CCMRPM
2013 Press Pass Signings Blue /1 #AA
2013 Press Pass Signings Gold /25 #AA
2013 Press Pass Signings Holofoil /10 #AA
2013 Press Pass Signings Printing Plates Black /1 #AA
2013 Press Pass Signings Printing Plates Cyan /1 #AA
2013 Press Pass Signings Printing Plates Magenta /1 #AA
2013 Press Pass Signings Printing Plates Yellow /1 #AA
2013 Press Pass Signings Silver /50 #AA
2013 Total Memorabilia #1
2013 Total Memorabilia Black and White /99 #1
2013 Total Memorabilia Dual Swatch Gold /199 #TMAA
2013 Total Memorabilia Gold /275 #1
2013 Total Memorabilia Red #1
2013 Total Memorabilia Single Swatch Silver /475 #TMAA
2014 Press Pass #1
2014 Press Pass American Thunder #3
2014 Press Pass American Thunder #58
2014 Press Pass American Thunder Autographs Blue /10 #ATAAA
2014 Press Pass American Thunder Autographs Red /5 #ATAAA
2014 Press Pass American Thunder Autographs White /25 #ATAAA
2014 Press Pass American Thunder Black and White /50 #3
2014 Press Pass American Thunder Black and White /50 #58
2014 Press Pass American Thunder Brothers In Arms Autographs Blue /5 #BARPM
2014 Press Pass American Thunder Brothers In Arms Autographs Red /1 #BARPM
2014 Press Pass American Thunder Brothers In Arms Autographs White /10 #BARPM
2014 Press Pass American Thunder Brothers In Arms Relics Blue /25 #BARPM
2014 Press Pass American Thunder Brothers In Arms Relics Red /5 #BARPM
2014 Press Pass American Thunder Brothers In Arms Relics Silver /50 #BARPM
2014 Press Pass American Thunder Class A Uniforms Blue /99 #CAUAA
2014 Press Pass American Thunder Class A Uniforms Red /10 #CAUAA
2014 Press Pass American Thunder Class A Uniforms Silver #CAUAA
2014 Press Pass American Thunder Cyan #3
2014 Press Pass American Thunder Cyan #58
2014 Press Pass American Thunder Magenta #3
2014 Press Pass American Thunder Magenta #58
2014 Press Pass American Thunder Yellow /5 #3
2014 Press Pass American Thunder Yellow /5 #58
2014 Press Pass Color Proofs Black /70 #1
2014 Press Pass Color Proofs Cyan /35 #1
2014 Press Pass Color Proofs Magenta #1
2014 Press Pass Color Proofs Yellow /5 #1
2014 Press Pass Five Star Classic Compilations Autographed Patch Booklet /1 #CCAA1
2014 Press Pass Five Star Classic Compilations Autographed Patch Booklet /1 #CCAA2
2014 Press Pass Five Star Classic Compilations Autographed Patch Booklet /1 #CCAA3
2014 Press Pass Five Star Classic Compilations Autographed Patch Booklet /1 #CCAA4
2014 Press Pass Five Star Classic Compilations Autographed Patch Booklet /1 #CCAA5
2014 Press Pass Five Star Classic Compilations Autographed Patch Booklet /1 #CCAA6
2014 Press Pass Five Star Classic Compilations Autographed Patch Booklet /1 #CCAA7
2014 Press Pass Five Star Classic Compilations Combo Autographs Blue /5 #CCRPM
2014 Press Pass Five Star Classic Compilations Combo Autographs Melting /1 #CCRPM
2014 Press Pass Gold #1
2014 Press Pass Redline #3
2014 Press Pass Redline Black /75 #3
2014 Press Pass Redline Blue Foil #3
2014 Press Pass Redline Cyan /50 #3
2014 Press Pass Redline Green National Convention /5 #3
2014 Press Pass Redline Magenta /10 #3
2014 Press Pass Redline Relic Autographs Blue /10 #RRSEAA
2014 Press Pass Redline Relic Autographs Gold /15 #RRSEAA
2014 Press Pass Redline Relic Autographs Melting /1 #RRSEAA
2014 Press Pass Redline Relic Autographs Red /25 #RRSEAA
2014 Press Pass Redline Relics Blue /25 #RRAA
2014 Press Pass Redline Relics Gold /50 #RRAA
2014 Press Pass Redline Relics Melting /1 #RRAA
2014 Press Pass Redline Relics Red /75 #RRAA
2014 Press Pass Redline Signatures Blue /10 #RSAA
2014 Press Pass Redline Signatures Gold /25 #RSAA
2014 Press Pass Redline Signatures Melting /1 #RSAA
2014 Press Pass Redline Signatures Red /50 #RSAA
2014 Press Pass Redline Yellow /1 #3
2014 Press Pass Signings Gold /25 #PPSAA
2014 Press Pass Signings Holofoil /10 #PPSAA
2014 Press Pass Signings Melting /1 #PPSAA
2014 Press Pass Signings Printing Plates Black /1 #PPSAA
2014 Press Pass Signings Printing Plates Cyan /1 #PPSAA
2014 Press Pass Signings Printing Plates Magenta /1 #PPSAA
2014 Press Pass Signings Printing Plates Yellow /1 #PPSAA
2014 Press Pass Signings Silver /50 #PPSAA
2014 Total Memorabilia #1
2014 Total Memorabilia Black and White /99 #1
2014 Total Memorabilia Dual Swatch Gold /150 #TMAA
2014 Total Memorabilia Gold /175 #1
2014 Total Memorabilia Quad Swatch Melting /25 #TMAA
2014 Total Memorabilia Red #1
2014 Total Memorabilia Single Swatch Silver /275 #TMAA
2014 Total Memorabilia Triple Swatch Blue /99 #TMAA
2015 Press Pass #3
2015 Press Pass #61
2015 Press Pass #100
2015 Press Pass Burning Rubber Blue /50 #BRAA
2015 Press Pass Burning Rubber Gold #BRAA
2015 Press Pass Burning Rubber Green /10 #BRAA
2015 Press Pass Burning Rubber Melting /1 #BRAA
2015 Press Pass Cup Chase #3
2015 Press Pass Cup Chase #61
2015 Press Pass Cup Chase #100
2015 Press Pass Cup Chase Blue /25 #3
2015 Press Pass Cup Chase Blue /25 #61
2015 Press Pass Cup Chase Blue /25 #100
2015 Press Pass Cup Chase Gold /75 #3
2015 Press Pass Cup Chase Gold /75 #61
2015 Press Pass Cup Chase Gold /75 #100
2015 Press Pass Cup Chase Green /10 #3
2015 Press Pass Cup Chase Green /10 #61
2015 Press Pass Cup Chase Green /10 #100
2015 Press Pass Cup Chase Melting /1 #3
2015 Press Pass Cup Chase Melting /1 #61
2015 Press Pass Cup Chase Melting /1 #100
2015 Press Pass Purple #3
2015 Press Pass Purple #61
2015 Press Pass Purple #100
2015 Press Pass Red #3
2015 Press Pass Red #61
2015 Press Pass Red #100
2015 Press Pass Signature Series Blue /25 #SSAA
2015 Press Pass Signature Series Gold /50 #SSAA
2015 Press Pass Signature Series Green /10 #SSAA
2015 Press Pass Signature Series Melting /1 #SSAA
2015 Press Pass Signings Blue /50 #PPSAA
2015 Press Pass Signings Gold #PPSAA
2015 Press Pass Signings Green /10 #PPSAA
2015 Press Pass Signings Melting /5 #PPSAA
2015 Press Pass Signings Red /25 #PPSAA
2016 Certified #23
2016 Certified Mirror Black /1 #23
2016 Certified Mirror Blue /50 #23
2016 Certified Mirror Gold /25 #23
2016 Certified Mirror Green /5 #23
2016 Certified Mirror Orange /99 #23
2016 Certified Mirror Purple /10 #23
2016 Certified Mirror Red /75 #23
2016 Certified Mirror Silver /99 #23
2016 Certified Signatures /204 #47
2016 Certified Signatures Mirror Black /1 #47
2016 Certified Signatures Mirror Blue /50 #47
2016 Certified Signatures Mirror Gold /25 #47
2016 Certified Signatures Mirror Green /5 #47
2016 Certified Signatures Mirror Orange /15 #47
2016 Certified Signatures Mirror Purple /10 #47
2016 Certified Signatures Mirror Red /75 #47
2016 Certified Signatures Mirror Silver /15 #47
2016 Certified Sprint Cup Swatches /299 #13
2016 Certified Sprint Cup Swatches Mirror Black /1 #13
2016 Certified Sprint Cup Swatches Mirror Blue /50 #13
2016 Certified Sprint Cup Swatches Mirror Gold /25 #13
2016 Certified Sprint Cup Swatches Mirror Green /5 #13
2016 Certified Sprint Cup Swatches Mirror Orange /99 #13
2016 Certified Sprint Cup Swatches Mirror Purple /10 #13
2016 Certified Sprint Cup Swatches Mirror Red /75 #13
2016 Certified Sprint Cup Swatches Mirror Silver /99 #13
2016 Panini National Treasures Combo Materials /25 #3
2016 Panini National Treasures Combo Materials Black /5 #3
2016 Panini National Treasures Combo Materials Blue /1 #3
2016 Panini National Treasures Combo Materials Gold /10 #3
2016 Panini National Treasures Combo Materials Printing Plates Black /1 #3
2016 Panini National Treasures Combo Materials Printing Plates Cyan /1 #3
2016 Panini National Treasures Combo Materials Printing Plates Magenta /1 #3
2016 Panini National Treasures Combo Materials Printing Plates Yellow /1 #3
2016 Panini National Treasures Combo Materials Silver /15 #3
2016 Panini National Treasures Jumbo Firesuit Patch Signature Booklet Associate Sponsor 1 /1 #1
2016 Panini National Treasures Jumbo Firesuit Patch Signature Booklet Associate Sponsor 10 /1 #1
2016 Panini National Treasures Jumbo Firesuit Patch Signature Booklet Associate Sponsor 11 /1 #1
2016 Panini National Treasures Jumbo Firesuit Patch Signature Booklet Associate Sponsor 12 /1 #1
2016 Panini National Treasures Jumbo Firesuit Patch Signature Booklet Associate Sponsor 13 /1 #1
2016 Panini National Treasures Jumbo Firesuit Patch Signature Booklet Associate Sponsor 14 /1 #1
2016 Panini National Treasures Jumbo Firesuit Patch Signature Booklet Associate Sponsor 15 /1 #1
2016 Panini National Treasures Jumbo Firesuit Patch Signature Booklet Associate Sponsor 2 /1 #1
2016 Panini National Treasures Jumbo Firesuit Patch Signature Booklet Associate Sponsor 3 /1 #1
2016 Panini National Treasures Jumbo Firesuit Patch Signature Booklet Associate Sponsor 4 /1 #1
2016 Panini National Treasures Jumbo Firesuit Patch Signature Booklet Associate Sponsor 5 /1 #1
2016 Panini National Treasures Jumbo Firesuit Patch Signature Booklet Associate Sponsor 6 /1 #1
2016 Panini National Treasures Jumbo Firesuit Patch Signature Booklet Associate Sponsor 7 /1 #1
2016 Panini National Treasures Jumbo Firesuit Patch Signature Booklet Associate Sponsor 8 /1 #1
2016 Panini National Treasures Jumbo Firesuit Patch Signature Booklet Associate Sponsor 9 /1 #1
2016 Panini National Treasures Jumbo Firesuit Patch Signature Booklet Goodyear /2 #1
2016 Panini National Treasures Jumbo Firesuit Patch Signature Booklet Manufacturers Logo /2 #1
2016 Panini National Treasures Jumbo Firesuit Patch Signature Booklet Nameplate /2 #1
2016 Panini National Treasures Jumbo Firesuit Patch Signature Booklet NASCAR /1 #1
2016 Panini National Treasures Jumbo Firesuit Patch Signature Booklet Sprint Cup Logo /1 #1
2016 Panini National Treasures Jumbo Firesuit Patch Signature Booklet Sunoco /1 #1
2016 Panini National Treasures Jumbo Firesuit Signatures /25 #1
2016 Panini National Treasures Jumbo Firesuit Signatures Black /5 #1
2016 Panini National Treasures Jumbo Firesuit Signatures Blue /1 #1
2016 Panini National Treasures Jumbo Firesuit Signatures Gold /10 #1
2016 Panini National Treasures Jumbo Firesuit Signatures Printing Plates Black /1 #1
2016 Panini National Treasures Jumbo Firesuit Signatures Printing Plates Cyan /1 #1
2016 Panini National Treasures Jumbo Firesuit Signatures Printing Plates Magenta /1 #1
2016 Panini National Treasures Jumbo Firesuit Signatures Printing Plates Yellow /1 #1

2016 Panini National Treasures Jumbo Firesuit Signatures Silver /15 #1
2016 Panini National Treasures Quad Driver Materials /25 #5
2016 Panini National Treasures Quad Driver Materials Black /5 #5
2016 Panini National Treasures Quad Driver Materials Blue /1 #5
2016 Panini National Treasures Quad Driver Materials Gold /10 #5
2016 Panini National Treasures Quad Driver Materials Printing Plates Black /1 #5
2016 Panini National Treasures Quad Driver Materials Printing Plates Cyan /1 #5
2016 Panini National Treasures Quad Driver Materials Printing Plates Magenta /1 #5
2016 Panini National Treasures Quad Driver Materials Printing Plates Yellow /1 #5
2016 Panini National Treasures Quad Driver Materials Silver /15 #5
2016 Panini National Treasures Signature Dual Materials /25 #1
2016 Panini National Treasures Signature Dual Materials Black /5 #1
2016 Panini National Treasures Signature Dual Materials Blue /1 #1
2016 Panini National Treasures Signature Dual Materials Gold /10 #1
2016 Panini National Treasures Signature Dual Materials Printing Plates Black /1 #1
2016 Panini National Treasures Signature Dual Materials Printing Plates Cyan /1 #1
2016 Panini National Treasures Signature Dual Materials Printing Plates Magenta /1 #1
2016 Panini National Treasures Signature Dual Materials Printing Plates Yellow /1 #1
2016 Panini National Treasures Signature Dual Materials Silver /15 #1
2016 Panini National Treasures Signature Firesuit Materials /25 #1
2016 Panini National Treasures Signature Firesuit Materials Blue /1 #1
2016 Panini National Treasures Signature Firesuit Materials Gold /10 #1
2016 Panini National Treasures Signature Firesuit Materials Laundry Tag /1 #1
2016 Panini National Treasures Signature Firesuit Materials Printing Plates Black /1 #1
2016 Panini National Treasures Signature Firesuit Materials Printing Plates Cyan /1 #1
2016 Panini National Treasures Signature Firesuit Materials Printing Plates Magenta /1 #1
2016 Panini National Treasures Signature Firesuit Materials Printing Plates Yellow /1 #1
2016 Panini National Treasures Signature Firesuit Materials Silver /15 #1
2016 Panini National Treasures Signature Quad Materials /25 #1
2016 Panini National Treasures Signature Quad Materials Black /5 #1
2016 Panini National Treasures Signature Quad Materials Blue /1 #1
2016 Panini National Treasures Signature Quad Materials Gold /10 #1
2016 Panini National Treasures Signature Quad Materials Printing Plates Black /1 #1
2016 Panini National Treasures Signature Quad Materials Printing Plates Cyan /1 #1
2016 Panini National Treasures Signature Quad Materials Printing Plates Magenta /1 #1
2016 Panini National Treasures Signature Quad Materials Printing Plates Yellow /1 #1
2016 Panini National Treasures Signature Quad Materials Silver /15 #1
2016 Panini National Treasures Six Signatures Black /10 #7
2016 Panini National Treasures Six Signatures Blue /1 #7
2016 Panini National Treasures Timelines /25 #1
2016 Panini National Treasures Timelines Black /5 #1
2016 Panini National Treasures Timelines Blue /1 #1
2016 Panini National Treasures Timelines Gold /10 #1
2016 Panini National Treasures Timelines Printing Plates Black /1 #1
2016 Panini National Treasures Timelines Printing Plates Cyan /1 #1
2016 Panini National Treasures Timelines Printing Plates Magenta /1 #1
2016 Panini National Treasures Timelines Printing Plates Yellow /1 #1
2016 Panini National Treasures Timelines Signatures Black /5 #1
2016 Panini National Treasures Timelines Signatures Printing Plates Black /1 #1
2016 Panini National Treasures Timelines Signatures Printing Plates Cyan /1 #1
2016 Panini National Treasures Timelines Signatures Printing Plates Magenta /1 #1
2016 Panini National Treasures Timelines Signatures Printing Plates Yellow /1 #1
2016 Panini National Treasures Timelines Signatures Silver /15 #1
2016 Panini National Treasures Timelines Silver /15 #1
2016 Panini Prizm #37
2016 Panini Prizm Autographs Prizms #3
2016 Panini Prizm Autographs Prizms Black /3 #3
2016 Panini Prizm Autographs Prizms Blue Flag /50 #3
2016 Panini Prizm Autographs Prizms Camo /43 #3
2016 Panini Prizm Autographs Prizms Checkered Flag /1 #3
2016 Panini Prizm Autographs Prizms Gold /10 #3
2016 Panini Prizm Autographs Prizms Green Flag /75 #3
2016 Panini Prizm Autographs Prizms Rainbow /24 #3
2016 Panini Prizm Autographs Prizms Red Flag /25 #3
2016 Panini Prizm Autographs Prizms Red White and Blue /49 #3
2016 Panini Prizm Autographs Prizms White Flag /5 #3
2016 Panini Prizm Firesuit Fabrics /149 #17
2016 Panini Prizm Firesuit Fabrics Prizms Blue Flag /75 #17
2016 Panini Prizm Firesuit Fabrics Prizms Checkered Flag /1 #17
2016 Panini Prizm Firesuit Fabrics Prizms Green Flag /99 #17
2016 Panini Prizm Firesuit Fabrics Prizms Red Flag /25 #17
2016 Panini Prizm Firesuit Fabrics Team /249 #17
2016 Panini Prizm Firesuit Fabrics Team Prizms Blue Flag /75 #17
2016 Panini Prizm Firesuit Fabrics Team Prizms Checkered Flag /1 #17
2016 Panini Prizm Firesuit Fabrics Team Prizms Green Flag /99 #17
2016 Panini Prizm Firesuit Fabrics Team Prizms Red Flag /25 #17
2016 Panini Prizm Prizms #37
2016 Panini Prizm Prizms Black /3 #37
2016 Panini Prizm Prizms Blue Flag /99 #37
2016 Panini Prizm Prizms Camo /43 #37
2016 Panini Prizm Prizms Checkered Flag /1 #37
2016 Panini Prizm Prizms Gold /10 #37
2016 Panini Prizm Prizms Green Flag /149 #37
2016 Panini Prizm Prizms Rainbow /24 #37
2016 Panini Prizm Prizms Red Flag /75 #37
2016 Panini Prizm Prizms Red White and Blue #37
2016 Panini Prizm Prizms White Flag /5 #37
2016 Panini Torque #15
2016 Panini Torque Artist Proof /50 #15
2016 Panini Torque Blackout /1 #15
2016 Panini Torque Blue /125 #15
2016 Panini Torque Gold #15
2016 Panini Torque Holo Gold /5 #15
2016 Panini Torque Holo Silver /10 #15
2016 Panini Torque Horsepower Heroes #17
2016 Panini Torque Horsepower Heroes Gold /199 #17
2016 Panini Torque Horsepower Heroes Holo Silver /99 #17
2016 Panini Torque Jumbo Firesuit Autographs /117 #20
2016 Panini Torque Jumbo Firesuit Autographs Blue /99 #20
2016 Panini Torque Jumbo Firesuit Autographs Green /25 #20
2016 Panini Torque Jumbo Firesuit Autographs Purple /10 #20
2016 Panini Torque Jumbo Firesuit Autographs Red /49 #20
2016 Panini Torque Metal Materials /43 #1
2016 Panini Torque Metal Materials Blue /99 #1
2016 Panini Torque Metal Materials Green /25 #1
2016 Panini Torque Metal Materials Purple /10 #1
2016 Panini Torque Metal Materials Red /49 #1
2016 Panini Torque Pairings Materials /125 #25
2016 Panini Torque Pairings Materials Blue /99 #25
2016 Panini Torque Pairings Materials Green /25 #25
2016 Panini Torque Pairings Materials Purple /10 #25
2016 Panini Torque Pairings Materials Red /49 #25
2016 Panini Torque Printing Plates Black /1 #15
2016 Panini Torque Printing Plates Cyan /1 #15
2016 Panini Torque Printing Plates Magenta /1 #15
2016 Panini Torque Printing Plates Yellow /1 #15
2016 Panini Torque Purple /25 #15
2016 Panini Torque Red /99 #15
2016 Panini Torque Test Proof Black /1 #15
2016 Panini Torque Test Proof Cyan /1 #15
2016 Panini Torque Test Proof Magenta /1 #15
2016 Panini Torque Test Proof Yellow /1 #15
2017 Donruss #179
2017 Donruss Artist Proof /25 #179
2017 Donruss Blue Foil /299 #179
2017 Donruss Gold Foil /499 #179
2017 Donruss Gold Press Proof /99 #179
2017 Donruss Green Foil /199 #179
2017 Donruss Press Proof /49 #179
2017 Donruss Printing Plates Black /1 #179
2017 Donruss Printing Plates Cyan /1 #179
2017 Donruss Printing Plates Magenta /1 #179
2017 Donruss Printing Plates Yellow /1 #179
2017 Donruss Retro Relics 1984 #2
2017 Donruss Retro Relics 1984 Holo Black /10 #2
2017 Donruss Retro Relics 1984 Holo Gold /25 #2
2017 Donruss Signature Series #4
2017 Donruss Signature Series Holo Black /1 #SSAA
2017 Donruss Signature Series Holo Gold /25 #SSAA
2017 Panini National Treasures Dual Firesuit Materials /25 #20
2017 Panini National Treasures Dual Firesuit Materials Black /1 #20
2017 Panini National Treasures Dual Firesuit Materials Gold /15 #20
2017 Panini National Treasures Dual Firesuit Materials Green /5 #20
2017 Panini National Treasures Dual Firesuit Materials Holo Gold /10 #20
2017 Panini National Treasures Dual Firesuit Materials Holo Silver /20 #20
2017 Panini National Treasures Dual Firesuit Materials Laundry Tag /1 #20
2017 Panini National Treasures Dual Firesuit Materials Printing Plates Black /1 #20
2017 Panini National Treasures Dual Firesuit Materials Printing Plates Cyan /1 #20
2017 Panini National Treasures Dual Firesuit Materials Printing Plates Magenta /1 #20
2017 Panini National Treasures Dual Firesuit Materials Printing Plates Yellow /1 #20
2017 Panini National Treasures Dual Firesuit Signatures /25 #20
2017 Panini National Treasures Dual Firesuit Signatures Black /1 #20
2017 Panini National Treasures Dual Firesuit Signatures Green /5 #20
2017 Panini National Treasures Dual Firesuit Signatures Holo Gold /9 #20
2017 Panini National Treasures Dual Firesuit Signatures Holo Silver /20 #20
2017 Panini National Treasures Dual Firesuit Signatures Laundry Tag /1 #20
2017 Panini National Treasures Dual Firesuit Signatures Printing Plates Black /1 #20
2017 Panini National Treasures Dual Firesuit Signatures Printing Plates Cyan /1 #20
2017 Panini National Treasures Dual Firesuit Signatures Printing Plates Magenta /1 #20
2017 Panini National Treasures Dual Firesuit Signatures Printing Plates Yellow /1 #20
2017 Panini National Treasures Hats Off /13 #5
2017 Panini National Treasures Hats Off Gold /2 #5
2017 Panini National Treasures Hats Off Holo Gold /5 #5
2017 Panini National Treasures Hats Off Holo Silver /1 #5
2017 Panini National Treasures Hats Off Laundry Tag /6 #5
2017 Panini National Treasures Hats Off New Era /1 #5
2017 Panini National Treasures Hats Off Printing Plates Black /1 #5
2017 Panini National Treasures Hats Off Printing Plates Cyan /1 #5
2017 Panini National Treasures Hats Off Printing Plates Magenta /1 #5
2017 Panini National Treasures Hats Off Printing Plates Yellow /1 #5
2017 Panini National Treasures Hats Off Sponsor /10 #5
2017 Panini Torque #18
2017 Panini Torque Artist Proof /75 #18
2017 Panini Torque Blackout /1 #18
2017 Panini Torque Blue /150 #18
2017 Panini Torque Clear Vision #27
2017 Panini Torque Clear Vision Blue /99 #27
2017 Panini Torque Clear Vision Gold /149 #27
2017 Panini Torque Clear Vision Green /25 #27
2017 Panini Torque Clear Vision Purple /10 #27
2017 Panini Torque Clear Vision Red /49 #27
2017 Panini Torque Combo Materials Signatures /57 #10
2017 Panini Torque Combo Materials Signatures Blue /43 #10
2017 Panini Torque Combo Materials Signatures Green /15 #10
2017 Panini Torque Combo Materials Signatures Purple /10 #10
2017 Panini Torque Combo Materials Signatures Red /25 #10
2017 Panini Torque Gold #18
2017 Panini Torque Holo Gold /10 #18
2017 Panini Torque Holo Silver /25 #18
2017 Panini Torque Horsepower Heroes #20
2017 Panini Torque Horsepower Heroes Gold /199 #20
2017 Panini Torque Horsepower Heroes Holo Silver /99 #20
2017 Panini Torque Jumbo Firesuit Signatures /57 #2
2017 Panini Torque Jumbo Firesuit Signatures Blue /43 #2
2017 Panini Torque Jumbo Firesuit Signatures Green /15 #2
2017 Panini Torque Jumbo Firesuit Signatures Purple /10 #2
2017 Panini Torque Jumbo Firesuit Signatures Red /25 #2
2017 Panini Torque Printing Plates Black /1 #18
2017 Panini Torque Printing Plates Cyan /1 #18
2017 Panini Torque Printing Plates Magenta /1 #18
2017 Panini Torque Printing Plates Yellow /1 #18
2017 Panini Torque Purple /50 #18
2017 Panini Torque Red /100 #18
2017 Panini Torque Special Paint #8
2017 Panini Torque Special Paint Gold /199 #8
2017 Panini Torque Special Paint Holo Silver /99 #8
2017 Panini Torque Test Proof Black /1 #18
2017 Panini Torque Test Proof Cyan /1 #18
2017 Panini Torque Test Proof Magenta /1 #18
2017 Panini Torque Test Proof Yellow /1 #18
2017 Select #35
2017 Select #36
2017 Select #128
2017 Select Prizms Black /3 #35
2017 Select Prizms Black /3 #36
2017 Select Prizms Black /3 #128
2017 Select Prizms Blue /199 #35
2017 Select Prizms Blue /199 #36
2017 Select Prizms Checkered Flag /1 #35
2017 Select Prizms Checkered Flag /1 #36
2017 Select Prizms Checkered Flag /1 #128
2017 Select Prizms Gold /10 #35
2017 Select Prizms Gold /10 #36
2017 Select Prizms Gold /10 #128
2017 Select Prizms Purple Pulsar #35
2017 Select Prizms Purple Pulsar #36
2017 Select Prizms Red /99 #35
2017 Select Prizms Red /99 #36
2017 Select Prizms Red White and Blue Pulsar /299 #35
2017 Select Prizms Red White and Blue Pulsar /299 #36
2017 Select Prizms Silver #35
2017 Select Prizms Silver #36
2017 Select Prizms Tie Dye /24 #35
2017 Select Prizms Tie Dye /24 #36
2017 Select Prizms Tie Dye /24 #128
2017 Select Prizms White /50 #35
2017 Select Prizms White /50 #36
2017 Select Prizms White /50 #128
2017 Select Select Swatches #2
2017 Select Select Swatches Prizms Blue /199 #2
2017 Select Select Swatches Prizms Checkered Flag /1 #2
2017 Select Select Swatches Prizms Gold /10 #2
2017 Select Select Swatches Prizms Red /99 #2
2017 Select Speed Merchants #23
2017 Select Speed Merchants Prizms Black /3 #23
2017 Select Speed Merchants Prizms Checkered Flag /1 #23
2017 Select Speed Merchants Prizms Gold /10 #23
2017 Select Speed Merchants Prizms Tie Dye /24 #23
2017 Select Speed Merchants Prizms White /50 #23
2018 Certified #43
2018 Certified Black /1 #43
2018 Certified Blue /99 #43
2018 Certified Cup Swatches /499 #2
2018 Certified Cup Swatches Black /1 #2
2018 Certified Cup Swatches Blue /49 #2
2018 Certified Cup Swatches Gold /25 #2
2018 Certified Cup Swatches Green /5 #2
2018 Certified Cup Swatches Purple /10 #2
2018 Certified Cup Swatches Red /199 #2
2018 Certified Gold /49 #43
2018 Certified Green /10 #43
2018 Certified Mirror Black /1 #43
2018 Certified Mirror Gold /25 #43
2018 Certified Mirror Green /5 #43
2018 Certified Mirror Purple /10 #43
2018 Certified Orange /249 #43
2018 Certified Piece of the Race /499 #19
2018 Certified Piece of the Race Black /1 #19
2018 Certified Piece of the Race Blue /49 #19
2018 Certified Piece of the Race Gold /25 #19
2018 Certified Piece of the Race Green /5 #19
2018 Certified Piece of the Race Purple /10 #19
2018 Certified Piece of the Race Red /199 #19
2018 Certified Purple /25 #43
2018 Certified Red /199 #43
2018 Certified Signature Swatches /99 #2
2018 Certified Signature Swatches Black /1 #2
2018 Certified Signature Swatches Blue /49 #2
2018 Certified Signature Swatches Gold /25 #2
2018 Certified Signature Swatches Green /5 #2
2018 Certified Signature Swatches Purple /10 #2
2018 Certified Signature Swatches Red /75 #2
2018 Certified Signatures /49 #1
2018 Certified Signatures Black /1 #1
2018 Certified Signatures Gold /15 #1
2018 Certified Signatures Green /5 #1
2018 Certified Signatures Purple /10 #1
2018 Certified Signatures Red /25 #1
2018 Certified Skills /199 #5
2018 Certified Skills Black /1 #5
2018 Certified Skills Blue /99 #5
2018 Certified Skills Gold /49 #5
2018 Certified Skills Green /10 #5
2018 Certified Skills Mirror Black /1 #5
2018 Certified Skills Mirror Gold /25 #5
2018 Certified Skills Mirror Green /5 #5
2018 Certified Skills Mirror Purple /10 #5
2018 Certified Skills Purple /25 #5
2018 Certified Skills Red /149 #5
2018 Certified Stars /199 #20
2018 Certified Stars Black /1 #20
2018 Certified Stars Blue /99 #20
2018 Certified Stars Gold /49 #20
2018 Certified Stars Green /10 #20
2018 Certified Stars Mirror Black /1 #20
2018 Certified Stars Mirror Gold /25 #20
2018 Certified Stars Mirror Green /5 #20
2018 Certified Stars Mirror Purple /10 #20
2018 Certified Stars Purple /25 #20
2018 Certified Stars Red /149 #20
2018 Donruss #54A
2018 Donruss #99
2018 Donruss #143
2018 Donruss #54B
2018 Donruss Artist Proofs /25 #54A
2018 Donruss Artist Proofs /25 #99
2018 Donruss Artist Proofs /25 #143
2018 Donruss Artist Proofs /25 #54B
2018 Donruss Gold Foil /499 #54A
2018 Donruss Gold Foil /499 #99
2018 Donruss Gold Foil /499 #143
2018 Donruss Gold Foil /499 #54B
2018 Donruss Gold Press Proofs /99 #54A
2018 Donruss Gold Press Proofs /99 #99
2018 Donruss Gold Press Proofs /99 #143
2018 Donruss Gold Press Proofs /99 #54B
2018 Donruss Green Foil /199 #54A
2018 Donruss Green Foil /199 #99
2018 Donruss Green Foil /199 #143
2018 Donruss Green Foil /199 #54B
2018 Donruss Press Proofs /49 #54A
2018 Donruss Press Proofs /49 #99
2018 Donruss Press Proofs /49 #143
2018 Donruss Press Proofs /49 #54B
2018 Donruss Printing Plates Black /1 #54
2018 Donruss Printing Plates Black /1 #99
2018 Donruss Printing Plates Black /1 #143
2018 Donruss Printing Plates Black /1 #54B
2018 Donruss Printing Plates Cyan /1 #54
2018 Donruss Printing Plates Cyan /1 #99
2018 Donruss Printing Plates Cyan /1 #143
2018 Donruss Printing Plates Cyan /1 #54B
2018 Donruss Printing Plates Magenta /1 #54
2018 Donruss Printing Plates Magenta /1 #99
2018 Donruss Printing Plates Magenta /1 #143
2018 Donruss Printing Plates Magenta /1 #54B
2018 Donruss Printing Plates Yellow /1 #54
2018 Donruss Printing Plates Yellow /1 #99
2018 Donruss Printing Plates Yellow /1 #143
2018 Donruss Printing Plates Yellow /1 #54B
2018 Donruss Red Foil /299 #54A
2018 Donruss Red Foil /299 #99
2018 Donruss Red Foil /299 #143
2018 Donruss Red Foil /299 #54B
2018 Donruss Retro Relics '85 #25
2018 Donruss Retro Relics '85 Black /10 #25
2018 Donruss Retro Relics '85 Holo Gold /75 #25
2018 Donruss Studio Signatures #2
2018 Donruss Studio Signatures Black /1 #2
2018 Donruss Studio Signatures Holo Gold /25 #2
2018 Panini Father's Day Racing Memorabilia #AA
2018 Panini Father's Day Racing Memorabilia Checkerboard /10 #AA
2018 Panini Father's Day Racing Memorabilia Cracked Ice /25 #AA
2018 Panini Father's Day Racing Memorabilia Escher Squares /5 #AA
2018 Panini Father's Day Racing Memorabilia Hyperplaid /1 #AA
2018 Panini Prime /50 #11
2018 Panini Prime /50 #45
2018 Panini Prime /50 #78
2018 Panini Prime Autograph Materials /25 #2
2018 Panini Prime Autograph Materials Black /1 #2
2018 Panini Prime Autograph Materials Holo Gold /10 #2
2018 Panini Prime Autograph Materials Laundry Tag /1 #2
2018 Panini Prime Black /1 #11
2018 Panini Prime Black /1 #45
2018 Panini Prime Black /1 #78
2018 Panini Prime Clear Silhouettes /99 #1
2018 Panini Prime Clear Silhouettes Black /1 #1
2018 Panini Prime Clear Silhouettes Dual /99 #1
2018 Panini Prime Clear Silhouettes Dual Black /1 #1
2018 Panini Prime Clear Silhouettes Dual Holo Gold /50 #1
2018 Panini Prime Clear Silhouettes Holo Gold /13 #1
2018 Panini Prime Dual Material Autographs /25 #16
2018 Panini Prime Dual Material Autographs Black /1 #16
2018 Panini Prime Dual Material Autographs Holo Gold /10 #16
2018 Panini Prime Dual Material Autographs Laundry Tag /1 #16
2018 Panini Prime Dual Signatures /50 #8
2018 Panini Prime Dual Signatures Black /1 #8
2018 Panini Prime Dual Signatures Holo Gold /25 #8
2018 Panini Prime Holo Gold /25 #11
2018 Panini Prime Holo Gold /25 #45
2018 Panini Prime Holo Gold /25 #78
2018 Panini Prime Prime Jumbo Associate Sponsor 1 /1 #2
2018 Panini Prime Prime Jumbo Associate Sponsor 2 /1 #2
2018 Panini Prime Prime Jumbo Associate Sponsor 3 /1 #2
2018 Panini Prime Prime Jumbo Associate Sponsor 4 /1 #2
2018 Panini Prime Prime Jumbo Associate Sponsor 5 /1 #2
2018 Panini Prime Prime Jumbo Associate Sponsor 6 /1 #2
2018 Panini Prime Prime Jumbo Associate Sponsor 7 /1 #2
2018 Panini Prime Prime Jumbo Associate Sponsor 8 /1 #2
2018 Panini Prime Prime Jumbo Associate Sponsor 9 /1 #2
2018 Panini Prime Prime Jumbo Car Manufacturer /1 #2
2018 Panini Prime Prime Jumbo Firesuit Manufacturer /1 #2
2018 Panini Prime Prime Jumbo Glove Manufacturer Patch /1 #2
2018 Panini Prime Prime Jumbo Glove Name Patch /1 #2
2018 Panini Prime Prime Jumbo Glove Number Patch /1 #2
2018 Panini Prime Prime Jumbo Goodyear /2 #2
2018 Panini Prime Prime Jumbo Nameplate /2 #2
2018 Panini Prime Prime Jumbo NASCAR /1 #2
2018 Panini Prime Prime Jumbo Series Sponsor /1 #2
2018 Panini Prime Prime Jumbo Shoe Brand Logo /1 #2
2018 Panini Prime Prime Jumbo Shoe Name Patch /1 #2
2018 Panini Prime Prime Jumbo Sunoco /1 #2
2018 Panini Prime Quad Material Autographs /39 #18
2018 Panini Prime Quad Material Autographs Black /1 #18
2018 Panini Prime Quad Material Autographs Holo Gold /10 #18
2018 Panini Prime Quad Material Autographs Laundry Tag /1 #18
2018 Panini Prime Race Used Duals Firesuit Black /1 #2
2018 Panini Prime Race Used Duals Firesuit Holo Gold /25 #2
2018 Panini Prime Race Used Duals Firesuit Laundry Tag /1 #2
2018 Panini Prime Race Used Duals Sheet Metal /50 #2
2018 Panini Prime Race Used Duals Sheet Metal Black /1 #2
2018 Panini Prime Race Used Duals Sheet Metal Holo Gold /25 #2
2018 Panini Prime Race Used Duals Tire /50 #2
2018 Panini Prime Race Used Duals Tire Black /1 #2
2018 Panini Prime Race Used Duals Tire Holo Gold /25 #2
2018 Panini Prime Race Used Firesuits Black /1 #1
2018 Panini Prime Race Used Firesuits Holo Gold /25 #1
2018 Panini Prime Race Used Firesuits Laundry Tag /1 #1
2018 Panini Prime Race Used Sheet Metal Black /1 #1
2018 Panini Prime Race Used Sheet Metal Holo Gold /25 #1
2018 Panini Prime Race Used Tires Black /1 #1
2018 Panini Prime Race Used Tires Holo Gold /25 #1
2018 Panini Prime Signature Swatches /25 #10
2018 Panini Prime Signature Swatches Black /1 #10
2018 Panini Prime Signature Swatches Holo Gold /10 #10
2018 Panini Prime Triple Material Autographs /25 #21
2018 Panini Prime Triple Material Autographs Black /1 #21
2018 Panini Prime Triple Material Autographs Holo Gold /10 #21
2018 Panini Prime Triple Material Autographs Laundry Tag /1 #21
2018 Panini Prizm #42
2018 Panini Prizm Autographs Prizms #13
2018 Panini Prizm Autographs Prizms Black /1 #13
2018 Panini Prizm Autographs Prizms Blue /75 #13
2018 Panini Prizm Autographs Prizms Camo #13
2018 Panini Prizm Autographs Prizms Gold /10 #13
2018 Panini Prizm Autographs Prizms Green /99 #13
2018 Panini Prizm Autographs Prizms Rainbow /24 #13
2018 Panini Prizm Autographs Prizms Red /50 #13
2018 Panini Prizm Autographs Prizms Red White and Blue /125 #13
2018 Panini Prizm Autographs Prizms White /5 #13
2018 Panini Prizm Prizms #42
2018 Panini Prizm Prizms Black /1 #42
2018 Panini Prizm Prizms Blue /99 #42
2018 Panini Prizm Prizms Camo #42
2018 Panini Prizm Prizms Gold /10 #42
2018 Panini Prizm Prizms Green /149 #42
2018 Panini Prizm Prizms Purple Flash #42
2018 Panini Prizm Prizms Rainbow /24 #42
2018 Panini Prizm Prizms Red /75 #42
2018 Panini Prizm Prizms Red White and Blue #42
2018 Panini Prizm Prizms White /5 #42
2018 Panini Prizm Stars and Stripes #5
2018 Panini Prizm Stars and Stripes Prizms #5
2018 Panini Prizm Stars and Stripes Prizms Black /1 #5
2018 Panini Prizm Stars and Stripes Prizms Gold /10 #5
2018 Panini Prizm Team Tandems #3
2018 Panini Prizm Team Tandems Prizms #3
2018 Panini Prizm Team Tandems Prizms Black /1 #3
2018 Panini Prizm Team Tandems Prizms Gold /10 #3
2018 Panini Victory Lane #20
2018 Panini Victory Lane Black /1 #20
2018 Panini Victory Lane Blue /25 #20
2018 Panini Victory Lane Gold /99 #20
2018 Panini Victory Lane Green /5 #20
2018 Panini Victory Lane Octane Autographs /125 #3
2018 Panini Victory Lane Octane Autographs Black /1 #3
2018 Panini Victory Lane Octane Autographs Gold /99 #3
2018 Panini Victory Lane Pedal to the Metal #3
2018 Panini Victory Lane Pedal to the Metal Black /1 #3
2018 Panini Victory Lane Pedal to the Metal Blue /25 #3
2018 Panini Victory Lane Pedal to the Metal Green /5 #3
2018 Panini Victory Lane Printing Plates Black /1 #20
2018 Panini Victory Lane Printing Plates Cyan /1 #20
2018 Panini Victory Lane Printing Plates Magenta /1 #20
2018 Panini Victory Lane Printing Plates Yellow /1 #20
2018 Panini Victory Lane Red /49 #20
2018 Panini Victory Lane Signatures /40 #6
2018 Panini Victory Lane Signatures Black /1 #6
2018 Panini Victory Lane Signatures Gold /10 #6
2018 Panini Victory Lane Silver #20
2018 Panini Victory Lane Victory Lane Prime Patches Associate Sponsor 1 /1 #22
2018 Panini Victory Lane Victory Lane Prime Patches Associate Sponsor 10 /1 #22
2018 Panini Victory Lane Victory Lane Prime Patches Associate Sponsor 2 /1 #22
2018 Panini Victory Lane Victory Lane Prime Patches Associate Sponsor 3 /1 #22
2018 Panini Victory Lane Victory Lane Prime Patches Associate Sponsor 4 /1 #22
2018 Panini Victory Lane Victory Lane Prime Patches Associate Sponsor 5 /1 #22
2018 Panini Victory Lane Victory Lane Prime Patches Associate Sponsor 6 /1 #22
2018 Panini Victory Lane Victory Lane Prime Patches Associate Sponsor 7 /1 #22
2018 Panini Victory Lane Victory Lane Prime Patches Associate Sponsor 8 /1 #22
2018 Panini Victory Lane Victory Lane Prime Patches Associate Sponsor 9 /1 #22
2018 Panini Victory Lane Victory Lane Prime Patches Car Manufacturer /1 #22
2018 Panini Victory Lane Victory Lane Prime Patches Firesuit Manufacturer /1 #22
2018 Panini Victory Lane Victory Lane Prime Patches Goodyear /1 #22
2018 Panini Victory Lane Victory Lane Prime Patches Nameplate /2 #22
2018 Panini Victory Lane Victory Lane Prime Patches NASCAR /1 #22
2018 Panini Victory Lane Victory Lane Prime Patches Series Sponsor /1 #22
2018 Panini Victory Lane Victory Lane Prime Patches Sunoco /1 #22
2019 Donruss #52
2019 Donruss #92
2019 Donruss #115
2019 Donruss Artist Proofs /25 #52
2019 Donruss Artist Proofs /25 #92
2019 Donruss Artist Proofs /25 #115
2019 Donruss Black /199 #52
2019 Donruss Black /199 #92
2019 Donruss Black /199 #115
2019 Donruss Contenders #6
2019 Donruss Contenders Cracked Ice /25 #6
2019 Donruss Contenders Holographic #6
2019 Donruss Contenders Xplosion /10 #6
2019 Donruss Gold /299 #52
2019 Donruss Gold /299 #92
2019 Donruss Gold /299 #115
2019 Donruss Gold Press Proofs /99 #52
2019 Donruss Gold Press Proofs /99 #92
2019 Donruss Gold Press Proofs /99 #115
2019 Donruss Optic #17
2019 Donruss Optic #79
2019 Donruss Optic Blue Pulsar #17
2019 Donruss Optic Blue Pulsar /1 #79
2019 Donruss Optic Gold /10 #17
2019 Donruss Optic Gold /10 #79
2019 Donruss Optic Gold Vinyl /1 #17
2019 Donruss Optic Gold Vinyl /1 #79
2019 Donruss Optic Holo #17
2019 Donruss Optic Holo #79
2019 Donruss Optic Red Wave #17
2019 Donruss Optic Red Wave /1 #79
2019 Donruss Optic Signatures Gold Vinyl /1 #79
2019 Donruss Optic Signatures Gold Vinyl /1 #17
2019 Donruss Optic Signatures Holo /75 #17
2019 Donruss Optic Signatures Holo /75 #79
2019 Donruss Originals #11
2019 Donruss Originals Cracked Ice /25 #11
2019 Donruss Originals Holographic #11
2019 Donruss Originals Xplosion /10 #11
2019 Donruss Press Proofs /49 #52
2019 Donruss Press Proofs /49 #92
2019 Donruss Press Proofs /49 #115
2019 Donruss Printing Plates Black /1 #52
2019 Donruss Printing Plates Black /1 #92
2019 Donruss Printing Plates Black /1 #115
2019 Donruss Printing Plates Cyan /1 #52
2019 Donruss Printing Plates Cyan /1 #92
2019 Donruss Printing Plates Cyan /1 #115
2019 Donruss Printing Plates Magenta /1 #52
2019 Donruss Printing Plates Magenta /1 #92
2019 Donruss Printing Plates Magenta /1 #115
2019 Donruss Printing Plates Yellow /1 #52
2019 Donruss Printing Plates Yellow /1 #92
2019 Donruss Printing Plates Yellow /1 #115
2019 Donruss Race Day Relics #2
2019 Donruss Race Day Relics Holo Black /10 #2
2019 Donruss Race Day Relics Holo Gold /25 #2
2019 Donruss Race Day Relics Red /185 #2
2019 Donruss Signature Series #2
2019 Donruss Signature Series Holo Black /10 #2
2019 Donruss Signature Series Holo Gold /25 #2
2019 Donruss Signature Series Red /149 #2
2019 Donruss Silver #52
2019 Donruss Silver #92
2019 Donruss Silver #115
2019 Panini Prime /50 #8
2019 Panini Prime /50 #42
2019 Panini Prime /50 #75
2019 Panini Prime Autograph Materials Black /5 #6
2019 Panini Prime Autograph Materials Holo Gold /10 #6
2019 Panini Prime Autograph Materials Platinum Blue /1 #6
2019 Panini Prime Black /10 #8
2019 Panini Prime Black /10 #42
2019 Panini Prime Black /10 #75
2019 Panini Prime Clear Silhouettes /99 #18
2019 Panini Prime Clear Silhouettes Black /10 #18
2019 Panini Prime Clear Silhouettes Dual /99 #4
2019 Panini Prime Clear Silhouettes Dual Black /10 #4
2019 Panini Prime Clear Silhouettes Dual Holo Gold /25 #4
2019 Panini Prime Clear Silhouettes Dual Platinum Blue /1 #4
2019 Panini Prime Clear Silhouettes Holo Gold /25 #18
2019 Panini Prime Clear Silhouettes Platinum Blue /1 #18
2019 Panini Prime Dual Material Autographs Black /5 #18
2019 Panini Prime Dual Material Autographs Holo Gold /10 #18
2019 Panini Prime Dual Material Autographs Laundry Tags /1 #18
2019 Panini Prime Emerald /5 #8
2019 Panini Prime Emerald /5 #42
2019 Panini Prime Emerald /5 #75
2019 Panini Prime Hats Off Button /1 #1
2019 Panini Prime Hats Off Driver Name /3 #1
2019 Panini Prime Hats Off Eyelets /6 #1
2019 Panini Prime Hats Off Headband /36 #1
2019 Panini Prime Hats Off Laundry Tags /2 #1
2019 Panini Prime Hats Off New Era /1 #1
2019 Panini Prime Hats Off Number /4 #1
2019 Panini Prime Hats Off Sponsor Logo /5 #1
2019 Panini Prime Jumbo Material Signatures Firesuit /5 #2
2019 Panini Prime Jumbo Material Signatures Firesuit Platinum Blue /1 #2
2019 Panini Prime Jumbo Material Signatures Sheet Metal /8 #2
2019 Panini Prime NASCAR Shadowbox Signatures Car Number /14 #7
2019 Panini Prime NASCAR Shadowbox Signatures Manufacturer /5 #7
2019 Panini Prime NASCAR Shadowbox Signatures Sponsor /9 #7
2019 Panini Prime NASCAR Shadowbox Signatures Team Owner /1 #7
2019 Panini Prime Platinum Blue /1 #8
2019 Panini Prime Platinum Blue /1 #42
2019 Panini Prime Platinum Blue /1 #75
2019 Panini Prime Prime Jumbo Associate Sponsor 1 /1 #2
2019 Panini Prime Prime Jumbo Associate Sponsor 2 /1 #2
2019 Panini Prime Prime Jumbo Associate Sponsor 3 /1 #2
2019 Panini Prime Prime Jumbo Associate Sponsor 4 /1 #2
2019 Panini Prime Prime Jumbo Associate Sponsor 5 /1 #2
2019 Panini Prime Prime Jumbo Associate Sponsor 6 /1 #2
2019 Panini Prime Prime Jumbo Car Manufacturer /1 #2
2019 Panini Prime Prime Jumbo Firesuit Manufacturer /1 #2
2019 Panini Prime Prime Jumbo Glove Manufacturer Patch /1 #2
2019 Panini Prime Prime Jumbo Goodyear /2 #2
2019 Panini Prime Prime Jumbo Nameplate /2 #2
2019 Panini Prime Prime Jumbo NASCAR /1 #2
2019 Panini Prime Prime Jumbo Prime Colors /6 #2
2019 Panini Prime Prime Jumbo Series Sponsor /1 #2
2019 Panini Prime Prime Jumbo Shoe Brand Logo /1 #2
2019 Panini Prime Prime Jumbo Sunoco /1 #2
2019 Panini Prime Prime Number Die Cut Signatures Black /5 #1
2019 Panini Prime Prime Number Die Cut Signatures Holo Gold /10 #1
2019 Panini Prime Prime Number Die Cut Signatures Platinum Blue /1 #1
2019 Panini Prime Quad Materials Autographs Black /5 #2
2019 Panini Prime Quad Materials Autographs Holo Gold /10 #2
2019 Panini Prime Quad Materials Autographs Laundry Tags /1 #2
2019 Panini Prime Race Used Duals Firesuits /50 #7
2019 Panini Prime Race Used Duals Firesuits Black /10 #7
2019 Panini Prime Race Used Duals Firesuits Holo Gold /25 #7
2019 Panini Prime Race Used Duals Firesuits Laundry Tags /1 #7
2019 Panini Prime Race Used Duals Sheet Metal Platinum Blue /1 #7
2019 Panini Prime Race Used Duals Tires /50 #7
2019 Panini Prime Race Used Duals Tires Black /10 #7
2019 Panini Prime Race Used Duals Tires Holo Gold /25 #7
2019 Panini Prime Race Used Duals Tires Platinum Blue /1 #7
2019 Panini Prime Race Used Firesuits /50 #7
2019 Panini Prime Race Used Firesuits Black /10 #7
2019 Panini Prime Race Used Firesuits Holo Gold /25 #7
2019 Panini Prime Race Used Firesuits Laundry Tags /1 #7
2019 Panini Prime Race Used Quads Firesuits /50 #3
2019 Panini Prime Race Used Quads Firesuits Black /10 #3
2019 Panini Prime Race Used Quads Firesuits Holo Gold /25 #3
2019 Panini Prime Race Used Quads Firesuits Laundry Tags /1 #3
2019 Panini Prime Race Used Quads Sheet Metal Platinum Blue /1 #3
2019 Panini Prime Race Used Quads Tires /50 #3
2019 Panini Prime Race Used Quads Tires Black /10 #3
2019 Panini Prime Race Used Quads Tires Holo Gold /25 #3
2019 Panini Prime Race Used Quads Tires Platinum Blue /1 #3
2019 Panini Prime Race Used Sheet Metal /50 #7
2019 Panini Prime Race Used Sheet Metal Black /10 #7
2019 Panini Prime Race Used Sheet Metal Holo Gold /25 #7
2019 Panini Prime Race Used Sheet Metal Platinum Blue /1 #7
2019 Panini Prime Race Used Tires /50 #7
2019 Panini Prime Race Used Tires Black /10 #7
2019 Panini Prime Race Used Tires Holo Gold /25 #7
2019 Panini Prime Race Used Tires Platinum Blue /1 #7
2019 Panini Prime Race Used Trios Firesuits /50 #7
2019 Panini Prime Race Used Trios Firesuits Black /10 #7
2019 Panini Prime Race Used Trios Firesuits Holo Gold /25 #7
2019 Panini Prime Race Used Trios Firesuits Laundry Tags /1 #7
2019 Panini Prime Race Used Trios Sheet Metal Platinum Blue /1 #7
2019 Panini Prime Race Used Trios Tires /50 #7
2019 Panini Prime Race Used Trios Tires Black /10 #7
2019 Panini Prime Race Used Trios Tires Holo Gold /25 #7
2019 Panini Prime Race Used Trios Tires Platinum Blue /1 #7
2019 Panini Prime Timeline Signatures Manufacturer /1 #15
2019 Panini Prime Timeline Signatures Name /10 #15
2019 Panini Prime Timeline Signatures Sponsor /5 #15
2019 Panini Prizm #8
2019 Panini Prizm #70
2019 Panini Prizm #87
2019 Panini Prizm Fireworks #9
2019 Panini Prizm Fireworks Prizms #9
2019 Panini Prizm Fireworks Prizms Black /1 #9
2019 Panini Prizm Fireworks Prizms Gold /10 #9
2019 Panini Prizm Fireworks Prizms White Sparkle #9
2019 Panini Prizm In the Groove #13
2019 Panini Prizm In the Groove Prizms #13
2019 Panini Prizm In the Groove Prizms Black /1 #13
2019 Panini Prizm In the Groove Prizms Gold /10 #13
2019 Panini Prizm In the Groove Prizms White Sparkle #13
2019 Panini Prizm Prizms #70
2019 Panini Prizm Prizms #87
2019 Panini Prizm Prizms #8
2019 Panini Prizm Prizms Black /1 #8
2019 Panini Prizm Prizms Black /1 #70
2019 Panini Prizm Prizms Black /1 #87
2019 Panini Prizm Prizms Blue /75 #8
2019 Panini Prizm Prizms Blue /75 #70
2019 Panini Prizm Prizms Blue /75 #87
2019 Panini Prizm Prizms Camo #8
2019 Panini Prizm Prizms Camo #70
2019 Panini Prizm Prizms Camo #87
2019 Panini Prizm Prizms Flash #8
2019 Panini Prizm Prizms Flash #70
2019 Panini Prizm Prizms Flash #87
2019 Panini Prizm Prizms Gold /10 #8
2019 Panini Prizm Prizms Gold /10 #70
2019 Panini Prizm Prizms Gold /10 #87
2019 Panini Prizm Prizms Green /99 #8
2019 Panini Prizm Prizms Green /99 #70
2019 Panini Prizm Prizms Green /99 #87
2019 Panini Prizm Prizms Rainbow /24 #8
2019 Panini Prizm Prizms Rainbow /24 #70
2019 Panini Prizm Prizms Rainbow /24 #87
2019 Panini Prizm Prizms Red /50 #8
2019 Panini Prizm Prizms Red /50 #70
2019 Panini Prizm Prizms Red /50 #87
2019 Panini Prizm Prizms Red White and Blue #8
2019 Panini Prizm Prizms Red White and Blue #70
2019 Panini Prizm Prizms Red White and Blue #87
2019 Panini Prizm Prizms White /5 #8
2019 Panini Prizm Prizms White /5 #70
2019 Panini Prizm Prizms White /5 #87
2019 Panini Prizm Prizms White Sparkle #8
2019 Panini Prizm Prizms White Sparkle #70
2019 Panini Prizm Prizms White Sparkle #87
2019 Panini Prizm Signing Sessions Prizms #2
2019 Panini Prizm Signing Sessions Prizms Black /1 #2
2019 Panini Prizm Signing Sessions Prizms Blue /35 #2
2019 Panini Prizm Signing Sessions Prizms Camo #2
2019 Panini Prizm Signing Sessions Prizms Gold /10 #2
2019 Panini Prizm Signing Sessions Prizms Rainbow /24 #2
2019 Panini Prizm Signing Sessions Prizms Red /25 #2
2019 Panini Prizm Signing Sessions Prizms Red White and Blue #2
2019 Panini Prizm Signing Sessions Prizms White /5 #2
2019 Panini Prizm Teammates #7
2019 Panini Prizm Teammates Prizms #7
2019 Panini Prizm Teammates Prizms Black /1 #7
2019 Panini Prizm Teammates Prizms Gold /10 #7
2019 Panini Prizm Teammates Prizms White Sparkle #7
2019 Panini Victory Lane #8
2019 Panini Victory Lane #55
2019 Panini Victory Lane Black /1 #8
2019 Panini Victory Lane Black /1 #55
2019 Panini Victory Lane Celebrations #10
2019 Panini Victory Lane Celebrations Black /1 #10
2019 Panini Victory Lane Celebrations Blue /99 #10
2019 Panini Victory Lane Celebrations Gold /25 #10
2019 Panini Victory Lane Celebrations Green /5 #10
2019 Panini Victory Lane Celebrations Printing Plates Black /1 #10
2019 Panini Victory Lane Celebrations Printing Plates Cyan /1 #10
2019 Panini Victory Lane Celebrations Printing Plates Magenta /1 #10
2019 Panini Victory Lane Celebrations Printing Plates Yellow /1 #10
2019 Panini Victory Lane Dual Swatches Gold /99 #21
2019 Panini Victory Lane Dual Swatches Laundry Tag /1 #21
2019 Panini Victory Lane Dual Swatches Platinum /1 #21
2019 Panini Victory Lane Dual Swatches Red /25 #21
2019 Panini Victory Lane Gold /25 #8
2019 Panini Victory Lane Gold /25 #55
2019 Panini Victory Lane Machines #19
2019 Panini Victory Lane Machines Black /1 #19
2019 Panini Victory Lane Machines Blue /99 #19
2019 Panini Victory Lane Machines Gold /25 #19
2019 Panini Victory Lane Machines Green /5 #19
2019 Panini Victory Lane Machines Printing Plates Black /1 #19
2019 Panini Victory Lane Machines Printing Plates Cyan /1 #19
2019 Panini Victory Lane Machines Printing Plates Magenta /1 #19
2019 Panini Victory Lane Machines Printing Plates Yellow /1 #19
2019 Panini Victory Lane Pedal to the Metal #25
2019 Panini Victory Lane Pedal to the Metal #56
2019 Panini Victory Lane Pedal to the Metal Black /1 #25
2019 Panini Victory Lane Pedal to the Metal Black /1 #56
2019 Panini Victory Lane Pedal to the Metal Gold /25 #25
2019 Panini Victory Lane Pedal to the Metal Gold /25 #56
2019 Panini Victory Lane Pedal to the Metal Green /5 #25
2019 Panini Victory Lane Pedal to the Metal Green /5 #56
2019 Panini Victory Lane Pedal to the Metal Red /3 #25
2019 Panini Victory Lane Pedal to the Metal Red /3 #56
2019 Panini Victory Lane Printing Plates Black /1 #8
2019 Panini Victory Lane Printing Plates Black /1 #55
2019 Panini Victory Lane Printing Plates Cyan /1 #8
2019 Panini Victory Lane Printing Plates Cyan /1 #55
2019 Panini Victory Lane Printing Plates Magenta /1 #8
2019 Panini Victory Lane Printing Plates Magenta /1 #55
2019 Panini Victory Lane Printing Plates Yellow /1 #8
2019 Panini Victory Lane Printing Plates Yellow /1 #55
2019 Panini Victory Lane Signature Swatches /0 #1

ini Victory Lane Signature Swatches Gold /49 #1
ini Victory Lane Signature Swatches Laundry Tag /1 #1
ini Victory Lane Signature Swatches Platinum /1 #1
ini Victory Lane Signature Swatches Red /25 #1
ini Victory Lane Starting Grid #13
ini Victory Lane Starting Grid Black /1 #13
ini Victory Lane Starting Grid Blue /99 #13
ini Victory Lane Starting Grid Gold /25 #13
ini Victory Lane Starting Grid Green /5 #13
ini Victory Lane Starting Grid Printing Plates Black /1 #13
ini Victory Lane Starting Grid Printing Plates Cyan /1 #13
ini Victory Lane Starting Grid Printing Plates Magenta /1 #13
ini Victory Lane Starting Grid Printing Plates Yellow /1 #13
ini Victory Lane Top 10 #5
ini Victory Lane Top 10 Black /1 #5
ini Victory Lane Top 10 Blue /99 #5
ini Victory Lane Top 10 Gold /25 #5
ini Victory Lane Top 10 Green /5 #5
ini Victory Lane Top 10 Printing Plates Black /1 #5
ini Victory Lane Top 10 Printing Plates Cyan /1 #5
ini Victory Lane Top 10 Printing Plates Magenta /1 #5
ini Victory Lane Top 10 Printing Plates Yellow /1 #5
onruss #24
onruss #109
onruss #130
onruss Black Numbers /10 #24
onruss Black Numbers /10 #109
onruss Black Numbers /10 #130
onruss Black Trophy Club /1 #24
onruss Black Trophy Club /1 #109
onruss Black Trophy Club /1 #130
onruss Blue /199 #109
onruss Blue /199 #130
onruss Blue /199 #24
onruss Carolina Blue #24
onruss Carolina Blue #109
onruss Carolina Blue #130
onruss Contenders #12
onruss Contenders Checkers #12
onruss Contenders Cracked Ice /25 #12
onruss Contenders Holographic /199 #12
onruss Contenders Xplosion /10 #12
onruss Green /99 #24
onruss Green /99 #109
onruss Green /99 #130
Donruss Optic #29
Donruss Optic #74
Donruss Optic Carolina Blue Wave #29
Donruss Optic Carolina Blue Wave #74
Donruss Optic Gold /10 #29
Donruss Optic Gold /10 #74
Donruss Optic Gold Vinyl /1 #29
Donruss Optic Gold Vinyl /1 #74
Donruss Optic Holo #29
Donruss Optic Holo #74
Donruss Optic Orange Pulsar #29
Donruss Optic Orange Pulsar #74
Donruss Optic Red Mojo #29
Donruss Optic Red Mojo #74
Donruss Optic Signatures Gold Vinyl /1 #29
Donruss Optic Signatures Gold Vinyl /1 #74
Donruss Optic Signatures Holo /99 #29
Donruss Optic Signatures Holo /99 #74
Donruss Orange #24
Donruss Orange #109
Donruss Orange #130
Donruss Pink /25 #24
Donruss Pink /25 #109
Donruss Pink /25 #130
Donruss Printing Plates Black /1 #24
Donruss Printing Plates Black /1 #109
Donruss Printing Plates Black /1 #130
Donruss Printing Plates Cyan /1 #24
Donruss Printing Plates Cyan /1 #109
Donruss Printing Plates Cyan /1 #130
Donruss Printing Plates Magenta /1 #24
Donruss Printing Plates Magenta /1 #109
Donruss Printing Plates Magenta /1 #130
Donruss Printing Plates Yellow /1 #130
Donruss Printing Plates Yellow /1 #24
Donruss Printing Plates Yellow /1 #109
Donruss Purple /49 #24
Donruss Purple /49 #109
Donruss Purple /49 #130
Donruss Race Day Relics #2
Donruss Race Day Relics Holo Black /10 #2
Donruss Race Day Relics Holo Gold /25 #2
Donruss Race Day Relics Red /250 #2
Donruss Red /299 #24
Donruss Red /299 #109
Donruss Red /299 #130
Donruss Retro Series #5
Donruss Retro Series Checkers #5
Donruss Retro Series Cracked Ice /25 #5
Donruss Retro Series Holographic /199 #5
Donruss Retro Series Xplosion /10 #5
Donruss Signature Series #18
Donruss Signature Series Holo Black /1 #18
Donruss Signature Series Holo Gold /25 #18
Donruss Signature Series Red /50 #18
Donruss Silver #24
Donruss Silver #109
Donruss Silver #130

revor Bayne

10 Element #98
10 Element Blue /35 #98
10 Element Green #98
10 Element Red Target #98
10 Element Undiscovered Elements Autographs /125 #UETB
10 Element Undiscovered Elements Autographs Red Ink Inscriptions /25 #UETB
10 Press Pass Signings Blue /10 #4
10 Press Pass Signings Gold /40 #4
10 Press Pass Signings Red /15 #4
10 Press Pass Signings Silver /75 #4
10 Press Pass Stealth #47
10 Press Pass Stealth Black and White #47
10 Press Pass Stealth Purple /25 #47
10 Wheels Main Event #85
10 Wheels Main Event Blue #85
10 Wheels Main Event Marks Autographs /71 #4
10 Wheels Main Event Marks Autographs Black /1 #4
10 Wheels Main Event Marks Autographs Blue /30 #4
10 Wheels Main Event Marks Autographs Red /25 #4
11 Element #51
11 Element Autographs /45 #4
11 Element Autographs Blue /5 #4
11 Element Autographs Gold /10 #4
11 Element Autographs Printing Plates Black /1 #4
11 Element Autographs Printing Plates Cyan /1 #4
11 Element Autographs Printing Plates Magenta /1 #4
11 Element Autographs Printing Plates Yellow /1 #4
11 Element Autographs Silver /15 #4
11 Element Black /35 #51
11 Element Green #51
2011 Element Previews /1 #EB51
2011 Element Purple /25 #51
2011 Element Red #51
2011 Press Pass #42
2011 Press Pass #97
2011 Press Pass Autographs Blue /10 #4
2011 Press Pass Autographs Bronze /75 #4
2011 Press Pass Autographs Gold /25 #4
2011 Press Pass Autographs Printing Plates Black /1 #4
2011 Press Pass Autographs Printing Plates Cyan /1 #4
2011 Press Pass Autographs Printing Plates Magenta /1 #4
2011 Press Pass Autographs Printing Plates Yellow /1 #4
2011 Press Pass Autographs Silver /50 #4
2011 Press Pass Blue Holofoil /10 #42
2011 Press Pass Blue Holofoil /10 #97
2011 Press Pass Blue Retail #42
2011 Press Pass Blue Retail #97
2011 Press Pass FanFare #3
2011 Press Pass FanFare #42
2011 Press Pass FanFare Autographs Blue /5 #5
2011 Press Pass FanFare Autographs Blue /5 #6
2011 Press Pass FanFare Autographs Bronze /60 #5
2011 Press Pass FanFare Autographs Bronze /115 #6
2011 Press Pass FanFare Autographs Gold /25 #5
2011 Press Pass FanFare Autographs Gold /75 #6
2011 Press Pass FanFare Autographs Printing Plates Black /1 #5
2011 Press Pass FanFare Autographs Printing Plates Black /1 #6
2011 Press Pass FanFare Autographs Printing Plates Cyan /1 #5
2011 Press Pass FanFare Autographs Printing Plates Cyan /1 #6
2011 Press Pass FanFare Autographs Printing Plates Magenta /1 #5
2011 Press Pass FanFare Autographs Printing Plates Magenta /1 #6
2011 Press Pass FanFare Autographs Printing Plates Yellow /1 #5
2011 Press Pass FanFare Autographs Printing Plates Yellow /1 #6
2011 Press Pass FanFare Autographs Silver /20 #5
2011 Press Pass FanFare Autographs Silver /25 #6
2011 Press Pass FanFare Blue Die Cuts #3
2011 Press Pass FanFare Blue Die Cuts #42
2011 Press Pass FanFare Dual Autographs /10 #NNO
2011 Press Pass FanFare Emerald /25 #3
2011 Press Pass FanFare Emerald /25 #42
2011 Press Pass FanFare Holofoil Die Cuts #3
2011 Press Pass FanFare Holofoil Die Cuts #42
2011 Press Pass FanFare Magnificent Materials /199 #MMTB
2011 Press Pass FanFare Magnificent Materials /199 #MMTB
2011 Press Pass FanFare Magnificent Materials Dual Swatches /50 #MMDTB
2011 Press Pass FanFare Magnificent Materials Dual Swatches /50 #MMDTB
2011 Press Pass FanFare Magnificent Materials Dual Swatches Holofoil /10 #MMDTB
2011 Press Pass FanFare Magnificent Materials Dual Swatches Holofoil /10 #MMDTB
2011 Press Pass FanFare Magnificent Materials Holofoil /50 #MMTB
2011 Press Pass FanFare Magnificent Materials Holofoil /50 #MMTB
2011 Press Pass FanFare Magnificent Materials Signatures /50 #MMSETB
2011 Press Pass FanFare Magnificent Materials Signatures Holofoil /25 #MMSETB
2011 Press Pass FanFare Rookie Standouts #RS1
2011 Press Pass FanFare Ruby Die Cuts /15 #3
2011 Press Pass FanFare Ruby Die Cuts /15 #42
2011 Press Pass FanFare Sapphire /10 #3
2011 Press Pass FanFare Sapphire /10 #42
2011 Press Pass FanFare Silver /25 #3
2011 Press Pass FanFare Silver /25 #42
2011 Press Pass Gold /50 #42
2011 Press Pass Gold /50 #97
2011 Press Pass Legends #37
2011 Press Pass Legends Autographs Blue /10 #LGATB
2011 Press Pass Legends Autographs Gold /50 #LGATB
2011 Press Pass Legends Autographs Printing Plates Black /1 #LGATB
2011 Press Pass Legends Autographs Printing Plates Cyan /1 #LGATB
2011 Press Pass Legends Autographs Printing Plates Magenta /1 #LGATB
2011 Press Pass Legends Autographs Printing Plates Yellow /1 #LGATB
2011 Press Pass Legends Autographs Silver /125 #LGATB
2011 Press Pass Legends Gold /250 #37
2011 Press Pass Legends Holofoil /25 #37
2011 Press Pass Legends Printing Plates Black /1 #37
2011 Press Pass Legends Printing Plates Cyan /1 #37
2011 Press Pass Legends Printing Plates Magenta /1 #37
2011 Press Pass Legends Printing Plates Yellow /1 #37
2011 Press Pass Legends Prominent Pieces Gold /50 #PPTB
2011 Press Pass Legends Prominent Pieces Holofoil /25 #PPTB
2011 Press Pass Legends Prominent Pieces Oversized Firesuit /25 #PPOETB
2011 Press Pass Legends Prominent Pieces Purple /15 #PPTB
2011 Press Pass Legends Prominent Pieces Silver /99 #PPTB
2011 Press Pass Legends Purple /25 #37
2011 Press Pass Legends Red /99 #37
2011 Press Pass Legends Solo /1 #37
2011 Press Pass Premium #54
2011 Press Pass Premium #56
2011 Press Pass Premium #65
2011 Press Pass Premium #3
2011 Press Pass Premium #38
2011 Press Pass Premium Crystal Ball #CB10
2011 Press Pass Premium Crystal Ball Autographs /10 #CBATB
2011 Press Pass Premium Pairings Firesuits /25 #PPCETB
2011 Press Pass Premium Pairings Signatures /5 #PPACETB
2011 Press Pass Premium Purple /25 #3
2011 Press Pass Premium Purple /25 #38
2011 Press Pass Premium Purple /25 #54
2011 Press Pass Premium Purple /25 #56
2011 Press Pass Premium Purple /25 #65
2011 Press Pass Premium Signatures /164 #PSTB
2011 Press Pass Premium Signatures Red Ink /15 #PSTB
2011 Press Pass Purple /25 #42
2011 Press Pass Showcase /99 #61
2011 Press Pass Showcase Gold /50 #61
2011 Press Pass Showcase Melting /1 #61
2011 Press Pass Signature Series /11 #SSTB
2011 Press Pass Signature Series /11 #SSMTB
2011 Press Pass Signings Black and White /10 #PPSTB1
2011 Press Pass Signings Brushed Metal /50 #PPSTB1
2011 Press Pass Signings Holofoil /25 #PPSTB1
2011 Press Pass Stealth #39
2011 Press Pass Stealth #57
2011 Press Pass Stealth #71
2011 Press Pass Stealth Black and White /25 #39
2011 Press Pass Stealth Black and White /25 #57
2011 Press Pass Stealth Black and White /25 #71
2011 Press Pass Stealth Holofoil /99 #39
2011 Press Pass Stealth Holofoil /99 #57
2011 Press Pass Stealth Holofoil /99 #71
2011 Press Pass Stealth Metal of Honor Medal of Honor /50 #BATB
2011 Press Pass Stealth Metal of Honor Purple Heart /25 #MHTB
2011 Press Pass Stealth Metal of Honor Silver Star /99 #BATB
2011 Press Pass Stealth Purple /25 #39
2011 Press Pass Stealth Purple /25 #57
2011 Wheels Main Event #3
2011 Wheels Main Event #39
2011 Wheels Main Event Black and White #3
2011 Wheels Main Event Black and White #39
2011 Wheels Main Event Blue /75 #3
2011 Wheels Main Event Blue /75 #39
2011 Wheels Main Event Gloves Off Holofoil /25 #GOTB
2011 Wheels Main Event Gloves Off Silver /99 #GOTB
2011 Wheels Main Event Green /1 #3
2011 Wheels Main Event Green /1 #39
2011 Wheels Main Event Headliners Holofoil /25 #HLTB
2011 Wheels Main Event Headliners Silver /50 #HLTB
2011 Wheels Main Event Marks Autographs Blue #METB
2011 Wheels Main Event Marks Autographs Gold /25 #METB
2011 Wheels Main Event Marks Autographs Silver /50 #METB
2011 Wheels Main Event Matchups Autographs /10 #MEMTBCE
2011 Wheels Main Event Materials Holofoil /25 #MEMTB
2011 Wheels Main Event Materials Silver /99 #MEMTB
2011 Wheels Main Event Red /20 #3
2011 Wheels Main Event Red /20 #39
2012 Press Pass #3
2012 Press Pass #39
2012 Press Pass #91
2012 Press Pass Autographs Blue /10 #PPATB1
2012 Press Pass Autographs Printing Plates Black /1 #PPATB1
2012 Press Pass Autographs Printing Plates Cyan /1 #PPATB1
2012 Press Pass Autographs Printing Plates Magenta /1 #PPATB1
2012 Press Pass Autographs Printing Plates Yellow /1 #PPATB1
2012 Press Pass Autographs Red /15 #PPATB1
2012 Press Pass Autographs Silver /35 #PPATB1
2012 Press Pass Blue #3
2012 Press Pass Blue #39
2012 Press Pass Blue #91
2012 Press Pass Blue Holofoil /35 #3
2012 Press Pass Blue Holofoil /35 #39
2012 Press Pass Blue Holofoil /35 #91
2012 Press Pass Burning Rubber Gold /99 #BRTB
2012 Press Pass Burning Rubber Holofoil /25 #BRTB
2012 Press Pass Burning Rubber Prime Cuts /25 #BRTB
2012 Press Pass Burning Rubber Purple /15 #BRTB
2012 Press Pass Fanfare #3
2012 Press Pass Fanfare #45
2012 Press Pass Fanfare Autographs Blue /5 #TB1
2012 Press Pass Fanfare Autographs Blue /5 #TB2
2012 Press Pass Fanfare Autographs Gold /25 #TB1
2012 Press Pass Fanfare Autographs Gold /75 #TB2
2012 Press Pass Fanfare Autographs Red /10 #TB1
2012 Press Pass Fanfare Autographs Red /20 #TB2
2012 Press Pass Fanfare Autographs Silver /75 #TB1
2012 Press Pass Fanfare Autographs Silver /99 #TB2
2012 Press Pass Fanfare Blue Foil Die Cuts #3
2012 Press Pass Fanfare Blue Foil Die Cuts #45
2012 Press Pass Fanfare Diamond /5 #3
2012 Press Pass Fanfare Diamond /5 #45
2012 Press Pass Fanfare Holofoil Die Cuts #3
2012 Press Pass Fanfare Holofoil Die Cuts #45
2012 Press Pass Fanfare Magnificent Materials /250 #MMTB
2012 Press Pass Fanfare Magnificent Materials /250 #MMTB2
2012 Press Pass Fanfare Magnificent Materials Dual Swatches /50 #MMTB
2012 Press Pass Fanfare Magnificent Materials Dual Swatches Melting /10 #MMTB
2012 Press Pass Fanfare Magnificent Materials Gold /125 #MMTB
2012 Press Pass Fanfare Magnificent Materials Gold /125 #MMTB2
2012 Press Pass Fanfare Magnificent Materials Signatures /99 #TB
2012 Press Pass Fanfare Magnificent Materials Signatures Blue /25 #TB
2012 Press Pass Fanfare Sapphire /20 #3
2012 Press Pass Fanfare Sapphire /20 #45
2012 Press Pass Fanfare Silver /25 #3
2012 Press Pass Fanfare Silver /25 #45
2012 Press Pass Gold #3
2012 Press Pass Gold #39
2012 Press Pass Gold #91
2012 Press Pass Ignite #4
2012 Press Pass Ignite #59
2012 Press Pass Ignite Materials Autographs Gun Metal /45 #IMTB
2012 Press Pass Ignite Materials Autographs Red /5 #IMTB
2012 Press Pass Ignite Materials Autographs Silver /150 #IMTB
2012 Press Pass Ignite Materials Gun Metal /99 #IMTB
2012 Press Pass Ignite Materials Gun Metal /99 #IMTB2
2012 Press Pass Ignite Materials Red /10 #IMTB
2012 Press Pass Ignite Materials Red /10 #IMTB2
2012 Press Pass Ignite Materials Silver #IMTB
2012 Press Pass Ignite Materials Silver #IMTB2
2012 Press Pass Ignite Profile #P5
2012 Press Pass Ignite Proofs Black and White /50 #4
2012 Press Pass Ignite Proofs Black and White /50 #59
2012 Press Pass Ignite Proofs Cyan #4
2012 Press Pass Ignite Proofs Cyan #59
2012 Press Pass Ignite Proofs Magenta #4
2012 Press Pass Ignite Proofs Magenta #59
2012 Press Pass Ignite Proofs Yellow /10 #4
2012 Press Pass Ignite Proofs Yellow /10 #59
2012 Press Pass Power Picks Blue /50 #1
2012 Press Pass Power Picks Blue /50 #52
2012 Press Pass Power Picks Gold /50 #1
2012 Press Pass Power Picks Gold /50 #52
2012 Press Pass Power Picks Holofoil /10 #1
2012 Press Pass Power Picks Holofoil /10 #52
2012 Press Pass Purple /35 #3
2012 Press Pass Purple /35 #39
2012 Press Pass Purple /35 #91
2012 Press Pass Redline #4
2012 Press Pass Redline Black /99 #4
2012 Press Pass Redline Cyan /50 #4
2012 Press Pass Redline Full Throttle Dual Relic Blue /5 #FTTB
2012 Press Pass Redline Full Throttle Dual Relic Gold /10 #FTTB
2012 Press Pass Redline Full Throttle Dual Relic Melting /1 #FTTB
2012 Press Pass Redline Full Throttle Dual Relic Red /25 #FTTB
2012 Press Pass Redline Full Throttle Dual Relic Silver /15 #FTTB
2012 Press Pass Redline Magenta /15 #4
2012 Press Pass Redline Relic Autographs Blue /10 #RLRTB
2012 Press Pass Redline Relic Autographs Gold /25 #RLRTB
2012 Press Pass Redline Relic Autographs Melting /1 #RLRTB
2012 Press Pass Redline Relic Autographs Red /75 #RLRTB
2012 Press Pass Redline Relic Autographs Silver /50 #RLRTB
2012 Press Pass Redline Relics Blue /5 #RLTB
2012 Press Pass Redline Relics Gold /10 #RLTB
2012 Press Pass Redline Relics Melting /1 #RLTB
2012 Press Pass Redline Relics Red /25 #RLTB
2012 Press Pass Redline Relics Silver /15 #RLTB
2012 Press Pass Redline Signatures Blue /4 #RSTB
2012 Press Pass Redline Signatures Gold /25 #RSTB
2012 Press Pass Redline Signatures Holofoil /10 #RSTB
2012 Press Pass Redline Signatures Melting /1 #RSTB
2012 Press Pass Redline Signatures Red /50 #RSTB
2012 Press Pass Redline Yellow /1 #4
2012 Press Pass Showcase /499 #2
2012 Press Pass Showcase Elite Exhibit Ink /50 #EEITB
2012 Press Pass Showcase Elite Exhibit Ink Gold /25 #EEITB
2012 Press Pass Showcase Elite Exhibit Ink Melting /1 #EEITB
2012 Press Pass Showcase Gold /125 #2
2012 Press Pass Showcase Green /5 #2
2012 Press Pass Showcase Masterpieces Ink /50 #MPITB
2012 Press Pass Showcase Masterpieces Ink Gold /25 #MPITB
2012 Press Pass Showcase Masterpieces Ink Melting /1 #MPITB
2012 Press Pass Showcase Masterpieces Memorabilia /99 #MPTB
2012 Press Pass Showcase Masterpieces Memorabilia Gold /50 #MPTB
2012 Press Pass Showcase Masterpieces Memorabilia Melting /5 #MPTB
2012 Press Pass Showcase Melting /1 #2
2012 Press Pass Showcase Prized Pieces Ink /50 #PPITB
2012 Press Pass Showcase Prized Pieces Ink Gold /25 #PPITB
2012 Press Pass Showcase Prized Pieces Ink Melting /1 #PPITB
2012 Press Pass Showcase Purple /1 #2
2012 Press Pass Showcase Red /25 #2
2012 Press Pass Signature Series Race Used /12 #PPATB1
2012 Press Pass Signature Series Race Used /12 #PPATB2
2012 Press Pass Snapshots #SS3
2012 Press Pass Snapshots #SS41
2012 Press Pass Target Snapshots #SSTG3
2012 Press Pass Ultimate Collection Blue Holofoil /25 #UCTB
2012 Press Pass Ultimate Collection Holofoil /50 #UCTB
2012 Total Memorabilia #2
2012 Total Memorabilia Black and White /99 #2
2012 Total Memorabilia Dual Swatch Gold /75 #TMTB
2012 Total Memorabilia Dual Swatch Holofoil /25 #TMTB
2012 Total Memorabilia Dual Swatch Melting /5 #TMTB
2012 Total Memorabilia Dual Swatch Silver /99 #TMTB
2012 Total Memorabilia Gold /275 #2
2012 Total Memorabilia Jumbo Swatch Gold /50 #TMTB
2012 Total Memorabilia Jumbo Swatch Holofoil /10 #TMTB
2012 Total Memorabilia Jumbo Swatch Melting /1 #TMTB
2012 Total Memorabilia Quad Swatch Gold /25 #TMTB
2012 Total Memorabilia Quad Swatch Holofoil /10 #TMTB
2012 Total Memorabilia Quad Swatch Melting /1 #TMTB
2012 Total Memorabilia Quad Swatch Silver /50 #TMTB
2012 Total Memorabilia Red Retail /250 #2
2012 Total Memorabilia Signature Collection Dual Swatch Silver /10 #SCTB
2012 Total Memorabilia Signature Collection Quad Swatch Holofoil /5 #SCTB
2012 Total Memorabilia Signature Collection Single Swatch Melting /1 #SCTB
2012 Total Memorabilia Signature Collection Triple Swatch Gold /10 #SCTB
2012 Total Memorabilia Single Swatch Gold /99 #TMTB
2012 Total Memorabilia Single Swatch Holofoil /50 #TMTB
2012 Total Memorabilia Single Swatch Melting /10 #TMTB
2012 Total Memorabilia Single Swatch Silver /199 #TMTB
2012 Total Memorabilia Triple Swatch Gold /50 #TMTB
2012 Total Memorabilia Triple Swatch Holofoil /25 #TMTB
2012 Total Memorabilia Triple Swatch Melting /1 #TMTB
2012 Total Memorabilia Triple Swatch Silver /99 #TMTB
2013 Press Pass #3
2013 Press Pass #46
2013 Press Pass Color Proofs Black #3
2013 Press Pass Color Proofs Black #46
2013 Press Pass Color Proofs Cyan /35 #3
2013 Press Pass Color Proofs Cyan /35 #46
2013 Press Pass Color Proofs Magenta #3
2013 Press Pass Color Proofs Magenta #46
2013 Press Pass Color Proofs Yellow /5 #3
2013 Press Pass Color Proofs Yellow /5 #46
2013 Press Pass Fanfare #4
2013 Press Pass Fanfare #62
2013 Press Pass Fanfare Autographs Blue /5 #TB
2013 Press Pass Fanfare Autographs Blue /1 #TB2
2013 Press Pass Fanfare Autographs Gold /25 #TB
2013 Press Pass Fanfare Autographs Gold /25 #TB2
2013 Press Pass Fanfare Autographs Green /5 #TB
2013 Press Pass Fanfare Autographs Green /5 #TB2
2013 Press Pass Fanfare Autographs Red /10 #TB
2013 Press Pass Fanfare Autographs Red /10 #TB2
2013 Press Pass Fanfare Autographs Silver /75 #TB
2013 Press Pass Fanfare Autographs Silver /50 #TB2
2013 Press Pass Fanfare Diamond Die Cuts /5 #4
2013 Press Pass Fanfare Diamond Die Cuts /5 #62
2013 Press Pass Fanfare Green /3 #4
2013 Press Pass Fanfare Green /3 #62
2013 Press Pass Fanfare Holofoil Die Cuts #4
2013 Press Pass Fanfare Holofoil Die Cuts #62
2013 Press Pass Fanfare Magnificent Materials Dual Swatches /50 #TB
2013 Press Pass Fanfare Magnificent Materials Dual Swatches Melting /10 #TB
2013 Press Pass Fanfare Magnificent Materials Gold /50 #TB
2013 Press Pass Fanfare Magnificent Materials Gold /50 #TB2
2013 Press Pass Fanfare Magnificent Materials Jumbo Swatches /25 #TB
2013 Press Pass Fanfare Magnificent Materials Silver /199 #TB
2013 Press Pass Fanfare Magnificent Materials Silver /199 #TB2
2013 Press Pass Fanfare Red Foil Die Cuts #4
2013 Press Pass Fanfare Red Foil Die Cuts #62
2013 Press Pass Fanfare Sapphire /20 #4
2013 Press Pass Fanfare Sapphire /20 #62
2013 Press Pass Fanfare Silver /25 #4
2013 Press Pass Fanfare Silver /25 #62
2013 Press Pass Ignite #3
2013 Press Pass Ignite #53
2013 Press Pass Ignite Hot Threads Blue Holofoil /99 #HTTB
2013 Press Pass Ignite Hot Threads Patch Red /10 #HTTB
2013 Press Pass Ignite Hot Threads Silver #HTTB
2013 Press Pass Ignite Ink Black /99 #ITB
2013 Press Pass Ignite Ink Blue /25 #ITB
2013 Press Pass Ignite Ink Red /5 #ITB
2013 Press Pass Ignite Proofs Black and White /50 #3
2013 Press Pass Ignite Proofs Black and White /50 #53
2013 Press Pass Ignite Proofs Cyan #3
2013 Press Pass Ignite Proofs Cyan #53
2013 Press Pass Ignite Proofs Magenta #3
2013 Press Pass Ignite Proofs Magenta #53
2013 Press Pass Ignite Proofs Yellow /5 #3
2013 Press Pass Ignite Proofs Yellow /5 #53
2013 Press Pass Power Picks Blue /99 #1
2013 Press Pass Power Picks Blue /99 #28
2013 Press Pass Power Picks Gold /50 #1
2013 Press Pass Power Picks Gold /50 #28
2013 Press Pass Power Picks Holofoil /10 #1
2013 Press Pass Power Picks Holofoil /10 #28
2013 Press Pass Redline #5
2013 Press Pass Redline Black /99 #5
2013 Press Pass Redline Cyan /50 #5
2013 Press Pass Redline Magenta /15 #5
2013 Press Pass Redline Yellow /1 #5
2013 Press Pass Showcase /349 #2
2013 Press Pass Showcase Black /1 #2
2013 Press Pass Showcase Blue /25 #2
2013 Press Pass Showcase Gold /99 #2
2013 Press Pass Showcase Green /20 #2
2013 Press Pass Showcase Prized Pieces /99 #PPMTB
2013 Press Pass Showcase Prized Pieces Blue /20 #PPMTB
2013 Press Pass Showcase Prized Pieces Gold /25 #PPMTB
2013 Press Pass Showcase Prized Pieces Ink /49 #PPITB
2013 Press Pass Showcase Prized Pieces Ink Gold /25 #PPITB
2013 Press Pass Showcase Prized Pieces Ink Melting /1 #PPITB
2013 Press Pass Showcase Prized Pieces Melting /5 #PPMTB
2013 Press Pass Showcase Purple /13 #2
2013 Press Pass Showcase Red /10 #2
2013 Press Pass Showcase Series Standouts Gold /50 #1
2013 Press Pass Showcase Studio Showcase /299 #1
2013 Press Pass Showcase Studio Showcase Blue /40 #1
2013 Press Pass Showcase Studio Showcase Green /25 #1
2013 Press Pass Showcase Studio Showcase Ink /25 #SSITB
2013 Press Pass Showcase Studio Showcase Ink Gold /10 #SSITB
2013 Press Pass Showcase Studio Showcase Ink Melting /1 #SSITB
2013 Press Pass Showcase Studio Showcase Ink Red /5 #SSITB
2013 Press Pass Showcase Studio Showcase Melting /1 #1
2013 Press Pass Showcase Studio Showcase Purple /13 #1
2013 Press Pass Showcase Studio Showcase Red /10 #1
2013 Press Pass Signings Blue /1 #TB
2013 Press Pass Signings Gold /15 #TB
2013 Press Pass Signings Holofoil /10 #TB
2013 Press Pass Signings Printing Plates Black /1 #TB
2013 Press Pass Signings Printing Plates Cyan /1 #TB
2013 Press Pass Signings Printing Plates Magenta /1 #TB
2013 Press Pass Signings Printing Plates Yellow /1 #TB
2013 Press Pass Signings Silver /25 #TB
2013 Total Memorabilia #3
2013 Total Memorabilia Black and White /99 #3
2013 Total Memorabilia Dual Swatch Gold /199 #TMTB
2013 Total Memorabilia Gold /275 #3
2013 Total Memorabilia Red #3
2013 Total Memorabilia Single Swatch Silver /475 #TMTB
2014 Press Pass #45
2014 Press Pass American Thunder #40
2014 Press Pass American Thunder Autographs Blue /10 #ATATB
2014 Press Pass American Thunder Autographs Red /5 #ATATB
2014 Press Pass American Thunder Autographs White /25 #ATATB
2014 Press Pass American Thunder Black and White /50 #40
2014 Press Pass American Thunder Class A Uniforms Blue /99 #CAUTB
2014 Press Pass American Thunder Class A Uniforms Red /10 #CAUTB
2014 Press Pass American Thunder Class A Uniforms Silver #CAUTB
2014 Press Pass American Thunder Cyan #40
2014 Press Pass American Thunder Magenta #40
2014 Press Pass American Thunder Yellow /5 #40
2014 Press Pass Color Proofs Black /70 #45
2014 Press Pass Color Proofs Cyan /35 #45
2014 Press Pass Color Proofs Magenta #45
2014 Press Pass Color Proofs Yellow /5 #45
2014 Press Pass Gold #45
2014 Press Pass Redline #57
2014 Press Pass Redline Black /75 #57
2014 Press Pass Redline Blue Foil #57
2014 Press Pass Redline Cyan /50 #57
2014 Press Pass Redline Green National Convention /5 #57
2014 Press Pass Redline Magenta /10 #57
2014 Press Pass Redline Relic Autographs Blue /10 #RRSETB
2014 Press Pass Redline Relic Autographs Gold /15 #RRSETB
2014 Press Pass Redline Relic Autographs Melting /1 #RRSETB
2014 Press Pass Redline Relic Autographs Red /25 #RRSETB
2014 Press Pass Redline Relics Blue /25 #RRTB
2014 Press Pass Redline Relics Gold /50 #RRTB
2014 Press Pass Redline Relics Melting /1 #RRTB
2014 Press Pass Redline Relics Red /75 #RRTB
2014 Press Pass Redline Signatures Blue /10 #RSTB
2014 Press Pass Redline Signatures Gold /25 #RSTB
2014 Press Pass Redline Signatures Melting /1 #RSTB
2014 Press Pass Redline Signatures Red /50 #RSTB
2014 Press Pass Redline Yellow /1 #57
2014 Total Memorabilia #34
2014 Total Memorabilia Black and White /99 #34
2014 Total Memorabilia Dual Swatch Gold /150 #TMTB
2014 Total Memorabilia Gold /175 #34
2014 Total Memorabilia Quad Swatch Melting /25 #TMTB
2014 Total Memorabilia Red #34
2014 Total Memorabilia Single Swatch Silver /275 #TMTB
2014 Total Memorabilia Triple Swatch Blue /99 #TMTB
2015 Press Pass #41
2015 Press Pass Cup Chase #41
2015 Press Pass Cup Chase Blue /25 #41
2015 Press Pass Cup Chase Gold /75 #41
2015 Press Pass Cup Chase Green /10 #41
2015 Press Pass Cup Chase Melting /1 #41
2015 Press Pass Purple #41
2015 Press Pass Red #41
2015 Press Pass Signings Blue /99 #PPSTBA
2015 Press Pass Signings Gold #PPSTBA
2015 Press Pass Signings Green /25 #PPSTBA
2015 Press Pass Signings Melting /10 #PPSTBA
2015 Press Pass Signings Red /50 #PPSTBA
2016 Certified #17
2016 Certified Mirror Black /1 #17
2016 Certified Mirror Blue /50 #17
2016 Certified Mirror Gold /25 #17
2016 Certified Mirror Green /5 #17
2016 Certified Mirror Orange /99 #17
2016 Certified Mirror Purple /10 #17
2016 Certified Mirror Red /75 #17
2016 Certified Mirror Silver /99 #17
2016 Certified Signatures /299 #45
2016 Certified Signatures Mirror Black /1 #45
2016 Certified Signatures Mirror Blue /50 #45
2016 Certified Signatures Mirror Gold /25 #45
2016 Certified Signatures Mirror Green /5 #45
2016 Certified Signatures Mirror Orange /60 #45
2016 Certified Signatures Mirror Purple /10 #45
2016 Certified Signatures Mirror Red /75 #45
2016 Certified Signatures Mirror Silver /50 #45
2016 Certified Skills /199 #14
2016 Certified Skills Mirror Black /1 #14
2016 Certified Skills Mirror Blue /50 #14
2016 Certified Skills Mirror Gold /25 #14
2016 Certified Skills Mirror Green /5 #14
2016 Certified Skills Mirror Orange /99 #14
2016 Certified Skills Mirror Purple /10 #14
2016 Certified Skills Mirror Red /75 #14
2016 Certified Skills Mirror Silver /99 #14
2016 Certified Sprint Cup Swatches /299 #35
2016 Certified Sprint Cup Swatches Mirror Black /1 #35
2016 Certified Sprint Cup Swatches Mirror Blue /50 #35
2016 Certified Sprint Cup Swatches Mirror Gold /25 #35
2016 Certified Sprint Cup Swatches Mirror Green /5 #35
2016 Certified Sprint Cup Swatches Mirror Orange /199 #35
2016 Certified Sprint Cup Swatches Mirror Purple /10 #35
2016 Certified Sprint Cup Swatches Mirror Red /75 #35
2016 Certified Sprint Cup Swatches Mirror Silver /199 #35
2016 Panini National Treasures /25 #14
2016 Panini National Treasures Black /5 #14
2016 Panini National Treasures Blue /1 #14
2016 Panini National Treasures Dual Driver Materials /25 #5
2016 Panini National Treasures Dual Driver Materials Black /5 #5
2016 Panini National Treasures Dual Driver Materials Blue /1 #5
2016 Panini National Treasures Dual Driver Materials Gold /10 #5
2016 Panini National Treasures Dual Driver Materials Printing Plates Black /1 #5
2016 Panini National Treasures Dual Driver Materials Printing Plates Cyan /1 #5
2016 Panini National Treasures Dual Driver Materials Printing Plates Magenta /1 #5
2016 Panini National Treasures Dual Driver Materials Printing Plates Yellow /1 #5
2016 Panini National Treasures Dual Driver Materials Silver /15 #5
2016 Panini National Treasures Dual Signatures /15 #18
2016 Panini National Treasures Dual Signatures Black /5 #7
2016 Panini National Treasures Dual Signatures Black /5 #18
2016 Panini National Treasures Dual Signatures Blue /1 #7
2016 Panini National Treasures Dual Signatures Blue /1 #18
2016 Panini National Treasures Dual Signatures Gold /10 #18
2016 Panini National Treasures Gold /15 #14
2016 Panini National Treasures Printing Plates Black /1 #14
2016 Panini National Treasures Printing Plates Cyan /1 #14
2016 Panini National Treasures Printing Plates Magenta /1 #14
2016 Panini National Treasures Printing Plates Yellow /1 #14
2016 Panini National Treasures Quad Driver Materials /25 #3
2016 Panini National Treasures Quad Driver Materials /25 #7
2016 Panini National Treasures Quad Driver Materials /25 #9
2016 Panini National Treasures Quad Driver Materials Black /5 #3
2016 Panini National Treasures Quad Driver Materials Black /5 #7
2016 Panini National Treasures Quad Driver Materials Black /5 #9
2016 Panini National Treasures Quad Driver Materials Blue /1 #3
2016 Panini National Treasures Quad Driver Materials Blue /1 #7
2016 Panini National Treasures Quad Driver Materials Blue /1 #9
2016 Panini National Treasures Quad Driver Materials Gold /10 #3
2016 Panini National Treasures Quad Driver Materials Gold /10 #7
2016 Panini National Treasures Quad Driver Materials Gold /10 #9
2016 Panini National Treasures Quad Driver Materials Printing Plates Black /1 #3
2016 Panini National Treasures Quad Driver Materials Printing Plates Black /1 #7
2016 Panini National Treasures Quad Driver Materials Printing Plates Black /1 #9
2016 Panini National Treasures Quad Driver Materials Printing Plates Cyan /1 #3
2016 Panini National Treasures Quad Driver Materials Printing Plates Cyan /1 #7
2016 Panini National Treasures Quad Driver Materials Printing Plates Cyan /1 #9
2016 Panini National Treasures Quad Driver Materials Printing Plates Magenta /1 #3
2016 Panini National Treasures Quad Driver Materials Printing Plates Magenta /1 #7
2016 Panini National Treasures Quad Driver Materials Printing Plates Magenta /1 #9
2016 Panini National Treasures Quad Driver Materials Printing Plates Yellow /1 #3
2016 Panini National Treasures Quad Driver Materials Printing Plates Yellow /1 #7
2016 Panini National Treasures Quad Driver Materials Printing Plates Yellow /1 #9
2016 Panini National Treasures Quad Driver Materials Silver /15 #3
2016 Panini National Treasures Quad Driver Materials Silver /15 #7
2016 Panini National Treasures Quad Driver Materials Silver /15 #9
2016 Panini National Treasures Silver /20 #14
2016 Panini National Treasures Six Signatures /25 #2
2016 Panini National Treasures Six Signatures Black /10 #2
2016 Panini National Treasures Six Signatures Black /10 #7
2016 Panini National Treasures Six Signatures Blue /1 #2
2016 Panini National Treasures Six Signatures Blue /1 #7
2016 Panini National Treasures Six Signatures Gold /15 #2
2016 Panini National Treasures Trio Driver Materials /25 #7
2016 Panini National Treasures Trio Driver Materials /25 #13
2016 Panini National Treasures Trio Driver Materials Black /5 #7
2016 Panini National Treasures Trio Driver Materials Black /5 #13
2016 Panini National Treasures Trio Driver Materials Blue /1 #7
2016 Panini National Treasures Trio Driver Materials Blue /1 #13
2016 Panini National Treasures Trio Driver Materials Gold /10 #7
2016 Panini National Treasures Trio Driver Materials Gold /10 #13
2016 Panini National Treasures Trio Driver Materials Printing Plates Black /1 #7
2016 Panini National Treasures Trio Driver Materials Printing Plates Black /1 #13
2016 Panini National Treasures Trio Driver Materials Printing Plates Cyan /1 #7
2016 Panini National Treasures Trio Driver Materials Printing Plates Cyan /1 #13
2016 Panini National Treasures Trio Driver Materials Printing Plates Magenta /1 #7
2016 Panini National Treasures Trio Driver Materials Printing Plates Magenta /1 #13
2016 Panini National Treasures Trio Driver Materials Printing Plates Yellow /1 #7
2016 Panini National Treasures Trio Driver Materials Printing Plates Yellow /1 #13
2016 Panini National Treasures Trio Driver Materials Silver /15 #7
2016 Panini National Treasures Trio Driver Materials Silver /15 #13
2016 Panini Prizm #6A
2016 Panini Prizm Autographs Prizms #56
2016 Panini Prizm Autographs Prizms Black /3 #56
2016 Panini Prizm Autographs Prizms Blue Flag /75 #56
2016 Panini Prizm Autographs Prizms Camo /6 #56
2016 Panini Prizm Autographs Prizms Checkered Flag /1 #56
2016 Panini Prizm Autographs Prizms Gold /10 #56
2016 Panini Prizm Autographs Prizms Green Flag /99 #56
2016 Panini Prizm Autographs Prizms Rainbow /24 #56
2016 Panini Prizm Autographs Prizms Red Flag /50 #56
2016 Panini Prizm Autographs Prizms Red White and Blue /49 #56
2016 Panini Prizm Autographs Prizms White Flag /5 #56
2016 Panini Prizm Prizms #6A
2016 Panini Prizm Prizms Black /3 #6
2016 Panini Prizm Prizms Blue Flag /99 #6
2016 Panini Prizm Prizms Camo /6 #6
2016 Panini Prizm Prizms Checkered Flag /1 #6A
2016 Panini Prizm Prizms Gold /10 #6A
2016 Panini Prizm Prizms Green Flag /149 #6
2016 Panini Prizm Prizms Rainbow /24 #6
2016 Panini Prizm Prizms Red Flag /75 #6
2016 Panini Prizm Prizms Red White and Blue #6
2016 Panini Prizm Prizms White Flag /5 #6
2016 Panini Torque #23
2016 Panini Torque Artist Proof /50 #23
2016 Panini Torque Blackout /1 #23
2016 Panini Torque Blue /125 #23
2016 Panini Torque Dual Materials /149 #19
2016 Panini Torque Dual Materials Blue /99 #19
2016 Panini Torque Dual Materials Green /25 #19
2016 Panini Torque Dual Materials Purple /10 #19
2016 Panini Torque Dual Materials Red /49 #19
2016 Panini Torque Gold #23
2016 Panini Torque Holo Gold /5 #23
2016 Panini Torque Holo Silver /10 #23
2016 Panini Torque Jumbo Firesuit Autographs /30 #17
2016 Panini Torque Jumbo Firesuit Autographs Blue /20 #17
2016 Panini Torque Jumbo Firesuit Autographs Green /10 #17
2016 Panini Torque Jumbo Firesuit Autographs Purple /5 #17
2016 Panini Torque Jumbo Firesuit Autographs Red /15 #17
2016 Panini Torque Jumbo Tire Autographs /35 #14
2016 Panini Torque Jumbo Tire Autographs Blue /20 #14
2016 Panini Torque Jumbo Tire Autographs Green /10 #14
2016 Panini Torque Jumbo Tire Autographs Purple /5 #14
2016 Panini Torque Jumbo Tire Autographs Red /15 #14
2016 Panini Torque Metal Materials /249 #20
2016 Panini Torque Metal Materials Blue /99 #20
2016 Panini Torque Metal Materials Green /25 #20
2016 Panini Torque Metal Materials Purple /10 #20
2016 Panini Torque Metal Materials Red /49 #20
2016 Panini Torque Pairings Materials /249 #21
2016 Panini Torque Pairings Materials /125 #22
2016 Panini Torque Pairings Materials Blue /99 #21
2016 Panini Torque Pairings Materials Blue /99 #22
2016 Panini Torque Pairings Materials Green /25 #21
2016 Panini Torque Pairings Materials Green /25 #22
2016 Panini Torque Pairings Materials Purple /10 #21
2016 Panini Torque Pairings Materials Purple /10 #22
2016 Panini Torque Pairings Materials Red /49 #21
2016 Panini Torque Pairings Materials Red /49 #22
2016 Panini Torque Pole Position #18
2016 Panini Torque Pole Position Blue /99 #18
2016 Panini Torque Pole Position Checkerboard /10 #18
2016 Panini Torque Pole Position Green /25 #18
2016 Panini Torque Pole Position Red /49 #18
2016 Panini Torque Printing Plates Black /1 #23
2016 Panini Torque Printing Plates Cyan /1 #23
2016 Panini Torque Printing Plates Magenta /1 #23
2016 Panini Torque Printing Plates Yellow /1 #23
2016 Panini Torque Purple /25 #23
2016 Panini Torque Red /99 #23
2016 Panini Torque Silhouettes Firesuit Autographs /35 #24
2016 Panini Torque Silhouettes Firesuit Autographs Blue /20 #24
2016 Panini Torque Silhouettes Firesuit Autographs Green /10 #24
2016 Panini Torque Silhouettes Firesuit Autographs Purple /5 #24
2016 Panini Torque Silhouettes Firesuit Autographs Red /15 #24
2016 Panini Torque Test Proof Black /1 #23
2016 Panini Torque Test Proof Cyan /1 #23
2016 Panini Torque Test Proof Magenta /1 #23
2016 Panini Torque Test Proof Yellow /1 #23
2016 Panini Torque Winning Vision #22
2016 Panini Torque Winning Vision Blue /99 #22

2016 Panini Torque Winning Vision Gold /149 #22
2016 Panini Torque Winning Vision Green /25 #22
2016 Panini Torque Winning Vision Purple /10 #22
2016 Panini Torque Winning Vision Red /49 #22
2017 Donruss #18
2017 Donruss #54
2017 Donruss #108
2017 Donruss Artist Proof /25 #18
2017 Donruss Artist Proof /25 #54
2017 Donruss Artist Proof /25 #108
2017 Donruss Blue Foil /299 #18
2017 Donruss Blue Foil /299 #54
2017 Donruss Blue Foil /299 #108
2017 Donruss Dual Rubber Relics Holo Black /1 #15
2017 Donruss Gold Foil /499 #18
2017 Donruss Gold Foil /499 #54
2017 Donruss Gold Foil /499 #108
2017 Donruss Gold Press Proof /99 #18
2017 Donruss Gold Press Proof /99 #54
2017 Donruss Gold Press Proof /99 #108
2017 Donruss Green Foil /199 #18
2017 Donruss Green Foil /199 #54
2017 Donruss Green Foil /199 #108
2017 Donruss Press Proof /49 #18
2017 Donruss Press Proof /49 #54
2017 Donruss Press Proof /49 #108
2017 Donruss Printing Plates Black /1 #18
2017 Donruss Printing Plates Black /1 #54
2017 Donruss Printing Plates Black /1 #108
2017 Donruss Printing Plates Cyan /1 #18
2017 Donruss Printing Plates Cyan /1 #54
2017 Donruss Printing Plates Cyan /1 #108
2017 Donruss Printing Plates Magenta /1 #18
2017 Donruss Printing Plates Magenta /1 #54
2017 Donruss Printing Plates Magenta /1 #108
2017 Donruss Printing Plates Yellow /1 #18
2017 Donruss Printing Plates Yellow /1 #54
2017 Donruss Printing Plates Yellow /1 #108
2017 Donruss Retro Relics 1984 #35
2017 Donruss Retro Relics 1984 Holo Black /10 #35
2017 Donruss Retro Relics 1984 Holo Gold /99 #35
2017 Donruss Rubber Relics #43
2017 Donruss Rubber Relics Holo Black /1 #43
2017 Donruss Rubber Relics Holo Gold /25 #43
2017 Donruss Speed #9
2017 Donruss Speed Cracked Ice /999 #9
2017 Donruss Studio Signatures Holo Black /1 #14
2017 Panini National Treasures Associate Sponsor Patch Signatures 1 /1 #25
2017 Panini National Treasures Associate Sponsor Patch Signatures 10 /1 #25
2017 Panini National Treasures Associate Sponsor Patch Signatures 11 /1 #25
2017 Panini National Treasures Associate Sponsor Patch Signatures 12 /1 #25
2017 Panini National Treasures Associate Sponsor Patch Signatures 13 /1 #25
2017 Panini National Treasures Associate Sponsor Patch Signatures 14 /1 #25
2017 Panini National Treasures Associate Sponsor Patch Signatures 2 /1 #25
2017 Panini National Treasures Associate Sponsor Patch Signatures 3 /1 #25
2017 Panini National Treasures Associate Sponsor Patch Signatures 4 /1 #25
2017 Panini National Treasures Associate Sponsor Patch Signatures 5 /1 #25
2017 Panini National Treasures Associate Sponsor Patch Signatures 6 /1 #25
2017 Panini National Treasures Associate Sponsor Patch Signatures 7 /1 #25
2017 Panini National Treasures Associate Sponsor Patch Signatures 8 /1 #25
2017 Panini National Treasures Associate Sponsor Patch Signatures 9 /1 #25
2017 Panini National Treasures Car Manufacturer Patch Signatures /1 #25
2017 Panini National Treasures Dual Firesuit Materials Black /1 #16
2017 Panini National Treasures Dual Firesuit Materials Green /5 #16
2017 Panini National Treasures Dual Firesuit Materials Laundry Tag /1 #16
2017 Panini National Treasures Dual Firesuit Materials Printing Plates Black /1 #16
2017 Panini National Treasures Dual Firesuit Materials Printing Plates Cyan /1 #16
2017 Panini National Treasures Dual Firesuit Materials Printing Plates Magenta /1 #16
2017 Panini National Treasures Dual Firesuit Materials Printing Plates Yellow /1 #16
2017 Panini National Treasures Dual Firesuit Signatures /25 #16
2017 Panini National Treasures Dual Firesuit Signatures Black /1 #16
2017 Panini National Treasures Dual Firesuit Signatures Gold /15 #16
2017 Panini National Treasures Dual Firesuit Signatures Green /5 #16
2017 Panini National Treasures Dual Firesuit Signatures Holo Gold /10 #16
2017 Panini National Treasures Dual Firesuit Signatures Holo Silver /20 #16
2017 Panini National Treasures Dual Firesuit Signatures Laundry Tag /1 #16
2017 Panini National Treasures Dual Firesuit Signatures Printing Plates Black /1 #16
2017 Panini National Treasures Dual Firesuit Signatures Printing Plates Cyan /1 #16
2017 Panini National Treasures Dual Firesuit Signatures Printing Plates Magenta /1 #16
2017 Panini National Treasures Dual Firesuit Signatures Printing Plates Yellow /1 #16
2017 Panini National Treasures Firesuit Manufacturer Patch Signatures /1 #25
2017 Panini National Treasures Goodyear Patch Signatures /2 #25
2017 Panini National Treasures Jumbo Firesuit Materials Black /1 #9
2017 Panini National Treasures Jumbo Firesuit Materials Green /5 #9
2017 Panini National Treasures Jumbo Firesuit Materials Laundry Tag /1 #9
2017 Panini National Treasures Jumbo Firesuit Materials Printing Plates Black /1 #9
2017 Panini National Treasures Jumbo Firesuit Materials Printing Plates Cyan /1 #9
2017 Panini National Treasures Jumbo Firesuit Materials Printing Plates Magenta /1 #9
2017 Panini National Treasures Jumbo Firesuit Materials Printing Plates Yellow /1 #9
2017 Panini National Treasures Nameplate Patch Signatures /2 #25
2017 Panini National Treasures NASCAR Patch Signatures /1 #25
2017 Panini National Treasures Series Sponsor Patch Signatures /1 #25
2017 Panini National Treasures Six Way Swatches Black /1 #1
2017 Panini National Treasures Six Way Swatches Green /5 #1
2017 Panini National Treasures Six Way Swatches Laundry Tag /1 #1
2017 Panini National Treasures Six Way Swatches Printing Plates Black /1 #1
2017 Panini National Treasures Six Way Swatches Printing Plates Cyan /1 #1
2017 Panini National Treasures Six Way Swatches Printing Plates Magenta /1 #1
2017 Panini National Treasures Six Way Swatches Printing Plates Yellow /1 #1
2017 Panini National Treasures Sunoco Patch Signatures /1 #25
2017 Panini National Treasures Teammates Dual Materials /25 #10
2017 Panini National Treasures Teammates Dual Materials Black /1 #10
2017 Panini National Treasures Teammates Dual Materials Gold /15 #10
2017 Panini National Treasures Teammates Dual Materials Green /5 #10
2017 Panini National Treasures Teammates Dual Materials Holo Gold /10 #10
2017 Panini National Treasures Teammates Dual Materials Holo Silver /20 #10
2017 Panini National Treasures Teammates Dual Materials Laundry Tag /1 #10
2017 Panini National Treasures Teammates Dual Materials Printing Plates Black /1 #10
2017 Panini National Treasures Teammates Dual Materials Printing Plates Cyan /1 #10
2017 Panini National Treasures Teammates Dual Materials Printing Plates Magenta /1 #10
2017 Panini National Treasures Teammates Dual Materials Printing Plates Yellow /1 #10
2017 Panini National Treasures Three Wide Black /1 #12
2017 Panini National Treasures Three Wide Green /5 #12
2017 Panini National Treasures Three Wide Laundry Tag /1 #12
2017 Panini National Treasures Three Wide Printing Plates Black /1 #12
2017 Panini National Treasures Three Wide Printing Plates Cyan /1 #12
2017 Panini National Treasures Three Wide Printing Plates Magenta /1 #12
2017 Panini National Treasures Three Wide Printing Plates Yellow /1 #12
2017 Panini Torque #5
2017 Panini Torque #62
2017 Panini Torque Artist Proof /75 #5
2017 Panini Torque Artist Proof /75 #62
2017 Panini Torque Blackout /1 #5
2017 Panini Torque Blackout /1 #62
2017 Panini Torque Blue /150 #5
2017 Panini Torque Blue /150 #62
2017 Panini Torque Clear Vision #31
2017 Panini Torque Clear Vision Blue /99 #31
2017 Panini Torque Clear Vision Gold /149 #31
2017 Panini Torque Clear Vision Green /25 #31
2017 Panini Torque Clear Vision Purple /10 #31
2017 Panini Torque Clear Vision Red /49 #31
2017 Panini Torque Dual Materials /499 #20
2017 Panini Torque Dual Materials Blue /99 #20
2017 Panini Torque Dual Materials Green /25 #20
2017 Panini Torque Dual Materials Purple /10 #20
2017 Panini Torque Dual Materials Red /49 #20
2017 Panini Torque Gold #5
2017 Panini Torque Gold #62
2017 Panini Torque Holo Gold /10 #5
2017 Panini Torque Holo Gold /10 #62
2017 Panini Torque Holo Silver /25 #5
2017 Panini Torque Holo Silver /25 #62
2017 Panini Torque Horsepower Heroes #6
2017 Panini Torque Horsepower Heroes Gold /199 #6
2017 Panini Torque Horsepower Heroes Holo Silver /99 #6
2017 Panini Torque Jumbo Tire Signatures /51 #18
2017 Panini Torque Jumbo Tire Signatures Blue /49 #18
2017 Panini Torque Jumbo Tire Signatures Green /15 #18
2017 Panini Torque Jumbo Tire Signatures Purple /10 #18
2017 Panini Torque Jumbo Tire Signatures Red /25 #18
2017 Panini Torque Pairings Materials /199 #8
2017 Panini Torque Pairings Materials Blue /99 #8
2017 Panini Torque Pairings Materials Green /25 #8
2017 Panini Torque Pairings Materials Purple /10 #8
2017 Panini Torque Pairings Materials Red /49 #8
2017 Panini Torque Printing Plates Black /1 #5
2017 Panini Torque Printing Plates Black /1 #62
2017 Panini Torque Printing Plates Cyan /1 #5
2017 Panini Torque Printing Plates Cyan /1 #62
2017 Panini Torque Printing Plates Magenta /1 #5
2017 Panini Torque Printing Plates Magenta /1 #62
2017 Panini Torque Printing Plates Yellow /1 #5
2017 Panini Torque Printing Plates Yellow /1 #62
2017 Panini Torque Purple /50 #5
2017 Panini Torque Purple /50 #62
2017 Panini Torque Red /100 #5
2017 Panini Torque Red /100 #62
2017 Panini Torque Silhouettes Firesuit Signatures /51 #8
2017 Panini Torque Silhouettes Firesuit Signatures Blue /49 #8
2017 Panini Torque Silhouettes Firesuit Signatures Green /15 #8
2017 Panini Torque Silhouettes Firesuit Signatures Purple /10 #8
2017 Panini Torque Silhouettes Firesuit Signatures Red /25 #8
2017 Panini Torque Superstar Vision #15
2017 Panini Torque Superstar Vision Blue /99 #15
2017 Panini Torque Superstar Vision Gold /149 #15
2017 Panini Torque Superstar Vision Green /25 #15
2017 Panini Torque Superstar Vision Purple /10 #15
2017 Panini Torque Superstar Vision Red /49 #15
2017 Panini Torque Test Proof Black /1 #5
2017 Panini Torque Test Proof Black /1 #62
2017 Panini Torque Test Proof Cyan /1 #5
2017 Panini Torque Test Proof Cyan /1 #62
2017 Panini Torque Test Proof Magenta /1 #5
2017 Panini Torque Test Proof Magenta /1 #62
2017 Panini Torque Test Proof Yellow /1 #5
2017 Panini Torque Test Proof Yellow /1 #62
2017 Select #19
2017 Select #20
2017 Select #101
2017 Select Prizms Black /3 #19
2017 Select Prizms Black /3 #20
2017 Select Prizms Black /3 #101
2017 Select Prizms Blue /199 #19
2017 Select Prizms Blue /199 #20
2017 Select Prizms Checkered Flag /1 #19
2017 Select Prizms Checkered Flag /1 #20
2017 Select Prizms Checkered Flag /1 #101
2017 Select Prizms Gold /10 #19
2017 Select Prizms Gold /10 #20
2017 Select Prizms Gold /10 #101
2017 Select Prizms Purple Pulsar #19
2017 Select Prizms Purple Pulsar #20
2017 Select Prizms Red /99 #19
2017 Select Prizms Red /99 #20
2017 Select Prizms Red White and Blue Pulsar /299 #19
2017 Select Prizms Red White and Blue Pulsar /299 #20
2017 Select Prizms Silver #19
2017 Select Prizms Silver #20
2017 Select Prizms Tie Dye /24 #19
2017 Select Prizms Tie Dye /24 #20
2017 Select Prizms Tie Dye /24 #101
2017 Select Prizms White /50 #19
2017 Select Prizms White /50 #20
2017 Select Prizms White /50 #101
2017 Select Select Pairs Materials #19
2017 Select Select Pairs Materials Prizms Blue /199 #19
2017 Select Select Pairs Materials Prizms Checkered Flag /1 #19
2017 Select Select Pairs Materials Prizms Gold /10 #19
2017 Select Select Pairs Materials Prizms Red /99 #19
2017 Select Select Stars #18
2017 Select Select Stars Prizms Black /3 #18
2017 Select Select Stars Prizms Checkered Flag /1 #18
2017 Select Select Stars Prizms Gold /10 #18
2017 Select Select Stars Prizms Tie Dye /24 #18
2017 Select Select Stars Prizms White /50 #18
2017 Select Select Swatches #42
2017 Select Select Swatches Prizms Blue /50 #42
2017 Select Select Swatches Prizms Checkered Flag /1 #42
2017 Select Select Swatches Prizms Gold /10 #42
2017 Select Select Swatches Prizms Red /25 #42
2017 Select Sheet Metal #24
2017 Select Sheet Metal Prizms Blue /199 #24
2017 Select Sheet Metal Prizms Checkered Flag /1 #24
2017 Select Sheet Metal Prizms Gold /10 #24
2017 Select Sheet Metal Prizms Red /99 #24
2017 Select Signature Paint Schemes #20
2017 Select Signature Paint Schemes Prizms Blue /50 #20
2017 Select Signature Paint Schemes Prizms Checkered Flag /1 #20
2017 Select Signature Paint Schemes Prizms Gold /10 #20
2017 Select Signature Paint Schemes Prizms Red /25 #20
2017 Select Signature Swatches #42
2017 Select Signature Swatches Prizms Checkered Flag /1 #42
2017 Select Signature Swatches Prizms Gold /10 #42
2017 Select Signature Swatches Prizms Tie Dye /24 #42
2017 Select Signature Swatches Prizms White /50 #42
2017 Select Signature Swatches Triple #25
2017 Select Signature Swatches Triple Prizms Checkered Flag /1 #25
2017 Select Signature Swatches Triple Prizms Gold /10 #25
2017 Select Signature Swatches Triple Prizms Tie Dye /24 #25
2017 Select Signature Swatches Triple Prizms White /50 #25
2017 Select Speed Merchants #14
2017 Select Speed Merchants Prizms Black /3 #14
2017 Select Speed Merchants Prizms Checkered Flag /1 #14
2017 Select Speed Merchants Prizms Gold /10 #14
2017 Select Speed Merchants Prizms Tie Dye /24 #14
2017 Select Speed Merchants Prizms White /50 #14
2018 Certified #39
2018 Certified All Certified Team /199 #13
2018 Certified All Certified Team Black /1 #13
2018 Certified All Certified Team Blue /99 #13
2018 Certified All Certified Team Gold /49 #13
2018 Certified All Certified Team Green /10 #13
2018 Certified All Certified Team Mirror Black /1 #13
2018 Certified All Certified Team Mirror Gold /25 #13
2018 Certified All Certified Team Mirror Green /5 #13
2018 Certified All Certified Team Mirror Purple /10 #13
2018 Certified All Certified Team Purple /25 #13
2018 Certified All Certified Team Red /149 #13
2018 Certified Black /1 #39
2018 Certified Blue /99 #39
2018 Certified Cup Swatches /499 #25
2018 Certified Cup Swatches Black /1 #25
2018 Certified Cup Swatches Blue /49 #25
2018 Certified Cup Swatches Gold /25 #25
2018 Certified Cup Swatches Green /5 #25
2018 Certified Cup Swatches Purple /10 #25
2018 Certified Cup Swatches Red /199 #25
2018 Certified Epix /199 #14
2018 Certified Epix Black /1 #14
2018 Certified Epix Blue /99 #14
2018 Certified Epix Gold /49 #14
2018 Certified Epix Green /10 #14
2018 Certified Epix Mirror Black /1 #14
2018 Certified Epix Mirror Gold /25 #14
2018 Certified Epix Mirror Green /5 #14
2018 Certified Epix Mirror Purple /10 #14
2018 Certified Epix Purple /25 #14
2018 Certified Epix Red /149 #14
2018 Certified Gold /49 #39
2018 Certified Green /10 #39
2018 Certified Mirror Black /1 #39
2018 Certified Mirror Gold /25 #39
2018 Certified Mirror Green /5 #39
2018 Certified Mirror Purple /10 #39
2018 Certified Orange /249 #39
2018 Certified Piece of the Race /499 #18
2018 Certified Piece of the Race Black /1 #18
2018 Certified Piece of the Race Blue /49 #18
2018 Certified Piece of the Race Gold /25 #18
2018 Certified Piece of the Race Green /5 #18
2018 Certified Piece of the Race Purple /10 #18
2018 Certified Piece of the Race Red /199 #18
2018 Certified Purple /25 #39
2018 Certified Red /199 #39
2018 Certified Signature Swatches /99 #19
2018 Certified Signature Swatches Black /1 #19
2018 Certified Signature Swatches Blue /49 #19
2018 Certified Signature Swatches Gold /25 #19
2018 Certified Signature Swatches Green /5 #19
2018 Certified Signature Swatches Purple /10 #19
2018 Certified Signature Swatches Red /75 #19
2018 Certified Signing Sessions /49 #26
2018 Certified Signing Sessions Black /1 #26
2018 Certified Signing Sessions Blue /20 #26
2018 Certified Signing Sessions Gold /15 #26
2018 Certified Signing Sessions Green /5 #26
2018 Certified Signing Sessions Purple /10 #26
2018 Certified Signing Sessions Red /25 #26
2018 Certified Stars /199 #5
2018 Certified Stars Black /1 #5
2018 Certified Stars Blue /99 #5
2018 Certified Stars Gold /49 #5
2018 Certified Stars Green /10 #5
2018 Certified Stars Mirror Black /1 #5
2018 Certified Stars Mirror Gold /25 #5
2018 Certified Stars Mirror Green /5 #5
2018 Certified Stars Mirror Purple /10 #5
2018 Certified Stars Purple /25 #5
2018 Certified Stars Red /149 #5
2018 Donruss #9
2018 Donruss #36
2018 Donruss #126
2018 Donruss Artist Proofs /25 #9
2018 Donruss Artist Proofs /25 #36
2018 Donruss Artist Proofs /25 #126
2018 Donruss Gold Foil /499 #9
2018 Donruss Gold Foil /499 #36
2018 Donruss Gold Foil /499 #126
2018 Donruss Gold Press Proofs /99 #9
2018 Donruss Gold Press Proofs /99 #36
2018 Donruss Gold Press Proofs /99 #126
2018 Donruss Green Foil /199 #9
2018 Donruss Green Foil /199 #36
2018 Donruss Green Foil /199 #126
2018 Donruss Press Proofs /49 #9
2018 Donruss Press Proofs /49 #36
2018 Donruss Press Proofs /49 #126
2018 Donruss Printing Plates Black /1 #9
2018 Donruss Printing Plates Black /1 #36
2018 Donruss Printing Plates Black /1 #126
2018 Donruss Printing Plates Cyan /1 #9
2018 Donruss Printing Plates Cyan /1 #36
2018 Donruss Printing Plates Cyan /1 #126
2018 Donruss Printing Plates Magenta /1 #9
2018 Donruss Printing Plates Magenta /1 #36
2018 Donruss Printing Plates Magenta /1 #126
2018 Donruss Printing Plates Yellow /1 #9
2018 Donruss Printing Plates Yellow /1 #36
2018 Donruss Printing Plates Yellow /1 #126
2018 Donruss Racing Relics #18
2018 Donruss Racing Relics Black /10 #18
2018 Donruss Racing Relics Holo Gold /99 #18
2018 Donruss Red Foil /299 #9
2018 Donruss Red Foil /299 #36
2018 Donruss Red Foil /299 #126
2018 Donruss Retro Relics '85 #16
2018 Donruss Retro Relics '85 Black /10 #16
2018 Donruss Retro Relics '85 Holo Gold /99 #16
2018 Donruss Retro Signatures '85 Black /1 #19
2018 Donruss Rubber Relics #38
2018 Donruss Rubber Relics Black /10 #38
2018 Donruss Rubber Relics Holo Gold /99 #38
2018 Donruss Studio #7
2018 Donruss Studio Cracked Ice /999 #7
2018 Donruss Studio Xplosion /99 #7
2018 Panini Prime /50 #23
2018 Panini Prime /50 #56
2018 Panini Prime /50 #89
2018 Panini Prime Black /1 #23
2018 Panini Prime Black /1 #56
2018 Panini Prime Black /1 #89
2018 Panini Prime Clear Silhouettes /99 #27
2018 Panini Prime Clear Silhouettes Black /1 #27
2018 Panini Prime Clear Silhouettes Holo Gold /50 #27
2018 Panini Prime Dual Material Autographs /10 #23
2018 Panini Prime Dual Material Autographs Black /1 #23
2018 Panini Prime Dual Material Autographs Holo Gold /5 #23
2018 Panini Prime Dual Material Autographs Laundry Tag /1 #23
2018 Panini Prime Dual Signatures /25 #14
2018 Panini Prime Dual Signatures Black /1 #14
2018 Panini Prime Dual Signatures Holo Gold /10 #14
2018 Panini Prime Holo Gold /25 #23
2018 Panini Prime Holo Gold /25 #56
2018 Panini Prime Holo Gold /25 #89
2018 Panini Prime Prime Jumbo Associate Sponsor 1 /1 #73
2018 Panini Prime Prime Jumbo Associate Sponsor 1 /1 #74
2018 Panini Prime Prime Jumbo Associate Sponsor 10 /1 #73
2018 Panini Prime Prime Jumbo Associate Sponsor 11 /1 #73
2018 Panini Prime Prime Jumbo Associate Sponsor 12 /1 #73
2018 Panini Prime Prime Jumbo Associate Sponsor 2 /1 #73
2018 Panini Prime Prime Jumbo Associate Sponsor 2 /1 #74
2018 Panini Prime Prime Jumbo Associate Sponsor 3 /1 #73
2018 Panini Prime Prime Jumbo Associate Sponsor 3 /1 #74
2018 Panini Prime Prime Jumbo Associate Sponsor 4 /1 #73
2018 Panini Prime Prime Jumbo Associate Sponsor 4 /1 #74
2018 Panini Prime Prime Jumbo Associate Sponsor 5 /1 #73
2018 Panini Prime Prime Jumbo Associate Sponsor 5 /1 #74
2018 Panini Prime Prime Jumbo Associate Sponsor 6 /1 #73
2018 Panini Prime Prime Jumbo Associate Sponsor 6 /1 #74
2018 Panini Prime Prime Jumbo Associate Sponsor 7 /1 #73
2018 Panini Prime Prime Jumbo Associate Sponsor 7 /1 #74
2018 Panini Prime Prime Jumbo Associate Sponsor 8 /1 #73
2018 Panini Prime Prime Jumbo Associate Sponsor 8 /1 #74
2018 Panini Prime Prime Jumbo Associate Sponsor 9 /1 #73
2018 Panini Prime Prime Jumbo Car Manufacturer /1 #73
2018 Panini Prime Prime Jumbo Car Manufacturer /1 #74
2018 Panini Prime Prime Jumbo Firesuit Manufacturer /1 #73
2018 Panini Prime Prime Jumbo Firesuit Manufacturer /1 #74
2018 Panini Prime Prime Jumbo Glove Manufacturer Patch /1 #73
2018 Panini Prime Prime Jumbo Glove Manufacturer Patch /1 #74
2018 Panini Prime Prime Jumbo Glove Name Patch /1 #73
2018 Panini Prime Prime Jumbo Glove Name Patch /1 #74
2018 Panini Prime Prime Jumbo Glove Number Patch /1 #73
2018 Panini Prime Prime Jumbo Glove Number Patch /1 #74
2018 Panini Prime Prime Jumbo Goodyear /2 #74
2018 Panini Prime Prime Jumbo Nameplate /2 #73
2018 Panini Prime Prime Jumbo Nameplate /2 #74
2018 Panini Prime Prime Jumbo NASCAR /1 #73
2018 Panini Prime Prime Jumbo NASCAR /1 #74
2018 Panini Prime Prime Jumbo Prime Colors /15 #74
2018 Panini Prime Prime Jumbo Series Sponsor /1 #73
2018 Panini Prime Prime Jumbo Series Sponsor /1 #74
2018 Panini Prime Prime Jumbo Shoe Brand Logo /1 #73
2018 Panini Prime Prime Jumbo Shoe Brand Logo /1 #74
2018 Panini Prime Prime Jumbo Shoe Name Patch /1 #73
2018 Panini Prime Prime Jumbo Shoe Name Patch /1 #74
2018 Panini Prime Prime Jumbo Sunoco /1 #73
2018 Panini Prime Prime Jumbo Sunoco /1 #74
2018 Panini Prime Prime Number Signatures /25 #18
2018 Panini Prime Prime Number Signatures Black /1 #18
2018 Panini Prime Prime Number Signatures Holo Gold /10 #18
2018 Panini Prime Quad Material Autographs /37 #23
2018 Panini Prime Quad Material Autographs Black /1 #23
2018 Panini Prime Quad Material Autographs Holo Gold /15 #23
2018 Panini Prime Quad Material Autographs Laundry Tag /1 #23
2018 Panini Prime Race Used Duals Firesuit Black /1 #29
2018 Panini Prime Race Used Duals Firesuit Holo Gold /25 #29
2018 Panini Prime Race Used Duals Firesuit Laundry Tag /1 #29
2018 Panini Prime Race Used Duals Sheet Metal /50 #29
2018 Panini Prime Race Used Duals Sheet Metal Black /1 #29
2018 Panini Prime Race Used Duals Sheet Metal Holo Gold /25 #29
2018 Panini Prime Race Used Duals Tire /50 #29
2018 Panini Prime Race Used Duals Tire Black /1 #29
2018 Panini Prime Race Used Duals Tire Holo Gold /25 #29
2018 Panini Prime Race Used Firesuits Black /1 #38
2018 Panini Prime Race Used Firesuits Holo Gold /25 #38
2018 Panini Prime Race Used Firesuits Laundry Tag /1 #38
2018 Panini Prime Race Used Sheet Metal /50 #38
2018 Panini Prime Race Used Sheet Metal Black /1 #38
2018 Panini Prime Race Used Sheet Metal Holo Gold /25 #38
2018 Panini Prime Race Used Tires Black /1 #38
2018 Panini Prime Race Used Tires Holo Gold /25 #38
2018 Panini Prime Signature Tires /10 #18
2018 Panini Prime Signature Tires Black /1 #18
2018 Panini Prime Signature Tires Holo Gold /5 #18
2018 Panini Prime Triple Material Autographs /25 #25
2018 Panini Prime Triple Material Autographs Black /1 #25
2018 Panini Prime Triple Material Autographs Holo Gold /10 #25
2018 Panini Prime Triple Material Autographs Laundry Tag /1 #25
2018 Panini Prizm #4
2018 Panini Prizm Fireworks #17
2018 Panini Prizm Fireworks Prizms #17
2018 Panini Prizm Fireworks Prizms Black /1 #17
2018 Panini Prizm Fireworks Prizms Gold /10 #17
2018 Panini Prizm Instant Impact #15
2018 Panini Prizm Instant Impact Prizms #15
2018 Panini Prizm Instant Impact Prizms Black /1 #15
2018 Panini Prizm Instant Impact Prizms Gold /10 #15
2018 Panini Prizm Prizms #4
2018 Panini Prizm Prizms Black /1 #4
2018 Panini Prizm Prizms Blue /99 #4
2018 Panini Prizm Prizms Camo #4
2018 Panini Prizm Prizms Gold /10 #4
2018 Panini Prizm Prizms Green /149 #4
2018 Panini Prizm Prizms Purple Flash #4
2018 Panini Prizm Prizms Rainbow /24 #4
2018 Panini Prizm Prizms Red /75 #4
2018 Panini Prizm Prizms Red White and Blue #4
2018 Panini Prizm Prizms White /5 #4
2018 Panini Prizm Scripted Signatures Prizms #6
2018 Panini Prizm Scripted Signatures Prizms Black /1 #6
2018 Panini Prizm Scripted Signatures Prizms Blue /75 #6
2018 Panini Prizm Scripted Signatures Prizms Camo #6
2018 Panini Prizm Scripted Signatures Prizms Gold /10 #6
2018 Panini Prizm Scripted Signatures Prizms Green /99 #6
2018 Panini Prizm Scripted Signatures Prizms Rainbow /24 #6
2018 Panini Prizm Scripted Signatures Prizms Red /50 #6
2018 Panini Prizm Scripted Signatures Prizms Red White and Blue /125 #6
2018 Panini Prizm Scripted Signatures Prizms White /5 #6
2018 Panini Prizm Team Tandems #8
2018 Panini Prizm Team Tandems Prizms #8
2018 Panini Prizm Team Tandems Prizms Black /1 #8
2018 Panini Prizm Team Tandems Prizms Gold /10 #8
2018 Panini Victory Lane #5
2018 Panini Victory Lane Black /1 #5
2018 Panini Victory Lane Blue /25 #5
2018 Panini Victory Lane Engineered to Perfection Materials Black /25 #24
2018 Panini Victory Lane Engineered to Perfection Materials Gold /199 #24
2018 Panini Victory Lane Engineered to Perfection Materials Green /99 #24
2018 Panini Victory Lane Engineered to Perfection Materials Laundry Tag /1 #24
2018 Panini Victory Lane Gold /99 #5
2018 Panini Victory Lane Green /5 #5
2018 Panini Victory Lane Octane Autographs /125 #37
2018 Panini Victory Lane Octane Autographs Black /1 #37
2018 Panini Victory Lane Octane Autographs Gold /99 #37
2018 Panini Victory Lane Pedal to the Metal #48
2018 Panini Victory Lane Pedal to the Metal #55
2018 Panini Victory Lane Pedal to the Metal Black /1 #48
2018 Panini Victory Lane Pedal to the Metal Black /1 #55
2018 Panini Victory Lane Pedal to the Metal Blue /25 #48
2018 Panini Victory Lane Pedal to the Metal Blue /25 #55
2018 Panini Victory Lane Pedal to the Metal Green /5 #48
2018 Panini Victory Lane Pedal to the Metal Green /5 #55
2018 Panini Victory Lane Printing Plates Black /1 #5
2018 Panini Victory Lane Printing Plates Cyan /1 #5
2018 Panini Victory Lane Printing Plates Magenta /1 #5
2018 Panini Victory Lane Printing Plates Yellow /1 #5
2018 Panini Victory Lane Red /49 #5
2018 Panini Victory Lane Signatures /125 #40
2018 Panini Victory Lane Signatures Black /1 #40
2018 Panini Victory Lane Signatures Gold /99 #40
2018 Panini Victory Lane Silver #5
2018 Panini Victory Lane Starting Grid #5
2018 Panini Victory Lane Starting Grid Black /1 #5
2018 Panini Victory Lane Starting Grid Blue /25 #5
2018 Panini Victory Lane Starting Grid Gold /99 #5
2018 Panini Victory Lane Starting Grid Green /5 #5
2018 Panini Victory Lane Starting Grid Printing Plates Black /1 #5
2018 Panini Victory Lane Starting Grid Printing Plates Cyan /1 #5
2018 Panini Victory Lane Starting Grid Printing Plates Magenta /1 #5
2018 Panini Victory Lane Starting Grid Printing Plates Yellow /1 #5
2018 Panini Victory Lane Starting Grid Red /49 #5
2019 Donruss #32
2019 Donruss #135
2019 Donruss Artist Proofs /25 #32
2019 Donruss Artist Proofs /25 #135
2019 Donruss Black /199 #32
2019 Donruss Black /199 #135
2019 Donruss Gold /299 #32
2019 Donruss Gold /299 #135
2019 Donruss Gold Press Proofs /99 #32
2019 Donruss Gold Press Proofs /99 #135
2019 Donruss Press Proofs /49 #32
2019 Donruss Press Proofs /49 #135
2019 Donruss Printing Plates Black /1 #32
2019 Donruss Printing Plates Black /1 #135
2019 Donruss Printing Plates Cyan /1 #32
2019 Donruss Printing Plates Cyan /1 #135
2019 Donruss Printing Plates Magenta /1 #135
2019 Donruss Printing Plates Magenta /1 #32
2019 Donruss Printing Plates Yellow /1 #32
2019 Donruss Printing Plates Yellow /1 #135
2019 Donruss Race Day Relics #24
2019 Donruss Race Day Relics Holo Black /10 #24
2019 Donruss Race Day Relics Holo Gold /25 #24
2019 Donruss Race Day Relics Red /185 #24
2019 Donruss Signature Series #36
2019 Donruss Signature Series Holo Black /10 #36
2019 Donruss Signature Series Holo Gold /25 #36
2019 Donruss Signature Series Red /199 #36
2019 Donruss Silver #32
2019 Donruss Silver #135
2019 Panini Prime Autograph Materials /99 #20
2019 Panini Prime Autograph Materials Black /10 #20
2019 Panini Prime Autograph Materials Holo Gold /25 #20
2019 Panini Prime Autograph Materials Platinum Blue /1 #20
2019 Panini Prime Clear Vision Signatures /99 #3
2019 Panini Prime Clear Vision Signatures Black /10 #3
2019 Panini Prime Clear Vision Signatures Holo Gold /25 #3
2019 Panini Prime Clear Vision Signatures Platinum Blue /1 #3
2019 Panini Prime Dual Material Autographs /99 #8
2019 Panini Prime Dual Material Autographs Black /10 #8
2019 Panini Prime Dual Material Autographs Holo Gold /25 #8
2019 Panini Prime Dual Material Autographs Laundry Tags /1 #8
2019 Panini Prime Prime Jumbo Associate Sponsor 1 /1 #78
2019 Panini Prime Prime Jumbo Associate Sponsor 1 /1 #79
2019 Panini Prime Prime Jumbo Associate Sponsor 2 /1 #78
2019 Panini Prime Prime Jumbo Associate Sponsor 3 /1 #78
2019 Panini Prime Prime Jumbo Associate Sponsor 4 /1 #78
2019 Panini Prime Prime Jumbo Car Manufacturer /1 #78
2019 Panini Prime Prime Jumbo Car Manufacturer /1 #79
2019 Panini Prime Prime Jumbo Firesuit Manufacturer /1 #78
2019 Panini Prime Prime Jumbo Firesuit Manufacturer /1 #79
2019 Panini Prime Prime Jumbo Glove Manufacturer Patch /1 #78
2019 Panini Prime Prime Jumbo Glove Manufacturer Patch /1 #79
2019 Panini Prime Prime Jumbo Glove Name Patch /1 #78
2019 Panini Prime Prime Jumbo Glove Name Patch /1 #79
2019 Panini Prime Prime Jumbo Glove Number Patch /1 #78
2019 Panini Prime Prime Jumbo Glove Number Patch /1 #79
2019 Panini Prime Prime Jumbo Nameplate /2 #78
2019 Panini Prime Prime Jumbo NASCAR /1 #78
2019 Panini Prime Prime Jumbo Prime Colors /11 #78
2019 Panini Prime Prime Jumbo Prime Colors /8 #79
2019 Panini Prime Prime Jumbo Shoe Brand Logo /1 #78
2019 Panini Prime Prime Jumbo Shoe Brand Logo /1 #79
2019 Panini Prime Prime Jumbo Shoe Name Patch /1 #78
2019 Panini Prime Prime Jumbo Shoe Name Patch /1 #79
2019 Panini Prime Prime Jumbo Sunoco /1 #78
2019 Panini Prime Prime Signatures Black /10 #19
2019 Panini Prime Prime Signatures Platinum Blue /1 #19
2019 Panini Prime Quad Materials Autographs /99 #24
2019 Panini Prime Quad Materials Autographs Black /10 #24
2019 Panini Prime Quad Materials Autographs Holo Gold /25 #24
2019 Panini Prime Quad Materials Autographs Laundry Tags /1 #24
2019 Panini Prime Race Used Duals Firesuits /50 #5
2019 Panini Prime Race Used Duals Firesuits Black /10 #5
2019 Panini Prime Race Used Duals Firesuits Holo Gold /25 #5
2019 Panini Prime Race Used Duals Firesuits Laundry Tags /1 #5
2019 Panini Prime Race Used Duals Sheet Metal /50 #5
2019 Panini Prime Race Used Duals Sheet Metal Black /10 #5
2019 Panini Prime Race Used Duals Sheet Metal Holo Gold /25 #5
2019 Panini Prime Race Used Duals Sheet Metal Platinum Blue /1 #5
2019 Panini Prime Race Used Duals Tires /50 #5
2019 Panini Prime Race Used Duals Tires Black /10 #5
2019 Panini Prime Race Used Duals Tires Holo Gold /25 #5
2019 Panini Prime Race Used Duals Tires Platinum Blue /1 #5
2019 Panini Prime Race Used Firesuits /50 #36
2019 Panini Prime Race Used Firesuits Black /10 #36
2019 Panini Prime Race Used Firesuits Holo Gold /25 #36
2019 Panini Prime Race Used Firesuits Laundry Tags /1 #36
2019 Panini Prime Race Used Sheet Metal /50 #36
2019 Panini Prime Race Used Sheet Metal Black /10 #36
2019 Panini Prime Race Used Sheet Metal Holo Gold /25 #36
2019 Panini Prime Race Used Sheet Metal Platinum Blue /1 #36
2019 Panini Prime Race Used Tires /50 #36
2019 Panini Prime Race Used Tires Black /10 #36
2019 Panini Prime Race Used Tires Holo Gold /25 #36
2019 Panini Prime Race Used Tires Platinum Blue /1 #36
2019 Panini Prizm Scripted Signatures Prizms #17
2019 Panini Prizm Scripted Signatures Prizms Black /1 #17
2019 Panini Prizm Scripted Signatures Prizms Blue /75 #17
2019 Panini Prizm Scripted Signatures Prizms Camo #17
2019 Panini Prizm Scripted Signatures Prizms Gold /10 #17
2019 Panini Prizm Scripted Signatures Prizms Green /99 #17
2019 Panini Prizm Scripted Signatures Prizms Rainbow /24 #17
2019 Panini Prizm Scripted Signatures Prizms Red /50 #17
2019 Panini Prizm Scripted Signatures Prizms Red White and Blue #17
2019 Panini Prizm Scripted Signatures Prizms White /5 #17

Greg Biffle

1999 Wheels #91
1999 Wheels Golden #91
1999 Wheels Solos #91
2000 Maxx #71
2000 SP Authentic Sign of the Times #BI
2000 SP Authentic Sign of the Times Gold /25 #BI
2001 Press Pass #73
2001 Press Pass Autographs #2
2001 Press Pass Millennium #73
2001 Press Pass Signings #3
2001 Press Pass Stealth #46
2001 Press Pass Stealth Holofoils #46
2001 Press Pass Trackside #57
2001 Press Pass Trackside Die Cuts #57
2001 Press Pass Trackside Golden #57
2002 Press Pass #37
2002 Press Pass Autographs #6
2002 Press Pass Optima #31
2002 Press Pass Optima Gold #31
2002 Press Pass Optima Promos /5 #31
2002 Press Pass Optima Samples #31
2002 Press Pass Platinum #37
2002 Press Pass Signings #4
2002 Press Pass Signings Gold /50 #5
2002 Press Pass Stealth #46
2002 Press Pass Stealth Gold #46
2002 Press Pass Stealth Samples #46
2002 Wheels High Gear Autographs #4
2003 eTopps /2802 #19
2003 Press Pass #34
2003 Press Pass Autographs #4
2003 Press Pass Gold Holofoil #P34
2003 Press Pass Optima #1
2003 Press Pass Optima Fan Favorite #FF17
2003 Press Pass Optima Gold #G1
2003 Press Pass Optima Previews /5 #1
2003 Press Pass Optima Q and A #QA5
2003 Press Pass Optima Samples #1
2003 Press Pass Premium #31
2003 Press Pass Premium #45
2003 Press Pass Premium Previews /5 #31
2003 Press Pass Premium Red Reflectors #31
2003 Press Pass Premium Red Reflectors #45
2003 Press Pass Premium Samples #31
2003 Press Pass Premium Samples #45
2003 Press Pass Samples #34
2003 Press Pass Signings #5
2003 Press Pass Signings Gold /50 #5
2003 Press Pass Stealth EFX #FX2
2003 Press Pass Stealth No Boundaries #NB9
2003 Press Pass Trackside #1
2003 Press Pass Trackside #66
2003 Press Pass Trackside #78
2003 Press Pass Trackside Gold Holofoil #P1
2003 Press Pass Trackside Gold Holofoil #P66
2003 Press Pass Trackside Gold Holofoil #P78
2003 Press Pass Trackside Golden /50 #G1
2003 Press Pass Trackside Hat Giveaway #PPH2
2003 Press Pass Trackside License to Drive #LD1
2003 Press Pass Trackside Previews /5 #1
2003 Press Pass Trackside Samples #1
2003 Press Pass Trackside Samples #66
2003 Press Pass Trackside Samples #78
2003 VIP Making the Show #MS7
2003 Wheels American Thunder Heads Up Manufacturer /90 #HUM24
2003 Wheels American Thunder Heads Up Team /90 #HUT22
2003 Wheels American Thunder Heads Up Winston /90 #HUW24
2003 Wheels American Thunder Rookie Class #RC2
2003 Wheels American Thunder Rookie Class Prizes #RC2
2003 Wheels American Thunder Rookie Thunder #RT2
2003 Wheels American Thunder Triple Hat /25 #TH14
2003 Wheels Autographs #3
2003 Wheels Autographs #4
2003 Wheels High Gear #41
2003 Wheels High Gear #69
2003 Wheels High Gear Blue Hawaii SCDA Promos #41
2003 Wheels High Gear Blue Hawaii SCDA Promos #69
2003 Wheels High Gear First Gear #F41
2003 Wheels High Gear First Gear #F69
2003 Wheels High Gear MPH /100 #M41
2003 Wheels High Gear MPH /100 #M69
2003 Wheels High Gear Previews /5 #41
2003 Wheels High Gear Samples #41
2003 Wheels High Gear Samples #69
2004 Post Cereal #1
2004 Press Pass #1
2004 Press Pass #80
2004 Press Pass #90
2004 Press Pass Autographs #3
2004 Press Pass Cup Chase #CCR17
2004 Press Pass Cup Chase Prizes #CCR17
2004 Press Pass Eclipse #19
2004 Press Pass Eclipse #68
2004 Press Pass Eclipse Destination WIN #18
2004 Press Pass Eclipse Maxim #MX11
2004 Press Pass Eclipse Previews /5 #19
2004 Press Pass Eclipse Samples #19
2004 Press Pass Eclipse Samples #68
2004 Press Pass Eclipse Skidmarks #SM12
2004 Press Pass Eclipse Skidmarks Holofoil /500 #SM12
2004 Press Pass Eclipse Teammates Autographs /25 #3
2004 Press Pass Hot Treads /1100 #HTR8
2004 Press Pass Hot Treads Holofoil /200 #HTR8
2004 Press Pass Making the Show Collector's Series #MS10
2004 Press Pass Optima #1
2004 Press Pass Optima #98
2004 Press Pass Optima Fan Favorite #FF1
2004 Press Pass Optima Gold #G1
2004 Press Pass Optima Gold #G98
2004 Press Pass Optima Previews /5 #EB1
2004 Press Pass Optima Samples #1
2004 Press Pass Optima Samples #98
2004 Press Pass Platinum #P1
2004 Press Pass Platinum #P80
2004 Press Pass Platinum #P90
2004 Press Pass Premium #11
2004 Press Pass Premium #49
2004 Press Pass Premium #68
2004 Press Pass Premium Previews /5 #11
2004 Press Pass Premium Samples #11
2004 Press Pass Premium Samples #49
2004 Press Pass Previews /5 #1
2004 Press Pass Samples #1
2004 Press Pass Samples #80
2004 Press Pass Samples #90
2004 Press Pass Signings #2
2004 Press Pass Signings #3
2004 Press Pass Signings Gold /50 #2
2004 Press Pass Signings Gold /50 #3
2004 Press Pass Snapshots #SN1
2004 Press Pass Stealth #43
2004 Press Pass Stealth #44
2004 Press Pass Stealth #45
2004 Press Pass Stealth #79
2004 Press Pass Stealth Gear Grippers Drivers /80 #GGD18

2004 Press Pass Stealth Gear Grippers Drivers Retail /120 #GGT18
2004 Press Pass Stealth Profile #P9
2004 Press Pass Stealth Samples #X43
2004 Press Pass Stealth Samples #X44
2004 Press Pass Stealth Samples #X45
2004 Press Pass Stealth Samples #X79
2004 Press Pass Stealth X-Ray /100 #43
2004 Press Pass Stealth X-Ray /100 #44
2004 Press Pass Stealth X-Ray /100 #45
2004 Press Pass Stealth X-Ray /100 #79
2004 Press Pass Trackside #12
2004 Press Pass Trackside #57
2004 Press Pass Trackside #68
2004 Press Pass Trackside #101
2004 Press Pass Trackside Golden /100 #G12
2004 Press Pass Trackside Golden /100 #G57
2004 Press Pass Trackside Golden /100 #G68
2004 Press Pass Trackside Golden /100 #G101
2004 Press Pass Trackside Hat Giveaway #PPH1
2004 Press Pass Trackside Hot Pass #HP1
2004 Press Pass Trackside Hot Pass #HP20
2004 Press Pass Trackside Hot Pass National #HP1
2004 Press Pass Trackside Hot Pass National #HP20
2004 Press Pass Trackside Previews /5 #EB12
2004 Press Pass Trackside Runnin n' Gunnin #RG8
2004 Press Pass Trackside Samples #12
2004 Press Pass Trackside Samples #57
2004 Press Pass Trackside Samples #68
2004 Press Pass Trackside Samples #101
2004 Team Caliber First Choice Beckett 1:24 #16
2004 Team Caliber First Choice Beckett 1:24 #60
2004 VIP #19
2004 VIP Making the Show #MS10
2004 VIP Previews /5 #EB19
2004 VIP Samples #19
2004 Wheels American Thunder American Eagle #AE7
2004 Wheels American Thunder Golden Eagle /250 #AE7
2004 Wheels American Thunder Post Mark #PM10
2004 Wheels American Thunder Pushin Pedal /275 #PP1
2004 Wheels American Thunder Triple Hat /160 #TH26
2004 Wheels Autographs #2
2004 Wheels High Gear #1
2004 Wheels High Gear High Groove #HG1
2004 Wheels High Gear MPH /100 #M1
2004 Wheels High Gear Previews /5 #1
2004 Wheels High Gear Samples #1
2005 Press Pass #11
2005 Press Pass #48
2005 Press Pass Autographs #2
2005 Press Pass Autographs #3
2005 Press Pass Cup Chase #CCR11
2005 Press Pass Cup Chase Prizes #CCP11
2005 Press Pass Eclipse #17
2005 Press Pass Eclipse #74
2005 Press Pass Eclipse Destination WIN #20
2005 Press Pass Eclipse Destination WIN #27
2005 Press Pass Eclipse Previews /5 #EB17
2005 Press Pass Eclipse Previews /1 #EB74
2005 Press Pass Eclipse Samples #17
2005 Press Pass Eclipse Samples #74
2005 Press Pass Optima #2
2005 Press Pass Optima #28
2005 Press Pass Optima #68
2005 Press Pass Optima #94
2005 Press Pass Optima Corporate Cuts Cars /160 #CCT5
2005 Press Pass Optima Corporate Cuts Drivers /120 #CCD5
2005 Press Pass Optima Fan Favorite #FF2
2005 Press Pass Optima Gold /100 #G2
2005 Press Pass Optima Gold /100 #G68
2005 Press Pass Optima Gold /100 #G94
2005 Press Pass Optima Previews /5 #2
2005 Press Pass Optima Samples #2
2005 Press Pass Optima Samples #68
2005 Press Pass Optima Samples #94
2005 Press Pass Platinum /100 #P11
2005 Press Pass Platinum /100 #P48
2005 Press Pass Premium #2
2005 Press Pass Premium Samples #2
2005 Press Pass Previews Green /5 #EB11
2005 Press Pass Samples #11
2005 Press Pass Samples #48
2005 Press Pass Snapshots #SN1
2005 Press Pass Stealth #28
2005 Press Pass Stealth #31
2005 Press Pass Stealth #34
2005 Press Pass Stealth Gear Grippers Cars /90 #GGT17
2005 Press Pass Stealth Gear Grippers Drivers /75 #GGD17
2005 Press Pass Stealth Previews /5 #28
2005 Press Pass Stealth Previews /5 #31
2005 Press Pass Stealth Previews /5 #34
2005 Press Pass Stealth Samples #28
2005 Press Pass Stealth Samples #31
2005 Press Pass Stealth Samples #34
2005 Press Pass Stealth X-Ray /100 #X28
2005 Press Pass Stealth X-Ray /100 #X31
2005 Press Pass Stealth X-Ray /100 #X34
2005 Press Pass Trackside #26
2005 Press Pass Trackside Golden /100 #G26
2005 Press Pass Trackside Hat Giveaway #PPH44
2005 Press Pass Trackside Previews /5 #26
2005 Press Pass Trackside Samples #26
2005 Press Pass UMI Cup Chase #1
2005 Press Pass UMI Cup Chase #3
2005 VIP #1
2005 VIP #44
2005 VIP #49
2005 VIP #52
2005 VIP Making The Show #10
2005 VIP Previews /5 #EB1
2005 VIP Samples #1
2005 VIP Samples #44
2005 VIP Samples #49
2005 VIP Samples #52
2005 Wheels American Thunder #2
2005 Wheels American Thunder American Eagle #AE12
2005 Wheels American Thunder American Muscle #AM7
2005 Wheels American Thunder Golden Eagle /250 #GE12
2005 Wheels American Thunder Head to Toe /125 #HT2
2005 Wheels American Thunder Previews /5 #2
2005 Wheels American Thunder Pushin Pedal /150 #PP1
2005 Wheels American Thunder Samples #2
2005 Wheels American Thunder Triple Hat /190 #TH1
2005 Wheels Autographs #2
2005 Wheels Autographs #3
2005 Wheels High Gear #9
2005 Wheels High Gear #31
2005 Wheels High Gear Flag to Flag #FF1
2005 Wheels High Gear MPH /100 #M9
2005 Wheels High Gear MPH /100 #M31
2005 Wheels High Gear Previews Green /5 #EB9
2005 Wheels High Gear Previews Green /5 #EB31
2005 Wheels High Gear Samples #9
2005 Wheels High Gear Samples #31
2005 Wheels High Gear Samples #44
2006 Press Pass #12
2006 Press Pass #78
2006 Press Pass #86
2006 Press Pass #92
2006 Press Pass #110
2006 Press Pass Blue #B12
2006 Press Pass Blue #B78
2006 Press Pass Blue #B86
2006 Press Pass Blue #B92
2006 Press Pass Blue #B110
2006 Press Pass Coca Cola AutoZone #GB
2006 Press Pass Collectors Series Making the Show #MS15
2006 Press Pass Cup Chase #CCR2
2006 Press Pass Eclipse #2
2006 Press Pass Eclipse #46
2006 Press Pass Eclipse #61
2006 Press Pass Eclipse #65
2006 Press Pass Eclipse #69
2006 Press Pass Eclipse Previews /5 #EB2
2006 Press Pass Eclipse Previews /1 #EB61
2006 Press Pass Eclipse Racing Champions #RC2
2006 Press Pass Eclipse Skidmarks #SM13
2006 Press Pass Eclipse Skidmarks Holofoil /250 #SM13
2006 Press Pass Eclipse Supernova #SU3
2006 Press Pass Eclipse Teammates Autographs /25 #1
2006 Press Pass Eclipse Under Cover Autographs /16 #GB
2006 Press Pass Eclipse Under Cover Cars /140 #UCT14
2006 Press Pass Eclipse Under Cover Double Cover /100 #DC3
2006 Press Pass Eclipse Under Cover Double Cover /100 #DC9
2006 Press Pass Eclipse Under Cover Double Cover Holofoil /25 #DC3
2006 Press Pass Eclipse Under Cover Double Cover Holofoil /25 #DC9
2006 Press Pass Eclipse Under Cover Drivers Gold /1 #UCD14
2006 Press Pass Eclipse Under Cover Drivers Holofoil /100 #UCD14
2006 Press Pass Eclipse Under Cover Drivers Red /225 #UCD14
2006 Press Pass Eclipse Under Cover Drivers Silver /400 #UCD14
2006 Press Pass Gold #G12
2006 Press Pass Gold #G78
2006 Press Pass Gold #G86
2006 Press Pass Gold #G92
2006 Press Pass Gold #G110
2006 Press Pass Legends Autographs Blue /50 #4
2006 Press Pass Optima #14
2006 Press Pass Optima Gold /100 #G14
2006 Press Pass Optima Pole Position #PP3
2006 Press Pass Optima Previews /5 #EB14
2006 Press Pass Platinum /100 #P12
2006 Press Pass Platinum /100 #P78
2006 Press Pass Platinum /100 #P86
2006 Press Pass Platinum /100 #P92
2006 Press Pass Platinum /100 #P110
2006 Press Pass Premium #1
2006 Press Pass Premium #40
2006 Press Pass Premium #64
2006 Press Pass Previews /5 #EB12
2006 Press Pass Signings #4
2006 Press Pass Signings Gold /50 #4
2006 Press Pass Signings Silver /100 #4
2006 Press Pass Stealth #1
2006 Press Pass Stealth #37
2006 Press Pass Stealth #48
2006 Press Pass Stealth #81
2006 Press Pass Stealth Autographed Hat Entry #PPH1
2006 Press Pass Stealth Corporate Cuts /250 #CCD1
2006 Press Pass Stealth EFX #EFX10
2006 Press Pass Stealth Hot Pass #HP1
2006 Press Pass Stealth Previews /5 #1
2006 Press Pass Stealth Retail #1
2006 Press Pass Stealth Retail #37
2006 Press Pass Stealth Retail #48
2006 Press Pass Stealth Retail #81
2006 Press Pass Stealth X-Ray /100 #X1
2006 Press Pass Stealth X-Ray /100 #X37
2006 Press Pass Stealth X-Ray /100 #X48
2006 Press Pass Stealth X-Ray /100 #X81
2006 Press Pass Top 25 Drivers & Rides #C10
2006 Press Pass Top 25 Drivers & Rides #D10
2006 TRAKS #1
2006 TRAKS #44
2006 TRAKS #103
2006 TRAKS Autographs #1
2006 TRAKS Autographs 100 /100 #1
2006 TRAKS Autographs 25 /25 #1
2006 TRAKS Previews /1 #1
2006 TRAKS Previews /1 #44
2006 TRAKS Previews /1 #103
2006 TRAKS Stickers #16
2006 VIP #1
2006 VIP #50
2006 VIP #63
2006 VIP #68
2006 VIP Making the Show #MS15
2006 Wheels American Thunder #1
2006 Wheels American Thunder #64
2006 Wheels American Thunder #84
2006 Wheels American Thunder Double Hat /99 #DH1
2006 Wheels American Thunder Previews /5 #EB1
2006 Wheels Autographs #4
2006 Wheels High Gear #2
2006 Wheels High Gear Flag to Flag #FF1
2006 Wheels High Gear MPH /100 #M2
2006 Wheels High Gear Previews Green /5 #EB2
2006 Wheels High Gear Top Tier #TT2
2007 Press Pass #12
2007 Press Pass #85
2007 Press Pass #102
2007 Press Pass Autographs #1
2007 Press Pass Autographs Press Plates Yellow /1 #1
2007 Press Pass Blue #B12
2007 Press Pass Blue #B85
2007 Press Pass Blue #B102
2007 Press Pass Burning Rubber Drivers /75 #BRD8
2007 Press Pass Burning Rubber Drivers Gold /1 #BRD8
2007 Press Pass Burning Rubber Team /325 #BRT8
2007 Press Pass Cup Chase #CCR9
2007 Press Pass Eclipse #13
2007 Press Pass Eclipse Gold /25 #G13
2007 Press Pass Eclipse Hyperdrive #HD3
2007 Press Pass Eclipse Previews /5 #EB13
2007 Press Pass Eclipse Racing Champions #RC6
2007 Press Pass Eclipse Racing Champions #RC22
2007 Press Pass Eclipse Red /1 #R13
2007 Press Pass Eclipse Skidmarks #SM15
2007 Press Pass Eclipse Skidmarks Holofoil /250 #SM15
2007 Press Pass Eclipse Teammates Autographs /25 #6
2007 Press Pass Eclipse Under Cover Autographs /16 #UCGB
2007 Press Pass Eclipse Under Cover Double Cover Name /25 #DC1
2007 Press Pass Eclipse Under Cover Double Cover NASCAR /99 #DC1
2007 Press Pass Eclipse Under Cover Drivers /450 #UCD6
2007 Press Pass Eclipse Under Cover Drivers Eclipse /1 #UCD6
2007 Press Pass Eclipse Under Cover Drivers Name /99 #UCD6
2007 Press Pass Eclipse Under Cover Drivers NASCAR /270 #UCD6
2007 Press Pass Eclipse Under Cover Teams /135 #UCT6
2007 Press Pass Eclipse Under Cover Teams NASCAR /25 #UCT6
2007 Press Pass Gold #G12
2007 Press Pass Gold #G85
2007 Press Pass Gold #G102
2007 Press Pass Platinum /100 #P12
2007 Press Pass Platinum /100 #P85
2007 Press Pass Platinum /100 #P102
2007 Press Pass Premium #14
2007 Press Pass Premium #60
2007 Press Pass Premium Red /15 #R14
2007 Press Pass Premium Red /15 #R60
2007 Press Pass Previews /5 #EB12
2007 Press Pass Signings #7
2007 Press Pass Signings Gold /50 #4
2007 Press Pass Signings Press Plates Black /1 #4
2007 Press Pass Signings Silver /100 #3
2007 Press Pass Snapshots #SN1
2007 Press Pass Stealth #1
2007 Press Pass Stealth #58
2007 Press Pass Stealth #69
2007 Press Pass Stealth #80
2007 Press Pass Stealth Battle Armor Drivers /150 #BAD2
2007 Press Pass Stealth Battle Armor Teams /85 #BAT2
2007 Press Pass Stealth Chrome #1
2007 Press Pass Stealth Chrome #58
2007 Press Pass Stealth Chrome #69
2007 Press Pass Stealth Chrome #80
2007 Press Pass Stealth Chrome Exclusives /99 #X58
2007 Press Pass Stealth Chrome Exclusives /99 #X69
2007 Press Pass Stealth Chrome Exclusives /99 #X80
2007 Press Pass Stealth Chrome Exclusives /99 #X1
2007 Press Pass Stealth Chrome Platinum /25 #P58
2007 Press Pass Stealth Chrome Platinum /25 #P69
2007 Press Pass Stealth Chrome Platinum /25 #P80
2007 Press Pass Stealth Chrome Platinum /25 #P1
2007 Press Pass Stealth Maximum Access #MA2
2007 Press Pass Stealth Maximum Access Autographs /25 #MA2
2007 Press Pass Stealth Previews /5 #EB1
2007 Traks #1
2007 Traks Corporate Cuts Driver /99 #CCD11
2007 Traks Corporate Cuts Patch /15 #CCD11
2007 Traks Corporate Cuts Team /180 #CCT11
2007 Traks Driver's Seat #DS16
2007 Traks Driver's Seat #DS16B
2007 Traks Driver's Seat National #DS16
2007 Traks Gold #G1
2007 Traks Holofoil /50 #H1
2007 Traks Previews /5 #EB1
2007 Traks Red /10 #R1
2007 VIP #2
2007 VIP Previews /5 #EB2
2007 Wheels American Thunder #2
2007 Wheels American Thunder #42
2007 Wheels American Thunder #67
2007 Wheels American Thunder Autographed Hat Instant Winner /1 #AH2
2007 Wheels American Thunder Previews /5 #EB2
2007 Wheels American Thunder Thunder Strokes #3
2007 Wheels American Thunder Thunder Strokes Press Plates Black /1 #3
2007 Wheels American Thunder Thunder Strokes Press Plates Cyan /1 #3
2007 Wheels American Thunder Thunder Strokes Press Plates Magenta /1 #3
2007 Wheels American Thunder Thunder Strokes Press Plates Yellow /1 #3
2007 Wheels American Thunder Triple Hat /99 #TH1
2007 Wheels Autographs #1
2007 Wheels Autographs Press Plates Black /1 #1
2007 Wheels Autographs Press Plates Cyan /1 #1
2007 Wheels Autographs Press Plates Magenta /1 #1
2007 Wheels High Gear #12
2007 Wheels High Gear #84
2007 Wheels High Gear Driven #DR10
2007 Wheels High Gear Final Standings Gold /13 #FS12
2007 Wheels High Gear MPH /100 #M12
2007 Wheels High Gear MPH /100 #M84
2007 Wheels High Gear Previews /5 #EB12
2008 Press Pass #15
2008 Press Pass Autographs #5
2008 Press Pass Autographs Press Plates Black /1 #4
2008 Press Pass Autographs Press Plates Cyan /1 #4
2008 Press Pass Autographs Press Plates Magenta /1 #4
2008 Press Pass Autographs Press Plates Yellow /1 #4
2008 Press Pass Blue #B15
2008 Press Pass Collector's Series Box Set #6
2008 Press Pass Cup Chase #CC17
2008 Press Pass Cup Chase Prizes #CC9
2008 Press Pass Eclipse #13
2008 Press Pass Eclipse #48
2008 Press Pass Eclipse Gold /25 #G13
2008 Press Pass Eclipse Gold /25 #G48
2008 Press Pass Eclipse Previews /5 #EB13
2008 Press Pass Eclipse Red /1 #R13
2008 Press Pass Eclipse Red /1 #R48
2008 Press Pass Eclipse Stellar #ST12
2008 Press Pass Gold #G15
2008 Press Pass Legends Prominent Pieces Metal-Tire-Net /50 #PP4GB
2008 Press Pass Legends Prominent Pieces Metal-Tire-Net Gold /25 #PP4GB
2008 Press Pass Platinum /100 #P15
2008 Press Pass Premium #13
2008 Press Pass Premium #81
2008 Press Pass Premium Previews /5 #EB13
2008 Press Pass Premium Red /15 #13
2008 Press Pass Premium Red /5 #81
2008 Press Pass Previews /5 #EB15
2008 Press Pass Signings Gold /50 #4
2008 Press Pass Signings Silver /100 #4
2008 Press Pass Speedway #21
2008 Press Pass Speedway Gold #G21
2008 Press Pass Speedway Holofoil /50 #H21
2008 Press Pass Speedway Previews /5 #EB21
2008 Press Pass Speedway Red /10 #R21
2008 Press Pass Starting Grid #SG6
2008 Press Pass Stealth #1
2008 Press Pass Stealth #58
2008 Press Pass Stealth #70
2008 Press Pass Stealth #73
2008 Press Pass Stealth Chrome #1
2008 Press Pass Stealth Chrome #58
2008 Press Pass Stealth Chrome #70
2008 Press Pass Stealth Chrome #73
2008 Press Pass Stealth Chrome Exclusives /25 #1
2008 Press Pass Stealth Chrome Exclusives /25 #58
2008 Press Pass Stealth Chrome Exclusives /25 #70
2008 Press Pass Stealth Chrome Exclusives /25 #73
2008 Press Pass Stealth Chrome Exclusives Gold /99 #1
2008 Press Pass Stealth Chrome Exclusives Gold /99 #58
2008 Press Pass Stealth Chrome Exclusives Gold /99 #70
2008 Press Pass Stealth Chrome Exclusives Gold /99 #73
2008 Press Pass Stealth Maximum Access #MA2
2008 Press Pass Stealth Maximum Access Autographs /25 #MA2
2008 Press Pass Stealth Previews /5 #1
2008 VIP #3
2008 VIP #55
2008 VIP #64
2008 VIP #79
2008 VIP Get a Grip Drivers /80 #GGD3
2008 VIP Get a Grip Teams /99 #GGT3
2008 VIP Previews /5 #EB3
2008 VIP Triple Grip /25 #TG3
2008 VIP Trophy Club #TC1
2008 VIP Trophy Club Transparent #TC1
2008 Wheels American Thunder #3
2008 Wheels American Thunder #58
2008 Wheels American Thunder #67
2008 Wheels American Thunder American Dreams #AD12
2008 Wheels American Thunder American Dreams Gold /250 #AD12
2008 Wheels American Thunder Autographed Hat Winner /1 #IWHGB
2008 Wheels American Thunder Head to Toe /99 #HT3
2008 Wheels American Thunder Previews /5 #3
2008 Wheels American Thunder Pushin' Pedal /99 #PP 3
2008 Wheels American Thunder Trackside Treasury Autographs #GB
2008 Wheels American Thunder Trackside Treasury Autographs Gold /25 #GB
2008 Wheels American Thunder Trackside Treasury Autographs Printing Plates Black /1 #GB
2008 Wheels American Thunder Trackside Treasury Autographs Printing Plates Cyan /1 #GB
2008 Wheels American Thunder Trackside Treasury Autographs Printing Plates Magenta /1 #GB
2008 Wheels American Thunder Trackside Treasury Autographs Printing Plates Yellow /1 #GB
2008 Wheels American Thunder Triple Hat /99 #TH1
2008 Wheels Autographs #3
2008 Wheels Autographs Press Plates Black /1 #3
2008 Wheels Autographs Press Plates Cyan /1 #3
2008 Wheels Autographs Press Plates Magenta /1 #3
2008 Wheels Autographs Press Plates Yellow /1 #3
2008 Wheels High Gear #14
2008 Wheels High Gear Driven #DR14
2008 Wheels High Gear Final Standings /14 #F14
2008 Wheels High Gear MPH /100 #M14
2008 Wheels High Gear Previews /5 #EB14
2009 Element #2
2009 Element #57
2009 Element 1-2-3 Finish /50 #RFR
2009 Element Kinetic Energy #KE11
2009 Element Lab Report #LR2
2009 Element Previews /5 #2
2009 Element Radioactive /100 #2
2009 Element Radioactive /100 #57
2009 Press Pass #9
2009 Press Pass #38
2009 Press Pass #66
2009 Press Pass #115
2009 Press Pass #0
2009 Press Pass #122
2009 Press Pass Autographs Chase Edition /25 #GB
2009 Press Pass Autographs Gold #5
2009 Press Pass Autographs Printing Plates Black /1 #3
2009 Press Pass Autographs Printing Plates Cyan /1 #3
2009 Press Pass Autographs Printing Plates Magenta /1 #3
2009 Press Pass Autographs Printing Plates Yellow /1 #3
2009 Press Pass Autographs Silver #3
2009 Press Pass Blue #9
2009 Press Pass Blue #38
2009 Press Pass Blue #66
2009 Press Pass Blue #115
2009 Press Pass Blue #122
2009 Press Pass Burning Rubber Drivers /320 #BRD27
2009 Press Pass Burning Rubber Drivers /320 #BRD28
2009 Press Pass Burning Rubber Prime Cut /25 #BRD27
2009 Press Pass Burning Rubber Prime Cut /25 #BRD28
2009 Press Pass Burning Rubber Teams /85 #BRT27
2009 Press Pass Burning Rubber Teams /85 #BRT28
2009 Press Pass Chase for the Sprint Cup #CC12
2009 Press Pass Cup Chase #CCR16
2009 Press Pass Cup Chase Prizes #CC12
2009 Press Pass Eclipse #11
2009 Press Pass Eclipse #42
2009 Press Pass Eclipse #55
2009 Press Pass Eclipse #66
2009 Press Pass Eclipse #75
2009 Press Pass Eclipse #82
2009 Press Pass Eclipse Black and White #11
2009 Press Pass Eclipse Black and White #42
2009 Press Pass Eclipse Black and White #55
2009 Press Pass Eclipse Black and White #66
2009 Press Pass Eclipse Black and White #75
2009 Press Pass Eclipse Black and White #82
2009 Press Pass Eclipse Blue #11
2009 Press Pass Eclipse Blue #42
2009 Press Pass Eclipse Blue #55
2009 Press Pass Eclipse Blue #66
2009 Press Pass Eclipse Blue #75
2009 Press Pass Eclipse Blue #82
2009 Press Pass Eclipse Ecliptic Path #EP17
2009 Press Pass Eclipse Solar System #SS3
2009 Press Pass Final Standings /110 #115
2009 Press Pass Four Wide Firesuit /50 #FWGB
2009 Press Pass Four Wide Tire /25 #FWGB
2009 Press Pass Fusion #63
2009 Press Pass Fusion Bronze /150 #63
2009 Press Pass Fusion Gold /50 #63
2009 Press Pass Fusion Green /25 #63
2009 Press Pass Fusion Onyx /1 #63
2009 Press Pass Fusion Revered Relics Gold /50 #RRGBMK
2009 Press Pass Fusion Revered Relics Holofoil /25 #RRGBMK
2009 Press Pass Fusion Revered Relics Premium Swatch /10 #RRGBMK
2009 Press Pass Fusion Revered Relics Silver /65 #RRGBMK
2009 Press Pass Fusion Silver /99 #63
2009 Press Pass Gold #9
2009 Press Pass Gold #38
2009 Press Pass Gold #66
2009 Press Pass Gold #115
2009 Press Pass Gold #122
2009 Press Pass Gold Holofoil /100 #9
2009 Press Pass Gold Holofoil /100 #38
2009 Press Pass Gold Holofoil /100 #66
2009 Press Pass Gold Holofoil /100 #115
2009 Press Pass Gold Holofoil /100 #122
2009 Press Pass Legends Prominent Pieces Bronze /150 #PPGB
2009 Press Pass Legends Prominent Pieces Gold /25 #PPGB
2009 Press Pass Legends Prominent Pieces Silver /50 #PPGB
2009 Press Pass Pocket Portraits #P1
2009 Press Pass Pocket Portraits Hometown #P1
2009 Press Pass Pocket Portraits Smoke #P1
2009 Press Pass Pocket Portraits Target #PPT13
2009 Press Pass Premium #14
2009 Press Pass Premium Hot Threads /299 #HTGB1
2009 Press Pass Premium Hot Threads /99 #HTGB2
2009 Press Pass Premium Hot Threads Multi-Color /25 #HTGB
2009 Press Pass Premium Previews /5 #EB14
2009 Press Pass Premium Signatures #4
2009 Press Pass Premium Signatures Gold /25 #4
2009 Press Pass Premium Win Streak #WS14
2009 Press Pass Premium Win Streak Victory Lane #WSVL-GB
2009 Press Pass Previews /5 #EB9
2009 Press Pass Previews /1 #EB115
2009 Press Pass Previews /5 #EB122
2009 Press Pass Red #9
2009 Press Pass Red #38
2009 Press Pass Red #66
2009 Press Pass Red #115
2009 Press Pass Red #122
2009 Press Pass Santa Hats /50 #SH2
2009 Press Pass Showcase /499 #21
2009 Press Pass Showcase /499 #35
2009 Press Pass Showcase 2nd Gear /125 #21
2009 Press Pass Showcase 2nd Gear /125 #35
2009 Press Pass Showcase 3rd Gear /50 #21
2009 Press Pass Showcase 3rd Gear /50 #35
2009 Press Pass Showcase 4th Gear /15 #21
2009 Press Pass Showcase 4th Gear /15 #35
2009 Press Pass Showcase Classic Collections Firesuit /25 #CCF8
2009 Press Pass Showcase Classic Collections Firesuit Patch /5 #CCF8
2009 Press Pass Showcase Classic Collections Ink /45 #9
2009 Press Pass Showcase Classic Collections Ink Gold /25 #9
2009 Press Pass Showcase Classic Collections Ink Green /5 #9
2009 Press Pass Showcase Classic Collections Ink Melting /1 #9
2009 Press Pass Showcase Classic Collections Sheet Metal /45 #CCS8
2009 Press Pass Showcase Classic Collections Tire /99 #CCT8
2009 Press Pass Showcase Printing Plates Black /1 #21
2009 Press Pass Showcase Printing Plates Black /1 #35
2009 Press Pass Showcase Printing Plates Cyan /1 #21
2009 Press Pass Showcase Printing Plates Cyan /1 #35
2009 Press Pass Showcase Printing Plates Magenta /1 #21
2009 Press Pass Showcase Printing Plates Magenta /1 #35
2009 Press Pass Showcase Printing Plates Yellow /1 #21
2009 Press Pass Showcase Printing Plates Yellow /1 #35
2009 Press Pass Showcase Prized Pieces Firesuit /25 #PPFGB
2009 Press Pass Showcase Prized Pieces Firesuit Patch /5 #PPFGB
2009 Press Pass Showcase Prized Pieces Sheet Metal /45 #PPSGB
2009 Press Pass Showcase Prized Pieces Tire /99 #PPTGB
2009 Press Pass Signings Blue /25 #5
2009 Press Pass Signings Gold #5
2009 Press Pass Signings Green /15 #5
2009 Press Pass Signings Orange /65 #5
2009 Press Pass Signings Printing Plates Black /1 #5
2009 Press Pass Signings Printing Plates Cyan /1 #5
2009 Press Pass Signings Purple /45 #5
2009 Press Pass Sponsor Swatches /200 #SSGB
2009 Press Pass Sponsor Swatches Select /8 #SSGB
2009 Press Pass Stealth #4
2009 Press Pass Stealth #48
2009 Press Pass Stealth #56
2009 Press Pass Stealth #66
2009 Press Pass Stealth #77
2009 Press Pass Stealth Battle Armor /425 #BAGB2
2009 Press Pass Stealth Battle Armor /125 #BAGB1
2009 Press Pass Stealth Battle Armor /50 #BAGB3
2009 Press Pass Stealth Battle Armor Autographs /16 #BASGB
2009 Press Pass Stealth Battle Armor Multi-Color /160 #BAGB
2009 Press Pass Stealth Chrome #4
2009 Press Pass Stealth Chrome #48
2009 Press Pass Stealth Chrome #56
2009 Press Pass Stealth Chrome #66
2009 Press Pass Stealth Chrome #77
2009 Press Pass Stealth Chrome Brushed Metal /25 #4
2009 Press Pass Stealth Chrome Brushed Metal /25 #48
2009 Press Pass Stealth Chrome Brushed Metal /25 #56
2009 Press Pass Stealth Chrome Brushed Metal /25 #66
2009 Press Pass Stealth Chrome Brushed Metal /25 #77
2009 Press Pass Stealth Chrome Gold /99 #4
2009 Press Pass Stealth Chrome Gold /99 #48
2009 Press Pass Stealth Chrome Gold /99 #56
2009 Press Pass Stealth Chrome Gold /99 #66
2009 Press Pass Stealth Chrome Gold /99 #77
2009 Press Pass Stealth Confidential Classified Bronze #PC21
2009 Press Pass Stealth Confidential Secret Silver #PC21
2009 Press Pass Stealth Confidential Top Secret Gold /25 #PC21
2009 Press Pass Stealth Previews /5 #EB4
2009 Press Pass Stealth Previews /1 #EB77
2009 Press Pass Tread Marks Autographs /15 #SSGB
2009 VIP #3
2009 VIP #52
2009 VIP Get A Grip /120 #GGGB
2009 VIP Get A Grip Holofoil /10 #GGGB
2009 VIP Hardware #H4
2009 VIP Hardware Transparent #H4
2009 VIP Leadfoot /150 #LFGB
2009 VIP Leadfoot Holofoil /10 #LFGB
2009 VIP Previews /5 #3
2009 VIP Purple /25 #3
2009 VIP Purple /25 #52
2009 Wheels Autographs #3
2009 Wheels Autographs Press Plates Black /1 #GB
2009 Wheels Autographs Press Plates Cyan /1 #GB
2009 Wheels Autographs Press Plates Magenta /1 #GB
2009 Wheels Autographs Press Plates Yellow /1 #GB
2009 Wheels Main Event #13
2009 Wheels Main Event #38
2009 Wheels Main Event Fast Pass Purple /25 #13
2009 Wheels Main Event Fast Pass Purple /25 #38
2009 Wheels Main Event Foil #13
2009 Wheels Main Event Hat Dance Patch /10 #HDGB
2009 Wheels Main Event Hat Dance Triple /99 #HDGB
2009 Wheels Main Event Marks Clubs #4
2009 Wheels Main Event Marks Diamonds /50 #4
2009 Wheels Main Event Marks Hearts /10 #4
2009 Wheels Main Event Marks Printing Plates Black /1 #4
2009 Wheels Main Event Marks Printing Plates Cyan /1 #4
2009 Wheels Main Event Marks Printing Plates Magenta /1 #4
2009 Wheels Main Event Marks Printing Plates Yellow /1 #4
2009 Wheels Main Event Marks Spades /1 #4
2009 Wheels Main Event Playing Cards Blue #JS
2009 Wheels Main Event Playing Cards Red #JS
2009 Wheels Main Event Previews /5 #13
2009 Wheels Main Event Wildcard Cuts /2 #WCCGB
2010 Element #8
2010 Element #47
2010 Element Blue /35 #8
2010 Element Blue /35 #47
2010 Element Green #8
2010 Element Green #47
2010 Element Previews /5 #EB8
2010 Element Purple /25 #8
2010 Element Purple /25 #47
2010 Element Red Target #8
2010 Element Red Target #47
2010 Press Pass #13
2010 Press Pass #59
2010 Press Pass #120
2010 Press Pass #0
2010 Press Pass Autographs #4
2010 Press Pass Autographs Chase Edition /25 #1
2010 Press Pass Autographs Printing Plates Black /1 #4
2010 Press Pass Autographs Printing Plates Cyan /1 #4
2010 Press Pass Autographs Printing Plates Magenta /1 #3
2010 Press Pass Autographs Printing Plates Yellow /1 #4
2010 Press Pass Blue #13
2010 Press Pass Blue #59
2010 Press Pass Blue #120
2010 Press Pass Cup Chase #CCR3
2010 Press Pass Cup Chase Prizes #CC7
2010 Press Pass Eclipse #10
2010 Press Pass Eclipse #33
2010 Press Pass Eclipse #57
2010 Press Pass Eclipse Blue #10
2010 Press Pass Eclipse Blue #33
2010 Press Pass Eclipse Blue #57
2010 Press Pass Eclipse Gold #10
2010 Press Pass Eclipse Gold #33
2010 Press Pass Eclipse Gold #57
2010 Press Pass Eclipse Previews /5 #10
2010 Press Pass Eclipse Previews /1 #33
2010 Press Pass Eclipse Purple /25 #10
2010 Press Pass Eclipse Purple /25 #33
2010 Press Pass Eclipse Purple /25 #57
2010 Press Pass Final Standings /90 #FS7
2010 Press Pass Five Star Classic Compilations Combos Firesuit Autographs /15 #CCMROU
2010 Press Pass Five Star Classic Compilations Combos Patches Autographs /1 #CCMROU
2010 Press Pass Gold #13
2010 Press Pass Gold #59
2010 Press Pass Gold #120
2010 Press Pass Holofoil /100 #13
2010 Press Pass Holofoil /100 #59
2010 Press Pass Holofoil /100 #120
2010 Press Pass Premium #12
2010 Press Pass Premium Purple /25 #12
2010 Press Pass Premium Rivals #R2
2010 Press Pass Premium Rivals Signatures /5 #RSHB
2010 Press Pass Premium Signatures #PSGB
2010 Press Pass Premium Signatures Red Ink /25 #PSGB
2010 Press Pass Previews /5 #13
2010 Press Pass Previews /1 #120
2010 Press Pass Purple /25 #13
2010 Press Pass Purple /25 #59
2010 Press Pass Purple /25 #120
2010 Press Pass Showcase /499 #12
2010 Press Pass Showcase /499 #34
2010 Press Pass Showcase Classic Collections Firesuit Green /25 #CCIRFR
2010 Press Pass Showcase Classic Collections Firesuit Patch Melting /5 #CCIRFR
2010 Press Pass Showcase Classic Collections Ink /15 #CCIRFR
2010 Press Pass Showcase Classic Collections Ink Gold /10 #CCIRFR
2010 Press Pass Showcase Classic Collections Ink Green /5 #CCIRFR
2010 Press Pass Showcase Classic Collections Ink Melting /1 #CCIRFR
2010 Press Pass Showcase Classic Collections Sheet Metal /99 #CCIRFR
2010 Press Pass Showcase Classic Collections Sheet Metal Gold /45 #CCIRFR
2010 Press Pass Showcase Gold /125 #12
2010 Press Pass Showcase Gold /125 #34
2010 Press Pass Showcase Green /50 #12
2010 Press Pass Showcase Green /50 #34
2010 Press Pass Showcase Melting /15 #12
2010 Press Pass Showcase Melting /15 #34
2010 Press Pass Showcase Platinum Holo /1 #12
2010 Press Pass Showcase Platinum Holo /1 #34
2010 Press Pass Signings Blue /10 #5
2010 Press Pass Signings Gold /35 #5
2010 Press Pass Signings Red /15 #5
2010 Press Pass Signings Silver /75 #5
2010 Press Pass Stealth #3
2010 Press Pass Stealth Battle Armor Holofoil /25 #BAGB
2010 Press Pass Stealth Battle Armor Silver /225 #BAGB
2010 Press Pass Stealth Black and White #3
2010 Press Pass Stealth Previews /5 #3
2010 Press Pass Stealth Purple /25 #3
2010 Press Pass Stealth Signature Series Sheet Metal /15 #SSMEGB
2010 Press Pass Top 12 Tires /16 #GB
2010 Press Pass Top 12 Tires 10 /10 #GB
2010 Wheels Autographs #5
2010 Wheels Autographs Printing Plates Black /1 #5
2010 Wheels Autographs Printing Plates Cyan /1 #5
2010 Wheels Autographs Printing Plates Magenta /1 #5
2010 Wheels Autographs Printing Plates Yellow /1 #5
2010 Wheels Autographs Target /10 #4
2010 Wheels Main Event #3
2010 Wheels Main Event Blue #3
2010 Wheels Main Event Fight Card #FC3
2010 Wheels Main Event Fight Card Checkered Flag #FC3
2010 Wheels Main Event Fight Card Full Color Retail #FC3
2010 Wheels Main Event Fight Card Gold /25 #FC3
2010 Wheels Main Event Marks Autographs /86 #5
2010 Wheels Main Event Marks Autographs Black /1 #5
2010 Wheels Main Event Marks Autographs Blue /50 #5
2010 Wheels Main Event Marks Autographs Red /5 #5
2010 Wheels Main Event Matchups Autographs /10 #KBGB
2010 Wheels Main Event Purple /25 #3
2011 Element #3
2011 Element #71
2011 Element #80
2011 Element Autographs /89 #5
2011 Element Autographs Blue /10 #5
2011 Element Autographs Gold /25 #5
2011 Element Autographs Printing Plates Black /1 #5
2011 Element Autographs Printing Plates Cyan /1 #5
2011 Element Autographs Printing Plates Magenta /1 #5
2011 Element Autographs Printing Plates Yellow /1 #5
2011 Element Autographs Silver /50 #5
2011 Element Black /35 #3
2011 Element Black /35 #71
2011 Element Black /35 #80
2011 Element Flagship Performers Career Wins White /50 #FPWGB
2011 Element Green #3
2011 Element Green #71
2011 Element Green #80
2011 Element High Octane Vehicle #HOV11
2011 Element Previews /5 #EB3
2011 Element Purple /25 #3
2011 Element Purple /25 #71
2011 Element Purple /25 #80
2011 Element Red #3
2011 Element Red #71
2011 Element Red #80
2011 Press Pass #3
2011 Press Pass #58
2011 Press Pass #132
2011 Press Pass #143
2011 Press Pass #173
2011 Press Pass #200
2011 Press Pass #0
2011 Press Pass Autographs Blue /10 #5
2011 Press Pass Autographs Bronze /75 #5
2011 Press Pass Autographs Gold /25 #5
2011 Press Pass Autographs Printing Plates Black /1 #5
2011 Press Pass Autographs Printing Plates Cyan /1 #5
2011 Press Pass Autographs Printing Plates Magenta /1 #5
2011 Press Pass Autographs Printing Plates Yellow /1 #5
2011 Press Pass Autographs Silver /50 #5
2011 Press Pass Blue Holofoil /10 #3
2011 Press Pass Blue Holofoil /10 #58
2011 Press Pass Blue Holofoil /10 #132
2011 Press Pass Blue Holofoil /10 #143
2011 Press Pass Blue Holofoil /10 #173
2011 Press Pass Blue Holofoil /10 #200
2011 Press Pass Blue Retail #3
2011 Press Pass Blue Retail #58
2011 Press Pass Blue Retail #132
2011 Press Pass Blue Retail #143
2011 Press Pass Blue Retail #173
2011 Press Pass Blue Retail #200
2011 Press Pass Burning Rubber Fast Pass /10 #BRGB
2011 Press Pass Burning Rubber Gold /150 #BRGB
2011 Press Pass Burning Rubber Gold /150 #BRCGB
2011 Press Pass Burning Rubber Holofoil /50 #BRGB
2011 Press Pass Burning Rubber Holofoil /50 #BRCGB
2011 Press Pass Burning Rubber Prime Cuts /25 #BRGB
2011 Press Pass Burning Rubber Prime Cuts /25 #BRCGB
2011 Press Pass Cup Chase #CCR7
2011 Press Pass Eclipse #3
2011 Press Pass Eclipse #39
2011 Press Pass Eclipse #70
2011 Press Pass Eclipse Blue #3
2011 Press Pass Eclipse Blue #39
2011 Press Pass Eclipse Blue #70
2011 Press Pass Eclipse Gold /55 #3
2011 Press Pass Eclipse Gold /55 #39
2011 Press Pass Eclipse Gold /55 #70
2011 Press Pass Eclipse In Focus #IF7
2011 Press Pass Eclipse Previews /5 #EB3

2011 Press Pass Eclipse Previews /1 #EB39
2011 Press Pass Eclipse Purple /25 #3
2011 Press Pass Eclipse Purple /25 #39
2011 Press Pass FanFare #4
2011 Press Pass FanFare Autographs Blue /5 #7
2011 Press Pass FanFare Autographs Bronze /65 #7
2011 Press Pass FanFare Autographs Gold /50 #7
2011 Press Pass FanFare Autographs Printing Plates Black /1 #7
2011 Press Pass FanFare Autographs Printing Plates Cyan /1 #7
2011 Press Pass FanFare Autographs Printing Plates Magenta /1 #7
2011 Press Pass FanFare Autographs Printing Plates Yellow /1 #7
2011 Press Pass FanFare Autographs Silver /25 #7
2011 Press Pass FanFare Blue Die Cuts #4
2011 Press Pass FanFare Emerald /25 #4
2011 Press Pass FanFare Holofoil Die Cuts #4
2011 Press Pass FanFare Magnificent Materials /199 #MMGB
2011 Press Pass FanFare Magnificent Materials Holofoil /50 #MMGB
2011 Press Pass FanFare Ruby Die Cuts /15 #4
2011 Press Pass FanFare Sapphire /10 #4
2011 Press Pass FanFare Silver /25 #4
2011 Press Pass Flashback #FB1
2011 Press Pass Geared Up Gold /50 #GUGB
2011 Press Pass Geared Up Holofoil /25 #GUGB
2011 Press Pass Gold /50 #3
2011 Press Pass Gold /50 #58
2011 Press Pass Gold /50 #132
2011 Press Pass Gold /50 #143
2011 Press Pass Gold /50 #173
2011 Press Pass Gold /50 #200
2011 Press Pass Premium #4
2011 Press Pass Premium #73
2011 Press Pass Premium Purple /25 #4
2011 Press Pass Premium Purple /25 #73
2011 Press Pass Premium Signatures /287 #PSGB
2011 Press Pass Previews /5 #EB3
2011 Press Pass Previews /1 #EB200
2011 Press Pass Purple /25 #3
2011 Press Pass Purple /25 #200
2011 Press Pass Showcase /499 #11
2011 Press Pass Showcase /499 #55
2011 Press Pass Showcase Classic Collections Firesuit /45 #CCMRFR
2011 Press Pass Showcase Classic Collections Firesuit Patches /5 #CCMRFR
2011 Press Pass Showcase Classic Collections Ink /25 #CCMRFR
2011 Press Pass Showcase Classic Collections Ink Gold /5 #CCMRFR
2011 Press Pass Showcase Classic Collections Ink Melting /1 #CCMRFR
2011 Press Pass Showcase Classic Collections Sheet Metal /99 #CCMRFR
2011 Press Pass Showcase Gold /125 #11
2011 Press Pass Showcase Gold /125 #55
2011 Press Pass Showcase Green /25 #11
2011 Press Pass Showcase Green /25 #55
2011 Press Pass Showcase Melting /1 #11
2011 Press Pass Showcase Melting /1 #55
2011 Press Pass Signature Series /11 #SSSGB
2011 Press Pass Signature Series /11 #SSFGB
2011 Press Pass Signature Series /11 #SSMGB
2011 Press Pass Signings Black and White /10 #PPSGB
2011 Press Pass Signings Brushed Metal /50 #PPSGB
2011 Press Pass Signings Holofoil /25 #PPSGB
2011 Press Pass Stealth #40
2011 Press Pass Stealth #81
2011 Press Pass Stealth Black and White /25 #40
2011 Press Pass Stealth Black and White /25 #81
2011 Press Pass Stealth Holofoil /99 #40
2011 Press Pass Stealth Holofoil /99 #81
2011 Press Pass Stealth Metal of Honor Medal of Honor /50 #BAGB
2011 Press Pass Stealth Metal of Honor Purple Heart /25 #MHGB
2011 Press Pass Stealth Metal of Honor Silver Star /99 #BAGB
2011 Press Pass Stealth Purple /25 #40
2011 Press Pass Wal-Mart Top 12 Tires /25 #T12GB
2011 Press Pass Winning Tickets #WT21
2011 Press Pass Winning Tickets #WT29
2011 Wheels Main Event #4
2011 Wheels Main Event #75
2011 Wheels Main Event All Stars #A5
2011 Wheels Main Event All Stars Brushed Foil /199 #A5
2011 Wheels Main Event All Stars Holofoil /50 #A5
2011 Wheels Main Event Black and White #4
2011 Wheels Main Event Black and White #75
2011 Wheels Main Event Blue /75 #4
2011 Wheels Main Event Blue /75 #75
2011 Wheels Main Event Green /1 #4
2011 Wheels Main Event Green /1 #75
2011 Wheels Main Event Marks Autographs Blue /10 #MEGB
2011 Wheels Main Event Marks Autographs Gold /25 #MEGB
2011 Wheels Main Event Marks Autographs Silver /50 #MEGB
2011 Wheels Main Event Red /20 #4
2011 Wheels Main Event Red /20 #75
2012 Press Pass #4
2012 Press Pass Autographs Blue /10 #PPAGB
2012 Press Pass Autographs Printing Plates Black /1 #PPAGB
2012 Press Pass Autographs Printing Plates Cyan /1 #PPAGB
2012 Press Pass Autographs Printing Plates Magenta /1 #PPAGB
2012 Press Pass Autographs Printing Plates Yellow /1 #PPAGB
2012 Press Pass Autographs Red /35 #PPAGB
2012 Press Pass Autographs Silver /199 #PPAGB
2012 Press Pass Blue #4
2012 Press Pass Blue Holofoil /35 #4
2012 Press Pass Cup Chase #CCR7
2012 Press Pass Cup Chase Prizes #CCP5
2012 Press Pass Fanfare #4
2012 Press Pass Fanfare Autographs Blue /10 #GB
2012 Press Pass Fanfare Autographs Red /75 #GB
2012 Press Pass Fanfare Blue Foil Die Cuts #4
2012 Press Pass Fanfare Diamond /5 #4
2012 Press Pass Fanfare Holofoil Die Cuts #4
2012 Press Pass Fanfare Magnificent Materials /250 #MMGB
2012 Press Pass Fanfare Magnificent Materials Dual Swatches /50 #MMGB
2012 Press Pass Fanfare Magnificent Materials Dual Swatches Melting /10 #MMGB
2012 Press Pass Fanfare Magnificent Materials Gold /125 #MMGB
2012 Press Pass Fanfare Power Rankings #PR1
2012 Press Pass Fanfare Sapphire /20 #4
2012 Press Pass Fanfare Silver /25 #4
2012 Press Pass Gold #4
2012 Press Pass Ignite #5
2012 Press Pass Ignite #52
2012 Press Pass Ignite Materials Autographs Gun Metal /20 #IMGB
2012 Press Pass Ignite Materials Autographs Red /5 #IMGB
2012 Press Pass Ignite Materials Autographs Silver /125 #IMGB
2012 Press Pass Ignite Materials Gun Metal /99 #IMGB
2012 Press Pass Ignite Materials Red /10 #IMGB
2012 Press Pass Ignite Materials Silver #IMGB
2012 Press Pass Ignite Proofs Black and White /50 #5
2012 Press Pass Ignite Proofs Black and White /50 #52
2012 Press Pass Ignite Proofs Cyan #5
2012 Press Pass Ignite Proofs Cyan #52
2012 Press Pass Ignite Proofs Magenta #5
2012 Press Pass Ignite Proofs Magenta #52
2012 Press Pass Ignite Proofs Yellow /10 #5
2012 Press Pass Ignite Proofs Yellow /10 #52
2012 Press Pass Power Picks Blue /50 #28
2012 Press Pass Power Picks Gold /50 #28
2012 Press Pass Power Picks Holofoil /10 #28
2012 Press Pass Purple /35 #4
2012 Press Pass Redline #5
2012 Press Pass Redline Black /99 #5
2012 Press Pass Redline Cyan /50 #5
2012 Press Pass Redline Magenta /15 #5
2012 Press Pass Redline Signatures Blue /5 #RSGB
2012 Press Pass Redline Signatures Gold /25 #RSGB
2012 Press Pass Redline Signatures Holofoil /10 #RSGB
2012 Press Pass Redline Signatures Melting /1 #RSGB
2012 Press Pass Redline Signatures Red /48 #RSGB
2012 Press Pass Redline Yellow /1 #5
2012 Press Pass Showcase /499 #3
2012 Press Pass Showcase /499 #54
2012 Press Pass Showcase Classic Collections Ink /10 #CCMRFR
2012 Press Pass Showcase Classic Collections Ink Gold /5 #CCMRFR
2012 Press Pass Showcase Classic Collections Ink Melting /1 #CCMRFR
2012 Press Pass Showcase Classic Collections Memorabilia /99 #CCMRFR
2012 Press Pass Showcase Classic Collections Memorabilia Gold /50 #CCMRFR
2012 Press Pass Showcase Classic Collections Memorabilia Melting /5 #CCMRFR
2012 Press Pass Showcase Gold /125 #3
2012 Press Pass Showcase Gold /125 #54
2012 Press Pass Showcase Green /5 #3
2012 Press Pass Showcase Green /5 #54
2012 Press Pass Showcase Melting /1 #3
2012 Press Pass Showcase Melting /1 #54
2012 Press Pass Showcase Purple /1 #3
2012 Press Pass Showcase Purple /1 #54
2012 Press Pass Showcase Red /25 #3
2012 Press Pass Showcase Red /25 #54
2012 Press Pass Snapshots #SS4
2012 Press Pass Target Snapshots #SSTG4
2012 Total Memorabilia #3
2012 Total Memorabilia Black and White /99 #3
2012 Total Memorabilia Gold /275 #3
2012 Total Memorabilia Red Retail /250 #3
2012 Total Memorabilia Single Swatch Gold /99 #TMGB
2012 Total Memorabilia Single Swatch Holofoil /50 #TMGB
2012 Total Memorabilia Single Swatch Melting /10 #TMGB
2012 Total Memorabilia Single Swatch Silver /199 #TMGB
2013 Press Pass #4
2013 Press Pass #0
2013 Press Pass Burning Rubber Blue /50 #BRGB
2013 Press Pass Burning Rubber Blue /50 #BRGB2
2013 Press Pass Burning Rubber Gold /199 #BRGB
2013 Press Pass Burning Rubber Gold /199 #BRGB2
2013 Press Pass Burning Rubber Holofoil /75 #BRGB
2013 Press Pass Burning Rubber Holofoil /75 #BRGB2
2013 Press Pass Burning Rubber Melting /10 #BRGB
2013 Press Pass Burning Rubber Melting /10 #BRGB2
2013 Press Pass Certified Winners Autographs Gold /10 #GB
2013 Press Pass Certified Winners Autographs Melting /5 #GB
2013 Press Pass Color Proofs Black #4
2013 Press Pass Color Proofs Cyan /35 #4
2013 Press Pass Color Proofs Magenta #4
2013 Press Pass Color Proofs Yellow /5 #4
2013 Press Pass Cup Chase #CC1
2013 Press Pass Cup Chase Prizes #CCP7
2013 Press Pass Fanfare #5
2013 Press Pass Fanfare #6
2013 Press Pass Fanfare Autographs Blue /1 #GB
2013 Press Pass Fanfare Autographs Gold /10 #GB
2013 Press Pass Fanfare Autographs Green /6 #GB
2013 Press Pass Fanfare Autographs Red /5 #GB
2013 Press Pass Fanfare Autographs Silver /25 #GB
2013 Press Pass Fanfare Diamond Die Cuts /5 #5
2013 Press Pass Fanfare Diamond Die Cuts /5 #6
2013 Press Pass Fanfare Green /3 #5
2013 Press Pass Fanfare Green /3 #6
2013 Press Pass Fanfare Holofoil Die Cuts #5
2013 Press Pass Fanfare Holofoil Die Cuts #6
2013 Press Pass Fanfare Magnificent Jumbo Materials Signatures /10 #GB
2013 Press Pass Fanfare Magnificent Materials Dual Swatches /50 #GB
2013 Press Pass Fanfare Magnificent Materials Dual Swatches Melting /10 #GB
2013 Press Pass Fanfare Magnificent Materials Gold /50 #GB
2013 Press Pass Fanfare Magnificent Materials Jumbo Swatches /25 #GB
2013 Press Pass Fanfare Magnificent Materials Signatures /99 #GB
2013 Press Pass Fanfare Magnificent Materials Signatures Blue /25 #GB
2013 Press Pass Fanfare Magnificent Materials Silver /199 #GB
2013 Press Pass Fanfare Red Foil Die Cuts #5
2013 Press Pass Fanfare Red Foil Die Cuts #6
2013 Press Pass Fanfare Sapphire /20 #5
2013 Press Pass Fanfare Sapphire /20 #6
2013 Press Pass Fanfare Signature Ride Autographs /25 #GB
2013 Press Pass Fanfare Signature Ride Autographs Blue /5 #GB
2013 Press Pass Fanfare Signature Ride Autographs Red /10 #GB
2013 Press Pass Fanfare Silver /25 #5
2013 Press Pass Fanfare Silver /25 #6
2013 Press Pass Ignite #4
2013 Press Pass Ignite Great American Treads Autographs Blue Holofoil /20 #GATGB
2013 Press Pass Ignite Great American Treads Autographs Red /1 #GATGB
2013 Press Pass Ignite Hot Threads Blue Holofoil /99 #HTGB
2013 Press Pass Ignite Hot Threads Patch Red /10 #HTGB
2013 Press Pass Ignite Hot Threads Silver #HTGB
2013 Press Pass Ignite Ink Black /50 #IIGB
2013 Press Pass Ignite Ink Blue /20 #IIGB
2013 Press Pass Ignite Ink Red /5 #IIGB
2013 Press Pass Ignite Proofs Black and White /50 #4
2013 Press Pass Ignite Proofs Cyan #4
2013 Press Pass Ignite Proofs Magenta #4
2013 Press Pass Ignite Proofs Yellow /5 #4
2013 Press Pass Power Picks Blue /99 #25
2013 Press Pass Power Picks Blue /99 #29
2013 Press Pass Power Picks Gold /50 #25
2013 Press Pass Power Picks Gold /50 #29
2013 Press Pass Power Picks Holofoil /10 #25
2013 Press Pass Power Picks Holofoil /10 #29
2013 Press Pass Racing Champions #RC7
2013 Press Pass Racing Champions #RC23
2013 Press Pass Redline #6
2013 Press Pass Redline Black /99 #6
2013 Press Pass Redline Cyan /50 #6
2013 Press Pass Redline Dynamic Duals Dual Relic Blue /5 #DDGB
2013 Press Pass Redline Dynamic Duals Dual Relic Gold /10 #DDGB
2013 Press Pass Redline Dynamic Duals Dual Relic Melting /1 #DDGB
2013 Press Pass Redline Dynamic Duals Dual Relic Red /75 #DDGB
2013 Press Pass Redline Dynamic Duals Dual Relic Silver /25 #DDGB
2013 Press Pass Redline Magenta /15 #6
2013 Press Pass Redline Signatures Blue /50 #RSGB
2013 Press Pass Redline Signatures Gold /5 #RSGB
2013 Press Pass Redline Signatures Holo /16 #RSGB
2013 Press Pass Redline Signatures Melting /1 #RSGB
2013 Press Pass Redline Signatures Red /99 #RSGB
2013 Press Pass Redline Yellow /1 #6
2013 Press Pass Showcase /349 #3
2013 Press Pass Showcase /349 #57
2013 Press Pass Showcase Black /1 #3
2013 Press Pass Showcase Black /1 #57
2013 Press Pass Showcase Blue /25 #3
2013 Press Pass Showcase Blue /25 #57
2013 Press Pass Showcase Classic Collections Ink Gold /5 #CCIRFR
2013 Press Pass Showcase Classic Collections Ink Melting /1 #CCIRFR
2013 Press Pass Showcase Classic Collections Ink Red /1 #CCIRFR
2013 Press Pass Showcase Classic Collections Memorabilia Gold /25 #CCMRFR
2013 Press Pass Showcase Classic Collections Memorabilia Melting /5 #CCMRFR
2013 Press Pass Showcase Classic Collections Memorabilia Silver /75 #CCMRFR
2013 Press Pass Showcase Gold /99 #3
2013 Press Pass Showcase Gold /99 #57
2013 Press Pass Showcase Green /20 #3
2013 Press Pass Showcase Green /20 #57
2013 Press Pass Showcase Purple /13 #3
2013 Press Pass Showcase Purple /13 #57
2013 Press Pass Showcase Red /10 #3
2013 Press Pass Showcase Red /10 #57
2013 Press Pass Showcase Series Standouts Gold /50 #2
2013 Press Pass Showcase Showcase Patches /5 #SPGB
2013 Press Pass Showcase Studio Showcase /299 #2
2013 Press Pass Showcase Studio Showcase Blue /40 #2
2013 Press Pass Showcase Studio Showcase Green /25 #2
2013 Press Pass Showcase Studio Showcase Ink /25 #SSIGB
2013 Press Pass Showcase Studio Showcase Ink Gold /10 #SSIGB
2013 Press Pass Showcase Studio Showcase Ink Melting /1 #SSIGB
2013 Press Pass Showcase Studio Showcase Ink Red /5 #SSIGB
2013 Press Pass Showcase Studio Showcase Melting /1 #2
2013 Press Pass Showcase Studio Showcase Purple /13 #2
2013 Press Pass Showcase Studio Showcase Red /10 #2
2013 Press Pass Signings Blue /1 #GB
2013 Press Pass Signings Gold /25 #GB
2013 Press Pass Signings Holofoil /9 #GB
2013 Press Pass Signings Printing Plates Black /1 #GB
2013 Press Pass Signings Printing Plates Cyan /1 #GB
2013 Press Pass Signings Printing Plates Magenta /1 #GB
2013 Press Pass Signings Printing Plates Yellow /1 #GB
2013 Press Pass Signings Silver /50 #GB
2013 Total Memorabilia #4
2013 Total Memorabilia Black and White /99 #4
2013 Total Memorabilia Dual Swatch Gold /199 #TMGB
2013 Total Memorabilia Gold /275 #4
2013 Total Memorabilia Quad Swatch Melting /10 #TMGB
2013 Total Memorabilia Red #4
2013 Total Memorabilia Single Swatch Silver /438 #TMGB
2013 Total Memorabilia Smooth Operators #SO8
2013 Total Memorabilia Triple Swatch Holofoil /99 #TMGB
2014 Press Pass #3
2014 Press Pass #75
2014 Press Pass American Thunder #6
2014 Press Pass American Thunder #53
2014 Press Pass American Thunder Autographs Blue /10 #ATAGB
2014 Press Pass American Thunder Autographs Red /5 #ATAGB
2014 Press Pass American Thunder Autographs White /25 #ATAGB
2014 Press Pass American Thunder Battle Armor Blue /25 #BAGB
2014 Press Pass American Thunder Battle Armor Red /1 #BAGB
2014 Press Pass American Thunder Battle Armor Silver /99 #BAGB
2014 Press Pass American Thunder Black and White /50 #6
2014 Press Pass American Thunder Black and White /50 #53
2014 Press Pass American Thunder Brothers In Arms Autographs Blue /5 #BARFR
2014 Press Pass American Thunder Brothers In Arms Autographs Red /1 #BARFR
2014 Press Pass American Thunder Brothers In Arms Autographs White /10 #BARFR
2014 Press Pass American Thunder Brothers In Arms Relics Blue /25 #BARFR
2014 Press Pass American Thunder Brothers In Arms Relics Red /5 #BARFR
2014 Press Pass American Thunder Brothers In Arms Relics Silver /50 #BARFR
2014 Press Pass American Thunder Class A Uniforms Blue /99 #CAUGB
2014 Press Pass American Thunder Class A Uniforms Red /10 #CAUGB
2014 Press Pass American Thunder Class A Uniforms Silver #CAUGB
2014 Press Pass American Thunder Cyan #6
2014 Press Pass American Thunder Cyan #53
2014 Press Pass American Thunder Great American Treads Autographs Blue /25 #GATGB
2014 Press Pass American Thunder Great American Treads Autographs Red /1 #GATGB
2014 Press Pass American Thunder Magenta #6
2014 Press Pass American Thunder Magenta #53
2014 Press Pass American Thunder Top Speed #TS3
2014 Press Pass American Thunder Yellow /5 #6
2014 Press Pass American Thunder Yellow /5 #53
2014 Press Pass Burning Rubber Blue /25 #BRGB
2014 Press Pass Burning Rubber Gold /75 #BRGB
2014 Press Pass Burning Rubber Holofoil /50 #BRGB
2014 Press Pass Burning Rubber Letterman /8 #BRLGB
2014 Press Pass Burning Rubber Melting /10 #BRGB
2014 Press Pass Certified Winners Memorabilia Autographs Gold /10 #CWGB
2014 Press Pass Certified Winners Memorabilia Autographs Melting /1 #CWGB
2014 Press Pass Color Proofs Black /70 #3
2014 Press Pass Color Proofs Black /70 #75
2014 Press Pass Color Proofs Cyan /35 #3
2014 Press Pass Color Proofs Cyan /35 #75
2014 Press Pass Color Proofs Magenta #3
2014 Press Pass Color Proofs Magenta #75
2014 Press Pass Color Proofs Yellow /5 #3
2014 Press Pass Color Proofs Yellow /5 #75
2014 Press Pass Cup Chase #1
2014 Press Pass Five Star Classic Compilations Combo Autographs Blue /5 #CCRFR
2014 Press Pass Five Star Classic Compilations Combo Autographs Melting /1 #CCRFR
2014 Press Pass Gold #3
2014 Press Pass Gold #75
2014 Press Pass Redline #7
2014 Press Pass Redline Black /75 #7
2014 Press Pass Redline Blue Foil #7
2014 Press Pass Redline Cyan /50 #7
2014 Press Pass Redline Green National Convention /5 #7
2014 Press Pass Redline Magenta /10 #7
2014 Press Pass Redline Muscle Car Sheet Metal Blue /10 #MCMGB
2014 Press Pass Redline Muscle Car Sheet Metal Gold /25 #MCMGB
2014 Press Pass Redline Muscle Car Sheet Metal Melting /1 #MCMGB
2014 Press Pass Redline Muscle Car Sheet Metal Red /50 #MCMGB
2014 Press Pass Redline Relic Autographs Blue /10 #RRSEGB
2014 Press Pass Redline Relic Autographs Gold /25 #RRSEGB
2014 Press Pass Redline Relic Autographs Melting /1 #RRSEGB
2014 Press Pass Redline Relic Autographs Red /50 #RRSEGB
2014 Press Pass Redline Relics Blue /25 #RRGB
2014 Press Pass Redline Relics Gold /50 #RRGB
2014 Press Pass Redline Relics Melting /1 #RRGB
2014 Press Pass Redline Relics Red /75 #RRGB
2014 Press Pass Redline Signatures Blue /25 #RSGB
2014 Press Pass Redline Signatures Gold /50 #RSGB
2014 Press Pass Redline Signatures Melting /10 #RSGB
2014 Press Pass Redline Signatures Red /65 #RSGB
2014 Press Pass Redline Yellow /1 #7
2014 Press Pass Replay #15
2014 Press Pass Signings Gold /50 #PPSGB
2014 Press Pass Signings Holofoil /10 #PPSGB
2014 Press Pass Signings Melting /1 #PPSGB
2014 Press Pass Signings Printing Plates Black /1 #PPSGB
2014 Press Pass Signings Printing Plates Cyan /1 #PPSGB
2014 Press Pass Signings Printing Plates Magenta /1 #PPSGB
2014 Press Pass Signings Printing Plates Yellow /1 #PPSGB
2014 Press Pass Signings Silver /100 #PPSGB
2014 Total Memorabilia #3
2014 Total Memorabilia Black and White /99 #3
2014 Total Memorabilia Dual Swatch Gold /150 #TMGB
2014 Total Memorabilia Gold /175 #3
2014 Total Memorabilia Quad Swatch Melting /25 #TMGB
2014 Total Memorabilia Red #3
2014 Total Memorabilia Single Swatch Silver /275 #TMGB
2014 Total Memorabilia Triple Swatch Blue /99 #TMGB
2015 Press Pass #6
2015 Press Pass #100
2015 Press Pass Cup Chase #6
2015 Press Pass Cup Chase #100
2015 Press Pass Cup Chase Blue /25 #6
2015 Press Pass Cup Chase Blue /25 #100
2015 Press Pass Cup Chase Gold /75 #6
2015 Press Pass Cup Chase Gold /75 #100
2015 Press Pass Cup Chase Green /10 #6
2015 Press Pass Cup Chase Green /10 #100
2015 Press Pass Cup Chase Melting /1 #6
2015 Press Pass Cup Chase Melting /1 #100
2015 Press Pass Cup Chase Upper Cuts /13 #UCGB
2015 Press Pass Pit Road Pieces Blue /25 #PPMGB
2015 Press Pass Pit Road Pieces Gold /50 #PPMGB
2015 Press Pass Pit Road Pieces Green /10 #PPMGB
2015 Press Pass Pit Road Pieces Melting /1 #PPMGB
2015 Press Pass Pit Road Pieces Signature Edition Blue /25 #PRPGB
2015 Press Pass Pit Road Pieces Signature Edition Gold /50 #PRPGB
2015 Press Pass Pit Road Pieces Signature Edition Green /10 #PRPGB
2015 Press Pass Pit Road Pieces Signature Edition Melting /1 #PRPGB
2015 Press Pass Purple #6
2015 Press Pass Purple #100
2015 Press Pass Red #6
2015 Press Pass Red #100
2015 Press Pass Signature Series Blue /25 #SSGB
2015 Press Pass Signature Series Gold /50 #SSGB
2015 Press Pass Signature Series Green /10 #SSGB
2015 Press Pass Signature Series Melting /1 #SSGB
2015 Press Pass Signings Blue /75 #PPSGB
2015 Press Pass Signings Gold #PPSGB
2015 Press Pass Signings Green /25 #PPSGB
2015 Press Pass Signings Melting /10 #PPSGB
2015 Press Pass Signings Red /50 #PPSGB
2016 Certified #22
2016 Certified Complete Materials /249 #8
2016 Certified Complete Materials Mirror Black /1 #8
2016 Certified Complete Materials Mirror Blue /50 #8
2016 Certified Complete Materials Mirror Gold /25 #8
2016 Certified Complete Materials Mirror Green /5 #8
2016 Certified Complete Materials Mirror Orange /99 #8
2016 Certified Complete Materials Mirror Purple /10 #8
2016 Certified Complete Materials Mirror Red /75 #8
2016 Certified Complete Materials Mirror Silver /99 #8
2016 Certified Mirror Black /1 #22
2016 Certified Mirror Blue /50 #22
2016 Certified Mirror Gold /25 #22
2016 Certified Mirror Green /5 #22
2016 Certified Mirror Orange /99 #22
2016 Certified Mirror Purple /10 #22
2016 Certified Mirror Red /75 #22
2016 Certified Mirror Silver /99 #22
2016 Certified Signatures /199 #9
2016 Certified Signatures Mirror Black /1 #9
2016 Certified Signatures Mirror Blue /50 #9
2016 Certified Signatures Mirror Gold /25 #9
2016 Certified Signatures Mirror Green /5 #9
2016 Certified Signatures Mirror Orange /25 #9
2016 Certified Signatures Mirror Purple /10 #9
2016 Certified Signatures Mirror Red /60 #9
2016 Certified Signatures Mirror Silver /25 #9
2016 Certified Skills /199 #8
2016 Certified Skills Mirror Black /1 #8
2016 Certified Skills Mirror Blue /50 #8
2016 Certified Skills Mirror Gold /25 #8
2016 Certified Skills Mirror Green /5 #8
2016 Certified Skills Mirror Orange /99 #8
2016 Certified Skills Mirror Purple /10 #8
2016 Certified Skills Mirror Red /75 #8
2016 Certified Skills Mirror Silver /99 #8
2016 Certified Sprint Cup Swatches /99 #10
2016 Certified Sprint Cup Swatches Mirror Black /1 #10
2016 Certified Sprint Cup Swatches Mirror Blue /50 #10
2016 Certified Sprint Cup Swatches Mirror Gold /25 #10
2016 Certified Sprint Cup Swatches Mirror Green /5 #10
2016 Certified Sprint Cup Swatches Mirror Orange /99 #10
2016 Certified Sprint Cup Swatches Mirror Purple /10 #10
2016 Certified Sprint Cup Swatches Mirror Red /75 #10
2016 Certified Sprint Cup Swatches Mirror Silver /99 #10
2016 Panini National Treasures /25 #12
2016 Panini National Treasures Black /5 #12
2016 Panini National Treasures Blue /1 #12
2016 Panini National Treasures Combo Materials /25 #8
2016 Panini National Treasures Combo Materials Black /5 #8
2016 Panini National Treasures Combo Materials Blue /1 #8
2016 Panini National Treasures Combo Materials Gold /10 #8
2016 Panini National Treasures Combo Materials Printing Plates Black /1 #8
2016 Panini National Treasures Combo Materials Printing Plates Cyan /1 #8
2016 Panini National Treasures Combo Materials Printing Plates Magenta /1 #8
2016 Panini National Treasures Combo Materials Printing Plates Yellow /1 #8
2016 Panini National Treasures Combo Materials Silver /15 #8
2016 Panini National Treasures Gold /15 #12
2016 Panini National Treasures Jumbo Firesuit Patch Signature Booklet Alpine Stars /1 #10
2016 Panini National Treasures Jumbo Firesuit Patch Signature Booklet Associate Sponsor 1 /1 #10
2016 Panini National Treasures Jumbo Firesuit Patch Signature Booklet Associate Sponsor 10 /1 #10
2016 Panini National Treasures Jumbo Firesuit Patch Signature Booklet Associate Sponsor 11 /1 #10
2016 Panini National Treasures Jumbo Firesuit Patch Signature Booklet Associate Sponsor 12 /1 #10
2016 Panini National Treasures Jumbo Firesuit Patch Signature Booklet Associate Sponsor 13 /1 #10
2016 Panini National Treasures Jumbo Firesuit Patch Signature Booklet Associate Sponsor 2 /1 #10
2016 Panini National Treasures Jumbo Firesuit Patch Signature Booklet Associate Sponsor 3 /1 #10
2016 Panini National Treasures Jumbo Firesuit Patch Signature Booklet Associate Sponsor 4 /1 #10
2016 Panini National Treasures Jumbo Firesuit Patch Signature Booklet Associate Sponsor 5 /1 #10
2016 Panini National Treasures Jumbo Firesuit Patch Signature Booklet Associate Sponsor 6 /1 #10
2016 Panini National Treasures Jumbo Firesuit Patch Signature Booklet Associate Sponsor 7 /1 #10
2016 Panini National Treasures Jumbo Firesuit Patch Signature Booklet Associate Sponsor 8 /1 #10
2016 Panini National Treasures Jumbo Firesuit Patch Signature Booklet Associate Sponsor 9 /1 #10
2016 Panini National Treasures Jumbo Firesuit Patch Signature Booklet Goodyear /2 #10
2016 Panini National Treasures Jumbo Firesuit Patch Signature Booklet Manufacturers Logo /1 #10
2016 Panini National Treasures Jumbo Firesuit Patch Signature Booklet Nameplate /1 #10
2016 Panini National Treasures Jumbo Firesuit Patch Signature Booklet NASCAR /1 #10
2016 Panini National Treasures Jumbo Firesuit Patch Signature Booklet Sprint Cup Logo /1 #10
2016 Panini National Treasures Jumbo Firesuit Patch Signature Booklet Sunoco /1 #10
2016 Panini National Treasures Jumbo Firesuit Signatures /25 #10
2016 Panini National Treasures Jumbo Firesuit Signatures Black /5 #10
2016 Panini National Treasures Jumbo Firesuit Signatures Blue /1 #10
2016 Panini National Treasures Jumbo Firesuit Signatures Gold /10 #10
2016 Panini National Treasures Jumbo Firesuit Signatures Printing Plates Black /1 #10
2016 Panini National Treasures Jumbo Firesuit Signatures Printing Plates Cyan /1 #10
2016 Panini National Treasures Jumbo Firesuit Signatures Printing Plates Magenta /1 #10
2016 Panini National Treasures Jumbo Firesuit Signatures Printing Plates Yellow /1 #10
2016 Panini National Treasures Jumbo Firesuit Signatures Silver /15 #10
2016 Panini National Treasures Jumbo Sheet Metal Signatures Blue /1 #5
2016 Panini National Treasures Jumbo Sheet Metal Signatures Printing Plates Black /1 #5
2016 Panini National Treasures Jumbo Sheet Metal Signatures Printing Plates Cyan /1 #5
2016 Panini National Treasures Jumbo Sheet Metal Signatures Printing Plates Magenta /1 #5
2016 Panini National Treasures Jumbo Sheet Metal Signatures Printing Plates Yellow /1 #5
2016 Panini National Treasures Printing Plates Black /1 #12
2016 Panini National Treasures Printing Plates Cyan /1 #12
2016 Panini National Treasures Printing Plates Magenta /1 #12
2016 Panini National Treasures Printing Plates Yellow /1 #12
2016 Panini National Treasures Quad Driver Materials /25 #3
2016 Panini National Treasures Quad Driver Materials /25 #9
2016 Panini National Treasures Quad Driver Materials Black /5 #3
2016 Panini National Treasures Quad Driver Materials Black /5 #9
2016 Panini National Treasures Quad Driver Materials Blue /1 #3
2016 Panini National Treasures Quad Driver Materials Blue /1 #9
2016 Panini National Treasures Quad Driver Materials Gold /10 #3
2016 Panini National Treasures Quad Driver Materials Gold /10 #9
2016 Panini National Treasures Quad Driver Materials Printing Plates Black /1 #3
2016 Panini National Treasures Quad Driver Materials Printing Plates Black /1 #9
2016 Panini National Treasures Quad Driver Materials Printing Plates Cyan /1 #3
2016 Panini National Treasures Quad Driver Materials Printing Plates Cyan /1 #9
2016 Panini National Treasures Quad Driver Materials Printing Plates Magenta /1 #3
2016 Panini National Treasures Quad Driver Materials Printing Plates Magenta /1 #9
2016 Panini National Treasures Quad Driver Materials Printing Plates Yellow /1 #3
2016 Panini National Treasures Quad Driver Materials Printing Plates Yellow /1 #9
2016 Panini National Treasures Quad Driver Materials Silver /15 #3
2016 Panini National Treasures Quad Driver Materials Silver /15 #9
2016 Panini National Treasures Signature Dual Materials Black /5 #10
2016 Panini National Treasures Signature Dual Materials Blue /1 #10
2016 Panini National Treasures Signature Dual Materials Printing Plates Black /1 #10
2016 Panini National Treasures Signature Dual Materials Printing Plates Cyan /1 #10
2016 Panini National Treasures Signature Dual Materials Printing Plates Magenta /1 #10
2016 Panini National Treasures Signature Dual Materials Printing Plates Yellow /1 #10
2016 Panini National Treasures Signature Firesuit Materials Black /5 #10
2016 Panini National Treasures Signature Firesuit Materials Blue /1 #10
2016 Panini National Treasures Signature Firesuit Materials Laundry Tag /1 #10
2016 Panini National Treasures Signature Firesuit Materials Printing Plates Black /1 #10
2016 Panini National Treasures Signature Firesuit Materials Printing Plates Cyan /1 #10
2016 Panini National Treasures Signature Firesuit Materials Printing Plates Magenta /1 #10
2016 Panini National Treasures Signature Firesuit Materials Printing Plates Yellow /1 #10
2016 Panini National Treasures Signature Quad Materials /25 #10
2016 Panini National Treasures Signature Quad Materials Black /5 #10
2016 Panini National Treasures Signature Quad Materials Blue /1 #10
2016 Panini National Treasures Signature Quad Materials Gold /10 #10
2016 Panini National Treasures Signature Quad Materials Printing Plates Black /1 #10
2016 Panini National Treasures Signature Quad Materials Printing Plates Cyan /1 #10
2016 Panini National Treasures Signature Quad Materials Printing Plates Magenta /1 #10
2016 Panini National Treasures Signature Quad Materials Printing Plates Yellow /1 #10
2016 Panini National Treasures Signature Quad Materials Silver /15 #10
2016 Panini National Treasures Signature Sheet Metal Materials Black /5 #10
2016 Panini National Treasures Signature Sheet Metal Materials Blue /1 #10
2016 Panini National Treasures Signature Sheet Metal Materials Printing Plates Black /1 #10
2016 Panini National Treasures Signature Sheet Metal Materials Printing Plates Cyan /1 #10
2016 Panini National Treasures Signature Sheet Metal Materials Printing Plates Magenta /1 #10
2016 Panini National Treasures Signature Sheet Metal Materials Printing Plates Yellow /1 #10
2016 Panini National Treasures Silver /20 #12
2016 Panini National Treasures Six Signatures /25 #2
2016 Panini National Treasures Six Signatures Black /10 #2
2016 Panini National Treasures Six Signatures Blue /1 #2
2016 Panini National Treasures Six Signatures Gold /15 #2
2016 Panini National Treasures Timelines Black /5 #5
2016 Panini National Treasures Timelines Blue /1 #5
2016 Panini National Treasures Timelines Gold /10 #5
2016 Panini National Treasures Timelines Printing Plates Black /1 #5
2016 Panini National Treasures Timelines Printing Plates Cyan /1 #5
2016 Panini National Treasures Timelines Printing Plates Magenta /1 #5
2016 Panini National Treasures Timelines Printing Plates Yellow /1 #5
2016 Panini National Treasures Timelines Signatures Black /5 #5
2016 Panini National Treasures Timelines Signatures Blue /1 #5
2016 Panini National Treasures Timelines Signatures Gold /10 #5
2016 Panini National Treasures Timelines Signatures Printing Plates Black /1 #5
2016 Panini National Treasures Timelines Signatures Printing Plates Cyan /1 #5
2016 Panini National Treasures Timelines Signatures Printing Plates Magenta /1 #5
2016 Panini National Treasures Timelines Signatures Printing Plates Yellow /1 #5
2016 Panini National Treasures Trio Driver Materials /25 #7
2016 Panini National Treasures Trio Driver Materials Black /5 #7
2016 Panini National Treasures Trio Driver Materials Blue /1 #7
2016 Panini National Treasures Trio Driver Materials Gold /10 #7
2016 Panini National Treasures Trio Driver Materials Printing Plates Black /1 #7
2016 Panini National Treasures Trio Driver Materials Printing Plates Cyan /1 #7
2016 Panini National Treasures Trio Driver Materials Printing Plates Magenta /1 #7
2016 Panini National Treasures Trio Driver Materials Printing Plates Yellow /1 #7
2016 Panini National Treasures Trio Driver Materials Silver /15 #7
2016 Panini Prizm #16
2016 Panini Prizm Autographs Prizms #28
2016 Panini Prizm Autographs Prizms Black /3 #28
2016 Panini Prizm Autographs Prizms Blue Flag /75 #28
2016 Panini Prizm Autographs Prizms Camo /16 #28
2016 Panini Prizm Autographs Prizms Checkered Flag /1 #28
2016 Panini Prizm Autographs Prizms Gold /10 #28
2016 Panini Prizm Autographs Prizms Green Flag /99 #28
2016 Panini Prizm Autographs Prizms Rainbow /24 #28
2016 Panini Prizm Autographs Prizms Red Flag /50 #28
2016 Panini Prizm Autographs Prizms Red White and Blue /25 #28
2016 Panini Prizm Autographs Prizms White Flag /5 #28
2016 Panini Prizm Firesuit Fabrics /149 #20
2016 Panini Prizm Firesuit Fabrics Prizms Blue Flag /75 #20
2016 Panini Prizm Firesuit Fabrics Prizms Checkered Flag /1 #20
2016 Panini Prizm Firesuit Fabrics Prizms Green Flag /99 #20
2016 Panini Prizm Firesuit Fabrics Prizms Red Flag /25 #20
2016 Panini Prizm Firesuit Fabrics Team /249 #20
2016 Panini Prizm Firesuit Fabrics Team Prizms Blue Flag /75 #20
2016 Panini Prizm Firesuit Fabrics Team Prizms Checkered Flag /1 #20
2016 Panini Prizm Firesuit Fabrics Team Prizms Green Flag /99 #20
2016 Panini Prizm Firesuit Fabrics Team Prizms Red Flag /25 #20
2016 Panini Prizm Prizms #16
2016 Panini Prizm Prizms Black /3 #16
2016 Panini Prizm Prizms Blue Flag /99 #16
2016 Panini Prizm Prizms Camo /16 #16
2016 Panini Prizm Prizms Checkered Flag /1 #16
2016 Panini Prizm Prizms Gold /10 #16
2016 Panini Prizm Prizms Green Flag /149 #16
2016 Panini Prizm Prizms Rainbow /24 #16
2016 Panini Prizm Prizms Red Flag /75 #16
2016 Panini Prizm Prizms Red White and Blue #16
2016 Panini Prizm Prizms White Flag /5 #16
2016 Panini Torque #29
2016 Panini Torque Artist Proof /50 #29
2016 Panini Torque Blackout /1 #29
2016 Panini Torque Blue /125 #29
2016 Panini Torque Gold #29
2016 Panini Torque Holo Gold /5 #29
2016 Panini Torque Holo Silver /10 #29
2016 Panini Torque Horsepower Heroes #20
2016 Panini Torque Horsepower Heroes Gold /199 #20
2016 Panini Torque Horsepower Heroes Holo Silver /99 #20
2016 Panini Torque Metal Materials /249 #13
2016 Panini Torque Metal Materials Blue /99 #13
2016 Panini Torque Metal Materials Green /25 #13
2016 Panini Torque Metal Materials Purple /10 #13
2016 Panini Torque Metal Materials Red /49 #13
2016 Panini Torque Painted to Perfection #17
2016 Panini Torque Painted to Perfection Blue /99 #17
2016 Panini Torque Painted to Perfection Checkerboard /10 #17
2016 Panini Torque Painted to Perfection Green /25 #17
2016 Panini Torque Painted to Perfection Red /49 #17
2016 Panini Torque Pairings Materials /249 #21
2016 Panini Torque Pairings Materials Blue /99 #21
2016 Panini Torque Pairings Materials Green /25 #21
2016 Panini Torque Pairings Materials Purple /10 #21
2016 Panini Torque Pairings Materials Red /49 #21
2016 Panini Torque Printing Plates Black /1 #29
2016 Panini Torque Printing Plates Cyan /1 #29
2016 Panini Torque Printing Plates Magenta /1 #29
2016 Panini Torque Printing Plates Yellow /1 #29
2016 Panini Torque Purple /25 #29
2016 Panini Torque Red /99 #29
2016 Panini Torque Rubber Relics /399 #10
2016 Panini Torque Rubber Relics Blue /99 #10
2016 Panini Torque Rubber Relics Green /25 #10
2016 Panini Torque Rubber Relics Purple /10 #10
2016 Panini Torque Rubber Relics Red /49 #10
2016 Panini Torque Silhouettes Firesuit Autographs /75 #9
2016 Panini Torque Silhouettes Firesuit Autographs Blue /50 #9
2016 Panini Torque Silhouettes Firesuit Autographs Green /15 #9
2016 Panini Torque Silhouettes Firesuit Autographs Purple /10 #9
2016 Panini Torque Silhouettes Firesuit Autographs Red /25 #9
2016 Panini Torque Silhouettes Sheet Metal Autographs /75 #10
2016 Panini Torque Silhouettes Sheet Metal Autographs Blue /50 #10
2016 Panini Torque Silhouettes Sheet Metal Autographs Green /15 #10
2016 Panini Torque Silhouettes Sheet Metal Autographs Purple /10 #10
2016 Panini Torque Silhouettes Sheet Metal Autographs Red /25 #10
2016 Panini Torque Special Paint #7
2016 Panini Torque Special Paint Gold /199 #7
2016 Panini Torque Special Paint Holo Silver /99 #7
2016 Panini Torque Test Proof Black /1 #29
2016 Panini Torque Test Proof Cyan /1 #29
2016 Panini Torque Test Proof Magenta /1 #29
2016 Panini Torque Test Proof Yellow /1 #29
2016 Panini Torque Winning Vision #15
2016 Panini Torque Winning Vision Blue /99 #15
2016 Panini Torque Winning Vision Gold /149 #15
2016 Panini Torque Winning Vision Green /25 #15
2016 Panini Torque Winning Vision Purple /10 #15
2016 Panini Torque Winning Vision Red /49 #15
2017 Donruss #15
2017 Donruss #57A
2017 Donruss #155
2017 Donruss #57B
2017 Donruss #119
2017 Donruss Artist Proof /25 #15
2017 Donruss Artist Proof /25 #57
2017 Donruss Artist Proof /25 #155
2017 Donruss Artist Proof /25 #57B
2017 Donruss Artist Proof /25 #119
2017 Donruss Blue Foil /299 #15
2017 Donruss Blue Foil /299 #57A
2017 Donruss Blue Foil /299 #155
2017 Donruss Blue Foil /299 #57B
2017 Donruss Blue Foil /299 #119
2017 Donruss Gold Foil /499 #15
2017 Donruss Gold Foil /499 #155
2017 Donruss Gold Foil /499 #57A
2017 Donruss Gold Foil /499 #57B
2017 Donruss Gold Foil /499 #119
2017 Donruss Gold Press Proof /99 #15
2017 Donruss Gold Press Proof /99 #57A
2017 Donruss Gold Press Proof /99 #155
2017 Donruss Gold Press Proof /99 #57B
2017 Donruss Gold Press Proof /99 #119
2017 Donruss Green Foil /199 #15
2017 Donruss Green Foil /199 #57A
2017 Donruss Green Foil /199 #155
2017 Donruss Green Foil /199 #57B
2017 Donruss Green Foil /199 #119
2017 Donruss Press Proof /49 #15
2017 Donruss Press Proof /49 #57A
2017 Donruss Press Proof /49 #155
2017 Donruss Press Proof /49 #57B
2017 Donruss Press Proof /49 #119
2017 Donruss Printing Plates Black /1 #15
2017 Donruss Printing Plates Black /1 #57A
2017 Donruss Printing Plates Black /1 #155
2017 Donruss Printing Plates Black /1 #57B
2017 Donruss Printing Plates Black /1 #119
2017 Donruss Printing Plates Cyan /1 #15
2017 Donruss Printing Plates Cyan /1 #57A
2017 Donruss Printing Plates Cyan /1 #155
2017 Donruss Printing Plates Cyan /1 #57B
2017 Donruss Printing Plates Cyan /1 #119
2017 Donruss Printing Plates Magenta /1 #15
2017 Donruss Printing Plates Magenta /1 #155
2017 Donruss Printing Plates Magenta /1 #57A
2017 Donruss Printing Plates Magenta /1 #57B
2017 Donruss Printing Plates Magenta /1 #119
2017 Donruss Printing Plates Yellow /1 #15
2017 Donruss Printing Plates Yellow /1 #155
2017 Donruss Printing Plates Yellow /1 #57A
2017 Donruss Printing Plates Yellow /1 #57B

2017 Donruss Printing Plates Yellow /1 #119
2017 Donruss Rubber Relics #20
2017 Donruss Rubber Relics Holo Black /10 #20
2017 Donruss Rubber Relics Holo Gold /25 #20
2017 Donruss Studio Signatures Holo Black /1 #8
2017 Panini National Treasures /25 #23
2017 Panini National Treasures Associate Sponsor Patch Signatures 1 /1 #21
2017 Panini National Treasures Associate Sponsor Patch Signatures 2 /1 #21
2017 Panini National Treasures Associate Sponsor Patch Signatures 3 /1 #21
2017 Panini National Treasures Associate Sponsor Patch Signatures 4 /1 #21
2017 Panini National Treasures Associate Sponsor Patch Signatures 5 /1 #21
2017 Panini National Treasures Associate Sponsor Patch Signatures 6 /1 #21
2017 Panini National Treasures Associate Sponsor Patch Signatures 7 /1 #21
2017 Panini National Treasures Associate Sponsor Patch Signatures 8 /1 #21
2017 Panini National Treasures Associate Sponsor Patch Signatures 9 /1 #21
2017 Panini National Treasures Car Manufacturer Patch Signatures /1 #21
2017 Panini National Treasures Century Black /1 #23
2017 Panini National Treasures Century Gold /15 #23
2017 Panini National Treasures Century Green /5 #23
2017 Panini National Treasures Century Holo Gold /10 #23
2017 Panini National Treasures Century Holo Silver /20 #23
2017 Panini National Treasures Dual Firesuit Materials /25 #6
2017 Panini National Treasures Dual Firesuit Materials Black /1 #6
2017 Panini National Treasures Dual Firesuit Materials Gold /15 #6
2017 Panini National Treasures Dual Firesuit Materials Green /5 #6
2017 Panini National Treasures Dual Firesuit Materials Holo Gold /10 #6
2017 Panini National Treasures Dual Firesuit Materials Holo Silver /20 #6
2017 Panini National Treasures Dual Firesuit Materials Laundry Tag /1 #6
2017 Panini National Treasures Dual Firesuit Materials Printing Plates Black /1 #6
2017 Panini National Treasures Dual Firesuit Materials Printing Plates Cyan /1 #6
2017 Panini National Treasures Dual Firesuit Materials Printing Plates Magenta /1 #6
2017 Panini National Treasures Dual Firesuit Materials Printing Plates Yellow /1 #6
2017 Panini National Treasures Dual Firesuit Signatures /25 #6
2017 Panini National Treasures Dual Firesuit Signatures Black /1 #6
2017 Panini National Treasures Dual Firesuit Signatures Gold /15 #6
2017 Panini National Treasures Dual Firesuit Signatures Green /5 #6
2017 Panini National Treasures Dual Firesuit Signatures Holo Gold /10 #6
2017 Panini National Treasures Dual Firesuit Signatures Holo Silver /20 #6
2017 Panini National Treasures Dual Firesuit Signatures Laundry Tag /1 #6
2017 Panini National Treasures Dual Firesuit Signatures Printing Plates Black /1 #6
2017 Panini National Treasures Dual Firesuit Signatures Printing Plates Cyan /1 #6
2017 Panini National Treasures Dual Firesuit Signatures Printing Plates Magenta /1 #6
2017 Panini National Treasures Dual Firesuit Signatures Printing Plates Yellow /1 #6
2017 Panini National Treasures Dual Sheet Metal Signatures /25 #13
2017 Panini National Treasures Dual Sheet Metal Signatures Black /1 #13
2017 Panini National Treasures Dual Sheet Metal Signatures Gold /15 #13
2017 Panini National Treasures Dual Sheet Metal Signatures Green /5 #13
2017 Panini National Treasures Dual Sheet Metal Signatures Holo Gold /10 #13
2017 Panini National Treasures Dual Sheet Metal Signatures Holo Silver /20 #13
2017 Panini National Treasures Dual Sheet Metal Signatures Printing Plates Black /1 #13
2017 Panini National Treasures Dual Sheet Metal Signatures Printing Plates Cyan /1 #13
2017 Panini National Treasures Dual Sheet Metal Signatures Printing Plates Magenta /1 #13
2017 Panini National Treasures Dual Sheet Metal Signatures Printing Plates Yellow /1 #13
2017 Panini National Treasures Dual Signature Materials /50 #1
2017 Panini National Treasures Dual Signature Materials Black /1 #1
2017 Panini National Treasures Dual Signature Materials Gold /15 #1
2017 Panini National Treasures Dual Signature Materials Green /5 #1
2017 Panini National Treasures Dual Signature Materials Holo Gold /10 #1
2017 Panini National Treasures Dual Signature Materials Holo Silver /25 #1
2017 Panini National Treasures Dual Signature Materials Laundry Tag /1 #1
2017 Panini National Treasures Firesuit Manufacturer Patch Signatures /1 #21
2017 Panini National Treasures Goodyear Patch Signatures /2 #21
2017 Panini National Treasures Jumbo Firesuit Signatures /25 #6
2017 Panini National Treasures Jumbo Firesuit Signatures Black /1 #6
2017 Panini National Treasures Jumbo Firesuit Signatures Gold /15 #6
2017 Panini National Treasures Jumbo Firesuit Signatures Green /5 #6
2017 Panini National Treasures Jumbo Firesuit Signatures Holo Gold /10 #6
2017 Panini National Treasures Jumbo Firesuit Signatures Holo Silver /20 #6
2017 Panini National Treasures Jumbo Firesuit Signatures Laundry Tag /1 #6
2017 Panini National Treasures Jumbo Firesuit Signatures Printing Plates Black /1 #6
2017 Panini National Treasures Jumbo Firesuit Signatures Printing Plates Cyan /1 #6
2017 Panini National Treasures Jumbo Firesuit Signatures Printing Plates Magenta /1 #6
2017 Panini National Treasures Jumbo Firesuit Signatures Printing Plates Yellow /1 #6
2017 Panini National Treasures Nameplate Patch Signatures /1 #21
2017 Panini National Treasures NASCAR Patch Signatures /1 #21
2017 Panini National Treasures Printing Plates Black /1 #23
2017 Panini National Treasures Printing Plates Cyan /1 #23
2017 Panini National Treasures Printing Plates Magenta /1 #23
2017 Panini National Treasures Printing Plates Yellow /1 #23
2017 Panini National Treasures Series Sponsor Patch Signatures /1 #21
2017 Panini National Treasures Sunoco Patch Signatures /1 #21
2017 Panini National Treasures Three Wide Signatures /25 #9
2017 Panini National Treasures Three Wide Signatures Black /1 #9
2017 Panini National Treasures Three Wide Signatures Gold /15 #9
2017 Panini National Treasures Three Wide Signatures Green /5 #9
2017 Panini National Treasures Three Wide Signatures Holo Gold /10 #9
2017 Panini National Treasures Three Wide Signatures Holo Silver /20 #9
2017 Panini National Treasures Three Wide Signatures Laundry Tag /1 #9
2017 Panini National Treasures Three Wide Signatures Printing Plates Black /1 #9
2017 Panini National Treasures Three Wide Signatures Printing Plates Cyan /1 #9
2017 Panini National Treasures Three Wide Signatures Printing Plates Magenta /1 #9
2017 Panini National Treasures Three Wide Signatures Printing Plates Yellow /1 #9
2017 Panini Torque #28
2017 Panini Torque Artist Proof /75 #28
2017 Panini Torque Blackout /1 #28
2017 Panini Torque Blue /150 #28
2017 Panini Torque Clear Vision #28
2017 Panini Torque Clear Vision Blue /99 #28
2017 Panini Torque Clear Vision Gold /149 #28
2017 Panini Torque Clear Vision Green /25 #28
2017 Panini Torque Clear Vision Purple /10 #28
2017 Panini Torque Clear Vision Red /49 #28
2017 Panini Torque Gold #28
2017 Panini Torque Holo Gold /10 #28
2017 Panini Torque Holo Silver /25 #28
2017 Panini Torque Printing Plates Black /1 #28
2017 Panini Torque Printing Plates Cyan /1 #28
2017 Panini Torque Printing Plates Magenta /1 #28
2017 Panini Torque Printing Plates Yellow /1 #28
2017 Panini Torque Purple /50 #28
2017 Panini Torque Red /100 #28
2017 Panini Torque Test Proof Black /1 #28
2017 Panini Torque Test Proof Cyan /1 #28
2017 Panini Torque Test Proof Magenta /1 #28
2017 Panini Torque Test Proof Yellow /1 #28
2017 Select #133
2017 Select Prizms Black /3 #133
2017 Select Prizms Checkered Flag /1 #133
2017 Select Prizms Gold /10 #133
2017 Select Prizms Tie Dye /24 #133
2017 Select Prizms White /50 #133
2017 Select Select Stars #20
2017 Select Select Stars Prizms Black /3 #20
2017 Select Select Stars Prizms Checkered Flag /1 #20
2017 Select Select Stars Prizms Gold /10 #20
2017 Select Select Stars Prizms Tie Dye /24 #20
2017 Select Select Stars Prizms White /50 #20
2017 Select Select Swatches #20
2017 Select Select Swatches Prizms Blue /199 #20
2017 Select Select Swatches Prizms Checkered Flag /1 #20
2017 Select Select Swatches Prizms Gold /10 #20
2017 Select Select Swatches Prizms Red /99 #20
2017 Select Signature Paint Schemes #19
2017 Select Signature Paint Schemes Prizms Blue /50 #19
2017 Select Signature Paint Schemes Prizms Checkered Flag /1 #19
2017 Select Signature Paint Schemes Prizms Gold /10 #19
2017 Select Signature Paint Schemes Prizms Red /25 #19
2017 Select Signature Swatches #20
2017 Select Signature Swatches Dual #16
2017 Select Signature Swatches Dual Prizms Checkered Flag /1 #16
2017 Select Signature Swatches Dual Prizms Gold /10 #16
2017 Select Signature Swatches Dual Prizms Tie Dye /24 #16
2017 Select Signature Swatches Dual Prizms White /50 #16
2017 Select Signature Swatches Prizms Checkered Flag /1 #20
2017 Select Signature Swatches Prizms Gold /10 #20
2017 Select Signature Swatches Prizms Tie Dye /24 #20
2017 Select Signature Swatches Prizms White /50 #20
2018 Certified Signing Sessions /199 #8
2018 Certified Signing Sessions Black /1 #8
2018 Certified Signing Sessions Blue /50 #8
2018 Certified Signing Sessions Gold /25 #8
2018 Certified Signing Sessions Green /5 #8
2018 Certified Signing Sessions Purple /10 #8
2018 Certified Signing Sessions Red /75 #8
2018 Donruss #120
2018 Donruss #166
2018 Donruss Artist Proofs /25 #120
2018 Donruss Artist Proofs /25 #166
2018 Donruss Gold Foil /499 #120
2018 Donruss Gold Foil /499 #166
2018 Donruss Gold Press Proofs /99 #120
2018 Donruss Gold Press Proofs /99 #166
2018 Donruss Green Foil /199 #120
2018 Donruss Green Foil /199 #166
2018 Donruss Press Proofs /49 #120
2018 Donruss Press Proofs /49 #166
2018 Donruss Printing Plates Black /1 #120
2018 Donruss Printing Plates Black /1 #166
2018 Donruss Printing Plates Cyan /1 #120
2018 Donruss Printing Plates Cyan /1 #166
2018 Donruss Printing Plates Magenta /1 #120
2018 Donruss Printing Plates Magenta /1 #166
2018 Donruss Printing Plates Yellow /1 #120
2018 Donruss Printing Plates Yellow /1 #166
2018 Donruss Racing Relics #12
2018 Donruss Racing Relics Black /10 #12
2018 Donruss Racing Relics Holo Gold /99 #12
2018 Donruss Red Foil /299 #120
2018 Donruss Red Foil /299 #166
2018 Donruss Retro Relics '85 #10
2018 Donruss Retro Relics '85 Black /10 #10
2018 Donruss Retro Relics '85 Holo Gold /99 #10
2018 Donruss Retro Signatures '85 #10
2018 Donruss Retro Signatures '85 Black /1 #10
2018 Donruss Retro Signatures '85 Holo Gold /25 #10
2018 Panini Prime Autograph Materials /49 #12
2018 Panini Prime Autograph Materials Black /1 #12
2018 Panini Prime Autograph Materials Holo Gold /25 #12
2018 Panini Prime Autograph Materials Laundry Tag /1 #12
2018 Panini Prime Driver Signatures /50 #21
2018 Panini Prime Driver Signatures Black /1 #21
2018 Panini Prime Driver Signatures Holo Gold /25 #21
2018 Panini Prime Dual Material Autographs /50 #15
2018 Panini Prime Dual Material Autographs Black /1 #15
2018 Panini Prime Dual Material Autographs Holo Gold /25 #15
2018 Panini Prime Dual Material Autographs Laundry Tag /1 #15
2018 Panini Prime Prime Jumbo Associate Sponsor 1 /1 #34
2018 Panini Prime Prime Jumbo Associate Sponsor 2 /1 #34
2018 Panini Prime Prime Jumbo Associate Sponsor 3 /1 #34
2018 Panini Prime Prime Jumbo Associate Sponsor 4 /1 #34
2018 Panini Prime Prime Jumbo Associate Sponsor 5 /1 #34
2018 Panini Prime Prime Jumbo Associate Sponsor 6 /1 #34
2018 Panini Prime Prime Jumbo Associate Sponsor 7 /1 #34
2018 Panini Prime Prime Jumbo Associate Sponsor 8 /1 #34
2018 Panini Prime Prime Jumbo Car Manufacturer /1 #34
2018 Panini Prime Prime Jumbo Firesuit Manufacturer /1 #34
2018 Panini Prime Prime Jumbo Glove Manufacturer Patch /1 #34
2018 Panini Prime Prime Jumbo Glove Name Patch /1 #34
2018 Panini Prime Prime Jumbo Nameplate /1 #34
2018 Panini Prime Prime Jumbo NASCAR /1 #34
2018 Panini Prime Prime Jumbo Prime Colors /4 #34
2018 Panini Prime Prime Jumbo Shoe Brand Logo /1 #34
2018 Panini Prime Prime Jumbo Shoe Name Patch /1 #34
2018 Panini Prime Prime Jumbo Sunoco /1 #34
2018 Panini Prime Prime Signatures /35 #9
2018 Panini Prime Prime Signatures Black /1 #9
2018 Panini Prime Prime Signatures Holo Gold /10 #9
2018 Panini Prime Signature Swatches /49 #4
2018 Panini Prime Signature Swatches Black /1 #4
2018 Panini Prime Signature Swatches Holo Gold /25 #4
2018 Panini Prizm #35
2018 Panini Prizm Autographs Prizms #2
2018 Panini Prizm Autographs Prizms Black /1 #2
2018 Panini Prizm Autographs Prizms Blue /50 #2
2018 Panini Prizm Autographs Prizms Camo #2
2018 Panini Prizm Autographs Prizms Gold /10 #2
2018 Panini Prizm Autographs Prizms Green /75 #2
2018 Panini Prizm Autographs Prizms Rainbow /24 #2
2018 Panini Prizm Autographs Prizms Red /35 #2
2018 Panini Prizm Autographs Prizms Red White and Blue /99 #2
2018 Panini Prizm Autographs Prizms White /5 #2
2018 Panini Prizm Prizms #35
2018 Panini Prizm Prizms Black /1 #35
2018 Panini Prizm Prizms Blue /99 #35
2018 Panini Prizm Prizms Camo #35
2018 Panini Prizm Prizms Gold /10 #35
2018 Panini Prizm Prizms Green /149 #35
2018 Panini Prizm Prizms Purple Flash #35
2018 Panini Prizm Prizms Rainbow /24 #35
2018 Panini Prizm Prizms Red /75 #35
2018 Panini Prizm Prizms Red White and Blue #35
2018 Panini Prizm Prizms White /5 #35
2018 Panini Prizm Scripted Signatures Prizms #2
2018 Panini Prizm Scripted Signatures Prizms Black /1 #2
2018 Panini Prizm Scripted Signatures Prizms Blue /50 #2
2018 Panini Prizm Scripted Signatures Prizms Camo #2
2018 Panini Prizm Scripted Signatures Prizms Gold /10 #2
2018 Panini Prizm Scripted Signatures Prizms Green /75 #2
2018 Panini Prizm Scripted Signatures Prizms Rainbow /24 #2
2018 Panini Prizm Scripted Signatures Prizms Red /35 #2
2018 Panini Prizm Scripted Signatures Prizms Red White and Blue /99 #2
2018 Panini Prizm Scripted Signatures Prizms White /5 #2
2018 Panini Victory Lane Engineered to Perfection Materials /399 #11
2018 Panini Victory Lane Engineered to Perfection Materials Black /25 #11
2018 Panini Victory Lane Engineered to Perfection Materials Gold /199 #11
2018 Panini Victory Lane Engineered to Perfection Materials Green /99 #11
2018 Panini Victory Lane Engineered to Perfection Materials Laundry Tag /1 #11
2018 Panini Victory Lane Pedal to the Metal #88
2018 Panini Victory Lane Pedal to the Metal Black /1 #88
2018 Panini Victory Lane Pedal to the Metal Blue /25 #88
2018 Panini Victory Lane Pedal to the Metal Green /5 #88
2018 Panini Victory Lane Race Ready Materials Black /5 #13
2018 Panini Victory Lane Race Ready Materials Laundry Tag /1 #13
2018 Panini Victory Lane Victory Marks /250 #6
2018 Panini Victory Lane Victory Marks Black /1 #6
2018 Panini Victory Lane Victory Marks Gold /99 #6
2019 Panini Prime Autograph Materials /99 #4
2019 Panini Prime Autograph Materials Black /10 #4
2019 Panini Prime Autograph Materials Holo Gold /25 #4
2019 Panini Prime Autograph Materials Platinum Blue /1 #4
2019 Panini Prime Prime Jumbo Associate Sponsor 1 /1 #32
2019 Panini Prime Prime Jumbo Associate Sponsor 2 /1 #32
2019 Panini Prime Prime Jumbo Associate Sponsor 3 /1 #32
2019 Panini Prime Prime Jumbo Glove Manufacturer Patch /1 #32
2019 Panini Prime Prime Jumbo Glove Name Patch /1 #32
2019 Panini Prime Prime Jumbo Glove Number Patch /1 #32
2019 Panini Prime Prime Jumbo Prime Colors /12 #32
2019 Panini Prime Prime Jumbo Shoe Brand Logo /1 #32
2019 Panini Prime Prime Jumbo Shoe Name Patch /1 #32
2019 Panini Prime Prime Jumbo Shoe Number Patch /1 #32
2019 Panini Prime Prime Jumbo Sunoco /1 #32
2019 Panini Prime Prime Names Die Cut Signatures /99 #18
2019 Panini Prime Prime Names Die Cut Signatures Black /10 #18
2019 Panini Prime Prime Names Die Cut Signatures Holo Gold /25 #18
2019 Panini Prime Prime Names Die Cut Signatures Platinum Blue /1 #18
2019 Panini Prime Prime Signatures /99 #7
2019 Panini Prime Prime Signatures Black /10 #7
2019 Panini Prime Prime Signatures Holo Gold /25 #7
2019 Panini Prime Prime Signatures Platinum Blue /1 #7
2019 Panini Prime Race Used Firesuits /39 #2
2019 Panini Prime Race Used Firesuits Black /10 #2
2019 Panini Prime Race Used Firesuits Laundry Tags /1 #2
2019 Panini Prime Race Used Sheet Metal /50 #2
2019 Panini Prime Race Used Sheet Metal Black /10 #2
2019 Panini Prime Race Used Sheet Metal Holo Gold /25 #2
2019 Panini Prime Race Used Sheet Metal Platinum Blue /1 #2
2019 Panini Prime Shadowbox Signatures /99 #16
2019 Panini Prime Shadowbox Signatures Black /10 #16
2019 Panini Prime Shadowbox Signatures Holo Gold /25 #16
2019 Panini Prizm Endorsements Prizms #7
2019 Panini Prizm Endorsements Prizms Black /1 #7
2019 Panini Prizm Endorsements Prizms Blue /75 #7
2019 Panini Prizm Endorsements Prizms Camo /0 #7
2019 Panini Prizm Endorsements Prizms Gold /10 #7
2019 Panini Prizm Endorsements Prizms Green /99 #7
2019 Panini Prizm Endorsements Prizms Rainbow /24 #7
2019 Panini Prizm Endorsements Prizms Red /50 #7
2019 Panini Prizm Endorsements Prizms Red White and Blue #7
2019 Panini Prizm Endorsements Prizms White /5 #7
2020 Donruss #88
2020 Donruss #169
2020 Donruss Black Numbers /16 #88
2020 Donruss Black Numbers /15 #169
2020 Donruss Black Trophy Club /1 #88
2020 Donruss Black Trophy Club /1 #169
2020 Donruss Blue /199 #88
2020 Donruss Blue /199 #169
2020 Donruss Carolina Blue #88
2020 Donruss Carolina Blue #169
2020 Donruss Classics #14
2020 Donruss Classics Checkers #14
2020 Donruss Classics Cracked Ice /25 #14
2020 Donruss Classics Holographic /199 #14
2020 Donruss Classics Xplosion /10 #14
2020 Donruss Green /99 #88
2020 Donruss Green /99 #169
2020 Donruss Orange #88
2020 Donruss Orange #169
2020 Donruss Pink /25 #88
2020 Donruss Pink /25 #169
2020 Donruss Printing Plates Black /1 #88
2020 Donruss Printing Plates Black /1 #169
2020 Donruss Printing Plates Cyan /1 #88
2020 Donruss Printing Plates Cyan /1 #169
2020 Donruss Printing Plates Magenta /1 #88
2020 Donruss Printing Plates Magenta /1 #169
2020 Donruss Printing Plates Yellow /1 #169
2020 Donruss Printing Plates Yellow /1 #88
2020 Donruss Purple /49 #88
2020 Donruss Purple /49 #169
2020 Donruss Red /299 #88
2020 Donruss Red /299 #169
2020 Donruss Retro Relics '87 #5
2020 Donruss Retro Relics '87 Holo Black /10 #5
2020 Donruss Retro Relics '87 Holo Gold /25 #5
2020 Donruss Retro Relics '87 Red /99 #5
2020 Donruss Silver #88
2020 Donruss Silver #169
2020 Donruss Timeless Treasures Signatures #3
2020 Donruss Timeless Treasures Signatures Holo Black /1 #3
2020 Donruss Timeless Treasures Signatures Holo Gold /5 #3
2020 Donruss Timeless Treasures Signatures Red /10 #3

Clint Bowyer

2004 Press Pass Optima #30
2004 Press Pass Optima Gold #G30
2004 Press Pass Optima Previews /5 #EB30
2004 Press Pass Optima Samples #30
2004 Press Pass Signings #6
2004 Press Pass Signings Gold /50 #6
2004 Press Pass Stealth No Boundaries #NB1
2004 Press Pass Top Prospects Memorabilia /350 #CBT
2004 Press Pass Top Prospects Memorabilia /200 #CBSM
2004 Press Pass Trackside #42
2004 Press Pass Trackside Golden /100 #G42
2004 Press Pass Trackside Previews /5 #EB42
2004 Press Pass Trackside Samples #42
2004 Wheels Autographs #7
2005 Press Pass Autographs #5
2005 Press Pass Optima #31
2005 Press Pass Optima #53
2005 Press Pass Optima Gold /100 #G31
2005 Press Pass Optima Gold /100 #G53
2005 Press Pass Optima Previews /5 #31
2005 Press Pass Optima Previews /1 #53
2005 Press Pass Optima Samples #31
2005 Press Pass Optima Samples #53
2005 Press Pass Panorama #PPP68
2005 Press Pass Signings #4
2005 Press Pass Signings Gold /50 #3
2005 Press Pass Stealth #65
2005 Press Pass Stealth No Boundaries #NB27
2005 Press Pass Stealth Previews /5 #65
2005 Press Pass Stealth Samples #65
2005 Press Pass Stealth X-Ray /100 #X65
2005 Press Pass Trackside #34
2005 Press Pass Trackside Golden /100 #G34
2005 Press Pass Trackside Previews /5 #34
2005 Press Pass Trackside Samples #34
2005 Wheels American Thunder License to Drive #7
2005 Wheels Autographs #5
2006 Press Pass #32
2006 Press Pass Autographs #5
2006 Press Pass Blue #B32
2006 Press Pass Burnouts /900 #HT8
2006 Press Pass Burnouts Holofoil /100 #HT8
2006 Press Pass Eclipse #29
2006 Press Pass Eclipse Previews /5 #EB29
2006 Press Pass Eclipse Racing Champions #RC23
2006 Press Pass Gold #G32
2006 Press Pass Optima #2
2006 Press Pass Optima #35
2006 Press Pass Optima #73
2006 Press Pass Optima Fan Favorite #FF1
2006 Press Pass Optima Gold /100 #G2
2006 Press Pass Optima Gold /100 #G35
2006 Press Pass Optima Gold /100 #G73
2006 Press Pass Optima Previews /5 #EB2
2006 Press Pass Optima Previews /1 #EB73
2006 Press Pass Optima Rookie Relics Cars /50 #RRT1
2006 Press Pass Optima Rookie Relics Drivers /50 #RRD1
2006 Press Pass Platinum /100 #P32
2006 Press Pass Premium #30
2006 Press Pass Premium #52
2006 Press Pass Previews /5 #EB32
2006 Press Pass Signings #6
2006 Press Pass Signings Gold /50 #6
2006 Press Pass Signings Gold Red Ink #6
2006 Press Pass Signings Red Ink #6
2006 Press Pass Signings Silver /100 #6
2006 Press Pass Stealth #36
2006 Press Pass Stealth #50
2006 Press Pass Stealth #76
2006 Press Pass Stealth #91
2006 Press Pass Stealth Autographed Hat Entry #PPH2
2006 Press Pass Stealth Corporate Cuts /250 #CCD12
2006 Press Pass Stealth Gear Grippers Autographs /7 #CB
2006 Press Pass Stealth Gear Grippers Cars Retail /99 #GGT14
2006 Press Pass Stealth Gear Grippers Drivers /99 #GGD14
2006 Press Pass Stealth Hot Pass #HP3
2006 Press Pass Stealth Previews /1 #91
2006 Press Pass Stealth Retail #36
2006 Press Pass Stealth Retail #50
2006 Press Pass Stealth Retail #76
2006 Press Pass Stealth Retail #91
2006 Press Pass Stealth X-Ray /100 #X36
2006 Press Pass Stealth X-Ray /100 #X50
2006 Press Pass Stealth X-Ray /100 #X76
2006 Press Pass Stealth X-Ray /100 #X91
2006 Press Pass Top 25 Drivers & Rides #C5
2006 Press Pass Top 25 Drivers & Rides #D5
2006 TRAKS #3
2006 TRAKS Autographs #3
2006 TRAKS Autographs 100 /100 #3
2006 TRAKS Autographs 25 /25 #3
2006 TRAKS Previews /1 #3
2006 TRAKS Stickers #7
2006 VIP #90
2006 VIP Rookie Stripes /100 #RS1
2006 VIP Rookie Stripes Autographs /25 #RSCB
2006 VIP Tradin' Paint Cars Bronze /145 #TPT1
2006 VIP Tradin' Paint Drivers Gold /50 #TPD1
2006 VIP Tradin' Paint Drivers Silver /80 #TPD1
2006 Wheels American Thunder /350 #90
2006 Wheels American Thunder Double Hat /99 #DH2
2006 Wheels American Thunder Thunder Strokes /100 #1
2006 Wheels Autographs #6
2006 Wheels High Gear #29
2006 Wheels High Gear MPH /100 #M29
2006 Wheels High Gear Previews Green /5 #EB29
2007 Press Pass #16
2007 Press Pass #37
2007 Press Pass #64
2007 Press Pass Autographs #3
2007 Press Pass Autographs Press Plates Black /1 #1
2007 Press Pass Autographs Press Plates Cyan /1 #1
2007 Press Pass Autographs Press Plates Magenta /1 #1
2007 Press Pass Autographs Press Plates Yellow /1 #2
2007 Press Pass Blue #B16
2007 Press Pass Blue #B37
2007 Press Pass Blue #B64
2007 Press Pass Collector's Series Box Set #SB1
2007 Press Pass Cup Chase Prizes #CC12
2007 Press Pass Eclipse #16
2007 Press Pass Eclipse Gold /25 #G16
2007 Press Pass Eclipse Previews /5 #EB16
2007 Press Pass Eclipse Racing Champions #RC21
2007 Press Pass Eclipse Red /1 #R16
2007 Press Pass Eclipse Skidmarks #SM14
2007 Press Pass Eclipse Skidmarks Holofoil /250 #SM14
2007 Press Pass Eclipse Teammates Autographs /25 #8
2007 Press Pass Gold #G16
2007 Press Pass Gold #G37
2007 Press Pass Gold #G64
2007 Press Pass Platinum /100 #P16
2007 Press Pass Platinum /100 #P37
2007 Press Pass Platinum /100 #P64
2007 Press Pass Premium #3
2007 Press Pass Premium Red /15 #R3
2007 Press Pass Previews /5 #EB16
2007 Press Pass Previews /5 #EB37
2007 Press Pass Signings #10
2007 Press Pass Signings Blue /25 #2
2007 Press Pass Signings Gold /50 #7
2007 Press Pass Signings Press Plates Black /1 #6
2007 Press Pass Signings Press Plates Cyan /1 #5
2007 Press Pass Signings Press Plates Magenta /1 #5
2007 Press Pass Signings Press Plates Yellow /1 #5
2007 Press Pass Signings Silver /100 #6
2007 Press Pass Stealth #2
2007 Press Pass Stealth #38
2007 Press Pass Stealth #64
2007 Press Pass Stealth Chrome #2
2007 Press Pass Stealth Chrome #38
2007 Press Pass Stealth Chrome #64
2007 Press Pass Stealth Chrome Exclusives /99 #X2
2007 Press Pass Stealth Chrome Exclusives /99 #X38
2007 Press Pass Stealth Chrome Exclusives /99 #X64
2007 Press Pass Stealth Chrome Platinum /25 #P2
2007 Press Pass Stealth Chrome Platinum /25 #P38
2007 Press Pass Stealth Chrome Platinum /25 #P64
2007 Press Pass Stealth Maximum Access #MA3
2007 Press Pass Stealth Maximum Access Autographs /25 #MA3
2007 Press Pass Stealth Previews /5 #EB2
2007 Press Pass Stealth Previews /5 #EB38
2007 VIP #3
2007 VIP Get A Grip Drivers /70 #GGD21
2007 VIP Get A Grip Teams /70 #GGT21
2007 VIP Previews /5 #EB3
2007 VIP Sunday Best #SB1
2007 Wheels American Thunder #4
2007 Wheels American Thunder Autographed Hat Instant Winner /1 #AH4
2007 Wheels American Thunder Previews /5 #EB4
2007 Wheels American Thunder Thunder Strokes #6
2007 Wheels American Thunder Thunder Strokes Press Plates Black /1 #6
2007 Wheels American Thunder Thunder Strokes Press Plates Cyan /1 #6
2007 Wheels American Thunder Thunder Strokes Press Plates Magenta /1 #6
2007 Wheels American Thunder Thunder Strokes Press Plates Yellow /1 #6
2007 Wheels American Thunder Triple Hat /99 #TH3
2007 Wheels Autographs #3
2007 Wheels Autographs Press Plates Black /1 #3
2007 Wheels Autographs Press Plates Cyan /1 #3
2007 Wheels Autographs Press Plates Magenta /1 #3
2007 Wheels High Gear #16
2007 Wheels High Gear #78
2007 Wheels High Gear Driven #DR13
2007 Wheels High Gear Final Standings Gold /17 #FS16
2007 Wheels High Gear MPH /100 #M16
2007 Wheels High Gear MPH /100 #M78
2007 Wheels High Gear Previews /5 #EB16
2008 Press Pass #9
2008 Press Pass #118
2008 Press Pass #0
2008 Press Pass Autographs #8
2008 Press Pass Autographs Press Plates Black /1 #7
2008 Press Pass Autographs Press Plates Cyan /1 #7
2008 Press Pass Autographs Press Plates Magenta /1 #7
2008 Press Pass Autographs Press Plates Yellow /1 #7
2008 Press Pass Blue #B9
2008 Press Pass Blue #B118
2008 Press Pass Collector's Series Box Set #12
2008 Press Pass Cup Chase #CC7
2008 Press Pass Cup Chase Prizes #CC5
2008 Press Pass Eclipse #3
2008 Press Pass Eclipse #31
2008 Press Pass Eclipse #44
2008 Press Pass Eclipse #46
2008 Press Pass Eclipse #75
2008 Press Pass Eclipse Gold /25 #G3
2008 Press Pass Eclipse Gold /25 #G31
2008 Press Pass Eclipse Gold /25 #G44
2008 Press Pass Eclipse Gold /25 #G46
2008 Press Pass Eclipse Gold /25 #G75
2008 Press Pass Eclipse Previews /5 #EB3
2008 Press Pass Eclipse Previews /5 #EB31
2008 Press Pass Eclipse Previews /1 #EB75
2008 Press Pass Eclipse Red /1 #R3
2008 Press Pass Eclipse Red /1 #R31
2008 Press Pass Eclipse Red /1 #R44
2008 Press Pass Eclipse Red /1 #R46
2008 Press Pass Eclipse Red /1 #R75
2008 Press Pass Eclipse Stellar #ST7
2008 Press Pass Eclipse Stellar #ST19
2008 Press Pass Eclipse Teammates Autographs /25 #BBH
2008 Press Pass Gillette Young Guns #1
2008 Press Pass Gold #G9
2008 Press Pass Gold #G118
2008 Press Pass Legends Prominent Pieces Firesuit-Glove Bronze /99 #PP1CB
2008 Press Pass Legends Prominent Pieces Firesuit-Glove Gold /25 #PP1CB
2008 Press Pass Legends Prominent Pieces Firesuit-Glove Silver /50 #PP1CB
2008 Press Pass Legends Prominent Pieces Metal-Tire-Net /50 #PP4CB
2008 Press Pass Legends Prominent Pieces Metal-Tire-Net Gold /25 #PP4CB
2008 Press Pass Legends Signature Series Memorabilia /25 #LSCB
2008 Press Pass Platinum /100 #P9
2008 Press Pass Platinum /100 #P118
2008 Press Pass Premium #3
2008 Press Pass Premium #76
2008 Press Pass Premium Previews /5 #EB3
2008 Press Pass Premium Red /15 #3
2008 Press Pass Premium Red /5 #76
2008 Press Pass Previews /5 #EB9
2008 Press Pass Previews /1 #EB118
2008 Press Pass Signings #8
2008 Press Pass Signings Blue /25 #4
2008 Press Pass Signings Gold /50 #7
2008 Press Pass Signings Press Plates Black /1 #6
2008 Press Pass Signings Press Plates Cyan /1 #6
2008 Press Pass Signings Press Plates Cyan /1 #CB
2008 Press Pass Signings Press Plates Magenta /1 #6
2008 Press Pass Signings Press Plates Yellow /1 #6
2008 Press Pass Signings Press Plates Yellow #CB
2008 Press Pass Signings Silver /100 #7
2008 Press Pass Speedway #2
2008 Press Pass Speedway #37
2008 Press Pass Speedway #96
2008 Press Pass Speedway Blur #B7
2008 Press Pass Speedway Cockpit #CP2
2008 Press Pass Speedway Gold #G2
2008 Press Pass Speedway Gold #G37
2008 Press Pass Speedway Gold #G96
2008 Press Pass Speedway Holofoil /50 #H2
2008 Press Pass Speedway Holofoil /50 #H37
2008 Press Pass Speedway Holofoil /50 #H96
2008 Press Pass Speedway Previews /5 #EB2
2008 Press Pass Speedway Previews /5 #EB37
2008 Press Pass Speedway Previews /1 #EB96
2008 Press Pass Speedway Red /10 #R2
2008 Press Pass Speedway Red /10 #R37
2008 Press Pass Speedway Red /10 #R96
2008 Press Pass Starting Grid #SG12
2008 Press Pass Stealth #3
2008 Press Pass Stealth #37
2008 Press Pass Stealth #69
2008 Press Pass Stealth #74
2008 Press Pass Stealth #82
2008 Press Pass Stealth Chrome #3
2008 Press Pass Stealth Chrome #37
2008 Press Pass Stealth Chrome #69A
2008 Press Pass Stealth Chrome #69B
2008 Press Pass Stealth Chrome #74
2008 Press Pass Stealth Chrome #82
2008 Press Pass Stealth Chrome Exclusives /25 #3
2008 Press Pass Stealth Chrome Exclusives /25 #37
2008 Press Pass Stealth Chrome Exclusives /25 #69
2008 Press Pass Stealth Chrome Exclusives /25 #74
2008 Press Pass Stealth Chrome Exclusives /25 #82
2008 Press Pass Stealth Chrome Exclusives Gold /99 #3
2008 Press Pass Stealth Chrome Exclusives Gold /99 #37
2008 Press Pass Stealth Chrome Exclusives Gold /99 #69
2008 Press Pass Stealth Chrome Exclusives Gold /99 #74
2008 Press Pass Stealth Chrome Exclusives Gold /99 #82
2008 Press Pass Stealth Maximum Access #MA4
2008 Press Pass Stealth Maximum Access Autographs /25 #MA4
2008 Press Pass Stealth Previews /5 #3
2008 Press Pass Stealth Previews /5 #37
2008 Press Pass Stealth Previews /1 #82
2008 Press Pass Stealth Synthesis #S2
2008 VIP #4
2008 VIP #45
2008 VIP #74
2008 VIP All Access #AA2
2008 VIP Gear Gallery #GG1
2008 VIP Gear Gallery Memorabilia /50 #GGCB
2008 VIP Gear Gallery Transparent #GG1
2008 VIP Get a Grip Autographs /7 #GGSCB
2008 VIP Previews /5 #EB4
2008 VIP Triple Grip /25 #TG2
2008 Wheels American Thunder #5
2008 Wheels American Thunder #45
2008 Wheels American Thunder #63
2008 Wheels American Thunder Autographed Hat Winner /1 #IWHCB
2008 Wheels American Thunder Campaign Trail #CT4
2008 Wheels American Thunder Delegates #D3
2008 Wheels American Thunder Motorcade #M6
2008 Wheels American Thunder Previews /5 #5
2008 Wheels American Thunder Trackside Treasury Autographs #CB
2008 Wheels American Thunder Trackside Treasury Autographs Gold /25 #CB
2008 Wheels American Thunder Trackside Treasury Autographs Printing Plates Black /1 #CB
2008 Wheels American Thunder Trackside Treasury Autographs Printing Plates Cyan /1 #CB
2008 Wheels American Thunder Trackside Treasury Autographs Printing Plates Magenta /1 #CB
2008 Wheels American Thunder Trackside Treasury Autographs Printing Plates Yellow /1 #CB
2008 Wheels American Thunder Triple Hat /125 #TH3
2008 Wheels Autographs #6
2008 Wheels Autographs Chase Edition /25 #1
2008 Wheels Autographs Press Plates Black /1 #6
2008 Wheels Autographs Press Plates Cyan /1 #6
2008 Wheels Autographs Press Plates Magenta /1 #6
2008 Wheels Autographs Press Plates Yellow /1 #6
2008 Wheels High Gear #3
2008 Wheels High Gear #30
2008 Wheels High Gear #48
2008 Wheels High Gear #77
2008 Wheels High Gear Driven #DR4
2008 Wheels High Gear Final Standings /3 #F3
2008 Wheels High Gear Last Lap /10 #LL7
2008 Wheels High Gear Last Lap Holofoil /5 #LL7
2008 Wheels High Gear MPH /100 #M3
2008 Wheels High Gear MPH /100 #M30
2008 Wheels High Gear MPH /100 #M48
2008 Wheels High Gear MPH /100 #M77
2008 Wheels High Gear Previews /5 #EB3
2008 Wheels High Gear The Chase #TC3
2009 Element #3
2009 Element #36
2009 Element #60
2009 Element #73
2009 Element 1-2-3 Finish /50 #RCR
2009 Element Green White Checker /25 #GWCCB
2009 Element Lab Report #LR3
2009 Element Previews /5 #3
2009 Element Radioactive /100 #3
2009 Element Radioactive /100 #36
2009 Element Radioactive /100 #60
2009 Element Radioactive /100 #73
2009 Element Taking the Checkers /45 #TCCB
2009 Press Pass #5
2009 Press Pass #39
2009 Press Pass #85
2009 Press Pass #111
2009 Press Pass #123
2009 Press Pass #0
2009 Press Pass Autographs Chase Edition /25 #CB
2009 Press Pass Autographs Printing Plates Black /1 #5
2009 Press Pass Autographs Printing Plates Cyan /1 #5
2009 Press Pass Autographs Printing Plates Magenta /1 #5
2009 Press Pass Autographs Printing Plates Yellow /1 #5
2009 Press Pass Autographs Silver #5
2009 Press Pass Blue #5
2009 Press Pass Blue #39
2009 Press Pass Blue #85
2009 Press Pass Blue #111
2009 Press Pass Blue #123
2009 Press Pass Burning Rubber Drivers /185 #BRD10
2009 Press Pass Burning Rubber Prime Cut /25 #BRD10
2009 Press Pass Burning Rubber Teams /250 #BRT10
2009 Press Pass Cup Chase #CCR7
2009 Press Pass Daytona 500 Tires /25 #TTCB
2009 Press Pass Eclipse #19
2009 Press Pass Eclipse #64
2009 Press Pass Eclipse Black and White #19
2009 Press Pass Eclipse Black and White #64
2009 Press Pass Eclipse Blue #19
2009 Press Pass Eclipse Blue #64
2009 Press Pass Eclipse Solar System #SS5
2009 Press Pass Final Standings /120 #111
2009 Press Pass Four Wide Checkered Flag /1 #FWCB
2009 Press Pass Four Wide Firesuit /50 #FWCB
2009 Press Pass Four Wide Firesuit /50 #FWCB2
2009 Press Pass Four Wide Sheet Metal /10 #FWCB
2009 Press Pass Four Wide Tire /25 #FWCB2
2009 Press Pass Four Wide Tire /25 #FWCB
2009 Press Pass Game Face #GF6
2009 Press Pass Gold #5
2009 Press Pass Gold #39
2009 Press Pass Gold #85
2009 Press Pass Gold #111
2009 Press Pass Gold #123
2009 Press Pass Gold Holofoil /100 #5
2009 Press Pass Gold Holofoil /100 #39
2009 Press Pass Gold Holofoil /100 #85
2009 Press Pass Gold Holofoil /100 #111
2009 Press Pass Gold Holofoil /100 #123
2009 Press Pass Legends Prominent Pieces Bronze /99 #PPCB
2009 Press Pass Legends Prominent Pieces Gold /25 #PPCB
2009 Press Pass Legends Prominent Pieces Silver /50 #PPCB
2009 Press Pass Pieces Race Used Memorabilia #CB
2009 Press Pass Pocket Portraits #P2
2009 Press Pass Pocket Portraits Checkered Flag #P2
2009 Press Pass Pocket Portraits Hometown #P2
2009 Press Pass Pocket Portraits Smoke #P2
2009 Press Pass Pocket Portraits Wal-Mart #PPW13
2009 Press Pass Premium #23
2009 Press Pass Premium #45
2009 Press Pass Premium Previews /5 #EB23
2009 Press Pass Premium Signatures #5
2009 Press Pass Premium Signatures Gold /25 #5
2009 Press Pass Premium Top Contenders #TC11
2009 Press Pass Premium Top Contenders Gold #TC11
2009 Press Pass Premium Win Streak #WS15
2009 Press Pass Premium Win Streak Victory Lane #WSVL-CB
2009 Press Pass Previews /5 #EB5
2009 Press Pass Previews /1 #EB111
2009 Press Pass Previews /5 #EB123
2009 Press Pass Red #5
2009 Press Pass Red #39
2009 Press Pass Red #85
2009 Press Pass Red #111
2009 Press Pass Red #123
2009 Press Pass Santa Hats /50 #SH3
2009 Press Pass Showcase /499 #13
2009 Press Pass Showcase /499 #33

2009 Press Pass Showcase 2nd Gear /125 #13
2009 Press Pass Showcase 2nd Gear /125 #33
2009 Press Pass Showcase 3rd Gear /50 #13
2009 Press Pass Showcase 3rd Gear /50 #33
2009 Press Pass Showcase 4th Gear /15 #13
2009 Press Pass Showcase 4th Gear /15 #33
2009 Press Pass Showcase Classic Collections Firesuit /25 #CCF7
2009 Press Pass Showcase Classic Collections Firesuit Patch /5 #CCF7
2009 Press Pass Showcase Classic Collections Ink /45 #7
2009 Press Pass Showcase Classic Collections Ink Gold /25 #7
2009 Press Pass Showcase Classic Collections Ink Green /5 #7
2009 Press Pass Showcase Classic Collections Ink Melting /1 #7
2009 Press Pass Showcase Classic Collections Sheet Metal /45 #CCS7
2009 Press Pass Showcase Classic Collections Tire /99 #CCT7
2009 Press Pass Showcase Printing Plates Black /1 #13
2009 Press Pass Showcase Printing Plates Black /1 #33
2009 Press Pass Showcase Printing Plates Cyan /1 #13
2009 Press Pass Showcase Printing Plates Cyan /1 #33
2009 Press Pass Showcase Printing Plates Magenta /1 #13
2009 Press Pass Showcase Printing Plates Magenta /1 #33
2009 Press Pass Showcase Printing Plates Yellow /1 #13
2009 Press Pass Showcase Printing Plates Yellow /1 #33
2009 Press Pass Signings Blue /25 #6
2009 Press Pass Signings Gold #6
2009 Press Pass Signings Green /15 #6
2009 Press Pass Signings Orange /65 #6
2009 Press Pass Signings Printing Plates Cyan /1 #6
2009 Press Pass Signings Printing Plates Yellow /1 #6
2009 Press Pass Signings Purple /45 #6
2009 Press Pass Stealth #5
2009 Press Pass Stealth #69
2009 Press Pass Stealth Chrome #5
2009 Press Pass Stealth Chrome #69
2009 Press Pass Stealth Chrome Brushed Metal /25 #5
2009 Press Pass Stealth Chrome Brushed Metal /25 #69
2009 Press Pass Stealth Chrome Gold /99 #5
2009 Press Pass Stealth Chrome Gold /99 #69
2009 Press Pass Stealth Confidential Classified Bronze #PC20
2009 Press Pass Stealth Confidential Secret Silver #PC20
2009 Press Pass Stealth Confidential Top Secret Gold /25 #PC20
2009 Press Pass Stealth Mach 09 #M7
2009 Press Pass Stealth Previews /5 #EB5
2009 Press Pass Target Victory Tires /50 #CBTT
2009 Press Pass Tread Marks Autographs /10 #SSCB
2009 Press Pass Unleashed #U6
2009 VIP #4
2009 VIP Get A Grip /120 #GGCB
2009 VIP Get A Grip Holofoil /10 #GGCB
2009 VIP Guest List #GG12
2009 VIP Previews /5 #4
2009 VIP Purple /25 #4
2009 Wheels Autographs #5
2009 Wheels Autographs Press Plates Black /1 #CB
2009 Wheels Autographs Press Plates Cyan /1 #CB
2009 Wheels Autographs Press Plates Magenta /1 #CB
2009 Wheels Autographs Press Plates Yellow /1 #CB
2009 Wheels Main Event #17
2009 Wheels Main Event #39
2009 Wheels Main Event Fast Pass Purple /25 #17
2009 Wheels Main Event Fast Pass Purple /25 #39
2009 Wheels Main Event Foil #17
2009 Wheels Main Event Hat Dance Patch /10 #HDCB
2009 Wheels Main Event Hat Dance Triple /99 #HDCB
2009 Wheels Main Event High Rollers #HR8
2009 Wheels Main Event Marks Clubs #5
2009 Wheels Main Event Marks Diamonds /10 #5
2009 Wheels Main Event Marks Hearts /5 #5
2009 Wheels Main Event Marks Printing Plates Black /1 #5
2009 Wheels Main Event Marks Printing Plates Cyan /1 #5
2009 Wheels Main Event Marks Printing Plates Magenta /1 #5
2009 Wheels Main Event Marks Printing Plates Yellow /1 #5
2009 Wheels Main Event Marks Spades /1 #5
2009 Wheels Main Event Playing Cards Blue #10S
2009 Wheels Main Event Playing Cards Red #10S
2009 Wheels Main Event Previews /5 #17
2009 Wheels Main Event Renegade Rounders Wanted #RR4
2009 Wheels Main Event Reward Copper /10 #RWCB
2009 Wheels Main Event Reward Holofoil /50 #RWCB
2009 Wheels Main Event Stop and Go Swatches Pit Banner /125 #SGBCB
2009 Wheels Main Event Stop and Go Swatches Pit Banner Green /10 #SGBCB
2009 Wheels Main Event Stop and Go Swatches Pit Banner Holofoil /75 #SGBCB
2009 Wheels Main Event Stop and Go Swatches Pit Banner Red /25 #SGBCB
2009 Wheels Main Event Wildcard Cuts /2 #WCCCB
2010 Element #14
2010 Element #50
2010 Element #87
2010 Element #88
2010 Element #90
2010 Element Blue /35 #14
2010 Element Blue /35 #50
2010 Element Blue /35 #87
2010 Element Blue /35 #88
2010 Element Blue /35 #90
2010 Element Green #14
2010 Element Green #50
2010 Element Green #87
2010 Element Green #88
2010 Element Green #90
2010 Element Previews /5 #EB14
2010 Element Purple /25 #14
2010 Element Purple /25 #50
2010 Element Red Target #14
2010 Element Red Target #50
2010 Element Red Target #87
2010 Element Red Target #88
2010 Element Red Target #90
2010 Press Pass #16
2010 Press Pass #64
2010 Press Pass #92
2010 Press Pass Autographs #5
2010 Press Pass Autographs Printing Plates Black /1 #5
2010 Press Pass Autographs Printing Plates Cyan /1 #5
2010 Press Pass Autographs Printing Plates Magenta /1 #4
2010 Press Pass Autographs Printing Plates Yellow /1 #5
2010 Press Pass Blue #16
2010 Press Pass Blue #64
2010 Press Pass Blue #92
2010 Press Pass Cup Chase #CCR15
2010 Press Pass Cup Chase Prizes #CC12
2010 Press Pass Eclipse #4
2010 Press Pass Eclipse Blue #4
2010 Press Pass Eclipse Gold #4
2010 Press Pass Eclipse Previews /5 #4
2010 Press Pass Eclipse Purple /25 #4
2010 Press Pass Five Star Classic Compilations Combos Firesuit Autographs /15 #CCMRCR
2010 Press Pass Five Star Classic Compilations Combos Patches Autographs /1 #CCMRCR
2010 Press Pass Gold #16
2010 Press Pass Gold #64
2010 Press Pass Gold #92
2010 Press Pass Holofoil /100 #16
2010 Press Pass Holofoil /100 #64
2010 Press Pass Holofoil /100 #92
2010 Press Pass Premium #15
2010 Press Pass Premium #65
2010 Press Pass Premium #74
2010 Press Pass Premium Hot Threads /299 #HTCB
2010 Press Pass Premium Hot Threads Holofoil /99 #HTCB
2010 Press Pass Premium Hot Threads Multi Color /25 #HTCB
2010 Press Pass Premium Hot Threads Two Color /125 #HTCB
2010 Press Pass Premium Purple /25 #15
2010 Press Pass Premium Purple /25 #65
2010 Press Pass Premium Rivals #R7
2010 Press Pass Premium Rivals Signatures /5 #RSBT
2010 Press Pass Premium Signature Series Firesuit /15 #SSFCB1
2010 Press Pass Premium Signature Series Firesuit /15 #SSFCB2
2010 Press Pass Premium Signatures #PSCB
2010 Press Pass Premium Signatures Red Ink /25 #PSCB
2010 Press Pass Previews /5 #16
2010 Press Pass Purple /25 #16
2010 Press Pass Purple /25 #64
2010 Press Pass Purple /25 #92
2010 Press Pass Showcase /499 #15
2010 Press Pass Showcase /499 #33
2010 Press Pass Showcase Classic Collections Firesuit Green /25 #CCIRCR
2010 Press Pass Showcase Classic Collections Firesuit Patch Melting /5 #CCIRCR
2010 Press Pass Showcase Classic Collections Ink /15 #CCIRCR
2010 Press Pass Showcase Classic Collections Ink Gold /10 #CCIRCR
2010 Press Pass Showcase Classic Collections Ink Green /5 #CCIRCR
2010 Press Pass Showcase Classic Collections Ink Melting /1 #CCIRCR
2010 Press Pass Showcase Classic Collections Sheet Metal /99 #CCIRCR
2010 Press Pass Showcase Classic Collections Sheet Metal Gold /45 #CCIRCR
2010 Press Pass Showcase Elite Exhibit Triple Memorabilia /99 #EEMCB
2010 Press Pass Showcase Elite Exhibit Triple Memorabilia Gold /45 #EEMCB
2010 Press Pass Showcase Elite Exhibit Triple Memorabilia Green /25 #EEMCB
2010 Press Pass Showcase Elite Exhibit Triple Memorabilia Melting /5 #EEMCB
2010 Press Pass Showcase Gold /125 #15
2010 Press Pass Showcase Gold /125 #33
2010 Press Pass Showcase Green /50 #15
2010 Press Pass Showcase Green /50 #33
2010 Press Pass Showcase Melting /15 #15
2010 Press Pass Showcase Melting /15 #33
2010 Press Pass Showcase Platinum Holo /1 #15
2010 Press Pass Showcase Platinum Holo /1 #33
2010 Press Pass Showcase Prized Pieces Firesuit Green /25 #PPMMCB
2010 Press Pass Showcase Prized Pieces Firesuit Ink Gold /25 #PPICB
2010 Press Pass Showcase Prized Pieces Firesuit Ink Melting /1 #PPICB
2010 Press Pass Showcase Prized Pieces Firesuit Patch Melting /5 #PPMMCB
2010 Press Pass Showcase Prized Pieces Memorabilia Ink Green /15 #PPICB
2010 Press Pass Showcase Prized Pieces Sheet Metal /99 #PPMMCB
2010 Press Pass Showcase Prized Pieces Sheet Metal Gold /45 #PPMMCB
2010 Press Pass Showcase Prized Pieces Sheet Metal Ink Silver /45 #PPICB
2010 Press Pass Signings Blue /10 #7
2010 Press Pass Signings Gold /50 #7
2010 Press Pass Signings Red /15 #7
2010 Press Pass Signings Silver /99 #7
2010 Press Pass Stealth #4
2010 Press Pass Stealth #81
2010 Press Pass Stealth Black and White #4
2010 Press Pass Stealth Black and White #81
2010 Press Pass Stealth Power Players #PP9
2010 Press Pass Stealth Previews /5 #4
2010 Press Pass Stealth Purple /25 #4
2010 Press Pass Stealth Signature Series Sheet Metal /15 #SSMECB
2010 Press Pass Tradin' Paint Sheet Metal /299 #TPCB
2010 Press Pass Tradin' Paint Sheet Metal Gold /50 #TPCB
2010 Press Pass Tradin' Paint Sheet Metal Holofoil /25 #TPCB
2010 Wheels Autographs #6
2010 Wheels Autographs Printing Plates Black /1 #6
2010 Wheels Autographs Printing Plates Cyan /1 #6
2010 Wheels Autographs Printing Plates Magenta /1 #6
2010 Wheels Autographs Printing Plates Yellow /1 #6
2010 Wheels Autographs Target /10 #5
2010 Wheels Main Event #4
2010 Wheels Main Event #54
2010 Wheels Main Event #100
2010 Wheels Main Event American Muscle #AM8
2010 Wheels Main Event Blue #4
2010 Wheels Main Event Blue #54
2010 Wheels Main Event Blue #100
2010 Wheels Main Event Fight Card #FC4
2010 Wheels Main Event Fight Card Checkered Flag #FC4
2010 Wheels Main Event Fight Card Full Color Retail #FC4
2010 Wheels Main Event Fight Card Gold /25 #FC4
2010 Wheels Main Event Marks Autographs /96 #6
2010 Wheels Main Event Marks Autographs Black /1 #6
2010 Wheels Main Event Marks Autographs Blue /50 #6
2010 Wheels Main Event Marks Autographs Red /5 #6
2010 Wheels Main Event Purple /25 #4
2010 Wheels Main Event Purple /25 #54
2010 Wheels Main Event Toe to Toe /10 #TTKHCB
2010 Wheels Main Event Upper Cuts Blue /50 #UCCB
2010 Wheels Main Event Upper Cuts Holofoil /5 #UCCB
2010 Wheels Main Event Upper Cuts Red /25 #UCCB
2011 Element #4
2011 Element Autographs /58 #6
2011 Element Autographs Blue /5 #6
2011 Element Autographs Gold /10 #6
2011 Element Autographs Printing Plates Black /1 #6
2011 Element Autographs Printing Plates Cyan /1 #6
2011 Element Autographs Printing Plates Magenta /1 #6
2011 Element Autographs Printing Plates Yellow /1 #6
2011 Element Autographs Silver /25 #6
2011 Element Black /35 #4
2011 Element Finish Line Checkered Flag /10 #FLCB
2011 Element Finish Line Green Flag /25 #FLCB
2011 Element Finish Line Tires /99 #FLCB
2011 Element Green #4
2011 Element Previews /5 #EB4
2011 Element Purple /25 #4
2011 Element Red #4
2011 Press Pass #4
2011 Press Pass #59
2011 Press Pass #174
2011 Press Pass #199
2011 Press Pass #0
2011 Press Pass Autographs Blue /10 #6
2011 Press Pass Autographs Bronze /99 #6
2011 Press Pass Autographs Gold /25 #6
2011 Press Pass Autographs Printing Plates Black /1 #6
2011 Press Pass Autographs Printing Plates Cyan /1 #6
2011 Press Pass Autographs Printing Plates Magenta /1 #6
2011 Press Pass Autographs Printing Plates Yellow /1 #6
2011 Press Pass Autographs Silver /50 #6
2011 Press Pass Blue Holofoil /10 #4
2011 Press Pass Blue Holofoil /10 #59
2011 Press Pass Blue Holofoil /10 #174
2011 Press Pass Blue Holofoil /10 #199
2011 Press Pass Blue Retail #4
2011 Press Pass Blue Retail #59
2011 Press Pass Blue Retail #174
2011 Press Pass Blue Retail #199
2011 Press Pass Burning Rubber Gold /150 #BRCCB1
2011 Press Pass Burning Rubber Gold /150 #BRCCB2
2011 Press Pass Burning Rubber Holofoil /50 #BRCCB1
2011 Press Pass Burning Rubber Holofoil /50 #BRCCB2
2011 Press Pass Burning Rubber Prime Cuts /25 #BRCCB1
2011 Press Pass Burning Rubber Prime Cuts /25 #BRCCB2
2011 Press Pass Cup Chase #CCR12
2011 Press Pass Eclipse #4
2011 Press Pass Eclipse #45
2011 Press Pass Eclipse #65
2011 Press Pass Eclipse #82
2011 Press Pass Eclipse Blue #4
2011 Press Pass Eclipse Blue #45
2011 Press Pass Eclipse Blue #65
2011 Press Pass Eclipse Blue #82
2011 Press Pass Eclipse Gold /55 #4
2011 Press Pass Eclipse Gold /55 #45
2011 Press Pass Eclipse Gold /55 #65
2011 Press Pass Eclipse Gold /55 #82
2011 Press Pass Eclipse Previews /5 #EB4
2011 Press Pass Eclipse Previews /1 #EB45
2011 Press Pass Eclipse Purple /25 #4
2011 Press Pass Eclipse Purple /25 #45
2011 Press Pass Eclipse Purple /25 #65
2011 Press Pass FanFare #5
2011 Press Pass FanFare Autographs Blue /5 #8
2011 Press Pass FanFare Autographs Bronze /65 #8
2011 Press Pass FanFare Autographs Gold /50 #8
2011 Press Pass FanFare Autographs Printing Plates Black /1 #8
2011 Press Pass FanFare Autographs Printing Plates Cyan /1 #8
2011 Press Pass FanFare Autographs Printing Plates Magenta /1 #8
2011 Press Pass FanFare Autographs Printing Plates Yellow /1 #8
2011 Press Pass FanFare Autographs Silver /25 #8
2011 Press Pass FanFare Blue Die Cuts #5
2011 Press Pass FanFare Championship Caliber #CC24
2011 Press Pass FanFare Emerald /25 #5
2011 Press Pass FanFare Holofoil Die Cuts #5
2011 Press Pass FanFare Magnificent Materials /199 #MMCB
2011 Press Pass FanFare Magnificent Materials Holofoil /50 #MMCB
2011 Press Pass FanFare Ruby Die Cuts /15 #5
2011 Press Pass FanFare Sapphire /10 #5
2011 Press Pass FanFare Silver /25 #5
2011 Press Pass Geared Up Gold /100 #GUCB
2011 Press Pass Geared Up Holofoil /50 #GUCB
2011 Press Pass Gold /50 #4
2011 Press Pass Gold /50 #59
2011 Press Pass Gold /50 #174
2011 Press Pass Gold /50 #199
2011 Press Pass Premium #5
2011 Press Pass Premium Purple /25 #5
2011 Press Pass Premium Signatures /189 #PSCB
2011 Press Pass Premium Signatures Red Ink /11 #PSCB
2011 Press Pass Previews /5 #EB4
2011 Press Pass Previews /1 #EB199
2011 Press Pass Purple /25 #4
2011 Press Pass Purple /25 #199
2011 Press Pass Showcase /499 #12
2011 Press Pass Showcase /499 #57
2011 Press Pass Showcase Classic Collections Firesuit /45 #CCMRCR
2011 Press Pass Showcase Classic Collections Firesuit Patches /5 #CCMRCR
2011 Press Pass Showcase Classic Collections Ink /25 #CCMRCR
2011 Press Pass Showcase Classic Collections Ink Gold /5 #CCMRCR
2011 Press Pass Showcase Classic Collections Ink Melting /1 #CCMRCR
2011 Press Pass Showcase Classic Collections Sheet Metal /99 #CCMRCR
2011 Press Pass Showcase Gold /125 #12
2011 Press Pass Showcase Gold /125 #57
2011 Press Pass Showcase Green /25 #12
2011 Press Pass Showcase Green /25 #57
2011 Press Pass Showcase Melting /1 #12
2011 Press Pass Showcase Melting /1 #57
2011 Press Pass Signature Series /11 #SSBCB
2011 Press Pass Signature Series /11 #SSTCB
2011 Press Pass Signings Black and White /10 #PPSCB
2011 Press Pass Signings Brushed Metal /60 #PPSCB
2011 Press Pass Signings Holofoil /25 #PPSCB
2011 Press Pass Signings Printing Plates Black /1 #PPSCB
2011 Press Pass Signings Printing Plates Cyan /1 #PPSCB
2011 Press Pass Signings Printing Plates Magenta /1 #PPSCB
2011 Press Pass Signings Printing Plates Yellow /1 #PPSCB
2011 Press Pass Stealth #41
2011 Press Pass Stealth #75
2011 Press Pass Stealth Black and White /25 #41
2011 Press Pass Stealth Black and White /25 #75
2011 Press Pass Stealth Holofoil /99 #41
2011 Press Pass Stealth Holofoil /99 #75
2011 Press Pass Stealth Metal of Honor Medal of Honor /50 #BACB
2011 Press Pass Stealth Metal of Honor Purple Heart /25 #MHCB
2011 Press Pass Stealth Metal of Honor Silver Star /99 #BACB
2011 Press Pass Stealth Purple /25 #41
2011 Press Pass Target Top 12 Tires /25 #T12CB
2011 Press Pass Winning Tickets #WT27
2011 Wheels Main Event #5
2011 Wheels Main Event #76
2011 Wheels Main Event All Stars #A16
2011 Wheels Main Event All Stars Brushed Foil /199 #A16
2011 Wheels Main Event All Stars Holofoil /50 #A16
2011 Wheels Main Event Black and White #5
2011 Wheels Main Event Black and White #76
2011 Wheels Main Event Blue /75 #5
2011 Wheels Main Event Blue /75 #76
2011 Wheels Main Event Green /1 #5
2011 Wheels Main Event Green /1 #76
2011 Wheels Main Event Marks Autographs Blue /8 #MECB
2011 Wheels Main Event Marks Autographs Gold /25 #MECB
2011 Wheels Main Event Marks Autographs Silver /45 #MECB
2011 Wheels Main Event Matchups Autographs /10 #MEMJJCB
2011 Wheels Main Event Materials Holofoil /25 #MEMCB
2011 Wheels Main Event Red /20 #5
2011 Wheels Main Event Red /20 #76
2012 Press Pass Autographs Blue /5 #PPACB
2012 Press Pass Autographs Printing Plates Black /1 #PPACB
2012 Press Pass Autographs Printing Plates Cyan /1 #PPACB
2012 Press Pass Autographs Printing Plates Magenta /1 #PPACB
2012 Press Pass Autographs Printing Plates Yellow /1 #PPACB
2012 Press Pass Autographs Red /15 #PPACB
2012 Press Pass Autographs Silver /25 #PPACB
2012 Press Pass Cup Chase Prizes #CCP6
2012 Press Pass Fanfare #6
2012 Press Pass Fanfare Autographs Blue /10 #CB
2012 Press Pass Fanfare Autographs Gold /75 #CB
2012 Press Pass Fanfare Autographs Red /50 #CB
2012 Press Pass Fanfare Autographs Silver /150 #CB
2012 Press Pass Fanfare Blue Foil Die Cuts #6
2012 Press Pass Fanfare Diamond /5 #6
2012 Press Pass Fanfare Holofoil Die Cuts #6
2012 Press Pass Fanfare Magnificent Materials /250 #MMCB
2012 Press Pass Fanfare Magnificent Materials Dual Swatches /50 #MMCB
2012 Press Pass Fanfare Magnificent Materials Dual Swatches Melting /10 #MMCB
2012 Press Pass Fanfare Magnificent Materials Gold /99 #MMCB
2012 Press Pass Fanfare Magnificent Materials Signatures /99 #CB
2012 Press Pass Fanfare Magnificent Materials Signatures Blue /25 #CB
2012 Press Pass Fanfare Power Rankings #PR13
2012 Press Pass Fanfare Sapphire /20 #6
2012 Press Pass Fanfare Silver /25 #6
2012 Press Pass Ignite #7
2012 Press Pass Ignite Limelight #L4
2012 Press Pass Ignite Materials Autographs Gun Metal /20 #IMCB
2012 Press Pass Ignite Materials Autographs Red /5 #IMCB
2012 Press Pass Ignite Materials Autographs Silver /125 #IMCB
2012 Press Pass Ignite Materials Gun Metal /99 #IMCB
2012 Press Pass Ignite Materials Red /10 #IMCB
2012 Press Pass Ignite Materials Silver #IMCB
2012 Press Pass Ignite Proofs Black and White /50 #7
2012 Press Pass Ignite Proofs Cyan #7
2012 Press Pass Ignite Proofs Magenta #7
2012 Press Pass Ignite Proofs Yellow /10 #7
2012 Press Pass Power Picks Blue /50 #29
2012 Press Pass Power Picks Gold /50 #29
2012 Press Pass Power Picks Holofoil /10 #29
2012 Press Pass Redline #7
2012 Press Pass Redline Black /99 #7
2012 Press Pass Redline Cyan /50 #7
2012 Press Pass Redline Full Throttle Dual Relic Blue /5 #FTCB
2012 Press Pass Redline Full Throttle Dual Relic Gold /10 #FTCB
2012 Press Pass Redline Full Throttle Dual Relic Melting /1 #FTCB
2012 Press Pass Redline Full Throttle Dual Relic Red /75 #FTCB
2012 Press Pass Redline Full Throttle Dual Relic Silver /25 #FTCB
2012 Press Pass Redline Magenta /15 #7
2012 Press Pass Redline Signatures Blue /5 #RSCB
2012 Press Pass Redline Signatures Gold /25 #RSCB
2012 Press Pass Redline Signatures Holofoil /10 #RSCB
2012 Press Pass Redline Signatures Melting /1 #RSCB
2012 Press Pass Redline Signatures Red /50 #RSCB
2012 Press Pass Redline Yellow /1 #7
2012 Press Pass Showcase /499 #4
2012 Press Pass Showcase /499 #60
2012 Press Pass Showcase Classic Collections Ink /10 #CCMMWR
2012 Press Pass Showcase Classic Collections Ink Gold /5 #CCMMWR
2012 Press Pass Showcase Classic Collections Ink Melting /1 #CCMMWR
2012 Press Pass Showcase Classic Collections Memorabilia /99 #CCMMWR
2012 Press Pass Showcase Classic Collections Memorabilia Gold /50 #CCMMWR
2012 Press Pass Showcase Classic Collections Memorabilia Melting /5 #CCMMWR
2012 Press Pass Showcase Gold /125 #4
2012 Press Pass Showcase Gold /125 #60
2012 Press Pass Showcase Green /5 #4
2012 Press Pass Showcase Green /5 #60
2012 Press Pass Showcase Melting /1 #4
2012 Press Pass Showcase Melting /1 #60
2012 Press Pass Showcase Purple /1 #4
2012 Press Pass Showcase Purple /1 #60
2012 Press Pass Showcase Red /25 #4
2012 Press Pass Showcase Red /25 #60
2012 Total Memorabilia #4
2012 Total Memorabilia Black and White /99 #4
2012 Total Memorabilia Gold /275 #4
2012 Total Memorabilia Red Retail /250 #4
2013 Press Pass #6
2013 Press Pass #0
2013 Press Pass Burning Rubber Blue /50 #BRCB
2013 Press Pass Burning Rubber Blue /50 #BRCB2
2013 Press Pass Burning Rubber Gold /199 #BRCB
2013 Press Pass Burning Rubber Gold /199 #BRCB2
2013 Press Pass Burning Rubber Holofoil /75 #BRCB
2013 Press Pass Burning Rubber Holofoil /75 #BRCB2
2013 Press Pass Burning Rubber Melting /10 #BRCB
2013 Press Pass Burning Rubber Melting /10 #BRCB2
2013 Press Pass Color Proofs Black #6
2013 Press Pass Color Proofs Cyan /35 #6
2013 Press Pass Color Proofs Magenta #6
2013 Press Pass Color Proofs Yellow /5 #6
2013 Press Pass Cup Chase Prizes #CCP10
2013 Press Pass Fanfare #7
2013 Press Pass Fanfare #8
2013 Press Pass Fanfare Autographs Blue /5 #CB
2013 Press Pass Fanfare Autographs Gold /10 #CB
2013 Press Pass Fanfare Autographs Green /8 #CB
2013 Press Pass Fanfare Autographs Red /5 #CB
2013 Press Pass Fanfare Autographs Silver /25 #CB
2013 Press Pass Fanfare Diamond Die Cuts /5 #7
2013 Press Pass Fanfare Diamond Die Cuts /5 #8
2013 Press Pass Fanfare Green /3 #7
2013 Press Pass Fanfare Green /3 #8
2013 Press Pass Fanfare Holofoil Die Cuts #7
2013 Press Pass Fanfare Holofoil Die Cuts #8
2013 Press Pass Fanfare Magnificent Jumbo Materials Signatures /10 #CB
2013 Press Pass Fanfare Magnificent Materials Dual Swatches /50 #CB
2013 Press Pass Fanfare Magnificent Materials Dual Swatches Melting /10 #CB
2013 Press Pass Fanfare Magnificent Materials Gold /50 #CB
2013 Press Pass Fanfare Magnificent Materials Jumbo Swatches /25 #CB
2013 Press Pass Fanfare Magnificent Materials Signatures /99 #CB
2013 Press Pass Fanfare Magnificent Materials Signatures Blue /25 #CB
2013 Press Pass Fanfare Magnificent Materials Silver /199 #CB
2013 Press Pass Fanfare Red Foil Die Cuts #7
2013 Press Pass Fanfare Red Foil Die Cuts #8
2013 Press Pass Fanfare Sapphire /20 #7
2013 Press Pass Fanfare Sapphire /20 #8
2013 Press Pass Fanfare Signature Ride Autographs /25 #CB
2013 Press Pass Fanfare Signature Ride Autographs Blue /5 #CB
2013 Press Pass Fanfare Signature Ride Autographs Red /10 #CB
2013 Press Pass Fanfare Silver /25 #7
2013 Press Pass Fanfare Silver /25 #8
2013 Press Pass Ignite #5
2013 Press Pass Ignite #68
2013 Press Pass Ignite Great American Treads Autographs Blue Holofoil /20 #GATCB
2013 Press Pass Ignite Great American Treads Autographs Red /1 #GATCB
2013 Press Pass Ignite Hot Threads Blue Holofoil /99 #HTCB
2013 Press Pass Ignite Hot Threads Patch Red /10 #HTCB
2013 Press Pass Ignite Hot Threads Silver #HTCB
2013 Press Pass Ignite Ink Black /50 #IICB
2013 Press Pass Ignite Ink Blue /20 #IICB
2013 Press Pass Ignite Ink Red /5 #IICB
2013 Press Pass Ignite Proofs Black and White /50 #5
2013 Press Pass Ignite Proofs Black and White /50 #68
2013 Press Pass Ignite Proofs Cyan #5
2013 Press Pass Ignite Proofs Cyan #68
2013 Press Pass Ignite Proofs Magenta #5
2013 Press Pass Ignite Proofs Magenta #68
2013 Press Pass Ignite Proofs Yellow /5 #5
2013 Press Pass Ignite Proofs Yellow /5 #68
2013 Press Pass Legends Prominent Pieces Gold /10 #PPCB
2013 Press Pass Legends Prominent Pieces Holofoil /5 #PPCB
2013 Press Pass Legends Prominent Pieces Oversized Firesuit /5 #PPCB
2013 Press Pass Legends Prominent Pieces Silver /25 #PPCB
2013 Press Pass Power Picks Blue /99 #24
2013 Press Pass Power Picks Gold /50 #24
2013 Press Pass Power Picks Holofoil /10 #24
2013 Press Pass Racing Champions #RC16
2013 Press Pass Racing Champions #RC26
2013 Press Pass Redline #7
2013 Press Pass Redline #8
2013 Press Pass Redline Black /99 #7
2013 Press Pass Redline Black /99 #8
2013 Press Pass Redline Cyan /50 #7
2013 Press Pass Redline Cyan /50 #8
2013 Press Pass Redline Dark Horse Relic Autographs Blue /5 #DHCB
2013 Press Pass Redline Dark Horse Relic Autographs Gold /25 #DHCB
2013 Press Pass Redline Dark Horse Relic Autographs Red /50 #DHCB
2013 Press Pass Redline Magenta /15 #7
2013 Press Pass Redline Magenta /15 #8
2013 Press Pass Redline Muscle Car Sheet Metal Blue /5 #MCMCB
2013 Press Pass Redline Muscle Car Sheet Metal Gold /10 #MCMCB
2013 Press Pass Redline Muscle Car Sheet Metal Melting /1 #MCMCB
2013 Press Pass Redline Muscle Car Sheet Metal Red /50 #MCMCB
2013 Press Pass Redline Muscle Car Sheet Metal Silver /25 #MCMCB
2013 Press Pass Redline Relics Blue /5 #RRCB
2013 Press Pass Redline Relics Gold /10 #RRCB
2013 Press Pass Redline Relics Melting /1 #RRCB
2013 Press Pass Redline Relics Red /50 #RRCB
2013 Press Pass Redline Relics Silver /25 #RRCB
2013 Press Pass Redline Signatures Blue /25 #RSCB
2013 Press Pass Redline Signatures Gold /3 #RSCB
2013 Press Pass Redline Signatures Holo /15 #RSCB
2013 Press Pass Redline Signatures Melting /1 #RSCB
2013 Press Pass Redline Signatures Red /75 #RSCB
2013 Press Pass Redline Yellow /1 #7
2013 Press Pass Redline Yellow /1 #8
2013 Press Pass Showcase /349 #4
2013 Press Pass Showcase /349 #60
2013 Press Pass Showcase Black /1 #4
2013 Press Pass Showcase Black /1 #60
2013 Press Pass Showcase Blue /25 #4
2013 Press Pass Showcase Blue /25 #60
2013 Press Pass Showcase Classic Collections Ink Gold /5 #CCIMWR
2013 Press Pass Showcase Classic Collections Ink Melting /1 #CCIMWR
2013 Press Pass Showcase Classic Collections Ink Red /1 #CCIMWR
2013 Press Pass Showcase Classic Collections Memorabilia Gold /25 #CCMMWR
2013 Press Pass Showcase Classic Collections Memorabilia Melting /5 #CCMMWR
2013 Press Pass Showcase Classic Collections Memorabilia Silver /75 #CCMMWR
2013 Press Pass Showcase Gold /99 #4
2013 Press Pass Showcase Gold /99 #60
2013 Press Pass Showcase Green /20 #4
2013 Press Pass Showcase Green /20 #60
2013 Press Pass Showcase Purple /13 #4
2013 Press Pass Showcase Purple /13 #60
2013 Press Pass Showcase Red /10 #4
2013 Press Pass Showcase Red /10 #60
2013 Press Pass Showcase Showcase Patches /5 #SPCB
2013 Press Pass Signings Gold /25 #CB
2013 Press Pass Signings Holofoil /10 #CB
2013 Press Pass Signings Printing Plates Black /1 #CB
2013 Press Pass Signings Printing Plates Cyan /1 #CB
2013 Press Pass Signings Printing Plates Magenta /1 #CB
2013 Press Pass Signings Printing Plates Yellow /1 #CB
2013 Press Pass Signings Silver /50 #CB
2013 Total Memorabilia #5
2013 Total Memorabilia Black and White /99 #5
2013 Total Memorabilia Burning Rubber Chase Edition Gold /75 #BRCCB
2013 Total Memorabilia Burning Rubber Chase Edition Holofoil /50 #BRCCB
2013 Total Memorabilia Burning Rubber Chase Edition Melting /5 #BRCCB
2013 Total Memorabilia Burning Rubber Chase Edition Silver /175 #BRCCB
2013 Total Memorabilia Dual Swatch Gold /199 #TMCB
2013 Total Memorabilia Gold /275 #5
2013 Total Memorabilia Quad Swatch Melting /10 #TMCB
2013 Total Memorabilia Red #5
2013 Total Memorabilia Single Swatch Silver /475 #TMCB
2013 Total Memorabilia Triple Swatch Holofoil /99 #TMCB
2014 Press Pass #4
2014 Press Pass American Thunder #8
2014 Press Pass American Thunder #52
2014 Press Pass American Thunder Autographs Blue /10 #ATACB
2014 Press Pass American Thunder Autographs Red /5 #ATACB
2014 Press Pass American Thunder Autographs White /15 #ATACB
2014 Press Pass American Thunder Black and White /50 #8
2014 Press Pass American Thunder Black and White /50 #52
2014 Press Pass American Thunder Brothers In Arms Autographs Blue /5 #BAMWR
2014 Press Pass American Thunder Brothers In Arms Autographs Red /1 #BAMWR
2014 Press Pass American Thunder Brothers In Arms Autographs White /10 #BAMWR
2014 Press Pass American Thunder Brothers In Arms Relics Blue /25 #BAMWR
2014 Press Pass American Thunder Brothers In Arms Relics Red /5 #BAMWR
2014 Press Pass American Thunder Brothers In Arms Relics Silver /50 #BAMWR
2014 Press Pass American Thunder Class A Uniforms Blue /99 #CAUCB
2014 Press Pass American Thunder Class A Uniforms Flag /1 #CAUCB
2014 Press Pass American Thunder Class A Uniforms Red /10 #CAUCB
2014 Press Pass American Thunder Class A Uniforms Silver #CAUCB
2014 Press Pass American Thunder Cyan #8
2014 Press Pass American Thunder Cyan #52
2014 Press Pass American Thunder Great American Treads Autographs Blue /25 #GATCB
2014 Press Pass American Thunder Great American Treads Autographs Red /1 #GATCB
2014 Press Pass American Thunder Magenta #8
2014 Press Pass American Thunder Magenta #52
2014 Press Pass American Thunder Yellow /5 #8
2014 Press Pass American Thunder Yellow /5 #52
2014 Press Pass Color Proofs Black /70 #4
2014 Press Pass Color Proofs Cyan /35 #4
2014 Press Pass Color Proofs Magenta #4
2014 Press Pass Color Proofs Yellow /5 #4
2014 Press Pass Five Star Classic Compilations Autographed Patch Booklet /1 #CCCB1
2014 Press Pass Five Star Classic Compilations Autographed Patch Booklet /1 #CCCB2
2014 Press Pass Five Star Classic Compilations Autographed Patch Booklet /1 #CCCB3
2014 Press Pass Five Star Classic Compilations Autographed Patch Booklet /1 #CCCB4
2014 Press Pass Five Star Classic Compilations Autographed Patch Booklet /1 #CCCB5
2014 Press Pass Five Star Classic Compilations Autographed Patch Booklet /1 #CCCB6
2014 Press Pass Five Star Classic Compilations Autographed Patch Booklet /1 #CCCB7
2014 Press Pass Five Star Classic Compilations Autographed Patch Booklet /1 #CCCB8
2014 Press Pass Five Star Classic Compilations Autographed Patch Booklet /1 #CCCB9
2014 Press Pass Five Star Classic Compilations Autographed Patch Booklet /1 #CCCB10
2014 Press Pass Five Star Paramount Pieces Blue /5 #PPCB
2014 Press Pass Five Star Paramount Pieces Gold /25 #PPCB
2014 Press Pass Five Star Paramount Pieces Holofoil /10 #PPCB
2014 Press Pass Five Star Paramount Pieces Melting /1 #PPCB
2014 Press Pass Five Star Paramount Pieces Melting Patch /1 #PPCB
2014 Press Pass Gold #4
2014 Press Pass Gold #90
2014 Press Pass Redline #9
2014 Press Pass Redline #10
2014 Press Pass Redline Black /75 #9
2014 Press Pass Redline Black /75 #10
2014 Press Pass Redline Blue Foil #9
2014 Press Pass Redline Blue Foil #10
2014 Press Pass Redline Cyan /50 #9
2014 Press Pass Redline Cyan /50 #10
2014 Press Pass Redline Green National Convention /5 #9
2014 Press Pass Redline Green National Convention /5 #10
2014 Press Pass Redline Magenta /10 #9
2014 Press Pass Redline Magenta /10 #10
2014 Press Pass Redline Muscle Car Sheet Metal Blue /10 #MCMCB
2014 Press Pass Redline Muscle Car Sheet Metal Gold /25 #MCMCB
2014 Press Pass Redline Muscle Car Sheet Metal Melting /1 #MCMCB
2014 Press Pass Redline Muscle Car Sheet Metal Red /50 #MCMCB
2014 Press Pass Redline Relic Autographs Blue /10 #RRSECB
2014 Press Pass Redline Relic Autographs Gold /25 #RRSECB
2014 Press Pass Redline Relic Autographs Melting /1 #RRSECB
2014 Press Pass Redline Relic Autographs Red /50 #RRSECB
2014 Press Pass Redline Relics Blue /25 #RRCB
2014 Press Pass Redline Relics Gold /50 #RRCB
2014 Press Pass Redline Relics Melting /1 #RRCB
2014 Press Pass Redline Relics Red /75 #RRCB
2014 Press Pass Redline Signatures Blue /25 #RSCB
2014 Press Pass Redline Signatures Gold /50 #RSCB
2014 Press Pass Redline Signatures Melting /10 #RSCB
2014 Press Pass Redline Signatures Red /65 #RSCB
2014 Press Pass Redline Yellow /1 #9
2014 Press Pass Redline Yellow /1 #10
2014 Press Pass Signings Gold /75 #PPSCB
2014 Press Pass Signings Holofoil /10 #PPSCB
2014 Press Pass Signings Melting /1 #PPSCB
2014 Press Pass Signings Printing Plates Black /1 #PPSCB
2014 Press Pass Signings Printing Plates Cyan /1 #PPSCB
2014 Press Pass Signings Printing Plates Magenta /1 #PPSCB
2014 Press Pass Signings Printing Plates Yellow /1 #PPSCB
2014 Press Pass Signings Silver /100 #PPSCB
2014 Press Pass Three Wide Gold /10 #TWCB
2014 Press Pass Three Wide Melting /1 #TWCB
2014 Total Memorabilia #4
2014 Total Memorabilia Acceleration #AC10
2014 Total Memorabilia Black and White /99 #4
2014 Total Memorabilia Dual Swatch Gold /150 #TMCB
2014 Total Memorabilia Gold /175 #4
2014 Total Memorabilia Quad Swatch Melting /25 #TMCB
2014 Total Memorabilia Red #4
2014 Total Memorabilia Single Swatch Silver /275 #TMCB
2014 Total Memorabilia Triple Swatch Blue /99 #TMCB
2015 Press Pass #8
2015 Press Pass Cup Chase #8
2015 Press Pass Cup Chase Blue /25 #8
2015 Press Pass Cup Chase Gold /75 #8
2015 Press Pass Cup Chase Green /10 #8
2015 Press Pass Cup Chase Melting /1 #8
2015 Press Pass Cup Chase Upper Cuts /13 #UCCB
2015 Press Pass Pit Road Pieces Blue /25 #PPMCB
2015 Press Pass Pit Road Pieces Gold /50 #PPMCB
2015 Press Pass Pit Road Pieces Green /10 #PPMCB
2015 Press Pass Pit Road Pieces Melting /1 #PPMCB
2015 Press Pass Pit Road Pieces Signature Edition Blue /25 #PRPCB
2015 Press Pass Pit Road Pieces Signature Edition Gold /50 #PRPCB
2015 Press Pass Pit Road Pieces Signature Edition Green /10 #PRPCB
2015 Press Pass Pit Road Pieces Signature Edition Melting /1 #PRPCB
2015 Press Pass Purple #8
2015 Press Pass Red #8
2015 Press Pass Signature Series Blue /25 #SSCB
2015 Press Pass Signature Series Gold /50 #SSCB
2015 Press Pass Signature Series Green /10 #SSCB
2015 Press Pass Signature Series Melting /1 #SSCB
2015 Press Pass Signings Blue /75 #PPSCB1
2015 Press Pass Signings Gold #PPSCB1
2015 Press Pass Signings Green /25 #PPSCB1
2015 Press Pass Signings Melting /10 #PPSCB
2015 Press Pass Signings Red /50 #PPSCB1
2016 Certified #24
2016 Certified Complete Materials /199 #5
2016 Certified Complete Materials Mirror Black /1 #5
2016 Certified Complete Materials Mirror Blue /50 #5
2016 Certified Complete Materials Mirror Gold /25 #5
2016 Certified Complete Materials Mirror Green /5 #5
2016 Certified Complete Materials Mirror Orange /99 #5
2016 Certified Complete Materials Mirror Purple /10 #5
2016 Certified Complete Materials Mirror Red /75 #5
2016 Certified Complete Materials Mirror Silver /99 #5
2016 Certified Epix /199 #14
2016 Certified Epix Mirror Black /1 #14
2016 Certified Epix Mirror Blue /50 #14
2016 Certified Epix Mirror Gold /25 #14
2016 Certified Epix Mirror Green /5 #14
2016 Certified Epix Mirror Orange /99 #14
2016 Certified Epix Mirror Purple /10 #14
2016 Certified Epix Mirror Red /75 #14
2016 Certified Epix Mirror Silver /99 #14
2016 Certified Gold Team /199 #20
2016 Certified Gold Team Mirror Black /1 #20
2016 Certified Gold Team Mirror Blue /50 #20
2016 Certified Gold Team Mirror Gold /25 #20
2016 Certified Gold Team Mirror Green /5 #20
2016 Certified Gold Team Mirror Orange /99 #20
2016 Certified Gold Team Mirror Purple /10 #20
2016 Certified Gold Team Mirror Red /75 #20
2016 Certified Gold Team Mirror Silver /99 #20
2016 Certified Mirror Black /1 #24
2016 Certified Mirror Blue /50 #24
2016 Certified Mirror Gold /25 #24
2016 Certified Mirror Green /5 #24
2016 Certified Mirror Orange /99 #24
2016 Certified Mirror Purple /10 #24
2016 Certified Mirror Red /75 #24
2016 Certified Mirror Silver /99 #24
2016 Certified Signatures /85 #6
2016 Certified Signatures Mirror Black /1 #6
2016 Certified Signatures Mirror Blue /49 #6
2016 Certified Signatures Mirror Gold /25 #6
2016 Certified Signatures Mirror Green /5 #6
2016 Certified Signatures Mirror Orange /25 #6
2016 Certified Signatures Mirror Purple /10 #6
2016 Certified Signatures Mirror Red /75 #6
2016 Certified Signatures Mirror Silver /25 #6
2016 Certified Sprint Cup Swatches /299 #19
2016 Certified Sprint Cup Swatches Mirror Black /1 #19
2016 Certified Sprint Cup Swatches Mirror Blue /50 #19
2016 Certified Sprint Cup Swatches Mirror Gold /25 #19
2016 Certified Sprint Cup Swatches Mirror Green /5 #19
2016 Certified Sprint Cup Swatches Mirror Orange /99 #19
2016 Certified Sprint Cup Swatches Mirror Purple /10 #19
2016 Certified Sprint Cup Swatches Mirror Red /75 #19
2016 Certified Sprint Cup Swatches Mirror Silver /99 #19
2016 Panini National Treasures /25 #22
2016 Panini National Treasures Black /5 #22
2016 Panini National Treasures Blue /1 #22
2016 Panini National Treasures Combo Materials /25 #6
2016 Panini National Treasures Combo Materials Black /5 #6
2016 Panini National Treasures Combo Materials Blue /1 #6
2016 Panini National Treasures Combo Materials Gold /10 #6
2016 Panini National Treasures Combo Materials Printing Plates Black /1 #6
2016 Panini National Treasures Combo Materials Printing Plates Cyan /1 #6
2016 Panini National Treasures Combo Materials Printing Plates Magenta /1 #6
2016 Panini National Treasures Combo Materials Printing Plates Yellow /1 #6
2016 Panini National Treasures Combo Materials Silver /15 #6
2016 Panini National Treasures Eight Signatures /15 #1
2016 Panini National Treasures Eight Signatures Black /5 #1
2016 Panini National Treasures Eight Signatures Blue /1 #1
2016 Panini National Treasures Eight Signatures Gold /10 #1
2016 Panini National Treasures Firesuit Materials /25 #4
2016 Panini National Treasures Firesuit Materials Black /5 #4
2016 Panini National Treasures Firesuit Materials Blue /1 #4
2016 Panini National Treasures Firesuit Materials Gold /10 #4

2016 Panini National Treasures Firesuit Materials Laundry Tag /1 #4
2016 Panini National Treasures Firesuit Materials Printing Plates Black /1 #4
2016 Panini National Treasures Firesuit Materials Printing Plates Cyan /1 #4
2016 Panini National Treasures Firesuit Materials Printing Plates Magenta /1 #4
2016 Panini National Treasures Firesuit Materials Printing Plates Yellow /1 #4
2016 Panini National Treasures Firesuit Materials Silver /15 #4
2016 Panini National Treasures Gold /15 #22
2016 Panini National Treasures Jumbo Firesuit Patch Signature Booklet Alpine Stars /4 #6
2016 Panini National Treasures Jumbo Firesuit Patch Signature Booklet Associate Sponsor 1 /1 #6
2016 Panini National Treasures Jumbo Firesuit Patch Signature Booklet Associate Sponsor 2 /1 #6
2016 Panini National Treasures Jumbo Firesuit Patch Signature Booklet Associate Sponsor 3 /1 #6
2016 Panini National Treasures Jumbo Firesuit Patch Signature Booklet Associate Sponsor 4 /1 #6
2016 Panini National Treasures Jumbo Firesuit Patch Signature Booklet Associate Sponsor 5 /1 #6
2016 Panini National Treasures Jumbo Firesuit Patch Signature Booklet Flag /1 #6
2016 Panini National Treasures Jumbo Firesuit Patch Signature Booklet Goodyear /2 #6
2016 Panini National Treasures Jumbo Firesuit Patch Signature Booklet Manufacturers Logo /1 #6
2016 Panini National Treasures Jumbo Firesuit Patch Signature Booklet Nameplate /1 #6
2016 Panini National Treasures Jumbo Firesuit Patch Signature Booklet NASCAR /1 #6
2016 Panini National Treasures Jumbo Firesuit Patch Signature Booklet Sprint Cup Logo /1 #6
2016 Panini National Treasures Jumbo Firesuit Patch Signature Booklet Sunoco /1 #6
2016 Panini National Treasures Jumbo Firesuit Signatures /25 #6
2016 Panini National Treasures Jumbo Firesuit Signatures Black /5 #6
2016 Panini National Treasures Jumbo Firesuit Signatures Blue /1 #6
2016 Panini National Treasures Jumbo Firesuit Signatures Gold /10 #6
2016 Panini National Treasures Jumbo Firesuit Signatures Printing Plates Black /1 #6
2016 Panini National Treasures Jumbo Firesuit Signatures Printing Plates Cyan /1 #6
2016 Panini National Treasures Jumbo Firesuit Signatures Printing Plates Magenta /1 #6
2016 Panini National Treasures Jumbo Firesuit Signatures Printing Plates Yellow /1 #6
2016 Panini National Treasures Jumbo Firesuit Signatures Silver /15 #6
2016 Panini National Treasures Jumbo Sheet Metal Signatures /25 #13
2016 Panini National Treasures Jumbo Sheet Metal Signatures Black /5 #13
2016 Panini National Treasures Jumbo Sheet Metal Signatures Blue /1 #13
2016 Panini National Treasures Jumbo Sheet Metal Signatures Gold /10 #13
2016 Panini National Treasures Jumbo Sheet Metal Signatures Printing Plates Black /1 #13
2016 Panini National Treasures Jumbo Sheet Metal Signatures Printing Plates Cyan /1 #13
2016 Panini National Treasures Jumbo Sheet Metal Signatures Printing Plates Magenta /1 #13
2016 Panini National Treasures Jumbo Sheet Metal Signatures Printing Plates Yellow /1 #13
2016 Panini National Treasures Jumbo Sheet Metal Signatures Silver /15 #13
2016 Panini National Treasures Printing Plates Black /1 #22
2016 Panini National Treasures Printing Plates Cyan /1 #22
2016 Panini National Treasures Printing Plates Magenta /1 #22
2016 Panini National Treasures Printing Plates Yellow /1 #22
2016 Panini National Treasures Quad Materials /25 #4
2016 Panini National Treasures Quad Materials Black /5 #4
2016 Panini National Treasures Quad Materials Blue /1 #4
2016 Panini National Treasures Quad Materials Gold /10 #4
2016 Panini National Treasures Quad Materials Printing Plates Black /1 #4
2016 Panini National Treasures Quad Materials Printing Plates Cyan /1 #4
2016 Panini National Treasures Quad Materials Printing Plates Magenta /1 #4
2016 Panini National Treasures Quad Materials Printing Plates Yellow /1 #4
2016 Panini National Treasures Quad Materials Silver /15 #4
2016 Panini National Treasures Sheet Metal Materials /25 #4
2016 Panini National Treasures Sheet Metal Materials Black /5 #4
2016 Panini National Treasures Sheet Metal Materials Blue /1 #4
2016 Panini National Treasures Sheet Metal Materials Gold /10 #4
2016 Panini National Treasures Sheet Metal Materials Printing Plates Black /1 #4
2016 Panini National Treasures Sheet Metal Materials Printing Plates Cyan /1 #4
2016 Panini National Treasures Sheet Metal Materials Printing Plates Magenta /1 #4
2016 Panini National Treasures Sheet Metal Materials Printing Plates Yellow /1 #4
2016 Panini National Treasures Sheet Metal Materials Silver /15 #4
2016 Panini National Treasures Signature Dual Materials /25 #6
2016 Panini National Treasures Signature Dual Materials Black /5 #6
2016 Panini National Treasures Signature Dual Materials Blue /1 #6
2016 Panini National Treasures Signature Dual Materials Gold /10 #6
2016 Panini National Treasures Signature Dual Materials Printing Plates Black /1 #6
2016 Panini National Treasures Signature Dual Materials Printing Plates Cyan /1 #6
2016 Panini National Treasures Signature Dual Materials Printing Plates Magenta /1 #6
2016 Panini National Treasures Signature Dual Materials Printing Plates Yellow /1 #6
2016 Panini National Treasures Signature Dual Materials Silver /15 #6
2016 Panini National Treasures Signature Firesuit Materials /25 #6
2016 Panini National Treasures Signature Firesuit Materials Black /5 #6
2016 Panini National Treasures Signature Firesuit Materials Blue /1 #6
2016 Panini National Treasures Signature Firesuit Materials Gold /10 #6
2016 Panini National Treasures Signature Firesuit Materials Laundry Tag /1 #6
2016 Panini National Treasures Signature Firesuit Materials Printing Plates Black /1 #6
2016 Panini National Treasures Signature Firesuit Materials Printing Plates Cyan /1 #6
2016 Panini National Treasures Signature Firesuit Materials Printing Plates Magenta /1 #6
2016 Panini National Treasures Signature Firesuit Materials Printing Plates Yellow /1 #6
2016 Panini National Treasures Signature Firesuit Materials Silver /15 #6
2016 Panini National Treasures Signature Quad Materials Black /5 #6
2016 Panini National Treasures Signature Quad Materials Blue /1 #6
2016 Panini National Treasures Signature Quad Materials Gold /10 #6
2016 Panini National Treasures Signature Quad Materials Printing Plates Black /1 #6
2016 Panini National Treasures Signature Quad Materials Printing Plates Cyan /1 #6
2016 Panini National Treasures Signature Quad Materials Printing Plates Magenta /1 #6
2016 Panini National Treasures Signature Quad Materials Printing Plates Yellow /1 #6
2016 Panini National Treasures Signature Sheet Metal Materials /25 #6
2016 Panini National Treasures Signature Sheet Metal Materials Black /5 #6
2016 Panini National Treasures Signature Sheet Metal Materials Blue /1 #6
2016 Panini National Treasures Signature Sheet Metal Materials Gold /10 #6
2016 Panini National Treasures Signature Sheet Metal Materials Printing Plates Black /1 #6
2016 Panini National Treasures Signature Sheet Metal Materials Printing Plates Cyan /1 #6
2016 Panini National Treasures Signature Sheet Metal Materials Printing Plates Magenta /1 #6
2016 Panini National Treasures Signature Sheet Metal Materials Printing Plates Yellow /1 #6
2016 Panini National Treasures Signature Sheet Metal Materials Silver /15 #6
2016 Panini National Treasures Signatures /25 #5
2016 Panini National Treasures Signatures Black /5 #5
2016 Panini National Treasures Signatures Blue /1 #5
2016 Panini National Treasures Signatures Gold /15 #5
2016 Panini National Treasures Signatures Printing Plates Black /1 #5
2016 Panini National Treasures Signatures Printing Plates Cyan /1 #5
2016 Panini National Treasures Signatures Printing Plates Magenta /1 #5
2016 Panini National Treasures Signatures Printing Plates Yellow /1 #5
2016 Panini National Treasures Signatures Silver /20 #5
2016 Panini National Treasures Silver /20 #22
2016 Panini National Treasures Timelines /25 #4
2016 Panini National Treasures Timelines Black /5 #4
2016 Panini National Treasures Timelines Blue /1 #4
2016 Panini National Treasures Timelines Gold /10 #4
2016 Panini National Treasures Timelines Printing Plates Black /1 #4
2016 Panini National Treasures Timelines Printing Plates Cyan /1 #4
2016 Panini National Treasures Timelines Printing Plates Magenta /1 #4
2016 Panini National Treasures Timelines Printing Plates Yellow /1 #4
2016 Panini National Treasures Timelines Signatures /25 #4
2016 Panini National Treasures Timelines Signatures Black /5 #4
2016 Panini National Treasures Timelines Signatures Blue /1 #4
2016 Panini National Treasures Timelines Signatures Gold /10 #4
2016 Panini National Treasures Timelines Signatures Printing Plates Black /1 #4
2016 Panini National Treasures Timelines Signatures Printing Plates Cyan /1 #4
2016 Panini National Treasures Timelines Signatures Printing Plates Magenta /1 #4
2016 Panini National Treasures Timelines Signatures Printing Plates Yellow /1 #4
2016 Panini National Treasures Timelines Signatures Silver /15 #4
2016 Panini National Treasures Timelines Silver /15 #4
2016 Panini Prizm #15
2016 Panini Prizm #86
2016 Panini Prizm Autographs Prizms #14
2016 Panini Prizm Autographs Prizms Black /3 #14
2016 Panini Prizm Autographs Prizms Blue Flag /35 #14
2016 Panini Prizm Autographs Prizms Camo /15 #14
2016 Panini Prizm Autographs Prizms Checkered Flag /1 #14
2016 Panini Prizm Autographs Prizms Gold /10 #14
2016 Panini Prizm Autographs Prizms Green Flag /50 #14
2016 Panini Prizm Autographs Prizms Rainbow /24 #14
2016 Panini Prizm Autographs Prizms Red Flag /25 #14
2016 Panini Prizm Autographs Prizms Red White and Blue /25 #14
2016 Panini Prizm Autographs Prizms White Flag /5 #14
2016 Panini Prizm Machinery #9
2016 Panini Prizm Machinery Prizms #9
2016 Panini Prizm Machinery Prizms Checkered Flag /1 #9
2016 Panini Prizm Machinery Prizms Gold /10 #9
2016 Panini Prizm Prizms #15
2016 Panini Prizm Prizms #86
2016 Panini Prizm Prizms Black /3 #15
2016 Panini Prizm Prizms Black /3 #86
2016 Panini Prizm Prizms Blue Flag /99 #15
2016 Panini Prizm Prizms Blue Flag /99 #86
2016 Panini Prizm Prizms Camo /15 #15
2016 Panini Prizm Prizms Camo /15 #86
2016 Panini Prizm Prizms Checkered Flag /1 #15
2016 Panini Prizm Prizms Checkered Flag /1 #86
2016 Panini Prizm Prizms Gold /10 #15
2016 Panini Prizm Prizms Gold /10 #86
2016 Panini Prizm Prizms Green Flag /149 #15
2016 Panini Prizm Prizms Green Flag /149 #86
2016 Panini Prizm Prizms Rainbow /24 #15
2016 Panini Prizm Prizms Rainbow /24 #86
2016 Panini Prizm Prizms Red Flag /75 #15
2016 Panini Prizm Prizms Red Flag /75 #86
2016 Panini Prizm Prizms Red White and Blue #15
2016 Panini Prizm Prizms Red White and Blue #86
2016 Panini Prizm Prizms White Flag /5 #15
2016 Panini Prizm Prizms White Flag /5 #86
2016 Panini Prizm Qualifying Times #3
2016 Panini Prizm Qualifying Times Prizms #3
2016 Panini Prizm Qualifying Times Prizms Checkered Flag /1 #3
2016 Panini Prizm Qualifying Times Prizms Gold /10 #3
2016 Panini Prizm Race Used Tire Team #14
2016 Panini Prizm Race Used Tire Team Prizms Blue Flag /75 #14
2016 Panini Prizm Race Used Tire Team Prizms Checkered Flag /1 #14
2016 Panini Prizm Race Used Tire Team Prizms Green Flag /149 #14
2016 Panini Prizm Race Used Tire Team Prizms Red Flag /10 #14
2016 Panini Torque #33
2016 Panini Torque Artist Proof /50 #33
2016 Panini Torque Blackout /1 #33
2016 Panini Torque Blue /125 #33
2016 Panini Torque Clear Vision #25
2016 Panini Torque Clear Vision Blue /99 #25
2016 Panini Torque Clear Vision Gold /149 #25
2016 Panini Torque Clear Vision Green /25 #25
2016 Panini Torque Clear Vision Purple /10 #25
2016 Panini Torque Clear Vision Red /49 #25
2016 Panini Torque Gold #33
2016 Panini Torque Holo Gold /5 #33
2016 Panini Torque Holo Silver /10 #33
2016 Panini Torque Horsepower Heroes #16
2016 Panini Torque Horsepower Heroes Gold /199 #16
2016 Panini Torque Horsepower Heroes Holo Silver /99 #16
2016 Panini Torque Metal Materials /249 #8
2016 Panini Torque Metal Materials Blue /99 #8
2016 Panini Torque Metal Materials Green /25 #8
2016 Panini Torque Metal Materials Purple /10 #8
2016 Panini Torque Metal Materials Red /49 #8
2016 Panini Torque Painted to Perfection #16
2016 Panini Torque Painted to Perfection Blue /99 #16
2016 Panini Torque Painted to Perfection Checkerboard /10 #16
2016 Panini Torque Painted to Perfection Green /25 #16
2016 Panini Torque Painted to Perfection Red /49 #16
2016 Panini Torque Pairings Materials /125 #26
2016 Panini Torque Pairings Materials Blue /99 #26
2016 Panini Torque Pairings Materials Green /25 #26
2016 Panini Torque Pairings Materials Purple /10 #26
2016 Panini Torque Pairings Materials Red /49 #26
2016 Panini Torque Pole Position #20
2016 Panini Torque Pole Position Blue /99 #20
2016 Panini Torque Pole Position Checkerboard /10 #20
2016 Panini Torque Pole Position Green /25 #20
2016 Panini Torque Pole Position Red /49 #20
2016 Panini Torque Printing Plates Black /1 #33
2016 Panini Torque Printing Plates Cyan /1 #33
2016 Panini Torque Printing Plates Magenta /1 #33
2016 Panini Torque Printing Plates Yellow /1 #33
2016 Panini Torque Purple /25 #33
2016 Panini Torque Red /99 #33
2016 Panini Torque Rubber Relics /399 #5
2016 Panini Torque Rubber Relics Blue /99 #5
2016 Panini Torque Rubber Relics Green /25 #5
2016 Panini Torque Rubber Relics Purple /10 #5
2016 Panini Torque Rubber Relics Red /49 #5
2016 Panini Torque Shades #7
2016 Panini Torque Shades Gold /199 #7
2016 Panini Torque Shades Holo Silver /99 #7
2016 Panini Torque Silhouettes Firesuit Autographs /60 #5
2016 Panini Torque Silhouettes Firesuit Autographs Blue /35 #5
2016 Panini Torque Silhouettes Firesuit Autographs Green /20 #5
2016 Panini Torque Silhouettes Firesuit Autographs Purple /10 #5
2016 Panini Torque Silhouettes Firesuit Autographs Red /25 #5
2016 Panini Torque Silhouettes Sheet Metal Autographs /60 #5
2016 Panini Torque Silhouettes Sheet Metal Autographs Blue /35 #5
2016 Panini Torque Silhouettes Sheet Metal Autographs Green /20 #5
2016 Panini Torque Silhouettes Sheet Metal Autographs Purple /10 #5
2016 Panini Torque Silhouettes Sheet Metal Autographs Red /25 #5
2016 Panini Torque Superstar Vision #14
2016 Panini Torque Superstar Vision Blue /99 #14
2016 Panini Torque Superstar Vision Gold /149 #14
2016 Panini Torque Superstar Vision Green /25 #14
2016 Panini Torque Superstar Vision Purple /10 #14
2016 Panini Torque Superstar Vision Red /49 #14
2016 Panini Torque Test Proof Black /1 #33
2016 Panini Torque Test Proof Cyan /1 #33
2016 Panini Torque Test Proof Magenta /1 #33
2016 Panini Torque Test Proof Yellow /1 #33
2016 Panini Torque Victory Laps #12
2016 Panini Torque Victory Laps Gold /199 #12
2016 Panini Torque Victory Laps Holo Silver /99 #12
2016 Panini Torque Winning Vision #17
2016 Panini Torque Winning Vision Blue /99 #17
2016 Panini Torque Winning Vision Gold /149 #17
2016 Panini Torque Winning Vision Green /25 #17
2016 Panini Torque Winning Vision Purple /10 #17
2016 Panini Torque Winning Vision Red /49 #17
2017 Donruss #5
2017 Donruss #55
2017 Donruss #113
2017 Donruss #154
2017 Donruss Artist Proof /25 #5
2017 Donruss Artist Proof /25 #55
2017 Donruss Artist Proof /25 #113
2017 Donruss Artist Proof /25 #154
2017 Donruss Blue Foil /299 #5
2017 Donruss Blue Foil /299 #55
2017 Donruss Blue Foil /299 #113
2017 Donruss Blue Foil /299 #154
2017 Donruss Gold Foil /499 #5
2017 Donruss Gold Foil /499 #55
2017 Donruss Gold Foil /499 #113
2017 Donruss Gold Foil /499 #154
2017 Donruss Gold Press Proof /99 #5
2017 Donruss Gold Press Proof /99 #55
2017 Donruss Gold Press Proof /99 #113
2017 Donruss Gold Press Proof /99 #154
2017 Donruss Green Foil /199 #5
2017 Donruss Green Foil /199 #55
2017 Donruss Green Foil /199 #113
2017 Donruss Green Foil /199 #154
2017 Donruss Press Proof /49 #5
2017 Donruss Press Proof /49 #55
2017 Donruss Press Proof /49 #113
2017 Donruss Press Proof /49 #154
2017 Donruss Printing Plates Black /1 #5
2017 Donruss Printing Plates Black /1 #55
2017 Donruss Printing Plates Black /1 #113
2017 Donruss Printing Plates Black /1 #154
2017 Donruss Printing Plates Cyan /1 #5
2017 Donruss Printing Plates Cyan /1 #55
2017 Donruss Printing Plates Cyan /1 #113
2017 Donruss Printing Plates Cyan /1 #154
2017 Donruss Printing Plates Magenta /1 #5
2017 Donruss Printing Plates Magenta /1 #55
2017 Donruss Printing Plates Magenta /1 #113
2017 Donruss Printing Plates Magenta /1 #154
2017 Donruss Printing Plates Yellow /1 #5
2017 Donruss Printing Plates Yellow /1 #55
2017 Donruss Printing Plates Yellow /1 #113
2017 Donruss Printing Plates Yellow /1 #154
2017 Donruss Retro Relics 1984 #10
2017 Donruss Retro Relics 1984 Holo Black /10 #10
2017 Donruss Retro Relics 1984 Holo Gold /99 #10
2017 Donruss Retro Signatures 1984 #5
2017 Donruss Retro Signatures 1984 Holo Black /1 #5
2017 Donruss Retro Signatures 1984 Holo Gold /25 #5
2017 Donruss Rubber Relics #12
2017 Donruss Rubber Relics Holo Black /1 #12
2017 Donruss Rubber Relics Holo Gold /25 #12
2017 Donruss Top Tier #8
2017 Donruss Top Tier Cracked Ice /999 #8
2017 Panini Black Friday Happy Holiday Memorabilia #HHCB
2017 Panini Black Friday Happy Holiday Memorabilia Cracked Ice /25 #HHCB
2017 Panini Black Friday Happy Holiday Memorabilia Galactic Windows /10 #HHCB
2017 Panini Black Friday Happy Holiday Memorabilia Hyperplaid /1 #HHCB
2017 Panini National Treasures /25 #12
2017 Panini National Treasures Associate Sponsor Patch Signatures 1 /1 #11
2017 Panini National Treasures Associate Sponsor Patch Signatures 2 /1 #11
2017 Panini National Treasures Associate Sponsor Patch Signatures 3 /1 #11
2017 Panini National Treasures Associate Sponsor Patch Signatures 4 /1 #11
2017 Panini National Treasures Associate Sponsor Patch Signatures 5 /1 #11
2017 Panini National Treasures Associate Sponsor Patch Signatures 6 /1 #11
2017 Panini National Treasures Associate Sponsor Patch Signatures 7 /1 #11
2017 Panini National Treasures Associate Sponsor Patch Signatures 8 /1 #11
2017 Panini National Treasures Car Manufacturer Patch Signatures /1 #11
2017 Panini National Treasures Century Black /1 #12
2017 Panini National Treasures Century Gold /15 #12
2017 Panini National Treasures Century Green /5 #12
2017 Panini National Treasures Century Holo Gold /10 #12
2017 Panini National Treasures Century Holo Silver /20 #12
2017 Panini National Treasures Century Laundry Tags /1 #12
2017 Panini National Treasures Dual Firesuit Materials Black /1 #5
2017 Panini National Treasures Dual Firesuit Materials Gold /15 #5
2017 Panini National Treasures Dual Firesuit Materials Green /5 #5
2017 Panini National Treasures Dual Firesuit Materials Holo Gold /10 #5
2017 Panini National Treasures Dual Firesuit Materials Laundry Tag /1 #5
2017 Panini National Treasures Dual Firesuit Materials Printing Plates Black /1 #5
2017 Panini National Treasures Dual Firesuit Materials Printing Plates Cyan /1 #5
2017 Panini National Treasures Dual Firesuit Materials Printing Plates Magenta /1 #5
2017 Panini National Treasures Dual Firesuit Materials Printing Plates Yellow /1 #5
2017 Panini National Treasures Dual Firesuit Signatures /25 #5
2017 Panini National Treasures Dual Firesuit Signatures Black /1 #5
2017 Panini National Treasures Dual Firesuit Signatures Gold /15 #5
2017 Panini National Treasures Dual Firesuit Signatures Green /5 #5
2017 Panini National Treasures Dual Firesuit Signatures Holo Gold /10 #5
2017 Panini National Treasures Dual Firesuit Signatures Holo Silver /20 #5
2017 Panini National Treasures Dual Firesuit Signatures Laundry Tag /1 #5
2017 Panini National Treasures Dual Firesuit Signatures Printing Plates Black /1 #5
2017 Panini National Treasures Dual Firesuit Signatures Printing Plates Cyan /1 #5
2017 Panini National Treasures Dual Firesuit Signatures Printing Plates Magenta /1 #5
2017 Panini National Treasures Dual Firesuit Signatures Printing Plates Yellow /1 #5
2017 Panini National Treasures Dual Sheet Metal Materials Black /1 #8
2017 Panini National Treasures Dual Sheet Metal Materials Green /5 #8
2017 Panini National Treasures Dual Sheet Metal Materials Printing Plates Black /1 #8
2017 Panini National Treasures Dual Sheet Metal Materials Printing Plates Cyan /1 #8
2017 Panini National Treasures Dual Sheet Metal Materials Printing Plates Magenta /1 #8
2017 Panini National Treasures Dual Sheet Metal Materials Printing Plates Yellow /1 #8
2017 Panini National Treasures Dual Sheet Metal Signatures /25 #4
2017 Panini National Treasures Dual Sheet Metal Signatures Black /1 #4
2017 Panini National Treasures Dual Sheet Metal Signatures Gold /15 #4
2017 Panini National Treasures Dual Sheet Metal Signatures Green /5 #4
2017 Panini National Treasures Dual Sheet Metal Signatures Holo Gold /10 #4
2017 Panini National Treasures Dual Sheet Metal Signatures Holo Silver /20 #4
2017 Panini National Treasures Dual Sheet Metal Signatures Printing Plates Black /1 #4
2017 Panini National Treasures Dual Sheet Metal Signatures Printing Plates Cyan /1 #4
2017 Panini National Treasures Dual Sheet Metal Signatures Printing Plates Magenta /1 #4
2017 Panini National Treasures Dual Sheet Metal Signatures Printing Plates Yellow /1 #4
2017 Panini National Treasures Dual Signature Materials /50 #5
2017 Panini National Treasures Dual Signature Materials Black /1 #5
2017 Panini National Treasures Dual Signature Materials Gold /15 #5
2017 Panini National Treasures Dual Signature Materials Green /5 #5
2017 Panini National Treasures Dual Signature Materials Holo Gold /10 #5
2017 Panini National Treasures Dual Signature Materials Holo Silver /25 #5
2017 Panini National Treasures Dual Signature Materials Laundry Tag /1 #5
2017 Panini National Treasures Firesuit Manufacturer Patch Signatures /1 #11
2017 Panini National Treasures Flag Patch Signatures /1 #11
2017 Panini National Treasures Goodyear Patch Signatures /2 #11
2017 Panini National Treasures Jumbo Firesuit Signatures /25 #2
2017 Panini National Treasures Jumbo Firesuit Signatures Black /1 #2
2017 Panini National Treasures Jumbo Firesuit Signatures Gold /15 #2
2017 Panini National Treasures Jumbo Firesuit Signatures Green /5 #2
2017 Panini National Treasures Jumbo Firesuit Signatures Holo Gold /10 #2
2017 Panini National Treasures Jumbo Firesuit Signatures Holo Silver /20 #2
2017 Panini National Treasures Jumbo Firesuit Signatures Laundry Tag /1 #2
2017 Panini National Treasures Jumbo Firesuit Signatures Printing Plates Black /1 #2
2017 Panini National Treasures Jumbo Firesuit Signatures Printing Plates Cyan /1 #2
2017 Panini National Treasures Jumbo Firesuit Signatures Printing Plates Magenta /1 #2
2017 Panini National Treasures Jumbo Firesuit Signatures Printing Plates Yellow /1 #2
2017 Panini National Treasures Jumbo Tire Signatures Black /1 #4
2017 Panini National Treasures Jumbo Tire Signatures Green /5 #4
2017 Panini National Treasures Jumbo Tire Signatures Holo Gold /15 #4
2017 Panini National Treasures Jumbo Tire Signatures Printing Plates Black /1 #4
2017 Panini National Treasures Jumbo Tire Signatures Printing Plates Cyan /1 #4
2017 Panini National Treasures Jumbo Tire Signatures Printing Plates Magenta /1 #4
2017 Panini National Treasures Jumbo Tire Signatures Printing Plates Yellow /1 #4
2017 Panini National Treasures Nameplate Patch Signatures /2 #11
2017 Panini National Treasures NASCAR Patch Signatures /1 #11
2017 Panini National Treasures Printing Plates Black /1 #12
2017 Panini National Treasures Printing Plates Cyan /1 #12
2017 Panini National Treasures Printing Plates Magenta /1 #12
2017 Panini National Treasures Printing Plates Yellow /1 #12
2017 Panini National Treasures Series Sponsor Patch Signatures /1 #11
2017 Panini National Treasures Signature Six Way Swatches /25 #9
2017 Panini National Treasures Signature Six Way Swatches Black /1 #9
2017 Panini National Treasures Signature Six Way Swatches Gold /15 #9
2017 Panini National Treasures Signature Six Way Swatches Green /5 #9
2017 Panini National Treasures Signature Six Way Swatches Holo Gold /10 #9
2017 Panini National Treasures Signature Six Way Swatches Holo Silver /20 #9
2017 Panini National Treasures Signature Six Way Swatches Laundry Tag /1 #9
2017 Panini National Treasures Sunoco Patch Signatures /1 #11
2017 Panini National Treasures Teammates Dual Materials /25 #4
2017 Panini National Treasures Teammates Dual Materials Black /1 #4
2017 Panini National Treasures Teammates Dual Materials Gold /15 #4
2017 Panini National Treasures Teammates Dual Materials Green /5 #4
2017 Panini National Treasures Teammates Dual Materials Holo Gold /10 #4
2017 Panini National Treasures Teammates Dual Materials Holo Silver /20 #4
2017 Panini National Treasures Teammates Dual Materials Laundry Tag /1 #4
2017 Panini National Treasures Teammates Dual Materials Printing Plates Black /1 #4
2017 Panini National Treasures Teammates Dual Materials Printing Plates Cyan /1 #4
2017 Panini National Treasures Teammates Dual Materials Printing Plates Magenta /1 #4
2017 Panini National Treasures Teammates Dual Materials Printing Plates Yellow /1 #4
2017 Panini National Treasures Teammates Quad Materials /25 #6
2017 Panini National Treasures Teammates Quad Materials Black /1 #6
2017 Panini National Treasures Teammates Quad Materials Gold /15 #6
2017 Panini National Treasures Teammates Quad Materials Green /5 #6
2017 Panini National Treasures Teammates Quad Materials Holo Gold /10 #6
2017 Panini National Treasures Teammates Quad Materials Holo Silver /20 #6
2017 Panini National Treasures Teammates Quad Materials Laundry Tag /1 #6
2017 Panini National Treasures Teammates Quad Materials Printing Plates Black /1 #6
2017 Panini National Treasures Teammates Quad Materials Printing Plates Cyan /1 #6
2017 Panini National Treasures Teammates Quad Materials Printing Plates Magenta /1 #6
2017 Panini National Treasures Teammates Quad Materials Printing Plates Yellow /1 #6
2017 Panini National Treasures Teammates Triple Materials /25 #2
2017 Panini National Treasures Teammates Triple Materials Black /1 #2
2017 Panini National Treasures Teammates Triple Materials Gold /15 #2
2017 Panini National Treasures Teammates Triple Materials Green /5 #2
2017 Panini National Treasures Teammates Triple Materials Holo Gold /10 #2
2017 Panini National Treasures Teammates Triple Materials Holo Silver /20 #2
2017 Panini National Treasures Teammates Triple Materials Laundry Tag /1 #2
2017 Panini National Treasures Teammates Triple Materials Printing Plates Black /1 #2
2017 Panini National Treasures Teammates Triple Materials Printing Plates Cyan /1 #2
2017 Panini National Treasures Teammates Triple Materials Printing Plates Magenta /1 #2
2017 Panini National Treasures Teammates Triple Materials Printing Plates Yellow /1 #2
2017 Panini National Treasures Three Wide Signatures /25 #14
2017 Panini National Treasures Three Wide Signatures Black /1 #14
2017 Panini National Treasures Three Wide Signatures Gold /15 #14
2017 Panini National Treasures Three Wide Signatures Green /5 #14
2017 Panini National Treasures Three Wide Signatures Holo Gold /10 #14
2017 Panini National Treasures Three Wide Signatures Holo Silver /20 #14
2017 Panini National Treasures Three Wide Signatures Laundry Tag /1 #14
2017 Panini National Treasures Three Wide Signatures Printing Plates Black /1 #14
2017 Panini National Treasures Three Wide Signatures Printing Plates Cyan /1 #14
2017 Panini National Treasures Three Wide Signatures Printing Plates Magenta /1 #14
2017 Panini National Treasures Three Wide Signatures Printing Plates Yellow /1 #14
2017 Panini Torque #23
2017 Panini Torque #60
2017 Panini Torque #90
2017 Panini Torque Artist Proof /75 #23
2017 Panini Torque Artist Proof /75 #60
2017 Panini Torque Artist Proof /75 #90
2017 Panini Torque Blackout /1 #23
2017 Panini Torque Blackout /1 #60
2017 Panini Torque Blackout /1 #90
2017 Panini Torque Blue /150 #23
2017 Panini Torque Blue /150 #60
2017 Panini Torque Blue /150 #90
2017 Panini Torque Clear Vision #23
2017 Panini Torque Clear Vision Blue /99 #23
2017 Panini Torque Clear Vision Gold /149 #23
2017 Panini Torque Clear Vision Green /25 #23
2017 Panini Torque Clear Vision Purple /10 #23
2017 Panini Torque Clear Vision Red /49 #23
2017 Panini Torque Dual Materials /25 #6
2017 Panini Torque Dual Materials Blue /20 #6
2017 Panini Torque Dual Materials Green /10 #6
2017 Panini Torque Dual Materials Purple /5 #6
2017 Panini Torque Dual Materials Red /15 #6
2017 Panini Torque Gold #23
2017 Panini Torque Gold #60
2017 Panini Torque Gold #90
2017 Panini Torque Holo Gold /10 #23
2017 Panini Torque Holo Gold /10 #60
2017 Panini Torque Holo Gold /10 #90
2017 Panini Torque Holo Silver /25 #23
2017 Panini Torque Holo Silver /25 #60
2017 Panini Torque Holo Silver /25 #90
2017 Panini Torque Horsepower Heroes #11
2017 Panini Torque Horsepower Heroes Gold /199 #11
2017 Panini Torque Horsepower Heroes Holo Silver /99 #11
2017 Panini Torque Jumbo Firesuit Signatures /50 #15
2017 Panini Torque Jumbo Firesuit Signatures Blue /25 #15
2017 Panini Torque Jumbo Firesuit Signatures Green /15 #15
2017 Panini Torque Jumbo Firesuit Signatures Purple /10 #15
2017 Panini Torque Jumbo Firesuit Signatures Red /20 #15
2017 Panini Torque Jumbo Tire Signatures /35 #8
2017 Panini Torque Jumbo Tire Signatures Blue /25 #8
2017 Panini Torque Jumbo Tire Signatures Green /15 #8
2017 Panini Torque Jumbo Tire Signatures Purple /10 #8
2017 Panini Torque Jumbo Tire Signatures Red /20 #8
2017 Panini Torque Pairings Materials /199 #4
2017 Panini Torque Pairings Materials Blue /99 #4
2017 Panini Torque Pairings Materials Green /25 #4
2017 Panini Torque Pairings Materials Purple /10 #4
2017 Panini Torque Pairings Materials Red /49 #4
2017 Panini Torque Primary Paint #2
2017 Panini Torque Primary Paint Blue /99 #2
2017 Panini Torque Primary Paint Checkerboard /10 #2
2017 Panini Torque Primary Paint Green /25 #2
2017 Panini Torque Primary Paint Red /49 #2
2017 Panini Torque Prime Associate Sponsors Jumbo Patches /1 #4A
2017 Panini Torque Prime Associate Sponsors Jumbo Patches /1 #4B
2017 Panini Torque Prime Associate Sponsors Jumbo Patches /1 #4C
2017 Panini Torque Prime Associate Sponsors Jumbo Patches /1 #4D
2017 Panini Torque Prime Associate Sponsors Jumbo Patches /1 #4E
2017 Panini Torque Prime Associate Sponsors Jumbo Patches /1 #4F
2017 Panini Torque Prime Associate Sponsors Jumbo Patches /1 #4G
2017 Panini Torque Prime Associate Sponsors Jumbo Patches /1 #4H
2017 Panini Torque Prime Associate Sponsors Jumbo Patches /1 #4I
2017 Panini Torque Prime Flag Jumbo Patches /1 #4
2017 Panini Torque Prime Goodyear Jumbo Patches /2 #4
2017 Panini Torque Prime Manufacturer Jumbo Patches /1 #4
2017 Panini Torque Prime Nameplates Jumbo Patches /1 #4
2017 Panini Torque Prime NASCAR Jumbo Patches /1 #4
2017 Panini Torque Prime Series Sponsor Jumbo Patches /1 #4
2017 Panini Torque Printing Plates Black /1 #23
2017 Panini Torque Printing Plates Black /1 #60
2017 Panini Torque Printing Plates Black /1 #90
2017 Panini Torque Printing Plates Cyan /1 #23
2017 Panini Torque Printing Plates Cyan /1 #60
2017 Panini Torque Printing Plates Cyan /1 #90
2017 Panini Torque Printing Plates Magenta /1 #23
2017 Panini Torque Printing Plates Magenta /1 #60
2017 Panini Torque Printing Plates Magenta /1 #90
2017 Panini Torque Printing Plates Yellow /1 #23
2017 Panini Torque Printing Plates Yellow /1 #60
2017 Panini Torque Printing Plates Yellow /1 #90
2017 Panini Torque Purple /50 #23
2017 Panini Torque Purple /50 #60
2017 Panini Torque Purple /50 #90
2017 Panini Torque Quad Materials /25 #5
2017 Panini Torque Quad Materials Blue /20 #5
2017 Panini Torque Quad Materials Green /10 #5
2017 Panini Torque Quad Materials Purple /5 #5
2017 Panini Torque Quad Materials Red /15 #5
2017 Panini Torque Raced Relics /199 #4
2017 Panini Torque Raced Relics Blue /99 #4
2017 Panini Torque Raced Relics Green /25 #4
2017 Panini Torque Raced Relics Purple /10 #4
2017 Panini Torque Raced Relics Red /49 #4
2017 Panini Torque Red /100 #23
2017 Panini Torque Red /100 #60
2017 Panini Torque Red /100 #90
2017 Panini Torque Silhouettes Sheet Metal Signatures /25 #1
2017 Panini Torque Silhouettes Sheet Metal Signatures Blue /20 #1
2017 Panini Torque Silhouettes Sheet Metal Signatures Green /10 #1
2017 Panini Torque Silhouettes Sheet Metal Signatures Purple /5 #1
2017 Panini Torque Silhouettes Sheet Metal Signatures Red /15 #1
2017 Panini Torque Superstar Vision #10
2017 Panini Torque Superstar Vision Blue /99 #10
2017 Panini Torque Superstar Vision Gold /149 #10
2017 Panini Torque Superstar Vision Green /25 #10
2017 Panini Torque Superstar Vision Purple /10 #10
2017 Panini Torque Superstar Vision Red /49 #10
2017 Panini Torque Test Proof Black /1 #23
2017 Panini Torque Test Proof Black /1 #60
2017 Panini Torque Test Proof Black /1 #90
2017 Panini Torque Test Proof Cyan /1 #23
2017 Panini Torque Test Proof Cyan /1 #60
2017 Panini Torque Test Proof Cyan /1 #90
2017 Panini Torque Test Proof Magenta /1 #23
2017 Panini Torque Test Proof Magenta /1 #60
2017 Panini Torque Test Proof Magenta /1 #90
2017 Panini Torque Test Proof Yellow /1 #23
2017 Panini Torque Test Proof Yellow /1 #60
2017 Panini Torque Test Proof Yellow /1 #90
2017 Select #61
2017 Select #121
2017 Select Prizms Black /3 #61
2017 Select Prizms Black /3 #121
2017 Select Prizms Blue /199 #61
2017 Select Prizms Checkered Flag /1 #61
2017 Select Prizms Checkered Flag /1 #121
2017 Select Prizms Gold /10 #61
2017 Select Prizms Gold /10 #121
2017 Select Prizms Purple Pulsar #61
2017 Select Prizms Red /99 #61
2017 Select Prizms Red White and Blue Pulsar /299 #61
2017 Select Prizms Silver #61
2017 Select Prizms Tie Dye /24 #61
2017 Select Prizms Tie Dye /24 #121
2017 Select Prizms White /50 #61
2017 Select Prizms White /50 #121
2017 Select Select Pairs Materials #7
2017 Select Select Pairs Materials #10
2017 Select Select Pairs Materials #11
2017 Select Select Pairs Materials Prizms Blue /199 #7
2017 Select Select Pairs Materials Prizms Blue /199 #10
2017 Select Select Pairs Materials Prizms Blue /199 #11
2017 Select Select Pairs Materials Prizms Checkered Flag /1 #7
2017 Select Select Pairs Materials Prizms Checkered Flag /1 #10
2017 Select Select Pairs Materials Prizms Checkered Flag /1 #11
2017 Select Select Pairs Materials Prizms Gold /10 #7
2017 Select Select Pairs Materials Prizms Gold /10 #10
2017 Select Select Pairs Materials Prizms Gold /10 #11
2017 Select Select Pairs Materials Prizms Red /99 #7
2017 Select Select Pairs Materials Prizms Red /99 #10
2017 Select Select Pairs Materials Prizms Red /99 #11
2017 Select Select Stars #8
2017 Select Select Stars Prizms Black /3 #8
2017 Select Select Stars Prizms Checkered Flag /1 #8
2017 Select Select Stars Prizms Gold /10 #8
2017 Select Select Stars Prizms Tie Dye /24 #8
2017 Select Select Stars Prizms White /50 #8
2017 Select Select Swatches #8
2017 Select Select Swatches Prizms Blue /199 #8
2017 Select Select Swatches Prizms Checkered Flag /1 #8
2017 Select Select Swatches Prizms Gold /10 #8
2017 Select Select Swatches Prizms Red /99 #8
2017 Select Sheet Metal #4
2017 Select Sheet Metal Prizms Blue /199 #4
2017 Select Sheet Metal Prizms Checkered Flag /1 #4
2017 Select Sheet Metal Prizms Gold /10 #4
2017 Select Sheet Metal Prizms Red /99 #4
2017 Select Signature Paint Schemes #7
2017 Select Signature Paint Schemes Prizms Blue /15 #7
2017 Select Signature Paint Schemes Prizms Checkered Flag /1 #7
2017 Select Signature Paint Schemes Prizms Gold /5 #7
2017 Select Signature Paint Schemes Prizms Red /10 #7
2017 Select Signature Swatches #8
2017 Select Signature Swatches Prizms Checkered Flag /1 #8
2017 Select Signature Swatches Prizms Gold /10 #8
2017 Select Signature Swatches Prizms Tie Dye /24 #8
2017 Select Signature Swatches Prizms White /50 #8
2017 Select Signature Swatches Triple #5
2017 Select Signature Swatches Triple Prizms Checkered Flag /1 #5
2017 Select Signature Swatches Triple Prizms Gold /10 #5
2017 Select Signature Swatches Triple Prizms Tie Dye /24 #5
2017 Select Signature Swatches Triple Prizms White /50 #5
2017 Select Speed Merchants #12
2017 Select Speed Merchants Prizms Black /3 #12
2017 Select Speed Merchants Prizms Checkered Flag /1 #12
2017 Select Speed Merchants Prizms Gold /10 #12
2017 Select Speed Merchants Prizms Tie Dye /24 #12
2017 Select Speed Merchants Prizms White /50 #12
2017 Select Up Close and Personal #9
2017 Select Up Close and Personal Prizms Black /3 #9
2017 Select Up Close and Personal Prizms Checkered Flag /1 #9
2017 Select Up Close and Personal Prizms Gold /10 #9
2017 Select Up Close and Personal Prizms Tie Dye /24 #9
2017 Select Up Close and Personal Prizms White /50 #9
2018 Certified #50
2018 Certified All Certified Team /199 #17
2018 Certified All Certified Team Black /1 #17
2018 Certified All Certified Team Blue /99 #17
2018 Certified All Certified Team Gold /49 #17
2018 Certified All Certified Team Green /10 #17
2018 Certified All Certified Team Mirror Black /1 #17
2018 Certified All Certified Team Mirror Gold /25 #17
2018 Certified All Certified Team Mirror Green /5 #17
2018 Certified All Certified Team Mirror Purple /10 #17
2018 Certified All Certified Team Purple /25 #17
2018 Certified All Certified Team Red /149 #17
2018 Certified Black /1 #50
2018 Certified Blue /99 #50
2018 Certified Cup Swatches Black /1 #7
2018 Certified Cup Swatches Blue /49 #7
2018 Certified Cup Swatches Gold /25 #7
2018 Certified Cup Swatches Green /5 #7
2018 Certified Cup Swatches Purple /10 #7
2018 Certified Epix /199 #19
2018 Certified Epix Black /1 #19
2018 Certified Epix Blue /99 #19
2018 Certified Epix Gold /49 #19
2018 Certified Epix Green /10 #19
2018 Certified Epix Mirror Black /1 #19
2018 Certified Epix Mirror Gold /25 #19
2018 Certified Epix Mirror Green /5 #19
2018 Certified Epix Mirror Purple /10 #19
2018 Certified Epix Purple /25 #19
2018 Certified Epix Red /149 #19
2018 Certified Gold /49 #50
2018 Certified Green /10 #50
2018 Certified Materials Signatures /75 #14
2018 Certified Materials Signatures Black /1 #14
2018 Certified Materials Signatures Blue /20 #14
2018 Certified Materials Signatures Gold /14 #14
2018 Certified Materials Signatures Green /5 #14
2018 Certified Materials Signatures Purple /10 #14
2018 Certified Materials Signatures Red /50 #14
2018 Certified Mirror Black /1 #50
2018 Certified Mirror Gold /25 #50
2018 Certified Mirror Green /5 #50
2018 Certified Mirror Purple /10 #50
2018 Certified Orange /249 #50
2018 Certified Purple /25 #50
2018 Certified Red /199 #50
2018 Certified Signing Sessions /49 #2
2018 Certified Signing Sessions Black /1 #2
2018 Certified Signing Sessions Blue /20 #2
2018 Certified Signing Sessions Gold /15 #2
2018 Certified Signing Sessions Green /5 #2
2018 Certified Signing Sessions Purple /10 #2
2018 Certified Signing Sessions Red /25 #2
2018 Certified Skills /199 #8
2018 Certified Skills Black /1 #8
2018 Certified Skills Blue /99 #8
2018 Certified Skills Gold /49 #8
2018 Certified Skills Green /10 #8
2018 Certified Skills Mirror Black /1 #8
2018 Certified Skills Mirror Gold /25 #8
2018 Certified Skills Mirror Green /5 #8
2018 Certified Skills Mirror Purple /10 #8
2018 Certified Skills Purple /25 #8
2018 Certified Skills Red /149 #8
2018 Certified Stars /199 #13

2018 Certified Stars Black /1 #13
2018 Certified Stars Blue /99 #13
2018 Certified Stars Gold /49 #13
2018 Certified Stars Green /10 #13
2018 Certified Stars Mirror Black /1 #13
2018 Certified Stars Mirror Gold /25 #13
2018 Certified Stars Mirror Green /5 #13
2018 Certified Stars Mirror Purple /10 #13
2018 Certified Stars Purple /25 #13
2018 Certified Stars Red /149 #13
2018 Donruss #13
2018 Donruss #40A
2018 Donruss #94
2018 Donruss #130
2018 Donruss #40B
2018 Donruss Artist Proofs /25 #13
2018 Donruss Artist Proofs /25 #40A
2018 Donruss Artist Proofs /25 #94
2018 Donruss Artist Proofs /25 #130
2018 Donruss Artist Proofs /25 #40B
2018 Donruss Gold Foil /499 #13
2018 Donruss Gold Foil /499 #40A
2018 Donruss Gold Foil /499 #94
2018 Donruss Gold Foil /499 #130
2018 Donruss Gold Foil /499 #40B
2018 Donruss Gold Press Proofs /99 #13
2018 Donruss Gold Press Proofs /99 #40A
2018 Donruss Gold Press Proofs /99 #94
2018 Donruss Gold Press Proofs /99 #130
2018 Donruss Gold Press Proofs /99 #40B
2018 Donruss Green Foil /199 #13
2018 Donruss Green Foil /199 #40A
2018 Donruss Green Foil /199 #94
2018 Donruss Green Foil /199 #130
2018 Donruss Green Foil /199 #40B
2018 Donruss Pole Position #5
2018 Donruss Pole Position Cracked Ice /999 #5
2018 Donruss Pole Position Xplosion /99 #5
2018 Donruss Press Proofs /49 #13
2018 Donruss Press Proofs /49 #40A
2018 Donruss Press Proofs /49 #94
2018 Donruss Press Proofs /49 #130
2018 Donruss Press Proofs /49 #40B
2018 Donruss Printing Plates Black /1 #13
2018 Donruss Printing Plates Black /1 #40
2018 Donruss Printing Plates Black /1 #94
2018 Donruss Printing Plates Black /1 #130
2018 Donruss Printing Plates Black /1 #40B
2018 Donruss Printing Plates Cyan /1 #13
2018 Donruss Printing Plates Cyan /1 #40
2018 Donruss Printing Plates Cyan /1 #94
2018 Donruss Printing Plates Cyan /1 #130
2018 Donruss Printing Plates Cyan /1 #40B
2018 Donruss Printing Plates Magenta /1 #13
2018 Donruss Printing Plates Magenta /1 #40
2018 Donruss Printing Plates Magenta /1 #94
2018 Donruss Printing Plates Magenta /1 #130
2018 Donruss Printing Plates Magenta /1 #40B
2018 Donruss Printing Plates Yellow /1 #13
2018 Donruss Printing Plates Yellow /1 #40
2018 Donruss Printing Plates Yellow /1 #94
2018 Donruss Printing Plates Yellow /1 #130
2018 Donruss Printing Plates Yellow /1 #40B
2018 Donruss Red Foil /299 #13
2018 Donruss Red Foil /299 #40A
2018 Donruss Red Foil /299 #94
2018 Donruss Red Foil /299 #130
2018 Donruss Red Foil /299 #40B
2018 Donruss Rubber Relic Signatures #4
2018 Donruss Rubber Relic Signatures Black /1 #4
2018 Donruss Rubber Relic Signatures Holo Gold /25 #4
2018 Donruss Rubber Relics #7
2018 Donruss Rubber Relics Black /10 #7
2018 Donruss Rubber Relics Holo Gold /99 #7
2018 Donruss Studio #15
2018 Donruss Studio Cracked Ice /999 #15
2018 Donruss Studio Xplosion /99 #15
2018 Donruss Top Tier #7
2018 Donruss Top Tier Cracked Ice /999 #7
2018 Donruss Top Tier Xplosion /99 #7
2018 Panini Prime /50 #4
2018 Panini Prime /50 #38
2018 Panini Prime /50 #71
2018 Panini Prime Autograph Materials /50 #6
2018 Panini Prime Autograph Materials Black /1 #6
2018 Panini Prime Autograph Materials Holo Gold /25 #6
2018 Panini Prime Autograph Materials Laundry Tag /1 #6
2018 Panini Prime Black /1 #4
2018 Panini Prime Black /1 #38
2018 Panini Prime Black /1 #71
2018 Panini Prime Clear Silhouettes /99 #6
2018 Panini Prime Clear Silhouettes Black /1 #6
2018 Panini Prime Clear Silhouettes Dual /99 #6
2018 Panini Prime Clear Silhouettes Dual Black /1 #6
2018 Panini Prime Clear Silhouettes Dual Holo Gold /50 #6
2018 Panini Prime Clear Silhouettes Holo Gold /50 #6
2018 Panini Prime Dual Signatures /50 #8
2018 Panini Prime Dual Signatures Black /1 #8
2018 Panini Prime Dual Signatures Holo Gold /25 #8
2018 Panini Prime Holo Gold /25 #4
2018 Panini Prime Holo Gold /25 #38
2018 Panini Prime Holo Gold /25 #71
2018 Panini Prime Prime Jumbo Associate Sponsor 1 /1 #18
2018 Panini Prime Prime Jumbo Associate Sponsor 1 /1 #19
2018 Panini Prime Prime Jumbo Associate Sponsor 10 /1 #19
2018 Panini Prime Prime Jumbo Associate Sponsor 2 /1 #18
2018 Panini Prime Prime Jumbo Associate Sponsor 2 /1 #19
2018 Panini Prime Prime Jumbo Associate Sponsor 3 /1 #18
2018 Panini Prime Prime Jumbo Associate Sponsor 3 /1 #19
2018 Panini Prime Prime Jumbo Associate Sponsor 4 /1 #18
2018 Panini Prime Prime Jumbo Associate Sponsor 4 /1 #19
2018 Panini Prime Prime Jumbo Associate Sponsor 5 /1 #18
2018 Panini Prime Prime Jumbo Associate Sponsor 5 /1 #19
2018 Panini Prime Prime Jumbo Associate Sponsor 6 /1 #18
2018 Panini Prime Prime Jumbo Associate Sponsor 6 /1 #19
2018 Panini Prime Prime Jumbo Associate Sponsor 7 /1 #18
2018 Panini Prime Prime Jumbo Associate Sponsor 7 /1 #19
2018 Panini Prime Prime Jumbo Associate Sponsor 8 /1 #18
2018 Panini Prime Prime Jumbo Associate Sponsor 8 /1 #19
2018 Panini Prime Prime Jumbo Associate Sponsor 9 /1 #19
2018 Panini Prime Prime Jumbo Car Manufacturer /1 #18
2018 Panini Prime Prime Jumbo Car Manufacturer /1 #19
2018 Panini Prime Prime Jumbo Firesuit Manufacturer /1 #18
2018 Panini Prime Prime Jumbo Firesuit Manufacturer /1 #19
2018 Panini Prime Prime Jumbo Flag Patch /1 #18
2018 Panini Prime Prime Jumbo Flag Patch /1 #19
2018 Panini Prime Prime Jumbo Glove Manufacturer Patch /1 #18
2018 Panini Prime Prime Jumbo Glove Manufacturer Patch /1 #19
2018 Panini Prime Prime Jumbo Glove Name Patch /1 #18
2018 Panini Prime Prime Jumbo Glove Name Patch /1 #19
2018 Panini Prime Prime Jumbo Glove Number Patch /1 #18
2018 Panini Prime Prime Jumbo Glove Number Patch /1 #19
2018 Panini Prime Prime Jumbo Goodyear /2 #18
2018 Panini Prime Prime Jumbo Goodyear /2 #19
2018 Panini Prime Prime Jumbo Nameplate /2 #18
2018 Panini Prime Prime Jumbo Nameplate /2 #19
2018 Panini Prime Prime Jumbo NASCAR /1 #18
2018 Panini Prime Prime Jumbo NASCAR /1 #19
2018 Panini Prime Prime Jumbo Prime Colors /10 #18
2018 Panini Prime Prime Jumbo Prime Colors /24 #19
2018 Panini Prime Prime Jumbo Series Sponsor /1 #18
2018 Panini Prime Prime Jumbo Series Sponsor /1 #19
2018 Panini Prime Prime Jumbo Shoe Brand Logo /1 #18
2018 Panini Prime Prime Jumbo Shoe Brand Logo /1 #19
2018 Panini Prime Prime Jumbo Shoe Name Patch /1 #18
2018 Panini Prime Prime Jumbo Sunoco /1 #18
2018 Panini Prime Prime Jumbo Sunoco /1 #19
2018 Panini Prime Prime Number Signatures /99 #4
2018 Panini Prime Prime Number Signatures Black /1 #4
2018 Panini Prime Prime Number Signatures Holo Gold /25 #4
2018 Panini Prime Quad Material Autographs /60 #5
2018 Panini Prime Quad Material Autographs Black /1 #5
2018 Panini Prime Quad Material Autographs Holo Gold /49 #5
2018 Panini Prime Quad Material Autographs Laundry Tag /1 #5
2018 Panini Prime Race Used Duals Firesuit /50 #9
2018 Panini Prime Race Used Duals Firesuit Black /1 #9
2018 Panini Prime Race Used Duals Firesuit Holo Gold /25 #9
2018 Panini Prime Race Used Duals Firesuit Laundry Tag /1 #9
2018 Panini Prime Race Used Duals Sheet Metal /50 #9
2018 Panini Prime Race Used Duals Sheet Metal Black /1 #9
2018 Panini Prime Race Used Duals Sheet Metal Holo Gold /25 #9
2018 Panini Prime Race Used Duals Tire /50 #9
2018 Panini Prime Race Used Duals Tire Black /1 #9
2018 Panini Prime Race Used Duals Tire Holo Gold /25 #9
2018 Panini Prime Race Used Firesuits /50 #7
2018 Panini Prime Race Used Firesuits Black /1 #7
2018 Panini Prime Race Used Firesuits Holo Gold /25 #7
2018 Panini Prime Race Used Firesuits Laundry Tag /1 #7
2018 Panini Prime Race Used Sheet Metal /50 #7
2018 Panini Prime Race Used Sheet Metal Black /1 #7
2018 Panini Prime Race Used Sheet Metal Holo Gold /25 #7
2018 Panini Prime Race Used Tires Black /1 #7
2018 Panini Prime Race Used Tires Holo Gold /25 #7
2018 Panini Prime Shadowbox Signatures /99 #17
2018 Panini Prime Shadowbox Signatures Black /1 #17
2018 Panini Prime Shadowbox Signatures Holo Gold /25 #17
2018 Panini Prime Signature Tires /99 #2
2018 Panini Prime Signature Tires Black /1 #2
2018 Panini Prime Signature Tires Holo Gold /25 #2
2018 Panini Prime Triple Material Autographs /60 #12
2018 Panini Prime Triple Material Autographs Black /1 #12
2018 Panini Prime Triple Material Autographs Holo Gold /25 #12
2018 Panini Prime Triple Material Autographs Laundry Tag /1 #12
2018 Panini Prizm #48
2018 Panini Prizm #64
2018 Panini Prizm Instant Impact #7
2018 Panini Prizm Instant Impact Prizms #7
2018 Panini Prizm Instant Impact Prizms Black /1 #7
2018 Panini Prizm Instant Impact Prizms Gold /10 #7
2018 Panini Prizm National Pride #10
2018 Panini Prizm National Pride Prizms #10
2018 Panini Prizm National Pride Prizms Black /1 #10
2018 Panini Prizm National Pride Prizms Gold /10 #10
2018 Panini Prizm Prizms #48
2018 Panini Prizm Prizms #64
2018 Panini Prizm Prizms Black /1 #48
2018 Panini Prizm Prizms Black /1 #64
2018 Panini Prizm Prizms Blue /99 #48
2018 Panini Prizm Prizms Blue /99 #64
2018 Panini Prizm Prizms Camo #48
2018 Panini Prizm Prizms Camo #64
2018 Panini Prizm Prizms Gold /10 #48
2018 Panini Prizm Prizms Gold /10 #64
2018 Panini Prizm Prizms Green /149 #48
2018 Panini Prizm Prizms Green /149 #64
2018 Panini Prizm Prizms Purple Flash #48
2018 Panini Prizm Prizms Purple Flash #64
2018 Panini Prizm Prizms Rainbow /24 #48
2018 Panini Prizm Prizms Rainbow /24 #64
2018 Panini Prizm Prizms Red /75 #48
2018 Panini Prizm Prizms Red /75 #64
2018 Panini Prizm Prizms Red White and Blue #48
2018 Panini Prizm Prizms Red White and Blue #64
2018 Panini Prizm Prizms White /5 #48
2018 Panini Prizm Prizms White /5 #64
2018 Panini Prizm Scripted Signatures Prizms #28
2018 Panini Prizm Scripted Signatures Prizms Black /1 #28
2018 Panini Prizm Scripted Signatures Prizms Blue /35 #28
2018 Panini Prizm Scripted Signatures Prizms Camo #28
2018 Panini Prizm Scripted Signatures Prizms Gold /10 #28
2018 Panini Prizm Scripted Signatures Prizms Green /50 #28
2018 Panini Prizm Scripted Signatures Prizms Rainbow /24 #28
2018 Panini Prizm Scripted Signatures Prizms Red /25 #28
2018 Panini Prizm Scripted Signatures Prizms Red White and Blue /60 #28
2018 Panini Prizm Scripted Signatures Prizms White /5 #28
2018 Panini Prizm Stars and Stripes #8
2018 Panini Prizm Stars and Stripes Prizms #8
2018 Panini Prizm Stars and Stripes Prizms Black /1 #8
2018 Panini Prizm Stars and Stripes Prizms Gold /10 #8
2018 Panini Prizm Team Tandems #4
2018 Panini Prizm Team Tandems Prizms #4
2018 Panini Prizm Team Tandems Prizms Black /1 #4
2018 Panini Prizm Team Tandems Prizms Gold /10 #4
2018 Panini Victory Lane #10
2018 Panini Victory Lane Black /1 #10
2018 Panini Victory Lane Blue /25 #10
2018 Panini Victory Lane Engineered to Perfection Materials Black /25 #5
2018 Panini Victory Lane Engineered to Perfection Materials Gold /199 #5
2018 Panini Victory Lane Engineered to Perfection Materials Green /99 #5
2018 Panini Victory Lane Engineered to Perfection Materials Laundry Tag /1 #5
2018 Panini Victory Lane Gold /99 #10
2018 Panini Victory Lane Green /5 #10
2018 Panini Victory Lane Octane Autographs /125 #8
2018 Panini Victory Lane Octane Autographs Black /1 #8
2018 Panini Victory Lane Octane Autographs Gold /99 #8
2018 Panini Victory Lane Pedal to the Metal #10
2018 Panini Victory Lane Pedal to the Metal #60
2018 Panini Victory Lane Pedal to the Metal Black /1 #10
2018 Panini Victory Lane Pedal to the Metal Black /1 #60
2018 Panini Victory Lane Pedal to the Metal Blue /25 #10
2018 Panini Victory Lane Pedal to the Metal Blue /25 #60
2018 Panini Victory Lane Pedal to the Metal Green /5 #10
2018 Panini Victory Lane Pedal to the Metal Green /5 #60
2018 Panini Victory Lane Printing Plates Black /1 #10
2018 Panini Victory Lane Printing Plates Cyan /1 #10
2018 Panini Victory Lane Printing Plates Magenta /1 #10
2018 Panini Victory Lane Printing Plates Yellow /1 #10
2018 Panini Victory Lane Race Day #4
2018 Panini Victory Lane Race Day Black /1 #4
2018 Panini Victory Lane Race Day Blue /25 #4
2018 Panini Victory Lane Race Day Gold /99 #4
2018 Panini Victory Lane Race Day Green /5 #4
2018 Panini Victory Lane Race Day Printing Plates Black /1 #4
2018 Panini Victory Lane Race Day Printing Plates Cyan /1 #4
2018 Panini Victory Lane Race Day Printing Plates Magenta /1 #4
2018 Panini Victory Lane Race Day Printing Plates Yellow /1 #4
2018 Panini Victory Lane Race Day Red /49 #4
2018 Panini Victory Lane Race Ready Dual Materials /399 #2
2018 Panini Victory Lane Race Ready Dual Materials Black /25 #2
2018 Panini Victory Lane Race Ready Dual Materials Gold /199 #2
2018 Panini Victory Lane Race Ready Dual Materials Green /99 #2
2018 Panini Victory Lane Race Ready Dual Materials Laundry Tag /1 #2
2018 Panini Victory Lane Race Ready Materials Black /25 #6
2018 Panini Victory Lane Red /49 #10
2018 Panini Victory Lane Silver #10
2018 Panini Victory Lane Starting Grid #10
2018 Panini Victory Lane Starting Grid Black /1 #10
2018 Panini Victory Lane Starting Grid Blue /25 #10
2018 Panini Victory Lane Starting Grid Gold /99 #10
2018 Panini Victory Lane Starting Grid Green /5 #10
2018 Panini Victory Lane Starting Grid Printing Plates Black /1 #10
2018 Panini Victory Lane Starting Grid Printing Plates Cyan /1 #10
2018 Panini Victory Lane Starting Grid Printing Plates Magenta /1 #10
2018 Panini Victory Lane Starting Grid Printing Plates Yellow /1 #10
2018 Panini Victory Lane Starting Grid Red /49 #10
2018 Panini Victory Lane Victory Lane Prime Patches Associate Sponsor 1 /1 #30
2018 Panini Victory Lane Victory Lane Prime Patches Associate Sponsor 10 /1 #30
2018 Panini Victory Lane Victory Lane Prime Patches Associate Sponsor 2 /1 #30
2018 Panini Victory Lane Victory Lane Prime Patches Associate Sponsor 3 /1 #30
2018 Panini Victory Lane Victory Lane Prime Patches Associate Sponsor 4 /1 #30
2018 Panini Victory Lane Victory Lane Prime Patches Associate Sponsor 5 /1 #30
2018 Panini Victory Lane Victory Lane Prime Patches Associate Sponsor 6 /1 #30
2018 Panini Victory Lane Victory Lane Prime Patches Associate Sponsor 7 /1 #30
2018 Panini Victory Lane Victory Lane Prime Patches Associate Sponsor 8 /1 #30
2018 Panini Victory Lane Victory Lane Prime Patches Associate Sponsor 9 /1 #30
2018 Panini Victory Lane Victory Lane Prime Patches Car Manufacturer /1 #30
2018 Panini Victory Lane Victory Lane Prime Patches Firesuit Manufacturer /1 #30
2018 Panini Victory Lane Victory Lane Prime Patches Goodyear /2 #30
2018 Panini Victory Lane Victory Lane Prime Patches Nameplate /2 #30
2018 Panini Victory Lane Victory Lane Prime Patches NASCAR /1 #30
2018 Panini Victory Lane Victory Lane Prime Patches Series Sponsor /1 #30
2018 Panini Victory Lane Victory Lane Prime Patches Sunoco /1 #30
2019 Donruss #43
2019 Donruss #98
2019 Donruss #120
2019 Donruss Artist Proofs /25 #43
2019 Donruss Artist Proofs /25 #98
2019 Donruss Artist Proofs /25 #120
2019 Donruss Black /199 #43
2019 Donruss Black /199 #98
2019 Donruss Black /199 #120
2019 Donruss Contenders #13
2019 Donruss Contenders Cracked Ice /25 #13
2019 Donruss Contenders Holographic #13
2019 Donruss Contenders Xplosion /10 #13
2019 Donruss Gold /299 #43
2019 Donruss Gold /299 #98
2019 Donruss Gold /299 #120
2019 Donruss Gold Press Proofs /99 #43
2019 Donruss Gold Press Proofs /99 #98
2019 Donruss Gold Press Proofs /99 #120
2019 Donruss Optic #26
2019 Donruss Optic #74
2019 Donruss Optic Blue Pulsar #26
2019 Donruss Optic Blue Pulsar /1 #74
2019 Donruss Optic Gold /10 #26
2019 Donruss Optic Gold /10 #74
2019 Donruss Optic Gold Vinyl /1 #26
2019 Donruss Optic Gold Vinyl /1 #74
2019 Donruss Optic Holo #26
2019 Donruss Optic Holo #74
2019 Donruss Optic Red Wave #26
2019 Donruss Optic Red Wave /1 #74
2019 Donruss Optic Signatures Gold Vinyl /1 #74
2019 Donruss Optic Signatures Gold Vinyl /1 #26
2019 Donruss Optic Signatures Holo /75 #26
2019 Donruss Optic Signatures Holo /75 #74
2019 Donruss Originals #5
2019 Donruss Originals Cracked Ice /25 #5
2019 Donruss Originals Holographic #5
2019 Donruss Originals Xplosion /10 #5
2019 Donruss Press Proofs /49 #43
2019 Donruss Press Proofs /49 #98
2019 Donruss Press Proofs /49 #120
2019 Donruss Printing Plates Black /1 #43
2019 Donruss Printing Plates Black /1 #98
2019 Donruss Printing Plates Black /1 #120
2019 Donruss Printing Plates Cyan /1 #43
2019 Donruss Printing Plates Cyan /1 #98
2019 Donruss Printing Plates Cyan /1 #120
2019 Donruss Printing Plates Magenta /1 #43
2019 Donruss Printing Plates Magenta /1 #98
2019 Donruss Printing Plates Magenta /1 #120
2019 Donruss Printing Plates Yellow /1 #43
2019 Donruss Printing Plates Yellow /1 #98
2019 Donruss Printing Plates Yellow /1 #120
2019 Donruss Retro Relics '86 #5
2019 Donruss Retro Relics '86 Holo Black /10 #5
2019 Donruss Retro Relics '86 Holo Gold /25 #5
2019 Donruss Retro Relics '86 Red /225 #5
2019 Donruss Silver #43
2019 Donruss Silver #98
2019 Donruss Silver #120
2019 Panini Prime /50 #12
2019 Panini Prime /50 #45
2019 Panini Prime /50 #78
2019 Panini Prime Black /10 #12
2019 Panini Prime Black /10 #45
2019 Panini Prime Black /10 #78
2019 Panini Prime Clear Silhouettes /99 #6
2019 Panini Prime Clear Silhouettes Black /10 #6
2019 Panini Prime Clear Silhouettes Dual /99 #8
2019 Panini Prime Clear Silhouettes Dual Black /10 #8
2019 Panini Prime Clear Silhouettes Dual Holo Gold /25 #8
2019 Panini Prime Clear Silhouettes Dual Platinum Blue /1 #8
2019 Panini Prime Clear Silhouettes Holo Gold /25 #6
2019 Panini Prime Clear Silhouettes Platinum Blue /1 #6
2019 Panini Prime Emerald /5 #12
2019 Panini Prime Emerald /5 #45
2019 Panini Prime Emerald /5 #78
2019 Panini Prime Hats Off Button /1 #11
2019 Panini Prime Hats Off Driver Name /2 #11
2019 Panini Prime Hats Off Eyelets /6 #11
2019 Panini Prime Hats Off Headband /31 #11
2019 Panini Prime Hats Off Laundry Tags /2 #11
2019 Panini Prime Hats Off New Era /1 #11
2019 Panini Prime Hats Off Number /4 #11
2019 Panini Prime Hats Off Sponsor Logo /10 #11
2019 Panini Prime Jumbo Material Signatures Firesuit /10 #7
2019 Panini Prime Jumbo Material Signatures Firesuit Platinum Blue /1 #7
2019 Panini Prime Jumbo Material Signatures Sheet Metal /25 #7
2019 Panini Prime Jumbo Material Signatures Tire /50 #7
2019 Panini Prime NASCAR Shadowbox Signatures Car Number /50 #12
2019 Panini Prime NASCAR Shadowbox Signatures Manufacturer /10 #12
2019 Panini Prime NASCAR Shadowbox Signatures Sponsor /25 #12
2019 Panini Prime NASCAR Shadowbox Signatures Team Owner /1 #12
2019 Panini Prime Platinum Blue /1 #12
2019 Panini Prime Platinum Blue /1 #45
2019 Panini Prime Platinum Blue /1 #78
2019 Panini Prime Prime Cars Die Cut Signatures /50 #15
2019 Panini Prime Prime Cars Die Cut Signatures Black /10 #15
2019 Panini Prime Prime Cars Die Cut Signatures Holo Gold /25 #15
2019 Panini Prime Prime Cars Die Cut Signatures Platinum Blue /1 #15
2019 Panini Prime Prime Jumbo Associate Sponsor 1 /1 #14
2019 Panini Prime Prime Jumbo Associate Sponsor 1 /1 #15
2019 Panini Prime Prime Jumbo Associate Sponsor 2 /1 #14
2019 Panini Prime Prime Jumbo Associate Sponsor 2 /1 #15
2019 Panini Prime Prime Jumbo Associate Sponsor 3 /1 #14
2019 Panini Prime Prime Jumbo Associate Sponsor 3 /1 #15
2019 Panini Prime Prime Jumbo Associate Sponsor 4 /1 #14
2019 Panini Prime Prime Jumbo Associate Sponsor 4 /1 #15
2019 Panini Prime Prime Jumbo Associate Sponsor 5 /1 #14
2019 Panini Prime Prime Jumbo Associate Sponsor 5 /1 #15
2019 Panini Prime Prime Jumbo Associate Sponsor 6 /1 #14
2019 Panini Prime Prime Jumbo Associate Sponsor 6 /1 #15
2019 Panini Prime Prime Jumbo Associate Sponsor 7 /1 #14
2019 Panini Prime Prime Jumbo Associate Sponsor 7 /1 #15
2019 Panini Prime Prime Jumbo Associate Sponsor 8 /1 #14
2019 Panini Prime Prime Jumbo Associate Sponsor 8 /1 #15
2019 Panini Prime Prime Jumbo Associate Sponsor 9 /1 #14
2019 Panini Prime Prime Jumbo Associate Sponsor 9 /1 #15
2019 Panini Prime Prime Jumbo Car Manufacturer /1 #14
2019 Panini Prime Prime Jumbo Car Manufacturer /1 #15
2019 Panini Prime Prime Jumbo Firesuit Manufacturer /1 #14
2019 Panini Prime Prime Jumbo Firesuit Manufacturer /1 #15
2019 Panini Prime Prime Jumbo Flag Patch /1 #14
2019 Panini Prime Prime Jumbo Flag Patch /1 #15
2019 Panini Prime Prime Jumbo Glove Manufacturer Patch /1 #14
2019 Panini Prime Prime Jumbo Glove Manufacturer Patch /1 #15
2019 Panini Prime Prime Jumbo Glove Name Patch /1 #14
2019 Panini Prime Prime Jumbo Glove Name Patch /1 #15
2019 Panini Prime Prime Jumbo Glove Number Patch /1 #14
2019 Panini Prime Prime Jumbo Goodyear /2 #14
2019 Panini Prime Prime Jumbo Goodyear /1 #15
2019 Panini Prime Prime Jumbo Nameplate /2 #14
2019 Panini Prime Prime Jumbo Nameplate /1 #15
2019 Panini Prime Prime Jumbo NASCAR /1 #14
2019 Panini Prime Prime Jumbo NASCAR /1 #15
2019 Panini Prime Prime Jumbo Prime Colors /20 #14
2019 Panini Prime Prime Jumbo Prime Colors /17 #15
2019 Panini Prime Prime Jumbo Series Sponsor /1 #14
2019 Panini Prime Prime Jumbo Series Sponsor /1 #15
2019 Panini Prime Prime Jumbo Shoe Brand Logo /1 #14
2019 Panini Prime Prime Jumbo Shoe Brand Logo /1 #15
2019 Panini Prime Prime Jumbo Shoe Name Patch /1 #14
2019 Panini Prime Prime Jumbo Sunoco /1 #14
2019 Panini Prime Prime Jumbo Sunoco /1 #15
2019 Panini Prime Prime Number Die Cut Signatures /49 #5
2019 Panini Prime Prime Number Die Cut Signatures Black /10 #5
2019 Panini Prime Prime Number Die Cut Signatures Holo Gold /25 #5
2019 Panini Prime Prime Number Die Cut Signatures Platinum Blue /1 #5
2019 Panini Prime Quad Materials Autographs /50 #7
2019 Panini Prime Quad Materials Autographs Black /10 #7
2019 Panini Prime Quad Materials Autographs Holo Gold /25 #7
2019 Panini Prime Quad Materials Autographs Laundry Tags /1 #7
2019 Panini Prime Race Used Duals Firesuits /50 #12
2019 Panini Prime Race Used Duals Firesuits Black /10 #12
2019 Panini Prime Race Used Duals Firesuits Holo Gold /25 #12
2019 Panini Prime Race Used Duals Firesuits Laundry Tags /1 #12
2019 Panini Prime Race Used Duals Sheet Metal /50 #12
2019 Panini Prime Race Used Duals Sheet Metal Black /10 #12
2019 Panini Prime Race Used Duals Sheet Metal Holo Gold /25 #12
2019 Panini Prime Race Used Duals Sheet Metal Platinum Blue /1 #12
2019 Panini Prime Race Used Duals Tires /50 #12
2019 Panini Prime Race Used Duals Tires Black /10 #12
2019 Panini Prime Race Used Duals Tires Holo Gold /25 #12
2019 Panini Prime Race Used Duals Tires Platinum Blue /1 #12
2019 Panini Prime Race Used Firesuits /50 #12
2019 Panini Prime Race Used Firesuits Black /10 #12
2019 Panini Prime Race Used Firesuits Holo Gold /25 #12
2019 Panini Prime Race Used Firesuits Laundry Tags /1 #12
2019 Panini Prime Race Used Sheet Metal /50 #12
2019 Panini Prime Race Used Sheet Metal Black /10 #12
2019 Panini Prime Race Used Sheet Metal Holo Gold /25 #12
2019 Panini Prime Race Used Sheet Metal Platinum Blue /1 #12
2019 Panini Prime Race Used Tires /50 #12
2019 Panini Prime Race Used Tires Black /10 #12
2019 Panini Prime Race Used Tires Holo Gold /25 #12
2019 Panini Prime Race Used Tires Platinum Blue /1 #12
2019 Panini Prime Race Used Trios Firesuits /50 #12
2019 Panini Prime Race Used Trios Firesuits Black /10 #12
2019 Panini Prime Race Used Trios Firesuits Holo Gold /25 #12
2019 Panini Prime Race Used Trios Firesuits Laundry Tags /1 #12
2019 Panini Prime Race Used Trios Sheet Metal /50 #12
2019 Panini Prime Race Used Trios Sheet Metal Black /10 #12
2019 Panini Prime Race Used Trios Sheet Metal Holo Gold /25 #12
2019 Panini Prime Race Used Trios Sheet Metal Platinum Blue /1 #12
2019 Panini Prime Race Used Trios Tires /50 #12
2019 Panini Prime Race Used Trios Tires Black /10 #12
2019 Panini Prime Race Used Trios Tires Holo Gold /25 #12
2019 Panini Prime Race Used Trios Tires Platinum Blue /1 #12
2019 Panini Prime Shadowbox Signatures /50 #4
2019 Panini Prime Shadowbox Signatures Black /10 #4
2019 Panini Prime Shadowbox Signatures Holo Gold /25 #4
2019 Panini Prime Shadowbox Signatures Platinum Blue /1 #4
2019 Panini Prime Timeline Signatures /49 #6
2019 Panini Prime Timeline Signatures Manufacturer /1 #6
2019 Panini Prime Timeline Signatures Name /25 #6
2019 Panini Prime Timeline Signatures Sponsor /10 #6
2019 Panini Prizm #12
2019 Panini Prizm Fireworks #15
2019 Panini Prizm Fireworks Prizms #15
2019 Panini Prizm Fireworks Prizms Black /1 #15
2019 Panini Prizm Fireworks Prizms Gold /10 #15
2019 Panini Prizm Fireworks Prizms White Sparkle #15
2019 Panini Prizm Prizms #12
2019 Panini Prizm Prizms Black /1 #12
2019 Panini Prizm Prizms Blue /75 #12
2019 Panini Prizm Prizms Camo #12
2019 Panini Prizm Prizms Flash #12
2019 Panini Prizm Prizms Gold /10 #12
2019 Panini Prizm Prizms Green /99 #12
2019 Panini Prizm Prizms Rainbow /24 #12
2019 Panini Prizm Prizms Red /50 #12
2019 Panini Prizm Prizms Red White and Blue #12
2019 Panini Prizm Prizms White /5 #12
2019 Panini Prizm Prizms White Sparkle #12
2019 Panini Prizm Signing Sessions Prizms #7
2019 Panini Prizm Signing Sessions Prizms Black /1 #7
2019 Panini Prizm Signing Sessions Prizms Blue /30 #7
2019 Panini Prizm Signing Sessions Prizms Camo #7
2019 Panini Prizm Signing Sessions Prizms Gold /10 #7
2019 Panini Prizm Signing Sessions Prizms Green /35 #7
2019 Panini Prizm Signing Sessions Prizms Rainbow /24 #7
2019 Panini Prizm Signing Sessions Prizms Red /25 #7
2019 Panini Prizm Signing Sessions Prizms Red White and Blue #7
2019 Panini Prizm Signing Sessions Prizms White /5 #7
2019 Panini Prizm Teammates #7
2019 Panini Prizm Teammates Prizms #7
2019 Panini Prizm Teammates Prizms Black /1 #7
2019 Panini Prizm Teammates Prizms Gold /10 #7
2019 Panini Prizm Teammates Prizms White Sparkle #7
2019 Panini Victory Lane #12
2019 Panini Victory Lane Black /1 #12
2019 Panini Victory Lane Celebrations #5
2019 Panini Victory Lane Celebrations Black /1 #5
2019 Panini Victory Lane Celebrations Blue /99 #5
2019 Panini Victory Lane Celebrations Gold /25 #5
2019 Panini Victory Lane Celebrations Green /5 #5
2019 Panini Victory Lane Celebrations Printing Plates Black /1 #5
2019 Panini Victory Lane Celebrations Printing Plates Cyan /1 #5
2019 Panini Victory Lane Celebrations Printing Plates Magenta /1 #5
2019 Panini Victory Lane Celebrations Printing Plates Yellow /1 #5
2019 Panini Victory Lane Dual Swatches #7
2019 Panini Victory Lane Dual Swatches Gold /99 #7
2019 Panini Victory Lane Dual Swatches Laundry Tag /1 #7
2019 Panini Victory Lane Dual Swatches Platinum /1 #7
2019 Panini Victory Lane Dual Swatches Red /25 #7
2019 Panini Victory Lane Gold /25 #12
2019 Panini Victory Lane Machines #17
2019 Panini Victory Lane Machines Black /1 #17
2019 Panini Victory Lane Machines Blue /99 #17
2019 Panini Victory Lane Machines Gold /25 #17
2019 Panini Victory Lane Machines Green /5 #17
2019 Panini Victory Lane Machines Printing Plates Black /1 #17
2019 Panini Victory Lane Machines Printing Plates Cyan /1 #17
2019 Panini Victory Lane Machines Printing Plates Magenta /1 #17
2019 Panini Victory Lane Machines Printing Plates Yellow /1 #17
2019 Panini Victory Lane Pedal to the Metal #29
2019 Panini Victory Lane Pedal to the Metal Black /1 #29
2019 Panini Victory Lane Pedal to the Metal Gold /25 #29
2019 Panini Victory Lane Pedal to the Metal Green /5 #29
2019 Panini Victory Lane Pedal to the Metal Red /3 #29
2019 Panini Victory Lane Printing Plates Black /1 #12
2019 Panini Victory Lane Printing Plates Cyan /1 #12
2019 Panini Victory Lane Printing Plates Magenta /1 #12
2019 Panini Victory Lane Printing Plates Yellow /1 #12
2019 Panini Victory Lane Starting Grid #15
2019 Panini Victory Lane Starting Grid Black /1 #15
2019 Panini Victory Lane Starting Grid Blue /99 #15
2019 Panini Victory Lane Starting Grid Gold /25 #15
2019 Panini Victory Lane Starting Grid Green /5 #15
2019 Panini Victory Lane Starting Grid Printing Plates Black /1 #15
2019 Panini Victory Lane Starting Grid Printing Plates Cyan /1 #15
2019 Panini Victory Lane Starting Grid Printing Plates Magenta /1 #15
2019 Panini Victory Lane Starting Grid Printing Plates Yellow /1 #15
2019 Panini Victory Lane Triple Swatch Signatures #4
2019 Panini Victory Lane Triple Swatch Signatures Gold /99 #4
2019 Panini Victory Lane Triple Swatch Signatures Laundry Tag /1 #4
2019 Panini Victory Lane Triple Swatch Signatures Platinum /1 #4
2019 Panini Victory Lane Triple Swatch Signatures Red /25 #4
2019 Panini Victory Lane Triple Swatches #4
2019 Panini Victory Lane Triple Swatches Gold /99 #4
2019 Panini Victory Lane Triple Swatches Laundry Tag /1 #4
2019 Panini Victory Lane Triple Swatches Platinum /1 #4
2019 Panini Victory Lane Triple Swatches Red /25 #4
2020 Donruss #30
2020 Donruss #108
2020 Donruss #154
2020 Donruss Black Numbers /14 #30
2020 Donruss Black Numbers /14 #108
2020 Donruss Black Numbers /14 #154
2020 Donruss Black Trophy Club /1 #30
2020 Donruss Black Trophy Club /1 #108
2020 Donruss Black Trophy Club /1 #154
2020 Donruss Blue /199 #108
2020 Donruss Blue /199 #154
2020 Donruss Blue /199 #30
2020 Donruss Carolina Blue #30
2020 Donruss Carolina Blue #108
2020 Donruss Carolina Blue #154
2020 Donruss Contenders #15
2020 Donruss Contenders Checkers #15
2020 Donruss Contenders Cracked Ice /25 #15
2020 Donruss Contenders Holographic /199 #15
2020 Donruss Contenders Xplosion /10 #15
2020 Donruss Green /99 #30
2020 Donruss Green /99 #108
2020 Donruss Green /99 #154
2020 Donruss Optic #32
2020 Donruss Optic #77
2020 Donruss Optic Carolina Blue Wave #32
2020 Donruss Optic Carolina Blue Wave #77
2020 Donruss Optic Gold /10 #32
2020 Donruss Optic Gold /10 #77
2020 Donruss Optic Gold Vinyl /1 #32
2020 Donruss Optic Gold Vinyl /1 #77
2020 Donruss Optic Holo #32
2020 Donruss Optic Holo #77
2020 Donruss Optic Orange Pulsar #32
2020 Donruss Optic Orange Pulsar #77
2020 Donruss Optic Red Mojo #32
2020 Donruss Optic Red Mojo #77
2020 Donruss Optic Signatures Gold Vinyl /1 #32
2020 Donruss Optic Signatures Gold Vinyl /1 #77
2020 Donruss Optic Signatures Holo /99 #32
2020 Donruss Optic Signatures Holo /99 #77
2020 Donruss Orange #30
2020 Donruss Orange #108
2020 Donruss Orange #154
2020 Donruss Pink /25 #30
2020 Donruss Pink /25 #108
2020 Donruss Pink /25 #154
2020 Donruss Printing Plates Black /1 #30
2020 Donruss Printing Plates Black /1 #108
2020 Donruss Printing Plates Black /1 #154
2020 Donruss Printing Plates Cyan /1 #30
2020 Donruss Printing Plates Cyan /1 #108
2020 Donruss Printing Plates Cyan /1 #154
2020 Donruss Printing Plates Magenta /1 #30
2020 Donruss Printing Plates Magenta /1 #108
2020 Donruss Printing Plates Magenta /1 #154
2020 Donruss Printing Plates Yellow /1 #154
2020 Donruss Printing Plates Yellow /1 #30
2020 Donruss Printing Plates Yellow /1 #108
2020 Donruss Purple /49 #30
2020 Donruss Purple /49 #108
2020 Donruss Purple /49 #154
2020 Donruss Race Day Relics #8
2020 Donruss Race Day Relics Holo Black /10 #8
2020 Donruss Race Day Relics Holo Gold /25 #8
2020 Donruss Race Day Relics Red /250 #8
2020 Donruss Red /299 #30
2020 Donruss Red /299 #108
2020 Donruss Red /299 #154
2020 Donruss Signature Series Holo Black /1 #21
2020 Donruss Signature Series Holo Gold /14 #21
2020 Donruss Signature Series Red /25 #21
2020 Donruss Silver #30
2020 Donruss Silver #108
2020 Donruss Silver #154

Kurt Busch

2000 Maxx #75
2000 SP Authentic #40
2000 SP Authentic Overdrive Gold /99 #40
2000 SP Authentic Overdrive Silver /250 #40
2000 SP Authentic Sign of the Times #KB
2000 SP Authentic Sign of the Times Gold /25 #KB
2001 Press Pass Hot Treads Rookie Rubber /1100 #RR2
2001 Press Pass Optima #4
2001 Press Pass Optima G Force #GF3
2001 Press Pass Optima Gold #4
2001 Press Pass Premium #46
2001 Press Pass Premium Gold #46
2001 Press Pass Signings #9
2001 Press Pass Signings Gold /50 #8
2001 Press Pass Trackside #18
2001 Press Pass Trackside Die Cuts #18
2001 Press Pass Trackside Golden #18
2002 Press Pass #7
2002 Press Pass Autographs #12
2002 Press Pass Eclipse #21
2002 Press Pass Eclipse #49
2002 Press Pass Eclipse Samples #21
2002 Press Pass Eclipse Samples #49
2002 Press Pass Eclipse Solar Eclipse #S21
2002 Press Pass Eclipse Solar Eclipse #S49
2002 Press Pass Hot Treads /1555 #HT16
2002 Press Pass Optima #5
2002 Press Pass Optima #49
2002 Press Pass Optima Fan Favorite #FF4
2002 Press Pass Optima Gold #5
2002 Press Pass Optima Gold #49
2002 Press Pass Optima Promos /5 #5
2002 Press Pass Optima Promos /5 #49
2002 Press Pass Optima Q and A #QA1
2002 Press Pass Optima Race Used Lugnuts Cars /100 #LNC3
2002 Press Pass Optima Race Used Lugnuts Drivers /100 #LND3
2002 Press Pass Optima Samples #5
2002 Press Pass Optima Samples #49
2002 Press Pass Platinum #7
2002 Press Pass Premium #5
2002 Press Pass Premium #58
2002 Press Pass Premium Red Reflectors #5
2002 Press Pass Premium Red Reflectors #58
2002 Press Pass Premium Samples #5
2002 Press Pass Signings #10
2002 Press Pass Signings Gold /50 #11
2002 Press Pass Stealth Lap Leaders #LL5
2002 Press Pass Trackside #19
2002 Press Pass Trackside #76
2002 Press Pass Trackside Generation Now #GN7
2002 Press Pass Trackside Golden /50 #G19
2002 Press Pass Trackside License to Drive #6
2002 Press Pass Trackside License to Drive Die Cuts #6
2002 Press Pass Trackside Samples #19
2002 Press Pass Trackside Samples #76
2002 Wheels High Gear #4
2002 Wheels High Gear Autographs #10
2002 Wheels High Gear First Gear #4
2002 Wheels High Gear High Groove #HG4
2002 Wheels High Gear MPH /100 #4
2003 Action Racing Collectables 1:24 #2
2003 eTopps /3000 #33
2003 Press Pass #7
2003 Press Pass #58
2003 Press Pass #63
2003 Press Pass #75
2003 Press Pass Autographs #9
2003 Press Pass Coca-Cola Racing Family #3
2003 Press Pass Coca-Cola Racing Family Scratch-off #2
2003 Press Pass Eclipse #3
2003 Press Pass Eclipse #42
2003 Press Pass Eclipse Double Hot Treads /999 #DT7
2003 Press Pass Eclipse Previews /5 #3
2003 Press Pass Eclipse Racing Champions #RC8
2003 Press Pass Eclipse Racing Champions #RC33
2003 Press Pass Eclipse Racing Champions #RC34
2003 Press Pass Eclipse Racing Champions #RC36
2003 Press Pass Eclipse Samples #3
2003 Press Pass Eclipse Samples #42
2003 Press Pass Eclipse Skidmarks #SM6
2003 Press Pass Eclipse Solar Eclipse #P3
2003 Press Pass Eclipse Solar Eclipse #P42
2003 Press Pass Eclipse Teammates Autographs /25 #JBKB
2003 Press Pass Gold Holofoil #P7
2003 Press Pass Gold Holofoil #P58
2003 Press Pass Gold Holofoil #P63
2003 Press Pass Gold Holofoil #P75
2003 Press Pass Optima #5
2003 Press Pass Optima #45
2003 Press Pass Optima Fan Favorite #FF13
2003 Press Pass Optima Gold #G5
2003 Press Pass Optima Gold #G45
2003 Press Pass Optima Previews /5 #5
2003 Press Pass Optima Q and A #QA8
2003 Press Pass Optima Samples #5
2003 Press Pass Optima Samples #45
2003 Press Pass Optima Thunder Bolts Cars /95 #TBT14
2003 Press Pass Optima Thunder Bolts Drivers /65 #TBD14
2003 Press Pass Optima Young Guns #YG6
2003 Press Pass Premium #5
2003 Press Pass Premium #35
2003 Press Pass Premium #58
2003 Press Pass Premium #69
2003 Press Pass Premium Performance Driven #PD5
2003 Press Pass Premium Previews /5 #5
2003 Press Pass Premium Red Reflectors #5
2003 Press Pass Premium Red Reflectors #35
2003 Press Pass Premium Red Reflectors #58
2003 Press Pass Premium Red Reflectors #69
2003 Press Pass Premium Samples #5
2003 Press Pass Premium Samples #35
2003 Press Pass Previews /5 #7
2003 Press Pass Samples #7
2003 Press Pass Samples #58
2003 Press Pass Samples #63
2003 Press Pass Samples #75
2003 Press Pass Signings #12
2003 Press Pass Signings Gold /50 #12
2003 Press Pass Signings Transparent /100 #1
2003 Press Pass Snapshots #SN18
2003 Press Pass Stealth #40
2003 Press Pass Stealth #41
2003 Press Pass Stealth #42
2003 Press Pass Stealth Previews /5 #40
2003 Press Pass Stealth Previews /5 #41
2003 Press Pass Stealth Previews /5 #42
2003 Press Pass Stealth Red #P40
2003 Press Pass Stealth Red #P41
2003 Press Pass Stealth Red #P42
2003 Press Pass Stealth Samples #40
2003 Press Pass Stealth Samples #41
2003 Press Pass Stealth Samples #42
2003 Press Pass Trackside #3
2003 Press Pass Trackside #78
2003 Press Pass Trackside Gold Holofoil #P3
2003 Press Pass Trackside Gold Holofoil #P78
2003 Press Pass Trackside Golden /50 #G3
2003 Press Pass Trackside Hat Giveaway #PPH5
2003 Press Pass Trackside Previews /5 #3
2003 Press Pass Trackside Samples #3
2003 Press Pass Trackside Samples #78
2003 VIP #3
2003 VIP #24
2003 VIP Explosives #X3
2003 VIP Explosives #X24
2003 VIP Laser Explosive #LX3
2003 VIP Laser Explosive #LX24
2003 VIP Previews /5 #3
2003 VIP Previews /5 #24
2003 VIP Samples #3

2003 VIP Samples #24
2003 VIP Tin #CT3
2003 VIP Tin #CT24
2003 VIP Tradin' Paint Cars /160 #TPT12
2003 VIP Tradin' Paint Drivers /110 #TPD12
2003 Wheels American Thunder #4
2003 Wheels American Thunder American Eagle #AE8
2003 Wheels American Thunder Born On /100 #BO4
2003 Wheels American Thunder Golden Eagle /100 #AEG8
2003 Wheels American Thunder Heads Up Goodyear /90 #HUG14
2003 Wheels American Thunder Heads Up Manufacturer /90 #HUM30
2003 Wheels American Thunder Heads Up Team /60 #HUT28
2003 Wheels American Thunder Heads Up Winston /90 #HUW30
2003 Wheels American Thunder Holofoil #P4
2003 Wheels American Thunder Post Mark #PM3
2003 Wheels American Thunder Previews /5 #4
2003 Wheels American Thunder Rookie Thunder #RT6
2003 Wheels American Thunder Samples #P4
2003 Wheels American Thunder Thunder Road #TR6
2003 Wheels Autographs #11
2003 Wheels High Gear #6
2003 Wheels High Gear #58
2003 Wheels High Gear Blue Hawaii SCDA Promos #6
2003 Wheels High Gear Blue Hawaii SCDA Promos #58
2003 Wheels High Gear First Gear #F6
2003 Wheels High Gear First Gear #F58
2003 Wheels High Gear Flag Chasers Black /90 #FC8
2003 Wheels High Gear Flag Chasers Blue-Yellow /45 #FC8
2003 Wheels High Gear Flag Chasers Checkered /25 #FC8
2003 Wheels High Gear Flag Chasers Green /90 #FC8
2003 Wheels High Gear Flag Chasers Red /90 #FC8
2003 Wheels High Gear Flag Chasers White /90 #FC8
2003 Wheels High Gear Flag Chasers Yellow /90 #FC8
2003 Wheels High Gear High Groove #HG4
2003 Wheels High Gear Hot Treads /425 #HT4
2003 Wheels High Gear MPH /100 #M6
2003 Wheels High Gear MPH /100 #M58
2003 Wheels High Gear Previews /5 #6
2003 Wheels High Gear Samples #6
2003 Wheels High Gear Samples #58
2003 Wheels High Gear Top Tier #TT3
2004 Post Cereal #3
2004 Press Pass #7
2004 Press Pass #75
2004 Press Pass #75B
2004 Press Pass #78
2004 Press Pass #80
2004 Press Pass #82
2004 Press Pass #94
2004 Press Pass Autographs #9
2004 Press Pass Burning Rubber Autographs /97 #BRKB
2004 Press Pass Burning Rubber Cars /140 #BRT5
2004 Press Pass Burning Rubber Drivers /70 #BRD5
2004 Press Pass Cup Chase #CCR6
2004 Press Pass Cup Chase Prizes #CCR6
2004 Press Pass Eclipse #10
2004 Press Pass Eclipse #36
2004 Press Pass Eclipse #67
2004 Press Pass Eclipse Destination WIN #8
2004 Press Pass Eclipse Destination WIN #12
2004 Press Pass Eclipse Maxim #MX8
2004 Press Pass Eclipse Previews /5 #10
2004 Press Pass Eclipse Samples #10
2004 Press Pass Eclipse Samples #36
2004 Press Pass Eclipse Samples #67
2004 Press Pass Eclipse Skidmarks #SM2
2004 Press Pass Eclipse Skidmarks Holofoil /500 #SM2
2004 Press Pass Eclipse Under Cover Cars /170 #UCD5
2004 Press Pass Eclipse Under Cover Double Cover /100 #DC12
2004 Press Pass Eclipse Under Cover Double Cover /100 #DC15
2004 Press Pass Eclipse Under Cover Driver Gold /325 #UCD5
2004 Press Pass Eclipse Under Cover Driver Red /100 #UCD5
2004 Press Pass Eclipse Under Cover Driver Silver /690 #UCD5
2004 Press Pass Hot Treads /1250 #HTR14
2004 Press Pass Hot Treads Holofoil /200 #HTR14
2004 Press Pass Optima #3
2004 Press Pass Optima #63
2004 Press Pass Optima #96
2004 Press Pass Optima Fan Favorite #FF3
2004 Press Pass Optima Gold #G3
2004 Press Pass Optima Gold #G63
2004 Press Pass Optima Gold #G96
2004 Press Pass Optima Previews /5 #EB3
2004 Press Pass Optima Q&A #QA7
2004 Press Pass Optima Samples #3
2004 Press Pass Optima Samples #63
2004 Press Pass Optima Samples #96
2004 Press Pass Optima Thunder Bolts Cars /120 #TBT16
2004 Press Pass Optima Thunder Bolts Drivers /70 #TBD16
2004 Press Pass Platinum #P7
2004 Press Pass Platinum #P75
2004 Press Pass Platinum #P78
2004 Press Pass Platinum #P80
2004 Press Pass Platinum #P82
2004 Press Pass Platinum #P94
2004 Press Pass Premium #13
2004 Press Pass Premium #45
2004 Press Pass Premium #81
2004 Press Pass Premium Hot Threads Drivers Bronze /125 #HTD5
2004 Press Pass Premium Hot Threads Drivers Bronze Retail /125 #HTT5
2004 Press Pass Premium Hot Threads Drivers Gold /50 #HTD5
2004 Press Pass Premium Hot Threads Drivers Silver /75 #HTD5
2004 Press Pass Premium Performance Driven #PD5
2004 Press Pass Premium Previews /5 #13
2004 Press Pass Premium Samples #13
2004 Press Pass Premium Samples #45
2004 Press Pass Previews /5 #7
2004 Press Pass Samples #7
2004 Press Pass Samples #75
2004 Press Pass Samples #78
2004 Press Pass Samples #80
2004 Press Pass Samples #82
2004 Press Pass Samples #94
2004 Press Pass Showcar #S2B
2004 Press Pass Showman #S2A
2004 Press Pass Signings #9
2004 Press Pass Signings Gold /50 #9
2004 Press Pass Snapshots #SN4
2004 Press Pass Stealth #1
2004 Press Pass Stealth #2
2004 Press Pass Stealth #3
2004 Press Pass Stealth #90
2004 Press Pass Stealth #95
2004 Press Pass Stealth EFX #EF6
2004 Press Pass Stealth Fusion #FU7
2004 Press Pass Stealth Gear Grippers Drivers /80 #GGD5
2004 Press Pass Stealth Gear Grippers Drivers Retail /120 #GGT5
2004 Press Pass Stealth Previews /5 #EB1
2004 Press Pass Stealth Previews /5 #EB2
2004 Press Pass Stealth Previews /5 #EB3
2004 Press Pass Stealth Profile #P4
2004 Press Pass Stealth Samples #X1
2004 Press Pass Stealth Samples #X2
2004 Press Pass Stealth Samples #X3
2004 Press Pass Stealth Samples #X90
2004 Press Pass Stealth Samples #X95
2004 Press Pass Stealth X-Ray /100 #1
2004 Press Pass Stealth X-Ray /100 #2
2004 Press Pass Stealth X-Ray /100 #3
2004 Press Pass Stealth X-Ray /100 #90
2004 Press Pass Stealth X-Ray /100 #95
2004 Press Pass Top Shelf #TS10
2004 Press Pass Trackside #13
2004 Press Pass Trackside #68
2004 Press Pass Trackside #96
2004 Press Pass Trackside Dialed In #DI9
2004 Press Pass Trackside Golden /100 #G13
2004 Press Pass Trackside Golden /100 #G68
2004 Press Pass Trackside Golden /100 #G96
2004 Press Pass Trackside Hat Giveaway #PPH5
2004 Press Pass Trackside Previews /5 #EB13
2004 Press Pass Trackside Samples #13
2004 Press Pass Trackside Samples #68
2004 Press Pass Trackside Samples #96
2004 Press Pass Velocity #VC9
2004 Team Caliber First Choice Beckett 1:24 #97
2004 VIP #3
2004 VIP #48
2004 VIP Previews /5 #EB3
2004 VIP Previews /5 #EB48
2004 VIP Samples #3
2004 VIP Samples #48
2004 VIP Tradin' Paint Bronze /130 #TPT10
2004 VIP Tradin' Paint Gold /50 #TPD10
2004 VIP Tradin' Paint Silver /70 #TPD10
2004 Wheels American Thunder #2
2004 Wheels American Thunder #63
2004 Wheels American Thunder #90
2004 Wheels American Thunder American Muscle #AM9
2004 Wheels American Thunder Previews /5 #EB2
2004 Wheels American Thunder Pushin Pedal /275 #PP4
2004 Wheels American Thunder Samples #2
2004 Wheels American Thunder Samples #63
2004 Wheels American Thunder Samples #90
2004 Wheels American Thunder Triple Hat /160 #TH1
2004 Wheels Autographs #10
2004 Wheels High Gear #4
2004 Wheels High Gear #30
2004 Wheels High Gear #64
2004 Wheels High Gear #68
2004 Wheels High Gear High Groove #HG3
2004 Wheels High Gear Machine #MM2B
2004 Wheels High Gear Man #MM2A
2004 Wheels High Gear MPH /100 #M4
2004 Wheels High Gear MPH /100 #M30
2004 Wheels High Gear MPH /100 #M64
2004 Wheels High Gear MPH /100 #M68
2004 Wheels High Gear Previews /5 #4
2004 Wheels High Gear Previews /5 #30
2004 Wheels High Gear Samples #4
2004 Wheels High Gear Samples #30
2004 Wheels High Gear Samples #64
2004 Wheels High Gear Samples #68
2005 Coca-Cola Racing Family AutoZone #1
2005 Press Pass #36
2005 Press Pass #69
2005 Press Pass #77
2005 Press Pass #97
2005 Press Pass #117
2005 Press Pass Autographs #7
2005 Press Pass Burning Rubber Cars /130 #BRT17
2005 Press Pass Burning Rubber Drivers /80 #BRD17
2005 Press Pass Burning Rubber Drivers Gold /1 #BRD17
2005 Press Pass Cup Chase #CCR1
2005 Press Pass Cup Chase Prizes #CCP1
2005 Press Pass Cup Chase Prizes #CCP18
2005 Press Pass Double Burner /100 #DB11
2005 Press Pass Double Burner Exchange /100 #DB11
2005 Press Pass Eclipse #1
2005 Press Pass Eclipse #52
2005 Press Pass Eclipse #54
2005 Press Pass Eclipse #67
2005 Press Pass Eclipse #88
2005 Press Pass Eclipse /200 #0
2005 Press Pass Eclipse /50 #0
2005 Press Pass Eclipse Destination WIN #5
2005 Press Pass Eclipse Destination WIN #17
2005 Press Pass Eclipse Hyperdrive #HD9
2005 Press Pass Eclipse Previews /5 #EB1
2005 Press Pass Eclipse Previews /5 #EB52
2005 Press Pass Eclipse Previews /5 #EB54
2005 Press Pass Eclipse Previews /5 #EB67
2005 Press Pass Eclipse Previews /5 #EB88
2005 Press Pass Eclipse Samples #1
2005 Press Pass Eclipse Samples #52
2005 Press Pass Eclipse Samples #54
2005 Press Pass Eclipse Samples #67
2005 Press Pass Eclipse Samples #88
2005 Press Pass Eclipse Skidmarks #SM2
2005 Press Pass Eclipse Skidmarks Holofoil /250 #SM2
2005 Press Pass Eclipse Teammates Autographs /25 #2
2005 Press Pass Eclipse Teammates Autographs /25 #8
2005 Press Pass Eclipse Under Cover Cars /120 #UCT5
2005 Press Pass Eclipse Under Cover Double Cover /340 #DC4
2005 Press Pass Eclipse Under Cover Double Cover /340 #DC6
2005 Press Pass Eclipse Under Cover Driver Red /400 #UCD5
2005 Press Pass Eclipse Under Cover Drivers Holofoil /100 #UCD5
2005 Press Pass Eclipse Under Cover Drivers Silver /690 #UCD5
2005 Press Pass Hot Treads /900 #HTR5
2005 Press Pass Hot Treads Holofoil /100 #HTR5
2005 Press Pass Legends #46
2005 Press Pass Legends Autographs Black /50 #13
2005 Press Pass Legends Blue /1890 #46B
2005 Press Pass Legends Double Threads Bronze /375 #DTBK
2005 Press Pass Legends Double Threads Bronze /375 #DTMB
2005 Press Pass Legends Double Threads Gold /99 #DTBK
2005 Press Pass Legends Double Threads Gold /99 #DTMB
2005 Press Pass Legends Double Threads Silver /225 #DTBK
2005 Press Pass Legends Double Threads Silver /225 #DTMB
2005 Press Pass Legends Gold /750 #46G
2005 Press Pass Legends Greatest Moments /640 #GM18
2005 Press Pass Legends Holofoil /100 #46H
2005 Press Pass Legends Press Plates Black /1 #46
2005 Press Pass Legends Press Plates Cyan /1 #46
2005 Press Pass Legends Press Plates Magenta /1 #46
2005 Press Pass Legends Press Plates Yellow /1 #46
2005 Press Pass Legends Previews /5 #46
2005 Press Pass Legends Solo /1 #46S
2005 Press Pass Optima #6
2005 Press Pass Optima #6B
2005 Press Pass Optima #63
2005 Press Pass Optima #81
2005 Press Pass Optima Corporate Cuts Cars /160 #CCT7
2005 Press Pass Optima Corporate Cuts Drivers /120 #CCD7
2005 Press Pass Optima Fan Favorite #FF5
2005 Press Pass Optima Gold /100 #G6
2005 Press Pass Optima Gold /100 #G63
2005 Press Pass Optima Gold /100 #G81
2005 Press Pass Optima Previews /5 #6
2005 Press Pass Optima Samples #6
2005 Press Pass Optima Samples #63
2005 Press Pass Optima Samples #81
2005 Press Pass Optima Thunder Bolts Autographs /97 #TBKB
2005 Press Pass Platinum /100 #P36
2005 Press Pass Platinum /100 #P69
2005 Press Pass Platinum /100 #P77
2005 Press Pass Platinum /100 #P97
2005 Press Pass Platinum /100 #P117
2005 Press Pass Premium #4
2005 Press Pass Premium #37
2005 Press Pass Premium #58
2005 Press Pass Premium #81
2005 Press Pass Premium Hot Threads Cars /85 #HTT1
2005 Press Pass Premium Hot Threads Drivers /275 #HTD1
2005 Press Pass Premium Hot Threads Drivers Gold /1 #HTD1
2005 Press Pass Premium Samples #4
2005 Press Pass Premium Samples #37
2005 Press Pass Previews Green /5 #EB36
2005 Press Pass Samples #36
2005 Press Pass Samples #69
2005 Press Pass Samples #77
2005 Press Pass Samples #97
2005 Press Pass Samples #117
2005 Press Pass Showcar #SC2
2005 Press Pass Showman #SM2
2005 Press Pass Signings #5
2005 Press Pass Signings Gold /50 #4
2005 Press Pass Signings Platinum /100 #4
2005 Press Pass Snapshots #SN4
2005 Press Pass Stealth #29
2005 Press Pass Stealth #32
2005 Press Pass Stealth #35
2005 Press Pass Stealth #90
2005 Press Pass Stealth Gear Grippers Cars /90 #GGT5
2005 Press Pass Stealth Gear Grippers Drivers /75 #GGD5
2005 Press Pass Stealth No Boundaries #NB16
2005 Press Pass Stealth Previews /5 #29
2005 Press Pass Stealth Previews /5 #32
2005 Press Pass Stealth Previews /5 #35
2005 Press Pass Stealth Samples #29
2005 Press Pass Stealth Samples #32
2005 Press Pass Stealth Samples #35
2005 Press Pass Stealth Samples #90
2005 Press Pass Stealth X-Ray /100 #X29
2005 Press Pass Stealth X-Ray /100 #X32
2005 Press Pass Stealth X-Ray /100 #X35
2005 Press Pass Stealth X-Ray /100 #X90
2005 Press Pass Top Ten #TT7
2005 Press Pass Total Memorabilia Power Pick #TM12
2005 Press Pass Trackside #27
2005 Press Pass Trackside #76
2005 Press Pass Trackside Golden /100 #G27
2005 Press Pass Trackside Golden /100 #G76
2005 Press Pass Trackside Hat Giveaway #PPH4
2005 Press Pass Trackside Previews /5 #27
2005 Press Pass Trackside Samples #27
2005 Press Pass Trackside Samples #76
2005 Press Pass Triple Burner /100 #TB11
2005 Press Pass Triple Burner Exchange /100 #TB11
2005 Press Pass UMI Cup Chase #1
2005 Press Pass UMI Cup Chase #6
2005 Sports Illustrated for Kids #459
2005 VIP #3
2005 VIP #36
2005 VIP #50
2005 VIP Previews /5 #EB3
2005 VIP Previews /5 #EB36
2005 VIP Samples #3
2005 VIP Samples #36
2005 VIP Samples #50
2005 VIP Tradin' Paint Cars /110 #TPT10
2005 VIP Tradin' Paint Drivers /90 #TPD10
2005 Wheels American Thunder #4
2005 Wheels American Thunder American Muscle #AM9
2005 Wheels American Thunder Cool Threads /475 #CT9
2005 Wheels American Thunder Head to Toe /125 #HT3
2005 Wheels American Thunder Previews /5 #4
2005 Wheels American Thunder Pushin Pedal /150 #PP2
2005 Wheels American Thunder Samples #4
2005 Wheels American Thunder Thunder Road #TR5
2005 Wheels American Thunder Triple Hat /190 #TH2
2005 Wheels Autographs #6
2005 Wheels High Gear #27
2005 Wheels High Gear #46
2005 Wheels High Gear #90
2005 Wheels High Gear #0
2005 Wheels High Gear MPH /100 #M27
2005 Wheels High Gear MPH /100 #M46
2005 Wheels High Gear MPH /100 #M90
2005 Wheels High Gear Previews Green /5 #EB27
2005 Wheels High Gear Samples #27
2005 Wheels High Gear Samples #46
2005 Wheels High Gear Samples #90
2005 Wheels High Gear Top Tier #TT1
2006 Press Pass #29
2006 Press Pass #82
2006 Press Pass #108
2006 Press Pass #114
2006 Press Pass Autographs #7
2006 Press Pass Blue #B29
2006 Press Pass Blue #B82
2006 Press Pass Blue #B108
2006 Press Pass Blue #B114
2006 Press Pass Burning Rubber Cars /370 #BRT1
2006 Press Pass Burning Rubber Drivers /100 #BRD1
2006 Press Pass Burning Rubber Drivers Gold /1 #BRD1
2006 Press Pass Collectors Series Making the Show #MS24
2006 Press Pass Cup Chase #CCR4
2006 Press Pass Eclipse #65
2006 Press Pass Gold #G29
2006 Press Pass Gold #G82
2006 Press Pass Gold #G108
2006 Press Pass Gold #G114
2006 Press Pass Legends #39
2006 Press Pass Legends Autographs Black /50 #20
2006 Press Pass Legends Blue /1999 #B39
2006 Press Pass Legends Bronze /999 #Z39
2006 Press Pass Legends Champion Threads and Treads Bronze /399 #CTTKB
2006 Press Pass Legends Champion Threads and Treads Gold /99 #CTTKB
2006 Press Pass Legends Champion Threads and Treads Silver /299 #CTTKB
2006 Press Pass Legends Champion Threads Bronze /399 #CTKB
2006 Press Pass Legends Champion Threads Gold /50 #CTKB
2006 Press Pass Legends Champion Threads Patch /25 #CTKB
2006 Press Pass Legends Champion Threads Silver /199 #CTKB
2006 Press Pass Legends Gold /299 #G39
2006 Press Pass Legends Holofoil /99 #H39
2006 Press Pass Legends Press Plates Black /1 #PPB39
2006 Press Pass Legends Press Plates Black Backs /1 #PPB39B
2006 Press Pass Legends Press Plates Cyan /1 #PPC39
2006 Press Pass Legends Press Plates Cyan Backs /1 #PPC39B
2006 Press Pass Legends Press Plates Magenta /1 #PPM39
2006 Press Pass Legends Press Plates Magenta Backs /1 #PPM39B
2006 Press Pass Legends Press Plates Yellow /1 #PPY39
2006 Press Pass Legends Press Plates Yellow Backs /1 #PPY39B
2006 Press Pass Legends Previews /5 #EB39
2006 Press Pass Legends Solo /1 #S39
2006 Press Pass Optima #4
2006 Press Pass Optima #56
2006 Press Pass Optima Fan Favorite #FF3
2006 Press Pass Optima Gold /100 #G4
2006 Press Pass Optima Gold /100 #G56
2006 Press Pass Optima Pole Position #PP2
2006 Press Pass Optima Previews /5 #EB4
2006 Press Pass Optima Q & A #QA6
2006 Press Pass Platinum /100 #P29
2006 Press Pass Platinum /100 #P82
2006 Press Pass Platinum /100 #P108
2006 Press Pass Platinum /100 #P114
2006 Press Pass Premium #4
2006 Press Pass Premium #56
2006 Press Pass Premium In the Zone #IZ6
2006 Press Pass Premium In the Zone Red /250 #IZ6
2006 Press Pass Previews /5 #EB29
2006 Press Pass Previews /1 #EB108
2006 Press Pass Signings #8
2006 Press Pass Signings Gold /50 #8
2006 Press Pass Signings Red Ink #8
2006 Press Pass Signings Silver /100 #8
2006 Press Pass Stealth #4
2006 Press Pass Stealth #55
2006 Press Pass Stealth Autographed Hat Entry #PPH4
2006 Press Pass Stealth Corporate Cuts /250 #CCD11
2006 Press Pass Stealth Hot Pass #HP5
2006 Press Pass Stealth Previews /5 #4
2006 Press Pass Stealth Retail #4
2006 Press Pass Stealth Retail #55
2006 Press Pass Stealth X-Ray /100 #X4
2006 Press Pass Stealth X-Ray /100 #X55
2006 Press Pass Top 25 Drivers & Rides #C2
2006 Press Pass Top 25 Drivers & Rides #D2
2006 TRAKS #5
2006 TRAKS #38
2006 TRAKS Autographs #5
2006 TRAKS Autographs 100 /100 #4
2006 TRAKS Autographs 25 /25 #5
2006 TRAKS Previews /1 #5
2006 TRAKS Previews /1 #38
2006 TRAKS Stickers #2
2006 VIP #3
2006 VIP #29
2006 VIP #44
2006 VIP #64
2006 VIP #69
2006 VIP #89
2006 VIP Head Gear #HG9
2006 VIP Head Gear Transparent #HG9
2006 VIP Lap Leader #LL8
2006 VIP Lap Leader Transparent #LL8
2006 VIP Making the Show #MS24
2006 VIP Tradin' Paint Cars Bronze /145 #TPT2
2006 VIP Tradin' Paint Drivers Gold /50 #TPD2
2006 VIP Tradin' Paint Drivers Silver /80 #TPD2
2006 Wheels American Thunder #4
2006 Wheels American Thunder Cool Threads /329 #CT6
2006 Wheels American Thunder Double Hat /99 #DH4
2006 Wheels American Thunder Grandstand #GS2
2006 Wheels American Thunder Previews /5 #EB4
2006 Wheels American Thunder Thunder Road #TR16
2006 Wheels American Thunder Thunder Strokes /100 #2
2006 Wheels Autographs #8
2007 Press Pass #14
2007 Press Pass #81
2007 Press Pass #87
2007 Press Pass #99
2007 Press Pass Autographs #4
2007 Press Pass Blue #B14
2007 Press Pass Blue #B81
2007 Press Pass Blue #B87
2007 Press Pass Blue #B99
2007 Press Pass Burning Rubber Autographs /2 #BRSKB
2007 Press Pass Collector's Series Box Set #SB3
2007 Press Pass Cup Chase #CCR13
2007 Press Pass Cup Chase Prizes #CC5
2007 Press Pass Double Burner Firesuit-Glove /100 #DB8
2007 Press Pass Double Burner Firesuit-Glove Exchange /100 #DB8
2007 Press Pass Eclipse #15
2007 Press Pass Eclipse #34
2007 Press Pass Eclipse Gold /25 #G15
2007 Press Pass Eclipse Gold /25 #G34
2007 Press Pass Eclipse Previews /5 #EB15
2007 Press Pass Eclipse Previews /5 #EB34
2007 Press Pass Eclipse Racing Champions #RC10
2007 Press Pass Eclipse Racing Champions #RC17
2007 Press Pass Eclipse Red /1 #R15
2007 Press Pass Eclipse Red /1 #R34
2007 Press Pass Eclipse Teammates Autographs /25 #5
2007 Press Pass Eclipse Under Cover Double Cover Name /25 #DC4
2007 Press Pass Eclipse Under Cover Double Cover NASCAR /99 #DC4
2007 Press Pass Eclipse Under Cover Drivers /450 #UCD14
2007 Press Pass Eclipse Under Cover Drivers Eclipse /1 #UCD14
2007 Press Pass Eclipse Under Cover Drivers Name /99 #UCD14
2007 Press Pass Eclipse Under Cover Drivers NASCAR /270 #UCD14
2007 Press Pass Eclipse Under Cover Teams /135 #UCT14
2007 Press Pass Eclipse Under Cover Teams NASCAR /25 #UCT14
2007 Press Pass Gold #G14
2007 Press Pass Gold #G81
2007 Press Pass Gold #G87
2007 Press Pass Gold #G99
2007 Press Pass Legends #47
2007 Press Pass Legends Autographs Blue /70 #4
2007 Press Pass Legends Blue /999 #B47
2007 Press Pass Legends Bronze /599 #Z47
2007 Press Pass Legends Gold /249 #G47
2007 Press Pass Legends Holofoil /99 #H47
2007 Press Pass Legends Press Plates Black /1 #PP47
2007 Press Pass Legends Press Plates Black Backs /1 #PP47
2007 Press Pass Legends Press Plates Cyan /1 #PP47
2007 Press Pass Legends Press Plates Cyan Backs /1 #PP47
2007 Press Pass Legends Press Plates Magenta /1 #PP47
2007 Press Pass Legends Press Plates Magenta Backs /1 #PP47
2007 Press Pass Legends Press Plates Yellow /1 #PP47
2007 Press Pass Legends Press Plates Yellow Backs /1 #PP47
2007 Press Pass Legends Previews /5 #EB47
2007 Press Pass Legends Signature Series /25 #KB
2007 Press Pass Legends Solo /1 #S47
2007 Press Pass Platinum /100 #P14
2007 Press Pass Platinum /100 #P81
2007 Press Pass Platinum /100 #P87
2007 Press Pass Platinum /100 #P99
2007 Press Pass Premium #5
2007 Press Pass Premium #38
2007 Press Pass Premium Hot Threads Autographs /2 #HTKB
2007 Press Pass Premium Hot Threads Drivers /145 #HTD7
2007 Press Pass Premium Hot Threads Drivers Gold /1 #HTD7
2007 Press Pass Premium Hot Threads Patch /10 #HTP15
2007 Press Pass Premium Hot Threads Team /160 #HTT7
2007 Press Pass Premium Performance Driven #PD7
2007 Press Pass Premium Performance Driven Red /250 #PD7
2007 Press Pass Premium Red /15 #R5
2007 Press Pass Premium Red /15 #R38
2007 Press Pass Previews /5 #EB14
2007 Press Pass Signings #12
2007 Press Pass Signings Blue /25 #4
2007 Press Pass Signings Gold /50 #9
2007 Press Pass Signings Silver /100 #8
2007 Press Pass Snapshots #SN4
2007 Press Pass Stealth #4
2007 Press Pass Stealth #56
2007 Press Pass Stealth #67
2007 Press Pass Stealth Battle Armor Drivers /150 #BAD11
2007 Press Pass Stealth Battle Armor Teams /85 #BAT11
2007 Press Pass Stealth Chrome #4
2007 Press Pass Stealth Chrome #56
2007 Press Pass Stealth Chrome #67
2007 Press Pass Stealth Chrome Exclusives /99 #X4
2007 Press Pass Stealth Chrome Exclusives /99 #X56
2007 Press Pass Stealth Chrome Exclusives /99 #X67
2007 Press Pass Stealth Chrome Platinum /25 #P4
2007 Press Pass Stealth Chrome Platinum /25 #P56
2007 Press Pass Stealth Chrome Platinum /25 #P67
2007 Press Pass Stealth Previews /5 #EB4
2007 Traks #4
2007 Traks #67
2007 Traks #92
2007 Traks Corporate Cuts Driver /99 #CCD8
2007 Traks Corporate Cuts Patch /6 #CCD8
2007 Traks Corporate Cuts Team /180 #CCT8
2007 Traks Driver's Seat #DS18
2007 Traks Driver's Seat #DS18B
2007 Traks Driver's Seat National #DS18
2007 Traks Gold #G4
2007 Traks Gold #G67
2007 Traks Gold #G92
2007 Traks Holofoil /50 #H4
2007 Traks Holofoil /50 #H67
2007 Traks Holofoil /50 #H92
2007 Traks Previews /5 #EB4
2007 Traks Red /10 #R4
2007 Traks Red /10 #R67
2007 Traks Red /10 #R92
2007 VIP #5
2007 VIP #42
2007 VIP Previews /5 #EB5
2007 VIP Sunday Best #SB3
2007 VIP Trophy Club #TC6
2007 VIP Trophy Club Transparent #TC6
2007 Wheels American Thunder #5
2007 Wheels American Thunder #77
2007 Wheels American Thunder Autographed Hat Instant Winner /1 #AH6
2007 Wheels American Thunder Cool Threads /299 #CT12
2007 Wheels American Thunder Previews /5 #EB5
2007 Wheels American Thunder Thunder Strokes #7
2007 Wheels American Thunder Thunder Strokes Press Plates Black /1 #7
2007 Wheels American Thunder Thunder Strokes Press Plates Cyan /1 #7
2007 Wheels American Thunder Thunder Strokes Press Plates Magenta /1 #7
2007 Wheels American Thunder Thunder Strokes Press Plates Yellow /1 #7
2007 Wheels American Thunder Triple Hat /99 #TH4
2007 Wheels Autographs #5
2007 Wheels Autographs Press Plates Black /1 #5
2007 Wheels Autographs Press Plates Cyan /1 #5
2007 Wheels Autographs Press Plates Magenta /1 #5
2007 Wheels High Gear #15
2007 Wheels High Gear Driven #DR17
2007 Wheels High Gear Final Standings Gold /16 #FS15
2007 Wheels High Gear MPH /100 #M15
2007 Wheels High Gear Previews /5 #EB15
2008 Press Pass #12
2008 Press Pass #111
2008 Press Pass #0
2008 Press Pass Autographs #9
2008 Press Pass Blue #B12
2008 Press Pass Blue #B111
2008 Press Pass Burning Rubber Drivers /60 #BRD20
2008 Press Pass Burning Rubber Drivers /60 #BRD22
2008 Press Pass Burning Rubber Drivers Gold /1 #BRD20
2008 Press Pass Burning Rubber Drivers Gold /1 #BRD22
2008 Press Pass Burning Rubber Drivers Prime Cuts /25 #BRD20
2008 Press Pass Burning Rubber Drivers Prime Cuts /25 #BRD22
2008 Press Pass Burning Rubber Teams /175 #BRT20
2008 Press Pass Burning Rubber Teams /175 #BRT22
2008 Press Pass Collector's Series Box Set #18
2008 Press Pass Cup Chase #CC16
2008 Press Pass Eclipse #6
2008 Press Pass Eclipse #33
2008 Press Pass Eclipse #40
2008 Press Pass Eclipse #65
2008 Press Pass Eclipse #75
2008 Press Pass Eclipse Gold /25 #G6
2008 Press Pass Eclipse Gold /25 #G33
2008 Press Pass Eclipse Gold /25 #G40
2008 Press Pass Eclipse Gold /25 #G65
2008 Press Pass Eclipse Gold /25 #G75
2008 Press Pass Eclipse Previews /5 #EB6
2008 Press Pass Eclipse Previews /5 #EB33
2008 Press Pass Eclipse Previews /1 #EB75
2008 Press Pass Eclipse Red /1 #R6
2008 Press Pass Eclipse Red /1 #R33
2008 Press Pass Eclipse Red /1 #R40
2008 Press Pass Eclipse Red /1 #R65
2008 Press Pass Eclipse Red /1 #R75
2008 Press Pass Eclipse Star Tracks #ST9
2008 Press Pass Eclipse Star Tracks Holofoil /250 #ST9
2008 Press Pass Eclipse Stellar #ST5
2008 Press Pass Eclipse Teammates Autographs /35 #BN
2008 Press Pass Eclipse Under Cover Autographs /2 #UCKB
2008 Press Pass Eclipse Under Cover Double Cover Name /25 #DC5
2008 Press Pass Eclipse Under Cover Double Cover NASCAR /99 #DC5
2008 Press Pass Eclipse Under Cover Drivers /250 #UCD4
2008 Press Pass Eclipse Under Cover Drivers Eclipse /1 #UCD4
2008 Press Pass Eclipse Under Cover Drivers Name /50 #UCD4
2008 Press Pass Eclipse Under Cover Drivers NASCAR /150 #UCD4
2008 Press Pass Eclipse Under Cover Teams /99 #UCT4
2008 Press Pass Eclipse Under Cover Teams NASCAR /25 #UCT4
2008 Press Pass Four Wide /50 #FWKB
2008 Press Pass Four Wide Checkered Flag /1 #FWKB
2008 Press Pass Gillette Young Guns #2
2008 Press Pass Gold #G12
2008 Press Pass Gold #G111
2008 Press Pass Legends #45
2008 Press Pass Legends Blue /599 #45
2008 Press Pass Legends Bronze /299 #45
2008 Press Pass Legends Gold /99 #45
2008 Press Pass Legends Holo /25 #45
2008 Press Pass Legends IROC Champions /380 #I23
2008 Press Pass Legends IROC Champions Gold /99 #I23
2008 Press Pass Legends Previews /5 #EB45
2008 Press Pass Legends Printing Plates Black /1 #45
2008 Press Pass Legends Printing Plates Cyan /1 #45
2008 Press Pass Legends Printing Plates Magenta /1 #45
2008 Press Pass Legends Printing Plates Yellow /1 #45
2008 Press Pass Legends Prominent Pieces Metal-Tire Bronze /99 #PP3KuB
2008 Press Pass Legends Prominent Pieces Metal-Tire Gold /25 #PP3KuB
2008 Press Pass Legends Prominent Pieces Metal-Tire Silver /50 #PP3KuB
2008 Press Pass Legends Solo /1 #45
2008 Press Pass Platinum /100 #P12
2008 Press Pass Platinum /100 #P111
2008 Press Pass Premium #5
2008 Press Pass Premium #54
2008 Press Pass Premium Hot Threads Drivers /120 #HTD12
2008 Press Pass Premium Hot Threads Drivers Gold /1 #HTD12
2008 Press Pass Premium Hot Threads Patches #HTP1
2008 Press Pass Premium Hot Threads Team /120 #HTT12
2008 Press Pass Premium Previews /5 #EB5
2008 Press Pass Premium Previews /1 #EB54
2008 Press Pass Premium Red /15 #5
2008 Press Pass Premium Red /15 #54
2008 Press Pass Previews /5 #EB12
2008 Press Pass Previews /1 #EB111
2008 Press Pass Signings #10
2008 Press Pass Signings Blue /25 #5
2008 Press Pass Signings Gold /50 #8
2008 Press Pass Signings Press Plates Black /1 #7
2008 Press Pass Signings Press Plates Black /1 #KB
2008 Press Pass Signings Press Plates Cyan /1 #7
2008 Press Pass Signings Press Plates Magenta /1 #7
2008 Press Pass Signings Press Plates Yellow /1 #7
2008 Press Pass Signings Press Plates Yellow #KB
2008 Press Pass Signings Silver /100 #9
2008 Press Pass Speedway #12
2008 Press Pass Speedway #93
2008 Press Pass Speedway Cockpit #CP4
2008 Press Pass Speedway Corporate Cuts Drivers /80 #CDKuB
2008 Press Pass Speedway Corporate Cuts Drivers Patches #CDKuB
2008 Press Pass Speedway Corporate Cuts Team /165 #CTKuB
2008 Press Pass Speedway Gold #G12
2008 Press Pass Speedway Gold #G93
2008 Press Pass Speedway Holofoil /50 #H12
2008 Press Pass Speedway Holofoil /50 #H93
2008 Press Pass Speedway Previews /5 #EB12
2008 Press Pass Speedway Previews /1 #EB93
2008 Press Pass Speedway Red /10 #R12
2008 Press Pass Speedway Red /10 #R93
2008 Press Pass Speedway Test Drive #TD2
2008 Press Pass Starting Grid #SG18
2008 Press Pass Stealth #5
2008 Press Pass Stealth Battle Armor Drivers /120 #BAD12
2008 Press Pass Stealth Battle Armor Teams /115 #BAT12
2008 Press Pass Stealth Chrome #5
2008 Press Pass Stealth Chrome Exclusives /25 #5
2008 Press Pass Stealth Chrome Exclusives Gold /99 #5
2008 Press Pass Stealth Maximum Access #MA6
2008 Press Pass Stealth Maximum Access Autographs /25 #MA6
2008 Press Pass Stealth Previews /5 #5
2008 VIP #6
2008 VIP #83
2008 VIP Previews /5 #EB6
2008 VIP Previews /1 #EB83
2008 Wheels American Thunder #7
2008 Wheels American Thunder #44
2008 Wheels American Thunder Autographed Hat Winner /1 #IWHKuB
2008 Wheels American Thunder Delegates #D5
2008 Wheels American Thunder Previews /5 #7
2008 Wheels American Thunder Trackside Treasury Autographs #KB
2008 Wheels American Thunder Trackside Treasury Autographs Gold /25 #KB
2008 Wheels American Thunder Trackside Treasury Autographs Printing Plates Black /1 #KB
2008 Wheels American Thunder Trackside Treasury Autographs Printing Plates Cyan /1 #KB
2008 Wheels American Thunder Trackside Treasury Autographs Printing Plates Magenta /1 #KB
2008 Wheels American Thunder Trackside Treasury Autographs Printing Plates Yellow /1 #KB
2008 Wheels American Thunder Triple Hat /99 #TH4
2008 Wheels Autographs #7
2008 Wheels Autographs Chase Edition /25 #2
2008 Wheels Autographs Press Plates Black /1 #7
2008 Wheels Autographs Press Plates Cyan /1 #7
2008 Wheels Autographs Press Plates Magenta /1 #7
2008 Wheels Autographs Press Plates Yellow /1 #7
2008 Wheels High Gear #7
2008 Wheels High Gear #65
2008 Wheels High Gear Driven #DR3
2008 Wheels High Gear Final Standings /7 #F7
2008 Wheels High Gear Last Lap /10 #LL12
2008 Wheels High Gear Last Lap Holofoil /5 #LL12
2008 Wheels High Gear MPH /100 #M7
2008 Wheels High Gear MPH /100 #M65
2008 Wheels High Gear Previews /5 #EB7
2008 Wheels High Gear The Chase #TC7
2009 Element #5
2009 Element #69
2009 Element Lab Report #LR5
2009 Element Previews /5 #5
2009 Element Radioactive /100 #5
2009 Element Radioactive /100 #69
2009 Press Pass #19
2009 Press Pass #75
2009 Press Pass #125
2009 Press Pass #175
2009 Press Pass #201
2009 Press Pass Autographs Gold #8
2009 Press Pass Autographs Printing Plates Black /1 #7
2009 Press Pass Autographs Printing Plates Cyan /1 #7
2009 Press Pass Autographs Printing Plates Magenta /1 #7
2009 Press Pass Autographs Printing Plates Yellow /1 #7
2009 Press Pass Autographs Silver #8
2009 Press Pass Blue #19
2009 Press Pass Blue #75
2009 Press Pass Blue #125
2009 Press Pass Blue #175
2009 Press Pass Blue #201
2009 Press Pass Burning Rubber Autographs /2 #BRSKuB
2009 Press Pass Burning Rubber Drivers /185 #BRD17
2009 Press Pass Burning Rubber Prime Cut /25 #BRD17
2009 Press Pass Burning Rubber Teams /250 #BRT17
2009 Press Pass Chase for the Sprint Cup #CC7
2009 Press Pass Cup Chase #CCR10
2009 Press Pass Cup Chase Prizes #CC7
2009 Press Pass Eclipse #3
2009 Press Pass Eclipse #41
2009 Press Pass Eclipse #69
2009 Press Pass Eclipse Black and White #3
2009 Press Pass Eclipse Black and White #41
2009 Press Pass Eclipse Black and White #69
2009 Press Pass Eclipse Blue #3
2009 Press Pass Eclipse Blue #41
2009 Press Pass Eclipse Blue #69
2009 Press Pass Gold #19
2009 Press Pass Gold #75
2009 Press Pass Gold #125
2009 Press Pass Gold #175
2009 Press Pass Gold #201
2009 Press Pass Gold Holofoil /100 #19
2009 Press Pass Gold Holofoil /100 #75
2009 Press Pass Gold Holofoil /100 #125
2009 Press Pass Gold Holofoil /100 #175
2009 Press Pass Gold Holofoil /100 #201
2009 Press Pass Legends #41
2009 Press Pass Legends Gold /399 #41
2009 Press Pass Legends Holofoil /50 #41
2009 Press Pass Legends Previews /5 #41
2009 Press Pass Legends Printing Plates Black /1 #41
2009 Press Pass Legends Printing Plates Cyan /1 #41
2009 Press Pass Legends Printing Plates Magenta /1 #41
2009 Press Pass Legends Printing Plates Yellow /1 #41
2009 Press Pass Legends Prominent Pieces Bronze /99 #PPKB
2009 Press Pass Legends Prominent Pieces Gold /25 #PPKB
2009 Press Pass Legends Prominent Pieces Silver /50 #PPKB
2009 Press Pass Legends Red /199 #41
2009 Press Pass Legends Solo /1 #41
2009 Press Pass Pocket Portraits #P5
2009 Press Pass Pocket Portraits Hometown #P5
2009 Press Pass Pocket Portraits Smoke #P5

2009 Press Pass Pocket Portraits Target #PPT9
2009 Press Pass Premium #5
2009 Press Pass Premium Hot Threads /299 #HTKB
2009 Press Pass Premium Hot Threads Multi-Color /25 #HTKB
2009 Press Pass Premium Hot Threads Patches /10 #HTP-KB
2009 Press Pass Premium Previews /5 #EB5
2009 Press Pass Premium Signatures #7
2009 Press Pass Premium Signatures Gold /25 #7
2009 Press Pass Previews /5 #EB19
2009 Press Pass Previews /5 #EB125
2009 Press Pass Red #19
2009 Press Pass Red #75
2009 Press Pass Red #125
2009 Press Pass Red #175
2009 Press Pass Red #201
2009 Press Pass Showcase /499 #9
2009 Press Pass Showcase /499 #31
2009 Press Pass Showcase /499 #47
2009 Press Pass Showcase 2nd Gear /125 #9
2009 Press Pass Showcase 2nd Gear /125 #31
2009 Press Pass Showcase 2nd Gear /125 #47
2009 Press Pass Showcase 3rd Gear /50 #9
2009 Press Pass Showcase 3rd Gear /50 #31
2009 Press Pass Showcase 3rd Gear /50 #47
2009 Press Pass Showcase 4th Gear /15 #9
2009 Press Pass Showcase 4th Gear /15 #31
2009 Press Pass Showcase 4th Gear /15 #47
2009 Press Pass Showcase Classic Collections Ink /45 #5
2009 Press Pass Showcase Classic Collections Ink Gold /25 #5
2009 Press Pass Showcase Classic Collections Ink Green /5 #5
2009 Press Pass Showcase Classic Collections Ink Melting /1 #5
2009 Press Pass Showcase Printing Plates Black /1 #9
2009 Press Pass Showcase Printing Plates Black /1 #31
2009 Press Pass Showcase Printing Plates Black /1 #47
2009 Press Pass Showcase Printing Plates Cyan /1 #9
2009 Press Pass Showcase Printing Plates Cyan /1 #31
2009 Press Pass Showcase Printing Plates Cyan /1 #47
2009 Press Pass Showcase Printing Plates Magenta /1 #9
2009 Press Pass Showcase Printing Plates Magenta /1 #31
2009 Press Pass Showcase Printing Plates Magenta /1 #47
2009 Press Pass Showcase Printing Plates Yellow /1 #9
2009 Press Pass Showcase Printing Plates Yellow /1 #31
2009 Press Pass Showcase Printing Plates Yellow /1 #47
2009 Press Pass Sponsor Swatches /200 #SSKB
2009 Press Pass Sponsor Swatches Select /10 #SSKB
2009 Press Pass Stealth #7
2009 Press Pass Stealth #75
2009 Press Pass Stealth Chrome #7
2009 Press Pass Stealth Chrome #75
2009 Press Pass Stealth Chrome Brushed Metal /25 #7
2009 Press Pass Stealth Chrome Brushed Metal /25 #75
2009 Press Pass Stealth Chrome Gold /99 #7
2009 Press Pass Stealth Chrome Gold /99 #75
2009 Press Pass Stealth Confidential Classified Bronze #PC25
2009 Press Pass Stealth Confidential Secret Silver #PC25
2009 Press Pass Stealth Confidential Top Secret Gold /25 #PC25
2009 Press Pass Stealth Previews /5 #EB7
2009 Press Pass Stealth Previews /1 #EB75
2009 Press Pass Target Victory Tires /50 #KuBTT
2009 Press Pass Wal-Mart Autographs Red #1
2009 VIP #6
2009 VIP #51
2009 VIP After Party #AP4
2009 VIP After Party Transparent #AP4
2009 VIP Previews /5 #6
2009 VIP Purple /25 #6
2009 VIP Purple /25 #51
2009 Wheels Autographs #8
2009 Wheels Autographs Press Plates Black /1 #KB
2009 Wheels Autographs Press Plates Cyan /1 #KB
2009 Wheels Autographs Press Plates Magenta /1 #KB
2009 Wheels Autographs Press Plates Yellow /1 #KB
2009 Wheels Main Event #12
2009 Wheels Main Event #42
2009 Wheels Main Event #52
2009 Wheels Main Event #60
2009 Wheels Main Event #66
2009 Wheels Main Event #80
2009 Wheels Main Event Fast Pass Purple /25 #12
2009 Wheels Main Event Fast Pass Purple /25 #42
2009 Wheels Main Event Fast Pass Purple /25 #52
2009 Wheels Main Event Fast Pass Purple /25 #60
2009 Wheels Main Event Fast Pass Purple /25 #66
2009 Wheels Main Event Fast Pass Purple /25 #80
2009 Wheels Main Event Foil #12
2009 Wheels Main Event Hat Dance Patch /10 #HDKuB
2009 Wheels Main Event Hat Dance Triple /99 #HDKB
2009 Wheels Main Event Marks Clubs #8
2009 Wheels Main Event Marks Diamonds /50 #8
2009 Wheels Main Event Marks Hearts /10 #8
2009 Wheels Main Event Marks Printing Plates Black /1 #8
2009 Wheels Main Event Marks Printing Plates Cyan /1 #8
2009 Wheels Main Event Marks Printing Plates Magenta /1 #8
2009 Wheels Main Event Marks Printing Plates Yellow /1 #8
2009 Wheels Main Event Marks Spades /1 #8
2009 Wheels Main Event Playing Cards Blue #QC
2009 Wheels Main Event Playing Cards Red #QC
2009 Wheels Main Event Poker Chips #10
2009 Wheels Main Event Previews /5 #12
2009 Wheels Main Event Stop and Go Swatches Pit Banner /125 #SGBKB
2009 Wheels Main Event Stop and Go Swatches Pit Banner Green /10 #SGBKB
2009 Wheels Main Event Stop and Go Swatches Pit Banner Holofoil /75 #SGBKB
2009 Wheels Main Event Stop and Go Swatches Pit Banner Red /25 #SGBKB
2009 Wheels Main Event Wildcard Cuts /2 #WCCKB
2010 Element #6
2010 Element #42
2010 Element Blue /35 #6
2010 Element Blue /35 #42
2010 Element Finish Line Checkered Flag /10 #FLKuB
2010 Element Finish Line Green Flag /20 #FLKuB
2010 Element Finish Line Tires /99 #FLKuB
2010 Element Flagship Performers Championships Black /25 #FPCKuB
2010 Element Flagship Performers Championships Blue-Orange /25 #FPCKuB
2010 Element Flagship Performers Championships Checkered /1 #FPCKuB
2010 Element Flagship Performers Championships Green /5 #FPCKuB
2010 Element Flagship Performers Championships Red /25 #FPCKuB
2010 Element Flagship Performers Championships White /15 #FPCKuB
2010 Element Flagship Performers Championships X /25 #FPCKuB
2010 Element Flagship Performers Championships Yellow /25 #FPCKuB
2010 Element Flagship Performers Wins Black /20 #FPWKuB
2010 Element Flagship Performers Wins Blue-Orange /20 #FPWKuB
2010 Element Flagship Performers Wins Checkered /1 #FPWKuB
2010 Element Flagship Performers Wins Green /5 #FPWKuB
2010 Element Flagship Performers Wins Red /20 #FPWKuB
2010 Element Flagship Performers Wins White /15 #FPWKuB
2010 Element Flagship Performers Wins X /10 #FPWKuB
2010 Element Flagship Performers Wins Yellow /20 #FPWKuB
2010 Element Green #6
2010 Element Green #42
2010 Element Green-White-Checkers Blue /10 #GWCKB
2010 Element Green-White-Checkers Green /50 #GWCKB
2010 Element High Octane Vehicle #HOV10
2010 Element Previews /5 #EB6
2010 Element Purple /25 #6
2010 Element Purple /25 #42
2010 Element Red Target #6
2010 Element Red Target #42
2010 Press Pass #8
2010 Press Pass #86
2010 Press Pass #105
2010 Press Pass #115
2010 Press Pass #125
2010 Press Pass #0
2010 Press Pass Autographs #9
2010 Press Pass Autographs Chase Edition /25 #2
2010 Press Pass Autographs Printing Plates Black /1 #7
2010 Press Pass Autographs Printing Plates Cyan /1 #9
2010 Press Pass Autographs Printing Plates Cyan /1 #10
2010 Press Pass Autographs Printing Plates Magenta /1 #7
2010 Press Pass Blue #8
2010 Press Pass Blue #86
2010 Press Pass Blue #105
2010 Press Pass Blue #115
2010 Press Pass Blue #125
2010 Press Pass Burning Rubber /250 #BR30
2010 Press Pass Burning Rubber Gold /99 #BR30
2010 Press Pass Burning Rubber Prime Cuts /25 #BRD30
2010 Press Pass Cup Chase #CCR2
2010 Press Pass Cup Chase Prizes #CC5
2010 Press Pass Eclipse #18
2010 Press Pass Eclipse #28
2010 Press Pass Eclipse Blue #18
2010 Press Pass Eclipse Blue #28
2010 Press Pass Eclipse Decade #D5
2010 Press Pass Eclipse Gold #18
2010 Press Pass Eclipse Gold #28
2010 Press Pass Eclipse Previews /5 #18
2010 Press Pass Eclipse Previews /1 #28
2010 Press Pass Eclipse Purple /25 #18
2010 Press Pass Eclipse Purple /25 #28
2010 Press Pass Final Standings /60 #FS4
2010 Press Pass Five Star /35 #10
2010 Press Pass Five Star Holofoil /10 #10
2010 Press Pass Five Star Melting /1 #10
2010 Press Pass Gold #8
2010 Press Pass Gold #86
2010 Press Pass Gold #105
2010 Press Pass Gold #115
2010 Press Pass Gold #125
2010 Press Pass Holofoil /100 #8
2010 Press Pass Holofoil /100 #86
2010 Press Pass Holofoil /100 #105
2010 Press Pass Holofoil /100 #115
2010 Press Pass Holofoil /100 #125
2010 Press Pass Legends Autographs Blue /10 #8
2010 Press Pass Legends Autographs Holofoil /25 #8
2010 Press Pass Legends Autographs Printing Plates Black /1 #7
2010 Press Pass Legends Autographs Printing Plates Cyan /1 #7
2010 Press Pass Legends Autographs Printing Plates Magenta /1 #7
2010 Press Pass Legends Autographs Printing Plates Yellow /1 #7
2010 Press Pass Legends Motorsports Masters #MMKUB
2010 Press Pass Legends Motorsports Masters Autographs Blue /1 #NNO
2010 Press Pass Legends Motorsports Masters Autographs Gold /50 #7
2010 Press Pass Legends Motorsports Masters Autographs Holofoil /25 #7
2010 Press Pass Legends Motorsports Masters Autographs Printing Plates Black /1 #7
2010 Press Pass Legends Motorsports Masters Autographs Printing Plates Cyan /1 #7
2010 Press Pass Legends Motorsports Masters Autographs Printing Plates Magenta /1 #7
2010 Press Pass Legends Motorsports Masters Autographs Printing Plates Yellow /1 #7
2010 Press Pass Legends Motorsports Masters Blue /10 #MMKUB
2010 Press Pass Legends Motorsports Masters Gold /299 #MMKUB
2010 Press Pass Legends Motorsports Masters Holofoil /149 #MMKUB
2010 Press Pass NASCAR Hall of Fame #NHOF49
2010 Press Pass NASCAR Hall of Fame Blue #NHOF49
2010 Press Pass NASCAR Hall of Fame Holofoil /50 #NHOF49
2010 Press Pass Premium #7
2010 Press Pass Premium #44
2010 Press Pass Premium Allies #A4
2010 Press Pass Premium Hot Threads /299 #HTKuB
2010 Press Pass Premium Hot Threads Holofoil /99 #HTKuB
2010 Press Pass Premium Hot Threads Multi Color /25 #HTKuB
2010 Press Pass Premium Hot Threads Two Color /125 #HTKuB
2010 Press Pass Premium Purple /25 #7
2010 Press Pass Premium Purple /25 #44
2010 Press Pass Premium Signatures #PSKUB
2010 Press Pass Premium Signatures Red Ink /25 #PSKUB
2010 Press Pass Previews /5 #8
2010 Press Pass Previews /1 #115
2010 Press Pass Purple /25 #8
2010 Press Pass Purple /25 #86
2010 Press Pass Purple /25 #105
2010 Press Pass Purple /25 #115
2010 Press Pass Purple /25 #125
2010 Press Pass Showcase /499 #7
2010 Press Pass Showcase /499 #36
2010 Press Pass Showcase /499 #47
2010 Press Pass Showcase Classic Collections Ink /15 #CCIPEN
2010 Press Pass Showcase Classic Collections Ink Gold /10 #CCIPEN
2010 Press Pass Showcase Classic Collections Ink Green /5 #CCIPEN
2010 Press Pass Showcase Classic Collections Ink Melting /1 #CCIPEN
2010 Press Pass Showcase Elite Exhibit Ink /20 #EEIKB1
2010 Press Pass Showcase Elite Exhibit Ink Gold /10 #EEIKB1
2010 Press Pass Showcase Elite Exhibit Ink Green /5 #EEIKB1
2010 Press Pass Showcase Elite Exhibit Ink Melting /1 #EEIKB1
2010 Press Pass Showcase Elite Exhibit Triple Memorabilia /99 #EEMKB1
2010 Press Pass Showcase Elite Exhibit Triple Memorabilia Gold /45 #EEMKB1
2010 Press Pass Showcase Elite Exhibit Triple Memorabilia Green /25 #EEMKB1
2010 Press Pass Showcase Elite Exhibit Triple Memorabilia Melting /5 #EEMKB1
2010 Press Pass Showcase Gold /125 #7
2010 Press Pass Showcase Gold /125 #36
2010 Press Pass Showcase Gold /125 #47
2010 Press Pass Showcase Green /50 #7
2010 Press Pass Showcase Green /50 #36
2010 Press Pass Showcase Green /50 #47
2010 Press Pass Showcase Melting /15 #7
2010 Press Pass Showcase Melting /15 #36
2010 Press Pass Showcase Melting /15 #47
2010 Press Pass Showcase Platinum Holo /1 #7
2010 Press Pass Showcase Platinum Holo /1 #36
2010 Press Pass Showcase Platinum Holo /1 #47
2010 Press Pass Showcase Prized Pieces Firesuit Ink Gold /25 #PPIKB1
2010 Press Pass Showcase Prized Pieces Firesuit Ink Melting /1 #PPIKB1
2010 Press Pass Showcase Prized Pieces Memorabilia Ink Green /15 #PPIKB1
2010 Press Pass Showcase Prized Pieces Sheet Metal Ink Silver /45 #PPIKB1
2010 Press Pass Signings Blue /10 #11
2010 Press Pass Signings Gold /50 #11
2010 Press Pass Signings Red /5 #11
2010 Press Pass Signings Silver /44 #11
2010 Press Pass Stealth #6
2010 Press Pass Stealth #59
2010 Press Pass Stealth Black and White #6
2010 Press Pass Stealth Black and White #59
2010 Press Pass Stealth Power Players #PP3
2010 Press Pass Stealth Previews /5 #6
2010 Press Pass Stealth Previews /5 #59
2010 Press Pass Stealth Purple /25 #6
2010 Press Pass Stealth Purple /25 #59
2010 Press Pass Top 12 Tires /2 #KB
2010 Press Pass Top 12 Tires 10 /10 #KB
2010 Wheels Autographs #8
2010 Wheels Autographs Printing Plates Black /1 #8
2010 Wheels Autographs Printing Plates Cyan /1 #8
2010 Wheels Autographs Printing Plates Magenta /1 #8
2010 Wheels Autographs Printing Plates Yellow /1 #8
2010 Wheels Autographs Special Ink /10 #1
2010 Wheels Autographs Target /10 #6
2010 Wheels Main Event #6
2010 Wheels Main Event #39
2010 Wheels Main Event #60
2010 Wheels Main Event #67
2010 Wheels Main Event #72
2010 Wheels Main Event American Muscle #AM1
2010 Wheels Main Event Blue #6
2010 Wheels Main Event Blue #39
2010 Wheels Main Event Blue #60
2010 Wheels Main Event Blue #67
2010 Wheels Main Event Blue #72
2010 Wheels Main Event Fight Card #FC6
2010 Wheels Main Event Fight Card Checkered Flag #FC6
2010 Wheels Main Event Fight Card Full Color Retail #FC6
2010 Wheels Main Event Fight Card Gold /25 #FC6
2010 Wheels Main Event Head to Head /150 #HHKBBK
2010 Wheels Main Event Head to Head Blue /75 #HHKBBK
2010 Wheels Main Event Head to Head Holofoil /10 #HHKBBK
2010 Wheels Main Event Head to Head Red /25 #HHKBBK
2010 Wheels Main Event Marks Autographs /91 #10
2010 Wheels Main Event Marks Autographs Black /1 #10
2010 Wheels Main Event Marks Autographs Blue /35 #10
2010 Wheels Main Event Marks Autographs Red /5 #10
2010 Wheels Main Event Matchups Autographs /10 #KBGB
2010 Wheels Main Event Matchups Autographs /10 #KBBK
2010 Wheels Main Event Purple /25 #6
2010 Wheels Main Event Purple /25 #39
2010 Wheels Main Event Upper Cuts Knock Out Patches /25 #UCKOKUB
2010 Wheels Main Event Wheel to Wheel /25 #WWKBBK
2010 Wheels Main Event Wheel to Wheel Holofoil /10 #WWKBBK
2011 Element #6
2011 Element #35
2011 Element #66
2011 Element #74
2011 Element #83
2011 Element Autographs /99 #10
2011 Element Autographs Blue /10 #10
2011 Element Autographs Gold /25 #10
2011 Element Autographs Printing Plates Black /1 #10
2011 Element Autographs Printing Plates Cyan /1 #10
2011 Element Autographs Printing Plates Magenta /1 #10
2011 Element Autographs Printing Plates Yellow /1 #10
2011 Element Autographs Silver /50 #10
2011 Element Black /35 #6
2011 Element Black /35 #35
2011 Element Black /35 #66
2011 Element Black /35 #74
2011 Element Black /35 #83
2011 Element Finish Line Checkered Flag /10 #FLKUB
2011 Element Finish Line Green Flag /25 #FLKUB
2011 Element Finish Line Tires /99 #FLKUB
2011 Element Flagship Performers Career Wins White /50 #FPWKuB
2011 Element Flagship Performers Championships Checkered /25 #FPCKuB
2011 Element Green #6
2011 Element Green #35
2011 Element Green #66
2011 Element Green #74
2011 Element Green #83
2011 Element Previews /5 #EB6
2011 Element Purple /25 #6
2011 Element Purple /25 #35
2011 Element Purple /25 #66
2011 Element Purple /25 #74
2011 Element Purple /25 #83
2011 Element Red #6
2011 Element Red #35
2011 Element Red #66
2011 Element Red #74
2011 Element Red #83
2011 Press Pass #6
2011 Press Pass #61
2011 Press Pass #119
2011 Press Pass #126
2011 Press Pass #138
2011 Press Pass #167
2011 Press Pass #176
2011 Press Pass #198
2011 Press Pass #0
2011 Press Pass Autographs Blue /10 #10
2011 Press Pass Autographs Bronze /70 #10
2011 Press Pass Autographs Gold /15 #10
2011 Press Pass Autographs Printing Plates Black /1 #10
2011 Press Pass Autographs Printing Plates Cyan /1 #10
2011 Press Pass Autographs Printing Plates Magenta /1 #10
2011 Press Pass Autographs Printing Plates Yellow /1 #10
2011 Press Pass Autographs Silver /50 #10
2011 Press Pass Blue Holofoil /10 #6
2011 Press Pass Blue Holofoil /10 #61
2011 Press Pass Blue Holofoil /10 #119
2011 Press Pass Blue Holofoil /10 #126
2011 Press Pass Blue Holofoil /10 #138
2011 Press Pass Blue Holofoil /10 #167
2011 Press Pass Blue Holofoil /10 #176
2011 Press Pass Blue Holofoil /10 #198
2011 Press Pass Blue Retail #6
2011 Press Pass Blue Retail #61
2011 Press Pass Blue Retail #119
2011 Press Pass Blue Retail #126
2011 Press Pass Blue Retail #138
2011 Press Pass Blue Retail #167
2011 Press Pass Blue Retail #176
2011 Press Pass Blue Retail #198
2011 Press Pass Burning Rubber Autographs /10 #BRKUB1
2011 Press Pass Burning Rubber Autographs /10 #BRKUB2
2011 Press Pass Burning Rubber Fast Pass /10 #BRKUB
2011 Press Pass Burning Rubber Gold /150 #BRKUB
2011 Press Pass Burning Rubber Holofoil /50 #BRKUB
2011 Press Pass Burning Rubber Prime Cuts /25 #BRKUB
2011 Press Pass Cup Chase #CCR5
2011 Press Pass Cup Chase Prizes #CC7
2011 Press Pass Eclipse #6
2011 Press Pass Eclipse #86
2011 Press Pass Eclipse Blue #6
2011 Press Pass Eclipse Blue #86
2011 Press Pass Eclipse Gold /55 #6
2011 Press Pass Eclipse Gold /55 #86
2011 Press Pass Eclipse Previews /5 #EB6
2011 Press Pass Eclipse Purple /25 #6
2011 Press Pass FanFare #7
2011 Press Pass FanFare Autographs Blue /5 #11
2011 Press Pass FanFare Autographs Bronze /50 #11
2011 Press Pass FanFare Autographs Gold /25 #11
2011 Press Pass FanFare Autographs Printing Plates Black /1 #11
2011 Press Pass FanFare Autographs Printing Plates Cyan /1 #11
2011 Press Pass FanFare Autographs Printing Plates Magenta /1 #11
2011 Press Pass FanFare Autographs Printing Plates Yellow /1 #11
2011 Press Pass FanFare Autographs Silver /15 #11
2011 Press Pass FanFare Blue Die Cuts #7
2011 Press Pass FanFare Championship Caliber #CC3
2011 Press Pass FanFare Emerald /25 #7
2011 Press Pass FanFare Holofoil Die Cuts #7
2011 Press Pass FanFare Magnificent Materials /199 #MMKB
2011 Press Pass FanFare Magnificent Materials Holofoil /50 #MMKB
2011 Press Pass FanFare Ruby Die Cuts /15 #7
2011 Press Pass FanFare Sapphire /10 #7
2011 Press Pass FanFare Silver /25 #7
2011 Press Pass Geared Up Gold /100 #GUKUB
2011 Press Pass Geared Up Holofoil /50 #GUKUB
2011 Press Pass Gold /50 #6
2011 Press Pass Gold /50 #61
2011 Press Pass Gold /50 #119
2011 Press Pass Gold /50 #126
2011 Press Pass Gold /50 #138
2011 Press Pass Gold /50 #167
2011 Press Pass Gold /50 #176
2011 Press Pass Gold /50 #198
2011 Press Pass Legends #38
2011 Press Pass Legends Autographs Gold /25 #LGAKUB
2011 Press Pass Legends Autographs Printing Plates Black /1 #LGAKUB
2011 Press Pass Legends Autographs Printing Plates Cyan /1 #LGAKUB
2011 Press Pass Legends Autographs Printing Plates Magenta /1 #LGAKUB
2011 Press Pass Legends Autographs Printing Plates Yellow /1 #LGAKUB
2011 Press Pass Legends Autographs Silver /50 #LGAKUB
2011 Press Pass Legends Gold /250 #38
2011 Press Pass Legends Holofoil /25 #38
2011 Press Pass Legends Printing Plates Black /1 #38
2011 Press Pass Legends Printing Plates Cyan /1 #38
2011 Press Pass Legends Printing Plates Magenta /1 #38
2011 Press Pass Legends Printing Plates Yellow /1 #38
2011 Press Pass Legends Purple /25 #38
2011 Press Pass Legends Red /99 #38
2011 Press Pass Legends Solo /1 #38
2011 Press Pass Premium #45
2011 Press Pass Premium #57
2011 Press Pass Premium #75
2011 Press Pass Premium #80
2011 Press Pass Premium #81
2011 Press Pass Premium #7A
2011 Press Pass Premium #7B
2011 Press Pass Premium Double Burner /25 #DBKUB
2011 Press Pass Premium Hot Threads /150 #HTKB1
2011 Press Pass Premium Hot Threads Fast Pass /25 #HTKUB
2011 Press Pass Premium Hot Threads Multi Color /25 #HTKB1
2011 Press Pass Premium Hot Threads Secondary Color /99 #HTKB1
2011 Press Pass Premium Pairings Firesuits /25 #PPBKKB
2011 Press Pass Premium Pairings Signatures /5 #PPABKKB
2011 Press Pass Premium Purple /25 #7
2011 Press Pass Premium Purple /25 #45
2011 Press Pass Premium Purple /25 #57
2011 Press Pass Premium Purple /25 #75
2011 Press Pass Premium Purple /25 #80
2011 Press Pass Premium Purple /25 #81
2011 Press Pass Premium Signatures /195 #PSKB1
2011 Press Pass Premium Signatures Red Ink /5 #PSKB
2011 Press Pass Previews /5 #EB6
2011 Press Pass Previews /1 #EB198
2011 Press Pass Purple /25 #6
2011 Press Pass Purple /25 #198
2011 Press Pass Showcase /499 #7
2011 Press Pass Showcase /499 #38
2011 Press Pass Showcase /499 #60
2011 Press Pass Showcase Champions /499 #CH5
2011 Press Pass Showcase Champions Gold /125 #CH5
2011 Press Pass Showcase Champions Ink /25 #CHIKUB
2011 Press Pass Showcase Champions Ink Gold /10 #CHIKUB
2011 Press Pass Showcase Champions Ink Melting /1 #CHIKUB
2011 Press Pass Showcase Champions Melting /1 #CH5
2011 Press Pass Showcase Champions Memorabilia Firesuit /99 #CHMKB
2011 Press Pass Showcase Champions Memorabilia Firesuit Gold /45 #CHMKB
2011 Press Pass Showcase Champions Memorabilia Firesuit Melting /5 #CHMKB
2011 Press Pass Showcase Classic Collections Firesuit /45 #CCMPEN
2011 Press Pass Showcase Classic Collections Firesuit Patches /5 #CCMPEN
2011 Press Pass Showcase Classic Collections Ink /25 #CCMPEN
2011 Press Pass Showcase Classic Collections Ink Gold /5 #CCMPEN
2011 Press Pass Showcase Classic Collections Ink Melting /1 #CCMPEN
2011 Press Pass Showcase Classic Collections Sheet Metal /99 #CCMPEN
2011 Press Pass Showcase Elite Exhibit Ink /50 #EEIKUB
2011 Press Pass Showcase Elite Exhibit Ink Gold /25 #EEIKUB
2011 Press Pass Showcase Elite Exhibit Ink Melting /1 #EEIKUB
2011 Press Pass Showcase Gold /125 #7
2011 Press Pass Showcase Gold /125 #38
2011 Press Pass Showcase Gold /125 #60
2011 Press Pass Showcase Green /25 #7
2011 Press Pass Showcase Green /25 #38
2011 Press Pass Showcase Green /25 #60
2011 Press Pass Showcase Melting /1 #7
2011 Press Pass Showcase Melting /1 #38
2011 Press Pass Showcase Melting /1 #60
2011 Press Pass Showcase Prized Pieces Firesuit /99 #PPMKUB
2011 Press Pass Showcase Prized Pieces Firesuit Gold /45 #PPMKUB
2011 Press Pass Showcase Prized Pieces Firesuit Ink /25 #PPIKUB
2011 Press Pass Showcase Prized Pieces Firesuit Patches Ink /1 #PPIKUB
2011 Press Pass Showcase Prized Pieces Firesuit Patches Melting /5 #PPMKUB
2011 Press Pass Showcase Prized Pieces Sheet Metal Ink /45 #PPIKUB
2011 Press Pass Signature Series /11 #SSTKB
2011 Press Pass Signature Series /11 #SSBKUB
2011 Press Pass Stealth #22
2011 Press Pass Stealth #23
2011 Press Pass Stealth #24
2011 Press Pass Stealth #90
2011 Press Pass Stealth Black and White /25 #22
2011 Press Pass Stealth Black and White /25 #23
2011 Press Pass Stealth Black and White /25 #24
2011 Press Pass Stealth Black and White /25 #90
2011 Press Pass Stealth Holofoil /99 #22
2011 Press Pass Stealth Holofoil /99 #23
2011 Press Pass Stealth Holofoil /99 #24
2011 Press Pass Stealth Holofoil /99 #90
2011 Press Pass Stealth Metal of Honor Medal of Honor /50 #BAKUB
2011 Press Pass Stealth Metal of Honor Purple Heart /25 #MHKUB
2011 Press Pass Stealth Metal of Honor Silver Star /99 #BAKUB
2011 Press Pass Stealth Purple /25 #22
2011 Press Pass Stealth Purple /25 #23
2011 Press Pass Stealth Purple /25 #24
2011 Press Pass Stealth Supersonic #SS4
2011 Press Pass Wal-Mart Top 12 Tires /25 #T12KUB
2011 Press Pass Wal-Mart Winning Tickets #WTW6
2011 Press Pass Winning Tickets #WT4
2011 Press Pass Winning Tickets #WT13
2011 Wheels Main Event #7
2011 Wheels Main Event #69
2011 Wheels Main Event #83
2011 Wheels Main Event All Stars #A13
2011 Wheels Main Event All Stars Brushed Foil /199 #A13
2011 Wheels Main Event All Stars Holofoil /50 #A13
2011 Wheels Main Event Black and White #7
2011 Wheels Main Event Black and White #69
2011 Wheels Main Event Black and White #83
2011 Wheels Main Event Blue /75 #7
2011 Wheels Main Event Blue /75 #69
2011 Wheels Main Event Blue /75 #83
2011 Wheels Main Event Green /1 #7
2011 Wheels Main Event Green /1 #69
2011 Wheels Main Event Green /1 #83
2011 Wheels Main Event Headliners Holofoil /25 #HLKUB
2011 Wheels Main Event Headliners Silver /50 #HLKUB
2011 Wheels Main Event Marks Autographs Blue /10 #MEKUB
2011 Wheels Main Event Marks Autographs Gold /25 #MEKUB
2011 Wheels Main Event Marks Autographs Silver /45 #MEKUB
2011 Wheels Main Event Materials Holofoil /25 #MEMKUB
2011 Wheels Main Event Materials Silver /99 #MEMKUB
2011 Wheels Main Event Rear View #R9
2011 Wheels Main Event Rear View Brushed Foil /199 #R9
2011 Wheels Main Event Rear View Holofoil /50 #R9
2011 Wheels Main Event Red /20 #7
2011 Wheels Main Event Red /20 #69
2011 Wheels Main Event Red /20 #83
2012 Press Pass #6
2012 Press Pass #70
2012 Press Pass #71
2012 Press Pass #85
2012 Press Pass Autographs Blue /5 #PPAKUB
2012 Press Pass Autographs Printing Plates Black /1 #PPAKUB
2012 Press Pass Autographs Printing Plates Cyan /1 #PPAKUB
2012 Press Pass Autographs Printing Plates Magenta /1 #PPAKUB
2012 Press Pass Autographs Printing Plates Yellow /1 #PPAKUB
2012 Press Pass Autographs Red /10 #PPAKUB
2012 Press Pass Autographs Silver /20 #PPAKUB
2012 Press Pass Blue #6
2012 Press Pass Blue #70
2012 Press Pass Blue #71
2012 Press Pass Blue #85
2012 Press Pass Blue Holofoil /35 #6
2012 Press Pass Blue Holofoil /35 #70
2012 Press Pass Blue Holofoil /35 #71
2012 Press Pass Blue Holofoil /35 #85
2012 Press Pass Burning Rubber Gold /99 #BRKUB
2012 Press Pass Burning Rubber Holofoil /25 #BRKUB
2012 Press Pass Burning Rubber Prime Cuts /25 #BRKUB
2012 Press Pass Burning Rubber Purple /15 #BRKUB
2012 Press Pass Cup Chase #CCR5
2012 Press Pass Fanfare #8
2012 Press Pass Fanfare #47
2012 Press Pass Fanfare Autographs Blue /10 #KB1
2012 Press Pass Fanfare Autographs Blue /5 #KB2
2012 Press Pass Fanfare Autographs Gold /75 #KB1
2012 Press Pass Fanfare Autographs Gold /75 #KB2
2012 Press Pass Fanfare Autographs Red /50 #KB1
2012 Press Pass Fanfare Autographs Red /25 #KB2
2012 Press Pass Fanfare Autographs Silver /175 #KB1
2012 Press Pass Fanfare Autographs Silver /99 #KB2
2012 Press Pass Fanfare Blue Foil Die Cuts #8
2012 Press Pass Fanfare Blue Foil Die Cuts #47
2012 Press Pass Fanfare Diamond /5 #8
2012 Press Pass Fanfare Diamond /5 #47
2012 Press Pass Fanfare Dual Autographs /10 #BB2
2012 Press Pass Fanfare Holofoil Die Cuts #8
2012 Press Pass Fanfare Holofoil Die Cuts #47
2012 Press Pass Fanfare Magnificent Materials /250 #MMKUB
2012 Press Pass Fanfare Magnificent Materials /75 #MMKUB2
2012 Press Pass Fanfare Magnificent Materials Dual Swatches /50 #MMKUB
2012 Press Pass Fanfare Magnificent Materials Dual Swatches Melting /10 #MMKUB
2012 Press Pass Fanfare Magnificent Materials Gold /125 #MMKUB
2012 Press Pass Fanfare Magnificent Materials Gold /10 #MMKUB2
2012 Press Pass Fanfare Sapphire /20 #8
2012 Press Pass Fanfare Sapphire /20 #47
2012 Press Pass Fanfare Silver /25 #8
2012 Press Pass Fanfare Silver /25 #47
2012 Press Pass Gold #6
2012 Press Pass Gold #70
2012 Press Pass Gold #71
2012 Press Pass Gold #85
2012 Press Pass Ignite #9
2012 Press Pass Ignite #38
2012 Press Pass Ignite Materials Autographs Gun Metal /20 #IMKUB
2012 Press Pass Ignite Materials Autographs Red /5 #IMKUB
2012 Press Pass Ignite Materials Autographs Silver /125 #IMKUB
2012 Press Pass Ignite Materials Gun Metal /99 #IMKUB
2012 Press Pass Ignite Materials Red /10 #IMKUB
2012 Press Pass Ignite Materials Silver #IMKUB
2012 Press Pass Ignite Proofs Black and White /50 #9
2012 Press Pass Ignite Proofs Black and White /50 #38
2012 Press Pass Ignite Proofs Cyan #9
2012 Press Pass Ignite Proofs Cyan #38
2012 Press Pass Ignite Proofs Magenta #9
2012 Press Pass Ignite Proofs Magenta #38
2012 Press Pass Ignite Proofs Yellow /10 #9
2012 Press Pass Ignite Proofs Yellow /10 #38
2012 Press Pass Power Picks Blue /50 #2
2012 Press Pass Power Picks Blue /50 #31
2012 Press Pass Power Picks Blue /50 #68
2012 Press Pass Power Picks Gold /50 #2
2012 Press Pass Power Picks Gold /50 #31
2012 Press Pass Power Picks Gold /50 #68
2012 Press Pass Power Picks Holofoil /10 #2
2012 Press Pass Power Picks Holofoil /10 #31
2012 Press Pass Power Picks Holofoil /10 #68
2012 Press Pass Purple /35 #6
2012 Press Pass Purple /35 #70
2012 Press Pass Purple /35 #71
2012 Press Pass Purple /35 #85
2012 Press Pass Redline #9
2012 Press Pass Redline #40
2012 Press Pass Redline Black /99 #9
2012 Press Pass Redline Black /99 #40
2012 Press Pass Redline Cyan /50 #9
2012 Press Pass Redline Cyan /50 #40
2012 Press Pass Redline Magenta /15 #9
2012 Press Pass Redline Magenta /15 #40
2012 Press Pass Redline Signatures Blue /5 #RSKUB
2012 Press Pass Redline Signatures Gold /25 #RSKUB
2012 Press Pass Redline Signatures Holofoil /10 #RSKUB
2012 Press Pass Redline Signatures Melting /1 #RSKUB
2012 Press Pass Redline Signatures Red /50 #RSKUB
2012 Press Pass Redline Yellow /1 #9
2012 Press Pass Redline Yellow /1 #40
2012 Press Pass Showcar #SC8
2012 Press Pass Showcase /499 #6
2012 Press Pass Showcase Gold /125 #6
2012 Press Pass Showcase Green /5 #6
2012 Press Pass Showcase Melting /1 #6
2012 Press Pass Showcase Purple /1 #6
2012 Press Pass Showcase Red /25 #6
2012 Press Pass Showman #SM8
2012 Press Pass Signature Series Race Used /12 #PPAKUB
2012 Press Pass Snapshots #SS6
2012 Press Pass Ultimate Collection Blue Holofoil /25 #UCKUB
2012 Press Pass Ultimate Collection Holofoil /50 #UCKUB
2013 Press Pass #8
2013 Press Pass #47
2013 Press Pass Color Proofs Black #8
2013 Press Pass Color Proofs Black #47
2013 Press Pass Color Proofs Cyan /35 #8
2013 Press Pass Color Proofs Cyan /35 #47
2013 Press Pass Color Proofs Magenta #8
2013 Press Pass Color Proofs Magenta #47
2013 Press Pass Color Proofs Yellow /5 #8
2013 Press Pass Color Proofs Yellow /5 #47
2013 Press Pass Cup Chase #CC3
2013 Press Pass Cup Chase Prizes #CCP9
2013 Press Pass Fanfare #11
2013 Press Pass Fanfare Autographs Blue /1 #KUB
2013 Press Pass Fanfare Autographs Gold /15 #KUB
2013 Press Pass Fanfare Autographs Green /7 #KUB
2013 Press Pass Fanfare Autographs Red /10 #KUB
2013 Press Pass Fanfare Autographs Silver /35 #KUB
2013 Press Pass Fanfare Diamond Die Cuts /5 #11
2013 Press Pass Fanfare Green /3 #11
2013 Press Pass Fanfare Holofoil Die Cuts #11
2013 Press Pass Fanfare Magnificent Materials Gold /50 #KUB
2013 Press Pass Fanfare Magnificent Materials Jumbo Swatches /25 #KUB
2013 Press Pass Fanfare Magnificent Materials Silver /199 #KUB
2013 Press Pass Fanfare Red Foil Die Cuts #11
2013 Press Pass Fanfare Sapphire /20 #11
2013 Press Pass Fanfare Signature Ride Autographs /50 #KUB
2013 Press Pass Fanfare Signature Ride Autographs Blue /10 #KUB
2013 Press Pass Fanfare Signature Ride Autographs Red /25 #KUB
2013 Press Pass Fanfare Silver /25 #11
2013 Press Pass Ignite #7
2013 Press Pass Ignite Ink Black /75 #IIKUB
2013 Press Pass Ignite Ink Blue /20 #IIKUB
2013 Press Pass Ignite Ink Red /5 #IIKUB
2013 Press Pass Ignite Profile #11
2013 Press Pass Ignite Proofs Black and White /50 #7
2013 Press Pass Ignite Proofs Cyan #7
2013 Press Pass Ignite Proofs Magenta #7
2013 Press Pass Ignite Proofs Yellow /5 #7
2013 Press Pass Power Picks Blue /99 #2
2013 Press Pass Power Picks Blue /99 #31
2013 Press Pass Power Picks Gold /50 #2
2013 Press Pass Power Picks Gold /50 #31
2013 Press Pass Power Picks Holofoil /10 #2
2013 Press Pass Power Picks Holofoil /10 #31
2013 Press Pass Redline #11
2013 Press Pass Redline Black /99 #11
2013 Press Pass Redline Cyan /50 #11
2013 Press Pass Redline Magenta /15 #11
2013 Press Pass Redline Muscle Car Sheet Metal Blue /5 #MCMKUB
2013 Press Pass Redline Muscle Car Sheet Metal Gold /10 #MCMKUB
2013 Press Pass Redline Muscle Car Sheet Metal Melting /1 #MCMKUB
2013 Press Pass Redline Muscle Car Sheet Metal Red /50 #MCMKUB
2013 Press Pass Redline Muscle Car Sheet Metal Silver /25 #MCMKUB
2013 Press Pass Redline Signatures Blue /78 #RSKUB
2013 Press Pass Redline Signatures Gold /5 #RSKUB
2013 Press Pass Redline Signatures Holo /25 #RSKUB
2013 Press Pass Redline Signatures Melting /1 #RSKUB
2013 Press Pass Redline Signatures Red /99 #RSKUB
2013 Press Pass Redline Yellow /1 #11
2013 Press Pass Showcase /349 #6
2013 Press Pass Showcase /349 #30
2013 Press Pass Showcase Black /1 #6
2013 Press Pass Showcase Black /1 #30
2013 Press Pass Showcase Blue /25 #6
2013 Press Pass Showcase Blue /25 #30
2013 Press Pass Showcase Elite Exhibit Ink /25 #EEIKUB
2013 Press Pass Showcase Elite Exhibit Ink Blue /30 #EEIKUB
2013 Press Pass Showcase Elite Exhibit Ink Gold /10 #EEIKUB
2013 Press Pass Showcase Elite Exhibit Ink Melting /1 #EEIKUB
2013 Press Pass Showcase Elite Exhibit Ink Red /5 #EEIKUB
2013 Press Pass Showcase Gold /99 #6
2013 Press Pass Showcase Gold /99 #30
2013 Press Pass Showcase Green /20 #6
2013 Press Pass Showcase Green /20 #30
2013 Press Pass Showcase Prized Pieces /99 #PPMKUB
2013 Press Pass Showcase Prized Pieces Blue /20 #PPMKUB
2013 Press Pass Showcase Prized Pieces Gold /25 #PPMKUB
2013 Press Pass Showcase Prized Pieces Melting /5 #PPMKUB
2013 Press Pass Showcase Purple /13 #6
2013 Press Pass Showcase Purple /13 #30
2013 Press Pass Showcase Red /10 #6
2013 Press Pass Showcase Red /10 #30
2013 Press Pass Signings Blue /1 #KUB
2013 Press Pass Signings Gold /15 #KUB
2013 Press Pass Signings Holofoil /10 #KUB
2013 Press Pass Signings Printing Plates Black /1 #KUB
2013 Press Pass Signings Printing Plates Cyan /1 #KUB
2013 Press Pass Signings Printing Plates Magenta /1 #KUB
2013 Press Pass Signings Printing Plates Yellow /1 #KUB
2013 Press Pass Signings Silver /25 #KUB
2013 Total Memorabilia #7
2013 Total Memorabilia Black and White /99 #7
2013 Total Memorabilia Gold /275 #7
2013 Total Memorabilia Red #7
2014 Press Pass #6
2014 Press Pass #77
2014 Press Pass American Thunder #9
2014 Press Pass American Thunder #50
2014 Press Pass American Thunder Autographs Blue /10 #ATAKUB
2014 Press Pass American Thunder Autographs Red /5 #ATAKUB
2014 Press Pass American Thunder Autographs White /25 #ATAKUB
2014 Press Pass American Thunder Battle Armor Blue /25 #BAKUB
2014 Press Pass American Thunder Battle Armor Red /1 #BAKUB
2014 Press Pass American Thunder Battle Armor Silver /99 #BAKUB
2014 Press Pass American Thunder Black and White /50 #9
2014 Press Pass American Thunder Black and White /50 #50
2014 Press Pass American Thunder Brothers In Arms Autographs Blue /5 #BASHR
2014 Press Pass American Thunder Brothers In Arms Autographs Red /1 #BASHR
2014 Press Pass American Thunder Brothers In Arms Autographs White /10 #BASHR
2014 Press Pass American Thunder Brothers In Arms Relics Blue /25 #BASHR
2014 Press Pass American Thunder Brothers In Arms Relics Red /5 #BASHR
2014 Press Pass American Thunder Brothers In Arms Relics Silver /50 #BASHR
2014 Press Pass American Thunder Cyan #9
2014 Press Pass American Thunder Cyan #50
2014 Press Pass American Thunder Great American Treads Autographs Blue /25 #GATKUB
2014 Press Pass American Thunder Great American Treads Autographs Red /1 #GATKUB
2014 Press Pass American Thunder Magenta #9
2014 Press Pass American Thunder Magenta #50
2014 Press Pass American Thunder Yellow /5 #9
2014 Press Pass American Thunder Yellow /5 #50
2014 Press Pass Color Proofs Black /70 #6
2014 Press Pass Color Proofs Black /70 #77
2014 Press Pass Color Proofs Cyan /35 #6
2014 Press Pass Color Proofs Cyan /35 #77
2014 Press Pass Color Proofs Magenta #6
2014 Press Pass Color Proofs Magenta #77
2014 Press Pass Color Proofs Yellow /5 #6
2014 Press Pass Color Proofs Yellow /5 #77
2014 Press Pass Cup Chase #2
2014 Press Pass Five Star /15 #2
2014 Press Pass Five Star Blue /5 #2
2014 Press Pass Five Star Holofoil /10 #2
2014 Press Pass Five Star Melting /1 #2
2014 Press Pass Gold #6
2014 Press Pass Gold #77
2014 Press Pass Redline #11
2014 Press Pass Redline Black /75 #11
2014 Press Pass Redline Blue Foil #11

2014 Press Pass Redline Cyan /50 #11
2014 Press Pass Redline Dynamic Duals Relic Autographs Blue /10 #DDKUB
2014 Press Pass Redline Dynamic Duals Relic Autographs Gold /5 #DDKUB
2014 Press Pass Redline Dynamic Duals Relic Autographs Melting /1 #DDKUB
2014 Press Pass Redline Dynamic Duals Relic Autographs Red /15 #DDKUB
2014 Press Pass Redline Green National Convention /5 #11
2014 Press Pass Redline Magenta /10 #11
2014 Press Pass Redline Muscle Car Sheet Metal Blue /10 #MCMKUB
2014 Press Pass Redline Muscle Car Sheet Metal Gold /25 #MCMKUB
2014 Press Pass Redline Muscle Car Sheet Metal Melting /1 #MCMKUB
2014 Press Pass Redline Muscle Car Sheet Metal Red /50 #MCMKUB
2014 Press Pass Redline Redline Racers #RR1
2014 Press Pass Redline Relic Autographs Blue /10 #RRSEKUB
2014 Press Pass Redline Relic Autographs Gold /15 #RRSEKUB
2014 Press Pass Redline Relic Autographs Melting /1 #RRSEKUB
2014 Press Pass Redline Relic Autographs Red /25 #RRSEKUB
2014 Press Pass Redline Relics Blue /25 #RRKUB
2014 Press Pass Redline Relics Gold /50 #RRKUB
2014 Press Pass Redline Relics Melting /1 #RRKUB
2014 Press Pass Redline Relics Red /75 #RRKUB
2014 Press Pass Redline Signatures Blue /10 #RSKUB
2014 Press Pass Redline Signatures Gold /15 #RSKUB
2014 Press Pass Redline Signatures Melting /5 #RSKUB
2014 Press Pass Redline Signatures Red /25 #RSKUB
2014 Press Pass Redline Yellow /1 #11
2014 Press Pass Signings Gold /10 #PPSKUB
2014 Press Pass Signings Holofoil /5 #PPSKUB
2014 Press Pass Signings Melting /1 #PPSKUB
2014 Press Pass Signings Silver /50 #PPSKUB
2014 Press Pass Velocity #4
2014 Total Memorabilia #5
2014 Total Memorabilia Black and White /99 #5
2014 Total Memorabilia Dual Swatch Gold /150 #TMKuB
2014 Total Memorabilia Gold /175 #5
2014 Total Memorabilia Red #5
2014 Total Memorabilia Single Swatch Silver /275 #TMKuB
2014 Total Memorabilia Triple Swatch Blue /99 #TMKuB
2015 Press Pass #9
2015 Press Pass #62
2015 Press Pass #100
2015 Press Pass Burning Rubber Blue /50 #BRKUB
2015 Press Pass Burning Rubber Gold #BRKUB
2015 Press Pass Burning Rubber Green /10 #BRKUB
2015 Press Pass Burning Rubber Melting /1 #BRKUB
2015 Press Pass Championship Caliber Dual /25 #CCMKUB
2015 Press Pass Championship Caliber Quad /1 #CCMKUB
2015 Press Pass Championship Caliber Signature Edition Blue /25 #CCKUB
2015 Press Pass Championship Caliber Signature Edition Gold /50 #CCKUB
2015 Press Pass Championship Caliber Signature Edition Green /10 #CCKUB
2015 Press Pass Championship Caliber Signature Edition Melting /1 #CCKUB
2015 Press Pass Championship Caliber Single /50 #CCMKUB
2015 Press Pass Championship Caliber Triple /10 #CCMKUB
2015 Press Pass Cup Chase #9
2015 Press Pass Cup Chase #62
2015 Press Pass Cup Chase #100
2015 Press Pass Cup Chase Blue /25 #9
2015 Press Pass Cup Chase Blue /25 #62
2015 Press Pass Cup Chase Blue /25 #100
2015 Press Pass Cup Chase Gold /75 #9
2015 Press Pass Cup Chase Gold /75 #62
2015 Press Pass Cup Chase Gold /75 #100
2015 Press Pass Cup Chase Green /10 #9
2015 Press Pass Cup Chase Green /10 #62
2015 Press Pass Cup Chase Green /10 #100
2015 Press Pass Cup Chase Melting /1 #9
2015 Press Pass Cup Chase Melting /1 #62
2015 Press Pass Cup Chase Melting /1 #100
2015 Press Pass Cup Chase Three Wide Blue /25 #3WKUB
2015 Press Pass Cup Chase Three Wide Gold /50 #3WKUB
2015 Press Pass Cup Chase Three Wide Green /10 #3WKUB
2015 Press Pass Cup Chase Three Wide Melting /1 #3WKUB
2015 Press Pass Cup Chase Upper Cuts /13 #UCKUB
2015 Press Pass Four Wide Signature Edition Blue /25 #4WKUB
2015 Press Pass Four Wide Signature Edition Gold /50 #4WKUB
2015 Press Pass Four Wide Signature Edition Green /10 #4WKUB
2015 Press Pass Four Wide Signature Edition Melting /1 #4WKUB
2015 Press Pass Pit Road Pieces Blue /25 #PPMKUB
2015 Press Pass Pit Road Pieces Gold /50 #PPMKUB
2015 Press Pass Pit Road Pieces Green /10 #PPMKUB
2015 Press Pass Pit Road Pieces Melting /1 #PPMKUB
2015 Press Pass Pit Road Pieces Signature Edition Blue /25 #PRPKUB
2015 Press Pass Pit Road Pieces Signature Edition Gold /50 #PRPKUB
2015 Press Pass Pit Road Pieces Signature Edition Green /10 #PRPKUB
2015 Press Pass Pit Road Pieces Signature Edition Melting /1 #PRPKUB
2015 Press Pass Purple #9
2015 Press Pass Purple #62
2015 Press Pass Purple #100
2015 Press Pass Red #9
2015 Press Pass Red #62
2015 Press Pass Red #100
2015 Press Pass Signings Blue /25 #PPSKUB
2015 Press Pass Signings Gold #PPSKUB
2015 Press Pass Signings Green /10 #PPSKUB
2015 Press Pass Signings Melting /5 #PPSKUB
2015 Press Pass Signings Red /15 #PPSKUB
2016 Certified #3
2016 Certified Gold Team /199 #12
2016 Certified Gold Team Mirror Black /1 #12
2016 Certified Gold Team Mirror Blue /50 #12
2016 Certified Gold Team Mirror Gold /25 #12
2016 Certified Gold Team Mirror Green /5 #12
2016 Certified Gold Team Mirror Orange /99 #12
2016 Certified Gold Team Mirror Purple /10 #12
2016 Certified Gold Team Mirror Red /75 #12
2016 Certified Gold Team Mirror Silver /99 #12
2016 Certified Mirror Black /1 #3
2016 Certified Mirror Blue /50 #3
2016 Certified Mirror Gold /25 #3
2016 Certified Mirror Green /5 #3
2016 Certified Mirror Orange /99 #3
2016 Certified Mirror Purple /10 #3
2016 Certified Mirror Red /75 #3
2016 Certified Mirror Silver /99 #3
2016 Certified Signatures /139 #14
2016 Certified Signatures Mirror Black /1 #14
2016 Certified Signatures Mirror Blue /50 #14
2016 Certified Signatures Mirror Gold /25 #14
2016 Certified Signatures Mirror Green /5 #14
2016 Certified Signatures Mirror Orange /5 #14
2016 Certified Signatures Mirror Purple /10 #14
2016 Certified Signatures Mirror Red /60 #14
2016 Certified Signatures Mirror Silver /5 #14
2016 Certified Skills /199 #11
2016 Certified Skills Mirror Black /1 #11
2016 Certified Skills Mirror Blue /50 #11
2016 Certified Skills Mirror Gold /25 #11
2016 Certified Skills Mirror Green /5 #11
2016 Certified Skills Mirror Orange /99 #11
2016 Certified Skills Mirror Purple /10 #11
2016 Certified Skills Mirror Red /75 #11
2016 Certified Skills Mirror Silver /99 #11
2016 Certified Sprint Cup Swatches /299 #37
2016 Certified Sprint Cup Swatches Mirror Black /1 #37
2016 Certified Sprint Cup Swatches Mirror Blue /50 #37
2016 Certified Sprint Cup Swatches Mirror Gold /25 #37
2016 Certified Sprint Cup Swatches Mirror Green /5 #37
2016 Certified Sprint Cup Swatches Mirror Orange /149 #37
2016 Certified Sprint Cup Swatches Mirror Purple /10 #37
2016 Certified Sprint Cup Swatches Mirror Red /75 #37
2016 Certified Sprint Cup Swatches Mirror Silver /149 #37
2016 Panini National Treasures /25 #16
2016 Panini National Treasures Black /5 #16
2016 Panini National Treasures Blue /1 #16
2016 Panini National Treasures Championship Signature Threads /25 #6
2016 Panini National Treasures Championship Signature Threads Black /5 #6
2016 Panini National Treasures Championship Signature Threads Blue /1 #6
2016 Panini National Treasures Championship Signature Threads Gold /10 #6
2016 Panini National Treasures Championship Signature Threads Printing Plates Black /1 #6
2016 Panini National Treasures Championship Signature Threads Printing Plates Cyan /1 #6
2016 Panini National Treasures Championship Signature Threads Printing Plates Magenta /1 #6
2016 Panini National Treasures Championship Signature Threads Printing Plates Yellow /1 #6
2016 Panini National Treasures Championship Signature Threads Silver /15 #6
2016 Panini National Treasures Championship Signatures Black /5 #5
2016 Panini National Treasures Championship Signatures Blue /1 #5
2016 Panini National Treasures Championship Signatures Printing Plates Black /1 #5
2016 Panini National Treasures Championship Signatures Printing Plates Cyan /1 #5
2016 Panini National Treasures Championship Signatures Printing Plates Magenta /1 #5
2016 Panini National Treasures Championship Signatures Printing Plates Yellow /1 #5
2016 Panini National Treasures Combo Materials /25 #10
2016 Panini National Treasures Combo Materials Black /5 #10
2016 Panini National Treasures Combo Materials Blue /1 #10
2016 Panini National Treasures Combo Materials Gold /10 #10
2016 Panini National Treasures Combo Materials Printing Plates Black /1 #10
2016 Panini National Treasures Combo Materials Printing Plates Cyan /1 #10
2016 Panini National Treasures Combo Materials Printing Plates Magenta /1 #10
2016 Panini National Treasures Combo Materials Printing Plates Yellow /1 #10
2016 Panini National Treasures Combo Materials Silver /15 #10
2016 Panini National Treasures Dual Signatures /25 #10
2016 Panini National Treasures Dual Signatures Black /10 #10
2016 Panini National Treasures Dual Signatures Blue /1 #10
2016 Panini National Treasures Dual Signatures Gold /15 #10
2016 Panini National Treasures Eight Signatures /15 #1
2016 Panini National Treasures Eight Signatures Black /5 #1
2016 Panini National Treasures Eight Signatures Blue /1 #1
2016 Panini National Treasures Eight Signatures Gold /10 #1
2016 Panini National Treasures Gold /15 #16
2016 Panini National Treasures Jumbo Firesuit Patch Signature Booklet Alpine Stars /2 #16
2016 Panini National Treasures Jumbo Firesuit Patch Signature Booklet Associate Sponsor 1 /1 #16
2016 Panini National Treasures Jumbo Firesuit Patch Signature Booklet Associate Sponsor 2 /1 #16
2016 Panini National Treasures Jumbo Firesuit Patch Signature Booklet Associate Sponsor 3 /1 #16
2016 Panini National Treasures Jumbo Firesuit Patch Signature Booklet Associate Sponsor 4 /1 #16
2016 Panini National Treasures Jumbo Firesuit Patch Signature Booklet Associate Sponsor 5 /1 #16
2016 Panini National Treasures Jumbo Firesuit Patch Signature Booklet Associate Sponsor 6 /1 #16
2016 Panini National Treasures Jumbo Firesuit Patch Signature Booklet Associate Sponsor 7 /1 #16
2016 Panini National Treasures Jumbo Firesuit Patch Signature Booklet Associate Sponsor 8 /1 #16
2016 Panini National Treasures Jumbo Firesuit Patch Signature Booklet Associate Sponsor 9 /1 #16
2016 Panini National Treasures Jumbo Firesuit Patch Signature Booklet Goodyear /2 #16
2016 Panini National Treasures Jumbo Firesuit Patch Signature Booklet Manufacturers Logo /1 #16
2016 Panini National Treasures Jumbo Firesuit Patch Signature Booklet Nameplate /2 #16
2016 Panini National Treasures Jumbo Firesuit Patch Signature Booklet NASCAR /1 #16
2016 Panini National Treasures Jumbo Firesuit Patch Signature Booklet Sprint Cup Logo /1 #16
2016 Panini National Treasures Jumbo Firesuit Patch Signature Booklet Sunoco /1 #16
2016 Panini National Treasures Jumbo Firesuit Signatures /25 #16
2016 Panini National Treasures Jumbo Firesuit Signatures Black /5 #16
2016 Panini National Treasures Jumbo Firesuit Signatures Blue /1 #16
2016 Panini National Treasures Jumbo Firesuit Signatures Gold /10 #16
2016 Panini National Treasures Jumbo Firesuit Signatures Printing Plates Black /1 #16
2016 Panini National Treasures Jumbo Firesuit Signatures Printing Plates Cyan /1 #16
2016 Panini National Treasures Jumbo Firesuit Signatures Printing Plates Magenta /1 #16
2016 Panini National Treasures Jumbo Firesuit Signatures Printing Plates Yellow /1 #16
2016 Panini National Treasures Jumbo Firesuit Signatures Silver /15 #16
2016 Panini National Treasures Printing Plates Black /1 #16
2016 Panini National Treasures Printing Plates Cyan /1 #16
2016 Panini National Treasures Printing Plates Magenta /1 #16
2016 Panini National Treasures Printing Plates Yellow /1 #16
2016 Panini National Treasures Quad Driver Materials /25 #10
2016 Panini National Treasures Quad Driver Materials Black /5 #10
2016 Panini National Treasures Quad Driver Materials Blue /1 #10
2016 Panini National Treasures Quad Driver Materials Gold /10 #10
2016 Panini National Treasures Quad Driver Materials Printing Plates Black /1 #10
2016 Panini National Treasures Quad Driver Materials Printing Plates Cyan /1 #10
2016 Panini National Treasures Quad Driver Materials Printing Plates Magenta /1 #10
2016 Panini National Treasures Quad Driver Materials Printing Plates Yellow /1 #10
2016 Panini National Treasures Quad Driver Materials Silver /15 #10
2016 Panini National Treasures Signature Dual Materials Black /5 #16
2016 Panini National Treasures Signature Dual Materials Blue /1 #16
2016 Panini National Treasures Signature Dual Materials Printing Plates Black /1 #16
2016 Panini National Treasures Signature Dual Materials Printing Plates Cyan /1 #16
2016 Panini National Treasures Signature Dual Materials Printing Plates Magenta /1 #16
2016 Panini National Treasures Signature Dual Materials Printing Plates Yellow /1 #16
2016 Panini National Treasures Signature Firesuit Materials /25 #16
2016 Panini National Treasures Signature Firesuit Materials Black /5 #16
2016 Panini National Treasures Signature Firesuit Materials Blue /1 #16
2016 Panini National Treasures Signature Firesuit Materials Gold /10 #16
2016 Panini National Treasures Signature Firesuit Materials Laundry Tag /1 #16
2016 Panini National Treasures Signature Firesuit Materials Printing Plates Black /1 #16
2016 Panini National Treasures Signature Firesuit Materials Printing Plates Cyan /1 #16
2016 Panini National Treasures Signature Firesuit Materials Printing Plates Magenta /1 #16
2016 Panini National Treasures Signature Firesuit Materials Printing Plates Yellow /1 #16
2016 Panini National Treasures Signature Firesuit Materials Silver /15 #16
2016 Panini National Treasures Signature Quad Materials /20 #16
2016 Panini National Treasures Signature Quad Materials Black /5 #16
2016 Panini National Treasures Signature Quad Materials Blue /1 #16
2016 Panini National Treasures Signature Quad Materials Gold /10 #16
2016 Panini National Treasures Signature Quad Materials Printing Plates Black /1 #16
2016 Panini National Treasures Signature Quad Materials Printing Plates Cyan /1 #16
2016 Panini National Treasures Signature Quad Materials Printing Plates Magenta /1 #16
2016 Panini National Treasures Signature Quad Materials Printing Plates Yellow /1 #16
2016 Panini National Treasures Signature Quad Materials Silver /15 #16
2016 Panini National Treasures Signature Sheet Metal Materials /25 #16
2016 Panini National Treasures Signature Sheet Metal Materials Black /5 #16
2016 Panini National Treasures Signature Sheet Metal Materials Blue /1 #16
2016 Panini National Treasures Signature Sheet Metal Materials Gold /10 #16
2016 Panini National Treasures Signature Sheet Metal Materials Printing Plates Black /1 #16
2016 Panini National Treasures Signature Sheet Metal Materials Printing Plates Cyan /1 #16
2016 Panini National Treasures Signature Sheet Metal Materials Printing Plates Magenta /1 #16
2016 Panini National Treasures Signature Sheet Metal Materials Printing Plates Yellow /1 #16
2016 Panini National Treasures Signature Sheet Metal Materials Silver /15 #16
2016 Panini National Treasures Signatures Blue /1 #12
2016 Panini National Treasures Signatures Printing Plates Black /1 #12
2016 Panini National Treasures Signatures Printing Plates Cyan /1 #12
2016 Panini National Treasures Signatures Printing Plates Magenta /1 #12
2016 Panini National Treasures Signatures Printing Plates Yellow /1 #12
2016 Panini National Treasures Silver /20 #16
2016 Panini National Treasures Six Signatures /25 #5
2016 Panini National Treasures Six Signatures Black /10 #5
2016 Panini National Treasures Six Signatures Blue /1 #5
2016 Panini National Treasures Six Signatures Gold /15 #5
2016 Panini National Treasures Timelines /25 #9
2016 Panini National Treasures Timelines Black /5 #9
2016 Panini National Treasures Timelines Blue /1 #9
2016 Panini National Treasures Timelines Gold /10 #9
2016 Panini National Treasures Timelines Printing Plates Black /1 #9
2016 Panini National Treasures Timelines Printing Plates Cyan /1 #9
2016 Panini National Treasures Timelines Printing Plates Magenta /1 #9
2016 Panini National Treasures Timelines Printing Plates Yellow /1 #9
2016 Panini National Treasures Timelines Signatures Black /5 #7
2016 Panini National Treasures Timelines Signatures Blue /1 #7
2016 Panini National Treasures Timelines Signatures Gold /10 #7
2016 Panini National Treasures Timelines Signatures Printing Plates Black /1 #7
2016 Panini National Treasures Timelines Signatures Printing Plates Cyan /1 #7
2016 Panini National Treasures Timelines Signatures Printing Plates Magenta /1 #7
2016 Panini National Treasures Timelines Signatures Printing Plates Yellow /1 #7
2016 Panini National Treasures Timelines Silver /15 #9
2016 Panini National Treasures Winning Signatures Blue /1 #9
2016 Panini National Treasures Winning Signatures Printing Plates Black /1 #9
2016 Panini National Treasures Winning Signatures Printing Plates Cyan /1 #9
2016 Panini National Treasures Winning Signatures Printing Plates Magenta /1 #9
2016 Panini National Treasures Winning Signatures Printing Plates Yellow /1 #9
2016 Panini Prizm #30
2016 Panini Prizm #46
2016 Panini Prizm #68
2016 Panini Prizm Autographs Prizms #39
2016 Panini Prizm Autographs Prizms Black /3 #39
2016 Panini Prizm Autographs Prizms Blue Flag /25 #39
2016 Panini Prizm Autographs Prizms Camo /41 #39
2016 Panini Prizm Autographs Prizms Checkered Flag /1 #39
2016 Panini Prizm Autographs Prizms Gold /10 #39
2016 Panini Prizm Autographs Prizms Green Flag /50 #39
2016 Panini Prizm Autographs Prizms Rainbow /24 #39
2016 Panini Prizm Autographs Prizms Red Flag /15 #39
2016 Panini Prizm Autographs Prizms Red White and Blue /25 #39
2016 Panini Prizm Autographs Prizms White Flag /5 #39
2016 Panini Prizm Prizms #30
2016 Panini Prizm Prizms #46
2016 Panini Prizm Prizms #68
2016 Panini Prizm Prizms Black /3 #30
2016 Panini Prizm Prizms Black /3 #46
2016 Panini Prizm Prizms Black /3 #68
2016 Panini Prizm Prizms Blue Flag /99 #30
2016 Panini Prizm Prizms Blue Flag /99 #46
2016 Panini Prizm Prizms Blue Flag /99 #68
2016 Panini Prizm Prizms Camo /41 #30
2016 Panini Prizm Prizms Camo /41 #46
2016 Panini Prizm Prizms Camo /41 #68
2016 Panini Prizm Prizms Checkered Flag /1 #30
2016 Panini Prizm Prizms Checkered Flag /1 #46
2016 Panini Prizm Prizms Checkered Flag /1 #68
2016 Panini Prizm Prizms Gold /10 #30
2016 Panini Prizm Prizms Gold /10 #46
2016 Panini Prizm Prizms Gold /10 #68
2016 Panini Prizm Prizms Green Flag /149 #30
2016 Panini Prizm Prizms Green Flag /149 #46
2016 Panini Prizm Prizms Green Flag /149 #68
2016 Panini Prizm Prizms Rainbow /24 #30
2016 Panini Prizm Prizms Rainbow /24 #46
2016 Panini Prizm Prizms Rainbow /24 #68
2016 Panini Prizm Prizms Red Flag /75 #30
2016 Panini Prizm Prizms Red Flag /75 #46
2016 Panini Prizm Prizms Red Flag /75 #68
2016 Panini Prizm Prizms Red White and Blue #30
2016 Panini Prizm Prizms Red White and Blue #46
2016 Panini Prizm Prizms Red White and Blue #68
2016 Panini Prizm Prizms White Flag /5 #30
2016 Panini Prizm Prizms White Flag /5 #46
2016 Panini Prizm Prizms White Flag /5 #68
2016 Panini Prizm Race Used Tire #14
2016 Panini Prizm Race Used Tire Prizms Blue Flag /49 #14
2016 Panini Prizm Race Used Tire Prizms Checkered Flag /1 #14
2016 Panini Prizm Race Used Tire Prizms Green Flag /99 #14
2016 Panini Prizm Race Used Tire Prizms Red Flag /25 #14
2016 Panini Prizm Race Used Tire Team #13
2016 Panini Prizm Race Used Tire Team Prizms Blue Flag /75 #13
2016 Panini Prizm Race Used Tire Team Prizms Checkered Flag /1 #13
2016 Panini Prizm Race Used Tire Team Prizms Green Flag /149 #13
2016 Panini Prizm Race Used Tire Team Prizms Red Flag /10 #13
2016 Panini Prizm Raising the Flag #12
2016 Panini Prizm Raising the Flag Prizms #12
2016 Panini Prizm Raising the Flag Prizms Checkered Flag /1 #12
2016 Panini Prizm Raising the Flag Prizms Gold /10 #12
2016 Panini Prizm Winner's Circle #9
2016 Panini Prizm Winner's Circle #15
2016 Panini Prizm Winner's Circle Prizms #9
2016 Panini Prizm Winner's Circle Prizms #15
2016 Panini Prizm Winner's Circle Prizms Checkered Flag /1 #9
2016 Panini Prizm Winner's Circle Prizms Checkered Flag /1 #15
2016 Panini Prizm Winner's Circle Prizms Gold /10 #9
2016 Panini Prizm Winner's Circle Prizms Gold /10 #15
2016 Panini Torque #9
2016 Panini Torque #85
2016 Panini Torque Artist Proof /50 #9
2016 Panini Torque Artist Proof /50 #85
2016 Panini Torque Blackout /1 #9
2016 Panini Torque Blackout /1 #85
2016 Panini Torque Blue /125 #9
2016 Panini Torque Blue /125 #85
2016 Panini Torque Championship Vision #9
2016 Panini Torque Championship Vision Blue /99 #9
2016 Panini Torque Championship Vision Gold /149 #9
2016 Panini Torque Championship Vision Green /25 #9
2016 Panini Torque Championship Vision Purple /10 #9
2016 Panini Torque Championship Vision Red /49 #9
2016 Panini Torque Clear Vision #9
2016 Panini Torque Clear Vision Blue /99 #9
2016 Panini Torque Clear Vision Gold /149 #9
2016 Panini Torque Clear Vision Green /25 #9
2016 Panini Torque Clear Vision Purple /10 #9
2016 Panini Torque Clear Vision Red /49 #9
2016 Panini Torque Gold #9
2016 Panini Torque Gold #85
2016 Panini Torque Holo Gold /5 #9
2016 Panini Torque Holo Gold /5 #85
2016 Panini Torque Holo Silver /10 #9
2016 Panini Torque Holo Silver /10 #85
2016 Panini Torque Horsepower Heroes #8
2016 Panini Torque Horsepower Heroes Gold /199 #8
2016 Panini Torque Horsepower Heroes Holo Silver /99 #8
2016 Panini Torque Jumbo Firesuit Autographs /30 #8
2016 Panini Torque Jumbo Firesuit Autographs Blue /25 #8
2016 Panini Torque Jumbo Firesuit Autographs Green /15 #8
2016 Panini Torque Jumbo Firesuit Autographs Purple /10 #8
2016 Panini Torque Jumbo Firesuit Autographs Red /20 #8
2016 Panini Torque Pole Position #9
2016 Panini Torque Pole Position Blue /99 #9
2016 Panini Torque Pole Position Checkerboard /10 #9
2016 Panini Torque Pole Position Green /25 #9
2016 Panini Torque Pole Position Red /49 #9
2016 Panini Torque Printing Plates Black /1 #9
2016 Panini Torque Printing Plates Black /1 #85
2016 Panini Torque Printing Plates Cyan /1 #9
2016 Panini Torque Printing Plates Cyan /1 #85
2016 Panini Torque Printing Plates Magenta /1 #9
2016 Panini Torque Printing Plates Magenta /1 #85
2016 Panini Torque Printing Plates Yellow /1 #9
2016 Panini Torque Printing Plates Yellow /1 #85
2016 Panini Torque Purple /25 #9
2016 Panini Torque Purple /25 #85
2016 Panini Torque Red /99 #9
2016 Panini Torque Red /99 #85
2016 Panini Torque Rubber Relics /399 #16
2016 Panini Torque Rubber Relics Blue /99 #16
2016 Panini Torque Rubber Relics Green /25 #16
2016 Panini Torque Rubber Relics Purple /10 #16
2016 Panini Torque Rubber Relics Red /49 #16
2016 Panini Torque Shades #13
2016 Panini Torque Shades Gold /199 #13
2016 Panini Torque Shades Holo Silver /99 #13
2016 Panini Torque Silhouettes Firesuit Autographs /30 #15
2016 Panini Torque Silhouettes Firesuit Autographs Blue /25 #15
2016 Panini Torque Silhouettes Firesuit Autographs Green /15 #15
2016 Panini Torque Silhouettes Firesuit Autographs Purple /10 #15
2016 Panini Torque Silhouettes Firesuit Autographs Red /20 #15
2016 Panini Torque Silhouettes Sheet Metal Autographs /30 #18
2016 Panini Torque Silhouettes Sheet Metal Autographs Blue /25 #18
2016 Panini Torque Silhouettes Sheet Metal Autographs Green /15 #18
2016 Panini Torque Silhouettes Sheet Metal Autographs Purple /10 #18
2016 Panini Torque Silhouettes Sheet Metal Autographs Red /20 #18
2016 Panini Torque Superstar Vision #19
2016 Panini Torque Superstar Vision Blue /99 #19
2016 Panini Torque Superstar Vision Gold /149 #19
2016 Panini Torque Superstar Vision Green /25 #19
2016 Panini Torque Superstar Vision Purple /10 #19
2016 Panini Torque Superstar Vision Red /49 #19
2016 Panini Torque Test Proof Black /1 #9
2016 Panini Torque Test Proof Black /1 #85
2016 Panini Torque Test Proof Cyan /1 #9
2016 Panini Torque Test Proof Cyan /1 #85
2016 Panini Torque Test Proof Magenta /1 #9
2016 Panini Torque Test Proof Magenta /1 #85
2016 Panini Torque Test Proof Yellow /1 #9
2016 Panini Torque Test Proof Yellow /1 #85
2016 Panini Torque Victory Laps #14
2016 Panini Torque Victory Laps Gold /199 #14
2016 Panini Torque Victory Laps Holo Silver /99 #14
2016 Panini Torque Winning Vision #9
2016 Panini Torque Winning Vision Blue /99 #9
2016 Panini Torque Winning Vision Gold /149 #9
2016 Panini Torque Winning Vision Green /25 #9
2016 Panini Torque Winning Vision Purple /10 #9
2016 Panini Torque Winning Vision Red /49 #9
2017 Donruss #11
2017 Donruss #48
2017 Donruss #128
2017 Donruss #175
2017 Donruss #48B
2017 Donruss Artist Proof /25 #11
2017 Donruss Artist Proof /25 #48A
2017 Donruss Artist Proof /25 #128
2017 Donruss Artist Proof /25 #175
2017 Donruss Artist Proof /25 #48B
2017 Donruss Blue Foil /299 #11
2017 Donruss Blue Foil /299 #128
2017 Donruss Blue Foil /299 #48A
2017 Donruss Blue Foil /299 #175
2017 Donruss Blue Foil /299 #48B
2017 Donruss Dual Rubber Relics #11
2017 Donruss Dual Rubber Relics Holo Black /1 #11
2017 Donruss Dual Rubber Relics Holo Gold /25 #11
2017 Donruss Gold Foil /499 #11
2017 Donruss Gold Foil /499 #128
2017 Donruss Gold Foil /499 #175
2017 Donruss Gold Foil /499 #48A
2017 Donruss Gold Foil /499 #48B
2017 Donruss Gold Press Proof /99 #11
2017 Donruss Gold Press Proof /99 #48A
2017 Donruss Gold Press Proof /99 #128
2017 Donruss Gold Press Proof /99 #175
2017 Donruss Gold Press Proof /99 #48B
2017 Donruss Green Foil /199 #11
2017 Donruss Green Foil /199 #48A
2017 Donruss Green Foil /199 #128
2017 Donruss Green Foil /199 #175
2017 Donruss Green Foil /199 #48B
2017 Donruss Press Proof /49 #11
2017 Donruss Press Proof /49 #48A
2017 Donruss Press Proof /49 #128
2017 Donruss Press Proof /49 #175
2017 Donruss Press Proof /49 #48B
2017 Donruss Printing Plates Black /1 #11
2017 Donruss Printing Plates Black /1 #48A
2017 Donruss Printing Plates Black /1 #128
2017 Donruss Printing Plates Black /1 #175
2017 Donruss Printing Plates Black /1 #48B
2017 Donruss Printing Plates Cyan /1 #11
2017 Donruss Printing Plates Cyan /1 #48A
2017 Donruss Printing Plates Cyan /1 #128
2017 Donruss Printing Plates Cyan /1 #175
2017 Donruss Printing Plates Cyan /1 #48B
2017 Donruss Printing Plates Magenta /1 #11
2017 Donruss Printing Plates Magenta /1 #128
2017 Donruss Printing Plates Magenta /1 #175
2017 Donruss Printing Plates Magenta /1 #48A
2017 Donruss Printing Plates Magenta /1 #48B
2017 Donruss Printing Plates Yellow /1 #11
2017 Donruss Printing Plates Yellow /1 #128
2017 Donruss Printing Plates Yellow /1 #175
2017 Donruss Printing Plates Yellow /1 #48A
2017 Donruss Printing Plates Yellow /1 #48B
2017 Donruss Retro Relics 1984 #27
2017 Donruss Retro Relics 1984 Holo Black /10 #27
2017 Donruss Retro Relics 1984 Holo Gold /99 #27
2017 Donruss Rubber Relics #32
2017 Donruss Rubber Relics Holo Black /1 #32
2017 Donruss Rubber Relics Holo Gold /35 #32
2017 Donruss Significant Signatures #9
2017 Donruss Significant Signatures Holo Black /1 #9
2017 Donruss Significant Signatures Holo Gold /25 #9
2017 Donruss Top Tier #12
2017 Donruss Top Tier Cracked Ice /999 #12
2017 Donruss Track Masters #10
2017 Donruss Track Masters Cracked Ice /999 #10
2017 Panini Black Friday Happy Holiday Memorabilia #HHKTB
2017 Panini Black Friday Happy Holiday Memorabilia Cracked Ice /25 #HHKTB
2017 Panini Black Friday Happy Holiday Memorabilia Galactic Windows /10 #HHKTB
2017 Panini Black Friday Happy Holiday Memorabilia Hyperplaid /1 #HHKTB
2017 Panini Day Memorabilia #41
2017 Panini Day Memorabilia Galactic Window /25 #41
2017 Panini Day Memorabilia Hyperplaid /1 #41
2017 Panini Father's Day /499 #KB
2017 Panini Father's Day Autographs /25 #KB
2017 Panini Father's Day Cracked Ice /25 #KB
2017 Panini Father's Day Foil /50 #KB
2017 Panini Father's Day Future Frames /10 #KB
2017 Panini Father's Day Hyperplaid /1 #KB
2017 Panini Father's Day Lava Flow /5 #KB
2017 Panini Father's Day Thick Stock /25 #KB
2017 Panini Instant Nascar /90 #1
2017 Panini Instant Nascar Black /1 #1
2017 Panini Instant Nascar Green /10 #1
2017 Panini National Convention #R11
2017 Panini National Convention Autographs #R11
2017 Panini National Convention Autographs Hyperplaid /1 #R11
2017 Panini National Convention Escher Squares /25 #R11
2017 Panini National Convention Escher Squares Thick Stock /10 #R11
2017 Panini National Convention Galatic Windows /5 #R11
2017 Panini National Convention Hyperplaid /1 #R11
2017 Panini National Convention Pyramids /10 #R11
2017 Panini National Convention Rainbow Spokes /49 #R11
2017 Panini National Convention Rainbow Spokes Thick Stock /25 #R11
2017 Panini National Convention Rapture /99 #R11
2017 Panini National Treasures Associate Sponsor Patch Signatures 1 /1 #22
2017 Panini National Treasures Associate Sponsor Patch Signatures 2 /1 #22
2017 Panini National Treasures Associate Sponsor Patch Signatures 3 /1 #22
2017 Panini National Treasures Associate Sponsor Patch Signatures 5 /1 #22
2017 Panini National Treasures Car Manufacturer Patch Signatures /1 #22
2017 Panini National Treasures Dual Sheet Metal Materials Black /1 #11
2017 Panini National Treasures Dual Sheet Metal Materials Printing Plates Black /1 #11
2017 Panini National Treasures Dual Sheet Metal Materials Printing Plates Cyan /1 #11
2017 Panini National Treasures Dual Sheet Metal Materials Printing Plates Magenta /1 #11
2017 Panini National Treasures Dual Sheet Metal Materials Printing Plates Yellow /1 #11
2017 Panini National Treasures Dual Tire Signatures /25 #7
2017 Panini National Treasures Dual Tire Signatures Black /1 #7
2017 Panini National Treasures Dual Tire Signatures Gold /15 #7
2017 Panini National Treasures Dual Tire Signatures Green /5 #7
2017 Panini National Treasures Dual Tire Signatures Holo Gold /10 #7
2017 Panini National Treasures Dual Tire Signatures Holo Silver /20 #7
2017 Panini National Treasures Dual Tire Signatures Printing Plates Black /1 #7
2017 Panini National Treasures Dual Tire Signatures Printing Plates Cyan /1 #7
2017 Panini National Treasures Dual Tire Signatures Printing Plates Magenta /1 #7
2017 Panini National Treasures Dual Tire Signatures Printing Plates Yellow /1 #7
2017 Panini National Treasures Firesuit Manufacturer Patch Signatures /1 #22
2017 Panini National Treasures Hats Off /13 #2
2017 Panini National Treasures Hats Off Gold /2 #2
2017 Panini National Treasures Hats Off Holo Gold /5 #2
2017 Panini National Treasures Hats Off Holo Silver /1 #2
2017 Panini National Treasures Hats Off Laundry Tag /6 #2
2017 Panini National Treasures Hats Off Monster Energy Cup /14 #1
2017 Panini National Treasures Hats Off Monster Energy Cup Gold /4 #1
2017 Panini National Treasures Hats Off Monster Energy Cup Holo Gold /5 #1
2017 Panini National Treasures Hats Off Monster Energy Cup Holo Silver /1 #1
2017 Panini National Treasures Hats Off Monster Energy Cup Laundry Tag /3 #1
2017 Panini National Treasures Hats Off Monster Energy Cup New Era /1 #1
2017 Panini National Treasures Hats Off Monster Energy Cup Printing Plates Black /1 #1
2017 Panini National Treasures Hats Off Monster Energy Cup Printing Plates Cyan /1 #1
2017 Panini National Treasures Hats Off Monster Energy Cup Printing Plates Magenta /1 #1
2017 Panini National Treasures Hats Off Monster Energy Cup Printing Plates Yellow /1 #1
2017 Panini National Treasures Hats Off Monster Energy Cup Sponsor /5 #1
2017 Panini National Treasures Hats Off New Era /1 #2
2017 Panini National Treasures Hats Off Printing Plates Black /1 #2
2017 Panini National Treasures Hats Off Printing Plates Cyan /1 #2
2017 Panini National Treasures Hats Off Printing Plates Magenta /1 #2
2017 Panini National Treasures Hats Off Sponsor /5 #2
2017 Panini National Treasures Jumbo Firesuit Signatures Black /1 #11
2017 Panini National Treasures Jumbo Firesuit Signatures Green /5 #11
2017 Panini National Treasures Jumbo Firesuit Signatures Holo Gold /10 #11
2017 Panini National Treasures Jumbo Firesuit Signatures Laundry Tag /1 #11
2017 Panini National Treasures Jumbo Firesuit Signatures Printing Plates Black /1 #11
2017 Panini National Treasures Jumbo Firesuit Signatures Printing Plates Cyan /1 #11
2017 Panini National Treasures Jumbo Firesuit Signatures Printing Plates Magenta /1 #11
2017 Panini National Treasures Jumbo Firesuit Signatures Printing Plates Yellow /1 #11
2017 Panini National Treasures Nameplate Patch Signatures /2 #22
2017 Panini National Treasures NASCAR Patch Signatures /1 #22
2017 Panini National Treasures Quad Material Signatures /25 #8
2017 Panini National Treasures Quad Material Signatures Black /1 #8
2017 Panini National Treasures Quad Material Signatures Gold /15 #8
2017 Panini National Treasures Quad Material Signatures Green /5 #8
2017 Panini National Treasures Quad Material Signatures Holo Gold /10 #8
2017 Panini National Treasures Quad Material Signatures Holo Silver /20 #8
2017 Panini National Treasures Quad Material Signatures Laundry Tag /1 #8
2017 Panini National Treasures Quad Material Signatures Printing Plates Black /1 #8
2017 Panini National Treasures Quad Material Signatures Printing Plates Cyan /1 #8
2017 Panini National Treasures Quad Material Signatures Printing Plates Magenta /1 #8
2017 Panini National Treasures Quad Material Signatures Printing Plates Yellow /1 #8
2017 Panini National Treasures Quad Materials Black /1 #9
2017 Panini National Treasures Quad Materials Laundry Tag /1 #9
2017 Panini National Treasures Quad Materials Printing Plates Black /1 #9
2017 Panini National Treasures Quad Materials Printing Plates Cyan /1 #9
2017 Panini National Treasures Quad Materials Printing Plates Magenta /1 #9
2017 Panini National Treasures Quad Materials Printing Plates Yellow /1 #9
2017 Panini National Treasures Series Sponsor Patch Signatures /1 #22
2017 Panini National Treasures Teammates Dual Materials /25 #3
2017 Panini National Treasures Teammates Dual Materials Black /1 #3
2017 Panini National Treasures Teammates Dual Materials Gold /15 #3
2017 Panini National Treasures Teammates Dual Materials Green /5 #3
2017 Panini National Treasures Teammates Dual Materials Holo Gold /10 #3
2017 Panini National Treasures Teammates Dual Materials Holo Silver /20 #3
2017 Panini National Treasures Teammates Dual Materials Laundry Tag /1 #3
2017 Panini National Treasures Teammates Dual Materials Printing Plates Black /1 #3
2017 Panini National Treasures Teammates Dual Materials Printing Plates Cyan /1 #3
2017 Panini National Treasures Teammates Dual Materials Printing Plates Magenta /1 #3
2017 Panini National Treasures Teammates Dual Materials Printing Plates Yellow /1 #3
2017 Panini National Treasures Teammates Quad Materials /25 #6
2017 Panini National Treasures Teammates Quad Materials Black /1 #6
2017 Panini National Treasures Teammates Quad Materials Gold /15 #6
2017 Panini National Treasures Teammates Quad Materials Green /5 #6
2017 Panini National Treasures Teammates Quad Materials Holo Gold /10 #6
2017 Panini National Treasures Teammates Quad Materials Holo Silver /20 #6
2017 Panini National Treasures Teammates Quad Materials Laundry Tag /1 #6
2017 Panini National Treasures Teammates Quad Materials Printing Plates Black /1 #6
2017 Panini National Treasures Teammates Quad Materials Printing Plates Cyan /1 #6
2017 Panini National Treasures Teammates Quad Materials Printing Plates Magenta /1 #6
2017 Panini National Treasures Teammates Quad Materials Printing Plates Yellow /1 #6
2017 Panini National Treasures Winning Material Signatures Black /1 #7
2017 Panini National Treasures Winning Material Signatures Gold /15 #7
2017 Panini National Treasures Winning Material Signatures Green /5 #7
2017 Panini National Treasures Winning Material Signatures Holo Gold /10 #7
2017 Panini National Treasures Winning Material Signatures Holo Silver /20 #7
2017 Panini National Treasures Winning Material Signatures Laundry Tag /1 #7
2017 Panini National Treasures Winning Material Signatures Printing Plates Black /1 #7
2017 Panini National Treasures Winning Material Signatures Printing Plates Cyan /1 #7
2017 Panini National Treasures Winning Material Signatures Printing Plates Magenta /1 #7
2017 Panini National Treasures Winning Material Signatures Printing Plates Yellow /1 #7
2017 Panini National Treasures Winning Signatures /25 #13
2017 Panini National Treasures Winning Signatures Black /1 #13
2017 Panini National Treasures Winning Signatures Gold /15 #13
2017 Panini National Treasures Winning Signatures Green /5 #13
2017 Panini National Treasures Winning Signatures Holo Gold /10 #13
2017 Panini National Treasures Winning Signatures Holo Silver /20 #13
2017 Panini National Treasures Winning Signatures Printing Plates Black /1 #13
2017 Panini National Treasures Winning Signatures Printing Plates Cyan /1 #13
2017 Panini National Treasures Winning Signatures Printing Plates Magenta /1 #13
2017 Panini National Treasures Winning Signatures Printing Plates Yellow /1 #13
2017 Panini Torque #26
2017 Panini Torque #84
2017 Panini Torque Artist Proof /75 #26
2017 Panini Torque Artist Proof /75 #84
2017 Panini Torque Blackout /1 #26
2017 Panini Torque Blackout /1 #84
2017 Panini Torque Blue /150 #26
2017 Panini Torque Blue /150 #84
2017 Panini Torque Clear Vision #26
2017 Panini Torque Clear Vision Blue /99 #26
2017 Panini Torque Clear Vision Gold /149 #26
2017 Panini Torque Clear Vision Green /25 #26
2017 Panini Torque Clear Vision Purple /10 #26
2017 Panini Torque Clear Vision Red /49 #26
2017 Panini Torque Combo Materials Signatures /51 #7
2017 Panini Torque Combo Materials Signatures Blue /49 #7
2017 Panini Torque Combo Materials Signatures Green /15 #7
2017 Panini Torque Combo Materials Signatures Purple /10 #7
2017 Panini Torque Combo Materials Signatures Red /25 #7
2017 Panini Torque Gold #26
2017 Panini Torque Gold #84
2017 Panini Torque Holo Gold /10 #26
2017 Panini Torque Holo Gold /10 #84
2017 Panini Torque Holo Silver /25 #26
2017 Panini Torque Holo Silver /25 #84
2017 Panini Torque Horsepower Heroes #24
2017 Panini Torque Horsepower Heroes Gold /199 #24
2017 Panini Torque Horsepower Heroes Holo Silver /99 #24
2017 Panini Torque Jumbo Firesuit Signatures /51 #18
2017 Panini Torque Jumbo Firesuit Signatures Blue /49 #18
2017 Panini Torque Jumbo Firesuit Signatures Green /15 #18
2017 Panini Torque Jumbo Firesuit Signatures Purple /10 #18
2017 Panini Torque Jumbo Firesuit Signatures Red /25 #18
2017 Panini Torque Manufacturer Marks #8
2017 Panini Torque Manufacturer Marks Gold /199 #8
2017 Panini Torque Manufacturer Marks Holo Silver /99 #8
2017 Panini Torque Metal Materials /299 #10
2017 Panini Torque Metal Materials Blue /49 #10
2017 Panini Torque Metal Materials Green /10 #10
2017 Panini Torque Metal Materials Purple /1 #10
2017 Panini Torque Metal Materials Red /25 #10
2017 Panini Torque Pairings Materials /199 #5
2017 Panini Torque Pairings Materials Blue /99 #5
2017 Panini Torque Pairings Materials Green /25 #5
2017 Panini Torque Pairings Materials Purple /10 #5

2017 Panini Torque Pairings Materials Red /49 #5
2017 Panini Torque Prime Associate Sponsors Jumbo Patches /1 #13A
2017 Panini Torque Prime Associate Sponsors Jumbo Patches /1 #13B
2017 Panini Torque Prime Associate Sponsors Jumbo Patches /1 #13C
2017 Panini Torque Prime Associate Sponsors Jumbo Patches /1 #13D
2017 Panini Torque Prime Associate Sponsors Jumbo Patches /1 #13E
2017 Panini Torque Prime Associate Sponsors Jumbo Patches /1 #13F
2017 Panini Torque Prime Associate Sponsors Jumbo Patches /1 #13G
2017 Panini Torque Prime Associate Sponsors Jumbo Patches /1 #13H
2017 Panini Torque Prime Associate Sponsors Jumbo Patches /1 #13I
2017 Panini Torque Prime Associate Sponsors Jumbo Patches /1 #13J
2017 Panini Torque Prime Associate Sponsors Jumbo Patches /1 #13K
2017 Panini Torque Prime Goodyear Jumbo Patches /2 #13
2017 Panini Torque Prime Manufacturer Jumbo Patches /1 #13
2017 Panini Torque Prime Nameplates Jumbo Patches /2 #13
2017 Panini Torque Prime NASCAR Jumbo Patches /1 #13
2017 Panini Torque Prime Series Sponsor Jumbo Patches /1 #13
2017 Panini Torque Printing Plates Black /1 #26
2017 Panini Torque Printing Plates Black /1 #84
2017 Panini Torque Printing Plates Cyan /1 #26
2017 Panini Torque Printing Plates Cyan /1 #84
2017 Panini Torque Printing Plates Magenta /1 #26
2017 Panini Torque Printing Plates Magenta /1 #84
2017 Panini Torque Printing Plates Yellow /1 #26
2017 Panini Torque Printing Plates Yellow /1 #84
2017 Panini Torque Purple /50 #26
2017 Panini Torque Purple /50 #84
2017 Panini Torque Quad Materials /99 #18
2017 Panini Torque Quad Materials Blue /49 #18
2017 Panini Torque Quad Materials Green /10 #18
2017 Panini Torque Quad Materials Purple /1 #18
2017 Panini Torque Quad Materials Red /25 #18
2017 Panini Torque Raced Relics /499 #14
2017 Panini Torque Raced Relics Blue /99 #14
2017 Panini Torque Raced Relics Green /25 #14
2017 Panini Torque Raced Relics Purple /10 #14
2017 Panini Torque Raced Relics Red /49 #14
2017 Panini Torque Red /100 #26
2017 Panini Torque Red /100 #84
2017 Panini Torque Running Order #7
2017 Panini Torque Running Order Blue /99 #7
2017 Panini Torque Running Order Checkerboard /10 #7
2017 Panini Torque Running Order Green /25 #7
2017 Panini Torque Running Order Red /49 #7
2017 Panini Torque Test Proof Black /1 #26
2017 Panini Torque Test Proof Black /1 #84
2017 Panini Torque Test Proof Cyan /1 #26
2017 Panini Torque Test Proof Cyan /1 #84
2017 Panini Torque Test Proof Magenta /1 #26
2017 Panini Torque Test Proof Magenta /1 #84
2017 Panini Torque Test Proof Yellow /1 #26
2017 Panini Torque Test Proof Yellow /1 #84
2017 Panini Torque Track Vision #5
2017 Panini Torque Track Vision Blue /99 #5
2017 Panini Torque Track Vision Gold /149 #5
2017 Panini Torque Track Vision Green /25 #5
2017 Panini Torque Track Vision Purple /10 #5
2017 Panini Torque Track Vision Red /49 #5
2017 Panini Torque Victory Laps #10
2017 Panini Torque Victory Laps Gold /199 #10
2017 Panini Torque Victory Laps Holo Silver /99 #10
2017 Panini Torque Visions of Greatness #23
2017 Panini Torque Visions of Greatness Blue /99 #23
2017 Panini Torque Visions of Greatness Gold /149 #23
2017 Panini Torque Visions of Greatness Green /25 #23
2017 Panini Torque Visions of Greatness Purple /10 #23
2017 Panini Torque Visions of Greatness Red /49 #23
2017 Select #17
2017 Select #18
2017 Select #113
2017 Select Prizms Black /3 #17
2017 Select Prizms Black /3 #18
2017 Select Prizms Black /3 #113
2017 Select Prizms Blue /199 #17
2017 Select Prizms Blue /199 #18
2017 Select Prizms Checkered Flag /1 #17
2017 Select Prizms Checkered Flag /1 #18
2017 Select Prizms Checkered Flag /1 #113
2017 Select Prizms Gold /10 #17
2017 Select Prizms Gold /10 #18
2017 Select Prizms Gold /10 #113
2017 Select Prizms Purple Pulsar #17
2017 Select Prizms Purple Pulsar #18
2017 Select Prizms Red /99 #17
2017 Select Prizms Red /99 #18
2017 Select Prizms Red White and Blue Pulsar /299 #17
2017 Select Prizms Red White and Blue Pulsar /299 #18
2017 Select Prizms Silver #17
2017 Select Prizms Silver #18
2017 Select Prizms Tie Dye /24 #17
2017 Select Prizms Tie Dye /24 #18
2017 Select Prizms Tie Dye /24 #113
2017 Select Prizms White /50 #17
2017 Select Prizms White /50 #18
2017 Select Prizms White /50 #113
2017 Select Select Pairs Materials #9
2017 Select Select Pairs Materials #11
2017 Select Select Pairs Materials #12
2017 Select Select Pairs Materials Prizms Blue /199 #9
2017 Select Select Pairs Materials Prizms Blue /199 #11
2017 Select Select Pairs Materials Prizms Blue /199 #12
2017 Select Select Pairs Materials Prizms Checkered Flag /1 #9
2017 Select Select Pairs Materials Prizms Checkered Flag /1 #11
2017 Select Select Pairs Materials Prizms Checkered Flag /1 #12
2017 Select Select Pairs Materials Prizms Gold /10 #9
2017 Select Select Pairs Materials Prizms Gold /10 #11
2017 Select Select Pairs Materials Prizms Gold /10 #12
2017 Select Select Pairs Materials Prizms Red /99 #9
2017 Select Select Pairs Materials Prizms Red /99 #11
2017 Select Select Pairs Materials Prizms Red /99 #12
2017 Select Select Stars #16
2017 Select Select Stars Prizms Black /3 #16
2017 Select Select Stars Prizms Checkered Flag /1 #16
2017 Select Select Stars Prizms Gold /10 #16
2017 Select Select Stars Prizms Tie Dye /24 #16
2017 Select Select Stars Prizms White /50 #16
2017 Select Select Swatches #28
2017 Select Select Swatches Prizms Blue /50 #28
2017 Select Select Swatches Prizms Checkered Flag /1 #28
2017 Select Select Swatches Prizms Gold /10 #28
2017 Select Select Swatches Prizms Red /25 #28
2017 Select Sheet Metal #16
2017 Select Sheet Metal Prizms Blue /99 #16
2017 Select Sheet Metal Prizms Checkered Flag /1 #16
2017 Select Sheet Metal Prizms Gold /10 #16
2017 Select Sheet Metal Prizms Red /49 #16
2017 Select Signature Paint Schemes #10
2017 Select Signature Paint Schemes Prizms Blue /50 #10
2017 Select Signature Paint Schemes Prizms Checkered Flag /1 #10
2017 Select Signature Paint Schemes Prizms Gold /10 #10
2017 Select Signature Paint Schemes Prizms Red /25 #10
2017 Select Signature Swatches #28
2017 Select Signature Swatches Prizms Checkered Flag /1 #28
2017 Select Signature Swatches Prizms Gold /10 #28
2017 Select Signature Swatches Prizms Tie Dye /24 #28
2017 Select Signature Swatches Prizms White /50 #28
2017 Select Signature Swatches Triple #17
2017 Select Signature Swatches Triple Prizms Checkered Flag /1 #17
2017 Select Signature Swatches Triple Prizms Gold /10 #17
2017 Select Signature Swatches Triple Prizms Tie Dye /24 #17
2017 Select Signature Swatches Triple Prizms White /50 #17
2017 Select Speed Merchants #8
2017 Select Speed Merchants Prizms Black /3 #8
2017 Select Speed Merchants Prizms Checkered Flag /1 #8
2017 Select Speed Merchants Prizms Gold /10 #8
2017 Select Speed Merchants Prizms Tie Dye /24 #8
2017 Select Speed Merchants Prizms White /50 #8
2017 Select Up Close and Personal #10
2017 Select Up Close and Personal Prizms Black /3 #10
2017 Select Up Close and Personal Prizms Checkered Flag /1 #10
2017 Select Up Close and Personal Prizms Gold /10 #10
2017 Select Up Close and Personal Prizms Tie Dye /24 #10
2017 Select Up Close and Personal Prizms White /50 #10
2018 Certified #46
2018 Certified All Certified Team /199 #20
2018 Certified All Certified Team Black /1 #20
2018 Certified All Certified Team Blue /99 #20
2018 Certified All Certified Team Gold /49 #20
2018 Certified All Certified Team Green /10 #20
2018 Certified All Certified Team Mirror Black /1 #20
2018 Certified All Certified Team Mirror Gold /25 #20
2018 Certified All Certified Team Mirror Green /5 #20
2018 Certified All Certified Team Mirror Purple /10 #20
2018 Certified All Certified Team Purple /25 #20
2018 Certified All Certified Team Red /149 #20
2018 Certified Black /1 #46
2018 Certified Blue /99 #46
2018 Certified Cup Swatches /499 #17
2018 Certified Cup Swatches Black /1 #17
2018 Certified Cup Swatches Blue /49 #17
2018 Certified Cup Swatches Gold /25 #17
2018 Certified Cup Swatches Green /5 #17
2018 Certified Cup Swatches Purple /10 #17
2018 Certified Cup Swatches Red /199 #17
2018 Certified Epix /199 #17
2018 Certified Epix Black /1 #17
2018 Certified Epix Blue /99 #17
2018 Certified Epix Gold /49 #17
2018 Certified Epix Green /10 #17
2018 Certified Epix Mirror Black /1 #17
2018 Certified Epix Mirror Gold /25 #17
2018 Certified Epix Mirror Green /5 #17
2018 Certified Epix Mirror Purple /10 #17
2018 Certified Epix Purple /25 #17
2018 Certified Epix Red /149 #17
2018 Certified Gold /49 #46
2018 Certified Green /10 #46
2018 Certified Mirror Black /1 #46
2018 Certified Mirror Gold /25 #46
2018 Certified Mirror Green /5 #46
2018 Certified Mirror Purple /10 #46
2018 Certified Orange /249 #46
2018 Certified Piece of the Race /399 #16
2018 Certified Piece of the Race Black /1 #16
2018 Certified Piece of the Race Blue /49 #16
2018 Certified Piece of the Race Gold /25 #16
2018 Certified Piece of the Race Green /5 #16
2018 Certified Piece of the Race Purple /10 #16
2018 Certified Piece of the Race Red /199 #16
2018 Certified Purple /25 #46
2018 Certified Red /199 #46
2018 Certified Signature Swatches /41 #12
2018 Certified Signature Swatches Black /1 #12
2018 Certified Signature Swatches Blue /30 #12
2018 Certified Signature Swatches Gold /25 #12
2018 Certified Signature Swatches Green /5 #12
2018 Certified Signature Swatches Purple /10 #12
2018 Certified Signature Swatches Red /35 #12
2018 Certified Signing Sessions Black /1 #14
2018 Certified Signing Sessions Blue /20 #14
2018 Certified Signing Sessions Gold /15 #14
2018 Certified Signing Sessions Green /5 #14
2018 Certified Signing Sessions Purple /10 #14
2018 Certified Signing Sessions Red /25 #14
2018 Certified Skills /199 #14
2018 Certified Skills Black /1 #14
2018 Certified Skills Blue /99 #14
2018 Certified Skills Gold /49 #14
2018 Certified Skills Green /10 #14
2018 Certified Skills Mirror Black /1 #14
2018 Certified Skills Mirror Gold /25 #14
2018 Certified Skills Mirror Green /5 #14
2018 Certified Skills Mirror Purple /10 #14
2018 Certified Skills Purple /25 #14
2018 Certified Skills Red /149 #14
2018 Donruss #15
2018 Donruss #42
2018 Donruss #86
2018 Donruss #132
2018 Donruss Artist Proofs /25 #15
2018 Donruss Artist Proofs /25 #42
2018 Donruss Artist Proofs /25 #86
2018 Donruss Artist Proofs /25 #132
2018 Donruss Classics #8
2018 Donruss Classics Cracked Ice /999 #8
2018 Donruss Classics Xplosion /99 #8
2018 Donruss Gold Foil /499 #15
2018 Donruss Gold Foil /499 #42
2018 Donruss Gold Foil /499 #86
2018 Donruss Gold Foil /499 #132
2018 Donruss Gold Press Proofs /99 #15
2018 Donruss Gold Press Proofs /99 #42
2018 Donruss Gold Press Proofs /99 #86
2018 Donruss Gold Press Proofs /99 #132
2018 Donruss Green Foil /199 #15
2018 Donruss Green Foil /199 #42
2018 Donruss Green Foil /199 #86
2018 Donruss Green Foil /199 #132
2018 Donruss Press Proofs /49 #15
2018 Donruss Press Proofs /49 #42
2018 Donruss Press Proofs /49 #86
2018 Donruss Press Proofs /49 #132
2018 Donruss Printing Plates Black /1 #15
2018 Donruss Printing Plates Black /1 #42
2018 Donruss Printing Plates Black /1 #86
2018 Donruss Printing Plates Black /1 #132
2018 Donruss Printing Plates Cyan /1 #15
2018 Donruss Printing Plates Cyan /1 #42
2018 Donruss Printing Plates Cyan /1 #86
2018 Donruss Printing Plates Cyan /1 #132
2018 Donruss Printing Plates Magenta /1 #15
2018 Donruss Printing Plates Magenta /1 #42
2018 Donruss Printing Plates Magenta /1 #86
2018 Donruss Printing Plates Magenta /1 #132
2018 Donruss Printing Plates Yellow /1 #15
2018 Donruss Printing Plates Yellow /1 #42
2018 Donruss Printing Plates Yellow /1 #86
2018 Donruss Printing Plates Yellow /1 #132
2018 Donruss Red Foil /299 #15
2018 Donruss Red Foil /299 #42
2018 Donruss Red Foil /299 #86
2018 Donruss Red Foil /299 #132
2018 Donruss Rubber Relics #22
2018 Donruss Rubber Relics Black /10 #22
2018 Donruss Rubber Relics Holo Gold /99 #22
2018 Donruss Studio Signatures #8
2018 Donruss Studio Signatures Black /1 #8
2018 Donruss Studio Signatures Holo Gold /25 #8
2018 Panini Prime /50 #5
2018 Panini Prime /50 #39
2018 Panini Prime /50 #72
2018 Panini Prime Autograph Materials /99 #17
2018 Panini Prime Autograph Materials Black /1 #17
2018 Panini Prime Autograph Materials Holo Gold /50 #17
2018 Panini Prime Autograph Materials Laundry Tag /1 #17
2018 Panini Prime Black /1 #5
2018 Panini Prime Black /1 #39
2018 Panini Prime Black /1 #72
2018 Panini Prime Clear Silhouettes /99 #19
2018 Panini Prime Clear Silhouettes Black /1 #19
2018 Panini Prime Clear Silhouettes Dual /99 #21
2018 Panini Prime Clear Silhouettes Dual Black /1 #21
2018 Panini Prime Clear Silhouettes Dual Holo Gold /50 #21
2018 Panini Prime Clear Silhouettes Holo Gold /50 #19
2018 Panini Prime Driver Signatures /99 #9
2018 Panini Prime Driver Signatures Black /1 #9
2018 Panini Prime Driver Signatures Holo Gold /50 #9
2018 Panini Prime Hats Off Button /1 #7
2018 Panini Prime Hats Off Driver Name /2 #7
2018 Panini Prime Hats Off Eyelet /6 #7
2018 Panini Prime Hats Off Headband /36 #7
2018 Panini Prime Hats Off Laundry Tag /1 #7
2018 Panini Prime Hats Off New Era /1 #7
2018 Panini Prime Hats Off Number /2 #7
2018 Panini Prime Hats Off Sponsor Logo /4 #7
2018 Panini Prime Holo Gold /25 #5
2018 Panini Prime Holo Gold /25 #39
2018 Panini Prime Holo Gold /25 #72
2018 Panini Prime Prime Jumbo Associate Sponsor 1 /1 #50
2018 Panini Prime Prime Jumbo Associate Sponsor 10 /1 #50
2018 Panini Prime Prime Jumbo Associate Sponsor 2 /1 #50
2018 Panini Prime Prime Jumbo Associate Sponsor 3 /1 #50
2018 Panini Prime Prime Jumbo Associate Sponsor 4 /1 #50
2018 Panini Prime Prime Jumbo Associate Sponsor 5 /1 #50
2018 Panini Prime Prime Jumbo Associate Sponsor 6 /1 #50
2018 Panini Prime Prime Jumbo Associate Sponsor 7 /1 #50
2018 Panini Prime Prime Jumbo Associate Sponsor 8 /1 #50
2018 Panini Prime Prime Jumbo Associate Sponsor 9 /1 #50
2018 Panini Prime Prime Jumbo Car Manufacturer /1 #50
2018 Panini Prime Prime Jumbo Firesuit Manufacturer /1 #50
2018 Panini Prime Prime Jumbo Glove Manufacturer Patch /1 #50
2018 Panini Prime Prime Jumbo Glove Name Patch /1 #50
2018 Panini Prime Prime Jumbo Goodyear /2 #50
2018 Panini Prime Prime Jumbo Nameplate /2 #50
2018 Panini Prime Prime Jumbo NASCAR /1 #50
2018 Panini Prime Prime Jumbo Series Sponsor /1 #50
2018 Panini Prime Prime Jumbo Shoe Brand Logo /1 #50
2018 Panini Prime Prime Jumbo Shoe Name Patch /1 #50
2018 Panini Prime Prime Jumbo Sunoco /1 #50
2018 Panini Prime Prime Number Signatures /99 #10
2018 Panini Prime Prime Number Signatures Black /1 #10
2018 Panini Prime Prime Number Signatures Holo Gold /50 #10
2018 Panini Prime Quad Material Autographs /99 #1
2018 Panini Prime Quad Material Autographs Black /1 #1
2018 Panini Prime Quad Material Autographs Holo Gold /50 #1
2018 Panini Prime Quad Material Autographs Laundry Tag /1 #1
2018 Panini Prime Race Used Firesuits Black /1 #24
2018 Panini Prime Race Used Firesuits Holo Gold /25 #24
2018 Panini Prime Race Used Firesuits Laundry Tag /1 #24
2018 Panini Prime Race Used Sheet Metal /50 #24
2018 Panini Prime Race Used Sheet Metal Black /1 #24
2018 Panini Prime Race Used Sheet Metal Holo Gold /25 #24
2018 Panini Prime Race Used Tires Black /1 #24
2018 Panini Prime Race Used Tires Holo Gold /25 #24
2018 Panini Prime Shadowbox Signatures /99 #5
2018 Panini Prime Shadowbox Signatures Black /1 #5
2018 Panini Prime Shadowbox Signatures Holo Gold /50 #5
2018 Panini Prime Triple Material Autographs /99 #9
2018 Panini Prime Triple Material Autographs Black /1 #9
2018 Panini Prime Triple Material Autographs Holo Gold /50 #9
2018 Panini Prime Triple Material Autographs Laundry Tag /1 #9
2018 Panini Prizm #9
2018 Panini Prizm #84
2018 Panini Prizm Autographs Prizms #24
2018 Panini Prizm Autographs Prizms Black /1 #24
2018 Panini Prizm Autographs Prizms Blue /25 #24
2018 Panini Prizm Autographs Prizms Camo #24
2018 Panini Prizm Autographs Prizms Gold /10 #24
2018 Panini Prizm Autographs Prizms Green /25 #24
2018 Panini Prizm Autographs Prizms Rainbow /24 #24
2018 Panini Prizm Autographs Prizms Red /25 #24
2018 Panini Prizm Autographs Prizms Red White and Blue /25 #24
2018 Panini Prizm Autographs Prizms White /5 #24
2018 Panini Prizm Prizms #9
2018 Panini Prizm Prizms #84
2018 Panini Prizm Prizms Black /1 #9
2018 Panini Prizm Prizms Black /1 #84
2018 Panini Prizm Prizms Blue /99 #9
2018 Panini Prizm Prizms Blue /99 #84
2018 Panini Prizm Prizms Camo #9
2018 Panini Prizm Prizms Camo #84
2018 Panini Prizm Prizms Gold /10 #9
2018 Panini Prizm Prizms Gold /10 #84
2018 Panini Prizm Prizms Green /149 #9
2018 Panini Prizm Prizms Green /149 #84
2018 Panini Prizm Prizms Purple Flash #9
2018 Panini Prizm Prizms Purple Flash #84
2018 Panini Prizm Prizms Rainbow /24 #9
2018 Panini Prizm Prizms Rainbow /24 #84
2018 Panini Prizm Prizms Red /75 #9
2018 Panini Prizm Prizms Red /75 #84
2018 Panini Prizm Prizms Red White and Blue #9
2018 Panini Prizm Prizms Red White and Blue #84
2018 Panini Prizm Prizms White /5 #9
2018 Panini Prizm Prizms White /5 #84
2018 Panini Prizm Stars and Stripes #12
2018 Panini Prizm Stars and Stripes Prizms #12
2018 Panini Prizm Stars and Stripes Prizms Black /1 #12
2018 Panini Prizm Stars and Stripes Prizms Gold /10 #12
2018 Panini Prizm Team Tandems #4
2018 Panini Prizm Team Tandems Prizms #4
2018 Panini Prizm Team Tandems Prizms Black /1 #4
2018 Panini Prizm Team Tandems Prizms Gold /10 #4
2018 Panini Victory Lane #22
2018 Panini Victory Lane #90
2018 Panini Victory Lane Black /1 #22
2018 Panini Victory Lane Black /1 #90
2018 Panini Victory Lane Blue /25 #22
2018 Panini Victory Lane Blue /25 #90
2018 Panini Victory Lane Celebrations #13
2018 Panini Victory Lane Celebrations Black /1 #13
2018 Panini Victory Lane Celebrations Blue /25 #13
2018 Panini Victory Lane Celebrations Gold /99 #13
2018 Panini Victory Lane Celebrations Green /5 #13
2018 Panini Victory Lane Celebrations Printing Plates Black /1 #13
2018 Panini Victory Lane Celebrations Printing Plates Cyan /1 #13
2018 Panini Victory Lane Celebrations Printing Plates Magenta /1 #13
2018 Panini Victory Lane Celebrations Printing Plates Yellow /1 #13
2018 Panini Victory Lane Celebrations Red /49 #13
2018 Panini Victory Lane Gold /99 #22
2018 Panini Victory Lane Gold /99 #90
2018 Panini Victory Lane Green /5 #22
2018 Panini Victory Lane Green /5 #90
2018 Panini Victory Lane Pedal to the Metal #34
2018 Panini Victory Lane Pedal to the Metal #67
2018 Panini Victory Lane Pedal to the Metal Black /1 #34
2018 Panini Victory Lane Pedal to the Metal Black /1 #67
2018 Panini Victory Lane Pedal to the Metal Blue /25 #34
2018 Panini Victory Lane Pedal to the Metal Blue /25 #67
2018 Panini Victory Lane Pedal to the Metal Green /5 #34
2018 Panini Victory Lane Pedal to the Metal Green /5 #67
2018 Panini Victory Lane Printing Plates Black /1 #22
2018 Panini Victory Lane Printing Plates Black /1 #90
2018 Panini Victory Lane Printing Plates Cyan /1 #22
2018 Panini Victory Lane Printing Plates Cyan /1 #90
2018 Panini Victory Lane Printing Plates Magenta /1 #22
2018 Panini Victory Lane Printing Plates Magenta /1 #90
2018 Panini Victory Lane Printing Plates Yellow /1 #22
2018 Panini Victory Lane Printing Plates Yellow /1 #90
2018 Panini Victory Lane Race Ready Materials Black /25 #20
2018 Panini Victory Lane Race Ready Materials Laundry Tag /1 #20
2018 Panini Victory Lane Red /49 #22
2018 Panini Victory Lane Red /49 #90
2018 Panini Victory Lane Signatures /50 #38
2018 Panini Victory Lane Signatures Black /1 #38
2018 Panini Victory Lane Signatures Gold /25 #38
2018 Panini Victory Lane Silver #22
2018 Panini Victory Lane Silver #90
2018 Panini Victory Lane Starting Grid #18
2018 Panini Victory Lane Starting Grid Black /1 #18
2018 Panini Victory Lane Starting Grid Blue /25 #18
2018 Panini Victory Lane Starting Grid Gold /99 #18
2018 Panini Victory Lane Starting Grid Green /5 #18
2018 Panini Victory Lane Starting Grid Printing Plates Black /1 #18
2018 Panini Victory Lane Starting Grid Printing Plates Cyan /1 #18
2018 Panini Victory Lane Starting Grid Printing Plates Magenta /1 #18
2018 Panini Victory Lane Starting Grid Printing Plates Yellow /1 #18
2018 Panini Victory Lane Starting Grid Red /49 #18
2019 Donruss #6
2019 Donruss #66
2019 Donruss #117
2019 Donruss Artist Proofs /25 #6
2019 Donruss Artist Proofs /25 #66
2019 Donruss Artist Proofs /25 #117
2019 Donruss Black /199 #6
2019 Donruss Black /199 #66
2019 Donruss Black /199 #117
2019 Donruss Contenders #8
2019 Donruss Contenders Cracked Ice /25 #8
2019 Donruss Contenders Holographic #8
2019 Donruss Contenders Xplosion /10 #8
2019 Donruss Gold /299 #6
2019 Donruss Gold /299 #66
2019 Donruss Gold /299 #117
2019 Donruss Gold Press Proofs /99 #6
2019 Donruss Gold Press Proofs /99 #66
2019 Donruss Gold Press Proofs /99 #117
2019 Donruss Optic #21
2019 Donruss Optic Blue Pulsar #21
2019 Donruss Optic Gold /10 #21
2019 Donruss Optic Gold Vinyl /1 #21
2019 Donruss Optic Holo #21
2019 Donruss Optic Red Wave #21
2019 Donruss Optic Signatures Gold Vinyl /1 #21
2019 Donruss Optic Signatures Holo /75 #21
2019 Donruss Originals #13
2019 Donruss Originals Cracked Ice /25 #13
2019 Donruss Originals Holographic #13
2019 Donruss Originals Xplosion /10 #13
2019 Donruss Press Proofs /49 #66
2019 Donruss Press Proofs /49 #117
2019 Donruss Press Proofs /49 #6
2019 Donruss Printing Plates Black /1 #6
2019 Donruss Printing Plates Black /1 #66
2019 Donruss Printing Plates Black /1 #117
2019 Donruss Printing Plates Cyan /1 #6
2019 Donruss Printing Plates Cyan /1 #66
2019 Donruss Printing Plates Cyan /1 #117
2019 Donruss Printing Plates Magenta /1 #66
2019 Donruss Printing Plates Magenta /1 #117
2019 Donruss Printing Plates Magenta /1 #6
2019 Donruss Printing Plates Yellow /1 #6
2019 Donruss Printing Plates Yellow /1 #66
2019 Donruss Printing Plates Yellow /1 #117
2019 Donruss Retro Relics '86 #15
2019 Donruss Retro Relics '86 Holo Black /10 #15
2019 Donruss Retro Relics '86 Holo Gold /25 #15
2019 Donruss Retro Relics '86 Red /225 #15
2019 Donruss Silver #6
2019 Donruss Silver #66
2019 Donruss Silver #117
2019 Panini National Convention NASCAR #R6
2019 Panini National Convention NASCAR Galatic Windows /25 #R6
2019 Panini National Convention NASCAR HyperPlaid /1 #R6
2019 Panini Prime /50 #1
2019 Panini Prime /50 #35
2019 Panini Prime /50 #68
2019 Panini Prime Black /10 #1
2019 Panini Prime Black /10 #35
2019 Panini Prime Black /10 #68
2019 Panini Prime Clear Silhouettes /99 #20
2019 Panini Prime Clear Silhouettes Black /10 #20
2019 Panini Prime Clear Silhouettes Dual /99 #1
2019 Panini Prime Clear Silhouettes Dual Black /10 #1
2019 Panini Prime Clear Silhouettes Dual Holo Gold /25 #1
2019 Panini Prime Clear Silhouettes Dual Platinum Blue /1 #1
2019 Panini Prime Clear Silhouettes Holo Gold /25 #20
2019 Panini Prime Clear Silhouettes Platinum Blue /1 #20
2019 Panini Prime Emerald /5 #1
2019 Panini Prime Emerald /5 #35
2019 Panini Prime Emerald /5 #68
2019 Panini Prime Jumbo Material Signatures Firesuit /10 #18
2019 Panini Prime Jumbo Material Signatures Firesuit Platinum Blue /1 #18
2019 Panini Prime Jumbo Material Signatures Sheet Metal /25 #18
2019 Panini Prime Jumbo Material Signatures Tire /99 #18
2019 Panini Prime NASCAR Shadowbox Signatures Car Number /99 #25
2019 Panini Prime NASCAR Shadowbox Signatures Manufacturer /10 #25
2019 Panini Prime NASCAR Shadowbox Signatures Sponsor /25 #25
2019 Panini Prime NASCAR Shadowbox Signatures Team Owner /1 #25
2019 Panini Prime Platinum Blue /1 #1
2019 Panini Prime Platinum Blue /1 #35
2019 Panini Prime Platinum Blue /1 #68
2019 Panini Prime Prime Cars Die Cut Signatures /99 #1
2019 Panini Prime Prime Cars Die Cut Signatures Black /10 #1
2019 Panini Prime Prime Cars Die Cut Signatures Holo Gold /25 #1
2019 Panini Prime Prime Cars Die Cut Signatures Platinum Blue /1 #1
2019 Panini Prime Prime Jumbo Associate Sponsor 1 /1 #45
2019 Panini Prime Prime Jumbo Associate Sponsor 1 /1 #46
2019 Panini Prime Prime Jumbo Associate Sponsor 2 /1 #45
2019 Panini Prime Prime Jumbo Associate Sponsor 2 /1 #46
2019 Panini Prime Prime Jumbo Associate Sponsor 3 /1 #45
2019 Panini Prime Prime Jumbo Associate Sponsor 3 /1 #46
2019 Panini Prime Prime Jumbo Associate Sponsor 4 /1 #45
2019 Panini Prime Prime Jumbo Associate Sponsor 4 /1 #46
2019 Panini Prime Prime Jumbo Associate Sponsor 5 /1 #45
2019 Panini Prime Prime Jumbo Associate Sponsor 5 /1 #46
2019 Panini Prime Prime Jumbo Associate Sponsor 6 /1 #45
2019 Panini Prime Prime Jumbo Associate Sponsor 6 /1 #46
2019 Panini Prime Prime Jumbo Associate Sponsor 7 /1 #46
2019 Panini Prime Prime Jumbo Associate Sponsor 8 /1 #46
2019 Panini Prime Prime Jumbo Car Manufacturer /1 #45
2019 Panini Prime Prime Jumbo Car Manufacturer /1 #46
2019 Panini Prime Prime Jumbo Firesuit Manufacturer /1 #45
2019 Panini Prime Prime Jumbo Firesuit Manufacturer /1 #46
2019 Panini Prime Prime Jumbo Glove Manufacturer Patch /1 #45
2019 Panini Prime Prime Jumbo Glove Manufacturer Patch /1 #46
2019 Panini Prime Prime Jumbo Glove Name Patch /1 #45
2019 Panini Prime Prime Jumbo Glove Name Patch /1 #46
2019 Panini Prime Prime Jumbo Nameplate /2 #45
2019 Panini Prime Prime Jumbo Nameplate /2 #46
2019 Panini Prime Prime Jumbo NASCAR /1 #45
2019 Panini Prime Prime Jumbo NASCAR /1 #46
2019 Panini Prime Prime Jumbo Prime Colors /16 #45
2019 Panini Prime Prime Jumbo Prime Colors /12 #46
2019 Panini Prime Prime Jumbo Series Sponsor /1 #45
2019 Panini Prime Prime Jumbo Series Sponsor /1 #46
2019 Panini Prime Prime Jumbo Shoe Brand Logo /1 #45
2019 Panini Prime Prime Jumbo Shoe Brand Logo /1 #46
2019 Panini Prime Prime Jumbo Shoe Name Patch /1 #45
2019 Panini Prime Prime Jumbo Shoe Name Patch /1 #46
2019 Panini Prime Prime Jumbo Sunoco /1 #45
2019 Panini Prime Prime Jumbo Sunoco /1 #46
2019 Panini Prime Race Used Duals Firesuits Black /10 #25
2019 Panini Prime Race Used Duals Firesuits Laundry Tags /1 #25
2019 Panini Prime Race Used Duals Sheet Metal Black /10 #25
2019 Panini Prime Race Used Duals Sheet Metal Platinum Blue /1 #25
2019 Panini Prime Race Used Duals Tires Black /10 #25
2019 Panini Prime Race Used Duals Tires Platinum Blue /1 #25
2019 Panini Prime Race Used Firesuits Black /10 #25
2019 Panini Prime Race Used Firesuits Laundry Tags /1 #25
2019 Panini Prime Race Used Sheet Metal Black /10 #25
2019 Panini Prime Race Used Sheet Metal Platinum Blue /1 #25
2019 Panini Prime Race Used Tires Black /10 #25
2019 Panini Prime Race Used Tires Platinum Blue /1 #25
2019 Panini Prizm #1
2019 Panini Prizm #55
2019 Panini Prizm #79
2019 Panini Prizm Expert Level #8
2019 Panini Prizm Expert Level Prizms #8
2019 Panini Prizm Expert Level Prizms Black /1 #8
2019 Panini Prizm Expert Level Prizms Gold /10 #8
2019 Panini Prizm Expert Level Prizms White Sparkle #8
2019 Panini Prizm In the Groove #10
2019 Panini Prizm In the Groove Prizms #10
2019 Panini Prizm In the Groove Prizms Black /1 #10
2019 Panini Prizm In the Groove Prizms Gold /10 #10
2019 Panini Prizm In the Groove Prizms White Sparkle #10
2019 Panini Prizm National Pride #12
2019 Panini Prizm National Pride Prizms #12
2019 Panini Prizm National Pride Prizms Black /1 #12
2019 Panini Prizm National Pride Prizms Gold /10 #12
2019 Panini Prizm National Pride Prizms White Sparkle #12
2019 Panini Prizm Patented Penmanship Prizms #7
2019 Panini Prizm Patented Penmanship Prizms Black /1 #7
2019 Panini Prizm Patented Penmanship Prizms Blue /75 #7
2019 Panini Prizm Patented Penmanship Prizms Camo #7
2019 Panini Prizm Patented Penmanship Prizms Gold /10 #7
2019 Panini Prizm Patented Penmanship Prizms Green /99 #7
2019 Panini Prizm Patented Penmanship Prizms Rainbow /24 #7
2019 Panini Prizm Patented Penmanship Prizms Red /50 #7
2019 Panini Prizm Patented Penmanship Prizms Red White and Blue #7
2019 Panini Prizm Patented Penmanship Prizms White /5 #7
2019 Panini Prizm Prizms #55
2019 Panini Prizm Prizms #79
2019 Panini Prizm Prizms #1
2019 Panini Prizm Prizms Black /1 #1
2019 Panini Prizm Prizms Black /1 #55
2019 Panini Prizm Prizms Black /1 #79
2019 Panini Prizm Prizms Blue /75 #1
2019 Panini Prizm Prizms Blue /75 #55
2019 Panini Prizm Prizms Blue /75 #79
2019 Panini Prizm Prizms Camo #1
2019 Panini Prizm Prizms Camo #55
2019 Panini Prizm Prizms Camo #79
2019 Panini Prizm Prizms Flash #1
2019 Panini Prizm Prizms Flash #55
2019 Panini Prizm Prizms Flash #79
2019 Panini Prizm Prizms Gold /10 #1
2019 Panini Prizm Prizms Gold /10 #55
2019 Panini Prizm Prizms Gold /10 #79
2019 Panini Prizm Prizms Green /99 #1
2019 Panini Prizm Prizms Green /99 #55
2019 Panini Prizm Prizms Green /99 #79
2019 Panini Prizm Prizms Rainbow /24 #1
2019 Panini Prizm Prizms Rainbow /24 #55
2019 Panini Prizm Prizms Rainbow /24 #79
2019 Panini Prizm Prizms Red /50 #1
2019 Panini Prizm Prizms Red /50 #55
2019 Panini Prizm Prizms Red /50 #79
2019 Panini Prizm Prizms Red White and Blue #1
2019 Panini Prizm Prizms Red White and Blue #55
2019 Panini Prizm Prizms Red White and Blue #79
2019 Panini Prizm Prizms White /5 #1
2019 Panini Prizm Prizms White /5 #55
2019 Panini Prizm Prizms White /5 #79
2019 Panini Prizm Prizms White Sparkle #1
2019 Panini Prizm Prizms White Sparkle #55
2019 Panini Prizm Prizms White Sparkle #79
2019 Panini Prizm Signing Sessions Prizms #14
2019 Panini Prizm Signing Sessions Prizms Black /1 #14
2019 Panini Prizm Signing Sessions Prizms Blue /25 #14
2019 Panini Prizm Signing Sessions Prizms Camo #14
2019 Panini Prizm Signing Sessions Prizms Gold /10 #14
2019 Panini Prizm Signing Sessions Prizms Green /25 #14
2019 Panini Prizm Signing Sessions Prizms Rainbow /24 #14
2019 Panini Prizm Signing Sessions Prizms Red /25 #14
2019 Panini Prizm Signing Sessions Prizms Red White and Blue #14
2019 Panini Prizm Signing Sessions Prizms White /5 #14
2019 Panini Prizm Stars and Stripes #6
2019 Panini Prizm Stars and Stripes Prizms #6
2019 Panini Prizm Stars and Stripes Prizms Black /1 #6
2019 Panini Prizm Stars and Stripes Prizms Gold /10 #6
2019 Panini Prizm Stars and Stripes Prizms White Sparkle #6
2019 Panini Prizm Teammates #8
2019 Panini Prizm Teammates Prizms #8
2019 Panini Prizm Teammates Prizms Black /1 #8
2019 Panini Prizm Teammates Prizms Gold /10 #8
2019 Panini Prizm Teammates Prizms White Sparkle #8
2019 Panini Victory Lane #1
2019 Panini Victory Lane Black /1 #1
2019 Panini Victory Lane Dual Swatch Signatures #12
2019 Panini Victory Lane Dual Swatch Signatures Gold /99 #12
2019 Panini Victory Lane Dual Swatch Signatures Laundry Tag /1 #12
2019 Panini Victory Lane Dual Swatch Signatures Platinum /1 #12
2019 Panini Victory Lane Dual Swatch Signatures Red /25 #12
2019 Panini Victory Lane Dual Swatches #15
2019 Panini Victory Lane Dual Swatches Gold /99 #15
2019 Panini Victory Lane Dual Swatches Laundry Tag /1 #15
2019 Panini Victory Lane Dual Swatches Platinum /1 #15
2019 Panini Victory Lane Dual Swatches Red /25 #15
2019 Panini Victory Lane Gold /25 #1
2019 Panini Victory Lane Machines #14
2019 Panini Victory Lane Machines Black /1 #14
2019 Panini Victory Lane Machines Blue /99 #14
2019 Panini Victory Lane Machines Gold /25 #14
2019 Panini Victory Lane Machines Green /5 #14
2019 Panini Victory Lane Machines Printing Plates Black /1 #14
2019 Panini Victory Lane Machines Printing Plates Cyan /1 #14
2019 Panini Victory Lane Machines Printing Plates Magenta /1 #14
2019 Panini Victory Lane Machines Printing Plates Yellow /1 #14
2019 Panini Victory Lane Pedal to the Metal #34
2019 Panini Victory Lane Pedal to the Metal Black /1 #34
2019 Panini Victory Lane Pedal to the Metal Gold /25 #34
2019 Panini Victory Lane Pedal to the Metal Green /5 #34
2019 Panini Victory Lane Pedal to the Metal Red /3 #34
2019 Panini Victory Lane Printing Plates Black /1 #1
2019 Panini Victory Lane Printing Plates Cyan /1 #1
2019 Panini Victory Lane Printing Plates Magenta /1 #1
2019 Panini Victory Lane Printing Plates Yellow /1 #1
2019 Panini Victory Lane Starting Grid #17
2019 Panini Victory Lane Starting Grid Black /1 #17
2019 Panini Victory Lane Starting Grid Blue /99 #17
2019 Panini Victory Lane Starting Grid Gold /25 #17
2019 Panini Victory Lane Starting Grid Green /5 #17
2019 Panini Victory Lane Starting Grid Printing Plates Black /1 #17
2019 Panini Victory Lane Starting Grid Printing Plates Cyan /1 #17
2019 Panini Victory Lane Starting Grid Printing Plates Magenta /1 #17
2019 Panini Victory Lane Starting Grid Printing Plates Yellow /1 #17
2019 Panini Victory Lane Triple Swatches #13
2019 Panini Victory Lane Triple Swatches Gold /99 #13
2019 Panini Victory Lane Triple Swatches Laundry Tag /1 #13
2019 Panini Victory Lane Triple Swatches Platinum /1 #13
2019 Panini Victory Lane Triple Swatches Red /25 #13
2020 Donruss #41
2020 Donruss #112
2020 Donruss #161
2020 Donruss #189
2020 Donruss Aero Package #4
2020 Donruss Aero Package Checkers #4
2020 Donruss Aero Package Cracked Ice /25 #4
2020 Donruss Aero Package Holographic /199 #4
2020 Donruss Aero Package Xplosion /10 #4
2020 Donruss Black Numbers /1 #41
2020 Donruss Black Numbers /1 #112
2020 Donruss Black Numbers /1 #161
2020 Donruss Black Numbers /1 #189
2020 Donruss Black Trophy Club /1 #41
2020 Donruss Black Trophy Club /1 #112
2020 Donruss Black Trophy Club /1 #161
2020 Donruss Black Trophy Club /1 #189
2020 Donruss Blue /199 #112
2020 Donruss Blue /199 #161
2020 Donruss Blue /199 #189
2020 Donruss Blue /199 #41
2020 Donruss Carolina Blue #41
2020 Donruss Carolina Blue #112
2020 Donruss Carolina Blue #161
2020 Donruss Carolina Blue #189
2020 Donruss Contenders #14
2020 Donruss Contenders Checkers #14
2020 Donruss Contenders Cracked Ice /25 #14
2020 Donruss Contenders Holographic /199 #14
2020 Donruss Contenders Xplosion /10 #14
2020 Donruss Green /99 #41
2020 Donruss Green /99 #112
2020 Donruss Green /99 #161
2020 Donruss Green /99 #189
2020 Donruss Optic #31
2020 Donruss Optic #76
2020 Donruss Optic Carolina Blue Wave #31
2020 Donruss Optic Carolina Blue Wave #76
2020 Donruss Optic Gold /10 #31
2020 Donruss Optic Gold /10 #76
2020 Donruss Optic Gold Vinyl /1 #31
2020 Donruss Optic Gold Vinyl /1 #76
2020 Donruss Optic Holo #31
2020 Donruss Optic Holo #76
2020 Donruss Optic Illusion #10
2020 Donruss Optic Illusion Carolina Blue Wave #10
2020 Donruss Optic Illusion Gold /10 #10
2020 Donruss Optic Illusion Gold Vinyl /1 #10
2020 Donruss Optic Illusion Holo #10
2020 Donruss Optic Illusion Orange Pulsar #10
2020 Donruss Optic Illusion Red Mojo #10
2020 Donruss Optic Illusion Signatures Gold Vinyl /1 #10
2020 Donruss Optic Illusion Signatures Holo /99 #10
2020 Donruss Optic Orange Pulsar #31
2020 Donruss Optic Orange Pulsar #76
2020 Donruss Optic Red Mojo #31
2020 Donruss Optic Red Mojo #76
2020 Donruss Optic Signatures Gold Vinyl /1 #31
2020 Donruss Optic Signatures Gold Vinyl /1 #76
2020 Donruss Optic Signatures Holo /99 #31
2020 Donruss Optic Signatures Holo /99 #76
2020 Donruss Orange #189
2020 Donruss Orange #41
2020 Donruss Orange #112
2020 Donruss Orange #161
2020 Donruss Pink /25 #41
2020 Donruss Pink /25 #112
2020 Donruss Pink /25 #161
2020 Donruss Pink /25 #189
2020 Donruss Printing Plates Black /1 #41
2020 Donruss Printing Plates Black /1 #112
2020 Donruss Printing Plates Black /1 #161
2020 Donruss Printing Plates Black /1 #189
2020 Donruss Printing Plates Cyan /1 #41
2020 Donruss Printing Plates Cyan /1 #112
2020 Donruss Printing Plates Cyan /1 #161
2020 Donruss Printing Plates Cyan /1 #189
2020 Donruss Printing Plates Magenta /1 #41
2020 Donruss Printing Plates Magenta /1 #112
2020 Donruss Printing Plates Magenta /1 #161
2020 Donruss Printing Plates Magenta /1 #189
2020 Donruss Printing Plates Yellow /1 #161
2020 Donruss Printing Plates Yellow /1 #189
2020 Donruss Printing Plates Yellow /1 #41
2020 Donruss Printing Plates Yellow /1 #112
2020 Donruss Purple /49 #41
2020 Donruss Purple /49 #112
2020 Donruss Purple /49 #161
2020 Donruss Purple /49 #189
2020 Donruss Race Day Relics #18
2020 Donruss Race Day Relics Holo Black /10 #18
2020 Donruss Race Day Relics Holo Gold /25 #18
2020 Donruss Race Day Relics Red /250 #18
2020 Donruss Red /299 #41
2020 Donruss Red /299 #112
2020 Donruss Red /299 #161
2020 Donruss Red /299 #189
2020 Donruss Silver #41
2020 Donruss Silver #112
2020 Donruss Silver #161
2020 Donruss Silver #189
2020 Donruss Timeless Treasures Signatures Holo Black /1 #4
2020 Donruss Timeless Treasures Signatures Holo Gold /25 #4
2020 Donruss Timeless Treasures Signatures Red /41 #4

Kyle Busch

2002 Choice Rising Stars #18
2004 Press Pass #38B
2004 Press Pass #38
2004 Press Pass Autographs #10
2004 Press Pass Optima #54
2004 Press Pass Optima Gold #G54
2004 Press Pass Optima Samples #54
2004 Press Pass Platinum #P38
2004 Press Pass Previews /5 #38
2004 Press Pass Samples #38
2004 Press Pass Signings #10
2004 Press Pass Signings Gold /50 #10
2004 Press Pass Stealth #65
2004 Press Pass Stealth No Boundaries #NB2
2004 Press Pass Stealth Samples #X65
2004 Press Pass Stealth X-Ray /100 #65
2004 Press Pass Top Prospects Memorabilia /350 #KBT
2004 Press Pass Top Prospects Memorabilia /100 #KBG
2004 Press Pass Top Prospects Memorabilia /200 #KBSM
2004 Press Pass Trackside #84
2004 Press Pass Trackside #92
2004 Press Pass Trackside #31
2004 Press Pass Trackside Golden /100 #G31
2004 Press Pass Trackside Golden /100 #G84
2004 Press Pass Trackside Golden /100 #G92
2004 Press Pass Trackside Previews /5 #EB31
2004 Press Pass Trackside Samples #31
2004 Press Pass Trackside Samples #84
2004 Press Pass Trackside Samples #92
2004 Wheels Autographs #11
2004 Wheels High Gear #45
2004 Wheels High Gear MPH /100 #M45
2004 Wheels High Gear Previews /5 #45
2004 Wheels High Gear Samples #45
2005 Press Pass #39
2005 Press Pass #97
2005 Press Pass Autographs #8
2005 Press Pass Autographs #9
2005 Press Pass Eclipse #38
2005 Press Pass Eclipse Previews /5 #EB38
2005 Press Pass Eclipse Samples #38
2005 Press Pass Legends #33
2005 Press Pass Legends Blue /1890 #33B
2005 Press Pass Legends Gold /750 #33G
2005 Press Pass Legends Holofoil /100 #33H
2005 Press Pass Legends Press Plates Black /1 #33
2005 Press Pass Legends Press Plates Cyan /1 #33
2005 Press Pass Legends Press Plates Magenta /1 #33
2005 Press Pass Legends Press Plates Yellow /1 #33
2005 Press Pass Legends Previews /5 #33
2005 Press Pass Legends Solo /1 #33S
2005 Press Pass Optima #7
2005 Press Pass Optima #54
2005 Press Pass Optima Fan Favorite #FF6
2005 Press Pass Optima Gold /100 #G7
2005 Press Pass Optima Gold /100 #G54
2005 Press Pass Optima Previews /5 #7
2005 Press Pass Optima Previews /1 #54
2005 Press Pass Optima Q & A #QA2
2005 Press Pass Optima Samples #7
2005 Press Pass Optima Samples #54
2005 Press Pass Platinum /100 #P39
2005 Press Pass Platinum /100 #P97
2005 Press Pass Premium #35
2005 Press Pass Premium Samples #35
2005 Press Pass Previews Green /5 #EB39
2005 Press Pass Samples #39
2005 Press Pass Samples #97
2005 Press Pass Signings #6
2005 Press Pass Signings Gold /50 #5
2005 Press Pass Signings Platinum /100 #5
2005 Press Pass Trackside #12
2005 Press Pass Trackside #75
2005 Press Pass Trackside #76
2005 Press Pass Trackside Golden /100 #G12
2005 Press Pass Trackside Golden /100 #G75
2005 Press Pass Trackside Golden /100 #G76
2005 Press Pass Trackside Hat Giveaway #PPH5
2005 Press Pass Trackside Previews /5 #12
2005 Press Pass Trackside Samples #12
2005 Press Pass Trackside Samples #75
2005 Press Pass Trackside Samples #76
2005 VIP #4
2005 VIP Previews /5 #EB4
2005 VIP Samples #4
2005 Wheels American Thunder #5
2005 Wheels American Thunder #61
2005 Wheels American Thunder #74
2005 Wheels American Thunder #85
2005 Wheels American Thunder #90
2005 Wheels American Thunder Medallion #MD2
2005 Wheels American Thunder Previews /5 #5
2005 Wheels American Thunder Previews /1 #85
2005 Wheels American Thunder Samples #5
2005 Wheels American Thunder Samples #61
2005 Wheels American Thunder Samples #74
2005 Wheels American Thunder Samples #85
2005 Wheels American Thunder Samples #90
2005 Wheels American Thunder Thunder Road #TR7
2005 Wheels American Thunder Triple Hat /190 #TH3
2005 Wheels Autographs #7
2005 Wheels Autographs #8
2005 Wheels High Gear #29
2005 Wheels High Gear #86
2005 Wheels High Gear MPH /100 #M29
2005 Wheels High Gear MPH /100 #M86
2005 Wheels High Gear Previews Green /5 #EB29
2005 Wheels High Gear Samples #29
2005 Wheels High Gear Samples #86
2006 Kellogg's All-Star Autographs #KB
2006 Kellogg's Racing #1
2006 Press Pass #67
2006 Press Pass #96
2006 Press Pass #5
2006 Press Pass Autographs #8
2006 Press Pass Blue #B5
2006 Press Pass Blue #B67
2006 Press Pass Blue #B96
2006 Press Pass Burning Rubber Autographs /5 #BRKB
2006 Press Pass Burning Rubber Cars /370 #BRT2
2006 Press Pass Burning Rubber Drivers /100 #BRD2
2006 Press Pass Burning Rubber Drivers Gold /1 #BRD2
2006 Press Pass Burnouts /900 #HT1
2006 Press Pass Burnouts Holofoil /100 #HT1
2006 Press Pass Collectors Series Making the Show #MS19
2006 Press Pass Cup Chase #CCR5
2006 Press Pass Cup Chase Prizes #CC10
2006 Press Pass Eclipse #19
2006 Press Pass Eclipse #38
2006 Press Pass Eclipse #83
2006 Press Pass Eclipse #87
2006 Press Pass Eclipse #87B
2006 Press Pass Eclipse Previews /5 #EB19
2006 Press Pass Eclipse Racing Champions #RC11
2006 Press Pass Eclipse Racing Champions #RC27
2006 Press Pass Eclipse Skidmarks #SM1
2006 Press Pass Eclipse Skidmarks Holofoil /250 #SM1
2006 Press Pass Eclipse Teammates Autographs /25 #2
2006 Press Pass Gold #G5
2006 Press Pass Gold #G67
2006 Press Pass Gold #G96
2006 Press Pass Optima #5
2006 Press Pass Optima #85
2006 Press Pass Optima #4B
2006 Press Pass Optima Gold /100 #G5
2006 Press Pass Optima Gold /100 #G85
2006 Press Pass Optima Pole Position #PP6
2006 Press Pass Optima Previews /5 #EB5
2006 Press Pass Optima Rookie Relics Cars /50 #RRT7
2006 Press Pass Optima Rookie Relics Drivers /50 #RRD7
2006 Press Pass Platinum /100 #P5
2006 Press Pass Platinum /100 #P67
2006 Press Pass Platinum /100 #P96
2006 Press Pass Premium #5
2006 Press Pass Premium #67
2006 Press Pass Premium Hot Threads Autographs /5 #HT-KB
2006 Press Pass Premium Hot Threads Cars /165 #HTT14
2006 Press Pass Premium Hot Threads Drivers /220 #HTD14
2006 Press Pass Premium Hot Threads Drivers Gold /1 #HTD14
2006 Press Pass Previews /5 #EB5
2006 Press Pass Signings #9
2006 Press Pass Signings Gold /50 #9
2006 Press Pass Signings Gold Red Ink #9
2006 Press Pass Signings Silver /100 #9
2006 Press Pass Signings Silver Red Ink #9
2006 Press Pass Stealth #5
2006 Press Pass Stealth #80
2006 Press Pass Stealth #54
2006 Press Pass Stealth EFX #EFX12
2006 Press Pass Stealth Hot Pass #HP6
2006 Press Pass Stealth Previews /5 #5
2006 Press Pass Stealth Retail #5
2006 Press Pass Stealth Retail #80
2006 Press Pass Stealth Retail #54
2006 Press Pass Stealth X-Ray /100 #X5
2006 Press Pass Stealth X-Ray /100 #X54
2006 Press Pass Stealth X-Ray /100 #X80
2006 Press Pass Top 25 Drivers & Rides #C3
2006 Press Pass Top 25 Drivers & Rides #D3
2006 TRAKS #6
2006 TRAKS Autographs #6
2006 TRAKS Autographs 25 /25 #6
2006 TRAKS Previews /1 #6
2006 TRAKS Stickers #5
2006 VIP #4
2006 VIP #77
2006 VIP Making the Show #MS19
2006 VIP Tradin' Paint Cars Bronze /145 #TPT3
2006 VIP Tradin' Paint Drivers Gold /50 #TPD3
2006 VIP Tradin' Paint Drivers Silver /80 #TPD3
2006 Wheels American Thunder #5
2006 Wheels American Thunder #38
2006 Wheels American Thunder Grandstand #GS3
2006 Wheels American Thunder Previews /5 #EB5
2006 Wheels Autographs #9
2006 Wheels High Gear #19
2006 Wheels High Gear #56
2006 Wheels High Gear Flag to Flag #FF4
2006 Wheels High Gear MPH /100 #M19
2006 Wheels High Gear MPH /100 #M56
2006 Wheels High Gear Previews Green /5 #EB19
2007 Press Pass #4
2007 Press Pass #92
2007 Press Pass #104
2007 Press Pass #111
2007 Press Pass Autographs #5
2007 Press Pass Blue #B4
2007 Press Pass Blue #B92
2007 Press Pass Blue #B104
2007 Press Pass Blue #B111
2007 Press Pass Burning Rubber Drivers /75 #BRD14
2007 Press Pass Burning Rubber Drivers Gold /1 #BRD14
2007 Press Pass Burning Rubber Team /325 #BRT14
2007 Press Pass Collector's Series Box Set #SB4
2007 Press Pass Cup Chase #CCR15
2007 Press Pass Cup Chase Prizes #CC9
2007 Press Pass Eclipse #0
2007 Press Pass Eclipse #45
2007 Press Pass Eclipse #10
2007 Press Pass Eclipse Gold /25 #G10
2007 Press Pass Eclipse Gold /25 #G45
2007 Press Pass Eclipse Previews /5 #EB10
2007 Press Pass Eclipse Racing Champions #RC23
2007 Press Pass Eclipse Racing Champions #RC11
2007 Press Pass Eclipse Red /1 #R10
2007 Press Pass Eclipse Red /1 #R45
2007 Press Pass Eclipse Skidmarks #SM7
2007 Press Pass Eclipse Skidmarks Holofoil /250 #SM7
2007 Press Pass Eclipse Teammates Autographs /25 #7
2007 Press Pass Gold #G4
2007 Press Pass Gold #G92
2007 Press Pass Gold #G104
2007 Press Pass Gold #G111
2007 Press Pass Platinum /100 #P4
2007 Press Pass Platinum /100 #P92
2007 Press Pass Platinum /100 #P104
2007 Press Pass Platinum /100 #P111
2007 Press Pass Premium #6
2007 Press Pass Premium Hot Threads Autographs /5 #HTKB
2007 Press Pass Premium Hot Threads Drivers /145 #HTD13
2007 Press Pass Premium Hot Threads Drivers Gold /1 #HTD13
2007 Press Pass Premium Hot Threads Patch /20 #HTP7
2007 Press Pass Premium Hot Threads Team /160 #HTT13
2007 Press Pass Premium Red /15 #R6
2007 Press Pass Previews /5 #EB4
2007 Press Pass Previews /1 #EB111
2007 Press Pass Signings #13
2007 Press Pass Signings Blue /25 #5
2007 Press Pass Signings Gold /50 #10
2007 Press Pass Signings Press Plates Black /1 #8
2007 Press Pass Signings Press Plates Cyan /1 #7
2007 Press Pass Signings Press Plates Magenta /1 #7
2007 Press Pass Signings Press Plates Yellow /1 #7
2007 Press Pass Signings Silver /100 #9
2007 Press Pass Stealth #5
2007 Press Pass Stealth #72
2007 Press Pass Stealth Battle Armor Drivers /150 #BAD14
2007 Press Pass Stealth Battle Armor Teams /85 #BAT14
2007 Press Pass Stealth Battle Armor Teams /85 #BASKB
2007 Press Pass Stealth Chrome #5
2007 Press Pass Stealth Chrome #72
2007 Press Pass Stealth Chrome Exclusives /99 #X5
2007 Press Pass Stealth Chrome Exclusives /99 #X72
2007 Press Pass Stealth Chrome Platinum /25 #P5
2007 Press Pass Stealth Chrome Platinum /25 #P72
2007 Press Pass Stealth Maximum Access #MA5
2007 Press Pass Stealth Maximum Access Autographs /25 #MA5
2007 Press Pass Stealth Previews /5 #EB5
2007 Traks #72
2007 Traks #3
2007 Traks Gold #G3
2007 Traks Gold #G72
2007 Traks Holofoil /50 #H3
2007 Traks Holofoil /50 #H72
2007 Traks Hot Pursuit #HP2
2007 Traks Previews /5 #EB3
2007 Traks Red /10 #R3
2007 Traks Red /10 #R72
2007 VIP #73
2007 VIP #6
2007 VIP Gear Gallery #GG12
2007 VIP Gear Gallery Transparent #GG12
2007 VIP Get A Grip Drivers /70 #GGD23
2007 VIP Get A Grip Teams /70 #GGT23
2007 VIP Previews /5 #EB6
2007 VIP Sunday Best #SB4
2007 Wheels American Thunder #83
2007 Wheels American Thunder #6
2007 Wheels American Thunder American Dreams #AD4
2007 Wheels American Thunder American Dreams Gold /250 #ADG4
2007 Wheels American Thunder American Muscle #AM5
2007 Wheels American Thunder Autographed Hat Instant Winner /1 #AH7
2007 Wheels American Thunder Previews /5 #EB6
2007 Wheels American Thunder Thunder Strokes #8
2007 Wheels American Thunder Thunder Strokes Press Plates Black /1 #8
2007 Wheels American Thunder Thunder Strokes Press Plates Cyan /1 #8
2007 Wheels American Thunder Thunder Strokes Press Plates Magenta /1 #8
2007 Wheels American Thunder Thunder Strokes Press Plates Yellow /1 #8
2007 Wheels American Thunder Triple Hat /99 #TH5
2007 Wheels Autographs #6
2007 Wheels Autographs Press Plates Black /1 #6
2007 Wheels Autographs Press Plates Cyan /1 #6
2007 Wheels Autographs Press Plates Magenta /1 #6
2007 Wheels High Gear #85
2007 Wheels High Gear #10
2007 Wheels High Gear Final Standings Gold /10 #FS10
2007 Wheels High Gear MPH /100 #M10
2007 Wheels High Gear MPH /100 #M85
2007 Wheels High Gear Previews /5 #EB10
2007 Wheels High Gear Top Tier #TT10
2008 Press Pass #0
2008 Press Pass #8
2008 Press Pass #94
2008 Press Pass #115
2008 Press Pass Autographs #10
2008 Press Pass Autographs Press Plates Black /1 #8
2008 Press Pass Autographs Press Plates Cyan /1 #8
2008 Press Pass Autographs Press Plates Magenta /1 #8
2008 Press Pass Autographs Press Plates Yellow /1 #8
2008 Press Pass Blue #B8
2008 Press Pass Blue #B94
2008 Press Pass Blue #B115
2008 Press Pass Burning Rubber Autographs /5 #BRKB
2008 Press Pass Burning Rubber Drivers /60 #BRD5
2008 Press Pass Burning Rubber Drivers Gold /1 #BRD5
2008 Press Pass Burning Rubber Drivers Prime Cuts /25 #BRD5
2008 Press Pass Burning Rubber Teams /175 #BRT5
2008 Press Pass Collector's Series Box Set #1
2008 Press Pass Cup Chase Prizes #CC10
2008 Press Pass Eclipse #88
2008 Press Pass Eclipse #75
2008 Press Pass Eclipse Gold /25 #G75
2008 Press Pass Eclipse Gold /25 #G88
2008 Press Pass Eclipse Previews /1 #EB75
2008 Press Pass Eclipse Red /1 #R75
2008 Press Pass Eclipse Red /1 #R88
2008 Press Pass Eclipse Teammates Autographs /35 #BHS
2008 Press Pass Gold #G8
2008 Press Pass Gold #G94
2008 Press Pass Gold #G115
2008 Press Pass Legends #46
2008 Press Pass Legends Autographs Black Inscriptions /10 #KB
2008 Press Pass Legends Autographs Blue /75 #KB
2008 Press Pass Legends Autographs Press Plates Black /1 #KB
2008 Press Pass Legends Autographs Press Plates Cyan /1 #KB
2008 Press Pass Legends Autographs Press Plates Magenta /1 #KB
2008 Press Pass Legends Autographs Press Plates Yellow /1 #KB
2008 Press Pass Legends Blue /599 #46
2008 Press Pass Legends Bronze /299 #46
2008 Press Pass Legends Gold /99 #46
2008 Press Pass Legends Holo /25 #46
2008 Press Pass Legends Previews /5 #EB46
2008 Press Pass Legends Printing Plates Black /1 #46
2008 Press Pass Legends Printing Plates Cyan /1 #46
2008 Press Pass Legends Printing Plates Magenta /1 #46
2008 Press Pass Legends Printing Plates Yellow /1 #46
2008 Press Pass Legends Prominent Pieces Firesuit-Glove Bronze /50 #PP1KB
2008 Press Pass Legends Prominent Pieces Firesuit-Glove Gold /10 #PP1KB
2008 Press Pass Legends Prominent Pieces Firesuit-Glove Silver /25 #PP1KB
2008 Press Pass Legends Prominent Pieces Metal-Tire Bronze /99 #PP3KyB
2008 Press Pass Legends Prominent Pieces Metal-Tire Gold /25 #PP3KyB
2008 Press Pass Legends Prominent Pieces Metal-Tire Silver /50 #PP3KyB
2008 Press Pass Legends Solo /1 #46
2008 Press Pass Legends Victory Lane Bronze /99 #VLKB
2008 Press Pass Legends Victory Lane Gold /25 #VLKB
2008 Press Pass Legends Victory Lane Silver /50 #VLKB
2008 Press Pass Platinum /100 #P8
2008 Press Pass Platinum /100 #P94
2008 Press Pass Platinum /100 #P115
2008 Press Pass Premium #15
2008 Press Pass Premium #44
2008 Press Pass Premium #63
2008 Press Pass Premium #80
2008 Press Pass Premium Previews /5 #EB15
2008 Press Pass Premium Previews /1 #EB63
2008 Press Pass Premium Red /15 #15
2008 Press Pass Premium Red /15 #44
2008 Press Pass Premium Red /15 #63
2008 Press Pass Premium Red /5 #80
2008 Press Pass Premium Team Signed Baseballs #EGIB
2008 Press Pass Premium Team Signed Baseballs #GIB
2008 Press Pass Previews /5 #EB8
2008 Press Pass Previews /1 #EB115
2008 Press Pass Signings #11
2008 Press Pass Signings Blue /25 #6
2008 Press Pass Signings Gold /50 #9
2008 Press Pass Signings Press Plates Cyan #KB
2008 Press Pass Signings Press Plates Magenta /1 #KB
2008 Press Pass Signings Press Plates Yellow #KB
2008 Press Pass Signings Silver /100 #10
2008 Press Pass Speedway #29
2008 Press Pass Speedway #47
2008 Press Pass Speedway #83
2008 Press Pass Speedway #94
2008 Press Pass Speedway #99
2008 Press Pass Speedway Cockpit #CP5
2008 Press Pass Speedway Corporate Cuts Drivers /80 #CDKyB
2008 Press Pass Speedway Corporate Cuts Drivers Patches /8 #CDKyB
2008 Press Pass Speedway Corporate Cuts Team /165 #CTKyB
2008 Press Pass Speedway Gold #G29
2008 Press Pass Speedway Gold #G47
2008 Press Pass Speedway Gold #G83
2008 Press Pass Speedway Gold #G94
2008 Press Pass Speedway Gold #G99
2008 Press Pass Speedway Holofoil /50 #H29
2008 Press Pass Speedway Holofoil /50 #H47
2008 Press Pass Speedway Holofoil /50 #H83
2008 Press Pass Speedway Holofoil /50 #H94
2008 Press Pass Speedway Holofoil /50 #H99
2008 Press Pass Speedway Previews /5 #EB29
2008 Press Pass Speedway Previews /5 #EB47
2008 Press Pass Speedway Previews /1 #EB94
2008 Press Pass Speedway Previews /1 #EB99
2008 Press Pass Speedway Red /10 #R29
2008 Press Pass Speedway Red /10 #R47
2008 Press Pass Speedway Red /10 #R83
2008 Press Pass Speedway Red /10 #R94
2008 Press Pass Speedway Red /10 #R99
2008 Press Pass Starting Grid #SG1
2008 Press Pass Stealth #75
2008 Press Pass Stealth #68
2008 Press Pass Stealth Battle Armor Drivers /120 #BAD16
2008 Press Pass Stealth Battle Armor Teams /115 #BAT16
2008 Press Pass Stealth Chrome #75
2008 Press Pass Stealth Chrome #68
2008 Press Pass Stealth Chrome Exclusives /25 #68
2008 Press Pass Stealth Chrome Exclusives /25 #75
2008 Press Pass Stealth Chrome Exclusives Gold /99 #68
2008 Press Pass Stealth Chrome Exclusives Gold /99 #75
2008 Press Pass Stealth Maximum Access #MA7
2008 Press Pass Stealth Maximum Access Autographs /25 #MA7
2008 Press Pass VIP National Convention Promo #4
2008 Sports Illustrated for Kids #269
2008 VIP #7
2008 VIP #46
2008 VIP #60
2008 VIP #68
2008 VIP #73
2008 VIP #75
2008 VIP #77
2008 VIP All Access #AA4
2008 VIP Gear Gallery #GG8
2008 VIP Gear Gallery Memorabilia /50 #GGKyB
2008 VIP Gear Gallery Transparent #GG8
2008 VIP National Promos #4
2008 VIP Previews /5 #EB7
2008 Wheels American Thunder #8
2008 Wheels American Thunder #55
2008 Wheels American Thunder #72
2008 Wheels American Thunder #42
2008 Wheels American Thunder American Dreams #AD4
2008 Wheels American Thunder American Dreams Gold /250 #AD4
2008 Wheels American Thunder Autographed Hat Winner /1 #IWHKyB
2008 Wheels American Thunder Campaign Buttons #KB
2008 Wheels American Thunder Campaign Buttons Blue #KB
2008 Wheels American Thunder Campaign Buttons Gold #KB
2008 Wheels American Thunder Campaign Trail #CT1
2008 Wheels American Thunder Previews /5 #8
2008 Wheels American Thunder Trackside Treasury Autographs #KB
2008 Wheels American Thunder Trackside Treasury Autographs Gold /25 #KB
2008 Wheels American Thunder Trackside Treasury Autographs Printing Plates Black /1 #KB
2008 Wheels American Thunder Trackside Treasury Autographs Printing Plates Cyan /1 #KB
2008 Wheels American Thunder Trackside Treasury Autographs Printing Plates Magenta /1 #KB
2008 Wheels American Thunder Trackside Treasury Autographs Printing Plates Yellow /1 #KB
2008 Wheels American Thunder Triple Hat /125 #TH5
2008 Wheels High Gear #5
2008 Wheels High Gear #89
2008 Wheels High Gear Final Standings /5 #F5
2008 Wheels High Gear MPH /100 #M5
2008 Wheels High Gear MPH /100 #M89
2008 Wheels High Gear Previews /5 #EB5
2008 Wheels High Gear Previews /1 #EB89
2008 Wheels High Gear The Chase #TC5
2009 Element #6
2009 Element #66
2009 Element #74
2009 Element #89
2009 Element Big Win /35 #BWKB
2009 Element Elements of the Race Black Flag /99 #ERBKB
2009 Element Elements of the Race Black-White Flag /50 #ERXKB
2009 Element Elements of the Race Blue-Yellow Flag /50 #ERBOKB
2009 Element Elements of the Race Checkered Flag /5 #ERCKB
2009 Element Elements of the Race Green Flag /50 #ERGKB
2009 Element Elements of the Race Red Flag /99 #ERRKB
2009 Element Elements of the Race White Flag /75 #ERWKB
2009 Element Elements of the Race Yellow Flag /99 #ERYKB
2009 Element Green White Checker /25 #GWCKB
2009 Element Kinetic Energy #KE5
2009 Element Lab Report #LR6
2009 Element Previews /5 #6
2009 Element Radioactive /100 #6
2009 Element Radioactive /100 #66
2009 Element Radioactive /100 #74
2009 Element Radioactive /100 #89
2009 Element Taking the Checkers /45 #TCKB
2009 Press Pass #0
2009 Press Pass #1
2009 Press Pass #62
2009 Press Pass #77
2009 Press Pass #107
2009 Press Pass #126
2009 Press Pass #157
2009 Press Pass #167
2009 Press Pass #207
2009 Press Pass Autographs Chase Edition /25 #KB
2009 Press Pass Autographs Gold #9
2009 Press Pass Autographs Printing Plates Black /1 #8
2009 Press Pass Autographs Printing Plates Cyan /1 #8
2009 Press Pass Autographs Printing Plates Magenta /1 #8
2009 Press Pass Autographs Printing Plates Yellow /1 #8
2009 Press Pass Autographs Silver #9
2009 Press Pass Autographs Track Edition /25 #KB
2009 Press Pass Blue #1
2009 Press Pass Blue #62
2009 Press Pass Blue #77
2009 Press Pass Blue #107
2009 Press Pass Blue #126
2009 Press Pass Blue #157
2009 Press Pass Blue #167
2009 Press Pass Blue #207
2009 Press Pass Burning Rubber Autographs /18 #BRSKyB
2009 Press Pass Burning Rubber Drivers /185 #BRD4
2009 Press Pass Burning Rubber Drivers /185 #BRD9
2009 Press Pass Burning Rubber Drivers /185 #BRD11
2009 Press Pass Burning Rubber Drivers /185 #BRD13
2009 Press Pass Burning Rubber Drivers /185 #BRD16
2009 Press Pass Burning Rubber Drivers /185 #BRD18
2009 Press Pass Burning Rubber Drivers /185 #BRD19
2009 Press Pass Burning Rubber Drivers /185 #BRD22
2009 Press Pass Burning Rubber Prime Cut /25 #BRD4
2009 Press Pass Burning Rubber Prime Cut /25 #BRD9
2009 Press Pass Burning Rubber Prime Cut /25 #BRD11
2009 Press Pass Burning Rubber Prime Cut /25 #BRD13
2009 Press Pass Burning Rubber Prime Cut /25 #BRD16
2009 Press Pass Burning Rubber Prime Cut /25 #BRD18
2009 Press Pass Burning Rubber Prime Cut /25 #BRD19
2009 Press Pass Burning Rubber Prime Cut /25 #BRD22
2009 Press Pass Burning Rubber Teams /250 #BRT4
2009 Press Pass Burning Rubber Teams /250 #BRT9
2009 Press Pass Burning Rubber Teams /250 #BRT11
2009 Press Pass Burning Rubber Teams /250 #BRT13
2009 Press Pass Burning Rubber Teams /250 #BRT16
2009 Press Pass Burning Rubber Teams /250 #BRT18
2009 Press Pass Burning Rubber Teams /250 #BRT19
2009 Press Pass Burning Rubber Teams /250 #BRT22
2009 Press Pass Cup Chase #CCR3
2009 Press Pass Eclipse #13
2009 Press Pass Eclipse #48
2009 Press Pass Eclipse #68
2009 Press Pass Eclipse #74
2009 Press Pass Eclipse #76
2009 Press Pass Eclipse Black and White #13
2009 Press Pass Eclipse Black and White #48
2009 Press Pass Eclipse Black and White #68
2009 Press Pass Eclipse Black and White #74
2009 Press Pass Eclipse Black and White #76
2009 Press Pass Eclipse Black Hole Firesuits /50 #BH6
2009 Press Pass Eclipse Blue #13
2009 Press Pass Eclipse Blue #48
2009 Press Pass Eclipse Blue #68
2009 Press Pass Eclipse Blue #74
2009 Press Pass Eclipse Blue #76
2009 Press Pass Eclipse Ecliptic Path #EP7
2009 Press Pass Final Standings /150 #107
2009 Press Pass Four Wide Autographs /5 #FWKB
2009 Press Pass Four Wide Checkered Flag /1 #FWKB
2009 Press Pass Four Wide Firesuit /50 #FWKB
2009 Press Pass Four Wide Sheet Metal /10 #FWKB
2009 Press Pass Four Wide Tire /25 #FWKB
2009 Press Pass Freeze Frame #FF3
2009 Press Pass Fusion #64
2009 Press Pass Fusion Bronze /150 #64
2009 Press Pass Fusion Gold /50 #64
2009 Press Pass Fusion Green /25 #64
2009 Press Pass Fusion Onyx /1 #64
2009 Press Pass Fusion Revered Relics Gold /50 #RRKB
2009 Press Pass Fusion Revered Relics Holofoil /25 #RRKB
2009 Press Pass Fusion Revered Relics Premium Swatch /10 #RRKB
2009 Press Pass Fusion Revered Relics Silver /65 #RRKB
2009 Press Pass Fusion Silver /99 #64
2009 Press Pass Game Face #GF4
2009 Press Pass Gold #1
2009 Press Pass Gold #62
2009 Press Pass Gold #77
2009 Press Pass Gold #107
2009 Press Pass Gold #126
2009 Press Pass Gold #157
2009 Press Pass Gold #167
2009 Press Pass Gold #207
2009 Press Pass Gold Holofoil /100 #1
2009 Press Pass Gold Holofoil /100 #62
2009 Press Pass Gold Holofoil /100 #77
2009 Press Pass Gold Holofoil /100 #107
2009 Press Pass Gold Holofoil /100 #126
2009 Press Pass Gold Holofoil /100 #157
2009 Press Pass Gold Holofoil /100 #167
2009 Press Pass Gold Holofoil /100 #207
2009 Press Pass Legends #42
2009 Press Pass Legends Autographs Gold /25 #7
2009 Press Pass Legends Autographs Holofoil /15 #7
2009 Press Pass Legends Autographs Printing Plates Black /1 #5
2009 Press Pass Legends Autographs Printing Plates Cyan /1 #5
2009 Press Pass Legends Autographs Printing Plates Magenta /1 #5
2009 Press Pass Legends Autographs Printing Plates Yellow /1 #5
2009 Press Pass Legends Gold /399 #42
2009 Press Pass Legends Holofoil /50 #42
2009 Press Pass Legends Previews /5 #42
2009 Press Pass Legends Printing Plates Black /1 #42
2009 Press Pass Legends Printing Plates Cyan /1 #42
2009 Press Pass Legends Printing Plates Magenta /1 #42
2009 Press Pass Legends Printing Plates Yellow /1 #42
2009 Press Pass Legends Prominent Pieces Bronze /99 #PPKB
2009 Press Pass Legends Prominent Pieces Gold /25 #PPKB
2009 Press Pass Legends Prominent Pieces Oversized /25 #PPOEKB
2009 Press Pass Legends Prominent Pieces Silver /50 #PPKB
2009 Press Pass Legends Red /199 #42
2009 Press Pass Legends Solo /1 #42
2009 Press Pass NASCAR Gallery #NG2
2009 Press Pass Pieces Race Used Memorabilia #KB
2009 Press Pass Pocket Portraits #P4
2009 Press Pass Pocket Portraits Checkered Flag #P4
2009 Press Pass Pocket Portraits Smoke #P4
2009 Press Pass Pocket Portraits Wal-Mart #PPW4
2009 Press Pass Premium #16
2009 Press Pass Premium #41
2009 Press Pass Premium #55
2009 Press Pass Premium Hot Threads /325 #HTKyB1
2009 Press Pass Premium Hot Threads /99 #HTKyB2
2009 Press Pass Premium Hot Threads Autographs /18 #KyB
2009 Press Pass Premium Hot Threads Multi-Color /25 #HTKyB
2009 Press Pass Premium Hot Threads Patches /8 #HTP-KyB
2009 Press Pass Premium Previews /5 #EB16
2009 Press Pass Premium Previews /1 #EB54
2009 Press Pass Premium Signatures #8
2009 Press Pass Premium Signatures Gold /25 #8
2009 Press Pass Premium Top Contenders #TC8
2009 Press Pass Premium Top Contenders Gold #TC8
2009 Press Pass Premium Win Streak #WS7
2009 Press Pass Premium Win Streak Victory Lane #WSVL-KB
2009 Press Pass Previews /5 #EB1
2009 Press Pass Previews /1 #EB107
2009 Press Pass Previews /5 #EB126
2009 Press Pass Red #1
2009 Press Pass Red #62
2009 Press Pass Red #77
2009 Press Pass Red #107
2009 Press Pass Red #126
2009 Press Pass Red #157
2009 Press Pass Red #167
2009 Press Pass Red #207
2009 Press Pass Santa Hats /50 #SH5
2009 Press Pass Showcase /499 #7
2009 Press Pass Showcase /499 #45
2009 Press Pass Showcase /499 #30
2009 Press Pass Showcase 2nd Gear /125 #7
2009 Press Pass Showcase 2nd Gear /125 #30
2009 Press Pass Showcase 2nd Gear /125 #45
2009 Press Pass Showcase 3rd Gear /50 #7
2009 Press Pass Showcase 3rd Gear /50 #30
2009 Press Pass Showcase 3rd Gear /50 #45
2009 Press Pass Showcase 4th Gear /15 #7
2009 Press Pass Showcase 4th Gear /15 #30
2009 Press Pass Showcase 4th Gear /15 #45
2009 Press Pass Showcase Classic Collections Firesuit /25 #CCF5
2009 Press Pass Showcase Classic Collections Firesuit Patch /5 #CCF5
2009 Press Pass Showcase Classic Collections Ink /45 #3
2009 Press Pass Showcase Classic Collections Ink Gold /25 #3
2009 Press Pass Showcase Classic Collections Ink Green /5 #3
2009 Press Pass Showcase Classic Collections Ink Melting /1 #3
2009 Press Pass Showcase Classic Collections Sheet Metal /45 #CCS5
2009 Press Pass Showcase Classic Collections Tire /99 #CCT5
2009 Press Pass Showcase Elite Exhibit Ink /45 #1
2009 Press Pass Showcase Elite Exhibit Ink Gold /25 #1
2009 Press Pass Showcase Elite Exhibit Ink Green /5 #1
2009 Press Pass Showcase Elite Exhibit Ink Melting /1 #1
2009 Press Pass Showcase Elite Exhibit Triple Memorabilia /99 #EEKB
2009 Press Pass Showcase Elite Exhibit Triple Memorabilia Gold /45 #EEKB
2009 Press Pass Showcase Elite Exhibit Triple Memorabilia Green /25 #EEKB
2009 Press Pass Showcase Elite Exhibit Triple Memorabilia Melting /5 #EEKB
2009 Press Pass Showcase Printing Plates Black /1 #7
2009 Press Pass Showcase Printing Plates Black /1 #30
2009 Press Pass Showcase Printing Plates Black /1 #45
2009 Press Pass Showcase Printing Plates Cyan /1 #7
2009 Press Pass Showcase Printing Plates Cyan /1 #30
2009 Press Pass Showcase Printing Plates Cyan /1 #45
2009 Press Pass Showcase Printing Plates Magenta /1 #7
2009 Press Pass Showcase Printing Plates Magenta /1 #30
2009 Press Pass Showcase Printing Plates Magenta /1 #45
2009 Press Pass Showcase Printing Plates Yellow /1 #7
2009 Press Pass Showcase Printing Plates Yellow /1 #30
2009 Press Pass Showcase Printing Plates Yellow /1 #45
2009 Press Pass Showcase Prized Pieces Firesuit /25 #PPFKB
2009 Press Pass Showcase Prized Pieces Firesuit Patch /5 #PPFKB
2009 Press Pass Showcase Prized Pieces Ink Firesuit /5 #1
2009 Press Pass Showcase Prized Pieces Ink Firesuit Patch /1 #1
2009 Press Pass Showcase Prized Pieces Ink Sheet Metal /25 #1
2009 Press Pass Showcase Prized Pieces Ink Tire /45 #1
2009 Press Pass Showcase Prized Pieces Sheet Metal /45 #PPSKB
2009 Press Pass Showcase Prized Pieces Tire /99 #PPTKB
2009 Press Pass Signature Series Archive Edition /1 #HTKB
2009 Press Pass Signature Series Archive Edition /1 #BRKB
2009 Press Pass Signings Blue /25 #8
2009 Press Pass Signings Gold #8
2009 Press Pass Signings Green /15 #8
2009 Press Pass Signings Orange /65 #8
2009 Press Pass Signings Printing Plates Cyan /1 #8
2009 Press Pass Signings Printing Plates Magenta /1 #8
2009 Press Pass Signings Purple /45 #8
2009 Press Pass Sponsor Swatches /225 #SSKB2
2009 Press Pass Sponsor Swatches Select /10 #SSKB2
2009 Press Pass Stealth #8
2009 Press Pass Stealth #50
2009 Press Pass Stealth #67
2009 Press Pass Stealth #81
2009 Press Pass Stealth #83
2009 Press Pass Stealth Battle Armor /250 #BAKB2
2009 Press Pass Stealth Battle Armor /50 #BAKB1
2009 Press Pass Stealth Battle Armor Autographs /18 #BASKB
2009 Press Pass Stealth Battle Armor Multi-Color /160 #BAKB
2009 Press Pass Stealth Chrome #8
2009 Press Pass Stealth Chrome #50
2009 Press Pass Stealth Chrome #67
2009 Press Pass Stealth Chrome #81
2009 Press Pass Stealth Chrome #83
2009 Press Pass Stealth Chrome Brushed Metal /25 #8
2009 Press Pass Stealth Chrome Brushed Metal /25 #50
2009 Press Pass Stealth Chrome Brushed Metal /25 #67
2009 Press Pass Stealth Chrome Brushed Metal /25 #81
2009 Press Pass Stealth Chrome Brushed Metal /25 #83
2009 Press Pass Stealth Chrome Gold /99 #8
2009 Press Pass Stealth Chrome Gold /99 #50
2009 Press Pass Stealth Chrome Gold /99 #67
2009 Press Pass Stealth Chrome Gold /99 #81
2009 Press Pass Stealth Chrome Gold /99 #83
2009 Press Pass Stealth Confidential Classified Bronze #PC7
2009 Press Pass Stealth Confidential Secret Silver #PC7
2009 Press Pass Stealth Confidential Top Secret Gold /25 #PC7
2009 Press Pass Stealth Previews /5 #EB8
2009 Press Pass Stealth Previews /1 #EB81
2009 Press Pass Stealth Previews /1 #EB83
2009 Press Pass Target #KBB
2009 Press Pass Total Tire /25 #TT3
2009 Press Pass Tradin' Paint #TP2
2009 Press Pass Tread Marks Autographs /10 #SSKYB
2009 Press Pass Unleashed #U4
2009 Press Pass Unleashed #U8
2009 Press Pass Wal-Mart #KBA
2009 Press Pass Wal-Mart Autographs Red #2
2009 Sportkings National Convention Memorabilia Gold /1 #SK5
2009 Sportkings National Convention Memorabilia Gold /1 #SK24
2009 Sportkings National Convention Memorabilia Gold /1 #SK43
2009 Sportkings National Convention Memorabilia Gold /1 #SK63
2009 Sportkings National Convention Memorabilia Silver /9 #SK5
2009 Sportkings National Convention Memorabilia Silver /9 #SK24
2009 Sportkings National Convention Memorabilia Silver /9 #SK43
2009 Sportkings National Convention Memorabilia Silver /9 #SK63
2009 VIP #7
2009 VIP #39
2009 VIP #65
2009 VIP After Party #AP3
2009 VIP After Party #AP5
2009 VIP After Party #AP10
2009 VIP After Party Transparent #AP3
2009 VIP After Party Transparent #AP5
2009 VIP After Party Transparent #AP10
2009 VIP Get A Grip /120 #GGKB
2009 VIP Get A Grip Holofoil /10 #GGKB
2009 VIP Get A Grip Logos /5 #GGLKB
2009 VIP Guest List #GG1
2009 VIP Hardware #H6
2009 VIP Hardware Transparent #H6
2009 VIP Leadfoot /150 #LFKB
2009 VIP Leadfoot Holofoil /10 #LFKB
2009 VIP Leadfoot Logos /5 #LFLKB
2009 VIP National Promos #1
2009 VIP Previews /5 #7
2009 VIP Purple /25 #7
2009 VIP Purple /25 #39
2009 VIP Purple /25 #65
2009 VIP Race Day Gear /25 #RDGKB
2009 Wheels Autographs /25 #10
2009 Wheels Autographs #9
2009 Wheels Autographs Press Plates Black /1 #KB
2009 Wheels Autographs Press Plates Cyan /1 #KB
2009 Wheels Autographs Press Plates Magenta /1 #KB
2009 Wheels Autographs Press Plates Yellow /1 #KB
2009 Wheels Main Event #5
2009 Wheels Main Event #48
2009 Wheels Main Event #59
2009 Wheels Main Event #65
2009 Wheels Main Event #40
2009 Wheels Main Event #51
2009 Wheels Main Event Buyback Archive Edition /1 #BAKB
2009 Wheels Main Event Buyback Archive Edition /1 #HTKB
2009 Wheels Main Event Fast Pass Purple /25 #5
2009 Wheels Main Event Fast Pass Purple /25 #40
2009 Wheels Main Event Fast Pass Purple /25 #48
2009 Wheels Main Event Fast Pass Purple /25 #51
2009 Wheels Main Event Fast Pass Purple /25 #59
2009 Wheels Main Event Fast Pass Purple /25 #65
2009 Wheels Main Event Foil #5
2009 Wheels Main Event Hat Dance Patch /10 #HDKyB
2009 Wheels Main Event Hat Dance Triple /99 #HDKYB
2009 Wheels Main Event Marks Clubs #9
2009 Wheels Main Event Marks Diamonds /10 #9
2009 Wheels Main Event Marks Hearts /5 #9
2009 Wheels Main Event Marks Printing Plates Black /1 #9
2009 Wheels Main Event Marks Printing Plates Cyan /1 #9
2009 Wheels Main Event Marks Printing Plates Magenta /1 #9
2009 Wheels Main Event Marks Printing Plates Yellow /1 #9
2009 Wheels Main Event Marks Spades /1 #9
2009 Wheels Main Event Playing Cards Blue #KS
2009 Wheels Main Event Playing Cards Blue #5H

2009 Wheels Main Event Playing Cards Red #KS
2009 Wheels Main Event Playing Cards Red #5H
2009 Wheels Main Event Previews /5 #5
2009 Wheels Main Event Renegade Rounders Wanted #RR6
2009 Wheels Main Event Reward Copper /10 #RWKB
2009 Wheels Main Event Reward Holofoil /50 #RWKB
2009 Wheels Main Event Wildcard Cuts /2 #WCCKYB
2010 Action Racing Collectables Platinum 1:24 /117 #18
2010 Action Racing Collectables Platinum 1:24 /71 #18
2010 Action Racing Collectables Platinum 1:24 /100 #18
2010 Action Racing Collectables Platinum 1:24 /56 #18
2010 Element #5
2010 Element #48
2010 Element #69
2010 Element 10 in '10 #TT9
2010 Element Blue /35 #5
2010 Element Blue /35 #48
2010 Element Blue /35 #69
2010 Element Finish Line Checkered Flag /10 #FLKyB
2010 Element Finish Line Green Flag /20 #FLKyB
2010 Element Finish Line Tires /99 #FLKyB
2010 Element Flagship Performers Wins Black /20 #FPWKyB
2010 Element Flagship Performers Wins Blue-Orange /20 #FPWKyB
2010 Element Flagship Performers Wins Checkered /1 #FPWKyB
2010 Element Flagship Performers Wins Green /5 #FPWKyB
2010 Element Flagship Performers Wins Red /20 #FPWKyB
2010 Element Flagship Performers Wins White /15 #FPWKyB
2010 Element Flagship Performers Wins X /10 #FPWKyB
2010 Element Flagship Performers Wins Yellow /20 #FPWKyB
2010 Element Green #5
2010 Element Green #48
2010 Element Green #69
2010 Element Green-White-Checkers Blue /10 #GWCKyB
2010 Element Green-White-Checkers Green /50 #GWCKyB
2010 Element Previews /5 #EB5
2010 Element Purple /25 #5
2010 Element Purple /25 #48
2010 Element Red Target #5
2010 Element Red Target #48
2010 Element Red Target #69
2010 Press Pass #14
2010 Press Pass #37
2010 Press Pass #107
2010 Press Pass #95
2010 Press Pass #92
2010 Press Pass Autographs #10
2010 Press Pass Autographs Printing Plates Black /1 #8
2010 Press Pass Autographs Printing Plates Cyan /1 #11
2010 Press Pass Autographs Printing Plates Magenta /1 #8
2010 Press Pass Autographs Printing Plates Yellow /1 #8
2010 Press Pass Autographs Track Edition /10 #1
2010 Press Pass Blue #14
2010 Press Pass Blue #37
2010 Press Pass Blue #92
2010 Press Pass Blue #95
2010 Press Pass Blue #107
2010 Press Pass Burning Rubber /250 #BR3
2010 Press Pass Burning Rubber /250 #BR4
2010 Press Pass Burning Rubber /250 #BR9
2010 Press Pass Burning Rubber /250 #BR20
2010 Press Pass Burning Rubber Gold /50 #BR3
2010 Press Pass Burning Rubber Gold /50 #BR4
2010 Press Pass Burning Rubber Gold /50 #BR9
2010 Press Pass Burning Rubber Gold /50 #BR20
2010 Press Pass Burning Rubber Prime Cuts /25 #BR4
2010 Press Pass By The Numbers #BN2
2010 Press Pass Cup Chase #CCR8
2010 Press Pass Cup Chase Prizes #CC4
2010 Press Pass Eclipse #19
2010 Press Pass Eclipse #34
2010 Press Pass Eclipse #83
2010 Press Pass Eclipse Blue #19
2010 Press Pass Eclipse Blue #34
2010 Press Pass Eclipse Blue #83
2010 Press Pass Eclipse Cars #C3
2010 Press Pass Eclipse Decade #D7
2010 Press Pass Eclipse Gold #19
2010 Press Pass Eclipse Gold #34
2010 Press Pass Eclipse Gold #83
2010 Press Pass Eclipse Previews /5 #19
2010 Press Pass Eclipse Previews /1 #34
2010 Press Pass Eclipse Purple /25 #19
2010 Press Pass Eclipse Purple /25 #34
2010 Press Pass Eclipse Signature Series Shoes Autographs /18 #SSSEKB
2010 Press Pass Eclipse Spellbound Swatches /299 #SSKB2
2010 Press Pass Eclipse Spellbound Swatches /299 #SSKB3
2010 Press Pass Eclipse Spellbound Swatches /299 #SSKB4
2010 Press Pass Eclipse Spellbound Swatches /299 #SSKB5
2010 Press Pass Eclipse Spellbound Swatches /299 #SSKB1
2010 Press Pass Eclipse Spellbound Swatches Holofoil /18 #SSKB2
2010 Press Pass Eclipse Spellbound Swatches Holofoil /18 #SSKB3
2010 Press Pass Eclipse Spellbound Swatches Holofoil /18 #SSKB4
2010 Press Pass Eclipse Spellbound Swatches Holofoil /18 #SSKB5
2010 Press Pass Eclipse Spellbound Swatches Holofoil /18 #SSKB1
2010 Press Pass Five Star /35 #13
2010 Press Pass Five Star Classic Compilations Combos Firesuit Autographs /15 #CCMJGR
2010 Press Pass Five Star Classic Compilations Combos Patches Autographs /1 #CCMJGR
2010 Press Pass Five Star Classic Compilations Dual Memorabilia Autographs /10 #KB
2010 Press Pass Five Star Classic Compilations Firesuit Autographs /15 #KB
2010 Press Pass Five Star Classic Compilations Patch Autographs /1 #CCPKyB1
2010 Press Pass Five Star Classic Compilations Patch Autographs /1 #CCPKyB2
2010 Press Pass Five Star Classic Compilations Patch Autographs /1 #CCPKyB3
2010 Press Pass Five Star Classic Compilations Patch Autographs /1 #CCPKyB4
2010 Press Pass Five Star Classic Compilations Patch Autographs /1 #CCPKyB5
2010 Press Pass Five Star Classic Compilations Patch Autographs /1 #CCPKyB6
2010 Press Pass Five Star Classic Compilations Patch Autographs /1 #CCPKyB7
2010 Press Pass Five Star Classic Compilations Patch Autographs /1 #CCPKyB8
2010 Press Pass Five Star Classic Compilations Patch Autographs /1 #CCPKyB9
2010 Press Pass Five Star Classic Compilations Patch Autographs /1 #CCPKyB10
2010 Press Pass Five Star Classic Compilations Patch Autographs /1 #CCPKyB11
2010 Press Pass Five Star Classic Compilations Patch Autographs /1 #CCPKyB12
2010 Press Pass Five Star Classic Compilations Patch Autographs /1 #CCPKyB13
2010 Press Pass Five Star Classic Compilations Patch Autographs /1 #CCPKyB14
2010 Press Pass Five Star Classic Compilations Patch Autographs /1 #CCPKyB15
2010 Press Pass Five Star Classic Compilations Patch Autographs /1 #CCPKyB16
2010 Press Pass Five Star Classic Compilations Patch Autographs /1 #CCPKyB17
2010 Press Pass Five Star Classic Compilations Patch Autographs /1 #CCPKyB18
2010 Press Pass Five Star Classic Compilations Sheet Metal Autographs /25 #KB
2010 Press Pass Five Star Classic Compilations Triple Memorabilia Autographs /5 #KB
2010 Press Pass Five Star Holofoil /10 #13
2010 Press Pass Five Star Melting /1 #13
2010 Press Pass Five Star Paramount Pieces Aluminum /20 #KBU
2010 Press Pass Five Star Paramount Pieces Blue /20 #KBU
2010 Press Pass Five Star Paramount Pieces Gold /15 #KBU
2010 Press Pass Five Star Paramount Pieces Holofoil /10 #KB
2010 Press Pass Five Star Paramount Pieces Melting /1 #KBU
2010 Press Pass Five Star Signature Souvenirs Aluminum /50 #SSKB
2010 Press Pass Five Star Signature Souvenirs Gold /25 #SSKB
2010 Press Pass Five Star Signature Souvenirs Holofoil /10 #SSKB
2010 Press Pass Five Star Signature Souvenirs Melting /1 #SSKB
2010 Press Pass Five Star Signatures Aluminum /35 #KB
2010 Press Pass Five Star Signatures Gold /20 #KB
2010 Press Pass Five Star Signatures Holofoil /5 #KB
2010 Press Pass Five Star Signatures Melting /1 #KB
2010 Press Pass Four Wide Autographs /5 #NNO
2010 Press Pass Four Wide Firesuit /25 #FWKB
2010 Press Pass Four Wide Sheet Metal /15 #FWKB
2010 Press Pass Four Wide Shoes /1 #FWKB
2010 Press Pass Four Wide Tires /10 #FWKB
2010 Press Pass Gold #14
2010 Press Pass Gold #37
2010 Press Pass Gold #92
2010 Press Pass Gold #95
2010 Press Pass Gold #107
2010 Press Pass Holofoil /100 #14
2010 Press Pass Holofoil /100 #37
2010 Press Pass Holofoil /100 #92
2010 Press Pass Holofoil /100 #95
2010 Press Pass Holofoil /100 #107
2010 Press Pass Legends #37
2010 Press Pass Legends Autographs Blue /9 #9
2010 Press Pass Legends Autographs Holofoil /25 #9
2010 Press Pass Legends Autographs Printing Plates Black /1 #8
2010 Press Pass Legends Autographs Printing Plates Cyan /1 #8
2010 Press Pass Legends Autographs Printing Plates Magenta /1 #8
2010 Press Pass Legends Autographs Printing Plates Yellow /1 #8
2010 Press Pass Legends Blue /1 #37
2010 Press Pass Legends Gold /399 #37
2010 Press Pass Legends Holofoil /50 #37
2010 Press Pass Legends Motorsports Masters #MMKYB
2010 Press Pass Legends Motorsports Masters Autographs Printing Plates Black /1 #8
2010 Press Pass Legends Motorsports Masters Autographs Printing Plates Cyan /1 #8
2010 Press Pass Legends Motorsports Masters Autographs Printing Plates Magenta /1 #8
2010 Press Pass Legends Motorsports Masters Autographs Printing Plates Yellow /1 #8
2010 Press Pass Legends Motorsports Masters Blue /10 #MMKYB
2010 Press Pass Legends Motorsports Masters Gold /299 #MMKYB
2010 Press Pass Legends Motorsports Masters Holofoil /149 #MMKYB
2010 Press Pass Legends Printing Plates Black /1 #37
2010 Press Pass Legends Printing Plates Cyan /1 #37
2010 Press Pass Legends Printing Plates Magenta /1 #37
2010 Press Pass Legends Printing Plates Yellow /1 #37
2010 Press Pass Legends Prominent Pieces Copper /99 #PPKYB
2010 Press Pass Legends Prominent Pieces Gold /50 #PPKYB
2010 Press Pass Legends Prominent Pieces Holofoil /25 #PPKYB
2010 Press Pass Legends Prominent Pieces Oversized Firesuit /25 #PPOEKYB
2010 Press Pass Legends Red /199 #37
2010 Press Pass Premium #13
2010 Press Pass Premium #36
2010 Press Pass Premium Allies #A10
2010 Press Pass Premium Hot Threads /299 #HTKyB
2010 Press Pass Premium Hot Threads Holofoil /99 #HTKyB
2010 Press Pass Premium Hot Threads Multi Color /25 #HTKyB
2010 Press Pass Premium Hot Threads Two Color /125 #HTKyB
2010 Press Pass Premium Pairings Firesuits /25 #PFBL
2010 Press Pass Premium Pairings Signatures /5 #PSBL
2010 Press Pass Premium Purple /25 #13
2010 Press Pass Premium Purple /25 #36
2010 Press Pass Premium Signature Series Firesuit /15 #SSFKB
2010 Press Pass Premium Signatures #PSKYB
2010 Press Pass Premium Signatures Red Ink /24 #PSKYB
2010 Press Pass Previews /5 #14
2010 Press Pass Purple /25 #14
2010 Press Pass Purple /25 #37
2010 Press Pass Purple /25 #92
2010 Press Pass Purple /25 #95
2010 Press Pass Purple /25 #107
2010 Press Pass Showcase /499 #45
2010 Press Pass Showcase /499 #35
2010 Press Pass Showcase /499 #13
2010 Press Pass Showcase Classic Collections Firesuit Green /25 #CCIJGR
2010 Press Pass Showcase Classic Collections Firesuit Patch Melting /5 #CCIJGR
2010 Press Pass Showcase Classic Collections Ink /15 #CCIJGR
2010 Press Pass Showcase Classic Collections Ink Gold /10 #CCIJGR
2010 Press Pass Showcase Classic Collections Ink Green /5 #CCIJGR
2010 Press Pass Showcase Classic Collections Ink Melting /1 #CCIJGR
2010 Press Pass Showcase Classic Collections Sheet Metal /99 #CCIJGR
2010 Press Pass Showcase Classic Collections Sheet Metal Gold /45 #CCIJGR
2010 Press Pass Showcase Elite Exhibit Ink /45 #EEIKB2
2010 Press Pass Showcase Elite Exhibit Ink Gold /25 #EEIKB2
2010 Press Pass Showcase Elite Exhibit Ink Green /5 #EEIKB2
2010 Press Pass Showcase Elite Exhibit Ink Melting /1 #EEIKB2
2010 Press Pass Showcase Elite Exhibit Triple Memorabilia /99 #EEMKB2
2010 Press Pass Showcase Elite Exhibit Triple Memorabilia Gold /45 #EEMKB2
2010 Press Pass Showcase Elite Exhibit Triple Memorabilia Green /25 #EEMKB2
2010 Press Pass Showcase Elite Exhibit Triple Memorabilia Melting /5 #EEMKB2
2010 Press Pass Showcase Gold /125 #13
2010 Press Pass Showcase Gold /125 #35
2010 Press Pass Showcase Gold /125 #45
2010 Press Pass Showcase Green /50 #13
2010 Press Pass Showcase Green /50 #35
2010 Press Pass Showcase Green /50 #45
2010 Press Pass Showcase Melting /15 #13
2010 Press Pass Showcase Melting /15 #35
2010 Press Pass Showcase Melting /15 #45
2010 Press Pass Showcase Platinum Holo /1 #13
2010 Press Pass Showcase Platinum Holo /1 #35
2010 Press Pass Showcase Platinum Holo /1 #45
2010 Press Pass Showcase Prized Pieces Firesuit Green /25 #PPMKB
2010 Press Pass Showcase Prized Pieces Firesuit Ink Gold /25 #PPIKB2
2010 Press Pass Showcase Prized Pieces Firesuit Ink Melting /1 #PPIKB2
2010 Press Pass Showcase Prized Pieces Firesuit Patch Melting /5 #PPMKB
2010 Press Pass Showcase Prized Pieces Memorabilia Ink Green /15 #PPIKB2
2010 Press Pass Showcase Prized Pieces Sheet Metal /99 #PPMKB
2010 Press Pass Showcase Prized Pieces Sheet Metal Gold /45 #PPMKB
2010 Press Pass Showcase Prized Pieces Sheet Metal Ink Silver /45 #PPIKB2
2010 Press Pass Signings Blue /10 #12
2010 Press Pass Signings Gold /30 #12
2010 Press Pass Signings Red /15 #12
2010 Press Pass Signings Silver /50 #12
2010 Press Pass Stealth #7
2010 Press Pass Stealth #57
2010 Press Pass Stealth #61
2010 Press Pass Stealth #71
2010 Press Pass Stealth Battle Armor Holofoil /25 #BAKB1
2010 Press Pass Stealth Battle Armor Silver /225 #BAKB1
2010 Press Pass Stealth Black and White #7
2010 Press Pass Stealth Black and White #57
2010 Press Pass Stealth Black and White #61
2010 Press Pass Stealth Black and White #71
2010 Press Pass Stealth Power Players #PP6
2010 Press Pass Stealth Previews /5 #7
2010 Press Pass Stealth Previews /5 #57
2010 Press Pass Stealth Previews /1 #61
2010 Press Pass Stealth Purple /25 #7
2010 Press Pass Stealth Purple /25 #57
2010 Press Pass Stealth Purple /25 #61
2010 Press Pass Stealth Signature Series Sheet Metal /15 #SSMEKB
2010 Press Pass Stealth Weekend Warriors Holofoil /25 #WWKB
2010 Press Pass Stealth Weekend Warriors Silver /199 #WWKB
2010 Press Pass Tradin' Paint #TP3
2010 Press Pass Tradin' Paint Sheet Metal /299 #TPKB
2010 Press Pass Tradin' Paint Sheet Metal Gold /50 #TPKB
2010 Press Pass Tradin' Paint Sheet Metal Holofoil /25 #TPKB
2010 Press Pass Unleashed #U3
2010 Wheels Autographs #9
2010 Wheels Autographs Printing Plates Black /1 #9
2010 Wheels Autographs Printing Plates Cyan /1 #9
2010 Wheels Autographs Printing Plates Magenta /1 #9
2010 Wheels Autographs Printing Plates Yellow /1 #9
2010 Wheels Autographs Special Ink /10 #2
2010 Wheels Autographs Target /10 #7
2010 Wheels Main Event #7
2010 Wheels Main Event #53
2010 Wheels Main Event #57
2010 Wheels Main Event #98
2010 Wheels Main Event Blue #7
2010 Wheels Main Event Blue #53
2010 Wheels Main Event Blue #57
2010 Wheels Main Event Blue #98
2010 Wheels Main Event Fight Card #FC7
2010 Wheels Main Event Fight Card Checkered Flag #FC7
2010 Wheels Main Event Fight Card Full Color Retail #FC7
2010 Wheels Main Event Fight Card Gold /25 #FC7
2010 Wheels Main Event Head to Head /150 #HHKBDH
2010 Wheels Main Event Head to Head /150 #HHKBJL
2010 Wheels Main Event Head to Head Blue /75 #HHKBDH
2010 Wheels Main Event Head to Head Blue /75 #HHKBJL
2010 Wheels Main Event Head to Head Holofoil /10 #HHKBDH
2010 Wheels Main Event Head to Head Holofoil /10 #HHKBJL
2010 Wheels Main Event Head to Head Red /25 #HHKBDH
2010 Wheels Main Event Head to Head Red /25 #HHKBJL
2010 Wheels Main Event Marks Autographs /56 #11
2010 Wheels Main Event Marks Autographs Black /1 #11
2010 Wheels Main Event Marks Autographs Blue /15 #11
2010 Wheels Main Event Marks Autographs Red /5 #11
2010 Wheels Main Event Purple /25 #7
2010 Wheels Main Event Purple /25 #53
2010 Wheels Main Event Tale of the Tape #TT3
2010 Wheels Main Event Toe to Toe /10 #TTKBDH
2010 Wheels Main Event Toe to Toe /10 #TTKBJL
2010 Wheels Main Event Upper Cuts Knock Out Patches /25 #UCKOKYB
2010 Wheels Main Event Wheel to Wheel /25 #WWKBDH
2010 Wheels Main Event Wheel to Wheel /25 #WWKBJL
2010 Wheels Main Event Wheel to Wheel Holofoil /10 #WWKBDH
2010 Wheels Main Event Wheel to Wheel Holofoil /10 #WWKBJL
2011 Element #7
2011 Element #41
2011 Element #65
2011 Element #81
2011 Element Autographs /25 #11
2011 Element Autographs Blue /5 #11
2011 Element Autographs Gold /5 #11
2011 Element Autographs Printing Plates Black /1 #11
2011 Element Autographs Printing Plates Cyan /1 #11
2011 Element Autographs Printing Plates Magenta /1 #11
2011 Element Autographs Printing Plates Yellow /1 #11
2011 Element Autographs Silver /15 #11
2011 Element Black /35 #7
2011 Element Black /35 #41
2011 Element Black /35 #65
2011 Element Black /35 #81
2011 Element Finish Line Checkered Flag /10 #FLKYB
2011 Element Finish Line Green Flag /25 #FLKYB
2011 Element Finish Line Tires /99 #FLKYB
2011 Element Finish Line Tires Purple Fast Pass /30 #FLKYB
2011 Element Flagship Performers 2010 Laps Completed Yellow /50 #FPLKyB
2011 Element Flagship Performers Career Wins White /50 #FPWKyB
2011 Element Flagstand Swatches /25 #FSSKB
2011 Element Green #7
2011 Element Green #41
2011 Element Green #65
2011 Element Green #81
2011 Element Previews /5 #EB7
2011 Element Purple /25 #7
2011 Element Purple /25 #41
2011 Element Purple /25 #65
2011 Element Purple /25 #81
2011 Element Red #7
2011 Element Red #41
2011 Element Red #65
2011 Element Red #81
2011 Press Pass #7
2011 Press Pass #62
2011 Press Pass #118
2011 Press Pass #141
2011 Press Pass #158
2011 Press Pass #160
2011 Press Pass #177
2011 Press Pass #190
2011 Press Pass #0
2011 Press Pass Autographs Blue /5 #11
2011 Press Pass Autographs Bronze /5 #11
2011 Press Pass Autographs Gold /5 #11
2011 Press Pass Autographs Printing Plates Black /1 #11
2011 Press Pass Autographs Printing Plates Cyan /1 #11
2011 Press Pass Autographs Printing Plates Magenta /1 #11
2011 Press Pass Autographs Printing Plates Yellow /1 #11
2011 Press Pass Autographs Silver /5 #11
2011 Press Pass Blue Holofoil /10 #7
2011 Press Pass Blue Holofoil /10 #62
2011 Press Pass Blue Holofoil /10 #118
2011 Press Pass Blue Holofoil /10 #141
2011 Press Pass Blue Holofoil /10 #158
2011 Press Pass Blue Holofoil /10 #160
2011 Press Pass Blue Holofoil /10 #177
2011 Press Pass Blue Holofoil /10 #190
2011 Press Pass Blue Retail #7
2011 Press Pass Blue Retail #62
2011 Press Pass Blue Retail #118
2011 Press Pass Blue Retail #141
2011 Press Pass Blue Retail #158
2011 Press Pass Blue Retail #160
2011 Press Pass Blue Retail #177
2011 Press Pass Blue Retail #190
2011 Press Pass Bristol Sweep Fast Pass /10 #BRKYB3
2011 Press Pass Bristol Sweep Holofoil /50 #BRKYB3
2011 Press Pass Burning Rubber Autographs /10 #BRKYB1
2011 Press Pass Burning Rubber Autographs /10 #BRKYB2
2011 Press Pass Burning Rubber Fast Pass /10 #BRKYB
2011 Press Pass Burning Rubber Gold /150 #BRKYB
2011 Press Pass Burning Rubber Holofoil /50 #BRKYB
2011 Press Pass Burning Rubber Prime Cuts /25 #BRKYB
2011 Press Pass Cup Chase #CCR4
2011 Press Pass Cup Chase Prizes #CC1
2011 Press Pass Eclipse #7
2011 Press Pass Eclipse #41
2011 Press Pass Eclipse #68
2011 Press Pass Eclipse #84
2011 Press Pass Eclipse Blue #7
2011 Press Pass Eclipse Blue #41
2011 Press Pass Eclipse Blue #68
2011 Press Pass Eclipse Blue #84
2011 Press Pass Eclipse Encore #E9
2011 Press Pass Eclipse Gold /55 #7
2011 Press Pass Eclipse Gold /55 #41
2011 Press Pass Eclipse Gold /55 #68
2011 Press Pass Eclipse Gold /55 #84
2011 Press Pass Eclipse Previews /5 #EB7
2011 Press Pass Eclipse Previews /1 #EB41
2011 Press Pass Eclipse Purple /25 #7
2011 Press Pass Eclipse Purple /25 #41
2011 Press Pass Eclipse Rides #R3
2011 Press Pass Eclipse Spellbound Swatches /150 #SBKB2
2011 Press Pass Eclipse Spellbound Swatches /250 #SBKB1
2011 Press Pass Eclipse Spellbound Swatches /75 #SBKB4
2011 Press Pass Eclipse Spellbound Swatches /100 #SBKB3
2011 Press Pass Eclipse Spellbound Swatches /50 #SBKB5
2011 Press Pass Eclipse Spellbound Swatches Signatures /10 #NNO
2011 Press Pass FanFare #8
2011 Press Pass FanFare Autographs Blue /5 #12
2011 Press Pass FanFare Autographs Bronze /20 #12
2011 Press Pass FanFare Autographs Gold /15 #12
2011 Press Pass FanFare Autographs Printing Plates Black /1 #12
2011 Press Pass FanFare Autographs Printing Plates Cyan /1 #12
2011 Press Pass FanFare Autographs Printing Plates Magenta /1 #12
2011 Press Pass FanFare Autographs Printing Plates Yellow /1 #12
2011 Press Pass FanFare Autographs Silver /10 #12
2011 Press Pass FanFare Blue Die Cuts #8
2011 Press Pass FanFare Championship Caliber #CC23
2011 Press Pass FanFare Dual Autographs /10 #NNO
2011 Press Pass FanFare Emerald /25 #8
2011 Press Pass FanFare Holofoil Die Cuts #8
2011 Press Pass FanFare Magnificent Materials /199 #MMKB
2011 Press Pass FanFare Magnificent Materials Dual Swatches /50 #MMDKB
2011 Press Pass FanFare Magnificent Materials Dual Swatches Holofoil /10 #MMDKB
2011 Press Pass FanFare Magnificent Materials Holofoil /50 #MMKB
2011 Press Pass FanFare Magnificent Materials Signatures /50 #MMSEKB
2011 Press Pass FanFare Magnificent Materials Signatures Holofoil /25 #MMSEKB
2011 Press Pass FanFare Rookie Standouts #RS5
2011 Press Pass FanFare Ruby Die Cuts /15 #8
2011 Press Pass FanFare Sapphire /10 #8
2011 Press Pass FanFare Silver /25 #8
2011 Press Pass Four Wide Firesuit /25 #FWKB
2011 Press Pass Four Wide Glove /1 #FWKB
2011 Press Pass Four Wide Sheet Metal /15 #FWKB
2011 Press Pass Four Wide Tire /10 #FWKB
2011 Press Pass Geared Up Gold /100 #GUKYB
2011 Press Pass Geared Up Holofoil /50 #GUKYB
2011 Press Pass Gold /50 #7
2011 Press Pass Gold /50 #62
2011 Press Pass Gold /50 #118
2011 Press Pass Gold /50 #141
2011 Press Pass Gold /50 #158
2011 Press Pass Gold /50 #160
2011 Press Pass Gold /50 #177
2011 Press Pass Gold /50 #190
2011 Press Pass Legends #39
2011 Press Pass Legends Autographs Blue /10 #LGAKYB
2011 Press Pass Legends Autographs Gold /25 #LGAKYB
2011 Press Pass Legends Autographs Printing Plates Black /1 #LGAKYB
2011 Press Pass Legends Autographs Printing Plates Cyan /1 #LGAKYB
2011 Press Pass Legends Autographs Printing Plates Magenta /1 #LGAKYB
2011 Press Pass Legends Autographs Printing Plates Yellow /1 #LGAKYB
2011 Press Pass Legends Autographs Silver /50 #LGAKYB
2011 Press Pass Legends Gold /250 #39
2011 Press Pass Legends Holofoil /25 #39
2011 Press Pass Legends Printing Plates Black /1 #39
2011 Press Pass Legends Printing Plates Cyan /1 #39
2011 Press Pass Legends Printing Plates Magenta /1 #39
2011 Press Pass Legends Printing Plates Yellow /1 #39
2011 Press Pass Legends Prominent Pieces Gold /50 #PPKYB
2011 Press Pass Legends Prominent Pieces Holofoil /25 #PPKYB
2011 Press Pass Legends Prominent Pieces Oversized Firesuit /25 #PPOEKYB
2011 Press Pass Legends Prominent Pieces Purple /15 #PPKYB
2011 Press Pass Legends Prominent Pieces Silver /99 #PPKYB
2011 Press Pass Legends Purple /25 #39
2011 Press Pass Legends Red /99 #39
2011 Press Pass Legends Solo /1 #39
2011 Press Pass Premium #37
2011 Press Pass Premium #58
2011 Press Pass Premium #76
2011 Press Pass Premium #8A
2011 Press Pass Premium #8B
2011 Press Pass Premium Crystal Ball #CB9
2011 Press Pass Premium Crystal Ball Autographs /10 #CBAKB
2011 Press Pass Premium Double Burner /25 #DBKYB
2011 Press Pass Premium Hot Pursuit 3D #HP10
2011 Press Pass Premium Hot Pursuit Autographs /10 #HPAKB
2011 Press Pass Premium Hot Pursuit National Convention #HP10
2011 Press Pass Premium Hot Threads /150 #HTKB2
2011 Press Pass Premium Hot Threads Fast Pass /25 #HTKB2
2011 Press Pass Premium Hot Threads Multi Color /25 #HTKB2
2011 Press Pass Premium Hot Threads Patches /12 #NNO
2011 Press Pass Premium Hot Threads Secondary Color /99 #HTKB2
2011 Press Pass Premium Pairings Firesuits /25 #PPKBDH
2011 Press Pass Premium Pairings Signatures /5 #PPAKBDH
2011 Press Pass Premium Purple /25 #8
2011 Press Pass Premium Purple /25 #37
2011 Press Pass Premium Purple /25 #58
2011 Press Pass Premium Purple /25 #76
2011 Press Pass Premium Signatures /32 #PSKB2
2011 Press Pass Previews /5 #EB7
2011 Press Pass Previews /1 #EB190
2011 Press Pass Purple /25 #7
2011 Press Pass Purple /25 #190
2011 Press Pass Showcase /499 #13
2011 Press Pass Showcase /499 #48
2011 Press Pass Showcase /499 #54
2011 Press Pass Showcase Classic Collections Firesuit /45 #CCMJGR
2011 Press Pass Showcase Classic Collections Firesuit Patches /5 #CCMJGR
2011 Press Pass Showcase Classic Collections Ink /25 #CCMJGR
2011 Press Pass Showcase Classic Collections Ink Gold /5 #CCMJGR
2011 Press Pass Showcase Classic Collections Ink Melting /1 #CCMJGR
2011 Press Pass Showcase Classic Collections Sheet Metal /99 #CCMJGR
2011 Press Pass Showcase Elite Exhibit Ink /50 #EEIKYB
2011 Press Pass Showcase Elite Exhibit Ink Gold /25 #EEIKYB
2011 Press Pass Showcase Elite Exhibit Ink Melting /1 #EEIKYB
2011 Press Pass Showcase Gold /125 #13
2011 Press Pass Showcase Gold /125 #48
2011 Press Pass Showcase Gold /125 #54
2011 Press Pass Showcase Green /25 #13
2011 Press Pass Showcase Green /25 #48
2011 Press Pass Showcase Green /25 #54
2011 Press Pass Showcase Masterpieces Ink /45 #MPIKYB
2011 Press Pass Showcase Masterpieces Ink Gold /25 #MPIKYB
2011 Press Pass Showcase Masterpieces Ink Melting /1 #MPIKYB
2011 Press Pass Showcase Masterpieces Memorabilia /99 #MPMKYB
2011 Press Pass Showcase Masterpieces Memorabilia Gold /45 #MPMKYB
2011 Press Pass Showcase Masterpieces Memorabilia Melting /5 #MPMKYB
2011 Press Pass Showcase Melting /1 #13
2011 Press Pass Showcase Melting /1 #48
2011 Press Pass Showcase Melting /1 #54
2011 Press Pass Showcase Prized Pieces Firesuit /99 #PPMKYB
2011 Press Pass Showcase Prized Pieces Firesuit Gold /45 #PPMKYB
2011 Press Pass Showcase Prized Pieces Firesuit Ink /25 #PPIKYB
2011 Press Pass Showcase Prized Pieces Firesuit Patches Ink /1 #PPIKYB
2011 Press Pass Showcase Prized Pieces Firesuit Patches Melting /5 #PPMKYB
2011 Press Pass Showcase Prized Pieces Sheet Metal Ink /45 #PPIKYB
2011 Press Pass Showcase Showroom /499 #SR6
2011 Press Pass Showcase Showroom Gold /125 #SR6
2011 Press Pass Showcase Showroom Melting /1 #SR6
2011 Press Pass Showcase Showroom Memorabilia Sheet Metal /45 #SRMKYB
2011 Press Pass Showcase Showroom Memorabilia Sheet Metal Gold /25 #SRMKYB
2011 Press Pass Showcase Showroom Memorabilia Sheet Metal Melting /5 #SRMKYB
2011 Press Pass Signature Series /11 #SSTKYB
2011 Press Pass Signature Series /11 #SSCKYB
2011 Press Pass Signature Series /11 #SSFKYB
2011 Press Pass Signature Series /11 #SSMKYB
2011 Press Pass Signings Black and White /10 #PPSKyB
2011 Press Pass Signings Brushed Metal /70 #PPSKyB
2011 Press Pass Signings Holofoil /25 #PPSKyB
2011 Press Pass Signings Printing Plates Black /1 #PPSKyB
2011 Press Pass Signings Printing Plates Cyan /1 #PPSKyB
2011 Press Pass Signings Printing Plates Magenta /1 #PPSKyB
2011 Press Pass Signings Printing Plates Yellow /1 #PPSKyB
2011 Press Pass Stealth #28
2011 Press Pass Stealth #29
2011 Press Pass Stealth #30
2011 Press Pass Stealth #98
2011 Press Pass Stealth #88
2011 Press Pass Stealth Afterburner /99 #ABKYB
2011 Press Pass Stealth Afterburner Gold /25 #ABKYB
2011 Press Pass Stealth Black and White /25 #28
2011 Press Pass Stealth Black and White /25 #29
2011 Press Pass Stealth Black and White /25 #30
2011 Press Pass Stealth Black and White /25 #88
2011 Press Pass Stealth Black and White /25 #98
2011 Press Pass Stealth Holofoil /99 #28
2011 Press Pass Stealth Holofoil /99 #29
2011 Press Pass Stealth Holofoil /99 #30
2011 Press Pass Stealth Holofoil /99 #88
2011 Press Pass Stealth Holofoil /99 #98
2011 Press Pass Stealth In Flight Report #IF6
2011 Press Pass Stealth Metal of Honor Medal of Honor /50 #BAKYB
2011 Press Pass Stealth Metal of Honor Purple Heart /25 #MHKYB
2011 Press Pass Stealth Metal of Honor Silver Star /99 #BAKYB
2011 Press Pass Stealth Purple /25 #28
2011 Press Pass Stealth Purple /25 #29
2011 Press Pass Stealth Purple /25 #30
2011 Press Pass Target Winning Tickets #WTT7
2011 Press Pass Tradin' Paint #TP2
2011 Press Pass Tradin' Paint Sheet Metal Blue /25 #TPKYB
2011 Press Pass Tradin' Paint Sheet Metal Holofoil /50 #TPKYB
2011 Press Pass Wal-Mart Top 12 Tires /25 #T12KYB
2011 Press Pass Wal-Mart Winning Tickets #WTW2
2011 Press Pass Wal-Mart Winning Tickets #WTW7
2011 Press Pass Wal-Mart Winning Tickets #WTW4
2011 Press Pass Winning Tickets #WTXTR
2011 Press Pass Winning Tickets #WT10
2011 Press Pass Winning Tickets #WT12
2011 Press Pass Winning Tickets #WT24
2011 Press Pass Winning Tickets #WT39
2011 Press Pass Winning Tickets #WT41
2011 Press Pass Winning Tickets #WT46
2011 Wheels Main Event #8
2011 Wheels Main Event #86
2011 Wheels Main Event All Stars #A2
2011 Wheels Main Event All Stars Brushed Foil /199 #A2
2011 Wheels Main Event All Stars Holofoil /50 #A2
2011 Wheels Main Event Black and White #8
2011 Wheels Main Event Black and White #86
2011 Wheels Main Event Blue /75 #8
2011 Wheels Main Event Blue /75 #86
2011 Wheels Main Event Gloves Off Holofoil /25 #GOKB
2011 Wheels Main Event Gloves Off Silver /99 #GOKB
2011 Wheels Main Event Green /1 #8
2011 Wheels Main Event Green /1 #86
2011 Wheels Main Event Headliners Holofoil /25 #HLKYB
2011 Wheels Main Event Headliners Silver /99 #HLKYB
2011 Wheels Main Event Joe Gibbs Racing 20th Anniversary #JGR5
2011 Wheels Main Event Joe Gibbs Racing 20th Anniversary Brushed Foil /199 #JGR5
2011 Wheels Main Event Joe Gibbs Racing 20th Anniversary Holofoil /50 #JGR5
2011 Wheels Main Event Marks Autographs Blue /5 #MEKYB
2011 Wheels Main Event Marks Autographs Gold /15 #MEKYB
2011 Wheels Main Event Marks Autographs Silver /30 #MEKYB
2011 Wheels Main Event Matchups Autographs /10 #MEMJGKB
2011 Wheels Main Event Matchups Autographs /10 #MEMKBCE
2011 Wheels Main Event Matchups Autographs /10 #MEMKBDH
2011 Wheels Main Event Materials Holofoil /25 #MEMKYB
2011 Wheels Main Event Materials Silver /99 #MEMKYB
2011 Wheels Main Event Rear View #R7
2011 Wheels Main Event Rear View Brushed Foil /199 #R7
2011 Wheels Main Event Rear View Holofoil /50 #R7
2011 Wheels Main Event Red /20 #8
2011 Wheels Main Event Red /20 #86
2012 Press Pass #7
2012 Press Pass #82
2012 Press Pass #64
2012 Press Pass #93
2012 Press Pass #99
2012 Press Pass Autographs Blue /5 #PPAKYB
2012 Press Pass Autographs Printing Plates Black /1 #PPAKYB
2012 Press Pass Autographs Printing Plates Cyan /1 #PPAKYB
2012 Press Pass Autographs Printing Plates Magenta /1 #PPAKYB
2012 Press Pass Autographs Printing Plates Yellow /1 #PPAKYB
2012 Press Pass Autographs Red /5 #PPAKYB
2012 Press Pass Autographs Silver /20 #PPAKYB
2012 Press Pass Blue #7
2012 Press Pass Blue #64
2012 Press Pass Blue #82
2012 Press Pass Blue #93
2012 Press Pass Blue #99
2012 Press Pass Blue Holofoil /35 #7
2012 Press Pass Blue Holofoil /35 #64
2012 Press Pass Blue Holofoil /35 #82
2012 Press Pass Blue Holofoil /35 #93
2012 Press Pass Blue Holofoil /35 #99
2012 Press Pass Burning Rubber Gold /99 #BRKYB3
2012 Press Pass Burning Rubber Gold /99 #BRKYB4
2012 Press Pass Burning Rubber Gold /99 #BRKYB2
2012 Press Pass Burning Rubber Gold /99 #BRKYB
2012 Press Pass Burning Rubber Holofoil /25 #BRKYB
2012 Press Pass Burning Rubber Holofoil /25 #BRKYB2
2012 Press Pass Burning Rubber Holofoil /25 #BRKYB3
2012 Press Pass Burning Rubber Holofoil /25 #BRKYB4
2012 Press Pass Burning Rubber Prime Cuts /25 #BRKYB
2012 Press Pass Burning Rubber Prime Cuts /25 #BRKYB2
2012 Press Pass Burning Rubber Prime Cuts /25 #BRKYB3
2012 Press Pass Burning Rubber Prime Cuts /25 #BRKYB4
2012 Press Pass Burning Rubber Purple /15 #BRKYB
2012 Press Pass Burning Rubber Purple /15 #BRKYB2
2012 Press Pass Burning Rubber Purple /15 #BRKYB3
2012 Press Pass Burning Rubber Purple /15 #BRKYB4
2012 Press Pass Cup Chase #CCR4
2012 Press Pass Fanfare #48
2012 Press Pass Fanfare #10
2012 Press Pass Fanfare #9
2012 Press Pass Fanfare Autographs Blue /5 #KB3
2012 Press Pass Fanfare Autographs Blue /5 #KB4
2012 Press Pass Fanfare Autographs Gold /15 #KB3
2012 Press Pass Fanfare Autographs Gold /75 #KB4
2012 Press Pass Fanfare Autographs Red /10 #KB3
2012 Press Pass Fanfare Autographs Red /25 #KB4
2012 Press Pass Fanfare Autographs Silver /50 #KB3
2012 Press Pass Fanfare Autographs Silver /99 #KB4
2012 Press Pass Fanfare Blue Foil Die Cuts #9
2012 Press Pass Fanfare Blue Foil Die Cuts #10
2012 Press Pass Fanfare Blue Foil Die Cuts #48
2012 Press Pass Fanfare Diamond /5 #9
2012 Press Pass Fanfare Diamond /5 #10
2012 Press Pass Fanfare Diamond /5 #48
2012 Press Pass Fanfare Dual Autographs /10 #BB2
2012 Press Pass Fanfare Holofoil Die Cuts #9
2012 Press Pass Fanfare Holofoil Die Cuts #10
2012 Press Pass Fanfare Holofoil Die Cuts #48
2012 Press Pass Fanfare Magnificent Materials /250 #MMKYB
2012 Press Pass Fanfare Magnificent Materials /99 #MMKYB3
2012 Press Pass Fanfare Magnificent Materials Dual Swatches /50 #MMKYB
2012 Press Pass Fanfare Magnificent Materials Dual Swatches Melting /10 #MMKYB
2012 Press Pass Fanfare Magnificent Materials Gold /99 #MMKYB
2012 Press Pass Fanfare Magnificent Materials Gold /75 #MMKYB3
2012 Press Pass Fanfare Magnificent Materials Signatures /25 #KB
2012 Press Pass Fanfare Magnificent Materials Signatures Blue /5 #KB
2012 Press Pass Fanfare Power Rankings #PR3
2012 Press Pass Fanfare Sapphire /20 #9
2012 Press Pass Fanfare Sapphire /20 #10
2012 Press Pass Fanfare Sapphire /20 #48
2012 Press Pass Fanfare Showtime #S8
2012 Press Pass Fanfare Silver /25 #9
2012 Press Pass Fanfare Silver /25 #10
2012 Press Pass Fanfare Silver /25 #48
2012 Press Pass Four Wide Autographs /5 #KB
2012 Press Pass Four Wide Firesuit /25 #FWKB
2012 Press Pass Four Wide Glove /1 #FWKB
2012 Press Pass Four Wide Sheet Metal /15 #FWKB
2012 Press Pass Four Wide Tire /10 #FWKB
2012 Press Pass Gold #7
2012 Press Pass Gold #64
2012 Press Pass Gold #82
2012 Press Pass Gold #93
2012 Press Pass Gold #99
2012 Press Pass Ignite #10
2012 Press Pass Ignite Double Burner Gun Metal /10 #DBKYB
2012 Press Pass Ignite Double Burner Red /1 #DBKYB
2012 Press Pass Ignite Double Burner Silver /25 #DBKYB
2012 Press Pass Ignite Materials Autographs Gun Metal /20 #IMKYB
2012 Press Pass Ignite Materials Autographs Red /5 #IMKYB
2012 Press Pass Ignite Materials Autographs Silver /125 #IMKYB
2012 Press Pass Ignite Materials Gun Metal /99 #IMKYB
2012 Press Pass Ignite Materials Red /10 #IMKYB
2012 Press Pass Ignite Materials Silver #IMKYB
2012 Press Pass Ignite Profile #P11
2012 Press Pass Ignite Proofs Black and White /50 #10
2012 Press Pass Ignite Proofs Cyan #10
2012 Press Pass Ignite Proofs Magenta #10
2012 Press Pass Ignite Proofs Yellow /10 #10
2012 Press Pass Ignite Steel Horses #SH9
2012 Press Pass Ignite Supercharged Signatures /5 #SSKYB
2012 Press Pass Legends #39
2012 Press Pass Legends Blue Holofoil /1 #39
2012 Press Pass Legends Gold /275 #39
2012 Press Pass Legends Green #39
2012 Press Pass Legends Prominent Pieces Gold /50 #KB
2012 Press Pass Legends Prominent Pieces Holofoil /25 #KB
2012 Press Pass Legends Prominent Pieces Oversized Firesuit /25 #KB
2012 Press Pass Legends Prominent Pieces Silver /99 #KB
2012 Press Pass Legends Rainbow Holofoil /50 #39
2012 Press Pass Legends Red /99 #39
2012 Press Pass Legends Silver Holofoil /25 #39
2012 Press Pass Power Picks Blue /50 #3
2012 Press Pass Power Picks Blue /50 #32
2012 Press Pass Power Picks Blue /50 #63
2012 Press Pass Power Picks Gold /50 #3
2012 Press Pass Power Picks Gold /50 #32
2012 Press Pass Power Picks Gold /50 #63
2012 Press Pass Power Picks Holofoil /10 #3
2012 Press Pass Power Picks Holofoil /10 #32
2012 Press Pass Power Picks Holofoil /10 #63
2012 Press Pass Purple /35 #7
2012 Press Pass Purple /35 #64
2012 Press Pass Purple /35 #82
2012 Press Pass Purple /35 #93
2012 Press Pass Purple /35 #99
2012 Press Pass Redline #10
2012 Press Pass Redline #41
2012 Press Pass Redline Black /99 #10
2012 Press Pass Redline Black /99 #41
2012 Press Pass Redline Cyan /50 #10
2012 Press Pass Redline Cyan /50 #41
2012 Press Pass Redline Full Throttle Dual Relic Blue /5 #FTKYB
2012 Press Pass Redline Full Throttle Dual Relic Gold /10 #FTKYB
2012 Press Pass Redline Full Throttle Dual Relic Melting /1 #FTKYB
2012 Press Pass Redline Full Throttle Dual Relic Red /75 #FTKYB
2012 Press Pass Redline Full Throttle Dual Relic Silver /25 #FTKYB
2012 Press Pass Redline Intensity #I1
2012 Press Pass Redline Magenta /15 #10
2012 Press Pass Redline Magenta /15 #41
2012 Press Pass Redline Muscle Car Sheet Metal Blue /5 #MCKYB
2012 Press Pass Redline Muscle Car Sheet Metal Gold /10 #MCKYB
2012 Press Pass Redline Muscle Car Sheet Metal Melting /1 #MCKYB
2012 Press Pass Redline Muscle Car Sheet Metal Red /75 #MCKYB
2012 Press Pass Redline Muscle Car Sheet Metal Silver /25 #MCKYB
2012 Press Pass Redline Performance Driven #PD1
2012 Press Pass Redline Pieces of the Action Blue /10 #PAKYB
2012 Press Pass Redline Pieces of the Action Gold /25 #PAKYB
2012 Press Pass Redline Pieces of the Action Melting /1 #PAKYB
2012 Press Pass Redline Pieces of the Action Red /75 #PAKYB
2012 Press Pass Redline Pieces of the Action Silver /50 #PAKYB
2012 Press Pass Redline Relic Autographs Blue /10 #RLRKYB
2012 Press Pass Redline Relic Autographs Gold /25 #RLRKYB
2012 Press Pass Redline Relic Autographs Melting /1 #RLRKYB
2012 Press Pass Redline Relic Autographs Red /75 #RLRKYB
2012 Press Pass Redline Relic Autographs Silver /50 #RLRKYB
2012 Press Pass Redline Relics Blue /5 #RLKYB
2012 Press Pass Redline Relics Gold /10 #RLKYB
2012 Press Pass Redline Relics Melting /1 #RLKYB

2012 Press Pass Redline Relics Red /75 #RLKYB
2012 Press Pass Redline Relics Silver /25 #RLKYB
2012 Press Pass Redline Rookie Year Relic Autographs Blue /5 #RYKYB
2012 Press Pass Redline Rookie Year Relic Autographs Gold /25 #RYKYB
2012 Press Pass Redline Rookie Year Relic Autographs Melting /1 #RYKYB
2012 Press Pass Redline Rookie Year Relic Autographs Red /50 #RYKYB
2012 Press Pass Redline RPM #RPM1
2012 Press Pass Redline Signatures Blue /5 #RSKYB
2012 Press Pass Redline Signatures Gold /23 #RSKYB
2012 Press Pass Redline Signatures Holofoil /10 #RSKYB
2012 Press Pass Redline Signatures Melting /1 #RSKYB
2012 Press Pass Redline Signatures Red /50 #RSKYB
2012 Press Pass Redline V8 Relics Blue /5 #V8KYB
2012 Press Pass Redline V8 Relics Gold /10 #V8KYB
2012 Press Pass Redline V8 Relics Melting /1 #V8KYB
2012 Press Pass Redline V8 Relics Red /25 #V8KYB
2012 Press Pass Redline Yellow /1 #10
2012 Press Pass Redline Yellow /1 #41
2012 Press Pass Showcar #SC9
2012 Press Pass Showcase /499 #56
2012 Press Pass Showcase /499 #49
2012 Press Pass Showcase /499 #34
2012 Press Pass Showcase /499 #7
2012 Press Pass Showcase Classic Collections Ink /10 #CCMJGR
2012 Press Pass Showcase Classic Collections Ink Gold /5 #CCMJGR
2012 Press Pass Showcase Classic Collections Ink Melting /1 #CCMJGR
2012 Press Pass Showcase Classic Collections Memorabilia /99 #CCMJGR
2012 Press Pass Showcase Classic Collections Memorabilia Gold /50 #CCMJGR
2012 Press Pass Showcase Classic Collections Memorabilia Melting /5 #CCMJGR
2012 Press Pass Showcase Elite Exhibit Ink /50 #EEIKYB
2012 Press Pass Showcase Elite Exhibit Ink Gold /25 #EEIKYB
2012 Press Pass Showcase Elite Exhibit Ink Melting /1 #EEIKYB
2012 Press Pass Showcase Gold /125 #7
2012 Press Pass Showcase Gold /125 #34
2012 Press Pass Showcase Gold /125 #49
2012 Press Pass Showcase Gold /125 #56
2012 Press Pass Showcase Green /5 #7
2012 Press Pass Showcase Green /5 #34
2012 Press Pass Showcase Green /5 #49
2012 Press Pass Showcase Green /5 #56
2012 Press Pass Showcase Masterpieces Ink /50 #MPIKYB
2012 Press Pass Showcase Masterpieces Ink Gold /25 #MPIKYB
2012 Press Pass Showcase Masterpieces Ink Melting /1 #MPIKYB
2012 Press Pass Showcase Masterpieces Memorabilia /99 #MPKYB
2012 Press Pass Showcase Masterpieces Memorabilia Gold /50 #MPKYB
2012 Press Pass Showcase Masterpieces Memorabilia Melting /5 #MPKYB
2012 Press Pass Showcase Melting /1 #7
2012 Press Pass Showcase Melting /1 #34
2012 Press Pass Showcase Melting /1 #49
2012 Press Pass Showcase Melting /1 #56
2012 Press Pass Showcase Prized Pieces /99 #PPKYB
2012 Press Pass Showcase Prized Pieces Gold /50 #PPKYB
2012 Press Pass Showcase Prized Pieces Ink /50 #PPIKYB
2012 Press Pass Showcase Prized Pieces Ink Gold /25 #PPIKYB
2012 Press Pass Showcase Prized Pieces Ink Melting /1 #PPIKYB
2012 Press Pass Showcase Prized Pieces Melting /5 #PPKYB
2012 Press Pass Showcase Purple /1 #7
2012 Press Pass Showcase Purple /1 #34
2012 Press Pass Showcase Purple /1 #49
2012 Press Pass Showcase Purple /1 #56
2012 Press Pass Showcase Red /25 #7
2012 Press Pass Showcase Red /25 #34
2012 Press Pass Showcase Red /25 #49
2012 Press Pass Showcase Red /25 #56
2012 Press Pass Showcase Richard Petty 75th Birthday Tribute /10 #RPKYB
2012 Press Pass Showcase Richard Petty 75th Birthday Tribute Melting /1 #RPKYB
2012 Press Pass Showcase Showcase Patches /5 #SSPKYB
2012 Press Pass Showcase Showcase Patches Melting /1 #SSPKYB
2012 Press Pass Showcase Showroom /499 #SR9
2012 Press Pass Showcase Showroom Gold /125 #SR9
2012 Press Pass Showcase Showroom Melting /1 #SR9
2012 Press Pass Showcase Showroom Memorabilia /99 #SRKYB
2012 Press Pass Showcase Showroom Memorabilia Gold /50 #SRKYB
2012 Press Pass Showcase Showroom Memorabilia Melting /5 #SRKYB
2012 Press Pass Showcase Signature Patches /1 #SSPKYB
2012 Press Pass Showman #SM9
2012 Press Pass Signature Series Race Used /12 #PPAKYB1
2012 Press Pass Signature Series Race Used /12 #PPAKYB2
2012 Press Pass Snapshots #SS7
2012 Press Pass Snapshots #SS69
2012 Press Pass Target Snapshots #SSTG5
2012 Press Pass Triple Gear 3 in 1 /5 #TGKYB
2012 Press Pass Triple Gear Firesuit and Sheet Metal /15 #TGKYB
2012 Press Pass Triple Gear Tire /25 #TGKYB
2012 Total Memorabilia #6A
2012 Total Memorabilia #6B
2012 Total Memorabilia Black and White /99 #6
2012 Total Memorabilia Dual Swatch Gold /75 #TMKYB
2012 Total Memorabilia Dual Swatch Holofoil /25 #TMKYB
2012 Total Memorabilia Dual Swatch Melting /5 #TMKYB
2012 Total Memorabilia Dual Swatch Silver /99 #TMKYB
2012 Total Memorabilia Gold /275 #6
2012 Total Memorabilia Hot Rod Relics Gold /50 #HRRKYN
2012 Total Memorabilia Hot Rod Relics Holofoil /10 #HRRKYN
2012 Total Memorabilia Hot Rod Relics Melting /1 #HRRKYN
2012 Total Memorabilia Hot Rod Relics Silver /99 #HRRKYN
2012 Total Memorabilia Jumbo Swatch Gold /50 #TMKYB
2012 Total Memorabilia Jumbo Swatch Holofoil /10 #TMKYB
2012 Total Memorabilia Jumbo Swatch Melting /1 #TMKYB
2012 Total Memorabilia Quad Swatch Gold /25 #TMKYB
2012 Total Memorabilia Quad Swatch Holofoil /10 #TMKYB
2012 Total Memorabilia Quad Swatch Melting /1 #TMKYB
2012 Total Memorabilia Quad Swatch Silver /50 #TMKYB
2012 Total Memorabilia Red Retail /250 #6
2012 Total Memorabilia Signature Collection Dual Swatch Silver /10 #SCKYB
2012 Total Memorabilia Signature Collection Quad Swatch Holofoil /5 #SCKYB
2012 Total Memorabilia Signature Collection Single Swatch Melting /1 #SCKYB
2012 Total Memorabilia Signature Collection Triple Swatch Gold /10 #SCKYB
2012 Total Memorabilia Single Swatch Gold /99 #TMKYB
2012 Total Memorabilia Single Swatch Holofoil /50 #TMKYB
2012 Total Memorabilia Single Swatch Melting /10 #TMKYB
2012 Total Memorabilia Single Swatch Silver /199 #TMKYB
2012 Total Memorabilia Tandem Treasures Dual Memorabilia Gold /75 #TTKBJG
2012 Total Memorabilia Tandem Treasures Dual Memorabilia Gold /75 #TTKBJD
2012 Total Memorabilia Tandem Treasures Dual Memorabilia Holofoil /25 #TTKBJG
2012 Total Memorabilia Tandem Treasures Dual Memorabilia Holofoil /25 #TTKBJD
2012 Total Memorabilia Tandem Treasures Dual Memorabilia Melting /5 #TTKBJG
2012 Total Memorabilia Tandem Treasures Dual Memorabilia Melting /5 #TTKBJD
2012 Total Memorabilia Tandem Treasures Dual Memorabilia Silver /99 #TTKBJG
2012 Total Memorabilia Tandem Treasures Dual Memorabilia Silver /99 #TTKBJD
2012 Total Memorabilia Triple Swatch Gold /50 #TMKYB
2012 Total Memorabilia Triple Swatch Holofoil /25 #TMKYB
2012 Total Memorabilia Triple Swatch Melting /1 #TMKYB
2012 Total Memorabilia Triple Swatch Silver /99 #TMKYB
2013 Press Pass #9
2013 Press Pass #10
2013 Press Pass #48
2013 Press Pass #92
2013 Press Pass #67
2013 Press Pass #77
2013 Press Pass #95
2013 Press Pass Aerodynamic Autographs Blue /1 #KB
2013 Press Pass Aerodynamic Autographs Holofoil /5 #KB
2013 Press Pass Aerodynamic Autographs Printing Plates Black /1 #KB
2013 Press Pass Aerodynamic Autographs Printing Plates Cyan /1 #KB
2013 Press Pass Aerodynamic Autographs Printing Plates Magenta /1 #KB
2013 Press Pass Aerodynamic Autographs Printing Plates Yellow /1 #KB
2013 Press Pass Burning Rubber Blue /50 #BRKB
2013 Press Pass Burning Rubber Gold /199 #BRKB
2013 Press Pass Burning Rubber Holofoil /75 #BRKB
2013 Press Pass Burning Rubber Letterman /8 #BRLKB
2013 Press Pass Burning Rubber Melting /10 #BRKB
2013 Press Pass Certified Winners Autographs Gold /10 #KYB
2013 Press Pass Certified Winners Autographs Melting /5 #KYB
2013 Press Pass Color Proofs Black #9
2013 Press Pass Color Proofs Black #10
2013 Press Pass Color Proofs Black #48
2013 Press Pass Color Proofs Black #67
2013 Press Pass Color Proofs Black #77
2013 Press Pass Color Proofs Black #92
2013 Press Pass Color Proofs Black #95
2013 Press Pass Color Proofs Cyan /35 #9
2013 Press Pass Color Proofs Cyan /35 #10
2013 Press Pass Color Proofs Cyan /35 #48
2013 Press Pass Color Proofs Cyan /35 #67
2013 Press Pass Color Proofs Cyan /35 #77
2013 Press Pass Color Proofs Cyan /35 #92
2013 Press Pass Color Proofs Cyan /35 #95
2013 Press Pass Color Proofs Magenta #9
2013 Press Pass Color Proofs Magenta #10
2013 Press Pass Color Proofs Magenta #48
2013 Press Pass Color Proofs Magenta #67
2013 Press Pass Color Proofs Magenta #77
2013 Press Pass Color Proofs Magenta #92
2013 Press Pass Color Proofs Magenta #95
2013 Press Pass Color Proofs Yellow /5 #9
2013 Press Pass Color Proofs Yellow /5 #10
2013 Press Pass Color Proofs Yellow /5 #48
2013 Press Pass Color Proofs Yellow /5 #67
2013 Press Pass Color Proofs Yellow /5 #77
2013 Press Pass Color Proofs Yellow /5 #92
2013 Press Pass Color Proofs Yellow /5 #95
2013 Press Pass Cup Chase #CC4
2013 Press Pass Cup Chase Prizes #CCP3
2013 Press Pass Fanfare #12
2013 Press Pass Fanfare #13
2013 Press Pass Fanfare Autographs Blue /1 #KYB
2013 Press Pass Fanfare Autographs Gold /10 #KYB
2013 Press Pass Fanfare Autographs Green /2 #KYB
2013 Press Pass Fanfare Autographs Red /5 #KYB
2013 Press Pass Fanfare Autographs Silver /10 #KYB
2013 Press Pass Fanfare Diamond Die Cuts /5 #12
2013 Press Pass Fanfare Diamond Die Cuts /5 #13
2013 Press Pass Fanfare Fan Following #FF7
2013 Press Pass Fanfare Green /3 #12
2013 Press Pass Fanfare Green /3 #13
2013 Press Pass Fanfare Holofoil Die Cuts #12
2013 Press Pass Fanfare Holofoil Die Cuts #13
2013 Press Pass Fanfare Magnificent Jumbo Materials Signatures /10 #KYB
2013 Press Pass Fanfare Magnificent Materials Dual Swatches /50 #KYB
2013 Press Pass Fanfare Magnificent Materials Dual Swatches Melting /10 #KYB
2013 Press Pass Fanfare Magnificent Materials Gold /50 #KYB
2013 Press Pass Fanfare Magnificent Materials Jumbo Swatches /25 #KYB
2013 Press Pass Fanfare Magnificent Materials Signatures /50 #KYB
2013 Press Pass Fanfare Magnificent Materials Signatures Blue /25 #KYB
2013 Press Pass Fanfare Magnificent Materials Silver /199 #KYB
2013 Press Pass Fanfare Red Foil Die Cuts #12
2013 Press Pass Fanfare Red Foil Die Cuts #13
2013 Press Pass Fanfare Sapphire /20 #12
2013 Press Pass Fanfare Sapphire /20 #13
2013 Press Pass Fanfare Showtime #S4
2013 Press Pass Fanfare Signature Ride Autographs /10 #KYB
2013 Press Pass Fanfare Signature Ride Autographs Blue /1 #KYB
2013 Press Pass Fanfare Signature Ride Autographs Red /5 #KYB
2013 Press Pass Fanfare Silver /25 #12
2013 Press Pass Fanfare Silver /25 #13
2013 Press Pass Four Wide Gold /10 #FWKB
2013 Press Pass Four Wide Melting /1 #FWKB
2013 Press Pass Ignite #8
2013 Press Pass Ignite #58
2013 Press Pass Ignite Convoy #10
2013 Press Pass Ignite Double Burner Blue Holofoil /10 #DBKYB
2013 Press Pass Ignite Double Burner Red /1 #DBKYB
2013 Press Pass Ignite Double Burner Silver /25 #DBKYB
2013 Press Pass Ignite Hot Threads Blue Holofoil /99 #HTKYB
2013 Press Pass Ignite Hot Threads Patch Red /10 #HTKYB
2013 Press Pass Ignite Hot Threads Patch Red Oversized /20 #HTPKYB
2013 Press Pass Ignite Hot Threads Silver #HTKYB
2013 Press Pass Ignite Ink Black /45 #IIKYB
2013 Press Pass Ignite Ink Blue /10 #IIKYB
2013 Press Pass Ignite Ink Red /5 #IIKYB
2013 Press Pass Ignite Profile #1
2013 Press Pass Ignite Proofs Black and White /50 #8
2013 Press Pass Ignite Proofs Black and White /50 #58
2013 Press Pass Ignite Proofs Cyan #8
2013 Press Pass Ignite Proofs Cyan #58
2013 Press Pass Ignite Proofs Magenta #8
2013 Press Pass Ignite Proofs Magenta #58
2013 Press Pass Ignite Proofs Yellow /5 #8
2013 Press Pass Ignite Proofs Yellow /5 #58
2013 Press Pass Ignite Supercharged Signatures Blue Holofoil /10 #SSKYB
2013 Press Pass Ignite Supercharged Signatures Red /1 #SSKYB
2013 Press Pass Ignite Turning Point #9
2013 Press Pass Legends #41
2013 Press Pass Legends Autographs Blue /5 #LGKYB
2013 Press Pass Legends Autographs Gold /4 #LGKYB
2013 Press Pass Legends Autographs Holofoil #LGKYB
2013 Press Pass Legends Autographs Printing Plates Black /1 #LGKYB
2013 Press Pass Legends Autographs Printing Plates Cyan /1 #LGKYB
2013 Press Pass Legends Autographs Printing Plates Magenta /1 #LGKYB
2013 Press Pass Legends Autographs Printing Plates Yellow /1 #LGKYB
2013 Press Pass Legends Autographs Silver #LGKYB
2013 Press Pass Legends Blue #41
2013 Press Pass Legends Blue Holofoil /1 #41
2013 Press Pass Legends Four Wide Memorabilia Autographs Gold /25 #FWSEKB
2013 Press Pass Legends Four Wide Memorabilia Autographs Melting /5 #FWSEKB
2013 Press Pass Legends Gold /149 #41
2013 Press Pass Legends Holofoil /10 #41
2013 Press Pass Legends Printing Plates Black /1 #41
2013 Press Pass Legends Printing Plates Cyan /1 #41
2013 Press Pass Legends Printing Plates Magenta /1 #41
2013 Press Pass Legends Printing Plates Yellow /1 #41
2013 Press Pass Legends Prominent Pieces Gold /10 #PPKB
2013 Press Pass Legends Prominent Pieces Holofoil /5 #PPKB
2013 Press Pass Legends Prominent Pieces Oversized Firesuit /5 #PPKB
2013 Press Pass Legends Prominent Pieces Silver /25 #PPKB
2013 Press Pass Legends Red /99 #41
2013 Press Pass Power Picks Blue /99 #3
2013 Press Pass Power Picks Blue /99 #32
2013 Press Pass Power Picks Gold /50 #3
2013 Press Pass Power Picks Gold /50 #32
2013 Press Pass Power Picks Holofoil /10 #3
2013 Press Pass Power Picks Holofoil /10 #32
2013 Press Pass Racing Champions #RC9
2013 Press Pass Racing Champions #RC27
2013 Press Pass Redline #12
2013 Press Pass Redline #13
2013 Press Pass Redline Black /99 #12
2013 Press Pass Redline Black /99 #13
2013 Press Pass Redline Cyan /50 #12
2013 Press Pass Redline Cyan /50 #13
2013 Press Pass Redline Dynamic Duals Dual Relic Blue /5 #DDKYB
2013 Press Pass Redline Dynamic Duals Dual Relic Gold /10 #DDKYB
2013 Press Pass Redline Dynamic Duals Dual Relic Melting /1 #DDKYB
2013 Press Pass Redline Dynamic Duals Dual Relic Red /50 #DDKYB
2013 Press Pass Redline Dynamic Duals Dual Relic Silver /25 #DDKYB
2013 Press Pass Redline Intensity #10
2013 Press Pass Redline Magenta /15 #12
2013 Press Pass Redline Magenta /15 #13
2013 Press Pass Redline Muscle Car Sheet Metal Blue /5 #MCMKYB
2013 Press Pass Redline Muscle Car Sheet Metal Gold /10 #MCMKYB
2013 Press Pass Redline Muscle Car Sheet Metal Melting /1 #MCMKYB
2013 Press Pass Redline Muscle Car Sheet Metal Red /50 #MCMKYB
2013 Press Pass Redline Muscle Car Sheet Metal Silver /25 #MCMKYB
2013 Press Pass Redline Pieces of the Action Blue /10 #PAKYB
2013 Press Pass Redline Pieces of the Action Gold /25 #PAKYB
2013 Press Pass Redline Pieces of the Action Melting /1 #PAKYB
2013 Press Pass Redline Pieces of the Action Red /75 #PAKYB
2013 Press Pass Redline Pieces of the Action Silver /50 #PAKYB
2013 Press Pass Redline Redline Racers #1
2013 Press Pass Redline Relic Autographs Blue /10 #RRSEKYB
2013 Press Pass Redline Relic Autographs Gold /18 #RRSEKYB
2013 Press Pass Redline Relic Autographs Melting /1 #RRSEKYB
2013 Press Pass Redline Relic Autographs Red /50 #RRSEKYB
2013 Press Pass Redline Relic Autographs Silver /26 #RRSEKYB
2013 Press Pass Redline Relics Blue /5 #RRKYB
2013 Press Pass Redline Relics Gold /10 #RRKYB
2013 Press Pass Redline Relics Melting /1 #RRKYB
2013 Press Pass Redline Relics Red /50 #RRKYB
2013 Press Pass Redline Relics Silver /25 #RRKYB
2013 Press Pass Redline RPM #9
2013 Press Pass Redline Signatures Blue /25 #RSKYB1
2013 Press Pass Redline Signatures Blue /10 #RSKYB2
2013 Press Pass Redline Signatures Gold /5 #RSKYB1
2013 Press Pass Redline Signatures Gold /5 #RSKYB2
2013 Press Pass Redline Signatures Holo /10 #RSKYB1
2013 Press Pass Redline Signatures Holo /5 #RSKYB2
2013 Press Pass Redline Signatures Melting /1 #RSKYB1
2013 Press Pass Redline Signatures Melting /1 #RSKYB2
2013 Press Pass Redline Signatures Red /10 #RSKYB2
2013 Press Pass Redline Signatures Red /75 #RSKYB1
2013 Press Pass Redline V8 Relics Blue /5 #V8KYB
2013 Press Pass Redline V8 Relics Gold /10 #V8KYB
2013 Press Pass Redline V8 Relics Melting /1 #V8KYB
2013 Press Pass Redline V8 Relics Red /25 #V8KYB
2013 Press Pass Redline Yellow /1 #12
2013 Press Pass Redline Yellow /1 #13
2013 Press Pass Showcase /349 #7
2013 Press Pass Showcase /349 #31
2013 Press Pass Showcase /349 #52
2013 Press Pass Showcase /349 #59
2013 Press Pass Showcase Black /1 #7
2013 Press Pass Showcase Black /1 #31
2013 Press Pass Showcase Black /1 #52
2013 Press Pass Showcase Black /1 #59
2013 Press Pass Showcase Blue /25 #7
2013 Press Pass Showcase Blue /25 #31
2013 Press Pass Showcase Blue /25 #52
2013 Press Pass Showcase Blue /25 #59
2013 Press Pass Showcase Classic Collections Ink Gold /5 #CCIJGR
2013 Press Pass Showcase Classic Collections Ink Melting /1 #CCIJGR
2013 Press Pass Showcase Classic Collections Ink Red /1 #CCIJGR
2013 Press Pass Showcase Classic Collections Memorabilia Gold /25 #CCMJGR
2013 Press Pass Showcase Classic Collections Memorabilia Melting /5 #CCMJGR
2013 Press Pass Showcase Classic Collections Memorabilia Silver /75 #CCMJGR
2013 Press Pass Showcase Elite Exhibit Ink /35 #EEIKYB
2013 Press Pass Showcase Elite Exhibit Ink Blue /30 #EEIKYB
2013 Press Pass Showcase Elite Exhibit Ink Gold /10 #EEIKYB
2013 Press Pass Showcase Elite Exhibit Ink Melting /1 #EEIKYB
2013 Press Pass Showcase Elite Exhibit Ink Red /5 #EEIKYB
2013 Press Pass Showcase Gold /99 #7
2013 Press Pass Showcase Gold /99 #31
2013 Press Pass Showcase Gold /99 #52
2013 Press Pass Showcase Gold /99 #59
2013 Press Pass Showcase Green /20 #7
2013 Press Pass Showcase Green /20 #31
2013 Press Pass Showcase Green /20 #52
2013 Press Pass Showcase Green /20 #59
2013 Press Pass Showcase Masterpieces Ink /25 #MPIKYB
2013 Press Pass Showcase Masterpieces Ink Gold /10 #MPIKYB
2013 Press Pass Showcase Masterpieces Ink Melting /1 #MPIKYB
2013 Press Pass Showcase Masterpieces Memorabilia /75 #MPKYB
2013 Press Pass Showcase Masterpieces Memorabilia Gold /25 #MPKYB
2013 Press Pass Showcase Masterpieces Memorabilia Melting /5 #MPKYB
2013 Press Pass Showcase Prized Pieces /99 #PPMKYB
2013 Press Pass Showcase Prized Pieces Blue /20 #PPMKYB
2013 Press Pass Showcase Prized Pieces Gold /25 #PPMKYB
2013 Press Pass Showcase Prized Pieces Ink /25 #PPIKYB
2013 Press Pass Showcase Prized Pieces Ink Gold /10 #PPIKYB
2013 Press Pass Showcase Prized Pieces Ink Melting /1 #PPIKYB
2013 Press Pass Showcase Prized Pieces Melting /5 #PPMKYB
2013 Press Pass Showcase Purple /13 #7
2013 Press Pass Showcase Purple /13 #31
2013 Press Pass Showcase Purple /13 #52
2013 Press Pass Showcase Purple /13 #59
2013 Press Pass Showcase Red /10 #7
2013 Press Pass Showcase Red /10 #31
2013 Press Pass Showcase Red /10 #52
2013 Press Pass Showcase Red /10 #59
2013 Press Pass Showcase Series Standouts Gold /50 #3
2013 Press Pass Showcase Series Standouts Memorabilia /75 #SSMKYB
2013 Press Pass Showcase Series Standouts Memorabilia Blue /20 #SSMKYB
2013 Press Pass Showcase Series Standouts Memorabilia Gold /25 #SSMKYB
2013 Press Pass Showcase Series Standouts Memorabilia Melting /5 #SSMKYB
2013 Press Pass Showcase Showcase Patches /5 #SPKYB
2013 Press Pass Showcase Showroom /299 #5
2013 Press Pass Showcase Showroom Blue /40 #5
2013 Press Pass Showcase Showroom Gold /50 #5
2013 Press Pass Showcase Showroom Green /20 #5
2013 Press Pass Showcase Showroom Melting /1 #5
2013 Press Pass Showcase Showroom Purple /13 #5
2013 Press Pass Showcase Showroom Red /10 #5
2013 Press Pass Showcase Signature Patches /15 #SSPKYB
2013 Press Pass Showcase Studio Showcase /299 #3
2013 Press Pass Showcase Studio Showcase Blue /40 #3
2013 Press Pass Showcase Studio Showcase Green /25 #3
2013 Press Pass Showcase Studio Showcase Ink /25 #SSIKYB
2013 Press Pass Showcase Studio Showcase Ink Gold /10 #SSIKYB
2013 Press Pass Showcase Studio Showcase Ink Melting /1 #SSIKYB
2013 Press Pass Showcase Studio Showcase Ink Red /5 #SSIKYB
2013 Press Pass Showcase Studio Showcase Melting /1 #3
2013 Press Pass Showcase Studio Showcase Purple /13 #3
2013 Press Pass Showcase Studio Showcase Red /10 #3
2013 Press Pass Signature Series Gold /5 #KYB
2013 Press Pass Signature Series Melting /1 #KYB
2013 Press Pass Signings Blue /1 #KYB
2013 Press Pass Signings Gold /5 #KYB
2013 Press Pass Signings Holofoil /1 #KYB
2013 Press Pass Signings Printing Plates Black /1 #KYB
2013 Press Pass Signings Printing Plates Cyan /1 #KYB
2013 Press Pass Signings Printing Plates Magenta /1 #KYB
2013 Press Pass Signings Printing Plates Yellow /1 #KYB
2013 Press Pass Signings Silver /5 #KYB
2013 Press Pass Three Wide Gold /10 #TWKB
2013 Press Pass Three Wide Melting /1 #TWKB
2013 Total Memorabilia #8
2013 Total Memorabilia #9
2013 Total Memorabilia Black and White /99 #8
2013 Total Memorabilia Black and White /99 #9
2013 Total Memorabilia Dual Swatch Gold /199 #TMKB
2013 Total Memorabilia Gold /275 #8
2013 Total Memorabilia Gold /275 #9
2013 Total Memorabilia Hot Rod Relics Gold /50 #HRRKB
2013 Total Memorabilia Hot Rod Relics Holofoil /10 #HRRKB
2013 Total Memorabilia Hot Rod Relics Melting /1 #HRRKB
2013 Total Memorabilia Hot Rod Relics Silver /99 #HRRKB
2013 Total Memorabilia Quad Swatch Melting /10 #TMKB
2013 Total Memorabilia Red #8
2013 Total Memorabilia Red #9
2013 Total Memorabilia Signature Collection Dual Swatch Gold /10 #SCKYB
2013 Total Memorabilia Signature Collection Quad Swatch Melting /1 #SCKYB
2013 Total Memorabilia Signature Collection Single Swatch Silver /10 #SCKYB
2013 Total Memorabilia Signature Collection Triple Swatch Holofoil /5 #SCKYB
2013 Total Memorabilia Single Swatch Silver /475 #TMKB
2013 Total Memorabilia Triple Swatch Holofoil /99 #TMKB
2014 Press Pass #7
2014 Press Pass #89
2014 Press Pass #94
2014 Press Pass #71
2014 Press Pass Aerodynamic Autographs Blue /1 #AAKYB
2014 Press Pass Aerodynamic Autographs Holofoil /5 #AAKYB
2014 Press Pass Aerodynamic Autographs Printing Plates Black /1 #AAKYB
2014 Press Pass Aerodynamic Autographs Printing Plates Cyan /1 #AAKYB
2014 Press Pass Aerodynamic Autographs Printing Plates Magenta /1 #AAKYB
2014 Press Pass Aerodynamic Autographs Printing Plates Yellow /1 #AAKYB
2014 Press Pass American Thunder #10
2014 Press Pass American Thunder #65
2014 Press Pass American Thunder #55
2014 Press Pass American Thunder Autographs Blue /10 #ATAKYB
2014 Press Pass American Thunder Autographs Red /5 #ATAKYB
2014 Press Pass American Thunder Autographs White /35 #ATAKYB
2014 Press Pass American Thunder Battle Armor Blue /25 #BAKYB
2014 Press Pass American Thunder Battle Armor Red /1 #BAKYB
2014 Press Pass American Thunder Battle Armor Silver /99 #BAKYB
2014 Press Pass American Thunder Black and White /50 #10
2014 Press Pass American Thunder Black and White /50 #55
2014 Press Pass American Thunder Black and White /50 #65
2014 Press Pass American Thunder Brothers In Arms Autographs Blue /5 #BAJGR
2014 Press Pass American Thunder Brothers In Arms Autographs Red /1 #BAJGR
2014 Press Pass American Thunder Brothers In Arms Autographs White /10 #BAJGR
2014 Press Pass American Thunder Brothers In Arms Relics Blue /25 #BAJGR
2014 Press Pass American Thunder Brothers In Arms Relics Red /5 #BAJGR
2014 Press Pass American Thunder Brothers In Arms Relics Silver /50 #BAJGR
2014 Press Pass American Thunder Class A Uniforms Blue /99 #CAUKYB
2014 Press Pass American Thunder Class A Uniforms Red /10 #CAUKYB
2014 Press Pass American Thunder Class A Uniforms Silver #CAUKYB
2014 Press Pass American Thunder Cyan #10
2014 Press Pass American Thunder Cyan #55
2014 Press Pass American Thunder Cyan #65
2014 Press Pass American Thunder Great American Treads Autographs Blue /25 #GATKYB
2014 Press Pass American Thunder Great American Treads Autographs Red /1 #GATKYB
2014 Press Pass American Thunder Magenta #10
2014 Press Pass American Thunder Magenta #55
2014 Press Pass American Thunder Magenta #65
2014 Press Pass American Thunder Yellow /5 #10
2014 Press Pass American Thunder Yellow /5 #55
2014 Press Pass Burning Rubber Blue /25 #BRKYB
2014 Press Pass Burning Rubber Blue /25 #BRKYB2
2014 Press Pass Burning Rubber Blue /25 #BRKYB3
2014 Press Pass Burning Rubber Blue /25 #BRKYB4
2014 Press Pass Burning Rubber Gold /75 #BRKYB
2014 Press Pass Burning Rubber Gold /75 #BRKYB2
2014 Press Pass Burning Rubber Gold /75 #BRKYB3
2014 Press Pass Burning Rubber Gold /75 #BRKYB4
2014 Press Pass Burning Rubber Holofoil /50 #BRKYB
2014 Press Pass Burning Rubber Holofoil /50 #BRKYB2
2014 Press Pass Burning Rubber Holofoil /50 #BRKYB3
2014 Press Pass Burning Rubber Holofoil /50 #BRKYB4
2014 Press Pass Burning Rubber Letterman /8 #BRLKYB
2014 Press Pass Burning Rubber Melting /10 #BRKYB
2014 Press Pass Burning Rubber Melting /10 #BRKYB2
2014 Press Pass Burning Rubber Melting /10 #BRKYB3
2014 Press Pass Burning Rubber Melting /10 #BRKYB4
2014 Press Pass Certified Winners Memorabilia Autographs Gold /10 #CWKYB
2014 Press Pass Certified Winners Memorabilia Autographs Melting /1 #CWKYB
2014 Press Pass Color Proofs Black /70 #7
2014 Press Pass Color Proofs Black /70 #71
2014 Press Pass Color Proofs Black /70 #89
2014 Press Pass Color Proofs Black /70 #94
2014 Press Pass Color Proofs Cyan /35 #7
2014 Press Pass Color Proofs Cyan /35 #71
2014 Press Pass Color Proofs Cyan /35 #89
2014 Press Pass Color Proofs Cyan /35 #94
2014 Press Pass Color Proofs Magenta #7
2014 Press Pass Color Proofs Magenta #71
2014 Press Pass Color Proofs Magenta #89
2014 Press Pass Color Proofs Magenta #94
2014 Press Pass Color Proofs Yellow /5 #7
2014 Press Pass Color Proofs Yellow /5 #71
2014 Press Pass Color Proofs Yellow /5 #89
2014 Press Pass Color Proofs Yellow /5 #94
2014 Press Pass Cup Chase #3
2014 Press Pass Five Star /15 #3
2014 Press Pass Five Star Blue /5 #3
2014 Press Pass Five Star Classic Compilation Autographs Blue Triple Swatch /5 #CCKYB
2014 Press Pass Five Star Classic Compilation Autographs Holofoil /9 #CCKYB
2014 Press Pass Five Star Classic Compilation Autographs Holofoil Dual Swatch /10 #CCKYB
2014 Press Pass Five Star Classic Compilation Autographs Melting Five Swatch /1 #CCKYB
2014 Press Pass Five Star Classic Compilation Autographs Melting Quad Swatch /1 #CCKYB
2014 Press Pass Five Star Classic Compilations Autographed Patch Booklet /1 #CCKYB1
2014 Press Pass Five Star Classic Compilations Autographed Patch Booklet /1 #CCKYB2
2014 Press Pass Five Star Classic Compilations Autographed Patch Booklet /1 #CCKYB3
2014 Press Pass Five Star Classic Compilations Autographed Patch Booklet /1 #CCKYB4
2014 Press Pass Five Star Classic Compilations Autographed Patch Booklet /1 #CCKYB5
2014 Press Pass Five Star Classic Compilations Autographed Patch Booklet /1 #CCKYB6
2014 Press Pass Five Star Classic Compilations Autographed Patch Booklet /1 #CCKYB7
2014 Press Pass Five Star Classic Compilations Autographed Patch Booklet /1 #CCKYB8
2014 Press Pass Five Star Classic Compilations Autographed Patch Booklet /1 #CCKYB9
2014 Press Pass Five Star Classic Compilations Autographed Patch Booklet /1 #CCKYB10
2014 Press Pass Five Star Classic Compilations Autographed Patch Booklet /1 #CCKYB11
2014 Press Pass Five Star Classic Compilations Autographed Patch Booklet /1 #CCKYB12
2014 Press Pass Five Star Classic Compilations Autographed Patch Booklet /1 #CCKYB13
2014 Press Pass Five Star Classic Compilations Autographed Patch Booklet /1 #CCKYB14
2014 Press Pass Five Star Classic Compilations Autographed Patch Booklet /1 #CCKYB15
2014 Press Pass Five Star Classic Compilations Combo Autographs Blue /5 #CCJGR
2014 Press Pass Five Star Classic Compilations Combo Autographs Melting /1 #CCJGR
2014 Press Pass Five Star Holofoil /10 #3
2014 Press Pass Five Star Melting /1 #3
2014 Press Pass Five Star Paramount Pieces Blue /5 #PPKYB
2014 Press Pass Five Star Paramount Pieces Gold /25 #PPKYB
2014 Press Pass Five Star Paramount Pieces Holofoil /10 #PPKYB
2014 Press Pass Five Star Paramount Pieces Melting /1 #PPKYB
2014 Press Pass Five Star Paramount Pieces Melting Patch /1 #PPKYB
2014 Press Pass Five Star Signature Souvenirs Blue /5 #SSKYB
2014 Press Pass Five Star Signature Souvenirs Gold /50 #SSKYB
2014 Press Pass Five Star Signature Souvenirs Holofoil /25 #SSKYB
2014 Press Pass Five Star Signature Souvenirs Melting /1 #SSKYB
2014 Press Pass Five Star Signatures Blue /5 #FSSKYB
2014 Press Pass Five Star Signatures Holofoil /10 #FSSKYB
2014 Press Pass Five Star Signatures Melting /1 #FSSKYB
2014 Press Pass Four Wide Gold /10 #FWKYB
2014 Press Pass Four Wide Melting /1 #FWKYB
2014 Press Pass Gold #7
2014 Press Pass Gold #71
2014 Press Pass Gold #89
2014 Press Pass Gold #94
2014 Press Pass Redline #12
2014 Press Pass Redline #13
2014 Press Pass Redline Black /75 #12
2014 Press Pass Redline Black /75 #13
2014 Press Pass Redline Blue Foil #12
2014 Press Pass Redline Blue Foil #13
2014 Press Pass Redline Cyan /50 #12
2014 Press Pass Redline Cyan /50 #13
2014 Press Pass Redline Dynamic Duals Relic Autographs Blue /10 #DDKYB
2014 Press Pass Redline Dynamic Duals Relic Autographs Gold /25 #DDKYB
2014 Press Pass Redline Dynamic Duals Relic Autographs Melting /1 #DDKYB
2014 Press Pass Redline Dynamic Duals Relic Autographs Red /50 #DDKYB
2014 Press Pass Redline Green National Convention /5 #12
2014 Press Pass Redline Green National Convention /5 #13
2014 Press Pass Redline Head to Head Blue /10 #HTHKBKL
2014 Press Pass Redline Head to Head Gold /25 #HTHKBKL
2014 Press Pass Redline Head to Head Melting /1 #HTHKBKL
2014 Press Pass Redline Head to Head Red /75 #HTHKBKL
2014 Press Pass Redline Intensity #I1
2014 Press Pass Redline Magenta /10 #12
2014 Press Pass Redline Magenta /10 #13
2014 Press Pass Redline Muscle Car Sheet Metal Blue /25 #MCMKYB
2014 Press Pass Redline Muscle Car Sheet Metal Gold /50 #MCMKYB
2014 Press Pass Redline Muscle Car Sheet Metal Melting /1 #MCMKYB
2014 Press Pass Redline Muscle Car Sheet Metal Red /75 #MCMKYB
2014 Press Pass Redline Pieces of the Action Blue /10 #PAKYB
2014 Press Pass Redline Pieces of the Action Gold /25 #PAKYB
2014 Press Pass Redline Pieces of the Action Melting /1 #PAKYB
2014 Press Pass Redline Pieces of the Action Red /75 #PAKYB
2014 Press Pass Redline Redline Racers #RR2
2014 Press Pass Redline Relic Autographs Blue /10 #RRSEKYB
2014 Press Pass Redline Relic Autographs Gold /25 #RRSEKYB
2014 Press Pass Redline Relic Autographs Melting /1 #RRSEKYB
2014 Press Pass Redline Relic Autographs Red /50 #RRSEKYB
2014 Press Pass Redline Relics Blue /25 #RRKYB
2014 Press Pass Redline Relics Gold /50 #RRKYB
2014 Press Pass Redline Relics Melting /1 #RRKYB
2014 Press Pass Redline Relics Red /75 #RRKYB
2014 Press Pass Redline RPM #RPM1
2014 Press Pass Redline Signatures Blue /10 #RSKYB
2014 Press Pass Redline Signatures Gold /15 #RSKYB
2014 Press Pass Redline Signatures Melting /5 #RSKYB
2014 Press Pass Redline Signatures Red /25 #RSKYB
2014 Press Pass Redline Yellow /1 #12
2014 Press Pass Redline Yellow /1 #13
2014 Press Pass Replay #5
2014 Press Pass Replay #23
2014 Press Pass Replay #20
2014 Press Pass Replay #7
2014 Press Pass Signature Series Gold /5 #SSKYB
2014 Press Pass Signature Series Melting /1 #SSKYB
2014 Press Pass Signings Gold /10 #PPSKYB
2014 Press Pass Signings Holofoil /5 #PPSKYB
2014 Press Pass Signings Melting /1 #PPSKYB
2014 Press Pass Signings Printing Plates Black /1 #PPSKYB
2014 Press Pass Signings Printing Plates Cyan /1 #PPSKYB
2014 Press Pass Signings Printing Plates Magenta /1 #PPSKYB
2014 Press Pass Signings Printing Plates Yellow /1 #PPSKYB
2014 Press Pass Signings Silver /10 #PPSKYB
2014 Press Pass Velocity #8
2014 Total Memorabilia #6
2014 Total Memorabilia Acceleration #AC8
2014 Total Memorabilia Autographed Memorabilia Blue /5 #SCKYB
2014 Total Memorabilia Autographed Memorabilia Gold /5 #SCKYB
2014 Total Memorabilia Autographed Memorabilia Melting /1 #SCKYB
2014 Total Memorabilia Autographed Memorabilia Silver /10 #SC-KYB
2014 Total Memorabilia Black and White /99 #6
2014 Total Memorabilia Dual Swatch Gold /150 #TMKyB
2014 Total Memorabilia Gold /175 #6
2014 Total Memorabilia Quad Swatch Melting /25 #TMKyB
2014 Total Memorabilia Red #6
2014 Total Memorabilia Single Swatch Silver /275 #TMKyB
2014 Total Memorabilia Triple Swatch Blue /99 #TMKyB
2015 Press Pass #10
2015 Press Pass #95
2015 Press Pass #86
2015 Press Pass #63
2015 Press Pass #100
2015 Press Pass Burning Rubber Blue /50 #BRKYB
2015 Press Pass Burning Rubber Gold #BRKYB
2015 Press Pass Burning Rubber Green /10 #BRKYB
2015 Press Pass Burning Rubber Letterman /8 #BRLEKYB
2015 Press Pass Burning Rubber Melting /1 #BRKYB
2015 Press Pass Championship Caliber Dual /25 #CCMKYB
2015 Press Pass Championship Caliber Quad /1 #CCMKYB
2015 Press Pass Championship Caliber Signature Edition Blue /25 #CCKYB
2015 Press Pass Championship Caliber Signature Edition Gold /50 #CCKYB
2015 Press Pass Championship Caliber Signature Edition Green /10 #CCKYB
2015 Press Pass Championship Caliber Signature Edition Melting /1 #CCKYB
2015 Press Pass Championship Caliber Single /50 #CCMKYB
2015 Press Pass Championship Caliber Triple /10 #CCMKYB
2015 Press Pass Cup Chase #10
2015 Press Pass Cup Chase #63
2015 Press Pass Cup Chase #86
2015 Press Pass Cup Chase #95
2015 Press Pass Cup Chase #100
2015 Press Pass Cup Chase Blue /25 #10
2015 Press Pass Cup Chase Blue /25 #63
2015 Press Pass Cup Chase Blue /25 #86
2015 Press Pass Cup Chase Blue /25 #95
2015 Press Pass Cup Chase Blue /25 #100
2015 Press Pass Cup Chase Gold /75 #10
2015 Press Pass Cup Chase Gold /75 #63
2015 Press Pass Cup Chase Gold /75 #86
2015 Press Pass Cup Chase Gold /75 #95
2015 Press Pass Cup Chase Gold /75 #100
2015 Press Pass Cup Chase Green /10 #10
2015 Press Pass Cup Chase Green /10 #63
2015 Press Pass Cup Chase Green /10 #86
2015 Press Pass Cup Chase Green /10 #95
2015 Press Pass Cup Chase Green /10 #100
2015 Press Pass Cup Chase Melting /1 #10
2015 Press Pass Cup Chase Melting /1 #63
2015 Press Pass Cup Chase Melting /1 #86
2015 Press Pass Cup Chase Melting /1 #95
2015 Press Pass Cup Chase Melting /1 #100
2015 Press Pass Cup Chase Three Wide Blue /25 #3WKYB
2015 Press Pass Cup Chase Three Wide Gold /50 #3WKYB
2015 Press Pass Cup Chase Three Wide Green /10 #3WKYB
2015 Press Pass Cup Chase Three Wide Melting /1 #3WKYB
2015 Press Pass Cup Chase Upper Cuts /13 #UCKYB
2015 Press Pass Cuts Blue /25 #CCCKYB
2015 Press Pass Cuts Gold /50 #CCCKYB
2015 Press Pass Cuts Green /10 #CCCKYB
2015 Press Pass Cuts Melting /1 #CCCKYB
2015 Press Pass Four Wide Signature Edition Blue /25 #4WKYB
2015 Press Pass Four Wide Signature Edition Gold /50 #4WKYB
2015 Press Pass Four Wide Signature Edition Green /10 #4WKYB
2015 Press Pass Four Wide Signature Edition Melting /1 #4WKYB
2015 Press Pass Purple #10
2015 Press Pass Purple #63
2015 Press Pass Purple #86
2015 Press Pass Purple #95
2015 Press Pass Purple #100
2015 Press Pass Red #10
2015 Press Pass Red #63
2015 Press Pass Red #86
2015 Press Pass Red #95
2015 Press Pass Red #100
2015 Press Pass Signature Series Blue /25 #SSKYB
2015 Press Pass Signature Series Gold /50 #SSKYB
2015 Press Pass Signature Series Green /10 #SSKYB
2015 Press Pass Signature Series Melting /1 #SSKYB
2015 Press Pass Signings Blue /25 #PPSKYB
2015 Press Pass Signings Gold #PPSKYB
2015 Press Pass Signings Green /10 #PPSKYB
2015 Press Pass Signings Melting /5 #PPSKYB
2015 Press Pass Signings Red /15 #PPSKYB
2016 Certified #55
2016 Certified #2
2016 Certified Complete Materials /199 #3
2016 Certified Complete Materials Mirror Black /1 #3
2016 Certified Complete Materials Mirror Blue /50 #3
2016 Certified Complete Materials Mirror Gold /25 #3
2016 Certified Complete Materials Mirror Green /5 #3
2016 Certified Complete Materials Mirror Orange /99 #3
2016 Certified Complete Materials Mirror Purple /10 #3
2016 Certified Complete Materials Mirror Red /75 #3
2016 Certified Complete Materials Mirror Silver /99 #3
2016 Certified Epix /199 #10
2016 Certified Epix Mirror Black /1 #10
2016 Certified Epix Mirror Blue /50 #10
2016 Certified Epix Mirror Gold /25 #10
2016 Certified Epix Mirror Green /5 #10
2016 Certified Epix Mirror Orange /99 #10
2016 Certified Epix Mirror Purple /10 #10
2016 Certified Epix Mirror Red /75 #10
2016 Certified Epix Mirror Silver /99 #10
2016 Certified Famed Rides /199 #11
2016 Certified Famed Rides Mirror Black /1 #11
2016 Certified Famed Rides Mirror Blue /50 #11
2016 Certified Famed Rides Mirror Gold /25 #11
2016 Certified Famed Rides Mirror Green /5 #11
2016 Certified Famed Rides Mirror Orange /99 #11
2016 Certified Famed Rides Mirror Purple /10 #11
2016 Certified Famed Rides Mirror Red /75 #11
2016 Certified Famed Rides Mirror Silver /99 #11
2016 Certified Gold Team /199 #18
2016 Certified Gold Team Mirror Black /1 #18
2016 Certified Gold Team Mirror Blue /50 #18
2016 Certified Gold Team Mirror Gold /25 #18
2016 Certified Gold Team Mirror Green /5 #18
2016 Certified Gold Team Mirror Orange /99 #18
2016 Certified Gold Team Mirror Purple /10 #18
2016 Certified Gold Team Mirror Red /75 #18
2016 Certified Gold Team Mirror Silver /99 #18
2016 Certified Gold Team Signatures /18 #13
2016 Certified Gold Team Signatures Mirror Black /1 #13
2016 Certified Gold Team Signatures Mirror Gold /5 #13
2016 Certified Mirror Black /1 #2
2016 Certified Mirror Black /1 #55
2016 Certified Mirror Blue /50 #2
2016 Certified Mirror Blue /50 #55
2016 Certified Mirror Gold /25 #2
2016 Certified Mirror Gold /25 #55
2016 Certified Mirror Green /5 #2
2016 Certified Mirror Green /5 #55
2016 Certified Mirror Orange /99 #2
2016 Certified Mirror Orange /99 #55
2016 Certified Mirror Purple /10 #2
2016 Certified Mirror Purple /10 #55
2016 Certified Mirror Red /75 #2
2016 Certified Mirror Red /75 #55
2016 Certified Mirror Silver /99 #2
2016 Certified Mirror Silver /99 #55
2016 Certified Signatures /28 #30
2016 Certified Signatures Mirror Black /1 #30
2016 Certified Signatures Mirror Blue /18 #30
2016 Certified Signatures Mirror Gold /15 #30
2016 Certified Signatures Mirror Green /5 #30
2016 Certified Signatures Mirror Orange /5 #30
2016 Certified Signatures Mirror Purple /10 #30
2016 Certified Signatures Mirror Red /25 #30
2016 Certified Signatures Mirror Silver /5 #30
2016 Certified Skills /199 #5

2016 Certified Skills Mirror Black /1 #5
2016 Certified Skills Mirror Blue /50 #5
2016 Certified Skills Mirror Gold /25 #5
2016 Certified Skills Mirror Green /5 #5
2016 Certified Skills Mirror Orange /99 #5
2016 Certified Skills Mirror Purple /10 #5
2016 Certified Skills Mirror Red /75 #5
2016 Certified Skills Mirror Silver /99 #5
2016 Certified Sprint Cup Signature Swatches /60 #12
2016 Certified Sprint Cup Signature Swatches Mirror Black /1 #12
2016 Certified Sprint Cup Signature Swatches Mirror Blue /25 #12
2016 Certified Sprint Cup Signature Swatches Mirror Gold /18 #12
2016 Certified Sprint Cup Signature Swatches Mirror Green /5 #12
2016 Certified Sprint Cup Signature Swatches Mirror Orange /5 #12
2016 Certified Sprint Cup Signature Swatches Mirror Purple /10 #12
2016 Certified Sprint Cup Signature Swatches Mirror Red /35 #12
2016 Certified Sprint Cup Signature Swatches Mirror Silver /5 #12
2016 Certified Sprint Cup Swatches /200 #7
2016 Certified Sprint Cup Swatches Mirror Black /1 #7
2016 Certified Sprint Cup Swatches Mirror Blue /25 #7
2016 Certified Sprint Cup Swatches Mirror Gold /15 #7
2016 Certified Sprint Cup Swatches Mirror Green /5 #7
2016 Certified Sprint Cup Swatches Mirror Orange /99 #7
2016 Certified Sprint Cup Swatches Mirror Purple /10 #7
2016 Certified Sprint Cup Swatches Mirror Red /75 #7
2016 Certified Sprint Cup Swatches Mirror Silver /99 #7
2016 Panini Black Friday Racing Memorabilia #R3
2016 Panini Black Friday Racing Memorabilia Cracked Ice /25 #R3
2016 Panini Black Friday Racing Memorabilia Galactic Window /10 #R3
2016 Panini Black Friday Racing Memorabilia Holo Plaid /1 #R3
2016 Panini Instant #10
2016 Panini Instant Black /1 #10
2016 Panini Instant Blue /25 #10
2016 Panini Instant Green /5 #10
2016 Panini Instant Orange /50 #10
2016 Panini Instant Purple /10 #10
2016 Panini National Treasures /25 #6
2016 Panini National Treasures /25 #31
2016 Panini National Treasures Black /5 #6
2016 Panini National Treasures Black /5 #31
2016 Panini National Treasures Blue /1 #6
2016 Panini National Treasures Blue /1 #31
2016 Panini National Treasures Championship Signature Threads Black /5 #3
2016 Panini National Treasures Championship Signature Threads Blue /1 #3
2016 Panini National Treasures Championship Signature Threads Gold /10 #3
2016 Panini National Treasures Championship Signature Threads Printing Plates Black /1 #3
2016 Panini National Treasures Championship Signature Threads Printing Plates Cyan /1 #3
2016 Panini National Treasures Championship Signature Threads Printing Plates Magenta /1 #3
2016 Panini National Treasures Championship Signature Threads Printing Plates Yellow /1 #3
2016 Panini National Treasures Championship Signature Threads Silver /15 #3
2016 Panini National Treasures Championship Signatures Blue /1 #6
2016 Panini National Treasures Championship Signatures Printing Plates Black /1 #6
2016 Panini National Treasures Championship Signatures Printing Plates Cyan /1 #6
2016 Panini National Treasures Championship Signatures Printing Plates Magenta /1 #6
2016 Panini National Treasures Championship Signatures Printing Plates Yellow /1 #6
2016 Panini National Treasures Dual Signatures /25 #11
2016 Panini National Treasures Dual Signatures Black /10 #11
2016 Panini National Treasures Dual Signatures Blue /1 #11
2016 Panini National Treasures Dual Signatures Gold /15 #11
2016 Panini National Treasures Eight Signatures /15 #2
2016 Panini National Treasures Eight Signatures /15 #3
2016 Panini National Treasures Eight Signatures Black /5 #2
2016 Panini National Treasures Eight Signatures Black /5 #3
2016 Panini National Treasures Eight Signatures Blue /1 #2
2016 Panini National Treasures Eight Signatures Blue /1 #3
2016 Panini National Treasures Eight Signatures Gold /10 #2
2016 Panini National Treasures Eight Signatures Gold /10 #3
2016 Panini National Treasures Firesuit Materials /25 #12
2016 Panini National Treasures Firesuit Materials Black /5 #12
2016 Panini National Treasures Firesuit Materials Blue /1 #12
2016 Panini National Treasures Firesuit Materials Gold /10 #12
2016 Panini National Treasures Firesuit Materials Laundry Tag /1 #12
2016 Panini National Treasures Firesuit Materials Printing Plates Black /1 #12
2016 Panini National Treasures Firesuit Materials Printing Plates Cyan /1 #12
2016 Panini National Treasures Firesuit Materials Printing Plates Magenta /1 #12
2016 Panini National Treasures Firesuit Materials Printing Plates Yellow /1 #12
2016 Panini National Treasures Firesuit Materials Silver /15 #12
2016 Panini National Treasures Gold /15 #6
2016 Panini National Treasures Gold /15 #31
2016 Panini National Treasures Jumbo Firesuit Patch Signature Booklet Alpine Stars /2 #17
2016 Panini National Treasures Jumbo Firesuit Patch Signature Booklet Associate Sponsor 1 /1 #17
2016 Panini National Treasures Jumbo Firesuit Patch Signature Booklet Associate Sponsor 10 /1 #17
2016 Panini National Treasures Jumbo Firesuit Patch Signature Booklet Associate Sponsor 11 /1 #17
2016 Panini National Treasures Jumbo Firesuit Patch Signature Booklet Associate Sponsor 12 /1 #17
2016 Panini National Treasures Jumbo Firesuit Patch Signature Booklet Associate Sponsor 13 /1 #17
2016 Panini National Treasures Jumbo Firesuit Patch Signature Booklet Associate Sponsor 14 /1 #17
2016 Panini National Treasures Jumbo Firesuit Patch Signature Booklet Associate Sponsor 15 /1 #17
2016 Panini National Treasures Jumbo Firesuit Patch Signature Booklet Associate Sponsor 2 /1 #17
2016 Panini National Treasures Jumbo Firesuit Patch Signature Booklet Associate Sponsor 3 /1 #17
2016 Panini National Treasures Jumbo Firesuit Patch Signature Booklet Associate Sponsor 4 /1 #17
2016 Panini National Treasures Jumbo Firesuit Patch Signature Booklet Associate Sponsor 5 /1 #17
2016 Panini National Treasures Jumbo Firesuit Patch Signature Booklet Associate Sponsor 6 /1 #17
2016 Panini National Treasures Jumbo Firesuit Patch Signature Booklet Associate Sponsor 7 /1 #17
2016 Panini National Treasures Jumbo Firesuit Patch Signature Booklet Associate Sponsor 8 /1 #17
2016 Panini National Treasures Jumbo Firesuit Patch Signature Booklet Associate Sponsor 9 /1 #17
2016 Panini National Treasures Jumbo Firesuit Patch Signature Booklet Flag /1 #17
2016 Panini National Treasures Jumbo Firesuit Patch Signature Booklet Goodyear /2 #17
2016 Panini National Treasures Jumbo Firesuit Patch Signature Booklet Manufacturers Logo /1 #17
2016 Panini National Treasures Jumbo Firesuit Patch Signature Booklet Nameplate /1 #17
2016 Panini National Treasures Jumbo Firesuit Patch Signature Booklet NASCAR /1 #17
2016 Panini National Treasures Jumbo Firesuit Patch Signature Booklet Sprint Cup Logo /1 #17
2016 Panini National Treasures Jumbo Firesuit Patch Signature Booklet Sunoco /1 #17
2016 Panini National Treasures Jumbo Firesuit Signatures Black /5 #17
2016 Panini National Treasures Jumbo Firesuit Signatures Blue /1 #17
2016 Panini National Treasures Jumbo Firesuit Signatures Gold /10 #17
2016 Panini National Treasures Jumbo Firesuit Signatures Printing Plates Black /1 #17
2016 Panini National Treasures Jumbo Firesuit Signatures Printing Plates Cyan /1 #17
2016 Panini National Treasures Jumbo Firesuit Signatures Printing Plates Magenta /1 #17
2016 Panini National Treasures Jumbo Firesuit Signatures Printing Plates Yellow /1 #17
2016 Panini National Treasures Jumbo Firesuit Signatures Silver /15 #17
2016 Panini National Treasures Jumbo Sheet Metal Signature Booklet /49 #6
2016 Panini National Treasures Jumbo Sheet Metal Signature Booklet Black /10 #6
2016 Panini National Treasures Jumbo Sheet Metal Signature Booklet Blue /1 #6
2016 Panini National Treasures Jumbo Sheet Metal Signature Booklet Gold /25 #6
2016 Panini National Treasures Jumbo Sheet Metal Signatures Black /5 #10
2016 Panini National Treasures Jumbo Sheet Metal Signatures Blue /1 #10
2016 Panini National Treasures Jumbo Sheet Metal Signatures Printing Plates Black /1 #10
2016 Panini National Treasures Jumbo Sheet Metal Signatures Printing Plates Cyan /1 #10
2016 Panini National Treasures Jumbo Sheet Metal Signatures Printing Plates Magenta /1 #10
2016 Panini National Treasures Jumbo Sheet Metal Signatures Printing Plates Yellow /1 #10
2016 Panini National Treasures Printing Plates Black /1 #6
2016 Panini National Treasures Printing Plates Black /1 #31
2016 Panini National Treasures Printing Plates Cyan /1 #6
2016 Panini National Treasures Printing Plates Cyan /1 #31
2016 Panini National Treasures Printing Plates Magenta /1 #6
2016 Panini National Treasures Printing Plates Magenta /1 #31
2016 Panini National Treasures Printing Plates Yellow /1 #6
2016 Panini National Treasures Printing Plates Yellow /1 #31
2016 Panini National Treasures Quad Driver Materials /25 #2
2016 Panini National Treasures Quad Driver Materials /25 #6
2016 Panini National Treasures Quad Driver Materials /25 #8
2016 Panini National Treasures Quad Driver Materials Black /5 #2
2016 Panini National Treasures Quad Driver Materials Black /5 #6
2016 Panini National Treasures Quad Driver Materials Black /5 #8
2016 Panini National Treasures Quad Driver Materials Blue /1 #2
2016 Panini National Treasures Quad Driver Materials Blue /1 #6
2016 Panini National Treasures Quad Driver Materials Blue /1 #8
2016 Panini National Treasures Quad Driver Materials Gold /10 #2
2016 Panini National Treasures Quad Driver Materials Gold /10 #6
2016 Panini National Treasures Quad Driver Materials Gold /10 #8
2016 Panini National Treasures Quad Driver Materials Printing Plates Black /1 #2
2016 Panini National Treasures Quad Driver Materials Printing Plates Black /1 #6
2016 Panini National Treasures Quad Driver Materials Printing Plates Black /1 #8
2016 Panini National Treasures Quad Driver Materials Printing Plates Cyan /1 #2
2016 Panini National Treasures Quad Driver Materials Printing Plates Cyan /1 #6
2016 Panini National Treasures Quad Driver Materials Printing Plates Cyan /1 #8
2016 Panini National Treasures Quad Driver Materials Printing Plates Magenta /1 #2
2016 Panini National Treasures Quad Driver Materials Printing Plates Magenta /1 #6
2016 Panini National Treasures Quad Driver Materials Printing Plates Magenta /1 #8
2016 Panini National Treasures Quad Driver Materials Printing Plates Yellow /1 #2
2016 Panini National Treasures Quad Driver Materials Printing Plates Yellow /1 #6
2016 Panini National Treasures Quad Driver Materials Printing Plates Yellow /1 #8
2016 Panini National Treasures Quad Driver Materials Silver /15 #2
2016 Panini National Treasures Quad Driver Materials Silver /15 #6
2016 Panini National Treasures Quad Driver Materials Silver /15 #8
2016 Panini National Treasures Quad Materials /25 #12
2016 Panini National Treasures Quad Materials Black /5 #12
2016 Panini National Treasures Quad Materials Blue /1 #12
2016 Panini National Treasures Quad Materials Gold /10 #12
2016 Panini National Treasures Quad Materials Printing Plates Black /1 #12
2016 Panini National Treasures Quad Materials Printing Plates Cyan /1 #12
2016 Panini National Treasures Quad Materials Printing Plates Magenta /1 #12
2016 Panini National Treasures Quad Materials Printing Plates Yellow /1 #12
2016 Panini National Treasures Quad Materials Silver /15 #12
2016 Panini National Treasures Sheet Metal Materials /25 #12
2016 Panini National Treasures Sheet Metal Materials Black /5 #12
2016 Panini National Treasures Sheet Metal Materials Blue /1 #12
2016 Panini National Treasures Sheet Metal Materials Gold /10 #12
2016 Panini National Treasures Sheet Metal Materials Printing Plates Black /1 #12
2016 Panini National Treasures Sheet Metal Materials Printing Plates Cyan /1 #12
2016 Panini National Treasures Sheet Metal Materials Printing Plates Magenta /1 #12
2016 Panini National Treasures Sheet Metal Materials Printing Plates Yellow /1 #12
2016 Panini National Treasures Sheet Metal Materials Silver /15 #12
2016 Panini National Treasures Signature Dual Materials Black /5 #17
2016 Panini National Treasures Signature Dual Materials Blue /1 #17
2016 Panini National Treasures Signature Dual Materials Gold /10 #17
2016 Panini National Treasures Signature Dual Materials Printing Plates Black /1 #17
2016 Panini National Treasures Signature Dual Materials Printing Plates Cyan /1 #17
2016 Panini National Treasures Signature Dual Materials Printing Plates Magenta /1 #17
2016 Panini National Treasures Signature Dual Materials Printing Plates Yellow /1 #17
2016 Panini National Treasures Signature Firesuit Materials Black /5 #17
2016 Panini National Treasures Signature Firesuit Materials Blue /1 #17
2016 Panini National Treasures Signature Firesuit Materials Gold /10 #17
2016 Panini National Treasures Signature Firesuit Materials Laundry Tag /1 #17
2016 Panini National Treasures Signature Firesuit Materials Printing Plates Black /1 #17
2016 Panini National Treasures Signature Firesuit Materials Printing Plates Cyan /1 #17
2016 Panini National Treasures Signature Firesuit Materials Printing Plates Magenta /1 #17
2016 Panini National Treasures Signature Firesuit Materials Printing Plates Yellow /1 #17
2016 Panini National Treasures Signature Quad Materials Black /5 #17
2016 Panini National Treasures Signature Quad Materials Blue /1 #17
2016 Panini National Treasures Signature Quad Materials Gold /10 #17
2016 Panini National Treasures Signature Quad Materials Printing Plates Black /1 #17
2016 Panini National Treasures Signature Quad Materials Printing Plates Cyan /1 #17
2016 Panini National Treasures Signature Quad Materials Printing Plates Magenta /1 #17
2016 Panini National Treasures Signature Quad Materials Printing Plates Yellow /1 #17
2016 Panini National Treasures Signature Quad Materials Silver /15 #17
2016 Panini National Treasures Signature Sheet Metal Materials Blue /1 #17
2016 Panini National Treasures Signature Sheet Metal Materials Printing Plates Black /1 #17
2016 Panini National Treasures Signature Sheet Metal Materials Printing Plates Cyan /1 #17
2016 Panini National Treasures Signature Sheet Metal Materials Printing Plates Magenta /1 #17
2016 Panini National Treasures Signature Sheet Metal Materials Printing Plates Yellow /1 #17
2016 Panini National Treasures Signatures Blue /1 #13
2016 Panini National Treasures Signatures Printing Plates Black /1 #13
2016 Panini National Treasures Signatures Printing Plates Cyan /1 #13
2016 Panini National Treasures Signatures Printing Plates Magenta /1 #13
2016 Panini National Treasures Signatures Printing Plates Yellow /1 #13
2016 Panini National Treasures Silver /20 #6
2016 Panini National Treasures Silver /20 #31
2016 Panini National Treasures Six Signatures /25 #1
2016 Panini National Treasures Six Signatures /25 #5
2016 Panini National Treasures Six Signatures Black /10 #1
2016 Panini National Treasures Six Signatures Black /10 #5
2016 Panini National Treasures Six Signatures Blue /1 #1
2016 Panini National Treasures Six Signatures Blue /1 #5
2016 Panini National Treasures Six Signatures Gold /15 #1
2016 Panini National Treasures Six Signatures Gold /15 #5
2016 Panini National Treasures Trio Driver Materials /25 #8
2016 Panini National Treasures Trio Driver Materials /25 #9
2016 Panini National Treasures Trio Driver Materials /25 #14
2016 Panini National Treasures Trio Driver Materials Black /5 #8
2016 Panini National Treasures Trio Driver Materials Black /5 #9
2016 Panini National Treasures Trio Driver Materials Black /5 #14
2016 Panini National Treasures Trio Driver Materials Blue /1 #8
2016 Panini National Treasures Trio Driver Materials Blue /1 #9
2016 Panini National Treasures Trio Driver Materials Blue /1 #14
2016 Panini National Treasures Trio Driver Materials Gold /10 #8
2016 Panini National Treasures Trio Driver Materials Gold /10 #9
2016 Panini National Treasures Trio Driver Materials Gold /10 #14
2016 Panini National Treasures Trio Driver Materials Printing Plates Black /1 #8
2016 Panini National Treasures Trio Driver Materials Printing Plates Black /1 #9
2016 Panini National Treasures Trio Driver Materials Printing Plates Black /1 #14
2016 Panini National Treasures Trio Driver Materials Printing Plates Cyan /1 #8
2016 Panini National Treasures Trio Driver Materials Printing Plates Cyan /1 #9
2016 Panini National Treasures Trio Driver Materials Printing Plates Cyan /1 #14
2016 Panini National Treasures Trio Driver Materials Printing Plates Magenta /1 #8
2016 Panini National Treasures Trio Driver Materials Printing Plates Magenta /1 #9
2016 Panini National Treasures Trio Driver Materials Printing Plates Magenta /1 #14
2016 Panini National Treasures Trio Driver Materials Printing Plates Yellow /1 #8
2016 Panini National Treasures Trio Driver Materials Printing Plates Yellow /1 #9
2016 Panini National Treasures Trio Driver Materials Printing Plates Yellow /1 #14
2016 Panini National Treasures Trio Driver Materials Silver /15 #8
2016 Panini National Treasures Trio Driver Materials Silver /15 #9
2016 Panini National Treasures Trio Driver Materials Silver /15 #14
2016 Panini Prizm #76
2016 Panini Prizm #66
2016 Panini Prizm #59
2016 Panini Prizm #18
2016 Panini Prizm Autographs Prizms #67
2016 Panini Prizm Autographs Prizms Black /3 #67
2016 Panini Prizm Autographs Prizms Blue Flag /35 #67
2016 Panini Prizm Autographs Prizms Camo /18 #67
2016 Panini Prizm Autographs Prizms Checkered Flag /1 #67
2016 Panini Prizm Autographs Prizms Gold /10 #67
2016 Panini Prizm Autographs Prizms Green Flag /50 #67
2016 Panini Prizm Autographs Prizms Rainbow /24 #67
2016 Panini Prizm Autographs Prizms Red Flag /25 #67
2016 Panini Prizm Autographs Prizms Red White and Blue /25 #67
2016 Panini Prizm Autographs Prizms White Flag /5 #67
2016 Panini Prizm Blowing Smoke #3
2016 Panini Prizm Blowing Smoke Prizms #3
2016 Panini Prizm Blowing Smoke Prizms Checkered Flag /1 #3
2016 Panini Prizm Blowing Smoke Prizms Gold /10 #3
2016 Panini Prizm Competitors #2
2016 Panini Prizm Competitors Prizms #2
2016 Panini Prizm Competitors Prizms Checkered Flag /1 #2
2016 Panini Prizm Competitors Prizms Gold /10 #2
2016 Panini Prizm Firesuit Fabrics /149 #3
2016 Panini Prizm Firesuit Fabrics Prizms Blue Flag /75 #3
2016 Panini Prizm Firesuit Fabrics Prizms Checkered Flag /1 #3
2016 Panini Prizm Firesuit Fabrics Prizms Green Flag /99 #3
2016 Panini Prizm Firesuit Fabrics Prizms Red Flag /25 #3
2016 Panini Prizm Firesuit Fabrics Team /249 #3
2016 Panini Prizm Firesuit Fabrics Team Prizms Blue Flag /75 #3
2016 Panini Prizm Firesuit Fabrics Team Prizms Checkered Flag /1 #3
2016 Panini Prizm Firesuit Fabrics Team Prizms Green Flag /99 #3
2016 Panini Prizm Firesuit Fabrics Team Prizms Red Flag /10 #3
2016 Panini Prizm Prizms #18
2016 Panini Prizm Prizms #59
2016 Panini Prizm Prizms #66
2016 Panini Prizm Prizms #76
2016 Panini Prizm Prizms Black /3 #18
2016 Panini Prizm Prizms Black /3 #59
2016 Panini Prizm Prizms Black /3 #66
2016 Panini Prizm Prizms Black /3 #76
2016 Panini Prizm Prizms Blue Flag /99 #18
2016 Panini Prizm Prizms Blue Flag /99 #59
2016 Panini Prizm Prizms Blue Flag /99 #66
2016 Panini Prizm Prizms Blue Flag /99 #76
2016 Panini Prizm Prizms Camo /18 #18
2016 Panini Prizm Prizms Camo /18 #59
2016 Panini Prizm Prizms Camo /18 #66
2016 Panini Prizm Prizms Camo /18 #76
2016 Panini Prizm Prizms Checkered Flag /1 #18
2016 Panini Prizm Prizms Checkered Flag /1 #59
2016 Panini Prizm Prizms Checkered Flag /1 #66
2016 Panini Prizm Prizms Checkered Flag /1 #76
2016 Panini Prizm Prizms Gold /10 #18
2016 Panini Prizm Prizms Gold /10 #59
2016 Panini Prizm Prizms Gold /10 #66
2016 Panini Prizm Prizms Gold /10 #76
2016 Panini Prizm Prizms Green Flag /149 #18
2016 Panini Prizm Prizms Green Flag /149 #59
2016 Panini Prizm Prizms Green Flag /149 #66
2016 Panini Prizm Prizms Green Flag /149 #76
2016 Panini Prizm Prizms Rainbow /24 #18
2016 Panini Prizm Prizms Rainbow /24 #59
2016 Panini Prizm Prizms Rainbow /24 #66
2016 Panini Prizm Prizms Rainbow /24 #76
2016 Panini Prizm Prizms Red Flag /75 #18
2016 Panini Prizm Prizms Red Flag /75 #59
2016 Panini Prizm Prizms Red Flag /75 #66
2016 Panini Prizm Prizms Red Flag /75 #76
2016 Panini Prizm Prizms Red White and Blue #18
2016 Panini Prizm Prizms Red White and Blue #59
2016 Panini Prizm Prizms Red White and Blue #66
2016 Panini Prizm Prizms Red White and Blue #76
2016 Panini Prizm Prizms White Flag /5 #18
2016 Panini Prizm Prizms White Flag /5 #59
2016 Panini Prizm Prizms White Flag /5 #66
2016 Panini Prizm Prizms White Flag /5 #76
2016 Panini Prizm Qualifying Times #2
2016 Panini Prizm Qualifying Times Prizms #2
2016 Panini Prizm Qualifying Times Prizms Checkered Flag /1 #2
2016 Panini Prizm Qualifying Times Prizms Gold /10 #2
2016 Panini Prizm Race Used Tire #3
2016 Panini Prizm Race Used Tire Prizms Blue Flag /49 #3
2016 Panini Prizm Race Used Tire Prizms Checkered Flag /1 #3
2016 Panini Prizm Race Used Tire Prizms Green Flag /99 #3
2016 Panini Prizm Race Used Tire Prizms Red Flag /25 #3
2016 Panini Prizm Race Used Tire Team #3
2016 Panini Prizm Race Used Tire Team Prizms Blue Flag /75 #3
2016 Panini Prizm Race Used Tire Team Prizms Checkered Flag /1 #3
2016 Panini Prizm Race Used Tire Team Prizms Green Flag /149 #3
2016 Panini Prizm Race Used Tire Team Prizms Red Flag /10 #3
2016 Panini Prizm Raising the Flag #3
2016 Panini Prizm Raising the Flag Prizms #3
2016 Panini Prizm Raising the Flag Prizms Checkered Flag /1 #3
2016 Panini Prizm Raising the Flag Prizms Gold /10 #3
2016 Panini Prizm Winner's Circle #36
2016 Panini Prizm Winner's Circle #20
2016 Panini Prizm Winner's Circle #19
2016 Panini Prizm Winner's Circle #18
2016 Panini Prizm Winner's Circle #16
2016 Panini Prizm Winner's Circle Prizms #16
2016 Panini Prizm Winner's Circle Prizms #18
2016 Panini Prizm Winner's Circle Prizms #19
2016 Panini Prizm Winner's Circle Prizms #20
2016 Panini Prizm Winner's Circle Prizms #36
2016 Panini Prizm Winner's Circle Prizms Checkered Flag /1 #16
2016 Panini Prizm Winner's Circle Prizms Checkered Flag /1 #18
2016 Panini Prizm Winner's Circle Prizms Checkered Flag /1 #19
2016 Panini Prizm Winner's Circle Prizms Checkered Flag /1 #20
2016 Panini Prizm Winner's Circle Prizms Checkered Flag /1 #36
2016 Panini Prizm Winner's Circle Prizms Gold /10 #16
2016 Panini Prizm Winner's Circle Prizms Gold /10 #18
2016 Panini Prizm Winner's Circle Prizms Gold /10 #19
2016 Panini Prizm Winner's Circle Prizms Gold /10 #20
2016 Panini Prizm Winner's Circle Prizms Gold /10 #36
2016 Panini Torque #7
2016 Panini Torque #56
2016 Panini Torque #72
2016 Panini Torque #84
2016 Panini Torque Artist Proof /50 #7
2016 Panini Torque Artist Proof /50 #56
2016 Panini Torque Artist Proof /50 #72
2016 Panini Torque Artist Proof /50 #84
2016 Panini Torque Blackout /1 #7
2016 Panini Torque Blackout /1 #56
2016 Panini Torque Blackout /1 #72
2016 Panini Torque Blackout /1 #84
2016 Panini Torque Blue /125 #7
2016 Panini Torque Blue /125 #56
2016 Panini Torque Blue /125 #72
2016 Panini Torque Blue /125 #84
2016 Panini Torque Championship Vision #6
2016 Panini Torque Championship Vision Blue /99 #6
2016 Panini Torque Championship Vision Gold /149 #6
2016 Panini Torque Championship Vision Green /25 #6
2016 Panini Torque Championship Vision Purple /10 #6
2016 Panini Torque Championship Vision Red /49 #6
2016 Panini Torque Clear Vision #7
2016 Panini Torque Clear Vision Blue /99 #7
2016 Panini Torque Clear Vision Gold /149 #7
2016 Panini Torque Clear Vision Green /25 #7
2016 Panini Torque Clear Vision Purple /10 #7
2016 Panini Torque Clear Vision Red /49 #7
2016 Panini Torque Gold #7
2016 Panini Torque Gold #56
2016 Panini Torque Gold #72
2016 Panini Torque Gold #84
2016 Panini Torque Helmets #9
2016 Panini Torque Helmets Blue /99 #9
2016 Panini Torque Helmets Checkerboard /10 #9
2016 Panini Torque Helmets Green /25 #9
2016 Panini Torque Helmets Red /49 #9
2016 Panini Torque Holo Gold /5 #7
2016 Panini Torque Holo Gold /5 #56
2016 Panini Torque Holo Gold /5 #72
2016 Panini Torque Holo Gold /5 #84
2016 Panini Torque Holo Silver /10 #7
2016 Panini Torque Holo Silver /10 #56
2016 Panini Torque Holo Silver /10 #72
2016 Panini Torque Holo Silver /10 #84
2016 Panini Torque Horsepower Heroes #1
2016 Panini Torque Horsepower Heroes Gold /199 #1
2016 Panini Torque Horsepower Heroes Holo Silver /99 #1
2016 Panini Torque Jumbo Tire Autographs /35 #9
2016 Panini Torque Jumbo Tire Autographs Blue /25 #9
2016 Panini Torque Jumbo Tire Autographs Green /15 #9
2016 Panini Torque Jumbo Tire Autographs Purple /5 #9
2016 Panini Torque Jumbo Tire Autographs Red /20 #9
2016 Panini Torque Metal Materials /249 #16
2016 Panini Torque Metal Materials Blue /99 #16
2016 Panini Torque Metal Materials Green /25 #16
2016 Panini Torque Metal Materials Purple /10 #16
2016 Panini Torque Metal Materials Red /49 #16
2016 Panini Torque Nicknames #9
2016 Panini Torque Nicknames Gold /199 #9
2016 Panini Torque Nicknames Holo Silver /99 #9
2016 Panini Torque Painted to Perfection #5
2016 Panini Torque Painted to Perfection Blue /99 #5
2016 Panini Torque Painted to Perfection Checkerboard /10 #5
2016 Panini Torque Painted to Perfection Green /25 #5
2016 Panini Torque Painted to Perfection Red /49 #5
2016 Panini Torque Pairings Materials /249 #14
2016 Panini Torque Pairings Materials /249 #13
2016 Panini Torque Pairings Materials /249 #12
2016 Panini Torque Pairings Materials Blue /99 #12
2016 Panini Torque Pairings Materials Blue /99 #13
2016 Panini Torque Pairings Materials Blue /99 #14
2016 Panini Torque Pairings Materials Green /25 #12
2016 Panini Torque Pairings Materials Green /25 #13
2016 Panini Torque Pairings Materials Green /25 #14
2016 Panini Torque Pairings Materials Purple /10 #12
2016 Panini Torque Pairings Materials Purple /10 #13
2016 Panini Torque Pairings Materials Purple /10 #14
2016 Panini Torque Pairings Materials Red /49 #12
2016 Panini Torque Pairings Materials Red /49 #13
2016 Panini Torque Pairings Materials Red /49 #14
2016 Panini Torque Pole Position #7
2016 Panini Torque Pole Position Blue /99 #7
2016 Panini Torque Pole Position Checkerboard /10 #7
2016 Panini Torque Pole Position Green /25 #7
2016 Panini Torque Pole Position Red /49 #7
2016 Panini Torque Printing Plates Black /1 #7
2016 Panini Torque Printing Plates Black /1 #56
2016 Panini Torque Printing Plates Black /1 #72
2016 Panini Torque Printing Plates Black /1 #84
2016 Panini Torque Printing Plates Cyan /1 #7
2016 Panini Torque Printing Plates Cyan /1 #56
2016 Panini Torque Printing Plates Cyan /1 #72
2016 Panini Torque Printing Plates Cyan /1 #84
2016 Panini Torque Printing Plates Magenta /1 #7
2016 Panini Torque Printing Plates Magenta /1 #56
2016 Panini Torque Printing Plates Magenta /1 #72
2016 Panini Torque Printing Plates Magenta /1 #84
2016 Panini Torque Printing Plates Yellow /1 #7
2016 Panini Torque Printing Plates Yellow /1 #56
2016 Panini Torque Printing Plates Yellow /1 #72
2016 Panini Torque Printing Plates Yellow /1 #84
2016 Panini Torque Purple /25 #7
2016 Panini Torque Purple /25 #56
2016 Panini Torque Purple /25 #72
2016 Panini Torque Purple /25 #84
2016 Panini Torque Red /99 #7
2016 Panini Torque Red /99 #56
2016 Panini Torque Red /99 #72
2016 Panini Torque Red /99 #84
2016 Panini Torque Rubber Relics /399 #17
2016 Panini Torque Rubber Relics Blue /99 #17
2016 Panini Torque Rubber Relics Green /25 #17
2016 Panini Torque Rubber Relics Purple /10 #17
2016 Panini Torque Rubber Relics Red /49 #17
2016 Panini Torque Shades #8
2016 Panini Torque Shades Gold /199 #8
2016 Panini Torque Shades Holo Silver /99 #8
2016 Panini Torque Silhouettes Firesuit Autographs /35 #16
2016 Panini Torque Silhouettes Firesuit Autographs Blue /25 #16
2016 Panini Torque Silhouettes Firesuit Autographs Green /15 #16
2016 Panini Torque Silhouettes Firesuit Autographs Purple /5 #16
2016 Panini Torque Silhouettes Firesuit Autographs Red /20 #16
2016 Panini Torque Silhouettes Sheet Metal Autographs /35 #19
2016 Panini Torque Silhouettes Sheet Metal Autographs Blue /25 #19
2016 Panini Torque Silhouettes Sheet Metal Autographs Green /15 #19
2016 Panini Torque Silhouettes Sheet Metal Autographs Purple /5 #19
2016 Panini Torque Silhouettes Sheet Metal Autographs Red /20 #19
2016 Panini Torque Special Paint #4
2016 Panini Torque Special Paint Gold /199 #4
2016 Panini Torque Special Paint Holo Silver /99 #4
2016 Panini Torque Superstar Vision #6
2016 Panini Torque Superstar Vision Blue /99 #6
2016 Panini Torque Superstar Vision Gold /149 #6
2016 Panini Torque Superstar Vision Green /25 #6
2016 Panini Torque Superstar Vision Purple /10 #6
2016 Panini Torque Superstar Vision Red /49 #6
2016 Panini Torque Test Proof Black /1 #7
2016 Panini Torque Test Proof Black /1 #56
2016 Panini Torque Test Proof Black /1 #72
2016 Panini Torque Test Proof Black /1 #84
2016 Panini Torque Test Proof Cyan /1 #7
2016 Panini Torque Test Proof Cyan /1 #56
2016 Panini Torque Test Proof Cyan /1 #72
2016 Panini Torque Test Proof Cyan /1 #84
2016 Panini Torque Test Proof Magenta /1 #7
2016 Panini Torque Test Proof Magenta /1 #56
2016 Panini Torque Test Proof Magenta /1 #72
2016 Panini Torque Test Proof Magenta /1 #84
2016 Panini Torque Test Proof Yellow /1 #7
2016 Panini Torque Test Proof Yellow /1 #56
2016 Panini Torque Test Proof Yellow /1 #72
2016 Panini Torque Test Proof Yellow /1 #84
2016 Panini Torque Victory Laps #3
2016 Panini Torque Victory Laps Gold /199 #3
2016 Panini Torque Victory Laps Holo Silver /99 #3
2016 Panini Torque Winning Vision #7
2016 Panini Torque Winning Vision Blue /99 #7
2016 Panini Torque Winning Vision Gold /149 #7
2016 Panini Torque Winning Vision Green /25 #7
2016 Panini Torque Winning Vision Purple /10 #7
2016 Panini Torque Winning Vision Red /49 #7
2017 Donruss #2
2017 Donruss #95
2017 Donruss #103
2017 Donruss #123
2017 Donruss #157
2017 Donruss #44A
2017 Donruss #44B
2017 Donruss Artist Proof /25 #2
2017 Donruss Artist Proof /25 #44A
2017 Donruss Artist Proof /25 #95
2017 Donruss Artist Proof /25 #123
2017 Donruss Artist Proof /25 #157
2017 Donruss Artist Proof /25 #44B
2017 Donruss Artist Proof /25 #103
2017 Donruss Blue Foil /299 #2
2017 Donruss Blue Foil /299 #95
2017 Donruss Blue Foil /299 #123
2017 Donruss Blue Foil /299 #44A
2017 Donruss Blue Foil /299 #157
2017 Donruss Blue Foil /299 #44B
2017 Donruss Blue Foil /299 #103
2017 Donruss Dual Rubber Relics #12
2017 Donruss Dual Rubber Relics Holo Black /1 #12
2017 Donruss Dual Rubber Relics Holo Gold /25 #12
2017 Donruss Elite Dominators /999 #5
2017 Donruss Gold Foil /499 #2
2017 Donruss Gold Foil /499 #95
2017 Donruss Gold Foil /499 #123
2017 Donruss Gold Foil /499 #157
2017 Donruss Gold Foil /499 #44A
2017 Donruss Gold Foil /499 #44B
2017 Donruss Gold Foil /499 #103
2017 Donruss Gold Press Proof /99 #2
2017 Donruss Gold Press Proof /99 #44A
2017 Donruss Gold Press Proof /99 #95
2017 Donruss Gold Press Proof /99 #123
2017 Donruss Gold Press Proof /99 #157
2017 Donruss Gold Press Proof /99 #44B
2017 Donruss Gold Press Proof /99 #103
2017 Donruss Green Foil /199 #2
2017 Donruss Green Foil /199 #44A
2017 Donruss Green Foil /199 #95
2017 Donruss Green Foil /199 #123
2017 Donruss Green Foil /199 #157
2017 Donruss Green Foil /199 #44B
2017 Donruss Green Foil /199 #103
2017 Donruss Pole Position #5
2017 Donruss Pole Position Cracked Ice /999 #5
2017 Donruss Press Proof /49 #2
2017 Donruss Press Proof /49 #44A
2017 Donruss Press Proof /49 #95
2017 Donruss Press Proof /49 #123
2017 Donruss Press Proof /49 #157
2017 Donruss Press Proof /49 #44B
2017 Donruss Press Proof /49 #103
2017 Donruss Printing Plates Black /1 #2
2017 Donruss Printing Plates Black /1 #44A
2017 Donruss Printing Plates Black /1 #95
2017 Donruss Printing Plates Black /1 #123
2017 Donruss Printing Plates Black /1 #157
2017 Donruss Printing Plates Black /1 #44B
2017 Donruss Printing Plates Black /1 #103
2017 Donruss Printing Plates Cyan /1 #2
2017 Donruss Printing Plates Cyan /1 #44A
2017 Donruss Printing Plates Cyan /1 #95
2017 Donruss Printing Plates Cyan /1 #123
2017 Donruss Printing Plates Cyan /1 #157
2017 Donruss Printing Plates Cyan /1 #44B
2017 Donruss Printing Plates Cyan /1 #103
2017 Donruss Printing Plates Magenta /1 #2
2017 Donruss Printing Plates Magenta /1 #95
2017 Donruss Printing Plates Magenta /1 #123
2017 Donruss Printing Plates Magenta /1 #157
2017 Donruss Printing Plates Magenta /1 #44A
2017 Donruss Printing Plates Magenta /1 #44B
2017 Donruss Printing Plates Magenta /1 #103
2017 Donruss Printing Plates Yellow /1 #2
2017 Donruss Printing Plates Yellow /1 #95
2017 Donruss Printing Plates Yellow /1 #123
2017 Donruss Printing Plates Yellow /1 #157
2017 Donruss Printing Plates Yellow /1 #44A
2017 Donruss Printing Plates Yellow /1 #44B
2017 Donruss Printing Plates Yellow /1 #103
2017 Donruss Retro Relics 1984 #29
2017 Donruss Retro Relics 1984 Holo Black /10 #29
2017 Donruss Retro Relics 1984 Holo Gold /99 #29
2017 Donruss Rubber Relics #33
2017 Donruss Rubber Relics #34
2017 Donruss Rubber Relics Holo Black /1 #33
2017 Donruss Rubber Relics Holo Black /1 #34
2017 Donruss Rubber Relics Holo Gold /25 #33
2017 Donruss Rubber Relics Holo Gold /7 #34
2017 Donruss Rubber Relics Signatures /5 #5
2017 Donruss Rubber Relics Signatures Holo Black /1 #5
2017 Donruss Rubber Relics Signatures Holo Gold /24 #5
2017 Donruss Significant Signatures #10
2017 Donruss Significant Signatures Holo Black /1 #10
2017 Donruss Significant Signatures Holo Gold /25 #10
2017 Donruss Speed #5
2017 Donruss Speed Cracked Ice /999 #5
2017 Panini Black Friday Happy Holiday Memorabilia #HHKYB
2017 Panini Black Friday Happy Holiday Memorabilia Cracked Ice /25 #HHKYB
2017 Panini Black Friday Happy Holiday Memorabilia Galactic Windows /10 #HHKYB
2017 Panini Black Friday Happy Holiday Memorabilia Hyperplaid /1 #HHKYB
2017 Panini Day #56
2017 Panini Day Cracked Ice /25 #56
2017 Panini Day Decoy /50 #56
2017 Panini Day Hyperplaid /1 #56
2017 Panini Day Memorabilia #39
2017 Panini Day Memorabilia Galactic Window /25 #39
2017 Panini Day Memorabilia Hyperplaid /1 #39
2017 Panini Day Rapture /10 #56
2017 Panini Day Wedges /50 #56
2017 Panini Father's Day Racing Memorabilia /100 #5
2017 Panini Father's Day Racing Memorabilia Cracked Ice /25 #5
2017 Panini Father's Day Racing Memorabilia Hyperplaid /1 #5
2017 Panini Father's Day Racing Memorabilia Shimmer /10 #5
2017 Panini Instant Nascar #11
2017 Panini Instant Nascar #20
2017 Panini Instant Nascar #23
2017 Panini Instant Nascar #27
2017 Panini Instant Nascar #31
2017 Panini Instant Nascar Black /1 #11
2017 Panini Instant Nascar Black /1 #20
2017 Panini Instant Nascar Black /1 #23
2017 Panini Instant Nascar Black /1 #27
2017 Panini Instant Nascar Black /1 #31
2017 Panini Instant Nascar Green /10 #11
2017 Panini Instant Nascar Green /10 #20
2017 Panini Instant Nascar Green /10 #23
2017 Panini Instant Nascar Green /10 #27
2017 Panini Instant Nascar Green /10 #31
2017 Panini National Convention #R6
2017 Panini National Convention Autographs #R6
2017 Panini National Convention Autographs Hyperplaid /1 #R6
2017 Panini National Convention Escher Squares /25 #R6
2017 Panini National Convention Escher Squares Thick Stock /10 #R6
2017 Panini National Convention Galatic Windows /5 #R6
2017 Panini National Convention Hyperplaid /1 #R6
2017 Panini National Convention Pyramids /10 #R6
2017 Panini National Convention Rainbow Spokes /49 #R6
2017 Panini National Convention Rainbow Spokes Thick Stock /25 #R6
2017 Panini National Convention Rapture /99 #R6
2017 Panini National Treasures /25 #5
2017 Panini National Treasures /25 #20
2017 Panini National Treasures Associate Sponsor Patch Signatures 1 /1 #4
2017 Panini National Treasures Associate Sponsor Patch Signatures 10 /1 #4
2017 Panini National Treasures Associate Sponsor Patch Signatures 11 /1 #4
2017 Panini National Treasures Associate Sponsor Patch Signatures 12 /1 #4
2017 Panini National Treasures Associate Sponsor Patch Signatures 13 /1 #4
2017 Panini National Treasures Associate Sponsor Patch Signatures 14 /1 #4
2017 Panini National Treasures Associate Sponsor Patch Signatures 15 /1 #4
2017 Panini National Treasures Associate Sponsor Patch Signatures 16 /1 #4
2017 Panini National Treasures Associate Sponsor Patch Signatures 17 /1 #4
2017 Panini National Treasures Associate Sponsor Patch Signatures 18 /1 #4
2017 Panini National Treasures Associate Sponsor Patch Signatures 2 /1 #4
2017 Panini National Treasures Associate Sponsor Patch Signatures 3 /1 #4
2017 Panini National Treasures Associate Sponsor Patch Signatures 4 /1 #4
2017 Panini National Treasures Associate Sponsor Patch Signatures 5 /1 #4
2017 Panini National Treasures Associate Sponsor Patch Signatures 6 /1 #4
2017 Panini National Treasures Associate Sponsor Patch Signatures 7 /1 #4
2017 Panini National Treasures Associate Sponsor Patch Signatures 9 /1 #4
2017 Panini National Treasures Car Manufacturer Patch Signatures /1 #4
2017 Panini National Treasures Century Black /1 #5
2017 Panini National Treasures Century Black /1 #20
2017 Panini National Treasures Century Gold /15 #5
2017 Panini National Treasures Century Gold /15 #20
2017 Panini National Treasures Century Green /5 #5
2017 Panini National Treasures Century Green /5 #20
2017 Panini National Treasures Century Holo Gold /10 #5
2017 Panini National Treasures Century Holo Gold /10 #20
2017 Panini National Treasures Century Holo Silver /20 #5
2017 Panini National Treasures Century Holo Silver /20 #20
2017 Panini National Treasures Century Laundry Tags /1 #5
2017 Panini National Treasures Championship Swatches /25 #3
2017 Panini National Treasures Championship Swatches Black /1 #3
2017 Panini National Treasures Championship Swatches Gold /15 #3
2017 Panini National Treasures Championship Swatches Green /5 #3
2017 Panini National Treasures Championship Swatches Holo Gold /10 #3
2017 Panini National Treasures Championship Swatches Holo Silver /20 #3
2017 Panini National Treasures Championship Swatches Laundry Tag /1 #3
2017 Panini National Treasures Championship Swatches Printing Plates Black /1 #3
2017 Panini National Treasures Championship Swatches Printing Plates Cyan /1 #3
2017 Panini National Treasures Championship Swatches Printing Plates Magenta /1 #3
2017 Panini National Treasures Championship Swatches Printing Plates Yellow /1 #3
2017 Panini National Treasures Combo Material Signatures /25 #4
2017 Panini National Treasures Combo Material Signatures Black /1 #4
2017 Panini National Treasures Combo Material Signatures Gold /15 #4
2017 Panini National Treasures Combo Material Signatures Green /5 #4
2017 Panini National Treasures Combo Material Signatures Holo Gold /10 #4
2017 Panini National Treasures Combo Material Signatures Holo Silver /20 #4
2017 Panini National Treasures Dual Tire Signatures /25 #15
2017 Panini National Treasures Dual Tire Signatures Black /1 #15

2017 Panini National Treasures Dual Tire Signatures Gold /15 #15
2017 Panini National Treasures Dual Tire Signatures Green /5 #15
2017 Panini National Treasures Dual Tire Signatures Holo Gold /10 #15
2017 Panini National Treasures Dual Tire Signatures Holo Silver /20 #15
2017 Panini National Treasures Dual Tire Signatures Printing Plates Black /1 #15
2017 Panini National Treasures Dual Tire Signatures Printing Plates Cyan /1 #15
2017 Panini National Treasures Dual Tire Signatures Printing Plates Magenta /1 #15
2017 Panini National Treasures Dual Tire Signatures Printing Plates Yellow /1 #15
2017 Panini National Treasures Firesuit Manufacturer Patch Signatures /1 #4
2017 Panini National Treasures Flag Patch Signatures /1 #4
2017 Panini National Treasures Goodyear Patch Signatures /2 #4
2017 Panini National Treasures Hats Off /14 #8
2017 Panini National Treasures Hats Off /15 #9
2017 Panini National Treasures Hats Off /13 #10
2017 Panini National Treasures Hats Off Gold /1 #8
2017 Panini National Treasures Hats Off Gold /4 #9
2017 Panini National Treasures Hats Off Gold /1 #10
2017 Panini National Treasures Hats Off Holo Gold /5 #8
2017 Panini National Treasures Hats Off Holo Gold /5 #9
2017 Panini National Treasures Hats Off Holo Gold /5 #10
2017 Panini National Treasures Hats Off Holo Silver /1 #8
2017 Panini National Treasures Hats Off Holo Silver /1 #9
2017 Panini National Treasures Hats Off Holo Silver /1 #10
2017 Panini National Treasures Hats Off Laundry Tag /6 #8
2017 Panini National Treasures Hats Off Laundry Tag /6 #9
2017 Panini National Treasures Hats Off Laundry Tag /6 #10
2017 Panini National Treasures Hats Off Monster Energy Cup /14 #4
2017 Panini National Treasures Hats Off Monster Energy Cup Gold /4 #4
2017 Panini National Treasures Hats Off Monster Energy Cup Holo Gold /5 #4
2017 Panini National Treasures Hats Off Monster Energy Cup Holo Silver /1 #4
2017 Panini National Treasures Hats Off Monster Energy Cup Laundry Tag /3 #4
2017 Panini National Treasures Hats Off Monster Energy Cup New Era /1 #4
2017 Panini National Treasures Hats Off Monster Energy Cup Printing Plates Black /1 #4
2017 Panini National Treasures Hats Off Monster Energy Cup Printing Plates Cyan /1 #4
2017 Panini National Treasures Hats Off Monster Energy Cup Printing Plates Magenta /1 #4
2017 Panini National Treasures Hats Off Monster Energy Cup Printing Plates Yellow /1 #4
2017 Panini National Treasures Hats Off Monster Energy Cup Sponsor /5 #4
2017 Panini National Treasures Hats Off New Era /1 #8
2017 Panini National Treasures Hats Off New Era /1 #9
2017 Panini National Treasures Hats Off New Era /1 #10
2017 Panini National Treasures Hats Off Printing Plates Black /1 #8
2017 Panini National Treasures Hats Off Printing Plates Black /1 #9
2017 Panini National Treasures Hats Off Printing Plates Black /1 #10
2017 Panini National Treasures Hats Off Printing Plates Cyan /1 #8
2017 Panini National Treasures Hats Off Printing Plates Cyan /1 #9
2017 Panini National Treasures Hats Off Printing Plates Cyan /1 #10
2017 Panini National Treasures Hats Off Printing Plates Magenta /1 #8
2017 Panini National Treasures Hats Off Printing Plates Magenta /1 #9
2017 Panini National Treasures Hats Off Printing Plates Magenta /1 #10
2017 Panini National Treasures Hats Off Printing Plates Yellow /1 #8
2017 Panini National Treasures Hats Off Printing Plates Yellow /1 #9
2017 Panini National Treasures Hats Off Printing Plates Yellow /1 #10
2017 Panini National Treasures Hats Off Sponsor /10 #8
2017 Panini National Treasures Hats Off Sponsor /10 #9
2017 Panini National Treasures Hats Off Sponsor /5 #10
2017 Panini National Treasures Jumbo Firesuit Materials Black /1 #1
2017 Panini National Treasures Jumbo Firesuit Materials Green /5 #1
2017 Panini National Treasures Jumbo Firesuit Materials Laundry Tag /1 #1
2017 Panini National Treasures Jumbo Firesuit Materials Printing Plates Black /1 #1
2017 Panini National Treasures Jumbo Firesuit Materials Printing Plates Cyan /1 #1
2017 Panini National Treasures Jumbo Firesuit Materials Printing Plates Magenta /1 #1
2017 Panini National Treasures Jumbo Firesuit Materials Printing Plates Yellow /1 #1
2017 Panini National Treasures Jumbo Tire Signatures Black /1 #12
2017 Panini National Treasures Jumbo Tire Signatures Gold /25 #12
2017 Panini National Treasures Jumbo Tire Signatures Green /5 #12
2017 Panini National Treasures Jumbo Tire Signatures Holo Gold /10 #12
2017 Panini National Treasures Jumbo Tire Signatures Printing Plates Black /1 #12
2017 Panini National Treasures Jumbo Tire Signatures Printing Plates Cyan /1 #12
2017 Panini National Treasures Jumbo Tire Signatures Printing Plates Magenta /1 #12
2017 Panini National Treasures Jumbo Tire Signatures Printing Plates Yellow /1 #12
2017 Panini National Treasures Nameplate Patch Signatures /2 #4
2017 Panini National Treasures NASCAR Patch Signatures /1 #4
2017 Panini National Treasures Printing Plates Black /1 #5
2017 Panini National Treasures Printing Plates Black /1 #20
2017 Panini National Treasures Printing Plates Cyan /1 #5
2017 Panini National Treasures Printing Plates Cyan /1 #20
2017 Panini National Treasures Printing Plates Magenta /1 #5
2017 Panini National Treasures Printing Plates Magenta /1 #20
2017 Panini National Treasures Printing Plates Yellow /1 #5
2017 Panini National Treasures Printing Plates Yellow /1 #20
2017 Panini National Treasures Quad Materials Black /1 #1
2017 Panini National Treasures Quad Materials Laundry Tag /1 #1
2017 Panini National Treasures Quad Materials Printing Plates Black /1 #1
2017 Panini National Treasures Quad Materials Printing Plates Cyan /1 #1
2017 Panini National Treasures Quad Materials Printing Plates Magenta /1 #1
2017 Panini National Treasures Quad Materials Printing Plates Yellow /1 #1
2017 Panini National Treasures Series Sponsor Patch Signatures /1 #4
2017 Panini National Treasures Signature Sheet Metal /25 #2
2017 Panini National Treasures Signature Sheet Metal Black /1 #2
2017 Panini National Treasures Signature Sheet Metal Gold /15 #2
2017 Panini National Treasures Signature Sheet Metal Green /5 #2
2017 Panini National Treasures Signature Sheet Metal Holo Gold /10 #2
2017 Panini National Treasures Signature Sheet Metal Holo Silver /20 #2
2017 Panini National Treasures Signature Six Way Swatches /25 #6
2017 Panini National Treasures Signature Six Way Swatches Black /1 #6
2017 Panini National Treasures Signature Six Way Swatches Gold /15 #6
2017 Panini National Treasures Signature Six Way Swatches Green /5 #6
2017 Panini National Treasures Signature Six Way Swatches Holo Gold /10 #6
2017 Panini National Treasures Signature Six Way Swatches Holo Silver /20 #6
2017 Panini National Treasures Signature Six Way Swatches Laundry Tag /1 #6
2017 Panini National Treasures Six Way Swatches Black /1 #3
2017 Panini National Treasures Six Way Swatches Laundry Tag /1 #3
2017 Panini National Treasures Six Way Swatches Printing Plates Black /1 #3
2017 Panini National Treasures Six Way Swatches Printing Plates Cyan /1 #3
2017 Panini National Treasures Six Way Swatches Printing Plates Magenta /1 #3
2017 Panini National Treasures Six Way Swatches Printing Plates Yellow /1 #3
2017 Panini National Treasures Sunoco Patch Signatures /1 #4
2017 Panini National Treasures Teammates Dual Materials /25 #6
2017 Panini National Treasures Teammates Dual Materials Black /1 #6
2017 Panini National Treasures Teammates Dual Materials Gold /15 #6
2017 Panini National Treasures Teammates Dual Materials Green /5 #6
2017 Panini National Treasures Teammates Dual Materials Holo Gold /10 #6
2017 Panini National Treasures Teammates Dual Materials Holo Silver /20 #6
2017 Panini National Treasures Teammates Dual Materials Laundry Tag /1 #6
2017 Panini National Treasures Teammates Dual Materials Printing Plates Black /1 #6
2017 Panini National Treasures Teammates Dual Materials Printing Plates Cyan /1 #6
2017 Panini National Treasures Teammates Dual Materials Printing Plates Magenta /1 #6
2017 Panini National Treasures Teammates Dual Materials Printing Plates Yellow /1 #6
2017 Panini National Treasures Teammates Quad Materials /25 #7
2017 Panini National Treasures Teammates Quad Materials Black /1 #7
2017 Panini National Treasures Teammates Quad Materials Gold /15 #7
2017 Panini National Treasures Teammates Quad Materials Green /5 #7
2017 Panini National Treasures Teammates Quad Materials Holo Gold /10 #7
2017 Panini National Treasures Teammates Quad Materials Holo Silver /20 #7
2017 Panini National Treasures Teammates Quad Materials Laundry Tag /1 #7
2017 Panini National Treasures Teammates Quad Materials Printing Plates Black /1 #7
2017 Panini National Treasures Teammates Quad Materials Printing Plates Cyan /1 #7
2017 Panini National Treasures Teammates Quad Materials Printing Plates Magenta /1 #7
2017 Panini National Treasures Teammates Quad Materials Printing Plates Yellow /1 #7
2017 Panini National Treasures Teammates Triple Materials /25 #3
2017 Panini National Treasures Teammates Triple Materials Black /1 #3
2017 Panini National Treasures Teammates Triple Materials Gold /15 #3
2017 Panini National Treasures Teammates Triple Materials Green /5 #3
2017 Panini National Treasures Teammates Triple Materials Holo Gold /10 #3
2017 Panini National Treasures Teammates Triple Materials Holo Silver /20 #3
2017 Panini National Treasures Teammates Triple Materials Laundry Tag /1 #3
2017 Panini National Treasures Teammates Triple Materials Printing Plates Black /1 #3
2017 Panini National Treasures Teammates Triple Materials Printing Plates Cyan /1 #3
2017 Panini National Treasures Teammates Triple Materials Printing Plates Magenta /1 #3
2017 Panini National Treasures Teammates Triple Materials Printing Plates Yellow /1 #3
2017 Panini National Treasures Winning Material Signatures /25 #4
2017 Panini National Treasures Winning Material Signatures Black /1 #4
2017 Panini National Treasures Winning Material Signatures Gold /15 #4
2017 Panini National Treasures Winning Material Signatures Green /5 #4
2017 Panini National Treasures Winning Material Signatures Holo Gold /10 #4
2017 Panini National Treasures Winning Material Signatures Holo Silver /20 #4
2017 Panini National Treasures Winning Material Signatures Laundry Tag /1 #4
2017 Panini National Treasures Winning Material Signatures Printing Plates Black /1 #4
2017 Panini National Treasures Winning Material Signatures Printing Plates Cyan /1 #4
2017 Panini National Treasures Winning Material Signatures Printing Plates Magenta /1 #4
2017 Panini National Treasures Winning Material Signatures Printing Plates Yellow /1 #4
2017 Panini National Treasures Winning Signatures /25 #9
2017 Panini National Treasures Winning Signatures Black /1 #9
2017 Panini National Treasures Winning Signatures Gold /15 #9
2017 Panini National Treasures Winning Signatures Green /5 #9
2017 Panini National Treasures Winning Signatures Holo Gold /10 #9
2017 Panini National Treasures Winning Signatures Holo Silver /20 #9
2017 Panini National Treasures Winning Signatures Printing Plates Black /1 #9
2017 Panini National Treasures Winning Signatures Printing Plates Cyan /1 #9
2017 Panini National Treasures Winning Signatures Printing Plates Magenta /1 #9
2017 Panini National Treasures Winning Signatures Printing Plates Yellow /1 #9
2017 Panini Torque #8
2017 Panini Torque #85
2017 Panini Torque #94
2017 Panini Torque Artist Proof /75 #8
2017 Panini Torque Artist Proof /75 #85
2017 Panini Torque Artist Proof /75 #94
2017 Panini Torque Blackout /1 #8
2017 Panini Torque Blackout /1 #85
2017 Panini Torque Blackout /1 #94
2017 Panini Torque Blue /150 #8
2017 Panini Torque Blue /150 #85
2017 Panini Torque Blue /150 #94
2017 Panini Torque Claiming The Chase #3
2017 Panini Torque Claiming The Chase Gold /199 #3
2017 Panini Torque Claiming The Chase Holo Silver /99 #3
2017 Panini Torque Clear Vision #18
2017 Panini Torque Clear Vision Blue /99 #18
2017 Panini Torque Clear Vision Gold /149 #18
2017 Panini Torque Clear Vision Green /25 #18
2017 Panini Torque Clear Vision Purple /10 #18
2017 Panini Torque Clear Vision Red /49 #18
2017 Panini Torque Dual Materials /499 #17
2017 Panini Torque Dual Materials Blue /99 #17
2017 Panini Torque Dual Materials Green /25 #17
2017 Panini Torque Dual Materials Purple /10 #17
2017 Panini Torque Dual Materials Red /49 #17
2017 Panini Torque Gold #8
2017 Panini Torque Gold #85
2017 Panini Torque Gold #94
2017 Panini Torque Holo Gold /10 #8
2017 Panini Torque Holo Gold /10 #85
2017 Panini Torque Holo Gold /10 #94
2017 Panini Torque Holo Silver /25 #8
2017 Panini Torque Holo Silver /25 #85
2017 Panini Torque Holo Silver /25 #94
2017 Panini Torque Horsepower Heroes #13
2017 Panini Torque Horsepower Heroes Gold /199 #13
2017 Panini Torque Horsepower Heroes Holo Silver /99 #13
2017 Panini Torque Jumbo Firesuit Signatures /51 #19
2017 Panini Torque Jumbo Firesuit Signatures Blue /49 #19
2017 Panini Torque Jumbo Firesuit Signatures Green /15 #19
2017 Panini Torque Jumbo Firesuit Signatures Purple /10 #19
2017 Panini Torque Jumbo Firesuit Signatures Red /25 #19
2017 Panini Torque Manufacturer Marks #2
2017 Panini Torque Manufacturer Marks Gold /199 #2
2017 Panini Torque Manufacturer Marks Holo Silver /99 #2
2017 Panini Torque Pairings Materials /199 #10
2017 Panini Torque Pairings Materials /75 #14
2017 Panini Torque Pairings Materials Blue /99 #10
2017 Panini Torque Pairings Materials Blue /49 #14
2017 Panini Torque Pairings Materials Green /25 #10
2017 Panini Torque Pairings Materials Green /10 #14
2017 Panini Torque Pairings Materials Purple /10 #10
2017 Panini Torque Pairings Materials Purple /1 #14
2017 Panini Torque Pairings Materials Red /49 #10
2017 Panini Torque Pairings Materials Red /25 #14
2017 Panini Torque Primary Paint #11
2017 Panini Torque Primary Paint Blue /99 #11
2017 Panini Torque Primary Paint Checkerboard /10 #11
2017 Panini Torque Primary Paint Green /25 #11
2017 Panini Torque Primary Paint Red /49 #11
2017 Panini Torque Prime Associate Sponsors Jumbo Patches /1 #14A
2017 Panini Torque Prime Associate Sponsors Jumbo Patches /1 #14B
2017 Panini Torque Prime Associate Sponsors Jumbo Patches /1 #14C
2017 Panini Torque Prime Associate Sponsors Jumbo Patches /1 #14D
2017 Panini Torque Prime Associate Sponsors Jumbo Patches /1 #14E
2017 Panini Torque Prime Associate Sponsors Jumbo Patches /1 #14F
2017 Panini Torque Prime Associate Sponsors Jumbo Patches /1 #14G
2017 Panini Torque Prime Associate Sponsors Jumbo Patches /1 #14H
2017 Panini Torque Prime Associate Sponsors Jumbo Patches /1 #14I
2017 Panini Torque Prime Associate Sponsors Jumbo Patches /1 #14J
2017 Panini Torque Prime Associate Sponsors Jumbo Patches /1 #14K
2017 Panini Torque Prime Associate Sponsors Jumbo Patches /1 #14L
2017 Panini Torque Prime Associate Sponsors Jumbo Patches /1 #14M
2017 Panini Torque Prime Associate Sponsors Jumbo Patches /1 #14N
2017 Panini Torque Prime Associate Sponsors Jumbo Patches /1 #14O
2017 Panini Torque Prime Goodyear Jumbo Patches /2 #14
2017 Panini Torque Prime Manufacturer Jumbo Patches /1 #14
2017 Panini Torque Prime Nameplates Jumbo Patches /1 #14
2017 Panini Torque Prime NASCAR Jumbo Patches /1 #14
2017 Panini Torque Prime Series Sponsor Jumbo Patches /1 #14
2017 Panini Torque Printing Plates Black /1 #8
2017 Panini Torque Printing Plates Black /1 #85
2017 Panini Torque Printing Plates Black /1 #94
2017 Panini Torque Printing Plates Cyan /1 #8
2017 Panini Torque Printing Plates Cyan /1 #85
2017 Panini Torque Printing Plates Cyan /1 #94
2017 Panini Torque Printing Plates Magenta /1 #8
2017 Panini Torque Printing Plates Magenta /1 #85
2017 Panini Torque Printing Plates Magenta /1 #94
2017 Panini Torque Printing Plates Yellow /1 #8
2017 Panini Torque Printing Plates Yellow /1 #85
2017 Panini Torque Printing Plates Yellow /1 #94
2017 Panini Torque Purple /50 #8
2017 Panini Torque Purple /50 #85
2017 Panini Torque Purple /50 #94
2017 Panini Torque Quad Materials /99 #19
2017 Panini Torque Quad Materials Blue /49 #19
2017 Panini Torque Quad Materials Green /10 #19
2017 Panini Torque Quad Materials Purple /5 #19
2017 Panini Torque Quad Materials Red /25 #19
2017 Panini Torque Raced Relics /499 #15
2017 Panini Torque Raced Relics Blue /99 #15
2017 Panini Torque Raced Relics Green /25 #15
2017 Panini Torque Raced Relics Purple /10 #15
2017 Panini Torque Raced Relics Red /49 #15
2017 Panini Torque Red /100 #8
2017 Panini Torque Red /100 #85
2017 Panini Torque Red /100 #94
2017 Panini Torque Running Order #3
2017 Panini Torque Running Order Blue /99 #3
2017 Panini Torque Running Order Checkerboard /10 #3
2017 Panini Torque Running Order Green /25 #3
2017 Panini Torque Running Order Red /49 #3
2017 Panini Torque Silhouettes Sheet Metal Signatures /51 #24
2017 Panini Torque Silhouettes Sheet Metal Signatures Blue /49 #24
2017 Panini Torque Silhouettes Sheet Metal Signatures Green /15 #24
2017 Panini Torque Silhouettes Sheet Metal Signatures Purple /10 #24
2017 Panini Torque Silhouettes Sheet Metal Signatures Red /25 #24
2017 Panini Torque Special Paint #3
2017 Panini Torque Special Paint Gold /199 #3
2017 Panini Torque Special Paint Holo Silver /99 #3
2017 Panini Torque Superstar Vision #12
2017 Panini Torque Superstar Vision Blue /99 #12
2017 Panini Torque Superstar Vision Gold /149 #12
2017 Panini Torque Superstar Vision Green /25 #12
2017 Panini Torque Superstar Vision Purple /10 #12
2017 Panini Torque Superstar Vision Red /49 #12
2017 Panini Torque Test Proof Black /1 #8
2017 Panini Torque Test Proof Black /1 #85
2017 Panini Torque Test Proof Black /1 #94
2017 Panini Torque Test Proof Cyan /1 #8
2017 Panini Torque Test Proof Cyan /1 #85
2017 Panini Torque Test Proof Cyan /1 #94
2017 Panini Torque Test Proof Magenta /1 #8
2017 Panini Torque Test Proof Magenta /1 #85
2017 Panini Torque Test Proof Magenta /1 #94
2017 Panini Torque Test Proof Yellow /1 #8
2017 Panini Torque Test Proof Yellow /1 #85
2017 Panini Torque Test Proof Yellow /1 #94
2017 Panini Torque Track Vision #8
2017 Panini Torque Track Vision Blue /99 #8
2017 Panini Torque Track Vision Gold /149 #8
2017 Panini Torque Track Vision Green /25 #8
2017 Panini Torque Track Vision Purple /10 #8
2017 Panini Torque Track Vision Red /49 #8
2017 Panini Torque Trackside #9
2017 Panini Torque Trackside Blue /99 #9
2017 Panini Torque Trackside Checkerboard /10 #9
2017 Panini Torque Trackside Green /25 #9
2017 Panini Torque Trackside Red /49 #9
2017 Panini Torque Victory Laps #2
2017 Panini Torque Victory Laps Gold /199 #2
2017 Panini Torque Victory Laps Holo Silver /99 #2
2017 Panini Torque Visions of Greatness #20
2017 Panini Torque Visions of Greatness Blue /99 #20
2017 Panini Torque Visions of Greatness Gold /149 #20
2017 Panini Torque Visions of Greatness Green /25 #20
2017 Panini Torque Visions of Greatness Purple /10 #20
2017 Panini Torque Visions of Greatness Red /49 #20
2017 Select #49
2017 Select #50
2017 Select #51
2017 Select #118
2017 Select Prizms Black /3 #49
2017 Select Prizms Black /3 #50
2017 Select Prizms Black /3 #51
2017 Select Prizms Black /3 #118
2017 Select Prizms Blue /199 #49
2017 Select Prizms Blue /199 #50
2017 Select Prizms Blue /199 #51
2017 Select Prizms Checkered Flag /1 #49
2017 Select Prizms Checkered Flag /1 #50
2017 Select Prizms Checkered Flag /1 #51
2017 Select Prizms Checkered Flag /1 #118
2017 Select Prizms Gold /10 #49
2017 Select Prizms Gold /10 #50
2017 Select Prizms Gold /10 #51
2017 Select Prizms Gold /10 #118
2017 Select Prizms Purple Pulsar #49
2017 Select Prizms Purple Pulsar #50
2017 Select Prizms Purple Pulsar #51
2017 Select Prizms Red /99 #49
2017 Select Prizms Red /99 #50
2017 Select Prizms Red /99 #51
2017 Select Prizms Red White and Blue Pulsar /299 #49
2017 Select Prizms Red White and Blue Pulsar /299 #50
2017 Select Prizms Red White and Blue Pulsar /299 #51
2017 Select Prizms Silver #49
2017 Select Prizms Silver #50
2017 Select Prizms Silver #51
2017 Select Prizms Tie Dye /24 #49
2017 Select Prizms Tie Dye /24 #50
2017 Select Prizms Tie Dye /24 #51
2017 Select Prizms Tie Dye /24 #118
2017 Select Prizms White /50 #49
2017 Select Prizms White /50 #50
2017 Select Prizms White /50 #51
2017 Select Prizms White /50 #118
2017 Select Select Pairs Materials #20
2017 Select Select Pairs Materials #23
2017 Select Select Pairs Materials #24
2017 Select Select Pairs Materials Prizms Blue /199 #20
2017 Select Select Pairs Materials Prizms Blue /199 #23
2017 Select Select Pairs Materials Prizms Blue /199 #24
2017 Select Select Pairs Materials Prizms Checkered Flag /1 #20
2017 Select Select Pairs Materials Prizms Checkered Flag /1 #23
2017 Select Select Pairs Materials Prizms Checkered Flag /1 #24
2017 Select Select Pairs Materials Prizms Gold /10 #20
2017 Select Select Pairs Materials Prizms Gold /10 #23
2017 Select Select Pairs Materials Prizms Gold /10 #24
2017 Select Select Pairs Materials Prizms Red /99 #20
2017 Select Select Pairs Materials Prizms Red /99 #23
2017 Select Select Pairs Materials Prizms Red /99 #24
2017 Select Select Stars #13
2017 Select Select Stars Prizms Black /3 #13
2017 Select Select Stars Prizms Checkered Flag /1 #13
2017 Select Select Stars Prizms Gold /10 #13
2017 Select Select Stars Prizms Tie Dye /24 #13
2017 Select Select Stars Prizms White /50 #13
2017 Select Select Swatches #29
2017 Select Select Swatches Prizms Blue /199 #29
2017 Select Select Swatches Prizms Checkered Flag /1 #29
2017 Select Select Swatches Prizms Gold /10 #29
2017 Select Select Swatches Prizms Red /99 #29
2017 Select Sheet Metal #17
2017 Select Sheet Metal Prizms Blue /49 #17
2017 Select Sheet Metal Prizms Checkered Flag /1 #17
2017 Select Sheet Metal Prizms Gold /10 #17
2017 Select Sheet Metal Prizms Red /25 #17
2017 Select Signature Paint Schemes #2
2017 Select Signature Paint Schemes Prizms Blue /50 #2
2017 Select Signature Paint Schemes Prizms Checkered Flag /1 #2
2017 Select Signature Paint Schemes Prizms Gold /10 #2
2017 Select Signature Paint Schemes Prizms Red /25 #2
2017 Select Signature Swatches #29
2017 Select Signature Swatches Prizms Checkered Flag /1 #29
2017 Select Signature Swatches Prizms Gold /10 #29
2017 Select Signature Swatches Prizms Tie Dye /24 #29
2017 Select Signature Swatches Prizms White /50 #29
2017 Select Signature Swatches Triple #18
2017 Select Signature Swatches Triple Prizms Checkered Flag /1 #18
2017 Select Signature Swatches Triple Prizms Gold /10 #18
2017 Select Signature Swatches Triple Prizms Tie Dye /24 #18
2017 Select Signature Swatches Triple Prizms White /50 #18
2017 Select Speed Merchants #24
2017 Select Speed Merchants Prizms Black /3 #24
2017 Select Speed Merchants Prizms Checkered Flag /1 #24
2017 Select Speed Merchants Prizms Gold /10 #24
2017 Select Speed Merchants Prizms Tie Dye /24 #24
2017 Select Speed Merchants Prizms White /50 #24
2018 Certified #4
2018 Certified All Certified Team /199 #11
2018 Certified All Certified Team Black /1 #11
2018 Certified All Certified Team Blue /99 #11
2018 Certified All Certified Team Gold /49 #11
2018 Certified All Certified Team Green /10 #11
2018 Certified All Certified Team Mirror Black /1 #11
2018 Certified All Certified Team Mirror Gold /25 #11
2018 Certified All Certified Team Mirror Green /5 #11
2018 Certified All Certified Team Mirror Purple /10 #11
2018 Certified All Certified Team Purple /25 #11
2018 Certified All Certified Team Red /149 #11
2018 Certified Black /1 #4
2018 Certified Blue /99 #4
2018 Certified Complete Materials /199 #9
2018 Certified Complete Materials Black /1 #9
2018 Certified Complete Materials Blue /49 #9
2018 Certified Complete Materials Gold /25 #9
2018 Certified Complete Materials Green /5 #9
2018 Certified Complete Materials Purple /10 #9
2018 Certified Complete Materials Red /99 #9
2018 Certified Cup Swatches /199 #18
2018 Certified Cup Swatches Black /1 #18
2018 Certified Cup Swatches Blue /49 #18
2018 Certified Cup Swatches Gold /25 #18
2018 Certified Cup Swatches Green /5 #18
2018 Certified Cup Swatches Purple /10 #18
2018 Certified Cup Swatches Red /99 #18
2018 Certified Epix /199 #1
2018 Certified Epix Black /1 #1
2018 Certified Epix Blue /99 #1
2018 Certified Epix Gold /49 #1
2018 Certified Epix Green /10 #1
2018 Certified Epix Mirror Black /1 #1
2018 Certified Epix Mirror Gold /25 #1
2018 Certified Epix Mirror Green /5 #1
2018 Certified Epix Mirror Purple /10 #1
2018 Certified Epix Purple /25 #1
2018 Certified Epix Red /149 #1
2018 Certified Gold /49 #4
2018 Certified Green /10 #4
2018 Certified Materials Signatures /75 #12
2018 Certified Materials Signatures Black /1 #12
2018 Certified Materials Signatures Blue /25 #12
2018 Certified Materials Signatures Gold /15 #12
2018 Certified Materials Signatures Green /5 #12
2018 Certified Materials Signatures Purple /10 #12
2018 Certified Materials Signatures Red /49 #12
2018 Certified Mirror Black /1 #4
2018 Certified Mirror Gold /25 #4
2018 Certified Mirror Green /5 #4
2018 Certified Mirror Purple /10 #4
2018 Certified Orange /249 #4
2018 Certified Piece of the Race /399 #9
2018 Certified Piece of the Race Black /1 #9
2018 Certified Piece of the Race Blue /49 #9
2018 Certified Piece of the Race Gold /25 #9
2018 Certified Piece of the Race Green /5 #9
2018 Certified Piece of the Race Purple /10 #9
2018 Certified Piece of the Race Red /199 #9
2018 Certified Purple /25 #4
2018 Certified Red /199 #4
2018 Certified Signing Sessions /25 #15
2018 Certified Signing Sessions Black /1 #15
2018 Certified Signing Sessions Blue /15 #15
2018 Certified Signing Sessions Gold /10 #15
2018 Certified Signing Sessions Green /3 #15
2018 Certified Signing Sessions Purple /5 #15
2018 Certified Signing Sessions Red /20 #15
2018 Certified Skills /199 #10
2018 Certified Skills Black /1 #10
2018 Certified Skills Blue /99 #10
2018 Certified Skills Gold /49 #10
2018 Certified Skills Green /10 #10
2018 Certified Skills Mirror Black /1 #10
2018 Certified Skills Mirror Gold /25 #10
2018 Certified Skills Mirror Green /5 #10
2018 Certified Skills Mirror Purple /10 #10
2018 Certified Skills Purple /25 #10
2018 Certified Skills Red /149 #10
2018 Certified Stars /199 #12
2018 Certified Stars Black /1 #12
2018 Certified Stars Blue /99 #12
2018 Certified Stars Gold /49 #12
2018 Certified Stars Green /10 #12
2018 Certified Stars Mirror Black /1 #12
2018 Certified Stars Mirror Gold /25 #12
2018 Certified Stars Mirror Green /5 #12
2018 Certified Stars Mirror Purple /10 #12
2018 Certified Stars Purple /25 #12
2018 Certified Stars Red /149 #12
2018 Donruss #14
2018 Donruss #41A
2018 Donruss #87
2018 Donruss #131
2018 Donruss #41B
2018 Donruss Artist Proofs /25 #14
2018 Donruss Artist Proofs /25 #41A
2018 Donruss Artist Proofs /25 #87
2018 Donruss Artist Proofs /25 #131
2018 Donruss Artist Proofs /25 #41B
2018 Donruss Classics #7
2018 Donruss Classics Cracked Ice /999 #7
2018 Donruss Classics Xplosion /99 #7
2018 Donruss Elite Series /999 #4
2018 Donruss Gold Foil /499 #14
2018 Donruss Gold Foil /499 #41A
2018 Donruss Gold Foil /499 #87
2018 Donruss Gold Foil /499 #131
2018 Donruss Gold Foil /499 #41B
2018 Donruss Gold Press Proofs /99 #14
2018 Donruss Gold Press Proofs /99 #41A
2018 Donruss Gold Press Proofs /99 #87
2018 Donruss Gold Press Proofs /99 #131
2018 Donruss Gold Press Proofs /99 #41B
2018 Donruss Green Foil /199 #14
2018 Donruss Green Foil /199 #41A
2018 Donruss Green Foil /199 #87
2018 Donruss Green Foil /199 #131
2018 Donruss Green Foil /199 #41B
2018 Donruss Pole Position #10
2018 Donruss Pole Position Cracked Ice /999 #10
2018 Donruss Pole Position Xplosion /99 #10
2018 Donruss Press Proofs /49 #14
2018 Donruss Press Proofs /49 #41A
2018 Donruss Press Proofs /49 #87
2018 Donruss Press Proofs /49 #131
2018 Donruss Press Proofs /49 #41B
2018 Donruss Printing Plates Black /1 #14
2018 Donruss Printing Plates Black /1 #41
2018 Donruss Printing Plates Black /1 #87
2018 Donruss Printing Plates Black /1 #131
2018 Donruss Printing Plates Black /1 #41B
2018 Donruss Printing Plates Cyan /1 #14
2018 Donruss Printing Plates Cyan /1 #41
2018 Donruss Printing Plates Cyan /1 #87
2018 Donruss Printing Plates Cyan /1 #131
2018 Donruss Printing Plates Cyan /1 #41B
2018 Donruss Printing Plates Magenta /1 #14
2018 Donruss Printing Plates Magenta /1 #41
2018 Donruss Printing Plates Magenta /1 #87
2018 Donruss Printing Plates Magenta /1 #131
2018 Donruss Printing Plates Magenta /1 #41B
2018 Donruss Printing Plates Yellow /1 #14
2018 Donruss Printing Plates Yellow /1 #41
2018 Donruss Printing Plates Yellow /1 #87
2018 Donruss Printing Plates Yellow /1 #131
2018 Donruss Printing Plates Yellow /1 #41B
2018 Donruss Red Foil /299 #14
2018 Donruss Red Foil /299 #41A
2018 Donruss Red Foil /299 #87
2018 Donruss Red Foil /299 #131
2018 Donruss Red Foil /299 #41B
2018 Donruss Rubber Relic Signatures #12
2018 Donruss Rubber Relic Signatures Black /1 #12
2018 Donruss Rubber Relic Signatures Holo Gold /25 #12
2018 Donruss Rubber Relics #23
2018 Donruss Rubber Relics Black /10 #23
2018 Donruss Rubber Relics Holo Gold /99 #23
2018 Donruss Studio #8
2018 Donruss Studio Cracked Ice /999 #8
2018 Donruss Studio Xplosion /99 #8
2018 Donruss Top Tier #5
2018 Donruss Top Tier Cracked Ice /999 #5
2018 Donruss Top Tier Xplosion /99 #5
2018 Panini Father's Day Racing Memorabilia #KB
2018 Panini Father's Day Racing Memorabilia Checkerboard /10 #KB
2018 Panini Father's Day Racing Memorabilia Cracked Ice /25 #KB
2018 Panini Father's Day Racing Memorabilia Escher Squares /5 #KB
2018 Panini Father's Day Racing Memorabilia Hyperplaid /1 #KB
2018 Panini Prime /50 #1
2018 Panini Prime /50 #35
2018 Panini Prime /50 #68
2018 Panini Prime Black /1 #1
2018 Panini Prime Black /1 #35
2018 Panini Prime Black /1 #68
2018 Panini Prime Clear Silhouettes /99 #20
2018 Panini Prime Clear Silhouettes Black /1 #20
2018 Panini Prime Clear Silhouettes Dual /99 #22
2018 Panini Prime Clear Silhouettes Dual Black /1 #22
2018 Panini Prime Clear Silhouettes Dual Holo Gold /50 #22
2018 Panini Prime Clear Silhouettes Holo Gold /50 #20
2018 Panini Prime Dual Material Autographs /25 #6
2018 Panini Prime Dual Material Autographs Black /1 #6
2018 Panini Prime Dual Material Autographs Holo Gold /10 #6
2018 Panini Prime Dual Material Autographs Laundry Tag /1 #6
2018 Panini Prime Dual Signatures /10 #12
2018 Panini Prime Dual Signatures Black /1 #12
2018 Panini Prime Dual Signatures Holo Gold /5 #12
2018 Panini Prime Hats Off Button /1 #8
2018 Panini Prime Hats Off Button /1 #9
2018 Panini Prime Hats Off Button /1 #10
2018 Panini Prime Hats Off Button /1 #11
2018 Panini Prime Hats Off Driver Name /1 #8
2018 Panini Prime Hats Off Driver Name /1 #9
2018 Panini Prime Hats Off Driver Name /1 #10
2018 Panini Prime Hats Off Driver Name /1 #11
2018 Panini Prime Hats Off Eyelet /6 #8
2018 Panini Prime Hats Off Eyelet /6 #9
2018 Panini Prime Hats Off Eyelet /6 #10
2018 Panini Prime Hats Off Eyelet /6 #11
2018 Panini Prime Hats Off Headband /36 #8
2018 Panini Prime Hats Off Headband /24 #9
2018 Panini Prime Hats Off Headband /30 #10
2018 Panini Prime Hats Off Headband /30 #11
2018 Panini Prime Hats Off Laundry Tag /1 #8
2018 Panini Prime Hats Off Laundry Tag /1 #9
2018 Panini Prime Hats Off Laundry Tag /1 #10
2018 Panini Prime Hats Off Laundry Tag /1 #11
2018 Panini Prime Hats Off New Era /1 #8
2018 Panini Prime Hats Off New Era /1 #9
2018 Panini Prime Hats Off New Era /1 #10
2018 Panini Prime Hats Off New Era /1 #11
2018 Panini Prime Hats Off Number /4 #8
2018 Panini Prime Hats Off Number /4 #9
2018 Panini Prime Hats Off Number /4 #10
2018 Panini Prime Hats Off Number /4 #11
2018 Panini Prime Hats Off Sponsor Logo /6 #8
2018 Panini Prime Hats Off Sponsor Logo /8 #9
2018 Panini Prime Hats Off Sponsor Logo /6 #10
2018 Panini Prime Hats Off Sponsor Logo /4 #11
2018 Panini Prime Hats Off Team Logo /2 #8
2018 Panini Prime Hats Off Team Logo /2 #9
2018 Panini Prime Hats Off Team Logo /2 #10
2018 Panini Prime Hats Off Team Logo /2 #11
2018 Panini Prime Holo Gold /25 #1
2018 Panini Prime Holo Gold /25 #35
2018 Panini Prime Holo Gold /25 #68
2018 Panini Prime Prime Jumbo Associate Sponsor 1 /1 #51
2018 Panini Prime Prime Jumbo Associate Sponsor 10 /1 #51
2018 Panini Prime Prime Jumbo Associate Sponsor 11 /1 #51
2018 Panini Prime Prime Jumbo Associate Sponsor 12 /1 #51
2018 Panini Prime Prime Jumbo Associate Sponsor 13 /1 #51
2018 Panini Prime Prime Jumbo Associate Sponsor 14 /1 #51
2018 Panini Prime Prime Jumbo Associate Sponsor 2 /1 #51
2018 Panini Prime Prime Jumbo Associate Sponsor 3 /1 #51
2018 Panini Prime Prime Jumbo Associate Sponsor 4 /1 #51
2018 Panini Prime Prime Jumbo Associate Sponsor 5 /1 #51
2018 Panini Prime Prime Jumbo Associate Sponsor 6 /1 #51
2018 Panini Prime Prime Jumbo Associate Sponsor 7 /1 #51
2018 Panini Prime Prime Jumbo Associate Sponsor 8 /1 #51
2018 Panini Prime Prime Jumbo Associate Sponsor 9 /1 #51
2018 Panini Prime Prime Jumbo Car Manufacturer /1 #51
2018 Panini Prime Prime Jumbo Firesuit Manufacturer /1 #51
2018 Panini Prime Prime Jumbo Flag Patch /1 #51
2018 Panini Prime Prime Jumbo Glove Manufacturer Patch /1 #51
2018 Panini Prime Prime Jumbo Goodyear /2 #51
2018 Panini Prime Prime Jumbo Laundry Tag /1 #51
2018 Panini Prime Prime Jumbo Nameplate /2 #51
2018 Panini Prime Prime Jumbo NASCAR /1 #51
2018 Panini Prime Prime Jumbo Prime Colors /20 #51
2018 Panini Prime Prime Jumbo Series Sponsor /1 #51
2018 Panini Prime Prime Jumbo Shoe Brand Logo /1 #51
2018 Panini Prime Prime Jumbo Shoe Name Patch /1 #51
2018 Panini Prime Prime Jumbo Sunoco /1 #51
2018 Panini Prime Prime Number Signatures /25 #11
2018 Panini Prime Prime Number Signatures Black /1 #11
2018 Panini Prime Prime Number Signatures Holo Gold /10 #11
2018 Panini Prime Quad Material Autographs /25 #8
2018 Panini Prime Quad Material Autographs Black /1 #8
2018 Panini Prime Quad Material Autographs Holo Gold /10 #8
2018 Panini Prime Quad Material Autographs Laundry Tag /1 #8
2018 Panini Prime Race Used Duals Firesuit Black /1 #26
2018 Panini Prime Race Used Duals Firesuit Holo Gold /25 #26
2018 Panini Prime Race Used Duals Firesuit Laundry Tag /1 #26
2018 Panini Prime Race Used Duals Sheet Metal /50 #26
2018 Panini Prime Race Used Duals Sheet Metal Black /1 #26
2018 Panini Prime Race Used Duals Sheet Metal Holo Gold /25 #26
2018 Panini Prime Race Used Duals Tire /50 #26
2018 Panini Prime Race Used Duals Tire Black /1 #26
2018 Panini Prime Race Used Duals Tire Holo Gold /25 #26
2018 Panini Prime Race Used Firesuits Black /1 #25
2018 Panini Prime Race Used Firesuits Holo Gold /25 #25
2018 Panini Prime Race Used Firesuits Laundry Tag /1 #25
2018 Panini Prime Race Used Sheet Metal /50 #25
2018 Panini Prime Race Used Sheet Metal Black /1 #25
2018 Panini Prime Race Used Sheet Metal Holo Gold /25 #25
2018 Panini Prime Race Used Tires /50 #25
2018 Panini Prime Race Used Tires Black /1 #25
2018 Panini Prime Race Used Tires Holo Gold /25 #25
2018 Panini Prime Race Used Trios Firesuit /50 #8
2018 Panini Prime Race Used Trios Firesuit Black /1 #8
2018 Panini Prime Race Used Trios Firesuit Holo Gold /25 #8
2018 Panini Prime Race Used Trios Firesuit Laundry Tag /1 #8
2018 Panini Prime Race Used Trios Sheet Metal /50 #8
2018 Panini Prime Race Used Trios Sheet Metal Black /1 #8
2018 Panini Prime Race Used Trios Sheet Metal Holo Gold /25 #8
2018 Panini Prime Race Used Trios Tire /50 #8
2018 Panini Prime Race Used Trios Tire Black /1 #8
2018 Panini Prime Race Used Trios Tire Holo Gold /25 #8
2018 Panini Prime Shadowbox Signatures /25 #20
2018 Panini Prime Shadowbox Signatures Black /1 #20
2018 Panini Prime Shadowbox Signatures Holo Gold /10 #20
2018 Panini Prime Signature Swatches /25 #13
2018 Panini Prime Signature Swatches Black /1 #13
2018 Panini Prime Signature Swatches Holo Gold /10 #13
2018 Panini Prime Signature Tires /25 #10
2018 Panini Prime Signature Tires Black /1 #10
2018 Panini Prime Signature Tires Holo Gold /10 #10
2018 Panini Prizm #29
2018 Panini Prizm #66
2018 Panini Prizm #87
2018 Panini Prizm Brilliance #1
2018 Panini Prizm Brilliance Prizms #1
2018 Panini Prizm Brilliance Prizms Black /1 #1
2018 Panini Prizm Brilliance Prizms Gold /10 #1
2018 Panini Prizm Fireworks #8
2018 Panini Prizm Fireworks Prizms #8
2018 Panini Prizm Fireworks Prizms Black /1 #8
2018 Panini Prizm Fireworks Prizms Gold /10 #8
2018 Panini Prizm National Pride #4
2018 Panini Prizm National Pride Prizms #4
2018 Panini Prizm National Pride Prizms Black /1 #4
2018 Panini Prizm National Pride Prizms Gold /10 #4
2018 Panini Prizm Prizms #29
2018 Panini Prizm Prizms #66
2018 Panini Prizm Prizms #87
2018 Panini Prizm Prizms Black /1 #29
2018 Panini Prizm Prizms Black /1 #66
2018 Panini Prizm Prizms Black /1 #87
2018 Panini Prizm Prizms Blue /99 #29
2018 Panini Prizm Prizms Blue /99 #66
2018 Panini Prizm Prizms Blue /99 #87
2018 Panini Prizm Prizms Camo #29
2018 Panini Prizm Prizms Camo #66
2018 Panini Prizm Prizms Camo #87
2018 Panini Prizm Prizms Gold /10 #29
2018 Panini Prizm Prizms Gold /10 #66
2018 Panini Prizm Prizms Gold /10 #87
2018 Panini Prizm Prizms Green /149 #29
2018 Panini Prizm Prizms Green /149 #66
2018 Panini Prizm Prizms Green /149 #87
2018 Panini Prizm Prizms Purple Flash #29
2018 Panini Prizm Prizms Purple Flash #66
2018 Panini Prizm Prizms Purple Flash #87
2018 Panini Prizm Prizms Rainbow /24 #29
2018 Panini Prizm Prizms Rainbow /24 #66
2018 Panini Prizm Prizms Rainbow /24 #87
2018 Panini Prizm Prizms Red /75 #29
2018 Panini Prizm Prizms Red /75 #66
2018 Panini Prizm Prizms Red /75 #87
2018 Panini Prizm Prizms Red White and Blue #29
2018 Panini Prizm Prizms Red White and Blue #66
2018 Panini Prizm Prizms Red White and Blue #87
2018 Panini Prizm Prizms White /5 #29
2018 Panini Prizm Prizms White /5 #66
2018 Panini Prizm Prizms White /5 #87
2018 Panini Prizm Scripted Signatures Prizms #37
2018 Panini Prizm Scripted Signatures Prizms Black /1 #37
2018 Panini Prizm Scripted Signatures Prizms Blue /25 #37
2018 Panini Prizm Scripted Signatures Prizms Camo #37
2018 Panini Prizm Scripted Signatures Prizms Gold /10 #37
2018 Panini Prizm Scripted Signatures Prizms Green /25 #37
2018 Panini Prizm Scripted Signatures Prizms Rainbow /24 #37
2018 Panini Prizm Scripted Signatures Prizms Red /25 #37
2018 Panini Prizm Scripted Signatures Prizms Red White and Blue /25 #37
2018 Panini Prizm Scripted Signatures Prizms White /5 #37

2018 Panini Prizm Stars and Stripes #11
2018 Panini Prizm Stars and Stripes Prizms #11
2018 Panini Prizm Stars and Stripes Prizms Black /1 #11
2018 Panini Prizm Stars and Stripes Prizms Gold /10 #11
2018 Panini Prizm Team Tandems #9
2018 Panini Prizm Team Tandems Prizms #9
2018 Panini Prizm Team Tandems Prizms Black /1 #9
2018 Panini Prizm Team Tandems Prizms Gold /10 #9
2018 Panini Victory Lane #12
2018 Panini Victory Lane #42
2018 Panini Victory Lane #43
2018 Panini Victory Lane #47
2018 Panini Victory Lane #96
2018 Panini Victory Lane Black /1 #12
2018 Panini Victory Lane Black /1 #42
2018 Panini Victory Lane Black /1 #43
2018 Panini Victory Lane Black /1 #47
2018 Panini Victory Lane Black /1 #96
2018 Panini Victory Lane Blue /25 #12
2018 Panini Victory Lane Blue /25 #42
2018 Panini Victory Lane Blue /25 #43
2018 Panini Victory Lane Blue /25 #47
2018 Panini Victory Lane Blue /25 #96
2018 Panini Victory Lane Celebrations #10
2018 Panini Victory Lane Celebrations Black /1 #10
2018 Panini Victory Lane Celebrations Blue /25 #10
2018 Panini Victory Lane Celebrations Gold /99 #10
2018 Panini Victory Lane Celebrations Green /5 #10
2018 Panini Victory Lane Celebrations Printing Plates Black /1 #10
2018 Panini Victory Lane Celebrations Printing Plates Cyan /1 #10
2018 Panini Victory Lane Celebrations Printing Plates Magenta /1 #10
2018 Panini Victory Lane Celebrations Printing Plates Yellow /1 #10
2018 Panini Victory Lane Celebrations Red /49 #10
2018 Panini Victory Lane Champions #14
2018 Panini Victory Lane Champions Black /1 #14
2018 Panini Victory Lane Champions Blue /25 #14
2018 Panini Victory Lane Champions Gold /99 #14
2018 Panini Victory Lane Champions Green /5 #14
2018 Panini Victory Lane Champions Printing Plates Black /1 #14
2018 Panini Victory Lane Champions Printing Plates Cyan /1 #14
2018 Panini Victory Lane Champions Printing Plates Magenta /1 #14
2018 Panini Victory Lane Champions Printing Plates Yellow /1 #14
2018 Panini Victory Lane Champions Red /49 #14
2018 Panini Victory Lane Chasing the Flag #8
2018 Panini Victory Lane Chasing the Flag Black /1 #8
2018 Panini Victory Lane Chasing the Flag Blue /25 #8
2018 Panini Victory Lane Chasing the Flag Gold /99 #8
2018 Panini Victory Lane Chasing the Flag Green /5 #8
2018 Panini Victory Lane Chasing the Flag Printing Plates Black /1 #8
2018 Panini Victory Lane Chasing the Flag Printing Plates Cyan /1 #8
2018 Panini Victory Lane Chasing the Flag Printing Plates Magenta /1 #8
2018 Panini Victory Lane Chasing the Flag Printing Plates Yellow /1 #8
2018 Panini Victory Lane Chasing the Flag Red /49 #8
2018 Panini Victory Lane Engineered to Perfection Materials /199 #15
2018 Panini Victory Lane Engineered to Perfection Materials Black /18 #15
2018 Panini Victory Lane Engineered to Perfection Materials Gold /99 #15
2018 Panini Victory Lane Engineered to Perfection Materials Green /49 #15
2018 Panini Victory Lane Engineered to Perfection Materials Laundry Tag /1 #15
2018 Panini Victory Lane Gold /99 #12
2018 Panini Victory Lane Gold /99 #42
2018 Panini Victory Lane Gold /99 #43
2018 Panini Victory Lane Gold /99 #47
2018 Panini Victory Lane Gold /99 #96
2018 Panini Victory Lane Green /5 #12
2018 Panini Victory Lane Green /5 #42
2018 Panini Victory Lane Green /5 #43
2018 Panini Victory Lane Green /5 #47
2018 Panini Victory Lane Green /5 #96
2018 Panini Victory Lane Octane Autographs /25 #1
2018 Panini Victory Lane Octane Autographs Black /1 #1
2018 Panini Victory Lane Octane Autographs Gold /18 #1
2018 Panini Victory Lane Pedal to the Metal #35
2018 Panini Victory Lane Pedal to the Metal #62
2018 Panini Victory Lane Pedal to the Metal Black /1 #35
2018 Panini Victory Lane Pedal to the Metal Black /1 #62
2018 Panini Victory Lane Pedal to the Metal Blue /25 #35
2018 Panini Victory Lane Pedal to the Metal Blue /25 #62
2018 Panini Victory Lane Pedal to the Metal Green /5 #35
2018 Panini Victory Lane Pedal to the Metal Green /5 #62
2018 Panini Victory Lane Printing Plates Black /1 #12
2018 Panini Victory Lane Printing Plates Black /1 #42
2018 Panini Victory Lane Printing Plates Black /1 #43
2018 Panini Victory Lane Printing Plates Black /1 #47
2018 Panini Victory Lane Printing Plates Black /1 #96
2018 Panini Victory Lane Printing Plates Cyan /1 #12
2018 Panini Victory Lane Printing Plates Cyan /1 #42
2018 Panini Victory Lane Printing Plates Cyan /1 #43
2018 Panini Victory Lane Printing Plates Cyan /1 #47
2018 Panini Victory Lane Printing Plates Cyan /1 #96
2018 Panini Victory Lane Printing Plates Magenta /1 #12
2018 Panini Victory Lane Printing Plates Magenta /1 #42
2018 Panini Victory Lane Printing Plates Magenta /1 #43
2018 Panini Victory Lane Printing Plates Magenta /1 #47
2018 Panini Victory Lane Printing Plates Magenta /1 #96
2018 Panini Victory Lane Printing Plates Yellow /1 #12
2018 Panini Victory Lane Printing Plates Yellow /1 #42
2018 Panini Victory Lane Printing Plates Yellow /1 #43
2018 Panini Victory Lane Printing Plates Yellow /1 #47
2018 Panini Victory Lane Printing Plates Yellow /1 #96
2018 Panini Victory Lane Race Day #6
2018 Panini Victory Lane Race Day Black /1 #6
2018 Panini Victory Lane Race Day Blue /25 #6
2018 Panini Victory Lane Race Day Gold /99 #6
2018 Panini Victory Lane Race Day Green /5 #6
2018 Panini Victory Lane Race Day Printing Plates Black /1 #6
2018 Panini Victory Lane Race Day Printing Plates Cyan /1 #6
2018 Panini Victory Lane Race Day Printing Plates Magenta /1 #6
2018 Panini Victory Lane Race Day Printing Plates Yellow /1 #6
2018 Panini Victory Lane Race Day Red /49 #6
2018 Panini Victory Lane Race Ready Dual Materials /49 #12
2018 Panini Victory Lane Race Ready Dual Materials Black /5 #12
2018 Panini Victory Lane Race Ready Dual Materials Gold /25 #12
2018 Panini Victory Lane Race Ready Dual Materials Green /18 #12
2018 Panini Victory Lane Race Ready Dual Materials Laundry Tag /1 #12
2018 Panini Victory Lane Red /49 #12
2018 Panini Victory Lane Red /49 #42
2018 Panini Victory Lane Red /49 #43
2018 Panini Victory Lane Red /49 #47
2018 Panini Victory Lane Red /49 #96
2018 Panini Victory Lane Remarkable Remnants Material Autographs /99 #8
2018 Panini Victory Lane Remarkable Remnants Material Autographs Black /18 #8
2018 Panini Victory Lane Remarkable Remnants Material Autographs Gold /49 #8
2018 Panini Victory Lane Remarkable Remnants Material Autographs Green /25 #8
2018 Panini Victory Lane Remarkable Remnants Material Autographs Laundry Tag /1 #8
2018 Panini Victory Lane Silver #12
2018 Panini Victory Lane Silver #42
2018 Panini Victory Lane Silver #43
2018 Panini Victory Lane Silver #47
2018 Panini Victory Lane Silver #96
2018 Panini Victory Lane Starting Grid #12
2018 Panini Victory Lane Starting Grid Black /1 #12
2018 Panini Victory Lane Starting Grid Blue /25 #12
2018 Panini Victory Lane Starting Grid Gold /99 #12
2018 Panini Victory Lane Starting Grid Green /5 #12
2018 Panini Victory Lane Starting Grid Printing Plates Black /1 #12
2018 Panini Victory Lane Starting Grid Printing Plates Cyan /1 #12
2018 Panini Victory Lane Starting Grid Printing Plates Magenta /1 #12
2018 Panini Victory Lane Starting Grid Printing Plates Yellow /1 #12
2018 Panini Victory Lane Starting Grid Red /49 #12
2018 Panini Victory Lane Victory Lane Prime Patches Associate Sponsor 1 /1 #2
2018 Panini Victory Lane Victory Lane Prime Patches Associate Sponsor 10 /1 #2
2018 Panini Victory Lane Victory Lane Prime Patches Associate Sponsor 2 /1 #2
2018 Panini Victory Lane Victory Lane Prime Patches Associate Sponsor 3 /1 #2
2018 Panini Victory Lane Victory Lane Prime Patches Associate Sponsor 4 /1 #2
2018 Panini Victory Lane Victory Lane Prime Patches Associate Sponsor 5 /1 #2
2018 Panini Victory Lane Victory Lane Prime Patches Associate Sponsor 6 /1 #2
2018 Panini Victory Lane Victory Lane Prime Patches Associate Sponsor 7 /1 #2
2018 Panini Victory Lane Victory Lane Prime Patches Associate Sponsor 8 /1 #2
2018 Panini Victory Lane Victory Lane Prime Patches Associate Sponsor 9 /1 #2
2018 Panini Victory Lane Victory Lane Prime Patches Car Manufacturer /1 #2
2018 Panini Victory Lane Victory Lane Prime Patches Firesuit Manufacturer /1 #2
2018 Panini Victory Lane Victory Lane Prime Patches Goodyear /2 #2
2018 Panini Victory Lane Victory Lane Prime Patches Nameplate /2 #2
2018 Panini Victory Lane Victory Lane Prime Patches NASCAR /1 #2
2018 Panini Victory Lane Victory Lane Prime Patches Series Sponsor /1 #2
2018 Panini Victory Lane Victory Lane Prime Patches Sunoco /1 #2
2018 Panini Victory Lane Victory Marks /25 #9
2018 Panini Victory Lane Victory Marks Black /1 #9
2018 Panini Victory Lane Victory Marks Gold /18 #9
2019 Donruss #5
2019 Donruss #50A
2019 Donruss #88
2019 Donruss #112
2019 Donruss #50B
2019 Donruss Artist Proofs /25 #5
2019 Donruss Artist Proofs /25 #50A
2019 Donruss Artist Proofs /25 #88
2019 Donruss Artist Proofs /25 #112
2019 Donruss Artist Proofs /25 #50B
2019 Donruss Black /199 #5
2019 Donruss Black /199 #50A
2019 Donruss Black /199 #88
2019 Donruss Black /199 #112
2019 Donruss Black /199 #50B
2019 Donruss Classics #12
2019 Donruss Classics Cracked Ice /25 #12
2019 Donruss Classics Holographic #12
2019 Donruss Classics Xplosion /10 #12
2019 Donruss Contenders #2
2019 Donruss Contenders Cracked Ice /25 #2
2019 Donruss Contenders Holographic #2
2019 Donruss Contenders Xplosion /10 #2
2019 Donruss Gold /299 #5
2019 Donruss Gold /299 #50A
2019 Donruss Gold /299 #88
2019 Donruss Gold /299 #112
2019 Donruss Gold /299 #50B
2019 Donruss Gold Press Proofs /99 #5
2019 Donruss Gold Press Proofs /99 #50A
2019 Donruss Gold Press Proofs /99 #88
2019 Donruss Gold Press Proofs /99 #112
2019 Donruss Gold Press Proofs /99 #50B
2019 Donruss Optic #5
2019 Donruss Optic #15
2019 Donruss Optic #78
2019 Donruss Optic Blue Pulsar #5
2019 Donruss Optic Blue Pulsar #15
2019 Donruss Optic Blue Pulsar /1 #78
2019 Donruss Optic Gold /10 #5
2019 Donruss Optic Gold /10 #15
2019 Donruss Optic Gold /10 #78
2019 Donruss Optic Gold Vinyl /1 #5
2019 Donruss Optic Gold Vinyl /1 #15
2019 Donruss Optic Gold Vinyl /1 #78
2019 Donruss Optic Holo #5
2019 Donruss Optic Holo #15
2019 Donruss Optic Holo #78
2019 Donruss Optic Illusion #9
2019 Donruss Optic Illusion Blue Pulsar #9
2019 Donruss Optic Illusion Gold /10 #9
2019 Donruss Optic Illusion Gold Vinyl /1 #9
2019 Donruss Optic Illusion Holo #9
2019 Donruss Optic Illusion Red Wave #9
2019 Donruss Optic Illusion Signatures Gold Vinyl /1 #9
2019 Donruss Optic Illusion Signatures Holo /25 #9
2019 Donruss Optic Red Wave #5
2019 Donruss Optic Red Wave #15
2019 Donruss Optic Red Wave /1 #78
2019 Donruss Optic Signatures Gold Vinyl /1 #78
2019 Donruss Optic Signatures Gold Vinyl /1 #5
2019 Donruss Optic Signatures Gold Vinyl /1 #15
2019 Donruss Optic Signatures Holo /25 #5
2019 Donruss Optic Signatures Holo /49 #15
2019 Donruss Optic Signatures Holo /49 #78
2019 Donruss Originals #4
2019 Donruss Originals Cracked Ice /25 #4
2019 Donruss Originals Holographic #4
2019 Donruss Originals Xplosion /10 #4
2019 Donruss Press Proofs /49 #50A
2019 Donruss Press Proofs /49 #88
2019 Donruss Press Proofs /49 #112
2019 Donruss Press Proofs /49 #50B
2019 Donruss Press Proofs /49 #5
2019 Donruss Printing Plates Black /1 #5
2019 Donruss Printing Plates Black /1 #50A
2019 Donruss Printing Plates Black /1 #88
2019 Donruss Printing Plates Black /1 #112
2019 Donruss Printing Plates Black /1 #50B
2019 Donruss Printing Plates Cyan /1 #5
2019 Donruss Printing Plates Cyan /1 #50A
2019 Donruss Printing Plates Cyan /1 #88
2019 Donruss Printing Plates Cyan /1 #112
2019 Donruss Printing Plates Cyan /1 #50B
2019 Donruss Printing Plates Magenta /1 #50A
2019 Donruss Printing Plates Magenta /1 #88
2019 Donruss Printing Plates Magenta /1 #112
2019 Donruss Printing Plates Magenta /1 #50B
2019 Donruss Printing Plates Magenta /1 #5
2019 Donruss Printing Plates Yellow /1 #5
2019 Donruss Printing Plates Yellow /1 #50A
2019 Donruss Printing Plates Yellow /1 #88
2019 Donruss Printing Plates Yellow /1 #112
2019 Donruss Printing Plates Yellow /1 #50B
2019 Donruss Race Day Relics #19
2019 Donruss Race Day Relics Holo Black /10 #19
2019 Donruss Race Day Relics Holo Gold /25 #19
2019 Donruss Race Day Relics Red /185 #19
2019 Donruss Retro Relics '86 #12
2019 Donruss Retro Relics '86 Holo Black /10 #12
2019 Donruss Retro Relics '86 Holo Gold /25 #12
2019 Donruss Retro Relics '86 Red /225 #12
2019 Donruss Signature Swatches #9
2019 Donruss Signature Swatches Holo Black /10 #9
2019 Donruss Signature Swatches Holo Gold /25 #9
2019 Donruss Signature Swatches Red /50 #9
2019 Donruss Silver #5
2019 Donruss Silver #50A
2019 Donruss Silver #88
2019 Donruss Silver #112
2019 Donruss Silver #50B
2019 Donruss Top Tier #7
2019 Donruss Top Tier Cracked Ice /25 #7
2019 Donruss Top Tier Holographic #7
2019 Donruss Top Tier Xplosion /10 #7
2019 Panini National Convention NASCAR #R4
2019 Panini National Convention NASCAR Galatic Windows /25 #R4
2019 Panini National Convention NASCAR HyperPlaid /1 #R4
2019 Panini Prime /50 #15
2019 Panini Prime /50 #47
2019 Panini Prime /50 #79
2019 Panini Prime Black /10 #15
2019 Panini Prime Black /10 #47
2019 Panini Prime Black /10 #79
2019 Panini Prime Clear Silhouettes /99 #8
2019 Panini Prime Clear Silhouettes Black /10 #8
2019 Panini Prime Clear Silhouettes Dual /99 #2
2019 Panini Prime Clear Silhouettes Dual Black /10 #2
2019 Panini Prime Clear Silhouettes Dual Holo Gold /25 #2
2019 Panini Prime Clear Silhouettes Dual Platinum Blue /1 #2
2019 Panini Prime Clear Silhouettes Holo Gold /25 #8
2019 Panini Prime Clear Silhouettes Platinum Blue /1 #8
2019 Panini Prime Dual Material Autographs /25 #25
2019 Panini Prime Dual Material Autographs Black /10 #25
2019 Panini Prime Dual Material Autographs Holo Gold /18 #25
2019 Panini Prime Dual Material Autographs Laundry Tags /1 #25
2019 Panini Prime Emerald /5 #15
2019 Panini Prime Emerald /5 #47
2019 Panini Prime Emerald /5 #79
2019 Panini Prime Jumbo Material Signatures Firesuit /10 #19
2019 Panini Prime Jumbo Material Signatures Firesuit Platinum Blue /1 #19
2019 Panini Prime Jumbo Material Signatures Sheet Metal /18 #19
2019 Panini Prime Jumbo Material Signatures Tire /25 #19
2019 Panini Prime NASCAR Shadowbox Signatures Car Number /25 #26
2019 Panini Prime NASCAR Shadowbox Signatures Manufacturer /10 #26
2019 Panini Prime NASCAR Shadowbox Signatures Sponsor /18 #26
2019 Panini Prime NASCAR Shadowbox Signatures Team Owner /1 #26
2019 Panini Prime Platinum Blue /1 #15
2019 Panini Prime Platinum Blue /1 #47
2019 Panini Prime Platinum Blue /1 #79
2019 Panini Prime Prime Cars Die Cut Signatures /25 #18
2019 Panini Prime Prime Cars Die Cut Signatures Black /10 #18
2019 Panini Prime Prime Cars Die Cut Signatures Holo Gold /18 #18
2019 Panini Prime Prime Cars Die Cut Signatures Platinum Blue /1 #18
2019 Panini Prime Prime Jumbo Associate Sponsor 1 /1 #47
2019 Panini Prime Prime Jumbo Associate Sponsor 10 /1 #47
2019 Panini Prime Prime Jumbo Associate Sponsor 11 /1 #47
2019 Panini Prime Prime Jumbo Associate Sponsor 12 /1 #47
2019 Panini Prime Prime Jumbo Associate Sponsor 2 /1 #47
2019 Panini Prime Prime Jumbo Associate Sponsor 3 /1 #47
2019 Panini Prime Prime Jumbo Associate Sponsor 4 /1 #47
2019 Panini Prime Prime Jumbo Associate Sponsor 5 /1 #47
2019 Panini Prime Prime Jumbo Associate Sponsor 6 /1 #47
2019 Panini Prime Prime Jumbo Associate Sponsor 7 /1 #47
2019 Panini Prime Prime Jumbo Associate Sponsor 8 /1 #47
2019 Panini Prime Prime Jumbo Associate Sponsor 9 /1 #47
2019 Panini Prime Prime Jumbo Car Manufacturer /1 #47
2019 Panini Prime Prime Jumbo Firesuit Manufacturer /1 #47
2019 Panini Prime Prime Jumbo Flag Patch /1 #47
2019 Panini Prime Prime Jumbo Glove Manufacturer Patch /1 #47
2019 Panini Prime Prime Jumbo Goodyear /2 #47
2019 Panini Prime Prime Jumbo Nameplate /2 #47
2019 Panini Prime Prime Jumbo NASCAR /1 #47
2019 Panini Prime Prime Jumbo Prime Colors /22 #47
2019 Panini Prime Prime Jumbo Series Sponsor /1 #47
2019 Panini Prime Prime Jumbo Shoe Brand Logo /1 #47
2019 Panini Prime Prime Jumbo Shoe Name Patch /1 #47
2019 Panini Prime Prime Jumbo Sunoco /1 #47
2019 Panini Prime Prime Number Die Cut Signatures /25 #7
2019 Panini Prime Prime Number Die Cut Signatures Black /10 #7
2019 Panini Prime Prime Number Die Cut Signatures Holo Gold /18 #7
2019 Panini Prime Prime Number Die Cut Signatures Platinum Blue /1 #7
2019 Panini Prime Quad Materials Autographs /25 #16
2019 Panini Prime Quad Materials Autographs Black /10 #16
2019 Panini Prime Quad Materials Autographs Holo Gold /18 #16
2019 Panini Prime Quad Materials Autographs Laundry Tags /1 #16
2019 Panini Prime Race Used Duals Firesuits /50 #26
2019 Panini Prime Race Used Duals Firesuits Black /10 #26
2019 Panini Prime Race Used Duals Firesuits Holo Gold /25 #26
2019 Panini Prime Race Used Duals Firesuits Laundry Tags /1 #26
2019 Panini Prime Race Used Duals Sheet Metal /50 #26
2019 Panini Prime Race Used Duals Sheet Metal Black /10 #26
2019 Panini Prime Race Used Duals Sheet Metal Holo Gold /25 #26
2019 Panini Prime Race Used Duals Sheet Metal Platinum Blue /1 #26
2019 Panini Prime Race Used Duals Tires /50 #26
2019 Panini Prime Race Used Duals Tires Black /10 #26
2019 Panini Prime Race Used Duals Tires Holo Gold /25 #26
2019 Panini Prime Race Used Duals Tires Platinum Blue /1 #26
2019 Panini Prime Race Used Firesuits /50 #26
2019 Panini Prime Race Used Firesuits Black /10 #26
2019 Panini Prime Race Used Firesuits Holo Gold /25 #26
2019 Panini Prime Race Used Firesuits Laundry Tags /1 #26
2019 Panini Prime Race Used Quads Firesuits /50 #10
2019 Panini Prime Race Used Quads Firesuits Black /10 #10
2019 Panini Prime Race Used Quads Firesuits Holo Gold /25 #10
2019 Panini Prime Race Used Quads Firesuits Laundry Tags /1 #10
2019 Panini Prime Race Used Quads Sheet Metal /50 #10
2019 Panini Prime Race Used Quads Sheet Metal Black /10 #10
2019 Panini Prime Race Used Quads Sheet Metal Holo Gold /25 #10
2019 Panini Prime Race Used Quads Sheet Metal Platinum Blue /1 #10
2019 Panini Prime Race Used Quads Tires /50 #10
2019 Panini Prime Race Used Quads Tires Black /10 #10
2019 Panini Prime Race Used Quads Tires Holo Gold /25 #10
2019 Panini Prime Race Used Quads Tires Platinum Blue /1 #10
2019 Panini Prime Race Used Sheet Metal /50 #26
2019 Panini Prime Race Used Sheet Metal Black /10 #26
2019 Panini Prime Race Used Sheet Metal Holo Gold /25 #26
2019 Panini Prime Race Used Sheet Metal Platinum Blue /1 #26
2019 Panini Prime Race Used Tires /50 #26
2019 Panini Prime Race Used Tires Black /10 #26
2019 Panini Prime Race Used Tires Holo Gold /25 #26
2019 Panini Prime Race Used Tires Platinum Blue /1 #26
2019 Panini Prime Race Used Trios Firesuits /50 #19
2019 Panini Prime Race Used Trios Firesuits Black /10 #19
2019 Panini Prime Race Used Trios Firesuits Holo Gold /25 #19
2019 Panini Prime Race Used Trios Firesuits Laundry Tags /1 #19
2019 Panini Prime Race Used Trios Sheet Metal /50 #19
2019 Panini Prime Race Used Trios Sheet Metal Black /10 #19
2019 Panini Prime Race Used Trios Sheet Metal Holo Gold /25 #19
2019 Panini Prime Race Used Trios Sheet Metal Platinum Blue /1 #19
2019 Panini Prime Race Used Trios Tires /50 #19
2019 Panini Prime Race Used Trios Tires Black /10 #19
2019 Panini Prime Race Used Trios Tires Holo Gold /25 #19
2019 Panini Prime Race Used Trios Tires Platinum Blue /1 #19
2019 Panini Prime Timeline Signatures /25 #7
2019 Panini Prime Timeline Signatures Manufacturer /1 #7
2019 Panini Prime Timeline Signatures Name /18 #7
2019 Panini Prime Timeline Signatures Sponsor /10 #7
2019 Panini Prizm #15A
2019 Panini Prizm #53
2019 Panini Prizm #67
2019 Panini Prizm #76
2019 Panini Prizm #83
2019 Panini Prizm #15B
2019 Panini Prizm Apex #9
2019 Panini Prizm Apex Prizms #9
2019 Panini Prizm Apex Prizms Black /1 #9
2019 Panini Prizm Apex Prizms Gold /10 #9
2019 Panini Prizm Apex Prizms White Sparkle #9
2019 Panini Prizm Expert Level #4
2019 Panini Prizm Expert Level Prizms #4
2019 Panini Prizm Expert Level Prizms Black /1 #4
2019 Panini Prizm Expert Level Prizms Gold /10 #4
2019 Panini Prizm Expert Level Prizms White Sparkle #4
2019 Panini Prizm Fireworks #11
2019 Panini Prizm Fireworks Prizms #11
2019 Panini Prizm Fireworks Prizms Black /1 #11
2019 Panini Prizm Fireworks Prizms Gold /10 #11
2019 Panini Prizm Fireworks Prizms White Sparkle #11
2019 Panini Prizm In the Groove #7
2019 Panini Prizm In the Groove Prizms #7
2019 Panini Prizm In the Groove Prizms Black /1 #7
2019 Panini Prizm In the Groove Prizms Gold /10 #7
2019 Panini Prizm In the Groove Prizms White Sparkle #7
2019 Panini Prizm National Pride #7
2019 Panini Prizm National Pride Prizms #7
2019 Panini Prizm National Pride Prizms Black /1 #7
2019 Panini Prizm National Pride Prizms Gold /10 #7
2019 Panini Prizm National Pride Prizms White Sparkle #7
2019 Panini Prizm Patented Penmanship Prizms #8
2019 Panini Prizm Patented Penmanship Prizms Black /1 #8
2019 Panini Prizm Patented Penmanship Prizms Blue /18 #8
2019 Panini Prizm Patented Penmanship Prizms Camo #8
2019 Panini Prizm Patented Penmanship Prizms Gold /10 #8
2019 Panini Prizm Patented Penmanship Prizms Rainbow /18 #8
2019 Panini Prizm Patented Penmanship Prizms Red White and Blue #8
2019 Panini Prizm Patented Penmanship Prizms White /5 #8
2019 Panini Prizm Prizms #53
2019 Panini Prizm Prizms #67
2019 Panini Prizm Prizms #76
2019 Panini Prizm Prizms #83
2019 Panini Prizm Prizms #15B
2019 Panini Prizm Prizms #15A
2019 Panini Prizm Prizms Black /1 #15A
2019 Panini Prizm Prizms Black /1 #53
2019 Panini Prizm Prizms Black /1 #67
2019 Panini Prizm Prizms Black /1 #76
2019 Panini Prizm Prizms Black /1 #83
2019 Panini Prizm Prizms Black /1 #15B
2019 Panini Prizm Prizms Blue /75 #15A
2019 Panini Prizm Prizms Blue /75 #53
2019 Panini Prizm Prizms Blue /75 #67
2019 Panini Prizm Prizms Blue /75 #76
2019 Panini Prizm Prizms Blue /75 #83
2019 Panini Prizm Prizms Blue /75 #15B
2019 Panini Prizm Prizms Camo #15A
2019 Panini Prizm Prizms Camo #53
2019 Panini Prizm Prizms Camo #67
2019 Panini Prizm Prizms Camo #76
2019 Panini Prizm Prizms Camo #83
2019 Panini Prizm Prizms Camo #15B
2019 Panini Prizm Prizms Flash #15A
2019 Panini Prizm Prizms Flash #53
2019 Panini Prizm Prizms Flash #67
2019 Panini Prizm Prizms Flash #76
2019 Panini Prizm Prizms Flash #83
2019 Panini Prizm Prizms Flash #15B
2019 Panini Prizm Prizms Gold /10 #15A
2019 Panini Prizm Prizms Gold /10 #53
2019 Panini Prizm Prizms Gold /10 #67
2019 Panini Prizm Prizms Gold /10 #76
2019 Panini Prizm Prizms Gold /10 #83
2019 Panini Prizm Prizms Gold /10 #15B
2019 Panini Prizm Prizms Green /99 #15A
2019 Panini Prizm Prizms Green /99 #53
2019 Panini Prizm Prizms Green /99 #67
2019 Panini Prizm Prizms Green /99 #76
2019 Panini Prizm Prizms Green /99 #83
2019 Panini Prizm Prizms Green /99 #15B
2019 Panini Prizm Prizms Rainbow /24 #15A
2019 Panini Prizm Prizms Rainbow /24 #53
2019 Panini Prizm Prizms Rainbow /24 #67
2019 Panini Prizm Prizms Rainbow /24 #76
2019 Panini Prizm Prizms Rainbow /24 #83
2019 Panini Prizm Prizms Rainbow /24 #15B
2019 Panini Prizm Prizms Red /50 #15A
2019 Panini Prizm Prizms Red /50 #53
2019 Panini Prizm Prizms Red /50 #67
2019 Panini Prizm Prizms Red /50 #76
2019 Panini Prizm Prizms Red /50 #83
2019 Panini Prizm Prizms Red /50 #15B
2019 Panini Prizm Prizms Red White and Blue #15A
2019 Panini Prizm Prizms Red White and Blue #53
2019 Panini Prizm Prizms Red White and Blue #67
2019 Panini Prizm Prizms Red White and Blue #76
2019 Panini Prizm Prizms Red White and Blue #83
2019 Panini Prizm Prizms Red White and Blue #15B
2019 Panini Prizm Prizms White /5 #15A
2019 Panini Prizm Prizms White /5 #53
2019 Panini Prizm Prizms White /5 #67
2019 Panini Prizm Prizms White /5 #76
2019 Panini Prizm Prizms White /5 #83
2019 Panini Prizm Prizms White /5 #15B
2019 Panini Prizm Prizms White Sparkle #15A
2019 Panini Prizm Prizms White Sparkle #53
2019 Panini Prizm Prizms White Sparkle #67
2019 Panini Prizm Prizms White Sparkle #76
2019 Panini Prizm Prizms White Sparkle #83
2019 Panini Prizm Prizms White Sparkle #15B
2019 Panini Prizm Scripted Signatures Prizms #10
2019 Panini Prizm Scripted Signatures Prizms Black /1 #10
2019 Panini Prizm Scripted Signatures Prizms Blue /18 #10
2019 Panini Prizm Scripted Signatures Prizms Camo #10
2019 Panini Prizm Scripted Signatures Prizms Gold /10 #10
2019 Panini Prizm Scripted Signatures Prizms Rainbow /18 #10
2019 Panini Prizm Scripted Signatures Prizms Red White and Blue #10
2019 Panini Prizm Scripted Signatures Prizms White /5 #10
2019 Panini Prizm Signing Sessions Prizms #15
2019 Panini Prizm Signing Sessions Prizms Black /1 #15
2019 Panini Prizm Signing Sessions Prizms Camo #15
2019 Panini Prizm Signing Sessions Prizms Gold /10 #15
2019 Panini Prizm Signing Sessions Prizms Rainbow /18 #15
2019 Panini Prizm Signing Sessions Prizms Red /18 #15
2019 Panini Prizm Signing Sessions Prizms Red White and Blue #15
2019 Panini Prizm Signing Sessions Prizms White /5 #15
2019 Panini Prizm Stars and Stripes #10
2019 Panini Prizm Stars and Stripes Prizms #10
2019 Panini Prizm Stars and Stripes Prizms Black /1 #10
2019 Panini Prizm Stars and Stripes Prizms Gold /10 #10
2019 Panini Prizm Stars and Stripes Prizms White Sparkle #10
2019 Panini Prizm Teammates #4
2019 Panini Prizm Teammates Prizms #4
2019 Panini Prizm Teammates Prizms Black /1 #4
2019 Panini Prizm Teammates Prizms Gold /10 #4
2019 Panini Prizm Teammates Prizms White Sparkle #4
2019 Panini Victory Lane #15
2019 Panini Victory Lane #52
2019 Panini Victory Lane #59
2019 Panini Victory Lane #64
2019 Panini Victory Lane #98
2019 Panini Victory Lane Black /1 #15
2019 Panini Victory Lane Black /1 #52
2019 Panini Victory Lane Black /1 #59
2019 Panini Victory Lane Black /1 #64
2019 Panini Victory Lane Black /1 #98
2019 Panini Victory Lane Celebrations #3
2019 Panini Victory Lane Celebrations Black /1 #3
2019 Panini Victory Lane Celebrations Blue /99 #3
2019 Panini Victory Lane Celebrations Gold /25 #3
2019 Panini Victory Lane Celebrations Green /5 #3
2019 Panini Victory Lane Celebrations Printing Plates Black /1 #3
2019 Panini Victory Lane Celebrations Printing Plates Cyan /1 #3
2019 Panini Victory Lane Celebrations Printing Plates Magenta /1 #3
2019 Panini Victory Lane Celebrations Printing Plates Yellow /1 #3
2019 Panini Victory Lane Dual Swatches Gold /99 #16
2019 Panini Victory Lane Dual Swatches Laundry Tag /1 #16
2019 Panini Victory Lane Dual Swatches Platinum /1 #16
2019 Panini Victory Lane Dual Swatches Red /25 #16
2019 Panini Victory Lane Gold /25 #15
2019 Panini Victory Lane Gold /25 #52
2019 Panini Victory Lane Gold /25 #59
2019 Panini Victory Lane Gold /25 #64
2019 Panini Victory Lane Gold /25 #98
2019 Panini Victory Lane Horsepower Heroes #2
2019 Panini Victory Lane Horsepower Heroes Black /1 #2
2019 Panini Victory Lane Horsepower Heroes Blue /99 #2
2019 Panini Victory Lane Horsepower Heroes Gold /25 #2
2019 Panini Victory Lane Horsepower Heroes Green /5 #2
2019 Panini Victory Lane Horsepower Heroes Printing Plates Black /1 #2
2019 Panini Victory Lane Horsepower Heroes Printing Plates Cyan /1 #2
2019 Panini Victory Lane Horsepower Heroes Printing Plates Magenta /1 #2
2019 Panini Victory Lane Horsepower Heroes Printing Plates Yellow /1 #2
2019 Panini Victory Lane Machines #4
2019 Panini Victory Lane Machines Black /1 #4
2019 Panini Victory Lane Machines Blue /99 #4
2019 Panini Victory Lane Machines Gold /25 #4
2019 Panini Victory Lane Machines Green /5 #4
2019 Panini Victory Lane Machines Printing Plates Black /1 #4
2019 Panini Victory Lane Machines Printing Plates Cyan /1 #4
2019 Panini Victory Lane Machines Printing Plates Magenta /1 #4
2019 Panini Victory Lane Machines Printing Plates Yellow /1 #4
2019 Panini Victory Lane Pedal to the Metal #35
2019 Panini Victory Lane Pedal to the Metal #59
2019 Panini Victory Lane Pedal to the Metal #79
2019 Panini Victory Lane Pedal to the Metal Black /1 #35
2019 Panini Victory Lane Pedal to the Metal Black /1 #59
2019 Panini Victory Lane Pedal to the Metal Black /1 #79
2019 Panini Victory Lane Pedal to the Metal Gold /25 #35
2019 Panini Victory Lane Pedal to the Metal Gold /25 #59
2019 Panini Victory Lane Pedal to the Metal Gold /25 #79
2019 Panini Victory Lane Pedal to the Metal Green /5 #35
2019 Panini Victory Lane Pedal to the Metal Green /5 #59
2019 Panini Victory Lane Pedal to the Metal Green /5 #79
2019 Panini Victory Lane Pedal to the Metal Red /3 #35
2019 Panini Victory Lane Pedal to the Metal Red /3 #59
2019 Panini Victory Lane Pedal to the Metal Red /3 #79
2019 Panini Victory Lane Printing Plates Black /1 #15
2019 Panini Victory Lane Printing Plates Black /1 #52
2019 Panini Victory Lane Printing Plates Black /1 #59
2019 Panini Victory Lane Printing Plates Black /1 #64
2019 Panini Victory Lane Printing Plates Black /1 #98
2019 Panini Victory Lane Printing Plates Cyan /1 #15
2019 Panini Victory Lane Printing Plates Cyan /1 #52
2019 Panini Victory Lane Printing Plates Cyan /1 #59
2019 Panini Victory Lane Printing Plates Cyan /1 #64
2019 Panini Victory Lane Printing Plates Cyan /1 #98
2019 Panini Victory Lane Printing Plates Magenta /1 #15
2019 Panini Victory Lane Printing Plates Magenta /1 #52
2019 Panini Victory Lane Printing Plates Magenta /1 #59
2019 Panini Victory Lane Printing Plates Magenta /1 #64
2019 Panini Victory Lane Printing Plates Magenta /1 #98
2019 Panini Victory Lane Printing Plates Yellow /1 #15
2019 Panini Victory Lane Printing Plates Yellow /1 #52
2019 Panini Victory Lane Printing Plates Yellow /1 #59
2019 Panini Victory Lane Printing Plates Yellow /1 #64
2019 Panini Victory Lane Printing Plates Yellow /1 #98
2019 Panini Victory Lane Quad Swatches #4
2019 Panini Victory Lane Quad Swatches Gold /99 #4
2019 Panini Victory Lane Quad Swatches Laundry Tag /1 #4
2019 Panini Victory Lane Quad Swatches Platinum /1 #4
2019 Panini Victory Lane Quad Swatches Red /25 #4
2019 Panini Victory Lane Starting Grid #8
2019 Panini Victory Lane Starting Grid Black /1 #8
2019 Panini Victory Lane Starting Grid Blue /99 #8
2019 Panini Victory Lane Starting Grid Gold /25 #8
2019 Panini Victory Lane Starting Grid Green /5 #8
2019 Panini Victory Lane Starting Grid Printing Plates Black /1 #8
2019 Panini Victory Lane Starting Grid Printing Plates Cyan /1 #8
2019 Panini Victory Lane Starting Grid Printing Plates Magenta /1 #8
2019 Panini Victory Lane Starting Grid Printing Plates Yellow /1 #8
2019 Panini Victory Lane Top 10 #4
2019 Panini Victory Lane Top 10 Black /1 #4
2019 Panini Victory Lane Top 10 Blue /99 #4
2019 Panini Victory Lane Top 10 Gold /25 #4
2019 Panini Victory Lane Top 10 Green /5 #4
2019 Panini Victory Lane Top 10 Printing Plates Black /1 #4
2019 Panini Victory Lane Top 10 Printing Plates Cyan /1 #4
2019 Panini Victory Lane Top 10 Printing Plates Magenta /1 #4
2019 Panini Victory Lane Top 10 Printing Plates Yellow /1 #4
2019 Panini Victory Lane Track Stars #4
2019 Panini Victory Lane Track Stars Black /1 #4
2019 Panini Victory Lane Track Stars Blue /99 #4
2019 Panini Victory Lane Track Stars Gold /25 #4
2019 Panini Victory Lane Track Stars Green /5 #4
2019 Panini Victory Lane Track Stars Printing Plates Black /1 #4
2019 Panini Victory Lane Track Stars Printing Plates Cyan /1 #4
2019 Panini Victory Lane Track Stars Printing Plates Magenta /1 #4
2019 Panini Victory Lane Track Stars Printing Plates Yellow /1 #4
2019 Panini Victory Lane Triple Swatch Signatures #10
2019 Panini Victory Lane Triple Swatch Signatures Gold /99 #10
2019 Panini Victory Lane Triple Swatch Signatures Laundry Tag /1 #10
2019 Panini Victory Lane Triple Swatch Signatures Platinum /1 #10
2019 Panini Victory Lane Triple Swatch Signatures Red /25 #10
2019 Panini Victory Lane Triple Swatches #7
2019 Panini Victory Lane Triple Swatches Gold /99 #7
2019 Panini Victory Lane Triple Swatches Laundry Tag /1 #7
2019 Panini Victory Lane Triple Swatches Platinum /1 #7
2019 Panini Victory Lane Triple Swatches Red /25 #7
2019-20 Funko Pop Vinyl NASCAR #8
2020 Donruss #5
2020 Donruss #42
2020 Donruss #102
2020 Donruss #182
2020 Donruss #196
2020 Donruss Aero Package #3
2020 Donruss Aero Package Checkers #3
2020 Donruss Aero Package Cracked Ice /25 #3
2020 Donruss Aero Package Holographic /199 #3
2020 Donruss Aero Package Xplosion /10 #3
2020 Donruss Black Numbers /18 #5
2020 Donruss Black Numbers /18 #42
2020 Donruss Black Numbers /18 #102
2020 Donruss Black Numbers /18 #182
2020 Donruss Black Numbers /18 #196
2020 Donruss Black Trophy Club /1 #5
2020 Donruss Black Trophy Club /1 #42
2020 Donruss Black Trophy Club /1 #102
2020 Donruss Black Trophy Club /1 #182
2020 Donruss Black Trophy Club /1 #196
2020 Donruss Blue /199 #102
2020 Donruss Blue /199 #182
2020 Donruss Blue /199 #196
2020 Donruss Blue /199 #5
2020 Donruss Blue /199 #42
2020 Donruss Carolina Blue #5
2020 Donruss Carolina Blue #42
2020 Donruss Carolina Blue #102
2020 Donruss Carolina Blue #182
2020 Donruss Carolina Blue #196
2020 Donruss Contenders #4
2020 Donruss Contenders Checkers #4
2020 Donruss Contenders Cracked Ice /25 #4
2020 Donruss Contenders Holographic /199 #4
2020 Donruss Contenders Xplosion /10 #4
2020 Donruss Dominators #3
2020 Donruss Dominators Checkers #3
2020 Donruss Dominators Cracked Ice /25 #3
2020 Donruss Dominators Holographic /199 #3
2020 Donruss Dominators Xplosion /10 #3
2020 Donruss Elite Series #1
2020 Donruss Elite Series Checkers #1
2020 Donruss Elite Series Cracked Ice /25 #1
2020 Donruss Elite Series Holographic /199 #1
2020 Donruss Elite Series Xplosion /10 #1
2020 Donruss Green /99 #5
2020 Donruss Green /99 #42
2020 Donruss Green /99 #102
2020 Donruss Green /99 #182
2020 Donruss Green /99 #196
2020 Donruss Optic #5
2020 Donruss Optic #21
2020 Donruss Optic #66
2020 Donruss Optic Carolina Blue Wave #21
2020 Donruss Optic Carolina Blue Wave #66
2020 Donruss Optic Carolina Blue Wave #5
2020 Donruss Optic Gold /10 #5
2020 Donruss Optic Gold /10 #21
2020 Donruss Optic Gold /10 #66
2020 Donruss Optic Gold Vinyl /1 #5
2020 Donruss Optic Gold Vinyl /1 #21
2020 Donruss Optic Gold Vinyl /1 #66
2020 Donruss Optic Holo #5
2020 Donruss Optic Holo #21
2020 Donruss Optic Holo #66
2020 Donruss Optic Illusion #1
2020 Donruss Optic Illusion Carolina Blue Wave #1
2020 Donruss Optic Illusion Gold /10 #1
2020 Donruss Optic Illusion Gold Vinyl /1 #1
2020 Donruss Optic Illusion Holo #1
2020 Donruss Optic Illusion Orange Pulsar #1
2020 Donruss Optic Illusion Red Mojo #1
2020 Donruss Optic Illusion Signatures Gold Vinyl /1 #1
2020 Donruss Optic Illusion Signatures Holo /99 #1
2020 Donruss Optic Orange Pulsar #5
2020 Donruss Optic Orange Pulsar #21
2020 Donruss Optic Orange Pulsar #66
2020 Donruss Optic Red Mojo #5
2020 Donruss Optic Red Mojo #21
2020 Donruss Optic Red Mojo #66
2020 Donruss Optic Signatures Gold Vinyl /1 #5
2020 Donruss Optic Signatures Gold Vinyl /1 #21
2020 Donruss Optic Signatures Gold Vinyl /1 #66
2020 Donruss Optic Signatures Holo /99 #5
2020 Donruss Optic Signatures Holo /99 #21
2020 Donruss Optic Signatures Holo /99 #66
2020 Donruss Orange #182
2020 Donruss Orange #196
2020 Donruss Orange #5
2020 Donruss Orange #42
2020 Donruss Orange #102
2020 Donruss Pink /25 #5
2020 Donruss Pink /25 #42
2020 Donruss Pink /25 #102
2020 Donruss Pink /25 #182
2020 Donruss Pink /25 #196
2020 Donruss Printing Plates Black /1 #5
2020 Donruss Printing Plates Black /1 #42
2020 Donruss Printing Plates Black /1 #102
2020 Donruss Printing Plates Black /1 #182
2020 Donruss Printing Plates Black /1 #196
2020 Donruss Printing Plates Cyan /1 #5
2020 Donruss Printing Plates Cyan /1 #42
2020 Donruss Printing Plates Cyan /1 #102
2020 Donruss Printing Plates Cyan /1 #182
2020 Donruss Printing Plates Cyan /1 #196
2020 Donruss Printing Plates Magenta /1 #42
2020 Donruss Printing Plates Magenta /1 #102
2020 Donruss Printing Plates Magenta /1 #182
2020 Donruss Printing Plates Magenta /1 #196
2020 Donruss Printing Plates Magenta /1 #5
2020 Donruss Printing Plates Yellow /1 #182
2020 Donruss Printing Plates Yellow /1 #196
2020 Donruss Printing Plates Yellow /1 #5
2020 Donruss Printing Plates Yellow /1 #42
2020 Donruss Printing Plates Yellow /1 #102
2020 Donruss Purple /49 #5
2020 Donruss Purple /49 #42
2020 Donruss Purple /49 #102
2020 Donruss Purple /49 #182
2020 Donruss Purple /49 #196
2020 Donruss Race Day Relics #19
2020 Donruss Race Day Relics Holo Black /10 #19
2020 Donruss Race Day Relics Holo Gold /25 #19
2020 Donruss Race Day Relics Red /250 #19
2020 Donruss Red /299 #5
2020 Donruss Red /299 #42
2020 Donruss Red /299 #102
2020 Donruss Red /299 #182
2020 Donruss Red /299 #196
2020 Donruss Retro Series #10
2020 Donruss Retro Series Checkers #10
2020 Donruss Retro Series Cracked Ice /25 #10
2020 Donruss Retro Series Holographic /199 #10
2020 Donruss Retro Series Xplosion /10 #10
2020 Donruss Silver #5
2020 Donruss Silver #42
2020 Donruss Silver #102
2020 Donruss Silver #182
2020 Donruss Silver #196
2020 Donruss Timeless Treasures Signatures Holo Black /1 #5
2020 Donruss Timeless Treasures Signatures Holo Gold /18 #5
2020 Donruss Timeless Treasures Signatures Red /25 #5
2020 Donruss Top Tier #7
2020 Donruss Top Tier Checkers #7
2020 Donruss Top Tier Cracked Ice /25 #7
2020 Donruss Top Tier Holographic /199 #7
2020 Donruss Top Tier Xplosion /10 #7

Hailie Deegan

2018 Certified NEXT Signatures /210 #3
2018 Certified NEXT Signatures Black /1 #3
2018 Certified NEXT Signatures Blue /50 #3
2018 Certified NEXT Signatures Gold /25 #3
2018 Certified NEXT Signatures Green /5 #3
2018 Certified NEXT Signatures Purple /10 #3
2018 Certified NEXT Signatures Red /149 #3
2018 Donruss NEXT in Line #3
2018 Donruss NEXT in Line Cracked Ice /999 #3
2018 Donruss NEXT in Line Xplosion /99 #3
2018 Donruss Signature Series #15
2018 Donruss Signature Series Black /1 #15
2018 Donruss Signature Series Holo Gold /25 #15
2018 Panini Prizm #30
2018 Panini Prizm Prizms #30
2018 Panini Prizm Prizms Black /1 #30
2018 Panini Prizm Prizms Blue /99 #30
2018 Panini Prizm Prizms Camo #30
2018 Panini Prizm Prizms Gold /10 #30
2018 Panini Prizm Prizms Green /149 #30
2018 Panini Prizm Prizms Purple Flash #30
2018 Panini Prizm Prizms Rainbow /24 #30
2018 Panini Prizm Prizms Red /75 #30
2018 Panini Prizm Prizms Red White and Blue #30
2018 Panini Prizm Prizms White /5 #30
2018 Panini Victory Lane #37
2018 Panini Victory Lane Black /1 #37
2018 Panini Victory Lane Blue /25 #37
2018 Panini Victory Lane Gold /99 #37
2018 Panini Victory Lane Green /5 #37
2018 Panini Victory Lane Printing Plates Black /1 #37
2018 Panini Victory Lane Printing Plates Cyan /1 #37
2018 Panini Victory Lane Printing Plates Magenta /1 #37
2018 Panini Victory Lane Printing Plates Yellow /1 #37
2018 Panini Victory Lane Red /49 #37
2018 Panini Victory Lane Silver #37
2019 Donruss NEXT in Line #1
2019 Donruss NEXT in Line Cracked Ice /25 #1
2019 Donruss NEXT in Line Holographic #1
2019 Donruss NEXT in Line Xplosion /10 #1
2019 Donruss Recollection Collection /50 #2
2019 Donruss Signature Series #18
2019 Donruss Signature Series Holo Black /10 #18
2019 Donruss Signature Series Holo Gold /25 #18
2019 Donruss Signature Series Red /99 #18
2019 Panini Prime /50 #34
2019 Panini Prime /50 #61
2019 Panini Prime /50 #88
2019 Panini Prime Autograph Materials /49 #11
2019 Panini Prime Autograph Materials Black /10 #11
2019 Panini Prime Autograph Materials Holo Gold /25 #11
2019 Panini Prime Autograph Materials Platinum Blue /1 #11
2019 Panini Prime Black /10 #34
2019 Panini Prime Black /10 #61
2019 Panini Prime Black /10 #88
2019 Panini Prime Clear Vision Signatures /75 #1
2019 Panini Prime Clear Vision Signatures Black /10 #1
2019 Panini Prime Clear Vision Signatures Holo Gold /25 #1
2019 Panini Prime Clear Vision Signatures Platinum Blue /1 #1
2019 Panini Prime Emerald /5 #34
2019 Panini Prime Emerald /5 #61
2019 Panini Prime Emerald /5 #88
2019 Panini Prime Platinum Blue /1 #34
2019 Panini Prime Platinum Blue /1 #61
2019 Panini Prime Platinum Blue /1 #88
2019 Panini Prime Prime Jumbo Associate Sponsor 1 /1 #33
2019 Panini Prime Prime Jumbo Associate Sponsor 2 /1 #33
2019 Panini Prime Prime Jumbo Associate Sponsor 3 /1 #33
2019 Panini Prime Prime Jumbo Associate Sponsor 4 /1 #33
2019 Panini Prime Prime Jumbo Associate Sponsor 5 /1 #33
2019 Panini Prime Prime Jumbo Associate Sponsor 6 /1 #33
2019 Panini Prime Prime Jumbo Car Manufacturer /1 #33
2019 Panini Prime Prime Jumbo Firesuit Manufacturer /1 #33
2019 Panini Prime Prime Jumbo Laundry Tag /1 #33
2019 Panini Prime Prime Jumbo NASCAR /1 #33
2019 Panini Prime Prime Jumbo Prime Colors /12 #33
2019 Panini Prime Prime Names Die Cut Signatures /49 #5
2019 Panini Prime Prime Names Die Cut Signatures Black /10 #5
2019 Panini Prime Prime Names Die Cut Signatures Holo Gold /25 #5
2019 Panini Prime Prime Names Die Cut Signatures Platinum Blue /1 #5
2019 Panini Prime Prime Signatures Black /10 #8
2019 Panini Prime Prime Signatures Holo Gold /25 #8
2019 Panini Prime Prime Signatures Platinum Blue /1 #8
2019 Panini Prime Shadowbox Signatures /75 #18
2019 Panini Prime Shadowbox Signatures Black /10 #18
2019 Panini Prime Shadowbox Signatures Holo Gold /25 #18
2019 Panini Prime Shadowbox Signatures Platinum Blue /1 #18
2019 Panini Prizm #39
2019 Panini Prizm Apex #7
2019 Panini Prizm Apex Prizms #7
2019 Panini Prizm Apex Prizms Black /1 #7
2019 Panini Prizm Apex Prizms Gold /10 #7
2019 Panini Prizm Apex Prizms White Sparkle #7
2019 Panini Prizm Fireworks #5
2019 Panini Prizm Fireworks Prizms #5
2019 Panini Prizm Fireworks Prizms Black /1 #5
2019 Panini Prizm Fireworks Prizms Gold /10 #5
2019 Panini Prizm Fireworks Prizms White Sparkle #5
2019 Panini Prizm Prizms #39
2019 Panini Prizm Prizms Black /1 #39
2019 Panini Prizm Prizms Blue /75 #39
2019 Panini Prizm Prizms Camo #39
2019 Panini Prizm Prizms Flash #39
2019 Panini Prizm Prizms Gold /10 #39
2019 Panini Prizm Prizms Green /99 #39
2019 Panini Prizm Prizms Rainbow /24 #39
2019 Panini Prizm Prizms Red /50 #39
2019 Panini Prizm Prizms Red White and Blue #39
2019 Panini Prizm Prizms White /5 #39
2019 Panini Prizm Prizms White Sparkle #39
2019 Panini Prizm Scripted Signatures Prizms #6
2019 Panini Prizm Scripted Signatures Prizms Black /1 #6
2019 Panini Prizm Scripted Signatures Prizms Blue /75 #6
2019 Panini Prizm Scripted Signatures Prizms Camo #6
2019 Panini Prizm Scripted Signatures Prizms Gold /10 #6
2019 Panini Prizm Scripted Signatures Prizms Green /99 #6
2019 Panini Prizm Scripted Signatures Prizms Rainbow /24 #6
2019 Panini Prizm Scripted Signatures Prizms Red /50 #6
2019 Panini Prizm Scripted Signatures Prizms Red White and Blue #6
2019 Panini Prizm Scripted Signatures Prizms White /5 #6
2019 Panini Victory Lane Pedal to the Metal #5
2019 Panini Victory Lane Pedal to the Metal Black /1 #5
2019 Panini Victory Lane Pedal to the Metal Gold /25 #5
2019 Panini Victory Lane Pedal to the Metal Green /5 #5
2019 Panini Victory Lane Pedal to the Metal Red /3 #5
2019 Panini Victory Lane Signature Swatches #8
2019 Panini Victory Lane Signature Swatches Gold /99 #8
2019 Panini Victory Lane Signature Swatches Laundry Tag /1 #8
2019 Panini Victory Lane Signature Swatches Platinum /1 #8
2019 Panini Victory Lane Signature Swatches Red /25 #8
2019 Upper Deck Goodwin Champions #17
2019 Upper Deck Goodwin Champions #67
2019 Upper Deck Goodwin Champions #117
2019 Upper Deck Goodwin Champions Autographs #AHD
2019 Upper Deck Goodwin Champions Autographs Inscriptions /25 #AHD
2019 Upper Deck Goodwin Champions Blank Back #17
2019 Upper Deck Goodwin Champions Blank Back #67
2019 Upper Deck Goodwin Champions Goudey #G11
2019 Upper Deck Goodwin Champions Goudey Autographs #GAHD
2019 Upper Deck Goodwin Champions Goudey Memorabilia #GMHD
2019 Upper Deck Goodwin Champions Goudey Memorabilia Premium /50 #GMHD
2019 Upper Deck Goodwin Champions Goudey Mini #G11
2019 Upper Deck Goodwin Champions Goudey Mini Wood Lumberjack #G11
2019 Upper Deck Goodwin Champions Goudey Mini Wood Lumberjack Black /8 #G11
2019 Upper Deck Goodwin Champions Goudey Printing Plates Black /1 #G11
2019 Upper Deck Goodwin Champions Goudey Printing Plates Cyan /1 #G11
2019 Upper Deck Goodwin Champions Goudey Printing Plates Magenta /1 #G11
2019 Upper Deck Goodwin Champions Goudey Printing Plates Yellow /1 #G11
2019 Upper Deck Goodwin Champions Memorabilia #MHD
2019 Upper Deck Goodwin Champions Memorabilia Premium /65 #MHD
2019 Upper Deck Goodwin Champions Mini #17
2019 Upper Deck Goodwin Champions Mini #67
2019 Upper Deck Goodwin Champions Mini Blank Back #17
2019 Upper Deck Goodwin Champions Mini Blank Back #67
2019 Upper Deck Goodwin Champions Mini Wood Lumberjack #17
2019 Upper Deck Goodwin Champions Mini Wood Lumberjack #67
2019 Upper Deck Goodwin Champions Mini Wood Lumberjack Black /8 #17
2019 Upper Deck Goodwin Champions Mini Wood Lumberjack Black /8 #67
2019 Upper Deck Goodwin Champions Printing Plates Black /1 #17
2019 Upper Deck Goodwin Champions Printing Plates Black /1 #67
2019 Upper Deck Goodwin Champions Printing Plates Black /1 #117
2019 Upper Deck Goodwin Champions Printing Plates Cyan /1 #17
2019 Upper Deck Goodwin Champions Printing Plates Cyan /1 #67
2019 Upper Deck Goodwin Champions Printing Plates Cyan /1 #117
2019 Upper Deck Goodwin Champions Printing Plates Magenta /1 #17
2019 Upper Deck Goodwin Champions Printing Plates Magenta /1 #67
2019 Upper Deck Goodwin Champions Printing Plates Magenta /1 #117
2019 Upper Deck Goodwin Champions Printing Plates Yellow /1 #17
2019 Upper Deck Goodwin Champions Printing Plates Yellow /1 #67
2019 Upper Deck Goodwin Champions Printing Plates Yellow /1 #117
2019 Upper Deck Goodwin Champions Splash of Color 3D #LSHD
2019 Upper Deck Goodwin Champions Splash of Color Memorabilia #SMHD
2019 Upper Deck Goodwin Champions Splash of Color Memorabilia Premium /25 #SMHD
2020 Donruss #16
2020 Donruss Black Numbers /19 #16
2020 Donruss Black Trophy Club /1 #16
2020 Donruss Blue /199 #16
2020 Donruss Carolina Blue #16
2020 Donruss Green /99 #16
2020 Donruss New Age #9
2020 Donruss New Age Checkers #9
2020 Donruss New Age Cracked Ice /25 #9
2020 Donruss New Age Holographic /199 #9
2020 Donruss New Age Xplosion /10 #9
2020 Donruss Optic #11
2020 Donruss Optic Carolina Blue Wave #11
2020 Donruss Optic Gold /10 #11
2020 Donruss Optic Gold Vinyl /1 #11
2020 Donruss Optic Holo #11
2020 Donruss Optic Orange Pulsar #11
2020 Donruss Optic Red Mojo #11
2020 Donruss Optic Signatures Gold Vinyl /1 #11
2020 Donruss Optic Signatures Holo /99 #11
2020 Donruss Orange #16
2020 Donruss Pink /25 #16
2020 Donruss Printing Plates Black /1 #16
2020 Donruss Printing Plates Cyan /1 #16
2020 Donruss Printing Plates Magenta /1 #16
2020 Donruss Printing Plates Yellow /1 #16
2020 Donruss Purple /49 #16
2020 Donruss Red /299 #16
2020 Donruss Silver #16

Austin Dillon

2009 Element #97
2009 Element Radioactive /100 #97
2009 Element Undiscovered Elements Autographs /130 #UEAD
2009 Element Undiscovered Elements Autographs Red Ink /25 #UEAD
2010 Press Pass Signings Blue /10 #16
2010 Press Pass Signings Gold /50 #16
2010 Press Pass Signings Red /15 #16
2010 Press Pass Signings Silver /75 #16
2010 Wheels Main Event #90
2010 Wheels Main Event Blue #90
2010 Wheels Main Event Marks Autographs /96 #15
2010 Wheels Main Event Marks Autographs Black /1 #15
2010 Wheels Main Event Marks Autographs Blue /30 #15
2010 Wheels Main Event Marks Autographs Red /25 #15
2011 Element #61
2011 Element Autographs /75 #14
2011 Element Autographs Blue /5 #14
2011 Element Autographs Gold /15 #14
2011 Element Autographs Printing Plates Black /1 #14
2011 Element Autographs Printing Plates Cyan /1 #14
2011 Element Autographs Printing Plates Magenta /1 #14
2011 Element Autographs Printing Plates Yellow /1 #14
2011 Element Autographs Silver /48 #14
2011 Element Black /35 #61
2011 Element Green #61
2011 Element Purple /25 #61
2011 Element Red #61
2011 Press Pass #54
2011 Press Pass #109
2011 Press Pass #151
2011 Press Pass Autographs Blue /10 #14
2011 Press Pass Autographs Bronze /150 #14
2011 Press Pass Autographs Gold /25 #14
2011 Press Pass Autographs Printing Plates Black /1 #14
2011 Press Pass Autographs Printing Plates Cyan /1 #14
2011 Press Pass Autographs Printing Plates Magenta /1 #14
2011 Press Pass Autographs Printing Plates Yellow /1 #14
2011 Press Pass Autographs Silver /50 #14
2011 Press Pass Blue Holofoil /10 #54
2011 Press Pass Blue Holofoil /10 #109
2011 Press Pass Blue Holofoil /10 #151
2011 Press Pass Blue Retail #54
2011 Press Pass Blue Retail #109
2011 Press Pass Blue Retail #151
2011 Press Pass Eclipse #58
2011 Press Pass Eclipse Blue #58
2011 Press Pass Eclipse Gold /55 #58
2011 Press Pass Eclipse Purple /25 #58
2011 Press Pass FanFare #60
2011 Press Pass FanFare Autographs Blue /5 #21
2011 Press Pass FanFare Autographs Bronze /245 #21
2011 Press Pass FanFare Autographs Gold /150 #21
2011 Press Pass FanFare Autographs Printing Plates Black /1 #21
2011 Press Pass FanFare Autographs Printing Plates Cyan /1 #21
2011 Press Pass FanFare Autographs Printing Plates Magenta /1 #21
2011 Press Pass FanFare Autographs Printing Plates Yellow /1 #21
2011 Press Pass FanFare Autographs Silver /75 #21
2011 Press Pass FanFare Blue Die Cuts #60
2011 Press Pass FanFare Dual Autographs /10 #NNO
2011 Press Pass FanFare Dual Autographs /10 #NNO
2011 Press Pass FanFare Emerald /25 #60
2011 Press Pass FanFare Holofoil Die Cuts #60
2011 Press Pass FanFare Magnificent Materials /199 #MMAD
2011 Press Pass FanFare Magnificent Materials Dual Swatches /50 #MMDAD
2011 Press Pass FanFare Magnificent Materials Dual Swatches Holofoil /10 #MMDAD
2011 Press Pass FanFare Magnificent Materials Holofoil /50 #MMAD
2011 Press Pass FanFare Ruby Die Cuts /15 #60
2011 Press Pass FanFare Sapphire /10 #60
2011 Press Pass FanFare Silver /25 #60
2011 Press Pass Gold /50 #54
2011 Press Pass Gold /50 #109
2011 Press Pass Gold /50 #151
2011 Press Pass Purple /25 #54
2011 Press Pass Signings Black and White /10 #PPSAD
2011 Press Pass Signings Brushed Metal /50 #PPSAD
2011 Press Pass Signings Holofoil /25 #PPSAD
2011 Press Pass Winning Tickets #WT43
2011 Wheels Main Event #51
2011 Wheels Main Event Black and White #51
2011 Wheels Main Event Blue /75 #51
2011 Wheels Main Event Green /1 #51
2011 Wheels Main Event Marks Autographs Blue /8 #MEAD
2011 Wheels Main Event Marks Autographs Gold /25 #MEAD
2011 Wheels Main Event Marks Autographs Silver /64 #MEAD
2011 Wheels Main Event Red /20 #51
2012 Press Pass #53
2012 Press Pass Blue #53
2012 Press Pass Blue Holofoil /35 #53
2012 Press Pass Fanfare #49
2012 Press Pass Fanfare Autographs Blue /20 #AD
2012 Press Pass Fanfare Autographs Gold /99 #AD
2012 Press Pass Fanfare Autographs Red /75 #AD
2012 Press Pass Fanfare Autographs Silver /165 #AD
2012 Press Pass Fanfare Blue Foil Die Cuts #49
2012 Press Pass Fanfare Diamond /5 #49
2012 Press Pass Fanfare Dual Autographs /10 #DD
2012 Press Pass Fanfare Holofoil Die Cuts #49
2012 Press Pass Fanfare Magnificent Materials /299 #MMAD
2012 Press Pass Fanfare Magnificent Materials Dual Swatches /50 #MMAD
2012 Press Pass Fanfare Magnificent Materials Dual Swatches Melting /10 #MMAD
2012 Press Pass Fanfare Magnificent Materials Gold /125 #MMAD
2012 Press Pass Fanfare Magnificent Materials Signatures /99 #AD
2012 Press Pass Fanfare Magnificent Materials Signatures Blue /25 #AD
2012 Press Pass Fanfare Sapphire /20 #49
2012 Press Pass Fanfare Silver /25 #49
2012 Press Pass Gold #53
2012 Press Pass Ignite #39
2012 Press Pass Ignite Proofs Black and White /50 #39
2012 Press Pass Ignite Proofs Cyan #39
2012 Press Pass Ignite Proofs Magenta #39
2012 Press Pass Ignite Proofs Yellow /10 #39
2012 Press Pass Purple /35 #53
2012 Press Pass Redline #42
2012 Press Pass Redline Black /99 #42
2012 Press Pass Redline Cyan /50 #42
2012 Press Pass Redline Magenta /15 #42
2012 Press Pass Redline Yellow /1 #42
2012 Press Pass Snapshots #SS56
2012 Total Memorabilia #36
2012 Total Memorabilia Black and White /99 #36
2012 Total Memorabilia Dual Swatch Gold /75 #TMAD
2012 Total Memorabilia Dual Swatch Holofoil /25 #TMAD
2012 Total Memorabilia Dual Swatch Melting /5 #TMAD
2012 Total Memorabilia Dual Swatch Silver /99 #TMAD
2012 Total Memorabilia Gold /275 #36
2012 Total Memorabilia Red Retail /250 #36
2012 Total Memorabilia Single Swatch Gold /99 #TMAD
2012 Total Memorabilia Single Swatch Holofoil /50 #TMAD
2012 Total Memorabilia Single Swatch Melting /10 #TMAD
2012 Total Memorabilia Single Swatch Silver /199 #TMAD
2012 Total Memorabilia Tandem Treasures Dual Memorabilia Gold /75 #TTADTD
2012 Total Memorabilia Tandem Treasures Dual Memorabilia Holofoil /25 #TTADTD
2012 Total Memorabilia Tandem Treasures Dual Memorabilia Melting /5 #TTADTD
2012 Total Memorabilia Tandem Treasures Dual Memorabilia Silver /99 #TTADTD
2013 Press Pass #49
2013 Press Pass Color Proofs Black #49
2013 Press Pass Color Proofs Cyan /35 #49
2013 Press Pass Color Proofs Magenta #49
2013 Press Pass Color Proofs Yellow /5 #49
2013 Press Pass Fanfare #63
2013 Press Pass Fanfare Autographs Blue /1 #AD
2013 Press Pass Fanfare Autographs Gold /10 #AD
2013 Press Pass Fanfare Autographs Green /5 #AD
2013 Press Pass Fanfare Autographs Red /5 #AD
2013 Press Pass Fanfare Autographs Silver /25 #AD
2013 Press Pass Fanfare Diamond Die Cuts /5 #63
2013 Press Pass Fanfare Fan Following #FF15
2013 Press Pass Fanfare Green /3 #63
2013 Press Pass Fanfare Holofoil Die Cuts #63
2013 Press Pass Fanfare Magnificent Jumbo Materials Signatures /10 #AD
2013 Press Pass Fanfare Magnificent Materials Dual Swatches /50 #AD
2013 Press Pass Fanfare Magnificent Materials Dual Swatches Melting /10 #AD
2013 Press Pass Fanfare Magnificent Materials Gold /50 #AD
2013 Press Pass Fanfare Magnificent Materials Jumbo Swatches /25 #AD
2013 Press Pass Fanfare Magnificent Materials Signatures /99 #AD
2013 Press Pass Fanfare Magnificent Materials Signatures Blue /25 #AD
2013 Press Pass Fanfare Magnificent Materials Silver /199 #AD
2013 Press Pass Fanfare Red Foil Die Cuts #63
2013 Press Pass Fanfare Sapphire /20 #63
2013 Press Pass Fanfare Signature Ride Autographs /10 #AD
2013 Press Pass Fanfare Signature Ride Autographs Blue /1 #AD
2013 Press Pass Fanfare Signature Ride Autographs Red /5 #AD
2013 Press Pass Fanfare Silver /25 #63
2013 Press Pass Ignite #41
2013 Press Pass Ignite #66
2013 Press Pass Ignite Hot Threads Blue Holofoil /99 #HTAD
2013 Press Pass Ignite Hot Threads Patch Red /10 #HTAD
2013 Press Pass Ignite Hot Threads Silver #HTAD
2013 Press Pass Ignite Ink Black /99 #IIAD
2013 Press Pass Ignite Ink Blue /25 #IIAD
2013 Press Pass Ignite Ink Red /5 #IIAD
2013 Press Pass Ignite Proofs Black and White /50 #41
2013 Press Pass Ignite Proofs Black and White /50 #66
2013 Press Pass Ignite Proofs Cyan #41
2013 Press Pass Ignite Proofs Cyan #66
2013 Press Pass Ignite Proofs Magenta #41
2013 Press Pass Ignite Proofs Magenta #66
2013 Press Pass Ignite Proofs Yellow /5 #41
2013 Press Pass Ignite Proofs Yellow /5 #66
2013 Press Pass Ignite Turning Point #2
2013 Press Pass Power Picks Blue /99 #20
2013 Press Pass Power Picks Gold /50 #20
2013 Press Pass Power Picks Holofoil /10 #20
2013 Press Pass Racing Champions #RC32
2013 Press Pass Redline #48
2013 Press Pass Redline Black /99 #48
2013 Press Pass Redline Cyan /50 #48
2013 Press Pass Redline Dynamic Duals Dual Relic Blue /5 #DDAD
2013 Press Pass Redline Dynamic Duals Dual Relic Gold /10 #DDAD
2013 Press Pass Redline Dynamic Duals Dual Relic Melting /1 #DDAD
2013 Press Pass Redline Dynamic Duals Dual Relic Red /75 #DDAD
2013 Press Pass Redline Dynamic Duals Dual Relic Silver /25 #DDAD
2013 Press Pass Redline Magenta /15 #48
2013 Press Pass Redline Muscle Car Sheet Metal Blue /5 #MCMAD
2013 Press Pass Redline Muscle Car Sheet Metal Gold /10 #MCMAD
2013 Press Pass Redline Muscle Car Sheet Metal Melting /1 #MCMAD
2013 Press Pass Redline Muscle Car Sheet Metal Red /50 #MCMAD
2013 Press Pass Redline Muscle Car Sheet Metal Silver /25 #MCMAD
2013 Press Pass Redline Yellow /1 #48
2013 Press Pass Showcase Prized Pieces /99 #PPMAD
2013 Press Pass Showcase Prized Pieces Blue /20 #PPMAD
2013 Press Pass Showcase Prized Pieces Gold /25 #PPMAD
2013 Press Pass Showcase Prized Pieces Ink /50 #PPIAD
2013 Press Pass Showcase Prized Pieces Ink Gold /25 #PPIAD
2013 Press Pass Showcase Prized Pieces Ink Melting /1 #PPIAD
2013 Press Pass Showcase Prized Pieces Melting /5 #PPMAD
2013 Press Pass Showcase Signature Patches /21 #SSPAD
2013 Press Pass Signings Blue /1 #AD
2013 Press Pass Signings Gold /25 #AD
2013 Press Pass Signings Holofoil /10 #AD
2013 Press Pass Signings Silver /65 #AD
2013 Total Memorabilia #39
2013 Total Memorabilia Black and White /99 #39
2013 Total Memorabilia Dual Swatch Gold /199 #TMAD
2013 Total Memorabilia Gold /275 #39
2013 Total Memorabilia Memory Lane #ML6
2013 Total Memorabilia Quad Swatch Melting /10 #TMAD
2013 Total Memorabilia Red #39
2013 Total Memorabilia Single Swatch Silver /475 #TMAD
2013 Total Memorabilia Triple Swatch Holofoil /99 #TMAD
2014 Press Pass #42
2014 Press Pass #46
2014 Press Pass #95
2014 Press Pass Aerodynamic Autographs Blue /1 #AAAD
2014 Press Pass Aerodynamic Autographs Holofoil /5 #AAAD
2014 Press Pass Aerodynamic Autographs Printing Plates Black /1 #AAAD
2014 Press Pass Aerodynamic Autographs Printing Plates Cyan /1 #AAAD
2014 Press Pass Aerodynamic Autographs Printing Plates Magenta /1 #AAAD
2014 Press Pass Aerodynamic Autographs Printing Plates Yellow /1 #AAAD
2014 Press Pass American Thunder #11
2014 Press Pass American Thunder #54
2014 Press Pass American Thunder #61
2014 Press Pass American Thunder Autographs Blue /10 #ATAAD
2014 Press Pass American Thunder Autographs Red /5 #ATAAD
2014 Press Pass American Thunder Autographs White /35 #ATAAD
2014 Press Pass American Thunder Battle Armor Blue /25 #BAAD
2014 Press Pass American Thunder Battle Armor Red /1 #BAAD
2014 Press Pass American Thunder Battle Armor Silver /99 #BAAD
2014 Press Pass American Thunder Black and White /50 #11
2014 Press Pass American Thunder Black and White /50 #54
2014 Press Pass American Thunder Black and White /50 #61
2014 Press Pass American Thunder Brothers In Arms Autographs Blue /5 #BARCR
2014 Press Pass American Thunder Brothers In Arms Autographs Red /1 #BARCR
2014 Press Pass American Thunder Brothers In Arms Autographs White /10 #BARCR
2014 Press Pass American Thunder Brothers In Arms Relics Blue /25 #BARCR
2014 Press Pass American Thunder Brothers In Arms Relics Red /5 #BARCR
2014 Press Pass American Thunder Brothers In Arms Relics Silver /50 #BARCR
2014 Press Pass American Thunder Class A Uniforms Blue /99 #CAUAD
2014 Press Pass American Thunder Class A Uniforms Flag /1 #CAUAD
2014 Press Pass American Thunder Class A Uniforms Red /10 #CAUAD
2014 Press Pass American Thunder Class A Uniforms Silver #CAUAD
2014 Press Pass American Thunder Climbing the Ranks #CR1
2014 Press Pass American Thunder Cyan #11
2014 Press Pass American Thunder Cyan #54
2014 Press Pass American Thunder Cyan #61
2014 Press Pass American Thunder Great American Treads Autographs Blue /10 #GATAD
2014 Press Pass American Thunder Great American Treads Autographs Red /1 #GATAD
2014 Press Pass American Thunder Magenta #11
2014 Press Pass American Thunder Magenta #54
2014 Press Pass American Thunder Magenta #61
2014 Press Pass American Thunder Top Speed #TS1
2014 Press Pass American Thunder With Honors #WH6
2014 Press Pass American Thunder Yellow /5 #11
2014 Press Pass American Thunder Yellow /5 #54
2014 Press Pass Color Proofs Black /70 #42
2014 Press Pass Color Proofs Black /70 #46
2014 Press Pass Color Proofs Black /70 #95
2014 Press Pass Color Proofs Cyan /35 #42
2014 Press Pass Color Proofs Cyan /35 #46
2014 Press Pass Color Proofs Cyan /35 #95
2014 Press Pass Color Proofs Magenta #42
2014 Press Pass Color Proofs Magenta #46
2014 Press Pass Color Proofs Magenta #95
2014 Press Pass Color Proofs Yellow /5 #42
2014 Press Pass Color Proofs Yellow /5 #46
2014 Press Pass Color Proofs Yellow /5 #95
2014 Press Pass Five Star /15 #17
2014 Press Pass Five Star Blue /5 #17
2014 Press Pass Five Star Classic Compilations Autographed Patch Booklet /1 #CCAD1
2014 Press Pass Five Star Classic Compilations Autographed Patch Booklet /1 #CCAD2
2014 Press Pass Five Star Classic Compilations Autographed Patch Booklet /1 #CCAD3
2014 Press Pass Five Star Classic Compilations Autographed Patch Booklet /1 #CCAD4
2014 Press Pass Five Star Classic Compilations Autographed Patch Booklet /1 #CCAD5
2014 Press Pass Five Star Classic Compilations Autographed Patch Booklet /1 #CCAD6
2014 Press Pass Five Star Classic Compilations Combo Autographs Blue /5 #CCDIL
2014 Press Pass Five Star Classic Compilations Combo Autographs Melting /1 #CCDIL
2014 Press Pass Five Star Holofoil /10 #17
2014 Press Pass Five Star Melting /1 #17
2014 Press Pass Five Star Paramount Pieces Blue /5 #PPAD
2014 Press Pass Five Star Paramount Pieces Gold /25 #PPAD
2014 Press Pass Five Star Paramount Pieces Holofoil /10 #PPAD
2014 Press Pass Five Star Paramount Pieces Melting /1 #PPAD
2014 Press Pass Five Star Paramount Pieces Melting Patch /1 #PPAD
2014 Press Pass Five Star Signatures Blue /5 #FSSAD
2014 Press Pass Five Star Signatures Holofoil /10 #FSSAD
2014 Press Pass Five Star Signatures Melting /1 #FSSAD
2014 Press Pass Gold #42
2014 Press Pass Gold #46
2014 Press Pass Gold #95
2014 Press Pass Redline #14
2014 Press Pass Redline #15
2014 Press Pass Redline Black /75 #14
2014 Press Pass Redline Black /75 #15
2014 Press Pass Redline Blue Foil #14
2014 Press Pass Redline Blue Foil #15
2014 Press Pass Redline Cyan /50 #14
2014 Press Pass Redline Cyan /50 #15
2014 Press Pass Redline Dynamic Duals Relic Autographs Blue /25 #DDAD
2014 Press Pass Redline Dynamic Duals Relic Autographs Gold /10 #DDAD
2014 Press Pass Redline Dynamic Duals Relic Autographs Melting /1 #DDAD
2014 Press Pass Redline Dynamic Duals Relic Autographs Red /50 #DDAD
2014 Press Pass Redline Full Throttle Relics Blue /10 #FTAD
2014 Press Pass Redline Full Throttle Relics Gold /25 #FTAD
2014 Press Pass Redline Full Throttle Relics Melting /1 #FTAD
2014 Press Pass Redline Full Throttle Relics Red /50 #FTAD
2014 Press Pass Redline Green National Convention /5 #14
2014 Press Pass Redline Green National Convention /5 #15
2014 Press Pass Redline Head to Head Blue /10 #HTHADDE
2014 Press Pass Redline Head to Head Gold /25 #HTHADDE
2014 Press Pass Redline Head to Head Melting /1 #HTHADDE
2014 Press Pass Redline Head to Head Red /75 #HTHADDE
2014 Press Pass Redline Intensity #I2
2014 Press Pass Redline Magenta /10 #14
2014 Press Pass Redline Magenta /10 #15
2014 Press Pass Redline Muscle Car Sheet Metal Blue /25 #MCMAD
2014 Press Pass Redline Muscle Car Sheet Metal Gold /50 #MCMAD
2014 Press Pass Redline Muscle Car Sheet Metal Melting /1 #MCMAD
2014 Press Pass Redline Muscle Car Sheet Metal Red /75 #MCMAD
2014 Press Pass Redline Redline Racers #RR3
2014 Press Pass Redline Signatures Blue /10 #RSAD
2014 Press Pass Redline Signatures Gold /25 #RSAD
2014 Press Pass Redline Signatures Melting /5 #RSAD
2014 Press Pass Redline Signatures Red /50 #RSAD
2014 Press Pass Redline Yellow /1 #14
2014 Press Pass Redline Yellow /1 #15
2014 Press Pass Signings Gold /10 #PPSAD
2014 Press Pass Signings Holofoil /1 #PPSAD
2014 Press Pass Signings Melting /1 #PPSAD
2014 Press Pass Signings Printing Plates Black /1 #PPSAD
2014 Press Pass Signings Printing Plates Cyan /1 #PPSAD
2014 Press Pass Signings Printing Plates Magenta /1 #PPSAD
2014 Press Pass Signings Printing Plates Yellow /1 #PPSAD
2014 Press Pass Signings Silver /50 #PPSAD
2014 Press Pass Three Wide Gold /10 #TWAD
2014 Press Pass Three Wide Melting /1 #TWAD
2014 Press Pass Velocity #9
2014 Total Memorabilia #32
2014 Total Memorabilia Black and White /99 #32
2014 Total Memorabilia Champions Collection Blue /25 #CCAD
2014 Total Memorabilia Champions Collection Gold /50 #CCAD
2014 Total Memorabilia Champions Collection Melting /5 #CCAD
2014 Total Memorabilia Champions Collection Silver /75 #CCAD
2014 Total Memorabilia Dirt Track Treads Blue /25 #DTTAD
2014 Total Memorabilia Dirt Track Treads Gold /50 #DTTAD
2014 Total Memorabilia Dirt Track Treads Melting /10 #DTTAD
2014 Total Memorabilia Dirt Track Treads Silver /99 #DTTAD
2014 Total Memorabilia Dual Swatch Gold /150 #TMAD
2014 Total Memorabilia Gold /175 #32
2014 Total Memorabilia Quad Swatch Melting /25 #TMAD
2014 Total Memorabilia Red #32
2014 Total Memorabilia Single Swatch Silver /275 #TMAD
2014 Total Memorabilia Triple Swatch Blue /99 #TMAD
2015 Press Pass #11
2015 Press Pass #64
2015 Press Pass #90
2015 Press Pass Championship Caliber Dual /25 #CCMAD
2015 Press Pass Championship Caliber Quad /1 #CCMAD
2015 Press Pass Championship Caliber Signature Edition Blue /15 #CCAD
2015 Press Pass Championship Caliber Signature Edition Gold /50 #CCAD
2015 Press Pass Championship Caliber Signature Edition Green /10 #CCAD
2015 Press Pass Championship Caliber Signature Edition Melting /1 #CCAD
2015 Press Pass Championship Caliber Single /50 #CCMAD
2015 Press Pass Championship Caliber Triple /10 #CCMAD
2015 Press Pass Cup Chase #11
2015 Press Pass Cup Chase #64
2015 Press Pass Cup Chase #90
2015 Press Pass Cup Chase Blue /25 #11
2015 Press Pass Cup Chase Blue /25 #64
2015 Press Pass Cup Chase Blue /25 #90
2015 Press Pass Cup Chase Gold /75 #11
2015 Press Pass Cup Chase Gold /75 #64
2015 Press Pass Cup Chase Gold /75 #90
2015 Press Pass Cup Chase Green /10 #11
2015 Press Pass Cup Chase Green /10 #64
2015 Press Pass Cup Chase Green /10 #90
2015 Press Pass Cup Chase Melting /1 #11
2015 Press Pass Cup Chase Melting /1 #64
2015 Press Pass Cup Chase Melting /1 #90
2015 Press Pass Cup Chase Three Wide Blue /25 #3WAD
2015 Press Pass Cup Chase Three Wide Gold /50 #3WAD
2015 Press Pass Cup Chase Three Wide Green /10 #3WAD
2015 Press Pass Cup Chase Three Wide Melting /1 #3WAD
2015 Press Pass Cup Chase Upper Cuts /13 #UCAD
2015 Press Pass Cuts Blue /25 #CCCAD
2015 Press Pass Cuts Gold /50 #CCCAD
2015 Press Pass Cuts Green /10 #CCCAD
2015 Press Pass Cuts Melting /1 #CCCAD
2015 Press Pass Four Wide Signature Edition Blue /25 #4WAD
2015 Press Pass Four Wide Signature Edition Gold /50 #4WAD
2015 Press Pass Four Wide Signature Edition Green /10 #4WAD
2015 Press Pass Four Wide Signature Edition Melting /1 #4WAD
2015 Press Pass Purple #11
2015 Press Pass Purple #64
2015 Press Pass Purple #90
2015 Press Pass Red #11
2015 Press Pass Red #64
2015 Press Pass Red #90
2015 Press Pass Signings Blue /15 #PPSAD
2015 Press Pass Signings Gold #PPSAD
2015 Press Pass Signings Green /5 #PPSAD
2015 Press Pass Signings Melting /1 #PPSAD
2015 Press Pass Signings Red /10 #PPSAD
2016 Certified #9
2016 Certified Complete Materials /199 #22
2016 Certified Complete Materials Mirror Black /1 #22
2016 Certified Complete Materials Mirror Blue /50 #22
2016 Certified Complete Materials Mirror Gold /25 #22
2016 Certified Complete Materials Mirror Green /5 #22
2016 Certified Complete Materials Mirror Orange /99 #22
2016 Certified Complete Materials Mirror Purple /10 #22
2016 Certified Complete Materials Mirror Red /75 #22
2016 Certified Complete Materials Mirror Silver /99 #22
2016 Certified Mirror Black /1 #9
2016 Certified Mirror Blue /50 #9
2016 Certified Mirror Gold /25 #9
2016 Certified Mirror Green /5 #9
2016 Certified Mirror Orange /99 #9
2016 Certified Mirror Purple /10 #9
2016 Certified Mirror Red /75 #9
2016 Certified Mirror Silver /99 #9
2016 Certified Potential Signatures /30 #1
2016 Certified Potential Signatures Mirror Black /1 #1
2016 Certified Potential Signatures Mirror Blue /15 #1
2016 Certified Potential Signatures Mirror Gold /10 #1
2016 Certified Potential Signatures Mirror Green /3 #1
2016 Certified Potential Signatures Mirror Orange /5 #1
2016 Certified Potential Signatures Mirror Purple /5 #1
2016 Certified Potential Signatures Mirror Red /20 #1
2016 Certified Potential Signatures Mirror Silver /5 #1
2016 Certified Skills /199 #6
2016 Certified Skills Mirror Black /1 #6
2016 Certified Skills Mirror Blue /50 #6
2016 Certified Skills Mirror Gold /25 #6
2016 Certified Skills Mirror Green /5 #6
2016 Certified Skills Mirror Orange /99 #6
2016 Certified Skills Mirror Purple /10 #6
2016 Certified Skills Mirror Red /75 #6
2016 Certified Skills Mirror Silver /99 #6
2016 Certified Sprint Cup Signature Swatches /75 #15
2016 Certified Sprint Cup Signature Swatches Mirror Black /1 #15
2016 Certified Sprint Cup Signature Swatches Mirror Blue /30 #15
2016 Certified Sprint Cup Signature Swatches Mirror Gold /25 #15
2016 Certified Sprint Cup Signature Swatches Mirror Green /3 #15
2016 Certified Sprint Cup Signature Swatches Mirror Orange /10 #15
2016 Certified Sprint Cup Signature Swatches Mirror Purple /10 #15
2016 Certified Sprint Cup Signature Swatches Mirror Red /50 #15
2016 Certified Sprint Cup Signature Swatches Mirror Silver /5 #15
2016 Certified Sprint Cup Swatches Mirror Black /1 #26
2016 Certified Sprint Cup Swatches Mirror Blue /50 #26
2016 Certified Sprint Cup Swatches Mirror Gold /25 #26
2016 Certified Sprint Cup Swatches Mirror Green /5 #26
2016 Certified Sprint Cup Swatches Mirror Orange /10 #26
2016 Certified Sprint Cup Swatches Mirror Purple /10 #26
2016 Certified Sprint Cup Swatches Mirror Red /75 #26
2016 Certified Sprint Cup Swatches Mirror Silver /10 #26
2016 Panini Black Friday #35
2016 Panini Black Friday Autographs /25 #35
2016 Panini Black Friday Cracked Ice /25 #35
2016 Panini Black Friday Holo Plaid /1 #35
2016 Panini Black Friday Rapture /10 #35
2016 Panini Black Friday Thick Stock /50 #35
2016 Panini Black Friday Wedges /50 #35
2016 Panini National Treasures /25 #25
2016 Panini National Treasures Black /5 #25
2016 Panini National Treasures Blue /1 #25
2016 Panini National Treasures Combo Materials /25 #1
2016 Panini National Treasures Combo Materials Black /5 #1
2016 Panini National Treasures Combo Materials Blue /1 #1
2016 Panini National Treasures Combo Materials Gold /10 #1
2016 Panini National Treasures Combo Materials Printing Plates Black /1 #1
2016 Panini National Treasures Combo Materials Printing Plates Cyan /1 #1
2016 Panini National Treasures Combo Materials Printing Plates Magenta /1 #1
2016 Panini National Treasures Combo Materials Printing Plates Yellow /1 #1
2016 Panini National Treasures Combo Materials Silver /15 #1
2016 Panini National Treasures Dual Driver Materials /25 #3
2016 Panini National Treasures Dual Driver Materials /25 #14
2016 Panini National Treasures Dual Driver Materials Black /5 #3
2016 Panini National Treasures Dual Driver Materials Black /5 #14
2016 Panini National Treasures Dual Driver Materials Blue /1 #3
2016 Panini National Treasures Dual Driver Materials Blue /1 #14
2016 Panini National Treasures Dual Driver Materials Gold /10 #3
2016 Panini National Treasures Dual Driver Materials Gold /10 #14
2016 Panini National Treasures Dual Driver Materials Printing Plates Black /1 #3
2016 Panini National Treasures Dual Driver Materials Printing Plates Black /1 #14
2016 Panini National Treasures Dual Driver Materials Printing Plates Cyan /1 #3
2016 Panini National Treasures Dual Driver Materials Printing Plates Cyan /1 #14
2016 Panini National Treasures Dual Driver Materials Printing Plates Magenta /1 #3
2016 Panini National Treasures Dual Driver Materials Printing Plates Magenta /1 #14
2016 Panini National Treasures Dual Driver Materials Printing Plates Yellow /1 #3
2016 Panini National Treasures Dual Driver Materials Printing Plates Yellow /1 #14
2016 Panini National Treasures Dual Driver Materials Silver /15 #3
2016 Panini National Treasures Dual Driver Materials Silver /15 #14
2016 Panini National Treasures Dual Signatures Black /5 #3
2016 Panini National Treasures Dual Signatures Blue /1 #3
2016 Panini National Treasures Dual Signatures Gold /10 #3
2016 Panini National Treasures Gold /15 #25
2016 Panini National Treasures Jumbo Firesuit Patch Signature Booklet Associate Sponsor 1 /1 #2
2016 Panini National Treasures Jumbo Firesuit Patch Signature Booklet Associate Sponsor 10 /1 #2
2016 Panini National Treasures Jumbo Firesuit Patch Signature Booklet Associate Sponsor 11 /1 #2
2016 Panini National Treasures Jumbo Firesuit Patch Signature Booklet Associate Sponsor 12 /1 #2
2016 Panini National Treasures Jumbo Firesuit Patch Signature Booklet Associate Sponsor 13 /1 #2
2016 Panini National Treasures Jumbo Firesuit Patch Signature Booklet Associate Sponsor 14 /1 #2
2016 Panini National Treasures Jumbo Firesuit Patch Signature Booklet Associate Sponsor 15 /1 #2
2016 Panini National Treasures Jumbo Firesuit Patch Signature Booklet Associate Sponsor 16 /1 #2
2016 Panini National Treasures Jumbo Firesuit Patch Signature Booklet Associate Sponsor 17 /1 #2
2016 Panini National Treasures Jumbo Firesuit Patch Signature Booklet Associate Sponsor 18 /1 #2
2016 Panini National Treasures Jumbo Firesuit Patch Signature Booklet Associate Sponsor 2 /1 #2
2016 Panini National Treasures Jumbo Firesuit Patch Signature Booklet Associate Sponsor 3 /1 #2
2016 Panini National Treasures Jumbo Firesuit Patch Signature Booklet Associate Sponsor 4 /1 #2
2016 Panini National Treasures Jumbo Firesuit Patch Signature Booklet Associate Sponsor 5 /1 #2
2016 Panini National Treasures Jumbo Firesuit Patch Signature Booklet Associate Sponsor 6 /1 #2
2016 Panini National Treasures Jumbo Firesuit Patch Signature Booklet Associate Sponsor 7 /1 #2
2016 Panini National Treasures Jumbo Firesuit Patch Signature Booklet Associate Sponsor 8 /1 #2
2016 Panini National Treasures Jumbo Firesuit Patch Signature Booklet Associate Sponsor 9 /1 #2
2016 Panini National Treasures Jumbo Firesuit Patch Signature Booklet Flag /1 #2
2016 Panini National Treasures Jumbo Firesuit Patch Signature Booklet Goodyear /1 #2
2016 Panini National Treasures Jumbo Firesuit Patch Signature Booklet Manufacturers Logo /2 #2
2016 Panini National Treasures Jumbo Firesuit Patch Signature Booklet Nameplate /2 #2
2016 Panini National Treasures Jumbo Firesuit Patch Signature Booklet NASCAR /1 #2
2016 Panini National Treasures Jumbo Firesuit Patch Signature Booklet Sprint Cup Logo /1 #2
2016 Panini National Treasures Jumbo Firesuit Patch Signature Booklet Sunoco /1 #2
2016 Panini National Treasures Jumbo Firesuit Signatures /25 #2
2016 Panini National Treasures Jumbo Firesuit Signatures Black /5 #2
2016 Panini National Treasures Jumbo Firesuit Signatures Blue /1 #2
2016 Panini National Treasures Jumbo Firesuit Signatures Gold /10 #2
2016 Panini National Treasures Jumbo Firesuit Signatures Printing Plates Black /1 #2
2016 Panini National Treasures Jumbo Firesuit Signatures Printing Plates Cyan /1 #2
2016 Panini National Treasures Jumbo Firesuit Signatures Printing Plates Magenta /1 #2
2016 Panini National Treasures Jumbo Firesuit Signatures Printing Plates Yellow /1 #2
2016 Panini National Treasures Jumbo Firesuit Signatures Silver /15 #2
2016 Panini National Treasures Jumbo Sheet Metal Signatures /25 #14
2016 Panini National Treasures Jumbo Sheet Metal Signatures Black /5 #14
2016 Panini National Treasures Jumbo Sheet Metal Signatures Blue /1 #14
2016 Panini National Treasures Jumbo Sheet Metal Signatures Gold /10 #14

2016 Panini National Treasures Jumbo Sheet Metal Signatures Printing Plates Black /1 #14
2016 Panini National Treasures Jumbo Sheet Metal Signatures Printing Plates Cyan /1 #14
2016 Panini National Treasures Jumbo Sheet Metal Signatures Printing Plates Magenta /1 #14
2016 Panini National Treasures Jumbo Sheet Metal Signatures Printing Plates Yellow /1 #14
2016 Panini National Treasures Jumbo Sheet Metal Signatures Silver /15 #14
2016 Panini National Treasures Printing Plates Black /1 #25
2016 Panini National Treasures Printing Plates Cyan /1 #25
2016 Panini National Treasures Printing Plates Magenta /1 #25
2016 Panini National Treasures Printing Plates Yellow /1 #25
2016 Panini National Treasures Signature Dual Materials /25 #2
2016 Panini National Treasures Signature Dual Materials Black /5 #2
2016 Panini National Treasures Signature Dual Materials Blue /1 #2
2016 Panini National Treasures Signature Dual Materials Gold /10 #2
2016 Panini National Treasures Signature Dual Materials Printing Plates Black /1 #2
2016 Panini National Treasures Signature Dual Materials Printing Plates Cyan /1 #2
2016 Panini National Treasures Signature Dual Materials Printing Plates Magenta /1 #2
2016 Panini National Treasures Signature Dual Materials Printing Plates Yellow /1 #2
2016 Panini National Treasures Signature Dual Materials Silver /15 #2
2016 Panini National Treasures Signature Firesuit Materials /25 #2
2016 Panini National Treasures Signature Firesuit Materials Black /5 #2
2016 Panini National Treasures Signature Firesuit Materials Blue /1 #2
2016 Panini National Treasures Signature Firesuit Materials Gold /10 #2
2016 Panini National Treasures Signature Firesuit Materials Laundry Tag /1 #2
2016 Panini National Treasures Signature Firesuit Materials Printing Plates Black /1 #2
2016 Panini National Treasures Signature Firesuit Materials Printing Plates Cyan /1 #2
2016 Panini National Treasures Signature Firesuit Materials Printing Plates Magenta /1 #2
2016 Panini National Treasures Signature Firesuit Materials Printing Plates Yellow /1 #2
2016 Panini National Treasures Signature Firesuit Materials Silver /15 #2
2016 Panini National Treasures Signature Quad Materials /25 #2
2016 Panini National Treasures Signature Quad Materials Black /5 #2
2016 Panini National Treasures Signature Quad Materials Blue /1 #2
2016 Panini National Treasures Signature Quad Materials Gold /10 #2
2016 Panini National Treasures Signature Quad Materials Printing Plates Black /1 #2
2016 Panini National Treasures Signature Quad Materials Printing Plates Cyan /1 #2
2016 Panini National Treasures Signature Quad Materials Printing Plates Magenta /1 #2
2016 Panini National Treasures Signature Quad Materials Printing Plates Yellow /1 #2
2016 Panini National Treasures Signature Quad Materials Silver /15 #2
2016 Panini National Treasures Signature Sheet Metal Materials Black /5 #2
2016 Panini National Treasures Signature Sheet Metal Materials Blue /1 #2
2016 Panini National Treasures Signature Sheet Metal Materials Gold /10 #2
2016 Panini National Treasures Signature Sheet Metal Materials Printing Plates Black /1 #2
2016 Panini National Treasures Signature Sheet Metal Materials Printing Plates Cyan /1 #2
2016 Panini National Treasures Signature Sheet Metal Materials Printing Plates Magenta /1 #2
2016 Panini National Treasures Signature Sheet Metal Materials Printing Plates Yellow /1 #2
2016 Panini National Treasures Signature Sheet Metal Materials Silver /15 #2
2016 Panini National Treasures Signatures Black /5 #2
2016 Panini National Treasures Signatures Blue /1 #2
2016 Panini National Treasures Signatures Printing Plates Black /1 #2
2016 Panini National Treasures Signatures Printing Plates Cyan /1 #2
2016 Panini National Treasures Signatures Printing Plates Magenta /1 #2
2016 Panini National Treasures Signatures Printing Plates Yellow /1 #2
2016 Panini National Treasures Silver /20 #25
2016 Panini National Treasures Six Signatures /25 #3
2016 Panini National Treasures Six Signatures Black /10 #3
2016 Panini National Treasures Six Signatures Blue /1 #3
2016 Panini National Treasures Six Signatures Gold /15 #3
2016 Panini National Treasures Timelines /25 #2
2016 Panini National Treasures Timelines Black /5 #2
2016 Panini National Treasures Timelines Blue /1 #2
2016 Panini National Treasures Timelines Gold /10 #2
2016 Panini National Treasures Timelines Printing Plates Black /1 #2
2016 Panini National Treasures Timelines Printing Plates Cyan /1 #2
2016 Panini National Treasures Timelines Printing Plates Magenta /1 #2
2016 Panini National Treasures Timelines Printing Plates Yellow /1 #2
2016 Panini National Treasures Timelines Signatures /25 #2
2016 Panini National Treasures Timelines Signatures Black /5 #2
2016 Panini National Treasures Timelines Signatures Blue /1 #2
2016 Panini National Treasures Timelines Signatures Gold /10 #2
2016 Panini National Treasures Timelines Signatures Printing Plates Black /1 #2
2016 Panini National Treasures Timelines Signatures Printing Plates Cyan /1 #2
2016 Panini National Treasures Timelines Signatures Printing Plates Magenta /1 #2
2016 Panini National Treasures Timelines Signatures Printing Plates Yellow /1 #2
2016 Panini National Treasures Timelines Signatures Silver /15 #2
2016 Panini National Treasures Timelines Silver /15 #2
2016 Panini National Treasures Trio Driver Materials /25 #6
2016 Panini National Treasures Trio Driver Materials /25 #15
2016 Panini National Treasures Trio Driver Materials Black /5 #6
2016 Panini National Treasures Trio Driver Materials Black /5 #15
2016 Panini National Treasures Trio Driver Materials Blue /1 #6
2016 Panini National Treasures Trio Driver Materials Blue /1 #15
2016 Panini National Treasures Trio Driver Materials Gold /10 #6
2016 Panini National Treasures Trio Driver Materials Gold /10 #15
2016 Panini National Treasures Trio Driver Materials Printing Plates Black /1 #6
2016 Panini National Treasures Trio Driver Materials Printing Plates Black /1 #15
2016 Panini National Treasures Trio Driver Materials Printing Plates Cyan /1 #6
2016 Panini National Treasures Trio Driver Materials Printing Plates Cyan /1 #15
2016 Panini National Treasures Trio Driver Materials Printing Plates Magenta /1 #6
2016 Panini National Treasures Trio Driver Materials Printing Plates Magenta /1 #15
2016 Panini National Treasures Trio Driver Materials Printing Plates Yellow /1 #6
2016 Panini National Treasures Trio Driver Materials Printing Plates Yellow /1 #15
2016 Panini National Treasures Trio Driver Materials Silver /15 #6
2016 Panini National Treasures Trio Driver Materials Silver /15 #15
2016 Panini Prizm #3
2016 Panini Prizm #50
2016 Panini Prizm #87
2016 Panini Prizm Autographs Prizms #4
2016 Panini Prizm Autographs Prizms Black /3 #4
2016 Panini Prizm Autographs Prizms Blue Flag /50 #4
2016 Panini Prizm Autographs Prizms Camo /3 #4
2016 Panini Prizm Autographs Prizms Checkered Flag /1 #4
2016 Panini Prizm Autographs Prizms Gold /10 #4
2016 Panini Prizm Autographs Prizms Green Flag /75 #4
2016 Panini Prizm Autographs Prizms Rainbow /24 #4
2016 Panini Prizm Autographs Prizms Red Flag /25 #4
2016 Panini Prizm Autographs Prizms Red White and Blue /25 #4
2016 Panini Prizm Autographs Prizms White Flag /5 #4
2016 Panini Prizm Prizms #3
2016 Panini Prizm Prizms #50
2016 Panini Prizm Prizms #87
2016 Panini Prizm Prizms Black /3 #3
2016 Panini Prizm Prizms Black /3 #50
2016 Panini Prizm Prizms Black /3 #87
2016 Panini Prizm Prizms Blue Flag /99 #3
2016 Panini Prizm Prizms Blue Flag /99 #50
2016 Panini Prizm Prizms Blue Flag /99 #87
2016 Panini Prizm Prizms Camo /3 #3
2016 Panini Prizm Prizms Camo /3 #50
2016 Panini Prizm Prizms Camo /3 #87
2016 Panini Prizm Prizms Checkered Flag /1 #3
2016 Panini Prizm Prizms Checkered Flag /1 #50
2016 Panini Prizm Prizms Checkered Flag /1 #87
2016 Panini Prizm Prizms Gold /10 #3
2016 Panini Prizm Prizms Gold /10 #50
2016 Panini Prizm Prizms Gold /10 #87
2016 Panini Prizm Prizms Green Flag /149 #3
2016 Panini Prizm Prizms Green Flag /149 #50
2016 Panini Prizm Prizms Green Flag /149 #87
2016 Panini Prizm Prizms Rainbow /24 #3
2016 Panini Prizm Prizms Rainbow /24 #50
2016 Panini Prizm Prizms Rainbow /24 #87
2016 Panini Prizm Prizms Red Flag /75 #3
2016 Panini Prizm Prizms Red Flag /75 #50
2016 Panini Prizm Prizms Red Flag /75 #87
2016 Panini Prizm Prizms Red White and Blue #3
2016 Panini Prizm Prizms Red White and Blue #50
2016 Panini Prizm Prizms Red White and Blue #87
2016 Panini Prizm Prizms White Flag /5 #3
2016 Panini Prizm Prizms White Flag /5 #50
2016 Panini Prizm Prizms White Flag /5 #87
2016 Panini Torque #12
2016 Panini Torque #58
2016 Panini Torque #88
2016 Panini Torque Artist Proof /50 #12
2016 Panini Torque Artist Proof /50 #58
2016 Panini Torque Artist Proof /50 #88
2016 Panini Torque Blackout /1 #12
2016 Panini Torque Blackout /1 #58
2016 Panini Torque Blackout /1 #88
2016 Panini Torque Blue /125 #12
2016 Panini Torque Blue /125 #58
2016 Panini Torque Blue /125 #88
2016 Panini Torque Clear Vision #12
2016 Panini Torque Clear Vision Blue /99 #12
2016 Panini Torque Clear Vision Gold /149 #12
2016 Panini Torque Clear Vision Green /25 #12
2016 Panini Torque Clear Vision Purple /10 #12
2016 Panini Torque Clear Vision Red /49 #12
2016 Panini Torque Gold #12
2016 Panini Torque Gold #58
2016 Panini Torque Gold #88
2016 Panini Torque Holo Gold /5 #12
2016 Panini Torque Holo Gold /5 #58
2016 Panini Torque Holo Gold /5 #88
2016 Panini Torque Holo Silver /10 #12
2016 Panini Torque Holo Silver /10 #58
2016 Panini Torque Holo Silver /10 #88
2016 Panini Torque Horsepower Heroes #21
2016 Panini Torque Horsepower Heroes Gold /199 #21
2016 Panini Torque Horsepower Heroes Holo Silver /99 #21
2016 Panini Torque Jumbo Firesuit Autographs /25 #1
2016 Panini Torque Jumbo Firesuit Autographs Blue /20 #1
2016 Panini Torque Jumbo Firesuit Autographs Green /5 #1
2016 Panini Torque Jumbo Firesuit Autographs Purple /1 #1
2016 Panini Torque Jumbo Firesuit Autographs Red /10 #1
2016 Panini Torque Jumbo Tire Autographs /49 #1
2016 Panini Torque Jumbo Tire Autographs Blue /25 #1
2016 Panini Torque Jumbo Tire Autographs Green /5 #1
2016 Panini Torque Jumbo Tire Autographs Purple /1 #1
2016 Panini Torque Jumbo Tire Autographs Red /10 #1
2016 Panini Torque Metal Materials /249 #2
2016 Panini Torque Metal Materials Blue /99 #2
2016 Panini Torque Metal Materials Green /25 #2
2016 Panini Torque Metal Materials Purple /10 #2
2016 Panini Torque Metal Materials Red /49 #2
2016 Panini Torque Pairings Materials /125 #16
2016 Panini Torque Pairings Materials /125 #28
2016 Panini Torque Pairings Materials /125 #29
2016 Panini Torque Pairings Materials Blue /99 #16
2016 Panini Torque Pairings Materials Blue /99 #28
2016 Panini Torque Pairings Materials Blue /99 #29
2016 Panini Torque Pairings Materials Green /25 #16
2016 Panini Torque Pairings Materials Green /25 #28
2016 Panini Torque Pairings Materials Green /25 #29
2016 Panini Torque Pairings Materials Purple /10 #16
2016 Panini Torque Pairings Materials Purple /10 #28
2016 Panini Torque Pairings Materials Purple /10 #29
2016 Panini Torque Pairings Materials Red /49 #16
2016 Panini Torque Pairings Materials Red /49 #28
2016 Panini Torque Pairings Materials Red /49 #29
2016 Panini Torque Pole Position #12
2016 Panini Torque Pole Position Blue /99 #12
2016 Panini Torque Pole Position Checkerboard /10 #12
2016 Panini Torque Pole Position Green /25 #12
2016 Panini Torque Pole Position Red /49 #12
2016 Panini Torque Printing Plates Black /1 #12
2016 Panini Torque Printing Plates Black /1 #58
2016 Panini Torque Printing Plates Black /1 #88
2016 Panini Torque Printing Plates Cyan /1 #12
2016 Panini Torque Printing Plates Cyan /1 #58
2016 Panini Torque Printing Plates Cyan /1 #88
2016 Panini Torque Printing Plates Magenta /1 #12
2016 Panini Torque Printing Plates Magenta /1 #58
2016 Panini Torque Printing Plates Magenta /1 #88
2016 Panini Torque Printing Plates Yellow /1 #12
2016 Panini Torque Printing Plates Yellow /1 #58
2016 Panini Torque Printing Plates Yellow /1 #88
2016 Panini Torque Purple /25 #12
2016 Panini Torque Purple /25 #58
2016 Panini Torque Purple /25 #88
2016 Panini Torque Red /99 #12
2016 Panini Torque Red /99 #58
2016 Panini Torque Red /99 #88
2016 Panini Torque Rubber Relics /399 #2
2016 Panini Torque Rubber Relics Blue /99 #2
2016 Panini Torque Rubber Relics Green /25 #2
2016 Panini Torque Rubber Relics Purple /10 #2
2016 Panini Torque Rubber Relics Red /49 #2
2016 Panini Torque Silhouettes Firesuit Autographs /25 #1
2016 Panini Torque Silhouettes Firesuit Autographs Blue /15 #1
2016 Panini Torque Silhouettes Firesuit Autographs Green /5 #1
2016 Panini Torque Silhouettes Firesuit Autographs Purple /1 #1
2016 Panini Torque Silhouettes Firesuit Autographs Red /10 #1
2016 Panini Torque Silhouettes Sheet Metal Autographs /49 #1
2016 Panini Torque Silhouettes Sheet Metal Autographs Blue /25 #1
2016 Panini Torque Silhouettes Sheet Metal Autographs Green /5 #1
2016 Panini Torque Silhouettes Sheet Metal Autographs Purple /1 #1
2016 Panini Torque Silhouettes Sheet Metal Autographs Red /10 #1
2016 Panini Torque Superstar Vision #9
2016 Panini Torque Superstar Vision Blue /99 #9
2016 Panini Torque Superstar Vision Gold /149 #9
2016 Panini Torque Superstar Vision Green /25 #9
2016 Panini Torque Superstar Vision Purple /10 #9
2016 Panini Torque Superstar Vision Red /49 #9
2016 Panini Torque Test Proof Black /1 #12
2016 Panini Torque Test Proof Black /1 #58
2016 Panini Torque Test Proof Black /1 #88
2016 Panini Torque Test Proof Cyan /1 #12
2016 Panini Torque Test Proof Cyan /1 #58
2016 Panini Torque Test Proof Cyan /1 #88
2016 Panini Torque Test Proof Magenta /1 #12
2016 Panini Torque Test Proof Magenta /1 #58
2016 Panini Torque Test Proof Magenta /1 #88
2016 Panini Torque Test Proof Yellow /1 #12
2016 Panini Torque Test Proof Yellow /1 #58
2016 Panini Torque Test Proof Yellow /1 #88
2017 Donruss #23
2017 Donruss #42
2017 Donruss #132
2017 Donruss #148
2017 Donruss Artist Proof /25 #23
2017 Donruss Artist Proof /25 #42
2017 Donruss Artist Proof /25 #132
2017 Donruss Artist Proof /25 #148
2017 Donruss Blue Foil /299 #23
2017 Donruss Blue Foil /299 #132
2017 Donruss Blue Foil /299 #42
2017 Donruss Blue Foil /299 #148
2017 Donruss Gold Foil /499 #23
2017 Donruss Gold Foil /499 #132
2017 Donruss Gold Foil /499 #148
2017 Donruss Gold Foil /499 #42
2017 Donruss Gold Press Proof /99 #23
2017 Donruss Gold Press Proof /99 #42
2017 Donruss Gold Press Proof /99 #132
2017 Donruss Gold Press Proof /99 #148
2017 Donruss Green Foil /199 #23
2017 Donruss Green Foil /199 #42
2017 Donruss Green Foil /199 #132
2017 Donruss Green Foil /199 #148
2017 Donruss Phenoms #10
2017 Donruss Phenoms Cracked Ice /999 #10
2017 Donruss Pole Position #8
2017 Donruss Pole Position Cracked Ice /999 #8
2017 Donruss Press Proof /49 #23
2017 Donruss Press Proof /49 #42
2017 Donruss Press Proof /49 #132
2017 Donruss Press Proof /49 #148
2017 Donruss Printing Plates Black /1 #23
2017 Donruss Printing Plates Black /1 #42
2017 Donruss Printing Plates Black /1 #132
2017 Donruss Printing Plates Black /1 #148
2017 Donruss Printing Plates Cyan /1 #23
2017 Donruss Printing Plates Cyan /1 #42
2017 Donruss Printing Plates Cyan /1 #132
2017 Donruss Printing Plates Cyan /1 #148
2017 Donruss Printing Plates Magenta /1 #23
2017 Donruss Printing Plates Magenta /1 #132
2017 Donruss Printing Plates Magenta /1 #148
2017 Donruss Printing Plates Magenta /1 #42
2017 Donruss Printing Plates Yellow /1 #23
2017 Donruss Printing Plates Yellow /1 #132
2017 Donruss Printing Plates Yellow /1 #148
2017 Donruss Printing Plates Yellow /1 #42
2017 Donruss Retro Signatures 1984 #1
2017 Donruss Retro Signatures 1984 Holo Black /1 #1
2017 Donruss Retro Signatures 1984 Holo Gold /25 #1
2017 Donruss Rubber Relics #1
2017 Donruss Rubber Relics Holo Black /10 #1
2017 Donruss Rubber Relics Holo Gold /99 #1
2017 Donruss Top Tier #11
2017 Donruss Top Tier Cracked Ice /999 #11
2017 Panini Day #60
2017 Panini Day Cracked Ice /25 #60
2017 Panini Day Decoy /50 #60
2017 Panini Day Hyperplaid /1 #60
2017 Panini Day Memorabilia #43
2017 Panini Day Memorabilia Galactic Window /25 #43
2017 Panini Day Memorabilia Hyperplaid /1 #43
2017 Panini Day Rapture /10 #60
2017 Panini Day Wedges /50 #60
2017 Panini Father's Day Racing Memorabilia /100 #8
2017 Panini Father's Day Racing Memorabilia Cracked Ice /25 #8
2017 Panini Father's Day Racing Memorabilia Hyperplaid /1 #8
2017 Panini Father's Day Racing Memorabilia Shimmer /10 #8
2017 Panini Instant Nascar /57 #12
2017 Panini Instant Nascar Black /1 #12
2017 Panini Instant Nascar Green /10 #12
2017 Panini National Convention #R8
2017 Panini National Convention Autographs #R8
2017 Panini National Convention Autographs Hyperplaid /1 #R8
2017 Panini National Convention Escher Squares /25 #R8
2017 Panini National Convention Escher Squares Thick Stock /10 #R8
2017 Panini National Convention Galatic Windows /5 #R8
2017 Panini National Convention Hyperplaid /1 #R8
2017 Panini National Convention Pyramids /10 #R8
2017 Panini National Convention Rainbow Spokes /49 #R8
2017 Panini National Convention Rainbow Spokes Thick Stock /25 #R8
2017 Panini National Convention Rapture /99 #R8
2017 Panini National Treasures /25 #9
2017 Panini National Treasures Associate Sponsor Patch Signatures 1 /1 #8
2017 Panini National Treasures Associate Sponsor Patch Signatures 10 /1 #8
2017 Panini National Treasures Associate Sponsor Patch Signatures 11 /1 #8
2017 Panini National Treasures Associate Sponsor Patch Signatures 12 /1 #8
2017 Panini National Treasures Associate Sponsor Patch Signatures 13 /1 #8
2017 Panini National Treasures Associate Sponsor Patch Signatures 2 /1 #8
2017 Panini National Treasures Associate Sponsor Patch Signatures 3 /1 #8
2017 Panini National Treasures Associate Sponsor Patch Signatures 4 /1 #8
2017 Panini National Treasures Associate Sponsor Patch Signatures 5 /1 #8
2017 Panini National Treasures Associate Sponsor Patch Signatures 6 /1 #8
2017 Panini National Treasures Associate Sponsor Patch Signatures 7 /1 #8
2017 Panini National Treasures Associate Sponsor Patch Signatures 8 /1 #8
2017 Panini National Treasures Associate Sponsor Patch Signatures 9 /1 #8
2017 Panini National Treasures Car Manufacturer Patch Signatures /1 #8
2017 Panini National Treasures Century Black /1 #9
2017 Panini National Treasures Century Gold /15 #9
2017 Panini National Treasures Century Green /5 #9
2017 Panini National Treasures Century Holo Gold /10 #9
2017 Panini National Treasures Century Holo Silver /20 #9
2017 Panini National Treasures Century Laundry Tags /1 #9
2017 Panini National Treasures Dual Firesuit Materials /25 #18
2017 Panini National Treasures Dual Firesuit Materials Black /1 #18
2017 Panini National Treasures Dual Firesuit Materials Gold /15 #18
2017 Panini National Treasures Dual Firesuit Materials Green /5 #18
2017 Panini National Treasures Dual Firesuit Materials Holo Gold /10 #18
2017 Panini National Treasures Dual Firesuit Materials Holo Silver /20 #18
2017 Panini National Treasures Dual Firesuit Materials Laundry Tag /1 #18
2017 Panini National Treasures Dual Firesuit Materials Printing Plates Black /1 #18
2017 Panini National Treasures Dual Firesuit Materials Printing Plates Cyan /1 #18
2017 Panini National Treasures Dual Firesuit Materials Printing Plates Magenta /1 #18
2017 Panini National Treasures Dual Firesuit Materials Printing Plates Yellow /1 #18
2017 Panini National Treasures Dual Firesuit Signatures /25 #18
2017 Panini National Treasures Dual Firesuit Signatures Black /1 #18
2017 Panini National Treasures Dual Firesuit Signatures Gold /15 #18
2017 Panini National Treasures Dual Firesuit Signatures Green /5 #18
2017 Panini National Treasures Dual Firesuit Signatures Holo Gold /10 #18
2017 Panini National Treasures Dual Firesuit Signatures Holo Silver /20 #18
2017 Panini National Treasures Dual Firesuit Signatures Laundry Tag /1 #18
2017 Panini National Treasures Dual Firesuit Signatures Printing Plates Black /1 #18
2017 Panini National Treasures Dual Firesuit Signatures Printing Plates Cyan /1 #18
2017 Panini National Treasures Dual Firesuit Signatures Printing Plates Magenta /1 #18
2017 Panini National Treasures Dual Firesuit Signatures Printing Plates Yellow /1 #18
2017 Panini National Treasures Dual Sheet Metal Signatures Black /1 #2
2017 Panini National Treasures Dual Sheet Metal Signatures Green /5 #2
2017 Panini National Treasures Dual Sheet Metal Signatures Holo Gold /10 #2
2017 Panini National Treasures Dual Sheet Metal Signatures Printing Plates Black /1 #2
2017 Panini National Treasures Dual Sheet Metal Signatures Printing Plates Cyan /1 #2
2017 Panini National Treasures Dual Sheet Metal Signatures Printing Plates Magenta /1 #2
2017 Panini National Treasures Dual Sheet Metal Signatures Printing Plates Yellow /1 #2
2017 Panini National Treasures Dual Tire Signatures /25 #5
2017 Panini National Treasures Dual Tire Signatures Black /1 #5
2017 Panini National Treasures Dual Tire Signatures Gold /15 #5
2017 Panini National Treasures Dual Tire Signatures Green /5 #5
2017 Panini National Treasures Dual Tire Signatures Holo Gold /10 #5
2017 Panini National Treasures Dual Tire Signatures Printing Plates Black /1 #5
2017 Panini National Treasures Dual Tire Signatures Printing Plates Cyan /1 #5
2017 Panini National Treasures Dual Tire Signatures Printing Plates Magenta /1 #5
2017 Panini National Treasures Dual Tire Signatures Printing Plates Yellow /1 #5
2017 Panini National Treasures Firesuit Manufacturer Patch Signatures /1 #8
2017 Panini National Treasures Flag Patch Signatures /1 #8
2017 Panini National Treasures Hats Off /13 #25
2017 Panini National Treasures Hats Off Gold /2 #25
2017 Panini National Treasures Hats Off Holo Gold /5 #25
2017 Panini National Treasures Hats Off Holo Silver /1 #25
2017 Panini National Treasures Hats Off Laundry Tag /6 #25
2017 Panini National Treasures Hats Off Monster Energy Cup /13 #13
2017 Panini National Treasures Hats Off Monster Energy Cup Gold /4 #13
2017 Panini National Treasures Hats Off Monster Energy Cup Holo Gold /5 #13
2017 Panini National Treasures Hats Off Monster Energy Cup Holo Silver /1 #13
2017 Panini National Treasures Hats Off Monster Energy Cup Laundry Tag /6 #13
2017 Panini National Treasures Hats Off Monster Energy Cup New Era /1 #13
2017 Panini National Treasures Hats Off Monster Energy Cup Printing Plates Black /1 #13
2017 Panini National Treasures Hats Off Monster Energy Cup Printing Plates Cyan /1 #13
2017 Panini National Treasures Hats Off Monster Energy Cup Printing Plates Magenta /1 #13
2017 Panini National Treasures Hats Off Monster Energy Cup Printing Plates Yellow /1 #13
2017 Panini National Treasures Hats Off Monster Energy Cup Sponsor /5 #13
2017 Panini National Treasures Hats Off New Era /1 #25
2017 Panini National Treasures Hats Off Printing Plates Black /1 #25
2017 Panini National Treasures Hats Off Printing Plates Cyan /1 #25
2017 Panini National Treasures Hats Off Printing Plates Magenta /1 #25
2017 Panini National Treasures Hats Off Sponsor /5 #25
2017 Panini National Treasures Nameplate Patch Signatures /2 #8
2017 Panini National Treasures NASCAR Patch Signatures /1 #8
2017 Panini National Treasures Printing Plates Black /1 #9
2017 Panini National Treasures Printing Plates Cyan /1 #9
2017 Panini National Treasures Printing Plates Magenta /1 #9
2017 Panini National Treasures Printing Plates Yellow /1 #9
2017 Panini National Treasures Quad Material Signatures Black /1 #3
2017 Panini National Treasures Quad Material Signatures Gold /15 #3
2017 Panini National Treasures Quad Material Signatures Green /5 #3
2017 Panini National Treasures Quad Material Signatures Holo Gold /10 #3
2017 Panini National Treasures Quad Material Signatures Holo Silver /20 #3
2017 Panini National Treasures Quad Material Signatures Laundry Tag /1 #3
2017 Panini National Treasures Quad Material Signatures Printing Plates Black /1 #3
2017 Panini National Treasures Quad Material Signatures Printing Plates Cyan /1 #3
2017 Panini National Treasures Quad Material Signatures Printing Plates Magenta /1 #3
2017 Panini National Treasures Quad Material Signatures Printing Plates Yellow /1 #3
2017 Panini National Treasures Quad Materials Black /1 #6
2017 Panini National Treasures Quad Materials Green /5 #6
2017 Panini National Treasures Quad Materials Laundry Tag /1 #6
2017 Panini National Treasures Quad Materials Printing Plates Black /1 #6
2017 Panini National Treasures Quad Materials Printing Plates Cyan /1 #6
2017 Panini National Treasures Quad Materials Printing Plates Magenta /1 #6
2017 Panini National Treasures Quad Materials Printing Plates Yellow /1 #6
2017 Panini National Treasures Series Sponsor Patch Signatures /1 #8
2017 Panini National Treasures Sunoco Patch Signatures /1 #8
2017 Panini National Treasures Teammates Dual Materials /25 #8
2017 Panini National Treasures Teammates Dual Materials Black /1 #8
2017 Panini National Treasures Teammates Dual Materials Gold /15 #8
2017 Panini National Treasures Teammates Dual Materials Green /5 #8
2017 Panini National Treasures Teammates Dual Materials Holo Gold /10 #8
2017 Panini National Treasures Teammates Dual Materials Holo Silver /20 #8
2017 Panini National Treasures Teammates Dual Materials Laundry Tag /1 #8
2017 Panini National Treasures Teammates Dual Materials Printing Plates Black /1 #8
2017 Panini National Treasures Teammates Dual Materials Printing Plates Cyan /1 #8
2017 Panini National Treasures Teammates Dual Materials Printing Plates Magenta /1 #8
2017 Panini National Treasures Teammates Dual Materials Printing Plates Yellow /1 #8
2017 Panini National Treasures Teammates Quad Materials /25 #10
2017 Panini National Treasures Teammates Quad Materials Black /1 #10
2017 Panini National Treasures Teammates Quad Materials Gold /15 #10
2017 Panini National Treasures Teammates Quad Materials Green /5 #10
2017 Panini National Treasures Teammates Quad Materials Holo Gold /10 #10
2017 Panini National Treasures Teammates Quad Materials Holo Silver /20 #10
2017 Panini National Treasures Teammates Quad Materials Laundry Tag /1 #10
2017 Panini National Treasures Teammates Quad Materials Printing Plates Black /1 #10
2017 Panini National Treasures Teammates Quad Materials Printing Plates Cyan /1 #10
2017 Panini National Treasures Teammates Quad Materials Printing Plates Magenta /1 #10
2017 Panini National Treasures Teammates Quad Materials Printing Plates Yellow /1 #10
2017 Panini National Treasures Teammates Triple Materials /25 #4
2017 Panini National Treasures Teammates Triple Materials Black /1 #4
2017 Panini National Treasures Teammates Triple Materials Gold /15 #4
2017 Panini National Treasures Teammates Triple Materials Green /5 #4
2017 Panini National Treasures Teammates Triple Materials Holo Gold /10 #4
2017 Panini National Treasures Teammates Triple Materials Holo Silver /20 #4
2017 Panini National Treasures Teammates Triple Materials Laundry Tag /1 #4
2017 Panini National Treasures Teammates Triple Materials Printing Plates Black /1 #4
2017 Panini National Treasures Teammates Triple Materials Printing Plates Cyan /1 #4
2017 Panini National Treasures Teammates Triple Materials Printing Plates Magenta /1 #4
2017 Panini National Treasures Teammates Triple Materials Printing Plates Yellow /1 #4
2017 Panini Torque #3
2017 Panini Torque #63
2017 Panini Torque Artist Proof /75 #3
2017 Panini Torque Artist Proof /75 #63
2017 Panini Torque Blackout /1 #3
2017 Panini Torque Blackout /1 #63
2017 Panini Torque Blue /150 #3
2017 Panini Torque Blue /150 #63
2017 Panini Torque Claiming The Chase #10
2017 Panini Torque Claiming The Chase Gold /199 #10
2017 Panini Torque Claiming The Chase Holo Silver /99 #10
2017 Panini Torque Clear Vision #3
2017 Panini Torque Clear Vision Blue /99 #3
2017 Panini Torque Clear Vision Gold /149 #3
2017 Panini Torque Clear Vision Green /25 #3
2017 Panini Torque Clear Vision Purple /10 #3
2017 Panini Torque Clear Vision Red /49 #3
2017 Panini Torque Dual Materials /499 #1
2017 Panini Torque Dual Materials Blue /99 #1
2017 Panini Torque Dual Materials Green /25 #1
2017 Panini Torque Dual Materials Purple /10 #1
2017 Panini Torque Dual Materials Red /49 #1
2017 Panini Torque Gold #3
2017 Panini Torque Gold #63
2017 Panini Torque Holo Gold /10 #3
2017 Panini Torque Holo Gold /10 #63
2017 Panini Torque Holo Silver /25 #3
2017 Panini Torque Holo Silver /25 #63
2017 Panini Torque Horsepower Heroes #3
2017 Panini Torque Horsepower Heroes Gold /199 #3
2017 Panini Torque Horsepower Heroes Holo Silver /99 #3
2017 Panini Torque Jumbo Tire Signatures /62 #1
2017 Panini Torque Jumbo Tire Signatures Blue /50 #1
2017 Panini Torque Jumbo Tire Signatures Green /10 #1
2017 Panini Torque Jumbo Tire Signatures Purple /3 #1
2017 Panini Torque Jumbo Tire Signatures Red /25 #1
2017 Panini Torque Metal Materials /499 #1
2017 Panini Torque Metal Materials Blue /49 #1
2017 Panini Torque Metal Materials Green /10 #1
2017 Panini Torque Metal Materials Purple /5 #1
2017 Panini Torque Metal Materials Red /25 #1
2017 Panini Torque Pairings Materials /199 #3
2017 Panini Torque Pairings Materials Blue /99 #3
2017 Panini Torque Pairings Materials Green /25 #3
2017 Panini Torque Pairings Materials Purple /10 #3
2017 Panini Torque Pairings Materials Red /49 #3
2017 Panini Torque Prime Associate Sponsors Jumbo Patches /1 #1A
2017 Panini Torque Prime Associate Sponsors Jumbo Patches /1 #1B
2017 Panini Torque Prime Associate Sponsors Jumbo Patches /1 #1C
2017 Panini Torque Prime Associate Sponsors Jumbo Patches /1 #1D
2017 Panini Torque Prime Associate Sponsors Jumbo Patches /1 #1E
2017 Panini Torque Prime Associate Sponsors Jumbo Patches /1 #1F
2017 Panini Torque Prime Associate Sponsors Jumbo Patches /1 #1G
2017 Panini Torque Prime Associate Sponsors Jumbo Patches /1 #1H
2017 Panini Torque Prime Associate Sponsors Jumbo Patches /1 #1I
2017 Panini Torque Prime Associate Sponsors Jumbo Patches /1 #1J
2017 Panini Torque Prime Associate Sponsors Jumbo Patches /1 #1K
2017 Panini Torque Prime Associate Sponsors Jumbo Patches /1 #1L
2017 Panini Torque Prime Associate Sponsors Jumbo Patches /1 #1M
2017 Panini Torque Prime Associate Sponsors Jumbo Patches /1 #1N
2017 Panini Torque Prime Associate Sponsors Jumbo Patches /1 #1O
2017 Panini Torque Prime Flag Jumbo Patches /1 #1
2017 Panini Torque Prime Goodyear Jumbo Patches /1 #1
2017 Panini Torque Prime Manufacturer Jumbo Patches /1 #1
2017 Panini Torque Prime Nameplates Jumbo Patches /2 #1
2017 Panini Torque Prime NASCAR Jumbo Patches /1 #1
2017 Panini Torque Prime Series Sponsor Jumbo Patches /1 #1
2017 Panini Torque Printing Plates Black /1 #3
2017 Panini Torque Printing Plates Black /1 #63
2017 Panini Torque Printing Plates Cyan /1 #3
2017 Panini Torque Printing Plates Cyan /1 #63
2017 Panini Torque Printing Plates Magenta /1 #3
2017 Panini Torque Printing Plates Magenta /1 #63
2017 Panini Torque Printing Plates Yellow /1 #3
2017 Panini Torque Printing Plates Yellow /1 #63
2017 Panini Torque Purple /50 #3
2017 Panini Torque Purple /50 #63
2017 Panini Torque Quad Materials /75 #1
2017 Panini Torque Quad Materials Blue /50 #1
2017 Panini Torque Quad Materials Green /10 #1
2017 Panini Torque Quad Materials Purple /5 #1
2017 Panini Torque Quad Materials Red /15 #1
2017 Panini Torque Raced Relics /499 #1
2017 Panini Torque Raced Relics Blue /99 #1
2017 Panini Torque Raced Relics Green /25 #1
2017 Panini Torque Raced Relics Purple /10 #1
2017 Panini Torque Raced Relics Red /49 #1
2017 Panini Torque Red /100 #3
2017 Panini Torque Red /100 #63
2017 Panini Torque Running Order #14
2017 Panini Torque Running Order Blue /99 #14
2017 Panini Torque Running Order Checkerboard /10 #14
2017 Panini Torque Running Order Green /25 #14
2017 Panini Torque Running Order Red /49 #14
2017 Panini Torque Silhouettes Sheet Metal Signatures /62 #5
2017 Panini Torque Silhouettes Sheet Metal Signatures Blue /50 #5
2017 Panini Torque Silhouettes Sheet Metal Signatures Green /10 #5
2017 Panini Torque Silhouettes Sheet Metal Signatures Purple /3 #5
2017 Panini Torque Silhouettes Sheet Metal Signatures Red /25 #5
2017 Panini Torque Test Proof Black /1 #3
2017 Panini Torque Test Proof Black /1 #63
2017 Panini Torque Test Proof Cyan /1 #3
2017 Panini Torque Test Proof Cyan /1 #63
2017 Panini Torque Test Proof Magenta /1 #3
2017 Panini Torque Test Proof Magenta /1 #63
2017 Panini Torque Test Proof Yellow /1 #3
2017 Panini Torque Test Proof Yellow /1 #63
2017 Panini Torque Track Vision #7
2017 Panini Torque Track Vision Blue /99 #7
2017 Panini Torque Track Vision Gold /149 #7
2017 Panini Torque Track Vision Green /25 #7
2017 Panini Torque Track Vision Purple /10 #7
2017 Panini Torque Track Vision Red /49 #7
2017 Panini Torque Trackside #7
2017 Panini Torque Trackside Blue /99 #7
2017 Panini Torque Trackside Checkerboard /10 #7
2017 Panini Torque Trackside Green /25 #7
2017 Panini Torque Trackside Red /49 #7
2017 Select #62
2017 Select #63
2017 Select #108
2017 Select Prizms Black /3 #62
2017 Select Prizms Black /3 #63
2017 Select Prizms Black /3 #108
2017 Select Prizms Blue /199 #62
2017 Select Prizms Blue /199 #63
2017 Select Prizms Checkered Flag /1 #62
2017 Select Prizms Checkered Flag /1 #63
2017 Select Prizms Checkered Flag /1 #108
2017 Select Prizms Gold /10 #62
2017 Select Prizms Gold /10 #63
2017 Select Prizms Gold /10 #108
2017 Select Prizms Purple Pulsar #62
2017 Select Prizms Purple Pulsar #63
2017 Select Prizms Red /99 #62
2017 Select Prizms Red /99 #63
2017 Select Prizms Red White and Blue Pulsar /299 #62
2017 Select Prizms Red White and Blue Pulsar /299 #63
2017 Select Prizms Silver #62
2017 Select Prizms Silver #63
2017 Select Prizms Tie Dye /24 #62
2017 Select Prizms Tie Dye /24 #63
2017 Select Prizms Tie Dye /24 #108
2017 Select Prizms White /50 #62
2017 Select Prizms White /50 #63
2017 Select Prizms White /50 #108
2017 Select Select Pairs Materials #5
2017 Select Select Pairs Materials #6
2017 Select Select Pairs Materials Prizms Blue /199 #5
2017 Select Select Pairs Materials Prizms Blue /199 #6
2017 Select Select Pairs Materials Prizms Checkered Flag /1 #5
2017 Select Select Pairs Materials Prizms Checkered Flag /1 #6
2017 Select Select Pairs Materials Prizms Gold /10 #5
2017 Select Select Pairs Materials Prizms Gold /10 #6
2017 Select Select Pairs Materials Prizms Red /99 #5
2017 Select Select Pairs Materials Prizms Red /99 #6
2017 Select Select Stars #17
2017 Select Select Stars Prizms Black /3 #17
2017 Select Select Stars Prizms Checkered Flag /1 #17
2017 Select Select Stars Prizms Gold /10 #17
2017 Select Select Stars Prizms Tie Dye /24 #17
2017 Select Select Stars Prizms White /50 #17
2017 Select Select Swatches #3
2017 Select Select Swatches Prizms Blue /199 #3
2017 Select Select Swatches Prizms Checkered Flag /1 #3
2017 Select Select Swatches Prizms Gold /10 #3
2017 Select Select Swatches Prizms Red /99 #3
2017 Select Sheet Metal #1
2017 Select Sheet Metal Prizms Blue /199 #1
2017 Select Sheet Metal Prizms Checkered Flag /1 #1
2017 Select Sheet Metal Prizms Gold /10 #1
2017 Select Sheet Metal Prizms Red /99 #1
2017 Select Signature Paint Schemes #18
2017 Select Signature Paint Schemes Prizms Blue /15 #18
2017 Select Signature Paint Schemes Prizms Checkered Flag /1 #18
2017 Select Signature Paint Schemes Prizms Gold /5 #18
2017 Select Signature Paint Schemes Prizms Red /10 #18
2017 Select Signature Swatches #3
2017 Select Signature Swatches Prizms Checkered Flag /1 #3
2017 Select Signature Swatches Prizms Gold /10 #3
2017 Select Signature Swatches Prizms Tie Dye /24 #3
2017 Select Signature Swatches Prizms White /50 #3
2017 Select Signature Swatches Triple #3
2017 Select Signature Swatches Triple Prizms Checkered Flag /1 #3
2017 Select Signature Swatches Triple Prizms Gold /10 #3
2017 Select Signature Swatches Triple Prizms Tie Dye /24 #3
2017 Select Signature Swatches Triple Prizms White /50 #3
2017 Select Speed Merchants #13
2017 Select Speed Merchants Prizms Black /3 #13
2017 Select Speed Merchants Prizms Checkered Flag /1 #13
2017 Select Speed Merchants Prizms Gold /10 #13
2017 Select Speed Merchants Prizms Tie Dye /24 #13
2017 Select Speed Merchants Prizms White /50 #13
2018 Certified #30
2018 Certified #97
2018 Certified All Certified Team /199 #14
2018 Certified All Certified Team Black /1 #14
2018 Certified All Certified Team Blue /99 #14
2018 Certified All Certified Team Gold /49 #14
2018 Certified All Certified Team Green /10 #14
2018 Certified All Certified Team Mirror Black /1 #14
2018 Certified All Certified Team Mirror Gold /25 #14
2018 Certified All Certified Team Mirror Green /5 #14
2018 Certified All Certified Team Mirror Purple /10 #14
2018 Certified All Certified Team Purple /25 #14
2018 Certified All Certified Team Red /149 #14
2018 Certified Black /1 #30
2018 Certified Black /1 #97
2018 Certified Blue /99 #30
2018 Certified Blue /99 #97
2018 Certified Cup Swatches /499 #3
2018 Certified Cup Swatches Black /1 #3
2018 Certified Cup Swatches Blue /49 #3
2018 Certified Cup Swatches Gold /25 #3
2018 Certified Cup Swatches Green /5 #3
2018 Certified Cup Swatches Purple /10 #3
2018 Certified Cup Swatches Red /199 #3
2018 Certified Epix /199 #4
2018 Certified Epix Black /1 #4
2018 Certified Epix Blue /99 #4
2018 Certified Epix Gold /49 #4
2018 Certified Epix Green /10 #4
2018 Certified Epix Mirror Black /1 #4
2018 Certified Epix Mirror Gold /25 #4
2018 Certified Epix Mirror Green /5 #4
2018 Certified Epix Mirror Purple /10 #4
2018 Certified Epix Purple /25 #4
2018 Certified Epix Red /149 #4
2018 Certified Fresh Faces /199 #14
2018 Certified Fresh Faces Black /1 #14
2018 Certified Fresh Faces Blue /99 #14
2018 Certified Fresh Faces Gold /49 #14
2018 Certified Fresh Faces Green /10 #14
2018 Certified Fresh Faces Mirror Black /1 #14
2018 Certified Fresh Faces Mirror Gold /25 #14
2018 Certified Fresh Faces Mirror Green /5 #14
2018 Certified Fresh Faces Mirror Purple /10 #14
2018 Certified Fresh Faces Purple /25 #14
2018 Certified Fresh Faces Red /149 #14
2018 Certified Fresh Faces Signatures /25 #2
2018 Certified Fresh Faces Signatures Black /1 #2
2018 Certified Fresh Faces Signatures Blue /15 #2
2018 Certified Fresh Faces Signatures Gold /10 #2
2018 Certified Fresh Faces Signatures Green /3 #2
2018 Certified Fresh Faces Signatures Purple /5 #2
2018 Certified Fresh Faces Signatures Red /20 #2
2018 Certified Gold /49 #30
2018 Certified Gold /49 #97
2018 Certified Green /10 #30
2018 Certified Green /10 #97
2018 Certified Mirror Black /1 #30
2018 Certified Mirror Black /1 #97
2018 Certified Mirror Gold /25 #30
2018 Certified Mirror Gold /25 #97
2018 Certified Mirror Green /5 #30
2018 Certified Mirror Green /5 #97
2018 Certified Mirror Purple /10 #30
2018 Certified Mirror Purple /10 #97
2018 Certified Orange /249 #30

2018 Certified Orange /249 #97
2018 Certified Purple /25 #30
2018 Certified Purple /25 #97
2018 Certified Red /199 #30
2018 Certified Red /199 #97
2018 Certified Signature Swatches /49 #3
2018 Certified Signature Swatches Black /1 #3
2018 Certified Signature Swatches Blue /20 #3
2018 Certified Signature Swatches Gold /15 #3
2018 Certified Signature Swatches Green /5 #3
2018 Certified Signature Swatches Purple /10 #3
2018 Certified Signature Swatches Red /25 #3
2018 Certified Skills /199 #2
2018 Certified Skills Black /1 #2
2018 Certified Skills Blue /99 #2
2018 Certified Skills Gold /49 #2
2018 Certified Skills Green /10 #2
2018 Certified Skills Mirror Black /1 #2
2018 Certified Skills Mirror Gold /25 #2
2018 Certified Skills Mirror Green /5 #2
2018 Certified Skills Mirror Purple /10 #2
2018 Certified Skills Purple /25 #2
2018 Certified Skills Red /149 #2
2018 Certified Stars /199 #4
2018 Certified Stars Black /1 #4
2018 Certified Stars Blue /99 #4
2018 Certified Stars Gold /49 #4
2018 Certified Stars Green /10 #4
2018 Certified Stars Mirror Black /1 #4
2018 Certified Stars Mirror Gold /25 #4
2018 Certified Stars Mirror Green /5 #4
2018 Certified Stars Mirror Purple /10 #4
2018 Certified Stars Purple /25 #4
2018 Certified Stars Red /149 #4
2018 Donruss #6
2018 Donruss #33A
2018 Donruss #93
2018 Donruss #123
2018 Donruss #33B
2018 Donruss Artist Proofs /25 #6
2018 Donruss Artist Proofs /25 #33A
2018 Donruss Artist Proofs /25 #93
2018 Donruss Artist Proofs /25 #123
2018 Donruss Artist Proofs /25 #33B
2018 Donruss Gold Foil /499 #6
2018 Donruss Gold Foil /499 #33A
2018 Donruss Gold Foil /499 #93
2018 Donruss Gold Foil /499 #123
2018 Donruss Gold Foil /499 #33B
2018 Donruss Gold Press Proofs /99 #6
2018 Donruss Gold Press Proofs /99 #33A
2018 Donruss Gold Press Proofs /99 #93
2018 Donruss Gold Press Proofs /99 #123
2018 Donruss Gold Press Proofs /99 #33B
2018 Donruss Green Foil /199 #6
2018 Donruss Green Foil /199 #33A
2018 Donruss Green Foil /199 #93
2018 Donruss Green Foil /199 #123
2018 Donruss Green Foil /199 #33B
2018 Donruss Press Proofs /49 #6
2018 Donruss Press Proofs /49 #33A
2018 Donruss Press Proofs /49 #93
2018 Donruss Press Proofs /49 #123
2018 Donruss Press Proofs /49 #33B
2018 Donruss Printing Plates Black /1 #6
2018 Donruss Printing Plates Black /1 #33
2018 Donruss Printing Plates Black /1 #93
2018 Donruss Printing Plates Black /1 #123
2018 Donruss Printing Plates Black /1 #33B
2018 Donruss Printing Plates Cyan /1 #6
2018 Donruss Printing Plates Cyan /1 #33
2018 Donruss Printing Plates Cyan /1 #93
2018 Donruss Printing Plates Cyan /1 #123
2018 Donruss Printing Plates Cyan /1 #33B
2018 Donruss Printing Plates Magenta /1 #6
2018 Donruss Printing Plates Magenta /1 #33
2018 Donruss Printing Plates Magenta /1 #93
2018 Donruss Printing Plates Magenta /1 #123
2018 Donruss Printing Plates Magenta /1 #33B
2018 Donruss Printing Plates Yellow /1 #6
2018 Donruss Printing Plates Yellow /1 #33
2018 Donruss Printing Plates Yellow /1 #93
2018 Donruss Printing Plates Yellow /1 #123
2018 Donruss Printing Plates Yellow /1 #33B
2018 Donruss Racing Relics #3
2018 Donruss Racing Relics Black /10 #3
2018 Donruss Racing Relics Holo Gold /99 #3
2018 Donruss Red Foil /299 #6
2018 Donruss Red Foil /299 #33A
2018 Donruss Red Foil /299 #93
2018 Donruss Red Foil /299 #123
2018 Donruss Red Foil /299 #33B
2018 Donruss Rubber Relics #5
2018 Donruss Rubber Relics Black /10 #5
2018 Donruss Rubber Relics Holo Gold /99 #5
2018 Donruss Studio Signatures #3
2018 Donruss Studio Signatures Black /1 #3
2018 Donruss Studio Signatures Holo Gold /25 #3
2018 Panini Black Friday VIP Gems /5 #AD
2018 Panini Black Friday VIP Gems Autographs /1 #AD
2018 Panini Black Friday VIP Gems One of One /1 #AD
2018 Panini Father's Day Panini Collection /399 #12
2018 Panini Father's Day Panini Collection Autographs #12
2018 Panini Father's Day Panini Collection Checkerboard /5 #12
2018 Panini Father's Day Panini Collection Crystal Shards /10 #12
2018 Panini Father's Day Panini Collection Escher Squares /25 #12
2018 Panini Father's Day Panini Collection Future Frames /50 #12
2018 Panini Father's Day Panini Collection Hyperplaid /1 #12
2018 Panini Father's Day Racing Memorabilia #AD
2018 Panini Father's Day Racing Memorabilia Checkerboard /10 #AD
2018 Panini Father's Day Racing Memorabilia Cracked Ice /25 #AD
2018 Panini Father's Day Racing Memorabilia Escher Squares /5 #AD
2018 Panini Father's Day Racing Memorabilia Hyperplaid /1 #AD
2018 Panini National Convention #72
2018 Panini National Convention Escher Squares /25 #72
2018 Panini National Convention Galatic Windows /5 #72
2018 Panini National Convention Hyperplaid /1 #72
2018 Panini National Convention Magnetic Fur /99 #72
2018 Panini National Convention Pyramids /10 #72
2018 Panini National Convention Rainbow Spokes /49 #72
2018 Panini Prime /50 #17
2018 Panini Prime /50 #50
2018 Panini Prime /50 #83
2018 Panini Prime Autograph Materials /50 #3
2018 Panini Prime Autograph Materials Black /1 #3
2018 Panini Prime Autograph Materials Holo Gold /25 #3
2018 Panini Prime Autograph Materials Laundry Tag /1 #3
2018 Panini Prime Black /1 #17
2018 Panini Prime Black /1 #50
2018 Panini Prime Black /1 #83
2018 Panini Prime Clear Silhouettes /99 #2
2018 Panini Prime Clear Silhouettes Black /1 #2
2018 Panini Prime Clear Silhouettes Dual /99 #2
2018 Panini Prime Clear Silhouettes Dual Black /1 #2
2018 Panini Prime Clear Silhouettes Dual Holo Gold /50 #2
2018 Panini Prime Clear Silhouettes Holo Gold /50 #2
2018 Panini Prime Driver Signatures /99 #11
2018 Panini Prime Driver Signatures Black /1 #11
2018 Panini Prime Driver Signatures Holo Gold /25 #11
2018 Panini Prime Dual Material Autographs /50 #3
2018 Panini Prime Dual Material Autographs Black /1 #3
2018 Panini Prime Dual Material Autographs Holo Gold /25 #3
2018 Panini Prime Dual Material Autographs Laundry Tag /1 #3
2018 Panini Prime Dual Signatures /50 #15
2018 Panini Prime Dual Signatures Black /1 #15
2018 Panini Prime Dual Signatures Holo Gold /25 #15
2018 Panini Prime Hats Off Button /1 #1
2018 Panini Prime Hats Off Eyelet /6 #1
2018 Panini Prime Hats Off Headband /36 #1
2018 Panini Prime Hats Off Laundry Tag /1 #1
2018 Panini Prime Hats Off New Era /1 #1
2018 Panini Prime Hats Off Number /2 #1
2018 Panini Prime Hats Off Sponsor Logo /3 #1
2018 Panini Prime Hats Off Team Logo /2 #1
2018 Panini Prime Holo Gold /25 #17
2018 Panini Prime Holo Gold /25 #50
2018 Panini Prime Holo Gold /25 #83
2018 Panini Prime Prime Jumbo Associate Sponsor 1 /1 #3
2018 Panini Prime Prime Jumbo Associate Sponsor 10 /1 #3
2018 Panini Prime Prime Jumbo Associate Sponsor 11 /1 #3
2018 Panini Prime Prime Jumbo Associate Sponsor 2 /1 #3
2018 Panini Prime Prime Jumbo Associate Sponsor 3 /1 #3
2018 Panini Prime Prime Jumbo Associate Sponsor 4 /1 #3
2018 Panini Prime Prime Jumbo Associate Sponsor 5 /1 #3
2018 Panini Prime Prime Jumbo Associate Sponsor 6 /1 #3
2018 Panini Prime Prime Jumbo Associate Sponsor 7 /1 #3
2018 Panini Prime Prime Jumbo Associate Sponsor 8 /1 #3
2018 Panini Prime Prime Jumbo Associate Sponsor 9 /1 #3
2018 Panini Prime Prime Jumbo Car Manufacturer /1 #3
2018 Panini Prime Prime Jumbo Firesuit Manufacturer /1 #3
2018 Panini Prime Prime Jumbo Flag Patch /1 #3
2018 Panini Prime Prime Jumbo Glove Manufacturer Patch /1 #3
2018 Panini Prime Prime Jumbo Glove Name Patch /1 #3
2018 Panini Prime Prime Jumbo Glove Number Patch /1 #3
2018 Panini Prime Prime Jumbo Goodyear /1 #3
2018 Panini Prime Prime Jumbo Nameplate /2 #3
2018 Panini Prime Prime Jumbo NASCAR /1 #3
2018 Panini Prime Prime Jumbo Prime Colors /14 #3
2018 Panini Prime Prime Jumbo Series Sponsor /1 #3
2018 Panini Prime Prime Jumbo Shoe Brand Logo /1 #3
2018 Panini Prime Prime Jumbo Shoe Name Patch /1 #3
2018 Panini Prime Prime Jumbo Sunoco /1 #3
2018 Panini Prime Prime Number Signatures /99 #1
2018 Panini Prime Prime Number Signatures Black /1 #1
2018 Panini Prime Prime Number Signatures Holo Gold /25 #1
2018 Panini Prime Quad Material Autographs /50 #3
2018 Panini Prime Quad Material Autographs Black /1 #3
2018 Panini Prime Quad Material Autographs Holo Gold /41 #3
2018 Panini Prime Quad Material Autographs Laundry Tag /1 #3
2018 Panini Prime Race Used Duals Firesuit /50 #3
2018 Panini Prime Race Used Duals Firesuit Black /1 #3
2018 Panini Prime Race Used Duals Firesuit Holo Gold /25 #3
2018 Panini Prime Race Used Duals Firesuit Laundry Tag /1 #3
2018 Panini Prime Race Used Duals Sheet Metal /50 #3
2018 Panini Prime Race Used Duals Sheet Metal Black /1 #3
2018 Panini Prime Race Used Duals Sheet Metal Holo Gold /25 #3
2018 Panini Prime Race Used Duals Tire /50 #3
2018 Panini Prime Race Used Duals Tire Black /1 #3
2018 Panini Prime Race Used Duals Tire Holo Gold /25 #3
2018 Panini Prime Race Used Firesuits Black /1 #2
2018 Panini Prime Race Used Firesuits Holo Gold /25 #2
2018 Panini Prime Race Used Firesuits Laundry Tag /1 #2
2018 Panini Prime Race Used Sheet Metal /50 #2
2018 Panini Prime Race Used Sheet Metal Black /1 #2
2018 Panini Prime Race Used Sheet Metal Holo Gold /25 #2
2018 Panini Prime Race Used Tires Black /1 #2
2018 Panini Prime Race Used Tires Holo Gold /25 #2
2018 Panini Prime Shadowbox Signatures /99 #14
2018 Panini Prime Shadowbox Signatures Black /1 #14
2018 Panini Prime Shadowbox Signatures Holo Gold /25 #14
2018 Panini Prime Triple Material Autographs /50 #10
2018 Panini Prime Triple Material Autographs Black /1 #10
2018 Panini Prime Triple Material Autographs Holo Gold /25 #10
2018 Panini Prime Triple Material Autographs Laundry Tag /1 #10
2018 Panini Prizm #20
2018 Panini Prizm Autographs Prizms #33
2018 Panini Prizm Autographs Prizms Black /1 #33
2018 Panini Prizm Autographs Prizms Blue /35 #33
2018 Panini Prizm Autographs Prizms Camo #33
2018 Panini Prizm Autographs Prizms Gold /10 #33
2018 Panini Prizm Autographs Prizms Green /50 #33
2018 Panini Prizm Autographs Prizms Rainbow /24 #33
2018 Panini Prizm Autographs Prizms Red /25 #33
2018 Panini Prizm Autographs Prizms Red White and Blue /75 #33
2018 Panini Prizm Autographs Prizms White /5 #33
2018 Panini Prizm Fireworks #10
2018 Panini Prizm Fireworks Prizms #10
2018 Panini Prizm Fireworks Prizms Black /1 #10
2018 Panini Prizm Fireworks Prizms Gold /10 #10
2018 Panini Prizm National Pride #9
2018 Panini Prizm National Pride Prizms #9
2018 Panini Prizm National Pride Prizms Black /1 #9
2018 Panini Prizm National Pride Prizms Gold /10 #9
2018 Panini Prizm Prizms #20
2018 Panini Prizm Prizms Black /1 #20
2018 Panini Prizm Prizms Blue /99 #20
2018 Panini Prizm Prizms Camo #20
2018 Panini Prizm Prizms Gold /10 #20
2018 Panini Prizm Prizms Green /149 #20
2018 Panini Prizm Prizms Purple Flash #20
2018 Panini Prizm Prizms Rainbow /24 #20
2018 Panini Prizm Prizms Red /75 #20
2018 Panini Prizm Prizms Red White and Blue #20
2018 Panini Prizm Prizms White /5 #20
2018 Panini Prizm Stars and Stripes #2
2018 Panini Prizm Stars and Stripes Prizms #2
2018 Panini Prizm Stars and Stripes Prizms Black /1 #2
2018 Panini Prizm Stars and Stripes Prizms Gold /10 #2
2018 Panini Victory Lane #3
2018 Panini Victory Lane Black /1 #3
2018 Panini Victory Lane Blue /25 #3
2018 Panini Victory Lane Celebrations #14
2018 Panini Victory Lane Celebrations Black /1 #14
2018 Panini Victory Lane Celebrations Blue /25 #14
2018 Panini Victory Lane Celebrations Gold /99 #14
2018 Panini Victory Lane Celebrations Green /5 #14
2018 Panini Victory Lane Celebrations Printing Plates Black /1 #14
2018 Panini Victory Lane Celebrations Printing Plates Cyan /1 #14
2018 Panini Victory Lane Celebrations Printing Plates Magenta /1 #14
2018 Panini Victory Lane Celebrations Printing Plates Yellow /1 #14
2018 Panini Victory Lane Celebrations Red /49 #14
2018 Panini Victory Lane Gold /99 #3
2018 Panini Victory Lane Green /5 #3
2018 Panini Victory Lane Octane Autographs /125 #4
2018 Panini Victory Lane Octane Autographs Black /1 #4
2018 Panini Victory Lane Octane Autographs Gold /99 #4
2018 Panini Victory Lane Pedal to the Metal #4
2018 Panini Victory Lane Pedal to the Metal #53
2018 Panini Victory Lane Pedal to the Metal Black /1 #4
2018 Panini Victory Lane Pedal to the Metal Black /1 #53
2018 Panini Victory Lane Pedal to the Metal Blue /25 #4
2018 Panini Victory Lane Pedal to the Metal Blue /25 #53
2018 Panini Victory Lane Pedal to the Metal Green /5 #4
2018 Panini Victory Lane Pedal to the Metal Green /5 #53
2018 Panini Victory Lane Printing Plates Black /1 #3
2018 Panini Victory Lane Printing Plates Cyan /1 #3
2018 Panini Victory Lane Printing Plates Magenta /1 #3
2018 Panini Victory Lane Printing Plates Yellow /1 #3
2018 Panini Victory Lane Red /49 #3
2018 Panini Victory Lane Silver #3
2018 Panini Victory Lane Starting Grid #3
2018 Panini Victory Lane Starting Grid Black /1 #3
2018 Panini Victory Lane Starting Grid Blue /25 #3
2018 Panini Victory Lane Starting Grid Gold /99 #3
2018 Panini Victory Lane Starting Grid Green /5 #3
2018 Panini Victory Lane Starting Grid Printing Plates Black /1 #3
2018 Panini Victory Lane Starting Grid Printing Plates Cyan /1 #3
2018 Panini Victory Lane Starting Grid Printing Plates Magenta /1 #3
2018 Panini Victory Lane Starting Grid Printing Plates Yellow /1 #3
2018 Panini Victory Lane Starting Grid Red /49 #3
2018 Panini Victory Lane Victory Lane Prime Patches Associate Sponsor 1 /1 #23
2018 Panini Victory Lane Victory Lane Prime Patches Associate Sponsor 10 /1 #23
2018 Panini Victory Lane Victory Lane Prime Patches Associate Sponsor 2 /1 #23
2018 Panini Victory Lane Victory Lane Prime Patches Associate Sponsor 3 /1 #23
2018 Panini Victory Lane Victory Lane Prime Patches Associate Sponsor 4 /1 #23
2018 Panini Victory Lane Victory Lane Prime Patches Associate Sponsor 5 /1 #23
2018 Panini Victory Lane Victory Lane Prime Patches Associate Sponsor 6 /1 #23
2018 Panini Victory Lane Victory Lane Prime Patches Associate Sponsor 7 /1 #23
2018 Panini Victory Lane Victory Lane Prime Patches Associate Sponsor 8 /1 #23
2018 Panini Victory Lane Victory Lane Prime Patches Associate Sponsor 9 /1 #23
2018 Panini Victory Lane Victory Lane Prime Patches Car Manufacturer /1 #23
2018 Panini Victory Lane Victory Lane Prime Patches Firesuit Manufacturer /1 #23
2018 Panini Victory Lane Victory Lane Prime Patches Nameplate /2 #23
2018 Panini Victory Lane Victory Lane Prime Patches NASCAR /1 #23
2018 Panini Victory Lane Victory Lane Prime Patches Series Sponsor /1 #23
2018 Panini Victory Lane Victory Lane Prime Patches Sunoco /1 #23
2019 Donruss #73
2019 Donruss #95
2019 Donruss #118
2019 Donruss Action #7
2019 Donruss Action Cracked Ice /25 #7
2019 Donruss Action Holographic #7
2019 Donruss Action Xplosion /10 #7
2019 Donruss Artist Proofs /25 #73
2019 Donruss Artist Proofs /25 #95
2019 Donruss Artist Proofs /25 #118
2019 Donruss Black /199 #73
2019 Donruss Black /199 #95
2019 Donruss Black /199 #118
2019 Donruss Classics #18
2019 Donruss Classics Cracked Ice /25 #18
2019 Donruss Classics Holographic #18
2019 Donruss Classics Xplosion /10 #18
2019 Donruss Contenders #10
2019 Donruss Contenders Cracked Ice /25 #10
2019 Donruss Contenders Holographic #10
2019 Donruss Contenders Xplosion /10 #10
2019 Donruss Gold /299 #73
2019 Donruss Gold /299 #95
2019 Donruss Gold /299 #118
2019 Donruss Gold Press Proofs /99 #73
2019 Donruss Gold Press Proofs /99 #95
2019 Donruss Gold Press Proofs /99 #118
2019 Donruss Optic #23
2019 Donruss Optic #67
2019 Donruss Optic Blue Pulsar #23
2019 Donruss Optic Blue Pulsar /1 #67
2019 Donruss Optic Gold /10 #23
2019 Donruss Optic Gold /10 #67
2019 Donruss Optic Gold Vinyl /1 #23
2019 Donruss Optic Gold Vinyl /1 #67
2019 Donruss Optic Holo #23
2019 Donruss Optic Holo #67
2019 Donruss Optic Red Wave #23
2019 Donruss Optic Red Wave /1 #67
2019 Donruss Optic Signatures Gold Vinyl /1 #67
2019 Donruss Optic Signatures Gold Vinyl /1 #23
2019 Donruss Optic Signatures Holo /75 #23
2019 Donruss Optic Signatures Holo /75 #67
2019 Donruss Originals #12
2019 Donruss Originals Cracked Ice /25 #12
2019 Donruss Originals Holographic #12
2019 Donruss Originals Xplosion /10 #12
2019 Donruss Press Proofs /49 #73
2019 Donruss Press Proofs /49 #95
2019 Donruss Press Proofs /49 #118
2019 Donruss Printing Plates Black /1 #73
2019 Donruss Printing Plates Black /1 #95
2019 Donruss Printing Plates Black /1 #118
2019 Donruss Printing Plates Cyan /1 #73
2019 Donruss Printing Plates Cyan /1 #95
2019 Donruss Printing Plates Cyan /1 #118
2019 Donruss Printing Plates Magenta /1 #73
2019 Donruss Printing Plates Magenta /1 #95
2019 Donruss Printing Plates Magenta /1 #118
2019 Donruss Printing Plates Yellow /1 #73
2019 Donruss Printing Plates Yellow /1 #95
2019 Donruss Printing Plates Yellow /1 #118
2019 Donruss Retro Relics '86 #4
2019 Donruss Retro Relics '86 Holo Black /10 #4
2019 Donruss Retro Relics '86 Holo Gold /25 #4
2019 Donruss Retro Relics '86 Red /225 #4
2019 Donruss Signature Series #3
2019 Donruss Signature Series Holo Black /10 #3
2019 Donruss Signature Series Holo Gold /25 #3
2019 Donruss Signature Series Red /99 #3
2019 Donruss Silver #73
2019 Donruss Silver #95
2019 Donruss Silver #118
2019 Donruss Top Tier #10
2019 Donruss Top Tier Cracked Ice /25 #10
2019 Donruss Top Tier Holographic #10
2019 Donruss Top Tier Xplosion /10 #10
2019 Panini National Convention NASCAR #R8
2019 Panini National Convention NASCAR Galatic Windows /25 #R8
2019 Panini National Convention NASCAR HyperPlaid /1 #R8
2019 Panini Prime /50 #3
2019 Panini Prime /50 #37
2019 Panini Prime /50 #70
2019 Panini Prime Autograph Materials /50 #23
2019 Panini Prime Autograph Materials Black /3 #23
2019 Panini Prime Autograph Materials Holo Gold /10 #23
2019 Panini Prime Autograph Materials Platinum Blue /1 #23
2019 Panini Prime Black /10 #3
2019 Panini Prime Black /10 #37
2019 Panini Prime Black /10 #70
2019 Panini Prime Clear Silhouettes /99 #7
2019 Panini Prime Clear Silhouettes Black /10 #7
2019 Panini Prime Clear Silhouettes Holo Gold /25 #7
2019 Panini Prime Clear Silhouettes Platinum Blue /1 #7
2019 Panini Prime Clear Vision Signatures /25 #4
2019 Panini Prime Clear Vision Signatures Black /3 #4
2019 Panini Prime Clear Vision Signatures Holo Gold /10 #4
2019 Panini Prime Clear Vision Signatures Platinum Blue /1 #4
2019 Panini Prime Dual Material Autographs /50 #22
2019 Panini Prime Dual Material Autographs Black /3 #22
2019 Panini Prime Dual Material Autographs Holo Gold /10 #22
2019 Panini Prime Dual Material Autographs Laundry Tags /1 #22
2019 Panini Prime Emerald /5 #3
2019 Panini Prime Emerald /5 #37
2019 Panini Prime Emerald /5 #70
2019 Panini Prime Hats Off Button /1 #10
2019 Panini Prime Hats Off Eyelets /4 #10
2019 Panini Prime Hats Off Headband /18 #10
2019 Panini Prime Hats Off Laundry Tags /3 #10
2019 Panini Prime Hats Off New Era /1 #10
2019 Panini Prime Hats Off Number /4 #10
2019 Panini Prime Hats Off Sponsor Logo /5 #10
2019 Panini Prime Hats Off Team Logo /2 #10
2019 Panini Prime Jumbo Material Signatures Firesuit /3 #3
2019 Panini Prime Jumbo Material Signatures Firesuit Platinum Blue /1 #3
2019 Panini Prime Jumbo Material Signatures Sheet Metal /10 #3
2019 Panini Prime Jumbo Material Signatures Tire /50 #3
2019 Panini Prime NASCAR Shadowbox Signatures Car Number /50 #8
2019 Panini Prime NASCAR Shadowbox Signatures Manufacturer /3 #8
2019 Panini Prime NASCAR Shadowbox Signatures Sponsor /10 #8
2019 Panini Prime NASCAR Shadowbox Signatures Team Owner /1 #8
2019 Panini Prime Platinum Blue /1 #3
2019 Panini Prime Platinum Blue /1 #37
2019 Panini Prime Platinum Blue /1 #70
2019 Panini Prime Prime Cars Die Cut Signatures /25 #3
2019 Panini Prime Prime Cars Die Cut Signatures Black /3 #3
2019 Panini Prime Prime Cars Die Cut Signatures Holo Gold /10 #3
2019 Panini Prime Prime Cars Die Cut Signatures Platinum Blue /1 #3
2019 Panini Prime Prime Jumbo Associate Sponsor 1 /1 #3
2019 Panini Prime Prime Jumbo Associate Sponsor 10 /1 #3
2019 Panini Prime Prime Jumbo Associate Sponsor 11 /1 #3
2019 Panini Prime Prime Jumbo Associate Sponsor 2 /1 #3
2019 Panini Prime Prime Jumbo Associate Sponsor 3 /1 #3
2019 Panini Prime Prime Jumbo Associate Sponsor 4 /1 #3
2019 Panini Prime Prime Jumbo Associate Sponsor 5 /1 #3
2019 Panini Prime Prime Jumbo Associate Sponsor 6 /1 #3
2019 Panini Prime Prime Jumbo Associate Sponsor 7 /1 #3
2019 Panini Prime Prime Jumbo Associate Sponsor 8 /1 #3
2019 Panini Prime Prime Jumbo Associate Sponsor 9 /1 #3
2019 Panini Prime Prime Jumbo Car Manufacturer /1 #3
2019 Panini Prime Prime Jumbo Firesuit Manufacturer /1 #3
2019 Panini Prime Prime Jumbo Flag Patch /1 #3
2019 Panini Prime Prime Jumbo Glove Manufacturer Patch /1 #3
2019 Panini Prime Prime Jumbo Glove Name Patch /1 #3
2019 Panini Prime Prime Jumbo Glove Number Patch /1 #3
2019 Panini Prime Prime Jumbo Goodyear /1 #3
2019 Panini Prime Prime Jumbo Nameplate /2 #3
2019 Panini Prime Prime Jumbo Prime Colors /8 #3
2019 Panini Prime Prime Jumbo Series Sponsor /1 #3
2019 Panini Prime Prime Jumbo Shoe Brand Logo /1 #3
2019 Panini Prime Prime Jumbo Shoe Name Patch /1 #3
2019 Panini Prime Quad Materials Autographs /50 #3
2019 Panini Prime Quad Materials Autographs Black /3 #3
2019 Panini Prime Quad Materials Autographs Holo Gold /10 #3
2019 Panini Prime Quad Materials Autographs Laundry Tags /1 #3
2019 Panini Prime Race Used Duals Firesuits /50 #8
2019 Panini Prime Race Used Duals Firesuits Black /10 #8
2019 Panini Prime Race Used Duals Firesuits Holo Gold /25 #8
2019 Panini Prime Race Used Duals Firesuits Laundry Tags /1 #8
2019 Panini Prime Race Used Duals Sheet Metal /50 #8
2019 Panini Prime Race Used Duals Sheet Metal Black /10 #8
2019 Panini Prime Race Used Duals Sheet Metal Holo Gold /25 #8
2019 Panini Prime Race Used Duals Sheet Metal Platinum Blue /1 #8
2019 Panini Prime Race Used Duals Tires /50 #8
2019 Panini Prime Race Used Duals Tires Black /10 #8
2019 Panini Prime Race Used Duals Tires Holo Gold /25 #8
2019 Panini Prime Race Used Duals Tires Platinum Blue /1 #8
2019 Panini Prime Race Used Firesuits /50 #8
2019 Panini Prime Race Used Firesuits Black /10 #8
2019 Panini Prime Race Used Firesuits Holo Gold /25 #8
2019 Panini Prime Race Used Firesuits Laundry Tags /1 #8
2019 Panini Prime Race Used Quads Firesuits /50 #4
2019 Panini Prime Race Used Quads Firesuits Black /10 #4
2019 Panini Prime Race Used Quads Firesuits Holo Gold /25 #4
2019 Panini Prime Race Used Quads Firesuits Laundry Tags /1 #4
2019 Panini Prime Race Used Quads Sheet Metal /50 #4
2019 Panini Prime Race Used Quads Sheet Metal Black /10 #4
2019 Panini Prime Race Used Quads Sheet Metal Holo Gold /25 #4
2019 Panini Prime Race Used Quads Sheet Metal Platinum Blue /1 #4
2019 Panini Prime Race Used Quads Tires /50 #4
2019 Panini Prime Race Used Quads Tires Black /10 #4
2019 Panini Prime Race Used Quads Tires Holo Gold /25 #4
2019 Panini Prime Race Used Quads Tires Platinum Blue /1 #4
2019 Panini Prime Race Used Sheet Metal /50 #8
2019 Panini Prime Race Used Sheet Metal Black /10 #8
2019 Panini Prime Race Used Sheet Metal Holo Gold /25 #8
2019 Panini Prime Race Used Sheet Metal Platinum Blue /1 #8
2019 Panini Prime Race Used Tires /50 #8
2019 Panini Prime Race Used Tires Black /10 #8
2019 Panini Prime Race Used Tires Holo Gold /25 #8
2019 Panini Prime Race Used Tires Platinum Blue /1 #8
2019 Panini Prime Race Used Trios Firesuits /50 #8
2019 Panini Prime Race Used Trios Firesuits Black /10 #8
2019 Panini Prime Race Used Trios Firesuits Holo Gold /25 #8
2019 Panini Prime Race Used Trios Firesuits Laundry Tags /1 #8
2019 Panini Prime Race Used Trios Sheet Metal /50 #8
2019 Panini Prime Race Used Trios Sheet Metal Black /10 #8
2019 Panini Prime Race Used Trios Sheet Metal Holo Gold /25 #8
2019 Panini Prime Race Used Trios Sheet Metal Platinum Blue /1 #8
2019 Panini Prime Race Used Trios Tires /50 #8
2019 Panini Prime Race Used Trios Tires Black /10 #8
2019 Panini Prime Race Used Trios Tires Holo Gold /25 #8
2019 Panini Prime Race Used Trios Tires Platinum Blue /1 #8
2019 Panini Prime Timeline Signatures /25 #11
2019 Panini Prime Timeline Signatures Manufacturer /1 #11
2019 Panini Prime Timeline Signatures Name /10 #11
2019 Panini Prime Timeline Signatures Sponsor /3 #11
2019 Panini Prizm #3A
2019 Panini Prizm #78
2019 Panini Prizm #3B
2019 Panini Prizm Fireworks #1
2019 Panini Prizm Fireworks Prizms #1
2019 Panini Prizm Fireworks Prizms Black /1 #1
2019 Panini Prizm Fireworks Prizms Gold /10 #1
2019 Panini Prizm Fireworks Prizms White Sparkle #1
2019 Panini Prizm In the Groove #12
2019 Panini Prizm In the Groove Prizms #12
2019 Panini Prizm In the Groove Prizms Black /1 #12
2019 Panini Prizm In the Groove Prizms Gold /10 #12
2019 Panini Prizm In the Groove Prizms White Sparkle #12
2019 Panini Prizm National Pride #15
2019 Panini Prizm National Pride Prizms #15
2019 Panini Prizm National Pride Prizms Black /1 #15
2019 Panini Prizm National Pride Prizms Gold /10 #15
2019 Panini Prizm National Pride Prizms White Sparkle #15
2019 Panini Prizm Prizms #78
2019 Panini Prizm Prizms #3B
2019 Panini Prizm Prizms #3A
2019 Panini Prizm Prizms Black /1 #3A
2019 Panini Prizm Prizms Black /1 #78
2019 Panini Prizm Prizms Black /1 #3B
2019 Panini Prizm Prizms Blue /75 #3A
2019 Panini Prizm Prizms Blue /75 #78
2019 Panini Prizm Prizms Blue /75 #3B
2019 Panini Prizm Prizms Camo #3A
2019 Panini Prizm Prizms Camo #78
2019 Panini Prizm Prizms Camo #3B
2019 Panini Prizm Prizms Flash #3A
2019 Panini Prizm Prizms Flash #78
2019 Panini Prizm Prizms Flash #3B
2019 Panini Prizm Prizms Gold /10 #3A
2019 Panini Prizm Prizms Gold /10 #78
2019 Panini Prizm Prizms Gold /10 #3B
2019 Panini Prizm Prizms Green /99 #3A
2019 Panini Prizm Prizms Green /99 #78
2019 Panini Prizm Prizms Green /99 #3B
2019 Panini Prizm Prizms Rainbow /24 #3A
2019 Panini Prizm Prizms Rainbow /24 #78
2019 Panini Prizm Prizms Rainbow /24 #3B
2019 Panini Prizm Prizms Red /50 #3A
2019 Panini Prizm Prizms Red /50 #78
2019 Panini Prizm Prizms Red /50 #3B
2019 Panini Prizm Prizms Red White and Blue #3A
2019 Panini Prizm Prizms Red White and Blue #78
2019 Panini Prizm Prizms Red White and Blue #3B
2019 Panini Prizm Prizms White /5 #3A
2019 Panini Prizm Prizms White /5 #78
2019 Panini Prizm Prizms White /5 #3B
2019 Panini Prizm Prizms White Sparkle #3A
2019 Panini Prizm Prizms White Sparkle #78
2019 Panini Prizm Prizms White Sparkle #3B
2019 Panini Prizm Signing Sessions Prizms #3
2019 Panini Prizm Signing Sessions Prizms Black /1 #3
2019 Panini Prizm Signing Sessions Prizms Blue /75 #3
2019 Panini Prizm Signing Sessions Prizms Camo #3
2019 Panini Prizm Signing Sessions Prizms Gold /10 #3
2019 Panini Prizm Signing Sessions Prizms Green /99 #3
2019 Panini Prizm Signing Sessions Prizms Rainbow /24 #3
2019 Panini Prizm Signing Sessions Prizms Red /50 #3
2019 Panini Prizm Signing Sessions Prizms Red White and Blue #3
2019 Panini Prizm Signing Sessions Prizms White /5 #3
2019 Panini Prizm Stars and Stripes #5
2019 Panini Prizm Stars and Stripes Prizms #5
2019 Panini Prizm Stars and Stripes Prizms Black /1 #5
2019 Panini Prizm Stars and Stripes Prizms Gold /10 #5
2019 Panini Prizm Stars and Stripes Prizms White Sparkle #5
2019 Panini Prizm Teammates #10
2019 Panini Prizm Teammates Prizms #10
2019 Panini Prizm Teammates Prizms Black /1 #10
2019 Panini Prizm Teammates Prizms Gold /10 #10
2019 Panini Prizm Teammates Prizms White Sparkle #10
2019 Panini Victory Lane #3
2019 Panini Victory Lane #77
2019 Panini Victory Lane #87
2019 Panini Victory Lane Black /1 #3
2019 Panini Victory Lane Black /1 #77
2019 Panini Victory Lane Black /1 #87
2019 Panini Victory Lane Celebrations #1
2019 Panini Victory Lane Celebrations Black /1 #1
2019 Panini Victory Lane Celebrations Blue /99 #1
2019 Panini Victory Lane Celebrations Gold /25 #1
2019 Panini Victory Lane Celebrations Green /5 #1
2019 Panini Victory Lane Celebrations Printing Plates Black /1 #1
2019 Panini Victory Lane Celebrations Printing Plates Cyan /1 #1
2019 Panini Victory Lane Celebrations Printing Plates Magenta /1 #1
2019 Panini Victory Lane Celebrations Printing Plates Yellow /1 #1
2019 Panini Victory Lane Dual Swatches #3
2019 Panini Victory Lane Dual Swatches Gold /99 #3
2019 Panini Victory Lane Dual Swatches Laundry Tag /1 #3
2019 Panini Victory Lane Dual Swatches Platinum /1 #3
2019 Panini Victory Lane Dual Swatches Red /25 #3
2019 Panini Victory Lane Gold /25 #3
2019 Panini Victory Lane Gold /25 #77
2019 Panini Victory Lane Gold /25 #87
2019 Panini Victory Lane Horsepower Heroes #10
2019 Panini Victory Lane Horsepower Heroes Black /1 #10
2019 Panini Victory Lane Horsepower Heroes Blue /99 #10
2019 Panini Victory Lane Horsepower Heroes Gold /25 #10
2019 Panini Victory Lane Horsepower Heroes Green /5 #10
2019 Panini Victory Lane Horsepower Heroes Printing Plates Black /1 #10
2019 Panini Victory Lane Horsepower Heroes Printing Plates Cyan /1 #10
2019 Panini Victory Lane Horsepower Heroes Printing Plates Magenta /1 #10
2019 Panini Victory Lane Horsepower Heroes Printing Plates Yellow /1 #10
2019 Panini Victory Lane Machines #12
2019 Panini Victory Lane Machines Black /1 #12
2019 Panini Victory Lane Machines Blue /99 #12
2019 Panini Victory Lane Machines Gold /25 #12
2019 Panini Victory Lane Machines Green /5 #12
2019 Panini Victory Lane Machines Printing Plates Black /1 #12
2019 Panini Victory Lane Machines Printing Plates Cyan /1 #12
2019 Panini Victory Lane Machines Printing Plates Magenta /1 #12
2019 Panini Victory Lane Machines Printing Plates Yellow /1 #12
2019 Panini Victory Lane Pedal to the Metal #49
2019 Panini Victory Lane Pedal to the Metal #63
2019 Panini Victory Lane Pedal to the Metal Black /1 #49
2019 Panini Victory Lane Pedal to the Metal Black /1 #63
2019 Panini Victory Lane Pedal to the Metal Gold /25 #49
2019 Panini Victory Lane Pedal to the Metal Gold /25 #63
2019 Panini Victory Lane Pedal to the Metal Green /5 #49
2019 Panini Victory Lane Pedal to the Metal Green /5 #63
2019 Panini Victory Lane Pedal to the Metal Red /3 #49
2019 Panini Victory Lane Pedal to the Metal Red /3 #63
2019 Panini Victory Lane Printing Plates Black /1 #3
2019 Panini Victory Lane Printing Plates Black /1 #77
2019 Panini Victory Lane Printing Plates Black /1 #87
2019 Panini Victory Lane Printing Plates Cyan /1 #3
2019 Panini Victory Lane Printing Plates Cyan /1 #77
2019 Panini Victory Lane Printing Plates Cyan /1 #87
2019 Panini Victory Lane Printing Plates Magenta /1 #3
2019 Panini Victory Lane Printing Plates Magenta /1 #77
2019 Panini Victory Lane Printing Plates Magenta /1 #87
2019 Panini Victory Lane Printing Plates Yellow /1 #3
2019 Panini Victory Lane Printing Plates Yellow /1 #77
2019 Panini Victory Lane Printing Plates Yellow /1 #87
2019 Panini Victory Lane Starting Grid #1
2019 Panini Victory Lane Starting Grid Black /1 #1
2019 Panini Victory Lane Starting Grid Blue /99 #1
2019 Panini Victory Lane Starting Grid Gold /25 #1
2019 Panini Victory Lane Starting Grid Green /5 #1
2019 Panini Victory Lane Starting Grid Printing Plates Black /1 #1
2019 Panini Victory Lane Starting Grid Printing Plates Cyan /1 #1
2019 Panini Victory Lane Starting Grid Printing Plates Magenta /1 #1
2019 Panini Victory Lane Starting Grid Printing Plates Yellow /1 #1
2019 Panini Victory Lane Track Stars #14
2019 Panini Victory Lane Track Stars Black /1 #14
2019 Panini Victory Lane Track Stars Blue /99 #14
2019 Panini Victory Lane Track Stars Gold /25 #14
2019 Panini Victory Lane Track Stars Green /5 #14
2019 Panini Victory Lane Track Stars Printing Plates Black /1 #14
2019 Panini Victory Lane Track Stars Printing Plates Cyan /1 #14
2019 Panini Victory Lane Track Stars Printing Plates Magenta /1 #14
2019 Panini Victory Lane Track Stars Printing Plates Yellow /1 #14
2019 Panini Victory Lane Triple Swatch Signatures #1
2019 Panini Victory Lane Triple Swatch Signatures Gold /99 #1
2019 Panini Victory Lane Triple Swatch Signatures Laundry Tag /1 #1
2019 Panini Victory Lane Triple Swatch Signatures Platinum /1 #1
2019 Panini Victory Lane Triple Swatch Signatures Red /25 #1
2019 Panini Victory Lane Triple Swatches #1
2019 Panini Victory Lane Triple Swatches Gold /99 #1
2019 Panini Victory Lane Triple Swatches Laundry Tag /1 #1
2019 Panini Victory Lane Triple Swatches Platinum /1 #1
2019 Panini Victory Lane Triple Swatches Red /25 #1
2020 Donruss #3
2020 Donruss #25
2020 Donruss #111
2020 Donruss #168
2020 Donruss #191
2020 Donruss Action Packed #1
2020 Donruss Action Packed Checkers #1
2020 Donruss Action Packed Cracked Ice /25 #1
2020 Donruss Action Packed Holographic /199 #1
2020 Donruss Action Packed Xplosion /10 #1
2020 Donruss Aero Package #11
2020 Donruss Aero Package Checkers #11
2020 Donruss Aero Package Cracked Ice /25 #11
2020 Donruss Aero Package Holographic /199 #11
2020 Donruss Aero Package Xplosion /10 #11
2020 Donruss Black Numbers /3 #3
2020 Donruss Black Numbers /3 #25
2020 Donruss Black Numbers /3 #111
2020 Donruss Black Numbers /3 #168
2020 Donruss Black Numbers /3 #191
2020 Donruss Black Trophy Club /1 #3
2020 Donruss Black Trophy Club /1 #25
2020 Donruss Black Trophy Club /1 #111
2020 Donruss Black Trophy Club /1 #168
2020 Donruss Black Trophy Club /1 #191
2020 Donruss Blue /199 #111
2020 Donruss Blue /199 #168
2020 Donruss Blue /199 #191
2020 Donruss Blue /199 #3
2020 Donruss Blue /199 #25
2020 Donruss Carolina Blue #3
2020 Donruss Carolina Blue #25
2020 Donruss Carolina Blue #111
2020 Donruss Carolina Blue #168
2020 Donruss Carolina Blue #191
2020 Donruss Elite Series #8
2020 Donruss Elite Series Checkers #8
2020 Donruss Elite Series Cracked Ice /25 #8
2020 Donruss Elite Series Holographic /199 #8
2020 Donruss Elite Series Xplosion /10 #8
2020 Donruss Green /99 #3
2020 Donruss Green /99 #25
2020 Donruss Green /99 #111
2020 Donruss Green /99 #168
2020 Donruss Green /99 #191
2020 Donruss Optic #3
2020 Donruss Optic #37
2020 Donruss Optic #81
2020 Donruss Optic Carolina Blue Wave #37
2020 Donruss Optic Carolina Blue Wave #81
2020 Donruss Optic Carolina Blue Wave #3
2020 Donruss Optic Gold /10 #3
2020 Donruss Optic Gold /10 #37
2020 Donruss Optic Gold /10 #81
2020 Donruss Optic Gold Vinyl /1 #3
2020 Donruss Optic Gold Vinyl /1 #37
2020 Donruss Optic Gold Vinyl /1 #81
2020 Donruss Optic Holo #3
2020 Donruss Optic Holo #37
2020 Donruss Optic Holo #81
2020 Donruss Optic Illusion #3
2020 Donruss Optic Illusion Carolina Blue Wave #3
2020 Donruss Optic Illusion Gold /10 #3
2020 Donruss Optic Illusion Gold Vinyl /1 #3
2020 Donruss Optic Illusion Holo #3
2020 Donruss Optic Illusion Orange Pulsar #3
2020 Donruss Optic Illusion Red Mojo #3
2020 Donruss Optic Illusion Signatures Gold Vinyl /1 #3
2020 Donruss Optic Illusion Signatures Holo /99 #3
2020 Donruss Optic Orange Pulsar #3
2020 Donruss Optic Orange Pulsar #37
2020 Donruss Optic Orange Pulsar #81
2020 Donruss Optic Red Mojo #3
2020 Donruss Optic Red Mojo #37
2020 Donruss Optic Red Mojo #81
2020 Donruss Optic Signatures Gold Vinyl /1 #3
2020 Donruss Optic Signatures Gold Vinyl /1 #37
2020 Donruss Optic Signatures Gold Vinyl /1 #81
2020 Donruss Optic Signatures Holo /99 #3
2020 Donruss Optic Signatures Holo /99 #37
2020 Donruss Optic Signatures Holo /99 #81
2020 Donruss Orange #191
2020 Donruss Orange #3
2020 Donruss Orange #25
2020 Donruss Orange #111
2020 Donruss Orange #168
2020 Donruss Pink /25 #3
2020 Donruss Pink /25 #25
2020 Donruss Pink /25 #111
2020 Donruss Pink /25 #168
2020 Donruss Pink /25 #191
2020 Donruss Printing Plates Black /1 #3
2020 Donruss Printing Plates Black /1 #25
2020 Donruss Printing Plates Black /1 #111
2020 Donruss Printing Plates Black /1 #168
2020 Donruss Printing Plates Black /1 #191
2020 Donruss Printing Plates Cyan /1 #3
2020 Donruss Printing Plates Cyan /1 #25
2020 Donruss Printing Plates Cyan /1 #111
2020 Donruss Printing Plates Cyan /1 #168
2020 Donruss Printing Plates Cyan /1 #191
2020 Donruss Printing Plates Magenta /1 #25
2020 Donruss Printing Plates Magenta /1 #111
2020 Donruss Printing Plates Magenta /1 #168
2020 Donruss Printing Plates Magenta /1 #191
2020 Donruss Printing Plates Magenta /1 #3
2020 Donruss Printing Plates Yellow /1 #168
2020 Donruss Printing Plates Yellow /1 #191
2020 Donruss Printing Plates Yellow /1 #3
2020 Donruss Printing Plates Yellow /1 #25
2020 Donruss Printing Plates Yellow /1 #111
2020 Donruss Purple /49 #3
2020 Donruss Purple /49 #25
2020 Donruss Purple /49 #111
2020 Donruss Purple /49 #168
2020 Donruss Purple /49 #191
2020 Donruss Race Day Relics #3
2020 Donruss Race Day Relics Holo Black /10 #3
2020 Donruss Race Day Relics Holo Gold /25 #3
2020 Donruss Race Day Relics Red /250 #3
2020 Donruss Red /299 #3
2020 Donruss Red /299 #25
2020 Donruss Red /299 #111
2020 Donruss Red /299 #168
2020 Donruss Red /299 #191
2020 Donruss Silver #3
2020 Donruss Silver #25
2020 Donruss Silver #111
2020 Donruss Silver #168
2020 Donruss Silver #191

Ty Dillon

2012 Press Pass Fantare #68
2012 Press Pass Fanfare Autographs Blue /25 #TD
2012 Press Pass Fanfare Autographs Gold /99 #TD
2012 Press Pass Fanfare Autographs Red /75 #TD
2012 Press Pass Fanfare Autographs Silver /175 #TD
2012 Press Pass Fanfare Blue Foil Die Cuts #68
2012 Press Pass Fanfare Diamond /5 #68
2012 Press Pass Fanfare Dual Autographs /10 #DD
2012 Press Pass Fanfare Holofoil Die Cuts #68
2012 Press Pass Fanfare Magnificent Materials /199 #MMTD
2012 Press Pass Fanfare Magnificent Materials Gold /75 #MMTD
2012 Press Pass Fanfare Magnificent Materials Signatures /99 #TD
2012 Press Pass Fanfare Magnificent Materials Signatures Blue /25 #TD
2012 Press Pass Fanfare Sapphire /20 #68
2012 Press Pass Fanfare Silver /25 #68
2012 Press Pass Ignite #50
2012 Press Pass Ignite Proofs Black and White /50 #50
2012 Press Pass Ignite Proofs Cyan #50
2012 Press Pass Ignite Proofs Magenta #50
2012 Press Pass Ignite Proofs Yellow /10 #50
2012 Total Memorabilia Rising Stars #RS2
2012 Total Memorabilia Rising Stars Autographed Memorabilia Gold /99 #RSTD
2012 Total Memorabilia Rising Stars Autographed Memorabilia Holofoil /25 #RSTD
2012 Total Memorabilia Rising Stars Autographed Memorabilia Melting /5 #RSTD
2012 Total Memorabilia Rising Stars Autographed Memorabilia Silver /125 #RSTD
2012 Total Memorabilia Tandem Treasures Dual Memorabilia Gold /75 #TTADTD
2012 Total Memorabilia Tandem Treasures Dual Memorabilia Holofoil /25 #TTADTD
2012 Total Memorabilia Tandem Treasures Dual Memorabilia Melting /5 #TTADTD
2012 Total Memorabilia Tandem Treasures Dual Memorabilia Silver /99 #TTADTD
2013 Press Pass #60
2013 Press Pass Color Proofs Black #60
2013 Press Pass Color Proofs Cyan /35 #60
2013 Press Pass Color Proofs Magenta #60
2013 Press Pass Color Proofs Yellow /5 #60
2013 Press Pass Fanfare #64
2013 Press Pass Fanfare #82
2013 Press Pass Fanfare Autographs Blue /1 #TD
2013 Press Pass Fanfare Autographs Gold /25 #TD
2013 Press Pass Fanfare Autographs Gold /5 #TD2
2013 Press Pass Fanfare Autographs Green /2 #TD
2013 Press Pass Fanfare Autographs Red /10 #TD
2013 Press Pass Fanfare Autographs Silver /50 #TD
2013 Press Pass Fanfare Diamond Die Cuts /5 #64
2013 Press Pass Fanfare Diamond Die Cuts /5 #82
2013 Press Pass Fanfare Green /3 #64
2013 Press Pass Fanfare Green /3 #82
2013 Press Pass Fanfare Holofoil Die Cuts #64
2013 Press Pass Fanfare Holofoil Die Cuts #82
2013 Press Pass Fanfare Magnificent Jumbo Materials Signatures /10 #TD
2013 Press Pass Fanfare Magnificent Materials Dual Swatches /50 #TD
2013 Press Pass Fanfare Magnificent Materials Dual Swatches Melting /10 #TD
2013 Press Pass Fanfare Magnificent Materials Gold /50 #TD
2013 Press Pass Fanfare Magnificent Materials Jumbo Swatches /25 #TD
2013 Press Pass Fanfare Magnificent Materials Signatures /99 #TD
2013 Press Pass Fanfare Magnificent Materials Signatures Blue /25 #TD
2013 Press Pass Fanfare Magnificent Materials Silver /199 #TD
2013 Press Pass Fanfare Red Foil Die Cuts #64
2013 Press Pass Fanfare Red Foil Die Cuts #82
2013 Press Pass Fanfare Sapphire /20 #64
2013 Press Pass Fanfare Sapphire /20 #82
2013 Press Pass Fanfare Signature Ride Autographs Red /5 #TD
2013 Press Pass Fanfare Silver /25 #64
2013 Press Pass Fanfare Silver /25 #82
2013 Press Pass Ignite #49
2013 Press Pass Ignite Ink Black /75 #IITD
2013 Press Pass Ignite Ink Blue /20 #IITD
2013 Press Pass Ignite Ink Red /5 #IITD
2013 Press Pass Ignite Proofs Black and White /50 #49
2013 Press Pass Ignite Proofs Cyan #49
2013 Press Pass Ignite Proofs Magenta #49
2013 Press Pass Ignite Proofs Yellow /5 #49
2013 Press Pass Power Picks Blue /99 #21
2013 Press Pass Power Picks Gold /50 #21
2013 Press Pass Power Picks Holofoil /10 #21
2013 Press Pass Redline #50
2013 Press Pass Redline Black /99 #50
2013 Press Pass Redline Cyan /50 #50
2013 Press Pass Redline Dark Horse Relic Autographs Red /75 #DHTD
2013 Press Pass Redline Dynamic Duals Dual Relic Blue /5 #DDTD
2013 Press Pass Redline Dynamic Duals Dual Relic Gold /10 #DDTD
2013 Press Pass Redline Dynamic Duals Dual Relic Melting /1 #DDTD
2013 Press Pass Redline Dynamic Duals Dual Relic Red /75 #DDTD
2013 Press Pass Redline Dynamic Duals Dual Relic Silver /25 #DDTD
2013 Press Pass Redline Magenta /15 #50
2013 Press Pass Redline Muscle Car Sheet Metal Blue /5 #MCMTD
2013 Press Pass Redline Muscle Car Sheet Metal Gold /10 #MCMTD
2013 Press Pass Redline Muscle Car Sheet Metal Melting /1 #MCMTD
2013 Press Pass Redline Muscle Car Sheet Metal Red /50 #MCMTD
2013 Press Pass Redline Muscle Car Sheet Metal Silver /25 #MCMTD
2013 Press Pass Redline Yellow /1 #50
2013 Press Pass Showcase Prized Pieces /52 #PPMTD
2013 Press Pass Showcase Prized Pieces Blue /20 #PPMTD
2013 Press Pass Showcase Prized Pieces Gold /25 #PPMTD
2013 Press Pass Showcase Prized Pieces Ink /50 #PPITD
2013 Press Pass Showcase Prized Pieces Ink Gold /25 #PPITD
2013 Press Pass Showcase Prized Pieces Ink Melting /1 #PPITD
2013 Press Pass Showcase Prized Pieces Melting /5 #PPMTD
2013 Press Pass Signings Blue /1 #TD
2013 Press Pass Signings Gold /25 #TD
2013 Press Pass Signings Holofoil /10 #TD
2013 Press Pass Signings Printing Plates Black /1 #TD
2013 Press Pass Signings Printing Plates Cyan /1 #TD
2013 Press Pass Signings Printing Plates Magenta /1 #TD
2013 Press Pass Signings Printing Plates Yellow /1 #TD
2013 Press Pass Signings Silver /65 #TD
2013 Total Memorabilia Memory Lane #ML7
2014 Press Pass #62
2014 Press Pass American Thunder #42
2014 Press Pass American Thunder Autographs Blue /10 #ATATD
2014 Press Pass American Thunder Autographs Red /5 #ATATD
2014 Press Pass American Thunder Autographs White /25 #ATATD
2014 Press Pass American Thunder Black and White /50 #42
2014 Press Pass American Thunder Class A Uniforms Blue /99 #CAUTD
2014 Press Pass American Thunder Class A Uniforms Flag /1 #CAUTD
2014 Press Pass American Thunder Class A Uniforms Red /10 #CAUTD
2014 Press Pass American Thunder Class A Uniforms Silver #CAUTD
2014 Press Pass American Thunder Climbing the Ranks #CR8
2014 Press Pass American Thunder Cyan #42
2014 Press Pass American Thunder Magenta #42
2014 Press Pass American Thunder Yellow /5 #42
2014 Press Pass Color Proofs Black /70 #62
2014 Press Pass Color Proofs Cyan /35 #62
2014 Press Pass Color Proofs Magenta #62
2014 Press Pass Color Proofs Yellow /5 #62
2014 Press Pass Five Star Classic Compilations Autographed Patch Booklet /1 #CCTD1
2014 Press Pass Five Star Classic Compilations Autographed Patch Booklet /1 #CCTD2
2014 Press Pass Five Star Classic Compilations Autographed Patch Booklet /1 #CCTD3
2014 Press Pass Five Star Classic Compilations Autographed Patch Booklet /1 #CCTD4
2014 Press Pass Five Star Classic Compilations Autographed Patch Booklet /1 #CCTD5
2014 Press Pass Five Star Classic Compilations Autographed Patch Booklet /1 #CCTD6
2014 Press Pass Five Star Classic Compilations Autographed Patch Booklet /1 #CCTD7
2014 Press Pass Five Star Classic Compilations Autographed Patch Booklet /1 #CCTD8
2014 Press Pass Five Star Classic Compilations Autographed Patch Booklet /1 #CCTD9
2014 Press Pass Five Star Classic Compilations Autographed Patch Booklet /1 #CCTD10
2014 Press Pass Five Star Classic Compilations Autographed Patch Booklet /1 #CCTD11
2014 Press Pass Five Star Classic Compilations Autographed Patch Booklet /1 #CCTD12
2014 Press Pass Five Star Classic Compilations Combo Autographs Blue /5 #CCDIL
2014 Press Pass Five Star Classic Compilations Combo Autographs Melting /1 #CCDIL
2014 Press Pass Gold #62
2014 Press Pass Redline #59
2014 Press Pass Redline #60
2014 Press Pass Redline Black /75 #59
2014 Press Pass Redline Black /75 #60
2014 Press Pass Redline Blue Foil #59
2014 Press Pass Redline Blue Foil #60
2014 Press Pass Redline Cyan /50 #59
2014 Press Pass Redline Cyan /50 #60
2014 Press Pass Redline Green National Convention /5 #59
2014 Press Pass Redline Green National Convention /5 #60
2014 Press Pass Redline Magenta /10 #59
2014 Press Pass Redline Magenta /10 #60
2014 Press Pass Redline Muscle Car Sheet Metal Blue /10 #MCMTD
2014 Press Pass Redline Muscle Car Sheet Metal Gold /25 #MCMTD
2014 Press Pass Redline Muscle Car Sheet Metal Melting /1 #MCMTD
2014 Press Pass Redline Muscle Car Sheet Metal Red /50 #MCMTD
2014 Press Pass Redline Relic Autographs Blue /10 #RRSETD
2014 Press Pass Redline Relic Autographs Gold /15 #RRSETD
2014 Press Pass Redline Relic Autographs Melting /1 #RRSETD
2014 Press Pass Redline Relic Autographs Red /25 #RRSETD
2014 Press Pass Redline Relics Blue /25 #RRTD
2014 Press Pass Redline Relics Gold /50 #RRTD
2014 Press Pass Redline Relics Melting /1 #RRTD
2014 Press Pass Redline Relics Red /75 #RRTD
2014 Press Pass Redline Signatures Blue /10 #RSTD
2014 Press Pass Redline Signatures Gold /25 #RSTD
2014 Press Pass Redline Signatures Melting /1 #RSTD
2014 Press Pass Redline Signatures Red /50 #RSTD
2014 Press Pass Redline Yellow /1 #59
2014 Press Pass Redline Yellow /1 #60
2014 Press Pass Signings Gold /10 #PPSTD
2014 Press Pass Signings Holofoil /1 #PPSTD
2014 Press Pass Signings Melting /1 #PPSTD
2014 Press Pass Signings Printing Plates Black /1 #PPSTD
2014 Press Pass Signings Printing Plates Cyan /1 #PPSTD
2014 Press Pass Signings Printing Plates Magenta /1 #PPSTD
2014 Press Pass Signings Printing Plates Yellow /1 #PPSTD
2014 Press Pass Signings Silver /50 #PPSTD
2014 Total Memorabilia #42
2014 Total Memorabilia Black and White /99 #42
2014 Total Memorabilia Dirt Track Treads Blue /25 #DTTTD
2014 Total Memorabilia Dirt Track Treads Gold /50 #DTTTD
2014 Total Memorabilia Dirt Track Treads Melting /10 #DTTTD
2014 Total Memorabilia Dirt Track Treads Silver /99 #DTTTD
2014 Total Memorabilia Dual Swatch Gold /150 #TMTD
2014 Total Memorabilia Gold /175 #42
2014 Total Memorabilia Quad Swatch Melting /25 #TMTD
2014 Total Memorabilia Red #42
2014 Total Memorabilia Single Swatch Silver /275 #TMTD
2014 Total Memorabilia Triple Swatch Blue /99 #TMTD
2015 Press Pass #45
2015 Press Pass #76
2015 Press Pass Championship Caliber Dual /25 #CCMTD
2015 Press Pass Championship Caliber Quad /1 #CCMTD
2015 Press Pass Championship Caliber Signature Edition Blue /25 #CCTD
2015 Press Pass Championship Caliber Signature Edition Gold /50 #CCTD
2015 Press Pass Championship Caliber Signature Edition Green /10 #CCTD
2015 Press Pass Championship Caliber Signature Edition Melting /1 #CCTD
2015 Press Pass Championship Caliber Single /50 #CCMTD
2015 Press Pass Championship Caliber Triple /10 #CCMTD
2015 Press Pass Cup Chase #45
2015 Press Pass Cup Chase #76
2015 Press Pass Cup Chase Blue /25 #45
2015 Press Pass Cup Chase Blue /25 #76
2015 Press Pass Cup Chase Gold /75 #45
2015 Press Pass Cup Chase Gold /75 #76
2015 Press Pass Cup Chase Green /10 #45
2015 Press Pass Cup Chase Green /10 #76
2015 Press Pass Cup Chase Melting /1 #45
2015 Press Pass Cup Chase Melting /1 #76
2015 Press Pass Cup Chase Three Wide Blue /25 #3WTD
2015 Press Pass Cup Chase Three Wide Gold /50 #3WTD
2015 Press Pass Cup Chase Three Wide Green /10 #3WTD
2015 Press Pass Cup Chase Three Wide Melting /1 #3WTD
2015 Press Pass Cup Chase Upper Cuts /13 #UCTD
2015 Press Pass Cuts Blue /25 #CCCTD
2015 Press Pass Cuts Gold /50 #CCCTD
2015 Press Pass Cuts Green /10 #CCCTD
2015 Press Pass Cuts Melting /1 #CCCTD
2015 Press Pass Four Wide Signature Edition Blue /15 #4WTD
2015 Press Pass Four Wide Signature Edition Gold /25 #4WTD
2015 Press Pass Four Wide Signature Edition Green /10 #4WTD
2015 Press Pass Four Wide Signature Edition Melting /1 #4WTD
2015 Press Pass Purple #45
2015 Press Pass Purple #76
2015 Press Pass Red #45
2015 Press Pass Red #76
2015 Press Pass Signature Series Blue /25 #SSTD
2015 Press Pass Signature Series Gold /35 #SSTD
2015 Press Pass Signature Series Green /10 #SSTD
2015 Press Pass Signature Series Melting /1 #SSTD
2015 Press Pass Signings Blue /25 #PPSTD
2015 Press Pass Signings Gold #PPSTD
2015 Press Pass Signings Green /10 #PPSTD
2015 Press Pass Signings Melting /5 #PPSTD
2015 Press Pass Signings Red /15 #PPSTD
2016 Certified #40
2016 Certified Complete Materials /199 #23
2016 Certified Complete Materials Mirror Black /1 #23
2016 Certified Complete Materials Mirror Blue /50 #23
2016 Certified Complete Materials Mirror Gold /25 #23
2016 Certified Complete Materials Mirror Green /5 #23
2016 Certified Complete Materials Mirror Orange /99 #23
2016 Certified Complete Materials Mirror Purple /10 #23
2016 Certified Complete Materials Mirror Red /75 #23
2016 Certified Complete Materials Mirror Silver /99 #23
2016 Certified Mirror Black /1 #40
2016 Certified Mirror Blue /50 #40
2016 Certified Mirror Gold /25 #40
2016 Certified Mirror Green /5 #40
2016 Certified Mirror Orange /99 #40
2016 Certified Mirror Purple /10 #40
2016 Certified Mirror Red /75 #40
2016 Certified Mirror Silver /99 #40
2016 Certified Potential Signatures /190 #29
2016 Certified Potential Signatures Mirror Black /1 #29
2016 Certified Potential Signatures Mirror Blue /20 #29
2016 Certified Potential Signatures Mirror Gold /15 #29
2016 Certified Potential Signatures Mirror Green /5 #29
2016 Certified Potential Signatures Mirror Orange /5 #29
2016 Certified Potential Signatures Mirror Purple /10 #29
2016 Certified Potential Signatures Mirror Red /50 #29
2016 Certified Potential Signatures Mirror Silver /5 #29
2016 Certified Skills /199 #15
2016 Certified Skills Mirror Black /1 #15
2016 Certified Skills Mirror Blue /50 #15
2016 Certified Skills Mirror Gold /25 #15
2016 Certified Skills Mirror Green /5 #15
2016 Certified Skills Mirror Orange /99 #15
2016 Certified Skills Mirror Purple /10 #15
2016 Certified Skills Mirror Red /75 #15
2016 Certified Skills Mirror Silver /99 #15
2016 Certified Xfinity Materials /299 #5
2016 Certified Xfinity Materials Mirror Black /1 #5
2016 Certified Xfinity Materials Mirror Blue /50 #5
2016 Certified Xfinity Materials Mirror Gold /25 #5
2016 Certified Xfinity Materials Mirror Green /5 #5
2016 Certified Xfinity Materials Mirror Orange /99 #5
2016 Certified Xfinity Materials Mirror Purple /10 #5
2016 Certified Xfinity Materials Mirror Red /75 #5
2016 Certified Xfinity Materials Mirror Silver /99 #5
2016 Panini National Treasures /25 #20
2016 Panini National Treasures Black /5 #20
2016 Panini National Treasures Blue /1 #20
2016 Panini National Treasures Combo Materials /25 #2
2016 Panini National Treasures Combo Materials Black /5 #2
2016 Panini National Treasures Combo Materials Blue /1 #2
2016 Panini National Treasures Combo Materials Gold /10 #2
2016 Panini National Treasures Combo Materials Printing Plates Black /1 #2
2016 Panini National Treasures Combo Materials Printing Plates Cyan /1 #2
2016 Panini National Treasures Combo Materials Printing Plates Magenta /1 #2
2016 Panini National Treasures Combo Materials Printing Plates Yellow /1 #2
2016 Panini National Treasures Combo Materials Silver /15 #2
2016 Panini National Treasures Dual Driver Materials /25 #14
2016 Panini National Treasures Dual Driver Materials Black /5 #14
2016 Panini National Treasures Dual Driver Materials Blue /1 #14
2016 Panini National Treasures Dual Driver Materials Gold /10 #14
2016 Panini National Treasures Dual Driver Materials Printing Plates Black /1 #14
2016 Panini National Treasures Dual Driver Materials Printing Plates Cyan /1 #14
2016 Panini National Treasures Dual Driver Materials Printing Plates Magenta /1 #14
2016 Panini National Treasures Dual Driver Materials Printing Plates Yellow /1 #14
2016 Panini National Treasures Dual Driver Materials Silver /15 #14
2016 Panini National Treasures Dual Signatures Black /5 #3
2016 Panini National Treasures Dual Signatures Blue /1 #3
2016 Panini National Treasures Dual Signatures Gold /10 #3
2016 Panini National Treasures Gold /15 #20
2016 Panini National Treasures Jumbo Firesuit Patch Signature Booklet Associate Sponsor 1 /1 #25
2016 Panini National Treasures Jumbo Firesuit Patch Signature Booklet Associate Sponsor 10 /1 #25
2016 Panini National Treasures Jumbo Firesuit Patch Signature Booklet Associate Sponsor 11 /1 #25
2016 Panini National Treasures Jumbo Firesuit Patch Signature Booklet Associate Sponsor 12 /1 #25
2016 Panini National Treasures Jumbo Firesuit Patch Signature Booklet Associate Sponsor 13 /1 #25
2016 Panini National Treasures Jumbo Firesuit Patch Signature Booklet Associate Sponsor 14 /1 #25
2016 Panini National Treasures Jumbo Firesuit Patch Signature Booklet Associate Sponsor 15 /1 #25
2016 Panini National Treasures Jumbo Firesuit Patch Signature Booklet Associate Sponsor 16 /1 #25
2016 Panini National Treasures Jumbo Firesuit Patch Signature Booklet Associate Sponsor 17 /1 #25
2016 Panini National Treasures Jumbo Firesuit Patch Signature Booklet Associate Sponsor 18 /1 #25
2016 Panini National Treasures Jumbo Firesuit Patch Signature Booklet Associate Sponsor 19 /1 #25
2016 Panini National Treasures Jumbo Firesuit Patch Signature Booklet Associate Sponsor 2 /1 #25
2016 Panini National Treasures Jumbo Firesuit Patch Signature Booklet Associate Sponsor 20 /1 #25
2016 Panini National Treasures Jumbo Firesuit Patch Signature Booklet Associate Sponsor 3 /1 #25
2016 Panini National Treasures Jumbo Firesuit Patch Signature Booklet Associate Sponsor 4 /1 #25
2016 Panini National Treasures Jumbo Firesuit Patch Signature Booklet Associate Sponsor 5 /1 #25
2016 Panini National Treasures Jumbo Firesuit Patch Signature Booklet Associate Sponsor 6 /1 #25
2016 Panini National Treasures Jumbo Firesuit Patch Signature Booklet Associate Sponsor 7 /1 #25
2016 Panini National Treasures Jumbo Firesuit Patch Signature Booklet Associate Sponsor 8 /1 #25
2016 Panini National Treasures Jumbo Firesuit Patch Signature Booklet Associate Sponsor 9 /1 #25
2016 Panini National Treasures Jumbo Firesuit Patch Signature Booklet Flag /1 #25
2016 Panini National Treasures Jumbo Firesuit Patch Signature Booklet Goodyear /1 #25
2016 Panini National Treasures Jumbo Firesuit Patch Signature Booklet Manufacturers Logo /2 #25
2016 Panini National Treasures Jumbo Firesuit Patch Signature Booklet Nameplate /2 #25
2016 Panini National Treasures Jumbo Firesuit Patch Signature Booklet NASCAR /1 #25
2016 Panini National Treasures Jumbo Firesuit Patch Signature Booklet Sprint Cup Logo /1 #25
2016 Panini National Treasures Jumbo Firesuit Patch Signature Booklet Sunoco /1 #25
2016 Panini National Treasures Jumbo Firesuit Signatures /25 #25
2016 Panini National Treasures Jumbo Firesuit Signatures Black /5 #25
2016 Panini National Treasures Jumbo Firesuit Signatures Blue /1 #25
2016 Panini National Treasures Jumbo Firesuit Signatures Gold /10 #25
2016 Panini National Treasures Jumbo Firesuit Signatures Printing Plates Black /1 #25
2016 Panini National Treasures Jumbo Firesuit Signatures Printing Plates Cyan /1 #25
2016 Panini National Treasures Jumbo Firesuit Signatures Printing Plates Magenta /1 #25
2016 Panini National Treasures Jumbo Firesuit Signatures Printing Plates Yellow /1 #25
2016 Panini National Treasures Jumbo Firesuit Signatures Silver /15 #25
2016 Panini National Treasures Printing Plates Black /1 #20
2016 Panini National Treasures Printing Plates Cyan /1 #20
2016 Panini National Treasures Printing Plates Magenta /1 #20
2016 Panini National Treasures Printing Plates Yellow /1 #20
2016 Panini National Treasures Signature Dual Materials /25 #22
2016 Panini National Treasures Signature Dual Materials Black /5 #22
2016 Panini National Treasures Signature Dual Materials Blue /1 #22
2016 Panini National Treasures Signature Dual Materials Gold /10 #22
2016 Panini National Treasures Signature Dual Materials Printing Plates Black /1 #22
2016 Panini National Treasures Signature Dual Materials Printing Plates Cyan /1 #22
2016 Panini National Treasures Signature Dual Materials Printing Plates Magenta /1 #22
2016 Panini National Treasures Signature Dual Materials Printing Plates Yellow /1 #22
2016 Panini National Treasures Signature Dual Materials Silver /15 #22
2016 Panini National Treasures Signature Firesuit Materials /25 #24
2016 Panini National Treasures Signature Firesuit Materials Black /3 #24
2016 Panini National Treasures Signature Firesuit Materials Blue /1 #24
2016 Panini National Treasures Signature Firesuit Materials Gold /10 #24
2016 Panini National Treasures Signature Firesuit Materials Laundry Tag /1 #24
2016 Panini National Treasures Signature Firesuit Materials Printing Plates Black /1 #24
2016 Panini National Treasures Signature Firesuit Materials Printing Plates Cyan /1 #24
2016 Panini National Treasures Signature Firesuit Materials Printing Plates Magenta /1 #24
2016 Panini National Treasures Signature Firesuit Materials Printing Plates Yellow /1 #24
2016 Panini National Treasures Signature Firesuit Materials Silver /15 #24
2016 Panini National Treasures Signature Quad Materials /25 #22
2016 Panini National Treasures Signature Quad Materials Black /5 #22
2016 Panini National Treasures Signature Quad Materials Blue /1 #22
2016 Panini National Treasures Signature Quad Materials Gold /10 #22
2016 Panini National Treasures Signature Quad Materials Printing Plates Black /1 #22
2016 Panini National Treasures Signature Quad Materials Printing Plates Cyan /1 #22
2016 Panini National Treasures Signature Quad Materials Printing Plates Magenta /1 #22
2016 Panini National Treasures Signature Quad Materials Printing Plates Yellow /1 #22
2016 Panini National Treasures Signature Quad Materials Silver /15 #22
2016 Panini National Treasures Signature Sheet Metal Materials /25 #22
2016 Panini National Treasures Signature Sheet Metal Materials Black /5 #22
2016 Panini National Treasures Signature Sheet Metal Materials Blue /1 #22
2016 Panini National Treasures Signature Sheet Metal Materials Gold /10 #22
2016 Panini National Treasures Signature Sheet Metal Materials Printing Plates Black /1 #22
2016 Panini National Treasures Signature Sheet Metal Materials Printing Plates Cyan /1 #22
2016 Panini National Treasures Signature Sheet Metal Materials Printing Plates Magenta /1 #22
2016 Panini National Treasures Signature Sheet Metal Materials Printing Plates Yellow /1 #22
2016 Panini National Treasures Signature Sheet Metal Materials Silver /15 #22
2016 Panini National Treasures Signatures Black /5 #21
2016 Panini National Treasures Signatures Blue /1 #21
2016 Panini National Treasures Signatures Gold /10 #21
2016 Panini National Treasures Signatures Printing Plates Black /1 #21
2016 Panini National Treasures Signatures Printing Plates Cyan /1 #21
2016 Panini National Treasures Signatures Printing Plates Magenta /1 #21
2016 Panini National Treasures Signatures Printing Plates Yellow /1 #21
2016 Panini National Treasures Signatures Silver /15 #21
2016 Panini National Treasures Silver /20 #20
2016 Panini National Treasures Six Signatures /25 #3
2016 Panini National Treasures Six Signatures Black /10 #3
2016 Panini National Treasures Six Signatures Blue /1 #3
2016 Panini National Treasures Six Signatures Gold /15 #3
2016 Panini National Treasures Timelines /25 #16
2016 Panini National Treasures Timelines Black /5 #16
2016 Panini National Treasures Timelines Blue /1 #16
2016 Panini National Treasures Timelines Gold /10 #16
2016 Panini National Treasures Timelines Printing Plates Black /1 #16
2016 Panini National Treasures Timelines Printing Plates Cyan /1 #16
2016 Panini National Treasures Timelines Printing Plates Magenta /1 #16
2016 Panini National Treasures Timelines Printing Plates Yellow /1 #16
2016 Panini National Treasures Timelines Signatures /25 #15
2016 Panini National Treasures Timelines Signatures Black /5 #15
2016 Panini National Treasures Timelines Signatures Blue /1 #15
2016 Panini National Treasures Timelines Signatures Gold /10 #15
2016 Panini National Treasures Timelines Signatures Printing Plates Black /1 #15
2016 Panini National Treasures Timelines Signatures Printing Plates Cyan /1 #15
2016 Panini National Treasures Timelines Signatures Printing Plates Magenta /1 #15
2016 Panini National Treasures Timelines Signatures Printing Plates Yellow /1 #15
2016 Panini National Treasures Timelines Signatures Silver /15 #15
2016 Panini National Treasures Timelines Silver /15 #16
2016 Panini National Treasures Trio Driver Materials /25 #12
2016 Panini National Treasures Trio Driver Materials /25 #15
2016 Panini National Treasures Trio Driver Materials Black /5 #12
2016 Panini National Treasures Trio Driver Materials Black /5 #15
2016 Panini National Treasures Trio Driver Materials Blue /1 #12
2016 Panini National Treasures Trio Driver Materials Blue /1 #15
2016 Panini National Treasures Trio Driver Materials Gold /10 #12
2016 Panini National Treasures Trio Driver Materials Gold /10 #15
2016 Panini National Treasures Trio Driver Materials Printing Plates Black /1 #12
2016 Panini National Treasures Trio Driver Materials Printing Plates Black /1 #15
2016 Panini National Treasures Trio Driver Materials Printing Plates Cyan /1 #12
2016 Panini National Treasures Trio Driver Materials Printing Plates Cyan /1 #15
2016 Panini National Treasures Trio Driver Materials Printing Plates Magenta /1 #12
2016 Panini National Treasures Trio Driver Materials Printing Plates Magenta /1 #15
2016 Panini National Treasures Trio Driver Materials Printing Plates Yellow /1 #12
2016 Panini National Treasures Trio Driver Materials Printing Plates Yellow /1 #15
2016 Panini National Treasures Trio Driver Materials Silver /15 #12
2016 Panini National Treasures Trio Driver Materials Silver /15 #15
2016 Panini Prizm #33
2016 Panini Prizm Autographs Prizms #57
2016 Panini Prizm Autographs Prizms Black /3 #57
2016 Panini Prizm Autographs Prizms Blue Flag /50 #57
2016 Panini Prizm Autographs Prizms Camo /3 #57
2016 Panini Prizm Autographs Prizms Checkered Flag /1 #57
2016 Panini Prizm Autographs Prizms Gold /10 #57
2016 Panini Prizm Autographs Prizms Green Flag /75 #57
2016 Panini Prizm Autographs Prizms Rainbow /24 #57
2016 Panini Prizm Autographs Prizms Red Flag /25 #57
2016 Panini Prizm Autographs Prizms Red White and Blue /25 #57
2016 Panini Prizm Autographs Prizms White Flag /5 #57
2016 Panini Prizm Prizms #33
2016 Panini Prizm Prizms Black /3 #33
2016 Panini Prizm Prizms Blue Flag /99 #33
2016 Panini Prizm Prizms Camo /95 #33
2016 Panini Prizm Prizms Checkered Flag /1 #33
2016 Panini Prizm Prizms Gold /10 #33
2016 Panini Prizm Prizms Green Flag /149 #33
2016 Panini Prizm Prizms Rainbow /24 #33
2016 Panini Prizm Prizms Red Flag /75 #33
2016 Panini Prizm Prizms Red White and Blue #33
2016 Panini Prizm Prizms White Flag /5 #33
2016 Panini Torque #45
2016 Panini Torque #50
2016 Panini Torque Artist Proof /50 #45
2016 Panini Torque Artist Proof /50 #50
2016 Panini Torque Blackout /1 #45
2016 Panini Torque Blackout /1 #50
2016 Panini Torque Blue /125 #45
2016 Panini Torque Blue /125 #50
2016 Panini Torque Clear Vision #30
2016 Panini Torque Clear Vision Blue /99 #30
2016 Panini Torque Clear Vision Gold /149 #30
2016 Panini Torque Clear Vision Green /25 #30
2016 Panini Torque Clear Vision Purple /10 #30
2016 Panini Torque Clear Vision Red /49 #30
2016 Panini Torque Dual Materials /199 #4
2016 Panini Torque Dual Materials Blue /99 #4
2016 Panini Torque Dual Materials Green /25 #4
2016 Panini Torque Dual Materials Purple /10 #4
2016 Panini Torque Dual Materials Red /49 #4
2016 Panini Torque Gold #45
2016 Panini Torque Gold #50
2016 Panini Torque Holo Gold /5 #45
2016 Panini Torque Holo Gold /5 #50
2016 Panini Torque Holo Silver /10 #45
2016 Panini Torque Holo Silver /10 #50
2016 Panini Torque Jumbo Firesuit Autographs /30 #9
2016 Panini Torque Jumbo Firesuit Autographs Blue /25 #9
2016 Panini Torque Jumbo Firesuit Autographs Green /15 #9
2016 Panini Torque Jumbo Firesuit Autographs Purple /10 #9
2016 Panini Torque Jumbo Firesuit Autographs Red /20 #9
2016 Panini Torque Pairings Materials /125 #16
2016 Panini Torque Pairings Materials Blue /99 #16
2016 Panini Torque Pairings Materials Green /25 #16
2016 Panini Torque Pairings Materials Purple /10 #16
2016 Panini Torque Pairings Materials Red /49 #16
2016 Panini Torque Printing Plates Black /1 #45
2016 Panini Torque Printing Plates Black /1 #50
2016 Panini Torque Printing Plates Cyan /1 #45
2016 Panini Torque Printing Plates Cyan /1 #50
2016 Panini Torque Printing Plates Magenta /1 #45
2016 Panini Torque Printing Plates Magenta /1 #50
2016 Panini Torque Printing Plates Yellow /1 #45
2016 Panini Torque Printing Plates Yellow /1 #50
2016 Panini Torque Purple /25 #45
2016 Panini Torque Purple /25 #50
2016 Panini Torque Red /99 #45
2016 Panini Torque Red /99 #50
2016 Panini Torque Silhouettes Firesuit Autographs /30 #25
2016 Panini Torque Silhouettes Firesuit Autographs Blue /25 #25
2016 Panini Torque Silhouettes Firesuit Autographs Green /15 #25
2016 Panini Torque Silhouettes Firesuit Autographs Purple /10 #25
2016 Panini Torque Silhouettes Firesuit Autographs Red /20 #25
2016 Panini Torque Silhouettes Sheet Metal Autographs /30 #25
2016 Panini Torque Silhouettes Sheet Metal Autographs Blue /25 #25
2016 Panini Torque Silhouettes Sheet Metal Autographs Green /15 #25
2016 Panini Torque Silhouettes Sheet Metal Autographs Purple /10 #25
2016 Panini Torque Silhouettes Sheet Metal Autographs Red /20 #25
2016 Panini Torque Superstar Vision #10
2016 Panini Torque Superstar Vision Blue /99 #10
2016 Panini Torque Superstar Vision Gold /149 #10
2016 Panini Torque Superstar Vision Green /25 #10
2016 Panini Torque Superstar Vision Purple /10 #10
2016 Panini Torque Superstar Vision Red /49 #10
2016 Panini Torque Test Proof Black /1 #45
2016 Panini Torque Test Proof Black /1 #50
2016 Panini Torque Test Proof Cyan /1 #45
2016 Panini Torque Test Proof Cyan /1 #50
2016 Panini Torque Test Proof Magenta /1 #45
2016 Panini Torque Test Proof Magenta /1 #50
2016 Panini Torque Test Proof Yellow /1 #45
2016 Panini Torque Test Proof Yellow /1 #50
2017 Donruss #28
2017 Donruss #81
2017 Donruss Artist Proof /25 #28
2017 Donruss Artist Proof /25 #81
2017 Donruss Blue Foil /299 #28
2017 Donruss Blue Foil /299 #81
2017 Donruss Gold Foil /499 #28
2017 Donruss Gold Foil /499 #81
2017 Donruss Gold Press Proof /99 #28
2017 Donruss Gold Press Proof /99 #81
2017 Donruss Green Foil /199 #28
2017 Donruss Green Foil /199 #81
2017 Donruss Phenoms #2
2017 Donruss Phenoms Cracked Ice /999 #2
2017 Donruss Press Proof /49 #28
2017 Donruss Press Proof /49 #81
2017 Donruss Printing Plates Black /1 #28
2017 Donruss Printing Plates Black /1 #81
2017 Donruss Printing Plates Cyan /1 #28
2017 Donruss Printing Plates Cyan /1 #81
2017 Donruss Printing Plates Magenta /1 #28
2017 Donruss Printing Plates Magenta /1 #81
2017 Donruss Printing Plates Yellow /1 #28
2017 Donruss Printing Plates Yellow /1 #81
2017 Donruss Rubber Relics #44
2017 Donruss Rubber Relics Holo Black /10 #44
2017 Donruss Rubber Relics Holo Gold /25 #44
2017 Donruss Studio Signatures #15
2017 Donruss Studio Signatures Holo Black /1 #15
2017 Donruss Studio Signatures Holo Gold /25 #15
2017 Panini Father's Day /499 #70
2017 Panini Father's Day Autographs /25 #70
2017 Panini Father's Day Cracked Ice /25 #70
2017 Panini Father's Day Foil /50 #70
2017 Panini Father's Day Future Frames /10 #70
2017 Panini Father's Day Hyperplaid /1 #70
2017 Panini Father's Day Lava Flow /5 #70
2017 Panini Father's Day Thick Stock /25 #70
2017 Panini National Convention /399 #R11
2017 Panini National Convention Autographs #R11
2017 Panini National Convention Autographs Hyperplaid /1 #R11
2017 Panini National Convention Escher Squares /25 #R11
2017 Panini National Convention Escher Squares Thick Stock /10 #R11
2017 Panini National Convention Galatic Windows /5 #R11
2017 Panini National Convention Hyperplaid /1 #R11
2017 Panini National Convention Pyramids /10 #R11
2017 Panini National Convention Rainbow Spokes /49 #R11
2017 Panini National Convention Rainbow Spokes Thick Stock /25 #R11
2017 Panini National Convention Rapture /99 #R11
2017 Panini National Treasures Associate Sponsor Patch Signatures 1 /1 #19
2017 Panini National Treasures Associate Sponsor Patch Signatures 2 /1 #19
2017 Panini National Treasures Associate Sponsor Patch Signatures 3 /1 #19
2017 Panini National Treasures Associate Sponsor Patch Signatures 4 /1 #19
2017 Panini National Treasures Associate Sponsor Patch Signatures 5 /1 #19
2017 Panini National Treasures Associate Sponsor Patch Signatures 6 /1 #19
2017 Panini National Treasures Associate Sponsor Patch Signatures 7 /1 #19
2017 Panini National Treasures Car Manufacturer Patch Signatures /1 #19
2017 Panini National Treasures Firesuit Manufacturer Patch Signatures /1 #19
2017 Panini National Treasures Flag Patch Signatures /1 #19
2017 Panini National Treasures Goodyear Patch Signatures /2 #19
2017 Panini National Treasures Nameplate Patch Signatures /1 #19
2017 Panini National Treasures NASCAR Patch Signatures /1 #19
2017 Panini National Treasures Rookie Material Signatures /25 #31
2017 Panini National Treasures Rookie Material Signatures Black /1 #31
2017 Panini National Treasures Rookie Material Signatures Gold /15 #31
2017 Panini National Treasures Rookie Material Signatures Green /5 #31
2017 Panini National Treasures Rookie Material Signatures Holo Gold /10 #31
2017 Panini National Treasures Rookie Material Signatures Holo Silver /20 #31
2017 Panini National Treasures Rookie Material Signatures Laundry Tag /1 #31
2017 Panini National Treasures Rookie Material Signatures Printing Plates Black /1 #31
2017 Panini National Treasures Rookie Material Signatures Printing Plates Cyan /1 #31
2017 Panini National Treasures Rookie Material Signatures Printing Plates Magenta /1 #31
2017 Panini National Treasures Rookie Material Signatures Printing Plates Yellow /1 #31
2017 Panini National Treasures Series Sponsor Patch Signatures /1 #19
2017 Panini National Treasures Sunoco Patch Signatures /1 #19
2017 Panini National Treasures Three Wide /25 #2
2017 Panini National Treasures Three Wide Black /1 #2
2017 Panini National Treasures Three Wide Gold /15 #2
2017 Panini National Treasures Three Wide Green /5 #2
2017 Panini National Treasures Three Wide Holo Gold /10 #2
2017 Panini National Treasures Three Wide Holo Silver /20 #2
2017 Panini National Treasures Three Wide Laundry Tag /1 #2
2017 Panini National Treasures Three Wide Printing Plates Black /1 #2
2017 Panini National Treasures Three Wide Printing Plates Cyan /1 #2
2017 Panini National Treasures Three Wide Printing Plates Magenta /1 #2
2017 Panini National Treasures Three Wide Printing Plates Yellow /1 #2
2017 Panini Torque #29
2017 Panini Torque #39
2017 Panini Torque Artist Proof /75 #29
2017 Panini Torque Artist Proof /75 #39
2017 Panini Torque Blackout /1 #29
2017 Panini Torque Blackout /1 #39
2017 Panini Torque Blue /150 #29
2017 Panini Torque Blue /150 #39
2017 Panini Torque Clear Vision #44
2017 Panini Torque Clear Vision Blue /99 #44
2017 Panini Torque Clear Vision Gold /149 #44
2017 Panini Torque Clear Vision Green /25 #44
2017 Panini Torque Clear Vision Purple /10 #44
2017 Panini Torque Clear Vision Red /49 #44
2017 Panini Torque Gold #29
2017 Panini Torque Gold #39
2017 Panini Torque Holo Gold /10 #29
2017 Panini Torque Holo Gold /10 #39
2017 Panini Torque Holo Silver /25 #29
2017 Panini Torque Holo Silver /25 #39
2017 Panini Torque Horsepower Heroes #10
2017 Panini Torque Horsepower Heroes Gold /199 #10
2017 Panini Torque Horsepower Heroes Holo Silver /99 #10
2017 Panini Torque Prime Associate Sponsors Jumbo Patches /1 #18A
2017 Panini Torque Prime Associate Sponsors Jumbo Patches /1 #18B
2017 Panini Torque Prime Associate Sponsors Jumbo Patches /1 #18C
2017 Panini Torque Prime Associate Sponsors Jumbo Patches /1 #18D
2017 Panini Torque Prime Associate Sponsors Jumbo Patches /1 #18E
2017 Panini Torque Prime Associate Sponsors Jumbo Patches /1 #18F
2017 Panini Torque Prime Associate Sponsors Jumbo Patches /1 #18G
2017 Panini Torque Prime Associate Sponsors Jumbo Patches /1 #18H
2017 Panini Torque Prime Associate Sponsors Jumbo Patches /1 #18I
2017 Panini Torque Prime Associate Sponsors Jumbo Patches /1 #18J
2017 Panini Torque Prime Associate Sponsors Jumbo Patches /1 #18K
2017 Panini Torque Prime Associate Sponsors Jumbo Patches /1 #18L
2017 Panini Torque Prime Associate Sponsors Jumbo Patches /1 #18M
2017 Panini Torque Prime Flag Jumbo Patches /1 #18
2017 Panini Torque Prime Goodyear Jumbo Patches /1 #18
2017 Panini Torque Prime Manufacturer Jumbo Patches /1 #18
2017 Panini Torque Prime Nameplates Jumbo Patches /2 #18
2017 Panini Torque Prime NASCAR Jumbo Patches /1 #18
2017 Panini Torque Prime Series Sponsor Jumbo Patches /1 #18
2017 Panini Torque Printing Plates Black /1 #29
2017 Panini Torque Printing Plates Black /1 #39
2017 Panini Torque Printing Plates Cyan /1 #29
2017 Panini Torque Printing Plates Cyan /1 #39
2017 Panini Torque Printing Plates Magenta /1 #29
2017 Panini Torque Printing Plates Magenta /1 #39
2017 Panini Torque Printing Plates Yellow /1 #29
2017 Panini Torque Printing Plates Yellow /1 #39
2017 Panini Torque Purple /50 #29
2017 Panini Torque Purple /50 #39
2017 Panini Torque Raced Relics /499 #20
2017 Panini Torque Raced Relics Blue /99 #20
2017 Panini Torque Raced Relics Green /25 #20
2017 Panini Torque Raced Relics Purple /10 #20
2017 Panini Torque Raced Relics Red /49 #20
2017 Panini Torque Red /100 #29
2017 Panini Torque Red /100 #39
2017 Panini Torque Rookie Stripes #2
2017 Panini Torque Rookie Stripes Gold /199 #2
2017 Panini Torque Rookie Stripes Holo Silver /99 #2
2017 Panini Torque Silhouettes Firesuit Signatures /51 #9
2017 Panini Torque Silhouettes Firesuit Signatures Blue /49 #9
2017 Panini Torque Silhouettes Firesuit Signatures Green /15 #9
2017 Panini Torque Silhouettes Firesuit Signatures Purple /10 #9
2017 Panini Torque Silhouettes Firesuit Signatures Red /25 #9
2017 Panini Torque Silhouettes Sheet Metal Signatures /51 #17
2017 Panini Torque Silhouettes Sheet Metal Signatures Blue /49 #17
2017 Panini Torque Silhouettes Sheet Metal Signatures Green /15 #17
2017 Panini Torque Silhouettes Sheet Metal Signatures Purple /10 #17
2017 Panini Torque Silhouettes Sheet Metal Signatures Red /25 #17
2017 Panini Torque Test Proof Black /1 #29
2017 Panini Torque Test Proof Black /1 #39
2017 Panini Torque Test Proof Cyan /1 #29
2017 Panini Torque Test Proof Cyan /1 #39
2017 Panini Torque Test Proof Magenta /1 #29
2017 Panini Torque Test Proof Magenta /1 #39
2017 Panini Torque Test Proof Yellow /1 #29
2017 Panini Torque Test Proof Yellow /1 #39
2017 Select #21
2017 Select Prizms Black /3 #21
2017 Select Prizms Blue /199 #21
2017 Select Prizms Checkered Flag /1 #21
2017 Select Prizms Gold /10 #21
2017 Select Prizms Purple Pulsar #21
2017 Select Prizms Red /99 #21
2017 Select Prizms Red White and Blue Pulsar /299 #21
2017 Select Prizms Silver #21
2017 Select Prizms Tie Dye /24 #21
2017 Select Prizms White /50 #21
2017 Select Select Swatches #43
2017 Select Select Swatches Prizms Blue /199 #43
2017 Select Select Swatches Prizms Checkered Flag /1 #43
2017 Select Select Swatches Prizms Gold /10 #43
2017 Select Select Swatches Prizms Red /99 #43
2017 Select Sheet Metal #25
2017 Select Sheet Metal Prizms Blue /149 #25
2017 Select Sheet Metal Prizms Checkered Flag /1 #25
2017 Select Sheet Metal Prizms Gold /10 #25
2017 Select Sheet Metal Prizms Red /99 #25
2017 Select Signature Paint Schemes #16
2017 Select Signature Paint Schemes Prizms Blue /10 #16
2017 Select Signature Paint Schemes Prizms Checkered Flag /1 #16
2017 Select Signature Paint Schemes Prizms Gold /3 #16

2017 Select Signature Paint Schemes Prizms Red /5 #16
2017 Select Signature Swatches #43
2017 Select Signature Swatches Dual #25
2017 Select Signature Swatches Dual Prizms Checkered Flag /1 #25
2017 Select Signature Swatches Dual Prizms Gold /10 #25
2017 Select Signature Swatches Dual Prizms Tie Dye /24 #25
2017 Select Signature Swatches Dual Prizms White /30 #25
2017 Select Signature Swatches Prizms Checkered Flag /1 #43
2017 Select Signature Swatches Prizms Gold /10 #43
2017 Select Signature Swatches Prizms Tie Dye /24 #43
2017 Select Signature Swatches Prizms White /30 #43
2018 Certified #20
2018 Certified Black /1 #20
2018 Certified Blue /99 #20
2018 Certified Fresh Faces /199 #13
2018 Certified Fresh Faces Black /1 #13
2018 Certified Fresh Faces Blue /99 #13
2018 Certified Fresh Faces Gold /49 #13
2018 Certified Fresh Faces Green /10 #13
2018 Certified Fresh Faces Mirror Black /1 #13
2018 Certified Fresh Faces Mirror Gold /25 #13
2018 Certified Fresh Faces Mirror Green /5 #13
2018 Certified Fresh Faces Mirror Purple /10 #13
2018 Certified Fresh Faces Purple /25 #13
2018 Certified Fresh Faces Red /149 #13
2018 Certified Gold /49 #20
2018 Certified Green /10 #20
2018 Certified Mirror Black /1 #20
2018 Certified Mirror Gold /25 #20
2018 Certified Mirror Green /5 #20
2018 Certified Mirror Purple /10 #20
2018 Certified Orange /249 #20
2018 Certified Purple /25 #20
2018 Certified Red /199 #20
2018 Donruss #55
2018 Donruss #144
2018 Donruss Artist Proofs /25 #55
2018 Donruss Artist Proofs /25 #144
2018 Donruss Gold Foil /499 #55
2018 Donruss Gold Foil /499 #144
2018 Donruss Gold Press Proofs /99 #55
2018 Donruss Gold Press Proofs /99 #144
2018 Donruss Green Foil /199 #55
2018 Donruss Green Foil /199 #144
2018 Donruss Press Proofs /49 #55
2018 Donruss Press Proofs /49 #144
2018 Donruss Printing Plates Black /1 #55
2018 Donruss Printing Plates Black /1 #144
2018 Donruss Printing Plates Cyan /1 #55
2018 Donruss Printing Plates Cyan /1 #144
2018 Donruss Printing Plates Magenta /1 #55
2018 Donruss Printing Plates Magenta /1 #144
2018 Donruss Printing Plates Yellow /1 #55
2018 Donruss Printing Plates Yellow /1 #144
2018 Donruss Red Foil /299 #55
2018 Donruss Red Foil /299 #144
2018 Donruss Retro Signatures '85 #20
2018 Donruss Retro Signatures '85 Black /1 #20
2018 Donruss Retro Signatures '85 Holo Gold /25 #20
2018 Donruss Rubber Relics #39
2018 Donruss Rubber Relics Black /10 #39
2018 Donruss Rubber Relics Holo Gold /99 #39
2018 Panini Prime /50 #21
2018 Panini Prime /50 #54
2018 Panini Prime /50 #87
2018 Panini Prime Black /1 #21
2018 Panini Prime Black /1 #54
2018 Panini Prime Black /1 #87
2018 Panini Prime Clear Silhouettes /99 #28
2018 Panini Prime Clear Silhouettes Black /1 #28
2018 Panini Prime Clear Silhouettes Holo Gold /50 #28
2018 Panini Prime Dual Material Autographs /50 #20
2018 Panini Prime Dual Material Autographs Black /1 #20
2018 Panini Prime Dual Material Autographs Holo Gold /15 #20
2018 Panini Prime Dual Material Autographs Laundry Tag /1 #20
2018 Panini Prime Holo Gold /25 #21
2018 Panini Prime Holo Gold /25 #54
2018 Panini Prime Holo Gold /25 #87
2018 Panini Prime Prime Jumbo Associate Sponsor 1 /1 #75
2018 Panini Prime Prime Jumbo Associate Sponsor 1 /1 #76
2018 Panini Prime Prime Jumbo Associate Sponsor 2 /1 #75
2018 Panini Prime Prime Jumbo Associate Sponsor 2 /1 #76
2018 Panini Prime Prime Jumbo Associate Sponsor 3 /1 #75
2018 Panini Prime Prime Jumbo Associate Sponsor 3 /1 #76
2018 Panini Prime Prime Jumbo Associate Sponsor 4 /1 #75
2018 Panini Prime Prime Jumbo Associate Sponsor 4 /1 #76
2018 Panini Prime Prime Jumbo Associate Sponsor 5 /1 #75
2018 Panini Prime Prime Jumbo Associate Sponsor 5 /1 #76
2018 Panini Prime Prime Jumbo Associate Sponsor 6 /1 #75
2018 Panini Prime Prime Jumbo Associate Sponsor 6 /1 #76
2018 Panini Prime Prime Jumbo Car Manufacturer /1 #75
2018 Panini Prime Prime Jumbo Car Manufacturer /1 #76
2018 Panini Prime Prime Jumbo Firesuit Manufacturer /1 #75
2018 Panini Prime Prime Jumbo Firesuit Manufacturer /1 #76
2018 Panini Prime Prime Jumbo Flag Patch /1 #75
2018 Panini Prime Prime Jumbo Flag Patch /1 #76
2018 Panini Prime Prime Jumbo Glove Manufacturer Patch /1 #75
2018 Panini Prime Prime Jumbo Glove Manufacturer Patch /1 #76
2018 Panini Prime Prime Jumbo Glove Name Patch /1 #75
2018 Panini Prime Prime Jumbo Glove Name Patch /1 #76
2018 Panini Prime Prime Jumbo Glove Number Patch /1 #75
2018 Panini Prime Prime Jumbo Glove Number Patch /1 #76
2018 Panini Prime Prime Jumbo Nameplate /1 #75
2018 Panini Prime Prime Jumbo Nameplate /1 #76
2018 Panini Prime Prime Jumbo NASCAR /1 #75
2018 Panini Prime Prime Jumbo NASCAR /1 #76
2018 Panini Prime Prime Jumbo Prime Colors /17 #75
2018 Panini Prime Prime Jumbo Prime Colors /10 #76
2018 Panini Prime Prime Jumbo Series Sponsor /1 #75
2018 Panini Prime Prime Jumbo Series Sponsor /1 #76
2018 Panini Prime Prime Jumbo Shoe Brand Logo /1 #75
2018 Panini Prime Prime Jumbo Shoe Brand Logo /1 #76
2018 Panini Prime Prime Jumbo Shoe Name Patch /1 #75
2018 Panini Prime Prime Jumbo Shoe Name Patch /1 #76
2018 Panini Prime Prime Jumbo Sunoco /1 #75
2018 Panini Prime Prime Jumbo Sunoco /1 #76
2018 Panini Prime Prime Number Signatures /25 #19
2018 Panini Prime Prime Number Signatures Black /1 #19
2018 Panini Prime Prime Number Signatures Holo Gold /10 #19
2018 Panini Prime Quad Material Autographs /54 #22
2018 Panini Prime Quad Material Autographs Black /1 #22
2018 Panini Prime Quad Material Autographs Holo Gold /25 #22
2018 Panini Prime Quad Material Autographs Laundry Tag /1 #22
2018 Panini Prime Race Used Firesuits /50 #39
2018 Panini Prime Race Used Firesuits Black /1 #39
2018 Panini Prime Race Used Firesuits Holo Gold /25 #39
2018 Panini Prime Race Used Firesuits Laundry Tag /1 #39
2018 Panini Prime Race Used Sheet Metal /50 #39
2018 Panini Prime Race Used Sheet Metal Black /1 #39
2018 Panini Prime Race Used Sheet Metal Holo Gold /25 #39
2018 Panini Prime Race Used Tires Black /1 #39
2018 Panini Prime Race Used Tires Holo Gold /25 #39
2018 Panini Prime Signature Tires /10 #19
2018 Panini Prime Signature Tires Black /1 #19
2018 Panini Prime Signature Tires Holo Gold /5 #19
2018 Panini Prizm #16
2018 Panini Prizm Prizms #16
2018 Panini Prizm Prizms Black /1 #16
2018 Panini Prizm Prizms Blue /99 #16
2018 Panini Prizm Prizms Camo #16
2018 Panini Prizm Prizms Gold /10 #16
2018 Panini Prizm Prizms Green /149 #16
2018 Panini Prizm Prizms Purple Flash #16
2018 Panini Prizm Prizms Rainbow /24 #16
2018 Panini Prizm Prizms Red /75 #16
2018 Panini Prizm Prizms Red White and Blue #16
2018 Panini Prizm Prizms White /5 #16
2018 Panini Prizm Scripted Signatures Prizms #18
2018 Panini Prizm Scripted Signatures Prizms Black /1 #18
2018 Panini Prizm Scripted Signatures Prizms Blue /75 #18
2018 Panini Prizm Scripted Signatures Prizms Camo #18
2018 Panini Prizm Scripted Signatures Prizms Gold /10 #18
2018 Panini Prizm Scripted Signatures Prizms Green /99 #18
2018 Panini Prizm Scripted Signatures Prizms Rainbow /24 #18
2018 Panini Prizm Scripted Signatures Prizms Red /50 #18
2018 Panini Prizm Scripted Signatures Prizms Red White and Blue /125 #18
2018 Panini Prizm Scripted Signatures Prizms White /5 #18
2018 Panini Victory Lane #9
2018 Panini Victory Lane Black /1 #9
2018 Panini Victory Lane Blue /25 #9
2018 Panini Victory Lane Engineered to Perfection Triple Materials /399 #19
2018 Panini Victory Lane Engineered to Perfection Triple Materials Black /25 #19
2018 Panini Victory Lane Engineered to Perfection Triple Materials Gold /199 #19
2018 Panini Victory Lane Engineered to Perfection Triple Materials Green /99 #19
2018 Panini Victory Lane Engineered to Perfection Triple Materials Laundry Tag /1 #19
2018 Panini Victory Lane Gold /99 #9
2018 Panini Victory Lane Green /5 #9
2018 Panini Victory Lane Octane Autographs /299 #38
2018 Panini Victory Lane Octane Autographs Black /1 #38
2018 Panini Victory Lane Octane Autographs Gold /99 #38
2018 Panini Victory Lane Pedal to the Metal #49
2018 Panini Victory Lane Pedal to the Metal #59
2018 Panini Victory Lane Pedal to the Metal Black /1 #49
2018 Panini Victory Lane Pedal to the Metal Black /1 #59
2018 Panini Victory Lane Pedal to the Metal Blue /25 #49
2018 Panini Victory Lane Pedal to the Metal Blue /25 #59
2018 Panini Victory Lane Pedal to the Metal Green /5 #49
2018 Panini Victory Lane Pedal to the Metal Green /5 #59
2018 Panini Victory Lane Printing Plates Black /1 #9
2018 Panini Victory Lane Printing Plates Cyan /1 #9
2018 Panini Victory Lane Printing Plates Magenta /1 #9
2018 Panini Victory Lane Printing Plates Yellow /1 #9
2018 Panini Victory Lane Race Ready Dual Materials /399 #20
2018 Panini Victory Lane Race Ready Dual Materials Black /25 #20
2018 Panini Victory Lane Race Ready Dual Materials Gold /199 #20
2018 Panini Victory Lane Race Ready Dual Materials Green /99 #20
2018 Panini Victory Lane Race Ready Dual Materials Laundry Tag /1 #20
2018 Panini Victory Lane Red /49 #9
2018 Panini Victory Lane Silver #9
2018 Panini Victory Lane Starting Grid #9
2018 Panini Victory Lane Starting Grid Black /1 #9
2018 Panini Victory Lane Starting Grid Blue /25 #9
2018 Panini Victory Lane Starting Grid Gold /99 #9
2018 Panini Victory Lane Starting Grid Green /5 #9
2018 Panini Victory Lane Starting Grid Printing Plates Black /1 #9
2018 Panini Victory Lane Starting Grid Printing Plates Cyan /1 #9
2018 Panini Victory Lane Starting Grid Printing Plates Magenta /1 #9
2018 Panini Victory Lane Starting Grid Printing Plates Yellow /1 #9
2018 Panini Victory Lane Starting Grid Red /49 #9
2018 Panini Victory Lane Victory Lane Prime Patches Associate Sponsor 1 /1 #44
2018 Panini Victory Lane Victory Lane Prime Patches Associate Sponsor 10 /1 #44
2018 Panini Victory Lane Victory Lane Prime Patches Associate Sponsor 2 /1 #44
2018 Panini Victory Lane Victory Lane Prime Patches Associate Sponsor 3 /1 #44
2018 Panini Victory Lane Victory Lane Prime Patches Associate Sponsor 4 /1 #44
2018 Panini Victory Lane Victory Lane Prime Patches Associate Sponsor 5 /1 #44
2018 Panini Victory Lane Victory Lane Prime Patches Associate Sponsor 6 /1 #44
2018 Panini Victory Lane Victory Lane Prime Patches Associate Sponsor 7 /1 #44
2018 Panini Victory Lane Victory Lane Prime Patches Associate Sponsor 8 /1 #44
2018 Panini Victory Lane Victory Lane Prime Patches Associate Sponsor 9 /1 #44
2018 Panini Victory Lane Victory Lane Prime Patches Car Manufacturer /1 #44
2018 Panini Victory Lane Victory Lane Prime Patches Firesuit Manufacturer /1 #44
2018 Panini Victory Lane Victory Lane Prime Patches Goodyear /1 #44
2018 Panini Victory Lane Victory Lane Prime Patches Nameplate /1 #44
2018 Panini Victory Lane Victory Lane Prime Patches NASCAR /1 #44
2018 Panini Victory Lane Victory Lane Prime Patches Series Sponsor /1 #44
2018 Panini Victory Lane Victory Lane Prime Patches Sunoco /1 #44
2019 Donruss #61
2019 Donruss #133
2019 Donruss Action #11
2019 Donruss Action Cracked Ice /25 #11
2019 Donruss Action Holographic #11
2019 Donruss Action Xplosion /10 #11
2019 Donruss Artist Proofs /25 #61
2019 Donruss Artist Proofs /25 #133
2019 Donruss Black /199 #61
2019 Donruss Black /199 #133
2019 Donruss Gold /299 #61
2019 Donruss Gold /299 #133
2019 Donruss Gold Press Proofs /99 #61
2019 Donruss Gold Press Proofs /99 #133
2019 Donruss Optic #38
2019 Donruss Optic #60
2019 Donruss Optic Blue Pulsar #38
2019 Donruss Optic Blue Pulsar /1 #60
2019 Donruss Optic Gold /10 #38
2019 Donruss Optic Gold /10 #60
2019 Donruss Optic Gold Vinyl /1 #38
2019 Donruss Optic Gold Vinyl /1 #60
2019 Donruss Optic Holo #38
2019 Donruss Optic Holo #60
2019 Donruss Optic Red Wave #38
2019 Donruss Optic Red Wave /1 #60
2019 Donruss Press Proofs /49 #61
2019 Donruss Press Proofs /49 #133
2019 Donruss Printing Plates Black /1 #61
2019 Donruss Printing Plates Black /1 #133
2019 Donruss Printing Plates Cyan /1 #61
2019 Donruss Printing Plates Cyan /1 #133
2019 Donruss Printing Plates Magenta /1 #61
2019 Donruss Printing Plates Magenta /1 #133
2019 Donruss Printing Plates Yellow /1 #61
2019 Donruss Printing Plates Yellow /1 #133
2019 Donruss Retro Relics '86 #3
2019 Donruss Retro Relics '86 Holo Black /10 #3
2019 Donruss Retro Relics '86 Holo Gold /25 #3
2019 Donruss Retro Relics '86 Red /250 #3
2019 Donruss Silver #61
2019 Donruss Silver #133
2019 Panini Prime /50 #11
2019 Panini Prime Autograph Materials /50 #21
2019 Panini Prime Autograph Materials Black /10 #21
2019 Panini Prime Autograph Materials Holo Gold /25 #21
2019 Panini Prime Autograph Materials Platinum Blue /1 #21
2019 Panini Prime Black /10 #11
2019 Panini Prime Clear Silhouettes Dual /99 #10
2019 Panini Prime Clear Silhouettes Dual Black /10 #10
2019 Panini Prime Clear Silhouettes Dual Holo Gold /25 #10
2019 Panini Prime Clear Silhouettes Dual Platinum Blue /1 #10
2019 Panini Prime Dual Material Autographs /99 #7
2019 Panini Prime Dual Material Autographs Black /10 #7
2019 Panini Prime Dual Material Autographs Holo Gold /25 #7
2019 Panini Prime Dual Material Autographs Laundry Tags /1 #7
2019 Panini Prime Emerald /5 #11
2019 Panini Prime NASCAR Shadowbox Signatures Car Number /99 #3
2019 Panini Prime NASCAR Shadowbox Signatures Manufacturer /10 #3
2019 Panini Prime NASCAR Shadowbox Signatures Sponsor /25 #3
2019 Panini Prime NASCAR Shadowbox Signatures Team Owner /1 #3
2019 Panini Prime Platinum Blue /1 #11
2019 Panini Prime Prime Jumbo Associate Sponsor 1 /1 #80
2019 Panini Prime Prime Jumbo Associate Sponsor 1 /1 #81
2019 Panini Prime Prime Jumbo Associate Sponsor 2 /1 #80
2019 Panini Prime Prime Jumbo Associate Sponsor 3 /1 #80
2019 Panini Prime Prime Jumbo Associate Sponsor 4 /1 #80
2019 Panini Prime Prime Jumbo Associate Sponsor 5 /1 #80
2019 Panini Prime Prime Jumbo Associate Sponsor 6 /1 #80
2019 Panini Prime Prime Jumbo Car Manufacturer /1 #80
2019 Panini Prime Prime Jumbo Car Manufacturer /1 #81
2019 Panini Prime Prime Jumbo Firesuit Manufacturer /1 #80
2019 Panini Prime Prime Jumbo Firesuit Manufacturer /1 #81
2019 Panini Prime Prime Jumbo Flag Patch /1 #80
2019 Panini Prime Prime Jumbo Glove Manufacturer Patch /1 #80
2019 Panini Prime Prime Jumbo Glove Manufacturer Patch /1 #81
2019 Panini Prime Prime Jumbo Glove Name Patch /1 #80
2019 Panini Prime Prime Jumbo Glove Name Patch /1 #81
2019 Panini Prime Prime Jumbo Glove Number Patch /1 #80
2019 Panini Prime Prime Jumbo Glove Number Patch /1 #81
2019 Panini Prime Prime Jumbo Nameplate /1 #80
2019 Panini Prime Prime Jumbo Nameplate /1 #81
2019 Panini Prime Prime Jumbo NASCAR /1 #80
2019 Panini Prime Prime Jumbo Prime Colors /10 #80
2019 Panini Prime Prime Jumbo Prime Colors /9 #81
2019 Panini Prime Prime Jumbo Shoe Brand Logo /1 #80
2019 Panini Prime Prime Jumbo Shoe Brand Logo /1 #81
2019 Panini Prime Prime Jumbo Shoe Name Patch /1 #80
2019 Panini Prime Prime Jumbo Shoe Name Patch /1 #81
2019 Panini Prime Prime Jumbo Sunoco /1 #80
2019 Panini Prime Prime Jumbo Sunoco /1 #81
2019 Panini Prime Prime Number Die Cut Signatures Black /10 #4
2019 Panini Prime Prime Number Die Cut Signatures Holo Gold /25 #4
2019 Panini Prime Prime Number Die Cut Signatures Platinum Blue /1 #4
2019 Panini Prime Prime Signatures Black /10 #20
2019 Panini Prime Prime Signatures Holo Gold /25 #20
2019 Panini Prime Prime Signatures Platinum Blue /1 #20
2019 Panini Prime Race Used Duals Firesuits Black /10 #2
2019 Panini Prime Race Used Duals Firesuits Laundry Tags /1 #2
2019 Panini Prime Race Used Duals Sheet Metal Black /10 #2
2019 Panini Prime Race Used Duals Sheet Metal Platinum Blue /1 #2
2019 Panini Prime Race Used Duals Tires Black /10 #2
2019 Panini Prime Race Used Duals Tires Platinum Blue /1 #2
2019 Panini Prime Race Used Firesuits Black /10 #37
2019 Panini Prime Race Used Firesuits Laundry Tags /1 #37
2019 Panini Prime Race Used Sheet Metal Black /10 #37
2019 Panini Prime Race Used Sheet Metal Platinum Blue /1 #37
2019 Panini Prime Race Used Tires Black /10 #37
2019 Panini Prime Race Used Tires Platinum Blue /1 #37
2019 Panini Prime Race Used Trios Firesuits Black /10 #2
2019 Panini Prime Race Used Trios Firesuits Laundry Tags /1 #2
2019 Panini Prime Race Used Trios Sheet Metal Black /10 #2
2019 Panini Prime Race Used Trios Sheet Metal Platinum Blue /1 #2
2019 Panini Prime Race Used Trios Tires Black /10 #2
2019 Panini Prime Race Used Trios Tires Platinum Blue /1 #2
2019 Panini Prizm #11
2019 Panini Prizm Patented Penmanship Prizms #19
2019 Panini Prizm Patented Penmanship Prizms Black /1 #19
2019 Panini Prizm Patented Penmanship Prizms Blue /30 #19
2019 Panini Prizm Patented Penmanship Prizms Camo #19
2019 Panini Prizm Patented Penmanship Prizms Gold /10 #19
2019 Panini Prizm Patented Penmanship Prizms Green /35 #19
2019 Panini Prizm Patented Penmanship Prizms Rainbow /24 #19
2019 Panini Prizm Patented Penmanship Prizms Red /25 #19
2019 Panini Prizm Patented Penmanship Prizms Red White and Blue #19
2019 Panini Prizm Patented Penmanship Prizms White /5 #19
2019 Panini Prizm Prizms #11
2019 Panini Prizm Prizms Black /1 #11
2019 Panini Prizm Prizms Blue /75 #11
2019 Panini Prizm Prizms Camo #11
2019 Panini Prizm Prizms Flash #11
2019 Panini Prizm Prizms Gold /10 #11
2019 Panini Prizm Prizms Green /99 #11
2019 Panini Prizm Prizms Rainbow /24 #11
2019 Panini Prizm Prizms Red /50 #11
2019 Panini Prizm Prizms Red White and Blue #11
2019 Panini Prizm Prizms White /5 #11
2019 Panini Prizm Prizms White Sparkle #11
2019 Panini Prizm Scripted Signatures Prizms #18
2019 Panini Prizm Scripted Signatures Prizms Black /1 #18
2019 Panini Prizm Scripted Signatures Prizms Blue /30 #18
2019 Panini Prizm Scripted Signatures Prizms Camo #18
2019 Panini Prizm Scripted Signatures Prizms Gold /10 #18
2019 Panini Prizm Scripted Signatures Prizms Green /35 #18
2019 Panini Prizm Scripted Signatures Prizms Rainbow /24 #18
2019 Panini Prizm Scripted Signatures Prizms Red /25 #18
2019 Panini Prizm Scripted Signatures Prizms Red White and Blue #18
2019 Panini Prizm Scripted Signatures Prizms White /5 #18
2019 Panini Victory Lane #11
2019 Panini Victory Lane Black /1 #11
2019 Panini Victory Lane Dual Swatches #13
2019 Panini Victory Lane Dual Swatches Gold /99 #13
2019 Panini Victory Lane Dual Swatches Laundry Tag /1 #13
2019 Panini Victory Lane Dual Swatches Platinum /1 #13
2019 Panini Victory Lane Dual Swatches Red /25 #13
2019 Panini Victory Lane Gold /25 #11
2019 Panini Victory Lane Machines #15
2019 Panini Victory Lane Machines Black /1 #15
2019 Panini Victory Lane Machines Blue /99 #15
2019 Panini Victory Lane Machines Gold /25 #15
2019 Panini Victory Lane Machines Green /5 #15
2019 Panini Victory Lane Machines Printing Plates Black /1 #15
2019 Panini Victory Lane Machines Printing Plates Cyan /1 #15
2019 Panini Victory Lane Machines Printing Plates Magenta /1 #15
2019 Panini Victory Lane Machines Printing Plates Yellow /1 #15
2019 Panini Victory Lane Pedal to the Metal #37
2019 Panini Victory Lane Pedal to the Metal #60
2019 Panini Victory Lane Pedal to the Metal Black /1 #37
2019 Panini Victory Lane Pedal to the Metal Black /1 #60
2019 Panini Victory Lane Pedal to the Metal Gold /25 #37
2019 Panini Victory Lane Pedal to the Metal Gold /25 #60
2019 Panini Victory Lane Pedal to the Metal Green /5 #37
2019 Panini Victory Lane Pedal to the Metal Green /5 #60
2019 Panini Victory Lane Pedal to the Metal Red /3 #37
2019 Panini Victory Lane Pedal to the Metal Red /3 #60
2019 Panini Victory Lane Printing Plates Black /1 #11
2019 Panini Victory Lane Printing Plates Cyan /1 #11
2019 Panini Victory Lane Printing Plates Magenta /1 #11
2019 Panini Victory Lane Printing Plates Yellow /1 #11
2019 Panini Victory Lane Signature Swatches #25
2019 Panini Victory Lane Signature Swatches Gold /99 #25
2019 Panini Victory Lane Signature Swatches Laundry Tag /1 #25
2019 Panini Victory Lane Signature Swatches Platinum /1 #25
2019 Panini Victory Lane Signature Swatches Red /25 #25
2019 Panini Victory Lane Starting Grid #5
2019 Panini Victory Lane Starting Grid Black /1 #5
2019 Panini Victory Lane Starting Grid Blue /99 #5
2019 Panini Victory Lane Starting Grid Gold /25 #5
2019 Panini Victory Lane Starting Grid Green /5 #5
2019 Panini Victory Lane Starting Grid Printing Plates Black /1 #5
2019 Panini Victory Lane Starting Grid Printing Plates Cyan /1 #5
2019 Panini Victory Lane Starting Grid Printing Plates Magenta /1 #5
2019 Panini Victory Lane Starting Grid Printing Plates Yellow /1 #5
2019 Panini Victory Lane Triple Swatches #10
2019 Panini Victory Lane Triple Swatches Gold /99 #10
2019 Panini Victory Lane Triple Swatches Laundry Tag /1 #10
2019 Panini Victory Lane Triple Swatches Platinum /1 #10
2019 Panini Victory Lane Triple Swatches Red /25 #10
2020 Donruss #54
2020 Donruss #138
2020 Donruss Black Numbers /13 #54
2020 Donruss Black Numbers /13 #138
2020 Donruss Black Trophy Club /1 #54
2020 Donruss Black Trophy Club /1 #138
2020 Donruss Blue /199 #138
2020 Donruss Blue /199 #54
2020 Donruss Carolina Blue #54
2020 Donruss Carolina Blue #138
2020 Donruss Green /99 #54
2020 Donruss Green /99 #138
2020 Donruss Optic #39
2020 Donruss Optic Carolina Blue Wave #39
2020 Donruss Optic Gold /10 #39
2020 Donruss Optic Gold Vinyl /1 #39
2020 Donruss Optic Holo #39
2020 Donruss Optic Orange Pulsar #39
2020 Donruss Optic Red Mojo #39
2020 Donruss Optic Signatures Gold Vinyl /1 #39
2020 Donruss Optic Signatures Holo /99 #39
2020 Donruss Orange #54
2020 Donruss Orange #138
2020 Donruss Pink /25 #54
2020 Donruss Pink /25 #138
2020 Donruss Printing Plates Black /1 #54
2020 Donruss Printing Plates Black /1 #138
2020 Donruss Printing Plates Cyan /1 #54
2020 Donruss Printing Plates Cyan /1 #138
2020 Donruss Printing Plates Magenta /1 #54
2020 Donruss Printing Plates Magenta /1 #138
2020 Donruss Printing Plates Yellow /1 #138
2020 Donruss Printing Plates Yellow /1 #54
2020 Donruss Purple /49 #54
2020 Donruss Purple /49 #138
2020 Donruss Race Day Relics #23
2020 Donruss Race Day Relics Holo Black /10 #23
2020 Donruss Race Day Relics Holo Gold /25 #23
2020 Donruss Race Day Relics Red /250 #23
2020 Donruss Red /299 #54
2020 Donruss Red /299 #138
2020 Donruss Signature Series #17
2020 Donruss Signature Series Holo Black /1 #17
2020 Donruss Signature Series Holo Gold /14 #17
2020 Donruss Signature Series Red /25 #17
2020 Donruss Silver #54
2020 Donruss Silver #138

Dale Earnhardt

1983 UNO Racing #27
1986 SportStars Photo-Graphics #4
1988 Maxx Charlotte #45
1988 Maxx Charlotte #38
1988 Maxx Charlotte #17
1988 Maxx Charlotte #13
1988 Maxx Charlotte #9
1988 Maxx Charlotte #54
1988 Maxx Charlotte #49
1988 Maxx Charlotte #84
1988 Maxx Charlotte #87
1988 Maxx Charlotte #99P
1989 Maxx #148
1989 Maxx #144
1989 Maxx #121
1989 Maxx #108
1989 Maxx #102
1989 Maxx #60
1989 Maxx #160
1969 Maxx #3
1989 Maxx Crisco #6
1990 AC Racing Proven Winners #3
1990 Maxx #191
1990 Maxx #116
1990 Maxx #3
1990 Maxx #179
1990 Maxx #183
1990 Maxx #195
1990 Maxx Glossy #195
1990 Maxx Glossy #191
1990 Maxx Glossy #183
1990 Maxx Glossy #179
1990 Maxx Glossy #116
1990 Maxx Glossy #3
1990 Maxx Holly Farms #HF1
1991 AC Racing #1
1991 Hickory Motor Speedway #6
1991 Hickory Motor Speedway #10
1991 IROC #12
1991 Maxx #178
1991 Maxx #179
1991 Maxx #184
1991 Maxx #185
1991 Maxx #187
1991 Maxx #198
1991 Maxx #220
1991 Maxx #174
1991 Maxx #173
1991 Maxx #3
1991 Maxx #191
1991 Maxx #192
1991 Maxx #200
1991 Maxx McDonald's #1A
1991 Maxx McDonald's #1B
1991 Maxx McDonald's #30
1991 Maxx Racing for Kids #1
1991 Maxx The Winston Acrylics #5
1991 Maxx Update #3
1991 Maxx Update #220
1991 Maxx Update #200
1991 Maxx Winston 20th Anniversary Foils #10
1991 Maxx Winston 20th Anniversary Foils #16
1991 Maxx Winston 20th Anniversary Foils #17
1991 Maxx Winston 20th Anniversary Foils #20
1991 Sports Legends Phil Parsons #PP18
1991 Sunbelt Racing Legends #3
1991 Traks #3A
1991 Traks #3B
1991 Traks #103A
1991 Traks #103B
1991 Traks #190A
1991 Traks #190B
1991 Traks Mom-n-Pop's Biscuits Dale Earnhardt #3
1991 Traks Mom-n-Pop's Biscuits Dale Earnhardt #4
1991 Traks Mom-n-Pop's Biscuits Dale Earnhardt #5
1991 Traks Mom-n-Pop's Biscuits Dale Earnhardt #6
1991 Traks Mom-n-Pop's Biscuits Dale Earnhardt #1
1991 Traks Mom-n-Pop's Biscuits Dale Earnhardt #2
1991 Traks Mom-n-Pop's Ham Dale Earnhardt #1
1991 Traks Mom-n-Pop's Ham Dale Earnhardt #2
1991 Traks Mom-n-Pop's Ham Dale Earnhardt #3
1991 Traks Mom-n-Pop's Ham Dale Earnhardt #4
1991 Traks Mom-n-Pop's Ham Dale Earnhardt #5
1991 Traks Mom-n-Pop's Ham Dale Earnhardt #6
1991 Traks Richard Petty #22
1992 AC Racing Postcards #1
1992 Maxx All-Pro Team #1
1992 Maxx Black #3
1992 Maxx Black #203
1992 Maxx Black #231
1992 Maxx Black #265
1992 Maxx Black #271
1992 Maxx Black #281
1992 Maxx Black #289
1992 Maxx Black #294
1992 Maxx McDonald's #2
1992 Maxx McDonald's #1
1992 Maxx Red #294
1992 Maxx Red #231
1992 Maxx Red #203
1992 Maxx Red #3
1992 Maxx Red #265
1992 Maxx Red #271
1992 Maxx Red #281
1992 Maxx Red #289
1992 Maxx Texaco Davey Allison #12
1992 Maxx The Winston #34
1992 Maxx The Winston #14
1992 Pro Set #161
1992 Pro Set #172
1992 Pro Set #182
1992 Pro Set #224
1992 Pro Set /5000 #NNO
1992 Pro Set /5000 #NNO
1992 Pro Set #1
1992 Pro Set #59
1992 Pro Set Prototypes #P1
1992 Sports Legends Alan Kulwicki #AK11
1992 Traks #3
1992 Traks #60
1992 Traks #103
1992 Traks #193
1992 Traks #175
1992 Traks #190
1992 Traks Autographs #A1
1992 Traks Goody's #19
1992 Traks Mom-n-Pop's Ham Dale Earnhardt #3
1992 Traks Mom-n-Pop's Ham Dale Earnhardt #4
1992 Traks Mom-n-Pop's Ham Dale Earnhardt #5
1992 Traks Mom-n-Pop's Ham Dale Earnhardt #6
1992 Traks Mom-n-Pop's Ham Dale Earnhardt #NNO
1992 Traks Mom-n-Pop's Ham Dale Earnhardt #1
1992 Traks Mom-n-Pop's Ham Dale Earnhardt #2
1992 Traks Racing Machines #1
1992 Traks Racing Machines #3
1992 Traks Racing Machines #9
1992 Traks Racing Machines #34
1992 Traks Racing Machines #44
1992 Traks Racing Machines #54
1992 Traks Racing Machines #84
1992 Traks Racing Machines #89
1992 Traks Racing Machines #91
1992 Traks Racing Machines #100
1992 Traks Racing Machines #P1
1992 Traks Racing Machines Bonus #3B
1992 Traks Team Sets #1
1992 Traks Team Sets #2
1992 Traks Team Sets #3
1992 Traks Team Sets #4
1992 Traks Team Sets #13
1992 Traks Team Sets #15
1992 Traks Team Sets #16
1992 Traks Team Sets #17
1992 Traks Team Sets #18
1992 Traks Team Sets #19
1992 Traks Team Sets #20
1992 Traks Team Sets #21
1992 Traks Team Sets #22
1992 Traks Team Sets #23
1992 Traks Team Sets #24
1992 Traks Team Sets #25
1992 Traks Team Sets #101
1992 Wheels Dale Earnhardt Tribute Hologram #1A
1992 Wheels Dale Earnhardt Tribute Hologram #1G
1992 Wheels Dale Earnhardt Tribute Hologram #1P
1992 Wheels Dale Earnhardt Tribute Hologram #1S
1993 AC Racing Foldouts #3
1993 Action Packed #95
1993 Action Packed #120
1993 Action Packed #121
1993 Action Packed #122
1993 Action Packed #123
1993 Action Packed #124
1993 Action Packed #125
1993 Action Packed #126
1993 Action Packed #127
1993 Action Packed #138
1993 Action Packed #139
1993 Action Packed #171
1993 Action Packed #198
1993 Action Packed #202
1993 Action Packed #207
1993 Action Packed #88
1993 Action Packed #89
1993 Action Packed #94
1993 Action Packed 24K Gold #18G
1993 Action Packed 24K Gold #19G
1993 Action Packed 24K Gold #20G
1993 Action Packed 24K Gold #21G
1993 Action Packed 24K Gold #53G
1993 Action Packed 24K Gold #24G
1993 Action Packed 24K Gold #25G
1993 Action Packed 24K Gold #37G
1993 Action Packed 24K Gold #38G
1993 Action Packed 24K Gold #22G
1993 Action Packed 24K Gold #23G
1993 Action Packed Prototypes #DE1
1993 Card Dynamics Gant Oil /6000 #8
1993 Card Dynamics Quik Chek /7000 #8
1993 Dayco Series 2 Rusty Wallace #12
1993 Hi-Tech Tire Test #1
1993 Maxx #3
1993 Maxx #56
1993 Maxx #274
1993 Maxx Premier Plus #56
1993 Maxx Premier Plus #189
1993 Maxx Premier Plus #3
1993 Maxx Premier Plus Jumbos #2
1993 Maxx Premier Series #3
1993 Maxx Premier Series #56
1993 Maxx Premier Series #274
1993 Maxx The Winston #1
1993 Maxx The Winston #21
1993 Maxx The Winston #49
1993 Maxx The Winston #50
1993 Maxx The Winston #51
1993 Wheels Mom-n-Pop's Dale Earnhardt #4
1993 Wheels Mom-n-Pop's Dale Earnhardt #5
1993 Wheels Mom-n-Pop's Dale Earnhardt #6
1993 Wheels Mom-n-Pop's Dale Earnhardt #3
1993 Wheels Mom-n-Pop's Dale Earnhardt #2
1993 Wheels Mom-n-Pop's Dale Earnhardt #1
1993-95 Card Dynamics Double Eagle Postcards #3
1993-95 Card Dynamics North State Chevrolet #2
1994 Action Packed #1
1994 Action Packed #8
1994 Action Packed #32
1994 Action Packed #41
1994 Action Packed #68
1994 Action Packed #99
1994 Action Packed #104
1994 Action Packed #126
1994 Action Packed #179
1994 Action Packed #180
1994 Action Packed #187
1994 Action Packed 24K Gold #2G
1994 Action Packed 24K Gold #11G
1994 Action Packed 24K Gold #22G
1994 Action Packed 24K Gold #179G
1994 Action Packed 24K Gold #180G
1994 Action Packed 24K Gold #187G
1994 Action Packed Champ and Challenger #21
1994 Action Packed Champ and Challenger #22
1994 Action Packed Champ and Challenger #23
1994 Action Packed Champ and Challenger #24
1994 Action Packed Champ and Challenger #25
1994 Action Packed Champ and Challenger #26
1994 Action Packed Champ and Challenger #27
1994 Action Packed Champ and Challenger #28
1994 Action Packed Champ and Challenger #29
1994 Action Packed Champ and Challenger #30
1994 Action Packed Champ and Challenger #31
1994 Action Packed Champ and Challenger #32
1994 Action Packed Champ and Challenger #33
1994 Action Packed Champ and Challenger #34
1994 Action Packed Champ and Challenger #35
1994 Action Packed Champ and Challenger #36
1994 Action Packed Champ and Challenger #37
1994 Action Packed Champ and Challenger #38
1994 Action Packed Champ and Challenger #39
1994 Action Packed Champ and Challenger #40
1994 Action Packed Champ and Challenger #41
1994 Action Packed Champ and Challenger #42
1994 Action Packed Champ and Challenger 24K Gold #22G
1994 Action Packed Champ and Challenger 24K Gold #28G
1994 Action Packed Champ and Challenger 24K Gold #30G
1994 Action Packed Champ and Challenger 24K Gold #32G
1994 Action Packed Champ and Challenger 24K Gold #39G
1994 Action Packed Champ and Challenger 24K Gold #41G
1994 Action Packed Champ and Challenger 24K Gold #42G
1994 Action Packed Coastars #2
1994 Action Packed Mint #99
1994 Action Packed Mint #104
1994 Action Packed Mint #126
1994 Action Packed Mint #179
1994 Action Packed Mint #180
1994 Action Packed Mint #187
1994 Action Packed Mint #1
1994 Action Packed Mint #8
1994 Action Packed Mint #32
1994 Action Packed Mint #41
1994 Action Packed Mint #68
1994 Action Packed Prototypes #2R941
1994 Action Packed Richard Childress Racing #RCR2
1994 Action Packed Richard Childress Racing #RCR3
1994 Action Packed Richard Childress Racing #RCR4
1994 Action Packed Richard Childress Racing #RCR5
1994 Action Packed Richard Childress Racing #RCR6
1994 Action Packed Select 24K Gold #W3
1994 Action Packed Select 24K Gold #W6
1994 Action Packed Select 24K Gold #W9
1994 Card Dynamics Black Top Busch Series /5000 #4
1994 Card Dynamics Double Eagle Dale Earnhardt /5000 #1
1994 Card Dynamics Double Eagle Dale Earnhardt /5000 #2
1994 Card Dynamics Double Eagle Dale Earnhardt /5000 #3
1994 Card Dynamics Double Eagle Dale Earnhardt /5000 #4
1994 Card Dynamics Double Eagle Dale Earnhardt /5000 #5
1994 Card Dynamics Double Eagle Dale Earnhardt /5000 #6
1994 Classic Dale Earnhardt 23K Gold /10000 #1
1994 Hi-Tech Brickyard 400 #9
1994 Hi-Tech Brickyard 400 #38
1994 Hi-Tech Brickyard 400 Artist Proofs #9
1994 Hi-Tech Brickyard 400 Artist Proofs #38
1994 Maxx #3
1994 Maxx #23
1994 Maxx #218
1994 Maxx #219
1994 Maxx #222
1994 Maxx #224
1994 Maxx #225
1994 Maxx #238
1994 Maxx #334
1994 Maxx #335
1994 Maxx #211
1994 Maxx Medallion #46
1994 Maxx Medallion /999 #99SP
1994 Maxx Premier Plus #3
1994 Maxx Premier Plus #23
1994 Maxx Premier Plus #165
1994 Maxx Premier Plus #170
1994 Maxx Premier Plus #177
1994 Maxx Premier Plus #178
1994 Maxx Premier Plus #181
1994 Maxx Premier Plus #183
1994 Maxx Premier Plus #184
1994 Maxx Premier Series #3
1994 Maxx Premier Series #23
1994 Maxx Premier Series #270
1994 Maxx Premier Series #277
1994 Maxx Premier Series #278
1994 Maxx Premier Series #281
1994 Maxx Premier Series #283
1994 Maxx Premier Series #284
1994 Maxx Premier Series #297
1994 Maxx Rookies of the Year #3
1994 Maxx The Select 25 #1
1994 Power #DB2
1994 Power #PW16
1994 Power #SL38
1994 Power #PR59
1994 Power /3500 #NNO
1994 Power #DB2
1994 Power Gold #DB2
1994 Power Gold #PW16
1994 Power Gold #SL38
1994 Power Gold #PR59
1994 Power Preview #31

1994 Press Pass #5
1994 Press Pass Checkered Flags #CF1
1994 Press Pass Cup Chase #CC5
1994 Press Pass Cup Chase #SPCL1
1994 Press Pass Holofoils #H1
1994 Press Pass Optima XL #4
1994 Press Pass Optima XL #41
1994 Press Pass Optima XL #43B
1994 Press Pass Optima XL Double Clutch #DC1
1994 Press Pass Optima XL Red Hot #4
1994 Press Pass Optima XL Red Hot #41
1994 Press Pass Optima XL Red Hot #43B
1994 Press Pass Race Day #RD10
1994 Score Board National Promos #20B
1994 Score Board National Promos #18
1994 Score Board National Promos #17
1994 Score Board National Promos #16
1994 Score Board National Promos #15
1994 Score Board National Promos #14
1994 SkyBox #1
1994 VIP #10
1994 VIP #42
1994 VIP Driver's Choice #DC1
1994 VIP Gold Signature #EC1
1994 Wheels High Gear #1
1994 Wheels High Gear #79
1994 Wheels High Gear #85
1994 Wheels High Gear #92
1994 Wheels High Gear #186
1994 Wheels High Gear #188
1994 Wheels High Gear Day One #186
1994 Wheels High Gear Day One #188
1994 Wheels High Gear Day One Gold #186
1994 Wheels High Gear Day One Gold #188
1994 Wheels High Gear Dominators /3000 #D3
1994 Wheels High Gear Gold #92
1994 Wheels High Gear Gold #186
1994 Wheels High Gear Gold #188
1994 Wheels High Gear Gold #1
1994 Wheels High Gear Gold #79
1994 Wheels High Gear Gold #85
1994 Wheels High Gear Mega Gold #MG1
1994 Wheels High Gear Mega Gold #MG1S
1994 Wheels High Gear Power Pak Teams #E3
1994 Wheels High Gear Power Pak Teams #E4
1994 Wheels High Gear Power Pak Teams #E5
1994 Wheels High Gear Power Pak Teams #E18
1994 Wheels High Gear Power Pak Teams #E19
1994 Wheels High Gear Power Pak Teams #E20
1994 Wheels High Gear Power Pak Teams #E21
1994 Wheels High Gear Power Pak Teams Gold #3E
1994 Wheels High Gear Power Pak Teams Gold #4E
1994 Wheels High Gear Power Pak Teams Gold #5E
1994 Wheels High Gear Power Pak Teams Gold #18E
1994 Wheels High Gear Power Pak Teams Gold #19E
1994 Wheels High Gear Power Pak Teams Gold #20E
1994 Wheels High Gear Rookie Thunder Update #104
1994 Wheels High Gear Rookie Thunder Update Platinum #104
1994-01 Story of America #124-9
1994-95 Assets #5
1994-95 Assets #30
1994-95 Assets Die Cuts #DC5
1994-95 Assets Phone Cards $1000 #1
1994-95 Assets Phone Cards $2 #5
1994-95 Assets Phone Cards $25 #1
1994-95 Assets Phone Cards One Minute #5
1994-95 Assets Silver Signature #5
1994-95 Highland Mint/VIP /5000 #1B
1994-95 Highland Mint/VIP /500 #1G
1994-95 Highland Mint/VIP /1000 #1S
1994-96 Bleachers NASCAR #2
1994-96 Bleachers NASCAR #3
1994-96 Bleachers NASCAR #4
1994-96 Bleachers NASCAR #5
1994-96 Bleachers NASCAR #6
1994-96 Bleachers NASCAR #7
1995 Action Packed Country #5
1995 Action Packed Country #11
1995 Action Packed Country #17
1995 Action Packed Country #25
1995 Action Packed Country #26
1995 Action Packed Country #27
1995 Action Packed Country #28
1995 Action Packed Country #29
1995 Action Packed Country #30
1995 Action Packed Country #31
1995 Action Packed Country #45
1995 Action Packed Country #54
1995 Action Packed Country #62
1995 Action Packed Country 24K Team #5
1995 Action Packed Country 24K Team #6
1995 Action Packed Country 24K Team #7
1995 Action Packed Country 2nd Career Choice #6
1995 Action Packed Country Silver Speed #5
1995 Action Packed Country Silver Speed #11
1995 Action Packed Country Silver Speed #17
1995 Action Packed Country Silver Speed #25
1995 Action Packed Country Silver Speed #26
1995 Action Packed Country Silver Speed #27
1995 Action Packed Country Silver Speed #28
1995 Action Packed Country Silver Speed #29
1995 Action Packed Country Silver Speed #30
1995 Action Packed Country Silver Speed #31
1995 Action Packed Country Silver Speed #45
1995 Action Packed Country Silver Speed #54
1995 Action Packed Country Silver Speed #62
1995 Action Packed Mammoth #MM1
1995 Action Packed Mammoth #MM6
1995 Action Packed Preview #7
1995 Action Packed Preview #33
1995 Action Packed Preview #48
1995 Action Packed Preview #59
1995 Action Packed Preview #BP1
1995 Action Packed Select 25 #1
1995 Action Packed Stars #23
1995 Action Packed Stars #31
1995 Action Packed Stars #52
1995 Action Packed Stars #NNO
1995 Action Packed Stars 24K Gold #16G
1995 Action Packed Stars 24K Gold #15G
1995 Action Packed Stars 24K Gold #14G
1995 Action Packed Stars 24K Gold #13G
1995 Action Packed Stars 24K Gold #12G
1995 Action Packed Stars 24K Gold #11G
1995 Action Packed Stars 24K Gold #10G
1995 Action Packed Stars 24K Gold #9G
1995 Action Packed Stars 24K Gold #7G
1995 Action Packed Stars Dale Earnhardt Race for Eight #DE1
1995 Action Packed Stars Dale Earnhardt Race for Eight #DE2
1995 Action Packed Stars Dale Earnhardt Race for Eight #DE3
1995 Action Packed Stars Dale Earnhardt Race for Eight #DE4
1995 Action Packed Stars Dale Earnhardt Race for Eight #DE5
1995 Action Packed Stars Dale Earnhardt Race for Eight #DE6
1995 Action Packed Stars Dale Earnhardt Race for Eight #DE7
1995 Action Packed Stars Dale Earnhardt Race for Eight #DE8
1995 Action Packed Stars Dale Earnhardt Silver Salute #1
1995 Action Packed Stars Dale Earnhardt Silver Salute #2
1995 Action Packed Stars Dale Earnhardt Silver Salute #3
1995 Action Packed Stars Dale Earnhardt Silver Salute #4
1995 Action Packed Stars Silver Speed #23
1995 Action Packed Stars Silver Speed #31
1995 Action Packed Stars Silver Speed #52
1995 Action Packed Sundrop Dale Earnhardt #SD1
1995 Action Packed Sundrop Dale Earnhardt #SD2
1995 Action Packed Sundrop Dale Earnhardt #SD3
1995 Assets #1
1995 Assets #29
1995 Assets #44
1995 Assets #46
1995 Assets #P1
1995 Assets $100 Phone Cards #P1
1995 Assets $100 Phone Cards #2
1995 Assets $1000 Phone Cards #2
1995 Assets $2 Phone Cards #4
1995 Assets $2 Phone Cards Gold Signature #4
1995 Assets $25 Phone Cards #2
1995 Assets $5 Phone Cards #2
1995 Assets 1-Minute Phone Cards #4
1995 Assets 1-Minute Phone Cards Gold Signature #4
1995 Assets Coca-Cola 600 Die Cut Phone Cards #1
1995 Assets Gold #1
1995 Assets Gold Die Cuts Gold #SDC10
1995 Assets Gold Die Cuts Silver #SDC10
1995 Assets Gold Phone Cards $1000 #2
1995 Assets Gold Phone Cards $2 #1
1995 Assets Gold Phone Cards $5 #12
1995 Assets Gold Phone Cards $5 Microlined #12
1995 Assets Gold Printer's Proofs #1
1995 Assets Gold Signature #1
1995 Assets Gold Signature #29
1995 Assets Gold Signature #44
1995 Assets Gold Signature #46
1995 Assets Gold Silver Signatures #1
1995 Assets Images Previews #RI1
1995 Classic Five Sport #161
1995 Classic Five Sport Autographs Numbered /225 #161
1995 Classic Five Sport Classic Standouts #CS3
1995 Classic Five Sport Hot Box Autographs /635 #3
1995 Classic Five Sport On Fire #H3
1995 Classic Five Sport Phone Cards $3 #1
1995 Classic Five Sport Phone Cards $4 #1
1995 Classic Five Sport Previews #SP1
1995 Classic Five Sport Printer's Proofs /795 #161
1995 Classic Five Sport Record Setters #RS4
1995 Classic Five Sport Red Die Cuts #161
1995 Classic Five Sport Silver Die Cuts #161
1995 Classic National #NC4
1995 Crown Jewels #1
1995 Crown Jewels #64
1995 Crown Jewels Diamond /599 #1
1995 Crown Jewels Diamond /599 #64
1995 Crown Jewels Dual Jewels #DJ1
1995 Crown Jewels Dual Jewels #DJ6
1995 Crown Jewels Dual Jewels Diamond #DJ1
1995 Crown Jewels Dual Jewels Diamond #DJ6
1995 Crown Jewels Dual Jewels Emerald #DJ1
1995 Crown Jewels Dual Jewels Emerald #DJ6
1995 Crown Jewels Emerald /1199 #1
1995 Crown Jewels Emerald /1199 #64
1995 Crown Jewels Sapphire /2500 #1
1995 Crown Jewels Sapphire /2500 #64
1995 Crown Jewels Signature Gems #SG3
1995 Finish Line #1
1995 Finish Line #89
1995 Finish Line #111
1995 Finish Line #CE1
1995 Finish Line #HP1
1995 Finish Line #RP1
1995 Finish Line /250 #89AUH
1995 Finish Line /250 #89AUR
1995 Finish Line /250 #111AU
1995 Finish Line Coca-Cola 600 #1
1995 Finish Line Coca-Cola 600 #29
1995 Finish Line Coca-Cola 600 #44
1995 Finish Line Coca-Cola 600 #46
1995 Finish Line Coca-Cola 600 Die Cuts #C1
1995 Finish Line Coca-Cola 600 Winners #CC2
1995 Finish Line Coca-Cola 600 Winners #CC8
1995 Finish Line Coca-Cola 600 Winners #CC9
1995 Finish Line Dale Earnhardt #DE1
1995 Finish Line Dale Earnhardt #DE2
1995 Finish Line Dale Earnhardt #DE3
1995 Finish Line Dale Earnhardt #DE4
1995 Finish Line Dale Earnhardt #DE5
1995 Finish Line Dale Earnhardt #DE6
1995 Finish Line Dale Earnhardt #DE7
1995 Finish Line Dale Earnhardt #DE8
1995 Finish Line Dale Earnhardt #DE9
1995 Finish Line Dale Earnhardt #DE10
1995 Finish Line Gold Signature #GS3
1995 Finish Line Printer's Proof /398 #1
1995 Finish Line Printer's Proof /398 #89
1995 Finish Line Printer's Proof /398 #111
1995 Finish Line Silver #1
1995 Finish Line Silver #89
1995 Finish Line Silver #111
1995 Finish Line Standout Cars #SC1
1995 Finish Line Standout Drivers #SD1
1995 Hi-Tech Brickyard 400 #2
1995 Hi-Tech Brickyard 400 #41
1995 Hi-Tech Brickyard 400 #56
1995 Hi-Tech Brickyard 400 #77
1995 Hi-Tech Brickyard 400 #87
1995 Hi-Tech Brickyard 400 Prototypes #P3
1995 Hi-Tech Brickyard 400 Top Ten #BY5
1995 Images #3
1995 Images #50
1995 Images #97
1995 Images #99
1995 Images Circuit Champions #8
1995 Images Driven #D1
1995 Images Gold #3
1995 Images Gold #50
1995 Images Gold #97
1995 Images Gold #99
1995 Images Hard Chargers #HC9
1995 Images Owner's Pride #OP13
1995 Images Race Reflections Dale Earnhardt #DE1
1995 Images Race Reflections Dale Earnhardt #DE2
1995 Images Race Reflections Dale Earnhardt #DE3
1995 Images Race Reflections Dale Earnhardt #DE4
1995 Images Race Reflections Dale Earnhardt #DE5
1995 Images Race Reflections Dale Earnhardt #DE6
1995 Images Race Reflections Dale Earnhardt #DE7
1995 Images Race Reflections Dale Earnhardt #DE8
1995 Images Race Reflections Dale Earnhardt #DE9
1995 Images Race Reflections Dale Earnhardt #DE10
1995 Images Race Reflections Dale Earnhardt Facsimile Signature #DE1
1995 Images Race Reflections Dale Earnhardt Facsimile Signature #DE2
1995 Images Race Reflections Dale Earnhardt Facsimile Signature #DE3
1995 Images Race Reflections Dale Earnhardt Facsimile Signature #DE4
1995 Images Race Reflections Dale Earnhardt Facsimile Signature #DE5
1995 Images Race Reflections Dale Earnhardt Facsimile Signature #DE6
1995 Images Race Reflections Dale Earnhardt Facsimile Signature #DE7
1995 Images Race Reflections Dale Earnhardt Facsimile Signature #DE8
1995 Images Race Reflections Dale Earnhardt Facsimile Signature #DE9
1995 Images Race Reflections Dale Earnhardt Facsimile Signature #DE10
1995 Matchbook Winston Cup Champions #10
1995 Matchbook Winston Cup Champions #16
1995 Matchbook Winston Cup Champions #17
1995 Matchbook Winston Cup Champions #20
1995 Matchbook Winston Cup Champions #21
1995 Matchbook Winston Cup Champions #23
1995 Matchbook Winston Cup Champions #24
1995 Maxx Chase the Champion #1
1995 Maxx Chase the Champion #2
1995 Maxx Chase the Champion #3
1995 Maxx Chase the Champion #4
1995 Maxx Chase the Champion #5
1995 Maxx Chase the Champion #6
1995 Maxx Chase the Champion #7
1995 Maxx Chase the Champion #8
1995 Maxx Chase the Champion #9
1995 Maxx Chase the Champion #10
1995 Maxx Larger than Life Dale Earnhardt #1
1995 Maxx Larger than Life Dale Earnhardt #2
1995 Maxx Larger than Life Dale Earnhardt #3
1995 Maxx Larger than Life Dale Earnhardt #4
1995 Maxx Larger than Life Dale Earnhardt #5
1995 Maxx Larger than Life Dale Earnhardt #6
1995 Maxx Larger than Life Dale Earnhardt #7
1995 Maxx Premier Plus /750 #SS1
1995 Metallic Impressions Classic Dale Earnhardt 10-Card Tin #1
1995 Metallic Impressions Classic Dale Earnhardt 10-Card Tin #2
1995 Metallic Impressions Classic Dale Earnhardt 10-Card Tin #3
1995 Metallic Impressions Classic Dale Earnhardt 10-Card Tin #4
1995 Metallic Impressions Classic Dale Earnhardt 10-Card Tin #5
1995 Metallic Impressions Classic Dale Earnhardt 10-Card Tin #6
1995 Metallic Impressions Classic Dale Earnhardt 10-Card Tin #7
1995 Metallic Impressions Classic Dale Earnhardt 10-Card Tin #8
1995 Metallic Impressions Classic Dale Earnhardt 10-Card Tin #9
1995 Metallic Impressions Classic Dale Earnhardt 10-Card Tin #10
1995 Metallic Impressions Classic Dale Earnhardt 21-Card Tin #1
1995 Metallic Impressions Classic Dale Earnhardt 21-Card Tin #2
1995 Metallic Impressions Classic Dale Earnhardt 21-Card Tin #3
1995 Metallic Impressions Classic Dale Earnhardt 21-Card Tin #4
1995 Metallic Impressions Classic Dale Earnhardt 21-Card Tin #5
1995 Metallic Impressions Classic Dale Earnhardt 21-Card Tin #6
1995 Metallic Impressions Classic Dale Earnhardt 21-Card Tin #7
1995 Metallic Impressions Classic Dale Earnhardt 21-Card Tin #8
1995 Metallic Impressions Classic Dale Earnhardt 21-Card Tin #9
1995 Metallic Impressions Classic Dale Earnhardt 21-Card Tin #10
1995 Metallic Impressions Classic Dale Earnhardt 21-Card Tin #11
1995 Metallic Impressions Classic Dale Earnhardt 21-Card Tin #12
1995 Metallic Impressions Classic Dale Earnhardt 21-Card Tin #13
1995 Metallic Impressions Classic Dale Earnhardt 21-Card Tin #14
1995 Metallic Impressions Classic Dale Earnhardt 21-Card Tin #15
1995 Metallic Impressions Classic Dale Earnhardt 21-Card Tin #16
1995 Metallic Impressions Classic Dale Earnhardt 21-Card Tin #17
1995 Metallic Impressions Classic Dale Earnhardt 21-Card Tin #18
1995 Metallic Impressions Classic Dale Earnhardt 21-Card Tin #19
1995 Metallic Impressions Classic Dale Earnhardt 21-Card Tin #20
1995 Metallic Impressions Classic Dale Earnhardt 21-Card Tin #E1
1995 Metallic Impressions Classic Dale Earnhardt 5-Card Tin #1
1995 Metallic Impressions Classic Dale Earnhardt 5-Card Tin #2
1995 Metallic Impressions Classic Dale Earnhardt 5-Card Tin #3
1995 Metallic Impressions Classic Dale Earnhardt 5-Card Tin #4
1995 Metallic Impressions Classic Dale Earnhardt 5-Card Tin #5
1995 Metallic Impressions Winston Cup Champions 10-Card Tin #4
1995 Press Pass #9
1995 Press Pass #41
1995 Press Pass #115
1995 Press Pass Checkered Flags #CF2
1995 Press Pass Cup Chase #9
1995 Press Pass Cup Chase Prizes #CCR2
1995 Press Pass Optima XL #6
1995 Press Pass Optima XL #51
1995 Press Pass Optima XL Cool Blue #6
1995 Press Pass Optima XL Cool Blue #51
1995 Press Pass Optima XL Die Cut #6
1995 Press Pass Optima XL Die Cut #51
1995 Press Pass Optima XL Red Hot #6
1995 Press Pass Optima XL Red Hot #51
1995 Press Pass Optima XL Stealth #XLS2
1995 Press Pass Premium #1
1995 Press Pass Premium Holofoil #1
1995 Press Pass Premium Hot Pursuit #HP2
1995 Press Pass Premium Red Hot #1
1995 Press Pass Race Day #RD3
1995 Press Pass Red Hot #9
1995 Press Pass Red Hot #41
1995 Press Pass Red Hot #115
1995 Race Call Phone Cards #3
1995 Race Call Phone Cards #4
1995 Race Call Phone Cards #5
1995 Race Call Phone Cards #6
1995 Race Call Phone Cards #7
1995 Race Call Phone Cards #8
1995 Select #41
1995 Select #151S
1995 Select Flat Out #41
1995 Select Flat Out #151FO
1995 Traks #27
1995 Traks 5th Anniversary #3
1995 Traks 5th Anniversary Clear Contenders #C1
1995 Traks 5th Anniversary Gold #3
1995 Traks 5th Anniversary Jumbos #E6
1995 Traks 5th Anniversary Jumbos Gold /100 #E6
1995 Traks 5th Anniversary Red #3
1995 Traks 5th Anniversary Retrospective #R2
1995 Traks First Run #27
1995 Traks Series Stars #SS19
1995 Traks Series Stars First Run #SS19
1995 VIP #9
1995 VIP Cool Blue #9
1995 VIP Emerald Proofs #9
1995 VIP Fan's Choice #FC1
1995 VIP Fan's Choice Gold #FC1
1995 VIP Red Hot #9
1995 Western Steer Earnhardt Next Generation #1
1995 Western Steer Earnhardt Next Generation #2
1995 Western Steer Earnhardt Next Generation #3
1995 Western Steer Earnhardt Next Generation #JUM
1995 Wheels High Gear #1
1995 Wheels High Gear #71
1995 Wheels High Gear #86
1995 Wheels High Gear Busch Clash #BC8
1995 Wheels High Gear Busch Clash Gold #BC8
1995 Wheels High Gear Day One #1
1995 Wheels High Gear Day One #71
1995 Wheels High Gear Day One #86
1995 Wheels High Gear Day One Gold #1
1995 Wheels High Gear Day One Gold #71
1995 Wheels High Gear Day One Gold #86
1995 Wheels High Gear Dominators /1750 #D3
1995 Wheels High Gear Dominators Jumbos /1750 #D3
1995 Wheels High Gear Gold #1
1995 Wheels High Gear Gold #71
1995 Wheels High Gear Gold #86
1995 Zenith #3
1995 Zenith #36
1995 Zenith #76
1995 Zenith #P3
1995 Zenith Helmets #1
1995 Zenith Tribute #1
1995 Zenith Winston Winners #7
1995 Zenith Winston Winners #10
1995 Zenith Winston Winners #19
1995 Zenith Winston Winners #24
1995 Zenith Z-Team #1
1995-96 Classic Five Sport Signings #79
1995-96 Classic Five Sport Signings Blue Signature #79
1995-96 Classic Five Sport Signings Die Cuts #79
1995-96 Classic Five Sport Signings Red Signature #79
1996 Action Packed Credentials #6
1996 Action Packed Credentials #7
1996 Action Packed Credentials #8
1996 Action Packed Credentials #9
1996 Action Packed Credentials #10
1996 Action Packed Credentials #17
1996 Action Packed Credentials #21
1996 Action Packed Credentials #57
1996 Action Packed Credentials #104
1996 Action Packed Credentials Fan Scan #1
1996 Action Packed Credentials Fan Scan #2
1996 Action Packed Credentials Jumbos #1
1996 Action Packed Credentials Leaders of the Pack #1
1996 Action Packed Credentials Leaders of the Pack #2
1996 Action Packed Credentials Leaders of the Pack #3
1996 Action Packed Credentials Leaders of the Pack #4
1996 Action Packed Credentials Silver Speed #6
1996 Action Packed Credentials Silver Speed #7
1996 Action Packed Credentials Silver Speed #8
1996 Action Packed Credentials Silver Speed #9
1996 Action Packed Credentials Silver Speed #10
1996 Action Packed Credentials Silver Speed #17
1996 Action Packed Credentials Silver Speed #21
1996 Action Packed McDonald's #2
1996 Action Packed McDonald's #12
1996 Action Packed Racing For Kids /5000 #RFK1
1996 Action Packed Racing For Kids #NNO
1996 Assets #9
1996 Assets A Cut Above Phone Cards #1
1996 Assets Crystal Phone Cards #3
1996 Assets Crystal Phone Cards $20 #3
1996 Assets Hot Prints #9
1996 Assets Phone Cards $1 #6
1996 Assets Phone Cards $10 #3
1996 Assets Phone Cards $100 #1
1996 Assets Phone Cards $1000 #1
1996 Assets Phone Cards $2 #6
1996 Assets Phone Cards $2 Hot Prints #6
1996 Assets Phone Cards $20 #1
1996 Assets Phone Cards $5 #6
1996 Assets Racing #1
1996 Assets Racing #38
1996 Assets Racing #44
1996 Assets Racing #P1
1996 Assets Racing #P2
1996 Assets Racing $10 Phone Cards #4
1996 Assets Racing $10 Phone Cards #9
1996 Assets Racing $100 Cup Champion Interactive Phone Cards #1
1996 Assets Racing $1000 Cup Champion Interactive Phone Cards #1
1996 Assets Racing $2 Phone Cards #1
1996 Assets Racing $2 Phone Cards #10
1996 Assets Racing $5 Phone Cards #6
1996 Assets Racing $5 Phone Cards #11
1996 Assets Racing Competitor's License #CL4
1996 Assets Racing Race Day #RD3
1996 Assets Silksations #3
1996 Autographed Racing #1
1996 Autographed Racing #25
1996 Autographed Racing Autographs #13
1996 Autographed Racing Autographs Certified Golds #13
1996 Autographed Racing Front Runners #13
1996 Autographed Racing Front Runners #14
1996 Autographed Racing Front Runners #19
1996 Autographed Racing Front Runners #20
1996 Autographed Racing Front Runners #21
1996 Autographed Racing Front Runners #22
1996 Autographed Racing High Performance #HP1
1996 Autographed Racing Kings of the Circuit $5 Phone Cards #KC6
1996 Autographed Racing Kings of the Circuit $5 Phone Cards #KC8
1996 Autographed Racing Kings of the Circuit $5 Phone Cards #KC10
1996 Classic #32
1996 Classic #53
1996 Classic #HP96
1996 Classic #RP96
1996 Classic Images Preview #RP5
1996 Classic Innerview #IV3
1996 Classic Innerview #IV7
1996 Classic Mark Martin's Challengers #MC3
1996 Classic Printer's Proof #32
1996 Classic Race Chase #RC3
1996 Classic Race Chase #RC13
1996 Classic Silver #32
1996 Clear Assets #64
1996 Clear Assets Phone Cards $1 #19
1996 Clear Assets Phone Cards $10 #3
1996 Clear Assets Phone Cards $2 #19
1996 Clear Assets Phone Cards $5 #4
1996 Crown Jewels Elite #1
1996 Crown Jewels Elite #27
1996 Crown Jewels Elite #56
1996 Crown Jewels Elite #57
1996 Crown Jewels Elite /300 #SD1
1996 Crown Jewels Elite /1500 #SG1
1996 Crown Jewels Elite /1500 #SGTC1
1996 Crown Jewels Elite Birthstones of the Champions #BC1
1996 Crown Jewels Elite Birthstones of the Champions Diamond Tribute #BC1
1996 Crown Jewels Elite Birthstones of the Champions Treasure Chest #BC1
1996 Crown Jewels Elite Crown Signature Amethyst #CS1
1996 Crown Jewels Elite Crown Signature Garnet #CS1
1996 Crown Jewels Elite Crown Signature Peridot #CS1
1996 Crown Jewels Elite Diamond Tribute /2500 #1
1996 Crown Jewels Elite Diamond Tribute /2500 #27
1996 Crown Jewels Elite Diamond Tribute /2500 #56
1996 Crown Jewels Elite Diamond Tribute /2500 #57
1996 Crown Jewels Elite Diamond Tribute Citrine /999 #1
1996 Crown Jewels Elite Diamond Tribute Citrine /999 #27
1996 Crown Jewels Elite Diamond Tribute Citrine /999 #56
1996 Crown Jewels Elite Diamond Tribute Citrine /999 #57
1996 Crown Jewels Elite Dual Jewels Amethyst #DJ1
1996 Crown Jewels Elite Dual Jewels Amethyst Diamond Tribute #DJ1
1996 Crown Jewels Elite Dual Jewels Amethyst Treasure Chest #DJ1
1996 Crown Jewels Elite Dual Jewels Garnet #DJ1
1996 Crown Jewels Elite Dual Jewels Garnet Diamond Tribute #DJ1
1996 Crown Jewels Elite Dual Jewels Garnet Treasure Chest #DJ1
1996 Crown Jewels Elite Dual Jewels Sapphire #DJ1
1996 Crown Jewels Elite Dual Jewels Sapphire Treasure Chest #DJ1
1996 Crown Jewels Elite Emerald /599 #1
1996 Crown Jewels Elite Emerald /599 #27
1996 Crown Jewels Elite Emerald /599 #56
1996 Crown Jewels Elite Emerald /599 #57
1996 Crown Jewels Elite Emerald Treasure Chest #1
1996 Crown Jewels Elite Emerald Treasure Chest #27
1996 Crown Jewels Elite Emerald Treasure Chest #56
1996 Crown Jewels Elite Emerald Treasure Chest #57
1996 Crown Jewels Elite Retail Blue #1
1996 Crown Jewels Elite Retail Blue #27
1996 Crown Jewels Elite Retail Blue #56
1996 Crown Jewels Elite Retail Blue #57
1996 Crown Jewels Elite Sapphire #1
1996 Crown Jewels Elite Sapphire #27
1996 Crown Jewels Elite Sapphire #56
1996 Crown Jewels Elite Sapphire #57
1996 Crown Jewels Elite Sapphire Treasure Chest /1099 #1
1996 Crown Jewels Elite Sapphire Treasure Chest /1099 #27
1996 Crown Jewels Elite Sapphire Treasure Chest /1099 #56
1996 Crown Jewels Elite Sapphire Treasure Chest /1099 #57
1996 Crown Jewels Elite Treasure Chest #1
1996 Crown Jewels Elite Treasure Chest #27
1996 Crown Jewels Elite Treasure Chest #56
1996 Crown Jewels Elite Treasure Chest #57
1996 Flair #10
1996 Flair #66
1996 Flair Autographs #2
1996 Flair Center Spotlight #2
1996 Flair Hot Numbers #1
1996 Flair Power Performance #2
1996 KnightQuest #1
1996 KnightQuest #22
1996 KnightQuest #25
1996 KnightQuest Black Knights #1
1996 KnightQuest Black Knights #22
1996 KnightQuest Black Knights #25
1996 KnightQuest First Knights #FK1
1996 KnightQuest Knights of the Round Table #KT2
1996 KnightQuest Protectors of the Crown /899 #PC2
1996 KnightQuest Red Knight Preview #1
1996 KnightQuest Red Knight Preview #22
1996 KnightQuest Red Knight Preview #25
1996 KnightQuest Royalty #1
1996 KnightQuest Royalty #22
1996 KnightQuest Royalty #25
1996 KnightQuest Santa Claus #SC1
1996 KnightQuest Santa Claus Green #SC1
1996 KnightQuest White Knights #1
1996 KnightQuest White Knights #22
1996 KnightQuest White Knights #25
1996 Maxx #3
1996 Maxx Odyssey #70
1996 Maxx Odyssey Millennium #MM1
1996 Maxx Premier Series #3
1996 Maxx Premier Series #73
1996 Maxx Premier Series #262
1996 Metallic Impressions 25th Anniversary Winston Cup Champions #10
1996 Metallic Impressions 25th Anniversary Winston Cup Champions #16
1996 Metallic Impressions 25th Anniversary Winston Cup Champions #17
1996 Metallic Impressions 25th Anniversary Winston Cup Champions #20
1996 Metallic Impressions 25th Anniversary Winston Cup Champions #21
1996 Metallic Impressions 25th Anniversary Winston Cup Champions #23
1996 Metallic Impressions 25th Anniversary Winston Cup Champions #24
1996 Metallic Impressions Avon All-Time Racing Greatest #1
1996 Metallic Impressions Dale Earnhardt Burger King #1
1996 Metallic Impressions Dale Earnhardt Burger King #2
1996 Metallic Impressions Dale Earnhardt Burger King #3
1996 Metallic Impressions Winston Cup Top Five #4
1996 M-Force #3
1996 M-Force #4
1996 M-Force #45
1996 M-Force Black #B3
1996 M-Force Black #B4
1996 M-Force Sheet Metal #M2
1996 M-Force Silvers #S3
1996 M-Force Silvers #S2
1996 Pinnacle #3
1996 Pinnacle #38
1996 Pinnacle #91
1996 Pinnacle Artist Proofs #3
1996 Pinnacle Artist Proofs #38
1996 Pinnacle Artist Proofs #91
1996 Pinnacle Checkered Flag #3
1996 Pinnacle Foil #3
1996 Pinnacle Foil #38
1996 Pinnacle Foil #91
1996 Pinnacle Pole Position #3
1996 Pinnacle Pole Position #27
1996 Pinnacle Pole Position #56
1996 Pinnacle Pole Position #57
1996 Pinnacle Pole Position #58
1996 Pinnacle Pole Position #59
1996 Pinnacle Pole Position #60
1996 Pinnacle Pole Position #72
1996 Pinnacle Pole Position Certified Strong #3
1996 Pinnacle Pole Position Lightning Fast #3
1996 Pinnacle Pole Position Lightning Fast #27
1996 Pinnacle Pole Position Lightning Fast #56
1996 Pinnacle Pole Position Lightning Fast #57
1996 Pinnacle Pole Position Lightning Fast #58
1996 Pinnacle Pole Position Lightning Fast #59
1996 Pinnacle Pole Position Lightning Fast #60
1996 Pinnacle Pole Position Lightning Fast #72
1996 Pinnacle Pole Position No Limit #3
1996 Pinnacle Pole Position No Limit Gold #3
1996 Pinnacle Team Pinnacle #3
1996 Pinnacle Team Pinnacle #11
1996 Pinnacle Winston Cup Collection Dufex #3
1996 Pinnacle Winston Cup Collection Dufex #38
1996 Pinnacle Winston Cup Collection Dufex #91
1996 Press Pass #40
1996 Press Pass #9
1996 Press Pass Burning Rubber /500 #BR3
1996 Press Pass Cup Chase #9
1996 Press Pass Cup Chase Foil Prizes #9
1996 Press Pass F.Q.S. #FQS1A
1996 Press Pass F.Q.S. #FQS1B
1996 Press Pass Focused #F1
1996 Press Pass Premium #2
1996 Press Pass Premium #35
1996 Press Pass Premium Burning Rubber II /500 #BR5
1996 Press Pass Premium Crystal Ball #CB3
1996 Press Pass Premium Emerald Proofs /380 #35
1996 Press Pass Premium Emerald Proofs /380 #2
1996 Press Pass Premium Holofoil #35
1996 Press Pass Premium Holofoil #2
1996 Press Pass Premium Hot Pursuit #HP1
1996 Press Pass R and N China #9
1996 Press Pass Scorchers #9
1996 Press Pass Scorchers #40
1996 Press Pass Torquers #9
1996 Press Pass Torquers #40
1996 Racer's Choice #3
1996 Racer's Choice #27
1996 Racer's Choice #56
1996 Racer's Choice #57
1996 Racer's Choice #58
1996 Racer's Choice #59
1996 Racer's Choice #60
1996 Racer's Choice #84
1996 Racer's Choice #89
1996 Racer's Choice #92
1996 Racer's Choice Racer's Review #6
1996 Racer's Choice Racer's Review #7
1996 Racer's Choice Racer's Review #8
1996 Racer's Choice Racer's Review #9
1996 Racer's Choice Racer's Review #10
1996 Racer's Choice Speedway Collection #3
1996 Racer's Choice Speedway Collection #27
1996 Racer's Choice Speedway Collection #56
1996 Racer's Choice Speedway Collection #57
1996 Racer's Choice Speedway Collection #58
1996 Racer's Choice Speedway Collection #59
1996 Racer's Choice Speedway Collection #60
1996 Racer's Choice Speedway Collection #84
1996 Racer's Choice Speedway Collection #89
1996 Racer's Choice Speedway Collection #92
1996 Racer's Choice Speedway Collection Artist's Proofs #3
1996 Racer's Choice Speedway Collection Artist's Proofs #27
1996 Racer's Choice Speedway Collection Artist's Proofs #56
1996 Racer's Choice Speedway Collection Artist's Proofs #57
1996 Racer's Choice Speedway Collection Artist's Proofs #58
1996 Racer's Choice Speedway Collection Artist's Proofs #59
1996 Racer's Choice Speedway Collection Artist's Proofs #60
1996 Racer's Choice Speedway Collection Artist's Proofs #84
1996 Racer's Choice Speedway Collection Artist's Proofs #89
1996 Racer's Choice Speedway Collection Artist's Proofs #92
1996 Racer's Choice Sundrop #SD1
1996 Racer's Choice Sundrop #SD2
1996 Racer's Choice Sundrop #SD3
1996 Racer's Choice Top Ten #2
1996 Racer's Choice Top Ten #P2
1996 Racer's Choice Up Close with Dale Earnhardt #1
1996 Racer's Choice Up Close with Dale Earnhardt #2
1996 Racer's Choice Up Close with Dale Earnhardt #3
1996 Racer's Choice Up Close with Dale Earnhardt #4
1996 Racer's Choice Up Close with Dale Earnhardt #5
1996 Racer's Choice Up Close with Dale Earnhardt #6
1996 Racer's Choice Up Close with Dale Earnhardt #7
1996 Score Board Dale Earnhardt #1
1996 Score Board Dale Earnhardt #2
1996 Score Board Dale Earnhardt #3
1996 Score Board Dale Earnhardt #4
1996 Score Board Dale Earnhardt #5
1996 Score Board Dale Earnhardt #6
1996 Score Board Dale Earnhardt #7
1996 Score Board Dale Earnhardt #8
1996 Score Board Dale Earnhardt #9
1996 Score Board Dale Earnhardt #10
1996 SP #3
1996 SP #KR1
1996 SP Holoview Maximum Effects #ME3
1996 SP Holoview Maximum Effects Die Cuts #ME3
1996 Speedflix #17
1996 Speedflix #37
1996 Speedflix #51
1996 Speedflix #52
1996 Speedflix #53
1996 Speedflix #54
1996 Speedflix #83
1996 Speedflix #85
1996 Speedflix Artist Proof's #85
1996 Speedflix Artist Proof's #83
1996 Speedflix Artist Proof's #54
1996 Speedflix Artist Proof's #53
1996 Speedflix Artist Proof's #52
1996 Speedflix Artist Proof's #51
1996 Speedflix Artist Proof's #37
1996 Speedflix Artist Proof's #17
1996 Speedflix Clear Shots #1
1996 Speedflix In Motion #1
1996 Speedflix ProMotion #1
1996 SPx #3
1996 SPx Gold #3
1996 Traks Review and Preview #37
1996 Traks Review and Preview First Run #37
1996 Traks Review and Preview Magnets #37
1996 Ultra #200
1996 Ultra #197
1996 Ultra #192
1996 Ultra #187
1996 Ultra #185
1996 Ultra #176
1996 Ultra #175
1996 Ultra #173
1996 Ultra #7
1996 Ultra #6
1996 Ultra #5
1996 Ultra Autographs #9
1996 Ultra Boxed Set #2
1996 Ultra Champions Club #2
1996 Ultra Flair Preview #2
1996 Ultra Golden Memories #4
1996 Ultra Season Crowns #15
1996 Ultra Season Crowns #12
1996 Ultra Season Crowns #9
1996 Ultra Season Crowns #5
1996 Ultra Season Crowns #3
1996 Ultra Thunder and Lightning #6
1996 Ultra Thunder and Lightning #5
1996 Ultra Update #96
1996 Ultra Update #56
1996 Ultra Update #45
1996 Ultra Update #10
1996 Ultra Update Autographs #2
1996 Ultra Update Proven Power #2
1996 Ultra Update Winner #16
1996 Ultra Update Winner #7
1996 Upper Deck Road To The Cup #DE1
1996 Upper Deck Road To The Cup #301
1996 Upper Deck Road To The Cup #RC42
1996 Upper Deck Road To The Cup Predictor Points Prizes #PR10
1996 VIP #38
1996 VIP #8
1996 VIP Autographs #6
1996 VIP Dale Earnhardt Firesuit #DE1B
1996 VIP Dale Earnhardt Firesuit #DE1S
1996 VIP Dale Earnhardt Firesuit #DE1GL
1996 VIP Dale Earnhardt Firesuit #DE1GR
1996 VIP Dale Earnhardt Firesuit #DE2B
1996 VIP Dale Earnhardt Firesuit #DE2S
1996 VIP Dale Earnhardt Firesuit #DE2GL
1996 VIP Dale Earnhardt Firesuit #DE2GR
1996 VIP Emerald Proofs #8
1996 VIP Emerald Proofs #38
1996 VIP Head Gear #HG2
1996 VIP Head Gear Die Cuts #HG2
1996 VIP Sam Bass Top Flight #SB1
1996 VIP Sam Bass Top Flight Gold #SB1
1996 VIP Torquers #8
1996 VIP Torquers #38
1996 VIP War Paint #WP2
1996 VIP War Paint Gold #WP2
1996 Viper #R3FS
1996 Viper #R3
1996 Viper #43
1996 Viper #1
1996 Viper Black Mamba #1
1996 Viper Black Mamba #43
1996 Viper Black Mamba #R3B
1996 Viper Black Mamba First Strike #1
1996 Viper Black Mamba First Strike #43
1996 Viper Busch Clash #B14
1996 Viper Busch Clash First Strike #B14
1996 Viper Cobra /1799 #C1
1996 Viper Cobra First Strike /1799 #C1

1996 Viper Copperhead Die Cuts #1
1996 Viper Copperhead Die Cuts #43
1996 Viper Copperhead Die Cuts First Strike #1
1996 Viper Copperhead Die Cuts First Strike #43
1996 Viper Dale Earnhardt #1
1996 Viper Dale Earnhardt #2
1996 Viper Dale Earnhardt #3
1996 Viper Dale Earnhardt Cobra Mom-n-Pop's #1
1996 Viper Dale Earnhardt Cobra Mom-n-Pop's #2
1996 Viper Dale Earnhardt Cobra Mom-n-Pop's #3
1996 Viper Diamondback #D2
1996 Viper Diamondback Authentic #DA2
1996 Viper Diamondback Authentic California #DA2
1996 Viper Diamondback Authentic Eastern #DA2
1996 Viper Diamondback Authentic First Strike #DA2
1996 Viper Diamondback First Strike #D2
1996 Viper First Strike #1
1996 Viper First Strike #43
1996 Viper Green Mamba #1
1996 Viper Green Mamba #43
1996 Viper Green Mamba #R3G
1996 Viper King Cobra /699 #KC1
1996 Viper King Cobra First Strike #KC1
1996 Viper Red Cobra /1799 #1
1996 Viper Red Cobra /1799 #43
1996 Visions #124
1996 Visions Signings #100
1996 Visions Signings Artistry #3
1996 Wheels Dale Earnhardt Mom-n-Pop's #MPC1
1996 Wheels Dale Earnhardt Mom-n-Pop's #MPC2
1996 Wheels Dale Earnhardt Mom-n-Pop's #MPC3
1996 Zenith #1
1996 Zenith #35
1996 Zenith #50
1996 Zenith #65
1996 Zenith #66
1996 Zenith #67
1996 Zenith #68
1996 Zenith #69
1996 Zenith /94 #WC1
1996 Zenith Artist Proofs #1
1996 Zenith Artist Proofs #35
1996 Zenith Artist Proofs #50
1996 Zenith Artist Proofs #65
1996 Zenith Artist Proofs #66
1996 Zenith Artist Proofs #67
1996 Zenith Artist Proofs #68
1996 Zenith Artist Proofs #69
1996 Zenith Champion Salute #2
1996 Zenith Champion Salute #3
1996 Zenith Champion Salute #5
1996 Zenith Champion Salute #6
1996 Zenith Champion Salute #9
1996 Zenith Champion Salute #10
1996 Zenith Champion Salute #16
1996 Zenith Highlights #1
1997 Action Packed #3
1997 Action Packed #45
1997 Action Packed #84
1997 Action Packed 24K Gold #2
1997 Action Packed Chevy Madness #1
1997 Action Packed Fifth Anniversary #6
1997 Action Packed First Impressions #3
1997 Action Packed First Impressions #45
1997 Action Packed First Impressions #84
1997 Action Packed Rolling Thunder #2
1997 ActionVision #3
1997 ActionVision #8
1997 ActionVision Precious Metal #6
1997 Autographed Racing #1
1997 Autographed Racing #36
1997 Autographed Racing #47
1997 Autographed Racing #49
1997 Autographed Racing Autographs #12
1997 Autographed Racing Mayne Street #KM1
1997 Collector's Choice #3
1997 Collector's Choice Upper Deck 500 #UD1
1997 Collector's Choice Victory Circle #VC2
1997 Jurassic Park Carnivore #C1
1997 Jurassic Park Pteranodon #P1
1997 Jurassic Park Thunder Lizard #TL8
1997 Jurassic Park T-Rex #TR5
1997 Maxx #48
1997 Maxx /50 #NNO
1997 Maxx #3
1997 Maxx #109
1997 Maxx Flag Firsts #FF14
1997 Pinnacle #3
1997 Pinnacle #32
1997 Pinnacle #66
1997 Pinnacle #68
1997 Pinnacle #69
1997 Pinnacle #70
1997 Pinnacle #82
1997 Pinnacle #84
1997 Pinnacle #91
1997 Pinnacle #95
1997 Pinnacle Artist Proofs #3
1997 Pinnacle Artist Proofs #32
1997 Pinnacle Artist Proofs #66
1997 Pinnacle Artist Proofs #68
1997 Pinnacle Artist Proofs #69
1997 Pinnacle Artist Proofs #70
1997 Pinnacle Artist Proofs #82
1997 Pinnacle Artist Proofs #84
1997 Pinnacle Artist Proofs #91
1997 Pinnacle Artist Proofs #95
1997 Pinnacle Certified #3
1997 Pinnacle Certified #37
1997 Pinnacle Certified #76
1997 Pinnacle Certified #93
1997 Pinnacle Certified Certified Team #1
1997 Pinnacle Certified Certified Team Gold #1
1997 Pinnacle Certified Epix #E1
1997 Pinnacle Certified Epix Emerald #E1
1997 Pinnacle Certified Epix Purple #E1
1997 Pinnacle Certified Mirror Blue #3
1997 Pinnacle Certified Mirror Blue #37
1997 Pinnacle Certified Mirror Blue #76
1997 Pinnacle Certified Mirror Blue #93
1997 Pinnacle Certified Mirror Gold #93
1997 Pinnacle Certified Mirror Gold #76
1997 Pinnacle Certified Mirror Gold #37
1997 Pinnacle Certified Mirror Gold #3
1997 Pinnacle Certified Mirror Red #93
1997 Pinnacle Certified Mirror Red #76
1997 Pinnacle Certified Mirror Red #37
1997 Pinnacle Certified Mirror Red #3
1997 Pinnacle Certified Red #93
1997 Pinnacle Certified Red #76
1997 Pinnacle Certified Red #37
1997 Pinnacle Certified Red #3
1997 Pinnacle Chevy Madness #13
1997 Pinnacle Mint #21
1997 Pinnacle Mint Bronze #21
1997 Pinnacle Mint Coins #21
1997 Pinnacle Mint Coins 24K Gold Plated #21
1997 Pinnacle Mint Coins Nickel-Silver #21
1997 Pinnacle Mint Gold #21
1997 Pinnacle Mint Silver #21
1997 Pinnacle Portraits #3
1997 Pinnacle Portraits #23
1997 Pinnacle Portraits 8x10 #DE1
1997 Pinnacle Portraits 8x10 #DE2
1997 Pinnacle Portraits 8x10 #DE3
1997 Pinnacle Portraits 8x10 #DE4
1997 Pinnacle Portraits 8x10 Dufex #DE4
1997 Pinnacle Portraits 8x10 Dufex #DE3
1997 Pinnacle Portraits 8x10 Dufex #DE2
1997 Pinnacle Portraits 8x10 Dufex #DE1
1997 Pinnacle Precision #15
1997 Pinnacle Precision #18
1997 Pinnacle Precision Bronze #13
1997 Pinnacle Precision Bronze #14
1997 Pinnacle Precision Bronze #15
1997 Pinnacle Precision Bronze #17
1997 Pinnacle Precision Bronze #18
1997 Pinnacle Precision Bronze #12
1997 Pinnacle Precision Gold #12
1997 Pinnacle Precision Gold #13
1997 Pinnacle Precision Gold #14
1997 Pinnacle Precision Gold #15
1997 Pinnacle Precision Gold #17
1997 Pinnacle Precision Gold #18
1997 Pinnacle Precision Silver #12
1997 Pinnacle Precision Silver #13
1997 Pinnacle Precision Silver #14
1997 Pinnacle Precision Silver #15
1997 Pinnacle Precision Silver #17
1997 Pinnacle Precision Silver #18
1997 Pinnacle Press Plates #3
1997 Pinnacle Press Plates #32
1997 Pinnacle Press Plates #66
1997 Pinnacle Press Plates #68
1997 Pinnacle Press Plates #69
1997 Pinnacle Press Plates #70
1997 Pinnacle Press Plates #82
1997 Pinnacle Press Plates #84
1997 Pinnacle Press Plates #91
1997 Pinnacle Press Plates #95
1997 Pinnacle Press Plates #S3S
1997 Pinnacle Press Plates #CM13
1997 Pinnacle Press Plates #TP3A
1997 Pinnacle Spellbound #3S
1997 Pinnacle Spellbound Autographs #3S
1997 Pinnacle Spellbound Promos #3S
1997 Pinnacle Team Pinnacle #3
1997 Pinnacle Team Pinnacle Red #3
1997 Pinnacle Totally Certified Platinum Blue #3
1997 Pinnacle Totally Certified Platinum Blue #37
1997 Pinnacle Totally Certified Platinum Blue #76
1997 Pinnacle Totally Certified Platinum Blue #93
1997 Pinnacle Totally Certified Platinum Gold #3
1997 Pinnacle Totally Certified Platinum Gold #37
1997 Pinnacle Totally Certified Platinum Gold #76
1997 Pinnacle Totally Certified Platinum Gold #93
1997 Pinnacle Totally Certified Platinum Red #3
1997 Pinnacle Totally Certified Platinum Red #37
1997 Pinnacle Totally Certified Platinum Red #76
1997 Pinnacle Totally Certified Platinum Red #93
1997 Pinnacle Trophy Collection #3
1997 Pinnacle Trophy Collection #32
1997 Pinnacle Trophy Collection #66
1997 Pinnacle Trophy Collection #68
1997 Pinnacle Trophy Collection #69
1997 Pinnacle Trophy Collection #70
1997 Pinnacle Trophy Collection #82
1997 Pinnacle Trophy Collection #84
1997 Pinnacle Trophy Collection #91
1997 Pinnacle Trophy Collection #95
1997 Predator #3
1997 Predator American Eagle #AE1
1997 Predator American Eagle First Slash #AE1
1997 Predator Black Wolf #3
1997 Predator Black Wolf First Slash /3750 #3
1997 Predator Eye of the Tiger #ET1
1997 Predator Eye of the Tiger First Slash #ET1
1997 Predator First Slash #3
1997 Predator Gatorback #GB1
1997 Predator Gatorback Authentic #GBA1
1997 Predator Gatorback Authentic First Slash #GBA1
1997 Predator Gatorback First Slash #GB1
1997 Predator Golden Eagle #GE1
1997 Predator Golden Eagle First Slash #GE1
1997 Predator Grizzly #3
1997 Predator Grizzly First Slash #3
1997 Predator Red Wolf #3
1997 Predator Red Wolf First Slash #3
1997 Press Pass #4
1997 Press Pass #32
1997 Press Pass #56
1997 Press Pass #95
1997 Press Pass Autographs #4
1997 Press Pass Banquet Bound #BB4
1997 Press Pass Burning Rubber /400 #BR2
1997 Press Pass Clear Cut #C1
1997 Press Pass Cup Chase #CC5
1997 Press Pass Cup Chase Gold Die Cuts #CC5
1997 Press Pass Lasers Silver #4
1997 Press Pass Lasers Silver #32
1997 Press Pass Lasers Silver #56
1997 Press Pass Lasers Silver #95
1997 Press Pass Oil Slicks /100 #4
1997 Press Pass Oil Slicks /100 #32
1997 Press Pass Oil Slicks /100 #56
1997 Press Pass Oil Slicks /100 #95
1997 Press Pass Premium #4
1997 Press Pass Premium #29
1997 Press Pass Premium Crystal Ball #CB2
1997 Press Pass Premium Crystal Ball Die Cut #CB2
1997 Press Pass Premium Double Burners /350 #DB1
1997 Press Pass Premium Emerald Proofs /380 #4
1997 Press Pass Premium Emerald Proofs /380 #29
1997 Press Pass Premium Lap Leaders #LL1
1997 Press Pass Premium Mirrors #4
1997 Press Pass Premium Mirrors #29
1997 Press Pass Premium Oil Slicks /100 #4
1997 Press Pass Premium Oil Slicks /100 #29
1997 Press Pass Torquers Blue #4
1997 Press Pass Torquers Blue #32
1997 Press Pass Torquers Blue #56
1997 Press Pass Torquers Blue #95
1997 Press Pass Victory Lane #VL1A
1997 Press Pass Victory Lane #VL1B
1997 Race Sharks #1
1997 Race Sharks First Bite #1
1997 Race Sharks Great White #1
1997 Race Sharks Great White Shark's Teeth #GW1
1997 Race Sharks Great White Shark's Teeth First Bite #GW1
1997 Race Sharks Hammerhead #1
1997 Race Sharks Hammerhead First Bite #1
1997 Race Sharks Shark Attack #SA1
1997 Race Sharks Shark Attack First Bite #SA1
1997 Race Sharks Shark Attack First Bite Previews #1
1997 Race Sharks Shark Tooth Signatures /300 #ST1
1997 Race Sharks Shark Tooth Signatures First Bite /400 #ST1
1997 Race Sharks Tiger Shark #1
1997 Race Sharks Tiger Shark First Bite #1
1997 Racer's Choice #3
1997 Racer's Choice #27
1997 Racer's Choice #38
1997 Racer's Choice #62
1997 Racer's Choice #90
1997 Racer's Choice #104
1997 Racer's Choice #106
1997 Racer's Choice Busch Clash #1
1997 Racer's Choice Busch Clash #11
1997 Racer's Choice Chevy Madness #8
1997 Racer's Choice High Octane #2
1997 Racer's Choice High Octane Glow in the Dark #2
1997 Racer's Choice Showcase Series #3
1997 Racer's Choice Showcase Series #27
1997 Racer's Choice Showcase Series #38
1997 Racer's Choice Showcase Series #62
1997 Racer's Choice Showcase Series #90
1997 Racer's Choice Showcase Series #104
1997 Racer's Choice Showcase Series #106
1997 SB Motorsports #1
1997 SB Motorsports #41
1997 SB Motorsports #47
1997 SB Motorsports #50
1997 SB Motorsports #92
1997 SB Motorsports Autographs /500 #1
1997 SB Motorsports Race Chat #RC1
1997 SB Motorsports Winston Cup Rewind #WC2
1997 SB Motorsports Winston Cup Rewind #WC20
1997 Score Board IQ #1
1997 Score Board IQ #27
1997 Score Board IQ #38
1997 Score Board IQ #40
1997 Score Board IQ $10 Phone Cards #PC1
1997 Score Board IQ $10 Phone Cards #PC4
1997 Score Board IQ Remarques #SB1
1997 Score Board IQ Remarques Sam Bass Finished #SB1
1997 Score Board Seven-Eleven Phone Cards #1
1997 SkyBox Profile #5
1997 SkyBox Profile #63
1997 SkyBox Profile Autographs /200 #5
1997 SkyBox Profile Pace Setters #E1
1997 SkyBox Profile Team #T4
1997 SP #3
1997 SP #45
1997 SP Race Film #RD3
1997 SP Super Series #3
1997 SP Super Series #45
1997 SportsCom FanScan #2
1997 SPx #3
1997 SPx Blue #3
1997 SPx Gold #3
1997 SPx Silver #3
1997 Ultra #10
1997 Ultra #43
1997 Ultra AKA #A1
1997 Ultra Inside Out #DC1
1997 Ultra Shoney's #3
1997 Ultra Update #2
1997 Ultra Update #77
1997 Ultra Update Autographs #2
1997 Ultra Update Driver View #D6
1997 Ultra Update Elite Seats #E2
1997 Ultra Winn Dixie #WD3
1997 Upper Deck Road To The Cup #4
1997 Upper Deck Road To The Cup #121
1997 Upper Deck Road To The Cup Cup Quest #CQ3
1997 Upper Deck Road To The Cup Cup Quest Checkered #CQ3
1997 Upper Deck Road To The Cup Cup Quest White #CQ3
1997 Upper Deck Road To The Cup Premiere Position #PP4
1997 Upper Deck Victory Circle #3
1997 Upper Deck Victory Circle Championship Reflections #CR4
1997 Upper Deck Victory Circle Driver's Seat #DS1
1997 Upper Deck Victory Circle Victory Lap #VL1
1997 VIP #6
1997 VIP Explosives #6
1997 VIP Head Gear #HG1
1997 VIP Head Gear Die Cuts #HG1
1997 VIP Knights of Thunder #KT1
1997 VIP Knights of Thunder Gold #KT1
1997 VIP Oil Slicks #6
1997 VIP Ring of Honor #RH2
1997 VIP Ring of Honor Die Cuts #RH2
1997 Viper #68
1997 Viper Anaconda Jumbos #A5
1997 Viper Black Racer #68
1997 Viper Black Racer First Strike #68
1997 Viper Cobra #C1
1997 Viper Cobra First Strike #C1
1997 Viper Diamondback #DB8
1997 Viper Diamondback Authentic #DBA8
1997 Viper Diamondback Authentic Eastern #DBA8
1997 Viper Diamondback Authentic Eastern First Strike #DBA8
1997 Viper Diamondback Authentic First Strike #DBA8
1997 Viper Diamondback First Strike #DB8
1997 Viper First Strike #68
1997 Viper King Cobra #KC1
1997 Viper Snake Eyes #SE1
1997 Viper Snake Eyes First Strike #SE1
1998 Big League Cards Creative Images #29
1998 Burger King Dale Earnhardt #4
1998 Burger King Dale Earnhardt #1
1998 Burger King Dale Earnhardt #2
1998 Burger King Dale Earnhardt #3
1998 Collector's Choice #3
1998 Collector's Choice #39
1998 Collector's Choice #103
1998 Collector's Choice Star Quest #SQ26
1998 Maxx #3
1998 Maxx #33
1998 Maxx #95
1998 Maxx 10th Anniversary #96
1998 Maxx 10th Anniversary #119
1998 Maxx 10th Anniversary Champions Past #CP3
1998 Maxx 10th Anniversary Champions Past Die Cuts /1000 #CP3
1998 Maxx 1997 Year In Review #9
1998 Maxx 1997 Year In Review #33
1998 Maxx 1997 Year In Review #53
1998 Maxx 1997 Year In Review #128
1998 Maxx 1997 Year In Review #P05
1998 Maxx Focus on a Champion #FC3
1998 Maxx Focus on a Champion Cel #FC3
1998 Maximum #3
1998 Maximum #28
1998 Maximum Battle Proven #B2
1998 Maximum Field Generals Four Star Autographs /1 #10
1998 Maximum Field Generals One Star /2000 #10
1998 Maximum Field Generals Three Star Autographs /100 #10
1998 Maximum Field Generals Two Star /1000 #10
1998 Pinnacle Mint #3
1998 Pinnacle Mint #17
1998 Pinnacle Mint Coins #3
1998 Pinnacle Mint Coins #17
1998 Pinnacle Mint Coins Bronze Proof #3
1998 Pinnacle Mint Coins Bronze Proof #17
1998 Pinnacle Mint Coins Gold Plated #3
1998 Pinnacle Mint Coins Gold Plated #17
1998 Pinnacle Mint Coins Gold Plated Proofs #3
1998 Pinnacle Mint Coins Gold Plated Proofs #17
1998 Pinnacle Mint Coins Nickel-Silver #3
1998 Pinnacle Mint Coins Nickel-Silver #17
1998 Pinnacle Mint Coins Silver Plated Proofs #3
1998 Pinnacle Mint Coins Silver Plated Proofs #17
1998 Pinnacle Mint Coins Solid Gold #3
1998 Pinnacle Mint Coins Solid Gold #17
1998 Pinnacle Mint Coins Solid Silver #3
1998 Pinnacle Mint Coins Solid Silver #17
1998 Pinnacle Mint Die Cuts #3
1998 Pinnacle Mint Die Cuts #17
1998 Pinnacle Mint Gold Team #3
1998 Pinnacle Mint Gold Team #17
1998 Pinnacle Mint Silver Team #3
1998 Pinnacle Mint Silver Team #17
1998 Press Pass #104
1998 Press Pass #29
1998 Press Pass #4
1998 Press Pass Autographs /63 #1
1998 Press Pass Cup Chase #CC5
1998 Press Pass Cup Chase Die Cut Prizes #CC5
1998 Press Pass Oil Cans #OC2
1998 Press Pass Oil Slicks /100 #4
1998 Press Pass Oil Slicks /100 #29
1998 Press Pass Pit Stop #PS2
1998 Press Pass Premium #32
1998 Press Pass Premium #15
1998 Press Pass Premium #0
1998 Press Pass Premium Flag Chasers #FC20
1998 Press Pass Premium Flag Chasers Reflectors #FC20
1998 Press Pass Premium Reflectors #15
1998 Press Pass Premium Reflectors #32
1998 Press Pass Premium Rivalries #6B
1998 Press Pass Premium Rivalries #3A
1998 Press Pass Premium Steel Horses #SH2
1998 Press Pass Premium Triple Gear Firesuit /150 #TGF2
1998 Press Pass Shockers #ST3A
1998 Press Pass Signings /402 #3
1998 Press Pass Signings Gold /10 #3B
1998 Press Pass Signings Gold /100 #3
1998 Press Pass Stealth #59
1998 Press Pass Stealth #1
1998 Press Pass Stealth #2
1998 Press Pass Stealth Fan Talk #1
1998 Press Pass Stealth Fan Talk Die Cuts #1
1998 Press Pass Stealth Fusion #1
1998 Press Pass Stealth Fusion #2
1998 Press Pass Stealth Fusion #59
1998 Press Pass Stealth Octane #10
1998 Press Pass Stealth Octane #9
1998 Press Pass Stealth Octane Die Cuts #9
1998 Press Pass Stealth Octane Die Cuts #10
1998 Press Pass Stealth Race Used Gloves /205 #G8
1998 Press Pass Torpedoes #ST3B
1998 Press Pass Triple Gear 3 in 1 /33 #STG2
1998 Press Pass Triple Gear Burning Rubber /250 #TG2
1998 SP Authentic #37
1998 SP Authentic #3
1998 SP Authentic Sign of the Times Red #ST3
1998 SP Authentic Traditions #T1
1998 SportsCom FanScan #1
1998 Upper Deck Diamond Vision #3
1998 Upper Deck Diamond Vision Signature Moves #3
1998 Upper Deck Diamond Vision Vision of a Champion #VC2
1998 Upper Deck Pop Weaver #PW2
1998 Upper Deck Road To The Cup #75
1998 Upper Deck Road To The Cup #3
1998 Upper Deck Road To The Cup 50th Anniversary #AN49
1998 Upper Deck Road To The Cup 50th Anniversary Autographs /50 #AN49
1998 Upper Deck Road To The Cup Cover Story #CS10
1998 Upper Deck Victory Circle #48
1998 Upper Deck Victory Circle #3
1998 Upper Deck Victory Circle Point Leaders #PL5
1998 Upper Deck Victory Circle Sparks of Brilliance #SB3
1998 VIP #38
1998 VIP #6
1998 VIP Driving Force #DF5
1998 VIP Driving Force Die Cuts #DF5
1998 VIP Explosives #6
1998 VIP Explosives #38
1998 VIP Head Gear #HG2
1998 VIP Head Gear Die Cuts #HG2
1998 VIP Lap Leaders #LL2
1998 VIP Lap Leaders Acetate #LL2
1998 VIP NASCAR Country #NC1
1998 VIP NASCAR Country Die Cuts #NC1
1998 VIP Solos #6
1998 VIP Solos #38
1998 VIP Triple Gear Sheet Metal /225 #TGS2
1998 Wheels #9
1998 Wheels #34
1998 Wheels #83
1998 Wheels #99
1998 Wheels 50th Anniversary #A3
1998 Wheels 50th Anniversary #A18
1998 Wheels Autographs #1
1998 Wheels Double Take #E2
1998 Wheels Golden #9
1998 Wheels Golden #34
1998 Wheels Golden #83
1998 Wheels Golden #99
1998 Wheels Green Flags #GF4
1998 Wheels High Gear #5
1998 Wheels High Gear #29
1998 Wheels High Gear #48
1998 Wheels High Gear #64
1998 Wheels High Gear Autographs /50 #6
1998 Wheels High Gear Custom Shop #CS1
1998 Wheels High Gear Custom Shop Prizes #DEA1
1998 Wheels High Gear Custom Shop Prizes #DEA2
1998 Wheels High Gear Custom Shop Prizes #DEA3
1998 Wheels High Gear Custom Shop Prizes #DEB1
1998 Wheels High Gear Custom Shop Prizes #DEB2
1998 Wheels High Gear Custom Shop Prizes #DEB3
1998 Wheels High Gear Custom Shop Prizes #43070
1998 Wheels High Gear Custom Shop Prizes #43071
1998 Wheels High Gear Custom Shop Prizes #43072
1998 Wheels High Gear First Gear #4
1998 Wheels High Gear First Gear #29
1998 Wheels High Gear First Gear #48
1998 Wheels High Gear First Gear #64
1998 Wheels High Gear Gear Jammers #GJ2
1998 Wheels High Gear High Groove #HG2
1998 Wheels High Gear Man and Machine Cars #7
1998 Wheels High Gear Man and Machine Drivers #MM7
1998 Wheels High Gear MPH /100 #4
1998 Wheels High Gear MPH /100 #29
1998 Wheels High Gear MPH /100 #48
1998 Wheels High Gear MPH /100 #64
1998 Wheels High Gear Pure Gold #PG1
1998 Wheels High Gear Top Tier #TT5
1998 Wheels Jackpot #J1
1999 Coca-Cola Racing Family #2
1999 Hasbro/Winner's Circle #NNO
1999 Maxx #88
1999 Maxx #89
1999 Maxx FANtastic Finishes #F10
1999 Maxx Focus on a Champion #FC2
1999 Maxx Focus on a Champion Gold #FC2
1999 Press Pass #8
1999 Press Pass #35
1999 Press Pass Autographs /75 #3
1999 Press Pass Burning Rubber /250 #BR9
1999 Press Pass Chase Cars #7B
1999 Press Pass Cup Chase #4
1999 Press Pass Cup Chase Die Cut Prizes #4
1999 Press Pass Pit Stop #3
1999 Press Pass Premium #6
1999 Press Pass Premium #35
1999 Press Pass Premium Badge of Honor #BH19
1999 Press Pass Premium Badge of Honor Reflectors #BH19
1999 Press Pass Premium Extreme Fire #FD2A
1999 Press Pass Premium Race Used Firesuit /250 #F3
1999 Press Pass Premium Reflectors /1975 #R6
1999 Press Pass Premium Reflectors /1975 #R35
1999 Press Pass Premium Steel Horses #SH2
1999 Press Pass Signings /400 #14
1999 Press Pass Signings Gold /100 #3
1999 Press Pass Skidmarks /250 #8
1999 Press Pass Skidmarks /250 #35
1999 Press Pass Stealth #7
1999 Press Pass Stealth #8
1999 Press Pass Stealth #53
1999 Press Pass Stealth Big Numbers #BN3
1999 Press Pass Stealth Big Numbers Die Cuts #BN3
1999 Press Pass Stealth Fusion #F7
1999 Press Pass Stealth Fusion #F8
1999 Press Pass Stealth Fusion #F53
1999 Press Pass Stealth Headlines #SH2
1999 Press Pass Stealth Octane SLX #O28
1999 Press Pass Stealth Octane SLX Die Cuts #O28
1999 Press Pass Stealth Race Used Gloves /30 #G3
1999 Press Pass Stealth SST Cars #SS2
1999 Press Pass Stealth SST Drivers #SS2
1999 Press Pass Triple Gear 3 in 1 /33 #TG9
1999 SP Authentic #2
1999 SP Authentic #53
1999 SP Authentic #79
1999 SP Authentic Driving Force #DF7
1999 SP Authentic In the Driver's Seat #DS1
1999 SP Authentic Overdrive #2
1999 SP Authentic Overdrive #53
1999 SP Authentic Overdrive /3 #79
1999 SP Authentic Sign of the Times #DE
1999 SportsCom FanScan #1
1999 Upper Deck Road to the Cup #26
1999 Upper Deck Road to the Cup #60
1999 Upper Deck Road to the Cup NASCAR Chronicles #NC11
1999 Upper Deck Road to the Cup Signature Collection #DE
1999 Upper Deck Road to the Cup Signature Collection Checkered Flag #DE
1999 Upper Deck Road to the Cup Upper Deck Profiles #P3
1999 Upper Deck Victory Circle #83
1999 Upper Deck Victory Circle Signature Collection #DE
1999 Upper Deck Victory Circle UD Exclusives #83
1999 Upper Deck Victory Circle Victory Circle #V1
1999 VIP #7
1999 VIP #41
1999 VIP Explosives #X7
1999 VIP Explosives #X41
1999 VIP Explosives Lasers #7
1999 VIP Explosives Lasers #41
1999 VIP Lap Leaders #LL3
1999 VIP Out of the Box #OB3
1999 VIP Rear View Mirror #RM3
1999 VIP Sheet Metal #SM2
1999 VIP Vintage Performance #8
1999 Wheels #9
1999 Wheels #56
1999 Wheels Circuit Breaker #CB3
1999 Wheels Dialed In #DI3
1999 Wheels Flag Chasers Daytona Seven #DS2
1999 Wheels Flag Chasers Daytona Seven Blue-Yellow #DS2
1999 Wheels Flag Chasers Daytona Seven Checkered #DS2
1999 Wheels Flag Chasers Daytona Seven Green #DS2
1999 Wheels Flag Chasers Daytona Seven Red #DS2
1999 Wheels Flag Chasers Daytona Seven White #DS2
1999 Wheels Flag Chasers Daytona Seven Yellow #DS2
1999 Wheels Golden #9
1999 Wheels Golden #56
1999 Wheels High Gear #8
1999 Wheels High Gear #29
1999 Wheels High Gear #48
1999 Wheels High Gear #64
1999 Wheels High Gear Autographs /55 #6
1999 Wheels High Gear Custom Shop #CSDE
1999 Wheels High Gear Custom Shop Prizes #DEA1
1999 Wheels High Gear Custom Shop Prizes #DEA2
1999 Wheels High Gear Custom Shop Prizes #DEA3
1999 Wheels High Gear Custom Shop Prizes #DEB1
1999 Wheels High Gear Custom Shop Prizes #DEB2
1999 Wheels High Gear Custom Shop Prizes #DEB3
1999 Wheels High Gear Custom Shop Prizes #43070
1999 Wheels High Gear Custom Shop Prizes #43071
1999 Wheels High Gear Custom Shop Prizes #43072
1999 Wheels High Gear First Gear #8
1999 Wheels High Gear First Gear #29
1999 Wheels High Gear First Gear #48
1999 Wheels High Gear First Gear #64
1999 Wheels High Gear Flag Chasers #FC5
1999 Wheels High Gear Flag Chasers Blue-Yellow #FC5
1999 Wheels High Gear Flag Chasers Checkered #FC5
1999 Wheels High Gear Flag Chasers Green #FC5
1999 Wheels High Gear Flag Chasers Red #FC5
1999 Wheels High Gear Flag Chasers White #FC5
1999 Wheels High Gear Flag Chasers Yellow #FC5
1999 Wheels High Gear Gear Shifters #GS8
1999 Wheels High Gear Hot Streaks #HS3
1999 Wheels High Gear MPH #8
1999 Wheels High Gear MPH #29
1999 Wheels High Gear MPH #48
1999 Wheels High Gear MPH #64
1999 Wheels High Gear Top Tier #TT8
1999 Wheels High Groove #HG4
1999 Wheels Runnin and Gunnin #RG3
1999 Wheels Runnin and Gunnin Foils #RG3
1999 Wheels Solos #9
1999 Wheels Solos #56
2000 Coca-Cola Racing Family #3
2000 Coca-Cola Racing Family #4
2000 Coca-Cola Racing Family #16
2000 Maxx #3
2000 Maxx #43
2000 Maxx Fantastic Finishes #FF1
2000 Maxx Oval Office #OO2
2000 Maxx Racer's Ink #DE
2000 Maximum #7
2000 Maximum Die Cuts /250 #7
2000 Maximum MPH /3 #7
2000 Maximum Roots of Racing #R1
2000 Maximum Signatures #DE
2000 Maximum Signatures #DE2
2000 Press Pass #7
2000 Press Pass Burning Rubber /200 #BR6
2000 Press Pass Cup Chase #CC4
2000 Press Pass Cup Chase Die Cut Prizes #CC4
2000 Press Pass Gatorade Front Runner Award #12
2000 Press Pass Millennium #7
2000 Press Pass Oil Cans #OC7
2000 Press Pass Optima #5
2000 Press Pass Optima Encore #EN6
2000 Press Pass Optima G Force #GF5
2000 Press Pass Optima On the Edge #OE1
2000 Press Pass Optima Platinum #5
2000 Press Pass Optima Race Used Lugnuts Cars /100 #LC15
2000 Press Pass Optima Race Used Lugnuts Drivers /55 #LD15
2000 Press Pass Pitstop #PS3
2000 Press Pass Premium #49
2000 Press Pass Premium #64
2000 Press Pass Premium Performance Driven #PD6
2000 Press Pass Premium Race Used Firesuit /130 #F3
2000 Press Pass Premium Reflectors #49
2000 Press Pass Premium Reflectors #64
2000 Press Pass Showcar #SC5
2000 Press Pass Showcar Die Cuts #SC5
2000 Press Pass Signings #14
2000 Press Pass Signings Gold /100 #9
2000 Press Pass Skidmarks #SK6
2000 Press Pass Stealth #7
2000 Press Pass Stealth #8
2000 Press Pass Stealth Intensity #IN6
2000 Press Pass Stealth Profile #PR10
2000 Press Pass Stealth Race Used Gloves /100 #G3
2000 Press Pass Techno-Retro #TR6
2000 Press Pass Trackside #2
2000 Press Pass Trackside #36
2000 Press Pass Trackside Dialed In #DI9
2000 Press Pass Trackside Die Cuts #2
2000 Press Pass Trackside Die Cuts #36
2000 Press Pass Trackside Golden #2
2000 Press Pass Trackside Golden #36
2000 Press Pass Trackside Panorama #P28
2000 Press Pass Trackside Pit Stoppers /200 #PS3
2000 Press Pass Trackside Too Tough To Tame #TT6
2000 SP Authentic #5
2000 SP Authentic /1000 #80
2000 SP Authentic Overdrive Gold /3 #5
2000 SP Authentic Overdrive Gold /3 #80
2000 SP Authentic Overdrive Silver /250 #5
2000 SP Authentic Overdrive Silver /250 #80
2000 SP Authentic Power Surge #PS1
2000 SP Authentic Sign of the Times #DE
2000 SP Authentic Sign of the Times Gold /25 #DE
2000 Upper Deck MVP #3
2000 Upper Deck MVP #87
2000 Upper Deck MVP Cup Quest 2000 #CQ1
2000 Upper Deck MVP Gold Script /125 #3
2000 Upper Deck MVP Gold Script /125 #87
2000 Upper Deck MVP NASCAR Stars #NS3
2000 Upper Deck MVP Silver Script #3
2000 Upper Deck MVP Silver Script #87
2000 Upper Deck MVP Super Script /3 #87
2000 Upper Deck MVP Super Script /3 #3
2000 Upper Deck Racing #7
2000 Upper Deck Racing Dale Earnhardt Tribute #DE1
2000 Upper Deck Racing Dale Earnhardt Tribute #DE2
2000 Upper Deck Racing Dale Earnhardt Tribute #DE3
2000 Upper Deck Racing Dale Earnhardt Tribute #DE4
2000 Upper Deck Racing Dale Earnhardt Tribute #DE5
2000 Upper Deck Racing Dale Earnhardt Tribute #DE6
2000 Upper Deck Racing Dale Earnhardt Tribute #DE7
2000 Upper Deck Racing Dale Earnhardt Tribute #DE8
2000 Upper Deck Racing Dale Earnhardt Tribute #DE9
2000 Upper Deck Racing Dale Earnhardt Tribute #DE10
2000 Upper Deck Racing Dale Earnhardt Tribute #DE11
2000 Upper Deck Racing Dale Earnhardt Tribute #DE12
2000 Upper Deck Racing Dale Earnhardt Tribute #DE13
2000 Upper Deck Racing Dale Earnhardt Tribute #DE14
2000 Upper Deck Racing Dale Earnhardt Tribute #DE15
2000 Upper Deck Racing Dale Earnhardt Tribute #DE16
2000 Upper Deck Racing Dale Earnhardt Tribute #DE17
2000 Upper Deck Racing Dale Earnhardt Tribute #DE18
2000 Upper Deck Racing Dale Earnhardt Tribute #DE19
2000 Upper Deck Racing Dale Earnhardt Tribute #DE20
2000 Upper Deck Racing Dale Earnhardt Tribute #DE21
2000 Upper Deck Racing Dale Earnhardt Tribute #DE22
2000 Upper Deck Racing Dale Earnhardt Tribute #DE23
2000 Upper Deck Racing Dale Earnhardt Tribute #DE24
2000 Upper Deck Racing Dale Earnhardt Tribute #DE25
2000 Upper Deck Racing High Groove #HG5
2000 Upper Deck Racing Record Pace #RP3
2000 Upper Deck Racing Road Signs #RSDE
2000 Upper Deck Racing Speeding Ticket #ST5
2000 Upper Deck Racing Trophy Dash #TD6
2000 Upper Deck Racing Winning Formula #WF3
2000 Upper Deck Victory Circle #9
2000 Upper Deck Victory Circle #55
2000 Upper Deck Victory Circle #70
2000 Upper Deck Victory Circle Exclusives Level 1 Silver /250 #9
2000 Upper Deck Victory Circle Exclusives Level 1 Silver /250 #55
2000 Upper Deck Victory Circle Exclusives Level 1 Silver /250 #70
2000 Upper Deck Victory Circle Exclusives Level 2 Gold /3 #70
2000 Upper Deck Victory Circle Exclusives Level 2 Gold /3 #55
2000 Upper Deck Victory Circle Exclusives Level 2 Gold /3 #9
2000 Upper Deck Victory Circle PowerDeck #PD1
2000 Upper Deck Victory Circle Winning Material Tire #TDE
2000 VIP #4
2000 VIP #41
2000 VIP #48
2000 VIP Explosives #X4
2000 VIP Explosives #X41
2000 VIP Explosives #X48
2000 VIP Explosives Lasers #LX4
2000 VIP Explosives Lasers #LX41
2000 VIP Explosives Lasers #LX48
2000 VIP Rear View Mirror #RM3
2000 VIP Rear View Mirror Explosives #RM3
2000 VIP Rear View Mirror Explosives Laser Die Cuts #RM3
2000 VIP Sheet Metal #SM3
2000 Wheels High Gear #7
2000 Wheels High Gear Autographs #9
2000 Wheels High Gear First Gear #7
2000 Wheels High Gear Flag Chasers #FC3
2000 Wheels High Gear Flag Chasers Blue-Yellow #FC3
2000 Wheels High Gear Flag Chasers Checkered #FC3
2000 Wheels High Gear Flag Chasers Checkered Blue/Orange #FC3
2000 Wheels High Gear Flag Chasers Green #FC3
2000 Wheels High Gear Flag Chasers Red #FC3
2000 Wheels High Gear Flag Chasers White #FC3
2000 Wheels High Gear Flag Chasers Yellow #FC3
2000 Wheels High Gear Gear Shifters #GS7
2000 Wheels High Gear MPH #7
2000 Wheels High Gear Sunday Sensation #OC7
2000 Wheels High Gear Top Tier #TT7
2000 Wheels High Gear Winning Edge #WE6
2001 Gold Collectibles Dale Earnhardt #1
2001 Gold Collectibles Dale Earnhardt #2
2001 Gold Collectibles Dale Earnhardt #3
2001 Gold Collectibles Dale Earnhardt #4
2001 Press Pass #2
2001 Press Pass #49
2001 Press Pass #67
2001 Press Pass Autographs #11
2001 Press Pass Burning Rubber Cars /105 #BRC3

2001 Press Pass Burning Rubber Drivers /90 #BRD3
2001 Press Pass Cup Chase #CC3
2001 Press Pass Cup Chase Die Cut Prizes #CC3
2001 Press Pass Double Burner /100 #DB3
2001 Press Pass Ground Zero #GZ3
2001 Press Pass Hot Treads /1000 #HT6
2001 Press Pass Millennium #2
2001 Press Pass Millennium #49
2001 Press Pass Millennium #67
2001 Press Pass Optima Race Used Lugnuts Cars /50 #LNC3
2001 Press Pass Optima Race Used Lugnuts Drivers /45 #LND0
2001 Press Pass Premium #3
2001 Press Pass Premium #30
2001 Press Pass Premium #51
2001 Press Pass Premium #77
2001 Press Pass Premium Gold #3
2001 Press Pass Premium Gold #30
2001 Press Pass Premium Gold #51
2001 Press Pass Premium Gold #77
2001 Press Pass Premium In The Zone #IZ3
2001 Press Pass Premium Performance Driven #PD3
2001 Press Pass Premium Race Used Firesuit Cars /110 #FC3
2001 Press Pass Premium Race Used Firesuit Drivers /100 #FD3
2001 Press Pass Showman/Showcar #S7A
2001 Press Pass Showman/Showcar #S7B
2001 Press Pass Total Memorabilia Power Pick #TM3
2001 Press Pass Trackside #3
2001 Press Pass Trackside Dialed In #D3
2001 Press Pass Trackside Die Cuts #3
2001 Press Pass Trackside Golden #3
2001 Press Pass Trackside Mirror Image #MI3
2001 Press Pass Trackside Pit Stoppers Cars #PSC3
2001 Press Pass Trackside Pit Stoppers Drivers /10 #PSD3
2001 Press Pass Triple Burner /100 #TB3A
2001 Press Pass Triple Burner /100 #TB3B
2001 Press Pass Velocity #VL9
2001 Press Pass Vintage #VN2
2001 VIP Sheet Metal Cars /120 #SC3
2001 VIP Sheet Metal Drivers /75 #SD3
2001 Wheels High Gear #2
2001 Wheels High Gear #61
2001 Wheels High Gear Autographs #8
2001 Wheels High Gear First Gear #2
2001 Wheels High Gear First Gear #61
2001 Wheels High Gear Flag Chasers #FC3
2001 Wheels High Gear Flag Chasers Blue-Yellow /45 #FC3
2001 Wheels High Gear Flag Chasers Checkered /35 #FC3
2001 Wheels High Gear Flag Chasers Checkered Blue/Orange /45 #FC3
2001 Wheels High Gear Flag Chasers Green /75 #FC3
2001 Wheels High Gear Flag Chasers Power Pick #FCPP
2001 Wheels High Gear Flag Chasers Red /75 #FC3
2001 Wheels High Gear Flag Chasers White /75 #FC3
2001 Wheels High Gear Flag Chasers Yellow /75 #FC3
2001 Wheels High Gear Gear Shifters #GS2
2001 Wheels High Gear Hot Streaks #HS3
2001 Wheels High Gear Man and Machine Cars #MM6B
2001 Wheels High Gear Man and Machine Drivers #MM6A
2001 Wheels High Gear MPH #2
2001 Wheels High Gear MPH #61
2001 Wheels High Gear Sunday Sensation #SS6
2001 Wheels High Gear Top Tier #TT2
2001 Wheels High Gear Top Tier Holofoils #TT2
2001-03 Press Pass Dale Earnhardt #DE1
2001-03 Press Pass Dale Earnhardt #DE2
2001-03 Press Pass Dale Earnhardt #DE3
2001-03 Press Pass Dale Earnhardt #DE4
2001-03 Press Pass Dale Earnhardt #DE5
2001-03 Press Pass Dale Earnhardt #DE6
2001-03 Press Pass Dale Earnhardt #DE7
2001-03 Press Pass Dale Earnhardt #DE8
2001-03 Press Pass Dale Earnhardt #DE9
2001-03 Press Pass Dale Earnhardt #DE10
2001-03 Press Pass Dale Earnhardt #DE11
2001-03 Press Pass Dale Earnhardt #DE12
2001-03 Press Pass Dale Earnhardt #DE13
2001-03 Press Pass Dale Earnhardt #DE14
2001-03 Press Pass Dale Earnhardt #DE15
2001-03 Press Pass Dale Earnhardt #DE16
2001-03 Press Pass Dale Earnhardt #DE17
2001-03 Press Pass Dale Earnhardt /90 #DE18
2001-03 Press Pass Dale Earnhardt #DE19
2001-03 Press Pass Dale Earnhardt #DE20
2001-03 Press Pass Dale Earnhardt #DE21
2001-03 Press Pass Dale Earnhardt #DE22
2001-03 Press Pass Dale Earnhardt #DE23
2001-03 Press Pass Dale Earnhardt #DE24
2001-03 Press Pass Dale Earnhardt #DE25
2001-03 Press Pass Dale Earnhardt #DE26
2001-03 Press Pass Dale Earnhardt #DE27
2001-03 Press Pass Dale Earnhardt #DE28
2001-03 Press Pass Dale Earnhardt #DE29
2001-03 Press Pass Dale Earnhardt #DE30
2001-03 Press Pass Dale Earnhardt #DE31
2001-03 Press Pass Dale Earnhardt #DE32
2001-03 Press Pass Dale Earnhardt #DE33
2001-03 Press Pass Dale Earnhardt #DE34
2001-03 Press Pass Dale Earnhardt #DE35
2001-03 Press Pass Dale Earnhardt #DE35B
2001-03 Press Pass Dale Earnhardt #DE36
2001-03 Press Pass Dale Earnhardt #DE36B
2001-03 Press Pass Dale Earnhardt #DE37
2001-03 Press Pass Dale Earnhardt #DE37B
2001-03 Press Pass Dale Earnhardt #DE38
2001-03 Press Pass Dale Earnhardt #DE38B
2001-03 Press Pass Dale Earnhardt #DE39
2001-03 Press Pass Dale Earnhardt #DE39B
2001-03 Press Pass Dale Earnhardt #DE40
2001-03 Press Pass Dale Earnhardt #DE40B
2001-03 Press Pass Dale Earnhardt #DE41
2001-03 Press Pass Dale Earnhardt #DE41B
2001-03 Press Pass Dale Earnhardt #DE42
2001-03 Press Pass Dale Earnhardt #DE42B
2001-03 Press Pass Dale Earnhardt #DE43
2001-03 Press Pass Dale Earnhardt #DE43B
2001-03 Press Pass Dale Earnhardt #DE44
2001-03 Press Pass Dale Earnhardt #DE45
2001-03 Press Pass Dale Earnhardt #DE46
2001-03 Press Pass Dale Earnhardt #DE47
2001-03 Press Pass Dale Earnhardt #DE48
2001-03 Press Pass Dale Earnhardt #DE49
2001-03 Press Pass Dale Earnhardt #DE50
2001-03 Press Pass Dale Earnhardt #DE51
2001-03 Press Pass Dale Earnhardt #DE52
2001-03 Press Pass Dale Earnhardt #DE53
2001-03 Press Pass Dale Earnhardt #DE54
2001-03 Press Pass Dale Earnhardt #DE55
2001-03 Press Pass Dale Earnhardt #DE56
2001-03 Press Pass Dale Earnhardt #DE57
2001-03 Press Pass Dale Earnhardt #DE58
2001-03 Press Pass Dale Earnhardt #DE59
2001-03 Press Pass Dale Earnhardt #DE60
2001-03 Press Pass Dale Earnhardt #DE61
2001-03 Press Pass Dale Earnhardt #DE62
2001-03 Press Pass Dale Earnhardt #DE63
2001-03 Press Pass Dale Earnhardt #DE64
2001-03 Press Pass Dale Earnhardt #DE65
2001-03 Press Pass Dale Earnhardt #DE66
2001-03 Press Pass Dale Earnhardt #DE67
2001-03 Press Pass Dale Earnhardt #DE68
2001-03 Press Pass Dale Earnhardt #DE69
2001-03 Press Pass Dale Earnhardt #DE70
2001-03 Press Pass Dale Earnhardt #DE71
2001-03 Press Pass Dale Earnhardt #DE72
2001-03 Press Pass Dale Earnhardt #DE73
2001-03 Press Pass Dale Earnhardt #DE74
2001-03 Press Pass Dale Earnhardt #DE75
2001-03 Press Pass Dale Earnhardt #DE76
2001-03 Press Pass Dale Earnhardt #DE77
2001-03 Press Pass Dale Earnhardt #DE78
2001-03 Press Pass Dale Earnhardt #DE79
2001-03 Press Pass Dale Earnhardt #DE80
2001-03 Press Pass Dale Earnhardt #DE81
2001-03 Press Pass Dale Earnhardt #DE82
2001-03 Press Pass Dale Earnhardt #DE83
2001-03 Press Pass Dale Earnhardt #DE84
2001-03 Press Pass Dale Earnhardt #DE85
2001-03 Press Pass Dale Earnhardt #DE86
2001-03 Press Pass Dale Earnhardt #DE87
2001-03 Press Pass Dale Earnhardt #DE88
2001-03 Press Pass Dale Earnhardt #DE89
2001-03 Press Pass Dale Earnhardt #DE90
2001-03 Press Pass Dale Earnhardt #DE91
2001-03 Press Pass Dale Earnhardt #DE92
2001-03 Press Pass Dale Earnhardt #DE93
2001-03 Press Pass Dale Earnhardt #DE94
2001-03 Press Pass Dale Earnhardt #DE95
2001-03 Press Pass Dale Earnhardt #DE96
2001-03 Press Pass Dale Earnhardt #DE97
2001-03 Press Pass Dale Earnhardt #DE98
2001-03 Press Pass Dale Earnhardt #DE99
2001-03 Press Pass Dale Earnhardt #DE100
2001-03 Press Pass Dale Earnhardt Celebration Foil #DE1
2001-03 Press Pass Dale Earnhardt Celebration Foil #DE2
2001-03 Press Pass Dale Earnhardt Celebration Foil #DE3
2001-03 Press Pass Dale Earnhardt Celebration Foil #DE4
2001-03 Press Pass Dale Earnhardt Celebration Foil #DE5
2001-03 Press Pass Dale Earnhardt Celebration Foil #DE6
2001-03 Press Pass Dale Earnhardt Celebration Foil #DE7
2001-03 Press Pass Dale Earnhardt Celebration Foil #DE8
2001-03 Press Pass Dale Earnhardt Celebration Foil #DE9
2001-03 Press Pass Dale Earnhardt Celebration Foil #DE10
2001-03 Press Pass Dale Earnhardt Celebration Foil #DE11
2001-03 Press Pass Dale Earnhardt Celebration Foil #DE12
2001-03 Press Pass Dale Earnhardt Celebration Foil #DE13
2001-03 Press Pass Dale Earnhardt Celebration Foil #DE14
2001-03 Press Pass Dale Earnhardt Celebration Foil #DE15
2001-03 Press Pass Dale Earnhardt Celebration Foil #DE16
2001-03 Press Pass Dale Earnhardt Celebration Foil #DE17
2001-03 Press Pass Dale Earnhardt Celebration Foil #DE18
2001-03 Press Pass Dale Earnhardt Celebration Foil #DE19
2001-03 Press Pass Dale Earnhardt Celebration Foil #DE20
2001-03 Press Pass Dale Earnhardt Celebration Foil #DE21
2001-03 Press Pass Dale Earnhardt Celebration Foil #DE22
2001-03 Press Pass Dale Earnhardt Celebration Foil #DE23
2001-03 Press Pass Dale Earnhardt Celebration Foil #DE24
2001-03 Press Pass Dale Earnhardt Celebration Foil #DE25
2001-03 Press Pass Dale Earnhardt Celebration Foil #DE26
2001-03 Press Pass Dale Earnhardt Celebration Foil #DE27
2001-03 Press Pass Dale Earnhardt Celebration Foil #DE28
2001-03 Press Pass Dale Earnhardt Celebration Foil #DE29
2001-03 Press Pass Dale Earnhardt Celebration Foil #DE30
2001-03 Press Pass Dale Earnhardt Celebration Foil #DE31
2001-03 Press Pass Dale Earnhardt Celebration Foil #DE32
2001-03 Press Pass Dale Earnhardt Celebration Foil #DE33
2001-03 Press Pass Dale Earnhardt Celebration Foil #DE34
2001-03 Press Pass Dale Earnhardt Celebration Foil #DE35
2001-03 Press Pass Dale Earnhardt Celebration Foil #DE35B
2001-03 Press Pass Dale Earnhardt Celebration Foil #DE36
2001-03 Press Pass Dale Earnhardt Celebration Foil #DE36B
2001-03 Press Pass Dale Earnhardt Celebration Foil #DE37
2001-03 Press Pass Dale Earnhardt Celebration Foil #DE37B
2001-03 Press Pass Dale Earnhardt Celebration Foil #DE38
2001-03 Press Pass Dale Earnhardt Celebration Foil #DE38B
2001-03 Press Pass Dale Earnhardt Celebration Foil #DE39
2001-03 Press Pass Dale Earnhardt Celebration Foil #DE39B
2001-03 Press Pass Dale Earnhardt Celebration Foil #DE40
2001-03 Press Pass Dale Earnhardt Celebration Foil #DE40B
2001-03 Press Pass Dale Earnhardt Celebration Foil #DE41
2001-03 Press Pass Dale Earnhardt Celebration Foil #DE41B
2001-03 Press Pass Dale Earnhardt Celebration Foil #DE42
2001-03 Press Pass Dale Earnhardt Celebration Foil #DE42B
2001-03 Press Pass Dale Earnhardt Celebration Foil #DE43
2001-03 Press Pass Dale Earnhardt Celebration Foil #DE43B
2001-03 Press Pass Dale Earnhardt Celebration Foil #DE44
2001-03 Press Pass Dale Earnhardt Celebration Foil #DE45
2001-03 Press Pass Dale Earnhardt Celebration Foil #DE46
2001-03 Press Pass Dale Earnhardt Celebration Foil #DE47
2001-03 Press Pass Dale Earnhardt Celebration Foil #DE48
2001-03 Press Pass Dale Earnhardt Celebration Foil #DE49
2001-03 Press Pass Dale Earnhardt Celebration Foil #DE50
2001-03 Press Pass Dale Earnhardt Celebration Foil #DE51
2001-03 Press Pass Dale Earnhardt Celebration Foil #DE52
2001-03 Press Pass Dale Earnhardt Celebration Foil #DE53
2001-03 Press Pass Dale Earnhardt Celebration Foil #DE54
2001-03 Press Pass Dale Earnhardt Celebration Foil #DE55
2001-03 Press Pass Dale Earnhardt Celebration Foil #DE56
2001-03 Press Pass Dale Earnhardt Celebration Foil #DE57
2001-03 Press Pass Dale Earnhardt Celebration Foil #DE58
2001-03 Press Pass Dale Earnhardt Celebration Foil #DE59
2001-03 Press Pass Dale Earnhardt Celebration Foil #DE60
2001-03 Press Pass Dale Earnhardt Celebration Foil #DE61
2001-03 Press Pass Dale Earnhardt Celebration Foil #DE62
2001-03 Press Pass Dale Earnhardt Celebration Foil #DE63
2001-03 Press Pass Dale Earnhardt Celebration Foil #DE64
2001-03 Press Pass Dale Earnhardt Celebration Foil #DE65
2001-03 Press Pass Dale Earnhardt Celebration Foil #DE66
2001-03 Press Pass Dale Earnhardt Celebration Foil #DE67
2001-03 Press Pass Dale Earnhardt Celebration Foil #DE68
2001-03 Press Pass Dale Earnhardt Celebration Foil #DE69
2001-03 Press Pass Dale Earnhardt Celebration Foil #DE70
2001-03 Press Pass Dale Earnhardt Celebration Foil #DE71
2001-03 Press Pass Dale Earnhardt Celebration Foil #DE72
2001-03 Press Pass Dale Earnhardt Celebration Foil #DE73
2001-03 Press Pass Dale Earnhardt Celebration Foil #DE74
2001-03 Press Pass Dale Earnhardt Celebration Foil #DE75
2001-03 Press Pass Dale Earnhardt Celebration Foil #DE76
2001-03 Press Pass Dale Earnhardt Celebration Foil #DE77
2001-03 Press Pass Dale Earnhardt Celebration Foil #DE78
2001-03 Press Pass Dale Earnhardt Celebration Foil #DE79
2001-03 Press Pass Dale Earnhardt Celebration Foil #DE80
2001-03 Press Pass Dale Earnhardt Celebration Foil #DE81
2001-03 Press Pass Dale Earnhardt Celebration Foil #DE82
2001-03 Press Pass Dale Earnhardt Celebration Foil #DE83
2001-03 Press Pass Dale Earnhardt Celebration Foil #DE84
2001-03 Press Pass Dale Earnhardt Celebration Foil #DE85
2001-03 Press Pass Dale Earnhardt Celebration Foil #DE86
2001-03 Press Pass Dale Earnhardt Celebration Foil #DE87
2001-03 Press Pass Dale Earnhardt Celebration Foil #DE88
2001-03 Press Pass Dale Earnhardt Celebration Foil #DE89
2001-03 Press Pass Dale Earnhardt Celebration Foil #DE90
2001-03 Press Pass Dale Earnhardt Celebration Foil #DE91
2001-03 Press Pass Dale Earnhardt Celebration Foil #DE92
2001-03 Press Pass Dale Earnhardt Celebration Foil #DE93
2001-03 Press Pass Dale Earnhardt Celebration Foil #DE94
2001-03 Press Pass Dale Earnhardt Celebration Foil #DE95
2001-03 Press Pass Dale Earnhardt Celebration Foil #DE96
2001-03 Press Pass Dale Earnhardt Celebration Foil #DE97
2001-03 Press Pass Dale Earnhardt Celebration Foil #DE98
2001-03 Press Pass Dale Earnhardt Celebration Foil #DE99
2001-03 Press Pass Dale Earnhardt Celebration Foil #DE100
2002 Press Pass Burning Rubber Cars /120 #BRC3
2002 Press Pass Burning Rubber Drivers /90 #BRD3
2002 Press Pass Optima Race Used Lugnuts Cars /10 #LNC4
2002 Press Pass Optima Race Used Lugnuts Drivers /10 #LND4
2002 Press Pass Premium Race Used Firesuit Cars /90 #FC11
2002 Press Pass Premium Race Used Firesuit Drivers /80 #FD11
2002 Press Pass Stealth Race Used Glove Cars /10 #GLC16
2002 Press Pass Stealth Race Used Glove Drivers /10 #GLD16
2002 Press Pass Total Memorabilia Power Pick #TM0
2002 Press Pass Trackside Pit Stoppers Cars /20 #PSC15
2002 Press Pass Trackside Pit Stoppers Drivers /20 #PSD15
2002 VIP Race Used Sheet Metal Cars #SC16
2002 VIP Race Used Sheet Metal Drivers /50 #SD16
2003 Press Pass Burning Rubber Cars /60 #BRT16
2003 Press Pass Burning Rubber Drivers /50 #BRD16
2003 Press Pass Optima Thunder Bolts Cars /3 #TBT11
2003 Press Pass Optima Thunder Bolts Drivers /3 #TBD11
2003 Press Pass Premium Hot Threads Cars /160 #HTT0
2003 Press Pass Premium Hot Threads Drivers /285 #HTD0
2003 Press Pass Snapshots #SN6
2003 Press Pass Stealth #0
2003 Press Pass Stealth Gear Grippers Cars /3 #GGT11
2003 Press Pass Stealth Gear Grippers Drivers /3 #GGD11
2003 Press Pass Trackside Dialed In #DI2
2003 Press Pass Trackside License to Drive #LD4
2003 Press Pass Trackside Pit Stoppers Cars /3 #PST9
2003 Press Pass Trackside Pit Stoppers Drivers /3 #PSD9
2003 Press Pass Velocity #VC1
2003 Press Pass Victory Lap #5
2003 VIP Tradin' Paint Cars /3 #TPT13
2003 VIP Tradin' Paint Drivers /110 #TPD13
2003 Wheels American Thunder Dale Earnhardt Retrospective #AT1
2003 Wheels American Thunder Dale Earnhardt Retrospective #AT2
2003 Wheels American Thunder Dale Earnhardt Retrospective #AT3
2003 Wheels American Thunder Dale Earnhardt Retrospective #AT4
2003 Wheels American Thunder Dale Earnhardt Retrospective #AT5
2003 Wheels American Thunder Dale Earnhardt Retrospective #AT6
2003 Wheels American Thunder Dale Earnhardt Retrospective #AT7
2003 Wheels American Thunder Dale Earnhardt Retrospective #AT8
2003 Wheels American Thunder Dale Earnhardt Retrospective #AT9
2003 Wheels American Thunder Dale Earnhardt Retrospective Foil #AT1
2003 Wheels American Thunder Dale Earnhardt Retrospective Foil #AT2
2003 Wheels American Thunder Dale Earnhardt Retrospective Foil #AT3
2003 Wheels American Thunder Dale Earnhardt Retrospective Foil #AT4
2003 Wheels American Thunder Dale Earnhardt Retrospective Foil #AT5
2003 Wheels American Thunder Dale Earnhardt Retrospective Foil #AT6
2003 Wheels American Thunder Dale Earnhardt Retrospective Foil #AT7
2003 Wheels American Thunder Dale Earnhardt Retrospective Foil #AT8
2003 Wheels American Thunder Dale Earnhardt Retrospective Foil #AT9
2003 Wheels High Gear Dale Earnhardt Retrospective #RT1
2003 Wheels High Gear Dale Earnhardt Retrospective #RT2
2003 Wheels High Gear Dale Earnhardt Retrospective #RT3
2003 Wheels High Gear Dale Earnhardt Retrospective #RT4
2003 Wheels High Gear Dale Earnhardt Retrospective #RT5
2003 Wheels High Gear Dale Earnhardt Retrospective #RT6
2003 Wheels High Gear Dale Earnhardt Retrospective #RT7
2003 Wheels High Gear Dale Earnhardt Retrospective #RT8
2003 Wheels High Gear Dale Earnhardt Retrospective #RT9
2003 Wheels High Gear Dale Earnhardt Retrospective Foil #RT1
2003 Wheels High Gear Dale Earnhardt Retrospective Foil #RT2
2003 Wheels High Gear Dale Earnhardt Retrospective Foil #RT3
2003 Wheels High Gear Dale Earnhardt Retrospective Foil #RT4
2003 Wheels High Gear Dale Earnhardt Retrospective Foil #RT5
2003 Wheels High Gear Dale Earnhardt Retrospective Foil #RT6
2003 Wheels High Gear Dale Earnhardt Retrospective Foil #RT7
2003 Wheels High Gear Dale Earnhardt Retrospective Foil #RT8
2003 Wheels High Gear Dale Earnhardt Retrospective Foil #RT9
2003-04 Press Pass 10th Anniversary Earnhardt #TA1
2003-04 Press Pass 10th Anniversary Earnhardt #TA2
2003-04 Press Pass 10th Anniversary Earnhardt #TA3
2003-04 Press Pass 10th Anniversary Earnhardt #TA4
2003-04 Press Pass 10th Anniversary Earnhardt #TA5
2003-04 Press Pass 10th Anniversary Earnhardt #TA6
2003-04 Press Pass 10th Anniversary Earnhardt #TA7
2003-04 Press Pass 10th Anniversary Earnhardt #TA8
2003-04 Press Pass 10th Anniversary Earnhardt #TA9
2003-04 Press Pass 10th Anniversary Earnhardt #TA10
2003-04 Press Pass 10th Anniversary Earnhardt #TA11
2003-04 Press Pass 10th Anniversary Earnhardt #TA12
2003-04 Press Pass 10th Anniversary Earnhardt #TA13
2003-04 Press Pass 10th Anniversary Earnhardt #TA14
2003-04 Press Pass 10th Anniversary Earnhardt #TA15
2003-04 Press Pass 10th Anniversary Earnhardt #TA16
2003-04 Press Pass 10th Anniversary Earnhardt #TA17
2003-04 Press Pass 10th Anniversary Earnhardt #TA18
2003-04 Press Pass 10th Anniversary Earnhardt #TA19
2003-04 Press Pass 10th Anniversary Earnhardt #TA20
2003-04 Press Pass 10th Anniversary Earnhardt #TA21
2003-04 Press Pass 10th Anniversary Earnhardt #TA22
2003-04 Press Pass 10th Anniversary Earnhardt #TA23
2003-04 Press Pass 10th Anniversary Earnhardt #TA24
2003-04 Press Pass 10th Anniversary Earnhardt #TA25
2003-04 Press Pass 10th Anniversary Earnhardt #TA26
2003-04 Press Pass 10th Anniversary Earnhardt #TA27
2003-04 Press Pass 10th Anniversary Earnhardt #TA28
2003-04 Press Pass 10th Anniversary Earnhardt #TA29
2003-04 Press Pass 10th Anniversary Earnhardt #TA30
2003-04 Press Pass 10th Anniversary Earnhardt #TA31
2003-04 Press Pass 10th Anniversary Earnhardt #TA32
2003-04 Press Pass 10th Anniversary Earnhardt #TA33
2003-04 Press Pass 10th Anniversary Earnhardt #TA34
2003-04 Press Pass 10th Anniversary Earnhardt #TA35
2003-04 Press Pass 10th Anniversary Earnhardt #TA36
2003-04 Press Pass 10th Anniversary Earnhardt #TA37
2003-04 Press Pass 10th Anniversary Earnhardt #TA38
2003-04 Press Pass 10th Anniversary Earnhardt #TA39
2003-04 Press Pass 10th Anniversary Earnhardt #TA40
2003-04 Press Pass 10th Anniversary Earnhardt #TA41
2003-04 Press Pass 10th Anniversary Earnhardt #TA42
2003-04 Press Pass 10th Anniversary Earnhardt #TA43
2003-04 Press Pass 10th Anniversary Earnhardt #TA44
2003-04 Press Pass 10th Anniversary Earnhardt #TA45
2003-04 Press Pass 10th Anniversary Earnhardt #TA46
2003-04 Press Pass 10th Anniversary Earnhardt #TA47
2003-04 Press Pass 10th Anniversary Earnhardt #TA48
2003-04 Press Pass 10th Anniversary Earnhardt #TA49
2003-04 Press Pass 10th Anniversary Earnhardt #TA50
2003-04 Press Pass 10th Anniversary Earnhardt #TA51
2003-04 Press Pass 10th Anniversary Earnhardt #TA52
2003-04 Press Pass 10th Anniversary Earnhardt #TA53
2003-04 Press Pass 10th Anniversary Earnhardt #TA54
2003-04 Press Pass 10th Anniversary Earnhardt #TA55
2003-04 Press Pass 10th Anniversary Earnhardt #TA56
2003-04 Press Pass 10th Anniversary Earnhardt #TA57
2003-04 Press Pass 10th Anniversary Earnhardt #TA58
2003-04 Press Pass 10th Anniversary Earnhardt #TA59
2003-04 Press Pass 10th Anniversary Earnhardt #TA60
2003-04 Press Pass 10th Anniversary Earnhardt #TA61
2003-04 Press Pass 10th Anniversary Earnhardt #TA62
2003-04 Press Pass 10th Anniversary Earnhardt #TA63
2003-04 Press Pass 10th Anniversary Earnhardt #TA64
2003-04 Press Pass 10th Anniversary Earnhardt #TA65
2003-04 Press Pass 10th Anniversary Earnhardt #TA66
2003-04 Press Pass 10th Anniversary Earnhardt #TA67
2003-04 Press Pass 10th Anniversary Earnhardt #TA68
2003-04 Press Pass 10th Anniversary Earnhardt #TA69
2003-04 Press Pass 10th Anniversary Earnhardt #TA70
2003-04 Press Pass 10th Anniversary Earnhardt #TA71
2003-04 Press Pass 10th Anniversary Earnhardt #TA72
2003-04 Press Pass 10th Anniversary Earnhardt #TA73
2003-04 Press Pass 10th Anniversary Earnhardt #TA74
2003-04 Press Pass 10th Anniversary Earnhardt #TA75
2003-04 Press Pass 10th Anniversary Earnhardt #TA76
2003-04 Press Pass 10th Anniversary Earnhardt #TA77
2003-04 Press Pass 10th Anniversary Earnhardt #TA78
2003-04 Press Pass 10th Anniversary Earnhardt #TA79
2003-04 Press Pass 10th Anniversary Earnhardt #TA80
2003-04 Press Pass 10th Anniversary Earnhardt #TA81
2003-04 Press Pass 10th Anniversary Earnhardt #TA82
2003-04 Press Pass 10th Anniversary Earnhardt #TA83
2003-04 Press Pass 10th Anniversary Earnhardt #TA84
2003-04 Press Pass 10th Anniversary Earnhardt #TA85
2003-04 Press Pass 10th Anniversary Earnhardt #TA86
2003-04 Press Pass 10th Anniversary Earnhardt #TA87
2003-04 Press Pass 10th Anniversary Earnhardt #TA88
2003-04 Press Pass 10th Anniversary Earnhardt #TA89
2003-04 Press Pass 10th Anniversary Earnhardt #TA90
2003-04 Press Pass 10th Anniversary Earnhardt #TA91
2003-04 Press Pass 10th Anniversary Earnhardt #TA92
2003-04 Press Pass 10th Anniversary Earnhardt #TA93
2003-04 Press Pass 10th Anniversary Earnhardt #TA94
2003-04 Press Pass 10th Anniversary Earnhardt #TA95
2003-04 Press Pass 10th Anniversary Earnhardt #TA96
2003-04 Press Pass 10th Anniversary Earnhardt #TA97
2003-04 Press Pass 10th Anniversary Earnhardt #TA98
2003-04 Press Pass 10th Anniversary Earnhardt #TA99
2003-04 Press Pass 10th Anniversary Earnhardt #TA100
2003-04 Press Pass 10th Anniversary Earnhardt Gold #TA1
2003-04 Press Pass 10th Anniversary Earnhardt Gold #TA2
2003-04 Press Pass 10th Anniversary Earnhardt Gold #TA3
2003-04 Press Pass 10th Anniversary Earnhardt Gold #TA4
2003-04 Press Pass 10th Anniversary Earnhardt Gold #TA5
2003-04 Press Pass 10th Anniversary Earnhardt Gold #TA6
2003-04 Press Pass 10th Anniversary Earnhardt Gold #TA7
2003-04 Press Pass 10th Anniversary Earnhardt Gold #TA8
2003-04 Press Pass 10th Anniversary Earnhardt Gold #TA9
2003-04 Press Pass 10th Anniversary Earnhardt Gold #TA10
2003-04 Press Pass 10th Anniversary Earnhardt Gold #TA11
2003-04 Press Pass 10th Anniversary Earnhardt Gold #TA12
2003-04 Press Pass 10th Anniversary Earnhardt Gold #TA13
2003-04 Press Pass 10th Anniversary Earnhardt Gold #TA14
2003-04 Press Pass 10th Anniversary Earnhardt Gold #TA15
2003-04 Press Pass 10th Anniversary Earnhardt Gold #TA16
2003-04 Press Pass 10th Anniversary Earnhardt Gold #TA17
2003-04 Press Pass 10th Anniversary Earnhardt Gold #TA18
2003-04 Press Pass 10th Anniversary Earnhardt Gold #TA19
2003-04 Press Pass 10th Anniversary Earnhardt Gold #TA20
2003-04 Press Pass 10th Anniversary Earnhardt Gold #TA21
2003-04 Press Pass 10th Anniversary Earnhardt Gold #TA22
2003-04 Press Pass 10th Anniversary Earnhardt Gold #TA23
2003-04 Press Pass 10th Anniversary Earnhardt Gold #TA24
2003-04 Press Pass 10th Anniversary Earnhardt Gold #TA25
2003-04 Press Pass 10th Anniversary Earnhardt Gold #TA26
2003-04 Press Pass 10th Anniversary Earnhardt Gold #TA27
2003-04 Press Pass 10th Anniversary Earnhardt Gold #TA28
2003-04 Press Pass 10th Anniversary Earnhardt Gold #TA29
2003-04 Press Pass 10th Anniversary Earnhardt Gold #TA30
2003-04 Press Pass 10th Anniversary Earnhardt Gold #TA31
2003-04 Press Pass 10th Anniversary Earnhardt Gold #TA32
2003-04 Press Pass 10th Anniversary Earnhardt Gold #TA33
2003-04 Press Pass 10th Anniversary Earnhardt Gold #TA34
2003-04 Press Pass 10th Anniversary Earnhardt Gold #TA35
2003-04 Press Pass 10th Anniversary Earnhardt Gold #TA36
2003-04 Press Pass 10th Anniversary Earnhardt Gold #TA37
2003-04 Press Pass 10th Anniversary Earnhardt Gold #TA38
2003-04 Press Pass 10th Anniversary Earnhardt Gold #TA39
2003-04 Press Pass 10th Anniversary Earnhardt Gold #TA40
2003-04 Press Pass 10th Anniversary Earnhardt Gold #TA41
2003-04 Press Pass 10th Anniversary Earnhardt Gold #TA42
2003-04 Press Pass 10th Anniversary Earnhardt Gold #TA43
2003-04 Press Pass 10th Anniversary Earnhardt Gold #TA44
2003-04 Press Pass 10th Anniversary Earnhardt Gold #TA45
2003-04 Press Pass 10th Anniversary Earnhardt Gold #TA46
2003-04 Press Pass 10th Anniversary Earnhardt Gold #TA47
2003-04 Press Pass 10th Anniversary Earnhardt Gold #TA48
2003-04 Press Pass 10th Anniversary Earnhardt Gold #TA49
2003-04 Press Pass 10th Anniversary Earnhardt Gold #TA50
2003-04 Press Pass 10th Anniversary Earnhardt Gold #TA51
2003-04 Press Pass 10th Anniversary Earnhardt Gold #TA52
2003-04 Press Pass 10th Anniversary Earnhardt Gold #TA53
2003-04 Press Pass 10th Anniversary Earnhardt Gold #TA54
2003-04 Press Pass 10th Anniversary Earnhardt Gold #TA55
2003-04 Press Pass 10th Anniversary Earnhardt Gold #TA56
2003-04 Press Pass 10th Anniversary Earnhardt Gold #TA57
2003-04 Press Pass 10th Anniversary Earnhardt Gold #TA58
2003-04 Press Pass 10th Anniversary Earnhardt Gold #TA59
2003-04 Press Pass 10th Anniversary Earnhardt Gold #TA60
2003-04 Press Pass 10th Anniversary Earnhardt Gold #TA61
2003-04 Press Pass 10th Anniversary Earnhardt Gold #TA62
2003-04 Press Pass 10th Anniversary Earnhardt Gold #TA63
2003-04 Press Pass 10th Anniversary Earnhardt Gold #TA64
2003-04 Press Pass 10th Anniversary Earnhardt Gold #TA65
2003-04 Press Pass 10th Anniversary Earnhardt Gold #TA66
2003-04 Press Pass 10th Anniversary Earnhardt Gold #TA67
2003-04 Press Pass 10th Anniversary Earnhardt Gold #TA68
2003-04 Press Pass 10th Anniversary Earnhardt Gold #TA69
2003-04 Press Pass 10th Anniversary Earnhardt Gold #TA70
2003-04 Press Pass 10th Anniversary Earnhardt Gold #TA71
2003-04 Press Pass 10th Anniversary Earnhardt Gold #TA72
2003-04 Press Pass 10th Anniversary Earnhardt Gold #TA73
2003-04 Press Pass 10th Anniversary Earnhardt Gold #TA74
2003-04 Press Pass 10th Anniversary Earnhardt Gold #TA75
2003-04 Press Pass 10th Anniversary Earnhardt Gold #TA76
2003-04 Press Pass 10th Anniversary Earnhardt Gold #TA77
2003-04 Press Pass 10th Anniversary Earnhardt Gold #TA78
2003-04 Press Pass 10th Anniversary Earnhardt Gold #TA79
2003-04 Press Pass 10th Anniversary Earnhardt Gold #TA80
2003-04 Press Pass 10th Anniversary Earnhardt Gold #TA81
2003-04 Press Pass 10th Anniversary Earnhardt Gold #TA82
2003-04 Press Pass 10th Anniversary Earnhardt Gold #TA83
2003-04 Press Pass 10th Anniversary Earnhardt Gold #TA84
2003-04 Press Pass 10th Anniversary Earnhardt Gold #TA85
2003-04 Press Pass 10th Anniversary Earnhardt Gold #TA86
2003-04 Press Pass 10th Anniversary Earnhardt Gold #TA87
2003-04 Press Pass 10th Anniversary Earnhardt Gold #TA88
2003-04 Press Pass 10th Anniversary Earnhardt Gold #TA89
2003-04 Press Pass 10th Anniversary Earnhardt Gold #TA90
2003-04 Press Pass 10th Anniversary Earnhardt Gold #TA91
2003-04 Press Pass 10th Anniversary Earnhardt Gold #TA92
2003-04 Press Pass 10th Anniversary Earnhardt Gold #TA93
2003-04 Press Pass 10th Anniversary Earnhardt Gold #TA94
2003-04 Press Pass 10th Anniversary Earnhardt Gold #TA95
2003-04 Press Pass 10th Anniversary Earnhardt Gold #TA96
2003-04 Press Pass 10th Anniversary Earnhardt Gold #TA97
2003-04 Press Pass 10th Anniversary Earnhardt Gold #TA98
2003-04 Press Pass 10th Anniversary Earnhardt Gold #TA99
2003-04 Press Pass 10th Anniversary Earnhardt Gold #TA100
2004 Press Pass Burning Rubber Cars /140 #BRT17
2004 Press Pass Burning Rubber Drivers /70 #BRD17
2004 Press Pass Dale Earnhardt Gallery #DEG1
2004 Press Pass Dale Earnhardt Gallery #DEG2
2004 Press Pass Dale Earnhardt Gallery #DEG3
2004 Press Pass Dale Earnhardt Gallery #DEG4
2004 Press Pass Dale Earnhardt Gallery #DEG5
2004 Press Pass Dale Earnhardt Gallery #DEG6
2004 Press Pass Dale Earnhardt Gallery #DEG7
2004 Press Pass Dale Earnhardt Gallery #DEG8
2004 Press Pass Dale Earnhardt Gallery #DEG9
2004 Press Pass Dale Earnhardt Gallery #DEG10
2004 Press Pass Dale Earnhardt Gallery #DEG11
2004 Press Pass Dale Earnhardt Gallery #DEG12
2004 Press Pass Dale Earnhardt Gallery #DEG13
2004 Press Pass Dale Earnhardt Gallery #DEG14
2004 Press Pass Dale Earnhardt Gallery #DEG15
2004 Press Pass Dale Earnhardt Gallery #DEG16
2004 Press Pass Dale Earnhardt Gallery #DEG17
2004 Press Pass Dale Earnhardt Gallery #DEG18
2004 Press Pass Dale Earnhardt Gallery #DEG19
2004 Press Pass Dale Earnhardt Gallery #DEG20
2004 Press Pass Dale Earnhardt Gallery #DEG21
2004 Press Pass Dale Earnhardt Gallery #DEG22
2004 Press Pass Dale Earnhardt Gallery #DEG23
2004 Press Pass Dale Earnhardt Gallery #DEG24
2004 Press Pass Dale Earnhardt Gallery #DEG25
2004 Press Pass Dale Earnhardt Gallery #DEG26
2004 Press Pass Dale Earnhardt Gallery #DEG27
2004 Press Pass Dale Earnhardt Gallery #DEG28
2004 Press Pass Dale Earnhardt Gallery #DEG29
2004 Press Pass Dale Earnhardt Gallery #DEG30
2004 Press Pass Dale Earnhardt Gallery #DEG31
2004 Press Pass Dale Earnhardt Gallery #DEG32
2004 Press Pass Dale Earnhardt Gallery #DEG33
2004 Press Pass Dale Earnhardt Gallery #DEG34
2004 Press Pass Dale Earnhardt Gallery #DEG35
2004 Press Pass Dale Earnhardt Gallery #DEG36
2004 Press Pass Dale Earnhardt Gallery #DEG37
2004 Press Pass Dale Earnhardt Gallery #DEG38
2004 Press Pass Dale Earnhardt Gallery #DEG39
2004 Press Pass Dale Earnhardt Gallery #DEG40
2004 Press Pass Dale Earnhardt Gallery #DEG41
2004 Press Pass Dale Earnhardt Gallery #DEG42
2004 Press Pass Dale Earnhardt Gallery #DEG43
2004 Press Pass Dale Earnhardt Gallery #DEG44
2004 Press Pass Dale Earnhardt Gallery #DEG45
2004 Press Pass Dale Earnhardt Gallery #DEG52
2004 Press Pass Dale Earnhardt Gallery #DEG48
2004 Press Pass Dale Earnhardt Gallery #DEG51
2004 Press Pass Dale Earnhardt Gallery #DEG53
2004 Press Pass Dale Earnhardt Gallery #DEG47
2004 Press Pass Dale Earnhardt Gallery #DEG49
2004 Press Pass Dale Earnhardt Gallery #DEG54
2004 Press Pass Dale Earnhardt Gallery #DEG50
2004 Press Pass Dale Earnhardt Gallery #DEG46
2004 Press Pass Dale Earnhardt Gallery Gold /200 #DEG1
2004 Press Pass Dale Earnhardt Gallery Gold /200 #DEG2
2004 Press Pass Dale Earnhardt Gallery Gold /200 #DEG3
2004 Press Pass Dale Earnhardt Gallery Gold /200 #DEG4
2004 Press Pass Dale Earnhardt Gallery Gold /200 #DEG5
2004 Press Pass Dale Earnhardt Gallery Gold /200 #DEG6
2004 Press Pass Dale Earnhardt Gallery Gold /200 #DEG7
2004 Press Pass Dale Earnhardt Gallery Gold /200 #DEG8
2004 Press Pass Dale Earnhardt Gallery Gold /200 #DEG9
2004 Press Pass Dale Earnhardt Gallery Gold /200 #DEG10
2004 Press Pass Dale Earnhardt Gallery Gold /200 #DEG11
2004 Press Pass Dale Earnhardt Gallery Gold /200 #DEG12
2004 Press Pass Dale Earnhardt Gallery Gold /200 #DEG13
2004 Press Pass Dale Earnhardt Gallery Gold /200 #DEG14
2004 Press Pass Dale Earnhardt Gallery Gold /200 #DEG15
2004 Press Pass Dale Earnhardt Gallery Gold /200 #DEG16
2004 Press Pass Dale Earnhardt Gallery Gold /200 #DEG17
2004 Press Pass Dale Earnhardt Gallery Gold /200 #DEG18
2004 Press Pass Dale Earnhardt Gallery Gold /200 #DEG19
2004 Press Pass Dale Earnhardt Gallery Gold /200 #DEG20
2004 Press Pass Dale Earnhardt Gallery Gold /200 #DEG21
2004 Press Pass Dale Earnhardt Gallery Gold /200 #DEG22
2004 Press Pass Dale Earnhardt Gallery Gold /200 #DEG23
2004 Press Pass Dale Earnhardt Gallery Gold /200 #DEG24
2004 Press Pass Dale Earnhardt Gallery Gold /200 #DEG25
2004 Press Pass Dale Earnhardt Gallery Gold /200 #DEG26
2004 Press Pass Dale Earnhardt Gallery Gold /200 #DEG27
2004 Press Pass Dale Earnhardt Gallery Gold /200 #DEG28
2004 Press Pass Dale Earnhardt Gallery Gold /200 #DEG29
2004 Press Pass Dale Earnhardt Gallery Gold /200 #DEG30
2004 Press Pass Dale Earnhardt Gallery Gold /200 #DEG31
2004 Press Pass Dale Earnhardt Gallery Gold /200 #DEG32
2004 Press Pass Dale Earnhardt Gallery Gold /200 #DEG33
2004 Press Pass Dale Earnhardt Gallery Gold /200 #DEG34
2004 Press Pass Dale Earnhardt Gallery Gold /200 #DEG35
2004 Press Pass Dale Earnhardt Gallery Gold /200 #DEG36
2004 Press Pass Dale Earnhardt Gallery Gold /200 #DEG37
2004 Press Pass Dale Earnhardt Gallery Gold /200 #DEG38
2004 Press Pass Dale Earnhardt Gallery Gold /200 #DEG39
2004 Press Pass Dale Earnhardt Gallery Gold /200 #DEG40
2004 Press Pass Dale Earnhardt Gallery Gold /200 #DEG41
2004 Press Pass Dale Earnhardt Gallery Gold /200 #DEG42
2004 Press Pass Dale Earnhardt Gallery Gold /200 #DEG43
2004 Press Pass Dale Earnhardt Gallery Gold /200 #DEG44
2004 Press Pass Dale Earnhardt Gallery Gold /200 #DEG45
2004 Press Pass Dale Earnhardt Gallery Gold /200 #DEG46
2004 Press Pass Dale Earnhardt Gallery Gold /200 #DEG47
2004 Press Pass Dale Earnhardt Gallery Gold /200 #DEG48
2004 Press Pass Dale Earnhardt Gallery Gold /200 #DEG49
2004 Press Pass Dale Earnhardt Gallery Gold /200 #DEG50
2004 Press Pass Dale Earnhardt Gallery Gold /200 #DEG51
2004 Press Pass Dale Earnhardt Gallery Gold /200 #DEG52
2004 Press Pass Dale Earnhardt Gallery Gold /200 #DEG53
2004 Press Pass Dale Earnhardt Gallery Gold /200 #DEG54
2004 Press Pass Dale Earnhardt Jr. #10
2004 Press Pass Dale Earnhardt Jr. #11
2004 Press Pass Dale Earnhardt Jr. #12
2004 Press Pass Dale Earnhardt Jr. #13
2004 Press Pass Dale Earnhardt Jr. #14
2004 Press Pass Dale Earnhardt Jr. #15
2004 Press Pass Dale Earnhardt Jr. #16
2004 Press Pass Dale Earnhardt Jr. #17
2004 Press Pass Dale Earnhardt Jr. #18
2004 Press Pass Dale Earnhardt Jr. Blue #C10
2004 Press Pass Dale Earnhardt Jr. Blue #C11
2004 Press Pass Dale Earnhardt Jr. Blue #C12
2004 Press Pass Dale Earnhardt Jr. Blue #C13
2004 Press Pass Dale Earnhardt Jr. Blue #C14
2004 Press Pass Dale Earnhardt Jr. Blue #C15
2004 Press Pass Dale Earnhardt Jr. Blue #C16
2004 Press Pass Dale Earnhardt Jr. Blue #C17
2004 Press Pass Dale Earnhardt Jr. Blue #C18
2004 Press Pass Dale Earnhardt Jr. Bronze #B10
2004 Press Pass Dale Earnhardt Jr. Bronze #B11
2004 Press Pass Dale Earnhardt Jr. Bronze #B12
2004 Press Pass Dale Earnhardt Jr. Bronze #B13
2004 Press Pass Dale Earnhardt Jr. Bronze #B14
2004 Press Pass Dale Earnhardt Jr. Bronze #B15
2004 Press Pass Dale Earnhardt Jr. Bronze #B16
2004 Press Pass Dale Earnhardt Jr. Bronze #B17
2004 Press Pass Dale Earnhardt Jr. Bronze #B18
2004 Press Pass Dale Earnhardt Jr. Gallery #G2
2004 Press Pass Dale Earnhardt Jr. Gold #D10
2004 Press Pass Dale Earnhardt Jr. Gold #D11
2004 Press Pass Dale Earnhardt Jr. Gold #D12
2004 Press Pass Dale Earnhardt Jr. Gold #D13
2004 Press Pass Dale Earnhardt Jr. Gold #D14
2004 Press Pass Dale Earnhardt Jr. Gold #D15
2004 Press Pass Dale Earnhardt Jr. Gold #D16
2004 Press Pass Dale Earnhardt Jr. Gold #D17
2004 Press Pass Dale Earnhardt Jr. Gold #D18
2004 Press Pass Dale Earnhardt The Legacy Victories #1
2004 Press Pass Dale Earnhardt The Legacy Victories #2
2004 Press Pass Dale Earnhardt The Legacy Victories #3
2004 Press Pass Dale Earnhardt The Legacy Victories #4
2004 Press Pass Dale Earnhardt The Legacy Victories #5
2004 Press Pass Dale Earnhardt The Legacy Victories #6
2004 Press Pass Dale Earnhardt The Legacy Victories #7
2004 Press Pass Dale Earnhardt The Legacy Victories #8
2004 Press Pass Dale Earnhardt The Legacy Victories #9
2004 Press Pass Dale Earnhardt The Legacy Victories #10
2004 Press Pass Dale Earnhardt The Legacy Victories #11
2004 Press Pass Dale Earnhardt The Legacy Victories #12
2004 Press Pass Dale Earnhardt The Legacy Victories #13
2004 Press Pass Dale Earnhardt The Legacy Victories #14
2004 Press Pass Dale Earnhardt The Legacy Victories #15
2004 Press Pass Dale Earnhardt The Legacy Victories #16
2004 Press Pass Dale Earnhardt The Legacy Victories #17
2004 Press Pass Dale Earnhardt The Legacy Victories #18
2004 Press Pass Dale Earnhardt The Legacy Victories #19
2004 Press Pass Dale Earnhardt The Legacy Victories #20
2004 Press Pass Dale Earnhardt The Legacy Victories #21
2004 Press Pass Dale Earnhardt The Legacy Victories #22
2004 Press Pass Dale Earnhardt The Legacy Victories #23
2004 Press Pass Dale Earnhardt The Legacy Victories #24
2004 Press Pass Dale Earnhardt The Legacy Victories #25
2004 Press Pass Dale Earnhardt The Legacy Victories #26
2004 Press Pass Dale Earnhardt The Legacy Victories #27
2004 Press Pass Dale Earnhardt The Legacy Victories #28
2004 Press Pass Dale Earnhardt The Legacy Victories #29
2004 Press Pass Dale Earnhardt The Legacy Victories #30
2004 Press Pass Dale Earnhardt The Legacy Victories #31
2004 Press Pass Dale Earnhardt The Legacy Victories #32
2004 Press Pass Dale Earnhardt The Legacy Victories #33
2004 Press Pass Dale Earnhardt The Legacy Victories #34
2004 Press Pass Dale Earnhardt The Legacy Victories #35
2004 Press Pass Dale Earnhardt The Legacy Victories #36
2004 Press Pass Dale Earnhardt The Legacy Victories #37
2004 Press Pass Dale Earnhardt The Legacy Victories #38
2004 Press Pass Dale Earnhardt The Legacy Victories #39
2004 Press Pass Dale Earnhardt The Legacy Victories #40
2004 Press Pass Dale Earnhardt The Legacy Victories #41
2004 Press Pass Dale Earnhardt The Legacy Victories #42
2004 Press Pass Dale Earnhardt The Legacy Victories #43
2004 Press Pass Dale Earnhardt The Legacy Victories #44
2004 Press Pass Dale Earnhardt The Legacy Victories #45
2004 Press Pass Dale Earnhardt The Legacy Victories #46
2004 Press Pass Dale Earnhardt The Legacy Victories #47
2004 Press Pass Dale Earnhardt The Legacy Victories #48
2004 Press Pass Dale Earnhardt The Legacy Victories #49
2004 Press Pass Dale Earnhardt The Legacy Victories #50
2004 Press Pass Dale Earnhardt The Legacy Victories #51
2004 Press Pass Dale Earnhardt The Legacy Victories #52
2004 Press Pass Dale Earnhardt The Legacy Victories #53
2004 Press Pass Dale Earnhardt The Legacy Victories #54
2004 Press Pass Dale Earnhardt The Legacy Victories #55
2004 Press Pass Dale Earnhardt The Legacy Victories #56
2004 Press Pass Dale Earnhardt The Legacy Victories #57
2004 Press Pass Dale Earnhardt The Legacy Victories #58
2004 Press Pass Dale Earnhardt The Legacy Victories #59
2004 Press Pass Dale Earnhardt The Legacy Victories #60
2004 Press Pass Dale Earnhardt The Legacy Victories #61
2004 Press Pass Dale Earnhardt The Legacy Victories #62
2004 Press Pass Dale Earnhardt The Legacy Victories #63
2004 Press Pass Dale Earnhardt The Legacy Victories #64
2004 Press Pass Dale Earnhardt The Legacy Victories #65
2004 Press Pass Dale Earnhardt The Legacy Victories #66
2004 Press Pass Dale Earnhardt The Legacy Victories #67
2004 Press Pass Dale Earnhardt The Legacy Victories #68
2004 Press Pass Dale Earnhardt The Legacy Victories #69
2004 Press Pass Dale Earnhardt The Legacy Victories #70
2004 Press Pass Dale Earnhardt The Legacy Victories #71
2004 Press Pass Dale Earnhardt The Legacy Victories #72
2004 Press Pass Dale Earnhardt The Legacy Victories #73
2004 Press Pass Dale Earnhardt The Legacy Victories #74
2004 Press Pass Dale Earnhardt The Legacy Victories #75
2004 Press Pass Dale Earnhardt The Legacy Victories #76
2004 Press Pass Dale Earnhardt The Legacy Victories Tin #NNO
2004 Press Pass Optima Thunder Bolts Cars /3 #TBT18
2004 Press Pass Optima Thunder Bolts Drivers /3 #TBD18
2004 Press Pass Premium Hot Threads Drivers Bronze /125 #HTD16
2004 Press Pass Premium Hot Threads Drivers Bronze Retail /125 #HTT16
2004 Press Pass Premium Hot Threads Drivers Gold /50 #HTD16
2004 Press Pass Premium Hot Threads Drivers Silver /75 #HTD16
2004 Press Pass Trackside Pit Stoppers Cars /150 #PST9
2004 Press Pass Trackside Pit Stoppers Drivers /95 #PSD9
2004 VIP #87
2004 VIP #0
2004 VIP Samples #87
2004 Wheels High Gear Winston Victory Lap Tribute #WVL4
2004 Wheels High Gear Winston Victory Lap Tribute Gold #WVL4
2005 Press Pass Dale Earnhardt Victories /825 #1
2005 Press Pass Dale Earnhardt Victories /825 #2
2005 Press Pass Dale Earnhardt Victories /825 #3
2005 Press Pass Dale Earnhardt Victories /825 #4
2005 Press Pass Dale Earnhardt Victories /825 #5
2005 Press Pass Dale Earnhardt Victories /825 #6
2005 Press Pass Dale Earnhardt Victories /825 #7
2005 Press Pass Dale Earnhardt Victories /825 #8
2005 Press Pass Dale Earnhardt Victories /825 #9
2005 Press Pass Dale Earnhardt Victories /825 #10
2005 Press Pass Dale Earnhardt Victories /825 #11
2005 Press Pass Dale Earnhardt Victories /825 #12
2005 Press Pass Dale Earnhardt Victories /825 #13
2005 Press Pass Dale Earnhardt Victories /825 #14
2005 Press Pass Dale Earnhardt Victories /825 #15
2005 Press Pass Dale Earnhardt Victories /825 #16
2005 Press Pass Dale Earnhardt Victories /825 #17
2005 Press Pass Dale Earnhardt Victories /825 #18
2005 Press Pass Dale Earnhardt Victories /825 #19
2005 Press Pass Dale Earnhardt Victories /825 #20
2005 Press Pass Dale Earnhardt Victories /825 #21
2005 Press Pass Dale Earnhardt Victories /825 #22
2005 Press Pass Dale Earnhardt Victories /825 #23
2005 Press Pass Dale Earnhardt Victories /825 #24
2005 Press Pass Dale Earnhardt Victories /825 #25
2005 Press Pass Dale Earnhardt Victories /825 #26
2005 Press Pass Dale Earnhardt Victories /825 #27
2005 Press Pass Dale Earnhardt Victories /825 #28
2005 Press Pass Dale Earnhardt Victories /825 #29
2005 Press Pass Dale Earnhardt Victories /825 #30
2005 Press Pass Dale Earnhardt Victories /825 #31
2005 Press Pass Dale Earnhardt Victories /825 #32
2005 Press Pass Dale Earnhardt Victories /825 #33
2005 Press Pass Dale Earnhardt Victories /825 #34
2005 Press Pass Dale Earnhardt Victories /825 #35
2005 Press Pass Dale Earnhardt Victories /825 #36
2005 Press Pass Dale Earnhardt Victories /825 #37
2005 Press Pass Dale Earnhardt Victories /825 #38
2005 Press Pass Dale Earnhardt Victories /825 #39
2005 Press Pass Dale Earnhardt Victories /825 #40
2005 Press Pass Dale Earnhardt Victories /825 #41
2005 Press Pass Dale Earnhardt Victories /825 #42
2005 Press Pass Dale Earnhardt Victories /825 #43

2005 Press Pass Dale Earnhardt Victories /825 #44
2005 Press Pass Dale Earnhardt Victories /825 #45
2005 Press Pass Dale Earnhardt Victories /825 #46
2005 Press Pass Dale Earnhardt Victories /825 #47
2005 Press Pass Dale Earnhardt Victories /825 #48
2005 Press Pass Dale Earnhardt Victories /825 #49
2005 Press Pass Dale Earnhardt Victories /825 #50
2005 Press Pass Dale Earnhardt Victories /825 #51
2005 Press Pass Dale Earnhardt Victories /825 #52
2005 Press Pass Dale Earnhardt Victories /825 #53
2005 Press Pass Dale Earnhardt Victories /825 #54
2005 Press Pass Dale Earnhardt Victories /825 #55
2005 Press Pass Dale Earnhardt Victories /825 #56
2005 Press Pass Dale Earnhardt Victories /825 #57
2005 Press Pass Dale Earnhardt Victories /825 #58
2005 Press Pass Dale Earnhardt Victories /825 #59
2005 Press Pass Dale Earnhardt Victories /825 #60
2005 Press Pass Dale Earnhardt Victories /825 #61
2005 Press Pass Dale Earnhardt Victories /825 #62
2005 Press Pass Dale Earnhardt Victories /825 #63
2005 Press Pass Dale Earnhardt Victories /825 #64
2005 Press Pass Dale Earnhardt Victories /825 #65
2005 Press Pass Dale Earnhardt Victories /825 #66
2005 Press Pass Dale Earnhardt Victories /825 #67
2005 Press Pass Dale Earnhardt Victories /825 #68
2005 Press Pass Dale Earnhardt Victories /825 #69
2005 Press Pass Dale Earnhardt Victories /825 #70
2005 Press Pass Dale Earnhardt Victories /825 #71
2005 Press Pass Dale Earnhardt Victories /825 #72
2005 Press Pass Dale Earnhardt Victories /825 #73
2005 Press Pass Dale Earnhardt Victories /825 #74
2005 Press Pass Dale Earnhardt Victories /825 #75
2005 Press Pass Dale Earnhardt Victories /825 #76
2005 Press Pass Legends #19
2005 Press Pass Legends #40
2005 Press Pass Legends Blue /1890 #19B
2005 Press Pass Legends Blue /1890 #40B
2005 Press Pass Legends Gold /750 #19G
2005 Press Pass Legends Gold /750 #40G
2005 Press Pass Legends Greatest Moments /640 #GM7
2005 Press Pass Legends Greatest Moments /640 #GM14
2005 Press Pass Legends Greatest Moments /640 #GM15
2005 Press Pass Legends Holofoil /100 #19H
2005 Press Pass Legends Holofoil /100 #40H
2005 Press Pass Legends Press Plates Black /1 #19
2005 Press Pass Legends Press Plates Black /1 #40
2005 Press Pass Legends Press Plates Cyan /1 #19
2005 Press Pass Legends Press Plates Cyan /1 #40
2005 Press Pass Legends Press Plates Magenta /1 #19
2005 Press Pass Legends Press Plates Magenta /1 #40
2005 Press Pass Legends Press Plates Yellow /1 #19
2005 Press Pass Legends Press Plates Yellow /1 #40
2005 Press Pass Legends Previews /5 #19
2005 Press Pass Legends Previews /5 #40
2005 Press Pass Legends Solo /1 #19S
2005 Press Pass Legends Solo /1 #40S
2005 Press Pass Legends Threads and Treads Bronze /375 #TTDE
2005 Press Pass Legends Threads and Treads Gold /99 #TTDE
2005 Press Pass Legends Threads and Treads Silver /225 #TTDE
2006 Press Pass Dominator Dale Earnhardt #1
2006 Press Pass Dominator Dale Earnhardt #2
2006 Press Pass Dominator Dale Earnhardt #3
2006 Press Pass Dominator Dale Earnhardt #4
2006 Press Pass Dominator Dale Earnhardt #5
2006 Press Pass Dominator Dale Earnhardt #6
2006 Press Pass Dominator Dale Earnhardt #7
2006 Press Pass Dominator Dale Earnhardt #8
2006 Press Pass Dominator Dale Earnhardt #9
2006 Press Pass Dominator Dale Earnhardt #10
2006 Press Pass Dominator Dale Earnhardt #11
2006 Press Pass Dominator Dale Earnhardt #12
2006 Press Pass Dominator Dale Earnhardt #13
2006 Press Pass Dominator Dale Earnhardt #14
2006 Press Pass Dominator Dale Earnhardt #15
2006 Press Pass Dominator Dale Earnhardt #16
2006 Press Pass Dominator Dale Earnhardt #17
2006 Press Pass Dominator Dale Earnhardt #18
2006 Press Pass Dominator Dale Earnhardt #19
2006 Press Pass Dominator Dale Earnhardt #20
2006 Press Pass Dominator Dale Earnhardt #21
2006 Press Pass Dominator Dale Earnhardt #22
2006 Press Pass Dominator Dale Earnhardt #23
2006 Press Pass Dominator Dale Earnhardt #24
2006 Press Pass Dominator Dale Earnhardt #25
2006 Press Pass Dominator Dale Earnhardt #26
2006 Press Pass Dominator Dale Earnhardt #27
2006 Press Pass Dominator Dale Earnhardt #28
2006 Press Pass Dominator Dale Earnhardt #29
2006 Press Pass Dominator Dale Earnhardt #30
2006 Press Pass Dominator Dale Earnhardt #31
2006 Press Pass Dominator Dale Earnhardt #32
2006 Press Pass Dominator Dale Earnhardt #33
2006 Press Pass Dominator Dale Earnhardt Jumbo #SR1
2006 Press Pass Dominator Dale Earnhardt Jumbo #SR2
2006 Press Pass Dominator Dale Earnhardt Jumbo #SR3
2006 Press Pass Dominator Tins #DE
2006 Press Pass Legends #24
2006 Press Pass Legends #47
2006 Press Pass Legends Blue /1999 #B24
2006 Press Pass Legends Blue /1999 #B47
2006 Press Pass Legends Bronze /999 #Z24
2006 Press Pass Legends Bronze /999 #Z47
2006 Press Pass Legends Gold /299 #G24
2006 Press Pass Legends Gold /299 #G47
2006 Press Pass Legends Heritage Gold /99 #HE6
2006 Press Pass Legends Heritage Gold /99 #HE15
2006 Press Pass Legends Heritage Silver /549 #HE6
2006 Press Pass Legends Heritage Silver /549 #HE15
2006 Press Pass Legends Holofoil /99 #H24
2006 Press Pass Legends Holofoil /99 #H47
2006 Press Pass Legends Memorable Moments Gold /199 #MM7
2006 Press Pass Legends Memorable Moments Silver /699 #MM7
2006 Press Pass Legends Press Plates Black /1 #PPB24
2006 Press Pass Legends Press Plates Black /1 #PPB47
2006 Press Pass Legends Press Plates Black Backs /1 #PPB24B
2006 Press Pass Legends Press Plates Black Backs /1 #PPB47B
2006 Press Pass Legends Press Plates Cyan /1 #PPC24
2006 Press Pass Legends Press Plates Cyan /1 #PPC47
2006 Press Pass Legends Press Plates Cyan Backs /1 #PPC24B
2006 Press Pass Legends Press Plates Cyan Backs /1 #PPC47B
2006 Press Pass Legends Press Plates Magenta /1 #PPM24
2006 Press Pass Legends Press Plates Magenta /1 #PPM47
2006 Press Pass Legends Press Plates Magenta Backs /1 #PPM24B
2006 Press Pass Legends Press Plates Magenta Backs /1 #PPM47B
2006 Press Pass Legends Press Plates Yellow /1 #PPY24
2006 Press Pass Legends Press Plates Yellow /1 #PPY47
2006 Press Pass Legends Press Plates Yellow Backs /1 #PPY24B
2006 Press Pass Legends Press Plates Yellow Backs /1 #PPY47B
2006 Press Pass Legends Previews /5 #EB24
2006 Press Pass Legends Previews /1 #EB47
2006 Press Pass Legends Racing Artifacts Firesuit Bronze /399 #DEF
2006 Press Pass Legends Racing Artifacts Firesuit Gold /50 #DEF
2006 Press Pass Legends Racing Artifacts Firesuit Patch /25 #DEF
2006 Press Pass Legends Racing Artifacts Firesuit Silver /199 #DEF
2006 Press Pass Legends Racing Artifacts Tire Bronze /399 #DET
2006 Press Pass Legends Racing Artifacts Tire Gold /50 #DET
2006 Press Pass Legends Racing Artifacts Tire Silver /199 #DET
2006 Press Pass Legends Racing Cuts /3 #DE
2006 Press Pass Legends Solo /1 #S24
2006 Press Pass Legends Solo /1 #S47
2006 Press Pass Stealth #82
2006 Press Pass Stealth #83
2006 Press Pass Stealth #84
2006 Press Pass Stealth #85
2006 Press Pass Stealth #86
2006 Press Pass Stealth #87
2006 Press Pass Stealth #88
2006 Press Pass Stealth #89
2006 Press Pass Stealth Retail #82
2006 Press Pass Stealth Retail #83
2006 Press Pass Stealth Retail #84
2006 Press Pass Stealth Retail #85
2006 Press Pass Stealth Retail #86
2006 Press Pass Stealth Retail #87
2006 Press Pass Stealth Retail #88
2006 Press Pass Stealth Retail #89
2006 Press Pass Stealth X-Ray /100 #X82
2006 Press Pass Stealth X-Ray /100 #X83
2006 Press Pass Stealth X-Ray /100 #X84
2006 Press Pass Stealth X-Ray /100 #X85
2006 Press Pass Stealth X-Ray /100 #X86
2006 Press Pass Stealth X-Ray /100 #X87
2006 Press Pass Stealth X-Ray /100 #X88
2006 Press Pass Stealth X-Ray /100 #X89
2006 TRAKS #74
2006 TRAKS Previews /1 #74
2007 Press Pass Dale The Movie #21
2007 Press Pass Dale The Movie #23
2007 Press Pass Dale The Movie #26
2007 Press Pass Dale The Movie #28
2007 Press Pass Dale The Movie #29
2007 Press Pass Dale The Movie #33
2007 Press Pass Dale The Movie #34
2007 Press Pass Dale The Movie #37
2007 Press Pass Dale The Movie #38
2007 Press Pass Dale The Movie #39
2007 Press Pass Dale The Movie #40
2007 Press Pass Dale The Movie #43
2007 Press Pass Dale The Movie #50
2007 Press Pass Dale The Movie #1
2007 Press Pass Dale The Movie #2
2007 Press Pass Dale The Movie #3
2007 Press Pass Dale The Movie #4
2007 Press Pass Dale The Movie #6
2007 Press Pass Dale The Movie #7
2007 Press Pass Dale The Movie #8
2007 Press Pass Dale The Movie #9
2007 Press Pass Dale The Movie #10
2007 Press Pass Dale The Movie #11
2007 Press Pass Dale The Movie #12
2007 Press Pass Dale The Movie #13
2007 Press Pass Dale The Movie #14
2007 Press Pass Dale The Movie #15
2007 Press Pass Dale The Movie #16
2007 Press Pass Dale The Movie #20
2007 Press Pass Dale The Movie #22
2007 Press Pass Dale The Movie #24
2007 Press Pass Dale The Movie #25
2007 Press Pass Dale The Movie #27
2007 Press Pass Dale The Movie #30
2007 Press Pass Dale The Movie #32
2007 Press Pass Dale The Movie #36
2007 Press Pass Dale The Movie #41
2007 Press Pass Dale The Movie #42
2007 Press Pass Dale The Movie #47
2007 Press Pass Dale The Movie #48
2007 Press Pass Dale The Movie #49
2007 Press Pass Dale The Movie #31
2007 Press Pass Dale The Movie #45
2007 Press Pass Dale The Movie #35
2007 Press Pass Legends #29
2007 Press Pass Legends #51
2007 Press Pass Legends #65
2007 Press Pass Legends #68
2007 Press Pass Legends Blue /999 #B29
2007 Press Pass Legends Blue /999 #B51
2007 Press Pass Legends Blue /999 #B65
2007 Press Pass Legends Blue /999 #B68
2007 Press Pass Legends Bronze /599 #Z29
2007 Press Pass Legends Bronze /599 #Z51
2007 Press Pass Legends Bronze /599 #Z65
2007 Press Pass Legends Bronze /599 #Z68
2007 Press Pass Legends Cut Signatures /2 #DE
2007 Press Pass Legends Dale Earnhardt Gold /99 #DE1
2007 Press Pass Legends Dale Earnhardt Gold /99 #DE2
2007 Press Pass Legends Dale Earnhardt Gold /99 #DE3
2007 Press Pass Legends Dale Earnhardt Gold /99 #DE4
2007 Press Pass Legends Dale Earnhardt Gold /99 #DE5
2007 Press Pass Legends Dale Earnhardt Gold /99 #DE6
2007 Press Pass Legends Dale Earnhardt Gold /99 #DE7
2007 Press Pass Legends Dale Earnhardt Gold /99 #DE8
2007 Press Pass Legends Dale Earnhardt Gold /99 #DE9
2007 Press Pass Legends Dale Earnhardt Silver /499 #DE1
2007 Press Pass Legends Dale Earnhardt Silver /499 #DE2
2007 Press Pass Legends Dale Earnhardt Silver /499 #DE3
2007 Press Pass Legends Dale Earnhardt Silver /499 #DE4
2007 Press Pass Legends Dale Earnhardt Silver /499 #DE5
2007 Press Pass Legends Dale Earnhardt Silver /499 #DE6
2007 Press Pass Legends Dale Earnhardt Silver /499 #DE7
2007 Press Pass Legends Dale Earnhardt Silver /499 #DE8
2007 Press Pass Legends Dale Earnhardt Silver /499 #DE9
2007 Press Pass Legends Gold /249 #G29
2007 Press Pass Legends Gold /249 #G51
2007 Press Pass Legends Gold /249 #G65
2007 Press Pass Legends Gold /249 #G68
2007 Press Pass Legends Holofoil /99 #H29
2007 Press Pass Legends Holofoil /99 #H51
2007 Press Pass Legends Holofoil /99 #H65
2007 Press Pass Legends Holofoil /99 #H68
2007 Press Pass Legends Legends Gallery Gold /99 #LG5
2007 Press Pass Legends Legends Gallery Silver /499 #LG5
2007 Press Pass Legends Memorable Moments Gold /169 #MM4
2007 Press Pass Legends Memorable Moments Gold /169 #MM8
2007 Press Pass Legends Memorable Moments Gold /169 #MM13
2007 Press Pass Legends Memorable Moments Gold /169 #MM15
2007 Press Pass Legends Memorable Moments Silver /499 #MM4
2007 Press Pass Legends Memorable Moments Silver /499 #MM8
2007 Press Pass Legends Memorable Moments Silver /499 #MM13
2007 Press Pass Legends Memorable Moments Silver /499 #MM15
2007 Press Pass Legends Press Plates Black /1 #PP29
2007 Press Pass Legends Press Plates Black /1 #PP51
2007 Press Pass Legends Press Plates Black /1 #PP65
2007 Press Pass Legends Press Plates Black /1 #PP68
2007 Press Pass Legends Press Plates Black Backs /1 #PP29
2007 Press Pass Legends Press Plates Black Backs /1 #PP51
2007 Press Pass Legends Press Plates Black Backs /1 #PP65
2007 Press Pass Legends Press Plates Black Backs /1 #PP68
2007 Press Pass Legends Press Plates Cyan /1 #PP29
2007 Press Pass Legends Press Plates Cyan /1 #PP51
2007 Press Pass Legends Press Plates Cyan /1 #PP65
2007 Press Pass Legends Press Plates Cyan /1 #PP68
2007 Press Pass Legends Press Plates Cyan Backs /1 #PP29
2007 Press Pass Legends Press Plates Cyan Backs /1 #PP51
2007 Press Pass Legends Press Plates Cyan Backs /1 #PP65
2007 Press Pass Legends Press Plates Cyan Backs /1 #PP68
2007 Press Pass Legends Press Plates Magenta /1 #PP29
2007 Press Pass Legends Press Plates Magenta /1 #PP51
2007 Press Pass Legends Press Plates Magenta /1 #PP65
2007 Press Pass Legends Press Plates Magenta /1 #PP68
2007 Press Pass Legends Press Plates Magenta Backs /1 #PP29
2007 Press Pass Legends Press Plates Magenta Backs /1 #PP51
2007 Press Pass Legends Press Plates Magenta Backs /1 #PP65
2007 Press Pass Legends Press Plates Magenta Backs /1 #PP68
2007 Press Pass Legends Press Plates Yellow /1 #PP29
2007 Press Pass Legends Press Plates Yellow /1 #PP51
2007 Press Pass Legends Press Plates Yellow /1 #PP65
2007 Press Pass Legends Press Plates Yellow /1 #PP68
2007 Press Pass Legends Press Plates Yellow Backs /1 #PP29
2007 Press Pass Legends Press Plates Yellow Backs /1 #PP51
2007 Press Pass Legends Press Plates Yellow Backs /1 #PP65
2007 Press Pass Legends Press Plates Yellow Backs /1 #PP68
2007 Press Pass Legends Previews /5 #EB29
2007 Press Pass Legends Previews /1 #EB65
2007 Press Pass Legends Previews /1 #EB68
2007 Press Pass Legends Racing Artifacts Firesuit Bronze /199 #DEF
2007 Press Pass Legends Racing Artifacts Firesuit Gold /50 #DEF
2007 Press Pass Legends Racing Artifacts Firesuit Patch /25 #DEF
2007 Press Pass Legends Racing Artifacts Firesuit Silver /99 #DEF
2007 Press Pass Legends Racing Artifacts Tire Bronze /299 #DET
2007 Press Pass Legends Racing Artifacts Tire Gold /99 #DET
2007 Press Pass Legends Racing Artifacts Tire Silver /199 #DET
2007 Press Pass Legends Solo /1 #S29
2007 Press Pass Legends Solo /1 #S51
2007 Press Pass Legends Solo /1 #S65
2007 Press Pass Legends Solo /1 #S68
2007 Press Pass Premium Hot Threads Patch /10 #HTP1
2008 Press Pass #61
2008 Press Pass Blue #B61
2008 Press Pass Daytona 500 50th Anniversary #48
2008 Press Pass Daytona 500 50th Anniversary #35
2008 Press Pass Gold #G61
2008 Press Pass Legends #10
2008 Press Pass Legends #58
2008 Press Pass Legends Blue /599 #10
2008 Press Pass Legends Blue /599 #58
2008 Press Pass Legends Bronze /299 #10
2008 Press Pass Legends Bronze /299 #58
2008 Press Pass Legends Dale Earnhardt Buyback /3 #DE
2008 Press Pass Legends Gold /99 #10
2008 Press Pass Legends Gold /99 #58
2008 Press Pass Legends Holo /25 #10
2008 Press Pass Legends Holo /25 #58
2008 Press Pass Legends IROC Champions /380 #I12
2008 Press Pass Legends IROC Champions /380 #I15
2008 Press Pass Legends IROC Champions /380 #I19
2008 Press Pass Legends IROC Champions /380 #I20
2008 Press Pass Legends IROC Champions Gold /99 #I12
2008 Press Pass Legends IROC Champions Gold /99 #I15
2008 Press Pass Legends IROC Champions Gold /99 #I19
2008 Press Pass Legends IROC Champions Gold /99 #I20
2008 Press Pass Legends Previews /5 #EB10
2008 Press Pass Legends Previews /1 #EB58
2008 Press Pass Legends Printing Plates Black /1 #10
2008 Press Pass Legends Printing Plates Black /1 #58
2008 Press Pass Legends Printing Plates Cyan /1 #10
2008 Press Pass Legends Printing Plates Cyan /1 #58
2008 Press Pass Legends Printing Plates Magenta /1 #10
2008 Press Pass Legends Printing Plates Magenta /1 #58
2008 Press Pass Legends Printing Plates Yellow /1 #10
2008 Press Pass Legends Printing Plates Yellow /1 #58
2008 Press Pass Legends Racing Artifacts Dual Memorabilia /25 #DEDM
2008 Press Pass Legends Racing Artifacts Firesuit Bronze /180 #DEF
2008 Press Pass Legends Racing Artifacts Firesuit Bronze /180 #DEF2
2008 Press Pass Legends Racing Artifacts Firesuit Gold /25 #DEF
2008 Press Pass Legends Racing Artifacts Firesuit Gold /25 #DEF2
2008 Press Pass Legends Racing Artifacts Firesuit Patch /10 #DEF
2008 Press Pass Legends Racing Artifacts Firesuit Patch /10 #DEF2
2008 Press Pass Legends Racing Artifacts Firesuit Silver /50 #DEF
2008 Press Pass Legends Racing Artifacts Firesuit Silver /50 #DEF2
2008 Press Pass Legends Racing Artifacts Sheet Metal Bronze /199 #DES
2008 Press Pass Legends Racing Artifacts Sheet Metal Gold /50 #DES
2008 Press Pass Legends Racing Artifacts Sheet Metal Silver /99 #DES
2008 Press Pass Legends Racing Artifacts Tire Bronze /199 #DET
2008 Press Pass Legends Racing Artifacts Tire Gold /50 #DET
2008 Press Pass Legends Racing Artifacts Tire Silver /99 #DET
2008 Press Pass Legends Solo /1 #10
2008 Press Pass Legends Solo /1 #58
2008 Press Pass Platinum /100 #P61
2008 SP Legendary Cuts Mystery Cut Signatures /22 #DE
2008 Upper Deck Goudey Cut Signatures /1 #3
2008 Upper Deck Heroes Cut Signatures /1 #HCDE
2008 VIP Gear Gallery Memorabilia /50 #GGDE
2008 Wheels American Thunder #47
2009 Element Missing Elements #ME3
2009 Element Missing Elements Exchange #ME3
2009 Press Pass Freeze Frame #FF23
2009 Press Pass Freeze Frame #FF31
2009 Press Pass Fusion #66
2009 Press Pass Fusion Bronze /150 #66
2009 Press Pass Fusion Gold /50 #66
2009 Press Pass Fusion Green /25 #66
2009 Press Pass Fusion Onyx /1 #66
2009 Press Pass Fusion Revered Relics Gold /50 #RRDES
2009 Press Pass Fusion Revered Relics Holofoil /25 #RRDES
2009 Press Pass Fusion Revered Relics Premium Swatch /10 #RRDES
2009 Press Pass Fusion Revered Relics Silver /65 #RRDES
2009 Press Pass Fusion Silver /99 #66
2009 Press Pass Legends #9
2009 Press Pass Legends #70
2009 Press Pass Legends #58
2009 Press Pass Legends Artifacts Firesuits Bronze /250 #DEF2
2009 Press Pass Legends Artifacts Firesuits Bronze /250 #DEF
2009 Press Pass Legends Artifacts Firesuits Gold /25 #DEF
2009 Press Pass Legends Artifacts Firesuits Gold /25 #DEF2
2009 Press Pass Legends Artifacts Firesuits Silver /50 #DEF
2009 Press Pass Legends Artifacts Firesuits Silver /50 #DEF2
2009 Press Pass Legends Artifacts Sheet Metal Bronze /199 #DES
2009 Press Pass Legends Artifacts Sheet Metal Gold /25 #DES
2009 Press Pass Legends Artifacts Sheet Metal Silver /50 #DES
2009 Press Pass Legends Artifacts Tires Bronze /199 #DET
2009 Press Pass Legends Artifacts Tires Gold /25 #DET
2009 Press Pass Legends Artifacts Tires Silver /50 #DET
2009 Press Pass Legends Family Cuts /1 #1
2009 Press Pass Legends Family Portraits /550 #FP12
2009 Press Pass Legends Family Portraits /550 #FP15
2009 Press Pass Legends Family Portraits /550 #FP14
2009 Press Pass Legends Family Portraits /550 #FP13
2009 Press Pass Legends Family Portraits /550 #FP11
2009 Press Pass Legends Family Portraits /550 #FP10
2009 Press Pass Legends Family Portraits Holofoil /99 #FP10
2009 Press Pass Legends Family Portraits Holofoil /99 #FP11
2009 Press Pass Legends Family Portraits Holofoil /99 #FP12
2009 Press Pass Legends Family Portraits Holofoil /99 #FP13
2009 Press Pass Legends Family Portraits Holofoil /99 #FP14
2009 Press Pass Legends Family Portraits Holofoil /99 #FP15
2009 Press Pass Legends Family Relics Bronze /99 #FREa
2009 Press Pass Legends Family Relics Gold /25 #FREa
2009 Press Pass Legends Family Relics Gold /25 #FREa4
2009 Press Pass Legends Family Relics Gold /25 #FREa3
2009 Press Pass Legends Family Relics Silver /50 #FREa
2009 Press Pass Legends Family Relics Silver /50 #FREa3
2009 Press Pass Legends Gold /399 #9
2009 Press Pass Legends Gold /399 #58
2009 Press Pass Legends Gold /399 #70
2009 Press Pass Legends Holofoil /50 #9
2009 Press Pass Legends Holofoil /50 #58
2009 Press Pass Legends Holofoil /50 #70
2009 Press Pass Legends Past and Present /550 #PP2
2009 Press Pass Legends Past and Present Holofoil /99 #PP2
2009 Press Pass Legends Previews /5 #9
2009 Press Pass Legends Previews /1 #58
2009 Press Pass Legends Printing Plates Black /1 #9
2009 Press Pass Legends Printing Plates Black /1 #58
2009 Press Pass Legends Printing Plates Black /1 #70
2009 Press Pass Legends Printing Plates Cyan /1 #9
2009 Press Pass Legends Printing Plates Cyan /1 #58
2009 Press Pass Legends Printing Plates Cyan /1 #70
2009 Press Pass Legends Printing Plates Magenta /1 #9
2009 Press Pass Legends Printing Plates Magenta /1 #58
2009 Press Pass Legends Printing Plates Magenta /1 #70
2009 Press Pass Legends Printing Plates Yellow /1 #9
2009 Press Pass Legends Printing Plates Yellow /1 #58
2009 Press Pass Legends Printing Plates Yellow /1 #70
2009 Press Pass Legends Racing Cuts /1 #RCDE
2009 Press Pass Legends Red /199 #9
2009 Press Pass Legends Red /199 #58
2009 Press Pass Legends Red /199 #70
2009 Press Pass Legends Solo /1 #9
2009 Press Pass Legends Solo /1 #58
2009 Press Pass Legends Solo /1 #70
2009 Press Pass Pocket Portraits #P28
2009 Press Pass Pocket Portraits Checkered Flag #P28
2009 Press Pass Pocket Portraits Hometown #P28
2009 Press Pass Pocket Portraits Smoke #P28
2009 Press Pass Showcase /499 #50
2009 Press Pass Showcase 2nd Gear /125 #50
2009 Press Pass Showcase 3rd Gear /50 #50
2009 Press Pass Showcase 4th Gear /15 #50
2009 Press Pass Showcase Dale Earnhardt Buybacks /20 #DE
2009 Press Pass Showcase Printing Plates Yellow /1 #37
2009 Press Pass Showcase Prized Pieces Firesuit /25 #PPFDE
2009 Press Pass Showcase Prized Pieces Firesuit Patch /5 #PPFDE
2009 Press Pass Showcase Prized Pieces Sheet Metal /45 #PPSDE
2009 Press Pass Showcase Prized Pieces Tire /25 #PPTDE
2009 Topps Sterling Cut Signatures /3 #MPS211
2009 Upper Deck Prominent Cuts Cut Signatures /49 #PCDE
2009 VIP #71
2009 VIP #73
2009 VIP National Promos #6
2009 VIP Previews /1 #71
2009 VIP Previews /1 #73
2009 VIP Purple /25 #71
2009 VIP Purple /25 #73
2009 Wheels Main Event Poker Chips #2
2010 Element High Octane Vehicle #HOV9
2010 Press Pass By The Numbers #BN7
2010 Press Pass By The Numbers #BN10
2010 Press Pass By The Numbers #BN16
2010 Press Pass Eclipse #45
2010 Press Pass Eclipse Blue #45
2010 Press Pass Eclipse Gold #45
2010 Press Pass Eclipse Previews /1 #45
2010 Press Pass Eclipse Purple /25 #45
2010 Press Pass Eclipse Spellbound Swatches Holofoil /3 #SSDE1
2010 Press Pass Eclipse Spellbound Swatches Holofoil /3 #SSDE2
2010 Press Pass Eclipse Spellbound Swatches Holofoil /3 #SSDE3
2010 Press Pass Eclipse Spellbound Swatches Holofoil /3 #SSDE4
2010 Press Pass Eclipse Spellbound Swatches Holofoil /3 #SSDE5
2010 Press Pass Eclipse Spellbound Swatches Holofoil /3 #SSDE6
2010 Press Pass Eclipse Spellbound Swatches Holofoil /3 #SSDE7
2010 Press Pass Eclipse Spellbound Swatches Holofoil /3 #SSDE8
2010 Press Pass Eclipse Spellbound Swatches Holofoil /3 #SSDE9
2010 Press Pass Five Star /35 #5
2010 Press Pass Five Star Classic Compilations Family Firesuit Autographs /1 #EE
2010 Press Pass Five Star Classic Compilations Firesuit Cut Signatures /2 #DE
2010 Press Pass Five Star Classic Compilations Wrangler Firesuit Dual /25 #EE
2010 Press Pass Five Star Cut Signatures /1 #DE
2010 Press Pass Five Star Holofoil /10 #5
2010 Press Pass Five Star Melting /1 #5
2010 Press Pass Five Star Paramount Pieces Aluminum /25 #DE
2010 Press Pass Five Star Paramount Pieces Blue /20 #DE
2010 Press Pass Five Star Paramount Pieces Gold /15 #DE
2010 Press Pass Five Star Paramount Pieces Holofoil /10 #DE
2010 Press Pass Five Star Paramount Pieces Melting /1 #DE
2010 Press Pass Legends #10
2010 Press Pass Legends #55
2010 Press Pass Legends #67
2010 Press Pass Legends #77
2010 Press Pass Legends 50 Win Club Memorabilia Gold /75 #50DE
2010 Press Pass Legends 50 Win Club Memorabilia Holofoil /25 #50DE
2010 Press Pass Legends Blue /1 #10
2010 Press Pass Legends Blue /1 #55
2010 Press Pass Legends Blue /1 #67
2010 Press Pass Legends Blue /1 #77
2010 Press Pass Legends Gold /399 #10
2010 Press Pass Legends Gold /399 #55
2010 Press Pass Legends Gold /399 #67
2010 Press Pass Legends Gold /399 #77
2010 Press Pass Legends Holofoil /50 #10
2010 Press Pass Legends Holofoil /50 #55
2010 Press Pass Legends Holofoil /50 #67
2010 Press Pass Legends Holofoil /50 #77
2010 Press Pass Legends Lasting Legacies Copper /175 #LLDE
2010 Press Pass Legends Lasting Legacies Gold /75 #LLDE1
2010 Press Pass Legends Lasting Legacies Gold /75 #LLDE2
2010 Press Pass Legends Lasting Legacies Holofoil /25 #LLDE3
2010 Press Pass Legends Lasting Legacies Holofoil /25 #LLDE1
2010 Press Pass Legends Lasting Legacies Holofoil /25 #LLDE2
2010 Press Pass Legends Lasting Legacies Holofoil /25 #LLDE4
2010 Press Pass Legends Legendary Links Gold /75 #LXDEJG
2010 Press Pass Legends Legendary Links Holofoil /25 #LXDEJG
2010 Press Pass Legends Memorable Matchups /25 #MMDETL
2010 Press Pass Legends Printing Plates Black /1 #10
2010 Press Pass Legends Printing Plates Black /1 #55
2010 Press Pass Legends Printing Plates Black /1 #67
2010 Press Pass Legends Printing Plates Black /1 #77
2010 Press Pass Legends Printing Plates Cyan /1 #10
2010 Press Pass Legends Printing Plates Cyan /1 #55
2010 Press Pass Legends Printing Plates Cyan /1 #67
2010 Press Pass Legends Printing Plates Cyan /1 #77
2010 Press Pass Legends Printing Plates Magenta /1 #10
2010 Press Pass Legends Printing Plates Magenta /1 #55
2010 Press Pass Legends Printing Plates Magenta /1 #67
2010 Press Pass Legends Printing Plates Magenta /1 #77
2010 Press Pass Legends Printing Plates Yellow /1 #10
2010 Press Pass Legends Printing Plates Yellow /1 #55
2010 Press Pass Legends Printing Plates Yellow /1 #67
2010 Press Pass Legends Printing Plates Yellow /1 #77
2010 Press Pass Legends Racing Cuts /1 #NNO
2010 Press Pass Legends Red /199 #10
2010 Press Pass Legends Red /199 #55
2010 Press Pass Legends Red /199 #67
2010 Press Pass Legends Red /199 #77
2010 Press Pass NASCAR Hall of Fame #NHOF32
2010 Press Pass NASCAR Hall of Fame #NHOF47
2010 Press Pass NASCAR Hall of Fame #NHOF71
2010 Press Pass NASCAR Hall of Fame #NHOF72
2010 Press Pass NASCAR Hall of Fame #NHOF74
2010 Press Pass NASCAR Hall of Fame #NHOF73
2010 Press Pass NASCAR Hall of Fame #NHOF75
2010 Press Pass NASCAR Hall of Fame #NHOF76
2010 Press Pass NASCAR Hall of Fame #NHOF77
2010 Press Pass NASCAR Hall of Fame #NHOF78
2010 Press Pass NASCAR Hall of Fame #NHOF79
2010 Press Pass NASCAR Hall of Fame #NHOF80
2010 Press Pass NASCAR Hall of Fame Blue #NHOF32
2010 Press Pass NASCAR Hall of Fame Blue #NHOF47
2010 Press Pass NASCAR Hall of Fame Blue #NHOF71
2010 Press Pass NASCAR Hall of Fame Blue #NHOF72
2010 Press Pass NASCAR Hall of Fame Blue #NHOF73
2010 Press Pass NASCAR Hall of Fame Blue #NHOF74
2010 Press Pass NASCAR Hall of Fame Blue #NHOF75
2010 Press Pass NASCAR Hall of Fame Blue #NHOF76
2010 Press Pass NASCAR Hall of Fame Blue #NHOF77
2010 Press Pass NASCAR Hall of Fame Blue #NHOF78
2010 Press Pass NASCAR Hall of Fame Blue #NHOF79
2010 Press Pass NASCAR Hall of Fame Blue #NHOF80
2010 Press Pass NASCAR Hall of Fame Holofoil /50 #NHOF32
2010 Press Pass NASCAR Hall of Fame Holofoil /50 #NHOF47
2010 Press Pass NASCAR Hall of Fame Holofoil /50 #NHOF71
2010 Press Pass NASCAR Hall of Fame Holofoil /50 #NHOF72
2010 Press Pass NASCAR Hall of Fame Holofoil /50 #NHOF73
2010 Press Pass NASCAR Hall of Fame Holofoil /50 #NHOF74
2010 Press Pass NASCAR Hall of Fame Holofoil /50 #NHOF75
2010 Press Pass NASCAR Hall of Fame Holofoil /50 #NHOF76
2010 Press Pass NASCAR Hall of Fame Holofoil /50 #NHOF77
2010 Press Pass NASCAR Hall of Fame Holofoil /50 #NHOF78
2010 Press Pass NASCAR Hall of Fame Holofoil /50 #NHOF79
2010 Press Pass NASCAR Hall of Fame Holofoil /50 #NHOF80
2010 Press Pass Showcase Elite Exhibit Triple Memorabilia /99 #EEMDE
2010 Press Pass Showcase Elite Exhibit Triple Memorabilia Gold /25 #EEMDE
2010 Press Pass Showcase Elite Exhibit Triple Memorabilia Green /10 #EEMDE
2010 Press Pass Showcase Elite Exhibit Triple Memorabilia Melting /5 #EEMDE
2010 Press Pass Showcase Prized Pieces Firesuit Green /10 #PPMDE
2010 Press Pass Showcase Prized Pieces Firesuit Patch Melting /5 #PPMDE
2010 Press Pass Showcase Prized Pieces Sheet Metal /45 #PPMDE
2010 Press Pass Showcase Prized Pieces Sheet Metal Gold /15 #PPMDE
2010 Press Pass Showcase Racing's Finest /499 #RF1
2010 Press Pass Showcase Racing's Finest Gold /125 #RF1
2010 Press Pass Showcase Racing's Finest Green /50 #RF1
2010 Press Pass Showcase Racing's Finest Melting /15 #RF1
2010 Press Pass Stealth Earnhardt Retail #DE2
2010 Press Pass Stealth Earnhardt Retail #DE3
2010 Press Pass Target By The Numbers #BNT2
2010 Press Pass Wal-Mart By The Numbers #BNW2
2010 Wheels Main Event Dog Tags #DE
2011 Press Pass Eclipse Spellbound Swatches /25 #SBDE1
2011 Press Pass Eclipse Spellbound Swatches /25 #SBDE2
2011 Press Pass Eclipse Spellbound Swatches /20 #SBDE3
2011 Press Pass Eclipse Spellbound Swatches /20 #SBDE4
2011 Press Pass Eclipse Spellbound Swatches /15 #SBDE5
2011 Press Pass Eclipse Spellbound Swatches /15 #SBDE6
2011 Press Pass Eclipse Spellbound Swatches /10 #SBDE7
2011 Press Pass Eclipse Spellbound Swatches /10 #SBDE8
2011 Press Pass Eclipse Spellbound Swatches /5 #SBDE9
2011 Press Pass FanFare #78
2011 Press Pass FanFare Blue Die Cuts #78
2011 Press Pass FanFare Championship Caliber #CC9
2011 Press Pass FanFare Emerald /25 #78
2011 Press Pass FanFare Holofoil Die Cuts #78
2011 Press Pass FanFare Rookie Standouts #RS14
2011 Press Pass FanFare Ruby Die Cuts /15 #78
2011 Press Pass FanFare Sapphire /10 #78
2011 Press Pass FanFare Silver /25 #78
2011 Press Pass Legends #9
2011 Press Pass Legends #63
2011 Press Pass Legends #64
2011 Press Pass Legends Dual Firesuits Gold /50 #DECM
2011 Press Pass Legends Dual Firesuits Holofoil /25 #DECM
2011 Press Pass Legends Dual Firesuits Purple /15 #DECM
2011 Press Pass Legends Dual Firesuits Silver /99 #DECM
2011 Press Pass Legends Famed Fabrics Gold /50 #HOFDE
2011 Press Pass Legends Famed Fabrics Holofoil /25 #HOFDE
2011 Press Pass Legends Famed Fabrics Purple /15 #HOFDE
2011 Press Pass Legends Gold /250 #9
2011 Press Pass Legends Gold /250 #63
2011 Press Pass Legends Gold /250 #64
2011 Press Pass Legends Holofoil /25 #9
2011 Press Pass Legends Holofoil /25 #63
2011 Press Pass Legends Holofoil /25 #64
2011 Press Pass Legends Lasting Legacies Memorabilia Gold /50 #LLDE
2011 Press Pass Legends Lasting Legacies Memorabilia Gold /50 #LLDE2
2011 Press Pass Legends Lasting Legacies Memorabilia Holofoil /25 #LLDE
2011 Press Pass Legends Lasting Legacies Memorabilia Holofoil /25 #LLDE2
2011 Press Pass Legends Lasting Legacies Memorabilia Purple /15 #LLDE
2011 Press Pass Legends Lasting Legacies Memorabilia Purple /15 #LLDE2
2011 Press Pass Legends Lasting Legacies Memorabilia Silver /199 #LLDE2
2011 Press Pass Legends Lasting Legacies Memorabilia Silver /199 #LLDE
2011 Press Pass Legends Motorsports Masters #MM1
2011 Press Pass Legends Motorsports Masters Brushed Foil /199 #MM1
2011 Press Pass Legends Motorsports Masters Holofoil /50 #MM1
2011 Press Pass Legends Pacing The Field #PF1
2011 Press Pass Legends Pacing The Field Brushed Foil /199 #PF1
2011 Press Pass Legends Pacing The Field Holofoil /50 #PF1
2011 Press Pass Legends Printing Plates Black /1 #9
2011 Press Pass Legends Printing Plates Black /1 #63
2011 Press Pass Legends Printing Plates Black /1 #64
2011 Press Pass Legends Printing Plates Cyan /1 #9
2011 Press Pass Legends Printing Plates Cyan /1 #63
2011 Press Pass Legends Printing Plates Cyan /1 #64
2011 Press Pass Legends Printing Plates Magenta /1 #9
2011 Press Pass Legends Printing Plates Magenta /1 #63
2011 Press Pass Legends Printing Plates Magenta /1 #64
2011 Press Pass Legends Printing Plates Yellow /1 #9
2011 Press Pass Legends Printing Plates Yellow /1 #63
2011 Press Pass Legends Printing Plates Yellow /1 #64
2011 Press Pass Legends Purple /25 #9
2011 Press Pass Legends Purple /25 #63
2011 Press Pass Legends Purple /25 #64
2011 Press Pass Legends Racing Cuts /1 #RCDE
2011 Press Pass Legends Red /99 #9
2011 Press Pass Legends Red /99 #63
2011 Press Pass Legends Red /99 #64
2011 Press Pass Legends Solo /1 #9
2011 Press Pass Legends Solo /1 #63
2011 Press Pass Legends Solo /1 #64
2011 Press Pass Legends Trophy Room Gold /50 #TRDE
2011 Press Pass Legends Trophy Room Holofoil /25 #TRDE
2011 Press Pass Legends Trophy Room Purple /15 #TRDE
2011 Press Pass Premium #0
2011 Press Pass Premium /25 #CTLDE
2011 Press Pass Showcase /499 #27
2011 Press Pass Showcase /499 #51
2011 Press Pass Showcase Champions /499 #CH11
2011 Press Pass Showcase Champions Gold /125 #CH11
2011 Press Pass Showcase Champions Melting /1 #CH11
2011 Press Pass Showcase Champions Memorabilia Firesuit /99 #CHMDE
2011 Press Pass Showcase Champions Memorabilia Firesuit Gold /45 #CHMDE
2011 Press Pass Showcase Champions Memorabilia Firesuit Melting /5 #CHMDE
2011 Press Pass Showcase Gold /125 #27
2011 Press Pass Showcase Gold /125 #51
2011 Press Pass Showcase Green /25 #27
2011 Press Pass Showcase Green /25 #51
2011 Press Pass Showcase Masterpieces Memorabilia /99 #MPMDE
2011 Press Pass Showcase Melting /1 #27
2011 Press Pass Showcase Melting /1 #51
2011 Press Pass Showcase Prized Pieces Firesuit /50 #PPMDE
2011 Press Pass Showcase Prized Pieces Firesuit Gold /25 #PPMDE
2011 Press Pass Showcase Prized Pieces Firesuit Patches Melting /5 #PPMDE
2011 Press Pass Showcase Showroom /499 #SR10
2011 Press Pass Showcase Showroom Gold /125 #SR10
2011 Press Pass Showcase Showroom Melting /1 #SR10
2011 Press Pass Showcase Showroom Memorabilia Sheet Metal Gold /25 #SRMDE
2011 Press Pass Showcase Showroom Memorabilia Sheet Metal Melting /5 #SRMDE
2011 Press Pass Winning Tickets #WT56
2011 Press Pass Winning Tickets #WT57
2012 Historic Autographs Peerless /9 #37
2012 Press Pass Fanfare #83
2012 Press Pass Fanfare Blue Foil Die Cuts #83
2012 Press Pass Fanfare Diamond /5 #83
2012 Press Pass Fanfare Holofoil Die Cuts #83
2012 Press Pass Fanfare Sapphire /20 #83
2012 Press Pass Fanfare Silver /25 #83
2012 Press Pass Ignite Materials Gun Metal /50 #IMDE
2012 Press Pass Ignite Materials Red /10 #IMDE
2012 Press Pass Ignite Materials Silver #IMDE
2012 Press Pass Legends #9
2012 Press Pass Legends Blue Holofoil /1 #9
2012 Press Pass Legends Gold /275 #9
2012 Press Pass Legends Green #9
2012 Press Pass Legends Pieces of History Memorabilia Gold /99 #DE1
2012 Press Pass Legends Pieces of History Memorabilia Gold /25 #DE2
2012 Press Pass Legends Pieces of History Memorabilia Gold /50 #DE3
2012 Press Pass Legends Pieces of History Memorabilia Holofoil /25 #DE1
2012 Press Pass Legends Pieces of History Memorabilia Holofoil /3 #DE2
2012 Press Pass Legends Pieces of History Memorabilia Holofoil /10 #DE3
2012 Press Pass Legends Pieces of History Memorabilia Silver /199 #DE1
2012 Press Pass Legends Racing Cuts /3 #DE
2012 Press Pass Legends Rainbow Holofoil /50 #9
2012 Press Pass Legends Red /99 #9
2012 Press Pass Legends Silver Holofoil /25 #9
2012 Press Pass Legends Trailblazers #TB7
2012 Press Pass Power Picks Blue /50 #17
2012 Press Pass Power Picks Blue /50 #74
2012 Press Pass Power Picks Gold /50 #17
2012 Press Pass Power Picks Gold /50 #74
2012 Press Pass Power Picks Holofoil /10 #17
2012 Press Pass Power Picks Holofoil /10 #74
2012 Press Pass Redline #50
2012 Press Pass Redline Black /99 #50
2012 Press Pass Redline Cyan /50 #50
2012 Press Pass Redline Magenta /15 #50
2012 Press Pass Redline Yellow /1 #50
2012 Press Pass Showcase /499 #25
2012 Press Pass Showcase /499 #46
2012 Press Pass Showcase Champions Memorabilia /99 #CHDE
2012 Press Pass Showcase Champions Memorabilia Gold /50 #CHDE
2012 Press Pass Showcase Champions Memorabilia Melting /5 #CHDE
2012 Press Pass Showcase Champions Showcase /499 #CH8
2012 Press Pass Showcase Champions Showcase Gold /125 #CH8
2012 Press Pass Showcase Champions Showcase Melting /1 #CH8
2012 Press Pass Showcase Gold /125 #25
2012 Press Pass Showcase Gold /125 #46
2012 Press Pass Showcase Green /5 #25
2012 Press Pass Showcase Green /5 #46
2012 Press Pass Showcase Masterpieces Memorabilia /50 #MPDE
2012 Press Pass Showcase Masterpieces Memorabilia Gold /10 #MPDE
2012 Press Pass Showcase Masterpieces Memorabilia Melting /5 #MPDE
2012 Press Pass Showcase Melting /1 #25
2012 Press Pass Showcase Melting /1 #46
2012 Press Pass Showcase Purple /1 #25
2012 Press Pass Showcase Purple /1 #46
2012 Press Pass Showcase Red /25 #25
2012 Press Pass Showcase Red /25 #46
2012 Press Pass Triple Gear 3 in 1 /5 #TGDE
2012 Press Pass Triple Gear Firesuit and Sheet Metal /15 #TGDE
2012 Press Pass Triple Gear Tire /25 #TGDE
2012 Sportkings Premium Back Redemption Paintings /1 #15
2012 Total Memorabilia #37
2012 Total Memorabilia Black and White /99 #37
2012 Total Memorabilia Gold /275 #37
2012 Total Memorabilia Red Retail /250 #37
2013 Press Pass Power Picks Blue /99 #17
2013 Press Pass Power Picks Gold /50 #17
2013 Press Pass Power Picks Holofoil /10 #17
2013 Press Pass Showcase Blue /25 #8
2013 Press Pass Showcase Blue /25 #32
2013 Press Pass Showcase Blue /25 #49
2014 Press Pass Five Star /15 #26
2014 Press Pass Five Star Blue /5 #26
2014 Press Pass Five Star Cut Signatures /5 #FSCDE
2014 Press Pass Five Star Holofoil /10 #26
2014 Press Pass Five Star Melting /1 #26
2014 Press Pass Five Star Paramount Pieces Blue /5 #PPDE
2014 Press Pass Five Star Paramount Pieces Gold /25 #PPDE
2014 Press Pass Five Star Paramount Pieces Holofoil /10 #PPDE
2014 Press Pass Five Star Paramount Pieces Melting /1 #PPDE
2015 Press Pass Dale Earnhardt Tribute #DE3
2015 Press Pass Dale Earnhardt Tribute #DE4
2015 Press Pass Dale Earnhardt Tribute #DE5
2015 Press Pass Dale Earnhardt Tribute #DE1
2015 Press Pass Dale Earnhardt Tribute #DE2
2015 Press Pass Dale Earnhardt Tribute Melting /30 #DE1
2015 Press Pass Dale Earnhardt Tribute Melting /30 #DE2
2015 Press Pass Dale Earnhardt Tribute Melting /30 #DE3
2015 Press Pass Dale Earnhardt Tribute Melting /30 #DE4
2015 Press Pass Dale Earnhardt Tribute Melting /30 #DE5
2016 Panini National Treasures Firesuit Materials /25 #5
2016 Panini National Treasures Firesuit Materials Black /5 #5
2016 Panini National Treasures Firesuit Materials Blue /1 #5
2016 Panini National Treasures Firesuit Materials Gold /10 #5
2016 Panini National Treasures Firesuit Materials Laundry Tag /1 #5
2016 Panini National Treasures Firesuit Materials Printing Plates Black /1 #5
2016 Panini National Treasures Firesuit Materials Printing Plates Cyan /1 #5
2016 Panini National Treasures Firesuit Materials Printing Plates Magenta /1 #5
2016 Panini National Treasures Firesuit Materials Printing Plates Yellow /1 #5
2016 Panini National Treasures Firesuit Materials Silver /15 #5
2016 Panini National Treasures Quad Driver Materials /25 #1
2016 Panini National Treasures Quad Driver Materials Black /5 #1
2016 Panini National Treasures Quad Driver Materials Blue /1 #1
2016 Panini National Treasures Quad Driver Materials Gold /10 #1
2016 Panini National Treasures Quad Driver Materials Printing Plates Black /1 #1
2016 Panini National Treasures Quad Driver Materials Printing Plates Cyan /1 #1
2016 Panini National Treasures Quad Driver Materials Printing Plates Magenta /1 #1
2016 Panini National Treasures Quad Driver Materials Printing Plates Yellow /1 #1
2016 Panini National Treasures Quad Driver Materials Silver /15 #1
2018 Panini Prime /50 #91
2018 Panini Prime /50 #58

2018 Panini Prime /50 #25
2018 Panini Prime Autograph Materials Black /1 #9
2018 Panini Prime Autograph Materials Laundry Tag /1 #9
2018 Panini Prime Black /1 #25
2018 Panini Prime Black /1 #58
2018 Panini Prime Black /1 #91
2018 Panini Prime Clear Silhouettes Black /1 #7
2018 Panini Prime Driver Signatures Black /1 #25
2018 Panini Prime Dual Material Autographs Black /1 #2
2018 Panini Prime Dual Material Autographs Laundry Tag /1 #2
2018 Panini Prime Dual Signatures /10 #7
2018 Panini Prime Dual Signatures Black /1 #7
2018 Panini Prime Dual Signatures Holo Gold /5 #7
2018 Panini Prime Holo Gold /25 #25
2018 Panini Prime Holo Gold /25 #58
2018 Panini Prime Holo Gold /25 #91
2018 Panini Prime Prime Jumbo Associate Sponsor 1 /1 #22
2018 Panini Prime Prime Jumbo Associate Sponsor 1 /1 #23
2018 Panini Prime Prime Jumbo Associate Sponsor 1 /1 #24
2018 Panini Prime Prime Jumbo Associate Sponsor 1 /1 #25
2018 Panini Prime Prime Jumbo Associate Sponsor 2 /1 #22
2018 Panini Prime Prime Jumbo Associate Sponsor 2 /1 #23
2018 Panini Prime Prime Jumbo Associate Sponsor 2 /1 #24
2018 Panini Prime Prime Jumbo Associate Sponsor 2 /1 #25
2018 Panini Prime Prime Jumbo Associate Sponsor 3 /1 #22
2018 Panini Prime Prime Jumbo Associate Sponsor 3 /1 #23
2018 Panini Prime Prime Jumbo Associate Sponsor 3 /1 #24
2018 Panini Prime Prime Jumbo Associate Sponsor 3 /1 #25
2018 Panini Prime Prime Jumbo Associate Sponsor 4 /1 #22
2018 Panini Prime Prime Jumbo Associate Sponsor 4 /1 #23
2018 Panini Prime Prime Jumbo Associate Sponsor 4 /1 #24
2018 Panini Prime Prime Jumbo Associate Sponsor 4 /1 #25
2018 Panini Prime Prime Jumbo Associate Sponsor 5 /1 #22
2018 Panini Prime Prime Jumbo Associate Sponsor 5 /1 #23
2018 Panini Prime Prime Jumbo Associate Sponsor 5 /1 #24
2018 Panini Prime Prime Jumbo Associate Sponsor 5 /1 #25
2018 Panini Prime Prime Jumbo Associate Sponsor 6 /1 #22
2018 Panini Prime Prime Jumbo Associate Sponsor 6 /1 #23
2018 Panini Prime Prime Jumbo Associate Sponsor 6 /1 #24
2018 Panini Prime Prime Jumbo Associate Sponsor 7 /1 #22
2018 Panini Prime Prime Jumbo Associate Sponsor 7 /1 #25
2018 Panini Prime Prime Jumbo Associate Sponsor 8 /1 #25
2018 Panini Prime Prime Jumbo Associate Sponsor 9 /1 #25
2018 Panini Prime Prime Jumbo Car Manufacturer /1 #22
2018 Panini Prime Prime Jumbo Car Manufacturer /1 #23
2018 Panini Prime Prime Jumbo Car Manufacturer /1 #24
2018 Panini Prime Prime Jumbo Car Manufacturer /1 #25
2018 Panini Prime Prime Jumbo Firesuit Manufacturer /1 #22
2018 Panini Prime Prime Jumbo Firesuit Manufacturer /1 #23
2018 Panini Prime Prime Jumbo Firesuit Manufacturer /1 #24
2018 Panini Prime Prime Jumbo Firesuit Manufacturer /1 #25
2018 Panini Prime Prime Jumbo Flag Patch /1 #24
2018 Panini Prime Prime Jumbo Glove Manufacturer Patch /1 #22
2018 Panini Prime Prime Jumbo Glove Manufacturer Patch /1 #23
2018 Panini Prime Prime Jumbo Glove Manufacturer Patch /1 #24
2018 Panini Prime Prime Jumbo Glove Manufacturer Patch /1 #25
2018 Panini Prime Prime Jumbo Goodyear /2 #22
2018 Panini Prime Prime Jumbo Goodyear /2 #23
2018 Panini Prime Prime Jumbo Goodyear /2 #24
2018 Panini Prime Prime Jumbo Goodyear /2 #25
2018 Panini Prime Prime Jumbo Nameplate /1 #22
2018 Panini Prime Prime Jumbo NASCAR /1 #22
2018 Panini Prime Prime Jumbo NASCAR /1 #23
2018 Panini Prime Prime Jumbo NASCAR /1 #24
2018 Panini Prime Prime Jumbo NASCAR /1 #25
2018 Panini Prime Prime Jumbo Prime Colors /11 #22
2018 Panini Prime Prime Jumbo Prime Colors /10 #23
2018 Panini Prime Prime Jumbo Series Sponsor /1 #22
2018 Panini Prime Prime Jumbo Series Sponsor /1 #23
2018 Panini Prime Prime Jumbo Series Sponsor /1 #24
2018 Panini Prime Prime Jumbo Series Sponsor /1 #25
2018 Panini Prime Prime Jumbo Shoe Brand Logo /1 #22
2018 Panini Prime Prime Jumbo Shoe Brand Logo /1 #23
2018 Panini Prime Prime Jumbo Shoe Brand Logo /1 #24
2018 Panini Prime Prime Jumbo Shoe Brand Logo /1 #25
2018 Panini Prime Prime Jumbo Shoe Name Patch /1 #22
2018 Panini Prime Prime Jumbo Sunoco /1 #22
2018 Panini Prime Prime Jumbo Sunoco /1 #23
2018 Panini Prime Prime Jumbo Sunoco /1 #24
2018 Panini Prime Prime Jumbo Sunoco /1 #25
2018 Panini Prime Prime Signatures Black /1 #4
2018 Panini Prime Race Used Duals Firesuit Black /1 #13
2018 Panini Prime Race Used Duals Firesuit Laundry Tag /1 #13
2018 Panini Prime Race Used Duals Sheet Metal Black /1 #13
2018 Panini Prime Race Used Firesuits Black /1 #10
2018 Panini Prime Race Used Firesuits Laundry Tag /1 #10
2018 Panini Prime Race Used Sheet Metal Black /1 #10
2018 Panini Prime Race Used Tires Black /1 #10
2018 Panini Prime Race Used Trios Firesuit Black /1 #3
2018 Panini Prime Race Used Trios Firesuit Laundry Tag /1 #3
2018 Panini Prime Race Used Trios Sheet Metal Black /1 #3
2018 Panini Prime Shadowbox Signatures Black /1 #3
2018 Panini Prime Signature Swatches /25 #11
2018 Panini Prime Signature Swatches Black /1 #11
2018 Panini Prime Signature Swatches Holo Gold /10 #11
2018 Panini Prime Triple Material Autographs Black /1 #1
2018 Panini Prime Triple Material Autographs Laundry Tag /1 #1
2018 Panini Victory Lane #53
2018 Panini Victory Lane #63
2018 Panini Victory Lane #67
2018 Panini Victory Lane #73
2018 Panini Victory Lane #88
2018 Panini Victory Lane #93
2018 Panini Victory Lane #98
2018 Panini Victory Lane Black /1 #53
2018 Panini Victory Lane Black /1 #63
2018 Panini Victory Lane Black /1 #67
2018 Panini Victory Lane Black /1 #73
2018 Panini Victory Lane Black /1 #88
2018 Panini Victory Lane Black /1 #93
2018 Panini Victory Lane Black /1 #98
2018 Panini Victory Lane Blue /25 #53
2018 Panini Victory Lane Blue /25 #63
2018 Panini Victory Lane Blue /25 #67
2018 Panini Victory Lane Blue /25 #73
2018 Panini Victory Lane Blue /25 #88
2018 Panini Victory Lane Blue /25 #93
2018 Panini Victory Lane Blue /25 #98
2018 Panini Victory Lane Celebrations #4
2018 Panini Victory Lane Celebrations Black /1 #4
2018 Panini Victory Lane Celebrations Blue /25 #4
2018 Panini Victory Lane Celebrations Gold /99 #4
2018 Panini Victory Lane Celebrations Green /5 #4
2018 Panini Victory Lane Celebrations Printing Plates Black /1 #4
2018 Panini Victory Lane Celebrations Printing Plates Cyan /1 #4
2018 Panini Victory Lane Celebrations Printing Plates Magenta /1 #4
2018 Panini Victory Lane Celebrations Printing Plates Yellow /1 #4
2018 Panini Victory Lane Celebrations Red /49 #4
2018 Panini Victory Lane Chasing the Flag #2
2018 Panini Victory Lane Chasing the Flag Black /1 #2
2018 Panini Victory Lane Chasing the Flag Blue /25 #2
2018 Panini Victory Lane Chasing the Flag Gold /99 #2
2018 Panini Victory Lane Chasing the Flag Green /5 #2
2018 Panini Victory Lane Chasing the Flag Printing Plates Black /1 #2
2018 Panini Victory Lane Chasing the Flag Printing Plates Cyan /1 #2
2018 Panini Victory Lane Chasing the Flag Printing Plates Magenta /1 #2
2018 Panini Victory Lane Chasing the Flag Printing Plates Yellow /1 #2
2018 Panini Victory Lane Chasing the Flag Red /49 #2
2018 Panini Victory Lane Foundations #1
2018 Panini Victory Lane Foundations Black /1 #1
2018 Panini Victory Lane Foundations Blue /25 #1
2018 Panini Victory Lane Foundations Gold /99 #1
2018 Panini Victory Lane Foundations Green /5 #1
2018 Panini Victory Lane Foundations Printing Plates Black /1 #1
2018 Panini Victory Lane Foundations Printing Plates Cyan /1 #1
2018 Panini Victory Lane Foundations Printing Plates Magenta /1 #1
2018 Panini Victory Lane Foundations Printing Plates Yellow /1 #1
2018 Panini Victory Lane Foundations Red /49 #1
2018 Panini Victory Lane Gold /99 #53
2018 Panini Victory Lane Gold /99 #63
2018 Panini Victory Lane Gold /99 #67
2018 Panini Victory Lane Gold /99 #73
2018 Panini Victory Lane Gold /99 #88
2018 Panini Victory Lane Gold /99 #93
2018 Panini Victory Lane Gold /99 #98
2018 Panini Victory Lane Green /5 #53
2018 Panini Victory Lane Green /5 #63
2018 Panini Victory Lane Green /5 #67
2018 Panini Victory Lane Green /5 #73
2018 Panini Victory Lane Green /5 #88
2018 Panini Victory Lane Green /5 #93
2018 Panini Victory Lane Green /5 #98
2018 Panini Victory Lane NASCAR at 70 #10
2018 Panini Victory Lane NASCAR at 70 Black /1 #10
2018 Panini Victory Lane NASCAR at 70 Blue /25 #10
2018 Panini Victory Lane NASCAR at 70 Gold /99 #10
2018 Panini Victory Lane NASCAR at 70 Green /5 #10
2018 Panini Victory Lane NASCAR at 70 Printing Plates Black /1 #10
2018 Panini Victory Lane NASCAR at 70 Printing Plates Cyan /1 #10
2018 Panini Victory Lane NASCAR at 70 Printing Plates Magenta /1 #10
2018 Panini Victory Lane NASCAR at 70 Printing Plates Yellow /1 #10
2018 Panini Victory Lane NASCAR at 70 Red /49 #10
2018 Panini Victory Lane Octane Autographs Black /1 #9
2018 Panini Victory Lane Octane Autographs Gold /5 #9
2018 Panini Victory Lane Pedal to the Metal #14
2018 Panini Victory Lane Pedal to the Metal #75
2018 Panini Victory Lane Pedal to the Metal Black /1 #14
2018 Panini Victory Lane Pedal to the Metal Black /1 #75
2018 Panini Victory Lane Pedal to the Metal Blue /25 #14
2018 Panini Victory Lane Pedal to the Metal Blue /25 #75
2018 Panini Victory Lane Pedal to the Metal Green /5 #14
2018 Panini Victory Lane Pedal to the Metal Green /5 #75
2018 Panini Victory Lane Printing Plates Black /1 #53
2018 Panini Victory Lane Printing Plates Black /1 #63
2018 Panini Victory Lane Printing Plates Black /1 #67
2018 Panini Victory Lane Printing Plates Black /1 #73
2018 Panini Victory Lane Printing Plates Black /1 #88
2018 Panini Victory Lane Printing Plates Black /1 #93
2018 Panini Victory Lane Printing Plates Black /1 #98
2018 Panini Victory Lane Printing Plates Cyan /1 #53
2018 Panini Victory Lane Printing Plates Cyan /1 #63
2018 Panini Victory Lane Printing Plates Cyan /1 #67
2018 Panini Victory Lane Printing Plates Cyan /1 #73
2018 Panini Victory Lane Printing Plates Cyan /1 #88
2018 Panini Victory Lane Printing Plates Cyan /1 #93
2018 Panini Victory Lane Printing Plates Cyan /1 #98
2018 Panini Victory Lane Printing Plates Magenta /1 #53
2018 Panini Victory Lane Printing Plates Magenta /1 #63
2018 Panini Victory Lane Printing Plates Magenta /1 #67
2018 Panini Victory Lane Printing Plates Magenta /1 #73
2018 Panini Victory Lane Printing Plates Magenta /1 #88
2018 Panini Victory Lane Printing Plates Magenta /1 #93
2018 Panini Victory Lane Printing Plates Magenta /1 #98
2018 Panini Victory Lane Printing Plates Yellow /1 #53
2018 Panini Victory Lane Printing Plates Yellow /1 #63
2018 Panini Victory Lane Printing Plates Yellow /1 #67
2018 Panini Victory Lane Printing Plates Yellow /1 #73
2018 Panini Victory Lane Printing Plates Yellow /1 #88
2018 Panini Victory Lane Printing Plates Yellow /1 #93
2018 Panini Victory Lane Printing Plates Yellow /1 #98
2018 Panini Victory Lane Race Day #10
2018 Panini Victory Lane Race Day Black /1 #10
2018 Panini Victory Lane Race Day Blue /25 #10
2018 Panini Victory Lane Race Day Gold /99 #10
2018 Panini Victory Lane Race Day Green /5 #10
2018 Panini Victory Lane Race Day Printing Plates Black /1 #10
2018 Panini Victory Lane Race Day Printing Plates Cyan /1 #10
2018 Panini Victory Lane Race Day Printing Plates Magenta /1 #10
2018 Panini Victory Lane Race Day Printing Plates Yellow /1 #10
2018 Panini Victory Lane Race Day Red /49 #10
2018 Panini Victory Lane Race Ready Dual Materials /399 #4
2018 Panini Victory Lane Race Ready Dual Materials Black /25 #4
2018 Panini Victory Lane Race Ready Dual Materials Gold /199 #4
2018 Panini Victory Lane Race Ready Dual Materials Green /99 #4
2018 Panini Victory Lane Race Ready Dual Materials Laundry Tag /1 #4
2018 Panini Victory Lane Race Ready Materials /399 #8
2018 Panini Victory Lane Race Ready Materials Black /25 #8
2018 Panini Victory Lane Race Ready Materials Gold /199 #8
2018 Panini Victory Lane Race Ready Materials Green /99 #8
2018 Panini Victory Lane Race Ready Materials Laundry Tag /1 #8
2018 Panini Victory Lane Red /49 #53
2018 Panini Victory Lane Red /49 #63
2018 Panini Victory Lane Red /49 #67
2018 Panini Victory Lane Red /49 #73
2018 Panini Victory Lane Red /49 #88
2018 Panini Victory Lane Red /49 #93
2018 Panini Victory Lane Red /49 #98
2018 Panini Victory Lane Remarkable Remnants Material Autographs /70 #1
2018 Panini Victory Lane Remarkable Remnants Material Autographs Black /10 #1
2018 Panini Victory Lane Remarkable Remnants Material Autographs Gold /50 #1
2018 Panini Victory Lane Remarkable Remnants Material Autographs Green /25 #1
2018 Panini Victory Lane Remarkable Remnants Material Autographs Laundry Tag /1 #1
2018 Panini Victory Lane Silver #53
2018 Panini Victory Lane Silver #63
2018 Panini Victory Lane Silver #67
2018 Panini Victory Lane Silver #73
2018 Panini Victory Lane Silver #88
2018 Panini Victory Lane Silver #93
2018 Panini Victory Lane Silver #98
2018 Panini Victory Lane Victory Lane Prime Patches Associate Sponsor 1 /1 #5
2018 Panini Victory Lane Victory Lane Prime Patches Associate Sponsor 10 /1 #5
2018 Panini Victory Lane Victory Lane Prime Patches Associate Sponsor 2 /1 #5
2018 Panini Victory Lane Victory Lane Prime Patches Associate Sponsor 3 /1 #5
2018 Panini Victory Lane Victory Lane Prime Patches Associate Sponsor 4 /1 #5
2018 Panini Victory Lane Victory Lane Prime Patches Associate Sponsor 5 /1 #5
2018 Panini Victory Lane Victory Lane Prime Patches Associate Sponsor 6 /1 #5
2018 Panini Victory Lane Victory Lane Prime Patches Associate Sponsor 7 /1 #5
2018 Panini Victory Lane Victory Lane Prime Patches Associate Sponsor 8 /1 #5
2018 Panini Victory Lane Victory Lane Prime Patches Associate Sponsor 9 /1 #5
2018 Panini Victory Lane Victory Lane Prime Patches Car Manufacturer /1 #5
2018 Panini Victory Lane Victory Lane Prime Patches Firesuit Manufacturer /1 #5
2018 Panini Victory Lane Victory Lane Prime Patches Goodyear /2 #5
2018 Panini Victory Lane Victory Lane Prime Patches NASCAR /1 #5
2018 Panini Victory Lane Victory Lane Prime Patches Series Sponsor /1 #5
2018 Panini Victory Lane Victory Lane Prime Patches Sunoco /1 #5
2018 Panini Victory Lane Victory Marks Black /1 #3
2018 Panini Victory Lane Victory Marks Gold /5 #3
2018 The Bar /1 #NNO

Dale Earnhardt Jr.

1993 Action Packed #139
1993 Maxx #274
1993 Maxx Premier Plus #189
1993 Maxx Premier Series #274
1994 Press Pass Optima XL #46
1994 Press Pass Optima XL Red Hot #46
1994 Wheels High Gear #180
1994 Wheels High Gear #183
1994 Wheels High Gear Day One #180
1994 Wheels High Gear Day One #183
1994 Wheels High Gear Day One Gold #180
1994 Wheels High Gear Day One Gold #183
1994 Wheels High Gear Gold #180
1994 Wheels High Gear Gold #183
1995 Action Packed Sundrop Dale Earnhardt #SD3
1995 Western Steer Earnhardt Next Generation #3
1995 Western Steer Earnhardt Next Generation #JUM
1998 Maxx 10th Anniversary #34
1998 Maxx 10th Anniversary #79
1998 Maxx 10th Anniversary #97
1998 Maximum #53
1998 Maximum #78
1998 Press Pass #46
1998 Press Pass Oil Slicks /100 #46
1998 Press Pass Premium #12
1998 Press Pass Premium Reflectors #12
1998 Press Pass Signings #39
1998 Press Pass Stealth #37
1998 Press Pass Stealth #60
1998 Press Pass Stealth Fusion #37
1998 Press Pass Stealth Fusion #60
1998 Press Pass Stealth Stars #3
1998 Press Pass Stealth Stars Die Cuts #3
1998 Upper Deck Road To The Cup #83
1998 Upper Deck Road To The Cup #94
1998 VIP #28
1998 VIP Explosives #28
1998 VIP Solos #28
1998 Wheels #47
1998 Wheels #60
1998 Wheels Golden #47
1998 Wheels Golden #60
1999 Maxx #19
1999 Maxx #20
1999 Maxx #21
1999 Maxx FANtastic Finishes #F15
1999 Maxx Focus on a Champion #FC3
1999 Maxx Focus on a Champion Gold #FC3
1999 Maxx Race Ticket #RT4
1999 Maxx Racer's Ink #DE
1999 Maxx Racing Images #RI28
1999 Press Pass #37
1999 Press Pass #58
1999 Press Pass #73
1999 Press Pass Autographs /250 #4
1999 Press Pass Premium #41
1999 Press Pass Premium #P1
1999 Press Pass Premium Badge of Honor #BH2
1999 Press Pass Premium Badge of Honor #BH26
1999 Press Pass Premium Badge of Honor Reflectors #BH2
1999 Press Pass Premium Badge of Honor Reflectors #BH26
1999 Press Pass Premium Burning Desire #FD2B
1999 Press Pass Premium Reflectors /1975 #R41
1999 Press Pass Premium Steel Horses #SH6
1999 Press Pass Showman #7A
1999 Press Pass Showman #P1
1999 Press Pass Signings /875 #15A
1999 Press Pass Signings Gold /85 #4A
1999 Press Pass Signings Gold /125 #4B
1999 Press Pass Skidmarks /250 #37
1999 Press Pass Skidmarks /250 #58
1999 Press Pass Skidmarks /250 #73
1999 Press Pass Stealth #39
1999 Press Pass Stealth Big Numbers #BN4
1999 Press Pass Stealth Big Numbers #BN5
1999 Press Pass Stealth Big Numbers Die Cuts #BN4
1999 Press Pass Stealth Big Numbers Die Cuts #BN5
1999 Press Pass Stealth Fusion #F39
1999 Press Pass Stealth Headlines #SH3
1999 Press Pass Stealth Headlines #SH7
1999 Press Pass Stealth Octane SLX #O4
1999 Press Pass Stealth Octane SLX #O5
1999 Press Pass Stealth Octane SLX #O24
1999 Press Pass Stealth Octane SLX #O25
1999 Press Pass Stealth Octane SLX Die Cuts #O4
1999 Press Pass Stealth Octane SLX Die Cuts #O5
1999 Press Pass Stealth Octane SLX Die Cuts #O24
1999 Press Pass Stealth Octane SLX Die Cuts #O25
1999 Press Pass Stealth SST Cars #SS1
1999 Press Pass Stealth SST Drivers #SS1
1999 SP Authentic #30
1999 SP Authentic #37
1999 SP Authentic #66
1999 SP Authentic #72
1999 SP Authentic /500 #83
1999 SP Authentic Driving Force #DF9
1999 SP Authentic In the Driver's Seat #DS7
1999 SP Authentic Overdrive #30
1999 SP Authentic Overdrive #37
1999 SP Authentic Overdrive #66
1999 SP Authentic Overdrive #72
1999 SP Authentic Overdrive /3 #83
1999 SP Authentic Sign of the Times #DEJ
1999 Upper Deck MVP ProSign #JR
1999 Upper Deck Road to the Cup #30
1999 Upper Deck Road to the Cup #37
1999 Upper Deck Road to the Cup #67
1999 Upper Deck Road to the Cup #90
1999 Upper Deck Road to the Cup NASCAR Chronicles #NC14
1999 Upper Deck Road to the Cup Road to the Cup Bronze Level 1 #RTTC10
1999 Upper Deck Road to the Cup Road to the Cup Gold Level 3 #RTTC10
1999 Upper Deck Road to the Cup Road to the Cup Silver Level 2 #RTTC10
1999 Upper Deck Road to the Cup Signature Collection #DEJR
1999 Upper Deck Road to the Cup Signature Collection Checkered Flag #DEJR
1999 Upper Deck Road to the Cup Upper Deck Profiles #P10
1999 Upper Deck Victory Circle #14
1999 Upper Deck Victory Circle #50
1999 Upper Deck Victory Circle #85
1999 Upper Deck Victory Circle Income Statement #IS15
1999 Upper Deck Victory Circle Signature Collection #DEJ
1999 Upper Deck Victory Circle Speed Zone #SZ10
1999 Upper Deck Victory Circle Track Masters #TM15
1999 Upper Deck Victory Circle UD Exclusives #14
1999 Upper Deck Victory Circle UD Exclusives #50
1999 Upper Deck Victory Circle UD Exclusives #85
1999 VIP #30
1999 VIP Double Take #DT4
1999 VIP Explosives #X30
1999 VIP Explosives Lasers #30
1999 VIP Head Gear #HG4
1999 VIP Head Gear Plastic #HG4
1999 VIP Head Gear Plastic #HG10
1999 VIP Lap Leaders #LL4
1999 VIP Out of the Box #OB4
1999 VIP Rear View Mirror #RM4
1999 Wheels #39
1999 Wheels #65
1999 Wheels #96
1999 Wheels Autographs /75 #6
1999 Wheels Custom Shop #CS3
1999 Wheels Custom Shop Prizes #DEA1
1999 Wheels Custom Shop Prizes #DEA2
1999 Wheels Custom Shop Prizes #DEA3
1999 Wheels Custom Shop Prizes #DEB1
1999 Wheels Custom Shop Prizes #DEB2
1999 Wheels Custom Shop Prizes #DEB3
1999 Wheels Custom Shop Prizes #43070
1999 Wheels Custom Shop Prizes #43071
1999 Wheels Custom Shop Prizes #43072
1999 Wheels Dialed In #DI4
1999 Wheels Golden #39
1999 Wheels Golden #65
1999 Wheels Golden #96
1999 Wheels High Gear #37
1999 Wheels High Gear Autographs /350 #7
1999 Wheels High Gear Custom Shop #CSJR
1999 Wheels High Gear Custom Shop Prizes #JRA1
1999 Wheels High Gear Custom Shop Prizes #JRA2
1999 Wheels High Gear Custom Shop Prizes #JRA2
1999 Wheels High Gear Custom Shop Prizes #JRB1
1999 Wheels High Gear Custom Shop Prizes #JRB2
1999 Wheels High Gear Custom Shop Prizes #JRB3
1999 Wheels High Gear Custom Shop Prizes #JRC1
1999 Wheels High Gear Custom Shop Prizes #JRC2
1999 Wheels High Gear Custom Shop Prizes #JRC3
1999 Wheels High Gear First Gear #37
1999 Wheels High Gear MPH #37
1999 Wheels Runnin and Gunnin #RG13
1999 Wheels Runnin and Gunnin Foils #RG13
1999 Wheels Solos #39
1999 Wheels Solos #65
1999 Wheels Solos #96
2000 Maxx #8
2000 Maxx #48
2000 Maxx Fantastic Finishes #FF2
2000 Maxx Racer's Ink #JR
2000 Maxx Speedway Boogie #SB5
2000 Maximum #31
2000 Maximum Cruise Control #CC5
2000 Maximum Die Cuts /250 #31
2000 Maximum MPH /8 #31
2000 Maximum Signatures #DE2
2000 Press Pass #39
2000 Press Pass #46
2000 Press Pass #62
2000 Press Pass #70
2000 Press Pass #85
2000 Press Pass #93
2000 Press Pass Burning Rubber /200 #BR9
2000 Press Pass Cup Chase #CC5
2000 Press Pass Cup Chase Die Cut Prizes #CC5
2000 Press Pass Millennium #39
2000 Press Pass Millennium #46
2000 Press Pass Millennium #62
2000 Press Pass Millennium #70
2000 Press Pass Millennium #85
2000 Press Pass Millennium #93
2000 Press Pass Optima #6
2000 Press Pass Optima #43
2000 Press Pass Optima Cool Persistence #CP1
2000 Press Pass Optima Encore #EN4
2000 Press Pass Optima G Force #GF6
2000 Press Pass Optima On the Edge #OE2
2000 Press Pass Optima Platinum #6
2000 Press Pass Optima Platinum #43
2000 Press Pass Optima Race Used Lugnuts Cars /50 #LC16
2000 Press Pass Optima Race Used Lugnuts Drivers /55 #LD16
2000 Press Pass Pitstop #PS17
2000 Press Pass Premium #43
2000 Press Pass Premium #53
2000 Press Pass Premium #66
2000 Press Pass Premium In The Zone #IZ9
2000 Press Pass Premium Performance Driven #PD4
2000 Press Pass Premium Race Used Firesuit /130 #F1
2000 Press Pass Premium Reflectors #43
2000 Press Pass Premium Reflectors #53
2000 Press Pass Premium Reflectors #66
2000 Press Pass Showcar #SC4
2000 Press Pass Showcar Die Cuts #SC4
2000 Press Pass Showman #SM4
2000 Press Pass Showman #SM5
2000 Press Pass Showman Die Cuts #SM4
2000 Press Pass Showman Die Cuts #SM5
2000 Press Pass Signings #15
2000 Press Pass Signings Gold /100 #10
2000 Press Pass Skidmarks #SK9
2000 Press Pass Stealth #16
2000 Press Pass Stealth #17
2000 Press Pass Stealth #70
2000 Press Pass Stealth Behind the Numbers #BN2
2000 Press Pass Stealth Fusion #FS16
2000 Press Pass Stealth Fusion #FS17
2000 Press Pass Stealth Fusion #FS18
2000 Press Pass Stealth Fusion Green /1000 #FS16
2000 Press Pass Stealth Fusion Green /1000 #FS17
2000 Press Pass Stealth Fusion Green /1000 #FS18
2000 Press Pass Stealth Fusion Red #FS16
2000 Press Pass Stealth Fusion Red #FS17
2000 Press Pass Stealth Fusion Red #FS18
2000 Press Pass Stealth Intensity #IN9
2000 Press Pass Stealth Profile #PR8
2000 Press Pass Stealth Race Used Gloves /50 #G8
2000 Press Pass Stealth SST #SST12
2000 Press Pass Techno-Retro #TR7
2000 Press Pass Trackside #6
2000 Press Pass Trackside #29
2000 Press Pass Trackside Dialed In #DI12
2000 Press Pass Trackside Die Cuts #6
2000 Press Pass Trackside Die Cuts #29
2000 Press Pass Trackside Generation.now #GN2
2000 Press Pass Trackside Golden #6
2000 Press Pass Trackside Golden #29
2000 Press Pass Trackside Pit Stoppers /200 #PS13
2000 Press Pass Trackside Runnin N' Gunnin #RG2
2000 Press Pass Trackside Too Tough To Tame #TT9
2000 SP Authentic #19
2000 SP Authentic /1000 #89
2000 SP Authentic Dominance #D2
2000 SP Authentic Overdrive Gold /8 #19
2000 SP Authentic Overdrive Gold /8 #89
2000 SP Authentic Overdrive Silver /250 #19
2000 SP Authentic Overdrive Silver /250 #89
2000 SP Authentic Power Surge #PS4
2000 SP Authentic Sign of the Times #JR
2000 SP Authentic Sign of the Times Gold /25 #JR
2000 Upper Deck MVP #93
2000 Upper Deck MVP #98
2000 Upper Deck MVP Cup Quest 2000 #CQ2
2000 Upper Deck MVP Gold Script /125 #93
2000 Upper Deck MVP Gold Script /125 #98
2000 Upper Deck MVP Legends in the Making #LM5
2000 Upper Deck MVP NASCAR Gallery #NG5
2000 Upper Deck MVP NASCAR Stars #NS11
2000 Upper Deck MVP ProSign #PSJR
2000 Upper Deck MVP Silver Script #93
2000 Upper Deck MVP Silver Script #98
2000 Upper Deck MVP Super Script /3 #93
2000 Upper Deck MVP Super Script /8 #98
2000 Upper Deck Racing #31
2000 Upper Deck Racing Dale Earnhardt Jr. Tribute #DEJ1
2000 Upper Deck Racing Dale Earnhardt Jr. Tribute #DEJ2
2000 Upper Deck Racing Dale Earnhardt Jr. Tribute #DEJ3
2000 Upper Deck Racing Dale Earnhardt Jr. Tribute #DEJ4
2000 Upper Deck Racing Dale Earnhardt Jr. Tribute #DEJ5
2000 Upper Deck Racing Dale Earnhardt Jr. Tribute #DEJ6
2000 Upper Deck Racing Dale Earnhardt Jr. Tribute #DEJ7
2000 Upper Deck Racing Dale Earnhardt Jr. Tribute #DEJ8
2000 Upper Deck Racing Dale Earnhardt Jr. Tribute #DEJ9
2000 Upper Deck Racing Dale Earnhardt Jr. Tribute #DEJ10
2000 Upper Deck Racing Dale Earnhardt Jr. Tribute #DEJ11
2000 Upper Deck Racing Dale Earnhardt Jr. Tribute #DEJ12
2000 Upper Deck Racing Dale Earnhardt Jr. Tribute #DEJ13
2000 Upper Deck Racing Dale Earnhardt Jr. Tribute #DEJ14
2000 Upper Deck Racing Dale Earnhardt Jr. Tribute #DEJ15
2000 Upper Deck Racing Dale Earnhardt Jr. Tribute #DEJ16
2000 Upper Deck Racing Dale Earnhardt Jr. Tribute #DEJ17
2000 Upper Deck Racing Dale Earnhardt Jr. Tribute #DEJ18
2000 Upper Deck Racing Dale Earnhardt Jr. Tribute #DEJ19
2000 Upper Deck Racing Dale Earnhardt Jr. Tribute #DEJ20
2000 Upper Deck Racing Dale Earnhardt Jr. Tribute #DEJ21
2000 Upper Deck Racing Dale Earnhardt Jr. Tribute #DEJ22
2000 Upper Deck Racing Dale Earnhardt Jr. Tribute #DEJ23
2000 Upper Deck Racing Dale Earnhardt Jr. Tribute #DEJ24
2000 Upper Deck Racing Dale Earnhardt Jr. Tribute #DEJ25
2000 Upper Deck Racing High Groove #HG2
2000 Upper Deck Racing Record Pace #RP6
2000 Upper Deck Racing Road Signs #RSJR
2000 Upper Deck Racing Speeding Ticket #ST3
2000 Upper Deck Racing Trophy Dash #TD2
2000 Upper Deck Victory Circle #37
2000 Upper Deck Victory Circle #56
2000 Upper Deck Victory Circle #78
2000 Upper Deck Victory Circle A Day in the Life #JR1
2000 Upper Deck Victory Circle A Day in the Life #JR2
2000 Upper Deck Victory Circle A Day in the Life #JR3
2000 Upper Deck Victory Circle A Day in the Life #JR4
2000 Upper Deck Victory Circle A Day in the Life #JR5
2000 Upper Deck Victory Circle A Day in the Life #JR6
2000 Upper Deck Victory Circle A Day in the Life LTD #JR1
2000 Upper Deck Victory Circle A Day in the Life LTD #JR2
2000 Upper Deck Victory Circle A Day in the Life LTD #JR3
2000 Upper Deck Victory Circle A Day in the Life LTD #JR4
2000 Upper Deck Victory Circle A Day in the Life LTD #JR5
2000 Upper Deck Victory Circle A Day in the Life LTD #JR6
2000 Upper Deck Victory Circle Exclusives Level 1 Silver /250 #37
2000 Upper Deck Victory Circle Exclusives Level 1 Silver /250 #56
2000 Upper Deck Victory Circle Exclusives Level 1 Silver /250 #78
2000 Upper Deck Victory Circle Exclusives Level 2 Gold /8 #37
2000 Upper Deck Victory Circle Exclusives Level 2 Gold /8 #56
2000 Upper Deck Victory Circle Exclusives Level 2 Gold /8 #78
2000 Upper Deck Victory Circle PowerDeck #PD2
2000 Upper Deck Victory Circle PowerDeck #PD6
2000 Upper Deck Victory Circle Victory Circle #V9
2000 Upper Deck Victory Circle Victory Circle LTD #V9
2000 Upper Deck Victory Circle Winning Material Tire #TJR
2000 VIP #17
2000 VIP #24
2000 VIP #P1
2000 VIP Explosives #X17
2000 VIP Explosives #X24
2000 VIP Explosives Lasers #LX17
2000 VIP Explosives Lasers #LX24
2000 VIP Head Gear #HG4
2000 VIP Head Gear Explosives #HG4
2000 VIP Head Gear Explosives Laser Die Cuts #HG4
2000 VIP Making the Show #MS4
2000 VIP Rear View Mirror #RM4
2000 VIP Rear View Mirror Explosives #RM4
2000 VIP Rear View Mirror Explosives Laser Die Cuts #RM4
2000 VIP Sheet Metal #SM7
2000 VIP Sheet Metal #SM10
2000 VIP Under the Lights #UL4
2000 VIP Under the Lights Explosives #UL4
2000 VIP Under the Lights Explosives Lasers #UL4
2000 Wheels High Gear #37
2000 Wheels High Gear #65
2000 Wheels High Gear Autographs #10
2000 Wheels High Gear Custom Shop #CSDE
2000 Wheels High Gear Custom Shop Prizes #DEA1
2000 Wheels High Gear Custom Shop Prizes #DEA2
2000 Wheels High Gear Custom Shop Prizes #DEA3
2000 Wheels High Gear Custom Shop Prizes #DEB1
2000 Wheels High Gear Custom Shop Prizes #DEB2
2000 Wheels High Gear Custom Shop Prizes #DEB3
2000 Wheels High Gear Custom Shop Prizes #43070
2000 Wheels High Gear Custom Shop Prizes #43071
2000 Wheels High Gear Custom Shop Prizes #43072
2000 Wheels High Gear First Gear #37
2000 Wheels High Gear First Gear #65
2000 Wheels High Gear Gear Shifters #GS23
2000 Wheels High Gear Man and Machine Cars #MM2B
2000 Wheels High Gear Man and Machine Drivers #MM2A
2000 Wheels High Gear MPH #37
2000 Wheels High Gear MPH #65
2000 Wheels High Gear Winning Edge #WE9
2001 Bud All-Star Promos #DEJ
2001 Gold Collectibles Dale Earnhardt Jr. #1
2001 Gold Collectibles Dale Earnhardt Jr. #2
2001 Gold Collectibles Dale Earnhardt Jr. #3
2001 Gold Collectibles Dale Earnhardt Jr. #4
2001 Press Pass #15
2001 Press Pass #64
2001 Press Pass #89
2001 Press Pass Autographs #12
2001 Press Pass Burning Rubber Cars /105 #BRC8
2001 Press Pass Burning Rubber Drivers /90 #BRD8
2001 Press Pass Cup Chase #CC7
2001 Press Pass Cup Chase Die Cut Prizes #CC7
2001 Press Pass Double Burner /100 #DB8
2001 Press Pass Ground Zero #GZ8
2001 Press Pass Hot Treads /2405 #HT16
2001 Press Pass Millennium #15
2001 Press Pass Millennium #64
2001 Press Pass Millennium #89
2001 Press Pass Optima #5
2001 Press Pass Optima #41
2001 Press Pass Optima Cool Persistence #CP3
2001 Press Pass Optima G Force #GF4
2001 Press Pass Optima Gold #5
2001 Press Pass Optima Gold #41
2001 Press Pass Optima On the Edge #OE1
2001 Press Pass Optima Race Used Lugnuts Cars /115 #LNC4
2001 Press Pass Optima Race Used Lugnuts Drivers /100 #LND3
2001 Press Pass Optima Up Close #UC1
2001 Press Pass Premium #5
2001 Press Pass Premium #32
2001 Press Pass Premium #59
2001 Press Pass Premium #72
2001 Press Pass Premium Gold #5
2001 Press Pass Premium Gold #32
2001 Press Pass Premium Gold #59
2001 Press Pass Premium Gold #72
2001 Press Pass Premium In The Zone #IZ2
2001 Press Pass Premium Performance Driven #PD2
2001 Press Pass Premium Race Used Firesuit Cars /110 #FC0
2001 Press Pass Premium Race Used Firesuit Drivers /100 #FD0
2001 Press Pass Showman/Showcar #S8A
2001 Press Pass Showman/Showcar #S8B
2001 Press Pass Signings #12
2001 Press Pass Signings Gold /50 #11
2001 Press Pass Signings Transparent /100 #3
2001 Press Pass Stealth #13
2001 Press Pass Stealth #14
2001 Press Pass Stealth #15
2001 Press Pass Stealth #66
2001 Press Pass Stealth Fusion #F1
2001 Press Pass Stealth Holofoils #13
2001 Press Pass Stealth Holofoils #14
2001 Press Pass Stealth Holofoils #15
2001 Press Pass Stealth Holofoils #66
2001 Press Pass Stealth Lap Leaders #LL4
2001 Press Pass Stealth Lap Leaders #LL22
2001 Press Pass Stealth Lap Leaders Clear Cars #LL22
2001 Press Pass Stealth Lap Leaders Clear Drivers #LL4
2001 Press Pass Stealth Profile #PR6
2001 Press Pass Stealth Race Used Glove Cars /50 #RGC8
2001 Press Pass Stealth Race Used Glove Drivers /50 #RGD8
2001 Press Pass Total Memorabilia Power Pick #TM8
2001 Press Pass Trackside #1
2001 Press Pass Trackside #43
2001 Press Pass Trackside Dialed In #D8
2001 Press Pass Trackside Die Cuts #1
2001 Press Pass Trackside Die Cuts #43
2001 Press Pass Trackside Golden #1
2001 Press Pass Trackside Golden #43
2001 Press Pass Trackside Mirror Image #MI8
2001 Press Pass Trackside Pit Stoppers Cars /250 #PSC1
2001 Press Pass Trackside Pit Stoppers Drivers /100 #PSD1
2001 Press Pass Trackside Runnin N' Gunnin #RG2
2001 Press Pass Triple Burner /100 #TB8
2001 Press Pass Velocity #VL8
2001 Press Pass Vintage #VN15
2001 VIP #17
2001 VIP #45
2001 VIP Driver's Choice #DC4
2001 VIP Driver's Choice Precious Metal /100 #DC4
2001 VIP Driver's Choice Transparent #DC4
2001 VIP Explosives #17
2001 VIP Explosives #45
2001 VIP Explosives Lasers /420 #LX17
2001 VIP Explosives Lasers /420 #LX45
2001 VIP Head Gear #HG4
2001 VIP Head Gear Die Cuts #HG4
2001 VIP Making the Show #5
2001 VIP Mile Masters #MM4
2001 VIP Mile Masters Precious Metal /325 #MM4
2001 VIP Mile Masters Transparent #MM4
2001 VIP Rear View Mirror #RV4
2001 VIP Rear View Mirror Die Cuts #RV4
2001 VIP Sheet Metal Cars /120 #SC8
2001 VIP Sheet Metal Drivers /75 #SD8
2001 Wheels High Gear #13
2001 Wheels High Gear #56
2001 Wheels High Gear Autographs #9
2001 Wheels High Gear Custom Shop #CSDEJ
2001 Wheels High Gear Custom Shop Prizes #DEJA1
2001 Wheels High Gear Custom Shop Prizes #DEJA2
2001 Wheels High Gear Custom Shop Prizes #DEJA3
2001 Wheels High Gear Custom Shop Prizes #DEJB1
2001 Wheels High Gear Custom Shop Prizes #DEJB2
2001 Wheels High Gear Custom Shop Prizes #DEJB3
2001 Wheels High Gear Custom Shop Prizes #DEJC1
2001 Wheels High Gear Custom Shop Prizes #DEJC2
2001 Wheels High Gear Custom Shop Prizes #DEJC3
2001 Wheels High Gear First Gear #13
2001 Wheels High Gear First Gear #56
2001 Wheels High Gear Flag Chasers #FC5
2001 Wheels High Gear Flag Chasers Blue-Yellow /45 #FC5
2001 Wheels High Gear Flag Chasers Checkered /35 #FC5
2001 Wheels High Gear Flag Chasers Checkered Blue/Orange /45 #FC5
2001 Wheels High Gear Flag Chasers Green /75 #FC5
2001 Wheels High Gear Flag Chasers Power Pick #FCPP
2001 Wheels High Gear Flag Chasers Red /75 #FC5
2001 Wheels High Gear Flag Chasers White /75 #FC5
2001 Wheels High Gear Flag Chasers Yellow /75 #FC5
2001 Wheels High Gear Gear Shifters #GS14
2001 Wheels High Gear Hot Streaks #HS8
2001 Wheels High Gear Man and Machine Cars #MM7B
2001 Wheels High Gear Man and Machine Drivers #MM7A
2001 Wheels High Gear MPH #13
2001 Wheels High Gear MPH #56
2002 Press Pass #10
2002 Press Pass #75
2002 Press Pass #100
2002 Press Pass Autographs #17
2002 Press Pass Burning Rubber Cars /120 #BRC9
2002 Press Pass Burning Rubber Drivers /90 #BRD9
2002 Press Pass Cup Chase #CC3
2002 Press Pass Cup Chase Prizes #CC3
2002 Press Pass Dale Earnhardt Jr. Firesuit #NNO
2002 Press Pass Double Burner /100 #DB1
2002 Press Pass Eclipse #8
2002 Press Pass Eclipse #40
2002 Press Pass Eclipse Racing Champions #RC17
2002 Press Pass Eclipse Racing Champions #RC27
2002 Press Pass Eclipse Racing Champions #RC31
2002 Press Pass Eclipse Samples #8
2002 Press Pass Eclipse Samples #40
2002 Press Pass Eclipse Skidmarks #SK2
2002 Press Pass Eclipse Solar Eclipse #S8
2002 Press Pass Eclipse Solar Eclipse #S40
2002 Press Pass Eclipse Supernova #SN2
2002 Press Pass Eclipse Supernova Numbered /250 #SN2
2002 Press Pass Eclipse Under Cover Double Cover /625 #DC8
2002 Press Pass Eclipse Under Cover Drivers #CD12
2002 Press Pass Eclipse Under Cover Gold Cars /300 #CD12
2002 Press Pass Eclipse Under Cover Gold Drivers /400 #CD12
2002 Press Pass Eclipse Under Cover Holofoil Drivers /100 #CD12
2002 Press Pass Eclipse Warp Speed #WS2
2002 Press Pass Hot Treads /2375 #HT25
2002 Press Pass Nabisco Albertsons #1
2002 Press Pass Optima #7
2002 Press Pass Optima #45
2002 Press Pass Optima Cool Persistence #CP2
2002 Press Pass Optima Fan Favorite #FF6
2002 Press Pass Optima Gold #7
2002 Press Pass Optima Gold #45
2002 Press Pass Optima Promos /5 #7

2002 Press Pass Optima Promos /5 #45
2002 Press Pass Optima Q and A #QA2
2002 Press Pass Optima Race Used Lugnuts Cars /100 #LNC5
2002 Press Pass Optima Race Used Lugnuts Drivers /100 #LND5
2002 Press Pass Optima Samples #7
2002 Press Pass Optima Samples #45
2002 Press Pass Optima Up Close #UC6
2002 Press Pass Platinum #10
2002 Press Pass Platinum #75
2002 Press Pass Platinum #100
2002 Press Pass Premium #7
2002 Press Pass Premium #36
2002 Press Pass Premium #60
2002 Press Pass Premium #71
2002 Press Pass Premium In The Zone #IZ3
2002 Press Pass Premium Performance Driven #PD1
2002 Press Pass Premium Race Used Firesuit Cars /90 #FC12
2002 Press Pass Premium Race Used Firesuit Drivers /80 #FD12
2002 Press Pass Premium Red Reflectors #7
2002 Press Pass Premium Red Reflectors #36
2002 Press Pass Premium Red Reflectors #60
2002 Press Pass Premium Red Reflectors #71
2002 Press Pass Premium Samples #7
2002 Press Pass Premium Samples #36
2002 Press Pass Showcar #S2B
2002 Press Pass Showman #S2A
2002 Press Pass Signings #14
2002 Press Pass Signings Gold /50 #14
2002 Press Pass Signings Transparent /100 #1
2002 Press Pass Stealth #10
2002 Press Pass Stealth #11
2002 Press Pass Stealth #12
2002 Press Pass Stealth #55
2002 Press Pass Stealth #64
2002 Press Pass Stealth EFX #FX4
2002 Press Pass Stealth Fusion #F2
2002 Press Pass Stealth Gold #10
2002 Press Pass Stealth Gold #11
2002 Press Pass Stealth Gold #12
2002 Press Pass Stealth Gold #55
2002 Press Pass Stealth Gold #64
2002 Press Pass Stealth Lap Leaders #LL6
2002 Press Pass Stealth Race Used Glove Cars /85 #GLC7
2002 Press Pass Stealth Race Used Glove Drivers /50 #GLD7
2002 Press Pass Stealth Samples #10
2002 Press Pass Stealth Samples #11
2002 Press Pass Stealth Samples #12
2002 Press Pass Stealth Samples #55
2002 Press Pass Stealth Samples #64
2002 Press Pass Top Shelf #TS1
2002 Press Pass Total Memorabilia Power Pick #TM1
2002 Press Pass Trackside #1
2002 Press Pass Trackside #52
2002 Press Pass Trackside #67
2002 Press Pass Trackside #73
2002 Press Pass Trackside #90
2002 Press Pass Trackside Dialed In #DI2
2002 Press Pass Trackside Generation Now #GN3
2002 Press Pass Trackside Golden /50 #G1
2002 Press Pass Trackside License to Drive #8
2002 Press Pass Trackside License to Drive Die Cuts #8
2002 Press Pass Trackside Mirror Image #MI1
2002 Press Pass Trackside Pit Stoppers Cars /50 #PSC4
2002 Press Pass Trackside Pit Stoppers Drivers /50 #PSD4
2002 Press Pass Trackside Runnin N' Gunnin #RG1
2002 Press Pass Trackside Samples #1
2002 Press Pass Trackside Samples #52
2002 Press Pass Trackside Samples #67
2002 Press Pass Trackside Samples #73
2002 Press Pass Trackside Samples #90
2002 Press Pass Triple Burner /100 #TB1
2002 Press Pass Velocity #VL2
2002 Press Pass Vintage #VN6
2002 Sports Illustrated for Kids #126
2002 VIP #5
2002 VIP #26
2002 VIP #33
2002 VIP Driver's Choice #DC4
2002 VIP Driver's Choice Transparent #DC4
2002 VIP Driver's Choice Transparent LTD #DC4
2002 VIP Explosives #X5
2002 VIP Explosives #X26
2002 VIP Explosives #X33
2002 VIP Explosives Lasers #LX5
2002 VIP Explosives Lasers #LX26
2002 VIP Explosives Lasers #LX33
2002 VIP Head Gear #HG4
2002 VIP Head Gear Die Cuts #HG4
2002 VIP Making the Show #MS6
2002 VIP Mile Masters #MM4
2002 VIP Mile Masters Transparent #MM4
2002 VIP Mile Masters Transparent LTD #MM4
2002 VIP Race Used Sheet Metal Cars #SC15
2002 VIP Race Used Sheet Metal Drivers /130 #SD15
2002 VIP Samples #5
2002 VIP Samples #26
2002 VIP Samples #33
2002 Wheels High Gear #6
2002 Wheels High Gear #46
2002 Wheels High Gear #55
2002 Wheels High Gear Autographs #14
2002 Wheels High Gear First Gear #6
2002 Wheels High Gear First Gear #46
2002 Wheels High Gear First Gear #55
2002 Wheels High Gear Flag Chasers /130 #FC1
2002 Wheels High Gear Flag Chasers Black /90 #FC1
2002 Wheels High Gear Flag Chasers Blue-Yellow /40 #FC1
2002 Wheels High Gear Flag Chasers Checkered /35 #FC1
2002 Wheels High Gear Flag Chasers Checkered Blue/Orange /10 #FC1
2002 Wheels High Gear Flag Chasers Green /90 #FC1
2002 Wheels High Gear Flag Chasers Red /90 #FC1
2002 Wheels High Gear Flag Chasers Yellow /110 #FC1
2002 Wheels High Gear High Groove #HG6
2002 Wheels High Gear Hot Streaks #HS2
2002 Wheels High Gear Man and Machine Cars #MM1B
2002 Wheels High Gear Man and Machine Drivers #MM1A
2002 Wheels High Gear MPH /100 #6
2002 Wheels High Gear MPH /100 #46
2002 Wheels High Gear MPH /100 #55
2003 Nilla Wafers Team Nabisco #1
2003 Nilla Wafers Team Nabisco #2
2003 Nilla Wafers Team Nabisco #4
2003 Press Pass #9
2003 Press Pass #55
2003 Press Pass #63
2003 Press Pass #99
2003 Press Pass Burning Rubber Cars /60 #BRT10
2003 Press Pass Burning Rubber Drivers /50 #BRD10
2003 Press Pass Cup Chase #CCR3
2003 Press Pass Cup Chase Prizes #CCR3
2003 Press Pass Double Burner /100 #DB10
2003 Press Pass Double Burner Exchange /100 #DB10
2003 Press Pass Eclipse #11
2003 Press Pass Eclipse #30
2003 Press Pass Eclipse #40
2003 Press Pass Eclipse #49
2003 Press Pass Eclipse Double Hot Treads /999 #DT10
2003 Press Pass Eclipse Previews /5 #11
2003 Press Pass Eclipse Previews /5 #30
2003 Press Pass Eclipse Racing Champions #RC11
2003 Press Pass Eclipse Racing Champions #RC31
2003 Press Pass Eclipse Samples #11
2003 Press Pass Eclipse Samples #30
2003 Press Pass Eclipse Samples #40
2003 Press Pass Eclipse Samples #49
2003 Press Pass Eclipse Solar Eclipse #P11
2003 Press Pass Eclipse Solar Eclipse #P30
2003 Press Pass Eclipse Solar Eclipse #P40
2003 Press Pass Eclipse Solar Eclipse #P49
2003 Press Pass Eclipse Supernova #SN2
2003 Press Pass Eclipse Under Cover Cars /215 #UCT7
2003 Press Pass Eclipse Under Cover Driver Gold /260 #UCD7
2003 Press Pass Eclipse Under Cover Driver Red /100 #UCD7
2003 Press Pass Eclipse Under Cover Driver Silver /450 #UCD7
2003 Press Pass Eclipse Warp Speed #WS2
2003 Press Pass Gold Holofoil #P9
2003 Press Pass Gold Holofoil #P55
2003 Press Pass Gold Holofoil #P63
2003 Press Pass Gold Holofoil #P99
2003 Press Pass Nabisco Albertsons #1
2003 Press Pass Optima #6
2003 Press Pass Optima #40
2003 Press Pass Optima #46
2003 Press Pass Optima #47
2003 Press Pass Optima #48
2003 Press Pass Optima #49
2003 Press Pass Optima Cool Persistence #CP1
2003 Press Pass Optima Fan Favorite #FF6
2003 Press Pass Optima Gold #G6
2003 Press Pass Optima Gold #G40
2003 Press Pass Optima Gold #G46
2003 Press Pass Optima Gold #G47
2003 Press Pass Optima Gold #G48
2003 Press Pass Optima Gold #G49
2003 Press Pass Optima Previews /5 #6
2003 Press Pass Optima Samples #6
2003 Press Pass Optima Samples #40
2003 Press Pass Optima Samples #46
2003 Press Pass Optima Samples #47
2003 Press Pass Optima Samples #48
2003 Press Pass Optima Samples #49
2003 Press Pass Optima Thunder Bolts Cars /95 #TBT10
2003 Press Pass Optima Thunder Bolts Drivers /65 #TBD10
2003 Press Pass Optima Young Guns #YG1
2003 Press Pass Premium #7
2003 Press Pass Premium #36
2003 Press Pass Premium #46
2003 Press Pass Premium #48
2003 Press Pass Premium #50
2003 Press Pass Premium #59
2003 Press Pass Premium #70
2003 Press Pass Premium Hot Threads Cars /160 #HTT10
2003 Press Pass Premium Hot Threads Drivers /285 #HTD10
2003 Press Pass Premium In the Zone #IZ1
2003 Press Pass Premium Performance Driven #PD1
2003 Press Pass Premium Previews /5 #7
2003 Press Pass Premium Red Reflectors #7
2003 Press Pass Premium Red Reflectors #36
2003 Press Pass Premium Red Reflectors #46
2003 Press Pass Premium Red Reflectors #48
2003 Press Pass Premium Red Reflectors #50
2003 Press Pass Premium Red Reflectors #59
2003 Press Pass Premium Red Reflectors #70
2003 Press Pass Premium Samples #7
2003 Press Pass Premium Samples #36
2003 Press Pass Premium Samples #46
2003 Press Pass Premium Samples #48
2003 Press Pass Premium Samples #50
2003 Press Pass Previews /5 #9
2003 Press Pass Race Exclusives #9
2003 Press Pass Samples #9
2003 Press Pass Samples #55
2003 Press Pass Samples #63
2003 Press Pass Samples #99
2003 Press Pass Signings #17
2003 Press Pass Signings Gold /50 #17
2003 Press Pass Stealth #10
2003 Press Pass Stealth #11
2003 Press Pass Stealth #12
2003 Press Pass Stealth #57
2003 Press Pass Stealth #72
2003 Press Pass Stealth EFX #FX3
2003 Press Pass Stealth Fusion #FU3
2003 Press Pass Stealth Gear Grippers Cars /150 #GGT10
2003 Press Pass Stealth Gear Grippers Drivers /75 #GGD10
2003 Press Pass Stealth No Boundaries #NB11
2003 Press Pass Stealth Previews /5 #10
2003 Press Pass Stealth Previews /5 #11
2003 Press Pass Stealth Previews /5 #12
2003 Press Pass Stealth Profile #PR1
2003 Press Pass Stealth Red #P10
2003 Press Pass Stealth Red #P11
2003 Press Pass Stealth Red #P12
2003 Press Pass Stealth Red #P57
2003 Press Pass Stealth Red #P72
2003 Press Pass Stealth Samples #10
2003 Press Pass Stealth Samples #11
2003 Press Pass Stealth Samples #12
2003 Press Pass Stealth Samples #57
2003 Press Pass Stealth Samples #72
2003 Press Pass Stealth Supercharged #SC3
2003 Press Pass Top Shelf #TS1
2003 Press Pass Total Memorabilia Power Pick #TM10
2003 Press Pass Trackside #19
2003 Press Pass Trackside #62
2003 Press Pass Trackside Gold Holofoil #P19
2003 Press Pass Trackside Gold Holofoil #P62
2003 Press Pass Trackside Golden /50 #G19
2003 Press Pass Trackside Hot Pursuit #HP2
2003 Press Pass Trackside Mirror Image #MI2
2003 Press Pass Trackside Pit Stoppers Cars /175 #PST18
2003 Press Pass Trackside Pit Stoppers Drivers /100 #PSD18
2003 Press Pass Trackside Previews /5 #19
2003 Press Pass Trackside Runnin n' Gunnin #RG2
2003 Press Pass Trackside Samples #19
2003 Press Pass Trackside Samples #62
2003 Press Pass Triple Burner /100 #TB10
2003 Press Pass Triple Burner Exchange /100 #TB10
2003 VIP #4
2003 VIP #26
2003 VIP #31
2003 VIP Driver's Choice #DC2
2003 VIP Driver's Choice Die Cuts #DC2
2003 VIP Driver's Choice National #DC2
2003 VIP Explosives #X4
2003 VIP Explosives #X26
2003 VIP Explosives #X31
2003 VIP Head Gear #HG2
2003 VIP Head Gear Die Cuts #HG2
2003 VIP Head Gear National #HG2
2003 VIP Lap Leaders #LL2
2003 VIP Lap Leaders National #LL2
2003 VIP Lap Leaders Transparent #LL2
2003 VIP Lap Leaders Transparent LTD #LL2
2003 VIP Laser Explosive #LX4
2003 VIP Laser Explosive #LX26
2003 VIP Laser Explosive #LX31
2003 VIP Making the Show #MS4
2003 VIP Mile Masters #MM2
2003 VIP Mile Masters National #MM2
2003 VIP Mile Masters Transparent #MM2
2003 VIP Mile Masters Transparent LTD #MM2
2003 VIP Previews /5 #4
2003 VIP Previews /5 #26
2003 VIP Previews /5 #31
2003 VIP Samples #4
2003 VIP Samples #26
2003 VIP Samples #31
2003 VIP Tin #CT4
2003 VIP Tin #CT26
2003 VIP Tin #CT31
2003 VIP Tradin' Paint Cars /160 #TPT10
2003 VIP Tradin' Paint Drivers /110 #TPD10
2003 Wheels American Thunder #5
2003 Wheels American Thunder #37
2003 Wheels American Thunder #46
2003 Wheels American Thunder American Muscle #AM1
2003 Wheels American Thunder Born On /100 #BO5
2003 Wheels American Thunder Born On /100 #BO37
2003 Wheels American Thunder Born On /100 #BO46
2003 Wheels American Thunder Heads Up Team /60 #HUT26
2003 Wheels American Thunder Holofoil #P5
2003 Wheels American Thunder Holofoil #P37
2003 Wheels American Thunder Holofoil #P46
2003 Wheels American Thunder Post Mark #PM4
2003 Wheels American Thunder Previews /5 #5
2003 Wheels American Thunder Rookie Thunder #RT8
2003 Wheels American Thunder Samples #P5
2003 Wheels American Thunder Samples #P37
2003 Wheels American Thunder Samples #P46
2003 Wheels American Thunder Thunder Road #TR1
2003 Wheels High Gear #8
2003 Wheels High Gear #52
2003 Wheels High Gear Blue Hawaii SCDA Promos #8
2003 Wheels High Gear Blue Hawaii SCDA Promos #52
2003 Wheels High Gear Custom Shop #CSDE
2003 Wheels High Gear Custom Shop Autograph Redemption #CSDE
2003 Wheels High Gear Custom Shop Prizes #DEA1
2003 Wheels High Gear Custom Shop Prizes #DEA2
2003 Wheels High Gear Custom Shop Prizes #DEA3
2003 Wheels High Gear Custom Shop Prizes #DEB1
2003 Wheels High Gear Custom Shop Prizes #DEB2
2003 Wheels High Gear Custom Shop Prizes #DEB3
2003 Wheels High Gear Custom Shop Prizes #43070
2003 Wheels High Gear Custom Shop Prizes #43071
2003 Wheels High Gear Custom Shop Prizes #43072
2003 Wheels High Gear First Gear #F8
2003 Wheels High Gear First Gear #F52
2003 Wheels High Gear Flag Chasers Black /90 #FC1
2003 Wheels High Gear Flag Chasers Blue-Yellow /45 #FC1
2003 Wheels High Gear Flag Chasers Checkered /25 #FC1
2003 Wheels High Gear Flag Chasers Green /90 #FC1
2003 Wheels High Gear Flag Chasers Red /90 #FC1
2003 Wheels High Gear Flag Chasers White /90 #FC1
2003 Wheels High Gear Flag Chasers Yellow /90 #FC1
2003 Wheels High Gear Full Throttle #FT7
2003 Wheels High Gear High Groove #HG6
2003 Wheels High Gear Hot Treads /425 #HT18
2003 Wheels High Gear Machine #MM6B
2003 Wheels High Gear Man #MM6A
2003 Wheels High Gear MPH /100 #M8
2003 Wheels High Gear MPH /100 #M52
2003 Wheels High Gear Previews /5 #8
2003 Wheels High Gear Samples #8
2003 Wheels High Gear Samples #52
2003 Wheels High Gear Sunday Sensation #SS9
2004 Bass Pro Shops Racing #1
2004 Bass Pro Shops Racing #3
2004 National Trading Card Day #PP4
2004 Post Cereal #4
2004 Press Pass #9B
2004 Press Pass #9
2004 Press Pass #66
2004 Press Pass #91
2004 Press Pass Autographs #16
2004 Press Pass Burning Rubber Cars /140 #BRT10
2004 Press Pass Burning Rubber Drivers /70 #BRD10
2004 Press Pass Cup Chase #CCR3
2004 Press Pass Cup Chase Prizes #CCR3
2004 Press Pass Dale Earnhardt Jr. #1
2004 Press Pass Dale Earnhardt Jr. #2
2004 Press Pass Dale Earnhardt Jr. #3
2004 Press Pass Dale Earnhardt Jr. #4
2004 Press Pass Dale Earnhardt Jr. #5
2004 Press Pass Dale Earnhardt Jr. #6
2004 Press Pass Dale Earnhardt Jr. #7
2004 Press Pass Dale Earnhardt Jr. #8
2004 Press Pass Dale Earnhardt Jr. #9
2004 Press Pass Dale Earnhardt Jr. #10
2004 Press Pass Dale Earnhardt Jr. #11
2004 Press Pass Dale Earnhardt Jr. #12
2004 Press Pass Dale Earnhardt Jr. #13
2004 Press Pass Dale Earnhardt Jr. #14
2004 Press Pass Dale Earnhardt Jr. #15
2004 Press Pass Dale Earnhardt Jr. #16
2004 Press Pass Dale Earnhardt Jr. #17
2004 Press Pass Dale Earnhardt Jr. #18
2004 Press Pass Dale Earnhardt Jr. #19
2004 Press Pass Dale Earnhardt Jr. #20
2004 Press Pass Dale Earnhardt Jr. #21
2004 Press Pass Dale Earnhardt Jr. #22
2004 Press Pass Dale Earnhardt Jr. #23
2004 Press Pass Dale Earnhardt Jr. #24
2004 Press Pass Dale Earnhardt Jr. #25
2004 Press Pass Dale Earnhardt Jr. #26
2004 Press Pass Dale Earnhardt Jr. #27
2004 Press Pass Dale Earnhardt Jr. #28
2004 Press Pass Dale Earnhardt Jr. #29
2004 Press Pass Dale Earnhardt Jr. #30
2004 Press Pass Dale Earnhardt Jr. #31
2004 Press Pass Dale Earnhardt Jr. #32
2004 Press Pass Dale Earnhardt Jr. #33
2004 Press Pass Dale Earnhardt Jr. #34
2004 Press Pass Dale Earnhardt Jr. #35
2004 Press Pass Dale Earnhardt Jr. #36
2004 Press Pass Dale Earnhardt Jr. #37
2004 Press Pass Dale Earnhardt Jr. #38
2004 Press Pass Dale Earnhardt Jr. #39
2004 Press Pass Dale Earnhardt Jr. #40
2004 Press Pass Dale Earnhardt Jr. #41
2004 Press Pass Dale Earnhardt Jr. #42
2004 Press Pass Dale Earnhardt Jr. #43
2004 Press Pass Dale Earnhardt Jr. #44
2004 Press Pass Dale Earnhardt Jr. #45
2004 Press Pass Dale Earnhardt Jr. #46
2004 Press Pass Dale Earnhardt Jr. #47
2004 Press Pass Dale Earnhardt Jr. #48
2004 Press Pass Dale Earnhardt Jr. #49
2004 Press Pass Dale Earnhardt Jr. #50
2004 Press Pass Dale Earnhardt Jr. #51
2004 Press Pass Dale Earnhardt Jr. #52
2004 Press Pass Dale Earnhardt Jr. #53
2004 Press Pass Dale Earnhardt Jr. #54
2004 Press Pass Dale Earnhardt Jr. #55
2004 Press Pass Dale Earnhardt Jr. #56
2004 Press Pass Dale Earnhardt Jr. #57
2004 Press Pass Dale Earnhardt Jr. #58
2004 Press Pass Dale Earnhardt Jr. #59
2004 Press Pass Dale Earnhardt Jr. #60
2004 Press Pass Dale Earnhardt Jr. #61
2004 Press Pass Dale Earnhardt Jr. #62
2004 Press Pass Dale Earnhardt Jr. #63
2004 Press Pass Dale Earnhardt Jr. #64
2004 Press Pass Dale Earnhardt Jr. #65
2004 Press Pass Dale Earnhardt Jr. #66
2004 Press Pass Dale Earnhardt Jr. #67
2004 Press Pass Dale Earnhardt Jr. #68
2004 Press Pass Dale Earnhardt Jr. #69
2004 Press Pass Dale Earnhardt Jr. #70
2004 Press Pass Dale Earnhardt Jr. #71
2004 Press Pass Dale Earnhardt Jr. #72
2004 Press Pass Dale Earnhardt Jr. Blue #C1
2004 Press Pass Dale Earnhardt Jr. Blue #C2
2004 Press Pass Dale Earnhardt Jr. Blue #C3
2004 Press Pass Dale Earnhardt Jr. Blue #C4
2004 Press Pass Dale Earnhardt Jr. Blue #C5
2004 Press Pass Dale Earnhardt Jr. Blue #C6
2004 Press Pass Dale Earnhardt Jr. Blue #C7
2004 Press Pass Dale Earnhardt Jr. Blue #C8
2004 Press Pass Dale Earnhardt Jr. Blue #C9
2004 Press Pass Dale Earnhardt Jr. Blue #C10
2004 Press Pass Dale Earnhardt Jr. Blue #C11
2004 Press Pass Dale Earnhardt Jr. Blue #C12
2004 Press Pass Dale Earnhardt Jr. Blue #C13
2004 Press Pass Dale Earnhardt Jr. Blue #C14
2004 Press Pass Dale Earnhardt Jr. Blue #C15
2004 Press Pass Dale Earnhardt Jr. Blue #C16
2004 Press Pass Dale Earnhardt Jr. Blue #C17
2004 Press Pass Dale Earnhardt Jr. Blue #C18
2004 Press Pass Dale Earnhardt Jr. Blue #C19
2004 Press Pass Dale Earnhardt Jr. Blue #C20
2004 Press Pass Dale Earnhardt Jr. Blue #C21
2004 Press Pass Dale Earnhardt Jr. Blue #C22
2004 Press Pass Dale Earnhardt Jr. Blue #C23
2004 Press Pass Dale Earnhardt Jr. Blue #C24
2004 Press Pass Dale Earnhardt Jr. Blue #C25
2004 Press Pass Dale Earnhardt Jr. Blue #C26
2004 Press Pass Dale Earnhardt Jr. Blue #C27
2004 Press Pass Dale Earnhardt Jr. Blue #C28
2004 Press Pass Dale Earnhardt Jr. Blue #C29
2004 Press Pass Dale Earnhardt Jr. Blue #C30
2004 Press Pass Dale Earnhardt Jr. Blue #C31
2004 Press Pass Dale Earnhardt Jr. Blue #C32
2004 Press Pass Dale Earnhardt Jr. Blue #C33
2004 Press Pass Dale Earnhardt Jr. Blue #C34
2004 Press Pass Dale Earnhardt Jr. Blue #C35
2004 Press Pass Dale Earnhardt Jr. Blue #C36
2004 Press Pass Dale Earnhardt Jr. Blue #C37
2004 Press Pass Dale Earnhardt Jr. Blue #C38
2004 Press Pass Dale Earnhardt Jr. Blue #C39
2004 Press Pass Dale Earnhardt Jr. Blue #C40
2004 Press Pass Dale Earnhardt Jr. Blue #C41
2004 Press Pass Dale Earnhardt Jr. Blue #C42
2004 Press Pass Dale Earnhardt Jr. Blue #C43
2004 Press Pass Dale Earnhardt Jr. Blue #C44
2004 Press Pass Dale Earnhardt Jr. Blue #C45
2004 Press Pass Dale Earnhardt Jr. Blue #C46
2004 Press Pass Dale Earnhardt Jr. Blue #C47
2004 Press Pass Dale Earnhardt Jr. Blue #C48
2004 Press Pass Dale Earnhardt Jr. Blue #C49
2004 Press Pass Dale Earnhardt Jr. Blue #C50
2004 Press Pass Dale Earnhardt Jr. Blue #C51
2004 Press Pass Dale Earnhardt Jr. Blue #C52
2004 Press Pass Dale Earnhardt Jr. Blue #C53
2004 Press Pass Dale Earnhardt Jr. Blue #C54
2004 Press Pass Dale Earnhardt Jr. Blue #C55
2004 Press Pass Dale Earnhardt Jr. Blue #C56
2004 Press Pass Dale Earnhardt Jr. Blue #C57
2004 Press Pass Dale Earnhardt Jr. Blue #C58
2004 Press Pass Dale Earnhardt Jr. Blue #C59
2004 Press Pass Dale Earnhardt Jr. Blue #C60
2004 Press Pass Dale Earnhardt Jr. Blue #C61
2004 Press Pass Dale Earnhardt Jr. Blue #C62
2004 Press Pass Dale Earnhardt Jr. Blue #C63
2004 Press Pass Dale Earnhardt Jr. Blue #C64
2004 Press Pass Dale Earnhardt Jr. Blue #C65
2004 Press Pass Dale Earnhardt Jr. Blue #C66
2004 Press Pass Dale Earnhardt Jr. Blue #C67
2004 Press Pass Dale Earnhardt Jr. Blue #C68
2004 Press Pass Dale Earnhardt Jr. Blue #C69
2004 Press Pass Dale Earnhardt Jr. Blue #C70
2004 Press Pass Dale Earnhardt Jr. Blue #C71
2004 Press Pass Dale Earnhardt Jr. Blue #C72
2004 Press Pass Dale Earnhardt Jr. Bronze #B1
2004 Press Pass Dale Earnhardt Jr. Bronze #B2
2004 Press Pass Dale Earnhardt Jr. Bronze #B3
2004 Press Pass Dale Earnhardt Jr. Bronze #B4
2004 Press Pass Dale Earnhardt Jr. Bronze #B5
2004 Press Pass Dale Earnhardt Jr. Bronze #B6
2004 Press Pass Dale Earnhardt Jr. Bronze #B7
2004 Press Pass Dale Earnhardt Jr. Bronze #B8
2004 Press Pass Dale Earnhardt Jr. Bronze #B9
2004 Press Pass Dale Earnhardt Jr. Bronze #B10
2004 Press Pass Dale Earnhardt Jr. Bronze #B11
2004 Press Pass Dale Earnhardt Jr. Bronze #B12
2004 Press Pass Dale Earnhardt Jr. Bronze #B13
2004 Press Pass Dale Earnhardt Jr. Bronze #B14
2004 Press Pass Dale Earnhardt Jr. Bronze #B15
2004 Press Pass Dale Earnhardt Jr. Bronze #B16
2004 Press Pass Dale Earnhardt Jr. Bronze #B17
2004 Press Pass Dale Earnhardt Jr. Bronze #B18
2004 Press Pass Dale Earnhardt Jr. Bronze #B19
2004 Press Pass Dale Earnhardt Jr. Bronze #B20
2004 Press Pass Dale Earnhardt Jr. Bronze #B21
2004 Press Pass Dale Earnhardt Jr. Bronze #B22
2004 Press Pass Dale Earnhardt Jr. Bronze #B23
2004 Press Pass Dale Earnhardt Jr. Bronze #B24
2004 Press Pass Dale Earnhardt Jr. Bronze #B25
2004 Press Pass Dale Earnhardt Jr. Bronze #B26
2004 Press Pass Dale Earnhardt Jr. Bronze #B27
2004 Press Pass Dale Earnhardt Jr. Bronze #B28
2004 Press Pass Dale Earnhardt Jr. Bronze #B29
2004 Press Pass Dale Earnhardt Jr. Bronze #B30
2004 Press Pass Dale Earnhardt Jr. Bronze #B31
2004 Press Pass Dale Earnhardt Jr. Bronze #B32
2004 Press Pass Dale Earnhardt Jr. Bronze #B33
2004 Press Pass Dale Earnhardt Jr. Bronze #B34
2004 Press Pass Dale Earnhardt Jr. Bronze #B35
2004 Press Pass Dale Earnhardt Jr. Bronze #B36
2004 Press Pass Dale Earnhardt Jr. Bronze #B37
2004 Press Pass Dale Earnhardt Jr. Bronze #B38
2004 Press Pass Dale Earnhardt Jr. Bronze #B39
2004 Press Pass Dale Earnhardt Jr. Bronze #B40
2004 Press Pass Dale Earnhardt Jr. Bronze #B41
2004 Press Pass Dale Earnhardt Jr. Bronze #B42
2004 Press Pass Dale Earnhardt Jr. Bronze #B43
2004 Press Pass Dale Earnhardt Jr. Bronze #B44
2004 Press Pass Dale Earnhardt Jr. Bronze #B45
2004 Press Pass Dale Earnhardt Jr. Bronze #B46
2004 Press Pass Dale Earnhardt Jr. Bronze #B47
2004 Press Pass Dale Earnhardt Jr. Bronze #B48
2004 Press Pass Dale Earnhardt Jr. Bronze #B49
2004 Press Pass Dale Earnhardt Jr. Bronze #B50
2004 Press Pass Dale Earnhardt Jr. Bronze #B51
2004 Press Pass Dale Earnhardt Jr. Bronze #B52
2004 Press Pass Dale Earnhardt Jr. Bronze #B53
2004 Press Pass Dale Earnhardt Jr. Bronze #B54
2004 Press Pass Dale Earnhardt Jr. Bronze #B55
2004 Press Pass Dale Earnhardt Jr. Bronze #B56
2004 Press Pass Dale Earnhardt Jr. Bronze #B57
2004 Press Pass Dale Earnhardt Jr. Bronze #B58
2004 Press Pass Dale Earnhardt Jr. Bronze #B59
2004 Press Pass Dale Earnhardt Jr. Bronze #B60
2004 Press Pass Dale Earnhardt Jr. Bronze #B61
2004 Press Pass Dale Earnhardt Jr. Bronze #B62
2004 Press Pass Dale Earnhardt Jr. Bronze #B63
2004 Press Pass Dale Earnhardt Jr. Bronze #B64
2004 Press Pass Dale Earnhardt Jr. Bronze #B65
2004 Press Pass Dale Earnhardt Jr. Bronze #B66
2004 Press Pass Dale Earnhardt Jr. Bronze #B67
2004 Press Pass Dale Earnhardt Jr. Bronze #B68
2004 Press Pass Dale Earnhardt Jr. Bronze #B69
2004 Press Pass Dale Earnhardt Jr. Bronze #B70
2004 Press Pass Dale Earnhardt Jr. Bronze #B71
2004 Press Pass Dale Earnhardt Jr. Bronze #B72
2004 Press Pass Dale Earnhardt Jr. Gallery #G1
2004 Press Pass Dale Earnhardt Jr. Gallery #G2
2004 Press Pass Dale Earnhardt Jr. Gallery #G3
2004 Press Pass Dale Earnhardt Jr. Gallery #G4
2004 Press Pass Dale Earnhardt Jr. Gallery #G5
2004 Press Pass Dale Earnhardt Jr. Gallery #G6
2004 Press Pass Dale Earnhardt Jr. Gallery #G7
2004 Press Pass Dale Earnhardt Jr. Gallery #G8
2004 Press Pass Dale Earnhardt Jr. Gold #D1
2004 Press Pass Dale Earnhardt Jr. Gold #D2
2004 Press Pass Dale Earnhardt Jr. Gold #D3
2004 Press Pass Dale Earnhardt Jr. Gold #D4
2004 Press Pass Dale Earnhardt Jr. Gold #D5
2004 Press Pass Dale Earnhardt Jr. Gold #D6
2004 Press Pass Dale Earnhardt Jr. Gold #D7
2004 Press Pass Dale Earnhardt Jr. Gold #D8
2004 Press Pass Dale Earnhardt Jr. Gold #D9
2004 Press Pass Dale Earnhardt Jr. Gold #D10
2004 Press Pass Dale Earnhardt Jr. Gold #D11
2004 Press Pass Dale Earnhardt Jr. Gold #D12
2004 Press Pass Dale Earnhardt Jr. Gold #D13
2004 Press Pass Dale Earnhardt Jr. Gold #D14
2004 Press Pass Dale Earnhardt Jr. Gold #D15
2004 Press Pass Dale Earnhardt Jr. Gold #D16
2004 Press Pass Dale Earnhardt Jr. Gold #D17
2004 Press Pass Dale Earnhardt Jr. Gold #D18
2004 Press Pass Dale Earnhardt Jr. Gold #D19
2004 Press Pass Dale Earnhardt Jr. Gold #D20
2004 Press Pass Dale Earnhardt Jr. Gold #D21
2004 Press Pass Dale Earnhardt Jr. Gold #D22
2004 Press Pass Dale Earnhardt Jr. Gold #D23
2004 Press Pass Dale Earnhardt Jr. Gold #D24
2004 Press Pass Dale Earnhardt Jr. Gold #D25
2004 Press Pass Dale Earnhardt Jr. Gold #D26
2004 Press Pass Dale Earnhardt Jr. Gold #D27
2004 Press Pass Dale Earnhardt Jr. Gold #D28
2004 Press Pass Dale Earnhardt Jr. Gold #D29
2004 Press Pass Dale Earnhardt Jr. Gold #D30
2004 Press Pass Dale Earnhardt Jr. Gold #D31
2004 Press Pass Dale Earnhardt Jr. Gold #D32
2004 Press Pass Dale Earnhardt Jr. Gold #D33
2004 Press Pass Dale Earnhardt Jr. Gold #D34
2004 Press Pass Dale Earnhardt Jr. Gold #D35
2004 Press Pass Dale Earnhardt Jr. Gold #D36
2004 Press Pass Dale Earnhardt Jr. Gold #D37
2004 Press Pass Dale Earnhardt Jr. Gold #D38
2004 Press Pass Dale Earnhardt Jr. Gold #D39
2004 Press Pass Dale Earnhardt Jr. Gold #D40
2004 Press Pass Dale Earnhardt Jr. Gold #D41
2004 Press Pass Dale Earnhardt Jr. Gold #D42
2004 Press Pass Dale Earnhardt Jr. Gold #D43
2004 Press Pass Dale Earnhardt Jr. Gold #D44
2004 Press Pass Dale Earnhardt Jr. Gold #D45
2004 Press Pass Dale Earnhardt Jr. Gold #D46
2004 Press Pass Dale Earnhardt Jr. Gold #D47
2004 Press Pass Dale Earnhardt Jr. Gold #D48
2004 Press Pass Dale Earnhardt Jr. Gold #D49
2004 Press Pass Dale Earnhardt Jr. Gold #D50
2004 Press Pass Dale Earnhardt Jr. Gold #D51
2004 Press Pass Dale Earnhardt Jr. Gold #D52
2004 Press Pass Dale Earnhardt Jr. Gold #D53
2004 Press Pass Dale Earnhardt Jr. Gold #D54
2004 Press Pass Dale Earnhardt Jr. Gold #D55
2004 Press Pass Dale Earnhardt Jr. Gold #D56
2004 Press Pass Dale Earnhardt Jr. Gold #D57
2004 Press Pass Dale Earnhardt Jr. Gold #D58
2004 Press Pass Dale Earnhardt Jr. Gold #D59
2004 Press Pass Dale Earnhardt Jr. Gold #D60
2004 Press Pass Dale Earnhardt Jr. Gold #D61
2004 Press Pass Dale Earnhardt Jr. Gold #D62
2004 Press Pass Dale Earnhardt Jr. Gold #D63
2004 Press Pass Dale Earnhardt Jr. Gold #D64
2004 Press Pass Dale Earnhardt Jr. Gold #D65
2004 Press Pass Dale Earnhardt Jr. Gold #D66
2004 Press Pass Dale Earnhardt Jr. Gold #D67
2004 Press Pass Dale Earnhardt Jr. Gold #D68
2004 Press Pass Dale Earnhardt Jr. Gold #D69
2004 Press Pass Dale Earnhardt Jr. Gold #D70
2004 Press Pass Dale Earnhardt Jr. Gold #D71
2004 Press Pass Dale Earnhardt Jr. Gold #D72
2004 Press Pass Dale Earnhardt Jr. Tins #NNO
2004 Press Pass Dale Earnhardt Jr. Tins #NNO
2004 Press Pass Dale Earnhardt Jr. Tins #NNO
2004 Press Pass Dale Earnhardt Jr. Tins #NNO
2004 Press Pass Double Burner /100 #DB10
2004 Press Pass Double Burner Exchange /100 #DB10
2004 Press Pass Eclipse #3
2004 Press Pass Eclipse #30
2004 Press Pass Eclipse #47
2004 Press Pass Eclipse #47B
2004 Press Pass Eclipse #52
2004 Press Pass Eclipse #56
2004 Press Pass Eclipse #73
2004 Press Pass Eclipse #78
2004 Press Pass Eclipse Destination WIN #1
2004 Press Pass Eclipse Destination WIN #2
2004 Press Pass Eclipse Destination WIN #10
2004 Press Pass Eclipse Destination WIN #27
2004 Press Pass Eclipse Hyperdrive #HP5
2004 Press Pass Eclipse Maxim #MX3
2004 Press Pass Eclipse Previews /5 #3
2004 Press Pass Eclipse Samples #3
2004 Press Pass Eclipse Samples #30
2004 Press Pass Eclipse Samples #47
2004 Press Pass Eclipse Samples #52
2004 Press Pass Eclipse Samples #56
2004 Press Pass Eclipse Samples #73
2004 Press Pass Eclipse Samples #78
2004 Press Pass Eclipse Skidmarks #SM7
2004 Press Pass Eclipse Skidmarks Holofoil /500 #SM7
2004 Press Pass Eclipse Under Cover Autographs /8 #UCDE
2004 Press Pass Eclipse Under Cover Cars /170 #UCD12
2004 Press Pass Eclipse Under Cover Double Cover /100 #DC1
2004 Press Pass Eclipse Under Cover Driver Gold /325 #UCD12
2004 Press Pass Eclipse Under Cover Driver Red /100 #UCD12
2004 Press Pass Eclipse Under Cover Driver Silver /690 #UCD12
2004 Press Pass Hot Treads /1100 #HTR2
2004 Press Pass Hot Treads Holofoil /200 #HTR2
2004 Press Pass Making the Show Collector's Series #MS5
2004 Press Pass Making the Show Collector's Series Tins #NNO
2004 Press Pass Nilla Wafers #1
2004 Press Pass Nilla Wafers #2
2004 Press Pass Nilla Wafers #3
2004 Press Pass Optima #4
2004 Press Pass Optima #55
2004 Press Pass Optima #73
2004 Press Pass Optima #83
2004 Press Pass Optima #88
2004 Press Pass Optima #NNO
2004 Press Pass Optima Cool Persistence #CP3
2004 Press Pass Optima Fan Favorite #FF4
2004 Press Pass Optima G Force #GF1
2004 Press Pass Optima Gold #G4
2004 Press Pass Optima Gold #G55
2004 Press Pass Optima Gold #G73
2004 Press Pass Optima Gold #G83
2004 Press Pass Optima Gold #G88
2004 Press Pass Optima Previews /5 #EB4
2004 Press Pass Optima Q&A #QA9
2004 Press Pass Optima Samples #4
2004 Press Pass Optima Samples #55
2004 Press Pass Optima Samples #73
2004 Press Pass Optima Samples #83
2004 Press Pass Optima Samples #88
2004 Press Pass Optima Thunder Bolts Autographs /8 #TBDE
2004 Press Pass Optima Thunder Bolts Cars /120 #TBT1
2004 Press Pass Optima Thunder Bolts Drivers /70 #TBD1
2004 Press Pass Platinum #P9
2004 Press Pass Platinum #P66
2004 Press Pass Platinum #P91
2004 Press Pass Premium #1
2004 Press Pass Premium #39
2004 Press Pass Premium #46
2004 Press Pass Premium #59
2004 Press Pass Premium #80
2004 Press Pass Premium #0
2004 Press Pass Premium Asphalt Jungle #A5
2004 Press Pass Premium Hot Threads Autographs /8 #HTDE
2004 Press Pass Premium Hot Threads Drivers Bronze /125 #HTD11
2004 Press Pass Premium Hot Threads Drivers Bronze Retail /125 #HTT11
2004 Press Pass Premium Hot Threads Drivers Gold /50 #HTD11
2004 Press Pass Premium Hot Threads Drivers Silver /75 #HTD11
2004 Press Pass Premium In the Zone #IZ2
2004 Press Pass Premium In the Zone Elite Edition #IZ2
2004 Press Pass Premium Performance Driven #PD9
2004 Press Pass Premium Previews /5 #1
2004 Press Pass Premium Samples #1
2004 Press Pass Premium Samples #39
2004 Press Pass Premium Samples #46
2004 Press Pass Previews /5 #9
2004 Press Pass Samples #9
2004 Press Pass Samples #66
2004 Press Pass Samples #91
2004 Press Pass Schedule #3
2004 Press Pass Showcar #S4B
2004 Press Pass Showman #S4A
2004 Press Pass Signings #17
2004 Press Pass Signings Gold /50 #16
2004 Press Pass Snapshots #SN6
2004 Press Pass Stealth #52
2004 Press Pass Stealth #53
2004 Press Pass Stealth #54
2004 Press Pass Stealth #83
2004 Press Pass Stealth #99
2004 Press Pass Stealth EFX #EF1
2004 Press Pass Stealth Fusion #FU3
2004 Press Pass Stealth Gear Grippers Autographs /8 #HTDE
2004 Press Pass Stealth Gear Grippers Drivers /80 #GGD9
2004 Press Pass Stealth Gear Grippers Drivers Retail /120 #GGT9
2004 Press Pass Stealth No Boundaries #NB11
2004 Press Pass Stealth Profile #P3
2004 Press Pass Stealth Samples #X52
2004 Press Pass Stealth Samples #X54
2004 Press Pass Stealth Samples #X53
2004 Press Pass Stealth Samples #X83
2004 Press Pass Stealth Samples #X99
2004 Press Pass Stealth X-Ray /100 #52
2004 Press Pass Stealth X-Ray /100 #53
2004 Press Pass Stealth X-Ray /100 #54
2004 Press Pass Stealth X-Ray /100 #83
2004 Press Pass Stealth X-Ray /100 #99
2004 Press Pass Top Shelf #TS3
2004 Press Pass Total Memorabilia Power Pick #TM10
2004 Press Pass Trackside #19
2004 Press Pass Trackside #53
2004 Press Pass Trackside #72
2004 Press Pass Trackside #100
2004 Press Pass Trackside #109
2004 Press Pass Trackside Dialed In #DI2
2004 Press Pass Trackside Golden /100 #G19
2004 Press Pass Trackside Golden /100 #G53
2004 Press Pass Trackside Golden /100 #G72
2004 Press Pass Trackside Golden /100 #G100
2004 Press Pass Trackside Golden /100 #G109
2004 Press Pass Trackside Hat Giveaway #PPH6
2004 Press Pass Trackside Hot Pass #HP5
2004 Press Pass Trackside Hot Pass National #HP5
2004 Press Pass Trackside Hot Pursuit #HP1
2004 Press Pass Trackside Pit Stoppers Autographs /8 #PSDE
2004 Press Pass Trackside Pit Stoppers Cars /150 #PST15
2004 Press Pass Trackside Pit Stoppers Drivers /95 #PSD15
2004 Press Pass Trackside Previews /5 #EB19
2004 Press Pass Trackside Runnin n' Gunnin #RG1
2004 Press Pass Trackside Samples #19
2004 Press Pass Trackside Samples #53
2004 Press Pass Trackside Samples #72
2004 Press Pass Trackside Samples #100
2004 Press Pass Trackside Samples #109
2004 Press Pass Triple Burner /100 #TB10
2004 Press Pass Triple Burner Exchange /100 #TB10
2004 Press Pass Velocity #VC8
2004 VIP #4
2004 VIP #28
2004 VIP #43
2004 VIP #46
2004 VIP #53
2004 VIP #55
2004 VIP #77
2004 VIP #90
2004 VIP Driver's Choice #DC2
2004 VIP Driver's Choice Die Cuts #DC2
2004 VIP Head Gear #HG1
2004 VIP Head Gear Transparent #HG1
2004 VIP Lap Leaders #LL2
2004 VIP Lap Leaders Transparent #LL2
2004 VIP Making the Show #MS5
2004 VIP Previews /5 #EB4
2004 VIP Previews /5 #EB43
2004 VIP Previews /5 #EB46
2004 VIP Previews /5 #EB28
2004 VIP Previews /5 #EB53
2004 VIP Samples #4
2004 VIP Samples #28
2004 VIP Samples #53
2004 VIP Samples #77
2004 VIP Samples #46
2004 VIP Samples #90
2004 VIP Samples #43
2004 VIP Samples #55
2004 VIP Tradin' Paint Autographs /8 #TPDE
2004 VIP Tradin' Paint Bronze /130 #TPT1

2004 VIP Tradin' Paint Gold /50 #TPD1
2004 VIP Tradin' Paint Silver /70 #TPD1
2004 Wheels American Thunder #4
2004 Wheels American Thunder #33
2004 Wheels American Thunder #41
2004 Wheels American Thunder #47
2004 Wheels American Thunder #62
2004 Wheels American Thunder #69
2004 Wheels American Thunder #77
2004 Wheels American Thunder American Muscle #AM1
2004 Wheels American Thunder Cool Threads /525 #CT2
2004 Wheels American Thunder Cup Quest #CQ2
2004 Wheels American Thunder Head to Toe /100 #HT3
2004 Wheels American Thunder Post Mark #PM6
2004 Wheels American Thunder Previews /5 #EB4
2004 Wheels American Thunder Previews /5 #EB33
2004 Wheels American Thunder Previews /5 #EB41
2004 Wheels American Thunder Pushin Pedal /275 #PP5
2004 Wheels American Thunder Samples #4
2004 Wheels American Thunder Samples #33
2004 Wheels American Thunder Samples #41
2004 Wheels American Thunder Samples #47
2004 Wheels American Thunder Samples #62
2004 Wheels American Thunder Samples #69
2004 Wheels American Thunder Samples #77
2004 Wheels American Thunder Thunder Road #TR4
2004 Wheels American Thunder Triple Hat /160 #TH33
2004 Wheels Autographs #17
2004 Wheels High Gear #6
2004 Wheels High Gear #29
2004 Wheels High Gear #50
2004 Wheels High Gear #61
2004 Wheels High Gear Custom Shop #CSDE
2004 Wheels High Gear Dale Earnhardt Jr. #DJR1
2004 Wheels High Gear Dale Earnhardt Jr. #DJR2
2004 Wheels High Gear Dale Earnhardt Jr. #DJR3
2004 Wheels High Gear Dale Earnhardt Jr. #DJR4
2004 Wheels High Gear Dale Earnhardt Jr. #DJR5
2004 Wheels High Gear Dale Earnhardt Jr. #DJR6
2004 Wheels High Gear Flag Chasers Black /100 #FC7
2004 Wheels High Gear Flag Chasers Blue /50 #FC7
2004 Wheels High Gear Flag Chasers Checkered /35 #FC7
2004 Wheels High Gear Flag Chasers Green /100 #FC7
2004 Wheels High Gear Flag Chasers Red /100 #FC7
2004 Wheels High Gear Flag Chasers White /100 #FC7
2004 Wheels High Gear Flag Chasers Yellow /100 #FC7
2004 Wheels High Gear High Groove #HG5
2004 Wheels High Gear Machine #MM9B
2004 Wheels High Gear Man #MM9A
2004 Wheels High Gear MPH /100 #M6
2004 Wheels High Gear MPH /100 #M29
2004 Wheels High Gear MPH /100 #M50
2004 Wheels High Gear MPH /100 #M61
2004 Wheels High Gear Previews /5 #6
2004 Wheels High Gear Previews /5 #29
2004 Wheels High Gear Previews /5 #50
2004 Wheels High Gear Samples #6
2004 Wheels High Gear Samples #29
2004 Wheels High Gear Samples #50
2004 Wheels High Gear Samples #61
2004 Wheels High Gear Sunday Sensation #SS3
2004 Wheels High Gear Top Ten #TT3
2005 NAPA #NNO
2005 Press Pass #6
2005 Press Pass #65
2005 Press Pass #73
2005 Press Pass #75
2005 Press Pass #78
2005 Press Pass #94
2005 Press Pass #102
2005 Press Pass #109
2005 Press Pass #113
2005 Press Pass #120
2005 Press Pass Autographs #14
2005 Press Pass Burning Rubber Autographs /8 #BRDE
2005 Press Pass Burning Rubber Cars /130 #BRT7
2005 Press Pass Burning Rubber Drivers /80 #BRD7
2005 Press Pass Burning Rubber Drivers Gold /1 #BRD7
2005 Press Pass Cup Chase #CCR15
2005 Press Pass Cup Chase Prizes #CCP15
2005 Press Pass Double Burner /100 #DB10
2005 Press Pass Double Burner Exchange /100 #DB10
2005 Press Pass Eclipse #5
2005 Press Pass Eclipse #30
2005 Press Pass Eclipse #53
2005 Press Pass Eclipse #56
2005 Press Pass Eclipse #71
2005 Press Pass Eclipse #73
2005 Press Pass Eclipse Destination WIN #1
2005 Press Pass Eclipse Destination WIN #3
2005 Press Pass Eclipse Destination WIN #10
2005 Press Pass Eclipse Destination WIN #21
2005 Press Pass Eclipse Destination WIN #23
2005 Press Pass Eclipse Destination WIN #26
2005 Press Pass Eclipse Hyperdrive #HD5
2005 Press Pass Eclipse Maxim #MX3
2005 Press Pass Eclipse Previews /5 #EB5
2005 Press Pass Eclipse Previews /5 #EB30
2005 Press Pass Eclipse Previews /5 #EB53
2005 Press Pass Eclipse Previews /5 #EB56
2005 Press Pass Eclipse Previews /5 #EB71
2005 Press Pass Eclipse Previews /1 #EB73
2005 Press Pass Eclipse Samples #5
2005 Press Pass Eclipse Samples #30
2005 Press Pass Eclipse Samples #53
2005 Press Pass Eclipse Samples #56
2005 Press Pass Eclipse Samples #71
2005 Press Pass Eclipse Samples #73
2005 Press Pass Eclipse Skidmarks #SM7
2005 Press Pass Eclipse Skidmarks Holofoil /250 #SM7
2005 Press Pass Eclipse Under Cover Autographs /8 #UCDE
2005 Press Pass Eclipse Under Cover Cars /120 #UCT11
2005 Press Pass Eclipse Under Cover Double Cover /340 #DC1
2005 Press Pass Eclipse Under Cover Driver Red /400 #UCD11
2005 Press Pass Eclipse Under Cover Drivers Holofoil /100 #UCD11
2005 Press Pass Eclipse Under Cover Drivers Silver /690 #UCD11
2005 Press Pass Game Face #GF3
2005 Press Pass Hot Treads /900 #HTR1
2005 Press Pass Hot Treads Holofoil /100 #HTR1
2005 Press Pass Legends #30
2005 Press Pass Legends Autographs Black /50 #14
2005 Press Pass Legends Blue /1890 #30B
2005 Press Pass Legends Double Threads Bronze /375 #DTEW
2005 Press Pass Legends Double Threads Gold /99 #DTEW
2005 Press Pass Legends Double Threads Silver /225 #DTEW
2005 Press Pass Legends Gold /750 #30G
2005 Press Pass Legends Greatest Moments /650 #GM17
2005 Press Pass Legends Holofoil /100 #30H
2005 Press Pass Legends Press Plates Black /1 #30
2005 Press Pass Legends Press Plates Cyan /1 #30
2005 Press Pass Legends Press Plates Magenta /1 #30
2005 Press Pass Legends Press Plates Yellow /1 #30
2005 Press Pass Legends Previews /5 #30
2005 Press Pass Legends Solo /1 #30S
2005 Press Pass Legends Threads and Treads Bronze /375 #TTJR
2005 Press Pass Legends Threads and Treads Gold /99 #TTJR
2005 Press Pass Legends Threads and Treads Silver /225 #TTJR
2005 Press Pass Optima #8
2005 Press Pass Optima #56
2005 Press Pass Optima #74
2005 Press Pass Optima #93
2005 Press Pass Optima Gold /100 #G8
2005 Press Pass Optima Gold /100 #G56
2005 Press Pass Optima Gold /100 #G74
2005 Press Pass Optima Gold /100 #G93
2005 Press Pass Optima Previews /5 #8
2005 Press Pass Optima Q & A #QA6
2005 Press Pass Optima Samples #8
2005 Press Pass Optima Samples #56
2005 Press Pass Optima Samples #74
2005 Press Pass Optima Samples #93
2005 Press Pass Optima Thunder Bolts Autographs /8 #TBDE
2005 Press Pass Panorama #PPP33
2005 Press Pass Platinum /100 #P6
2005 Press Pass Platinum /100 #P65
2005 Press Pass Platinum /100 #P73
2005 Press Pass Platinum /100 #P75
2005 Press Pass Platinum /100 #P78
2005 Press Pass Platinum /100 #P94
2005 Press Pass Platinum /100 #P102
2005 Press Pass Platinum /100 #P109
2005 Press Pass Platinum /100 #P113
2005 Press Pass Platinum /100 #P120
2005 Press Pass Premium #5
2005 Press Pass Premium #61
2005 Press Pass Premium #71
2005 Press Pass Premium Hot Threads Autographs /8 #HTDE
2005 Press Pass Premium Hot Threads Cars /85 #HTT4
2005 Press Pass Premium Hot Threads Drivers /275 #HTD4
2005 Press Pass Premium Hot Threads Drivers Gold /1 #HTD4
2005 Press Pass Premium In the Zone #IZ10
2005 Press Pass Premium In the Zone Elite Edition /250 #IZ10
2005 Press Pass Premium Performance Driven #PD1
2005 Press Pass Premium Samples #5
2005 Press Pass Previews Green /5 #EB6
2005 Press Pass Previews Silver /1 #EB102
2005 Press Pass Samples #6
2005 Press Pass Samples #65
2005 Press Pass Samples #73
2005 Press Pass Samples #75
2005 Press Pass Samples #78
2005 Press Pass Samples #94
2005 Press Pass Samples #102
2005 Press Pass Samples #109
2005 Press Pass Samples #113
2005 Press Pass Samples #120
2005 Press Pass Showcar #SC4
2005 Press Pass Showman #SM4
2005 Press Pass Signings #13
2005 Press Pass Signings Platinum /100 #11
2005 Press Pass Snapshots #SN5
2005 Press Pass Snapshots Extra #SS1
2005 Press Pass Stealth #38
2005 Press Pass Stealth #41
2005 Press Pass Stealth #44
2005 Press Pass Stealth #83
2005 Press Pass Stealth Gear Grippers Autographs /8 #GGDE
2005 Press Pass Stealth Gear Grippers Cars /90 #GGT18
2005 Press Pass Stealth Gear Grippers Drivers /75 #GGD18
2005 Press Pass Stealth No Boundaries #NB15
2005 Press Pass Stealth Previews /5 #38
2005 Press Pass Stealth Previews /5 #41
2005 Press Pass Stealth Previews /5 #44
2005 Press Pass Stealth Profile #PR3
2005 Press Pass Stealth Samples #38
2005 Press Pass Stealth Samples #41
2005 Press Pass Stealth Samples #44
2005 Press Pass Stealth Samples #83
2005 Press Pass Stealth X-Ray /100 #X38
2005 Press Pass Stealth X-Ray /100 #X41
2005 Press Pass Stealth X-Ray /100 #X44
2005 Press Pass Stealth X-Ray /100 #X83
2005 Press Pass Top Ten #TT3
2005 Press Pass Total Memorabilia Power Pick #TM10
2005 Press Pass Trackside #2
2005 Press Pass Trackside #2B
2005 Press Pass Trackside #82
2005 Press Pass Trackside #94
2005 Press Pass Trackside #100
2005 Press Pass Trackside Golden /100 #G2
2005 Press Pass Trackside Golden /100 #G82
2005 Press Pass Trackside Golden /100 #G94
2005 Press Pass Trackside Golden /100 #G100
2005 Press Pass Trackside Hat Giveaway #PPH6
2005 Press Pass Trackside Hot Pass #3
2005 Press Pass Trackside Hot Pass National #3
2005 Press Pass Trackside Pit Stoppers Autographs /8 #PSDE
2005 Press Pass Trackside Pit Stoppers Cars /85 #PST14
2005 Press Pass Trackside Pit Stoppers Drivers /85 #PSD14
2005 Press Pass Trackside Previews /5 #2
2005 Press Pass Trackside Previews /1 #82
2005 Press Pass Trackside Runnin n' Gunnin #RG1
2005 Press Pass Trackside Samples #2
2005 Press Pass Trackside Samples #82
2005 Press Pass Trackside Samples #94
2005 Press Pass Trackside Samples #100
2005 Press Pass Triple Burner /100 #TB10
2005 Press Pass Triple Burner Exchange /100 #TB10
2005 Press Pass Velocity #V7
2005 VIP #5
2005 VIP #33
2005 VIP #73
2005 VIP Driver's Choice #DC2
2005 VIP Driver's Choice Die Cuts #DC2
2005 VIP Lap Leaders #2
2005 VIP Lap Leaders Transparent #2
2005 VIP Making The Show #5
2005 VIP Previews /5 #EB5
2005 VIP Previews /5 #EB33
2005 VIP Samples #5
2005 VIP Samples #33
2005 VIP Samples #73
2005 VIP Tradin' Paint Autographs /8 #DE
2005 VIP Tradin' Paint Cars /110 #TPT1
2005 VIP Tradin' Paint Drivers /90 #TPD1
2005 Wheels American Thunder #6
2005 Wheels American Thunder #36
2005 Wheels American Thunder #38
2005 Wheels American Thunder #57
2005 Wheels American Thunder #69
2005 Wheels American Thunder #77
2005 Wheels American Thunder American Eagle #AE2
2005 Wheels American Thunder American Muscle #AM6
2005 Wheels American Thunder Cool Threads /475 #CT4
2005 Wheels American Thunder Golden Eagle /250 #GE2
2005 Wheels American Thunder Head to Toe /125 #HT4
2005 Wheels American Thunder Previews /5 #6
2005 Wheels American Thunder Previews /5 #77
2005 Wheels American Thunder Pushin Pedal /150 #PP3
2005 Wheels American Thunder Samples #6
2005 Wheels American Thunder Samples #36
2005 Wheels American Thunder Samples #38
2005 Wheels American Thunder Samples #57
2005 Wheels American Thunder Samples #69
2005 Wheels American Thunder Samples #77
2005 Wheels American Thunder Thunder Road #TR4
2005 Wheels American Thunder Triple Hat /190 #TH4
2005 Wheels Autographs #13
2005 Wheels High Gear #4
2005 Wheels High Gear #52
2005 Wheels High Gear #61
2005 Wheels High Gear #65
2005 Wheels High Gear #67
2005 Wheels High Gear #72
2005 Wheels High Gear #75
2005 Wheels High Gear #84
2005 Wheels High Gear Flag Chasers Black /55 #FC7
2005 Wheels High Gear Flag Chasers Blue-Yellow /25 #FC7
2005 Wheels High Gear Flag Chasers Checkered /10 #FC7
2005 Wheels High Gear Flag Chasers Green /55 #FC7
2005 Wheels High Gear Flag Chasers Red /55 #FC7
2005 Wheels High Gear Flag Chasers White /55 #FC7
2005 Wheels High Gear Flag Chasers Yellow /55 #FC7
2005 Wheels High Gear Flag to Flag #FF3
2005 Wheels High Gear Full Throttle #FT1
2005 Wheels High Gear Machine #MMB4
2005 Wheels High Gear Man #MMA4
2005 Wheels High Gear MPH /100 #M4
2005 Wheels High Gear MPH /100 #M52
2005 Wheels High Gear MPH /100 #M61
2005 Wheels High Gear MPH /100 #M65
2005 Wheels High Gear MPH /100 #M67
2005 Wheels High Gear MPH /100 #M72
2005 Wheels High Gear MPH /100 #M75
2005 Wheels High Gear MPH /100 #M84
2005 Wheels High Gear Previews Green /5 #EB4
2005 Wheels High Gear Previews Silver /1 #EB75
2005 Wheels High Gear Samples #4
2005 Wheels High Gear Samples #52
2005 Wheels High Gear Samples #61
2005 Wheels High Gear Samples #65
2005 Wheels High Gear Samples #67
2005 Wheels High Gear Samples #72
2005 Wheels High Gear Samples #75
2005 Wheels High Gear Samples #84
2005 Wheels High Gear Top Tier #TT5
2006 Press Pass #9
2006 Press Pass #76
2006 Press Pass #97
2006 Press Pass Blaster Kmart #DEC
2006 Press Pass Blaster Target #DEB
2006 Press Pass Blaster Wal-Mart #DEA
2006 Press Pass Blue #B9
2006 Press Pass Blue #B76
2006 Press Pass Blue #B97
2006 Press Pass Burning Rubber Cars /370 #BRT3
2006 Press Pass Burning Rubber Drivers /100 #BRD3
2006 Press Pass Burning Rubber Drivers Gold /1 #BRD3
2006 Press Pass Burnouts /1050 #HT11
2006 Press Pass Burnouts Holofoil /125 #HT11
2006 Press Pass Collectors Series Making the Show #MS23
2006 Press Pass Cup Chase #CCR12
2006 Press Pass Cup Chase Prizes #CC5
2006 Press Pass Dominator Dale Earnhardt Jr. #1
2006 Press Pass Dominator Dale Earnhardt Jr. #2
2006 Press Pass Dominator Dale Earnhardt Jr. #3
2006 Press Pass Dominator Dale Earnhardt Jr. #4
2006 Press Pass Dominator Dale Earnhardt Jr. #5
2006 Press Pass Dominator Dale Earnhardt Jr. #6
2006 Press Pass Dominator Dale Earnhardt Jr. #7
2006 Press Pass Dominator Dale Earnhardt Jr. #8
2006 Press Pass Dominator Dale Earnhardt Jr. #9
2006 Press Pass Dominator Dale Earnhardt Jr. #10
2006 Press Pass Dominator Dale Earnhardt Jr. #11
2006 Press Pass Dominator Dale Earnhardt Jr. #12
2006 Press Pass Dominator Dale Earnhardt Jr. #13
2006 Press Pass Dominator Dale Earnhardt Jr. #14
2006 Press Pass Dominator Dale Earnhardt Jr. #15
2006 Press Pass Dominator Dale Earnhardt Jr. #16
2006 Press Pass Dominator Dale Earnhardt Jr. #17
2006 Press Pass Dominator Dale Earnhardt Jr. #18
2006 Press Pass Dominator Dale Earnhardt Jr. #19
2006 Press Pass Dominator Dale Earnhardt Jr. #20
2006 Press Pass Dominator Dale Earnhardt Jr. #21
2006 Press Pass Dominator Dale Earnhardt Jr. #22
2006 Press Pass Dominator Dale Earnhardt Jr. #23
2006 Press Pass Dominator Dale Earnhardt Jr. #24
2006 Press Pass Dominator Dale Earnhardt Jr. #25
2006 Press Pass Dominator Dale Earnhardt Jr. #26
2006 Press Pass Dominator Dale Earnhardt Jr. #27
2006 Press Pass Dominator Dale Earnhardt Jr. #28
2006 Press Pass Dominator Dale Earnhardt Jr. #29
2006 Press Pass Dominator Dale Earnhardt Jr. #30
2006 Press Pass Dominator Dale Earnhardt Jr. #31
2006 Press Pass Dominator Dale Earnhardt Jr. #32
2006 Press Pass Dominator Dale Earnhardt Jr. #33
2006 Press Pass Dominator Dale Earnhardt Jr. Jumbo #JR1
2006 Press Pass Dominator Dale Earnhardt Jr. Jumbo #JR2
2006 Press Pass Dominator Dale Earnhardt Jr. Jumbo #JR3
2006 Press Pass Dominator Tins #JR
2006 Press Pass Double Burner Firesuit-Glove /100 #DB6
2006 Press Pass Double Burner Metal-Tire /100 #DB2
2006 Press Pass Eclipse #18
2006 Press Pass Eclipse #63
2006 Press Pass Eclipse #73
2006 Press Pass Eclipse #90
2006 Press Pass Eclipse Hyperdrive #HP3
2006 Press Pass Eclipse Previews /5 #EB18
2006 Press Pass Eclipse Previews /1 #EB63
2006 Press Pass Eclipse Racing Champions #RC8
2006 Press Pass Eclipse Skidmarks #SM2
2006 Press Pass Eclipse Skidmarks Holofoil /250 #SM2
2006 Press Pass Eclipse Supernova #SU10
2006 Press Pass Eclipse Under Cover Cars /140 #UCT3
2006 Press Pass Eclipse Under Cover Drivers Gold /1 #UCD3
2006 Press Pass Eclipse Under Cover Drivers Holofoil /100 #UCD3
2006 Press Pass Eclipse Under Cover Drivers Red /225 #UCD3
2006 Press Pass Eclipse Under Cover Drivers Silver /400 #UCD3
2006 Press Pass Four Wide /50 #FWDE
2006 Press Pass Four Wide Checkered Flag /1 #FWDE
2006 Press Pass Game Face #GF4
2006 Press Pass Gold #G9
2006 Press Pass Gold #G76
2006 Press Pass Gold #G97
2006 Press Pass Legends #37
2006 Press Pass Legends #47
2006 Press Pass Legends Autographs Black /50 #21
2006 Press Pass Legends Blue /1999 #B37
2006 Press Pass Legends Blue /1999 #B47
2006 Press Pass Legends Bronze /999 #Z37
2006 Press Pass Legends Bronze /999 #Z47
2006 Press Pass Legends Gold /299 #G37
2006 Press Pass Legends Gold /299 #G47
2006 Press Pass Legends Heritage Gold /99 #HE12
2006 Press Pass Legends Heritage Gold /99 #HE15
2006 Press Pass Legends Heritage Silver /549 #HE12
2006 Press Pass Legends Heritage Silver /549 #HE15
2006 Press Pass Legends Holofoil /99 #H37
2006 Press Pass Legends Holofoil /99 #H47
2006 Press Pass Legends Press Plates Black /1 #PPB37
2006 Press Pass Legends Press Plates Black /1 #PPB47
2006 Press Pass Legends Press Plates Black Backs /1 #PPB37B
2006 Press Pass Legends Press Plates Black Backs /1 #PPB47B
2006 Press Pass Legends Press Plates Cyan /1 #PPC37
2006 Press Pass Legends Press Plates Cyan /1 #PPC47
2006 Press Pass Legends Press Plates Cyan Backs /1 #PPC37B
2006 Press Pass Legends Press Plates Cyan Backs /1 #PPC47B
2006 Press Pass Legends Press Plates Magenta /1 #PPM37
2006 Press Pass Legends Press Plates Magenta /1 #PPM47
2006 Press Pass Legends Press Plates Magenta Backs /1 #PPM37B
2006 Press Pass Legends Press Plates Magenta Backs /1 #PPM47B
2006 Press Pass Legends Press Plates Yellow /1 #PPY37
2006 Press Pass Legends Press Plates Yellow /1 #PPY47
2006 Press Pass Legends Press Plates Yellow Backs /1 #PPY37B
2006 Press Pass Legends Press Plates Yellow Backs /1 #PPY47B
2006 Press Pass Legends Previews /5 #EB37
2006 Press Pass Legends Previews /1 #EB47
2006 Press Pass Legends Solo /1 #S37
2006 Press Pass Legends Solo /1 #S47
2006 Press Pass Legends Triple Threads /50 #TTDE
2006 Press Pass Optima #8
2006 Press Pass Optima #60
2006 Press Pass Optima #68
2006 Press Pass Optima #8B
2006 Press Pass Optima Fan Favorite #FF4
2006 Press Pass Optima Gold /100 #G8
2006 Press Pass Optima Gold /100 #G60
2006 Press Pass Optima Gold /100 #G68
2006 Press Pass Optima Previews /5 #EB8
2006 Press Pass Optima Q & A #QA7
2006 Press Pass Platinum /100 #P9
2006 Press Pass Platinum /100 #P76
2006 Press Pass Platinum /100 #P97
2006 Press Pass Premium #6
2006 Press Pass Premium #63
2006 Press Pass Premium #80
2006 Press Pass Premium Asphalt Jungle #AJ1
2006 Press Pass Premium Hot Threads Cars /165 #HTT3
2006 Press Pass Premium Hot Threads Drivers /220 #HTD3
2006 Press Pass Premium Hot Threads Drivers Gold /1 #HTD3
2006 Press Pass Premium In the Zone #IZ1
2006 Press Pass Premium In the Zone Red /250 #IZ1
2006 Press Pass Previews /5 #EB9
2006 Press Pass Previews /1 #EB97
2006 Press Pass Signings #NNO
2006 Press Pass Signings #14
2006 Press Pass Signings Gold /50 #14
2006 Press Pass Signings Gold Red Ink #14
2006 Press Pass Signings Red Ink #14
2006 Press Pass Signings Silver /100 #14
2006 Press Pass Signings Silver Red Ink #14
2006 Press Pass Snapshots #SN11
2006 Press Pass Stealth #6
2006 Press Pass Stealth #47
2006 Press Pass Stealth #57
2006 Press Pass Stealth #71
2006 Press Pass Stealth #52
2006 Press Pass Stealth Autographed Hat Entry #PPH5
2006 Press Pass Stealth Corporate Cuts /250 #CCD3
2006 Press Pass Stealth EFX #EFX2
2006 Press Pass Stealth Gear Grippers Autographs /8 #DE
2006 Press Pass Stealth Gear Grippers Cars Retail /99 #GGT6
2006 Press Pass Stealth Gear Grippers Drivers /99 #GGD6
2006 Press Pass Stealth Hot Pass #HP7
2006 Press Pass Stealth Previews /5 #6
2006 Press Pass Stealth Profile #P1
2006 Press Pass Stealth Retail #6
2006 Press Pass Stealth Retail #47
2006 Press Pass Stealth Retail #57
2006 Press Pass Stealth Retail #71
2006 Press Pass Stealth Retail #52
2006 Press Pass Stealth X-Ray /100 #X6
2006 Press Pass Stealth X-Ray /100 #X47
2006 Press Pass Stealth X-Ray /100 #X52
2006 Press Pass Stealth X-Ray /100 #X57
2006 Press Pass Stealth X-Ray /100 #X71
2006 Press Pass Top 25 Drivers & Rides #C6
2006 Press Pass Top 25 Drivers & Rides #D6
2006 Press Pass Velocity #VE1
2006 TRAKS #7
2006 TRAKS #40
2006 TRAKS Autographs #8
2006 TRAKS Autographs 25 /25 #8
2006 TRAKS Previews /1 #7
2006 TRAKS Previews /1 #40
2006 TRAKS Stickers #8
2006 VIP #5
2006 VIP #49
2006 VIP #54
2006 VIP #83
2006 VIP Lap Leader #LL3
2006 VIP Lap Leader Transparent #LL3
2006 VIP Making the Show #MS23
2006 VIP Tradin' Paint Autographs /8 #TPDE
2006 VIP Tradin' Paint Cars Bronze /145 #TPT4
2006 VIP Tradin' Paint Drivers Gold /50 #TPD4
2006 VIP Tradin' Paint Drivers Silver /80 #TPD4
2006 Wheels American Thunder #6
2006 Wheels American Thunder #32
2006 Wheels American Thunder #47
2006 Wheels American Thunder #74
2006 Wheels American Thunder #85
2006 Wheels American Thunder American Muscle #AM7
2006 Wheels American Thunder American Racing Idol #RI3
2006 Wheels American Thunder American Racing Idol Golden /250 #RI3
2006 Wheels American Thunder Cool Threads /329 #CT4
2006 Wheels American Thunder Double Hat /99 #DH5
2006 Wheels American Thunder Grandstand #GS4
2006 Wheels American Thunder Head to Toe /99 #HT9
2006 Wheels American Thunder Previews /5 #EB6
2006 Wheels American Thunder Previews /1 #EB74
2006 Wheels American Thunder Pushin' Pedal /199 #PP1
2006 Wheels American Thunder Thunder Road #TR2
2006 Wheels American Thunder Thunder Strokes /100 #3
2006 Wheels High Gear #18
2006 Wheels High Gear #18B
2006 Wheels High Gear #47
2006 Wheels High Gear #79
2006 Wheels High Gear Flag Chasers Black /110 #FC3
2006 Wheels High Gear Flag Chasers Blue-Yellow /65 #FC3
2006 Wheels High Gear Flag Chasers Checkered /3 #FC3
2006 Wheels High Gear Flag Chasers Green /110 #FC3
2006 Wheels High Gear Flag Chasers Red /110 #FC3
2006 Wheels High Gear Flag Chasers White /110 #FC3
2006 Wheels High Gear Flag Chasers Yellow /110 #FC3
2006 Wheels High Gear Flag to Flag #FF5
2006 Wheels High Gear Full Throttle #FT4
2006 Wheels High Gear Man & Machine Cars #MMB4
2006 Wheels High Gear Man & Machine Drivers #MMA4
2006 Wheels High Gear MPH /100 #M18
2006 Wheels High Gear MPH /100 #M47
2006 Wheels High Gear MPH /100 #M79
2006 Wheels High Gear Previews Green /5 #EB18
2006 Wheels High Gear Previews Silver /1 #EB79
2007 Press Pass #6
2007 Press Pass #66
2007 Press Pass #106
2007 Press Pass #113
2007 Press Pass Autographs #11
2007 Press Pass Blue #B6
2007 Press Pass Blue #B66
2007 Press Pass Blue #B106
2007 Press Pass Blue #B113
2007 Press Pass Burning Rubber Drivers /75 #BRD7
2007 Press Pass Burning Rubber Drivers Gold /1 #BRD7
2007 Press Pass Burning Rubber Team /325 #BRT7
2007 Press Pass Burnouts #BO2
2007 Press Pass Burnouts Blue /99 #BO2
2007 Press Pass Burnouts Gold /299 #BO2
2007 Press Pass Collector's Series Box Set #SB5
2007 Press Pass Cup Chase #CCR14
2007 Press Pass Dale The Movie #18
2007 Press Pass Dale The Movie #31
2007 Press Pass Dale The Movie #46
2007 Press Pass Double Burner Firesuit-Glove /100 #DB2
2007 Press Pass Double Burner Firesuit-Glove Exchange /100 #DB2
2007 Press Pass Double Burner Metal-Tire /100 #DBDE
2007 Press Pass Double Burner Metal-Tire Exchange /100 #DBDE
2007 Press Pass Eclipse #0
2007 Press Pass Eclipse #5A
2007 Press Pass Eclipse #41
2007 Press Pass Eclipse #77
2007 Press Pass Eclipse #CL
2007 Press Pass Eclipse #5B
2007 Press Pass Eclipse Ecliptic #EC8
2007 Press Pass Eclipse Gold /25 #G5
2007 Press Pass Eclipse Gold /25 #G41
2007 Press Pass Eclipse Gold /25 #G77
2007 Press Pass Eclipse Gold /25 #GCL
2007 Press Pass Eclipse Hyperdrive #HD9
2007 Press Pass Eclipse Previews /5 #EB5
2007 Press Pass Eclipse Racing Champions #RC12
2007 Press Pass Eclipse Racing Champions #RC18
2007 Press Pass Eclipse Red /1 #R5
2007 Press Pass Eclipse Red /1 #R41
2007 Press Pass Eclipse Red /1 #R77
2007 Press Pass Eclipse Red /1 #RCL
2007 Press Pass Eclipse Skidmarks #SM1
2007 Press Pass Eclipse Skidmarks Holofoil /250 #SM1
2007 Press Pass Eclipse Teammates Autographs /25 #1
2007 Press Pass Eclipse Under Cover Autographs /8 #UCDE
2007 Press Pass Eclipse Under Cover Double Cover Name /25 #DC6
2007 Press Pass Eclipse Under Cover Double Cover NASCAR /99 #DC6
2007 Press Pass Eclipse Under Cover Drivers /450 #UCD1
2007 Press Pass Eclipse Under Cover Drivers Eclipse /1 #UCD1
2007 Press Pass Eclipse Under Cover Drivers Name /99 #UCD1
2007 Press Pass Eclipse Under Cover Drivers NASCAR /270 #UCD1
2007 Press Pass Eclipse Under Cover Teams /135 #UCT1
2007 Press Pass Eclipse Under Cover Teams NASCAR /25 #UCT1
2007 Press Pass Four Wide /50 #FWDE
2007 Press Pass Four Wide Checkered Flag /1 #FWDE
2007 Press Pass Four Wide Checkered Flag Exchange /1 #FWDE
2007 Press Pass Four Wide Exchange /50 #FWDE
2007 Press Pass Gold #G6
2007 Press Pass Gold #G66
2007 Press Pass Gold #G106
2007 Press Pass Gold #G113
2007 Press Pass Hot Treads #HT5
2007 Press Pass Hot Treads Blue /99 #HT5
2007 Press Pass Hot Treads Gold /299 #HT5
2007 Press Pass K-Mart #DEC
2007 Press Pass Legends #42
2007 Press Pass Legends Autographs Blue /59 #5
2007 Press Pass Legends Autographs Inscriptions Blue /8 #3
2007 Press Pass Legends Autographs Inscriptions Blue /1 #4
2007 Press Pass Legends Blue /999 #B42
2007 Press Pass Legends Bronze /599 #Z42
2007 Press Pass Legends Gold /249 #G42
2007 Press Pass Legends Holofoil /99 #H42
2007 Press Pass Legends Press Plates Black /1 #PP42
2007 Press Pass Legends Press Plates Black Backs /1 #PP42
2007 Press Pass Legends Press Plates Cyan /1 #PP42
2007 Press Pass Legends Press Plates Cyan Backs /1 #PP42
2007 Press Pass Legends Press Plates Magenta /1 #PP42
2007 Press Pass Legends Press Plates Magenta Backs /1 #PP42
2007 Press Pass Legends Press Plates Yellow /1 #PP42
2007 Press Pass Legends Press Plates Yellow Backs /1 #PP42
2007 Press Pass Legends Previews /5 #EB42
2007 Press Pass Legends Solo /1 #S42
2007 Press Pass Legends Sunday Swatches Bronze /199 #DESS
2007 Press Pass Legends Sunday Swatches Gold /50 #DESS
2007 Press Pass Legends Sunday Swatches Silver /99 #DESS
2007 Press Pass Legends Victory Lane Bronze /199 #VL1
2007 Press Pass Legends Victory Lane Gold /25 #VL1
2007 Press Pass Legends Victory Lane Silver /99 #VL1
2007 Press Pass Platinum /100 #P6
2007 Press Pass Platinum /100 #P86
2007 Press Pass Platinum /100 #P106
2007 Press Pass Platinum /100 #P113
2007 Press Pass Premium #7
2007 Press Pass Premium #52
2007 Press Pass Premium #65
2007 Press Pass Premium #73
2007 Press Pass Premium #77
2007 Press Pass Premium Concrete Chaos #CC2
2007 Press Pass Premium Hot Threads Autographs /8 #HTDE
2007 Press Pass Premium Hot Threads Drivers /145 #HTD11
2007 Press Pass Premium Hot Threads Drivers Gold /1 #HTD11
2007 Press Pass Premium Hot Threads Patch /8 #HTP14
2007 Press Pass Premium Hot Threads Patch /10 #HTP13
2007 Press Pass Premium Hot Threads Team /160 #HTT11
2007 Press Pass Premium Performance Driven #PD3
2007 Press Pass Premium Performance Driven Red /250 #PD3
2007 Press Pass Premium Red /15 #7
2007 Press Pass Premium Red /15 #52
2007 Press Pass Premium Red /15 #65
2007 Press Pass Premium Red /5 #73
2007 Press Pass Premium Red /5 #77
2007 Press Pass Previews /5 #EB6
2007 Press Pass Previews /1 #EB113
2007 Press Pass Race Day #RD6
2007 Press Pass Signings #17
2007 Press Pass Signings Blue /25 #6
2007 Press Pass Signings Gold /50 #14
2007 Press Pass Signings Press Plates Black /1 #11
2007 Press Pass Signings Press Plates Cyan /1 #10
2007 Press Pass Signings Press Plates Magenta /1 #10
2007 Press Pass Signings Press Plates Yellow /1 #10
2007 Press Pass Signings Silver /100 #13
2007 Press Pass Snapshots #SN5
2007 Press Pass Stealth #6
2007 Press Pass Stealth #47
2007 Press Pass Stealth #57
2007 Press Pass Stealth #82
2007 Press Pass Stealth #90
2007 Press Pass Stealth #71
2007 Press Pass Stealth Battle Armor Autographs /8 #BASDE
2007 Press Pass Stealth Battle Armor Drivers /150 #BAD6
2007 Press Pass Stealth Battle Armor Teams /85 #BAT6
2007 Press Pass Stealth Chrome #6A
2007 Press Pass Stealth Chrome #47
2007 Press Pass Stealth Chrome #57
2007 Press Pass Stealth Chrome #82
2007 Press Pass Stealth Chrome #90
2007 Press Pass Stealth Chrome #6B
2007 Press Pass Stealth Chrome #6C
2007 Press Pass Stealth Chrome #71
2007 Press Pass Stealth Chrome Exclusives /99 #X6
2007 Press Pass Stealth Chrome Exclusives /99 #X47
2007 Press Pass Stealth Chrome Exclusives /99 #X57
2007 Press Pass Stealth Chrome Exclusives /99 #X71
2007 Press Pass Stealth Chrome Exclusives /99 #X82
2007 Press Pass Stealth Chrome Exclusives /99 #X90
2007 Press Pass Stealth Chrome Platinum /25 #P6
2007 Press Pass Stealth Chrome Platinum /25 #P47
2007 Press Pass Stealth Chrome Platinum /25 #P57
2007 Press Pass Stealth Chrome Platinum /25 #P71
2007 Press Pass Stealth Chrome Platinum /25 #P82
2007 Press Pass Stealth Chrome Platinum /25 #P90
2007 Press Pass Stealth Fusion #F7
2007 Press Pass Stealth Mach 07 #M7-1
2007 Press Pass Stealth Maximum Access #MA6
2007 Press Pass Stealth Maximum Access Autographs /25 #MA6
2007 Press Pass Stealth Previews /1 #EB90
2007 Press Pass Stealth Previews /1 #EB82
2007 Press Pass Stealth Previews /5 #EB6
2007 Press Pass Target #DEB
2007 Press Pass Target Race Win Tires #RW3
2007 Press Pass Velocity #V4
2007 Press Pass Wal-Mart #DEA
2007 Traks #5
2007 Traks #73
2007 Traks #79
2007 Traks #83
2007 Traks #93
2007 Traks Corporate Cuts Driver /99 #CCD12
2007 Traks Corporate Cuts Patch /8 #CCD12
2007 Traks Corporate Cuts Team /180 #CCT12
2007 Traks Driver's Seat #DS14B
2007 Traks Driver's Seat #DS14
2007 Traks Driver's Seat National #DS14
2007 Traks Gold #G5
2007 Traks Gold #G73
2007 Traks Gold #G79
2007 Traks Gold #G83
2007 Traks Gold #G93
2007 Traks Holofoil /50 #H5
2007 Traks Holofoil /50 #H73
2007 Traks Holofoil /50 #H79
2007 Traks Holofoil /50 #H83
2007 Traks Holofoil /50 #H93
2007 Traks Hot Pursuit #HP10
2007 Traks Previews /5 #EB5
2007 Traks Previews /1 #EB79
2007 Traks Red /10 #R5
2007 Traks Red /10 #R73
2007 Traks Red /10 #R79
2007 Traks Red /10 #R83
2007 Traks Red /10 #R93
2007 Traks Target Exclusives #DEA
2007 Traks Track Time #TT1
2007 Traks Wal-Mart Exclusives #DEB
2007 VIP #7
2007 VIP #50
2007 VIP #67
2007 VIP Get A Grip Autographs /8 #GGDE
2007 VIP Get A Grip Drivers /70 #GGD27
2007 VIP Get A Grip Teams /70 #GGT27
2007 VIP Pedal To The Metal /50 #PM3
2007 VIP Previews /5 #EB7
2007 VIP Sunday Best #SB5
2007 VIP Trophy Club #TC4
2007 VIP Trophy Club Transparent #TC4
2007 Wheels American Thunder #7
2007 Wheels American Thunder #39
2007 Wheels American Thunder #57
2007 Wheels American Thunder #80
2007 Wheels American Thunder American Dreams #AD10
2007 Wheels American Thunder American Dreams Gold /250 #ADG10
2007 Wheels American Thunder Autographed Hat Instant Winner /1 #AH8
2007 Wheels American Thunder Cool Threads /299 #CT6
2007 Wheels American Thunder Head to Toe /99 #HT5
2007 Wheels American Thunder Previews /5 #EB7
2007 Wheels American Thunder Previews /1 #EB57
2007 Wheels American Thunder Pushin' Pedal /99 #PP1
2007 Wheels American Thunder Starting Grid #SG2
2007 Wheels American Thunder Thunder Road #TR10
2007 Wheels American Thunder Thunder Strokes #12
2007 Wheels American Thunder Thunder Strokes Press Plates Black /1 #12
2007 Wheels American Thunder Thunder Strokes Press Plates Cyan /1 #12
2007 Wheels American Thunder Thunder Strokes Press Plates Magenta /1 #12
2007 Wheels American Thunder Thunder Strokes Press Plates Yellow /1 #12
2007 Wheels American Thunder Triple Hat /99 #TH6
2007 Wheels Autographs #10
2007 Wheels Autographs Press Plates Black /1 #9
2007 Wheels Autographs Press Plates Cyan /1 #9
2007 Wheels Autographs Press Plates Magenta /1 #9
2007 Wheels High Gear #5A
2007 Wheels High Gear #5B
2007 Wheels High Gear Driven #DR18
2007 Wheels High Gear Final Standings Gold /5 #FS5
2007 Wheels High Gear Flag Chasers Black /89 #FC1
2007 Wheels High Gear Flag Chasers Blue-Yellow /50 #FC1
2007 Wheels High Gear Flag Chasers Checkered /10 #FC1
2007 Wheels High Gear Flag Chasers Green /89 #FC1
2007 Wheels High Gear Flag Chasers Red /89 #FC1
2007 Wheels High Gear Flag Chasers White /89 #FC1
2007 Wheels High Gear Flag Chasers Yellow /89 #FC1
2007 Wheels High Gear Full Throttle #FT4
2007 Wheels High Gear Last Lap /10 #LL8
2007 Wheels High Gear MPH /100 #M5
2007 Wheels High Gear Previews /5 #EB5
2007 Wheels High Gear Top Tier #TT5
2008 Go Daddy Promos #DEJ
2008 Press Pass #13
2008 Press Pass #96
2008 Press Pass #97
2008 Press Pass #98
2008 Press Pass #99
2008 Press Pass #100
2008 Press Pass #101
2008 Press Pass #102
2008 Press Pass #103
2008 Press Pass #104
2008 Press Pass #105
2008 Press Pass #106
2008 Press Pass Autographs #14
2008 Press Pass Autographs Press Plates Black /1 #10
2008 Press Pass Autographs Press Plates Cyan /1 #10
2008 Press Pass Autographs Press Plates Magenta /1 #10
2008 Press Pass Autographs Press Plates Yellow /1 #10
2008 Press Pass Blue #B13
2008 Press Pass Blue #B96
2008 Press Pass Blue #B97
2008 Press Pass Blue #B98
2008 Press Pass Blue #B99
2008 Press Pass Blue #B100
2008 Press Pass Blue #B101
2008 Press Pass Blue #B102
2008 Press Pass Blue #B103
2008 Press Pass Blue #B104
2008 Press Pass Blue #B105
2008 Press Pass Blue #B106
2008 Press Pass Burning Rubber Autographs /8 #BRDE
2008 Press Pass Collector's Series Box Set #4
2008 Press Pass Cup Chase #CC4
2008 Press Pass Cup Chase Prizes #CC4

2008 Press Pass Daytona 500 50th Anniversary #41
2008 Press Pass Double Burner Metal-Tire /100 #DBDE
2008 Press Pass Eclipse #67A
2008 Press Pass Eclipse #86
2008 Press Pass Eclipse #90
2008 Press Pass Eclipse #67B
2008 Press Pass Eclipse Gold /25 #G67
2008 Press Pass Eclipse Gold /25 #G86
2008 Press Pass Eclipse Gold /25 #G90
2008 Press Pass Eclipse Red /1 #R67
2008 Press Pass Eclipse Red /1 #R86
2008 Press Pass Eclipse Red /1 #R90
2008 Press Pass Eclipse Star Tracks #ST15
2008 Press Pass Eclipse Star Tracks Holofoil /250 #ST15
2008 Press Pass Eclipse Teammates Autographs /25 #EG
2008 Press Pass Eclipse Teammates Autographs /25 #EJ
2008 Press Pass Eclipse Teammates Autographs /25 #EM
2008 Press Pass Eclipse Teammates Autographs /25 #EGJM
2008 Press Pass Eclipse Under Cover Autographs /8 #UCDE
2008 Press Pass Four Wide /50 #FWDE1
2008 Press Pass Four Wide /50 #FWDE3
2008 Press Pass Four Wide /50 #FWDE2
2008 Press Pass Four Wide Checkered Flag /1 #FWDE
2008 Press Pass Four Wide Checkered Flag /1 #FWDE2
2008 Press Pass Four Wide Checkered Flag /1 #FWDE3
2008 Press Pass Gold #G13
2008 Press Pass Gold #G96
2008 Press Pass Gold #G97
2008 Press Pass Gold #G98
2008 Press Pass Gold #G99
2008 Press Pass Gold #G100
2008 Press Pass Gold #G101
2008 Press Pass Gold #G102
2008 Press Pass Gold #G103
2008 Press Pass Gold #G104
2008 Press Pass Gold #G105
2008 Press Pass Gold #G106
2008 Press Pass Legends #47
2008 Press Pass Legends Autographs Black #DE
2008 Press Pass Legends Autographs Blue #DE
2008 Press Pass Legends Autographs Press Plates Black /1 #DE
2008 Press Pass Legends Autographs Press Plates Cyan /1 #DE
2008 Press Pass Legends Autographs Press Plates Magenta /1 #DE
2008 Press Pass Legends Autographs Press Plates Yellow /1 #DE
2008 Press Pass Legends Blue /599 #47
2008 Press Pass Legends Bronze /299 #47
2008 Press Pass Legends Gold /99 #47
2008 Press Pass Legends Holo /25 #47
2008 Press Pass Legends Previews /5 #EB47
2008 Press Pass Legends Printing Plates Black /1 #47
2008 Press Pass Legends Printing Plates Cyan /1 #47
2008 Press Pass Legends Printing Plates Magenta /1 #47
2008 Press Pass Legends Printing Plates Yellow /1 #47
2008 Press Pass Legends Prominent Pieces Metal-Tire Bronze /99 #PP3DE
2008 Press Pass Legends Prominent Pieces Metal-Tire Gold /25 #PP3DE
2008 Press Pass Legends Prominent Pieces Metal-Tire Silver /50 #PP3DE
2008 Press Pass Legends Solo /1 #47
2008 Press Pass Legends Victory Lane Bronze /99 #VLDE
2008 Press Pass Legends Victory Lane Gold /25 #VLDE
2008 Press Pass Legends Victory Lane Silver /50 #VLDE
2008 Press Pass Platinum /100 #P13
2008 Press Pass Platinum /100 #P96
2008 Press Pass Platinum /100 #P97
2008 Press Pass Platinum /100 #P98
2008 Press Pass Platinum /100 #P99
2008 Press Pass Platinum /100 #P100
2008 Press Pass Platinum /100 #P101
2008 Press Pass Platinum /100 #P102
2008 Press Pass Platinum /100 #P103
2008 Press Pass Platinum /100 #P104
2008 Press Pass Platinum /100 #P105
2008 Press Pass Platinum /100 #P106
2008 Press Pass Premium #1
2008 Press Pass Premium #34
2008 Press Pass Premium #37
2008 Press Pass Premium #49
2008 Press Pass Premium #51
2008 Press Pass Premium #57
2008 Press Pass Premium #71
2008 Press Pass Premium #75
2008 Press Pass Premium #84
2008 Press Pass Premium Clean Air #CA4
2008 Press Pass Premium Going Global #GG1
2008 Press Pass Premium Going Global Red /250 #GG1
2008 Press Pass Premium Hot Threads Drivers /120 #HTD19
2008 Press Pass Premium Hot Threads Drivers /120 #HTD18
2008 Press Pass Premium Hot Threads Drivers Gold /1 #HTD18
2008 Press Pass Premium Hot Threads Drivers Gold /1 #HTD19
2008 Press Pass Premium Hot Threads Team /120 #HTT18
2008 Press Pass Premium Hot Threads Team /120 #HTT19
2008 Press Pass Premium Previews /5 #EB1
2008 Press Pass Premium Previews /5 #EB34
2008 Press Pass Premium Previews /1 #EB57
2008 Press Pass Premium Red /15 #1
2008 Press Pass Premium Red /15 #34
2008 Press Pass Premium Red /15 #37
2008 Press Pass Premium Red /15 #49
2008 Press Pass Premium Red /15 #51
2008 Press Pass Premium Red /15 #57
2008 Press Pass Premium Red /15 #71
2008 Press Pass Premium Red /5 #75
2008 Press Pass Premium Red /5 #84
2008 Press Pass Premium Target #TA5
2008 Press Pass Premium Team Signed Baseballs #HMS
2008 Press Pass Premium Team Signed Baseballs #EHMS
2008 Press Pass Premium Wal-Mart #WM1
2008 Press Pass Previews /5 #EB13
2008 Press Pass Previews /5 #EB96
2008 Press Pass Previews /5 #EB97
2008 Press Pass Previews /5 #EB98
2008 Press Pass Previews /5 #EB99
2008 Press Pass Previews /5 #EB100
2008 Press Pass Previews /5 #EB101
2008 Press Pass Previews /5 #EB102
2008 Press Pass Previews /5 #EB103
2008 Press Pass Race Day #RD8
2008 Press Pass Signings #17
2008 Press Pass Signings #18
2008 Press Pass Signings Blue /8 #7
2008 Press Pass Signings Gold /25 #15
2008 Press Pass Signings Gold /25 #16
2008 Press Pass Signings Press Plates Black /1 #10
2008 Press Pass Signings Press Plates Black /1 #11
2008 Press Pass Signings Press Plates Black /1 #DE
2008 Press Pass Signings Press Plates Cyan /1 #10
2008 Press Pass Signings Press Plates Cyan /1 #11
2008 Press Pass Signings Press Plates Cyan #DE
2008 Press Pass Signings Press Plates Magenta /1 #10
2008 Press Pass Signings Press Plates Magenta /1 #11
2008 Press Pass Signings Press Plates Magenta #DE
2008 Press Pass Signings Press Plates Yellow /1 #10
2008 Press Pass Signings Press Plates Yellow /1 #11
2008 Press Pass Signings Press Plates Yellow /1 #DE
2008 Press Pass Signings Silver /50 #16
2008 Press Pass Signings Silver /50 #17
2008 Press Pass Slideshow #SS12
2008 Press Pass Slideshow #SS36
2008 Press Pass Speedway #4
2008 Press Pass Speedway #62
2008 Press Pass Speedway #68
2008 Press Pass Speedway #77
2008 Press Pass Speedway #91
2008 Press Pass Speedway Blur #B3
2008 Press Pass Speedway Garage Graphs Duals /50 #EE
2008 Press Pass Speedway Gold #G4
2008 Press Pass Speedway Gold #G62
2008 Press Pass Speedway Gold #G68
2008 Press Pass Speedway Gold #G77
2008 Press Pass Speedway Gold #G91
2008 Press Pass Speedway Holofoil /50 #H4
2008 Press Pass Speedway Holofoil /50 #H62
2008 Press Pass Speedway Holofoil /50 #H68
2008 Press Pass Speedway Holofoil /50 #H77
2008 Press Pass Speedway Holofoil /50 #H91
2008 Press Pass Speedway Previews /5 #EB4
2008 Press Pass Speedway Previews /1 #EB91
2008 Press Pass Speedway Red /10 #R4
2008 Press Pass Speedway Red /10 #R62
2008 Press Pass Speedway Red /10 #R68
2008 Press Pass Speedway Red /10 #R77
2008 Press Pass Speedway Red /10 #R91
2008 Press Pass Speedway Test Drive #TD7
2008 Press Pass Starting Grid #SG4
2008 Press Pass Stealth #8
2008 Press Pass Stealth #53
2008 Press Pass Stealth #83
2008 Press Pass Stealth #67
2008 Press Pass Stealth Battle Armor Drivers /120 #BAD23
2008 Press Pass Stealth Battle Armor Teams /115 #BAT23
2008 Press Pass Stealth Chrome #8
2008 Press Pass Stealth Chrome #53
2008 Press Pass Stealth Chrome #83A
2008 Press Pass Stealth Chrome #83B
2008 Press Pass Stealth Chrome #67
2008 Press Pass Stealth Chrome Exclusives /25 #8
2008 Press Pass Stealth Chrome Exclusives /25 #53
2008 Press Pass Stealth Chrome Exclusives /25 #67
2008 Press Pass Stealth Chrome Exclusives /25 #83
2008 Press Pass Stealth Chrome Exclusives Gold /99 #8
2008 Press Pass Stealth Chrome Exclusives Gold /99 #53
2008 Press Pass Stealth Chrome Exclusives Gold /99 #67
2008 Press Pass Stealth Chrome Exclusives Gold /99 #83
2008 Press Pass Stealth Mach 08 #M8-2
2008 Press Pass Stealth Maximum Access #MA8
2008 Press Pass Stealth Maximum Access Autographs /25 #MA8
2008 Press Pass Stealth Previews /5 #8
2008 Press Pass Stealth Previews /1 #83
2008 Press Pass Stealth Synthesis #S7
2008 Press Pass Stealth Target #TA7
2008 Press Pass Stealth Wal-Mart #WM11
2008 Press Pass Target #DEB
2008 Press Pass VIP National Convention Promo #3
2008 Press Pass Wal-Mart #DEA
2008 Press Pass Wal-Mart Autographs /50 #1
2008 Press Pass Weekend Warriors #WW5
2008 VIP #9
2008 VIP #48
2008 VIP All Access #AA5
2008 VIP Gear Gallery #GG11
2008 VIP Gear Gallery Memorabilia /50 #GGDE
2008 VIP Gear Gallery Transparent #GG11
2008 VIP Get a Grip Autographs /88 #GGSDE
2008 VIP National Promos #3
2008 VIP Previews /5 #EB9
2008 VIP Triple Grip /25 #TG1
2008 VIP Trophy Club #TC6
2008 VIP Trophy Club Transparent #TC6
2008 Wheels American Thunder #9
2008 Wheels American Thunder #57
2008 Wheels American Thunder #70
2008 Wheels American Thunder #74
2008 Wheels American Thunder #41
2008 Wheels American Thunder American Dreams #AD1
2008 Wheels American Thunder American Dreams Gold /250 #AD1
2008 Wheels American Thunder Autographed Hat Winner /1 #WHDE
2008 Wheels American Thunder Campaign Trail #CT6
2008 Wheels American Thunder Delegates #D6
2008 Wheels American Thunder Head to Toe /150 #HT10
2008 Wheels American Thunder Motorcade #M8
2008 Wheels American Thunder Previews /5 #9
2008 Wheels American Thunder Previews /1 #74
2008 Wheels American Thunder Pushin' Pedal /150 #PP 10
2008 Wheels American Thunder Triple Hat /125 #TH7
2008 Wheels Autographs #10
2008 Wheels Autographs Press Plates Black /1 #10
2008 Wheels Autographs Press Plates Cyan /1 #10
2008 Wheels Autographs Press Plates Magenta /1 #10
2008 Wheels Autographs Press Plates Yellow /1 #10
2008 Wheels High Gear #80
2008 Wheels High Gear #81
2008 Wheels High Gear #82A
2008 Wheels High Gear #83
2008 Wheels High Gear #84
2008 Wheels High Gear #85A
2008 Wheels High Gear #90
2008 Wheels High Gear #82B
2008 Wheels High Gear #85B
2008 Wheels High Gear MPH /100 #M80
2008 Wheels High Gear MPH /100 #M81
2008 Wheels High Gear MPH /100 #M82
2008 Wheels High Gear MPH /100 #M83
2008 Wheels High Gear MPH /100 #M84
2008 Wheels High Gear MPH /100 #M85
2008 Wheels High Gear MPH /100 #M90
2008 Wheels High Gear Previews /5 #EB80
2008 Wheels High Gear Previews /5 #EB81
2008 Wheels High Gear Previews /5 #EB82
2008 Wheels High Gear Previews /5 #EB83
2008 Wheels High Gear Previews /5 #EB84
2008 Wheels High Gear Previews /5 #EB85
2009 Element #7
2009 Element #39
2009 Element #50
2009 Element #63
2009 Element #75
2009 Element #93
2009 Element Big Win /35 #BWDE
2009 Element Elements of the Race Black Flag /99 #ERBDE
2009 Element Elements of the Race Black-White Flag /50 #ERXDE
2009 Element Elements of the Race Blue-Yellow Flag /50 #ERBODE
2009 Element Elements of the Race Checkered Flag /5 #ERCDE
2009 Element Elements of the Race Green Flag /50 #ERGDE
2009 Element Elements of the Race Red Flag /99 #ERRDE
2009 Element Elements of the Race White Flag /75 #ERWDE
2009 Element Elements of the Race Yellow Flag /99 #ERYDE
2009 Element Green White Checker /25 #GWCDE
2009 Element Kinetic Energy #KE1
2009 Element Kinetic Energy #KE9
2009 Element Lab Report #LR8
2009 Element Missing Elements #ME1
2009 Element Missing Elements Exchange #ME1
2009 Element Nobel Prize #NP2
2009 Element Previews /5 #7
2009 Element Previews /1 #50
2009 Element Radioactive /100 #7
2009 Element Radioactive /100 #39
2009 Element Radioactive /100 #50
2009 Element Radioactive /100 #63
2009 Element Radioactive /100 #75
2009 Element Radioactive /100 #93
2009 Element Taking the Checkers /45 #TCDE
2009 Press Pass #0
2009 Press Pass #4
2009 Press Pass #42
2009 Press Pass #56
2009 Press Pass #67
2009 Press Pass #74
2009 Press Pass #110
2009 Press Pass #127
2009 Press Pass #159
2009 Press Pass #180
2009 Press Pass #198
2009 Press Pass #211
2009 Press Pass #216
2009 Press Pass #200
2009 Press Pass Autographs Chase Edition /25 #DE
2009 Press Pass Autographs Gold #12
2009 Press Pass Autographs Printing Plates Black /1 #15
2009 Press Pass Autographs Printing Plates Cyan /1 #15
2009 Press Pass Autographs Printing Plates Magenta /1 #15
2009 Press Pass Autographs Printing Plates Yellow /1 #15
2009 Press Pass Autographs Silver #16
2009 Press Pass Autographs Track Edition /25 #DE
2009 Press Pass Blue #4
2009 Press Pass Blue #42
2009 Press Pass Blue #56
2009 Press Pass Blue #67
2009 Press Pass Blue #74
2009 Press Pass Blue #110
2009 Press Pass Blue #127
2009 Press Pass Blue #159
2009 Press Pass Blue #180
2009 Press Pass Blue #198
2009 Press Pass Blue #200
2009 Press Pass Blue #211
2009 Press Pass Blue #216
2009 Press Pass Burning Rubber Autographs /8 #BRSDE
2009 Press Pass Burning Rubber Drivers /185 #BRD15
2009 Press Pass Burning Rubber Prime Cut /25 #BRD15
2009 Press Pass Burning Rubber Teams /250 #BRT15
2009 Press Pass Cup Chase #CCR12
2009 Press Pass Daytona 500 Tires /25 #TTDEJR
2009 Press Pass Eclipse #28
2009 Press Pass Eclipse #35
2009 Press Pass Eclipse #54
2009 Press Pass Eclipse #67
2009 Press Pass Eclipse #86
2009 Press Pass Eclipse Black and White #28
2009 Press Pass Eclipse Black and White #35
2009 Press Pass Eclipse Black and White #54
2009 Press Pass Eclipse Black and White #67
2009 Press Pass Eclipse Black and White #86
2009 Press Pass Eclipse Black Hole Firesuits /50 #BH1
2009 Press Pass Eclipse Black Hole Firesuits /50 #BH2
2009 Press Pass Eclipse Blue #28
2009 Press Pass Eclipse Blue #35
2009 Press Pass Eclipse Blue #54
2009 Press Pass Eclipse Blue #67
2009 Press Pass Eclipse Blue #86
2009 Press Pass Eclipse Ecliptic Path #EP12
2009 Press Pass Eclipse Solar Swatches /10 #SSDE1
2009 Press Pass Eclipse Solar Swatches /15 #SSDE4
2009 Press Pass Eclipse Solar Swatches /15 #SSDE7
2009 Press Pass Eclipse Solar Swatches /15 #SSDE10
2009 Press Pass Eclipse Solar Swatches /25 #SSDE9
2009 Press Pass Eclipse Solar Swatches /25 #SSDE6
2009 Press Pass Eclipse Solar Swatches /25 #SSDE3
2009 Press Pass Eclipse Solar Swatches /20 #SSDE8
2009 Press Pass Eclipse Solar Swatches /20 #SSDE11
2009 Press Pass Eclipse Solar Swatches /20 #SSDE2
2009 Press Pass Eclipse Solar Swatches /20 #SSDE5
2009 Press Pass Final Standings /170 #110
2009 Press Pass Four Wide Autographs /3 #FWDE1
2009 Press Pass Four Wide Autographs /3 #FWDE2
2009 Press Pass Four Wide Checkered Flag /1 #FWDE
2009 Press Pass Four Wide Firesuit /50 #FWDE
2009 Press Pass Four Wide Firesuit /50 #FWDE2
2009 Press Pass Four Wide Sheet Metal /10 #FWDE
2009 Press Pass Four Wide Sheet Metal /10 #FWDE2
2009 Press Pass Four Wide Tire /25 #FWDE2
2009 Press Pass Four Wide Tire /25 #FWDE
2009 Press Pass Freeze Frame #FF6
2009 Press Pass Freeze Frame #FF21
2009 Press Pass Fusion #65
2009 Press Pass Fusion Bronze /150 #65
2009 Press Pass Fusion Gold /50 #65
2009 Press Pass Fusion Green /25 #65
2009 Press Pass Fusion Onyx /1 #65
2009 Press Pass Fusion Revered Relics Gold /50 #RRDEJ
2009 Press Pass Fusion Revered Relics Holofoil /25 #RRDEJ
2009 Press Pass Fusion Revered Relics Premium Swatch /10 #RRDEJ
2009 Press Pass Fusion Revered Relics Silver /65 #RRDEJ
2009 Press Pass Fusion Silver /99 #65
2009 Press Pass Game Face #GF1
2009 Press Pass Gold #4
2009 Press Pass Gold #42
2009 Press Pass Gold #56
2009 Press Pass Gold #67
2009 Press Pass Gold #74
2009 Press Pass Gold #110
2009 Press Pass Gold #127
2009 Press Pass Gold #159
2009 Press Pass Gold #180
2009 Press Pass Gold #198
2009 Press Pass Gold #200
2009 Press Pass Gold #211
2009 Press Pass Gold #216
2009 Press Pass Gold Holofoil /100 #4
2009 Press Pass Gold Holofoil /100 #42
2009 Press Pass Gold Holofoil /100 #56
2009 Press Pass Gold Holofoil /100 #67
2009 Press Pass Gold Holofoil /100 #74
2009 Press Pass Gold Holofoil /100 #110
2009 Press Pass Gold Holofoil /100 #127
2009 Press Pass Gold Holofoil /100 #159
2009 Press Pass Gold Holofoil /100 #180
2009 Press Pass Gold Holofoil /100 #198
2009 Press Pass Gold Holofoil /100 #200
2009 Press Pass Gold Holofoil /100 #211
2009 Press Pass Gold Holofoil /100 #216
2009 Press Pass Legends #43
2009 Press Pass Legends #58
2009 Press Pass Legends Autographs Gold /40 #8
2009 Press Pass Legends Autographs Inscriptions /20 #5
2009 Press Pass Legends Autographs Printing Plates Black /1 #6
2009 Press Pass Legends Autographs Printing Plates Cyan /1 #6
2009 Press Pass Legends Autographs Printing Plates Magenta /1 #6
2009 Press Pass Legends Autographs Printing Plates Yellow /1 #6
2009 Press Pass Legends Family Cuts /1 #1
2009 Press Pass Legends Family Portraits /550 #FP10
2009 Press Pass Legends Family Portraits /550 #FP11
2009 Press Pass Legends Family Portraits /550 #FP13
2009 Press Pass Legends Family Portraits /550 #FP14
2009 Press Pass Legends Family Portraits /550 #FP15
2009 Press Pass Legends Family Portraits Holofoil /99 #FP10
2009 Press Pass Legends Family Portraits Holofoil /99 #FP11
2009 Press Pass Legends Family Portraits Holofoil /99 #FP13
2009 Press Pass Legends Family Portraits Holofoil /99 #FP14
2009 Press Pass Legends Family Portraits Holofoil /99 #FP15
2009 Press Pass Legends Family Relics Bronze /99 #FREa5
2009 Press Pass Legends Family Relics Bronze /99 #FREa
2009 Press Pass Legends Family Relics Gold /25 #FREa
2009 Press Pass Legends Family Relics Gold /25 #FREa5
2009 Press Pass Legends Family Relics Gold /25 #FREa4
2009 Press Pass Legends Family Relics Gold /25 #FREa3
2009 Press Pass Legends Family Relics Silver /50 #FREa
2009 Press Pass Legends Family Relics Silver /50 #FREa5
2009 Press Pass Legends Family Relics Silver /50 #FREa3
2009 Press Pass Legends Gold /399 #43
2009 Press Pass Legends Gold /399 #58
2009 Press Pass Legends Holofoil /50 #43
2009 Press Pass Legends Holofoil /50 #58
2009 Press Pass Legends Past and Present /550 #PP2
2009 Press Pass Legends Past and Present Holofoil /99 #PP2
2009 Press Pass Legends Previews /5 #43
2009 Press Pass Legends Previews /1 #58
2009 Press Pass Legends Printing Plates Black /1 #43
2009 Press Pass Legends Printing Plates Black /1 #58
2009 Press Pass Legends Printing Plates Cyan /1 #43
2009 Press Pass Legends Printing Plates Cyan /1 #58
2009 Press Pass Legends Printing Plates Magenta /1 #43
2009 Press Pass Legends Printing Plates Magenta /1 #58
2009 Press Pass Legends Printing Plates Yellow /1 #43
2009 Press Pass Legends Printing Plates Yellow /1 #58
2009 Press Pass Legends Prominent Pieces Bronze /99 #PPDE1
2009 Press Pass Legends Prominent Pieces Bronze /99 #PPDE2
2009 Press Pass Legends Prominent Pieces Gold /25 #PPDE1
2009 Press Pass Legends Prominent Pieces Gold /25 #PPDE2
2009 Press Pass Legends Prominent Pieces Oversized /25 #PPOEDE
2009 Press Pass Legends Prominent Pieces Oversized /25 #PPOEDE2
2009 Press Pass Legends Prominent Pieces Silver /50 #PPDE1
2009 Press Pass Legends Prominent Pieces Silver /50 #PPDE2
2009 Press Pass Legends Red /199 #43
2009 Press Pass Legends Red /199 #58
2009 Press Pass Legends Solo /1 #43
2009 Press Pass Legends Solo /1 #58
2009 Press Pass Pieces Race Used Memorabilia #DE
2009 Press Pass Pocket Portraits #P6
2009 Press Pass Pocket Portraits Checkered Flag #P6
2009 Press Pass Pocket Portraits Hometown #P6
2009 Press Pass Pocket Portraits Smoke #P6
2009 Press Pass Pocket Portraits Target #PPT1
2009 Press Pass Pocket Portraits Target #PPT6
2009 Press Pass Pocket Portraits Wal-Mart #PPW1
2009 Press Pass Premium #1
2009 Press Pass Premium #32
2009 Press Pass Premium #49
2009 Press Pass Premium #62
2009 Press Pass Premium #77
2009 Press Pass Premium #87
2009 Press Pass Premium Gold #87
2009 Press Pass Premium Hot Threads /99 #HTDE2
2009 Press Pass Premium Hot Threads /325 #HTDE1
2009 Press Pass Premium Hot Threads /325 #HTDE1
2009 Press Pass Premium Hot Threads /99 #HTDE2
2009 Press Pass Premium Hot Threads Autographs /8 #DE2
2009 Press Pass Premium Hot Threads Autographs /8 #DE1
2009 Press Pass Premium Hot Threads Multi-Color /25 #HTDE1
2009 Press Pass Premium Hot Threads Multi-Color /25 #HTDE2
2009 Press Pass Premium Hot Threads Patches /10 #HTP-DE1
2009 Press Pass Premium Hot Threads Patches /10 #HTP-DE2
2009 Press Pass Premium Hot Threads Patches /10 #HTP-DE3
2009 Press Pass Premium Hot Threads Patches /10 #HTP-DE4
2009 Press Pass Premium Previews /5 #EB1
2009 Press Pass Premium Previews /5 #EB32
2009 Press Pass Premium Signatures #9
2009 Press Pass Premium Signatures Gold /25 #9
2009 Press Pass Premium Top Contenders #TC1
2009 Press Pass Premium Top Contenders Gold #TC1
2009 Press Pass Premium Win Streak #WS4
2009 Press Pass Premium Win Streak Victory Lane #WSVL-DE
2009 Press Pass Previews /5 #EB4
2009 Press Pass Previews /1 #EB110
2009 Press Pass Previews /5 #EB127
2009 Press Pass Previews /1 #EB198
2009 Press Pass Previews /1 #EB200
2009 Press Pass Red #4
2009 Press Pass Red #42
2009 Press Pass Red #56
2009 Press Pass Red #67
2009 Press Pass Red #74
2009 Press Pass Red #110
2009 Press Pass Red #127
2009 Press Pass Red #159
2009 Press Pass Red #180
2009 Press Pass Red #198
2009 Press Pass Red #200
2009 Press Pass Red #211
2009 Press Pass Red #216
2009 Press Pass Shifting Gears #1
2009 Press Pass Shifting Gears #2
2009 Press Pass Shifting Gears #3
2009 Press Pass Shifting Gears #4
2009 Press Pass Shifting Gears #5
2009 Press Pass Shifting Gears #6
2009 Press Pass Shifting Gears #7
2009 Press Pass Shifting Gears #8
2009 Press Pass Shifting Gears #9
2009 Press Pass Shifting Gears #10
2009 Press Pass Shifting Gears #11
2009 Press Pass Shifting Gears #12
2009 Press Pass Shifting Gears #13
2009 Press Pass Shifting Gears #14
2009 Press Pass Shifting Gears #15
2009 Press Pass Shifting Gears #16
2009 Press Pass Shifting Gears #17
2009 Press Pass Shifting Gears #18
2009 Press Pass Shifting Gears #19
2009 Press Pass Shifting Gears #20
2009 Press Pass Shifting Gears #21
2009 Press Pass Shifting Gears #22
2009 Press Pass Shifting Gears #23
2009 Press Pass Shifting Gears #24
2009 Press Pass Shifting Gears #25
2009 Press Pass Showcase /499 #3
2009 Press Pass Showcase /499 #37
2009 Press Pass Showcase /499 #29
2009 Press Pass Showcase 2nd Gear /125 #3
2009 Press Pass Showcase 2nd Gear /125 #29
2009 Press Pass Showcase 2nd Gear /125 #37
2009 Press Pass Showcase 3rd Gear /50 #3
2009 Press Pass Showcase 3rd Gear /50 #29
2009 Press Pass Showcase 3rd Gear /50 #37
2009 Press Pass Showcase 4th Gear /15 #3
2009 Press Pass Showcase 4th Gear /15 #29
2009 Press Pass Showcase 4th Gear /15 #37
2009 Press Pass Showcase Classic Collections Firesuit /25 #CCF1
2009 Press Pass Showcase Classic Collections Firesuit /25 #CCF2
2009 Press Pass Showcase Classic Collections Firesuit /25 #CCF3
2009 Press Pass Showcase Classic Collections Firesuit Patch /5 #CCF1
2009 Press Pass Showcase Classic Collections Firesuit Patch /5 #CCF2
2009 Press Pass Showcase Classic Collections Firesuit Patch /5 #CCF3
2009 Press Pass Showcase Classic Collections Ink /45 #2
2009 Press Pass Showcase Classic Collections Ink Gold /25 #2
2009 Press Pass Showcase Classic Collections Ink Green /5 #2
2009 Press Pass Showcase Classic Collections Ink Melting /1 #2
2009 Press Pass Showcase Classic Collections Sheet Metal /45 #CCS1
2009 Press Pass Showcase Classic Collections Sheet Metal /45 #CCS2
2009 Press Pass Showcase Classic Collections Sheet Metal /45 #CCS3
2009 Press Pass Showcase Classic Collections Tire /99 #CCT1
2009 Press Pass Showcase Classic Collections Tire /99 #CCT2
2009 Press Pass Showcase Classic Collections Tire /99 #CCT3
2009 Press Pass Showcase Elite Exhibit Ink /45 #2
2009 Press Pass Showcase Elite Exhibit Ink Gold /25 #2
2009 Press Pass Showcase Elite Exhibit Ink Green /5 #2
2009 Press Pass Showcase Elite Exhibit Ink Melting /1 #2
2009 Press Pass Showcase Elite Exhibit Triple Memorabilia /99 #EEDEJ
2009 Press Pass Showcase Elite Exhibit Triple Memorabilia Gold /45 #EEDEJ
2009 Press Pass Showcase Elite Exhibit Triple Memorabilia Green /25 #EEDEJ
2009 Press Pass Showcase Elite Exhibit Triple Memorabilia Melting /5 #EEDEJ
2009 Press Pass Showcase Printing Plates Black /1 #3
2009 Press Pass Showcase Printing Plates Black /1 #29
2009 Press Pass Showcase Printing Plates Black /1 #37
2009 Press Pass Showcase Printing Plates Black /1 #50
2009 Press Pass Showcase Printing Plates Cyan /1 #3
2009 Press Pass Showcase Printing Plates Cyan /1 #29
2009 Press Pass Showcase Printing Plates Cyan /1 #37
2009 Press Pass Showcase Printing Plates Cyan /1 #50
2009 Press Pass Showcase Printing Plates Magenta /1 #3
2009 Press Pass Showcase Printing Plates Magenta /1 #29
2009 Press Pass Showcase Printing Plates Magenta /1 #37
2009 Press Pass Showcase Printing Plates Magenta /1 #50
2009 Press Pass Showcase Printing Plates Yellow /1 #3
2009 Press Pass Showcase Printing Plates Yellow /1 #29
2009 Press Pass Showcase Printing Plates Yellow /1 #37
2009 Press Pass Showcase Printing Plates Yellow /1 #50
2009 Press Pass Showcase Prized Pieces Firesuit /25 #PPFDEJ
2009 Press Pass Showcase Prized Pieces Firesuit /25 #PPFDEJ2
2009 Press Pass Showcase Prized Pieces Firesuit Patch /5 #PPFDEJ
2009 Press Pass Showcase Prized Pieces Firesuit Patch /5 #PPFDEJ2
2009 Press Pass Showcase Prized Pieces Ink Firesuit /5 #2
2009 Press Pass Showcase Prized Pieces Ink Firesuit Patch /1 #2
2009 Press Pass Showcase Prized Pieces Ink Sheet Metal /25 #2
2009 Press Pass Showcase Prized Pieces Ink Tire /45 #2
2009 Press Pass Showcase Prized Pieces Sheet Metal /45 #PPSDEJ
2009 Press Pass Showcase Prized Pieces Sheet Metal /45 #PPSDEJ2
2009 Press Pass Showcase Prized Pieces Tire /99 #PPTDEJ
2009 Press Pass Showcase Prized Pieces Tire /99 #PPTDEJ2
2009 Press Pass Signature Series Archive Edition /1 #HTDE
2009 Press Pass Signature Series Archive Edition /1 #UCDE
2009 Press Pass Signature Series Archive Edition /1 #HTDE
2009 Press Pass Signature Series Archive Edition /1 #UCDE
2009 Press Pass Signature Series Archive Edition /1 #GGDE
2009 Press Pass Signature Series Archive Edition /1 #HTDE
2009 Press Pass Signings Blue /25 #11
2009 Press Pass Signings Gold #11
2009 Press Pass Signings Green /15 #11
2009 Press Pass Signings Orange /65 #11
2009 Press Pass Signings Printing Plates Magenta /1 #11
2009 Press Pass Signings Printing Plates Yellow /1 #11
2009 Press Pass Signings Purple /45 #11
2009 Press Pass Sponsor Swatches /250 #SSDEJR
2009 Press Pass Sponsor Swatches Select /10 #SSDEJR
2009 Press Pass Stealth #9A
2009 Press Pass Stealth #53
2009 Press Pass Stealth #63
2009 Press Pass Stealth #64
2009 Press Pass Stealth #79
2009 Press Pass Stealth #9B
2009 Press Pass Stealth Battle Armor /299 #BADE1C
2009 Press Pass Stealth Battle Armor /25 #BADE1B
2009 Press Pass Stealth Battle Armor /35 #BADE2B
2009 Press Pass Stealth Battle Armor /20 #BADE2A
2009 Press Pass Stealth Battle Armor /3 #BADE1A
2009 Press Pass Stealth Battle Armor Autographs /8 #BASDE2
2009 Press Pass Stealth Battle Armor Autographs /8 #BASDE1
2009 Press Pass Stealth Battle Armor Multi-Color /110 #BADE2
2009 Press Pass Stealth Battle Armor Multi-Color /185 #BADE1
2009 Press Pass Stealth Chrome #9A
2009 Press Pass Stealth Chrome #53
2009 Press Pass Stealth Chrome #63
2009 Press Pass Stealth Chrome #64
2009 Press Pass Stealth Chrome #79
2009 Press Pass Stealth Chrome #9B
2009 Press Pass Stealth Chrome #9C
2009 Press Pass Stealth Chrome Brushed Metal /25 #9
2009 Press Pass Stealth Chrome Brushed Metal /25 #53
2009 Press Pass Stealth Chrome Brushed Metal /25 #63
2009 Press Pass Stealth Chrome Brushed Metal /25 #64
2009 Press Pass Stealth Chrome Brushed Metal /25 #79
2009 Press Pass Stealth Chrome Gold /99 #9
2009 Press Pass Stealth Chrome Gold /99 #53
2009 Press Pass Stealth Chrome Gold /99 #63
2009 Press Pass Stealth Chrome Gold /99 #64
2009 Press Pass Stealth Chrome Gold /99 #79
2009 Press Pass Stealth Confidential Classified Bronze #PC1
2009 Press Pass Stealth Confidential Secret Silver #PC1
2009 Press Pass Stealth Confidential Top Secret Gold /25 #PC1
2009 Press Pass Stealth Mach 09 #M11
2009 Press Pass Stealth Previews /5 #EB9
2009 Press Pass Stealth Previews /1 #EB79
2009 Press Pass Target #DEB
2009 Press Pass Target Victory Tires /50 #DETT
2009 Press Pass Total Tire /25 #TT1
2009 Press Pass Tradin' Paint #TP1
2009 Press Pass Tread Marks Autographs /10 #SSDEJR
2009 Press Pass Unleashed #U1
2009 Press Pass Unleashed #U11
2009 Press Pass Wal-Mart #DEA
2009 Press Pass Wal-Mart Autographs Red #3
2009 Topps Sterling Cut Signatures /3 #MPS211
2009 Upper Deck Prominent Cuts Cut Signatures /2 #PCDEJ
2009 VIP #8
2009 VIP #47
2009 VIP #56
2009 VIP #76
2009 VIP #88
2009 VIP #90
2009 VIP Get A Grip /100 #GGDE
2009 VIP Get A Grip Autographs /8 #GGSDE2
2009 VIP Get A Grip Autographs /8 #GGSDE1
2009 VIP Get A Grip Holofoil /10 #GGDE
2009 VIP Get A Grip Logos /5 #GGLDE
2009 VIP Guest List #GG22
2009 VIP Hardware #H1
2009 VIP Hardware Transparent #H1
2009 VIP Leadfoot /150 #LFDE
2009 VIP Leadfoot Holofoil /10 #LFDE
2009 VIP National Promos #6
2009 VIP Previews /5 #8
2009 VIP Previews /1 #76
2009 VIP Purple /25 #8
2009 VIP Purple /25 #47
2009 VIP Purple /25 #56
2009 VIP Purple /25 #76
2009 VIP Purple /25 #88
2009 VIP Purple /25 #90
2009 VIP Race Day Gear /25 #RDGJG
2009 Wheels Autographs #16
2009 Wheels Autographs /25 #17
2009 Wheels Autographs Press Plates Black /1 #DE
2009 Wheels Autographs Press Plates Cyan /1 #DE
2009 Wheels Autographs Press Plates Magenta /1 #DE
2009 Wheels Autographs Press Plates Yellow /1 #DE
2009 Wheels Main Event #1
2009 Wheels Main Event #14
2009 Wheels Main Event #43
2009 Wheels Main Event #37
2009 Wheels Main Event Buyback Archive Edition /1 #PSDE
2009 Wheels Main Event Buyback Archive Edition /1 #PSDE
2009 Wheels Main Event Buyback Archive Edition /1 #TBDE
2009 Wheels Main Event Buyback Archive Edition /1 #BRDE
2009 Wheels Main Event Buyback Archive Edition /1 #GGDE
2009 Wheels Main Event Buyback Archive Edition /1 #BRDE
2009 Wheels Main Event Fast Pass Purple /25 #1
2009 Wheels Main Event Fast Pass Purple /25 #14
2009 Wheels Main Event Fast Pass Purple /25 #37
2009 Wheels Main Event Fast Pass Purple /25 #43
2009 Wheels Main Event Foil #1
2009 Wheels Main Event Foil #14
2009 Wheels Main Event Hat Dance Patch /10 #HDDEJR
2009 Wheels Main Event Hat Dance Triple /99 #HDDEJR
2009 Wheels Main Event High Rollers #HR1
2009 Wheels Main Event Marks Clubs #17
2009 Wheels Main Event Marks Diamonds /10 #17
2009 Wheels Main Event Marks Hearts /5 #17
2009 Wheels Main Event Marks Printing Plates Black /1 #14
2009 Wheels Main Event Marks Printing Plates Cyan /1 #14
2009 Wheels Main Event Marks Printing Plates Magenta /1 #14
2009 Wheels Main Event Marks Printing Plates Yellow /1 #14
2009 Wheels Main Event Marks Spades /1 #17
2009 Wheels Main Event Playing Cards Blue #AS
2009 Wheels Main Event Playing Cards Blue #5D
2009 Wheels Main Event Playing Cards Red #AS
2009 Wheels Main Event Playing Cards Red #5D
2009 Wheels Main Event Poker Chips #1
2009 Wheels Main Event Previews /5 #1
2009 Wheels Main Event Previews /5 #14
2009 Wheels Main Event Spark Plugs /8 #DE1
2009 Wheels Main Event Spark Plugs /8 #DE2
2009 Wheels Main Event Stop and Go Swatches Lugnut /88 #SGLDEJ
2009 Wheels Main Event Wildcard Cuts /2 #WCCDE
2010 Action Racing Collectables Platinum 1:24 /163 #88
2010 Action Racing Collectables Platinum 1:24 /88 #88
2010 Action Racing Collectables Platinum 1:24 /87 #88
2010 Element #52
2010 Element #16
2010 Element #85
2010 Element #79
2010 Element 10 in '10 #TT6
2010 Element Blue /35 #16
2010 Element Blue /35 #52
2010 Element Blue /35 #79
2010 Element Blue /35 #85
2010 Element Flagship Performers Consecutive Starts Black /20 #FPSDJr
2010 Element Flagship Performers Consecutive Starts Blue-Orange /20 #FPSDJr
2010 Element Flagship Performers Consecutive Starts Checkered /1 #FPSDJr
2010 Element Flagship Performers Consecutive Starts Green /5 #FPSDJr
2010 Element Flagship Performers Consecutive Starts Red /20 #FPSDJr
2010 Element Flagship Performers Consecutive Starts White /10 #FPSDJr
2010 Element Flagship Performers Consecutive Starts X /10 #FPSDJr
2010 Element Flagship Performers Consecutive Starts Yellow /20 #FPSDJr
2010 Element Flagship Performers Wins Black /20 #FPWDJr
2010 Element Flagship Performers Wins Blue-Orange /20 #FPWDJr
2010 Element Flagship Performers Wins Checkered /1 #FPWDJr
2010 Element Flagship Performers Wins Green /5 #FPWDJr
2010 Element Flagship Performers Wins Red /20 #FPWDJr
2010 Element Flagship Performers Wins White /15 #FPWDJr
2010 Element Flagship Performers Wins X /10 #FPWDJr
2010 Element Flagship Performers Wins Yellow /20 #FPWDJr
2010 Element Green #16
2010 Element Green #52
2010 Element Green #79
2010 Element Green #85
2010 Element Previews /5 #EB16
2010 Element Previews /1 #EB85
2010 Element Purple /25 #16
2010 Element Purple /25 #52
2010 Element Recycled Materials Blue /25 #RMDEJr
2010 Element Recycled Materials Green /125 #RMDEJr
2010 Element Red Target #16
2010 Element Red Target #52
2010 Element Red Target #79
2010 Element Red Target #85
2010 Press Pass #22
2010 Press Pass #68
2010 Press Pass Autographs #14
2010 Press Pass Autographs Track Edition /10 #2
2010 Press Pass Blue #22
2010 Press Pass Blue #68
2010 Press Pass Burning Rubber Autographs /8 #STEDE
2010 Press Pass By The Numbers #BN18
2010 Press Pass Cup Chase #CCR4
2010 Press Pass Eclipse #5
2010 Press Pass Eclipse #71
2010 Press Pass Eclipse #77
2010 Press Pass Eclipse Blue #5
2010 Press Pass Eclipse Blue #71
2010 Press Pass Eclipse Blue #77
2010 Press Pass Eclipse Cars #C8
2010 Press Pass Eclipse Decade #D6
2010 Press Pass Eclipse Element Inserts #3
2010 Press Pass Eclipse Focus #F1
2010 Press Pass Eclipse Gold #5
2010 Press Pass Eclipse Gold #71
2010 Press Pass Eclipse Gold #77
2010 Press Pass Eclipse Previews /5 #5
2010 Press Pass Eclipse Purple /25 #5
2010 Press Pass Eclipse Spellbound Swatches /250 #SSDEJ2
2010 Press Pass Eclipse Spellbound Swatches /250 #SSDEJ3
2010 Press Pass Eclipse Spellbound Swatches /250 #SSDEJ4
2010 Press Pass Eclipse Spellbound Swatches /250 #SSDEJ5
2010 Press Pass Eclipse Spellbound Swatches /250 #SSDEJ6
2010 Press Pass Eclipse Spellbound Swatches /250 #SSDEJ7
2010 Press Pass Eclipse Spellbound Swatches /250 #SSDEJ8
2010 Press Pass Eclipse Spellbound Swatches /250 #SSDEJ9
2010 Press Pass Eclipse Spellbound Swatches /250 #SSDEJ10
2010 Press Pass Eclipse Spellbound Swatches /250 #SSDEJ11
2010 Press Pass Eclipse Spellbound Swatches /250 #SSDEJ1
2010 Press Pass Eclipse Spellbound Swatches Holofoil /88 #SSDEJ2
2010 Press Pass Eclipse Spellbound Swatches Holofoil /88 #SSDEJ3
2010 Press Pass Eclipse Spellbound Swatches Holofoil /88 #SSDEJ4
2010 Press Pass Eclipse Spellbound Swatches Holofoil /88 #SSDEJ5
2010 Press Pass Eclipse Spellbound Swatches Holofoil /88 #SSDEJ6
2010 Press Pass Eclipse Spellbound Swatches Holofoil /88 #SSDEJ7
2010 Press Pass Eclipse Spellbound Swatches Holofoil /88 #SSDEJ8
2010 Press Pass Eclipse Spellbound Swatches Holofoil /88 #SSDEJ9
2010 Press Pass Eclipse Spellbound Swatches Holofoil /88 #SSDEJ10
2010 Press Pass Eclipse Spellbound Swatches Holofoil /88 #SSDEJ11
2010 Press Pass Eclipse Spellbound Swatches Holofoil /88 #SSDEJ1
2010 Press Pass Five Star /35 #14
2010 Press Pass Five Star Classic Compilations Combos Firesuit Autographs /15 #CCMTSDE

2010 Press Pass Five Star Classic Compilations Combos Firesuit Autographs /15 #CCMHMS
2010 Press Pass Five Star Classic Compilations Combos Firesuit Autographs /15 #CCMDPDE
2010 Press Pass Five Star Classic Compilations Combos Firesuit Autographs /15 #CCMDEJG
2010 Press Pass Five Star Classic Compilations Combos Patches Autographs /1 #CCMGJME
2010 Press Pass Five Star Classic Compilations Combos Patches Autographs /1 #CCMDPDE
2010 Press Pass Five Star Classic Compilations Combos Patches Autographs /1 #CCMDEJG
2010 Press Pass Five Star Classic Compilations Combos Patches Autographs /1 #CCMTSDE
2010 Press Pass Five Star Classic Compilations Dual Memorabilia Autographs /10 #DEJ
2010 Press Pass Five Star Classic Compilations Family Firesuit Autographs /1 #EE
2010 Press Pass Five Star Classic Compilations Firesuit Autographs /15 #DEJ
2010 Press Pass Five Star Classic Compilations Patch Autographs /1 #CCPDEJ1
2010 Press Pass Five Star Classic Compilations Patch Autographs /1 #CCPDEJ2
2010 Press Pass Five Star Classic Compilations Patch Autographs /1 #CCPDEJ3
2010 Press Pass Five Star Classic Compilations Patch Autographs /1 #CCPDEJ4
2010 Press Pass Five Star Classic Compilations Patch Autographs /1 #CCPDEJ5
2010 Press Pass Five Star Classic Compilations Patch Autographs /1 #CCPDEJ6
2010 Press Pass Five Star Classic Compilations Patch Autographs /1 #CCPDEJ7
2010 Press Pass Five Star Classic Compilations Patch Autographs /1 #CCPDEJ8
2010 Press Pass Five Star Classic Compilations Patch Autographs /1 #CCPDEJ9
2010 Press Pass Five Star Classic Compilations Patch Autographs /1 #CCPDEJ10
2010 Press Pass Five Star Classic Compilations Patch Autographs /1 #CCPDEJ11
2010 Press Pass Five Star Classic Compilations Patch Autographs /1 #CCPDEJ12
2010 Press Pass Five Star Classic Compilations Patch Autographs /1 #CCPDEJ13
2010 Press Pass Five Star Classic Compilations Patch Autographs /1 #CCPDEJ14
2010 Press Pass Five Star Classic Compilations Sheet Metal Autographs /25 #DEJ
2010 Press Pass Five Star Classic Compilations Triple Memorabilia Autographs /5 #DEJ
2010 Press Pass Five Star Classic Compilations Wrangler Firesuit Dual /25 #EE
2010 Press Pass Five Star Holofoil /10 #14
2010 Press Pass Five Star Melting /1 #14
2010 Press Pass Five Star Paramount Pieces Aluminum /25 #DEJ1
2010 Press Pass Five Star Paramount Pieces Aluminum /25 #DEJ2
2010 Press Pass Five Star Paramount Pieces Blue /20 #DEJ1
2010 Press Pass Five Star Paramount Pieces Blue /20 #DEJ2
2010 Press Pass Five Star Paramount Pieces Gold /15 #DEJ1
2010 Press Pass Five Star Paramount Pieces Gold /15 #DEJ2
2010 Press Pass Five Star Paramount Pieces Holofoil /10 #DEJ
2010 Press Pass Five Star Paramount Pieces Melting /1 #DEJ1
2010 Press Pass Five Star Paramount Pieces Melting /1 #DEJ2
2010 Press Pass Five Star Signature Souvenirs Aluminum /50 #SSDE
2010 Press Pass Five Star Signature Souvenirs Gold /25 #SSDE
2010 Press Pass Five Star Signature Souvenirs Holofoil /10 #SSDE
2010 Press Pass Five Star Signature Souvenirs Melting /1 #SSDE
2010 Press Pass Five Star Signatures Aluminum /35 #DEJ
2010 Press Pass Five Star Signatures Gold /20 #DEJ
2010 Press Pass Five Star Signatures Holofoil /5 #DEJ
2010 Press Pass Five Star Signatures Melting /1 #DEJ
2010 Press Pass Four Wide Autographs /5 #NNO
2010 Press Pass Four Wide Firesuit /25 #FWDE1
2010 Press Pass Four Wide Firesuit /25 #FWDE2
2010 Press Pass Four Wide Sheet Metal /15 #FWDE1
2010 Press Pass Four Wide Sheet Metal /15 #FWDE2
2010 Press Pass Four Wide Tires /10 #FWDE1
2010 Press Pass Four Wide Tires /10 #FWDE2
2010 Press Pass Gold #22
2010 Press Pass Gold #68
2010 Press Pass Holofoil /100 #22
2010 Press Pass Holofoil /100 #68
2010 Press Pass Legends #40
2010 Press Pass Legends Autographs Blue /10 #14
2010 Press Pass Legends Autographs Holofoil /25 #14
2010 Press Pass Legends Autographs Printing Plates Black /1 #13
2010 Press Pass Legends Autographs Printing Plates Cyan /1 #13
2010 Press Pass Legends Autographs Printing Plates Magenta /1 #13
2010 Press Pass Legends Autographs Printing Plates Yellow /1 #13
2010 Press Pass Legends Blue /1 #40
2010 Press Pass Legends Gold /399 #40
2010 Press Pass Legends Holofoil /50 #40
2010 Press Pass Legends Legendary Links Gold /75 #LXBEDEJ
2010 Press Pass Legends Legendary Links Holofoil /25 #LXBEDEJ
2010 Press Pass Legends Motorsports Masters Autographs Printing Plates Black /1 #13
2010 Press Pass Legends Motorsports Masters Autographs Printing Plates Cyan /1 #13
2010 Press Pass Legends Motorsports Masters Autographs Printing Plates Magenta /1 #13
2010 Press Pass Legends Motorsports Masters Autographs Printing Plates Yellow /1 #13
2010 Press Pass Legends Printing Plates Black /1 #40
2010 Press Pass Legends Printing Plates Cyan /1 #40
2010 Press Pass Legends Printing Plates Magenta /1 #40
2010 Press Pass Legends Printing Plates Yellow /1 #40
2010 Press Pass Legends Prominent Pieces Copper /99 #PPDEJR
2010 Press Pass Legends Prominent Pieces Gold /50 #PPDEJR
2010 Press Pass Legends Prominent Pieces Holofoil /25 #PPDEJR
2010 Press Pass Legends Prominent Pieces Oversized Firesuit /25 #PPOEDEJR
2010 Press Pass Legends Red /199 #40
2010 Press Pass Premium #37
2010 Press Pass Premium #54
2010 Press Pass Premium #20
2010 Press Pass Premium #93
2010 Press Pass Premium #60
2010 Press Pass Premium #72
2010 Press Pass Premium Allies #A2
2010 Press Pass Premium Allies #A6
2010 Press Pass Premium Allies Signatures /5 #ASSE
2010 Press Pass Premium Allies Signatures /5 #ASEM
2010 Press Pass Premium Hot Threads /299 #HTDE2
2010 Press Pass Premium Hot Threads /299 #HTDE1
2010 Press Pass Premium Hot Threads Holofoil /99 #HTDE1
2010 Press Pass Premium Hot Threads Holofoil /99 #HTDE2
2010 Press Pass Premium Hot Threads Multi Color /25 #HTDE1
2010 Press Pass Premium Hot Threads Multi Color /25 #HTDE2
2010 Press Pass Premium Hot Threads Patches /32 #HTPDE
2010 Press Pass Premium Hot Threads Two Color /125 #HTDE1
2010 Press Pass Premium Hot Threads Two Color /125 #HTDE2
2010 Press Pass Premium Iron On Patch #2
2010 Press Pass Premium Pairings Firesuits /25 #PFPE
2010 Press Pass Premium Pairings Signatures /5 #PSPE
2010 Press Pass Premium Purple /25 #20
2010 Press Pass Premium Purple /25 #37
2010 Press Pass Premium Purple /25 #54
2010 Press Pass Premium Purple /25 #60
2010 Press Pass Premium Rivals #R1
2010 Press Pass Premium Rivals Signatures /5 #RSEG
2010 Press Pass Premium Signature Series Firesuit /15 #SSFDE1
2010 Press Pass Premium Signature Series Firesuit /15 #SSFDE2
2010 Press Pass Premium Signatures #PSDE
2010 Press Pass Previews /5 #22
2010 Press Pass Purple /25 #22
2010 Press Pass Purple /25 #68
2010 Press Pass Showcase /499 #30
2010 Press Pass Showcase /499 #31
2010 Press Pass Showcase /499 #20
2010 Press Pass Showcase /499 #37
2010 Press Pass Showcase /499 #32
2010 Press Pass Showcase Classic Collections Firesuit Green /25 #CCIHMS
2010 Press Pass Showcase Classic Collections Firesuit Green /25 #CCIFAN
2010 Press Pass Showcase Classic Collections Firesuit Green /25 #CCIJRM
2010 Press Pass Showcase Classic Collections Firesuit Patch Melting /5 #CCIFAN
2010 Press Pass Showcase Classic Collections Firesuit Patch Melting /5 #CCIJRM
2010 Press Pass Showcase Classic Collections Firesuit Patch Melting /5 #CCIHMS
2010 Press Pass Showcase Classic Collections Ink /15 #CCIJRM
2010 Press Pass Showcase Classic Collections Ink /15 #CCIHMS
2010 Press Pass Showcase Classic Collections Ink /15 #CCIFAN
2010 Press Pass Showcase Classic Collections Ink Gold /10 #CCIFAN
2010 Press Pass Showcase Classic Collections Ink Gold /10 #CCIJRM
2010 Press Pass Showcase Classic Collections Ink Gold /10 #CCIHMS
2010 Press Pass Showcase Classic Collections Ink Green /5 #CCIFAN
2010 Press Pass Showcase Classic Collections Ink Green /5 #CCIJRM
2010 Press Pass Showcase Classic Collections Ink Green /5 #CCIHMS
2010 Press Pass Showcase Classic Collections Ink Melting /1 #CCIFAN
2010 Press Pass Showcase Classic Collections Ink Melting /1 #CCIJRM
2010 Press Pass Showcase Classic Collections Ink Melting /1 #CCIHMS
2010 Press Pass Showcase Classic Collections Sheet Metal /99 #CCIFAN
2010 Press Pass Showcase Classic Collections Sheet Metal /99 #CCIHMS
2010 Press Pass Showcase Classic Collections Sheet Metal /99 #CCIJRM
2010 Press Pass Showcase Classic Collections Sheet Metal Gold /45 #CCIFAN
2010 Press Pass Showcase Classic Collections Sheet Metal Gold /45 #CCIJRM
2010 Press Pass Showcase Classic Collections Sheet Metal Gold /45 #CCIHMS
2010 Press Pass Showcase Elite Exhibit Ink /45 #EEIDE
2010 Press Pass Showcase Elite Exhibit Ink Gold /25 #EEIDE
2010 Press Pass Showcase Elite Exhibit Ink Green /5 #EEIDE
2010 Press Pass Showcase Elite Exhibit Ink Melting /1 #EEIDE
2010 Press Pass Showcase Elite Exhibit Triple Memorabilia /99 #EEMDEJ
2010 Press Pass Showcase Elite Exhibit Triple Memorabilia Gold /45 #EEMDEJ
2010 Press Pass Showcase Elite Exhibit Triple Memorabilia Green /25 #EEMDEJ
2010 Press Pass Showcase Elite Exhibit Triple Memorabilia Melting /5 #EEMDEJ
2010 Press Pass Showcase Gold /125 #20
2010 Press Pass Showcase Gold /125 #30
2010 Press Pass Showcase Gold /125 #31
2010 Press Pass Showcase Gold /125 #32
2010 Press Pass Showcase Gold /125 #37
2010 Press Pass Showcase Green /50 #20
2010 Press Pass Showcase Green /50 #30
2010 Press Pass Showcase Green /50 #31
2010 Press Pass Showcase Green /50 #32
2010 Press Pass Showcase Green /50 #37
2010 Press Pass Showcase Melting /15 #20
2010 Press Pass Showcase Melting /15 #30
2010 Press Pass Showcase Melting /15 #31
2010 Press Pass Showcase Melting /15 #32
2010 Press Pass Showcase Melting /15 #37
2010 Press Pass Showcase Platinum Holo /1 #20
2010 Press Pass Showcase Platinum Holo /1 #30
2010 Press Pass Showcase Platinum Holo /1 #31
2010 Press Pass Showcase Platinum Holo /1 #32
2010 Press Pass Showcase Platinum Holo /1 #37
2010 Press Pass Showcase Prized Pieces Firesuit Green /25 #PPMDEJR
2010 Press Pass Showcase Prized Pieces Firesuit Ink Gold /25 #PPIDEJR
2010 Press Pass Showcase Prized Pieces Firesuit Ink Melting /1 #PPIDEJR
2010 Press Pass Showcase Prized Pieces Firesuit Patch Melting /5 #PPMDEJR
2010 Press Pass Showcase Prized Pieces Memorabilia Ink Green /15 #PPIDEJR
2010 Press Pass Showcase Prized Pieces Sheet Metal /99 #PPMDEJR
2010 Press Pass Showcase Prized Pieces Sheet Metal Gold /45 #PPMDEJR
2010 Press Pass Showcase Prized Pieces Sheet Metal Ink Silver /45 #PPIDEJR
2010 Press Pass Signings Blue /10 #17
2010 Press Pass Signings Gold /50 #17
2010 Press Pass Signings Red /15 #17
2010 Press Pass Signings Silver /99 #17
2010 Press Pass Stealth #67
2010 Press Pass Stealth #8
2010 Press Pass Stealth #77
2010 Press Pass Stealth #49
2010 Press Pass Stealth #52
2010 Press Pass Stealth Battle Armor Fast Pass /25 #BADE1
2010 Press Pass Stealth Battle Armor Fast Pass /25 #BADE2
2010 Press Pass Stealth Battle Armor Holofoil /25 #BADE1
2010 Press Pass Stealth Battle Armor Holofoil /25 #BADE2
2010 Press Pass Stealth Battle Armor Silver /225 #BADE1
2010 Press Pass Stealth Battle Armor Silver /225 #BADE2
2010 Press Pass Stealth Black and White #8
2010 Press Pass Stealth Black and White #49
2010 Press Pass Stealth Black and White #52
2010 Press Pass Stealth Black and White #67
2010 Press Pass Stealth Black and White #77
2010 Press Pass Stealth Earnhardt Retail #DE1
2010 Press Pass Stealth Earnhardt Retail #DE3
2010 Press Pass Stealth National Convention #VIP1
2010 Press Pass Stealth Previews /5 #8
2010 Press Pass Stealth Previews /5 #52
2010 Press Pass Stealth Previews /1 #67
2010 Press Pass Stealth Purple /25 #8
2010 Press Pass Stealth Purple /25 #49
2010 Press Pass Stealth Purple /25 #52
2010 Press Pass Stealth Signature Series Sheet Metal /15 #SSMEDE
2010 Press Pass Stealth Weekend Warriors Holofoil /25 #WWDE
2010 Press Pass Stealth Weekend Warriors Silver /99 #WWDE
2010 Press Pass Target By The Numbers #BNT1
2010 Press Pass Target Top Numbers Tires /50 #TNT-DE
2010 Press Pass Tradin' Paint #TP8
2010 Press Pass Tradin' Paint Sheet Metal /299 #TPDE
2010 Press Pass Tradin' Paint Sheet Metal Gold /50 #TPDE
2010 Press Pass Tradin' Paint Sheet Metal Holofoil /25 #TPDE
2010 Press Pass Wal-Mart By The Numbers #BNW1
2010 Press Pass Wal-Mart Top Numbers Tires /50 #TNW-DE
2010 Wheels Autographs #13
2010 Wheels Autographs Printing Plates Black /1 #13
2010 Wheels Autographs Printing Plates Cyan /1 #13
2010 Wheels Autographs Printing Plates Magenta /1 #13
2010 Wheels Autographs Printing Plates Yellow /1 #13
2010 Wheels Autographs Special Ink /10 #3
2010 Wheels Autographs Target /10 #8
2010 Wheels Main Event #42
2010 Wheels Main Event #9
2010 Wheels Main Event #92
2010 Wheels Main Event #64
2010 Wheels Main Event #46
2010 Wheels Main Event American Muscle #AM11
2010 Wheels Main Event Blue #9
2010 Wheels Main Event Blue #42
2010 Wheels Main Event Blue #46
2010 Wheels Main Event Blue #64
2010 Wheels Main Event Blue #92
2010 Wheels Main Event Dog Tags #JR
2010 Wheels Main Event Fight Card #FC8
2010 Wheels Main Event Fight Card Checkered Flag #FC8
2010 Wheels Main Event Fight Card Full Color Retail #FC8
2010 Wheels Main Event Fight Card Gold /25 #FC8
2010 Wheels Main Event Head to Head /150 #HHDEDP
2010 Wheels Main Event Head to Head /150 #HHTSDE
2010 Wheels Main Event Head to Head /150 #HHDEJG
2010 Wheels Main Event Head to Head Blue /75 #HHDEDP
2010 Wheels Main Event Head to Head Blue /75 #HHDEJG
2010 Wheels Main Event Head to Head Blue /75 #HHTSDE
2010 Wheels Main Event Head to Head Holofoil /10 #HHDEDP
2010 Wheels Main Event Head to Head Holofoil /10 #HHDEJG
2010 Wheels Main Event Head to Head Holofoil /10 #HHTSDE
2010 Wheels Main Event Head to Head Red /25 #HHDEDP
2010 Wheels Main Event Head to Head Red /25 #HHDEJG
2010 Wheels Main Event Head to Head Red /25 #HHTSDE
2010 Wheels Main Event Marks Autographs /22 #17
2010 Wheels Main Event Marks Autographs Black /1 #17
2010 Wheels Main Event Marks Autographs Blue /10 #17
2010 Wheels Main Event Marks Autographs Red /5 #17
2010 Wheels Main Event Matchups Autographs /10 #JMJR
2010 Wheels Main Event Purple /25 #9
2010 Wheels Main Event Purple /25 #42
2010 Wheels Main Event Purple /25 #46
2010 Wheels Main Event Upper Cuts /199 #UCDE
2010 Wheels Main Event Upper Cuts Blue /75 #UCDE
2010 Wheels Main Event Upper Cuts Holofoil /10 #UCDE
2010 Wheels Main Event Upper Cuts Knock Out Patches /25 #UCKODE
2010 Wheels Main Event Upper Cuts Red /25 #UCDE
2010 Wheels Main Event Wheel to Wheel /25 #WWJGDE
2010 Wheels Main Event Wheel to Wheel /25 #WWDETS
2010 Wheels Main Event Wheel to Wheel Holofoil /10 #WWJGDE
2010 Wheels Main Event Wheel to Wheel Holofoil /10 #WWDETS
2011 Element #8
2011 Element #36
2011 Element #94
2011 Element #79
2011 Element Autographs /45 #16
2011 Element Autographs Blue /5 #16
2011 Element Autographs Gold /10 #15
2011 Element Autographs Printing Plates Black /1 #16
2011 Element Autographs Printing Plates Cyan /1 #16
2011 Element Autographs Printing Plates Magenta /1 #16
2011 Element Autographs Printing Plates Yellow /1 #16
2011 Element Autographs Silver /15 #15
2011 Element Black /35 #8
2011 Element Black /35 #36
2011 Element Black /35 #79
2011 Element Black /35 #94
2011 Element Cut and Collect Exclusives #NNO
2011 Element Finish Line Checkered Flag /10 #FLDE
2011 Element Finish Line Green Flag /25 #FLDE
2011 Element Finish Line Tires /99 #FLDE
2011 Element Finish Line Tires Purple Fast Pass /30 #FLDE
2011 Element Flagship Performers 2010 Green Flag Passes Blue-Yellow /50 #FPPDE
2011 Element Flagship Performers 2010 Laps Completed Yellow /50 #FPLDE
2011 Element Flagship Performers Career Wins White /50 #FPWDEJ
2011 Element Flagship Performers Race Streak Without DNF Red /50 #FPDDE
2011 Element Flagstand Swatches /25 #FSSDE
2011 Element Green #8
2011 Element Green #36
2011 Element Green #79
2011 Element Green #94
2011 Element Previews /5 #EB8
2011 Element Purple /25 #8
2011 Element Purple /25 #36
2011 Element Purple /25 #79
2011 Element Purple /25 #94
2011 Element Red #8
2011 Element Red #36
2011 Element Red #79
2011 Element Red #94
2011 Press Pass #169
2011 Press Pass #8
2011 Press Pass #178
2011 Press Pass #156
2011 Press Pass #148
2011 Press Pass #111
2011 Press Pass #63
2011 Press Pass #131
2011 Press Pass Autographs Blue /5 #16
2011 Press Pass Autographs Bronze /20 #15
2011 Press Pass Autographs Gold /5 #15
2011 Press Pass Autographs Printing Plates Black /1 #16
2011 Press Pass Autographs Printing Plates Cyan /1 #16
2011 Press Pass Autographs Printing Plates Magenta /1 #16
2011 Press Pass Autographs Printing Plates Yellow /1 #16
2011 Press Pass Autographs Silver /10 #16
2011 Press Pass Blue Holofoil /10 #8
2011 Press Pass Blue Holofoil /10 #63
2011 Press Pass Blue Holofoil /10 #111
2011 Press Pass Blue Holofoil /10 #131
2011 Press Pass Blue Holofoil /10 #148
2011 Press Pass Blue Holofoil /10 #156
2011 Press Pass Blue Holofoil /10 #169
2011 Press Pass Blue Holofoil /10 #178
2011 Press Pass Blue Retail #8
2011 Press Pass Blue Retail #63
2011 Press Pass Blue Retail #111
2011 Press Pass Blue Retail #131
2011 Press Pass Blue Retail #148
2011 Press Pass Blue Retail #156
2011 Press Pass Blue Retail #169
2011 Press Pass Blue Retail #178
2011 Press Pass Burning Rubber Fast Pass /10 #BRDE
2011 Press Pass Burning Rubber Gold /150 #BRDE
2011 Press Pass Burning Rubber Holofoil /50 #BRDE
2011 Press Pass Burning Rubber Prime Cuts /25 #BRDE
2011 Press Pass Cup Chase #CCR13
2011 Press Pass Cup Chase Prizes #CC10
2011 Press Pass Eclipse #53
2011 Press Pass Eclipse #8
2011 Press Pass Eclipse #50
2011 Press Pass Eclipse #72
2011 Press Pass Eclipse #83
2011 Press Pass Eclipse Blue #8
2011 Press Pass Eclipse Blue #50
2011 Press Pass Eclipse Blue #53
2011 Press Pass Eclipse Blue #72
2011 Press Pass Eclipse Blue #83
2011 Press Pass Eclipse Encore #E1
2011 Press Pass Eclipse Gold /55 #8
2011 Press Pass Eclipse Gold /55 #50
2011 Press Pass Eclipse Gold /55 #53
2011 Press Pass Eclipse Gold /55 #72
2011 Press Pass Eclipse Gold /55 #83
2011 Press Pass Eclipse Previews /5 #EB8
2011 Press Pass Eclipse Purple /25 #8
2011 Press Pass Eclipse Purple /25 #50
2011 Press Pass Eclipse Purple /25 #53
2011 Press Pass Eclipse Rides #R1
2011 Press Pass Eclipse Spellbound Swatches /125 #SBDEJR2
2011 Press Pass Eclipse Spellbound Swatches /125 #SBDEJR3
2011 Press Pass Eclipse Spellbound Swatches /125 #SBDEJR4
2011 Press Pass Eclipse Spellbound Swatches /125 #SBDEJR5
2011 Press Pass Eclipse Spellbound Swatches /100 #SBDEJR6
2011 Press Pass Eclipse Spellbound Swatches /100 #SBDEJR7
2011 Press Pass Eclipse Spellbound Swatches /75 #SBDEJR8
2011 Press Pass Eclipse Spellbound Swatches /75 #SBDEJR9
2011 Press Pass Eclipse Spellbound Swatches /35 #SBDEJR10
2011 Press Pass Eclipse Spellbound Swatches /35 #SBDEJR11
2011 Press Pass Eclipse Spellbound Swatches /125 #SBDEJR1
2011 Press Pass Eclipse Spellbound Swatches Signatures /10 #NNO
2011 Press Pass FanFare #11
2011 Press Pass FanFare Autographs Blue /5 #22
2011 Press Pass FanFare Autographs Bronze /10 #22
2011 Press Pass FanFare Autographs Gold /10 #22
2011 Press Pass FanFare Autographs Printing Plates Black /1 #22
2011 Press Pass FanFare Autographs Printing Plates Cyan /1 #22
2011 Press Pass FanFare Autographs Printing Plates Magenta /1 #22
2011 Press Pass FanFare Autographs Printing Plates Yellow /1 #22
2011 Press Pass FanFare Autographs Silver /5 #22
2011 Press Pass FanFare Blue Die Cuts #11
2011 Press Pass FanFare Dual Autographs /10 #NNO
2011 Press Pass FanFare Emerald /25 #11
2011 Press Pass FanFare Holofoil Die Cuts #11
2011 Press Pass FanFare Magnificent Materials /199 #MMDE
2011 Press Pass FanFare Magnificent Materials Dual Swatches /50 #MMDDE
2011 Press Pass FanFare Magnificent Materials Dual Swatches Holofoil /10 #MMDDE
2011 Press Pass FanFare Magnificent Materials Holofoil /50 #MMDE
2011 Press Pass FanFare Magnificent Materials Signatures /25 #MMSEDE
2011 Press Pass FanFare Magnificent Materials Signatures Holofoil /10 #MMSEDE
2011 Press Pass FanFare Promotional Memorabilia /25 #PMDE
2011 Press Pass FanFare Ruby Die Cuts /15 #11
2011 Press Pass FanFare Sapphire /10 #11
2011 Press Pass FanFare Silver /25 #11
2011 Press Pass Flashback #FB4
2011 Press Pass Four Wide Firesuit /25 #FWDE
2011 Press Pass Four Wide Glove /1 #FWDE
2011 Press Pass Four Wide Sheet Metal /15 #FWDE
2011 Press Pass Four Wide Shoes /1 #FWDE
2011 Press Pass Four Wide Tire /10 #FWDE
2011 Press Pass Geared Up Holofoil /50 #GUDE
2011 Press Pass Gold /50 #8
2011 Press Pass Gold /50 #63
2011 Press Pass Gold /50 #111
2011 Press Pass Gold /50 #131
2011 Press Pass Gold /50 #148
2011 Press Pass Gold /50 #156
2011 Press Pass Gold /50 #169
2011 Press Pass Gold /50 #178
2011 Press Pass Legends #40
2011 Press Pass Legends Autographs Blue /5 #LDADE
2011 Press Pass Legends Autographs Gold /24 #LDADE
2011 Press Pass Legends Autographs Printing Plates Black /1 #LDADE
2011 Press Pass Legends Autographs Printing Plates Cyan /1 #LDADE
2011 Press Pass Legends Autographs Printing Plates Magenta /1 #LDADE
2011 Press Pass Legends Autographs Printing Plates Yellow /1 #LDADE
2011 Press Pass Legends Gold /250 #40
2011 Press Pass Legends Holofoil /25 #40
2011 Press Pass Legends Printing Plates Black /1 #40
2011 Press Pass Legends Printing Plates Cyan /1 #40
2011 Press Pass Legends Printing Plates Magenta /1 #40
2011 Press Pass Legends Printing Plates Yellow /1 #40
2011 Press Pass Legends Prominent Pieces Gold /50 #PPDE
2011 Press Pass Legends Prominent Pieces Holofoil /25 #PPDE
2011 Press Pass Legends Prominent Pieces Oversized Firesuit /25 #PPOEDEJR
2011 Press Pass Legends Prominent Pieces Purple /15 #PPDE
2011 Press Pass Legends Prominent Pieces Silver /99 #PPDE
2011 Press Pass Legends Purple /25 #40
2011 Press Pass Legends Red /99 #40
2011 Press Pass Legends Solo /1 #40
2011 Press Pass Premium #9B
2011 Press Pass Premium #9A
2011 Press Pass Premium #38
2011 Press Pass Premium #59
2011 Press Pass Premium #49
2011 Press Pass Premium #67
2011 Press Pass Premium Crystal Ball #CB3
2011 Press Pass Premium Crystal Ball Autographs /10 #CBADEJ
2011 Press Pass Premium Double Burner /25 #DBDEJ
2011 Press Pass Premium Hot Pursuit 3D #HP1
2011 Press Pass Premium Hot Pursuit Autographs /10 #HPADEJ
2011 Press Pass Premium Hot Pursuit National Convention #HP1
2011 Press Pass Premium Hot Threads /150 #HTDJR
2011 Press Pass Premium Hot Threads Fast Pass /25 #HTDJR
2011 Press Pass Premium Hot Threads Multi Color /25 #HTDJR
2011 Press Pass Premium Hot Threads Patches /20 #HTPDEJ
2011 Press Pass Premium Hot Threads Secondary Color /99 #HTDJR
2011 Press Pass Premium Pairings Firesuits /25 #PPDEJJG
2011 Press Pass Premium Pairings Signatures /5 #PPADEJJG
2011 Press Pass Premium Purple /25 #9
2011 Press Pass Premium Purple /25 #38
2011 Press Pass Premium Purple /25 #49
2011 Press Pass Premium Purple /25 #59
2011 Press Pass Premium Purple /25 #67
2011 Press Pass Premium Signatures /22 #PSDEJ
2011 Press Pass Previews /5 #EB8
2011 Press Pass Purple /25 #8
2011 Press Pass Showcase /499 #1
2011 Press Pass Showcase /499 #49
2011 Press Pass Showcase /499 #34
2011 Press Pass Showcase /499 #53
2011 Press Pass Showcase Classic Collections Firesuit /45 #CCMHMS
2011 Press Pass Showcase Classic Collections Firesuit Patches /5 #CCMHMS
2011 Press Pass Showcase Classic Collections Ink /25 #CCMHMS
2011 Press Pass Showcase Classic Collections Ink Gold /5 #CCMHMS
2011 Press Pass Showcase Classic Collections Ink Melting /1 #CCMHMS
2011 Press Pass Showcase Classic Collections Sheet Metal /99 #CCMHMS
2011 Press Pass Showcase Elite Exhibit Ink /50 #EEIDEJ
2011 Press Pass Showcase Elite Exhibit Ink Gold /25 #EEIDEJ
2011 Press Pass Showcase Elite Exhibit Ink Melting /1 #EEIDEJ
2011 Press Pass Showcase Gold /125 #1
2011 Press Pass Showcase Gold /125 #34
2011 Press Pass Showcase Gold /125 #49
2011 Press Pass Showcase Gold /125 #53
2011 Press Pass Showcase Green /25 #1
2011 Press Pass Showcase Green /25 #34
2011 Press Pass Showcase Green /25 #49
2011 Press Pass Showcase Green /25 #53
2011 Press Pass Showcase Masterpieces Ink /45 #MPIDEJ
2011 Press Pass Showcase Masterpieces Ink Gold /25 #MPIDEJ
2011 Press Pass Showcase Masterpieces Ink Melting /1 #MPIDEJ
2011 Press Pass Showcase Masterpieces Memorabilia /99 #MPMDEJ
2011 Press Pass Showcase Masterpieces Memorabilia Gold /45 #MPMDEJ
2011 Press Pass Showcase Masterpieces Memorabilia Melting /5 #MPMDEJ
2011 Press Pass Showcase Melting /1 #1
2011 Press Pass Showcase Melting /1 #34
2011 Press Pass Showcase Melting /1 #49
2011 Press Pass Showcase Melting /1 #53
2011 Press Pass Showcase Prized Pieces Firesuit /99 #PPMDEJ
2011 Press Pass Showcase Prized Pieces Firesuit Gold /45 #PPMDEJ
2011 Press Pass Showcase Prized Pieces Firesuit Ink /25 #PPIDEJ
2011 Press Pass Showcase Prized Pieces Firesuit Patches Ink /1 #PPIDEJ
2011 Press Pass Showcase Prized Pieces Firesuit Patches Melting /5 #PPMDEJ
2011 Press Pass Showcase Prized Pieces Sheet Metal Ink /45 #PPIDEJ
2011 Press Pass Showcase Showroom /499 #SR7
2011 Press Pass Showcase Showroom Gold /125 #SR7
2011 Press Pass Showcase Showroom Melting /1 #SR7
2011 Press Pass Showcase Showroom Memorabilia Sheet Metal /45 #SRMDEJ
2011 Press Pass Showcase Showroom Memorabilia Sheet Metal Gold /25 #SRMDEJ
2011 Press Pass Showcase Showroom Memorabilia Sheet Metal Melting /5 #SRMDEJ
2011 Press Pass Signature Series /11 #SSTDE
2011 Press Pass Signature Series /11 #SSCDE
2011 Press Pass Signature Series /11 #SSFDE
2011 Press Pass Signature Series /11 #SSMDEJ
2011 Press Pass Signings Black and White /5 #PPSDE
2011 Press Pass Signings Brushed Metal /20 #PPSDE
2011 Press Pass Signings Holofoil /10 #PPSDE
2011 Press Pass Signings Printing Plates Black /1 #PPSDE
2011 Press Pass Signings Printing Plates Cyan /1 #PPSDE
2011 Press Pass Stealth #1
2011 Press Pass Stealth #3
2011 Press Pass Stealth #2
2011 Press Pass Stealth #87
2011 Press Pass Stealth #70
2011 Press Pass Stealth #93
2011 Press Pass Stealth Afterburner /99 #ABDE
2011 Press Pass Stealth Afterburner Gold /25 #ABDE
2011 Press Pass Stealth Black and White /25 #1
2011 Press Pass Stealth Black and White /25 #2
2011 Press Pass Stealth Black and White /25 #3
2011 Press Pass Stealth Black and White /25 #70
2011 Press Pass Stealth Black and White /25 #87
2011 Press Pass Stealth Black and White /25 #93
2011 Press Pass Stealth Holofoil /99 #1
2011 Press Pass Stealth Holofoil /99 #2
2011 Press Pass Stealth Holofoil /99 #3
2011 Press Pass Stealth Holofoil /99 #70
2011 Press Pass Stealth Holofoil /99 #87
2011 Press Pass Stealth Holofoil /99 #93
2011 Press Pass Stealth In Flight Report #IF1
2011 Press Pass Stealth Metal of Honor Medal of Honor /50 #BADE
2011 Press Pass Stealth Metal of Honor Purple Heart /25 #MHDE
2011 Press Pass Stealth Metal of Honor Silver Star /99 #BADE
2011 Press Pass Stealth Purple /25 #1
2011 Press Pass Stealth Purple /25 #2
2011 Press Pass Stealth Purple /25 #3
2011 Press Pass Stealth Supersonic #SS7
2011 Press Pass Tradin' Paint #TP9
2011 Press Pass Tradin' Paint #TP3
2011 Press Pass Tradin' Paint Sheet Metal Blue /25 #TPDE
2011 Press Pass Tradin' Paint Sheet Metal Holofoil /50 #TPDE
2011 Press Pass Winning Tickets #WT34
2011 Press Pass Winning Tickets #WT36
2011 Wheels Main Event #61
2011 Wheels Main Event #70
2011 Wheels Main Event #10
2011 Wheels Main Event All Stars #A14
2011 Wheels Main Event All Stars Brushed Foil /199 #A14
2011 Wheels Main Event All Stars Holofoil /50 #A14
2011 Wheels Main Event Black and White #10
2011 Wheels Main Event Black and White #61
2011 Wheels Main Event Black and White #70
2011 Wheels Main Event Blue /75 #10
2011 Wheels Main Event Blue /75 #61
2011 Wheels Main Event Blue /75 #70
2011 Wheels Main Event Green /1 #10
2011 Wheels Main Event Green /1 #61
2011 Wheels Main Event Green /1 #70
2011 Wheels Main Event Headliners Holofoil /25 #HLDE
2011 Wheels Main Event Headliners Silver /99 #HLDE
2011 Wheels Main Event Lead Foot Holofoil /25 #LFDE
2011 Wheels Main Event Lead Foot Silver /99 #LFDE
2011 Wheels Main Event Marks Autographs Blue /6 #MEDE
2011 Wheels Main Event Marks Autographs Gold /10 #MEDE
2011 Wheels Main Event Marks Autographs Silver /15 #MEDE
2011 Wheels Main Event Matchups Autographs /10 #MEMKHDE
2011 Wheels Main Event Materials Holofoil /25 #MEMDE
2011 Wheels Main Event Materials Silver /99 #MEMDE
2011 Wheels Main Event Rear View #R1
2011 Wheels Main Event Rear View Brushed Foil /199 #R1
2011 Wheels Main Event Rear View Holofoil /50 #R1
2011 Wheels Main Event Red /20 #10
2011 Wheels Main Event Red /20 #61
2011 Wheels Main Event Red /20 #70
2012 Press Pass #10
2012 Press Pass #68
2012 Press Pass #75
2012 Press Pass #97
2012 Press Pass Autographs Blue /5 #PPADE
2012 Press Pass Autographs Printing Plates Black /1 #PPADE
2012 Press Pass Autographs Printing Plates Cyan /1 #PPADE
2012 Press Pass Autographs Printing Plates Magenta /1 #PPADE
2012 Press Pass Autographs Printing Plates Yellow /1 #PPADE
2012 Press Pass Autographs Red /5 #PPADE
2012 Press Pass Autographs Silver /15 #PPADE
2012 Press Pass Blue #10
2012 Press Pass Blue #68
2012 Press Pass Blue #75
2012 Press Pass Blue #97
2012 Press Pass Blue Holofoil /35 #10
2012 Press Pass Blue Holofoil /35 #68
2012 Press Pass Blue Holofoil /35 #75
2012 Press Pass Blue Holofoil /35 #97
2012 Press Pass Cup Chase #CCR13
2012 Press Pass Cup Chase Prizes #CCP7
2012 Press Pass Fanfare #12
2012 Press Pass Fanfare #13
2012 Press Pass Fanfare #100
2012 Press Pass Fanfare Autographs Blue /1 #DE
2012 Press Pass Fanfare Autographs Gold /5 #DE
2012 Press Pass Fanfare Autographs Red /1 #DE
2012 Press Pass Fanfare Autographs Silver /5 #DE
2012 Press Pass Fanfare Blue Foil Die Cuts #12
2012 Press Pass Fanfare Blue Foil Die Cuts #13
2012 Press Pass Fanfare Blue Foil Die Cuts #100
2012 Press Pass Fanfare Diamond /5 #12
2012 Press Pass Fanfare Diamond /5 #13
2012 Press Pass Fanfare Diamond /5 #100
2012 Press Pass Fanfare Holofoil Die Cuts #12
2012 Press Pass Fanfare Holofoil Die Cuts #13
2012 Press Pass Fanfare Holofoil Die Cuts #100
2012 Press Pass Fanfare Magnificent Materials /250 #MMDEJR
2012 Press Pass Fanfare Magnificent Materials /235 #MMDEJR2
2012 Press Pass Fanfare Magnificent Materials Dual Swatches /50 #MMDEJR
2012 Press Pass Fanfare Magnificent Materials Dual Swatches /50 #MMDEJR2
2012 Press Pass Fanfare Magnificent Materials Dual Swatches Melting /10 #MMDEJR
2012 Press Pass Fanfare Magnificent Materials Dual Swatches Melting /10 #MMDEJR2
2012 Press Pass Fanfare Magnificent Materials Gold /99 #MMDEJR
2012 Press Pass Fanfare Magnificent Materials Gold /125 #MMDEJR2
2012 Press Pass Fanfare Magnificent Materials Signatures /25 #DE
2012 Press Pass Fanfare Magnificent Materials Signatures Blue /5 #DE
2012 Press Pass Fanfare Power Rankings #PR6
2012 Press Pass Fanfare Sapphire /20 #12
2012 Press Pass Fanfare Sapphire /20 #13
2012 Press Pass Fanfare Sapphire /20 #100
2012 Press Pass Fanfare Showtime #S1
2012 Press Pass Fanfare Silver /25 #12
2012 Press Pass Fanfare Silver /25 #13
2012 Press Pass Fanfare Silver /25 #100
2012 Press Pass Four Wide Autographs /5 #DEJ
2012 Press Pass Four Wide Firesuit /25 #FWDEJR
2012 Press Pass Four Wide Glove /1 #FWDEJR
2012 Press Pass Four Wide Sheet Metal /15 #FWDEJR
2012 Press Pass Four Wide Tire /10 #FWDEJR
2012 Press Pass Gold #10
2012 Press Pass Gold #68
2012 Press Pass Gold #75
2012 Press Pass Gold #97
2012 Press Pass Ignite #12
2012 Press Pass Ignite #53
2012 Press Pass Ignite Double Burner Gun Metal /10 #DBDE
2012 Press Pass Ignite Double Burner Red /1 #DBDE
2012 Press Pass Ignite Double Burner Silver /25 #DBDE
2012 Press Pass Ignite Limelight #L7
2012 Press Pass Ignite Materials Autographs Red /5 #IMDE
2012 Press Pass Ignite Materials Autographs Silver /64 #IMDE
2012 Press Pass Ignite Materials Gun Metal /99 #IMDEJR1
2012 Press Pass Ignite Materials Gun Metal /99 #IMDEJR2
2012 Press Pass Ignite Materials Red /10 #IMDEJR1
2012 Press Pass Ignite Materials Red /10 #IMDEJR2
2012 Press Pass Ignite Materials Silver #IMDEJR1
2012 Press Pass Ignite Materials Silver #IMDEJR2
2012 Press Pass Ignite Profile #P6
2012 Press Pass Ignite Proofs Black and White /50 #12
2012 Press Pass Ignite Proofs Black and White /50 #53
2012 Press Pass Ignite Proofs Cyan #12
2012 Press Pass Ignite Proofs Cyan #53
2012 Press Pass Ignite Proofs Magenta #12
2012 Press Pass Ignite Proofs Magenta #53
2012 Press Pass Ignite Proofs Yellow /10 #12
2012 Press Pass Ignite Proofs Yellow /10 #53
2012 Press Pass Ignite Steel Horses #SH1
2012 Press Pass Ignite Supercharged Signatures /5 #SSDE
2012 Press Pass Legends #40
2012 Press Pass Legends Blue Holofoil /1 #40
2012 Press Pass Legends Gold /275 #40
2012 Press Pass Legends Green #40
2012 Press Pass Legends Prominent Pieces Gold /50 #DEJ
2012 Press Pass Legends Prominent Pieces Holofoil /25 #DEJ
2012 Press Pass Legends Prominent Pieces Oversized Firesuit /25 #DEJ
2012 Press Pass Legends Prominent Pieces Silver /99 #DEJ
2012 Press Pass Legends Rainbow Holofoil /50 #40
2012 Press Pass Legends Red /99 #40
2012 Press Pass Legends Silver Holofoil /25 #40
2012 Press Pass Power Picks Blue /50 #4
2012 Press Pass Power Picks Blue /50 #33
2012 Press Pass Power Picks Blue /50 #55
2012 Press Pass Power Picks Gold /50 #4
2012 Press Pass Power Picks Gold /50 #33
2012 Press Pass Power Picks Gold /50 #55
2012 Press Pass Power Picks Holofoil /10 #4
2012 Press Pass Power Picks Holofoil /10 #33
2012 Press Pass Power Picks Holofoil /10 #55
2012 Press Pass Preferred Line #PL5
2012 Press Pass Purple /35 #10
2012 Press Pass Purple /35 #68
2012 Press Pass Purple /35 #75
2012 Press Pass Purple /35 #97
2012 Press Pass Redline #12
2012 Press Pass Redline Black /99 #12
2012 Press Pass Redline Cyan /50 #12
2012 Press Pass Redline Full Throttle Dual Relic Blue /5 #FTDEJR
2012 Press Pass Redline Full Throttle Dual Relic Gold /10 #FTDEJR
2012 Press Pass Redline Full Throttle Dual Relic Melting /1 #FTDEJR
2012 Press Pass Redline Full Throttle Dual Relic Red /75 #FTDEJR
2012 Press Pass Redline Full Throttle Dual Relic Silver /25 #FTDEJR
2012 Press Pass Redline Intensity #I2
2012 Press Pass Redline Magenta /15 #12
2012 Press Pass Redline Muscle Car Sheet Metal Blue /5 #MCDEJ1
2012 Press Pass Redline Muscle Car Sheet Metal Blue /5 #MCDEJ2
2012 Press Pass Redline Muscle Car Sheet Metal Gold /10 #MCDEJ1
2012 Press Pass Redline Muscle Car Sheet Metal Gold /10 #MCDEJ2
2012 Press Pass Redline Muscle Car Sheet Metal Melting /1 #MCDEJ1
2012 Press Pass Redline Muscle Car Sheet Metal Melting /1 #MCDEJ2
2012 Press Pass Redline Muscle Car Sheet Metal Red /75 #MCDEJ1
2012 Press Pass Redline Muscle Car Sheet Metal Red /75 #MCDEJ2
2012 Press Pass Redline Muscle Car Sheet Metal Silver /25 #MCDEJ1
2012 Press Pass Redline Muscle Car Sheet Metal Silver /25 #MCDEJ2
2012 Press Pass Redline Performance Driven #PD2
2012 Press Pass Redline Pieces of the Action Blue /10 #PADEJR
2012 Press Pass Redline Pieces of the Action Gold /25 #PADEJR
2012 Press Pass Redline Pieces of the Action Melting /1 #PADEJR
2012 Press Pass Redline Pieces of the Action Red /75 #PADEJR
2012 Press Pass Redline Pieces of the Action Silver /50 #PADEJR
2012 Press Pass Redline Relic Autographs Blue /5 #RLRDEJ
2012 Press Pass Redline Relic Autographs Gold /10 #RLRDEJ
2012 Press Pass Redline Relic Autographs Melting /1 #RLRDEJ
2012 Press Pass Redline Relic Autographs Red /50 #RLRDEJ
2012 Press Pass Redline Relic Autographs Silver /23 #RLRDEJ
2012 Press Pass Redline Relics Blue /5 #RLDEJR
2012 Press Pass Redline Relics Gold /10 #RLDEJR
2012 Press Pass Redline Relics Melting /1 #RLDEJR
2012 Press Pass Redline Relics Red /75 #RLDEJR
2012 Press Pass Redline Relics Silver /25 #RLDEJR
2012 Press Pass Redline Rookie Year Relic Autographs Blue /5 #RYDEJR
2012 Press Pass Redline Rookie Year Relic Autographs Gold /25 #RYDEJR
2012 Press Pass Redline Rookie Year Relic Autographs Melting /1 #RYDEJR
2012 Press Pass Redline Rookie Year Relic Autographs Red /50 #RYDEJR
2012 Press Pass Redline RPM #RPM2
2012 Press Pass Redline Signatures Blue /5 #RSDEJ1
2012 Press Pass Redline Signatures Blue /5 #RSDEJ2
2012 Press Pass Redline Signatures Gold /15 #RSDEJ1
2012 Press Pass Redline Signatures Holofoil /10 #RSDEJ1
2012 Press Pass Redline Signatures Melting /1 #RSDEJ1
2012 Press Pass Redline Signatures Melting /1 #RSDEJ2
2012 Press Pass Redline Signatures Red /31 #RSDEJ1
2012 Press Pass Redline V8 Relics Blue /5 #V8DEJR
2012 Press Pass Redline V8 Relics Gold /10 #V8DEJR
2012 Press Pass Redline V8 Relics Melting /1 #V8DEJR
2012 Press Pass Redline V8 Relics Red /25 #V8DEJR
2012 Press Pass Redline Yellow /1 #12
2012 Press Pass Showcar #SC1
2012 Press Pass Showcase /499 #8
2012 Press Pass Showcase /499 #35
2012 Press Pass Showcase /499 #52
2012 Press Pass Showcase Classic Collections Ink /10 #CCMHMS
2012 Press Pass Showcase Classic Collections Ink Gold /5 #CCMHMS
2012 Press Pass Showcase Classic Collections Ink Melting /1 #CCMHMS
2012 Press Pass Showcase Classic Collections Memorabilia /50 #CCMHMS
2012 Press Pass Showcase Classic Collections Memorabilia Gold /25 #CCMHMS

2012 Press Pass Showcase Classic Collections Memorabilia Melting /5 #CCMHMS
2012 Press Pass Showcase Elite Exhibit Ink /25 #EEIDE
2012 Press Pass Showcase Elite Exhibit Ink Gold /10 #EEIDE
2012 Press Pass Showcase Elite Exhibit Ink Melting /1 #EEIDE
2012 Press Pass Showcase Gold /125 #8
2012 Press Pass Showcase Gold /125 #35
2012 Press Pass Showcase Gold /125 #52
2012 Press Pass Showcase Green /5 #8
2012 Press Pass Showcase Green /5 #35
2012 Press Pass Showcase Green /5 #52
2012 Press Pass Showcase Masterpieces Ink /50 #MPIDE
2012 Press Pass Showcase Masterpieces Ink Gold /25 #MPIDE
2012 Press Pass Showcase Masterpieces Ink Melting /1 #MPIDE
2012 Press Pass Showcase Masterpieces Memorabilia /99 #MPDEJR
2012 Press Pass Showcase Masterpieces Memorabilia Gold /50 #MPDEJR
2012 Press Pass Showcase Masterpieces Memorabilia Melting /5 #MPDEJR
2012 Press Pass Showcase Melting /1 #8
2012 Press Pass Showcase Melting /1 #35
2012 Press Pass Showcase Melting /1 #52
2012 Press Pass Showcase Prized Pieces /88 #PPDE
2012 Press Pass Showcase Prized Pieces /99 #PPDE2
2012 Press Pass Showcase Prized Pieces Gold /10 #PPDE
2012 Press Pass Showcase Prized Pieces Gold /50 #PPDE2
2012 Press Pass Showcase Prized Pieces Ink /50 #PPIDE
2012 Press Pass Showcase Prized Pieces Ink Gold /25 #PPIDE
2012 Press Pass Showcase Prized Pieces Ink Melting /1 #PPIDE
2012 Press Pass Showcase Prized Pieces Melting /5 #PPDE
2012 Press Pass Showcase Prized Pieces Melting /5 #PPDE2
2012 Press Pass Showcase Purple /1 #8
2012 Press Pass Showcase Purple /1 #35
2012 Press Pass Showcase Purple /1 #52
2012 Press Pass Showcase Red /25 #8
2012 Press Pass Showcase Red /25 #35
2012 Press Pass Showcase Red /25 #52
2012 Press Pass Showcase Richard Petty 75th Birthday Tribute /10 #RPDE
2012 Press Pass Showcase Richard Petty 75th Birthday Tribute Melting /1 #RPDE
2012 Press Pass Showcase Showcase Patches /5 #SSPDE
2012 Press Pass Showcase Showcase Patches Melting /1 #SSPDE
2012 Press Pass Showcase Showroom /499 #SR1
2012 Press Pass Showcase Showroom Gold /125 #SR1
2012 Press Pass Showcase Showroom Melting /1 #SR1
2012 Press Pass Showcase Showroom Memorabilia /99 #SRDEJR
2012 Press Pass Showcase Showroom Memorabilia Gold /50 #SRDEJR
2012 Press Pass Showcase Showroom Memorabilia Melting /5 #SRDEJR
2012 Press Pass Showcase Signature Patches /1 #SSPDE
2012 Press Pass Showman #SM1
2012 Press Pass Signature Series Race Used /12 #PPADE1
2012 Press Pass Signature Series Race Used /12 #PPADE2
2012 Press Pass Snapshots #SS10
2012 Press Pass Snapshots #SS66
2012 Press Pass Snapshots #SS70
2012 Press Pass Triple Gear 3 in 1 /5 #TGDEJr
2012 Press Pass Triple Gear Firesuit and Sheet Metal /15 #TGDEJr
2012 Press Pass Triple Gear Tire /25 #TGDEJr
2012 Press Pass Ultimate Collection Blue Holofoil /25 #UCDEJR
2012 Press Pass Ultimate Collection Holofoil /50 #UCDEJR
2012 Press Pass Wal-Mart Snapshots #SSWM3
2012 Sportkings Premium Back Redemption Paintings /1 #15
2012 Sports Illustrated for Kids #189
2012 Total Memorabilia #7A
2012 Total Memorabilia #7B
2012 Total Memorabilia Black and White /99 #7
2012 Total Memorabilia Dual Swatch Gold /75 #TMDEJ
2012 Total Memorabilia Dual Swatch Holofoil /25 #TMDEJ
2012 Total Memorabilia Dual Swatch Melting /5 #TMDEJ
2012 Total Memorabilia Dual Swatch Silver /99 #TMDEJ
2012 Total Memorabilia Gold /275 #7
2012 Total Memorabilia Hot Rod Relics Gold /50 #HRRDEJ
2012 Total Memorabilia Hot Rod Relics Holofoil /10 #HRRDEJ
2012 Total Memorabilia Hot Rod Relics Melting /1 #HRRDEJ
2012 Total Memorabilia Hot Rod Relics Silver /99 #HRRDEJ
2012 Total Memorabilia Jumbo Swatch Gold /50 #TMDEJ
2012 Total Memorabilia Jumbo Swatch Holofoil /10 #TMDEJ
2012 Total Memorabilia Jumbo Swatch Melting /1 #TMDEJ
2012 Total Memorabilia Memory Lane #ML7
2012 Total Memorabilia Quad Swatch Gold /25 #TMDEJ
2012 Total Memorabilia Quad Swatch Holofoil /10 #TMDEJ
2012 Total Memorabilia Quad Swatch Melting /1 #TMDEJ
2012 Total Memorabilia Quad Swatch Silver /50 #TMDEJ
2012 Total Memorabilia Red Retail /250 #7
2012 Total Memorabilia Signature Collection Dual Swatch Silver /10 #SCDEJ
2012 Total Memorabilia Signature Collection Quad Swatch Holofoil /5 #SCDEJ
2012 Total Memorabilia Signature Collection Single Swatch Melting /1 #SCDEJ
2012 Total Memorabilia Signature Collection Triple Swatch Gold /10 #SCDEJ
2012 Total Memorabilia Single Swatch Gold /99 #TMDEJ
2012 Total Memorabilia Single Swatch Holofoil /50 #TMDEJ
2012 Total Memorabilia Single Swatch Melting /10 #TMDEJ
2012 Total Memorabilia Single Swatch Silver /199 #TMDEJ
2012 Total Memorabilia Tandem Treasures Dual Memorabilia Gold /75 #TTDEKK
2012 Total Memorabilia Tandem Treasures Dual Memorabilia Holofoil /25 #TTDEKK
2012 Total Memorabilia Tandem Treasures Dual Memorabilia Melting /5 #TTDEKK
2012 Total Memorabilia Tandem Treasures Dual Memorabilia Silver /99 #TTDEKK
2012 Total Memorabilia Triple Swatch Gold /50 #TMDEJ
2012 Total Memorabilia Triple Swatch Holofoil /25 #TMDEJ
2012 Total Memorabilia Triple Swatch Melting /1 #TMDEJ
2012 Total Memorabilia Triple Swatch Silver /99 #TMDEJ
2013 Press Pass #12
2013 Press Pass #13
2013 Press Pass #68
2013 Press Pass #99
2013 Press Pass #81
2013 Press Pass #84
2013 Press Pass #0
2013 Press Pass Aerodynamic Autographs Blue /1 #DEJ
2013 Press Pass Aerodynamic Autographs Holofoil /5 #DEJ
2013 Press Pass Aerodynamic Autographs Printing Plates Black /1 #DEJ
2013 Press Pass Aerodynamic Autographs Printing Plates Cyan /1 #DEJ
2013 Press Pass Aerodynamic Autographs Printing Plates Magenta /1 #DEJ
2013 Press Pass Aerodynamic Autographs Printing Plates Yellow /1 #DEJ
2013 Press Pass Burning Rubber Blue /50 #BRDE
2013 Press Pass Burning Rubber Blue /50 #BRDE2
2013 Press Pass Burning Rubber Gold /199 #BRDE
2013 Press Pass Burning Rubber Gold /199 #BRDE2
2013 Press Pass Burning Rubber Holofoil /75 #BRDE
2013 Press Pass Burning Rubber Holofoil /75 #BRDE2
2013 Press Pass Burning Rubber Letterman /8 #BRLDE
2013 Press Pass Burning Rubber Melting /10 #BRDE
2013 Press Pass Burning Rubber Melting /10 #BRDE2
2013 Press Pass Certified Winners Autographs Gold /10 #DEJ
2013 Press Pass Certified Winners Autographs Melting /5 #DEJ
2013 Press Pass Color Proofs Black #12
2013 Press Pass Color Proofs Black #13
2013 Press Pass Color Proofs Black #68
2013 Press Pass Color Proofs Black #81
2013 Press Pass Color Proofs Black #84
2013 Press Pass Color Proofs Black #99
2013 Press Pass Color Proofs Cyan /35 #12
2013 Press Pass Color Proofs Cyan /35 #13
2013 Press Pass Color Proofs Cyan /35 #68
2013 Press Pass Color Proofs Cyan /35 #81
2013 Press Pass Color Proofs Cyan /35 #84
2013 Press Pass Color Proofs Cyan /35 #99
2013 Press Pass Color Proofs Magenta #12
2013 Press Pass Color Proofs Magenta #13
2013 Press Pass Color Proofs Magenta #68
2013 Press Pass Color Proofs Magenta #81
2013 Press Pass Color Proofs Magenta #84
2013 Press Pass Color Proofs Magenta #99
2013 Press Pass Color Proofs Yellow /5 #12
2013 Press Pass Color Proofs Yellow /5 #13
2013 Press Pass Color Proofs Yellow /5 #68
2013 Press Pass Color Proofs Yellow /5 #81
2013 Press Pass Color Proofs Yellow /5 #84
2013 Press Pass Color Proofs Yellow /5 #99
2013 Press Pass Cool Persistence #CP7
2013 Press Pass Cup Chase #CC5
2013 Press Pass Cup Chase Prizes #CCP8
2013 Press Pass Fanfare #14
2013 Press Pass Fanfare #15
2013 Press Pass Fanfare Autographs Blue /1 #DEJ
2013 Press Pass Fanfare Autographs Gold /1 #DEJ
2013 Press Pass Fanfare Autographs Green /1 #DEJ
2013 Press Pass Fanfare Autographs Red /1 #DEJ
2013 Press Pass Fanfare Autographs Silver /1 #DEJ
2013 Press Pass Fanfare Diamond Die Cuts /5 #14
2013 Press Pass Fanfare Diamond Die Cuts /5 #15
2013 Press Pass Fanfare Fan Following #FF1
2013 Press Pass Fanfare Fan Following National Convention VIP #FFN1
2013 Press Pass Fanfare Green /3 #14
2013 Press Pass Fanfare Green /3 #15
2013 Press Pass Fanfare Holofoil Die Cuts #14
2013 Press Pass Fanfare Holofoil Die Cuts #15
2013 Press Pass Fanfare Magnificent Jumbo Materials Signatures /10 #DEJ
2013 Press Pass Fanfare Magnificent Materials Dual Swatches /50 #DEJ
2013 Press Pass Fanfare Magnificent Materials Dual Swatches Melting /10 #DEJ
2013 Press Pass Fanfare Magnificent Materials Gold /50 #DEJ
2013 Press Pass Fanfare Magnificent Materials Jumbo Swatches /25 #DEJ
2013 Press Pass Fanfare Magnificent Materials Signatures /10 #DEJ
2013 Press Pass Fanfare Magnificent Materials Signatures Blue /5 #DEJ
2013 Press Pass Fanfare Magnificent Materials Silver /199 #DEJ
2013 Press Pass Fanfare Red Foil Die Cuts #14
2013 Press Pass Fanfare Red Foil Die Cuts #15
2013 Press Pass Fanfare Sapphire /20 #14
2013 Press Pass Fanfare Sapphire /20 #15
2013 Press Pass Fanfare Showtime #S9
2013 Press Pass Fanfare Silver /25 #14
2013 Press Pass Fanfare Silver /25 #15
2013 Press Pass Four Wide Gold /10 #FWDE
2013 Press Pass Four Wide Melting /1 #FWDE
2013 Press Pass Ignite #9
2013 Press Pass Ignite #61
2013 Press Pass Ignite Convoy #2
2013 Press Pass Ignite Double Burner Blue Holofoil /10 #DBDE
2013 Press Pass Ignite Double Burner Red /1 #DBDE
2013 Press Pass Ignite Double Burner Silver /25 #DBDE
2013 Press Pass Ignite Great American Treads Autographs Blue Holofoil /10 #GATDE
2013 Press Pass Ignite Great American Treads Autographs Red /1 #GATDE
2013 Press Pass Ignite Hot Threads Blue Holofoil /99 #HTDEJR
2013 Press Pass Ignite Hot Threads Patch Red /10 #HTDEJR
2013 Press Pass Ignite Hot Threads Patch Red Oversized /20 #HTPDEJR
2013 Press Pass Ignite Hot Threads Silver #HTDEJR
2013 Press Pass Ignite Ink Black /20 #IIDE
2013 Press Pass Ignite Ink Blue /5 #IIDE
2013 Press Pass Ignite Ink Red /1 #IIDE
2013 Press Pass Ignite Proofs Black and White /50 #9
2013 Press Pass Ignite Proofs Black and White /50 #61
2013 Press Pass Ignite Proofs Cyan #9
2013 Press Pass Ignite Proofs Cyan #61
2013 Press Pass Ignite Proofs Magenta #9
2013 Press Pass Ignite Proofs Magenta #61
2013 Press Pass Ignite Proofs Yellow /5 #9
2013 Press Pass Ignite Proofs Yellow /5 #61
2013 Press Pass Ignite Supercharged Signatures Blue Holofoil /10 #SSDE
2013 Press Pass Ignite Supercharged Signatures Red /1 #SSDE
2013 Press Pass Ignite Turning Point #3
2013 Press Pass Legends #42
2013 Press Pass Legends Autographs Blue #LGDEJ
2013 Press Pass Legends Autographs Gold /4 #LGDEJ
2013 Press Pass Legends Autographs Holofoil /2 #LGDEJ
2013 Press Pass Legends Autographs Printing Plates Black /1 #LGDEJ
2013 Press Pass Legends Autographs Printing Plates Cyan /1 #LGDEJ
2013 Press Pass Legends Autographs Printing Plates Magenta /1 #LGDEJ
2013 Press Pass Legends Autographs Printing Plates Yellow /1 #LGDEJ
2013 Press Pass Legends Autographs Silver #LGDEJ
2013 Press Pass Legends Blue #42
2013 Press Pass Legends Blue Holofoil /1 #42
2013 Press Pass Legends Four Wide Memorabilia Autographs Gold /25 #FWSEDE
2013 Press Pass Legends Four Wide Memorabilia Autographs Melting /5 #FWSEDE
2013 Press Pass Legends Gold /149 #42
2013 Press Pass Legends Holofoil /10 #42
2013 Press Pass Legends Printing Plates Black /1 #42
2013 Press Pass Legends Printing Plates Cyan /1 #42
2013 Press Pass Legends Printing Plates Magenta /1 #42
2013 Press Pass Legends Printing Plates Yellow /1 #42
2013 Press Pass Legends Prominent Pieces Gold /10 #PPDE
2013 Press Pass Legends Prominent Pieces Holofoil /5 #PPDE
2013 Press Pass Legends Prominent Pieces Oversized Firesuit /5 #PPDE
2013 Press Pass Legends Prominent Pieces Silver /25 #PPDE
2013 Press Pass Legends Red /99 #42
2013 Press Pass Power Picks Blue /99 #4
2013 Press Pass Power Picks Blue /99 #33
2013 Press Pass Power Picks Gold /50 #4
2013 Press Pass Power Picks Gold /50 #33
2013 Press Pass Power Picks Holofoil /10 #4
2013 Press Pass Power Picks Holofoil /10 #33
2013 Press Pass Racing Champions #RC15
2013 Press Pass Racing Champions #RC30
2013 Press Pass Redline #14
2013 Press Pass Redline Black /99 #14
2013 Press Pass Redline Cyan /50 #14
2013 Press Pass Redline Dynamic Duals Dual Relic Blue /5 #DDDEJR
2013 Press Pass Redline Dynamic Duals Dual Relic Gold /10 #DDDEJR
2013 Press Pass Redline Dynamic Duals Dual Relic Melting /1 #DDDEJR
2013 Press Pass Redline Dynamic Duals Dual Relic Red /50 #DDDEJR
2013 Press Pass Redline Dynamic Duals Dual Relic Silver /25 #DDDEJR
2013 Press Pass Redline Intensity #2
2013 Press Pass Redline Magenta /15 #14
2013 Press Pass Redline Muscle Car Sheet Metal Blue /5 #MCMDEJR
2013 Press Pass Redline Muscle Car Sheet Metal Gold /10 #MCMDEJR
2013 Press Pass Redline Muscle Car Sheet Metal Melting /1 #MCMDEJR
2013 Press Pass Redline Muscle Car Sheet Metal Red /50 #MCMDEJR
2013 Press Pass Redline Muscle Car Sheet Metal Silver /25 #MCMDEJR
2013 Press Pass Redline Pieces of the Action Blue /10 #PADE
2013 Press Pass Redline Pieces of the Action Gold /25 #PADE
2013 Press Pass Redline Pieces of the Action Melting /1 #PADE
2013 Press Pass Redline Pieces of the Action Red /75 #PADE
2013 Press Pass Redline Pieces of the Action Silver /50 #PADE
2013 Press Pass Redline Redline Racers #11
2013 Press Pass Redline Relic Autographs Blue /5 #RRSETS
2013 Press Pass Redline Relic Autographs Gold /10 #RRSEDEJ
2013 Press Pass Redline Relic Autographs Melting /1 #RRSETS
2013 Press Pass Redline Relic Autographs Red /88 #RRSEDEJ
2013 Press Pass Redline Relic Autographs Silver /25 #RRSEDEJ
2013 Press Pass Redline Relics Blue /5 #RRDEJR1
2013 Press Pass Redline Relics Gold /10 #RRDEJR1
2013 Press Pass Redline Relics Melting /1 #RRDEJR1
2013 Press Pass Redline Relics Red /50 #RRDEJR1
2013 Press Pass Redline Relics Silver /25 #RRDEJR1
2013 Press Pass Redline RPM #3
2013 Press Pass Redline Signatures Blue /25 #RSDEJR1
2013 Press Pass Redline Signatures Gold /5 #RSDEJR1
2013 Press Pass Redline Signatures Holo /10 #RSDEJR1
2013 Press Pass Redline Signatures Melting /1 #RSDEJR1
2013 Press Pass Redline Signatures Red /50 #RSDEJR1
2013 Press Pass Redline V8 Relics Blue /5 #V8DE
2013 Press Pass Redline V8 Relics Gold /10 #V8DE
2013 Press Pass Redline V8 Relics Melting /1 #V8DE
2013 Press Pass Redline V8 Relics Red /25 #V8DE
2013 Press Pass Redline Yellow /1 #14
2013 Press Pass Showcase /349 #8
2013 Press Pass Showcase /349 #32
2013 Press Pass Showcase /349 #49
2013 Press Pass Showcase /349 #55
2013 Press Pass Showcase Black /1 #8
2013 Press Pass Showcase Black /1 #32
2013 Press Pass Showcase Black /1 #49
2013 Press Pass Showcase Black /1 #55
2013 Press Pass Showcase Blue /25 #55
2013 Press Pass Showcase Classic Collections Ink Gold /5 #CCIHMS
2013 Press Pass Showcase Classic Collections Ink Melting /1 #CCIHMS
2013 Press Pass Showcase Classic Collections Ink Red /1 #CCIHMS
2013 Press Pass Showcase Classic Collections Memorabilia Gold /25 #CCMHMS
2013 Press Pass Showcase Classic Collections Memorabilia Melting /5 #CCMHMS
2013 Press Pass Showcase Classic Collections Memorabilia Silver /75 #CCMHMS
2013 Press Pass Showcase Elite Exhibit Ink /25 #EEIDEJR
2013 Press Pass Showcase Elite Exhibit Ink Blue /30 #EEIDEJR
2013 Press Pass Showcase Elite Exhibit Ink Gold /10 #EEIDEJR
2013 Press Pass Showcase Elite Exhibit Ink Melting /1 #EEIDEJR
2013 Press Pass Showcase Elite Exhibit Ink Red /5 #EEIDEJR
2013 Press Pass Showcase Gold /99 #8
2013 Press Pass Showcase Gold /99 #32
2013 Press Pass Showcase Gold /99 #49
2013 Press Pass Showcase Gold /99 #55
2013 Press Pass Showcase Green /20 #8
2013 Press Pass Showcase Green /20 #32
2013 Press Pass Showcase Green /20 #49
2013 Press Pass Showcase Green /20 #55
2013 Press Pass Showcase Masterpieces Ink /25 #MPIDEJR
2013 Press Pass Showcase Masterpieces Ink Gold /10 #MPIDEJR
2013 Press Pass Showcase Masterpieces Ink Melting /1 #MPIDEJR
2013 Press Pass Showcase Masterpieces Memorabilia /75 #MPDEJR
2013 Press Pass Showcase Masterpieces Memorabilia Gold /25 #MPDEJR
2013 Press Pass Showcase Masterpieces Memorabilia Melting /5 #MPDEJR
2013 Press Pass Showcase Prized Pieces /99 #PPMDEJR
2013 Press Pass Showcase Prized Pieces Blue /20 #PPMDEJR
2013 Press Pass Showcase Prized Pieces Gold /25 #PPMDEJR
2013 Press Pass Showcase Prized Pieces Ink /10 #PPIDEJR
2013 Press Pass Showcase Prized Pieces Ink Blue /25 #PPIDEJR
2013 Press Pass Showcase Prized Pieces Ink Gold /5 #PPIDEJR
2013 Press Pass Showcase Prized Pieces Ink Melting /1 #PPIDEJR
2013 Press Pass Showcase Prized Pieces Melting /5 #PPMDEJR
2013 Press Pass Showcase Purple /13 #8
2013 Press Pass Showcase Purple /13 #32
2013 Press Pass Showcase Purple /13 #49
2013 Press Pass Showcase Purple /13 #55
2013 Press Pass Showcase Red /10 #8
2013 Press Pass Showcase Red /10 #32
2013 Press Pass Showcase Red /10 #49
2013 Press Pass Showcase Red /10 #55
2013 Press Pass Showcase Series Standouts Gold /50 #4
2013 Press Pass Showcase Series Standouts Memorabilia /75 #SSMDEJR
2013 Press Pass Showcase Series Standouts Memorabilia Blue /80 #SSMDEJR
2013 Press Pass Showcase Series Standouts Memorabilia Gold /25 #SSMDEJR
2013 Press Pass Showcase Series Standouts Memorabilia Melting /5 #SSMDEJR
2013 Press Pass Showcase Showcase Patches /5 #SPDEJR
2013 Press Pass Showcase Showroom /299 #1
2013 Press Pass Showcase Showroom Blue /40 #1
2013 Press Pass Showcase Showroom Gold /50 #1
2013 Press Pass Showcase Showroom Green /20 #1
2013 Press Pass Showcase Showroom Melting /1 #1
2013 Press Pass Showcase Showroom Purple /13 #1
2013 Press Pass Showcase Showroom Red /10 #1
2013 Press Pass Showcase Signature Patches /7 #SSPDEJR
2013 Press Pass Showcase Studio Showcase /299 #4
2013 Press Pass Showcase Studio Showcase Blue /40 #4
2013 Press Pass Showcase Studio Showcase Green /25 #4
2013 Press Pass Showcase Studio Showcase Ink /25 #SSIDEJR
2013 Press Pass Showcase Studio Showcase Ink Gold /10 #SSIDEJR
2013 Press Pass Showcase Studio Showcase Ink Melting /1 #SSIDEJR
2013 Press Pass Showcase Studio Showcase Ink Red /5 #SSIDEJR
2013 Press Pass Showcase Studio Showcase Melting /1 #4
2013 Press Pass Showcase Studio Showcase Purple /13 #4
2013 Press Pass Showcase Studio Showcase Red /10 #4
2013 Press Pass Signature Series Gold /5 #DEJ
2013 Press Pass Signature Series Melting /1 #DEJ
2013 Press Pass Signings Blue /1 #DEJ
2013 Press Pass Signings Gold /1 #DEJ
2013 Press Pass Signings Holofoil /1 #DEJ
2013 Press Pass Signings Printing Plates Black /1 #DEJ
2013 Press Pass Signings Printing Plates Cyan /1 #DEJ
2013 Press Pass Signings Printing Plates Magenta /1 #DEJ
2013 Press Pass Signings Printing Plates Yellow /1 #DEJ
2013 Press Pass Signings Silver /1 #DEJ
2013 Total Memorabilia #11
2013 Total Memorabilia #12
2013 Total Memorabilia Black and White /99 #11
2013 Total Memorabilia Black and White /99 #12
2013 Total Memorabilia Dual Swatch Gold /199 #TMDE
2013 Total Memorabilia Gold /275 #11
2013 Total Memorabilia Gold /275 #12
2013 Total Memorabilia Hot Rod Relics Gold /50 #HRRDEJR
2013 Total Memorabilia Hot Rod Relics Holofoil /10 #HRRDEJR
2013 Total Memorabilia Hot Rod Relics Melting /1 #HRRDEJR
2013 Total Memorabilia Hot Rod Relics Silver /99 #HRRDEJR
2013 Total Memorabilia Memory Lane #ML1
2013 Total Memorabilia Quad Swatch Melting /10 #TMDE
2013 Total Memorabilia Red #11
2013 Total Memorabilia Red #12
2013 Total Memorabilia Signature Collection Dual Swatch Gold /5 #SCDE
2013 Total Memorabilia Signature Collection Quad Swatch Melting /1 #SCDE
2013 Total Memorabilia Signature Collection Single Swatch Silver /5 #SCDE
2013 Total Memorabilia Signature Collection Triple Swatch Holofoil /5 #SCDE
2013 Total Memorabilia Single Swatch Silver /475 #TMDE
2013 Total Memorabilia Smooth Operators #SO2
2013 Total Memorabilia Triple Swatch Holofoil /99 #TMDE
2014 Press Pass #0
2014 Press Pass #8
2014 Press Pass #9
2014 Press Pass #100
2014 Press Pass #67
2014 Press Pass #99
2014 Press Pass #78
2014 Press Pass #81
2014 Press Pass Aerodynamic Autographs Blue /1 #AADE
2014 Press Pass Aerodynamic Autographs Holofoil /3 #AADE
2014 Press Pass Aerodynamic Autographs Printing Plates Black /1 #AADE
2014 Press Pass Aerodynamic Autographs Printing Plates Cyan /1 #AADE
2014 Press Pass Aerodynamic Autographs Printing Plates Magenta /1 #AADE
2014 Press Pass Aerodynamic Autographs Printing Plates Yellow /1 #AADE
2014 Press Pass American Thunder #12
2014 Press Pass American Thunder #70
2014 Press Pass American Thunder #68
2014 Press Pass American Thunder #51
2014 Press Pass American Thunder Autographs Blue /5 #ATADEJ
2014 Press Pass American Thunder Autographs Red /1 #ATADEJ
2014 Press Pass American Thunder Autographs White /15 #ATADEJ
2014 Press Pass American Thunder Battle Armor Blue /25 #BADEJ
2014 Press Pass American Thunder Battle Armor Silver /99 #BADEJ
2014 Press Pass American Thunder Black and White /50 #12
2014 Press Pass American Thunder Black and White /50 #51
2014 Press Pass American Thunder Black and White /50 #68
2014 Press Pass American Thunder Black and White /50 #70
2014 Press Pass American Thunder Brothers In Arms Autographs Blue /5 #BAHMS
2014 Press Pass American Thunder Brothers In Arms Autographs Red /1 #BAHMS
2014 Press Pass American Thunder Brothers In Arms Autographs White /10 #BAHMS
2014 Press Pass American Thunder Brothers In Arms Relics Blue /25 #BAHMS
2014 Press Pass American Thunder Brothers In Arms Relics Red /5 #BAHMS
2014 Press Pass American Thunder Brothers In Arms Relics Silver /50 #BAHMS
2014 Press Pass American Thunder Class A Uniforms Blue /99 #CAUDEJ
2014 Press Pass American Thunder Class A Uniforms Red /10 #CAUDEJ
2014 Press Pass American Thunder Class A Uniforms Silver #CAUDEJ
2014 Press Pass American Thunder Cyan #12
2014 Press Pass American Thunder Cyan #51
2014 Press Pass American Thunder Cyan #68
2014 Press Pass American Thunder Cyan #70
2014 Press Pass American Thunder Great American Treads Autographs Blue /10 #GATDEJ
2014 Press Pass American Thunder Great American Treads Autographs Red /1 #GATDEJ
2014 Press Pass American Thunder Magenta #12
2014 Press Pass American Thunder Magenta #51
2014 Press Pass American Thunder Magenta #68
2014 Press Pass American Thunder Magenta #70
2014 Press Pass American Thunder Top Speed #TS7
2014 Press Pass American Thunder With Honors #WH1
2014 Press Pass American Thunder Yellow /5 #12
2014 Press Pass American Thunder Yellow /5 #51
2014 Press Pass American Thunder Yellow /5 #70
2014 Press Pass Color Proofs Black /70 #8
2014 Press Pass Color Proofs Black /70 #9
2014 Press Pass Color Proofs Black /70 #67
2014 Press Pass Color Proofs Black /70 #78
2014 Press Pass Color Proofs Black /70 #81
2014 Press Pass Color Proofs Black /70 #99
2014 Press Pass Color Proofs Black /70 #100
2014 Press Pass Color Proofs Cyan /35 #8
2014 Press Pass Color Proofs Cyan /35 #9
2014 Press Pass Color Proofs Cyan /35 #67
2014 Press Pass Color Proofs Cyan /35 #78
2014 Press Pass Color Proofs Cyan /35 #81
2014 Press Pass Color Proofs Cyan /35 #99
2014 Press Pass Color Proofs Cyan /35 #100
2014 Press Pass Color Proofs Magenta #8
2014 Press Pass Color Proofs Magenta #9
2014 Press Pass Color Proofs Magenta #67
2014 Press Pass Color Proofs Magenta #78
2014 Press Pass Color Proofs Magenta #81
2014 Press Pass Color Proofs Magenta #99
2014 Press Pass Color Proofs Magenta #100
2014 Press Pass Color Proofs Yellow /5 #8
2014 Press Pass Color Proofs Yellow /5 #9
2014 Press Pass Color Proofs Yellow /5 #67
2014 Press Pass Color Proofs Yellow /5 #78
2014 Press Pass Color Proofs Yellow /5 #81
2014 Press Pass Color Proofs Yellow /5 #99
2014 Press Pass Color Proofs Yellow /5 #100
2014 Press Pass Cup Chase #4
2014 Press Pass Five Star /15 #4
2014 Press Pass Five Star Blue /5 #4
2014 Press Pass Five Star Classic Compilation Autographs Blue Triple Swatch /5 #CCDEJR
2014 Press Pass Five Star Classic Compilation Autographs Holofoil /10 #CCDEJR
2014 Press Pass Five Star Classic Compilation Autographs Holofoil Dual Swatch /10 #CCDEJR
2014 Press Pass Five Star Classic Compilation Autographs Melting Five Swatch /1 #CCDEJR
2014 Press Pass Five Star Classic Compilation Autographs Melting Quad Swatch /1 #CCDEJR
2014 Press Pass Five Star Classic Compilations Autographed Patch Booklet /1 #CCDEJR1
2014 Press Pass Five Star Classic Compilations Autographed Patch Booklet /1 #CCDEJR2
2014 Press Pass Five Star Classic Compilations Autographed Patch Booklet /1 #CCDEJR3
2014 Press Pass Five Star Classic Compilations Autographed Patch Booklet /1 #CCDEJR4
2014 Press Pass Five Star Classic Compilations Autographed Patch Booklet /1 #CCDEJR5
2014 Press Pass Five Star Classic Compilations Autographed Patch Booklet /1 #CCDEJR6
2014 Press Pass Five Star Classic Compilations Autographed Patch Booklet /1 #CCDEJR7
2014 Press Pass Five Star Classic Compilations Autographed Patch Booklet /1 #CCDEJR8
2014 Press Pass Five Star Classic Compilations Autographed Patch Booklet /1 #CCDEJR9
2014 Press Pass Five Star Classic Compilations Autographed Patch Booklet /1 #CCDEJR10
2014 Press Pass Five Star Classic Compilations Autographed Patch Booklet /1 #CCDEJR11
2014 Press Pass Five Star Classic Compilations Autographed Patch Booklet /1 #CCDEJR12
2014 Press Pass Five Star Classic Compilations Autographed Patch Booklet /1 #CCDEJR13
2014 Press Pass Five Star Classic Compilations Autographed Patch Booklet /1 #CCDEJR14
2014 Press Pass Five Star Classic Compilations Autographed Patch Booklet /1 #CCDEJR15
2014 Press Pass Five Star Classic Compilations Combo Autographs Blue /5 #CCHMS
2014 Press Pass Five Star Classic Compilations Combo Autographs Blue /5 #CCTSDE
2014 Press Pass Five Star Classic Compilations Combo Autographs Melting /1 #CCHMS
2014 Press Pass Five Star Classic Compilations Combo Autographs Melting /1 #CCTSDE
2014 Press Pass Five Star Holofoil /10 #4
2014 Press Pass Five Star Melting /1 #4
2014 Press Pass Five Star Paramount Pieces Blue /5 #PPDEJR
2014 Press Pass Five Star Paramount Pieces Gold /25 #PPDEJR
2014 Press Pass Five Star Paramount Pieces Holofoil /10 #PPDEJR
2014 Press Pass Five Star Paramount Pieces Melting /1 #PPDEJR
2014 Press Pass Five Star Paramount Pieces Melting Patch /1 #PPDEJR
2014 Press Pass Five Star Signature Souvenirs Blue /5 #SSDE
2014 Press Pass Five Star Signature Souvenirs Gold /50 #SSDE
2014 Press Pass Five Star Signature Souvenirs Holofoil /25 #SSDE
2014 Press Pass Five Star Signature Souvenirs Melting /1 #SSDE
2014 Press Pass Five Star Signatures Blue /5 #FSSDE
2014 Press Pass Five Star Signatures Holofoil /10 #FSSDE
2014 Press Pass Five Star Signatures Melting /1 #FSSDE
2014 Press Pass Four Wide Gold /10 #FWDEJ
2014 Press Pass Four Wide Melting /1 #FWDEJ
2014 Press Pass Gold #8
2014 Press Pass Gold #9
2014 Press Pass Gold #67
2014 Press Pass Gold #78
2014 Press Pass Gold #81
2014 Press Pass Gold #99
2014 Press Pass Gold #100
2014 Press Pass Intensity National Convention VIP #NE1
2014 Press Pass Redline #16
2014 Press Pass Redline #17
2014 Press Pass Redline Black /75 #16
2014 Press Pass Redline Black /75 #17
2014 Press Pass Redline Blue Foil #16
2014 Press Pass Redline Blue Foil #17
2014 Press Pass Redline Cyan /50 #16
2014 Press Pass Redline Cyan /50 #17
2014 Press Pass Redline Dynamic Duals Relic Autographs Blue /10 #DDDEJ
2014 Press Pass Redline Dynamic Duals Relic Autographs Gold /5 #DDDEJ
2014 Press Pass Redline Dynamic Duals Relic Autographs Melting /1 #DDDEJ
2014 Press Pass Redline Dynamic Duals Relic Autographs Red /15 #DDDEJ
2014 Press Pass Redline Green National Convention /5 #16
2014 Press Pass Redline Green National Convention /5 #17
2014 Press Pass Redline Head to Head Blue /10 #HTHADDE
2014 Press Pass Redline Head to Head Gold /25 #HTHADDE
2014 Press Pass Redline Head to Head Melting /1 #HTHADDE
2014 Press Pass Redline Head to Head Red /75 #HTHADDE
2014 Press Pass Redline Intensity #I3
2014 Press Pass Redline Magenta /10 #16
2014 Press Pass Redline Magenta /10 #17
2014 Press Pass Redline Muscle Car Sheet Metal Blue /25 #MCMDEJ
2014 Press Pass Redline Muscle Car Sheet Metal Gold /50 #MCMDEJ
2014 Press Pass Redline Muscle Car Sheet Metal Melting /1 #MCMDEJ
2014 Press Pass Redline Muscle Car Sheet Metal Red /75 #MCMDEJ
2014 Press Pass Redline Pieces of the Action Blue /10 #PADEJ
2014 Press Pass Redline Pieces of the Action Gold /25 #PADEJ
2014 Press Pass Redline Pieces of the Action Melting /1 #PADEJ
2014 Press Pass Redline Pieces of the Action Red /75 #PADEJ
2014 Press Pass Redline Redline Racers #RR4
2014 Press Pass Redline Relic Autographs Blue /5 #RRSEDEJ
2014 Press Pass Redline Relic Autographs Gold /10 #RRSEDEJ
2014 Press Pass Redline Relic Autographs Melting /1 #RRSEDEJ
2014 Press Pass Redline Relic Autographs Red /15 #RRSEDEJ
2014 Press Pass Redline Relics Blue /25 #RRDEJ
2014 Press Pass Redline Relics Gold /50 #RRDEJ
2014 Press Pass Redline Relics Melting /1 #RRDEJ
2014 Press Pass Redline Relics Red /75 #RRDEJ
2014 Press Pass Redline RPM #RPM2
2014 Press Pass Redline Signatures Blue /5 #RSDEJ
2014 Press Pass Redline Signatures Gold /10 #RSDEJ
2014 Press Pass Redline Signatures Melting /1 #RSDEJ
2014 Press Pass Redline Signatures Red /15 #RSDEJ
2014 Press Pass Redline Yellow /1 #16
2014 Press Pass Redline Yellow /1 #17
2014 Press Pass Signature Series Gold /3 #SSDE
2014 Press Pass Signature Series Melting /1 #SSDE
2014 Press Pass Signings Gold /2 #PPSDE
2014 Press Pass Signings Holofoil /2 #PPSDE
2014 Press Pass Signings Melting /1 #PPSDE
2014 Press Pass Signings Printing Plates Black /1 #PPSDE
2014 Press Pass Signings Printing Plates Cyan /1 #PPSDE
2014 Press Pass Signings Printing Plates Magenta /1 #PPSDE
2014 Press Pass Signings Printing Plates Yellow /1 #PPSDE
2014 Press Pass Signings Silver /2 #PPSDE
2014 Press Pass Velocity #1
2014 Sports Illustrated for Kids #367
2014 Total Memorabilia #7
2014 Total Memorabilia Acceleration #AC5
2014 Total Memorabilia Autographed Memorabilia Blue /5 #SCDE
2014 Total Memorabilia Autographed Memorabilia Gold /5 #SCDE
2014 Total Memorabilia Autographed Memorabilia Melting /1 #SCDE
2014 Total Memorabilia Autographed Memorabilia Silver /5 #SC-DE
2014 Total Memorabilia Black and White /99 #7
2014 Total Memorabilia Clear Cuts Blue /175 #CCUDEJ
2014 Total Memorabilia Clear Cuts Melting /25 #CCUDEJ
2014 Total Memorabilia Dual Swatch Gold /150 #TMDE
2014 Total Memorabilia Gold /175 #7
2014 Total Memorabilia Quad Swatch Melting /25 #TMDE
2014 Total Memorabilia Red #7
2014 Total Memorabilia Single Swatch Silver /275 #TMDE
2014 Total Memorabilia Triple Swatch Blue /99 #TMDE
2015 Press Pass #12
2015 Press Pass #91
2015 Press Pass #79
2015 Press Pass #65
2015 Press Pass #100
2015 Press Pass Burning Rubber Blue /50 #BRDEJ1
2015 Press Pass Burning Rubber Blue /50 #BRDEJ2
2015 Press Pass Burning Rubber Blue /50 #BRDEJ3
2015 Press Pass Burning Rubber Gold #BRDEJ1
2015 Press Pass Burning Rubber Gold #BRDEJ2
2015 Press Pass Burning Rubber Gold #BRDEJ3
2015 Press Pass Burning Rubber Green /10 #BRDEJ1
2015 Press Pass Burning Rubber Green /10 #BRDEJ2
2015 Press Pass Burning Rubber Green /10 #BRDEJ3
2015 Press Pass Burning Rubber Letterman /8 #BRLEDEJ
2015 Press Pass Burning Rubber Melting /1 #BRDEJ1
2015 Press Pass Burning Rubber Melting /1 #BRDEJ2
2015 Press Pass Burning Rubber Melting /1 #BRDEJ3
2015 Press Pass Championship Caliber Dual /25 #CCMDEJ
2015 Press Pass Championship Caliber Quad /1 #CCMDEJ
2015 Press Pass Championship Caliber Signature Edition Blue /1 #CCDEJ
2015 Press Pass Championship Caliber Signature Edition Gold /25 #CCDEJ
2015 Press Pass Championship Caliber Signature Edition Green /5 #CCDEJ
2015 Press Pass Championship Caliber Signature Edition Melting /1 #CCDEJ
2015 Press Pass Championship Caliber Single /50 #CCMDEJ
2015 Press Pass Championship Caliber Triple /10 #CCMDEJ
2015 Press Pass Cup Chase #12
2015 Press Pass Cup Chase #65
2015 Press Pass Cup Chase #79
2015 Press Pass Cup Chase #91
2015 Press Pass Cup Chase #100
2015 Press Pass Cup Chase Blue /25 #12
2015 Press Pass Cup Chase Blue /25 #65
2015 Press Pass Cup Chase Blue /25 #79
2015 Press Pass Cup Chase Blue /25 #91
2015 Press Pass Cup Chase Blue /25 #100
2015 Press Pass Cup Chase Gold /75 #12
2015 Press Pass Cup Chase Gold /75 #65
2015 Press Pass Cup Chase Gold /75 #79
2015 Press Pass Cup Chase Gold /75 #91
2015 Press Pass Cup Chase Gold /75 #100
2015 Press Pass Cup Chase Green /10 #12
2015 Press Pass Cup Chase Green /10 #65
2015 Press Pass Cup Chase Green /10 #79
2015 Press Pass Cup Chase Green /10 #91
2015 Press Pass Cup Chase Green /10 #100
2015 Press Pass Cup Chase Melting /1 #12
2015 Press Pass Cup Chase Melting /1 #65
2015 Press Pass Cup Chase Melting /1 #79
2015 Press Pass Cup Chase Melting /1 #91
2015 Press Pass Cup Chase Melting /1 #100
2015 Press Pass Cup Chase Three Wide Blue /25 #3WDEJ
2015 Press Pass Cup Chase Three Wide Gold /50 #3WDEJ
2015 Press Pass Cup Chase Three Wide Green /10 #3WDEJ
2015 Press Pass Cup Chase Three Wide Melting /1 #3WDEJ
2015 Press Pass Cup Chase Upper Cuts /14 #UCDEJ
2015 Press Pass Cuts Blue /25 #CCCDEJ
2015 Press Pass Cuts Gold /50 #CCCDEJ
2015 Press Pass Cuts Green /10 #CCCDEJ
2015 Press Pass Cuts Melting /1 #CCCDEJ
2015 Press Pass Four Wide Signature Edition Blue /15 #4WDEJ
2015 Press Pass Four Wide Signature Edition Gold /35 #4WDEJ
2015 Press Pass Four Wide Signature Edition Green /10 #4WDEJ
2015 Press Pass Four Wide Signature Edition Melting /1 #4WDEJ
2015 Press Pass Pit Road Pieces Blue /25 #PPMDEJ
2015 Press Pass Pit Road Pieces Gold /50 #PPMDEJ
2015 Press Pass Pit Road Pieces Green /10 #PPMDEJ
2015 Press Pass Pit Road Pieces Melting /1 #PPMDEJ
2015 Press Pass Pit Road Pieces Signature Edition Blue /10 #PRPDEJ
2015 Press Pass Pit Road Pieces Signature Edition Gold /25 #PRPDEJ
2015 Press Pass Pit Road Pieces Signature Edition Green /5 #PRPDEJ
2015 Press Pass Pit Road Pieces Signature Edition Melting /1 #PRPDEJ
2015 Press Pass Purple #12
2015 Press Pass Purple #65
2015 Press Pass Purple #79
2015 Press Pass Purple #91
2015 Press Pass Purple #100
2015 Press Pass Red #12
2015 Press Pass Red #65
2015 Press Pass Red #79
2015 Press Pass Red #91
2015 Press Pass Red #100
2015 Press Pass Signings Blue /15 #PPSDE
2015 Press Pass Signings Gold #PPSDE
2015 Press Pass Signings Green /5 #PPSDE
2015 Press Pass Signings Melting /1 #PPSDE
2015 Press Pass Signings Red /10 #PPSDE
2016 Certified #50
2016 Certified #10
2016 Certified Complete Materials /199 #6
2016 Certified Complete Materials Mirror Black /1 #6
2016 Certified Complete Materials Mirror Blue /50 #6
2016 Certified Complete Materials Mirror Gold /25 #6
2016 Certified Complete Materials Mirror Green /5 #6
2016 Certified Complete Materials Mirror Orange /99 #6
2016 Certified Complete Materials Mirror Purple /10 #6
2016 Certified Complete Materials Mirror Red /75 #6
2016 Certified Complete Materials Mirror Silver /99 #6
2016 Certified Epix /199 #2
2016 Certified Epix Mirror Black /1 #2
2016 Certified Epix Mirror Blue /50 #2
2016 Certified Epix Mirror Gold /25 #2
2016 Certified Epix Mirror Green /5 #2
2016 Certified Epix Mirror Orange /99 #2
2016 Certified Epix Mirror Purple /10 #2
2016 Certified Epix Mirror Red /75 #2
2016 Certified Epix Mirror Silver /99 #2
2016 Certified Famed Rides /199 #16
2016 Certified Famed Rides /199 #1
2016 Certified Famed Rides Mirror Black /1 #1
2016 Certified Famed Rides Mirror Black /1 #16
2016 Certified Famed Rides Mirror Blue /50 #1
2016 Certified Famed Rides Mirror Blue /50 #16
2016 Certified Famed Rides Mirror Gold /25 #1
2016 Certified Famed Rides Mirror Gold /25 #16
2016 Certified Famed Rides Mirror Green /5 #1
2016 Certified Famed Rides Mirror Green /5 #16
2016 Certified Famed Rides Mirror Orange /99 #1
2016 Certified Famed Rides Mirror Orange /99 #16
2016 Certified Famed Rides Mirror Purple /10 #1
2016 Certified Famed Rides Mirror Purple /10 #16
2016 Certified Famed Rides Mirror Red /75 #1
2016 Certified Famed Rides Mirror Red /75 #16
2016 Certified Famed Rides Mirror Silver /99 #1
2016 Certified Famed Rides Mirror Silver /99 #16
2016 Certified Gold Team /199 #8
2016 Certified Gold Team Mirror Black /1 #8
2016 Certified Gold Team Mirror Blue /50 #8
2016 Certified Gold Team Mirror Gold /25 #8
2016 Certified Gold Team Mirror Green /5 #8
2016 Certified Gold Team Mirror Orange /99 #8
2016 Certified Gold Team Mirror Purple /10 #8
2016 Certified Gold Team Mirror Red /75 #8
2016 Certified Gold Team Mirror Silver /99 #8
2016 Certified Gold Team Signatures /50 #7
2016 Certified Gold Team Signatures Mirror Black /1 #7
2016 Certified Gold Team Signatures Mirror Gold /25 #7
2016 Certified Mirror Black /1 #10
2016 Certified Mirror Black /1 #50
2016 Certified Mirror Blue /50 #10
2016 Certified Mirror Blue /50 #50
2016 Certified Mirror Gold /25 #10
2016 Certified Mirror Gold /25 #50
2016 Certified Mirror Green /5 #10
2016 Certified Mirror Green /5 #50
2016 Certified Mirror Orange /99 #10
2016 Certified Mirror Orange /99 #50
2016 Certified Mirror Purple /10 #10
2016 Certified Mirror Purple /10 #50
2016 Certified Mirror Red /75 #10
2016 Certified Mirror Red /75 #50
2016 Certified Mirror Silver /99 #10
2016 Certified Mirror Silver /99 #50
2016 Certified Signatures /25 #24
2016 Certified Signatures Mirror Black /1 #24
2016 Certified Signatures Mirror Blue /15 #24
2016 Certified Signatures Mirror Gold /10 #24
2016 Certified Signatures Mirror Green /3 #24
2016 Certified Signatures Mirror Orange /3 #24
2016 Certified Signatures Mirror Purple /8 #24
2016 Certified Signatures Mirror Red /20 #24
2016 Certified Signatures Mirror Silver /3 #24
2016 Certified Sprint Cup Signature Swatches /50 #4
2016 Certified Sprint Cup Signature Swatches Mirror Black /1 #4
2016 Certified Sprint Cup Signature Swatches Mirror Blue /20 #4
2016 Certified Sprint Cup Signature Swatches Mirror Gold /15 #4
2016 Certified Sprint Cup Signature Swatches Mirror Green /5 #4
2016 Certified Sprint Cup Signature Swatches Mirror Orange /10 #4
2016 Certified Sprint Cup Signature Swatches Mirror Purple /10 #4
2016 Certified Sprint Cup Signature Swatches Mirror Red /35 #4
2016 Certified Sprint Cup Signature Swatches Mirror Silver /5 #4
2016 Certified Sprint Cup Swatches /125 #30
2016 Certified Sprint Cup Swatches Mirror Black /1 #30
2016 Certified Sprint Cup Swatches Mirror Blue /50 #30
2016 Certified Sprint Cup Swatches Mirror Gold /25 #30
2016 Certified Sprint Cup Swatches Mirror Green /5 #30
2016 Certified Sprint Cup Swatches Mirror Orange /99 #30
2016 Certified Sprint Cup Swatches Mirror Purple /10 #30
2016 Certified Sprint Cup Swatches Mirror Red /75 #30
2016 Certified Sprint Cup Swatches Mirror Silver /99 #30
2016 Panini Black Friday #28
2016 Panini Black Friday Autographs /25 #28
2016 Panini Black Friday Cracked Ice /25 #28

2016 Panini Black Friday Holo Plaid /1 #28
2016 Panini Black Friday Manufactured Patches #7
2016 Panini Black Friday Manufactured Patches Cracked Ice /25 #7
2016 Panini Black Friday Manufactured Patches Galactic Window /10 #7
2016 Panini Black Friday Manufactured Patches Holo Plaid /1 #7
2016 Panini Black Friday Panini Collection #16
2016 Panini Black Friday Panini Collection Autographs /25 #16
2016 Panini Black Friday Panini Collection Cracked Ice /25 #16
2016 Panini Black Friday Panini Collection Holo Plaid /1 #16
2016 Panini Black Friday Panini Collection Rapture /10 #16
2016 Panini Black Friday Panini Collection Thick Stock /50 #16
2016 Panini Black Friday Panini Collection Wedges /50 #16
2016 Panini Black Friday Racing Memorabilia #R1
2016 Panini Black Friday Racing Memorabilia Cracked Ice /25 #R1
2016 Panini Black Friday Racing Memorabilia Galactic Window /10 #R1
2016 Panini Black Friday Racing Memorabilia Holo Plaid /1 #R1
2016 Panini Black Friday Rapture /10 #28
2016 Panini Black Friday Thick Stock /50 #28
2016 Panini Black Friday Wedges /50 #28
2016 Panini Cyber Monday #26
2016 Panini National Convention #36
2016 Panini National Convention Autographs /25 #36
2016 Panini National Convention Cracked Ice /25 #36
2016 Panini National Convention Decoy Cracked Ice /25 #36
2016 Panini National Convention Decoy Escher Squares /10 #36
2016 Panini National Convention Decoy Rapture /1 #36
2016 Panini National Convention Decoy Wedges /99 #36
2016 Panini National Convention Diamond Awe /49 #36
2016 Panini National Convention Escher Squares /10 #36
2016 Panini National Convention Rapture /1 #36
2016 Panini National Convention VIP #91
2016 Panini National Convention VIP Autographs Gold Vinyl /1 #91
2016 Panini National Convention VIP Autographs Kaleidoscope Red /25 #91
2016 Panini National Convention VIP Blue Wave Gold /10 #91
2016 Panini National Convention VIP Cracked Ice /25 #91
2016 Panini National Convention VIP Flash Green /5 #91
2016 Panini National Convention VIP Gold Vinyl /1 #91
2016 Panini National Convention VIP Memorabilia Gold Vinyl /1 #91
2016 Panini National Convention VIP Memorabilia Kaleidoscope Blue /25 #91
2016 Panini National Convention VIP Prizm /99 #91
2016 Panini National Convention VIP Purple Pulsar /50 #91
2016 Panini National Convention Wedges /99 #36
2016 Panini National Treasures /25 #2
2016 Panini National Treasures /25 #27
2016 Panini National Treasures Black /5 #2
2016 Panini National Treasures Black /5 #27
2016 Panini National Treasures Blue /1 #2
2016 Panini National Treasures Blue /1 #27
2016 Panini National Treasures Dual Driver Materials /25 #1
2016 Panini National Treasures Dual Driver Materials Black /5 #1
2016 Panini National Treasures Dual Driver Materials Blue /1 #1
2016 Panini National Treasures Dual Driver Materials Gold /10 #1
2016 Panini National Treasures Dual Driver Materials Printing Plates Black /1 #1
2016 Panini National Treasures Dual Driver Materials Printing Plates Cyan /1 #1
2016 Panini National Treasures Dual Driver Materials Printing Plates Magenta /1 #1
2016 Panini National Treasures Dual Driver Materials Printing Plates Yellow /1 #1
2016 Panini National Treasures Dual Driver Materials Silver /15 #1
2016 Panini National Treasures Dual Signatures /24 #6
2016 Panini National Treasures Dual Signatures /25 #22
2016 Panini National Treasures Dual Signatures Black /10 #6
2016 Panini National Treasures Dual Signatures Black /10 #22
2016 Panini National Treasures Dual Signatures Blue /1 #6
2016 Panini National Treasures Dual Signatures Blue /1 #22
2016 Panini National Treasures Dual Signatures Gold /15 #6
2016 Panini National Treasures Dual Signatures Gold /15 #22
2016 Panini National Treasures Eight Signatures /15 #1
2016 Panini National Treasures Eight Signatures Black /5 #1
2016 Panini National Treasures Eight Signatures Blue /1 #1
2016 Panini National Treasures Eight Signatures Gold /10 #1
2016 Panini National Treasures Firesuit Materials /25 #5
2016 Panini National Treasures Firesuit Materials Black /5 #5
2016 Panini National Treasures Firesuit Materials Blue /1 #5
2016 Panini National Treasures Firesuit Materials Gold /10 #5
2016 Panini National Treasures Firesuit Materials Laundry Tag /1 #5
2016 Panini National Treasures Firesuit Materials Printing Plates Black /1 #5
2016 Panini National Treasures Firesuit Materials Printing Plates Cyan /1 #5
2016 Panini National Treasures Firesuit Materials Printing Plates Magenta /1 #5
2016 Panini National Treasures Firesuit Materials Printing Plates Yellow /1 #5
2016 Panini National Treasures Firesuit Materials Silver /15 #5
2016 Panini National Treasures Gold /15 #2
2016 Panini National Treasures Gold /15 #27
2016 Panini National Treasures Jumbo Firesuit Patch Signature Booklet Alpine Stars /1 #7
2016 Panini National Treasures Jumbo Firesuit Patch Signature Booklet Associate Sponsor 1 /1 #7
2016 Panini National Treasures Jumbo Firesuit Patch Signature Booklet Associate Sponsor 2 /1 #7
2016 Panini National Treasures Jumbo Firesuit Patch Signature Booklet Associate Sponsor 3 /1 #7
2016 Panini National Treasures Jumbo Firesuit Patch Signature Booklet Associate Sponsor 4 /1 #7
2016 Panini National Treasures Jumbo Firesuit Patch Signature Booklet Associate Sponsor 5 /1 #7
2016 Panini National Treasures Jumbo Firesuit Patch Signature Booklet Associate Sponsor 6 /1 #7
2016 Panini National Treasures Jumbo Firesuit Patch Signature Booklet Associate Sponsor 7 /1 #7
2016 Panini National Treasures Jumbo Firesuit Patch Signature Booklet Associate Sponsor 8 /1 #7
2016 Panini National Treasures Jumbo Firesuit Patch Signature Booklet Associate Sponsor 9 /1 #7
2016 Panini National Treasures Jumbo Firesuit Patch Signature Booklet Goodyear /2 #7
2016 Panini National Treasures Jumbo Firesuit Patch Signature Booklet Manufacturers Logo /1 #7
2016 Panini National Treasures Jumbo Firesuit Patch Signature Booklet NASCAR /1 #7
2016 Panini National Treasures Jumbo Firesuit Patch Signature Booklet Sprint Cup Logo /1 #7
2016 Panini National Treasures Jumbo Firesuit Patch Signature Booklet Sunoco /1 #7
2016 Panini National Treasures Jumbo Firesuit Signatures /25 #7
2016 Panini National Treasures Jumbo Firesuit Signatures Black /5 #7
2016 Panini National Treasures Jumbo Firesuit Signatures Blue /1 #7
2016 Panini National Treasures Jumbo Firesuit Signatures Gold /10 #7
2016 Panini National Treasures Jumbo Firesuit Signatures Printing Plates Black /1 #7
2016 Panini National Treasures Jumbo Firesuit Signatures Printing Plates Cyan /1 #7
2016 Panini National Treasures Jumbo Firesuit Signatures Printing Plates Magenta /1 #7
2016 Panini National Treasures Jumbo Firesuit Signatures Printing Plates Yellow /1 #7
2016 Panini National Treasures Jumbo Firesuit Signatures Silver /15 #7
2016 Panini National Treasures Jumbo Sheet Metal Signature Booklet /49 #1
2016 Panini National Treasures Jumbo Sheet Metal Signature Booklet Black /10 #1
2016 Panini National Treasures Jumbo Sheet Metal Signature Booklet Blue /1 #1
2016 Panini National Treasures Jumbo Sheet Metal Signature Booklet Gold /25 #1
2016 Panini National Treasures Jumbo Sheet Metal Signatures Black /5 #3
2016 Panini National Treasures Jumbo Sheet Metal Signatures Blue /1 #3
2016 Panini National Treasures Jumbo Sheet Metal Signatures Gold /10 #3
2016 Panini National Treasures Jumbo Sheet Metal Signatures Printing Plates Black /1 #3
2016 Panini National Treasures Jumbo Sheet Metal Signatures Printing Plates Cyan /1 #3
2016 Panini National Treasures Jumbo Sheet Metal Signatures Printing Plates Magenta /1 #3
2016 Panini National Treasures Jumbo Sheet Metal Signatures Printing Plates Yellow /1 #3
2016 Panini National Treasures Printing Plates Black /1 #2
2016 Panini National Treasures Printing Plates Black /1 #27
2016 Panini National Treasures Printing Plates Cyan /1 #2
2016 Panini National Treasures Printing Plates Cyan /1 #27
2016 Panini National Treasures Printing Plates Magenta /1 #2
2016 Panini National Treasures Printing Plates Magenta /1 #27
2016 Panini National Treasures Printing Plates Yellow /1 #2
2016 Panini National Treasures Printing Plates Yellow /1 #27
2016 Panini National Treasures Quad Driver Materials /25 #1
2016 Panini National Treasures Quad Driver Materials Black /5 #1
2016 Panini National Treasures Quad Driver Materials Blue /1 #1
2016 Panini National Treasures Quad Driver Materials Gold /10 #1
2016 Panini National Treasures Quad Driver Materials Printing Plates Black /1 #1
2016 Panini National Treasures Quad Driver Materials Printing Plates Cyan /1 #1
2016 Panini National Treasures Quad Driver Materials Printing Plates Magenta /1 #1
2016 Panini National Treasures Quad Driver Materials Printing Plates Yellow /1 #1
2016 Panini National Treasures Quad Driver Materials Silver /15 #1
2016 Panini National Treasures Quad Materials /25 #5
2016 Panini National Treasures Quad Materials Black /5 #5
2016 Panini National Treasures Quad Materials Blue /1 #5
2016 Panini National Treasures Quad Materials Gold /10 #5
2016 Panini National Treasures Quad Materials Printing Plates Black /1 #5
2016 Panini National Treasures Quad Materials Printing Plates Cyan /1 #5
2016 Panini National Treasures Quad Materials Printing Plates Magenta /1 #5
2016 Panini National Treasures Quad Materials Printing Plates Yellow /1 #5
2016 Panini National Treasures Quad Materials Silver /15 #5
2016 Panini National Treasures Sheet Metal Materials /25 #5
2016 Panini National Treasures Sheet Metal Materials Black /5 #5
2016 Panini National Treasures Sheet Metal Materials Blue /1 #5
2016 Panini National Treasures Sheet Metal Materials Gold /10 #5
2016 Panini National Treasures Sheet Metal Materials Printing Plates Black /1 #5
2016 Panini National Treasures Sheet Metal Materials Printing Plates Cyan /1 #5
2016 Panini National Treasures Sheet Metal Materials Printing Plates Magenta /1 #5
2016 Panini National Treasures Sheet Metal Materials Printing Plates Yellow /1 #5
2016 Panini National Treasures Sheet Metal Materials Silver /15 #5
2016 Panini National Treasures Signature Dual Materials Black /5 #7
2016 Panini National Treasures Signature Dual Materials Blue /1 #7
2016 Panini National Treasures Signature Dual Materials Gold /10 #7
2016 Panini National Treasures Signature Dual Materials Printing Plates Black /1 #7
2016 Panini National Treasures Signature Dual Materials Printing Plates Cyan /1 #7
2016 Panini National Treasures Signature Dual Materials Printing Plates Magenta /1 #7
2016 Panini National Treasures Signature Dual Materials Printing Plates Yellow /1 #7
2016 Panini National Treasures Signature Dual Materials Silver /15 #7
2016 Panini National Treasures Signature Firesuit Materials /25 #7
2016 Panini National Treasures Signature Firesuit Materials Black /5 #7
2016 Panini National Treasures Signature Firesuit Materials Blue /1 #7
2016 Panini National Treasures Signature Firesuit Materials Gold /10 #7
2016 Panini National Treasures Signature Firesuit Materials Printing Plates Black /1 #7
2016 Panini National Treasures Signature Firesuit Materials Printing Plates Cyan /1 #7
2016 Panini National Treasures Signature Firesuit Materials Printing Plates Magenta /1 #7
2016 Panini National Treasures Signature Firesuit Materials Printing Plates Yellow /1 #7
2016 Panini National Treasures Signature Firesuit Materials Silver /15 #7
2016 Panini National Treasures Signature Quad Materials Black /5 #7
2016 Panini National Treasures Signature Quad Materials Blue /1 #7
2016 Panini National Treasures Signature Quad Materials Gold /10 #7
2016 Panini National Treasures Signature Quad Materials Printing Plates Black /1 #7
2016 Panini National Treasures Signature Quad Materials Printing Plates Cyan /1 #7
2016 Panini National Treasures Signature Quad Materials Printing Plates Magenta /1 #7
2016 Panini National Treasures Signature Quad Materials Printing Plates Yellow /1 #7
2016 Panini National Treasures Signature Sheet Metal Materials Black /5 #7
2016 Panini National Treasures Signature Sheet Metal Materials Blue /1 #7
2016 Panini National Treasures Signature Sheet Metal Materials Gold /10 #7
2016 Panini National Treasures Signature Sheet Metal Materials Printing Plates Black /1 #7
2016 Panini National Treasures Signature Sheet Metal Materials Printing Plates Cyan /1 #7
2016 Panini National Treasures Signature Sheet Metal Materials Printing Plates Magenta /1 #7
2016 Panini National Treasures Signature Sheet Metal Materials Printing Plates Yellow /1 #7
2016 Panini National Treasures Silver /20 #2
2016 Panini National Treasures Silver /20 #27
2016 Panini National Treasures Six Signatures /25 #8
2016 Panini National Treasures Six Signatures Black /10 #8
2016 Panini National Treasures Six Signatures Blue /1 #8
2016 Panini National Treasures Six Signatures Gold /15 #8
2016 Panini National Treasures Trio Driver Materials /25 #4
2016 Panini National Treasures Trio Driver Materials Black /5 #4
2016 Panini National Treasures Trio Driver Materials Blue /1 #4
2016 Panini National Treasures Trio Driver Materials Gold /10 #4
2016 Panini National Treasures Trio Driver Materials Printing Plates Black /1 #4
2016 Panini National Treasures Trio Driver Materials Printing Plates Cyan /1 #4
2016 Panini National Treasures Trio Driver Materials Printing Plates Magenta /1 #4
2016 Panini National Treasures Trio Driver Materials Printing Plates Yellow /1 #4
2016 Panini National Treasures Trio Driver Materials Silver /15 #4
2016 Panini Prizm #73
2016 Panini Prizm #63
2016 Panini Prizm #8
2016 Panini Prizm Autographs Prizms #74
2016 Panini Prizm Autographs Prizms Black /3 #74
2016 Panini Prizm Autographs Prizms Blue Flag /25 #74
2016 Panini Prizm Autographs Prizms Camo /8 #74
2016 Panini Prizm Autographs Prizms Checkered Flag /1 #74
2016 Panini Prizm Autographs Prizms Gold /10 #74
2016 Panini Prizm Autographs Prizms Green Flag /35 #74
2016 Panini Prizm Autographs Prizms Rainbow /24 #74
2016 Panini Prizm Autographs Prizms Red Flag /15 #74
2016 Panini Prizm Autographs Prizms Red White and Blue /10 #74
2016 Panini Prizm Autographs Prizms White Flag /5 #74
2016 Panini Prizm Blowing Smoke #4
2016 Panini Prizm Blowing Smoke Prizms #4
2016 Panini Prizm Blowing Smoke Prizms Checkered Flag /1 #4
2016 Panini Prizm Blowing Smoke Prizms Gold /10 #4
2016 Panini Prizm Competitors #1
2016 Panini Prizm Competitors Prizms #1
2016 Panini Prizm Competitors Prizms Checkered Flag /1 #1
2016 Panini Prizm Competitors Prizms Gold /10 #1
2016 Panini Prizm Firesuit Fabrics /50 #1
2016 Panini Prizm Firesuit Fabrics Prizms Blue Flag /15 #1
2016 Panini Prizm Firesuit Fabrics Prizms Checkered Flag /1 #1
2016 Panini Prizm Firesuit Fabrics Prizms Green Flag /25 #1
2016 Panini Prizm Firesuit Fabrics Prizms Red Flag /10 #1
2016 Panini Prizm Firesuit Fabrics Team /149 #1
2016 Panini Prizm Firesuit Fabrics Team Prizms Blue Flag /10 #1
2016 Panini Prizm Firesuit Fabrics Team Prizms Checkered Flag /1 #1
2016 Panini Prizm Firesuit Fabrics Team Prizms Green Flag /25 #1
2016 Panini Prizm Firesuit Fabrics Team Prizms Red Flag /5 #1
2016 Panini Prizm Machinery #1
2016 Panini Prizm Machinery Prizms Checkered Flag /1 #1
2016 Panini Prizm Machinery Prizms Gold /10 #1
2016 Panini Prizm Patented Penmanship Prizms #2
2016 Panini Prizm Patented Penmanship Prizms Black /3 #2
2016 Panini Prizm Patented Penmanship Prizms Blue Flag /25 #2
2016 Panini Prizm Patented Penmanship Prizms Camo /8 #2
2016 Panini Prizm Patented Penmanship Prizms Checkered Flag /1 #2
2016 Panini Prizm Patented Penmanship Prizms Gold /10 #2
2016 Panini Prizm Patented Penmanship Prizms Green Flag /35 #2
2016 Panini Prizm Patented Penmanship Prizms Rainbow /24 #2
2016 Panini Prizm Patented Penmanship Prizms Red Flag /15 #2
2016 Panini Prizm Patented Penmanship Prizms Red White and Blue /10 #2
2016 Panini Prizm Patented Penmanship Prizms White Flag /5 #2
2016 Panini Prizm Prizms #8
2016 Panini Prizm Prizms #63
2016 Panini Prizm Prizms #73
2016 Panini Prizm Prizms Black /3 #8
2016 Panini Prizm Prizms Black /3 #63
2016 Panini Prizm Prizms Black /3 #73
2016 Panini Prizm Prizms Blue Flag /99 #8
2016 Panini Prizm Prizms Blue Flag /99 #63
2016 Panini Prizm Prizms Blue Flag /99 #73
2016 Panini Prizm Prizms Camo /88 #8
2016 Panini Prizm Prizms Camo /88 #63
2016 Panini Prizm Prizms Camo /88 #73
2016 Panini Prizm Prizms Checkered Flag /1 #8
2016 Panini Prizm Prizms Checkered Flag /1 #63
2016 Panini Prizm Prizms Checkered Flag /1 #73
2016 Panini Prizm Prizms Gold /10 #8
2016 Panini Prizm Prizms Gold /10 #63
2016 Panini Prizm Prizms Gold /10 #73
2016 Panini Prizm Prizms Green Flag /149 #8
2016 Panini Prizm Prizms Green Flag /149 #63
2016 Panini Prizm Prizms Green Flag /149 #73
2016 Panini Prizm Prizms Rainbow /24 #8
2016 Panini Prizm Prizms Rainbow /24 #63
2016 Panini Prizm Prizms Rainbow /24 #73
2016 Panini Prizm Prizms Red Flag /75 #8
2016 Panini Prizm Prizms Red Flag /75 #63
2016 Panini Prizm Prizms Red Flag /75 #73
2016 Panini Prizm Prizms Red White and Blue #8
2016 Panini Prizm Prizms Red White and Blue #63
2016 Panini Prizm Prizms Red White and Blue #73
2016 Panini Prizm Prizms White Flag /5 #8
2016 Panini Prizm Prizms White Flag /5 #63
2016 Panini Prizm Prizms White Flag /5 #73
2016 Panini Prizm Qualifying Times #6
2016 Panini Prizm Qualifying Times Prizms #6
2016 Panini Prizm Qualifying Times Prizms Checkered Flag /1 #6
2016 Panini Prizm Qualifying Times Prizms Gold /10 #6
2016 Panini Prizm Race Used Tire #1
2016 Panini Prizm Race Used Tire Prizms Blue Flag /49 #1
2016 Panini Prizm Race Used Tire Prizms Checkered Flag /1 #1
2016 Panini Prizm Race Used Tire Prizms Green Flag /99 #1
2016 Panini Prizm Race Used Tire Prizms Red Flag /25 #1
2016 Panini Prizm Race Used Tire Team #1
2016 Panini Prizm Race Used Tire Team Prizms Blue Flag /75 #1
2016 Panini Prizm Race Used Tire Team Prizms Green Flag /149 #1
2016 Panini Prizm Race Used Tire Team Prizms Red Flag /10 #1
2016 Panini Prizm Raising the Flag #5
2016 Panini Prizm Raising the Flag Prizms #5
2016 Panini Prizm Raising the Flag Prizms Checkered Flag /1 #5
2016 Panini Prizm Raising the Flag Prizms Gold /10 #5
2016 Panini Prizm Winner's Circle #17
2016 Panini Prizm Winner's Circle #10
2016 Panini Prizm Winner's Circle #35
2016 Panini Prizm Winner's Circle Prizms #10
2016 Panini Prizm Winner's Circle Prizms #17
2016 Panini Prizm Winner's Circle Prizms #35
2016 Panini Prizm Winner's Circle Prizms Checkered Flag /1 #10
2016 Panini Prizm Winner's Circle Prizms Checkered Flag /1 #17
2016 Panini Prizm Winner's Circle Prizms Checkered Flag /1 #35
2016 Panini Prizm Winner's Circle Prizms Gold /10 #10
2016 Panini Prizm Winner's Circle Prizms Gold /10 #17
2016 Panini Prizm Winner's Circle Prizms Gold /10 #35
2016 Panini Torque #10
2016 Panini Torque #48
2016 Panini Torque #73
2016 Panini Torque Artist Proof /50 #10
2016 Panini Torque Artist Proof /50 #48
2016 Panini Torque Artist Proof /50 #73
2016 Panini Torque Blackout /1 #10
2016 Panini Torque Blackout /1 #48
2016 Panini Torque Blackout /1 #73
2016 Panini Torque Blue /125 #10
2016 Panini Torque Blue /125 #48
2016 Panini Torque Blue /125 #73
2016 Panini Torque Clear Vision #10
2016 Panini Torque Clear Vision Blue /99 #10
2016 Panini Torque Clear Vision Gold /149 #10
2016 Panini Torque Clear Vision Green /25 #10
2016 Panini Torque Clear Vision Purple /10 #10
2016 Panini Torque Clear Vision Red /49 #10
2016 Panini Torque Combo Materials Autographs /25 #8
2016 Panini Torque Combo Materials Autographs Blue /20 #8
2016 Panini Torque Combo Materials Autographs Green /10 #8
2016 Panini Torque Combo Materials Autographs Purple /5 #8
2016 Panini Torque Combo Materials Autographs Red /15 #8
2016 Panini Torque Gas N Go #8
2016 Panini Torque Gas N Go Gold /199 #8
2016 Panini Torque Gas N Go Holo Silver /99 #8
2016 Panini Torque Gold #10
2016 Panini Torque Gold #48
2016 Panini Torque Gold #73
2016 Panini Torque Helmets #3
2016 Panini Torque Helmets Blue /99 #3
2016 Panini Torque Helmets Checkerboard /10 #3
2016 Panini Torque Helmets Green /25 #3
2016 Panini Torque Helmets Red /49 #3
2016 Panini Torque Holo Gold /5 #10
2016 Panini Torque Holo Gold /5 #48
2016 Panini Torque Holo Gold /5 #73
2016 Panini Torque Holo Silver /10 #10
2016 Panini Torque Holo Silver /10 #48
2016 Panini Torque Holo Silver /10 #73
2016 Panini Torque Horsepower Heroes #12
2016 Panini Torque Horsepower Heroes Gold /199 #12
2016 Panini Torque Horsepower Heroes Holo Silver /99 #12
2016 Panini Torque Jumbo Tire Autographs /25 #7
2016 Panini Torque Jumbo Tire Autographs Blue /20 #7
2016 Panini Torque Jumbo Tire Autographs Green /10 #7
2016 Panini Torque Jumbo Tire Autographs Purple /5 #7
2016 Panini Torque Jumbo Tire Autographs Red /15 #7
2016 Panini Torque Metal Materials /249 #9
2016 Panini Torque Metal Materials Blue /99 #9
2016 Panini Torque Metal Materials Green /25 #9
2016 Panini Torque Metal Materials Purple /10 #9
2016 Panini Torque Metal Materials Red /49 #9
2016 Panini Torque Nicknames #2
2016 Panini Torque Nicknames Gold /199 #2
2016 Panini Torque Nicknames Holo Silver /99 #2
2016 Panini Torque Painted to Perfection #7
2016 Panini Torque Painted to Perfection Blue /99 #7
2016 Panini Torque Painted to Perfection Checkerboard /10 #7
2016 Panini Torque Painted to Perfection Green /25 #7
2016 Panini Torque Painted to Perfection Red /49 #7
2016 Panini Torque Pairings Materials /249 #1
2016 Panini Torque Pairings Materials /125 #3
2016 Panini Torque Pairings Materials /125 #2
2016 Panini Torque Pairings Materials /125 #7
2016 Panini Torque Pairings Materials Blue /99 #1
2016 Panini Torque Pairings Materials Blue /99 #2
2016 Panini Torque Pairings Materials Blue /99 #3
2016 Panini Torque Pairings Materials Blue /99 #7
2016 Panini Torque Pairings Materials Green /25 #1
2016 Panini Torque Pairings Materials Green /25 #2
2016 Panini Torque Pairings Materials Green /25 #3
2016 Panini Torque Pairings Materials Green /10 #7
2016 Panini Torque Pairings Materials Purple /10 #1
2016 Panini Torque Pairings Materials Purple /10 #2
2016 Panini Torque Pairings Materials Purple /10 #3
2016 Panini Torque Pairings Materials Red /49 #1
2016 Panini Torque Pairings Materials Red /49 #2
2016 Panini Torque Pairings Materials Red /49 #3
2016 Panini Torque Pairings Materials Red /25 #7
2016 Panini Torque Pole Position #10
2016 Panini Torque Pole Position Blue /99 #10
2016 Panini Torque Pole Position Checkerboard /10 #10
2016 Panini Torque Pole Position Green /25 #10
2016 Panini Torque Pole Position Red /49 #10
2016 Panini Torque Printing Plates Black /1 #10
2016 Panini Torque Printing Plates Black /1 #48
2016 Panini Torque Printing Plates Black /1 #73
2016 Panini Torque Printing Plates Cyan /1 #10
2016 Panini Torque Printing Plates Cyan /1 #48
2016 Panini Torque Printing Plates Cyan /1 #73
2016 Panini Torque Printing Plates Magenta /1 #10
2016 Panini Torque Printing Plates Magenta /1 #48
2016 Panini Torque Printing Plates Magenta /1 #73
2016 Panini Torque Printing Plates Yellow /1 #10
2016 Panini Torque Printing Plates Yellow /1 #48
2016 Panini Torque Printing Plates Yellow /1 #73
2016 Panini Torque Purple /25 #10
2016 Panini Torque Purple /25 #48
2016 Panini Torque Purple /25 #73
2016 Panini Torque Quad Materials /149 #2
2016 Panini Torque Quad Materials Blue /99 #2
2016 Panini Torque Quad Materials Green /25 #2
2016 Panini Torque Quad Materials Purple /10 #2
2016 Panini Torque Quad Materials Red /49 #2
2016 Panini Torque Red /99 #10
2016 Panini Torque Red /99 #48
2016 Panini Torque Red /99 #73
2016 Panini Torque Rubber Relics /399 #7
2016 Panini Torque Rubber Relics /49 #6
2016 Panini Torque Rubber Relics Blue /25 #6
2016 Panini Torque Rubber Relics Blue /99 #7
2016 Panini Torque Rubber Relics Green /3 #6
2016 Panini Torque Rubber Relics Green /25 #7
2016 Panini Torque Rubber Relics Purple /10 #7
2016 Panini Torque Rubber Relics Red /10 #6
2016 Panini Torque Rubber Relics Red /49 #7
2016 Panini Torque Shades #3
2016 Panini Torque Shades Gold /199 #3
2016 Panini Torque Shades Holo Silver /99 #3
2016 Panini Torque Silhouettes Firesuit Autographs /25 #6
2016 Panini Torque Silhouettes Firesuit Autographs Blue /20 #6
2016 Panini Torque Silhouettes Firesuit Autographs Green /10 #6
2016 Panini Torque Silhouettes Firesuit Autographs Purple /5 #6
2016 Panini Torque Silhouettes Firesuit Autographs Red /15 #6
2016 Panini Torque Silhouettes Sheet Metal Autographs /25 #6
2016 Panini Torque Silhouettes Sheet Metal Autographs Blue /20 #6
2016 Panini Torque Silhouettes Sheet Metal Autographs Green /10 #6
2016 Panini Torque Silhouettes Sheet Metal Autographs Purple /5 #6
2016 Panini Torque Silhouettes Sheet Metal Autographs Red /15 #6
2016 Panini Torque Special Paint #2
2016 Panini Torque Special Paint Gold /199 #2
2016 Panini Torque Special Paint Holo Silver /99 #2
2016 Panini Torque Superstar Vision #3
2016 Panini Torque Superstar Vision Blue /99 #3
2016 Panini Torque Superstar Vision Gold /149 #3
2016 Panini Torque Superstar Vision Green /25 #3
2016 Panini Torque Superstar Vision Purple /10 #3
2016 Panini Torque Superstar Vision Red /49 #3
2016 Panini Torque Test Proof Black /1 #10
2016 Panini Torque Test Proof Black /1 #48
2016 Panini Torque Test Proof Black /1 #73
2016 Panini Torque Test Proof Cyan /1 #10
2016 Panini Torque Test Proof Cyan /1 #48
2016 Panini Torque Test Proof Cyan /1 #73
2016 Panini Torque Test Proof Magenta /1 #10
2016 Panini Torque Test Proof Magenta /1 #48
2016 Panini Torque Test Proof Magenta /1 #73
2016 Panini Torque Test Proof Yellow /1 #10
2016 Panini Torque Test Proof Yellow /1 #48
2016 Panini Torque Test Proof Yellow /1 #73
2016 Panini Torque Victory Laps #2
2016 Panini Torque Victory Laps Gold /199 #2
2016 Panini Torque Victory Laps Holo Silver /99 #2
2016 Panini Torque Winning Vision #10
2016 Panini Torque Winning Vision Blue /99 #10
2016 Panini Torque Winning Vision Gold /149 #10
2016 Panini Torque Winning Vision Green /25 #10
2016 Panini Torque Winning Vision Purple /10 #10
2016 Panini Torque Winning Vision Red /49 #10
2017 Donruss #3
2017 Donruss #93
2017 Donruss #100
2017 Donruss #137
2017 Donruss #37A
2017 Donruss #37B
2017 Donruss Artist Proof /25 #3
2017 Donruss Artist Proof /25 #37A
2017 Donruss Artist Proof /25 #93
2017 Donruss Artist Proof /25 #137
2017 Donruss Artist Proof /25 #37B
2017 Donruss Artist Proof /25 #100
2017 Donruss Blue Foil /299 #3
2017 Donruss Blue Foil /299 #93
2017 Donruss Blue Foil /299 #37A
2017 Donruss Blue Foil /299 #137
2017 Donruss Blue Foil /299 #37B
2017 Donruss Blue Foil /299 #100
2017 Donruss Classics #1
2017 Donruss Classics Cracked Ice /999 #1
2017 Donruss Dual Rubber Relics #4
2017 Donruss Dual Rubber Relics Holo Black /1 #4
2017 Donruss Dual Rubber Relics Holo Gold /25 #4
2017 Donruss Elite Dominators /999 #3
2017 Donruss Elite Series /999 #5
2017 Donruss Gold Foil /499 #3
2017 Donruss Gold Foil /499 #93
2017 Donruss Gold Foil /499 #137
2017 Donruss Gold Foil /499 #37A
2017 Donruss Gold Foil /499 #37B
2017 Donruss Gold Foil /499 #100
2017 Donruss Gold Press Proof /99 #3
2017 Donruss Gold Press Proof /99 #37A
2017 Donruss Gold Press Proof /99 #93
2017 Donruss Gold Press Proof /99 #137
2017 Donruss Gold Press Proof /99 #37B
2017 Donruss Gold Press Proof /99 #100
2017 Donruss Green Foil /199 #3
2017 Donruss Green Foil /199 #37A
2017 Donruss Green Foil /199 #93
2017 Donruss Green Foil /199 #137
2017 Donruss Green Foil /199 #37B
2017 Donruss Green Foil /199 #100
2017 Donruss Press Proof /49 #3
2017 Donruss Press Proof /49 #37A
2017 Donruss Press Proof /49 #93
2017 Donruss Press Proof /49 #137
2017 Donruss Press Proof /49 #37B
2017 Donruss Press Proof /49 #100
2017 Donruss Printing Plates Black /1 #3
2017 Donruss Printing Plates Black /1 #37A
2017 Donruss Printing Plates Black /1 #93
2017 Donruss Printing Plates Black /1 #137
2017 Donruss Printing Plates Black /1 #37B
2017 Donruss Printing Plates Black /1 #100
2017 Donruss Printing Plates Cyan /1 #3
2017 Donruss Printing Plates Cyan /1 #37A
2017 Donruss Printing Plates Cyan /1 #93
2017 Donruss Printing Plates Cyan /1 #137
2017 Donruss Printing Plates Cyan /1 #37B
2017 Donruss Printing Plates Cyan /1 #100
2017 Donruss Printing Plates Magenta /1 #3
2017 Donruss Printing Plates Magenta /1 #93
2017 Donruss Printing Plates Magenta /1 #137
2017 Donruss Printing Plates Magenta /1 #37A
2017 Donruss Printing Plates Magenta /1 #37B
2017 Donruss Printing Plates Magenta /1 #100
2017 Donruss Printing Plates Yellow /1 #3
2017 Donruss Printing Plates Yellow /1 #93
2017 Donruss Printing Plates Yellow /1 #137
2017 Donruss Printing Plates Yellow /1 #37A
2017 Donruss Printing Plates Yellow /1 #37B
2017 Donruss Printing Plates Yellow /1 #100
2017 Donruss Retro Relics 1984 #13
2017 Donruss Retro Relics 1984 Holo Black /5 #13
2017 Donruss Retro Relics 1984 Holo Gold /99 #13
2017 Donruss Retro Signatures 1984 #6
2017 Donruss Retro Signatures 1984 Holo Black /1 #6
2017 Donruss Retro Signatures 1984 Holo Gold /25 #6
2017 Donruss Rubber Relics #13
2017 Donruss Rubber Relics #14
2017 Donruss Rubber Relics Holo Black /1 #13
2017 Donruss Rubber Relics Holo Black /1 #14
2017 Donruss Rubber Relics Holo Gold /50 #13
2017 Donruss Rubber Relics Holo Gold /50 #14
2017 Donruss Rubber Relics Signatures /99 #1
2017 Donruss Rubber Relics Signatures Holo Black /1 #1
2017 Donruss Rubber Relics Signatures Holo Gold /25 #1
2017 Donruss Significant Signatures #4
2017 Donruss Significant Signatures Holo Black /1 #4
2017 Donruss Significant Signatures Holo Gold /25 #4
2017 Donruss Speed #2
2017 Donruss Speed Cracked Ice /999 #2
2017 Donruss Studio Signatures #5
2017 Donruss Studio Signatures Holo Black /1 #5
2017 Donruss Studio Signatures Holo Gold /25 #5
2017 Donruss Top Tier #7
2017 Donruss Top Tier Cracked Ice /999 #7
2017 Donruss Track Masters #3
2017 Donruss Track Masters Cracked Ice /999 #3
2017 Panini Black Friday Happy Holiday Memorabilia #HHDE
2017 Panini Black Friday Happy Holiday Memorabilia Cracked Ice /25 #HHDE
2017 Panini Black Friday Happy Holiday Memorabilia Galactic Windows /10 #HHDE
2017 Panini Black Friday Happy Holiday Memorabilia Hyperplaid /1 #HHDE
2017 Panini Black Friday Panini Collection #22
2017 Panini Black Friday Panini Collection Autographs /25 #22
2017 Panini Black Friday Panini Collection Cracked Ice /25 #22
2017 Panini Black Friday Panini Collection Decoy /50 #22
2017 Panini Black Friday Panini Collection Hyperplaid /1 #22
2017 Panini Black Friday Panini Collection Rapture /10 #22
2017 Panini Black Friday Panini Collection Wedges /50 #22
2017 Panini Day #52
2017 Panini Day Cracked Ice /25 #52
2017 Panini Day Decoy /50 #52
2017 Panini Day Hyperplaid /1 #52
2017 Panini Day Memorabilia #36
2017 Panini Day Memorabilia Galactic Window /25 #36
2017 Panini Day Memorabilia Hyperplaid /1 #36
2017 Panini Day Rapture /10 #52
2017 Panini Day Wedges /50 #52
2017 Panini Father's Day #34
2017 Panini Father's Day Cracked Ice /25 #34
2017 Panini Father's Day Foil /50 #34
2017 Panini Father's Day Hyperplaid /1 #34
2017 Panini Instant Nascar #35
2017 Panini Instant Nascar Black /1 #35
2017 Panini Instant Nascar Green /10 #35
2017 Panini National Convention #R1
2017 Panini National Convention #DE
2017 Panini National Convention Autographs #R1
2017 Panini National Convention Autographs #DE
2017 Panini National Convention Autographs Hyperplaid /1 #R1
2017 Panini National Convention Autographs Hyperplaid /1 #DE
2017 Panini National Convention Escher Squares /25 #R1
2017 Panini National Convention Escher Squares /25 #DE
2017 Panini National Convention Escher Squares Thick Stock /10 #R1
2017 Panini National Convention Escher Squares Thick Stock /10 #DE
2017 Panini National Convention Galatic Windows /5 #R1
2017 Panini National Convention Galatic Windows /5 #DE
2017 Panini National Convention Hyperplaid /1 #R1
2017 Panini National Convention Hyperplaid /1 #DE
2017 Panini National Convention Legends /299 #SP4
2017 Panini National Convention Legends Escher Squares /25 #SP4
2017 Panini National Convention Legends Escher Squares Thick Stock /10 #SP4
2017 Panini National Convention Legends Galatic Windows /5 #SP4
2017 Panini National Convention Legends Hyperplaid /1 #SP4
2017 Panini National Convention Legends Pyramids /10 #SP4
2017 Panini National Convention Legends Rainbow Spokes /49 #SP4
2017 Panini National Convention Legends Rainbow Spokes Thick Stock /25 #SP4
2017 Panini National Convention Legends Rapture #SP4
2017 Panini National Convention Memorabilia #DE
2017 Panini National Convention Memorabilia Escher Squares /10 #DE
2017 Panini National Convention Memorabilia Hyperplaid /1 #DE
2017 Panini National Convention Memorabilia Pyramids /5 #DE
2017 Panini National Convention Memorabilia Rainbow Spokes /25 #DE
2017 Panini National Convention Memorabilia Rapture /49 #DE
2017 Panini National Convention Pyramids /10 #R1
2017 Panini National Convention Pyramids /10 #DE
2017 Panini National Convention Rainbow Spokes /49 #R1
2017 Panini National Convention Rainbow Spokes /49 #DE
2017 Panini National Convention Rainbow Spokes Thick Stock /25 #R1
2017 Panini National Convention Rainbow Spokes Thick Stock /25 #DE
2017 Panini National Convention Rapture /99 #R1
2017 Panini National Convention Rapture /99 #DE
2017 Panini National Convention VIP #80
2017 Panini National Convention VIP Autographs /2 #80
2017 Panini National Convention VIP Autographs Black /1 #80
2017 Panini National Convention VIP Gems #DE
2017 Panini National Convention VIP Gems Autographs /1 #DE
2017 Panini National Convention VIP Gems Gold /1 #DE
2017 Panini National Convention VIP Memorabilia /25 #80
2017 Panini National Convention VIP Memorabilia Black /1 #80
2017 Panini National Convention VIP Prizm #80
2017 Panini National Convention VIP Prizm Black /1 #80
2017 Panini National Convention VIP Prizm Cracked Ice /25 #80
2017 Panini National Convention VIP Prizm Gold /15 #80
2017 Panini National Convention VIP Prizm Green /5 #80
2017 Panini National Treasures /25 #3
2017 Panini National Treasures /25 #17
2017 Panini National Treasures Associate Sponsor Patch Signatures 1 /1 #3
2017 Panini National Treasures Associate Sponsor Patch Signatures 10 /1 #3
2017 Panini National Treasures Associate Sponsor Patch Signatures 2 /1 #3
2017 Panini National Treasures Associate Sponsor Patch Signatures 3 /1 #3
2017 Panini National Treasures Associate Sponsor Patch Signatures 4 /1 #3
2017 Panini National Treasures Associate Sponsor Patch Signatures 5 /1 #3
2017 Panini National Treasures Associate Sponsor Patch Signatures 6 /1 #3
2017 Panini National Treasures Associate Sponsor Patch Signatures 7 /1 #3
2017 Panini National Treasures Associate Sponsor Patch Signatures 8 /1 #3
2017 Panini National Treasures Associate Sponsor Patch Signatures 9 /1 #3
2017 Panini National Treasures Car Manufacturer Patch Signatures /1 #3
2017 Panini National Treasures Century Black /1 #3
2017 Panini National Treasures Century Black /1 #17
2017 Panini National Treasures Century Gold /15 #3
2017 Panini National Treasures Century Gold /15 #17
2017 Panini National Treasures Century Green /5 #3
2017 Panini National Treasures Century Green /5 #17
2017 Panini National Treasures Century Holo Gold /10 #3
2017 Panini National Treasures Century Holo Gold /10 #17
2017 Panini National Treasures Century Holo Silver /20 #3
2017 Panini National Treasures Century Holo Silver /20 #17
2017 Panini National Treasures Century Laundry Tags /1 #3
2017 Panini National Treasures Dual Firesuit Materials Black /1 #2
2017 Panini National Treasures Dual Firesuit Materials Gold /15 #2
2017 Panini National Treasures Dual Firesuit Materials Green /5 #2
2017 Panini National Treasures Dual Firesuit Materials Holo Gold /10 #2
2017 Panini National Treasures Dual Firesuit Materials Laundry Tag /1 #2
2017 Panini National Treasures Dual Firesuit Materials Printing Plates Black /1 #2
2017 Panini National Treasures Dual Firesuit Materials Printing Plates Cyan /1 #2
2017 Panini National Treasures Dual Firesuit Materials Printing Plates Magenta /1 #2
2017 Panini National Treasures Dual Firesuit Materials Printing Plates Yellow /1 #2
2017 Panini National Treasures Dual Firesuit Signatures Black /1 #2
2017 Panini National Treasures Dual Firesuit Signatures Gold /15 #2
2017 Panini National Treasures Dual Firesuit Signatures Green /5 #2
2017 Panini National Treasures Dual Firesuit Signatures Holo Gold /10 #2
2017 Panini National Treasures Dual Firesuit Signatures Holo Silver /20 #2
2017 Panini National Treasures Dual Firesuit Signatures Laundry Tag /1 #2
2017 Panini National Treasures Dual Firesuit Signatures Printing Plates Black /1 #2
2017 Panini National Treasures Dual Firesuit Signatures Printing Plates Cyan /1 #2
2017 Panini National Treasures Dual Firesuit Signatures Printing Plates Magenta /1 #2
2017 Panini National Treasures Dual Firesuit Signatures Printing Plates Yellow /1 #2
2017 Panini National Treasures Dual Sheet Metal Materials Black /1 #13
2017 Panini National Treasures Dual Sheet Metal Materials Gold /15 #13
2017 Panini National Treasures Dual Sheet Metal Materials Green /5 #13
2017 Panini National Treasures Dual Sheet Metal Materials Holo Gold /10 #13
2017 Panini National Treasures Dual Sheet Metal Materials Printing Plates Black /1 #13
2017 Panini National Treasures Dual Sheet Metal Materials Printing Plates Cyan /1 #13
2017 Panini National Treasures Dual Sheet Metal Materials Printing Plates Magenta /1 #13
2017 Panini National Treasures Dual Sheet Metal Materials Printing Plates Yellow /1 #13
2017 Panini National Treasures Dual Sheet Metal Signatures Black /1 #5
2017 Panini National Treasures Dual Sheet Metal Signatures Gold /15 #5
2017 Panini National Treasures Dual Sheet Metal Signatures Green /5 #5
2017 Panini National Treasures Dual Sheet Metal Signatures Holo Gold /8 #5
2017 Panini National Treasures Dual Sheet Metal Signatures Holo Silver /2 #5
2017 Panini National Treasures Dual Sheet Metal Signatures Printing Plates Black /1 #5
2017 Panini National Treasures Dual Sheet Metal Signatures Printing Plates Cyan /1 #5
2017 Panini National Treasures Dual Sheet Metal Signatures Printing Plates Magenta /1 #5
2017 Panini National Treasures Dual Sheet Metal Signatures Printing Plates Yellow /1 #5
2017 Panini National Treasures Dual Signature Materials /25 #2
2017 Panini National Treasures Dual Signature Materials /50 #3
2017 Panini National Treasures Dual Signature Materials Black /1 #2
2017 Panini National Treasures Dual Signature Materials Black /1 #3
2017 Panini National Treasures Dual Signature Materials Gold /15 #2
2017 Panini National Treasures Dual Signature Materials Gold /15 #3
2017 Panini National Treasures Dual Signature Materials Green /5 #2
2017 Panini National Treasures Dual Signature Materials Green /5 #3
2017 Panini National Treasures Dual Signature Materials Holo Gold /10 #2
2017 Panini National Treasures Dual Signature Materials Holo Gold /10 #3
2017 Panini National Treasures Dual Signature Materials Holo Silver /20 #2
2017 Panini National Treasures Dual Signature Materials Holo Silver /25 #3
2017 Panini National Treasures Dual Signature Materials Laundry Tag /1 #2
2017 Panini National Treasures Dual Signature Materials Laundry Tag /1 #3
2017 Panini National Treasures Dual Tire Signatures Black /1 #1
2017 Panini National Treasures Dual Tire Signatures Green /5 #1
2017 Panini National Treasures Dual Tire Signatures Holo Gold /10 #1
2017 Panini National Treasures Dual Tire Signatures Printing Plates Black / #1
2017 Panini National Treasures Dual Tire Signatures Printing Plates Cyan / #1
2017 Panini National Treasures Dual Tire Signatures Printing Plates Magenta /1 #1
2017 Panini National Treasures Dual Tire Signatures Printing Plates Yellow /1 #1
2017 Panini National Treasures Firesuit Manufacturer Patch Signatures /1 #3
2017 Panini National Treasures Goodyear Patch Signatures /2 #3
2017 Panini National Treasures Hats Off /13 #29
2017 Panini National Treasures Hats Off /13 #30
2017 Panini National Treasures Hats Off Gold /2 #29
2017 Panini National Treasures Hats Off Gold /2 #30
2017 Panini National Treasures Hats Off Holo Gold /5 #29
2017 Panini National Treasures Hats Off Holo Gold /5 #30
2017 Panini National Treasures Hats Off Holo Silver /1 #29
2017 Panini National Treasures Hats Off Holo Silver /1 #30
2017 Panini National Treasures Hats Off Laundry Tag /6 #29

Panini National Treasures Hats Off Laundry Tag /6 #30
Panini National Treasures Hats Off New Era /1 #29
Panini National Treasures Hats Off New Era /1 #30
Panini National Treasures Hats Off Printing Plates Black /1 #29
Panini National Treasures Hats Off Printing Plates Black /1 #30
Panini National Treasures Hats Off Printing Plates Cyan /1 #29
Panini National Treasures Hats Off Printing Plates Cyan /1 #30
Panini National Treasures Hats Off Printing Plates Magenta /1 #29
Panini National Treasures Hats Off Printing Plates Magenta /1 #30
Panini National Treasures Hats Off Printing Plates Yellow /1 #29
Panini National Treasures Hats Off Printing Plates Yellow /1 #30
Panini National Treasures Hats Off Sponsor /5 #29
Panini National Treasures Hats Off Sponsor /5 #30
Panini National Treasures Jumbo Firesuit Signatures Black /1 #4
Panini National Treasures Jumbo Firesuit Signatures Gold /15 #4
Panini National Treasures Jumbo Firesuit Signatures Green /5 #4
Panini National Treasures Jumbo Firesuit Signatures Holo Gold /8 #4
Panini National Treasures Jumbo Firesuit Signatures Holo Silver /20 #4
Panini National Treasures Jumbo Firesuit Signatures Laundry Tag /1 #4
Panini National Treasures Jumbo Firesuit Signatures Printing Plates Black /1 #4
Panini National Treasures Jumbo Firesuit Signatures Printing Plates Cyan /1 #4
Panini National Treasures Jumbo Firesuit Signatures Printing Plates Magenta /1 #4
Panini National Treasures Jumbo Firesuit Signatures Printing Plates Yellow /1 #4
Panini National Treasures Jumbo Sheet Metal Materials Black /1 #2
Panini National Treasures Jumbo Sheet Metal Materials Gold /15 #2
Panini National Treasures Jumbo Sheet Metal Materials Green /5 #2
Panini National Treasures Jumbo Sheet Metal Materials Holo Gold /10 #2
Panini National Treasures Jumbo Sheet Metal Materials Printing Plates Black /1 #2
Panini National Treasures Jumbo Sheet Metal Materials Printing Plates Cyan /1 #2
Panini National Treasures Jumbo Sheet Metal Materials Printing Plates Magenta /1 #2
Panini National Treasures Jumbo Sheet Metal Materials Printing Plates Yellow /1 #2
Panini National Treasures Nameplate Patch Signatures /1 #3
Panini National Treasures NASCAR Patch Signatures /1 #3
Panini National Treasures Printing Plates Black /1 #3
Panini National Treasures Printing Plates Black /1 #17
Panini National Treasures Printing Plates Cyan /1 #3
Panini National Treasures Printing Plates Cyan /1 #17
Panini National Treasures Printing Plates Magenta /1 #3
Panini National Treasures Printing Plates Magenta /1 #17
Panini National Treasures Printing Plates Yellow /1 #3
Panini National Treasures Printing Plates Yellow /1 #17
Panini National Treasures Quad Material Signatures Black /1 #10
Panini National Treasures Quad Material Signatures Gold /15 #10
Panini National Treasures Quad Material Signatures Green /5 #10
Panini National Treasures Quad Material Signatures Holo Gold /8 #10
Panini National Treasures Quad Material Signatures Laundry Tag /1 #10
Panini National Treasures Quad Material Signatures Printing Plates Black /1 #10
Panini National Treasures Quad Material Signatures Printing Plates Cyan /1 #10
Panini National Treasures Quad Material Signatures Printing Plates Magenta /1 #10
Panini National Treasures Quad Material Signatures Printing Plates Yellow /1 #10
Panini National Treasures Series Sponsor Patch Signatures /1 #3
Panini National Treasures Signature Six Way Swatches /25 #5
Panini National Treasures Signature Six Way Swatches Black /1 #5
Panini National Treasures Signature Six Way Swatches Gold /15 #5
Panini National Treasures Signature Six Way Swatches Green /5 #5
Panini National Treasures Signature Six Way Swatches Holo Gold /10 #5
Panini National Treasures Signature Six Way Swatches Holo Silver /20 #5
Panini National Treasures Signature Six Way Swatches Laundry Tag /1 #5
Panini National Treasures Six Way Swatches Black /1 #2
Panini National Treasures Six Way Swatches Gold /15 #2
Panini National Treasures Six Way Swatches Green /5 #2
Panini National Treasures Six Way Swatches Holo Gold /10 #2
Panini National Treasures Six Way Swatches Holo Silver /20 #2
Panini National Treasures Six Way Swatches Laundry Tag /1 #2
Panini National Treasures Six Way Swatches Printing Plates Black /1 #2
Panini National Treasures Six Way Swatches Printing Plates Cyan /1 #2
Panini National Treasures Six Way Swatches Printing Plates Magenta /1 #2
Panini National Treasures Six Way Swatches Printing Plates Yellow /1 #2
Panini National Treasures Sunoco Patch Signatures /1 #3
Panini National Treasures Teammates Dual Materials /25 #2
Panini National Treasures Teammates Dual Materials Black /1 #2
Panini National Treasures Teammates Dual Materials Gold /15 #2
Panini National Treasures Teammates Dual Materials Green /5 #2
Panini National Treasures Teammates Dual Materials Holo Gold /10 #2
Panini National Treasures Teammates Dual Materials Holo Silver /20 #2
Panini National Treasures Teammates Dual Materials Laundry Tag /1 #2
Panini National Treasures Teammates Dual Materials Printing Plates Black /1 #2
Panini National Treasures Teammates Dual Materials Printing Plates Cyan /1 #2
Panini National Treasures Teammates Dual Materials Printing Plates Magenta /1 #2
Panini National Treasures Teammates Dual Materials Printing Plates Yellow /1 #2
Panini National Treasures Teammates Quad Materials /25 #4
Panini National Treasures Teammates Quad Materials Black /1 #4
Panini National Treasures Teammates Quad Materials Gold /15 #4
Panini National Treasures Teammates Quad Materials Green /5 #4
Panini National Treasures Teammates Quad Materials Holo Gold /10 #4
Panini National Treasures Teammates Quad Materials Holo Silver /20 #4
Panini National Treasures Teammates Quad Materials Laundry Tag /1 #4
Panini National Treasures Teammates Quad Materials Printing Plates Black /1 #4
Panini National Treasures Teammates Quad Materials Printing Plates Cyan /1 #4
Panini National Treasures Teammates Quad Materials Printing Plates Magenta /1 #4
Panini National Treasures Teammates Quad Materials Printing Plates Yellow /1 #4
Panini National Treasures Teammates Triple Materials /25 #1
Panini National Treasures Teammates Triple Materials /25 #5
Panini National Treasures Teammates Triple Materials Black /1 #1
Panini National Treasures Teammates Triple Materials Black /1 #5
Panini National Treasures Teammates Triple Materials Gold /15 #1
Panini National Treasures Teammates Triple Materials Gold /15 #5
Panini National Treasures Teammates Triple Materials Green /5 #1
Panini National Treasures Teammates Triple Materials Green /5 #5
Panini National Treasures Teammates Triple Materials Holo Gold /10 #1
2017 Panini National Treasures Teammates Triple Materials Holo Gold /10 #5
2017 Panini National Treasures Teammates Triple Materials Holo Silver /20 #1
2017 Panini National Treasures Teammates Triple Materials Holo Silver /20 #5
2017 Panini National Treasures Teammates Triple Materials Laundry Tag /1 #1
2017 Panini National Treasures Teammates Triple Materials Laundry Tag /1 #5
2017 Panini National Treasures Teammates Triple Materials Printing Plates Black /1 #1
2017 Panini National Treasures Teammates Triple Materials Printing Plates Black /1 #5
2017 Panini National Treasures Teammates Triple Materials Printing Plates Cyan /1 #1
2017 Panini National Treasures Teammates Triple Materials Printing Plates Cyan /1 #5
2017 Panini National Treasures Teammates Triple Materials Printing Plates Magenta /1 #1
2017 Panini National Treasures Teammates Triple Materials Printing Plates Magenta /1 #5
2017 Panini National Treasures Teammates Triple Materials Printing Plates Yellow /1 #1
2017 Panini National Treasures Teammates Triple Materials Printing Plates Yellow /1 #5
2017 Panini National Treasures Three Wide Black /1 #6
2017 Panini National Treasures Three Wide Gold /15 #6
2017 Panini National Treasures Three Wide Green /5 #6
2017 Panini National Treasures Three Wide Holo Gold /10 #6
2017 Panini National Treasures Three Wide Laundry Tag /1 #6
2017 Panini National Treasures Three Wide Printing Plates Black /1 #6
2017 Panini National Treasures Three Wide Printing Plates Cyan /1 #6
2017 Panini National Treasures Three Wide Printing Plates Magenta /1 #6
2017 Panini National Treasures Three Wide Printing Plates Yellow /1 #6
2017 Panini National Treasures Three Wide Signatures Black /1 #8
2017 Panini National Treasures Three Wide Signatures Gold /15 #8
2017 Panini National Treasures Three Wide Signatures Green /5 #8
2017 Panini National Treasures Three Wide Signatures Holo Gold /8 #8
2017 Panini National Treasures Three Wide Signatures Holo Silver /20 #8
2017 Panini National Treasures Three Wide Signatures Laundry Tag /1 #8
2017 Panini National Treasures Three Wide Signatures Printing Plates Black /1 #8
2017 Panini National Treasures Three Wide Signatures Printing Plates Cyan /1 #8
2017 Panini National Treasures Three Wide Signatures Printing Plates Magenta /1 #8
2017 Panini National Treasures Three Wide Signatures Printing Plates Yellow /1 #8
2017 Panini Torque #27
2017 Panini Torque #58
2017 Panini Torque #73
2017 Panini Torque #97
2017 Panini Torque Artist Proof /75 #27
2017 Panini Torque Artist Proof /75 #58
2017 Panini Torque Artist Proof /75 #73
2017 Panini Torque Artist Proof /75 #97
2017 Panini Torque Blackout /1 #27
2017 Panini Torque Blackout /1 #58
2017 Panini Torque Blackout /1 #73
2017 Panini Torque Blackout /1 #97
2017 Panini Torque Blue /150 #27
2017 Panini Torque Blue /150 #58
2017 Panini Torque Blue /150 #73
2017 Panini Torque Blue /150 #97
2017 Panini Torque Claiming The Chase #6
2017 Panini Torque Claiming The Chase Gold /199 #6
2017 Panini Torque Claiming The Chase Holo Silver /99 #6
2017 Panini Torque Clear Vision #8
2017 Panini Torque Clear Vision Blue /99 #8
2017 Panini Torque Clear Vision Gold /149 #8
2017 Panini Torque Clear Vision Green /25 #8
2017 Panini Torque Clear Vision Purple /10 #8
2017 Panini Torque Clear Vision Red /49 #8
2017 Panini Torque Dual Materials /199 #7
2017 Panini Torque Dual Materials Blue /99 #7
2017 Panini Torque Dual Materials Green /25 #7
2017 Panini Torque Dual Materials Purple /10 #7
2017 Panini Torque Dual Materials Red /49 #7
2017 Panini Torque Gold #27
2017 Panini Torque Gold #58
2017 Panini Torque Gold #73
2017 Panini Torque Gold #97
2017 Panini Torque Holo Gold /10 #27
2017 Panini Torque Holo Gold /10 #58
2017 Panini Torque Holo Gold /10 #73
2017 Panini Torque Holo Gold /10 #97
2017 Panini Torque Holo Silver /25 #27
2017 Panini Torque Holo Silver /25 #58
2017 Panini Torque Holo Silver /25 #73
2017 Panini Torque Holo Silver /25 #97
2017 Panini Torque Horsepower Heroes #7
2017 Panini Torque Horsepower Heroes Gold /199 #7
2017 Panini Torque Horsepower Heroes Holo Silver /99 #7
2017 Panini Torque Jumbo Tire Signatures /35 #19
2017 Panini Torque Jumbo Tire Signatures Blue /25 #19
2017 Panini Torque Jumbo Tire Signatures Green /15 #19
2017 Panini Torque Jumbo Tire Signatures Purple /10 #19
2017 Panini Torque Jumbo Tire Signatures Red /20 #19
2017 Panini Torque Manufacturer Marks #4
2017 Panini Torque Manufacturer Marks Gold /199 #4
2017 Panini Torque Manufacturer Marks Holo Silver /99 #4
2017 Panini Torque Metal Materials /25 #19
2017 Panini Torque Metal Materials Blue /15 #19
2017 Panini Torque Metal Materials Green /5 #19
2017 Panini Torque Metal Materials Purple /1 #19
2017 Panini Torque Metal Materials Red /10 #19
2017 Panini Torque Pairings Materials /99 #7
2017 Panini Torque Pairings Materials /49 #15
2017 Panini Torque Pairings Materials Blue /49 #7
2017 Panini Torque Pairings Materials Blue /25 #15
2017 Panini Torque Pairings Materials Green /10 #7
2017 Panini Torque Pairings Materials Green /5 #15
2017 Panini Torque Pairings Materials Purple /5 #7
2017 Panini Torque Pairings Materials Purple /1 #15
2017 Panini Torque Pairings Materials Red /25 #7
2017 Panini Torque Pairings Materials Red /10 #15
2017 Panini Torque Primary Paint #4
2017 Panini Torque Primary Paint Blue /99 #4
2017 Panini Torque Primary Paint Checkerboard /10 #4
2017 Panini Torque Primary Paint Green /25 #4
2017 Panini Torque Primary Paint Red /49 #4
2017 Panini Torque Prime Associate Sponsors Jumbo Patches /1 #5A
2017 Panini Torque Prime Associate Sponsors Jumbo Patches /1 #5B
2017 Panini Torque Prime Associate Sponsors Jumbo Patches /1 #5C
2017 Panini Torque Prime Associate Sponsors Jumbo Patches /1 #5D
2017 Panini Torque Prime Associate Sponsors Jumbo Patches /1 #5E
2017 Panini Torque Prime Associate Sponsors Jumbo Patches /1 #5F
2017 Panini Torque Prime Associate Sponsors Jumbo Patches /1 #5G
2017 Panini Torque Prime Associate Sponsors Jumbo Patches /1 #5H
2017 Panini Torque Prime Associate Sponsors Jumbo Patches /1 #5I
2017 Panini Torque Prime Associate Sponsors Jumbo Patches /1 #5J
2017 Panini Torque Prime Associate Sponsors Jumbo Patches /1 #5K
2017 Panini Torque Prime Associate Sponsors Jumbo Patches /1 #5L
2017 Panini Torque Prime Associate Sponsors Jumbo Patches /1 #5M
2017 Panini Torque Prime Goodyear Jumbo Patches /2 #5
2017 Panini Torque Prime Manufacturer Jumbo Patches /1 #5
2017 Panini Torque Prime NASCAR Jumbo Patches /1 #5
2017 Panini Torque Prime Series Sponsor Jumbo Patches /1 #5
2017 Panini Torque Printing Plates Black /1 #27
2017 Panini Torque Printing Plates Black /1 #58
2017 Panini Torque Printing Plates Black /1 #73
2017 Panini Torque Printing Plates Black /1 #97
2017 Panini Torque Printing Plates Cyan /1 #27
2017 Panini Torque Printing Plates Cyan /1 #58
2017 Panini Torque Printing Plates Cyan /1 #73
2017 Panini Torque Printing Plates Cyan /1 #97
2017 Panini Torque Printing Plates Magenta /1 #27
2017 Panini Torque Printing Plates Magenta /1 #58
2017 Panini Torque Printing Plates Magenta /1 #73
2017 Panini Torque Printing Plates Magenta /1 #97
2017 Panini Torque Printing Plates Yellow /1 #27
2017 Panini Torque Printing Plates Yellow /1 #58
2017 Panini Torque Printing Plates Yellow /1 #73
2017 Panini Torque Printing Plates Yellow /1 #97
2017 Panini Torque Purple /50 #27
2017 Panini Torque Purple /50 #58
2017 Panini Torque Purple /50 #73
2017 Panini Torque Purple /50 #97
2017 Panini Torque Quad Materials /99 #6
2017 Panini Torque Quad Materials Blue /49 #6
2017 Panini Torque Quad Materials Green /10 #6
2017 Panini Torque Quad Materials Purple /5 #6
2017 Panini Torque Quad Materials Red /25 #6
2017 Panini Torque Raced Relics /399 #5
2017 Panini Torque Raced Relics Blue /99 #5
2017 Panini Torque Raced Relics Green /25 #5
2017 Panini Torque Raced Relics Purple /10 #5
2017 Panini Torque Raced Relics Red /49 #5
2017 Panini Torque Red /100 #27
2017 Panini Torque Red /100 #58
2017 Panini Torque Red /100 #73
2017 Panini Torque Red /100 #97
2017 Panini Torque Silhouettes Firesuit Signatures /50 #14
2017 Panini Torque Silhouettes Firesuit Signatures Blue /25 #14
2017 Panini Torque Silhouettes Firesuit Signatures Green /15 #14
2017 Panini Torque Silhouettes Firesuit Signatures Purple /10 #14
2017 Panini Torque Silhouettes Firesuit Signatures Red /20 #14
2017 Panini Torque Silhouettes Sheet Metal Signatures /25 #11
2017 Panini Torque Silhouettes Sheet Metal Signatures Blue /20 #11
2017 Panini Torque Silhouettes Sheet Metal Signatures Green /10 #11
2017 Panini Torque Silhouettes Sheet Metal Signatures Purple /5 #11
2017 Panini Torque Silhouettes Sheet Metal Signatures Red /15 #11
2017 Panini Torque Special Paint #10
2017 Panini Torque Special Paint Gold /199 #10
2017 Panini Torque Special Paint Holo Silver /99 #10
2017 Panini Torque Superstar Vision #1
2017 Panini Torque Superstar Vision Blue /99 #1
2017 Panini Torque Superstar Vision Gold /149 #1
2017 Panini Torque Superstar Vision Green /25 #1
2017 Panini Torque Superstar Vision Purple /10 #1
2017 Panini Torque Superstar Vision Red /49 #1
2017 Panini Torque Test Proof Black /1 #27
2017 Panini Torque Test Proof Black /1 #58
2017 Panini Torque Test Proof Black /1 #73
2017 Panini Torque Test Proof Black /1 #97
2017 Panini Torque Test Proof Cyan /1 #27
2017 Panini Torque Test Proof Cyan /1 #58
2017 Panini Torque Test Proof Cyan /1 #73
2017 Panini Torque Test Proof Cyan /1 #97
2017 Panini Torque Test Proof Magenta /1 #27
2017 Panini Torque Test Proof Magenta /1 #58
2017 Panini Torque Test Proof Magenta /1 #73
2017 Panini Torque Test Proof Magenta /1 #97
2017 Panini Torque Test Proof Yellow /1 #27
2017 Panini Torque Test Proof Yellow /1 #58
2017 Panini Torque Test Proof Yellow /1 #73
2017 Panini Torque Test Proof Yellow /1 #97
2017 Panini Torque Track Vision #1
2017 Panini Torque Track Vision Blue /99 #1
2017 Panini Torque Track Vision Gold /149 #1
2017 Panini Torque Track Vision Green /25 #1
2017 Panini Torque Track Vision Purple /10 #1
2017 Panini Torque Track Vision Red /49 #1
2017 Panini Torque Trackside #1
2017 Panini Torque Trackside Blue /99 #1
2017 Panini Torque Trackside Checkerboard /10 #1
2017 Panini Torque Trackside Green /25 #1
2017 Panini Torque Trackside Red /49 #1
2017 Panini Torque Victory Laps #8
2017 Panini Torque Victory Laps Gold /199 #8
2017 Panini Torque Victory Laps Holo Silver /99 #8
2017 Select #124
2017 Select #66
2017 Select #65
2017 Select #64
2017 Select Endorsements #27
2017 Select Endorsements Prizms Blue /20 #27
2017 Select Endorsements Prizms Checkered Flag /1 #27
2017 Select Endorsements Prizms Gold /10 #27
2017 Select Endorsements Prizms Red /15 #27
2017 Select Prizms Black /3 #64
2017 Select Prizms Black /3 #65
2017 Select Prizms Black /3 #66
2017 Select Prizms Black /3 #124
2017 Select Prizms Blue /199 #64
2017 Select Prizms Blue /199 #65
2017 Select Prizms Blue /199 #66
2017 Select Prizms Checkered Flag /1 #64
2017 Select Prizms Checkered Flag /1 #65
2017 Select Prizms Checkered Flag /1 #66
2017 Select Prizms Checkered Flag /1 #124
2017 Select Prizms Gold /10 #64
2017 Select Prizms Gold /10 #65
2017 Select Prizms Gold /10 #66
2017 Select Prizms Gold /10 #124
2017 Select Prizms Purple Pulsar #64
2017 Select Prizms Purple Pulsar #65
2017 Select Prizms Purple Pulsar #66
2017 Select Prizms Red /99 #64
2017 Select Prizms Red /99 #65
2017 Select Prizms Red /99 #66
2017 Select Prizms Red White and Blue Pulsar /299 #64
2017 Select Prizms Red White and Blue Pulsar /299 #65
2017 Select Prizms Red White and Blue Pulsar /299 #66
2017 Select Prizms Silver #64
2017 Select Prizms Silver #65
2017 Select Prizms Silver #66
2017 Select Prizms Tie Dye /24 #64
2017 Select Prizms Tie Dye /24 #65
2017 Select Prizms Tie Dye /24 #66
2017 Select Prizms Tie Dye /24 #124
2017 Select Prizms White /50 #64
2017 Select Prizms White /50 #65
2017 Select Prizms White /50 #66
2017 Select Prizms White /50 #124
2017 Select Select Pairs Materials #13
2017 Select Select Pairs Materials #16
2017 Select Select Pairs Materials Prizms Blue /199 #13
2017 Select Select Pairs Materials Prizms Blue /199 #16
2017 Select Select Pairs Materials Prizms Blue /30 #17
2017 Select Select Pairs Materials Prizms Checkered Flag /1 #13
2017 Select Select Pairs Materials Prizms Checkered Flag /1 #16
2017 Select Select Pairs Materials Prizms Checkered Flag /1 #17
2017 Select Select Pairs Materials Prizms Gold /10 #13
2017 Select Select Pairs Materials Prizms Gold /10 #16
2017 Select Select Pairs Materials Prizms Gold /10 #17
2017 Select Select Pairs Materials Prizms Red /99 #13
2017 Select Select Pairs Materials Prizms Red /99 #16
2017 Select Select Pairs Materials Prizms Red /25 #17
2017 Select Select Stars #15
2017 Select Select Stars Prizms Black /3 #15
2017 Select Select Stars Prizms Checkered Flag /1 #15
2017 Select Select Stars Prizms Gold /10 #15
2017 Select Select Stars Prizms Tie Dye /24 #15
2017 Select Select Stars Prizms White /50 #15
2017 Select Select Swatches #12
2017 Select Select Swatches Prizms Blue /199 #12
2017 Select Select Swatches Prizms Checkered Flag /1 #12
2017 Select Select Swatches Prizms Gold /10 #12
2017 Select Select Swatches Prizms Red /99 #12
2017 Select Sheet Metal #5
2017 Select Sheet Metal Prizms Blue /199 #5
2017 Select Sheet Metal Prizms Checkered Flag /1 #5
2017 Select Sheet Metal Prizms Gold /10 #5
2017 Select Sheet Metal Prizms Red /99 #5
2017 Select Signature Paint Schemes #3
2017 Select Signature Paint Schemes Prizms Blue /20 #3
2017 Select Signature Paint Schemes Prizms Checkered Flag /1 #3
2017 Select Signature Paint Schemes Prizms Gold /10 #3
2017 Select Signature Paint Schemes Prizms Red /15 #3
2017 Select Signature Swatches #12
2017 Select Signature Swatches Prizms Checkered Flag /1 #12
2017 Select Signature Swatches Prizms Gold /10 #12
2017 Select Signature Swatches Prizms Tie Dye /24 #12
2017 Select Signature Swatches Prizms White /50 #12
2017 Select Signature Swatches Triple #7
2017 Select Signature Swatches Triple Prizms Checkered Flag /1 #7
2017 Select Signature Swatches Triple Prizms Gold /10 #7
2017 Select Signature Swatches Triple Prizms Tie Dye /24 #7
2017 Select Signature Swatches Triple Prizms White /50 #7
2017 Select Speed Merchants #16
2017 Select Speed Merchants Prizms Black /3 #16
2017 Select Speed Merchants Prizms Checkered Flag /1 #16
2017 Select Speed Merchants Prizms Gold /10 #16
2017 Select Speed Merchants Prizms Tie Dye /24 #16
2017 Select Speed Merchants Prizms White /50 #16
2017 Select Up Close and Personal #2
2017 Select Up Close and Personal Prizms Black /3 #2
2017 Select Up Close and Personal Prizms Checkered Flag /1 #2
2017 Select Up Close and Personal Prizms Gold /10 #2
2017 Select Up Close and Personal Prizms Tie Dye /24 #2
2017 Select Up Close and Personal Prizms White /50 #2
2017 Topps Transcendent Cut Signatures /1 #TCSDES
2018 Certified #11
2018 Certified #86
2018 Certified All Certified Team /199 #2
2018 Certified All Certified Team Black /1 #2
2018 Certified All Certified Team Blue /99 #2
2018 Certified All Certified Team Gold /49 #2
2018 Certified All Certified Team Green /10 #2
2018 Certified All Certified Team Mirror Black /1 #2
2018 Certified All Certified Team Mirror Gold /25 #2
2018 Certified All Certified Team Mirror Green /5 #2
2018 Certified All Certified Team Mirror Purple /10 #2
2018 Certified All Certified Team Purple /25 #2
2018 Certified All Certified Team Red /149 #2
2018 Certified Black /1 #11
2018 Certified Black /1 #86
2018 Certified Blue /99 #11
2018 Certified Blue /99 #86
2018 Certified Complete Materials /299 #2
2018 Certified Complete Materials Black /1 #2
2018 Certified Complete Materials Blue /49 #2
2018 Certified Complete Materials Gold /25 #2
2018 Certified Complete Materials Green /5 #2
2018 Certified Complete Materials Purple /10 #2
2018 Certified Complete Materials Red /199 #2
2018 Certified Cup Swatches /499 #8
2018 Certified Cup Swatches Black /1 #8
2018 Certified Cup Swatches Blue /49 #8
2018 Certified Cup Swatches Gold /25 #8
2018 Certified Cup Swatches Green /5 #8
2018 Certified Cup Swatches Purple /10 #8
2018 Certified Cup Swatches Red /199 #8
2018 Certified Epix /199 #11
2018 Certified Epix Black /1 #11
2018 Certified Epix Blue /99 #11
2018 Certified Epix Gold /49 #11
2018 Certified Epix Green /10 #11
2018 Certified Epix Mirror Black /1 #11
2018 Certified Epix Mirror Gold /25 #11
2018 Certified Epix Mirror Green /5 #11
2018 Certified Epix Mirror Purple /10 #11
2018 Certified Epix Purple /25 #11
2018 Certified Epix Red /149 #11
2018 Certified Gold /49 #11
2018 Certified Gold /49 #86
2018 Certified Green /10 #11
2018 Certified Green /10 #86
2018 Certified Materials Signatures Black /1 #4
2018 Certified Materials Signatures Blue /49 #4
2018 Certified Materials Signatures Gold /25 #4
2018 Certified Materials Signatures Green /5 #4
2018 Certified Materials Signatures Purple /10 #4
2018 Certified Materials Signatures Red /50 #4
2018 Certified Mirror Black /1 #11
2018 Certified Mirror Black /1 #86
2018 Certified Mirror Gold /25 #11
2018 Certified Mirror Gold /25 #86
2018 Certified Mirror Green /5 #11
2018 Certified Mirror Green /5 #86
2018 Certified Mirror Purple /10 #11
2018 Certified Mirror Purple /10 #86
2018 Certified Orange /249 #11
2018 Certified Orange /249 #86
2018 Certified Piece of the Race /199 #2
2018 Certified Piece of the Race Black /1 #2
2018 Certified Piece of the Race Blue /49 #2
2018 Certified Piece of the Race Gold /25 #2
2018 Certified Piece of the Race Green /5 #2
2018 Certified Piece of the Race Purple /10 #2
2018 Certified Piece of the Race Red /99 #2
2018 Certified Purple /25 #11
2018 Certified Purple /25 #86
2018 Certified Red /199 #11
2018 Certified Red /199 #86
2018 Certified Signature Swatches Black /1 #5
2018 Certified Signature Swatches Blue /49 #5
2018 Certified Signature Swatches Gold /25 #5
2018 Certified Signature Swatches Green /5 #5
2018 Certified Signature Swatches Purple /10 #5
2018 Certified Signature Swatches Red /50 #5
2018 Certified Signing Sessions /25 #3
2018 Certified Signing Sessions Black /1 #3
2018 Certified Signing Sessions Blue /10 #3
2018 Certified Signing Sessions Gold /8 #3
2018 Certified Signing Sessions Green /3 #3
2018 Certified Signing Sessions Purple /5 #3
2018 Certified Signing Sessions Red /15 #3
2018 Certified Stars /199 #22
2018 Certified Stars Black /1 #22
2018 Certified Stars Blue /99 #22
2018 Certified Stars Gold /49 #22
2018 Certified Stars Green /10 #22
2018 Certified Stars Mirror Black /1 #22
2018 Certified Stars Mirror Gold /25 #22
2018 Certified Stars Mirror Green /5 #22
2018 Certified Stars Mirror Purple /10 #22
2018 Certified Stars Purple /25 #22
2018 Certified Stars Red /149 #22
2018 Donruss #2
2018 Donruss #53A
2018 Donruss #100
2018 Donruss #150
2018 Donruss #153
2018 Donruss #53B
2018 Donruss #101B
2018 Donruss Artist Proofs /25 #2
2018 Donruss Artist Proofs /25 #53A
2018 Donruss Artist Proofs /25 #100
2018 Donruss Artist Proofs /25 #150
2018 Donruss Artist Proofs /25 #153
2018 Donruss Artist Proofs /25 #53B
2018 Donruss Artist Proofs /25 #101B
2018 Donruss Classics #1
2018 Donruss Classics Cracked Ice /999 #1
2018 Donruss Classics Xplosion /99 #1
2018 Donruss Gold Foil /499 #2
2018 Donruss Gold Foil /499 #53A
2018 Donruss Gold Foil /499 #100
2018 Donruss Gold Foil /499 #150
2018 Donruss Gold Foil /499 #153
2018 Donruss Gold Foil /499 #53B
2018 Donruss Gold Foil /499 #101B
2018 Donruss Gold Press Proofs /99 #2
2018 Donruss Gold Press Proofs /99 #53A
2018 Donruss Gold Press Proofs /99 #100
2018 Donruss Gold Press Proofs /99 #150
2018 Donruss Gold Press Proofs /99 #153
2018 Donruss Gold Press Proofs /99 #53B
2018 Donruss Gold Press Proofs /99 #101B
2018 Donruss Green Foil /199 #2
2018 Donruss Green Foil /199 #53A
2018 Donruss Green Foil /199 #100
2018 Donruss Green Foil /199 #150
2018 Donruss Green Foil /199 #153
2018 Donruss Green Foil /199 #53B
2018 Donruss Green Foil /199 #101B
2018 Donruss Masters of the Track #5
2018 Donruss Masters of the Track Cracked Ice /999 #5
2018 Donruss Masters of the Track Xplosion /99 #5
2018 Donruss Pole Position #7
2018 Donruss Pole Position Cracked Ice /999 #7
2018 Donruss Pole Position Xplosion /99 #7
2018 Donruss Press Proofs /49 #2
2018 Donruss Press Proofs /49 #53A
2018 Donruss Press Proofs /49 #100
2018 Donruss Press Proofs /49 #150
2018 Donruss Press Proofs /49 #153
2018 Donruss Press Proofs /49 #53B
2018 Donruss Press Proofs /49 #101B
2018 Donruss Printing Plates Black /1 #2
2018 Donruss Printing Plates Black /1 #53
2018 Donruss Printing Plates Black /1 #100
2018 Donruss Printing Plates Black /1 #150
2018 Donruss Printing Plates Black /1 #153
2018 Donruss Printing Plates Black /1 #53B
2018 Donruss Printing Plates Black /1 #101B
2018 Donruss Printing Plates Cyan /1 #2
2018 Donruss Printing Plates Cyan /1 #53
2018 Donruss Printing Plates Cyan /1 #100
2018 Donruss Printing Plates Cyan /1 #150
2018 Donruss Printing Plates Cyan /1 #153
2018 Donruss Printing Plates Cyan /1 #53B
2018 Donruss Printing Plates Cyan /1 #101B
2018 Donruss Printing Plates Magenta /1 #2
2018 Donruss Printing Plates Magenta /1 #53
2018 Donruss Printing Plates Magenta /1 #100
2018 Donruss Printing Plates Magenta /1 #150
2018 Donruss Printing Plates Magenta /1 #153
2018 Donruss Printing Plates Magenta /1 #53B
2018 Donruss Printing Plates Magenta /1 #101B
2018 Donruss Printing Plates Yellow /1 #2
2018 Donruss Printing Plates Yellow /1 #53
2018 Donruss Printing Plates Yellow /1 #100
2018 Donruss Printing Plates Yellow /1 #150
2018 Donruss Printing Plates Yellow /1 #153
2018 Donruss Printing Plates Yellow /1 #53B
2018 Donruss Printing Plates Yellow /1 #101B
2018 Donruss Racing Relics #9
2018 Donruss Racing Relics Black /10 #9
2018 Donruss Racing Relics Holo Gold /99 #9
2018 Donruss Red Foil /299 #2
2018 Donruss Red Foil /299 #53A
2018 Donruss Red Foil /299 #100
2018 Donruss Red Foil /299 #150
2018 Donruss Red Foil /299 #153
2018 Donruss Red Foil /299 #53B
2018 Donruss Red Foil /299 #101B
2018 Donruss Retro Relics '85 #4
2018 Donruss Retro Relics '85 Black /10 #4
2018 Donruss Retro Relics '85 Holo Gold /99 #4
2018 Donruss Rubber Relic Signatures #5
2018 Donruss Rubber Relic Signatures Black /1 #5
2018 Donruss Rubber Relic Signatures Holo Gold /25 #5
2018 Donruss Rubber Relics Black /10 #9
2018 Donruss Rubber Relics Holo Gold /7 #9
2018 Donruss Slingshot #SS4
2018 Donruss Studio #4
2018 Donruss Studio Cracked Ice /999 #4
2018 Donruss Studio Xplosion /99 #4
2018 Panini Father's Day Patches #FDDE
2018 Panini National Convention Black Boxes #DE
2018 Panini National Convention Black Boxes 1/1 #DE
2018 Panini National Convention Legends /299 #L18
2018 Panini National Convention Legends Escher Squares /25 #L18
2018 Panini National Convention Legends Galatic Windows /5 #L18
2018 Panini National Convention Legends Hyperplaid /1 #L18
2018 Panini National Convention Legends Magnetic Fur /99 #L18
2018 Panini National Convention Legends Pyramids /10 #L18
2018 Panini National Convention Legends Rainbow Spokes /49 #L18
2018 Panini Prime /50 #91
2018 Panini Prime /50 #58
2018 Panini Prime /50 #25
2018 Panini Prime Autograph Materials /25 #9
2018 Panini Prime Autograph Materials Black /1 #9
2018 Panini Prime Autograph Materials Holo Gold /10 #9
2018 Panini Prime Autograph Materials Laundry Tag /1 #9
2018 Panini Prime Black /1 #25
2018 Panini Prime Black /1 #58
2018 Panini Prime Black /1 #91
2018 Panini Prime Clear Silhouettes /99 #7
2018 Panini Prime Clear Silhouettes Black /1 #7
2018 Panini Prime Clear Silhouettes Dual /99 #7
2018 Panini Prime Clear Silhouettes Dual Black /1 #7
2018 Panini Prime Clear Silhouettes Dual Holo Gold /50 #7
2018 Panini Prime Clear Silhouettes Holo Gold /50 #7
2018 Panini Prime Driver Signatures /25 #25
2018 Panini Prime Driver Signatures Black /1 #25
2018 Panini Prime Driver Signatures Holo Gold /10 #25
2018 Panini Prime Dual Material Autographs /25 #2
2018 Panini Prime Dual Material Autographs Black /1 #2
2018 Panini Prime Dual Material Autographs Holo Gold /10 #2
2018 Panini Prime Dual Material Autographs Laundry Tag /1 #2
2018 Panini Prime Dual Signatures /10 #7
2018 Panini Prime Dual Signatures Black /1 #7
2018 Panini Prime Dual Signatures Holo Gold /5 #7
2018 Panini Prime Holo Gold /25 #25
2018 Panini Prime Holo Gold /25 #58
2018 Panini Prime Holo Gold /25 #91
2018 Panini Prime Prime Jumbo Associate Sponsor 1 /1 #22
2018 Panini Prime Prime Jumbo Associate Sponsor 1 /1 #23
2018 Panini Prime Prime Jumbo Associate Sponsor 1 /1 #24
2018 Panini Prime Prime Jumbo Associate Sponsor 1 /1 #25
2018 Panini Prime Prime Jumbo Associate Sponsor 2 /1 #22
2018 Panini Prime Prime Jumbo Associate Sponsor 2 /1 #23
2018 Panini Prime Prime Jumbo Associate Sponsor 2 /1 #24
2018 Panini Prime Prime Jumbo Associate Sponsor 2 /1 #25
2018 Panini Prime Prime Jumbo Associate Sponsor 3 /1 #22
2018 Panini Prime Prime Jumbo Associate Sponsor 3 /1 #23
2018 Panini Prime Prime Jumbo Associate Sponsor 3 /1 #24
2018 Panini Prime Prime Jumbo Associate Sponsor 3 /1 #25
2018 Panini Prime Prime Jumbo Associate Sponsor 4 /1 #22
2018 Panini Prime Prime Jumbo Associate Sponsor 4 /1 #23
2018 Panini Prime Prime Jumbo Associate Sponsor 4 /1 #24
2018 Panini Prime Prime Jumbo Associate Sponsor 4 /1 #25
2018 Panini Prime Prime Jumbo Associate Sponsor 5 /1 #22
2018 Panini Prime Prime Jumbo Associate Sponsor 5 /1 #23
2018 Panini Prime Prime Jumbo Associate Sponsor 5 /1 #24
2018 Panini Prime Prime Jumbo Associate Sponsor 5 /1 #25
2018 Panini Prime Prime Jumbo Associate Sponsor 6 /1 #22
2018 Panini Prime Prime Jumbo Associate Sponsor 6 /1 #23
2018 Panini Prime Prime Jumbo Associate Sponsor 6 /1 #24
2018 Panini Prime Prime Jumbo Associate Sponsor 7 /1 #22
2018 Panini Prime Prime Jumbo Associate Sponsor 7 /1 #25
2018 Panini Prime Prime Jumbo Associate Sponsor 8 /1 #25
2018 Panini Prime Prime Jumbo Associate Sponsor 9 /1 #25
2018 Panini Prime Prime Jumbo Car Manufacturer /1 #22
2018 Panini Prime Prime Jumbo Car Manufacturer /1 #23
2018 Panini Prime Prime Jumbo Car Manufacturer /1 #24
2018 Panini Prime Prime Jumbo Car Manufacturer /1 #25
2018 Panini Prime Prime Jumbo Firesuit Manufacturer /1 #22
2018 Panini Prime Prime Jumbo Firesuit Manufacturer /1 #23
2018 Panini Prime Prime Jumbo Firesuit Manufacturer /1 #24
2018 Panini Prime Prime Jumbo Firesuit Manufacturer /1 #25
2018 Panini Prime Prime Jumbo Flag Patch /1 #24
2018 Panini Prime Prime Jumbo Glove Manufacturer Patch /1 #22
2018 Panini Prime Prime Jumbo Glove Manufacturer Patch /1 #23
2018 Panini Prime Prime Jumbo Glove Manufacturer Patch /1 #24
2018 Panini Prime Prime Jumbo Glove Manufacturer Patch /1 #25
2018 Panini Prime Prime Jumbo Goodyear /2 #22
2018 Panini Prime Prime Jumbo Goodyear /2 #23
2018 Panini Prime Prime Jumbo Goodyear /2 #24
2018 Panini Prime Prime Jumbo Goodyear /2 #25
2018 Panini Prime Prime Jumbo Nameplate /1 #22
2018 Panini Prime Prime Jumbo NASCAR /1 #22
2018 Panini Prime Prime Jumbo NASCAR /1 #23
2018 Panini Prime Prime Jumbo NASCAR /1 #24
2018 Panini Prime Prime Jumbo NASCAR /1 #25
2018 Panini Prime Prime Jumbo Prime Colors /11 #22
2018 Panini Prime Prime Jumbo Prime Colors /10 #23
2018 Panini Prime Prime Jumbo Series Sponsor /1 #22
2018 Panini Prime Prime Jumbo Series Sponsor /1 #23
2018 Panini Prime Prime Jumbo Series Sponsor /1 #24
2018 Panini Prime Prime Jumbo Series Sponsor /1 #25
2018 Panini Prime Prime Jumbo Shoe Brand Logo /1 #22
2018 Panini Prime Prime Jumbo Shoe Brand Logo /1 #23
2018 Panini Prime Prime Jumbo Shoe Brand Logo /1 #24
2018 Panini Prime Prime Jumbo Shoe Brand Logo /1 #25
2018 Panini Prime Prime Jumbo Shoe Name Patch /1 #22
2018 Panini Prime Prime Jumbo Sunoco /1 #22
2018 Panini Prime Prime Jumbo Sunoco /1 #23
2018 Panini Prime Prime Jumbo Sunoco /1 #24
2018 Panini Prime Prime Jumbo Sunoco /1 #25
2018 Panini Prime Prime Signatures /25 #4
2018 Panini Prime Prime Signatures Black /1 #4
2018 Panini Prime Prime Signatures Holo Gold /10 #4
2018 Panini Prime Race Used Duals Firesuit Black /1 #13
2018 Panini Prime Race Used Duals Firesuit Holo Gold /25 #13
2018 Panini Prime Race Used Duals Firesuit Laundry Tag /1 #13
2018 Panini Prime Race Used Duals Sheet Metal /50 #13
2018 Panini Prime Race Used Duals Sheet Metal Black /1 #13
2018 Panini Prime Race Used Duals Sheet Metal Holo Gold /25 #13
2018 Panini Prime Race Used Firesuits Black /1 #10
2018 Panini Prime Race Used Firesuits Holo Gold /25 #10
2018 Panini Prime Race Used Firesuits Laundry Tag /1 #10
2018 Panini Prime Race Used Sheet Metal /50 #10
2018 Panini Prime Race Used Sheet Metal Black /1 #10
2018 Panini Prime Race Used Sheet Metal Holo Gold /25 #10
2018 Panini Prime Race Used Tires /50 #10
2018 Panini Prime Race Used Tires Black /1 #10
2018 Panini Prime Race Used Tires Holo Gold /25 #10
2018 Panini Prime Race Used Trios Firesuit Black /1 #3
2018 Panini Prime Race Used Trios Firesuit Holo Gold /25 #3
2018 Panini Prime Race Used Trios Firesuit Laundry Tag /1 #3
2018 Panini Prime Race Used Trios Sheet Metal /50 #3
2018 Panini Prime Race Used Trios Sheet Metal Black /1 #3
2018 Panini Prime Race Used Trios Sheet Metal Holo Gold /25 #3
2018 Panini Prime Shadowbox Signatures /25 #3
2018 Panini Prime Shadowbox Signatures Black /1 #3
2018 Panini Prime Shadowbox Signatures Holo Gold /10 #3
2018 Panini Prime Signature Swatches /25 #11
2018 Panini Prime Signature Swatches Black /1 #11
2018 Panini Prime Signature Swatches Holo Gold /10 #11
2018 Panini Prime Triple Material Autographs /25 #1
2018 Panini Prime Triple Material Autographs Black /1 #1
2018 Panini Prime Triple Material Autographs Holo Gold /10 #1
2018 Panini Prime Triple Material Autographs Laundry Tag /1 #1
2018 Panini Prizm #22A
2018 Panini Prizm #22B
2018 Panini Prizm #56
2018 Panini Prizm #69
2018 Panini Prizm #72
2018 Panini Prizm #83
2018 Panini Prizm Brilliance #6
2018 Panini Prizm Brilliance Prizms #6
2018 Panini Prizm Brilliance Prizms Black /1 #6
2018 Panini Prizm Brilliance Prizms Gold /10 #6
2018 Panini Prizm Fireworks #3
2018 Panini Prizm Fireworks Prizms #3
2018 Panini Prizm Fireworks Prizms Black /1 #3
2018 Panini Prizm Fireworks Prizms Gold /10 #3
2018 Panini Prizm Illumination #1
2018 Panini Prizm Illumination Prizms #1
2018 Panini Prizm Illumination Prizms Black /1 #1
2018 Panini Prizm Illumination Prizms Gold /10 #1
2018 Panini Prizm National Pride #2
2018 Panini Prizm National Pride Prizms #2
2018 Panini Prizm National Pride Prizms Black /1 #2
2018 Panini Prizm National Pride Prizms Gold /10 #2
2018 Panini Prizm Patented Penmanship Prizms #17
2018 Panini Prizm Patented Penmanship Prizms Black /1 #17
2018 Panini Prizm Patented Penmanship Prizms Blue /10 #17
2018 Panini Prizm Patented Penmanship Prizms Camo #17
2018 Panini Prizm Patented Penmanship Prizms Gold /8 #17
2018 Panini Prizm Patented Penmanship Prizms Green /10 #17
2018 Panini Prizm Patented Penmanship Prizms Rainbow /24 #17
2018 Panini Prizm Patented Penmanship Prizms Red /10 #17

2018 Panini Prizm Patented Penmanship Prizms Red White and Blue /20 #17
2018 Panini Prizm Patented Penmanship Prizms White /3 #17
2018 Panini Prizm Prizms #22A
2018 Panini Prizm Prizms #22B
2018 Panini Prizm Prizms #56
2018 Panini Prizm Prizms #69
2018 Panini Prizm Prizms #72
2018 Panini Prizm Prizms #83
2018 Panini Prizm Prizms Black /1 #22A
2018 Panini Prizm Prizms Black /1 #22B
2018 Panini Prizm Prizms Black /1 #56
2018 Panini Prizm Prizms Black /1 #69
2018 Panini Prizm Prizms Black /1 #72
2018 Panini Prizm Prizms Black /1 #83
2018 Panini Prizm Prizms Blue /99 #22A
2018 Panini Prizm Prizms Blue /99 #22B
2018 Panini Prizm Prizms Blue /99 #56
2018 Panini Prizm Prizms Blue /99 #69
2018 Panini Prizm Prizms Blue /99 #72
2018 Panini Prizm Prizms Blue /99 #83
2018 Panini Prizm Prizms Camo #22A
2018 Panini Prizm Prizms Camo #22B
2018 Panini Prizm Prizms Camo #56
2018 Panini Prizm Prizms Camo #69
2018 Panini Prizm Prizms Camo #72
2018 Panini Prizm Prizms Camo #83
2018 Panini Prizm Prizms Gold /10 #22A
2018 Panini Prizm Prizms Gold /10 #22B
2018 Panini Prizm Prizms Gold /10 #56
2018 Panini Prizm Prizms Gold /10 #69
2018 Panini Prizm Prizms Gold /10 #72
2018 Panini Prizm Prizms Gold /10 #83
2018 Panini Prizm Prizms Green /149 #22A
2018 Panini Prizm Prizms Green /149 #22B
2018 Panini Prizm Prizms Green /149 #56
2018 Panini Prizm Prizms Green /149 #69
2018 Panini Prizm Prizms Green /149 #72
2018 Panini Prizm Prizms Green /149 #83
2018 Panini Prizm Prizms Purple Flash #22A
2018 Panini Prizm Prizms Purple Flash #22B
2018 Panini Prizm Prizms Purple Flash #56
2018 Panini Prizm Prizms Purple Flash #69
2018 Panini Prizm Prizms Purple Flash #72
2018 Panini Prizm Prizms Purple Flash #83
2018 Panini Prizm Prizms Rainbow /24 #22A
2018 Panini Prizm Prizms Rainbow /24 #22B
2018 Panini Prizm Prizms Rainbow /24 #56
2018 Panini Prizm Prizms Rainbow /24 #69
2018 Panini Prizm Prizms Rainbow /24 #72
2018 Panini Prizm Prizms Rainbow /24 #83
2018 Panini Prizm Prizms Red /75 #22A
2018 Panini Prizm Prizms Red /75 #22B
2018 Panini Prizm Prizms Red /75 #56
2018 Panini Prizm Prizms Red /75 #69
2018 Panini Prizm Prizms Red /75 #72
2018 Panini Prizm Prizms Red /75 #83
2018 Panini Prizm Prizms Red White and Blue #22A
2018 Panini Prizm Prizms Red White and Blue #22B
2018 Panini Prizm Prizms Red White and Blue #56
2018 Panini Prizm Prizms Red White and Blue #69
2018 Panini Prizm Prizms Red White and Blue #72
2018 Panini Prizm Prizms Red White and Blue #83
2018 Panini Prizm Prizms White /5 #22A
2018 Panini Prizm Prizms White /5 #22B
2018 Panini Prizm Prizms White /5 #56
2018 Panini Prizm Prizms White /5 #69
2018 Panini Prizm Prizms White /5 #72
2018 Panini Prizm Prizms White /5 #83
2018 Panini Prizm Scripted Signatures Prizms #19
2018 Panini Prizm Scripted Signatures Prizms Black /1 #19
2018 Panini Prizm Scripted Signatures Prizms Blue /10 #19
2018 Panini Prizm Scripted Signatures Prizms Camo #19
2018 Panini Prizm Scripted Signatures Prizms Gold /8 #19
2018 Panini Prizm Scripted Signatures Prizms Green /10 #19
2018 Panini Prizm Scripted Signatures Prizms Rainbow /24 #19
2018 Panini Prizm Scripted Signatures Prizms Red /10 #19
2018 Panini Prizm Scripted Signatures Prizms Red White and Blue /20 #19
2018 Panini Prizm Scripted Signatures Prizms White /3 #19
2018 Panini Prizm Stars and Stripes #10
2018 Panini Prizm Stars and Stripes Prizms #10
2018 Panini Prizm Stars and Stripes Prizms Black /1 #10
2018 Panini Prizm Stars and Stripes Prizms Gold /10 #10
2018 Panini Victory Lane #53
2018 Panini Victory Lane #63
2018 Panini Victory Lane #67
2018 Panini Victory Lane #73
2018 Panini Victory Lane #88
2018 Panini Victory Lane #93
2018 Panini Victory Lane #98
2018 Panini Victory Lane Black /1 #53
2018 Panini Victory Lane Black /1 #63
2018 Panini Victory Lane Black /1 #67
2018 Panini Victory Lane Black /1 #73
2018 Panini Victory Lane Black /1 #88
2018 Panini Victory Lane Black /1 #93
2018 Panini Victory Lane Black /1 #98
2018 Panini Victory Lane Blue /25 #53
2018 Panini Victory Lane Blue /25 #63
2018 Panini Victory Lane Blue /25 #67
2018 Panini Victory Lane Blue /25 #73
2018 Panini Victory Lane Blue /25 #88
2018 Panini Victory Lane Blue /25 #93
2018 Panini Victory Lane Blue /25 #98
2018 Panini Victory Lane Celebrations #4
2018 Panini Victory Lane Celebrations Black /1 #4
2018 Panini Victory Lane Celebrations Blue /25 #4
2018 Panini Victory Lane Celebrations Gold /99 #4
2018 Panini Victory Lane Celebrations Green /5 #4
2018 Panini Victory Lane Celebrations Printing Plates Black /1 #4
2018 Panini Victory Lane Celebrations Printing Plates Cyan /1 #4
2018 Panini Victory Lane Celebrations Printing Plates Magenta /1 #4
2018 Panini Victory Lane Celebrations Printing Plates Yellow /1 #4
2018 Panini Victory Lane Celebrations Red /49 #4
2018 Panini Victory Lane Chasing the Flag #2
2018 Panini Victory Lane Chasing the Flag Black /1 #2
2018 Panini Victory Lane Chasing the Flag Blue /25 #2
2018 Panini Victory Lane Chasing the Flag Gold /99 #2
2018 Panini Victory Lane Chasing the Flag Green /5 #2
2018 Panini Victory Lane Chasing the Flag Printing Plates Black /1 #2
2018 Panini Victory Lane Chasing the Flag Printing Plates Cyan /1 #2
2018 Panini Victory Lane Chasing the Flag Printing Plates Magenta /1 #2
2018 Panini Victory Lane Chasing the Flag Printing Plates Yellow /1 #2
2018 Panini Victory Lane Chasing the Flag Red /49 #2
2018 Panini Victory Lane Foundations #1
2018 Panini Victory Lane Foundations Black /1 #1
2018 Panini Victory Lane Foundations Blue /25 #1
2018 Panini Victory Lane Foundations Gold /99 #1
2018 Panini Victory Lane Foundations Green /5 #1
2018 Panini Victory Lane Foundations Printing Plates Black /1 #1
2018 Panini Victory Lane Foundations Printing Plates Cyan /1 #1
2018 Panini Victory Lane Foundations Printing Plates Magenta /1 #1
2018 Panini Victory Lane Foundations Printing Plates Yellow /1 #1
2018 Panini Victory Lane Foundations Red /49 #1
2018 Panini Victory Lane Gold /99 #53
2018 Panini Victory Lane Gold /99 #63
2018 Panini Victory Lane Gold /99 #67
2018 Panini Victory Lane Gold /99 #73
2018 Panini Victory Lane Gold /99 #88
2018 Panini Victory Lane Gold /99 #93
2018 Panini Victory Lane Gold /99 #98
2018 Panini Victory Lane Green /5 #53
2018 Panini Victory Lane Green /5 #63
2018 Panini Victory Lane Green /5 #67
2018 Panini Victory Lane Green /5 #73
2018 Panini Victory Lane Green /5 #88
2018 Panini Victory Lane Green /5 #93
2018 Panini Victory Lane Green /5 #98
2018 Panini Victory Lane NASCAR at 70 #10
2018 Panini Victory Lane NASCAR at 70 Black /1 #10
2018 Panini Victory Lane NASCAR at 70 Blue /25 #10
2018 Panini Victory Lane NASCAR at 70 Gold /99 #10
2018 Panini Victory Lane NASCAR at 70 Green /5 #10
2018 Panini Victory Lane NASCAR at 70 Printing Plates Black /1 #10
2018 Panini Victory Lane NASCAR at 70 Printing Plates Cyan /1 #10
2018 Panini Victory Lane NASCAR at 70 Printing Plates Magenta /1 #10
2018 Panini Victory Lane NASCAR at 70 Printing Plates Yellow /1 #10
2018 Panini Victory Lane NASCAR at 70 Red /49 #10
2018 Panini Victory Lane Octane Autographs Black /1 #9
2018 Panini Victory Lane Octane Autographs Gold /5 #9
2018 Panini Victory Lane Pedal to the Metal #14
2018 Panini Victory Lane Pedal to the Metal #75
2018 Panini Victory Lane Pedal to the Metal Black /1 #14
2018 Panini Victory Lane Pedal to the Metal Black /1 #75
2018 Panini Victory Lane Pedal to the Metal Blue /25 #14
2018 Panini Victory Lane Pedal to the Metal Blue /25 #75
2018 Panini Victory Lane Pedal to the Metal Green /5 #14
2018 Panini Victory Lane Pedal to the Metal Green /5 #75
2018 Panini Victory Lane Printing Plates Black /1 #53
2018 Panini Victory Lane Printing Plates Black /1 #63
2018 Panini Victory Lane Printing Plates Black /1 #67
2018 Panini Victory Lane Printing Plates Black /1 #73
2018 Panini Victory Lane Printing Plates Black /1 #88
2018 Panini Victory Lane Printing Plates Black /1 #93
2018 Panini Victory Lane Printing Plates Black /1 #98
2018 Panini Victory Lane Printing Plates Cyan /1 #53
2018 Panini Victory Lane Printing Plates Cyan /1 #63
2018 Panini Victory Lane Printing Plates Cyan /1 #67
2018 Panini Victory Lane Printing Plates Cyan /1 #73
2018 Panini Victory Lane Printing Plates Cyan /1 #88
2018 Panini Victory Lane Printing Plates Cyan /1 #93
2018 Panini Victory Lane Printing Plates Cyan /1 #98
2018 Panini Victory Lane Printing Plates Magenta /1 #53
2018 Panini Victory Lane Printing Plates Magenta /1 #63
2018 Panini Victory Lane Printing Plates Magenta /1 #67
2018 Panini Victory Lane Printing Plates Magenta /1 #73
2018 Panini Victory Lane Printing Plates Magenta /1 #88
2018 Panini Victory Lane Printing Plates Magenta /1 #93
2018 Panini Victory Lane Printing Plates Magenta /1 #98
2018 Panini Victory Lane Printing Plates Yellow /1 #53
2018 Panini Victory Lane Printing Plates Yellow /1 #63
2018 Panini Victory Lane Printing Plates Yellow /1 #67
2018 Panini Victory Lane Printing Plates Yellow /1 #73
2018 Panini Victory Lane Printing Plates Yellow /1 #88
2018 Panini Victory Lane Printing Plates Yellow /1 #93
2018 Panini Victory Lane Printing Plates Yellow /1 #98
2018 Panini Victory Lane Race Day #10
2018 Panini Victory Lane Race Day Black /1 #10
2018 Panini Victory Lane Race Day Blue /25 #10
2018 Panini Victory Lane Race Day Gold /99 #10
2018 Panini Victory Lane Race Day Green /5 #10
2018 Panini Victory Lane Race Day Printing Plates Black /1 #10
2018 Panini Victory Lane Race Day Printing Plates Cyan /1 #10
2018 Panini Victory Lane Race Day Printing Plates Magenta /1 #10
2018 Panini Victory Lane Race Day Printing Plates Yellow /1 #10
2018 Panini Victory Lane Race Day Red /49 #10
2018 Panini Victory Lane Race Ready Dual Materials /399 #4
2018 Panini Victory Lane Race Ready Dual Materials Black /25 #4
2018 Panini Victory Lane Race Ready Dual Materials Gold /199 #4
2018 Panini Victory Lane Race Ready Dual Materials Green /99 #4
2018 Panini Victory Lane Race Ready Dual Materials Laundry Tag /1 #4
2018 Panini Victory Lane Race Ready Materials /399 #8
2018 Panini Victory Lane Race Ready Materials Black /25 #8
2018 Panini Victory Lane Race Ready Materials Gold /199 #8
2018 Panini Victory Lane Race Ready Materials Green /99 #8
2018 Panini Victory Lane Race Ready Materials Laundry Tag /1 #8
2018 Panini Victory Lane Red /49 #53
2018 Panini Victory Lane Red /49 #63
2018 Panini Victory Lane Red /49 #67
2018 Panini Victory Lane Red /49 #73
2018 Panini Victory Lane Red /49 #88
2018 Panini Victory Lane Red /49 #93
2018 Panini Victory Lane Red /49 #98
2018 Panini Victory Lane Remarkable Remnants Material Autographs /70 #1
2018 Panini Victory Lane Remarkable Remnants Material Autographs Black /10 #1
2018 Panini Victory Lane Remarkable Remnants Material Autographs Gold /50 #1
2018 Panini Victory Lane Remarkable Remnants Material Autographs Green /25 #1
2018 Panini Victory Lane Remarkable Remnants Material Autographs Laundry Tag /1 #1
2018 Panini Victory Lane Silver #53
2018 Panini Victory Lane Silver #63
2018 Panini Victory Lane Silver #67
2018 Panini Victory Lane Silver #73
2018 Panini Victory Lane Silver #88
2018 Panini Victory Lane Silver #93
2018 Panini Victory Lane Silver #98
2018 Panini Victory Lane Victory Lane Prime Patches Associate Sponsor 1 /1 #5
2018 Panini Victory Lane Victory Lane Prime Patches Associate Sponsor 10 /1 #5
2018 Panini Victory Lane Victory Lane Prime Patches Associate Sponsor 2 /1 #5
2018 Panini Victory Lane Victory Lane Prime Patches Associate Sponsor 3 /1 #5
2018 Panini Victory Lane Victory Lane Prime Patches Associate Sponsor 4 /1 #5
2018 Panini Victory Lane Victory Lane Prime Patches Associate Sponsor 5 /1 #5
2018 Panini Victory Lane Victory Lane Prime Patches Associate Sponsor 6 /1 #5
2018 Panini Victory Lane Victory Lane Prime Patches Associate Sponsor 7 /1 #5
2018 Panini Victory Lane Victory Lane Prime Patches Associate Sponsor 8 /1 #5
2018 Panini Victory Lane Victory Lane Prime Patches Associate Sponsor 9 /1 #5
2018 Panini Victory Lane Victory Lane Prime Patches Car Manufacturer /1 #5
2018 Panini Victory Lane Victory Lane Prime Patches Firesuit Manufacturer /1 #5
2018 Panini Victory Lane Victory Lane Prime Patches Goodyear /2 #5
2018 Panini Victory Lane Victory Lane Prime Patches NASCAR /1 #5
2018 Panini Victory Lane Victory Lane Prime Patches Series Sponsor /1 #5
2018 Panini Victory Lane Victory Lane Prime Patches Sunoco /1 #5
2018 Panini Victory Lane Victory Marks Black /1 #3
2018 Panini Victory Lane Victory Marks Gold /5 #3
2019 Donruss #8
2019 Donruss #72A
2019 Donruss #102A
2019 Donruss #162
2019 Donruss #72B
2019 Donruss #102B
2019 Donruss Artist Proofs /25 #8
2019 Donruss Artist Proofs /25 #72A
2019 Donruss Artist Proofs /25 #102A
2019 Donruss Artist Proofs /25 #162
2019 Donruss Artist Proofs /25 #72B
2019 Donruss Artist Proofs /25 #102B
2019 Donruss Black /199 #8
2019 Donruss Black /199 #72A
2019 Donruss Black /199 #102A
2019 Donruss Black /199 #162
2019 Donruss Black /199 #72B
2019 Donruss Black /199 #102B
2019 Donruss Classics #2
2019 Donruss Classics Cracked Ice /25 #2
2019 Donruss Classics Holographic #2
2019 Donruss Classics Xplosion /10 #2
2019 Donruss Decades of Speed #2
2019 Donruss Decades of Speed Cracked Ice /25 #2
2019 Donruss Decades of Speed Holographic #2
2019 Donruss Decades of Speed Xplosion /10 #2
2019 Donruss Gold /299 #8
2019 Donruss Gold /299 #72A
2019 Donruss Gold /299 #102A
2019 Donruss Gold /299 #162
2019 Donruss Gold /299 #72B
2019 Donruss Gold /299 #102B
2019 Donruss Gold Press Proofs /99 #8
2019 Donruss Gold Press Proofs /99 #72A
2019 Donruss Gold Press Proofs /99 #102A
2019 Donruss Gold Press Proofs /99 #162
2019 Donruss Gold Press Proofs /99 #72B
2019 Donruss Gold Press Proofs /99 #102B
2019 Donruss Icons #3
2019 Donruss Icons Cracked Ice /25 #3
2019 Donruss Icons Holographic #3
2019 Donruss Icons Xplosion /10 #3
2019 Donruss Optic #4
2019 Donruss Optic #11
2019 Donruss Optic #57
2019 Donruss Optic Blue Pulsar #4
2019 Donruss Optic Blue Pulsar #11
2019 Donruss Optic Blue Pulsar /1 #57
2019 Donruss Optic Gold /10 #4
2019 Donruss Optic Gold /10 #11
2019 Donruss Optic Gold /10 #57
2019 Donruss Optic Gold Vinyl /1 #4
2019 Donruss Optic Gold Vinyl /1 #11
2019 Donruss Optic Gold Vinyl /1 #57
2019 Donruss Optic Holo #4
2019 Donruss Optic Holo #11
2019 Donruss Optic Holo #57
2019 Donruss Optic Red Wave #4
2019 Donruss Optic Red Wave #11
2019 Donruss Optic Red Wave /1 #57
2019 Donruss Optic Signatures Gold Vinyl /1 #57
2019 Donruss Optic Signatures Gold Vinyl /1 #4
2019 Donruss Optic Signatures Gold Vinyl /1 #11
2019 Donruss Optic Signatures Holo /25 #4
2019 Donruss Optic Signatures Holo /75 #11
2019 Donruss Optic Signatures Holo /75 #57
2019 Donruss Press Proofs /49 #72A
2019 Donruss Press Proofs /49 #102A
2019 Donruss Press Proofs /49 #162
2019 Donruss Press Proofs /49 #72B
2019 Donruss Press Proofs /49 #102B
2019 Donruss Press Proofs /49 #8
2019 Donruss Printing Plates Black /1 #8
2019 Donruss Printing Plates Black /1 #72A
2019 Donruss Printing Plates Black /1 #102A
2019 Donruss Printing Plates Black /1 #162
2019 Donruss Printing Plates Black /1 #72B
2019 Donruss Printing Plates Black /1 #102B
2019 Donruss Printing Plates Cyan /1 #8
2019 Donruss Printing Plates Cyan /1 #72A
2019 Donruss Printing Plates Cyan /1 #102A
2019 Donruss Printing Plates Cyan /1 #162
2019 Donruss Printing Plates Cyan /1 #72B
2019 Donruss Printing Plates Cyan /1 #102B
2019 Donruss Printing Plates Magenta /1 #72A
2019 Donruss Printing Plates Magenta /1 #102A
2019 Donruss Printing Plates Magenta /1 #162
2019 Donruss Printing Plates Magenta /1 #72B
2019 Donruss Printing Plates Magenta /1 #102B
2019 Donruss Printing Plates Magenta /1 #8
2019 Donruss Printing Plates Yellow /1 #8
2019 Donruss Printing Plates Yellow /1 #72A
2019 Donruss Printing Plates Yellow /1 #102A
2019 Donruss Printing Plates Yellow /1 #162
2019 Donruss Printing Plates Yellow /1 #72B
2019 Donruss Printing Plates Yellow /1 #102B
2019 Donruss Race Day Relics #8
2019 Donruss Race Day Relics Holo Black /10 #8
2019 Donruss Race Day Relics Holo Gold /25 #8
2019 Donruss Race Day Relics Red /185 #8
2019 Donruss Retro Relics '86 #13
2019 Donruss Retro Relics '86 Holo Black /10 #13
2019 Donruss Retro Relics '86 Holo Gold /25 #13
2019 Donruss Retro Relics '86 Red /140 #13
2019 Donruss Signature Swatches #2
2019 Donruss Signature Swatches Holo Black /10 #2
2019 Donruss Signature Swatches Holo Gold /25 #2
2019 Donruss Signature Swatches Red /49 #2
2019 Donruss Silver #8
2019 Donruss Silver #72A
2019 Donruss Silver #102A
2019 Donruss Silver #162
2019 Donruss Silver #72B
2019 Donruss Silver #102B
2019 Panini National Convention NASCAR #R1
2019 Panini National Convention NASCAR Galatic Windows /25 #R1
2019 Panini National Convention NASCAR HyperPlaid /1 #R1
2019 Panini National Convention VIP Party #80
2019 Panini National Convention VIP Party Blue /15 #80
2019 Panini National Convention VIP Party Gold /10 #80
2019 Panini National Convention VIP Party Green /5 #80
2019 Panini National Convention VIP Party Lazer #80
2019 Panini National Convention VIP Party Memorabilia Gold /5 #80
2019 Panini National Convention VIP Party Pink /50 #80
2019 Panini National Convention VIP Party Prizms #80
2019 Panini National Convention VIP Party Purple /99 #80
2019 Panini National Convention VIP Party Red /25 #80
2019 Panini National Convention VIP Party Red, White, and Blue #80
2019 Panini National Convention VIP Party Tiger Stripes #80
2019 Panini Prime /50 #62
2019 Panini Prime /50 #90
2019 Panini Prime Black /10 #62
2019 Panini Prime Black /10 #90
2019 Panini Prime Clear Silhouettes /99 #4
2019 Panini Prime Clear Silhouettes Black /10 #4
2019 Panini Prime Clear Silhouettes Dual /99 #7
2019 Panini Prime Clear Silhouettes Dual Black /10 #7
2019 Panini Prime Clear Silhouettes Dual Holo Gold /25 #7
2019 Panini Prime Clear Silhouettes Dual Platinum Blue /1 #7
2019 Panini Prime Clear Silhouettes Holo Gold /25 #4
2019 Panini Prime Clear Silhouettes Platinum Blue /1 #4
2019 Panini Prime Emerald /5 #62
2019 Panini Prime Emerald /5 #90
2019 Panini Prime Jumbo Material Signatures Firesuit /10 #8
2019 Panini Prime Jumbo Material Signatures Firesuit Platinum Blue /1 #8
2019 Panini Prime Jumbo Material Signatures Sheet Metal /25 #8
2019 Panini Prime NASCAR Shadowbox Signatures Car Number /25 #14
2019 Panini Prime NASCAR Shadowbox Signatures Manufacturer /3 #14
2019 Panini Prime NASCAR Shadowbox Signatures Team Owner /1 #14
2019 Panini Prime Platinum Blue /1 #62
2019 Panini Prime Platinum Blue /1 #90
2019 Panini Prime Prime Cars Die Cut Signatures /25 #10
2019 Panini Prime Prime Cars Die Cut Signatures Black /3 #10
2019 Panini Prime Prime Cars Die Cut Signatures Holo Gold /8 #10
2019 Panini Prime Prime Cars Die Cut Signatures Platinum Blue /1 #10
2019 Panini Prime Prime Jumbo Associate Sponsor 1 /1 #18
2019 Panini Prime Prime Jumbo Associate Sponsor 1 /1 #19
2019 Panini Prime Prime Jumbo Associate Sponsor 1 /1 #20
2019 Panini Prime Prime Jumbo Associate Sponsor 2 /1 #18
2019 Panini Prime Prime Jumbo Associate Sponsor 2 /1 #19
2019 Panini Prime Prime Jumbo Associate Sponsor 2 /1 #20
2019 Panini Prime Prime Jumbo Associate Sponsor 3 /1 #18
2019 Panini Prime Prime Jumbo Associate Sponsor 3 /1 #20
2019 Panini Prime Prime Jumbo Associate Sponsor 4 /1 #18
2019 Panini Prime Prime Jumbo Associate Sponsor 4 /1 #20
2019 Panini Prime Prime Jumbo Associate Sponsor 5 /1 #18
2019 Panini Prime Prime Jumbo Associate Sponsor 5 /1 #20
2019 Panini Prime Prime Jumbo Associate Sponsor 6 /1 #18
2019 Panini Prime Prime Jumbo Associate Sponsor 6 /1 #20
2019 Panini Prime Prime Jumbo Associate Sponsor 7 /1 #18
2019 Panini Prime Prime Jumbo Associate Sponsor 7 /1 #20
2019 Panini Prime Prime Jumbo Car Manufacturer /1 #18
2019 Panini Prime Prime Jumbo Car Manufacturer /1 #19
2019 Panini Prime Prime Jumbo Car Manufacturer /1 #20
2019 Panini Prime Prime Jumbo Firesuit Manufacturer /1 #18
2019 Panini Prime Prime Jumbo Firesuit Manufacturer /1 #19
2019 Panini Prime Prime Jumbo Firesuit Manufacturer /1 #20
2019 Panini Prime Prime Jumbo Glove Manufacturer Patch /1 #18
2019 Panini Prime Prime Jumbo Glove Manufacturer Patch /1 #19
2019 Panini Prime Prime Jumbo Glove Manufacturer Patch /1 #20
2019 Panini Prime Prime Jumbo Goodyear /2 #18
2019 Panini Prime Prime Jumbo Goodyear /2 #20
2019 Panini Prime Prime Jumbo NASCAR /1 #18
2019 Panini Prime Prime Jumbo NASCAR /1 #20
2019 Panini Prime Prime Jumbo Prime Colors /8 #19
2019 Panini Prime Prime Jumbo Prime Colors /12 #20
2019 Panini Prime Prime Jumbo Prime Colors /16 #18
2019 Panini Prime Prime Jumbo Series Sponsor /1 #18
2019 Panini Prime Prime Jumbo Series Sponsor /1 #20
2019 Panini Prime Prime Jumbo Shoe Brand Logo /1 #18
2019 Panini Prime Prime Jumbo Shoe Brand Logo /1 #19
2019 Panini Prime Prime Jumbo Shoe Brand Logo /1 #20
2019 Panini Prime Prime Jumbo Sunoco /1 #18
2019 Panini Prime Prime Jumbo Sunoco /1 #20
2019 Panini Prime Prime Names Die Cut Signatures /25 #21
2019 Panini Prime Prime Names Die Cut Signatures Black /3 #21
2019 Panini Prime Prime Names Die Cut Signatures Holo Gold /8 #21
2019 Panini Prime Prime Names Die Cut Signatures Platinum Blue /1 #21
2019 Panini Prime Quad Materials Autographs /25 #8
2019 Panini Prime Quad Materials Autographs Black /3 #8
2019 Panini Prime Quad Materials Autographs Holo Gold /8 #8
2019 Panini Prime Quad Materials Autographs Laundry Tags /1 #8
2019 Panini Prime Race Used Firesuits /50 #14
2019 Panini Prime Race Used Firesuits Black /10 #14
2019 Panini Prime Race Used Firesuits Holo Gold /25 #14
2019 Panini Prime Race Used Firesuits Laundry Tags /1 #14
2019 Panini Prime Race Used Sheet Metal /50 #14
2019 Panini Prime Race Used Sheet Metal Black /10 #14
2019 Panini Prime Race Used Sheet Metal Holo Gold /25 #14
2019 Panini Prime Race Used Sheet Metal Platinum Blue /1 #14
2019 Panini Prime Shadowbox Signatures /25 #20
2019 Panini Prime Shadowbox Signatures /25 #5
2019 Panini Prime Shadowbox Signatures Black /3 #5
2019 Panini Prime Shadowbox Signatures Black /3 #20
2019 Panini Prime Shadowbox Signatures Holo Gold /8 #5
2019 Panini Prime Shadowbox Signatures Holo Gold /8 #20
2019 Panini Prime Shadowbox Signatures Platinum Blue /1 #5
2019 Panini Prime Shadowbox Signatures Platinum Blue /1 #20
2019 Panini Prime Timeline Signatures /25 #4
2019 Panini Prime Timeline Signatures Manufacturer /1 #4
2019 Panini Prime Timeline Signatures Name /8 #4
2019 Panini Prime Timeline Signatures Sponsor /3 #4
2019 Panini Prizm #41A
2019 Panini Prizm #41B
2019 Panini Prizm Apex #5
2019 Panini Prizm Apex Prizms #5
2019 Panini Prizm Apex Prizms Black /1 #5
2019 Panini Prizm Apex Prizms Gold /10 #5
2019 Panini Prizm Apex Prizms White Sparkle #5
2019 Panini Prizm Endorsements Prizms #3
2019 Panini Prizm Endorsements Prizms Black /1 #3
2019 Panini Prizm Endorsements Prizms Blue /5 #3
2019 Panini Prizm Endorsements Prizms Camo #3
2019 Panini Prizm Endorsements Prizms Gold /10 #3
2019 Panini Prizm Endorsements Prizms Green /5 #3
2019 Panini Prizm Endorsements Prizms Rainbow /5 #3
2019 Panini Prizm Endorsements Prizms Red /5 #3
2019 Panini Prizm Endorsements Prizms Red White and Blue #3
2019 Panini Prizm Endorsements Prizms White /5 #3
2019 Panini Prizm Expert Level #10
2019 Panini Prizm Expert Level Prizms #10
2019 Panini Prizm Expert Level Prizms Black /1 #10
2019 Panini Prizm Expert Level Prizms Gold /10 #10
2019 Panini Prizm Expert Level Prizms White Sparkle #10
2019 Panini Prizm Fireworks #3
2019 Panini Prizm Fireworks Prizms #3
2019 Panini Prizm Fireworks Prizms Black /1 #3
2019 Panini Prizm Fireworks Prizms Gold /10 #3
2019 Panini Prizm Fireworks Prizms White Sparkle #3
2019 Panini Prizm National Pride #2
2019 Panini Prizm National Pride Prizms #2
2019 Panini Prizm National Pride Prizms Black /1 #2
2019 Panini Prizm National Pride Prizms Gold /10 #2
2019 Panini Prizm National Pride Prizms White Sparkle #2
2019 Panini Prizm Patented Penmanship Prizms #2
2019 Panini Prizm Patented Penmanship Prizms Black /1 #2
2019 Panini Prizm Patented Penmanship Prizms Blue /5 #2
2019 Panini Prizm Patented Penmanship Prizms Camo #2
2019 Panini Prizm Patented Penmanship Prizms Gold /10 #2
2019 Panini Prizm Patented Penmanship Prizms Green /5 #2
2019 Panini Prizm Patented Penmanship Prizms Rainbow /5 #2
2019 Panini Prizm Patented Penmanship Prizms Red /5 #2
2019 Panini Prizm Patented Penmanship Prizms Red White and Blue #2
2019 Panini Prizm Patented Penmanship Prizms White /5 #2
2019 Panini Prizm Prizms #41B
2019 Panini Prizm Prizms #41A
2019 Panini Prizm Prizms Black /1 #41A
2019 Panini Prizm Prizms Black /1 #41B
2019 Panini Prizm Prizms Blue /75 #41A
2019 Panini Prizm Prizms Blue /75 #41B
2019 Panini Prizm Prizms Camo #41A
2019 Panini Prizm Prizms Camo #41B
2019 Panini Prizm Prizms Flash #41A
2019 Panini Prizm Prizms Flash #41B
2019 Panini Prizm Prizms Gold /10 #41A
2019 Panini Prizm Prizms Gold /10 #41B
2019 Panini Prizm Prizms Green /99 #41A
2019 Panini Prizm Prizms Green /99 #41B
2019 Panini Prizm Prizms Rainbow /24 #41A
2019 Panini Prizm Prizms Rainbow /24 #41B
2019 Panini Prizm Prizms Red /50 #41A
2019 Panini Prizm Prizms Red /50 #41B
2019 Panini Prizm Prizms Red White and Blue #41A
2019 Panini Prizm Prizms Red White and Blue #41B
2019 Panini Prizm Prizms White /5 #41A
2019 Panini Prizm Prizms White /5 #41B
2019 Panini Prizm Prizms White Sparkle #41A
2019 Panini Prizm Prizms White Sparkle #41B
2019 Panini Prizm Scripted Signatures Prizms #3
2019 Panini Prizm Scripted Signatures Prizms Black /1 #3
2019 Panini Prizm Scripted Signatures Prizms Blue /5 #3
2019 Panini Prizm Scripted Signatures Prizms Camo #3
2019 Panini Prizm Scripted Signatures Prizms Gold /10 #3
2019 Panini Prizm Scripted Signatures Prizms Green /5 #3
2019 Panini Prizm Scripted Signatures Prizms Rainbow /5 #3
2019 Panini Prizm Scripted Signatures Prizms Red /5 #3
2019 Panini Prizm Scripted Signatures Prizms Red White and Blue #3
2019 Panini Prizm Scripted Signatures Prizms White /5 #3
2019 Panini Prizm Stars and Stripes #11
2019 Panini Prizm Stars and Stripes Prizms #11
2019 Panini Prizm Stars and Stripes Prizms Black /1 #11
2019 Panini Prizm Stars and Stripes Prizms Gold /10 #11
2019 Panini Prizm Stars and Stripes Prizms White Sparkle #11
2019 Panini Victory Lane #46
2019 Panini Victory Lane #81
2019 Panini Victory Lane #91
2019 Panini Victory Lane Black /1 #46
2019 Panini Victory Lane Black /1 #81
2019 Panini Victory Lane Black /1 #91
2019 Panini Victory Lane Dual Swatch Signatures #5
2019 Panini Victory Lane Dual Swatch Signatures Gold /99 #5
2019 Panini Victory Lane Dual Swatch Signatures Laundry Tag /1 #5
2019 Panini Victory Lane Dual Swatch Signatures Platinum /1 #5
2019 Panini Victory Lane Dual Swatch Signatures Red /25 #5
2019 Panini Victory Lane Dual Swatches Gold /99 #8
2019 Panini Victory Lane Dual Swatches Laundry Tag /1 #8
2019 Panini Victory Lane Dual Swatches Platinum /1 #8
2019 Panini Victory Lane Dual Swatches Red /25 #8
2019 Panini Victory Lane Gold /25 #46
2019 Panini Victory Lane Gold /25 #81
2019 Panini Victory Lane Gold /25 #91
2019 Panini Victory Lane Horsepower Heroes #7
2019 Panini Victory Lane Horsepower Heroes Black /1 #7
2019 Panini Victory Lane Horsepower Heroes Blue /99 #7
2019 Panini Victory Lane Horsepower Heroes Gold /25 #7
2019 Panini Victory Lane Horsepower Heroes Green /5 #7
2019 Panini Victory Lane Horsepower Heroes Printing Plates Black /1 #7
2019 Panini Victory Lane Horsepower Heroes Printing Plates Cyan /1 #7
2019 Panini Victory Lane Horsepower Heroes Printing Plates Magenta /1 #7
2019 Panini Victory Lane Horsepower Heroes Printing Plates Yellow /1 #7
2019 Panini Victory Lane Printing Plates Black /1 #46
2019 Panini Victory Lane Printing Plates Black /1 #81
2019 Panini Victory Lane Printing Plates Black /1 #91
2019 Panini Victory Lane Printing Plates Cyan /1 #46
2019 Panini Victory Lane Printing Plates Cyan /1 #81
2019 Panini Victory Lane Printing Plates Cyan /1 #91
2019 Panini Victory Lane Printing Plates Magenta /1 #46
2019 Panini Victory Lane Printing Plates Magenta /1 #81
2019 Panini Victory Lane Printing Plates Magenta /1 #91
2019 Panini Victory Lane Printing Plates Yellow /1 #46
2019 Panini Victory Lane Printing Plates Yellow /1 #81
2019 Panini Victory Lane Printing Plates Yellow /1 #91
2019 Panini Victory Lane Quad Swatches #1
2019 Panini Victory Lane Quad Swatches Gold /99 #1
2019 Panini Victory Lane Quad Swatches Laundry Tag /1 #1
2019 Panini Victory Lane Quad Swatches Platinum /1 #1
2019 Panini Victory Lane Quad Swatches Red /25 #1
2019 Panini Victory Lane Track Stars #10
2019 Panini Victory Lane Track Stars Black /1 #10
2019 Panini Victory Lane Track Stars Blue /99 #10
2019 Panini Victory Lane Track Stars Gold /25 #10
2019 Panini Victory Lane Track Stars Green /5 #10
2019 Panini Victory Lane Track Stars Printing Plates Black /1 #10
2019 Panini Victory Lane Track Stars Printing Plates Cyan /1 #10
2019 Panini Victory Lane Track Stars Printing Plates Magenta /1 #10
2019 Panini Victory Lane Track Stars Printing Plates Yellow /1 #10
2019-20 Funko Pop Vinyl NASCAR #4
2020 Donruss #8
2020 Donruss #94
2020 Donruss #170
2020 Donruss Black Numbers /88 #8
2020 Donruss Black Numbers /88 #94
2020 Donruss Black Numbers /88 #170
2020 Donruss Black Trophy Club /1 #8
2020 Donruss Black Trophy Club /1 #94
2020 Donruss Black Trophy Club /1 #170
2020 Donruss Blue /199 #94
2020 Donruss Blue /199 #170
2020 Donruss Blue /199 #8
2020 Donruss Carolina Blue #8
2020 Donruss Carolina Blue #94
2020 Donruss Carolina Blue #170
2020 Donruss Classics #1
2020 Donruss Classics Checkers #1
2020 Donruss Classics Cracked Ice /25 #1
2020 Donruss Classics Holographic /199 #1
2020 Donruss Classics Xplosion /10 #1
2020 Donruss Green /99 #8
2020 Donruss Green /99 #94
2020 Donruss Green /99 #170
2020 Donruss Optic #8
2020 Donruss Optic #62
2020 Donruss Optic #89
2020 Donruss Optic Carolina Blue Wave #62
2020 Donruss Optic Carolina Blue Wave #89
2020 Donruss Optic Carolina Blue Wave #8
2020 Donruss Optic Gold /10 #8
2020 Donruss Optic Gold /10 #62
2020 Donruss Optic Gold /10 #89
2020 Donruss Optic Gold Vinyl /1 #8
2020 Donruss Optic Gold Vinyl /1 #62
2020 Donruss Optic Gold Vinyl /1 #89
2020 Donruss Optic Holo #8
2020 Donruss Optic Holo #62
2020 Donruss Optic Holo #89
2020 Donruss Optic Orange Pulsar #8
2020 Donruss Optic Orange Pulsar #62
2020 Donruss Optic Orange Pulsar #89
2020 Donruss Optic Red Mojo #8
2020 Donruss Optic Red Mojo #62
2020 Donruss Optic Red Mojo #89
2020 Donruss Optic Signatures Gold Vinyl /1 #8
2020 Donruss Optic Signatures Gold Vinyl /1 #62
2020 Donruss Optic Signatures Gold Vinyl /1 #89
2020 Donruss Optic Signatures Holo /99 #8
2020 Donruss Optic Signatures Holo /99 #62
2020 Donruss Optic Signatures Holo /99 #89
2020 Donruss Orange #8
2020 Donruss Orange #94
2020 Donruss Orange #170
2020 Donruss Pink /25 #8
2020 Donruss Pink /25 #94
2020 Donruss Pink /25 #170
2020 Donruss Printing Plates Black /1 #8
2020 Donruss Printing Plates Black /1 #94
2020 Donruss Printing Plates Black /1 #170
2020 Donruss Printing Plates Cyan /1 #8
2020 Donruss Printing Plates Cyan /1 #94
2020 Donruss Printing Plates Cyan /1 #170
2020 Donruss Printing Plates Magenta /1 #94
2020 Donruss Printing Plates Magenta /1 #170
2020 Donruss Printing Plates Magenta /1 #8
2020 Donruss Printing Plates Yellow /1 #170
2020 Donruss Printing Plates Yellow /1 #8
2020 Donruss Printing Plates Yellow /1 #94
2020 Donruss Purple /49 #8
2020 Donruss Purple /49 #94
2020 Donruss Purple /49 #170
2020 Donruss Red /299 #8
2020 Donruss Red /299 #94
2020 Donruss Red /299 #170
2020 Donruss Retro Relics '87 #3
2020 Donruss Retro Relics '87 Holo Black /10 #3
2020 Donruss Retro Relics '87 Holo Gold /25 #3
2020 Donruss Retro Relics '87 Red /99 #3
2020 Donruss Silver #8
2020 Donruss Silver #94
2020 Donruss Silver #170
2020 Donruss Timeless Treasures Material Signatures Holo Black /1 #1
2020 Donruss Timeless Treasures Material Signatures Holo Gold /8 #1
2020 Donruss Timeless Treasures Material Signatures Red /25 #1
2020 Donruss Timeless Treasures Signatures Holo Black /1 #10
2020 Donruss Timeless Treasures Signatures Holo Gold /8 #10
2020 Donruss Timeless Treasures Signatures Red /25 #10
2020 Donruss Top Tier #3
2020 Donruss Top Tier Checkers #3
2020 Donruss Top Tier Cracked Ice /25 #3
2020 Donruss Top Tier Holographic /199 #3
2020 Donruss Top Tier Xplosion /10 #3

Carl Edwards

2003 Press Pass Signings #19
2003 Press Pass Signings Gold /50 #19
2003 Press Pass Trackside #48
2003 Press Pass Trackside Gold Holofoil #P48
2003 Press Pass Trackside Samples #48
2004 Press Pass #51
2004 Press Pass Autographs #18
2004 Press Pass Optima #42
2004 Press Pass Optima Gold #G42
2004 Press Pass Optima Previews /5 #EB42
2004 Press Pass Optima Samples #42
2004 Press Pass Platinum #P51
2004 Press Pass Samples #51
2004 Press Pass Signings #18
2004 Press Pass Signings Gold /50 #17
2004 Wheels Autographs #19
2005 Press Pass #57
2005 Press Pass Autographs #16
2005 Press Pass Eclipse Teammates Autographs /25 #8
2005 Press Pass Optima #9
2005 Press Pass Optima #9B
2005 Press Pass Optima #32
2005 Press Pass Optima #50
2005 Press Pass Optima #61
2005 Press Pass Optima #84
2005 Press Pass Optima #NNO
2005 Press Pass Optima Cool Persistence #CP6
2005 Press Pass Optima Fan Favorite #FF7
2005 Press Pass Optima Gold /100 #G9
2005 Press Pass Optima Gold /100 #G32
2005 Press Pass Optima Gold /100 #G50
2005 Press Pass Optima Gold /100 #G61
2005 Press Pass Optima Gold /100 #G84
2005 Press Pass Optima Previews /5 #9
2005 Press Pass Optima Previews /5 #32
2005 Press Pass Optima Previews /1 #50
2005 Press Pass Optima Q & A #QA4
2005 Press Pass Optima Samples #9
2005 Press Pass Optima Samples #32
2005 Press Pass Optima Samples #50
2005 Press Pass Optima Samples #61
2005 Press Pass Optima Samples #84
2005 Press Pass Platinum /100 #P57
2005 Press Pass Premium #6
2005 Press Pass Premium Samples #6
2005 Press Pass Samples #57
2005 Press Pass Signings #15
2005 Press Pass Signings #14
2005 Press Pass Signings Gold /50 #13
2005 Press Pass Signings Gold /50 #14
2005 Press Pass Signings Platinum /100 #13
2005 Press Pass Signings Platinum /100 #14
2005 Press Pass Snapshots #SN6
2005 Press Pass Top Prospects Memorabilia /50 #CESM
2005 Press Pass Top Prospects Memorabilia /350 #CET
2005 Press Pass Top Prospects Memorabilia /100 #CEG
2005 Press Pass Top Prospects Memorabilia /200 #CES
2005 Press Pass Trackside #28
2005 Press Pass Trackside #28B
2005 Press Pass Trackside Golden /100 #G28
2005 Press Pass Trackside Hat Giveaway #PPH7
2005 Press Pass Trackside Previews /5 #28
2005 Press Pass Trackside Samples #28
2005 Press Pass UMI Cup Chase #1
2005 Press Pass UMI Cup Chase #10
2005 VIP #6
2005 VIP #46
2005 VIP Head Gear #8
2005 VIP Head Gear Transparent #8
2005 VIP Previews /5 #EB6
2005 VIP Samples #6
2005 VIP Samples #46
2005 Wheels American Thunder #7
2005 Wheels American Thunder #55
2005 Wheels American Thunder #64
2005 Wheels American Thunder #87
2005 Wheels American Thunder #90
2005 Wheels American Thunder American Muscle #AM5
2005 Wheels American Thunder Double Hat /190 #DH3
2005 Wheels American Thunder Head to Toe /125 #HT1
2005 Wheels American Thunder License to Drive #1
2005 Wheels American Thunder Previews /5 #7
2005 Wheels American Thunder Previews /1 #87
2005 Wheels American Thunder Pushin Pedal /150 #PP9
2005 Wheels American Thunder Samples #7
2005 Wheels American Thunder Samples #55
2005 Wheels American Thunder Samples #64
2005 Wheels American Thunder Samples #87
2005 Wheels American Thunder Samples #90
2005 Wheels American Thunder Thunder Road #TR13
2006 Press Pass #30
2006 Press Pass #42
2006 Press Pass #69
2006 Press Pass #83
2006 Press Pass #87
2006 Press Pass #101
2006 Press Pass #116
2006 Press Pass Autographs #13
2006 Press Pass Autographs #14
2006 Press Pass Blaster Kmart #CEC
2006 Press Pass Blaster Target #CEB
2006 Press Pass Blaster Wal-Mart #CEA
2006 Press Pass Blue #B30
2006 Press Pass Blue #B42
2006 Press Pass Blue #B69
2006 Press Pass Blue #B83

2006 Press Pass Blue #B87
2006 Press Pass Blue #B101
2006 Press Pass Blue #B116
2006 Press Pass Burning Rubber Autographs /99 #BRCE
2006 Press Pass Burning Rubber Cars /370 #BRT4
2006 Press Pass Burning Rubber Drivers /100 #BRD4
2006 Press Pass Burning Rubber Drivers Gold /1 #BRD4
2006 Press Pass Burnouts /900 #HT7
2006 Press Pass Burnouts Holofoil /100 #HT7
2006 Press Pass Collectors Series Making the Show #MS11
2006 Press Pass Cup Chase #CCR6
2006 Press Pass Double Burner Firesuit-Glove /100 #DB7
2006 Press Pass Double Burner Metal-Tire /100 #DB1
2006 Press Pass Eclipse #3
2006 Press Pass Eclipse #30
2006 Press Pass Eclipse #57
2006 Press Pass Eclipse #64
2006 Press Pass Eclipse #76
2006 Press Pass Eclipse #88
2006 Press Pass Eclipse #57B
2006 Press Pass Eclipse #65
2006 Press Pass Eclipse #69
2006 Press Pass Eclipse Hyperdrive #HP1
2006 Press Pass Eclipse Previews /5 #EB3
2006 Press Pass Eclipse Previews /5 #EB30
2006 Press Pass Eclipse Racing Champions #RC4
2006 Press Pass Eclipse Racing Champions #RC18
2006 Press Pass Eclipse Skidmarks #SM15
2006 Press Pass Eclipse Skidmarks Holofoil /250 #SM15
2006 Press Pass Eclipse Supernova #SU7
2006 Press Pass Eclipse Teammates Autographs /25 #3
2006 Press Pass Eclipse Under Cover Cars /140 #UCT10
2006 Press Pass Eclipse Under Cover Double Cover /100 #DC6
2006 Press Pass Eclipse Under Cover Double Cover /100 #DC7
2006 Press Pass Eclipse Under Cover Double Cover /100 #DC9
2006 Press Pass Eclipse Under Cover Double Cover Holofoil /25 #DC6
2006 Press Pass Eclipse Under Cover Double Cover Holofoil /25 #DC7
2006 Press Pass Eclipse Under Cover Double Cover Holofoil /25 #DC9
2006 Press Pass Eclipse Under Cover Drivers Gold /1 #UCD10
2006 Press Pass Eclipse Under Cover Drivers Holofoil /100 #UCD10
2006 Press Pass Eclipse Under Cover Drivers Red /225 #UCD10
2006 Press Pass Eclipse Under Cover Drivers Silver /400 #UCD10
2006 Press Pass Gold #G30
2006 Press Pass Gold #G42
2006 Press Pass Gold #G69
2006 Press Pass Gold #G83
2006 Press Pass Gold #G87
2006 Press Pass Gold #G101
2006 Press Pass Gold #G116
2006 Press Pass Legends #44
2006 Press Pass Legends Autographs Black /50 #22
2006 Press Pass Legends Blue /1999 #B44
2006 Press Pass Legends Bronze /999 #Z44
2006 Press Pass Legends Gold /299 #G44
2006 Press Pass Legends Holofoil /99 #H44
2006 Press Pass Legends Press Plates Black /1 #PPB44
2006 Press Pass Legends Press Plates Black Backs /1 #PPB44B
2006 Press Pass Legends Press Plates Cyan /1 #PPC44
2006 Press Pass Legends Press Plates Cyan Backs /1 #PPC44B
2006 Press Pass Legends Press Plates Magenta /1 #PPM44
2006 Press Pass Legends Press Plates Magenta Backs /1 #PPM44B
2006 Press Pass Legends Press Plates Yellow /1 #PPY44
2006 Press Pass Legends Press Plates Yellow Backs /1 #PPY44B
2006 Press Pass Legends Previews /5 #EB44
2006 Press Pass Legends Solo /1 #S44
2006 Press Pass Legends Triple Threads /50 #TTCE
2006 Press Pass Optima #33
2006 Press Pass Optima #43
2006 Press Pass Optima Fan Favorite #FF5
2006 Press Pass Optima Gold /100 #G33
2006 Press Pass Optima Gold /100 #G43
2006 Press Pass Optima Previews /5 #EB33
2006 Press Pass Platinum /100 #P30
2006 Press Pass Platinum /100 #P42
2006 Press Pass Platinum /100 #P69
2006 Press Pass Platinum /100 #P83
2006 Press Pass Platinum /100 #P87
2006 Press Pass Platinum /100 #P101
2006 Press Pass Platinum /100 #P116
2006 Press Pass Premium #7
2006 Press Pass Premium #41
2006 Press Pass Premium #60
2006 Press Pass Premium #79
2006 Press Pass Premium Hot Threads Cars /165 #HTT4
2006 Press Pass Premium Hot Threads Drivers /220 #HTD4
2006 Press Pass Premium Hot Threads Drivers Gold /1 #HTD4
2006 Press Pass Premium In the Zone #IZ2
2006 Press Pass Premium In the Zone Red /250 #IZ2
2006 Press Pass Previews /5 #EB30
2006 Press Pass Previews /5 #EB42
2006 Press Pass Previews /1 #EB101
2006 Press Pass Signings #15
2006 Press Pass Signings Red Ink #15
2006 Press Pass Signings Silver /100 #15
2006 Press Pass Stealth #7
2006 Press Pass Stealth #46
2006 Press Pass Stealth #62
2006 Press Pass Stealth #72
2006 Press Pass Stealth #48
2006 Press Pass Stealth Autographed Hat Entry #PPH6
2006 Press Pass Stealth Corporate Cuts /250 #CCD4
2006 Press Pass Stealth EFX #EFX8
2006 Press Pass Stealth Gear Grippers Cars Retail /99 #GGT17
2006 Press Pass Stealth Gear Grippers Drivers /99 #GGD17
2006 Press Pass Stealth Hot Pass #HP8
2006 Press Pass Stealth Previews /5 #7
2006 Press Pass Stealth Retail #7
2006 Press Pass Stealth Retail #46
2006 Press Pass Stealth Retail #62
2006 Press Pass Stealth Retail #72
2006 Press Pass Stealth Retail #48
2006 Press Pass Stealth X-Ray /100 #X7
2006 Press Pass Stealth X-Ray /100 #X46
2006 Press Pass Stealth X-Ray /100 #X48
2006 Press Pass Stealth X-Ray /100 #X62
2006 Press Pass Stealth X-Ray /100 #X72
2006 Press Pass Top 25 Drivers & Rides #C25
2006 Press Pass Top 25 Drivers & Rides #D25
2006 Press Pass Velocity #VE3
2006 TRAKS #8
2006 TRAKS #54
2006 TRAKS #109
2006 TRAKS Autographs #9
2006 TRAKS Previews /1 #8
2006 TRAKS Previews /1 #54
2006 TRAKS Previews /1 #109
2006 TRAKS Stickers #99
2006 VIP #6
2006 VIP #36
2006 VIP #56
2006 VIP #85
2006 VIP Making the Show #MS11
2006 VIP Tradin' Paint Cars Bronze /145 #TPT5
2006 VIP Tradin' Paint Drivers Gold /50 #TPD5
2006 VIP Tradin' Paint Drivers Silver /80 #TPD5
2006 Wheels American Thunder #7
2006 Wheels American Thunder #36
2006 Wheels American Thunder #58
2006 Wheels American Thunder #78
2006 Wheels American Thunder Double Hat /99 #DH6
2006 Wheels American Thunder Grandstand #GS5
2006 Wheels American Thunder Head to Toe /99 #HT15
2006 Wheels American Thunder Previews /5 #EB7
2006 Wheels American Thunder Previews /1 #EB78
2006 Wheels American Thunder Pushin' Pedal /199 #PP12
2006 Wheels American Thunder Thunder Road #TR18
2006 Wheels Autographs #14
2006 Wheels Autographs #15
2006 Wheels High Gear #3
2006 Wheels High Gear #31
2006 Wheels High Gear #50
2006 Wheels High Gear #58
2006 Wheels High Gear #64
2006 Wheels High Gear Flag Chasers Black /110 #FC1
2006 Wheels High Gear Flag Chasers Blue-Yellow /65 #FC1
2006 Wheels High Gear Flag Chasers Checkered /3 #FC1
2006 Wheels High Gear Flag Chasers Green /110 #FC1
2006 Wheels High Gear Flag Chasers Red /110 #FC1
2006 Wheels High Gear Flag Chasers White /110 #FC1
2006 Wheels High Gear Flag Chasers Yellow /110 #FC1
2006 Wheels High Gear Flag to Flag #FF6
2006 Wheels High Gear MPH /100 #M3
2006 Wheels High Gear MPH /100 #M31
2006 Wheels High Gear MPH /100 #M50
2006 Wheels High Gear MPH /100 #M58
2006 Wheels High Gear MPH /100 #M64
2006 Wheels High Gear Previews Green /5 #EB3
2006 Wheels High Gear Previews Green /5 #EB31
2006 Wheels High Gear Top Tier #TT3
2007 Press Pass #13
2007 Press Pass #35
2007 Press Pass #82
2007 Press Pass #88
2007 Press Pass Autographs #12
2007 Press Pass Autographs Press Plates Magenta /1 #3
2007 Press Pass Autographs Press Plates Yellow /1 #40
2007 Press Pass Blue #B13
2007 Press Pass Blue #B35
2007 Press Pass Blue #B82
2007 Press Pass Blue #B88
2007 Press Pass Collector's Series Box Set #SB6
2007 Press Pass Cup Chase #CCR17
2007 Press Pass Cup Chase Prizes #CC4
2007 Press Pass Double Burner Firesuit-Glove /100 #DB9
2007 Press Pass Double Burner Firesuit-Glove Exchange /100 #DB9
2007 Press Pass Double Burner Metal-Tire /100 #DBCE
2007 Press Pass Double Burner Metal-Tire Exchange /100 #DBCE
2007 Press Pass Eclipse #12
2007 Press Pass Eclipse Ecliptic #EC12
2007 Press Pass Eclipse Gold /25 #G12
2007 Press Pass Eclipse Previews /5 #EB12
2007 Press Pass Eclipse Racing Champions #RC14
2007 Press Pass Eclipse Red /1 #R12
2007 Press Pass Eclipse Skidmarks #SM13
2007 Press Pass Eclipse Skidmarks Holofoil /250 #SM13
2007 Press Pass Eclipse Teammates Autographs /25 #6
2007 Press Pass Eclipse Under Cover Double Cover Name /25 #DC1
2007 Press Pass Eclipse Under Cover Double Cover Name /25 #DC5
2007 Press Pass Eclipse Under Cover Double Cover NASCAR /99 #DC1
2007 Press Pass Eclipse Under Cover Double Cover NASCAR /99 #DC5
2007 Press Pass Eclipse Under Cover Drivers /450 #UCD11
2007 Press Pass Eclipse Under Cover Drivers Eclipse /1 #UCD11
2007 Press Pass Eclipse Under Cover Drivers Name /99 #UCD11
2007 Press Pass Eclipse Under Cover Drivers NASCAR /270 #UCD11
2007 Press Pass Eclipse Under Cover Teams /135 #UCT11
2007 Press Pass Eclipse Under Cover Teams NASCAR /25 #UCT11
2007 Press Pass Gold #G13
2007 Press Pass Gold #G35
2007 Press Pass Gold #G82
2007 Press Pass Gold #G88
2007 Press Pass Legends #48
2007 Press Pass Legends Autographs Blue /71 #6
2007 Press Pass Legends Blue /999 #B48
2007 Press Pass Legends Bronze /599 #Z48
2007 Press Pass Legends Gold /249 #G48
2007 Press Pass Legends Holofoil /99 #H48
2007 Press Pass Legends Press Plates Black /1 #PP48
2007 Press Pass Legends Press Plates Black Backs /1 #PP48
2007 Press Pass Legends Press Plates Cyan /1 #PP48
2007 Press Pass Legends Press Plates Cyan Backs /1 #PP48
2007 Press Pass Legends Press Plates Magenta /1 #PP48
2007 Press Pass Legends Press Plates Magenta Backs /1 #PP48
2007 Press Pass Legends Press Plates Yellow /1 #PP48
2007 Press Pass Legends Press Plates Yellow Backs /1 #PP48
2007 Press Pass Legends Previews /5 #EB48
2007 Press Pass Legends Signature Series /25 #CE
2007 Press Pass Legends Solo /1 #S48
2007 Press Pass Platinum /100 #P13
2007 Press Pass Platinum /100 #P35
2007 Press Pass Platinum /100 #P82
2007 Press Pass Platinum /100 #P88
2007 Press Pass Premium #33
2007 Press Pass Premium #44
2007 Press Pass Premium #55
2007 Press Pass Premium Hot Threads Drivers /145 #HTD14
2007 Press Pass Premium Hot Threads Drivers Gold /1 #HTD14
2007 Press Pass Premium Hot Threads Patch /8 #HTP21
2007 Press Pass Premium Hot Threads Patch /8 #HTP20
2007 Press Pass Premium Hot Threads Team /160 #HTT14
2007 Press Pass Premium Red /15 #R33
2007 Press Pass Premium Red /15 #R44
2007 Press Pass Premium Red /15 #R55
2007 Press Pass Previews /5 #EB13
2007 Press Pass Previews /5 #EB35
2007 Press Pass Signings #18
2007 Press Pass Signings Gold /50 #15
2007 Press Pass Signings Silver /100 #14
2007 Press Pass Snapshots #SN6
2007 Press Pass Stealth #7
2007 Press Pass Stealth #39
2007 Press Pass Stealth #79
2007 Press Pass Stealth #69
2007 Press Pass Stealth Battle Armor Drivers /150 #BAD7
2007 Press Pass Stealth Battle Armor Teams /85 #BAT7
2007 Press Pass Stealth Chrome #7
2007 Press Pass Stealth Chrome #39
2007 Press Pass Stealth Chrome #79
2007 Press Pass Stealth Chrome #69
2007 Press Pass Stealth Chrome Exclusives /99 #X7
2007 Press Pass Stealth Chrome Exclusives /99 #X39
2007 Press Pass Stealth Chrome Exclusives /99 #X69
2007 Press Pass Stealth Chrome Exclusives /99 #X79
2007 Press Pass Stealth Chrome Platinum /25 #P7
2007 Press Pass Stealth Chrome Platinum /25 #P39
2007 Press Pass Stealth Chrome Platinum /25 #P69
2007 Press Pass Stealth Chrome Platinum /25 #P79
2007 Press Pass Stealth Maximum Access #MA7
2007 Press Pass Stealth Maximum Access Autographs /25 #MA7
2007 Press Pass Stealth Previews /5 #EB39
2007 Press Pass Stealth Previews /5 #EB7
2007 Press Pass Wal-Mart Autographs /50 #CE
2007 Traks #6
2007 Traks #56
2007 Traks Corporate Cuts Driver /99 #CCD10
2007 Traks Corporate Cuts Patch /12 #CCD10
2007 Traks Corporate Cuts Team /180 #CCT10
2007 Traks Driver's Seat #DS24B
2007 Traks Driver's Seat #DS24
2007 Traks Driver's Seat National #DS24
2007 Traks Gold #G6
2007 Traks Gold #G56
2007 Traks Holofoil /50 #H6
2007 Traks Holofoil /50 #H56
2007 Traks Hot Pursuit #HP6
2007 Traks Previews /5 #EB6
2007 Traks Red /10 #R6
2007 Traks Red /10 #R56
2007 VIP #8
2007 VIP #83
2007 VIP Get A Grip Drivers /70 #GGD2
2007 VIP Get A Grip Teams /70 #GGT2
2007 VIP Pedal To The Metal /50 #PM6
2007 VIP Previews /5 #EB8
2007 VIP Sunday Best #SB6
2007 Wheels American Thunder #8
2007 Wheels American Thunder #49
2007 Wheels American Thunder #64
2007 Wheels American Thunder American Dreams #AD9
2007 Wheels American Thunder American Dreams Gold /250 #ADG9
2007 Wheels American Thunder Autographed Hat Instant Winner /1 #AH9
2007 Wheels American Thunder Cool Threads /299 #CT10
2007 Wheels American Thunder Previews /5 #EB8
2007 Wheels American Thunder Previews /1 #EB49
2007 Wheels American Thunder Pushin' Pedal /99 #PP8
2007 Wheels American Thunder Thunder Strokes #13
2007 Wheels American Thunder Thunder Strokes Press Plates Black /1 #13
2007 Wheels American Thunder Thunder Strokes Press Plates Cyan /1 #13
2007 Wheels American Thunder Thunder Strokes Press Plates Magenta /1 #13
2007 Wheels American Thunder Thunder Strokes Press Plates Yellow /1 #13
2007 Wheels American Thunder Triple Hat /99 #TH7
2007 Wheels Autographs #11
2007 Wheels Autographs Press Plates Black /1 #10
2007 Wheels Autographs Press Plates Cyan /1 #10
2007 Wheels Autographs Press Plates Magenta /1 #10
2007 Wheels High Gear #13
2007 Wheels High Gear #33
2007 Wheels High Gear #74
2007 Wheels High Gear Driven #DR20
2007 Wheels High Gear Final Standings Gold /12 #FS13
2007 Wheels High Gear Flag Chasers Black /89 #FC2
2007 Wheels High Gear Flag Chasers Blue-Yellow /50 #FC2
2007 Wheels High Gear Flag Chasers Checkered /10 #FC2
2007 Wheels High Gear Flag Chasers Green /89 #FC2
2007 Wheels High Gear Flag Chasers Red /89 #FC2
2007 Wheels High Gear Flag Chasers White /89 #FC2
2007 Wheels High Gear Flag Chasers Yellow /89 #FC2
2007 Wheels High Gear MPH /100 #M13
2007 Wheels High Gear MPH /100 #M33
2007 Wheels High Gear MPH /100 #M74
2007 Wheels High Gear Previews /5 #EB13
2007 Wheels High Gear Previews /5 #EB33
2008 Press Pass #0
2008 Press Pass #5
2008 Press Pass #37
2008 Press Pass #110
2008 Press Pass Blue #B5
2008 Press Pass Blue #B37
2008 Press Pass Blue #B110
2008 Press Pass Burning Rubber Autographs /99 #BRCE
2008 Press Pass Burning Rubber Drivers /60 #BRD14
2008 Press Pass Burning Rubber Drivers /60 #BRD23
2008 Press Pass Burning Rubber Drivers Gold /1 #BRD14
2008 Press Pass Burning Rubber Drivers Gold /1 #BRD23
2008 Press Pass Burning Rubber Drivers Prime Cuts /25 #BRD14
2008 Press Pass Burning Rubber Drivers Prime Cuts /25 #BRD23
2008 Press Pass Burning Rubber Teams /175 #BRT14
2008 Press Pass Burning Rubber Teams /175 #BRT23
2008 Press Pass Burnouts #BO2
2008 Press Pass Burnouts Blue /99 #BO2
2008 Press Pass Burnouts Gold /299 #BO2
2008 Press Pass Collector's Series Box Set #2
2008 Press Pass Cup Chase #CC15
2008 Press Pass Cup Chase Prizes #CC2
2008 Press Pass Double Burner Firesuit-Glove /100 #DBCE
2008 Press Pass Double Burner Metal-Tire /100 #DBCE
2008 Press Pass Eclipse #8
2008 Press Pass Eclipse #47
2008 Press Pass Eclipse #58
2008 Press Pass Eclipse #76
2008 Press Pass Eclipse #75
2008 Press Pass Eclipse Gold /25 #G8
2008 Press Pass Eclipse Gold /25 #G47
2008 Press Pass Eclipse Gold /25 #G58
2008 Press Pass Eclipse Gold /25 #G75
2008 Press Pass Eclipse Gold /25 #G76
2008 Press Pass Eclipse Previews /5 #EB8
2008 Press Pass Eclipse Previews /1 #EB75
2008 Press Pass Eclipse Previews /1 #EB76
2008 Press Pass Eclipse Red /1 #R8
2008 Press Pass Eclipse Red /1 #R47
2008 Press Pass Eclipse Red /1 #R58
2008 Press Pass Eclipse Red /1 #R75
2008 Press Pass Eclipse Red /1 #R76
2008 Press Pass Eclipse Star Tracks #ST14
2008 Press Pass Eclipse Star Tracks Holofoil /250 #ST14
2008 Press Pass Eclipse Stellar #ST3
2008 Press Pass Eclipse Stellar #ST17
2008 Press Pass Eclipse Under Cover Double Cover Name /25 #DC3
2008 Press Pass Eclipse Under Cover Double Cover Name /25 #DC7
2008 Press Pass Eclipse Under Cover Double Cover NASCAR /99 #DC3
2008 Press Pass Eclipse Under Cover Double Cover NASCAR /99 #DC7
2008 Press Pass Eclipse Under Cover Drivers /250 #UCD5
2008 Press Pass Eclipse Under Cover Drivers Eclipse /1 #UCD5
2008 Press Pass Eclipse Under Cover Drivers Name /50 #UCD5
2008 Press Pass Eclipse Under Cover Drivers NASCAR /150 #UCD5
2008 Press Pass Eclipse Under Cover Teams /99 #UCT5
2008 Press Pass Eclipse Under Cover Teams NASCAR /25 #UCT5
2008 Press Pass Four Wide /50 #FWCE
2008 Press Pass Four Wide Checkered Flag /1 #FWCE
2008 Press Pass Gillette Young Guns #3
2008 Press Pass Gold #G5
2008 Press Pass Gold #G37
2008 Press Pass Gold #G110
2008 Press Pass Hot Treads #HT6
2008 Press Pass Hot Treads Blue /99 #HT6
2008 Press Pass Hot Treads Gold /299 #HT6
2008 Press Pass Legends #48
2008 Press Pass Legends Autographs Black Inscriptions /9 #CE
2008 Press Pass Legends Autographs Blue /75 #CE
2008 Press Pass Legends Autographs Press Plates Black /1 #CE
2008 Press Pass Legends Autographs Press Plates Cyan /1 #CE
2008 Press Pass Legends Autographs Press Plates Magenta /1 #CE
2008 Press Pass Legends Autographs Press Plates Yellow /1 #CE
2008 Press Pass Legends Blue /599 #48
2008 Press Pass Legends Bronze /299 #48
2008 Press Pass Legends Gold /99 #48
2008 Press Pass Legends Holo /25 #48
2008 Press Pass Legends Previews /5 #EB48
2008 Press Pass Legends Printing Plates Black /1 #48
2008 Press Pass Legends Printing Plates Cyan /1 #48
2008 Press Pass Legends Printing Plates Magenta /1 #48
2008 Press Pass Legends Printing Plates Yellow /1 #48
2008 Press Pass Legends Prominent Pieces Firesuit-Glove Bronze /99 #PP1CE
2008 Press Pass Legends Prominent Pieces Firesuit-Glove Gold /10 #PP1CE
2008 Press Pass Legends Prominent Pieces Firesuit-Glove Silver /30 #PP1CE
2008 Press Pass Legends Prominent Pieces Metal-Tire-Net /50 #PP4CE
2008 Press Pass Legends Prominent Pieces Metal-Tire-Net Gold /25 #PP4CE
2008 Press Pass Legends Signature Series Memorabilia /25 #LSCE
2008 Press Pass Legends Solo /1 #48
2008 Press Pass Platinum /100 #P5
2008 Press Pass Platinum /100 #P37
2008 Press Pass Platinum /100 #P110
2008 Press Pass Premium #36
2008 Press Pass Premium #56
2008 Press Pass Premium #70
2008 Press Pass Premium #78
2008 Press Pass Premium #86
2008 Press Pass Premium Hot Threads Drivers /120 #HTD8
2008 Press Pass Premium Hot Threads Drivers Gold /1 #HTD8
2008 Press Pass Premium Hot Threads Patches #HTP4
2008 Press Pass Premium Hot Threads Patches /6 #HTP3
2008 Press Pass Premium Hot Threads Patches #HTP2
2008 Press Pass Premium Hot Threads Team /120 #HTT8
2008 Press Pass Premium Previews /5 #EB36
2008 Press Pass Premium Previews /1 #EB56
2008 Press Pass Premium Red /15 #36
2008 Press Pass Premium Red /15 #56
2008 Press Pass Premium Red /15 #70
2008 Press Pass Premium Red /5 #78
2008 Press Pass Premium Red /5 #86
2008 Press Pass Premium Team Signed Baseballs #ROU
2008 Press Pass Premium Team Signed Baseballs #EROU
2008 Press Pass Premium Wal-Mart #WM4
2008 Press Pass Previews /5 #EB5
2008 Press Pass Previews /1 #EB110
2008 Press Pass Race Day #RD11
2008 Press Pass Signings #19
2008 Press Pass Signings Gold /50 #17
2008 Press Pass Signings Press Plates Black /1 #12
2008 Press Pass Signings Press Plates Cyan /1 #12
2008 Press Pass Signings Press Plates Magenta /1 #12
2008 Press Pass Signings Press Plates Yellow /1 #12
2008 Press Pass Signings Silver /100 #18
2008 Press Pass Speedway #22
2008 Press Pass Speedway #45
2008 Press Pass Speedway #79
2008 Press Pass Speedway #90
2008 Press Pass Speedway #95
2008 Press Pass Speedway Corporate Cuts Drivers /80 #CDCE
2008 Press Pass Speedway Corporate Cuts Drivers Patches /13 #CDCE
2008 Press Pass Speedway Corporate Cuts Team /165 #CTCE
2008 Press Pass Speedway Gold #G22
2008 Press Pass Speedway Gold #G45
2008 Press Pass Speedway Gold #G79
2008 Press Pass Speedway Gold #G90
2008 Press Pass Speedway Gold #G95
2008 Press Pass Speedway Holofoil /50 #H22
2008 Press Pass Speedway Holofoil /50 #H45
2008 Press Pass Speedway Holofoil /50 #H79
2008 Press Pass Speedway Holofoil /50 #H90
2008 Press Pass Speedway Holofoil /50 #H95
2008 Press Pass Speedway Previews /5 #EB22
2008 Press Pass Speedway Previews /5 #EB45
2008 Press Pass Speedway Previews /1 #EB95
2008 Press Pass Speedway Red /10 #R22
2008 Press Pass Speedway Red /10 #R45
2008 Press Pass Speedway Red /10 #R79
2008 Press Pass Speedway Red /10 #R90
2008 Press Pass Speedway Red /10 #R95
2008 Press Pass Speedway Test Drive #TD10
2008 Press Pass Starting Grid #SG2
2008 Press Pass Stealth #9
2008 Press Pass Stealth #39
2008 Press Pass Stealth #54
2008 Press Pass Stealth #76
2008 Press Pass Stealth #70
2008 Press Pass Stealth Battle Armor Drivers /120 #BAD5
2008 Press Pass Stealth Battle Armor Teams /115 #BAT5
2008 Press Pass Stealth Chrome #9
2008 Press Pass Stealth Chrome #39
2008 Press Pass Stealth Chrome #54
2008 Press Pass Stealth Chrome #76
2008 Press Pass Stealth Chrome #70
2008 Press Pass Stealth Chrome Exclusives /25 #9
2008 Press Pass Stealth Chrome Exclusives /25 #39
2008 Press Pass Stealth Chrome Exclusives /25 #54
2008 Press Pass Stealth Chrome Exclusives /25 #70
2008 Press Pass Stealth Chrome Exclusives /25 #76
2008 Press Pass Stealth Chrome Exclusives Gold /99 #9
2008 Press Pass Stealth Chrome Exclusives Gold /99 #39
2008 Press Pass Stealth Chrome Exclusives Gold /99 #54
2008 Press Pass Stealth Chrome Exclusives Gold /99 #70
2008 Press Pass Stealth Chrome Exclusives Gold /99 #76
2008 Press Pass Stealth Maximum Access #MA9
2008 Press Pass Stealth Maximum Access Autographs /25 #MA9
2008 Press Pass Stealth Previews /5 #9
2008 Press Pass Stealth Previews /5 #39
2008 Press Pass Stealth Target #TA10
2008 Press Pass Target Victory Tires /50 #TTCE
2008 Press Pass VIP National Convention Promo #5
2008 Press Pass Wal-Mart Autographs /50 #2
2008 VIP #10
2008 VIP #66
2008 VIP #67
2008 VIP #71
2008 VIP Gear Gallery #GG6
2008 VIP Gear Gallery Memorabilia /50 #GGCE
2008 VIP Gear Gallery Transparent #GG6
2008 VIP Get a Grip Drivers /80 #GGD7
2008 VIP Get a Grip Teams /99 #GGT7
2008 VIP National Promos #5
2008 VIP Previews /5 #EB10
2008 VIP Triple Grip /25 #TG3
2008 VIP Trophy Club #TC7
2008 VIP Trophy Club Transparent #TC7
2008 Wheels American Thunder #10
2008 Wheels American Thunder #38
2008 Wheels American Thunder Autographed Hat Winner /1 #WHCE
2008 Wheels American Thunder Campaign Buttons #CE
2008 Wheels American Thunder Campaign Buttons Blue #CE
2008 Wheels American Thunder Campaign Buttons Gold #CE
2008 Wheels American Thunder Cool Threads /325 #CT6
2008 Wheels American Thunder Head to Toe /125 #HT8
2008 Wheels American Thunder Previews /5 #10
2008 Wheels American Thunder Pushin' Pedal /99 #PP 8
2008 Wheels American Thunder Triple Hat /125 #TH8
2008 Wheels High Gear #9
2008 Wheels High Gear #32
2008 Wheels High Gear #54
2008 Wheels High Gear #72A
2008 Wheels High Gear #72B
2008 Wheels High Gear Driven #DR25
2008 Wheels High Gear Final Standings /9 #F9
2008 Wheels High Gear Flag Chasers Black /89 #FC7
2008 Wheels High Gear Flag Chasers Blue-Yellow /50 #FC7
2008 Wheels High Gear Flag Chasers Checkered /20 #FC7
2008 Wheels High Gear Flag Chasers Green /60 #FC7
2008 Wheels High Gear Flag Chasers Red /89 #FC7
2008 Wheels High Gear Flag Chasers White /65 #FC7
2008 Wheels High Gear Flag Chasers Yellow /89 #FC7
2008 Wheels High Gear Full Throttle #FT5
2008 Wheels High Gear Last Lap /10 #LL3
2008 Wheels High Gear Last Lap Holofoil /5 #LL3
2008 Wheels High Gear MPH /100 #M9
2008 Wheels High Gear MPH /100 #M32
2008 Wheels High Gear MPH /100 #M54
2008 Wheels High Gear MPH /100 #M72
2008 Wheels High Gear Previews /5 #EB9
2008 Wheels High Gear The Chase #TC9
2009 Element #8
2009 Element #40
2009 Element #52
2009 Element #55
2009 Element #76
2009 Element #80
2009 Element #94
2009 Element 1-2-3 Finish /50 #RFR
2009 Element Big Win /35 #BWCE
2009 Element Elements of the Race Black Flag /99 #ERBCE
2009 Element Elements of the Race Black-White Flag /50 #ERXCE
2009 Element Elements of the Race Blue-Yellow Flag /50 #ERBOCE
2009 Element Elements of the Race Checkered Flag /5 #ERCCE
2009 Element Elements of the Race Green Flag /50 #ERGCE
2009 Element Elements of the Race Red Flag /99 #ERRCE
2009 Element Elements of the Race White Flag /75 #ERWCE
2009 Element Elements of the Race Yellow Flag /99 #ERYCE
2009 Element Green White Checker /25 #GWCCE
2009 Element Kinetic Energy #KE3
2009 Element Lab Report #LR9
2009 Element Nobel Prize #NP1
2009 Element Previews /5 #8
2009 Element Previews /1 #52
2009 Element Radioactive /100 #8
2009 Element Radioactive /100 #40
2009 Element Radioactive /100 #52
2009 Element Radioactive /100 #55
2009 Element Radioactive /100 #76
2009 Element Radioactive /100 #80
2009 Element Radioactive /100 #94
2009 Element Taking the Checkers /45 #TCCE
2009 Element Taking the Checkers /45 #TCCE
2009 Press Pass #0
2009 Press Pass #2
2009 Press Pass #43
2009 Press Pass #58
2009 Press Pass #71
2009 Press Pass #78
2009 Press Pass #81
2009 Press Pass #108
2009 Press Pass #128
2009 Press Pass #160
2009 Press Pass #183
2009 Press Pass #212
2009 Press Pass Autographs Chase Edition /25 #CE
2009 Press Pass Autographs Gold #13
2009 Press Pass Autographs Silver #17
2009 Press Pass Autographs Track Edition /25 #CE
2009 Press Pass Blue #2
2009 Press Pass Blue #43
2009 Press Pass Blue #58
2009 Press Pass Blue #71
2009 Press Pass Blue #78
2009 Press Pass Blue #81
2009 Press Pass Blue #108
2009 Press Pass Blue #128
2009 Press Pass Blue #160
2009 Press Pass Blue #183
2009 Press Pass Blue #212
2009 Press Pass Burning Rubber Drivers /185 #BRD2
2009 Press Pass Burning Rubber Drivers /185 #BRD3
2009 Press Pass Burning Rubber Drivers /185 #BRD7
2009 Press Pass Burning Rubber Drivers /185 #BRD21
2009 Press Pass Burning Rubber Drivers /185 #BRD23
2009 Press Pass Burning Rubber Drivers /185 #BRD24
2009 Press Pass Burning Rubber Drivers /320 #BRD33
2009 Press Pass Burning Rubber Drivers /320 #BRD34
2009 Press Pass Burning Rubber Drivers /320 #BRD36
2009 Press Pass Burning Rubber Prime Cut /25 #BRD2
2009 Press Pass Burning Rubber Prime Cut /25 #BRD3
2009 Press Pass Burning Rubber Prime Cut /25 #BRD7
2009 Press Pass Burning Rubber Prime Cut /25 #BRD21
2009 Press Pass Burning Rubber Prime Cut /25 #BRD23
2009 Press Pass Burning Rubber Prime Cut /25 #BRD24
2009 Press Pass Burning Rubber Prime Cut /25 #BRD33
2009 Press Pass Burning Rubber Prime Cut /25 #BRD34
2009 Press Pass Burning Rubber Prime Cut /25 #BRD36
2009 Press Pass Burning Rubber Teams /250 #BRT2
2009 Press Pass Burning Rubber Teams /250 #BRT3
2009 Press Pass Burning Rubber Teams /250 #BRT7
2009 Press Pass Burning Rubber Teams /250 #BRT21
2009 Press Pass Burning Rubber Teams /250 #BRT23
2009 Press Pass Burning Rubber Teams /250 #BRT24
2009 Press Pass Burning Rubber Teams /85 #BRT33
2009 Press Pass Burning Rubber Teams /85 #BRT34
2009 Press Pass Burning Rubber Teams /85 #BRT36
2009 Press Pass Chase for the Sprint Cup #CC9
2009 Press Pass Cup Chase #CCR6
2009 Press Pass Cup Chase Prizes #CC9
2009 Press Pass Daytona 500 Tires /25 #TTCE
2009 Press Pass Eclipse #29
2009 Press Pass Eclipse #49
2009 Press Pass Eclipse #59
2009 Press Pass Eclipse #72
2009 Press Pass Eclipse #89
2009 Press Pass Eclipse Black and White #29
2009 Press Pass Eclipse Black and White #49
2009 Press Pass Eclipse Black and White #59
2009 Press Pass Eclipse Black and White #72
2009 Press Pass Eclipse Black and White #89
2009 Press Pass Eclipse Blue #29
2009 Press Pass Eclipse Blue #49
2009 Press Pass Eclipse Blue #59
2009 Press Pass Eclipse Blue #72
2009 Press Pass Eclipse Blue #89
2009 Press Pass Eclipse Ecliptic Path #EP9
2009 Press Pass Eclipse Solar Swatches /299 #SSCE4
2009 Press Pass Eclipse Solar Swatches /299 #SSCE1
2009 Press Pass Eclipse Solar Swatches /50 #SSCE3
2009 Press Pass Eclipse Solar Swatches /99 #SSCE5
2009 Press Pass Eclipse Solar Swatches /299 #SSCE2
2009 Press Pass Eclipse Solar Swatches /250 #SSCE6
2009 Press Pass Eclipse Solar Swatches /299 #SSCE7
2009 Press Pass Eclipse Solar System #SS2
2009 Press Pass Final Standings /99 #108
2009 Press Pass Four Wide Autographs /5 #FWCE2
2009 Press Pass Four Wide Checkered Flag /1 #FWCE
2009 Press Pass Four Wide Firesuit /50 #FWCE
2009 Press Pass Four Wide Sheet Metal /10 #FWCE
2009 Press Pass Four Wide Tire /25 #FWCE2
2009 Press Pass Four Wide Tire /25 #FWCE
2009 Press Pass Freeze Frame #FF16
2009 Press Pass Fusion #67
2009 Press Pass Fusion Bronze /150 #67
2009 Press Pass Fusion Gold /50 #67
2009 Press Pass Fusion Green /25 #67
2009 Press Pass Fusion Onyx /1 #67
2009 Press Pass Fusion Revered Relics Gold /50 #RRCE
2009 Press Pass Fusion Revered Relics Holofoil /25 #RRCE
2009 Press Pass Fusion Revered Relics Premium Swatch /10 #RRCE
2009 Press Pass Fusion Revered Relics Silver /65 #RRCE
2009 Press Pass Fusion Silver /99 #67
2009 Press Pass Game Face #GF3
2009 Press Pass Gold #2
2009 Press Pass Gold #43
2009 Press Pass Gold #58
2009 Press Pass Gold #71
2009 Press Pass Gold #78
2009 Press Pass Gold #81
2009 Press Pass Gold #108
2009 Press Pass Gold #128
2009 Press Pass Gold #160
2009 Press Pass Gold #183
2009 Press Pass Gold #212
2009 Press Pass Gold Holofoil /100 #2
2009 Press Pass Gold Holofoil /100 #43
2009 Press Pass Gold Holofoil /100 #58
2009 Press Pass Gold Holofoil /100 #71
2009 Press Pass Gold Holofoil /100 #78
2009 Press Pass Gold Holofoil /100 #81
2009 Press Pass Gold Holofoil /100 #108
2009 Press Pass Gold Holofoil /100 #128
2009 Press Pass Gold Holofoil /100 #160
2009 Press Pass Gold Holofoil /100 #183
2009 Press Pass Gold Holofoil /100 #212
2009 Press Pass Legends #44
2009 Press Pass Legends Gold /399 #44
2009 Press Pass Legends Holofoil /50 #44
2009 Press Pass Legends Past and Present /550 #PP7
2009 Press Pass Legends Past and Present /550 #PP10
2009 Press Pass Legends Past and Present Holofoil /99 #PP7
2009 Press Pass Legends Past and Present Holofoil /99 #PP10
2009 Press Pass Legends Previews /5 #44
2009 Press Pass Legends Printing Plates Black /1 #44
2009 Press Pass Legends Printing Plates Cyan /1 #44
2009 Press Pass Legends Printing Plates Magenta /1 #44
2009 Press Pass Legends Printing Plates Yellow /1 #44
2009 Press Pass Legends Prominent Pieces Bronze /99 #PPCE
2009 Press Pass Legends Prominent Pieces Gold /25 #PPCE
2009 Press Pass Legends Prominent Pieces Oversized /25 #PPOECE
2009 Press Pass Legends Prominent Pieces Silver /50 #PPCE
2009 Press Pass Legends Red /199 #44
2009 Press Pass Legends Solo /1 #44
2009 Press Pass NASCAR Gallery #NG5
2009 Press Pass Pocket Portraits #P7
2009 Press Pass Pocket Portraits Checkered Flag #P7
2009 Press Pass Pocket Portraits Hometown #P7
2009 Press Pass Pocket Portraits Smoke #P7
2009 Press Pass Pocket Portraits Wal-Mart #PPW3
2009 Press Pass Premium #35
2009 Press Pass Premium #50
2009 Press Pass Premium #60
2009 Press Pass Premium #66
2009 Press Pass Premium Hot Threads /325 #HTCE1
2009 Press Pass Premium Hot Threads /99 #HTCE2
2009 Press Pass Premium Hot Threads Multi-Color /25 #HTCE
2009 Press Pass Premium Previews /5 #EB35
2009 Press Pass Premium Signatures #10
2009 Press Pass Premium Signatures Gold /25 #10
2009 Press Pass Premium Top Contenders #TC7
2009 Press Pass Premium Top Contenders Gold #TC7
2009 Press Pass Premium Win Streak #WS2
2009 Press Pass Premium Win Streak Victory Lane #WSVL-CE
2009 Press Pass Previews /5 #EB2
2009 Press Pass Previews /1 #EB108
2009 Press Pass Previews /5 #EB128
2009 Press Pass Red #2
2009 Press Pass Red #43
2009 Press Pass Red #58
2009 Press Pass Red #71
2009 Press Pass Red #78
2009 Press Pass Red #81
2009 Press Pass Red #108
2009 Press Pass Red #128
2009 Press Pass Red #160
2009 Press Pass Red #183
2009 Press Pass Red #212
2009 Press Pass Santa Hats /50 #SH6
2009 Press Pass Showcase /499 #22
2009 Press Pass Showcase /499 #35
2009 Press Pass Showcase /499 #42
2009 Press Pass Showcase 2nd Gear /125 #22
2009 Press Pass Showcase 2nd Gear /125 #35
2009 Press Pass Showcase 2nd Gear /125 #42
2009 Press Pass Showcase 3rd Gear /50 #22
2009 Press Pass Showcase 3rd Gear /50 #35
2009 Press Pass Showcase 3rd Gear /50 #42
2009 Press Pass Showcase 4th Gear /15 #22
2009 Press Pass Showcase 4th Gear /15 #35
2009 Press Pass Showcase 4th Gear /15 #42
2009 Press Pass Showcase Classic Collections Firesuit /25 #CCF8
2009 Press Pass Showcase Classic Collections Firesuit Patch /5 #CCF8
2009 Press Pass Showcase Classic Collections Ink /45 #9
2009 Press Pass Showcase Classic Collections Ink Gold /25 #9
2009 Press Pass Showcase Classic Collections Ink Green /5 #9
2009 Press Pass Showcase Classic Collections Ink Melting /1 #9
2009 Press Pass Showcase Classic Collections Sheet Metal /45 #CCS8
2009 Press Pass Showcase Classic Collections Tire /99 #CCT8
2009 Press Pass Showcase Elite Exhibit Ink /45 #3
2009 Press Pass Showcase Elite Exhibit Ink Gold /25 #3
2009 Press Pass Showcase Elite Exhibit Ink Green /5 #3
2009 Press Pass Showcase Elite Exhibit Ink Melting /1 #3
2009 Press Pass Showcase Elite Exhibit Triple Memorabilia /99 #EECE
2009 Press Pass Showcase Elite Exhibit Triple Memorabilia Gold /45 #EECE
2009 Press Pass Showcase Elite Exhibit Triple Memorabilia Green /25 #EECE
2009 Press Pass Showcase Elite Exhibit Triple Memorabilia Melting /5 #EECE
2009 Press Pass Showcase Printing Plates Black /1 #22
2009 Press Pass Showcase Printing Plates Black /1 #35
2009 Press Pass Showcase Printing Plates Black /1 #42
2009 Press Pass Showcase Printing Plates Cyan /1 #22
2009 Press Pass Showcase Printing Plates Cyan /1 #35
2009 Press Pass Showcase Printing Plates Cyan /1 #42
2009 Press Pass Showcase Printing Plates Magenta /1 #22
2009 Press Pass Showcase Printing Plates Magenta /1 #35
2009 Press Pass Showcase Printing Plates Magenta /1 #42
2009 Press Pass Showcase Printing Plates Yellow /1 #22
2009 Press Pass Showcase Printing Plates Yellow /1 #35
2009 Press Pass Showcase Printing Plates Yellow /1 #42
2009 Press Pass Showcase Prized Pieces Firesuit /25 #PPFCE
2009 Press Pass Showcase Prized Pieces Firesuit Patch /5 #PPFCE
2009 Press Pass Showcase Prized Pieces Ink Firesuit /5 #3
2009 Press Pass Showcase Prized Pieces Ink Firesuit Patch /1 #3
2009 Press Pass Showcase Prized Pieces Ink Sheet Metal /25 #3
2009 Press Pass Showcase Prized Pieces Ink Tire /45 #3
2009 Press Pass Showcase Prized Pieces Sheet Metal /45 #PPSCE
2009 Press Pass Showcase Prized Pieces Tire /99 #PPTCE
2009 Press Pass Sponsor Swatches /250 #SSCE
2009 Press Pass Sponsor Swatches Select /7 #SSCE
2009 Press Pass Stealth #10
2009 Press Pass Stealth #44
2009 Press Pass Stealth #54

2009 Press Pass Stealth #71A
2009 Press Pass Stealth #76
2009 Press Pass Stealth #71B
2009 Press Pass Stealth Battle Armor /185 #BACE1
2009 Press Pass Stealth Battle Armor /50 #BACE3
2009 Press Pass Stealth Battle Armor /115 #BACE2
2009 Press Pass Stealth Battle Armor Multi-Color /160 #BACE
2009 Press Pass Stealth Chrome #10
2009 Press Pass Stealth Chrome #44
2009 Press Pass Stealth Chrome #54
2009 Press Pass Stealth Chrome #71A
2009 Press Pass Stealth Chrome #76
2009 Press Pass Stealth Chrome #71B
2009 Press Pass Stealth Chrome Brushed Metal /25 #10
2009 Press Pass Stealth Chrome Brushed Metal /25 #44
2009 Press Pass Stealth Chrome Brushed Metal /25 #54
2009 Press Pass Stealth Chrome Brushed Metal /25 #71
2009 Press Pass Stealth Chrome Brushed Metal /25 #76
2009 Press Pass Stealth Chrome Gold /99 #10
2009 Press Pass Stealth Chrome Gold /99 #44
2009 Press Pass Stealth Chrome Gold /99 #54
2009 Press Pass Stealth Chrome Gold /99 #71
2009 Press Pass Stealth Chrome Gold /99 #76
2009 Press Pass Stealth Confidential Classified Bronze #PC4
2009 Press Pass Stealth Confidential Secret Silver #PC4
2009 Press Pass Stealth Confidential Top Secret Gold /25 #PC4
2009 Press Pass Stealth Mach 09 #M6
2009 Press Pass Stealth Previews /5 #EB10
2009 Press Pass Stealth Previews /1 #EB76
2009 Press Pass Target #CEB
2009 Press Pass Target Victory Tires /50 #CETT
2009 Press Pass Tread Marks Autographs /10 #SSCE
2009 Press Pass Unleashed #U3
2009 Press Pass Unleashed #U10
2009 Press Pass Wal-Mart #CEA
2009 Press Pass Wal-Mart Autographs Red #4
2009 Sportkings National Convention Memorabilia Gold /1 #SK5
2009 Sportkings National Convention Memorabilia Gold /1 #SK24
2009 Sportkings National Convention Memorabilia Gold /1 #SK43
2009 Sportkings National Convention Memorabilia Silver /9 #SK5
2009 Sportkings National Convention Memorabilia Silver /9 #SK24
2009 Sportkings National Convention Memorabilia Silver /9 #SK43
2009 VIP #9
2009 VIP #48
2009 VIP Get A Grip /120 #GGCE
2009 VIP Get A Grip Holofoil /10 #GGCE
2009 VIP Guest List #GG14
2009 VIP Hardware #H8
2009 VIP Hardware Transparent #H8
2009 VIP Leadfoot /150 #LFCE
2009 VIP Leadfoot Holofoil /10 #LFCE
2009 VIP Leadfoot Logos /5 #LFLCE
2009 VIP Previews /5 #9
2009 VIP Purple /25 #9
2009 VIP Purple /25 #48
2009 Wheels Autographs /25 #19
2009 Wheels Autographs #18
2009 Wheels Autographs Press Plates Black /1 #CE
2009 Wheels Autographs Press Plates Cyan /1 #CE
2009 Wheels Autographs Press Plates Magenta /1 #CE
2009 Wheels Autographs Press Plates Yellow /1 #CE
2009 Wheels Main Event #7
2009 Wheels Main Event #38
2009 Wheels Main Event #47
2009 Wheels Main Event #53
2009 Wheels Main Event #55
2009 Wheels Main Event #79
2009 Wheels Main Event Fast Pass Purple /25 #7
2009 Wheels Main Event Fast Pass Purple /25 #38
2009 Wheels Main Event Fast Pass Purple /25 #47
2009 Wheels Main Event Fast Pass Purple /25 #53
2009 Wheels Main Event Fast Pass Purple /25 #55
2009 Wheels Main Event Fast Pass Purple /25 #79
2009 Wheels Main Event Foil #7
2009 Wheels Main Event Hat Dance Patch /10 #HDCE
2009 Wheels Main Event Hat Dance Triple /99 #HDCE
2009 Wheels Main Event High Rollers #HR6
2009 Wheels Main Event Marks Clubs #18
2009 Wheels Main Event Marks Diamonds /10 #18
2009 Wheels Main Event Marks Hearts /5 #18
2009 Wheels Main Event Marks Printing Plates Black /1 #15
2009 Wheels Main Event Marks Printing Plates Cyan /1 #15
2009 Wheels Main Event Marks Printing Plates Magenta /1 #15
2009 Wheels Main Event Marks Printing Plates Yellow /1 #15
2009 Wheels Main Event Marks Spades /1 #18
2009 Wheels Main Event Playing Cards Blue #KD
2009 Wheels Main Event Playing Cards Blue #5C
2009 Wheels Main Event Playing Cards Red #KD
2009 Wheels Main Event Playing Cards Red #5C
2009 Wheels Main Event Poker Chips #9
2009 Wheels Main Event Previews /5 #7
2009 Wheels Main Event Renegade Rounders Wanted #RR1
2009 Wheels Main Event Reward Copper /10 #RWCE
2009 Wheels Main Event Reward Holofoil /50 #RWCE
2009 Wheels Main Event Stop and Go Swatches Pit Banner /175 #SGBCE
2009 Wheels Main Event Stop and Go Swatches Pit Banner Blue All Season's Sports Cards /1 #SGBCE
2009 Wheels Main Event Stop and Go Swatches Pit Banner Blue Arena /1 #SGBCE
2009 Wheels Main Event Stop and Go Swatches Pit Banner Blue Card Stadium /1 #SGBCE
2009 Wheels Main Event Stop and Go Swatches Pit Banner Blue Chicagoland Sportscards /1 #SGBCE
2009 Wheels Main Event Stop and Go Swatches Pit Banner Blue Chris Comics /1 #SGBCE
2009 Wheels Main Event Stop and Go Swatches Pit Banner Blue Chuck's Field of Dreams /1 #SGBCE
2009 Wheels Main Event Stop and Go Swatches Pit Banner Blue Collector's Heaven /1 #SGBCE
2009 Wheels Main Event Stop and Go Swatches Pit Banner Blue D&S Racing /1 #SGBCE
2009 Wheels Main Event Stop and Go Swatches Pit Banner Blue Dave's Pitstop /1 #SGBCE
2009 Wheels Main Event Stop and Go Swatches Pit Banner Blue Diamond King Sports /1 #SGBCE
2009 Wheels Main Event Stop and Go Swatches Pit Banner Blue Georgetown Card Exchange /1 #SGBCE
2009 Wheels Main Event Stop and Go Swatches Pit Banner Blue Jaimie's Field of Dreams /1 #SGBCE
2009 Wheels Main Event Stop and Go Swatches Pit Banner Blue Juniata Cards /1 #SGBCE
2009 Wheels Main Event Stop and Go Swatches Pit Banner Blue Main Steet Sportscards /1 #SGBCE
2009 Wheels Main Event Stop and Go Swatches Pit Banner Blue Matt's Sports Cards /1 #SGBCE
2009 Wheels Main Event Stop and Go Swatches Pit Banner Blue P&T Sportscards /1 #SGBCE
2009 Wheels Main Event Stop and Go Swatches Pit Banner Blue Republic Jewelry /1 #SGBCE
2009 Wheels Main Event Stop and Go Swatches Pit Banner Blue Ron's Racing /1 #SGBCE
2009 Wheels Main Event Stop and Go Swatches Pit Banner Blue Shelby Collectibles /1 #SGBCE
2009 Wheels Main Event Stop and Go Swatches Pit Banner Blue Spectator Sportscards /1 #SGBCE
2009 Wheels Main Event Stop and Go Swatches Pit Banner Blue Squeeze Play /1 #SGBCE
2009 Wheels Main Event Stop and Go Swatches Pit Banner Blue TBJ Sports Cards /1 #SGBCE
2009 Wheels Main Event Stop and Go Swatches Pit Banner Blue TCI Sports Fan /1 #SGBCE
2009 Wheels Main Event Stop and Go Swatches Pit Banner Blue The Card Cellar /1 #SGBCE
2009 Wheels Main Event Stop and Go Swatches Pit Banner Blue TJ Warner Ballcards /1 #SGBCE
2009 Wheels Main Event Stop and Go Swatches Pit Banner Blue Trademark Sports /1 #SGBCE
2009 Wheels Main Event Stop and Go Swatches Pit Banner Blue Triple I Sportscards /1 #SGBCE
2009 Wheels Main Event Stop and Go Swatches Pit Banner Blue Triple Play /1 #SGBCE
2009 Wheels Main Event Stop and Go Swatches Pit Banner Blue West Allis /1 #SGBCE
2009 Wheels Main Event Stop and Go Swatches Pit Banner Green /10 #SGBCE
2009 Wheels Main Event Stop and Go Swatches Pit Banner Holofoil /75 #SGBCE
2009 Wheels Main Event Stop and Go Swatches Pit Banner Red /25 #SGBCE
2009 Wheels Main Event Wildcard Cuts /2 #WCCCE
2010 Element #10
2010 Element #44
2010 Element #84
2010 Element 10 in '10 #TT8
2010 Element Blue /35 #10
2010 Element Blue /35 #44
2010 Element Blue /35 #84
2010 Element Flagship Performers Wins Black /20 #FPWCE
2010 Element Flagship Performers Wins Blue-Orange /20 #FPWCE
2010 Element Flagship Performers Wins Checkered /1 #FPWCE
2010 Element Flagship Performers Wins Green /5 #FPWCE
2010 Element Flagship Performers Wins Red /20 #FPWCE
2010 Element Flagship Performers Wins White /15 #FPWCE
2010 Element Flagship Performers Wins X /10 #FPWCE
2010 Element Flagship Performers Wins Yellow /20 #FPWCE
2010 Element Green #10
2010 Element Green #44
2010 Element Green #84
2010 Element Previews /5 #EB10
2010 Element Purple /25 #10
2010 Element Purple /25 #44
2010 Element Recycled Materials Blue /25 #RMCE
2010 Element Recycled Materials Green /125 #RMCE
2010 Element Red Target #10
2010 Element Red Target #44
2010 Element Red Target #84
2010 Press Pass #10
2010 Press Pass #38
2010 Press Pass #117
2010 Press Pass #69
2010 Press Pass #0
2010 Press Pass Autographs #15
2010 Press Pass Autographs Chase Edition /25 #3
2010 Press Pass Autographs Printing Plates Black /1 #11
2010 Press Pass Autographs Printing Plates Cyan /1 #14
2010 Press Pass Autographs Printing Plates Magenta /1 #11
2010 Press Pass Autographs Printing Plates Yellow /1 #11
2010 Press Pass Autographs Track Edition /10 #3
2010 Press Pass Blue #10
2010 Press Pass Blue #38
2010 Press Pass Blue #69
2010 Press Pass Blue #117
2010 Press Pass By The Numbers #BN22
2010 Press Pass Cup Chase #CCR9
2010 Press Pass Cup Chase Prizes #CC9
2010 Press Pass Eclipse #3
2010 Press Pass Eclipse #44
2010 Press Pass Eclipse #63
2010 Press Pass Eclipse Blue #3
2010 Press Pass Eclipse Blue #44
2010 Press Pass Eclipse Blue #63
2010 Press Pass Eclipse Cars #C9
2010 Press Pass Eclipse Decade #D4
2010 Press Pass Eclipse Gold #3
2010 Press Pass Eclipse Gold #44
2010 Press Pass Eclipse Gold #63
2010 Press Pass Eclipse Previews /5 #3
2010 Press Pass Eclipse Previews /1 #44
2010 Press Pass Eclipse Purple /25 #3
2010 Press Pass Eclipse Purple /25 #44
2010 Press Pass Eclipse Purple /25 #63
2010 Press Pass Eclipse Spellbound Swatches Holofoil /99 #SSCE2
2010 Press Pass Eclipse Spellbound Swatches Holofoil /99 #SSCE3
2010 Press Pass Eclipse Spellbound Swatches Holofoil /99 #SSCE4
2010 Press Pass Eclipse Spellbound Swatches Holofoil /99 #SSCE5
2010 Press Pass Eclipse Spellbound Swatches Holofoil /99 #SSCE6
2010 Press Pass Eclipse Spellbound Swatches Holofoil /99 #SSCE7
2010 Press Pass Eclipse Spellbound Swatches Holofoil /99 #SSCE1
2010 Press Pass Final Standings /130 #FS11
2010 Press Pass Five Star /35 #16
2010 Press Pass Five Star Classic Compilations Combos Firesuit Autographs /15 #CCMROU
2010 Press Pass Five Star Classic Compilations Combos Patches Autographs /1 #CCMROU
2010 Press Pass Five Star Classic Compilations Dual Memorabilia Autographs /10 #CE
2010 Press Pass Five Star Classic Compilations Firesuit Autographs /15 #CE
2010 Press Pass Five Star Classic Compilations Patch Autographs /1 #CCPCE1
2010 Press Pass Five Star Classic Compilations Patch Autographs /1 #CCPCE2
2010 Press Pass Five Star Classic Compilations Patch Autographs /1 #CCPCE3
2010 Press Pass Five Star Classic Compilations Patch Autographs /1 #CCPCE4
2010 Press Pass Five Star Classic Compilations Patch Autographs /1 #CCPCE5
2010 Press Pass Five Star Classic Compilations Patch Autographs /1 #CCPCE6
2010 Press Pass Five Star Classic Compilations Patch Autographs /1 #CCPCE7
2010 Press Pass Five Star Classic Compilations Patch Autographs /1 #CCPCE8
2010 Press Pass Five Star Classic Compilations Patch Autographs /1 #CCPCE9
2010 Press Pass Five Star Classic Compilations Patch Autographs /1 #CCPCE10
2010 Press Pass Five Star Classic Compilations Patch Autographs /1 #CCPCE11
2010 Press Pass Five Star Classic Compilations Patch Autographs /1 #CCPCE12
2010 Press Pass Five Star Classic Compilations Patch Autographs /1 #CCPCE13
2010 Press Pass Five Star Classic Compilations Patch Autographs /1 #CCPCE14
2010 Press Pass Five Star Classic Compilations Patch Autographs /1 #CCPCE15
2010 Press Pass Five Star Classic Compilations Sheet Metal Autographs /25 #CE
2010 Press Pass Five Star Classic Compilations Triple Memorabilia Autographs /5 #CE
2010 Press Pass Five Star Holofoil /10 #16
2010 Press Pass Five Star Melting /1 #16
2010 Press Pass Five Star Paramount Pieces Aluminum /20 #CE
2010 Press Pass Five Star Paramount Pieces Blue /20 #CE
2010 Press Pass Five Star Paramount Pieces Gold /10 #CE
2010 Press Pass Five Star Paramount Pieces Holofoil /5 #CE
2010 Press Pass Five Star Paramount Pieces Melting /1 #CE
2010 Press Pass Five Star Signature Souvenirs Aluminum /50 #SSCE
2010 Press Pass Five Star Signature Souvenirs Gold /25 #SSCE
2010 Press Pass Five Star Signature Souvenirs Holofoil /10 #SSCE
2010 Press Pass Five Star Signature Souvenirs Melting /1 #SSCE
2010 Press Pass Five Star Signatures Aluminum /35 #CE
2010 Press Pass Five Star Signatures Gold /20 #CE
2010 Press Pass Five Star Signatures Holofoil /5 #CE
2010 Press Pass Five Star Signatures Melting /1 #CE
2010 Press Pass Four Wide Autographs /5 #NNO
2010 Press Pass Four Wide Firesuit /25 #FWCE
2010 Press Pass Four Wide Sheet Metal /15 #FWCE
2010 Press Pass Four Wide Shoes /1 #FWCE
2010 Press Pass Four Wide Tires /10 #FWCE
2010 Press Pass Gold #10
2010 Press Pass Gold #38
2010 Press Pass Gold #69
2010 Press Pass Gold #117
2010 Press Pass Holofoil /100 #10
2010 Press Pass Holofoil /100 #38
2010 Press Pass Holofoil /100 #69
2010 Press Pass Holofoil /100 #117
2010 Press Pass Legends #41
2010 Press Pass Legends Autographs Blue /10 #15
2010 Press Pass Legends Autographs Holofoil /25 #15
2010 Press Pass Legends Blue /1 #41
2010 Press Pass Legends Gold /399 #41
2010 Press Pass Legends Holofoil /50 #41
2010 Press Pass Legends Motorsports Masters #MMCE
2010 Press Pass Legends Motorsports Masters Blue /10 #MMCE
2010 Press Pass Legends Motorsports Masters Gold /299 #MMCE
2010 Press Pass Legends Motorsports Masters Holofoil /149 #MMCE
2010 Press Pass Legends Printing Plates Black /1 #41
2010 Press Pass Legends Printing Plates Cyan /1 #41
2010 Press Pass Legends Printing Plates Magenta /1 #41
2010 Press Pass Legends Printing Plates Yellow /1 #41
2010 Press Pass Legends Prominent Pieces Copper /99 #PPCE
2010 Press Pass Legends Prominent Pieces Gold /50 #PPCE
2010 Press Pass Legends Prominent Pieces Holofoil /25 #PPCE
2010 Press Pass Legends Prominent Pieces Oversized Firesuit /25 #PPOECE
2010 Press Pass Legends Red /199 #41
2010 Press Pass Premium #9
2010 Press Pass Premium #43
2010 Press Pass Premium #58
2010 Press Pass Premium #95
2010 Press Pass Premium Hot Threads /299 #HTCE
2010 Press Pass Premium Hot Threads Holofoil /99 #HTCE
2010 Press Pass Premium Hot Threads Multi Color /25 #HTCE
2010 Press Pass Premium Hot Threads Patches /30 #HTPCE
2010 Press Pass Premium Hot Threads Two Color /125 #HTCE
2010 Press Pass Premium Pairings Firesuits /25 #PFKE
2010 Press Pass Premium Pairings Signatures /5 #PSKE
2010 Press Pass Premium Purple /25 #9
2010 Press Pass Premium Purple /25 #43
2010 Press Pass Premium Purple /25 #58
2010 Press Pass Premium Signature Series Firesuit /15 #SSFCE
2010 Press Pass Premium Signatures #PSCE
2010 Press Pass Premium Signatures Red Ink /24 #PSCE
2010 Press Pass Previews /5 #10
2010 Press Pass Previews /1 #117
2010 Press Pass Purple /25 #10
2010 Press Pass Purple /25 #38
2010 Press Pass Purple /25 #69
2010 Press Pass Purple /25 #117
2010 Press Pass Showcase /499 #9
2010 Press Pass Showcase /499 #42
2010 Press Pass Showcase /499 #34
2010 Press Pass Showcase Classic Collections Firesuit Green /25 #CCIRFR
2010 Press Pass Showcase Classic Collections Firesuit Patch Melting /5 #CCIRFR
2010 Press Pass Showcase Classic Collections Ink /15 #CCIRFR
2010 Press Pass Showcase Classic Collections Ink Gold /10 #CCIRFR
2010 Press Pass Showcase Classic Collections Ink Green /5 #CCIRFR
2010 Press Pass Showcase Classic Collections Ink Melting /1 #CCIRFR
2010 Press Pass Showcase Classic Collections Sheet Metal /99 #CCIRFR
2010 Press Pass Showcase Classic Collections Sheet Metal Gold /45 #CCIRFR
2010 Press Pass Showcase Elite Exhibit Ink /45 #EEICE
2010 Press Pass Showcase Elite Exhibit Ink Gold /25 #EEICE
2010 Press Pass Showcase Elite Exhibit Ink Green /5 #EEICE
2010 Press Pass Showcase Elite Exhibit Ink Melting /1 #EEICE
2010 Press Pass Showcase Elite Exhibit Triple Memorabilia /99 #EEMCE
2010 Press Pass Showcase Elite Exhibit Triple Memorabilia Gold /45 #EEMCE
2010 Press Pass Showcase Elite Exhibit Triple Memorabilia Green /25 #EEMCE
2010 Press Pass Showcase Elite Exhibit Triple Memorabilia Melting /5 #EEMCE
2010 Press Pass Showcase Gold /125 #9
2010 Press Pass Showcase Gold /125 #34
2010 Press Pass Showcase Gold /125 #42
2010 Press Pass Showcase Green /50 #9
2010 Press Pass Showcase Green /50 #34
2010 Press Pass Showcase Green /50 #42
2010 Press Pass Showcase Melting /15 #9
2010 Press Pass Showcase Melting /15 #34
2010 Press Pass Showcase Melting /15 #42
2010 Press Pass Showcase Platinum Holo /1 #9
2010 Press Pass Showcase Platinum Holo /1 #34
2010 Press Pass Showcase Platinum Holo /1 #42
2010 Press Pass Showcase Prized Pieces Firesuit Green /25 #PPMCE
2010 Press Pass Showcase Prized Pieces Firesuit Ink Gold /25 #PPICE
2010 Press Pass Showcase Prized Pieces Firesuit Ink Melting /1 #PPICE
2010 Press Pass Showcase Prized Pieces Firesuit Patch Melting /5 #PPMCE
2010 Press Pass Showcase Prized Pieces Memorabilia Ink Green /15 #PPICE
2010 Press Pass Showcase Prized Pieces Sheet Metal /99 #PPMCE
2010 Press Pass Showcase Prized Pieces Sheet Metal Gold /45 #PPMCE
2010 Press Pass Showcase Prized Pieces Sheet Metal Ink Silver /45 #PPICE
2010 Press Pass Signings Blue /10 #18
2010 Press Pass Signings Gold /25 #18
2010 Press Pass Signings Red /15 #18
2010 Press Pass Signings Silver /50 #18
2010 Press Pass Stealth #9
2010 Press Pass Stealth #60
2010 Press Pass Stealth #74
2010 Press Pass Stealth Battle Armor Holofoil /25 #BACE
2010 Press Pass Stealth Battle Armor Silver /225 #BACE
2010 Press Pass Stealth Black and White #9
2010 Press Pass Stealth Black and White #60
2010 Press Pass Stealth Black and White #74
2010 Press Pass Stealth Mach 10 #MT3
2010 Press Pass Stealth Previews /5 #9
2010 Press Pass Stealth Previews /1 #60
2010 Press Pass Stealth Purple /25 #9
2010 Press Pass Stealth Purple /25 #60
2010 Press Pass Stealth Signature Series Sheet Metal /20 #SSMECE
2010 Press Pass Top 12 Tires /99 #CE
2010 Press Pass Top 12 Tires 10 /10 #CE
2010 Press Pass Tradin' Paint #TP6
2010 Press Pass Tradin' Paint Sheet Metal /299 #TPCE
2010 Press Pass Tradin' Paint Sheet Metal Gold /50 #TPCE
2010 Press Pass Tradin' Paint Sheet Metal Holofoil /25 #TPCE
2010 Wheels Autographs #14
2010 Wheels Autographs Printing Plates Black /1 #14
2010 Wheels Autographs Printing Plates Cyan /1 #14
2010 Wheels Autographs Printing Plates Magenta /1 #14
2010 Wheels Autographs Printing Plates Yellow /1 #14
2010 Wheels Autographs Special Ink /10 #4
2010 Wheels Autographs Target /10 #9
2010 Wheels Main Event #10
2010 Wheels Main Event #38
2010 Wheels Main Event #59
2010 Wheels Main Event #97
2010 Wheels Main Event #66
2010 Wheels Main Event American Muscle #AM12
2010 Wheels Main Event Blue #10
2010 Wheels Main Event Blue #38
2010 Wheels Main Event Blue #59
2010 Wheels Main Event Blue #66
2010 Wheels Main Event Blue #97
2010 Wheels Main Event Fight Card #FC9
2010 Wheels Main Event Fight Card Checkered Flag #FC9
2010 Wheels Main Event Fight Card Full Color Retail #FC9
2010 Wheels Main Event Fight Card Gold /25 #FC9
2010 Wheels Main Event Head to Head /150 #HHKKCE
2010 Wheels Main Event Head to Head /150 #HHCEMK
2010 Wheels Main Event Head to Head Blue /75 #HHKKCE
2010 Wheels Main Event Head to Head Blue /75 #HHCEMK
2010 Wheels Main Event Head to Head Holofoil /10 #HHKKCE
2010 Wheels Main Event Head to Head Holofoil /10 #HHCEMK
2010 Wheels Main Event Head to Head Red /25 #HHKKCE
2010 Wheels Main Event Head to Head Red /25 #HHCEMK
2010 Wheels Main Event Marks Autographs /73 #18
2010 Wheels Main Event Marks Autographs Blue /25 #18
2010 Wheels Main Event Marks Autographs Red /5 #18
2010 Wheels Main Event Matchups Autographs /10 #CEBK
2010 Wheels Main Event Purple /25 #10
2010 Wheels Main Event Purple /25 #38
2010 Wheels Main Event Tale of the Tape #TT5
2010 Wheels Main Event Toe to Toe /10 #TTKKCE
2010 Wheels Main Event Toe to Toe /10 #TTCEMK
2010 Wheels Main Event Upper Cuts /150 #UCCE
2010 Wheels Main Event Upper Cuts Blue /75 #UCCE
2010 Wheels Main Event Upper Cuts Holofoil /10 #UCCE
2010 Wheels Main Event Upper Cuts Holofoil /5 #UCCE
2010 Wheels Main Event Upper Cuts Knock Out Patches /25 #UCKOCE
2010 Wheels Main Event Upper Cuts Red /25 #UCCE
2010 Wheels Main Event Wheel to Wheel /25 #WWCEMK
2010 Wheels Main Event Wheel to Wheel Holofoil /10 #WWCEMK
2011 Element #9
2011 Element #42
2011 Element #72
2011 Element #76
2011 Element #80
2011 Element Autographs /60 #17
2011 Element Autographs Blue /5 #17
2011 Element Autographs Gold /10 #16
2011 Element Autographs Printing Plates Black /1 #17
2011 Element Autographs Printing Plates Cyan /1 #17
2011 Element Autographs Printing Plates Magenta /1 #17
2011 Element Autographs Printing Plates Yellow /1 #17
2011 Element Autographs Silver /25 #16
2011 Element Black /35 #9
2011 Element Black /35 #42
2011 Element Black /35 #72
2011 Element Black /35 #76
2011 Element Black /35 #80
2011 Element Flagship Performers 2010 Laps Completed Yellow /50 #FPLCE
2011 Element Flagship Performers Career Wins White /50 #FPWCE
2011 Element Flagship Performers Race Streak Without DNF Red /50 #FPDCE
2011 Element Green #9
2011 Element Green #42
2011 Element Green #72
2011 Element Green #76
2011 Element Green #80
2011 Element High Octane Vehicle #HOV4
2011 Element High Octane Vehicle #HOV6
2011 Element Previews /5 #EB9
2011 Element Purple /25 #9
2011 Element Purple /25 #42
2011 Element Purple /25 #72
2011 Element Purple /25 #76
2011 Element Purple /25 #80
2011 Element Red #9
2011 Element Red #42
2011 Element Red #72
2011 Element Red #76
2011 Element Red #80
2011 Element Trackside Treasures Holofoil /25 #TTCE
2011 Element Trackside Treasures Silver /85 #TTCE
2011 Press Pass #9
2011 Press Pass #64
2011 Press Pass #114
2011 Press Pass #147
2011 Press Pass #179
2011 Press Pass #192
2011 Press Pass #0
2011 Press Pass Autographs Blue /10 #17
2011 Press Pass Autographs Bronze /99 #16
2011 Press Pass Autographs Gold /25 #16
2011 Press Pass Autographs Printing Plates Black /1 #17
2011 Press Pass Autographs Printing Plates Cyan /1 #17
2011 Press Pass Autographs Printing Plates Magenta /1 #17
2011 Press Pass Autographs Printing Plates Yellow /1 #17
2011 Press Pass Autographs Silver /50 #17
2011 Press Pass Blue Holofoil /10 #9
2011 Press Pass Blue Holofoil /10 #64
2011 Press Pass Blue Holofoil /10 #114
2011 Press Pass Blue Holofoil /10 #147
2011 Press Pass Blue Holofoil /10 #179
2011 Press Pass Blue Holofoil /10 #192
2011 Press Pass Blue Retail #9
2011 Press Pass Blue Retail #64
2011 Press Pass Blue Retail #114
2011 Press Pass Blue Retail #147
2011 Press Pass Blue Retail #179
2011 Press Pass Blue Retail #192
2011 Press Pass Burning Rubber Gold /150 #BRCCE
2011 Press Pass Burning Rubber Gold /150 #BRCCE1
2011 Press Pass Burning Rubber Holofoil /50 #BRCCE
2011 Press Pass Burning Rubber Holofoil /50 #BRCCE1
2011 Press Pass Burning Rubber Prime Cuts /25 #BRCCE
2011 Press Pass Burning Rubber Prime Cuts /25 #BRCCE1
2011 Press Pass Cup Chase #CCR9
2011 Press Pass Cup Chase Prizes #CC5
2011 Press Pass Eclipse #9
2011 Press Pass Eclipse #51
2011 Press Pass Eclipse #78
2011 Press Pass Eclipse #69
2011 Press Pass Eclipse Blue #9
2011 Press Pass Eclipse Blue #51
2011 Press Pass Eclipse Blue #69
2011 Press Pass Eclipse Blue #78
2011 Press Pass Eclipse Encore #E5
2011 Press Pass Eclipse Gold /55 #9
2011 Press Pass Eclipse Gold /55 #51
2011 Press Pass Eclipse Gold /55 #69
2011 Press Pass Eclipse Gold /55 #78
2011 Press Pass Eclipse In Focus #IF9
2011 Press Pass Eclipse Previews /5 #EB9
2011 Press Pass Eclipse Purple /25 #9
2011 Press Pass Eclipse Purple /25 #51
2011 Press Pass Eclipse Spellbound Swatches /150 #SBCE2
2011 Press Pass Eclipse Spellbound Swatches /150 #SBCE3
2011 Press Pass Eclipse Spellbound Swatches /250 #SBCE1
2011 Press Pass Eclipse Spellbound Swatches /100 #SBCE5
2011 Press Pass Eclipse Spellbound Swatches /100 #SBCE4
2011 Press Pass Eclipse Spellbound Swatches /50 #SBCE7
2011 Press Pass Eclipse Spellbound Swatches /75 #SBCE6
2011 Press Pass Eclipse Spellbound Swatches Signatures /10 #NNO
2011 Press Pass FanFare #12
2011 Press Pass FanFare #100
2011 Press Pass FanFare Autographs Blue /5 #23
2011 Press Pass FanFare Autographs Bronze /25 #23
2011 Press Pass FanFare Autographs Gold /15 #23
2011 Press Pass FanFare Autographs Printing Plates Black /1 #23
2011 Press Pass FanFare Autographs Printing Plates Cyan /1 #23
2011 Press Pass FanFare Autographs Printing Plates Magenta /1 #23
2011 Press Pass FanFare Autographs Printing Plates Yellow /1 #23
2011 Press Pass FanFare Autographs Silver /10 #23
2011 Press Pass FanFare Blue Die Cuts #12
2011 Press Pass FanFare Blue Die Cuts #100
2011 Press Pass FanFare Championship Caliber #CC25
2011 Press Pass FanFare Dual Autographs /10 #NNO
2011 Press Pass FanFare Dual Autographs /10 #NNO
2011 Press Pass FanFare Emerald /25 #12
2011 Press Pass FanFare Emerald /25 #100
2011 Press Pass FanFare Holofoil Die Cuts #12
2011 Press Pass FanFare Holofoil Die Cuts #100
2011 Press Pass FanFare Magnificent Materials /199 #MMCE
2011 Press Pass FanFare Magnificent Materials Dual Swatches /50 #MMDCE
2011 Press Pass FanFare Magnificent Materials Dual Swatches Holofoil /10 #MMDCE
2011 Press Pass FanFare Magnificent Materials Holofoil /50 #MMCE
2011 Press Pass FanFare Magnificent Materials Signatures /50 #MMSECE
2011 Press Pass FanFare Magnificent Materials Signatures Holofoil /25 #MMSECE
2011 Press Pass FanFare Ruby Die Cuts /15 #12
2011 Press Pass FanFare Ruby Die Cuts /15 #100
2011 Press Pass FanFare Sapphire /10 #12
2011 Press Pass FanFare Sapphire /10 #100
2011 Press Pass FanFare Silver /25 #12
2011 Press Pass FanFare Silver /25 #100
2011 Press Pass Flashback #FB5
2011 Press Pass Four Wide Firesuit /25 #FWCE
2011 Press Pass Four Wide Glove /1 #FWCE
2011 Press Pass Four Wide Sheet Metal /15 #FWCE
2011 Press Pass Four Wide Shoes /1 #FWCE
2011 Press Pass Four Wide Tire /10 #FWCE
2011 Press Pass Geared Up Gold /75 #GUCE
2011 Press Pass Geared Up Holofoil /50 #GUCE
2011 Press Pass Gold /50 #9
2011 Press Pass Gold /50 #64
2011 Press Pass Gold /50 #114
2011 Press Pass Gold /50 #147
2011 Press Pass Gold /50 #179
2011 Press Pass Gold /50 #192
2011 Press Pass Legends #41
2011 Press Pass Legends Autographs Blue /10 #LGACE
2011 Press Pass Legends Autographs Gold /50 #LGACE
2011 Press Pass Legends Autographs Printing Plates Black /1 #LGACE
2011 Press Pass Legends Autographs Printing Plates Cyan /1 #LGACE
2011 Press Pass Legends Autographs Printing Plates Magenta /1 #LGACE
2011 Press Pass Legends Autographs Printing Plates Yellow /1 #LGACE
2011 Press Pass Legends Autographs Silver /125 #LGACE
2011 Press Pass Legends Gold /250 #41
2011 Press Pass Legends Holofoil /25 #41
2011 Press Pass Legends Printing Plates Black /1 #41
2011 Press Pass Legends Printing Plates Cyan /1 #41
2011 Press Pass Legends Printing Plates Magenta /1 #41
2011 Press Pass Legends Printing Plates Yellow /1 #41
2011 Press Pass Legends Prominent Pieces Gold /50 #PPCE
2011 Press Pass Legends Prominent Pieces Holofoil /25 #PPCE
2011 Press Pass Legends Prominent Pieces Oversized Firesuit /25 #PPOECE
2011 Press Pass Legends Prominent Pieces Purple /15 #PPCE
2011 Press Pass Legends Prominent Pieces Silver /99 #PPCE
2011 Press Pass Legends Purple /25 #41
2011 Press Pass Legends Red /99 #41
2011 Press Pass Legends Solo /1 #41
2011 Press Pass Premium #44
2011 Press Pass Premium #60
2011 Press Pass Premium #77
2011 Press Pass Premium #10A
2011 Press Pass Premium #10B
2011 Press Pass Premium Crystal Ball #CB8
2011 Press Pass Premium Crystal Ball Autographs /10 #CBACE
2011 Press Pass Premium Double Burner /25 #DBCE
2011 Press Pass Premium Hot Pursuit 3D #HP5
2011 Press Pass Premium Hot Pursuit Autographs /10 #HPACE
2011 Press Pass Premium Hot Pursuit National Convention #HP5
2011 Press Pass Premium Hot Threads /150 #HTCE
2011 Press Pass Premium Hot Threads Fast Pass /25 #HTCE
2011 Press Pass Premium Hot Threads Multi Color /25 #HTCE
2011 Press Pass Premium Hot Threads Patches /25 #HTPCE
2011 Press Pass Premium Hot Threads Secondary Color /99 #HTCE
2011 Press Pass Premium Pairings Firesuits /25 #PPCETB
2011 Press Pass Premium Pairings Signatures /5 #PPACETB
2011 Press Pass Premium Purple /25 #10
2011 Press Pass Premium Purple /25 #44
2011 Press Pass Premium Purple /25 #60
2011 Press Pass Premium Purple /25 #77
2011 Press Pass Premium Signatures /160 #PSCE
2011 Press Pass Previews /5 #EB9
2011 Press Pass Previews /1 #EB192
2011 Press Pass Purple /25 #9
2011 Press Pass Purple /25 #192
2011 Press Pass Showcase /499 #10
2011 Press Pass Showcase /499 #39
2011 Press Pass Showcase /499 #46
2011 Press Pass Showcase /499 #55
2011 Press Pass Showcase Classic Collections Firesuit /45 #CCMRFR
2011 Press Pass Showcase Classic Collections Firesuit Patches /5 #CCMRFR
2011 Press Pass Showcase Classic Collections Ink /25 #CCMRFR
2011 Press Pass Showcase Classic Collections Ink Gold /5 #CCMRFR
2011 Press Pass Showcase Classic Collections Ink Melting /1 #CCMRFR
2011 Press Pass Showcase Classic Collections Sheet Metal /99 #CCMRFR
2011 Press Pass Showcase Elite Exhibit Ink /50 #EEICE
2011 Press Pass Showcase Elite Exhibit Ink Gold /25 #EEICE
2011 Press Pass Showcase Elite Exhibit Ink Melting /1 #EEICE
2011 Press Pass Showcase Gold /125 #10
2011 Press Pass Showcase Gold /125 #39
2011 Press Pass Showcase Gold /125 #46
2011 Press Pass Showcase Gold /125 #55
2011 Press Pass Showcase Green /25 #10
2011 Press Pass Showcase Green /25 #39
2011 Press Pass Showcase Green /25 #46
2011 Press Pass Showcase Green /25 #55
2011 Press Pass Showcase Masterpieces Ink /45 #MPICE
2011 Press Pass Showcase Masterpieces Ink Gold /25 #MPICE
2011 Press Pass Showcase Masterpieces Ink Melting /1 #MPICE
2011 Press Pass Showcase Masterpieces Memorabilia /99 #MPMCE
2011 Press Pass Showcase Masterpieces Memorabilia Gold /45 #MPMCE
2011 Press Pass Showcase Masterpieces Memorabilia Melting /5 #MPMCE
2011 Press Pass Showcase Melting /1 #10
2011 Press Pass Showcase Melting /1 #39
2011 Press Pass Showcase Melting /1 #46
2011 Press Pass Showcase Melting /1 #55
2011 Press Pass Showcase Prized Pieces Firesuit /99 #PPMCE
2011 Press Pass Showcase Prized Pieces Firesuit Gold /45 #PPMCE
2011 Press Pass Showcase Prized Pieces Firesuit Ink /25 #PPICE
2011 Press Pass Showcase Prized Pieces Firesuit Patches Ink /1 #PPICE
2011 Press Pass Showcase Prized Pieces Firesuit Patches Melting /5 #PPMCE
2011 Press Pass Showcase Prized Pieces Sheet Metal Ink /45 #PPICE
2011 Press Pass Showcase Showroom /499 #SR4
2011 Press Pass Showcase Showroom Gold /125 #SR4
2011 Press Pass Showcase Showroom Melting /1 #SR4
2011 Press Pass Showcase Showroom Memorabilia Sheet Metal /45 #SRMCE
2011 Press Pass Showcase Showroom Memorabilia Sheet Metal Gold /25 #SRMCE
2011 Press Pass Showcase Showroom Memorabilia Sheet Metal Melting /5 #SRMCE
2011 Press Pass Signature Series /11 #SSTCE
2011 Press Pass Signature Series /11 #SSBCE
2011 Press Pass Signature Series /11 #SSFCE
2011 Press Pass Signature Series /11 #SSMCE
2011 Press Pass Signings Black and White /10 #PPSCE
2011 Press Pass Signings Brushed Metal /70 #PPSCE
2011 Press Pass Signings Holofoil /25 #PPSCE
2011 Press Pass Signings Printing Plates Black /1 #PPSCE
2011 Press Pass Signings Printing Plates Cyan /1 #PPSCE
2011 Press Pass Signings Printing Plates Magenta /1 #PPSCE
2011 Press Pass Signings Printing Plates Yellow /1 #PPSCE
2011 Press Pass Stealth #25
2011 Press Pass Stealth #26
2011 Press Pass Stealth #27
2011 Press Pass Stealth #80
2011 Press Pass Stealth #91
2011 Press Pass Stealth Afterburner /99 #ABCE
2011 Press Pass Stealth Afterburner Gold /25 #ABCE
2011 Press Pass Stealth Black and White /25 #25
2011 Press Pass Stealth Black and White /25 #26
2011 Press Pass Stealth Black and White /25 #27
2011 Press Pass Stealth Black and White /25 #80
2011 Press Pass Stealth Black and White /25 #91
2011 Press Pass Stealth Holofoil /99 #25
2011 Press Pass Stealth Holofoil /99 #26
2011 Press Pass Stealth Holofoil /99 #27
2011 Press Pass Stealth Holofoil /99 #80
2011 Press Pass Stealth Holofoil /99 #91
2011 Press Pass Stealth In Flight Report #IF5
2011 Press Pass Stealth Metal of Honor Medal of Honor /50 #BACE
2011 Press Pass Stealth Metal of Honor Purple Heart /25 #MHCE
2011 Press Pass Stealth Metal of Honor Silver Star /99 #BACE
2011 Press Pass Stealth Purple /25 #25
2011 Press Pass Stealth Purple /25 #26
2011 Press Pass Stealth Purple /25 #27
2011 Press Pass Target Top 12 Tires /25 #T12CE
2011 Press Pass Target Winning Tickets #WTT4
2011 Press Pass Tradin' Paint #TP6
2011 Press Pass Tradin' Paint Sheet Metal Blue /25 #TPCE
2011 Press Pass Tradin' Paint Sheet Metal Holofoil /50 #TPCE
2011 Press Pass Winning Tickets #WT37
2011 Wheels Main Event #11
2011 Wheels Main Event #62
2011 Wheels Main Event #85
2011 Wheels Main Event All Stars #A1
2011 Wheels Main Event All Stars Brushed Foil /199 #A1
2011 Wheels Main Event All Stars Holofoil /50 #A1
2011 Wheels Main Event Black and White #11
2011 Wheels Main Event Black and White #62
2011 Wheels Main Event Black and White #85
2011 Wheels Main Event Blue /75 #11
2011 Wheels Main Event Blue /75 #62
2011 Wheels Main Event Blue /75 #85
2011 Wheels Main Event Green /1 #11
2011 Wheels Main Event Green /1 #62
2011 Wheels Main Event Green /1 #85
2011 Wheels Main Event Headliners Holofoil /25 #HLCE
2011 Wheels Main Event Headliners Silver /99 #HLCE
2011 Wheels Main Event Lead Foot Holofoil /25 #LFCE
2011 Wheels Main Event Lead Foot Silver /99 #LFCE
2011 Wheels Main Event Marks Autographs Blue /10 #MECE
2011 Wheels Main Event Marks Autographs Gold /25 #MECE
2011 Wheels Main Event Marks Autographs Silver /50 #MECE
2011 Wheels Main Event Matchups Autographs /10 #MEMTBCE
2011 Wheels Main Event Matchups Autographs /10 #MEMKBCE
2011 Wheels Main Event Materials Holofoil /25 #MEMCE
2011 Wheels Main Event Rear View #R6
2011 Wheels Main Event Rear View Brushed Foil /199 #R6
2011 Wheels Main Event Rear View Holofoil /50 #R6
2011 Wheels Main Event Red /20 #11
2011 Wheels Main Event Red /20 #62
2011 Wheels Main Event Red /20 #85
2012 Press Pass #11
2012 Press Pass #72
2012 Press Pass #83
2012 Press Pass #65
2012 Press Pass #100
2012 Press Pass Blue #11
2012 Press Pass Blue #65
2012 Press Pass Blue #72
2012 Press Pass Blue #83
2012 Press Pass Blue #100
2012 Press Pass Blue Holofoil /35 #11
2012 Press Pass Blue Holofoil /35 #65
2012 Press Pass Blue Holofoil /35 #72
2012 Press Pass Blue Holofoil /35 #83
2012 Press Pass Blue Holofoil /35 #100
2012 Press Pass Burning Rubber Gold /99 #BRCE
2012 Press Pass Burning Rubber Holofoil /25 #BRCE
2012 Press Pass Burning Rubber Prime Cuts /25 #BRCE
2012 Press Pass Burning Rubber Purple /15 #BRCE
2012 Press Pass Cup Chase #CCR9
2012 Press Pass Fanfare #14
2012 Press Pass Fanfare Autographs Blue /5 #CE
2012 Press Pass Fanfare Autographs Gold /25 #CE
2012 Press Pass Fanfare Autographs Red /10 #CE
2012 Press Pass Fanfare Autographs Silver /75 #CE
2012 Press Pass Fanfare Blue Foil Die Cuts #14
2012 Press Pass Fanfare Diamond /5 #14
2012 Press Pass Fanfare Holofoil Die Cuts #14
2012 Press Pass Fanfare Magnificent Materials /250 #MMCE
2012 Press Pass Fanfare Magnificent Materials Dual Swatches /50 #MMCE
2012 Press Pass Fanfare Magnificent Materials Dual Swatches Melting /10 #MMCE
2012 Press Pass Fanfare Magnificent Materials Gold /125 #MMCE
2012 Press Pass Fanfare Magnificent Materials Signatures /25 #CE
2012 Press Pass Fanfare Magnificent Materials Signatures Blue /5 #CE
2012 Press Pass Fanfare Power Rankings #PR10
2012 Press Pass Fanfare Sapphire /20 #14
2012 Press Pass Fanfare Showtime #S7
2012 Press Pass Fanfare Silver /25 #14
2012 Press Pass Four Wide Firesuit /25 #FWCE
2012 Press Pass Four Wide Glove /1 #FWCE
2012 Press Pass Four Wide Sheet Metal /15 #FWCE
2012 Press Pass Four Wide Tire /10 #FWCE
2012 Press Pass Gold #11
2012 Press Pass Gold #65
2012 Press Pass Gold #72
2012 Press Pass Gold #83

s Pass Gold #100
s Pass Ignite #13
ss Pass Ignite #51
ss Pass Ignite Double Burner Gun Metal /10 #DBCE
s Pass Ignite Double Burner Red /1 #DBCE
s Pass Ignite Double Burner Silver /25 #DBCE
s Pass Ignite Limelight #L3
s Pass Ignite Materials Autographs Gun Metal /20 #IMCE
s Pass Ignite Materials Autographs Red /5 #IMCE
s Pass Ignite Materials Autographs Silver /125 #IMCE
ss Pass Ignite Materials Gun Metal /99 #IMCE
s Pass Ignite Materials Red /10 #IMCE
ss Pass Ignite Materials Silver #IMCE
s Pass Ignite Profile #P10
s Pass Ignite Proofs Black and White /50 #13
s Pass Ignite Proofs Black and White /50 #51
s Pass Ignite Proofs Cyan #13
s Pass Ignite Proofs Cyan #51
s Pass Ignite Proofs Magenta #13
s Pass Ignite Proofs Magenta #51
s Pass Ignite Proofs Yellow /10 #13
s Pass Ignite Proofs Yellow /10 #51
s Pass Ignite Steel Horses #SH6
s Pass Ignite Supercharged Signatures /5 #SSCE
s Pass Legends #41
ss Pass Legends Blue Holofoil /1 #41
ss Pass Legends Gold /275 #41
s Pass Legends Green #41
ss Pass Legends Prominent Pieces Gold /50 #CE
ss Pass Legends Prominent Pieces Holofoil /25 #CE
ss Pass Legends Prominent Pieces Silver /99 #CE
ss Pass Legends Rainbow Holofoil /50 #41
ss Pass Legends Red /99 #41
ss Pass Legends Silver Holofoil /25 #41
ss Pass Power Picks Blue /50 #5
ss Pass Power Picks Blue /50 #34
ss Pass Power Picks Blue /50 #62
ss Pass Power Picks Gold /50 #5
ss Pass Power Picks Gold /50 #34
ss Pass Power Picks Gold /50 #62
ss Pass Power Picks Holofoil /10 #5
ss Pass Power Picks Holofoil /10 #34
ss Pass Power Picks Holofoil /10 #62
ss Pass Preferred Line #PL8
ss Pass Purple /35 #11
ss Pass Purple /35 #65
ss Pass Purple /35 #72
ss Pass Purple /35 #83
ss Pass Purple /35 #100
ss Pass Redline #13
ss Pass Redline Black /99 #13
ss Pass Redline Cyan /50 #13
ss Pass Redline Full Throttle Dual Relic Blue /5 #FTCE
ss Pass Redline Full Throttle Dual Relic Gold /10 #FTCE
ss Pass Redline Full Throttle Dual Relic Melting /1 #FTCE
ss Pass Redline Full Throttle Dual Relic Red /75 #FTCE
ss Pass Redline Full Throttle Dual Relic Silver /25 #FTCE
ss Pass Redline Intensity #I3
ss Pass Redline Magenta /15 #13
ss Pass Redline Muscle Car Sheet Metal Blue /5 #MCCE
ss Pass Redline Muscle Car Sheet Metal Gold /10 #MCCE
ss Pass Redline Muscle Car Sheet Metal Melting /1 #MCCE
ss Pass Redline Muscle Car Sheet Metal Red /75 #MCCE
ss Pass Redline Muscle Car Sheet Metal Silver /25 #MCCE
ss Pass Redline Performance Driven #PD3
ss Pass Redline Pieces of the Action Blue /10 #PACE
ss Pass Redline Pieces of the Action Gold /25 #PACE
ss Pass Redline Pieces of the Action Melting /1 #PACE
ss Pass Redline Pieces of the Action Red /75 #PACE
ss Pass Redline Pieces of the Action Silver /50 #PACE
ss Pass Redline Relic Autographs Blue /10 #RLRCE
ss Pass Redline Relic Autographs Gold /25 #RLRCE
ss Pass Redline Relic Autographs Melting /1 #RLRCE
ss Pass Redline Relic Autographs Red /75 #RLRCE
ss Pass Redline Relic Autographs Silver /50 #RLRCE
ss Pass Redline Relics Blue /5 #RLCE
ss Pass Redline Relics Gold /10 #RLCE
ss Pass Redline Relics Melting /1 #RLCE
ss Pass Redline Relics Red /75 #RLCE
ss Pass Redline Relics Silver /25 #RLCE
ss Pass Redline RPM #RPM3
ss Pass Redline Signatures Blue /5 #RSCE1
ss Pass Redline Signatures Blue /5 #RSCE2
ss Pass Redline Signatures Gold /25 #RSCE1
ss Pass Redline Signatures Gold /15 #RSCE2
ss Pass Redline Signatures Holofoil /10 #RSCE1
ss Pass Redline Signatures Holofoil /10 #RSCE2
ss Pass Redline Signatures Melting /1 #RSCE1
ss Pass Redline Signatures Melting /1 #RSCE2
ss Pass Redline Signatures Red /50 #RSCE1
ss Pass Redline Signatures Red /25 #RSCE2
ss Pass Redline V8 Relics Blue /5 #V8CE
ss Pass Redline V8 Relics Gold /10 #V8CE
ss Pass Redline V8 Relics Melting /1 #V8CE
ss Pass Redline V8 Relics Red /25 #V8CE
ss Pass Redline Yellow /1 #13
ess Pass Showcar #SC6
ss Pass Showcase /499 #54
ss Pass Showcase /499 #47
ss Pass Showcase /499 #36
ss Pass Showcase /499 #9
ess Pass Showcase Classic Collections Ink /10 #CCMRFR
ss Pass Showcase Classic Collections Ink Gold /5 #CCMRFR
ss Pass Showcase Classic Collections Ink Melting /1 #CCMRFR
ss Pass Showcase Classic Collections Memorabilia /99 #CCMRFR
ss Pass Showcase Classic Collections Memorabilia Gold /50
CMRFR
ss Pass Showcase Classic Collections Memorabilia Melting /5
CMRFR
ss Pass Showcase Elite Exhibit Ink /25 #EEICE
ss Pass Showcase Elite Exhibit Ink Gold /10 #EEICE
ess Pass Showcase Elite Exhibit Ink Melting /1 #EEICE
ess Pass Showcase Gold /125 #9
ess Pass Showcase Gold /125 #36
ess Pass Showcase Gold /125 #47
ess Pass Showcase Gold /125 #54
ess Pass Showcase Green /5 #9
ess Pass Showcase Green /5 #36
ess Pass Showcase Green /5 #47
ess Pass Showcase Green /5 #54
ess Pass Showcase Masterpieces Ink /50 #MPICE
ess Pass Showcase Masterpieces Ink Gold /25 #MPICE
ess Pass Showcase Masterpieces Ink Melting /1 #MPICE
ess Pass Showcase Masterpieces Memorabilia /99 #MPCE
ess Pass Showcase Masterpieces Memorabilia Gold /50 #MPCE
ess Pass Showcase Masterpieces Memorabilia Melting /5 #MPCE
ess Pass Showcase Melting /1 #9
ess Pass Showcase Melting /1 #36
ess Pass Showcase Melting /1 #47
ess Pass Showcase Melting /1 #54
ess Pass Showcase Prized Pieces /99 #PPCE
ess Pass Showcase Prized Pieces Gold /50 #PPCE
ess Pass Showcase Prized Pieces Ink /50 #PPICE
ess Pass Showcase Prized Pieces Ink Gold /25 #PPICE
ess Pass Showcase Prized Pieces Ink Melting /1 #PPICE
ess Pass Showcase Prized Pieces Melting /5 #PPCE
ess Pass Showcase Purple /1 #9
ess Pass Showcase Purple /1 #36
2012 Press Pass Showcase Purple /1 #47
2012 Press Pass Showcase Purple /1 #54
2012 Press Pass Showcase Red /25 #9
2012 Press Pass Showcase Red /25 #36
2012 Press Pass Showcase Red /25 #47
2012 Press Pass Showcase Red /25 #54
2012 Press Pass Showcase Richard Petty 75th Birthday Tribute /10 #RPCE
2012 Press Pass Showcase Richard Petty 75th Birthday Tribute Melting /1 #RPCE
2012 Press Pass Showcase Showcase Patches /5 #SSPCE
2012 Press Pass Showcase Showcase Patches Melting /1 #SSPCE
2012 Press Pass Showcase Showroom /499 #SR6
2012 Press Pass Showcase Showroom Gold /125 #SR6
2012 Press Pass Showcase Showroom Melting /1 #SR6
2012 Press Pass Showcase Showroom Memorabilia /99 #SRCE
2012 Press Pass Showcase Showroom Memorabilia Gold /50 #SRCE
2012 Press Pass Showcase Showroom Memorabilia Melting /5 #SRCE
2012 Press Pass Showcase Signature Patches /1 #SSPCE
2012 Press Pass Showman #SM6
2012 Press Pass Snapshots #SS11
2012 Press Pass Target Snapshots #SSTG6
2012 Press Pass Ultimate Collection Blue Holofoil /25 #UCCE
2012 Press Pass Ultimate Collection Holofoil /50 #UCCE
2012 Total Memorabilia #8A
2012 Total Memorabilia #8B
2012 Total Memorabilia Black and White /99 #8
2012 Total Memorabilia Dual Swatch Gold /75 #TMCE
2012 Total Memorabilia Dual Swatch Holofoil /25 #TMCE
2012 Total Memorabilia Dual Swatch Melting /5 #TMCE
2012 Total Memorabilia Dual Swatch Silver /99 #TMCE
2012 Total Memorabilia Gold /275 #8
2012 Total Memorabilia Hot Rod Relics Gold /50 #HRRCE
2012 Total Memorabilia Hot Rod Relics Holofoil /10 #HRRCE
2012 Total Memorabilia Hot Rod Relics Melting /1 #HRRCE
2012 Total Memorabilia Hot Rod Relics Silver /99 #HRRCE
2012 Total Memorabilia Jumbo Swatch Gold /50 #TMCE
2012 Total Memorabilia Jumbo Swatch Holofoil /10 #TMCE
2012 Total Memorabilia Jumbo Swatch Melting /1 #TMCE
2012 Total Memorabilia Quad Swatch Gold /25 #TMCE
2012 Total Memorabilia Quad Swatch Holofoil /10 #TMCE
2012 Total Memorabilia Quad Swatch Melting /1 #TMCE
2012 Total Memorabilia Quad Swatch Silver /50 #TMCE
2012 Total Memorabilia Red Retail /250 #8
2012 Total Memorabilia Signature Collection Dual Swatch Silver /10 #SCCE
2012 Total Memorabilia Signature Collection Quad Swatch Holofoil /5 #SCCE
2012 Total Memorabilia Signature Collection Single Swatch Melting /1 #SCCE
2012 Total Memorabilia Signature Collection Triple Swatch Gold /10 #SCCE
2012 Total Memorabilia Single Swatch Gold /99 #TMCE
2012 Total Memorabilia Single Swatch Holofoil /50 #TMCE
2012 Total Memorabilia Single Swatch Melting /10 #TMCE
2012 Total Memorabilia Single Swatch Silver /199 #TMCE
2012 Total Memorabilia Triple Swatch Gold /50 #TMCE
2012 Total Memorabilia Triple Swatch Holofoil /25 #TMCE
2012 Total Memorabilia Triple Swatch Melting /1 #TMCE
2012 Total Memorabilia Triple Swatch Silver /99 #TMCE
2013 Press Pass #14
2013 Press Pass #89
2013 Press Pass #96
2013 Press Pass #79
2013 Press Pass Aerodynamic Autographs Blue /5 #CE
2013 Press Pass Aerodynamic Autographs Holofoil /20 #CE
2013 Press Pass Color Proofs Black #14
2013 Press Pass Color Proofs Black #79
2013 Press Pass Color Proofs Black #89
2013 Press Pass Color Proofs Black #96
2013 Press Pass Color Proofs Cyan /35 #14
2013 Press Pass Color Proofs Cyan /35 #79
2013 Press Pass Color Proofs Cyan /35 #89
2013 Press Pass Color Proofs Cyan /35 #96
2013 Press Pass Color Proofs Magenta #14
2013 Press Pass Color Proofs Magenta #79
2013 Press Pass Color Proofs Magenta #89
2013 Press Pass Color Proofs Magenta #96
2013 Press Pass Color Proofs Yellow /5 #14
2013 Press Pass Color Proofs Yellow /5 #79
2013 Press Pass Color Proofs Yellow /5 #89
2013 Press Pass Color Proofs Yellow /5 #96
2013 Press Pass Cool Persistence #CP3
2013 Press Pass Cup Chase #CC6
2013 Press Pass Cup Chase Prizes #CCP5
2013 Press Pass Fanfare #16
2013 Press Pass Fanfare #17
2013 Press Pass Fanfare Autographs Blue /1 #CE
2013 Press Pass Fanfare Autographs Gold /5 #CE
2013 Press Pass Fanfare Autographs Green /2 #CE
2013 Press Pass Fanfare Autographs Red /5 #CE
2013 Press Pass Fanfare Autographs Silver /10 #CE
2013 Press Pass Fanfare Diamond Die Cuts /5 #16
2013 Press Pass Fanfare Diamond Die Cuts /5 #17
2013 Press Pass Fanfare Fan Following #FF6
2013 Press Pass Fanfare Green /3 #16
2013 Press Pass Fanfare Green /3 #17
2013 Press Pass Fanfare Holofoil Die Cuts #16
2013 Press Pass Fanfare Holofoil Die Cuts #17
2013 Press Pass Fanfare Magnificent Jumbo Materials Signatures /10 #CE
2013 Press Pass Fanfare Magnificent Materials Dual Swatches /50 #CE
2013 Press Pass Fanfare Magnificent Materials Dual Swatches Melting /10 #CE
2013 Press Pass Fanfare Magnificent Materials Gold /50 #CE
2013 Press Pass Fanfare Magnificent Materials Jumbo Swatches /25 #CE
2013 Press Pass Fanfare Magnificent Materials Signatures /99 #CE
2013 Press Pass Fanfare Magnificent Materials Signatures Blue /25 #CE
2013 Press Pass Fanfare Magnificent Materials Silver /199 #CE
2013 Press Pass Fanfare Red Foil Die Cuts #16
2013 Press Pass Fanfare Red Foil Die Cuts #17
2013 Press Pass Fanfare Sapphire /20 #16
2013 Press Pass Fanfare Sapphire /20 #17
2013 Press Pass Fanfare Showtime #S10
2013 Press Pass Fanfare Signature Ride Autographs /10 #CE
2013 Press Pass Fanfare Signature Ride Autographs Blue /1 #CE
2013 Press Pass Fanfare Signature Ride Autographs Red /5 #CE
2013 Press Pass Fanfare Silver /25 #16
2013 Press Pass Fanfare Silver /25 #17
2013 Press Pass Four Wide Gold /10 #FWCE
2013 Press Pass Four Wide Melting /1 #FWCE
2013 Press Pass Ignite #10
2013 Press Pass Ignite #67
2013 Press Pass Ignite Double Burner Blue Holofoil /10 #DBCE
2013 Press Pass Ignite Double Burner Red /1 #DBCE
2013 Press Pass Ignite Double Burner Silver /25 #DBCE
2013 Press Pass Ignite Hot Threads Blue Holofoil /99 #HTCE
2013 Press Pass Ignite Hot Threads Patch Red /10 #HTCE
2013 Press Pass Ignite Hot Threads Patch Red Oversized /20 #HTPCE
2013 Press Pass Ignite Hot Threads Silver #HTCE
2013 Press Pass Ignite Ink Black /60 #IICE
2013 Press Pass Ignite Ink Blue /25 #IICE
2013 Press Pass Ignite Ink Red /5 #IICE
2013 Press Pass Ignite Profile #3
2013 Press Pass Ignite Proofs Black and White /50 #10
2013 Press Pass Ignite Proofs Black and White /50 #67
2013 Press Pass Ignite Proofs Cyan #10
2013 Press Pass Ignite Proofs Cyan #67
2013 Press Pass Ignite Proofs Magenta #10
2013 Press Pass Ignite Proofs Magenta #67
2013 Press Pass Ignite Proofs Yellow /5 #10
2013 Press Pass Ignite Proofs Yellow /5 #67
2013 Press Pass Ignite Supercharged Signatures Blue Holofoil /10 #SSCE
2013 Press Pass Ignite Supercharged Signatures Red /1 #SSCE
2013 Press Pass Ignite Turning Point #4
2013 Press Pass Legends #43
2013 Press Pass Legends Autographs Blue #LGCE
2013 Press Pass Legends Autographs Gold /4 #LGCE
2013 Press Pass Legends Autographs Holofoil #LGCE
2013 Press Pass Legends Autographs Printing Plates Black /1 #LGCE
2013 Press Pass Legends Autographs Printing Plates Cyan /1 #LGCE
2013 Press Pass Legends Autographs Printing Plates Magenta /1 #LGCE
2013 Press Pass Legends Autographs Printing Plates Yellow /1 #LGCE
2013 Press Pass Legends Autographs Silver #LGCE
2013 Press Pass Legends Blue #43
2013 Press Pass Legends Blue Holofoil /1 #43
2013 Press Pass Legends Four Wide Memorabilia Autographs Gold /25 #FWSECE
2013 Press Pass Legends Four Wide Memorabilia Autographs Melting /4 #FWSECE
2013 Press Pass Legends Gold /149 #43
2013 Press Pass Legends Holofoil /10 #43
2013 Press Pass Legends Printing Plates Black /1 #43
2013 Press Pass Legends Printing Plates Cyan /1 #43
2013 Press Pass Legends Printing Plates Magenta /1 #43
2013 Press Pass Legends Printing Plates Yellow /1 #43
2013 Press Pass Legends Prominent Pieces Gold /10 #PPCE
2013 Press Pass Legends Prominent Pieces Holofoil /5 #PPCE
2013 Press Pass Legends Prominent Pieces Oversized Firesuit /5 #PPCE
2013 Press Pass Legends Prominent Pieces Silver /25 #PPCE
2013 Press Pass Legends Red /99 #43
2013 Press Pass Legends Signature Style #SS14
2013 Press Pass Legends Signature Style Blue /5 #SS14
2013 Press Pass Legends Signature Style Holofoil /99 #SS14
2013 Press Pass Legends Signature Style Melting /10 #SS14
2013 Press Pass Power Picks Blue /99 #5
2013 Press Pass Power Picks Blue /99 #34
2013 Press Pass Power Picks Gold /50 #5
2013 Press Pass Power Picks Gold /50 #34
2013 Press Pass Power Picks Holofoil /10 #5
2013 Press Pass Power Picks Holofoil /10 #34
2013 Press Pass Racing Champions #RC34
2013 Press Pass Redline #15
2013 Press Pass Redline #16
2013 Press Pass Redline Black /99 #15
2013 Press Pass Redline Black /99 #16
2013 Press Pass Redline Cyan /50 #15
2013 Press Pass Redline Cyan /50 #16
2013 Press Pass Redline Dynamic Duals Dual Relic Blue /5 #DDCE
2013 Press Pass Redline Dynamic Duals Dual Relic Gold /10 #DDCE
2013 Press Pass Redline Dynamic Duals Dual Relic Melting /1 #DDCE
2013 Press Pass Redline Dynamic Duals Dual Relic Red /75 #DDCE
2013 Press Pass Redline Dynamic Duals Dual Relic Silver /25 #DDCE
2013 Press Pass Redline Magenta /15 #15
2013 Press Pass Redline Magenta /15 #16
2013 Press Pass Redline Muscle Car Sheet Metal Blue /5 #MCMCE
2013 Press Pass Redline Muscle Car Sheet Metal Gold /10 #MCMCE
2013 Press Pass Redline Muscle Car Sheet Metal Melting /1 #MCMCE
2013 Press Pass Redline Muscle Car Sheet Metal Red /50 #MCMCE
2013 Press Pass Redline Muscle Car Sheet Metal Silver /25 #MCMCE
2013 Press Pass Redline Pieces of the Action Blue /10 #PACE
2013 Press Pass Redline Pieces of the Action Gold /25 #PACE
2013 Press Pass Redline Pieces of the Action Melting /1 #PACE
2013 Press Pass Redline Pieces of the Action Red /75 #PACE
2013 Press Pass Redline Pieces of the Action Silver /50 #PACE
2013 Press Pass Redline Redline Racers #3
2013 Press Pass Redline Relic Autographs Blue /5 #RRSECE
2013 Press Pass Redline Relic Autographs Gold /10 #RRSECE
2013 Press Pass Redline Relic Autographs Melting /1 #RRSECE
2013 Press Pass Redline Relic Autographs Red /99 #RRSECE
2013 Press Pass Redline Relic Autographs Silver /50 #RRSECE
2013 Press Pass Redline Relics Blue /5 #RRCE
2013 Press Pass Redline Relics Gold /10 #RRCE
2013 Press Pass Redline Relics Melting /1 #RRCE
2013 Press Pass Redline Relics Red /50 #RRCE
2013 Press Pass Redline Relics Silver /25 #RRCE
2013 Press Pass Redline RPM #4
2013 Press Pass Redline Signatures Blue /15 #RSCE1
2013 Press Pass Redline Signatures Blue /10 #RSCE2
2013 Press Pass Redline Signatures Gold /5 #RSCE1
2013 Press Pass Redline Signatures Gold /5 #RSCE2
2013 Press Pass Redline Signatures Holo /10 #RSCE1
2013 Press Pass Redline Signatures Holo /5 #RSCE2
2013 Press Pass Redline Signatures Melting /1 #RSCE1
2013 Press Pass Redline Signatures Melting /1 #RSCE2
2013 Press Pass Redline Signatures Red /10 #RSCE2
2013 Press Pass Redline Signatures Red /25 #RSCE1
2013 Press Pass Redline V8 Relics Blue /5 #V8CE
2013 Press Pass Redline V8 Relics Gold /10 #V8CE
2013 Press Pass Redline V8 Relics Melting /1 #V8CE
2013 Press Pass Redline V8 Relics Red /25 #V8CE
2013 Press Pass Redline Yellow /1 #15
2013 Press Pass Redline Yellow /1 #16
2013 Press Pass Showcase /349 #9
2013 Press Pass Showcase /349 #33
2013 Press Pass Showcase /349 #57
2013 Press Pass Showcase Black /1 #9
2013 Press Pass Showcase Black /1 #33
2013 Press Pass Showcase Black /1 #57
2013 Press Pass Showcase Blue /25 #9
2013 Press Pass Showcase Blue /25 #33
2013 Press Pass Showcase Blue /25 #57
2013 Press Pass Showcase Classic Collections Ink Gold /5 #CCIRFR
2013 Press Pass Showcase Classic Collections Ink Melting /1 #CCIRFR
2013 Press Pass Showcase Classic Collections Ink Red /1 #CCIRFR
2013 Press Pass Showcase Classic Collections Memorabilia Gold /25 #CCMRFR
2013 Press Pass Showcase Classic Collections Memorabilia Melting /5 #CCMRFR
2013 Press Pass Showcase Classic Collections Memorabilia Silver /75 #CCMRFR
2013 Press Pass Showcase Elite Exhibit Ink /25 #EEICE
2013 Press Pass Showcase Elite Exhibit Ink Blue /30 #EEICE
2013 Press Pass Showcase Elite Exhibit Ink Gold /10 #EEICE
2013 Press Pass Showcase Elite Exhibit Ink Melting /1 #EEICE
2013 Press Pass Showcase Elite Exhibit Ink Red /5 #EEICE
2013 Press Pass Showcase Gold /99 #9
2013 Press Pass Showcase Gold /99 #33
2013 Press Pass Showcase Gold /99 #57
2013 Press Pass Showcase Green /20 #9
2013 Press Pass Showcase Green /20 #33
2013 Press Pass Showcase Green /20 #57
2013 Press Pass Showcase Masterpieces Ink /25 #MPICE
2013 Press Pass Showcase Masterpieces Ink Gold /10 #MPICE
2013 Press Pass Showcase Masterpieces Ink Melting /1 #MPICE
2013 Press Pass Showcase Masterpieces Memorabilia /75 #MPCE
2013 Press Pass Showcase Masterpieces Memorabilia Gold /25 #MPCE
2013 Press Pass Showcase Masterpieces Memorabilia Melting /5 #MPCE
2013 Press Pass Showcase Prized Pieces /99 #PPMCE
2013 Press Pass Showcase Prized Pieces Blue /20 #PPMCE
2013 Press Pass Showcase Prized Pieces Gold /25 #PPMCE
2013 Press Pass Showcase Prized Pieces Ink /25 #PPICE
2013 Press Pass Showcase Prized Pieces Ink Gold /10 #PPICE
2013 Press Pass Showcase Prized Pieces Ink Melting /1 #PPICE
2013 Press Pass Showcase Prized Pieces Melting /5 #PPMCE
2013 Press Pass Showcase Purple /13 #9
2013 Press Pass Showcase Purple /13 #33
2013 Press Pass Showcase Purple /13 #57
2013 Press Pass Showcase Red /10 #9
2013 Press Pass Showcase Red /10 #33
2013 Press Pass Showcase Red /10 #57
2013 Press Pass Showcase Series Standouts Gold /50 #5
2013 Press Pass Showcase Showcase Patches /5 #SPCE
2013 Press Pass Showcase Showroom /299 #7
2013 Press Pass Showcase Showroom Blue /40 #7
2013 Press Pass Showcase Showroom Gold /50 #7
2013 Press Pass Showcase Showroom Green /20 #7
2013 Press Pass Showcase Showroom Melting /1 #7
2013 Press Pass Showcase Showroom Purple /13 #7
2013 Press Pass Showcase Showroom Red /10 #7
2013 Press Pass Showcase Signature Patches /19 #SSPCE
2013 Press Pass Showcase Studio Showcase /299 #5
2013 Press Pass Showcase Studio Showcase Blue /40 #5
2013 Press Pass Showcase Studio Showcase Green /25 #5
2013 Press Pass Showcase Studio Showcase Melting /1 #5
2013 Press Pass Showcase Studio Showcase Purple /13 #5
2013 Press Pass Showcase Studio Showcase Red /10 #5
2013 Press Pass Signings Blue /1 #CE
2013 Press Pass Signings Gold /15 #CE
2013 Press Pass Signings Holofoil /5 #CE
2013 Press Pass Signings Printing Plates Black /1 #CE
2013 Press Pass Signings Printing Plates Cyan /1 #CE
2013 Press Pass Signings Printing Plates Magenta /1 #CE
2013 Press Pass Signings Printing Plates Yellow /1 #CE
2013 Press Pass Signings Silver /35 #CE
2013 Press Pass Three Wide Gold /10 #TWCE
2013 Press Pass Three Wide Melting /1 #TWCE
2013 Total Memorabilia #13
2013 Total Memorabilia Black and White /99 #13
2013 Total Memorabilia Dual Swatch Gold /199 #TMCE
2013 Total Memorabilia Gold /275 #13
2013 Total Memorabilia Hot Rod Relics Gold /50 #HRRCE
2013 Total Memorabilia Hot Rod Relics Holofoil /10 #HRRCE
2013 Total Memorabilia Hot Rod Relics Melting /1 #HRRCE
2013 Total Memorabilia Hot Rod Relics Silver /99 #HRRCE
2013 Total Memorabilia Quad Swatch Melting /10 #TMCE
2013 Total Memorabilia Red #13
2013 Total Memorabilia Signature Collection Dual Swatch Gold /10 #SCCE
2013 Total Memorabilia Signature Collection Quad Swatch Melting /1 #SCCE
2013 Total Memorabilia Signature Collection Single Swatch Silver /10 #SCCE
2013 Total Memorabilia Signature Collection Triple Swatch Holofoil /5 #SCCE
2013 Total Memorabilia Single Swatch Silver /475 #TMCE
2013 Total Memorabilia Smooth Operators #SO9
2013 Total Memorabilia Triple Swatch Holofoil /99 #TMCE
2014 Press Pass #10
2014 Press Pass #70
2014 Press Pass #86
2014 Press Pass #91
2014 Press Pass Aerodynamic Autographs Blue /1 #AACE
2014 Press Pass Aerodynamic Autographs Holofoil /20 #AACE
2014 Press Pass Aerodynamic Autographs Printing Plates Black /1 #AACE
2014 Press Pass Aerodynamic Autographs Printing Plates Cyan /1 #AACE
2014 Press Pass Aerodynamic Autographs Printing Plates Magenta /1 #AACE
2014 Press Pass Aerodynamic Autographs Printing Plates Yellow /1 #AACE
2014 Press Pass American Thunder #13
2014 Press Pass American Thunder #69
2014 Press Pass American Thunder #53
2014 Press Pass American Thunder Autographs Blue /10 #ATACE1
2014 Press Pass American Thunder Autographs Red /5 #ATACE1
2014 Press Pass American Thunder Autographs White /35 #ATACE1
2014 Press Pass American Thunder Battle Armor Blue /25 #BACE
2014 Press Pass American Thunder Battle Armor Red /1 #BACE
2014 Press Pass American Thunder Battle Armor Silver /99 #BACE
2014 Press Pass American Thunder Black and White /50 #13
2014 Press Pass American Thunder Black and White /50 #53
2014 Press Pass American Thunder Black and White /50 #69
2014 Press Pass American Thunder Brothers In Arms Autographs Blue /5 #BARFR
2014 Press Pass American Thunder Brothers In Arms Autographs Red /1 #BARFR
2014 Press Pass American Thunder Brothers In Arms Autographs White /10 #BARFR
2014 Press Pass American Thunder Brothers In Arms Relics Blue /25 #BARFR
2014 Press Pass American Thunder Brothers In Arms Relics Red /5 #BARFR
2014 Press Pass American Thunder Brothers In Arms Relics Silver /50 #BARFR
2014 Press Pass American Thunder Class A Uniforms Blue /99 #CAUCE
2014 Press Pass American Thunder Class A Uniforms Red /10 #CAUCE
2014 Press Pass American Thunder Class A Uniforms Silver #CAUCE
2014 Press Pass American Thunder Cyan #13
2014 Press Pass American Thunder Cyan #53
2014 Press Pass American Thunder Cyan #69
2014 Press Pass American Thunder Great American Treads Autographs Blue /25 #GATCE
2014 Press Pass American Thunder Great American Treads Autographs Red /1 #GATCE
2014 Press Pass American Thunder Magenta #13
2014 Press Pass American Thunder Magenta #53
2014 Press Pass American Thunder Magenta #69
2014 Press Pass American Thunder Top Speed #TS4
2014 Press Pass American Thunder Yellow /5 #13
2014 Press Pass American Thunder Yellow /5 #53
2014 Press Pass Burning Rubber Blue /25 #BRCE
2014 Press Pass Burning Rubber Blue /25 #BRCE2
2014 Press Pass Burning Rubber Gold /75 #BRCE2
2014 Press Pass Burning Rubber Gold /75 #BRCE
2014 Press Pass Burning Rubber Holofoil /50 #BRCE
2014 Press Pass Burning Rubber Holofoil /50 #BRCE2
2014 Press Pass Burning Rubber Letterman /8 #BRLCE
2014 Press Pass Burning Rubber Melting /10 #BRCE
2014 Press Pass Burning Rubber Melting /10 #BRCE2
2014 Press Pass Certified Winners Memorabilia Autographs Gold /10 #CWCE
2014 Press Pass Certified Winners Memorabilia Autographs Melting /1 #CWCE
2014 Press Pass Color Proofs Black /70 #10
2014 Press Pass Color Proofs Black /70 #70
2014 Press Pass Color Proofs Black /70 #86
2014 Press Pass Color Proofs Black /70 #91
2014 Press Pass Color Proofs Cyan /35 #10
2014 Press Pass Color Proofs Cyan /35 #70
2014 Press Pass Color Proofs Cyan /35 #86
2014 Press Pass Color Proofs Cyan /35 #91
2014 Press Pass Color Proofs Magenta #10
2014 Press Pass Color Proofs Magenta #70
2014 Press Pass Color Proofs Magenta #86
2014 Press Pass Color Proofs Magenta #91
2014 Press Pass Color Proofs Yellow /5 #10
2014 Press Pass Color Proofs Yellow /5 #70
2014 Press Pass Color Proofs Yellow /5 #86
2014 Press Pass Color Proofs Yellow /5 #91
2014 Press Pass Cup Chase #5
2014 Press Pass Five Star /15 #5
2014 Press Pass Five Star Blue /5 #5
2014 Press Pass Five Star Classic Compilation Autographs Blue Triple Swatch /5 #CCCE
2014 Press Pass Five Star Classic Compilation Autographs Holofoil /10 #CCCE
2014 Press Pass Five Star Classic Compilation Autographs Holofoil Dual Swatch /10 #CCCE
2014 Press Pass Five Star Classic Compilation Autographs Melting Five Swatch /1 #CCCE
2014 Press Pass Five Star Classic Compilation Autographs Melting Quad Swatch /1 #CCCE
2014 Press Pass Five Star Classic Compilations Autographed Patch Booklet /1 #CCCE1
2014 Press Pass Five Star Classic Compilations Autographed Patch Booklet /1 #CCCE2
2014 Press Pass Five Star Classic Compilations Autographed Patch Booklet /1 #CCCE3
2014 Press Pass Five Star Classic Compilations Autographed Patch Booklet /1 #CCCE4
2014 Press Pass Five Star Classic Compilations Autographed Patch Booklet /1 #CCCE5
2014 Press Pass Five Star Classic Compilations Autographed Patch Booklet /1 #CCCE6
2014 Press Pass Five Star Classic Compilations Autographed Patch Booklet /1 #CCCE7
2014 Press Pass Five Star Classic Compilations Autographed Patch Booklet /1 #CCCE8
2014 Press Pass Five Star Classic Compilations Autographed Patch Booklet /1 #CCCE9
2014 Press Pass Five Star Classic Compilations Autographed Patch Booklet /1 #CCCE10
2014 Press Pass Five Star Classic Compilations Autographed Patch Booklet /1 #CCCE11
2014 Press Pass Five Star Classic Compilations Autographed Patch Booklet /1 #CCCE12
2014 Press Pass Five Star Classic Compilations Autographed Patch Booklet /1 #CCCE13
2014 Press Pass Five Star Classic Compilations Autographed Patch Booklet /1 #CCCE14
2014 Press Pass Five Star Classic Compilations Autographed Patch Booklet /1 #CCCE15
2014 Press Pass Five Star Classic Compilations Combo Autographs Blue /5 #CCRFR
2014 Press Pass Five Star Classic Compilations Combo Autographs Melting /1 #CCRFR
2014 Press Pass Five Star Holofoil /10 #5
2014 Press Pass Five Star Melting /1 #5
2014 Press Pass Five Star Paramount Pieces Blue /5 #PPCE
2014 Press Pass Five Star Paramount Pieces Gold /25 #PPCE
2014 Press Pass Five Star Paramount Pieces Holofoil /10 #PPCE
2014 Press Pass Five Star Paramount Pieces Melting /1 #PPCE
2014 Press Pass Five Star Paramount Pieces Melting Patch /1 #PPCE
2014 Press Pass Five Star Signature Souvenirs Blue /5 #SSCE
2014 Press Pass Five Star Signature Souvenirs Gold /50 #SSCE
2014 Press Pass Five Star Signature Souvenirs Holofoil /25 #SSCE
2014 Press Pass Five Star Signature Souvenirs Melting /1 #SSCE
2014 Press Pass Five Star Signatures Blue /5 #FSSCE
2014 Press Pass Five Star Signatures Holofoil /10 #FSSCE
2014 Press Pass Five Star Signatures Melting /1 #FSSCE
2014 Press Pass Four Wide Gold /10 #FWCE
2014 Press Pass Four Wide Melting /1 #FWCE
2014 Press Pass Gold #10
2014 Press Pass Gold #70
2014 Press Pass Gold #86
2014 Press Pass Gold #91
2014 Press Pass Redline #18
2014 Press Pass Redline #19
2014 Press Pass Redline Black /75 #18
2014 Press Pass Redline Black /75 #19
2014 Press Pass Redline Blue Foil #18
2014 Press Pass Redline Blue Foil #19
2014 Press Pass Redline Cyan /50 #18
2014 Press Pass Redline Cyan /50 #19
2014 Press Pass Redline Dynamic Duals Relic Autographs Blue /25 #DDCE
2014 Press Pass Redline Dynamic Duals Relic Autographs Gold /10 #DDCE
2014 Press Pass Redline Dynamic Duals Relic Autographs Melting /1 #DDCE
2014 Press Pass Redline Dynamic Duals Relic Autographs Red /50 #DDCE
2014 Press Pass Redline Green National Convention /5 #18
2014 Press Pass Redline Green National Convention /5 #19
2014 Press Pass Redline Magenta /10 #18
2014 Press Pass Redline Magenta /10 #19
2014 Press Pass Redline Muscle Car Sheet Metal Blue /25 #MCMCE1
2014 Press Pass Redline Muscle Car Sheet Metal Gold /50 #MCMCE1
2014 Press Pass Redline Muscle Car Sheet Metal Melting /1 #MCMCE1
2014 Press Pass Redline Muscle Car Sheet Metal Red /75 #MCMCE1
2014 Press Pass Redline Pieces of the Action Blue /10 #PACE
2014 Press Pass Redline Pieces of the Action Gold /25 #PACE
2014 Press Pass Redline Pieces of the Action Melting /1 #PACE
2014 Press Pass Redline Pieces of the Action Red /75 #PACE
2014 Press Pass Redline Redline Racers #RR5
2014 Press Pass Redline Relic Autographs Blue /10 #RRSECE1
2014 Press Pass Redline Relic Autographs Gold /25 #RRSECE1
2014 Press Pass Redline Relic Autographs Melting /1 #RRSECE1
2014 Press Pass Redline Relic Autographs Red /50 #RRSECE1
2014 Press Pass Redline Relics Blue /25 #RRCE1
2014 Press Pass Redline Relics Gold /50 #RRCE1
2014 Press Pass Redline Relics Melting /1 #RRCE1
2014 Press Pass Redline Relics Red /75 #RRCE1
2014 Press Pass Redline Signatures Blue /10 #RSCE1
2014 Press Pass Redline Signatures Gold /15 #RSCE1
2014 Press Pass Redline Signatures Melting /5 #RSCE1
2014 Press Pass Redline Signatures Red /30 #RSCE1
2014 Press Pass Redline Yellow /1 #18
2014 Press Pass Redline Yellow /1 #19
2014 Press Pass Replay #2
2014 Press Pass Replay #24
2014 Press Pass Signature Series Gold /5 #SSCE
2014 Press Pass Signature Series Melting /1 #SSCE
2014 Press Pass Signings Gold /10 #PPSCE
2014 Press Pass Signings Holofoil /5 #PPSCE
2014 Press Pass Signings Melting /1 #PPSCE
2014 Press Pass Signings Printing Plates Black /1 #PPSCE
2014 Press Pass Signings Printing Plates Cyan /1 #PPSCE
2014 Press Pass Signings Printing Plates Magenta /1 #PPSCE
2014 Press Pass Signings Printing Plates Yellow /1 #PPSCE
2014 Press Pass Signings Silver /25 #PPSCE
2014 Total Memorabilia #8
2014 Total Memorabilia Acceleration #AC3
2014 Total Memorabilia Autographed Memorabilia Blue /5 #SCCE
2014 Total Memorabilia Autographed Memorabilia Gold /10 #SCCE
2014 Total Memorabilia Autographed Memorabilia Melting /1 #SCCE
2014 Total Memorabilia Autographed Memorabilia Silver /10 #SC-CE
2014 Total Memorabilia Black and White /99 #8
2014 Total Memorabilia Clear Cuts Blue /175 #CCUCE
2014 Total Memorabilia Clear Cuts Melting /25 #CCUCE
2014 Total Memorabilia Dual Swatch Gold /150 #TMCE
2014 Total Memorabilia Gold /175 #8
2014 Total Memorabilia Quad Swatch Melting /25 #TMCE
2014 Total Memorabilia Red #8
2014 Total Memorabilia Single Swatch Silver /275 #TMCE
2014 Total Memorabilia Triple Swatch Blue /99 #TMCE
2015 Press Pass #13
2015 Press Pass #84
2015 Press Pass #66
2015 Press Pass #100
2015 Press Pass Burning Rubber Blue /50 #BRCE1
2015 Press Pass Burning Rubber Blue /50 #BRCE2
2015 Press Pass Burning Rubber Gold #BRCE1
2015 Press Pass Burning Rubber Gold #BRCE2
2015 Press Pass Burning Rubber Green /10 #BRCE1
2015 Press Pass Burning Rubber Green /10 #BRCE2
2015 Press Pass Burning Rubber Letterman /8 #BRLECE
2015 Press Pass Burning Rubber Melting /1 #BRCE1
2015 Press Pass Burning Rubber Melting /1 #BRCE2
2015 Press Pass Championship Caliber Dual /25 #CCMCE
2015 Press Pass Championship Caliber Quad /1 #CCMCE
2015 Press Pass Championship Caliber Signature Edition Blue /25 #CCCE
2015 Press Pass Championship Caliber Signature Edition Gold /30 #CCCE
2015 Press Pass Championship Caliber Signature Edition Green /10 #CCCE
2015 Press Pass Championship Caliber Signature Edition Melting /1 #CCCE
2015 Press Pass Championship Caliber Single /50 #CCMCE
2015 Press Pass Championship Caliber Triple /10 #CCMCE
2015 Press Pass Cup Chase #13
2015 Press Pass Cup Chase #66
2015 Press Pass Cup Chase #84
2015 Press Pass Cup Chase #100
2015 Press Pass Cup Chase Blue /25 #13
2015 Press Pass Cup Chase Blue /25 #66
2015 Press Pass Cup Chase Blue /25 #84
2015 Press Pass Cup Chase Blue /25 #100
2015 Press Pass Cup Chase Gold /75 #13
2015 Press Pass Cup Chase Gold /75 #66
2015 Press Pass Cup Chase Gold /75 #84
2015 Press Pass Cup Chase Gold /75 #100
2015 Press Pass Cup Chase Green /10 #13
2015 Press Pass Cup Chase Green /10 #66
2015 Press Pass Cup Chase Green /10 #84
2015 Press Pass Cup Chase Green /10 #100
2015 Press Pass Cup Chase Melting /1 #13
2015 Press Pass Cup Chase Melting /1 #66
2015 Press Pass Cup Chase Melting /1 #84
2015 Press Pass Cup Chase Melting /1 #100
2015 Press Pass Cup Chase Upper Cuts /13 #UCCE
2015 Press Pass Cuts Blue /25 #CCCCE
2015 Press Pass Cuts Gold /50 #CCCCE
2015 Press Pass Cuts Green /10 #CCCCE
2015 Press Pass Cuts Melting /1 #CCCCE
2015 Press Pass Pit Road Pieces Blue /25 #PPMCE
2015 Press Pass Pit Road Pieces Gold /50 #PPMCE
2015 Press Pass Pit Road Pieces Green /10 #PPMCE
2015 Press Pass Pit Road Pieces Melting /1 #PPMCE
2015 Press Pass Pit Road Pieces Signature Edition Blue /25 #PRPCE
2015 Press Pass Pit Road Pieces Signature Edition Gold /50 #PRPCE
2015 Press Pass Pit Road Pieces Signature Edition Green /10 #PRPCE
2015 Press Pass Pit Road Pieces Signature Edition Melting /1 #PRPCE
2015 Press Pass Purple #13
2015 Press Pass Purple #66
2015 Press Pass Purple #84
2015 Press Pass Purple #100
2015 Press Pass Red #13
2015 Press Pass Red #66
2015 Press Pass Red #84
2015 Press Pass Red #100
2015 Press Pass Signature Series Blue /25 #SSCE
2015 Press Pass Signature Series Gold /50 #SSCE
2015 Press Pass Signature Series Green /10 #SSCE
2015 Press Pass Signature Series Melting /1 #SSCE
2015 Press Pass Signings Blue /25 #PPSCED
2015 Press Pass Signings Gold #PPSCED
2015 Press Pass Signings Green /10 #PPSCED
2015 Press Pass Signings Melting /5 #PPSCED
2015 Press Pass Signings Red /15 #PPSCED
2016 Certified #56
2016 Certified #4
2016 Certified Complete Materials /199 #15
2016 Certified Complete Materials Mirror Black /1 #15
2016 Certified Complete Materials Mirror Blue /50 #15
2016 Certified Complete Materials Mirror Gold /25 #15
2016 Certified Complete Materials Mirror Green /5 #15
2016 Certified Complete Materials Mirror Orange /99 #15
2016 Certified Complete Materials Mirror Purple /10 #15
2016 Certified Complete Materials Mirror Red /75 #15
2016 Certified Complete Materials Mirror Silver /99 #15
2016 Certified Epix /199 #9
2016 Certified Epix Mirror Black /1 #9
2016 Certified Epix Mirror Blue /50 #9
2016 Certified Epix Mirror Gold /25 #9
2016 Certified Epix Mirror Green /5 #9
2016 Certified Epix Mirror Orange /99 #9
2016 Certified Epix Mirror Purple /10 #9
2016 Certified Epix Mirror Red /75 #9
2016 Certified Epix Mirror Silver /99 #9
2016 Certified Gold Team /199 #11
2016 Certified Gold Team Mirror Black /1 #11
2016 Certified Gold Team Mirror Blue /50 #11
2016 Certified Gold Team Mirror Gold /25 #11
2016 Certified Gold Team Mirror Green /5 #11
2016 Certified Gold Team Mirror Orange /99 #11
2016 Certified Gold Team Mirror Purple /10 #11
2016 Certified Gold Team Mirror Red /75 #11
2016 Certified Gold Team Mirror Silver /99 #11
2016 Certified Mirror Black /1 #4
2016 Certified Mirror Black /1 #56
2016 Certified Mirror Blue /50 #4
2016 Certified Mirror Blue /50 #56
2016 Certified Mirror Gold /25 #4
2016 Certified Mirror Gold /25 #56
2016 Certified Mirror Green /5 #4
2016 Certified Mirror Green /5 #56
2016 Certified Mirror Orange /99 #4
2016 Certified Mirror Orange /99 #56
2016 Certified Mirror Purple /10 #4
2016 Certified Mirror Purple /10 #56
2016 Certified Mirror Red /75 #4
2016 Certified Mirror Red /75 #56
2016 Certified Mirror Silver /99 #4
2016 Certified Mirror Silver /99 #56
2016 Certified Signatures /33 #3
2016 Certified Signatures Mirror Black /1 #3
2016 Certified Signatures Mirror Blue /20 #3
2016 Certified Signatures Mirror Gold /15 #3
2016 Certified Signatures Mirror Green /5 #3
2016 Certified Signatures Mirror Orange /15 #3
2016 Certified Signatures Mirror Purple /10 #3
2016 Certified Signatures Mirror Red /25 #3
2016 Certified Signatures Mirror Silver /10 #3
2016 Certified Skills /199 #17
2016 Certified Skills Mirror Black /1 #17
2016 Certified Skills Mirror Blue /50 #17
2016 Certified Skills Mirror Gold /25 #17
2016 Certified Skills Mirror Green /5 #17
2016 Certified Skills Mirror Orange /99 #17
2016 Certified Skills Mirror Purple /10 #17
2016 Certified Skills Mirror Red /75 #17
2016 Certified Skills Mirror Silver /99 #17
2016 Certified Sprint Cup Signature Swatches /50 #1
2016 Certified Sprint Cup Signature Swatches Mirror Black /1 #1
2016 Certified Sprint Cup Signature Swatches Mirror Blue /25 #1
2016 Certified Sprint Cup Signature Swatches Mirror Gold /15 #1
2016 Certified Sprint Cup Signature Swatches Mirror Green /5 #1
2016 Certified Sprint Cup Signature Swatches Mirror Orange /15 #1
2016 Certified Sprint Cup Signature Swatches Mirror Purple /10 #1
2016 Certified Sprint Cup Signature Swatches Mirror Red /35 #1
2016 Certified Sprint Cup Signature Swatches Mirror Silver /10 #1
2016 Certified Sprint Cup Swatches /299 #9
2016 Certified Sprint Cup Swatches Mirror Black /1 #8
2016 Certified Sprint Cup Swatches Mirror Black /1 #9
2016 Certified Sprint Cup Swatches Mirror Blue /50 #8
2016 Certified Sprint Cup Swatches Mirror Blue /50 #9
2016 Certified Sprint Cup Swatches Mirror Gold /25 #8
2016 Certified Sprint Cup Swatches Mirror Gold /25 #9
2016 Certified Sprint Cup Swatches Mirror Green /5 #8
2016 Certified Sprint Cup Swatches Mirror Green /5 #9

2016 Certified Sprint Cup Swatches Mirror Orange /99 #8
2016 Certified Sprint Cup Swatches Mirror Orange /99 #9
2016 Certified Sprint Cup Swatches Mirror Purple /10 #9
2016 Certified Sprint Cup Swatches Mirror Red /31 #8
2016 Certified Sprint Cup Swatches Mirror Red /75 #9
2016 Certified Sprint Cup Swatches Mirror Silver /99 #8
2016 Certified Sprint Cup Swatches Mirror Silver /99 #9
2016 Panini Black Friday #33
2016 Panini Black Friday Autographs /25 #33
2016 Panini Black Friday Cracked Ice /25 #33
2016 Panini Black Friday Holo Plaid /1 #33
2016 Panini Black Friday Rapture /10 #33
2016 Panini Black Friday Thick Stock /50 #33
2016 Panini Black Friday Wedges /50 #33
2016 Panini Instant #8
2016 Panini Instant #11
2016 Panini Instant Black /1 #8
2016 Panini Instant Black /1 #11
2016 Panini Instant Blue /25 #8
2016 Panini Instant Blue /25 #11
2016 Panini Instant Green /5 #8
2016 Panini Instant Green /5 #11
2016 Panini Instant Orange /50 #8
2016 Panini Instant Orange /50 #11
2016 Panini Instant Purple /10 #8
2016 Panini Instant Purple /10 #11
2016 Panini National Convention #40
2016 Panini National Convention Autographs /25 #40
2016 Panini National Convention Cracked Ice /25 #40
2016 Panini National Convention Decoy Cracked Ice /25 #40
2016 Panini National Convention Decoy Escher Squares /10 #40
2016 Panini National Convention Decoy Rapture /1 #40
2016 Panini National Convention Decoy Wedges /99 #40
2016 Panini National Convention Diamond Awe /49 #40
2016 Panini National Convention Escher Squares /10 #40
2016 Panini National Convention Rapture /1 #40
2016 Panini National Convention Wedges /99 #40
2016 Panini National Treasures /25 #23
2016 Panini National Treasures Black /5 #23
2016 Panini National Treasures Blue /1 #23
2016 Panini National Treasures Dual Driver Materials /25 #6
2016 Panini National Treasures Dual Driver Materials Black /5 #6
2016 Panini National Treasures Dual Driver Materials Blue /1 #6
2016 Panini National Treasures Dual Driver Materials Gold /10 #6
2016 Panini National Treasures Dual Driver Materials Printing Plates Black /1 #6
2016 Panini National Treasures Dual Driver Materials Printing Plates Cyan /1 #6
2016 Panini National Treasures Dual Driver Materials Printing Plates Magenta /1 #6
2016 Panini National Treasures Dual Driver Materials Printing Plates Yellow /1 #6
2016 Panini National Treasures Dual Driver Materials Silver /15 #6
2016 Panini National Treasures Dual Signatures /50 #12
2016 Panini National Treasures Dual Signatures Black /10 #12
2016 Panini National Treasures Dual Signatures Blue /1 #12
2016 Panini National Treasures Dual Signatures Gold /30 #12
2016 Panini National Treasures Eight Signatures /15 #2
2016 Panini National Treasures Eight Signatures Black /5 #2
2016 Panini National Treasures Eight Signatures Blue /1 #2
2016 Panini National Treasures Eight Signatures Gold /10 #2
2016 Panini National Treasures Firesuit Materials /25 #2
2016 Panini National Treasures Firesuit Materials Black /5 #2
2016 Panini National Treasures Firesuit Materials Blue /1 #2
2016 Panini National Treasures Firesuit Materials Gold /10 #2
2016 Panini National Treasures Firesuit Materials Laundry Tag /1 #2
2016 Panini National Treasures Firesuit Materials Printing Plates Black /1 #2
2016 Panini National Treasures Firesuit Materials Printing Plates Cyan /1 #2
2016 Panini National Treasures Firesuit Materials Printing Plates Magenta /1 #2
2016 Panini National Treasures Firesuit Materials Printing Plates Yellow /1 #2
2016 Panini National Treasures Firesuit Materials Silver /15 #2
2016 Panini National Treasures Gold /15 #23
2016 Panini National Treasures Jumbo Firesuit Patch Signature Booklet Associate Sponsor 1 /1 #4
2016 Panini National Treasures Jumbo Firesuit Patch Signature Booklet Associate Sponsor 2 /1 #4
2016 Panini National Treasures Jumbo Firesuit Patch Signature Booklet Associate Sponsor 3 /1 #4
2016 Panini National Treasures Jumbo Firesuit Patch Signature Booklet Associate Sponsor 4 /1 #4
2016 Panini National Treasures Jumbo Firesuit Patch Signature Booklet Associate Sponsor 5 /1 #4
2016 Panini National Treasures Jumbo Firesuit Patch Signature Booklet Associate Sponsor 6 /1 #4
2016 Panini National Treasures Jumbo Firesuit Patch Signature Booklet Associate Sponsor 7 /1 #4
2016 Panini National Treasures Jumbo Firesuit Patch Signature Booklet Associate Sponsor 8 /1 #4
2016 Panini National Treasures Jumbo Firesuit Patch Signature Booklet Associate Sponsor 9 /1 #4
2016 Panini National Treasures Jumbo Firesuit Patch Signature Booklet Goodyear /1 #4
2016 Panini National Treasures Jumbo Firesuit Patch Signature Booklet Manufacturers Logo /3 #4
2016 Panini National Treasures Jumbo Firesuit Patch Signature Booklet Nameplate /2 #4
2016 Panini National Treasures Jumbo Firesuit Patch Signature Booklet NASCAR /1 #4
2016 Panini National Treasures Jumbo Firesuit Patch Signature Booklet Sprint Cup Logo /1 #4
2016 Panini National Treasures Jumbo Firesuit Patch Signature Booklet Sunoco /1 #4
2016 Panini National Treasures Jumbo Firesuit Signatures /25 #4
2016 Panini National Treasures Jumbo Firesuit Signatures Black /5 #4
2016 Panini National Treasures Jumbo Firesuit Signatures Blue /1 #4
2016 Panini National Treasures Jumbo Firesuit Signatures Gold /10 #4
2016 Panini National Treasures Jumbo Firesuit Signatures Printing Plates Black /1 #4
2016 Panini National Treasures Jumbo Firesuit Signatures Printing Plates Cyan /1 #4
2016 Panini National Treasures Jumbo Firesuit Signatures Printing Plates Magenta /1 #4
2016 Panini National Treasures Jumbo Firesuit Signatures Silver /15 #4
2016 Panini National Treasures Jumbo Sheet Metal Signatures /25 #1
2016 Panini National Treasures Jumbo Sheet Metal Signatures Black /5 #1
2016 Panini National Treasures Jumbo Sheet Metal Signatures Blue /1 #1
2016 Panini National Treasures Jumbo Sheet Metal Signatures Gold /10 #1
2016 Panini National Treasures Jumbo Sheet Metal Signatures Printing Plates Black /1 #1
2016 Panini National Treasures Jumbo Sheet Metal Signatures Printing Plates Cyan /1 #1
2016 Panini National Treasures Jumbo Sheet Metal Signatures Printing Plates Magenta /1 #1
2016 Panini National Treasures Jumbo Sheet Metal Signatures Printing Plates Yellow /1 #1
2016 Panini National Treasures Jumbo Sheet Metal Signatures Silver /15 #1
2016 Panini National Treasures Printing Plates Black /1 #23
2016 Panini National Treasures Printing Plates Cyan /1 #23
2016 Panini National Treasures Printing Plates Magenta /1 #23
2016 Panini National Treasures Printing Plates Yellow /1 #23
2016 Panini National Treasures Quad Driver Materials /25 #2
2016 Panini National Treasures Quad Driver Materials Black /5 #2
2016 Panini National Treasures Quad Driver Materials Blue /1 #2
2016 Panini National Treasures Quad Driver Materials Gold /10 #2
2016 Panini National Treasures Quad Driver Materials Printing Plates Black /1 #2
2016 Panini National Treasures Quad Driver Materials Printing Plates Cyan /1 #2
2016 Panini National Treasures Quad Driver Materials Printing Plates Magenta /1 #2
2016 Panini National Treasures Quad Driver Materials Printing Plates Yellow /1 #2
2016 Panini National Treasures Quad Driver Materials Silver /15 #2
2016 Panini National Treasures Quad Materials /25 #2
2016 Panini National Treasures Quad Materials Black /5 #2
2016 Panini National Treasures Quad Materials Blue /1 #2
2016 Panini National Treasures Quad Materials Gold /10 #2
2016 Panini National Treasures Quad Materials Printing Plates Black /1 #2
2016 Panini National Treasures Quad Materials Printing Plates Cyan /1 #2
2016 Panini National Treasures Quad Materials Printing Plates Magenta /1 #2
2016 Panini National Treasures Quad Materials Printing Plates Yellow /1 #2
2016 Panini National Treasures Quad Materials Silver /15 #2
2016 Panini National Treasures Sheet Metal Materials /25 #2
2016 Panini National Treasures Sheet Metal Materials Black /5 #2
2016 Panini National Treasures Sheet Metal Materials Blue /1 #2
2016 Panini National Treasures Sheet Metal Materials Gold /10 #2
2016 Panini National Treasures Sheet Metal Materials Printing Plates Black /1 #2
2016 Panini National Treasures Sheet Metal Materials Printing Plates Cyan /1 #2
2016 Panini National Treasures Sheet Metal Materials Printing Plates Magenta /1 #2
2016 Panini National Treasures Sheet Metal Materials Printing Plates Yellow /1 #2
2016 Panini National Treasures Sheet Metal Materials Silver /15 #2
2016 Panini National Treasures Signature Dual Materials /25 #4
2016 Panini National Treasures Signature Dual Materials Black /5 #4
2016 Panini National Treasures Signature Dual Materials Gold /10 #4
2016 Panini National Treasures Signature Dual Materials Silver /15 #4
2016 Panini National Treasures Signature Firesuit Materials /25 #4
2016 Panini National Treasures Signature Firesuit Materials Black /5 #4
2016 Panini National Treasures Signature Firesuit Materials Blue /1 #4
2016 Panini National Treasures Signature Firesuit Materials Gold /10 #4
2016 Panini National Treasures Signature Firesuit Materials Laundry Tag /1 #4
2016 Panini National Treasures Signature Firesuit Materials Printing Plates Black /1 #4
2016 Panini National Treasures Signature Firesuit Materials Printing Plates Cyan /1 #4
2016 Panini National Treasures Signature Firesuit Materials Printing Plates Magenta /1 #4
2016 Panini National Treasures Signature Firesuit Materials Printing Plates Yellow /1 #4
2016 Panini National Treasures Signature Firesuit Materials Silver /15 #4
2016 Panini National Treasures Signature Quad Materials /25 #4
2016 Panini National Treasures Signature Quad Materials Black /5 #4
2016 Panini National Treasures Signature Quad Materials Blue /1 #4
2016 Panini National Treasures Signature Quad Materials Gold /10 #4
2016 Panini National Treasures Signature Quad Materials Printing Plates Black /1 #4
2016 Panini National Treasures Signature Quad Materials Printing Plates Cyan /1 #4
2016 Panini National Treasures Signature Quad Materials Printing Plates Magenta /1 #4
2016 Panini National Treasures Signature Quad Materials Printing Plates Yellow /1 #4
2016 Panini National Treasures Signature Quad Materials Silver /15 #4
2016 Panini National Treasures Signatures Black /5 #4
2016 Panini National Treasures Signatures Blue /1 #4
2016 Panini National Treasures Signatures Printing Plates Black /1 #4
2016 Panini National Treasures Signatures Printing Plates Cyan /1 #4
2016 Panini National Treasures Signatures Printing Plates Magenta /1 #4
2016 Panini National Treasures Signatures Printing Plates Yellow /1 #4
2016 Panini National Treasures Silver /20 #23
2016 Panini National Treasures Six Signatures /25 #1
2016 Panini National Treasures Six Signatures Black /10 #1
2016 Panini National Treasures Six Signatures Blue /1 #1
2016 Panini National Treasures Six Signatures Gold /15 #1
2016 Panini National Treasures Trio Driver Materials /25 #8
2016 Panini National Treasures Trio Driver Materials /25 #9
2016 Panini National Treasures Trio Driver Materials Black /5 #8
2016 Panini National Treasures Trio Driver Materials Black /5 #9
2016 Panini National Treasures Trio Driver Materials Blue /1 #8
2016 Panini National Treasures Trio Driver Materials Blue /1 #9
2016 Panini National Treasures Trio Driver Materials Gold /10 #8
2016 Panini National Treasures Trio Driver Materials Gold /10 #9
2016 Panini National Treasures Trio Driver Materials Printing Plates Black /1 #8
2016 Panini National Treasures Trio Driver Materials Printing Plates Black /1 #9
2016 Panini National Treasures Trio Driver Materials Printing Plates Cyan /1 #8
2016 Panini National Treasures Trio Driver Materials Printing Plates Cyan /1 #9
2016 Panini National Treasures Trio Driver Materials Printing Plates Magenta /1 #8
2016 Panini National Treasures Trio Driver Materials Printing Plates Magenta /1 #9
2016 Panini National Treasures Trio Driver Materials Printing Plates Yellow /1 #8
2016 Panini National Treasures Trio Driver Materials Printing Plates Yellow /1 #9
2016 Panini National Treasures Trio Driver Materials Silver /15 #8
2016 Panini National Treasures Trio Driver Materials Silver /15 #9
2016 Panini National Treasures Winning Signatures Black /5 #3
2016 Panini National Treasures Winning Signatures Blue /1 #3
2016 Panini National Treasures Winning Signatures Printing Plates Black /1 #3
2016 Panini National Treasures Winning Signatures Printing Plates Cyan /1 #3
2016 Panini National Treasures Winning Signatures Printing Plates Magenta /1 #3
2016 Panini National Treasures Winning Signatures Printing Plates Yellow /1 #3
2016 Panini Prizm #100
2016 Panini Prizm #88
2016 Panini Prizm #47
2016 Panini Prizm #19
2016 Panini Prizm Autographs Prizms #62
2016 Panini Prizm Autographs Prizms Black /3 #62
2016 Panini Prizm Autographs Prizms Blue Flag /25 #62
2016 Panini Prizm Autographs Prizms Camo /19 #62
2016 Panini Prizm Autographs Prizms Checkered Flag /1 #62
2016 Panini Prizm Autographs Prizms Gold /10 #62
2016 Panini Prizm Autographs Prizms Rainbow /24 #62
2016 Panini Prizm Autographs Prizms Red Flag /15 #62
2016 Panini Prizm Autographs Prizms Red White and Blue /10 #62
2016 Panini Prizm Autographs Prizms White Flag /5 #62
2016 Panini Prizm Blowing Smoke #9
2016 Panini Prizm Blowing Smoke Prizms #9
2016 Panini Prizm Blowing Smoke Prizms Checkered Flag /1 #9
2016 Panini Prizm Blowing Smoke Prizms Gold /10 #9
2016 Panini Prizm Competitors #6
2016 Panini Prizm Competitors Prizms #6
2016 Panini Prizm Competitors Prizms Checkered Flag /1 #6
2016 Panini Prizm Competitors Prizms Gold /10 #6
2016 Panini Prizm Firesuit Fabrics /149 #8
2016 Panini Prizm Firesuit Fabrics Prizms Blue Flag /75 #8
2016 Panini Prizm Firesuit Fabrics Prizms Checkered Flag /1 #8
2016 Panini Prizm Firesuit Fabrics Prizms Green Flag /99 #8
2016 Panini Prizm Firesuit Fabrics Prizms Red Flag /25 #8
2016 Panini Prizm Firesuit Fabrics Team /249 #8
2016 Panini Prizm Firesuit Fabrics Team Prizms Blue Flag /75 #8
2016 Panini Prizm Firesuit Fabrics Team Prizms Checkered Flag /1 #8
2016 Panini Prizm Firesuit Fabrics Team Prizms Green Flag /99 #8
2016 Panini Prizm Firesuit Fabrics Team Prizms Red Flag /3 #8
2016 Panini Prizm Patented Penmanship Prizms #14
2016 Panini Prizm Patented Penmanship Prizms Black /3 #14
2016 Panini Prizm Patented Penmanship Prizms Blue Flag /25 #14
2016 Panini Prizm Patented Penmanship Prizms Camo /19 #14
2016 Panini Prizm Patented Penmanship Prizms Checkered Flag /1 #14
2016 Panini Prizm Patented Penmanship Prizms Gold /10 #14
2016 Panini Prizm Patented Penmanship Prizms Rainbow /24 #14
2016 Panini Prizm Patented Penmanship Prizms Red Flag /15 #14
2016 Panini Prizm Patented Penmanship Prizms Red White and Blue /25 #14
2016 Panini Prizm Patented Penmanship Prizms White Flag /5 #14
2016 Panini Prizm Prizms #19
2016 Panini Prizm Prizms #47
2016 Panini Prizm Prizms #88
2016 Panini Prizm Prizms #100
2016 Panini Prizm Prizms Black /3 #19
2016 Panini Prizm Prizms Black /3 #47
2016 Panini Prizm Prizms Black /3 #88
2016 Panini Prizm Prizms Black /3 #100
2016 Panini Prizm Prizms Blue Flag /99 #19
2016 Panini Prizm Prizms Blue Flag /99 #47
2016 Panini Prizm Prizms Blue Flag /99 #88
2016 Panini Prizm Prizms Blue Flag /99 #100
2016 Panini Prizm Prizms Camo /19 #19
2016 Panini Prizm Prizms Camo /19 #47
2016 Panini Prizm Prizms Camo /19 #88
2016 Panini Prizm Prizms Camo /18 #100
2016 Panini Prizm Prizms Checkered Flag /1 #19
2016 Panini Prizm Prizms Checkered Flag /1 #47
2016 Panini Prizm Prizms Checkered Flag /1 #88
2016 Panini Prizm Prizms Checkered Flag /1 #100
2016 Panini Prizm Prizms Gold /10 #19
2016 Panini Prizm Prizms Gold /10 #47
2016 Panini Prizm Prizms Gold /10 #88
2016 Panini Prizm Prizms Gold /10 #100
2016 Panini Prizm Prizms Green Flag /149 #19
2016 Panini Prizm Prizms Green Flag /149 #47
2016 Panini Prizm Prizms Green Flag /149 #88
2016 Panini Prizm Prizms Green Flag /149 #100
2016 Panini Prizm Prizms Rainbow /24 #19
2016 Panini Prizm Prizms Rainbow /24 #47
2016 Panini Prizm Prizms Rainbow /24 #88
2016 Panini Prizm Prizms Rainbow /24 #100
2016 Panini Prizm Prizms Red Flag /75 #19
2016 Panini Prizm Prizms Red Flag /75 #47
2016 Panini Prizm Prizms Red Flag /75 #88
2016 Panini Prizm Prizms Red Flag /75 #100
2016 Panini Prizm Prizms Red White and Blue #19
2016 Panini Prizm Prizms Red White and Blue #47
2016 Panini Prizm Prizms Red White and Blue #88
2016 Panini Prizm Prizms Red White and Blue #100
2016 Panini Prizm Prizms White Flag /5 #19
2016 Panini Prizm Prizms White Flag /5 #47
2016 Panini Prizm Prizms White Flag /5 #88
2016 Panini Prizm Prizms White Flag /5 #100
2016 Panini Prizm Qualifying Times #1
2016 Panini Prizm Qualifying Times Prizms #1
2016 Panini Prizm Qualifying Times Prizms Checkered Flag /1 #1
2016 Panini Prizm Qualifying Times Prizms Gold /10 #1
2016 Panini Prizm Race Used Tire #7
2016 Panini Prizm Race Used Tire Prizms Blue Flag /49 #7
2016 Panini Prizm Race Used Tire Prizms Checkered Flag /1 #7
2016 Panini Prizm Race Used Tire Prizms Green Flag /99 #7
2016 Panini Prizm Race Used Tire Prizms Red Flag /25 #7
2016 Panini Prizm Race Used Tire Team #6
2016 Panini Prizm Race Used Tire Team Prizms Blue Flag /75 #6
2016 Panini Prizm Race Used Tire Team Prizms Checkered Flag /1 #6
2016 Panini Prizm Race Used Tire Team Prizms Green Flag /149 #6
2016 Panini Prizm Race Used Tire Team Prizms Red Flag /10 #6
2016 Panini Prizm Raising the Flag #6
2016 Panini Prizm Raising the Flag Prizms #6
2016 Panini Prizm Raising the Flag Prizms Checkered Flag /1 #6
2016 Panini Prizm Raising the Flag Prizms Gold /10 #6
2016 Panini Prizm Winner's Circle #25
2016 Panini Prizm Winner's Circle #12
2016 Panini Prizm Winner's Circle Prizms #12
2016 Panini Prizm Winner's Circle Prizms #25
2016 Panini Prizm Winner's Circle Prizms Checkered Flag /1 #12
2016 Panini Prizm Winner's Circle Prizms Checkered Flag /1 #25
2016 Panini Prizm Winner's Circle Prizms Gold /10 #12
2016 Panini Prizm Winner's Circle Prizms Gold /10 #25
2016 Panini Torque #5
2016 Panini Torque #82
2016 Panini Torque Artist Proof /50 #5
2016 Panini Torque Artist Proof /50 #82
2016 Panini Torque Blackout /1 #5
2016 Panini Torque Blackout /1 #82
2016 Panini Torque Blue /125 #5
2016 Panini Torque Blue /125 #82
2016 Panini Torque Clear Vision #5
2016 Panini Torque Clear Vision Blue /99 #5
2016 Panini Torque Clear Vision Gold /149 #5
2016 Panini Torque Clear Vision Green /25 #5
2016 Panini Torque Clear Vision Purple /10 #5
2016 Panini Torque Clear Vision Red /49 #5
2016 Panini Torque Gas N Go #4
2016 Panini Torque Gas N Go Gold /199 #4
2016 Panini Torque Gas N Go Holo Silver /99 #4
2016 Panini Torque Gold #5
2016 Panini Torque Gold #82
2016 Panini Torque Helmets #10
2016 Panini Torque Helmets Blue /99 #10
2016 Panini Torque Helmets Checkerboard /10 #10
2016 Panini Torque Helmets Green /25 #10
2016 Panini Torque Helmets Red /49 #10
2016 Panini Torque Holo Gold /5 #5
2016 Panini Torque Holo Gold /5 #82
2016 Panini Torque Holo Silver /10 #5
2016 Panini Torque Holo Silver /10 #82
2016 Panini Torque Horsepower Heroes #5
2016 Panini Torque Horsepower Heroes Gold /199 #5
2016 Panini Torque Horsepower Heroes Holo Silver /99 #5
2016 Panini Torque Jumbo Tire Autographs /49 #16
2016 Panini Torque Jumbo Tire Autographs Blue /25 #16
2016 Panini Torque Jumbo Tire Autographs Green /10 #16
2016 Panini Torque Jumbo Tire Autographs Purple /1 #16
2016 Panini Torque Jumbo Tire Autographs Red /15 #16
2016 Panini Torque Metal Materials /249 #5
2016 Panini Torque Metal Materials Blue /99 #5
2016 Panini Torque Metal Materials Green /25 #5
2016 Panini Torque Metal Materials Purple /10 #5
2016 Panini Torque Metal Materials Red /49 #5
2016 Panini Torque Painted to Perfection #11
2016 Panini Torque Painted to Perfection Blue /99 #11
2016 Panini Torque Painted to Perfection Checkerboard /10 #11
2016 Panini Torque Painted to Perfection Green /25 #11
2016 Panini Torque Painted to Perfection Red /49 #11
2016 Panini Torque Pairings Materials /249 #13
2016 Panini Torque Pairings Materials /249 #11
2016 Panini Torque Pairings Materials Blue /99 #11
2016 Panini Torque Pairings Materials Blue /99 #13
2016 Panini Torque Pairings Materials Green /25 #11
2016 Panini Torque Pairings Materials Green /25 #13
2016 Panini Torque Pairings Materials Purple /10 #11
2016 Panini Torque Pairings Materials Purple /10 #13
2016 Panini Torque Pairings Materials Red /49 #11
2016 Panini Torque Pairings Materials Red /49 #13
2016 Panini Torque Pole Position #5
2016 Panini Torque Pole Position Blue /99 #5
2016 Panini Torque Pole Position Checkerboard /10 #5
2016 Panini Torque Pole Position Green /25 #5
2016 Panini Torque Pole Position Red /49 #5
2016 Panini Torque Printing Plates Black /1 #5
2016 Panini Torque Printing Plates Black /1 #82
2016 Panini Torque Printing Plates Cyan /1 #5
2016 Panini Torque Printing Plates Cyan /1 #82
2016 Panini Torque Printing Plates Magenta /1 #5
2016 Panini Torque Printing Plates Magenta /1 #82
2016 Panini Torque Printing Plates Yellow /1 #5
2016 Panini Torque Printing Plates Yellow /1 #82
2016 Panini Torque Purple /25 #5
2016 Panini Torque Purple /25 #82
2016 Panini Torque Red /99 #5
2016 Panini Torque Red /99 #82
2016 Panini Torque Rubber Relics /399 #4
2016 Panini Torque Rubber Relics Blue /99 #4
2016 Panini Torque Rubber Relics Green /25 #4
2016 Panini Torque Rubber Relics Purple /10 #4
2016 Panini Torque Rubber Relics Red /49 #4
2016 Panini Torque Shades #12
2016 Panini Torque Shades Gold /199 #12
2016 Panini Torque Shades Holo Silver /99 #12
2016 Panini Torque Silhouettes Firesuit Autographs /49 #3
2016 Panini Torque Silhouettes Firesuit Autographs Blue /25 #3
2016 Panini Torque Silhouettes Firesuit Autographs Green /10 #3
2016 Panini Torque Silhouettes Firesuit Autographs Purple /1 #3
2016 Panini Torque Silhouettes Firesuit Autographs Red /15 #3
2016 Panini Torque Silhouettes Sheet Metal Autographs /49 #3
2016 Panini Torque Silhouettes Sheet Metal Autographs Blue /25 #3
2016 Panini Torque Silhouettes Sheet Metal Autographs Green /10 #3
2016 Panini Torque Silhouettes Sheet Metal Autographs Purple /1 #3
2016 Panini Torque Silhouettes Sheet Metal Autographs Red /15 #3
2016 Panini Torque Superstar Vision #15
2016 Panini Torque Superstar Vision Blue /99 #15
2016 Panini Torque Superstar Vision Gold /149 #15
2016 Panini Torque Superstar Vision Green /25 #15
2016 Panini Torque Superstar Vision Purple /10 #15
2016 Panini Torque Superstar Vision Red /49 #15
2016 Panini Torque Test Proof Black /1 #5
2016 Panini Torque Test Proof Black /1 #82
2016 Panini Torque Test Proof Cyan /1 #5
2016 Panini Torque Test Proof Cyan /1 #82
2016 Panini Torque Test Proof Magenta /1 #5
2016 Panini Torque Test Proof Magenta /1 #82
2016 Panini Torque Test Proof Yellow /1 #5
2016 Panini Torque Test Proof Yellow /1 #82
2016 Panini Torque Victory Laps #5
2016 Panini Torque Victory Laps Gold /199 #5
2016 Panini Torque Victory Laps Holo Silver /99 #5
2016 Panini Torque Winning Vision #5
2016 Panini Torque Winning Vision Blue /99 #5
2016 Panini Torque Winning Vision Gold /149 #5
2016 Panini Torque Winning Vision Green /25 #5
2016 Panini Torque Winning Vision Purple /10 #5
2016 Panini Torque Winning Vision Red /49 #5
2017 Donruss #12
2017 Donruss #130
2017 Donruss #144
2017 Donruss #45A
2017 Donruss #45B
2017 Donruss Artist Proof /25 #12
2017 Donruss Artist Proof /25 #45A
2017 Donruss Artist Proof /25 #130
2017 Donruss Artist Proof /25 #144
2017 Donruss Artist Proof /25 #45B
2017 Donruss Blue Foil /299 #12
2017 Donruss Blue Foil /299 #130
2017 Donruss Blue Foil /299 #45A
2017 Donruss Blue Foil /299 #144
2017 Donruss Blue Foil /299 #45B
2017 Donruss Cut to The Chase #8
2017 Donruss Cut to The Chase Cracked Ice /999 #8
2017 Donruss Dual Rubber Relics #2
2017 Donruss Dual Rubber Relics Holo Black /1 #2
2017 Donruss Dual Rubber Relics Holo Gold /25 #2
2017 Donruss Gold Foil /499 #12
2017 Donruss Gold Foil /499 #130
2017 Donruss Gold Foil /499 #144
2017 Donruss Gold Foil /499 #45A
2017 Donruss Gold Foil /499 #45B
2017 Donruss Gold Press Proof /99 #12
2017 Donruss Gold Press Proof /99 #45A
2017 Donruss Gold Press Proof /99 #130
2017 Donruss Gold Press Proof /99 #144
2017 Donruss Gold Press Proof /99 #45B
2017 Donruss Green Foil /199 #12
2017 Donruss Green Foil /199 #45A
2017 Donruss Green Foil /199 #130
2017 Donruss Green Foil /199 #144
2017 Donruss Green Foil /199 #45B
2017 Donruss Pole Position #1
2017 Donruss Pole Position Cracked Ice /999 #1
2017 Donruss Press Proof /49 #12
2017 Donruss Press Proof /49 #45A
2017 Donruss Press Proof /49 #130
2017 Donruss Press Proof /49 #144
2017 Donruss Press Proof /49 #45B
2017 Donruss Printing Plates Black /1 #12
2017 Donruss Printing Plates Black /1 #45A
2017 Donruss Printing Plates Black /1 #130
2017 Donruss Printing Plates Black /1 #144
2017 Donruss Printing Plates Black /1 #45B
2017 Donruss Printing Plates Cyan /1 #12
2017 Donruss Printing Plates Cyan /1 #45A
2017 Donruss Printing Plates Cyan /1 #130
2017 Donruss Printing Plates Cyan /1 #144
2017 Donruss Printing Plates Cyan /1 #45B
2017 Donruss Printing Plates Magenta /1 #12
2017 Donruss Printing Plates Magenta /1 #130
2017 Donruss Printing Plates Magenta /1 #144
2017 Donruss Printing Plates Magenta /1 #45A
2017 Donruss Printing Plates Magenta /1 #45B
2017 Donruss Printing Plates Yellow /1 #12
2017 Donruss Printing Plates Yellow /1 #130
2017 Donruss Printing Plates Yellow /1 #144
2017 Donruss Printing Plates Yellow /1 #45A
2017 Donruss Printing Plates Yellow /1 #45B
2017 Donruss Retro Relics 1984 #9
2017 Donruss Retro Relics 1984 Holo Black /1 #9
2017 Donruss Retro Relics 1984 Holo Gold /25 #9
2017 Donruss Rubber Relics #7
2017 Donruss Rubber Relics #8
2017 Donruss Rubber Relics Holo Black /1 #7
2017 Donruss Rubber Relics Holo Black /1 #8
2017 Donruss Rubber Relics Holo Gold /20 #7
2017 Donruss Rubber Relics Holo Gold /25 #8
2017 Donruss Speed #10
2017 Donruss Speed Cracked Ice /999 #10
2017 Donruss Top Tier #10
2017 Donruss Top Tier Cracked Ice /999 #10
2017 Donruss Track Masters #2
2017 Donruss Track Masters Cracked Ice /999 #2
2017 Panini Day #57
2017 Panini Day Cracked Ice /25 #57
2017 Panini Day Decoy /50 #57
2017 Panini Day Hyperplaid /1 #57
2017 Panini Day Rapture /10 #57
2017 Panini Day Wedges /50 #57
2017 Panini National Treasures /25 #22
2017 Panini National Treasures Associate Sponsor Patch Signatures 1 /1 #20
2017 Panini National Treasures Associate Sponsor Patch Signatures 2 /1 #20
2017 Panini National Treasures Associate Sponsor Patch Signatures 3 /1 #20
2017 Panini National Treasures Associate Sponsor Patch Signatures 4 /1 #20
2017 Panini National Treasures Associate Sponsor Patch Signatures 5 /1 #20
2017 Panini National Treasures Associate Sponsor Patch Signatures 6 /1 #20
2017 Panini National Treasures Associate Sponsor Patch Signatures 7 /1 #20
2017 Panini National Treasures Associate Sponsor Patch Signatures 8 /1 #20
2017 Panini National Treasures Car Manufacturer Patch Signatures /1 #20
2017 Panini National Treasures Century Black /1 #22
2017 Panini National Treasures Century Gold /15 #22
2017 Panini National Treasures Century Green /5 #22
2017 Panini National Treasures Century Holo Gold /10 #22
2017 Panini National Treasures Century Holo Silver /20 #22
2017 Panini National Treasures Combo Material Signatures /25 #1
2017 Panini National Treasures Combo Material Signatures Black /1 #1
2017 Panini National Treasures Combo Material Signatures Gold /15 #1
2017 Panini National Treasures Combo Material Signatures Green /5 #1
2017 Panini National Treasures Combo Material Signatures Holo Gold /10 #1
2017 Panini National Treasures Combo Material Signatures Holo Silver /20 #1
2017 Panini National Treasures Dual Signature Materials /50 #1
2017 Panini National Treasures Dual Signature Materials Black /1 #1
2017 Panini National Treasures Dual Signature Materials Gold /15 #1
2017 Panini National Treasures Dual Signature Materials Green /5 #1
2017 Panini National Treasures Dual Signature Materials Holo Gold /10 #1
2017 Panini National Treasures Dual Signature Materials Holo Silver /25 #1
2017 Panini National Treasures Dual Signature Materials Laundry Tag /1 #1
2017 Panini National Treasures Dual Tire Signatures /25 #12
2017 Panini National Treasures Dual Tire Signatures Black /1 #12
2017 Panini National Treasures Dual Tire Signatures Gold /15 #12
2017 Panini National Treasures Dual Tire Signatures Green /5 #12
2017 Panini National Treasures Dual Tire Signatures Holo Gold /10 #12
2017 Panini National Treasures Dual Tire Signatures Holo Silver /20 #12
2017 Panini National Treasures Dual Tire Signatures Printing Plates Black /1 #12
2017 Panini National Treasures Dual Tire Signatures Printing Plates Cyan /1 #12
2017 Panini National Treasures Dual Tire Signatures Printing Plates Magenta /1 #12
2017 Panini National Treasures Dual Tire Signatures Printing Plates Yellow /1 #12
2017 Panini National Treasures Firesuit Manufacturer Patch Signatures /1 #20
2017 Panini National Treasures Goodyear Patch Signatures /2 #20
2017 Panini National Treasures Jumbo Tire Signatures Gold /15 #6
2017 Panini National Treasures Jumbo Tire Signatures Green /5 #6
2017 Panini National Treasures Jumbo Tire Signatures Holo Gold /10 #6
2017 Panini National Treasures Jumbo Tire Signatures Printing Plates Black /1 #6
2017 Panini National Treasures Jumbo Tire Signatures Printing Plates Cyan /1 #6
2017 Panini National Treasures Jumbo Tire Signatures Printing Plates Magenta /1 #6
2017 Panini National Treasures Jumbo Tire Signatures Printing Plates Yellow /1 #6
2017 Panini National Treasures Legendary Material Signatures Black /1 #10
2017 Panini National Treasures Legendary Material Signatures Gold /15 #10
2017 Panini National Treasures Legendary Material Signatures Green /5 #10
2017 Panini National Treasures Legendary Material Signatures Holo Gold /10 #10
2017 Panini National Treasures Legendary Material Signatures Holo Silver /20 #10
2017 Panini National Treasures Legendary Material Signatures Laundry Tag /1 #10
2017 Panini National Treasures Legendary Material Signatures Printing Plates Black /1 #10
2017 Panini National Treasures Legendary Material Signatures Printing Plates Cyan /1 #10
2017 Panini National Treasures Legendary Material Signatures Printing Plates Magenta /1 #10
2017 Panini National Treasures Legendary Material Signatures Printing Plates Yellow /1 #10
2017 Panini National Treasures Nameplate Patch Signatures /2 #20
2017 Panini National Treasures NASCAR Patch Signatures /1 #20
2017 Panini National Treasures Printing Plates Black /1 #22
2017 Panini National Treasures Printing Plates Cyan /1 #22
2017 Panini National Treasures Printing Plates Magenta /1 #22
2017 Panini National Treasures Printing Plates Yellow /1 #22
2017 Panini National Treasures Series Sponsor Patch Signatures /1 #20
2017 Panini National Treasures Signature Six Way Swatches /25 #10
2017 Panini National Treasures Signature Six Way Swatches Black /1 #10
2017 Panini National Treasures Signature Six Way Swatches Gold /15 #10
2017 Panini National Treasures Signature Six Way Swatches Green /5 #10
2017 Panini National Treasures Signature Six Way Swatches Holo Gold /10 #10
2017 Panini National Treasures Signature Six Way Swatches Holo Silver /20 #10
2017 Panini National Treasures Signature Six Way Swatches Laundry Tag /1 #10
2017 Panini National Treasures Sunoco Patch Signatures /1 #20
2017 Panini National Treasures Winning Material Signatures /25 #9
2017 Panini National Treasures Winning Material Signatures Black /1 #9
2017 Panini National Treasures Winning Material Signatures Gold /15 #9
2017 Panini National Treasures Winning Material Signatures Green /5 #9
2017 Panini National Treasures Winning Material Signatures Holo Gold /10 #9
2017 Panini National Treasures Winning Material Signatures Holo Silver /20 #9
2017 Panini National Treasures Winning Material Signatures Laundry Tag /1 #9
2017 Panini National Treasures Winning Material Signatures Printing Plates Black /1 #9
2017 Panini National Treasures Winning Material Signatures Printing Plates Cyan /1 #9
2017 Panini National Treasures Winning Material Signatures Printing Plates Magenta /1 #9
2017 Panini National Treasures Winning Material Signatures Printing Plates Yellow /1 #9
2017 Panini National Treasures Winning Signatures /99 #15
2017 Panini National Treasures Winning Signatures Black /1 #15
2017 Panini National Treasures Winning Signatures Gold /25 #15
2017 Panini National Treasures Winning Signatures Green /5 #15
2017 Panini National Treasures Winning Signatures Holo Gold /15 #15
2017 Panini National Treasures Winning Signatures Holo Silver /50 #15
2017 Panini National Treasures Winning Signatures Printing Plates Black /1 #15
2017 Panini National Treasures Winning Signatures Printing Plates Cyan /1 #15
2017 Panini National Treasures Winning Signatures Printing Plates Magenta /1 #15
2017 Panini National Treasures Winning Signatures Printing Plates /1 #15
2017 Panini Torque #93
2017 Panini Torque Artist Proof /75 #93
2017 Panini Torque Blackout /1 #93
2017 Panini Torque Blue /150 #93
2017 Panini Torque Clear Vision #39
2017 Panini Torque Clear Vision Blue /99 #39
2017 Panini Torque Clear Vision Gold /149 #39
2017 Panini Torque Clear Vision Green /25 #39
2017 Panini Torque Clear Vision Purple /10 #39
2017 Panini Torque Clear Vision Red /49 #39
2017 Panini Torque Driver Scripts #32
2017 Panini Torque Driver Scripts Blue /99 #32
2017 Panini Torque Driver Scripts Checkerboard /10 #32
2017 Panini Torque Driver Scripts Green /25 #32
2017 Panini Torque Driver Scripts Red /49 #32
2017 Panini Torque Gold #93
2017 Panini Torque Holo Gold /10 #93
2017 Panini Torque Holo Silver /25 #93
2017 Panini Torque Primary Paint #19
2017 Panini Torque Primary Paint Blue /99 #19
2017 Panini Torque Primary Paint Checkerboard /10 #19
2017 Panini Torque Primary Paint Green /25 #19
2017 Panini Torque Primary Paint Red /49 #19
2017 Panini Torque Printing Plates Black /1 #93
2017 Panini Torque Printing Plates Cyan /1 #93
2017 Panini Torque Printing Plates Magenta /1 #93
2017 Panini Torque Printing Plates Yellow /1 #93
2017 Panini Torque Purple /50 #93
2017 Panini Torque Red /100 #93
2017 Panini Torque Running Order #4
2017 Panini Torque Running Order Blue /99 #4
2017 Panini Torque Running Order Checkerboard /10 #4
2017 Panini Torque Running Order Green /25 #4
2017 Panini Torque Running Order Red /49 #4
2017 Panini Torque Silhouettes Firesuit Signatures /30 #19
2017 Panini Torque Silhouettes Firesuit Signatures Blue /25 #19
2017 Panini Torque Silhouettes Firesuit Signatures Green /15 #19
2017 Panini Torque Silhouettes Firesuit Signatures Purple /10 #19
2017 Panini Torque Silhouettes Firesuit Signatures Red /20 #19
2017 Panini Torque Superstar Vision #6
2017 Panini Torque Superstar Vision Blue /99 #6
2017 Panini Torque Superstar Vision Gold /149 #6
2017 Panini Torque Superstar Vision Green /25 #6
2017 Panini Torque Superstar Vision Purple /10 #6
2017 Panini Torque Superstar Vision Red /49 #6
2017 Panini Torque Test Proof Black /1 #93
2017 Panini Torque Test Proof Cyan /1 #93
2017 Panini Torque Test Proof Magenta /1 #93
2017 Panini Torque Test Proof Yellow /1 #93
2017 Panini Torque Victory Laps #14
2017 Panini Torque Victory Laps Gold /199 #14
2017 Panini Torque Victory Laps Holo Silver /99 #14
2017 Panini Torque Visions of Greatness #2
2017 Panini Torque Visions of Greatness Blue /99 #2
2017 Panini Torque Visions of Greatness Gold /149 #2
2017 Panini Torque Visions of Greatness Green /25 #2
2017 Panini Torque Visions of Greatness Purple /10 #2
2017 Panini Torque Visions of Greatness Red /49 #2
2017 Select #134
2017 Select Prizms Black /3 #134
2017 Select Prizms Checkered Flag /1 #134
2017 Select Prizms Gold /10 #134
2017 Select Prizms Tie Dye /24 #134
2017 Select Prizms White /50 #134
2017 Select Select Stars #3
2017 Select Select Stars Prizms Black /3 #3
2017 Select Select Stars Prizms Checkered Flag /1 #3
2017 Select Select Stars Prizms Gold /10 #3
2017 Select Select Stars Prizms Tie Dye /24 #3
2017 Select Select Stars Prizms White /50 #3
2017 Select Signature Swatches #45
2017 Select Signature Swatches Dual #23
2017 Select Signature Swatches Dual Prizms Checkered Flag /1 #23
2017 Select Signature Swatches Dual Prizms Gold /10 #23
2017 Select Signature Swatches Dual Prizms Tie Dye /24 #23
2017 Select Signature Swatches Dual Prizms White /50 #23
2017 Select Signature Swatches Prizms Checkered Flag /1 #45
2017 Select Signature Swatches Prizms Gold /10 #45
2017 Select Signature Swatches Prizms Tie Dye /24 #45
2017 Select Signature Swatches Prizms White /50 #45
2017 Select Signatures #48
2017 Select Signatures Prizms Blue /50 #48
2017 Select Signatures Prizms Checkered Flag /1 #48
2017 Select Signatures Prizms Gold /10 #48
2017 Select Signatures Prizms Red /25 #48
2018 Certified #13
2018 Certified #85
2018 Certified All Certified Team /199 #4
2018 Certified All Certified Team Black /1 #4
2018 Certified All Certified Team Blue /99 #4
2018 Certified All Certified Team Gold /49 #4
2018 Certified All Certified Team Green /10 #4
2018 Certified All Certified Team Mirror Black /1 #4
2018 Certified All Certified Team Mirror Gold /25 #4
2018 Certified All Certified Team Mirror Green /5 #4
2018 Certified All Certified Team Mirror Purple /10 #4
2018 Certified All Certified Team Purple /25 #4
2018 Certified All Certified Team Red /149 #4
2018 Certified Black /1 #13
2018 Certified Black /1 #85
2018 Certified Blue /99 #13
2018 Certified Blue /99 #85
2018 Certified Epix /199 #18
2018 Certified Epix Black /1 #18
2018 Certified Epix Blue /99 #18
2018 Certified Epix Gold /49 #18
2018 Certified Epix Green /10 #18
2018 Certified Epix Mirror Black /1 #18
2018 Certified Epix Mirror Gold /25 #18
2018 Certified Epix Mirror Green /5 #18
2018 Certified Epix Mirror Purple /10 #18
2018 Certified Epix Purple /25 #18
2018 Certified Epix Red /149 #18
2018 Certified Gold /49 #13
2018 Certified Gold /49 #85
2018 Certified Green /10 #13
2018 Certified Green /10 #85
2018 Certified Mirror Black /1 #13
2018 Certified Mirror Black /1 #85
2018 Certified Mirror Gold /25 #13
2018 Certified Mirror Gold /25 #85
2018 Certified Mirror Green /5 #13
2018 Certified Mirror Green /5 #85
2018 Certified Mirror Purple /10 #13
2018 Certified Mirror Purple /10 #85
2018 Certified Orange /249 #13
2018 Certified Orange /249 #85
2018 Certified Piece of the Race Black /1 #11
2018 Certified Piece of the Race Blue /49 #11
2018 Certified Piece of the Race Gold /25 #11
2018 Certified Piece of the Race Green /5 #11
2018 Certified Piece of the Race Purple /10 #11
2018 Certified Piece of the Race Red /125 #11
2018 Certified Purple /25 #13
2018 Certified Purple /25 #85
2018 Certified Red /199 #13

8 Certified Red /199 #85
8 Certified Signing Sessions /99 #1
8 Certified Signing Sessions Black /1 #1
8 Certified Signing Sessions Blue /25 #1
8 Certified Signing Sessions Gold /20 #1
8 Certified Signing Sessions Green /5 #1
8 Certified Signing Sessions Purple /10 #1
8 Certified Signing Sessions Red /50 #1
8 Certified Stars /199 #24
8 Certified Stars Black /1 #24
8 Certified Stars Blue /99 #24
8 Certified Stars Gold /49 #24
8 Certified Stars Green /10 #24
8 Certified Stars Mirror Black /1 #24
8 Certified Stars Mirror Gold /25 #24
8 Certified Stars Mirror Green /5 #24
8 Certified Stars Mirror Purple /10 #24
8 Certified Stars Purple /25 #24
8 Certified Stars Red /149 #24
18 Donruss #3
8 Donruss #103
8 Donruss #152
8 Donruss Artist Proofs /25 #3
8 Donruss Artist Proofs /25 #103
8 Donruss Artist Proofs /25 #152
8 Donruss Gold Foil /499 #3
8 Donruss Gold Foil /499 #103
8 Donruss Gold Foil /499 #152
8 Donruss Gold Press Proofs /99 #3
8 Donruss Gold Press Proofs /99 #103
8 Donruss Gold Press Proofs /99 #152
18 Donruss Green Foil /199 #3
8 Donruss Green Foil /199 #103
8 Donruss Green Foil /199 #152
8 Donruss Masters of the Track #7
8 Donruss Masters of the Track Cracked Ice /999 #7
8 Donruss Masters of the Track Xplosion /99 #7
8 Donruss Press Proofs /49 #3
8 Donruss Press Proofs /49 #103
8 Donruss Press Proofs /49 #152
8 Donruss Printing Plates Black /1 #3
8 Donruss Printing Plates Black /1 #103
8 Donruss Printing Plates Black /1 #152
8 Donruss Printing Plates Cyan /1 #3
8 Donruss Printing Plates Cyan /1 #103
8 Donruss Printing Plates Cyan /1 #152
8 Donruss Printing Plates Magenta /1 #3
8 Donruss Printing Plates Magenta /1 #103
8 Donruss Printing Plates Magenta /1 #152
8 Donruss Printing Plates Yellow /1 #3
8 Donruss Printing Plates Yellow /1 #103
18 Donruss Printing Plates Yellow /1 #152
18 Donruss Red Foil /299 #3
18 Donruss Red Foil /299 #103
18 Donruss Red Foil /299 #152
18 Donruss Retro Relics '85 #18
18 Donruss Retro Relics '85 Black /10 #18
18 Donruss Retro Relics '85 Holo Gold /99 #18
18 Donruss Retro Signatures '85 #2
18 Donruss Retro Signatures '85 Black /1 #2
18 Donruss Retro Signatures '85 Holo Gold /25 #2
18 Donruss Slingshot #SS2
18 Panini Prime /50 #27
18 Panini Prime /50 #60
18 Panini Prime /50 #93
18 Panini Prime Black /1 #27
18 Panini Prime Black /1 #60
18 Panini Prime Black /1 #93
18 Panini Prime Driver Signatures /25 #3
18 Panini Prime Driver Signatures Black /1 #3
18 Panini Prime Driver Signatures Holo Gold /10 #3
18 Panini Prime Holo Gold /25 #27
18 Panini Prime Holo Gold /25 #60
18 Panini Prime Holo Gold /25 #93
18 Panini Prime Prime Signatures /25 #3
18 Panini Prime Prime Signatures Black /1 #3
18 Panini Prime Prime Signatures Holo Gold /10 #3
18 Panini Prime Shadowbox Signatures /25 #7
18 Panini Prime Shadowbox Signatures Black /1 #7
18 Panini Prime Shadowbox Signatures Holo Gold /10 #7
18 Panini Prime Signature Swatches /25 #SSCE
18 Panini Prime Signature Swatches Black /1 #1
18 Panini Prime Signature Swatches Holo Gold /10 #1
18 Panini Prizm #23A
18 Panini Prizm #23B
18 Panini Prizm #74
18 Panini Prizm Brilliance #9
18 Panini Prizm Brilliance Prizms #9
18 Panini Prizm Brilliance Prizms Black /1 #9
18 Panini Prizm Brilliance Prizms Gold /10 #9
18 Panini Prizm Illumination #5
18 Panini Prizm Illumination Prizms #5
18 Panini Prizm Illumination Prizms Black /1 #5
18 Panini Prizm Illumination Prizms Gold /10 #5
18 Panini Prizm Patented Penmanship Prizms #12
18 Panini Prizm Patented Penmanship Prizms Black /1 #12
18 Panini Prizm Patented Penmanship Prizms Blue /35 #12
18 Panini Prizm Patented Penmanship Prizms Camo #12
18 Panini Prizm Patented Penmanship Prizms Gold /10 #12
18 Panini Prizm Patented Penmanship Prizms Green /50 #12
18 Panini Prizm Patented Penmanship Prizms Rainbow /24 #12
18 Panini Prizm Patented Penmanship Prizms Red /25 #12
18 Panini Prizm Patented Penmanship Prizms Red White and Blue /60 #12
18 Panini Prizm Patented Penmanship Prizms White /5 #12
018 Panini Prizm Prizms #23A
018 Panini Prizm Prizms #23B
018 Panini Prizm Prizms #74
018 Panini Prizm Prizms Black /1 #23A
018 Panini Prizm Prizms Black /1 #23B
018 Panini Prizm Prizms Black /1 #74
018 Panini Prizm Prizms Blue /99 #23A
018 Panini Prizm Prizms Blue /99 #23B
018 Panini Prizm Prizms Blue /99 #74
018 Panini Prizm Prizms Camo #23A
018 Panini Prizm Prizms Camo #23B
018 Panini Prizm Prizms Camo #74
018 Panini Prizm Prizms Gold /10 #23A
018 Panini Prizm Prizms Gold /10 #23B
018 Panini Prizm Prizms Gold /10 #74
018 Panini Prizm Prizms Green /149 #23A
018 Panini Prizm Prizms Green /149 #23B
018 Panini Prizm Prizms Green /149 #74
018 Panini Prizm Prizms Purple Flash #23A
018 Panini Prizm Prizms Purple Flash #23B
018 Panini Prizm Prizms Purple Flash #74
018 Panini Prizm Prizms Rainbow /24 #23A
018 Panini Prizm Prizms Rainbow /24 #23B
018 Panini Prizm Prizms Rainbow /24 #74
018 Panini Prizm Prizms Red /75 #23A
018 Panini Prizm Prizms Red /75 #23B
018 Panini Prizm Prizms Red /75 #74
018 Panini Prizm Prizms Red White and Blue #23A
018 Panini Prizm Prizms Red White and Blue #23B
018 Panini Prizm Prizms Red White and Blue #74
018 Panini Prizm Prizms White /5 #23A
018 Panini Prizm Prizms White /5 #23B
018 Panini Prizm Prizms White /5 #74

2018 Panini Victory Lane #64
2018 Panini Victory Lane Black /1 #64
2018 Panini Victory Lane Blue /25 #64
2018 Panini Victory Lane Celebrations #1
2018 Panini Victory Lane Celebrations Black /1 #1
2018 Panini Victory Lane Celebrations Blue /25 #1
2018 Panini Victory Lane Celebrations Gold /99 #1
2018 Panini Victory Lane Celebrations Green /5 #1
2018 Panini Victory Lane Celebrations Printing Plates Black /1 #1
2018 Panini Victory Lane Celebrations Printing Plates Cyan /1 #1
2018 Panini Victory Lane Celebrations Printing Plates Magenta /1 #1
2018 Panini Victory Lane Celebrations Printing Plates Yellow /1 #1
2018 Panini Victory Lane Celebrations Red /49 #1
2018 Panini Victory Lane Chasing the Flag #6
2018 Panini Victory Lane Chasing the Flag Black /1 #6
2018 Panini Victory Lane Chasing the Flag Blue /25 #6
2018 Panini Victory Lane Chasing the Flag Gold /99 #6
2018 Panini Victory Lane Chasing the Flag Green /5 #6
2018 Panini Victory Lane Chasing the Flag Printing Plates Black /1 #6
2018 Panini Victory Lane Chasing the Flag Printing Plates Cyan /1 #6
2018 Panini Victory Lane Chasing the Flag Printing Plates Magenta /1 #6
2018 Panini Victory Lane Chasing the Flag Printing Plates Yellow /1 #6
2018 Panini Victory Lane Chasing the Flag Red /49 #6
2018 Panini Victory Lane Foundations #3
2018 Panini Victory Lane Foundations Black /1 #3
2018 Panini Victory Lane Foundations Blue /25 #3
2018 Panini Victory Lane Foundations Gold /99 #3
2018 Panini Victory Lane Foundations Green /5 #3
2018 Panini Victory Lane Foundations Printing Plates Black /1 #3
2018 Panini Victory Lane Foundations Printing Plates Cyan /1 #3
2018 Panini Victory Lane Foundations Printing Plates Magenta /1 #3
2018 Panini Victory Lane Foundations Printing Plates Yellow /1 #3
2018 Panini Victory Lane Foundations Red /49 #3
2018 Panini Victory Lane Gold /99 #64
2018 Panini Victory Lane Green /5 #64
2018 Panini Victory Lane Pedal to the Metal #83
2018 Panini Victory Lane Pedal to the Metal Black /1 #83
2018 Panini Victory Lane Pedal to the Metal Blue /25 #83
2018 Panini Victory Lane Pedal to the Metal Green /5 #83
2018 Panini Victory Lane Printing Plates Black /1 #64
2018 Panini Victory Lane Printing Plates Cyan /1 #64
2018 Panini Victory Lane Printing Plates Magenta /1 #64
2018 Panini Victory Lane Printing Plates Yellow /1 #64
2018 Panini Victory Lane Red /49 #64
2018 Panini Victory Lane Remarkable Remnants Material Autographs /89 #6
2018 Panini Victory Lane Remarkable Remnants Material Autographs Black /25 #6
2018 Panini Victory Lane Remarkable Remnants Material Autographs Gold /49 #6
2018 Panini Victory Lane Remarkable Remnants Material Autographs Green /50 #6
2018 Panini Victory Lane Remarkable Remnants Material Autographs Laundry Tag /1 #6
2018 Panini Victory Lane Silver #64
2018 Panini Victory Lane Victory Marks /25 #19
2018 Panini Victory Lane Victory Marks Black /1 #19
2018 Panini Victory Lane Victory Marks Gold /10 #19
2019 Donruss #22
2019 Donruss #84
2019 Donruss #103
2019 Donruss #161
2019 Donruss Artist Proofs /25 #22
2019 Donruss Artist Proofs /25 #84
2019 Donruss Artist Proofs /25 #103
2019 Donruss Artist Proofs /25 #161
2019 Donruss Black /199 #22
2019 Donruss Black /199 #84
2019 Donruss Black /199 #103
2019 Donruss Black /199 #161
2019 Donruss Classics #6
2019 Donruss Classics Cracked Ice /25 #6
2019 Donruss Classics Holographic #6
2019 Donruss Classics Xplosion /10 #6
2019 Donruss Gold /299 #22
2019 Donruss Gold /299 #84
2019 Donruss Gold /299 #103
2019 Donruss Gold /299 #161
2019 Donruss Gold Press Proofs /99 #22
2019 Donruss Gold Press Proofs /99 #84
2019 Donruss Gold Press Proofs /99 #103
2019 Donruss Gold Press Proofs /99 #161
2019 Donruss Optic #47
2019 Donruss Optic #76
2019 Donruss Optic Blue Pulsar #47
2019 Donruss Optic Blue Pulsar /1 #76
2019 Donruss Optic Gold /10 #47
2019 Donruss Optic Gold /10 #76
2019 Donruss Optic Gold Vinyl /1 #47
2019 Donruss Optic Gold Vinyl /1 #76
2019 Donruss Optic Holo #47
2019 Donruss Optic Holo #76
2019 Donruss Optic Red Wave #47
2019 Donruss Optic Red Wave /1 #76
2019 Donruss Optic Signatures Gold Vinyl /1 #47
2019 Donruss Optic Signatures Gold Vinyl /1 #76
2019 Donruss Optic Signatures Holo /75 #47
2019 Donruss Optic Signatures Holo /75 #76
2019 Donruss Press Proofs /49 #22
2019 Donruss Press Proofs /49 #84
2019 Donruss Press Proofs /49 #103
2019 Donruss Press Proofs /49 #161
2019 Donruss Printing Plates Black /1 #22
2019 Donruss Printing Plates Black /1 #84
2019 Donruss Printing Plates Black /1 #103
2019 Donruss Printing Plates Black /1 #161
2019 Donruss Printing Plates Cyan /1 #22
2019 Donruss Printing Plates Cyan /1 #84
2019 Donruss Printing Plates Cyan /1 #103
2019 Donruss Printing Plates Cyan /1 #161
2019 Donruss Printing Plates Magenta /1 #84
2019 Donruss Printing Plates Magenta /1 #103
2019 Donruss Printing Plates Magenta /1 #161
2019 Donruss Printing Plates Magenta /1 #22
2019 Donruss Printing Plates Yellow /1 #22
2019 Donruss Printing Plates Yellow /1 #84
2019 Donruss Printing Plates Yellow /1 #103
2019 Donruss Printing Plates Yellow /1 #161
2019 Donruss Silver #22
2019 Donruss Silver #84
2019 Donruss Silver #103
2019 Donruss Silver #161
2019 Panini Prime /50 #65
2019 Panini Prime /50 #92
2019 Panini Prime Black /10 #65
2019 Panini Prime Black /10 #92
2019 Panini Prime Dual Material Autographs Black /10 #6
2019 Panini Prime Dual Material Autographs Holo Gold /25 #6
2019 Panini Prime Dual Material Autographs Laundry Tags /1 #6
2019 Panini Prime Emerald /5 #65
2019 Panini Prime Emerald /5 #92
2019 Panini Prime Platinum Blue /1 #65
2019 Panini Prime Platinum Blue /1 #92
2019 Panini Prime Prime Names Die Cut Signatures Black /10 #19
2019 Panini Prime Prime Names Die Cut Signatures Holo Gold /25 #19
2019 Panini Prime Prime Names Die Cut Signatures Platinum Blue /1 #19
2019 Panini Prime Race Used Firesuits /11 #39

2019 Panini Prime Race Used Firesuits Black /5 #39
2019 Panini Prime Race Used Firesuits Holo Gold /10 #39
2019 Panini Prime Race Used Firesuits Laundry Tags /1 #39
2019 Panini Prime Race Used Sheet Metal /50 #39
2019 Panini Prime Race Used Sheet Metal Black /10 #39
2019 Panini Prime Race Used Sheet Metal Holo Gold /25 #39
2019 Panini Prime Race Used Sheet Metal Platinum Blue /1 #39
2019 Panini Prime Race Used Tires /50 #39
2019 Panini Prime Race Used Tires Black /5 #39
2019 Panini Prime Race Used Tires Holo Gold /10 #39
2019 Panini Prime Race Used Tires Platinum Blue /1 #39
2019 Panini Prime Shadowbox Signatures /99 #3
2019 Panini Prime Shadowbox Signatures Black /10 #3
2019 Panini Prime Shadowbox Signatures Holo Gold /25 #3
2019 Panini Prime Shadowbox Signatures Platinum Blue /1 #3
2019 Panini Prizm #46
2019 Panini Prizm Apex #10
2019 Panini Prizm Apex Prizms #10
2019 Panini Prizm Apex Prizms Black /1 #10
2019 Panini Prizm Apex Prizms Gold /10 #10
2019 Panini Prizm Apex Prizms White Sparkle #10
2019 Panini Prizm Endorsements Prizms #2
2019 Panini Prizm Endorsements Prizms Black /1 #2
2019 Panini Prizm Endorsements Prizms Blue /5 #2
2019 Panini Prizm Endorsements Prizms Camo #2
2019 Panini Prizm Endorsements Prizms Gold /10 #2
2019 Panini Prizm Endorsements Prizms Green /5 #2
2019 Panini Prizm Endorsements Prizms Rainbow /5 #2
2019 Panini Prizm Endorsements Prizms Red /5 #2
2019 Panini Prizm Endorsements Prizms Red White and Blue #2
2019 Panini Prizm Endorsements Prizms White /5 #2
2019 Panini Prizm Fireworks #19
2019 Panini Prizm Fireworks Prizms #19
2019 Panini Prizm Fireworks Prizms Black /1 #19
2019 Panini Prizm Fireworks Prizms Gold /10 #19
2019 Panini Prizm Fireworks Prizms White Sparkle #19
2019 Panini Prizm National Pride #11
2019 Panini Prizm National Pride Prizms #11
2019 Panini Prizm National Pride Prizms Black /1 #11
2019 Panini Prizm National Pride Prizms Gold /10 #11
2019 Panini Prizm National Pride Prizms White Sparkle #11
2019 Panini Prizm Prizms #46
2019 Panini Prizm Prizms Black /1 #46
2019 Panini Prizm Prizms Blue /75 #46
2019 Panini Prizm Prizms Camo #46
2019 Panini Prizm Prizms Flash #46
2019 Panini Prizm Prizms Gold /10 #46
2019 Panini Prizm Prizms Green /99 #46
2019 Panini Prizm Prizms Rainbow /24 #46
2019 Panini Prizm Prizms Red /50 #46
2019 Panini Prizm Prizms Red White and Blue #46
2019 Panini Prizm Prizms White /5 #46
2019 Panini Prizm Prizms White Sparkle #46
2019 Panini Prizm Scripted Signatures Prizms #1
2019 Panini Prizm Scripted Signatures Prizms Black /1 #1
2019 Panini Prizm Scripted Signatures Prizms Blue /5 #1
2019 Panini Prizm Scripted Signatures Prizms Camo #1
2019 Panini Prizm Scripted Signatures Prizms Gold /10 #1
2019 Panini Prizm Scripted Signatures Prizms Green /5 #1
2019 Panini Prizm Scripted Signatures Prizms Rainbow /5 #1
2019 Panini Prizm Scripted Signatures Prizms Red /5 #1
2019 Panini Prizm Scripted Signatures Prizms Red White and Blue #1
2019 Panini Prizm Scripted Signatures Prizms White /5 #1
2019 Panini Prizm Stars and Stripes #4
2019 Panini Prizm Stars and Stripes Prizms #4
2019 Panini Prizm Stars and Stripes Prizms Black /1 #4
2019 Panini Prizm Stars and Stripes Prizms Gold /10 #4
2019 Panini Prizm Stars and Stripes Prizms White Sparkle #4
2019 Panini Victory Lane Signature Swatches #4
2019 Panini Victory Lane Signature Swatches Gold /25 #4
2019 Panini Victory Lane Signature Swatches Laundry Tag /1 #4
2019 Panini Victory Lane Signature Swatches Platinum /1 #4
2019 Panini Victory Lane Signature Swatches Red /10 #4
2020 Donruss #83
2020 Donruss #171
2020 Donruss Black Numbers /99 #83
2020 Donruss Black Numbers /99 #171
2020 Donruss Black Trophy Club /1 #83
2020 Donruss Black Trophy Club /1 #171
2020 Donruss Blue /199 #171
2020 Donruss Blue /199 #83
2020 Donruss Carolina Blue #83
2020 Donruss Carolina Blue #171
2020 Donruss Classics #13
2020 Donruss Classics Checkers #13
2020 Donruss Classics Cracked Ice /25 #13
2020 Donruss Classics Holographic /199 #13
2020 Donruss Classics Xplosion /10 #13
2020 Donruss Green /99 #83
2020 Donruss Green /99 #171
2020 Donruss Optic #61
2020 Donruss Optic #88
2020 Donruss Optic Carolina Blue Wave #61
2020 Donruss Optic Carolina Blue Wave #88
2020 Donruss Optic Gold /10 #61
2020 Donruss Optic Gold /10 #88
2020 Donruss Optic Gold Vinyl /1 #61
2020 Donruss Optic Gold Vinyl /1 #88
2020 Donruss Optic Holo #61
2020 Donruss Optic Holo #88
2020 Donruss Optic Orange Pulsar #61
2020 Donruss Optic Orange Pulsar #88
2020 Donruss Optic Red Mojo #61
2020 Donruss Optic Red Mojo #88
2020 Donruss Optic Signatures Gold Vinyl /1 #61
2020 Donruss Optic Signatures Gold Vinyl /1 #88
2020 Donruss Optic Signatures Holo /99 #61
2020 Donruss Optic Signatures Holo /99 #88
2020 Donruss Orange #83
2020 Donruss Orange #171
2020 Donruss Pink /25 #83
2020 Donruss Pink /25 #171
2020 Donruss Printing Plates Black /1 #83
2020 Donruss Printing Plates Black /1 #171
2020 Donruss Printing Plates Cyan /1 #83
2020 Donruss Printing Plates Cyan /1 #171
2020 Donruss Printing Plates Magenta /1 #83
2020 Donruss Printing Plates Magenta /1 #171
2020 Donruss Printing Plates Yellow /1 #171
2020 Donruss Printing Plates Yellow /1 #83
2020 Donruss Purple /49 #83
2020 Donruss Purple /49 #171
2020 Donruss Red /299 #83
2020 Donruss Red /299 #171
2020 Donruss Retro Relics '87 #2
2020 Donruss Retro Relics '87 Holo Black /10 #2
2020 Donruss Retro Relics '87 Holo Gold /25 #2
2020 Donruss Retro Relics '87 Red /99 #2
2020 Donruss Silver #83
2020 Donruss Silver #171
2020 Donruss Top Tier #2
2020 Donruss Top Tier Checkers #2
2020 Donruss Top Tier Cracked Ice /25 #2
2020 Donruss Top Tier Holographic /199 #2
2020 Donruss Top Tier Xplosion /10 #2

Chase Elliott

2011 Element #99
2011 Element Black /35 #99
2011 Element Green #99
2011 Element Purple /25 #99
2011 Element Red #99
2011 Elements Undiscovered Elements Autographs /225 #2
2011 Elements Undiscovered Elements Autographs Red Ink /25 #2
2014 Press Pass American Thunder #44
2014 Press Pass American Thunder Autographs Blue /10 #ATACE2
2014 Press Pass American Thunder Autographs Red /5 #ATACE2
2014 Press Pass American Thunder Autographs White /25 #ATACE2
2014 Press Pass American Thunder Black and White /50 #44
2014 Press Pass American Thunder Cyan #44
2014 Press Pass American Thunder Magenta #44
2014 Press Pass American Thunder Yellow /5 #44
2014 Press Pass Redline #62
2014 Press Pass Redline Black /75 #62
2014 Press Pass Redline Blue Foil #62
2014 Press Pass Redline Cyan /50 #62
2014 Press Pass Redline Dynamic Duals Relic Autographs Blue /15 #DDCE
2014 Press Pass Redline Dynamic Duals Relic Autographs Gold /10 #DDCE
2014 Press Pass Redline Dynamic Duals Relic Autographs Melting /1 #DDCE
2014 Press Pass Redline Dynamic Duals Relic Autographs Red /25 #DDCE
2014 Press Pass Redline First Win Relic Autographs Blue /5 #RRFWCE
2014 Press Pass Redline First Win Relic Autographs Gold /15 #RRFWCE
2014 Press Pass Redline First Win Relic Autographs Melting /1 #RRFWCE
2014 Press Pass Redline First Win Relic Autographs Red /25 #RRFWCE
2014 Press Pass Redline Green National Convention /5 #62
2014 Press Pass Redline Magenta /10 #62
2014 Press Pass Redline Muscle Car Sheet Metal Blue /25 #MCMCE2
2014 Press Pass Redline Muscle Car Sheet Metal Gold /50 #MCMCE2
2014 Press Pass Redline Muscle Car Sheet Metal Melting /1 #MCMCE2
2014 Press Pass Redline Muscle Car Sheet Metal Red /75 #MCMCE2
2014 Press Pass Redline Relic Autographs Blue /10 #RRSECE2
2014 Press Pass Redline Relic Autographs Gold /15 #RRSECE2
2014 Press Pass Redline Relic Autographs Melting /1 #RRSECE2
2014 Press Pass Redline Relic Autographs Red /25 #RRSECE2
2014 Press Pass Redline Relics Blue /25 #RRCE2
2014 Press Pass Redline Relics Gold /50 #RRCE2
2014 Press Pass Redline Relics Melting /1 #RRCE2
2014 Press Pass Redline Relics Red /75 #RRCE2
2014 Press Pass Redline Signatures Blue /5 #RSCE2
2014 Press Pass Redline Signatures Gold /10 #RSCE2
2014 Press Pass Redline Signatures Melting /1 #RSCE2
2014 Press Pass Redline Signatures Red /25 #RSCE2
2014 Press Pass Redline Yellow /1 #62
2015 Press Pass #47
2015 Press Pass #77
2015 Press Pass #99
2015 Press Pass Championship Caliber Dual /25 #CCMCE2
2015 Press Pass Championship Caliber Quad /1 #CCMCE2
2015 Press Pass Championship Caliber Signature Edition Blue /15 #CCCE2
2015 Press Pass Championship Caliber Signature Edition Gold /30 #CCCE2
2015 Press Pass Championship Caliber Signature Edition Green /5 #CCCE2
2015 Press Pass Championship Caliber Signature Edition Melting /1 #CCCE2
2015 Press Pass Championship Caliber Single /50 #CCMCE2
2015 Press Pass Championship Caliber Triple /10 #CCMCE2
2015 Press Pass Cup Chase #47
2015 Press Pass Cup Chase #77
2015 Press Pass Cup Chase #99
2015 Press Pass Cup Chase Blue /25 #47
2015 Press Pass Cup Chase Blue /25 #77
2015 Press Pass Cup Chase Blue /25 #99
2015 Press Pass Cup Chase Gold /75 #47
2015 Press Pass Cup Chase Gold /75 #77
2015 Press Pass Cup Chase Gold /75 #99
2015 Press Pass Cup Chase Green /10 #47
2015 Press Pass Cup Chase Green /10 #77
2015 Press Pass Cup Chase Green /10 #99
2015 Press Pass Cup Chase Melting /1 #47
2015 Press Pass Cup Chase Melting /1 #77
2015 Press Pass Cup Chase Melting /1 #99
2015 Press Pass Cup Chase Three Wide Blue /25 #3WCE
2015 Press Pass Cup Chase Three Wide Gold /50 #3WCE
2015 Press Pass Cup Chase Three Wide Green /10 #3WCE
2015 Press Pass Cup Chase Three Wide Melting /1 #3WCE
2015 Press Pass Cup Chase Upper Cuts /13 #UCCE2
2015 Press Pass Cuts Blue /25 #CCCCE
2015 Press Pass Cuts Gold /50 #CCCCE
2015 Press Pass Cuts Green /10 #CCCCE
2015 Press Pass Cuts Melting /1 #CCCCE
2015 Press Pass Four Wide Signature Edition Blue /10 #4WCE
2015 Press Pass Four Wide Signature Edition Gold /15 #4WCE
2015 Press Pass Four Wide Signature Edition Green /5 #4WCE
2015 Press Pass Four Wide Signature Edition Melting /1 #4WCE
2015 Press Pass Pit Road Pieces Blue /25 #PPMBECE
2015 Press Pass Pit Road Pieces Gold /50 #PPMBECE
2015 Press Pass Pit Road Pieces Green /10 #PPMBECE
2015 Press Pass Pit Road Pieces Melting /1 #PPMBECE
2015 Press Pass Pit Road Pieces Signature Edition Blue /15 #PRPBECE
2015 Press Pass Pit Road Pieces Signature Edition Gold /25 #PRPBECE
2015 Press Pass Pit Road Pieces Signature Edition Green /5 #PRPBECE
2015 Press Pass Pit Road Pieces Signature Edition Melting /1 #PRPBECE
2015 Press Pass Purple #47
2015 Press Pass Purple #77
2015 Press Pass Purple #99
2015 Press Pass Red #47
2015 Press Pass Red #77
2015 Press Pass Red #99
2015 Press Pass Signature Series Blue /15 #SSCE2
2015 Press Pass Signature Series Gold /25 #SSCE2
2015 Press Pass Signature Series Green /10 #SSCE2
2015 Press Pass Signature Series Melting /1 #SSCE2
2015 Press Pass Signings Blue /15 #PPSCEL
2015 Press Pass Signings Gold #PPSCEL
2015 Press Pass Signings Green /5 #PPSCEL
2015 Press Pass Signings Melting /1 #PPSCEL
2015 Press Pass Signings Red /10 #PPSCEL
2016 Certified /99 #101
2016 Certified Complete Materials /199 #20
2016 Certified Complete Materials Mirror Black /1 #20
2016 Certified Complete Materials Mirror Blue /50 #20
2016 Certified Complete Materials Mirror Gold /25 #20
2016 Certified Complete Materials Mirror Green /5 #20
2016 Certified Complete Materials Mirror Orange /99 #20
2016 Certified Complete Materials Mirror Purple /10 #20
2016 Certified Complete Materials Mirror Red /75 #20
2016 Certified Complete Materials Mirror Silver /99 #20
2016 Certified Epix /199 #6
2016 Certified Epix Mirror Black /1 #6
2016 Certified Epix Mirror Blue /50 #6
2016 Certified Epix Mirror Gold /25 #6
2016 Certified Epix Mirror Green /5 #6
2016 Certified Epix Mirror Orange /99 #6
2016 Certified Epix Mirror Purple /10 #6
2016 Certified Epix Mirror Red /75 #6
2016 Certified Epix Mirror Silver /99 #6
2016 Certified Famed Rides /199 #19
2016 Certified Famed Rides Mirror Black /1 #19
2016 Certified Famed Rides Mirror Blue /50 #19
2016 Certified Famed Rides Mirror Gold /25 #19
2016 Certified Famed Rides Mirror Green /5 #19
2016 Certified Famed Rides Mirror Orange /99 #19

2016 Certified Famed Rides Mirror Purple /10 #19
2016 Certified Famed Rides Mirror Red /75 #19
2016 Certified Famed Rides Mirror Silver /99 #19
2016 Certified Mirror Black /1 #101
2016 Certified Mirror Blue /20 #101
2016 Certified Mirror Gold /15 #101
2016 Certified Mirror Green /5 #101
2016 Certified Mirror Orange /15 #101
2016 Certified Mirror Purple /10 #101
2016 Certified Mirror Red /25 #101
2016 Certified Mirror Silver /15 #101
2016 Certified Potential Signatures /25 #4
2016 Certified Potential Signatures Mirror Black /1 #4
2016 Certified Potential Signatures Mirror Blue /20 #4
2016 Certified Potential Signatures Mirror Gold /15 #4
2016 Certified Potential Signatures Mirror Green /5 #4
2016 Certified Potential Signatures Mirror Orange /5 #4
2016 Certified Potential Signatures Mirror Purple /10 #4
2016 Certified Potential Signatures Mirror Red /24 #4
2016 Certified Potential Signatures Mirror Silver /5 #4
2016 Certified Skills /199 #4
2016 Certified Skills Mirror Black /1 #4
2016 Certified Skills Mirror Blue /50 #4
2016 Certified Skills Mirror Gold /25 #4
2016 Certified Skills Mirror Green /5 #4
2016 Certified Skills Mirror Orange /99 #4
2016 Certified Skills Mirror Purple /10 #4
2016 Certified Skills Mirror Red /75 #4
2016 Certified Skills Mirror Silver /99 #4
2016 Certified Sprint Cup Swatches /125 #27
2016 Certified Sprint Cup Swatches Mirror Black /1 #27
2016 Certified Sprint Cup Swatches Mirror Blue /50 #27
2016 Certified Sprint Cup Swatches Mirror Gold /25 #27
2016 Certified Sprint Cup Swatches Mirror Green /5 #27
2016 Certified Sprint Cup Swatches Mirror Orange /99 #27
2016 Certified Sprint Cup Swatches Mirror Purple /10 #27
2016 Certified Sprint Cup Swatches Mirror Red /75 #27
2016 Certified Sprint Cup Swatches Mirror Silver /99 #27
2016 Panini Black Friday /499 #75
2016 Panini Black Friday Autographs /25 #75
2016 Panini Black Friday Cracked Ice /25 #75
2016 Panini Black Friday Holo Plaid /1 #75
2016 Panini Black Friday Racing Memorabilia #R5
2016 Panini Black Friday Racing Memorabilia Cracked Ice /25 #R5
2016 Panini Black Friday Racing Memorabilia Galactic Window /10 #R5
2016 Panini Black Friday Racing Memorabilia Holo Plaid /1 #R5
2016 Panini Black Friday Rapture /10 #75
2016 Panini Black Friday Thick Stock /50 #75
2016 Panini Black Friday Wedges /50 #75
2016 Panini Cyber Monday #49
2016 Panini Cyber Monday Memorabilia #20
2016 Panini Cyber Monday Memorabilia Cracked Ice /25 #20
2016 Panini Cyber Monday Memorabilia Galactic Window /10 #20
2016 Panini Cyber Monday Memorabilia Holo Plaid /1 #20
2016 Panini National Convention #41
2016 Panini National Convention Autographs /25 #41
2016 Panini National Convention Cracked Ice /25 #41
2016 Panini National Convention Decoy Cracked Ice /25 #41
2016 Panini National Convention Decoy Escher Squares /10 #41
2016 Panini National Convention Decoy Rapture /1 #41
2016 Panini National Convention Decoy Wedges /99 #41
2016 Panini National Convention Diamond Awe /49 #41
2016 Panini National Convention Escher Squares /10 #41
2016 Panini National Convention Rapture /1 #41
2016 Panini National Convention Wedges /99 #41
2016 Panini National Treasures /25 #46
2016 Panini National Treasures Black /5 #46
2016 Panini National Treasures Blue /1 #46
2016 Panini National Treasures Dual Driver Materials /25 #7
2016 Panini National Treasures Dual Driver Materials Black /5 #7
2016 Panini National Treasures Dual Driver Materials Blue /1 #7
2016 Panini National Treasures Dual Driver Materials Gold /10 #7
2016 Panini National Treasures Dual Driver Materials Printing Plates Black /1 #7
2016 Panini National Treasures Dual Driver Materials Printing Plates Cyan /1 #7
2016 Panini National Treasures Dual Driver Materials Printing Plates Magenta /1 #7
2016 Panini National Treasures Dual Driver Materials Printing Plates Yellow /1 #7
2016 Panini National Treasures Dual Driver Materials Silver /15 #7
2016 Panini National Treasures Dual Signatures /25 #5
2016 Panini National Treasures Dual Signatures /25 #27
2016 Panini National Treasures Dual Signatures Black /10 #5
2016 Panini National Treasures Dual Signatures Black /10 #27
2016 Panini National Treasures Dual Signatures Blue /1 #5
2016 Panini National Treasures Dual Signatures Blue /1 #27
2016 Panini National Treasures Dual Signatures Gold /20 #5
2016 Panini National Treasures Dual Signatures Gold /15 #27
2016 Panini National Treasures Eight Signatures /15 #1
2016 Panini National Treasures Eight Signatures Black /5 #1
2016 Panini National Treasures Eight Signatures Blue /1 #1
2016 Panini National Treasures Eight Signatures Gold /10 #1
2016 Panini National Treasures Firesuit Materials /25 #3
2016 Panini National Treasures Firesuit Materials Black /5 #3
2016 Panini National Treasures Firesuit Materials Blue /1 #3
2016 Panini National Treasures Firesuit Materials Gold /10 #3
2016 Panini National Treasures Firesuit Materials Laundry Tag /1 #3
2016 Panini National Treasures Firesuit Materials Printing Plates Black /1 #3
2016 Panini National Treasures Firesuit Materials Printing Plates Cyan /1 #3
2016 Panini National Treasures Firesuit Materials Printing Plates Magenta /1 #3
2016 Panini National Treasures Firesuit Materials Printing Plates Yellow /1 #3
2016 Panini National Treasures Firesuit Materials Silver /15 #3
2016 Panini National Treasures Gold /10 #46
2016 Panini National Treasures Jumbo Firesuit Patch Signature Booklet Alpine Stars /2 #5
2016 Panini National Treasures Jumbo Firesuit Patch Signature Booklet Associate Sponsor 1 /1 #5
2016 Panini National Treasures Jumbo Firesuit Patch Signature Booklet Associate Sponsor 10 /1 #5
2016 Panini National Treasures Jumbo Firesuit Patch Signature Booklet Associate Sponsor 3 /1 #5
2016 Panini National Treasures Jumbo Firesuit Patch Signature Booklet Associate Sponsor 4 /1 #5
2016 Panini National Treasures Jumbo Firesuit Patch Signature Booklet Associate Sponsor 5 /1 #5
2016 Panini National Treasures Jumbo Firesuit Patch Signature Booklet Associate Sponsor 6 /1 #5
2016 Panini National Treasures Jumbo Firesuit Patch Signature Booklet Associate Sponsor 7 /1 #5
2016 Panini National Treasures Jumbo Firesuit Patch Signature Booklet Associate Sponsor 8 /1 #5
2016 Panini National Treasures Jumbo Firesuit Patch Signature Booklet Associate Sponsor 9 /1 #5
2016 Panini National Treasures Jumbo Firesuit Patch Signature Booklet Goodyear /2 #5
2016 Panini National Treasures Jumbo Firesuit Patch Signature Booklet Manufacturers Logo /1 #5
2016 Panini National Treasures Jumbo Firesuit Patch Signature Booklet Nameplate /2 #5
2016 Panini National Treasures Jumbo Firesuit Patch Signature Booklet NASCAR /1 #5
2016 Panini National Treasures Jumbo Firesuit Patch Signature Booklet Sprint Cup Logo /1 #5

2016 Panini National Treasures Jumbo Firesuit Patch Signature Booklet Sunoco /1 #5
2016 Panini National Treasures Jumbo Firesuit Signatures Black /5 #5
2016 Panini National Treasures Jumbo Firesuit Signatures Blue /1 #5
2016 Panini National Treasures Jumbo Firesuit Signatures Gold /10 #5
2016 Panini National Treasures Jumbo Firesuit Signatures Printing Plates Black /1 #5
2016 Panini National Treasures Jumbo Firesuit Signatures Printing Plates Cyan /1 #5
2016 Panini National Treasures Jumbo Firesuit Signatures Printing Plates Magenta /1 #5
2016 Panini National Treasures Jumbo Firesuit Signatures Printing Plates Yellow /1 #5
2016 Panini National Treasures Jumbo Firesuit Signatures Silver /15 #5
2016 Panini National Treasures Jumbo Sheet Metal Signatures Black /5 #2
2016 Panini National Treasures Jumbo Sheet Metal Signatures Blue /1 #2
2016 Panini National Treasures Jumbo Sheet Metal Signatures Printing Plates Black /1 #2
2016 Panini National Treasures Jumbo Sheet Metal Signatures Printing Plates Cyan /1 #2
2016 Panini National Treasures Jumbo Sheet Metal Signatures Printing Plates Magenta /1 #2
2016 Panini National Treasures Jumbo Sheet Metal Signatures Printing Plates Yellow /1 #2
2016 Panini National Treasures Printing Plates Black /1 #46
2016 Panini National Treasures Printing Plates Cyan /1 #46
2016 Panini National Treasures Printing Plates Magenta /1 #46
2016 Panini National Treasures Printing Plates Yellow /1 #46
2016 Panini National Treasures Quad Driver Materials /25 #1
2016 Panini National Treasures Quad Driver Materials Black /5 #1
2016 Panini National Treasures Quad Driver Materials Blue /1 #1
2016 Panini National Treasures Quad Driver Materials Gold /10 #1
2016 Panini National Treasures Quad Driver Materials Printing Plates Black /1 #1
2016 Panini National Treasures Quad Driver Materials Printing Plates Cyan /1 #1
2016 Panini National Treasures Quad Driver Materials Printing Plates Magenta /1 #1
2016 Panini National Treasures Quad Driver Materials Printing Plates Yellow /1 #1
2016 Panini National Treasures Quad Driver Materials Silver /15 #1
2016 Panini National Treasures Quad Materials /25 #3
2016 Panini National Treasures Quad Materials Black /5 #3
2016 Panini National Treasures Quad Materials Blue /1 #3
2016 Panini National Treasures Quad Materials Gold /10 #3
2016 Panini National Treasures Quad Materials Printing Plates Black /1 #3
2016 Panini National Treasures Quad Materials Printing Plates Cyan /1 #3
2016 Panini National Treasures Quad Materials Printing Plates Magenta /1 #3
2016 Panini National Treasures Quad Materials Printing Plates Yellow /1 #3
2016 Panini National Treasures Quad Materials Silver /15 #3
2016 Panini National Treasures Rookie Signature Materials Laundry Tag /1 #46
2016 Panini National Treasures Signature Dual Materials /24 #5
2016 Panini National Treasures Signature Dual Materials Black /5 #5
2016 Panini National Treasures Signature Dual Materials Blue /1 #5
2016 Panini National Treasures Signature Dual Materials Gold /10 #5
2016 Panini National Treasures Signature Dual Materials Printing Plates Black /1 #5
2016 Panini National Treasures Signature Dual Materials Printing Plates Cyan /1 #5
2016 Panini National Treasures Signature Dual Materials Printing Plates Magenta /1 #5
2016 Panini National Treasures Signature Dual Materials Printing Plates Yellow /1 #5
2016 Panini National Treasures Signature Dual Materials Silver /15 #5
2016 Panini National Treasures Signature Firesuit Materials Black /5 #5
2016 Panini National Treasures Signature Firesuit Materials Blue /1 #5
2016 Panini National Treasures Signature Firesuit Materials Gold /10 #5
2016 Panini National Treasures Signature Firesuit Materials Laundry Tag /1 #5
2016 Panini National Treasures Signature Firesuit Materials Printing Plates Black /1 #5
2016 Panini National Treasures Signature Firesuit Materials Printing Plates Cyan /1 #5
2016 Panini National Treasures Signature Firesuit Materials Printing Plates Magenta /1 #5
2016 Panini National Treasures Signature Firesuit Materials Printing Plates Yellow /1 #5
2016 Panini National Treasures Signature Firesuit Materials Silver /15 #5
2016 Panini National Treasures Signature Quad Materials Black /5 #5
2016 Panini National Treasures Signature Quad Materials Blue /1 #5
2016 Panini National Treasures Signature Quad Materials Gold /10 #5
2016 Panini National Treasures Signature Quad Materials Printing Plates Black /1 #5
2016 Panini National Treasures Signature Quad Materials Printing Plates Cyan /1 #5
2016 Panini National Treasures Signature Quad Materials Printing Plates Magenta /1 #5
2016 Panini National Treasures Signature Quad Materials Printing Plates Yellow /1 #5
2016 Panini National Treasures Signature Quad Materials Silver /15 #5
2016 Panini National Treasures Signature Sheet Metal Materials Black /5 #5
2016 Panini National Treasures Signature Sheet Metal Materials Blue /1 #5
2016 Panini National Treasures Signature Sheet Metal Materials Printing Plates Black /1 #5
2016 Panini National Treasures Signature Sheet Metal Materials Printing Plates Cyan /1 #5
2016 Panini National Treasures Signature Sheet Metal Materials Printing Plates Magenta /1 #5
2016 Panini National Treasures Signature Sheet Metal Materials Printing Plates Yellow /1 #5
2016 Panini National Treasures Silver /15 #46
2016 Panini National Treasures Six Signatures /25 #6
2016 Panini National Treasures Six Signatures Black /10 #6
2016 Panini National Treasures Six Signatures Blue /1 #6
2016 Panini National Treasures Six Signatures Gold /15 #6
2016 Panini National Treasures Timelines Black /5 #3
2016 Panini National Treasures Timelines Blue /1 #3
2016 Panini National Treasures Timelines Printing Plates Black /1 #3
2016 Panini National Treasures Timelines Printing Plates Cyan /1 #3
2016 Panini National Treasures Timelines Printing Plates Magenta /1 #3
2016 Panini National Treasures Timelines Printing Plates Yellow /1 #3
2016 Panini National Treasures Trio Driver Materials /25 #11
2016 Panini National Treasures Trio Driver Materials Black /5 #11
2016 Panini National Treasures Trio Driver Materials Blue /1 #11
2016 Panini National Treasures Trio Driver Materials Gold /10 #11
2016 Panini National Treasures Trio Driver Materials Printing Plates Black /1 #11
2016 Panini National Treasures Trio Driver Materials Printing Plates Cyan /1 #11
2016 Panini National Treasures Trio Driver Materials Printing Plates Magenta /1 #11
2016 Panini National Treasures Trio Driver Materials Printing Plates Yellow /1 #11
2016 Panini National Treasures Trio Driver Materials Silver /15 #11
2016 Panini Prizm #24
2016 Panini Prizm #49
2016 Panini Prizm Autographs Prizms #63
2016 Panini Prizm Autographs Prizms Black /3 #63
2016 Panini Prizm Autographs Prizms Blue Flag /50 #63
2016 Panini Prizm Autographs Prizms Camo /24 #63
2016 Panini Prizm Autographs Prizms Checkered Flag /1 #63
2016 Panini Prizm Autographs Prizms Gold /10 #63
2016 Panini Prizm Autographs Prizms Green Flag /75 #63
2016 Panini Prizm Autographs Prizms Rainbow /24 #63
2016 Panini Prizm Autographs Prizms Red Flag /35 #63
2016 Panini Prizm Autographs Prizms Red White and Blue /25 #63

2016 Panini Prizm Autographs Prizms White Flag /5 #63
2016 Panini Prizm Firesuit Fabrics /50 #9
2016 Panini Prizm Firesuit Fabrics Prizms Blue Flag /15 #9
2016 Panini Prizm Firesuit Fabrics Prizms Checkered Flag /1 #9
2016 Panini Prizm Firesuit Fabrics Prizms Green Flag /35 #9
2016 Panini Prizm Firesuit Fabrics Prizms Red Flag /5 #9
2016 Panini Prizm Firesuit Fabrics Team /149 #7
2016 Panini Prizm Firesuit Fabrics Team Prizms Blue Flag /10 #7
2016 Panini Prizm Firesuit Fabrics Team Prizms Checkered Flag /1 #7
2016 Panini Prizm Firesuit Fabrics Team Prizms Green Flag /25 #7
2016 Panini Prizm Firesuit Fabrics Team Prizms Red Flag /5 #7
2016 Panini Prizm Prizms #24
2016 Panini Prizm Prizms #49
2016 Panini Prizm Prizms Black /3 #24
2016 Panini Prizm Prizms Black /3 #49
2016 Panini Prizm Prizms Blue Flag /99 #24
2016 Panini Prizm Prizms Blue Flag /99 #49
2016 Panini Prizm Prizms Camo /24 #24
2016 Panini Prizm Prizms Camo /24 #49
2016 Panini Prizm Prizms Checkered Flag /1 #24
2016 Panini Prizm Prizms Checkered Flag /1 #49
2016 Panini Prizm Prizms Gold /10 #24
2016 Panini Prizm Prizms Gold /10 #49
2016 Panini Prizm Prizms Green Flag /149 #24
2016 Panini Prizm Prizms Green Flag /149 #49
2016 Panini Prizm Prizms Rainbow /24 #24
2016 Panini Prizm Prizms Rainbow /24 #49
2016 Panini Prizm Prizms Red Flag /75 #24
2016 Panini Prizm Prizms Red Flag /75 #49
2016 Panini Prizm Prizms Red White and Blue #24
2016 Panini Prizm Prizms Red White and Blue #49
2016 Panini Prizm Prizms White Flag /5 #24
2016 Panini Prizm Prizms White Flag /5 #49
2016 Panini Torque #18
2016 Panini Torque #57
2016 Panini Torque #77
2016 Panini Torque Artist Proof /50 #18
2016 Panini Torque Artist Proof /50 #57
2016 Panini Torque Artist Proof /50 #77
2016 Panini Torque Blackout /1 #18
2016 Panini Torque Blackout /1 #57
2016 Panini Torque Blackout /1 #77
2016 Panini Torque Blue /125 #18
2016 Panini Torque Blue /125 #57
2016 Panini Torque Blue /125 #77
2016 Panini Torque Clear Vision #17
2016 Panini Torque Clear Vision Blue /99 #17
2016 Panini Torque Clear Vision Gold /149 #17
2016 Panini Torque Clear Vision Green /25 #17
2016 Panini Torque Clear Vision Purple /10 #17
2016 Panini Torque Clear Vision Red /49 #17
2016 Panini Torque Combo Materials Autographs /35 #6
2016 Panini Torque Combo Materials Autographs Blue /24 #6
2016 Panini Torque Combo Materials Autographs Green /5 #6
2016 Panini Torque Combo Materials Autographs Purple /1 #6
2016 Panini Torque Combo Materials Autographs Red /10 #6
2016 Panini Torque Dual Materials /149 #3
2016 Panini Torque Dual Materials Blue /99 #3
2016 Panini Torque Dual Materials Green /25 #3
2016 Panini Torque Dual Materials Purple /10 #3
2016 Panini Torque Dual Materials Red /49 #3
2016 Panini Torque Gold #18
2016 Panini Torque Gold #57
2016 Panini Torque Gold #77
2016 Panini Torque Helmets #7
2016 Panini Torque Helmets Blue /99 #7
2016 Panini Torque Helmets Checkerboard /10 #7
2016 Panini Torque Helmets Green /25 #7
2016 Panini Torque Helmets Red /49 #7
2016 Panini Torque Holo Gold /5 #18
2016 Panini Torque Holo Gold /5 #57
2016 Panini Torque Holo Gold /5 #77
2016 Panini Torque Holo Silver /10 #18
2016 Panini Torque Holo Silver /10 #57
2016 Panini Torque Holo Silver /10 #77
2016 Panini Torque Horsepower Heroes #3
2016 Panini Torque Horsepower Heroes Gold /199 #3
2016 Panini Torque Horsepower Heroes Holo Silver /99 #3
2016 Panini Torque Jumbo Tire Autographs /35 #2
2016 Panini Torque Jumbo Tire Autographs Blue /24 #2
2016 Panini Torque Jumbo Tire Autographs Green /5 #2
2016 Panini Torque Jumbo Tire Autographs Purple /1 #2
2016 Panini Torque Jumbo Tire Autographs Red /10 #2
2016 Panini Torque Metal Materials /249 #7
2016 Panini Torque Metal Materials Blue /99 #7
2016 Panini Torque Metal Materials Green /25 #7
2016 Panini Torque Metal Materials Purple /10 #7
2016 Panini Torque Metal Materials Red /49 #7
2016 Panini Torque Pairings Materials /125 #2
2016 Panini Torque Pairings Materials /125 #4
2016 Panini Torque Pairings Materials Blue /99 #2
2016 Panini Torque Pairings Materials Blue /99 #4
2016 Panini Torque Pairings Materials Green /25 #2
2016 Panini Torque Pairings Materials Green /25 #4
2016 Panini Torque Pairings Materials Purple /10 #2
2016 Panini Torque Pairings Materials Purple /10 #4
2016 Panini Torque Pairings Materials Red /49 #2
2016 Panini Torque Pairings Materials Red /49 #4
2016 Panini Torque Pole Position #15
2016 Panini Torque Pole Position Blue /99 #15
2016 Panini Torque Pole Position Checkerboard /10 #15
2016 Panini Torque Pole Position Green /25 #15
2016 Panini Torque Pole Position Red /49 #15
2016 Panini Torque Printing Plates Black /1 #18
2016 Panini Torque Printing Plates Black /1 #57
2016 Panini Torque Printing Plates Black /1 #77
2016 Panini Torque Printing Plates Cyan /1 #18
2016 Panini Torque Printing Plates Cyan /1 #57
2016 Panini Torque Printing Plates Cyan /1 #77
2016 Panini Torque Printing Plates Magenta /1 #18
2016 Panini Torque Printing Plates Magenta /1 #57
2016 Panini Torque Printing Plates Magenta /1 #77
2016 Panini Torque Printing Plates Yellow /1 #18
2016 Panini Torque Printing Plates Yellow /1 #57
2016 Panini Torque Printing Plates Yellow /1 #77
2016 Panini Torque Purple /25 #18
2016 Panini Torque Purple /25 #57
2016 Panini Torque Purple /25 #77
2016 Panini Torque Quad Materials /199 #3
2016 Panini Torque Quad Materials Blue /99 #3
2016 Panini Torque Quad Materials Green /25 #3
2016 Panini Torque Quad Materials Purple /10 #3
2016 Panini Torque Quad Materials Red /49 #3
2016 Panini Torque Red /99 #18
2016 Panini Torque Red /99 #57
2016 Panini Torque Red /99 #77
2016 Panini Torque Silhouettes Firesuit Autographs /35 #4
2016 Panini Torque Silhouettes Firesuit Autographs Blue /24 #4
2016 Panini Torque Silhouettes Firesuit Autographs Green /5 #4
2016 Panini Torque Silhouettes Firesuit Autographs Purple /1 #4
2016 Panini Torque Silhouettes Firesuit Autographs Red /10 #4
2016 Panini Torque Silhouettes Sheet Metal Autographs /35 #4
2016 Panini Torque Silhouettes Sheet Metal Autographs Blue /24 #4
2016 Panini Torque Silhouettes Sheet Metal Autographs Green /5 #4
2016 Panini Torque Silhouettes Sheet Metal Autographs Purple /1 #4
2016 Panini Torque Silhouettes Sheet Metal Autographs Red /10 #4
2016 Panini Torque Special Paint #8
2016 Panini Torque Special Paint Gold /199 #8
2016 Panini Torque Special Paint Holo Silver /99 #8
2016 Panini Torque Superstar Vision #8
2016 Panini Torque Superstar Vision Blue /99 #8
2016 Panini Torque Superstar Vision Gold /149 #8
2016 Panini Torque Superstar Vision Green /25 #8
2016 Panini Torque Superstar Vision Purple /10 #8
2016 Panini Torque Superstar Vision Red /49 #8
2016 Panini Torque Test Proof Black /1 #18
2016 Panini Torque Test Proof Black /1 #57
2016 Panini Torque Test Proof Black /1 #77
2016 Panini Torque Test Proof Cyan /1 #18
2016 Panini Torque Test Proof Cyan /1 #57
2016 Panini Torque Test Proof Cyan /1 #77
2016 Panini Torque Test Proof Magenta /1 #18
2016 Panini Torque Test Proof Magenta /1 #57
2016 Panini Torque Test Proof Magenta /1 #77
2016 Panini Torque Test Proof Yellow /1 #18
2016 Panini Torque Test Proof Yellow /1 #57
2016 Panini Torque Test Proof Yellow /1 #77
2017 Donruss #14
2017 Donruss #46
2017 Donruss #126
2017 Donruss #141
2017 Donruss #118
2017 Donruss Artist Proof /25 #14
2017 Donruss Artist Proof /25 #46
2017 Donruss Artist Proof /25 #126
2017 Donruss Artist Proof /25 #141
2017 Donruss Artist Proof /25 #118
2017 Donruss Blue Foil /299 #14
2017 Donruss Blue Foil /299 #126
2017 Donruss Blue Foil /299 #46
2017 Donruss Blue Foil /299 #141
2017 Donruss Blue Foil /299 #118
2017 Donruss Dual Rubber Relics #3
2017 Donruss Dual Rubber Relics Holo Black /1 #3
2017 Donruss Dual Rubber Relics Holo Gold /25 #3
2017 Donruss Gold Foil /499 #14
2017 Donruss Gold Foil /499 #126
2017 Donruss Gold Foil /499 #141
2017 Donruss Gold Foil /499 #46
2017 Donruss Gold Foil /499 #118
2017 Donruss Gold Press Proof /99 #14
2017 Donruss Gold Press Proof /99 #46
2017 Donruss Gold Press Proof /99 #126
2017 Donruss Gold Press Proof /99 #141
2017 Donruss Gold Press Proof /99 #118
2017 Donruss Green Foil /199 #14
2017 Donruss Green Foil /199 #46
2017 Donruss Green Foil /199 #126
2017 Donruss Green Foil /199 #141
2017 Donruss Green Foil /199 #118
2017 Donruss Phenoms #1
2017 Donruss Phenoms Cracked Ice /999 #1
2017 Donruss Pole Position #4
2017 Donruss Pole Position Cracked Ice /999 #4
2017 Donruss Press Proof /49 #14
2017 Donruss Press Proof /49 #46
2017 Donruss Press Proof /49 #126
2017 Donruss Press Proof /49 #141
2017 Donruss Press Proof /49 #118
2017 Donruss Printing Plates Black /1 #14
2017 Donruss Printing Plates Black /1 #46
2017 Donruss Printing Plates Black /1 #126
2017 Donruss Printing Plates Black /1 #141
2017 Donruss Printing Plates Black /1 #118
2017 Donruss Printing Plates Cyan /1 #14
2017 Donruss Printing Plates Cyan /1 #46
2017 Donruss Printing Plates Cyan /1 #126
2017 Donruss Printing Plates Cyan /1 #141
2017 Donruss Printing Plates Cyan /1 #118
2017 Donruss Printing Plates Magenta /1 #14
2017 Donruss Printing Plates Magenta /1 #126
2017 Donruss Printing Plates Magenta /1 #141
2017 Donruss Printing Plates Magenta /1 #46
2017 Donruss Printing Plates Magenta /1 #118
2017 Donruss Printing Plates Yellow /1 #14
2017 Donruss Printing Plates Yellow /1 #126
2017 Donruss Printing Plates Yellow /1 #141
2017 Donruss Printing Plates Yellow /1 #46
2017 Donruss Printing Plates Yellow /1 #118
2017 Donruss Retro Signatures 1984 #3
2017 Donruss Retro Signatures 1984 Holo Black /1 #3
2017 Donruss Retro Signatures 1984 Holo Gold /25 #3
2017 Donruss Rubber Relics #10
2017 Donruss Rubber Relics Holo Black /1 #10
2017 Donruss Rubber Relics Holo Gold /25 #10
2017 Donruss Studio Signatures #4
2017 Donruss Studio Signatures Holo Black /1 #4
2017 Donruss Studio Signatures Holo Gold /25 #4
2017 Donruss Top Tier #2
2017 Donruss Top Tier Cracked Ice /999 #2
2017 Panini Black Friday Happy Holiday Memorabilia #HHCE
2017 Panini Black Friday Happy Holiday Memorabilia Cracked Ice /25 #HHCE
2017 Panini Black Friday Happy Holiday Memorabilia Galactic Windows /10 #HHCE
2017 Panini Black Friday Happy Holiday Memorabilia Hyperplaid /1 #HHCE
2017 Panini Day #58
2017 Panini Day Cracked Ice /25 #58
2017 Panini Day Decoy /50 #58
2017 Panini Day Hyperplaid /1 #58
2017 Panini Day Memorabilia #42
2017 Panini Day Memorabilia Galactic Window /25 #42
2017 Panini Day Memorabilia Hyperplaid /1 #42
2017 Panini Day Rapture /10 #58
2017 Panini Day Wedges /50 #58
2017 Panini National Convention #R3
2017 Panini National Convention Autographs #R3
2017 Panini National Convention Autographs Hyperplaid /1 #R3
2017 Panini National Convention Escher Squares /25 #R3
2017 Panini National Convention Escher Squares Thick Stock /10 #R3
2017 Panini National Convention Galatic Windows /5 #R3
2017 Panini National Convention Hyperplaid /1 #R3
2017 Panini National Convention Pyramids /10 #R3
2017 Panini National Convention Rainbow Spokes /49 #R3
2017 Panini National Convention Rainbow Spokes Thick Stock /25 #R3
2017 Panini National Convention Rapture /99 #R3
2017 Panini National Convention VIP #82
2017 Panini National Convention VIP Prizm #82
2017 Panini National Convention VIP Prizm Black /1 #82
2017 Panini National Convention VIP Prizm Cracked Ice /25 #82
2017 Panini National Convention VIP Prizm Gold /15 #82
2017 Panini National Convention VIP Prizm Green /5 #82
2017 Panini National Treasures /25 #10
2017 Panini National Treasures Associate Sponsor Patch Signatures 1 /1 #9
2017 Panini National Treasures Associate Sponsor Patch Signatures 2 /1 #9
2017 Panini National Treasures Associate Sponsor Patch Signatures 3 /1 #9
2017 Panini National Treasures Associate Sponsor Patch Signatures 4 /1 #9
2017 Panini National Treasures Associate Sponsor Patch Signatures 5 /1 #9
2017 Panini National Treasures Associate Sponsor Patch Signatures 6 /1 #9
2017 Panini National Treasures Associate Sponsor Patch Signatures 7 /1 #9
2017 Panini National Treasures Associate Sponsor Patch Signatures 8 /1 #9
2017 Panini National Treasures Associate Sponsor Patch Signatures 9 /1 #9
2017 Panini National Treasures Century Black /1 #10
2017 Panini National Treasures Century Gold /15 #10
2017 Panini National Treasures Century Green /5 #10
2017 Panini National Treasures Century Holo Gold /10 #10
2017 Panini National Treasures Century Holo Silver /20 #10
2017 Panini National Treasures Century Laundry Tags /1 #10
2017 Panini National Treasures Dual Firesuit Materials /25 #4
2017 Panini National Treasures Dual Firesuit Materials Black /1 #4
2017 Panini National Treasures Dual Firesuit Materials Gold /15 #4
2017 Panini National Treasures Dual Firesuit Materials Green /5 #4
2017 Panini National Treasures Dual Firesuit Materials Holo Gold /10 #4
2017 Panini National Treasures Dual Firesuit Materials Holo Silver /20 #4
2017 Panini National Treasures Dual Firesuit Materials Laundry Tag /1 #4
2017 Panini National Treasures Dual Firesuit Materials Printing Plates Black /1 #4
2017 Panini National Treasures Dual Firesuit Materials Printing Plates Cyan /1 #4
2017 Panini National Treasures Dual Firesuit Materials Printing Plates Magenta /1 #4
2017 Panini National Treasures Dual Firesuit Materials Printing Plates Yellow /1 #4
2017 Panini National Treasures Dual Firesuit Signatures Black /1 #4
2017 Panini National Treasures Dual Firesuit Signatures Green /5 #4
2017 Panini National Treasures Dual Firesuit Signatures Holo Gold /10 #4
2017 Panini National Treasures Dual Firesuit Signatures Laundry Tag /1 #4
2017 Panini National Treasures Dual Firesuit Signatures Printing Plates Black /1 #4
2017 Panini National Treasures Dual Firesuit Signatures Printing Plates Cyan /1 #4
2017 Panini National Treasures Dual Firesuit Signatures Printing Plates Magenta /1 #4
2017 Panini National Treasures Dual Firesuit Signatures Printing Plates Yellow /1 #4
2017 Panini National Treasures Dual Sheet Metal Materials /25 #2
2017 Panini National Treasures Dual Sheet Metal Materials Black /1 #2
2017 Panini National Treasures Dual Sheet Metal Materials Gold /15 #2
2017 Panini National Treasures Dual Sheet Metal Materials Green /5 #2
2017 Panini National Treasures Dual Sheet Metal Materials Holo Gold /10 #2
2017 Panini National Treasures Dual Sheet Metal Materials Holo Silver /20 #2
2017 Panini National Treasures Dual Sheet Metal Materials Printing Plates Black /1 #2
2017 Panini National Treasures Dual Sheet Metal Materials Printing Plates Cyan /1 #2
2017 Panini National Treasures Dual Sheet Metal Materials Printing Plates Magenta /1 #2
2017 Panini National Treasures Dual Sheet Metal Materials Printing Plates Yellow /1 #2
2017 Panini National Treasures Dual Sheet Metal Signatures /24 #12
2017 Panini National Treasures Dual Sheet Metal Signatures Black /1 #12
2017 Panini National Treasures Dual Sheet Metal Signatures Gold /15 #12
2017 Panini National Treasures Dual Sheet Metal Signatures Green /5 #12
2017 Panini National Treasures Dual Sheet Metal Signatures Holo Gold /10 #12
2017 Panini National Treasures Dual Sheet Metal Signatures Holo Silver /20 #12
2017 Panini National Treasures Dual Sheet Metal Signatures Printing Plates Black /1 #12
2017 Panini National Treasures Dual Sheet Metal Signatures Printing Plates Cyan /1 #12
2017 Panini National Treasures Dual Sheet Metal Signatures Printing Plates Magenta /1 #12
2017 Panini National Treasures Dual Sheet Metal Signatures Printing Plates Yellow /1 #12
2017 Panini National Treasures Dual Signature Materials /50 #4
2017 Panini National Treasures Dual Signature Materials Black /1 #4
2017 Panini National Treasures Dual Signature Materials Gold /15 #4
2017 Panini National Treasures Dual Signature Materials Green /5 #4
2017 Panini National Treasures Dual Signature Materials Holo Gold /10 #4
2017 Panini National Treasures Dual Signature Materials Holo Silver /25 #4
2017 Panini National Treasures Dual Signature Materials Laundry Tag /1 #4
2017 Panini National Treasures Hats Off /13 #15
2017 Panini National Treasures Hats Off Gold /2 #15
2017 Panini National Treasures Hats Off Holo Gold /5 #15
2017 Panini National Treasures Hats Off Holo Silver /1 #15
2017 Panini National Treasures Hats Off Laundry Tag /6 #15
2017 Panini National Treasures Hats Off Printing Plates Black /1 #15
2017 Panini National Treasures Hats Off Printing Plates Cyan /1 #15
2017 Panini National Treasures Hats Off Printing Plates Magenta /1 #15
2017 Panini National Treasures Hats Off Printing Plates Yellow /1 #15
2017 Panini National Treasures Hats Off Sponsor /5 #15
2017 Panini National Treasures Jumbo Sheet Metal Materials Black /1 #5
2017 Panini National Treasures Jumbo Sheet Metal Materials Gold /15 #5
2017 Panini National Treasures Jumbo Sheet Metal Materials Green /5 #5
2017 Panini National Treasures Jumbo Sheet Metal Materials Holo Gold /10 #5
2017 Panini National Treasures Jumbo Sheet Metal Materials Printing Plates Black /1 #5
2017 Panini National Treasures Jumbo Sheet Metal Materials Printing Plates Cyan /1 #5
2017 Panini National Treasures Jumbo Sheet Metal Materials Printing Plates Magenta /1 #5
2017 Panini National Treasures Jumbo Sheet Metal Materials Printing Plates Yellow /1 #5
2017 Panini National Treasures Jumbo Tire Signatures /24 #3
2017 Panini National Treasures Jumbo Tire Signatures Black /1 #3
2017 Panini National Treasures Jumbo Tire Signatures Gold /15 #3
2017 Panini National Treasures Jumbo Tire Signatures Green /5 #3
2017 Panini National Treasures Jumbo Tire Signatures Holo Gold /10 #3
2017 Panini National Treasures Jumbo Tire Signatures Holo Silver /20 #3
2017 Panini National Treasures Jumbo Tire Signatures Printing Plates Black /1 #3
2017 Panini National Treasures Jumbo Tire Signatures Printing Plates Cyan /1 #3
2017 Panini National Treasures Jumbo Tire Signatures Printing Plates Magenta /1 #3
2017 Panini National Treasures Jumbo Tire Signatures Printing Plates Yellow /1 #3
2017 Panini National Treasures Nameplate Patch Signatures /2 #9
2017 Panini National Treasures NASCAR Patch Signatures /1 #9
2017 Panini National Treasures Printing Plates Black /1 #10
2017 Panini National Treasures Printing Plates Cyan /1 #10
2017 Panini National Treasures Printing Plates Magenta /1 #10
2017 Panini National Treasures Printing Plates Yellow /1 #10
2017 Panini National Treasures Series Sponsor Patch Signatures /1 #9
2017 Panini National Treasures Signature Sheet Metal /25 #6
2017 Panini National Treasures Signature Sheet Metal Black /1 #6
2017 Panini National Treasures Signature Sheet Metal Gold /15 #6
2017 Panini National Treasures Signature Sheet Metal Green /5 #6
2017 Panini National Treasures Signature Sheet Metal Holo Gold /10 #6
2017 Panini National Treasures Signature Sheet Metal Holo Silver /20 #6
2017 Panini National Treasures Signature Six Way Swatches /25 #1
2017 Panini National Treasures Signature Six Way Swatches Black /1 #1
2017 Panini National Treasures Signature Six Way Swatches Gold /15 #1
2017 Panini National Treasures Signature Six Way Swatches Green /5 #1
2017 Panini National Treasures Signature Six Way Swatches Holo Gold /10 #1
2017 Panini National Treasures Signature Six Way Swatches Holo Silver /20 #1
2017 Panini National Treasures Signature Six Way Swatches Laundry Tag /1 #1
2017 Panini National Treasures Sunoco Patch Signatures /1 #9
2017 Panini National Treasures Teammates Dual Materials /25 #1
2017 Panini National Treasures Teammates Dual Materials Black /1 #1
2017 Panini National Treasures Teammates Dual Materials Gold /15 #1
2017 Panini National Treasures Teammates Dual Materials Green /5 #1
2017 Panini National Treasures Teammates Dual Materials Holo Gold /10 #1
2017 Panini National Treasures Teammates Dual Materials Laundry Tag /1 #1
2017 Panini National Treasures Teammates Dual Materials Printing Plates Black /1 #1
2017 Panini National Treasures Teammates Dual Materials Printing Plates Cyan /1 #1
2017 Panini National Treasures Teammates Dual Materials Printing Plates Magenta /1 #1
2017 Panini National Treasures Teammates Dual Materials Printing Plates Yellow /1 #1
2017 Panini National Treasures Teammates Quad Materials /25 #8
2017 Panini National Treasures Teammates Quad Materials Black /1 #8
2017 Panini National Treasures Teammates Quad Materials Gold /15 #8
2017 Panini National Treasures Teammates Quad Materials Green /5 #8
2017 Panini National Treasures Teammates Quad Materials Holo Gold /10 #8
2017 Panini National Treasures Teammates Quad Materials Holo Silver /20 #8
2017 Panini National Treasures Teammates Quad Materials Laundry Tag /1 #8
2017 Panini National Treasures Teammates Quad Materials Printing Plates Black /1 #8
2017 Panini National Treasures Teammates Quad Materials Printing Plates Cyan /1 #8
2017 Panini National Treasures Teammates Quad Materials Printing Plates Magenta /1 #8
2017 Panini National Treasures Teammates Quad Materials Printing Plates Yellow /1 #8
2017 Panini National Treasures Teammates Triple Materials /25 #1
2017 Panini National Treasures Teammates Triple Materials /25 #5
2017 Panini National Treasures Teammates Triple Materials Black /1 #1
2017 Panini National Treasures Teammates Triple Materials Black /1 #5
2017 Panini National Treasures Teammates Triple Materials Gold /15 #1
2017 Panini National Treasures Teammates Triple Materials Gold /15 #5
2017 Panini National Treasures Teammates Triple Materials Green /5 #1
2017 Panini National Treasures Teammates Triple Materials Green /5 #5
2017 Panini National Treasures Teammates Triple Materials Holo Gold /10 #1
2017 Panini National Treasures Teammates Triple Materials Holo Gold /10 #5
2017 Panini National Treasures Teammates Triple Materials Holo Silver /20 #1
2017 Panini National Treasures Teammates Triple Materials Holo Silver /20 #5
2017 Panini National Treasures Teammates Triple Materials Laundry Tag /1 #1
2017 Panini National Treasures Teammates Triple Materials Laundry Tag /1 #5
2017 Panini National Treasures Teammates Triple Materials Printing Plates Black /1 #1
2017 Panini National Treasures Teammates Triple Materials Printing Plates Black /1 #5
2017 Panini National Treasures Teammates Triple Materials Printing Plates Cyan /1 #1
2017 Panini National Treasures Teammates Triple Materials Printing Plates Cyan /1 #5
2017 Panini National Treasures Teammates Triple Materials Printing Plates Magenta /1 #1
2017 Panini National Treasures Teammates Triple Materials Printing Plates Magenta /1 #5
2017 Panini National Treasures Teammates Triple Materials Printing Plates Yellow /1 #1
2017 Panini National Treasures Teammates Triple Materials Printing Plates Yellow /1 #5
2017 Panini National Treasures Three Wide /25 #8
2017 Panini National Treasures Three Wide Black /1 #8
2017 Panini National Treasures Three Wide Gold /15 #8
2017 Panini National Treasures Three Wide Green /5 #8
2017 Panini National Treasures Three Wide Holo Gold /10 #8
2017 Panini National Treasures Three Wide Holo Silver /20 #8
2017 Panini National Treasures Three Wide Laundry Tag /1 #8
2017 Panini National Treasures Three Wide Printing Plates Black /1 #8
2017 Panini National Treasures Three Wide Printing Plates Cyan /1 #8
2017 Panini National Treasures Three Wide Printing Plates Magenta /1 #8
2017 Panini National Treasures Three Wide Printing Plates Yellow /1 #8
2017 Panini National Treasures Three Wide Signatures /24 #15
2017 Panini National Treasures Three Wide Signatures Black /1 #15
2017 Panini National Treasures Three Wide Signatures Gold /15 #15
2017 Panini National Treasures Three Wide Signatures Green /5 #15
2017 Panini National Treasures Three Wide Signatures Holo Gold /10 #15
2017 Panini National Treasures Three Wide Signatures Holo Silver /20 #15
2017 Panini National Treasures Three Wide Signatures Laundry Tag /1 #15
2017 Panini National Treasures Three Wide Signatures Printing Plates Black /1 #15
2017 Panini National Treasures Three Wide Signatures Printing Plates Cyan /1 #15
2017 Panini National Treasures Three Wide Signatures Printing Plates Magenta /1 #15
2017 Panini National Treasures Three Wide Signatures Printing Plates Yellow /1 #15
2017 Panini Torque #13
2017 Panini Torque #61
2017 Panini Torque #98
2017 Panini Torque Artist Proof /75 #13
2017 Panini Torque Artist Proof /75 #61
2017 Panini Torque Artist Proof /75 #98
2017 Panini Torque Blackout /1 #13
2017 Panini Torque Blackout /1 #61
2017 Panini Torque Blackout /1 #98
2017 Panini Torque Blue /150 #13
2017 Panini Torque Blue /150 #61
2017 Panini Torque Blue /150 #98
2017 Panini Torque Clear Vision #13
2017 Panini Torque Clear Vision Blue /99 #13
2017 Panini Torque Clear Vision Gold /149 #13
2017 Panini Torque Clear Vision Green /25 #13
2017 Panini Torque Clear Vision Purple /10 #13
2017 Panini Torque Clear Vision Red /49 #13
2017 Panini Torque Dual Materials /49 #4
2017 Panini Torque Dual Materials Blue /25 #4
2017 Panini Torque Dual Materials Green /10 #4
2017 Panini Torque Dual Materials Purple /5 #4
2017 Panini Torque Dual Materials Red /15 #4
2017 Panini Torque Gold #13
2017 Panini Torque Gold #61
2017 Panini Torque Gold #98
2017 Panini Torque Holo Gold /10 #13
2017 Panini Torque Holo Gold /10 #61
2017 Panini Torque Holo Gold /10 #98
2017 Panini Torque Holo Silver /25 #13
2017 Panini Torque Holo Silver /25 #61
2017 Panini Torque Holo Silver /25 #98
2017 Panini Torque Horsepower Heroes #17
2017 Panini Torque Horsepower Heroes Gold /199 #17
2017 Panini Torque Horsepower Heroes Holo Silver /99 #17
2017 Panini Torque Jumbo Firesuit Signatures /41 #5
2017 Panini Torque Jumbo Firesuit Signatures Blue /40 #5
2017 Panini Torque Jumbo Firesuit Signatures Green /24 #5
2017 Panini Torque Jumbo Firesuit Signatures Purple /10 #5
2017 Panini Torque Jumbo Firesuit Signatures Red /35 #5
2017 Panini Torque Manufacturer Marks #7
2017 Panini Torque Manufacturer Marks Gold /199 #7
2017 Panini Torque Manufacturer Marks Holo Silver /99 #7
2017 Panini Torque Pairings Materials #7
2017 Panini Torque Pairings Materials Blue /49 #7
2017 Panini Torque Pairings Materials Green /10 #7
2017 Panini Torque Pairings Materials Purple /5 #7
2017 Panini Torque Pairings Materials Red /25 #7
2017 Panini Torque Primary Paint #9
2017 Panini Torque Primary Paint Blue /99 #9
2017 Panini Torque Primary Paint Checkerboard /10 #9
2017 Panini Torque Primary Paint Green /25 #9
2017 Panini Torque Primary Paint Red /49 #9
2017 Panini Torque Prime Associate Sponsors Jumbo Patches /1 #3A
2017 Panini Torque Prime Associate Sponsors Jumbo Patches /1 #3B
2017 Panini Torque Prime Associate Sponsors Jumbo Patches /1 #3C
2017 Panini Torque Prime Associate Sponsors Jumbo Patches /1 #3D
2017 Panini Torque Prime Associate Sponsors Jumbo Patches /1 #3E
2017 Panini Torque Prime Associate Sponsors Jumbo Patches /1 #3F
2017 Panini Torque Prime Associate Sponsors Jumbo Patches /1 #3G
2017 Panini Torque Prime Associate Sponsors Jumbo Patches /1 #3H
2017 Panini Torque Prime Associate Sponsors Jumbo Patches /1 #3I
2017 Panini Torque Prime Associate Sponsors Jumbo Patches /1 #3J
2017 Panini Torque Prime Associate Sponsors Jumbo Patches /1 #3K
2017 Panini Torque Prime Associate Sponsors Jumbo Patches /1 #3L
2017 Panini Torque Prime Nameplates Jumbo Patches /2 #3
2017 Panini Torque Prime NASCAR Jumbo Patches /1 #3
2017 Panini Torque Prime Series Sponsor Jumbo Patches /1 #3
2017 Panini Torque Printing Plates Black /1 #13
2017 Panini Torque Printing Plates Black /1 #61
2017 Panini Torque Printing Plates Black /1 #98
2017 Panini Torque Printing Plates Cyan /1 #13
2017 Panini Torque Printing Plates Cyan /1 #61
2017 Panini Torque Printing Plates Cyan /1 #98
2017 Panini Torque Printing Plates Magenta /1 #13
2017 Panini Torque Printing Plates Magenta /1 #61
2017 Panini Torque Printing Plates Magenta /1 #98
2017 Panini Torque Printing Plates Yellow /1 #13
2017 Panini Torque Printing Plates Yellow /1 #61
2017 Panini Torque Printing Plates Yellow /1 #98
2017 Panini Torque Purple /50 #13
2017 Panini Torque Purple /50 #61
2017 Panini Torque Purple /50 #98
2017 Panini Torque Quad Materials Blue /99 #3
2017 Panini Torque Quad Materials Green /25 #3
2017 Panini Torque Quad Materials Purple /10 #3
2017 Panini Torque Quad Materials Red /49 #3
2017 Panini Torque Raced Relics /499 #3
2017 Panini Torque Raced Relics Blue /49 #3
2017 Panini Torque Raced Relics Green /10 #3
2017 Panini Torque Raced Relics Purple /5 #3
2017 Panini Torque Raced Relics Red /25 #3
2017 Panini Torque Red /100 #13
2017 Panini Torque Red /100 #61
2017 Panini Torque Red /100 #98
2017 Panini Torque Rookie Stripes #8
2017 Panini Torque Rookie Stripes Gold /199 #8
2017 Panini Torque Rookie Stripes Holo Silver /99 #8
2017 Panini Torque Running Order #10
2017 Panini Torque Running Order Blue /99 #10
2017 Panini Torque Running Order Checkerboard /10 #10
2017 Panini Torque Running Order Green /25 #10
2017 Panini Torque Running Order Red /49 #10
2017 Panini Torque Silhouettes Sheet Metal Signatures /41 #6
2017 Panini Torque Silhouettes Sheet Metal Signatures Blue /40 #6
2017 Panini Torque Silhouettes Sheet Metal Signatures Green /24 #6
2017 Panini Torque Silhouettes Sheet Metal Signatures Purple /10 #6
2017 Panini Torque Silhouettes Sheet Metal Signatures Red /35 #6
2017 Panini Torque Superstar Vision #9
2017 Panini Torque Superstar Vision Blue /99 #9
2017 Panini Torque Superstar Vision Gold /149 #9
2017 Panini Torque Superstar Vision Green /25 #9
2017 Panini Torque Superstar Vision Purple /10 #9
2017 Panini Torque Superstar Vision Red /49 #9
2017 Panini Torque Test Proof Black /1 #13
2017 Panini Torque Test Proof Black /1 #61
2017 Panini Torque Test Proof Black /1 #98
2017 Panini Torque Test Proof Cyan /1 #13
2017 Panini Torque Test Proof Cyan /1 #61
2017 Panini Torque Test Proof Cyan /1 #98
2017 Panini Torque Test Proof Magenta /1 #13
2017 Panini Torque Test Proof Magenta /1 #61
2017 Panini Torque Test Proof Magenta /1 #98
2017 Panini Torque Test Proof Yellow /1 #13
2017 Panini Torque Test Proof Yellow /1 #61
2017 Panini Torque Test Proof Yellow /1 #98
2017 Panini Torque Trackside #8
2017 Panini Torque Trackside Blue /99 #8
2017 Panini Torque Trackside Checkerboard /10 #8
2017 Panini Torque Trackside Green /25 #8
2017 Panini Torque Trackside Red /49 #8
2017 Select #52
2017 Select #53
2017 Select #54
2017 Select #55
2017 Select #123
2017 Select Prizms Black /3 #52
2017 Select Prizms Black /3 #53
2017 Select Prizms Black /3 #54
2017 Select Prizms Black /3 #55
2017 Select Prizms Black /3 #123
2017 Select Prizms Blue /199 #52
2017 Select Prizms Blue /199 #53
2017 Select Prizms Blue /199 #54
2017 Select Prizms Blue /199 #55
2017 Select Prizms Checkered Flag /1 #52
2017 Select Prizms Checkered Flag /1 #53
2017 Select Prizms Checkered Flag /1 #54
2017 Select Prizms Checkered Flag /1 #55
2017 Select Prizms Checkered Flag /1 #123
2017 Select Prizms Gold /10 #52
2017 Select Prizms Gold /10 #53
2017 Select Prizms Gold /10 #54
2017 Select Prizms Gold /10 #55
2017 Select Prizms Gold /10 #123
2017 Select Prizms Purple Pulsar #52
2017 Select Prizms Purple Pulsar #53
2017 Select Prizms Purple Pulsar #54
2017 Select Prizms Purple Pulsar #55
2017 Select Prizms Red /99 #52
2017 Select Prizms Red /99 #53
2017 Select Prizms Red /99 #54
2017 Select Prizms Red /99 #55
2017 Select Prizms Red White and Blue Pulsar /299 #52
2017 Select Prizms Red White and Blue Pulsar /299 #53
2017 Select Prizms Red White and Blue Pulsar /299 #54
2017 Select Prizms Red White and Blue Pulsar /299 #55
2017 Select Prizms Silver #52
2017 Select Prizms Silver #53
2017 Select Prizms Silver #54
2017 Select Prizms Silver #55
2017 Select Prizms Tie Dye /24 #52
2017 Select Prizms Tie Dye /24 #53
2017 Select Prizms Tie Dye /24 #54
2017 Select Prizms Tie Dye /24 #55
2017 Select Prizms Tie Dye /24 #123
2017 Select Prizms White /50 #52
2017 Select Prizms White /50 #53
2017 Select Prizms White /50 #54
2017 Select Prizms White /50 #55
2017 Select Prizms White /50 #123
2017 Select Select Pairs Materials Prizms Blue /30 #15
2017 Select Select Pairs Materials Prizms Blue /30 #17
2017 Select Select Pairs Materials Prizms Blue /28 #18
2017 Select Select Pairs Materials Prizms Checkered Flag /1 #15
2017 Select Select Pairs Materials Prizms Checkered Flag /1 #17
2017 Select Select Pairs Materials Prizms Checkered Flag /1 #18
2017 Select Select Pairs Materials Prizms Gold /10 #15
2017 Select Select Pairs Materials Prizms Gold /10 #17
2017 Select Select Pairs Materials Prizms Gold /10 #18
2017 Select Select Pairs Materials Prizms Red /25 #15
2017 Select Select Pairs Materials Prizms Red /25 #17
2017 Select Select Pairs Materials Prizms Red /25 #18
2017 Select Select Swatches #6
2017 Select Select Swatches Prizms Blue /199 #6
2017 Select Select Swatches Prizms Checkered Flag /1 #6
2017 Select Select Swatches Prizms Gold /10 #6
2017 Select Select Swatches Prizms Red /99 #6
2017 Select Sheet Metal #3
2017 Select Sheet Metal Prizms Blue /99 #3
2017 Select Sheet Metal Prizms Checkered Flag /1 #3
2017 Select Sheet Metal Prizms Gold /10 #3
2017 Select Sheet Metal Prizms Red /50 #3
2017 Select Signature Paint Schemes #6
2017 Select Signature Paint Schemes Prizms Blue /15 #6
2017 Select Signature Paint Schemes Prizms Checkered Flag /1 #6
2017 Select Signature Paint Schemes Prizms Gold /5 #6
2017 Select Signature Paint Schemes Prizms Red /10 #6
2017 Select Signature Swatches #6
2017 Select Signature Swatches Dual #9
2017 Select Signature Swatches Dual Prizms Checkered Flag /1 #9
2017 Select Signature Swatches Dual Prizms Gold /10 #9
2017 Select Signature Swatches Dual Prizms Tie Dye /24 #9
2017 Select Signature Swatches Dual Prizms White /50 #9
2017 Select Signature Swatches Prizms Checkered Flag /1 #6
2017 Select Signature Swatches Prizms Gold /10 #6
2017 Select Signature Swatches Prizms Tie Dye /24 #6
2017 Select Signature Swatches Prizms White /50 #6
2017 Select Speed Merchants #22
2017 Select Speed Merchants Prizms Black /3 #22
2017 Select Speed Merchants Prizms Checkered Flag /1 #22
2017 Select Speed Merchants Prizms Gold /10 #22
2017 Select Speed Merchants Prizms Tie Dye /24 #22
2017 Select Speed Merchants Prizms White /50 #22
2017 Select Up Close and Personal #5
2017 Select Up Close and Personal Prizms Black /3 #5
2017 Select Up Close and Personal Prizms Checkered Flag /1 #5
2017 Select Up Close and Personal Prizms Gold /10 #5
2017 Select Up Close and Personal Prizms Tie Dye /24 #5
2017 Select Up Close and Personal Prizms White /50 #5
2018 Certified #29
2018 Certified #91
2018 Certified All Certified Team /199 #7
2018 Certified All Certified Team Black /1 #7
2018 Certified All Certified Team Blue /99 #7
2018 Certified All Certified Team Gold /49 #7
2018 Certified All Certified Team Green /10 #7
2018 Certified All Certified Team Mirror Black /1 #7
2018 Certified All Certified Team Mirror Gold /25 #7
2018 Certified All Certified Team Mirror Green /5 #7
2018 Certified All Certified Team Mirror Purple /10 #7
2018 Certified All Certified Team Purple /25 #7
2018 Certified All Certified Team Red /149 #7
2018 Certified Black /1 #29
2018 Certified Black /1 #91
2018 Certified Blue /99 #29
2018 Certified Blue /99 #91
2018 Certified Complete Materials /299 #4
2018 Certified Complete Materials Black /1 #4
2018 Certified Complete Materials Blue /49 #4
2018 Certified Complete Materials Gold /25 #4
2018 Certified Complete Materials Green /5 #4
2018 Certified Complete Materials Purple /10 #4
2018 Certified Complete Materials Red /199 #4
2018 Certified Cup Swatches /499 #6
2018 Certified Cup Swatches Black /1 #6
2018 Certified Cup Swatches Blue /49 #6
2018 Certified Cup Swatches Gold /25 #6
2018 Certified Cup Swatches Green /5 #6
2018 Certified Cup Swatches Purple /10 #6
2018 Certified Cup Swatches Red /199 #6
2018 Certified Epix /199 #6
2018 Certified Epix Black /1 #6
2018 Certified Epix Blue /99 #6
2018 Certified Epix Gold /49 #6
2018 Certified Epix Green /10 #6
2018 Certified Epix Mirror Black /1 #6
2018 Certified Epix Mirror Gold /25 #6
2018 Certified Epix Mirror Green /5 #6
2018 Certified Epix Mirror Purple /10 #6
2018 Certified Epix Purple /25 #6
2018 Certified Epix Red /149 #6
2018 Certified Fresh Faces /199 #1
2018 Certified Fresh Faces Black /1 #1
2018 Certified Fresh Faces Blue /99 #1
2018 Certified Fresh Faces Gold /49 #1
2018 Certified Fresh Faces Green /10 #1
2018 Certified Fresh Faces Mirror Black /1 #1
2018 Certified Fresh Faces Mirror Gold /25 #1
2018 Certified Fresh Faces Mirror Green /5 #1
2018 Certified Fresh Faces Mirror Purple /10 #1
2018 Certified Fresh Faces Purple /25 #1
2018 Certified Fresh Faces Red /149 #1
2018 Certified Fresh Faces Signatures /25 #8
2018 Certified Fresh Faces Signatures Black /1 #8
2018 Certified Fresh Faces Signatures Blue /15 #8
2018 Certified Fresh Faces Signatures Gold /10 #8
2018 Certified Fresh Faces Signatures Green /2 #8
2018 Certified Fresh Faces Signatures Purple /5 #8
2018 Certified Fresh Faces Signatures Red /20 #8
2018 Certified Gold /49 #29
2018 Certified Gold /49 #91
2018 Certified Green /10 #29
2018 Certified Green /10 #91
2018 Certified Materials Signatures /75 #3
2018 Certified Materials Signatures Black /1 #3
2018 Certified Materials Signatures Blue /24 #3
2018 Certified Materials Signatures Gold /15 #3
2018 Certified Materials Signatures Green /5 #3
2018 Certified Materials Signatures Purple /10 #3
2018 Certified Materials Signatures Red /50 #3
2018 Certified Mirror Black /1 #29
2018 Certified Mirror Black /1 #91
2018 Certified Mirror Gold /25 #29
2018 Certified Mirror Gold /25 #91
2018 Certified Mirror Green /5 #29
2018 Certified Mirror Green /5 #91
2018 Certified Mirror Purple /10 #29
2018 Certified Mirror Purple /10 #91
2018 Certified Orange /249 #29
2018 Certified Orange /249 #91
2018 Certified Piece of the Race /499 #4
2018 Certified Piece of the Race Black /1 #4
2018 Certified Piece of the Race Blue /49 #4
2018 Certified Piece of the Race Gold /25 #4
2018 Certified Piece of the Race Green /5 #4
2018 Certified Piece of the Race Purple /10 #4
2018 Certified Piece of the Race Red /199 #4
2018 Certified Purple /25 #29
2018 Certified Purple /25 #91
2018 Certified Red /199 #29
2018 Certified Red /199 #91
2018 Certified Skills /199 #4
2018 Certified Skills Black /1 #4
2018 Certified Skills Blue /99 #4
2018 Certified Skills Gold /49 #4

2018 Certified Skills Green /10 #4
2018 Certified Skills Mirror Black /1 #4
2018 Certified Skills Mirror Gold /25 #4
2018 Certified Skills Mirror Green /5 #4
2018 Certified Skills Mirror Purple /10 #4
2018 Certified Skills Purple /25 #4
2018 Certified Skills Red /149 #4
2018 Certified Stars /199 #1
2018 Certified Stars Black /1 #1
2018 Certified Stars Blue /99 #1
2018 Certified Stars Gold /49 #1
2018 Certified Stars Green /10 #1
2018 Certified Stars Mirror Black /1 #1
2018 Certified Stars Mirror Gold /25 #1
2018 Certified Stars Mirror Green /5 #1
2018 Certified Stars Mirror Purple /10 #1
2018 Certified Stars Purple /25 #1
2018 Certified Stars Red /149 #1
2018 Donruss #10
2018 Donruss #37A
2018 Donruss #90
2018 Donruss #127
2018 Donruss #37B
2018 Donruss Artist Proofs /25 #10
2018 Donruss Artist Proofs /25 #37A
2018 Donruss Artist Proofs /25 #90
2018 Donruss Artist Proofs /25 #127
2018 Donruss Artist Proofs /25 #37B
2018 Donruss Gold Foil /499 #10
2018 Donruss Gold Foil /499 #37A
2018 Donruss Gold Foil /499 #90
2018 Donruss Gold Foil /499 #127
2018 Donruss Gold Foil /499 #37B
2018 Donruss Gold Press Proofs /99 #10
2018 Donruss Gold Press Proofs /99 #37A
2018 Donruss Gold Press Proofs /99 #90
2018 Donruss Gold Press Proofs /99 #127
2018 Donruss Gold Press Proofs /99 #37B
2018 Donruss Green Foil /199 #10
2018 Donruss Green Foil /199 #37A
2018 Donruss Green Foil /199 #90
2018 Donruss Green Foil /199 #127
2018 Donruss Green Foil /199 #37B
2018 Donruss Pole Position #1
2018 Donruss Pole Position Cracked Ice /999 #1
2018 Donruss Pole Position Xplosion /99 #1
2018 Donruss Press Proofs /49 #10
2018 Donruss Press Proofs /49 #37A
2018 Donruss Press Proofs /49 #90
2018 Donruss Press Proofs /49 #127
2018 Donruss Press Proofs /49 #37B
2018 Donruss Printing Plates Black /1 #10
2018 Donruss Printing Plates Black /1 #37
2018 Donruss Printing Plates Black /1 #90
2018 Donruss Printing Plates Black /1 #127
2018 Donruss Printing Plates Black /1 #37B
2018 Donruss Printing Plates Cyan /1 #10
2018 Donruss Printing Plates Cyan /1 #37
2018 Donruss Printing Plates Cyan /1 #90
2018 Donruss Printing Plates Cyan /1 #127
2018 Donruss Printing Plates Cyan /1 #37B
2018 Donruss Printing Plates Magenta /1 #10
2018 Donruss Printing Plates Magenta /1 #37
2018 Donruss Printing Plates Magenta /1 #90
2018 Donruss Printing Plates Magenta /1 #127
2018 Donruss Printing Plates Magenta /1 #37B
2018 Donruss Printing Plates Yellow /1 #10
2018 Donruss Printing Plates Yellow /1 #37
2018 Donruss Printing Plates Yellow /1 #90
2018 Donruss Printing Plates Yellow /1 #127
2018 Donruss Printing Plates Yellow /1 #37B
2018 Donruss Racing Relics #7
2018 Donruss Racing Relics Black /10 #7
2018 Donruss Racing Relics Holo Gold /99 #7
2018 Donruss Red Foil /299 #10
2018 Donruss Red Foil /299 #37A
2018 Donruss Red Foil /299 #90
2018 Donruss Red Foil /299 #127
2018 Donruss Red Foil /299 #37B
2018 Donruss Retro Relics '85 #5
2018 Donruss Retro Relics '85 Black /10 #5
2018 Donruss Retro Relics '85 Holo Gold /99 #5
2018 Donruss Rubber Relic Signatures #3
2018 Donruss Rubber Relic Signatures Black /1 #3
2018 Donruss Rubber Relic Signatures Holo Gold /25 #3
2018 Donruss Rubber Relics #6
2018 Donruss Rubber Relics Black /10 #6
2018 Donruss Rubber Relics Holo Gold /99 #6
2018 Donruss Studio #5
2018 Donruss Studio Cracked Ice /999 #5
2018 Donruss Studio Xplosion /99 #5
2018 Donruss Top Tier #3
2018 Donruss Top Tier Cracked Ice /999 #3
2018 Donruss Top Tier Xplosion /99 #3
2018 Panini National Convention #73
2018 Panini National Convention Escher Squares /25 #73
2018 Panini National Convention Galatic Windows /5 #73
2018 Panini National Convention Hyperplaid /1 #73
2018 Panini National Convention Magnetic Fur /99 #73
2018 Panini National Convention Pyramids /10 #73
2018 Panini National Convention Rainbow Spokes /49 #73
2018 Panini Prime /50 #18
2018 Panini Prime /50 #51
2018 Panini Prime /50 #84
2018 Panini Prime Black /1 #18
2018 Panini Prime Black /1 #51
2018 Panini Prime Black /1 #84
2018 Panini Prime Clear Silhouettes /99 #5
2018 Panini Prime Clear Silhouettes Black /1 #5
2018 Panini Prime Clear Silhouettes Dual /99 #CSCE
2018 Panini Prime Clear Silhouettes Dual Black /1 #CSCE
2018 Panini Prime Clear Silhouettes Dual Holo Gold /50 #CSCE
2018 Panini Prime Clear Silhouettes Holo Gold /50 #5
2018 Panini Prime Dual Signatures /24 #3
2018 Panini Prime Dual Signatures Black /1 #3
2018 Panini Prime Dual Signatures Holo Gold /9 #3
2018 Panini Prime Hats Off Button /1 #18
2018 Panini Prime Hats Off Driver Name /2 #18
2018 Panini Prime Hats Off Eyelet /6 #18
2018 Panini Prime Hats Off Headband /34 #18
2018 Panini Prime Hats Off Laundry Tag /1 #18
2018 Panini Prime Hats Off New Era /1 #18
2018 Panini Prime Hats Off Number /2 #18
2018 Panini Prime Hats Off Sponsor Logo /4 #18
2018 Panini Prime Holo Gold /25 #18
2018 Panini Prime Holo Gold /25 #51
2018 Panini Prime Holo Gold /25 #84
2018 Panini Prime Prime Jumbo Associate Sponsor 1 /1 #14
2018 Panini Prime Prime Jumbo Associate Sponsor 1 /1 #15
2018 Panini Prime Prime Jumbo Associate Sponsor 10 /1 #14
2018 Panini Prime Prime Jumbo Associate Sponsor 2 /1 #14
2018 Panini Prime Prime Jumbo Associate Sponsor 2 /1 #15
2018 Panini Prime Prime Jumbo Associate Sponsor 3 /1 #14
2018 Panini Prime Prime Jumbo Associate Sponsor 3 /1 #15
2018 Panini Prime Prime Jumbo Associate Sponsor 4 /1 #14
2018 Panini Prime Prime Jumbo Associate Sponsor 4 /1 #15
2018 Panini Prime Prime Jumbo Associate Sponsor 5 /1 #14
2018 Panini Prime Prime Jumbo Associate Sponsor 5 /1 #15
2018 Panini Prime Prime Jumbo Associate Sponsor 6 /1 #14
2018 Panini Prime Prime Jumbo Associate Sponsor 6 /1 #15
2018 Panini Prime Prime Jumbo Associate Sponsor 7 /1 #14
2018 Panini Prime Prime Jumbo Associate Sponsor 7 /1 #15
2018 Panini Prime Prime Jumbo Associate Sponsor 8 /1 #14
2018 Panini Prime Prime Jumbo Associate Sponsor 9 /1 #14
2018 Panini Prime Prime Jumbo Car Manufacturer /1 #14
2018 Panini Prime Prime Jumbo Car Manufacturer /1 #15
2018 Panini Prime Prime Jumbo Firesuit Manufacturer /1 #14
2018 Panini Prime Prime Jumbo Firesuit Manufacturer /1 #15
2018 Panini Prime Prime Jumbo Glove Manufacturer Patch /1 #14
2018 Panini Prime Prime Jumbo Glove Manufacturer Patch /1 #15
2018 Panini Prime Prime Jumbo Glove Number Patch /1 #14
2018 Panini Prime Prime Jumbo Glove Number Patch /1 #15
2018 Panini Prime Prime Jumbo Nameplate /2 #14
2018 Panini Prime Prime Jumbo Nameplate /2 #15
2018 Panini Prime Prime Jumbo NASCAR /1 #14
2018 Panini Prime Prime Jumbo NASCAR /1 #15
2018 Panini Prime Prime Jumbo Series Sponsor /1 #14
2018 Panini Prime Prime Jumbo Series Sponsor /1 #15
2018 Panini Prime Prime Jumbo Shoe Brand Logo /1 #14
2018 Panini Prime Prime Jumbo Shoe Brand Logo /1 #15
2018 Panini Prime Prime Jumbo Shoe Name Patch /1 #14
2018 Panini Prime Prime Jumbo Shoe Name Patch /1 #15
2018 Panini Prime Prime Jumbo Shoe Number Patch /1 #14
2018 Panini Prime Prime Jumbo Shoe Number Patch /1 #15
2018 Panini Prime Prime Jumbo Sunoco /1 #14
2018 Panini Prime Prime Jumbo Sunoco /1 #15
2018 Panini Prime Prime Number Signatures /25 #3
2018 Panini Prime Prime Number Signatures Black /1 #3
2018 Panini Prime Prime Number Signatures Holo Gold /10 #3
2018 Panini Prime Quad Material Autographs /25 #17
2018 Panini Prime Quad Material Autographs Black /1 #17
2018 Panini Prime Quad Material Autographs Holo Gold /10 #17
2018 Panini Prime Quad Material Autographs Laundry Tag /1 #17
2018 Panini Prime Race Used Duals Firesuit Black /1 #6
2018 Panini Prime Race Used Duals Firesuit Holo Gold /25 #6
2018 Panini Prime Race Used Duals Firesuit Laundry Tag /1 #6
2018 Panini Prime Race Used Duals Sheet Metal /50 #6
2018 Panini Prime Race Used Duals Sheet Metal Black /1 #6
2018 Panini Prime Race Used Duals Sheet Metal Holo Gold /25 #6
2018 Panini Prime Race Used Duals Tire /50 #6
2018 Panini Prime Race Used Duals Tire Black /1 #6
2018 Panini Prime Race Used Duals Tire Holo Gold /25 #6
2018 Panini Prime Race Used Firesuits Black /1 #5
2018 Panini Prime Race Used Firesuits Holo Gold /25 #5
2018 Panini Prime Race Used Firesuits Laundry Tag /1 #5
2018 Panini Prime Race Used Sheet Metal /50 #5
2018 Panini Prime Race Used Sheet Metal Black /1 #5
2018 Panini Prime Race Used Sheet Metal Holo Gold /25 #5
2018 Panini Prime Race Used Tires /50 #5
2018 Panini Prime Race Used Tires Black /1 #5
2018 Panini Prime Race Used Tires Holo Gold /25 #5
2018 Panini Prime Race Used Trios Firesuit Black /1 #5
2018 Panini Prime Race Used Trios Firesuit Holo Gold /25 #5
2018 Panini Prime Race Used Trios Firesuit Laundry Tag /1 #5
2018 Panini Prime Race Used Trios Sheet Metal /50 #5
2018 Panini Prime Race Used Trios Sheet Metal Black /1 #5
2018 Panini Prime Race Used Trios Sheet Metal Holo Gold /25 #5
2018 Panini Prime Race Used Trios Tire /50 #5
2018 Panini Prime Race Used Trios Tire Black /1 #5
2018 Panini Prime Race Used Trios Tire Holo Gold /25 #5
2018 Panini Prime Signature Swatches /25 #9
2018 Panini Prime Signature Swatches Black /1 #9
2018 Panini Prime Signature Swatches Holo Gold /10 #9
2018 Panini Prime Signature Tires /25 #1
2018 Panini Prime Signature Tires Black /1 #1
2018 Panini Prime Signature Tires Holo Gold /10 #1
2018 Panini Prime Triple Material Autographs /25 #20
2018 Panini Prime Triple Material Autographs Black /1 #20
2018 Panini Prime Triple Material Autographs Holo Gold /10 #20
2018 Panini Prime Triple Material Autographs Laundry Tag /1 #20
2018 Panini Prizm #1
2018 Panini Prizm #54
2018 Panini Prizm #68
2018 Panini Prizm #80
2018 Panini Prizm #82
2018 Panini Prizm Fireworks #6
2018 Panini Prizm Fireworks Prizms #6
2018 Panini Prizm Fireworks Prizms Black /1 #6
2018 Panini Prizm Fireworks Prizms Gold /10 #6
2018 Panini Prizm Illumination #7
2018 Panini Prizm Illumination Prizms #7
2018 Panini Prizm Illumination Prizms Black /1 #7
2018 Panini Prizm Illumination Prizms Gold /10 #7
2018 Panini Prizm Instant Impact #9
2018 Panini Prizm Instant Impact Prizms #9
2018 Panini Prizm Instant Impact Prizms Black /1 #9
2018 Panini Prizm Instant Impact Prizms Gold /10 #9
2018 Panini Prizm National Pride #5
2018 Panini Prizm National Pride Prizms #5
2018 Panini Prizm National Pride Prizms Black /1 #5
2018 Panini Prizm National Pride Prizms Gold /10 #5
2018 Panini Prizm Patented Penmanship Prizms #16
2018 Panini Prizm Patented Penmanship Prizms Black /1 #16
2018 Panini Prizm Patented Penmanship Prizms Blue /25 #16
2018 Panini Prizm Patented Penmanship Prizms Camo #16
2018 Panini Prizm Patented Penmanship Prizms Gold /9 #16
2018 Panini Prizm Patented Penmanship Prizms Green /25 #16
2018 Panini Prizm Patented Penmanship Prizms Rainbow /24 #16
2018 Panini Prizm Patented Penmanship Prizms Red /25 #16
2018 Panini Prizm Patented Penmanship Prizms Red White and Blue /25 #16
2018 Panini Prizm Patented Penmanship Prizms White /5 #16
2018 Panini Prizm Prizms #1
2018 Panini Prizm Prizms #54
2018 Panini Prizm Prizms #68
2018 Panini Prizm Prizms #80
2018 Panini Prizm Prizms #82
2018 Panini Prizm Prizms Black /1 #1
2018 Panini Prizm Prizms Black /1 #54
2018 Panini Prizm Prizms Black /1 #68
2018 Panini Prizm Prizms Black /1 #80
2018 Panini Prizm Prizms Black /1 #82
2018 Panini Prizm Prizms Blue /99 #1
2018 Panini Prizm Prizms Blue /99 #54
2018 Panini Prizm Prizms Blue /99 #68
2018 Panini Prizm Prizms Blue /99 #80
2018 Panini Prizm Prizms Blue /99 #82
2018 Panini Prizm Prizms Camo #1
2018 Panini Prizm Prizms Camo #54
2018 Panini Prizm Prizms Camo #68
2018 Panini Prizm Prizms Camo #80
2018 Panini Prizm Prizms Camo #82
2018 Panini Prizm Prizms Gold /10 #1
2018 Panini Prizm Prizms Gold /10 #54
2018 Panini Prizm Prizms Gold /10 #68
2018 Panini Prizm Prizms Gold /10 #80
2018 Panini Prizm Prizms Gold /10 #82
2018 Panini Prizm Prizms Green /149 #1
2018 Panini Prizm Prizms Green /149 #54
2018 Panini Prizm Prizms Green /149 #68
2018 Panini Prizm Prizms Green /149 #80
2018 Panini Prizm Prizms Green /149 #82
2018 Panini Prizm Prizms Purple Flash #1
2018 Panini Prizm Prizms Purple Flash #54
2018 Panini Prizm Prizms Purple Flash #68
2018 Panini Prizm Prizms Purple Flash #80
2018 Panini Prizm Prizms Purple Flash #82
2018 Panini Prizm Prizms Rainbow /24 #1
2018 Panini Prizm Prizms Rainbow /24 #54
2018 Panini Prizm Prizms Rainbow /24 #68
2018 Panini Prizm Prizms Rainbow /24 #80
2018 Panini Prizm Prizms Rainbow /24 #82
2018 Panini Prizm Prizms Red /75 #1
2018 Panini Prizm Prizms Red /75 #54
2018 Panini Prizm Prizms Red /75 #68
2018 Panini Prizm Prizms Red /75 #80
2018 Panini Prizm Prizms Red /75 #82
2018 Panini Prizm Prizms Red White and Blue #1
2018 Panini Prizm Prizms Red White and Blue #54
2018 Panini Prizm Prizms Red White and Blue #68
2018 Panini Prizm Prizms Red White and Blue #80
2018 Panini Prizm Prizms Red White and Blue #82
2018 Panini Prizm Prizms White /5 #1
2018 Panini Prizm Prizms White /5 #54
2018 Panini Prizm Prizms White /5 #68
2018 Panini Prizm Prizms White /5 #80
2018 Panini Prizm Prizms White /5 #82
2018 Panini Prizm Stars and Stripes #4
2018 Panini Prizm Stars and Stripes Prizms #4
2018 Panini Prizm Stars and Stripes Prizms Black /1 #4
2018 Panini Prizm Stars and Stripes Prizms Gold /10 #4
2018 Panini Prizm Team Tandems #2
2018 Panini Prizm Team Tandems Prizms #2
2018 Panini Prizm Team Tandems Prizms Black /1 #2
2018 Panini Prizm Team Tandems Prizms Gold /10 #2
2018 Panini Victory Lane #6
2018 Panini Victory Lane Black /1 #6
2018 Panini Victory Lane Blue /25 #6
2018 Panini Victory Lane Celebrations #6
2018 Panini Victory Lane Celebrations Black /1 #6
2018 Panini Victory Lane Celebrations Blue /25 #6
2018 Panini Victory Lane Celebrations Gold /99 #6
2018 Panini Victory Lane Celebrations Green /5 #6
2018 Panini Victory Lane Celebrations Printing Plates Black /1 #6
2018 Panini Victory Lane Celebrations Printing Plates Cyan /1 #6
2018 Panini Victory Lane Celebrations Printing Plates Magenta /1 #6
2018 Panini Victory Lane Celebrations Printing Plates Yellow /1 #6
2018 Panini Victory Lane Celebrations Red /49 #6
2018 Panini Victory Lane Chasing the Flag #10
2018 Panini Victory Lane Chasing the Flag Black /1 #10
2018 Panini Victory Lane Chasing the Flag Blue /25 #10
2018 Panini Victory Lane Chasing the Flag Gold /99 #10
2018 Panini Victory Lane Chasing the Flag Green /5 #10
2018 Panini Victory Lane Chasing the Flag Printing Plates Black /1 #10
2018 Panini Victory Lane Chasing the Flag Printing Plates Cyan /1 #10
2018 Panini Victory Lane Chasing the Flag Printing Plates Magenta /1 #10
2018 Panini Victory Lane Chasing the Flag Printing Plates Yellow /1 #10
2018 Panini Victory Lane Chasing the Flag Red /49 #10
2018 Panini Victory Lane Gold /99 #6
2018 Panini Victory Lane Green /5 #6
2018 Panini Victory Lane Octane Autographs /25 #6
2018 Panini Victory Lane Octane Autographs Black /1 #6
2018 Panini Victory Lane Octane Autographs Gold /10 #6
2018 Panini Victory Lane Pedal to the Metal #8
2018 Panini Victory Lane Pedal to the Metal #56
2018 Panini Victory Lane Pedal to the Metal Black /1 #8
2018 Panini Victory Lane Pedal to the Metal Black /1 #56
2018 Panini Victory Lane Pedal to the Metal Blue /25 #8
2018 Panini Victory Lane Pedal to the Metal Blue /25 #56
2018 Panini Victory Lane Pedal to the Metal Green /5 #8
2018 Panini Victory Lane Pedal to the Metal Green /5 #56
2018 Panini Victory Lane Printing Plates Black /1 #6
2018 Panini Victory Lane Printing Plates Cyan /1 #6
2018 Panini Victory Lane Printing Plates Magenta /1 #6
2018 Panini Victory Lane Printing Plates Yellow /1 #6
2018 Panini Victory Lane Race Day #3
2018 Panini Victory Lane Race Day Black /1 #3
2018 Panini Victory Lane Race Day Blue /25 #3
2018 Panini Victory Lane Race Day Gold /99 #3
2018 Panini Victory Lane Race Day Green /5 #3
2018 Panini Victory Lane Race Day Printing Plates Black /1 #3
2018 Panini Victory Lane Race Day Printing Plates Cyan /1 #3
2018 Panini Victory Lane Race Day Printing Plates Magenta /1 #3
2018 Panini Victory Lane Race Day Printing Plates Yellow /1 #3
2018 Panini Victory Lane Race Day Red /49 #3
2018 Panini Victory Lane Race Ready Materials /399 #5
2018 Panini Victory Lane Race Ready Materials Black /25 #5
2018 Panini Victory Lane Race Ready Materials Gold /199 #5
2018 Panini Victory Lane Race Ready Materials Green /99 #5
2018 Panini Victory Lane Red /49 #6
2018 Panini Victory Lane Remarkable Remnants Material Autographs /100 #4
2018 Panini Victory Lane Remarkable Remnants Material Autographs Black /25 #4
2018 Panini Victory Lane Remarkable Remnants Material Autographs Gold /75 #4
2018 Panini Victory Lane Remarkable Remnants Material Autographs Green /50 #4
2018 Panini Victory Lane Remarkable Remnants Material Autographs Laundry Tag /1 #4
2018 Panini Victory Lane Silver #6
2018 Panini Victory Lane Starting Grid #6
2018 Panini Victory Lane Starting Grid Black /1 #6
2018 Panini Victory Lane Starting Grid Blue /25 #6
2018 Panini Victory Lane Starting Grid Gold /99 #6
2018 Panini Victory Lane Starting Grid Green /5 #6
2018 Panini Victory Lane Starting Grid Printing Plates Black /1 #6
2018 Panini Victory Lane Starting Grid Printing Plates Cyan /1 #6
2018 Panini Victory Lane Starting Grid Printing Plates Magenta /1 #6
2018 Panini Victory Lane Starting Grid Printing Plates Yellow /1 #6
2018 Panini Victory Lane Starting Grid Red /49 #6
2019 Donruss #31A
2019 Donruss #94
2019 Donruss #108A
2019 Donruss #31B
2019 Donruss #108B
2019 Donruss Artist Proofs /25 #31A
2019 Donruss Artist Proofs /25 #94
2019 Donruss Artist Proofs /25 #108A
2019 Donruss Artist Proofs /25 #31B
2019 Donruss Artist Proofs /25 #108B
2019 Donruss Black /199 #31A
2019 Donruss Black /199 #94
2019 Donruss Black /199 #108A
2019 Donruss Black /199 #31B
2019 Donruss Black /199 #108B
2019 Donruss Classics #15
2019 Donruss Classics Cracked Ice /25 #15
2019 Donruss Classics Holographic #15
2019 Donruss Classics Xplosion /10 #15
2019 Donruss Contenders #9
2019 Donruss Contenders Cracked Ice /25 #9
2019 Donruss Contenders Holographic #9
2019 Donruss Contenders Xplosion /10 #9
2019 Donruss Gold /299 #31A
2019 Donruss Gold /299 #94
2019 Donruss Gold /299 #108A
2019 Donruss Gold /299 #31B
2019 Donruss Gold /299 #108B
2019 Donruss Gold Press Proofs /99 #31A
2019 Donruss Gold Press Proofs /99 #94
2019 Donruss Gold Press Proofs /99 #108A
2019 Donruss Gold Press Proofs /99 #31B
2019 Donruss Gold Press Proofs /99 #108B
2019 Donruss Optic #22
2019 Donruss Optic Blue Pulsar #22
2019 Donruss Optic Gold /10 #22
2019 Donruss Optic Gold Vinyl /1 #22
2019 Donruss Optic Holo #22
2019 Donruss Optic Illusion #5
2019 Donruss Optic Illusion Blue Pulsar #5
2019 Donruss Optic Illusion Gold /10 #5
2019 Donruss Optic Illusion Gold Vinyl /1 #5
2019 Donruss Optic Illusion Holo #5
2019 Donruss Optic Illusion Red Wave #5
2019 Donruss Optic Illusion Signatures Gold Vinyl /1 #5
2019 Donruss Optic Illusion Signatures Holo /25 #5
2019 Donruss Optic Red Wave #22
2019 Donruss Optic Signatures Gold Vinyl /1 #22
2019 Donruss Optic Signatures Holo /25 #22
2019 Donruss Originals #6
2019 Donruss Originals Cracked Ice /25 #6
2019 Donruss Originals Holographic #6
2019 Donruss Originals Xplosion /10 #6
2019 Donruss Press Proofs /49 #31A
2019 Donruss Press Proofs /49 #94
2019 Donruss Press Proofs /49 #108A
2019 Donruss Press Proofs /49 #31B
2019 Donruss Press Proofs /49 #108B
2019 Donruss Printing Plates Black /1 #31A
2019 Donruss Printing Plates Black /1 #94
2019 Donruss Printing Plates Black /1 #108A
2019 Donruss Printing Plates Black /1 #31B
2019 Donruss Printing Plates Black /1 #108B
2019 Donruss Printing Plates Cyan /1 #31A
2019 Donruss Printing Plates Cyan /1 #94
2019 Donruss Printing Plates Cyan /1 #108A
2019 Donruss Printing Plates Cyan /1 #31B
2019 Donruss Printing Plates Cyan /1 #108B
2019 Donruss Printing Plates Magenta /1 #94
2019 Donruss Printing Plates Magenta /1 #108A
2019 Donruss Printing Plates Magenta /1 #31B
2019 Donruss Printing Plates Magenta /1 #108B
2019 Donruss Printing Plates Magenta /1 #31A
2019 Donruss Printing Plates Yellow /1 #31A
2019 Donruss Printing Plates Yellow /1 #94
2019 Donruss Printing Plates Yellow /1 #108A
2019 Donruss Printing Plates Yellow /1 #31B
2019 Donruss Printing Plates Yellow /1 #108B
2019 Donruss Race Day Relics #5
2019 Donruss Race Day Relics Holo Black /10 #5
2019 Donruss Race Day Relics Holo Gold /25 #5
2019 Donruss Race Day Relics Red /185 #5
2019 Donruss Signature Swatches #5
2019 Donruss Signature Swatches Holo Black /10 #5
2019 Donruss Signature Swatches Holo Gold /25 #5
2019 Donruss Signature Swatches Red /49 #5
2019 Donruss Silver #31A
2019 Donruss Silver #94
2019 Donruss Silver #108A
2019 Donruss Silver #31B
2019 Donruss Silver #108B
2019 Donruss Top Tier #3
2019 Donruss Top Tier Cracked Ice /25 #3
2019 Donruss Top Tier Holographic #3
2019 Donruss Top Tier Xplosion /10 #3
2019 Panini National Convention NASCAR #R7
2019 Panini National Convention NASCAR Galatic Windows /25 #R7
2019 Panini National Convention NASCAR HyperPlaid /1 #R7
2019 Panini Prime /50 #7
2019 Panini Prime /50 #41
2019 Panini Prime /50 #74
2019 Panini Prime Black /10 #7
2019 Panini Prime Black /10 #41
2019 Panini Prime Black /10 #74
2019 Panini Prime Clear Silhouettes /99 #3
2019 Panini Prime Clear Silhouettes Black /10 #3
2019 Panini Prime Clear Silhouettes Dual /99 #5
2019 Panini Prime Clear Silhouettes Dual Black /10 #5
2019 Panini Prime Clear Silhouettes Dual Holo Gold /25 #5
2019 Panini Prime Clear Silhouettes Dual Platinum Blue /1 #5
2019 Panini Prime Clear Silhouettes Holo Gold /18 #3
2019 Panini Prime Clear Silhouettes Platinum Blue /1 #3
2019 Panini Prime Emerald /5 #7
2019 Panini Prime Emerald /5 #41
2019 Panini Prime Emerald /5 #74
2019 Panini Prime Hats Off Button /1 #6
2019 Panini Prime Hats Off Button /1 #16
2019 Panini Prime Hats Off Eyelets /6 #16
2019 Panini Prime Hats Off Headband /25 #6
2019 Panini Prime Hats Off Headband /30 #16
2019 Panini Prime Hats Off Laundry Tags /2 #6
2019 Panini Prime Hats Off Laundry Tags /2 #16
2019 Panini Prime Hats Off New Era /1 #6
2019 Panini Prime Hats Off New Era /1 #16
2019 Panini Prime Hats Off Number /4 #6
2019 Panini Prime Hats Off Number /4 #16
2019 Panini Prime Hats Off Sponsor Logo /5 #6
2019 Panini Prime Hats Off Sponsor Logo /5 #16
2019 Panini Prime Hats Off Team Logo /3 #6
2019 Panini Prime Hats Off Team Logo /3 #16
2019 Panini Prime Jumbo Material Signatures Firesuit /5 #6
2019 Panini Prime Jumbo Material Signatures Firesuit Platinum Blue /1 #6
2019 Panini Prime Jumbo Material Signatures Sheet Metal /9 #6
2019 Panini Prime Jumbo Material Signatures Tire /25 #6
2019 Panini Prime NASCAR Shadowbox Signatures Car Number /25 #11
2019 Panini Prime NASCAR Shadowbox Signatures Manufacturer /5 #11
2019 Panini Prime NASCAR Shadowbox Signatures Sponsor /9 #11
2019 Panini Prime NASCAR Shadowbox Signatures Team Owner /1 #11
2019 Panini Prime Platinum Blue /1 #7
2019 Panini Prime Platinum Blue /1 #41
2019 Panini Prime Platinum Blue /1 #74
2019 Panini Prime Prime Cars Die Cut Signatures /25 #7
2019 Panini Prime Prime Cars Die Cut Signatures Black /5 #7
2019 Panini Prime Prime Cars Die Cut Signatures Holo Gold /9 #7
2019 Panini Prime Prime Cars Die Cut Signatures Platinum Blue /1 #7
2019 Panini Prime Prime Jumbo Associate Sponsor 1 /1 #8
2019 Panini Prime Prime Jumbo Associate Sponsor 1 /1 #9
2019 Panini Prime Prime Jumbo Associate Sponsor 2 /1 #8
2019 Panini Prime Prime Jumbo Associate Sponsor 2 /1 #9
2019 Panini Prime Prime Jumbo Associate Sponsor 3 /1 #8
2019 Panini Prime Prime Jumbo Associate Sponsor 3 /1 #9
2019 Panini Prime Prime Jumbo Associate Sponsor 4 /1 #8
2019 Panini Prime Prime Jumbo Associate Sponsor 4 /1 #9
2019 Panini Prime Prime Jumbo Associate Sponsor 5 /1 #9
2019 Panini Prime Prime Jumbo Associate Sponsor 6 /1 #9
2019 Panini Prime Prime Jumbo Associate Sponsor 7 /1 #9
2019 Panini Prime Prime Jumbo Associate Sponsor 8 /1 #9
2019 Panini Prime Prime Jumbo Associate Sponsor 9 /1 #9
2019 Panini Prime Prime Jumbo Car Manufacturer /1 #8
2019 Panini Prime Prime Jumbo Car Manufacturer /1 #9
2019 Panini Prime Prime Jumbo Firesuit Manufacturer /1 #8
2019 Panini Prime Prime Jumbo Firesuit Manufacturer /1 #9
2019 Panini Prime Prime Jumbo Glove Manufacturer Patch /1 #8
2019 Panini Prime Prime Jumbo Glove Manufacturer Patch /1 #9
2019 Panini Prime Prime Jumbo Glove Number Patch /1 #8
2019 Panini Prime Prime Jumbo Nameplate /2 #8
2019 Panini Prime Prime Jumbo Nameplate /4 #9
2019 Panini Prime Prime Jumbo NASCAR /1 #9
2019 Panini Prime Prime Jumbo Prime Colors /10 #8
2019 Panini Prime Prime Jumbo Prime Colors /22 #9
2019 Panini Prime Prime Jumbo Series Sponsor /1 #9
2019 Panini Prime Prime Jumbo Shoe Brand Logo /1 #8
2019 Panini Prime Prime Jumbo Shoe Brand Logo /1 #9
2019 Panini Prime Prime Jumbo Shoe Number Patch /1 #8
2019 Panini Prime Prime Jumbo Shoe Number Patch /1 #9
2019 Panini Prime Prime Jumbo Sunoco /1 #9
2019 Panini Prime Prime Names Die Cut Signatures /25 #24
2019 Panini Prime Prime Names Die Cut Signatures Black /5 #24
2019 Panini Prime Prime Names Die Cut Signatures Holo Gold /9 #24
2019 Panini Prime Prime Names Die Cut Signatures Platinum Blue /1 #24
2019 Panini Prime Quad Materials Autographs /25 #6
2019 Panini Prime Quad Materials Autographs Black /5 #6
2019 Panini Prime Quad Materials Autographs Holo Gold /9 #6
2019 Panini Prime Quad Materials Autographs Laundry Tags /1 #6
2019 Panini Prime Race Used Duals Firesuits /50 #11
2019 Panini Prime Race Used Duals Firesuits Black /10 #11
2019 Panini Prime Race Used Duals Firesuits Holo Gold /25 #11
2019 Panini Prime Race Used Duals Firesuits Laundry Tags /1 #11
2019 Panini Prime Race Used Duals Sheet Metal Black /10 #11
2019 Panini Prime Race Used Duals Sheet Metal Platinum Blue /1 #11
2019 Panini Prime Race Used Duals Tires /50 #11
2019 Panini Prime Race Used Duals Tires Black /10 #11
2019 Panini Prime Race Used Duals Tires Holo Gold /25 #11
2019 Panini Prime Race Used Duals Tires Platinum Blue /1 #11
2019 Panini Prime Race Used Firesuits /50 #11
2019 Panini Prime Race Used Firesuits Black /10 #11
2019 Panini Prime Race Used Firesuits Holo Gold /25 #11
2019 Panini Prime Race Used Firesuits Laundry Tags /1 #11
2019 Panini Prime Race Used Quads Firesuits /50 #5
2019 Panini Prime Race Used Quads Firesuits Black /10 #5
2019 Panini Prime Race Used Quads Firesuits Holo Gold /25 #5
2019 Panini Prime Race Used Quads Firesuits Laundry Tags /1 #5
2019 Panini Prime Race Used Quads Sheet Metal Black /10 #5
2019 Panini Prime Race Used Quads Sheet Metal Platinum Blue /1 #5
2019 Panini Prime Race Used Quads Tires /50 #5
2019 Panini Prime Race Used Quads Tires Black /10 #5
2019 Panini Prime Race Used Quads Tires Holo Gold /25 #5
2019 Panini Prime Race Used Quads Tires Platinum Blue /1 #5
2019 Panini Prime Race Used Sheet Metal /50 #11
2019 Panini Prime Race Used Sheet Metal Black /10 #11
2019 Panini Prime Race Used Sheet Metal Holo Gold /25 #11
2019 Panini Prime Race Used Sheet Metal Platinum Blue /1 #11
2019 Panini Prime Race Used Tires /50 #11
2019 Panini Prime Race Used Tires Black /10 #11
2019 Panini Prime Race Used Tires Holo Gold /25 #11
2019 Panini Prime Race Used Tires Platinum Blue /1 #11
2019 Panini Prime Race Used Trios Firesuits /50 #11
2019 Panini Prime Race Used Trios Firesuits Black /10 #11
2019 Panini Prime Race Used Trios Firesuits Holo Gold /25 #11
2019 Panini Prime Race Used Trios Firesuits Laundry Tags /1 #11
2019 Panini Prime Race Used Trios Sheet Metal Black /10 #11
2019 Panini Prime Race Used Trios Sheet Metal Platinum Blue /1 #11
2019 Panini Prime Race Used Trios Tires /50 #11
2019 Panini Prime Race Used Trios Tires Black /10 #11
2019 Panini Prime Race Used Trios Tires Holo Gold /25 #11
2019 Panini Prime Race Used Trios Tires Platinum Blue /1 #11
2019 Panini Prime Timeline Signatures /25 #5
2019 Panini Prime Timeline Signatures Manufacturer /1 #5
2019 Panini Prime Timeline Signatures Name /9 #5
2019 Panini Prime Timeline Signatures Sponsor /5 #5
2019 Panini Prizm #7A
2019 Panini Prizm #58
2019 Panini Prizm #65
2019 Panini Prizm #71
2019 Panini Prizm #84
2019 Panini Prizm #7B
2019 Panini Prizm Apex #2
2019 Panini Prizm Apex Prizms #2
2019 Panini Prizm Apex Prizms Black /1 #2
2019 Panini Prizm Apex Prizms Gold /10 #2
2019 Panini Prizm Apex Prizms White Sparkle #2
2019 Panini Prizm Fireworks #4
2019 Panini Prizm Fireworks Prizms #4
2019 Panini Prizm Fireworks Prizms Black /1 #4
2019 Panini Prizm Fireworks Prizms Gold /10 #4
2019 Panini Prizm Fireworks Prizms White Sparkle #4
2019 Panini Prizm In the Groove #3
2019 Panini Prizm In the Groove Prizms #3
2019 Panini Prizm In the Groove Prizms Black /1 #3
2019 Panini Prizm In the Groove Prizms Gold /10 #3
2019 Panini Prizm In the Groove Prizms White Sparkle #3
2019 Panini Prizm National Pride #3
2019 Panini Prizm National Pride Prizms #3
2019 Panini Prizm National Pride Prizms Black /1 #3
2019 Panini Prizm National Pride Prizms Gold /10 #3
2019 Panini Prizm National Pride Prizms White Sparkle #3
2019 Panini Prizm Prizms #58
2019 Panini Prizm Prizms #65
2019 Panini Prizm Prizms #71
2019 Panini Prizm Prizms #84
2019 Panini Prizm Prizms #7B
2019 Panini Prizm Prizms #7A
2019 Panini Prizm Prizms Black /1 #7A
2019 Panini Prizm Prizms Black /1 #58
2019 Panini Prizm Prizms Black /1 #65
2019 Panini Prizm Prizms Black /1 #71
2019 Panini Prizm Prizms Black /1 #84
2019 Panini Prizm Prizms Black /1 #7B
2019 Panini Prizm Prizms Blue /75 #7A
2019 Panini Prizm Prizms Blue /75 #58
2019 Panini Prizm Prizms Blue /75 #65
2019 Panini Prizm Prizms Blue /75 #71
2019 Panini Prizm Prizms Blue /75 #84
2019 Panini Prizm Prizms Blue /75 #7B
2019 Panini Prizm Prizms Camo #7A
2019 Panini Prizm Prizms Camo #58
2019 Panini Prizm Prizms Camo #65
2019 Panini Prizm Prizms Camo #71
2019 Panini Prizm Prizms Camo #84
2019 Panini Prizm Prizms Camo #7B
2019 Panini Prizm Prizms Flash #7A
2019 Panini Prizm Prizms Flash #58
2019 Panini Prizm Prizms Flash #65
2019 Panini Prizm Prizms Flash #71
2019 Panini Prizm Prizms Flash #84
2019 Panini Prizm Prizms Flash #7B
2019 Panini Prizm Prizms Gold /10 #7A
2019 Panini Prizm Prizms Gold /10 #58
2019 Panini Prizm Prizms Gold /10 #65
2019 Panini Prizm Prizms Gold /10 #71
2019 Panini Prizm Prizms Gold /10 #84
2019 Panini Prizm Prizms Gold /10 #7B
2019 Panini Prizm Prizms Green /99 #7A
2019 Panini Prizm Prizms Green /99 #58
2019 Panini Prizm Prizms Green /99 #65
2019 Panini Prizm Prizms Green /99 #71
2019 Panini Prizm Prizms Green /99 #84
2019 Panini Prizm Prizms Green /99 #7B
2019 Panini Prizm Prizms Rainbow /24 #7A
2019 Panini Prizm Prizms Rainbow /24 #58
2019 Panini Prizm Prizms Rainbow /24 #65
2019 Panini Prizm Prizms Rainbow /24 #71
2019 Panini Prizm Prizms Rainbow /24 #84
2019 Panini Prizm Prizms Rainbow /24 #7B
2019 Panini Prizm Prizms Red /50 #7A
2019 Panini Prizm Prizms Red /50 #58
2019 Panini Prizm Prizms Red /50 #65
2019 Panini Prizm Prizms Red /50 #71
2019 Panini Prizm Prizms Red /50 #84
2019 Panini Prizm Prizms Red /50 #7B
2019 Panini Prizm Prizms Red White and Blue #7A
2019 Panini Prizm Prizms Red White and Blue #58
2019 Panini Prizm Prizms Red White and Blue #65
2019 Panini Prizm Prizms Red White and Blue #71
2019 Panini Prizm Prizms Red White and Blue #84
2019 Panini Prizm Prizms Red White and Blue #7B
2019 Panini Prizm Prizms White /5 #7A
2019 Panini Prizm Prizms White /5 #58
2019 Panini Prizm Prizms White /5 #65
2019 Panini Prizm Prizms White /5 #71
2019 Panini Prizm Prizms White /5 #84
2019 Panini Prizm Prizms White /5 #7B
2019 Panini Prizm Prizms White Sparkle #7A
2019 Panini Prizm Prizms White Sparkle #58
2019 Panini Prizm Prizms White Sparkle #65
2019 Panini Prizm Prizms White Sparkle #71
2019 Panini Prizm Prizms White Sparkle #84
2019 Panini Prizm Prizms White Sparkle #7B
2019 Panini Prizm Scripted Signatures Prizms #2
2019 Panini Prizm Scripted Signatures Prizms Black /1 #2
2019 Panini Prizm Scripted Signatures Prizms Blue /25 #2
2019 Panini Prizm Scripted Signatures Prizms Camo #2
2019 Panini Prizm Scripted Signatures Prizms Gold /10 #2
2019 Panini Prizm Scripted Signatures Prizms Rainbow /24 #2
2019 Panini Prizm Scripted Signatures Prizms Red /25 #2
2019 Panini Prizm Scripted Signatures Prizms Red White and Blue #2
2019 Panini Prizm Scripted Signatures Prizms White /5 #2
2019 Panini Prizm Signing Sessions Prizms #6
2019 Panini Prizm Signing Sessions Prizms Black /1 #6
2019 Panini Prizm Signing Sessions Prizms Blue /25 #6
2019 Panini Prizm Signing Sessions Prizms Camo #6
2019 Panini Prizm Signing Sessions Prizms Gold /10 #6
2019 Panini Prizm Signing Sessions Prizms Rainbow /24 #6
2019 Panini Prizm Signing Sessions Prizms Red /25 #6
2019 Panini Prizm Signing Sessions Prizms Red White and Blue #6
2019 Panini Prizm Signing Sessions Prizms White /5 #6
2019 Panini Prizm Stars and Stripes #15
2019 Panini Prizm Stars and Stripes Prizms #15
2019 Panini Prizm Stars and Stripes Prizms Black /1 #15
2019 Panini Prizm Stars and Stripes Prizms Gold /10 #15
2019 Panini Prizm Stars and Stripes Prizms White Sparkle #15
2019 Panini Prizm Teammates #2
2019 Panini Prizm Teammates Prizms #2
2019 Panini Prizm Teammates Prizms Black /1 #2
2019 Panini Prizm Teammates Prizms Gold /10 #2
2019 Panini Prizm Teammates Prizms White Sparkle #2
2019 Panini Victory Lane #7
2019 Panini Victory Lane #54
2019 Panini Victory Lane #56
2019 Panini Victory Lane #80
2019 Panini Victory Lane Black /1 #7
2019 Panini Victory Lane Black /1 #54
2019 Panini Victory Lane Black /1 #56
2019 Panini Victory Lane Black /1 #80
2019 Panini Victory Lane Celebrations #7
2019 Panini Victory Lane Celebrations Black /1 #7
2019 Panini Victory Lane Celebrations Blue /99 #7
2019 Panini Victory Lane Celebrations Gold /25 #7
2019 Panini Victory Lane Celebrations Green /5 #7
2019 Panini Victory Lane Celebrations Printing Plates Black /1 #7
2019 Panini Victory Lane Celebrations Printing Plates Cyan /1 #7
2019 Panini Victory Lane Celebrations Printing Plates Magenta /1 #7
2019 Panini Victory Lane Celebrations Printing Plates Yellow /1 #7
2019 Panini Victory Lane Dual Swatches #6
2019 Panini Victory Lane Dual Swatches Gold /99 #6
2019 Panini Victory Lane Dual Swatches Laundry Tag /1 #6
2019 Panini Victory Lane Dual Swatches Platinum /1 #6
2019 Panini Victory Lane Dual Swatches Red /25 #6
2019 Panini Victory Lane Gold /25 #7
2019 Panini Victory Lane Gold /25 #54
2019 Panini Victory Lane Gold /25 #56
2019 Panini Victory Lane Gold /25 #80
2019 Panini Victory Lane Horsepower Heroes #14
2019 Panini Victory Lane Horsepower Heroes Black /1 #14
2019 Panini Victory Lane Horsepower Heroes Blue /99 #14
2019 Panini Victory Lane Horsepower Heroes Gold /25 #14
2019 Panini Victory Lane Horsepower Heroes Green /5 #14
2019 Panini Victory Lane Horsepower Heroes Printing Plates Black /1 #14
2019 Panini Victory Lane Horsepower Heroes Printing Plates Cyan /1 #14
2019 Panini Victory Lane Horsepower Heroes Printing Plates Magenta /1 #14
2019 Panini Victory Lane Horsepower Heroes Printing Plates Yellow /1 #14
2019 Panini Victory Lane Machines #3
2019 Panini Victory Lane Machines Black /1 #3
2019 Panini Victory Lane Machines Blue /99 #3
2019 Panini Victory Lane Machines Gold /25 #3
2019 Panini Victory Lane Machines Green /5 #3
2019 Panini Victory Lane Machines Printing Plates Black /1 #3
2019 Panini Victory Lane Machines Printing Plates Cyan /1 #3
2019 Panini Victory Lane Machines Printing Plates Magenta /1 #3
2019 Panini Victory Lane Machines Printing Plates Yellow /1 #3
2019 Panini Victory Lane Pedal to the Metal #22
2019 Panini Victory Lane Pedal to the Metal #55
2019 Panini Victory Lane Pedal to the Metal Black /1 #22
2019 Panini Victory Lane Pedal to the Metal Black /1 #55
2019 Panini Victory Lane Pedal to the Metal Gold /25 #22
2019 Panini Victory Lane Pedal to the Metal Gold /25 #55
2019 Panini Victory Lane Pedal to the Metal Green /5 #22
2019 Panini Victory Lane Pedal to the Metal Green /5 #55
2019 Panini Victory Lane Pedal to the Metal Red /3 #22
2019 Panini Victory Lane Pedal to the Metal Red /3 #55
2019 Panini Victory Lane Printing Plates Black /1 #7
2019 Panini Victory Lane Printing Plates Black /1 #54
2019 Panini Victory Lane Printing Plates Black /1 #56
2019 Panini Victory Lane Printing Plates Black /1 #80
2019 Panini Victory Lane Printing Plates Cyan /1 #7
2019 Panini Victory Lane Printing Plates Cyan /1 #54
2019 Panini Victory Lane Printing Plates Cyan /1 #56
2019 Panini Victory Lane Printing Plates Cyan /1 #80
2019 Panini Victory Lane Printing Plates Magenta /1 #7
2019 Panini Victory Lane Printing Plates Magenta /1 #54
2019 Panini Victory Lane Printing Plates Magenta /1 #56
2019 Panini Victory Lane Printing Plates Magenta /1 #80
2019 Panini Victory Lane Printing Plates Yellow /1 #7
2019 Panini Victory Lane Printing Plates Yellow /1 #54
2019 Panini Victory Lane Printing Plates Yellow /1 #56
2019 Panini Victory Lane Printing Plates Yellow /1 #80
2019 Panini Victory Lane Quad Swatches #7
2019 Panini Victory Lane Quad Swatches Gold /99 #7
2019 Panini Victory Lane Quad Swatches Laundry Tag /1 #7
2019 Panini Victory Lane Quad Swatches Platinum /1 #7
2019 Panini Victory Lane Quad Swatches Red /25 #7
2019 Panini Victory Lane Starting Grid #19
2019 Panini Victory Lane Starting Grid Black /1 #19
2019 Panini Victory Lane Starting Grid Blue /99 #19
2019 Panini Victory Lane Starting Grid Gold /25 #19
2019 Panini Victory Lane Starting Grid Green /5 #19
2019 Panini Victory Lane Starting Grid Printing Plates Black /1 #19
2019 Panini Victory Lane Starting Grid Printing Plates Cyan /1 #19
2019 Panini Victory Lane Starting Grid Printing Plates Magenta /1 #19
2019 Panini Victory Lane Starting Grid Printing Plates Yellow /1 #19
2019 Panini Victory Lane Top 10 #6
2019 Panini Victory Lane Top 10 Black /1 #6
2019 Panini Victory Lane Top 10 Blue /99 #6
2019 Panini Victory Lane Top 10 Gold /25 #6
2019 Panini Victory Lane Top 10 Green /5 #6
2019 Panini Victory Lane Top 10 Printing Plates Black /1 #6

2019 Panini Victory Lane Top 10 Printing Plates Cyan /1 #6
2019 Panini Victory Lane Top 10 Printing Plates Magenta /1 #6
2019 Panini Victory Lane Top 10 Printing Plates Yellow /1 #6
2019 Panini Victory Lane Track Stars #3
2019 Panini Victory Lane Track Stars Black /1 #3
2019 Panini Victory Lane Track Stars Blue /99 #3
2019 Panini Victory Lane Track Stars Gold /25 #3
2019 Panini Victory Lane Track Stars Green /5 #3
2019 Panini Victory Lane Track Stars Printing Plates Black /1 #3
2019 Panini Victory Lane Track Stars Printing Plates Cyan /1 #3
2019 Panini Victory Lane Track Stars Printing Plates Magenta /1 #3
2019 Panini Victory Lane Track Stars Printing Plates Yellow /1 #3
2019 Panini Victory Lane Triple Swatch Signatures #2
2019 Panini Victory Lane Triple Swatch Signatures Gold /75 #2
2019 Panini Victory Lane Triple Swatch Signatures Laundry Tag /1 #2
2019 Panini Victory Lane Triple Swatch Signatures Platinum /1 #2
2019 Panini Victory Lane Triple Swatch Signatures Red /25 #2
2019-20 Funko Pop Vinyl NASCAR #6
2020 Donruss #1
2020 Donruss #28
2020 Donruss #99
2020 Donruss #135
2020 Donruss #193
2020 Donruss Action Packed #5
2020 Donruss Action Packed Checkers #5
2020 Donruss Action Packed Cracked Ice /25 #5
2020 Donruss Action Packed Holographic /199 #5
2020 Donruss Action Packed Xplosion /10 #5
2020 Donruss Aero Package #7
2020 Donruss Aero Package Checkers #7
2020 Donruss Aero Package Cracked Ice /25 #7
2020 Donruss Aero Package Holographic /199 #7
2020 Donruss Aero Package Xplosion /10 #7
2020 Donruss Black Numbers /9 #1
2020 Donruss Black Numbers /9 #28
2020 Donruss Black Numbers /9 #99
2020 Donruss Black Numbers /9 #135
2020 Donruss Black Numbers /9 #193
2020 Donruss Black Trophy Club /1 #1
2020 Donruss Black Trophy Club /1 #28
2020 Donruss Black Trophy Club /1 #99
2020 Donruss Black Trophy Club /1 #135
2020 Donruss Black Trophy Club /1 #193
2020 Donruss Blue /199 #99
2020 Donruss Blue /199 #135
2020 Donruss Blue /199 #193
2020 Donruss Blue /199 #1
2020 Donruss Blue /199 #28
2020 Donruss Carolina Blue #1
2020 Donruss Carolina Blue #28
2020 Donruss Carolina Blue #99
2020 Donruss Carolina Blue #135
2020 Donruss Carolina Blue #193
2020 Donruss Contenders #6
2020 Donruss Contenders Checkers #6
2020 Donruss Contenders Cracked Ice /25 #6
2020 Donruss Contenders Holographic /199 #6
2020 Donruss Contenders Xplosion /10 #6
2020 Donruss Elite Series #5
2020 Donruss Elite Series Checkers #5
2020 Donruss Elite Series Cracked Ice /25 #5
2020 Donruss Elite Series Holographic /199 #5
2020 Donruss Elite Series Xplosion /10 #5
2020 Donruss Green /99 #1
2020 Donruss Green /99 #28
2020 Donruss Green /99 #99
2020 Donruss Green /99 #135
2020 Donruss Green /99 #193
2020 Donruss New Age #3
2020 Donruss New Age Checkers #3
2020 Donruss New Age Cracked Ice /25 #3
2020 Donruss New Age Holographic /199 #3
2020 Donruss New Age Xplosion /10 #3
2020 Donruss Optic #1
2020 Donruss Optic #23
2020 Donruss Optic #68
2020 Donruss Optic Carolina Blue Wave #23
2020 Donruss Optic Carolina Blue Wave #68
2020 Donruss Optic Carolina Blue Wave #1
2020 Donruss Optic Gold /10 #1
2020 Donruss Optic Gold /10 #23
2020 Donruss Optic Gold /10 #68
2020 Donruss Optic Gold Vinyl /1 #1
2020 Donruss Optic Gold Vinyl /1 #23
2020 Donruss Optic Gold Vinyl /1 #68
2020 Donruss Optic Holo #1
2020 Donruss Optic Holo #23
2020 Donruss Optic Holo #68
2020 Donruss Optic Illusion #6
2020 Donruss Optic Illusion Carolina Blue Wave #6
2020 Donruss Optic Illusion Gold /10 #6
2020 Donruss Optic Illusion Gold Vinyl /1 #6
2020 Donruss Optic Illusion Holo #6
2020 Donruss Optic Illusion Orange Pulsar #6
2020 Donruss Optic Illusion Red Mojo #6
2020 Donruss Optic Illusion Signatures Gold Vinyl /1 #6
2020 Donruss Optic Illusion Signatures Holo /25 #6
2020 Donruss Optic Orange Pulsar #1
2020 Donruss Optic Orange Pulsar #23
2020 Donruss Optic Orange Pulsar #68
2020 Donruss Optic Red Mojo #1
2020 Donruss Optic Red Mojo #23
2020 Donruss Optic Red Mojo #68
2020 Donruss Optic Signatures Gold Vinyl /1 #1
2020 Donruss Optic Signatures Gold Vinyl /1 #23
2020 Donruss Optic Signatures Gold Vinyl /1 #68
2020 Donruss Optic Signatures Holo /25 #1
2020 Donruss Optic Signatures Holo /25 #23
2020 Donruss Optic Signatures Holo /25 #68
2020 Donruss Orange #193
2020 Donruss Orange #1
2020 Donruss Orange #28
2020 Donruss Orange #99
2020 Donruss Orange #135
2020 Donruss Pink /25 #1
2020 Donruss Pink /25 #28
2020 Donruss Pink /25 #99
2020 Donruss Pink /25 #135
2020 Donruss Pink /25 #193
2020 Donruss Printing Plates Black /1 #1
2020 Donruss Printing Plates Black /1 #28
2020 Donruss Printing Plates Black /1 #99
2020 Donruss Printing Plates Black /1 #135
2020 Donruss Printing Plates Black /1 #193
2020 Donruss Printing Plates Cyan /1 #1
2020 Donruss Printing Plates Cyan /1 #28
2020 Donruss Printing Plates Cyan /1 #99
2020 Donruss Printing Plates Cyan /1 #135
2020 Donruss Printing Plates Cyan /1 #193
2020 Donruss Printing Plates Magenta /1 #28
2020 Donruss Printing Plates Magenta /1 #99
2020 Donruss Printing Plates Magenta /1 #135
2020 Donruss Printing Plates Magenta /1 #193
2020 Donruss Printing Plates Magenta /1 #1
2020 Donruss Printing Plates Yellow /1 #135
2020 Donruss Printing Plates Yellow /1 #193
2020 Donruss Printing Plates Yellow /1 #1
2020 Donruss Printing Plates Yellow /1 #28
2020 Donruss Printing Plates Yellow /1 #99
2020 Donruss Purple /49 #1
2020 Donruss Purple /49 #28
2020 Donruss Purple /49 #99
2020 Donruss Purple /49 #135
2020 Donruss Purple /49 #193
2020 Donruss Race Day Relics #6
2020 Donruss Race Day Relics Holo Black /10 #6
2020 Donruss Race Day Relics Holo Gold /25 #6
2020 Donruss Race Day Relics Red /250 #6
2020 Donruss Red /299 #1
2020 Donruss Red /299 #28
2020 Donruss Red /299 #99
2020 Donruss Red /299 #135
2020 Donruss Red /299 #193
2020 Donruss Retro Relics '87 #15
2020 Donruss Retro Relics '87 Holo Black /10 #15
2020 Donruss Retro Relics '87 Holo Gold /25 #15
2020 Donruss Retro Relics '87 Red /99 #15
2020 Donruss Retro Series #7
2020 Donruss Retro Series Checkers #7
2020 Donruss Retro Series Cracked Ice /25 #7
2020 Donruss Retro Series Holographic /199 #7
2020 Donruss Retro Series Xplosion /10 #7
2020 Donruss Silver #1
2020 Donruss Silver #28
2020 Donruss Silver #99
2020 Donruss Silver #135
2020 Donruss Silver #193
2020 Donruss Timeless Treasures Material Signatures #3
2020 Donruss Timeless Treasures Material Signatures Holo Black /1 #3
2020 Donruss Timeless Treasures Material Signatures Holo Gold /9 #3
2020 Donruss Timeless Treasures Material Signatures Red /24 #3

Jeff Gordon

1987 World of Outlaws #52
1988 World of Outlaws #54
1991 Traks #1
1992 Limited Editions Jeff Gordon #12
1992 Limited Editions Jeff Gordon #11
1992 Limited Editions Jeff Gordon #10
1992 Limited Editions Jeff Gordon #9
1992 Limited Editions Jeff Gordon #8
1992 Limited Editions Jeff Gordon #7
1992 Limited Editions Jeff Gordon #6
1992 Limited Editions Jeff Gordon #5
1992 Limited Editions Jeff Gordon #4
1992 Limited Editions Jeff Gordon #3
1992 Limited Editions Jeff Gordon #2
1992 Limited Editions Jeff Gordon /300 #AU2
1992 Limited Editions Promos #4
1992 Maxx Black #50
1992 Maxx Black #29
1992 Maxx Black Update #U6
1992 Maxx Red #29
1992 Maxx Red #50
1992 Maxx Red Update #U6
1992 Pro Set #128
1992 Traks #101
1992 Traks Autographs #A7
1992 Traks Baby Ruth Jeff Gordon #2
1992 Traks Baby Ruth Jeff Gordon #3
1992 Traks Baby Ruth Jeff Gordon #4
1992 Traks Baby Ruth Jeff Gordon #1
1992 Traks Goody's #9
1992 Traks Racing Machines #40
1992 Traks Racing Machines Bonus #20B
1992 Winner's Choice Busch #76
1992 Winner's Choice Busch #77
1993 AC Racing Foldouts #24
1993 Action Packed #32
1993 Action Packed #61
1993 Action Packed #63
1993 Action Packed #86
1993 Action Packed #87
1993 Action Packed #93
1993 Action Packed #150
1993 Action Packed #153
1993 Action Packed #156
1993 Action Packed #173
1993 Action Packed #205
1993 Action Packed 24K Gold #55G
1993 Action Packed 24K Gold #10G
1993 Action Packed 24K Gold #12G
1993 Action Packed 24K Gold #26G
1993 Action Packed 24K Gold #29G
1993 Action Packed 24K Gold #32G
1993 Action Packed 24K Gold #36G
1993 Action Packed Prototypes #JG1
1993 Card Dynamics Gant Oil /6000 #6
1993 Card Dynamics Quik Chek /7000 #9
1993 Finish Line #14
1993 Finish Line #83
1993 Finish Line #110
1993 Finish Line Commemorative Sheets #10
1993 Finish Line Commemorative Sheets #11
1993 Finish Line Commemorative Sheets #23
1993 Finish Line Promos #P2
1993 Finish Line Silver #14
1993 Finish Line Silver #83
1993 Finish Line Silver #110
1993 Maxwell House #24
1993 Maxwell House #25
1993 Maxx #24
1993 Maxx #168
1993 Maxx Club Sam Bass Chromium #7
1993 Maxx Club Sam Bass Chromium #10
1993 Maxx Jeff Gordon #7
1993 Maxx Jeff Gordon #8
1993 Maxx Jeff Gordon #9
1993 Maxx Jeff Gordon #10
1993 Maxx Jeff Gordon #11
1993 Maxx Jeff Gordon #12
1993 Maxx Jeff Gordon #13
1993 Maxx Jeff Gordon #14
1993 Maxx Jeff Gordon #15
1993 Maxx Jeff Gordon #16
1993 Maxx Jeff Gordon #17
1993 Maxx Jeff Gordon #18
1993 Maxx Jeff Gordon #19
1993 Maxx Jeff Gordon #20
1993 Maxx Jeff Gordon #6
1993 Maxx Jeff Gordon #5
1993 Maxx Jeff Gordon #4
1993 Maxx Jeff Gordon #3
1993 Maxx Jeff Gordon #2
1993 Maxx Jeff Gordon #1
1993 Maxx Jeff Gordon #NNO
1993 Maxx Lowes Foods Stickers #2
1993 Maxx Premier Plus #24
1993 Maxx Premier Plus #39
1993 Maxx Premier Plus #NNO
1993 Maxx Premier Series #24
1993 Maxx Premier Series #168
1993 Maxx Winnebago Motorsports #2
1993 Press Pass Previews #17
1993 Press Pass Previews #18A
1993 Press Pass Previews #18B
1993 Press Pass Previews #26
1993 Stove Top #1
1993 Traks #24
1993 Traks #39
1993 Traks #151
1993 Traks #P1
1993 Traks First Run #24
1993 Traks First Run #39
1993 Traks First Run #151
1993 Traks Trivia #2
1993 Traks Trivia #24
1993 Traks Trivia #36
1993 Traks Trivia #38
1993 Traks Trivia #45
1993 Wheels Rookie Thunder #32
1993 Wheels Rookie Thunder #37
1993 Wheels Rookie Thunder #50
1993 Wheels Rookie Thunder #51
1993 Wheels Rookie Thunder #62
1993 Wheels Rookie Thunder #70
1993 Wheels Rookie Thunder #71
1993 Wheels Rookie Thunder #82
1993 Wheels Rookie Thunder #93
1993 Wheels Rookie Thunder #97
1993 Wheels Rookie Thunder #98
1993 Wheels Rookie Thunder Platinum #32
1993 Wheels Rookie Thunder Platinum #37
1993 Wheels Rookie Thunder Platinum #50
1993 Wheels Rookie Thunder Platinum #51
1993 Wheels Rookie Thunder Platinum #62
1993 Wheels Rookie Thunder Platinum #70
1993 Wheels Rookie Thunder Platinum #71
1993 Wheels Rookie Thunder Platinum #82
1993 Wheels Rookie Thunder Platinum #93
1993 Wheels Rookie Thunder Platinum #97
1993 Wheels Rookie Thunder Platinum #98
1993 Wheels Rookie Thunder Promos #P2
1993-95 Card Dynamics Double Eagle Postcards #1
1993-95 Card Dynamics Double Eagle Postcards #7
1994 Action Packed #14
1994 Action Packed #30
1994 Action Packed #73
1994 Action Packed #103
1994 Action Packed #131
1994 Action Packed #146
1994 Action Packed #189
1994 Action Packed #209
1994 Action Packed 24K Gold #27G
1994 Action Packed 24K Gold #189G
1994 Action Packed Champ and Challenger #1
1994 Action Packed Champ and Challenger #3
1994 Action Packed Champ and Challenger #4
1994 Action Packed Champ and Challenger #5
1994 Action Packed Champ and Challenger #6
1994 Action Packed Champ and Challenger #7
1994 Action Packed Champ and Challenger #8
1994 Action Packed Champ and Challenger #9
1994 Action Packed Champ and Challenger #10
1994 Action Packed Champ and Challenger #11
1994 Action Packed Champ and Challenger #13
1994 Action Packed Champ and Challenger #14
1994 Action Packed Champ and Challenger #15
1994 Action Packed Champ and Challenger #16
1994 Action Packed Champ and Challenger #17
1994 Action Packed Champ and Challenger #18
1994 Action Packed Champ and Challenger #19
1994 Action Packed Champ and Challenger #20
1994 Action Packed Champ and Challenger #41
1994 Action Packed Champ and Challenger #42
1994 Action Packed Champ and Challenger 24K Gold #1G
1994 Action Packed Champ and Challenger 24K Gold #5G
1994 Action Packed Champ and Challenger 24K Gold #9G
1994 Action Packed Champ and Challenger 24K Gold #17G
1994 Action Packed Champ and Challenger 24K Gold #20G
1994 Action Packed Champ and Challenger 24K Gold #41G
1994 Action Packed Champ and Challenger 24K Gold #42G
1994 Action Packed Coastars #5
1994 Action Packed Mammoth #14
1994 Action Packed Mint #14
1994 Action Packed Mint #30
1994 Action Packed Mint #73
1994 Action Packed Mint #103
1994 Action Packed Mint #131
1994 Action Packed Mint #146
1994 Action Packed Mint #189
1994 Action Packed Mint #209
1994 Action Packed Mint Collection Jeff Gordon #11
1994 Action Packed Mint Collection Jeff Gordon #11
1994 Action Packed Mint Collection Jeff Gordon #19
1994 Action Packed Mint Collection Jeff Gordon #19
1994 Action Packed Prototypes #3R94S
1994 Action Packed Prototypes #2R942
1994 Action Packed Prototypes #2R942G
1994 Card Dynamics Black Top Busch Series /5000 #2
1994 Card Dynamics Gant Oil /6000 #4
1994 Card Dynamics Jeff Gordon Fan Club /1200 #1
1994 Card Dynamics Jeff Gordon Fan Club /1200 #2
1994 Card Dynamics Jeff Gordon Fan Club /1200 #3
1994 Finish Line #36
1994 Finish Line #75
1994 Finish Line #123
1994 Finish Line #NNO
1994 Finish Line Gold #11
1994 Finish Line Gold #28
1994 Finish Line Gold #60
1994 Finish Line Gold #65
1994 Finish Line Gold #88
1994 Finish Line Gold Phone Cards /3000 #2
1994 Finish Line Gold Promos #P1
1994 Finish Line Gold Teamwork #TG6
1994 Finish Line Phone Cards #2
1994 Finish Line Phone Cards #8
1994 Finish Line Silver #36
1994 Finish Line Silver #75
1994 Finish Line Silver #123
1994 Hi-Tech Brickyard 400 #20
1994 Hi-Tech Brickyard 400 #52
1994 Hi-Tech Brickyard 400 #69
1994 Hi-Tech Brickyard 400 Artist Proofs #20
1994 Hi-Tech Brickyard 400 Artist Proofs #52
1994 Hi-Tech Brickyard 400 Artist Proofs #69
1994 Hi-Tech Brickyard 400 Prototypes #2
1994 Maxx #13
1994 Maxx #24
1994 Maxx #65
1994 Maxx #201
1994 Maxx #327
1994 Maxx #328
1994 Maxx #335
1994 Maxx #S24
1994 Maxx Autographs #24
1994 Maxx Medallion #1
1994 Maxx Medallion #46
1994 Maxx Medallion #47
1994 Maxx Medallion #48
1994 Maxx Medallion #49
1994 Maxx Medallion #50
1994 Maxx Medallion #52
1994 Maxx Medallion #53
1994 Maxx Medallion #56
1994 Maxx Premier Plus #13
1994 Maxx Premier Plus #24
1994 Maxx Premier Plus #46
1994 Maxx Premier Plus #65
1994 Maxx Premier Series #13
1994 Maxx Premier Series #24
1994 Maxx Premier Series #65
1994 Maxx Premier Series #260
1994 Maxx Premier Series Jumbos #8
1994 Maxx Racing Champions #1
1994 Maxx Rookies of the Year #16
1994 Maxx The Select 25 #14
1994 MW Windows #5
1994 MW Windows #1
1994 Power #DB5
1994 Power #89
1994 Power #90
1994 Power #132
1994 Power #P1
1994 Power Gold #DB5
1994 Power Gold #89
1994 Power Gold #90
1994 Power Gold #132
1994 Power Preview #12
1994 Power Preview #22
1994 Press Pass #7
1994 Press Pass #40
1994 Press Pass #124
1994 Press Pass Authentics /1500 #1
1994 Press Pass Authentics Autographs /1000 #1
1994 Press Pass Cup Chase #CC7
1994 Press Pass Holofoils #H2
1994 Press Pass Optima XL #6
1994 Press Pass Optima XL #26
1994 Press Pass Optima XL #38
1994 Press Pass Optima XL #56
1994 Press Pass Optima XL #62
1994 Press Pass Optima XL #CC1
1994 Press Pass Optima XL Prototypes #3
1994 Press Pass Optima XL Red Hot #6
1994 Press Pass Optima XL Red Hot #26
1994 Press Pass Optima XL Red Hot #38
1994 Press Pass Optima XL Red Hot #56
1994 Press Pass Optima XL Red Hot #62
1994 Press Pass Race Day #RD7
1994 SkyBox #4
1994 SkyBox #NNO
1994 Traks #10
1994 Traks #24
1994 Traks #36
1994 Traks #86
1994 Traks #106
1994 Traks #171
1994 Traks #200
1994 Traks Auto Value #25
1994 Traks Autographs #A4
1994 Traks Cartoons #C5
1994 Traks First Run #200
1994 Traks First Run #171
1994 Traks First Run #106
1994 Traks First Run #86
1994 Traks First Run #36
1994 Traks First Run #24
1994 Traks First Run #10
1994 Traks Preferred Collector #33
1994 Traks Winners #W8
1994 Traks Winners #W21
1994 Traks Winners #W22
1994 VIP #12
1994 VIP #38
1994 VIP #74
1994 VIP #P1
1994 VIP Gold Signature #EC3
1994 Wheels Harry Gant #66
1994 Wheels Harry Gant #1994
1994 Wheels Harry Gant Gold #66
1994 Wheels High Gear #73
1994 Wheels High Gear #97
1994 Wheels High Gear #101
1994 Wheels High Gear /1500 #NNO
1994 Wheels High Gear Day One #101
1994 Wheels High Gear Day One Gold #101
1994 Wheels High Gear Dominators /1750 #D5
1994 Wheels High Gear Gold #73
1994 Wheels High Gear Gold #97
1994 Wheels High Gear Gold #101
1994 Wheels High Gear Mega Gold #MG5
1994 Wheels High Gear Promos #P1
1994 Wheels High Gear Promos Gold #P1
1994 Wheels High Gear Rookie Thunder Update #102
1994 Wheels High Gear Rookie Thunder Update Platinum #102
1994-95 Assets #68
1994-95 Assets #93
1994-95 Assets Die Cuts #DC19
1994-95 Assets Phone Cards $2 #30
1994-95 Assets Phone Cards $5 #9
1994-95 Assets Phone Cards One Minute #30
1994-95 Assets Silver Signature #68
1994-95 Highland Mint/VIP /5000 #3B
1994-95 Highland Mint/VIP /1000 #3S
1994-96 Bleachers NASCAR #8
1994-96 Bleachers NASCAR #9
1994-96 Bleachers NASCAR #10
1995 Action Packed Country #6
1995 Action Packed Country #14
1995 Action Packed Country #22
1995 Action Packed Country #50
1995 Action Packed Country #51
1995 Action Packed Country #63
1995 Action Packed Country #99
1995 Action Packed Country #P1
1995 Action Packed Country 24K Team #1
1995 Action Packed Country 24K Team #2
1995 Action Packed Country 24K Team #3
1995 Action Packed Country Silver Speed #6
1995 Action Packed Country Silver Speed #14
1995 Action Packed Country Silver Speed #22
1995 Action Packed Country Silver Speed #50
1995 Action Packed Country Silver Speed #51
1995 Action Packed Country Silver Speed #63
1995 Action Packed Country Team Rainbow #1
1995 Action Packed Country Team Rainbow #2
1995 Action Packed Country Team Rainbow #3
1995 Action Packed Country Team Rainbow #5
1995 Action Packed Country Team Rainbow #6
1995 Action Packed Country Team Rainbow #7
1995 Action Packed Country Team Rainbow #8
1995 Action Packed Country Team Rainbow #9
1995 Action Packed Country Team Rainbow #10
1995 Action Packed Country Team Rainbow #11
1995 Action Packed Country Team Rainbow #12
1995 Action Packed Country Team Rainbow #P1
1995 Action Packed Hendrick Motorsports #1
1995 Action Packed Mammoth #MM4
1995 Action Packed Preview #9
1995 Action Packed Preview #36
1995 Action Packed Preview #50
1995 Action Packed Preview #66
1995 Action Packed Preview #70
1995 Action Packed Preview 24K Gold #2G
1995 Action Packed Select 25 #8
1995 Action Packed Stars #24
1995 Action Packed Stars #40
1995 Action Packed Stars #49
1995 Action Packed Stars #51
1995 Action Packed Stars #60
1995 Action Packed Stars #61
1995 Action Packed Stars #62
1995 Action Packed Stars #63
1995 Action Packed Stars #64
1995 Action Packed Stars #65
1995 Action Packed Stars #86
1995 Action Packed Stars #47
1995 Action Packed Stars 24K Gold #2G
1995 Action Packed Stars 24K Gold #4G
1995 Action Packed Stars 24K Gold #6G
1995 Action Packed Stars 24K Gold #19G
1995 Action Packed Stars 24K Gold #20G
1995 Action Packed Stars Silver Speed #24
1995 Action Packed Stars Silver Speed #40
1995 Action Packed Stars Silver Speed #47
1995 Action Packed Stars Silver Speed #49
1995 Action Packed Stars Silver Speed #51
1995 Action Packed Stars Silver Speed #60
1995 Action Packed Stars Silver Speed #61
1995 Action Packed Stars Silver Speed #62
1995 Action Packed Stars Silver Speed #63
1995 Action Packed Stars Silver Speed #64
1995 Action Packed Stars Silver Speed #65
1995 Action Packed Stars Silver Speed #86
1995 Action Packed Stars Trucks That Haul #1
1995 Assets #3
1995 Assets #31
1995 Assets #49
1995 Assets $100 Phone Cards #3
1995 Assets $1000 Phone Cards #3
1995 Assets $2 Phone Cards #9
1995 Assets $2 Phone Cards Gold Signature #9
1995 Assets $25 Phone Cards #4
1995 Assets $5 Phone Cards #4
1995 Assets 1-Minute Phone Cards #9
1995 Assets 1-Minute Phone Cards Gold Signature #9
1995 Assets Coca-Cola 600 Die Cut Phone Cards #3
1995 Assets Gold Signature #3
1995 Assets Gold Signature #31
1995 Assets Gold Signature #49
1995 Assets Images Previews #RI4
1995 Crown Jewels #2
1995 Crown Jewels #68
1995 Crown Jewels #73
1995 Crown Jewels #75
1995 Crown Jewels #77
1995 Crown Jewels #DT1
1995 Crown Jewels Diamond /599 #2
1995 Crown Jewels Diamond /599 #68
1995 Crown Jewels Diamond /599 #73
1995 Crown Jewels Diamond /599 #75
1995 Crown Jewels Diamond /599 #77
1995 Crown Jewels Dual Jewels #DJ1
1995 Crown Jewels Dual Jewels Diamond #DJ1
1995 Crown Jewels Dual Jewels Emerald #DJ1
1995 Crown Jewels Emerald /1199 #2
1995 Crown Jewels Emerald /1199 #68
1995 Crown Jewels Emerald /1199 #73
1995 Crown Jewels Emerald /1199 #75
1995 Crown Jewels Emerald /1199 #77
1995 Crown Jewels Promos /3000 #PD1
1995 Crown Jewels Promos /6000 #PE1
1995 Crown Jewels Promos /12000 #PR1
1995 Crown Jewels Sapphire /2500 #2
1995 Crown Jewels Sapphire /2500 #68
1995 Crown Jewels Sapphire /2500 #73
1995 Crown Jewels Sapphire /2500 #75
1995 Crown Jewels Sapphire /2500 #77
1995 Crown Jewels Signature Gems #SG1
1995 Finish Line #24
1995 Finish Line #53
1995 Finish Line #67
1995 Finish Line #105
1995 Finish Line Coca-Cola 600 #3
1995 Finish Line Coca-Cola 600 #31
1995 Finish Line Coca-Cola 600 #49
1995 Finish Line Coca-Cola 600 Die Cuts #C3
1995 Finish Line Coca-Cola 600 Winners #CC10
1995 Finish Line Gold Signature #GS1
1995 Finish Line Phone Card of the Month /1500 #1
1995 Finish Line Platinum 5-Unit Phone Cards #1
1995 Finish Line Printer's Proof /398 #24
1995 Finish Line Printer's Proof /398 #53
1995 Finish Line Printer's Proof /398 #67
1995 Finish Line Printer's Proof /398 #105
1995 Finish Line Silver #24
1995 Finish Line Silver #53
1995 Finish Line Silver #67
1995 Finish Line Silver #105
1995 Finish Line Standout Cars #SC7
1995 Finish Line Standout Drivers #SD7
1995 Finish Line SuperTrucks #17
1995 Finish Line SuperTrucks Rainbow Foil #17
1995 Finish Line SuperTrucks Super Signature #SS1
1995 Hi-Tech Brickyard 400 #P1
1995 Hi-Tech Brickyard 400 #3
1995 Hi-Tech Brickyard 400 #40
1995 Hi-Tech Brickyard 400 #53
1995 Hi-Tech Brickyard 400 #88
1995 Hi-Tech Brickyard 400 #89
1995 Hi-Tech Brickyard 400 /1000 #NNO
1995 Hi-Tech Brickyard 400 /10000 #NNO
1995 Hi-Tech Brickyard 400 Top Ten #BY1
1995 Images #24
1995 Images #48
1995 Images #72
1995 Images #100
1995 Images #P1
1995 Images Driven #D2
1995 Images Gold #24
1995 Images Gold #48
1995 Images Gold #72
1995 Images Gold #100
1995 Images Hard Chargers #HC8
1995 Images Owner's Pride #OP5
1995 Images Race Reflections Jeff Gordon #JG1
1995 Images Race Reflections Jeff Gordon #JG2
1995 Images Race Reflections Jeff Gordon #JG3
1995 Images Race Reflections Jeff Gordon #JG4
1995 Images Race Reflections Jeff Gordon #JG5
1995 Images Race Reflections Jeff Gordon #JG6
1995 Images Race Reflections Jeff Gordon #JG7
1995 Images Race Reflections Jeff Gordon #JG8
1995 Images Race Reflections Jeff Gordon #JG9
1995 Images Race Reflections Jeff Gordon #JG10
1995 Images Race Reflections Jeff Gordon Facsimile Signature #JG1
1995 Images Race Reflections Jeff Gordon Facsimile Signature #JG2
1995 Images Race Reflections Jeff Gordon Facsimile Signature #JG3
1995 Images Race Reflections Jeff Gordon Facsimile Signature #JG4
1995 Images Race Reflections Jeff Gordon Facsimile Signature #JG5
1995 Images Race Reflections Jeff Gordon Facsimile Signature #JG6
1995 Images Race Reflections Jeff Gordon Facsimile Signature #JG7
1995 Images Race Reflections Jeff Gordon Facsimile Signature #JG8
1995 Images Race Reflections Jeff Gordon Facsimile Signature #JG9
1995 Images Race Reflections Jeff Gordon Facsimile Signature #JG10
1995 Maxx #3
1995 Maxx #24
1995 Maxx #72
1995 Maxx #80
1995 Maxx #105
1995 Maxx #139
1995 Maxx #169
1995 Maxx #236
1995 Maxx #237
1995 Maxx #P1G
1995 Maxx #P1R
1995 Maxx Autographs #24
1995 Maxx Medallion #17
1995 Maxx Medallion #47
1995 Maxx Medallion Blue #17
1995 Maxx Medallion Blue #47
1995 Maxx Medallion Jeff Gordon Puzzle #1
1995 Maxx Medallion Jeff Gordon Puzzle #2
1995 Maxx Medallion Jeff Gordon Puzzle #3
1995 Maxx Medallion Jeff Gordon Puzzle #4
1995 Maxx Medallion Jeff Gordon Puzzle #5
1995 Maxx Medallion Jeff Gordon Puzzle #6
1995 Maxx Medallion Jeff Gordon Puzzle #7
1995 Maxx Medallion Jeff Gordon Puzzle #8
1995 Maxx Medallion Jeff Gordon Puzzle #9
1995 Maxx Medallion Jeff Gordon Puzzle /999 #NNO
1995 Maxx Medallion On the Road Again #OTR2
1995 Maxx Over the Wall #1
1995 Maxx Premier Plus #24
1995 Maxx Premier Plus #64
1995 Maxx Premier Plus #147
1995 Maxx Premier Plus #158
1995 Maxx Premier Plus #160
1995 Maxx Premier Plus #168
1995 Maxx Premier Plus Crown Chrome #24
1995 Maxx Premier Plus Crown Chrome #64
1995 Maxx Premier Plus Crown Chrome #147
1995 Maxx Premier Plus Crown Chrome #158
1995 Maxx Premier Plus Crown Chrome #160
1995 Maxx Premier Plus Crown Chrome #168
1995 Maxx Premier Plus PaceSetters #PS7
1995 Maxx Premier Plus PaceSetters Crown Chrome #PS7
1995 Maxx Premier Series #3
1995 Maxx Premier Series #24
1995 Maxx Premier Series #64
1995 Maxx Premier Series #257
1995 Maxx Premier Series #262
1995 Maxx Premier Series #273
1995 Maxx Premier Series #275
1995 Maxx Premier Series #283
1995 Press Pass #10
1995 Press Pass #38
1995 Press Pass #102
1995 Press Pass #129
1995 Press Pass #136
1995 Press Pass Checkered Flags #CF3
1995 Press Pass Cup Chase #10
1995 Press Pass Cup Chase Prizes #CCR3
1995 Press Pass Cup Chase Prizes #CCR4
1995 Press Pass Optima XL #8
1995 Press Pass Optima XL #31
1995 Press Pass Optima XL #50
1995 Press Pass Optima XL #56
1995 Press Pass Optima XL Cool Blue #8
1995 Press Pass Optima XL Cool Blue #31
1995 Press Pass Optima XL Cool Blue #50
1995 Press Pass Optima XL Cool Blue #56
1995 Press Pass Optima XL Die Cut #8
1995 Press Pass Optima XL Die Cut #31
1995 Press Pass Optima XL Die Cut #50
1995 Press Pass Optima XL Die Cut #56
1995 Press Pass Optima XL JG/XL #1
1995 Press Pass Optima XL JG/XL #2
1995 Press Pass Optima XL JG/XL #3
1995 Press Pass Optima XL JG/XL #4
1995 Press Pass Optima XL Red Hot #8
1995 Press Pass Optima XL Red Hot #31
1995 Press Pass Optima XL Red Hot #50
1995 Press Pass Optima XL Red Hot #56
1995 Press Pass Optima XL Stealth #XLS4
1995 Press Pass Premium #8
1995 Press Pass Premium #33
1995 Press Pass Premium Holofoil #8
1995 Press Pass Premium Holofoil #33
1995 Press Pass Premium Hot Pursuit #HP3
1995 Press Pass Premium Phone Cards $5 #2
1995 Press Pass Premium Phone Cards $5 #10
1995 Press Pass Premium Phone Cards $50 #2
1995 Press Pass Premium Red Hot #8
1995 Press Pass Premium Red Hot #33
1995 Press Pass Prototypes #3
1995 Press Pass Race Day #RD4
1995 Press Pass Red Hot #10
1995 Press Pass Red Hot #38
1995 Press Pass Red Hot #102
1995 Press Pass Red Hot #129
1995 Press Pass Red Hot #136
1995 Select #12
1995 Select #38
1995 Select #118
1995 Select #141
1995 Select #NNO
1995 Select Dream Machines #DM8
1995 Select Flat Out #12
1995 Select Flat Out #38
1995 Select Flat Out #118
1995 Select Flat Out #141
1995 Select Promos #12
1995 Select Promos #DM8
1995 Select Skills #SS3
1995 SP #18
1995 SP #55
1995 SP #56
1995 SP #97
1995 SP #100
1995 SP #JG1
1995 SP Die Cuts #18
1995 SP Die Cuts #55
1995 SP Die Cuts #56
1995 SP Die Cuts #97
1995 SP Die Cuts #100
1995 SP Speed Merchants #SM24
1995 SP Speed Merchants Die Cuts #SM24
1995 Traks #4
1995 Traks #26
1995 Traks #52
1995 Traks #58
1995 Traks #68
1995 Traks #P26

1995 Traks 5th Anniversary #4
1995 Traks 5th Anniversary #38
1995 Traks 5th Anniversary #49
1995 Traks 5th Anniversary Clear Contenders #C3
1995 Traks 5th Anniversary Gold #4
1995 Traks 5th Anniversary Gold #38
1995 Traks 5th Anniversary Gold #49
1995 Traks 5th Anniversary Jumbos #E1
1995 Traks 5th Anniversary Jumbos Gold /100 #E1
1995 Traks 5th Anniversary Limited Production /1600 #2
1995 Traks 5th Anniversary Red #4
1995 Traks 5th Anniversary Red #38
1995 Traks 5th Anniversary Red #49
1995 Traks 5th Anniversary Retrospective #R3
1995 Traks Auto Value #1
1995 Traks Challengers #C1
1995 Traks Challengers First Run #C1
1995 Traks First Run #4
1995 Traks First Run #26
1995 Traks First Run #52
1995 Traks First Run #58
1995 Traks First Run #68
1995 Traks Racing Machines #RM7
1995 Traks Racing Machines First Run #RM7
1995 Traks Series Stars #SS8
1995 Traks Series Stars First Run #SS8
1995 Traks Valvoline #100
1995 Upper Deck #2
1995 Upper Deck #45
1995 Upper Deck #70
1995 Upper Deck #138
1995 Upper Deck #163
1995 Upper Deck #202
1995 Upper Deck #246
1995 Upper Deck #281
1995 Upper Deck #UD2
1995 Upper Deck #UD2A
1995 Upper Deck Autographs #202
1995 Upper Deck Gold Signature/Electric Gold #2
1995 Upper Deck Gold Signature/Electric Gold #45
1995 Upper Deck Gold Signature/Electric Gold #70
1995 Upper Deck Gold Signature/Electric Gold #138
1995 Upper Deck Gold Signature/Electric Gold #163
1995 Upper Deck Gold Signature/Electric Gold #202
1995 Upper Deck Gold Signature/Electric Gold #246
1995 Upper Deck Gold Signature/Electric Gold #281
1995 Upper Deck Illustrations #I9
1995 Upper Deck Jeff Gordon Phone Cards #1
1995 Upper Deck Jeff Gordon Phone Cards #2
1995 Upper Deck Jeff Gordon Phone Cards #3
1995 Upper Deck Jeff Gordon Phone Cards #4
1995 Upper Deck Jeff Gordon Phone Cards #5
1995 Upper Deck Jumbos #OS3
1995 Upper Deck Predictor Race Winners #P4
1995 Upper Deck Predictor Race Winners Coca-Cola 600 #P4
1995 Upper Deck Predictor Race Winners Daytona 500 #P4
1995 Upper Deck Predictor Race Winners Prizes #P4
1995 Upper Deck Predictor Series Points #PP6
1995 Upper Deck Predictor Series Points Prizes #PP6
1995 Upper Deck Silver Signature/Electric Silver #2
1995 Upper Deck Silver Signature/Electric Silver #45
1995 Upper Deck Silver Signature/Electric Silver #70
1995 Upper Deck Silver Signature/Electric Silver #138
1995 Upper Deck Silver Signature/Electric Silver #163
1995 Upper Deck Silver Signature/Electric Silver #202
1995 Upper Deck Silver Signature/Electric Silver #246
1995 Upper Deck Silver Signature/Electric Silver #281
1995 VIP #11
1995 VIP #31
1995 VIP #61
1995 VIP Autographs #11
1995 VIP Cool Blue #61
1995 VIP Cool Blue #31
1995 VIP Cool Blue #11
1995 VIP Emerald Proofs #61
1995 VIP Emerald Proofs #31
1995 VIP Emerald Proofs #11
1995 VIP Fan's Choice #FC3
1995 VIP Fan's Choice Gold #FC3
1995 VIP Helmets #H4
1995 VIP Helmets Gold #H4
1995 VIP Red Hot #61
1995 VIP Red Hot #31
1995 VIP Red Hot #11
1995 VIP Reflections #R2
1995 VIP Reflections Gold #R2
1995 Wheels High Gear #6
1995 Wheels High Gear #78
1995 Wheels High Gear #91
1995 Wheels High Gear #98
1995 Wheels High Gear Busch Clash #BC7
1995 Wheels High Gear Busch Clash Gold #BC7
1995 Wheels High Gear Day One #6
1995 Wheels High Gear Day One #78
1995 Wheels High Gear Day One #91
1995 Wheels High Gear Day One #98
1995 Wheels High Gear Day One Gold #6
1995 Wheels High Gear Day One Gold #78
1995 Wheels High Gear Day One Gold #91
1995 Wheels High Gear Day One Gold #98
1995 Wheels High Gear Gold #6
1995 Wheels High Gear Gold #78
1995 Wheels High Gear Gold #91
1995 Wheels High Gear Gold #98
1995 Wheels High Gear Promos #P2
1995 Zenith #23
1995 Zenith #51
1995 Zenith #64
1995 Zenith #77
1995 Zenith #78
1995 Zenith #79
1995 Zenith #80
1995 Zenith #81
1995 Zenith #82
1995 Zenith #83
1995 Zenith Helmets #3
1995 Zenith Tribute #2
1995 Zenith Winston Winners #2
1995 Zenith Winston Winners #4
1995 Zenith Winston Winners #6
1995 Zenith Winston Winners #15
1995 Zenith Winston Winners #16
1995 Zenith Winston Winners #23
1995 Zenith Winston Winners #25
1995 Zenith Z-Team #2
1996 Action Packed Credentials #1
1996 Action Packed Credentials #2
1996 Action Packed Credentials #3
1996 Action Packed Credentials #4
1996 Action Packed Credentials #5
1996 Action Packed Credentials #20
1996 Action Packed Credentials #99
1996 Action Packed Credentials #105
1996 Action Packed Credentials Fan Scan #4
1996 Action Packed Credentials Jumbos #2
1996 Action Packed Credentials Leaders of the Pack #5
1996 Action Packed Credentials Leaders of the Pack #6
1996 Action Packed Credentials Leaders of the Pack #7
1996 Action Packed Credentials Leaders of the Pack #8
1996 Action Packed Credentials Promos #5
1996 Action Packed Credentials Silver Speed #1
1996 Action Packed Credentials Silver Speed #2
1996 Action Packed Credentials Silver Speed #3
1996 Action Packed Credentials Silver Speed #4
1996 Action Packed Credentials Silver Speed #5
1996 Action Packed Credentials Silver Speed #20
1996 Action Packed McDonald's #3
1996 Action Packed McDonald's #13
1996 Action Packed Racing For Kids /5000 #RFK1
1996 Action Packed Racing For Kids #NNO
1996 Assets Racing #2
1996 Assets Racing $100 Cup Champion Interactive Phone Cards #2
1996 Autographed Racing #2
1996 Autographed Racing Autographs #16
1996 Autographed Racing Autographs Certified Golds #16
1996 Classic Winston Cup Champion #J1
1996 Classic Winston Cup Champion #J2
1996 Classic Winston Cup Champion #J3
1996 Classic Winston Cup Champion #J4
1996 Classic Winston Cup Champion #J5
1996 Crown Jewels Elite #2
1996 Crown Jewels Elite #28
1996 Crown Jewels Elite #29
1996 Crown Jewels Elite #30
1996 Crown Jewels Elite Birthstones of the Champions #BC2
1996 Crown Jewels Elite Birthstones of the Champions Diamond Tribute #BC2
1996 Crown Jewels Elite Birthstones of the Champions Treasure Chest #BC2
1996 Crown Jewels Elite Crown Signature Amethyst #CS2
1996 Crown Jewels Elite Crown Signature Garnet #CS2
1996 Crown Jewels Elite Crown Signature Peridot #CS2
1996 Crown Jewels Elite Diamond Tribute /2500 #2
1996 Crown Jewels Elite Diamond Tribute /2500 #28
1996 Crown Jewels Elite Diamond Tribute /2500 #29
1996 Crown Jewels Elite Diamond Tribute /2500 #30
1996 Crown Jewels Elite Diamond Tribute Citrine /999 #2
1996 Crown Jewels Elite Diamond Tribute Citrine /999 #28
1996 Crown Jewels Elite Diamond Tribute Citrine /999 #29
1996 Crown Jewels Elite Diamond Tribute Citrine /999 #30
1996 Crown Jewels Elite Dual Jewels Amethyst #DJ1
1996 Crown Jewels Elite Dual Jewels Amethyst Diamond Tribute #DJ1
1996 Crown Jewels Elite Dual Jewels Amethyst Treasure Chest #DJ1
1996 Crown Jewels Elite Dual Jewels Garnet #DJ1
1996 Crown Jewels Elite Dual Jewels Garnet Diamond Tribute #DJ1
1996 Crown Jewels Elite Dual Jewels Garnet Treasure Chest #DJ1
1996 Crown Jewels Elite Dual Jewels Sapphire #DJ1
1996 Crown Jewels Elite Dual Jewels Sapphire Treasure Chest #DJ1
1996 Crown Jewels Elite Emerald /599 #2
1996 Crown Jewels Elite Emerald /599 #28
1996 Crown Jewels Elite Emerald /599 #29
1996 Crown Jewels Elite Emerald /599 #30
1996 Crown Jewels Elite Emerald Treasure Chest #2
1996 Crown Jewels Elite Emerald Treasure Chest #28
1996 Crown Jewels Elite Emerald Treasure Chest #29
1996 Crown Jewels Elite Emerald Treasure Chest #30
1996 Crown Jewels Elite Retail Blue #2
1996 Crown Jewels Elite Retail Blue #28
1996 Crown Jewels Elite Retail Blue #29
1996 Crown Jewels Elite Retail Blue #30
1996 Crown Jewels Elite Sapphire #2
1996 Crown Jewels Elite Sapphire #28
1996 Crown Jewels Elite Sapphire #29
1996 Crown Jewels Elite Sapphire #30
1996 Crown Jewels Elite Sapphire Treasure Chest /1099 #2
1996 Crown Jewels Elite Sapphire Treasure Chest /1099 #28
1996 Crown Jewels Elite Sapphire Treasure Chest /1099 #29
1996 Crown Jewels Elite Sapphire Treasure Chest /1099 #30
1996 Crown Jewels Elite Treasure Chest #2
1996 Crown Jewels Elite Treasure Chest #28
1996 Crown Jewels Elite Treasure Chest #29
1996 Crown Jewels Elite Treasure Chest #30
1996 Finish Line #1
1996 Finish Line #87
1996 Finish Line #95
1996 Finish Line Black Gold #C1
1996 Finish Line Black Gold #D1
1996 Finish Line Black Gold #SG1
1996 Finish Line Black Gold #JPC2
1996 Finish Line Diamond Collection $5 Phone Cards #1
1996 Finish Line Gold Signature #GS1
1996 Finish Line Man and Machine #MM1
1996 Finish Line Mega-Phone XL Phone Cards /8000 #1
1996 Finish Line Phone Pak #11
1996 Finish Line Phone Pak #12
1996 Finish Line Phone Pak $10 #3
1996 Finish Line Phone Pak $100 #2
1996 Finish Line Phone Pak $1000 #K1
1996 Finish Line Phone Pak $2 Signature #11
1996 Finish Line Phone Pak $2 Signature #12
1996 Finish Line Phone Pak $5 #9
1996 Finish Line Phone Pak $50 #2
1996 Finish Line Printer's Proof #1
1996 Finish Line Printer's Proof #87
1996 Finish Line Printer's Proof #95
1996 Finish Line Rise To The Top Jeff Gordon #JG1
1996 Finish Line Rise To The Top Jeff Gordon #JG2
1996 Finish Line Rise To The Top Jeff Gordon #JG3
1996 Finish Line Rise To The Top Jeff Gordon #JG4
1996 Finish Line Rise To The Top Jeff Gordon #JG5
1996 Finish Line Rise To The Top Jeff Gordon #JG6
1996 Finish Line Rise To The Top Jeff Gordon #JG7
1996 Finish Line Rise To The Top Jeff Gordon #JG8
1996 Finish Line Rise To The Top Jeff Gordon #JG9
1996 Finish Line Rise To The Top Jeff Gordon #JG10
1996 Finish Line Silver #1
1996 Finish Line Silver #87
1996 Finish Line Silver #95
1996 Flair #12
1996 Flair #68
1996 Flair #99
1996 Flair #P1
1996 Flair Autographs #4
1996 Flair Center Spotlight #4
1996 Flair Hot Numbers #3
1996 Flair Power Performance #4
1996 KnightQuest #2
1996 KnightQuest #21
1996 KnightQuest #30
1996 KnightQuest #31
1996 KnightQuest Black Knights #2
1996 KnightQuest Black Knights #21
1996 KnightQuest Black Knights #30
1996 KnightQuest Black Knights #31
1996 KnightQuest First Knights #FK3
1996 KnightQuest Knights of the Round Table #KT1
1996 KnightQuest Protectors of the Crown /899 #PC6
1996 KnightQuest Red Knight Preview #2
1996 KnightQuest Red Knight Preview #21
1996 KnightQuest Red Knight Preview #30
1996 KnightQuest Red Knight Preview #31
1996 KnightQuest Royalty #2
1996 KnightQuest Royalty #21
1996 KnightQuest Royalty #30
1996 KnightQuest Royalty #31
1996 KnightQuest White Knights #2
1996 KnightQuest White Knights #21
1996 KnightQuest White Knights #30
1996 KnightQuest White Knights #31
1996 Maxx #24
1996 Maxx #88
1996 Maxx Autographs #24
1996 Maxx Chase the Champion #1
1996 Maxx Chase the Champion #2
1996 Maxx Chase the Champion #3
1996 Maxx Chase the Champion #4
1996 Maxx Chase the Champion #5
1996 Maxx Chase the Champion #6
1996 Maxx Chase the Champion #7
1996 Maxx Chase the Champion #8
1996 Maxx Chase the Champion #9
1996 Maxx Chase the Champion #10
1996 Maxx Chase the Champion #11
1996 Maxx Chase the Champion #12
1996 Maxx Chase the Champion #13
1996 Maxx Chase the Champion #14
1996 Maxx Made in America #24
1996 Maxx Odyssey #24
1996 Maxx Odyssey Millennium #MM6
1996 Maxx Premier Series #24
1996 Maxx Premier Series #296
1996 Maxx Sam Bass #1
1996 Maxx Sam Bass #2
1996 Metallic Impressions 25th Anniversary Winston Cup Champions #25
1996 Metallic Impressions Jeff Gordon Winston Cup Champ 10-Card Tin #1
1996 Metallic Impressions Jeff Gordon Winston Cup Champ 10-Card Tin #2
1996 Metallic Impressions Jeff Gordon Winston Cup Champ 10-Card Tin #3
1996 Metallic Impressions Jeff Gordon Winston Cup Champ 10-Card Tin #4
1996 Metallic Impressions Jeff Gordon Winston Cup Champ 10-Card Tin #5
1996 Metallic Impressions Jeff Gordon Winston Cup Champ 10-Card Tin #6
1996 Metallic Impressions Jeff Gordon Winston Cup Champ 10-Card Tin #7
1996 Metallic Impressions Jeff Gordon Winston Cup Champ 10-Card Tin #8
1996 Metallic Impressions Jeff Gordon Winston Cup Champ 10-Card Tin #9
1996 Metallic Impressions Jeff Gordon Winston Cup Champ 10-Card Tin #10
1996 Metallic Impressions Jeff Gordon Winston Cup Champ 5-Card Tin #1
1996 Metallic Impressions Jeff Gordon Winston Cup Champ 5-Card Tin #2
1996 Metallic Impressions Jeff Gordon Winston Cup Champ 5-Card Tin #3
1996 Metallic Impressions Jeff Gordon Winston Cup Champ 5-Card Tin #4
1996 Metallic Impressions Jeff Gordon Winston Cup Champ 5-Card Tin #5
1996 Metallic Impressions Winston Cup Top Five #2
1996 M-Force #19
1996 M-Force #20
1996 M-Force #40
1996 M-Force #P1
1996 M-Force #P2
1996 M-Force #P3
1996 M-Force Black #B7
1996 M-Force Black #B8
1996 M-Force Black #B12
1996 M-Force Sheet Metal #M5
1996 M-Force Silvers #S10
1996 M-Force Silvers #S14
1996 Pinnacle #24
1996 Pinnacle #51
1996 Pinnacle #66
1996 Pinnacle #67
1996 Pinnacle #68
1996 Pinnacle #69
1996 Pinnacle #70
1996 Pinnacle #71
1996 Pinnacle #72
1996 Pinnacle #73
1996 Pinnacle #85
1996 Pinnacle #92
1996 Pinnacle #95
1996 Pinnacle Artist Proofs #24
1996 Pinnacle Artist Proofs #51
1996 Pinnacle Artist Proofs #66
1996 Pinnacle Artist Proofs #67
1996 Pinnacle Artist Proofs #68
1996 Pinnacle Artist Proofs #69
1996 Pinnacle Artist Proofs #70
1996 Pinnacle Artist Proofs #71
1996 Pinnacle Artist Proofs #72
1996 Pinnacle Artist Proofs #73
1996 Pinnacle Artist Proofs #85
1996 Pinnacle Artist Proofs #92
1996 Pinnacle Artist Proofs #95
1996 Pinnacle Checkered Flag #1
1996 Pinnacle Cut Above #1
1996 Pinnacle Foil #24
1996 Pinnacle Foil #51
1996 Pinnacle Foil #66
1996 Pinnacle Foil #67
1996 Pinnacle Foil #68
1996 Pinnacle Foil #69
1996 Pinnacle Foil #70
1996 Pinnacle Foil #71
1996 Pinnacle Foil #72
1996 Pinnacle Foil #73
1996 Pinnacle Foil #85
1996 Pinnacle Foil #92
1996 Pinnacle Foil #95
1996 Pinnacle Pole Position #24
1996 Pinnacle Pole Position #40
1996 Pinnacle Pole Position #51
1996 Pinnacle Pole Position #52
1996 Pinnacle Pole Position #53
1996 Pinnacle Pole Position #54
1996 Pinnacle Pole Position #55
1996 Pinnacle Pole Position #68
1996 Pinnacle Pole Position #69
1996 Pinnacle Pole Position #73
1996 Pinnacle Pole Position Certified Strong #1
1996 Pinnacle Pole Position Lightning Fast #24
1996 Pinnacle Pole Position Lightning Fast #40
1996 Pinnacle Pole Position Lightning Fast #51
1996 Pinnacle Pole Position Lightning Fast #52
1996 Pinnacle Pole Position Lightning Fast #53
1996 Pinnacle Pole Position Lightning Fast #54
1996 Pinnacle Pole Position Lightning Fast #55
1996 Pinnacle Pole Position Lightning Fast #68
1996 Pinnacle Pole Position Lightning Fast #69
1996 Pinnacle Pole Position Lightning Fast #73
1996 Pinnacle Pole Position No Limit #1
1996 Pinnacle Pole Position No Limit Gold #1
1996 Pinnacle Team Pinnacle #1
1996 Pinnacle Team Pinnacle #10
1996 Pinnacle Winston Cup Collection Dufex #24
1996 Pinnacle Winston Cup Collection Dufex #51
1996 Pinnacle Winston Cup Collection Dufex #66
1996 Pinnacle Winston Cup Collection Dufex #67
1996 Pinnacle Winston Cup Collection Dufex #68
1996 Pinnacle Winston Cup Collection Dufex #69
1996 Pinnacle Winston Cup Collection Dufex #70
1996 Pinnacle Winston Cup Collection Dufex #71
1996 Pinnacle Winston Cup Collection Dufex #72
1996 Pinnacle Winston Cup Collection Dufex #73
1996 Pinnacle Winston Cup Collection Dufex #85
1996 Pinnacle Winston Cup Collection Dufex #92
1996 Pinnacle Winston Cup Collection Dufex #95
1996 Press Pass #11
1996 Press Pass #38
1996 Press Pass #78
1996 Press Pass #93
1996 Press Pass #100
1996 Press Pass #111
1996 Press Pass #0
1996 Press Pass Burning Rubber /500 #BR2
1996 Press Pass Checkered Flags #CF1
1996 Press Pass Cup Chase #11
1996 Press Pass Cup Chase Foil Prizes #11
1996 Press Pass F.Q.S. #FQS3A
1996 Press Pass F.Q.S. #FQS3B
1996 Press Pass Focused #F3
1996 Press Pass Focused #P1
1996 Press Pass Premium #1
1996 Press Pass Premium #34
1996 Press Pass Premium Burning Rubber II /500 #BR1
1996 Press Pass Premium Crystal Ball #CB5
1996 Press Pass Premium Emerald Proofs /380 #1
1996 Press Pass Premium Emerald Proofs /380 #34
1996 Press Pass Premium Holofoil #1
1996 Press Pass Premium Holofoil #34
1996 Press Pass Premium Hot Pursuit #HP3
1996 Press Pass R and N China #11
1996 Press Pass R and N China #38
1996 Press Pass Scorchers #11
1996 Press Pass Scorchers #38
1996 Press Pass Scorchers #78
1996 Press Pass Scorchers #93
1996 Press Pass Scorchers #100
1996 Press Pass Scorchers #111
1996 Press Pass Torquers #11
1996 Press Pass Torquers #38
1996 Press Pass Torquers #78
1996 Press Pass Torquers #93
1996 Press Pass Torquers #100
1996 Press Pass Torquers #111
1996 Racer's Choice #9
1996 Racer's Choice #40
1996 Racer's Choice #51
1996 Racer's Choice #52
1996 Racer's Choice #53
1996 Racer's Choice #54
1996 Racer's Choice #55
1996 Racer's Choice #83
1996 Racer's Choice #90
1996 Racer's Choice #110
1996 Racer's Choice #J52
1996 Racer's Choice #P9
1996 Racer's Choice Racer's Review #1
1996 Racer's Choice Racer's Review #2
1996 Racer's Choice Racer's Review #3
1996 Racer's Choice Racer's Review #4
1996 Racer's Choice Racer's Review #5
1996 Racer's Choice Speedway Collection #9
1996 Racer's Choice Speedway Collection #40
1996 Racer's Choice Speedway Collection #51
1996 Racer's Choice Speedway Collection #52
1996 Racer's Choice Speedway Collection #53
1996 Racer's Choice Speedway Collection #54
1996 Racer's Choice Speedway Collection #55
1996 Racer's Choice Speedway Collection #83
1996 Racer's Choice Speedway Collection #90
1996 Racer's Choice Speedway Collection #110
1996 Racer's Choice Speedway Collection Artist's Proofs #9
1996 Racer's Choice Speedway Collection Artist's Proofs #40
1996 Racer's Choice Speedway Collection Artist's Proofs #51
1996 Racer's Choice Speedway Collection Artist's Proofs #52
1996 Racer's Choice Speedway Collection Artist's Proofs #53
1996 Racer's Choice Speedway Collection Artist's Proofs #54
1996 Racer's Choice Speedway Collection Artist's Proofs #55
1996 Racer's Choice Speedway Collection Artist's Proofs #83
1996 Racer's Choice Speedway Collection Artist's Proofs #90
1996 Racer's Choice Speedway Collection Artist's Proofs #110
1996 Racer's Choice Top Ten #1
1996 Racer's Choice Up Close with Jeff Gordon #1
1996 Racer's Choice Up Close with Jeff Gordon #2
1996 Racer's Choice Up Close with Jeff Gordon #3
1996 Racer's Choice Up Close with Jeff Gordon #4
1996 Racer's Choice Up Close with Jeff Gordon #5
1996 Racer's Choice Up Close with Jeff Gordon #6
1996 Racer's Choice Up Close with Jeff Gordon #7
1996 SP #24
1996 SP #43
1996 SP #80
1996 SP #KR1
1996 SP Holoview Maximum Effects #ME1
1996 SP Holoview Maximum Effects Die Cuts #ME1
1996 SP Racing Legends #RL24
1996 Speedflix #9
1996 Speedflix #16
1996 Speedflix #44
1996 Speedflix #55
1996 Speedflix #56
1996 Speedflix #57
1996 Speedflix #58
1996 Speedflix #59
1996 Speedflix #60
1996 Speedflix #61
1996 Speedflix #62
1996 Speedflix #84
1996 Speedflix #86
1996 Speedflix Artist Proof's #9
1996 Speedflix Artist Proof's #16
1996 Speedflix Artist Proof's #44
1996 Speedflix Artist Proof's #55
1996 Speedflix Artist Proof's #56
1996 Speedflix Artist Proof's #57
1996 Speedflix Artist Proof's #58
1996 Speedflix Artist Proof's #59
1996 Speedflix Artist Proof's #60
1996 Speedflix Artist Proof's #61
1996 Speedflix Artist Proof's #62
1996 Speedflix Artist Proof's #84
1996 Speedflix Artist Proof's #86
1996 Speedflix Clear Shots #2
1996 Speedflix In Motion #2
1996 Speedflix ProMotion #2
1996 SPx #1
1996 SPx #T1
1996 SPx #T1A
1996 SPx #S1
1996 SPx Elite #E1
1996 SPx Gold #1
1996 Traks Review and Preview #15
1996 Traks Review and Preview First Run #15
1996 Traks Review and Preview Liquid Gold #LG18
1996 Traks Review and Preview Magnets #15
1996 Ultra #1
1996 Ultra #2
1996 Ultra #3
1996 Ultra #152
1996 Ultra #157
1996 Ultra #168
1996 Ultra #170
1996 Ultra #172
1996 Ultra #181
1996 Ultra #182
1996 Ultra #191
1996 Ultra #200
1996 Ultra #P1
1996 Ultra Autographs #11
1996 Ultra Boxed Set #1
1996 Ultra Champions Club #5
1996 Ultra Flair Preview #1
1996 Ultra Season Crowns #2
1996 Ultra Season Crowns #4
1996 Ultra Season Crowns #7
1996 Ultra Season Crowns #10
1996 Ultra Season Crowns #11
1996 Ultra Season Crowns #12
1996 Ultra Thunder and Lightning #3
1996 Ultra Thunder and Lightning #4
1996 Ultra Update #12
1996 Ultra Update #46
1996 Ultra Update #58
1996 Ultra Update Autographs #4
1996 Ultra Update Proven Power #4
1996 Ultra Update Winner #1
1996 Ultra Update Winner #4
1996 Ultra Update Winner #10
1996 Upper Deck #22
1996 Upper Deck #72
1996 Upper Deck #73
1996 Upper Deck #98
1996 Upper Deck #102
1996 Upper Deck #138
1996 Upper Deck #150
1996 Upper Deck #C1
1996 Upper Deck #C2
1996 Upper Deck #JG1
1996 Upper Deck All-Pro #AP1
1996 Upper Deck Jeff Gordon Profiles #1
1996 Upper Deck Jeff Gordon Profiles #2
1996 Upper Deck Jeff Gordon Profiles #3
1996 Upper Deck Jeff Gordon Profiles #4
1996 Upper Deck Jeff Gordon Profiles #5
1996 Upper Deck Jeff Gordon Profiles #6
1996 Upper Deck Jeff Gordon Profiles #7
1996 Upper Deck Jeff Gordon Profiles #8
1996 Upper Deck Jeff Gordon Profiles #9
1996 Upper Deck Jeff Gordon Profiles #10
1996 Upper Deck Jeff Gordon Profiles #11
1996 Upper Deck Jeff Gordon Profiles #12
1996 Upper Deck Jeff Gordon Profiles #13
1996 Upper Deck Jeff Gordon Profiles #14
1996 Upper Deck Jeff Gordon Profiles #15
1996 Upper Deck Jeff Gordon Profiles #16
1996 Upper Deck Jeff Gordon Profiles #17
1996 Upper Deck Jeff Gordon Profiles #18
1996 Upper Deck Jeff Gordon Profiles #19
1996 Upper Deck Jeff Gordon Profiles #20
1996 Upper Deck Meet the Stars Trivia Challenge #41
1996 Upper Deck Meet the Stars Trivia Challenge #42
1996 Upper Deck Meet the Stars Trivia Challenge #43
1996 Upper Deck Meet the Stars Trivia Challenge #44
1996 Upper Deck Meet the Stars Trivia Challenge #45
1996 Upper Deck Meet the Stars Trivia Challenge #46
1996 Upper Deck Meet the Stars Trivia Challenge #47
1996 Upper Deck Meet the Stars Trivia Challenge #48
1996 Upper Deck Meet the Stars Trivia Challenge #49
1996 Upper Deck Meet the Stars Trivia Challenge #50
1996 Upper Deck Meet the Stars Trivia Challenge #51
1996 Upper Deck Meet the Stars Trivia Challenge #52
1996 Upper Deck Meet the Stars Trivia Challenge #53
1996 Upper Deck Meet the Stars Trivia Challenge #54
1996 Upper Deck Meet the Stars Trivia Challenge #55
1996 Upper Deck Meet the Stars Trivia Challenge #56
1996 Upper Deck Meet the Stars Trivia Challenge #57
1996 Upper Deck Meet the Stars Trivia Challenge #58
1996 Upper Deck Meet the Stars Trivia Challenge #59
1996 Upper Deck Meet the Stars Trivia Challenge #60
1996 Upper Deck Meet the Stars Trivia Challenge #61
1996 Upper Deck Meet the Stars Trivia Challenge #62
1996 Upper Deck Meet the Stars Trivia Challenge #63
1996 Upper Deck Meet the Stars Trivia Challenge #64
1996 Upper Deck Meet the Stars Trivia Challenge #65
1996 Upper Deck Meet the Stars Trivia Challenge #66
1996 Upper Deck Meet the Stars Trivia Challenge #67
1996 Upper Deck Meet the Stars Trivia Challenge #68
1996 Upper Deck Meet the Stars Trivia Challenge #69
1996 Upper Deck Meet the Stars Trivia Challenge #70
1996 Upper Deck Meet the Stars Trivia Challenge #71
1996 Upper Deck Meet the Stars Trivia Challenge #72
1996 Upper Deck Meet the Stars Trivia Challenge #5
1996 Upper Deck Meet the Stars Trivia Challenge #6
1996 Upper Deck Meet the Stars Trivia Challenge #7
1996 Upper Deck Meet the Stars Trivia Challenge #8
1996 Upper Deck Meet the Stars Trivia Challenge #9
1996 Upper Deck Meet the Stars Trivia Challenge #10
1996 Upper Deck Meet the Stars Trivia Challenge #11
1996 Upper Deck Meet the Stars Trivia Challenge #12
1996 Upper Deck Meet the Stars Trivia Challenge #13
1996 Upper Deck Meet the Stars Trivia Challenge #14
1996 Upper Deck Meet the Stars Trivia Challenge #15
1996 Upper Deck Meet the Stars Trivia Challenge #16
1996 Upper Deck Meet the Stars Trivia Challenge #17
1996 Upper Deck Meet the Stars Trivia Challenge #18
1996 Upper Deck Meet the Stars Trivia Challenge #19
1996 Upper Deck Meet the Stars Trivia Challenge #20
1996 Upper Deck Meet the Stars Trivia Challenge #21
1996 Upper Deck Meet the Stars Trivia Challenge #22
1996 Upper Deck Meet the Stars Trivia Challenge #23
1996 Upper Deck Meet the Stars Trivia Challenge #24
1996 Upper Deck Meet the Stars Trivia Challenge #25
1996 Upper Deck Meet the Stars Trivia Challenge #26
1996 Upper Deck Meet the Stars Trivia Challenge #27
1996 Upper Deck Meet the Stars Trivia Challenge #28
1996 Upper Deck Meet the Stars Trivia Challenge #29
1996 Upper Deck Meet the Stars Trivia Challenge #30
1996 Upper Deck Meet the Stars Trivia Challenge #1
1996 Upper Deck Meet the Stars Trivia Challenge #2
1996 Upper Deck Meet the Stars Trivia Challenge #3
1996 Upper Deck Meet the Stars Trivia Challenge #31
1996 Upper Deck Meet the Stars Trivia Challenge #32
1996 Upper Deck Meet the Stars Trivia Challenge #33
1996 Upper Deck Meet the Stars Trivia Challenge #34
1996 Upper Deck Meet the Stars Trivia Challenge #35
1996 Upper Deck Meet the Stars Trivia Challenge #36
1996 Upper Deck Meet the Stars Trivia Challenge #37
1996 Upper Deck Meet the Stars Trivia Challenge #38
1996 Upper Deck Meet the Stars Trivia Challenge #39
1996 Upper Deck Meet the Stars Trivia Challenge #40
1996 Upper Deck Meet the Stars Trivia Challenge #4
1996 Upper Deck Meet the Stars Trivia Challenge #73
1996 Upper Deck Meet the Stars Trivia Challenge #74
1996 Upper Deck Meet the Stars Trivia Challenge #75
1996 Upper Deck Meet the Stars Trivia Challenge #76
1996 Upper Deck Meet the Stars Trivia Challenge #77
1996 Upper Deck Meet the Stars Trivia Challenge #78
1996 Upper Deck Meet the Stars Trivia Challenge #79
1996 Upper Deck Meet the Stars Trivia Challenge #80
1996 Upper Deck Meet the Stars Trivia Challenge #81
1996 Upper Deck Meet the Stars Trivia Challenge #82
1996 Upper Deck Meet the Stars Trivia Challenge #83
1996 Upper Deck Meet the Stars Trivia Challenge #84
1996 Upper Deck Meet the Stars Trivia Challenge #85
1996 Upper Deck Meet the Stars Trivia Challenge #86
1996 Upper Deck Meet the Stars Trivia Challenge #87
1996 Upper Deck Meet the Stars Trivia Challenge #88
1996 Upper Deck Meet the Stars Trivia Challenge #89
1996 Upper Deck Meet the Stars Trivia Challenge #90
1996 Upper Deck Predictor Poles #RP1
1996 Upper Deck Predictor Poles Prizes #RP1
1996 Upper Deck Predictor Wins #HP1
1996 Upper Deck Predictor Wins Prizes #HP1
1996 Upper Deck Road To The Cup #RC1
1996 Upper Deck Road To The Cup #RC51
1996 Upper Deck Road To The Cup #RC121
1996 Upper Deck Road To The Cup #RC124
1996 Upper Deck Road To The Cup #RC148
1996 Upper Deck Road To The Cup #JG1
1996 Upper Deck Road To The Cup Autographs #H1
1996 Upper Deck Road To The Cup Diary of a Champion #DC1
1996 Upper Deck Road To The Cup Diary of a Champion #DC2
1996 Upper Deck Road To The Cup Diary of a Champion #DC3
1996 Upper Deck Road To The Cup Diary of a Champion #DC4
1996 Upper Deck Road To The Cup Diary of a Champion #DC5
1996 Upper Deck Road To The Cup Diary of a Champion #DC6
1996 Upper Deck Road To The Cup Diary of a Champion #DC7
1996 Upper Deck Road To The Cup Diary of a Champion #DC8
1996 Upper Deck Road To The Cup Diary of a Champion #DC9
1996 Upper Deck Road To The Cup Diary of a Champion #DC10
1996 Upper Deck Road To The Cup Game Face #GF1
1996 Upper Deck Road To The Cup Jumbos #WC1
1996 Upper Deck Road To The Cup Leaders of the Pack #LP1
1996 Upper Deck Road To The Cup Predictor Points #PP1
1996 Upper Deck Road To The Cup Predictor Points Prizes #PR1
1996 Upper Deck Road To The Cup Predictor Top 3 #T1
1996 Upper Deck Road To The Cup Predictor Top 3 #T3
1996 Upper Deck Road To The Cup Predictor Top 3 #T6
1996 Upper Deck Road To The Cup Predictor Top 3 #T7
1996 Upper Deck Road To The Cup Predictor Top 3 Prizes #R1
1996 Upper Deck Virtual Velocity #VV1
1996 Upper Deck Virtual Velocity Gold #VV1
1996 VIP #10
1996 VIP #30
1996 VIP #37
1996 VIP Autographs #8
1996 VIP Emerald Proofs #10
1996 VIP Emerald Proofs #30
1996 VIP Emerald Proofs #37
1996 VIP Head Gear #HG3
1996 VIP Head Gear Die Cuts #HG3
1996 VIP Torquers #10
1996 VIP Torquers #30
1996 VIP Torquers #37
1996 VIP War Paint #WP12
1996 VIP War Paint Gold #WP12
1996 Viper #2
1996 Viper #40
1996 Viper #42
1996 Viper Black Mamba #2
1996 Viper Black Mamba #40
1996 Viper Black Mamba #42
1996 Viper Black Mamba First Strike #2
1996 Viper Black Mamba First Strike #40
1996 Viper Black Mamba First Strike #42
1996 Viper Busch Clash #B5
1996 Viper Busch Clash First Strike #B5
1996 Viper Cobra /1799 #C2
1996 Viper Cobra First Strike /1799 #C2
1996 Viper Copperhead Die Cuts #2
1996 Viper Copperhead Die Cuts #40
1996 Viper Copperhead Die Cuts #42
1996 Viper Copperhead Die Cuts First Strike #2
1996 Viper Copperhead Die Cuts First Strike #40
1996 Viper Copperhead Die Cuts First Strike #42
1996 Viper Diamondback #D1
1996 Viper Diamondback Authentic #DA1
1996 Viper Diamondback Authentic California #DA1
1996 Viper Diamondback Authentic First Strike #DA1
1996 Viper Diamondback First Strike #D1
1996 Viper First Strike #2
1996 Viper First Strike #40
1996 Viper First Strike #42
1996 Viper Green Mamba #2
1996 Viper Green Mamba #40
1996 Viper Green Mamba #42
1996 Viper King Cobra /699 #KC2
1996 Viper King Cobra First Strike #KC2
1996 Viper Promos #P3
1996 Viper Red Cobra /1799 #2
1996 Viper Red Cobra /1799 #40
1996 Viper Red Cobra /1799 #42
1996 Zenith #2
1996 Zenith #36
1996 Zenith #51
1996 Zenith #73
1996 Zenith #74
1996 Zenith #75
1996 Zenith #76
1996 Zenith #77
1996 Zenith #78
1996 Zenith #79
1996 Zenith #80
1996 Zenith #91
1996 Zenith #92
1996 Zenith #98
1996 Zenith #99
1996 Zenith Artist Proofs #2
1996 Zenith Artist Proofs #36
1996 Zenith Artist Proofs #51
1996 Zenith Artist Proofs #73
1996 Zenith Artist Proofs #74
1996 Zenith Artist Proofs #75
1996 Zenith Artist Proofs #76
1996 Zenith Artist Proofs #77
1996 Zenith Artist Proofs #78
1996 Zenith Artist Proofs #79
1996 Zenith Artist Proofs #80
1996 Zenith Artist Proofs #91
1996 Zenith Artist Proofs #92
1996 Zenith Artist Proofs #98
1996 Zenith Artist Proofs #99
1996 Zenith Champion Salute #1
1996 Zenith Highlights #2
1997 Action Packed #8
1997 Action Packed #29
1997 Action Packed #P8
1997 Action Packed 24K Gold #3
1997 Action Packed Chevy Madness #4
1997 Action Packed Fifth Anniversary #8
1997 Action Packed First Impressions #8
1997 Action Packed First Impressions #29
1997 Action Packed Rolling Thunder #3
1997 ActionVision #2
1997 ActionVision #5
1997 ActionVision #6
1997 ActionVision #10
1997 Autographed Racing #4
1997 Autographed Racing Autographs #16
1997 Autographed Racing Mayne Street #KM4
1997 Autographed Racing Take the Checkered Flag /325 #TF1
1997 Collector's Choice #24

1997 Collector's Choice #74
1997 Collector's Choice #101
1997 Collector's Choice #127
1997 Collector's Choice #128
1997 Collector's Choice #129
1997 Collector's Choice #154
1997 Collector's Choice #NNO
1997 Collector's Choice #NNO
1997 Collector's Choice Speedecals #S47
1997 Collector's Choice Speedecals #S48
1997 Collector's Choice Triple Force #F1
1997 Collector's Choice Triple Force #G2
1997 Collector's Choice Triple Force #G3
1997 Collector's Choice Upper Deck 500 #UD48
1997 Collector's Choice Upper Deck 500 #UD49
1997 Collector's Choice Victory Circle #VC9
1997 Finish Line Phone Pak II #1
1997 Finish Line Phone Pak II #39
1997 Finish Line Phone Pak II #80
1997 Finish Line Phone Pak II #87
1997 Finish Line Phone Pak II #95
1997 Finish Line Phone Pak II #P1
1997 Jurassic Park #1
1997 Jurassic Park #48
1997 Jurassic Park #51
1997 Jurassic Park Carnivore #C2
1997 Jurassic Park Pteranodon #P2
1997 Jurassic Park Raptors #R2
1997 Jurassic Park The Ride Jeff Gordon #1
1997 Jurassic Park The Ride Jeff Gordon #2
1997 Jurassic Park The Ride Jeff Gordon #3
1997 Jurassic Park The Ride Jeff Gordon #4
1997 Jurassic Park The Ride Jeff Gordon #5
1997 Jurassic Park Thunder Lizard #TL1
1997 Jurassic Park T-Rex #TR2
1997 Jurassic Park Triceratops #1
1997 Jurassic Park Triceratops #48
1997 Jurassic Park Triceratops #51
1997 Maxx #24
1997 Maxx #69
1997 Maxx Chase the Champion #C1
1997 Maxx Chase the Champion Gold Die Cuts #C1
1997 Maxx Flag Firsts #FF24
1997 Maxx Rookies of the Year #MR6
1997 Pinnacle #24
1997 Pinnacle #53
1997 Pinnacle Artist Proofs #24
1997 Pinnacle Artist Proofs #53
1997 Pinnacle Certified #24
1997 Pinnacle Certified #58
1997 Pinnacle Certified #74
1997 Pinnacle Certified #89
1997 Pinnacle Certified Certified Team #2
1997 Pinnacle Certified Certified Team Gold #2
1997 Pinnacle Certified Epix #E2
1997 Pinnacle Certified Epix Emerald #E2
1997 Pinnacle Certified Epix Purple #E2
1997 Pinnacle Certified Mirror Blue #24
1997 Pinnacle Certified Mirror Blue #58
1997 Pinnacle Certified Mirror Blue #74
1997 Pinnacle Certified Mirror Blue #89
1997 Pinnacle Certified Mirror Gold #24
1997 Pinnacle Certified Mirror Gold #58
1997 Pinnacle Certified Mirror Gold #74
1997 Pinnacle Certified Mirror Gold #89
1997 Pinnacle Certified Mirror Red #24
1997 Pinnacle Certified Mirror Red #58
1997 Pinnacle Certified Mirror Red #74
1997 Pinnacle Certified Mirror Red #89
1997 Pinnacle Certified Red #24
1997 Pinnacle Certified Red #58
1997 Pinnacle Certified Red #74
1997 Pinnacle Certified Red #89
1997 Pinnacle Chevy Madness #15
1997 Pinnacle Collectibles Club #RC4
1997 Pinnacle Mint #2
1997 Pinnacle Mint #24
1997 Pinnacle Mint Bronze #2
1997 Pinnacle Mint Bronze #24
1997 Pinnacle Mint Coins #2
1997 Pinnacle Mint Coins #24
1997 Pinnacle Mint Coins 24K Gold Plated #2
1997 Pinnacle Mint Coins 24K Gold Plated #24
1997 Pinnacle Mint Coins Nickel-Silver #2
1997 Pinnacle Mint Coins Nickel-Silver #24
1997 Pinnacle Mint Gold #2
1997 Pinnacle Mint Gold #24
1997 Pinnacle Mint Silver #2
1997 Pinnacle Mint Silver #24
1997 Pinnacle Pepsi Jeff Gordon #1
1997 Pinnacle Pepsi Jeff Gordon #2
1997 Pinnacle Pepsi Jeff Gordon #3
1997 Pinnacle Portraits #1
1997 Pinnacle Portraits #21
1997 Pinnacle Portraits 8x10 #JG1
1997 Pinnacle Portraits 8x10 #JG2
1997 Pinnacle Portraits 8x10 #JG3
1997 Pinnacle Portraits 8x10 #JG4
1997 Pinnacle Portraits 8x10 Dufex #JG1
1997 Pinnacle Portraits 8x10 Dufex #JG2
1997 Pinnacle Portraits 8x10 Dufex #JG3
1997 Pinnacle Portraits 8x10 Dufex #JG4
1997 Pinnacle Precision #3
1997 Pinnacle Precision #4
1997 Pinnacle Precision #5
1997 Pinnacle Precision #6
1997 Pinnacle Precision #8
1997 Pinnacle Precision #9
1997 Pinnacle Precision Bronze #3
1997 Pinnacle Precision Bronze #4
1997 Pinnacle Precision Bronze #5
1997 Pinnacle Precision Bronze #6
1997 Pinnacle Precision Bronze #8
1997 Pinnacle Precision Bronze #9
1997 Pinnacle Precision Gold #3
1997 Pinnacle Precision Gold #4
1997 Pinnacle Precision Gold #5
1997 Pinnacle Precision Gold #6
1997 Pinnacle Precision Gold #8
1997 Pinnacle Precision Gold #9
1997 Pinnacle Precision Silver #3
1997 Pinnacle Precision Silver #4
1997 Pinnacle Precision Silver #5
1997 Pinnacle Precision Silver #6
1997 Pinnacle Precision Silver #8
1997 Pinnacle Precision Silver #9
1997 Pinnacle Press Plates #24
1997 Pinnacle Press Plates #53
1997 Pinnacle Press Plates #S6R
1997 Pinnacle Press Plates #CM15
1997 Pinnacle Press Plates #TP1A
1997 Pinnacle Spellbound #6R
1997 Pinnacle Spellbound Autographs #6R
1997 Pinnacle Spellbound Autographs #6RAU
1997 Pinnacle Spellbound Promos #6R
1997 Pinnacle Team Pinnacle #1
1997 Pinnacle Team Pinnacle Red #1
1997 Pinnacle Totally Certified Platinum Blue #24
1997 Pinnacle Totally Certified Platinum Blue #58
1997 Pinnacle Totally Certified Platinum Blue #74
1997 Pinnacle Totally Certified Platinum Blue #89
1997 Pinnacle Totally Certified Platinum Gold #24
1997 Pinnacle Totally Certified Platinum Gold #58
1997 Pinnacle Totally Certified Platinum Gold #74
1997 Pinnacle Totally Certified Platinum Gold #89
1997 Pinnacle Totally Certified Platinum Red #24
1997 Pinnacle Totally Certified Platinum Red #58
1997 Pinnacle Totally Certified Platinum Red #74
1997 Pinnacle Totally Certified Platinum Red #89
1997 Pinnacle Trophy Collection #24
1997 Pinnacle Trophy Collection #53
1997 Predator #1
1997 Predator #44
1997 Predator American Eagle #AE2
1997 Predator American Eagle First Slash #AE2
1997 Predator Black Wolf #1
1997 Predator Black Wolf #44
1997 Predator Black Wolf First Slash /3750 #1
1997 Predator Black Wolf First Slash /3750 #44
1997 Predator Eye of the Tiger #ET2
1997 Predator Eye of the Tiger First Slash #ET2
1997 Predator First Slash #1
1997 Predator First Slash #44
1997 Predator Gatorback #GB2
1997 Predator Gatorback Authentic #GBA2
1997 Predator Gatorback Authentic First Slash #GBA2
1997 Predator Gatorback First Slash #GB2
1997 Predator Golden Eagle #GE2
1997 Predator Golden Eagle First Slash #GE2
1997 Predator Grizzly #1
1997 Predator Grizzly #44
1997 Predator Grizzly First Slash #1
1997 Predator Grizzly First Slash #44
1997 Predator Promos #P1
1997 Predator Promos #P1
1997 Predator Promos #P2
1997 Predator Promos #P2
1997 Predator Promos #P3
1997 Predator Promos #P3
1997 Predator Red Wolf #1
1997 Predator Red Wolf #44
1997 Predator Red Wolf First Slash #1
1997 Predator Red Wolf First Slash #44
1997 Press Pass #2
1997 Press Pass #39
1997 Press Pass #57
1997 Press Pass #96
1997 Press Pass #104
1997 Press Pass #105
1997 Press Pass #134
1997 Press Pass #135
1997 Press Pass #136
1997 Press Pass #137
1997 Press Pass #138
1997 Press Pass #SB1
1997 Press Pass Autographs #2
1997 Press Pass Banquet Bound #BB2
1997 Press Pass Burning Rubber /400 #BR5
1997 Press Pass Clear Cut #C2
1997 Press Pass Cup Chase #CC7
1997 Press Pass Cup Chase Gold Die Cuts #CC7
1997 Press Pass Lasers Silver #2
1997 Press Pass Lasers Silver #39
1997 Press Pass Lasers Silver #57
1997 Press Pass Lasers Silver #96
1997 Press Pass Lasers Silver #104
1997 Press Pass Lasers Silver #105
1997 Press Pass Lasers Silver #134
1997 Press Pass Lasers Silver #135
1997 Press Pass Lasers Silver #136
1997 Press Pass Lasers Silver #137
1997 Press Pass Lasers Silver #138
1997 Press Pass Oil Slicks /100 #2
1997 Press Pass Oil Slicks /100 #39
1997 Press Pass Oil Slicks /100 #57
1997 Press Pass Oil Slicks /100 #96
1997 Press Pass Oil Slicks /100 #104
1997 Press Pass Oil Slicks /100 #105
1997 Press Pass Oil Slicks /100 #134
1997 Press Pass Oil Slicks /100 #135
1997 Press Pass Oil Slicks /100 #136
1997 Press Pass Oil Slicks /100 #137
1997 Press Pass Oil Slicks /100 #138
1997 Press Pass Premium #2
1997 Press Pass Premium #33
1997 Press Pass Premium #38
1997 Press Pass Premium #P1
1997 Press Pass Premium Crystal Ball #CB4
1997 Press Pass Premium Crystal Ball Die Cut #CB4
1997 Press Pass Premium Double Burners /350 #DB2
1997 Press Pass Premium Emerald Proofs /380 #2
1997 Press Pass Premium Emerald Proofs /380 #33
1997 Press Pass Premium Emerald Proofs /380 #38
1997 Press Pass Premium Lap Leaders #LL3
1997 Press Pass Premium Mirrors #2
1997 Press Pass Premium Mirrors #33
1997 Press Pass Premium Mirrors #38
1997 Press Pass Premium Oil Slicks /100 #2
1997 Press Pass Premium Oil Slicks /100 #27
1997 Press Pass Premium Oil Slicks /100 #33
1997 Press Pass Premium Oil Slicks /100 #38
1997 Press Pass Torquers Blue #2
1997 Press Pass Torquers Blue #39
1997 Press Pass Torquers Blue #57
1997 Press Pass Torquers Blue #96
1997 Press Pass Torquers Blue #104
1997 Press Pass Torquers Blue #105
1997 Press Pass Torquers Blue #134
1997 Press Pass Torquers Blue #135
1997 Press Pass Torquers Blue #136
1997 Press Pass Torquers Blue #137
1997 Press Pass Torquers Blue #138
1997 Press Pass Victory Lane #VL2A
1997 Press Pass Victory Lane #VL2B
1997 Race Sharks #2
1997 Race Sharks #35
1997 Race Sharks #36
1997 Race Sharks #40
1997 Race Sharks #43
1997 Race Sharks #P1
1997 Race Sharks First Bite #2
1997 Race Sharks First Bite #35
1997 Race Sharks First Bite #36
1997 Race Sharks First Bite #40
1997 Race Sharks First Bite #43
1997 Race Sharks Great White #2
1997 Race Sharks Great White #35
1997 Race Sharks Great White #36
1997 Race Sharks Great White #40
1997 Race Sharks Great White #43
1997 Race Sharks Great White Shark's Teeth #GW2
1997 Race Sharks Great White Shark's Teeth First Bite #GW2
1997 Race Sharks Hammerhead #2
1997 Race Sharks Hammerhead #35
1997 Race Sharks Hammerhead #36
1997 Race Sharks Hammerhead #40
1997 Race Sharks Hammerhead #43
1997 Race Sharks Hammerhead First Bite #2
1997 Race Sharks Hammerhead First Bite #35
1997 Race Sharks Hammerhead First Bite #36
1997 Race Sharks Hammerhead First Bite #40
1997 Race Sharks Hammerhead First Bite #43
1997 Race Sharks Shark Attack #SA2
1997 Race Sharks Shark Attack First Bite #SA2
1997 Race Sharks Shark Attack First Bite Previews #2
1997 Race Sharks Shark Tooth Signatures /400 #ST2
1997 Race Sharks Shark Tooth Signatures First Bite /400 #ST2
1997 Race Sharks Tiger Shark #2
1997 Race Sharks Tiger Shark #35
1997 Race Sharks Tiger Shark #36
1997 Race Sharks Tiger Shark #40
1997 Race Sharks Tiger Shark #43
1997 Race Sharks Tiger Shark First Bite #2
1997 Race Sharks Tiger Shark First Bite #35
1997 Race Sharks Tiger Shark First Bite #36
1997 Race Sharks Tiger Shark First Bite #40
1997 Race Sharks Tiger Shark First Bite #43
1997 Racer's Choice #24
1997 Racer's Choice Busch Clash #8
1997 Racer's Choice Chevy Madness #7
1997 Racer's Choice High Octane #3
1997 Racer's Choice High Octane Glow in the Dark #3
1997 Racer's Choice Showcase Series #24
1997 SB Motorsports #2
1997 SB Motorsports #63
1997 SB Motorsports Autographs /250 #2
1997 Score Board IQ #2
1997 Score Board IQ #26
1997 Score Board IQ #37
1997 Score Board IQ #45
1997 Score Board IQ #50
1997 Score Board IQ Jeff Gordon #1
1997 Score Board IQ Jeff Gordon #2
1997 Score Board IQ Jeff Gordon #3
1997 Score Board IQ Jeff Gordon #4
1997 Score Board IQ Jeff Gordon #5
1997 Score Board IQ Remarques #SB2
1997 Score Board IQ Remarques Sam Bass Finished #SB2
1997 SkyBox Profile #7
1997 SkyBox Profile #70
1997 SkyBox Profile #D1
1997 SkyBox Profile #P1
1997 SkyBox Profile Autographs /200 #7
1997 SkyBox Profile Break Out #B1
1997 SkyBox Profile Pace Setters #E5
1997 SkyBox Profile Team #T2
1997 SP #24
1997 SP #66
1997 SP #102
1997 SP #122
1997 SP #S24
1997 SP Race Film #RD1
1997 SP SPx Force Autographs #SF1
1997 SP Super Series #24
1997 SP Super Series #66
1997 SP Super Series #102
1997 SP Super Series #122
1997 Sports Illustrated for Kids II #602
1997 SportsCom FanScan #3
1997 SPx #24
1997 SPx Blue #24
1997 SPx Gold #24
1997 SPx Silver #24
1997 SPx SpeedView Autographs #SV1
1997 SPx Tag Team #TT1
1997 SPx Tag Team #TT4
1997 SPx Tag Team Autographs #TA4
1997 SPx Tag Team Autographs #TA1
1997 UDA Jeff Gordon Commemorative Cards #NNO
1997 UDA Jeff Gordon Commemorative Cards #NNO
1997 UDA Jeff Gordon Commemorative Cards /2400 #NNO
1997 UDA Jeff Gordon Commemorative Cards /2373 #NNO
1997 UDA Jeff Gordon Commemorative Cards /2500 #NNO
1997 Ultra #12
1997 Ultra #41
1997 Ultra AKA #A2
1997 Ultra Inside Out #DC2
1997 Ultra Shoney's #4
1997 Ultra Update #1
1997 Ultra Update #86
1997 Ultra Update Autographs #1
1997 Ultra Update Driver View #D1
1997 Ultra Update Elite Seats #E1
1997 Ultra Winn Dixie #WD4
1997 Upper Deck Road To The Cup #2
1997 Upper Deck Road To The Cup #45
1997 Upper Deck Road To The Cup #87
1997 Upper Deck Road To The Cup #107
1997 Upper Deck Road To The Cup Cup Quest #CQ2
1997 Upper Deck Road To The Cup Cup Quest Checkered #CQ2
1997 Upper Deck Road To The Cup Cup Quest White #CQ2
1997 Upper Deck Road To The Cup Million Dollar Memoirs #MM5
1997 Upper Deck Road To The Cup Million Dollar Memoirs #MM6
1997 Upper Deck Road To The Cup Million Dollar Memoirs #MM7
1997 Upper Deck Road To The Cup Million Dollar Memoirs #MM8
1997 Upper Deck Road To The Cup Million Dollar Memoirs Autographs #MM5
1997 Upper Deck Road To The Cup Million Dollar Memoirs Autographs #MM6
1997 Upper Deck Road To The Cup Million Dollar Memoirs Autographs #MM7
1997 Upper Deck Road To The Cup Million Dollar Memoirs Autographs #MM8
1997 Upper Deck Road To The Cup Piece of the Action #HS6
1997 Upper Deck Road To The Cup Piece of the Action #HS5
1997 Upper Deck Road To The Cup Piece of the Action #HS4
1997 Upper Deck Road To The Cup Predictor Plus #2
1997 Upper Deck Road To The Cup Predictor Plus #11
1997 Upper Deck Road To The Cup Predictor Plus #28
1997 Upper Deck Road To The Cup Predictor Plus Cel Die Cuts #2
1997 Upper Deck Road To The Cup Predictor Plus Cel Die Cuts #11
1997 Upper Deck Road To The Cup Predictor Plus Cel Die Cuts #28
1997 Upper Deck Road To The Cup Predictor Plus Cels #2
1997 Upper Deck Road To The Cup Predictor Plus Cels #11
1997 Upper Deck Road To The Cup Predictor Plus Cels #28
1997 Upper Deck Road To The Cup Premiere Position #PP2
1997 Upper Deck Road To The Cup Premiere Position #PP11
1997 Upper Deck Road To The Cup Premiere Position #PP12
1997 Upper Deck Road To The Cup Premiere Position #PP20
1997 Upper Deck Road To The Cup Premiere Position #PP21
1997 Upper Deck Road To The Cup Premiere Position #PP28
1997 Upper Deck Road To The Cup Premiere Position #PP32
1997 Upper Deck Road To The Cup Premiere Position #PP42
1997 Upper Deck Victory Circle #24
1997 Upper Deck Victory Circle #74
1997 Upper Deck Victory Circle #111
1997 Upper Deck Victory Circle Championship Reflections #CR2
1997 Upper Deck Victory Circle Driver's Seat #DS2
1997 Upper Deck Victory Circle Generation Excitement #GE1
1997 Upper Deck Victory Circle Piece of the Action #FS1
1997 Upper Deck Victory Circle Piece of the Action #FS2
1997 Upper Deck Victory Circle Piece of the Action #FS3
1997 Upper Deck Victory Circle Predictor #PE1
1997 Upper Deck Victory Circle Predictor Winner Cels #PH1
1997 Upper Deck Victory Circle Victory Lap #VL2
1997 VIP #8
1997 VIP Explosives #8
1997 VIP Head Gear #HG3
1997 VIP Head Gear Die Cuts #HG3
1997 VIP Knights of Thunder #KT2
1997 VIP Knights of Thunder Gold #KT2
1997 VIP Oil Slicks #8
1997 VIP Precious Metal #SM1
1997 VIP Ring of Honor #RH8
1997 VIP Ring of Honor Die Cuts #RH8
1997 Viper #1
1997 Viper #51
1997 Viper #74
1997 Viper #P2
1997 Viper Anaconda Jumbos #A2
1997 Viper Black Racer #1
1997 Viper Black Racer #51
1997 Viper Black Racer #74
1997 Viper Black Racer First Strike #1
1997 Viper Black Racer First Strike #51
1997 Viper Black Racer First Strike #74
1997 Viper Cobra #C2
1997 Viper Cobra First Strike #C2
1997 Viper Diamondback #DB1
1997 Viper Diamondback Authentic #DBA1
1997 Viper Diamondback Authentic Eastern #DBA1
1997 Viper Diamondback Authentic Eastern First Strike #DBA1
1997 Viper Diamondback Authentic First Strike #DBA1
1997 Viper Diamondback First Strike #DB1
1997 Viper First Strike #1
1997 Viper First Strike #51
1997 Viper First Strike #74
1997 Viper King Cobra #KC2
1997 Viper Sidewinder #S2
1997 Viper Sidewinder First Strike #S2
1997 Viper Snake Eyes #SE2
1997 Viper Snake Eyes First Strike #SE2
1998 Big League Cards Creative Images #30
1998 Collector's Choice #24
1998 Collector's Choice #60
1998 Collector's Choice #88
1998 Collector's Choice #98
1998 Collector's Choice Star Quest #SQ36
1998 Collector's Choice Star Quest #SQ41
1998 Maxx #24
1998 Maxx #54
1998 Maxx #64
1998 Maxx #91
1998 Maxx 10th Anniversary #24
1998 Maxx 10th Anniversary #69
1998 Maxx 10th Anniversary #124
1998 Maxx 10th Anniversary #125
1998 Maxx 10th Anniversary #126
1998 Maxx 10th Anniversary Buy Back Autographs #21
1998 Maxx 10th Anniversary Buy Back Autographs /10 #22
1998 Maxx 10th Anniversary Buy Back Autographs /10 #23
1998 Maxx 10th Anniversary Buy Back Autographs /10 #24
1998 Maxx 10th Anniversary Buy Back Autographs #25
1998 Maxx 10th Anniversary Card of the Year #CY5
1998 Maxx 10th Anniversary Card of the Year #CY10
1998 Maxx 10th Anniversary Champions Past #CP1
1998 Maxx 10th Anniversary Champions Past Die Cuts /1000 #CP1
1998 Maxx 10th Anniversary Maxximum Preview #P24
1998 Maxx 1997 Year In Review #1
1998 Maxx 1997 Year In Review #5
1998 Maxx 1997 Year In Review #6
1998 Maxx 1997 Year In Review #29
1998 Maxx 1997 Year In Review #31
1998 Maxx 1997 Year In Review #36
1998 Maxx 1997 Year In Review #51
1998 Maxx 1997 Year In Review #52
1998 Maxx 1997 Year In Review #61
1998 Maxx 1997 Year In Review #71
1998 Maxx 1997 Year In Review #96
1998 Maxx 1997 Year In Review #111
1998 Maxx 1997 Year In Review #121
1998 Maxx 1997 Year In Review #130
1998 Maxx 1997 Year In Review #AW1
1998 Maxx 1997 Year In Review #P01
1998 Maxx Focus on a Champion #FC1
1998 Maxx Focus on a Champion Cel #FC1
1998 Maxx Signed, Sealed, and Delivered /250 #S3
1998 Maxx Teamwork #TW1
1998 Maxximum #24
1998 Maxximum #49
1998 Maxximum #74
1998 Maxximum #99
1998 Maxximum #S24
1998 Maxximum Battle Proven #B5
1998 Maxximum Field Generals Four Star Autographs /1 #3
1998 Maxximum Field Generals One Star /2000 #3
1998 Maxximum Field Generals Three Star Autographs /100 #3
1998 Maxximum Field Generals Two Star /1000 #3
1998 Maxximum First Class #F1
1998 Pinnacle Mint #1
1998 Pinnacle Mint #13
1998 Pinnacle Mint #27
1998 Pinnacle Mint Championship Mint #1
1998 Pinnacle Mint Championship Mint #2
1998 Pinnacle Mint Championship Mint Coins #1A
1998 Pinnacle Mint Championship Mint Coins #1B
1998 Pinnacle Mint Championship Mint Coins #2A
1998 Pinnacle Mint Championship Mint Coins #2B
1998 Pinnacle Mint Coins #1
1998 Pinnacle Mint Coins #13
1998 Pinnacle Mint Coins #3
1998 Pinnacle Mint Coins Bronze Proof #1
1998 Pinnacle Mint Coins Bronze Proof #13
1998 Pinnacle Mint Coins Bronze Proof #3
1998 Pinnacle Mint Coins Gold Plated #1
1998 Pinnacle Mint Coins Gold Plated #13
1998 Pinnacle Mint Coins Gold Plated #27
1998 Pinnacle Mint Coins Gold Plated Proofs #1
1998 Pinnacle Mint Coins Gold Plated Proofs #13
1998 Pinnacle Mint Coins Gold Plated Proofs #27
1998 Pinnacle Mint Coins Nickel-Silver #1
1998 Pinnacle Mint Coins Nickel-Silver #13
1998 Pinnacle Mint Coins Nickel-Silver #27
1998 Pinnacle Mint Coins Silver Plated Proofs #1
1998 Pinnacle Mint Coins Silver Plated Proofs #13
1998 Pinnacle Mint Coins Silver Plated Proofs #27
1998 Pinnacle Mint Coins Solid Gold #1
1998 Pinnacle Mint Coins Solid Gold #13
1998 Pinnacle Mint Coins Solid Gold #27
1998 Pinnacle Mint Coins Solid Silver #1
1998 Pinnacle Mint Coins Solid Silver #13
1998 Pinnacle Mint Coins Solid Silver #27
1998 Pinnacle Mint Die Cuts #1
1998 Pinnacle Mint Die Cuts #13
1998 Pinnacle Mint Die Cuts #27
1998 Pinnacle Mint Gold Team #1
1998 Pinnacle Mint Gold Team #13
1998 Pinnacle Mint Gold Team #27
1998 Pinnacle Mint Silver Team #1
1998 Pinnacle Mint Silver Team #13
1998 Pinnacle Mint Silver Team #27
1998 Press Pass #1
1998 Press Pass #34
1998 Press Pass #101
1998 Press Pass #P1
1998 Press Pass #0
1998 Press Pass Autographs /60 #2
1998 Press Pass Cup Chase #CC7
1998 Press Pass Cup Chase Die Cut Prizes #CC7
1998 Press Pass Oil Cans #OC3
1998 Press Pass Oil Slicks /100 #1
1998 Press Pass Oil Slicks /100 #34
1998 Press Pass Pit Stop #PS12
1998 Press Pass Premium #21
1998 Press Pass Premium #28
1998 Press Pass Premium #P1
1998 Press Pass Premium Flag Chasers #FC1
1998 Press Pass Premium Flag Chasers #FC24
1998 Press Pass Premium Flag Chasers Reflectors #FC1
1998 Press Pass Premium Flag Chasers Reflectors #FC24
1998 Press Pass Premium Reflectors #21
1998 Press Pass Premium Reflectors #28
1998 Press Pass Premium Rivalries #1B
1998 Press Pass Premium Rivalries #6A
1998 Press Pass Premium Steel Horses #SH7
1998 Press Pass Premium Triple Gear Firesuit /150 #TGF6
1998 Press Pass Shockers #ST2A
1998 Press Pass Signings /400 #1
1998 Press Pass Signings Gold /100 #1
1998 Press Pass Stealth #10
1998 Press Pass Stealth #11
1998 Press Pass Stealth #47
1998 Press Pass Stealth #P1
1998 Press Pass Stealth #0
1998 Press Pass Stealth #0
1998 Press Pass Stealth #0
1998 Press Pass Stealth Awards #5
1998 Press Pass Stealth Awards #7
1998 Press Pass Stealth Fan Talk #3
1998 Press Pass Stealth Fan Talk Die Cuts #3
1998 Press Pass Stealth Fusion #10
1998 Press Pass Stealth Fusion #11
1998 Press Pass Stealth Fusion #47
1998 Press Pass Stealth Octane #13
1998 Press Pass Stealth Octane #14
1998 Press Pass Stealth Octane Die Cuts #13
1998 Press Pass Stealth Octane Die Cuts #14
1998 Press Pass Stealth Race Used Gloves /205 #G6
1998 Press Pass Stealth Stars #5
1998 Press Pass Stealth Stars Die Cuts #5
1998 Press Pass Torpedoes #ST2B
1998 Press Pass Triple Gear 3 in 1 /33 #STG6
1998 Press Pass Triple Gear Burning Rubber /250 #TG6
1998 SP Authentic #24
1998 SP Authentic #58
1998 SP Authentic #72
1998 SP Authentic Behind the Wheel #BW1
1998 SP Authentic Behind the Wheel Die Cuts #BW1
1998 SP Authentic Behind the Wheel Gold #BW1
1998 SP Authentic Sign of the Times Red /45 #ST1
1998 SP Authentic Traditions #T2
1998 Sports Illustrated for Kids II #735
1998 SportsCom FanScan #2
1998 Upper Deck Diamond Vision #1
1998 Upper Deck Diamond Vision #RT1
1998 Upper Deck Diamond Vision Signature Moves #RT1
1998 Upper Deck Diamond Vision Signature Moves #1
1998 Upper Deck Diamond Vision Vision of a Champion #VC3
1998 Upper Deck Pop Weaver #PW1
1998 Upper Deck Road To The Cup #24
1998 Upper Deck Road To The Cup #66
1998 Upper Deck Road To The Cup #88
1998 Upper Deck Road To The Cup 50th Anniversary #AN43
1998 Upper Deck Road To The Cup 50th Anniversary #AN47
1998 Upper Deck Road To The Cup 50th Anniversary Autographs /50 #AN47
1998 Upper Deck Road To The Cup Cover Story #CS8
1998 Upper Deck Road To The Cup Cover Story #CS13
1998 Upper Deck Road To The Cup Cover Story #CS15
1998 Upper Deck Road To The Cup Cover Story #CS16
1998 Upper Deck Road To The Cup Cup Quest Turn 1 #CQ1
1998 Upper Deck Road To The Cup Cup Quest Turn 2 #CQ1
1998 Upper Deck Road To The Cup Cup Quest Turn 3 #CQ1
1998 Upper Deck Road To The Cup Cup Quest Turn 4 #CQ1
1998 Upper Deck Road To The Cup Cup Quest Victory Lane #CQ1
1998 Upper Deck Victory Circle #24
1998 Upper Deck Victory Circle #69
1998 Upper Deck Victory Circle #92
1998 Upper Deck Victory Circle #93
1998 Upper Deck Victory Circle #100
1998 Upper Deck Victory Circle #105
1998 Upper Deck Victory Circle #119
1998 Upper Deck Victory Circle #120
1998 Upper Deck Victory Circle 32 Days of Speed #D2
1998 Upper Deck Victory Circle 32 Days of Speed #D11
1998 Upper Deck Victory Circle 32 Days of Speed #D32
1998 Upper Deck Victory Circle 32 Days of Speed Gold #D2
1998 Upper Deck Victory Circle 32 Days of Speed Gold #D11
1998 Upper Deck Victory Circle 32 Days of Speed Gold #D32
1998 Upper Deck Victory Circle Autographs #AG1
1998 Upper Deck Victory Circle Point Leaders #PL1
1998 Upper Deck Victory Circle Sparks of Brilliance #SB1
1998 VIP #8
1998 VIP #40
1998 VIP Driving Force #DF7
1998 VIP Driving Force Die Cuts #DF7
1998 VIP Explosives #8
1998 VIP Explosives #40
1998 VIP Head Gear #HG4
1998 VIP Head Gear Die Cuts #HG4
1998 VIP Lap Leaders #LL3
1998 VIP Lap Leaders Acetate #LL3
1998 VIP NASCAR Country #NC3
1998 VIP NASCAR Country Die Cuts #NC3
1998 VIP Solos #8
1998 VIP Solos #40
1998 VIP Triple Gear Sheet Metal /225 #TGS6
1998 Wheels #11
1998 Wheels #36
1998 Wheels #85
1998 Wheels 50th Anniversary #A5
1998 Wheels 50th Anniversary #A20
1998 Wheels Autographs /200 #2
1998 Wheels Custom Shop #CSJG
1998 Wheels Custom Shop Prizes #JGA1
1998 Wheels Custom Shop Prizes #JGA2
1998 Wheels Custom Shop Prizes #JGA3
1998 Wheels Custom Shop Prizes #JGB1
1998 Wheels Custom Shop Prizes #JGB2
1998 Wheels Custom Shop Prizes #JGB3
1998 Wheels Custom Shop Prizes #JGC1
1998 Wheels Custom Shop Prizes #JGC2
1998 Wheels Custom Shop Prizes #JGC3
1998 Wheels Double Take #E4
1998 Wheels Golden #11
1998 Wheels Golden #36
1998 Wheels Golden #85
1998 Wheels Green Flags #GF6
1998 Wheels High Gear #1
1998 Wheels High Gear #33
1998 Wheels High Gear #50
1998 Wheels High Gear #69
1998 Wheels High Gear Autographs /50 #8
1998 Wheels High Gear Custom Shop #CS2
1998 Wheels High Gear Custom Shop Prizes #JGA1
1998 Wheels High Gear Custom Shop Prizes #JGA2
1998 Wheels High Gear Custom Shop Prizes #JGA3
1998 Wheels High Gear Custom Shop Prizes #JGB1
1998 Wheels High Gear Custom Shop Prizes #JGB2
1998 Wheels High Gear Custom Shop Prizes #JGB3
1998 Wheels High Gear Custom Shop Prizes #JGC1
1998 Wheels High Gear Custom Shop Prizes #JGC2
1998 Wheels High Gear Custom Shop Prizes #JGC3
1998 Wheels High Gear First Gear #1
1998 Wheels High Gear First Gear #33
1998 Wheels High Gear First Gear #50
1998 Wheels High Gear First Gear #69
1998 Wheels High Gear Gear Jammers #GJ12
1998 Wheels High Gear High Groove #HG5
1998 Wheels High Gear Man and Machine Cars #1
1998 Wheels High Gear Man and Machine Drivers #MM1
1998 Wheels High Gear MPH /100 #1
1998 Wheels High Gear MPH /100 #33
1998 Wheels High Gear MPH /100 #50
1998 Wheels High Gear MPH /100 #69
1998 Wheels High Gear Pure Gold #PG3
1998 Wheels High Gear Top Tier #TT1
1998 Wheels Jackpot #J3
1999 Maxx #1
1999 Maxx #2
1999 Maxx #3
1999 Maxx #90
1999 Maxx FANtastic Finishes #F1
1999 Maxx Focus on a Champion #FC1
1999 Maxx Focus on a Champion Gold #FC1
1999 Maxx Race Ticket #RT22
1999 Maxx Racer's Ink /250 #JG
1999 Maxx Racing Images #RI24
1999 Press Pass #1
1999 Press Pass #28
1999 Press Pass #79
1999 Press Pass #99
1999 Press Pass #101
1999 Press Pass #P1
1999 Press Pass /800 #0
1999 Press Pass Autographs /75 #7
1999 Press Pass Burning Rubber /250 #BR7
1999 Press Pass Chase Cars #11B
1999 Press Pass Cup Chase #6
1999 Press Pass Cup Chase Die Cut Prizes #6
1999 Press Pass Cup Chase Die Cut Prizes #20
1999 Press Pass Jeff Gordon Fan Club #JG
1999 Press Pass Oil Cans #6
1999 Press Pass Pit Stop #12
1999 Press Pass Premium #8
1999 Press Pass Premium #28
1999 Press Pass Premium #43
1999 Press Pass Premium #0
1999 Press Pass Premium Badge of Honor #BH10
1999 Press Pass Premium Badge of Honor #BH24
1999 Press Pass Premium Badge of Honor Reflectors #BH10
1999 Press Pass Premium Badge of Honor Reflectors #BH24
1999 Press Pass Premium Burning Desire #FD1B
1999 Press Pass Premium Extreme Fire #FD1A
1999 Press Pass Premium Race Used Firesuit /250 #F1
1999 Press Pass Premium Reflectors /1975 #R8
1999 Press Pass Premium Reflectors /1975 #R28
1999 Press Pass Premium Reflectors /1975 #R43
1999 Press Pass Premium Steel Horses #SH9
1999 Press Pass Showman #11A
1999 Press Pass Signings /400 #19
1999 Press Pass Signings Gold /100 #5
1999 Press Pass Skidmarks /250 #1
1999 Press Pass Skidmarks /250 #28
1999 Press Pass Skidmarks /250 #79
1999 Press Pass Skidmarks /250 #99
1999 Press Pass Stealth #10
1999 Press Pass Stealth #11
1999 Press Pass Stealth #40
1999 Press Pass Stealth #50
1999 Press Pass Stealth Big Numbers #BN7
1999 Press Pass Stealth Big Numbers #BN8
1999 Press Pass Stealth Big Numbers Die Cuts #BN7
1999 Press Pass Stealth Big Numbers Die Cuts #BN8
1999 Press Pass Stealth Fusion #F10
1999 Press Pass Stealth Fusion #F11
1999 Press Pass Stealth Fusion #F40
1999 Press Pass Stealth Fusion #F50
1999 Press Pass Stealth Headlines #SH1
1999 Press Pass Stealth Octane SLX #O6
1999 Press Pass Stealth Octane SLX #O7
1999 Press Pass Stealth Octane SLX #O26
1999 Press Pass Stealth Octane SLX #O34
1999 Press Pass Stealth Octane SLX Die Cuts #O6
1999 Press Pass Stealth Octane SLX Die Cuts #O7
1999 Press Pass Stealth Octane SLX Die Cuts #O26
1999 Press Pass Stealth Octane SLX Die Cuts #O34
1999 Press Pass Stealth Race Used Gloves /24 #G2
1999 Press Pass Stealth SST Cars #SS3
1999 Press Pass Stealth SST Drivers #SS3
1999 Press Pass Triple Gear 3 in 1 /33 #TG3
1999 SP Authentic #1
1999 SP Authentic #51
1999 SP Authentic #65
1999 SP Authentic #82
1999 SP Authentic Cup Challengers #CC1
1999 SP Authentic Driving Force #DF8
1999 SP Authentic In the Driver's Seat #DS10
1999 SP Authentic Overdrive #1
1999 SP Authentic Overdrive #51
1999 SP Authentic Overdrive #65
1999 SP Authentic Overdrive /24 #82
1999 SP Authentic Sign of the Times #JG
1999 SportsCom FanScan #2
1999 Upper Deck MVP ProSign #JGH
1999 Upper Deck MVP ProSign #JGR
1999 Upper Deck Road to the Cup #24
1999 Upper Deck Road to the Cup #43
1999 Upper Deck Road to the Cup #61
1999 Upper Deck Road to the Cup #77
1999 Upper Deck Road to the Cup A Day in the Life #JG1
1999 Upper Deck Road to the Cup A Day in the Life #JG2
1999 Upper Deck Road to the Cup A Day in the Life #JG3
1999 Upper Deck Road to the Cup A Day in the Life #JG4
1999 Upper Deck Road to the Cup A Day in the Life #JG5
1999 Upper Deck Road to the Cup A Day in the Life #JG6
1999 Upper Deck Road to the Cup A Day in the Life #JG7
1999 Upper Deck Road to the Cup A Day in the Life #JG8
1999 Upper Deck Road to the Cup A Day in the Life #JG9
1999 Upper Deck Road to the Cup A Day in the Life #JG10
1999 Upper Deck Road to the Cup NASCAR Chronicles #NC2
1999 Upper Deck Road to the Cup Road to the Cup Bronze Level 1 #RTTC1
1999 Upper Deck Road to the Cup Road to the Cup Gold Level 3 #RTTC1
1999 Upper Deck Road to the Cup Road to the Cup Silver Level 2 #RTTC1
1999 Upper Deck Road to the Cup Signature Collection #JG
1999 Upper Deck Road to the Cup Signature Collection Checkered Flag #JG
1999 Upper Deck Road to the Cup Tires of Daytona #T1
1999 Upper Deck Road to the Cup Tires of Daytona Autographed /24 #TS1
1999 Upper Deck Road to the Cup Upper Deck Profiles #P15

1999 Upper Deck Victory Circle #3
1999 Upper Deck Victory Circle #41
1999 Upper Deck Victory Circle #76
1999 Upper Deck Victory Circle #80
1999 Upper Deck Victory Circle #84
1999 Upper Deck Victory Circle Income Statement #IS1
1999 Upper Deck Victory Circle Signature Collection #JG
1999 Upper Deck Victory Circle Speed Zone #SZ3
1999 Upper Deck Victory Circle Track Masters #TM1
1999 Upper Deck Victory Circle UD Exclusives #3
1999 Upper Deck Victory Circle UD Exclusives #41
1999 Upper Deck Victory Circle UD Exclusives #76
1999 Upper Deck Victory Circle UD Exclusives #80
1999 Upper Deck Victory Circle UD Exclusives #84
1999 Upper Deck Victory Circle Victory Circle #V8
1999 VIP #8
1999 VIP #31
1999 VIP #42
1999 VIP Double Take #DT1
1999 VIP Explosives #X8
1999 VIP Explosives #X31
1999 VIP Explosives #X42
1999 VIP Explosives Lasers #8
1999 VIP Explosives Lasers #31
1999 VIP Explosives Lasers #42
1999 VIP Head Gear #HG1
1999 VIP Head Gear Plastic #HG1
1999 VIP Lap Leaders #LL1
1999 VIP Out of the Box #OB1
1999 VIP Rear View Mirror #RM1
1999 VIP Sheet Metal #SM3
1999 VIP Vintage Performance #4
1999 Wheels #12
1999 Wheels #42
1999 Wheels #60
1999 Wheels #72
1999 Wheels #P2
1999 Wheels Autographs /75 #8
1999 Wheels Circuit Breaker #CB5
1999 Wheels Custom Shop #CS2
1999 Wheels Custom Shop Prizes #JGA1
1999 Wheels Custom Shop Prizes #JGA2
1999 Wheels Custom Shop Prizes #JGA3
1999 Wheels Custom Shop Prizes #JGB1
1999 Wheels Custom Shop Prizes #JGB2
1999 Wheels Custom Shop Prizes #JGB3
1999 Wheels Custom Shop Prizes #JGC1
1999 Wheels Custom Shop Prizes #JGC2
1999 Wheels Custom Shop Prizes #JGC3
1999 Wheels Dialed In #DI1
1999 Wheels Flag Chasers Daytona Seven #DS1
1999 Wheels Flag Chasers Daytona Seven Blue-Yellow #DS1
1999 Wheels Flag Chasers Daytona Seven Checkered #DS1
1999 Wheels Flag Chasers Daytona Seven Green #DS1
1999 Wheels Flag Chasers Daytona Seven Red #DS1
1999 Wheels Flag Chasers Daytona Seven White #DS1
1999 Wheels Flag Chasers Daytona Seven Yellow #DS1
1999 Wheels Golden #12
1999 Wheels Golden #42
1999 Wheels Golden #60
1999 Wheels Golden #72
1999 Wheels High Gear #1
1999 Wheels High Gear #33
1999 Wheels High Gear #46
1999 Wheels High Gear #54
1999 Wheels High Gear #58
1999 Wheels High Gear #69
1999 Wheels High Gear #72
1999 Wheels High Gear #P1
1999 Wheels High Gear Autographs /100 #9
1999 Wheels High Gear Custom Shop #CSJG
1999 Wheels High Gear Custom Shop Prizes #JGA1
1999 Wheels High Gear Custom Shop Prizes #JGA2
1999 Wheels High Gear Custom Shop Prizes #JGA3
1999 Wheels High Gear Custom Shop Prizes #JGB1
1999 Wheels High Gear Custom Shop Prizes #JGB2
1999 Wheels High Gear Custom Shop Prizes #JGB3
1999 Wheels High Gear Custom Shop Prizes #JGC1
1999 Wheels High Gear Custom Shop Prizes #JGC2
1999 Wheels High Gear Custom Shop Prizes #JGC3
1999 Wheels High Gear First Gear #1
1999 Wheels High Gear First Gear #33
1999 Wheels High Gear First Gear #46
1999 Wheels High Gear First Gear #54
1999 Wheels High Gear First Gear #58
1999 Wheels High Gear First Gear #69
1999 Wheels High Gear First Gear #72
1999 Wheels High Gear Flag Chasers #FC1
1999 Wheels High Gear Flag Chasers Blue-Yellow #FC1
1999 Wheels High Gear Flag Chasers Checkered #FC1
1999 Wheels High Gear Flag Chasers Green #FC1
1999 Wheels High Gear Flag Chasers Red #FC1
1999 Wheels High Gear Flag Chasers White #FC1
1999 Wheels High Gear Flag Chasers Yellow #FC1
1999 Wheels High Gear Gear Shifters #GS1
1999 Wheels High Gear Hot Streaks #HS1
1999 Wheels High Gear Man and Machine Cars #MM1B
1999 Wheels High Gear Man and Machine Drivers #MM1A
1999 Wheels High Gear MPH #1
1999 Wheels High Gear MPH #33
1999 Wheels High Gear MPH #46
1999 Wheels High Gear MPH #54
1999 Wheels High Gear MPH #58
1999 Wheels High Gear MPH #69
1999 Wheels High Gear MPH #72
1999 Wheels High Gear Top Tier #TT1
1999 Wheels High Groove #HG3
1999 Wheels High Groove #HG7
1999 Wheels Runnin and Gunnin #RG9
1999 Wheels Runnin and Gunnin #RG29
1999 Wheels Runnin and Gunnin Foils #RG9
1999 Wheels Runnin and Gunnin Foils #RG29
1999 Wheels Solos #12
1999 Wheels Solos #42
1999 Wheels Solos #60
1999 Wheels Solos #72
2000 Maxx #24
2000 Maxx #59
2000 Maxx #77
2000 Maxx Drive Time #DT2
2000 Maxx Fantastic Finishes #FF9
2000 Maxx Focus On A Champion #FC5
2000 Maxx Oval Office #003
2000 Maxx Racer's Ink #JG
2000 Maxx Speedway Boogie #SB1
2000 Maximum #6
2000 Maximum #44
2000 Maximum Cruise Control #CC9
2000 Maximum Dialed In #DI3
2000 Maximum Die Cuts /250 #6
2000 Maximum Die Cuts /250 #44
2000 Maximum MPH /24 #6
2000 Maximum MPH /24 #44
2000 Maximum Roots of Racing #R5
2000 Press Pass #6
2000 Press Pass #37
2000 Press Pass #53
2000 Press Pass #63
2000 Press Pass Burning Rubber /200 #BR5
2000 Press Pass Cup Chase #CC6
2000 Press Pass Cup Chase Die Cut Prizes #CC6
2000 Press Pass Gatorade Front Runner Award #8
2000 Press Pass Millennium #6
2000 Press Pass Millennium #37
2000 Press Pass Millennium #53
2000 Press Pass Millennium #63
2000 Press Pass Oil Cans #OC6
2000 Press Pass Optima #7
2000 Press Pass Optima Cool Persistence #CP2
2000 Press Pass Optima Encore #EN5
2000 Press Pass Optima G Force #GF7
2000 Press Pass Optima On the Edge #OE3
2000 Press Pass Optima Overdrive #OD4
2000 Press Pass Optima Overdrive Square Cut #OD4
2000 Press Pass Optima Platinum #7
2000 Press Pass Optima Race Used Lugnuts Cars /50 #LC17
2000 Press Pass Optima Race Used Lugnuts Drivers /55 #LD17
2000 Press Pass Pitstop #PS12
2000 Press Pass Premium #13
2000 Press Pass Premium #36
2000 Press Pass Premium #47
2000 Press Pass Premium #65
2000 Press Pass Premium In The Zone #IZ4
2000 Press Pass Premium Performance Driven #PD2
2000 Press Pass Premium Race Used Firesuit /130 #F4
2000 Press Pass Premium Reflectors #13
2000 Press Pass Premium Reflectors #36
2000 Press Pass Premium Reflectors #47
2000 Press Pass Premium Reflectors #65
2000 Press Pass Showcar #SC7
2000 Press Pass Showcar Die Cuts #SC7
2000 Press Pass Showman #SM7
2000 Press Pass Showman Die Cuts #SM7
2000 Press Pass Signings #20
2000 Press Pass Signings Gold /100 #12
2000 Press Pass Skidmarks #SK5
2000 Press Pass Stealth #34
2000 Press Pass Stealth #35
2000 Press Pass Stealth #65
2000 Press Pass Stealth Behind the Numbers #BN7
2000 Press Pass Stealth Fusion #FS13
2000 Press Pass Stealth Fusion #FS14
2000 Press Pass Stealth Fusion #FS15
2000 Press Pass Stealth Fusion Green /1000 #FS13
2000 Press Pass Stealth Fusion Green /1000 #FS14
2000 Press Pass Stealth Fusion Green /1000 #FS15
2000 Press Pass Stealth Fusion Red #FS13
2000 Press Pass Stealth Fusion Red #FS14
2000 Press Pass Stealth Fusion Red #FS15
2000 Press Pass Stealth Intensity #IN5
2000 Press Pass Stealth Profile #PR9
2000 Press Pass Stealth Race Used Gloves /100 #G7
2000 Press Pass Stealth SST #SST4
2000 Press Pass Techno-Retro #TR8
2000 Press Pass Trackside #7
2000 Press Pass Trackside #30
2000 Press Pass Trackside Dialed In #DI4
2000 Press Pass Trackside Die Cuts #7
2000 Press Pass Trackside Die Cuts #30
2000 Press Pass Trackside Generation.now #GN6
2000 Press Pass Trackside Golden #7
2000 Press Pass Trackside Golden #30
2000 Press Pass Trackside Panorama #P31
2000 Press Pass Trackside Runnin N' Gunnin #RG6
2000 Press Pass Trackside Too Tough To Tame #TT5
2000 SP Authentic #12
2000 SP Authentic /1000 #87
2000 SP Authentic Driver's Seat #DS6
2000 SP Authentic Overdrive Gold /24 #12
2000 SP Authentic Overdrive Gold /24 #87
2000 SP Authentic Overdrive Silver /250 #12
2000 SP Authentic Overdrive Silver /250 #87
2000 SP Authentic Power Surge #PS2
2000 SP Authentic Race for the Cup #R1
2000 SP Authentic Sign of the Times #JG
2000 SP Authentic Sign of the Times Gold /25 #JG
2000 Upper Deck MVP #24
2000 Upper Deck MVP #65
2000 Upper Deck MVP #102
2000 Upper Deck MVP Cup Quest 2000 #CQ9
2000 Upper Deck MVP Gold Script /125 #24
2000 Upper Deck MVP Gold Script /125 #65
2000 Upper Deck MVP Gold Script /125 #102
2000 Upper Deck MVP Legends in the Making #LM1
2000 Upper Deck MVP NASCAR Gallery #NG9
2000 Upper Deck MVP NASCAR Stars #NS2
2000 Upper Deck MVP ProSign #PSJG
2000 Upper Deck MVP Silver Script #24
2000 Upper Deck MVP Silver Script #65
2000 Upper Deck MVP Silver Script #102
2000 Upper Deck MVP Super Script /24 #24
2000 Upper Deck MVP Super Script /24 #65
2000 Upper Deck MVP Super Script /24 #102
2000 Upper Deck Racing #6
2000 Upper Deck Racing Brickyard's Best #BB6
2000 Upper Deck Racing High Groove #HG6
2000 Upper Deck Racing Record Pace #RP5
2000 Upper Deck Racing Road Signs #RSJG
2000 Upper Deck Racing Speeding Ticket #ST1
2000 Upper Deck Racing Thunder Road #TR5
2000 Upper Deck Racing Trophy Dash #TD7
2000 Upper Deck Racing Winning Formula #WF6
2000 Upper Deck Victory Circle #16
2000 Upper Deck Victory Circle #59
2000 Upper Deck Victory Circle #65
2000 Upper Deck Victory Circle #66
2000 Upper Deck Victory Circle #73
2000 Upper Deck Victory Circle Exclusives Level 1 Silver /250 #16
2000 Upper Deck Victory Circle Exclusives Level 1 Silver /250 #59
2000 Upper Deck Victory Circle Exclusives Level 1 Silver /250 #65
2000 Upper Deck Victory Circle Exclusives Level 1 Silver /250 #66
2000 Upper Deck Victory Circle Exclusives Level 1 Silver /250 #73
2000 Upper Deck Victory Circle Exclusives Level 2 Gold /24 #16
2000 Upper Deck Victory Circle Exclusives Level 2 Gold /24 #59
2000 Upper Deck Victory Circle Exclusives Level 2 Gold /24 #65
2000 Upper Deck Victory Circle Exclusives Level 2 Gold /24 #66
2000 Upper Deck Victory Circle Exclusives Level 2 Gold /24 #73
2000 Upper Deck Victory Circle Income Statement #IS1
2000 Upper Deck Victory Circle Income Statement LTD #IS1
2000 Upper Deck Victory Circle PowerDeck #PD5
2000 Upper Deck Victory Circle Signature Collection #JG
2000 Upper Deck Victory Circle Signature Collection Gold /24 #3
2000 Upper Deck Victory Circle Winning Material Tire #TJG
2000 VIP #12
2000 VIP #26
2000 VIP #29
2000 VIP #32
2000 VIP #34
2000 VIP #45
2000 VIP #49
2000 VIP Explosives #X12
2000 VIP Explosives #X26
2000 VIP Explosives #X29
2000 VIP Explosives #X32
2000 VIP Explosives #X34
2000 VIP Explosives #X45
2000 VIP Explosives #X49
2000 VIP Explosives Lasers #LX12
2000 VIP Explosives Lasers #LX26
2000 VIP Explosives Lasers #LX29
2000 VIP Explosives Lasers #LX32
2000 VIP Explosives Lasers #LX34
2000 VIP Explosives Lasers #LX45
2000 VIP Explosives Lasers #LX49
2000 VIP Head Gear #HG1
2000 VIP Head Gear Explosives #HG1
2000 VIP Head Gear Explosives Laser Die Cuts #HG1
2000 VIP Lap Leaders #LL1
2000 VIP Lap Leaders Explosives #LL1
2000 VIP Lap Leaders Explosives Lasers #LL1
2000 VIP Making the Show #MS7
2000 VIP Sheet Metal #SM9
2000 VIP Under the Lights #UL1
2000 VIP Under the Lights Explosives #UL1
2000 VIP Under the Lights Explosives Lasers #UL1
2000 Wheels High Gear #4
2000 Wheels High Gear #33
2000 Wheels High Gear #41
2000 Wheels High Gear #46
2000 Wheels High Gear #48
2000 Wheels High Gear #59
2000 Wheels High Gear Custom Shop #CSJG
2000 Wheels High Gear Custom Shop Prizes #JGA1
2000 Wheels High Gear Custom Shop Prizes #JGA2
2000 Wheels High Gear Custom Shop Prizes #JGA3
2000 Wheels High Gear Custom Shop Prizes #JGB1
2000 Wheels High Gear Custom Shop Prizes #JGB2
2000 Wheels High Gear Custom Shop Prizes #JGB3
2000 Wheels High Gear Custom Shop Prizes #JGC1
2000 Wheels High Gear Custom Shop Prizes #JGC2
2000 Wheels High Gear Custom Shop Prizes #JGC3
2000 Wheels High Gear First Gear #4
2000 Wheels High Gear First Gear #33
2000 Wheels High Gear First Gear #41
2000 Wheels High Gear First Gear #46
2000 Wheels High Gear First Gear #48
2000 Wheels High Gear First Gear #59
2000 Wheels High Gear Flag Chasers #FC2
2000 Wheels High Gear Flag Chasers Blue-Yellow #FC2
2000 Wheels High Gear Flag Chasers Checkered #FC2
2000 Wheels High Gear Flag Chasers Checkered Blue/Orange #FC2
2000 Wheels High Gear Flag Chasers Green #FC2
2000 Wheels High Gear Flag Chasers Red #FC2
2000 Wheels High Gear Flag Chasers White #FC2
2000 Wheels High Gear Flag Chasers Yellow #FC2
2000 Wheels High Gear Gear Shifters #GS6
2000 Wheels High Gear Man and Machine Cars #MM6B
2000 Wheels High Gear Man and Machine Drivers #MM6A
2000 Wheels High Gear MPH #4
2000 Wheels High Gear MPH #33
2000 Wheels High Gear MPH #41
2000 Wheels High Gear MPH #46
2000 Wheels High Gear MPH #48
2000 Wheels High Gear MPH #59
2000 Wheels High Gear Sunday Sensation #OC6
2000 Wheels High Gear Top Tier #TT4
2000 Wheels High Gear Winning Edge #WE5
2001 Press Pass #9
2001 Press Pass #56
2001 Press Pass #88
2001 Press Pass Autographs #14
2001 Press Pass Burning Rubber Cars /105 #BRC1
2001 Press Pass Burning Rubber Drivers /90 #BRD1
2001 Press Pass Cup Chase #CC4
2001 Press Pass Cup Chase Die Cut Prizes /400 #CCC1
2001 Press Pass Cup Chase Die Cut Prizes #CC4
2001 Press Pass Double Burner /100 #DB1
2001 Press Pass Gatorade Front Runner Award #3
2001 Press Pass Ground Zero #GZ4
2001 Press Pass Hot Treads /1665 #HT11
2001 Press Pass Millennium #9
2001 Press Pass Millennium #56
2001 Press Pass Millennium #88
2001 Press Pass Optima #6
2001 Press Pass Optima #42
2001 Press Pass Optima Cool Persistence #CP4
2001 Press Pass Optima G Force #GF5
2001 Press Pass Optima Gold #6
2001 Press Pass Optima Gold #42
2001 Press Pass Optima On the Edge #OE2
2001 Press Pass Optima Race Used Lugnuts Cars /115 #LNC5
2001 Press Pass Optima Race Used Lugnuts Drivers /100 #LND4
2001 Press Pass Optima Up Close #UC2
2001 Press Pass Premium #6
2001 Press Pass Premium #36
2001 Press Pass Premium #52
2001 Press Pass Premium #73
2001 Press Pass Premium #0
2001 Press Pass Premium Gold #6
2001 Press Pass Premium Gold #36
2001 Press Pass Premium Gold #52
2001 Press Pass Premium Gold #73
2001 Press Pass Premium In The Zone #IZ5
2001 Press Pass Premium Performance Driven #PD4
2001 Press Pass Premium Race Used Firesuit Cars /110 #FC1
2001 Press Pass Premium Race Used Firesuit Drivers /100 #FD1
2001 Press Pass Showman/Showcar #S4A
2001 Press Pass Showman/Showcar #S4B
2001 Press Pass Signings #15
2001 Press Pass Signings Gold /50 #13
2001 Press Pass Stealth #28
2001 Press Pass Stealth #29
2001 Press Pass Stealth #30
2001 Press Pass Stealth #55
2001 Press Pass Stealth #56
2001 Press Pass Stealth #57
2001 Press Pass Stealth #58
2001 Press Pass Stealth #59
2001 Press Pass Stealth #60
2001 Press Pass Stealth #61
2001 Press Pass Stealth #62
2001 Press Pass Stealth #63
2001 Press Pass Stealth #65
2001 Press Pass Stealth Fusion #F2
2001 Press Pass Stealth Holofoils #28
2001 Press Pass Stealth Holofoils #29
2001 Press Pass Stealth Holofoils #30
2001 Press Pass Stealth Holofoils #55
2001 Press Pass Stealth Holofoils #56
2001 Press Pass Stealth Holofoils #57
2001 Press Pass Stealth Holofoils #58
2001 Press Pass Stealth Holofoils #59
2001 Press Pass Stealth Holofoils #60
2001 Press Pass Stealth Holofoils #61
2001 Press Pass Stealth Holofoils #62
2001 Press Pass Stealth Holofoils #63
2001 Press Pass Stealth Holofoils #65
2001 Press Pass Stealth Lap Leaders #LL10
2001 Press Pass Stealth Lap Leaders #LL28
2001 Press Pass Stealth Lap Leaders Clear Cars #LL28
2001 Press Pass Stealth Lap Leaders Clear Drivers #LL10
2001 Press Pass Stealth Profile #PR5
2001 Press Pass Stealth Race Used Glove Cars /50 #RGC1
2001 Press Pass Stealth Race Used Glove Drivers /50 #RGD1
2001 Press Pass Total Memorabilia Power Pick #TM1
2001 Press Pass Trackside #2
2001 Press Pass Trackside #48
2001 Press Pass Trackside #85
2001 Press Pass Trackside Dialed In #D4
2001 Press Pass Trackside Die Cuts #2
2001 Press Pass Trackside Die Cuts #48
2001 Press Pass Trackside Die Cuts #85
2001 Press Pass Trackside Golden #2
2001 Press Pass Trackside Golden #48
2001 Press Pass Trackside Mirror Image #MI5
2001 Press Pass Trackside Runnin N' Gunnin #RG6
2001 Press Pass Triple Burner /100 #TB1
2001 Press Pass Velocity #VL1
2001 Press Pass Vintage #VN9
2001 Super Shots Hendrick Motorsports #H8
2001 Super Shots Hendrick Motorsports #H9
2001 Super Shots Hendrick Motorsports #H10
2001 Super Shots Hendrick Motorsports #H11
2001 Super Shots Hendrick Motorsports #H14
2001 Super Shots Hendrick Motorsports #H15
2001 Super Shots Hendrick Motorsports #H17
2001 Super Shots Hendrick Motorsports #H19
2001 Super Shots Hendrick Motorsports #HR22
2001 Super Shots Hendrick Motorsports #NNO
2001 Super Shots Hendrick Motorsports Autographs /71 #HSA1
2001 Super Shots Hendrick Motorsports Gold /100 #HG8
2001 Super Shots Hendrick Motorsports Gold /100 #HG9
2001 Super Shots Hendrick Motorsports Gold /100 #HG10
2001 Super Shots Hendrick Motorsports Gold /100 #HG11
2001 Super Shots Hendrick Motorsports Gold /100 #HG14
2001 Super Shots Hendrick Motorsports Gold /100 #HG15
2001 Super Shots Hendrick Motorsports Gold /100 #HG17
2001 Super Shots Hendrick Motorsports Gold /100 #HG19
2001 Super Shots Hendrick Motorsports Silver /500 #HS8
2001 Super Shots Hendrick Motorsports Silver /500 #HS9
2001 Super Shots Hendrick Motorsports Silver /500 #HS10
2001 Super Shots Hendrick Motorsports Silver /500 #HS11
2001 Super Shots Hendrick Motorsports Silver /500 #HS14
2001 Super Shots Hendrick Motorsports Silver /500 #HS15
2001 Super Shots Hendrick Motorsports Silver /500 #HS17
2001 Super Shots Hendrick Motorsports Silver /500 #HS19
2001 Super Shots Hendrick Motorsports Victory Banners /775 #HRB2
2001 Super Shots Hendrick Motorsports Victory Banners /500 #HSB1
2001 Super Shots Hendrick Motorsports Victory Banners /500 #HSB2
2001 Super Shots Race Used Tire Jumbos /2001 #JGG1
2001 Super Shots Race Used Tire Jumbos /2001 #JGS1
2001 Super Shots Sears Point CHP #SP4
2001 VIP #12
2001 VIP #21
2001 VIP #33
2001 VIP #43
2001 VIP #50
2001 VIP Driver's Choice #DC1
2001 VIP Driver's Choice Precious Metal /100 #DC1
2001 VIP Driver's Choice Transparent #DC1
2001 VIP Explosives #12
2001 VIP Explosives #21
2001 VIP Explosives #33
2001 VIP Explosives #43
2001 VIP Explosives #50
2001 VIP Explosives Lasers /420 #LX12
2001 VIP Explosives Lasers /420 #LX21
2001 VIP Explosives Lasers /420 #LX33
2001 VIP Explosives Lasers /420 #LX43
2001 VIP Explosives Lasers /420 #LX50
2001 VIP Head Gear #HG1
2001 VIP Head Gear Die Cuts #HG1
2001 VIP Making the Show #12
2001 VIP Mile Masters #MM1
2001 VIP Mile Masters Precious Metal /325 #MM1
2001 VIP Mile Masters Transparent #MM1
2001 VIP Sheet Metal Cars /120 #SC9
2001 VIP Sheet Metal Drivers /75 #SD9
2001 Wheels High Gear Autographs #10
2001 Wheels High Gear Custom Shop #CSJG
2001 Wheels High Gear Custom Shop Prizes #JGA1
2001 Wheels High Gear Custom Shop Prizes #JGA2
2001 Wheels High Gear Custom Shop Prizes #JGA3
2001 Wheels High Gear Custom Shop Prizes #JGB1
2001 Wheels High Gear Custom Shop Prizes #JGB2
2001 Wheels High Gear Custom Shop Prizes #JGB3
2001 Wheels High Gear Custom Shop Prizes #JGC1
2001 Wheels High Gear Custom Shop Prizes #JGC2
2001 Wheels High Gear Custom Shop Prizes #JGC3
2002 Press Pass #11
2002 Press Pass #66
2002 Press Pass #83
2002 Press Pass #99
2002 Press Pass #0
2002 Press Pass Autographs #22
2002 Press Pass Burning Rubber Cars /120 #BRC1
2002 Press Pass Burning Rubber Drivers /90 #BRD1
2002 Press Pass Cup Chase #CC4
2002 Press Pass Cup Chase Prizes #CC4
2002 Press Pass Cup Chase Prizes #CC18
2002 Press Pass Delphi #D2
2002 Press Pass Double Burner /100 #DB2
2002 Press Pass Eclipse #1
2002 Press Pass Eclipse #29
2002 Press Pass Eclipse #30
2002 Press Pass Eclipse #31
2002 Press Pass Eclipse #32
2002 Press Pass Eclipse #33
2002 Press Pass Eclipse #35
2002 Press Pass Eclipse #38
2002 Press Pass Eclipse #36
2002 Press Pass Eclipse #P1
2002 Press Pass Eclipse Racing Champions #RC3
2002 Press Pass Eclipse Racing Champions #RC13
2002 Press Pass Eclipse Racing Champions #RC14
2002 Press Pass Eclipse Racing Champions #RC21
2002 Press Pass Eclipse Racing Champions #RC22
2002 Press Pass Eclipse Racing Champions #RC28
2002 Press Pass Eclipse Samples #1
2002 Press Pass Eclipse Samples #29
2002 Press Pass Eclipse Samples #30
2002 Press Pass Eclipse Samples #31
2002 Press Pass Eclipse Samples #32
2002 Press Pass Eclipse Samples #33
2002 Press Pass Eclipse Samples #35
2002 Press Pass Eclipse Samples #36
2002 Press Pass Eclipse Samples #38
2002 Press Pass Eclipse Skidmarks #SK4
2002 Press Pass Eclipse Solar Eclipse #S1
2002 Press Pass Eclipse Solar Eclipse #S29
2002 Press Pass Eclipse Solar Eclipse #S30
2002 Press Pass Eclipse Solar Eclipse #S31
2002 Press Pass Eclipse Solar Eclipse #S32
2002 Press Pass Eclipse Solar Eclipse #S33
2002 Press Pass Eclipse Solar Eclipse #S35
2002 Press Pass Eclipse Solar Eclipse #S36
2002 Press Pass Eclipse Solar Eclipse #S38
2002 Press Pass Eclipse Supernova #SN5
2002 Press Pass Eclipse Supernova Numbered /250 #SN5
2002 Press Pass Eclipse Under Cover Double Cover /625 #DC3
2002 Press Pass Eclipse Under Cover Double Cover /625 #DC1
2002 Press Pass Eclipse Under Cover Double Cover /625 #DC2
2002 Press Pass Eclipse Under Cover Drivers #CD3
2002 Press Pass Eclipse Under Cover Gold Cars /300 #CD3
2002 Press Pass Eclipse Under Cover Gold Drivers /400 #CD3
2002 Press Pass Eclipse Under Cover Holofoil Drivers /100 #CD3
2002 Press Pass Eclipse Warp Speed #WS1
2002 Press Pass Hot Treads /2425 #HT17
2002 Press Pass Optima #8
2002 Press Pass Optima #0
2002 Press Pass Optima Cool Persistence #CP3
2002 Press Pass Optima Fan Favorite #FF7
2002 Press Pass Optima Gold #8
2002 Press Pass Optima Promos /5 #8
2002 Press Pass Optima Race Used Lugnuts Autographs /24 #LNDA6
2002 Press Pass Optima Race Used Lugnuts Cars /100 #LNC6
2002 Press Pass Optima Race Used Lugnuts Drivers /100 #LND6
2002 Press Pass Optima Samples #8
2002 Press Pass Optima Up Close #UC2
2002 Press Pass Platinum #11
2002 Press Pass Platinum #66
2002 Press Pass Platinum #83
2002 Press Pass Platinum #99
2002 Press Pass Premium #8
2002 Press Pass Premium #38
2002 Press Pass Premium #46
2002 Press Pass Premium #51
2002 Press Pass Premium #72
2002 Press Pass Premium In The Zone #IZ4
2002 Press Pass Premium Performance Driven #PD2
2002 Press Pass Premium Race Used Firesuit Cars /90 #FC1
2002 Press Pass Premium Race Used Firesuit Drivers /80 #FD1
2002 Press Pass Premium Red Reflectors #8
2002 Press Pass Premium Red Reflectors #38
2002 Press Pass Premium Red Reflectors #46
2002 Press Pass Premium Red Reflectors #51
2002 Press Pass Premium Red Reflectors #72
2002 Press Pass Premium Samples #8
2002 Press Pass Premium Samples #38
2002 Press Pass Premium Samples #46
2002 Press Pass Showcar #S3B
2002 Press Pass Showman #S3A
2002 Press Pass Signings #18
2002 Press Pass Signings Gold /50 #18
2002 Press Pass Signings Transparent /100 #2
2002 Press Pass Stealth #28
2002 Press Pass Stealth #29
2002 Press Pass Stealth #30
2002 Press Pass Stealth #60
2002 Press Pass Stealth #71
2002 Press Pass Stealth Behind the Numbers #BN9
2002 Press Pass Stealth EFX #FX5
2002 Press Pass Stealth Fusion #F3
2002 Press Pass Stealth Gold #28
2002 Press Pass Stealth Gold #29
2002 Press Pass Stealth Gold #30
2002 Press Pass Stealth Gold #60
2002 Press Pass Stealth Gold #71
2002 Press Pass Stealth Lap Leaders #LL7
2002 Press Pass Stealth Profile #P1
2002 Press Pass Stealth Race Used Glove Cars /85 #GLC1
2002 Press Pass Stealth Race Used Glove Drivers /50 #GLD1
2002 Press Pass Stealth Samples #28
2002 Press Pass Stealth Samples #29
2002 Press Pass Stealth Samples #30
2002 Press Pass Stealth Samples #60
2002 Press Pass Stealth Samples #71
2002 Press Pass Top Shelf #TS2
2002 Press Pass Total Memorabilia Power Pick #TM2
2002 Press Pass Trackside #2
2002 Press Pass Trackside #53
2002 Press Pass Trackside #72
2002 Press Pass Trackside #82
2002 Press Pass Trackside Dialed In #DI3
2002 Press Pass Trackside Golden /50 #G2
2002 Press Pass Trackside License to Drive #9
2002 Press Pass Trackside License to Drive Die Cuts #9
2002 Press Pass Trackside Mirror Image #MI2
2002 Press Pass Trackside Runnin N' Gunnin #RG2
2002 Press Pass Trackside Samples #2
2002 Press Pass Trackside Samples #53
2002 Press Pass Trackside Samples #72
2002 Press Pass Trackside Samples #82
2002 Press Pass Triple Burner /100 #TB2
2002 Press Pass Velocity #VL3
2002 Press Pass Vintage #VN7
2002 Sports Illustrated for Kids #160
2002 VIP #11
2002 VIP #28
2002 VIP #50
2002 VIP #48
2002 VIP Driver's Choice #DC1
2002 VIP Driver's Choice Transparent #DC1
2002 VIP Driver's Choice Transparent LTD #DC1
2002 VIP Explosives #X11
2002 VIP Explosives #X28
2002 VIP Explosives #X48
2002 VIP Explosives #X50
2002 VIP Explosives Lasers #LX11
2002 VIP Explosives Lasers #LX28
2002 VIP Explosives Lasers #LX48
2002 VIP Explosives Lasers #LX50
2002 VIP Head Gear #HG1
2002 VIP Head Gear Die Cuts #HG1
2002 VIP Making the Show #MS13
2002 VIP Mile Masters #MM1
2002 VIP Mile Masters Transparent #MM1
2002 VIP Mile Masters Transparent LTD #MM1
2002 VIP Race Used Sheet Metal Cars #SC1
2002 VIP Race Used Sheet Metal Drivers /130 #SD1
2002 VIP Rear View Mirror #RM5
2002 VIP Rear View Mirror Die Cuts #RM5
2002 VIP Samples #11
2002 VIP Samples #28
2002 VIP Samples #48
2002 VIP Samples #50
2002 Wheels High Gear #7
2002 Wheels High Gear #28
2002 Wheels High Gear #47
2002 Wheels High Gear #56
2002 Wheels High Gear #61
2002 Wheels High Gear #62
2002 Wheels High Gear #65
2002 Wheels High Gear #71
2002 Wheels High Gear Autographs #17
2002 Wheels High Gear Custom Shop #CSJG
2002 Wheels High Gear Custom Shop Prizes #JGA1
2002 Wheels High Gear Custom Shop Prizes #JGA2
2002 Wheels High Gear Custom Shop Prizes #JGA3
2002 Wheels High Gear Custom Shop Prizes #JGB1
2002 Wheels High Gear Custom Shop Prizes #JGB2
2002 Wheels High Gear Custom Shop Prizes #JGB3
2002 Wheels High Gear Custom Shop Prizes #JGC1
2002 Wheels High Gear Custom Shop Prizes #JGC2
2002 Wheels High Gear Custom Shop Prizes #JGC3
2002 Wheels High Gear First Gear #7
2002 Wheels High Gear First Gear #28
2002 Wheels High Gear First Gear #47
2002 Wheels High Gear First Gear #56
2002 Wheels High Gear First Gear #61
2002 Wheels High Gear First Gear #62
2002 Wheels High Gear First Gear #65
2002 Wheels High Gear First Gear #71
2002 Wheels High Gear Flag Chasers /130 #FC2
2002 Wheels High Gear Flag Chasers Black /90 #FC2
2002 Wheels High Gear Flag Chasers Blue-Yellow /40 #FC2
2002 Wheels High Gear Flag Chasers Checkered /35 #FC2
2002 Wheels High Gear Flag Chasers Checkered Blue/Orange /10 #FC2
2002 Wheels High Gear Flag Chasers Green /90 #FC2
2002 Wheels High Gear Flag Chasers Red /90 #FC2
2002 Wheels High Gear Flag Chasers Yellow /110 #FC2
2002 Wheels High Gear High Groove #HG7
2002 Wheels High Gear Hot Streaks #HS3
2002 Wheels High Gear Man and Machine Cars #MM2B
2002 Wheels High Gear Man and Machine Drivers #MM2A
2002 Wheels High Gear MPH /100 #7
2002 Wheels High Gear MPH /100 #28
2002 Wheels High Gear MPH /100 #47
2002 Wheels High Gear MPH /100 #56
2002 Wheels High Gear MPH /100 #61
2002 Wheels High Gear MPH /100 #62
2002 Wheels High Gear MPH /100 #65
2002 Wheels High Gear MPH /100 #71
2002 Wheels High Gear Sunday Sensation #SS4
2002 Wheels High Gear Top Tier #TT1
2002 Wheels High Gear Top Tier Numbered /250 #TT1
2003 eTopps /6000 #4
2003 Press Pass #10
2003 Press Pass #60
2003 Press Pass #78
2003 Press Pass #98
2003 Press Pass #100
2003 Press Pass Autographs #16
2003 Press Pass Burning Rubber Cars /60 #BRT1
2003 Press Pass Burning Rubber Cars Autographs /24 #BRTJG
2003 Press Pass Burning Rubber Drivers /50 #BRD1
2003 Press Pass Burning Rubber Drivers Autographs /24 #BRDJG
2003 Press Pass Cup Chase #CCR4
2003 Press Pass Cup Chase Prizes #CCR4
2003 Press Pass Double Burner /100 #DB1
2003 Press Pass Double Burner Exchange /100 #DB1
2003 Press Pass Eclipse #4
2003 Press Pass Eclipse #35
2003 Press Pass Eclipse #38
2003 Press Pass Eclipse #42
2003 Press Pass Eclipse #46
2003 Press Pass Eclipse Double Hot Treads /999 #DT8
2003 Press Pass Eclipse Previews /5 #4
2003 Press Pass Eclipse Previews /5 #35
2003 Press Pass Eclipse Racing Champions #RC25
2003 Press Pass Eclipse Racing Champions #RC26
2003 Press Pass Eclipse Racing Champions #RC30
2003 Press Pass Eclipse Samples #4
2003 Press Pass Eclipse Samples #35
2003 Press Pass Eclipse Samples #38
2003 Press Pass Eclipse Samples #42
2003 Press Pass Eclipse Samples #46
2003 Press Pass Eclipse Skidmarks #SM2
2003 Press Pass Eclipse Solar Eclipse #P4
2003 Press Pass Eclipse Solar Eclipse #P35
2003 Press Pass Eclipse Solar Eclipse #P38
2003 Press Pass Eclipse Solar Eclipse #P42
2003 Press Pass Eclipse Solar Eclipse #P46
2003 Press Pass Eclipse Supernova #SN3
2003 Press Pass Eclipse Teammates Autographs /25 #JGJJ
2003 Press Pass Eclipse Under Cover Cars /215 #UCT1
2003 Press Pass Eclipse Under Cover Cars Autographs /24 #UCTJG
2003 Press Pass Eclipse Under Cover Double Cover /530 #DC1
2003 Press Pass Eclipse Under Cover Double Cover /530 #DC2
2003 Press Pass Eclipse Under Cover Double Cover /530 #DC3
2003 Press Pass Eclipse Under Cover Driver Autographs /24 #UCDJG
2003 Press Pass Eclipse Under Cover Driver Gold /260 #UCD1
2003 Press Pass Eclipse Under Cover Driver Red /100 #UCD1
2003 Press Pass Eclipse Under Cover Driver Silver /450 #UCD1
2003 Press Pass Eclipse Warp Speed #WS1
2003 Press Pass Gold Holofoil #P10
2003 Press Pass Gold Holofoil #P60
2003 Press Pass Gold Holofoil #P78
2003 Press Pass Gold Holofoil #P98
2003 Press Pass Gold Holofoil #P100
2003 Press Pass Optima #7
2003 Press Pass Optima Cool Persistence #CP8
2003 Press Pass Optima Fan Favorite #FF7
2003 Press Pass Optima Gold #G7
2003 Press Pass Optima Previews /5 #7
2003 Press Pass Optima Q and A #QA3
2003 Press Pass Optima Samples #7
2003 Press Pass Optima Thunder Bolts Cars /95 #TBT1
2003 Press Pass Optima Thunder Bolts Cars Autographs /24 #TBTJG
2003 Press Pass Optima Thunder Bolts Drivers /60 #TBD1
2003 Press Pass Optima Thunder Bolts Drivers Autographs /24 #TBDJG
2003 Press Pass Premium #8
2003 Press Pass Premium #37
2003 Press Pass Premium #53
2003 Press Pass Premium #71
2003 Press Pass Premium Hot Threads Cars /160 #HTT1
2003 Press Pass Premium Hot Threads Cars Autographs /24 #HTDJG
2003 Press Pass Premium Hot Threads Drivers /285 #HTD1
2003 Press Pass Premium Hot Threads Drivers Autographs /24 #HTTJG
2003 Press Pass Premium In the Zone #IZ2
2003 Press Pass Premium Performance Driven #PD2
2003 Press Pass Premium Previews /5 #8
2003 Press Pass Premium Red Reflectors #8
2003 Press Pass Premium Red Reflectors #37
2003 Press Pass Premium Red Reflectors #53
2003 Press Pass Premium Red Reflectors #71
2003 Press Pass Premium Samples #8
2003 Press Pass Premium Samples #37
2003 Press Pass Previews /5 #10
2003 Press Pass Samples #10
2003 Press Pass Samples #60
2003 Press Pass Samples #78
2003 Press Pass Samples #98
2003 Press Pass Samples #100
2003 Press Pass Showcar #S3B
2003 Press Pass Showman #S3A
2003 Press Pass Signings #23
2003 Press Pass Signings Gold /50 #23
2003 Press Pass Signings Transparent /100 #2
2003 Press Pass Snapshots #SN7
2003 Press Pass Stealth #31
2003 Press Pass Stealth #32
2003 Press Pass Stealth #33
2003 Press Pass Stealth #62
2003 Press Pass Stealth #64
2003 Press Pass Stealth EFX #FX4
2003 Press Pass Stealth Fusion #FU4
2003 Press Pass Stealth Gear Grippers Cars /150 #GGT1
2003 Press Pass Stealth Gear Grippers Cars Autographs /24 #JG
2003 Press Pass Stealth Gear Grippers Drivers /75 #GGD1
2003 Press Pass Stealth Gear Grippers Drivers Autographs /24 #JG
2003 Press Pass Stealth No Boundaries #NB12
2003 Press Pass Stealth Previews /5 #31
2003 Press Pass Stealth Previews /5 #32
2003 Press Pass Stealth Previews /5 #33
2003 Press Pass Stealth Profile #PR2
2003 Press Pass Stealth Red #P31
2003 Press Pass Stealth Red #P32

2003 Press Pass Stealth Red #P33
2003 Press Pass Stealth Red #P62
2003 Press Pass Stealth Red #P64
2003 Press Pass Stealth Samples #31
2003 Press Pass Stealth Samples #32
2003 Press Pass Stealth Samples #33
2003 Press Pass Stealth Samples #62
2003 Press Pass Stealth Samples #64
2003 Press Pass Stealth Supercharged #SC1
2003 Press Pass Top Shelf #TS2
2003 Press Pass Total Memorabilia Power Pick #TM1
2003 Press Pass Trackside #20
2003 Press Pass Trackside #79
2003 Press Pass Trackside Dialed In #DI3
2003 Press Pass Trackside Gold Holofoil #P20
2003 Press Pass Trackside Gold Holofoil #P79
2003 Press Pass Trackside Golden /50 #G20
2003 Press Pass Trackside Hat Giveaway #PPH7
2003 Press Pass Trackside License to Drive #LD5
2003 Press Pass Trackside Mirror Image #MI3
2003 Press Pass Trackside Pit Stoppers Cars /175 #PST1
2003 Press Pass Trackside Pit Stoppers Drivers /100 #PSD1
2003 Press Pass Trackside Previews /5 #20
2003 Press Pass Trackside Runnin n' Gunnin #RG3
2003 Press Pass Trackside Samples #20
2003 Press Pass Trackside Samples #79
2003 Press Pass Triple Burner /100 #TB1
2003 Press Pass Triple Burner Exchange /100 #TB1
2003 Press Pass Velocity #VC2
2003 Press Pass Victory Lap #11
2003 VIP #5
2003 VIP #27
2003 VIP #30
2003 VIP #34
2003 VIP #36
2003 VIP Driver's Choice #DC3
2003 VIP Driver's Choice Die Cuts #DC3
2003 VIP Driver's Choice National #DC3
2003 VIP Explosives #X5
2003 VIP Explosives #X27
2003 VIP Explosives #X30
2003 VIP Explosives #X34
2003 VIP Explosives #X36
2003 VIP Head Gear #HG3
2003 VIP Head Gear Die Cuts #HG3
2003 VIP Head Gear National #HG3
2003 VIP Lap Leaders #LL1
2003 VIP Lap Leaders National #LL1
2003 VIP Lap Leaders Transparent #LL1
2003 VIP Lap Leaders Transparent LTD #LL1
2003 VIP Laser Explosive #LX5
2003 VIP Laser Explosive #LX27
2003 VIP Laser Explosive #LX30
2003 VIP Laser Explosive #LX34
2003 VIP Laser Explosive #LX36
2003 VIP Making the Show #MS14
2003 VIP Mile Masters #MM3
2003 VIP Mile Masters National #MM3
2003 VIP Mile Masters Transparent #MM3
2003 VIP Mile Masters Transparent LTD #MM3
2003 VIP Previews /5 #5
2003 VIP Previews /5 #27
2003 VIP Previews /5 #30
2003 VIP Previews /5 #34
2003 VIP Previews /5 #36
2003 VIP Samples #5
2003 VIP Samples #27
2003 VIP Samples #30
2003 VIP Samples #34
2003 VIP Samples #36
2003 VIP Tin #CT5
2003 VIP Tin #CT27
2003 VIP Tin #CT30
2003 VIP Tin #CT34
2003 VIP Tin #CT36
2003 VIP Tradin' Paint Cars /160 #TPT1
2003 VIP Tradin' Paint Drivers /110 #TPD1
2003 Wheels American Thunder #6
2003 Wheels American Thunder #22
2003 Wheels American Thunder #43
2003 Wheels American Thunder #P1
2003 Wheels American Thunder American Eagle #AE5
2003 Wheels American Thunder American Muscle #AM2
2003 Wheels American Thunder Born On /100 #BO6
2003 Wheels American Thunder Born On /100 #BO22
2003 Wheels American Thunder Born On /100 #BO43
2003 Wheels American Thunder Cool Threads /285 #CT6
2003 Wheels American Thunder Golden Eagle /100 #AEG5
2003 Wheels American Thunder Heads Up Manufacturer /90 #HUM4
2003 Wheels American Thunder Heads Up Team /60 #HUT3
2003 Wheels American Thunder Heads Up Winston /90 #HUW4
2003 Wheels American Thunder Holofoil #P6
2003 Wheels American Thunder Holofoil #P22
2003 Wheels American Thunder Holofoil #P43
2003 Wheels American Thunder Post Mark #PM5
2003 Wheels American Thunder Previews /5 #6
2003 Wheels American Thunder Previews /5 #22
2003 Wheels American Thunder Pushin Pedal /285 #PP2
2003 Wheels American Thunder Rookie Thunder #RT9
2003 Wheels American Thunder Samples #P6
2003 Wheels American Thunder Samples #P22
2003 Wheels American Thunder Samples #P43
2003 Wheels American Thunder Thunder Road #TR2
2003 Wheels American Thunder Thunder Road #TR17
2003 Wheels American Thunder Triple Hat /25 #TH7
2003 Wheels Autographs #16
2003 Wheels High Gear #10
2003 Wheels High Gear #49
2003 Wheels High Gear #61
2003 Wheels High Gear #62
2003 Wheels High Gear Blue Hawaii SCDA Promos #10
2003 Wheels High Gear Blue Hawaii SCDA Promos #49
2003 Wheels High Gear Blue Hawaii SCDA Promos #61
2003 Wheels High Gear Blue Hawaii SCDA Promos #62
2003 Wheels High Gear Custom Shop #CSJG
2003 Wheels High Gear Custom Shop Autograph Redemption #CSJG
2003 Wheels High Gear Custom Shop Autographs /10 #JGB2
2003 Wheels High Gear Custom Shop Prizes #JGA1
2003 Wheels High Gear Custom Shop Prizes #JGA2
2003 Wheels High Gear Custom Shop Prizes #JGA3
2003 Wheels High Gear Custom Shop Prizes #JGB1
2003 Wheels High Gear Custom Shop Prizes #JGB2
2003 Wheels High Gear Custom Shop Prizes #JGB3
2003 Wheels High Gear Custom Shop Prizes #JGC1
2003 Wheels High Gear Custom Shop Prizes #JGC2
2003 Wheels High Gear Custom Shop Prizes #JGC3
2003 Wheels High Gear First Gear #F10
2003 Wheels High Gear First Gear #F49
2003 Wheels High Gear First Gear #F61
2003 Wheels High Gear First Gear #F62
2003 Wheels High Gear Flag Chasers Black /90 #FC2
2003 Wheels High Gear Flag Chasers Blue-Yellow /45 #FC2
2003 Wheels High Gear Flag Chasers Checkered /25 #FC2
2003 Wheels High Gear Flag Chasers Green /90 #FC2
2003 Wheels High Gear Flag Chasers Red /90 #FC2
2003 Wheels High Gear Flag Chasers White /90 #FC2
2003 Wheels High Gear Flag Chasers Yellow /90 #FC2
2003 Wheels High Gear Full Throttle #FT2
2003 Wheels High Gear High Groove #HG7
2003 Wheels High Gear Hot Treads /425 #HT5
2003 Wheels High Gear Machine #MM9B
2003 Wheels High Gear Man #MM9A
2003 Wheels High Gear MPH /100 #M10
2003 Wheels High Gear MPH /100 #M49
2003 Wheels High Gear MPH /100 #M61
2003 Wheels High Gear MPH /100 #M62
2003 Wheels High Gear Previews /5 #10
2003 Wheels High Gear Samples #10
2003 Wheels High Gear Samples #49
2003 Wheels High Gear Samples #61
2003 Wheels High Gear Samples #62
2003 Wheels High Gear Sunday Sensation #SS4
2003 Wheels High Gear Top Tier #TT4
2004 National Trading Card Day #PP2
2004 Press Pass #10B
2004 Press Pass #10
2004 Press Pass #93
2004 Press Pass Autographs #21
2004 Press Pass Burning Rubber Autographs /24 #BRJG
2004 Press Pass Burning Rubber Cars /140 #BRT4
2004 Press Pass Burning Rubber Drivers /70 #BRD4
2004 Press Pass Cup Chase #CCR2
2004 Press Pass Cup Chase Prizes #CCR2
2004 Press Pass Double Burner /100 #DB1
2004 Press Pass Double Burner Exchange /100 #DB1
2004 Press Pass Eclipse #4
2004 Press Pass Eclipse #53
2004 Press Pass Eclipse #57
2004 Press Pass Eclipse #75
2004 Press Pass Eclipse Destination WIN #11
2004 Press Pass Eclipse Destination WIN #26
2004 Press Pass Eclipse Hyperdrive #HP7
2004 Press Pass Eclipse Maxim #MX4
2004 Press Pass Eclipse Previews /5 #4
2004 Press Pass Eclipse Samples #4
2004 Press Pass Eclipse Samples #53
2004 Press Pass Eclipse Samples #57
2004 Press Pass Eclipse Samples #75
2004 Press Pass Eclipse Skidmarks #SM1
2004 Press Pass Eclipse Skidmarks Holofoil /500 #SM1
2004 Press Pass Eclipse Teammates Autographs /25 #2
2004 Press Pass Eclipse Under Cover Autographs /24 #UCJG
2004 Press Pass Eclipse Under Cover Cars /170 #UCD4
2004 Press Pass Eclipse Under Cover Double Cover /100 #DC3
2004 Press Pass Eclipse Under Cover Double Cover /100 #DC7
2004 Press Pass Eclipse Under Cover Double Cover /100 #DC4
2004 Press Pass Eclipse Under Cover Driver Gold /325 #UCD4
2004 Press Pass Eclipse Under Cover Driver Red /100 #UCD4
2004 Press Pass Eclipse Under Cover Driver Silver /690 #UCD4
2004 Press Pass Hot Treads /1250 #HTR11
2004 Press Pass Hot Treads Holofoil /200 #HTR11
2004 Press Pass Making the Show Collector's Series #MS16
2004 Press Pass Making the Show Collector's Series Tins #NNO
2004 Press Pass Optima #6
2004 Press Pass Optima #62
2004 Press Pass Optima #68
2004 Press Pass Optima #76
2004 Press Pass Optima #94
2004 Press Pass Optima #100
2004 Press Pass Optima Cool Persistence #CP1
2004 Press Pass Optima Fan Favorite #FF6
2004 Press Pass Optima G Force #GF2
2004 Press Pass Optima Gold #G6
2004 Press Pass Optima Gold #G62
2004 Press Pass Optima Gold #G68
2004 Press Pass Optima Gold #G76
2004 Press Pass Optima Gold #G94
2004 Press Pass Optima Gold #G100
2004 Press Pass Optima Previews /5 #EB6
2004 Press Pass Optima Q&A #QA1
2004 Press Pass Optima Samples #6
2004 Press Pass Optima Samples #62
2004 Press Pass Optima Samples #68
2004 Press Pass Optima Samples #76
2004 Press Pass Optima Samples #94
2004 Press Pass Optima Samples #100
2004 Press Pass Optima Thunder Bolts Autographs /24 #TBJG
2004 Press Pass Optima Thunder Bolts Cars /120 #TBT13
2004 Press Pass Optima Thunder Bolts Drivers /70 #TBD13
2004 Press Pass Platinum #P10
2004 Press Pass Platinum #P93
2004 Press Pass Premium #7
2004 Press Pass Premium #42
2004 Press Pass Premium #53
2004 Press Pass Premium #79
2004 Press Pass Premium Asphalt Jungle #A2
2004 Press Pass Premium Hot Threads Autographs /24 #HTJG
2004 Press Pass Premium Hot Threads Drivers Bronze /125 #HTD4
2004 Press Pass Premium Hot Threads Drivers Bronze Retail /125 #HTT4
2004 Press Pass Premium Hot Threads Drivers Gold /50 #HTD4
2004 Press Pass Premium Hot Threads Drivers Silver /75 #HTD4
2004 Press Pass Premium In the Zone #IZ4
2004 Press Pass Premium In the Zone Elite Edition #IZ4
2004 Press Pass Premium Performance Driven #PD7
2004 Press Pass Premium Previews /5 #7
2004 Press Pass Premium Samples #7
2004 Press Pass Premium Samples #42
2004 Press Pass Previews /5 #10
2004 Press Pass Samples #10
2004 Press Pass Samples #93
2004 Press Pass Schedule #1
2004 Press Pass Showcar #S5B
2004 Press Pass Showman #S5A
2004 Press Pass Signings #21
2004 Press Pass Signings Gold /50 #20
2004 Press Pass Signings Transparent /100 #1
2004 Press Pass Snapshots #SN7
2004 Press Pass Stealth #25
2004 Press Pass Stealth #26
2004 Press Pass Stealth #27
2004 Press Pass Stealth #86
2004 Press Pass Stealth EFX #EF2
2004 Press Pass Stealth Fusion #FU1
2004 Press Pass Stealth Gear Grippers Autographs /24 #HTJG
2004 Press Pass Stealth Gear Grippers Drivers /80 #GGD4
2004 Press Pass Stealth Gear Grippers Drivers Retail /120 #GGT4
2004 Press Pass Stealth No Boundaries #NB12
2004 Press Pass Stealth Previews /5 #EB25
2004 Press Pass Stealth Previews /5 #EB26
2004 Press Pass Stealth Previews /5 #EB27
2004 Press Pass Stealth Profile #P1
2004 Press Pass Stealth Samples #X26
2004 Press Pass Stealth Samples #X25
2004 Press Pass Stealth Samples #X27
2004 Press Pass Stealth Samples #X86
2004 Press Pass Stealth X-Ray /100 #25
2004 Press Pass Stealth X-Ray /100 #26
2004 Press Pass Stealth X-Ray /100 #27
2004 Press Pass Stealth X-Ray /100 #86
2004 Press Pass Top Shelf #TS6
2004 Press Pass Total Memorabilia Power Pick #TM1
2004 Press Pass Trackside #20
2004 Press Pass Trackside #20B
2004 Press Pass Trackside #69
2004 Press Pass Trackside #89
2004 Press Pass Trackside #108
2004 Press Pass Trackside #111
2004 Press Pass Trackside #120
2004 Press Pass Trackside Dialed In #DI3
2004 Press Pass Trackside Golden /100 #G20
2004 Press Pass Trackside Golden /100 #G69
2004 Press Pass Trackside Golden /100 #G89
2004 Press Pass Trackside Golden /100 #G108
2004 Press Pass Trackside Golden /100 #G111
2004 Press Pass Trackside Golden /100 #G120
2004 Press Pass Trackside Hat Giveaway #PPH8
2004 Press Pass Trackside Hot Pass #HP7
2004 Press Pass Trackside Hot Pass National #HP7
2004 Press Pass Trackside Hot Pursuit #HP4
2004 Press Pass Trackside Pit Stoppers Cars /150 #PST1
2004 Press Pass Trackside Pit Stoppers Drivers /95 #PSD1
2004 Press Pass Trackside Previews /5 #EB20
2004 Press Pass Trackside Runnin n' Gunnin #RG2
2004 Press Pass Trackside Samples #20
2004 Press Pass Trackside Samples #69
2004 Press Pass Trackside Samples #89
2004 Press Pass Trackside Samples #108
2004 Press Pass Trackside Samples #111
2004 Press Pass Trackside Samples #120
2004 Press Pass Triple Burner /100 #TB1
2004 Press Pass Triple Burner Exchange /100 #TB1
2004 Press Pass Velocity #VC7
2004 Super Shots CHP Sonoma #1
2004 VIP #5
2004 VIP #38
2004 VIP #51
2004 VIP #52
2004 VIP #56
2004 VIP #74
2004 VIP #88
2004 VIP Driver's Choice #DC3
2004 VIP Driver's Choice Die Cuts #DC3
2004 VIP Head Gear #HG2
2004 VIP Head Gear Transparent #HG2
2004 VIP Lap Leaders #LL7
2004 VIP Lap Leaders Transparent #LL7
2004 VIP Making the Show #MS16
2004 VIP Previews /5 #EB38
2004 VIP Previews /5 #EB51
2004 VIP Previews /5 #EB52
2004 VIP Previews /5 #EB5
2004 VIP Samples #5
2004 VIP Samples #52
2004 VIP Samples #56
2004 VIP Samples #38
2004 VIP Samples #88
2004 VIP Samples #74
2004 VIP Samples #51
2004 VIP Tradin' Paint Autographs /24 #TPJG
2004 VIP Tradin' Paint Bronze /130 #TPT2
2004 VIP Tradin' Paint Gold /50 #TPD2
2004 VIP Tradin' Paint Silver /70 #TPD2
2004 Wheels American Thunder #5
2004 Wheels American Thunder #34
2004 Wheels American Thunder #42
2004 Wheels American Thunder #52
2004 Wheels American Thunder #65
2004 Wheels American Thunder #76
2004 Wheels American Thunder American Eagle #AE2
2004 Wheels American Thunder American Muscle #AM4
2004 Wheels American Thunder Cool Threads /525 #CT3
2004 Wheels American Thunder Cup Quest #CQ3
2004 Wheels American Thunder Golden Eagle /250 #AE2
2004 Wheels American Thunder Head to Toe /50 #HT4
2004 Wheels American Thunder Post Mark #PM16
2004 Wheels American Thunder Previews /5 #EB5
2004 Wheels American Thunder Previews /5 #EB34
2004 Wheels American Thunder Previews /5 #EB42
2004 Wheels American Thunder Pushin Pedal /200 #PP6
2004 Wheels American Thunder Samples #5
2004 Wheels American Thunder Samples #34
2004 Wheels American Thunder Samples #42
2004 Wheels American Thunder Samples #52
2004 Wheels American Thunder Samples #65
2004 Wheels American Thunder Samples #76
2004 Wheels American Thunder Thunder Road #TR12
2004 Wheels American Thunder Triple Hat /160 #TH3
2004 Wheels Autographs #24
2004 Wheels High Gear #8
2004 Wheels High Gear #34
2004 Wheels High Gear #52
2004 Wheels High Gear #59
2004 Wheels High Gear Custom Shop #CSJG
2004 Wheels High Gear Flag Chasers Black /100 #FC6
2004 Wheels High Gear Flag Chasers Blue /50 #FC6
2004 Wheels High Gear Flag Chasers Checkered /35 #FC6
2004 Wheels High Gear Flag Chasers Green /100 #FC6
2004 Wheels High Gear Flag Chasers Red /100 #FC6
2004 Wheels High Gear Flag Chasers White /100 #FC6
2004 Wheels High Gear Flag Chasers Yellow /100 #FC6
2004 Wheels High Gear Full Throttle #FT2
2004 Wheels High Gear High Groove #HG6
2004 Wheels High Gear Machine #MM3B
2004 Wheels High Gear Man #MM3A
2004 Wheels High Gear MPH /100 #M8
2004 Wheels High Gear MPH /100 #M34
2004 Wheels High Gear MPH /100 #M52
2004 Wheels High Gear MPH /100 #M59
2004 Wheels High Gear Previews /5 #8
2004 Wheels High Gear Previews /5 #34
2004 Wheels High Gear Previews /5 #52
2004 Wheels High Gear Previews /5 #59
2004 Wheels High Gear Samples #8
2004 Wheels High Gear Samples #34
2004 Wheels High Gear Samples #52
2004 Wheels High Gear Samples #59
2004 Wheels High Gear Sunday Sensation #SS9
2004 Wheels High Gear Top Ten #TT4
2004 Wheels High Gear Winston Victory Lap Tribute #WVL1
2004 Wheels High Gear Winston Victory Lap Tribute Gold #WVL1
2005 Press Pass #19
2005 Press Pass #80
2005 Press Pass #84
2005 Press Pass #95
2005 Press Pass #105
2005 Press Pass #112
2005 Press Pass #92
2005 Press Pass #120
2005 Press Pass Autographs #19
2005 Press Pass Burning Rubber Cars /130 #BRT4
2005 Press Pass Burning Rubber Drivers /80 #BRD4
2005 Press Pass Burning Rubber Drivers Gold /1 #BRD4
2005 Press Pass Cup Chase #CCR7
2005 Press Pass Cup Chase Prizes #CCP7
2005 Press Pass Double Burner /100 #DB1
2005 Press Pass Double Burner Exchange /100 #DB1
2005 Press Pass Eclipse #3
2005 Press Pass Eclipse #48
2005 Press Pass Eclipse #57
2005 Press Pass Eclipse #65
2005 Press Pass Eclipse #70
2005 Press Pass Eclipse #72
2005 Press Pass Eclipse #75
2005 Press Pass Eclipse #85
2005 Press Pass Eclipse Destination WIN #8
2005 Press Pass Eclipse Destination WIN #9
2005 Press Pass Eclipse Destination WIN #15
2005 Press Pass Eclipse Destination WIN #18
2005 Press Pass Eclipse Hyperdrive #HD7
2005 Press Pass Eclipse Maxim #MX4
2005 Press Pass Eclipse Previews /5 #EB3
2005 Press Pass Eclipse Previews /5 #EB48
2005 Press Pass Eclipse Previews /5 #EB57
2005 Press Pass Eclipse Previews /5 #EB65
2005 Press Pass Eclipse Previews /5 #EB70
2005 Press Pass Eclipse Previews /5 #EB72
2005 Press Pass Eclipse Previews /1 #EB75
2005 Press Pass Eclipse Samples #3
2005 Press Pass Eclipse Samples #48
2005 Press Pass Eclipse Samples #57
2005 Press Pass Eclipse Samples #65
2005 Press Pass Eclipse Samples #70
2005 Press Pass Eclipse Samples #72
2005 Press Pass Eclipse Samples #75
2005 Press Pass Eclipse Skidmarks #SM1
2005 Press Pass Eclipse Skidmarks Holofoil /250 #SM1
2005 Press Pass Eclipse Teammates Autographs /25 #6
2005 Press Pass Eclipse Under Cover Autographs /24 #UCJG
2005 Press Pass Eclipse Under Cover Cars /120 #UCT4
2005 Press Pass Eclipse Under Cover Double Cover /340 #DC3
2005 Press Pass Eclipse Under Cover Double Cover /340 #DC9
2005 Press Pass Eclipse Under Cover Driver Red /400 #UCD4
2005 Press Pass Eclipse Under Cover Drivers Holofoil /100 #UCD4
2005 Press Pass Eclipse Under Cover Drivers Silver /690 #UCD4
2005 Press Pass Game Face #GF6
2005 Press Pass Hot Treads /900 #HTR10
2005 Press Pass Hot Treads Holofoil /100 #HTR10
2005 Press Pass Legends #28
2005 Press Pass Legends #43
2005 Press Pass Legends #50
2005 Press Pass Legends Autographs Black /50 #15
2005 Press Pass Legends Blue /1890 #28B
2005 Press Pass Legends Blue /1890 #43B
2005 Press Pass Legends Blue /1890 #50B
2005 Press Pass Legends Double Threads Bronze /375 #DTLG
2005 Press Pass Legends Double Threads Bronze /375 #DTGJ
2005 Press Pass Legends Double Threads Gold /99 #DTGJ
2005 Press Pass Legends Double Threads Gold /99 #DTLG
2005 Press Pass Legends Double Threads Silver /225 #DTGJ
2005 Press Pass Legends Double Threads Silver /225 #DTLG
2005 Press Pass Legends Gold /750 #28G
2005 Press Pass Legends Gold /750 #43G
2005 Press Pass Legends Gold /750 #50G
2005 Press Pass Legends Greatest Moments /640 #GM12
2005 Press Pass Legends Heritage /480 #HE2
2005 Press Pass Legends Holofoil /100 #28H
2005 Press Pass Legends Holofoil /100 #43H
2005 Press Pass Legends Holofoil /100 #50H
2005 Press Pass Legends Press Plates Black /1 #28
2005 Press Pass Legends Press Plates Black /1 #43
2005 Press Pass Legends Press Plates Black /1 #50
2005 Press Pass Legends Press Plates Cyan /1 #28
2005 Press Pass Legends Press Plates Cyan /1 #43
2005 Press Pass Legends Press Plates Cyan /1 #50
2005 Press Pass Legends Press Plates Magenta /1 #28
2005 Press Pass Legends Press Plates Magenta /1 #43
2005 Press Pass Legends Press Plates Magenta /1 #50
2005 Press Pass Legends Press Plates Yellow /1 #28
2005 Press Pass Legends Press Plates Yellow /1 #43
2005 Press Pass Legends Press Plates Yellow /1 #50
2005 Press Pass Legends Previews /5 #28
2005 Press Pass Legends Previews /5 #43
2005 Press Pass Legends Previews /5 #50
2005 Press Pass Legends Solo /1 #28S
2005 Press Pass Legends Solo /1 #43S
2005 Press Pass Legends Solo /1 #50S
2005 Press Pass Legends Threads and Treads Bronze /375 #TTJG
2005 Press Pass Legends Threads and Treads Gold /99 #TTJG
2005 Press Pass Legends Threads and Treads Silver /225 #TTJG
2005 Press Pass Optima #10
2005 Press Pass Optima #58
2005 Press Pass Optima #88
2005 Press Pass Optima Cool Persistence #CP1
2005 Press Pass Optima Fan Favorite #FF8
2005 Press Pass Optima G Force #GF5
2005 Press Pass Optima Gold /100 #G10
2005 Press Pass Optima Gold /100 #G58
2005 Press Pass Optima Gold /100 #G88
2005 Press Pass Optima Previews /5 #10
2005 Press Pass Optima Q & A #QA5
2005 Press Pass Optima Samples #10
2005 Press Pass Optima Samples #58
2005 Press Pass Optima Samples #88
2005 Press Pass Optima Thunder Bolts Autographs /24 #TBJG
2005 Press Pass Panorama #PPP3
2005 Press Pass Panorama #PPP20
2005 Press Pass Panorama #PPP27
2005 Press Pass Panorama #PPP30
2005 Press Pass Panorama #PPP37
2005 Press Pass Panorama #PPP38
2005 Press Pass Panorama #PPP39
2005 Press Pass Platinum /100 #P19
2005 Press Pass Platinum /100 #P80
2005 Press Pass Platinum /100 #P84
2005 Press Pass Platinum /100 #P92
2005 Press Pass Platinum /100 #P95
2005 Press Pass Platinum /100 #P105
2005 Press Pass Platinum /100 #P112
2005 Press Pass Platinum /100 #P120
2005 Press Pass Premium #7
2005 Press Pass Premium #40
2005 Press Pass Premium #53
2005 Press Pass Premium #72
2005 Press Pass Premium #0
2005 Press Pass Premium Asphalt Jungle #AJ3
2005 Press Pass Premium Hot Threads Autographs /24 #HTJG
2005 Press Pass Premium Hot Threads Cars /85 #HTT3
2005 Press Pass Premium Hot Threads Drivers /275 #HTD3
2005 Press Pass Premium Hot Threads Drivers Gold /1 #HTD3
2005 Press Pass Premium In the Zone #IZ9
2005 Press Pass Premium In the Zone Elite Edition /250 #IZ9
2005 Press Pass Premium Performance Driven #PD4
2005 Press Pass Premium Samples #7
2005 Press Pass Premium Samples #40
2005 Press Pass Previews Green /5 #EB19
2005 Press Pass Previews Silver /1 #EB105
2005 Press Pass Samples #19
2005 Press Pass Samples #80
2005 Press Pass Samples #84
2005 Press Pass Samples #92
2005 Press Pass Samples #95
2005 Press Pass Samples #105
2005 Press Pass Samples #112
2005 Press Pass Samples #120
2005 Press Pass Showcar #SC5
2005 Press Pass Showman #SM5
2005 Press Pass Signings #18
2005 Press Pass Signings Gold /50 #17
2005 Press Pass Signings Platinum /100 #17
2005 Press Pass Snapshots #SN8
2005 Press Pass Snapshots Extra #SS2
2005 Press Pass Stealth #48
2005 Press Pass Stealth #51
2005 Press Pass Stealth #54
2005 Press Pass Stealth #87
2005 Press Pass Stealth #97
2005 Press Pass Stealth #100
2005 Press Pass Stealth EFX #EFX1
2005 Press Pass Stealth Fusion #FU1
2005 Press Pass Stealth Gear Grippers Autographs /24 #GGJG
2005 Press Pass Stealth Gear Grippers Cars /90 #GGT4
2005 Press Pass Stealth Gear Grippers Drivers /75 #GGD4
2005 Press Pass Stealth No Boundaries #NB14
2005 Press Pass Stealth Previews /5 #48
2005 Press Pass Stealth Previews /5 #51
2005 Press Pass Stealth Previews /5 #54
2005 Press Pass Stealth Previews /5 #97
2005 Press Pass Stealth Profile #PR1
2005 Press Pass Stealth Samples #48
2005 Press Pass Stealth Samples #51
2005 Press Pass Stealth Samples #54
2005 Press Pass Stealth Samples #87
2005 Press Pass Stealth Samples #97
2005 Press Pass Stealth Samples #100
2005 Press Pass Stealth X-Ray #X48
2005 Press Pass Stealth X-Ray /100 #X51
2005 Press Pass Stealth X-Ray /100 #X54
2005 Press Pass Stealth X-Ray /100 #X87
2005 Press Pass Stealth X-Ray /100 #X97
2005 Press Pass Stealth X-Ray /100 #X100
2005 Press Pass Top Ten #TT1
2005 Press Pass Total Memorabilia Power Pick #TM1
2005 Press Pass Trackside #3
2005 Press Pass Trackside #61
2005 Press Pass Trackside #61B
2005 Press Pass Trackside #70
2005 Press Pass Trackside #83
2005 Press Pass Trackside #95
2005 Press Pass Trackside Dialed In #DI3
2005 Press Pass Trackside Golden /100 #G3
2005 Press Pass Trackside Golden /100 #G61
2005 Press Pass Trackside Golden /100 #G70
2005 Press Pass Trackside Golden /100 #G83
2005 Press Pass Trackside Golden /100 #G95
2005 Press Pass Trackside Hat Giveaway #PPH8
2005 Press Pass Trackside Hot Pass #4
2005 Press Pass Trackside Hot Pass National #4
2005 Press Pass Trackside Hot Pursuit #HP4
2005 Press Pass Trackside Pit Stoppers Autographs /24 #PSJG
2005 Press Pass Trackside Pit Stoppers Cars /85 #PST1
2005 Press Pass Trackside Pit Stoppers Drivers /85 #PSD1
2005 Press Pass Trackside Previews /5 #3
2005 Press Pass Trackside Previews /1 #83
2005 Press Pass Trackside Runnin n' Gunnin #RG2
2005 Press Pass Trackside Samples #3
2005 Press Pass Trackside Samples #61
2005 Press Pass Trackside Samples #70
2005 Press Pass Trackside Samples #83
2005 Press Pass Trackside Samples #95
2005 Press Pass Triple Burner /100 #TB1
2005 Press Pass Triple Burner Exchange /100 #TB1
2005 Press Pass Velocity #V3
2005 Sports Illustrated for Kids #495
2005 VIP #7
2005 VIP #43
2005 VIP #48
2005 VIP #51
2005 VIP #63
2005 VIP #74
2005 VIP #85
2005 VIP Driver's Choice #DC3
2005 VIP Driver's Choice Die Cuts #DC3
2005 VIP Head Gear #2
2005 VIP Head Gear Transparent #2
2005 VIP Lap Leaders #7
2005 VIP Lap Leaders Transparent #7
2005 VIP Making The Show #16
2005 VIP Previews /5 #EB7
2005 VIP Samples #7
2005 VIP Samples #43
2005 VIP Samples #48
2005 VIP Samples #51
2005 VIP Samples #63
2005 VIP Samples #74
2005 VIP Samples #85
2005 VIP Tradin' Paint Cars /110 #TPT2
2005 VIP Tradin' Paint Drivers /90 #TPD2
2005 Wheels American Thunder #8
2005 Wheels American Thunder #34
2005 Wheels American Thunder #40
2005 Wheels American Thunder #52
2005 Wheels American Thunder #63
2005 Wheels American Thunder #65
2005 Wheels American Thunder American Eagle #AE7
2005 Wheels American Thunder American Muscle #AM4
2005 Wheels American Thunder Cool Threads /475 #CT1
2005 Wheels American Thunder Golden Eagle /250 #GE7
2005 Wheels American Thunder Head to Toe /125 #HT10
2005 Wheels American Thunder Medallion #MD14
2005 Wheels American Thunder Previews /5 #8
2005 Wheels American Thunder Pushin Pedal /150 #PP12
2005 Wheels American Thunder Samples #8
2005 Wheels American Thunder Samples #34
2005 Wheels American Thunder Samples #40
2005 Wheels American Thunder Samples #52
2005 Wheels American Thunder Samples #63
2005 Wheels American Thunder Samples #65
2005 Wheels American Thunder Thunder Road #TR12
2005 Wheels American Thunder Triple Hat /190 #TH5
2005 Wheels Autographs #17
2005 Wheels High Gear #16
2005 Wheels High Gear #53
2005 Wheels High Gear #59
2005 Wheels High Gear #66
2005 Wheels High Gear #77
2005 Wheels High Gear #80
2005 Wheels High Gear Flag Chasers Black /55 #FC8
2005 Wheels High Gear Flag Chasers Blue-Yellow /25 #FC8
2005 Wheels High Gear Flag Chasers Checkered /10 #FC8
2005 Wheels High Gear Flag Chasers Green /55 #FC8
2005 Wheels High Gear Flag Chasers Red /55 #FC8
2005 Wheels High Gear Flag Chasers White /55 #FC8
2005 Wheels High Gear Flag Chasers Yellow /55 #FC8
2005 Wheels High Gear Flag to Flag #FF5
2005 Wheels High Gear Full Throttle #FT4
2005 Wheels High Gear Machine #MMB7
2005 Wheels High Gear Man #MMA7
2005 Wheels High Gear MPH /100 #M16
2005 Wheels High Gear MPH /100 #M53
2005 Wheels High Gear MPH /100 #M59
2005 Wheels High Gear MPH /100 #M66
2005 Wheels High Gear MPH /100 #M77
2005 Wheels High Gear MPH /100 #M80
2005 Wheels High Gear Previews Green /5 #EB16
2005 Wheels High Gear Previews Silver /1 #EB77
2005 Wheels High Gear Samples #16
2005 Wheels High Gear Samples #53
2005 Wheels High Gear Samples #59
2005 Wheels High Gear Samples #66
2005 Wheels High Gear Samples #77
2005 Wheels High Gear Samples #80
2005 Wheels High Gear Top Tier #TT3
2006 Press Pass #18
2006 Press Pass #77
2006 Press Pass #85
2006 Press Pass #104
2006 Press Pass Autographs #16
2006 Press Pass Blaster Kmart #JGC
2006 Press Pass Blaster Target #JGB
2006 Press Pass Blaster Wal-Mart #JGA
2006 Press Pass Blue #B18
2006 Press Pass Blue #B77
2006 Press Pass Blue #B85
2006 Press Pass Blue #B104
2006 Press Pass Burning Rubber Autographs /24 #BRJG
2006 Press Pass Burning Rubber Cars /370 #BRT5
2006 Press Pass Burning Rubber Drivers /100 #BRD5
2006 Press Pass Burning Rubber Drivers Gold /1 #BRD5
2006 Press Pass Burnouts /900 #HT2
2006 Press Pass Burnouts Holofoil /100 #HT2
2006 Press Pass Collectors Series Making the Show #MS2
2006 Press Pass Cup Chase #CCR10
2006 Press Pass Cup Chase Prizes #CC6
2006 Press Pass Dominator Jeff Gordon #1
2006 Press Pass Dominator Jeff Gordon #2
2006 Press Pass Dominator Jeff Gordon #3
2006 Press Pass Dominator Jeff Gordon #4
2006 Press Pass Dominator Jeff Gordon #5
2006 Press Pass Dominator Jeff Gordon #6
2006 Press Pass Dominator Jeff Gordon #7
2006 Press Pass Dominator Jeff Gordon #8
2006 Press Pass Dominator Jeff Gordon #9
2006 Press Pass Dominator Jeff Gordon #10
2006 Press Pass Dominator Jeff Gordon #11
2006 Press Pass Dominator Jeff Gordon #12
2006 Press Pass Dominator Jeff Gordon #13
2006 Press Pass Dominator Jeff Gordon #14
2006 Press Pass Dominator Jeff Gordon #15
2006 Press Pass Dominator Jeff Gordon #16
2006 Press Pass Dominator Jeff Gordon #17
2006 Press Pass Dominator Jeff Gordon #18
2006 Press Pass Dominator Jeff Gordon #19
2006 Press Pass Dominator Jeff Gordon #20
2006 Press Pass Dominator Jeff Gordon #21
2006 Press Pass Dominator Jeff Gordon #22
2006 Press Pass Dominator Jeff Gordon #23
2006 Press Pass Dominator Jeff Gordon #24
2006 Press Pass Dominator Jeff Gordon #25
2006 Press Pass Dominator Jeff Gordon #26
2006 Press Pass Dominator Jeff Gordon #27
2006 Press Pass Dominator Jeff Gordon #28
2006 Press Pass Dominator Jeff Gordon #29
2006 Press Pass Dominator Jeff Gordon #30
2006 Press Pass Dominator Jeff Gordon #31
2006 Press Pass Dominator Jeff Gordon #32
2006 Press Pass Dominator Jeff Gordon #33
2006 Press Pass Dominator Jeff Gordon Jumbo #JG1
2006 Press Pass Dominator Jeff Gordon Jumbo #JG2
2006 Press Pass Dominator Jeff Gordon Jumbo #JG3
2006 Press Pass Dominator Tins #JG
2006 Press Pass Double Burner Firesuit-Glove /100 #DB1
2006 Press Pass Double Burner Metal-Tire /100 #DB3
2006 Press Pass Eclipse #10
2006 Press Pass Eclipse #42
2006 Press Pass Eclipse #56
2006 Press Pass Eclipse #74
2006 Press Pass Eclipse Hyperdrive #HP7
2006 Press Pass Eclipse Previews /5 #EB10
2006 Press Pass Eclipse Racing Champions #RC1
2006 Press Pass Eclipse Skidmarks #SM14
2006 Press Pass Eclipse Skidmarks Holofoil /250 #SM14
2006 Press Pass Eclipse Supernova #SU2
2006 Press Pass Eclipse Teammates Autographs /25 #5
2006 Press Pass Eclipse Under Cover Autographs /24 #JG
2006 Press Pass Eclipse Under Cover Cars /140 #UCT11
2006 Press Pass Eclipse Under Cover Double Cover /100 #DC1
2006 Press Pass Eclipse Under Cover Double Cover /100 #DC5
2006 Press Pass Eclipse Under Cover Double Cover Holofoil /25 #DC5
2006 Press Pass Eclipse Under Cover Double Cover Holofoil /25 #DC1
2006 Press Pass Eclipse Under Cover Drivers Gold /1 #UCD11
2006 Press Pass Eclipse Under Cover Drivers Holofoil /100 #UCD11
2006 Press Pass Eclipse Under Cover Drivers Red /225 #UCD11
2006 Press Pass Eclipse Under Cover Drivers Silver /400 #UCD11
2006 Press Pass Four Wide /50 #FWJG
2006 Press Pass Four Wide Checkered Flag /1 #FWJG
2006 Press Pass Game Face #GF1
2006 Press Pass Gold #G18
2006 Press Pass Gold #G77
2006 Press Pass Gold #G85
2006 Press Pass Gold #G104
2006 Press Pass Legends #35
2006 Press Pass Legends #46
2006 Press Pass Legends #48
2006 Press Pass Legends #49
2006 Press Pass Legends Autographs Black /50 #23
2006 Press Pass Legends Blue /1999 #B35
2006 Press Pass Legends Blue /1999 #B46
2006 Press Pass Legends Blue /1999 #B48
2006 Press Pass Legends Blue /1999 #B49
2006 Press Pass Legends Bronze /999 #Z35
2006 Press Pass Legends Bronze /999 #Z46
2006 Press Pass Legends Bronze /999 #Z48
2006 Press Pass Legends Bronze /999 #Z49
2006 Press Pass Legends Champion Threads and Treads Bronze /399 #CTTJG
2006 Press Pass Legends Champion Threads and Treads Gold /99 #CTTJG
2006 Press Pass Legends Champion Threads and Treads Silver /299 #CTTJG
2006 Press Pass Legends Champion Threads Bronze /399 #CTJG
2006 Press Pass Legends Champion Threads Gold /50 #CTJG
2006 Press Pass Legends Champion Threads Patch /25 #CTJG
2006 Press Pass Legends Champion Threads Silver /199 #CTJG
2006 Press Pass Legends Gold /299 #G35
2006 Press Pass Legends Gold /299 #G46
2006 Press Pass Legends Gold /299 #G48
2006 Press Pass Legends Gold /299 #G49
2006 Press Pass Legends Heritage Gold /99 #HE7
2006 Press Pass Legends Heritage Silver /549 #HE7
2006 Press Pass Legends Holofoil /99 #H35
2006 Press Pass Legends Holofoil /99 #H46
2006 Press Pass Legends Holofoil /99 #H48
2006 Press Pass Legends Holofoil /99 #H49
2006 Press Pass Legends Memorable Moments Gold /199 #MM3
2006 Press Pass Legends Memorable Moments Gold /199 #MM6
2006 Press Pass Legends Memorable Moments Gold /199 #MM8
2006 Press Pass Legends Memorable Moments Gold /199 #MM11
2006 Press Pass Legends Memorable Moments Silver /699 #MM3
2006 Press Pass Legends Memorable Moments Silver /699 #MM6
2006 Press Pass Legends Memorable Moments Silver /699 #MM8
2006 Press Pass Legends Memorable Moments Silver /699 #MM11
2006 Press Pass Legends Press Plates Black /1 #PPB35
2006 Press Pass Legends Press Plates Black /1 #PPB46
2006 Press Pass Legends Press Plates Black /1 #PPB48
2006 Press Pass Legends Press Plates Black /1 #PPB49
2006 Press Pass Legends Press Plates Black Backs /1 #PPB35B
2006 Press Pass Legends Press Plates Black Backs /1 #PPB46B
2006 Press Pass Legends Press Plates Black Backs /1 #PPB48B
2006 Press Pass Legends Press Plates Black Backs /1 #PPB49B

s Pass Legends Press Plates Cyan /1 #PPC35
s Pass Legends Press Plates Cyan /1 #PPC46
s Pass Legends Press Plates Cyan /1 #PPC48
s Pass Legends Press Plates Cyan /1 #PPC49
s Pass Legends Press Plates Cyan Backs /1 #PPC35B
s Pass Legends Press Plates Cyan Backs /1 #PPC46B
s Pass Legends Press Plates Cyan Backs /1 #PPC48B
s Pass Legends Press Plates Cyan Backs /1 #PPC49B
s Pass Legends Press Plates Magenta /1 #PPM35
s Pass Legends Press Plates Magenta /1 #PPM46
s Pass Legends Press Plates Magenta /1 #PPM48
s Pass Legends Press Plates Magenta /1 #PPM49
s Pass Legends Press Plates Magenta Backs /1 #PPM35B
s Pass Legends Press Plates Magenta Backs /1 #PPM46B
s Pass Legends Press Plates Magenta Backs /1 #PPM48B
s Pass Legends Press Plates Magenta Backs /1 #PPM49B
s Pass Legends Press Plates Yellow /1 #PPY35
s Pass Legends Press Plates Yellow /1 #PPY46
s Pass Legends Press Plates Yellow /1 #PPY48
s Pass Legends Press Plates Yellow /1 #PPY49
s Pass Legends Press Plates Yellow Backs /1 #PPY35B
s Pass Legends Press Plates Yellow Backs /1 #PPY46B
s Pass Legends Press Plates Yellow Backs /1 #PPY48B
s Pass Legends Press Plates Yellow Backs /1 #PPY49B
ss Pass Legends Previews /5 #EB35
ss Pass Legends Previews /1 #EB46
ss Pass Legends Previews /1 #EB48
ss Pass Legends Previews /1 #EB49
ss Pass Legends Solo /1 #S35
ss Pass Legends Solo /1 #S46
ss Pass Legends Solo /1 #S48
ss Pass Legends Solo /1 #S49
ss Pass Legends Triple Threads /50 #TTJG
ss Pass Optima #19
ss Pass Optima #53
ss Pass Optima #64
ss Pass Optima #82
ss Pass Optima #84
ss Pass Optima #19B
ess Pass Optima Fan Favorite #FF6
ess Pass Optima Gold /100 #G19
ess Pass Optima Gold /100 #G53
ess Pass Optima Gold /100 #G64
ess Pass Optima Gold /100 #G82
ess Pass Optima Gold /100 #G84
ess Pass Optima Previews /5 #EB19
ess Pass Optima Q & A #QA11
ess Pass Optima Rookie Relics Cars /50 #RRT15
ess Pass Optima Rookie Relics Drivers /50 #RRD15
ess Pass Platinum /100 #P18
ress Pass Platinum /100 #P77
ress Pass Platinum /100 #P85
ress Pass Platinum /100 #P104
ress Pass Premium #8
ress Pass Premium #37
ress Pass Premium #48
ress Pass Premium #57
ress Pass Premium #76
ress Pass Premium Asphalt Jungle #AJ3
ress Pass Premium Hot Threads Cars /165 #HTT11
ress Pass Premium Hot Threads Drivers /220 #HTD11
ress Pass Premium Hot Threads Drivers Gold /1 #HTD11
ress Pass Premium In the Zone #IZ10
ress Pass Premium In the Zone Red /250 #IZ10
ress Pass Previews /5 #EB18
ress Pass Previews /1 #EB104
ress Pass Signings #17
ress Pass Signings Gold /50 #17
ress Pass Signings Silver /50 #17
ress Pass Snapshots #SN30
ress Pass Stealth #8
ress Pass Stealth #45
ress Pass Stealth #58
ress Pass Stealth #54
ress Pass Stealth #90
ress Pass Stealth Autographed Hat Entry #PPH7
ress Pass Stealth EFX #EFX3
ress Pass Stealth Gear Grippers Autographs /24 #JG
ress Pass Stealth Gear Grippers Cars Retail /99 #GGT1
ress Pass Stealth Gear Grippers Drivers /99 #GGD1
ress Pass Stealth Hot Pass #HP9
ress Pass Stealth Previews /5 #8
ress Pass Stealth Profile #P3
Press Pass Stealth Retail #8
Press Pass Stealth Retail #45
Press Pass Stealth Retail #58
Press Pass Stealth Retail #90
Press Pass Stealth Retail #54
Press Pass Stealth X-Ray /100 #X8
Press Pass Stealth X-Ray /100 #X45
Press Pass Stealth X-Ray /100 #X54
Press Pass Stealth X-Ray /100 #X58
Press Pass Stealth X-Ray /100 #X90
Press Pass Top 25 Drivers & Rides #C14
Press Pass Top 25 Drivers & Rides #D14
Press Pass Velocity #VE4
TRAKS #9
TRAKS #47
TRAKS Autographs #10
TRAKS Autographs 25 /25 #9
TRAKS Previews /1 #47
TRAKS Previews /1 #9
TRAKS Stickers #24
6 VIP #7
6 VIP #28
6 VIP #60
6 VIP #67
6 VIP #88
6 VIP #CL
6 VIP Head Gear #HG7
6 VIP Head Gear Transparent #HG7
6 VIP Lap Leader #LL7
6 VIP Lap Leader Transparent #LL7
6 VIP Making the Show #MS2
6 VIP Tradin' Paint Autographs /24 #TPJG
6 VIP Tradin' Paint Cars Bronze /145 #TPT6
6 VIP Tradin' Paint Drivers Gold /50 #TPD6
6 VIP Tradin' Paint Drivers Silver /80 #TPD6
06 Wheels American Thunder #8
06 Wheels American Thunder #37
06 Wheels American Thunder #43
06 Wheels American Thunder #70
06 Wheels American Thunder #73
06 Wheels American Thunder #CL
06 Wheels American Thunder American Muscle #AM2
06 Wheels American Thunder American Racing Idol #RI6
06 Wheels American Thunder American Racing Idol Golden /250 #RI6
06 Wheels American Thunder Cool Threads /329 #CT7
06 Wheels American Thunder Double Hat /99 #DH7
06 Wheels American Thunder Grandstand #GS6
06 Wheels American Thunder Head to Toe /99 #HT14
06 Wheels American Thunder Previews /5 #EB8
06 Wheels American Thunder Previews /1 #EB73
06 Wheels American Thunder Pushin' Pedal /199 #PP13
06 Wheels American Thunder Thunder Road #TR10
06 Wheels Autographs #17
06 Wheels High Gear #10
06 Wheels High Gear #16B
2006 Wheels High Gear #67
2006 Wheels High Gear #80
2006 Wheels High Gear #90
2006 Wheels High Gear Flag Chasers Black /110 #FC2
2006 Wheels High Gear Flag Chasers Blue-Yellow /65 #FC2
2006 Wheels High Gear Flag Chasers Checkered /3 #FC2
2006 Wheels High Gear Flag Chasers Green /110 #FC2
2006 Wheels High Gear Flag Chasers Red /110 #FC2
2006 Wheels High Gear Flag Chasers White /110 #FC2
2006 Wheels High Gear Flag Chasers Yellow /110 #FC2
2006 Wheels High Gear Flag to Flag #FF7
2006 Wheels High Gear Full Throttle #FT3
2006 Wheels High Gear Man & Machine Cars #MMB2
2006 Wheels High Gear Man & Machine Drivers #MMA2
2006 Wheels High Gear MPH /100 #M10
2006 Wheels High Gear MPH /100 #M67
2006 Wheels High Gear MPH /100 #M80
2006 Wheels High Gear MPH /100 #M90
2006 Wheels High Gear Previews Green /5 #EB10
2006 Wheels High Gear Previews Silver /1 #EB80
2007 Press Pass #9
2007 Press Pass #73
2007 Press Pass #100
2007 Press Pass #116
2007 Press Pass Autographs #13
2007 Press Pass Blue #B9
2007 Press Pass Blue #B73
2007 Press Pass Blue #B100
2007 Press Pass Blue #B116
2007 Press Pass Burning Rubber Autographs /24 #BRSJG
2007 Press Pass Burning Rubber Drivers /75 #BRD11
2007 Press Pass Burning Rubber Drivers /75 #BRD13
2007 Press Pass Burning Rubber Drivers Gold /1 #BRD11
2007 Press Pass Burning Rubber Drivers Gold /1 #BRD13
2007 Press Pass Burning Rubber Team /325 #BRT11
2007 Press Pass Burning Rubber Team /325 #BRT13
2007 Press Pass Burnouts #BO6
2007 Press Pass Burnouts Blue /99 #BO6
2007 Press Pass Burnouts Gold /299 #BO6
2007 Press Pass Collector's Series Box Set #SB7
2007 Press Pass Cup Chase #CCR1
2007 Press Pass Cup Chase Prizes #CC2
2007 Press Pass Dale The Movie #35
2007 Press Pass Dale The Movie #45
2007 Press Pass Double Burner Firesuit-Glove /100 #DB6
2007 Press Pass Double Burner Firesuit-Glove Exchange /100 #DB6
2007 Press Pass Double Burner Metal-Tire /100 #DBJG
2007 Press Pass Double Burner Metal-Tire Exchange /100 #DBJG
2007 Press Pass Eclipse #0
2007 Press Pass Eclipse #6A
2007 Press Pass Eclipse #33
2007 Press Pass Eclipse #47
2007 Press Pass Eclipse #55
2007 Press Pass Eclipse #6B
2007 Press Pass Eclipse Ecliptic #EC5
2007 Press Pass Eclipse Gold /25 #G6
2007 Press Pass Eclipse Gold /25 #G33
2007 Press Pass Eclipse Gold /25 #G47
2007 Press Pass Eclipse Gold /25 #G55
2007 Press Pass Eclipse Hyperdrive #HD7
2007 Press Pass Eclipse Previews /5 #EB6
2007 Press Pass Eclipse Previews /5 #EB33
2007 Press Pass Eclipse Racing Champions #RC7
2007 Press Pass Eclipse Red /1 #R6
2007 Press Pass Eclipse Red /1 #R33
2007 Press Pass Eclipse Red /1 #R47
2007 Press Pass Eclipse Red /1 #R55
2007 Press Pass Eclipse Skidmarks #SM16
2007 Press Pass Eclipse Skidmarks Holofoil /250 #SM16
2007 Press Pass Eclipse Teammates Autographs /25 #7
2007 Press Pass Eclipse Under Cover Autographs /24 #UCJG
2007 Press Pass Eclipse Under Cover Double Cover Name /25 #DC3
2007 Press Pass Eclipse Under Cover Double Cover NASCAR /99 #DC3
2007 Press Pass Eclipse Under Cover Drivers /450 #UCD13
2007 Press Pass Eclipse Under Cover Drivers Eclipse /1 #UCD13
2007 Press Pass Eclipse Under Cover Drivers Name /99 #UCD13
2007 Press Pass Eclipse Under Cover Drivers NASCAR /270 #UCD13
2007 Press Pass Eclipse Under Cover Teams /135 #UCT13
2007 Press Pass Eclipse Under Cover Teams NASCAR /25 #UCT13
2007 Press Pass Four Wide /50 #FWJG
2007 Press Pass Four Wide Checkered Flag /1 #FWJG
2007 Press Pass Four Wide Checkered Flag Exchange /1 #FWJG
2007 Press Pass Four Wide Exchange /50 #FWJG
2007 Press Pass Gold #G9
2007 Press Pass Gold #G73
2007 Press Pass Gold #G100
2007 Press Pass Gold #G116
2007 Press Pass Hot Treads #HT3
2007 Press Pass Hot Treads Blue /99 #HT3
2007 Press Pass Hot Treads Gold /299 #HT3
2007 Press Pass K-Mart #JGC
2007 Press Pass Legends #40
2007 Press Pass Legends #68
2007 Press Pass Legends Autographs Blue /48 #8
2007 Press Pass Legends Autographs Inscriptions Blue /9 #6
2007 Press Pass Legends Blue /999 #B40
2007 Press Pass Legends Blue /999 #B68
2007 Press Pass Legends Bronze /599 #Z40
2007 Press Pass Legends Bronze /599 #Z68
2007 Press Pass Legends Gold /249 #G40
2007 Press Pass Legends Gold /249 #G68
2007 Press Pass Legends Holofoil /99 #H40
2007 Press Pass Legends Holofoil /99 #H68
2007 Press Pass Legends Memorable Moments Gold /169 #MM3
2007 Press Pass Legends Memorable Moments Silver /499 #MM3
2007 Press Pass Legends Press Plates Black /1 #PP40
2007 Press Pass Legends Press Plates Black /1 #PP68
2007 Press Pass Legends Press Plates Black Backs /1 #PP40
2007 Press Pass Legends Press Plates Black Backs /1 #PP68
2007 Press Pass Legends Press Plates Cyan /1 #PP40
2007 Press Pass Legends Press Plates Cyan /1 #PP68
2007 Press Pass Legends Press Plates Cyan Backs /1 #PP40
2007 Press Pass Legends Press Plates Cyan Backs /1 #PP68
2007 Press Pass Legends Press Plates Magenta /1 #PP40
2007 Press Pass Legends Press Plates Magenta /1 #PP68
2007 Press Pass Legends Press Plates Magenta Backs /1 #PP40
2007 Press Pass Legends Press Plates Magenta Backs /1 #PP68
2007 Press Pass Legends Press Plates Yellow /1 #PP40
2007 Press Pass Legends Press Plates Yellow /1 #PP68
2007 Press Pass Legends Press Plates Yellow Backs /1 #PP40
2007 Press Pass Legends Press Plates Yellow Backs /1 #PP68
2007 Press Pass Legends Previews /5 #EB40
2007 Press Pass Legends Previews /1 #EB68
2007 Press Pass Legends Signature Series /25 #JG
2007 Press Pass Legends Solo /1 #S40
2007 Press Pass Legends Solo /1 #S68
2007 Press Pass Legends Sunday Swatches Bronze /199 #JGSS
2007 Press Pass Legends Sunday Swatches Gold /50 #JGSS
2007 Press Pass Legends Sunday Swatches Silver /99 #JGSS
2007 Press Pass Legends Victory Lane Bronze /199 #VL2
2007 Press Pass Legends Victory Lane Bronze /199 #VL3
2007 Press Pass Legends Victory Lane Gold /25 #VL2
2007 Press Pass Legends Victory Lane Gold /25 #VL3
2007 Press Pass Legends Victory Lane Silver /99 #VL2
2007 Press Pass Legends Victory Lane Silver /99 #VL3
2007 Press Pass Platinum /100 #P9
2007 Press Pass Platinum /100 #P73
2007 Press Pass Platinum /100 #P100
2007 Press Pass Platinum /100 #P116
2007 Press Pass Premium #21
2007 Press Pass Premium #35
2007 Press Pass Premium #49
2007 Press Pass Premium #57
2007 Press Pass Premium #69
2007 Press Pass Premium #72
2007 Press Pass Premium #78
2007 Press Pass Premium Concrete Chaos #CC1
2007 Press Pass Premium Hot Threads Autographs /24 #HTJG
2007 Press Pass Premium Hot Threads Drivers /145 #HTD8
2007 Press Pass Premium Hot Threads Drivers Gold /1 #HTD8
2007 Press Pass Premium Hot Threads Patch /8 #HTP3
2007 Press Pass Premium Hot Threads Patch /15 #HTP2
2007 Press Pass Premium Hot Threads Team /160 #HTT8
2007 Press Pass Premium Performance Driven #PD10
2007 Press Pass Premium Performance Driven Red /250 #PD10
2007 Press Pass Premium Red /15 #R21
2007 Press Pass Premium Red /15 #R35
2007 Press Pass Premium Red /15 #R49
2007 Press Pass Premium Red /15 #R57
2007 Press Pass Premium Red /15 #R69
2007 Press Pass Premium Red /5 #R72
2007 Press Pass Premium Red /5 #R78
2007 Press Pass Previews /5 #EB9
2007 Press Pass Previews /1 #EB116
2007 Press Pass Race Day #RD1
2007 Press Pass Signings #22
2007 Press Pass Signings Blue /25 #8
2007 Press Pass Signings Gold /50 #18
2007 Press Pass Signings Press Plates Black /1 #15
2007 Press Pass Signings Press Plates Cyan /1 #14
2007 Press Pass Signings Press Plates Magenta /1 #14
2007 Press Pass Signings Press Plates Yellow /1 #14
2007 Press Pass Signings Silver /100 #17
2007 Press Pass Snapshots #SN7
2007 Press Pass Stealth #8
2007 Press Pass Stealth #52
2007 Press Pass Stealth #60
2007 Press Pass Stealth #89
2007 Press Pass Stealth #72
2007 Press Pass Stealth Battle Armor Autographs /24 #BASJG
2007 Press Pass Stealth Battle Armor Drivers /150 #BAD1
2007 Press Pass Stealth Battle Armor Teams /85 #BAT1
2007 Press Pass Stealth Chrome #8A
2007 Press Pass Stealth Chrome #52
2007 Press Pass Stealth Chrome #60
2007 Press Pass Stealth Chrome #89
2007 Press Pass Stealth Chrome #8B
2007 Press Pass Stealth Chrome #8C
2007 Press Pass Stealth Chrome #72
2007 Press Pass Stealth Chrome Exclusives /99 #X8
2007 Press Pass Stealth Chrome Exclusives /99 #X52
2007 Press Pass Stealth Chrome Exclusives /99 #X60
2007 Press Pass Stealth Chrome Exclusives /99 #X72
2007 Press Pass Stealth Chrome Exclusives /99 #X89
2007 Press Pass Stealth Chrome Platinum /25 #P8
2007 Press Pass Stealth Chrome Platinum /25 #P52
2007 Press Pass Stealth Chrome Platinum /25 #P60
2007 Press Pass Stealth Chrome Platinum /25 #P72
2007 Press Pass Stealth Chrome Platinum /25 #P89
2007 Press Pass Stealth Fusion #F2
2007 Press Pass Stealth Mach 07 #M7-2
2007 Press Pass Stealth Maximum Access #MA8
2007 Press Pass Stealth Maximum Access Autographs /25 #MA8
2007 Press Pass Stealth Previews /1 #EB89
2007 Press Pass Stealth Previews /5 #EB8
2007 Press Pass Target #JGB
2007 Press Pass Target Race Win Tires #RW6
2007 Press Pass Target Race Win Tires #RW8
2007 Press Pass Velocity #V5
2007 Press Pass Wal-Mart #JGA
2007 Press Pass Wal-Mart Autographs /45 #JG
2007 Traks #8
2007 Traks #58
2007 Traks #74
2007 Traks #87
2007 Traks #94
2007 Traks Driver's Seat #DS2B
2007 Traks Driver's Seat #DS2
2007 Traks Driver's Seat National #DS2
2007 Traks Gold #G8
2007 Traks Gold #G58
2007 Traks Gold #G74
2007 Traks Gold #G87
2007 Traks Gold #G94
2007 Traks Holofoil /50 #H8
2007 Traks Holofoil /50 #H58
2007 Traks Holofoil /50 #H74
2007 Traks Holofoil /50 #H87
2007 Traks Holofoil /50 #H94
2007 Traks Hot Pursuit #HP1
2007 Traks Previews /5 #EB8
2007 Traks Red /10 #R8
2007 Traks Red /10 #R58
2007 Traks Red /10 #R74
2007 Traks Red /10 #R87
2007 Traks Red /10 #R94
2007 Traks Target Exclusives #JGA
2007 Traks Track Time #TT6
2007 Traks Wal-Mart Exclusives #JGB
2007 VIP #9
2007 VIP #43
2007 VIP #53
2007 VIP #76
2007 VIP #77
2007 VIP #79
2007 VIP #82
2007 VIP Gear Gallery #GG4
2007 VIP Gear Gallery Transparent #GG4
2007 VIP Get A Grip Drivers /70 #GGD13
2007 VIP Get A Grip Teams /70 #GGT13
2007 VIP Pedal To The Metal /50 #PM8
2007 VIP Previews /5 #EB9
2007 VIP Sunday Best #SB7
2007 VIP Trophy Club #TC9
2007 VIP Trophy Club Transparent #TC9
2007 Wheels American Thunder #1
2007 Wheels American Thunder #9
2007 Wheels American Thunder #45
2007 Wheels American Thunder #50
2007 Wheels American Thunder #60
2007 Wheels American Thunder #70
2007 Wheels American Thunder #76
2007 Wheels American Thunder American Dreams #AD6
2007 Wheels American Thunder American Dreams Gold /250 #ADG6
2007 Wheels American Thunder American Muscle #AM9
2007 Wheels American Thunder Autographed Hat Instant Winner /1 #AH10
2007 Wheels American Thunder Cool Threads /299 #CT13
2007 Wheels American Thunder Head to Toe /99 #HT14
2007 Wheels American Thunder Previews /5 #EB1
2007 Wheels American Thunder Previews /5 #EB9
2007 Wheels American Thunder Previews /1 #EB50
2007 Wheels American Thunder Pushin' Pedal /99 #PP16
2007 Wheels American Thunder Starting Grid #SG3
2007 Wheels American Thunder Thunder Road #TR7
2007 Wheels American Thunder Thunder Strokes #14
2007 Wheels American Thunder Thunder Strokes Press Plates Black /1 #14
2007 Wheels American Thunder Thunder Strokes Press Plates Cyan /1 #14
2007 Wheels American Thunder Thunder Strokes Press Plates Magenta /1 #14
2007 Wheels American Thunder Thunder Strokes Press Plates Yellow /1 #14
2007 Wheels American Thunder Triple Hat /99 #TH8
2007 Wheels High Gear #6A
2007 Wheels High Gear #77
2007 Wheels High Gear #82
2007 Wheels High Gear #CL
2007 Wheels High Gear #6B
2007 Wheels High Gear Driven #DR14
2007 Wheels High Gear Final Standings Gold /6 #FS6
2007 Wheels High Gear Flag Chasers Black /89 #FC8
2007 Wheels High Gear Flag Chasers Blue-Yellow /50 #FC8
2007 Wheels High Gear Flag Chasers Checkered /10 #FC8
2007 Wheels High Gear Flag Chasers Green /89 #FC8
2007 Wheels High Gear Flag Chasers Red /89 #FC8
2007 Wheels High Gear Flag Chasers White /89 #FC8
2007 Wheels High Gear Flag Chasers Yellow /89 #FC8
2007 Wheels High Gear Full Throttle #FT1
2007 Wheels High Gear Last Lap /10 #LL6
2007 Wheels High Gear MPH /100 #M6
2007 Wheels High Gear MPH /100 #M77
2007 Wheels High Gear MPH /100 #M82
2007 Wheels High Gear MPH /100 #MCL
2007 Wheels High Gear Previews /5 #EB6
2007 Wheels High Gear Top Tier #TT6
2008 Press Pass #0
2008 Press Pass #1
2008 Press Pass #64
2008 Press Pass #92
2008 Press Pass #108
2008 Press Pass Autographs #15
2008 Press Pass Autographs Press Plates Black /1 #11
2008 Press Pass Autographs Press Plates Cyan /1 #11
2008 Press Pass Autographs Press Plates Magenta /1 #11
2008 Press Pass Autographs Press Plates Yellow /1 #11
2008 Press Pass Blue #B92
2008 Press Pass Blue #B108
2008 Press Pass Blue #B64
2008 Press Pass Blue #B1
2008 Press Pass Burning Rubber Autographs /24 #BRJG
2008 Press Pass Burning Rubber Drivers /60 #BRD8
2008 Press Pass Burning Rubber Drivers /60 #BRD9
2008 Press Pass Burning Rubber Drivers /60 #BRD13
2008 Press Pass Burning Rubber Drivers Gold /1 #BRD13
2008 Press Pass Burning Rubber Drivers Gold /1 #BRD9
2008 Press Pass Burning Rubber Drivers Gold /1 #BRD8
2008 Press Pass Burning Rubber Drivers Prime Cuts /25 #BRD13
2008 Press Pass Burning Rubber Drivers Prime Cuts /25 #BRD9
2008 Press Pass Burning Rubber Drivers Prime Cuts /25 #BRD8
2008 Press Pass Burning Rubber Teams /175 #BRT13
2008 Press Pass Burning Rubber Teams /175 #BRT9
2008 Press Pass Burning Rubber Teams /175 #BRT8
2008 Press Pass Burnouts #BO1
2008 Press Pass Burnouts Blue /99 #BO1
2008 Press Pass Burnouts Gold /299 #BO1
2008 Press Pass Collector's Series Box Set #10
2008 Press Pass Cup Chase #CC3
2008 Press Pass Cup Chase Prizes #CC3
2008 Press Pass Daytona 500 50th Anniversary #34
2008 Press Pass Daytona 500 50th Anniversary #36
2008 Press Pass Daytona 500 50th Anniversary #42
2008 Press Pass Double Burner Firesuit-Glove /100 #DBJG
2008 Press Pass Double Burner Metal-Tire /100 #DBJG
2008 Press Pass Eclipse #2
2008 Press Pass Eclipse #28A
2008 Press Pass Eclipse #38
2008 Press Pass Eclipse #49
2008 Press Pass Eclipse #50
2008 Press Pass Eclipse #55
2008 Press Pass Eclipse #79
2008 Press Pass Eclipse #28B
2008 Press Pass Eclipse #75
2008 Press Pass Eclipse Escape Velocity #EV1
2008 Press Pass Eclipse Gold /25 #G2
2008 Press Pass Eclipse Gold /25 #G28
2008 Press Pass Eclipse Gold /25 #G38
2008 Press Pass Eclipse Gold /25 #G49
2008 Press Pass Eclipse Gold /25 #G50
2008 Press Pass Eclipse Gold /25 #G55
2008 Press Pass Eclipse Gold /25 #G75
2008 Press Pass Eclipse Gold /25 #G79
2008 Press Pass Eclipse Hyperdrive #HP3
2008 Press Pass Eclipse Previews /5 #EB2
2008 Press Pass Eclipse Previews /5 #EB28
2008 Press Pass Eclipse Previews /1 #EB75
2008 Press Pass Eclipse Previews /1 #EB79
2008 Press Pass Eclipse Red /1 #R79
2008 Press Pass Eclipse Red /1 #R2
2008 Press Pass Eclipse Red /1 #R28
2008 Press Pass Eclipse Red /1 #R38
2008 Press Pass Eclipse Red /1 #R49
2008 Press Pass Eclipse Red /1 #R50
2008 Press Pass Eclipse Red /1 #R55
2008 Press Pass Eclipse Red /1 #R75
2008 Press Pass Eclipse Star Tracks #ST4
2008 Press Pass Eclipse Star Tracks Holofoil /250 #ST4
2008 Press Pass Eclipse Stellar #ST2
2008 Press Pass Eclipse Teammates Autographs /25 #EG
2008 Press Pass Eclipse Teammates Autographs /25 #EGJM
2008 Press Pass Eclipse Under Cover Autographs /24 #UCJG
2008 Press Pass Eclipse Under Cover Double Cover Name /25 #DC6
2008 Press Pass Eclipse Under Cover Double Cover NASCAR /99 #DC6
2008 Press Pass Eclipse Under Cover Drivers /250 #UCD15
2008 Press Pass Eclipse Under Cover Drivers Eclipse /1 #UCD15
2008 Press Pass Eclipse Under Cover Drivers Name /50 #UCD15
2008 Press Pass Eclipse Under Cover Drivers NASCAR /150 #UCD15
2008 Press Pass Eclipse Under Cover Teams /99 #UCT15
2008 Press Pass Eclipse Under Cover Teams NASCAR /25 #UCT15
2008 Press Pass Four Wide /50 #FWJG
2008 Press Pass Four Wide Checkered Flag /1 #FWJG
2008 Press Pass Gold #G108
2008 Press Pass Gold #G92
2008 Press Pass Gold #G64
2008 Press Pass Gold #G1
2008 Press Pass Hot Treads #HT5
2008 Press Pass Hot Treads Blue /99 #HT5
2008 Press Pass Hot Treads Gold /299 #HT5
2008 Press Pass Legends #49
2008 Press Pass Legends #59
2008 Press Pass Legends 500 Club /560 #5C6
2008 Press Pass Legends 500 Club Gold /99 #5C6
2008 Press Pass Legends Autographs Black Inscriptions /10 #JG
2008 Press Pass Legends Autographs Blue /75 #JG
2008 Press Pass Legends Autographs Press Plates Black /1 #JG
2008 Press Pass Legends Autographs Press Plates Cyan /1 #JG
2008 Press Pass Legends Autographs Press Plates Magenta /1 #JG
2008 Press Pass Legends Autographs Press Plates Yellow /1 #JG
2008 Press Pass Legends Blue /599 #49
2008 Press Pass Legends Blue /599 #59
2008 Press Pass Legends Bronze /299 #49
2008 Press Pass Legends Bronze /299 #59
2008 Press Pass Legends Gold /99 #49
2008 Press Pass Legends Gold /99 #59
2008 Press Pass Legends Holo /25 #49
2008 Press Pass Legends Holo /25 #59
2008 Press Pass Legends Previews /5 #EB49
2008 Press Pass Legends Previews /1 #EB59
2008 Press Pass Legends Printing Plates Black /1 #49
2008 Press Pass Legends Printing Plates Black /1 #59
2008 Press Pass Legends Printing Plates Cyan /1 #49
2008 Press Pass Legends Printing Plates Cyan /1 #59
2008 Press Pass Legends Printing Plates Magenta /1 #49
2008 Press Pass Legends Printing Plates Magenta /1 #59
2008 Press Pass Legends Printing Plates Yellow /1 #49
2008 Press Pass Legends Printing Plates Yellow /1 #59
2008 Press Pass Legends Prominent Pieces Firesuit-Glove Gold /10 #PP1JG
2008 Press Pass Legends Prominent Pieces Metal-Tire Bronze /99 #PP3JG
2008 Press Pass Legends Prominent Pieces Metal-Tire Gold /25 #PP3JG
2008 Press Pass Legends Prominent Pieces Metal-Tire Silver /50 #PP3JG
2008 Press Pass Legends Signature Series Memorabilia /25 #LSJG
2008 Press Pass Legends Solo /1 #49
2008 Press Pass Legends Solo /1 #59
2008 Press Pass Platinum /100 #P108
2008 Press Pass Platinum /100 #P92
2008 Press Pass Platinum /100 #P64
2008 Press Pass Platinum /100 #P1
2008 Press Pass Premium #19
2008 Press Pass Premium #43
2008 Press Pass Premium #59
2008 Press Pass Premium #79
2008 Press Pass Premium #82
2008 Press Pass Premium Clean Air #CA1
2008 Press Pass Premium Going Global #GG5
2008 Press Pass Premium Going Global Red /250 #GG5
2008 Press Pass Premium Hot Threads Autographs /24 #HTJG
2008 Press Pass Premium Hot Threads Drivers /120 #HTD9
2008 Press Pass Premium Hot Threads Drivers Gold /1 #HTD9
2008 Press Pass Premium Hot Threads Patches #HTP7
2008 Press Pass Premium Hot Threads Patches #HTP6
2008 Press Pass Premium Hot Threads Patches /8 #HTP5
2008 Press Pass Premium Hot Threads Team /120 #HTT9
2008 Press Pass Premium Previews /5 #EB19
2008 Press Pass Premium Previews /1 #EB59
2008 Press Pass Premium Red /15 #19
2008 Press Pass Premium Red /15 #43
2008 Press Pass Premium Red /15 #59
2008 Press Pass Premium Red /5 #79
2008 Press Pass Premium Red /5 #82
2008 Press Pass Premium Team Signed Baseballs #HMS
2008 Press Pass Premium Team Signed Baseballs #EHMS
2008 Press Pass Premium Wal-Mart #WM5
2008 Press Pass Previews /1 #EB108
2008 Press Pass Previews /5 #EB1
2008 Press Pass Race Day #RD4
2008 Press Pass Signings #23
2008 Press Pass Signings Blue /25 #8
2008 Press Pass Signings Gold /50 #21
2008 Press Pass Signings Press Plates Black /1 #14
2008 Press Pass Signings Press Plates Black /1 #JG
2008 Press Pass Signings Press Plates Cyan /1 #14
2008 Press Pass Signings Press Plates Magenta /1 #14
2008 Press Pass Signings Press Plates Magenta #JG
2008 Press Pass Signings Press Plates Yellow /1 #14
2008 Press Pass Speedway #5
2008 Press Pass Speedway #61
2008 Press Pass Speedway #73
2008 Press Pass Speedway #78
2008 Press Pass Speedway #85
2008 Press Pass Speedway Blur #B5
2008 Press Pass Speedway Cockpit #CP7
2008 Press Pass Speedway Garage Graphs Duals /50 #GL
2008 Press Pass Speedway Gold #G85
2008 Press Pass Speedway Gold #G78
2008 Press Pass Speedway Gold #G73
2008 Press Pass Speedway Gold #G61
2008 Press Pass Speedway Gold #G5
2008 Press Pass Speedway Holofoil /50 #H85
2008 Press Pass Speedway Holofoil /50 #H78
2008 Press Pass Speedway Holofoil /50 #H73
2008 Press Pass Speedway Holofoil /50 #H61
2008 Press Pass Speedway Holofoil /50 #H5
2008 Press Pass Speedway Previews /5 #EB5
2008 Press Pass Speedway Red /10 #R78
2008 Press Pass Speedway Red /10 #R73
2008 Press Pass Speedway Red /10 #R61
2008 Press Pass Speedway Red /10 #R5
2008 Press Pass Speedway Red /10 #R85
2008 Press Pass Speedway Test Drive #TD1
2008 Press Pass Starting Grid #SG10
2008 Press Pass Stealth #11
2008 Press Pass Stealth #60
2008 Press Pass Stealth #84
2008 Press Pass Stealth #67
2008 Press Pass Stealth Battle Armor Autographs /24 #BASJG
2008 Press Pass Stealth Battle Armor Drivers /120 #BAD3
2008 Press Pass Stealth Battle Armor Teams /115 #BAT3
2008 Press Pass Stealth Chrome #11A
2008 Press Pass Stealth Chrome #60
2008 Press Pass Stealth Chrome #84
2008 Press Pass Stealth Chrome #11B
2008 Press Pass Stealth Chrome #67
2008 Press Pass Stealth Chrome Exclusives /25 #11
2008 Press Pass Stealth Chrome Exclusives /25 #60
2008 Press Pass Stealth Chrome Exclusives /25 #67
2008 Press Pass Stealth Chrome Exclusives /25 #84
2008 Press Pass Stealth Chrome Exclusives Gold /99 #11
2008 Press Pass Stealth Chrome Exclusives Gold /99 #60
2008 Press Pass Stealth Chrome Exclusives Gold /99 #67
2008 Press Pass Stealth Chrome Exclusives Gold /99 #84
2008 Press Pass Stealth Mach 08 #M8-1
2008 Press Pass Stealth Maximum Access #MA10
2008 Press Pass Stealth Maximum Access Autographs /25 #MA10
2008 Press Pass Stealth Previews /1 #84
2008 Press Pass Stealth Previews /5 #11
2008 Press Pass Stealth Synthesis #S9
2008 Press Pass Stealth Target #TA11
2008 Press Pass Target #JGB
2008 Press Pass Target Victory Tires /50 #TTJG
2008 Press Pass VIP National Convention Promo #6
2008 Press Pass Wal-Mart #JGA
2008 Press Pass Wal-Mart Autographs /50 #3
2008 Press Pass Weekend Warriors #WW1
2008 VIP #12
2008 VIP #50
2008 VIP All Access #AA6
2008 VIP Gear Gallery #GG10
2008 VIP Gear Gallery Memorabilia /50 #GGJG
2008 VIP Gear Gallery Transparent #GG10
2008 VIP Get a Grip Autographs /24 #GGSJG
2008 VIP Get a Grip Drivers /80 #GGD2
2008 VIP Get a Grip Teams /99 #GGT2
2008 VIP National Promos #6
2008 VIP Previews /5 #EB12
2008 VIP Triple Grip /25 #TG1
2008 VIP Trophy Club #TC9
2008 VIP Trophy Club Transparent #TC9
2008 Wheels American Thunder #1
2008 Wheels American Thunder #12
2008 Wheels American Thunder #56
2008 Wheels American Thunder #75
2008 Wheels American Thunder #41
2008 Wheels American Thunder American Dreams #AD5
2008 Wheels American Thunder American Dreams Gold /250 #AD5
2008 Wheels American Thunder Autographed Hat Winner /1 #WHJG
2008 Wheels American Thunder Campaign Buttons #JG
2008 Wheels American Thunder Campaign Buttons Blue #JG
2008 Wheels American Thunder Campaign Buttons Gold #JG
2008 Wheels American Thunder Campaign Trail #CT15
2008 Wheels American Thunder Delegates #D7
2008 Wheels American Thunder Head to Toe /99 #HT9
2008 Wheels American Thunder Motorcade #M1
2008 Wheels American Thunder Previews /5 #1
2008 Wheels American Thunder Previews /5 #12
2008 Wheels American Thunder Previews /1 #75
2008 Wheels American Thunder Pushin' Pedal /99 #PP 9
2008 Wheels American Thunder Trackside Treasury Autographs #JG
2008 Wheels American Thunder Trackside Treasury Autographs Gold /25 #JG
2008 Wheels American Thunder Trackside Treasury Autographs Printing Plates Black /1 #JG
2008 Wheels American Thunder Trackside Treasury Autographs Printing Plates Cyan /1 #JG
2008 Wheels American Thunder Trackside Treasury Autographs Printing Plates Magenta /1 #JG
2008 Wheels American Thunder Trackside Treasury Autographs Printing Plates Yellow /1 #JG
2008 Wheels American Thunder Triple Hat /125 #TH9
2008 Wheels Autographs #11
2008 Wheels Autographs Chase Edition /25 #3
2008 Wheels Autographs Press Plates Black /1 #11
2008 Wheels Autographs Press Plates Cyan /1 #11
2008 Wheels Autographs Press Plates Magenta /1 #11
2008 Wheels Autographs Press Plates Yellow /1 #11
2008 Wheels High Gear #2
2008 Wheels High Gear #52
2008 Wheels High Gear #56
2008 Wheels High Gear #58
2008 Wheels High Gear #60A
2008 Wheels High Gear #62
2008 Wheels High Gear #67
2008 Wheels High Gear #60B
2008 Wheels High Gear Driven #DR22
2008 Wheels High Gear Final Standings /2 #F2
2008 Wheels High Gear Flag Chasers Black /89 #FC3
2008 Wheels High Gear Flag Chasers Blue-Yellow /50 #FC3
2008 Wheels High Gear Flag Chasers Checkered /20 #FC3
2008 Wheels High Gear Flag Chasers Green /60 #FC3
2008 Wheels High Gear Flag Chasers Red /89 #FC3
2008 Wheels High Gear Flag Chasers White /65 #FC3
2008 Wheels High Gear Flag Chasers Yellow /89 #FC3
2008 Wheels High Gear Full Throttle #FT1
2008 Wheels High Gear Last Lap /10 #LL2
2008 Wheels High Gear Last Lap Holofoil /5 #LL2
2008 Wheels High Gear MPH /100 #M2
2008 Wheels High Gear MPH /100 #M52
2008 Wheels High Gear MPH /100 #M56
2008 Wheels High Gear MPH /100 #M58
2008 Wheels High Gear MPH /100 #M60
2008 Wheels High Gear MPH /100 #M62
2008 Wheels High Gear MPH /100 #M67
2008 Wheels High Gear Previews /5 #EB2
2008 Wheels High Gear The Chase #TC2
2009 Action/RCCA Elite 1:24 /240 #24
2009 Element #10
2009 Element #51
2009 Element #62
2009 Element #77
2009 Element #90
2009 Element Elements of the Race Black Flag /99 #ERBJG
2009 Element Elements of the Race Black-White Flag /50 #ERXJG
2009 Element Elements of the Race Blue-Yellow Flag /50 #ERBOJG
2009 Element Elements of the Race Checkered Flag /5 #ERCJG
2009 Element Elements of the Race Green Flag /50 #ERGJG
2009 Element Elements of the Race Red Flag /99 #ERRJG
2009 Element Elements of the Race White Flag /75 #ERWJG
2009 Element Elements of the Race Yellow Flag /99 #ERYJG
2009 Element Kinetic Energy #KE2
2009 Element Lab Report #LR10
2009 Element Missing Elements #ME2
2009 Element Missing Elements Exchange #ME2
2009 Element Previews /5 #10
2009 Element Previews /1 #51
2009 Element Radioactive /100 #10
2009 Element Radioactive /100 #51
2009 Element Radioactive /100 #62
2009 Element Radioactive /100 #77
2009 Element Radioactive /100 #90
2009 Press Pass #0
2009 Press Pass #10
2009 Press Pass #55
2009 Press Pass #116
2009 Press Pass #129
2009 Press Pass #181
2009 Press Pass #194
2009 Press Pass #195
2009 Press Pass #196
2009 Press Pass #209
2009 Press Pass #215
2009 Press Pass #218
2009 Press Pass #CL2
2009 Press Pass #200
2009 Press Pass Autographs Chase Edition /25 #JG
2009 Press Pass Autographs Gold #17
2009 Press Pass Autographs Printing Plates Black /1 #17
2009 Press Pass Autographs Printing Plates Cyan /1 #17
2009 Press Pass Autographs Printing Plates Magenta /1 #17
2009 Press Pass Autographs Printing Plates Yellow /1 #17
2009 Press Pass Autographs Silver #20
2009 Press Pass Autographs Track Edition /25 #JG
2009 Press Pass Blue #10
2009 Press Pass Blue #55
2009 Press Pass Blue #116
2009 Press Pass Blue #129
2009 Press Pass Blue #181
2009 Press Pass Blue #194
2009 Press Pass Blue #195
2009 Press Pass Blue #196
2009 Press Pass Blue #200
2009 Press Pass Blue #209
2009 Press Pass Blue #215
2009 Press Pass Blue #218
2009 Press Pass Blue #CL2
2009 Press Pass Burning Rubber Autographs /24 #BRSJG
2009 Press Pass Chase for the Sprint Cup #CC6
2009 Press Pass Cup Chase #CCR13
2009 Press Pass Cup Chase Prizes #CC6
2009 Press Pass Daytona 500 Tires /25 #TTJG
2009 Press Pass Eclipse #15
2009 Press Pass Eclipse #31
2009 Press Pass Eclipse #38
2009 Press Pass Eclipse #51
2009 Press Pass Eclipse #60
2009 Press Pass Eclipse #71
2009 Press Pass Eclipse Black and White #15
2009 Press Pass Eclipse Black and White #31
2009 Press Pass Eclipse Black and White #38
2009 Press Pass Eclipse Black and White #51
2009 Press Pass Eclipse Black and White #60
2009 Press Pass Eclipse Black and White #71
2009 Press Pass Eclipse Black Hole Firesuits /50 #BH3
2009 Press Pass Eclipse Blue #15

2009 Press Pass Eclipse Blue #31
2009 Press Pass Eclipse Blue #38
2009 Press Pass Eclipse Blue #51
2009 Press Pass Eclipse Blue #60
2009 Press Pass Eclipse Blue #71
2009 Press Pass Eclipse Solar Swatches /50 #SSJG4
2009 Press Pass Eclipse Solar Swatches /299 #SSJG1
2009 Press Pass Eclipse Solar Swatches /250 #SSJG2
2009 Press Pass Eclipse Solar Swatches /299 #SSJG3
2009 Press Pass Eclipse Solar Swatches /299 #SSJG5
2009 Press Pass Eclipse Solar Swatches /99 #SSJG6
2009 Press Pass Eclipse Solar System #SS7
2009 Press Pass Eclipse Under Cover Autographs /24 #UCSJG
2009 Press Pass Final Standings /130 #116
2009 Press Pass Four Wide Autographs /5 #FWJG
2009 Press Pass Four Wide Checkered Flag /1 #FWJG
2009 Press Pass Four Wide Firesuit /50 #FWJG
2009 Press Pass Four Wide Sheet Metal /10 #FWJG
2009 Press Pass Four Wide Tire /25 #FWJG
2009 Press Pass Freeze Frame #FF1
2009 Press Pass Freeze Frame #FF14
2009 Press Pass Fusion #68
2009 Press Pass Fusion Bronze /150 #68
2009 Press Pass Fusion Gold /50 #68
2009 Press Pass Fusion Green /25 #68
2009 Press Pass Fusion Onyx /1 #68
2009 Press Pass Fusion Revered Relics Gold /50 #RRJG
2009 Press Pass Fusion Revered Relics Holofoil /25 #RRJG
2009 Press Pass Fusion Revered Relics Premium Swatch /10 #RRJG
2009 Press Pass Fusion Revered Relics Silver /65 #RRJG
2009 Press Pass Fusion Silver /99 #68
2009 Press Pass Game Face #GF2
2009 Press Pass Gold #10
2009 Press Pass Gold #55
2009 Press Pass Gold #116
2009 Press Pass Gold #129
2009 Press Pass Gold #181
2009 Press Pass Gold #194
2009 Press Pass Gold #195
2009 Press Pass Gold #196
2009 Press Pass Gold #200
2009 Press Pass Gold #209
2009 Press Pass Gold #215
2009 Press Pass Gold #218
2009 Press Pass Gold #CL2
2009 Press Pass Gold Holofoil /100 #10
2009 Press Pass Gold Holofoil /100 #55
2009 Press Pass Gold Holofoil /100 #116
2009 Press Pass Gold Holofoil /100 #129
2009 Press Pass Gold Holofoil /100 #181
2009 Press Pass Gold Holofoil /100 #194
2009 Press Pass Gold Holofoil /100 #195
2009 Press Pass Gold Holofoil /100 #196
2009 Press Pass Gold Holofoil /100 #200
2009 Press Pass Gold Holofoil /100 #209
2009 Press Pass Gold Holofoil /100 #215
2009 Press Pass Gold Holofoil /100 #218
2009 Press Pass Gold Holofoil /100 #CL2
2009 Press Pass Legends #46
2009 Press Pass Legends Autographs Gold /35 #13
2009 Press Pass Legends Autographs Holofoil /10 #12
2009 Press Pass Legends Autographs Printing Plates Black /1 #10
2009 Press Pass Legends Autographs Printing Plates Cyan /1 #10
2009 Press Pass Legends Autographs Printing Plates Magenta /1 #10
2009 Press Pass Legends Autographs Printing Plates Yellow /1 #10
2009 Press Pass Legends Gold /399 #46
2009 Press Pass Legends Holofoil /50 #46
2009 Press Pass Legends Past and Present /550 #PP8
2009 Press Pass Legends Past and Present /550 #PP5
2009 Press Pass Legends Past and Present /550 #PP1
2009 Press Pass Legends Past and Present Holofoil /99 #PP1
2009 Press Pass Legends Past and Present Holofoil /99 #PP5
2009 Press Pass Legends Past and Present Holofoil /99 #PP8
2009 Press Pass Legends Previews /5 #46
2009 Press Pass Legends Printing Plates Black /1 #46
2009 Press Pass Legends Printing Plates Cyan /1 #46
2009 Press Pass Legends Printing Plates Magenta /1 #46
2009 Press Pass Legends Printing Plates Yellow /1 #46
2009 Press Pass Legends Prominent Pieces Bronze /99 #PPJG
2009 Press Pass Legends Prominent Pieces Gold /25 #PPJG
2009 Press Pass Legends Prominent Pieces Oversized /25 #PPOEJG
2009 Press Pass Legends Prominent Pieces Silver /50 #PPJG
2009 Press Pass Legends Red /199 #46
2009 Press Pass Legends Solo /1 #46
2009 Press Pass NASCAR Gallery #NG9
2009 Press Pass Pieces Race Used Memorabilia #JG
2009 Press Pass Pocket Portraits #P8
2009 Press Pass Pocket Portraits Checkered Flag #P8
2009 Press Pass Pocket Portraits Hometown #P8
2009 Press Pass Pocket Portraits Smoke #P8
2009 Press Pass Pocket Portraits Target #PPT2
2009 Press Pass Premium #18
2009 Press Pass Premium #43
2009 Press Pass Premium #54
2009 Press Pass Premium #63
2009 Press Pass Premium #73
2009 Press Pass Premium #81
2009 Press Pass Premium Gold #81
2009 Press Pass Premium Hot Threads /325 #HTJG1
2009 Press Pass Premium Hot Threads /99 #HTJG2
2009 Press Pass Premium Hot Threads Multi-Color /25 #HTJG
2009 Press Pass Premium Hot Threads Patches /10 #HTP-JG1
2009 Press Pass Premium Hot Threads Patches /9 #HTP-JG2
2009 Press Pass Premium Previews /5 #EB18
2009 Press Pass Premium Previews /1 #EB53
2009 Press Pass Premium Signatures #11
2009 Press Pass Premium Signatures Gold /25 #11
2009 Press Pass Premium Top Contenders #TC6
2009 Press Pass Premium Top Contenders Gold #TC6
2009 Press Pass Premium Win Streak #WS3
2009 Press Pass Premium Win Streak Victory Lane #WSVL-JG
2009 Press Pass Previews /5 #EB10
2009 Press Pass Previews /1 #EB116
2009 Press Pass Previews /5 #EB129
2009 Press Pass Previews /1 #EB194
2009 Press Pass Previews /1 #EB195
2009 Press Pass Previews /1 #EB196
2009 Press Pass Previews /1 #EB200
2009 Press Pass Red #10
2009 Press Pass Red #55
2009 Press Pass Red #116
2009 Press Pass Red #129
2009 Press Pass Red #181
2009 Press Pass Red #194
2009 Press Pass Red #195
2009 Press Pass Red #196
2009 Press Pass Red #200
2009 Press Pass Red #209
2009 Press Pass Red #215
2009 Press Pass Red #218
2009 Press Pass Red #CL2
2009 Press Pass Showcase /499 #4
2009 Press Pass Showcase /499 #38
2009 Press Pass Showcase /499 #29
2009 Press Pass Showcase 2nd Gear /125 #4
2009 Press Pass Showcase 2nd Gear /125 #29
2009 Press Pass Showcase 2nd Gear /125 #38
2009 Press Pass Showcase 3rd Gear /50 #4
2009 Press Pass Showcase 3rd Gear /50 #29
2009 Press Pass Showcase 3rd Gear /50 #38
2009 Press Pass Showcase 4th Gear /15 #4
2009 Press Pass Showcase 4th Gear /15 #29
2009 Press Pass Showcase 4th Gear /15 #38
2009 Press Pass Showcase Classic Collections Firesuit /25 #CCF1
2009 Press Pass Showcase Classic Collections Firesuit /25 #CCF2
2009 Press Pass Showcase Classic Collections Firesuit /25 #CCF4
2009 Press Pass Showcase Classic Collections Firesuit Patch /5 #CCF1
2009 Press Pass Showcase Classic Collections Firesuit Patch /5 #CCF2
2009 Press Pass Showcase Classic Collections Firesuit Patch /5 #CCF4
2009 Press Pass Showcase Classic Collections Ink /45 #2
2009 Press Pass Showcase Classic Collections Ink Gold /25 #2
2009 Press Pass Showcase Classic Collections Ink Green /5 #2
2009 Press Pass Showcase Classic Collections Ink Melting /1 #2
2009 Press Pass Showcase Classic Collections Sheet Metal /45 #CCS1
2009 Press Pass Showcase Classic Collections Sheet Metal /45 #CCS2
2009 Press Pass Showcase Classic Collections Sheet Metal /45 #CCS4
2009 Press Pass Showcase Classic Collections Tire /99 #CCT1
2009 Press Pass Showcase Classic Collections Tire /99 #CCT2
2009 Press Pass Showcase Classic Collections Tire /99 #CCT4
2009 Press Pass Showcase Elite Exhibit Ink /45 #4
2009 Press Pass Showcase Elite Exhibit Ink Gold /25 #4
2009 Press Pass Showcase Elite Exhibit Ink Green /5 #4
2009 Press Pass Showcase Elite Exhibit Ink Melting /1 #4
2009 Press Pass Showcase Elite Exhibit Triple Memorabilia /99 #EEJG
2009 Press Pass Showcase Elite Exhibit Triple Memorabilia Gold /45 #EEJG
2009 Press Pass Showcase Elite Exhibit Triple Memorabilia Green /25 #EEJG
2009 Press Pass Showcase Elite Exhibit Triple Memorabilia Melting /5 #EEJG
2009 Press Pass Showcase Printing Plates Black /1 #4
2009 Press Pass Showcase Printing Plates Black /1 #29
2009 Press Pass Showcase Printing Plates Black /1 #38
2009 Press Pass Showcase Printing Plates Cyan /1 #4
2009 Press Pass Showcase Printing Plates Cyan /1 #29
2009 Press Pass Showcase Printing Plates Cyan /1 #38
2009 Press Pass Showcase Printing Plates Magenta /1 #4
2009 Press Pass Showcase Printing Plates Magenta /1 #29
2009 Press Pass Showcase Printing Plates Magenta /1 #38
2009 Press Pass Showcase Printing Plates Yellow /1 #4
2009 Press Pass Showcase Printing Plates Yellow /1 #29
2009 Press Pass Showcase Printing Plates Yellow /1 #38
2009 Press Pass Showcase Prized Pieces Firesuit /25 #PPFJG
2009 Press Pass Showcase Prized Pieces Firesuit Patch /5 #PPFJG
2009 Press Pass Showcase Prized Pieces Ink Firesuit /5 #4
2009 Press Pass Showcase Prized Pieces Ink Firesuit Patch /1 #4
2009 Press Pass Showcase Prized Pieces Ink Sheet Metal /25 #4
2009 Press Pass Showcase Prized Pieces Ink Tire /45 #4
2009 Press Pass Showcase Prized Pieces Sheet Metal /45 #PPSJG
2009 Press Pass Showcase Prized Pieces Tire /99 #PPTJG
2009 Press Pass Signature Series Archive Edition /1 #GGTJG
2009 Press Pass Signature Series Archive Edition /1 #HTTJG
2009 Press Pass Signature Series Archive Edition /1 #UCDJG
2009 Press Pass Signature Series Archive Edition /1 #UCJG
2009 Press Pass Signature Series Archive Edition /1 #BRJG
2009 Press Pass Signature Series Archive Edition /1 #PSJG
2009 Press Pass Signature Series Archive Edition /1 #BRJG
2009 Press Pass Signature Series Archive Edition /1 #GGJG
2009 Press Pass Signings Blue /25 #10
2009 Press Pass Signings Gold #13
2009 Press Pass Signings Green /15 #13
2009 Press Pass Signings Orange /25 #13
2009 Press Pass Signings Printing Plates Black /1 #13
2009 Press Pass Signings Printing Plates Cyan /1 #13
2009 Press Pass Signings Purple /15 #13
2009 Press Pass Sponsor Swatches /250 #SSJG
2009 Press Pass Sponsor Swatches Select /10 #SSJG
2009 Press Pass Stealth #11A
2009 Press Pass Stealth #51
2009 Press Pass Stealth #59
2009 Press Pass Stealth #73
2009 Press Pass Stealth #80
2009 Press Pass Stealth #11B
2009 Press Pass Stealth Battle Armor /135 #BAJG1
2009 Press Pass Stealth Battle Armor /135 #BAJG2
2009 Press Pass Stealth Battle Armor /40 #BAJG3
2009 Press Pass Stealth Battle Armor Multi-Color /170 #BAJG
2009 Press Pass Stealth Chrome #11A
2009 Press Pass Stealth Chrome #51
2009 Press Pass Stealth Chrome #59
2009 Press Pass Stealth Chrome #73
2009 Press Pass Stealth Chrome #80
2009 Press Pass Stealth Chrome #11B
2009 Press Pass Stealth Chrome #11C
2009 Press Pass Stealth Chrome Brushed Metal /25 #11
2009 Press Pass Stealth Chrome Brushed Metal /25 #51
2009 Press Pass Stealth Chrome Brushed Metal /25 #59
2009 Press Pass Stealth Chrome Brushed Metal /25 #73
2009 Press Pass Stealth Chrome Brushed Metal /25 #80
2009 Press Pass Stealth Chrome Gold /99 #11
2009 Press Pass Stealth Chrome Gold /99 #51
2009 Press Pass Stealth Chrome Gold /99 #59
2009 Press Pass Stealth Chrome Gold /99 #73
2009 Press Pass Stealth Chrome Gold /99 #80
2009 Press Pass Stealth Confidential Classified Bronze #PC16
2009 Press Pass Stealth Confidential Secret Silver #PC16
2009 Press Pass Stealth Confidential Top Secret Gold /25 #PC16
2009 Press Pass Stealth Mach 09 #M8
2009 Press Pass Stealth Previews /5 #EB11
2009 Press Pass Stealth Previews /1 #EB73
2009 Press Pass Stealth Previews /1 #EB80
2009 Press Pass Target #JGB
2009 Press Pass Total Tire /25 #TT2
2009 Press Pass Tradin' Paint #TP9
2009 Press Pass Tread Marks Autographs /10 #SSJG
2009 Press Pass Wal-Mart #JGA
2009 Press Pass Wal-Mart Autographs Red #5
2009 Press Pass Wal-Mart Signature Edition /15 #JG
2009 Sportkings National Convention Memorabilia Gold /1 #SK6
2009 Sportkings National Convention Memorabilia Gold /1 #SK25
2009 Sportkings National Convention Memorabilia Silver /9 #SK6
2009 Sportkings National Convention Memorabilia Silver /9 #SK25
2009 VIP #10
2009 VIP #41
2009 VIP #50
2009 VIP #66
2009 VIP #77
2009 VIP #86
2009 VIP After Party #AP7
2009 VIP After Party Transparent #AP7
2009 VIP Get A Grip /100 #GGJG
2009 VIP Get A Grip Holofoil /10 #GGJG
2009 VIP Guest List #GG7
2009 VIP Hardware #H3
2009 VIP Hardware Transparent #H3
2009 VIP Leadfoot /150 #LFJG
2009 VIP Leadfoot Holofoil /10 #LFJG
2009 VIP National Promos #2
2009 VIP Previews /5 #10
2009 VIP Previews /1 #77
2009 VIP Purple /25 #10
2009 VIP Purple /25 #41
2009 VIP Purple /25 #50
2009 VIP Purple /25 #66
2009 VIP Purple /25 #77
2009 VIP Purple /25 #86
2009 VIP Race Day Gear /25 #RDGJG
2009 Wheels Autographs /25 #22
2009 Wheels Autographs #23
2009 Wheels Autographs Press Plates Black /1 #JG
2009 Wheels Autographs Press Plates Cyan /1 #JG
2009 Wheels Autographs Press Plates Magenta /1 #JG
2009 Wheels Autographs Press Plates Yellow /1 #JG
2009 Wheels Main Event #2
2009 Wheels Main Event #50
2009 Wheels Main Event #58
2009 Wheels Main Event #67
2009 Wheels Main Event #74
2009 Wheels Main Event #37
2009 Wheels Main Event Buyback Archive Edition /1 #TBJG
2009 Wheels Main Event Buyback Archive Edition /1 #TBTJG
2009 Wheels Main Event Buyback Archive Edition /1 #HTJG
2009 Wheels Main Event Buyback Archive Edition /1 #GGJG
2009 Wheels Main Event Buyback Archive Edition /1 #TPJG
2009 Wheels Main Event Buyback Archive Edition /1 #UCJG
2009 Wheels Main Event Buyback Archive Edition /1 #TPJG
2009 Wheels Main Event Buyback Archive Edition /1 #BRJG
2009 Wheels Main Event Fast Pass Purple /25 #2
2009 Wheels Main Event Fast Pass Purple /25 #37
2009 Wheels Main Event Fast Pass Purple /25 #50
2009 Wheels Main Event Fast Pass Purple /25 #58
2009 Wheels Main Event Fast Pass Purple /25 #67
2009 Wheels Main Event Fast Pass Purple /25 #74
2009 Wheels Main Event Foil #2
2009 Wheels Main Event Hat Dance Double /99 #HDJG
2009 Wheels Main Event Hat Dance Patch /10 #HDJG
2009 Wheels Main Event High Rollers #HR5
2009 Wheels Main Event Marks Clubs #21
2009 Wheels Main Event Marks Diamonds /10 #21
2009 Wheels Main Event Marks Hearts /5 #21
2009 Wheels Main Event Marks Printing Plates Black /1 #18
2009 Wheels Main Event Marks Printing Plates Cyan /1 #18
2009 Wheels Main Event Marks Printing Plates Magenta /1 #18
2009 Wheels Main Event Marks Printing Plates Yellow /1 #18
2009 Wheels Main Event Marks Spades /1 #21
2009 Wheels Main Event Playing Cards Blue #AH
2009 Wheels Main Event Playing Cards Red #AH
2009 Wheels Main Event Poker Chips #3
2009 Wheels Main Event Previews /5 #2
2009 Wheels Main Event Spark Plugs /8 #JG1
2009 Wheels Main Event Spark Plugs /8 #JG2
2009 Wheels Main Event Stop and Go Swatches Pit Banner /175 #SGBJG
2009 Wheels Main Event Stop and Go Swatches Pit Banner Blue All Season's Sports Cards /1 #SGBJG
2009 Wheels Main Event Stop and Go Swatches Pit Banner Blue Arena /1 #SGBJG
2009 Wheels Main Event Stop and Go Swatches Pit Banner Blue Card Stadium /1 #SGBJG
2009 Wheels Main Event Stop and Go Swatches Pit Banner Blue Chicagoland Sportscards /1 #SGBJG
2009 Wheels Main Event Stop and Go Swatches Pit Banner Blue Chris Comics /1 #SGBJG
2009 Wheels Main Event Stop and Go Swatches Pit Banner Blue Chuck's Field of Dreams /1 #SGBJG
2009 Wheels Main Event Stop and Go Swatches Pit Banner Blue Collector's Heaven /1 #SGBJG
2009 Wheels Main Event Stop and Go Swatches Pit Banner Blue D&S Racing /1 #SGBJG
2009 Wheels Main Event Stop and Go Swatches Pit Banner Blue Dave's Pitstop /1 #SGBJG
2009 Wheels Main Event Stop and Go Swatches Pit Banner Blue Diamond King Sports /1 #SGBJG
2009 Wheels Main Event Stop and Go Swatches Pit Banner Blue Georgetown Card Exchange /1 #SGBJG
2009 Wheels Main Event Stop and Go Swatches Pit Banner Blue Jaimie's Field of Dreams /1 #SGBJG
2009 Wheels Main Event Stop and Go Swatches Pit Banner Blue Juniata Cards /1 #SGBJG
2009 Wheels Main Event Stop and Go Swatches Pit Banner Blue Main Steet Sportscards /1 #SGBJG
2009 Wheels Main Event Stop and Go Swatches Pit Banner Blue Matt's Sports Cards /1 #SGBJG
2009 Wheels Main Event Stop and Go Swatches Pit Banner Blue P&T Sportscards /1 #SGBJG
2009 Wheels Main Event Stop and Go Swatches Pit Banner Blue Republic Jewelry /1 #SGBJG
2009 Wheels Main Event Stop and Go Swatches Pit Banner Blue Ron's Racing /1 #SGBJG
2009 Wheels Main Event Stop and Go Swatches Pit Banner Blue Shelby Collectibles /1 #SGBJG
2009 Wheels Main Event Stop and Go Swatches Pit Banner Blue Spectator Sportscards /1 #SGBJG
2009 Wheels Main Event Stop and Go Swatches Pit Banner Blue Squeeze Play /1 #SGBJG
2009 Wheels Main Event Stop and Go Swatches Pit Banner Blue TBJ Sports Cards /1 #SGBJG
2009 Wheels Main Event Stop and Go Swatches Pit Banner Blue TCI Sports Fan /1 #SGBJG
2009 Wheels Main Event Stop and Go Swatches Pit Banner Blue The Card Cellar /1 #SGBJG
2009 Wheels Main Event Stop and Go Swatches Pit Banner Blue TJ Warner Ballcards /1 #SGBJG
2009 Wheels Main Event Stop and Go Swatches Pit Banner Blue Trademark Sports /1 #SGBJG
2009 Wheels Main Event Stop and Go Swatches Pit Banner Blue Triple I Sportscards /1 #SGBJG
2009 Wheels Main Event Stop and Go Swatches Pit Banner Blue Triple Play /1 #SGBJG
2009 Wheels Main Event Stop and Go Swatches Pit Banner Blue West Allis /1 #SGBJG
2009 Wheels Main Event Stop and Go Swatches Pit Banner Green /10 #SGBJG
2009 Wheels Main Event Stop and Go Swatches Pit Banner Holofoil /75 #SGBJG
2009 Wheels Main Event Stop and Go Swatches Pit Banner Red /25 #SGBJG
2009 Wheels Main Event Stop and Go Swatches Wheel Covers /175 #SGCJG
2009 Wheels Main Event Stop and Go Swatches Wheel Covers Green /10 #SGCJG
2009 Wheels Main Event Stop and Go Swatches Wheel Covers Holofoil /75 #SGCJG
2009 Wheels Main Event Stop and Go Swatches Wheel Covers Red /25 #SGCJG
2009 Wheels Main Event Wildcard Cuts /2 #WCCJG
2010 Action Racing Collectables Platinum 1:24 /250 #24
2010 Element #9
2010 Element #41
2010 Element #70
2010 Element #83
2010 Element 10 in '10 #TT5
2010 Element Blue /35 #9
2010 Element Blue /35 #41
2010 Element Blue /35 #70
2010 Element Blue /35 #83
2010 Element Finish Line Checkered Flag /10 #FLJG
2010 Element Finish Line Green Flag /20 #FLJG
2010 Element Finish Line Tires /99 #FLJG
2010 Element Flagship Performers Championships Black /25 #FPCJG
2010 Element Flagship Performers Championships Blue-Orange /25 #FPCJG
2010 Element Flagship Performers Championships Checkered /1 #FPCJG
2010 Element Flagship Performers Championships Green /5 #FPCJG
2010 Element Flagship Performers Championships Red /25 #FPCJG
2010 Element Flagship Performers Championships White /15 #FPCJG
2010 Element Flagship Performers Championships X /25 #FPCJG
2010 Element Flagship Performers Championships Yellow /25 #FPCJG
2010 Element Flagship Performers Consecutive Starts Black /20 #FPSJG
2010 Element Flagship Performers Consecutive Starts Blue-Orange /20 #FPSJG
2010 Element Flagship Performers Consecutive Starts Checkered /1 #FPSJG
2010 Element Flagship Performers Consecutive Starts Green /5 #FPSJG
2010 Element Flagship Performers Consecutive Starts Red /20 #FPSJG
2010 Element Flagship Performers Consecutive Starts White /10 #FPSJG
2010 Element Flagship Performers Consecutive Starts X /10 #FPSJG
2010 Element Flagship Performers Consecutive Starts Yellow /20 #FPSJG
2010 Element Flagship Performers Wins Black /20 #FPWJG
2010 Element Flagship Performers Wins Blue-Orange /20 #FPWJG
2010 Element Flagship Performers Wins Checkered /1 #FPWJG
2010 Element Flagship Performers Wins Green /5 #FPWJG
2010 Element Flagship Performers Wins Red /20 #FPWJG
2010 Element Flagship Performers Wins White /15 #FPWJG
2010 Element Flagship Performers Wins X /10 #FPWJG
2010 Element Flagship Performers Wins Yellow /20 #FPWJG
2010 Element Green #9
2010 Element Green #41
2010 Element Green #70
2010 Element Green #83
2010 Element Previews /5 #EB9
2010 Element Previews /1 #EB70
2010 Element Purple /25 #9
2010 Element Purple /25 #41
2010 Element Recycled Materials Blue /25 #RMJG
2010 Element Recycled Materials Green /125 #RMJG
2010 Element Red Target #9
2010 Element Red Target #41
2010 Element Red Target #70
2010 Element Red Target #83
2010 Press Pass #7
2010 Press Pass #114
2010 Press Pass #121
2010 Press Pass #61
2010 Press Pass #84
2010 Press Pass #0
2010 Press Pass Autographs #18
2010 Press Pass Autographs Chase Edition /25 #4
2010 Press Pass Autographs Track Edition /10 #4
2010 Press Pass Blue #7
2010 Press Pass Blue #61
2010 Press Pass Blue #84
2010 Press Pass Blue #114
2010 Press Pass Blue #123
2010 Press Pass Burning Rubber /250 #BR6
2010 Press Pass Burning Rubber Autographs /24 #SSTEJG
2010 Press Pass Burning Rubber Gold /50 #BR6
2010 Press Pass Burning Rubber Prime Cuts /25 #BR6
2010 Press Pass By The Numbers #BN1
2010 Press Pass By The Numbers #BN13
2010 Press Pass By The Numbers #BN21
2010 Press Pass Cup Chase #CCR6
2010 Press Pass Cup Chase Prizes #CC8
2010 Press Pass Eclipse #11
2010 Press Pass Eclipse #37
2010 Press Pass Eclipse #47
2010 Press Pass Eclipse #50
2010 Press Pass Eclipse #51
2010 Press Pass Eclipse #54
2010 Press Pass Eclipse #56
2010 Press Pass Eclipse #61
2010 Press Pass Eclipse #62
2010 Press Pass Eclipse #74
2010 Press Pass Eclipse #78
2010 Press Pass Eclipse Blue #78
2010 Press Pass Eclipse Blue #74
2010 Press Pass Eclipse Blue #62
2010 Press Pass Eclipse Blue #61
2010 Press Pass Eclipse Blue #56
2010 Press Pass Eclipse Blue #54
2010 Press Pass Eclipse Blue #51
2010 Press Pass Eclipse Blue #50
2010 Press Pass Eclipse Blue #47
2010 Press Pass Eclipse Blue #37
2010 Press Pass Eclipse Blue #11
2010 Press Pass Eclipse Cars #C5
2010 Press Pass Eclipse Decade #D2
2010 Press Pass Eclipse Element Inserts #2
2010 Press Pass Eclipse Focus #F3
2010 Press Pass Eclipse Gold #78
2010 Press Pass Eclipse Gold #74
2010 Press Pass Eclipse Gold #62
2010 Press Pass Eclipse Gold #61
2010 Press Pass Eclipse Gold #56
2010 Press Pass Eclipse Gold #54
2010 Press Pass Eclipse Gold #51
2010 Press Pass Eclipse Gold #50
2010 Press Pass Eclipse Gold #47
2010 Press Pass Eclipse Gold #37
2010 Press Pass Eclipse Gold #11
2010 Press Pass Eclipse Previews /1 #37
2010 Press Pass Eclipse Previews /5 #11
2010 Press Pass Eclipse Purple /25 #62
2010 Press Pass Eclipse Purple /25 #61
2010 Press Pass Eclipse Purple /25 #56
2010 Press Pass Eclipse Purple /25 #54
2010 Press Pass Eclipse Purple /25 #51
2010 Press Pass Eclipse Purple /25 #50
2010 Press Pass Eclipse Purple /25 #47
2010 Press Pass Eclipse Purple /25 #37
2010 Press Pass Eclipse Purple /25 #11
2010 Press Pass Eclipse Signature Series Shoes Autographs /24 #SSSEJG
2010 Press Pass Eclipse Spellbound Swatches /125 #SSJG2
2010 Press Pass Eclipse Spellbound Swatches /125 #SSJG3
2010 Press Pass Eclipse Spellbound Swatches /125 #SSJG4
2010 Press Pass Eclipse Spellbound Swatches /125 #SSJG5
2010 Press Pass Eclipse Spellbound Swatches /125 #SSJG6
2010 Press Pass Eclipse Spellbound Swatches /125 #SSJG1
2010 Press Pass Eclipse Spellbound Swatches Holofoil /24 #SSJG2
2010 Press Pass Eclipse Spellbound Swatches Holofoil /24 #SSJG3
2010 Press Pass Eclipse Spellbound Swatches Holofoil /24 #SSJG4
2010 Press Pass Eclipse Spellbound Swatches Holofoil /24 #SSJG5
2010 Press Pass Eclipse Spellbound Swatches Holofoil /24 #SSJG6
2010 Press Pass Eclipse Spellbound Swatches Holofoil /24 #SSJG1
2010 Press Pass Final Standings /50 #FS3
2010 Press Pass Five Star /35 #4
2010 Press Pass Five Star Classic Compilations Combos Firesuit Autographs /15 #CCMKKJG
2010 Press Pass Five Star Classic Compilations Combos Firesuit Autographs /15 #CCMHMS
2010 Press Pass Five Star Classic Compilations Combos Firesuit Autographs /15 #CCMJJJG
2010 Press Pass Five Star Classic Compilations Combos Firesuit Autographs /15 #CCMDEJG
2010 Press Pass Five Star Classic Compilations Combos Patches Autographs /1 #CCMGJME
2010 Press Pass Five Star Classic Compilations Combos Patches Autographs /1 #CCMJJJG
2010 Press Pass Five Star Classic Compilations Combos Patches Autographs /1 #CCMDEJG
2010 Press Pass Five Star Classic Compilations Combos Patches Autographs /1 #CCMKKJG
2010 Press Pass Five Star Classic Compilations Dual Memorabilia Autographs /10 #JG
2010 Press Pass Five Star Classic Compilations Firesuit Autographs /15 #JG
2010 Press Pass Five Star Classic Compilations Patch Autographs /1 #CCPJG1
2010 Press Pass Five Star Classic Compilations Patch Autographs /1 #CCPJG2
2010 Press Pass Five Star Classic Compilations Patch Autographs /1 #CCPJG3
2010 Press Pass Five Star Classic Compilations Patch Autographs /1 #CCPJG4
2010 Press Pass Five Star Classic Compilations Patch Autographs /1 #CCPJG5
2010 Press Pass Five Star Classic Compilations Patch Autographs /1 #CCPJG6
2010 Press Pass Five Star Classic Compilations Patch Autographs /1 #CCPJG7
2010 Press Pass Five Star Classic Compilations Patch Autographs /1 #CCPJG8
2010 Press Pass Five Star Classic Compilations Patch Autographs /1 #CCPJG9
2010 Press Pass Five Star Classic Compilations Patch Autographs /1 #CCPJG10
2010 Press Pass Five Star Classic Compilations Patch Autographs /1 #CCPJG11
2010 Press Pass Five Star Classic Compilations Patch Autographs /1 #CCPJG12
2010 Press Pass Five Star Classic Compilations Patch Autographs /1 #CCPJG13
2010 Press Pass Five Star Classic Compilations Sheet Metal Autographs /25 #JG
2010 Press Pass Five Star Classic Compilations Triple Memorabilia Autographs /5 #JG
2010 Press Pass Five Star Holofoil /10 #4
2010 Press Pass Five Star Melting /1 #4
2010 Press Pass Five Star Paramount Pieces Aluminum /25 #JG
2010 Press Pass Five Star Paramount Pieces Blue /20 #JG
2010 Press Pass Five Star Paramount Pieces Gold /15 #JG
2010 Press Pass Five Star Paramount Pieces Holofoil /10 #JG
2010 Press Pass Five Star Paramount Pieces Melting /1 #JG
2010 Press Pass Five Star Signature Souvenirs Aluminum /50 #SSJG
2010 Press Pass Five Star Signature Souvenirs Gold /25 #SSJG
2010 Press Pass Five Star Signature Souvenirs Holofoil /10 #SSJG
2010 Press Pass Five Star Signature Souvenirs Melting /1 #SSJG
2010 Press Pass Five Star Signatures Aluminum /45 #JG
2010 Press Pass Five Star Signatures Gold /20 #JG
2010 Press Pass Five Star Signatures Holofoil /5 #JG
2010 Press Pass Five Star Signatures Melting /1 #JG
2010 Press Pass Four Wide Autographs /5 #NNO
2010 Press Pass Four Wide Firesuit /25 #FWJG
2010 Press Pass Four Wide Sheet Metal /15 #FWJG
2010 Press Pass Four Wide Shoes /1 #FWJG
2010 Press Pass Four Wide Tires /10 #FWJG
2010 Press Pass Gold #7
2010 Press Pass Gold #61
2010 Press Pass Gold #84
2010 Press Pass Gold #114
2010 Press Pass Gold #123
2010 Press Pass Holofoil /100 #7
2010 Press Pass Holofoil /100 #61
2010 Press Pass Holofoil /100 #84
2010 Press Pass Holofoil /100 #114
2010 Press Pass Holofoil /100 #123
2010 Press Pass Legends #45
2010 Press Pass Legends #66
2010 Press Pass Legends #76
2010 Press Pass Legends 50 Win Club Memorabilia Gold /75 #50JG
2010 Press Pass Legends 50 Win Club Memorabilia Holofoil /25 #50JG
2010 Press Pass Legends Autographs Blue /10 #24
2010 Press Pass Legends Autographs Holofoil /25 #24
2010 Press Pass Legends Autographs Printing Plates Black /1 #21
2010 Press Pass Legends Autographs Printing Plates Cyan /1 #21
2010 Press Pass Legends Autographs Printing Plates Magenta /1 #21
2010 Press Pass Legends Autographs Printing Plates Yellow /1 #21
2010 Press Pass Legends Blue /1 #76
2010 Press Pass Legends Blue /1 #66
2010 Press Pass Legends Blue /1 #45
2010 Press Pass Legends Gold /399 #76
2010 Press Pass Legends Gold /399 #66
2010 Press Pass Legends Gold /399 #45
2010 Press Pass Legends Holofoil /50 #76
2010 Press Pass Legends Holofoil /50 #66
2010 Press Pass Legends Holofoil /50 #45
2010 Press Pass Legends Legendary Links Gold /75 #LXDAJG
2010 Press Pass Legends Legendary Links Gold /75 #LXDEJG
2010 Press Pass Legends Legendary Links Holofoil /25 #LXDEJG
2010 Press Pass Legends Legendary Links Holofoil /25 #LXDAJG
2010 Press Pass Legends Make and Model Blue /99 #9
2010 Press Pass Legends Make and Model Gold /299 #9
2010 Press Pass Legends Make and Model Holofoil /199 #9
2010 Press Pass Legends Motorsports Masters #MMJG
2010 Press Pass Legends Motorsports Masters Autographs Blue /1 #NNO
2010 Press Pass Legends Motorsports Masters Autographs Gold /25 #14
2010 Press Pass Legends Motorsports Masters Autographs Holofoil /10 #14
2010 Press Pass Legends Motorsports Masters Autographs Printing Plates Black /1 #21
2010 Press Pass Legends Motorsports Masters Autographs Printing Plates Cyan /1 #21
2010 Press Pass Legends Motorsports Masters Autographs Printing Plates Magenta /1 #21
2010 Press Pass Legends Motorsports Masters Autographs Printing Plates Yellow /1 #21
2010 Press Pass Legends Motorsports Masters Blue /10 #MMJG
2010 Press Pass Legends Motorsports Masters Gold /299 #MMJG
2010 Press Pass Legends Motorsports Masters Holofoil /149 #MMJG
2010 Press Pass Legends Printing Plates Black /1 #45
2010 Press Pass Legends Printing Plates Black /1 #66
2010 Press Pass Legends Printing Plates Black /1 #76
2010 Press Pass Legends Printing Plates Cyan /1 #45
2010 Press Pass Legends Printing Plates Cyan /1 #66
2010 Press Pass Legends Printing Plates Cyan /1 #76
2010 Press Pass Legends Printing Plates Magenta /1 #45
2010 Press Pass Legends Printing Plates Magenta /1 #66
2010 Press Pass Legends Printing Plates Magenta /1 #76
2010 Press Pass Legends Printing Plates Yellow /1 #45
2010 Press Pass Legends Printing Plates Yellow /1 #66
2010 Press Pass Legends Printing Plates Yellow /1 #76
2010 Press Pass Legends Prominent Pieces Copper /99 #PPJG
2010 Press Pass Legends Prominent Pieces Gold /50 #PPJG
2010 Press Pass Legends Prominent Pieces Holofoil /25 #PPJG
2010 Press Pass Legends Prominent Pieces Oversized Firesuit /25 #PPOEJG
2010 Press Pass Legends Red /199 #76
2010 Press Pass Legends Red /199 #66
2010 Press Pass Legends Red /199 #45
2010 Press Pass NASCAR Hall of Fame #NHOF31
2010 Press Pass NASCAR Hall of Fame Blue #NHOF31
2010 Press Pass NASCAR Hall of Fame Holofoil /50 #NHOF31
2010 Press Pass Premium #6
2010 Press Pass Premium #38
2010 Press Pass Premium #53
2010 Press Pass Premium #57
2010 Press Pass Premium #67
2010 Press Pass Premium #78
2010 Press Pass Premium Allies #A1
2010 Press Pass Premium Allies Signatures /5 #ASJG
2010 Press Pass Premium Hot Threads /299 #HTJG
2010 Press Pass Premium Hot Threads Holofoil /99 #HTJG
2010 Press Pass Premium Hot Threads Multi Color /25 #HTJG
2010 Press Pass Premium Hot Threads Patches /39 #HTPJG
2010 Press Pass Premium Hot Threads Two Color /125 #HTJG
2010 Press Pass Premium Iron On Patch #1
2010 Press Pass Premium Pairings Firesuits /25 #PFGJ
2010 Press Pass Premium Pairings Signatures /5 #PSGJ
2010 Press Pass Premium Purple /25 #53
2010 Press Pass Premium Purple /25 #57
2010 Press Pass Premium Purple /25 #6
2010 Press Pass Premium Purple /25 #38
2010 Press Pass Premium Rivals #R1
2010 Press Pass Premium Rivals #R6
2010 Press Pass Premium Rivals #R5
2010 Press Pass Premium Rivals Signatures /5 #RSGK
2010 Press Pass Premium Rivals Signatures /5 #RSEG
2010 Press Pass Premium Signature Series Firesuit /15 #SSFJG
2010 Press Pass Premium Signatures #PSJG
2010 Press Pass Previews /5 #7
2010 Press Pass Previews /1 #114
2010 Press Pass Purple /25 #7
2010 Press Pass Purple /25 #61
2010 Press Pass Purple /25 #84
2010 Press Pass Purple /25 #114
2010 Press Pass Purple /25 #123
2010 Press Pass Showcase /499 #6
2010 Press Pass Showcase /499 #38
2010 Press Pass Showcase /499 #30
2010 Press Pass Showcase /499 #28
2010 Press Pass Showcase /499 #32
2010 Press Pass Showcase Classic Collections Firesuit Green /25 #CCIHMS
2010 Press Pass Showcase Classic Collections Firesuit Green /25 #C
2010 Press Pass Showcase Classic Collections Firesuit Green /25 #C
2010 Press Pass Showcase Classic Collections Firesuit Patch Melting #CCIWIN
2010 Press Pass Showcase Classic Collections Firesuit Patch Melting #CCIFAN
2010 Press Pass Showcase Classic Collections Firesuit Patch Melting #CCIHMS
2010 Press Pass Showcase Classic Collections Ink /15 #CCIWIN
2010 Press Pass Showcase Classic Collections Ink /15 #CCIHMS
2010 Press Pass Showcase Classic Collections Ink /15 #CCIFAN
2010 Press Pass Showcase Classic Collections Ink Gold /10 #CCIWIN
2010 Press Pass Showcase Classic Collections Ink Gold /10 #CCIFAN
2010 Press Pass Showcase Classic Collections Ink Gold /10 #CCIHM
2010 Press Pass Showcase Classic Collections Ink Green /5 #CCIWIN
2010 Press Pass Showcase Classic Collections Ink Green /5 #CCIFAN
2010 Press Pass Showcase Classic Collections Ink Green /5 #CCIHM
2010 Press Pass Showcase Classic Collections Ink Melting /1 #CCIW
2010 Press Pass Showcase Classic Collections Ink Melting /1 #CCIF
2010 Press Pass Showcase Classic Collections Ink Melting /1 #CCIH
2010 Press Pass Showcase Classic Collections Sheet Metal /99 #CCI
2010 Press Pass Showcase Classic Collections Sheet Metal /99 #CCI
2010 Press Pass Showcase Classic Collections Sheet Metal /99 #CCI
2010 Press Pass Showcase Classic Collections Sheet Metal Gold /45 #CCIWIN
2010 Press Pass Showcase Classic Collections Sheet Metal Gold /45 #CCIFAN
2010 Press Pass Showcase Classic Collections Sheet Metal Gold /45 #CCIHMS
2010 Press Pass Showcase Elite Exhibit Ink /45 #EEIJG
2010 Press Pass Showcase Elite Exhibit Ink Gold /25 #EEIJG
2010 Press Pass Showcase Elite Exhibit Ink Green /5 #EEIJG
2010 Press Pass Showcase Elite Exhibit Ink Melting /1 #EEIJG
2010 Press Pass Showcase Elite Exhibit Triple Memorabilia /99 #EEM
2010 Press Pass Showcase Elite Exhibit Triple Memorabilia Gold /45 #EEMJG
2010 Press Pass Showcase Elite Exhibit Triple Memorabilia Green /25 #EEMJG
2010 Press Pass Showcase Elite Exhibit Triple Memorabilia Melting /5 #EEMJG
2010 Press Pass Showcase Gold /125 #6
2010 Press Pass Showcase Gold /125 #28
2010 Press Pass Showcase Gold /125 #30
2010 Press Pass Showcase Gold /125 #32
2010 Press Pass Showcase Gold /125 #38
2010 Press Pass Showcase Green /50 #28
2010 Press Pass Showcase Green /50 #30
2010 Press Pass Showcase Green /50 #32
2010 Press Pass Showcase Green /50 #38
2010 Press Pass Showcase Green /50 #6
2010 Press Pass Showcase Melting /15 #6
2010 Press Pass Showcase Melting /15 #28
2010 Press Pass Showcase Melting /15 #30
2010 Press Pass Showcase Melting /15 #32
2010 Press Pass Showcase Melting /15 #38
2010 Press Pass Showcase Platinum Holo /1 #6
2010 Press Pass Showcase Platinum Holo /1 #28
2010 Press Pass Showcase Platinum Holo /1 #30
2010 Press Pass Showcase Platinum Holo /1 #32
2010 Press Pass Showcase Platinum Holo /1 #38
2010 Press Pass Showcase Prized Pieces Firesuit Green /25 #PPMJG
2010 Press Pass Showcase Prized Pieces Firesuit Ink Gold /25 #PPIJG
2010 Press Pass Showcase Prized Pieces Firesuit Ink Melting /1 #PPIJG
2010 Press Pass Showcase Prized Pieces Firesuit Patch Melting /5 #PP
2010 Press Pass Showcase Prized Pieces Memorabilia Ink Green /15 #PPIJG
2010 Press Pass Showcase Prized Pieces Sheet Metal /99 #PPMJG
2010 Press Pass Showcase Prized Pieces Sheet Metal Gold /45 #PPMJG
2010 Press Pass Showcase Prized Pieces Sheet Metal Ink Silver /45 #PP
2010 Press Pass Showcase Racing's Finest /499 #RF10
2010 Press Pass Showcase Racing's Finest Gold /125 #RF10
2010 Press Pass Showcase Racing's Finest Green /50 #RF10
2010 Press Pass Showcase Racing's Finest Melting /15 #RF10
2010 Press Pass Signings Blue /10 #20
2010 Press Pass Signings Gold /15 #20
2010 Press Pass Signings Red /15 #20
2010 Press Pass Signings Silver /25 #20
2010 Press Pass Stealth #10
2010 Press Pass Stealth #51
2010 Press Pass Stealth #72
2010 Press Pass Stealth Battle Armor Fast Pass /25 #BAJG
2010 Press Pass Stealth Battle Armor Holofoil /25 #BAJG
2010 Press Pass Stealth Battle Armor Silver /225 #BAJG
2010 Press Pass Stealth Black and White #10
2010 Press Pass Stealth Black and White #51
2010 Press Pass Stealth Black and White #72
2010 Press Pass Stealth National Convention #VIP2
2010 Press Pass Stealth Power Players #PP5
2010 Press Pass Stealth Previews /5 #10
2010 Press Pass Stealth Previews /5 #51
2010 Press Pass Stealth Purple /25 #10
2010 Press Pass Stealth Purple /25 #51
2010 Press Pass Stealth Signature Series Sheet Metal /15 #SSMEJG
2010 Press Pass Target By The Numbers #BNT4
2010 Press Pass Top 12 Tires /24 #JG
2010 Press Pass Top 12 Tires 10 /10 #JG
2010 Press Pass Tradin' Paint #TP1
2010 Press Pass Tradin' Paint Sheet Metal /299 #TPJG
2010 Press Pass Tradin' Paint Sheet Metal /299 #TPJG2
2010 Press Pass Tradin' Paint Sheet Metal Gold /50 #TPJG
2010 Press Pass Tradin' Paint Sheet Metal Gold /50 #TPJG2
2010 Press Pass Tradin' Paint Sheet Metal Holofoil /25 #TPJG
2010 Press Pass Tradin' Paint Sheet Metal Holofoil /25 #TPJG2
2010 Press Pass Unleashed #U2
2010 Press Pass Wal-Mart By The Numbers #BNW4
2010 Wheels Autographs #17
2010 Wheels Autographs Printing Plates Black /1 #17
2010 Wheels Autographs Printing Plates Cyan /1 #17
2010 Wheels Autographs Printing Plates Magenta /1 #17
2010 Wheels Autographs Printing Plates Yellow /1 #17

2010 Wheels Autographs Special Ink /10 #5
2010 Wheels Autographs Target /10 #10
2010 Wheels Main Event #11
2010 Wheels Main Event #45
2010 Wheels Main Event #58
2010 Wheels Main Event #94
2010 Wheels Main Event #65
2010 Wheels Main Event #47
2010 Wheels Main Event American Muscle #AM5
2010 Wheels Main Event Blue #11
2010 Wheels Main Event Blue #45
2010 Wheels Main Event Blue #47
2010 Wheels Main Event Blue #58
2010 Wheels Main Event Blue #65
2010 Wheels Main Event Blue #94
2010 Wheels Main Event Dog Tags #JG
2010 Wheels Main Event Fight Card #FC10
2010 Wheels Main Event Fight Card Checkered Flag #FC10
2010 Wheels Main Event Fight Card Full Color Retail #FC10
2010 Wheels Main Event Fight Card Gold /25 #FC10
2010 Wheels Main Event Head to Head /150 #HHKKJG
2010 Wheels Main Event Head to Head /150 #HHJGJJ
2010 Wheels Main Event Head to Head /150 #HHDEJG
2010 Wheels Main Event Head to Head /150 #HHMMJG
2010 Wheels Main Event Head to Head Blue /75 #HHJGJJ
2010 Wheels Main Event Head to Head Blue /75 #HHDEJG
2010 Wheels Main Event Head to Head Blue /75 #HHMMJG
2010 Wheels Main Event Head to Head Blue /75 #HHKKJG
2010 Wheels Main Event Head to Head Holofoil /10 #HHJGJJ
2010 Wheels Main Event Head to Head Holofoil /10 #HHDEJG
2010 Wheels Main Event Head to Head Holofoil /10 #HHMMJG
2010 Wheels Main Event Head to Head Holofoil /10 #HHKKJG
2010 Wheels Main Event Head to Head Red /25 #HHJGJJ
2010 Wheels Main Event Head to Head Red /25 #HHDEJG
2010 Wheels Main Event Head to Head Red /25 #HHMMJG
2010 Wheels Main Event Head to Head Red /25 #HHKKJG
2010 Wheels Main Event Marks Autographs /25 #20
2010 Wheels Main Event Marks Autographs Black /1 #19
2010 Wheels Main Event Marks Autographs Blue /10 #20
2010 Wheels Main Event Marks Autographs Red /5 #20
2010 Wheels Main Event Matchups Autographs /10 #JJJG
2010 Wheels Main Event Purple /25 #11
2010 Wheels Main Event Purple /25 #45
2010 Wheels Main Event Purple /25 #47
2010 Wheels Main Event Tale of the Tape #TT9
2010 Wheels Main Event Upper Cuts /199 #UCJG
2010 Wheels Main Event Upper Cuts Blue /75 #UCJG
2010 Wheels Main Event Upper Cuts Holofoil /10 #UCJG
2010 Wheels Main Event Upper Cuts Knock Out Patches /25 #UCKOJG
2010 Wheels Main Event Upper Cuts Red /25 #UCJG
2010 Wheels Main Event Wheel to Wheel /25 #WWJGDE
2010 Wheels Main Event Wheel to Wheel /25 #WWJJJG
2010 Wheels Main Event Wheel to Wheel Holofoil /10 #WWJJJG
2010 Wheels Main Event Wheel to Wheel Holofoil /10 #WWJGDE
2011 Element #11
2011 Element #37
2011 Element #93
2011 Element #79
2011 Element Autographs /25 #19
2011 Element Autographs Blue /5 #19
2011 Element Autographs Gold /5 #18
2011 Element Autographs Printing Plates Black /1 #19
2011 Element Autographs Printing Plates Cyan /1 #19
2011 Element Autographs Printing Plates Magenta /1 #19
2011 Element Autographs Printing Plates Yellow /1 #19
2011 Element Autographs Silver /15 #18
2011 Element Black /35 #11
2011 Element Black /35 #37
2011 Element Black /35 #79
2011 Element Black /35 #93
2011 Element Cut and Collect Exclusives #NNO
2011 Element Flagship Performers Career Starts Green /25 #FPSJG
2011 Element Flagship Performers Career Wins White /50 #FPWJG
2011 Element Flagship Performers Championships Checkered /25 #FPCJG
2011 Element Flagstand Swatches /25 #FSSJG
2011 Element Green #11
2011 Element Green #37
2011 Element Green #79
2011 Element Green #93
2011 Element Previews /5 #EB11
2011 Element Purple /25 #11
2011 Element Purple /25 #37
2011 Element Purple /25 #79
2011 Element Purple /25 #93
2011 Element Red #11
2011 Element Red #37
2011 Element Red #79
2011 Element Red #93
2011 Press Pass #11
2011 Press Pass #66
2011 Press Pass #161
2011 Press Pass #180
2011 Press Pass #191
2011 Press Pass #0
2011 Press Pass Autographs Blue /5 #19
2011 Press Pass Autographs Bronze /20 #18
2011 Press Pass Autographs Gold /5 #18
2011 Press Pass Autographs Printing Plates Black /1 #19
2011 Press Pass Autographs Printing Plates Cyan /1 #19
2011 Press Pass Autographs Printing Plates Magenta /1 #19
2011 Press Pass Autographs Printing Plates Yellow /1 #19
2011 Press Pass Autographs Silver /10 #19
2011 Press Pass Blue Holofoil /10 #11
2011 Press Pass Blue Holofoil /10 #66
2011 Press Pass Blue Holofoil /10 #161
2011 Press Pass Blue Holofoil /10 #180
2011 Press Pass Blue Holofoil /10 #191
2011 Press Pass Blue Retail #191
2011 Press Pass Blue Retail #180
2011 Press Pass Blue Retail #161
2011 Press Pass Blue Retail #66
2011 Press Pass Blue Retail #11
2011 Press Pass Cup Chase #CCR8
2011 Press Pass Cup Chase Prizes #CC3
2011 Press Pass Eclipse #11
2011 Press Pass Eclipse #43
2011 Press Pass Eclipse #64
2011 Press Pass Eclipse #76
2011 Press Pass Eclipse #90
2011 Press Pass Eclipse Blue #11
2011 Press Pass Eclipse Blue #43
2011 Press Pass Eclipse Blue #64
2011 Press Pass Eclipse Blue #76
2011 Press Pass Eclipse Blue #90
2011 Press Pass Eclipse Encore #E2
2011 Press Pass Eclipse Gold /55 #11
2011 Press Pass Eclipse Gold /55 #43
2011 Press Pass Eclipse Gold /55 #64
2011 Press Pass Eclipse Gold /55 #76
2011 Press Pass Eclipse Gold /55 #90
2011 Press Pass Eclipse In Focus #IF1
2011 Press Pass Eclipse Previews /1 #EB43
2011 Press Pass Eclipse Previews /5 #EB11
2011 Press Pass Eclipse Purple /25 #64
2011 Press Pass Eclipse Purple /25 #43
2011 Press Pass Eclipse Purple /25 #76
2011 Press Pass Eclipse Purple /25 #11
2011 Press Pass Eclipse Spellbound Swatches /150 #SBJG3
2011 Press Pass Eclipse Spellbound Swatches /250 #SBJG1
2011 Press Pass Eclipse Spellbound Swatches /150 #SBJG2
2011 Press Pass Eclipse Spellbound Swatches /100 #SBJG4
2011 Press Pass Eclipse Spellbound Swatches /75 #SBJG5
2011 Press Pass Eclipse Spellbound Swatches /50 #SBJG6
2011 Press Pass Eclipse Spellbound Swatches Signatures /10 #NNO
2011 Press Pass FanFare #14
2011 Press Pass FanFare Autographs Blue /5 #29
2011 Press Pass FanFare Autographs Bronze /15 #29
2011 Press Pass FanFare Autographs Gold /10 #29
2011 Press Pass FanFare Autographs Printing Plates Black /1 #29
2011 Press Pass FanFare Autographs Printing Plates Cyan /1 #29
2011 Press Pass FanFare Autographs Printing Plates Magenta /1 #29
2011 Press Pass FanFare Autographs Printing Plates Yellow /1 #29
2011 Press Pass FanFare Autographs Silver /10 #29
2011 Press Pass FanFare Blue Die Cuts #14
2011 Press Pass FanFare Championship Caliber #CC5
2011 Press Pass FanFare Emerald /25 #14
2011 Press Pass FanFare Holofoil Die Cuts #14
2011 Press Pass FanFare Magnificent Materials /199 #MMJG
2011 Press Pass FanFare Magnificent Materials Dual Swatches /50 #MMDJG
2011 Press Pass FanFare Magnificent Materials Dual Swatches Holofoil /10 #MMDJG
2011 Press Pass FanFare Magnificent Materials Holofoil /50 #MMJG
2011 Press Pass FanFare Magnificent Materials Signatures /25 #MMSEJG
2011 Press Pass FanFare Magnificent Materials Signatures Holofoil /10 #MMSEJG
2011 Press Pass FanFare Promotional Memorabilia /50 #PMJG
2011 Press Pass FanFare Rookie Standouts #RS13
2011 Press Pass FanFare Ruby Die Cuts /15 #14
2011 Press Pass FanFare Sapphire /10 #14
2011 Press Pass FanFare Silver /25 #14
2011 Press Pass Flashback #FB7
2011 Press Pass Four Wide Firesuit /25 #FWJG
2011 Press Pass Four Wide Glove /1 #FWJG
2011 Press Pass Four Wide Sheet Metal /15 #FWJG
2011 Press Pass Four Wide Shoes /1 #FWJG
2011 Press Pass Four Wide Tire /10 #FWJG
2011 Press Pass Geared Up Gold /75 #GUJG
2011 Press Pass Geared Up Holofoil /50 #GUJG
2011 Press Pass Gold /50 #11
2011 Press Pass Gold /50 #66
2011 Press Pass Gold /50 #161
2011 Press Pass Gold /50 #180
2011 Press Pass Gold /50 #191
2011 Press Pass Legends #42
2011 Press Pass Legends #59
2011 Press Pass Legends #70
2011 Press Pass Legends Autographs Blue /5 #LGAJG
2011 Press Pass Legends Autographs Gold /25 #LGAJG
2011 Press Pass Legends Autographs Printing Plates Black /1 #LGAJG
2011 Press Pass Legends Autographs Printing Plates Cyan /1 #LGAJG
2011 Press Pass Legends Autographs Printing Plates Magenta /1 #LGAJG
2011 Press Pass Legends Autographs Printing Plates Yellow /1 #LGAJG
2011 Press Pass Legends Gold /250 #42
2011 Press Pass Legends Gold /250 #59
2011 Press Pass Legends Gold /250 #70
2011 Press Pass Legends Holofoil /25 #42
2011 Press Pass Legends Holofoil /25 #59
2011 Press Pass Legends Holofoil /25 #70
2011 Press Pass Legends Motorsports Masters #MM18
2011 Press Pass Legends Motorsports Masters Brushed Foil /199 #MM18
2011 Press Pass Legends Motorsports Masters Holofoil /50 #MM18
2011 Press Pass Legends Pacing The Field #PF8
2011 Press Pass Legends Pacing The Field Autographs Silver /50 #PFAJG
2011 Press Pass Legends Pacing The Field Brushed Foil /199 #PF8
2011 Press Pass Legends Pacing The Field Holofoil /50 #PF8
2011 Press Pass Legends Printing Plates Black /1 #42
2011 Press Pass Legends Printing Plates Black /1 #59
2011 Press Pass Legends Printing Plates Black /1 #70
2011 Press Pass Legends Printing Plates Cyan /1 #42
2011 Press Pass Legends Printing Plates Cyan /1 #59
2011 Press Pass Legends Printing Plates Cyan /1 #70
2011 Press Pass Legends Printing Plates Magenta /1 #42
2011 Press Pass Legends Printing Plates Magenta /1 #59
2011 Press Pass Legends Printing Plates Magenta /1 #70
2011 Press Pass Legends Printing Plates Yellow /1 #42
2011 Press Pass Legends Printing Plates Yellow /1 #59
2011 Press Pass Legends Printing Plates Yellow /1 #70
2011 Press Pass Legends Prominent Pieces Gold /50 #PPJG
2011 Press Pass Legends Prominent Pieces Holofoil /25 #PPJG
2011 Press Pass Legends Prominent Pieces Oversized Firesuit /25 #PPOEJG
2011 Press Pass Legends Prominent Pieces Purple /15 #PPJG
2011 Press Pass Legends Prominent Pieces Silver /99 #PPJG
2011 Press Pass Legends Purple /25 #42
2011 Press Pass Legends Purple /25 #59
2011 Press Pass Legends Purple /25 #70
2011 Press Pass Legends Red /99 #42
2011 Press Pass Legends Red /99 #59
2011 Press Pass Legends Red /99 #70
2011 Press Pass Legends Solo /1 #42
2011 Press Pass Legends Solo /1 #59
2011 Press Pass Legends Solo /1 #70
2011 Press Pass Legends Trophy Room Gold /50 #TRJG
2011 Press Pass Legends Trophy Room Holofoil /25 #TRJG
2011 Press Pass Legends Trophy Room Purple /15 #TRJG
2011 Press Pass Premium #39
2011 Press Pass Premium #50
2011 Press Pass Premium #61
2011 Press Pass Premium #68
2011 Press Pass Premium #13A
2011 Press Pass Premium #13B
2011 Press Pass Premium Crystal Ball #CB4
2011 Press Pass Premium Crystal Ball Autographs /10 #CBAJG
2011 Press Pass Premium Double Burner /25 #DBJG
2011 Press Pass Premium Hot Pursuit 3D #HP3
2011 Press Pass Premium Hot Pursuit Autographs /10 #HPAJG
2011 Press Pass Premium Hot Pursuit National Convention #HP3
2011 Press Pass Premium Hot Threads /150 #HTJG
2011 Press Pass Premium Hot Threads Fast Pass /25 #HTJG
2011 Press Pass Premium Hot Threads Multi Color /25 #HTJG
2011 Press Pass Premium Hot Threads Patches /10 #HTPJG
2011 Press Pass Premium Hot Threads Secondary Color /99 #HTJG
2011 Press Pass Premium Pairings Firesuits /25 #PPDEJJG
2011 Press Pass Premium Pairings Signatures /5 #PPADEJJG
2011 Press Pass Premium Purple /25 #13
2011 Press Pass Premium Purple /25 #39
2011 Press Pass Premium Purple /25 #50
2011 Press Pass Premium Purple /25 #61
2011 Press Pass Premium Purple /25 #68
2011 Press Pass Premium Signatures /17 #PSJG
2011 Press Pass Premium Signatures Red Ink /4 #PSJG
2011 Press Pass Previews /1 #EB191
2011 Press Pass Previews /5 #EB11
2011 Press Pass Purple /25 #11
2011 Press Pass Purple /25 #191
2011 Press Pass Showcase /499 #2
2011 Press Pass Showcase /499 #36
2011 Press Pass Showcase /499 #44
2011 Press Pass Showcase /499 #53
2011 Press Pass Showcase Champions /499 #CH4
2011 Press Pass Showcase Champions Gold /125 #CH4
2011 Press Pass Showcase Champions Ink /25 #CHJG
2011 Press Pass Showcase Champions Ink Gold /10 #CHJG
2011 Press Pass Showcase Champions Ink Melting /1 #CHJG
2011 Press Pass Showcase Champions Melting /1 #CH4
2011 Press Pass Showcase Champions Memorabilia Firesuit /99 #CHMJG
2011 Press Pass Showcase Champions Memorabilia Firesuit Gold /45 #CHMJG
2011 Press Pass Showcase Champions Memorabilia Firesuit Melting /5 #CHMJG
2011 Press Pass Showcase Classic Collections Firesuit /45 #CCMHMS
2011 Press Pass Showcase Classic Collections Firesuit Patches /5 #CCMHMS
2011 Press Pass Showcase Classic Collections Ink /25 #CCMHMS
2011 Press Pass Showcase Classic Collections Ink Gold /5 #CCMHMS
2011 Press Pass Showcase Classic Collections Ink Melting /1 #CCMHMS
2011 Press Pass Showcase Classic Collections Sheet Metal /99 #CCMHMS
2011 Press Pass Showcase Elite Exhibit Ink /50 #EEIJG
2011 Press Pass Showcase Elite Exhibit Ink Gold /25 #EEIJG
2011 Press Pass Showcase Elite Exhibit Ink Melting /1 #EEIJG
2011 Press Pass Showcase Gold /125 #2
2011 Press Pass Showcase Gold /125 #36
2011 Press Pass Showcase Gold /125 #44
2011 Press Pass Showcase Gold /125 #53
2011 Press Pass Showcase Green /25 #2
2011 Press Pass Showcase Green /25 #36
2011 Press Pass Showcase Green /25 #44
2011 Press Pass Showcase Green /25 #53
2011 Press Pass Showcase Masterpieces Ink /45 #MPIJG
2011 Press Pass Showcase Masterpieces Ink Gold /25 #MPIJG
2011 Press Pass Showcase Masterpieces Ink Melting /1 #MPIJG
2011 Press Pass Showcase Masterpieces Memorabilia /99 #MPMJG
2011 Press Pass Showcase Masterpieces Memorabilia Gold /45 #MPMJG
2011 Press Pass Showcase Masterpieces Memorabilia Melting /5 #MPMJG
2011 Press Pass Showcase Melting /1 #2
2011 Press Pass Showcase Melting /1 #36
2011 Press Pass Showcase Melting /1 #44
2011 Press Pass Showcase Melting /1 #53
2011 Press Pass Showcase Prized Pieces Firesuit /99 #PPMJG
2011 Press Pass Showcase Prized Pieces Firesuit Gold /45 #PPMJG
2011 Press Pass Showcase Prized Pieces Firesuit Ink /25 #PPIJG
2011 Press Pass Showcase Prized Pieces Firesuit Patches Ink /1 #PPIJG
2011 Press Pass Showcase Prized Pieces Firesuit Patches Melting /5 #PPMJG
2011 Press Pass Showcase Prized Pieces Sheet Metal Ink /45 #PPIJG
2011 Press Pass Showcase Showroom /499 #SR2
2011 Press Pass Showcase Showroom Gold /125 #SR2
2011 Press Pass Showcase Showroom Melting /1 #SR2
2011 Press Pass Showcase Showroom Memorabilia Sheet Metal /45 #SRMJG
2011 Press Pass Showcase Showroom Memorabilia Sheet Metal Gold /25 #SRMJG
2011 Press Pass Showcase Showroom Memorabilia Sheet Metal Melting /5 #SRMJG
2011 Press Pass Signature Series /11 #SSTJG
2011 Press Pass Signature Series /11 #SSCJG
2011 Press Pass Signature Series /11 #SSFJG
2011 Press Pass Signature Series /11 #SSMJG
2011 Press Pass Signings Black and White /5 #PPSJG
2011 Press Pass Signings Brushed Metal /25 #PPSJG
2011 Press Pass Signings Holofoil /10 #PPSJG
2011 Press Pass Signings Printing Plates Black /1 #PPSJG
2011 Press Pass Signings Printing Plates Cyan /1 #PPSJG
2011 Press Pass Signings Printing Plates Magenta /1 #PPSJG
2011 Press Pass Signings Printing Plates Yellow /1 #PPSJG
2011 Press Pass Stealth #4
2011 Press Pass Stealth #5
2011 Press Pass Stealth #6
2011 Press Pass Stealth #83
2011 Press Pass Stealth #100
2011 Press Pass Stealth #76
2011 Press Pass Stealth Afterburner /99 #ABJG
2011 Press Pass Stealth Afterburner Gold /25 #ABJG
2011 Press Pass Stealth Black and White /25 #100
2011 Press Pass Stealth Black and White /25 #83
2011 Press Pass Stealth Black and White /25 #76
2011 Press Pass Stealth Black and White /25 #6
2011 Press Pass Stealth Black and White /25 #5
2011 Press Pass Stealth Black and White /25 #4
2011 Press Pass Stealth Holofoil /99 #100
2011 Press Pass Stealth Holofoil /99 #83
2011 Press Pass Stealth Holofoil /99 #76
2011 Press Pass Stealth Holofoil /99 #6
2011 Press Pass Stealth Holofoil /99 #5
2011 Press Pass Stealth Holofoil /99 #4
2011 Press Pass Stealth Metal of Honor Medal of Honor /50 #BAJG
2011 Press Pass Stealth Metal of Honor Purple Heart /25 #MHJG
2011 Press Pass Stealth Metal of Honor Silver Star /99 #BAJG
2011 Press Pass Stealth Purple /25 #6
2011 Press Pass Stealth Purple /25 #5
2011 Press Pass Stealth Purple /25 #4
2011 Press Pass Stealth Supersonic #SS1
2011 Press Pass Target Top 12 Tires /25 #T12JG
2011 Press Pass Tradin' Paint #TP5
2011 Press Pass Tradin' Paint Sheet Metal Blue /25 #TPJG
2011 Press Pass Tradin' Paint Sheet Metal Holofoil /50 #TPJG
2011 Press Pass Winning Tickets #WTXTRSP
2011 Press Pass Winning Tickets #WT55
2011 Press Pass Winning Tickets #WT62
2011 Wheels Main Event #66
2011 Wheels Main Event #71
2011 Wheels Main Event #13
2011 Wheels Main Event All Stars #A15
2011 Wheels Main Event All Stars Brushed Foil /199 #A15
2011 Wheels Main Event All Stars Holofoil /50 #A15
2011 Wheels Main Event Black and White #13
2011 Wheels Main Event Black and White #66
2011 Wheels Main Event Black and White #71
2011 Wheels Main Event Blue /75 #13
2011 Wheels Main Event Blue /75 #66
2011 Wheels Main Event Blue /75 #71
2011 Wheels Main Event Gloves Off Holofoil /25 #GOJG
2011 Wheels Main Event Gloves Off Silver /99 #GOJG
2011 Wheels Main Event Green /1 #13
2011 Wheels Main Event Green /1 #66
2011 Wheels Main Event Green /1 #71
2011 Wheels Main Event Headliners Holofoil /25 #HLJG
2011 Wheels Main Event Headliners Silver /99 #HLJG
2011 Wheels Main Event Lead Foot Holofoil /25 #LFJG
2011 Wheels Main Event Lead Foot Silver /99 #LFJG
2011 Wheels Main Event Marks Autographs Blue /5 #MEJG
2011 Wheels Main Event Marks Autographs Gold /10 #MEJG
2011 Wheels Main Event Marks Autographs Silver /15 #MEJG
2011 Wheels Main Event Matchups Autographs /10 #MEMJGKB
2011 Wheels Main Event Materials Holofoil /25 #MEMJG
2011 Wheels Main Event Materials Silver /99 #MEMJG
2011 Wheels Main Event Rear View #R2
2011 Wheels Main Event Rear View Brushed Foil /199 #R2
2011 Wheels Main Event Rear View Holofoil /50 #R2
2011 Wheels Main Event Red /20 #13
2011 Wheels Main Event Red /20 #66
2011 Wheels Main Event Red /20 #71
2012 Press Pass #13
2012 Press Pass #76
2012 Press Pass #86
2012 Press Pass #63
2012 Press Pass #96
2012 Press Pass Autographs Blue /5 #PPAJG
2012 Press Pass Autographs Printing Plates Black /1 #PPAJG
2012 Press Pass Autographs Printing Plates Cyan /1 #PPAJG
2012 Press Pass Autographs Printing Plates Magenta /1 #PPAJG
2012 Press Pass Autographs Printing Plates Yellow /1 #PPAJG
2012 Press Pass Autographs Silver /15 #PPAJG
2012 Press Pass Blue #13
2012 Press Pass Blue #63
2012 Press Pass Blue #76
2012 Press Pass Blue #86
2012 Press Pass Blue #96
2012 Press Pass Blue Holofoil /35 #13
2012 Press Pass Blue Holofoil /35 #63
2012 Press Pass Blue Holofoil /35 #76
2012 Press Pass Blue Holofoil /35 #86
2012 Press Pass Blue Holofoil /35 #96
2012 Press Pass Burning Rubber Gold /99 #BRJG
2012 Press Pass Burning Rubber Gold /99 #BRJG2
2012 Press Pass Burning Rubber Gold /99 #BRJG3
2012 Press Pass Burning Rubber Holofoil /25 #BRJG
2012 Press Pass Burning Rubber Holofoil /25 #BRJG2
2012 Press Pass Burning Rubber Holofoil /25 #BRJG3
2012 Press Pass Burning Rubber Prime Cuts /25 #BRJG
2012 Press Pass Burning Rubber Prime Cuts /25 #BRJG2
2012 Press Pass Burning Rubber Prime Cuts /25 #BRJG3
2012 Press Pass Burning Rubber Purple /15 #BRJG
2012 Press Pass Burning Rubber Purple /15 #BRJG2
2012 Press Pass Burning Rubber Purple /15 #BRJG3
2012 Press Pass Cup Chase #CCR8
2012 Press Pass Cup Chase Prizes #CCP12
2012 Press Pass Fanfare #16
2012 Press Pass Fanfare #17
2012 Press Pass Fanfare Autographs Blue /1 #JG
2012 Press Pass Fanfare Autographs Gold /10 #JG
2012 Press Pass Fanfare Autographs Red /5 #JG
2012 Press Pass Fanfare Autographs Silver /20 #JG
2012 Press Pass Fanfare Blue Foil Die Cuts #16
2012 Press Pass Fanfare Blue Foil Die Cuts #17
2012 Press Pass Fanfare Diamond /5 #16
2012 Press Pass Fanfare Diamond /5 #17
2012 Press Pass Fanfare Holofoil Die Cuts #16
2012 Press Pass Fanfare Holofoil Die Cuts #17
2012 Press Pass Fanfare Magnificent Materials /250 #MMJG
2012 Press Pass Fanfare Magnificent Materials /250 #MMJG2
2012 Press Pass Fanfare Magnificent Materials Dual Swatches /50 #MMJG
2012 Press Pass Fanfare Magnificent Materials Dual Swatches /50 #MMJG2
2012 Press Pass Fanfare Magnificent Materials Dual Swatches Melting /10 #MMJG
2012 Press Pass Fanfare Magnificent Materials Dual Swatches Melting /10 #MMJG2
2012 Press Pass Fanfare Magnificent Materials Gold /99 #MMJG
2012 Press Pass Fanfare Magnificent Materials Gold /99 #MMJG2
2012 Press Pass Fanfare Magnificent Materials Signatures /25 #JG
2012 Press Pass Fanfare Magnificent Materials Signatures Blue /5 #JG
2012 Press Pass Fanfare Sapphire /20 #16
2012 Press Pass Fanfare Sapphire /20 #17
2012 Press Pass Fanfare Showtime #S2
2012 Press Pass Fanfare Silver /25 #16
2012 Press Pass Fanfare Silver /25 #17
2012 Press Pass Four Wide Autographs /5 #JG
2012 Press Pass Four Wide Firesuit /25 #FWJG
2012 Press Pass Four Wide Glove /1 #FWJG
2012 Press Pass Four Wide Sheet Metal /15 #FWJG
2012 Press Pass Four Wide Tire /10 #FWJG
2012 Press Pass Gold #13
2012 Press Pass Gold #63
2012 Press Pass Gold #76
2012 Press Pass Gold #86
2012 Press Pass Gold #96
2012 Press Pass Ignite #15
2012 Press Pass Ignite #56
2012 Press Pass Ignite Double Burner Gun Metal /10 #DBJG
2012 Press Pass Ignite Double Burner Red /1 #DBJG
2012 Press Pass Ignite Double Burner Silver /25 #DBJG
2012 Press Pass Ignite Limelight #L5
2012 Press Pass Ignite Materials Autographs Red /5 #IMJG
2012 Press Pass Ignite Materials Autographs Silver /65 #IMJG
2012 Press Pass Ignite Materials Gun Metal /99 #IMJG1
2012 Press Pass Ignite Materials Gun Metal /99 #IMJG2
2012 Press Pass Ignite Materials Red /10 #IMJG1
2012 Press Pass Ignite Materials Red /10 #IMJG2
2012 Press Pass Ignite Materials Silver #IMJG1
2012 Press Pass Ignite Materials Silver #IMJG2
2012 Press Pass Ignite Profile #P7
2012 Press Pass Ignite Proofs Black and White /50 #15
2012 Press Pass Ignite Proofs Black and White /50 #56
2012 Press Pass Ignite Proofs Cyan #15
2012 Press Pass Ignite Proofs Cyan #56
2012 Press Pass Ignite Proofs Magenta #15
2012 Press Pass Ignite Proofs Magenta #56
2012 Press Pass Ignite Proofs Yellow /10 #15
2012 Press Pass Ignite Proofs Yellow /10 #56
2012 Press Pass Ignite Steel Horses #SH2
2012 Press Pass Ignite Supercharged Signatures /5 #SSJG
2012 Press Pass Legends #42
2012 Press Pass Legends Blue Holofoil /1 #42
2012 Press Pass Legends Gold /275 #42
2012 Press Pass Legends Green #42
2012 Press Pass Legends Prominent Pieces Gold /50 #JG
2012 Press Pass Legends Prominent Pieces Holofoil /25 #JG
2012 Press Pass Legends Prominent Pieces Oversized Firesuit /25 #JG
2012 Press Pass Legends Prominent Pieces Silver /99 #JG
2012 Press Pass Legends Rainbow Holofoil /50 #42
2012 Press Pass Legends Red /99 #42
2012 Press Pass Legends Silver Holofoil /25 #42
2012 Press Pass Power Picks Blue /50 #6
2012 Press Pass Power Picks Blue /50 #35
2012 Press Pass Power Picks Blue /50 #56
2012 Press Pass Power Picks Gold /50 #6
2012 Press Pass Power Picks Gold /50 #35
2012 Press Pass Power Picks Gold /50 #56
2012 Press Pass Power Picks Holofoil /10 #6
2012 Press Pass Power Picks Holofoil /10 #35
2012 Press Pass Power Picks Holofoil /10 #56
2012 Press Pass Preferred Line #PL4
2012 Press Pass Purple /35 #13
2012 Press Pass Purple /35 #63
2012 Press Pass Purple /35 #76
2012 Press Pass Purple /35 #86
2012 Press Pass Purple /35 #96
2012 Press Pass Redline #15
2012 Press Pass Redline Black /99 #15
2012 Press Pass Redline Cyan /50 #15
2012 Press Pass Redline Full Throttle Dual Relic Blue /5 #FTJG
2012 Press Pass Redline Full Throttle Dual Relic Gold /10 #FTJG
2012 Press Pass Redline Full Throttle Dual Relic Melting /1 #FTJG
2012 Press Pass Redline Full Throttle Dual Relic Red /75 #FTJG
2012 Press Pass Redline Full Throttle Dual Relic Silver /25 #FTJG
2012 Press Pass Redline Intensity #I4
2012 Press Pass Redline Magenta /15 #15
2012 Press Pass Redline Muscle Car Sheet Metal Blue /5 #MCJG1
2012 Press Pass Redline Muscle Car Sheet Metal Blue /5 #MCJG2
2012 Press Pass Redline Muscle Car Sheet Metal Gold /10 #MCJG1
2012 Press Pass Redline Muscle Car Sheet Metal Gold /10 #MCJG2
2012 Press Pass Redline Muscle Car Sheet Metal Melting /1 #MCJG1
2012 Press Pass Redline Muscle Car Sheet Metal Melting /1 #MCJG2
2012 Press Pass Redline Muscle Car Sheet Metal Red /10 #MCJG1
2012 Press Pass Redline Muscle Car Sheet Metal Red /45 #MCJG2
2012 Press Pass Redline Muscle Car Sheet Metal Silver /25 #MCJG1
2012 Press Pass Redline Muscle Car Sheet Metal Silver /20 #MCJG2
2012 Press Pass Redline Performance Driven #PD4
2012 Press Pass Redline Pieces of the Action Blue /10 #PAJG
2012 Press Pass Redline Pieces of the Action Gold /25 #PAJG
2012 Press Pass Redline Pieces of the Action Melting /1 #PAJG
2012 Press Pass Redline Pieces of the Action Red /75 #PAJG
2012 Press Pass Redline Pieces of the Action Silver /50 #PAJG
2012 Press Pass Redline Relic Autographs Blue /5 #RLRJG
2012 Press Pass Redline Relic Autographs Gold /10 #RLRJG
2012 Press Pass Redline Relic Autographs Melting /1 #RLRJG
2012 Press Pass Redline Relic Autographs Red /50 #RLRJG
2012 Press Pass Redline Relic Autographs Silver /25 #RLRJG
2012 Press Pass Redline Relics Blue /5 #RLJG
2012 Press Pass Redline Relics Gold /10 #RLJG
2012 Press Pass Redline Relics Melting /1 #RLJG
2012 Press Pass Redline Relics Red /75 #RLJG
2012 Press Pass Redline Relics Silver /25 #RLJG
2012 Press Pass Redline Rookie Year Relic Autographs Blue /5 #RYJG
2012 Press Pass Redline Rookie Year Relic Autographs Gold /25 #RYJG
2012 Press Pass Redline Rookie Year Relic Autographs Melting /1 #RYJG
2012 Press Pass Redline Rookie Year Relic Autographs Red /50 #RYJG
2012 Press Pass Redline RPM #RPM4
2012 Press Pass Redline Signatures Blue /5 #RSJG1
2012 Press Pass Redline Signatures Blue /5 #RSJG2
2012 Press Pass Redline Signatures Gold /15 #RSJG1
2012 Press Pass Redline Signatures Holofoil /10 #RSJG1
2012 Press Pass Redline Signatures Melting /1 #RSJG1
2012 Press Pass Redline Signatures Melting /1 #RSJG2
2012 Press Pass Redline Signatures Red /30 #RSJG1
2012 Press Pass Redline V8 Relics Blue /5 #V8JG
2012 Press Pass Redline V8 Relics Gold /10 #V8JG
2012 Press Pass Redline V8 Relics Melting /1 #V8JG
2012 Press Pass Redline V8 Relics Red /25 #V8JG
2012 Press Pass Redline Yellow /1 #15
2012 Press Pass Showcar #SC2
2012 Press Pass Showcase /499 #45
2012 Press Pass Showcase /499 #37
2012 Press Pass Showcase /499 #10
2012 Press Pass Showcase /499 #52
2012 Press Pass Showcase Champions Memorabilia /99 #CHJG
2012 Press Pass Showcase Champions Memorabilia Gold /50 #CHJG
2012 Press Pass Showcase Champions Memorabilia Melting /5 #CHJG
2012 Press Pass Showcase Champions Showcase /499 #CH2
2012 Press Pass Showcase Champions Showcase Gold /125 #CH2
2012 Press Pass Showcase Champions Showcase Ink /50 #CHSJG
2012 Press Pass Showcase Champions Showcase Ink Gold /25 #CHSJG
2012 Press Pass Showcase Champions Showcase Ink Melting /1 #CHSJG
2012 Press Pass Showcase Champions Showcase Melting /1 #CH2
2012 Press Pass Showcase Classic Collections Ink /10 #CCMHMS
2012 Press Pass Showcase Classic Collections Ink Gold /5 #CCMHMS
2012 Press Pass Showcase Classic Collections Ink Melting /1 #CCMHMS
2012 Press Pass Showcase Classic Collections Memorabilia /50 #CCMHMS
2012 Press Pass Showcase Classic Collections Memorabilia Gold /25 #CCMHMS
2012 Press Pass Showcase Classic Collections Memorabilia Melting /5 #CCMHMS
2012 Press Pass Showcase Elite Exhibit Ink /25 #EEIJG
2012 Press Pass Showcase Elite Exhibit Ink Gold /10 #EEIJG
2012 Press Pass Showcase Elite Exhibit Ink Melting /1 #EEIJG
2012 Press Pass Showcase Gold /125 #10
2012 Press Pass Showcase Gold /125 #37
2012 Press Pass Showcase Gold /125 #45
2012 Press Pass Showcase Gold /125 #52
2012 Press Pass Showcase Green /5 #10
2012 Press Pass Showcase Green /5 #37
2012 Press Pass Showcase Green /5 #45
2012 Press Pass Showcase Green /5 #52
2012 Press Pass Showcase Masterpieces Ink /50 #MPIJG
2012 Press Pass Showcase Masterpieces Ink Gold /25 #MPIJG
2012 Press Pass Showcase Masterpieces Ink Melting /1 #MPIJG
2012 Press Pass Showcase Masterpieces Memorabilia /99 #MPJG
2012 Press Pass Showcase Masterpieces Memorabilia Gold /50 #MPJG
2012 Press Pass Showcase Masterpieces Memorabilia Melting /5 #MPJG
2012 Press Pass Showcase Melting /1 #10
2012 Press Pass Showcase Melting /1 #37
2012 Press Pass Showcase Melting /1 #45
2012 Press Pass Showcase Melting /1 #52
2012 Press Pass Showcase Prized Pieces /24 #PPJG1
2012 Press Pass Showcase Prized Pieces /24 #PPJG2
2012 Press Pass Showcase Prized Pieces Gold /10 #PPJG1
2012 Press Pass Showcase Prized Pieces Gold /10 #PPJG2
2012 Press Pass Showcase Prized Pieces Melting /5 #PPJG1
2012 Press Pass Showcase Prized Pieces Melting /5 #PPJG2
2012 Press Pass Showcase Purple /1 #10
2012 Press Pass Showcase Purple /1 #37
2012 Press Pass Showcase Purple /1 #45
2012 Press Pass Showcase Purple /1 #52
2012 Press Pass Showcase Red /25 #10
2012 Press Pass Showcase Red /25 #37
2012 Press Pass Showcase Red /25 #45
2012 Press Pass Showcase Red /25 #52
2012 Press Pass Showcase Richard Petty 75th Birthday Tribute /10 #RPJG
2012 Press Pass Showcase Richard Petty 75th Birthday Tribute Melting /1 #RPJG
2012 Press Pass Showcase Showcase Patches /5 #SSPJG
2012 Press Pass Showcase Showcase Patches Melting /1 #SSPJG
2012 Press Pass Showcase Showroom /499 #SR2
2012 Press Pass Showcase Showroom Gold /125 #SR2
2012 Press Pass Showcase Showroom Melting /1 #SR2
2012 Press Pass Showcase Showroom Memorabilia /99 #SRJG
2012 Press Pass Showcase Showroom Memorabilia Gold /50 #SRJG
2012 Press Pass Showcase Showroom Memorabilia Melting /5 #SRJG
2012 Press Pass Showcase Signature Patches /1 #SSPJG
2012 Press Pass Showman #SM2
2012 Press Pass Signature Series Race Used /12 #PPAJG1
2012 Press Pass Signature Series Race Used /12 #PPAJG2
2012 Press Pass Snapshots #SS13
2012 Press Pass Snapshots #SS71
2012 Press Pass Triple Gear 3 in 1 /5 #TGJG
2012 Press Pass Triple Gear Firesuit and Sheet Metal /15 #TGJG
2012 Press Pass Triple Gear Tire /25 #TGJG
2012 Press Pass Ultimate Collection Blue Holofoil /25 #UCJG
2012 Press Pass Ultimate Collection Holofoil /50 #UCJG
2012 Press Pass Wal-Mart Snapshots #SSWM4
2012 Total Memorabilia #10A
2012 Total Memorabilia #10B
2012 Total Memorabilia Black and White /99 #10
2012 Total Memorabilia Dual Swatch Gold /75 #TMJG1
2012 Total Memorabilia Dual Swatch Holofoil /25 #TMJG1
2012 Total Memorabilia Dual Swatch Melting /5 #TMJG1
2012 Total Memorabilia Dual Swatch Silver /99 #TMJG1
2012 Total Memorabilia Gold /275 #10
2012 Total Memorabilia Hot Rod Relics Gold /50 #HRRJG
2012 Total Memorabilia Hot Rod Relics Holofoil /10 #HRRJG
2012 Total Memorabilia Hot Rod Relics Melting /1 #HRRJG
2012 Total Memorabilia Hot Rod Relics Silver /99 #HRRJG
2012 Total Memorabilia Jumbo Swatch Gold /50 #TMJG1
2012 Total Memorabilia Jumbo Swatch Holofoil /10 #TMJG1
2012 Total Memorabilia Jumbo Swatch Melting /1 #TMJG1
2012 Total Memorabilia Jumbo Swatch Silver /50 #TMJG1
2012 Total Memorabilia Quad Swatch Gold /25 #TMJG1
2012 Total Memorabilia Quad Swatch Holofoil /10 #TMJG1
2012 Total Memorabilia Quad Swatch Melting /1 #TMJG1
2012 Total Memorabilia Quad Swatch Silver /50 #TMJG1
2012 Total Memorabilia Red Retail /250 #10
2012 Total Memorabilia Signature Collection Dual Swatch Silver /10 #SCJG
2012 Total Memorabilia Signature Collection Quad Swatch Holofoil /5 #SCJG
2012 Total Memorabilia Signature Collection Single Swatch Melting /1 #SCJG
2012 Total Memorabilia Signature Collection Triple Swatch Gold /10 #SCJG
2012 Total Memorabilia Single Swatch Gold /99 #TMJG1
2012 Total Memorabilia Single Swatch Holofoil /50 #TMJG1
2012 Total Memorabilia Single Swatch Melting /10 #TMJG1
2012 Total Memorabilia Single Swatch Silver /199 #TMJG1
2012 Total Memorabilia Tandem Treasures Dual Memorabilia Gold /75 #TTJGKK
2012 Total Memorabilia Tandem Treasures Dual Memorabilia Holofoil /25 #TTJGKK
2012 Total Memorabilia Tandem Treasures Dual Memorabilia Melting /5 #TTJGKK
2012 Total Memorabilia Tandem Treasures Dual Memorabilia Silver /99 #TTJGKK
2012 Total Memorabilia Triple Swatch Gold /50 #TMJG1
2012 Total Memorabilia Triple Swatch Holofoil /25 #TMJG1
2012 Total Memorabilia Triple Swatch Melting /1 #TMJG1
2012 Total Memorabilia Triple Swatch Silver /99 #TMJG1
2013 Press Pass #16
2013 Press Pass #17
2013 Press Pass #85
2013 Press Pass #69
2013 Press Pass #97
2013 Press Pass #0
2013 Press Pass Aerodynamic Autographs Blue /5 #JG
2013 Press Pass Aerodynamic Autographs Holofoil /10 #JG
2013 Press Pass Aerodynamic Autographs Printing Plates Black /1 #JG
2013 Press Pass Aerodynamic Autographs Printing Plates Cyan /1 #JG
2013 Press Pass Aerodynamic Autographs Printing Plates Magenta /1 #JG
2013 Press Pass Aerodynamic Autographs Printing Plates Yellow /1 #JG
2013 Press Pass Burning Rubber Blue /50 #BRJG
2013 Press Pass Burning Rubber Gold /199 #BRJG
2013 Press Pass Burning Rubber Holofoil /75 #BRJG
2013 Press Pass Burning Rubber Melting /10 #BRJG
2013 Press Pass Color Proofs Black #16
2013 Press Pass Color Proofs Black #17
2013 Press Pass Color Proofs Black #69
2013 Press Pass Color Proofs Black #85
2013 Press Pass Color Proofs Black #97
2013 Press Pass Color Proofs Cyan /35 #16
2013 Press Pass Color Proofs Cyan /35 #17
2013 Press Pass Color Proofs Cyan /35 #69
2013 Press Pass Color Proofs Cyan /35 #85
2013 Press Pass Color Proofs Cyan /35 #97
2013 Press Pass Color Proofs Magenta #16
2013 Press Pass Color Proofs Magenta #17
2013 Press Pass Color Proofs Magenta #69
2013 Press Pass Color Proofs Magenta #85
2013 Press Pass Color Proofs Magenta #97
2013 Press Pass Color Proofs Yellow /5 #16
2013 Press Pass Color Proofs Yellow /5 #17
2013 Press Pass Color Proofs Yellow /5 #69
2013 Press Pass Color Proofs Yellow /5 #85
2013 Press Pass Color Proofs Yellow /5 #97
2013 Press Pass Cool Persistence #CP8
2013 Press Pass Cup Chase #CC7
2013 Press Pass Cup Chase Prizes #CCE13
2013 Press Pass Fanfare #19
2013 Press Pass Fanfare #20
2013 Press Pass Fanfare Autographs Blue /1 #JG
2013 Press Pass Fanfare Autographs Gold /1 #JG
2013 Press Pass Fanfare Autographs Green /1 #JG
2013 Press Pass Fanfare Autographs Red /1 #JG
2013 Press Pass Fanfare Autographs Silver /1 #JG
2013 Press Pass Fanfare Diamond Die Cuts /5 #19
2013 Press Pass Fanfare Diamond Die Cuts /5 #20
2013 Press Pass Fanfare Fan Following #FF2
2013 Press Pass Fanfare Fan Following National Convention VIP #FFN2
2013 Press Pass Fanfare Green /3 #19
2013 Press Pass Fanfare Green /3 #20
2013 Press Pass Fanfare Holofoil Die Cuts #19
2013 Press Pass Fanfare Holofoil Die Cuts #20
2013 Press Pass Fanfare Magnificent Jumbo Materials Signatures /10 #JG
2013 Press Pass Fanfare Magnificent Materials Dual Swatches /50 #JG
2013 Press Pass Fanfare Magnificent Materials Dual Swatches Melting /10 #JG
2013 Press Pass Fanfare Magnificent Materials Gold /50 #JG
2013 Press Pass Fanfare Magnificent Materials Jumbo Swatches /25 #JG
2013 Press Pass Fanfare Magnificent Materials Signatures /25 #JG
2013 Press Pass Fanfare Magnificent Materials Signatures Blue /5 #JG
2013 Press Pass Fanfare Magnificent Materials Silver /199 #JG
2013 Press Pass Fanfare Red Foil Die Cuts #19
2013 Press Pass Fanfare Red Foil Die Cuts #20
2013 Press Pass Fanfare Sapphire /20 #19
2013 Press Pass Fanfare Sapphire /20 #20
2013 Press Pass Fanfare Showtime #S6
2013 Press Pass Fanfare Silver /25 #19
2013 Press Pass Fanfare Silver /25 #20
2013 Press Pass Four Wide Gold /10 #FWJG
2013 Press Pass Four Wide Melting /1 #FWJG
2013 Press Pass Ignite #12
2013 Press Pass Ignite #52
2013 Press Pass Ignite Convoy #3
2013 Press Pass Ignite Double Burner Blue Holofoil /10 #DBJG
2013 Press Pass Ignite Double Burner Red /1 #DBJG
2013 Press Pass Ignite Double Burner Silver /25 #DBJG
2013 Press Pass Ignite Great American Treads Autographs Blue Holofoil /10 #GATJG
2013 Press Pass Ignite Great American Treads Autographs Red /1 #GATJG
2013 Press Pass Ignite Hot Threads Blue Holofoil /99 #HTJG
2013 Press Pass Ignite Hot Threads Blue Holofoil /99 #HTJG2
2013 Press Pass Ignite Hot Threads Patch Red /10 #HTJG
2013 Press Pass Ignite Hot Threads Patch Red /10 #HTJG2
2013 Press Pass Ignite Hot Threads Patch Red Oversized /20 #HTPJG
2013 Press Pass Ignite Hot Threads Silver #HTJG2
2013 Press Pass Ignite Hot Threads Silver #HTJG
2013 Press Pass Ignite Ink Black /17 #IIJG
2013 Press Pass Ignite Ink Blue /5 #IIJG
2013 Press Pass Ignite Ink Red /1 #IIJG
2013 Press Pass Ignite Profile #4
2013 Press Pass Ignite Proofs Black and White /50 #12
2013 Press Pass Ignite Proofs Black and White /50 #52
2013 Press Pass Ignite Proofs Cyan #12
2013 Press Pass Ignite Proofs Cyan #52
2013 Press Pass Ignite Proofs Magenta #12
2013 Press Pass Ignite Proofs Magenta #52
2013 Press Pass Ignite Proofs Yellow /5 #12
2013 Press Pass Ignite Proofs Yellow /5 #52
2013 Press Pass Ignite Supercharged Signatures Blue Holofoil /10 #SSJG
2013 Press Pass Ignite Supercharged Signatures Red /1 #SSJG
2013 Press Pass Ignite Turning Point #1
2013 Press Pass Legends #44
2013 Press Pass Legends Autographs Blue #LGJG
2013 Press Pass Legends Autographs Gold /4 #LGJG
2013 Press Pass Legends Autographs Holofoil /2 #LGJG
2013 Press Pass Legends Autographs Printing Plates Black /1 #LGJG
2013 Press Pass Legends Autographs Printing Plates Cyan /1 #LGJG
2013 Press Pass Legends Autographs Printing Plates Magenta /1 #LGJG
2013 Press Pass Legends Autographs Printing Plates Yellow /1 #LGJG
2013 Press Pass Legends Autographs Silver #LGJG
2013 Press Pass Legends Blue #44
2013 Press Pass Legends Blue Holofoil /1 #44
2013 Press Pass Legends Four Wide Memorabilia Autographs Gold /25 #FWSEJG
2013 Press Pass Legends Four Wide Memorabilia Autographs Melting /5 #FWSEJG
2013 Press Pass Legends Gold /149 #44
2013 Press Pass Legends Holofoil /10 #44
2013 Press Pass Legends Printing Plates Black /1 #44
2013 Press Pass Legends Printing Plates Cyan /1 #44
2013 Press Pass Legends Printing Plates Magenta /1 #44
2013 Press Pass Legends Printing Plates Yellow /1 #44

2013 Press Pass Legends Prominent Pieces Gold /10 #PPJG
2013 Press Pass Legends Prominent Pieces Holofoil /5 #PPJG
2013 Press Pass Legends Prominent Pieces Oversized Firesuit /5 #PPJG
2013 Press Pass Legends Prominent Pieces Silver /25 #PPJG
2013 Press Pass Legends Red /99 #44
2013 Press Pass Power Picks Blue /99 #6
2013 Press Pass Power Picks Blue /99 #35
2013 Press Pass Power Picks Gold /50 #6
2013 Press Pass Power Picks Gold /50 #35
2013 Press Pass Power Picks Holofoil /10 #6
2013 Press Pass Power Picks Holofoil /10 #35
2013 Press Pass Racing Champions #RC21
2013 Press Pass Redline #17
2013 Press Pass Redline #18
2013 Press Pass Redline Black /99 #17
2013 Press Pass Redline Black /99 #18
2013 Press Pass Redline Cyan /50 #17
2013 Press Pass Redline Cyan /50 #18
2013 Press Pass Redline Dynamic Duals Dual Relic Blue /5 #DDJG
2013 Press Pass Redline Dynamic Duals Dual Relic Gold /10 #DDJG
2013 Press Pass Redline Dynamic Duals Dual Relic Melting /1 #DDJG
2013 Press Pass Redline Dynamic Duals Dual Relic Red /50 #DDJG
2013 Press Pass Redline Dynamic Duals Dual Relic Silver /25 #DDJG
2013 Press Pass Redline Intensity #3
2013 Press Pass Redline Magenta /15 #17
2013 Press Pass Redline Magenta /15 #18
2013 Press Pass Redline Muscle Car Sheet Metal Blue /5 #MCMJG
2013 Press Pass Redline Muscle Car Sheet Metal Gold /10 #MCMJG
2013 Press Pass Redline Muscle Car Sheet Metal Melting /1 #MCMJG
2013 Press Pass Redline Muscle Car Sheet Metal Red /50 #MCMJG
2013 Press Pass Redline Muscle Car Sheet Metal Silver /25 #MCMJG
2013 Press Pass Redline Pieces of the Action Blue /10 #PAJG
2013 Press Pass Redline Pieces of the Action Gold /25 #PAJG
2013 Press Pass Redline Pieces of the Action Melting /1 #PAJG
2013 Press Pass Redline Pieces of the Action Red /75 #PAJG
2013 Press Pass Redline Pieces of the Action Silver /50 #PAJG
2013 Press Pass Redline Redline Racers #4
2013 Press Pass Redline Relic Autographs Blue /5 #RRSEJG
2013 Press Pass Redline Relic Autographs Gold /24 #RRSEJG
2013 Press Pass Redline Relic Autographs Melting /1 #RRSEJG
2013 Press Pass Redline Relic Autographs Red /95 #RRSEJG
2013 Press Pass Redline Relic Autographs Silver /50 #RRSEJG
2013 Press Pass Redline Relics Blue /5 #RRJG1
2013 Press Pass Redline Relics Blue /5 #RRJG2
2013 Press Pass Redline Relics Gold /10 #RRJG1
2013 Press Pass Redline Relics Gold /10 #RRJG2
2013 Press Pass Redline Relics Melting /1 #RRJG1
2013 Press Pass Redline Relics Melting /1 #RRJG2
2013 Press Pass Redline Relics Red /50 #RRJG1
2013 Press Pass Redline Relics Red /50 #RRJG2
2013 Press Pass Redline Relics Silver /25 #RRJG1
2013 Press Pass Redline Relics Silver /25 #RRJG2
2013 Press Pass Redline RPM #2
2013 Press Pass Redline Signatures Blue /5 #RSJG2
2013 Press Pass Redline Signatures Gold /5 #RSJG1
2013 Press Pass Redline Signatures Gold /5 #RSJG2
2013 Press Pass Redline Signatures Holo /5 #RSJG1
2013 Press Pass Redline Signatures Holo /5 #RSJG2
2013 Press Pass Redline Signatures Melting /1 #RSJG1
2013 Press Pass Redline Signatures Melting /1 #RSJG2
2013 Press Pass Redline Signatures Red /24 #RSJG1
2013 Press Pass Redline Signatures Red /24 #RSJG2
2013 Press Pass Redline V8 Relics Blue /5 #V8JG
2013 Press Pass Redline V8 Relics Gold /10 #V8JG
2013 Press Pass Redline V8 Relics Melting /1 #V8JG
2013 Press Pass Redline V8 Relics Red /25 #V8JG
2013 Press Pass Redline Yellow /1 #17
2013 Press Pass Redline Yellow /1 #18
2013 Press Pass Showcase /349 #10
2013 Press Pass Showcase /349 #34
2013 Press Pass Showcase /349 #45
2013 Press Pass Showcase /349 #55
2013 Press Pass Showcase Black /1 #10
2013 Press Pass Showcase Black /1 #34
2013 Press Pass Showcase Black /1 #45
2013 Press Pass Showcase Black /1 #55
2013 Press Pass Showcase Blue /25 #10
2013 Press Pass Showcase Blue /25 #34
2013 Press Pass Showcase Blue /25 #45
2013 Press Pass Showcase Blue /25 #55
2013 Press Pass Showcase Classic Collections Ink Gold /5 #CCIHMS
2013 Press Pass Showcase Classic Collections Ink Melting /1 #CCIHMS
2013 Press Pass Showcase Classic Collections Ink Red /1 #CCIHMS
2013 Press Pass Showcase Classic Collections Memorabilia Gold /25 #CCMHMS
2013 Press Pass Showcase Classic Collections Memorabilia Melting /5 #CCMHMS
2013 Press Pass Showcase Classic Collections Memorabilia Silver /75 #CCMHMS
2013 Press Pass Showcase Elite Exhibit Ink /25 #EEIJG
2013 Press Pass Showcase Elite Exhibit Ink Blue /30 #EEIJG
2013 Press Pass Showcase Elite Exhibit Ink Gold /10 #EEIJG
2013 Press Pass Showcase Elite Exhibit Ink Melting /1 #EEIJG
2013 Press Pass Showcase Elite Exhibit Ink Red /5 #EEIJG
2013 Press Pass Showcase Gold /99 #10
2013 Press Pass Showcase Gold /99 #34
2013 Press Pass Showcase Gold /99 #45
2013 Press Pass Showcase Gold /99 #55
2013 Press Pass Showcase Green /20 #10
2013 Press Pass Showcase Green /20 #34
2013 Press Pass Showcase Green /20 #45
2013 Press Pass Showcase Green /20 #55
2013 Press Pass Showcase Masterpieces Ink /25 #MPIJG
2013 Press Pass Showcase Masterpieces Ink Gold /10 #MPIJG
2013 Press Pass Showcase Masterpieces Ink Melting /1 #MPIJG
2013 Press Pass Showcase Masterpieces Memorabilia /75 #MPJG
2013 Press Pass Showcase Masterpieces Memorabilia Gold /25 #MPJG
2013 Press Pass Showcase Masterpieces Memorabilia Melting /5 #MPJG
2013 Press Pass Showcase Prized Pieces /99 #PPMJG
2013 Press Pass Showcase Prized Pieces Blue /20 #PPMJG
2013 Press Pass Showcase Prized Pieces Gold /25 #PPMJG
2013 Press Pass Showcase Prized Pieces Ink /25 #PPIJG
2013 Press Pass Showcase Prized Pieces Ink Gold /10 #PPIJG
2013 Press Pass Showcase Prized Pieces Ink Melting /1 #PPIJG
2013 Press Pass Showcase Prized Pieces Melting /5 #PPMJG
2013 Press Pass Showcase Purple /13 #10
2013 Press Pass Showcase Purple /13 #34
2013 Press Pass Showcase Purple /13 #45
2013 Press Pass Showcase Purple /13 #55
2013 Press Pass Showcase Red /10 #10
2013 Press Pass Showcase Red /10 #34
2013 Press Pass Showcase Red /10 #45
2013 Press Pass Showcase Red /10 #55
2013 Press Pass Showcase Series Standouts Gold /50 #6
2013 Press Pass Showcase Series Standouts Memorabilia /75 #SSMJG
2013 Press Pass Showcase Series Standouts Memorabilia Blue /50 #SSMJG
2013 Press Pass Showcase Series Standouts Memorabilia Gold /25 #SSMJG
2013 Press Pass Showcase Series Standouts Memorabilia Melting /5 #SSMJG
2013 Press Pass Showcase Showcase Patches /5 #SPJG
2013 Press Pass Showcase Showroom /299 #3
2013 Press Pass Showcase Showroom Blue /40 #3
2013 Press Pass Showcase Showroom Gold /50 #3
2013 Press Pass Showcase Showroom Green /20 #3
2013 Press Pass Showcase Showroom Melting /1 #3
2013 Press Pass Showcase Showroom Purple /13 #3
2013 Press Pass Showcase Showroom Red /10 #3
2013 Press Pass Showcase Signature Patches /11 #SSPJG
2013 Press Pass Showcase Studio Showcase /299 #6
2013 Press Pass Showcase Studio Showcase Blue /40 #6
2013 Press Pass Showcase Studio Showcase Green /25 #6
2013 Press Pass Showcase Studio Showcase Ink /25 #SSIJG
2013 Press Pass Showcase Studio Showcase Ink Gold /10 #SSIJG
2013 Press Pass Showcase Studio Showcase Ink Melting /1 #SSIJG
2013 Press Pass Showcase Studio Showcase Ink Red /5 #SSIJG
2013 Press Pass Showcase Studio Showcase Melting /1 #6
2013 Press Pass Showcase Studio Showcase Purple /13 #6
2013 Press Pass Showcase Studio Showcase Red /10 #6
2013 Press Pass Signature Series Gold /10 #JG
2013 Press Pass Signature Series Melting /5 #JG
2013 Press Pass Signings Blue /1 #JG
2013 Press Pass Signings Gold /5 #JG
2013 Press Pass Signings Holofoil /5 #JG
2013 Press Pass Signings Printing Plates Black /1 #JG
2013 Press Pass Signings Printing Plates Cyan /1 #JG
2013 Press Pass Signings Printing Plates Magenta /1 #JG
2013 Press Pass Signings Printing Plates Yellow /1 #JG
2013 Press Pass Signings Silver /5 #JG
2013 Total Memorabilia #14
2013 Total Memorabilia #15
2013 Total Memorabilia Black and White /99 #14
2013 Total Memorabilia Black and White /99 #15
2013 Total Memorabilia Burning Rubber Chase Edition Gold /75 #BRCJG
2013 Total Memorabilia Burning Rubber Chase Edition Holofoil /50 #BRCJG
2013 Total Memorabilia Burning Rubber Chase Edition Melting /5 #BRCJG
2013 Total Memorabilia Burning Rubber Chase Edition Silver /175 #BRCJG
2013 Total Memorabilia Dual Swatch Gold /199 #TMJG
2013 Total Memorabilia Gold /275 #14
2013 Total Memorabilia Gold /275 #15
2013 Total Memorabilia Hot Rod Relics Gold /50 #HRRJG
2013 Total Memorabilia Hot Rod Relics Holofoil /10 #HRRJG
2013 Total Memorabilia Hot Rod Relics Melting /1 #HRRJG
2013 Total Memorabilia Hot Rod Relics Silver /99 #HRRJG
2013 Total Memorabilia Memory Lane #ML4
2013 Total Memorabilia Quad Swatch Melting /10 #TMJG
2013 Total Memorabilia Red #14
2013 Total Memorabilia Red #15
2013 Total Memorabilia Signature Collection Dual Swatch Gold /5 #SCJG
2013 Total Memorabilia Signature Collection Quad Swatch Melting /1 #SCJG
2013 Total Memorabilia Signature Collection Single Swatch Silver /10 #SCJG
2013 Total Memorabilia Signature Collection Triple Swatch Holofoil /5 #SCJG
2013 Total Memorabilia Single Swatch Silver /475 #TMJG
2013 Total Memorabilia Triple Swatch Holofoil /99 #TMJG
2014 Press Pass #12
2014 Press Pass #13
2014 Press Pass #68
2014 Press Pass #82
2014 Press Pass Aerodynamic Autographs Blue /1 #AAJG
2014 Press Pass Aerodynamic Autographs Holofoil /5 #AAJG
2014 Press Pass Aerodynamic Autographs Printing Plates Black /1 #AAJG
2014 Press Pass Aerodynamic Autographs Printing Plates Cyan /1 #AAJG
2014 Press Pass Aerodynamic Autographs Printing Plates Magenta /1 #AAJG
2014 Press Pass Aerodynamic Autographs Printing Plates Yellow /1 #AAJG
2014 Press Pass American Thunder #15
2014 Press Pass American Thunder #66
2014 Press Pass American Thunder #51
2014 Press Pass American Thunder Autographs Blue /5 #ATAJG
2014 Press Pass American Thunder Autographs Red /1 #ATAJG
2014 Press Pass American Thunder Autographs White /15 #ATAJG
2014 Press Pass American Thunder Battle Armor Blue /25 #BAJG
2014 Press Pass American Thunder Battle Armor Red /1 #BAJG
2014 Press Pass American Thunder Battle Armor Silver /99 #BAJG
2014 Press Pass American Thunder Black and White /50 #66
2014 Press Pass American Thunder Black and White /50 #51
2014 Press Pass American Thunder Black and White /50 #15
2014 Press Pass American Thunder Brothers In Arms Autographs Blue /5 #BAHMS
2014 Press Pass American Thunder Brothers In Arms Autographs Red /1 #BAHMS
2014 Press Pass American Thunder Brothers In Arms Autographs White /10 #BAHMS
2014 Press Pass American Thunder Brothers In Arms Relics Blue /25 #BAHMS
2014 Press Pass American Thunder Brothers In Arms Relics Red /5 #BAHMS
2014 Press Pass American Thunder Brothers In Arms Relics Silver /50 #BAHMS
2014 Press Pass American Thunder Class A Uniforms Blue /99 #CAUJG
2014 Press Pass American Thunder Class A Uniforms Red /10 #CAUJG
2014 Press Pass American Thunder Class A Uniforms Silver #CAUJG
2014 Press Pass American Thunder Cyan #15
2014 Press Pass American Thunder Cyan #51
2014 Press Pass American Thunder Cyan #66
2014 Press Pass American Thunder Great American Treads Autographs Blue /10 #GATJG
2014 Press Pass American Thunder Great American Treads Autographs Red /1 #GATJG
2014 Press Pass American Thunder Magenta #15
2014 Press Pass American Thunder Magenta #51
2014 Press Pass American Thunder Magenta #66
2014 Press Pass American Thunder Top Speed #TS8
2014 Press Pass American Thunder Yellow /5 #51
2014 Press Pass American Thunder Yellow /5 #15
2014 Press Pass Burning Rubber Chase Edition Blue /25 #BRCJG
2014 Press Pass Burning Rubber Chase Edition Gold /50 #BRCJG
2014 Press Pass Burning Rubber Chase Edition Melting /10 #BRCJG
2014 Press Pass Burning Rubber Chase Edition Silver /99 #BRCJG
2014 Press Pass Color Proofs Black /70 #12
2014 Press Pass Color Proofs Black /70 #13
2014 Press Pass Color Proofs Black /70 #68
2014 Press Pass Color Proofs Black /70 #82
2014 Press Pass Color Proofs Cyan /35 #12
2014 Press Pass Color Proofs Cyan /35 #13
2014 Press Pass Color Proofs Cyan /35 #68
2014 Press Pass Color Proofs Cyan /35 #82
2014 Press Pass Color Proofs Magenta #12
2014 Press Pass Color Proofs Magenta #13
2014 Press Pass Color Proofs Magenta #68
2014 Press Pass Color Proofs Magenta #82
2014 Press Pass Color Proofs Yellow /5 #12
2014 Press Pass Color Proofs Yellow /5 #13
2014 Press Pass Color Proofs Yellow /5 #68
2014 Press Pass Color Proofs Yellow /5 #82
2014 Press Pass Cup Chase #6
2014 Press Pass Five Star /15 #6
2014 Press Pass Five Star Blue /5 #6
2014 Press Pass Five Star Classic Compilation Autographs Blue Triple Swatch /5 #CCJG
2014 Press Pass Five Star Classic Compilation Autographs Holofoil /10 #CCJG
2014 Press Pass Five Star Classic Compilation Autographs Holofoil Dual Swatch /10 #CCJG
2014 Press Pass Five Star Classic Compilation Autographs Melting Five Swatch /1 #CCJG
2014 Press Pass Five Star Classic Compilation Autographs Melting Quad Swatch /1 #CCJG
2014 Press Pass Five Star Classic Compilations Autographed Patch Booklet /1 #CCJG1
2014 Press Pass Five Star Classic Compilations Autographed Patch Booklet /1 #CCJG2
2014 Press Pass Five Star Classic Compilations Autographed Patch Booklet /1 #CCJG3
2014 Press Pass Five Star Classic Compilations Autographed Patch Booklet /1 #CCJG4
2014 Press Pass Five Star Classic Compilations Autographed Patch Booklet /1 #CCJG5
2014 Press Pass Five Star Classic Compilations Autographed Patch Booklet /1 #CCJG6
2014 Press Pass Five Star Classic Compilations Autographed Patch Booklet /1 #CCJG7
2014 Press Pass Five Star Classic Compilations Autographed Patch Booklet /1 #CCJG8
2014 Press Pass Five Star Classic Compilations Autographed Patch Booklet /1 #CCJG9
2014 Press Pass Five Star Classic Compilations Autographed Patch Booklet /1 #CCJG10
2014 Press Pass Five Star Classic Compilations Autographed Patch Booklet /1 #CCJG11
2014 Press Pass Five Star Classic Compilations Autographed Patch Booklet /1 #CCJG12
2014 Press Pass Five Star Classic Compilations Autographed Patch Booklet /1 #CCJG13
2014 Press Pass Five Star Classic Compilations Autographed Patch Booklet /1 #CCJG14
2014 Press Pass Five Star Classic Compilations Combo Autographs Blue /5 #CCHMS
2014 Press Pass Five Star Classic Compilations Combo Autographs Blue /5 #CCWINS
2014 Press Pass Five Star Classic Compilations Combo Autographs Melting /1 #CCHMS
2014 Press Pass Five Star Classic Compilations Combo Autographs Melting /1 #CCWINS
2014 Press Pass Five Star Holofoil /10 #6
2014 Press Pass Five Star Melting /1 #6
2014 Press Pass Five Star Paramount Pieces Blue /5 #PPJG
2014 Press Pass Five Star Paramount Pieces Gold /25 #PPJG
2014 Press Pass Five Star Paramount Pieces Holofoil /10 #PPJG
2014 Press Pass Five Star Paramount Pieces Melting /1 #PPJG
2014 Press Pass Five Star Paramount Pieces Melting Patch /1 #PPJG
2014 Press Pass Five Star Signature Souvenirs Blue /5 #SSJG
2014 Press Pass Five Star Signature Souvenirs Gold /50 #SSJG
2014 Press Pass Five Star Signature Souvenirs Holofoil /25 #SSJG
2014 Press Pass Five Star Signature Souvenirs Melting /1 #SSJG
2014 Press Pass Five Star Signatures Blue /5 #FSSJG
2014 Press Pass Five Star Signatures Holofoil /10 #FSSJG
2014 Press Pass Five Star Signatures Melting /1 #FSSJG
2014 Press Pass Four Wide Gold /10 #FWJG
2014 Press Pass Four Wide Melting /1 #FWJG
2014 Press Pass Gold #12
2014 Press Pass Gold #13
2014 Press Pass Gold #68
2014 Press Pass Gold #82
2014 Press Pass Intensity National Convention VIP #NE2
2014 Press Pass Redline #21
2014 Press Pass Redline #22
2014 Press Pass Redline Black /75 #21
2014 Press Pass Redline Black /75 #22
2014 Press Pass Redline Blue Foil #21
2014 Press Pass Redline Blue Foil #22
2014 Press Pass Redline Cyan /50 #21
2014 Press Pass Redline Cyan /50 #22
2014 Press Pass Redline Dynamic Duals Relic Autographs Blue /10 #DDJG
2014 Press Pass Redline Dynamic Duals Relic Autographs Gold /5 #DDJG
2014 Press Pass Redline Dynamic Duals Relic Autographs Melting /1 #DDJG
2014 Press Pass Redline Dynamic Duals Relic Autographs Red /15 #DDJG
2014 Press Pass Redline Green National Convention /5 #21
2014 Press Pass Redline Green National Convention /5 #22
2014 Press Pass Redline Head to Head Blue /10 #HTHJGKH
2014 Press Pass Redline Head to Head Gold /25 #HTHJGKH
2014 Press Pass Redline Head to Head Melting /1 #HTHJGKH
2014 Press Pass Redline Head to Head Red /75 #HTHJGKH
2014 Press Pass Redline Intensity #I4
2014 Press Pass Redline Magenta /10 #21
2014 Press Pass Redline Magenta /10 #22
2014 Press Pass Redline Muscle Car Sheet Metal Blue /25 #MCMJG
2014 Press Pass Redline Muscle Car Sheet Metal Gold /50 #MCMJG
2014 Press Pass Redline Muscle Car Sheet Metal Melting /1 #MCMJG
2014 Press Pass Redline Muscle Car Sheet Metal Red /75 #MCMJG
2014 Press Pass Redline Pieces of the Action Blue /10 #PAJG
2014 Press Pass Redline Pieces of the Action Gold /25 #PAJG
2014 Press Pass Redline Pieces of the Action Melting /1 #PAJG
2014 Press Pass Redline Pieces of the Action Red /75 #PAJG
2014 Press Pass Redline Redline Racers #RR6
2014 Press Pass Redline Relic Autographs Blue /5 #RRSEJG
2014 Press Pass Redline Relic Autographs Gold /10 #RRSEJG
2014 Press Pass Redline Relic Autographs Melting /1 #RRSEJG
2014 Press Pass Redline Relic Autographs Red /15 #RRSEJG
2014 Press Pass Redline Relics Blue /25 #RRJG
2014 Press Pass Redline Relics Gold /50 #RRJG
2014 Press Pass Redline Relics Melting /1 #RRJG
2014 Press Pass Redline Relics Red /75 #RRJG
2014 Press Pass Redline RPM #RPM3
2014 Press Pass Redline Signatures Blue /5 #RSJG
2014 Press Pass Redline Signatures Gold /10 #RSJG
2014 Press Pass Redline Signatures Melting /1 #RSJG
2014 Press Pass Redline Signatures Red /15 #RSJG
2014 Press Pass Redline Yellow /1 #21
2014 Press Pass Redline Yellow /1 #22
2014 Press Pass Signature Series Gold /5 #SSJG
2014 Press Pass Signature Series Melting /1 #SSJG
2014 Press Pass Signings Gold /1 #PPSJG
2014 Press Pass Signings Holofoil /1 #PPSJG
2014 Press Pass Signings Melting /1 #PPSJG
2014 Press Pass Signings Printing Plates Black /1 #PPSJG
2014 Press Pass Signings Printing Plates Cyan /1 #PPSJG
2014 Press Pass Signings Printing Plates Magenta /1 #PPSJG
2014 Press Pass Signings Printing Plates Yellow /1 #PPSJG
2014 Press Pass Signings Silver /1 #PPSJG
2014 Total Memorabilia #9
2014 Total Memorabilia Acceleration #AC6
2014 Total Memorabilia Autographed Memorabilia Blue /5 #SCJG
2014 Total Memorabilia Autographed Memorabilia Gold /5 #SCJG
2014 Total Memorabilia Autographed Memorabilia Melting /1 #SCJG
2014 Total Memorabilia Autographed Memorabilia Silver /5 #SC-JG
2014 Total Memorabilia Black and White /99 #9
2014 Total Memorabilia Clear Cuts Blue /175 #CCUJG
2014 Total Memorabilia Clear Cuts Melting /25 #CCUJG
2014 Total Memorabilia Dual Swatch Gold /150 #TMJG
2014 Total Memorabilia Gold /175 #9
2014 Total Memorabilia Quad Swatch Melting /25 #TMJG
2014 Total Memorabilia Red #9
2014 Total Memorabilia Single Swatch Silver /275 #TMJG
2014 Total Memorabilia Triple Swatch Blue /99 #TMJG
2015 Press Pass #15
2015 Press Pass #92
2015 Press Pass #82
2015 Press Pass #67
2015 Press Pass #100
2015 Press Pass Burning Rubber Blue /50 #BRJG1
2015 Press Pass Burning Rubber Blue /50 #BRJG2
2015 Press Pass Burning Rubber Blue /50 #BRJG3
2015 Press Pass Burning Rubber Gold #BRJG2
2015 Press Pass Burning Rubber Gold #BRJG1
2015 Press Pass Burning Rubber Gold #BRJG3
2015 Press Pass Burning Rubber Green /10 #BRJG1
2015 Press Pass Burning Rubber Green /10 #BRJG2
2015 Press Pass Burning Rubber Green /10 #BRJG3
2015 Press Pass Burning Rubber Letterman /8 #BRLEJG
2015 Press Pass Burning Rubber Melting /1 #BRJG1
2015 Press Pass Burning Rubber Melting /1 #BRJG2
2015 Press Pass Burning Rubber Melting /1 #BRJG3
2015 Press Pass Championship Caliber Dual /25 #CCMJG
2015 Press Pass Championship Caliber Quad /1 #CCMJG
2015 Press Pass Championship Caliber Signature Edition Blue /10 #CCJG
2015 Press Pass Championship Caliber Signature Edition Gold /25 #CCJG
2015 Press Pass Championship Caliber Signature Edition Green /5 #CCJG
2015 Press Pass Championship Caliber Signature Edition Melting /1 #CCJG
2015 Press Pass Championship Caliber Single /50 #CCMJG
2015 Press Pass Championship Caliber Triple /10 #CCMJG
2015 Press Pass Cup Chase #15
2015 Press Pass Cup Chase #67
2015 Press Pass Cup Chase #82
2015 Press Pass Cup Chase #92
2015 Press Pass Cup Chase #100
2015 Press Pass Cup Chase Blue /25 #15
2015 Press Pass Cup Chase Blue /25 #67
2015 Press Pass Cup Chase Blue /25 #82
2015 Press Pass Cup Chase Blue /25 #92
2015 Press Pass Cup Chase Blue /25 #100
2015 Press Pass Cup Chase Gold /75 #15
2015 Press Pass Cup Chase Gold /75 #67
2015 Press Pass Cup Chase Gold /75 #82
2015 Press Pass Cup Chase Gold /75 #92
2015 Press Pass Cup Chase Gold /75 #100
2015 Press Pass Cup Chase Green /10 #15
2015 Press Pass Cup Chase Green /10 #67
2015 Press Pass Cup Chase Green /10 #82
2015 Press Pass Cup Chase Green /10 #92
2015 Press Pass Cup Chase Green /10 #100
2015 Press Pass Cup Chase Melting /1 #15
2015 Press Pass Cup Chase Melting /1 #67
2015 Press Pass Cup Chase Melting /1 #82
2015 Press Pass Cup Chase Melting /1 #92
2015 Press Pass Cup Chase Melting /1 #100
2015 Press Pass Cup Chase Three Wide Blue /25 #3WJG
2015 Press Pass Cup Chase Three Wide Gold /50 #3WJG
2015 Press Pass Cup Chase Three Wide Green /10 #3WJG
2015 Press Pass Cup Chase Three Wide Melting /1 #3WJG
2015 Press Pass Cup Chase Upper Cuts /13 #UCJG
2015 Press Pass Cuts Blue /25 #CCCJG
2015 Press Pass Cuts Gold /50 #CCCJG
2015 Press Pass Cuts Green /10 #CCCJG
2015 Press Pass Cuts Melting /1 #CCCJG
2015 Press Pass Four Wide Signature Edition Blue /10 #4WJG
2015 Press Pass Four Wide Signature Edition Gold /15 #4WJG
2015 Press Pass Four Wide Signature Edition Green /5 #4WJG
2015 Press Pass Four Wide Signature Edition Melting /1 #4WJG
2015 Press Pass Pit Road Pieces Blue /25 #PPMJG
2015 Press Pass Pit Road Pieces Gold /50 #PPMJG
2015 Press Pass Pit Road Pieces Green /10 #PPMJG
2015 Press Pass Pit Road Pieces Melting /1 #PPMJG
2015 Press Pass Pit Road Pieces Signature Edition Blue /10 #PRPJG
2015 Press Pass Pit Road Pieces Signature Edition Gold /25 #PRPJG
2015 Press Pass Pit Road Pieces Signature Edition Green /5 #PRPJG
2015 Press Pass Pit Road Pieces Signature Edition Melting /1 #PRPJG
2015 Press Pass Purple #15
2015 Press Pass Purple #67
2015 Press Pass Purple #82
2015 Press Pass Purple #92
2015 Press Pass Purple #100
2015 Press Pass Red #15
2015 Press Pass Red #67
2015 Press Pass Red #82
2015 Press Pass Red #92
2015 Press Pass Red #100
2015 Press Pass Signings Blue /15 #PPSJG
2015 Press Pass Signings Gold #PPSJG
2015 Press Pass Signings Green /5 #PPSJG
2015 Press Pass Signings Melting /1 #PPSJG
2015 Press Pass Signings Red /10 #PPSJG
2015 Sports Illustrated for Kids #418
2016 Panini Prizm #100
2016 Panini Prizm Prizms #100
2016 Panini Prizm Prizms Black /3 #100
2016 Panini Prizm Prizms Blue Flag /99 #100
2016 Panini Prizm Prizms Camo /18 #100
2016 Panini Prizm Prizms Checkered Flag /1 #100
2016 Panini Prizm Prizms Gold /10 #100
2016 Panini Prizm Prizms Green Flag /149 #100
2016 Panini Prizm Prizms Rainbow /24 #100
2016 Panini Prizm Prizms Red Flag /75 #100
2016 Panini Prizm Prizms Red White and Blue #100
2016 Panini Prizm Prizms White Flag /5 #100

Denny Hamlin

2005 Press Pass Optima #34
2005 Press Pass Optima Gold /100 #G34
2005 Press Pass Optima Previews /5 #34
2005 Press Pass Optima Samples #34
2005 Press Pass Panorama #PPP4
2005 Press Pass Panorama #PPP76
2005 Press Pass Signings #21
2005 Press Pass Signings Gold /50 #20
2005 Press Pass Signings Platinum /100 #20
2005 Press Pass Stealth No Boundaries #NB24
2005 Press Pass Top Prospects Memorabilia /200 #DHS
2005 Press Pass Top Prospects Memorabilia /50 #DHSM
2005 Press Pass Top Prospects Memorabilia /350 #DHT
2005 Press Pass Trackside #37
2005 Press Pass Trackside Golden /100 #G37
2005 Press Pass Trackside Hot Pass #19
2005 Press Pass Trackside Hot Pass National #19
2005 Press Pass Trackside Previews /5 #37
2005 Press Pass Trackside Samples #37
2005 Wheels American Thunder #89
2005 Wheels American Thunder License to Drive #8
2005 Wheels American Thunder Previews /1 #89
2005 Wheels American Thunder Samples #89
2006 Press Pass #35
2006 Press Pass #70
2006 Press Pass Autographs #20
2006 Press Pass Blue #B35
2006 Press Pass Blue #B70
2006 Press Pass Burnouts /900 #HT5
2006 Press Pass Burnouts Holofoil /100 #HT5
2006 Press Pass Collectors Series Making the Show #MS5
2006 Press Pass Cup Chase Prizes #CC3
2006 Press Pass Eclipse #32
2006 Press Pass Eclipse Previews /5 #EB32
2006 Press Pass Gold #G35
2006 Press Pass Gold #G70
2006 Press Pass Legends #45
2006 Press Pass Legends Blue /1999 #B45
2006 Press Pass Legends Bronze /999 #Z45
2006 Press Pass Legends Gold /299 #G45
2006 Press Pass Legends Holofoil /99 #H45
2006 Press Pass Legends Press Plates Black /1 #PPB45
2006 Press Pass Legends Press Plates Black Backs /1 #PPB45B
2006 Press Pass Legends Press Plates Cyan /1 #PPC45
2006 Press Pass Legends Press Plates Cyan Backs /1 #PPC45B
2006 Press Pass Legends Press Plates Magenta /1 #PPM45
2006 Press Pass Legends Press Plates Magenta Backs /1 #PPM45B
2006 Press Pass Legends Press Plates Yellow /1 #PPY45
2006 Press Pass Legends Press Plates Yellow Backs /1 #PPY45B
2006 Press Pass Legends Previews /5 #EB45
2006 Press Pass Legends Solo /1 #S45
2006 Press Pass Optima #11
2006 Press Pass Optima #37
2006 Press Pass Optima #74
2006 Press Pass Optima #80
2006 Press Pass Optima #86
2006 Press Pass Optima #11B
2006 Press Pass Optima Fan Favorite #FF7
2006 Press Pass Optima Gold /100 #G11
2006 Press Pass Optima Gold /100 #G37
2006 Press Pass Optima Gold /100 #G74
2006 Press Pass Optima Gold /100 #G80
2006 Press Pass Optima Gold /100 #G86
2006 Press Pass Optima Pole Position #PP8
2006 Press Pass Optima Previews /5 #EB11
2006 Press Pass Optima Previews /1 #EB74
2006 Press Pass Optima Rookie Relics Cars /50 #RRT2
2006 Press Pass Optima Rookie Relics Drivers /50 #RRD2
2006 Press Pass Platinum /100 #P35
2006 Press Pass Platinum /100 #P70
2006 Press Pass Premium #31
2006 Press Pass Premium #50
2006 Press Pass Premium Hot Threads Cars /165 #HTT12
2006 Press Pass Premium Hot Threads Drivers /220 #HTD12
2006 Press Pass Premium Hot Threads Drivers Gold /1 #HTD12
2006 Press Pass Previews /5 #EB35
2006 Press Pass Signings #21
2006 Press Pass Signings Gold /50 #21
2006 Press Pass Signings Silver /100 #21
2006 Press Pass Stealth #49
2006 Press Pass Stealth #73
2006 Press Pass Stealth #92
2006 Press Pass Stealth Autographed Hat Entry #PPH9
2006 Press Pass Stealth Gear Grippers Autographs /11 #DH
2006 Press Pass Stealth Gear Grippers Cars Retail /99 #GGT9
2006 Press Pass Stealth Gear Grippers Drivers /99 #GGD9
2006 Press Pass Stealth Hot Pass #HP11
2006 Press Pass Stealth Previews /1 #92
2006 Press Pass Stealth Retail #49
2006 Press Pass Stealth Retail #73
2006 Press Pass Stealth Retail #92
2006 Press Pass Stealth X-Ray /100 #X49
2006 Press Pass Stealth X-Ray /100 #X73
2006 Press Pass Stealth X-Ray /100 #X92
2006 Press Pass Top 25 Drivers & Rides #C8
2006 Press Pass Top 25 Drivers & Rides #D8
2006 TRAKS #12
2006 TRAKS #42
2006 TRAKS Autographs #13
2006 TRAKS Previews /1 #12
2006 TRAKS Previews /1 #42
2006 TRAKS Stickers #11
2006 VIP #91
2006 VIP Head Gear #HG5
2006 VIP Head Gear Transparent #HG5
2006 VIP Making the Show #MS5
2006 VIP Rookie Stripes /100 #RS2
2006 VIP Rookie Stripes Autographs /25 #RSDH
2006 VIP Tradin' Paint Cars Bronze /145 #TPT8
2006 VIP Tradin' Paint Drivers Gold /50 #TPD8
2006 VIP Tradin' Paint Drivers Silver /80 #TPD8
2006 Wheels American Thunder /350 #91
2006 Wheels American Thunder Double Hat /99 #DH8
2006 Wheels American Thunder Grandstand #GS7
2006 Wheels Autographs #21
2006 Wheels High Gear #32
2006 Wheels High Gear MPH /100 #M32
2006 Wheels High Gear Previews Green /5 #EB32
2007 Press Pass #5
2007 Press Pass #36
2007 Press Pass #65
2007 Press Pass #80
2007 Press Pass #90
2007 Press Pass #98
2007 Press Pass #112
2007 Press Pass Autographs #16
2007 Press Pass Autographs Press Plates Black /1 #4
2007 Press Pass Autographs Press Plates Cyan /1 #4
2007 Press Pass Autographs Press Plates Magenta /1 #5
2007 Press Pass Autographs Press Plates Yellow /1 #5
2007 Press Pass Blue #B5
2007 Press Pass Blue #B36
2007 Press Pass Blue #B65
2007 Press Pass Blue #B80
2007 Press Pass Blue #B90
2007 Press Pass Blue #B98
2007 Press Pass Blue #B112
2007 Press Pass Burning Rubber Drivers /75 #BRD10
2007 Press Pass Burning Rubber Drivers /75 #BRD15
2007 Press Pass Burning Rubber Drivers Gold /1 #BRD10
2007 Press Pass Burning Rubber Drivers Gold /1 #BRD15
2007 Press Pass Burning Rubber Team /325 #BRT10
2007 Press Pass Burning Rubber Team /325 #BRT15
2007 Press Pass Collector's Series Box Set #SB8
2007 Press Pass Cup Chase #CCR12
2007 Press Pass Cup Chase Prizes #CC6
2007 Press Pass Double Burner Firesuit-Glove /100 #DB3
2007 Press Pass Double Burner Firesuit-Glove Exchange /100 #DB3
2007 Press Pass Double Burner Metal-Tire /100 #DBDH
2007 Press Pass Double Burner Metal-Tire Exchange /100 #DBDH
2007 Press Pass Eclipse #3
2007 Press Pass Eclipse #38
2007 Press Pass Eclipse #57
2007 Press Pass Eclipse #75
2007 Press Pass Eclipse #80
2007 Press Pass Eclipse #0
2007 Press Pass Eclipse Ecliptic #EC9
2007 Press Pass Eclipse Gold /25 #G3
2007 Press Pass Eclipse Gold /25 #G38
2007 Press Pass Eclipse Gold /25 #G57
2007 Press Pass Eclipse Gold /25 #G75
2007 Press Pass Eclipse Gold /25 #G80
2007 Press Pass Eclipse Previews /5 #EB3
2007 Press Pass Eclipse Previews /5 #EB38
2007 Press Pass Eclipse Racing Champions #RC8
2007 Press Pass Eclipse Racing Champions #RC19
2007 Press Pass Eclipse Red /1 #R3
2007 Press Pass Eclipse Red /1 #R38
2007 Press Pass Eclipse Red /1 #R57
2007 Press Pass Eclipse Red /1 #R75
2007 Press Pass Eclipse Red /1 #R80
2007 Press Pass Eclipse Skidmarks #SM5
2007 Press Pass Eclipse Skidmarks Holofoil /250 #SM5
2007 Press Pass Eclipse Teammates Autographs /25 #4
2007 Press Pass Four Wide /50 #FWDH
2007 Press Pass Four Wide Checkered Flag /1 #FWDH
2007 Press Pass Four Wide Checkered Flag Exchange /1 #FWDH
2007 Press Pass Four Wide Exchange /50 #FWDH
2007 Press Pass Gold #G5
2007 Press Pass Gold #G36
2007 Press Pass Gold #G65
2007 Press Pass Gold #G80
2007 Press Pass Gold #G90
2007 Press Pass Gold #G98
2007 Press Pass Gold #G112
2007 Press Pass Legends #50
2007 Press Pass Legends Autographs Blue /59 #10
2007 Press Pass Legends Autographs Inscriptions Blue /9 #8
2007 Press Pass Legends Blue /999 #B50
2007 Press Pass Legends Bronze /599 #Z50
2007 Press Pass Legends Gold /249 #G50
2007 Press Pass Legends Holofoil /99 #H50
2007 Press Pass Legends Press Plates Black /1 #PP50
2007 Press Pass Legends Press Plates Black Backs /1 #PP50
2007 Press Pass Legends Press Plates Cyan /1 #PP50
2007 Press Pass Legends Press Plates Cyan Backs /1 #PP50
2007 Press Pass Legends Press Plates Magenta /1 #PP50
2007 Press Pass Legends Press Plates Magenta Backs /1 #PP50
2007 Press Pass Legends Press Plates Yellow /1 #PP50
2007 Press Pass Legends Press Plates Yellow Backs /1 #PP50
2007 Press Pass Legends Previews /5 #EB50
2007 Press Pass Legends Signature Series /25 #DH
2007 Press Pass Legends Solo /1 #S50
2007 Press Pass Legends Sunday Swatches Bronze /199 #DHSS
2007 Press Pass Legends Sunday Swatches Gold /50 #DHSS
2007 Press Pass Legends Sunday Swatches Silver /99 #DHSS
2007 Press Pass Legends Victory Lane Bronze /199 #VL4
2007 Press Pass Legends Victory Lane Gold /25 #VL4
2007 Press Pass Legends Victory Lane Silver /99 #VL4
2007 Press Pass Platinum /100 #P5
2007 Press Pass Platinum /100 #P36
2007 Press Pass Platinum /100 #P65
2007 Press Pass Platinum /100 #P80
2007 Press Pass Platinum /100 #P90
2007 Press Pass Platinum /100 #P98
2007 Press Pass Platinum /100 #P112
2007 Press Pass Premium #10
2007 Press Pass Premium #39
2007 Press Pass Premium #53
2007 Press Pass Premium Hot Threads Drivers /145 #HTD6
2007 Press Pass Premium Hot Threads Drivers Gold /1 #HTD6
2007 Press Pass Premium Hot Threads Patch /15 #HTP5
2007 Press Pass Premium Hot Threads Patch /8 #HTP6
2007 Press Pass Premium Hot Threads Team /160 #HTT6
2007 Press Pass Premium Performance Driven #PD4
2007 Press Pass Premium Performance Driven Red /250 #PD4
2007 Press Pass Premium Red /15 #R10
2007 Press Pass Premium Red /15 #R39
2007 Press Pass Premium Red /15 #R53
2007 Press Pass Previews /5 #EB5
2007 Press Pass Previews /5 #EB36
2007 Press Pass Previews /1 #EB112
2007 Press Pass Race Day #RD7
2007 Press Pass Signings #25
2007 Press Pass Signings Blue /25 #10
2007 Press Pass Signings Gold /50 #20
2007 Press Pass Signings Press Plates Black /1 #18
2007 Press Pass Signings Press Plates Cyan /1 #17
2007 Press Pass Signings Press Plates Magenta /1 #17
2007 Press Pass Signings Press Plates Yellow /1 #17
2007 Press Pass Signings Silver /100 #19
2007 Press Pass Snapshots #SN10
2007 Press Pass Stealth #9
2007 Press Pass Stealth #49
2007 Press Pass Stealth #65
2007 Press Pass Stealth #75
2007 Press Pass Stealth Battle Armor Drivers /150 #BAD3
2007 Press Pass Stealth Battle Armor Teams /85 #BAT3
2007 Press Pass Stealth Chrome #9
2007 Press Pass Stealth Chrome #49
2007 Press Pass Stealth Chrome #65
2007 Press Pass Stealth Chrome #75
2007 Press Pass Stealth Chrome Exclusives /99 #X9
2007 Press Pass Stealth Chrome Exclusives /99 #X49
2007 Press Pass Stealth Chrome Exclusives /99 #X65
2007 Press Pass Stealth Chrome Exclusives /99 #X75
2007 Press Pass Stealth Chrome Platinum /25 #P9
2007 Press Pass Stealth Chrome Platinum /25 #P49
2007 Press Pass Stealth Chrome Platinum /25 #P65
2007 Press Pass Stealth Chrome Platinum /25 #P75
2007 Press Pass Stealth Fusion #F6
2007 Press Pass Stealth Mach 07 #M7-8
2007 Press Pass Stealth Maximum Access #MA10
2007 Press Pass Stealth Maximum Access Autographs /25 #MA10
2007 Press Pass Stealth Previews /5 #EB9
2007 Press Pass Target Race Win Tires #RW4
2007 Press Pass Velocity #V9
2007 Sports Illustrated for Kids #153
2007 Traks #9
2007 Traks #95
2007 Traks Corporate Cuts Driver /99 #CCD6
2007 Traks Corporate Cuts Patch /10 #CCD6
2007 Traks Corporate Cuts Team /180 #CCT6
2007 Traks Gold #G9
2007 Traks Gold #G95
2007 Traks Holofoil /50 #H9
2007 Traks Holofoil /50 #H95
2007 Traks Previews /5 #EB9
2007 Traks Red /10 #R9
2007 Traks Red /10 #R95
2007 VIP #11
2007 VIP Get A Grip Drivers /70 #GGD17
2007 VIP Get A Grip Teams /70 #GGT17
2007 VIP Previews /5 #EB11
2007 VIP Sunday Best #SB8
2007 VIP Trophy Club #TC7
2007 VIP Trophy Club Transparent #TC7
2007 Wheels American Thunder #11
2007 Wheels American Thunder #56
2007 Wheels American Thunder Autographed Hat Instant Winner /1 #AH12
2007 Wheels American Thunder Previews /5 #EB11
2007 Wheels American Thunder Previews /1 #EB56
2007 Wheels American Thunder Pushin' Pedal /99 #PP4
2007 Wheels American Thunder Thunder Road #TR11
2007 Wheels American Thunder Thunder Strokes #17
2007 Wheels American Thunder Thunder Strokes Press Plates Black /1 #17
2007 Wheels American Thunder Thunder Strokes Press Plates Cyan /1 #17
2007 Wheels American Thunder Thunder Strokes Press Plates Magenta /1 #17
2007 Wheels American Thunder Thunder Strokes Press Plates Yellow /1 #17
2007 Wheels American Thunder Triple Hat /99 #TH10
2007 Wheels Autographs #14
2007 Wheels Autographs Press Plates Black /1 #13
2007 Wheels Autographs Press Plates Cyan /1 #13
2007 Wheels Autographs Press Plates Magenta /1 #13
2007 Wheels High Gear #3A
2007 Wheels High Gear #34
2007 Wheels High Gear #60
2007 Wheels High Gear #65
2007 Wheels High Gear #66
2007 Wheels High Gear #3B
2007 Wheels High Gear Driven #DR9
2007 Wheels High Gear Final Standings Gold /3 #FS3
2007 Wheels High Gear Flag Chasers Black /89 #FC6
2007 Wheels High Gear Flag Chasers Blue-Yellow /50 #FC6
2007 Wheels High Gear Flag Chasers Checkered /10 #FC6
2007 Wheels High Gear Flag Chasers Green /89 #FC6
2007 Wheels High Gear Flag Chasers Red /89 #FC6
2007 Wheels High Gear Flag Chasers White /89 #FC6
2007 Wheels High Gear Flag Chasers Yellow /89 #FC6
2007 Wheels High Gear Last Lap /10 #LL7
2007 Wheels High Gear MPH /100 #M3
2007 Wheels High Gear MPH /100 #M34
2007 Wheels High Gear MPH /100 #M60

' Wheels High Gear MPH /100 #M65
' Wheels High Gear MPH /100 #M66
' Wheels High Gear Previews /5 #EB3
' Wheels High Gear Previews /5 #EB34
' Wheels High Gear Previews /5 #EB60
' Wheels High Gear Previews /5 #EB65
7 Wheels High Gear Top Tier #TT3
3 Press Pass #3
8 Press Pass #112
8 Press Pass #0
8 Press Pass Autographs #16
8 Press Pass Autographs Press Plates Black /1 #12
8 Press Pass Autographs Press Plates Cyan /1 #12
8 Press Pass Autographs Press Plates Magenta /1 #12
8 Press Pass Autographs Press Plates Yellow /1 #12
8 Press Pass Blue #B3
8 Press Pass Blue #B112
8 Press Pass Burning Rubber Autographs /11 #BRDH
8 Press Pass Burning Rubber Drivers /60 #BRD16
8 Press Pass Burning Rubber Drivers Gold /1 #BRD16
8 Press Pass Burning Rubber Drivers Prime Cuts /25 #BRD16
8 Press Pass Burning Rubber Teams /175 #BRT16
8 Press Pass Burnouts #B04
8 Press Pass Burnouts Blue /99 #B04
8 Press Pass Burnouts Gold /299 #B04
8 Press Pass Collector's Series Box Set #11
8 Press Pass Cup Chase #CC5
8 Press Pass Cup Chase Prizes #CC6
08 Press Pass Double Burner Metal-Tire /100 #DBDH
08 Press Pass Eclipse #11
08 Press Pass Eclipse #34
08 Press Pass Eclipse #39
08 Press Pass Eclipse Gold /25 #G11
08 Press Pass Eclipse Gold /25 #G34
08 Press Pass Eclipse Gold /25 #G39
08 Press Pass Eclipse Previews /5 #EB11
08 Press Pass Eclipse Previews /5 #EB34
08 Press Pass Eclipse Red /1 #R11
08 Press Pass Eclipse Red /1 #R34
08 Press Pass Eclipse Red /1 #R39
08 Press Pass Eclipse Stellar #ST10
08 Press Pass Eclipse Stellar #ST18
08 Press Pass Eclipse Teammates Autographs /35 #BHS
08 Press Pass Four Wide /50 #FWDH
08 Press Pass Four Wide Checkered Flag /1 #FWDH
08 Press Pass Gillette Young Guns #4
08 Press Pass Gold #G3
08 Press Pass Gold #G112
08 Press Pass Hot Treads #HT1
08 Press Pass Hot Treads Blue /99 #HT1
08 Press Pass Hot Treads Gold /299 #HT1
08 Press Pass Legends Autographs Black Inscriptions /10 #DH
08 Press Pass Legends Autographs Blue /75 #DH
08 Press Pass Legends Autographs Press Plates Black /1 #DH
08 Press Pass Legends Autographs Press Plates Cyan /1 #DH
08 Press Pass Legends Autographs Press Plates Magenta /1 #DH
08 Press Pass Legends Autographs Press Plates Yellow /1 #DH
08 Press Pass Legends Prominent Pieces Firesuit-Glove Bronze /99 #PP1DH
008 Press Pass Legends Prominent Pieces Firesuit-Glove Gold /25 #PP1DH
008 Press Pass Legends Prominent Pieces Firesuit-Glove Silver /50 #PP1DH
008 Press Pass Legends Prominent Pieces Metal-Tire Bronze /99 #PP3 DH
008 Press Pass Legends Prominent Pieces Metal-Tire Gold /25 #PP3 DH
008 Press Pass Legends Prominent Pieces Metal-Tire Silver /50 #PP3 DH
008 Press Pass Platinum /100 #P3
008 Press Pass Platinum /100 #P112
008 Press Pass Premium #10
2008 Press Pass Premium #42
2008 Press Pass Premium #52
2008 Press Pass Premium #65
2008 Press Pass Premium Hot Threads Autographs /11 #HTDH
2008 Press Pass Premium Hot Threads Drivers /120 #HTD5
2008 Press Pass Premium Hot Threads Drivers Gold /1 #HTD5
2008 Press Pass Premium Hot Threads Patches /4 #HTP8
2008 Press Pass Premium Hot Threads Team /120 #HTT5
2008 Press Pass Premium Previews /5 #EB10
2008 Press Pass Premium Previews /1 #EB65
2008 Press Pass Premium Red /15 #10
2008 Press Pass Premium Red /15 #42
2008 Press Pass Premium Red /15 #52
2008 Press Pass Premium Red /15 #65
2008 Press Pass Premium Target #TA2
2008 Press Pass Premium Team Signed Baseballs #GIB
2008 Press Pass Premium Team Signed Baseballs #EGIB
2008 Press Pass Previews /5 #EB3
2008 Press Pass Previews /1 #EB112
2008 Press Pass Signings #25
2008 Press Pass Signings Blue /25 #9
2008 Press Pass Signings Gold /50 #22
2008 Press Pass Signings Press Plates Black /1 #16
2008 Press Pass Signings Press Plates Cyan /1 #16
2008 Press Pass Signings Press Plates Magenta /1 #16
2008 Press Pass Signings Press Plates Yellow /1 #16
2008 Press Pass Signings Press Plates Yellow /1 #DH
2008 Press Pass Signings Silver /100 #22
2008 Press Pass Speedway #30
2008 Press Pass Speedway #76
2008 Press Pass Speedway Corporate Cuts Drivers /80 #CDDH
2008 Press Pass Speedway Corporate Cuts Drivers Patches /8 #CDDH
2008 Press Pass Speedway Corporate Cuts Team /165 #CTDH
2008 Press Pass Speedway Gold #G30
2008 Press Pass Speedway Gold #G76
2008 Press Pass Speedway Holofoil /50 #H30
2008 Press Pass Speedway Holofoil /50 #H76
2008 Press Pass Speedway Previews /5 #EB30
2008 Press Pass Speedway Red /10 #R30
2008 Press Pass Speedway Red /10 #R76
2008 Press Pass Starting Grid #SG11
2008 Press Pass Stealth #12
2008 Press Pass Stealth #57
2008 Press Pass Stealth #68
2008 Press Pass Stealth #85
2008 Press Pass Stealth Battle Armor Autographs /11 #BASDH
2008 Press Pass Stealth Battle Armor Drivers /120 #BAD18
2008 Press Pass Stealth Battle Armor Teams /115 #BAT18
2008 Press Pass Stealth Chrome #12
2008 Press Pass Stealth Chrome #57
2008 Press Pass Stealth Chrome #68
2008 Press Pass Stealth Chrome #85
2008 Press Pass Stealth Chrome Exclusives /25 #12
2008 Press Pass Stealth Chrome Exclusives /25 #57
2008 Press Pass Stealth Chrome Exclusives /25 #68
2008 Press Pass Stealth Chrome Exclusives /25 #85
2008 Press Pass Stealth Chrome Exclusives Gold /99 #12
2008 Press Pass Stealth Chrome Exclusives Gold /99 #57
2008 Press Pass Stealth Chrome Exclusives Gold /99 #68
2008 Press Pass Stealth Chrome Exclusives Gold /99 #85
2008 Press Pass Stealth Maximum Access #MA11
2008 Press Pass Stealth Maximum Access Autographs /25 #MA11
2008 Press Pass Stealth Previews /5 #12
2008 Press Pass Stealth Previews /1 #85
2008 Press Pass Stealth Wal-Mart #WM8
2008 Press Pass Target Victory Tires /50 #TTDH
2008 Press Pass Wal-Mart Autographs /50 #4
2008 VIP #13
2008 VIP #70
2008 VIP All Access #AA8
2008 VIP Get a Grip Drivers /80 #GGD13
2008 VIP Get a Grip Teams /99 #GGT13
2008 VIP Previews /5 #EB13
2008 Wheels American Thunder #13
2008 Wheels American Thunder #42
2008 Wheels American Thunder American Dreams #AD8
2008 Wheels American Thunder American Dreams Gold /250 #AD8
2008 Wheels American Thunder Autographed Hat Winner /1 #IWHDH
2008 Wheels American Thunder Campaign Trail #CT12
2008 Wheels American Thunder Double Hat /99 #DH4
2008 Wheels American Thunder Head to Toe /125 #HT16
2008 Wheels American Thunder Previews /5 #13
2008 Wheels American Thunder Pushin' Pedal /99 #PP 16
2008 Wheels American Thunder Trackside Treasury Autographs #DH
2008 Wheels American Thunder Trackside Treasury Autographs Gold /25 #DH
2008 Wheels American Thunder Trackside Treasury Autographs Printing Plates Black /1 #DH
2008 Wheels American Thunder Trackside Treasury Autographs Printing Plates Cyan /1 #DH
2008 Wheels American Thunder Trackside Treasury Autographs Printing Plates Magenta /1 #DH
2008 Wheels American Thunder Trackside Treasury Autographs Printing Plates Yellow /1 #DH
2008 Wheels Autographs #12
2008 Wheels Autographs Chase Edition /25 #4
2008 Wheels Autographs Press Plates Black /1 #12
2008 Wheels Autographs Press Plates Cyan /1 #12
2008 Wheels Autographs Press Plates Magenta /1 #12
2008 Wheels Autographs Press Plates Yellow /1 #12
2008 Wheels High Gear #12
2008 Wheels High Gear #33
2008 Wheels High Gear #63
2008 Wheels High Gear Driven #DR18
2008 Wheels High Gear Final Standings /12 #F12
2008 Wheels High Gear Last Lap /10 #LL10
2008 Wheels High Gear Last Lap Holofoil /5 #LL10
2008 Wheels High Gear MPH /100 #M12
2008 Wheels High Gear MPH /100 #M33
2008 Wheels High Gear MPH /100 #M63
2008 Wheels High Gear Previews /5 #EB12
2008 Wheels High Gear The Chase #TC12
2009 Element #11
2009 Element #41
2009 Element #65
2009 Element #86
2009 Element Big Win /35 #BWDH
2009 Element Lab Report #LR11
2009 Element Previews /5 #11
2009 Element Radioactive /100 #11
2009 Element Radioactive /100 #41
2009 Element Radioactive /100 #65
2009 Element Radioactive /100 #86
2009 Element Taking the Checkers /45 #TCDH
2009 Press Pass #6
2009 Press Pass #57
2009 Press Pass #70
2009 Press Pass #112
2009 Press Pass #0
2009 Press Pass #131
2009 Press Pass #204
2009 Press Pass Autographs Chase Edition /25 #DH
2009 Press Pass Autographs Gold #18
2009 Press Pass Autographs Silver #21
2009 Press Pass Blue #6
2009 Press Pass Blue #57
2009 Press Pass Blue #70
2009 Press Pass Blue #112
2009 Press Pass Blue #131
2009 Press Pass Blue #204
2009 Press Pass Burning Rubber Autographs /11 #BRSDH
2009 Press Pass Burning Rubber Drivers /185 #BRD6
2009 Press Pass Burning Rubber Prime Cut /25 #BRD6
2009 Press Pass Burning Rubber Teams /250 #BRT6
2009 Press Pass Chase for the Sprint Cup #CC4
2009 Press Pass Cup Chase #CCR2
2009 Press Pass Cup Chase Prizes #CC4
2009 Press Pass Daytona 500 Tires /25 #TTDH
2009 Press Pass Eclipse #9
2009 Press Pass Eclipse #43
2009 Press Pass Eclipse #63
2009 Press Pass Eclipse Black and White #9
2009 Press Pass Eclipse Black and White #43
2009 Press Pass Eclipse Black and White #63
2009 Press Pass Eclipse Blue #9
2009 Press Pass Eclipse Blue #43
2009 Press Pass Eclipse Blue #63
2009 Press Pass Eclipse Ecliptic Path #EP2
2009 Press Pass Eclipse Solar System #SS8
2009 Press Pass Final Standings /135 #112
2009 Press Pass Four Wide Firesuit /50 #FWDH
2009 Press Pass Four Wide Tire /25 #FWDH
2009 Press Pass Gold #6
2009 Press Pass Gold #57
2009 Press Pass Gold #70
2009 Press Pass Gold #112
2009 Press Pass Gold #131
2009 Press Pass Gold #204
2009 Press Pass Gold Holofoil /100 #6
2009 Press Pass Gold Holofoil /100 #57
2009 Press Pass Gold Holofoil /100 #70
2009 Press Pass Gold Holofoil /100 #112
2009 Press Pass Gold Holofoil /100 #131
2009 Press Pass Gold Holofoil /100 #204
2009 Press Pass Legends Autographs Gold /20 #14
2009 Press Pass Legends Autographs Holofoil /15 #13
2009 Press Pass Legends Autographs Printing Plates Black /1 #11
2009 Press Pass Legends Autographs Printing Plates Magenta /1 #11
2009 Press Pass Legends Autographs Printing Plates Yellow /1 #11
2009 Press Pass Legends Prominent Pieces Bronze /99 #PPDH
2009 Press Pass Legends Prominent Pieces Gold /25 #PPDH
2009 Press Pass Legends Prominent Pieces Silver /50 #PPDH
2009 Press Pass Pocket Portraits #P9
2009 Press Pass Pocket Portraits Checkered Flag #P9
2009 Press Pass Pocket Portraits Hometown #P9
2009 Press Pass Pocket Portraits Smoke #P9
2009 Press Pass Pocket Portraits Target #PPT10
2009 Press Pass Premium #11
2009 Press Pass Premium #38
2009 Press Pass Premium Hot Threads /299 #HTDH1
2009 Press Pass Premium Hot Threads /99 #HTDH2
2009 Press Pass Premium Hot Threads Multi-Color /25 #HTDH
2009 Press Pass Premium Hot Threads Patches /10 #HTP-DH
2009 Press Pass Premium Previews /5 #EB11
2009 Press Pass Premium Signatures #13
2009 Press Pass Premium Top Contenders #TC5
2009 Press Pass Premium Top Contenders Gold #TC5
2009 Press Pass Premium Win Streak #WS11
2009 Press Pass Premium Win Streak Victory Lane #WSVL-DH
2009 Press Pass Previews /5 #EB6
2009 Press Pass Previews /1 #EB112
2009 Press Pass Previews /5 #EB131
2009 Press Pass Red #6
2009 Press Pass Red #57
2009 Press Pass Red #70
2009 Press Pass Red #112
2009 Press Pass Red #131
2009 Press Pass Red #204
2009 Press Pass Santa Hats /50 #SH7
2009 Press Pass Showcase /499 #8
2009 Press Pass Showcase /499 #30
2009 Press Pass Showcase 2nd Gear /125 #8
2009 Press Pass Showcase 2nd Gear /125 #30
2009 Press Pass Showcase 3rd Gear /50 #8
2009 Press Pass Showcase 3rd Gear /50 #30
2009 Press Pass Showcase 4th Gear /15 #8
2009 Press Pass Showcase 4th Gear /15 #30
2009 Press Pass Showcase Classic Collections Firesuit /25 #CCF5
2009 Press Pass Showcase Classic Collections Firesuit Patch /5 #CCF5
2009 Press Pass Showcase Classic Collections Ink /45 #3
2009 Press Pass Showcase Classic Collections Ink Gold /25 #3
2009 Press Pass Showcase Classic Collections Ink Green /5 #3
2009 Press Pass Showcase Classic Collections Ink Melting /1 #3
2009 Press Pass Showcase Classic Collections Sheet Metal /45 #CCS5
2009 Press Pass Showcase Classic Collections Tire /99 #CCT5
2009 Press Pass Showcase Printing Plates Black /1 #8
2009 Press Pass Showcase Printing Plates Black /1 #30
2009 Press Pass Showcase Printing Plates Cyan /1 #8
2009 Press Pass Showcase Printing Plates Cyan /1 #30
2009 Press Pass Showcase Printing Plates Magenta /1 #8
2009 Press Pass Showcase Printing Plates Magenta /1 #30
2009 Press Pass Showcase Printing Plates Yellow /1 #8
2009 Press Pass Showcase Printing Plates Yellow /1 #30
2009 Press Pass Signature Series Archive Edition /1 #GGDH
2009 Press Pass Signature Series Archive Edition /1 #HTDH
2009 Press Pass Signings Blue /25 #15
2009 Press Pass Signings Gold #15
2009 Press Pass Signings Green /15 #15
2009 Press Pass Signings Orange /65 #15
2009 Press Pass Signings Printing Plates Black /1 #15
2009 Press Pass Signings Printing Plates Magenta /1 #15
2009 Press Pass Signings Purple /45 #15
2009 Press Pass Sponsor Swatches /200 #SSDH
2009 Press Pass Sponsor Swatches Select /6 #SSDH
2009 Press Pass Stealth #13
2009 Press Pass Stealth Battle Armor /420 #BADH1
2009 Press Pass Stealth Battle Armor /30 #BADH2
2009 Press Pass Stealth Battle Armor Autographs /11 #BASDH
2009 Press Pass Stealth Battle Armor Multi-Color /160 #BADH
2009 Press Pass Stealth Chrome #13
2009 Press Pass Stealth Chrome Brushed Metal /25 #13
2009 Press Pass Stealth Chrome Gold /99 #13
2009 Press Pass Stealth Confidential Classified Bronze #PC2
2009 Press Pass Stealth Confidential Secret Silver #PC2
2009 Press Pass Stealth Confidential Top Secret Gold /25 #PC2
2009 Press Pass Stealth Previews /5 #EB13
2009 Press Pass Target Victory Tires /50 #DHTT
2009 Press Pass Tread Marks Autographs /10 #SSDH
2009 VIP #12
2009 VIP #38
2009 VIP Get A Grip /120 #GGDH
2009 VIP Get A Grip Holofoil /10 #GGDH
2009 VIP Guest List #GG24
2009 VIP Leadfoot /150 #LFDH
2009 VIP Leadfoot Holofoil /10 #LFDH
2009 VIP Previews /5 #12
2009 VIP Purple /25 #12
2009 VIP Purple /25 #38
2009 Wheels Autographs /25 #24
2009 Wheels Autographs #25
2009 Wheels Autographs Press Plates Black /1 #DH
2009 Wheels Autographs Press Plates Cyan /1 #DH
2009 Wheels Autographs Press Plates Yellow /1 #DH
2009 Wheels Main Event #15
2009 Wheels Main Event #40
2009 Wheels Main Event Buyback Archive Edition /1 #BADH
2009 Wheels Main Event Buyback Archive Edition /1 #BADH
2009 Wheels Main Event Fast Pass Purple /25 #15
2009 Wheels Main Event Fast Pass Purple /25 #40
2009 Wheels Main Event Foil #15
2009 Wheels Main Event Hat Dance Patch /10 #HDDH
2009 Wheels Main Event Hat Dance Triple /99 #HDDH
2009 Wheels Main Event Marks Clubs #24
2009 Wheels Main Event Marks Diamonds /10 #24
2009 Wheels Main Event Marks Hearts /5 #24
2009 Wheels Main Event Marks Printing Plates Black /1 #20
2009 Wheels Main Event Marks Printing Plates Cyan /1 #20
2009 Wheels Main Event Marks Printing Plates Magenta /1 #20
2009 Wheels Main Event Marks Printing Plates Yellow /1 #20
2009 Wheels Main Event Marks Spades /1 #24
2009 Wheels Main Event Playing Cards Blue #JD
2009 Wheels Main Event Playing Cards Red #JD
2009 Wheels Main Event Previews /5 #15
2009 Wheels Main Event Stop and Go Swatches Pit Banner /175 #SGBDH
2009 Wheels Main Event Stop and Go Swatches Pit Banner Green /10 #SGBDH
2009 Wheels Main Event Stop and Go Swatches Pit Banner Holofoil /75 #SGBDH
2009 Wheels Main Event Stop and Go Swatches Pit Banner Red /25 #SGBDH
2010 Element #2
2010 Element #40
2010 Element #92
2010 Element Blue /35 #2
2010 Element Blue /35 #40
2010 Element Blue /35 #92
2010 Element Finish Line Checkered Flag /10 #FLCE
2010 Element Finish Line Green Flag /20 #FLCE
2010 Element Finish Line Tires /99 #FLCE
2010 Element Green #2
2010 Element Green #40
2010 Element Green #92
2010 Element High Octane Vehicle #HOV11
2010 Element Previews /5 #EB2
2010 Element Purple /25 #2
2010 Element Purple /25 #40
2010 Element Red Target #2
2010 Element Red Target #40
2010 Element Red Target #92
2010 Press Pass #5
2010 Press Pass #83
2010 Press Pass #92
2010 Press Pass #112
2010 Press Pass #127
2010 Press Pass #0
2010 Press Pass Autographs #20
2010 Press Pass Autographs Chase Edition /25 #5
2010 Press Pass Autographs Printing Plates Black /1 #15
2010 Press Pass Autographs Printing Plates Cyan /1 #17
2010 Press Pass Autographs Printing Plates Magenta /1 #15
2010 Press Pass Autographs Printing Plates Yellow /1 #16
2010 Press Pass Blue #5
2010 Press Pass Blue #83
2010 Press Pass Blue #92
2010 Press Pass Blue #112
2010 Press Pass Blue #129
2010 Press Pass Burning Rubber /250 #BR18
2010 Press Pass Burning Rubber /250 #BR22
2010 Press Pass Burning Rubber /250 #BR28
2010 Press Pass Burning Rubber /250 #BR32
2010 Press Pass Burning Rubber Gold /50 #BR18
2010 Press Pass Burning Rubber Gold /50 #BR22
2010 Press Pass Burning Rubber Gold /99 #BR28
2010 Press Pass Burning Rubber Gold /99 #BR32
2010 Press Pass Burning Rubber Prime Cuts /25 #BRD28
2010 Press Pass Burning Rubber Prime Cuts /25 #BRD32
2010 Press Pass Cup Chase #CCR14
2010 Press Pass Cup Chase Prizes #CC1
2010 Press Pass Eclipse #8
2010 Press Pass Eclipse #31
2010 Press Pass Eclipse #82
2010 Press Pass Eclipse Blue #8
2010 Press Pass Eclipse Blue #31
2010 Press Pass Eclipse Blue #82
2010 Press Pass Eclipse Gold #8
2010 Press Pass Eclipse Gold #31
2010 Press Pass Eclipse Gold #82
2010 Press Pass Eclipse Previews /5 #8
2010 Press Pass Eclipse Previews /1 #31
2010 Press Pass Eclipse Purple /25 #8
2010 Press Pass Eclipse Purple /25 #31
2010 Press Pass Eclipse Signature Series Shoes Autographs /11 #SSSEDH
2010 Press Pass Final Standings /70 #FS5
2010 Press Pass Five Star /35 #17
2010 Press Pass Five Star Classic Compilations Combos Firesuit Autographs /15 #CCMJGR
2010 Press Pass Five Star Classic Compilations Combos Patches Autographs /1 #CCMJGR
2010 Press Pass Five Star Classic Compilations Dual Memorabilia Autographs /10 #DH
2010 Press Pass Five Star Classic Compilations Patch Autographs /1 #CCPDH1
2010 Press Pass Five Star Classic Compilations Patch Autographs /1 #CCPDH2
2010 Press Pass Five Star Classic Compilations Patch Autographs /1 #CCPDH3
2010 Press Pass Five Star Classic Compilations Patch Autographs /1 #CCPDH4
2010 Press Pass Five Star Classic Compilations Patch Autographs /1 #CCPDH5
2010 Press Pass Five Star Classic Compilations Patch Autographs /1 #CCPDH6
2010 Press Pass Five Star Classic Compilations Patch Autographs /1 #CCPDH7
2010 Press Pass Five Star Classic Compilations Triple Memorabilia Autographs /5 #DH
2010 Press Pass Five Star Holofoil /10 #17
2010 Press Pass Five Star Melting /1 #17
2010 Press Pass Five Star Paramount Pieces Aluminum /10 #DH
2010 Press Pass Five Star Paramount Pieces Blue /20 #DH
2010 Press Pass Five Star Paramount Pieces Gold /15 #DH
2010 Press Pass Five Star Paramount Pieces Holofoil /10 #DH
2010 Press Pass Five Star Paramount Pieces Melting /1 #DH
2010 Press Pass Five Star Signatures Aluminum /35 #DH
2010 Press Pass Five Star Signatures Gold /20 #DH
2010 Press Pass Five Star Signatures Holofoil /5 #DH
2010 Press Pass Five Star Signatures Melting /1 #DH
2010 Press Pass Gold #5
2010 Press Pass Gold #83
2010 Press Pass Gold #92
2010 Press Pass Gold #112
2010 Press Pass Gold #129
2010 Press Pass Holofoil /100 #5
2010 Press Pass Holofoil /100 #83
2010 Press Pass Holofoil /100 #92
2010 Press Pass Holofoil /100 #112
2010 Press Pass Holofoil /100 #129
2010 Press Pass Legends Autographs Blue /10 #25
2010 Press Pass Legends Autographs Holofoil /25 #25
2010 Press Pass Legends Autographs Printing Plates Black /1 #22
2010 Press Pass Legends Autographs Printing Plates Cyan /1 #22
2010 Press Pass Legends Autographs Printing Plates Magenta /1 #22
2010 Press Pass Legends Autographs Printing Plates Yellow /1 #22
2010 Press Pass Legends Motorsports Masters Autographs Printing Plates Black /1 #22
2010 Press Pass Legends Motorsports Masters Autographs Printing Plates Cyan /1 #22
2010 Press Pass Legends Motorsports Masters Autographs Printing Plates Magenta /1 #22
2010 Press Pass Legends Motorsports Masters Autographs Printing Plates Yellow /1 #22
2010 Press Pass Premium #4
2010 Press Pass Premium Allies #A10
2010 Press Pass Premium Hot Threads /299 #HTDH
2010 Press Pass Premium Hot Threads Holofoil /99 #HTDH
2010 Press Pass Premium Hot Threads Multi Color /25 #HTDH
2010 Press Pass Premium Hot Threads Two Color /125 #HTDH
2010 Press Pass Premium Purple /25 #4
2010 Press Pass Premium Signatures #PSDH
2010 Press Pass Premium Signatures Red Ink /24 #PSDH
2010 Press Pass Previews /5 #5
2010 Press Pass Previews /1 #112
2010 Press Pass Purple /25 #5
2010 Press Pass Purple /25 #83
2010 Press Pass Purple /25 #92
2010 Press Pass Purple /25 #112
2010 Press Pass Purple /25 #129
2010 Press Pass Showcase /499 #4
2010 Press Pass Showcase /499 #35
2010 Press Pass Showcase Classic Collections Firesuit Green /25 #CCIJGR
2010 Press Pass Showcase Classic Collections Firesuit Patch Melting /5 #CCIJGR
2010 Press Pass Showcase Classic Collections Ink /15 #CCIJGR
2010 Press Pass Showcase Classic Collections Ink Gold /10 #CCIJGR
2010 Press Pass Showcase Classic Collections Ink Green /5 #CCIJGR
2010 Press Pass Showcase Classic Collections Ink Melting /1 #CCIJGR
2010 Press Pass Showcase Classic Collections Sheet Metal /99 #CCIJGR
2010 Press Pass Showcase Classic Collections Sheet Metal Gold /45 #CCIJGR
2010 Press Pass Showcase Elite Exhibit Ink /20 #EEIDH
2010 Press Pass Showcase Elite Exhibit Ink Gold /10 #EEIDH
2010 Press Pass Showcase Elite Exhibit Ink Green /5 #EEIDH
2010 Press Pass Showcase Elite Exhibit Ink Melting /1 #EEIDH
2010 Press Pass Showcase Elite Exhibit Triple Memorabilia /99 #EEMDH
2010 Press Pass Showcase Elite Exhibit Triple Memorabilia Gold /45 #EEMDH
2010 Press Pass Showcase Elite Exhibit Triple Memorabilia Green /25 #EEMDH
2010 Press Pass Showcase Elite Exhibit Triple Memorabilia Melting /5 #EEMDH
2010 Press Pass Showcase Gold /125 #4
2010 Press Pass Showcase Gold /125 #35
2010 Press Pass Showcase Green /50 #4
2010 Press Pass Showcase Green /50 #35
2010 Press Pass Showcase Melting /15 #4
2010 Press Pass Showcase Melting /15 #35
2010 Press Pass Showcase Platinum Holo /1 #4
2010 Press Pass Showcase Platinum Holo /1 #35
2010 Press Pass Signings Blue /10 #22
2010 Press Pass Signings Gold /25 #22
2010 Press Pass Signings Red /15 #22
2010 Press Pass Signings Silver /45 #22
2010 Press Pass Stealth #12
2010 Press Pass Stealth #65
2010 Press Pass Stealth #80
2010 Press Pass Stealth Battle Armor Holofoil /25 #BADH
2010 Press Pass Stealth Battle Armor Silver /225 #BADH
2010 Press Pass Stealth Black and White #12
2010 Press Pass Stealth Black and White #65
2010 Press Pass Stealth Black and White #80
2010 Press Pass Stealth Power Players #PP4
2010 Press Pass Stealth Previews /5 #12
2010 Press Pass Stealth Previews /1 #65
2010 Press Pass Stealth Purple /25 #12
2010 Press Pass Stealth Purple /25 #65
2010 Press Pass Stealth Signature Series Sheet Metal /15 #SSMEDH
2010 Press Pass Top 12 Tires /11 #DH
2010 Press Pass Top 12 Tires 10 /10 #DH
2010 Sports Illustrated for Kids #490
2010 Wheels Autographs #19
2010 Wheels Autographs Printing Plates Black /1 #19
2010 Wheels Autographs Printing Plates Cyan /1 #19
2010 Wheels Autographs Printing Plates Magenta /1 #19
2010 Wheels Autographs Printing Plates Yellow /1 #19
2010 Wheels Autographs Special Ink /10 #6
2010 Wheels Autographs Target /10 #12
2010 Wheels Main Event #13
2010 Wheels Main Event #68
2010 Wheels Main Event #73
2010 Wheels Main Event Blue #13
2010 Wheels Main Event Blue #68
2010 Wheels Main Event Blue #73
2010 Wheels Main Event Fight Card #FC11
2010 Wheels Main Event Fight Card Checkered Flag #FC11
2010 Wheels Main Event Fight Card Full Color Retail #FC11
2010 Wheels Main Event Fight Card Gold /25 #FC11
2010 Wheels Main Event Head to Head /150 #HHJBDH
2010 Wheels Main Event Head to Head /150 #HHKBDH
2010 Wheels Main Event Head to Head Blue /75 #HHJBDH
2010 Wheels Main Event Head to Head Blue /75 #HHKBDH
2010 Wheels Main Event Head to Head Holofoil /10 #HHJBDH
2010 Wheels Main Event Head to Head Holofoil /10 #HHKBDH
2010 Wheels Main Event Head to Head Red /25 #HHJBDH
2010 Wheels Main Event Head to Head Red /25 #HHKBDH
2010 Wheels Main Event Marks Autographs /40 #22
2010 Wheels Main Event Marks Autographs Black /1 #21
2010 Wheels Main Event Marks Autographs Blue /20 #22
2010 Wheels Main Event Marks Autographs Red /5 #22
2010 Wheels Main Event Matchups Autographs /10 #DHJB
2010 Wheels Main Event Matchups Autographs /10 #KHDH
2010 Wheels Main Event Purple /25 #13
2010 Wheels Main Event Tale of the Tape #TT4
2010 Wheels Main Event Toe to Toe /10 #TTKBDH
2010 Wheels Main Event Upper Cuts Knock Out Patches /25 #UCKODH
2010 Wheels Main Event Wheel to Wheel /25 #WWKBDH
2010 Wheels Main Event Wheel to Wheel Holofoil /10 #WWKBDH
2011 Element #13
2011 Element #44
2011 Element #68
2011 Element #81
2011 Element #87
2011 Element Autographs /40 #21
2011 Element Autographs Blue /5 #21
2011 Element Autographs Gold /10 #20
2011 Element Autographs Printing Plates Black /1 #21
2011 Element Autographs Printing Plates Cyan /1 #21
2011 Element Autographs Printing Plates Magenta /1 #21
2011 Element Autographs Printing Plates Yellow /1 #21
2011 Element Autographs Silver /15 #20
2011 Element Black /35 #13
2011 Element Black /35 #44
2011 Element Black /35 #68
2011 Element Black /35 #81
2011 Element Black /35 #87
2011 Element Finish Line Checkered Flag /10 #FLDH
2011 Element Finish Line Green Flag /25 #FLDH
2011 Element Finish Line Tires /99 #FLDH
2011 Element Green #13
2011 Element Green #44
2011 Element Green #68
2011 Element Green #81
2011 Element Green #87
2011 Element High Octane Vehicle #HOV2
2011 Element Previews /5 #EB13
2011 Element Purple /25 #13
2011 Element Purple /25 #44
2011 Element Purple /25 #68
2011 Element Purple /25 #81
2011 Element Purple /25 #87
2011 Element Red #13
2011 Element Red #44
2011 Element Red #68
2011 Element Red #81
2011 Element Red #87
2011 Press Pass #13
2011 Press Pass #68
2011 Press Pass #126
2011 Press Pass #139
2011 Press Pass #170
2011 Press Pass #181
2011 Press Pass #197
2011 Press Pass #0
2011 Press Pass Autographs Blue /10 #21
2011 Press Pass Autographs Bronze /75 #20
2011 Press Pass Autographs Gold /25 #20
2011 Press Pass Autographs Printing Plates Black /1 #21
2011 Press Pass Autographs Printing Plates Cyan /1 #21
2011 Press Pass Autographs Printing Plates Magenta /1 #21
2011 Press Pass Autographs Printing Plates Yellow /1 #21
2011 Press Pass Autographs Silver /50 #21
2011 Press Pass Blue Holofoil /10 #13
2011 Press Pass Blue Holofoil /10 #68
2011 Press Pass Blue Holofoil /10 #126
2011 Press Pass Blue Holofoil /10 #139
2011 Press Pass Blue Holofoil /10 #170
2011 Press Pass Blue Holofoil /10 #181
2011 Press Pass Blue Holofoil /10 #197
2011 Press Pass Blue Retail #13
2011 Press Pass Blue Retail #68
2011 Press Pass Blue Retail #126
2011 Press Pass Blue Retail #139
2011 Press Pass Blue Retail #170
2011 Press Pass Blue Retail #181
2011 Press Pass Blue Retail #197
2011 Press Pass Burning Rubber Autographs /10 #BRDH1
2011 Press Pass Burning Rubber Autographs /10 #BRDH2
2011 Press Pass Burning Rubber Autographs /10 #BRDH3
2011 Press Pass Burning Rubber Fast Pass /10 #BRDH
2011 Press Pass Burning Rubber Gold /150 #BRDH
2011 Press Pass Burning Rubber Gold /150 #BRCDH2
2011 Press Pass Burning Rubber Gold /150 #BRCDH1
2011 Press Pass Burning Rubber Holofoil /50 #BRDH
2011 Press Pass Burning Rubber Holofoil /50 #BRCDH1
2011 Press Pass Burning Rubber Holofoil /50 #BRCDH2
2011 Press Pass Burning Rubber Prime Cuts /25 #BRDH
2011 Press Pass Burning Rubber Prime Cuts /25 #BRCDH1
2011 Press Pass Burning Rubber Prime Cuts /25 #BRCDH2
2011 Press Pass Cup Chase #CCR1
2011 Press Pass Cup Chase Prizes #CC12
2011 Press Pass Eclipse #12
2011 Press Pass Eclipse #37
2011 Press Pass Eclipse #55
2011 Press Pass Eclipse #67
2011 Press Pass Eclipse #71
2011 Press Pass Eclipse #74
2011 Press Pass Eclipse Blue #12
2011 Press Pass Eclipse Blue #37
2011 Press Pass Eclipse Blue #55
2011 Press Pass Eclipse Blue #67
2011 Press Pass Eclipse Blue #71
2011 Press Pass Eclipse Blue #74
2011 Press Pass Eclipse Gold /55 #12
2011 Press Pass Eclipse Gold /55 #37
2011 Press Pass Eclipse Gold /55 #55
2011 Press Pass Eclipse Gold /55 #67
2011 Press Pass Eclipse Gold /55 #71
2011 Press Pass Eclipse Gold /55 #74
2011 Press Pass Eclipse Previews /5 #EB12
2011 Press Pass Eclipse Previews /1 #EB37
2011 Press Pass Eclipse Purple /25 #12
2011 Press Pass Eclipse Purple /25 #37
2011 Press Pass Eclipse Purple /25 #55
2011 Press Pass Eclipse Spellbound Swatches /250 #SBDH1
2011 Press Pass Eclipse Spellbound Swatches /150 #SBDH2
2011 Press Pass Eclipse Spellbound Swatches /150 #SBDH3
2011 Press Pass Eclipse Spellbound Swatches /100 #SBDH4
2011 Press Pass Eclipse Spellbound Swatches /75 #SBDH5
2011 Press Pass Eclipse Spellbound Swatches /50 #SBDH6
2011 Press Pass Eclipse Spellbound Swatches Signatures /10 #NNO
2011 Press Pass FanFare #16
2011 Press Pass FanFare Autographs Blue /5 #31
2011 Press Pass FanFare Autographs Bronze /10 #31
2011 Press Pass FanFare Autographs Gold /10 #31
2011 Press Pass FanFare Autographs Printing Plates Black /1 #31
2011 Press Pass FanFare Autographs Printing Plates Cyan /1 #31
2011 Press Pass FanFare Autographs Printing Plates Magenta /1 #31
2011 Press Pass FanFare Autographs Printing Plates Yellow /1 #31
2011 Press Pass FanFare Autographs Silver /5 #31
2011 Press Pass FanFare Blue Die Cuts #16
2011 Press Pass FanFare Dual Autographs /10 #NNO
2011 Press Pass FanFare Emerald /25 #16
2011 Press Pass FanFare Holofoil Die Cuts #16
2011 Press Pass FanFare Magnificent Materials /199 #MMDH
2011 Press Pass FanFare Magnificent Materials Dual Swatches /50 #MMDDH
2011 Press Pass FanFare Magnificent Materials Dual Swatches Holofoil /10 #MMDDH
2011 Press Pass FanFare Magnificent Materials Holofoil /50 #MMDH
2011 Press Pass FanFare Magnificent Materials Signatures /99 #MMSEDH
2011 Press Pass FanFare Magnificent Materials Signatures Holofoil /25 #MMSEDH
2011 Press Pass FanFare Rookie Standouts #RS4
2011 Press Pass FanFare Ruby Die Cuts /15 #16
2011 Press Pass FanFare Sapphire /10 #16
2011 Press Pass FanFare Silver /25 #16
2011 Press Pass Four Wide Firesuit /25 #FWDH
2011 Press Pass Four Wide Glove /1 #FWDH
2011 Press Pass Four Wide Sheet Metal /15 #FWDH
2011 Press Pass Four Wide Shoes /1 #FWDH
2011 Press Pass Four Wide Tire /10 #FWDH
2011 Press Pass Geared Up Holofoil /25 #GUDH
2011 Press Pass Gold /50 #13
2011 Press Pass Gold /50 #68
2011 Press Pass Gold /50 #126
2011 Press Pass Gold /50 #139
2011 Press Pass Gold /50 #170
2011 Press Pass Gold /50 #181
2011 Press Pass Gold /50 #197
2011 Press Pass Legends #43
2011 Press Pass Legends Autographs Blue /10 #LGADH
2011 Press Pass Legends Autographs Gold /50 #LGADH
2011 Press Pass Legends Autographs Printing Plates Black /1 #LGADH
2011 Press Pass Legends Autographs Printing Plates Cyan /1 #LGADH
2011 Press Pass Legends Autographs Printing Plates Magenta /1 #LGADH
2011 Press Pass Legends Autographs Printing Plates Yellow /1 #LGADH
2011 Press Pass Legends Autographs Silver /125 #LGADH
2011 Press Pass Legends Gold /250 #43
2011 Press Pass Legends Holofoil /25 #43
2011 Press Pass Legends Printing Plates Black /1 #43
2011 Press Pass Legends Printing Plates Cyan /1 #43
2011 Press Pass Legends Printing Plates Magenta /1 #43
2011 Press Pass Legends Printing Plates Yellow /1 #43
2011 Press Pass Legends Purple /25 #43
2011 Press Pass Legends Red /99 #43
2011 Press Pass Legends Solo /1 #43
2011 Press Pass Premium #15
2011 Press Pass Premium #47
2011 Press Pass Premium #62
2011 Press Pass Premium #78
2011 Press Pass Premium Crystal Ball #CB5
2011 Press Pass Premium Crystal Ball Autographs /10 #CBADH
2011 Press Pass Premium Hot Pursuit 3D #HP7
2011 Press Pass Premium Hot Pursuit Autographs /10 #HPADH
2011 Press Pass Premium Hot Pursuit National Convention #HP7
2011 Press Pass Premium Hot Threads /150 #HTDH
2011 Press Pass Premium Hot Threads Fast Pass /25 #HTDH
2011 Press Pass Premium Hot Threads Multi Color /25 #HTDH
2011 Press Pass Premium Hot Threads Secondary Color /99 #HTDH
2011 Press Pass Premium Pairings Firesuits /25 #PPKBDH
2011 Press Pass Premium Pairings Signatures /5 #PPAKBDH
2011 Press Pass Premium Purple /25 #15
2011 Press Pass Premium Purple /25 #47
2011 Press Pass Premium Purple /25 #62
2011 Press Pass Premium Purple /25 #78
2011 Press Pass Premium Signatures /66 #PSDH
2011 Press Pass Previews /5 #EB13
2011 Press Pass Previews /1 #EB197
2011 Press Pass Purple /25 #13
2011 Press Pass Purple /25 #197
2011 Press Pass Showcase /499 #14
2011 Press Pass Showcase /499 #42
2011 Press Pass Showcase /499 #54
2011 Press Pass Showcase Classic Collections Firesuit /45 #CCMJGR
2011 Press Pass Showcase Classic Collections Firesuit Patches /5 #CCMJGR
2011 Press Pass Showcase Classic Collections Ink /25 #CCMJGR
2011 Press Pass Showcase Classic Collections Ink Gold /5 #CCMJGR
2011 Press Pass Showcase Classic Collections Ink Melting /1 #CCMJGR
2011 Press Pass Showcase Classic Collections Sheet Metal /99 #CCMJGR
2011 Press Pass Showcase Elite Exhibit Ink /50 #EEIDH
2011 Press Pass Showcase Elite Exhibit Ink Gold /25 #EEIDH
2011 Press Pass Showcase Elite Exhibit Ink Melting /1 #EEIDH
2011 Press Pass Showcase Gold /125 #14
2011 Press Pass Showcase Gold /125 #42
2011 Press Pass Showcase Gold /125 #54
2011 Press Pass Showcase Green /25 #14
2011 Press Pass Showcase Green /25 #42
2011 Press Pass Showcase Green /25 #54
2011 Press Pass Showcase Masterpieces Ink /45 #MPIDH
2011 Press Pass Showcase Masterpieces Ink Gold /25 #MPIDH
2011 Press Pass Showcase Masterpieces Ink Melting /1 #MPIDH
2011 Press Pass Showcase Masterpieces Memorabilia /99 #MPMDH
2011 Press Pass Showcase Masterpieces Memorabilia Gold /45 #MPMDH
2011 Press Pass Showcase Masterpieces Memorabilia Melting /5 #MPMDH
2011 Press Pass Showcase Melting /1 #14
2011 Press Pass Showcase Melting /1 #42
2011 Press Pass Showcase Melting /1 #54
2011 Press Pass Showcase Prized Pieces Firesuit /99 #PPMDH
2011 Press Pass Showcase Prized Pieces Firesuit Gold /45 #PPMDH
2011 Press Pass Showcase Prized Pieces Firesuit Ink /25 #PPIDH
2011 Press Pass Showcase Prized Pieces Firesuit Patches Ink /1 #PPIDH
2011 Press Pass Showcase Prized Pieces Firesuit Patches Melting /5 #PPMDH
2011 Press Pass Showcase Prized Pieces Sheet Metal Ink /45 #PPIDH
2011 Press Pass Signature Series /11 #SSTDH
2011 Press Pass Signature Series /11 #SSBDH
2011 Press Pass Signature Series /11 #SSFDH
2011 Press Pass Stealth #43
2011 Press Pass Stealth #77

2011 Press Pass Stealth #88
2011 Press Pass Stealth Black and White /25 #43
2011 Press Pass Stealth Black and White /25 #77
2011 Press Pass Stealth Black and White /25 #88
2011 Press Pass Stealth Holofoil /99 #43
2011 Press Pass Stealth Holofoil /99 #77
2011 Press Pass Stealth Holofoil /99 #88
2011 Press Pass Stealth Metal of Honor Medal of Honor /50 #BADH
2011 Press Pass Stealth Metal of Honor Purple Heart /25 #MHDH
2011 Press Pass Stealth Metal of Honor Silver Star /99 #BADH
2011 Press Pass Stealth Purple /25 #43
2011 Press Pass Target Top 12 Tires /25 #T12DH
2011 Press Pass Winning Tickets #WT6
2011 Press Pass Winning Tickets #WT8
2011 Press Pass Winning Tickets #WT11
2011 Press Pass Winning Tickets #WT14
2011 Press Pass Winning Tickets #WT15
2011 Press Pass Winning Tickets #WT26
2011 Press Pass Winning Tickets #WT32
2011 Wheels Main Event #15
2011 Wheels Main Event #87
2011 Wheels Main Event All Stars #A7
2011 Wheels Main Event All Stars Brushed Foil /199 #A7
2011 Wheels Main Event All Stars Holofoil /50 #A7
2011 Wheels Main Event Black and White #15
2011 Wheels Main Event Black and White #87
2011 Wheels Main Event Blue /75 #15
2011 Wheels Main Event Blue /75 #87
2011 Wheels Main Event Green /1 #15
2011 Wheels Main Event Green /1 #87
2011 Wheels Main Event Headliners Holofoil /25 #HLDH
2011 Wheels Main Event Headliners Silver /50 #HLDH
2011 Wheels Main Event Joe Gibbs Racing 20th Anniversary #JGR5
2011 Wheels Main Event Joe Gibbs Racing 20th Anniversary Brushed Foil /199 #JGR5
2011 Wheels Main Event Joe Gibbs Racing 20th Anniversary Holofoil /50 #JGR5
2011 Wheels Main Event Marks Autographs Blue /10 #MEDH
2011 Wheels Main Event Marks Autographs Gold /25 #MEDH
2011 Wheels Main Event Marks Autographs Silver /50 #MEDH
2011 Wheels Main Event Matchups Autographs /10 #MEMKBDH
2011 Wheels Main Event Red /20 #15
2011 Wheels Main Event Red /20 #87
2012 Press Pass #15
2012 Press Pass Blue #15
2012 Press Pass Blue Holofoil /35 #15
2012 Press Pass Burning Rubber Gold /99 #BRDH
2012 Press Pass Burning Rubber Holofoil /25 #BRDH
2012 Press Pass Burning Rubber Prime Cuts /25 #BRDH
2012 Press Pass Burning Rubber Purple /15 #BRDH
2012 Press Pass Cup Chase #CCR1
2012 Press Pass Cup Chase Prizes #CCP1
2012 Press Pass Fanfare #18
2012 Press Pass Fanfare Autographs Blue /5 #DH
2012 Press Pass Fanfare Autographs Gold /15 #DH
2012 Press Pass Fanfare Autographs Red /10 #DH
2012 Press Pass Fanfare Autographs Silver /50 #DH
2012 Press Pass Fanfare Blue Foil Die Cuts #18
2012 Press Pass Fanfare Diamond /5 #18
2012 Press Pass Fanfare Holofoil Die Cuts #18
2012 Press Pass Fanfare Magnificent Materials /250 #MMDH
2012 Press Pass Fanfare Magnificent Materials Dual Swatches /50 #MMDH
2012 Press Pass Fanfare Magnificent Materials Dual Swatches Melting /10 #MMDH
2012 Press Pass Fanfare Magnificent Materials Gold /99 #MMDH
2012 Press Pass Fanfare Magnificent Materials Signatures /99 #DH
2012 Press Pass Fanfare Magnificent Materials Signatures Blue /25 #DH
2012 Press Pass Fanfare Power Rankings #PR4
2012 Press Pass Fanfare Sapphire /20 #18
2012 Press Pass Fanfare Showtime #S9
2012 Press Pass Fanfare Silver /25 #18
2012 Press Pass Gold #15
2012 Press Pass Ignite #16
2012 Press Pass Ignite Materials Autographs Gun Metal /20 #IMDH
2012 Press Pass Ignite Materials Autographs Red /5 #IMDH
2012 Press Pass Ignite Materials Autographs Silver /125 #IMDH
2012 Press Pass Ignite Materials Gun Metal /99 #IMDH
2012 Press Pass Ignite Materials Red /10 #IMDH
2012 Press Pass Ignite Materials Silver #IMDH
2012 Press Pass Ignite Proofs Black and White /50 #16
2012 Press Pass Ignite Proofs Cyan #16
2012 Press Pass Ignite Proofs Magenta #16
2012 Press Pass Ignite Proofs Yellow /10 #16
2012 Press Pass Power Picks Blue /50 #53
2012 Press Pass Power Picks Gold /50 #53
2012 Press Pass Power Picks Holofoil /10 #53
2012 Press Pass Purple /35 #15
2012 Press Pass Redline #16
2012 Press Pass Redline Black /99 #16
2012 Press Pass Redline Cyan /50 #16
2012 Press Pass Redline Full Throttle Dual Relic Blue /5 #FTDH
2012 Press Pass Redline Full Throttle Dual Relic Gold /10 #FTDH
2012 Press Pass Redline Full Throttle Dual Relic Melting /1 #FTDH
2012 Press Pass Redline Full Throttle Dual Relic Red /75 #FTDH
2012 Press Pass Redline Full Throttle Dual Relic Silver /25 #FTDH
2012 Press Pass Redline Magenta /15 #16
2012 Press Pass Redline Muscle Car Sheet Metal Blue /5 #MCDH
2012 Press Pass Redline Muscle Car Sheet Metal Gold /10 #MCDH
2012 Press Pass Redline Muscle Car Sheet Metal Melting /1 #MCDH
2012 Press Pass Redline Muscle Car Sheet Metal Red /75 #MCDH
2012 Press Pass Redline Muscle Car Sheet Metal Silver /25 #MCDH
2012 Press Pass Redline Relics Blue /5 #RLDH
2012 Press Pass Redline Relics Gold /10 #RLDH
2012 Press Pass Redline Relics Melting /1 #RLDH
2012 Press Pass Redline Relics Red /75 #RLDH
2012 Press Pass Redline Relics Silver /25 #RLDH
2012 Press Pass Redline RPM #RPM5
2012 Press Pass Redline Yellow /1 #16
2012 Press Pass Showcase /499 #11
2012 Press Pass Showcase /499 #56
2012 Press Pass Showcase Classic Collections Ink /10 #CCMJGR
2012 Press Pass Showcase Classic Collections Ink Gold /5 #CCMJGR
2012 Press Pass Showcase Classic Collections Ink Melting /1 #CCMJGR
2012 Press Pass Showcase Classic Collections Memorabilia /99 #CCMJGR
2012 Press Pass Showcase Classic Collections Memorabilia Gold /50 #CCMJGR
2012 Press Pass Showcase Classic Collections Memorabilia Melting /5 #CCMJGR
2012 Press Pass Showcase Elite Exhibit Ink /50 #EEIDH
2012 Press Pass Showcase Elite Exhibit Ink Gold /25 #EEIDH
2012 Press Pass Showcase Elite Exhibit Ink Melting /1 #EEIDH
2012 Press Pass Showcase Gold /125 #11
2012 Press Pass Showcase Gold /125 #56
2012 Press Pass Showcase Green /5 #11
2012 Press Pass Showcase Green /5 #56
2012 Press Pass Showcase Masterpieces Ink /50 #MPIDH
2012 Press Pass Showcase Masterpieces Ink Gold /25 #MPIDH
2012 Press Pass Showcase Masterpieces Ink Melting /1 #MPIDH
2012 Press Pass Showcase Masterpieces Memorabilia /99 #MPDH
2012 Press Pass Showcase Masterpieces Memorabilia Gold /50 #MPDH
2012 Press Pass Showcase Masterpieces Memorabilia Melting /5 #MPDH
2012 Press Pass Showcase Melting /1 #11
2012 Press Pass Showcase Melting /1 #56
2012 Press Pass Showcase Prized Pieces /11 #PPDH
2012 Press Pass Showcase Prized Pieces Gold /10 #PPDH
2012 Press Pass Showcase Prized Pieces Melting /5 #PPDH
2012 Press Pass Showcase Purple /1 #11
2012 Press Pass Showcase Purple /1 #56
2012 Press Pass Showcase Red /25 #11
2012 Press Pass Showcase Red /25 #56
2012 Press Pass Snapshots #SS15
2012 Press Pass Snapshots #SS72
2012 Press Pass Target Snapshots #SSTG7
2012 Press Pass Ultimate Collection Blue Holofoil /25 #UCDH
2012 Press Pass Ultimate Collection Holofoil /50 #UCDH
2012 Total Memorabilia #12
2012 Total Memorabilia Black and White /99 #12
2012 Total Memorabilia Dual Swatch Gold /75 #TMDH
2012 Total Memorabilia Dual Swatch Holofoil /25 #TMDH
2012 Total Memorabilia Dual Swatch Melting /5 #TMDH
2012 Total Memorabilia Dual Swatch Silver /99 #TMDH
2012 Total Memorabilia Gold /275 #12
2012 Total Memorabilia Jumbo Swatch Gold /50 #TMDH
2012 Total Memorabilia Jumbo Swatch Holofoil /10 #TMDH
2012 Total Memorabilia Jumbo Swatch Melting /1 #TMDH
2012 Total Memorabilia Red Retail /250 #12
2012 Total Memorabilia Single Swatch Gold /99 #TMDH
2012 Total Memorabilia Single Swatch Holofoil /50 #TMDH
2012 Total Memorabilia Single Swatch Melting /10 #TMDH
2012 Total Memorabilia Single Swatch Silver /199 #TMDH
2012 Total Memorabilia Triple Swatch Gold /50 #TMDH
2012 Total Memorabilia Triple Swatch Holofoil /25 #TMDH
2012 Total Memorabilia Triple Swatch Melting /1 #TMDH
2012 Total Memorabilia Triple Swatch Silver /99 #TMDH
2013 Press Pass #18
2013 Press Pass #73
2013 Press Pass #100
2013 Press Pass #0
2013 Press Pass Burning Rubber Blue /50 #BRDH
2013 Press Pass Burning Rubber Blue /50 #BRDH2
2013 Press Pass Burning Rubber Blue /50 #BRDH3
2013 Press Pass Burning Rubber Gold /199 #BRDH
2013 Press Pass Burning Rubber Gold /199 #BRDH2
2013 Press Pass Burning Rubber Gold /199 #BRDH3
2013 Press Pass Burning Rubber Holofoil /75 #BRDH
2013 Press Pass Burning Rubber Holofoil /75 #BRDH2
2013 Press Pass Burning Rubber Holofoil /75 #BRDH3
2013 Press Pass Burning Rubber Letterman /8 #BRLDH
2013 Press Pass Burning Rubber Melting /10 #BRDH
2013 Press Pass Burning Rubber Melting /10 #BRDH2
2013 Press Pass Burning Rubber Melting /10 #BRDH3
2013 Press Pass Certified Winners Autographs Gold /10 #DH
2013 Press Pass Certified Winners Autographs Melting /5 #DH
2013 Press Pass Color Proofs Black #18
2013 Press Pass Color Proofs Black #73
2013 Press Pass Color Proofs Black #100
2013 Press Pass Color Proofs Cyan /35 #18
2013 Press Pass Color Proofs Cyan /35 #73
2013 Press Pass Color Proofs Cyan /35 #100
2013 Press Pass Color Proofs Magenta #18
2013 Press Pass Color Proofs Magenta #73
2013 Press Pass Color Proofs Magenta #100
2013 Press Pass Color Proofs Yellow /5 #18
2013 Press Pass Color Proofs Yellow /5 #73
2013 Press Pass Color Proofs Yellow /5 #100
2013 Press Pass Cool Persistence #CP6
2013 Press Pass Cup Chase #CC8
2013 Press Pass Fanfare #21
2013 Press Pass Fanfare #22
2013 Press Pass Fanfare Autographs Blue /1 #DH
2013 Press Pass Fanfare Autographs Gold /10 #DH
2013 Press Pass Fanfare Autographs Green /6 #DH
2013 Press Pass Fanfare Autographs Red /5 #DH
2013 Press Pass Fanfare Autographs Silver /10 #DH
2013 Press Pass Fanfare Diamond Die Cuts /5 #21
2013 Press Pass Fanfare Diamond Die Cuts /5 #22
2013 Press Pass Fanfare Green /3 #21
2013 Press Pass Fanfare Green /3 #22
2013 Press Pass Fanfare Holofoil Die Cuts #21
2013 Press Pass Fanfare Holofoil Die Cuts #22
2013 Press Pass Fanfare Magnificent Jumbo Materials Signatures /10 #DH
2013 Press Pass Fanfare Magnificent Materials Dual Swatches /50 #DH
2013 Press Pass Fanfare Magnificent Materials Dual Swatches Melting /10 #DH
2013 Press Pass Fanfare Magnificent Materials Gold /50 #DH
2013 Press Pass Fanfare Magnificent Materials Jumbo Swatches /25 #DH
2013 Press Pass Fanfare Magnificent Materials Signatures /99 #DH
2013 Press Pass Fanfare Magnificent Materials Signatures Blue /25 #DH
2013 Press Pass Fanfare Magnificent Materials Silver /199 #DH
2013 Press Pass Fanfare Red Foil Die Cuts #21
2013 Press Pass Fanfare Red Foil Die Cuts #22
2013 Press Pass Fanfare Sapphire /20 #21
2013 Press Pass Fanfare Sapphire /20 #22
2013 Press Pass Fanfare Signature Ride Autographs /10 #DH
2013 Press Pass Fanfare Signature Ride Autographs Blue /1 #DH
2013 Press Pass Fanfare Signature Ride Autographs Red /5 #DH
2013 Press Pass Fanfare Silver /25 #21
2013 Press Pass Fanfare Silver /25 #22
2013 Press Pass Ignite #13
2013 Press Pass Ignite #57
2013 Press Pass Ignite Hot Threads Blue Holofoil /99 #HTDH
2013 Press Pass Ignite Hot Threads Patch Red /10 #HTDH
2013 Press Pass Ignite Hot Threads Silver #HTDH
2013 Press Pass Ignite Profile #5
2013 Press Pass Ignite Proofs Black and White /50 #13
2013 Press Pass Ignite Proofs Black and White /50 #57
2013 Press Pass Ignite Proofs Cyan #13
2013 Press Pass Ignite Proofs Cyan #57
2013 Press Pass Ignite Proofs Magenta #13
2013 Press Pass Ignite Proofs Magenta #57
2013 Press Pass Ignite Proofs Yellow /5 #13
2013 Press Pass Ignite Proofs Yellow /5 #57
2013 Press Pass Power Picks Blue /99 #22
2013 Press Pass Power Picks Blue /99 #36
2013 Press Pass Power Picks Gold /50 #22
2013 Press Pass Power Picks Gold /50 #36
2013 Press Pass Power Picks Holofoil /10 #22
2013 Press Pass Power Picks Holofoil /10 #36
2013 Press Pass Racing Champions #RC2
2013 Press Pass Racing Champions #RC8
2013 Press Pass Racing Champions #RC24
2013 Press Pass Racing Champions #RC25
2013 Press Pass Redline #19
2013 Press Pass Redline #20
2013 Press Pass Redline Black /99 #19
2013 Press Pass Redline Black /99 #20
2013 Press Pass Redline Cyan /50 #19
2013 Press Pass Redline Cyan /50 #20
2013 Press Pass Redline Dynamic Duals Dual Relic Blue /5 #DDDH
2013 Press Pass Redline Dynamic Duals Dual Relic Gold /10 #DDDH
2013 Press Pass Redline Dynamic Duals Dual Relic Melting /1 #DDDH
2013 Press Pass Redline Dynamic Duals Dual Relic Red /75 #DDDH
2013 Press Pass Redline Dynamic Duals Dual Relic Silver /25 #DDDH
2013 Press Pass Redline Magenta /15 #19
2013 Press Pass Redline Magenta /15 #20
2013 Press Pass Redline Redline Racers #5
2013 Press Pass Redline Relic Autographs Blue /10 #RRSEDH
2013 Press Pass Redline Relic Autographs Gold /25 #RRSEDH
2013 Press Pass Redline Relic Autographs Melting /1 #RRSEDH
2013 Press Pass Redline Relic Autographs Red /99 #RRSEDH
2013 Press Pass Redline Relic Autographs Silver /50 #RRSEDH
2013 Press Pass Redline Relics Blue /5 #RRDH
2013 Press Pass Redline Relics Gold /10 #RRDH
2013 Press Pass Redline Relics Melting /1 #RRDH
2013 Press Pass Redline Relics Red /50 #RRDH
2013 Press Pass Redline Relics Silver /25 #RRDH
2013 Press Pass Redline Signatures Blue /15 #RSDH1
2013 Press Pass Redline Signatures Blue /10 #RSDH2
2013 Press Pass Redline Signatures Gold /5 #RSDH1
2013 Press Pass Redline Signatures Gold /5 #RSDH2
2013 Press Pass Redline Signatures Holo /11 #RSDH1
2013 Press Pass Redline Signatures Holo /5 #RSDH2
2013 Press Pass Redline Signatures Melting /1 #RSDH1
2013 Press Pass Redline Signatures Melting /1 #RSDH2
2013 Press Pass Redline Signatures Red /25 #RSDH1
2013 Press Pass Redline Signatures Red /10 #RSDH2
2013 Press Pass Redline Yellow /1 #19
2013 Press Pass Redline Yellow /1 #20
2013 Press Pass Showcase /349 #11
2013 Press Pass Showcase /349 #35
2013 Press Pass Showcase /349 #59
2013 Press Pass Showcase Black /1 #11
2013 Press Pass Showcase Black /1 #35
2013 Press Pass Showcase Black /1 #59
2013 Press Pass Showcase Blue /25 #11
2013 Press Pass Showcase Blue /25 #35
2013 Press Pass Showcase Blue /25 #59
2013 Press Pass Showcase Classic Collections Ink Gold /5 #CCIJGR
2013 Press Pass Showcase Classic Collections Ink Melting /1 #CCIJGR
2013 Press Pass Showcase Classic Collections Ink Red /1 #CCIJGR
2013 Press Pass Showcase Classic Collections Memorabilia Gold /25 #CCMJGR
2013 Press Pass Showcase Classic Collections Memorabilia Melting /5 #CCMJGR
2013 Press Pass Showcase Classic Collections Memorabilia Silver /75 #CCMJGR
2013 Press Pass Showcase Elite Exhibit Ink /25 #EEIDH
2013 Press Pass Showcase Elite Exhibit Ink Blue /30 #EEIDH
2013 Press Pass Showcase Elite Exhibit Ink Gold /10 #EEIDH
2013 Press Pass Showcase Elite Exhibit Ink Melting /1 #EEIDH
2013 Press Pass Showcase Elite Exhibit Ink Red /5 #EEIDH
2013 Press Pass Showcase Gold /99 #11
2013 Press Pass Showcase Gold /99 #35
2013 Press Pass Showcase Gold /99 #59
2013 Press Pass Showcase Green /20 #11
2013 Press Pass Showcase Green /20 #35
2013 Press Pass Showcase Green /20 #59
2013 Press Pass Showcase Masterpieces Ink /35 #MPIDH
2013 Press Pass Showcase Masterpieces Ink Gold /10 #MPIDH
2013 Press Pass Showcase Masterpieces Ink Melting /1 #MPIDH
2013 Press Pass Showcase Masterpieces Memorabilia /75 #MPDH
2013 Press Pass Showcase Masterpieces Memorabilia Gold /25 #MPDH
2013 Press Pass Showcase Masterpieces Memorabilia Melting /5 #MPDH
2013 Press Pass Showcase Prized Pieces /99 #PPMDH
2013 Press Pass Showcase Prized Pieces Blue /20 #PPMDH
2013 Press Pass Showcase Prized Pieces Gold /25 #PPMDH
2013 Press Pass Showcase Prized Pieces Ink /50 #PPIDH
2013 Press Pass Showcase Prized Pieces Ink Gold /25 #PPIDH
2013 Press Pass Showcase Prized Pieces Ink Melting /1 #PPIDH
2013 Press Pass Showcase Prized Pieces Melting /5 #PPMDH
2013 Press Pass Showcase Purple /13 #11
2013 Press Pass Showcase Purple /13 #35
2013 Press Pass Showcase Purple /13 #59
2013 Press Pass Showcase Red /10 #11
2013 Press Pass Showcase Red /10 #35
2013 Press Pass Showcase Red /10 #59
2013 Press Pass Showcase Series Standouts Gold /50 #7
2013 Press Pass Showcase Showcase Patches /5 #SPDH
2013 Press Pass Showcase Signature Patches /11 #SSPDH
2013 Press Pass Showcase Studio Showcase /299 #7
2013 Press Pass Showcase Studio Showcase Blue /40 #7
2013 Press Pass Showcase Studio Showcase Green /25 #7
2013 Press Pass Showcase Studio Showcase Ink /20 #SSIDH
2013 Press Pass Showcase Studio Showcase Ink Gold /10 #SSIDH
2013 Press Pass Showcase Studio Showcase Ink Melting /1 #SSIDH
2013 Press Pass Showcase Studio Showcase Ink Red /5 #SSIDH
2013 Press Pass Showcase Studio Showcase Melting /1 #7
2013 Press Pass Showcase Studio Showcase Purple /13 #7
2013 Press Pass Showcase Studio Showcase Red /10 #7
2013 Press Pass Signings Blue /1 #DH
2013 Press Pass Signings Gold /50 #DH
2013 Press Pass Signings Holofoil /5 #DH
2013 Press Pass Signings Silver /99 #DH
2013 Press Pass Three Wide Gold /10 #TWDH
2013 Press Pass Three Wide Melting /1 #TWDH
2013 Total Memorabilia #16
2013 Total Memorabilia Black and White /99 #16
2013 Total Memorabilia Burning Rubber Chase Edition Gold /75 #BRCDH
2013 Total Memorabilia Burning Rubber Chase Edition Holofoil /50 #BRCDH
2013 Total Memorabilia Burning Rubber Chase Edition Melting /5 #BRCDH
2013 Total Memorabilia Burning Rubber Chase Edition Silver /175 #BRCDH
2013 Total Memorabilia Dual Swatch Gold /199 #TMDH
2013 Total Memorabilia Gold /275 #16
2013 Total Memorabilia Quad Swatch Melting /10 #TMDH
2013 Total Memorabilia Red #16
2013 Total Memorabilia Single Swatch Silver /475 #TMDH
2013 Total Memorabilia Triple Swatch Holofoil /99 #TMDH
2014 Press Pass #14
2014 Press Pass #73
2014 Press Pass #98
2014 Press Pass American Thunder #16
2014 Press Pass American Thunder #55
2014 Press Pass American Thunder Autographs Blue /10 #ATADH
2014 Press Pass American Thunder Autographs Red /5 #ATADH
2014 Press Pass American Thunder Autographs White /60 #ATADH
2014 Press Pass American Thunder Black and White /50 #16
2014 Press Pass American Thunder Black and White /50 #55
2014 Press Pass American Thunder Brothers In Arms Autographs Blue /5 #BAJGR
2014 Press Pass American Thunder Brothers In Arms Autographs Red /1 #BAJGR
2014 Press Pass American Thunder Brothers In Arms Autographs White /10 #BAJGR
2014 Press Pass American Thunder Brothers In Arms Relics Blue /25 #BAJGR
2014 Press Pass American Thunder Brothers In Arms Relics Red /5 #BAJGR
2014 Press Pass American Thunder Brothers In Arms Relics Silver /50 #BAJGR
2014 Press Pass American Thunder Class A Uniforms Blue /99 #CAUDH
2014 Press Pass American Thunder Class A Uniforms Red /10 #CAUDH
2014 Press Pass American Thunder Class A Uniforms Silver #CAUDH
2014 Press Pass American Thunder Cyan #16
2014 Press Pass American Thunder Cyan #55
2014 Press Pass American Thunder Great American Treads Autographs Blue /25 #GATDH
2014 Press Pass American Thunder Great American Treads Autographs Red /1 #GATDH
2014 Press Pass American Thunder Magenta #16
2014 Press Pass American Thunder Magenta #55
2014 Press Pass American Thunder Yellow /5 #16
2014 Press Pass American Thunder Yellow /5 #55
2014 Press Pass Burning Rubber Chase Edition Blue /25 #BRCDH
2014 Press Pass Burning Rubber Chase Edition Gold /50 #BRCDH
2014 Press Pass Burning Rubber Chase Edition Melting /10 #BRCDH
2014 Press Pass Burning Rubber Chase Edition Silver /99 #BRCDH
2014 Press Pass Color Proofs Black /70 #14
2014 Press Pass Color Proofs Black /70 #73
2014 Press Pass Color Proofs Black /70 #98
2014 Press Pass Color Proofs Cyan /35 #14
2014 Press Pass Color Proofs Cyan /35 #73
2014 Press Pass Color Proofs Cyan /35 #98
2014 Press Pass Color Proofs Magenta #14
2014 Press Pass Color Proofs Magenta #73
2014 Press Pass Color Proofs Magenta #98
2014 Press Pass Color Proofs Yellow /5 #14
2014 Press Pass Color Proofs Yellow /5 #73
2014 Press Pass Color Proofs Yellow /5 #98
2014 Press Pass Cup Chase #7
2014 Press Pass Five Star /15 #7
2014 Press Pass Five Star Blue /5 #7
2014 Press Pass Five Star Classic Compilation Autographs Blue Triple Swatch /5 #CCDH
2014 Press Pass Five Star Classic Compilation Autographs Holofoil /10 #CCDH
2014 Press Pass Five Star Classic Compilation Autographs Holofoil Dual Swatch /10 #CCDH
2014 Press Pass Five Star Classic Compilation Autographs Melting Five Swatch /1 #CCDH
2014 Press Pass Five Star Classic Compilation Autographs Melting Quad Swatch /1 #CCDH
2014 Press Pass Five Star Classic Compilations Autographed Patch Booklet /1 #CCDH1
2014 Press Pass Five Star Classic Compilations Autographed Patch Booklet /1 #CCDH2
2014 Press Pass Five Star Classic Compilations Autographed Patch Booklet /1 #CCDH3
2014 Press Pass Five Star Classic Compilations Autographed Patch Booklet /1 #CCDH4
2014 Press Pass Five Star Classic Compilations Autographed Patch Booklet /1 #CCDH5
2014 Press Pass Five Star Classic Compilations Autographed Patch Booklet /1 #CCDH6
2014 Press Pass Five Star Classic Compilations Autographed Patch Booklet /1 #CCDH7
2014 Press Pass Five Star Classic Compilations Autographed Patch Booklet /1 #CCDH8
2014 Press Pass Five Star Classic Compilations Autographed Patch Booklet /1 #CCDH9
2014 Press Pass Five Star Classic Compilations Autographed Patch Booklet /1 #CCDH10
2014 Press Pass Five Star Classic Compilations Autographed Patch Booklet /1 #CCDH11
2014 Press Pass Five Star Classic Compilations Autographed Patch Booklet /1 #CCDH12
2014 Press Pass Five Star Classic Compilations Combo Autographs Blue /5 #CCJGR
2014 Press Pass Five Star Classic Compilations Combo Autographs Melting /1 #CCJGR
2014 Press Pass Five Star Holofoil /10 #7
2014 Press Pass Five Star Melting /1 #7
2014 Press Pass Five Star Paramount Pieces Blue /5 #PPDH
2014 Press Pass Five Star Paramount Pieces Gold /25 #PPDH
2014 Press Pass Five Star Paramount Pieces Holofoil /10 #PPDH
2014 Press Pass Five Star Paramount Pieces Melting /1 #PPDH
2014 Press Pass Five Star Paramount Pieces Melting Patch /1 #PPDH
2014 Press Pass Five Star Signature Souvenirs Blue /5 #SSDH
2014 Press Pass Five Star Signature Souvenirs Gold /50 #SSDH
2014 Press Pass Five Star Signature Souvenirs Holofoil /25 #SSDH
2014 Press Pass Five Star Signature Souvenirs Melting /1 #SSDH
2014 Press Pass Five Star Signatures Blue /5 #FSSDH
2014 Press Pass Five Star Signatures Holofoil /10 #FSSDH
2014 Press Pass Five Star Signatures Melting /1 #FSSDH
2014 Press Pass Four Wide Gold /10 #FWDH
2014 Press Pass Four Wide Melting /1 #FWDH
2014 Press Pass Gold #14
2014 Press Pass Gold #73
2014 Press Pass Gold #98
2014 Press Pass Redline #23
2014 Press Pass Redline #24
2014 Press Pass Redline Black /75 #23
2014 Press Pass Redline Black /75 #24
2014 Press Pass Redline Blue Foil #23
2014 Press Pass Redline Blue Foil #24
2014 Press Pass Redline Cyan /50 #23
2014 Press Pass Redline Cyan /50 #24
2014 Press Pass Redline Dynamic Duals Relic Autographs Blue /25 #DDDH
2014 Press Pass Redline Dynamic Duals Relic Autographs Gold /10 #DDDH
2014 Press Pass Redline Dynamic Duals Relic Autographs Melting /1 #DDDH
2014 Press Pass Redline Dynamic Duals Relic Autographs Red /50 #DDDH
2014 Press Pass Redline Green National Convention /5 #23
2014 Press Pass Redline Green National Convention /5 #24
2014 Press Pass Redline Magenta /10 #23
2014 Press Pass Redline Magenta /10 #24
2014 Press Pass Redline Muscle Car Sheet Metal Blue /25 #MCMDH
2014 Press Pass Redline Muscle Car Sheet Metal Gold /50 #MCMDH
2014 Press Pass Redline Muscle Car Sheet Metal Melting /1 #MCMDH
2014 Press Pass Redline Muscle Car Sheet Metal Red /75 #MCMDH
2014 Press Pass Redline Pieces of the Action Blue /10 #PADH
2014 Press Pass Redline Pieces of the Action Gold /25 #PADH
2014 Press Pass Redline Pieces of the Action Melting /1 #PADH
2014 Press Pass Redline Pieces of the Action Red /75 #PADH
2014 Press Pass Redline Redline Racers #RR7
2014 Press Pass Redline Relic Autographs Blue /10 #RRSEDH
2014 Press Pass Redline Relic Autographs Gold /25 #RRSEDH
2014 Press Pass Redline Relic Autographs Melting /1 #RRSEDH
2014 Press Pass Redline Relic Autographs Red /50 #RRSEDH
2014 Press Pass Redline Relics Blue /25 #RRDH
2014 Press Pass Redline Relics Gold /50 #RRDH
2014 Press Pass Redline Relics Melting /1 #RRDH
2014 Press Pass Redline Relics Red /75 #RRDH
2014 Press Pass Redline RPM #RPM4
2014 Press Pass Redline Signatures Blue /10 #RSDH
2014 Press Pass Redline Signatures Gold /15 #RSDH
2014 Press Pass Redline Signatures Melting /5 #RSDH
2014 Press Pass Redline Signatures Red /30 #RSDH
2014 Press Pass Redline Yellow /1 #23
2014 Press Pass Redline Yellow /1 #24
2014 Press Pass Velocity #3
2014 Sports Illustrated for Kids #334
2014 Total Memorabilia #10
2014 Total Memorabilia Autographed Memorabilia Blue /5 #SCDH
2014 Total Memorabilia Autographed Memorabilia Gold /5 #SCDH
2014 Total Memorabilia Autographed Memorabilia Melting /1 #SCDH
2014 Total Memorabilia Autographed Memorabilia Silver /10 #SC-DH
2014 Total Memorabilia Black and White /99 #10
2014 Total Memorabilia Dual Swatch Gold /150 #TMDH
2014 Total Memorabilia Gold /175 #10
2014 Total Memorabilia Quad Swatch Melting /25 #TMDH
2014 Total Memorabilia Red #10
2014 Total Memorabilia Single Swatch Silver /275 #TMDH
2014 Total Memorabilia Triple Swatch Blue /99 #TMDH
2015 Press Pass #16
2015 Press Pass #68
2015 Press Pass #100
2015 Press Pass Burning Rubber Blue /50 #BRDH
2015 Press Pass Burning Rubber Gold #BRDH
2015 Press Pass Burning Rubber Green /10 #BRDH
2015 Press Pass Burning Rubber Letterman /8 #BRLEDH
2015 Press Pass Burning Rubber Melting /1 #BRDH
2015 Press Pass Championship Caliber Dual /25 #CCMDH
2015 Press Pass Championship Caliber Quad /1 #CCMDH
2015 Press Pass Championship Caliber Signature Edition Blue /25 #CCDH
2015 Press Pass Championship Caliber Signature Edition Gold /50 #CCDH
2015 Press Pass Championship Caliber Signature Edition Green /10 #CCDH
2015 Press Pass Championship Caliber Signature Edition Melting /1 #CCDH
2015 Press Pass Championship Caliber Single /50 #CCMDH
2015 Press Pass Championship Caliber Triple /10 #CCMDH
2015 Press Pass Cup Chase #16
2015 Press Pass Cup Chase #68
2015 Press Pass Cup Chase #100
2015 Press Pass Cup Chase Blue /25 #16
2015 Press Pass Cup Chase Blue /25 #68
2015 Press Pass Cup Chase Blue /25 #100
2015 Press Pass Cup Chase Gold /75 #16
2015 Press Pass Cup Chase Gold /75 #68
2015 Press Pass Cup Chase Gold /75 #100
2015 Press Pass Cup Chase Green /10 #16
2015 Press Pass Cup Chase Green /10 #68
2015 Press Pass Cup Chase Green /10 #100
2015 Press Pass Cup Chase Melting /1 #16
2015 Press Pass Cup Chase Melting /1 #68
2015 Press Pass Cup Chase Melting /1 #100
2015 Press Pass Cup Chase Three Wide Blue /25 #3WDH
2015 Press Pass Cup Chase Three Wide Gold /50 #3WDH
2015 Press Pass Cup Chase Three Wide Green /10 #3WDH
2015 Press Pass Cup Chase Three Wide Melting /1 #3WDH
2015 Press Pass Cup Chase Upper Cuts /13 #UCDH
2015 Press Pass Cuts Blue /25 #CCCDH
2015 Press Pass Cuts Gold /50 #CCCDH
2015 Press Pass Cuts Green /10 #CCCDH
2015 Press Pass Cuts Melting /1 #CCCDH
2015 Press Pass Four Wide Signature Edition Blue /25 #4WDH
2015 Press Pass Four Wide Signature Edition Gold /50 #4WDH
2015 Press Pass Four Wide Signature Edition Green /10 #4WDH
2015 Press Pass Four Wide Signature Edition Melting /1 #4WDH
2015 Press Pass Pit Road Pieces Blue /25 #PPMDH
2015 Press Pass Pit Road Pieces Gold /50 #PPMDH
2015 Press Pass Pit Road Pieces Green /10 #PPMDH
2015 Press Pass Pit Road Pieces Melting /1 #PPMDH
2015 Press Pass Pit Road Pieces Signature Edition Blue /25 #PRPDH
2015 Press Pass Pit Road Pieces Signature Edition Gold /50 #PRPDH
2015 Press Pass Pit Road Pieces Signature Edition Green /10 #PRPDH
2015 Press Pass Pit Road Pieces Signature Edition Melting /1 #PRPDH
2015 Press Pass Purple #16
2015 Press Pass Purple #68
2015 Press Pass Purple #100
2015 Press Pass Red #16
2015 Press Pass Red #68
2015 Press Pass Red #100
2015 Press Pass Signings Blue /15 #PPSDH
2015 Press Pass Signings Gold #PPSDH
2015 Press Pass Signings Green /5 #PPSDH
2015 Press Pass Signings Melting /1 #PPSDH
2015 Press Pass Signings Red /10 #PPSDH
2016 Certified #12
2016 Certified #62
2016 Certified Complete Materials /199 #7
2016 Certified Complete Materials Mirror Black /1 #7
2016 Certified Complete Materials Mirror Blue /50 #7
2016 Certified Complete Materials Mirror Gold /25 #7
2016 Certified Complete Materials Mirror Green /5 #7
2016 Certified Complete Materials Mirror Orange /99 #7
2016 Certified Complete Materials Mirror Purple /10 #7
2016 Certified Complete Materials Mirror Red /75 #7
2016 Certified Complete Materials Mirror Silver /99 #7
2016 Certified Epix /199 #13
2016 Certified Epix Mirror Black /1 #13
2016 Certified Epix Mirror Blue /50 #13
2016 Certified Epix Mirror Gold /25 #13
2016 Certified Epix Mirror Green /5 #13
2016 Certified Epix Mirror Orange /99 #13
2016 Certified Epix Mirror Purple /10 #13
2016 Certified Epix Mirror Red /75 #13
2016 Certified Epix Mirror Silver /99 #13
2016 Certified Mirror Black /1 #12
2016 Certified Mirror Black /1 #62
2016 Certified Mirror Blue /50 #12
2016 Certified Mirror Blue /50 #62
2016 Certified Mirror Gold /25 #12
2016 Certified Mirror Gold /25 #62
2016 Certified Mirror Green /5 #12
2016 Certified Mirror Green /5 #62
2016 Certified Mirror Orange /99 #12
2016 Certified Mirror Orange /99 #62
2016 Certified Mirror Purple /10 #12
2016 Certified Mirror Purple /10 #62
2016 Certified Mirror Red /75 #12
2016 Certified Mirror Red /75 #62
2016 Certified Mirror Silver /99 #12
2016 Certified Mirror Silver /99 #62
2016 Certified Skills /199 #18
2016 Certified Skills Mirror Black /1 #18
2016 Certified Skills Mirror Blue /50 #18
2016 Certified Skills Mirror Gold /25 #18
2016 Certified Skills Mirror Green /5 #18
2016 Certified Skills Mirror Orange /99 #18
2016 Certified Skills Mirror Purple /10 #18
2016 Certified Skills Mirror Red /75 #18
2016 Certified Skills Mirror Silver /99 #18
2016 Certified Sprint Cup Signature Swatches /50 #6
2016 Certified Sprint Cup Signature Swatches Mirror Black /1 #6
2016 Certified Sprint Cup Signature Swatches Mirror Blue /25 #6
2016 Certified Sprint Cup Signature Swatches Mirror Gold /15 #6
2016 Certified Sprint Cup Signature Swatches Mirror Green /5 #6
2016 Certified Sprint Cup Signature Swatches Mirror Orange /11 #6
2016 Certified Sprint Cup Signature Swatches Mirror Purple /10 #6
2016 Certified Sprint Cup Signature Swatches Mirror Red /35 #6
2016 Certified Sprint Cup Signature Swatches Mirror Silver /5 #6
2016 Certified Sprint Cup Swatches /249 #2
2016 Certified Sprint Cup Swatches Mirror Black /1 #2
2016 Certified Sprint Cup Swatches Mirror Blue /50 #2
2016 Certified Sprint Cup Swatches Mirror Gold /25 #2
2016 Certified Sprint Cup Swatches Mirror Green /5 #2
2016 Certified Sprint Cup Swatches Mirror Orange /99 #2
2016 Certified Sprint Cup Swatches Mirror Purple /10 #2
2016 Certified Sprint Cup Swatches Mirror Red /75 #2
2016 Certified Sprint Cup Swatches Mirror Silver /99 #2
2016 Panini National Treasures /25 #21
2016 Panini National Treasures Black /5 #21
2016 Panini National Treasures Blue /1 #21
2016 Panini National Treasures Dual Signatures /25 #11
2016 Panini National Treasures Dual Signatures Black /10 #11
2016 Panini National Treasures Dual Signatures Blue /1 #11
2016 Panini National Treasures Dual Signatures Gold /15 #11
2016 Panini National Treasures Eight Signatures /15 #2
2016 Panini National Treasures Eight Signatures Black /5 #2
2016 Panini National Treasures Eight Signatures Blue /1 #2
2016 Panini National Treasures Eight Signatures Gold /10 #2
2016 Panini National Treasures Firesuit Materials /25 #7
2016 Panini National Treasures Firesuit Materials Black /5 #7
2016 Panini National Treasures Firesuit Materials Blue /1 #7
2016 Panini National Treasures Firesuit Materials Gold /10 #7
2016 Panini National Treasures Firesuit Materials Laundry Tag /1 #7
2016 Panini National Treasures Firesuit Materials Printing Plates Black /1 #7
2016 Panini National Treasures Firesuit Materials Printing Plates Cyan /1 #7
2016 Panini National Treasures Firesuit Materials Printing Plates Magenta /1 #7
2016 Panini National Treasures Firesuit Materials Printing Plates Yellow /1 #7
2016 Panini National Treasures Firesuit Materials Silver /15 #7
2016 Panini National Treasures Gold /15 #21
2016 Panini National Treasures Jumbo Firesuit Patch Signature Booklet Alpine Stars /1 #9
2016 Panini National Treasures Jumbo Firesuit Patch Signature Booklet Associate Sponsor 1 /1 #9
2016 Panini National Treasures Jumbo Firesuit Patch Signature Booklet Associate Sponsor 2 /1 #9
2016 Panini National Treasures Jumbo Firesuit Patch Signature Booklet Associate Sponsor 3 /1 #9
2016 Panini National Treasures Jumbo Firesuit Patch Signature Booklet Associate Sponsor 4 /1 #9
2016 Panini National Treasures Jumbo Firesuit Patch Signature Booklet Associate Sponsor 5 /1 #9
2016 Panini National Treasures Jumbo Firesuit Patch Signature Booklet Associate Sponsor 6 /1 #9
2016 Panini National Treasures Jumbo Firesuit Patch Signature Booklet F[illegible] /1 #9
2016 Panini National Treasures Jumbo Firesuit Patch Signature Booklet Goodyear /2 #9
2016 Panini National Treasures Jumbo Firesuit Patch Signature Booklet Manufacturers Logo /1 #9
2016 Panini National Treasures Jumbo Firesuit Patch Signature Booklet Nameplate /2 #9
2016 Panini National Treasures Jumbo Firesuit Patch Signature Booklet NASCAR /1 #9
2016 Panini National Treasures Jumbo Firesuit Patch Signature Booklet Sprint Cup Logo /1 #9
2016 Panini National Treasures Jumbo Firesuit Patch Signature Booklet Sunoco /1 #9
2016 Panini National Treasures Jumbo Firesuit Signatures /25 #9
2016 Panini National Treasures Jumbo Firesuit Signatures Black /5 #9
2016 Panini National Treasures Jumbo Firesuit Signatures Blue /1 #9
2016 Panini National Treasures Jumbo Firesuit Signatures Gold /10 #9
2016 Panini National Treasures Jumbo Firesuit Signatures Printing Plates Black /1 #9
2016 Panini National Treasures Jumbo Firesuit Signatures Printing Plates Cyan /1 #9
2016 Panini National Treasures Jumbo Firesuit Signatures Printing Plates Magenta /1 #9
2016 Panini National Treasures Jumbo Firesuit Signatures Printing Plates Yellow /1 #9
2016 Panini National Treasures Jumbo Firesuit Signatures Silver /15 #9
2016 Panini National Treasures Jumbo Sheet Metal Signatures Black /5 #[illegible]
2016 Panini National Treasures Jumbo Sheet Metal Signatures Blue /1 #1[illegible]
2016 Panini National Treasures Jumbo Sheet Metal Signatures Printing Plates Black /1 #11
2016 Panini National Treasures Jumbo Sheet Metal Signatures Printing Plates Cyan /1 #11
2016 Panini National Treasures Jumbo Sheet Metal Signatures Printing Plates Magenta /1 #11
2016 Panini National Treasures Jumbo Sheet Metal Signatures Printing Plates Yellow /1 #11
2016 Panini National Treasures Printing Plates Black /1 #21
2016 Panini National Treasures Printing Plates Cyan /1 #21
2016 Panini National Treasures Printing Plates Magenta /1 #21
2016 Panini National Treasures Printing Plates Yellow /1 #21
2016 Panini National Treasures Quad Driver Materials /25 #2
2016 Panini National Treasures Quad Driver Materials Black /5 #2
2016 Panini National Treasures Quad Driver Materials Blue /1 #2
2016 Panini National Treasures Quad Driver Materials Gold /10 #2
2016 Panini National Treasures Quad Driver Materials Printing Plates Black /1 #2
2016 Panini National Treasures Quad Driver Materials Printing Plates Cyan /1 #2
2016 Panini National Treasures Quad Driver Materials Printing Plates Magenta /1 #2
2016 Panini National Treasures Quad Driver Materials Printing Plates Yellow /1 #2
2016 Panini National Treasures Quad Driver Materials Silver /15 #2
2016 Panini National Treasures Sheet Metal Materials /25 #7
2016 Panini National Treasures Sheet Metal Materials Black /5 #7
2016 Panini National Treasures Sheet Metal Materials Blue /1 #7
2016 Panini National Treasures Sheet Metal Materials Gold /10 #7
2016 Panini National Treasures Sheet Metal Materials Printing Plates Black /1 #7
2016 Panini National Treasures Sheet Metal Materials Printing Plates Cyan /1 #7
2016 Panini National Treasures Sheet Metal Materials Printing Plates Magenta /1 #7
2016 Panini National Treasures Sheet Metal Materials Printing Plates Yellow /1 #7
2016 Panini National Treasures Sheet Metal Materials Silver /15 #7
2016 Panini National Treasures Signature Dual Materials /25 #9
2016 Panini National Treasures Signature Dual Materials Black /5 #9
2016 Panini National Treasures Signature Dual Materials Blue /1 #9
2016 Panini National Treasures Signature Dual Materials Gold /10 #9
2016 Panini National Treasures Signature Dual Materials Printing Plates Black /1 #9
2016 Panini National Treasures Signature Dual Materials Printing Plates Cyan /1 #9
2016 Panini National Treasures Signature Dual Materials Printing Plates Magenta /1 #9
2016 Panini National Treasures Signature Dual Materials Printing Plates Yellow /1 #9
2016 Panini National Treasures Signature Dual Materials Silver /15 #9
2016 Panini National Treasures Signature Firesuit Materials Black /5 #9
2016 Panini National Treasures Signature Firesuit Materials Blue /1 #9
2016 Panini National Treasures Signature Firesuit Materials Gold /10 #9
2016 Panini National Treasures Signature Firesuit Materials Laundry Tag /1 #9
2016 Panini National Treasures Signature Firesuit Materials Printing Plates Black /1 #9
2016 Panini National Treasures Signature Firesuit Materials Printing Plates Cyan /1 #9
2016 Panini National Treasures Signature Firesuit Materials Printing Plates Magenta /1 #9
2016 Panini National Treasures Signature Firesuit Materials Printing Plates Yellow /1 #9
2016 Panini National Treasures Signature Firesuit Materials Silver /15 #9
2016 Panini National Treasures Signature Quad Materials /25 #9
2016 Panini National Treasures Signature Quad Materials Black /5 #9
2016 Panini National Treasures Signature Quad Materials Blue /1 #9
2016 Panini National Treasures Signature Quad Materials Gold /10 #9
2016 Panini National Treasures Signature Quad Materials Printing Plates Black /1 #9
2016 Panini National Treasures Signature Quad Materials Printing Plates Cyan /1 #9
2016 Panini National Treasures Signature Quad Materials Printing Plates Magenta /1 #9
2016 Panini National Treasures Signature Quad Materials Printing Plates Yellow /1 #9
2016 Panini National Treasures Signature Quad Materials Silver /15 #9
2016 Panini National Treasures Signature Sheet Metal Materials Black /5 #9
2016 Panini National Treasures Signature Sheet Metal Materials Blue /1 #9
2016 Panini National Treasures Signature Sheet Metal Materials Gold /10 #9
2016 Panini National Treasures Signature Sheet Metal Materials Printing Plates Black /1 #9
2016 Panini National Treasures Signature Sheet Metal Materials Printing Plates Cyan /1 #9
2016 Panini National Treasures Signature Sheet Metal Materials Printing Plates Magenta /1 #9
2016 Panini National Treasures Signature Sheet Metal Materials Printing Plates Yellow /1 #9
2016 Panini National Treasures Signature Sheet Metal Materials Silver /15 #9
2016 Panini National Treasures Silver /20 #21
2016 Panini National Treasures Six Signatures /25 #1
2016 Panini National Treasures Six Signatures Black /10 #1
2016 Panini National Treasures Six Signatures Blue /1 #1
2016 Panini National Treasures Six Signatures Gold /15 #1
2016 Panini National Treasures Trio Driver Materials /25 #8
2016 Panini National Treasures Trio Driver Materials Black /5 #8
2016 Panini National Treasures Trio Driver Materials Blue /1 #8

2016 Panini National Treasures Trio Driver Materials Gold /10 #8
2016 Panini National Treasures Trio Driver Materials Printing Plates Black /1 #8
2016 Panini National Treasures Trio Driver Materials Printing Plates Cyan /1 #8
2016 Panini National Treasures Trio Driver Materials Printing Plates Magenta /1 #8
2016 Panini National Treasures Trio Driver Materials Printing Plates Yellow /1 #8
2016 Panini National Treasures Trio Driver Materials Silver /15 #8
2016 Panini Prizm #11
2016 Panini Prizm #52
2016 Panini Prizm #74
2016 Panini Prizm #100
2016 Panini Prizm Autographs Prizms #64
2016 Panini Prizm Autographs Prizms Black /3 #64
2016 Panini Prizm Autographs Prizms Blue Flag /50 #64
2016 Panini Prizm Autographs Prizms Camo /11 #64
2016 Panini Prizm Autographs Prizms Checkered Flag /1 #64
2016 Panini Prizm Autographs Prizms Gold /10 #64
2016 Panini Prizm Autographs Prizms Green Flag /99 #64
2016 Panini Prizm Autographs Prizms Rainbow /24 #64
2016 Panini Prizm Autographs Prizms Red Flag /35 #64
2016 Panini Prizm Autographs Prizms Red White and Blue /10 #64
2016 Panini Prizm Autographs Prizms White Flag /5 #64
2016 Panini Prizm Competitors #8
2016 Panini Prizm Competitors Prizms #8
2016 Panini Prizm Competitors Prizms Checkered Flag /1 #8
2016 Panini Prizm Competitors Prizms Gold /10 #8
2016 Panini Prizm Firesuit Fabrics /149 #11
2016 Panini Prizm Firesuit Fabrics Prizms Blue Flag /75 #11
2016 Panini Prizm Firesuit Fabrics Prizms Checkered Flag /1 #11
2016 Panini Prizm Firesuit Fabrics Prizms Green Flag /99 #11
2016 Panini Prizm Firesuit Fabrics Prizms Red Flag /25 #11
2016 Panini Prizm Firesuit Fabrics Team /249 #11
2016 Panini Prizm Firesuit Fabrics Team Prizms Blue Flag /50 #11
2016 Panini Prizm Firesuit Fabrics Team Prizms Checkered Flag /1 #11
2016 Panini Prizm Firesuit Fabrics Team Prizms Green Flag /99 #11
2016 Panini Prizm Firesuit Fabrics Team Prizms Red Flag /11 #11
2016 Panini Prizm Prizms #11
2016 Panini Prizm Prizms #52
2016 Panini Prizm Prizms #74
2016 Panini Prizm Prizms #100
2016 Panini Prizm Prizms Black /3 #11
2016 Panini Prizm Prizms Black /3 #52
2016 Panini Prizm Prizms Black /3 #74
2016 Panini Prizm Prizms Black /3 #100
2016 Panini Prizm Prizms Blue Flag /99 #11
2016 Panini Prizm Prizms Blue Flag /99 #52
2016 Panini Prizm Prizms Blue Flag /99 #74
2016 Panini Prizm Prizms Blue Flag /99 #100
2016 Panini Prizm Prizms Camo /11 #11
2016 Panini Prizm Prizms Camo /11 #52
2016 Panini Prizm Prizms Camo /11 #74
2016 Panini Prizm Prizms Camo /18 #100
2016 Panini Prizm Prizms Checkered Flag /1 #11
2016 Panini Prizm Prizms Checkered Flag /1 #52
2016 Panini Prizm Prizms Checkered Flag /1 #74
2016 Panini Prizm Prizms Checkered Flag /1 #100
2016 Panini Prizm Prizms Gold /10 #11
2016 Panini Prizm Prizms Gold /10 #52
2016 Panini Prizm Prizms Gold /10 #74
2016 Panini Prizm Prizms Gold /10 #100
2016 Panini Prizm Prizms Green Flag /149 #11
2016 Panini Prizm Prizms Green Flag /149 #52
2016 Panini Prizm Prizms Green Flag /149 #74
2016 Panini Prizm Prizms Green Flag /149 #100
2016 Panini Prizm Prizms Rainbow /24 #11
2016 Panini Prizm Prizms Rainbow /24 #52
2016 Panini Prizm Prizms Rainbow /24 #74
2016 Panini Prizm Prizms Rainbow /24 #100
2016 Panini Prizm Prizms Red Flag /75 #11
2016 Panini Prizm Prizms Red Flag /75 #52
2016 Panini Prizm Prizms Red Flag /75 #74
2016 Panini Prizm Prizms Red Flag /75 #100
2016 Panini Prizm Prizms Red White and Blue #11
2016 Panini Prizm Prizms Red White and Blue #52
2016 Panini Prizm Prizms Red White and Blue #74
2016 Panini Prizm Prizms Red White and Blue #100
2016 Panini Prizm Prizms White Flag /5 #11
2016 Panini Prizm Prizms White Flag /5 #52
2016 Panini Prizm Prizms White Flag /5 #74
2016 Panini Prizm Prizms White Flag /5 #100
2016 Panini Prizm Raising the Flag #11
2016 Panini Prizm Raising the Flag Prizms #11
2016 Panini Prizm Raising the Flag Prizms Checkered Flag /1 #11
2016 Panini Prizm Raising the Flag Prizms Gold /10 #11
2016 Panini Prizm Winner's Circle #6
2016 Panini Prizm Winner's Circle #27
2016 Panini Prizm Winner's Circle #33
2016 Panini Prizm Winner's Circle Prizms #6
2016 Panini Prizm Winner's Circle Prizms #27
2016 Panini Prizm Winner's Circle Prizms #33
2016 Panini Prizm Winner's Circle Prizms Checkered Flag /1 #6
2016 Panini Prizm Winner's Circle Prizms Checkered Flag /1 #27
2016 Panini Prizm Winner's Circle Prizms Checkered Flag /1 #33
2016 Panini Prizm Winner's Circle Prizms Gold /10 #6
2016 Panini Prizm Winner's Circle Prizms Gold /10 #27
2016 Panini Prizm Winner's Circle Prizms Gold /10 #33
2016 Panini Torque #6
2016 Panini Torque #83
2016 Panini Torque Artist Proof /50 #6
2016 Panini Torque Artist Proof /50 #83
2016 Panini Torque Blackout /1 #6
2016 Panini Torque Blackout /1 #83
2016 Panini Torque Blue /125 #6
2016 Panini Torque Blue /125 #83
2016 Panini Torque Clear Vision #6
2016 Panini Torque Clear Vision Blue /99 #6
2016 Panini Torque Clear Vision Gold /149 #6
2016 Panini Torque Clear Vision Green /25 #6
2016 Panini Torque Clear Vision Purple /10 #6
2016 Panini Torque Clear Vision Red /49 #6
2016 Panini Torque Combo Materials Autographs /50 #3
2016 Panini Torque Combo Materials Autographs Blue /35 #3
2016 Panini Torque Combo Materials Autographs Green /10 #3
2016 Panini Torque Combo Materials Autographs Purple /5 #3
2016 Panini Torque Combo Materials Autographs Red /25 #3
2016 Panini Torque Gold #6
2016 Panini Torque Gold #83
2016 Panini Torque Holo Gold /5 #6
2016 Panini Torque Holo Gold /5 #83
2016 Panini Torque Holo Silver /10 #6
2016 Panini Torque Holo Silver /10 #83
2016 Panini Torque Horsepower Heroes #9
2016 Panini Torque Horsepower Heroes Gold /199 #9
2016 Panini Torque Horsepower Heroes Holo Silver /99 #9
2016 Panini Torque Jumbo Tire Autographs /50 #10
2016 Panini Torque Jumbo Tire Autographs Blue /25 #10
2016 Panini Torque Jumbo Tire Autographs Green /10 #10
2016 Panini Torque Jumbo Tire Autographs Purple /5 #10
2016 Panini Torque Jumbo Tire Autographs Red /15 #10
2016 Panini Torque Metal Materials /249 #11
2016 Panini Torque Metal Materials Blue /99 #11
2016 Panini Torque Metal Materials Green /25 #11
2016 Panini Torque Metal Materials Purple /10 #11
2016 Panini Torque Metal Materials Red /49 #11
2016 Panini Torque Painted to Perfection #9
2016 Panini Torque Painted to Perfection Blue /99 #9
2016 Panini Torque Painted to Perfection Checkerboard /10 #9
2016 Panini Torque Painted to Perfection Green /25 #9
2016 Panini Torque Painted to Perfection Red /49 #9
2016 Panini Torque Pairings Materials /249 #11
2016 Panini Torque Pairings Materials /249 #12
2016 Panini Torque Pairings Materials Blue /99 #11
2016 Panini Torque Pairings Materials Blue /99 #12
2016 Panini Torque Pairings Materials Green /25 #11
2016 Panini Torque Pairings Materials Green /25 #12
2016 Panini Torque Pairings Materials Purple /10 #11
2016 Panini Torque Pairings Materials Purple /10 #12
2016 Panini Torque Pairings Materials Red /49 #11
2016 Panini Torque Pairings Materials Red /49 #12
2016 Panini Torque Pole Position #6
2016 Panini Torque Pole Position Blue /99 #6
2016 Panini Torque Pole Position Checkerboard /10 #6
2016 Panini Torque Pole Position Green /25 #6
2016 Panini Torque Pole Position Red /49 #6
2016 Panini Torque Printing Plates Black /1 #6
2016 Panini Torque Printing Plates Black /1 #83
2016 Panini Torque Printing Plates Cyan /1 #6
2016 Panini Torque Printing Plates Cyan /1 #83
2016 Panini Torque Printing Plates Magenta /1 #6
2016 Panini Torque Printing Plates Magenta /1 #83
2016 Panini Torque Printing Plates Yellow /1 #6
2016 Panini Torque Printing Plates Yellow /1 #83
2016 Panini Torque Purple /25 #6
2016 Panini Torque Purple /25 #83
2016 Panini Torque Red /99 #6
2016 Panini Torque Red /99 #83
2016 Panini Torque Rubber Relics /399 #9
2016 Panini Torque Rubber Relics Blue /99 #9
2016 Panini Torque Rubber Relics Green /25 #9
2016 Panini Torque Rubber Relics Purple /10 #9
2016 Panini Torque Rubber Relics Red /49 #9
2016 Panini Torque Shades #15
2016 Panini Torque Shades Gold /199 #15
2016 Panini Torque Shades Holo Silver /99 #15
2016 Panini Torque Silhouettes Firesuit Autographs /35 #8
2016 Panini Torque Silhouettes Firesuit Autographs Blue /25 #8
2016 Panini Torque Silhouettes Firesuit Autographs Green /10 #8
2016 Panini Torque Silhouettes Firesuit Autographs Purple /5 #8
2016 Panini Torque Silhouettes Firesuit Autographs Red /15 #8
2016 Panini Torque Silhouettes Sheet Metal Autographs /50 #8
2016 Panini Torque Silhouettes Sheet Metal Autographs Blue /25 #8
2016 Panini Torque Silhouettes Sheet Metal Autographs Green /10 #8
2016 Panini Torque Silhouettes Sheet Metal Autographs Purple /5 #8
2016 Panini Torque Silhouettes Sheet Metal Autographs Red /15 #8
2016 Panini Torque Special Paint #3
2016 Panini Torque Special Paint Gold /199 #3
2016 Panini Torque Special Paint Holo Silver /99 #3
2016 Panini Torque Superstar Vision #16
2016 Panini Torque Superstar Vision Blue /99 #16
2016 Panini Torque Superstar Vision Gold /149 #16
2016 Panini Torque Superstar Vision Green /25 #16
2016 Panini Torque Superstar Vision Purple /10 #16
2016 Panini Torque Superstar Vision Red /49 #16
2016 Panini Torque Test Proof Black /1 #6
2016 Panini Torque Test Proof Black /1 #83
2016 Panini Torque Test Proof Cyan /1 #6
2016 Panini Torque Test Proof Cyan /1 #83
2016 Panini Torque Test Proof Magenta /1 #6
2016 Panini Torque Test Proof Magenta /1 #83
2016 Panini Torque Test Proof Yellow /1 #6
2016 Panini Torque Test Proof Yellow /1 #83
2016 Panini Torque Victory Laps #1
2016 Panini Torque Victory Laps Gold /199 #1
2016 Panini Torque Victory Laps Holo Silver /99 #1
2016 Panini Torque Winning Vision #6
2016 Panini Torque Winning Vision Blue /99 #6
2016 Panini Torque Winning Vision Gold /149 #6
2016 Panini Torque Winning Vision Green /25 #6
2016 Panini Torque Winning Vision Purple /10 #6
2016 Panini Torque Winning Vision Red /49 #6
2017 Donruss #6
2017 Donruss #41
2017 Donruss #129
2017 Donruss #146
2017 Donruss #112
2017 Donruss Artist Proof /25 #6
2017 Donruss Artist Proof /25 #41
2017 Donruss Artist Proof /25 #129
2017 Donruss Artist Proof /25 #146
2017 Donruss Artist Proof /25 #112
2017 Donruss Blue Foil /299 #6
2017 Donruss Blue Foil /299 #129
2017 Donruss Blue Foil /299 #41
2017 Donruss Blue Foil /299 #146
2017 Donruss Blue Foil /299 #112
2017 Donruss Dual Rubber Relics #6
2017 Donruss Dual Rubber Relics Holo Black /1 #6
2017 Donruss Dual Rubber Relics Holo Gold /25 #6
2017 Donruss Gold Foil /499 #6
2017 Donruss Gold Foil /499 #129
2017 Donruss Gold Foil /499 #146
2017 Donruss Gold Foil /499 #41
2017 Donruss Gold Foil /499 #112
2017 Donruss Gold Press Proof /99 #6
2017 Donruss Gold Press Proof /99 #41
2017 Donruss Gold Press Proof /99 #129
2017 Donruss Gold Press Proof /99 #146
2017 Donruss Gold Press Proof /99 #112
2017 Donruss Green Foil /199 #6
2017 Donruss Green Foil /199 #41
2017 Donruss Green Foil /199 #129
2017 Donruss Green Foil /199 #146
2017 Donruss Green Foil /199 #112
2017 Donruss Press Proof /49 #6
2017 Donruss Press Proof /49 #41
2017 Donruss Press Proof /49 #129
2017 Donruss Press Proof /49 #146
2017 Donruss Press Proof /49 #112
2017 Donruss Printing Plates Black /1 #6
2017 Donruss Printing Plates Black /1 #41
2017 Donruss Printing Plates Black /1 #129
2017 Donruss Printing Plates Black /1 #146
2017 Donruss Printing Plates Black /1 #112
2017 Donruss Printing Plates Cyan /1 #6
2017 Donruss Printing Plates Cyan /1 #41
2017 Donruss Printing Plates Cyan /1 #129
2017 Donruss Printing Plates Cyan /1 #146
2017 Donruss Printing Plates Cyan /1 #112
2017 Donruss Printing Plates Magenta /1 #6
2017 Donruss Printing Plates Magenta /1 #129
2017 Donruss Printing Plates Magenta /1 #146
2017 Donruss Printing Plates Magenta /1 #41
2017 Donruss Printing Plates Magenta /1 #112
2017 Donruss Printing Plates Yellow /1 #6
2017 Donruss Printing Plates Yellow /1 #129
2017 Donruss Printing Plates Yellow /1 #146
2017 Donruss Printing Plates Yellow /1 #41
2017 Donruss Printing Plates Yellow /1 #112
2017 Donruss Retro Relics 1984 #15
2017 Donruss Retro Relics 1984 Holo Black /5 #15
2017 Donruss Retro Relics 1984 Holo Gold /99 #15
2017 Donruss Retro Signatures 1984 #8
2017 Donruss Retro Signatures 1984 Holo Black /1 #8
2017 Donruss Retro Signatures 1984 Holo Gold /25 #8
2017 Donruss Rubber Relics #18
2017 Donruss Rubber Relics Holo Black /1 #18
2017 Donruss Rubber Relics Holo Gold /25 #18
2017 Donruss Speed #7
2017 Donruss Speed Cracked Ice /999 #7
2017 Donruss Top Tier #9
2017 Donruss Top Tier Cracked Ice /999 #9
2017 Donruss Track Masters #1
2017 Donruss Track Masters Cracked Ice /999 #1
2017 Panini Black Friday Happy Holiday Memorabilia #HHDH
2017 Panini Black Friday Happy Holiday Memorabilia Cracked Ice /25 #HHDH
2017 Panini Black Friday Happy Holiday Memorabilia Galactic Windows /10 #HHDH
2017 Panini Black Friday Happy Holiday Memorabilia Hyperplaid /1 #HHDH
2017 Panini Instant Nascar #18
2017 Panini Instant Nascar Black /1 #18
2017 Panini Instant Nascar Green /10 #18
2017 Panini National Treasures /25 #6
2017 Panini National Treasures Associate Sponsor Patch Signatures 1 /1 #5
2017 Panini National Treasures Associate Sponsor Patch Signatures 2 /1 #5
2017 Panini National Treasures Associate Sponsor Patch Signatures 3 /1 #5
2017 Panini National Treasures Associate Sponsor Patch Signatures 4 /1 #5
2017 Panini National Treasures Associate Sponsor Patch Signatures 5 /1 #5
2017 Panini National Treasures Car Manufacturer Patch Signatures /1 #5
2017 Panini National Treasures Century Black /1 #6
2017 Panini National Treasures Century Gold /15 #6
2017 Panini National Treasures Century Green /5 #6
2017 Panini National Treasures Century Holo Gold /10 #6
2017 Panini National Treasures Century Holo Silver /20 #6
2017 Panini National Treasures Century Laundry Tags /1 #6
2017 Panini National Treasures Combo Material Signatures /25 #6
2017 Panini National Treasures Combo Material Signatures Black /1 #6
2017 Panini National Treasures Combo Material Signatures Gold /15 #6
2017 Panini National Treasures Combo Material Signatures Green /5 #6
2017 Panini National Treasures Combo Material Signatures Holo Gold /10 #6
2017 Panini National Treasures Combo Material Signatures Holo Silver /20 #6
2017 Panini National Treasures Dual Sheet Metal Materials Black /1 #6
2017 Panini National Treasures Dual Sheet Metal Materials Printing Plates Black /1 #6
2017 Panini National Treasures Dual Sheet Metal Materials Printing Plates Cyan /1 #6
2017 Panini National Treasures Dual Sheet Metal Materials Printing Plates Magenta /1 #6
2017 Panini National Treasures Dual Sheet Metal Materials Printing Plates Yellow /1 #6
2017 Panini National Treasures Dual Sheet Metal Signatures Black /1 #14
2017 Panini National Treasures Dual Sheet Metal Signatures Green /5 #14
2017 Panini National Treasures Dual Sheet Metal Signatures Holo Gold /10 #14
2017 Panini National Treasures Dual Sheet Metal Signatures Printing Plates Black /1 #14
2017 Panini National Treasures Dual Sheet Metal Signatures Printing Plates Cyan /1 #14
2017 Panini National Treasures Dual Sheet Metal Signatures Printing Plates Magenta /1 #14
2017 Panini National Treasures Dual Sheet Metal Signatures Printing Plates Yellow /1 #14
2017 Panini National Treasures Dual Tire Signatures /25 #2
2017 Panini National Treasures Dual Tire Signatures Black /1 #2
2017 Panini National Treasures Dual Tire Signatures Gold /15 #2
2017 Panini National Treasures Dual Tire Signatures Green /5 #2
2017 Panini National Treasures Dual Tire Signatures Holo Gold /10 #2
2017 Panini National Treasures Dual Tire Signatures Holo Silver /20 #2
2017 Panini National Treasures Dual Tire Signatures Printing Plates Black /1 #2
2017 Panini National Treasures Dual Tire Signatures Printing Plates Cyan /1 #2
2017 Panini National Treasures Dual Tire Signatures Printing Plates Magenta /1 #2
2017 Panini National Treasures Dual Tire Signatures Printing Plates Yellow /1 #2
2017 Panini National Treasures Firesuit Manufacturer Patch Signatures /1 #5
2017 Panini National Treasures Flag Patch Signatures /1 #5
2017 Panini National Treasures Hats Off /14 #22
2017 Panini National Treasures Hats Off /14 #23
2017 Panini National Treasures Hats Off Gold /4 #22
2017 Panini National Treasures Hats Off Gold /2 #23
2017 Panini National Treasures Hats Off Holo Gold /5 #22
2017 Panini National Treasures Hats Off Holo Gold /5 #23
2017 Panini National Treasures Hats Off Holo Silver /1 #22
2017 Panini National Treasures Hats Off Holo Silver /1 #23
2017 Panini National Treasures Hats Off Laundry Tag /6 #22
2017 Panini National Treasures Hats Off Laundry Tag /6 #23
2017 Panini National Treasures Hats Off Monster Energy Cup /14 #11
2017 Panini National Treasures Hats Off Monster Energy Cup Gold /4 #11
2017 Panini National Treasures Hats Off Monster Energy Cup Holo Gold /5 #11
2017 Panini National Treasures Hats Off Monster Energy Cup Holo Silver /1 #11
2017 Panini National Treasures Hats Off Monster Energy Cup Laundry Tag /6 #11
2017 Panini National Treasures Hats Off Monster Energy Cup New Era /1 #11
2017 Panini National Treasures Hats Off Monster Energy Cup Printing Plates Black /1 #11
2017 Panini National Treasures Hats Off Monster Energy Cup Printing Plates Cyan /1 #11
2017 Panini National Treasures Hats Off Monster Energy Cup Printing Plates Magenta /1 #11
2017 Panini National Treasures Hats Off Monster Energy Cup Printing Plates Yellow /1 #11
2017 Panini National Treasures Hats Off Monster Energy Cup Sponsor /5 #11
2017 Panini National Treasures Hats Off New Era /1 #22
2017 Panini National Treasures Hats Off New Era /1 #23
2017 Panini National Treasures Hats Off Printing Plates Black /1 #22
2017 Panini National Treasures Hats Off Printing Plates Black /1 #23
2017 Panini National Treasures Hats Off Printing Plates Cyan /1 #22
2017 Panini National Treasures Hats Off Printing Plates Cyan /1 #23
2017 Panini National Treasures Hats Off Printing Plates Magenta /1 #22
2017 Panini National Treasures Hats Off Printing Plates Magenta /1 #23
2017 Panini National Treasures Hats Off Printing Plates Yellow /1 #22
2017 Panini National Treasures Hats Off Sponsor /10 #22
2017 Panini National Treasures Hats Off Sponsor /5 #23
2017 Panini National Treasures Jumbo Firesuit Materials /25 #4
2017 Panini National Treasures Jumbo Firesuit Materials Black /1 #4
2017 Panini National Treasures Jumbo Firesuit Materials Gold /15 #4
2017 Panini National Treasures Jumbo Firesuit Materials Green /5 #4
2017 Panini National Treasures Jumbo Firesuit Materials Holo Gold /10 #4
2017 Panini National Treasures Jumbo Firesuit Materials Holo Silver /20 #4
2017 Panini National Treasures Jumbo Firesuit Materials Laundry Tag /1 #4
2017 Panini National Treasures Jumbo Firesuit Materials Printing Plates Black /1 #4
2017 Panini National Treasures Jumbo Firesuit Materials Printing Plates Cyan /1 #4
2017 Panini National Treasures Jumbo Firesuit Materials Printing Plates Magenta /1 #4
2017 Panini National Treasures Jumbo Firesuit Materials Printing Plates Yellow /1 #4
2017 Panini National Treasures Jumbo Sheet Metal Materials Black /1 #9
2017 Panini National Treasures Jumbo Sheet Metal Materials Printing Plates Black /1 #9
2017 Panini National Treasures Jumbo Sheet Metal Materials Printing Plates Cyan /1 #9
2017 Panini National Treasures Jumbo Sheet Metal Materials Printing Plates Magenta /1 #9
2017 Panini National Treasures Jumbo Sheet Metal Materials Printing Plates Yellow /1 #9
2017 Panini National Treasures Nameplate Patch Signatures /2 #5
2017 Panini National Treasures NASCAR Patch Signatures /1 #5
2017 Panini National Treasures Printing Plates Black /1 #6
2017 Panini National Treasures Printing Plates Cyan /1 #6
2017 Panini National Treasures Printing Plates Magenta /1 #6
2017 Panini National Treasures Printing Plates Yellow /1 #6
2017 Panini National Treasures Quad Material Signatures Black /1 #5
2017 Panini National Treasures Quad Material Signatures Green /5 #5
2017 Panini National Treasures Quad Material Signatures Laundry Tag /1 #5
2017 Panini National Treasures Quad Material Signatures Printing Plates Black /1 #5
2017 Panini National Treasures Quad Material Signatures Printing Plates Cyan /1 #5
2017 Panini National Treasures Quad Material Signatures Printing Plates Magenta /1 #5
2017 Panini National Treasures Quad Material Signatures Printing Plates Yellow /1 #5
2017 Panini National Treasures Quad Materials /25 #3
2017 Panini National Treasures Quad Materials Black /1 #3
2017 Panini National Treasures Quad Materials Gold /15 #3
2017 Panini National Treasures Quad Materials Green /5 #3
2017 Panini National Treasures Quad Materials Holo Gold /10 #3
2017 Panini National Treasures Quad Materials Holo Silver /20 #3
2017 Panini National Treasures Quad Materials Laundry Tag /1 #3
2017 Panini National Treasures Quad Materials Printing Plates Black /1 #3
2017 Panini National Treasures Quad Materials Printing Plates Cyan /1 #3
2017 Panini National Treasures Quad Materials Printing Plates Magenta /1 #3
2017 Panini National Treasures Quad Materials Printing Plates Yellow /1 #3
2017 Panini National Treasures Series Sponsor Patch Signatures /1 #5
2017 Panini National Treasures Signature Sheet Metal Black /1 #1
2017 Panini National Treasures Signature Sheet Metal Green /5 #1
2017 Panini National Treasures Signature Sheet Metal Holo Gold /10 #1
2017 Panini National Treasures Signature Six Way Swatches /25 #8
2017 Panini National Treasures Signature Six Way Swatches Black /1 #8
2017 Panini National Treasures Signature Six Way Swatches Gold /15 #8
2017 Panini National Treasures Signature Six Way Swatches Green /5 #8
2017 Panini National Treasures Signature Six Way Swatches Holo Gold /10 #8
2017 Panini National Treasures Signature Six Way Swatches Holo Silver /20 #8
2017 Panini National Treasures Signature Six Way Swatches Laundry Tag /1 #8
2017 Panini National Treasures Sunoco Patch Signatures /1 #5
2017 Panini National Treasures Teammates Dual Materials /25 #7
2017 Panini National Treasures Teammates Dual Materials Black /1 #7
2017 Panini National Treasures Teammates Dual Materials Gold /15 #7
2017 Panini National Treasures Teammates Dual Materials Green /5 #7
2017 Panini National Treasures Teammates Dual Materials Holo Gold /10 #7
2017 Panini National Treasures Teammates Dual Materials Holo Silver /20 #7
2017 Panini National Treasures Teammates Dual Materials Laundry Tag /1 #7
2017 Panini National Treasures Teammates Dual Materials Printing Plates Black /1 #7
2017 Panini National Treasures Teammates Dual Materials Printing Plates Cyan /1 #7
2017 Panini National Treasures Teammates Dual Materials Printing Plates Magenta /1 #7
2017 Panini National Treasures Teammates Dual Materials Printing Plates Yellow /1 #7
2017 Panini National Treasures Teammates Quad Materials /25 #7
2017 Panini National Treasures Teammates Quad Materials Black /1 #7
2017 Panini National Treasures Teammates Quad Materials Gold /15 #7
2017 Panini National Treasures Teammates Quad Materials Green /5 #7
2017 Panini National Treasures Teammates Quad Materials Holo Gold /10 #7
2017 Panini National Treasures Teammates Quad Materials Holo Silver /20 #7
2017 Panini National Treasures Teammates Quad Materials Laundry Tag /1 #7
2017 Panini National Treasures Teammates Quad Materials Printing Plates Black /1 #7
2017 Panini National Treasures Teammates Quad Materials Printing Plates Cyan /1 #7
2017 Panini National Treasures Teammates Quad Materials Printing Plates Magenta /1 #7
2017 Panini National Treasures Teammates Quad Materials Printing Plates Yellow /1 #7
2017 Panini National Treasures Teammates Triple Materials /25 #3
2017 Panini National Treasures Teammates Triple Materials Black /1 #3
2017 Panini National Treasures Teammates Triple Materials Gold /15 #3
2017 Panini National Treasures Teammates Triple Materials Green /5 #3
2017 Panini National Treasures Teammates Triple Materials Holo Gold /10 #3
2017 Panini National Treasures Teammates Triple Materials Holo Silver /20 #3
2017 Panini National Treasures Teammates Triple Materials Laundry Tag /1 #3
2017 Panini National Treasures Teammates Triple Materials Printing Plates Black /1 #3
2017 Panini National Treasures Teammates Triple Materials Printing Plates Cyan /1 #3
2017 Panini National Treasures Teammates Triple Materials Printing Plates Magenta /1 #3
2017 Panini National Treasures Teammates Triple Materials Printing Plates Yellow /1 #3
2017 Panini National Treasures Winning Material Signatures Black /1 #8
2017 Panini National Treasures Winning Material Signatures Green /5 #8
2017 Panini National Treasures Winning Material Signatures Holo Gold /10 #8
2017 Panini National Treasures Winning Material Signatures Laundry Tag /1 #8
2017 Panini National Treasures Winning Material Signatures Printing Plates Black /1 #8
2017 Panini National Treasures Winning Material Signatures Printing Plates Cyan /1 #8
2017 Panini National Treasures Winning Material Signatures Printing Plates Magenta /1 #8
2017 Panini National Treasures Winning Material Signatures Printing Plates Yellow /1 #8
2017 Panini National Treasures Winning Signatures /99 #14
2017 Panini National Treasures Winning Signatures Black /1 #14
2017 Panini National Treasures Winning Signatures Gold /25 #14
2017 Panini National Treasures Winning Signatures Green /5 #14
2017 Panini National Treasures Winning Signatures Holo Gold /15 #14
2017 Panini National Treasures Winning Signatures Holo Silver /50 #14
2017 Panini National Treasures Winning Signatures Printing Plates Black /1 #14
2017 Panini National Treasures Winning Signatures Printing Plates Cyan /1 #14
2017 Panini National Treasures Winning Signatures Printing Plates Magenta /1 #14
2017 Panini National Treasures Winning Signatures Printing Plates Yellow /1 #14
2017 Panini Torque #6
2017 Panini Torque #67
2017 Panini Torque #80
2017 Panini Torque #89
2017 Panini Torque #99
2017 Panini Torque Artist Proof /75 #6
2017 Panini Torque Artist Proof /75 #67
2017 Panini Torque Artist Proof /75 #80
2017 Panini Torque Artist Proof /75 #89
2017 Panini Torque Artist Proof /75 #99
2017 Panini Torque Blackout /1 #6
2017 Panini Torque Blackout /1 #67
2017 Panini Torque Blackout /1 #80
2017 Panini Torque Blackout /1 #89
2017 Panini Torque Blackout /1 #99
2017 Panini Torque Blue /150 #6
2017 Panini Torque Blue /150 #67
2017 Panini Torque Blue /150 #80
2017 Panini Torque Blue /150 #89
2017 Panini Torque Blue /150 #99
2017 Panini Torque Claiming The Chase #7
2017 Panini Torque Claiming The Chase Gold /199 #7
2017 Panini Torque Claiming The Chase Holo Silver /99 #7
2017 Panini Torque Clear Vision #11
2017 Panini Torque Clear Vision Blue /99 #11
2017 Panini Torque Clear Vision Gold /149 #11
2017 Panini Torque Clear Vision Green /25 #11
2017 Panini Torque Clear Vision Purple /10 #11
2017 Panini Torque Clear Vision Red /49 #11
2017 Panini Torque Combo Materials Signatures /51 #3
2017 Panini Torque Combo Materials Signatures Blue /49 #3
2017 Panini Torque Combo Materials Signatures Green /15 #3
2017 Panini Torque Combo Materials Signatures Purple /10 #3
2017 Panini Torque Combo Materials Signatures Red /25 #3
2017 Panini Torque Dual Materials /49 #11
2017 Panini Torque Dual Materials Blue /25 #11
2017 Panini Torque Dual Materials Green /10 #11
2017 Panini Torque Dual Materials Purple /1 #11
2017 Panini Torque Dual Materials Red /15 #11
2017 Panini Torque Gold #6
2017 Panini Torque Gold #67
2017 Panini Torque Gold #80
2017 Panini Torque Gold #89
2017 Panini Torque Gold #99
2017 Panini Torque Holo Gold /10 #6
2017 Panini Torque Holo Gold /10 #67
2017 Panini Torque Holo Gold /10 #80
2017 Panini Torque Holo Gold /10 #89
2017 Panini Torque Holo Gold /10 #99
2017 Panini Torque Holo Silver /25 #6
2017 Panini Torque Holo Silver /25 #67
2017 Panini Torque Holo Silver /25 #80
2017 Panini Torque Holo Silver /25 #89
2017 Panini Torque Holo Silver /25 #99
2017 Panini Torque Horsepower Heroes #9
2017 Panini Torque Horsepower Heroes Gold /199 #9
2017 Panini Torque Horsepower Heroes Holo Silver /99 #9
2017 Panini Torque Jumbo Firesuit Signatures /51 #7
2017 Panini Torque Jumbo Firesuit Signatures Blue /49 #7
2017 Panini Torque Jumbo Firesuit Signatures Green /15 #7
2017 Panini Torque Jumbo Firesuit Signatures Purple /10 #7
2017 Panini Torque Jumbo Firesuit Signatures Red /25 #7
2017 Panini Torque Manufacturer Marks #12
2017 Panini Torque Manufacturer Marks Gold /199 #12
2017 Panini Torque Manufacturer Marks Holo Silver /99 #12
2017 Panini Torque Pairings Materials /99 #9
2017 Panini Torque Pairings Materials Blue /49 #9
2017 Panini Torque Pairings Materials Green /10 #9
2017 Panini Torque Pairings Materials Purple /1 #9
2017 Panini Torque Pairings Materials Red /25 #9
2017 Panini Torque Primary Paint #14
2017 Panini Torque Primary Paint Blue /99 #14
2017 Panini Torque Primary Paint Checkerboard /10 #14
2017 Panini Torque Primary Paint Green /25 #14
2017 Panini Torque Primary Paint Red /49 #14
2017 Panini Torque Printing Plates Black /1 #6
2017 Panini Torque Printing Plates Black /1 #67
2017 Panini Torque Printing Plates Black /1 #80
2017 Panini Torque Printing Plates Black /1 #89
2017 Panini Torque Printing Plates Black /1 #99
2017 Panini Torque Printing Plates Cyan /1 #6
2017 Panini Torque Printing Plates Cyan /1 #67
2017 Panini Torque Printing Plates Cyan /1 #80
2017 Panini Torque Printing Plates Cyan /1 #89
2017 Panini Torque Printing Plates Cyan /1 #99
2017 Panini Torque Printing Plates Magenta /1 #6
2017 Panini Torque Printing Plates Magenta /1 #67
2017 Panini Torque Printing Plates Magenta /1 #80
2017 Panini Torque Printing Plates Magenta /1 #89
2017 Panini Torque Printing Plates Magenta /1 #99
2017 Panini Torque Printing Plates Yellow /1 #6
2017 Panini Torque Printing Plates Yellow /1 #67
2017 Panini Torque Printing Plates Yellow /1 #80
2017 Panini Torque Printing Plates Yellow /1 #89
2017 Panini Torque Printing Plates Yellow /1 #99
2017 Panini Torque Purple /50 #6
2017 Panini Torque Purple /50 #67
2017 Panini Torque Purple /50 #80
2017 Panini Torque Purple /50 #89
2017 Panini Torque Purple /50 #99
2017 Panini Torque Quad Materials Blue /15 #10
2017 Panini Torque Quad Materials Green /5 #10
2017 Panini Torque Quad Materials Purple /1 #10
2017 Panini Torque Quad Materials Red /10 #10
2017 Panini Torque Red /100 #6
2017 Panini Torque Red /100 #67
2017 Panini Torque Red /100 #80
2017 Panini Torque Red /100 #89
2017 Panini Torque Red /100 #99
2017 Panini Torque Running Order #6
2017 Panini Torque Running Order Blue /99 #6
2017 Panini Torque Running Order Checkerboard /10 #6
2017 Panini Torque Running Order Green /25 #6
2017 Panini Torque Running Order Red /49 #6
2017 Panini Torque Superstar Vision #8
2017 Panini Torque Superstar Vision Blue /99 #8
2017 Panini Torque Superstar Vision Gold /149 #8
2017 Panini Torque Superstar Vision Green /25 #8
2017 Panini Torque Superstar Vision Purple /10 #8
2017 Panini Torque Superstar Vision Red /49 #8
2017 Panini Torque Test Proof Black /1 #6
2017 Panini Torque Test Proof Black /1 #67
2017 Panini Torque Test Proof Black /1 #80
2017 Panini Torque Test Proof Black /1 #89
2017 Panini Torque Test Proof Black /1 #99
2017 Panini Torque Test Proof Cyan /1 #6
2017 Panini Torque Test Proof Cyan /1 #67
2017 Panini Torque Test Proof Cyan /1 #80
2017 Panini Torque Test Proof Cyan /1 #89
2017 Panini Torque Test Proof Cyan /1 #99
2017 Panini Torque Test Proof Magenta /1 #6
2017 Panini Torque Test Proof Magenta /1 #67
2017 Panini Torque Test Proof Magenta /1 #80
2017 Panini Torque Test Proof Magenta /1 #89
2017 Panini Torque Test Proof Magenta /1 #99
2017 Panini Torque Test Proof Yellow /1 #6
2017 Panini Torque Test Proof Yellow /1 #67
2017 Panini Torque Test Proof Yellow /1 #80
2017 Panini Torque Test Proof Yellow /1 #89
2017 Panini Torque Test Proof Yellow /1 #99
2017 Panini Torque Trackside #5
2017 Panini Torque Trackside Blue /99 #5
2017 Panini Torque Trackside Checkerboard /10 #5
2017 Panini Torque Trackside Green /25 #5
2017 Panini Torque Trackside Red /49 #5
2017 Panini Torque Victory Laps #7
2017 Panini Torque Victory Laps Gold /199 #7
2017 Panini Torque Victory Laps Holo Silver /99 #7
2017 Select #91
2017 Select #112
2017 Select Prizms Black /3 #91
2017 Select Prizms Black /3 #112
2017 Select Prizms Blue /199 #91
2017 Select Prizms Checkered Flag /1 #91
2017 Select Prizms Checkered Flag /1 #112
2017 Select Prizms Gold /10 #91
2017 Select Prizms Gold /10 #112
2017 Select Prizms Purple Pulsar #91
2017 Select Prizms Red /99 #91
2017 Select Prizms Red White and Blue Pulsar /299 #91
2017 Select Prizms Silver #91
2017 Select Prizms Tie Dye /24 #91
2017 Select Prizms Tie Dye /24 #112
2017 Select Prizms White /50 #91
2017 Select Prizms White /50 #112
2017 Select Select Pairs Materials #20
2017 Select Select Pairs Materials #21
2017 Select Select Pairs Materials #22
2017 Select Select Pairs Materials Prizms Blue /199 #20
2017 Select Select Pairs Materials Prizms Blue /199 #21
2017 Select Select Pairs Materials Prizms Blue /199 #22
2017 Select Select Pairs Materials Prizms Checkered Flag /1 #20
2017 Select Select Pairs Materials Prizms Checkered Flag /1 #21
2017 Select Select Pairs Materials Prizms Checkered Flag /1 #22
2017 Select Select Pairs Materials Prizms Gold /10 #20
2017 Select Select Pairs Materials Prizms Gold /10 #21
2017 Select Select Pairs Materials Prizms Gold /10 #22
2017 Select Select Pairs Materials Prizms Red /99 #20
2017 Select Select Pairs Materials Prizms Red /99 #21
2017 Select Select Pairs Materials Prizms Red /99 #22
2017 Select Select Swatches #17
2017 Select Select Swatches Prizms Blue /199 #17
2017 Select Select Swatches Prizms Checkered Flag /1 #17
2017 Select Select Swatches Prizms Gold /10 #17
2017 Select Select Swatches Prizms Red /99 #17
2017 Select Sheet Metal #8
2017 Select Sheet Metal Prizms Blue /150 #8
2017 Select Sheet Metal Prizms Checkered Flag /1 #8
2017 Select Sheet Metal Prizms Gold /10 #8
2017 Select Sheet Metal Prizms Red /99 #8
2017 Select Signature Paint Schemes #4
2017 Select Signature Paint Schemes Prizms Blue /50 #4
2017 Select Signature Paint Schemes Prizms Checkered Flag /1 #4
2017 Select Signature Paint Schemes Prizms Gold /10 #4
2017 Select Signature Paint Schemes Prizms Red /25 #4
2017 Select Signature Swatches #17
2017 Select Signature Swatches Prizms Checkered Flag /1 #17
2017 Select Signature Swatches Prizms Gold /10 #17
2017 Select Signature Swatches Prizms Tie Dye /24 #17
2017 Select Signature Swatches Prizms White /50 #17
2017 Select Signature Swatches Triple #10
2017 Select Signature Swatches Triple Prizms Checkered Flag /1 #10
2017 Select Signature Swatches Triple Prizms Gold /10 #10
2017 Select Signature Swatches Triple Prizms Tie Dye /24 #10
2017 Select Signature Swatches Triple Prizms White /50 #10
2017 Select Speed Merchants #20
2017 Select Speed Merchants Prizms Black /3 #20
2017 Select Speed Merchants Prizms Checkered Flag /1 #20
2017 Select Speed Merchants Prizms Gold /10 #20
2017 Select Speed Merchants Prizms Tie Dye /24 #20
2017 Select Speed Merchants Prizms White /50 #20
2018 Certified #69
2018 Certified #100
2018 Certified All Certified Team /199 #18
2018 Certified All Certified Team Black /1 #18
2018 Certified All Certified Team Blue /99 #18
2018 Certified All Certified Team Gold /49 #18
2018 Certified All Certified Team Green /10 #18
2018 Certified All Certified Team Mirror Black /1 #18
2018 Certified All Certified Team Mirror Gold /25 #18
2018 Certified All Certified Team Mirror Green /5 #18
2018 Certified All Certified Team Mirror Purple /10 #18
2018 Certified All Certified Team Purple /25 #18
2018 Certified All Certified Team Red /149 #18
2018 Certified Black /1 #69
2018 Certified Black /1 #100
2018 Certified Blue /99 #69
2018 Certified Blue /99 #100
2018 Certified Cup Swatches /299 #10
2018 Certified Cup Swatches Black /1 #10
2018 Certified Cup Swatches Blue /49 #10
2018 Certified Cup Swatches Gold /25 #10
2018 Certified Cup Swatches Green /5 #10
2018 Certified Cup Swatches Purple /10 #10
2018 Certified Cup Swatches Red /199 #10
2018 Certified Epix /199 #5
2018 Certified Epix Black /1 #5
2018 Certified Epix Blue /99 #5
2018 Certified Epix Gold /49 #5
2018 Certified Epix Green /10 #5
2018 Certified Epix Mirror Black /1 #5
2018 Certified Epix Mirror Gold /25 #5
2018 Certified Epix Mirror Green /5 #5
2018 Certified Epix Mirror Purple /10 #5
2018 Certified Epix Purple /25 #5
2018 Certified Epix Red /149 #5
2018 Certified Gold /49 #69
2018 Certified Gold /49 #100
2018 Certified Green /10 #69
2018 Certified Green /10 #100
2018 Certified Mirror Black /1 #69
2018 Certified Mirror Black /1 #100
2018 Certified Mirror Gold /25 #69
2018 Certified Mirror Gold /25 #100
2018 Certified Mirror Green /5 #69
2018 Certified Mirror Green /5 #100
2018 Certified Mirror Purple /10 #69
2018 Certified Mirror Purple /10 #100
2018 Certified Orange /249 #69
2018 Certified Orange /249 #100
2018 Certified Piece of the Race Black /1 #15
2018 Certified Piece of the Race Blue /49 #15
2018 Certified Piece of the Race Gold /25 #15
2018 Certified Piece of the Race Green /5 #15
2018 Certified Piece of the Race Purple /10 #15
2018 Certified Piece of the Race Red /199 #15
2018 Certified Purple /25 #69
2018 Certified Purple /25 #100
2018 Certified Red /199 #69
2018 Certified Red /199 #100
2018 Certified Signature Swatches /99 #7
2018 Certified Signature Swatches Black /1 #7
2018 Certified Signature Swatches Blue /49 #7
2018 Certified Signature Swatches Gold /25 #7
2018 Certified Signature Swatches Green /5 #7
2018 Certified Signature Swatches Purple /10 #7
2018 Certified Signature Swatches Red /75 #7
2018 Certified Signing Sessions /49 #6
2018 Certified Signing Sessions Black /1 #6
2018 Certified Signing Sessions Gold /15 #6
2018 Certified Signing Sessions Green /5 #6
2018 Certified Signing Sessions Purple /10 #6
2018 Certified Signing Sessions Red /25 #6

2018 Certified Skills /199 #6
2018 Certified Skills Black /1 #6
2018 Certified Skills Blue /99 #6
2018 Certified Skills Gold /49 #6
2018 Certified Skills Green /10 #6
2018 Certified Skills Mirror Black /1 #6
2018 Certified Skills Mirror Gold /25 #6
2018 Certified Skills Mirror Green /5 #6
2018 Certified Skills Mirror Purple /10 #6
2018 Certified Skills Purple /25 #6
2018 Certified Skills Red /149 #6
2018 Certified Stars /199 #2
2018 Certified Stars Black /1 #2
2018 Certified Stars Blue /99 #2
2018 Certified Stars Gold /49 #2
2018 Certified Stars Green /10 #2
2018 Certified Stars Mirror Black /1 #2
2018 Certified Stars Mirror Gold /25 #2
2018 Certified Stars Mirror Green /5 #2
2018 Certified Stars Mirror Purple /10 #2
2018 Certified Stars Purple /25 #2
2018 Certified Stars Red /149 #2
2018 Donruss #11
2018 Donruss #38
2018 Donruss #92
2018 Donruss #128
2018 Donruss Artist Proofs /25 #11
2018 Donruss Artist Proofs /25 #38
2018 Donruss Artist Proofs /25 #92
2018 Donruss Artist Proofs /25 #128
2018 Donruss Elite Series /999 #5
2018 Donruss Gold Foil /499 #11
2018 Donruss Gold Foil /499 #38
2018 Donruss Gold Foil /499 #92
2018 Donruss Gold Foil /499 #128
2018 Donruss Gold Press Proofs /99 #11
2018 Donruss Gold Press Proofs /99 #38
2018 Donruss Gold Press Proofs /99 #92
2018 Donruss Gold Press Proofs /99 #128
2018 Donruss Green Foil /199 #11
2018 Donruss Green Foil /199 #38
2018 Donruss Green Foil /199 #92
2018 Donruss Green Foil /199 #128
2018 Donruss Press Proofs /49 #11
2018 Donruss Press Proofs /49 #38
2018 Donruss Press Proofs /49 #92
2018 Donruss Press Proofs /49 #128
2018 Donruss Printing Plates Black /1 #11
2018 Donruss Printing Plates Black /1 #38
2018 Donruss Printing Plates Black /1 #92
2018 Donruss Printing Plates Black /1 #128
2018 Donruss Printing Plates Cyan /1 #11
2018 Donruss Printing Plates Cyan /1 #38
2018 Donruss Printing Plates Cyan /1 #92
2018 Donruss Printing Plates Cyan /1 #128
2018 Donruss Printing Plates Magenta /1 #11
2018 Donruss Printing Plates Magenta /1 #38
2018 Donruss Printing Plates Magenta /1 #92
2018 Donruss Printing Plates Magenta /1 #128
2018 Donruss Printing Plates Yellow /1 #11
2018 Donruss Printing Plates Yellow /1 #38
2018 Donruss Printing Plates Yellow /1 #92
2018 Donruss Printing Plates Yellow /1 #128
2018 Donruss Racing Relics #11
2018 Donruss Racing Relics Black /5 #11
2018 Donruss Racing Relics Holo Gold /99 #11
2018 Donruss Red Foil /299 #11
2018 Donruss Red Foil /299 #38
2018 Donruss Red Foil /299 #92
2018 Donruss Red Foil /299 #128
2018 Donruss Retro Relics '85 #8
2018 Donruss Retro Relics '85 Black /10 #8
2018 Donruss Retro Relics '85 Holo Gold /99 #8
2018 Donruss Rubber Relic Signatures #7
2018 Donruss Rubber Relic Signatures Black /1 #7
2018 Donruss Rubber Relic Signatures Holo Gold /25 #7
2018 Donruss Rubber Relics #18
2018 Donruss Rubber Relics Black /10 #18
2018 Donruss Rubber Relics Holo Gold /99 #18
2018 Donruss Studio #16
2018 Donruss Studio Cracked Ice /999 #16
2018 Donruss Studio Xplosion /99 #16
2018 Panini Father's Day Racing Memorabilia #DH
2018 Panini Father's Day Racing Memorabilia Checkerboard /10 #DH
2018 Panini Father's Day Racing Memorabilia Cracked Ice /25 #DH
2018 Panini Father's Day Racing Memorabilia Escher Squares /5 #DH
2018 Panini Father's Day Racing Memorabilia Hyperplaid /1 #DH
2018 Panini Prime /50 #7
2018 Panini Prime /50 #41
2018 Panini Prime /50 #74
2018 Panini Prime Autograph Materials /50 #10
2018 Panini Prime Autograph Materials Black /1 #10
2018 Panini Prime Autograph Materials Holo Gold /25 #10
2018 Panini Prime Autograph Materials Laundry Tag /1 #10
2018 Panini Prime Black /1 #7
2018 Panini Prime Black /1 #41
2018 Panini Prime Black /1 #74
2018 Panini Prime Clear Silhouettes /99 #10
2018 Panini Prime Clear Silhouettes Black /1 #10
2018 Panini Prime Clear Silhouettes Dual /99 #10
2018 Panini Prime Clear Silhouettes Dual Black /1 #10
2018 Panini Prime Clear Silhouettes Dual Holo Gold /50 #10
2018 Panini Prime Clear Silhouettes Holo Gold /50 #10
2018 Panini Prime Dual Material Autographs /99 #4
2018 Panini Prime Dual Material Autographs Black /1 #4
2018 Panini Prime Dual Material Autographs Holo Gold /50 #4
2018 Panini Prime Dual Material Autographs Laundry Tag /1 #4
2018 Panini Prime Dual Signatures /10 #12
2018 Panini Prime Dual Signatures Black /1 #12
2018 Panini Prime Dual Signatures Holo Gold /5 #12
2018 Panini Prime Hats Off Button /1 #3
2018 Panini Prime Hats Off Driver Name /1 #3
2018 Panini Prime Hats Off Eyelet /6 #3
2018 Panini Prime Hats Off Headband /36 #3
2018 Panini Prime Hats Off Laundry Tag /1 #3
2018 Panini Prime Hats Off New Era /1 #3
2018 Panini Prime Hats Off Number /2 #3
2018 Panini Prime Hats Off Sponsor Logo /6 #3
2018 Panini Prime Hats Off Team Logo /2 #3
2018 Panini Prime Holo Gold /25 #7
2018 Panini Prime Holo Gold /25 #41
2018 Panini Prime Holo Gold /25 #74
2018 Panini Prime Prime Jumbo Associate Sponsor 1 /1 #28
2018 Panini Prime Prime Jumbo Associate Sponsor 2 /1 #28
2018 Panini Prime Prime Jumbo Associate Sponsor 3 /1 #28
2018 Panini Prime Prime Jumbo Associate Sponsor 4 /1 #28
2018 Panini Prime Prime Jumbo Associate Sponsor 5 /1 #28
2018 Panini Prime Prime Jumbo Associate Sponsor 6 /1 #28
2018 Panini Prime Prime Jumbo Car Manufacturer /1 #28
2018 Panini Prime Prime Jumbo Firesuit Manufacturer /1 #28
2018 Panini Prime Prime Jumbo Flag Patch /1 #28
2018 Panini Prime Prime Jumbo Glove Manufacturer Patch /1 #28
2018 Panini Prime Prime Jumbo Glove Name Patch /1 #28
2018 Panini Prime Prime Jumbo Glove Number Patch /1 #28
2018 Panini Prime Prime Jumbo Goodyear /2 #28
2018 Panini Prime Prime Jumbo Nameplate /2 #28
2018 Panini Prime Prime Jumbo NASCAR /1 #28
2018 Panini Prime Prime Jumbo Prime Colors /6 #28
2018 Panini Prime Prime Jumbo Series Sponsor /1 #28
2018 Panini Prime Prime Jumbo Shoe Brand Logo /1 #28
2018 Panini Prime Prime Jumbo Shoe Name Patch /1 #28
2018 Panini Prime Prime Jumbo Shoe Number Patch /1 #28
2018 Panini Prime Prime Jumbo Sunoco /1 #28
2018 Panini Prime Prime Number Signatures /50 #5
2018 Panini Prime Prime Number Signatures Black /1 #5
2018 Panini Prime Prime Number Signatures Holo Gold /11 #5
2018 Panini Prime Race Used Duals Firesuit /50 #16
2018 Panini Prime Race Used Duals Firesuit Black /1 #16
2018 Panini Prime Race Used Duals Firesuit Holo Gold /25 #16
2018 Panini Prime Race Used Duals Firesuit Laundry Tag /1 #16
2018 Panini Prime Race Used Duals Sheet Metal /50 #16
2018 Panini Prime Race Used Duals Sheet Metal Black /1 #16
2018 Panini Prime Race Used Duals Sheet Metal Holo Gold /25 #16
2018 Panini Prime Race Used Duals Tire /50 #16
2018 Panini Prime Race Used Duals Tire Black /1 #16
2018 Panini Prime Race Used Duals Tire Holo Gold /25 #16
2018 Panini Prime Race Used Firesuits Black /1 #13
2018 Panini Prime Race Used Firesuits Holo Gold /25 #13
2018 Panini Prime Race Used Firesuits Laundry Tag /1 #13
2018 Panini Prime Race Used Sheet Metal /50 #13
2018 Panini Prime Race Used Sheet Metal Black /1 #13
2018 Panini Prime Race Used Sheet Metal Holo Gold /25 #13
2018 Panini Prime Race Used Tires Black /1 #13
2018 Panini Prime Race Used Tires Holo Gold /25 #13
2018 Panini Prime Race Used Trios Firesuit Black /1 #11
2018 Panini Prime Race Used Trios Firesuit Laundry Tag /1 #11
2018 Panini Prime Race Used Trios Sheet Metal /50 #11
2018 Panini Prime Race Used Trios Sheet Metal Black /1 #11
2018 Panini Prime Race Used Trios Sheet Metal Holo Gold /25 #11
2018 Panini Prime Race Used Trios Tire /50 #11
2018 Panini Prime Race Used Trios Tire Black /1 #11
2018 Panini Prime Race Used Trios Tire Holo Gold /25 #11
2018 Panini Prime Shadowbox Signatures /99 #16
2018 Panini Prime Shadowbox Signatures Black /1 #16
2018 Panini Prime Shadowbox Signatures Holo Gold /50 #16
2018 Panini Prime Signature Tires /50 #5
2018 Panini Prime Signature Tires Black /1 #5
2018 Panini Prime Signature Tires Holo Gold /25 #5
2018 Panini Prime Triple Material Autographs /99 #4
2018 Panini Prime Triple Material Autographs Black /1 #4
2018 Panini Prime Triple Material Autographs Holo Gold /50 #4
2018 Panini Prime Triple Material Autographs Laundry Tag /1 #4
2018 Panini Prizm #26
2018 Panini Prizm #59
2018 Panini Prizm Brilliance #2
2018 Panini Prizm Brilliance Prizms #2
2018 Panini Prizm Brilliance Prizms Black /1 #2
2018 Panini Prizm Brilliance Prizms Gold /10 #2
2018 Panini Prizm Fireworks #11
2018 Panini Prizm Fireworks Prizms #11
2018 Panini Prizm Fireworks Prizms Black /1 #11
2018 Panini Prizm Fireworks Prizms Gold /10 #11
2018 Panini Prizm National Pride #7
2018 Panini Prizm National Pride Prizms #7
2018 Panini Prizm National Pride Prizms Black /1 #7
2018 Panini Prizm National Pride Prizms Gold /10 #7
2018 Panini Prizm Prizms #26
2018 Panini Prizm Prizms #59
2018 Panini Prizm Prizms Black /1 #26
2018 Panini Prizm Prizms Black /1 #59
2018 Panini Prizm Prizms Blue /99 #26
2018 Panini Prizm Prizms Blue /99 #59
2018 Panini Prizm Prizms Camo #26
2018 Panini Prizm Prizms Camo #59
2018 Panini Prizm Prizms Gold /10 #26
2018 Panini Prizm Prizms Gold /10 #59
2018 Panini Prizm Prizms Green /149 #26
2018 Panini Prizm Prizms Green /149 #59
2018 Panini Prizm Prizms Purple Flash #26
2018 Panini Prizm Prizms Purple Flash #59
2018 Panini Prizm Prizms Rainbow /24 #26
2018 Panini Prizm Prizms Rainbow /24 #59
2018 Panini Prizm Prizms Red /75 #26
2018 Panini Prizm Prizms Red /75 #59
2018 Panini Prizm Prizms Red White and Blue #26
2018 Panini Prizm Prizms Red White and Blue #59
2018 Panini Prizm Prizms White /5 #26
2018 Panini Prizm Prizms White /5 #59
2018 Panini Prizm Scripted Signatures Prizms #30
2018 Panini Prizm Scripted Signatures Prizms Black /1 #30
2018 Panini Prizm Scripted Signatures Prizms Blue /35 #30
2018 Panini Prizm Scripted Signatures Prizms Camo #30
2018 Panini Prizm Scripted Signatures Prizms Gold /10 #30
2018 Panini Prizm Scripted Signatures Prizms Green /50 #30
2018 Panini Prizm Scripted Signatures Prizms Rainbow /24 #30
2018 Panini Prizm Scripted Signatures Prizms Red /25 #30
2018 Panini Prizm Scripted Signatures Prizms Red White and Blue /75 #30
2018 Panini Prizm Scripted Signatures Prizms White /5 #30
2018 Panini Prizm Stars and Stripes #6
2018 Panini Prizm Stars and Stripes Prizms #6
2018 Panini Prizm Stars and Stripes Prizms Black /1 #6
2018 Panini Prizm Stars and Stripes Prizms Gold /10 #6
2018 Panini Prizm Team Tandems #9
2018 Panini Prizm Team Tandems Prizms #9
2018 Panini Prizm Team Tandems Prizms Black /1 #9
2018 Panini Prizm Team Tandems Prizms Gold /10 #9
2018 Panini Victory Lane #7
2018 Panini Victory Lane #68
2018 Panini Victory Lane #86
2018 Panini Victory Lane Black /1 #7
2018 Panini Victory Lane Black /1 #68
2018 Panini Victory Lane Black /1 #86
2018 Panini Victory Lane Blue /25 #7
2018 Panini Victory Lane Blue /25 #68
2018 Panini Victory Lane Blue /25 #86
2018 Panini Victory Lane Celebrations #12
2018 Panini Victory Lane Celebrations Black /1 #12
2018 Panini Victory Lane Celebrations Blue /25 #12
2018 Panini Victory Lane Celebrations Gold /99 #12
2018 Panini Victory Lane Celebrations Green /5 #12
2018 Panini Victory Lane Celebrations Printing Plates Black /1 #12
2018 Panini Victory Lane Celebrations Printing Plates Cyan /1 #12
2018 Panini Victory Lane Celebrations Printing Plates Magenta /1 #12
2018 Panini Victory Lane Celebrations Printing Plates Yellow /1 #12
2018 Panini Victory Lane Celebrations Red /49 #12
2018 Panini Victory Lane Engineered to Perfection Triple Materials /399 #5
2018 Panini Victory Lane Engineered to Perfection Triple Materials Black /25 #5
2018 Panini Victory Lane Engineered to Perfection Triple Materials Gold /199 #5
2018 Panini Victory Lane Engineered to Perfection Triple Materials Green /99 #5
2018 Panini Victory Lane Engineered to Perfection Triple Materials Laundry Tag /1 #5
2018 Panini Victory Lane Gold /99 #7
2018 Panini Victory Lane Gold /99 #68
2018 Panini Victory Lane Gold /99 #86
2018 Panini Victory Lane Green /5 #7
2018 Panini Victory Lane Green /5 #68
2018 Panini Victory Lane Green /5 #86
2018 Panini Victory Lane Octane Autographs /125 #13
2018 Panini Victory Lane Octane Autographs Black /1 #13
2018 Panini Victory Lane Octane Autographs Gold /99 #13
2018 Panini Victory Lane Pedal to the Metal #19
2018 Panini Victory Lane Pedal to the Metal #57
2018 Panini Victory Lane Pedal to the Metal Black /1 #19
2018 Panini Victory Lane Pedal to the Metal Black /1 #57
2018 Panini Victory Lane Pedal to the Metal Blue /25 #19
2018 Panini Victory Lane Pedal to the Metal Blue /25 #57
2018 Panini Victory Lane Pedal to the Metal Green /5 #19
2018 Panini Victory Lane Pedal to the Metal Green /5 #57
2018 Panini Victory Lane Printing Plates Black /1 #7
2018 Panini Victory Lane Printing Plates Black /1 #68
2018 Panini Victory Lane Printing Plates Black /1 #86
2018 Panini Victory Lane Printing Plates Cyan /1 #7
2018 Panini Victory Lane Printing Plates Cyan /1 #68
2018 Panini Victory Lane Printing Plates Cyan /1 #86
2018 Panini Victory Lane Printing Plates Magenta /1 #7
2018 Panini Victory Lane Printing Plates Magenta /1 #68
2018 Panini Victory Lane Printing Plates Magenta /1 #86
2018 Panini Victory Lane Printing Plates Yellow /1 #7
2018 Panini Victory Lane Printing Plates Yellow /1 #68
2018 Panini Victory Lane Printing Plates Yellow /1 #86
2018 Panini Victory Lane Race Day #5
2018 Panini Victory Lane Race Day Black /1 #5
2018 Panini Victory Lane Race Day Blue /25 #5
2018 Panini Victory Lane Race Day Gold /99 #5
2018 Panini Victory Lane Race Day Green /5 #5
2018 Panini Victory Lane Race Day Printing Plates Black /1 #5
2018 Panini Victory Lane Race Day Printing Plates Cyan /1 #5
2018 Panini Victory Lane Race Day Printing Plates Magenta /1 #5
2018 Panini Victory Lane Race Day Printing Plates Yellow /1 #5
2018 Panini Victory Lane Race Day Red /49 #5
2018 Panini Victory Lane Race Ready Dual Materials /399 #5
2018 Panini Victory Lane Race Ready Dual Materials Black /25 #5
2018 Panini Victory Lane Race Ready Dual Materials Gold /199 #5
2018 Panini Victory Lane Race Ready Dual Materials Green /99 #5
2018 Panini Victory Lane Race Ready Dual Materials Laundry Tag /1 #5
2018 Panini Victory Lane Race Ready Materials Black /25 #11
2018 Panini Victory Lane Red /49 #7
2018 Panini Victory Lane Red /49 #68
2018 Panini Victory Lane Red /49 #86
2018 Panini Victory Lane Silver #7
2018 Panini Victory Lane Silver #68
2018 Panini Victory Lane Silver #86
2018 Panini Victory Lane Starting Grid #7
2018 Panini Victory Lane Starting Grid Black /1 #7
2018 Panini Victory Lane Starting Grid Blue /25 #7
2018 Panini Victory Lane Starting Grid Gold /99 #7
2018 Panini Victory Lane Starting Grid Green /5 #7
2018 Panini Victory Lane Starting Grid Printing Plates Black /1 #7
2018 Panini Victory Lane Starting Grid Printing Plates Cyan /1 #7
2018 Panini Victory Lane Starting Grid Printing Plates Magenta /1 #7
2018 Panini Victory Lane Starting Grid Printing Plates Yellow /1 #7
2018 Panini Victory Lane Starting Grid Red /49 #7
2018 Panini Victory Lane Victory Lane Prime Patches Associate Sponsor 1 /1 #34
2018 Panini Victory Lane Victory Lane Prime Patches Associate Sponsor 2 /1 #34
2018 Panini Victory Lane Victory Lane Prime Patches Associate Sponsor 3 /1 #34
2018 Panini Victory Lane Victory Lane Prime Patches Associate Sponsor 4 /1 #34
2018 Panini Victory Lane Victory Lane Prime Patches Associate Sponsor 5 /1 #34
2018 Panini Victory Lane Victory Lane Prime Patches Associate Sponsor 6 /1 #34
2018 Panini Victory Lane Victory Lane Prime Patches Associate Sponsor 7 /1 #34
2018 Panini Victory Lane Victory Lane Prime Patches Associate Sponsor 8 /1 #34
2018 Panini Victory Lane Victory Lane Prime Patches Car Manufacturer /1 #34
2018 Panini Victory Lane Victory Lane Prime Patches Firesuit Manufacturer /1 #34
2018 Panini Victory Lane Victory Lane Prime Patches Nameplate /2 #34
2018 Panini Victory Lane Victory Lane Prime Patches NASCAR /1 #34
2018 Panini Victory Lane Victory Lane Prime Patches Series Sponsor /1 #34
2018 Panini Victory Lane Victory Lane Prime Patches Sunoco /1 #34
2019 Donruss #63
2019 Donruss #122
2019 Donruss Artist Proofs /25 #63
2019 Donruss Artist Proofs /25 #122
2019 Donruss Black /199 #63
2019 Donruss Black /199 #122
2019 Donruss Classics #1
2019 Donruss Classics Cracked Ice /25 #1
2019 Donruss Classics Holographic #1
2019 Donruss Classics Xplosion /10 #1
2019 Donruss Contenders #16
2019 Donruss Contenders Cracked Ice /25 #16
2019 Donruss Contenders Holographic #16
2019 Donruss Contenders Xplosion /10 #16
2019 Donruss Gold /299 #63
2019 Donruss Gold /299 #122
2019 Donruss Gold Press Proofs /99 #63
2019 Donruss Gold Press Proofs /99 #122
2019 Donruss Optic #12
2019 Donruss Optic #65
2019 Donruss Optic Blue Pulsar #12
2019 Donruss Optic Blue Pulsar /1 #65
2019 Donruss Optic Gold /10 #12
2019 Donruss Optic Gold /10 #65
2019 Donruss Optic Gold Vinyl /1 #12
2019 Donruss Optic Gold Vinyl /1 #65
2019 Donruss Optic Holo #12
2019 Donruss Optic Holo #65
2019 Donruss Optic Illusion #10
2019 Donruss Optic Illusion Blue Pulsar #10
2019 Donruss Optic Illusion Gold /10 #10
2019 Donruss Optic Illusion Gold Vinyl /1 #10
2019 Donruss Optic Illusion Holo #10
2019 Donruss Optic Illusion Red Wave #10
2019 Donruss Optic Illusion Signatures Gold Vinyl /1 #10
2019 Donruss Optic Illusion Signatures Holo /75 #10
2019 Donruss Optic Red Wave #12
2019 Donruss Optic Red Wave /1 #65
2019 Donruss Optic Signatures Gold Vinyl /1 #65
2019 Donruss Optic Signatures Gold Vinyl /1 #12
2019 Donruss Optic Signatures Holo /75 #12
2019 Donruss Optic Signatures Holo /75 #65
2019 Donruss Originals #3
2019 Donruss Originals Cracked Ice /25 #3
2019 Donruss Originals Holographic #3
2019 Donruss Originals Xplosion /10 #3
2019 Donruss Press Proofs /49 #63
2019 Donruss Press Proofs /49 #122
2019 Donruss Printing Plates Black /1 #63
2019 Donruss Printing Plates Black /1 #122
2019 Donruss Printing Plates Cyan /1 #63
2019 Donruss Printing Plates Cyan /1 #122
2019 Donruss Printing Plates Magenta /1 #63
2019 Donruss Printing Plates Magenta /1 #122
2019 Donruss Printing Plates Yellow /1 #63
2019 Donruss Printing Plates Yellow /1 #122
2019 Donruss Race Day Relics #10
2019 Donruss Race Day Relics Holo Black /10 #10
2019 Donruss Race Day Relics Holo Gold /25 #10
2019 Donruss Race Day Relics Red /185 #10
2019 Donruss Silver #63
2019 Donruss Silver #122
2019 Donruss Top Tier #8
2019 Donruss Top Tier Cracked Ice /25 #8
2019 Donruss Top Tier Holographic #8
2019 Donruss Top Tier Xplosion /10 #8
2019 Panini Prime /50 #9
2019 Panini Prime /50 #43
2019 Panini Prime /50 #76
2019 Panini Prime Black /10 #9
2019 Panini Prime Black /10 #43
2019 Panini Prime Black /10 #76
2019 Panini Prime Clear Silhouettes /99 #12
2019 Panini Prime Clear Silhouettes Black /10 #12
2019 Panini Prime Clear Silhouettes Dual /99 #6
2019 Panini Prime Clear Silhouettes Dual Black /10 #6
2019 Panini Prime Clear Silhouettes Dual Holo Gold /25 #6
2019 Panini Prime Clear Silhouettes Dual Platinum Blue /1 #6
2019 Panini Prime Clear Silhouettes Holo Gold /25 #12
2019 Panini Prime Clear Silhouettes Platinum Blue /1 #12
2019 Panini Prime Emerald /5 #9
2019 Panini Prime Emerald /5 #43
2019 Panini Prime Emerald /5 #76
2019 Panini Prime Hats Off Button /1 #9
2019 Panini Prime Hats Off Eyelets /6 #9
2019 Panini Prime Hats Off Headband /26 #9
2019 Panini Prime Hats Off Laundry Tags /3 #9
2019 Panini Prime Hats Off New Era /1 #9
2019 Panini Prime Hats Off Sponsor Logo /5 #9
2019 Panini Prime Hats Off Team Logo /2 #9
2019 Panini Prime Jumbo Material Signatures Firesuit /10 #11
2019 Panini Prime Jumbo Material Signatures Firesuit Platinum Blue /1 #11
2019 Panini Prime Jumbo Material Signatures Sheet Metal /25 #11
2019 Panini Prime Jumbo Material Signatures Tire /75 #11
2019 Panini Prime NASCAR Shadowbox Signatures Car Number /99 #16
2019 Panini Prime NASCAR Shadowbox Signatures Manufacturer /10 #16
2019 Panini Prime NASCAR Shadowbox Signatures Team Owner /1 #16
2019 Panini Prime Platinum Blue /1 #9
2019 Panini Prime Platinum Blue /1 #43
2019 Panini Prime Platinum Blue /1 #76
2019 Panini Prime Prime Jumbo Associate Sponsor 1 /1 #27
2019 Panini Prime Prime Jumbo Associate Sponsor 2 /1 #27
2019 Panini Prime Prime Jumbo Associate Sponsor 3 /1 #27
2019 Panini Prime Prime Jumbo Associate Sponsor 4 /1 #27
2019 Panini Prime Prime Jumbo Associate Sponsor 5 /1 #27
2019 Panini Prime Prime Jumbo Associate Sponsor 6 /1 #27
2019 Panini Prime Prime Jumbo Car Manufacturer /1 #27
2019 Panini Prime Prime Jumbo Firesuit Manufacturer /1 #27
2019 Panini Prime Prime Jumbo Flag Patch /1 #27
2019 Panini Prime Prime Jumbo Glove Manufacturer Patch /1 #27
2019 Panini Prime Prime Jumbo Glove Name Patch /1 #27
2019 Panini Prime Prime Jumbo Goodyear /2 #27
2019 Panini Prime Prime Jumbo Nameplate /2 #27
2019 Panini Prime Prime Jumbo NASCAR /1 #27
2019 Panini Prime Prime Jumbo Prime Colors /10 #27
2019 Panini Prime Prime Jumbo Series Sponsor /1 #27
2019 Panini Prime Prime Jumbo Shoe Brand Logo /1 #27
2019 Panini Prime Prime Jumbo Shoe Name Patch /1 #27
2019 Panini Prime Prime Jumbo Shoe Number Patch /1 #27
2019 Panini Prime Prime Jumbo Sunoco /1 #27
2019 Panini Prime Prime Number Die Cut Signatures /49 #2
2019 Panini Prime Prime Number Die Cut Signatures Black /10 #2
2019 Panini Prime Prime Number Die Cut Signatures Holo Gold /25 #2
2019 Panini Prime Prime Number Die Cut Signatures Platinum Blue /1 #2
2019 Panini Prime Quad Materials Autographs /49 #10
2019 Panini Prime Quad Materials Autographs Black /10 #10
2019 Panini Prime Quad Materials Autographs Holo Gold /25 #10
2019 Panini Prime Quad Materials Autographs Laundry Tags /1 #10
2019 Panini Prime Race Used Duals Firesuits /50 #16
2019 Panini Prime Race Used Duals Firesuits Black /10 #16
2019 Panini Prime Race Used Duals Firesuits Holo Gold /25 #16
2019 Panini Prime Race Used Duals Firesuits Laundry Tags /1 #16
2019 Panini Prime Race Used Duals Sheet Metal /50 #16
2019 Panini Prime Race Used Duals Sheet Metal Black /10 #16
2019 Panini Prime Race Used Duals Sheet Metal Holo Gold /25 #16
2019 Panini Prime Race Used Duals Sheet Metal Platinum Blue /1 #16
2019 Panini Prime Race Used Duals Tires /50 #16
2019 Panini Prime Race Used Duals Tires Black /10 #16
2019 Panini Prime Race Used Duals Tires Holo Gold /25 #16
2019 Panini Prime Race Used Duals Tires Platinum Blue /1 #16
2019 Panini Prime Race Used Firesuits /50 #16
2019 Panini Prime Race Used Firesuits Black /10 #16
2019 Panini Prime Race Used Firesuits Holo Gold /25 #16
2019 Panini Prime Race Used Firesuits Laundry Tags /1 #16
2019 Panini Prime Race Used Sheet Metal /50 #16
2019 Panini Prime Race Used Sheet Metal Black /10 #16
2019 Panini Prime Race Used Sheet Metal Holo Gold /25 #16
2019 Panini Prime Race Used Sheet Metal Platinum Blue /1 #16
2019 Panini Prime Race Used Tires /50 #16
2019 Panini Prime Race Used Tires Black /10 #16
2019 Panini Prime Race Used Tires Holo Gold /25 #16
2019 Panini Prime Race Used Tires Platinum Blue /1 #16
2019 Panini Prime Timeline Signatures /49 #8
2019 Panini Prime Timeline Signatures Manufacturer /1 #8
2019 Panini Prime Timeline Signatures Name /25 #8
2019 Panini Prime Timeline Signatures Sponsor /10 #8
2019 Panini Prizm #9
2019 Panini Prizm #68
2019 Panini Prizm #72
2019 Panini Prizm #86
2019 Panini Prizm Apex #13
2019 Panini Prizm Apex Prizms #13
2019 Panini Prizm Apex Prizms Black /1 #13
2019 Panini Prizm Apex Prizms Gold /10 #13
2019 Panini Prizm Apex Prizms White Sparkle #13
2019 Panini Prizm Fireworks #16
2019 Panini Prizm Fireworks Prizms #16
2019 Panini Prizm Fireworks Prizms Black /1 #16
2019 Panini Prizm Fireworks Prizms Gold /10 #16
2019 Panini Prizm Fireworks Prizms White Sparkle #16
2019 Panini Prizm National Pride #8
2019 Panini Prizm National Pride Prizms #8
2019 Panini Prizm National Pride Prizms Black /1 #8
2019 Panini Prizm National Pride Prizms Gold /10 #8
2019 Panini Prizm National Pride Prizms White Sparkle #8
2019 Panini Prizm Prizms #68
2019 Panini Prizm Prizms #72
2019 Panini Prizm Prizms #86
2019 Panini Prizm Prizms #9
2019 Panini Prizm Prizms Black /1 #9
2019 Panini Prizm Prizms Black /1 #68
2019 Panini Prizm Prizms Black /1 #72
2019 Panini Prizm Prizms Black /1 #86
2019 Panini Prizm Prizms Blue /75 #9
2019 Panini Prizm Prizms Blue /75 #68
2019 Panini Prizm Prizms Blue /75 #72
2019 Panini Prizm Prizms Blue /75 #86
2019 Panini Prizm Prizms Camo #9
2019 Panini Prizm Prizms Camo #68
2019 Panini Prizm Prizms Camo #72
2019 Panini Prizm Prizms Camo #86
2019 Panini Prizm Prizms Flash #9
2019 Panini Prizm Prizms Flash #68
2019 Panini Prizm Prizms Flash #72
2019 Panini Prizm Prizms Flash #86
2019 Panini Prizm Prizms Gold /10 #9
2019 Panini Prizm Prizms Gold /10 #68
2019 Panini Prizm Prizms Gold /10 #72
2019 Panini Prizm Prizms Gold /10 #86
2019 Panini Prizm Prizms Green /99 #9
2019 Panini Prizm Prizms Green /99 #68
2019 Panini Prizm Prizms Green /99 #72
2019 Panini Prizm Prizms Green /99 #86
2019 Panini Prizm Prizms Rainbow /24 #9
2019 Panini Prizm Prizms Rainbow /24 #68
2019 Panini Prizm Prizms Rainbow /24 #72
2019 Panini Prizm Prizms Rainbow /24 #86
2019 Panini Prizm Prizms Red /50 #9
2019 Panini Prizm Prizms Red /50 #68
2019 Panini Prizm Prizms Red /50 #72
2019 Panini Prizm Prizms Red /50 #86
2019 Panini Prizm Prizms Red White and Blue #9
2019 Panini Prizm Prizms Red White and Blue #68
2019 Panini Prizm Prizms Red White and Blue #72
2019 Panini Prizm Prizms Red White and Blue #86
2019 Panini Prizm Prizms White /5 #9
2019 Panini Prizm Prizms White /5 #68
2019 Panini Prizm Prizms White /5 #72
2019 Panini Prizm Prizms White /5 #86
2019 Panini Prizm Prizms White Sparkle #9
2019 Panini Prizm Prizms White Sparkle #68
2019 Panini Prizm Prizms White Sparkle #72
2019 Panini Prizm Prizms White Sparkle #86
2019 Panini Prizm Signing Sessions Prizms #9
2019 Panini Prizm Signing Sessions Prizms Black /1 #9
2019 Panini Prizm Signing Sessions Prizms Blue /75 #9
2019 Panini Prizm Signing Sessions Prizms Camo #9
2019 Panini Prizm Signing Sessions Prizms Gold /10 #9
2019 Panini Prizm Signing Sessions Prizms Green /99 #9
2019 Panini Prizm Signing Sessions Prizms Rainbow /24 #9
2019 Panini Prizm Signing Sessions Prizms Red /50 #9
2019 Panini Prizm Signing Sessions Prizms Red White and Blue #9
2019 Panini Prizm Signing Sessions Prizms White /5 #9
2019 Panini Prizm Stars and Stripes #14
2019 Panini Prizm Stars and Stripes Prizms #14
2019 Panini Prizm Stars and Stripes Prizms Black /1 #14
2019 Panini Prizm Stars and Stripes Prizms Gold /10 #14
2019 Panini Prizm Stars and Stripes Prizms White Sparkle #14
2019 Panini Prizm Teammates #3
2019 Panini Prizm Teammates Prizms #3
2019 Panini Prizm Teammates Prizms Black /1 #3
2019 Panini Prizm Teammates Prizms Gold /10 #3
2019 Panini Prizm Teammates Prizms White Sparkle #3
2019 Panini Victory Lane #9
2019 Panini Victory Lane Black /1 #9
2019 Panini Victory Lane Dual Swatch Signatures #7
2019 Panini Victory Lane Dual Swatch Signatures Gold /99 #7
2019 Panini Victory Lane Dual Swatch Signatures Laundry Tag /1 #7
2019 Panini Victory Lane Dual Swatch Signatures Platinum /1 #7
2019 Panini Victory Lane Dual Swatch Signatures Red /25 #7
2019 Panini Victory Lane Dual Swatches #10
2019 Panini Victory Lane Dual Swatches Gold /99 #10
2019 Panini Victory Lane Dual Swatches Laundry Tag /1 #10
2019 Panini Victory Lane Dual Swatches Platinum /1 #10
2019 Panini Victory Lane Dual Swatches Red /25 #10
2019 Panini Victory Lane Gold /25 #9
2019 Panini Victory Lane Horsepower Heroes #8
2019 Panini Victory Lane Horsepower Heroes Black /1 #8
2019 Panini Victory Lane Horsepower Heroes Blue /99 #8
2019 Panini Victory Lane Horsepower Heroes Gold /25 #8
2019 Panini Victory Lane Horsepower Heroes Green /5 #8
2019 Panini Victory Lane Horsepower Heroes Printing Plates Black /1 #8
2019 Panini Victory Lane Horsepower Heroes Printing Plates Cyan /1 #8
2019 Panini Victory Lane Horsepower Heroes Printing Plates Magenta /1 #8
2019 Panini Victory Lane Horsepower Heroes Printing Plates Yellow /1 #8
2019 Panini Victory Lane Machines #10
2019 Panini Victory Lane Machines Black /1 #10
2019 Panini Victory Lane Machines Blue /99 #10
2019 Panini Victory Lane Machines Gold /25 #10
2019 Panini Victory Lane Machines Green /5 #10
2019 Panini Victory Lane Machines Printing Plates Black /1 #10
2019 Panini Victory Lane Machines Printing Plates Cyan /1 #10
2019 Panini Victory Lane Machines Printing Plates Magenta /1 #10
2019 Panini Victory Lane Machines Printing Plates Yellow /1 #10
2019 Panini Victory Lane Pedal to the Metal #31
2019 Panini Victory Lane Pedal to the Metal #57
2019 Panini Victory Lane Pedal to the Metal Black /1 #31
2019 Panini Victory Lane Pedal to the Metal Black /1 #57
2019 Panini Victory Lane Pedal to the Metal Gold /25 #31
2019 Panini Victory Lane Pedal to the Metal Gold /25 #57
2019 Panini Victory Lane Pedal to the Metal Green /5 #31
2019 Panini Victory Lane Pedal to the Metal Green /5 #57
2019 Panini Victory Lane Pedal to the Metal Red /3 #31
2019 Panini Victory Lane Pedal to the Metal Red /3 #57
2019 Panini Victory Lane Printing Plates Black /1 #9
2019 Panini Victory Lane Printing Plates Cyan /1 #9
2019 Panini Victory Lane Printing Plates Magenta /1 #9
2019 Panini Victory Lane Printing Plates Yellow /1 #9
2019 Panini Victory Lane Starting Grid #22
2019 Panini Victory Lane Starting Grid Black /1 #22
2019 Panini Victory Lane Starting Grid Blue /99 #22
2019 Panini Victory Lane Starting Grid Gold /25 #22
2019 Panini Victory Lane Starting Grid Green /5 #22
2019 Panini Victory Lane Starting Grid Printing Plates Black /1 #22
2019 Panini Victory Lane Starting Grid Printing Plates Cyan /1 #22
2019 Panini Victory Lane Starting Grid Printing Plates Magenta /1 #22
2019 Panini Victory Lane Starting Grid Printing Plates Yellow /1 #22
2019 Panini Victory Lane Top 10 #7
2019 Panini Victory Lane Top 10 Black /1 #7
2019 Panini Victory Lane Top 10 Blue /99 #7
2019 Panini Victory Lane Top 10 Gold /25 #7
2019 Panini Victory Lane Top 10 Green /5 #7
2019 Panini Victory Lane Top 10 Printing Plates Black /1 #7
2019 Panini Victory Lane Top 10 Printing Plates Cyan /1 #7
2019 Panini Victory Lane Top 10 Printing Plates Magenta /1 #7
2019 Panini Victory Lane Top 10 Printing Plates Yellow /1 #7
2019 Panini Victory Lane Track Stars #12
2019 Panini Victory Lane Track Stars Black /1 #12
2019 Panini Victory Lane Track Stars Blue /99 #12
2019 Panini Victory Lane Track Stars Gold /25 #12
2019 Panini Victory Lane Track Stars Green /5 #12
2019 Panini Victory Lane Track Stars Printing Plates Black /1 #12
2019 Panini Victory Lane Track Stars Printing Plates Cyan /1 #12
2019 Panini Victory Lane Track Stars Printing Plates Magenta /1 #12
2019 Panini Victory Lane Track Stars Printing Plates Yellow /1 #12
2020 Donruss #12
2020 Donruss #35
2020 Donruss #101
2020 Donruss #174
2020 Donruss #194
2020 Donruss Action Packed #8
2020 Donruss Action Packed Checkers #8
2020 Donruss Action Packed Cracked Ice /25 #8
2020 Donruss Action Packed Holographic /199 #8
2020 Donruss Action Packed Xplosion /10 #8
2020 Donruss Aero Package #1
2020 Donruss Aero Package Checkers #1
2020 Donruss Aero Package Cracked Ice /25 #1
2020 Donruss Aero Package Holographic /199 #1
2020 Donruss Aero Package Xplosion /10 #1
2020 Donruss Black Numbers /11 #12
2020 Donruss Black Numbers /11 #35
2020 Donruss Black Numbers /11 #101
2020 Donruss Black Numbers /11 #174
2020 Donruss Black Numbers /11 #194
2020 Donruss Black Trophy Club /1 #12
2020 Donruss Black Trophy Club /1 #35
2020 Donruss Black Trophy Club /1 #101
2020 Donruss Black Trophy Club /1 #174
2020 Donruss Black Trophy Club /1 #194
2020 Donruss Blue /199 #101
2020 Donruss Blue /199 #174
2020 Donruss Blue /199 #194
2020 Donruss Blue /199 #12
2020 Donruss Blue /199 #35
2020 Donruss Carolina Blue #12
2020 Donruss Carolina Blue #35
2020 Donruss Carolina Blue #101
2020 Donruss Carolina Blue #174
2020 Donruss Carolina Blue #194
2020 Donruss Contenders #7
2020 Donruss Contenders Checkers #7
2020 Donruss Contenders Cracked Ice /25 #7
2020 Donruss Contenders Holographic /199 #7
2020 Donruss Contenders Xplosion /10 #7
2020 Donruss Elite Series #7
2020 Donruss Elite Series Checkers #7
2020 Donruss Elite Series Cracked Ice /25 #7
2020 Donruss Elite Series Holographic /199 #7
2020 Donruss Elite Series Xplosion /10 #7
2020 Donruss Green /99 #12
2020 Donruss Green /99 #35
2020 Donruss Green /99 #101
2020 Donruss Green /99 #174
2020 Donruss Green /99 #194
2020 Donruss Optic #24
2020 Donruss Optic #69
2020 Donruss Optic Carolina Blue Wave #24
2020 Donruss Optic Carolina Blue Wave #69
2020 Donruss Optic Gold /10 #24
2020 Donruss Optic Gold /10 #69
2020 Donruss Optic Gold Vinyl /1 #24
2020 Donruss Optic Gold Vinyl /1 #69
2020 Donruss Optic Holo #24
2020 Donruss Optic Holo #69
2020 Donruss Optic Orange Pulsar #24
2020 Donruss Optic Orange Pulsar #69
2020 Donruss Optic Red Mojo #24
2020 Donruss Optic Red Mojo #69
2020 Donruss Optic Signatures Gold Vinyl /1 #24
2020 Donruss Optic Signatures Gold Vinyl /1 #69
2020 Donruss Optic Signatures Holo /99 #24
2020 Donruss Optic Signatures Holo /99 #69
2020 Donruss Orange #194
2020 Donruss Orange #12
2020 Donruss Orange #35
2020 Donruss Orange #101
2020 Donruss Orange #174
2020 Donruss Pink /25 #12
2020 Donruss Pink /25 #35
2020 Donruss Pink /25 #101
2020 Donruss Pink /25 #174
2020 Donruss Pink /25 #194
2020 Donruss Printing Plates Black /1 #12
2020 Donruss Printing Plates Black /1 #35
2020 Donruss Printing Plates Black /1 #101
2020 Donruss Printing Plates Black /1 #174
2020 Donruss Printing Plates Black /1 #194
2020 Donruss Printing Plates Cyan /1 #12
2020 Donruss Printing Plates Cyan /1 #35
2020 Donruss Printing Plates Cyan /1 #101
2020 Donruss Printing Plates Cyan /1 #174
2020 Donruss Printing Plates Cyan /1 #194
2020 Donruss Printing Plates Magenta /1 #35
2020 Donruss Printing Plates Magenta /1 #101
2020 Donruss Printing Plates Magenta /1 #174
2020 Donruss Printing Plates Magenta /1 #194
2020 Donruss Printing Plates Magenta /1 #12
2020 Donruss Printing Plates Yellow /1 #174
2020 Donruss Printing Plates Yellow /1 #194
2020 Donruss Printing Plates Yellow /1 #12
2020 Donruss Printing Plates Yellow /1 #35
2020 Donruss Printing Plates Yellow /1 #101
2020 Donruss Purple /49 #12
2020 Donruss Purple /49 #35
2020 Donruss Purple /49 #101
2020 Donruss Purple /49 #174
2020 Donruss Purple /49 #194
2020 Donruss Race Day Relics #10
2020 Donruss Race Day Relics Holo Black /10 #10
2020 Donruss Race Day Relics Holo Gold /25 #10
2020 Donruss Race Day Relics Red /250 #10
2020 Donruss Red /299 #12
2020 Donruss Red /299 #35
2020 Donruss Red /299 #101
2020 Donruss Red /299 #174
2020 Donruss Red /299 #194
2020 Donruss Retro Relics '87 #14
2020 Donruss Retro Relics '87 Holo Black /10 #14
2020 Donruss Retro Relics '87 Holo Gold /25 #14
2020 Donruss Retro Relics '87 Red /250 #14
2020 Donruss Silver #12
2020 Donruss Silver #35
2020 Donruss Silver #101
2020 Donruss Silver #174
2020 Donruss Silver #194

Kevin Harvick

1999 Press Pass #76
1999 Press Pass Skidmarks /250 #76
1999 Wheels #88
1999 Wheels Golden #88
1999 Wheels Solos #88
2000 Maxx #63
2000 Maximum #39
2000 Maximum Die Cuts /250 #39
2000 Maximum MPH /2 #39
2000 Maximum Signatures #KH
2000 Maximum Young Lions #YL10
2000 Press Pass Optima #32
2000 Press Pass Optima Platinum #32
2000 Press Pass Stealth #62
2000 SP Authentic #44
2000 SP Authentic /2500 #74
2000 SP Authentic Overdrive Gold /2 #44
2000 SP Authentic Overdrive Gold /2 #74
2000 SP Authentic Overdrive Silver /250 #44
2000 SP Authentic Overdrive Silver /250 #74
2000 SP Authentic Sign of the Times #KH
2000 SP Authentic Sign of the Times Gold /25 #KH
2000 Upper Deck Racing #39
2000 Upper Deck Racing Road Signs #RSKH
2001 Press Pass #37
2001 Press Pass Autographs #20
2001 Press Pass Hot Treads Rookie Rubber /1100 #RR5
2001 Press Pass Millennium #37
2001 Press Pass Optima #8
2001 Press Pass Optima #31
2001 Press Pass Optima #43
2001 Press Pass Optima /550 #0
2001 Press Pass Optima Cool Persistence #CP5
2001 Press Pass Optima G Force #GF7
2001 Press Pass Optima Gold #8
2001 Press Pass Optima Gold #31
2001 Press Pass Optima Gold #43
2001 Press Pass Optima On the Edge #OE3
2001 Press Pass Optima Race Used Lugnuts Cars /115 #LNC6

2001 Press Pass Optima Race Used Lugnuts Drivers /100 #LND5
2001 Press Pass Optima Up Close #UC3
2001 Press Pass Premium #43
2001 Press Pass Premium #49
2001 Press Pass Premium Gold #43
2001 Press Pass Premium Gold #49
2001 Press Pass Signings #21
2001 Press Pass Signings #22
2001 Press Pass Signings Gold /50 #14
2001 Press Pass Stealth #34
2001 Press Pass Stealth #35
2001 Press Pass Stealth #36
2001 Press Pass Stealth #50
2001 Press Pass Stealth #68
2001 Press Pass Stealth Behind The Numbers #BN1
2001 Press Pass Stealth Holofoils #34
2001 Press Pass Stealth Holofoils #35
2001 Press Pass Stealth Holofoils #36
2001 Press Pass Stealth Holofoils #50
2001 Press Pass Stealth Holofoils #68
2001 Press Pass Stealth Lap Leaders #LL12
2001 Press Pass Stealth Lap Leaders #LL30
2001 Press Pass Stealth Lap Leaders Clear Cars #LL30
2001 Press Pass Stealth Lap Leaders Clear Drivers #LL12
2001 Press Pass Stealth Profile #PR2
2001 Press Pass Stealth Race Used Glove Cars /120 #RGC11
2001 Press Pass Stealth Race Used Glove Drivers /120 #RGD11
2001 Press Pass Trackside #5
2001 Press Pass Trackside #53
2001 Press Pass Trackside #64
2001 Press Pass Trackside Die Cuts #5
2001 Press Pass Trackside Die Cuts #53
2001 Press Pass Trackside Die Cuts #64
2001 Press Pass Trackside Golden #5
2001 Press Pass Trackside Golden #53
2001 Press Pass Trackside Runnin N' Gunnin #RG8
2001 Super Shots Sears Point CHP #SP5
2001 VIP #10
2001 VIP #22
2001 VIP Driver's Choice #DC7
2001 VIP Driver's Choice Precious Metal /100 #DC7
2001 VIP Driver's Choice Transparent #DC7
2001 VIP Explosives #10
2001 VIP Explosives #22
2001 VIP Explosives Lasers /420 #LX10
2001 VIP Explosives Lasers /420 #LX22
2001 VIP Head Gear #HG3
2001 VIP Head Gear Die Cuts #HG3
2001 VIP Making the Show #15
2001 VIP Mile Masters #MM12
2001 VIP Mile Masters Precious Metal /325 #MM12
2001 VIP Mile Masters Transparent #MM12
2001 VIP Rear View Mirror #RV3
2001 VIP Rear View Mirror Die Cuts #RV3
2001 VIP Sheet Metal Cars /120 #SC11
2001 VIP Sheet Metal Drivers /75 #SD11
2001 Wheels High Gear #38
2001 Wheels High Gear Autographs #15
2001 Wheels High Gear First Gear #38
2001 Wheels High Gear MPH #38
2002 Authentic Images Gold Signature /5029 #S9
2002 Authentic Images Gold Signature /5029 #S13
2002 Authentic Images Gold Signature /5029 #S16
2002 Authentic Images Gold Signature Metal Set /2902 #NAS13
2002 Press Pass #13
2002 Press Pass #43
2002 Press Pass #65
2002 Press Pass #85
2002 Press Pass #98
2002 Press Pass Autographs #26
2002 Press Pass Burning Rubber Cars /120 #BRC4
2002 Press Pass Burning Rubber Drivers /90 #BRD4
2002 Press Pass Cup Chase #CC5
2002 Press Pass Cup Chase Prizes #CC5
2002 Press Pass Double Burner /100 #DB3
2002 Press Pass Eclipse #9
2002 Press Pass Eclipse Racing Champions #RC4
2002 Press Pass Eclipse Racing Champions #RC18
2002 Press Pass Eclipse Samples #9
2002 Press Pass Eclipse Skidmarks #SK3
2002 Press Pass Eclipse Solar Eclipse #S9
2002 Press Pass Eclipse Supernova #SN3
2002 Press Pass Eclipse Supernova Numbered /250 #SN3
2002 Press Pass Eclipse Warp Speed #WS6
2002 Press Pass Hot Treads /1555 #HT9
2002 Press Pass Hot Treads /900 #HT38
2002 Press Pass Nabisco Albertsons #2
2002 Press Pass Optima #12
2002 Press Pass Optima #48
2002 Press Pass Optima Cool Persistence #CP4
2002 Press Pass Optima Fan Favorite #FF9
2002 Press Pass Optima Gold #12
2002 Press Pass Optima Gold #48
2002 Press Pass Optima Promos /5 #12
2002 Press Pass Optima Promos /5 #48
2002 Press Pass Optima Race Used Lugnuts Autographs /29 #LNDA7
2002 Press Pass Optima Race Used Lugnuts Cars /100 #LNC7
2002 Press Pass Optima Race Used Lugnuts Drivers /100 #LND7
2002 Press Pass Optima Samples #12
2002 Press Pass Optima Samples #48
2002 Press Pass Platinum #13
2002 Press Pass Platinum #43
2002 Press Pass Platinum #65
2002 Press Pass Platinum #85
2002 Press Pass Platinum #98
2002 Press Pass Premium #11
2002 Press Pass Premium #39
2002 Press Pass Premium #61
2002 Press Pass Premium #73
2002 Press Pass Premium In The Zone #IZ5
2002 Press Pass Premium Performance Driven #PD3
2002 Press Pass Premium Red Reflectors #11
2002 Press Pass Premium Red Reflectors #39
2002 Press Pass Premium Red Reflectors #61
2002 Press Pass Premium Red Reflectors #73
2002 Press Pass Premium Samples #11
2002 Press Pass Premium Samples #39
2002 Press Pass Showcar #S4B
2002 Press Pass Showman #S4A
2002 Press Pass Signings #26
2002 Press Pass Signings Gold /50 #24
2002 Press Pass Signings Transparent /100 #3
2002 Press Pass Stealth #31
2002 Press Pass Stealth #32
2002 Press Pass Stealth #33
2002 Press Pass Stealth #53
2002 Press Pass Stealth #65
2002 Press Pass Stealth Behind the Numbers #BN1
2002 Press Pass Stealth EFX #FX6
2002 Press Pass Stealth Fusion #F4
2002 Press Pass Stealth Gold #31
2002 Press Pass Stealth Gold #32
2002 Press Pass Stealth Gold #33
2002 Press Pass Stealth Gold #53
2002 Press Pass Stealth Gold #65
2002 Press Pass Stealth Lap Leaders #LL11
2002 Press Pass Stealth Profile #P4
2002 Press Pass Stealth Race Used Glove Cars /85 #GLC10
2002 Press Pass Stealth Race Used Glove Drivers /50 #GLD10
2002 Press Pass Stealth Samples #31
2002 Press Pass Stealth Samples #32
2002 Press Pass Stealth Samples #33
2002 Press Pass Stealth Samples #53
2002 Press Pass Stealth Samples #65
2002 Press Pass Top Shelf #TS3
2002 Press Pass Total Memorabilia Power Pick #TM3
2002 Press Pass Trackside #6
2002 Press Pass Trackside #54
2002 Press Pass Trackside Dialed In #DI4
2002 Press Pass Trackside Generation Now #GN1
2002 Press Pass Trackside Golden /50 #G6
2002 Press Pass Trackside License to Drive #13
2002 Press Pass Trackside License to Drive Die Cuts #13
2002 Press Pass Trackside Mirror Image #MI3
2002 Press Pass Trackside Pit Stoppers Cars /200 #PSC5
2002 Press Pass Trackside Pit Stoppers Drivers /100 #PSD5
2002 Press Pass Trackside Runnin N' Gunnin #RG3
2002 Press Pass Trackside Samples #6
2002 Press Pass Trackside Samples #54
2002 Press Pass Triple Burner /100 #TB3
2002 Press Pass Velocity #VL4
2002 Press Pass Vintage #VN9
2002 Super Shots California Speedway #CS1
2002 Upper Deck Twizzlers #9
2002 Upper Deck Twizzlers #10
2002 VIP #13
2002 VIP #29
2002 VIP Driver's Choice #DC7
2002 VIP Driver's Choice Transparent #DC7
2002 VIP Driver's Choice Transparent LTD #DC7
2002 VIP Explosives #X13
2002 VIP Explosives #X29
2002 VIP Explosives Lasers #LX13
2002 VIP Explosives Lasers #LX29
2002 VIP Head Gear #HG3
2002 VIP Head Gear Die Cuts #HG3
2002 VIP Making the Show #MS15
2002 VIP Mile Masters #MM12
2002 VIP Mile Masters Transparent #MM12
2002 VIP Mile Masters Transparent LTD #MM12
2002 VIP Race Used Sheet Metal Cars #SC2
2002 VIP Race Used Sheet Metal Drivers /130 #SD2
2002 VIP Rear View Mirror #RM3
2002 VIP Rear View Mirror Die Cuts #RM3
2002 VIP Samples #13
2002 VIP Samples #29
2002 Wheels High Gear #9
2002 Wheels High Gear #29
2002 Wheels High Gear #37
2002 Wheels High Gear #48
2002 Wheels High Gear #57
2002 Wheels High Gear #64
2002 Wheels High Gear #66
2002 Wheels High Gear #72
2002 Wheels High Gear Autographs #21
2002 Wheels High Gear Custom Shop #CSKH
2002 Wheels High Gear Custom Shop Prizes #KHA1
2002 Wheels High Gear Custom Shop Prizes #KHA2
2002 Wheels High Gear Custom Shop Prizes #KHA3
2002 Wheels High Gear Custom Shop Prizes #KHB1
2002 Wheels High Gear Custom Shop Prizes #KHB2
2002 Wheels High Gear Custom Shop Prizes #KHB3
2002 Wheels High Gear Custom Shop Prizes #KHC1
2002 Wheels High Gear Custom Shop Prizes #KHC2
2002 Wheels High Gear Custom Shop Prizes #KHC3
2002 Wheels High Gear First Gear #9
2002 Wheels High Gear First Gear #29
2002 Wheels High Gear First Gear #37
2002 Wheels High Gear First Gear #48
2002 Wheels High Gear First Gear #57
2002 Wheels High Gear First Gear #64
2002 Wheels High Gear First Gear #66
2002 Wheels High Gear First Gear #72
2002 Wheels High Gear Flag Chasers /130 #FC3
2002 Wheels High Gear Flag Chasers Black /90 #FC3
2002 Wheels High Gear Flag Chasers Blue-Yellow /40 #FC3
2002 Wheels High Gear Flag Chasers Checkered /35 #FC3
2002 Wheels High Gear Flag Chasers Checkered Blue/Orange /10 #FC3
2002 Wheels High Gear Flag Chasers Green /90 #FC3
2002 Wheels High Gear Flag Chasers Red /90 #FC3
2002 Wheels High Gear Flag Chasers Yellow /110 #FC3
2002 Wheels High Gear High Groove #HG9
2002 Wheels High Gear Hot Streaks #HS4
2002 Wheels High Gear Man and Machine Cars #MM3B
2002 Wheels High Gear Man and Machine Drivers #MM3A
2002 Wheels High Gear MPH /100 #9
2002 Wheels High Gear MPH /100 #29
2002 Wheels High Gear MPH /100 #37
2002 Wheels High Gear MPH /100 #48
2002 Wheels High Gear MPH /100 #57
2002 Wheels High Gear MPH /100 #64
2002 Wheels High Gear MPH /100 #66
2002 Wheels High Gear MPH /100 #72
2002 Wheels High Gear Sunday Sensation #SS5
2003 eTopps /4000 #21
2003 Nilla Wafers Team Nabisco #4
2003 Press Pass #14
2003 Press Pass #56
2003 Press Pass #83
2003 Press Pass #93
2003 Press Pass Autographs #22
2003 Press Pass Burning Rubber Cars /60 #BRT3
2003 Press Pass Burning Rubber Cars Autographs /29 #BRTKH
2003 Press Pass Burning Rubber Drivers /50 #BRD3
2003 Press Pass Burning Rubber Drivers Autographs /29 #BRDKH
2003 Press Pass Coca-Cola Racing Family #5
2003 Press Pass Coca-Cola Racing Family Regional #4
2003 Press Pass Cup Chase #CCR5
2003 Press Pass Cup Chase Prizes #CCR5
2003 Press Pass Double Burner /100 #DB3
2003 Press Pass Double Burner Exchange /100 #DB3
2003 Press Pass Eclipse #20
2003 Press Pass Eclipse Double Hot Treads /999 #DT2
2003 Press Pass Eclipse Previews /5 #20
2003 Press Pass Eclipse Racing Champions #RC21
2003 Press Pass Eclipse Samples #20
2003 Press Pass Eclipse Skidmarks #SM13
2003 Press Pass Eclipse Solar Eclipse #P20
2003 Press Pass Eclipse Supernova #SN4
2003 Press Pass Eclipse Teammates Autographs /25 #KHRG
2003 Press Pass Eclipse Under Cover Cars /215 #UCT3
2003 Press Pass Eclipse Under Cover Double Cover /530 #DC8
2003 Press Pass Eclipse Under Cover Double Cover /530 #DC9
2003 Press Pass Eclipse Under Cover Driver Gold /260 #UCD3
2003 Press Pass Eclipse Under Cover Driver Red /100 #UCD3
2003 Press Pass Eclipse Under Cover Driver Silver /450 #UCD3
2003 Press Pass Gold Holofoil #P14
2003 Press Pass Gold Holofoil #P56
2003 Press Pass Gold Holofoil #P83
2003 Press Pass Gold Holofoil #P93
2003 Press Pass Optima #9
2003 Press Pass Optima #43
2003 Press Pass Optima Cool Persistence #CP12
2003 Press Pass Optima Fan Favorite #FF9
2003 Press Pass Optima Gold #G9
2003 Press Pass Optima Gold #G43
2003 Press Pass Optima Previews /5 #9
2003 Press Pass Optima Samples #9
2003 Press Pass Optima Samples #43
2003 Press Pass Optima Thunder Bolts Cars /20 #TBT3
2003 Press Pass Optima Thunder Bolts Cars Autographs /29 #TBTKH
2003 Press Pass Optima Thunder Bolts Drivers /15 #TBD3
2003 Press Pass Optima Thunder Bolts Drivers Autographs /29 #TBDKH
2003 Press Pass Optima Young Guns #YG4
2003 Press Pass Premium #11
2003 Press Pass Premium #38
2003 Press Pass Premium #60
2003 Press Pass Premium Hot Threads Cars /160 #HTT3
2003 Press Pass Premium Hot Threads Cars Autographs /29 #HTDKH
2003 Press Pass Premium Hot Threads Drivers /285 #HTD3
2003 Press Pass Premium Hot Threads Drivers Autographs /29 #HTTKH
2003 Press Pass Premium Previews /5 #11
2003 Press Pass Premium Red Reflectors #11
2003 Press Pass Premium Red Reflectors #38
2003 Press Pass Premium Red Reflectors #60
2003 Press Pass Premium Samples #11
2003 Press Pass Premium Samples #38
2003 Press Pass Previews /5 #14
2003 Press Pass Samples #14
2003 Press Pass Samples #56
2003 Press Pass Samples #83
2003 Press Pass Samples #93
2003 Press Pass Showcar #S4B
2003 Press Pass Showman #S4A
2003 Press Pass Signings #29
2003 Press Pass Signings Gold /50 #29
2003 Press Pass Signings Transparent /100 #3
2003 Press Pass Snapshots #SN9
2003 Press Pass Stealth Fusion #FU5
2003 Press Pass Stealth Gear Grippers Cars /150 #GGT3
2003 Press Pass Stealth Gear Grippers Cars Autographs /29 #KH
2003 Press Pass Stealth Gear Grippers Drivers /75 #GGD3
2003 Press Pass Stealth Gear Grippers Drivers Autographs /29 #KH
2003 Press Pass Stealth No Boundaries #NB13
2003 Press Pass Top Shelf #TS10
2003 Press Pass Total Memorabilia Power Pick #TM3
2003 Press Pass Trackside #23
2003 Press Pass Trackside #68
2003 Press Pass Trackside Gold Holofoil #P23
2003 Press Pass Trackside Gold Holofoil #P68
2003 Press Pass Trackside Golden /50 #G23
2003 Press Pass Trackside Hat Giveaway #PPH10
2003 Press Pass Trackside Hot Pursuit #HP4
2003 Press Pass Trackside Pit Stoppers Cars /175 #PST3
2003 Press Pass Trackside Pit Stoppers Cars Autographs /29 #KH
2003 Press Pass Trackside Pit Stoppers Drivers /100 #PSD3
2003 Press Pass Trackside Pit Stoppers Drivers Autographs /29 #PSDKH
2003 Press Pass Trackside Previews /5 #23
2003 Press Pass Trackside Runnin n' Gunnin #RG11
2003 Press Pass Trackside Samples #23
2003 Press Pass Trackside Samples #68
2003 Press Pass Triple Burner /100 #TB3
2003 Press Pass Triple Burner Exchange /100 #TB3
2003 VIP #6
2003 VIP Explosives #X6
2003 VIP Laser Explosive #LX6
2003 VIP Making the Show #MS15
2003 VIP Previews /5 #6
2003 VIP Samples #6
2003 VIP Tin #CT6
2003 VIP Tradin' Paint Car Autographs /29 #KH
2003 VIP Tradin' Paint Cars /160 #TPT3
2003 VIP Tradin' Paint Driver Autographs /29 #KH
2003 VIP Tradin' Paint Drivers /110 #TPD3
2003 Wheels American Thunder #8
2003 Wheels American Thunder American Muscle #AM3
2003 Wheels American Thunder Born On /100 #BO8
2003 Wheels American Thunder Cool Threads /285 #CT2
2003 Wheels American Thunder Heads Up Goodyear /90 #HUG3
2003 Wheels American Thunder Heads Up Manufacturer /90 #HUM7
2003 Wheels American Thunder Heads Up Team /60 #HUT6
2003 Wheels American Thunder Heads Up Winston /90 #HUW7
2003 Wheels American Thunder Holofoil #P8
2003 Wheels American Thunder Post Mark #PM7
2003 Wheels American Thunder Previews /5 #8
2003 Wheels American Thunder Rookie Thunder #RT12
2003 Wheels American Thunder Samples #P8
2003 Wheels American Thunder Thunder Road #TR13
2003 Wheels American Thunder Triple Hat /25 #TH8
2003 Wheels Autographs #22
2003 Wheels High Gear #12
2003 Wheels High Gear #56
2003 Wheels High Gear #71
2003 Wheels High Gear Blue Hawaii SCDA Promos #12
2003 Wheels High Gear Blue Hawaii SCDA Promos #56
2003 Wheels High Gear Blue Hawaii SCDA Promos #71
2003 Wheels High Gear First Gear #F12
2003 Wheels High Gear First Gear #F56
2003 Wheels High Gear First Gear #F71
2003 Wheels High Gear Full Throttle #FT1
2003 Wheels High Gear High Groove #HG10
2003 Wheels High Gear Hot Treads /425 #HT6
2003 Wheels High Gear Machine #MM2B
2003 Wheels High Gear Man #MM2A
2003 Wheels High Gear MPH /100 #M12
2003 Wheels High Gear MPH /100 #M56
2003 Wheels High Gear MPH /100 #M71
2003 Wheels High Gear Previews /5 #12
2003 Wheels High Gear Samples #12
2003 Wheels High Gear Samples #56
2003 Wheels High Gear Samples #71
2004 Press Pass #12
2004 Press Pass #70
2004 Press Pass #99
2004 Press Pass Autographs #25
2004 Press Pass Burning Rubber Autographs /29 #BRKH
2004 Press Pass Burning Rubber Cars /140 #BRT3
2004 Press Pass Burning Rubber Drivers /70 #BRD3
2004 Press Pass Cup Chase #CCR9
2004 Press Pass Cup Chase Prizes #CCR9
2004 Press Pass Double Burner /100 #DB3
2004 Press Pass Double Burner Exchange /100 #DB3
2004 Press Pass Eclipse #5
2004 Press Pass Eclipse #35
2004 Press Pass Eclipse #59
2004 Press Pass Eclipse #71
2004 Press Pass Eclipse #74
2004 Press Pass Eclipse #82
2004 Press Pass Eclipse Destination WIN #21
2004 Press Pass Eclipse Maxim #MX5
2004 Press Pass Eclipse Previews /5 #5
2004 Press Pass Eclipse Samples #5
2004 Press Pass Eclipse Samples #35
2004 Press Pass Eclipse Samples #59
2004 Press Pass Eclipse Samples #71
2004 Press Pass Eclipse Samples #74
2004 Press Pass Eclipse Samples #82
2004 Press Pass Eclipse Skidmarks #SM9
2004 Press Pass Eclipse Skidmarks Holofoil /500 #SM9
2004 Press Pass Eclipse Teammates Autographs /25 #1
2004 Press Pass Eclipse Under Cover Autographs /29 #UCKH
2004 Press Pass Eclipse Under Cover Cars /170 #UCD3
2004 Press Pass Eclipse Under Cover Double Cover /100 #DC11
2004 Press Pass Eclipse Under Cover Driver Gold /325 #UCD3
2004 Press Pass Eclipse Under Cover Driver Red /100 #UCD3
2004 Press Pass Eclipse Under Cover Driver Silver /690 #UCD3
2004 Press Pass Hot Treads /1100 #HTR6
2004 Press Pass Hot Treads Holofoil /200 #HTR6
2004 Press Pass Making the Show Collector's Series #MS18
2004 Press Pass Optima #8
2004 Press Pass Optima #85
2004 Press Pass Optima #89
2004 Press Pass Optima Fan Favorite #FF8
2004 Press Pass Optima Gold #G8
2004 Press Pass Optima Gold #G85
2004 Press Pass Optima Gold #G89
2004 Press Pass Optima Previews /5 #EB8
2004 Press Pass Optima Samples #8
2004 Press Pass Optima Samples #85
2004 Press Pass Optima Samples #89
2004 Press Pass Optima Thunder Bolts Cars /120 #TBT6
2004 Press Pass Optima Thunder Bolts Drivers /70 #TBD6
2004 Press Pass Platinum #P12
2004 Press Pass Platinum #P70
2004 Press Pass Platinum #P99
2004 Press Pass Premium #3
2004 Press Pass Premium #43
2004 Press Pass Premium #60
2004 Press Pass Premium #77
2004 Press Pass Premium Asphalt Jungle #A6
2004 Press Pass Premium Hot Threads Autographs /29 #HTKH
2004 Press Pass Premium Hot Threads Drivers Bronze /125 #HTD3
2004 Press Pass Premium Hot Threads Drivers Bronze Retail /125 #HTT3
2004 Press Pass Premium Hot Threads Drivers Gold /50 #HTD3
2004 Press Pass Premium Hot Threads Drivers Silver /75 #HTD3
2004 Press Pass Premium Previews /5 #3
2004 Press Pass Premium Samples #3
2004 Press Pass Premium Samples #43
2004 Press Pass Previews /5 #12
2004 Press Pass Samples #12
2004 Press Pass Samples #70
2004 Press Pass Samples #99
2004 Press Pass Signings #26
2004 Press Pass Signings Gold /50 #24
2004 Press Pass Signings Transparent /100 #2
2004 Press Pass Snapshots #SN9
2004 Press Pass Stealth #19
2004 Press Pass Stealth #20
2004 Press Pass Stealth #21
2004 Press Pass Stealth #76
2004 Press Pass Stealth #87
2004 Press Pass Stealth #93
2004 Press Pass Stealth #100
2004 Press Pass Stealth Gear Grippers Autographs /29 #HTKH
2004 Press Pass Stealth Gear Grippers Drivers /80 #GGD3
2004 Press Pass Stealth Gear Grippers Drivers Retail /120 #GGT3
2004 Press Pass Stealth No Boundaries #NB13
2004 Press Pass Stealth Previews /5 #EB19
2004 Press Pass Stealth Previews /5 #EB20
2004 Press Pass Stealth Previews /5 #EB21
2004 Press Pass Stealth Samples #X20
2004 Press Pass Stealth Samples #X76
2004 Press Pass Stealth Samples #X100
2004 Press Pass Stealth Samples #X21
2004 Press Pass Stealth Samples #X19
2004 Press Pass Stealth Samples #X93
2004 Press Pass Stealth Samples #X87
2004 Press Pass Stealth X-Ray /100 #19
2004 Press Pass Stealth X-Ray /100 #20
2004 Press Pass Stealth X-Ray /100 #21
2004 Press Pass Stealth X-Ray /100 #76
2004 Press Pass Stealth X-Ray /100 #87
2004 Press Pass Stealth X-Ray /100 #93
2004 Press Pass Stealth X-Ray /100 #100
2004 Press Pass Top Shelf #TS2
2004 Press Pass Total Memorabilia Power Pick #TM3
2004 Press Pass Trackside #22
2004 Press Pass Trackside #59
2004 Press Pass Trackside #71
2004 Press Pass Trackside #102
2004 Press Pass Trackside #115
2004 Press Pass Trackside #115B
2004 Press Pass Trackside Golden /100 #G22
2004 Press Pass Trackside Golden /100 #G59
2004 Press Pass Trackside Golden /100 #G71
2004 Press Pass Trackside Golden /100 #G102
2004 Press Pass Trackside Golden /100 #G115
2004 Press Pass Trackside Hat Giveaway #PPH10
2004 Press Pass Trackside Hot Pass #HP21
2004 Press Pass Trackside Hot Pass National #HP21
2004 Press Pass Trackside Hot Pursuit #HP9
2004 Press Pass Trackside Pit Stoppers Autographs /29 #PSKH
2004 Press Pass Trackside Pit Stoppers Cars /150 #PST3
2004 Press Pass Trackside Pit Stoppers Drivers /40 #PSD3
2004 Press Pass Trackside Previews /5 #EB22
2004 Press Pass Trackside Samples #22
2004 Press Pass Trackside Samples #59
2004 Press Pass Trackside Samples #71
2004 Press Pass Trackside Samples #102
2004 Press Pass Trackside Samples #115
2004 Press Pass Triple Burner /100 #TB3
2004 Press Pass Triple Burner Exchange /100 #TB3
2004 Press Pass Velocity #VC3
2004 VIP #6
2004 VIP #30
2004 VIP Head Gear #HG3
2004 VIP Head Gear Transparent #HG3
2004 VIP Making the Show #MS18
2004 VIP Previews /5 #EB6
2004 VIP Previews /5 #EB30
2004 VIP Samples #6
2004 VIP Samples #30
2004 VIP Tradin' Paint Autographs /29 #TPKH
2004 VIP Tradin' Paint Bronze /130 #TPT6
2004 VIP Tradin' Paint Gold /50 #TPD6
2004 VIP Tradin' Paint Silver /70 #TPD6
2004 Wheels American Thunder #8
2004 Wheels American Thunder #61
2004 Wheels American Thunder #75
2004 Wheels American Thunder American Muscle #AM2
2004 Wheels American Thunder Cool Threads /525 #CT4
2004 Wheels American Thunder Post Mark #PM18
2004 Wheels American Thunder Previews /5 #EB8
2004 Wheels American Thunder Pushin Pedal /275 #PP8
2004 Wheels American Thunder Samples #8
2004 Wheels American Thunder Samples #61
2004 Wheels American Thunder Samples #75
2004 Wheels Autographs #29
2004 Wheels High Gear #9
2004 Wheels High Gear #58
2004 Wheels High Gear Custom Shop #CSKH
2004 Wheels High Gear Flag Chasers Black /100 #FC2
2004 Wheels High Gear Flag Chasers Blue /50 #FC2
2004 Wheels High Gear Flag Chasers Checkered /35 #FC2
2004 Wheels High Gear Flag Chasers Green /100 #FC2
2004 Wheels High Gear Flag Chasers Red /100 #FC2
2004 Wheels High Gear Flag Chasers White /100 #FC2
2004 Wheels High Gear Flag Chasers Yellow /100 #FC2
2004 Wheels High Gear Full Throttle #FT6
2004 Wheels High Gear High Groove #HG8
2004 Wheels High Gear Machine #MM5B
2004 Wheels High Gear Man #MM5A
2004 Wheels High Gear MPH /100 #M9
2004 Wheels High Gear MPH /100 #M58
2004 Wheels High Gear Previews /5 #9
2004 Wheels High Gear Previews /5 #58
2004 Wheels High Gear Samples #9
2004 Wheels High Gear Samples #58
2004 Wheels High Gear Sunday Sensation #SS7
2004 Wheels High Gear Top Ten #TT5
2005 Coca-Cola Racing Family AutoZone #4
2005 Press Pass #21
2005 Press Pass #70
2005 Press Pass #93
2005 Press Pass Autographs #23
2005 Press Pass Burning Rubber Autographs /29 #BRKH
2005 Press Pass Burning Rubber Cars /130 #BRT3
2005 Press Pass Burning Rubber Drivers /80 #BRD3
2005 Press Pass Burning Rubber Drivers Gold /1 #BRD3
2005 Press Pass Cup Chase #CCR6
2005 Press Pass Cup Chase Prizes #CCP6
2005 Press Pass Double Burner /100 #DB3
2005 Press Pass Double Burner Exchange /100 #DB3
2005 Press Pass Eclipse #14
2005 Press Pass Eclipse #59
2005 Press Pass Eclipse Hyperdrive #HD4
2005 Press Pass Eclipse Previews /5 #EB14
2005 Press Pass Eclipse Previews /5 #EB59
2005 Press Pass Eclipse Samples #14
2005 Press Pass Eclipse Samples #59
2005 Press Pass Eclipse Skidmarks #SM9
2005 Press Pass Eclipse Skidmarks Holofoil /250 #SM9
2005 Press Pass Eclipse Under Cover Autographs /29 #UCKH
2005 Press Pass Eclipse Under Cover Cars /120 #UCT3
2005 Press Pass Eclipse Under Cover Driver Red /400 #UCD3
2005 Press Pass Eclipse Under Cover Drivers Holofoil /100 #UCD3
2005 Press Pass Eclipse Under Cover Drivers Silver /690 #UCD3
2005 Press Pass Game Face #GF4
2005 Press Pass Hot Treads /900 #HTR8
2005 Press Pass Hot Treads Holofoil /100 #HTR8
2005 Press Pass Legends Autographs Black /50 #16
2005 Press Pass Legends Greatest Moments /640 #GM16
2005 Press Pass Optima #11
2005 Press Pass Optima #91
2005 Press Pass Optima Cool Persistence #CP9
2005 Press Pass Optima Fan Favorite #FF10
2005 Press Pass Optima Gold /100 #G11
2005 Press Pass Optima Gold /100 #G91
2005 Press Pass Optima Previews /5 #11
2005 Press Pass Optima Samples #11
2005 Press Pass Optima Samples #91
2005 Press Pass Panorama #PPP11
2005 Press Pass Panorama #PPP28
2005 Press Pass Platinum /100 #P21
2005 Press Pass Platinum /100 #P70
2005 Press Pass Platinum /100 #P93
2005 Press Pass Premium #9
2005 Press Pass Premium #43
2005 Press Pass Premium #66
2005 Press Pass Premium #78
2005 Press Pass Premium Hot Threads Cars /85 #HTT8
2005 Press Pass Premium Hot Threads Drivers /275 #HTD8
2005 Press Pass Premium Hot Threads Drivers Gold /1 #HTD8
2005 Press Pass Premium In the Zone #IZ6
2005 Press Pass Premium In the Zone Elite Edition /250 #IZ6
2005 Press Pass Premium Performance Driven #PD3
2005 Press Pass Premium Samples #9
2005 Press Pass Premium Samples #43
2005 Press Pass Previews Green /5 #EB21
2005 Press Pass Samples #21
2005 Press Pass Samples #70
2005 Press Pass Samples #93
2005 Press Pass Showcar #SC8
2005 Press Pass Showman #SM8
2005 Press Pass Signings #22
2005 Press Pass Signings Gold /50 #21
2005 Press Pass Signings Platinum /100 #21
2005 Press Pass Snapshots #SN10
2005 Press Pass Stealth #47
2005 Press Pass Stealth #50
2005 Press Pass Stealth #53
2005 Press Pass Stealth #88
2005 Press Pass Stealth #99
2005 Press Pass Stealth EFX #EFX9
2005 Press Pass Stealth Fusion #FU10
2005 Press Pass Stealth Gear Grippers Autographs /29 #GGKH
2005 Press Pass Stealth Gear Grippers Cars /90 #GGT3
2005 Press Pass Stealth Gear Grippers Drivers /75 #GGD3
2005 Press Pass Stealth No Boundaries #NB13
2005 Press Pass Stealth Previews /5 #47
2005 Press Pass Stealth Previews /5 #50
2005 Press Pass Stealth Previews /5 #53
2005 Press Pass Stealth Profile #PR7
2005 Press Pass Stealth Samples #47
2005 Press Pass Stealth Samples #50
2005 Press Pass Stealth Samples #53
2005 Press Pass Stealth Samples #88
2005 Press Pass Stealth Samples #99
2005 Press Pass Stealth X-Ray /100 #X47
2005 Press Pass Stealth X-Ray /100 #X50
2005 Press Pass Stealth X-Ray /100 #X53
2005 Press Pass Stealth X-Ray /100 #X88
2005 Press Pass Stealth X-Ray /100 #X99
2005 Press Pass Total Memorabilia Power Pick #TM3
2005 Press Pass Trackside #4
2005 Press Pass Trackside #62
2005 Press Pass Trackside #72
2005 Press Pass Trackside #85
2005 Press Pass Trackside Dialed In #DI2
2005 Press Pass Trackside Golden /100 #G4
2005 Press Pass Trackside Golden /100 #G62
2005 Press Pass Trackside Golden /100 #G72
2005 Press Pass Trackside Golden /100 #G85
2005 Press Pass Trackside Hat Giveaway #PPH10
2005 Press Pass Trackside Hot Pass #6
2005 Press Pass Trackside Hot Pass National #6
2005 Press Pass Trackside Hot Pursuit #HP1
2005 Press Pass Trackside Previews /5 #4
2005 Press Pass Trackside Previews /1 #85
2005 Press Pass Trackside Runnin n' Gunnin #RG11
2005 Press Pass Trackside Samples #4
2005 Press Pass Trackside Samples #62
2005 Press Pass Trackside Samples #72
2005 Press Pass Trackside Samples #85
2005 Press Pass Triple Burner /100 #TB3
2005 Press Pass Triple Burner Exchange /100 #TB3
2005 VIP #9
2005 VIP #47
2005 VIP Head Gear #3
2005 VIP Head Gear Transparent #3
2005 VIP Making The Show #18
2005 VIP Previews /5 #EB9
2005 VIP Samples #9
2005 VIP Samples #47
2005 VIP Tradin' Paint Autographs /29 #KH
2005 VIP Tradin' Paint Cars /110 #TPT6
2005 VIP Tradin' Paint Drivers /90 #TPD6
2005 Wheels American Thunder #10
2005 Wheels American Thunder #35
2005 Wheels American Thunder #46
2005 Wheels American Thunder American Muscle #AM2
2005 Wheels American Thunder Cool Threads /475 #CT11
2005 Wheels American Thunder Medallion #MD15
2005 Wheels American Thunder Previews /5 #10
2005 Wheels American Thunder Pushin Pedal /150 #PP5
2005 Wheels American Thunder Samples #10
2005 Wheels American Thunder Samples #35
2005 Wheels American Thunder Samples #46
2005 Wheels American Thunder Triple Hat /190 #TH7
2005 Wheels Autographs #22
2005 Wheels High Gear #18
2005 Wheels High Gear #41
2005 Wheels High Gear Flag Chasers Black /55 #FC6
2005 Wheels High Gear Flag Chasers Blue-Yellow /25 #FC6
2005 Wheels High Gear Flag Chasers Checkered /10 #FC6
2005 Wheels High Gear Flag Chasers Green /55 #FC6
2005 Wheels High Gear Flag Chasers Red /55 #FC6
2005 Wheels High Gear Flag Chasers White /55 #FC6
2005 Wheels High Gear Flag Chasers Yellow /55 #FC6
2005 Wheels High Gear Flag to Flag #FF7
2005 Wheels High Gear Full Throttle #FT3
2005 Wheels High Gear MPH /100 #M18
2005 Wheels High Gear MPH /100 #M41
2005 Wheels High Gear Previews Green /5 #EB18
2005 Wheels High Gear Samples #18
2005 Wheels High Gear Samples #41
2006 Press Pass #20
2006 Press Pass #79
2006 Press Pass #88
2006 Press Pass #107
2006 Press Pass Autographs #21
2006 Press Pass Blaster Kmart #KHC
2006 Press Pass Blaster Target #KHB
2006 Press Pass Blaster Wal-Mart #KHA
2006 Press Pass Blue #B20
2006 Press Pass Blue #B79
2006 Press Pass Blue #B88
2006 Press Pass Blue #B107
2006 Press Pass Burning Rubber Autographs /29 #BRKH
2006 Press Pass Burning Rubber Cars /370 #BRT6
2006 Press Pass Burning Rubber Drivers /100 #BRD6
2006 Press Pass Burning Rubber Drivers Gold /1 #BRD6
2006 Press Pass Burnouts /900 #HT4
2006 Press Pass Burnouts Holofoil /100 #HT4
2006 Press Pass Collectors Series Making the Show #MS16
2006 Press Pass Cup Chase #CCR14
2006 Press Pass Cup Chase Prizes #CC4
2006 Press Pass Double Burner Firesuit-Glove /100 #DB5
2006 Press Pass Eclipse #13
2006 Press Pass Eclipse #43
2006 Press Pass Eclipse #84
2006 Press Pass Eclipse Previews /5 #EB13
2006 Press Pass Eclipse Racing Champions #RC5
2006 Press Pass Eclipse Racing Champions #RC19
2006 Press Pass Eclipse Skidmarks #SM17
2006 Press Pass Eclipse Skidmarks Holofoil /250 #SM17
2006 Press Pass Eclipse Teammates Autographs /25 #8
2006 Press Pass Eclipse Under Cover Autographs /29 #KH
2006 Press Pass Eclipse Under Cover Cars /140 #UCT12
2006 Press Pass Eclipse Under Cover Drivers Gold /1 #UCD12
2006 Press Pass Eclipse Under Cover Drivers Holofoil /100 #UCD12
2006 Press Pass Eclipse Under Cover Drivers Red /225 #UCD12
2006 Press Pass Eclipse Under Cover Drivers Silver /400 #UCD12
2006 Press Pass Four Wide /50 #FWKH
2006 Press Pass Four Wide Checkered Flag /1 #FWKH
2006 Press Pass Gold #G20
2006 Press Pass Gold #G79
2006 Press Pass Gold #G88
2006 Press Pass Gold #G107
2006 Press Pass Legends #40
2006 Press Pass Legends Autographs Blue /50 #7
2006 Press Pass Legends Blue /1999 #B40
2006 Press Pass Legends Bronze /999 #Z40
2006 Press Pass Legends Gold /299 #G40
2006 Press Pass Legends Holofoil /99 #H40
2006 Press Pass Legends Press Plates Black /1 #PPB40
2006 Press Pass Legends Press Plates Black Backs /1 #PPB40B
2006 Press Pass Legends Press Plates Cyan /1 #PPC40
2006 Press Pass Legends Press Plates Cyan Backs /1 #PPC40B
2006 Press Pass Legends Press Plates Magenta /1 #PPM40
2006 Press Pass Legends Press Plates Magenta Backs /1 #PPM40B
2006 Press Pass Legends Press Plates Yellow /1 #PPY40
2006 Press Pass Legends Press Plates Yellow Backs /1 #PPY40B
2006 Press Pass Legends Previews /5 #EB40
2006 Press Pass Legends Solo /1 #S40
2006 Press Pass Legends Triple Threads /50 #TTKH
2006 Press Pass Optima #22
2006 Press Pass Optima #38
2006 Press Pass Optima #88
2006 Press Pass Optima #22B
2006 Press Pass Optima Fan Favorite #FF8
2006 Press Pass Optima Gold /100 #G22
2006 Press Pass Optima Gold /100 #G38
2006 Press Pass Optima Gold /100 #G88
2006 Press Pass Optima Previews /5 #EB22
2006 Press Pass Optima Q & A #QA5
2006 Press Pass Optima Rookie Relics Cars /50 #RRT11
2006 Press Pass Optima Rookie Relics Drivers /50 #RRD11
2006 Press Pass Platinum /100 #P20
2006 Press Pass Platinum /100 #P79
2006 Press Pass Platinum /100 #P88
2006 Press Pass Platinum /100 #P107
2006 Press Pass Premium #10
2006 Press Pass Premium #44
2006 Press Pass Premium #68
2006 Press Pass Premium Hot Threads Autographs /29 #HTKH
2006 Press Pass Premium Hot Threads Cars /165 #HTT6
2006 Press Pass Premium Hot Threads Drivers /220 #HTD6
2006 Press Pass Premium Hot Threads Drivers Gold /1 #HTD6
2006 Press Pass Premium In the Zone #IZ8
2006 Press Pass Premium In the Zone Red /250 #IZ8
2006 Press Pass Previews /5 #EB20
2006 Press Pass Previews /1 #EB107
2006 Press Pass Signings #22
2006 Press Pass Signings Gold /50 #22
2006 Press Pass Signings Gold Red Ink #22
2006 Press Pass Signings Red Ink #22
2006 Press Pass Signings Silver /100 #22
2006 Press Pass Stealth #11
2006 Press Pass Stealth #39
2006 Press Pass Stealth #50
2006 Press Pass Stealth #66
2006 Press Pass Stealth #69
2006 Press Pass Stealth Autographed Hat Entry #PPH8
2006 Press Pass Stealth Gear Grippers Autographs /29 #KH
2006 Press Pass Stealth Gear Grippers Cars Retail /99 #GGT8
2006 Press Pass Stealth Gear Grippers Drivers /99 #GGD8
2006 Press Pass Stealth Hot Pass #HP12
2006 Press Pass Stealth Previews /5 #11
2006 Press Pass Stealth Profile #P9
2006 Press Pass Stealth Retail #11
2006 Press Pass Stealth Retail #39
2006 Press Pass Stealth Retail #66
2006 Press Pass Stealth Retail #69
2006 Press Pass Stealth Retail #50
2006 Press Pass Stealth X-Ray /100 #X11
2006 Press Pass Stealth X-Ray /100 #X39
2006 Press Pass Stealth X-Ray /100 #X50

2006 Press Pass Stealth X-Ray /100 #X66
2006 Press Pass Stealth X-Ray /100 #X69
2006 Press Pass Top 25 Drivers & Rides #C15
2006 Press Pass Top 25 Drivers & Rides #D15
2006 TRAKS #13
2006 TRAKS #48
2006 TRAKS #105
2006 TRAKS Autographs #14
2006 TRAKS Autographs 100 /100 #8
2006 TRAKS Autographs 25 /25 #12
2006 TRAKS Previews /1 #13
2006 TRAKS Previews /1 #48
2006 TRAKS Previews /1 #105
2006 TRAKS Stickers #29
2006 VIP #9
2006 VIP #31
2006 VIP #47
2006 VIP #78
2006 VIP #87
2006 VIP Head Gear #HG10
2006 VIP Head Gear Transparent #HG10
2006 VIP Making the Show #MS16
2006 VIP Tradin' Paint Cars Bronze /145 #TPT7
2006 VIP Tradin' Paint Drivers Gold /50 #TPD7
2006 VIP Tradin' Paint Drivers Silver /80 #TPD7
2006 Wheels American Thunder #11
2006 Wheels American Thunder #54
2006 Wheels American Thunder #68
2006 Wheels American Thunder #89
2006 Wheels American Thunder American Racing Idol #RI8
2006 Wheels American Thunder American Racing Idol Golden /250 #RI8
2006 Wheels American Thunder Cool Threads /329 #CT12
2006 Wheels American Thunder Double Hat /99 #DH9
2006 Wheels American Thunder Grandstand #GS8
2006 Wheels American Thunder Head to Toe /99 #HT10
2006 Wheels American Thunder Previews /5 #EB11
2006 Wheels American Thunder Pushin' Pedal /199 #PP7
2006 Wheels American Thunder Thunder Road #TR5
2006 Wheels Autographs #22
2006 Wheels High Gear #13
2006 Wheels High Gear #52
2006 Wheels High Gear Flag Chasers Black /110 #FC7
2006 Wheels High Gear Flag Chasers Blue-Yellow /65 #FC7
2006 Wheels High Gear Flag Chasers Checkered /3 #FC7
2006 Wheels High Gear Flag Chasers Green /110 #FC7
2006 Wheels High Gear Flag Chasers Red /110 #FC7
2006 Wheels High Gear Flag Chasers White /110 #FC7
2006 Wheels High Gear Flag Chasers Yellow /110 #FC7
2006 Wheels High Gear Flag to Flag #FF9
2006 Wheels High Gear MPH /100 #M13
2006 Wheels High Gear MPH /100 #M52
2006 Wheels High Gear Previews Green /5 #EB13
2007 Press Pass #3
2007 Press Pass #34
2007 Press Pass #76
2007 Press Pass #93
2007 Press Pass #97
2007 Press Pass #110
2007 Press Pass Autographs #17
2007 Press Pass Autographs Press Plates Black /1 #5
2007 Press Pass Autographs Press Plates Cyan /1 #5
2007 Press Pass Autographs Press Plates Magenta /1 #6
2007 Press Pass Autographs Press Plates Yellow /1 #6
2007 Press Pass Blue #B3
2007 Press Pass Blue #B34
2007 Press Pass Blue #B76
2007 Press Pass Blue #B93
2007 Press Pass Blue #B97
2007 Press Pass Blue #B110
2007 Press Pass Burning Rubber Autographs /29 #BRSKH
2007 Press Pass Burning Rubber Drivers /75 #BRD5
2007 Press Pass Burning Rubber Drivers /75 #BRD17
2007 Press Pass Burning Rubber Drivers Gold /1 #BRD5
2007 Press Pass Burning Rubber Drivers Gold /1 #BRD17
2007 Press Pass Burning Rubber Team /325 #BRT5
2007 Press Pass Burning Rubber Team /325 #BRT17
2007 Press Pass Burnouts #BO3
2007 Press Pass Burnouts Blue /99 #BO3
2007 Press Pass Burnouts Gold /299 #BO3
2007 Press Pass Collector's Series Box Set #SB9
2007 Press Pass Cup Chase #CCR16
2007 Press Pass Cup Chase Prizes #CC11
2007 Press Pass Dale The Movie #45
2007 Press Pass Dale The Movie #46
2007 Press Pass Double Burner Metal-Tire /100 #DBKH
2007 Press Pass Double Burner Metal-Tire Exchange /100 #DBKH
2007 Press Pass Eclipse #0
2007 Press Pass Eclipse #4
2007 Press Pass Eclipse #39
2007 Press Pass Eclipse #44A
2007 Press Pass Eclipse #51
2007 Press Pass Eclipse #65
2007 Press Pass Eclipse #76
2007 Press Pass Eclipse #81
2007 Press Pass Eclipse #44B
2007 Press Pass Eclipse Ecliptic #EC11
2007 Press Pass Eclipse Gold /25 #G4
2007 Press Pass Eclipse Gold /25 #G39
2007 Press Pass Eclipse Gold /25 #G44
2007 Press Pass Eclipse Gold /25 #G51
2007 Press Pass Eclipse Gold /25 #G65
2007 Press Pass Eclipse Gold /25 #G76
2007 Press Pass Eclipse Gold /25 #G81
2007 Press Pass Eclipse Hyperdrive #HD4
2007 Press Pass Eclipse Previews /5 #EB4
2007 Press Pass Eclipse Previews /5 #EB39
2007 Press Pass Eclipse Racing Champions #RC2
2007 Press Pass Eclipse Racing Champions #RC13
2007 Press Pass Eclipse Red /1 #R4
2007 Press Pass Eclipse Red /1 #R39
2007 Press Pass Eclipse Red /1 #R44
2007 Press Pass Eclipse Red /1 #R51
2007 Press Pass Eclipse Red /1 #R65
2007 Press Pass Eclipse Red /1 #R76
2007 Press Pass Eclipse Red /1 #R81
2007 Press Pass Eclipse Skidmarks #SM3
2007 Press Pass Eclipse Skidmarks Holofoil /250 #SM3
2007 Press Pass Eclipse Teammates Autographs /25 #8
2007 Press Pass Eclipse Under Cover Drivers /450 #UCD5
2007 Press Pass Eclipse Under Cover Drivers Eclipse /1 #UCD5
2007 Press Pass Eclipse Under Cover Drivers Name /99 #UCD5
2007 Press Pass Eclipse Under Cover Drivers NASCAR /270 #UCD5
2007 Press Pass Eclipse Under Cover Teams /135 #UCT5
2007 Press Pass Eclipse Under Cover Teams NASCAR /25 #UCT5
2007 Press Pass Four Wide /50 #FWKH
2007 Press Pass Four Wide Checkered Flag /1 #FWKH
2007 Press Pass Four Wide Checkered Flag Exchange /1 #FWKH
2007 Press Pass Four Wide Exchange /50 #FWKH
2007 Press Pass Gold #G3
2007 Press Pass Gold #G34
2007 Press Pass Gold #G76
2007 Press Pass Gold #G93
2007 Press Pass Gold #G97
2007 Press Pass Gold #G110
2007 Press Pass Hot Treads #HT6
2007 Press Pass Hot Treads Blue /99 #HT6
2007 Press Pass Hot Treads Gold /299 #HT6
2007 Press Pass K-Mart #KHC
2007 Press Pass Legends #45
2007 Press Pass Legends #59
2007 Press Pass Legends Autographs Blue /71 #11
2007 Press Pass Legends Blue /999 #B45
2007 Press Pass Legends Blue /999 #B59
2007 Press Pass Legends Bronze /599 #Z45
2007 Press Pass Legends Bronze /599 #Z59
2007 Press Pass Legends Gold /249 #G45
2007 Press Pass Legends Gold /249 #G59
2007 Press Pass Legends Holofoil /99 #H45
2007 Press Pass Legends Holofoil /99 #H59
2007 Press Pass Legends Press Plates Black /1 #PP45
2007 Press Pass Legends Press Plates Black /1 #PP59
2007 Press Pass Legends Press Plates Black Backs /1 #PP45
2007 Press Pass Legends Press Plates Black Backs /1 #PP59
2007 Press Pass Legends Press Plates Cyan /1 #PP45
2007 Press Pass Legends Press Plates Cyan /1 #PP59
2007 Press Pass Legends Press Plates Cyan Backs /1 #PP45
2007 Press Pass Legends Press Plates Cyan Backs /1 #PP59
2007 Press Pass Legends Press Plates Magenta /1 #PP45
2007 Press Pass Legends Press Plates Magenta /1 #PP59
2007 Press Pass Legends Press Plates Magenta Backs /1 #PP45
2007 Press Pass Legends Press Plates Magenta Backs /1 #PP59
2007 Press Pass Legends Press Plates Yellow /1 #PP45
2007 Press Pass Legends Press Plates Yellow /1 #PP59
2007 Press Pass Legends Press Plates Yellow Backs /1 #PP45
2007 Press Pass Legends Press Plates Yellow Backs /1 #PP59
2007 Press Pass Legends Previews /5 #EB45
2007 Press Pass Legends Signature Series /25 #KH
2007 Press Pass Legends Solo /1 #S45
2007 Press Pass Legends Solo /1 #S59
2007 Press Pass Legends Sunday Swatches Bronze /199 #KHSS
2007 Press Pass Legends Sunday Swatches Gold /50 #KHSS
2007 Press Pass Legends Sunday Swatches Silver /99 #KHSS
2007 Press Pass Legends Victory Lane Bronze /199 #VL5
2007 Press Pass Legends Victory Lane Gold /25 #VL5
2007 Press Pass Legends Victory Lane Silver /99 #VL5
2007 Press Pass Platinum /100 #P3
2007 Press Pass Platinum /100 #P34
2007 Press Pass Platinum /100 #P76
2007 Press Pass Platinum /100 #P93
2007 Press Pass Platinum /100 #P97
2007 Press Pass Platinum /100 #P110
2007 Press Pass Premium #0
2007 Press Pass Premium #23
2007 Press Pass Premium #36
2007 Press Pass Premium #51
2007 Press Pass Premium Red /15 #R23
2007 Press Pass Premium Red /15 #R36
2007 Press Pass Premium Red /15 #R51
2007 Press Pass Previews /5 #EB3
2007 Press Pass Previews /5 #EB34
2007 Press Pass Previews /1 #EB110
2007 Press Pass Race Day #RD4
2007 Press Pass Signings #26
2007 Press Pass Signings Blue /25 #11
2007 Press Pass Signings Gold /50 #21
2007 Press Pass Signings Press Plates Black /1 #19
2007 Press Pass Signings Press Plates Cyan /1 #18
2007 Press Pass Signings Press Plates Magenta /1 #18
2007 Press Pass Signings Press Plates Yellow /1 #18
2007 Press Pass Signings Silver /100 #20
2007 Press Pass Snapshots #SN11
2007 Press Pass Stealth #10
2007 Press Pass Stealth #40
2007 Press Pass Stealth #77
2007 Press Pass Stealth #86
2007 Press Pass Stealth #64
2007 Press Pass Stealth Chrome #10
2007 Press Pass Stealth Chrome #40
2007 Press Pass Stealth Chrome #77A
2007 Press Pass Stealth Chrome #86
2007 Press Pass Stealth Chrome #77B
2007 Press Pass Stealth Chrome #64
2007 Press Pass Stealth Chrome Exclusives /99 #X10
2007 Press Pass Stealth Chrome Exclusives /99 #X40
2007 Press Pass Stealth Chrome Exclusives /99 #X64
2007 Press Pass Stealth Chrome Exclusives /99 #X77
2007 Press Pass Stealth Chrome Exclusives /99 #X86
2007 Press Pass Stealth Chrome Platinum /25 #P10
2007 Press Pass Stealth Chrome Platinum /25 #P40
2007 Press Pass Stealth Chrome Platinum /25 #P64
2007 Press Pass Stealth Chrome Platinum /25 #P77
2007 Press Pass Stealth Chrome Platinum /25 #P86
2007 Press Pass Stealth Fusion #F9
2007 Press Pass Stealth Mach 07 #M7-7
2007 Press Pass Stealth Maximum Access #MA11
2007 Press Pass Stealth Maximum Access Autographs /25 #MA11
2007 Press Pass Stealth Previews /1 #EB86
2007 Press Pass Stealth Previews /5 #EB40
2007 Press Pass Stealth Previews /5 #EB10
2007 Press Pass Target #KHB
2007 Press Pass Target Race Win Tires #RW2
2007 Press Pass Wal-Mart #KHA
2007 Press Pass Wal-Mart Autographs /50 #KH
2007 Traks #10
2007 Traks #78
2007 Traks #88
2007 Traks Driver's Seat #DS12B
2007 Traks Driver's Seat #DS12
2007 Traks Driver's Seat National #DS12
2007 Traks Gold #G10
2007 Traks Gold #G78
2007 Traks Gold #G88
2007 Traks Holofoil /50 #H10
2007 Traks Holofoil /50 #H78
2007 Traks Holofoil /50 #H88
2007 Traks Hot Pursuit #HP12
2007 Traks Previews /5 #EB10
2007 Traks Previews /1 #EB78
2007 Traks Red /10 #R10
2007 Traks Red /10 #R78
2007 Traks Red /10 #R88
2007 Traks Target Exclusives #KHA
2007 Traks Track Time #TT3
2007 Traks Wal-Mart Exclusives #KHB
2007 VIP #12
2007 VIP #59
2007 VIP #69
2007 VIP Gear Gallery #GG2
2007 VIP Gear Gallery Transparent #GG2
2007 VIP Get A Grip Autographs /29 #GGKH
2007 VIP Get A Grip Drivers /70 #GGD18
2007 VIP Get A Grip Teams /70 #GGT18
2007 VIP Pedal To The Metal /50 #PM9
2007 VIP Previews /5 #EB12
2007 VIP Sunday Best #SB9
2007 Wheels American Thunder #12
2007 Wheels American Thunder #53
2007 Wheels American Thunder #66
2007 Wheels American Thunder American Dreams #AD1
2007 Wheels American Thunder American Dreams Gold /250 #ADG1
2007 Wheels American Thunder American Muscle #AM7
2007 Wheels American Thunder Autographed Hat Instant Winner /1 #AH13
2007 Wheels American Thunder Previews /5 #EB12
2007 Wheels American Thunder Previews /1 #EB53
2007 Wheels American Thunder Thunder Road #TR8
2007 Wheels American Thunder Thunder Strokes #18
2007 Wheels American Thunder Thunder Strokes Press Plates Black /1 #18
2007 Wheels American Thunder Thunder Strokes Press Plates Cyan /1 #18
2007 Wheels American Thunder Thunder Strokes Press Plates Magenta /1 #18
2007 Wheels American Thunder Thunder Strokes Press Plates Yellow /1 #18
2007 Wheels American Thunder Triple Hat /99 #TH11
2007 Wheels Autographs #15
2007 Wheels Autographs Press Plates Black /1 #14
2007 Wheels Autographs Press Plates Cyan /1 #14
2007 Wheels Autographs Press Plates Magenta /1 #14
2007 Wheels High Gear #4
2007 Wheels High Gear #32
2007 Wheels High Gear #59
2007 Wheels High Gear #64
2007 Wheels High Gear #71A
2007 Wheels High Gear #76
2007 Wheels High Gear #83
2007 Wheels High Gear #71B
2007 Wheels High Gear Driven #DR7
2007 Wheels High Gear Final Standings Gold /4 #FS4
2007 Wheels High Gear Flag Chasers Black /89 #FC3
2007 Wheels High Gear Flag Chasers Blue-Yellow /50 #FC3
2007 Wheels High Gear Flag Chasers Checkered /10 #FC3
2007 Wheels High Gear Flag Chasers Green /89 #FC3
2007 Wheels High Gear Flag Chasers Red /89 #FC3
2007 Wheels High Gear Flag Chasers White /89 #FC3
2007 Wheels High Gear Flag Chasers Yellow /89 #FC3
2007 Wheels High Gear Full Throttle #FT3
2007 Wheels High Gear Last Lap /10 #LL4
2007 Wheels High Gear MPH /100 #M4
2007 Wheels High Gear MPH /100 #M32
2007 Wheels High Gear MPH /100 #M59
2007 Wheels High Gear MPH /100 #M64
2007 Wheels High Gear MPH /100 #M71
2007 Wheels High Gear MPH /100 #M76
2007 Wheels High Gear MPH /100 #M83
2007 Wheels High Gear Previews /5 #EB4
2007 Wheels High Gear Previews /5 #EB32
2007 Wheels High Gear Previews /5 #EB59
2007 Wheels High Gear Previews /5 #EB64
2007 Wheels High Gear Top Tier #TT4
2008 Press Pass #0
2008 Press Pass #10
2008 Press Pass #76
2008 Press Pass #88
2008 Press Pass #117
2008 Press Pass #80
2008 Press Pass #75
2008 Press Pass Autographs #17
2008 Press Pass Autographs Press Plates Black /1 #13
2008 Press Pass Autographs Press Plates Cyan /1 #13
2008 Press Pass Autographs Press Plates Magenta /1 #13
2008 Press Pass Autographs Press Plates Yellow /1 #13
2008 Press Pass Blue #B10
2008 Press Pass Blue #B75
2008 Press Pass Blue #B76
2008 Press Pass Blue #B80
2008 Press Pass Blue #B88
2008 Press Pass Blue #B117
2008 Press Pass Burning Rubber Autographs /29 #BRKH
2008 Press Pass Burning Rubber Drivers /60 #BRD1
2008 Press Pass Burning Rubber Drivers Gold /1 #BRD1
2008 Press Pass Burning Rubber Drivers Prime Cuts /25 #BRD1
2008 Press Pass Burning Rubber Teams /175 #BRT1
2008 Press Pass Burnouts #BO3
2008 Press Pass Burnouts Blue /99 #BO3
2008 Press Pass Burnouts Gold /299 #BO3
2008 Press Pass Collector's Series Box Set #7
2008 Press Pass Cup Chase #CC6
2008 Press Pass Cup Chase Prizes #CC11
2008 Press Pass Daytona 500 50th Anniversary #44
2008 Press Pass Daytona 500 50th Anniversary #49
2008 Press Pass Eclipse #9
2008 Press Pass Eclipse #77
2008 Press Pass Eclipse #75
2008 Press Pass Eclipse Escape Velocity #EV9
2008 Press Pass Eclipse Gold /25 #G9
2008 Press Pass Eclipse Gold /25 #G75
2008 Press Pass Eclipse Gold /25 #G77
2008 Press Pass Eclipse Hyperdrive #HP5
2008 Press Pass Eclipse Previews /5 #EB9
2008 Press Pass Eclipse Previews /1 #EB75
2008 Press Pass Eclipse Previews /1 #EB77
2008 Press Pass Eclipse Red /1 #R9
2008 Press Pass Eclipse Red /1 #R75
2008 Press Pass Eclipse Red /1 #R77
2008 Press Pass Eclipse Star Tracks #ST7
2008 Press Pass Eclipse Star Tracks Holofoil /250 #ST7
2008 Press Pass Eclipse Stellar #ST9
2008 Press Pass Eclipse Stellar #ST15
2008 Press Pass Eclipse Teammates Autographs /25 #BBH
2008 Press Pass Eclipse Under Cover Double Cover Name /25 #DC2
2008 Press Pass Eclipse Under Cover Double Cover NASCAR /99 #DC2
2008 Press Pass Eclipse Under Cover Drivers /250 #UCD3
2008 Press Pass Eclipse Under Cover Drivers Eclipse /1 #UCD3
2008 Press Pass Eclipse Under Cover Drivers Name /50 #UCD3
2008 Press Pass Eclipse Under Cover Drivers NASCAR /150 #UCD3
2008 Press Pass Eclipse Under Cover Teams /99 #UCT3
2008 Press Pass Eclipse Under Cover Teams NASCAR /25 #UCT3
2008 Press Pass Four Wide /50 #FWKH
2008 Press Pass Four Wide Checkered Flag /1 #FWKH
2008 Press Pass Gold #G10
2008 Press Pass Gold #G75
2008 Press Pass Gold #G76
2008 Press Pass Gold #G80
2008 Press Pass Gold #G88
2008 Press Pass Gold #G117
2008 Press Pass Hot Treads #HT7
2008 Press Pass Hot Treads Blue /99 #HT7
2008 Press Pass Hot Treads Gold /299 #HT7
2008 Press Pass Legends #50
2008 Press Pass Legends Autographs Black /10 #KH
2008 Press Pass Legends Autographs Blue /75 #KH
2008 Press Pass Legends Autographs Press Plates Black /1 #KH
2008 Press Pass Legends Autographs Press Plates Cyan /1 #KH
2008 Press Pass Legends Autographs Press Plates Magenta /1 #KH
2008 Press Pass Legends Autographs Press Plates Yellow /1 #KH
2008 Press Pass Legends Blue /599 #50
2008 Press Pass Legends Bronze /299 #50
2008 Press Pass Legends Gold /99 #50
2008 Press Pass Legends Holo /25 #50
2008 Press Pass Legends IROC Champions /380 #I22
2008 Press Pass Legends IROC Champions Gold /99 #I22
2008 Press Pass Legends Previews /5 #EB50
2008 Press Pass Legends Printing Plates Black /1 #50
2008 Press Pass Legends Printing Plates Cyan /1 #50
2008 Press Pass Legends Printing Plates Magenta /1 #50
2008 Press Pass Legends Printing Plates Yellow /1 #50
2008 Press Pass Legends Prominent Pieces Firesuit-Glove Bronze /50 #PP1KH
2008 Press Pass Legends Prominent Pieces Firesuit-Glove Gold /10 #PP1KH
2008 Press Pass Legends Prominent Pieces Firesuit-Glove Silver /25 #PP1KH
2008 Press Pass Legends Prominent Pieces Metal-Tire-Net /50 #PP4KH
2008 Press Pass Legends Prominent Pieces Metal-Tire-Net Gold /25 #PP4KH
2008 Press Pass Legends Signature Series Memorabilia /25 #LSKH
2008 Press Pass Legends Solo /1 #50
2008 Press Pass Legends Victory Lane Bronze /99 #VLKH
2008 Press Pass Legends Victory Lane Gold /25 #VLKH
2008 Press Pass Legends Victory Lane Silver /50 #VLKH
2008 Press Pass Platinum /100 #P10
2008 Press Pass Platinum /100 #P75
2008 Press Pass Platinum /100 #P76
2008 Press Pass Platinum /100 #P80
2008 Press Pass Platinum /100 #P88
2008 Press Pass Platinum /100 #P117
2008 Press Pass Premium #22
2008 Press Pass Premium #38
2008 Press Pass Premium #66
2008 Press Pass Premium Clean Air #CA6
2008 Press Pass Premium Hot Threads Autographs /29 #HTKH
2008 Press Pass Premium Hot Threads Drivers /120 #HTD1
2008 Press Pass Premium Hot Threads Drivers Gold /1 #HTD1
2008 Press Pass Premium Hot Threads Patches /6 #HTP11
2008 Press Pass Premium Hot Threads Patches /6 #HTP10
2008 Press Pass Premium Hot Threads Patches /14 #HTP9
2008 Press Pass Premium Hot Threads Team /120 #HTT1
2008 Press Pass Premium Previews /5 #EB22
2008 Press Pass Premium Previews /1 #EB66
2008 Press Pass Premium Red /15 #22
2008 Press Pass Premium Red /15 #38
2008 Press Pass Premium Red /15 #66
2008 Press Pass Premium Target #TA3
2008 Press Pass Previews /5 #EB10
2008 Press Pass Previews /1 #EB117
2008 Press Pass Signings #26
2008 Press Pass Signings Blue /25 #10
2008 Press Pass Signings Gold /50 #23
2008 Press Pass Signings Press Plates Black /1 #17
2008 Press Pass Signings Press Plates Cyan /1 #17
2008 Press Pass Signings Press Plates Cyan /1 #KH
2008 Press Pass Signings Press Plates Magenta /1 #17
2008 Press Pass Signings Press Plates Magenta #KH
2008 Press Pass Signings Press Plates Yellow /1 #17
2008 Press Pass Signings Silver /100 #23
2008 Press Pass Speedway #6
2008 Press Pass Speedway #59
2008 Press Pass Speedway #67
2008 Press Pass Speedway #96
2008 Press Pass Speedway Blur #B9
2008 Press Pass Speedway Cockpit #CP8
2008 Press Pass Speedway Corporate Cuts Drivers /80 #CDKH
2008 Press Pass Speedway Corporate Cuts Drivers Patches #CDKH
2008 Press Pass Speedway Corporate Cuts Team /165 #CTKH
2008 Press Pass Speedway Gold #G6
2008 Press Pass Speedway Gold #G59
2008 Press Pass Speedway Gold #G67
2008 Press Pass Speedway Gold #G96
2008 Press Pass Speedway Holofoil /50 #H6
2008 Press Pass Speedway Holofoil /50 #H59
2008 Press Pass Speedway Holofoil /50 #H67
2008 Press Pass Speedway Holofoil /50 #H96
2008 Press Pass Speedway Previews /5 #EB6
2008 Press Pass Speedway Previews /1 #EB96
2008 Press Pass Speedway Red /10 #R6
2008 Press Pass Speedway Red /10 #R59
2008 Press Pass Speedway Red /10 #R67
2008 Press Pass Speedway Red /10 #R96
2008 Press Pass Starting Grid #SG7
2008 Press Pass Stealth #13
2008 Press Pass Stealth #42
2008 Press Pass Stealth #51
2008 Press Pass Stealth #78
2008 Press Pass Stealth #86
2008 Press Pass Stealth #69
2008 Press Pass Stealth Battle Armor Autographs /29 #BASKH
2008 Press Pass Stealth Battle Armor Drivers /120 #BAD17
2008 Press Pass Stealth Battle Armor Teams /115 #BAT17
2008 Press Pass Stealth Chrome #13
2008 Press Pass Stealth Chrome #42
2008 Press Pass Stealth Chrome #51
2008 Press Pass Stealth Chrome #78
2008 Press Pass Stealth Chrome #86
2008 Press Pass Stealth Chrome #69A
2008 Press Pass Stealth Chrome #69B
2008 Press Pass Stealth Chrome Exclusives /25 #13
2008 Press Pass Stealth Chrome Exclusives /25 #42
2008 Press Pass Stealth Chrome Exclusives /25 #51
2008 Press Pass Stealth Chrome Exclusives /25 #69
2008 Press Pass Stealth Chrome Exclusives /25 #78
2008 Press Pass Stealth Chrome Exclusives /25 #86
2008 Press Pass Stealth Chrome Exclusives Gold /99 #13
2008 Press Pass Stealth Chrome Exclusives Gold /99 #42
2008 Press Pass Stealth Chrome Exclusives Gold /99 #51
2008 Press Pass Stealth Chrome Exclusives Gold /99 #69
2008 Press Pass Stealth Chrome Exclusives Gold /99 #78
2008 Press Pass Stealth Chrome Exclusives Gold /99 #86
2008 Press Pass Stealth Mach 08 #M8-7
2008 Press Pass Stealth Maximum Access #MA12
2008 Press Pass Stealth Maximum Access Autographs /25 #MA12
2008 Press Pass Stealth Previews /5 #13
2008 Press Pass Stealth Previews /5 #42
2008 Press Pass Stealth Previews /1 #86
2008 Press Pass Stealth Wal-Mart #WM9
2008 Press Pass Target Victory Tires /50 #TTKH
2008 Press Pass Wal-Mart Autographs /50 #5
2008 Press Pass Weekend Warriors #WW4
2008 VIP #14
2008 VIP All Access #AA9
2008 VIP Gear Gallery #GG2
2008 VIP Gear Gallery Memorabilia /50 #GGKH
2008 VIP Gear Gallery Transparent #GG2
2008 VIP Previews /5 #EB14
2008 VIP Triple Grip /25 #TG2
2008 Wheels American Thunder #14
2008 Wheels American Thunder #79
2008 Wheels American Thunder #45
2008 Wheels American Thunder American Dreams #AD9
2008 Wheels American Thunder American Dreams Gold /250 #AD9
2008 Wheels American Thunder Autographed Hat Winner /1 #IWHKH
2008 Wheels American Thunder Campaign Trail #CT7
2008 Wheels American Thunder Cool Threads /325 #CT7
2008 Wheels American Thunder Previews /5 #14
2008 Wheels American Thunder Previews /1 #79
2008 Wheels American Thunder Trackside Treasury Autographs #KH
2008 Wheels American Thunder Trackside Treasury Autographs Gold /25 #KH
2008 Wheels American Thunder Trackside Treasury Autographs Printing Plates Black /1 #KH
2008 Wheels American Thunder Trackside Treasury Autographs Printing Plates Cyan /1 #KH
2008 Wheels American Thunder Trackside Treasury Autographs Printing Plates Magenta /1 #KH
2008 Wheels American Thunder Trackside Treasury Autographs Printing Plates Yellow /1 #KH
2008 Wheels American Thunder Triple Hat /125 #TH10
2008 Wheels Autographs #13
2008 Wheels Autographs Chase Edition /25 #5
2008 Wheels Autographs Press Plates Black /1 #13
2008 Wheels Autographs Press Plates Cyan /1 #13
2008 Wheels Autographs Press Plates Magenta /1 #13
2008 Wheels Autographs Press Plates Yellow /1 #13
2008 Wheels High Gear #10
2008 Wheels High Gear #34
2008 Wheels High Gear #43
2008 Wheels High Gear #44
2008 Wheels High Gear #51
2008 Wheels High Gear #68
2008 Wheels High Gear Driven #DR9
2008 Wheels High Gear Final Standings /10 #F10
2008 Wheels High Gear Flag Chasers Black /89 #FC4
2008 Wheels High Gear Flag Chasers Blue-Yellow /50 #FC4
2008 Wheels High Gear Flag Chasers Checkered /20 #FC4
2008 Wheels High Gear Flag Chasers Green /60 #FC4
2008 Wheels High Gear Flag Chasers Red /89 #FC4
2008 Wheels High Gear Flag Chasers White /65 #FC4
2008 Wheels High Gear Flag Chasers Yellow /89 #FC4
2008 Wheels High Gear Full Throttle #FT3
2008 Wheels High Gear Last Lap /10 #LL6
2008 Wheels High Gear Last Lap Holofoil /5 #LL6
2008 Wheels High Gear MPH /100 #M10
2008 Wheels High Gear MPH /100 #M34
2008 Wheels High Gear MPH /100 #M43
2008 Wheels High Gear MPH /100 #M44
2008 Wheels High Gear MPH /100 #M51
2008 Wheels High Gear MPH /100 #M68
2008 Wheels High Gear Previews /5 #EB10
2008 Wheels High Gear The Chase #TC10
2009 Element #12
2009 Element #42
2009 Element #59
2009 Element 1-2-3 Finish /50 #RCR
2009 Element Elements of the Race Black Flag /99 #ERBKH
2009 Element Elements of the Race Black-White Flag /50 #ERXKH
2009 Element Elements of the Race Blue-Yellow Flag /50 #ERBOKH
2009 Element Elements of the Race Checkered Flag /5 #ERCKH
2009 Element Elements of the Race Green Flag /50 #ERGKH
2009 Element Elements of the Race Red Flag /99 #ERRKH
2009 Element Elements of the Race White Flag /75 #ERWKH
2009 Element Elements of the Race Yellow Flag /99 #ERYKH
2009 Element Kinetic Energy #KE8
2009 Element Lab Report #LR12
2009 Element Previews /5 #12
2009 Element Radioactive /100 #12
2009 Element Radioactive /100 #42
2009 Element Radioactive /100 #59
2009 Press Pass #0
2009 Press Pass #11
2009 Press Pass #46
2009 Press Pass #61
2009 Press Pass #117
2009 Press Pass #132
2009 Press Pass #162
2009 Press Pass Autographs Chase Edition /25 #KH
2009 Press Pass Autographs Gold #19
2009 Press Pass Autographs Printing Plates Black /1 #18
2009 Press Pass Autographs Printing Plates Cyan /1 #18
2009 Press Pass Autographs Printing Plates Magenta /1 #18
2009 Press Pass Autographs Printing Plates Yellow /1 #18
2009 Press Pass Autographs Silver #22
2009 Press Pass Autographs Track Edition /25 #KH
2009 Press Pass Blue #11
2009 Press Pass Blue #46
2009 Press Pass Blue #61
2009 Press Pass Blue #117
2009 Press Pass Blue #132
2009 Press Pass Blue #162
2009 Press Pass Burning Rubber Autographs /29 #BRSKH
2009 Press Pass Cup Chase #CCR9
2009 Press Pass Daytona 500 Tires /25 #TTKH
2009 Press Pass Eclipse #17
2009 Press Pass Eclipse #53
2009 Press Pass Eclipse #65
2009 Press Pass Eclipse #84
2009 Press Pass Eclipse Black and White #17
2009 Press Pass Eclipse Black and White #53
2009 Press Pass Eclipse Black and White #65
2009 Press Pass Eclipse Black and White #84
2009 Press Pass Eclipse Blue #17
2009 Press Pass Eclipse Blue #53
2009 Press Pass Eclipse Blue #65
2009 Press Pass Eclipse Blue #84
2009 Press Pass Eclipse Ecliptic Path #EP3
2009 Press Pass Eclipse Solar Swatches /299 #SSKH2
2009 Press Pass Eclipse Solar Swatches /299 #SSKH5
2009 Press Pass Eclipse Solar Swatches /50 #SSKH4
2009 Press Pass Eclipse Solar Swatches /99 #SSKH6
2009 Press Pass Eclipse Solar Swatches /250 #SSKH3
2009 Press Pass Eclipse Solar Swatches /299 #SSKH7
2009 Press Pass Eclipse Solar Swatches /250 #SSKH1
2009 Press Pass Eclipse Solar System #SS4
2009 Press Pass Eclipse Under Cover Autographs /29 #UCSKH
2009 Press Pass Final Standings /115 #117
2009 Press Pass Four Wide Autographs /5 #FWKH
2009 Press Pass Four Wide Checkered Flag /1 #FWKH
2009 Press Pass Four Wide Firesuit /50 #FWKH
2009 Press Pass Four Wide Sheet Metal /10 #FWKH
2009 Press Pass Four Wide Tire /25 #FWKH
2009 Press Pass Freeze Frame #FF15
2009 Press Pass Fusion #69
2009 Press Pass Fusion Bronze /150 #69
2009 Press Pass Fusion Gold /50 #69
2009 Press Pass Fusion Green /25 #69
2009 Press Pass Fusion Onyx /1 #69
2009 Press Pass Fusion Revered Relics Gold /50 #RRKH
2009 Press Pass Fusion Revered Relics Holofoil /25 #RRKH
2009 Press Pass Fusion Revered Relics Premium Swatch /10 #RRKH
2009 Press Pass Fusion Revered Relics Silver /65 #RRKH
2009 Press Pass Fusion Silver /99 #69
2009 Press Pass Gold #11
2009 Press Pass Gold #46
2009 Press Pass Gold #61
2009 Press Pass Gold #117
2009 Press Pass Gold #132
2009 Press Pass Gold #162
2009 Press Pass Gold Holofoil /100 #11
2009 Press Pass Gold Holofoil /100 #46
2009 Press Pass Gold Holofoil /100 #61
2009 Press Pass Gold Holofoil /100 #117
2009 Press Pass Gold Holofoil /100 #132
2009 Press Pass Gold Holofoil /100 #162
2009 Press Pass Legends #47
2009 Press Pass Legends Autographs Gold /40 #15
2009 Press Pass Legends Autographs Holofoil /15 #14
2009 Press Pass Legends Autographs Printing Plates Black /1 #12
2009 Press Pass Legends Autographs Printing Plates Cyan /1 #11
2009 Press Pass Legends Autographs Printing Plates Magenta /1 #12
2009 Press Pass Legends Autographs Printing Plates Yellow /1 #12
2009 Press Pass Legends Gold /399 #47
2009 Press Pass Legends Holofoil /50 #47
2009 Press Pass Legends Previews /5 #47
2009 Press Pass Legends Printing Plates Black /1 #47
2009 Press Pass Legends Printing Plates Cyan /1 #47
2009 Press Pass Legends Printing Plates Magenta /1 #47
2009 Press Pass Legends Printing Plates Yellow /1 #47
2009 Press Pass Legends Prominent Pieces Bronze /99 #PPKH
2009 Press Pass Legends Prominent Pieces Gold /25 #PPKH
2009 Press Pass Legends Prominent Pieces Oversized /25 #PPOEKH
2009 Press Pass Legends Prominent Pieces Silver /50 #PPKH
2009 Press Pass Legends Red /199 #47
2009 Press Pass Legends Solo /1 #47
2009 Press Pass NASCAR Gallery #NG10
2009 Press Pass Pocket Portraits #P10
2009 Press Pass Pocket Portraits Checkered Flag #P10
2009 Press Pass Pocket Portraits Hometown #P10
2009 Press Pass Pocket Portraits Smoke #P10
2009 Press Pass Pocket Portraits Target #PPT5
2009 Press Pass Premium #21
2009 Press Pass Premium #52
2009 Press Pass Premium #70
2009 Press Pass Premium Hot Threads /325 #HTKH1
2009 Press Pass Premium Hot Threads /99 #HTKH2
2009 Press Pass Premium Hot Threads Autographs /29 #KH
2009 Press Pass Premium Hot Threads Multi-Color /25 #HTKH
2009 Press Pass Premium Hot Threads Patches /5 #HTP-KH
2009 Press Pass Premium Hot Threads Patches /9 #HTP-KH
2009 Press Pass Premium Previews /5 #EB21
2009 Press Pass Premium Previews /1 #EB51
2009 Press Pass Premium Signatures #14
2009 Press Pass Premium Signatures Gold /25 #13
2009 Press Pass Premium Top Contenders #TC2
2009 Press Pass Premium Top Contenders Gold #TC2
2009 Press Pass Premium Win Streak #WS5
2009 Press Pass Premium Win Streak Victory Lane #WSVL-KH
2009 Press Pass Previews /5 #EB11
2009 Press Pass Previews /1 #EB117
2009 Press Pass Previews /5 #EB132
2009 Press Pass Red #11
2009 Press Pass Red #46
2009 Press Pass Red #61
2009 Press Pass Red #117
2009 Press Pass Red #132
2009 Press Pass Red #162
2009 Press Pass Santa Hats /50 #SH8
2009 Press Pass Showcase /499 #15
2009 Press Pass Showcase /499 #41
2009 Press Pass Showcase /499 #33
2009 Press Pass Showcase 2nd Gear /125 #15
2009 Press Pass Showcase 2nd Gear /125 #33
2009 Press Pass Showcase 2nd Gear /125 #41
2009 Press Pass Showcase 3rd Gear /50 #15
2009 Press Pass Showcase 3rd Gear /50 #33
2009 Press Pass Showcase 3rd Gear /50 #41
2009 Press Pass Showcase 4th Gear /15 #15
2009 Press Pass Showcase 4th Gear /15 #33
2009 Press Pass Showcase 4th Gear /15 #41
2009 Press Pass Showcase Classic Collections Firesuit /25 #CCF7
2009 Press Pass Showcase Classic Collections Firesuit Patch /5 #CCF7
2009 Press Pass Showcase Classic Collections Ink /45 #7
2009 Press Pass Showcase Classic Collections Ink Gold /25 #7
2009 Press Pass Showcase Classic Collections Ink Green /5 #7
2009 Press Pass Showcase Classic Collections Ink Melting /1 #7
2009 Press Pass Showcase Classic Collections Sheet Metal /45 #CCS7
2009 Press Pass Showcase Classic Collections Tire /99 #CCT7
2009 Press Pass Showcase Elite Exhibit Ink /45 #5
2009 Press Pass Showcase Elite Exhibit Ink Gold /25 #5
2009 Press Pass Showcase Elite Exhibit Ink Green /5 #5
2009 Press Pass Showcase Elite Exhibit Ink Melting /1 #5
2009 Press Pass Showcase Elite Exhibit Triple Memorabilia /99 #EEKH
2009 Press Pass Showcase Elite Exhibit Triple Memorabilia Gold /45 #EEKH
2009 Press Pass Showcase Elite Exhibit Triple Memorabilia Green /25 #EEKH
2009 Press Pass Showcase Elite Exhibit Triple Memorabilia Melting /5 #EEKH
2009 Press Pass Showcase Printing Plates Black /1 #15
2009 Press Pass Showcase Printing Plates Black /1 #33
2009 Press Pass Showcase Printing Plates Black /1 #41
2009 Press Pass Showcase Printing Plates Cyan /1 #15
2009 Press Pass Showcase Printing Plates Cyan /1 #33
2009 Press Pass Showcase Printing Plates Cyan /1 #41
2009 Press Pass Showcase Printing Plates Magenta /1 #15
2009 Press Pass Showcase Printing Plates Magenta /1 #33
2009 Press Pass Showcase Printing Plates Magenta /1 #41
2009 Press Pass Showcase Printing Plates Yellow /1 #15
2009 Press Pass Showcase Printing Plates Yellow /1 #33
2009 Press Pass Showcase Printing Plates Yellow /1 #41
2009 Press Pass Showcase Prized Pieces Firesuit /25 #PPFKH
2009 Press Pass Showcase Prized Pieces Firesuit Patch /5 #PPFKH
2009 Press Pass Showcase Prized Pieces Ink Firesuit /5 #5
2009 Press Pass Showcase Prized Pieces Ink Firesuit Patch /1 #5
2009 Press Pass Showcase Prized Pieces Ink Sheet Metal /25 #5
2009 Press Pass Showcase Prized Pieces Ink Tire /45 #5
2009 Press Pass Showcase Prized Pieces Sheet Metal /45 #PPSKH
2009 Press Pass Showcase Prized Pieces Tire /99 #PPTKH
2009 Press Pass Signature Series Archive Edition /1 #GGKH
2009 Press Pass Signature Series Archive Edition /1 #TPKH
2009 Press Pass Signature Series Archive Edition /1 #TPKH
2009 Press Pass Signature Series Archive Edition /1 #BAKH
2009 Press Pass Signings Blue /25 #16
2009 Press Pass Signings Gold #16
2009 Press Pass Signings Green /15 #16
2009 Press Pass Signings Orange /65 #16
2009 Press Pass Signings Printing Plates Magenta /1 #16
2009 Press Pass Signings Printing Plates Yellow /1 #16
2009 Press Pass Signings Purple /45 #16
2009 Press Pass Sponsor Swatches /225 #SSKH
2009 Press Pass Sponsor Swatches Select /10 #SSKH
2009 Press Pass Stealth #14
2009 Press Pass Stealth #46
2009 Press Pass Stealth #52
2009 Press Pass Stealth #60
2009 Press Pass Stealth #70
2009 Press Pass Stealth Battle Armor /99 #BAKH1
2009 Press Pass Stealth Battle Armor /65 #BAKH2
2009 Press Pass Stealth Battle Armor Multi-Color /150 #BAKH
2009 Press Pass Stealth Chrome #14
2009 Press Pass Stealth Chrome #46
2009 Press Pass Stealth Chrome #52
2009 Press Pass Stealth Chrome #60
2009 Press Pass Stealth Chrome #70
2009 Press Pass Stealth Chrome Brushed Metal /25 #14
2009 Press Pass Stealth Chrome Brushed Metal /25 #46
2009 Press Pass Stealth Chrome Brushed Metal /25 #52
2009 Press Pass Stealth Chrome Brushed Metal /25 #60
2009 Press Pass Stealth Chrome Brushed Metal /25 #70
2009 Press Pass Stealth Chrome Gold /99 #14
2009 Press Pass Stealth Chrome Gold /99 #46
2009 Press Pass Stealth Chrome Gold /99 #52
2009 Press Pass Stealth Chrome Gold /99 #60
2009 Press Pass Stealth Chrome Gold /99 #70
2009 Press Pass Stealth Confidential Classified Bronze #PC14
2009 Press Pass Stealth Confidential Secret Silver #PC14
2009 Press Pass Stealth Confidential Top Secret Gold /25 #PC14
2009 Press Pass Stealth Mach 09 #M2
2009 Press Pass Stealth Previews /5 #EB14
2009 Press Pass Tradin' Paint #TP6
2009 Press Pass Tread Marks Autographs /10 #SSKH
2009 Press Pass Wal-Mart Autographs Red #6
2009 Press Pass Wal-Mart Signature Edition /50 #KH
2009 VIP #13
2009 VIP #54
2009 VIP #83
2009 VIP Get A Grip /120 #GGKH
2009 VIP Get A Grip Autographs /29 #GGSKH
2009 VIP Get A Grip Holofoil /10 #GGKH
2009 VIP Get A Grip Logos /5 #GGLKH
2009 VIP Guest List #GG20
2009 VIP Hardware #H5
2009 VIP Hardware Transparent #H5
2009 VIP Leadfoot /150 #LFKH

2009 VIP Leadfoot Holofoil /10 #LFKH
2009 VIP Leadfoot Logos /5 #LFLKH
2009 VIP Previews /5 #13
2009 VIP Purple /25 #13
2009 VIP Purple /25 #54
2009 VIP Purple /25 #83
2009 Wheels Autographs #26
2009 Wheels Autographs /50 #27
2009 Wheels Autographs /25 #28
2009 Wheels Autographs Press Plates Black /1 #KH
2009 Wheels Autographs Press Plates Cyan /1 #KH
2009 Wheels Autographs Press Plates Magenta /1 #KH
2009 Wheels Autographs Press Plates Yellow /1 #KH
2009 Wheels Main Event #10
2009 Wheels Main Event #39
2009 Wheels Main Event Buyback Archive Edition /1 #TBKH
2009 Wheels Main Event Buyback Archive Edition /1 #TBTKH
2009 Wheels Main Event Buyback Archive Edition /1 #BRKH
2009 Wheels Main Event Buyback Archive Edition /1 #PSKH
2009 Wheels Main Event Buyback Archive Edition /1 #BRKH
2009 Wheels Main Event Fast Pass Purple /25 #10
2009 Wheels Main Event Fast Pass Purple /25 #39
2009 Wheels Main Event Foil #10
2009 Wheels Main Event Hat Dance Patch /10 #HDKH
2009 Wheels Main Event Hat Dance Triple /99 #HDKH
2009 Wheels Main Event High Rollers #HR9
2009 Wheels Main Event Marks Clubs #25
2009 Wheels Main Event Marks Diamonds /10 #25
2009 Wheels Main Event Marks Hearts /5 #25
2009 Wheels Main Event Marks Printing Plates Black /1 #21
2009 Wheels Main Event Marks Printing Plates Cyan /1 #21
2009 Wheels Main Event Marks Printing Plates Magenta /1 #21
2009 Wheels Main Event Marks Printing Plates Yellow /1 #21
2009 Wheels Main Event Marks Spades /1 #25
2009 Wheels Main Event Playing Cards Blue #QH
2009 Wheels Main Event Playing Cards Blue #4H
2009 Wheels Main Event Playing Cards Red #QH
2009 Wheels Main Event Playing Cards Red #4H
2009 Wheels Main Event Poker Chips #7
2009 Wheels Main Event Previews /5 #10
2009 Wheels Main Event Renegade Rounders Wanted #RR5
2009 Wheels Main Event Reward Copper /10 #RWKH
2009 Wheels Main Event Reward Holofoil /50 #RWKH
2009 Wheels Main Event Stop and Go Swatches Pit Banner /175 #SGBKH
2009 Wheels Main Event Stop and Go Swatches Pit Banner Green /10 #SGBKH
2009 Wheels Main Event Stop and Go Swatches Pit Banner Holofoil /75 #SGBKH
2009 Wheels Main Event Stop and Go Swatches Pit Banner Red /25 #SGBKH
2009 Wheels Main Event Wildcard Cuts /2 #WCCKH
2010 Action Racing Collectables Platinum 1:24 /507 #33
2010 Element #7
2010 Element #87
2010 Element #88
2010 Element Blue /35 #7
2010 Element Blue /35 #87
2010 Element Blue /35 #88
2010 Element Green #7
2010 Element Green #87
2010 Element Green #88
2010 Element Previews /5 #EB7
2010 Element Purple /25 #7
2010 Element Recycled Materials Blue /25 #RMKH
2010 Element Recycled Materials Green /125 #RMKH
2010 Element Red Target #7
2010 Element Red Target #87
2010 Element Red Target #88
2010 Press Pass #23
2010 Press Pass #63
2010 Press Pass Autographs #21
2010 Press Pass Autographs Printing Plates Black /1 #16
2010 Press Pass Autographs Printing Plates Cyan /1 #18
2010 Press Pass Autographs Printing Plates Magenta /1 #16
2010 Press Pass Autographs Printing Plates Yellow /1 #17
2010 Press Pass Autographs Track Edition /10 #5
2010 Press Pass Blue #23
2010 Press Pass Blue #63
2010 Press Pass Burning Rubber Autographs /29 #SSTEKH
2010 Press Pass By The Numbers #BN36
2010 Press Pass Cup Chase #CCR11
2010 Press Pass Cup Chase Prizes #CC3
2010 Press Pass Eclipse #17
2010 Press Pass Eclipse #38
2010 Press Pass Eclipse #49
2010 Press Pass Eclipse Blue #17
2010 Press Pass Eclipse Blue #38
2010 Press Pass Eclipse Blue #49
2010 Press Pass Eclipse Gold #17
2010 Press Pass Eclipse Gold #38
2010 Press Pass Eclipse Gold #49
2010 Press Pass Eclipse Previews /5 #17
2010 Press Pass Eclipse Previews /1 #38
2010 Press Pass Eclipse Purple /25 #17
2010 Press Pass Eclipse Purple /25 #38
2010 Press Pass Eclipse Purple /25 #49
2010 Press Pass Eclipse Signature Series Shoes Autographs /29 #SSSEKH
2010 Press Pass Five Star /35 #18
2010 Press Pass Five Star Classic Compilations Combos Firesuit Autographs /15 #CCMRCR
2010 Press Pass Five Star Classic Compilations Combos Patches Autographs /1 #CCMRCR
2010 Press Pass Five Star Classic Compilations Dual Memorabilia Autographs /10 #KH
2010 Press Pass Five Star Classic Compilations Firesuit Autographs /15 #KH
2010 Press Pass Five Star Classic Compilations Patch Autographs /1 #CCPKH1
2010 Press Pass Five Star Classic Compilations Patch Autographs /1 #CCPKH2
2010 Press Pass Five Star Classic Compilations Patch Autographs /1 #CCPKH3
2010 Press Pass Five Star Classic Compilations Patch Autographs /1 #CCPKH4
2010 Press Pass Five Star Classic Compilations Patch Autographs /1 #CCPKH5
2010 Press Pass Five Star Classic Compilations Patch Autographs /1 #CCPKH6
2010 Press Pass Five Star Classic Compilations Patch Autographs /1 #CCPKH7
2010 Press Pass Five Star Classic Compilations Patch Autographs /1 #CCPKH8
2010 Press Pass Five Star Classic Compilations Patch Autographs /1 #CCPKH9
2010 Press Pass Five Star Classic Compilations Patch Autographs /1 #CCPKH10
2010 Press Pass Five Star Classic Compilations Patch Autographs /1 #CCPKH11
2010 Press Pass Five Star Classic Compilations Patch Autographs /1 #CCPKH12
2010 Press Pass Five Star Classic Compilations Patch Autographs /1 #CCPKH13
2010 Press Pass Five Star Classic Compilations Patch Autographs /1 #CCPKH14
2010 Press Pass Five Star Classic Compilations Patch Autographs /1 #CCPKH15
2010 Press Pass Five Star Classic Compilations Patch Autographs /1 #CCPKH16
2010 Press Pass Five Star Classic Compilations Patch Autographs /1 #CCPKH17
2010 Press Pass Five Star Classic Compilations Patch Autographs /1 #CCPKH18
2010 Press Pass Five Star Classic Compilations Sheet Metal Autographs /25 #KH
2010 Press Pass Five Star Classic Compilations Triple Memorabilia Autographs /5 #KH
2010 Press Pass Five Star Holofoil /10 #18
2010 Press Pass Five Star Melting /1 #18
2010 Press Pass Five Star Paramount Pieces Aluminum /20 #KH
2010 Press Pass Five Star Paramount Pieces Blue /15 #KH
2010 Press Pass Five Star Paramount Pieces Gold /10 #KH
2010 Press Pass Five Star Paramount Pieces Holofoil /5 #KH
2010 Press Pass Five Star Paramount Pieces Melting /1 #KH
2010 Press Pass Five Star Signature Souvenirs Aluminum /50 #SSKH
2010 Press Pass Five Star Signature Souvenirs Gold /25 #SSKH
2010 Press Pass Five Star Signature Souvenirs Holofoil /10 #SSKH
2010 Press Pass Five Star Signature Souvenirs Melting /1 #SSKH
2010 Press Pass Five Star Signatures Aluminum /35 #KH
2010 Press Pass Five Star Signatures Gold /20 #KH
2010 Press Pass Five Star Signatures Holofoil /5 #KH
2010 Press Pass Five Star Signatures Melting /1 #KH
2010 Press Pass Four Wide Autographs /5 #NNO
2010 Press Pass Four Wide Firesuit /25 #FWKH
2010 Press Pass Four Wide Sheet Metal /15 #FWKH
2010 Press Pass Four Wide Shoes /1 #FWKH
2010 Press Pass Four Wide Tires /10 #FWKH
2010 Press Pass Gold #23
2010 Press Pass Gold #63
2010 Press Pass Holofoil /100 #23
2010 Press Pass Holofoil /100 #63
2010 Press Pass Legends Autographs Blue /10 #26
2010 Press Pass Legends Autographs Holofoil /25 #26
2010 Press Pass Legends Autographs Printing Plates Black /1 #23
2010 Press Pass Legends Autographs Printing Plates Cyan /1 #23
2010 Press Pass Legends Autographs Printing Plates Magenta /1 #23
2010 Press Pass Legends Autographs Printing Plates Yellow /1 #23
2010 Press Pass Legends Motorsports Masters #MMKH
2010 Press Pass Legends Motorsports Masters Autographs Printing Plates Black /1 #23
2010 Press Pass Legends Motorsports Masters Autographs Printing Plates Cyan /1 #23
2010 Press Pass Legends Motorsports Masters Autographs Printing Plates Magenta /1 #23
2010 Press Pass Legends Motorsports Masters Autographs Printing Plates Yellow /1 #23
2010 Press Pass Legends Motorsports Masters Blue /10 #MMKH
2010 Press Pass Legends Motorsports Masters Gold /299 #MMKH
2010 Press Pass Legends Motorsports Masters Holofoil /149 #MMKH
2010 Press Pass Legends Prominent Pieces Copper /99 #PPKH
2010 Press Pass Legends Prominent Pieces Gold /50 #PPKH
2010 Press Pass Legends Prominent Pieces Holofoil /25 #PPKH
2010 Press Pass Legends Prominent Pieces Oversized Firesuit /25 #PPOEKH
2010 Press Pass Premium #21
2010 Press Pass Premium #48
2010 Press Pass Premium #61
2010 Press Pass Premium #80
2010 Press Pass Premium Allies #A9
2010 Press Pass Premium Allies #A5
2010 Press Pass Premium Allies Signatures /5 #ASKH
2010 Press Pass Premium Hot Threads /299 #HTKH
2010 Press Pass Premium Hot Threads Holofoil /99 #HTKH
2010 Press Pass Premium Hot Threads Multi Color /25 #HTKH
2010 Press Pass Premium Hot Threads Two Color /125 #HTKH
2010 Press Pass Premium Purple /25 #21
2010 Press Pass Premium Purple /25 #48
2010 Press Pass Premium Purple /25 #61
2010 Press Pass Premium Rivals #R2
2010 Press Pass Premium Rivals #R4
2010 Press Pass Premium Rivals Signatures /5 #RSHB
2010 Press Pass Premium Rivals Signatures /5 #RSHM
2010 Press Pass Premium Signature Series Firesuit /15 #SSFKH
2010 Press Pass Premium Signatures #PSKH
2010 Press Pass Premium Signatures Red Ink /23 #PSKH
2010 Press Pass Previews /5 #23
2010 Press Pass Purple /25 #23
2010 Press Pass Purple /25 #63
2010 Press Pass Showcase /499 #21
2010 Press Pass Showcase /499 #41
2010 Press Pass Showcase /499 #33
2010 Press Pass Showcase Classic Collections Firesuit Green /25 #CCIRCR
2010 Press Pass Showcase Classic Collections Firesuit Patch Melting /5 #CCIRCR
2010 Press Pass Showcase Classic Collections Ink /15 #CCIRCR
2010 Press Pass Showcase Classic Collections Ink Gold /10 #CCIRCR
2010 Press Pass Showcase Classic Collections Ink Green /5 #CCIRCR
2010 Press Pass Showcase Classic Collections Ink Melting /1 #CCIRCR
2010 Press Pass Showcase Classic Collections Sheet Metal /99 #CCIRCR
2010 Press Pass Showcase Classic Collections Sheet Metal Gold /45 #CCIRCR
2010 Press Pass Showcase Elite Exhibit Ink /45 #EEIKH
2010 Press Pass Showcase Elite Exhibit Ink Gold /25 #EEIKH
2010 Press Pass Showcase Elite Exhibit Ink Green /5 #EEIKH
2010 Press Pass Showcase Elite Exhibit Ink Melting /1 #EEIKH
2010 Press Pass Showcase Elite Exhibit Triple Memorabilia /99 #EEMKH
2010 Press Pass Showcase Elite Exhibit Triple Memorabilia Gold /45 #EEMKH
2010 Press Pass Showcase Elite Exhibit Triple Memorabilia Green /25 #EEMKH
2010 Press Pass Showcase Elite Exhibit Triple Memorabilia Melting /5 #EEMKH
2010 Press Pass Showcase Gold /125 #21
2010 Press Pass Showcase Gold /125 #33
2010 Press Pass Showcase Gold /125 #41
2010 Press Pass Showcase Green /50 #21
2010 Press Pass Showcase Green /50 #33
2010 Press Pass Showcase Green /50 #41
2010 Press Pass Showcase Melting /15 #21
2010 Press Pass Showcase Melting /15 #33
2010 Press Pass Showcase Melting /15 #41
2010 Press Pass Showcase Platinum Holo /1 #21
2010 Press Pass Showcase Platinum Holo /1 #33
2010 Press Pass Showcase Platinum Holo /1 #41
2010 Press Pass Showcase Prized Pieces Firesuit Green /25 #PPMKH
2010 Press Pass Showcase Prized Pieces Firesuit Ink Gold /25 #PPIKH
2010 Press Pass Showcase Prized Pieces Firesuit Ink Melting /1 #PPIKH
2010 Press Pass Showcase Prized Pieces Firesuit Patch Melting /5 #PPMKH
2010 Press Pass Showcase Prized Pieces Memorabilia Ink Green /15 #PPIKH
2010 Press Pass Showcase Prized Pieces Sheet Metal /99 #PPMKH
2010 Press Pass Showcase Prized Pieces Sheet Metal Gold /45 #PPMKH
2010 Press Pass Showcase Prized Pieces Sheet Metal Ink Silver /45 #PPIKH
2010 Press Pass Signings Blue /10 #23
2010 Press Pass Signings Gold /15 #23
2010 Press Pass Signings Red /15 #23
2010 Press Pass Signings Silver /30 #23
2010 Press Pass Stealth #13
2010 Press Pass Stealth #53
2010 Press Pass Stealth #63
2010 Press Pass Stealth #75
2010 Press Pass Stealth Battle Armor Holofoil /25 #BAKH
2010 Press Pass Stealth Battle Armor Silver /275 #BAKH
2010 Press Pass Stealth Black and White #13
2010 Press Pass Stealth Black and White #53
2010 Press Pass Stealth Black and White #63
2010 Press Pass Stealth Black and White #75
2010 Press Pass Stealth Mach 10 #MT7
2010 Press Pass Stealth National Convention #VIP5
2010 Press Pass Stealth Previews /5 #13
2010 Press Pass Stealth Previews /5 #53
2010 Press Pass Stealth Previews /1 #63
2010 Press Pass Stealth Purple /25 #13
2010 Press Pass Stealth Purple /25 #53
2010 Press Pass Stealth Purple /25 #63
2010 Press Pass Stealth Signature Series Sheet Metal /15 #SSMEKH
2010 Press Pass Stealth Weekend Warriors Holofoil /25 #WWKH
2010 Press Pass Stealth Weekend Warriors Silver /199 #WWKH
2010 Press Pass Tradin' Paint #TP7
2010 Wheels Autographs #20
2010 Wheels Autographs Printing Plates Black /1 #20
2010 Wheels Autographs Printing Plates Cyan /1 #20
2010 Wheels Autographs Printing Plates Magenta /1 #20
2010 Wheels Autographs Printing Plates Yellow /1 #20
2010 Wheels Autographs Special Ink /10 #7
2010 Wheels Autographs Target /10 #13
2010 Wheels Main Event #14
2010 Wheels Main Event #40
2010 Wheels Main Event #61
2010 Wheels Main Event #99
2010 Wheels Main Event #69
2010 Wheels Main Event #75
2010 Wheels Main Event American Muscle #AM6
2010 Wheels Main Event Blue #14
2010 Wheels Main Event Blue #40
2010 Wheels Main Event Blue #61
2010 Wheels Main Event Blue #69
2010 Wheels Main Event Blue #75
2010 Wheels Main Event Blue #99
2010 Wheels Main Event Dual Firesuit /200 #KHDH
2010 Wheels Main Event Dual Firesuit Purple /200 #KHDH
2010 Wheels Main Event Fight Card #FC12
2010 Wheels Main Event Fight Card Checkered Flag #FC12
2010 Wheels Main Event Fight Card Full Color Retail #FC12
2010 Wheels Main Event Fight Card Gold /25 #FC12
2010 Wheels Main Event Head to Head /150 #HHKHJL
2010 Wheels Main Event Head to Head /150 #HHKHJB
2010 Wheels Main Event Head to Head Blue /75 #HHKHJL
2010 Wheels Main Event Head to Head Blue /75 #HHKHJB
2010 Wheels Main Event Head to Head Holofoil /10 #HHKHJL
2010 Wheels Main Event Head to Head Holofoil /10 #HHKHJB
2010 Wheels Main Event Head to Head Red /25 #HHKHJL
2010 Wheels Main Event Head to Head Red /25 #HHKHJB
2010 Wheels Main Event Marks Autographs /14 #23
2010 Wheels Main Event Marks Autographs Black /1 #22
2010 Wheels Main Event Marks Autographs Blue /5 #23
2010 Wheels Main Event Marks Autographs Red /5 #23
2010 Wheels Main Event Matchups Autographs /10 #JJKH
2010 Wheels Main Event Matchups Autographs /10 #KHDH
2010 Wheels Main Event Matchups Autographs /10 #KHRH
2010 Wheels Main Event Matchups Autographs /10 #KHJM
2010 Wheels Main Event Purple /25 #14
2010 Wheels Main Event Purple /25 #40
2010 Wheels Main Event Toe to Toe /10 #TTKHCB
2010 Wheels Main Event Toe to Toe /10 #TTXTR
2010 Wheels Main Event Upper Cuts Blue /50 #UCKH
2010 Wheels Main Event Upper Cuts Holofoil /10 #UCKH
2010 Wheels Main Event Upper Cuts Knock Out Patches /25 #UCKOKH
2010 Wheels Main Event Upper Cuts Red /25 #UCKH
2011 Element #14
2011 Element #43
2011 Element #67
2011 Element #75
2011 Element #89
2011 Element Autographs /45 #22
2011 Element Autographs Blue /5 #22
2011 Element Autographs Gold /10 #21
2011 Element Autographs Printing Plates Black /1 #22
2011 Element Autographs Printing Plates Cyan /1 #22
2011 Element Autographs Printing Plates Magenta /1 #22
2011 Element Autographs Printing Plates Yellow /1 #22
2011 Element Autographs Silver /15 #21
2011 Element Black /35 #14
2011 Element Black /35 #43
2011 Element Black /35 #67
2011 Element Black /35 #75
2011 Element Black /35 #89
2011 Element Finish Line Checkered Flag /10 #FLKH
2011 Element Finish Line Green Flag /25 #FLKH
2011 Element Finish Line Tires /99 #FLKH
2011 Element Finish Line Tires Purple Fast Pass /30 #FLKH
2011 Element Flagship Performers 2010 Laps Completed Yellow /50 #FPLKH
2011 Element Flagstand Swatches /25 #FSSKH
2011 Element Green #14
2011 Element Green #43
2011 Element Green #67
2011 Element Green #75
2011 Element Green #89
2011 Element Previews /5 #EB14
2011 Element Purple /25 #14
2011 Element Purple /25 #43
2011 Element Purple /25 #67
2011 Element Purple /25 #75
2011 Element Purple /25 #89
2011 Element Red #14
2011 Element Red #43
2011 Element Red #67
2011 Element Red #75
2011 Element Red #89
2011 Element Trackside Treasures Holofoil /25 #TTKH
2011 Element Trackside Treasures Silver /85 #TTKH
2011 Press Pass #14
2011 Press Pass #69
2011 Press Pass #135
2011 Press Pass #189
2011 Press Pass #0
2011 Press Pass Autographs Blue /5 #22
2011 Press Pass Autographs Bronze /10 #21
2011 Press Pass Autographs Gold /5 #21
2011 Press Pass Autographs Printing Plates Black /1 #22
2011 Press Pass Autographs Printing Plates Cyan /1 #22
2011 Press Pass Autographs Printing Plates Magenta /1 #22
2011 Press Pass Autographs Printing Plates Yellow /1 #22
2011 Press Pass Autographs Silver /10 #22
2011 Press Pass Blue Holofoil /10 #14
2011 Press Pass Blue Holofoil /10 #69
2011 Press Pass Blue Holofoil /10 #135
2011 Press Pass Blue Holofoil /10 #189
2011 Press Pass Blue Retail #14
2011 Press Pass Blue Retail #69
2011 Press Pass Blue Retail #135
2011 Press Pass Blue Retail #189
2011 Press Pass Burning Rubber Autographs /10 #BRKH
2011 Press Pass Burning Rubber Fast Pass /10 #BRKH
2011 Press Pass Burning Rubber Fast Pass /10 #BRKH2
2011 Press Pass Burning Rubber Gold /150 #BRKH
2011 Press Pass Burning Rubber Gold /150 #BRKH2
2011 Press Pass Burning Rubber Holofoil /50 #BRKH
2011 Press Pass Burning Rubber Holofoil /50 #BRKH2
2011 Press Pass Burning Rubber Prime Cuts /25 #BRKH
2011 Press Pass Cup Chase #CCR3
2011 Press Pass Cup Chase Prizes #CC2
2011 Press Pass Eclipse #13
2011 Press Pass Eclipse #66
2011 Press Pass Eclipse #87
2011 Press Pass Eclipse Blue #13
2011 Press Pass Eclipse Blue #66
2011 Press Pass Eclipse Blue #87
2011 Press Pass Eclipse Gold /55 #13
2011 Press Pass Eclipse Gold /55 #66
2011 Press Pass Eclipse Gold /55 #87
2011 Press Pass Eclipse Previews /5 #EB13
2011 Press Pass Eclipse Purple /25 #13
2011 Press Pass Eclipse Spellbound Swatches /150 #SBKH2
2011 Press Pass Eclipse Spellbound Swatches /150 #SBKH3
2011 Press Pass Eclipse Spellbound Swatches /250 #SBKH1
2011 Press Pass Eclipse Spellbound Swatches /100 #SBKH5
2011 Press Pass Eclipse Spellbound Swatches /100 #SBKH4
2011 Press Pass Eclipse Spellbound Swatches /75 #SBKH6
2011 Press Pass Eclipse Spellbound Swatches /50 #SBKH7
2011 Press Pass Eclipse Spellbound Swatches Signatures /10 #NNO
2011 Press Pass FanFare #17
2011 Press Pass FanFare Autographs Blue /5 #32
2011 Press Pass FanFare Autographs Bronze /25 #32
2011 Press Pass FanFare Autographs Gold /15 #32
2011 Press Pass FanFare Autographs Printing Plates Black /1 #32
2011 Press Pass FanFare Autographs Printing Plates Cyan /1 #32
2011 Press Pass FanFare Autographs Printing Plates Magenta /1 #32
2011 Press Pass FanFare Autographs Printing Plates Yellow /1 #32
2011 Press Pass FanFare Autographs Silver /10 #32
2011 Press Pass FanFare Blue Die Cuts #17
2011 Press Pass FanFare Championship Caliber #CC26
2011 Press Pass FanFare Dual Autographs /10 #NNO
2011 Press Pass FanFare Dual Autographs /10 #NNO
2011 Press Pass FanFare Emerald /25 #17
2011 Press Pass FanFare Holofoil Die Cuts #17
2011 Press Pass FanFare Magnificent Materials /199 #MMKH
2011 Press Pass FanFare Magnificent Materials Dual Swatches /50 #MMDKH
2011 Press Pass FanFare Magnificent Materials Dual Swatches Holofoil /10 #MMDKH
2011 Press Pass FanFare Magnificent Materials Holofoil /50 #MMKH
2011 Press Pass FanFare Magnificent Materials Signatures /50 #MMSEKH
2011 Press Pass FanFare Magnificent Materials Signatures Holofoil /25 #MMSEKH
2011 Press Pass FanFare Rookie Standouts #RS9
2011 Press Pass FanFare Ruby Die Cuts /15 #17
2011 Press Pass FanFare Sapphire /10 #17
2011 Press Pass FanFare Silver /25 #17
2011 Press Pass Flashback #FB6
2011 Press Pass Four Wide Firesuit /25 #FWKH
2011 Press Pass Four Wide Glove /1 #FWKH
2011 Press Pass Four Wide Sheet Metal /15 #FWKH
2011 Press Pass Four Wide Tire /10 #FWKH
2011 Press Pass Geared Up Holofoil /50 #GUKH
2011 Press Pass Gold /50 #14
2011 Press Pass Gold /50 #69
2011 Press Pass Gold /50 #135
2011 Press Pass Gold /50 #189
2011 Press Pass Legends #44
2011 Press Pass Legends Autographs Blue /10 #LGAKH
2011 Press Pass Legends Autographs Gold /25 #LGAKH
2011 Press Pass Legends Autographs Printing Plates Black /1 #LGAKH
2011 Press Pass Legends Autographs Printing Plates Cyan /1 #LGAKH
2011 Press Pass Legends Autographs Printing Plates Magenta /1 #LGAKH
2011 Press Pass Legends Autographs Printing Plates Yellow /1 #LGAKH
2011 Press Pass Legends Autographs Silver /50 #LGAKH
2011 Press Pass Legends Gold /250 #44
2011 Press Pass Legends Holofoil /25 #44
2011 Press Pass Legends Printing Plates Black /1 #44
2011 Press Pass Legends Printing Plates Cyan /1 #44
2011 Press Pass Legends Printing Plates Magenta /1 #44
2011 Press Pass Legends Printing Plates Yellow /1 #44
2011 Press Pass Legends Prominent Pieces Gold /50 #PPKH
2011 Press Pass Legends Prominent Pieces Holofoil /25 #PPKH
2011 Press Pass Legends Prominent Pieces Oversized Firesuit /25 #PPOEKH
2011 Press Pass Legends Prominent Pieces Purple /15 #PPKH
2011 Press Pass Legends Prominent Pieces Silver /99 #PPKH
2011 Press Pass Legends Purple /25 #44
2011 Press Pass Legends Red /99 #44
2011 Press Pass Legends Solo /1 #44
2011 Press Pass Premium #48
2011 Press Pass Premium #51
2011 Press Pass Premium #63
2011 Press Pass Premium #70
2011 Press Pass Premium #16A
2011 Press Pass Premium #16B
2011 Press Pass Premium Hot Pursuit 3D #HP2
2011 Press Pass Premium Hot Pursuit Autographs /10 #HPAKH
2011 Press Pass Premium Hot Pursuit National Convention #HP2
2011 Press Pass Premium Hot Threads /150 #HTKH
2011 Press Pass Premium Hot Threads Fast Pass /25 #HTKH
2011 Press Pass Premium Hot Threads Multi Color /25 #HTKH
2011 Press Pass Premium Hot Threads Secondary Color /25 #HTKH
2011 Press Pass Premium Purple /25 #16
2011 Press Pass Premium Purple /25 #48
2011 Press Pass Premium Purple /25 #51
2011 Press Pass Premium Purple /25 #63
2011 Press Pass Premium Purple /25 #70
2011 Press Pass Premium Signatures /256 #PSKH
2011 Press Pass Premium Signatures Red Ink /20 #PSKH
2011 Press Pass Previews /5 #EB14
2011 Press Pass Previews /1 #EB189
2011 Press Pass Purple /25 #14
2011 Press Pass Purple /25 #189
2011 Press Pass Showcase /499 #5
2011 Press Pass Showcase /499 #50
2011 Press Pass Showcase /499 #57
2011 Press Pass Showcase Classic Collections Firesuit /45 #CCMRCR
2011 Press Pass Showcase Classic Collections Firesuit Patches /5 #CCMRCR
2011 Press Pass Showcase Classic Collections Ink /25 #CCMRCR
2011 Press Pass Showcase Classic Collections Ink Gold /5 #CCMRCR
2011 Press Pass Showcase Classic Collections Ink Melting /1 #CCMRCR
2011 Press Pass Showcase Classic Collections Sheet Metal /99 #CCMRCR
2011 Press Pass Showcase Elite Exhibit Ink /50 #EEIKH
2011 Press Pass Showcase Elite Exhibit Ink Gold /25 #EEIKH
2011 Press Pass Showcase Elite Exhibit Ink Melting /1 #EEIKH
2011 Press Pass Showcase Gold /125 #5
2011 Press Pass Showcase Gold /125 #50
2011 Press Pass Showcase Gold /125 #57
2011 Press Pass Showcase Green /25 #5
2011 Press Pass Showcase Green /25 #50
2011 Press Pass Showcase Green /25 #57
2011 Press Pass Showcase Masterpieces Ink /45 #MPIKH
2011 Press Pass Showcase Masterpieces Ink Gold /25 #MPIKH
2011 Press Pass Showcase Masterpieces Ink Melting /1 #MPIKH
2011 Press Pass Showcase Masterpieces Memorabilia /99 #MPMKH
2011 Press Pass Showcase Masterpieces Memorabilia Gold /45 #MPMKH
2011 Press Pass Showcase Masterpieces Memorabilia Melting /5 #MPMKH
2011 Press Pass Showcase Melting /1 #5
2011 Press Pass Showcase Melting /1 #50
2011 Press Pass Showcase Melting /1 #57
2011 Press Pass Showcase Prized Pieces Firesuit /99 #PPMKH
2011 Press Pass Showcase Prized Pieces Firesuit Gold /45 #PPMKH
2011 Press Pass Showcase Prized Pieces Firesuit Ink /25 #PPIKH
2011 Press Pass Showcase Prized Pieces Firesuit Patches Ink /1 #PPIKH
2011 Press Pass Showcase Prized Pieces Firesuit Patches Melting /5 #PPMKH
2011 Press Pass Showcase Prized Pieces Sheet Metal Ink /45 #PPIKH
2011 Press Pass Signature Series /11 #SSFKH
2011 Press Pass Signature Series /11 #SSMKH
2011 Press Pass Signature Series /11 #SSTKH
2011 Press Pass Signature Series /11 #SSBKH
2011 Press Pass Signings Black and White /10 #PPSKH
2011 Press Pass Signings Brushed Metal /50 #PPSKH
2011 Press Pass Signings Holofoil /25 #PPSKH
2011 Press Pass Signings Printing Plates Black /1 #PPSKH
2011 Press Pass Signings Printing Plates Cyan /1 #PPSKH
2011 Press Pass Signings Printing Plates Magenta /1 #PPSKH
2011 Press Pass Signings Printing Plates Yellow /1 #PPSKH
2011 Press Pass Stealth #16
2011 Press Pass Stealth #17
2011 Press Pass Stealth #18
2011 Press Pass Stealth Afterburner /99 #ABKH
2011 Press Pass Stealth Afterburner Gold /25 #ABKH
2011 Press Pass Stealth Black and White /25 #16
2011 Press Pass Stealth Black and White /25 #17
2011 Press Pass Stealth Black and White /25 #18
2011 Press Pass Stealth Holofoil /99 #16
2011 Press Pass Stealth Holofoil /99 #17
2011 Press Pass Stealth Holofoil /99 #18
2011 Press Pass Stealth In Flight Report #IF4
2011 Press Pass Stealth Metal of Honor Medal of Honor /50 #BAKH
2011 Press Pass Stealth Metal of Honor Purple Heart /25 #MHKH
2011 Press Pass Stealth Metal of Honor Silver Star /99 #BAKH
2011 Press Pass Stealth Purple /25 #16
2011 Press Pass Stealth Purple /25 #17
2011 Press Pass Stealth Purple /25 #18
2011 Press Pass Target Top 12 Tires /25 #T12KH
2011 Press Pass Target Winning Tickets #WTT1
2011 Press Pass Target Winning Tickets #WTT6
2011 Press Pass Wal-Mart Winning Tickets #WTW1
2011 Press Pass Winning Tickets #WT9
2011 Press Pass Winning Tickets #WT18
2011 Press Pass Winning Tickets #WT23
2011 Press Pass Winning Tickets #WT59
2011 Press Pass Winning Tickets #WT31
2011 Press Pass Winning Tickets #WT40
2011 Press Pass Winning Tickets #WT44
2011 Press Pass Winning Tickets #WT61
2011 Sports Illustrated for Kids #69
2011 Wheels Main Event #16
2011 Wheels Main Event #72
2011 Wheels Main Event All Stars #A9
2011 Wheels Main Event All Stars Brushed Foil /199 #A9
2011 Wheels Main Event All Stars Holofoil /50 #A9
2011 Wheels Main Event Black and White #16
2011 Wheels Main Event Black and White #72
2011 Wheels Main Event Blue /75 #16
2011 Wheels Main Event Blue /75 #72
2011 Wheels Main Event Gloves Off Holofoil /25 #GOKH
2011 Wheels Main Event Gloves Off Silver /99 #GOKH
2011 Wheels Main Event Green /1 #16
2011 Wheels Main Event Green /1 #72
2011 Wheels Main Event Headliners Holofoil /25 #HLKH
2011 Wheels Main Event Headliners Silver /99 #HLKH
2011 Wheels Main Event Marks Autographs Blue /5 #MEKH
2011 Wheels Main Event Marks Autographs Gold /15 #MEKH
2011 Wheels Main Event Marks Autographs Silver /30 #MEKH
2011 Wheels Main Event Matchups Autographs /10 #MEMKHJJ
2011 Wheels Main Event Matchups Autographs /10 #MEMKHDE
2011 Wheels Main Event Materials Holofoil /25 #MEMKH
2011 Wheels Main Event Materials Silver /99 #MEMKH
2011 Wheels Main Event Rear View #R8
2011 Wheels Main Event Rear View Brushed Foil /199 #R8
2011 Wheels Main Event Rear View Holofoil /50 #R8
2011 Wheels Main Event Red /20 #16
2011 Wheels Main Event Red /20 #72
2012 Press Pass #16
2012 Press Pass #81
2012 Press Pass #95
2012 Press Pass Autographs Blue /5 #PPAKH
2012 Press Pass Autographs Printing Plates Black /1 #PPAKH
2012 Press Pass Autographs Printing Plates Cyan /1 #PPAKH
2012 Press Pass Autographs Printing Plates Magenta /1 #PPAKH
2012 Press Pass Autographs Printing Plates Yellow /1 #PPAKH
2012 Press Pass Autographs Red /10 #PPAKH
2012 Press Pass Autographs Silver /25 #PPAKH
2012 Press Pass Blue #16
2012 Press Pass Blue #81
2012 Press Pass Blue #95
2012 Press Pass Blue Holofoil /35 #16
2012 Press Pass Blue Holofoil /35 #81
2012 Press Pass Blue Holofoil /35 #95
2012 Press Pass Burning Rubber Gold /99 #BRKH
2012 Press Pass Burning Rubber Gold /99 #BRKH2
2012 Press Pass Burning Rubber Gold /99 #BRKH3
2012 Press Pass Burning Rubber Gold /99 #BRKH4
2012 Press Pass Burning Rubber Holofoil /25 #BRKH
2012 Press Pass Burning Rubber Holofoil /25 #BRKH2
2012 Press Pass Burning Rubber Holofoil /25 #BRKH3
2012 Press Pass Burning Rubber Holofoil /25 #BRKH4
2012 Press Pass Burning Rubber Prime Cuts /25 #BRKH
2012 Press Pass Burning Rubber Prime Cuts /25 #BRKH2
2012 Press Pass Burning Rubber Prime Cuts /25 #BRKH3
2012 Press Pass Burning Rubber Prime Cuts /25 #BRKH4
2012 Press Pass Burning Rubber Purple /15 #BRKH
2012 Press Pass Burning Rubber Purple /15 #BRKH2
2012 Press Pass Burning Rubber Purple /15 #BRKH3
2012 Press Pass Burning Rubber Purple /15 #BRKH4
2012 Press Pass Cup Chase #CCR3
2012 Press Pass Cup Chase Prizes #CCP9
2012 Press Pass Fanfare #19
2012 Press Pass Fanfare Autographs Blue /5 #KH
2012 Press Pass Fanfare Autographs Gold /15 #KH
2012 Press Pass Fanfare Autographs Red /10 #KH
2012 Press Pass Fanfare Autographs Silver /50 #KH
2012 Press Pass Fanfare Blue Foil Die Cuts #19
2012 Press Pass Fanfare Diamond /5 #19
2012 Press Pass Fanfare Holofoil Die Cuts #19
2012 Press Pass Fanfare Magnificent Materials /250 #MMKH
2012 Press Pass Fanfare Magnificent Materials Dual Swatches /50 #MMKH
2012 Press Pass Fanfare Magnificent Materials Dual Swatches Melting /10 #MMKH
2012 Press Pass Fanfare Magnificent Materials Gold /125 #MMKH
2012 Press Pass Fanfare Magnificent Materials Signatures /25 #KH
2012 Press Pass Fanfare Magnificent Materials Signatures Blue /5 #KH
2012 Press Pass Fanfare Power Rankings #PR12
2012 Press Pass Fanfare Sapphire /20 #19
2012 Press Pass Fanfare Silver /25 #19
2012 Press Pass Four Wide Firesuit /25 #FWKH
2012 Press Pass Four Wide Glove /1 #FWKH
2012 Press Pass Four Wide Sheet Metal /15 #FWKH
2012 Press Pass Four Wide Tire /10 #FWKH
2012 Press Pass Gold #16
2012 Press Pass Gold #81
2012 Press Pass Gold #95
2012 Press Pass Ignite #17
2012 Press Pass Ignite Double Burner Gun Metal /10 #DBKH
2012 Press Pass Ignite Double Burner Red /1 #DBKH
2012 Press Pass Ignite Double Burner Silver /25 #DBKH
2012 Press Pass Ignite Materials Autographs Gun Metal /20 #IMKH
2012 Press Pass Ignite Materials Autographs Red /5 #IMKH
2012 Press Pass Ignite Materials Autographs Silver /125 #IMKH
2012 Press Pass Ignite Materials Gun Metal /99 #IMKH
2012 Press Pass Ignite Materials Red /10 #IMKH
2012 Press Pass Ignite Materials Silver #IMKH
2012 Press Pass Ignite Proofs Black and White /50 #17
2012 Press Pass Ignite Proofs Cyan #17
2012 Press Pass Ignite Proofs Magenta #17
2012 Press Pass Ignite Proofs Yellow /10 #17
2012 Press Pass Ignite Steel Horses #SH5
2012 Press Pass Ignite Supercharged Signatures /5 #SSKH
2012 Press Pass Legends #43
2012 Press Pass Legends Blue Holofoil /1 #43
2012 Press Pass Legends Gold /275 #43
2012 Press Pass Legends Green #43
2012 Press Pass Legends Prominent Pieces Gold /50 #KH
2012 Press Pass Legends Prominent Pieces Holofoil /25 #KH
2012 Press Pass Legends Prominent Pieces Silver /99 #KH
2012 Press Pass Legends Rainbow Holofoil /50 #43
2012 Press Pass Legends Red /99 #43
2012 Press Pass Legends Silver Holofoil /25 #43
2012 Press Pass Power Picks Blue /50 #7
2012 Press Pass Power Picks Blue /50 #65
2012 Press Pass Power Picks Gold /50 #7
2012 Press Pass Power Picks Gold /50 #65
2012 Press Pass Power Picks Holofoil /10 #7
2012 Press Pass Power Picks Holofoil /10 #65
2012 Press Pass Preferred Line #PL9
2012 Press Pass Purple /35 #16
2012 Press Pass Purple /35 #81
2012 Press Pass Purple /35 #95
2012 Press Pass Redline #17
2012 Press Pass Redline Black /99 #17
2012 Press Pass Redline Cyan /50 #17
2012 Press Pass Redline Full Throttle Dual Relic Blue /5 #FTKH
2012 Press Pass Redline Full Throttle Dual Relic Gold /10 #FTKH
2012 Press Pass Redline Full Throttle Dual Relic Melting /1 #FTKH
2012 Press Pass Redline Full Throttle Dual Relic Red /25 #FTKH
2012 Press Pass Redline Full Throttle Dual Relic Silver /15 #FTKH
2012 Press Pass Redline Intensity #I5
2012 Press Pass Redline Magenta /15 #17
2012 Press Pass Redline Muscle Car Sheet Metal Blue /5 #MCKH
2012 Press Pass Redline Muscle Car Sheet Metal Gold /10 #MCKH
2012 Press Pass Redline Muscle Car Sheet Metal Melting /1 #MCKH
2012 Press Pass Redline Muscle Car Sheet Metal Red /75 #MCKH
2012 Press Pass Redline Muscle Car Sheet Metal Silver /25 #MCKH
2012 Press Pass Redline Pieces of the Action Blue /10 #PAKH
2012 Press Pass Redline Pieces of the Action Gold /25 #PAKH
2012 Press Pass Redline Pieces of the Action Melting /1 #PAKH
2012 Press Pass Redline Pieces of the Action Red /75 #PAKH
2012 Press Pass Redline Pieces of the Action Silver /50 #PAKH
2012 Press Pass Redline Relic Autographs Blue /10 #RLRKH
2012 Press Pass Redline Relic Autographs Gold /25 #RLRKH
2012 Press Pass Redline Relic Autographs Melting /1 #RLRKH
2012 Press Pass Redline Relic Autographs Red /75 #RLRKH
2012 Press Pass Redline Relic Autographs Silver /47 #RLRKH
2012 Press Pass Redline Relics Blue /5 #RLKH
2012 Press Pass Redline Relics Gold /10 #RLKH
2012 Press Pass Redline Relics Melting /1 #RLKH
2012 Press Pass Redline Relics Red /25 #RLKH
2012 Press Pass Redline Relics Silver /15 #RLKH
2012 Press Pass Redline Rookie Year Relic Autographs Blue /5 #RYKH
2012 Press Pass Redline Rookie Year Relic Autographs Gold /25 #RYKH
2012 Press Pass Redline Rookie Year Relic Autographs Melting /1 #RYKH
2012 Press Pass Redline Rookie Year Relic Autographs Red /50 #RYKH
2012 Press Pass Redline Signatures Blue /5 #RSKH1
2012 Press Pass Redline Signatures Blue /5 #RSKH2
2012 Press Pass Redline Signatures Gold /25 #RSKH1
2012 Press Pass Redline Signatures Gold /15 #RSKH2
2012 Press Pass Redline Signatures Holofoil /10 #RSKH1
2012 Press Pass Redline Signatures Holofoil /10 #RSKH2
2012 Press Pass Redline Signatures Melting /1 #RSKH1
2012 Press Pass Redline Signatures Melting /1 #RSKH2
2012 Press Pass Redline Signatures Red /50 #RSKH1
2012 Press Pass Redline Signatures Red /25 #RSKH2
2012 Press Pass Redline V8 Relics Blue /5 #V8KH
2012 Press Pass Redline V8 Relics Gold /10 #V8KH
2012 Press Pass Redline V8 Relics Melting /1 #V8KH
2012 Press Pass Redline V8 Relics Red /25 #V8KH
2012 Press Pass Redline Yellow /1 #17
2012 Press Pass Showcar #SC7
2012 Press Pass Showcase /499 #55
2012 Press Pass Showcase /499 #38
2012 Press Pass Showcase /499 #12
2012 Press Pass Showcase Classic Collections Ink /10 #CCMRCR
2012 Press Pass Showcase Classic Collections Ink Gold /5 #CCMRCR
2012 Press Pass Showcase Classic Collections Ink Melting /1 #CCMRCR
2012 Press Pass Showcase Classic Collections Memorabilia /99 #CCMRCR
2012 Press Pass Showcase Classic Collections Memorabilia Gold /50 #CCMRCR
2012 Press Pass Showcase Classic Collections Memorabilia Melting /5 #CCMRCR
2012 Press Pass Showcase Elite Exhibit Ink /50 #EEIKH
2012 Press Pass Showcase Elite Exhibit Ink Gold /25 #EEIKH
2012 Press Pass Showcase Elite Exhibit Ink Melting /1 #EEIKH
2012 Press Pass Showcase Gold /125 #12
2012 Press Pass Showcase Gold /125 #38
2012 Press Pass Showcase Gold /125 #55
2012 Press Pass Showcase Green /5 #12
2012 Press Pass Showcase Green /5 #38
2012 Press Pass Showcase Green /5 #55
2012 Press Pass Showcase Masterpieces Ink /50 #MPIKH
2012 Press Pass Showcase Masterpieces Ink Gold /25 #MPIKH
2012 Press Pass Showcase Masterpieces Ink Melting /1 #MPIKH
2012 Press Pass Showcase Masterpieces Memorabilia /99 #MPKH
2012 Press Pass Showcase Masterpieces Memorabilia Gold /50 #MPKH
2012 Press Pass Showcase Masterpieces Memorabilia Melting /5 #MPKH
2012 Press Pass Showcase Melting /1 #12
2012 Press Pass Showcase Melting /1 #38
2012 Press Pass Showcase Melting /1 #55
2012 Press Pass Showcase Prized Pieces /99 #PPKH
2012 Press Pass Showcase Prized Pieces Gold /50 #PPKH
2012 Press Pass Showcase Prized Pieces Ink /50 #PPIKH
2012 Press Pass Showcase Prized Pieces Ink Gold /25 #PPIKH
2012 Press Pass Showcase Prized Pieces Ink Melting /1 #PPIKH
2012 Press Pass Showcase Prized Pieces Melting /5 #PPKH
2012 Press Pass Showcase Purple /1 #12
2012 Press Pass Showcase Purple /1 #38
2012 Press Pass Showcase Purple /1 #55
2012 Press Pass Showcase Red /25 #12
2012 Press Pass Showcase Red /25 #38
2012 Press Pass Showcase Red /25 #55
2012 Press Pass Showcase Richard Petty 75th Birthday Tribute /10 #RPKH
2012 Press Pass Showcase Richard Petty 75th Birthday Tribute Melting /1 #RPKH
2012 Press Pass Showcase Showcase Patches /5 #SSPKH
2012 Press Pass Showcase Showcase Patches Melting /1 #SSPKH
2012 Press Pass Showcase Showroom /499 #SR7
2012 Press Pass Showcase Showroom Gold /125 #SR7
2012 Press Pass Showcase Showroom Melting /1 #SR7
2012 Press Pass Showcase Showroom Memorabilia /99 #SRKH
2012 Press Pass Showcase Showroom Memorabilia Gold /50 #SRKH
2012 Press Pass Showcase Showroom Memorabilia Melting /5 #SRKH
2012 Press Pass Showcase Signature Patches /1 #SSPKH
2012 Press Pass Showman #SM7
2012 Press Pass Signature Series Race Used /12 #PPAKH1
2012 Press Pass Signature Series Race Used /12 #PPAKH2
2012 Press Pass Snapshots #SS16
2012 Press Pass Triple Gear 3 in 1 /5 #TGKH
2012 Press Pass Triple Gear Firesuit and Sheet Metal /15 #TGKH
2012 Press Pass Triple Gear Tire /25 #TGKH
2012 Press Pass Wal-Mart Snapshots #SSWM5
2012 Total Memorabilia #13A

2012 Total Memorabilia #13B
2012 Total Memorabilia Black and White /99 #13
2012 Total Memorabilia Dual Swatch Gold /75 #TMKH
2012 Total Memorabilia Dual Swatch Holofoil /25 #TMKH
2012 Total Memorabilia Dual Swatch Melting /5 #TMKH
2012 Total Memorabilia Dual Swatch Silver /99 #TMKH
2012 Total Memorabilia Gold /275 #13
2012 Total Memorabilia Hot Rod Relics Gold /50 #HRRKH
2012 Total Memorabilia Hot Rod Relics Holofoil /10 #HRRKH
2012 Total Memorabilia Hot Rod Relics Melting /1 #HRRKH
2012 Total Memorabilia Hot Rod Relics Silver /99 #HRRKH
2012 Total Memorabilia Jumbo Swatch Holofoil /10 #TMKH
2012 Total Memorabilia Jumbo Swatch Melting /1 #TMKH
2012 Total Memorabilia Quad Swatch Gold /25 #TMKH
2012 Total Memorabilia Quad Swatch Holofoil /10 #TMKH
2012 Total Memorabilia Quad Swatch Melting /1 #TMKH
2012 Total Memorabilia Quad Swatch Silver /50 #TMKH
2012 Total Memorabilia Red Retail /250 #13
2012 Total Memorabilia Signature Collection Dual Swatch Silver /10 #SCKH
2012 Total Memorabilia Signature Collection Quad Swatch Holofoil /5 #SCKH
2012 Total Memorabilia Signature Collection Single Swatch Melting /1 #SCKH
2012 Total Memorabilia Signature Collection Triple Swatch Gold /10 #SCKH
2012 Total Memorabilia Single Swatch Gold /99 #TMKH
2012 Total Memorabilia Single Swatch Holofoil /50 #TMKH
2012 Total Memorabilia Single Swatch Melting /10 #TMKH
2012 Total Memorabilia Single Swatch Silver /199 #TMKH
2012 Total Memorabilia Tandem Treasures Dual Memorabilia Gold /75 #TTKHRC
2012 Total Memorabilia Tandem Treasures Dual Memorabilia Gold /75 #TTKHSW
2012 Total Memorabilia Tandem Treasures Dual Memorabilia Holofoil /25 #TTKHRC
2012 Total Memorabilia Tandem Treasures Dual Memorabilia Holofoil /25 #TTKHSW
2012 Total Memorabilia Tandem Treasures Dual Memorabilia Melting /5 #TTKHRC
2012 Total Memorabilia Tandem Treasures Dual Memorabilia Melting /5 #TTKHSW
2012 Total Memorabilia Tandem Treasures Dual Memorabilia Silver /99 #TTKHRC
2012 Total Memorabilia Tandem Treasures Dual Memorabilia Silver /99 #TTKHSW
2012 Total Memorabilia Triple Swatch Gold /50 #TMKH
2012 Total Memorabilia Triple Swatch Holofoil /25 #TMKH
2012 Total Memorabilia Triple Swatch Melting /1 #TMKH
2012 Total Memorabilia Triple Swatch Silver /99 #TMKH
2013 Press Pass #19
2013 Press Pass #20
2013 Press Pass #87
2013 Press Pass #93
2013 Press Pass #74
2013 Press Pass #0
2013 Press Pass Aerodynamic Autographs Blue /5 #KH
2013 Press Pass Aerodynamic Autographs Holofoil /20 #KH
2013 Press Pass Color Proofs Black #19
2013 Press Pass Color Proofs Black #20
2013 Press Pass Color Proofs Black #74
2013 Press Pass Color Proofs Black #87
2013 Press Pass Color Proofs Black #93
2013 Press Pass Color Proofs Cyan /35 #19
2013 Press Pass Color Proofs Cyan /35 #20
2013 Press Pass Color Proofs Cyan /35 #74
2013 Press Pass Color Proofs Cyan /35 #87
2013 Press Pass Color Proofs Cyan /35 #93
2013 Press Pass Color Proofs Magenta #19
2013 Press Pass Color Proofs Magenta #20
2013 Press Pass Color Proofs Magenta #74
2013 Press Pass Color Proofs Magenta #87
2013 Press Pass Color Proofs Magenta #93
2013 Press Pass Color Proofs Yellow /5 #19
2013 Press Pass Color Proofs Yellow /5 #20
2013 Press Pass Color Proofs Yellow /5 #74
2013 Press Pass Color Proofs Yellow /5 #87
2013 Press Pass Color Proofs Yellow /5 #93
2013 Press Pass Cool Persistence #CP4
2013 Press Pass Cup Chase #CC9
2013 Press Pass Cup Chase Prizes #CCP4
2013 Press Pass Fanfare #23
2013 Press Pass Fanfare #24
2013 Press Pass Fanfare Autographs Blue /1 #KH
2013 Press Pass Fanfare Autographs Gold /5 #KH
2013 Press Pass Fanfare Autographs Green /2 #KH
2013 Press Pass Fanfare Autographs Red /1 #KH
2013 Press Pass Fanfare Autographs Silver /5 #KH
2013 Press Pass Fanfare Diamond Die Cuts /5 #23
2013 Press Pass Fanfare Diamond Die Cuts /5 #24
2013 Press Pass Fanfare Fan Following #FF11
2013 Press Pass Fanfare Green /3 #23
2013 Press Pass Fanfare Green /3 #24
2013 Press Pass Fanfare Holofoil Die Cuts #23
2013 Press Pass Fanfare Holofoil Die Cuts #24
2013 Press Pass Fanfare Magnificent Jumbo Materials Signatures /10 #KH
2013 Press Pass Fanfare Magnificent Materials Dual Swatches /50 #KH
2013 Press Pass Fanfare Magnificent Materials Dual Swatches Melting /10 #KH
2013 Press Pass Fanfare Magnificent Materials Gold /50 #KH
2013 Press Pass Fanfare Magnificent Materials Jumbo Swatches /25 #KH
2013 Press Pass Fanfare Magnificent Materials Signatures /50 #KH
2013 Press Pass Fanfare Magnificent Materials Signatures Blue /1 #KH
2013 Press Pass Fanfare Magnificent Materials Silver /199 #KH
2013 Press Pass Fanfare Red Foil Die Cuts #23
2013 Press Pass Fanfare Red Foil Die Cuts #24
2013 Press Pass Fanfare Sapphire /20 #23
2013 Press Pass Fanfare Sapphire /20 #24
2013 Press Pass Fanfare Showtime #S7
2013 Press Pass Fanfare Signature Ride Autographs /10 #KH
2013 Press Pass Fanfare Signature Ride Autographs Blue /1 #KH
2013 Press Pass Fanfare Signature Ride Autographs Red /5 #KH
2013 Press Pass Fanfare Silver /25 #23
2013 Press Pass Fanfare Silver /25 #24
2013 Press Pass Four Wide Gold /10 #FWKH
2013 Press Pass Four Wide Melting /1 #FWKH
2013 Press Pass Ignite #14
2013 Press Pass Ignite Double Burner Blue Holofoil /10 #DBKH
2013 Press Pass Ignite Double Burner Red /1 #DBKH
2013 Press Pass Ignite Double Burner Silver /25 #DBKH
2013 Press Pass Ignite Hot Threads Blue Holofoil /99 #HTKH
2013 Press Pass Ignite Hot Threads Patch Red /10 #HTKH
2013 Press Pass Ignite Hot Threads Patch Red Oversized /20 #HTPKH
2013 Press Pass Ignite Hot Threads Silver #HTKH
2013 Press Pass Ignite Ink Black /45 #IIKH
2013 Press Pass Ignite Ink Blue /10 #IIKH
2013 Press Pass Ignite Ink Red /5 #IIKH
2013 Press Pass Ignite Profile #6
2013 Press Pass Ignite Proofs Black and White /50 #14
2013 Press Pass Ignite Proofs Cyan #14
2013 Press Pass Ignite Proofs Magenta #14
2013 Press Pass Ignite Proofs Yellow /5 #14
2013 Press Pass Ignite Supercharged Signatures Blue Holofoil /10 #SSKH
2013 Press Pass Ignite Supercharged Signatures Red /1 #SSKH
2013 Press Pass Ignite Turning Point #8
2013 Press Pass Legends #45
2013 Press Pass Legends Autographs Blue #LGKH
2013 Press Pass Legends Autographs Gold /4 #LGKH
2013 Press Pass Legends Autographs Holofoil #LGKH
2013 Press Pass Legends Autographs Printing Plates Black /1 #LGKH
2013 Press Pass Legends Autographs Printing Plates Cyan /1 #LGKH
2013 Press Pass Legends Autographs Printing Plates Magenta /1 #LGKH
2013 Press Pass Legends Autographs Printing Plates Yellow /1 #LGKH
2013 Press Pass Legends Autographs Silver #LGKH
2013 Press Pass Legends Blue #45
2013 Press Pass Legends Blue Holofoil /1 #45
2013 Press Pass Legends Four Wide Memorabilia Autographs Gold /25 #FWSEKH
2013 Press Pass Legends Four Wide Memorabilia Autographs Melting /5 #FWSEKH
2013 Press Pass Legends Gold /149 #45
2013 Press Pass Legends Holofoil /10 #45
2013 Press Pass Legends Printing Plates Black /1 #45
2013 Press Pass Legends Printing Plates Cyan /1 #45
2013 Press Pass Legends Printing Plates Magenta /1 #45
2013 Press Pass Legends Printing Plates Yellow /1 #45
2013 Press Pass Legends Prominent Pieces Gold /10 #PPKH
2013 Press Pass Legends Prominent Pieces Holofoil /5 #PPKH
2013 Press Pass Legends Prominent Pieces Oversized Firesuit /5 #PPKH
2013 Press Pass Legends Prominent Pieces Silver /25 #PPKH
2013 Press Pass Legends Red /99 #45
2013 Press Pass Legends Signature Style #SS13
2013 Press Pass Legends Signature Style Blue /5 #SS13
2013 Press Pass Legends Signature Style Holofoil /99 #SS13
2013 Press Pass Legends Signature Style Melting /10 #SS13
2013 Press Pass Power Picks Blue /99 #7
2013 Press Pass Power Picks Blue /99 #37
2013 Press Pass Power Picks Gold /50 #7
2013 Press Pass Power Picks Gold /50 #37
2013 Press Pass Power Picks Holofoil /10 #7
2013 Press Pass Power Picks Holofoil /10 #37
2013 Press Pass Racing Champions #RC35
2013 Press Pass Redline #21
2013 Press Pass Redline #22
2013 Press Pass Redline Black /99 #21
2013 Press Pass Redline Black /99 #22
2013 Press Pass Redline Cyan /50 #21
2013 Press Pass Redline Cyan /50 #22
2013 Press Pass Redline Dynamic Duals Dual Relic Blue /5 #DDKH
2013 Press Pass Redline Dynamic Duals Dual Relic Gold /10 #DDKH
2013 Press Pass Redline Dynamic Duals Dual Relic Melting /1 #DDKH
2013 Press Pass Redline Dynamic Duals Dual Relic Red /50 #DDKH
2013 Press Pass Redline Dynamic Duals Dual Relic Silver /25 #DDKH
2013 Press Pass Redline Intensity #4
2013 Press Pass Redline Magenta /15 #21
2013 Press Pass Redline Magenta /15 #22
2013 Press Pass Redline Muscle Car Sheet Metal Blue /5 #MCMKH
2013 Press Pass Redline Muscle Car Sheet Metal Gold /10 #MCMKH
2013 Press Pass Redline Muscle Car Sheet Metal Melting /1 #MCMKH
2013 Press Pass Redline Muscle Car Sheet Metal Red /50 #MCMKH
2013 Press Pass Redline Muscle Car Sheet Metal Silver /25 #MCMKH
2013 Press Pass Redline Pieces of the Action Blue /10 #PAKH
2013 Press Pass Redline Pieces of the Action Gold /25 #PAKH
2013 Press Pass Redline Pieces of the Action Melting /1 #PAKH
2013 Press Pass Redline Pieces of the Action Red /75 #PAKH
2013 Press Pass Redline Pieces of the Action Silver /50 #PAKH
2013 Press Pass Redline Redline Racers #6
2013 Press Pass Redline Relic Autographs Blue /10 #RRSEKH
2013 Press Pass Redline Relic Autographs Gold /25 #RRSEKH
2013 Press Pass Redline Relic Autographs Melting /1 #RRSEKH
2013 Press Pass Redline Relic Autographs Red /75 #RRSEKH
2013 Press Pass Redline Relic Autographs Silver /50 #RRSEKH
2013 Press Pass Redline Relics Blue /5 #RRKH
2013 Press Pass Redline Relics Gold /10 #RRKH
2013 Press Pass Redline Relics Melting /1 #RRKH
2013 Press Pass Redline Relics Red /50 #RRKH
2013 Press Pass Redline Relics Silver /25 #RRKH
2013 Press Pass Redline RPM #8
2013 Press Pass Redline Signatures Blue /10 #RSKH1
2013 Press Pass Redline Signatures Blue /10 #RSKH2
2013 Press Pass Redline Signatures Gold /5 #RSKH1
2013 Press Pass Redline Signatures Gold /5 #RSKH2
2013 Press Pass Redline Signatures Holo /5 #RSKH1
2013 Press Pass Redline Signatures Holo /5 #RSKH2
2013 Press Pass Redline Signatures Melting /1 #RSKH1
2013 Press Pass Redline Signatures Melting /1 #RSKH2
2013 Press Pass Redline Signatures Red /10 #RSKH2
2013 Press Pass Redline Signatures Red /29 #RSKH1
2013 Press Pass Redline V8 Relics Blue /5 #V8KH
2013 Press Pass Redline V8 Relics Gold /10 #V8KH
2013 Press Pass Redline V8 Relics Melting /1 #V8KH
2013 Press Pass Redline V8 Relics Red /25 #V8KH
2013 Press Pass Redline Yellow /1 #21
2013 Press Pass Redline Yellow /1 #22
2013 Press Pass Showcase /349 #12
2013 Press Pass Showcase /349 #36
2013 Press Pass Showcase /349 #58
2013 Press Pass Showcase Black /1 #12
2013 Press Pass Showcase Black /1 #36
2013 Press Pass Showcase Black /1 #58
2013 Press Pass Showcase Blue /25 #12
2013 Press Pass Showcase Blue /25 #36
2013 Press Pass Showcase Blue /25 #58
2013 Press Pass Showcase Classic Collections Ink Gold /5 #CCIRCR
2013 Press Pass Showcase Classic Collections Ink Melting /1 #CCIRCR
2013 Press Pass Showcase Classic Collections Ink Red /1 #CCIRCR
2013 Press Pass Showcase Classic Collections Memorabilia Gold /25 #CCMRCR
2013 Press Pass Showcase Classic Collections Memorabilia Melting /5 #CCMRCR
2013 Press Pass Showcase Classic Collections Memorabilia Silver /75 #CCMRCR
2013 Press Pass Showcase Elite Exhibit Ink /25 #EEIKH
2013 Press Pass Showcase Elite Exhibit Ink Blue /30 #EEIKH
2013 Press Pass Showcase Elite Exhibit Ink Gold /10 #EEIKH
2013 Press Pass Showcase Elite Exhibit Ink Melting /1 #EEIKH
2013 Press Pass Showcase Elite Exhibit Ink Red /5 #EEIKH
2013 Press Pass Showcase Gold /99 #12
2013 Press Pass Showcase Gold /99 #36
2013 Press Pass Showcase Gold /99 #58
2013 Press Pass Showcase Green /20 #12
2013 Press Pass Showcase Green /20 #36
2013 Press Pass Showcase Green /20 #58
2013 Press Pass Showcase Masterpieces Ink /25 #MPIKH
2013 Press Pass Showcase Masterpieces Ink Gold /10 #MPIKH
2013 Press Pass Showcase Masterpieces Ink Melting /1 #MPIKH
2013 Press Pass Showcase Masterpieces Memorabilia /75 #MPKH
2013 Press Pass Showcase Masterpieces Memorabilia Gold /25 #MPKH
2013 Press Pass Showcase Masterpieces Memorabilia Melting /5 #MPKH
2013 Press Pass Showcase Prized Pieces /99 #PPMKH
2013 Press Pass Showcase Prized Pieces Blue /20 #PPMKH
2013 Press Pass Showcase Prized Pieces Gold /25 #PPMKH
2013 Press Pass Showcase Prized Pieces Ink /25 #PPIKH
2013 Press Pass Showcase Prized Pieces Ink Gold /10 #PPIKH
2013 Press Pass Showcase Prized Pieces Ink Melting /1 #PPIKH
2013 Press Pass Showcase Prized Pieces Melting /5 #PPMKH
2013 Press Pass Showcase Purple /13 #12
2013 Press Pass Showcase Purple /13 #36
2013 Press Pass Showcase Purple /13 #58
2013 Press Pass Showcase Red /10 #12
2013 Press Pass Showcase Red /10 #36
2013 Press Pass Showcase Red /10 #58
2013 Press Pass Showcase Showcase Patches /5 #SPKH
2013 Press Pass Showcase Showroom /299 #8
2013 Press Pass Showcase Showroom Blue /40 #8
2013 Press Pass Showcase Showroom Gold /50 #8
2013 Press Pass Showcase Showroom Green /20 #8
2013 Press Pass Showcase Showroom Melting /1 #8
2013 Press Pass Showcase Showroom Purple /13 #8
2013 Press Pass Showcase Showroom Red /10 #8
2013 Press Pass Showcase Signature Patches /5 #SSPKH
2013 Press Pass Signings Blue /1 #KH
2013 Press Pass Signings Gold /5 #KH
2013 Press Pass Signings Holofoil /5 #KH
2013 Press Pass Signings Printing Plates Black /1 #KH
2013 Press Pass Signings Printing Plates Cyan /1 #KH
2013 Press Pass Signings Printing Plates Magenta /1 #KH
2013 Press Pass Signings Printing Plates Yellow /1 #KH
2013 Press Pass Signings Silver /10 #KH
2013 Press Pass Three Wide Gold /10 #TWKH
2013 Press Pass Three Wide Melting /1 #TWKH
2013 Topps Allen and Ginter #35
2013 Topps Allen and Ginter Autographs #KH
2013 Topps Allen and Ginter Autographs Red Ink /10 #KH
2013 Topps Allen and Ginter Framed Mini Relics #KH
2013 Topps Allen and Ginter Glossy /1 #35
2013 Topps Allen and Ginter Mini #35
2013 Topps Allen and Ginter Mini A and G Back #35
2013 Topps Allen and Ginter Mini A and G Red Back /25 #35
2013 Topps Allen and Ginter Mini Black #35
2013 Topps Allen and Ginter Mini Framed Printing Plates Black /1 #35
2013 Topps Allen and Ginter Mini Framed Printing Plates Cyan /1 #35
2013 Topps Allen and Ginter Mini Framed Printing Plates Magenta /1 #35
2013 Topps Allen and Ginter Mini Framed Printing Plates Yellow /1 #35
2013 Topps Allen and Ginter Mini No Card Number /50 #35
2013 Topps Allen and Ginter Mini Wood /1 #35
2013 Total Memorabilia #17
2013 Total Memorabilia #18
2013 Total Memorabilia Black and White /99 #17
2013 Total Memorabilia Black and White /99 #18
2013 Total Memorabilia Burning Rubber Chase Edition Gold /75 #BRCKC
2013 Total Memorabilia Burning Rubber Chase Edition Holofoil /50 #BRCKC
2013 Total Memorabilia Burning Rubber Chase Edition Melting /5 #BRCKC
2013 Total Memorabilia Burning Rubber Chase Edition Silver /175 #BRCKC
2013 Total Memorabilia Dual Swatch Gold /199 #TMKH
2013 Total Memorabilia Gold /275 #17
2013 Total Memorabilia Gold /275 #18
2013 Total Memorabilia Hot Rod Relics Gold /50 #HRRKH
2013 Total Memorabilia Hot Rod Relics Holofoil /10 #HRRKH
2013 Total Memorabilia Hot Rod Relics Melting /1 #HRRKH
2013 Total Memorabilia Hot Rod Relics Silver /99 #HRRKH
2013 Total Memorabilia Memory Lane #ML5
2013 Total Memorabilia Quad Swatch Melting /10 #TMKH
2013 Total Memorabilia Red #17
2013 Total Memorabilia Red #18
2013 Total Memorabilia Signature Collection Dual Swatch Gold /10 #SCKH
2013 Total Memorabilia Signature Collection Quad Swatch Melting /1 #SCKH
2013 Total Memorabilia Signature Collection Single Swatch Silver /10 #SCKH
2013 Total Memorabilia Signature Collection Triple Swatch Holofoil /5 #SCKH
2013 Total Memorabilia Single Swatch Silver /475 #TMKH
2013 Total Memorabilia Smooth Operators #SO5
2013 Total Memorabilia Triple Swatch Holofoil /99 #TMKH
2014 Press Pass #15
2014 Press Pass #80
2014 Press Pass Aerodynamic Autographs Blue /1 #AAKH
2014 Press Pass Aerodynamic Autographs Holofoil /5 #AAKH
2014 Press Pass Aerodynamic Autographs Printing Plates Black /1 #AAKH
2014 Press Pass Aerodynamic Autographs Printing Plates Cyan /1 #AAKH
2014 Press Pass Aerodynamic Autographs Printing Plates Magenta /1 #AAKH
2014 Press Pass Aerodynamic Autographs Printing Plates Yellow /1 #AAKH
2014 Press Pass American Thunder #17
2014 Press Pass American Thunder #50
2014 Press Pass American Thunder Autographs Blue /10 #ATAKH
2014 Press Pass American Thunder Autographs Red /5 #ATAKH
2014 Press Pass American Thunder Autographs White /35 #ATAKH
2014 Press Pass American Thunder Battle Armor Blue /25 #BAKH
2014 Press Pass American Thunder Battle Armor Red /1 #BAKH
2014 Press Pass American Thunder Battle Armor Silver /99 #BAKH
2014 Press Pass American Thunder Black and White /50 #17
2014 Press Pass American Thunder Black and White /50 #50
2014 Press Pass American Thunder Brothers In Arms Autographs Blue /5 #BASHR
2014 Press Pass American Thunder Brothers In Arms Autographs Red /1 #BASHR
2014 Press Pass American Thunder Brothers In Arms Autographs White /10 #BASHR
2014 Press Pass American Thunder Brothers In Arms Relics Blue /25 #BASHR
2014 Press Pass American Thunder Brothers In Arms Relics Red /5 #BASHR
2014 Press Pass American Thunder Brothers In Arms Relics Silver /50 #BASHR
2014 Press Pass American Thunder Class A Uniforms Blue /99 #CAUKH
2014 Press Pass American Thunder Class A Uniforms Red /10 #CAUKH
2014 Press Pass American Thunder Class A Uniforms Silver #CAUKH
2014 Press Pass American Thunder Cyan #17
2014 Press Pass American Thunder Cyan #50
2014 Press Pass American Thunder Magenta #17
2014 Press Pass American Thunder Magenta #50
2014 Press Pass American Thunder Yellow /5 #17
2014 Press Pass American Thunder Yellow /5 #50
2014 Press Pass Burning Rubber Blue /25 #BRKH
2014 Press Pass Burning Rubber Blue /25 #BRKH2
2014 Press Pass Burning Rubber Chase Edition Blue /25 #BRCKH
2014 Press Pass Burning Rubber Chase Edition Blue /25 #BRCKH2
2014 Press Pass Burning Rubber Chase Edition Gold /50 #BRCKH
2014 Press Pass Burning Rubber Chase Edition Gold /50 #BRCKH2
2014 Press Pass Burning Rubber Chase Edition Melting /10 #BRCKH
2014 Press Pass Burning Rubber Chase Edition Melting /10 #BRCKH2
2014 Press Pass Burning Rubber Chase Edition Silver /99 #BRCKH2
2014 Press Pass Burning Rubber Chase Edition Silver /99 #BRCKH
2014 Press Pass Burning Rubber Gold /75 #BRKH
2014 Press Pass Burning Rubber Gold /75 #BRKH2
2014 Press Pass Burning Rubber Holofoil /50 #BRKH
2014 Press Pass Burning Rubber Holofoil /50 #BRKH2
2014 Press Pass Burning Rubber Letterman /8 #BRLKH
2014 Press Pass Burning Rubber Melting /10 #BRKH
2014 Press Pass Burning Rubber Melting /10 #BRKH2
2014 Press Pass Certified Winners Memorabilia Autographs Gold /10 #CWKH
2014 Press Pass Certified Winners Memorabilia Autographs Melting /1 #CWKH
2014 Press Pass Color Proofs Black /70 #15
2014 Press Pass Color Proofs Black /70 #80
2014 Press Pass Color Proofs Cyan /35 #15
2014 Press Pass Color Proofs Cyan /35 #80
2014 Press Pass Color Proofs Magenta #15
2014 Press Pass Color Proofs Magenta #80
2014 Press Pass Color Proofs Yellow /5 #15
2014 Press Pass Color Proofs Yellow /5 #80
2014 Press Pass Five Star /15 #8
2014 Press Pass Five Star Blue /5 #8
2014 Press Pass Five Star Classic Compilation Autographs Blue Triple Swatch /4 #CCKH
2014 Press Pass Five Star Classic Compilation Autographs Holofoil /10 #CCKH
2014 Press Pass Five Star Classic Compilation Autographs Holofoil Dual Swatch /10 #CCKH
2014 Press Pass Five Star Classic Compilation Autographs Melting Five Swatch /1 #CCKH
2014 Press Pass Five Star Classic Compilation Autographs Melting Quad Swatch /1 #CCKH
2014 Press Pass Five Star Classic Compilations Autographed Patch Booklet /1 #CCKH1
2014 Press Pass Five Star Classic Compilations Autographed Patch Booklet /1 #CCKH2
2014 Press Pass Five Star Classic Compilations Autographed Patch Booklet /1 #CCKH3
2014 Press Pass Five Star Classic Compilations Autographed Patch Booklet /1 #CCKH4
2014 Press Pass Five Star Classic Compilations Autographed Patch Booklet /1 #CCKH5
2014 Press Pass Five Star Classic Compilations Autographed Patch Booklet /1 #CCKH6
2014 Press Pass Five Star Classic Compilations Autographed Patch Booklet /1 #CCKH7
2014 Press Pass Five Star Classic Compilations Autographed Patch Booklet /1 #CCKH8
2014 Press Pass Five Star Classic Compilations Autographed Patch Booklet /1 #CCKH9
2014 Press Pass Five Star Classic Compilations Autographed Patch Booklet /1 #CCKH10
2014 Press Pass Five Star Classic Compilations Autographed Patch Booklet /1 #CCKH11
2014 Press Pass Five Star Classic Compilations Autographed Patch Booklet /1 #CCKH12
2014 Press Pass Five Star Classic Compilations Autographed Patch Booklet /1 #CCKH13
2014 Press Pass Five Star Classic Compilations Autographed Patch Booklet /1 #CCKH14
2014 Press Pass Five Star Classic Compilations Autographed Patch Booklet /1 #CCKH15
2014 Press Pass Five Star Classic Compilations Combo Autographs Blue /5 #CCRCR
2014 Press Pass Five Star Classic Compilations Combo Autographs Melting /1 #CCRCR
2014 Press Pass Five Star Holofoil /10 #8
2014 Press Pass Five Star Melting /1 #8
2014 Press Pass Five Star Paramount Pieces Blue /5 #PPKH
2014 Press Pass Five Star Paramount Pieces Gold /25 #PPKH
2014 Press Pass Five Star Paramount Pieces Holofoil /10 #PPKH
2014 Press Pass Five Star Paramount Pieces Melting /1 #PPKH
2014 Press Pass Five Star Paramount Pieces Melting Patch /1 #PPKH
2014 Press Pass Five Star Signature Souvenirs Blue /5 #SSKH
2014 Press Pass Five Star Signature Souvenirs Gold /50 #SSKH
2014 Press Pass Five Star Signature Souvenirs Holofoil /25 #SSKH
2014 Press Pass Five Star Signature Souvenirs Melting /1 #SSKH
2014 Press Pass Five Star Signatures Blue /5 #FSSKH
2014 Press Pass Five Star Signatures Holofoil /10 #FSSKH
2014 Press Pass Five Star Signatures Melting /1 #FSSKH
2014 Press Pass Gold #15
2014 Press Pass Gold #80
2014 Press Pass Redline #25
2014 Press Pass Redline Black /75 #25
2014 Press Pass Redline Blue Foil #25
2014 Press Pass Redline Cyan /50 #25
2014 Press Pass Redline Dynamic Duals Relic Autographs Blue /15 #DDKH
2014 Press Pass Redline Dynamic Duals Relic Autographs Gold /5 #DDKH
2014 Press Pass Redline Dynamic Duals Relic Autographs Melting /1 #DDKH
2014 Press Pass Redline Dynamic Duals Relic Autographs Red /25 #DDKH
2014 Press Pass Redline Green National Convention /5 #25
2014 Press Pass Redline Head to Head Blue /10 #HTHJGKH
2014 Press Pass Redline Head to Head Gold /25 #HTHJGKH
2014 Press Pass Redline Head to Head Melting /1 #HTHJGKH
2014 Press Pass Redline Head to Head Red /75 #HTHJGKH
2014 Press Pass Redline Intensity #I5
2014 Press Pass Redline Magenta /10 #25
2014 Press Pass Redline Muscle Car Sheet Metal Blue /10 #MCMKH
2014 Press Pass Redline Muscle Car Sheet Metal Gold /25 #MCMKH
2014 Press Pass Redline Muscle Car Sheet Metal Melting /1 #MCMKH
2014 Press Pass Redline Muscle Car Sheet Metal Red /50 #MCMKH
2014 Press Pass Redline Pieces of the Action Blue /10 #PAKH
2014 Press Pass Redline Pieces of the Action Gold /25 #PAKH
2014 Press Pass Redline Pieces of the Action Melting /1 #PAKH
2014 Press Pass Redline Pieces of the Action Red /75 #PAKH
2014 Press Pass Redline Redline Racers #RR8
2014 Press Pass Redline Relic Autographs Blue /5 #RRSEKH
2014 Press Pass Redline Relic Autographs Gold /15 #RRSEKH
2014 Press Pass Redline Relic Autographs Melting /1 #RRSEKH
2014 Press Pass Redline Relic Autographs Red /25 #RRSEKH
2014 Press Pass Redline Relics Blue /25 #RRKH
2014 Press Pass Redline Relics Gold /50 #RRKH
2014 Press Pass Redline Relics Melting /1 #RRKH
2014 Press Pass Redline Relics Red /75 #RRKH
2014 Press Pass Redline RPM #RPM5
2014 Press Pass Redline Signatures Blue /5 #RSKH
2014 Press Pass Redline Signatures Gold /15 #RSKH
2014 Press Pass Redline Signatures Melting /1 #RSKH
2014 Press Pass Redline Signatures Red /25 #RSKH
2014 Press Pass Redline Yellow /1 #25
2014 Press Pass Replay #9
2014 Press Pass Replay #12
2014 Press Pass Signature Series Gold /5 #SSKH
2014 Press Pass Signature Series Melting /1 #SSKH
2014 Press Pass Signings Gold /5 #PPSKH
2014 Press Pass Signings Holofoil /1 #PPSKH
2014 Press Pass Signings Melting /1 #PPSKH
2014 Press Pass Signings Printing Plates Black /1 #PPSKH
2014 Press Pass Signings Printing Plates Cyan /1 #PPSKH
2014 Press Pass Signings Printing Plates Magenta /1 #PPSKH
2014 Press Pass Signings Printing Plates Yellow /1 #PPSKH
2014 Press Pass Signings Silver /10 #PPSKH
2014 Press Pass Three Wide Gold /10 #TWKH
2014 Press Pass Three Wide Melting /1 #TWKH
2014 Total Memorabilia #11
2014 Total Memorabilia Autographed Memorabilia Blue /5 #SCKH
2014 Total Memorabilia Autographed Memorabilia Gold /5 #SCKH
2014 Total Memorabilia Autographed Memorabilia Melting /1 #SCKH
2014 Total Memorabilia Autographed Memorabilia Silver /10 #SC-KH
2014 Total Memorabilia Black and White /99 #11
2014 Total Memorabilia Gold /175 #11
2014 Total Memorabilia Red #11
2015 Press Pass #17
2015 Press Pass #94
2015 Press Pass #85
2015 Press Pass #69
2015 Press Pass #100
2015 Press Pass Burning Rubber Blue /50 #BRKH1
2015 Press Pass Burning Rubber Blue /50 #BRKH2
2015 Press Pass Burning Rubber Gold #BRKH2
2015 Press Pass Burning Rubber Gold #BRKH1
2015 Press Pass Burning Rubber Green /10 #BRKH1
2015 Press Pass Burning Rubber Green /10 #BRKH2
2015 Press Pass Burning Rubber Letterman /8 #BRLEKH
2015 Press Pass Burning Rubber Melting /1 #BRKH1
2015 Press Pass Burning Rubber Melting /1 #BRKH2
2015 Press Pass Championship Caliber Dual /25 #CCMKH
2015 Press Pass Championship Caliber Quad /1 #CCMKH
2015 Press Pass Championship Caliber Signature Edition Blue /25 #CCKH
2015 Press Pass Championship Caliber Signature Edition Gold /50 #CCKH
2015 Press Pass Championship Caliber Signature Edition Green /10 #CCKH
2015 Press Pass Championship Caliber Signature Edition Melting /1 #CCKH
2015 Press Pass Championship Caliber Single /50 #CCMKH
2015 Press Pass Championship Caliber Triple /10 #CCMKH
2015 Press Pass Cup Chase #17
2015 Press Pass Cup Chase #69
2015 Press Pass Cup Chase #85
2015 Press Pass Cup Chase #94
2015 Press Pass Cup Chase #100
2015 Press Pass Cup Chase Blue /25 #17
2015 Press Pass Cup Chase Blue /25 #69
2015 Press Pass Cup Chase Blue /25 #85
2015 Press Pass Cup Chase Blue /25 #94
2015 Press Pass Cup Chase Blue /25 #100
2015 Press Pass Cup Chase Gold /75 #17
2015 Press Pass Cup Chase Gold /75 #69
2015 Press Pass Cup Chase Gold /75 #85
2015 Press Pass Cup Chase Gold /75 #94
2015 Press Pass Cup Chase Gold /75 #100
2015 Press Pass Cup Chase Green /10 #17
2015 Press Pass Cup Chase Green /10 #69
2015 Press Pass Cup Chase Green /10 #85
2015 Press Pass Cup Chase Green /10 #94
2015 Press Pass Cup Chase Green /10 #100
2015 Press Pass Cup Chase Melting /1 #17
2015 Press Pass Cup Chase Melting /1 #69
2015 Press Pass Cup Chase Melting /1 #85
2015 Press Pass Cup Chase Melting /1 #94
2015 Press Pass Cup Chase Melting /1 #100
2015 Press Pass Cup Chase Three Wide Blue /25 #3WKH
2015 Press Pass Cup Chase Three Wide Gold /50 #3WKH
2015 Press Pass Cup Chase Three Wide Green /10 #3WKH
2015 Press Pass Cup Chase Three Wide Melting /1 #3WKH
2015 Press Pass Cup Chase Upper Cuts /13 #UCKH
2015 Press Pass Cuts Blue /25 #CCCKH
2015 Press Pass Cuts Gold /50 #CCCKH
2015 Press Pass Cuts Green /10 #CCCKH
2015 Press Pass Cuts Melting /1 #CCCKH
2015 Press Pass Four Wide Signature Edition Blue /10 #4WKH
2015 Press Pass Four Wide Signature Edition Gold /15 #4WKH
2015 Press Pass Four Wide Signature Edition Green /5 #4WKH
2015 Press Pass Four Wide Signature Edition Melting /1 #4WKH
2015 Press Pass Purple #17
2015 Press Pass Purple #69
2015 Press Pass Purple #85
2015 Press Pass Purple #94
2015 Press Pass Purple #100
2015 Press Pass Red #17
2015 Press Pass Red #69
2015 Press Pass Red #85
2015 Press Pass Red #94
2015 Press Pass Red #100
2015 Press Pass Signature Series Blue /25 #SSKH
2015 Press Pass Signature Series Gold /50 #SSKH
2015 Press Pass Signature Series Green /10 #SSKH
2015 Press Pass Signature Series Melting /1 #SSKH
2015 Press Pass Signings Blue /15 #PPSKH
2015 Press Pass Signings Gold #PPSKH
2015 Press Pass Signings Green /5 #PPSKH
2015 Press Pass Signings Melting /1 #PPSKH
2015 Press Pass Signings Red /10 #PPSKH
2015 Sports Illustrated for Kids #394
2015-16 Upper Deck Contours High Profile Fans Jersey Autographs /149 #HPAJKH
2015-16 Upper Deck Contours High Profile Fans Jersey Autographs Patch /25 #HPJKH
2015-16 Upper Deck Contours High Profile Fans Jerseys #HPJKH
2015-16 Upper Deck Contours High Profile Fans Jerseys Patch /65 #HPJKH
2016 Certified #52
2016 Certified #1
2016 Certified Complete Materials /199 #2
2016 Certified Complete Materials Mirror Black /1 #2
2016 Certified Complete Materials Mirror Blue /50 #2
2016 Certified Complete Materials Mirror Gold /25 #2
2016 Certified Complete Materials Mirror Green /5 #2
2016 Certified Complete Materials Mirror Orange /99 #2
2016 Certified Complete Materials Mirror Purple /10 #2
2016 Certified Complete Materials Mirror Red /75 #2
2016 Certified Complete Materials Mirror Silver /99 #2
2016 Certified Epix /199 #4
2016 Certified Epix Mirror Black /1 #4
2016 Certified Epix Mirror Blue /50 #4
2016 Certified Epix Mirror Gold /25 #4
2016 Certified Epix Mirror Green /5 #4
2016 Certified Epix Mirror Orange /99 #4
2016 Certified Epix Mirror Purple /10 #4
2016 Certified Epix Mirror Red /75 #4
2016 Certified Epix Mirror Silver /99 #4
2016 Certified Famed Rides /199 #17
2016 Certified Famed Rides Mirror Black /1 #17
2016 Certified Famed Rides Mirror Blue /50 #17
2016 Certified Famed Rides Mirror Gold /25 #17
2016 Certified Famed Rides Mirror Green /5 #17
2016 Certified Famed Rides Mirror Orange /99 #17
2016 Certified Famed Rides Mirror Purple /10 #17
2016 Certified Famed Rides Mirror Red /75 #17
2016 Certified Famed Rides Mirror Silver /99 #17
2016 Certified Gold Team /199 #4
2016 Certified Gold Team Mirror Black /1 #4
2016 Certified Gold Team Mirror Blue /50 #4
2016 Certified Gold Team Mirror Gold /25 #4
2016 Certified Gold Team Mirror Green /5 #4
2016 Certified Gold Team Mirror Orange /99 #4
2016 Certified Gold Team Mirror Purple /10 #4
2016 Certified Gold Team Mirror Red /75 #4
2016 Certified Gold Team Mirror Silver /99 #4
2016 Certified Gold Team Signatures /25 #12
2016 Certified Gold Team Signatures Mirror Black /1 #12
2016 Certified Gold Team Signatures Mirror Gold /4 #12
2016 Certified Mirror Black /1 #1
2016 Certified Mirror Black /1 #52
2016 Certified Mirror Blue /50 #1
2016 Certified Mirror Blue /50 #52
2016 Certified Mirror Gold /25 #1
2016 Certified Mirror Gold /25 #52
2016 Certified Mirror Green /5 #1
2016 Certified Mirror Green /5 #52
2016 Certified Mirror Orange /99 #1
2016 Certified Mirror Orange /99 #52
2016 Certified Mirror Purple /10 #1
2016 Certified Mirror Purple /10 #52
2016 Certified Mirror Red /75 #1
2016 Certified Mirror Red /75 #52
2016 Certified Mirror Silver /99 #1
2016 Certified Mirror Silver /99 #52
2016 Certified Signatures /50 #29
2016 Certified Signatures Mirror Black /1 #29
2016 Certified Signatures Mirror Blue /20 #29
2016 Certified Signatures Mirror Gold /15 #29
2016 Certified Signatures Mirror Green /5 #29
2016 Certified Signatures Mirror Orange /5 #29
2016 Certified Signatures Mirror Purple /10 #29
2016 Certified Signatures Mirror Red /25 #29
2016 Certified Signatures Mirror Silver /4 #29
2016 Certified Skills /199 #9
2016 Certified Skills Mirror Black /1 #9
2016 Certified Skills Mirror Blue /50 #9
2016 Certified Skills Mirror Gold /25 #9
2016 Certified Skills Mirror Green /5 #9
2016 Certified Skills Mirror Orange /99 #9
2016 Certified Skills Mirror Purple /10 #9
2016 Certified Skills Mirror Red /75 #9
2016 Certified Skills Mirror Silver /99 #9
2016 Certified Sprint Cup Signature Swatches /50 #11
2016 Certified Sprint Cup Signature Swatches Mirror Black /1 #11
2016 Certified Sprint Cup Signature Swatches Mirror Blue /20 #11
2016 Certified Sprint Cup Signature Swatches Mirror Gold /15 #11
2016 Certified Sprint Cup Signature Swatches Mirror Green /5 #11
2016 Certified Sprint Cup Signature Swatches Mirror Orange /5 #11
2016 Certified Sprint Cup Signature Swatches Mirror Purple /10 #11
2016 Certified Sprint Cup Signature Swatches Mirror Red /25 #11
2016 Certified Sprint Cup Signature Swatches Mirror Silver /4 #11
2016 Certified Sprint Cup Swatches /299 #36
2016 Certified Sprint Cup Swatches Mirror Black /1 #36
2016 Certified Sprint Cup Swatches Mirror Blue /50 #36
2016 Certified Sprint Cup Swatches Mirror Gold /25 #36
2016 Certified Sprint Cup Swatches Mirror Green /5 #36
2016 Certified Sprint Cup Swatches Mirror Orange /149 #36
2016 Certified Sprint Cup Swatches Mirror Purple /10 #36
2016 Certified Sprint Cup Swatches Mirror Red /75 #36
2016 Certified Sprint Cup Swatches Mirror Silver /149 #36
2016 Panini Black Friday #27
2016 Panini Black Friday Autographs /25 #27
2016 Panini Black Friday Cracked Ice /25 #27
2016 Panini Black Friday Holo Plaid /1 #27
2016 Panini Black Friday Rapture /10 #27
2016 Panini Black Friday Thick Stock /50 #27
2016 Panini Black Friday Wedges /50 #27
2016 Panini Cyber Monday #29
2016 Panini Instant #2
2016 Panini Instant #5
2016 Panini Instant Black /1 #2
2016 Panini Instant Black /1 #5
2016 Panini Instant Blue /25 #2
2016 Panini Instant Blue /25 #5
2016 Panini Instant Green /5 #2
2016 Panini Instant Green /5 #5
2016 Panini Instant Orange /50 #2
2016 Panini Instant Orange /50 #5
2016 Panini Instant Purple /10 #2
2016 Panini Instant Purple /10 #5
2016 Panini National Convention #38
2016 Panini National Convention Autographs /25 #38
2016 Panini National Convention Cracked Ice /25 #38
2016 Panini National Convention Decoy Cracked Ice /25 #38
2016 Panini National Convention Decoy Escher Squares /10 #38
2016 Panini National Convention Decoy Rapture /1 #38
2016 Panini National Convention Decoy Wedges /99 #38
2016 Panini National Convention Diamond Awe /49 #38
2016 Panini National Convention Escher Squares /10 #38
2016 Panini National Convention Rapture /1 #38
2016 Panini National Convention VIP #94
2016 Panini National Convention VIP Autographs Gold Vinyl /1 #94
2016 Panini National Convention VIP Autographs Kaleidoscope Red /25 #94
2016 Panini National Convention VIP Blue Wave Gold /10 #94
2016 Panini National Convention VIP Cracked Ice /25 #94
2016 Panini National Convention VIP Flash Green /5 #94
2016 Panini National Convention VIP Gold Vinyl /1 #94
2016 Panini National Convention VIP Memorabilia Gold Vinyl /1 #94
2016 Panini National Convention VIP Memorabilia Kaleidoscope Blue /25 #94
2016 Panini National Convention VIP Prizm /99 #94
2016 Panini National Convention VIP Purple Pulsar /50 #94
2016 Panini National Convention Wedges /99 #38
2016 Panini National Treasures /25 #3
2016 Panini National Treasures /25 #28
2016 Panini National Treasures Black /5 #3
2016 Panini National Treasures Black /5 #28
2016 Panini National Treasures Blue /1 #3
2016 Panini National Treasures Blue /1 #28
2016 Panini National Treasures Championship Signature Threads Black /5 #4
2016 Panini National Treasures Championship Signature Threads Blue /1 #4
2016 Panini National Treasures Championship Signature Threads Gold /10 #4
2016 Panini National Treasures Championship Signature Threads Printing Plates Black /1 #4
2016 Panini National Treasures Championship Signature Threads Printing Plates Cyan /1 #4
2016 Panini National Treasures Championship Signature Threads Printing Plates Magenta /1 #4
2016 Panini National Treasures Championship Signature Threads Printing Plates Yellow /1 #4
2016 Panini National Treasures Championship Signature Threads Silver /15 #4
2016 Panini National Treasures Championship Signatures Black /4 #4
2016 Panini National Treasures Championship Signatures Blue /1 #4
2016 Panini National Treasures Championship Signatures Printing Plates Black /1 #4
2016 Panini National Treasures Championship Signatures Printing Plates Cyan /1 #4
2016 Panini National Treasures Championship Signatures Printing Plates Magenta /1 #4
2016 Panini National Treasures Championship Signatures Printing Plates Yellow /1 #4
2016 Panini National Treasures Dual Driver Materials /25 #4
2016 Panini National Treasures Dual Driver Materials Black /5 #4
2016 Panini National Treasures Dual Driver Materials Blue /1 #4
2016 Panini National Treasures Dual Driver Materials Gold /10 #4
2016 Panini National Treasures Dual Driver Materials Printing Plates Black /1 #4
2016 Panini National Treasures Dual Driver Materials Printing Plates Cyan /1 #4
2016 Panini National Treasures Dual Driver Materials Printing Plates Magenta /1 #4
2016 Panini National Treasures Dual Driver Materials Printing Plates Yellow /1 #4
2016 Panini National Treasures Dual Driver Materials Silver /15 #4
2016 Panini National Treasures Dual Signatures /26 #9
2016 Panini National Treasures Dual Signatures /25 #10
2016 Panini National Treasures Dual Signatures Black /10 #9
2016 Panini National Treasures Dual Signatures Black /10 #10
2016 Panini National Treasures Dual Signatures Blue /1 #9
2016 Panini National Treasures Dual Signatures Blue /1 #10
2016 Panini National Treasures Dual Signatures Gold /15 #9
2016 Panini National Treasures Dual Signatures Gold /15 #10
2016 Panini National Treasures Eight Signatures /15 #1
2016 Panini National Treasures Eight Signatures /15 #3
2016 Panini National Treasures Eight Signatures Black /5 #1
2016 Panini National Treasures Eight Signatures Black /5 #3
2016 Panini National Treasures Eight Signatures Blue /1 #1
2016 Panini National Treasures Eight Signatures Blue /1 #3
2016 Panini National Treasures Eight Signatures Gold /10 #1
2016 Panini National Treasures Eight Signatures Gold /10 #3
2016 Panini National Treasures Firesuit Materials /25 #11
2016 Panini National Treasures Firesuit Materials Black /5 #11
2016 Panini National Treasures Firesuit Materials Blue /1 #11
2016 Panini National Treasures Firesuit Materials Gold /10 #11
2016 Panini National Treasures Firesuit Materials Laundry Tag /1 #11
2016 Panini National Treasures Firesuit Materials Printing Plates Black /1 #11
2016 Panini National Treasures Firesuit Materials Printing Plates Cyan /1 #11
2016 Panini National Treasures Firesuit Materials Printing Plates Magenta /1 #11
2016 Panini National Treasures Firesuit Materials Printing Plates Yellow /1 #11
2016 Panini National Treasures Firesuit Materials Silver /15 #11
2016 Panini National Treasures Gold /15 #3
2016 Panini National Treasures Gold /15 #28
2016 Panini National Treasures Jumbo Firesuit Patch Signature Booklet Associate Sponsor 1 /1 #15
2016 Panini National Treasures Jumbo Firesuit Patch Signature Booklet Associate Sponsor 10 /1 #15

2016 Panini National Treasures Jumbo Firesuit Patch Signature Booklet Associate Sponsor 11 /1 #15
2016 Panini National Treasures Jumbo Firesuit Patch Signature Booklet Associate Sponsor 12 /1 #15
2016 Panini National Treasures Jumbo Firesuit Patch Signature Booklet Associate Sponsor 13 /1 #15
2016 Panini National Treasures Jumbo Firesuit Patch Signature Booklet Associate Sponsor 14 /1 #15
2016 Panini National Treasures Jumbo Firesuit Patch Signature Booklet Associate Sponsor 15 /1 #15
2016 Panini National Treasures Jumbo Firesuit Patch Signature Booklet Associate Sponsor 16 /1 #15
2016 Panini National Treasures Jumbo Firesuit Patch Signature Booklet Associate Sponsor 17 /1 #15
2016 Panini National Treasures Jumbo Firesuit Patch Signature Booklet Associate Sponsor 2 /1 #15
2016 Panini National Treasures Jumbo Firesuit Patch Signature Booklet Associate Sponsor 3 /1 #15
2016 Panini National Treasures Jumbo Firesuit Patch Signature Booklet Associate Sponsor 4 /1 #15
2016 Panini National Treasures Jumbo Firesuit Patch Signature Booklet Associate Sponsor 5 /1 #15
2016 Panini National Treasures Jumbo Firesuit Patch Signature Booklet Associate Sponsor 6 /1 #15
2016 Panini National Treasures Jumbo Firesuit Patch Signature Booklet Associate Sponsor 7 /1 #15
2016 Panini National Treasures Jumbo Firesuit Patch Signature Booklet Associate Sponsor 8 /1 #15
2016 Panini National Treasures Jumbo Firesuit Patch Signature Booklet Associate Sponsor 9 /1 #15
2016 Panini National Treasures Jumbo Firesuit Patch Signature Booklet Goodyear /2 #15
2016 Panini National Treasures Jumbo Firesuit Patch Signature Booklet Manufacturers Logo /1 #15
2016 Panini National Treasures Jumbo Firesuit Patch Signature Booklet Nameplate /2 #15
2016 Panini National Treasures Jumbo Firesuit Patch Signature Booklet NASCAR /1 #15
2016 Panini National Treasures Jumbo Firesuit Patch Signature Booklet Sprint Cup Logo /1 #15
2016 Panini National Treasures Jumbo Firesuit Patch Signature Booklet Sunoco /1 #15
2016 Panini National Treasures Jumbo Firesuit Signatures Black /4 #15
2016 Panini National Treasures Jumbo Firesuit Signatures Blue /1 #15
2016 Panini National Treasures Jumbo Firesuit Signatures Printing Plates Black /1 #15
2016 Panini National Treasures Jumbo Firesuit Signatures Printing Plates Cyan /1 #15
2016 Panini National Treasures Jumbo Firesuit Signatures Printing Plates Magenta /1 #15
2016 Panini National Treasures Jumbo Firesuit Signatures Printing Plates Yellow /1 #15
2016 Panini National Treasures Jumbo Sheet Metal Signature Booklet /49 #5
2016 Panini National Treasures Jumbo Sheet Metal Signature Booklet Black /10 #5
2016 Panini National Treasures Jumbo Sheet Metal Signature Booklet Blue /1 #5
2016 Panini National Treasures Jumbo Sheet Metal Signature Booklet Gold /25 #5
2016 Panini National Treasures Jumbo Sheet Metal Signatures Black /5 #9
2016 Panini National Treasures Jumbo Sheet Metal Signatures Blue /1 #9
2016 Panini National Treasures Jumbo Sheet Metal Signatures Printing Plates Black /1 #9
2016 Panini National Treasures Jumbo Sheet Metal Signatures Printing Plates Cyan /1 #9
2016 Panini National Treasures Jumbo Sheet Metal Signatures Printing Plates Magenta /1 #9
2016 Panini National Treasures Jumbo Sheet Metal Signatures Printing Plates Yellow /1 #9
2016 Panini National Treasures Printing Plates Black /1 #3
2016 Panini National Treasures Printing Plates Black /1 #28
2016 Panini National Treasures Printing Plates Cyan /1 #3
2016 Panini National Treasures Printing Plates Cyan /1 #28
2016 Panini National Treasures Printing Plates Magenta /1 #3
2016 Panini National Treasures Printing Plates Magenta /1 #28
2016 Panini National Treasures Printing Plates Yellow /1 #3
2016 Panini National Treasures Printing Plates Yellow /1 #28
2016 Panini National Treasures Quad Driver Materials /25 #10
2016 Panini National Treasures Quad Driver Materials Black /5 #10
2016 Panini National Treasures Quad Driver Materials Blue /1 #10
2016 Panini National Treasures Quad Driver Materials Gold /10 #10
2016 Panini National Treasures Quad Driver Materials Printing Plates Black /1 #10
2016 Panini National Treasures Quad Driver Materials Printing Plates Cyan /1 #10
2016 Panini National Treasures Quad Driver Materials Printing Plates Magenta /1 #10
2016 Panini National Treasures Quad Driver Materials Printing Plates Yellow /1 #10
2016 Panini National Treasures Quad Driver Materials Silver /15 #10
2016 Panini National Treasures Quad Materials /25 #11
2016 Panini National Treasures Quad Materials Black /5 #11
2016 Panini National Treasures Quad Materials Blue /1 #11
2016 Panini National Treasures Quad Materials Gold /10 #11
2016 Panini National Treasures Quad Materials Printing Plates Black /1 #11
2016 Panini National Treasures Quad Materials Printing Plates Cyan /1 #11
2016 Panini National Treasures Quad Materials Printing Plates Magenta /1 #11
2016 Panini National Treasures Quad Materials Printing Plates Yellow /1 #11
2016 Panini National Treasures Quad Materials Silver /15 #11
2016 Panini National Treasures Sheet Metal Materials /25 #11
2016 Panini National Treasures Sheet Metal Materials Black /5 #11
2016 Panini National Treasures Sheet Metal Materials Blue /1 #11
2016 Panini National Treasures Sheet Metal Materials Gold /10 #11
2016 Panini National Treasures Sheet Metal Materials Printing Plates Black /1 #11
2016 Panini National Treasures Sheet Metal Materials Printing Plates Cyan /1 #11
2016 Panini National Treasures Sheet Metal Materials Printing Plates Magenta /1 #11
2016 Panini National Treasures Sheet Metal Materials Printing Plates Yellow /1 #11
2016 Panini National Treasures Sheet Metal Materials Silver /15 #11
2016 Panini National Treasures Signature Dual Materials Black /4 #15
2016 Panini National Treasures Signature Dual Materials Blue /1 #15
2016 Panini National Treasures Signature Dual Materials Printing Plates Black /1 #15
2016 Panini National Treasures Signature Dual Materials Printing Plates Cyan /1 #15
2016 Panini National Treasures Signature Dual Materials Printing Plates Magenta /1 #15
2016 Panini National Treasures Signature Dual Materials Printing Plates Yellow /1 #15
2016 Panini National Treasures Signature Firesuit Materials Black /5 #15
2016 Panini National Treasures Signature Firesuit Materials Blue /1 #15
2016 Panini National Treasures Signature Firesuit Materials Gold /10 #15
2016 Panini National Treasures Signature Firesuit Materials Laundry Tag /1 #15
2016 Panini National Treasures Signature Firesuit Materials Printing Plates Black /1 #15
2016 Panini National Treasures Signature Firesuit Materials Printing Plates Cyan /1 #15
2016 Panini National Treasures Signature Firesuit Materials Printing Plates Magenta /1 #15
2016 Panini National Treasures Signature Firesuit Materials Printing Plates Yellow /1 #15
2016 Panini National Treasures Signature Firesuit Materials Silver /15 #15
2016 Panini National Treasures Signature Quad Materials /25 #15
2016 Panini National Treasures Signature Quad Materials Black /5 #15
2016 Panini National Treasures Signature Quad Materials Blue /1 #15
2016 Panini National Treasures Signature Quad Materials Gold /10 #15
2016 Panini National Treasures Signature Quad Materials Printing Plates Black /1 #15
2016 Panini National Treasures Signature Quad Materials Printing Plates Cyan /1 #15
2016 Panini National Treasures Signature Quad Materials Printing Plates Magenta /1 #15
2016 Panini National Treasures Signature Quad Materials Printing Plates Yellow /1 #15
2016 Panini National Treasures Signature Quad Materials Silver /15 #15
2016 Panini National Treasures Signature Sheet Metal Materials Black /4 #15
2016 Panini National Treasures Signature Sheet Metal Materials Blue /1 #15
2016 Panini National Treasures Signature Sheet Metal Materials Printing Plates Black /1 #15
2016 Panini National Treasures Signature Sheet Metal Materials Printing Plates Cyan /1 #15
2016 Panini National Treasures Signature Sheet Metal Materials Printing Plates Magenta /1 #15
2016 Panini National Treasures Signature Sheet Metal Materials Printing Plates Yellow /1 #15
2016 Panini National Treasures Silver /20 #3
2016 Panini National Treasures Silver /20 #28
2016 Panini National Treasures Six Signatures /25 #8
2016 Panini National Treasures Six Signatures Black /10 #8
2016 Panini National Treasures Six Signatures Blue /1 #8
2016 Panini National Treasures Six Signatures Gold /15 #8
2016 Panini National Treasures Trio Driver Materials /25 #1
2016 Panini National Treasures Trio Driver Materials Black /5 #1
2016 Panini National Treasures Trio Driver Materials Blue /1 #1
2016 Panini National Treasures Trio Driver Materials Gold /10 #1
2016 Panini National Treasures Trio Driver Materials Printing Plates Black /1 #1
2016 Panini National Treasures Trio Driver Materials Printing Plates Cyan /1 #1
2016 Panini National Treasures Trio Driver Materials Printing Plates Magenta /1 #1
2016 Panini National Treasures Trio Driver Materials Printing Plates Yellow /1 #1
2016 Panini National Treasures Trio Driver Materials Silver /15 #1
2016 Panini Prizm #78
2016 Panini Prizm #64
2016 Panini Prizm #55
2016 Panini Prizm #4
2016 Panini Prizm Autographs Prizms #72
2016 Panini Prizm Autographs Prizms Black /3 #72
2016 Panini Prizm Autographs Prizms Blue Flag /25 #72
2016 Panini Prizm Autographs Prizms Camo /4 #72
2016 Panini Prizm Autographs Prizms Checkered Flag /1 #72
2016 Panini Prizm Autographs Prizms Gold /10 #72
2016 Panini Prizm Autographs Prizms Green Flag /35 #72
2016 Panini Prizm Autographs Prizms Rainbow /24 #72
2016 Panini Prizm Autographs Prizms Red Flag /15 #72
2016 Panini Prizm Autographs Prizms Red White and Blue /5 #72
2016 Panini Prizm Autographs Prizms White Flag /5 #72
2016 Panini Prizm Blowing Smoke #2
2016 Panini Prizm Blowing Smoke Prizms #2
2016 Panini Prizm Blowing Smoke Prizms Checkered Flag /1 #2
2016 Panini Prizm Blowing Smoke Prizms Gold /10 #2
2016 Panini Prizm Machinery #6
2016 Panini Prizm Machinery Prizms #6
2016 Panini Prizm Machinery Prizms Checkered Flag /1 #6
2016 Panini Prizm Machinery Prizms Gold /10 #6
2016 Panini Prizm Patented Pennmanship Prizms #4
2016 Panini Prizm Patented Pennmanship Prizms Black /3 #4
2016 Panini Prizm Patented Pennmanship Prizms Blue Flag /25 #4
2016 Panini Prizm Patented Pennmanship Prizms Camo /4 #4
2016 Panini Prizm Patented Pennmanship Prizms Checkered Flag /1 #4
2016 Panini Prizm Patented Pennmanship Prizms Gold /10 #4
2016 Panini Prizm Patented Pennmanship Prizms Green Flag /35 #4
2016 Panini Prizm Patented Pennmanship Prizms Rainbow /24 #4
2016 Panini Prizm Patented Pennmanship Prizms Red Flag /15 #4
2016 Panini Prizm Patented Pennmanship Prizms Red White and Blue /10 #4
2016 Panini Prizm Patented Pennmanship Prizms White Flag /5 #4
2016 Panini Prizm Prizms #4
2016 Panini Prizm Prizms #55
2016 Panini Prizm Prizms #64
2016 Panini Prizm Prizms #78
2016 Panini Prizm Prizms Black /3 #4
2016 Panini Prizm Prizms Black /3 #55
2016 Panini Prizm Prizms Black /3 #64
2016 Panini Prizm Prizms Black /3 #78
2016 Panini Prizm Prizms Blue Flag /99 #4
2016 Panini Prizm Prizms Blue Flag /99 #55
2016 Panini Prizm Prizms Blue Flag /99 #64
2016 Panini Prizm Prizms Blue Flag /99 #78
2016 Panini Prizm Prizms Camo /4 #4
2016 Panini Prizm Prizms Camo /4 #55
2016 Panini Prizm Prizms Camo /4 #64
2016 Panini Prizm Prizms Camo /4 #78
2016 Panini Prizm Prizms Checkered Flag /1 #4
2016 Panini Prizm Prizms Checkered Flag /1 #55
2016 Panini Prizm Prizms Checkered Flag /1 #64
2016 Panini Prizm Prizms Checkered Flag /1 #78
2016 Panini Prizm Prizms Gold /10 #4
2016 Panini Prizm Prizms Gold /10 #55
2016 Panini Prizm Prizms Gold /10 #64
2016 Panini Prizm Prizms Gold /10 #78
2016 Panini Prizm Prizms Green Flag /149 #4
2016 Panini Prizm Prizms Green Flag /149 #55
2016 Panini Prizm Prizms Green Flag /149 #64
2016 Panini Prizm Prizms Green Flag /149 #78
2016 Panini Prizm Prizms Rainbow /24 #4
2016 Panini Prizm Prizms Rainbow /24 #55
2016 Panini Prizm Prizms Rainbow /24 #64
2016 Panini Prizm Prizms Rainbow /24 #78
2016 Panini Prizm Prizms Red Flag /75 #4
2016 Panini Prizm Prizms Red Flag /75 #55
2016 Panini Prizm Prizms Red Flag /75 #64
2016 Panini Prizm Prizms Red Flag /75 #78
2016 Panini Prizm Prizms Red White and Blue #4
2016 Panini Prizm Prizms Red White and Blue #55
2016 Panini Prizm Prizms Red White and Blue #64
2016 Panini Prizm Prizms Red White and Blue #78
2016 Panini Prizm Prizms White Flag /5 #4
2016 Panini Prizm Prizms White Flag /5 #55
2016 Panini Prizm Prizms White Flag /5 #64
2016 Panini Prizm Prizms White Flag /5 #78
2016 Panini Prizm Qualifying Times #4
2016 Panini Prizm Qualifying Times Prizms #4
2016 Panini Prizm Qualifying Times Prizms Checkered Flag /1 #4
2016 Panini Prizm Qualifying Times Prizms Gold /10 #4
2016 Panini Prizm Race Used Tire #6
2016 Panini Prizm Race Used Tire Prizms Blue Flag /49 #6
2016 Panini Prizm Race Used Tire Prizms Checkered Flag /1 #6
2016 Panini Prizm Race Used Tire Prizms Green Flag /99 #6
2016 Panini Prizm Race Used Tire Prizms Red Flag /25 #6
2016 Panini Prizm Race Used Tire Team #5
2016 Panini Prizm Race Used Tire Team Prizms Blue Flag /75 #5
2016 Panini Prizm Race Used Tire Team Prizms Green Flag /149 #5
2016 Panini Prizm Race Used Tire Team Prizms Red Flag /10 #5
2016 Panini Prizm Raising the Flag #10
2016 Panini Prizm Raising the Flag Prizms #10
2016 Panini Prizm Raising the Flag Prizms Checkered Flag /1 #10
2016 Panini Prizm Raising the Flag Prizms Gold /10 #10
2016 Panini Prizm Winner's Circle #29
2016 Panini Prizm Winner's Circle #4
2016 Panini Prizm Winner's Circle #3
2016 Panini Prizm Winner's Circle Prizms #3
2016 Panini Prizm Winner's Circle Prizms #4
2016 Panini Prizm Winner's Circle Prizms #29
2016 Panini Prizm Winner's Circle Prizms Checkered Flag /1 #3
2016 Panini Prizm Winner's Circle Prizms Checkered Flag /1 #4
2016 Panini Prizm Winner's Circle Prizms Checkered Flag /1 #29
2016 Panini Prizm Winner's Circle Prizms Gold /10 #3
2016 Panini Prizm Winner's Circle Prizms Gold /10 #4
2016 Panini Prizm Winner's Circle Prizms Gold /10 #29
2016 Panini Torque #3
2016 Panini Torque #62
2016 Panini Torque #80
2016 Panini Torque Artist Proof /50 #3
2016 Panini Torque Artist Proof /50 #62
2016 Panini Torque Artist Proof /50 #80
2016 Panini Torque Blackout /1 #3
2016 Panini Torque Blackout /1 #62
2016 Panini Torque Blackout /1 #80
2016 Panini Torque Blue /125 #3
2016 Panini Torque Blue /125 #62
2016 Panini Torque Blue /125 #80
2016 Panini Torque Championship Vision #7
2016 Panini Torque Championship Vision Blue /99 #7
2016 Panini Torque Championship Vision Gold /149 #7
2016 Panini Torque Championship Vision Green /25 #7
2016 Panini Torque Championship Vision Purple /10 #7
2016 Panini Torque Championship Vision Red /49 #7
2016 Panini Torque Clear Vision #3
2016 Panini Torque Clear Vision Blue /99 #3
2016 Panini Torque Clear Vision Gold /149 #3
2016 Panini Torque Clear Vision Green /25 #3
2016 Panini Torque Clear Vision Purple /10 #3
2016 Panini Torque Clear Vision Red /49 #3
2016 Panini Torque Gas N Go #6
2016 Panini Torque Gas N Go Gold /199 #6
2016 Panini Torque Gas N Go Holo Silver /99 #6
2016 Panini Torque Gold #3
2016 Panini Torque Gold #62
2016 Panini Torque Gold #80
2016 Panini Torque Helmets #2
2016 Panini Torque Helmets Blue /99 #2
2016 Panini Torque Helmets Checkerboard /10 #2
2016 Panini Torque Helmets Green /25 #2
2016 Panini Torque Helmets Red /49 #2
2016 Panini Torque Holo Gold /5 #3
2016 Panini Torque Holo Gold /5 #62
2016 Panini Torque Holo Gold /5 #80
2016 Panini Torque Holo Silver /10 #3
2016 Panini Torque Holo Silver /10 #62
2016 Panini Torque Holo Silver /10 #80
2016 Panini Torque Horsepower Heroes #2
2016 Panini Torque Horsepower Heroes Gold /199 #2
2016 Panini Torque Horsepower Heroes Holo Silver /99 #2
2016 Panini Torque Jumbo Firesuit Autographs /35 #19
2016 Panini Torque Jumbo Firesuit Autographs Blue /25 #19
2016 Panini Torque Jumbo Firesuit Autographs Green /15 #19
2016 Panini Torque Jumbo Firesuit Autographs Purple /5 #19
2016 Panini Torque Jumbo Firesuit Autographs Red /20 #19
2016 Panini Torque Metal Materials /249 #15
2016 Panini Torque Metal Materials Blue /99 #15
2016 Panini Torque Metal Materials Green /25 #15
2016 Panini Torque Metal Materials Purple /10 #15
2016 Panini Torque Metal Materials Red /49 #15
2016 Panini Torque Nicknames #3
2016 Panini Torque Nicknames Gold /199 #3
2016 Panini Torque Nicknames Holo Silver /99 #3
2016 Panini Torque Painted to Perfection #6
2016 Panini Torque Painted to Perfection Blue /99 #6
2016 Panini Torque Painted to Perfection Checkerboard /10 #6
2016 Panini Torque Painted to Perfection Green /25 #6
2016 Panini Torque Painted to Perfection Red /49 #6
2016 Panini Torque Pairings Materials /249 #30
2016 Panini Torque Pairings Materials /125 #17
2016 Panini Torque Pairings Materials Blue /99 #17
2016 Panini Torque Pairings Materials Blue /99 #30
2016 Panini Torque Pairings Materials Green /25 #17
2016 Panini Torque Pairings Materials Green /25 #30
2016 Panini Torque Pairings Materials Purple /10 #17
2016 Panini Torque Pairings Materials Purple /10 #30
2016 Panini Torque Pairings Materials Red /49 #17
2016 Panini Torque Pairings Materials Red /49 #30
2016 Panini Torque Pole Position #3
2016 Panini Torque Pole Position Blue /99 #3
2016 Panini Torque Pole Position Checkerboard /10 #3
2016 Panini Torque Pole Position Green /25 #3
2016 Panini Torque Pole Position Red /49 #3
2016 Panini Torque Printing Plates Black /1 #3
2016 Panini Torque Printing Plates Black /1 #62
2016 Panini Torque Printing Plates Black /1 #80
2016 Panini Torque Printing Plates Cyan /1 #3
2016 Panini Torque Printing Plates Cyan /1 #62
2016 Panini Torque Printing Plates Cyan /1 #80
2016 Panini Torque Printing Plates Magenta /1 #3
2016 Panini Torque Printing Plates Magenta /1 #62
2016 Panini Torque Printing Plates Magenta /1 #80
2016 Panini Torque Printing Plates Yellow /1 #3
2016 Panini Torque Printing Plates Yellow /1 #62
2016 Panini Torque Printing Plates Yellow /1 #80
2016 Panini Torque Purple /25 #3
2016 Panini Torque Purple /25 #62
2016 Panini Torque Purple /25 #80
2016 Panini Torque Quad Materials /199 #7
2016 Panini Torque Quad Materials Blue /99 #7
2016 Panini Torque Quad Materials Green /25 #7
2016 Panini Torque Quad Materials Purple /10 #7
2016 Panini Torque Quad Materials Red /49 #7
2016 Panini Torque Red /99 #3
2016 Panini Torque Red /99 #62
2016 Panini Torque Red /99 #80
2016 Panini Torque Rubber Relics /399 #15
2016 Panini Torque Rubber Relics Blue /99 #15
2016 Panini Torque Rubber Relics Green /25 #15
2016 Panini Torque Rubber Relics Purple /10 #15
2016 Panini Torque Rubber Relics Red /49 #15
2016 Panini Torque Shades #1
2016 Panini Torque Shades Gold /199 #1
2016 Panini Torque Shades Holo Silver /99 #1
2016 Panini Torque Silhouettes Firesuit Autographs /35 #14
2016 Panini Torque Silhouettes Firesuit Autographs Blue /25 #14
2016 Panini Torque Silhouettes Firesuit Autographs Green /15 #14
2016 Panini Torque Silhouettes Firesuit Autographs Purple /5 #14
2016 Panini Torque Silhouettes Firesuit Autographs Red /20 #14
2016 Panini Torque Silhouettes Sheet Metal Autographs /35 #17
2016 Panini Torque Silhouettes Sheet Metal Autographs Blue /25 #17
2016 Panini Torque Silhouettes Sheet Metal Autographs Green /2 #17
2016 Panini Torque Silhouettes Sheet Metal Autographs Purple /5 #17
2016 Panini Torque Silhouettes Sheet Metal Autographs Red /20 #17
2016 Panini Torque Superstar Vision #7
2016 Panini Torque Superstar Vision Blue /99 #7
2016 Panini Torque Superstar Vision Gold /149 #7
2016 Panini Torque Superstar Vision Green /25 #7
2016 Panini Torque Superstar Vision Purple /10 #7
2016 Panini Torque Superstar Vision Red /49 #7
2016 Panini Torque Test Proof Black /1 #3
2016 Panini Torque Test Proof Black /1 #62
2016 Panini Torque Test Proof Black /1 #80
2016 Panini Torque Test Proof Cyan /1 #3
2016 Panini Torque Test Proof Cyan /1 #62
2016 Panini Torque Test Proof Cyan /1 #80
2016 Panini Torque Test Proof Magenta /1 #3
2016 Panini Torque Test Proof Magenta /1 #62
2016 Panini Torque Test Proof Magenta /1 #80
2016 Panini Torque Test Proof Yellow /1 #3
2016 Panini Torque Test Proof Yellow /1 #62
2016 Panini Torque Test Proof Yellow /1 #80
2016 Panini Torque Victory Laps #11
2016 Panini Torque Victory Laps Gold /199 #11
2016 Panini Torque Victory Laps Holo Silver /99 #11
2016 Panini Torque Winning Vision #3
2016 Panini Torque Winning Vision Blue /99 #3
2016 Panini Torque Winning Vision Gold /149 #3
2016 Panini Torque Winning Vision Green /25 #3
2016 Panini Torque Winning Vision Purple /10 #3
2016 Panini Torque Winning Vision Red /49 #3
2016 Upper Deck Goodwin Champions #8
2016 Upper Deck Goodwin Champions #58
2016 Upper Deck Goodwin Champions #112
2016 Upper Deck Goodwin Champions Goudey #34
2016 Upper Deck Goodwin Champions Goudey Autographs #GAKH
2016 Upper Deck Goodwin Champions Goudey Printing Plates Black /1 #34
2016 Upper Deck Goodwin Champions Goudey Printing Plates Cyan /1 #34
2016 Upper Deck Goodwin Champions Goudey Printing Plates Magenta /1 #34
2016 Upper Deck Goodwin Champions Goudey Printing Plates Yellow /1 #34
2016 Upper Deck Goodwin Champions Goudey Sport Royalty Autographs #SRKH
2016 Upper Deck Goodwin Champions Mini #8
2016 Upper Deck Goodwin Champions Mini #58
2016 Upper Deck Goodwin Champions Mini #112
2016 Upper Deck Goodwin Champions Mini Black Metal Magician /16 #8
2016 Upper Deck Goodwin Champions Mini Black Metal Magician /16 #58
2016 Upper Deck Goodwin Champions Mini Black Metal Magician /16 #112
2016 Upper Deck Goodwin Champions Mini Canvas #8
2016 Upper Deck Goodwin Champions Mini Canvas #58
2016 Upper Deck Goodwin Champions Mini Canvas #112
2016 Upper Deck Goodwin Champions Mini Cloth Lady Luck /25 #8
2016 Upper Deck Goodwin Champions Mini Cloth Lady Luck /25 #58
2016 Upper Deck Goodwin Champions Mini Cloth Lady Luck /25 #112
2016 Upper Deck Goodwin Champions Mini Gold Presidential /1 #8
2016 Upper Deck Goodwin Champions Mini Gold Presidential /1 #58
2016 Upper Deck Goodwin Champions Mini Gold Presidential /1 #112
2016 Upper Deck Goodwin Champions Mini Royal Red #8
2016 Upper Deck Goodwin Champions Mini Royal Red #58
2016 Upper Deck Goodwin Champions Mini Royal Red #112
2016 Upper Deck Goodwin Champions Mini Wood Lumberjack /8 #8
2016 Upper Deck Goodwin Champions Mini Wood Lumberjack /8 #58
2016 Upper Deck Goodwin Champions Mini Wood Lumberjack /8 #112
2016 Upper Deck Goodwin Champions Printing Plates Black /1 #8
2016 Upper Deck Goodwin Champions Printing Plates Black /1 #58
2016 Upper Deck Goodwin Champions Printing Plates Black /1 #112
2016 Upper Deck Goodwin Champions Printing Plates Cyan /1 #8
2016 Upper Deck Goodwin Champions Printing Plates Cyan /1 #58
2016 Upper Deck Goodwin Champions Printing Plates Cyan /1 #112
2016 Upper Deck Goodwin Champions Printing Plates Magenta /1 #8
2016 Upper Deck Goodwin Champions Printing Plates Magenta /1 #58
2016 Upper Deck Goodwin Champions Printing Plates Magenta /1 #112
2016 Upper Deck Goodwin Champions Printing Plates Yellow /1 #8
2016 Upper Deck Goodwin Champions Printing Plates Yellow /1 #58
2016 Upper Deck Goodwin Champions Printing Plates Yellow /1 #112
2016 Upper Deck Goodwin Champions Royal Red #8
2016 Upper Deck Goodwin Champions Royal Red #58
2016 Upper Deck Goodwin Champions Royal Red #112
2017 Donruss #4
2017 Donruss #92
2017 Donruss #101
2017 Donruss #122
2017 Donruss #147
2017 Donruss #40A
2017 Donruss #40B
2017 Donruss Artist Proof /25 #4
2017 Donruss Artist Proof /25 #40A
2017 Donruss Artist Proof /25 #92
2017 Donruss Artist Proof /25 #122
2017 Donruss Artist Proof /25 #147
2017 Donruss Artist Proof /25 #40B
2017 Donruss Artist Proof /25 #101
2017 Donruss Blue Foil /299 #4
2017 Donruss Blue Foil /299 #92
2017 Donruss Blue Foil /299 #122
2017 Donruss Blue Foil /299 #40A
2017 Donruss Blue Foil /299 #147
2017 Donruss Blue Foil /299 #40B
2017 Donruss Blue Foil /299 #101
2017 Donruss Classics #9
2017 Donruss Classics Cracked Ice /999 #9
2017 Donruss Cut to The Chase #2
2017 Donruss Cut to The Chase #5
2017 Donruss Cut to The Chase Cracked Ice /999 #2
2017 Donruss Cut to The Chase Cracked Ice /999 #5
2017 Donruss Dual Rubber Relics #10
2017 Donruss Dual Rubber Relics Holo Black /1 #10
2017 Donruss Dual Rubber Relics Holo Gold /25 #10
2017 Donruss Elite Dominators /999 #2
2017 Donruss Gold Foil /499 #4
2017 Donruss Gold Foil /499 #92
2017 Donruss Gold Foil /499 #122
2017 Donruss Gold Foil /499 #147
2017 Donruss Gold Foil /499 #40A
2017 Donruss Gold Foil /499 #40B
2017 Donruss Gold Foil /499 #101
2017 Donruss Gold Press Proof /99 #4
2017 Donruss Gold Press Proof /99 #40A
2017 Donruss Gold Press Proof /99 #92
2017 Donruss Gold Press Proof /99 #122
2017 Donruss Gold Press Proof /99 #147
2017 Donruss Gold Press Proof /99 #40B
2017 Donruss Gold Press Proof /99 #101
2017 Donruss Green Foil /199 #4
2017 Donruss Green Foil /199 #40A
2017 Donruss Green Foil /199 #92
2017 Donruss Green Foil /199 #122
2017 Donruss Green Foil /199 #147
2017 Donruss Green Foil /199 #40B
2017 Donruss Green Foil /199 #101
2017 Donruss Pole Position #9
2017 Donruss Pole Position Cracked Ice /999 #9
2017 Donruss Press Proof /49 #4
2017 Donruss Press Proof /49 #40A
2017 Donruss Press Proof /49 #92
2017 Donruss Press Proof /49 #122
2017 Donruss Press Proof /49 #147
2017 Donruss Press Proof /49 #40B
2017 Donruss Press Proof /49 #101
2017 Donruss Printing Plates Black /1 #4
2017 Donruss Printing Plates Black /1 #40A
2017 Donruss Printing Plates Black /1 #92
2017 Donruss Printing Plates Black /1 #122
2017 Donruss Printing Plates Black /1 #147
2017 Donruss Printing Plates Black /1 #40B
2017 Donruss Printing Plates Black /1 #101
2017 Donruss Printing Plates Cyan /1 #4
2017 Donruss Printing Plates Cyan /1 #40A
2017 Donruss Printing Plates Cyan /1 #92
2017 Donruss Printing Plates Cyan /1 #122
2017 Donruss Printing Plates Cyan /1 #147
2017 Donruss Printing Plates Cyan /1 #40B
2017 Donruss Printing Plates Cyan /1 #101
2017 Donruss Printing Plates Magenta /1 #4
2017 Donruss Printing Plates Magenta /1 #92
2017 Donruss Printing Plates Magenta /1 #122
2017 Donruss Printing Plates Magenta /1 #147
2017 Donruss Printing Plates Magenta /1 #40A
2017 Donruss Printing Plates Magenta /1 #40B
2017 Donruss Printing Plates Magenta /1 #101
2017 Donruss Printing Plates Yellow /1 #4
2017 Donruss Printing Plates Yellow /1 #92
2017 Donruss Printing Plates Yellow /1 #122
2017 Donruss Printing Plates Yellow /1 #147
2017 Donruss Printing Plates Yellow /1 #40A
2017 Donruss Printing Plates Yellow /1 #40B
2017 Donruss Printing Plates Yellow /1 #101
2017 Donruss Retro Relics 1984 #26
2017 Donruss Retro Relics 1984 Holo Black /10 #26
2017 Donruss Retro Relics 1984 Holo Gold /99 #26
2017 Donruss Retro Signatures 1984 #15
2017 Donruss Retro Signatures 1984 Holo Black /1 #15
2017 Donruss Retro Signatures 1984 Holo Gold /25 #15
2017 Donruss Rubber Relics #30
2017 Donruss Rubber Relics #31
2017 Donruss Rubber Relics Holo Black /1 #30
2017 Donruss Rubber Relics Holo Black /1 #31
2017 Donruss Rubber Relics Holo Gold /99 #30
2017 Donruss Rubber Relics Holo Gold /22 #31
2017 Donruss Rubber Relics Signatures /99 #4
2017 Donruss Rubber Relics Signatures Holo Black /1 #4
2017 Donruss Rubber Relics Signatures Holo Gold /25 #4
2017 Donruss Significant Signatures #8
2017 Donruss Significant Signatures Holo Black /1 #8
2017 Donruss Significant Signatures Holo Gold /25 #8
2017 Donruss Speed #3
2017 Donruss Speed Cracked Ice /999 #3
2017 Donruss Top Tier #4
2017 Donruss Top Tier Cracked Ice /999 #4
2017 Donruss Track Masters #4
2017 Donruss Track Masters Cracked Ice /999 #4
2017 Panini Black Friday Happy Holiday Memorabilia #HHKH
2017 Panini Black Friday Happy Holiday Memorabilia Cracked Ice /25 #HHKH
2017 Panini Black Friday Happy Holiday Memorabilia Galactic Windows /10 #HHKH
2017 Panini Black Friday Happy Holiday Memorabilia Hyperplaid /1 #HHKH
2017 Panini Day #53
2017 Panini Day Cracked Ice /25 #53
2017 Panini Day Decoy /50 #53
2017 Panini Day Hyperplaid /1 #53
2017 Panini Day Rapture /10 #53
2017 Panini Day Wedges /50 #53
2017 Panini Father's Day Racing Memorabilia /100 #10
2017 Panini Father's Day Racing Memorabilia Cracked Ice /25 #10
2017 Panini Father's Day Racing Memorabilia Hyperplaid /1 #10
2017 Panini Father's Day Racing Memorabilia Shimmer /10 #10
2017 Panini Instant Nascar #15
2017 Panini Instant Nascar #32
2017 Panini Instant Nascar Black /1 #15
2017 Panini Instant Nascar Black /1 #32
2017 Panini Instant Nascar Green /10 #15
2017 Panini Instant Nascar Green /10 #32
2017 Panini National Convention #R5
2017 Panini National Convention Autographs #R5
2017 Panini National Convention Autographs Hyperplaid /1 #R5
2017 Panini National Convention Escher Squares /25 #R5
2017 Panini National Convention Escher Squares Thick Stock /10 #R5
2017 Panini National Convention Galatic Windows /5 #R5
2017 Panini National Convention Hyperplaid /1 #R5
2017 Panini National Convention Pyramids /10 #R5
2017 Panini National Convention Rainbow Spokes /49 #R5
2017 Panini National Convention Rainbow Spokes Thick Stock /25 #R5
2017 Panini National Convention Rapture /99 #R5
2017 Panini National Convention VIP #83
2017 Panini National Convention VIP Autographs /8 #83
2017 Panini National Convention VIP Autographs Black /1 #83
2017 Panini National Convention VIP Gems #KH
2017 Panini National Convention VIP Gems Gold /1 #KH
2017 Panini National Convention VIP Prizm #83
2017 Panini National Convention VIP Prizm Black /1 #83
2017 Panini National Convention VIP Prizm Cracked Ice /25 #83
2017 Panini National Convention VIP Prizm Gold /15 #83
2017 Panini National Convention VIP Prizm Green /5 #83
2017 Panini National Treasures /25 #2
2017 Panini National Treasures /25 #18
2017 Panini National Treasures Associate Sponsor Patch Signatures 1 /1 #2
2017 Panini National Treasures Associate Sponsor Patch Signatures 10 /1 #2
2017 Panini National Treasures Associate Sponsor Patch Signatures 11 /1 #2
2017 Panini National Treasures Associate Sponsor Patch Signatures 12 /1 #2
2017 Panini National Treasures Associate Sponsor Patch Signatures 13 /1 #2
2017 Panini National Treasures Associate Sponsor Patch Signatures 14 /1 #2
2017 Panini National Treasures Associate Sponsor Patch Signatures 15 /1 #2
2017 Panini National Treasures Associate Sponsor Patch Signatures 2 /1 #2
2017 Panini National Treasures Associate Sponsor Patch Signatures 3 /1 #2
2017 Panini National Treasures Associate Sponsor Patch Signatures 4 /1 #2
2017 Panini National Treasures Associate Sponsor Patch Signatures 5 /1 #2
2017 Panini National Treasures Associate Sponsor Patch Signatures 6 /1 #2
2017 Panini National Treasures Associate Sponsor Patch Signatures 7 /1 #2
2017 Panini National Treasures Associate Sponsor Patch Signatures 8 /1 #2
2017 Panini National Treasures Associate Sponsor Patch Signatures 9 /1 #2
2017 Panini National Treasures Car Manufacturer Patch Signatures /1 #2
2017 Panini National Treasures Century Black /1 #2
2017 Panini National Treasures Century Black /1 #18
2017 Panini National Treasures Century Gold /15 #2
2017 Panini National Treasures Century Gold /15 #18
2017 Panini National Treasures Century Green /5 #2
2017 Panini National Treasures Century Green /5 #18
2017 Panini National Treasures Century Holo Gold /10 #2
2017 Panini National Treasures Century Holo Gold /10 #18
2017 Panini National Treasures Century Holo Silver /20 #2
2017 Panini National Treasures Century Holo Silver /20 #18
2017 Panini National Treasures Century Laundry Tags /1 #2
2017 Panini National Treasures Championship Swatches /25 #2
2017 Panini National Treasures Championship Swatches Black /1 #2
2017 Panini National Treasures Championship Swatches Gold /15 #2
2017 Panini National Treasures Championship Swatches Green /5 #2
2017 Panini National Treasures Championship Swatches Holo Gold /10 #2
2017 Panini National Treasures Championship Swatches Holo Silver /20 #2
2017 Panini National Treasures Championship Swatches Laundry Tag /1 #2
2017 Panini National Treasures Championship Swatches Printing Plates Black /1 #2
2017 Panini National Treasures Championship Swatches Printing Plates Cyan /1 #2
2017 Panini National Treasures Championship Swatches Printing Plates Magenta /1 #2
2017 Panini National Treasures Championship Swatches Printing Plates Yellow /1 #2
2017 Panini National Treasures Combo Material Signatures /25 #3
2017 Panini National Treasures Combo Material Signatures Black /1 #3
2017 Panini National Treasures Combo Material Signatures Gold /15 #3
2017 Panini National Treasures Combo Material Signatures Green /5 #3
2017 Panini National Treasures Combo Material Signatures Holo Gold /10 #3
2017 Panini National Treasures Combo Material Signatures Holo Silver /20 #3
2017 Panini National Treasures Dual Sheet Metal Materials Black /1 #14
2017 Panini National Treasures Dual Sheet Metal Materials Gold /15 #14
2017 Panini National Treasures Dual Sheet Metal Materials Green /5 #14
2017 Panini National Treasures Dual Sheet Metal Materials Holo Gold /10 #14
2017 Panini National Treasures Dual Sheet Metal Materials Printing Plates Black /1 #14
2017 Panini National Treasures Dual Sheet Metal Materials Printing Plates Cyan /1 #14
2017 Panini National Treasures Dual Sheet Metal Materials Printing Plates Magenta /1 #14
2017 Panini National Treasures Dual Sheet Metal Materials Printing Plates Yellow /1 #14
2017 Panini National Treasures Dual Signature Materials /50 #5
2017 Panini National Treasures Dual Signature Materials Black /1 #5
2017 Panini National Treasures Dual Signature Materials Gold /15 #5
2017 Panini National Treasures Dual Signature Materials Green /5 #5
2017 Panini National Treasures Dual Signature Materials Holo Gold /10 #5
2017 Panini National Treasures Dual Signature Materials Holo Silver /25 #5
2017 Panini National Treasures Dual Signature Materials Laundry Tag /1 #5
2017 Panini National Treasures Dual Tire Signatures /25 #13
2017 Panini National Treasures Dual Tire Signatures Black /1 #13
2017 Panini National Treasures Dual Tire Signatures Gold /15 #13
2017 Panini National Treasures Dual Tire Signatures Green /5 #13
2017 Panini National Treasures Dual Tire Signatures Holo Gold /10 #13
2017 Panini National Treasures Dual Tire Signatures Holo Silver /20 #13
2017 Panini National Treasures Dual Tire Signatures Printing Plates Black /1 #13
2017 Panini National Treasures Dual Tire Signatures Printing Plates Cyan /1 #13
2017 Panini National Treasures Dual Tire Signatures Printing Plates Magenta /1 #13
2017 Panini National Treasures Dual Tire Signatures Printing Plates Yellow /1 #13
2017 Panini National Treasures Firesuit Manufacturer Patch Signatures /1 #2
2017 Panini National Treasures Goodyear Patch Signatures /2 #2
2017 Panini National Treasures Hats Off /16 #11
2017 Panini National Treasures Hats Off /13 #12
2017 Panini National Treasures Hats Off Gold /2 #11
2017 Panini National Treasures Hats Off Gold /2 #12
2017 Panini National Treasures Hats Off Holo Gold /5 #11
2017 Panini National Treasures Hats Off Holo Gold /5 #12
2017 Panini National Treasures Hats Off Holo Silver /1 #11
2017 Panini National Treasures Hats Off Holo Silver /1 #12
2017 Panini National Treasures Hats Off Laundry Tag /6 #11
2017 Panini National Treasures Hats Off Laundry Tag /6 #12
2017 Panini National Treasures Hats Off Monster Energy Cup /16 #5
2017 Panini National Treasures Hats Off Monster Energy Cup Gold /4 #5
2017 Panini National Treasures Hats Off Monster Energy Cup Holo Gold /5 #5
2017 Panini National Treasures Hats Off Monster Energy Cup Holo Silver /1 #5
2017 Panini National Treasures Hats Off Monster Energy Cup Laundry Tag /3 #5
2017 Panini National Treasures Hats Off Monster Energy Cup New Era /1 #5
2017 Panini National Treasures Hats Off Monster Energy Cup Printing Plates Black /1 #5
2017 Panini National Treasures Hats Off Monster Energy Cup Printing Plates Cyan /1 #5
2017 Panini National Treasures Hats Off Monster Energy Cup Printing Plates Magenta /1 #5
2017 Panini National Treasures Hats Off Monster Energy Cup Printing Plates Yellow /1 #5
2017 Panini National Treasures Hats Off Monster Energy Cup Sponsor /5 #5
2017 Panini National Treasures Hats Off New Era /1 #11
2017 Panini National Treasures Hats Off New Era /1 #12
2017 Panini National Treasures Hats Off Printing Plates Black /1 #11
2017 Panini National Treasures Hats Off Printing Plates Black /1 #12
2017 Panini National Treasures Hats Off Printing Plates Cyan /1 #12
2017 Panini National Treasures Hats Off Printing Plates Magenta /1 #11
2017 Panini National Treasures Hats Off Printing Plates Magenta /1 #12
2017 Panini National Treasures Hats Off Printing Plates Yellow /1 #11
2017 Panini National Treasures Hats Off Printing Plates Yellow /1 #12
2017 Panini National Treasures Hats Off Sponsor /5 #11
2017 Panini National Treasures Hats Off Sponsor /10 #12
2017 Panini National Treasures Jumbo Sheet Metal Materials Black /1 #3
2017 Panini National Treasures Jumbo Sheet Metal Materials Green /5 #3
2017 Panini National Treasures Jumbo Sheet Metal Materials Holo Gold /10 #3
2017 Panini National Treasures Jumbo Sheet Metal Materials Printing Plates Black /1 #3
2017 Panini National Treasures Jumbo Sheet Metal Materials Printing Plates Cyan /1 #3
2017 Panini National Treasures Jumbo Sheet Metal Materials Printing Plates Magenta /1 #3
2017 Panini National Treasures Jumbo Sheet Metal Materials Printing Plates Yellow /1 #3
2017 Panini National Treasures Jumbo Tire Signatures Black /1 #11
2017 Panini National Treasures Jumbo Tire Signatures Gold /25 #11
2017 Panini National Treasures Jumbo Tire Signatures Green /5 #11
2017 Panini National Treasures Jumbo Tire Signatures Holo Gold /15 #11
2017 Panini National Treasures Jumbo Tire Signatures Printing Plates Black /1 #11
2017 Panini National Treasures Jumbo Tire Signatures Printing Plates Cyan /1 #11
2017 Panini National Treasures Jumbo Tire Signatures Printing Plates Magenta /1 #11
2017 Panini National Treasures Jumbo Tire Signatures Printing Plates Yellow /1 #11
2017 Panini National Treasures Nameplate Patch Signatures /2 #2
2017 Panini National Treasures NASCAR Patch Signatures /1 #2
2017 Panini National Treasures Printing Plates Black /1 #2
2017 Panini National Treasures Printing Plates Black /1 #18
2017 Panini National Treasures Printing Plates Cyan /1 #2
2017 Panini National Treasures Printing Plates Cyan /1 #18
2017 Panini National Treasures Printing Plates Magenta /1 #2
2017 Panini National Treasures Printing Plates Magenta /1 #18
2017 Panini National Treasures Printing Plates Yellow /1 #2
2017 Panini National Treasures Printing Plates Yellow /1 #18
2017 Panini National Treasures Series Sponsor Patch Signatures /1 #2
2017 Panini National Treasures Signature Six Way Swatches /25 #2
2017 Panini National Treasures Signature Six Way Swatches Black /1 #2
2017 Panini National Treasures Signature Six Way Swatches Gold /15 #2
2017 Panini National Treasures Signature Six Way Swatches Green /5 #2
2017 Panini National Treasures Signature Six Way Swatches Holo Gold /10 #2
2017 Panini National Treasures Signature Six Way Swatches Holo Silver /20 #2
2017 Panini National Treasures Signature Six Way Swatches Laundry Tag /1 #2
2017 Panini National Treasures Sunoco Patch Signatures /1 #2
2017 Panini National Treasures Teammates Dual Materials /25 #4
2017 Panini National Treasures Teammates Dual Materials Black /1 #4
2017 Panini National Treasures Teammates Dual Materials Gold /15 #4
2017 Panini National Treasures Teammates Dual Materials Green /5 #4
2017 Panini National Treasures Teammates Dual Materials Holo Gold /10 #4
2017 Panini National Treasures Teammates Dual Materials Holo Silver /20 #4

2017 Panini National Treasures Teammates Dual Materials Laundry Tag /1 #4
2017 Panini National Treasures Teammates Dual Materials Printing Plates Black /1 #4
2017 Panini National Treasures Teammates Dual Materials Printing Plates Cyan /1 #4
2017 Panini National Treasures Teammates Dual Materials Printing Plates Magenta /1 #4
2017 Panini National Treasures Teammates Dual Materials Printing Plates Yellow /1 #4
2017 Panini National Treasures Teammates Quad Materials /25 #5
2017 Panini National Treasures Teammates Quad Materials Black /1 #5
2017 Panini National Treasures Teammates Quad Materials Gold /15 #5
2017 Panini National Treasures Teammates Quad Materials Green /5 #5
2017 Panini National Treasures Teammates Quad Materials Holo Gold /10 #5
2017 Panini National Treasures Teammates Quad Materials Holo Silver /20 #5
2017 Panini National Treasures Teammates Quad Materials Laundry Tag /1 #5
2017 Panini National Treasures Teammates Quad Materials Printing Plates Black /1 #5
2017 Panini National Treasures Teammates Quad Materials Printing Plates Cyan /1 #5
2017 Panini National Treasures Teammates Quad Materials Printing Plates Magenta /1 #5
2017 Panini National Treasures Teammates Quad Materials Printing Plates Yellow /1 #5
2017 Panini National Treasures Teammates Triple Materials /25 #2
2017 Panini National Treasures Teammates Triple Materials Black /1 #2
2017 Panini National Treasures Teammates Triple Materials Gold /15 #2
2017 Panini National Treasures Teammates Triple Materials Green /5 #2
2017 Panini National Treasures Teammates Triple Materials Holo Gold /10 #2
2017 Panini National Treasures Teammates Triple Materials Holo Silver /20 #2
2017 Panini National Treasures Teammates Triple Materials Laundry Tag /1 #2
2017 Panini National Treasures Teammates Triple Materials Printing Plates Black /1 #2
2017 Panini National Treasures Teammates Triple Materials Printing Plates Cyan /1 #2
2017 Panini National Treasures Teammates Triple Materials Printing Plates Magenta /1 #2
2017 Panini National Treasures Teammates Triple Materials Printing Plates Yellow /1 #2
2017 Panini National Treasures Three Wide /25 #7
2017 Panini National Treasures Three Wide Black /1 #7
2017 Panini National Treasures Three Wide Gold /15 #7
2017 Panini National Treasures Three Wide Green /5 #7
2017 Panini National Treasures Three Wide Holo Gold /10 #7
2017 Panini National Treasures Three Wide Holo Silver /20 #7
2017 Panini National Treasures Three Wide Laundry Tag /1 #7
2017 Panini National Treasures Three Wide Printing Plates Black /1 #7
2017 Panini National Treasures Three Wide Printing Plates Cyan /1 #7
2017 Panini National Treasures Three Wide Printing Plates Magenta /1 #7
2017 Panini National Treasures Three Wide Printing Plates Yellow /1 #7
2017 Panini National Treasures Winning Material Signatures /25 #6
2017 Panini National Treasures Winning Material Signatures Black /1 #6
2017 Panini National Treasures Winning Material Signatures Gold /15 #6
2017 Panini National Treasures Winning Material Signatures Green /5 #6
2017 Panini National Treasures Winning Material Signatures Holo Gold /10 #6
2017 Panini National Treasures Winning Material Signatures Holo Silver /20 #6
2017 Panini National Treasures Winning Material Signatures Laundry Tag /1 #6
2017 Panini National Treasures Winning Material Signatures Printing Plates Black /1 #6
2017 Panini National Treasures Winning Material Signatures Printing Plates Cyan /1 #6
2017 Panini National Treasures Winning Material Signatures Printing Plates Magenta /1 #6
2017 Panini National Treasures Winning Material Signatures Printing Plates Yellow /1 #6
2017 Panini National Treasures Winning Signatures Black /1 #11
2017 Panini National Treasures Winning Signatures Gold /25 #11
2017 Panini National Treasures Winning Signatures Green /5 #11
2017 Panini National Treasures Winning Signatures Holo Gold /15 #11
2017 Panini National Treasures Winning Signatures Printing Plates Black /1 #11
2017 Panini National Treasures Winning Signatures Printing Plates Cyan /1 #11
2017 Panini National Treasures Winning Signatures Printing Plates Magenta /1 #11
2017 Panini National Treasures Winning Signatures Printing Plates Yellow /1 #11
2017 Panini Torque #21
2017 Panini Torque #57
2017 Panini Torque #76
2017 Panini Torque #83
2017 Panini Torque #96
2017 Panini Torque Artist Proof /75 #21
2017 Panini Torque Artist Proof /75 #57
2017 Panini Torque Artist Proof /75 #76
2017 Panini Torque Artist Proof /75 #83
2017 Panini Torque Artist Proof /75 #96
2017 Panini Torque Blackout /1 #21
2017 Panini Torque Blackout /1 #57
2017 Panini Torque Blackout /1 #76
2017 Panini Torque Blackout /1 #83
2017 Panini Torque Blackout /1 #96
2017 Panini Torque Blue /150 #21
2017 Panini Torque Blue /150 #57
2017 Panini Torque Blue /150 #76
2017 Panini Torque Blue /150 #83
2017 Panini Torque Blue /150 #96
2017 Panini Torque Claiming The Chase #2
2017 Panini Torque Claiming The Chase Gold /199 #2
2017 Panini Torque Claiming The Chase Holo Silver /99 #2
2017 Panini Torque Clear Vision #4
2017 Panini Torque Clear Vision Blue /99 #4
2017 Panini Torque Clear Vision Gold /149 #4
2017 Panini Torque Clear Vision Green /25 #4
2017 Panini Torque Clear Vision Purple /10 #4
2017 Panini Torque Clear Vision Red /49 #4
2017 Panini Torque Dual Materials /199 #16
2017 Panini Torque Dual Materials Blue /99 #16
2017 Panini Torque Dual Materials Green /25 #16
2017 Panini Torque Dual Materials Purple /10 #16
2017 Panini Torque Dual Materials Red /49 #16
2017 Panini Torque Gold #21
2017 Panini Torque Gold #57
2017 Panini Torque Gold #76
2017 Panini Torque Gold #83
2017 Panini Torque Gold #96
2017 Panini Torque Holo Gold /10 #21
2017 Panini Torque Holo Gold /10 #57
2017 Panini Torque Holo Gold /10 #76
2017 Panini Torque Holo Gold /10 #83
2017 Panini Torque Holo Gold /10 #96
2017 Panini Torque Holo Silver /25 #21
2017 Panini Torque Holo Silver /25 #57
2017 Panini Torque Holo Silver /25 #76
2017 Panini Torque Holo Silver /25 #83
2017 Panini Torque Holo Silver /25 #96
2017 Panini Torque Horsepower Heroes #4
2017 Panini Torque Horsepower Heroes Gold /199 #4
2017 Panini Torque Horsepower Heroes Holo Silver /99 #4
2017 Panini Torque Jumbo Firesuit Signatures /51 #17
2017 Panini Torque Jumbo Firesuit Signatures Blue /49 #17
2017 Panini Torque Jumbo Firesuit Signatures Green /15 #17
2017 Panini Torque Jumbo Firesuit Signatures Purple /10 #17
2017 Panini Torque Jumbo Firesuit Signatures Red /25 #17
2017 Panini Torque Manufacturer Marks #3
2017 Panini Torque Manufacturer Marks Gold /199 #3
2017 Panini Torque Manufacturer Marks Holo Silver /99 #3
2017 Panini Torque Metal Materials /199 #18
2017 Panini Torque Metal Materials Blue /99 #18
2017 Panini Torque Metal Materials Green /25 #18
2017 Panini Torque Metal Materials Purple /10 #18
2017 Panini Torque Metal Materials Red /49 #18
2017 Panini Torque Pairings Materials /199 #4
2017 Panini Torque Pairings Materials Blue /99 #4
2017 Panini Torque Pairings Materials Green /25 #4
2017 Panini Torque Pairings Materials Purple /10 #4
2017 Panini Torque Pairings Materials Red /49 #4
2017 Panini Torque Primary Paint #8
2017 Panini Torque Primary Paint Blue /99 #8
2017 Panini Torque Primary Paint Checkerboard /10 #8
2017 Panini Torque Primary Paint Green /25 #8
2017 Panini Torque Primary Paint Red /49 #8
2017 Panini Torque Prime Associate Sponsors Jumbo Patches /1 #12A
2017 Panini Torque Prime Associate Sponsors Jumbo Patches /1 #12B
2017 Panini Torque Prime Associate Sponsors Jumbo Patches /1 #12C
2017 Panini Torque Prime Associate Sponsors Jumbo Patches /1 #12D
2017 Panini Torque Prime Associate Sponsors Jumbo Patches /1 #12E
2017 Panini Torque Prime Associate Sponsors Jumbo Patches /1 #12F
2017 Panini Torque Prime Associate Sponsors Jumbo Patches /1 #12G
2017 Panini Torque Prime Associate Sponsors Jumbo Patches /1 #12H
2017 Panini Torque Prime Associate Sponsors Jumbo Patches /1 #12I
2017 Panini Torque Prime Associate Sponsors Jumbo Patches /1 #12J
2017 Panini Torque Prime Associate Sponsors Jumbo Patches /1 #12K
2017 Panini Torque Prime Associate Sponsors Jumbo Patches /1 #12L
2017 Panini Torque Prime Associate Sponsors Jumbo Patches /1 #12M
2017 Panini Torque Prime Associate Sponsors Jumbo Patches /1 #12N
2017 Panini Torque Prime Associate Sponsors Jumbo Patches /1 #12O
2017 Panini Torque Prime Goodyear Jumbo Patches /2 #12
2017 Panini Torque Prime Manufacturer Jumbo Patches /1 #12
2017 Panini Torque Prime Nameplates Jumbo Patches /2 #12
2017 Panini Torque Prime Series Sponsor Jumbo Patches /1 #12
2017 Panini Torque Printing Plates Black /1 #21
2017 Panini Torque Printing Plates Black /1 #57
2017 Panini Torque Printing Plates Black /1 #76
2017 Panini Torque Printing Plates Black /1 #83
2017 Panini Torque Printing Plates Black /1 #96
2017 Panini Torque Printing Plates Cyan /1 #21
2017 Panini Torque Printing Plates Cyan /1 #57
2017 Panini Torque Printing Plates Cyan /1 #76
2017 Panini Torque Printing Plates Cyan /1 #83
2017 Panini Torque Printing Plates Cyan /1 #96
2017 Panini Torque Printing Plates Magenta /1 #21
2017 Panini Torque Printing Plates Magenta /1 #57
2017 Panini Torque Printing Plates Magenta /1 #76
2017 Panini Torque Printing Plates Magenta /1 #83
2017 Panini Torque Printing Plates Magenta /1 #96
2017 Panini Torque Printing Plates Yellow /1 #21
2017 Panini Torque Printing Plates Yellow /1 #57
2017 Panini Torque Printing Plates Yellow /1 #76
2017 Panini Torque Printing Plates Yellow /1 #83
2017 Panini Torque Printing Plates Yellow /1 #96
2017 Panini Torque Purple /50 #21
2017 Panini Torque Purple /50 #57
2017 Panini Torque Purple /50 #76
2017 Panini Torque Purple /50 #83
2017 Panini Torque Purple /50 #96
2017 Panini Torque Quad Materials /99 #17
2017 Panini Torque Quad Materials Blue /49 #17
2017 Panini Torque Quad Materials Green /10 #17
2017 Panini Torque Quad Materials Purple /1 #17
2017 Panini Torque Quad Materials Red /25 #17
2017 Panini Torque Raced Relics /499 #13
2017 Panini Torque Raced Relics Blue /99 #13
2017 Panini Torque Raced Relics Green /25 #13
2017 Panini Torque Raced Relics Purple /10 #13
2017 Panini Torque Raced Relics Red /49 #13
2017 Panini Torque Red /100 #21
2017 Panini Torque Red /100 #57
2017 Panini Torque Red /100 #76
2017 Panini Torque Red /100 #83
2017 Panini Torque Red /100 #96
2017 Panini Torque Running Order #8
2017 Panini Torque Running Order Blue /99 #8
2017 Panini Torque Running Order Checkerboard /10 #8
2017 Panini Torque Running Order Green /25 #8
2017 Panini Torque Running Order Red /49 #8
2017 Panini Torque Silhouettes Sheet Metal Signatures /51 #9
2017 Panini Torque Silhouettes Sheet Metal Signatures Blue /49 #9
2017 Panini Torque Silhouettes Sheet Metal Signatures Green /15 #9
2017 Panini Torque Silhouettes Sheet Metal Signatures Purple /10 #9
2017 Panini Torque Silhouettes Sheet Metal Signatures Red /25 #9
2017 Panini Torque Superstar Vision #4
2017 Panini Torque Superstar Vision Blue /99 #4
2017 Panini Torque Superstar Vision Gold /149 #4
2017 Panini Torque Superstar Vision Green /25 #4
2017 Panini Torque Superstar Vision Purple /10 #4
2017 Panini Torque Superstar Vision Red /49 #4
2017 Panini Torque Test Proof Black /1 #21
2017 Panini Torque Test Proof Black /1 #57
2017 Panini Torque Test Proof Black /1 #76
2017 Panini Torque Test Proof Black /1 #83
2017 Panini Torque Test Proof Black /1 #96
2017 Panini Torque Test Proof Cyan /1 #21
2017 Panini Torque Test Proof Cyan /1 #57
2017 Panini Torque Test Proof Cyan /1 #76
2017 Panini Torque Test Proof Cyan /1 #83
2017 Panini Torque Test Proof Cyan /1 #96
2017 Panini Torque Test Proof Magenta /1 #21
2017 Panini Torque Test Proof Magenta /1 #57
2017 Panini Torque Test Proof Magenta /1 #76
2017 Panini Torque Test Proof Magenta /1 #83
2017 Panini Torque Test Proof Magenta /1 #96
2017 Panini Torque Test Proof Yellow /1 #21
2017 Panini Torque Test Proof Yellow /1 #57
2017 Panini Torque Test Proof Yellow /1 #76
2017 Panini Torque Test Proof Yellow /1 #83
2017 Panini Torque Test Proof Yellow /1 #96
2017 Panini Torque Track Vision #3
2017 Panini Torque Track Vision Blue /99 #3
2017 Panini Torque Track Vision Gold /149 #3
2017 Panini Torque Track Vision Green /25 #3
2017 Panini Torque Track Vision Purple /10 #3
2017 Panini Torque Track Vision Red /49 #3
2017 Panini Torque Trackside #3
2017 Panini Torque Trackside Blue /99 #3
2017 Panini Torque Trackside Checkerboard /10 #3
2017 Panini Torque Trackside Green /25 #3
2017 Panini Torque Trackside Red /49 #3
2017 Panini Torque Victory Laps #3
2017 Panini Torque Victory Laps Gold /199 #3
2017 Panini Torque Victory Laps Holo Silver /99 #3
2017 Panini Torque Visions of Greatness #24
2017 Panini Torque Visions of Greatness Blue /99 #24
2017 Panini Torque Visions of Greatness Gold /149 #24
2017 Panini Torque Visions of Greatness Green /25 #24
2017 Panini Torque Visions of Greatness Purple /10 #24
2017 Panini Torque Visions of Greatness Red /49 #24
2017 Select #78
2017 Select #79
2017 Select #80
2017 Select #114
2017 Select Endorsements #24
2017 Select Endorsements Prizms Blue /50 #24
2017 Select Endorsements Prizms Checkered Flag /1 #24
2017 Select Endorsements Prizms Gold /10 #24
2017 Select Endorsements Prizms Red /25 #24
2017 Select Prizms Black /3 #78
2017 Select Prizms Black /3 #79
2017 Select Prizms Black /3 #80
2017 Select Prizms Black /3 #114
2017 Select Prizms Blue /199 #78
2017 Select Prizms Blue /199 #79
2017 Select Prizms Blue /199 #80
2017 Select Prizms Checkered Flag /1 #78
2017 Select Prizms Checkered Flag /1 #79
2017 Select Prizms Checkered Flag /1 #80
2017 Select Prizms Checkered Flag /1 #114
2017 Select Prizms Gold /10 #78
2017 Select Prizms Gold /10 #79
2017 Select Prizms Gold /10 #80
2017 Select Prizms Gold /10 #114
2017 Select Prizms Purple Pulsar #78
2017 Select Prizms Purple Pulsar #79
2017 Select Prizms Purple Pulsar #80
2017 Select Prizms Red /99 #78
2017 Select Prizms Red /99 #79
2017 Select Prizms Red /99 #80
2017 Select Prizms Red White and Blue Pulsar /299 #78
2017 Select Prizms Red White and Blue Pulsar /299 #79
2017 Select Prizms Red White and Blue Pulsar /299 #80
2017 Select Prizms Silver #78
2017 Select Prizms Silver #79
2017 Select Prizms Silver #80
2017 Select Prizms Tie Dye /24 #78
2017 Select Prizms Tie Dye /24 #79
2017 Select Prizms Tie Dye /24 #80
2017 Select Prizms Tie Dye /24 #114
2017 Select Prizms White /50 #78
2017 Select Prizms White /50 #79
2017 Select Prizms White /50 #80
2017 Select Prizms White /50 #114
2017 Select Select Pairs Materials #7
2017 Select Select Pairs Materials #8
2017 Select Select Pairs Materials #9
2017 Select Select Pairs Materials Prizms Blue /199 #7
2017 Select Select Pairs Materials Prizms Blue /199 #8
2017 Select Select Pairs Materials Prizms Blue /199 #9
2017 Select Select Pairs Materials Prizms Checkered Flag /1 #7
2017 Select Select Pairs Materials Prizms Checkered Flag /1 #8
2017 Select Select Pairs Materials Prizms Checkered Flag /1 #9
2017 Select Select Pairs Materials Prizms Gold /10 #7
2017 Select Select Pairs Materials Prizms Gold /10 #8
2017 Select Select Pairs Materials Prizms Gold /10 #9
2017 Select Select Pairs Materials Prizms Red /99 #7
2017 Select Select Pairs Materials Prizms Red /99 #8
2017 Select Select Pairs Materials Prizms Red /99 #9
2017 Select Select Stars #7
2017 Select Select Stars Prizms Black /3 #7
2017 Select Select Stars Prizms Checkered Flag /1 #7
2017 Select Select Stars Prizms Gold /10 #7
2017 Select Select Stars Prizms Tie Dye /24 #7
2017 Select Select Stars Prizms White /50 #7
2017 Select Select Swatches #27
2017 Select Select Swatches Prizms Blue /199 #27
2017 Select Select Swatches Prizms Checkered Flag /1 #27
2017 Select Select Swatches Prizms Gold /10 #27
2017 Select Select Swatches Prizms Red /99 #27
2017 Select Sheet Metal #15
2017 Select Sheet Metal Prizms Blue /199 #15
2017 Select Sheet Metal Prizms Checkered Flag /1 #15
2017 Select Sheet Metal Prizms Gold /10 #15
2017 Select Sheet Metal Prizms Red /99 #15
2017 Select Signature Swatches #27
2017 Select Signature Swatches Prizms Checkered Flag /1 #27
2017 Select Signature Swatches Prizms Gold /10 #27
2017 Select Signature Swatches Prizms Tie Dye /24 #27
2017 Select Signature Swatches Prizms White /50 #27
2017 Select Signature Swatches Triple #16
2017 Select Signature Swatches Triple Prizms Checkered Flag /1 #16
2017 Select Signature Swatches Triple Prizms Gold /10 #16
2017 Select Signature Swatches Triple Prizms Tie Dye /24 #16
2017 Select Signature Swatches Triple Prizms White /50 #16
2017 Select Speed Merchants #15
2017 Select Speed Merchants Prizms Black /3 #15
2017 Select Speed Merchants Prizms Checkered Flag /1 #15
2017 Select Speed Merchants Prizms Gold /10 #15
2017 Select Speed Merchants Prizms Tie Dye /24 #15
2017 Select Speed Merchants Prizms White /50 #15
2017 Select Up Close and Personal #6
2017 Select Up Close and Personal Prizms Black /3 #6
2017 Select Up Close and Personal Prizms Checkered Flag /1 #6
2017 Select Up Close and Personal Prizms Gold /10 #6
2017 Select Up Close and Personal Prizms Tie Dye /24 #6
2017 Select Up Close and Personal Prizms White /50 #6
2018 Certified #8
2018 Certified #93
2018 Certified All Certified Team /199 #6
2018 Certified All Certified Team Black /1 #6
2018 Certified All Certified Team Blue /99 #6
2018 Certified All Certified Team Gold /49 #6
2018 Certified All Certified Team Green /10 #6
2018 Certified All Certified Team Mirror Black /1 #6
2018 Certified All Certified Team Mirror Gold /25 #6
2018 Certified All Certified Team Mirror Green /5 #6
2018 Certified All Certified Team Mirror Purple /10 #6
2018 Certified All Certified Team Purple /25 #6
2018 Certified All Certified Team Red /149 #6
2018 Certified Black /1 #8
2018 Certified Black /1 #93
2018 Certified Blue /99 #8
2018 Certified Blue /99 #93
2018 Certified Complete Materials /199 #3
2018 Certified Complete Materials Black /1 #3
2018 Certified Complete Materials Blue /49 #3
2018 Certified Complete Materials Gold /25 #3
2018 Certified Complete Materials Green /5 #3
2018 Certified Complete Materials Purple /10 #3
2018 Certified Complete Materials Red /99 #3
2018 Certified Cup Swatches /499 #16
2018 Certified Cup Swatches Black /1 #16
2018 Certified Cup Swatches Blue /49 #16
2018 Certified Cup Swatches Gold /25 #16
2018 Certified Cup Swatches Green /5 #16
2018 Certified Cup Swatches Purple /10 #16
2018 Certified Cup Swatches Red /199 #16
2018 Certified Epix /199 #7
2018 Certified Epix Black /1 #7
2018 Certified Epix Blue /99 #7
2018 Certified Epix Gold /49 #7
2018 Certified Epix Green /10 #7
2018 Certified Epix Mirror Black /1 #7
2018 Certified Epix Mirror Gold /25 #7
2018 Certified Epix Mirror Green /5 #7
2018 Certified Epix Mirror Purple /10 #7
2018 Certified Epix Purple /25 #7
2018 Certified Epix Red /149 #7
2018 Certified Gold /49 #8
2018 Certified Gold /49 #93
2018 Certified Green /10 #8
2018 Certified Green /10 #93
2018 Certified Materials Signatures /75 #6
2018 Certified Materials Signatures Black /1 #6
2018 Certified Materials Signatures Blue /20 #6
2018 Certified Materials Signatures Gold /15 #6
2018 Certified Materials Signatures Green /4 #6
2018 Certified Materials Signatures Purple /10 #6
2018 Certified Materials Signatures Red /50 #6
2018 Certified Mirror Black /1 #8
2018 Certified Mirror Black /1 #93
2018 Certified Mirror Gold /25 #8
2018 Certified Mirror Gold /25 #93
2018 Certified Mirror Green /5 #8
2018 Certified Mirror Green /5 #93
2018 Certified Mirror Purple /10 #8
2018 Certified Mirror Purple /10 #93
2018 Certified Orange /249 #8
2018 Certified Orange /249 #93
2018 Certified Piece of the Race /499 #3
2018 Certified Piece of the Race Black /1 #3
2018 Certified Piece of the Race Blue /49 #3
2018 Certified Piece of the Race Gold /25 #3
2018 Certified Piece of the Race Green /5 #3
2018 Certified Piece of the Race Purple /10 #3
2018 Certified Piece of the Race Red /199 #3
2018 Certified Purple /25 #8
2018 Certified Purple /25 #93
2018 Certified Red /199 #8
2018 Certified Red /199 #93
2018 Certified Signing Sessions Black /1 #13
2018 Certified Signing Sessions Blue /20 #13
2018 Certified Signing Sessions Gold /15 #13
2018 Certified Signing Sessions Green /4 #13
2018 Certified Signing Sessions Purple /10 #13
2018 Certified Signing Sessions Red /25 #13
2018 Certified Skills /199 #3
2018 Certified Skills Black /1 #3
2018 Certified Skills Blue /99 #3
2018 Certified Skills Gold /49 #3
2018 Certified Skills Green /10 #3
2018 Certified Skills Mirror Black /1 #3
2018 Certified Skills Mirror Gold /25 #3
2018 Certified Skills Mirror Green /5 #3
2018 Certified Skills Mirror Purple /10 #3
2018 Certified Skills Purple /25 #3
2018 Certified Skills Red /149 #3
2018 Certified Stars /199 #11
2018 Certified Stars Black /1 #11
2018 Certified Stars Blue /99 #11
2018 Certified Stars Gold /49 #11
2018 Certified Stars Green /10 #11
2018 Certified Stars Mirror Black /1 #11
2018 Certified Stars Mirror Gold /25 #11
2018 Certified Stars Mirror Green /5 #11
2018 Certified Stars Mirror Purple /10 #11
2018 Certified Stars Purple /25 #11
2018 Certified Stars Red /149 #11
2018 Donruss #7
2018 Donruss #34A
2018 Donruss #81
2018 Donruss #124A
2018 Donruss #34B
2018 Donruss #124B
2018 Donruss Artist Proofs /25 #7
2018 Donruss Artist Proofs /25 #34A
2018 Donruss Artist Proofs /25 #81
2018 Donruss Artist Proofs /25 #124
2018 Donruss Artist Proofs /25 #34B
2018 Donruss Artist Proofs /25 #124B
2018 Donruss Classics #6
2018 Donruss Classics Cracked Ice /999 #6
2018 Donruss Classics Xplosion /99 #6
2018 Donruss Elite Series /999 #2
2018 Donruss Gold Foil /499 #7
2018 Donruss Gold Foil /499 #34A
2018 Donruss Gold Foil /499 #81
2018 Donruss Gold Foil /499 #124
2018 Donruss Gold Foil /499 #34B
2018 Donruss Gold Foil /499 #124B
2018 Donruss Gold Press Proofs /99 #7
2018 Donruss Gold Press Proofs /99 #34A
2018 Donruss Gold Press Proofs /99 #81
2018 Donruss Gold Press Proofs /99 #124
2018 Donruss Gold Press Proofs /99 #34B
2018 Donruss Gold Press Proofs /99 #124B
2018 Donruss Green Foil /199 #7
2018 Donruss Green Foil /199 #34A
2018 Donruss Green Foil /199 #81
2018 Donruss Green Foil /199 #124
2018 Donruss Green Foil /199 #34B
2018 Donruss Green Foil /199 #124B
2018 Donruss Pole Position #2
2018 Donruss Pole Position Cracked Ice /999 #2
2018 Donruss Pole Position Xplosion /99 #2
2018 Donruss Press Proofs /49 #7
2018 Donruss Press Proofs /49 #34A
2018 Donruss Press Proofs /49 #81
2018 Donruss Press Proofs /49 #124A
2018 Donruss Press Proofs /49 #34B
2018 Donruss Press Proofs /49 #124B
2018 Donruss Printing Plates Black /1 #7
2018 Donruss Printing Plates Black /1 #34
2018 Donruss Printing Plates Black /1 #81
2018 Donruss Printing Plates Black /1 #124
2018 Donruss Printing Plates Black /1 #34B
2018 Donruss Printing Plates Black /1 #124B
2018 Donruss Printing Plates Cyan /1 #7
2018 Donruss Printing Plates Cyan /1 #34
2018 Donruss Printing Plates Cyan /1 #81
2018 Donruss Printing Plates Cyan /1 #124
2018 Donruss Printing Plates Cyan /1 #34B
2018 Donruss Printing Plates Cyan /1 #124B
2018 Donruss Printing Plates Magenta /1 #7
2018 Donruss Printing Plates Magenta /1 #34
2018 Donruss Printing Plates Magenta /1 #81
2018 Donruss Printing Plates Magenta /1 #124
2018 Donruss Printing Plates Magenta /1 #34B
2018 Donruss Printing Plates Magenta /1 #124B
2018 Donruss Printing Plates Yellow /1 #7
2018 Donruss Printing Plates Yellow /1 #34
2018 Donruss Printing Plates Yellow /1 #81
2018 Donruss Printing Plates Yellow /1 #124
2018 Donruss Printing Plates Yellow /1 #34B
2018 Donruss Printing Plates Yellow /1 #124B
2018 Donruss Racing Relics #13
2018 Donruss Racing Relics Black /4 #13
2018 Donruss Racing Relics Holo Gold /10 #13
2018 Donruss Red Foil /299 #7
2018 Donruss Red Foil /299 #34A
2018 Donruss Red Foil /299 #81
2018 Donruss Red Foil /299 #124A
2018 Donruss Red Foil /299 #34B
2018 Donruss Red Foil /299 #124B
2018 Donruss Retro Relics '85 #1
2018 Donruss Retro Relics '85 Black /4 #1
2018 Donruss Retro Relics '85 Holo Gold /10 #1
2018 Donruss Rubber Relic Signatures #11
2018 Donruss Rubber Relic Signatures Black /1 #11
2018 Donruss Rubber Relic Signatures Holo Gold /25 #11
2018 Donruss Rubber Relics #21
2018 Donruss Rubber Relics Black /10 #21
2018 Donruss Rubber Relics Holo Gold /99 #21
2018 Donruss Studio #2
2018 Donruss Studio Cracked Ice /999 #2
2018 Donruss Studio Xplosion /99 #2
2018 Donruss Top Tier #4
2018 Donruss Top Tier Cracked Ice /999 #4
2018 Donruss Top Tier Xplosion /99 #4
2018 Panini Prime /50 #3
2018 Panini Prime /50 #37
2018 Panini Prime /50 #70
2018 Panini Prime Autograph Materials /25 #16
2018 Panini Prime Autograph Materials Black /1 #16
2018 Panini Prime Autograph Materials Holo Gold /10 #16
2018 Panini Prime Autograph Materials Laundry Tag /1 #16
2018 Panini Prime Black /1 #3
2018 Panini Prime Black /1 #37
2018 Panini Prime Black /1 #70
2018 Panini Prime Clear Silhouettes /99 #18
2018 Panini Prime Clear Silhouettes Black /1 #18
2018 Panini Prime Clear Silhouettes Dual /99 #20
2018 Panini Prime Clear Silhouettes Dual Black /1 #20
2018 Panini Prime Clear Silhouettes Dual Holo Gold /50 #20
2018 Panini Prime Clear Silhouettes Holo Gold /50 #18
2018 Panini Prime Dual Signatures /10 #6
2018 Panini Prime Dual Signatures Black /1 #6
2018 Panini Prime Dual Signatures Holo Gold /5 #6
2018 Panini Prime Hats Off Button /1 #19
2018 Panini Prime Hats Off Driver Name /3 #19
2018 Panini Prime Hats Off Eyelet /6 #19
2018 Panini Prime Hats Off Headband /34 #19
2018 Panini Prime Hats Off Laundry Tag /1 #19
2018 Panini Prime Hats Off New Era /1 #19
2018 Panini Prime Hats Off Number /2 #19
2018 Panini Prime Hats Off Sponsor Logo /4 #19
2018 Panini Prime Holo Gold /25 #3
2018 Panini Prime Holo Gold /25 #37
2018 Panini Prime Holo Gold /25 #70
2018 Panini Prime Prime Jumbo Associate Sponsor 1 /1 #49
2018 Panini Prime Prime Jumbo Associate Sponsor 10 /1 #49
2018 Panini Prime Prime Jumbo Associate Sponsor 11 /1 #49
2018 Panini Prime Prime Jumbo Associate Sponsor 12 /1 #49
2018 Panini Prime Prime Jumbo Associate Sponsor 13 /1 #49
2018 Panini Prime Prime Jumbo Associate Sponsor 14 /1 #49
2018 Panini Prime Prime Jumbo Associate Sponsor 15 /1 #49
2018 Panini Prime Prime Jumbo Associate Sponsor 2 /1 #49
2018 Panini Prime Prime Jumbo Associate Sponsor 3 /1 #49
2018 Panini Prime Prime Jumbo Associate Sponsor 4 /1 #49
2018 Panini Prime Prime Jumbo Associate Sponsor 5 /1 #49
2018 Panini Prime Prime Jumbo Associate Sponsor 6 /1 #49
2018 Panini Prime Prime Jumbo Associate Sponsor 7 /1 #49
2018 Panini Prime Prime Jumbo Associate Sponsor 8 /1 #49
2018 Panini Prime Prime Jumbo Associate Sponsor 9 /1 #49
2018 Panini Prime Prime Jumbo Car Manufacturer /1 #49
2018 Panini Prime Prime Jumbo Firesuit Manufacturer /1 #49
2018 Panini Prime Prime Jumbo Nameplate /2 #49
2018 Panini Prime Prime Jumbo NASCAR /1 #49
2018 Panini Prime Prime Jumbo Prime Colors /16 #49
2018 Panini Prime Prime Jumbo Series Sponsor /1 #49
2018 Panini Prime Prime Jumbo Shoe Brand Logo /1 #49
2018 Panini Prime Prime Jumbo Shoe Name Patch /1 #49
2018 Panini Prime Prime Jumbo Sunoco /1 #49
2018 Panini Prime Prime Number Signatures /25 #9
2018 Panini Prime Prime Number Signatures Black /1 #9
2018 Panini Prime Prime Number Signatures Holo Gold /10 #9
2018 Panini Prime Quad Material Autographs /25 #4
2018 Panini Prime Quad Material Autographs Black /1 #4
2018 Panini Prime Quad Material Autographs Holo Gold /10 #4
2018 Panini Prime Quad Material Autographs Laundry Tag /1 #4
2018 Panini Prime Race Used Duals Firesuit /50 #25
2018 Panini Prime Race Used Duals Firesuit Black /1 #25
2018 Panini Prime Race Used Duals Firesuit Holo Gold /25 #25
2018 Panini Prime Race Used Duals Firesuit Laundry Tag /1 #25
2018 Panini Prime Race Used Duals Sheet Metal /50 #25
2018 Panini Prime Race Used Duals Sheet Metal Black /1 #25
2018 Panini Prime Race Used Duals Sheet Metal Holo Gold /25 #25
2018 Panini Prime Race Used Duals Tire /50 #25
2018 Panini Prime Race Used Duals Tire Black /1 #25
2018 Panini Prime Race Used Duals Tire Holo Gold /25 #25
2018 Panini Prime Race Used Firesuits Black /1 #23
2018 Panini Prime Race Used Firesuits Holo Gold /25 #23
2018 Panini Prime Race Used Firesuits Laundry Tag /1 #23
2018 Panini Prime Race Used Sheet Metal /50 #23
2018 Panini Prime Race Used Sheet Metal Black /1 #23
2018 Panini Prime Race Used Sheet Metal Holo Gold /25 #23
2018 Panini Prime Race Used Tires /50 #23
2018 Panini Prime Race Used Tires Black /1 #23
2018 Panini Prime Race Used Tires Holo Gold /25 #23
2018 Panini Prime Race Used Trios Firesuit /50 #1
2018 Panini Prime Race Used Trios Firesuit Black /1 #1
2018 Panini Prime Race Used Trios Firesuit Holo Gold /25 #1
2018 Panini Prime Race Used Trios Firesuit Laundry Tag /1 #1
2018 Panini Prime Race Used Trios Sheet Metal /50 #1
2018 Panini Prime Race Used Trios Sheet Metal Black /1 #1
2018 Panini Prime Race Used Trios Sheet Metal Holo Gold /25 #1
2018 Panini Prime Race Used Trios Tire /50 #1
2018 Panini Prime Race Used Trios Tire Black /1 #1
2018 Panini Prime Race Used Trios Tire Holo Gold /25 #1
2018 Panini Prime Shadowbox Signatures /25 #15
2018 Panini Prime Shadowbox Signatures Black /1 #15
2018 Panini Prime Shadowbox Signatures Holo Gold /10 #15
2018 Panini Prime Signature Swatches /25 #20
2018 Panini Prime Signature Swatches Black /1 #20
2018 Panini Prime Signature Swatches Holo Gold /10 #20
2018 Panini Prime Signature Tires /25 #9
2018 Panini Prime Signature Tires Black /1 #9
2018 Panini Prime Signature Tires Holo Gold /10 #9
2018 Panini Prime Triple Material Autographs /25 #11
2018 Panini Prime Triple Material Autographs Black /1 #11
2018 Panini Prime Triple Material Autographs Holo Gold /10 #11
2018 Panini Prime Triple Material Autographs Laundry Tag /1 #11
2018 Panini Prizm #46
2018 Panini Prizm #51
2018 Panini Prizm #70
2018 Panini Prizm #77
2018 Panini Prizm #81
2018 Panini Prizm Brilliance #5
2018 Panini Prizm Brilliance Prizms #5
2018 Panini Prizm Brilliance Prizms Black /1 #5
2018 Panini Prizm Brilliance Prizms Gold /10 #5
2018 Panini Prizm Fireworks #5
2018 Panini Prizm Fireworks Prizms #5
2018 Panini Prizm Fireworks Prizms Black /1 #5
2018 Panini Prizm Fireworks Prizms Gold /10 #5
2018 Panini Prizm Illumination #6
2018 Panini Prizm Illumination Prizms #6
2018 Panini Prizm Illumination Prizms Black /1 #6
2018 Panini Prizm Illumination Prizms Gold /10 #6
2018 Panini Prizm Instant Impact #6
2018 Panini Prizm Instant Impact Prizms #6
2018 Panini Prizm Instant Impact Prizms Black /1 #6
2018 Panini Prizm Instant Impact Prizms Gold /10 #6
2018 Panini Prizm National Pride #3
2018 Panini Prizm National Pride Prizms #3
2018 Panini Prizm National Pride Prizms Black /1 #3
2018 Panini Prizm National Pride Prizms Gold /10 #3
2018 Panini Prizm Prizms #46
2018 Panini Prizm Prizms #51
2018 Panini Prizm Prizms #70
2018 Panini Prizm Prizms #77
2018 Panini Prizm Prizms #81
2018 Panini Prizm Prizms Black /1 #46
2018 Panini Prizm Prizms Black /1 #51
2018 Panini Prizm Prizms Black /1 #70
2018 Panini Prizm Prizms Black /1 #77
2018 Panini Prizm Prizms Black /1 #81
2018 Panini Prizm Prizms Blue /99 #46
2018 Panini Prizm Prizms Blue /99 #51
2018 Panini Prizm Prizms Blue /99 #70
2018 Panini Prizm Prizms Blue /99 #77
2018 Panini Prizm Prizms Blue /99 #81
2018 Panini Prizm Prizms Camo #46
2018 Panini Prizm Prizms Camo #51
2018 Panini Prizm Prizms Camo #70
2018 Panini Prizm Prizms Camo #77
2018 Panini Prizm Prizms Camo #81
2018 Panini Prizm Prizms Gold /10 #46
2018 Panini Prizm Prizms Gold /10 #51
2018 Panini Prizm Prizms Gold /10 #70
2018 Panini Prizm Prizms Gold /10 #77
2018 Panini Prizm Prizms Gold /10 #81
2018 Panini Prizm Prizms Green /149 #46
2018 Panini Prizm Prizms Green /149 #51
2018 Panini Prizm Prizms Green /149 #70
2018 Panini Prizm Prizms Green /149 #77
2018 Panini Prizm Prizms Green /149 #81
2018 Panini Prizm Prizms Purple Flash #46
2018 Panini Prizm Prizms Purple Flash #51
2018 Panini Prizm Prizms Purple Flash #70
2018 Panini Prizm Prizms Purple Flash #77
2018 Panini Prizm Prizms Purple Flash #81
2018 Panini Prizm Prizms Rainbow /24 #46
2018 Panini Prizm Prizms Rainbow /24 #51
2018 Panini Prizm Prizms Rainbow /24 #70
2018 Panini Prizm Prizms Rainbow /24 #77
2018 Panini Prizm Prizms Rainbow /24 #81
2018 Panini Prizm Prizms Red /75 #46
2018 Panini Prizm Prizms Red /75 #51
2018 Panini Prizm Prizms Red /75 #70
2018 Panini Prizm Prizms Red /75 #77
2018 Panini Prizm Prizms Red /75 #81
2018 Panini Prizm Prizms Red White and Blue #46
2018 Panini Prizm Prizms Red White and Blue #51
2018 Panini Prizm Prizms Red White and Blue #70
2018 Panini Prizm Prizms Red White and Blue #77
2018 Panini Prizm Prizms Red White and Blue #81
2018 Panini Prizm Prizms White /5 #46
2018 Panini Prizm Prizms White /5 #51
2018 Panini Prizm Prizms White /5 #70
2018 Panini Prizm Prizms White /5 #77
2018 Panini Prizm Prizms White /5 #81
2018 Panini Prizm Scripted Signatures Prizms #40
2018 Panini Prizm Scripted Signatures Prizms Black /1 #40
2018 Panini Prizm Scripted Signatures Prizms Blue /25 #40
2018 Panini Prizm Scripted Signatures Prizms Camo #40
2018 Panini Prizm Scripted Signatures Prizms Gold /10 #40
2018 Panini Prizm Scripted Signatures Prizms Green /25 #40
2018 Panini Prizm Scripted Signatures Prizms Rainbow /24 #40
2018 Panini Prizm Scripted Signatures Prizms Red /25 #40
2018 Panini Prizm Scripted Signatures Prizms Red White and Blue /25 #40
2018 Panini Prizm Scripted Signatures Prizms White /5 #40
2018 Panini Prizm Stars and Stripes #3
2018 Panini Prizm Stars and Stripes Prizms #3
2018 Panini Prizm Stars and Stripes Prizms Black /1 #3
2018 Panini Prizm Stars and Stripes Prizms Gold /10 #3
2018 Panini Prizm Team Tandems #3
2018 Panini Prizm Team Tandems Prizms #3
2018 Panini Prizm Team Tandems Prizms Black /1 #3
2018 Panini Prizm Team Tandems Prizms Gold /10 #3
2018 Panini Victory Lane #4
2018 Panini Victory Lane #48
2018 Panini Victory Lane #65
2018 Panini Victory Lane #95
2018 Panini Victory Lane Black /1 #4
2018 Panini Victory Lane Black /1 #48
2018 Panini Victory Lane Black /1 #65
2018 Panini Victory Lane Black /1 #95
2018 Panini Victory Lane Blue /25 #4
2018 Panini Victory Lane Blue /25 #48
2018 Panini Victory Lane Blue /25 #65
2018 Panini Victory Lane Blue /25 #95
2018 Panini Victory Lane Celebrations #3
2018 Panini Victory Lane Celebrations Black /1 #3
2018 Panini Victory Lane Celebrations Blue /25 #3
2018 Panini Victory Lane Celebrations Gold /99 #3
2018 Panini Victory Lane Celebrations Green /5 #3
2018 Panini Victory Lane Celebrations Printing Plates Black /1 #3
2018 Panini Victory Lane Celebrations Printing Plates Cyan /1 #3
2018 Panini Victory Lane Celebrations Printing Plates Magenta /1 #3
2018 Panini Victory Lane Celebrations Printing Plates Yellow /1 #3
2018 Panini Victory Lane Celebrations Red /49 #3
2018 Panini Victory Lane Champions #13
2018 Panini Victory Lane Champions Black /1 #13
2018 Panini Victory Lane Champions Blue /25 #13
2018 Panini Victory Lane Champions Gold /99 #13
2018 Panini Victory Lane Champions Green /5 #13
2018 Panini Victory Lane Champions Printing Plates Black /1 #13
2018 Panini Victory Lane Champions Printing Plates Cyan /1 #13
2018 Panini Victory Lane Champions Printing Plates Magenta /1 #13
2018 Panini Victory Lane Champions Printing Plates Yellow /1 #13
2018 Panini Victory Lane Champions Red /49 #13
2018 Panini Victory Lane Chasing the Flag #3
2018 Panini Victory Lane Chasing the Flag Black /1 #3
2018 Panini Victory Lane Chasing the Flag Blue /25 #3
2018 Panini Victory Lane Chasing the Flag Gold /99 #3
2018 Panini Victory Lane Chasing the Flag Green /5 #3
2018 Panini Victory Lane Chasing the Flag Printing Plates Black /1 #3
2018 Panini Victory Lane Chasing the Flag Printing Plates Cyan /1 #3
2018 Panini Victory Lane Chasing the Flag Printing Plates Magenta /1 #3
2018 Panini Victory Lane Chasing the Flag Printing Plates Yellow /1 #3
2018 Panini Victory Lane Chasing the Flag Red /49 #3
2018 Panini Victory Lane Gold /99 #4
2018 Panini Victory Lane Gold /99 #48
2018 Panini Victory Lane Gold /99 #65
2018 Panini Victory Lane Gold /99 #95
2018 Panini Victory Lane Green /5 #4
2018 Panini Victory Lane Green /5 #48
2018 Panini Victory Lane Green /5 #65
2018 Panini Victory Lane Green /5 #95
2018 Panini Victory Lane Pedal to the Metal #33
2018 Panini Victory Lane Pedal to the Metal #54
2018 Panini Victory Lane Pedal to the Metal Black /1 #33
2018 Panini Victory Lane Pedal to the Metal Black /1 #54
2018 Panini Victory Lane Pedal to the Metal Blue /25 #33
2018 Panini Victory Lane Pedal to the Metal Blue /25 #54
2018 Panini Victory Lane Pedal to the Metal Green /5 #33
2018 Panini Victory Lane Pedal to the Metal Green /5 #54
2018 Panini Victory Lane Printing Plates Black /1 #4
2018 Panini Victory Lane Printing Plates Black /1 #48

2018 Panini Victory Lane Printing Plates Black /1 #65
2018 Panini Victory Lane Printing Plates Black /1 #95
2018 Panini Victory Lane Printing Plates Cyan /1 #4
2018 Panini Victory Lane Printing Plates Cyan /1 #48
2018 Panini Victory Lane Printing Plates Cyan /1 #65
2018 Panini Victory Lane Printing Plates Cyan /1 #95
2018 Panini Victory Lane Printing Plates Magenta /1 #4
2018 Panini Victory Lane Printing Plates Magenta /1 #48
2018 Panini Victory Lane Printing Plates Magenta /1 #65
2018 Panini Victory Lane Printing Plates Magenta /1 #95
2018 Panini Victory Lane Printing Plates Yellow /1 #4
2018 Panini Victory Lane Printing Plates Yellow /1 #48
2018 Panini Victory Lane Printing Plates Yellow /1 #65
2018 Panini Victory Lane Printing Plates Yellow /1 #95
2018 Panini Victory Lane Race Day #2
2018 Panini Victory Lane Race Day Black /1 #2
2018 Panini Victory Lane Race Day Blue /25 #2
2018 Panini Victory Lane Race Day Gold /99 #2
2018 Panini Victory Lane Race Day Green /5 #2
2018 Panini Victory Lane Race Day Printing Plates Black /1 #2
2018 Panini Victory Lane Race Day Printing Plates Cyan /1 #2
2018 Panini Victory Lane Race Day Printing Plates Magenta /1 #2
2018 Panini Victory Lane Race Day Printing Plates Yellow /1 #2
2018 Panini Victory Lane Race Day Red /49 #2
2018 Panini Victory Lane Race Ready Materials /49 #19
2018 Panini Victory Lane Race Ready Materials Black /4 #19
2018 Panini Victory Lane Race Ready Materials Gold /25 #19
2018 Panini Victory Lane Race Ready Materials Green /10 #19
2018 Panini Victory Lane Red /49 #4
2018 Panini Victory Lane Red /49 #48
2018 Panini Victory Lane Red /49 #65
2018 Panini Victory Lane Red /49 #95
2018 Panini Victory Lane Remarkable Remnants Material Autographs /150 #3
2018 Panini Victory Lane Remarkable Remnants Material Autographs Black /25 #3
2018 Panini Victory Lane Remarkable Remnants Material Autographs Gold /99 #3
2018 Panini Victory Lane Remarkable Remnants Material Autographs Green /75 #3
2018 Panini Victory Lane Remarkable Remnants Material Autographs Laundry Tag /1 #3
2018 Panini Victory Lane Silver #4
2018 Panini Victory Lane Silver #48
2018 Panini Victory Lane Silver #65
2018 Panini Victory Lane Silver #95
2018 Panini Victory Lane Starting Grid #4
2018 Panini Victory Lane Starting Grid Black /1 #4
2018 Panini Victory Lane Starting Grid Blue /25 #4
2018 Panini Victory Lane Starting Grid Gold /99 #4
2018 Panini Victory Lane Starting Grid Green /5 #4
2018 Panini Victory Lane Starting Grid Printing Plates Black /1 #4
2018 Panini Victory Lane Starting Grid Printing Plates Cyan /1 #4
2018 Panini Victory Lane Starting Grid Printing Plates Magenta /1 #4
2018 Panini Victory Lane Starting Grid Printing Plates Yellow /1 #4
2018 Panini Victory Lane Starting Grid Red /49 #4
2018 Panini Victory Lane Victory Lane Prime Patches Associate Sponsor 1 /1 #17
2018 Panini Victory Lane Victory Lane Prime Patches Associate Sponsor 10 /1 #17
2018 Panini Victory Lane Victory Lane Prime Patches Associate Sponsor 2 /1 #17
2018 Panini Victory Lane Victory Lane Prime Patches Associate Sponsor 3 /1 #17
2018 Panini Victory Lane Victory Lane Prime Patches Associate Sponsor 4 /1 #17
2018 Panini Victory Lane Victory Lane Prime Patches Associate Sponsor 5 /1 #17
2018 Panini Victory Lane Victory Lane Prime Patches Associate Sponsor 6 /1 #17
2018 Panini Victory Lane Victory Lane Prime Patches Associate Sponsor 7 /1 #17
2018 Panini Victory Lane Victory Lane Prime Patches Associate Sponsor 8 /1 #17
2018 Panini Victory Lane Victory Lane Prime Patches Associate Sponsor 9 /1 #17
2018 Panini Victory Lane Victory Lane Prime Patches Car Manufacturer /1 #17
2018 Panini Victory Lane Victory Lane Prime Patches Firesuit Manufacturer- /1 #17
2018 Panini Victory Lane Victory Lane Prime Patches Nameplate /2 #17
2018 Panini Victory Lane Victory Lane Prime Patches NASCAR /1 #17
2018 Panini Victory Lane Victory Lane Prime Patches Series Sponsor /1 #17
2018 Panini Victory Lane Victory Lane Prime Patches Sunoco /1 #17
2018 Panini Victory Lane Victory Marks /25 #8
2018 Panini Victory Lane Victory Marks Black /1 #8
2018 Panini Victory Lane Victory Marks Gold /10 #8
2019 Donruss #4
2019 Donruss #60A
2019 Donruss #89
2019 Donruss #107A
2019 Donruss #60B
2019 Donruss #107B
2019 Donruss Artist Proofs /25 #4
2019 Donruss Artist Proofs /25 #60A
2019 Donruss Artist Proofs /25 #89
2019 Donruss Artist Proofs /25 #107A
2019 Donruss Artist Proofs /25 #60B
2019 Donruss Artist Proofs /25 #107B
2019 Donruss Black /199 #4
2019 Donruss Black /199 #60A
2019 Donruss Black /199 #89
2019 Donruss Black /199 #107A
2019 Donruss Black /199 #60B
2019 Donruss Black /199 #107B
2019 Donruss Classics #9
2019 Donruss Classics Cracked Ice /25 #9
2019 Donruss Classics Holographic #9
2019 Donruss Classics Xplosion /10 #9
2019 Donruss Contenders #3
2019 Donruss Contenders Cracked Ice /25 #3
2019 Donruss Contenders Holographic #3
2019 Donruss Contenders Xplosion /10 #3
2019 Donruss Gold /299 #4
2019 Donruss Gold /299 #60A
2019 Donruss Gold /299 #89
2019 Donruss Gold /299 #107A
2019 Donruss Gold /299 #60B
2019 Donruss Gold /299 #107B
2019 Donruss Gold Press Proofs /99 #4
2019 Donruss Gold Press Proofs /99 #60A
2019 Donruss Gold Press Proofs /99 #89
2019 Donruss Gold Press Proofs /99 #107A
2019 Donruss Gold Press Proofs /99 #60B
2019 Donruss Gold Press Proofs /99 #107B
2019 Donruss Optic #3
2019 Donruss Optic #16
2019 Donruss Optic #66
2019 Donruss Optic Blue Pulsar #3
2019 Donruss Optic Blue Pulsar #16
2019 Donruss Optic Blue Pulsar /1 #66
2019 Donruss Optic Gold /10 #3
2019 Donruss Optic Gold /10 #16
2019 Donruss Optic Gold /10 #66
2019 Donruss Optic Gold Vinyl /1 #3
2019 Donruss Optic Gold Vinyl /1 #16
2019 Donruss Optic Gold Vinyl /1 #66
2019 Donruss Optic Holo #3
2019 Donruss Optic Holo #16
2019 Donruss Optic Holo #66
2019 Donruss Optic Illusion #2
2019 Donruss Optic Illusion Blue Pulsar #2
2019 Donruss Optic Illusion Gold /10 #2
2019 Donruss Optic Illusion Gold Vinyl /1 #2
2019 Donruss Optic Illusion Holo #2
2019 Donruss Optic Illusion Red Wave #2
2019 Donruss Optic Illusion Signatures Gold Vinyl /1 #2
2019 Donruss Optic Illusion Signatures Holo /25 #2
2019 Donruss Optic Red Wave #3
2019 Donruss Optic Red Wave #16
2019 Donruss Optic Red Wave /1 #66
2019 Donruss Optic Signatures Gold Vinyl /1 #66
2019 Donruss Optic Signatures Gold Vinyl /1 #3
2019 Donruss Optic Signatures Gold Vinyl /1 #16
2019 Donruss Optic Signatures Holo /25 #3
2019 Donruss Optic Signatures Holo /49 #16
2019 Donruss Optic Signatures Holo /25 #66
2019 Donruss Originals #2
2019 Donruss Originals Cracked Ice /25 #2
2019 Donruss Originals Holographic #2
2019 Donruss Originals Xplosion /10 #2
2019 Donruss Press Proofs /49 #60A
2019 Donruss Press Proofs /49 #89
2019 Donruss Press Proofs /49 #107A
2019 Donruss Press Proofs /49 #60B
2019 Donruss Press Proofs /49 #107B
2019 Donruss Press Proofs /49 #4
2019 Donruss Printing Plates Black /1 #4
2019 Donruss Printing Plates Black /1 #60A
2019 Donruss Printing Plates Black /1 #89
2019 Donruss Printing Plates Black /1 #107A
2019 Donruss Printing Plates Black /1 #60B
2019 Donruss Printing Plates Black #107B
2019 Donruss Printing Plates Cyan /1 #4
2019 Donruss Printing Plates Cyan /1 #60A
2019 Donruss Printing Plates Cyan /1 #89
2019 Donruss Printing Plates Cyan /1 #107A
2019 Donruss Printing Plates Cyan /1 #60B
2019 Donruss Printing Plates Cyan #107B
2019 Donruss Printing Plates Magenta /1 #60A
2019 Donruss Printing Plates Magenta /1 #89
2019 Donruss Printing Plates Magenta /1 #107A
2019 Donruss Printing Plates Magenta /1 #60B
2019 Donruss Printing Plates Magenta #107B
2019 Donruss Printing Plates Magenta /1 #4
2019 Donruss Printing Plates Yellow /1 #4
2019 Donruss Printing Plates Yellow /1 #60A
2019 Donruss Printing Plates Yellow /1 #89
2019 Donruss Printing Plates Yellow /1 #107A
2019 Donruss Printing Plates Yellow /1 #60B
2019 Donruss Printing Plates Yellow #107B
2019 Donruss Race Day Relics #18
2019 Donruss Race Day Relics Holo Black /10 #18
2019 Donruss Race Day Relics Holo Gold /25 #18
2019 Donruss Race Day Relics Red /185 #18
2019 Donruss Retro Relics '86 #14
2019 Donruss Retro Relics '86 Holo Black /10 #14
2019 Donruss Retro Relics '86 Holo Gold /25 #14
2019 Donruss Retro Relics '86 Red /225 #14
2019 Donruss Signature Swatches #7
2019 Donruss Signature Swatches Holo Black /10 #7
2019 Donruss Signature Swatches Holo Gold /25 #7
2019 Donruss Signature Swatches Red /50 #7
2019 Donruss Silver #4
2019 Donruss Silver #60A
2019 Donruss Silver #89
2019 Donruss Silver #107A
2019 Donruss Silver #60B
2019 Donruss Silver #107B
2019 Donruss Top Tier #2
2019 Donruss Top Tier Cracked Ice /25 #2
2019 Donruss Top Tier Holographic #2
2019 Donruss Top Tier Xplosion /10 #2
2019 Panini Prime /50 #4
2019 Panini Prime /50 #38
2019 Panini Prime /50 #71
2019 Panini Prime Black /10 #4
2019 Panini Prime Black /10 #38
2019 Panini Prime Black /10 #71
2019 Panini Prime Clear Silhouettes /99 #2
2019 Panini Prime Clear Silhouettes Black /10 #2
2019 Panini Prime Clear Silhouettes Dual /99 #3
2019 Panini Prime Clear Silhouettes Dual Black /10 #3
2019 Panini Prime Clear Silhouettes Dual Holo Gold /25 #3
2019 Panini Prime Clear Silhouettes Dual Platinum Blue /1 #3
2019 Panini Prime Clear Silhouettes Holo Gold /25 #2
2019 Panini Prime Clear Silhouettes Platinum Blue /1 #2
2019 Panini Prime Dual Material Autographs /25 #19
2019 Panini Prime Dual Material Autographs Black /4 #19
2019 Panini Prime Dual Material Autographs Holo Gold /10 #19
2019 Panini Prime Dual Material Autographs Laundry Tags /1 #19
2019 Panini Prime Emerald /5 #4
2019 Panini Prime Emerald /5 #38
2019 Panini Prime Emerald /5 #71
2019 Panini Prime Hats Off Button /1 #2
2019 Panini Prime Hats Off Button /1 #3
2019 Panini Prime Hats Off Button /1 #8
2019 Panini Prime Hats Off Driver Name /3 #2
2019 Panini Prime Hats Off Driver Name /3 #3
2019 Panini Prime Hats Off Driver Name /3 #8
2019 Panini Prime Hats Off Eyelets /6 #2
2019 Panini Prime Hats Off Eyelets /6 #3
2019 Panini Prime Hats Off Eyelets /6 #8
2019 Panini Prime Hats Off Headband /26 #2
2019 Panini Prime Hats Off Headband /36 #3
2019 Panini Prime Hats Off Headband /26 #8
2019 Panini Prime Hats Off Laundry Tags /2 #2
2019 Panini Prime Hats Off Laundry Tags /2 #3
2019 Panini Prime Hats Off Laundry Tags /2 #8
2019 Panini Prime Hats Off New Era /1 #2
2019 Panini Prime Hats Off New Era /1 #3
2019 Panini Prime Hats Off New Era /1 #8
2019 Panini Prime Hats Off Number /3 #2
2019 Panini Prime Hats Off Number /3 #3
2019 Panini Prime Hats Off Number /3 #8
2019 Panini Prime Hats Off Sponsor Logo /12 #2
2019 Panini Prime Hats Off Sponsor Logo /5 #3
2019 Panini Prime Hats Off Sponsor Logo /6 #8
2019 Panini Prime Jumbo Material Signatures Firesuit /4 #17
2019 Panini Prime Jumbo Material Signatures Firesuit Platinum Blue /1 #17
2019 Panini Prime Jumbo Material Signatures Tire /35 #17
2019 Panini Prime NASCAR Shadowbox Signatures Car Number /25 #24
2019 Panini Prime NASCAR Shadowbox Signatures Manufacturer /4 #24
2019 Panini Prime NASCAR Shadowbox Signatures Sponsor /10 #24
2019 Panini Prime NASCAR Shadowbox Signatures Team Owner /1 #24
2019 Panini Prime Platinum Blue /1 #4
2019 Panini Prime Platinum Blue /1 #38
2019 Panini Prime Platinum Blue /1 #71
2019 Panini Prime Prime Cars Die Cut Signatures /25 #4
2019 Panini Prime Prime Cars Die Cut Signatures Black /4 #4
2019 Panini Prime Prime Cars Die Cut Signatures Holo Gold /10 #4
2019 Panini Prime Prime Cars Die Cut Signatures Platinum Blue /1 #4
2019 Panini Prime Prime Jumbo Associate Sponsor 1 /1 #44
2019 Panini Prime Prime Jumbo Associate Sponsor 10 /1 #44
2019 Panini Prime Prime Jumbo Associate Sponsor 11 /1 #44
2019 Panini Prime Prime Jumbo Associate Sponsor 12 /1 #44
2019 Panini Prime Prime Jumbo Associate Sponsor 2 /1 #44
2019 Panini Prime Prime Jumbo Associate Sponsor 3 /1 #44
2019 Panini Prime Prime Jumbo Associate Sponsor 4 /1 #44
2019 Panini Prime Prime Jumbo Associate Sponsor 5 /1 #44
2019 Panini Prime Prime Jumbo Associate Sponsor 6 /1 #44
2019 Panini Prime Prime Jumbo Associate Sponsor 7 /1 #44
2019 Panini Prime Prime Jumbo Associate Sponsor 8 /1 #44
2019 Panini Prime Prime Jumbo Associate Sponsor 9 /1 #44
2019 Panini Prime Prime Jumbo Car Manufacturer /1 #44
2019 Panini Prime Prime Jumbo Firesuit Manufacturer /1 #44
2019 Panini Prime Prime Jumbo Goodyear /2 #44
2019 Panini Prime Prime Jumbo Nameplate /2 #44
2019 Panini Prime Prime Jumbo NASCAR /1 #44
2019 Panini Prime Prime Jumbo Prime Colors /19 #44
2019 Panini Prime Prime Jumbo Series Sponsor /1 #44
2019 Panini Prime Prime Jumbo Shoe Brand Logo /1 #44
2019 Panini Prime Prime Jumbo Shoe Name Patch /1 #44
2019 Panini Prime Prime Jumbo Sunoco /1 #44
2019 Panini Prime Prime Names Die Cut Signatures /25 #25
2019 Panini Prime Prime Names Die Cut Signatures Black /4 #25
2019 Panini Prime Prime Names Die Cut Signatures Holo Gold /10 #25
2019 Panini Prime Prime Names Die Cut Signatures Platinum Blue /1 #25
2019 Panini Prime Quad Materials Autographs /25 #15
2019 Panini Prime Quad Materials Autographs Black /4 #15
2019 Panini Prime Quad Materials Autographs Holo Gold /10 #15
2019 Panini Prime Quad Materials Autographs Laundry Tags /1 #15
2019 Panini Prime Race Used Duals Firesuits /50 #24
2019 Panini Prime Race Used Duals Firesuits Black /10 #24
2019 Panini Prime Race Used Duals Firesuits Holo Gold /25 #24
2019 Panini Prime Race Used Duals Firesuits Laundry Tags /1 #24
2019 Panini Prime Race Used Duals Sheet Metal /50 #24
2019 Panini Prime Race Used Duals Sheet Metal Black /10 #24
2019 Panini Prime Race Used Duals Sheet Metal Holo Gold /25 #24
2019 Panini Prime Race Used Duals Sheet Metal Platinum Blue /1 #24
2019 Panini Prime Race Used Duals Tires /50 #24
2019 Panini Prime Race Used Duals Tires Black /10 #24
2019 Panini Prime Race Used Duals Tires Holo Gold /25 #24
2019 Panini Prime Race Used Duals Tires Platinum Blue /1 #24
2019 Panini Prime Race Used Firesuits /50 #24
2019 Panini Prime Race Used Firesuits Black /10 #24
2019 Panini Prime Race Used Firesuits Holo Gold /25 #24
2019 Panini Prime Race Used Firesuits Laundry Tags /1 #24
2019 Panini Prime Race Used Quads Firesuits /50 #9
2019 Panini Prime Race Used Quads Firesuits Black /10 #9
2019 Panini Prime Race Used Quads Firesuits Holo Gold /25 #9
2019 Panini Prime Race Used Quads Firesuits Laundry Tags /1 #9
2019 Panini Prime Race Used Quads Sheet Metal /50 #9
2019 Panini Prime Race Used Quads Sheet Metal Black /10 #9
2019 Panini Prime Race Used Quads Sheet Metal Holo Gold /25 #9
2019 Panini Prime Race Used Quads Sheet Metal Platinum Blue /1 #9
2019 Panini Prime Race Used Quads Tires /50 #9
2019 Panini Prime Race Used Quads Tires Black /10 #9
2019 Panini Prime Race Used Quads Tires Holo Gold /25 #9
2019 Panini Prime Race Used Quads Tires Platinum Blue /1 #9
2019 Panini Prime Race Used Sheet Metal /50 #24
2019 Panini Prime Race Used Sheet Metal Black /10 #24
2019 Panini Prime Race Used Sheet Metal Holo Gold /25 #24
2019 Panini Prime Race Used Sheet Metal Platinum Blue /1 #24
2019 Panini Prime Race Used Tires /50 #24
2019 Panini Prime Race Used Tires Black /10 #24
2019 Panini Prime Race Used Tires Holo Gold /25 #24
2019 Panini Prime Race Used Tires Platinum Blue /1 #24
2019 Panini Prime Race Used Trios Firesuits /50 #16
2019 Panini Prime Race Used Trios Firesuits Black /10 #16
2019 Panini Prime Race Used Trios Firesuits Holo Gold /25 #16
2019 Panini Prime Race Used Trios Firesuits Laundry Tags /1 #16
2019 Panini Prime Race Used Trios Sheet Metal /50 #16
2019 Panini Prime Race Used Trios Sheet Metal Black /10 #16
2019 Panini Prime Race Used Trios Sheet Metal Holo Gold /25 #16
2019 Panini Prime Race Used Trios Sheet Metal Platinum Blue /1 #16
2019 Panini Prime Race Used Trios Tires /50 #16
2019 Panini Prime Race Used Trios Tires Black /10 #16
2019 Panini Prime Race Used Trios Tires Holo Gold /25 #16
2019 Panini Prime Race Used Trios Tires Platinum Blue /1 #16
2019 Panini Prime Timeline Signatures /25 #2
2019 Panini Prime Timeline Signatures Manufacturer /1 #2
2019 Panini Prime Timeline Signatures Name /10 #2
2019 Panini Prime Timeline Signatures Sponsor /4 #2
2019 Panini Prizm #4A
2019 Panini Prizm #51
2019 Panini Prizm #64
2019 Panini Prizm #75
2019 Panini Prizm #82
2019 Panini Prizm #4B
2019 Panini Prizm Apex #1
2019 Panini Prizm Apex Prizms #1
2019 Panini Prizm Apex Prizms Black /1 #1
2019 Panini Prizm Apex Prizms Gold /10 #1
2019 Panini Prizm Apex Prizms White Sparkle #1
2019 Panini Prizm Expert Level #6
2019 Panini Prizm Expert Level Prizms #6
2019 Panini Prizm Expert Level Prizms Black /1 #6
2019 Panini Prizm Expert Level Prizms Gold /10 #6
2019 Panini Prizm Expert Level Prizms White Sparkle #6
2019 Panini Prizm Fireworks #8
2019 Panini Prizm Fireworks Prizms #8
2019 Panini Prizm Fireworks Prizms Black /1 #8
2019 Panini Prizm Fireworks Prizms Gold /10 #8
2019 Panini Prizm Fireworks Prizms White Sparkle #8
2019 Panini Prizm In the Groove #2
2019 Panini Prizm In the Groove Prizms #2
2019 Panini Prizm In the Groove Prizms Black /1 #2
2019 Panini Prizm In the Groove Prizms Gold /10 #2
2019 Panini Prizm In the Groove Prizms White Sparkle #2
2019 Panini Prizm National Pride #4
2019 Panini Prizm National Pride Prizms #4
2019 Panini Prizm National Pride Prizms Black /1 #4
2019 Panini Prizm National Pride Prizms Gold /10 #4
2019 Panini Prizm National Pride Prizms White Sparkle #4
2019 Panini Prizm Patented Penmanship Prizms #6
2019 Panini Prizm Patented Penmanship Prizms Black /1 #6
2019 Panini Prizm Patented Penmanship Prizms Blue /5 #6
2019 Panini Prizm Patented Penmanship Prizms Camo #6
2019 Panini Prizm Patented Penmanship Prizms Gold /10 #6
2019 Panini Prizm Patented Penmanship Prizms Rainbow /5 #6
2019 Panini Prizm Patented Penmanship Prizms Red /5 #6
2019 Panini Prizm Patented Penmanship Prizms Red White and Blue #6
2019 Panini Prizm Patented Penmanship Prizms White /5 #6
2019 Panini Prizm Prizms #51
2019 Panini Prizm Prizms #64
2019 Panini Prizm Prizms #75
2019 Panini Prizm Prizms #82
2019 Panini Prizm Prizms #4B
2019 Panini Prizm Prizms #4A
2019 Panini Prizm Prizms Black /1 #4A
2019 Panini Prizm Prizms Black /1 #51
2019 Panini Prizm Prizms Black /1 #64
2019 Panini Prizm Prizms Black /1 #75
2019 Panini Prizm Prizms Black /1 #82
2019 Panini Prizm Prizms Black /1 #4B
2019 Panini Prizm Prizms Blue /75 #4A
2019 Panini Prizm Prizms Blue /75 #51
2019 Panini Prizm Prizms Blue /75 #64
2019 Panini Prizm Prizms Blue /75 #75
2019 Panini Prizm Prizms Blue /75 #82
2019 Panini Prizm Prizms Blue /75 #4B
2019 Panini Prizm Prizms Camo #4A
2019 Panini Prizm Prizms Camo #51
2019 Panini Prizm Prizms Camo #64
2019 Panini Prizm Prizms Camo #75
2019 Panini Prizm Prizms Camo #82
2019 Panini Prizm Prizms Camo #4B
2019 Panini Prizm Prizms Flash #4A
2019 Panini Prizm Prizms Flash #51
2019 Panini Prizm Prizms Flash #64
2019 Panini Prizm Prizms Flash #75
2019 Panini Prizm Prizms Flash #82
2019 Panini Prizm Prizms Flash #4B
2019 Panini Prizm Prizms Gold /10 #4A
2019 Panini Prizm Prizms Gold /10 #51
2019 Panini Prizm Prizms Gold /10 #64
2019 Panini Prizm Prizms Gold /10 #75
2019 Panini Prizm Prizms Gold /10 #82
2019 Panini Prizm Prizms Gold /10 #4B
2019 Panini Prizm Prizms Green /99 #4A
2019 Panini Prizm Prizms Green /99 #51
2019 Panini Prizm Prizms Green /99 #64
2019 Panini Prizm Prizms Green /99 #75
2019 Panini Prizm Prizms Green /99 #82
2019 Panini Prizm Prizms Green /99 #4B
2019 Panini Prizm Prizms Rainbow /24 #4A
2019 Panini Prizm Prizms Rainbow /24 #51
2019 Panini Prizm Prizms Rainbow /24 #64
2019 Panini Prizm Prizms Rainbow /24 #75
2019 Panini Prizm Prizms Rainbow /24 #82
2019 Panini Prizm Prizms Rainbow /24 #4B
2019 Panini Prizm Prizms Red /50 #4A
2019 Panini Prizm Prizms Red /50 #51
2019 Panini Prizm Prizms Red /50 #64
2019 Panini Prizm Prizms Red /50 #75
2019 Panini Prizm Prizms Red /50 #82
2019 Panini Prizm Prizms Red /50 #4B
2019 Panini Prizm Prizms Red White and Blue #4A
2019 Panini Prizm Prizms Red White and Blue #51
2019 Panini Prizm Prizms Red White and Blue #64
2019 Panini Prizm Prizms Red White and Blue #75
2019 Panini Prizm Prizms Red White and Blue #82
2019 Panini Prizm Prizms Red White and Blue #4B
2019 Panini Prizm Prizms White /5 #4A
2019 Panini Prizm Prizms White /5 #51
2019 Panini Prizm Prizms White /5 #64
2019 Panini Prizm Prizms White /5 #75
2019 Panini Prizm Prizms White /5 #82
2019 Panini Prizm Prizms White /5 #4B
2019 Panini Prizm Prizms White Sparkle #4A
2019 Panini Prizm Prizms White Sparkle #51
2019 Panini Prizm Prizms White Sparkle #64
2019 Panini Prizm Prizms White Sparkle #75
2019 Panini Prizm Prizms White Sparkle #82
2019 Panini Prizm Prizms White Sparkle #4B
2019 Panini Prizm Scripted Signatures Prizms #9
2019 Panini Prizm Scripted Signatures Prizms Black /1 #9
2019 Panini Prizm Scripted Signatures Prizms Blue /5 #9
2019 Panini Prizm Scripted Signatures Prizms Camo #9
2019 Panini Prizm Scripted Signatures Prizms Gold /10 #9
2019 Panini Prizm Scripted Signatures Prizms Rainbow /5 #9
2019 Panini Prizm Scripted Signatures Prizms Red /5 #9
2019 Panini Prizm Scripted Signatures Prizms Red White and Blue #9
2019 Panini Prizm Scripted Signatures Prizms White /5 #9
2019 Panini Prizm Signing Sessions Prizms #13
2019 Panini Prizm Signing Sessions Prizms Black /1 #13
2019 Panini Prizm Signing Sessions Prizms Blue /5 #13
2019 Panini Prizm Signing Sessions Prizms Camo #13
2019 Panini Prizm Signing Sessions Prizms Gold /10 #13
2019 Panini Prizm Signing Sessions Prizms Rainbow /5 #13
2019 Panini Prizm Signing Sessions Prizms Red /5 #13
2019 Panini Prizm Signing Sessions Prizms Red White and Blue #13
2019 Panini Prizm Signing Sessions Prizms White /5 #13
2019 Panini Prizm Stars and Stripes #1
2019 Panini Prizm Stars and Stripes Prizms #1
2019 Panini Prizm Stars and Stripes Prizms Black /1 #1
2019 Panini Prizm Stars and Stripes Prizms Gold /10 #1
2019 Panini Prizm Stars and Stripes Prizms White Sparkle #1
2019 Panini Prizm Teammates #6
2019 Panini Prizm Teammates Prizms #6
2019 Panini Prizm Teammates Prizms Black /1 #6
2019 Panini Prizm Teammates Prizms Gold /10 #6
2019 Panini Prizm Teammates Prizms White Sparkle #6
2019 Panini Victory Lane #4
2019 Panini Victory Lane #58
2019 Panini Victory Lane #65
2019 Panini Victory Lane #85
2019 Panini Victory Lane Black /1 #4
2019 Panini Victory Lane Black /1 #58
2019 Panini Victory Lane Black /1 #65
2019 Panini Victory Lane Black /1 #85
2019 Panini Victory Lane Celebrations #2
2019 Panini Victory Lane Celebrations #12
2019 Panini Victory Lane Celebrations Black /1 #2
2019 Panini Victory Lane Celebrations Black /1 #12
2019 Panini Victory Lane Celebrations Blue /99 #2
2019 Panini Victory Lane Celebrations Blue /99 #12
2019 Panini Victory Lane Celebrations Gold /25 #2
2019 Panini Victory Lane Celebrations Gold /25 #12
2019 Panini Victory Lane Celebrations Green /5 #2
2019 Panini Victory Lane Celebrations Green /5 #12
2019 Panini Victory Lane Celebrations Printing Plates Black /1 #2
2019 Panini Victory Lane Celebrations Printing Plates Black /1 #12
2019 Panini Victory Lane Celebrations Printing Plates Cyan /1 #2
2019 Panini Victory Lane Celebrations Printing Plates Cyan /1 #12
2019 Panini Victory Lane Celebrations Printing Plates Magenta /1 #2
2019 Panini Victory Lane Celebrations Printing Plates Magenta /1 #12
2019 Panini Victory Lane Celebrations Printing Plates Yellow /1 #2
2019 Panini Victory Lane Celebrations Printing Plates Yellow /1 #12
2019 Panini Victory Lane Dual Swatch Signatures #11
2019 Panini Victory Lane Dual Swatch Signatures Gold /99 #11
2019 Panini Victory Lane Dual Swatch Signatures Laundry Tag /1 #11
2019 Panini Victory Lane Dual Swatch Signatures Platinum /1 #11
2019 Panini Victory Lane Dual Swatch Signatures Red /25 #11
2019 Panini Victory Lane Dual Swatches #14
2019 Panini Victory Lane Dual Swatches Gold /99 #14
2019 Panini Victory Lane Dual Swatches Laundry Tag /1 #14
2019 Panini Victory Lane Dual Swatches Platinum /1 #14
2019 Panini Victory Lane Dual Swatches Red /25 #14
2019 Panini Victory Lane Gold /25 #4
2019 Panini Victory Lane Gold /25 #58
2019 Panini Victory Lane Gold /25 #65
2019 Panini Victory Lane Gold /25 #85
2019 Panini Victory Lane Horsepower Heroes #15
2019 Panini Victory Lane Horsepower Heroes Black /1 #15
2019 Panini Victory Lane Horsepower Heroes Blue /99 #15
2019 Panini Victory Lane Horsepower Heroes Gold /25 #15
2019 Panini Victory Lane Horsepower Heroes Green /5 #15
2019 Panini Victory Lane Horsepower Heroes Printing Plates Black /1 #15
2019 Panini Victory Lane Horsepower Heroes Printing Plates Cyan /1 #15
2019 Panini Victory Lane Horsepower Heroes Printing Plates Magenta /1 #15
2019 Panini Victory Lane Horsepower Heroes Printing Plates Yellow /1 #15
2019 Panini Victory Lane Machines #2
2019 Panini Victory Lane Machines Black /1 #2
2019 Panini Victory Lane Machines Blue /99 #2
2019 Panini Victory Lane Machines Gold /25 #2
2019 Panini Victory Lane Machines Green /5 #2
2019 Panini Victory Lane Machines Printing Plates Black /1 #2
2019 Panini Victory Lane Machines Printing Plates Cyan /1 #2
2019 Panini Victory Lane Machines Printing Plates Magenta /1 #2
2019 Panini Victory Lane Machines Printing Plates Yellow /1 #2
2019 Panini Victory Lane Pedal to the Metal #41
2019 Panini Victory Lane Pedal to the Metal #61
2019 Panini Victory Lane Pedal to the Metal #80
2019 Panini Victory Lane Pedal to the Metal Black /1 #41
2019 Panini Victory Lane Pedal to the Metal Black /1 #61
2019 Panini Victory Lane Pedal to the Metal Black /1 #80
2019 Panini Victory Lane Pedal to the Metal Gold /25 #41
2019 Panini Victory Lane Pedal to the Metal Gold /25 #61
2019 Panini Victory Lane Pedal to the Metal Gold /25 #80
2019 Panini Victory Lane Pedal to the Metal Green /5 #41
2019 Panini Victory Lane Pedal to the Metal Green /5 #61
2019 Panini Victory Lane Pedal to the Metal Green /5 #80
2019 Panini Victory Lane Pedal to the Metal Red /3 #41
2019 Panini Victory Lane Pedal to the Metal Red /3 #61
2019 Panini Victory Lane Pedal to the Metal Red /3 #80
2019 Panini Victory Lane Printing Plates Black /1 #4
2019 Panini Victory Lane Printing Plates Black /1 #58
2019 Panini Victory Lane Printing Plates Black /1 #65
2019 Panini Victory Lane Printing Plates Black /1 #85
2019 Panini Victory Lane Printing Plates Cyan /1 #4
2019 Panini Victory Lane Printing Plates Cyan /1 #58
2019 Panini Victory Lane Printing Plates Cyan /1 #65
2019 Panini Victory Lane Printing Plates Cyan /1 #85
2019 Panini Victory Lane Printing Plates Magenta /1 #4
2019 Panini Victory Lane Printing Plates Magenta /1 #58
2019 Panini Victory Lane Printing Plates Magenta /1 #65
2019 Panini Victory Lane Printing Plates Magenta /1 #85
2019 Panini Victory Lane Printing Plates Yellow /1 #4
2019 Panini Victory Lane Printing Plates Yellow /1 #58
2019 Panini Victory Lane Printing Plates Yellow /1 #65
2019 Panini Victory Lane Printing Plates Yellow /1 #85
2019 Panini Victory Lane Quad Swatches #3
2019 Panini Victory Lane Quad Swatches Gold /99 #3
2019 Panini Victory Lane Quad Swatches Laundry Tag /1 #3
2019 Panini Victory Lane Quad Swatches Platinum /1 #3
2019 Panini Victory Lane Quad Swatches Red /25 #3
2019 Panini Victory Lane Starting Grid #4
2019 Panini Victory Lane Starting Grid Black /1 #4
2019 Panini Victory Lane Starting Grid Blue /99 #4
2019 Panini Victory Lane Starting Grid Gold /25 #4
2019 Panini Victory Lane Starting Grid Green /5 #4
2019 Panini Victory Lane Starting Grid Printing Plates Black /1 #4
2019 Panini Victory Lane Starting Grid Printing Plates Cyan /1 #4
2019 Panini Victory Lane Starting Grid Printing Plates Magenta /1 #4
2019 Panini Victory Lane Starting Grid Printing Plates Yellow /1 #4
2019 Panini Victory Lane Top 10 #3
2019 Panini Victory Lane Top 10 Black /1 #3
2019 Panini Victory Lane Top 10 Blue /99 #3
2019 Panini Victory Lane Top 10 Gold /25 #3
2019 Panini Victory Lane Top 10 Green /5 #3
2019 Panini Victory Lane Top 10 Printing Plates Black /1 #3
2019 Panini Victory Lane Top 10 Printing Plates Cyan /1 #3
2019 Panini Victory Lane Top 10 Printing Plates Magenta /1 #3
2019 Panini Victory Lane Top 10 Printing Plates Yellow /1 #3
2019 Panini Victory Lane Track Stars #2
2019 Panini Victory Lane Track Stars Black /1 #2
2019 Panini Victory Lane Track Stars Blue /99 #2
2019 Panini Victory Lane Track Stars Gold /25 #2
2019 Panini Victory Lane Track Stars Green /5 #2
2019 Panini Victory Lane Track Stars Printing Plates Black /1 #2
2019 Panini Victory Lane Track Stars Printing Plates Cyan /1 #2
2019 Panini Victory Lane Track Stars Printing Plates Magenta /1 #2
2019 Panini Victory Lane Track Stars Printing Plates Yellow /1 #2
2019-20 Funko Pop Vinyl NASCAR #7
2020 Donruss #40
2020 Donruss #107
2020 Donruss #140
2020 Donruss Action Packed #4
2020 Donruss Action Packed Checkers #4
2020 Donruss Action Packed Cracked Ice /25 #4
2020 Donruss Action Packed Holographic /199 #4
2020 Donruss Action Packed Xplosion /10 #4
2020 Donruss Black Numbers /4 #40
2020 Donruss Black Numbers /4 #107
2020 Donruss Black Numbers /4 #140
2020 Donruss Black Trophy Club /1 #40
2020 Donruss Black Trophy Club /1 #107
2020 Donruss Black Trophy Club /1 #140
2020 Donruss Blue /199 #107
2020 Donruss Blue /199 #140
2020 Donruss Blue /199 #40
2020 Donruss Carolina Blue #40
2020 Donruss Carolina Blue #107
2020 Donruss Carolina Blue #140
2020 Donruss Contenders #2
2020 Donruss Contenders Checkers #2
2020 Donruss Contenders Cracked Ice /25 #2
2020 Donruss Contenders Holographic /199 #2
2020 Donruss Contenders Xplosion /10 #2
2020 Donruss Dominators #9
2020 Donruss Dominators Checkers #9
2020 Donruss Dominators Cracked Ice /25 #9
2020 Donruss Dominators Holographic /199 #9
2020 Donruss Dominators Xplosion /10 #9
2020 Donruss Downtown #3
2020 Donruss Elite Series #2
2020 Donruss Elite Series Checkers #2
2020 Donruss Elite Series Cracked Ice /25 #2
2020 Donruss Elite Series Holographic /199 #2
2020 Donruss Elite Series Xplosion /10 #2
2020 Donruss Green /99 #40
2020 Donruss Green /99 #107
2020 Donruss Green /99 #140
2020 Donruss Optic #20
2020 Donruss Optic #65
2020 Donruss Optic Carolina Blue Wave #20
2020 Donruss Optic Carolina Blue Wave #65
2020 Donruss Optic Gold /10 #20
2020 Donruss Optic Gold /10 #65
2020 Donruss Optic Gold Vinyl /1 #20
2020 Donruss Optic Gold Vinyl /1 #65
2020 Donruss Optic Holo #20
2020 Donruss Optic Holo #65
2020 Donruss Optic Illusion #7
2020 Donruss Optic Illusion Carolina Blue Wave #7
2020 Donruss Optic Illusion Gold /10 #7
2020 Donruss Optic Illusion Gold Vinyl /1 #7
2020 Donruss Optic Illusion Holo #7
2020 Donruss Optic Illusion Orange Pulsar #7
2020 Donruss Optic Illusion Red Mojo #7
2020 Donruss Optic Illusion Signatures Gold Vinyl /1 #7
2020 Donruss Optic Illusion Signatures Holo /99 #7
2020 Donruss Optic Orange Pulsar #20
2020 Donruss Optic Orange Pulsar #65
2020 Donruss Optic Red Mojo #20
2020 Donruss Optic Red Mojo #65
2020 Donruss Optic Signatures Gold Vinyl /1 #20
2020 Donruss Optic Signatures Gold Vinyl /1 #65
2020 Donruss Optic Signatures Holo /99 #20
2020 Donruss Optic Signatures Holo /99 #65
2020 Donruss Orange #40
2020 Donruss Orange #107
2020 Donruss Pink /25 #40
2020 Donruss Pink /25 #107
2020 Donruss Pink /25 #140
2020 Donruss Printing Plates Black /1 #40
2020 Donruss Printing Plates Black /1 #107
2020 Donruss Printing Plates Black /1 #140
2020 Donruss Printing Plates Cyan /1 #40
2020 Donruss Printing Plates Cyan /1 #107
2020 Donruss Printing Plates Cyan /1 #140
2020 Donruss Printing Plates Magenta /1 #40
2020 Donruss Printing Plates Magenta /1 #107
2020 Donruss Printing Plates Magenta /1 #140
2020 Donruss Printing Plates Yellow /1 #140
2020 Donruss Printing Plates Yellow /1 #40
2020 Donruss Printing Plates Yellow /1 #107
2020 Donruss Purple /49 #40
2020 Donruss Purple /49 #107
2020 Donruss Purple /49 #140
2020 Donruss Race Day Relics #17
2020 Donruss Race Day Relics Holo Black /10 #17
2020 Donruss Race Day Relics Holo Gold /25 #17
2020 Donruss Race Day Relics Red /250 #17
2020 Donruss Red /299 #40
2020 Donruss Red /299 #107
2020 Donruss Red /299 #140
2020 Donruss Retro Relics '87 #12
2020 Donruss Retro Relics '87 Holo Black /10 #12
2020 Donruss Retro Relics '87 Holo Gold /25 #12
2020 Donruss Retro Relics '87 Red /250 #12
2020 Donruss Retro Series #4
2020 Donruss Retro Series Checkers #4
2020 Donruss Retro Series Cracked Ice /25 #4
2020 Donruss Retro Series Holographic /199 #4
2020 Donruss Retro Series Xplosion /10 #4
2020 Donruss Silver #40
2020 Donruss Silver #107
2020 Donruss Silver #140
2020 Donruss Timeless Treasures Material Signatures #4
2020 Donruss Timeless Treasures Material Signatures Holo Black /1 #4
2020 Donruss Timeless Treasures Material Signatures Holo Gold /4 #4
2020 Donruss Timeless Treasures Material Signatures Red /10 #4
2020 Donruss Top Tier #6
2020 Donruss Top Tier Checkers #6
2020 Donruss Top Tier Cracked Ice /25 #6
2020 Donruss Top Tier Holographic /199 #6
2020 Donruss Top Tier Xplosion /10 #6

Sam Hornish Jr.

2002 Indianapolis 500 #8
2006 Sports Illustrated for Kids #85
2007 Press Pass Signings #29
2007 Press Pass Signings Gold /50 #23
2007 Press Pass Signings Press Plates Magenta /1 #20
2007 Press Pass Signings Silver /100 #22
2007 Press Pass Top Prospects Tire Autographs /25 #SHOA
2007 Press Pass Top Prospects Tires Gold /99 #SHoT
2007 Press Pass Top Prospects Tires Silver /250 #SHoT
2007 Traks #41
2007 Traks Gold #G41
2007 Traks Holofoil /50 #H41
2007 Traks Previews /5 #EB41
2007 Traks Red /10 #R41
2007 Wheels American Thunder Thunder Strokes #19
2007 Wheels American Thunder Thunder Strokes Press Plates Black /1 #19
2007 Wheels American Thunder Thunder Strokes Press Plates Cyan /1 #19
2007 Wheels American Thunder Thunder Strokes Press Plates Magenta /1 #19
2007 Wheels American Thunder Thunder Strokes Press Plates Yellow /1 #19
2008 Press Pass #44
2008 Press Pass Blue #B44
2008 Press Pass Eclipse #84
2008 Press Pass Eclipse Gold /25 #G84
2008 Press Pass Eclipse Red /1 #R84
2008 Press Pass Gold #G44
2008 Press Pass Legends #68
2008 Press Pass Legends Blue /599 #68
2008 Press Pass Legends Bronze /299 #68
2008 Press Pass Legends Gold /99 #68
2008 Press Pass Legends Holo /25 #68
2008 Press Pass Legends Printing Plates Black /1 #68
2008 Press Pass Legends Printing Plates Cyan /1 #68
2008 Press Pass Legends Printing Plates Magenta /1 #68
2008 Press Pass Legends Printing Plates Yellow /1 #68
2008 Press Pass Legends Solo /1 #68
2008 Press Pass Platinum /100 #P44
2008 Press Pass Platinum /100 #P119
2008 Press Pass Premium #89
2008 Press Pass Premium Red /5 #89
2008 Press Pass Signings #28
2008 Press Pass Signings Blue /25 #11
2008 Press Pass Signings Gold /50 #25
2008 Press Pass Signings Press Plates Black /1 #19
2008 Press Pass Signings Press Plates Black #SH
2008 Press Pass Signings Press Plates Cyan /1 #19
2008 Press Pass Signings Press Plates Magenta /1 #19
2008 Press Pass Signings Press Plates Magenta /1 #SH
2008 Press Pass Signings Press Plates Yellow /1 #19
2008 Press Pass Signings Press Plates Yellow #SH
2008 Press Pass Signings Silver /100 #25
2008 Press Pass Slideshow #SS5
2008 Press Pass Speedway #15
2008 Press Pass Speedway Gold #G15
2008 Press Pass Speedway Holofoil /50 #H15
2008 Press Pass Speedway Previews /5 #EB15
2008 Press Pass Speedway Red /10 #R15
2008 Press Pass Stealth #14
2008 Press Pass Stealth Chrome #14
2008 Press Pass Stealth Chrome Exclusives /25 #14
2008 Press Pass Stealth Chrome Exclusives Gold /99 #14
2008 Press Pass Stealth Previews /5 #14
2008 VIP #15
2008 VIP #59
2008 VIP Previews /5 #EB15
2008 VIP Rookie Stripes /100 #RS3
2008 VIP Rookie Stripes Autographs /25 #RSSH
2008 Wheels American Thunder #44
2008 Wheels American Thunder /362 #89
2008 Wheels American Thunder Autographed Hat Winner /1 #IWHSH
2008 Wheels American Thunder Double Hat /99 #DH5
2008 Wheels High Gear #87
2008 Wheels High Gear MPH /100 #M87
2008 Wheels High Gear Previews /1 #EB87
2009 Element #13
2009 Element #72
2009 Element Previews /5 #13
2009 Element Radioactive /100 #13
2009 Element Radioactive /100 #72
2009 Press Pass #29
2009 Press Pass #133
2009 Press Pass Autographs Gold #21
2009 Press Pass Autographs Printing Plates Black /1 #20
2009 Press Pass Autographs Printing Plates Cyan /1 #20
2009 Press Pass Autographs Printing Plates Magenta /1 #20
2009 Press Pass Autographs Printing Plates Yellow /1 #20
2009 Press Pass Autographs Silver #24
2009 Press Pass Blue #29
2009 Press Pass Blue #133
2009 Press Pass Eclipse #24
2009 Press Pass Eclipse Black and White #24
2009 Press Pass Eclipse Blue #24
2009 Press Pass Gold #29

2009 Press Pass Gold #133
2009 Press Pass Gold Holofoil /100 #29
2009 Press Pass Gold Holofoil /100 #133
2009 Press Pass Premium #30
2009 Press Pass Premium Previews /5 #EB30
2009 Press Pass Premium Signatures #15
2009 Press Pass Premium Signatures Gold /25 #14
2009 Press Pass Previews /5 #EB29
2009 Press Pass Previews /5 #EB133
2009 Press Pass Red #29
2009 Press Pass Red #133
2009 Press Pass Showcase /499 #10
2009 Press Pass Showcase /499 #31
2009 Press Pass Showcase 2nd Gear /125 #10
2009 Press Pass Showcase 2nd Gear /125 #31
2009 Press Pass Showcase 3rd Gear /50 #10
2009 Press Pass Showcase 3rd Gear /50 #31
2009 Press Pass Showcase 4th Gear /15 #10
2009 Press Pass Showcase 4th Gear /15 #31
2009 Press Pass Showcase Classic Collections Ink /45 #5
2009 Press Pass Showcase Classic Collections Ink Gold /25 #5
2009 Press Pass Showcase Classic Collections Ink Green /5 #5
2009 Press Pass Showcase Classic Collections Ink Melting /1 #5
2009 Press Pass Showcase Printing Plates Black /1 #10
2009 Press Pass Showcase Printing Plates Black /1 #31
2009 Press Pass Showcase Printing Plates Cyan /1 #10
2009 Press Pass Showcase Printing Plates Cyan /1 #31
2009 Press Pass Showcase Printing Plates Magenta /1 #10
2009 Press Pass Showcase Printing Plates Magenta /1 #31
2009 Press Pass Showcase Printing Plates Yellow /1 #10
2009 Press Pass Showcase Printing Plates Yellow /1 #31
2009 Press Pass Signings Blue /25 #18
2009 Press Pass Signings Gold #18
2009 Press Pass Signings Green /15 #18
2009 Press Pass Signings Orange /65 #18
2009 Press Pass Signings Printing Plates Black /1 #18
2009 Press Pass Signings Printing Plates Cyan /1 #18
2009 Press Pass Signings Purple /45 #18
2009 Press Pass Stealth #15
2009 Press Pass Stealth Chrome #15
2009 Press Pass Stealth Chrome Brushed Metal /25 #15
2009 Press Pass Stealth Chrome Gold /99 #15
2009 Press Pass Stealth Confidential Classified Bronze #PC17
2009 Press Pass Stealth Confidential Secret Silver #PC17
2009 Press Pass Stealth Confidential Top Secret Gold /25 #PC17
2009 Press Pass Stealth Previews /5 #EB15
2009 VIP #14
2009 VIP #62
2009 VIP Guest List #GG13
2009 VIP Previews /5 #14
2009 VIP Purple /25 #14
2009 VIP Purple /25 #62
2009 Wheels Autographs #30
2009 Wheels Autographs Press Plates Black /1 #SH
2009 Wheels Autographs Press Plates Cyan /1 #SH
2009 Wheels Autographs Press Plates Magenta /1 #SH
2009 Wheels Autographs Press Plates Yellow /1 #SH
2009 Wheels Main Event #33
2009 Wheels Main Event #42
2009 Wheels Main Event Fast Pass Purple /25 #33
2009 Wheels Main Event Fast Pass Purple /25 #42
2009 Wheels Main Event Hat Dance Patch /10 #HDSH
2009 Wheels Main Event Hat Dance Triple /99 #HDSH
2009 Wheels Main Event Marks Clubs #27
2009 Wheels Main Event Marks Diamonds /50 #27
2009 Wheels Main Event Marks Hearts /10 #27
2009 Wheels Main Event Marks Printing Plates Black /1 #23
2009 Wheels Main Event Marks Printing Plates Cyan /1 #23
2009 Wheels Main Event Marks Printing Plates Magenta /1 #23
2009 Wheels Main Event Marks Printing Plates Yellow /1 #23
2009 Wheels Main Event Marks Spades /1 #27
2009 Wheels Main Event Playing Cards Blue #6D
2009 Wheels Main Event Playing Cards Red #6D
2009 Wheels Main Event Previews /5 #33
2009 Wheels Main Event Wildcard Cuts /2 #WCGSH
2010 Element #19
2010 Element Blue /35 #19
2010 Element Green #19
2010 Element Previews /5 #EB19
2010 Element Purple /25 #19
2010 Element Red Target #19
2010 Press Pass #27
2010 Press Pass Autographs #23
2010 Press Pass Autographs Printing Plates Black /1 #17
2010 Press Pass Autographs Printing Plates Cyan /1 #20
2010 Press Pass Autographs Printing Plates Magenta /1 #18
2010 Press Pass Autographs Printing Plates Yellow /1 #19
2010 Press Pass Blue #27
2010 Press Pass Gold #27
2010 Press Pass Holofoil /100 #27
2010 Press Pass Premium #25
2010 Press Pass Premium Allies #A4
2010 Press Pass Premium Purple /25 #25
2010 Press Pass Premium Signatures #PSSH
2010 Press Pass Premium Signatures Red Ink /150 #PSSH
2010 Press Pass Previews /5 #27
2010 Press Pass Purple /25 #27
2010 Press Pass Showcase /499 #36
2010 Press Pass Showcase Classic Collections Ink /15 #CCIPEN
2010 Press Pass Showcase Classic Collections Ink Gold /10 #CCIPEN
2010 Press Pass Showcase Classic Collections Ink Green /5 #CCIPEN
2010 Press Pass Showcase Classic Collections Ink Melting /1 #CCIPEN
2010 Press Pass Showcase Gold /125 #36
2010 Press Pass Showcase Green /50 #36
2010 Press Pass Showcase Melting /15 #36
2010 Press Pass Showcase Platinum Holo /1 #36
2010 Press Pass Signings Blue /10 #25
2010 Press Pass Signings Gold /50 #25
2010 Press Pass Signings Red /15 #25
2010 Press Pass Signings Silver /75 #25
2010 Press Pass Stealth #14
2010 Press Pass Stealth Black and White #14
2010 Press Pass Stealth Previews /5 #14
2010 Press Pass Stealth Purple /25 #14
2010 Wheels Autographs #22
2010 Wheels Autographs Printing Plates Black /1 #22
2010 Wheels Autographs Printing Plates Cyan /1 #22
2010 Wheels Autographs Printing Plates Magenta /1 #22
2010 Wheels Autographs Printing Plates Yellow /1 #22
2010 Wheels Autographs Target /10 #14
2010 Wheels Main Event Marks Autographs /50 #25
2010 Wheels Main Event Marks Autographs Black /1 #24
2010 Wheels Main Event Marks Autographs Blue /25 #25
2010 Wheels Main Event Marks Autographs Red /25 #25
2011 Element #83
2011 Element Autographs /100 #24
2011 Element Autographs Blue /10 #24
2011 Element Autographs Gold /25 #23
2011 Element Autographs Printing Plates Black /1 #24
2011 Element Autographs Printing Plates Cyan /1 #24
2011 Element Autographs Printing Plates Magenta /1 #24
2011 Element Autographs Printing Plates Yellow /1 #24
2011 Element Autographs Silver /50 #23
2011 Element Black /35 #83
2011 Element Green #83
2011 Element Purple /25 #83
2011 Element Red #83
2011 Press Pass #15
2011 Press Pass #70
2011 Press Pass #182
2011 Press Pass Autographs Blue /10 #24
2011 Press Pass Autographs Bronze /75 #23
2011 Press Pass Autographs Gold /25 #23
2011 Press Pass Autographs Printing Plates Black /1 #24
2011 Press Pass Autographs Printing Plates Cyan /1 #24
2011 Press Pass Autographs Printing Plates Magenta /1 #24
2011 Press Pass Autographs Printing Plates Yellow /1 #24
2011 Press Pass Autographs Silver /50 #24
2011 Press Pass Blue Holofoil /10 #15
2011 Press Pass Blue Holofoil /10 #70
2011 Press Pass Blue Holofoil /10 #182
2011 Press Pass Blue Retail #15
2011 Press Pass Blue Retail #70
2011 Press Pass Blue Retail #182
2011 Press Pass Geared Up Holofoil /50 #GUSH
2011 Press Pass Gold /50 #15
2011 Press Pass Gold /50 #70
2011 Press Pass Gold /50 #182
2011 Press Pass Previews /5 #EB15
2011 Press Pass Purple /25 #15
2012 Press Pass Fanfare #51
2012 Press Pass Fanfare Autographs Blue /25 #SH
2012 Press Pass Fanfare Autographs Gold /99 #SH
2012 Press Pass Fanfare Autographs Red /75 #SH
2012 Press Pass Fanfare Autographs Silver /299 #SH
2012 Press Pass Fanfare Blue Foil Die Cuts #51
2012 Press Pass Fanfare Diamond /5 #51
2012 Press Pass Fanfare Holofoil Die Cuts #51
2012 Press Pass Fanfare Magnificent Materials /250 #MMSH
2012 Press Pass Fanfare Magnificent Materials Gold /125 #MMSH
2012 Press Pass Fanfare Sapphire /20 #51
2012 Press Pass Fanfare Silver /25 #51
2012 Press Pass Ignite #40
2012 Press Pass Ignite Proofs Black and White /50 #40
2012 Press Pass Ignite Proofs Cyan #40
2012 Press Pass Ignite Proofs Magenta #40
2012 Press Pass Ignite Proofs Yellow /10 #40
2013 Press Pass #50
2013 Press Pass Color Proofs Black #50
2013 Press Pass Color Proofs Cyan /35 #50
2013 Press Pass Color Proofs Magenta #50
2013 Press Pass Color Proofs Yellow /5 #50
2013 Press Pass Fanfare #66
2013 Press Pass Fanfare Autographs Blue /10 #SHJ
2013 Press Pass Fanfare Autographs Gold /99 #SHJ
2013 Press Pass Fanfare Autographs Green /6 #SHJ
2013 Press Pass Fanfare Autographs Red /50 #SHJ
2013 Press Pass Fanfare Autographs Silver /199 #SHJ
2013 Press Pass Fanfare Diamond Die Cuts /5 #66
2013 Press Pass Fanfare Green /3 #66
2013 Press Pass Fanfare Holofoil Die Cuts #66
2013 Press Pass Fanfare Magnificent Materials Gold /50 #SH
2013 Press Pass Fanfare Magnificent Materials Silver /199 #SH
2013 Press Pass Fanfare Red Foil Die Cuts #66
2013 Press Pass Fanfare Sapphire /20 #66
2013 Press Pass Fanfare Silver /25 #66
2013 Press Pass Ignite #43
2013 Press Pass Ignite Ink Black /75 #IISH
2013 Press Pass Ignite Ink Blue /20 #IISH
2013 Press Pass Ignite Ink Red /5 #IISH
2013 Press Pass Ignite Proofs Black and White /50 #43
2013 Press Pass Ignite Proofs Cyan #43
2013 Press Pass Ignite Proofs Magenta #43
2013 Press Pass Ignite Proofs Yellow /5 #43
2013 Total Memorabilia #40
2013 Total Memorabilia Black and White /99 #40
2013 Total Memorabilia Gold /275 #40
2013 Total Memorabilia Red #40
2014 Press Pass #48
2014 Press Pass Color Proofs Black /70 #48
2014 Press Pass Color Proofs Cyan /35 #48
2014 Press Pass Color Proofs Magenta #48
2014 Press Pass Color Proofs Yellow /5 #48
2014 Press Pass Gold #48
2014 Press Pass Redline #64
2014 Press Pass Redline Black /75 #64
2014 Press Pass Redline Blue Foil #64
2014 Press Pass Redline Cyan /50 #64
2014 Press Pass Redline Green National Convention /5 #64
2014 Press Pass Redline Magenta /10 #64
2014 Press Pass Redline Yellow /1 #64
2014 Press Pass Signings Gold /5 #PPSSH
2014 Press Pass Signings Holofoil /1 #PPSSH
2014 Press Pass Signings Melting /1 #PPSSH
2014 Press Pass Signings Printing Plates Black /1 #PPSSH
2014 Press Pass Signings Printing Plates Cyan /1 #PPSSH
2014 Press Pass Signings Printing Plates Magenta /1 #PPSSH
2014 Press Pass Signings Printing Plates Yellow /1 #PPSSH
2014 Press Pass Signings Silver /10 #PPSSH
2015 Press Pass #49
2015 Press Pass Cup Chase #49
2015 Press Pass Cup Chase Blue /25 #49
2015 Press Pass Cup Chase Gold /75 #49
2015 Press Pass Cup Chase Green /10 #49
2015 Press Pass Cup Chase Melting /1 #49
2015 Press Pass Purple #49
2015 Press Pass Red #49
2015 Press Pass Signings Blue /125 #PPSSH
2015 Press Pass Signings Gold #PPSSH
2015 Press Pass Signings Green /50 #PPSSH
2015 Press Pass Signings Melting /10 #PPSSH
2015 Press Pass Signings Red /75 #PPSSH
2016 Panini Prizm #9A
2016 Panini Prizm Prizms #9A
2016 Panini Prizm Prizms Black /3 #9
2016 Panini Prizm Prizms Blue Flag /99 #9
2016 Panini Prizm Prizms Camo /9 #9
2016 Panini Prizm Prizms Checkered Flag /1 #9A
2016 Panini Prizm Prizms Gold /10 #9A
2016 Panini Prizm Prizms Green Flag /149 #9
2016 Panini Prizm Prizms Rainbow /24 #9
2016 Panini Prizm Prizms Red Flag /75 #9
2016 Panini Prizm Prizms Red White and Blue #9
2016 Panini Prizm Prizms White Flag /5 #9

Jimmie Johnson

2000 Maxx #60
2000 Maximum #38
2000 Maximum Die Cuts /250 #38
2000 Maximum MPH /92 #38
2000 Maximum Signatures #JO
2000 Maximum Young Lions #YL9
2000 SP Authentic #39
2000 SP Authentic /2500 #67
2000 SP Authentic Overdrive Gold /92 #67
2000 SP Authentic Overdrive Gold /92 #39
2000 SP Authentic Overdrive Silver /250 #39
2000 SP Authentic Overdrive Silver /250 #67
2000 SP Authentic Sign of the Times #JI
2000 SP Authentic Sign of the Times Gold /25 #JI
2000 Upper Deck Racing #38
2001 Press Pass Optima #32
2001 Press Pass Optima Gold #32
2002 Press Pass #44
2002 Press Pass Autographs #31
2002 Press Pass Delphi #D4
2002 Press Pass Eclipse Under Cover Double Cover /625 #DC4
2002 Press Pass Eclipse Under Cover Double Cover /625 #DC5
2002 Press Pass Eclipse Under Cover Double Cover /625 #DC2
2002 Press Pass Eclipse Under Cover Drivers #CD1
2002 Press Pass Eclipse Under Cover Gold Cars /300 #CD1
2002 Press Pass Eclipse Under Cover Gold Drivers /400 #CD1
2002 Press Pass Eclipse Under Cover Holofoil Drivers /100 #CD1
2002 Press Pass Hot Treads /1555 #HT14
2002 Press Pass Hot Treads /2375 #HT30
2002 Press Pass Optima #14
2002 Press Pass Optima #47
2002 Press Pass Optima #0
2002 Press Pass Optima Cool Persistence #CP6
2002 Press Pass Optima Fan Favorite #FF11
2002 Press Pass Optima Gold #14
2002 Press Pass Optima Gold #47
2002 Press Pass Optima Promos /5 #14
2002 Press Pass Optima Promos /5 #47
2002 Press Pass Optima Q and A #QA3
2002 Press Pass Optima Race Used Lugnuts Autographs /48 #LNDA9
2002 Press Pass Optima Race Used Lugnuts Cars /100 #LNC9
2002 Press Pass Optima Race Used Lugnuts Drivers /100 #LND9
2002 Press Pass Optima Samples #14
2002 Press Pass Optima Samples #47
2002 Press Pass Optima Up Close #UC4
2002 Press Pass Platinum #44
2002 Press Pass Premium #13
2002 Press Pass Premium #34
2002 Press Pass Premium #49
2002 Press Pass Premium #62
2002 Press Pass Premium #75
2002 Press Pass Premium Red Reflectors #13
2002 Press Pass Premium Red Reflectors #34
2002 Press Pass Premium Red Reflectors #49
2002 Press Pass Premium Red Reflectors #62
2002 Press Pass Premium Red Reflectors #75
2002 Press Pass Premium Samples #13
2002 Press Pass Premium Samples #34
2002 Press Pass Premium Samples #49
2002 Press Pass Signings #29
2002 Press Pass Signings Gold /50 #27
2002 Press Pass Stealth #37
2002 Press Pass Stealth #38
2002 Press Pass Stealth #39
2002 Press Pass Stealth #52
2002 Press Pass Stealth #69
2002 Press Pass Stealth Behind the Numbers #BN7
2002 Press Pass Stealth EFX #FX11
2002 Press Pass Stealth Fusion #F6
2002 Press Pass Stealth Gold #37
2002 Press Pass Stealth Gold #38
2002 Press Pass Stealth Gold #39
2002 Press Pass Stealth Gold #52
2002 Press Pass Stealth Gold #69
2002 Press Pass Stealth Lap Leaders #LL13
2002 Press Pass Stealth Profile #P6
2002 Press Pass Stealth Race Used Glove Cars /85 #GLC13
2002 Press Pass Stealth Race Used Glove Drivers /50 #GLD13
2002 Press Pass Stealth Samples #37
2002 Press Pass Stealth Samples #38
2002 Press Pass Stealth Samples #39
2002 Press Pass Stealth Samples #52
2002 Press Pass Stealth Samples #69
2002 Press Pass Trackside #7
2002 Press Pass Trackside #56
2002 Press Pass Trackside #83
2002 Press Pass Trackside Dialed In #DI6
2002 Press Pass Trackside Generation Now #GN4
2002 Press Pass Trackside Golden /50 #G7
2002 Press Pass Trackside License to Drive #15
2002 Press Pass Trackside License to Drive Die Cuts #15
2002 Press Pass Trackside Samples #7
2002 Press Pass Trackside Samples #56
2002 Press Pass Trackside Samples #83
2002 VIP #16
2002 VIP #23
2002 VIP #34
2002 VIP #50
2002 VIP Driver's Choice #DC9
2002 VIP Driver's Choice Transparent #DC9
2002 VIP Driver's Choice Transparent LTD #DC9
2002 VIP Explosives #X16
2002 VIP Explosives #X23
2002 VIP Explosives #X34
2002 VIP Explosives #X50
2002 VIP Explosives Lasers #LX16
2002 VIP Explosives Lasers #LX23
2002 VIP Explosives Lasers #LX34
2002 VIP Explosives Lasers #LX50
2002 VIP Making the Show #MS21
2002 VIP Mile Masters #MM3
2002 VIP Mile Masters Transparent #MM3
2002 VIP Mile Masters Transparent LTD #MM3
2002 VIP Race Used Sheet Metal Cars #SC12
2002 VIP Race Used Sheet Metal Drivers /130 #SD12
2002 VIP Samples #16
2002 VIP Samples #23
2002 VIP Samples #34
2002 VIP Samples #50
2002 Wheels High Gear #38
2002 Wheels High Gear #70
2002 Wheels High Gear Autographs #26
2002 Wheels High Gear First Gear #38
2002 Wheels High Gear First Gear #70
2002 Wheels High Gear MPH /100 #38
2002 Wheels High Gear MPH /100 #70
2003 eTopps /2945 #5
2003 Press Pass #16
2003 Press Pass #59
2003 Press Pass #63
2003 Press Pass #64
2003 Press Pass #65
2003 Press Pass #66
2003 Press Pass #67
2003 Press Pass #78
2003 Press Pass #79
2003 Press Pass Autographs #27
2003 Press Pass Burning Rubber Cars /60 #BRT4
2003 Press Pass Burning Rubber Cars Autographs /48 #BRTJJ
2003 Press Pass Burning Rubber Drivers /50 #BRD4
2003 Press Pass Burning Rubber Drivers Autographs /48 #BRDJJ
2003 Press Pass Cup Chase #CCR7
2003 Press Pass Cup Chase Prizes #CCR7
2003 Press Pass Double Burner /100 #DB4
2003 Press Pass Double Burner Exchange /100 #DB4
2003 Press Pass Eclipse #5
2003 Press Pass Eclipse #37
2003 Press Pass Eclipse #43
2003 Press Pass Eclipse #48
2003 Press Pass Eclipse Double Hot Treads /999 #DT8
2003 Press Pass Eclipse Previews /5 #5
2003 Press Pass Eclipse Racing Champions #RC2
2003 Press Pass Eclipse Racing Champions #RC12
2003 Press Pass Eclipse Racing Champions #RC16
2003 Press Pass Eclipse Racing Champions #RC29
2003 Press Pass Eclipse Samples #5
2003 Press Pass Eclipse Samples #37
2003 Press Pass Eclipse Samples #43
2003 Press Pass Eclipse Samples #48
2003 Press Pass Eclipse Skidmarks #SM8
2003 Press Pass Eclipse Solar Eclipse #P5
2003 Press Pass Eclipse Solar Eclipse #P37
2003 Press Pass Eclipse Solar Eclipse #P43
2003 Press Pass Eclipse Solar Eclipse #P48
2003 Press Pass Eclipse Supernova #SN8
2003 Press Pass Eclipse Teammates Autographs /25 #JGJJ
2003 Press Pass Eclipse Under Cover Cars /215 #UCT4
2003 Press Pass Eclipse Under Cover Cars Autographs /48 #UCTJJ
2003 Press Pass Eclipse Under Cover Double Cover /530 #DC2
2003 Press Pass Eclipse Under Cover Double Cover /530 #DC4
2003 Press Pass Eclipse Under Cover Double Cover /530 #DC5
2003 Press Pass Eclipse Under Cover Driver Autographs /48 #UCDJJ
2003 Press Pass Eclipse Under Cover Driver Gold /260 #UCD4
2003 Press Pass Eclipse Under Cover Driver Red /100 #UCD4
2003 Press Pass Eclipse Under Cover Driver Silver /450 #UCD4
2003 Press Pass Eclipse Warp Speed #WS6
2003 Press Pass Gatorade Jumbos #1
2003 Press Pass Gold Holofoil #P16
2003 Press Pass Gold Holofoil #P59
2003 Press Pass Gold Holofoil #P63
2003 Press Pass Gold Holofoil #P64
2003 Press Pass Gold Holofoil #P65
2003 Press Pass Gold Holofoil #P66
2003 Press Pass Gold Holofoil #P67
2003 Press Pass Gold Holofoil #P78
2003 Press Pass Gold Holofoil #P79
2003 Press Pass Optima #11
2003 Press Pass Optima Cool Persistence #CP2
2003 Press Pass Optima Fan Favorite #FF1
2003 Press Pass Optima Gold #G11
2003 Press Pass Optima Previews /5 #11
2003 Press Pass Optima Samples #11
2003 Press Pass Optima Thunder Bolts Cars /95 #TBT4
2003 Press Pass Optima Thunder Bolts Cars Autographs /48 #TBTJJ
2003 Press Pass Optima Thunder Bolts Drivers /50 #TBD4
2003 Press Pass Optima Thunder Bolts Drivers Autographs /48 #TBDJJ
2003 Press Pass Optima Young Guns #YG5
2003 Press Pass Premium #13
2003 Press Pass Premium #40
2003 Press Pass Premium #73
2003 Press Pass Premium #61
2003 Press Pass Premium Hot Threads Cars /160 #HTT4
2003 Press Pass Premium Hot Threads Cars Autographs /48 #HTDJJ
2003 Press Pass Premium Hot Threads Drivers /285 #HTD4
2003 Press Pass Premium Hot Threads Drivers Autographs /48 #HTTJJ
2003 Press Pass Premium In the Zone #IZ4
2003 Press Pass Premium Performance Driven #PD3
2003 Press Pass Premium Previews /5 #13
2003 Press Pass Premium Red Reflectors #13
2003 Press Pass Premium Red Reflectors #40
2003 Press Pass Premium Red Reflectors #61
2003 Press Pass Premium Red Reflectors #73
2003 Press Pass Premium Samples #13
2003 Press Pass Premium Samples #40
2003 Press Pass Previews /5 #16
2003 Press Pass Samples #16
2003 Press Pass Samples #59
2003 Press Pass Samples #63
2003 Press Pass Samples #64
2003 Press Pass Samples #65
2003 Press Pass Samples #66
2003 Press Pass Samples #67
2003 Press Pass Samples #78
2003 Press Pass Samples #79
2003 Press Pass Showcar #S6B
2003 Press Pass Showman #S6A
2003 Press Pass Signings #35
2003 Press Pass Signings Gold /50 #35
2003 Press Pass Signings Transparent /100 #5
2003 Press Pass Snapshots #SN11
2003 Press Pass Stealth #34
2003 Press Pass Stealth #35
2003 Press Pass Stealth #36
2003 Press Pass Stealth #63
2003 Press Pass Stealth #67
2003 Press Pass Stealth EFX #FX6
2003 Press Pass Stealth Fusion #FU7
2003 Press Pass Stealth Gear Grippers Cars /150 #GGT4
2003 Press Pass Stealth Gear Grippers Cars Autographs /48 #JJ
2003 Press Pass Stealth Gear Grippers Drivers /75 #GGD4
2003 Press Pass Stealth Gear Grippers Drivers Autographs /48 #JJ
2003 Press Pass Stealth No Boundaries #NB16
2003 Press Pass Stealth Previews /5 #34
2003 Press Pass Stealth Previews /5 #35
2003 Press Pass Stealth Previews /5 #36
2003 Press Pass Stealth Profile #PR4
2003 Press Pass Stealth Red #P34
2003 Press Pass Stealth Red #P35
2003 Press Pass Stealth Red #P36
2003 Press Pass Stealth Red #P63
2003 Press Pass Stealth Red #P67
2003 Press Pass Stealth Samples #34
2003 Press Pass Stealth Samples #35
2003 Press Pass Stealth Samples #36
2003 Press Pass Stealth Samples #63
2003 Press Pass Stealth Samples #67
2003 Press Pass Stealth Supercharged #SC2
2003 Press Pass Top Shelf #TS4
2003 Press Pass Total Memorabilia Power Pick #TM4
2003 Press Pass Trackside #24
2003 Press Pass Trackside #79
2003 Press Pass Trackside Dialed In #DI5
2003 Press Pass Trackside Gold Holofoil #P24
2003 Press Pass Trackside Gold Holofoil #P79
2003 Press Pass Trackside Golden /50 #G24
2003 Press Pass Trackside Hat Giveaway #PPH12
2003 Press Pass Trackside Hot Pursuit #HP3
2003 Press Pass Trackside Pit Stoppers Cars /175 #PST4
2003 Press Pass Trackside Pit Stoppers Cars Autographs /48 #JJ
2003 Press Pass Trackside Pit Stoppers Drivers /100 #PSD4
2003 Press Pass Trackside Pit Stoppers Drivers Autographs /48 #PSDJJ
2003 Press Pass Trackside Previews /5 #24
2003 Press Pass Trackside Runnin n' Gunnin #RG6
2003 Press Pass Trackside Samples #24
2003 Press Pass Trackside Samples #79
2003 Press Pass Triple Burner /100 #TB4
2003 Press Pass Triple Burner Exchange /100 #TB4
2003 Press Pass Velocity #VC4
2003 Sports Illustrated for Kids #243
2003 VIP #8
2003 VIP #28
2003 VIP #48
2003 VIP Driver's Choice #DC1
2003 VIP Driver's Choice Die Cuts #DC1
2003 VIP Driver's Choice National #DC1
2003 VIP Explosives #X8
2003 VIP Explosives #X28
2003 VIP Explosives #X48
2003 VIP Head Gear #HG1
2003 VIP Head Gear Die Cuts #HG1
2003 VIP Head Gear National #HG1
2003 VIP Lap Leaders #LL5
2003 VIP Lap Leaders National #LL5
2003 VIP Lap Leaders Transparent #LL5
2003 VIP Lap Leaders Transparent LTD #LL5
2003 VIP Laser Explosive #LX8
2003 VIP Laser Explosive #LX28
2003 VIP Laser Explosive #LX48
2003 VIP Making the Show #MS20
2003 VIP Mile Masters #MM5
2003 VIP Mile Masters National #MM5
2003 VIP Mile Masters Transparent #MM5
2003 VIP Mile Masters Transparent LTD #MM5
2003 VIP Previews /5 #8
2003 VIP Previews /5 #28
2003 VIP Samples #8
2003 VIP Samples #28
2003 VIP Samples #48
2003 VIP Tin #CT8
2003 VIP Tin #CT28
2003 VIP Tin #CT48
2003 VIP Tradin' Paint Car Autographs /48 #JJ
2003 VIP Tradin' Paint Cars /160 #TPT4
2003 VIP Tradin' Paint Driver Autographs /48 #JJ
2003 VIP Tradin' Paint Drivers /110 #TPD4
2003 Wheels American Thunder #10
2003 Wheels American Thunder #34
2003 Wheels American Thunder #48
2003 Wheels American Thunder American Eagle #AE6
2003 Wheels American Thunder American Muscle #AM4
2003 Wheels American Thunder Born On /100 #BO10
2003 Wheels American Thunder Born On /100 #BO34
2003 Wheels American Thunder Born On /100 #BO48
2003 Wheels American Thunder Golden Eagle /100 #AEG6
2003 Wheels American Thunder Heads Up Manufacturer /90 #HUM9
2003 Wheels American Thunder Heads Up Team /90 #HUT8
2003 Wheels American Thunder Heads Up Winston /90 #HUW9
2003 Wheels American Thunder Holofoil #P10
2003 Wheels American Thunder Holofoil #P34
2003 Wheels American Thunder Holofoil #P48
2003 Wheels American Thunder Post Mark #PM9
2003 Wheels American Thunder Previews /5 #10
2003 Wheels American Thunder Previews /5 #34
2003 Wheels American Thunder Pushin Pedal /285 #PP11
2003 Wheels American Thunder Rookie Thunder #RT14
2003 Wheels American Thunder Samples #P10
2003 Wheels American Thunder Samples #P34
2003 Wheels American Thunder Samples #P48
2003 Wheels American Thunder Thunder Road #TR8
2003 Wheels American Thunder Triple Hat /25 #TH9
2003 Wheels Autographs #26
2003 Wheels High Gear #14
2003 Wheels High Gear #33
2003 Wheels High Gear #61
2003 Wheels High Gear Blue Hawaii SCDA Promos #14
2003 Wheels High Gear Blue Hawaii SCDA Promos #33
2003 Wheels High Gear Blue Hawaii SCDA Promos #61
2003 Wheels High Gear Custom Shop #CSJJ
2003 Wheels High Gear Custom Shop Autograph Redemption #CSJJ
2003 Wheels High Gear Custom Shop Autographs /10 #JJB2
2003 Wheels High Gear Custom Shop Prizes #JJA1
2003 Wheels High Gear Custom Shop Prizes #JJA2
2003 Wheels High Gear Custom Shop Prizes #JJA3
2003 Wheels High Gear Custom Shop Prizes #JJB1
2003 Wheels High Gear Custom Shop Prizes #JJB2
2003 Wheels High Gear Custom Shop Prizes #JJB3
2003 Wheels High Gear Custom Shop Prizes #JJC1
2003 Wheels High Gear Custom Shop Prizes #JJC2
2003 Wheels High Gear Custom Shop Prizes #JJC3
2003 Wheels High Gear First Gear #F14
2003 Wheels High Gear First Gear #F33
2003 Wheels High Gear First Gear #F61
2003 Wheels High Gear Flag Chasers Black /90 #FC3
2003 Wheels High Gear Flag Chasers Blue-Yellow /45 #FC3
2003 Wheels High Gear Flag Chasers Checkered /25 #FC3
2003 Wheels High Gear Flag Chasers Green /90 #FC3
2003 Wheels High Gear Flag Chasers Red /90 #FC3
2003 Wheels High Gear Flag Chasers White /90 #FC3
2003 Wheels High Gear Flag Chasers Yellow /90 #FC3
2003 Wheels High Gear Full Throttle #FT4
2003 Wheels High Gear High Groove #HG12
2003 Wheels High Gear Hot Treads /425 #HT7
2003 Wheels High Gear Machine #MM1B
2003 Wheels High Gear Man #MM1A
2003 Wheels High Gear MPH /100 #M14
2003 Wheels High Gear MPH /100 #M33
2003 Wheels High Gear MPH /100 #M61
2003 Wheels High Gear Previews /5 #14
2003 Wheels High Gear Samples #14
2003 Wheels High Gear Samples #33
2003 Wheels High Gear Samples #61
2003 Wheels High Gear Sunday Sensation #SS5
2003 Wheels High Gear Top Tier #TT5
2004 National Trading Card Day #PP3
2004 Press Pass #95B
2004 Press Pass #14
2004 Press Pass #83
2004 Press Pass #84
2004 Press Pass #86
2004 Press Pass #95
2004 Press Pass Autographs #29
2004 Press Pass Burning Rubber Autographs /48 #BRJJ
2004 Press Pass Burning Rubber Cars /140 #BRT1
2004 Press Pass Burning Rubber Drivers /70 #BRD1
2004 Press Pass Cup Chase #CCR7
2004 Press Pass Cup Chase Prizes #CCR7
2004 Press Pass Double Burner /100 #DB4
2004 Press Pass Double Burner Exchange /100 #DB4
2004 Press Pass Eclipse #2
2004 Press Pass Eclipse #2B
2004 Press Pass Eclipse #48
2004 Press Pass Eclipse #58
2004 Press Pass Eclipse #78
2004 Press Pass Eclipse #85
2004 Press Pass Eclipse Destination WIN #14
2004 Press Pass Eclipse Destination WIN #19
2004 Press Pass Eclipse Hyperdrive #HP8
2004 Press Pass Eclipse Maxim #MX2
2004 Press Pass Eclipse Previews /5 #2
2004 Press Pass Eclipse Samples #2
2004 Press Pass Eclipse Samples #48
2004 Press Pass Eclipse Samples #58
2004 Press Pass Eclipse Samples #78
2004 Press Pass Eclipse Samples #85
2004 Press Pass Eclipse Skidmarks #SM3
2004 Press Pass Eclipse Skidmarks Holofoil /500 #SM3
2004 Press Pass Eclipse Teammates Autographs /25 #2
2004 Press Pass Eclipse Under Cover Autographs /48 #UCJJ
2004 Press Pass Eclipse Under Cover Cars /170 #UCD1
2004 Press Pass Eclipse Under Cover Double Cover /100 #DC3
2004 Press Pass Eclipse Under Cover Double Cover /100 #DC8
2004 Press Pass Eclipse Under Cover Double Cover /100 #DC5
2004 Press Pass Eclipse Under Cover Driver Gold /325 #UCD1
2004 Press Pass Eclipse Under Cover Driver Red /100 #UCD1
2004 Press Pass Eclipse Under Cover Driver Silver /690 #UCD1
2004 Press Pass Hot Treads /1100 #HTR3
2004 Press Pass Hot Treads Holofoil /200 #HTR3
2004 Press Pass Making the Show Collector's Series #MS23
2004 Press Pass Optima #10
2004 Press Pass Optima #58
2004 Press Pass Optima #77
2004 Press Pass Optima #90
2004 Press Pass Optima Cool Persistence #CP6
2004 Press Pass Optima Fan Favorite #FF10
2004 Press Pass Optima G Force #GF5
2004 Press Pass Optima Gold #G10
2004 Press Pass Optima Gold #G58
2004 Press Pass Optima Gold #G77
2004 Press Pass Optima Gold #G90
2004 Press Pass Optima Previews /5 #EB10
2004 Press Pass Optima Q&A #QA6
2004 Press Pass Optima Samples #10
2004 Press Pass Optima Samples #58
2004 Press Pass Optima Samples #77
2004 Press Pass Optima Samples #90
2004 Press Pass Optima Thunder Bolts Cars /120 #TBT9
2004 Press Pass Optima Thunder Bolts Drivers /70 #TBD9
2004 Press Pass Platinum #P14
2004 Press Pass Platinum #P83
2004 Press Pass Platinum #P84
2004 Press Pass Platinum #P86
2004 Press Pass Platinum #P95
2004 Press Pass Premium #4
2004 Press Pass Premium #44
2004 Press Pass Premium #58
2004 Press Pass Premium #75
2004 Press Pass Premium Asphalt Jungle #A4
2004 Press Pass Premium Hot Threads Autographs /48 #HTJJ
2004 Press Pass Premium Hot Threads Drivers Bronze /125 #HTD1
2004 Press Pass Premium Hot Threads Drivers Bronze Retail /125 #HTT1
2004 Press Pass Premium Hot Threads Drivers Gold /50 #HTD1
2004 Press Pass Premium Hot Threads Drivers Silver /75 #HTD1
2004 Press Pass Premium In the Zone #IZ5
2004 Press Pass Premium In the Zone Elite Edition #IZ5
2004 Press Pass Premium Performance Driven #PD6
2004 Press Pass Premium Previews /5 #4
2004 Press Pass Premium Samples #4
2004 Press Pass Premium Samples #44
2004 Press Pass Previews /5 #14
2004 Press Pass Samples #14
2004 Press Pass Samples #83
2004 Press Pass Samples #84
2004 Press Pass Samples #86
2004 Press Pass Samples #95
2004 Press Pass Schedule #2
2004 Press Pass Showcar #S7B
2004 Press Pass Showman #S7A
2004 Press Pass Signings #32
2004 Press Pass Signings Gold /50 #29
2004 Press Pass Signings Transparent /100 #3
2004 Press Pass Snapshots #SN11
2004 Press Pass Stealth #7
2004 Press Pass Stealth #8
2004 Press Pass Stealth #9
2004 Press Pass Stealth #88
2004 Press Pass Stealth #94
2004 Press Pass Stealth EFX #EF3
2004 Press Pass Stealth Gear Grippers Autographs /48 #HTJJ
2004 Press Pass Stealth Gear Grippers Drivers /80 #GGD1
2004 Press Pass Stealth Gear Grippers Drivers Retail /120 #GGT1
2004 Press Pass Stealth No Boundaries #NB15
2004 Press Pass Stealth Previews /5 #EB7
2004 Press Pass Stealth Previews /5 #EB8
2004 Press Pass Stealth Previews /5 #EB9
2004 Press Pass Stealth Profile #P2
2004 Press Pass Stealth Samples #X8
2004 Press Pass Stealth Samples #X88
2004 Press Pass Stealth Samples #X9
2004 Press Pass Stealth Samples #X7
2004 Press Pass Stealth Samples #X94
2004 Press Pass Stealth X-Ray /100 #7
2004 Press Pass Stealth X-Ray /100 #8
2004 Press Pass Stealth X-Ray /100 #9
2004 Press Pass Stealth X-Ray /100 #88
2004 Press Pass Stealth X-Ray /100 #94
2004 Press Pass Top Shelf #TS5
2004 Press Pass Total Memorabilia Power Pick #TM4
2004 Press Pass Trackside #23
2004 Press Pass Trackside #63
2004 Press Pass Trackside #69
2004 Press Pass Trackside #85
2004 Press Pass Trackside #108
2004 Press Pass Trackside #112
2004 Press Pass Trackside #120
2004 Press Pass Trackside Dialed In #DI1
2004 Press Pass Trackside Golden /100 #G23
2004 Press Pass Trackside Golden /100 #G63
2004 Press Pass Trackside Golden /100 #G69
2004 Press Pass Trackside Golden /100 #G85
2004 Press Pass Trackside Golden /100 #G108
2004 Press Pass Trackside Golden /100 #G112
2004 Press Pass Trackside Golden /100 #G120
2004 Press Pass Trackside Hat Giveaway #PPH13
2004 Press Pass Trackside Hot Pass #HP9
2004 Press Pass Trackside Hot Pass National #HP9
2004 Press Pass Trackside Hot Pursuit #HP2
2004 Press Pass Trackside Pit Stoppers Cars /150 #PST4
2004 Press Pass Trackside Pit Stoppers Drivers /95 #PSD4
2004 Press Pass Trackside Previews /5 #EB23
2004 Press Pass Trackside Runnin n' Gunnin #RG3
2004 Press Pass Trackside Samples #23
2004 Press Pass Trackside Samples #63
2004 Press Pass Trackside Samples #69
2004 Press Pass Trackside Samples #85
2004 Press Pass Trackside Samples #108
2004 Press Pass Trackside Samples #112
2004 Press Pass Trackside Samples #120
2004 Press Pass Triple Burner /100 #TB4
2004 Press Pass Triple Burner Exchange /100 #TB4
2004 Press Pass Velocity #VC6
2004 Super Shots CHP Sonoma #2
2004 VIP #8
2004 VIP #39
2004 VIP #47
2004 VIP #57
2004 VIP #80
2004 VIP Driver's Choice #DC1
2004 VIP Driver's Choice Die Cuts #DC1
2004 VIP Head Gear #HG4
2004 VIP Head Gear Transparent #HG4
2004 VIP Making the Show #MS23
2004 VIP Previews /5 #EB8
2004 VIP Previews /5 #EB39
2004 VIP Previews /5 #EB47
2004 VIP Samples #8
2004 VIP Samples #57
2004 VIP Samples #80
2004 VIP Samples #39
2004 VIP Samples #47
2004 VIP Tradin' Paint Autographs /48 #TPJJ
2004 VIP Tradin' Paint Bronze /130 #TPT3
2004 VIP Tradin' Paint Gold /50 #TPD3
2004 VIP Tradin' Paint Silver /70 #TPD3
2004 Wheels American Thunder #10
2004 Wheels American Thunder #31
2004 Wheels American Thunder #54
2004 Wheels American Thunder #72
2004 Wheels American Thunder #84
2004 Wheels American Thunder American Eagle #AE4
2004 Wheels American Thunder American Muscle #AM3

2004 Wheels American Thunder Cup Quest #CQ1
2004 Wheels American Thunder Golden Eagle /250 #AE4
2004 Wheels American Thunder Post Mark #PM24
2004 Wheels American Thunder Previews /5 #EB10
2004 Wheels American Thunder Previews /5 #EB31
2004 Wheels American Thunder Pushin Pedal /275 #PP9
2004 Wheels American Thunder Samples #10
2004 Wheels American Thunder Samples #31
2004 Wheels American Thunder Samples #54
2004 Wheels American Thunder Samples #72
2004 Wheels American Thunder Samples #84
2004 Wheels American Thunder Thunder Road #TR16
2004 Wheels American Thunder Triple Hat /160 #TH6
2004 Wheels Autographs #33
2004 Wheels High Gear #11
2004 Wheels High Gear #36
2004 Wheels High Gear #51
2004 Wheels High Gear #57
2004 Wheels High Gear #72
2004 Wheels High Gear Custom Shop #CSJJ
2004 Wheels High Gear Flag Chasers Black /100 #FC1
2004 Wheels High Gear Flag Chasers Blue /50 #FC1
2004 Wheels High Gear Flag Chasers Checkered /35 #FC1
2004 Wheels High Gear Flag Chasers Green /100 #FC1
2004 Wheels High Gear Flag Chasers Red /100 #FC1
2004 Wheels High Gear Flag Chasers White /100 #FC1
2004 Wheels High Gear Flag Chasers Yellow /100 #FC1
2004 Wheels High Gear Full Throttle #FT1
2004 Wheels High Gear High Groove #HG10
2004 Wheels High Gear Machine #MM6B
2004 Wheels High Gear Man #MM6A
2004 Wheels High Gear MPH /100 #M11
2004 Wheels High Gear MPH /100 #M36
2004 Wheels High Gear MPH /100 #M51
2004 Wheels High Gear MPH /100 #M57
2004 Wheels High Gear MPH /100 #M72
2004 Wheels High Gear Previews /5 #11
2004 Wheels High Gear Previews /5 #36
2004 Wheels High Gear Previews /5 #51
2004 Wheels High Gear Previews /5 #57
2004 Wheels High Gear Samples #11
2004 Wheels High Gear Samples #36
2004 Wheels High Gear Samples #51
2004 Wheels High Gear Samples #57
2004 Wheels High Gear Samples #72
2004 Wheels High Gear Sunday Sensation #SS4
2004 Wheels High Gear Top Ten #TT2
2005 Press Pass #32
2005 Press Pass #76
2005 Press Pass #82
2005 Press Pass #92
2005 Press Pass #106
2005 Press Pass #114
2005 Press Pass #118
2005 Press Pass #120
2005 Press Pass Autographs #27
2005 Press Pass Burning Rubber Autographs /48 #BRJJ
2005 Press Pass Burning Rubber Cars /130 #BRT1
2005 Press Pass Burning Rubber Drivers /80 #BRD1
2005 Press Pass Burning Rubber Drivers Gold /1 #BRD1
2005 Press Pass Cup Chase #CCR3
2005 Press Pass Cup Chase Prizes #CCP3
2005 Press Pass Double Burner /100 #DB4
2005 Press Pass Double Burner Exchange /100 #DB4
2005 Press Pass Eclipse #2
2005 Press Pass Eclipse #46
2005 Press Pass Eclipse #49
2005 Press Pass Eclipse #50
2005 Press Pass Eclipse #58
2005 Press Pass Eclipse #65
2005 Press Pass Eclipse #68
2005 Press Pass Eclipse #72
2005 Press Pass Eclipse #90
2005 Press Pass Eclipse #85
2005 Press Pass Eclipse Destination WIN #4
2005 Press Pass Eclipse Destination WIN #11
2005 Press Pass Eclipse Destination WIN #13
2005 Press Pass Eclipse Destination WIN #25
2005 Press Pass Eclipse Hyperdrive #HD8
2005 Press Pass Eclipse Maxim #MX2
2005 Press Pass Eclipse Previews /5 #EB2
2005 Press Pass Eclipse Previews /5 #EB46
2005 Press Pass Eclipse Previews /5 #EB49
2005 Press Pass Eclipse Previews /5 #EB50
2005 Press Pass Eclipse Previews /5 #EB58
2005 Press Pass Eclipse Previews /5 #EB65
2005 Press Pass Eclipse Previews /5 #EB68
2005 Press Pass Eclipse Previews /5 #EB72
2005 Press Pass Eclipse Previews /1 #EB85
2005 Press Pass Eclipse Previews /5 #EB90
2005 Press Pass Eclipse Samples #2
2005 Press Pass Eclipse Samples #46
2005 Press Pass Eclipse Samples #49
2005 Press Pass Eclipse Samples #50
2005 Press Pass Eclipse Samples #58
2005 Press Pass Eclipse Samples #65
2005 Press Pass Eclipse Samples #68
2005 Press Pass Eclipse Samples #72
2005 Press Pass Eclipse Samples #85
2005 Press Pass Eclipse Samples #90
2005 Press Pass Eclipse Skidmarks #SM3
2005 Press Pass Eclipse Skidmarks Holofoil /250 #SM3
2005 Press Pass Eclipse Teammates Autographs /25 #6
2005 Press Pass Eclipse Under Cover Autographs /48 #UCJJ
2005 Press Pass Eclipse Under Cover Cars /120 #UCT1
2005 Press Pass Eclipse Under Cover Double Cover /340 #DC3
2005 Press Pass Eclipse Under Cover Double Cover /340 #DC8
2005 Press Pass Eclipse Under Cover Driver Red /400 #UCD1
2005 Press Pass Eclipse Under Cover Drivers Holofoil /100 #UCD1
2005 Press Pass Eclipse Under Cover Drivers Silver /690 #UCD1
2005 Press Pass Game Face #GF2
2005 Press Pass Hot Treads /900 #HTR18
2005 Press Pass Hot Treads Holofoil /100 #HTR18
2005 Press Pass Legends #31
2005 Press Pass Legends Autographs Black /50 #18
2005 Press Pass Legends Blue /1890 #31B
2005 Press Pass Legends Double Threads Bronze /375 #DTGJ
2005 Press Pass Legends Double Threads Gold /99 #DTGJ
2005 Press Pass Legends Double Threads Silver /225 #DTGJ
2005 Press Pass Legends Gold /750 #31G
2005 Press Pass Legends Holofoil /100 #31H
2005 Press Pass Legends Press Plates Black /1 #31
2005 Press Pass Legends Press Plates Cyan /1 #31
2005 Press Pass Legends Press Plates Magenta /1 #31
2005 Press Pass Legends Press Plates Yellow /1 #31
2005 Press Pass Legends Previews /5 #31
2005 Press Pass Legends Solo /1 #31S
2005 Press Pass Legends Threads and Treads Bronze /375 #TTJJ
2005 Press Pass Legends Threads and Treads Gold /99 #TTJJ
2005 Press Pass Legends Threads and Treads Silver /225 #TTJJ
2005 Press Pass Optima #13
2005 Press Pass Optima #13B
2005 Press Pass Optima #62
2005 Press Pass Optima #67
2005 Press Pass Optima #85
2005 Press Pass Optima #92
2005 Press Pass Optima #95
2005 Press Pass Optima Cool Persistence #CP4
2005 Press Pass Optima Fan Favorite #FF12
2005 Press Pass Optima G Force #GF2
2005 Press Pass Optima Gold /100 #G13
2005 Press Pass Optima Gold /100 #G62
2005 Press Pass Optima Gold /100 #G67
2005 Press Pass Optima Gold /100 #G85
2005 Press Pass Optima Gold /100 #G92
2005 Press Pass Optima Gold /100 #G95
2005 Press Pass Optima Previews /5 #13
2005 Press Pass Optima Samples #13
2005 Press Pass Optima Samples #62
2005 Press Pass Optima Samples #67
2005 Press Pass Optima Samples #85
2005 Press Pass Optima Samples #92
2005 Press Pass Optima Samples #95
2005 Press Pass Optima Thunder Bolts Autographs /48 #TBJJ
2005 Press Pass Panorama #PPP12
2005 Press Pass Panorama #PPP21
2005 Press Pass Panorama #PPP25
2005 Press Pass Panorama #PPP36
2005 Press Pass Panorama #PPP43
2005 Press Pass Panorama #PPP44
2005 Press Pass Panorama #PPP59
2005 Press Pass Platinum /100 #P32
2005 Press Pass Platinum /100 #P76
2005 Press Pass Platinum /100 #P82
2005 Press Pass Platinum /100 #P92
2005 Press Pass Platinum /100 #P106
2005 Press Pass Platinum /100 #P114
2005 Press Pass Platinum /100 #P118
2005 Press Pass Platinum /100 #P120
2005 Press Pass Premium #11
2005 Press Pass Premium #38
2005 Press Pass Premium #48
2005 Press Pass Premium #59
2005 Press Pass Premium #74
2005 Press Pass Premium Asphalt Jungle #AJ1
2005 Press Pass Premium Hot Threads Autographs /48 #HTJJ
2005 Press Pass Premium Hot Threads Cars /85 #HTT2
2005 Press Pass Premium Hot Threads Drivers /275 #HTD2
2005 Press Pass Premium Hot Threads Drivers Gold /1 #HTD2
2005 Press Pass Premium In the Zone #IZ7
2005 Press Pass Premium In the Zone Elite Edition /250 #IZ7
2005 Press Pass Premium Performance Driven #PD5
2005 Press Pass Premium Samples #11
2005 Press Pass Premium Samples #38
2005 Press Pass Premium Samples #48
2005 Press Pass Previews Green /5 #EB32
2005 Press Pass Previews Silver /1 #EB106
2005 Press Pass Samples #32
2005 Press Pass Samples #76
2005 Press Pass Samples #82
2005 Press Pass Samples #92
2005 Press Pass Samples #106
2005 Press Pass Samples #114
2005 Press Pass Samples #118
2005 Press Pass Samples #120
2005 Press Pass Showcar #SC3
2005 Press Pass Showman #SM3
2005 Press Pass Signings #26
2005 Press Pass Signings Gold /50 #25
2005 Press Pass Signings Platinum /100 #25
2005 Press Pass Snapshots #SN12
2005 Press Pass Snapshots Extra #SS3
2005 Press Pass Stealth #39
2005 Press Pass Stealth #42
2005 Press Pass Stealth #45
2005 Press Pass Stealth #89
2005 Press Pass Stealth #96
2005 Press Pass Stealth EFX #EFX2
2005 Press Pass Stealth Fusion #FU2
2005 Press Pass Stealth No Boundaries #NB11
2005 Press Pass Stealth Previews /5 #39
2005 Press Pass Stealth Previews /5 #42
2005 Press Pass Stealth Previews /5 #45
2005 Press Pass Stealth Profile #PR2
2005 Press Pass Stealth Samples #39
2005 Press Pass Stealth Samples #42
2005 Press Pass Stealth Samples #45
2005 Press Pass Stealth Samples #89
2005 Press Pass Stealth Samples #96
2005 Press Pass Stealth X-Ray /100 #X39
2005 Press Pass Stealth X-Ray /100 #X42
2005 Press Pass Stealth X-Ray /100 #X45
2005 Press Pass Stealth X-Ray /100 #X89
2005 Press Pass Stealth X-Ray /100 #X96
2005 Press Pass Top Ten #TT2
2005 Press Pass Total Memorabilia Power Pick #TM4
2005 Press Pass Trackside #5
2005 Press Pass Trackside #65
2005 Press Pass Trackside #70
2005 Press Pass Trackside #86
2005 Press Pass Trackside #86B
2005 Press Pass Trackside #96
2005 Press Pass Trackside Dialed In #DI1
2005 Press Pass Trackside Golden /100 #G5
2005 Press Pass Trackside Golden /100 #G65
2005 Press Pass Trackside Golden /100 #G70
2005 Press Pass Trackside Golden /100 #G86
2005 Press Pass Trackside Golden /100 #G96
2005 Press Pass Trackside Hat Giveaway #PPH12
2005 Press Pass Trackside Hot Pass #8
2005 Press Pass Trackside Hot Pass National #8
2005 Press Pass Trackside Hot Pursuit #HP2
2005 Press Pass Trackside Pit Stoppers Autographs /48 #PSJJ
2005 Press Pass Trackside Pit Stoppers Cars /85 #PST3
2005 Press Pass Trackside Pit Stoppers Drivers /85 #PSD3
2005 Press Pass Trackside Previews /5 #5
2005 Press Pass Trackside Previews /1 #86
2005 Press Pass Trackside Runnin n' Gunnin #RG3
2005 Press Pass Trackside Samples #5
2005 Press Pass Trackside Samples #65
2005 Press Pass Trackside Samples #70
2005 Press Pass Trackside Samples #86
2005 Press Pass Trackside Samples #96
2005 Press Pass Triple Burner /100 #TB4
2005 Press Pass Triple Burner Exchange /100 #TB4
2005 Press Pass UMI Cup Chase #1
2005 Press Pass UMI Cup Chase #5
2005 Press Pass Velocity #V2
2005 VIP #11
2005 VIP #42
2005 VIP #45
2005 VIP #54
2005 VIP #76
2005 VIP Driver's Choice #DC1
2005 VIP Driver's Choice Die Cuts #DC1
2005 VIP Head Gear #4
2005 VIP Head Gear Transparent #4
2005 VIP Making The Show #23
2005 VIP Previews /5 #EB11
2005 VIP Previews /5 #EB42
2005 VIP Samples #11
2005 VIP Samples #42
2005 VIP Samples #45
2005 VIP Samples #54
2005 VIP Samples #76
2005 VIP Tradin' Paint Autographs /48 #JJ
2005 VIP Tradin' Paint Cars /110 #TPT3
2005 VIP Tradin' Paint Drivers /90 #TPD3
2005 Wheels American Thunder #12
2005 Wheels American Thunder #31
2005 Wheels American Thunder #53
2005 Wheels American Thunder #60
2005 Wheels American Thunder #67
2005 Wheels American Thunder #84
2005 Wheels American Thunder American Eagle #AE11
2005 Wheels American Thunder American Muscle #AM3
2005 Wheels American Thunder Golden Eagle /250 #GE11
2005 Wheels American Thunder Head to Toe /60 #HT13
2005 Wheels American Thunder Medallion #MD20
2005 Wheels American Thunder Previews /5 #12
2005 Wheels American Thunder Previews /5 #84
2005 Wheels American Thunder Pushin Pedal /60 #PP13
2005 Wheels American Thunder Samples #12
2005 Wheels American Thunder Samples #31
2005 Wheels American Thunder Samples #53
2005 Wheels American Thunder Samples #60
2005 Wheels American Thunder Samples #67
2005 Wheels American Thunder Samples #84
2005 Wheels American Thunder Thunder Road #TR16
2005 Wheels American Thunder Triple Hat /190 #TH9
2005 Wheels Autographs #26
2005 Wheels High Gear #23
2005 Wheels High Gear #54
2005 Wheels High Gear #55
2005 Wheels High Gear #70
2005 Wheels High Gear #73
2005 Wheels High Gear #83
2005 Wheels High Gear Flag Chasers Black /55 #FC4
2005 Wheels High Gear Flag Chasers Blue-Yellow /25 #FC4
2005 Wheels High Gear Flag Chasers Checkered /10 #FC4
2005 Wheels High Gear Flag Chasers Green /55 #FC4
2005 Wheels High Gear Flag Chasers Red /55 #FC4
2005 Wheels High Gear Flag Chasers White /55 #FC4
2005 Wheels High Gear Flag Chasers Yellow /55 #FC4
2005 Wheels High Gear Flag to Flag #FF9
2005 Wheels High Gear Full Throttle #FT6
2005 Wheels High Gear Machine #MMB5
2005 Wheels High Gear Man #MMA5
2005 Wheels High Gear MPH /100 #M23
2005 Wheels High Gear MPH /100 #M54
2005 Wheels High Gear MPH /100 #M55
2005 Wheels High Gear MPH /100 #M70
2005 Wheels High Gear MPH /100 #M73
2005 Wheels High Gear MPH /100 #M83
2005 Wheels High Gear Previews Green /5 #EB23
2005 Wheels High Gear Previews Silver /1 #EB73
2005 Wheels High Gear Samples #23
2005 Wheels High Gear Samples #54
2005 Wheels High Gear Samples #55
2005 Wheels High Gear Samples #70
2005 Wheels High Gear Samples #73
2005 Wheels High Gear Samples #83
2005 Wheels High Gear Top Tier #TT2
2006 Press Pass #27
2006 Press Pass #73
2006 Press Pass #91
2006 Press Pass #103
2006 Press Pass #111
2006 Press Pass Autographs #24
2006 Press Pass Blue #B27
2006 Press Pass Blue #B73
2006 Press Pass Blue #B91
2006 Press Pass Blue #B103
2006 Press Pass Blue #B111
2006 Press Pass Burning Rubber Autographs /48 #BRJJ
2006 Press Pass Burning Rubber Cars /370 #BRT8
2006 Press Pass Burning Rubber Drivers /100 #BRD8
2006 Press Pass Burning Rubber Drivers Gold /1 #BRD8
2006 Press Pass Burnouts /1050 #HT10
2006 Press Pass Burnouts Holofoil /125 #HT10
2006 Press Pass Collectors Series Making the Show #MS7
2006 Press Pass Cup Chase #CCR3
2006 Press Pass Cup Chase Prizes /475 #CCP1
2006 Press Pass Cup Chase Prizes #CC1
2006 Press Pass Double Burner Firesuit-Glove /100 #DB4
2006 Press Pass Double Burner Metal-Tire /100 #DB5
2006 Press Pass Eclipse #5
2006 Press Pass Eclipse #40
2006 Press Pass Eclipse #55
2006 Press Pass Eclipse #65
2006 Press Pass Eclipse #69
2006 Press Pass Eclipse #81
2006 Press Pass Eclipse Hyperdrive #HP4
2006 Press Pass Eclipse Previews /5 #EB5
2006 Press Pass Eclipse Racing Champions #RC3
2006 Press Pass Eclipse Skidmarks #SM7
2006 Press Pass Eclipse Skidmarks Holofoil /250 #SM7
2006 Press Pass Eclipse Supernova #SU12
2006 Press Pass Eclipse Teammates Autographs /25 #5
2006 Press Pass Eclipse Under Cover Autographs /48 #JJ
2006 Press Pass Eclipse Under Cover Cars /140 #UCT7
2006 Press Pass Eclipse Under Cover Double Cover /100 #DC1
2006 Press Pass Eclipse Under Cover Double Cover /100 #DC8
2006 Press Pass Eclipse Under Cover Double Cover Holofoil /25 #DC1
2006 Press Pass Eclipse Under Cover Double Cover Holofoil /25 #DC8
2006 Press Pass Eclipse Under Cover Drivers Gold /1 #UCD7
2006 Press Pass Eclipse Under Cover Drivers Holofoil /100 #UCD7
2006 Press Pass Eclipse Under Cover Drivers Red /225 #UCD7
2006 Press Pass Eclipse Under Cover Drivers Silver /400 #UCD7
2006 Press Pass Four Wide /50 #FWJJ
2006 Press Pass Four Wide Checkered Flag /1 #FWJJ
2006 Press Pass Game Face #GF6
2006 Press Pass Gold #G27
2006 Press Pass Gold #G73
2006 Press Pass Gold #G91
2006 Press Pass Gold #G103
2006 Press Pass Gold #G111
2006 Press Pass Legends #41
2006 Press Pass Legends Autographs Black /50 #25
2006 Press Pass Legends Blue /1999 #B41
2006 Press Pass Legends Bronze /999 #Z41
2006 Press Pass Legends Gold /299 #G41
2006 Press Pass Legends Heritage Gold /99 #HE11
2006 Press Pass Legends Heritage Silver /549 #HE11
2006 Press Pass Legends Holofoil /99 #H41
2006 Press Pass Legends Memorable Moments Gold /199 #MM4
2006 Press Pass Legends Memorable Moments Silver /699 #MM4
2006 Press Pass Legends Press Plates Black /1 #PPB41
2006 Press Pass Legends Press Plates Black Backs /1 #PPB41B
2006 Press Pass Legends Press Plates Cyan /1 #PPC41
2006 Press Pass Legends Press Plates Cyan Backs /1 #PPC41B
2006 Press Pass Legends Press Plates Magenta /1 #PPM41
2006 Press Pass Legends Press Plates Magenta Backs /1 #PPM41B
2006 Press Pass Legends Press Plates Yellow /1 #PPY41
2006 Press Pass Legends Press Plates Yellow Backs /1 #PPY41B
2006 Press Pass Legends Previews /5 #EB41
2006 Press Pass Legends Solo /1 #S41
2006 Press Pass Legends Triple Threads /50 #TTJJ
2006 Press Pass Optima #30
2006 Press Pass Optima #61
2006 Press Pass Optima #66
2006 Press Pass Optima #87
2006 Press Pass Optima #98
2006 Press Pass Optima #30B
2006 Press Pass Optima Fan Favorite #FF10
2006 Press Pass Optima Gold /100 #G30
2006 Press Pass Optima Gold /100 #G61
2006 Press Pass Optima Gold /100 #G66
2006 Press Pass Optima Gold /100 #G87
2006 Press Pass Optima Gold /100 #G98
2006 Press Pass Optima Pole Position #PP5
2006 Press Pass Optima Previews /5 #EB30
2006 Press Pass Optima Q & A #QA1
2006 Press Pass Platinum /100 #P27
2006 Press Pass Platinum /100 #P73
2006 Press Pass Platinum /100 #P91
2006 Press Pass Platinum /100 #P103
2006 Press Pass Platinum /100 #P111
2006 Press Pass Premium #0
2006 Press Pass Premium #12
2006 Press Pass Premium #45
2006 Press Pass Premium #61
2006 Press Pass Premium #73
2006 Press Pass Premium Asphalt Jungle #AJ5
2006 Press Pass Premium Hot Threads Autographs /48 #HTJJ
2006 Press Pass Premium Hot Threads Cars /165 #HTT5
2006 Press Pass Premium Hot Threads Drivers /220 #HTD5
2006 Press Pass Premium Hot Threads Drivers Gold /1 #HTD5
2006 Press Pass Premium In the Zone #IZ7
2006 Press Pass Premium In the Zone Red /250 #IZ7
2006 Press Pass Previews /5 #EB27
2006 Press Pass Previews /1 #EB103
2006 Press Pass Signings #26
2006 Press Pass Signings Gold /50 #26
2006 Press Pass Signings Silver /100 #26
2006 Press Pass Snapshots #SN7
2006 Press Pass Snapshots #SN17
2006 Press Pass Stealth #13
2006 Press Pass Stealth #40
2006 Press Pass Stealth #54
2006 Press Pass Stealth #65
2006 Press Pass Stealth #90
2006 Press Pass Stealth Autographed Hat Entry #PPH11
2006 Press Pass Stealth EFX #EFX4
2006 Press Pass Stealth Gear Grippers Cars Retail /99 #GGT13
2006 Press Pass Stealth Gear Grippers Drivers /99 #GGD13
2006 Press Pass Stealth Hot Pass #HP14
2006 Press Pass Stealth Previews /5 #13
2006 Press Pass Stealth Profile #P6
2006 Press Pass Stealth Retail #13
2006 Press Pass Stealth Retail #40
2006 Press Pass Stealth Retail #65
2006 Press Pass Stealth Retail #90
2006 Press Pass Stealth Retail #54
2006 Press Pass Stealth X-Ray /100 #X13
2006 Press Pass Stealth X-Ray /100 #X40
2006 Press Pass Stealth X-Ray /100 #X54
2006 Press Pass Stealth X-Ray /100 #X65
2006 Press Pass Stealth X-Ray /100 #X90
2006 Press Pass Top 25 Drivers & Rides #C22
2006 Press Pass Top 25 Drivers & Rides #D22
2006 Press Pass Velocity #VE8
2006 TRAKS #15
2006 TRAKS #52
2006 TRAKS Autographs #17
2006 TRAKS Autographs 25 /25 #15
2006 TRAKS Previews /1 #15
2006 TRAKS Previews /1 #52
2006 TRAKS Stickers #48
2006 VIP #11
2006 VIP #35
2006 VIP #40
2006 VIP #42
2006 VIP #48
2006 VIP #52
2006 VIP #71
2006 VIP #79
2006 VIP #84
2006 VIP Head Gear #HG2
2006 VIP Head Gear Transparent #HG2
2006 VIP Lap Leader #LL5
2006 VIP Lap Leader Transparent #LL5
2006 VIP Making the Show #MS7
2006 VIP Tradin' Paint Autographs /48 #TPJJ
2006 VIP Tradin' Paint Cars Bronze /145 #TPT10
2006 VIP Tradin' Paint Drivers Gold /50 #TPD10
2006 VIP Tradin' Paint Drivers Silver /80 #TPD10
2006 Wheels American Thunder #13
2006 Wheels American Thunder #34
2006 Wheels American Thunder #48
2006 Wheels American Thunder #66
2006 Wheels American Thunder #72
2006 Wheels American Thunder #83
2006 Wheels American Thunder American Muscle #AM9
2006 Wheels American Thunder American Racing Idol #RI1
2006 Wheels American Thunder American Racing Idol Golden /250 #RI1
2006 Wheels American Thunder Double Hat /99 #DH11
2006 Wheels American Thunder Grandstand #GS10
2006 Wheels American Thunder Head to Toe /35 #HT12
2006 Wheels American Thunder Previews /5 #EB13
2006 Wheels American Thunder Previews /1 #EB72
2006 Wheels American Thunder Pushin' Pedal /35 #PP14
2006 Wheels American Thunder Thunder Road #TR4
2006 Wheels Autographs #26
2006 Wheels High Gear #5
2006 Wheels High Gear #68
2006 Wheels High Gear #78
2006 Wheels High Gear Flag Chasers Black /110 #FC9
2006 Wheels High Gear Flag Chasers Blue-Yellow /65 #FC9
2006 Wheels High Gear Flag Chasers Checkered /3 #FC9
2006 Wheels High Gear Flag Chasers Green /110 #FC9
2006 Wheels High Gear Flag Chasers Red /110 #FC9
2006 Wheels High Gear Flag Chasers White /110 #FC9
2006 Wheels High Gear Flag Chasers Yellow /110 #FC9
2006 Wheels High Gear Flag to Flag #FF11
2006 Wheels High Gear Full Throttle #FT2
2006 Wheels High Gear Man & Machine Cars #MMB3
2006 Wheels High Gear Man & Machine Drivers #MMA3
2006 Wheels High Gear MPH /100 #M5
2006 Wheels High Gear MPH /100 #M68
2006 Wheels High Gear MPH /100 #M78
2006 Wheels High Gear Previews Green /5 #EB5
2006 Wheels High Gear Previews Silver /1 #EB78
2006 Wheels High Gear Top Tier #TT5
2007 Press Pass #2
2007 Press Pass #77
2007 Press Pass #94
2007 Press Pass #96
2007 Press Pass #109
2007 Press Pass #CL
2007 Press Pass Autographs #20
2007 Press Pass Blue #B2
2007 Press Pass Blue #B77
2007 Press Pass Blue #B94
2007 Press Pass Blue #B96
2007 Press Pass Blue #B109
2007 Press Pass Blue #BCL
2007 Press Pass Burning Rubber Autographs /48 #BRSJJ
2007 Press Pass Burning Rubber Drivers /75 #BRD1
2007 Press Pass Burning Rubber Drivers /75 #BRD6
2007 Press Pass Burning Rubber Drivers /75 #BRD16
2007 Press Pass Burning Rubber Drivers Gold /1 #BRD1
2007 Press Pass Burning Rubber Drivers Gold /1 #BRD6
2007 Press Pass Burning Rubber Drivers Gold /1 #BRD16
2007 Press Pass Burning Rubber Team /325 #BRT1
2007 Press Pass Burning Rubber Team /325 #BRT6
2007 Press Pass Burning Rubber Team /325 #BRT16
2007 Press Pass Burnouts #BO1
2007 Press Pass Burnouts Blue /99 #BO1
2007 Press Pass Burnouts Gold /299 #BO1
2007 Press Pass Collector's Series Box Set #SB11
2007 Press Pass Cup Chase #CCR8
2007 Press Pass Cup Chase Prizes #CCP1
2007 Press Pass Cup Chase Prizes #CC1
2007 Press Pass Dale The Movie #46
2007 Press Pass Double Burner Firesuit-Glove /100 #DB4
2007 Press Pass Double Burner Firesuit-Glove Exchange /100 #DB4
2007 Press Pass Double Burner Metal-Tire /100 #DBJJ
2007 Press Pass Double Burner Metal-Tire Exchange /100 #DBJJ
2007 Press Pass Eclipse #1
2007 Press Pass Eclipse #35
2007 Press Pass Eclipse #50
2007 Press Pass Eclipse #69
2007 Press Pass Eclipse #71
2007 Press Pass Eclipse #72
2007 Press Pass Eclipse #73A
2007 Press Pass Eclipse #79
2007 Press Pass Eclipse #73B
2007 Press Pass Eclipse Ecliptic #EC1
2007 Press Pass Eclipse Gold /25 #G1
2007 Press Pass Eclipse Gold /25 #G35
2007 Press Pass Eclipse Gold /25 #G50
2007 Press Pass Eclipse Gold /25 #G69
2007 Press Pass Eclipse Gold /25 #G71
2007 Press Pass Eclipse Gold /25 #G72
2007 Press Pass Eclipse Gold /25 #G73
2007 Press Pass Eclipse Gold /25 #G79
2007 Press Pass Eclipse Hyperdrive #HD5
2007 Press Pass Eclipse Previews /5 #EB1
2007 Press Pass Eclipse Previews /5 #EB35
2007 Press Pass Eclipse Racing Champions #RC3
2007 Press Pass Eclipse Red /1 #R1
2007 Press Pass Eclipse Red /1 #R35
2007 Press Pass Eclipse Red /1 #R50
2007 Press Pass Eclipse Red /1 #R69
2007 Press Pass Eclipse Red /1 #R71
2007 Press Pass Eclipse Red /1 #R72
2007 Press Pass Eclipse Red /1 #R73
2007 Press Pass Eclipse Red /1 #R79
2007 Press Pass Eclipse Skidmarks #SM6
2007 Press Pass Eclipse Skidmarks Holofoil /250 #SM6
2007 Press Pass Eclipse Teammates Autographs /25 #7
2007 Press Pass Eclipse Under Cover Autographs /48 #UCJJ
2007 Press Pass Eclipse Under Cover Double Cover Name /25 #DC3
2007 Press Pass Eclipse Under Cover Double Cover NASCAR /99 #DC3
2007 Press Pass Eclipse Under Cover Drivers /450 #UCD7
2007 Press Pass Eclipse Under Cover Drivers Eclipse /1 #UCD7
2007 Press Pass Eclipse Under Cover Drivers Name /99 #UCD7
2007 Press Pass Eclipse Under Cover Drivers NASCAR /270 #UCD7
2007 Press Pass Eclipse Under Cover Teams /135 #UCT7
2007 Press Pass Eclipse Under Cover Teams NASCAR /25 #UCT7
2007 Press Pass Four Wide /50 #FWJJ
2007 Press Pass Four Wide Checkered Flag /1 #FWJJ
2007 Press Pass Four Wide Checkered Flag Exchange /1 #FWJJ
2007 Press Pass Four Wide Exchange /50 #FWJJ
2007 Press Pass Gold #G2
2007 Press Pass Gold #G77
2007 Press Pass Gold #G94
2007 Press Pass Gold #G96
2007 Press Pass Gold #G109
2007 Press Pass Gold #G120
2007 Press Pass Hot Treads #HT4
2007 Press Pass Hot Treads Blue /99 #HT4
2007 Press Pass Hot Treads Gold /299 #HT4
2007 Press Pass K-Mart #JJC
2007 Press Pass Legends #43
2007 Press Pass Legends Autographs Blue /71 #15
2007 Press Pass Legends Blue /999 #B43
2007 Press Pass Legends Bronze /599 #Z43
2007 Press Pass Legends Gold /249 #G43
2007 Press Pass Legends Holofoil /99 #H43
2007 Press Pass Legends Press Plates Black /1 #PP43
2007 Press Pass Legends Press Plates Black Backs /1 #PP43
2007 Press Pass Legends Press Plates Cyan /1 #PP43
2007 Press Pass Legends Press Plates Cyan Backs /1 #PP43
2007 Press Pass Legends Press Plates Magenta /1 #PP43
2007 Press Pass Legends Press Plates Magenta Backs /1 #PP43
2007 Press Pass Legends Press Plates Yellow /1 #PP43
2007 Press Pass Legends Press Plates Yellow Backs /1 #PP43
2007 Press Pass Legends Previews /5 #EB43
2007 Press Pass Legends Signature Series /25 #JJ
2007 Press Pass Legends Solo /1 #S43
2007 Press Pass Legends Sunday Swatches Bronze /199 #JJSS
2007 Press Pass Legends Sunday Swatches Gold /50 #JJSS
2007 Press Pass Legends Sunday Swatches Silver /99 #JJSS
2007 Press Pass Legends Victory Lane Bronze /199 #VL6
2007 Press Pass Legends Victory Lane Gold /25 #VL6
2007 Press Pass Legends Victory Lane Silver /99 #VL6
2007 Press Pass Platinum /100 #P2
2007 Press Pass Platinum /100 #P77
2007 Press Pass Platinum /100 #P94
2007 Press Pass Platinum /100 #P96
2007 Press Pass Platinum /100 #P109
2007 Press Pass Platinum /100 #PCL
2007 Press Pass Premium #1
2007 Press Pass Premium #30
2007 Press Pass Premium #45
2007 Press Pass Premium #59
2007 Press Pass Premium #62
2007 Press Pass Premium #71
2007 Press Pass Premium #82
2007 Press Pass Premium Concrete Chaos #CC3
2007 Press Pass Premium Hot Threads Autographs /48 #HTJJ
2007 Press Pass Premium Hot Threads Drivers /145 #HTD15
2007 Press Pass Premium Hot Threads Drivers Gold /1 #HTD15
2007 Press Pass Premium Hot Threads Patch /10 #HTP12
2007 Press Pass Premium Hot Threads Patch /15 #HTP11
2007 Press Pass Premium Hot Threads Team /160 #HTT15
2007 Press Pass Premium Performance Driven #PD6
2007 Press Pass Premium Performance Driven Red /250 #PD6
2007 Press Pass Premium Red /15 #R1
2007 Press Pass Premium Red /15 #R30
2007 Press Pass Premium Red /15 #R45
2007 Press Pass Premium Red /15 #R59
2007 Press Pass Premium Red /15 #R62
2007 Press Pass Premium Red /5 #R71
2007 Press Pass Premium Red /5 #R82
2007 Press Pass Previews /5 #EB2
2007 Press Pass Previews /1 #EB109
2007 Press Pass Race Day #RD5
2007 Press Pass Signings #32
2007 Press Pass Signings Blue /25 #13
2007 Press Pass Signings Gold /50 #25
2007 Press Pass Signings Press Plates Black /1 #22
2007 Press Pass Signings Press Plates Cyan /1 #21
2007 Press Pass Signings Press Plates Magenta /1 #23
2007 Press Pass Signings Press Plates Yellow /1 #21
2007 Press Pass Signings Silver /100 #24
2007 Press Pass Snapshots #SN13
2007 Press Pass Stealth #12
2007 Press Pass Stealth #54
2007 Press Pass Stealth #63
2007 Press Pass Stealth #72
2007 Press Pass Stealth #83
2007 Press Pass Stealth Battle Armor Autographs /48 #BASJJ
2007 Press Pass Stealth Battle Armor Drivers /150 #BAD8
2007 Press Pass Stealth Battle Armor Teams /85 #BAT8
2007 Press Pass Stealth Chrome #12
2007 Press Pass Stealth Chrome #54
2007 Press Pass Stealth Chrome #63A
2007 Press Pass Stealth Chrome #72
2007 Press Pass Stealth Chrome #83
2007 Press Pass Stealth Chrome #63B
2007 Press Pass Stealth Chrome Exclusives /99 #X12
2007 Press Pass Stealth Chrome Exclusives /99 #X54
2007 Press Pass Stealth Chrome Exclusives /99 #X63
2007 Press Pass Stealth Chrome Exclusives /99 #X72
2007 Press Pass Stealth Chrome Exclusives /99 #X83
2007 Press Pass Stealth Chrome Platinum /25 #P12
2007 Press Pass Stealth Chrome Platinum /25 #P54
2007 Press Pass Stealth Chrome Platinum /25 #P63
2007 Press Pass Stealth Chrome Platinum /25 #P72
2007 Press Pass Stealth Chrome Platinum /25 #P83
2007 Press Pass Stealth Fusion #F5
2007 Press Pass Stealth Mach 07 #M7-6
2007 Press Pass Stealth Maximum Access #MA13
2007 Press Pass Stealth Maximum Access Autographs /25 #MA13
2007 Press Pass Stealth Previews /1 #EB83
2007 Press Pass Stealth Previews /5 #EB12
2007 Press Pass Target #JJB
2007 Press Pass Target Race Win Tires #RW1
2007 Press Pass Velocity #V2
2007 Press Pass Wal-Mart #JJA
2007 Sunoco OCC Postcards #JJ
2007 Traks #12
2007 Traks #62
2007 Traks #71
2007 Traks #81
2007 Traks #89
2007 Traks #96
2007 Traks Driver's Seat #DS8B
2007 Traks Driver's Seat #DS8
2007 Traks Driver's Seat National #DS8
2007 Traks Gold #G12
2007 Traks Gold #G62
2007 Traks Gold #G71
2007 Traks Gold #G81
2007 Traks Gold #G89
2007 Traks Gold #G96
2007 Traks Holofoil /50 #H12
2007 Traks Holofoil /50 #H62
2007 Traks Holofoil /50 #H71
2007 Traks Holofoil /50 #H81
2007 Traks Holofoil /50 #H89
2007 Traks Holofoil /50 #H96
2007 Traks Hot Pursuit #HP7
2007 Traks Previews /5 #EB12
2007 Traks Previews /1 #EB81
2007 Traks Red /10 #R12
2007 Traks Red /10 #R62
2007 Traks Red /10 #R71
2007 Traks Red /10 #R81
2007 Traks Red /10 #R89
2007 Traks Red /10 #R96
2007 Traks Target Exclusives #JJA
2007 Traks Track Time #TT4
2007 Traks Wal-Mart Exclusives #JJB
2007 VIP #14
2007 VIP #55
2007 VIP #60
2007 VIP #71
2007 VIP #72
2007 VIP #74
2007 VIP #78
2007 VIP Gear Gallery #GG10
2007 VIP Gear Gallery Transparent #GG10
2007 VIP Get A Grip Drivers /70 #GGD29
2007 VIP Get A Grip Teams /70 #GGT29
2007 VIP Previews /5 #EB14
2007 VIP Sunday Best #SB11
2007 VIP Trophy Club #TC3
2007 VIP Trophy Club Transparent #TC3
2007 Wheels American Thunder #14
2007 Wheels American Thunder #48
2007 Wheels American Thunder #54
2007 Wheels American Thunder American Dreams #AD3
2007 Wheels American Thunder American Dreams Gold /250 #ADG3
2007 Wheels American Thunder American Muscle #AM4
2007 Wheels American Thunder Autographed Hat Instant Winner /1 #AH15
2007 Wheels American Thunder Cool Threads /299 #CT16
2007 Wheels American Thunder Previews /5 #EB14
2007 Wheels American Thunder Previews /1 #EB54
2007 Wheels American Thunder Pushin' Pedal /99 #PP14
2007 Wheels American Thunder Starting Grid #SG5
2007 Wheels American Thunder Thunder Road #TR1
2007 Wheels American Thunder Thunder Strokes #21
2007 Wheels American Thunder Thunder Strokes Press Plates Black /1 #21
2007 Wheels American Thunder Thunder Strokes Press Plates Cyan /1 #21
2007 Wheels American Thunder Thunder Strokes Press Plates Magenta /1 #21
2007 Wheels American Thunder Thunder Strokes Press Plates Yellow /1 #21
2007 Wheels American Thunder Triple Hat /99 #TH13
2007 Wheels Autographs #17
2007 Wheels Autographs Press Plates Black /1 #16
2007 Wheels Autographs Press Plates Cyan /1 #16
2007 Wheels Autographs Press Plates Magenta /1 #16
2007 Wheels High Gear #0
2007 Wheels High Gear #1
2007 Wheels High Gear #56
2007 Wheels High Gear #73A
2007 Wheels High Gear #73B
2007 Wheels High Gear Driven #DR4
2007 Wheels High Gear Final Standings Gold /1 #FS1
2007 Wheels High Gear Flag Chasers Black /89 #FC5
2007 Wheels High Gear Flag Chasers Blue-Yellow /50 #FC5
2007 Wheels High Gear Flag Chasers Checkered /10 #FC5
2007 Wheels High Gear Flag Chasers Green /89 #FC5
2007 Wheels High Gear Flag Chasers Red /89 #FC5
2007 Wheels High Gear Flag Chasers White /89 #FC5
2007 Wheels High Gear Flag Chasers Yellow /89 #FC5
2007 Wheels High Gear Full Throttle #FT6
2007 Wheels High Gear Last Lap /10 #LL3
2007 Wheels High Gear MPH /100 #M1
2007 Wheels High Gear MPH /100 #M56
2007 Wheels High Gear MPH /100 #M73
2007 Wheels High Gear Previews /5 #EB1
2007 Wheels High Gear Previews /5 #EB56
2007 Wheels High Gear Top Tier #TT1
2008 Press Pass #0
2008 Press Pass #6
2008 Press Pass #68
2008 Press Pass #81
2008 Press Pass #107
2008 Press Pass Autographs #20
2008 Press Pass Autographs Press Plates Black /1 #16
2008 Press Pass Autographs Press Plates Cyan /1 #16
2008 Press Pass Autographs Press Plates Magenta /1 #16
2008 Press Pass Autographs Press Plates Yellow /1 #16

2008 Press Pass Blue #B6
2008 Press Pass Blue #B68
2008 Press Pass Blue #B81
2008 Press Pass Blue #B107
2008 Press Pass Burning Rubber Drivers /60 #BRD3
2008 Press Pass Burning Rubber Drivers /60 #BRD4
2008 Press Pass Burning Rubber Drivers /60 #BRD6
2008 Press Pass Burning Rubber Drivers /60 #BRD10
2008 Press Pass Burning Rubber Drivers /60 #BRD24
2008 Press Pass Burning Rubber Drivers /60 #BRD25
2008 Press Pass Burning Rubber Drivers Gold /1 #BRD3
2008 Press Pass Burning Rubber Drivers Gold /1 #BRD4
2008 Press Pass Burning Rubber Drivers Gold /1 #BRD6
2008 Press Pass Burning Rubber Drivers Gold /1 #BRD10
2008 Press Pass Burning Rubber Drivers Gold /1 #BRD24
2008 Press Pass Burning Rubber Drivers Gold /1 #BRD25
2008 Press Pass Burning Rubber Drivers Prime Cuts /25 #BRD3
2008 Press Pass Burning Rubber Drivers Prime Cuts /25 #BRD4
2008 Press Pass Burning Rubber Drivers Prime Cuts /25 #BRD6
2008 Press Pass Burning Rubber Drivers Prime Cuts /25 #BRD10
2008 Press Pass Burning Rubber Drivers Prime Cuts /25 #BRD24
2008 Press Pass Burning Rubber Drivers Prime Cuts /25 #BRD25
2008 Press Pass Burning Rubber Teams /175 #BRT3
2008 Press Pass Burning Rubber Teams /175 #BRT4
2008 Press Pass Burning Rubber Teams /175 #BRT6
2008 Press Pass Burning Rubber Teams /175 #BRT10
2008 Press Pass Burning Rubber Teams /175 #BRT24
2008 Press Pass Burning Rubber Teams /175 #BRT25
2008 Press Pass Burnouts #B07
2008 Press Pass Burnouts Blue /99 #B07
2008 Press Pass Burnouts Gold /299 #B07
2008 Press Pass Collector's Series Box Set #3
2008 Press Pass Cup Chase #CC14
2008 Press Pass Cup Chase Prizes #CCJJ
2008 Press Pass Cup Chase Prizes #CC1
2008 Press Pass Daytona 500 50th Anniversary #43
2008 Press Pass Double Burner Firesuit-Glove /100 #DBJJ
2008 Press Pass Double Burner Metal-Tire /100 #DBJJ
2008 Press Pass Eclipse #1
2008 Press Pass Eclipse #30
2008 Press Pass Eclipse #37B
2008 Press Pass Eclipse #51
2008 Press Pass Eclipse #52
2008 Press Pass Eclipse #53
2008 Press Pass Eclipse #64
2008 Press Pass Eclipse #73
2008 Press Pass Eclipse #75
2008 Press Pass Eclipse #81
2008 Press Pass Eclipse #37A
2008 Press Pass Eclipse Escape Velocity #EV7
2008 Press Pass Eclipse Gold /25 #G1
2008 Press Pass Eclipse Gold /25 #G30
2008 Press Pass Eclipse Gold /25 #G37
2008 Press Pass Eclipse Gold /25 #G51
2008 Press Pass Eclipse Gold /25 #G52
2008 Press Pass Eclipse Gold /25 #G53
2008 Press Pass Eclipse Gold /25 #G64
2008 Press Pass Eclipse Gold /25 #G73
2008 Press Pass Eclipse Gold /25 #G75
2008 Press Pass Eclipse Gold /25 #G81
2008 Press Pass Eclipse Hyperdrive #HP8
2008 Press Pass Eclipse Previews /5 #EB1
2008 Press Pass Eclipse Previews /5 #EB30
2008 Press Pass Eclipse Previews /1 #EB73
2008 Press Pass Eclipse Previews /1 #EB75
2008 Press Pass Eclipse Previews /1 #EB81
2008 Press Pass Eclipse Red /1 #R1
2008 Press Pass Eclipse Red /1 #R30
2008 Press Pass Eclipse Red /1 #R37
2008 Press Pass Eclipse Red /1 #R51
2008 Press Pass Eclipse Red /1 #R52
2008 Press Pass Eclipse Red /1 #R53
2008 Press Pass Eclipse Red /1 #R64
2008 Press Pass Eclipse Red /1 #R73
2008 Press Pass Eclipse Red /1 #R75
2008 Press Pass Eclipse Red /1 #R81
2008 Press Pass Eclipse Star Tracks #ST10
2008 Press Pass Eclipse Star Tracks Holofoil /250 #ST10
2008 Press Pass Eclipse Stellar #ST1
2008 Press Pass Eclipse Teammates Autographs /25 #EJ
2008 Press Pass Eclipse Teammates Autographs /25 #EGJM
2008 Press Pass Eclipse Under Cover Autographs /48 #UCJJ
2008 Press Pass Eclipse Under Cover Double Cover Name /25 #DC6
2008 Press Pass Eclipse Under Cover Double Cover NASCAR /99 #DC6
2008 Press Pass Eclipse Under Cover Drivers /250 #UCD14
2008 Press Pass Eclipse Under Cover Drivers Eclipse /1 #UCD14
2008 Press Pass Eclipse Under Cover Drivers Name /50 #UCD14
2008 Press Pass Eclipse Under Cover Drivers NASCAR /150 #UCD14
2008 Press Pass Eclipse Under Cover Teams /99 #UCT14
2008 Press Pass Eclipse Under Cover Teams NASCAR /25 #UCT14
2008 Press Pass Four Wide /50 #FWJJ
2008 Press Pass Four Wide Checkered Flag /1 #FWJJ
2008 Press Pass Gold #G6
2008 Press Pass Gold #G68
2008 Press Pass Gold #G81
2008 Press Pass Gold #G107
2008 Press Pass Hot Treads #HT3
2008 Press Pass Hot Treads Blue /99 #HT3
2008 Press Pass Hot Treads Gold /299 #HT3
2008 Press Pass Legends #51
2008 Press Pass Legends Autographs Black Inscriptions /10 #JJ
2008 Press Pass Legends Autographs Blue /75 #JJ
2008 Press Pass Legends Autographs Press Plates Black /1 #JJ
2008 Press Pass Legends Autographs Press Plates Cyan /1 #JJ
2008 Press Pass Legends Autographs Press Plates Magenta /1 #JJ
2008 Press Pass Legends Autographs Press Plates Yellow /1 #JJ
2008 Press Pass Legends Blue /599 #51
2008 Press Pass Legends Bronze /299 #51
2008 Press Pass Legends Gold /99 #51
2008 Press Pass Legends Holo /25 #51
2008 Press Pass Legends Previews /5 #EB51
2008 Press Pass Legends Printing Plates Black /1 #51
2008 Press Pass Legends Printing Plates Cyan /1 #51
2008 Press Pass Legends Printing Plates Magenta /1 #51
2008 Press Pass Legends Printing Plates Yellow /1 #51
2008 Press Pass Legends Prominent Pieces Firesuit-Glove Bronze /50 #PP1JJ
2008 Press Pass Legends Prominent Pieces Firesuit-Glove Gold /10 #PP1JJ
2008 Press Pass Legends Prominent Pieces Firesuit-Glove Silver /25 #PP1JJ
2008 Press Pass Legends Prominent Pieces Metal-Tire Bronze /99 #PP3JJ
2008 Press Pass Legends Prominent Pieces Metal-Tire Gold /25 #PP3JJ
2008 Press Pass Legends Prominent Pieces Metal-Tire Silver /50 #PP3JJ
2008 Press Pass Legends Signature Series Memorabilia /25 #LSJJ
2008 Press Pass Legends Solo /1 #51
2008 Press Pass Legends Victory Lane Bronze /99 #VLJJ
2008 Press Pass Legends Victory Lane Gold /25 #VLJJ
2008 Press Pass Legends Victory Lane Silver /50 #VLJJ
2008 Press Pass Platinum /100 #P6
2008 Press Pass Platinum /100 #P68
2008 Press Pass Platinum /100 #P81
2008 Press Pass Platinum /100 #P107
2008 Press Pass Premium #29
2008 Press Pass Premium #41
2008 Press Pass Premium #50
2008 Press Pass Premium #55
2008 Press Pass Premium #69
2008 Press Pass Premium #74
2008 Press Pass Premium #83
2008 Press Pass Premium Clean Air #CA10
2008 Press Pass Premium Hot Threads Drivers /120 #HTD4
2008 Press Pass Premium Hot Threads Drivers Gold /1 #HTD4
2008 Press Pass Premium Hot Threads Patches /6 #HTP17
2008 Press Pass Premium Hot Threads Patches /6 #HTP16
2008 Press Pass Premium Hot Threads Patches /8 #HTP15
2008 Press Pass Premium Hot Threads Team /120 #HTT4
2008 Press Pass Premium Previews /5 #EB29
2008 Press Pass Premium Previews /1 #EB55
2008 Press Pass Premium Red /15 #29
2008 Press Pass Premium Red /15 #41
2008 Press Pass Premium Red /15 #50
2008 Press Pass Premium Red /15 #55
2008 Press Pass Premium Red /15 #69
2008 Press Pass Premium Red /5 #74
2008 Press Pass Premium Red /5 #83
2008 Press Pass Premium Team Signed Baseballs #HMS
2008 Press Pass Premium Team Signed Baseballs #EHMS
2008 Press Pass Premium Wal-Mart #WM2
2008 Press Pass Previews /5 #EB6
2008 Press Pass Previews /1 #EB107
2008 Press Pass Signings #31
2008 Press Pass Signings Blue /25 #13
2008 Press Pass Signings Gold /50 #27
2008 Press Pass Signings Press Plates Black /1 #21
2008 Press Pass Signings Press Plates Cyan /1 #21
2008 Press Pass Signings Press Plates Magenta /1 #21
2008 Press Pass Signings Press Plates Magenta /1 #JJ
2008 Press Pass Signings Press Plates Yellow /1 #21
2008 Press Pass Slideshow #SS6
2008 Press Pass Speedway #7
2008 Press Pass Speedway #71
2008 Press Pass Speedway #88
2008 Press Pass Speedway Blur #B1
2008 Press Pass Speedway Cockpit #CP10
2008 Press Pass Speedway Garage Graphs Duals /50 #JK
2008 Press Pass Speedway Gold #G7
2008 Press Pass Speedway Gold #G71
2008 Press Pass Speedway Gold #G88
2008 Press Pass Speedway Holofoil /50 #H7
2008 Press Pass Speedway Holofoil /50 #H71
2008 Press Pass Speedway Holofoil /50 #H88
2008 Press Pass Speedway Previews /5 #EB7
2008 Press Pass Speedway Red /10 #R7
2008 Press Pass Speedway Red /10 #R71
2008 Press Pass Speedway Red /10 #R88
2008 Press Pass Speedway Test Drive #TD11
2008 Press Pass Starting Grid #SG3
2008 Press Pass Stealth #16
2008 Press Pass Stealth #63
2008 Press Pass Stealth #67
2008 Press Pass Stealth #90
2008 Press Pass Stealth Battle Armor Autographs /48 #BASJJ
2008 Press Pass Stealth Battle Armor Drivers /120 #BAD15
2008 Press Pass Stealth Battle Armor Teams /115 #BAT15
2008 Press Pass Stealth Chrome #16
2008 Press Pass Stealth Chrome #63A
2008 Press Pass Stealth Chrome #67
2008 Press Pass Stealth Chrome #90
2008 Press Pass Stealth Chrome #63B
2008 Press Pass Stealth Chrome Exclusives /25 #16
2008 Press Pass Stealth Chrome Exclusives /25 #63
2008 Press Pass Stealth Chrome Exclusives /25 #67
2008 Press Pass Stealth Chrome Exclusives /25 #90
2008 Press Pass Stealth Chrome Exclusives Gold /99 #16
2008 Press Pass Stealth Chrome Exclusives Gold /99 #63
2008 Press Pass Stealth Chrome Exclusives Gold /99 #67
2008 Press Pass Stealth Chrome Exclusives Gold /99 #90
2008 Press Pass Stealth Mach 08 #M8-4
2008 Press Pass Stealth Maximum Access #MA14
2008 Press Pass Stealth Maximum Access Autographs /25 #MA14
2008 Press Pass Stealth Previews /5 #16
2008 Press Pass Stealth Previews /1 #90
2008 Press Pass Stealth Synthesis #S1
2008 Press Pass Stealth Target #TA8
2008 Press Pass Target #JJB
2008 Press Pass Target Victory Tires /50 #TTJJ
2008 Press Pass VIP National Convention Promo #1
2008 Press Pass Wal-Mart #JJA
2008 Press Pass Wal-Mart Autographs /50 #6
2008 Press Pass Weekend Warriors #WW8
2008 VIP #16
2008 VIP #44
2008 VIP #56
2008 VIP #72
2008 VIP #82
2008 VIP All Access #AA10
2008 VIP Gear Gallery #GG5
2008 VIP Gear Gallery Memorabilia /50 #GGJJ
2008 VIP Gear Gallery Transparent #GG5
2008 VIP Get a Grip Drivers /80 #GGD12
2008 VIP Get a Grip Teams /99 #GGT12
2008 VIP National Promos #1
2008 VIP Previews /5 #EB16
2008 VIP Previews /1 #EB82
2008 VIP Triple Grip /25 #TG1
2008 VIP Trophy Club #TC3
2008 VIP Trophy Club Transparent #TC3
2008 Wheels American Thunder #15
2008 Wheels American Thunder #41
2008 Wheels American Thunder #59
2008 Wheels American Thunder #81
2008 Wheels American Thunder #83
2008 Wheels American Thunder American Dreams #AD11
2008 Wheels American Thunder American Dreams Gold /250 #AD11
2008 Wheels American Thunder Autographed Hat Winner /1 #IWHJJ
2008 Wheels American Thunder Campaign Buttons #JJ
2008 Wheels American Thunder Campaign Buttons Blue #JJ
2008 Wheels American Thunder Campaign Buttons Gold #JJ
2008 Wheels American Thunder Campaign Trail #CT3
2008 Wheels American Thunder Delegates #D8
2008 Wheels American Thunder Motorcade #M3
2008 Wheels American Thunder Previews /5 #15
2008 Wheels American Thunder Previews /1 #81
2008 Wheels American Thunder Trackside Treasury Autographs #JJ
2008 Wheels American Thunder Trackside Treasury Autographs Gold /25 #JJ
2008 Wheels American Thunder Trackside Treasury Autographs Printing Plates Black /1 #JJ
2008 Wheels American Thunder Trackside Treasury Autographs Printing Plates Cyan /1 #JJ
2008 Wheels American Thunder Trackside Treasury Autographs Printing Plates Magenta /1 #JJ
2008 Wheels American Thunder Trackside Treasury Autographs Printing Plates Yellow /1 #JJ
2008 Wheels American Thunder Triple Hat /125 #TH12
2008 Wheels Autographs #16
2008 Wheels Autographs Chase Edition /25 #6
2008 Wheels Autographs Press Plates Black /1 #16
2008 Wheels Autographs Press Plates Cyan /1 #16
2008 Wheels Autographs Press Plates Magenta /1 #16
2008 Wheels Autographs Press Plates Yellow /1 #16
2008 Wheels High Gear #0
2008 Wheels High Gear #1A
2008 Wheels High Gear #55
2008 Wheels High Gear #61
2008 Wheels High Gear #71
2008 Wheels High Gear #78
2008 Wheels High Gear #1B
2008 Wheels High Gear Driven #DR1
2008 Wheels High Gear Final Standings /1 #F1
2008 Wheels High Gear Flag Chasers Black /89 #FC6
2008 Wheels High Gear Flag Chasers Blue-Yellow /50 #FC6
2008 Wheels High Gear Flag Chasers Checkered /20 #FC6
2008 Wheels High Gear Flag Chasers Green /60 #FC6
2008 Wheels High Gear Flag Chasers Red /89 #FC6
2008 Wheels High Gear Flag Chasers White /65 #FC6
2008 Wheels High Gear Flag Chasers Yellow /89 #FC6
2008 Wheels High Gear Full Throttle #FT7
2008 Wheels High Gear Last Lap /10 #LL4
2008 Wheels High Gear Last Lap Holofoil /5 #LL4
2008 Wheels High Gear MPH /100 #M1
2008 Wheels High Gear MPH /100 #M55
2008 Wheels High Gear MPH /100 #M61
2008 Wheels High Gear MPH /100 #M71
2008 Wheels High Gear MPH /100 #M78
2008 Wheels High Gear Previews /5 #EB1
2008 Wheels High Gear The Chase #TC1
2009 Element #14
2009 Element #54
2009 Element #56
2009 Element #91
2009 Element Big Win /35 #BWJJ
2009 Element Elements of the Race Black Flag /99 #ERBJJ
2009 Element Elements of the Race Black-White Flag /50 #ERXJJ
2009 Element Elements of the Race Blue-Yellow Flag /50 #ERBOJJ
2009 Element Elements of the Race Checkered Flag /5 #ERCJJ
2009 Element Elements of the Race Green Flag /50 #ERGJJ
2009 Element Elements of the Race Red Flag /99 #ERRJJ
2009 Element Elements of the Race White Flag /75 #ERWJJ
2009 Element Elements of the Race Yellow Flag /99 #ERYJJ
2009 Element Jimmie Johnson 3-Time Champ Tires /48 #JJ1
2009 Element Jimmie Johnson 3-Time Champ Tires /48 #JJ2
2009 Element Jimmie Johnson 3-Time Champ Tires /48 #JJ3
2009 Element Kinetic Energy #KE6
2009 Element Kinetic Energy #KE12
2009 Element Lab Report #LR14
2009 Element Nobel Prize #NP6
2009 Element Previews /5 #14
2009 Element Previews /1 #54
2009 Element Radioactive /100 #14
2009 Element Radioactive /100 #54
2009 Element Radioactive /100 #56
2009 Element Radioactive /100 #91
2009 Press Pass #0
2009 Press Pass #3
2009 Press Pass #59
2009 Press Pass #72
2009 Press Pass #76
2009 Press Pass #109
2009 Press Pass #CL
2009 Press Pass #134
2009 Press Pass #186
2009 Press Pass #187
2009 Press Pass #188
2009 Press Pass #190
2009 Press Pass #191
2009 Press Pass #193
2009 Press Pass #197
2009 Press Pass #200
2009 Press Pass #210
2009 Press Pass Autographs Chase Edition /25 #JJ
2009 Press Pass Autographs Gold #22
2009 Press Pass Autographs Printing Plates Black /1 #21
2009 Press Pass Autographs Printing Plates Cyan /1 #21
2009 Press Pass Autographs Printing Plates Magenta /1 #21
2009 Press Pass Autographs Printing Plates Yellow /1 #21
2009 Press Pass Autographs Silver #25
2009 Press Pass Autographs Track Edition /25 #JJ
2009 Press Pass Blue #3
2009 Press Pass Blue #59
2009 Press Pass Blue #72
2009 Press Pass Blue #76
2009 Press Pass Blue #109
2009 Press Pass Blue #CL
2009 Press Pass Blue #134
2009 Press Pass Blue #186
2009 Press Pass Blue #187
2009 Press Pass Blue #188
2009 Press Pass Blue #190
2009 Press Pass Blue #191
2009 Press Pass Blue #193
2009 Press Pass Blue #197
2009 Press Pass Blue #200
2009 Press Pass Blue #210
2009 Press Pass Burning Rubber Autographs /48 #BRSJJ
2009 Press Pass Burning Rubber Drivers /185 #BRD8
2009 Press Pass Burning Rubber Drivers /185 #BRD20
2009 Press Pass Burning Rubber Drivers /185 #BRD25
2009 Press Pass Burning Rubber Drivers /185 #BRD26
2009 Press Pass Burning Rubber Drivers /320 #BRD29
2009 Press Pass Burning Rubber Drivers /320 #BRD32
2009 Press Pass Burning Rubber Drivers /320 #BRD35
2009 Press Pass Burning Rubber Drivers /320 #BRDCH
2009 Press Pass Burning Rubber Prime Cut /25 #BRD8
2009 Press Pass Burning Rubber Prime Cut /25 #BRD20
2009 Press Pass Burning Rubber Prime Cut /25 #BRD25
2009 Press Pass Burning Rubber Prime Cut /25 #BRD26
2009 Press Pass Burning Rubber Prime Cut /25 #BRD29
2009 Press Pass Burning Rubber Prime Cut /25 #BRD32
2009 Press Pass Burning Rubber Prime Cut /25 #BRD35
2009 Press Pass Burning Rubber Prime Cut /25 #BRDCH
2009 Press Pass Burning Rubber Teams /250 #BRT8
2009 Press Pass Burning Rubber Teams /250 #BRT20
2009 Press Pass Burning Rubber Teams /250 #BRT25
2009 Press Pass Burning Rubber Teams /250 #BRT26
2009 Press Pass Burning Rubber Teams /85 #BRT29
2009 Press Pass Burning Rubber Teams /85 #BRT32
2009 Press Pass Burning Rubber Teams /85 #BRT35
2009 Press Pass Burning Rubber Teams /85 #BRTCH
2009 Press Pass Chase for the Sprint Cup #CC3
2009 Press Pass Cup Chase #CCR1
2009 Press Pass Cup Chase Prizes #CC3
2009 Press Pass Cup Chase Prizes #CCJJ
2009 Press Pass Daytona 500 Tires /25 #TTJJ
2009 Press Pass Eclipse #22
2009 Press Pass Eclipse #34
2009 Press Pass Eclipse #40
2009 Press Pass Eclipse #46
2009 Press Pass Eclipse #58
2009 Press Pass Eclipse #70
2009 Press Pass Eclipse #77
2009 Press Pass Eclipse #85
2009 Press Pass Eclipse #88
2009 Press Pass Eclipse #90
2009 Press Pass Eclipse Black and White #22
2009 Press Pass Eclipse Black and White #34
2009 Press Pass Eclipse Black and White #40
2009 Press Pass Eclipse Black and White #46
2009 Press Pass Eclipse Black and White #58
2009 Press Pass Eclipse Black and White #70
2009 Press Pass Eclipse Black and White #77
2009 Press Pass Eclipse Black and White #85
2009 Press Pass Eclipse Black and White #88
2009 Press Pass Eclipse Black and White #90
2009 Press Pass Eclipse Black Hole Firesuits /50 #BH4
2009 Press Pass Eclipse Blue #22
2009 Press Pass Eclipse Blue #34
2009 Press Pass Eclipse Blue #40
2009 Press Pass Eclipse Blue #46
2009 Press Pass Eclipse Blue #58
2009 Press Pass Eclipse Blue #70
2009 Press Pass Eclipse Blue #77
2009 Press Pass Eclipse Blue #85
2009 Press Pass Eclipse Blue #88
2009 Press Pass Eclipse Blue #90
2009 Press Pass Eclipse Ecliptic Path #EP5
2009 Press Pass Eclipse Solar Swatches /99 #SSJJ1
2009 Press Pass Eclipse Solar Swatches /65 #SSJJ3
2009 Press Pass Eclipse Solar Swatches /200 #SSJJ4
2009 Press Pass Eclipse Solar Swatches /50 #SSJJ5
2009 Press Pass Eclipse Solar Swatches /200 #SSJJ6
2009 Press Pass Eclipse Solar Swatches /200 #SSJJ2
2009 Press Pass Eclipse Solar Swatches /200 #SSJJ7
2009 Press Pass Eclipse Solar System #SS1
2009 Press Pass Eclipse Under Cover Autographs /48 #UCSJJ
2009 Press Pass Final Standings /48 #109
2009 Press Pass Four Wide Autographs /2 #FWJJ
2009 Press Pass Four Wide Checkered Flag /1 #FWJJ
2009 Press Pass Four Wide Firesuit /50 #FWJJ
2009 Press Pass Four Wide Sheet Metal /10 #FWJJ
2009 Press Pass Four Wide Tire /25 #FWJJ
2009 Press Pass Freeze Frame #FF9
2009 Press Pass Freeze Frame #FF29
2009 Press Pass Fusion #70
2009 Press Pass Fusion Bronze /150 #70
2009 Press Pass Fusion Gold /50 #70
2009 Press Pass Fusion Green /25 #70
2009 Press Pass Fusion Onyx /1 #70
2009 Press Pass Fusion Revered Relics Gold /50 #RRJJ
2009 Press Pass Fusion Revered Relics Holofoil /25 #RRJJ
2009 Press Pass Fusion Revered Relics Premium Swatch /10 #RRJJ
2009 Press Pass Fusion Revered Relics Silver /65 #RRJJ
2009 Press Pass Fusion Silver /99 #70
2009 Press Pass Game Face #GF5
2009 Press Pass Gold #3
2009 Press Pass Gold #59
2009 Press Pass Gold #72
2009 Press Pass Gold #76
2009 Press Pass Gold #109
2009 Press Pass Gold #CL
2009 Press Pass Gold #134
2009 Press Pass Gold #186
2009 Press Pass Gold #187
2009 Press Pass Gold #188
2009 Press Pass Gold #190
2009 Press Pass Gold #191
2009 Press Pass Gold #193
2009 Press Pass Gold #197
2009 Press Pass Gold #200
2009 Press Pass Gold #210
2009 Press Pass Gold Holofoil /100 #3
2009 Press Pass Gold Holofoil /100 #59
2009 Press Pass Gold Holofoil /100 #72
2009 Press Pass Gold Holofoil /100 #76
2009 Press Pass Gold Holofoil /100 #109
2009 Press Pass Gold Holofoil /100 #CL
2009 Press Pass Gold Holofoil /100 #134
2009 Press Pass Gold Holofoil /100 #186
2009 Press Pass Gold Holofoil /100 #187
2009 Press Pass Gold Holofoil /100 #188
2009 Press Pass Gold Holofoil /100 #190
2009 Press Pass Gold Holofoil /100 #191
2009 Press Pass Gold Holofoil /100 #193
2009 Press Pass Gold Holofoil /100 #197
2009 Press Pass Gold Holofoil /100 #200
2009 Press Pass Gold Holofoil /100 #210
2009 Press Pass Legends #48
2009 Press Pass Legends Autographs Gold /35 #18
2009 Press Pass Legends Autographs Holofoil #17
2009 Press Pass Legends Gold /399 #48
2009 Press Pass Legends Holofoil /50 #48
2009 Press Pass Legends Past and Present /550 #PP3
2009 Press Pass Legends Past and Present /550 #PP11
2009 Press Pass Legends Past and Present Holofoil /99 #PP3
2009 Press Pass Legends Past and Present Holofoil /99 #PP11
2009 Press Pass Legends Previews /5 #48
2009 Press Pass Legends Printing Plates Black /1 #48
2009 Press Pass Legends Printing Plates Cyan /1 #48
2009 Press Pass Legends Printing Plates Magenta /1 #48
2009 Press Pass Legends Printing Plates Yellow /1 #48
2009 Press Pass Legends Prominent Pieces Bronze /99 #PPJJ
2009 Press Pass Legends Prominent Pieces Gold /25 #PPJJ
2009 Press Pass Legends Prominent Pieces Oversized /25 #PPOEJJ
2009 Press Pass Legends Prominent Pieces Silver /50 #PPJJ
2009 Press Pass Legends Red /199 #48
2009 Press Pass Legends Solo /1 #48
2009 Press Pass NASCAR Gallery #NG11
2009 Press Pass Pocket Portraits #P11
2009 Press Pass Pocket Portraits Checkered Flag #P11
2009 Press Pass Pocket Portraits Hometown #P11
2009 Press Pass Pocket Portraits Smoke #P11
2009 Press Pass Pocket Portraits Target #PPT3
2009 Press Pass Premium #28
2009 Press Pass Premium #48
2009 Press Pass Premium #61
2009 Press Pass Premium #80
2009 Press Pass Premium #82
2009 Press Pass Premium Gold #82
2009 Press Pass Premium Hot Threads /99 #HTJJ1
2009 Press Pass Premium Hot Threads /325 #HTJJ2
2009 Press Pass Premium Hot Threads Multi-Color /25 #HTJJ
2009 Press Pass Premium Hot Threads Patches /8 #HTP-JJ1
2009 Press Pass Premium Hot Threads Patches /10 #HTP-JJ2
2009 Press Pass Premium Previews /5 #EB28
2009 Press Pass Premium Signatures #16
2009 Press Pass Premium Signatures Gold /25 #15
2009 Press Pass Premium Top Contenders #TC9
2009 Press Pass Premium Top Contenders Gold #TC9
2009 Press Pass Premium Win Streak #WS1
2009 Press Pass Premium Win Streak Victory Lane #WSVL-JJ
2009 Press Pass Previews /5 #EB3
2009 Press Pass Previews /1 #EB109
2009 Press Pass Previews /5 #EB134
2009 Press Pass Previews /1 #EB193
2009 Press Pass Previews /1 #EB197
2009 Press Pass Previews /1 #EB200
2009 Press Pass Red #3
2009 Press Pass Red #59
2009 Press Pass Red #72
2009 Press Pass Red #76
2009 Press Pass Red #109
2009 Press Pass Red #134
2009 Press Pass Red #186
2009 Press Pass Red #187
2009 Press Pass Red #188
2009 Press Pass Red #190
2009 Press Pass Red #191
2009 Press Pass Red #193
2009 Press Pass Red #197
2009 Press Pass Red #200
2009 Press Pass Red #210
2009 Press Pass Red #CL
2009 Press Pass Santa Hats /50 #SH9
2009 Press Pass Showcase /499 #5
2009 Press Pass Showcase /499 #29
2009 Press Pass Showcase /499 #39
2009 Press Pass Showcase 2nd Gear /125 #5
2009 Press Pass Showcase 2nd Gear /125 #29
2009 Press Pass Showcase 2nd Gear /125 #39
2009 Press Pass Showcase 3rd Gear /50 #5
2009 Press Pass Showcase 3rd Gear /50 #29
2009 Press Pass Showcase 3rd Gear /50 #39
2009 Press Pass Showcase 4th Gear /15 #5
2009 Press Pass Showcase 4th Gear /15 #29
2009 Press Pass Showcase 4th Gear /15 #39
2009 Press Pass Showcase Classic Collections Firesuit /25 #CCF1
2009 Press Pass Showcase Classic Collections Firesuit /25 #CCF3
2009 Press Pass Showcase Classic Collections Firesuit /25 #CCF4
2009 Press Pass Showcase Classic Collections Firesuit Patch /5 #CCF1
2009 Press Pass Showcase Classic Collections Firesuit Patch /5 #CCF3
2009 Press Pass Showcase Classic Collections Firesuit Patch /5 #CCF4
2009 Press Pass Showcase Classic Collections Ink /45 #2
2009 Press Pass Showcase Classic Collections Ink Gold /25 #2
2009 Press Pass Showcase Classic Collections Ink Green /5 #2
2009 Press Pass Showcase Classic Collections Ink Melting /1 #2
2009 Press Pass Showcase Classic Collections Sheet Metal /45 #CCS1
2009 Press Pass Showcase Classic Collections Sheet Metal /45 #CCS3
2009 Press Pass Showcase Classic Collections Sheet Metal /45 #CCS4
2009 Press Pass Showcase Classic Collections Tire /99 #CCT1
2009 Press Pass Showcase Classic Collections Tire /99 #CCT3
2009 Press Pass Showcase Classic Collections Tire /99 #CCT4
2009 Press Pass Showcase Elite Exhibit Ink /45 #6
2009 Press Pass Showcase Elite Exhibit Ink Gold /25 #6
2009 Press Pass Showcase Elite Exhibit Ink Green /5 #6
2009 Press Pass Showcase Elite Exhibit Ink Melting /1 #6
2009 Press Pass Showcase Elite Exhibit Triple Memorabilia /99 #EEJJ
2009 Press Pass Showcase Elite Exhibit Triple Memorabilia Gold /45 #EEJJ
2009 Press Pass Showcase Elite Exhibit Triple Memorabilia Green /25 #EEJJ
2009 Press Pass Showcase Elite Exhibit Triple Memorabilia Melting /5 #EEJJ
2009 Press Pass Showcase Printing Plates Black /1 #5
2009 Press Pass Showcase Printing Plates Black /1 #29
2009 Press Pass Showcase Printing Plates Black /1 #39
2009 Press Pass Showcase Printing Plates Cyan /1 #5
2009 Press Pass Showcase Printing Plates Cyan /1 #29
2009 Press Pass Showcase Printing Plates Cyan /1 #39
2009 Press Pass Showcase Printing Plates Magenta /1 #5
2009 Press Pass Showcase Printing Plates Magenta /1 #29
2009 Press Pass Showcase Printing Plates Magenta /1 #39
2009 Press Pass Showcase Printing Plates Yellow /1 #5
2009 Press Pass Showcase Printing Plates Yellow /1 #29
2009 Press Pass Showcase Printing Plates Yellow /1 #39
2009 Press Pass Showcase Prized Pieces Firesuit /25 #PPFJJ
2009 Press Pass Showcase Prized Pieces Firesuit Patch /5 #PPFJJ
2009 Press Pass Showcase Prized Pieces Ink Firesuit /5 #6
2009 Press Pass Showcase Prized Pieces Ink Firesuit Patch /1 #6
2009 Press Pass Showcase Prized Pieces Ink Sheet Metal /25 #6
2009 Press Pass Showcase Prized Pieces Ink Tire /45 #6
2009 Press Pass Showcase Prized Pieces Sheet Metal /45 #PPSJJ
2009 Press Pass Showcase Prized Pieces Tire /99 #PPTJJ
2009 Press Pass Signature Series Archive Edition /1 #BRDJJ
2009 Press Pass Signature Series Archive Edition /1 #GGTJJ
2009 Press Pass Signature Series Archive Edition /1 #THDJJ
2009 Press Pass Signature Series Archive Edition /1 #UCTJJ
2009 Press Pass Signature Series Archive Edition /1 #GGJJ
2009 Press Pass Signature Series Archive Edition /1 #HTJJ
2009 Press Pass Signature Series Archive Edition /1 #BRJJ
2009 Press Pass Signature Series Archive Edition /1 #HTJJ
2009 Press Pass Signings Blue /25 #19
2009 Press Pass Signings Gold #19
2009 Press Pass Signings Green /15 #19
2009 Press Pass Signings Orange /25 #19
2009 Press Pass Signings Printing Plates Magenta /1 #19
2009 Press Pass Signings Printing Plates Yellow /1 #19
2009 Press Pass Signings Purple /45 #19
2009 Press Pass Sponsor Swatches /250 #SSJJ
2009 Press Pass Sponsor Swatches Select /10 #SSJJ
2009 Press Pass Stealth #16
2009 Press Pass Stealth #61
2009 Press Pass Stealth #74A
2009 Press Pass Stealth #78
2009 Press Pass Stealth #90
2009 Press Pass Stealth #74B
2009 Press Pass Stealth Battle Armor /199 #BAJJ2
2009 Press Pass Stealth Battle Armor /135 #BAJJ1
2009 Press Pass Stealth Battle Armor /25 #BAJJ3
2009 Press Pass Stealth Battle Armor Autographs /48 #BASJJ
2009 Press Pass Stealth Battle Armor Multi-Color /150 #BAJJ
2009 Press Pass Stealth Chrome #16
2009 Press Pass Stealth Chrome #61
2009 Press Pass Stealth Chrome #74A
2009 Press Pass Stealth Chrome #78
2009 Press Pass Stealth Chrome #90
2009 Press Pass Stealth Chrome #74B
2009 Press Pass Stealth Chrome #74C
2009 Press Pass Stealth Chrome Brushed Metal /25 #16
2009 Press Pass Stealth Chrome Brushed Metal /25 #61
2009 Press Pass Stealth Chrome Brushed Metal /25 #74
2009 Press Pass Stealth Chrome Brushed Metal /25 #78
2009 Press Pass Stealth Chrome Brushed Metal /25 #90
2009 Press Pass Stealth Chrome Gold /99 #16
2009 Press Pass Stealth Chrome Gold /99 #61
2009 Press Pass Stealth Chrome Gold /99 #74
2009 Press Pass Stealth Chrome Gold /99 #78
2009 Press Pass Stealth Chrome Gold /99 #90
2009 Press Pass Stealth Confidential Classified Bronze #PC11
2009 Press Pass Stealth Confidential Secret Silver #PC11
2009 Press Pass Stealth Confidential Top Secret Gold /25 #PC11
2009 Press Pass Stealth Mach 09 #M5
2009 Press Pass Stealth Previews /5 #EB16
2009 Press Pass Stealth Previews /1 #EB74
2009 Press Pass Stealth Previews /1 #EB78
2009 Press Pass Target #JJB
2009 Press Pass Target Victory Tires /50 #JJTT
2009 Press Pass Total Tire /25 #TT5
2009 Press Pass Tread Marks Autographs /10 #SSJJ
2009 Press Pass Unleashed #U9
2009 Press Pass Unleashed #U5
2009 Press Pass Wal-Mart #JJA
2009 Press Pass Wal-Mart Autographs Red #7
2009 Press Pass Wal-Mart Signature Edition /15 #JJ
2009 Sportkings National Convention Memorabilia Gold /1 #SK5
2009 Sportkings National Convention Memorabilia Gold /1 #SK24
2009 Sportkings National Convention Memorabilia Gold /1 #SK43
2009 Sportkings National Convention Memorabilia Gold /1 #SK63
2009 Sportkings National Convention Memorabilia Silver /9 #SK5
2009 Sportkings National Convention Memorabilia Silver /9 #SK24
2009 Sportkings National Convention Memorabilia Silver /9 #SK43
2009 Sportkings National Convention Memorabilia Silver /9 #SK63
2009 Upper Deck Prominent Cuts Cut Signatures /3 #PCJMJ
2009 VIP #15
2009 VIP #45
2009 VIP #57
2009 VIP #61
2009 VIP #64
2009 VIP #78
2009 VIP #85
2009 VIP After Party #AP6
2009 VIP After Party Transparent #AP6
2009 VIP Get A Grip /120 #GGJJ
2009 VIP Get A Grip Holofoil /10 #GGJJ
2009 VIP Get A Grip Logos /5 #GGLJJ
2009 VIP Guest List #GG17
2009 VIP Hardware Transparent #H2
2009 VIP Leadfoot /150 #LFJJ
2009 VIP Leadfoot Holofoil /10 #LFJJ
2009 VIP Leadfoot Logos /5 #LFLJJ
2009 VIP National Promos #3
2009 VIP Previews /5 #15
2009 VIP Previews /1 #78
2009 VIP Purple /25 #15
2009 VIP Purple /25 #45
2009 VIP Purple /25 #57
2009 VIP Purple /25 #61
2009 VIP Purple /25 #64
2009 VIP Purple /25 #78
2009 VIP Purple /25 #85
2009 VIP Race Day Gear /25 #RDGJJ
2009 Wheels Autographs /25 #31
2009 Wheels Autographs #32
2009 Wheels Autographs Press Plates Black /1 #JJ
2009 Wheels Autographs Press Plates Cyan /1 #JJ
2009 Wheels Autographs Press Plates Magenta /1 #JJ
2009 Wheels Autographs Press Plates Yellow /1 #JJ
2009 Wheels Main Event #4
2009 Wheels Main Event #37
2009 Wheels Main Event #46
2009 Wheels Main Event #49
2009 Wheels Main Event #57
2009 Wheels Main Event #71
2009 Wheels Main Event #76
2009 Wheels Main Event Buyback Archive Edition /1 #TBTJJ
2009 Wheels Main Event Buyback Archive Edition /1 #BRJJ
2009 Wheels Main Event Buyback Archive Edition /1 #HTJJ
2009 Wheels Main Event Buyback Archive Edition /1 #PSJJ
2009 Wheels Main Event Buyback Archive Edition /1 #TPJJ
2009 Wheels Main Event Buyback Archive Edition /1 #UCJJ
2009 Wheels Main Event Buyback Archive Edition /1 #TPJJ
2009 Wheels Main Event Fast Pass Purple /25 #4
2009 Wheels Main Event Fast Pass Purple /25 #37
2009 Wheels Main Event Fast Pass Purple /25 #46
2009 Wheels Main Event Fast Pass Purple /25 #49
2009 Wheels Main Event Fast Pass Purple /25 #57
2009 Wheels Main Event Fast Pass Purple /25 #71
2009 Wheels Main Event Fast Pass Purple /25 #76
2009 Wheels Main Event Foil #4
2009 Wheels Main Event Hat Dance Patch /10 #HDJJ
2009 Wheels Main Event Hat Dance Triple /99 #HDJJ
2009 Wheels Main Event High Rollers #HR11
2009 Wheels Main Event Marks Clubs #28
2009 Wheels Main Event Marks Diamonds /10 #28
2009 Wheels Main Event Marks Hearts /5 #28
2009 Wheels Main Event Marks Printing Plates Black /1 #24
2009 Wheels Main Event Marks Printing Plates Cyan /1 #24
2009 Wheels Main Event Marks Printing Plates Magenta /1 #24
2009 Wheels Main Event Marks Printing Plates Yellow /1 #24
2009 Wheels Main Event Marks Spades /1 #28
2009 Wheels Main Event Playing Cards Blue #AC
2009 Wheels Main Event Playing Cards Red #AC
2009 Wheels Main Event Poker Chips #6
2009 Wheels Main Event Previews /5 #4
2009 Wheels Main Event Spark Plugs /8 #JJ1
2009 Wheels Main Event Spark Plugs /8 #JJ2
2009 Wheels Main Event Stop and Go Swatches Pit Banner /175 #SGBJJ
2009 Wheels Main Event Stop and Go Swatches Pit Banner Blue All Season's Sports Cards /1 #SGBJJ
2009 Wheels Main Event Stop and Go Swatches Pit Banner Blue Arena /1 #SGBJJ
2009 Wheels Main Event Stop and Go Swatches Pit Banner Blue Card Stadium /1 #SGBJJ
2009 Wheels Main Event Stop and Go Swatches Pit Banner Blue Chicagoland Sportscards /1 #SGBJJ
2009 Wheels Main Event Stop and Go Swatches Pit Banner Blue Chris Comics /1 #SGBJJ
2009 Wheels Main Event Stop and Go Swatches Pit Banner Blue Chuck's Field of Dreams /1 #SGBJJ
2009 Wheels Main Event Stop and Go Swatches Pit Banner Blue Collector's Heaven /1 #SGBJJ
2009 Wheels Main Event Stop and Go Swatches Pit Banner Blue D&S Racing /1 #SGBJJ
2009 Wheels Main Event Stop and Go Swatches Pit Banner Blue Dave's Pitstop /1 #SGBJJ
2009 Wheels Main Event Stop and Go Swatches Pit Banner Blue Diamond King Sports /1 #SGBJJ
2009 Wheels Main Event Stop and Go Swatches Pit Banner Blue Georgetown Card Exchange /1 #SGBJJ
2009 Wheels Main Event Stop and Go Swatches Pit Banner Blue Jaimie's Field of Dreams /1 #SGBJJ
2009 Wheels Main Event Stop and Go Swatches Pit Banner Blue Juniata Cards /1 #SGBJJ
2009 Wheels Main Event Stop and Go Swatches Pit Banner Blue Main Steet Sportscards /1 #SGBJJ
2009 Wheels Main Event Stop and Go Swatches Pit Banner Blue Matt's Sports Cards /1 #SGBJJ
2009 Wheels Main Event Stop and Go Swatches Pit Banner Blue P&T Sportscards /1 #SGBJJ
2009 Wheels Main Event Stop and Go Swatches Pit Banner Blue Republic Jewelry /1 #SGBJJ
2009 Wheels Main Event Stop and Go Swatches Pit Banner Blue Ron's Racing /1 #SGBJJ
2009 Wheels Main Event Stop and Go Swatches Pit Banner Blue Shelby Collectibles /1 #SGBJJ
2009 Wheels Main Event Stop and Go Swatches Pit Banner Blue Spectator Sportscards /1 #SGBJJ
2009 Wheels Main Event Stop and Go Swatches Pit Banner Blue Squeeze Play /1 #SGBJJ
2009 Wheels Main Event Stop and Go Swatches Pit Banner Blue TBJ Sports Cards /1 #SGBJJ
2009 Wheels Main Event Stop and Go Swatches Pit Banner Blue TCI Sports Fan /1 #SGBJJ
2009 Wheels Main Event Stop and Go Swatches Pit Banner Blue The Card Cellar /1 #SGBJJ
2009 Wheels Main Event Stop and Go Swatches Pit Banner Blue TJ Warner Ballcards /1 #SGBJJ
2009 Wheels Main Event Stop and Go Swatches Pit Banner Blue Trademark Sports /1 #SGBJJ
2009 Wheels Main Event Stop and Go Swatches Pit Banner Blue Triple I Sportscards /1 #SGBJJ
2009 Wheels Main Event Stop and Go Swatches Pit Banner Blue Triple Play /1 #SGBJJ
2009 Wheels Main Event Stop and Go Swatches Pit Banner Blue West Allis /1 #SGBJJ
2009 Wheels Main Event Stop and Go Swatches Pit Banner Green /10 #SGB=JJ
2009 Wheels Main Event Stop and Go Swatches Pit Banner Holofoil /75 #SGBJJ
2009 Wheels Main Event Stop and Go Swatches Pit Banner Red /25 #SGBJJ
2009 Wheels Main Event Wildcard Cuts /2 #WCCJJ
2010 Element #4
2010 Element #39
2010 Element #73
2010 Element #78
2010 Element #82
2010 Element 10 in '10 #TT3
2010 Element Blue /35 #4
2010 Element Blue /35 #39
2010 Element Blue /35 #73

2010 Element Blue /35 #78
2010 Element Blue /35 #82
2010 Element Finish Line Checkered Flag /10 #FLJJ
2010 Element Finish Line Green Flag /20 #FLJJ
2010 Element Finish Line Tires /99 #FLJJ
2010 Element Flagship Performers Championships Black /25 #FPCJJ
2010 Element Flagship Performers Championships Blue-Orange /25 #FPCJJ
2010 Element Flagship Performers Championships Checkered /1 #FPCJJ
2010 Element Flagship Performers Championships Green /5 #FPCJJ
2010 Element Flagship Performers Championships Red /25 #FPCJJ
2010 Element Flagship Performers Championships White /15 #FPCJJ
2010 Element Flagship Performers Championships X /25 #FPCJJ
2010 Element Flagship Performers Championships Yellow /25 #FPCJJ
2010 Element Flagship Performers Consecutive Starts Black /20 #FPSJJ
2010 Element Flagship Performers Consecutive Starts Blue-Orange /20 #FPSJJ
2010 Element Flagship Performers Consecutive Starts Checkered /1 #FPSJJ
2010 Element Flagship Performers Consecutive Starts Green /5 #FPSJJ
2010 Element Flagship Performers Consecutive Starts Red /20 #FPSJJ
2010 Element Flagship Performers Consecutive Starts White /10 #FPSJJ
2010 Element Flagship Performers Consecutive Starts X /10 #FPSJJ
2010 Element Flagship Performers Consecutive Starts Yellow /20 #FPSJJ
2010 Element Flagship Performers Wins Black /20 #FPWJJ
2010 Element Flagship Performers Wins Blue-Orange /20 #FPWJJ
2010 Element Flagship Performers Wins Checkered /1 #FPWJJ
2010 Element Flagship Performers Wins Green /5 #FPWJJ
2010 Element Flagship Performers Wins Red /20 #FPWJJ
2010 Element Flagship Performers Wins White /15 #FPWJJ
2010 Element Flagship Performers Wins X /10 #FPWJJ
2010 Element Flagship Performers Wins Yellow /20 #FPWJJ
2010 Element Green #4
2010 Element Green #39
2010 Element Green #73
2010 Element Green #78
2010 Element Green #82
2010 Element High Octane Vehicle #HOV12
2010 Element Previews /5 #EB4
2010 Element Previews /1 #EB78
2010 Element Purple /25 #4
2010 Element Purple /25 #39
2010 Element Recycled Materials Blue /25 #RMJJ
2010 Element Recycled Materials Green /125 #RMJJ
2010 Element Red Target #4
2010 Element Red Target #39
2010 Element Red Target #73
2010 Element Red Target #78
2010 Element Red Target #82
2010 Press Pass #4
2010 Press Pass #111
2010 Press Pass #123
2010 Press Pass #66
2010 Press Pass #89
2010 Press Pass #96
2010 Press Pass #0
2010 Press Pass Autographs #24
2010 Press Pass Autographs Chase Edition /25 #6
2010 Press Pass Autographs Track Edition /10 #6
2010 Press Pass Blue #4
2010 Press Pass Blue #66
2010 Press Pass Blue #89
2010 Press Pass Blue #96
2010 Press Pass Blue #111
2010 Press Pass Blue #121
2010 Press Pass Burning Rubber /250 #BR5
2010 Press Pass Burning Rubber /250 #BR17
2010 Press Pass Burning Rubber /250 #BR24
2010 Press Pass Burning Rubber /250 #BR26
2010 Press Pass Burning Rubber /250 #BR27
2010 Press Pass Burning Rubber /250 #BR31
2010 Press Pass Burning Rubber Autographs /48 #SSTEJJ
2010 Press Pass Burning Rubber Gold /50 #BR5
2010 Press Pass Burning Rubber Gold /50 #BR17
2010 Press Pass Burning Rubber Gold /99 #BR24
2010 Press Pass Burning Rubber Gold /99 #BR26
2010 Press Pass Burning Rubber Gold /99 #BR27
2010 Press Pass Burning Rubber Gold /99 #BR31
2010 Press Pass Burning Rubber Prime Cuts /25 #BR17
2010 Press Pass Burning Rubber Prime Cuts /25 #BRD24
2010 Press Pass Burning Rubber Prime Cuts /25 #BRD26
2010 Press Pass Burning Rubber Prime Cuts /25 #BRD27
2010 Press Pass Burning Rubber Prime Cuts /25 #BRD31
2010 Press Pass By The Numbers #BN3
2010 Press Pass Cup Chase #CCR12
2010 Press Pass Cup Chase Prizes #CCP
2010 Press Pass Cup Chase Prizes #CC2
2010 Press Pass Eclipse #13
2010 Press Pass Eclipse #42
2010 Press Pass Eclipse #48
2010 Press Pass Eclipse #52
2010 Press Pass Eclipse #53
2010 Press Pass Eclipse #55
2010 Press Pass Eclipse #60
2010 Press Pass Eclipse #65
2010 Press Pass Eclipse #66
2010 Press Pass Eclipse #67
2010 Press Pass Eclipse #68
2010 Press Pass Eclipse #69
2010 Press Pass Eclipse #79
2010 Press Pass Eclipse Blue #13
2010 Press Pass Eclipse Blue #42
2010 Press Pass Eclipse Blue #48
2010 Press Pass Eclipse Blue #52
2010 Press Pass Eclipse Blue #53
2010 Press Pass Eclipse Blue #55
2010 Press Pass Eclipse Blue #60
2010 Press Pass Eclipse Blue #65
2010 Press Pass Eclipse Blue #66
2010 Press Pass Eclipse Blue #67
2010 Press Pass Eclipse Blue #68
2010 Press Pass Eclipse Blue #69
2010 Press Pass Eclipse Blue #79
2010 Press Pass Eclipse Cars #C7
2010 Press Pass Eclipse Decade #D1
2010 Press Pass Eclipse Element Inserts #1
2010 Press Pass Eclipse Focus #F6
2010 Press Pass Eclipse Gold #13
2010 Press Pass Eclipse Gold #42
2010 Press Pass Eclipse Gold #48
2010 Press Pass Eclipse Gold #52
2010 Press Pass Eclipse Gold #53
2010 Press Pass Eclipse Gold #55
2010 Press Pass Eclipse Gold #60
2010 Press Pass Eclipse Gold #65
2010 Press Pass Eclipse Gold #66
2010 Press Pass Eclipse Gold #67
2010 Press Pass Eclipse Gold #68
2010 Press Pass Eclipse Gold #69
2010 Press Pass Eclipse Gold #79
2010 Press Pass Eclipse Previews /5 #13
2010 Press Pass Eclipse Previews /1 #42
2010 Press Pass Eclipse Purple /25 #13
2010 Press Pass Eclipse Purple /25 #42
2010 Press Pass Eclipse Purple /25 #48
2010 Press Pass Eclipse Purple /25 #52
2010 Press Pass Eclipse Purple /25 #53
2010 Press Pass Eclipse Purple /25 #55
2010 Press Pass Eclipse Purple /25 #60
2010 Press Pass Eclipse Spellbound Swatches /250 #SSJJ2
2010 Press Pass Eclipse Spellbound Swatches /250 #SSJJ3
2010 Press Pass Eclipse Spellbound Swatches /250 #SSJJ4
2010 Press Pass Eclipse Spellbound Swatches /250 #SSJJ5
2010 Press Pass Eclipse Spellbound Swatches /250 #SSJJ6
2010 Press Pass Eclipse Spellbound Swatches /250 #SSJJ7
2010 Press Pass Eclipse Spellbound Swatches /250 #SSJJ1
2010 Press Pass Eclipse Spellbound Swatches Holofoil /48 #SSJJ2
2010 Press Pass Eclipse Spellbound Swatches Holofoil /48 #SSJJ3
2010 Press Pass Eclipse Spellbound Swatches Holofoil /48 #SSJJ4
2010 Press Pass Eclipse Spellbound Swatches Holofoil /48 #SSJJ5
2010 Press Pass Eclipse Spellbound Swatches Holofoil /48 #SSJJ6
2010 Press Pass Eclipse Spellbound Swatches Holofoil /48 #SSJJ7
2010 Press Pass Eclipse Spellbound Swatches Holofoil /48 #SSJJ1
2010 Press Pass Final Standings /25 #FS1
2010 Press Pass Five Star /35 #6
2010 Press Pass Five Star Classic Compilations Combos Firesuit Autographs /15 #CCMHMS
2010 Press Pass Five Star Classic Compilations Combos Firesuit Autographs /15 #CCMJJG
2010 Press Pass Five Star Classic Compilations Combos Patches Autographs /1 #CCMGJME
2010 Press Pass Five Star Classic Compilations Combos Patches Autographs /1 #CCMJJG
2010 Press Pass Five Star Classic Compilations Dual Memorabilia Autographs /10 #JJ
2010 Press Pass Five Star Classic Compilations Firesuit Autographs /15 #JJ
2010 Press Pass Five Star Classic Compilations Patch Autographs /1 #CCPJJ1
2010 Press Pass Five Star Classic Compilations Patch Autographs /1 #CCPJJ2
2010 Press Pass Five Star Classic Compilations Patch Autographs /1 #CCPJJ3
2010 Press Pass Five Star Classic Compilations Patch Autographs /1 #CCPJJ4
2010 Press Pass Five Star Classic Compilations Patch Autographs /1 #CCPJJ5
2010 Press Pass Five Star Classic Compilations Patch Autographs /1 #CCPJJ6
2010 Press Pass Five Star Classic Compilations Patch Autographs /1 #CCPJJ7
2010 Press Pass Five Star Classic Compilations Patch Autographs /1 #CCPJJ8
2010 Press Pass Five Star Classic Compilations Sheet Metal Autographs /25 #JJ
2010 Press Pass Five Star Classic Compilations Triple Memorabilia Autographs /5 #JJ
2010 Press Pass Five Star Holofoil /10 #6
2010 Press Pass Five Star Melting /1 #6
2010 Press Pass Five Star Paramount Pieces Aluminum /25 #JJ
2010 Press Pass Five Star Paramount Pieces Blue /20 #JJ
2010 Press Pass Five Star Paramount Pieces Gold /15 #JJ
2010 Press Pass Five Star Paramount Pieces Holofoil /5 #JJ
2010 Press Pass Five Star Paramount Pieces Melting /1 #JJ
2010 Press Pass Five Star Signature Souvenirs Aluminum /50 #SSJJ
2010 Press Pass Five Star Signature Souvenirs Gold /25 #SSJJ
2010 Press Pass Five Star Signature Souvenirs Holofoil /10 #SSJJ
2010 Press Pass Five Star Signature Souvenirs Melting /1 #SSJJ
2010 Press Pass Five Star Signatures Aluminum /35 #JJ
2010 Press Pass Five Star Signatures Gold /20 #JJ
2010 Press Pass Five Star Signatures Holofoil /5 #JJ
2010 Press Pass Five Star Signatures Melting /1 #JJ
2010 Press Pass Four Wide Autographs /5 #NNO
2010 Press Pass Four Wide Firesuit /25 #FWJJ
2010 Press Pass Four Wide Sheet Metal /15 #FWJJ
2010 Press Pass Four Wide Shoes /1 #FWJJ
2010 Press Pass Four Wide Tires /10 #FWJJ
2010 Press Pass Gold #4
2010 Press Pass Gold #66
2010 Press Pass Gold #89
2010 Press Pass Gold #96
2010 Press Pass Gold #111
2010 Press Pass Gold #121
2010 Press Pass Holofoil /100 #4
2010 Press Pass Holofoil /100 #66
2010 Press Pass Holofoil /100 #89
2010 Press Pass Holofoil /100 #96
2010 Press Pass Holofoil /100 #111
2010 Press Pass Holofoil /100 #121
2010 Press Pass Legends #47
2010 Press Pass Legends #70
2010 Press Pass Legends #79
2010 Press Pass Legends 50 Win Club Memorabilia Gold /75 #50JJ
2010 Press Pass Legends 50 Win Club Memorabilia Holofoil /25 #50JJ
2010 Press Pass Legends Autographs Blue /10 #31
2010 Press Pass Legends Autographs Holofoil /25 #31
2010 Press Pass Legends Autographs Printing Plates Black /1 #27
2010 Press Pass Legends Autographs Printing Plates Cyan /1 #27
2010 Press Pass Legends Autographs Printing Plates Magenta /1 #27
2010 Press Pass Legends Autographs Printing Plates Yellow /1 #27
2010 Press Pass Legends Blue /1 #47
2010 Press Pass Legends Blue /1 #70
2010 Press Pass Legends Blue /1 #79
2010 Press Pass Legends Gold /399 #47
2010 Press Pass Legends Gold /399 #70
2010 Press Pass Legends Gold /399 #79
2010 Press Pass Legends Holofoil /50 #47
2010 Press Pass Legends Holofoil /50 #70
2010 Press Pass Legends Holofoil /50 #79
2010 Press Pass Legends Legendary Links Gold /75 #LXCYJJ
2010 Press Pass Legends Legendary Links Holofoil /25 #LXCYJJ
2010 Press Pass Legends Motorsports Masters #MMJJ
2010 Press Pass Legends Motorsports Masters Autographs Gold /25 #17
2010 Press Pass Legends Motorsports Masters Autographs Holofoil /10 #17
2010 Press Pass Legends Motorsports Masters Autographs Printing Plates Black /1 #27
2010 Press Pass Legends Motorsports Masters Autographs Printing Plates Cyan /1 #27
2010 Press Pass Legends Motorsports Masters Autographs Printing Plates Magenta /1 #27
2010 Press Pass Legends Motorsports Masters Autographs Printing Plates Yellow /1 #27
2010 Press Pass Legends Motorsports Masters Blue /10 #MMJJ
2010 Press Pass Legends Motorsports Masters Gold /299 #MMJJ
2010 Press Pass Legends Motorsports Masters Holofoil /149 #MMJJ
2010 Press Pass Legends Printing Plates Black /1 #47
2010 Press Pass Legends Printing Plates Black /1 #70
2010 Press Pass Legends Printing Plates Black /1 #79
2010 Press Pass Legends Printing Plates Cyan /1 #47
2010 Press Pass Legends Printing Plates Cyan /1 #70
2010 Press Pass Legends Printing Plates Cyan /1 #79
2010 Press Pass Legends Printing Plates Magenta /1 #47
2010 Press Pass Legends Printing Plates Magenta /1 #70
2010 Press Pass Legends Printing Plates Magenta /1 #79
2010 Press Pass Legends Printing Plates Yellow /1 #47
2010 Press Pass Legends Printing Plates Yellow /1 #70
2010 Press Pass Legends Printing Plates Yellow /1 #79
2010 Press Pass Legends Prominent Pieces Copper /99 #PPJJ
2010 Press Pass Legends Prominent Pieces Gold /50 #PPJJ
2010 Press Pass Legends Prominent Pieces Holofoil /25 #PPJJ
2010 Press Pass Legends Prominent Pieces Oversized Firesuit /25 #PPOEJJ
2010 Press Pass Legends Red /199 #47
2010 Press Pass Legends Red /199 #70
2010 Press Pass Legends Red /199 #79
2010 Press Pass NASCAR Hall of Fame #NHOF50
2010 Press Pass NASCAR Hall of Fame Blue #NHOF50
2010 Press Pass NASCAR Hall of Fame Holofoil /50 #NHOF50
2010 Press Pass Premium #3
2010 Press Pass Premium #39
2010 Press Pass Premium #51
2010 Press Pass Premium #56
2010 Press Pass Premium #68
2010 Press Pass Premium #77
2010 Press Pass Premium #82
2010 Press Pass Premium Allies #A1
2010 Press Pass Premium Allies Signatures /5 #ASJG
2010 Press Pass Premium Hot Threads /299 #HTJJ
2010 Press Pass Premium Hot Threads Holofoil /99 #HTJJ
2010 Press Pass Premium Hot Threads Multi Color /25 #HTJJ
2010 Press Pass Premium Hot Threads Patches /28 #HTPJJ
2010 Press Pass Premium Hot Threads Two Color /125 #HTJJ
2010 Press Pass Premium Pairings Firesuits /25 #PFGJ
2010 Press Pass Premium Pairings Signatures /5 #PSGJ
2010 Press Pass Premium Purple /25 #3
2010 Press Pass Premium Purple /25 #39
2010 Press Pass Premium Purple /25 #51
2010 Press Pass Premium Purple /25 #56
2010 Press Pass Premium Rivals #R5
2010 Press Pass Premium Signature Series Firesuit /15 #SSFJJ
2010 Press Pass Premium Signatures #PSJJ
2010 Press Pass Previews /5 #4
2010 Press Pass Previews /1 #111
2010 Press Pass Purple /25 #4
2010 Press Pass Purple /25 #66
2010 Press Pass Purple /25 #89
2010 Press Pass Purple /25 #96
2010 Press Pass Purple /25 #111
2010 Press Pass Purple /25 #121
2010 Press Pass Showcase /499 #3
2010 Press Pass Showcase /499 #39
2010 Press Pass Showcase /499 #28
2010 Press Pass Showcase /499 #32
2010 Press Pass Showcase Classic Collections Firesuit Green /25 #CCIHMS
2010 Press Pass Showcase Classic Collections Firesuit Green /25 #CCIWIN
2010 Press Pass Showcase Classic Collections Firesuit Patch Melting /5 #CCIWIN
2010 Press Pass Showcase Classic Collections Firesuit Patch Melting /5 #CCIHMS
2010 Press Pass Showcase Classic Collections Ink /15 #CCIWIN
2010 Press Pass Showcase Classic Collections Ink /15 #CCIHMS
2010 Press Pass Showcase Classic Collections Ink Gold /10 #CCIWIN
2010 Press Pass Showcase Classic Collections Ink Gold /10 #CCIHMS
2010 Press Pass Showcase Classic Collections Ink Green /5 #CCIWIN
2010 Press Pass Showcase Classic Collections Ink Green /5 #CCIHMS
2010 Press Pass Showcase Classic Collections Ink Melting /1 #CCIWIN
2010 Press Pass Showcase Classic Collections Ink Melting /1 #CCIHMS
2010 Press Pass Showcase Classic Collections Sheet Metal /99 #CCIWIN
2010 Press Pass Showcase Classic Collections Sheet Metal /99 #CCIHMS
2010 Press Pass Showcase Classic Collections Sheet Metal Gold /45 #CCIWIN
2010 Press Pass Showcase Classic Collections Sheet Metal Gold /45 #CCIHMS
2010 Press Pass Showcase Elite Exhibit Ink /45 #EEIJJ
2010 Press Pass Showcase Elite Exhibit Ink Gold /25 #EEIJJ
2010 Press Pass Showcase Elite Exhibit Ink Green /5 #EEIJJ
2010 Press Pass Showcase Elite Exhibit Ink Melting /1 #EEIJJ
2010 Press Pass Showcase Elite Exhibit Triple Memorabilia /99 #EEMJJ
2010 Press Pass Showcase Elite Exhibit Triple Memorabilia Gold /45 #EEMJJ
2010 Press Pass Showcase Elite Exhibit Triple Memorabilia Green /25 #EEMJJ
2010 Press Pass Showcase Elite Exhibit Triple Memorabilia Melting /5 #EEMJJ
2010 Press Pass Showcase Gold /125 #3
2010 Press Pass Showcase Gold /125 #28
2010 Press Pass Showcase Gold /125 #32
2010 Press Pass Showcase Gold /125 #39
2010 Press Pass Showcase Green /50 #3
2010 Press Pass Showcase Green /50 #28
2010 Press Pass Showcase Green /50 #32
2010 Press Pass Showcase Green /50 #39
2010 Press Pass Showcase Melting /15 #3
2010 Press Pass Showcase Melting /15 #28
2010 Press Pass Showcase Melting /15 #32
2010 Press Pass Showcase Melting /15 #39
2010 Press Pass Showcase Platinum Holo /1 #3
2010 Press Pass Showcase Platinum Holo /1 #28
2010 Press Pass Showcase Platinum Holo /1 #32
2010 Press Pass Showcase Platinum Holo /1 #39
2010 Press Pass Showcase Prized Pieces Firesuit Green /25 #PPMJJ
2010 Press Pass Showcase Prized Pieces Firesuit Ink Gold /25 #PPIJJ
2010 Press Pass Showcase Prized Pieces Firesuit Ink Melting /1 #PPIJJ
2010 Press Pass Showcase Prized Pieces Firesuit Patch Melting /5 #PPMJJ
2010 Press Pass Showcase Prized Pieces Memorabilia Ink Green /15 #PPIJJ
2010 Press Pass Showcase Prized Pieces Sheet Metal /99 #PPMJJ
2010 Press Pass Showcase Prized Pieces Sheet Metal Gold /45 #PPMJJ
2010 Press Pass Showcase Prized Pieces Sheet Metal Ink Silver /45 #PPIJJ
2010 Press Pass Showcase Racing's Finest /499 #RF12
2010 Press Pass Showcase Racing's Finest Gold /125 #RF12
2010 Press Pass Showcase Racing's Finest Green /50 #RF12
2010 Press Pass Showcase Racing's Finest Melting /15 #RF12
2010 Press Pass Signings Blue /10 #27
2010 Press Pass Signings Gold /50 #27
2010 Press Pass Signings Red /15 #27
2010 Press Pass Signings Silver /20 #27
2010 Press Pass Stealth #15
2010 Press Pass Stealth #55
2010 Press Pass Stealth Battle Armor Fast Pass /25 #BAJJ
2010 Press Pass Stealth Battle Armor Holofoil /25 #BAJJ
2010 Press Pass Stealth Battle Armor Silver /225 #BAJJ
2010 Press Pass Stealth Black and White #15
2010 Press Pass Stealth Black and White #55
2010 Press Pass Stealth National Convention #VIP4
2010 Press Pass Stealth Power Players #PP1
2010 Press Pass Stealth Previews /5 #15
2010 Press Pass Stealth Previews /5 #55
2010 Press Pass Stealth Purple /25 #15
2010 Press Pass Stealth Purple /25 #55
2010 Press Pass Stealth Signature Series Sheet Metal /15 #SSMEJJ
2010 Press Pass Target By The Numbers #BNT6
2010 Press Pass Top 12 Tires /48 #JJ
2010 Press Pass Top 12 Tires 10 /10 #JJ
2010 Press Pass Tradin' Paint #TP9
2010 Press Pass Tradin' Paint Sheet Metal /299 #TPJJ
2010 Press Pass Tradin' Paint Sheet Metal Gold /50 #TPJJ
2010 Press Pass Tradin' Paint Sheet Metal Holofoil /25 #TPJJ
2010 Press Pass Unleashed #U6
2010 Press Pass Unleashed #U11
2010 Press Pass Wal-Mart By The Numbers #BNW6
2010 Sports Illustrated for Kids #470
2010 Wheels Autographs #23
2010 Wheels Autographs Printing Plates Black /1 #23
2010 Wheels Autographs Printing Plates Cyan /1 #23
2010 Wheels Autographs Printing Plates Magenta /1 #23
2010 Wheels Autographs Printing Plates Yellow /1 #23
2010 Wheels Autographs Special Ink /10 #8
2010 Wheels Autographs Target /10 #15
2010 Wheels Main Event #15
2010 Wheels Main Event #44
2010 Wheels Main Event #48
2010 Wheels Main Event #63
2010 Wheels Main Event #71
2010 Wheels Main Event #95
2010 Wheels Main Event #65
2010 Wheels Main Event American Muscle #AM9
2010 Wheels Main Event Blue #15
2010 Wheels Main Event Blue #44
2010 Wheels Main Event Blue #48
2010 Wheels Main Event Blue #63
2010 Wheels Main Event Blue #65
2010 Wheels Main Event Blue #71
2010 Wheels Main Event Blue #95
2010 Wheels Main Event Dog Tags #JJ
2010 Wheels Main Event Fight Card #FC13
2010 Wheels Main Event Fight Card Checkered Flag #FC13
2010 Wheels Main Event Fight Card Full Color Retail #FC13
2010 Wheels Main Event Fight Card Gold /25 #FC13
2010 Wheels Main Event Head to Head /150 #HHJGJJ
2010 Wheels Main Event Head to Head /150 #HHJJMM
2010 Wheels Main Event Head to Head Blue /75 #HHJGJJ
2010 Wheels Main Event Head to Head Blue /75 #HHJJMM
2010 Wheels Main Event Head to Head Holofoil /10 #HHJGJJ
2010 Wheels Main Event Head to Head Holofoil /10 #HHJJMM
2010 Wheels Main Event Head to Head Red /25 #HHJGJJ
2010 Wheels Main Event Head to Head Red /25 #HHJJMM
2010 Wheels Main Event Marks Autographs Black /1 #26
2010 Wheels Main Event Marks Autographs Blue /10 #27
2010 Wheels Main Event Marks Autographs Red /5 #27
2010 Wheels Main Event Matchups Autographs /10 #JJKH
2010 Wheels Main Event Matchups Autographs /10 #JJJG
2010 Wheels Main Event Purple /25 #15
2010 Wheels Main Event Purple /25 #44
2010 Wheels Main Event Purple /25 #48
2010 Wheels Main Event Tale of the Tape #TT8
2010 Wheels Main Event Upper Cuts Blue /50 #UCJJ
2010 Wheels Main Event Upper Cuts Holofoil /10 #UCJJ
2010 Wheels Main Event Upper Cuts Knock Out Patches /25 #UCKOJJ
2010 Wheels Main Event Upper Cuts Red /25 #UCJJ
2010 Wheels Main Event Wheel to Wheel /25 #WWJJJG
2010 Wheels Main Event Wheel to Wheel Holofoil /10 #WWJJJG
2011 Element #15
2011 Element #38
2011 Element #64
2011 Element #87
2011 Element #90
2011 Element #92
2011 Element #79
2011 Element Autographs /15 #26
2011 Element Autographs Blue /5 #26
2011 Element Autographs Gold /5 #25
2011 Element Autographs Printing Plates Black /1 #26
2011 Element Autographs Printing Plates Cyan /1 #26
2011 Element Autographs Printing Plates Magenta /1 #26
2011 Element Autographs Printing Plates Yellow /1 #26
2011 Element Autographs Silver /10 #25
2011 Element Black /35 #15
2011 Element Black /35 #38
2011 Element Black /35 #64
2011 Element Black /35 #79
2011 Element Black /35 #87
2011 Element Black /35 #90
2011 Element Black /35 #92
2011 Element Cut and Collect Exclusives #NNO
2011 Element Finish Line Checkered Flag /10 #FLJJ
2011 Element Finish Line Green Flag /25 #FLJJ
2011 Element Finish Line Tires /99 #FLJJ
2011 Element Finish Line Tires Purple Fast Pass /30 #FLJJ
2011 Element Flagship Performers Career Wins White /50 #FPWJJ
2011 Element Flagship Performers Championships Checkered /25 #FPCJJ
2011 Element Flagship Performers Race Streak Without DNF Red /50 #FPDJJ
2011 Element Flagstand Swatches /25 #FSSJJ
2011 Element Green #15
2011 Element Green #38
2011 Element Green #64
2011 Element Green #79
2011 Element Green #87
2011 Element Green #90
2011 Element Green #92
2011 Element High Octane Vehicle #HOV1
2011 Element Previews /5 #EB15
2011 Element Purple /25 #15
2011 Element Purple /25 #38
2011 Element Purple /25 #64
2011 Element Purple /25 #79
2011 Element Purple /25 #87
2011 Element Purple /25 #90
2011 Element Purple /25 #92
2011 Element Red #15
2011 Element Red #38
2011 Element Red #64
2011 Element Red #79
2011 Element Red #87
2011 Element Red #90
2011 Element Red #92
2011 Press Pass #16
2011 Press Pass #71
2011 Press Pass #113
2011 Press Pass #136
2011 Press Pass #162
2011 Press Pass #164
2011 Press Pass #183
2011 Press Pass #193
2011 Press Pass #132
2011 Press Pass #0
2011 Press Pass #126
2011 Press Pass Autographs Blue /5 #26
2011 Press Pass Autographs Bronze /5 #25
2011 Press Pass Autographs Gold /5 #25
2011 Press Pass Autographs Printing Plates Black /1 #26
2011 Press Pass Autographs Printing Plates Cyan /1 #26
2011 Press Pass Autographs Printing Plates Magenta /1 #26
2011 Press Pass Autographs Printing Plates Yellow /1 #26
2011 Press Pass Autographs Silver /5 #26
2011 Press Pass Blue Holofoil /10 #16
2011 Press Pass Blue Holofoil /10 #71
2011 Press Pass Blue Holofoil /10 #113
2011 Press Pass Blue Holofoil /10 #126
2011 Press Pass Blue Holofoil /10 #132
2011 Press Pass Blue Holofoil /10 #136
2011 Press Pass Blue Holofoil /10 #162
2011 Press Pass Blue Holofoil /10 #164
2011 Press Pass Blue Holofoil /10 #183
2011 Press Pass Blue Holofoil /10 #193
2011 Press Pass Blue Retail #16
2011 Press Pass Blue Retail #71
2011 Press Pass Blue Retail #113
2011 Press Pass Blue Retail #126
2011 Press Pass Blue Retail #132
2011 Press Pass Blue Retail #136
2011 Press Pass Blue Retail #162
2011 Press Pass Blue Retail #164
2011 Press Pass Blue Retail #183
2011 Press Pass Blue Retail #193
2011 Press Pass Burning Rubber Autographs /10 #BRJJ1
2011 Press Pass Burning Rubber Autographs /10 #BRJJ2
2011 Press Pass Burning Rubber Autographs /10 #BRJJ3
2011 Press Pass Burning Rubber Fast Pass /10 #BRJJ
2011 Press Pass Burning Rubber Fast Pass /10 #BRJJ2
2011 Press Pass Burning Rubber Fast Pass /10 #BRJJ3
2011 Press Pass Burning Rubber Gold /150 #BRJJ2
2011 Press Pass Burning Rubber Gold /150 #BRJJ
2011 Press Pass Burning Rubber Gold /150 #BRJJ3
2011 Press Pass Burning Rubber Gold /150 #BRCJJ
2011 Press Pass Burning Rubber Holofoil /50 #BRJJ
2011 Press Pass Burning Rubber Holofoil /50 #BRJJ2
2011 Press Pass Burning Rubber Holofoil /50 #BRJJ3
2011 Press Pass Burning Rubber Holofoil /50 #BRCJJ
2011 Press Pass Burning Rubber Prime Cuts /25 #BRJJ
2011 Press Pass Burning Rubber Prime Cuts /25 #BRCJJ
2011 Press Pass Cup Chase #CCR2
2011 Press Pass Cup Chase Prizes #CC6
2011 Press Pass Eclipse #14
2011 Press Pass Eclipse #47
2011 Press Pass Eclipse #52
2011 Press Pass Eclipse #62
2011 Press Pass Eclipse #63
2011 Press Pass Eclipse #71
2011 Press Pass Eclipse #77
2011 Press Pass Eclipse Blue #14
2011 Press Pass Eclipse Blue #47
2011 Press Pass Eclipse Blue #52
2011 Press Pass Eclipse Blue #62
2011 Press Pass Eclipse Blue #63
2011 Press Pass Eclipse Blue #71
2011 Press Pass Eclipse Blue #77
2011 Press Pass Eclipse Encore #E4
2011 Press Pass Eclipse Gold /55 #14
2011 Press Pass Eclipse Gold /55 #47
2011 Press Pass Eclipse Gold /55 #52
2011 Press Pass Eclipse Gold /55 #62
2011 Press Pass Eclipse Gold /55 #63
2011 Press Pass Eclipse Gold /55 #71
2011 Press Pass Eclipse Gold /55 #77
2011 Press Pass Eclipse Previews /5 #EB14
2011 Press Pass Eclipse Purple /25 #14
2011 Press Pass Eclipse Purple /25 #47
2011 Press Pass Eclipse Purple /25 #52
2011 Press Pass Eclipse Purple /25 #62
2011 Press Pass Eclipse Purple /25 #63
2011 Press Pass Eclipse Rides #R2
2011 Press Pass Eclipse Spellbound Swatches /150 #SBJJ2
2011 Press Pass Eclipse Spellbound Swatches /150 #SBJJ3
2011 Press Pass Eclipse Spellbound Swatches /250 #SBJJ1
2011 Press Pass Eclipse Spellbound Swatches /100 #SBJJ5
2011 Press Pass Eclipse Spellbound Swatches /100 #SBJJ4
2011 Press Pass Eclipse Spellbound Swatches /50 #SBJJ7
2011 Press Pass Eclipse Spellbound Swatches /75 #SBJJ6
2011 Press Pass Eclipse Spellbound Swatches Signatures /10 #NNO
2011 Press Pass FanFare #18
2011 Press Pass FanFare Autographs Blue /5 #34
2011 Press Pass FanFare Autographs Bronze /15 #34
2011 Press Pass FanFare Autographs Gold /10 #34
2011 Press Pass FanFare Autographs Printing Plates Black /1 #34
2011 Press Pass FanFare Autographs Printing Plates Cyan /1 #34
2011 Press Pass FanFare Autographs Printing Plates Magenta /1 #34
2011 Press Pass FanFare Autographs Printing Plates Yellow /1 #34
2011 Press Pass FanFare Autographs Silver /10 #34
2011 Press Pass FanFare Blue Die Cuts #18
2011 Press Pass FanFare Championship Caliber #CC1
2011 Press Pass FanFare Emerald /25 #18
2011 Press Pass FanFare Holofoil Die Cuts #18
2011 Press Pass FanFare Magnificent Materials /199 #MMJJ
2011 Press Pass FanFare Magnificent Materials Dual Swatches /50 #MMDJJ
2011 Press Pass FanFare Magnificent Materials Dual Swatches Holofoil /10 #MMDJJ
2011 Press Pass FanFare Magnificent Materials Holofoil /50 #MMJJ
2011 Press Pass FanFare Magnificent Materials Signatures /25 #MMSEJJ
2011 Press Pass FanFare Magnificent Materials Signatures Holofoil /10 #MMSEJJ
2011 Press Pass FanFare Promotional Memorabilia /199 #PMJJ
2011 Press Pass FanFare Ruby Die Cuts /15 #18
2011 Press Pass FanFare Sapphire /10 #18
2011 Press Pass FanFare Silver /25 #18
2011 Press Pass Flashback #FB8
2011 Press Pass Four Wide Firesuit /25 #FWJJ
2011 Press Pass Four Wide Glove /1 #FWJJ
2011 Press Pass Four Wide Sheet Metal /15 #FWJJ
2011 Press Pass Four Wide Tire /10 #FWJJ
2011 Press Pass Geared Up Holofoil /50 #GUJJ
2011 Press Pass Gold /50 #16
2011 Press Pass Gold /50 #71
2011 Press Pass Gold /50 #113
2011 Press Pass Gold /50 #126
2011 Press Pass Gold /50 #132
2011 Press Pass Gold /50 #136
2011 Press Pass Gold /50 #162
2011 Press Pass Gold /50 #164
2011 Press Pass Gold /50 #183
2011 Press Pass Gold /50 #193
2011 Press Pass Legends #45
2011 Press Pass Legends #71
2011 Press Pass Legends Autographs Blue /5 #LGAJJ
2011 Press Pass Legends Autographs Gold /25 #LGAJJ
2011 Press Pass Legends Autographs Printing Plates Black /1 #LGAJJ
2011 Press Pass Legends Autographs Printing Plates Cyan /1 #LGAJJ
2011 Press Pass Legends Autographs Printing Plates Magenta /1 #LGAJJ
2011 Press Pass Legends Autographs Printing Plates Yellow /1 #LGAJJ
2011 Press Pass Legends Gold /250 #45
2011 Press Pass Legends Gold /250 #71
2011 Press Pass Legends Holofoil /25 #45
2011 Press Pass Legends Holofoil /25 #71
2011 Press Pass Legends Motorsports Masters #MM19
2011 Press Pass Legends Motorsports Masters Brushed Foil /199 #MM19
2011 Press Pass Legends Motorsports Masters Holofoil /50 #MM19
2011 Press Pass Legends Pacing The Field Autographs Silver /25 #PFAJJ
2011 Press Pass Legends Printing Plates Black /1 #45
2011 Press Pass Legends Printing Plates Black /1 #71
2011 Press Pass Legends Printing Plates Cyan /1 #45
2011 Press Pass Legends Printing Plates Cyan /1 #71
2011 Press Pass Legends Printing Plates Magenta /1 #45
2011 Press Pass Legends Printing Plates Magenta /1 #71
2011 Press Pass Legends Printing Plates Yellow /1 #45
2011 Press Pass Legends Printing Plates Yellow /1 #71
2011 Press Pass Legends Prominent Pieces Gold /50 #PPJJ
2011 Press Pass Legends Prominent Pieces Holofoil /25 #PPJJ
2011 Press Pass Legends Prominent Pieces Oversized Firesuit /25 #PPOEJJ
2011 Press Pass Legends Prominent Pieces Purple /15 #PPJJ
2011 Press Pass Legends Prominent Pieces Silver /99 #PPJJ
2011 Press Pass Legends Purple /25 #45
2011 Press Pass Legends Purple /25 #71
2011 Press Pass Legends Red /99 #45
2011 Press Pass Legends Red /99 #71
2011 Press Pass Legends Solo /1 #45
2011 Press Pass Legends Solo /1 #71
2011 Press Pass Premium #17
2011 Press Pass Premium #40
2011 Press Pass Premium #64
2011 Press Pass Premium #71
2011 Press Pass Premium Crystal Ball #CB2
2011 Press Pass Premium Crystal Ball Autographs /10 #CBAJJ
2011 Press Pass Premium Double Burner /25 #DBJJ
2011 Press Pass Premium Hot Pursuit 3D #HP4
2011 Press Pass Premium Hot Pursuit Autographs /10 #HPAJJ
2011 Press Pass Premium Hot Pursuit National Convention #HP4
2011 Press Pass Premium Hot Threads /150 #HTJJ
2011 Press Pass Premium Hot Threads Fast Pass /25 #HTJJ
2011 Press Pass Premium Hot Threads Multi Color /25 #HTJJ
2011 Press Pass Premium Hot Threads Patches /25 #HTPJJ
2011 Press Pass Premium Hot Threads Secondary Color /99 #HTJJ
2011 Press Pass Premium Pairings Firesuits /25 #PPJJMM
2011 Press Pass Premium Pairings Signatures /5 #PPAJJMM
2011 Press Pass Premium Purple /25 #17
2011 Press Pass Premium Purple /25 #40
2011 Press Pass Premium Purple /25 #64
2011 Press Pass Premium Purple /25 #71
2011 Press Pass Premium Signatures /22 #PSJJ
2011 Press Pass Previews /5 #EB16
2011 Press Pass Previews /1 #EB193
2011 Press Pass Purple /25 #16
2011 Press Pass Purple /25 #193
2011 Press Pass Showcase /499 #3
2011 Press Pass Showcase /499 #37
2011 Press Pass Showcase /499 #43
2011 Press Pass Showcase /499 #53
2011 Press Pass Showcase Champions /499 #CH1
2011 Press Pass Showcase Champions Gold /125 #CH1
2011 Press Pass Showcase Champions Ink /25 #CHIJJ
2011 Press Pass Showcase Champions Ink Gold /10 #CHIJJ
2011 Press Pass Showcase Champions Ink Melting /1 #CHIJJ
2011 Press Pass Showcase Champions Melting /1 #CH1
2011 Press Pass Showcase Champions Memorabilia Firesuit /99 #CHMJJ
2011 Press Pass Showcase Champions Memorabilia Firesuit Gold /45 #CHMJJ
2011 Press Pass Showcase Champions Memorabilia Firesuit Melting /5 #CHMJJ
2011 Press Pass Showcase Classic Collections Firesuit /45 #CCMHMS
2011 Press Pass Showcase Classic Collections Firesuit Patches /5 #CCMHMS
2011 Press Pass Showcase Classic Collections Ink /25 #CCMHMS
2011 Press Pass Showcase Classic Collections Ink Gold /5 #CCMHMS
2011 Press Pass Showcase Classic Collections Ink Melting /1 #CCMHMS
2011 Press Pass Showcase Classic Collections Sheet Metal /99 #CCMHMS
2011 Press Pass Showcase Elite Exhibit Ink /50 #EEIJJ
2011 Press Pass Showcase Elite Exhibit Ink Gold /25 #EEIJJ
2011 Press Pass Showcase Elite Exhibit Ink Melting /1 #EEIJJ
2011 Press Pass Showcase Gold /125 #3
2011 Press Pass Showcase Gold /125 #37
2011 Press Pass Showcase Gold /125 #43
2011 Press Pass Showcase Gold /125 #53
2011 Press Pass Showcase Green /25 #3
2011 Press Pass Showcase Green /25 #37
2011 Press Pass Showcase Green /25 #43
2011 Press Pass Showcase Green /25 #53
2011 Press Pass Showcase Masterpieces Ink /45 #MPIJJ
2011 Press Pass Showcase Masterpieces Ink Gold /25 #MPIJJ
2011 Press Pass Showcase Masterpieces Ink Melting /1 #MPIJJ
2011 Press Pass Showcase Masterpieces Memorabilia /99 #MPMJJ
2011 Press Pass Showcase Masterpieces Memorabilia Gold /45 #MPMJJ
2011 Press Pass Showcase Masterpieces Memorabilia Melting /5 #MPMJJ
2011 Press Pass Showcase Melting /1 #3
2011 Press Pass Showcase Melting /1 #37
2011 Press Pass Showcase Melting /1 #43
2011 Press Pass Showcase Melting /1 #53
2011 Press Pass Showcase Prized Pieces Firesuit /99 #PPMJJ
2011 Press Pass Showcase Prized Pieces Firesuit Gold /45 #PPMJJ
2011 Press Pass Showcase Prized Pieces Firesuit Ink /25 #PPIJJ
2011 Press Pass Showcase Prized Pieces Firesuit Patches Ink /1 #PPIJJ
2011 Press Pass Showcase Prized Pieces Firesuit Patches Melting /5 #PPMJJ
2011 Press Pass Showcase Prized Pieces Sheet Metal Ink /45 #PPIJJ
2011 Press Pass Showcase Showroom /499 #SR1
2011 Press Pass Showcase Showroom Gold /125 #SR1
2011 Press Pass Showcase Showroom Melting /1 #SR1
2011 Press Pass Showcase Showroom Memorabilia Sheet Metal /45 #SRMJJ
2011 Press Pass Showcase Showroom Memorabilia Sheet Metal Gold /25 #SRMJJ
2011 Press Pass Showcase Showroom Memorabilia Sheet Metal Melting /5 #SRMJJ
2011 Press Pass Signature Series /11 #SSTJJ
2011 Press Pass Signature Series /11 #SSBJJ
2011 Press Pass Signature Series /11 #SSFJJ
2011 Press Pass Signature Series /11 #SSMJJ
2011 Press Pass Signings Black and White /5 #PPSJJ1
2011 Press Pass Signings Brushed Metal /30 #PPSJJ1
2011 Press Pass Signings Holofoil /10 #PPSJJ1
2011 Press Pass Signings Printing Plates Black /1 #PPSJJ1
2011 Press Pass Signings Printing Plates Cyan /1 #PPSJJ1
2011 Press Pass Signings Printing Plates Magenta /1 #PPSJJ1
2011 Press Pass Signings Printing Plates Yellow /1 #PPSJJ1
2011 Press Pass Stealth #8
2011 Press Pass Stealth #9
2011 Press Pass Stealth #82
2011 Press Pass Stealth #99
2011 Press Pass Stealth #7
2011 Press Pass Stealth Afterburner /99 #ABJJ
2011 Press Pass Stealth Afterburner Gold /25 #ABJJ
2011 Press Pass Stealth Black and White /25 #7
2011 Press Pass Stealth Black and White /25 #8
2011 Press Pass Stealth Black and White /25 #9
2011 Press Pass Stealth Black and White /25 #82
2011 Press Pass Stealth Black and White /25 #99
2011 Press Pass Stealth Holofoil /99 #7
2011 Press Pass Stealth Holofoil /99 #8
2011 Press Pass Stealth Holofoil /99 #9
2011 Press Pass Stealth Holofoil /99 #82
2011 Press Pass Stealth Holofoil /99 #99
2011 Press Pass Stealth In Flight Report #IF2
2011 Press Pass Stealth Metal of Honor Medal of Honor /50 #BAJJ
2011 Press Pass Stealth Metal of Honor Purple Heart /25 #MHJJ
2011 Press Pass Stealth Metal of Honor Silver Star /99 #BAJJ
2011 Press Pass Stealth Purple /25 #7
2011 Press Pass Stealth Purple /25 #8
2011 Press Pass Stealth Purple /25 #9
2011 Press Pass Target Winning Tickets #WTT2
2011 Press Pass Tradin' Paint #TP4
2011 Press Pass Tradin' Paint Sheet Metal Blue /25 #TPJJ
2011 Press Pass Tradin' Paint Sheet Metal Holofoil /50 #TPJJ
2011 Press Pass Wal-Mart Top 12 Tires /25 #T12JJ
2011 Press Pass Winning Tickets #WT2
2011 Press Pass Winning Tickets #WT3
2011 Press Pass Winning Tickets #WT5
2011 Press Pass Winning Tickets #WT16
2011 Press Pass Winning Tickets #WT17
2011 Press Pass Winning Tickets #WT28
2011 Press Pass Winning Tickets #WT60
2011 Wheels Main Event #17
2011 Wheels Main Event #77
2011 Wheels Main Event #80
2011 Wheels Main Event All Stars #A11
2011 Wheels Main Event All Stars Brushed Foil /199 #A11
2011 Wheels Main Event All Stars Holofoil /50 #A11
2011 Wheels Main Event Black and White #17
2011 Wheels Main Event Black and White #77
2011 Wheels Main Event Black and White #80
2011 Wheels Main Event Blue /75 #17
2011 Wheels Main Event Blue /75 #77
2011 Wheels Main Event Blue /75 #80
2011 Wheels Main Event Gloves Off Holofoil /25 #GOJJ
2011 Wheels Main Event Gloves Off Silver /99 #GOJJ
2011 Wheels Main Event Green /1 #17
2011 Wheels Main Event Green /1 #77
2011 Wheels Main Event Green /1 #80
2011 Wheels Main Event Headliners Holofoil /25 #HLJJ
2011 Wheels Main Event Headliners Silver /99 #HLJJ
2011 Wheels Main Event Marks Autographs Blue /5 #MEJJ
2011 Wheels Main Event Marks Autographs Gold /10 #MEJJ

2011 Wheels Main Event Marks Autographs Silver /15 #MEJJ
2011 Wheels Main Event Matchups Autographs /10 #MEMKHJJ
2011 Wheels Main Event Matchups Autographs /10 #MEMJJCB
2011 Wheels Main Event Materials Holofoil /25 #MEMJJ
2011 Wheels Main Event Materials Silver /99 #MEMJJ
2011 Wheels Main Event Rear View #R3
2011 Wheels Main Event Rear View Brushed Foil /199 #R3
2011 Wheels Main Event Rear View Holofoil /50 #R3
2011 Wheels Main Event Red /20 #17
2011 Wheels Main Event Red /20 #77
2011 Wheels Main Event Red /20 #80
2012 Press Pass #17
2012 Press Pass #84
2012 Press Pass #69
2012 Press Pass Autographs Blue /5 #PPAJJ1
2012 Press Pass Autographs Printing Plates Black /1 #PPAJJ1
2012 Press Pass Autographs Printing Plates Cyan /1 #PPAJJ1
2012 Press Pass Autographs Printing Plates Magenta /1 #PPAJJ1
2012 Press Pass Autographs Printing Plates Yellow /1 #PPAJJ1
2012 Press Pass Autographs Red /5 #PPAJJ1
2012 Press Pass Autographs Silver /15 #PPAJJ1
2012 Press Pass Blue #17
2012 Press Pass Blue #69
2012 Press Pass Blue #84
2012 Press Pass Blue Holofoil /35 #17
2012 Press Pass Blue Holofoil /35 #69
2012 Press Pass Blue Holofoil /35 #84
2012 Press Pass Burning Rubber Gold /99 #BRJJ
2012 Press Pass Burning Rubber Holofoil /25 #BRJJ
2012 Press Pass Burning Rubber Prime Cuts /25 #BRJJ
2012 Press Pass Burning Rubber Purple /15 #BRJJ
2012 Press Pass Cup Chase #CCR2
2012 Press Pass Cup Chase Prizes #CCP2
2012 Press Pass Fanfare #20
2012 Press Pass Fanfare #21
2012 Press Pass Fanfare Autographs Blue /1 #JJ
2012 Press Pass Fanfare Autographs Gold /10 #JJ
2012 Press Pass Fanfare Autographs Red /5 #JJ
2012 Press Pass Fanfare Autographs Silver /20 #JJ
2012 Press Pass Fanfare Blue Foil Die Cuts #20
2012 Press Pass Fanfare Blue Foil Die Cuts #21
2012 Press Pass Fanfare Diamond /5 #20
2012 Press Pass Fanfare Diamond /5 #21
2012 Press Pass Fanfare Holofoil Die Cuts #20
2012 Press Pass Fanfare Holofoil Die Cuts #21
2012 Press Pass Fanfare Magnificent Materials /125 #MMJJ
2012 Press Pass Fanfare Magnificent Materials Dual Swatches /50 #MMJJ
2012 Press Pass Fanfare Magnificent Materials Dual Swatches Melting /10 #MMJJ
2012 Press Pass Fanfare Magnificent Materials Gold /75 #MMJJ
2012 Press Pass Fanfare Magnificent Materials Signatures /25 #JJ
2012 Press Pass Fanfare Magnificent Materials Signatures Blue /5 #JJ
2012 Press Pass Fanfare Power Rankings #PR5
2012 Press Pass Fanfare Sapphire /20 #20
2012 Press Pass Fanfare Sapphire /20 #21
2012 Press Pass Fanfare Showtime #S3
2012 Press Pass Fanfare Silver /25 #20
2012 Press Pass Fanfare Silver /25 #21
2012 Press Pass Four Wide Autographs /5 #JJ
2012 Press Pass Four Wide Firesuit /25 #FWJJ
2012 Press Pass Four Wide Glove /1 #FWJJ
2012 Press Pass Four Wide Sheet Metal /15 #FWJJ
2012 Press Pass Four Wide Tire /10 #FWJJ
2012 Press Pass Gold #17
2012 Press Pass Gold #69
2012 Press Pass Gold #84
2012 Press Pass Ignite #18
2012 Press Pass Ignite #62
2012 Press Pass Ignite Double Burner Gun Metal /10 #DBJJ
2012 Press Pass Ignite Double Burner Red /1 #DBJJ
2012 Press Pass Ignite Double Burner Silver /25 #DBJJ
2012 Press Pass Ignite Limelight #L8
2012 Press Pass Ignite Materials Autographs Red /5 #IMJJ
2012 Press Pass Ignite Materials Autographs Silver /65 #IMJJ
2012 Press Pass Ignite Materials Gun Metal /99 #IMJJ
2012 Press Pass Ignite Materials Red /10 #IMJJ
2012 Press Pass Ignite Materials Silver #IMJJ
2012 Press Pass Ignite Profile #P8
2012 Press Pass Ignite Proofs Black and White /50 #18
2012 Press Pass Ignite Proofs Black and White /50 #62
2012 Press Pass Ignite Proofs Cyan #18
2012 Press Pass Ignite Proofs Cyan #62
2012 Press Pass Ignite Proofs Magenta #18
2012 Press Pass Ignite Proofs Magenta #62
2012 Press Pass Ignite Proofs Yellow /10 #18
2012 Press Pass Ignite Proofs Yellow /10 #62
2012 Press Pass Ignite Steel Horses #SH7
2012 Press Pass Ignite Supercharged Signatures /5 #SSJJ
2012 Press Pass Legends #44
2012 Press Pass Legends Blue Holofoil /1 #44
2012 Press Pass Legends Gold /275 #44
2012 Press Pass Legends Green #44
2012 Press Pass Legends Prominent Pieces Gold /50 #JJ
2012 Press Pass Legends Prominent Pieces Holofoil /25 #JJ
2012 Press Pass Legends Prominent Pieces Oversized Firesuit /25 #JJ
2012 Press Pass Legends Prominent Pieces Silver /99 #JJ
2012 Press Pass Legends Rainbow Holofoil /50 #44
2012 Press Pass Legends Red /99 #44
2012 Press Pass Legends Silver Holofoil /25 #44
2012 Press Pass Legends Trailblazers #TB14
2012 Press Pass Legends Trailblazers Holofoil /99 #TB14
2012 Press Pass Legends Trailblazers Melting /10 #TB14
2012 Press Pass Power Picks Blue /50 #8
2012 Press Pass Power Picks Blue /50 #36
2012 Press Pass Power Picks Blue /50 #57
2012 Press Pass Power Picks Gold /50 #8
2012 Press Pass Power Picks Gold /50 #36
2012 Press Pass Power Picks Gold /50 #57
2012 Press Pass Power Picks Holofoil /10 #8
2012 Press Pass Power Picks Holofoil /10 #36
2012 Press Pass Power Picks Holofoil /10 #57
2012 Press Pass Purple /35 #17
2012 Press Pass Purple /35 #69
2012 Press Pass Purple /35 #84
2012 Press Pass Redline #18
2012 Press Pass Redline Black /99 #18
2012 Press Pass Redline Cyan /50 #18
2012 Press Pass Redline Full Throttle Dual Relic Blue /5 #FTJJ
2012 Press Pass Redline Full Throttle Dual Relic Gold /10 #FTJJ
2012 Press Pass Redline Full Throttle Dual Relic Melting /1 #FTJJ
2012 Press Pass Redline Full Throttle Dual Relic Red /75 #FTJJ
2012 Press Pass Redline Full Throttle Dual Relic Silver /25 #FTJJ
2012 Press Pass Redline Intensity #I6
2012 Press Pass Redline Magenta /15 #18
2012 Press Pass Redline Muscle Car Sheet Metal Blue /5 #MCJJ
2012 Press Pass Redline Muscle Car Sheet Metal Gold /10 #MCJJ
2012 Press Pass Redline Muscle Car Sheet Metal Melting /1 #MCJJ
2012 Press Pass Redline Muscle Car Sheet Metal Red /75 #MCJJ
2012 Press Pass Redline Muscle Car Sheet Metal Silver /25 #MCJJ
2012 Press Pass Redline Performance Driven #PD5
2012 Press Pass Redline Pieces of the Action Blue /10 #PAJJ
2012 Press Pass Redline Pieces of the Action Gold /25 #PAJJ
2012 Press Pass Redline Pieces of the Action Melting /1 #PAJJ
2012 Press Pass Redline Pieces of the Action Red /75 #PAJJ
2012 Press Pass Redline Pieces of the Action Silver /50 #PAJJ
2012 Press Pass Redline Relic Autographs Blue /10 #RLRJJ
2012 Press Pass Redline Relic Autographs Gold /25 #RLRJJ
2012 Press Pass Redline Relic Autographs Melting /1 #RLRJJ
2012 Press Pass Redline Relic Autographs Red /75 #RLRJJ
2012 Press Pass Redline Relic Autographs Silver /50 #RLRJJ
2012 Press Pass Redline Relics Blue /5 #RLJJ
2012 Press Pass Redline Relics Gold /10 #RLJJ
2012 Press Pass Redline Relics Melting /1 #RLJJ
2012 Press Pass Redline Relics Red /75 #RLJJ
2012 Press Pass Redline Relics Silver /25 #RLJJ
2012 Press Pass Redline Rookie Year Relic Autographs Blue /5 #RYJJ
2012 Press Pass Redline Rookie Year Relic Autographs Gold /25 #RYJJ
2012 Press Pass Redline Rookie Year Relic Autographs Melting /1 #RYJJ
2012 Press Pass Redline Rookie Year Relic Autographs Red /50 #RYJJ
2012 Press Pass Redline RPM #RPM6
2012 Press Pass Redline Signatures Blue /5 #RSJJ1
2012 Press Pass Redline Signatures Blue /5 #RSJJ2
2012 Press Pass Redline Signatures Gold /15 #RSJJ1
2012 Press Pass Redline Signatures Holofoil /10 #RSJJ1
2012 Press Pass Redline Signatures Melting /1 #RSJJ1
2012 Press Pass Redline Signatures Melting /1 #RSJJ2
2012 Press Pass Redline Signatures Red /30 #RSJJ1
2012 Press Pass Redline V8 Relics Blue /5 #V8JJ
2012 Press Pass Redline V8 Relics Gold /10 #V8JJ
2012 Press Pass Redline V8 Relics Melting /1 #V8JJ
2012 Press Pass Redline V8 Relics Red /25 #V8JJ
2012 Press Pass Redline Yellow /1 #18
2012 Press Pass Showcar #SC4
2012 Press Pass Showcase /499 #50
2012 Press Pass Showcase /499 #39
2012 Press Pass Showcase /499 #13
2012 Press Pass Showcase /499 #52
2012 Press Pass Showcase Champions Memorabilia /99 #CHJJ
2012 Press Pass Showcase Champions Memorabilia Gold /50 #CHJJ
2012 Press Pass Showcase Champions Memorabilia Melting /5 #CHJJ
2012 Press Pass Showcase Champions Showcase /499 #CH4
2012 Press Pass Showcase Champions Showcase Gold /125 #CH4
2012 Press Pass Showcase Champions Showcase Ink /50 #CHSJJ
2012 Press Pass Showcase Champions Showcase Ink Gold /25 #CHSJJ
2012 Press Pass Showcase Champions Showcase Ink Melting /1 #CHSJJ
2012 Press Pass Showcase Champions Showcase Melting /1 #CH4
2012 Press Pass Showcase Classic Collections Ink /10 #CCMHMS
2012 Press Pass Showcase Classic Collections Ink Gold /5 #CCMHMS
2012 Press Pass Showcase Classic Collections Ink Melting /1 #CCMHMS
2012 Press Pass Showcase Classic Collections Memorabilia /50 #CCMHMS
2012 Press Pass Showcase Classic Collections Memorabilia Gold /25 #CCMHMS
2012 Press Pass Showcase Classic Collections Memorabilia Melting /5 #CCMHMS
2012 Press Pass Showcase Elite Exhibit Ink /50 #EEIJJ
2012 Press Pass Showcase Elite Exhibit Ink Gold /25 #EEIJJ
2012 Press Pass Showcase Elite Exhibit Ink Melting /1 #EEIJJ
2012 Press Pass Showcase Gold /125 #13
2012 Press Pass Showcase Gold /125 #39
2012 Press Pass Showcase Gold /125 #50
2012 Press Pass Showcase Gold /125 #52
2012 Press Pass Showcase Green /5 #13
2012 Press Pass Showcase Green /5 #39
2012 Press Pass Showcase Green /5 #50
2012 Press Pass Showcase Green /5 #52
2012 Press Pass Showcase Masterpieces Ink /50 #MPIJJ
2012 Press Pass Showcase Masterpieces Ink Gold /25 #MPIJJ
2012 Press Pass Showcase Masterpieces Ink Melting /1 #MPIJJ
2012 Press Pass Showcase Masterpieces Memorabilia /99 #MPJJ
2012 Press Pass Showcase Masterpieces Memorabilia Gold /50 #MPJJ
2012 Press Pass Showcase Masterpieces Memorabilia Melting /5 #MPJJ
2012 Press Pass Showcase Melting /1 #13
2012 Press Pass Showcase Melting /1 #39
2012 Press Pass Showcase Melting /1 #50
2012 Press Pass Showcase Melting /1 #52
2012 Press Pass Showcase Purple /1 #13
2012 Press Pass Showcase Purple /1 #39
2012 Press Pass Showcase Purple /1 #50
2012 Press Pass Showcase Purple /1 #52
2012 Press Pass Showcase Red /25 #13
2012 Press Pass Showcase Red /25 #39
2012 Press Pass Showcase Red /25 #50
2012 Press Pass Showcase Red /25 #52
2012 Press Pass Showcase Richard Petty 75th Birthday Tribute /10 #RPJJ
2012 Press Pass Showcase Richard Petty 75th Birthday Tribute Melting /1 #RPJJ
2012 Press Pass Showcase Showcase Patches /5 #SSPJJ
2012 Press Pass Showcase Showcase Patches Melting /1 #SSPJJ
2012 Press Pass Showcase Showroom /499 #SR4
2012 Press Pass Showcase Showroom Gold /125 #SR4
2012 Press Pass Showcase Showroom Melting /1 #SR4
2012 Press Pass Showcase Showroom Memorabilia /99 #SRJJ
2012 Press Pass Showcase Showroom Memorabilia Gold /50 #SRJJ
2012 Press Pass Showcase Showroom Memorabilia Melting /5 #SRJJ
2012 Press Pass Showcase Signature Patches /1 #SSPJJ
2012 Press Pass Showman #SM4
2012 Press Pass Signature Series Race Used /12 #PPAJJ1
2012 Press Pass Signature Series Race Used /12 #PPAJJ2
2012 Press Pass Snapshots #SS17
2012 Press Pass Snapshots #SS73
2012 Press Pass Triple Gear 3 in 1 /5 #TGJJ
2012 Press Pass Triple Gear Firesuit and Sheet Metal /15 #TGJJ
2012 Press Pass Triple Gear Tire /25 #TGJJ
2012 Press Pass Wal-Mart Snapshots #SSWM6
2012 Total Memorabilia #14A
2012 Total Memorabilia #14B
2012 Total Memorabilia Black and White /99 #14
2012 Total Memorabilia Dual Swatch Gold /75 #TMJJ
2012 Total Memorabilia Dual Swatch Holofoil /25 #TMJJ
2012 Total Memorabilia Dual Swatch Melting /5 #TMJJ
2012 Total Memorabilia Dual Swatch Silver /99 #TMJJ
2012 Total Memorabilia Gold /275 #14
2012 Total Memorabilia Hot Rod Relics Gold /50 #HRRJJ
2012 Total Memorabilia Hot Rod Relics Holofoil /10 #HRRJJ
2012 Total Memorabilia Hot Rod Relics Melting /1 #HRRJJ
2012 Total Memorabilia Hot Rod Relics Silver /99 #HRRJJ
2012 Total Memorabilia Jumbo Swatch Gold /50 #TMJJ
2012 Total Memorabilia Jumbo Swatch Holofoil /10 #TMJJ
2012 Total Memorabilia Jumbo Swatch Melting /1 #TMJJ
2012 Total Memorabilia Memory Lane #ML6
2012 Total Memorabilia Quad Swatch Gold /25 #TMJJ
2012 Total Memorabilia Quad Swatch Holofoil /10 #TMJJ
2012 Total Memorabilia Quad Swatch Melting /1 #TMJJ
2012 Total Memorabilia Quad Swatch Silver /50 #TMJJ
2012 Total Memorabilia Red Retail /250 #14
2012 Total Memorabilia Signature Collection Dual Swatch Silver /10 #SCJJ
2012 Total Memorabilia Signature Collection Quad Swatch Holofoil /5 #SCJJ
2012 Total Memorabilia Signature Collection Single Swatch Melting /1 #SCJJ
2012 Total Memorabilia Signature Collection Triple Swatch Gold /10 #SCJJ
2012 Total Memorabilia Single Swatch Gold /99 #TMJJ
2012 Total Memorabilia Single Swatch Holofoil /50 #TMJJ
2012 Total Memorabilia Single Swatch Melting /10 #TMJJ
2012 Total Memorabilia Single Swatch Silver /199 #TMJJ
2012 Total Memorabilia Triple Swatch Gold /50 #TMJJ
2012 Total Memorabilia Triple Swatch Holofoil /25 #TMJJ
2012 Total Memorabilia Triple Swatch Melting /1 #TMJJ
2012 Total Memorabilia Triple Swatch Silver /99 #TMJJ
2013 Press Pass #21
2013 Press Pass #22
2013 Press Pass #86
2013 Press Pass #100
2013 Press Pass #70
2013 Press Pass #75
2013 Press Pass #0
2013 Press Pass Aerodynamic Autographs Blue /1 #JJ
2013 Press Pass Aerodynamic Autographs Holofoil /5 #JJ
2013 Press Pass Burning Rubber Blue /50 #BRJJ
2013 Press Pass Burning Rubber Blue /50 #BRJJ2
2013 Press Pass Burning Rubber Blue /50 #BRJJ3
2013 Press Pass Burning Rubber Gold /199 #BRJJ
2013 Press Pass Burning Rubber Gold /199 #BRJJ3
2013 Press Pass Burning Rubber Gold /199 #BRJJ2
2013 Press Pass Burning Rubber Holofoil /75 #BRJJ
2013 Press Pass Burning Rubber Holofoil /75 #BRJJ2
2013 Press Pass Burning Rubber Holofoil /75 #BRJJ3
2013 Press Pass Burning Rubber Letterman /8 #BRLJJ
2013 Press Pass Burning Rubber Melting /10 #BRJJ
2013 Press Pass Burning Rubber Melting /10 #BRJJ2
2013 Press Pass Burning Rubber Melting /10 #BRJJ3
2013 Press Pass Certified Winners Autographs Gold /10 #JJ
2013 Press Pass Certified Winners Autographs Melting /5 #JJ
2013 Press Pass Color Proofs Black #21
2013 Press Pass Color Proofs Black #22
2013 Press Pass Color Proofs Black #70
2013 Press Pass Color Proofs Black #75
2013 Press Pass Color Proofs Black #86
2013 Press Pass Color Proofs Black #100
2013 Press Pass Color Proofs Cyan /35 #21
2013 Press Pass Color Proofs Cyan /35 #22
2013 Press Pass Color Proofs Cyan /35 #70
2013 Press Pass Color Proofs Cyan /35 #75
2013 Press Pass Color Proofs Cyan /35 #86
2013 Press Pass Color Proofs Cyan /35 #100
2013 Press Pass Color Proofs Magenta #21
2013 Press Pass Color Proofs Magenta #22
2013 Press Pass Color Proofs Magenta #70
2013 Press Pass Color Proofs Magenta #75
2013 Press Pass Color Proofs Magenta #86
2013 Press Pass Color Proofs Magenta #100
2013 Press Pass Color Proofs Yellow /5 #21
2013 Press Pass Color Proofs Yellow /5 #22
2013 Press Pass Color Proofs Yellow /5 #70
2013 Press Pass Color Proofs Yellow /5 #75
2013 Press Pass Color Proofs Yellow /5 #86
2013 Press Pass Color Proofs Yellow /5 #100
2013 Press Pass Cool Persistence #CP9
2013 Press Pass Cup Chase #CC10
2013 Press Pass Cup Chase Prizes /200 #CCPJJ
2013 Press Pass Cup Chase Prizes #CCP2
2013 Press Pass Fanfare #25
2013 Press Pass Fanfare Autographs Blue /1 #JJ
2013 Press Pass Fanfare Autographs Gold /1 #JJ
2013 Press Pass Fanfare Autographs Green /1 #JJ
2013 Press Pass Fanfare Autographs Red /1 #JJ
2013 Press Pass Fanfare Autographs Silver /1 #JJ
2013 Press Pass Fanfare Diamond Die Cuts /5 #25
2013 Press Pass Fanfare Fan Following #FF3
2013 Press Pass Fanfare Fan Following National Convention VIP #FFN3
2013 Press Pass Fanfare Green /3 #25
2013 Press Pass Fanfare Holofoil Die Cuts #25
2013 Press Pass Fanfare Magnificent Jumbo Materials Signatures /10 #JJ
2013 Press Pass Fanfare Magnificent Materials Dual Swatches /50 #JJ
2013 Press Pass Fanfare Magnificent Materials Dual Swatches Melting /10 #JJ
2013 Press Pass Fanfare Magnificent Materials Gold /50 #JJ
2013 Press Pass Fanfare Magnificent Materials Jumbo Swatches /25 #JJ
2013 Press Pass Fanfare Magnificent Materials Signatures /25 #JJ
2013 Press Pass Fanfare Magnificent Materials Signatures Blue /5 #JJ
2013 Press Pass Fanfare Magnificent Materials Silver /199 #JJ
2013 Press Pass Fanfare Red Foil Die Cuts #25
2013 Press Pass Fanfare Sapphire /20 #25
2013 Press Pass Fanfare Showtime #S8
2013 Press Pass Fanfare Silver /25 #25
2013 Press Pass Four Wide Gold /10 #FWJJ
2013 Press Pass Four Wide Melting /1 #FWJJ
2013 Press Pass Ignite #15
2013 Press Pass Ignite Convoy #5
2013 Press Pass Ignite Double Burner Blue Holofoil /10 #DBJJ
2013 Press Pass Ignite Double Burner Red /1 #DBJJ
2013 Press Pass Ignite Double Burner Silver /25 #DBJJ
2013 Press Pass Ignite Great American Treads Autographs Blue Holofoil /10 #GATJJ
2013 Press Pass Ignite Great American Treads Autographs Red /1 #GATJJ
2013 Press Pass Ignite Hot Threads Blue Holofoil /99 #HTJJ
2013 Press Pass Ignite Hot Threads Patch Red /10 #HTJJ
2013 Press Pass Ignite Hot Threads Patch Red Oversized /20 #HTPJJ
2013 Press Pass Ignite Hot Threads Silver #HTJJ
2013 Press Pass Ignite Ink Black /20 #IJJ
2013 Press Pass Ignite Ink Blue /5 #IJJ
2013 Press Pass Ignite Ink Red /1 #IJJ
2013 Press Pass Ignite Profile #7
2013 Press Pass Ignite Proofs Black and White /50 #15
2013 Press Pass Ignite Proofs Cyan #15
2013 Press Pass Ignite Proofs Magenta #15
2013 Press Pass Ignite Proofs Yellow /5 #15
2013 Press Pass Ignite Supercharged Signatures Blue Holofoil /10 #SSJJ
2013 Press Pass Ignite Supercharged Signatures Red /1 #SSJJ
2013 Press Pass Ignite Turning Point #5
2013 Press Pass Legends #46
2013 Press Pass Legends Autographs Blue #LGJJ
2013 Press Pass Legends Autographs Gold /4 #LGJJ
2013 Press Pass Legends Autographs Holofoil /2 #LGJJ
2013 Press Pass Legends Autographs Printing Plates Black /1 #LGJJ
2013 Press Pass Legends Autographs Printing Plates Cyan /1 #LGJJ
2013 Press Pass Legends Autographs Printing Plates Magenta /1 #LGJJ
2013 Press Pass Legends Autographs Printing Plates Yellow /1 #LGJJ
2013 Press Pass Legends Autographs Silver #LGJJ
2013 Press Pass Legends Blue #46
2013 Press Pass Legends Blue Holofoil /1 #46
2013 Press Pass Legends Four Wide Memorabilia Autographs Gold /25 #FWSEJJ
2013 Press Pass Legends Four Wide Memorabilia Autographs Melting /5 #FWSEJJ
2013 Press Pass Legends Gold /149 #46
2013 Press Pass Legends Holofoil /10 #46
2013 Press Pass Legends Printing Plates Black /1 #46
2013 Press Pass Legends Printing Plates Cyan /1 #46
2013 Press Pass Legends Printing Plates Magenta /1 #46
2013 Press Pass Legends Printing Plates Yellow /1 #46
2013 Press Pass Legends Prominent Pieces Gold /10 #PPJJ
2013 Press Pass Legends Prominent Pieces Holofoil /5 #PPJJ
2013 Press Pass Legends Prominent Pieces Oversized Firesuit /5 #PPJJ
2013 Press Pass Legends Prominent Pieces Silver /25 #PPJJ
2013 Press Pass Legends Red /99 #46
2013 Press Pass Power Picks Blue /99 #8
2013 Press Pass Power Picks Blue /99 #38
2013 Press Pass Power Picks Gold /50 #8
2013 Press Pass Power Picks Gold /50 #38
2013 Press Pass Power Picks Holofoil /10 #8
2013 Press Pass Power Picks Holofoil /10 #38
2013 Press Pass Racing Champions #RC20
2013 Press Pass Racing Champions #RC11
2013 Press Pass Racing Champions #RC13
2013 Press Pass Racing Champions #RC31
2013 Press Pass Redline #23
2013 Press Pass Redline #24
2013 Press Pass Redline Black /99 #23
2013 Press Pass Redline Black /99 #24
2013 Press Pass Redline Career Wins Relic Autographs Blue /5 #CWJJ
2013 Press Pass Redline Career Wins Relic Autographs Gold /10 #CWJJ
2013 Press Pass Redline Career Wins Relic Autographs Melting /1 #CWJJ
2013 Press Pass Redline Career Wins Relic Autographs Red /48 #CWJJ
2013 Press Pass Redline Cyan /50 #23
2013 Press Pass Redline Cyan /50 #24
2013 Press Pass Redline Dynamic Duals Dual Relic Blue /5 #DDJJ
2013 Press Pass Redline Dynamic Duals Dual Relic Gold /10 #DDJJ
2013 Press Pass Redline Dynamic Duals Dual Relic Melting /1 #DDJJ
2013 Press Pass Redline Dynamic Duals Dual Relic Red /50 #DDJJ
2013 Press Pass Redline Dynamic Duals Dual Relic Silver /25 #DDJJ
2013 Press Pass Redline Intensity #5
2013 Press Pass Redline Magenta /15 #23
2013 Press Pass Redline Magenta /15 #24
2013 Press Pass Redline Muscle Car Sheet Metal Blue /5 #MCMJJ
2013 Press Pass Redline Muscle Car Sheet Metal Gold /10 #MCMJJ
2013 Press Pass Redline Muscle Car Sheet Metal Melting /1 #MCMJJ
2013 Press Pass Redline Muscle Car Sheet Metal Red /50 #MCMJJ
2013 Press Pass Redline Muscle Car Sheet Metal Silver /25 #MCMJJ
2013 Press Pass Redline Pieces of the Action Blue /10 #PAJJ
2013 Press Pass Redline Pieces of the Action Gold /25 #PAJJ
2013 Press Pass Redline Pieces of the Action Melting /1 #PAJJ
2013 Press Pass Redline Pieces of the Action Red /75 #PAJJ
2013 Press Pass Redline Pieces of the Action Silver /50 #PAJJ
2013 Press Pass Redline Redline Racers #7
2013 Press Pass Redline Relic Autographs Blue /5 #RRSEJJ
2013 Press Pass Redline Relic Autographs Gold /10 #RRSEJJ
2013 Press Pass Redline Relic Autographs Melting /1 #RRSEJJ
2013 Press Pass Redline Relic Autographs Red /48 #RRSEJJ
2013 Press Pass Redline Relic Autographs Silver /10 #RRSEJJ
2013 Press Pass Redline Relics Blue /5 #RRJJ
2013 Press Pass Redline Relics Gold /10 #RRJJ
2013 Press Pass Redline Relics Melting /1 #RRJJ
2013 Press Pass Redline Relics Red /50 #RRJJ
2013 Press Pass Redline Relics Silver /25 #RRJJ
2013 Press Pass Redline RPM #5
2013 Press Pass Redline Signatures Blue /25 #RSJJ1
2013 Press Pass Redline Signatures Blue /10 #RSJJ2
2013 Press Pass Redline Signatures Gold /5 #RSJJ1
2013 Press Pass Redline Signatures Gold /5 #RSJJ2
2013 Press Pass Redline Signatures Holo /5 #RSJJ1
2013 Press Pass Redline Signatures Holo /5 #RSJJ2
2013 Press Pass Redline Signatures Melting /1 #RSJJ1
2013 Press Pass Redline Signatures Melting /1 #RSJJ2
2013 Press Pass Redline Signatures Red /10 #RSJJ2
2013 Press Pass Redline Signatures Red /48 #RSJJ1
2013 Press Pass Redline Yellow /1 #23
2013 Press Pass Redline Yellow /1 #24
2013 Press Pass Showcase /349 #13
2013 Press Pass Showcase /349 #37
2013 Press Pass Showcase /349 #46
2013 Press Pass Showcase /349 #55
2013 Press Pass Showcase Black /1 #13
2013 Press Pass Showcase Black /1 #37
2013 Press Pass Showcase Black /1 #46
2013 Press Pass Showcase Black /1 #55
2013 Press Pass Showcase Blue /25 #13
2013 Press Pass Showcase Blue /25 #37
2013 Press Pass Showcase Blue /25 #46
2013 Press Pass Showcase Blue /25 #55
2013 Press Pass Showcase Classic Collections Ink Gold /5 #CCIHMS
2013 Press Pass Showcase Classic Collections Ink Melting /1 #CCIHMS
2013 Press Pass Showcase Classic Collections Ink Red /1 #CCIHMS
2013 Press Pass Showcase Classic Collections Memorabilia Gold /25 #CCMHMS
2013 Press Pass Showcase Classic Collections Memorabilia Melting /5 #CCMHMS
2013 Press Pass Showcase Classic Collections Memorabilia Silver /75 #CCMHMS
2013 Press Pass Showcase Elite Exhibit Ink /25 #EEIJJ
2013 Press Pass Showcase Elite Exhibit Ink Blue /30 #EEIJJ
2013 Press Pass Showcase Elite Exhibit Ink Gold /10 #EEIJJ
2013 Press Pass Showcase Elite Exhibit Ink Melting /1 #EEIJJ
2013 Press Pass Showcase Elite Exhibit Ink Red /5 #EEIJJ
2013 Press Pass Showcase Gold /99 #13
2013 Press Pass Showcase Gold /99 #37
2013 Press Pass Showcase Gold /99 #46
2013 Press Pass Showcase Gold /99 #55
2013 Press Pass Showcase Green /20 #13
2013 Press Pass Showcase Green /20 #37
2013 Press Pass Showcase Green /20 #46
2013 Press Pass Showcase Green /20 #55
2013 Press Pass Showcase Masterpieces Ink /25 #MPIJJ
2013 Press Pass Showcase Masterpieces Ink Gold /10 #MPIJJ
2013 Press Pass Showcase Masterpieces Ink Melting /1 #MPIJJ
2013 Press Pass Showcase Masterpieces Memorabilia /75 #MPJJ
2013 Press Pass Showcase Masterpieces Memorabilia Gold /25 #MPJJ
2013 Press Pass Showcase Masterpieces Memorabilia Melting /5 #MPJJ
2013 Press Pass Showcase Prized Pieces /99 #PPMJJ
2013 Press Pass Showcase Prized Pieces Blue /20 #PPMJJ
2013 Press Pass Showcase Prized Pieces Gold /25 #PPMJJ
2013 Press Pass Showcase Prized Pieces Ink /25 #PPIJJ
2013 Press Pass Showcase Prized Pieces Ink Gold /10 #PPIJJ
2013 Press Pass Showcase Prized Pieces Ink Melting /1 #PPIJJ
2013 Press Pass Showcase Prized Pieces Melting /5 #PPMJJ
2013 Press Pass Showcase Purple /13 #13
2013 Press Pass Showcase Purple /13 #37
2013 Press Pass Showcase Purple /13 #46
2013 Press Pass Showcase Purple /13 #55
2013 Press Pass Showcase Red /10 #13
2013 Press Pass Showcase Red /10 #37
2013 Press Pass Showcase Red /10 #46
2013 Press Pass Showcase Red /10 #55
2013 Press Pass Showcase Series Standouts Gold /50 #9
2013 Press Pass Showcase Series Standouts Memorabilia /75 #SSMJJ
2013 Press Pass Showcase Series Standouts Memorabilia Blue /20 #SSMJJ
2013 Press Pass Showcase Series Standouts Memorabilia Gold /25 #SSMJJ
2013 Press Pass Showcase Series Standouts Memorabilia Melting /5 #SSMJJ
2013 Press Pass Showcase Showcase Patches /5 #SPJJ
2013 Press Pass Showcase Showroom /299 #2
2013 Press Pass Showcase Showroom Blue /40 #2
2013 Press Pass Showcase Showroom Gold /50 #2
2013 Press Pass Showcase Showroom Green /20 #2
2013 Press Pass Showcase Showroom Melting /1 #2
2013 Press Pass Showcase Showroom Purple /13 #2
2013 Press Pass Showcase Showroom Red /10 #2
2013 Press Pass Showcase Signature Patches /2 #SSPJJ
2013 Press Pass Showcase Studio Showcase /299 #9
2013 Press Pass Showcase Studio Showcase Blue /40 #9
2013 Press Pass Showcase Studio Showcase Green /25 #9
2013 Press Pass Showcase Studio Showcase Ink /25 #SSIJJ
2013 Press Pass Showcase Studio Showcase Ink Gold /10 #SSIJJ
2013 Press Pass Showcase Studio Showcase Ink Melting /1 #SSIJJ
2013 Press Pass Showcase Studio Showcase Ink Red /5 #SSIJJ
2013 Press Pass Showcase Studio Showcase Melting /1 #9
2013 Press Pass Showcase Studio Showcase Purple /13 #9
2013 Press Pass Showcase Studio Showcase Red /10 #9
2013 Press Pass Signature Series Gold /10 #JJ
2013 Press Pass Signature Series Melting /5 #JJ
2013 Press Pass Signings Blue /1 #JJ
2013 Press Pass Signings Gold /5 #JJ
2013 Press Pass Signings Printing Plates Black /1 #JJ
2013 Press Pass Signings Printing Plates Cyan /1 #JJ
2013 Press Pass Signings Printing Plates Magenta /1 #JJ
2013 Press Pass Signings Printing Plates Yellow /1 #JJ
2013 Press Pass Signings Silver /5 #JJ
2013 Press Pass Three Wide Gold /10 #TWJJ
2013 Press Pass Three Wide Melting /1 #TWJJ
2013 Sportkings National Convention Spectacular Patch /1 #SKFR93
2013 Total Memorabilia #19
2013 Total Memorabilia #20
2013 Total Memorabilia Black and White /99 #19
2013 Total Memorabilia Black and White /99 #20
2013 Total Memorabilia Burning Rubber Chase Edition Gold /75 #BRCJJ
2013 Total Memorabilia Burning Rubber Chase Edition Gold /75 #BRCJJ2
2013 Total Memorabilia Burning Rubber Chase Edition Holofoil /50 #BRCJJ
2013 Total Memorabilia Burning Rubber Chase Edition Holofoil /50 #BRCJJ2
2013 Total Memorabilia Burning Rubber Chase Edition Melting /5 #BRCJJ
2013 Total Memorabilia Burning Rubber Chase Edition Melting /5 #BRCJJ2
2013 Total Memorabilia Burning Rubber Chase Edition Silver /175 #BRCJJ
2013 Total Memorabilia Burning Rubber Chase Edition Silver /175 #BRCJJ2
2013 Total Memorabilia Dual Swatch Gold /99 #TMJJ
2013 Total Memorabilia Gold /275 #19
2013 Total Memorabilia Gold /275 #20
2013 Total Memorabilia Hot Rod Relics Gold /50 #HRRJJ
2013 Total Memorabilia Hot Rod Relics Holofoil /10 #HRRJJ
2013 Total Memorabilia Hot Rod Relics Melting /1 #HRRJJ
2013 Total Memorabilia Hot Rod Relics Silver /99 #HRRJJ
2013 Total Memorabilia Quad Swatch Melting /10 #TMJJ
2013 Total Memorabilia Red #19
2013 Total Memorabilia Red #20
2013 Total Memorabilia Signature Collection Dual Swatch Gold /5 #SCJJ
2013 Total Memorabilia Signature Collection Quad Swatch Melting /1 #SCJJ
2013 Total Memorabilia Signature Collection Single Swatch Silver /10 #SCJJ
2013 Total Memorabilia Signature Collection Triple Swatch Holofoil /5 #SCJJ
2013 Total Memorabilia Single Swatch Silver /475 #TMJJ
2013 Total Memorabilia Smooth Operators #SO4
2013 Total Memorabilia Triple Swatch Holofoil /99 #TMJJ
2014 Press Pass #16
2014 Press Pass #17
2014 Press Pass #69
2014 Press Pass #93
2014 Press Pass #76
2014 Press Pass #83
2014 Press Pass American Thunder #18
2014 Press Pass American Thunder #67
2014 Press Pass American Thunder #51
2014 Press Pass American Thunder Autographs Blue /5 #ATAJJ
2014 Press Pass American Thunder Autographs Red /1 #ATAJJ
2014 Press Pass American Thunder Autographs White /15 #ATAJJ
2014 Press Pass American Thunder Battle Armor Blue /25 #BAJJ
2014 Press Pass American Thunder Battle Armor Red /1 #BAJJ
2014 Press Pass American Thunder Battle Armor Silver /99 #BAJJ
2014 Press Pass American Thunder Black and White /50 #18
2014 Press Pass American Thunder Black and White /50 #51
2014 Press Pass American Thunder Black and White /50 #67
2014 Press Pass American Thunder Brothers In Arms Autographs Blue /5 #BAHMS
2014 Press Pass American Thunder Brothers In Arms Autographs Red /1 #BAHMS
2014 Press Pass American Thunder Brothers In Arms Autographs White /10 #BAHMS
2014 Press Pass American Thunder Brothers In Arms Relics Blue /25 #BAHMS
2014 Press Pass American Thunder Brothers In Arms Relics Red /5 #BAHMS
2014 Press Pass American Thunder Brothers In Arms Relics Silver /50 #BAHMS
2014 Press Pass American Thunder Class A Uniforms Blue /99 #CAUJJ
2014 Press Pass American Thunder Class A Uniforms Red /10 #CAUJJ
2014 Press Pass American Thunder Class A Uniforms Silver #CAUJJ
2014 Press Pass American Thunder Cyan #18
2014 Press Pass American Thunder Cyan #51
2014 Press Pass American Thunder Cyan #67
2014 Press Pass American Thunder Great American Treads Autographs Blue /10 #GATJJ
2014 Press Pass American Thunder Great American Treads Autographs Red /1 #GATJJ
2014 Press Pass American Thunder Magenta #18
2014 Press Pass American Thunder Magenta #51
2014 Press Pass American Thunder Magenta #67
2014 Press Pass American Thunder Yellow /5 #18
2014 Press Pass American Thunder Yellow /5 #51
2014 Press Pass Burning Rubber Blue /25 #BRJJ
2014 Press Pass Burning Rubber Blue /25 #BRJJ2
2014 Press Pass Burning Rubber Blue /25 #BRJJ3
2014 Press Pass Burning Rubber Blue /25 #BRJJ4
2014 Press Pass Burning Rubber Chase Edition Blue /25 #BRCJJ
2014 Press Pass Burning Rubber Chase Edition Blue /25 #BRCJJ2
2014 Press Pass Burning Rubber Chase Edition Gold /50 #BRCJJ
2014 Press Pass Burning Rubber Chase Edition Gold /50 #BRCJJ2
2014 Press Pass Burning Rubber Chase Edition Melting /10 #BRCJJ
2014 Press Pass Burning Rubber Chase Edition Melting /10 #BRCJJ2
2014 Press Pass Burning Rubber Chase Edition Silver /99 #BRCJJ
2014 Press Pass Burning Rubber Chase Edition Silver /99 #BRCJJ2
2014 Press Pass Burning Rubber Gold /75 #BRJJ
2014 Press Pass Burning Rubber Gold /75 #BRJJ2
2014 Press Pass Burning Rubber Gold /75 #BRJJ3
2014 Press Pass Burning Rubber Gold /75 #BRJJ4
2014 Press Pass Burning Rubber Holofoil /50 #BRJJ
2014 Press Pass Burning Rubber Holofoil /50 #BRJJ2
2014 Press Pass Burning Rubber Holofoil /50 #BRJJ3
2014 Press Pass Burning Rubber Holofoil /50 #BRJJ4
2014 Press Pass Burning Rubber Letterman /8 #BRLJJ
2014 Press Pass Burning Rubber Melting /10 #BRJJ
2014 Press Pass Burning Rubber Melting /10 #BRJJ2
2014 Press Pass Burning Rubber Melting /10 #BRJJ3
2014 Press Pass Burning Rubber Melting /10 #BRJJ4
2014 Press Pass Certified Winners Memorabilia Autographs Gold /5 #CWJJ
2014 Press Pass Certified Winners Memorabilia Autographs Melting /1 #CWJJ
2014 Press Pass Color Proofs Black /70 #16
2014 Press Pass Color Proofs Black /70 #17
2014 Press Pass Color Proofs Black /70 #69
2014 Press Pass Color Proofs Black /70 #76
2014 Press Pass Color Proofs Black /70 #83
2014 Press Pass Color Proofs Black /70 #93
2014 Press Pass Color Proofs Cyan /35 #16
2014 Press Pass Color Proofs Cyan /35 #17
2014 Press Pass Color Proofs Cyan /35 #69
2014 Press Pass Color Proofs Cyan /35 #76
2014 Press Pass Color Proofs Cyan /35 #83
2014 Press Pass Color Proofs Cyan /35 #93
2014 Press Pass Color Proofs Magenta #16
2014 Press Pass Color Proofs Magenta #17
2014 Press Pass Color Proofs Magenta #69
2014 Press Pass Color Proofs Magenta #76
2014 Press Pass Color Proofs Magenta #83
2014 Press Pass Color Proofs Magenta #93
2014 Press Pass Color Proofs Yellow /5 #16
2014 Press Pass Color Proofs Yellow /5 #17
2014 Press Pass Color Proofs Yellow /5 #69
2014 Press Pass Color Proofs Yellow /5 #76
2014 Press Pass Color Proofs Yellow /5 #83
2014 Press Pass Color Proofs Yellow /5 #93
2014 Press Pass Cup Chase #8
2014 Press Pass Five Star /15 #9
2014 Press Pass Five Star Blue /5 #9
2014 Press Pass Five Star Classic Compilation Autographs Blue Triple Swatch /5 #CCJJ
2014 Press Pass Five Star Classic Compilation Autographs Holofoil /10 #CCJJ
2014 Press Pass Five Star Classic Compilation Autographs Holofoil Dual Swatch /10 #CCJJ
2014 Press Pass Five Star Classic Compilation Autographs Melting Five Swatch /1 #CCJJ
2014 Press Pass Five Star Classic Compilation Autographs Melting Quad Swatch /1 #CCJJ
2014 Press Pass Five Star Classic Compilations Autographed Patch Booklet /1 #CCJJ1
2014 Press Pass Five Star Classic Compilations Autographed Patch Booklet /1 #CCJJ2
2014 Press Pass Five Star Classic Compilations Autographed Patch Booklet /1 #CCJJ3
2014 Press Pass Five Star Classic Compilations Autographed Patch Booklet /1 #CCJJ4
2014 Press Pass Five Star Classic Compilations Autographed Patch Booklet /1 #CCJJ5
2014 Press Pass Five Star Classic Compilations Autographed Patch Booklet /1 #CCJJ6
2014 Press Pass Five Star Classic Compilations Autographed Patch Booklet /1 #CCJJ7
2014 Press Pass Five Star Classic Compilations Autographed Patch Booklet /1 #CCJJ8
2014 Press Pass Five Star Classic Compilations Autographed Patch Booklet /1 #CCJJ9
2014 Press Pass Five Star Classic Compilations Autographed Patch Booklet /1 #CCJJ10
2014 Press Pass Five Star Classic Compilations Autographed Patch Booklet /1 #CCJJ11
2014 Press Pass Five Star Classic Compilations Autographed Patch Booklet /1 #CCJJ12
2014 Press Pass Five Star Classic Compilations Autographed Patch Booklet /1 #CCJJ13
2014 Press Pass Five Star Classic Compilations Autographed Patch Booklet /1 #CCJJ14
2014 Press Pass Five Star Classic Compilations Combo Autographs Blue /5 #CCHMS
2014 Press Pass Five Star Classic Compilations Combo Autographs Melting /1 #CCHMS
2014 Press Pass Five Star Holofoil /10 #9
2014 Press Pass Five Star Melting /1 #9
2014 Press Pass Five Star Paramount Pieces Blue /5 #PPJJ
2014 Press Pass Five Star Paramount Pieces Gold /25 #PPJJ
2014 Press Pass Five Star Paramount Pieces Holofoil /10 #PPJJ
2014 Press Pass Five Star Paramount Pieces Melting /1 #PPJJ
2014 Press Pass Five Star Paramount Pieces Melting Patch /1 #PPJJ
2014 Press Pass Five Star Signature Souvenirs Blue /5 #SSJJ
2014 Press Pass Five Star Signature Souvenirs Gold /50 #SSJJ
2014 Press Pass Five Star Signature Souvenirs Holofoil /25 #SSJJ
2014 Press Pass Five Star Signature Souvenirs Melting /1 #SSJJ
2014 Press Pass Five Star Signatures Blue /5 #FSSJJ
2014 Press Pass Five Star Signatures Holofoil /10 #FSSJJ
2014 Press Pass Five Star Signatures Melting /1 #FSSJJ
2014 Press Pass Four Wide Gold /10 #FWJJ
2014 Press Pass Four Wide Melting /1 #FWJJ
2014 Press Pass Gold #16
2014 Press Pass Gold #17
2014 Press Pass Gold #69
2014 Press Pass Gold #76
2014 Press Pass Gold #83
2014 Press Pass Gold #93
2014 Press Pass Intensity National Convention VIP #NE3
2014 Press Pass Redline #26
2014 Press Pass Redline #27
2014 Press Pass Redline Black /75 #26
2014 Press Pass Redline Black /75 #27
2014 Press Pass Redline Blue Foil #26
2014 Press Pass Redline Blue Foil #27
2014 Press Pass Redline Cyan /50 #26
2014 Press Pass Redline Cyan /50 #27
2014 Press Pass Redline Dynamic Duals Relic Autographs Blue /10 #DDJJ
2014 Press Pass Redline Dynamic Duals Relic Autographs Gold /5 #DDJJ
2014 Press Pass Redline Dynamic Duals Relic Autographs Melting /1 #DDJJ
2014 Press Pass Redline Dynamic Duals Relic Autographs Red /15 #DDJJ
2014 Press Pass Redline Green National Convention /5 #26
2014 Press Pass Redline Green National Convention /5 #27
2014 Press Pass Redline Head to Head Blue /10 #HTHJJTS
2014 Press Pass Redline Head to Head Gold /25 #HTHJJTS
2014 Press Pass Redline Head to Head Melting /1 #HTHJJTS
2014 Press Pass Redline Head to Head Red /75 #HTHJJTS
2014 Press Pass Redline Intensity #I6
2014 Press Pass Redline Magenta /10 #26
2014 Press Pass Redline Magenta /10 #27
2014 Press Pass Redline Muscle Car Sheet Metal Blue /25 #MCMJJ
2014 Press Pass Redline Muscle Car Sheet Metal Gold /50 #MCMJJ
2014 Press Pass Redline Muscle Car Sheet Metal Melting /1 #MCMJJ
2014 Press Pass Redline Muscle Car Sheet Metal Red /75 #MCMJJ
2014 Press Pass Redline Pieces of the Action Blue /10 #PAJJ
2014 Press Pass Redline Pieces of the Action Gold /25 #PAJJ
2014 Press Pass Redline Pieces of the Action Melting /1 #PAJJ
2014 Press Pass Redline Pieces of the Action Red /75 #PAJJ
2014 Press Pass Redline Redline Racers #RR9
2014 Press Pass Redline Relic Autographs Blue /5 #RRSEJJ
2014 Press Pass Redline Relic Autographs Gold /10 #RRSEJJ
2014 Press Pass Redline Relic Autographs Melting /1 #RRSEJJ
2014 Press Pass Redline Relic Autographs Red /15 #RRSEJJ
2014 Press Pass Redline Relics Blue /25 #RRJJ
2014 Press Pass Redline Relics Gold /50 #RRJJ
2014 Press Pass Redline Relics Melting /1 #RRJJ
2014 Press Pass Redline Relics Red /75 #RRJJ
2014 Press Pass Redline RPM #RPM6
2014 Press Pass Redline Signatures Blue /5 #RSJJ
2014 Press Pass Redline Signatures Gold /10 #RSJJ
2014 Press Pass Redline Signatures Melting /1 #RSJJ
2014 Press Pass Redline Signatures Red /15 #RSJJ
2014 Press Pass Redline Yellow /1 #26
2014 Press Pass Redline Yellow /1 #27
2014 Press Pass Replay #14
2014 Press Pass Replay #6
2014 Press Pass Replay #18
2014 Press Pass Replay #1
2014 Press Pass Signature Series Gold /9 #SSJJ
2014 Press Pass Signature Series Melting /1 #SSJJ
2014 Press Pass Signings Gold /10 #PPSJJ
2014 Press Pass Signings Holofoil /1 #PPSJJ
2014 Press Pass Signings Melting /1 #PPSJJ
2014 Press Pass Signings Printing Plates Black /1 #PPSJJ
2014 Press Pass Signings Printing Plates Cyan /1 #PPSJJ
2014 Press Pass Signings Printing Plates Magenta /1 #PPSJJ
2014 Press Pass Signings Printing Plates Yellow /1 #PPSJJ
2014 Press Pass Signings Silver /5 #PPSJJ
2014 Press Pass Velocity #5
2014 Total Memorabilia #12
2014 Total Memorabilia #50
2014 Total Memorabilia Acceleration #AC2
2014 Total Memorabilia Autographed Memorabilia Blue /5 #SCJJ
2014 Total Memorabilia Autographed Memorabilia Gold /5 #SCJJ
2014 Total Memorabilia Autographed Memorabilia Melting /1 #SCJJ
2014 Total Memorabilia Autographed Memorabilia Silver /5 #SC-JJ
2014 Total Memorabilia Black and White /99 #12
2014 Total Memorabilia Black and White /99 #50
2014 Total Memorabilia Champions Collection Blue /25 #CCJJ
2014 Total Memorabilia Champions Collection Gold /50 #CCJJ
2014 Total Memorabilia Champions Collection Melting /5 #CCJJ
2014 Total Memorabilia Champions Collection Silver /75 #CCJJ
2014 Total Memorabilia Clear Cuts Blue /175 #CCUJJ
2014 Total Memorabilia Clear Cuts Melting /25 #CCUJJ
2014 Total Memorabilia Dual Swatch Gold /150 #TMJJ

2014 Total Memorabilia Gold /175 #12
2014 Total Memorabilia Gold /175 #50
2014 Total Memorabilia Quad Swatch Melting /25 #TMJJ
2014 Total Memorabilia Red #12
2014 Total Memorabilia Red #50
2014 Total Memorabilia Single Swatch Silver /275 #TMJJ
2014 Total Memorabilia Triple Swatch Blue /99 #TMJJ
2015 Press Pass #18
2015 Press Pass #93
2015 Press Pass #81
2015 Press Pass #70
2015 Press Pass #100
2015 Press Pass Burning Rubber Blue /50 #BRJJ1
2015 Press Pass Burning Rubber Blue /50 #BRJJ2
2015 Press Pass Burning Rubber Blue /50 #BRJJ3
2015 Press Pass Burning Rubber Gold #BRJJ3
2015 Press Pass Burning Rubber Gold #BRJJ1
2015 Press Pass Burning Rubber Gold #BRJJ2
2015 Press Pass Burning Rubber Green /10 #BRJJ1
2015 Press Pass Burning Rubber Green /10 #BRJJ2
2015 Press Pass Burning Rubber Green /10 #BRJJ3
2015 Press Pass Burning Rubber Letterman /8 #BRLEJJ
2015 Press Pass Burning Rubber Melting /1 #BRJJ1
2015 Press Pass Burning Rubber Melting /1 #BRJJ2
2015 Press Pass Burning Rubber Melting /1 #BRJJ3
2015 Press Pass Championship Caliber Dual /25 #CCMJJ
2015 Press Pass Championship Caliber Quad /1 #CCMJJ
2015 Press Pass Championship Caliber Signature Edition Blue /10 #CCJJ
2015 Press Pass Championship Caliber Signature Edition Gold /25 #CCJJ
2015 Press Pass Championship Caliber Signature Edition Green /5 #CCJJ
2015 Press Pass Championship Caliber Signature Edition Melting /1 #CCJJ
2015 Press Pass Championship Caliber Single /50 #CCMJJ
2015 Press Pass Championship Caliber Triple /10 #CCMJJ
2015 Press Pass Cup Chase #18
2015 Press Pass Cup Chase #70
2015 Press Pass Cup Chase #81
2015 Press Pass Cup Chase #93
2015 Press Pass Cup Chase #100
2015 Press Pass Cup Chase Blue /25 #18
2015 Press Pass Cup Chase Blue /25 #70
2015 Press Pass Cup Chase Blue /25 #81
2015 Press Pass Cup Chase Blue /25 #93
2015 Press Pass Cup Chase Blue /25 #100
2015 Press Pass Cup Chase Gold /75 #18
2015 Press Pass Cup Chase Gold /75 #70
2015 Press Pass Cup Chase Gold /75 #81
2015 Press Pass Cup Chase Gold /75 #93
2015 Press Pass Cup Chase Gold /75 #100
2015 Press Pass Cup Chase Green /10 #18
2015 Press Pass Cup Chase Green /10 #70
2015 Press Pass Cup Chase Green /10 #81
2015 Press Pass Cup Chase Green /10 #93
2015 Press Pass Cup Chase Green /10 #100
2015 Press Pass Cup Chase Melting /1 #18
2015 Press Pass Cup Chase Melting /1 #70
2015 Press Pass Cup Chase Melting /1 #81
2015 Press Pass Cup Chase Melting /1 #93
2015 Press Pass Cup Chase Melting /1 #100
2015 Press Pass Cup Chase Three Wide Blue /25 #3WJJ
2015 Press Pass Cup Chase Three Wide Gold /50 #3WJJ
2015 Press Pass Cup Chase Three Wide Green /10 #3WJJ
2015 Press Pass Cup Chase Three Wide Melting /1 #3WJJ
2015 Press Pass Cup Chase Upper Cuts /13 #UCJJ
2015 Press Pass Cuts Blue /25 #CCCJJ
2015 Press Pass Cuts Gold /50 #CCCJJ
2015 Press Pass Cuts Green /10 #CCCJJ
2015 Press Pass Cuts Melting /1 #CCCJJ
2015 Press Pass Four Wide Signature Edition Blue /10 #4WJJ
2015 Press Pass Four Wide Signature Edition Gold /15 #4WJJ
2015 Press Pass Four Wide Signature Edition Green /5 #4WJJ
2015 Press Pass Four Wide Signature Edition Melting /1 #4WJJ
2015 Press Pass Pit Road Pieces Blue /25 #PPMJJ
2015 Press Pass Pit Road Pieces Gold /50 #PPMJJ
2015 Press Pass Pit Road Pieces Green /10 #PPMJJ
2015 Press Pass Pit Road Pieces Melting /1 #PPMJJ
2015 Press Pass Pit Road Pieces Signature Edition Blue /10 #PRPJJ
2015 Press Pass Pit Road Pieces Signature Edition Gold /25 #PRPJJ
2015 Press Pass Pit Road Pieces Signature Edition Green /5 #PRPJJ
2015 Press Pass Pit Road Pieces Signature Edition Melting /1 #PRPJJ
2015 Press Pass Purple #18
2015 Press Pass Purple #70
2015 Press Pass Purple #81
2015 Press Pass Purple #93
2015 Press Pass Purple #100
2015 Press Pass Red #18
2015 Press Pass Red #70
2015 Press Pass Red #81
2015 Press Pass Red #93
2015 Press Pass Red #100
2015 Press Pass Signings Blue /15 #PPSJJ
2015 Press Pass Signings Gold #PPSJJ
2015 Press Pass Signings Green /5 #PPSJJ
2015 Press Pass Signings Melting /1 #PPSJJ
2015 Press Pass Signings Red /9 #PPSJJ
2016 Certified #51
2016 Certified #5
2016 Certified Complete Materials /199 #1
2016 Certified Complete Materials Mirror Black /1 #1
2016 Certified Complete Materials Mirror Blue /50 #1
2016 Certified Complete Materials Mirror Gold /25 #1
2016 Certified Complete Materials Mirror Green /5 #1
2016 Certified Complete Materials Mirror Orange /99 #1
2016 Certified Complete Materials Mirror Purple /10 #1
2016 Certified Complete Materials Mirror Red /75 #1
2016 Certified Complete Materials Mirror Silver /99 #1
2016 Certified Epix /199 #1
2016 Certified Epix Mirror Black /1 #1
2016 Certified Epix Mirror Blue /50 #1
2016 Certified Epix Mirror Gold /25 #1
2016 Certified Epix Mirror Green /5 #1
2016 Certified Epix Mirror Orange /99 #1
2016 Certified Epix Mirror Purple /10 #1
2016 Certified Epix Mirror Red /75 #1
2016 Certified Epix Mirror Silver /99 #1
2016 Certified Famed Rides /199 #7
2016 Certified Famed Rides Mirror Black /1 #7
2016 Certified Famed Rides Mirror Blue /50 #7
2016 Certified Famed Rides Mirror Gold /25 #7
2016 Certified Famed Rides Mirror Green /5 #7
2016 Certified Famed Rides Mirror Orange /99 #7
2016 Certified Famed Rides Mirror Purple /10 #7
2016 Certified Famed Rides Mirror Red /75 #7
2016 Certified Famed Rides Mirror Silver /99 #7
2016 Certified Gold Team /199 #10
2016 Certified Gold Team Mirror Black /1 #10
2016 Certified Gold Team Mirror Blue /50 #10
2016 Certified Gold Team Mirror Gold /25 #10
2016 Certified Gold Team Mirror Green /5 #10
2016 Certified Gold Team Mirror Orange /99 #10
2016 Certified Gold Team Mirror Purple /10 #10
2016 Certified Gold Team Mirror Red /75 #10
2016 Certified Gold Team Mirror Silver /99 #10
2016 Certified Gold Team Signatures /25 #11
2016 Certified Gold Team Signatures Mirror Black /1 #11
2016 Certified Gold Team Signatures Mirror Gold /10 #11
2016 Certified Mirror Black /1 #5
2016 Certified Mirror Black /1 #51
2016 Certified Mirror Blue /50 #5
2016 Certified Mirror Blue /50 #51
2016 Certified Mirror Gold /25 #5
2016 Certified Mirror Gold /25 #51
2016 Certified Mirror Green /5 #5
2016 Certified Mirror Green /5 #51
2016 Certified Mirror Orange /99 #5
2016 Certified Mirror Orange /99 #51
2016 Certified Mirror Purple /10 #5
2016 Certified Mirror Purple /10 #51
2016 Certified Mirror Red /75 #5
2016 Certified Mirror Red /75 #51
2016 Certified Mirror Silver /99 #5
2016 Certified Mirror Silver /99 #51
2016 Certified Signatures /25 #28
2016 Certified Signatures Mirror Black /1 #28
2016 Certified Signatures Mirror Blue /15 #28
2016 Certified Signatures Mirror Gold /10 #28
2016 Certified Signatures Mirror Green /2 #28
2016 Certified Signatures Mirror Orange /1 #28
2016 Certified Signatures Mirror Purple /5 #28
2016 Certified Signatures Mirror Red /20 #28
2016 Certified Signatures Mirror Silver /1 #28
2016 Certified Skills /199 #2
2016 Certified Skills Mirror Black /1 #2
2016 Certified Skills Mirror Blue /50 #2
2016 Certified Skills Mirror Gold /25 #2
2016 Certified Skills Mirror Green /5 #2
2016 Certified Skills Mirror Orange /99 #2
2016 Certified Skills Mirror Purple /10 #2
2016 Certified Skills Mirror Red /75 #2
2016 Certified Skills Mirror Silver /99 #2
2016 Certified Sprint Cup Signature Swatches /30 #8
2016 Certified Sprint Cup Signature Swatches Mirror Black /1 #8
2016 Certified Sprint Cup Signature Swatches Mirror Blue /15 #8
2016 Certified Sprint Cup Signature Swatches Mirror Gold /10 #8
2016 Certified Sprint Cup Signature Swatches Mirror Green /3 #8
2016 Certified Sprint Cup Signature Swatches Mirror Orange /1 #8
2016 Certified Sprint Cup Signature Swatches Mirror Purple /5 #8
2016 Certified Sprint Cup Signature Swatches Mirror Red /20 #8
2016 Certified Sprint Cup Signature Swatches Mirror Silver /1 #8
2016 Certified Sprint Cup Swatches /125 #28
2016 Certified Sprint Cup Swatches Mirror Black /1 #28
2016 Certified Sprint Cup Swatches Mirror Blue /50 #28
2016 Certified Sprint Cup Swatches Mirror Gold /25 #28
2016 Certified Sprint Cup Swatches Mirror Green /5 #28
2016 Certified Sprint Cup Swatches Mirror Orange /99 #28
2016 Certified Sprint Cup Swatches Mirror Purple /10 #28
2016 Certified Sprint Cup Swatches Mirror Red /75 #28
2016 Certified Sprint Cup Swatches Mirror Silver /99 #28
2016 Panini Black Friday #32
2016 Panini Black Friday Autographs /25 #32
2016 Panini Black Friday Cracked Ice /25 #32
2016 Panini Black Friday Holo Plaid /1 #32
2016 Panini Black Friday Panini Collection #15
2016 Panini Black Friday Panini Collection Autographs /25 #15
2016 Panini Black Friday Panini Collection Cracked Ice /25 #15
2016 Panini Black Friday Panini Collection Holo Plaid /1 #15
2016 Panini Black Friday Panini Collection Rapture /10 #15
2016 Panini Black Friday Panini Collection Thick Stock /50 #15
2016 Panini Black Friday Panini Collection Wedges /50 #15
2016 Panini Black Friday Racing Memorabilia #R2
2016 Panini Black Friday Racing Memorabilia Cracked Ice /25 #R2
2016 Panini Black Friday Racing Memorabilia Galactic Window /10 #R2
2016 Panini Black Friday Racing Memorabilia Holo Plaid /1 #R2
2016 Panini Black Friday Rapture /10 #32
2016 Panini Black Friday Thick Stock /50 #32
2016 Panini Black Friday Wedges /50 #32
2016 Panini Cyber Monday #27
2016 Panini Instant #4
2016 Panini Instant #7
2016 Panini Instant #12
2016 Panini Instant #15
2016 Panini Instant Black /1 #4
2016 Panini Instant Black /1 #7
2016 Panini Instant Black /1 #12
2016 Panini Instant Black /1 #15
2016 Panini Instant Blue /25 #4
2016 Panini Instant Blue /25 #7
2016 Panini Instant Blue /25 #12
2016 Panini Instant Blue /25 #15
2016 Panini Instant Green /5 #4
2016 Panini Instant Green /5 #7
2016 Panini Instant Green /5 #12
2016 Panini Instant Green /5 #15
2016 Panini Instant Orange /50 #4
2016 Panini Instant Orange /50 #7
2016 Panini Instant Orange /50 #12
2016 Panini Instant Orange /50 #15
2016 Panini Instant Purple /10 #4
2016 Panini Instant Purple /10 #7
2016 Panini Instant Purple /10 #12
2016 Panini Instant Purple /10 #15
2016 Panini National Treasures /25 #1
2016 Panini National Treasures /25 #26
2016 Panini National Treasures Black /5 #1
2016 Panini National Treasures Black /5 #26
2016 Panini National Treasures Blue /1 #1
2016 Panini National Treasures Blue /1 #26
2016 Panini National Treasures Championship Signature Threads Blue /1 #1
2016 Panini National Treasures Championship Signature Threads Printing Plates Black /1 #1
2016 Panini National Treasures Championship Signature Threads Printing Plates Cyan /1 #1
2016 Panini National Treasures Championship Signature Threads Printing Plates Magenta /1 #1
2016 Panini National Treasures Championship Signature Threads Printing Plates Yellow /1 #1
2016 Panini National Treasures Dual Driver Materials /25 #1
2016 Panini National Treasures Dual Driver Materials Black /5 #1
2016 Panini National Treasures Dual Driver Materials Blue /1 #1
2016 Panini National Treasures Dual Driver Materials Gold /10 #1
2016 Panini National Treasures Dual Driver Materials Printing Plates Black /1 #1
2016 Panini National Treasures Dual Driver Materials Printing Plates Cyan /1 #1
2016 Panini National Treasures Dual Driver Materials Printing Plates Magenta /1 #1
2016 Panini National Treasures Dual Driver Materials Printing Plates Yellow /1 #1
2016 Panini National Treasures Dual Driver Materials Silver /15 #1
2016 Panini National Treasures Dual Signatures /24 #6
2016 Panini National Treasures Dual Signatures /25 #27
2016 Panini National Treasures Dual Signatures Black /10 #6
2016 Panini National Treasures Dual Signatures Black /10 #27
2016 Panini National Treasures Dual Signatures Blue /1 #6
2016 Panini National Treasures Dual Signatures Blue /1 #27
2016 Panini National Treasures Dual Signatures Gold /15 #6
2016 Panini National Treasures Dual Signatures Gold /15 #27
2016 Panini National Treasures Eight Signatures /15 #1
2016 Panini National Treasures Eight Signatures /15 #3
2016 Panini National Treasures Eight Signatures Black /5 #1
2016 Panini National Treasures Eight Signatures Black /5 #3
2016 Panini National Treasures Eight Signatures Blue /1 #1
2016 Panini National Treasures Eight Signatures Blue /1 #3
2016 Panini National Treasures Eight Signatures Gold /10 #1
2016 Panini National Treasures Eight Signatures Gold /10 #3
2016 Panini National Treasures Firesuit Materials /25 #8
2016 Panini National Treasures Firesuit Materials Black /5 #8
2016 Panini National Treasures Firesuit Materials Blue /1 #8
2016 Panini National Treasures Firesuit Materials Gold /10 #8
2016 Panini National Treasures Firesuit Materials Laundry Tag /1 #8
2016 Panini National Treasures Firesuit Materials Printing Plates Black /1 #8
2016 Panini National Treasures Firesuit Materials Printing Plates Cyan /1 #8
2016 Panini National Treasures Firesuit Materials Printing Plates Magenta /1 #8
2016 Panini National Treasures Firesuit Materials Printing Plates Yellow /1 #8
2016 Panini National Treasures Firesuit Materials Silver /15 #8
2016 Panini National Treasures Gold /15 #1
2016 Panini National Treasures Gold /15 #26
2016 Panini National Treasures Jumbo Firesuit Patch Signature Booklet Alpine Stars /2 #12
2016 Panini National Treasures Jumbo Firesuit Patch Signature Booklet Associate Sponsor 1 /1 #12
2016 Panini National Treasures Jumbo Firesuit Patch Signature Booklet Associate Sponsor 10 /1 #12
2016 Panini National Treasures Jumbo Firesuit Patch Signature Booklet Associate Sponsor 2 /1 #12
2016 Panini National Treasures Jumbo Firesuit Patch Signature Booklet Associate Sponsor 3 /1 #12
2016 Panini National Treasures Jumbo Firesuit Patch Signature Booklet Associate Sponsor 4 /1 #12
2016 Panini National Treasures Jumbo Firesuit Patch Signature Booklet Associate Sponsor 5 /1 #12
2016 Panini National Treasures Jumbo Firesuit Patch Signature Booklet Associate Sponsor 6 /1 #12
2016 Panini National Treasures Jumbo Firesuit Patch Signature Booklet Associate Sponsor 7 /1 #12
2016 Panini National Treasures Jumbo Firesuit Patch Signature Booklet Associate Sponsor 8 /1 #12
2016 Panini National Treasures Jumbo Firesuit Patch Signature Booklet Associate Sponsor 9 /1 #12
2016 Panini National Treasures Jumbo Firesuit Patch Signature Booklet Manufacturers Logo /1 #12
2016 Panini National Treasures Jumbo Firesuit Patch Signature Booklet Nameplate /2 #12
2016 Panini National Treasures Jumbo Firesuit Patch Signature Booklet NASCAR /1 #12
2016 Panini National Treasures Jumbo Firesuit Patch Signature Booklet Sprint Cup Logo /1 #12
2016 Panini National Treasures Jumbo Firesuit Patch Signature Booklet Sunoco /1 #12
2016 Panini National Treasures Printing Plates Black /1 #1
2016 Panini National Treasures Printing Plates Black /1 #26
2016 Panini National Treasures Printing Plates Cyan /1 #1
2016 Panini National Treasures Printing Plates Cyan /1 #26
2016 Panini National Treasures Printing Plates Magenta /1 #1
2016 Panini National Treasures Printing Plates Magenta /1 #26
2016 Panini National Treasures Printing Plates Yellow /1 #1
2016 Panini National Treasures Printing Plates Yellow /1 #26
2016 Panini National Treasures Quad Driver Materials /25 #1
2016 Panini National Treasures Quad Driver Materials Black /5 #1
2016 Panini National Treasures Quad Driver Materials Blue /1 #1
2016 Panini National Treasures Quad Driver Materials Gold /10 #1
2016 Panini National Treasures Quad Driver Materials Printing Plates Black /1 #1
2016 Panini National Treasures Quad Driver Materials Printing Plates Cyan /1 #1
2016 Panini National Treasures Quad Driver Materials Printing Plates Magenta /1 #1
2016 Panini National Treasures Quad Driver Materials Printing Plates Yellow /1 #1
2016 Panini National Treasures Quad Driver Materials Silver /15 #1
2016 Panini National Treasures Quad Materials /25 #8
2016 Panini National Treasures Quad Materials Black /5 #8
2016 Panini National Treasures Quad Materials Blue /1 #8
2016 Panini National Treasures Quad Materials Gold /10 #8
2016 Panini National Treasures Quad Materials Printing Plates Black /1 #8
2016 Panini National Treasures Quad Materials Printing Plates Cyan /1 #8
2016 Panini National Treasures Quad Materials Printing Plates Magenta /1 #8
2016 Panini National Treasures Quad Materials Printing Plates Yellow /1 #8
2016 Panini National Treasures Quad Materials Silver /15 #8
2016 Panini National Treasures Sheet Metal Materials /25 #8
2016 Panini National Treasures Sheet Metal Materials Black /5 #8
2016 Panini National Treasures Sheet Metal Materials Blue /1 #8
2016 Panini National Treasures Sheet Metal Materials Gold /10 #8
2016 Panini National Treasures Sheet Metal Materials Printing Plates Black /1 #8
2016 Panini National Treasures Sheet Metal Materials Printing Plates Cyan /1 #8
2016 Panini National Treasures Sheet Metal Materials Printing Plates Magenta /1 #8
2016 Panini National Treasures Sheet Metal Materials Printing Plates Yellow /1 #8
2016 Panini National Treasures Sheet Metal Materials Silver /15 #8
2016 Panini National Treasures Signature Firesuit Materials Laundry Tag /1 #12
2016 Panini National Treasures Signature Firesuit Materials Printing Plates Black /1 #12
2016 Panini National Treasures Signature Firesuit Materials Printing Plates Cyan /1 #12
2016 Panini National Treasures Signature Firesuit Materials Printing Plates Magenta /1 #12
2016 Panini National Treasures Signature Firesuit Materials Printing Plates Yellow /1 #12
2016 Panini National Treasures Signature Quad Materials Printing Plates Black /1 #12
2016 Panini National Treasures Signature Quad Materials Printing Plates Cyan /1 #12
2016 Panini National Treasures Signature Quad Materials Printing Plates Magenta /1 #12
2016 Panini National Treasures Signature Quad Materials Printing Plates Yellow /1 #12
2016 Panini National Treasures Signature Sheet Metal Materials Printing Plates Black /1 #12
2016 Panini National Treasures Signature Sheet Metal Materials Printing Plates Cyan /1 #12
2016 Panini National Treasures Signature Sheet Metal Materials Printing Plates Magenta /1 #12
2016 Panini National Treasures Signature Sheet Metal Materials Printing Plates Yellow /1 #12
2016 Panini National Treasures Silver /20 #1
2016 Panini National Treasures Silver /20 #26
2016 Panini National Treasures Six Signatures /25 #8
2016 Panini National Treasures Six Signatures Black /10 #8
2016 Panini National Treasures Six Signatures Blue /1 #8
2016 Panini National Treasures Six Signatures Gold /15 #8
2016 Panini National Treasures Trio Driver Materials /25 #4
2016 Panini National Treasures Trio Driver Materials /25 #11
2016 Panini National Treasures Trio Driver Materials Black /5 #4
2016 Panini National Treasures Trio Driver Materials Black /5 #11
2016 Panini National Treasures Trio Driver Materials Blue /1 #4
2016 Panini National Treasures Trio Driver Materials Blue /1 #11
2016 Panini National Treasures Trio Driver Materials Gold /10 #4
2016 Panini National Treasures Trio Driver Materials Gold /10 #11
2016 Panini National Treasures Trio Driver Materials Printing Plates Black /1 #4
2016 Panini National Treasures Trio Driver Materials Printing Plates Black /1 #11
2016 Panini National Treasures Trio Driver Materials Printing Plates Cyan /1 #4
2016 Panini National Treasures Trio Driver Materials Printing Plates Cyan /1 #11
2016 Panini National Treasures Trio Driver Materials Printing Plates Magenta /1 #4
2016 Panini National Treasures Trio Driver Materials Printing Plates Magenta /1 #11
2016 Panini National Treasures Trio Driver Materials Printing Plates Yellow /1 #4
2016 Panini National Treasures Trio Driver Materials Printing Plates Yellow /1 #11
2016 Panini National Treasures Trio Driver Materials Silver /15 #4
2016 Panini National Treasures Trio Driver Materials Silver /15 #11
2016 Panini Prizm #100
2016 Panini Prizm #81
2016 Panini Prizm #65
2016 Panini Prizm #61
2016 Panini Prizm #40
2016 Panini Prizm Autographs Prizms #83
2016 Panini Prizm Autographs Prizms Black /3 #83
2016 Panini Prizm Autographs Prizms Checkered Flag /1 #83
2016 Panini Prizm Autographs Prizms Gold /10 #83
2016 Panini Prizm Autographs Prizms Red White and Blue /1 #83
2016 Panini Prizm Autographs Prizms White Flag /5 #83
2016 Panini Prizm Blowing Smoke #5
2016 Panini Prizm Blowing Smoke Prizms #5
2016 Panini Prizm Blowing Smoke Prizms Checkered Flag /1 #5
2016 Panini Prizm Blowing Smoke Prizms Gold /10 #5
2016 Panini Prizm Champions #3
2016 Panini Prizm Champions Prizms #3
2016 Panini Prizm Champions Prizms Checkered Flag /1 #3
2016 Panini Prizm Champions Prizms Gold /10 #3
2016 Panini Prizm Competitors #4
2016 Panini Prizm Competitors Prizms #4
2016 Panini Prizm Competitors Prizms Checkered Flag /1 #4
2016 Panini Prizm Competitors Prizms Gold /10 #4
2016 Panini Prizm Firesuit Fabrics /50 #2
2016 Panini Prizm Firesuit Fabrics Prizms Blue Flag /10 #2
2016 Panini Prizm Firesuit Fabrics Prizms Checkered Flag /1 #2
2016 Panini Prizm Firesuit Fabrics Prizms Green Flag /25 #2
2016 Panini Prizm Firesuit Fabrics Prizms Red Flag /5 #2
2016 Panini Prizm Firesuit Fabrics Team /199 #2
2016 Panini Prizm Firesuit Fabrics Team Prizms Blue Flag /25 #2
2016 Panini Prizm Firesuit Fabrics Team Prizms Checkered Flag /1 #2
2016 Panini Prizm Firesuit Fabrics Team Prizms Green Flag /49 #2
2016 Panini Prizm Firesuit Fabrics Team Prizms Red Flag /5 #2
2016 Panini Prizm Machinery #3
2016 Panini Prizm Machinery Prizms #3
2016 Panini Prizm Machinery Prizms Checkered Flag /1 #3
2016 Panini Prizm Machinery Prizms Gold /10 #3
2016 Panini Prizm Patented Penmanship Prizms #3
2016 Panini Prizm Patented Penmanship Prizms Black /3 #3
2016 Panini Prizm Patented Penmanship Prizms Checkered Flag /1 #3
2016 Panini Prizm Patented Penmanship Prizms Gold /10 #3
2016 Panini Prizm Patented Penmanship Prizms Red White and Blue /1 #3
2016 Panini Prizm Patented Penmanship Prizms White Flag /5 #3
2016 Panini Prizm Prizms #40
2016 Panini Prizm Prizms #61
2016 Panini Prizm Prizms #65
2016 Panini Prizm Prizms #81
2016 Panini Prizm Prizms #100
2016 Panini Prizm Prizms Black /3 #40
2016 Panini Prizm Prizms Black /3 #61
2016 Panini Prizm Prizms Black /3 #65
2016 Panini Prizm Prizms Black /3 #81
2016 Panini Prizm Prizms Black /3 #100
2016 Panini Prizm Prizms Blue Flag /99 #40
2016 Panini Prizm Prizms Blue Flag /99 #61
2016 Panini Prizm Prizms Blue Flag /99 #65
2016 Panini Prizm Prizms Blue Flag /99 #81
2016 Panini Prizm Prizms Blue Flag /99 #100
2016 Panini Prizm Prizms Camo /48 #40
2016 Panini Prizm Prizms Camo /48 #61
2016 Panini Prizm Prizms Camo /48 #65
2016 Panini Prizm Prizms Camo /48 #81
2016 Panini Prizm Prizms Camo /18 #100
2016 Panini Prizm Prizms Checkered Flag /1 #40
2016 Panini Prizm Prizms Checkered Flag /1 #61
2016 Panini Prizm Prizms Checkered Flag /1 #65
2016 Panini Prizm Prizms Checkered Flag /1 #81
2016 Panini Prizm Prizms Checkered Flag /1 #100
2016 Panini Prizm Prizms Gold /10 #40
2016 Panini Prizm Prizms Gold /10 #61
2016 Panini Prizm Prizms Gold /10 #65
2016 Panini Prizm Prizms Gold /10 #81
2016 Panini Prizm Prizms Gold /10 #100
2016 Panini Prizm Prizms Green Flag /149 #40
2016 Panini Prizm Prizms Green Flag /149 #61
2016 Panini Prizm Prizms Green Flag /149 #65
2016 Panini Prizm Prizms Green Flag /149 #81
2016 Panini Prizm Prizms Green Flag /149 #100
2016 Panini Prizm Prizms Rainbow /24 #40
2016 Panini Prizm Prizms Rainbow /24 #61
2016 Panini Prizm Prizms Rainbow /24 #65
2016 Panini Prizm Prizms Rainbow /24 #81
2016 Panini Prizm Prizms Rainbow /24 #100
2016 Panini Prizm Prizms Red Flag /75 #40
2016 Panini Prizm Prizms Red Flag /75 #61
2016 Panini Prizm Prizms Red Flag /75 #65
2016 Panini Prizm Prizms Red Flag /75 #81
2016 Panini Prizm Prizms Red Flag /75 #100
2016 Panini Prizm Prizms Red White and Blue #40
2016 Panini Prizm Prizms Red White and Blue #61
2016 Panini Prizm Prizms Red White and Blue #65
2016 Panini Prizm Prizms Red White and Blue #81
2016 Panini Prizm Prizms Red White and Blue #100
2016 Panini Prizm Prizms White Flag /5 #40
2016 Panini Prizm Prizms White Flag /5 #61
2016 Panini Prizm Prizms White Flag /5 #65
2016 Panini Prizm Prizms White Flag /5 #81
2016 Panini Prizm Prizms White Flag /5 #100
2016 Panini Prizm Qualifying Times #7
2016 Panini Prizm Qualifying Times Prizms #7
2016 Panini Prizm Qualifying Times Prizms Checkered Flag /1 #7
2016 Panini Prizm Qualifying Times Prizms Gold /10 #7
2016 Panini Prizm Race Used Tire #2
2016 Panini Prizm Race Used Tire Prizms Blue Flag /49 #2
2016 Panini Prizm Race Used Tire Prizms Checkered Flag /1 #2
2016 Panini Prizm Race Used Tire Prizms Green Flag /99 #2
2016 Panini Prizm Race Used Tire Prizms Red Flag /25 #2
2016 Panini Prizm Race Used Tire Team #2
2016 Panini Prizm Race Used Tire Team Prizms Blue Flag /75 #2
2016 Panini Prizm Race Used Tire Team Prizms Checkered Flag /1 #2
2016 Panini Prizm Race Used Tire Team Prizms Green Flag /149 #2
2016 Panini Prizm Race Used Tire Team Prizms Red Flag /10 #2
2016 Panini Prizm Raising the Flag #1
2016 Panini Prizm Raising the Flag Prizms #1
2016 Panini Prizm Raising the Flag Prizms Checkered Flag /1 #1
2016 Panini Prizm Raising the Flag Prizms Gold /10 #1
2016 Panini Prizm Winner's Circle #34
2016 Panini Prizm Winner's Circle #13
2016 Panini Prizm Winner's Circle #11
2016 Panini Prizm Winner's Circle #7
2016 Panini Prizm Winner's Circle #2
2016 Panini Prizm Winner's Circle Prizms #2
2016 Panini Prizm Winner's Circle Prizms #7
2016 Panini Prizm Winner's Circle Prizms #11
2016 Panini Prizm Winner's Circle Prizms #13
2016 Panini Prizm Winner's Circle Prizms #34
2016 Panini Prizm Winner's Circle Prizms Checkered Flag /1 #2
2016 Panini Prizm Winner's Circle Prizms Checkered Flag /1 #7
2016 Panini Prizm Winner's Circle Prizms Checkered Flag /1 #11
2016 Panini Prizm Winner's Circle Prizms Checkered Flag /1 #13
2016 Panini Prizm Winner's Circle Prizms Checkered Flag /1 #34
2016 Panini Prizm Winner's Circle Prizms Gold /10 #2
2016 Panini Prizm Winner's Circle Prizms Gold /10 #7
2016 Panini Prizm Winner's Circle Prizms Gold /10 #11
2016 Panini Prizm Winner's Circle Prizms Gold /10 #13
2016 Panini Prizm Winner's Circle Prizms Gold /10 #34
2016 Panini Torque #4
2016 Panini Torque #74
2016 Panini Torque Artist Proof /50 #4
2016 Panini Torque Artist Proof /50 #74
2016 Panini Torque Blackout /1 #4
2016 Panini Torque Blackout /1 #74
2016 Panini Torque Blue /125 #4
2016 Panini Torque Blue /125 #74
2016 Panini Torque Championship Vision #3
2016 Panini Torque Championship Vision Blue /99 #3
2016 Panini Torque Championship Vision Gold /149 #3
2016 Panini Torque Championship Vision Green /25 #3
2016 Panini Torque Championship Vision Purple /10 #3
2016 Panini Torque Championship Vision Red /49 #3
2016 Panini Torque Clear Vision #4
2016 Panini Torque Clear Vision Blue /99 #4
2016 Panini Torque Clear Vision Gold /149 #4
2016 Panini Torque Clear Vision Green /25 #4
2016 Panini Torque Clear Vision Purple /10 #4
2016 Panini Torque Clear Vision Red /49 #4
2016 Panini Torque Gas N Go #7
2016 Panini Torque Gas N Go Gold /199 #7
2016 Panini Torque Gas N Go Holo Silver /99 #7
2016 Panini Torque Gold #4
2016 Panini Torque Gold #74
2016 Panini Torque Helmets #1
2016 Panini Torque Helmets Blue /99 #1
2016 Panini Torque Helmets Checkerboard /10 #1
2016 Panini Torque Helmets Green /25 #1
2016 Panini Torque Helmets Red /49 #1
2016 Panini Torque Holo Gold /5 #4
2016 Panini Torque Holo Gold /5 #74
2016 Panini Torque Holo Silver /10 #4
2016 Panini Torque Holo Silver /10 #74
2016 Panini Torque Horsepower Heroes #10
2016 Panini Torque Horsepower Heroes Gold /199 #10
2016 Panini Torque Horsepower Heroes Holo Silver /99 #10
2016 Panini Torque Jumbo Tire Autographs /25 #6
2016 Panini Torque Jumbo Tire Autographs Blue /20 #6
2016 Panini Torque Jumbo Tire Autographs Green /5 #6
2016 Panini Torque Jumbo Tire Autographs Purple /1 #6
2016 Panini Torque Jumbo Tire Autographs Red /15 #6
2016 Panini Torque Metal Materials /249 #18
2016 Panini Torque Metal Materials Blue /99 #18
2016 Panini Torque Metal Materials Green /25 #18
2016 Panini Torque Metal Materials Purple /10 #18
2016 Panini Torque Metal Materials Red /49 #18
2016 Panini Torque Pairings Materials /249 #1
2016 Panini Torque Pairings Materials /125 #4
2016 Panini Torque Pairings Materials Blue /99 #1
2016 Panini Torque Pairings Materials Blue /99 #4
2016 Panini Torque Pairings Materials Green /25 #1
2016 Panini Torque Pairings Materials Green /25 #4
2016 Panini Torque Pairings Materials Purple /10 #1
2016 Panini Torque Pairings Materials Purple /10 #4
2016 Panini Torque Pairings Materials Red /49 #1
2016 Panini Torque Pairings Materials Red /49 #4
2016 Panini Torque Pole Position #4
2016 Panini Torque Pole Position Blue /99 #4
2016 Panini Torque Pole Position Checkerboard /10 #4
2016 Panini Torque Pole Position Green /25 #4
2016 Panini Torque Pole Position Red /49 #4
2016 Panini Torque Printing Plates Black /1 #4
2016 Panini Torque Printing Plates Black /1 #74
2016 Panini Torque Printing Plates Cyan /1 #4
2016 Panini Torque Printing Plates Cyan /1 #74
2016 Panini Torque Printing Plates Magenta /1 #4
2016 Panini Torque Printing Plates Magenta /1 #74
2016 Panini Torque Printing Plates Yellow /1 #4
2016 Panini Torque Printing Plates Yellow /1 #74
2016 Panini Torque Purple /25 #4
2016 Panini Torque Purple /25 #74
2016 Panini Torque Quad Materials /48 #1
2016 Panini Torque Quad Materials Blue /99 #1
2016 Panini Torque Quad Materials Green /25 #1
2016 Panini Torque Quad Materials Purple /10 #1
2016 Panini Torque Quad Materials Red /49 #1
2016 Panini Torque Race Kings #13
2016 Panini Torque Race Kings Gold /199 #13
2016 Panini Torque Race Kings Holo Silver /99 #13
2016 Panini Torque Red /99 #4
2016 Panini Torque Red /99 #74
2016 Panini Torque Rubber Relics /399 #12
2016 Panini Torque Rubber Relics Blue /99 #12
2016 Panini Torque Rubber Relics Green /25 #12
2016 Panini Torque Rubber Relics Purple /10 #12
2016 Panini Torque Rubber Relics Red /49 #12
2016 Panini Torque Shades #2
2016 Panini Torque Shades Gold /199 #2
2016 Panini Torque Shades Holo Silver /99 #2
2016 Panini Torque Silhouettes Firesuit Autographs /25 #11
2016 Panini Torque Silhouettes Firesuit Autographs Blue /20 #11
2016 Panini Torque Silhouettes Firesuit Autographs Green /5 #11
2016 Panini Torque Silhouettes Firesuit Autographs Purple /1 #11
2016 Panini Torque Silhouettes Firesuit Autographs Red /15 #11
2016 Panini Torque Silhouettes Sheet Metal Autographs /25 #14
2016 Panini Torque Silhouettes Sheet Metal Autographs Blue /20 #14
2016 Panini Torque Silhouettes Sheet Metal Autographs Green /5 #14
2016 Panini Torque Silhouettes Sheet Metal Autographs Purple /1 #14
2016 Panini Torque Silhouettes Sheet Metal Autographs Red /15 #14
2016 Panini Torque Special Paint #1
2016 Panini Torque Special Paint Gold /199 #1
2016 Panini Torque Special Paint Holo Silver /99 #1
2016 Panini Torque Superstar Vision #2
2016 Panini Torque Superstar Vision Blue /99 #2
2016 Panini Torque Superstar Vision Gold /149 #2
2016 Panini Torque Superstar Vision Green /25 #2
2016 Panini Torque Superstar Vision Purple /10 #2
2016 Panini Torque Superstar Vision Red /49 #2
2016 Panini Torque Test Proof Black /1 #4
2016 Panini Torque Test Proof Black /1 #74
2016 Panini Torque Test Proof Cyan /1 #4
2016 Panini Torque Test Proof Cyan /1 #74
2016 Panini Torque Test Proof Magenta /1 #4
2016 Panini Torque Test Proof Magenta /1 #74
2016 Panini Torque Test Proof Yellow /1 #4
2016 Panini Torque Test Proof Yellow /1 #74
2016 Panini Torque Victory Laps #4
2016 Panini Torque Victory Laps Gold /199 #4
2016 Panini Torque Victory Laps Holo Silver /99 #4
2016 Panini Torque Winning Vision #4
2016 Panini Torque Winning Vision Blue /99 #4
2016 Panini Torque Winning Vision Gold /149 #4
2016 Panini Torque Winning Vision Green /25 #4
2016 Panini Torque Winning Vision Purple /10 #4
2016 Panini Torque Winning Vision Red /49 #4
2017 Donruss #1
2017 Donruss #47
2017 Donruss #91
2017 Donruss #102
2017 Donruss #131
2017 Donruss #139
2017 Donruss #47B
2017 Donruss Artist Proof /25 #1
2017 Donruss Artist Proof /25 #47A
2017 Donruss Artist Proof /25 #91
2017 Donruss Artist Proof /25 #131
2017 Donruss Artist Proof /25 #139
2017 Donruss Artist Proof /25 #47B
2017 Donruss Artist Proof /25 #102
2017 Donruss Blue Foil /299 #1
2017 Donruss Blue Foil /299 #91
2017 Donruss Blue Foil /299 #131
2017 Donruss Blue Foil /299 #47A
2017 Donruss Blue Foil /299 #139
2017 Donruss Blue Foil /299 #47B
2017 Donruss Blue Foil /299 #102
2017 Donruss Classics #2
2017 Donruss Classics Cracked Ice /999 #2
2017 Donruss Cut to The Chase #4
2017 Donruss Cut to The Chase #7
2017 Donruss Cut to The Chase #10
2017 Donruss Cut to The Chase Cracked Ice /999 #4
2017 Donruss Cut to The Chase Cracked Ice /999 #7
2017 Donruss Cut to The Chase Cracked Ice /999 #10
2017 Donruss Dual Rubber Relics #7
2017 Donruss Dual Rubber Relics Holo Black /1 #7
2017 Donruss Dual Rubber Relics Holo Gold /25 #7
2017 Donruss Elite Dominators /999 #1
2017 Donruss Elite Series /999 #1
2017 Donruss Gold Foil /499 #1
2017 Donruss Gold Foil /499 #91
2017 Donruss Gold Foil /499 #131
2017 Donruss Gold Foil /499 #139
2017 Donruss Gold Foil /499 #47A
2017 Donruss Gold Foil /499 #47B
2017 Donruss Gold Foil /499 #102
2017 Donruss Gold Press Proof /99 #1
2017 Donruss Gold Press Proof /99 #47A
2017 Donruss Gold Press Proof /99 #91
2017 Donruss Gold Press Proof /99 #131
2017 Donruss Gold Press Proof /99 #139
2017 Donruss Gold Press Proof /99 #47B
2017 Donruss Gold Press Proof /99 #102
2017 Donruss Green Foil /199 #1
2017 Donruss Green Foil /199 #47A
2017 Donruss Green Foil /199 #91
2017 Donruss Green Foil /199 #131
2017 Donruss Green Foil /199 #139
2017 Donruss Green Foil /199 #47B
2017 Donruss Green Foil /199 #102
2017 Donruss Pole Position #6
2017 Donruss Pole Position Cracked Ice /999 #6
2017 Donruss Press Proof /49 #1
2017 Donruss Press Proof /49 #47A
2017 Donruss Press Proof /49 #91
2017 Donruss Press Proof /49 #131
2017 Donruss Press Proof /49 #139
2017 Donruss Press Proof /49 #47B
2017 Donruss Press Proof /49 #102
2017 Donruss Printing Plates Black /1 #1
2017 Donruss Printing Plates Black /1 #47A
2017 Donruss Printing Plates Black /1 #91
2017 Donruss Printing Plates Black /1 #131
2017 Donruss Printing Plates Black /1 #139
2017 Donruss Printing Plates Black /1 #47B
2017 Donruss Printing Plates Black /1 #102
2017 Donruss Printing Plates Cyan /1 #1
2017 Donruss Printing Plates Cyan /1 #47A
2017 Donruss Printing Plates Cyan /1 #91
2017 Donruss Printing Plates Cyan /1 #131
2017 Donruss Printing Plates Cyan /1 #139
2017 Donruss Printing Plates Cyan /1 #47B
2017 Donruss Printing Plates Cyan /1 #102
2017 Donruss Printing Plates Magenta /1 #1
2017 Donruss Printing Plates Magenta /1 #91
2017 Donruss Printing Plates Magenta /1 #131
2017 Donruss Printing Plates Magenta /1 #139
2017 Donruss Printing Plates Magenta /1 #47A
2017 Donruss Printing Plates Magenta /1 #47B
2017 Donruss Printing Plates Magenta /1 #102
2017 Donruss Printing Plates Yellow /1 #1
2017 Donruss Printing Plates Yellow /1 #91
2017 Donruss Printing Plates Yellow /1 #131
2017 Donruss Printing Plates Yellow /1 #139
2017 Donruss Printing Plates Yellow /1 #47A
2017 Donruss Printing Plates Yellow /1 #47B
2017 Donruss Printing Plates Yellow /1 #102
2017 Donruss Retro Relics 1984 #21
2017 Donruss Retro Relics 1984 Holo Black /5 #21
2017 Donruss Retro Relics 1984 Holo Gold /99 #21
2017 Donruss Retro Signatures 1984 Holo Black /1 #12
2017 Donruss Rubber Relics #25
2017 Donruss Rubber Relics Holo Black /1 #24
2017 Donruss Rubber Relics Holo Black /1 #25
2017 Donruss Rubber Relics Holo Gold /99 #24
2017 Donruss Rubber Relics Holo Gold /99 #25
2017 Donruss Rubber Relics Signatures /99 #3
2017 Donruss Rubber Relics Signatures Holo Black /1 #3
2017 Donruss Rubber Relics Signatures Holo Gold /22 #3
2017 Donruss Significant Signatures Holo Black /1 #7
2017 Donruss Speed #1
2017 Donruss Speed Cracked Ice /999 #1
2017 Donruss Top Tier #6
2017 Donruss Top Tier Cracked Ice /999 #6
2017 Donruss Track Masters #9
2017 Donruss Track Masters Cracked Ice /999 #9
2017 Panini Black Friday Happy Holiday Memorabilia #HHJJN
2017 Panini Black Friday Happy Holiday Memorabilia Cracked Ice /25 #HHJJN
2017 Panini Black Friday Happy Holiday Memorabilia Galactic Windows /10 #HHJJN
2017 Panini Black Friday Happy Holiday Memorabilia Hyperplaid /1 #HHJJN
2017 Panini Black Friday Panini Collection #23
2017 Panini Black Friday Panini Collection Autographs /25 #23
2017 Panini Black Friday Panini Collection Cracked Ice /25 #23
2017 Panini Black Friday Panini Collection Decoy /50 #23
2017 Panini Black Friday Panini Collection Hyperplaid /1 #23
2017 Panini Black Friday Panini Collection Rapture /10 #23
2017 Panini Black Friday Panini Collection Wedges /50 #23
2017 Panini Day /299 #98
2017 Panini Day Cracked Ice /25 #98
2017 Panini Day Decoy /50 #98
2017 Panini Day Hyperplaid /1 #98
2017 Panini Day Memorabilia #38
2017 Panini Day Memorabilia Galactic Window /25 #38
2017 Panini Day Memorabilia Hyperplaid /1 #38
2017 Panini Day Rapture /10 #98
2017 Panini Day Wedges /50 #98
2017 Panini Father's Day #35
2017 Panini Father's Day Cracked Ice /25 #35
2017 Panini Father's Day Foil /50 #35
2017 Panini Father's Day Hyperplaid /1 #35
2017 Panini Father's Day Racing Memorabilia /100 #6
2017 Panini Father's Day Racing Memorabilia Cracked Ice /25 #6
2017 Panini Father's Day Racing Memorabilia Hyperplaid /1 #6
2017 Panini Father's Day Racing Memorabilia Shimmer /10 #6

2017 Panini Instant Nascar /68 #7
2017 Panini Instant Nascar /69 #8
2017 Panini Instant Nascar /64 #13
2017 Panini Instant Nascar Black /1 #7
2017 Panini Instant Nascar Black /1 #8
2017 Panini Instant Nascar Black /1 #13
2017 Panini Instant Nascar Green /10 #7
2017 Panini Instant Nascar Green /10 #8
2017 Panini Instant Nascar Green /10 #13
2017 Panini National Convention #R4
2017 Panini National Convention Autographs #R4
2017 Panini National Convention Autographs Hyperplaid /1 #R4
2017 Panini National Convention Escher Squares /25 #R4
2017 Panini National Convention Escher Squares Thick Stock /10 #R4
2017 Panini National Convention Galatic Windows /5 #R4
2017 Panini National Convention Hyperplaid /1 #R4
2017 Panini National Convention Memorabilia #JJ
2017 Panini National Convention Memorabilia Escher Squares /10 #JJ
2017 Panini National Convention Memorabilia Hyperplaid /1 #JJ
2017 Panini National Convention Memorabilia Pyramids /5 #JJ
2017 Panini National Convention Memorabilia Rainbow Spokes /25 #JJ
2017 Panini National Convention Memorabilia Rapture /49 #JJ
2017 Panini National Convention Pyramids /10 #R4
2017 Panini National Convention Rainbow Spokes /49 #R4
2017 Panini National Convention Rainbow Spokes Thick Stock /25 #R4
2017 Panini National Convention Rapture /99 #R4
2017 Panini National Convention VIP #81
2017 Panini National Convention VIP Gems #JJ
2017 Panini National Convention VIP Gems Autographs /1 #JJ
2017 Panini National Convention VIP Gems Gold /1 #JJ
2017 Panini National Convention VIP Memorabilia /25 #81
2017 Panini National Convention VIP Memorabilia Black /1 #81
2017 Panini National Convention VIP Prizm #81
2017 Panini National Convention VIP Prizm Black /1 #81
2017 Panini National Convention VIP Prizm Cracked Ice /25 #81
2017 Panini National Convention VIP Prizm Gold /15 #81
2017 Panini National Convention VIP Prizm Green /5 #81
2017 Panini National Treasures /25 #1
2017 Panini National Treasures /25 #16
2017 Panini National Treasures Associate Sponsor Patch Signatures 1 /1 #1
2017 Panini National Treasures Associate Sponsor Patch Signatures 2 /1 #1
2017 Panini National Treasures Associate Sponsor Patch Signatures 3 /1 #1
2017 Panini National Treasures Associate Sponsor Patch Signatures 4 /1 #1
2017 Panini National Treasures Associate Sponsor Patch Signatures 5 /1 #1
2017 Panini National Treasures Associate Sponsor Patch Signatures 6 /1 #1
2017 Panini National Treasures Associate Sponsor Patch Signatures 7 /1 #1
2017 Panini National Treasures Associate Sponsor Patch Signatures 8 /1 #1
2017 Panini National Treasures Car Manufacturer Patch Signatures /1 #1
2017 Panini National Treasures Century Black /1 #1
2017 Panini National Treasures Century Black /1 #16
2017 Panini National Treasures Century Gold /15 #1
2017 Panini National Treasures Century Gold /15 #16
2017 Panini National Treasures Century Green /5 #1
2017 Panini National Treasures Century Green /5 #16
2017 Panini National Treasures Century Holo Gold /10 #1
2017 Panini National Treasures Century Holo Gold /10 #16
2017 Panini National Treasures Century Holo Silver /20 #1
2017 Panini National Treasures Century Holo Silver /20 #16
2017 Panini National Treasures Century Laundry Tags /1 #1
2017 Panini National Treasures Championship Signatures Black /1 #1
2017 Panini National Treasures Championship Signatures Printing Plates Black /1 #1
2017 Panini National Treasures Championship Signatures Printing Plates Cyan /1 #1
2017 Panini National Treasures Championship Signatures Printing Plates Magenta /1 #1
2017 Panini National Treasures Championship Signatures Printing Plates Yellow /1 #1
2017 Panini National Treasures Dual Sheet Metal Materials /25 #12
2017 Panini National Treasures Dual Sheet Metal Materials Black /1 #12
2017 Panini National Treasures Dual Sheet Metal Materials Gold /15 #12
2017 Panini National Treasures Dual Sheet Metal Materials Green /5 #12
2017 Panini National Treasures Dual Sheet Metal Materials Holo Gold /10 #12
2017 Panini National Treasures Dual Sheet Metal Materials Holo Silver /20 #12
2017 Panini National Treasures Dual Sheet Metal Materials Printing Plates Black /1 #12
2017 Panini National Treasures Dual Sheet Metal Materials Printing Plates Cyan /1 #12
2017 Panini National Treasures Dual Sheet Metal Materials Printing Plates Magenta /1 #12
2017 Panini National Treasures Dual Sheet Metal Materials Printing Plates Yellow /1 #12
2017 Panini National Treasures Dual Signature Materials /25 #2
2017 Panini National Treasures Dual Signature Materials /25 #9
2017 Panini National Treasures Dual Signature Materials /25 #10
2017 Panini National Treasures Dual Signature Materials Black /1 #2
2017 Panini National Treasures Dual Signature Materials Black /1 #9
2017 Panini National Treasures Dual Signature Materials Black /1 #10
2017 Panini National Treasures Dual Signature Materials Gold /15 #2
2017 Panini National Treasures Dual Signature Materials Gold /15 #9
2017 Panini National Treasures Dual Signature Materials Gold /15 #10
2017 Panini National Treasures Dual Signature Materials Green /5 #2
2017 Panini National Treasures Dual Signature Materials Green /5 #9
2017 Panini National Treasures Dual Signature Materials Green /5 #10
2017 Panini National Treasures Dual Signature Materials Holo Gold /10 #2
2017 Panini National Treasures Dual Signature Materials Holo Gold /7 #9
2017 Panini National Treasures Dual Signature Materials Holo Gold /7 #10
2017 Panini National Treasures Dual Signature Materials Holo Silver /20 #2
2017 Panini National Treasures Dual Signature Materials Holo Silver /20 #9
2017 Panini National Treasures Dual Signature Materials Holo Silver /20 #10
2017 Panini National Treasures Dual Signature Materials Laundry Tag /1 #2
2017 Panini National Treasures Dual Signature Materials Laundry Tag /1 #9
2017 Panini National Treasures Dual Signature Materials Laundry Tag /1 #10
2017 Panini National Treasures Goodyear Patch Signatures /2 #1
2017 Panini National Treasures Hats Off /13 #13
2017 Panini National Treasures Hats Off /12 #14
2017 Panini National Treasures Hats Off Gold /4 #13
2017 Panini National Treasures Hats Off Gold /4 #14
2017 Panini National Treasures Hats Off Holo Gold /5 #13
2017 Panini National Treasures Hats Off Holo Gold /5 #14
2017 Panini National Treasures Hats Off Holo Silver /1 #13
2017 Panini National Treasures Hats Off Holo Silver /1 #14
2017 Panini National Treasures Hats Off Laundry Tag /6 #13
2017 Panini National Treasures Hats Off Laundry Tag /6 #14
2017 Panini National Treasures Hats Off New Era /1 #13
2017 Panini National Treasures Hats Off New Era /1 #14
2017 Panini National Treasures Hats Off Printing Plates Black /1 #13
2017 Panini National Treasures Hats Off Printing Plates Black /1 #14
2017 Panini National Treasures Hats Off Printing Plates Cyan /1 #13
2017 Panini National Treasures Hats Off Printing Plates Cyan /1 #14
2017 Panini National Treasures Hats Off Printing Plates Magenta /1 #13
2017 Panini National Treasures Hats Off Printing Plates Magenta /1 #14
2017 Panini National Treasures Hats Off Printing Plates Yellow /1 #13
2017 Panini National Treasures Hats Off Printing Plates Yellow /1 #14
2017 Panini National Treasures Hats Off Sponsor /5 #13
2017 Panini National Treasures Hats Off Sponsor /10 #14
2017 Panini National Treasures Jumbo Sheet Metal Materials /25 #1
2017 Panini National Treasures Jumbo Sheet Metal Materials Black /1 #1
2017 Panini National Treasures Jumbo Sheet Metal Materials Gold /15 #1
2017 Panini National Treasures Jumbo Sheet Metal Materials Green /5 #1
2017 Panini National Treasures Jumbo Sheet Metal Materials Holo Gold /10 #1
2017 Panini National Treasures Jumbo Sheet Metal Materials Holo Silver /20 #1
2017 Panini National Treasures Jumbo Sheet Metal Materials Printing Plates Black /1 #1
2017 Panini National Treasures Jumbo Sheet Metal Materials Printing Plates Cyan /1 #1
2017 Panini National Treasures Jumbo Sheet Metal Materials Printing Plates Magenta /1 #1
2017 Panini National Treasures Jumbo Sheet Metal Materials Printing Plates Yellow /1 #1
2017 Panini National Treasures Nameplate Patch Signatures /2 #1
2017 Panini National Treasures NASCAR Patch Signatures /1 #1
2017 Panini National Treasures Printing Plates Black /1 #1
2017 Panini National Treasures Printing Plates Black /1 #16
2017 Panini National Treasures Printing Plates Cyan /1 #1
2017 Panini National Treasures Printing Plates Cyan /1 #16
2017 Panini National Treasures Printing Plates Magenta /1 #1
2017 Panini National Treasures Printing Plates Magenta /1 #16
2017 Panini National Treasures Printing Plates Yellow /1 #1
2017 Panini National Treasures Printing Plates Yellow /1 #16
2017 Panini National Treasures Quad Material Signatures Black /1 #9
2017 Panini National Treasures Quad Material Signatures Laundry Tag /1 #9
2017 Panini National Treasures Quad Material Signatures Printing Plates Black /1 #9
2017 Panini National Treasures Quad Material Signatures Printing Plates Cyan /1 #9
2017 Panini National Treasures Quad Material Signatures Printing Plates Magenta /1 #9
2017 Panini National Treasures Quad Material Signatures Printing Plates Yellow /1 #9
2017 Panini National Treasures Signature Six Way Swatches /16 #4
2017 Panini National Treasures Signature Six Way Swatches Black /1 #4
2017 Panini National Treasures Signature Six Way Swatches Gold /10 #4
2017 Panini National Treasures Signature Six Way Swatches Green /5 #4
2017 Panini National Treasures Signature Six Way Swatches Holo Gold /7 #4
2017 Panini National Treasures Signature Six Way Swatches Holo Silver /15 #4
2017 Panini National Treasures Signature Six Way Swatches Laundry Tag /1 #4
2017 Panini National Treasures Sunoco Patch Signatures /1 #1
2017 Panini National Treasures Teammates Dual Materials /25 #1
2017 Panini National Treasures Teammates Dual Materials Black /1 #1
2017 Panini National Treasures Teammates Dual Materials Gold /15 #1
2017 Panini National Treasures Teammates Dual Materials Green /5 #1
2017 Panini National Treasures Teammates Dual Materials Holo Gold /10 #1
2017 Panini National Treasures Teammates Dual Materials Holo Silver /20 #1
2017 Panini National Treasures Teammates Dual Materials Laundry Tag /1 #1
2017 Panini National Treasures Teammates Dual Materials Printing Plates Black /1 #1
2017 Panini National Treasures Teammates Dual Materials Printing Plates Cyan /1 #1
2017 Panini National Treasures Teammates Dual Materials Printing Plates Magenta /1 #1
2017 Panini National Treasures Teammates Dual Materials Printing Plates Yellow /1 #1
2017 Panini National Treasures Teammates Quad Materials /25 #4
2017 Panini National Treasures Teammates Quad Materials Black /1 #4
2017 Panini National Treasures Teammates Quad Materials Gold /15 #4
2017 Panini National Treasures Teammates Quad Materials Green /5 #4
2017 Panini National Treasures Teammates Quad Materials Holo Gold /10 #4
2017 Panini National Treasures Teammates Quad Materials Holo Silver /20 #4
2017 Panini National Treasures Teammates Quad Materials Laundry Tag /1 #4
2017 Panini National Treasures Teammates Quad Materials Printing Plates Black /1 #4
2017 Panini National Treasures Teammates Quad Materials Printing Plates Cyan /1 #4
2017 Panini National Treasures Teammates Quad Materials Printing Plates Magenta /1 #4
2017 Panini National Treasures Teammates Quad Materials Printing Plates Yellow /1 #4
2017 Panini National Treasures Teammates Triple Materials /25 #1
2017 Panini National Treasures Teammates Triple Materials Black /1 #1
2017 Panini National Treasures Teammates Triple Materials Gold /15 #1
2017 Panini National Treasures Teammates Triple Materials Green /5 #1
2017 Panini National Treasures Teammates Triple Materials Holo Gold /10 #1
2017 Panini National Treasures Teammates Triple Materials Holo Silver /20 #1
2017 Panini National Treasures Teammates Triple Materials Laundry Tag /1 #1
2017 Panini National Treasures Teammates Triple Materials Printing Plates Black /1 #1
2017 Panini National Treasures Teammates Triple Materials Printing Plates Cyan /1 #1
2017 Panini National Treasures Teammates Triple Materials Printing Plates Magenta /1 #1
2017 Panini National Treasures Teammates Triple Materials Printing Plates Yellow /1 #1
2017 Panini National Treasures Three Wide /25 #5
2017 Panini National Treasures Three Wide Black /1 #5
2017 Panini National Treasures Three Wide Gold /15 #5
2017 Panini National Treasures Three Wide Green /5 #5
2017 Panini National Treasures Three Wide Holo Gold /10 #5
2017 Panini National Treasures Three Wide Holo Silver /20 #5
2017 Panini National Treasures Three Wide Laundry Tag /1 #5
2017 Panini National Treasures Three Wide Printing Plates Black /1 #5
2017 Panini National Treasures Three Wide Printing Plates Cyan /1 #5
2017 Panini National Treasures Three Wide Printing Plates Magenta /1 #5
2017 Panini National Treasures Three Wide Printing Plates Yellow /1 #5
2017 Panini Torque #20
2017 Panini Torque #55
2017 Panini Torque #74
2017 Panini Torque #82
2017 Panini Torque #91
2017 Panini Torque Artist Proof /75 #20
2017 Panini Torque Artist Proof /75 #55
2017 Panini Torque Artist Proof /75 #74
2017 Panini Torque Artist Proof /75 #82
2017 Panini Torque Artist Proof /75 #91
2017 Panini Torque Blackout /1 #20
2017 Panini Torque Blackout /1 #55
2017 Panini Torque Blackout /1 #74
2017 Panini Torque Blackout /1 #82
2017 Panini Torque Blackout /1 #91
2017 Panini Torque Blue /150 #20
2017 Panini Torque Blue /150 #55
2017 Panini Torque Blue /150 #74
2017 Panini Torque Blue /150 #82
2017 Panini Torque Blue /150 #91
2017 Panini Torque Claiming The Chase #1
2017 Panini Torque Claiming The Chase Gold /199 #1
2017 Panini Torque Claiming The Chase Holo Silver /99 #1
2017 Panini Torque Clear Vision #22
2017 Panini Torque Clear Vision Blue /99 #22
2017 Panini Torque Clear Vision Gold /149 #22
2017 Panini Torque Clear Vision Green /25 #22
2017 Panini Torque Clear Vision Purple /10 #22
2017 Panini Torque Clear Vision Red /49 #22
2017 Panini Torque Dual Materials Blue /14 #13
2017 Panini Torque Dual Materials Green /5 #13
2017 Panini Torque Dual Materials Purple /1 #13
2017 Panini Torque Dual Materials Red /10 #13
2017 Panini Torque Gold #20
2017 Panini Torque Gold #55
2017 Panini Torque Gold #74
2017 Panini Torque Gold #82
2017 Panini Torque Gold #91
2017 Panini Torque Holo Gold /10 #20
2017 Panini Torque Holo Gold /10 #55
2017 Panini Torque Holo Gold /10 #74
2017 Panini Torque Holo Gold /10 #82
2017 Panini Torque Holo Gold /10 #91
2017 Panini Torque Holo Silver /25 #20
2017 Panini Torque Holo Silver /25 #55
2017 Panini Torque Holo Silver /25 #74
2017 Panini Torque Holo Silver /25 #82
2017 Panini Torque Holo Silver /25 #91
2017 Panini Torque Horsepower Heroes #21
2017 Panini Torque Horsepower Heroes Gold /199 #21
2017 Panini Torque Horsepower Heroes Holo Silver /99 #21
2017 Panini Torque Jumbo Firesuit Signatures /19 #12
2017 Panini Torque Jumbo Firesuit Signatures Blue /15 #12
2017 Panini Torque Jumbo Firesuit Signatures Green /5 #12
2017 Panini Torque Jumbo Firesuit Signatures Purple /1 #12
2017 Panini Torque Jumbo Firesuit Signatures Red /10 #12
2017 Panini Torque Manufacturer Marks #1
2017 Panini Torque Manufacturer Marks Gold /199 #1
2017 Panini Torque Manufacturer Marks Holo Silver /99 #1
2017 Panini Torque Metal Materials /25 #20
2017 Panini Torque Metal Materials Blue /15 #20
2017 Panini Torque Metal Materials Green /5 #20
2017 Panini Torque Metal Materials Purple /1 #20
2017 Panini Torque Metal Materials Red /10 #20
2017 Panini Torque Pairings Materials /199 #6
2017 Panini Torque Pairings Materials /49 #15
2017 Panini Torque Pairings Materials Blue /99 #6
2017 Panini Torque Pairings Materials Blue /25 #15
2017 Panini Torque Pairings Materials Green /25 #6
2017 Panini Torque Pairings Materials Green /5 #15
2017 Panini Torque Pairings Materials Purple /10 #6
2017 Panini Torque Pairings Materials Purple /1 #15
2017 Panini Torque Pairings Materials Red /49 #6
2017 Panini Torque Pairings Materials Red /10 #15
2017 Panini Torque Primary Paint #1
2017 Panini Torque Primary Paint Blue /99 #1
2017 Panini Torque Primary Paint Checkerboard /10 #1
2017 Panini Torque Primary Paint Green /25 #1
2017 Panini Torque Primary Paint Red /49 #1
2017 Panini Torque Prime Associate Sponsors Jumbo Patches /1 #9A
2017 Panini Torque Prime Associate Sponsors Jumbo Patches /1 #9B
2017 Panini Torque Prime Associate Sponsors Jumbo Patches /1 #9C
2017 Panini Torque Prime Associate Sponsors Jumbo Patches /1 #9D
2017 Panini Torque Prime Associate Sponsors Jumbo Patches /1 #9E
2017 Panini Torque Prime Associate Sponsors Jumbo Patches /1 #9F
2017 Panini Torque Prime Associate Sponsors Jumbo Patches /1 #9G
2017 Panini Torque Prime Associate Sponsors Jumbo Patches /1 #9H
2017 Panini Torque Prime Associate Sponsors Jumbo Patches /1 #9I
2017 Panini Torque Prime Associate Sponsors Jumbo Patches /1 #9J
2017 Panini Torque Prime Associate Sponsors Jumbo Patches /1 #9K
2017 Panini Torque Prime Associate Sponsors Jumbo Patches /1 #9L
2017 Panini Torque Prime Associate Sponsors Jumbo Patches /1 #9M
2017 Panini Torque Prime Goodyear Jumbo Patches /2 #9
2017 Panini Torque Prime Manufacturer Jumbo Patches /1 #9
2017 Panini Torque Prime Nameplates Jumbo Patches /2 #9
2017 Panini Torque Prime NASCAR Jumbo Patches /1 #9
2017 Panini Torque Prime Series Sponsor Jumbo Patches /1 #9
2017 Panini Torque Printing Plates Black /1 #20
2017 Panini Torque Printing Plates Black /1 #55
2017 Panini Torque Printing Plates Black /1 #74
2017 Panini Torque Printing Plates Black /1 #82
2017 Panini Torque Printing Plates Black /1 #91
2017 Panini Torque Printing Plates Cyan /1 #20
2017 Panini Torque Printing Plates Cyan /1 #55
2017 Panini Torque Printing Plates Cyan /1 #74
2017 Panini Torque Printing Plates Cyan /1 #82
2017 Panini Torque Printing Plates Cyan /1 #91
2017 Panini Torque Printing Plates Magenta /1 #20
2017 Panini Torque Printing Plates Magenta /1 #55
2017 Panini Torque Printing Plates Magenta /1 #74
2017 Panini Torque Printing Plates Magenta /1 #82
2017 Panini Torque Printing Plates Magenta /1 #91
2017 Panini Torque Printing Plates Yellow /1 #20
2017 Panini Torque Printing Plates Yellow /1 #55
2017 Panini Torque Printing Plates Yellow /1 #74
2017 Panini Torque Printing Plates Yellow /1 #82
2017 Panini Torque Printing Plates Yellow /1 #91
2017 Panini Torque Purple /50 #20
2017 Panini Torque Purple /50 #55
2017 Panini Torque Purple /50 #74
2017 Panini Torque Purple /50 #82
2017 Panini Torque Purple /50 #91
2017 Panini Torque Quad Materials /49 #14
2017 Panini Torque Quad Materials Blue /25 #14
2017 Panini Torque Quad Materials Green /5 #14
2017 Panini Torque Quad Materials Purple /1 #14
2017 Panini Torque Quad Materials Red /10 #14
2017 Panini Torque Raced Relics /499 #10
2017 Panini Torque Raced Relics Blue /99 #10
2017 Panini Torque Raced Relics Green /25 #10
2017 Panini Torque Raced Relics Purple /10 #10
2017 Panini Torque Raced Relics Red /49 #10
2017 Panini Torque Red /100 #20
2017 Panini Torque Red /100 #55
2017 Panini Torque Red /100 #74
2017 Panini Torque Red /100 #82
2017 Panini Torque Red /100 #91
2017 Panini Torque Running Order #1
2017 Panini Torque Running Order Blue /99 #1
2017 Panini Torque Running Order Checkerboard /10 #1
2017 Panini Torque Running Order Green /25 #1
2017 Panini Torque Running Order Red /49 #1
2017 Panini Torque Silhouettes Sheet Metal Signatures /19 #18
2017 Panini Torque Silhouettes Sheet Metal Signatures Blue /15 #18
2017 Panini Torque Silhouettes Sheet Metal Signatures Green /5 #18
2017 Panini Torque Silhouettes Sheet Metal Signatures Purple /1 #18
2017 Panini Torque Silhouettes Sheet Metal Signatures Red /10 #18
2017 Panini Torque Special Paint #9
2017 Panini Torque Special Paint Gold /199 #9
2017 Panini Torque Special Paint Holo Silver /99 #9
2017 Panini Torque Superstar Vision #2
2017 Panini Torque Superstar Vision Blue /99 #2
2017 Panini Torque Superstar Vision Gold /149 #2
2017 Panini Torque Superstar Vision Green /25 #2
2017 Panini Torque Superstar Vision Purple /10 #2
2017 Panini Torque Superstar Vision Red /49 #2
2017 Panini Torque Test Proof Black /1 #20
2017 Panini Torque Test Proof Black /1 #55
2017 Panini Torque Test Proof Black /1 #74
2017 Panini Torque Test Proof Black /1 #82
2017 Panini Torque Test Proof Black /1 #91
2017 Panini Torque Test Proof Cyan /1 #20
2017 Panini Torque Test Proof Cyan /1 #55
2017 Panini Torque Test Proof Cyan /1 #74
2017 Panini Torque Test Proof Cyan /1 #82
2017 Panini Torque Test Proof Cyan /1 #91
2017 Panini Torque Test Proof Magenta /1 #20
2017 Panini Torque Test Proof Magenta /1 #55
2017 Panini Torque Test Proof Magenta /1 #74
2017 Panini Torque Test Proof Magenta /1 #82
2017 Panini Torque Test Proof Magenta /1 #91
2017 Panini Torque Test Proof Yellow /1 #20
2017 Panini Torque Test Proof Yellow /1 #55
2017 Panini Torque Test Proof Yellow /1 #74
2017 Panini Torque Test Proof Yellow /1 #82
2017 Panini Torque Test Proof Yellow /1 #91
2017 Panini Torque Track Vision #2
2017 Panini Torque Track Vision Blue /99 #2
2017 Panini Torque Track Vision Gold /149 #2
2017 Panini Torque Track Vision Green /25 #2
2017 Panini Torque Track Vision Purple /10 #2
2017 Panini Torque Track Vision Red /49 #2
2017 Panini Torque Trackside #2
2017 Panini Torque Trackside Blue /99 #2
2017 Panini Torque Trackside Checkerboard /10 #2
2017 Panini Torque Trackside Green /25 #2
2017 Panini Torque Trackside Red /49 #2
2017 Panini Torque Victory Laps #1
2017 Panini Torque Victory Laps Gold /199 #1
2017 Panini Torque Victory Laps Holo Silver /99 #1
2017 Panini Torque Visions of Greatness #19
2017 Panini Torque Visions of Greatness Blue /99 #19
2017 Panini Torque Visions of Greatness Gold /149 #19
2017 Panini Torque Visions of Greatness Green /25 #19
2017 Panini Torque Visions of Greatness Purple /10 #19
2017 Panini Torque Visions of Greatness Red /49 #19
2017 Select #1
2017 Select #2
2017 Select #117
2017 Select Endorsements Prizms Checkered Flag /1 #23
2017 Select Endorsements Prizms Gold /5 #23
2017 Select Endorsements Prizms Red /7 #23
2017 Select Prizms Black /3 #1
2017 Select Prizms Black /3 #2
2017 Select Prizms Black /3 #117
2017 Select Prizms Blue /199 #1
2017 Select Prizms Blue /199 #2
2017 Select Prizms Checkered Flag /1 #1
2017 Select Prizms Checkered Flag /1 #2
2017 Select Prizms Checkered Flag /1 #117
2017 Select Prizms Gold /10 #1
2017 Select Prizms Gold /10 #2
2017 Select Prizms Gold /10 #117
2017 Select Prizms Purple Pulsar #1
2017 Select Prizms Purple Pulsar #2
2017 Select Prizms Red /99 #1
2017 Select Prizms Red /99 #2
2017 Select Prizms Red White and Blue Pulsar /299 #1
2017 Select Prizms Red White and Blue Pulsar /299 #2
2017 Select Prizms Silver #1
2017 Select Prizms Silver #2
2017 Select Prizms Tie Dye /24 #1
2017 Select Prizms Tie Dye /24 #2
2017 Select Prizms Tie Dye /24 #117
2017 Select Prizms White /50 #1
2017 Select Prizms White /50 #2
2017 Select Prizms White /50 #117
2017 Select Select Pairs Materials #13
2017 Select Select Pairs Materials #14
2017 Select Select Pairs Materials Prizms Blue /199 #13
2017 Select Select Pairs Materials Prizms Blue /199 #14
2017 Select Select Pairs Materials Prizms Blue /30 #15
2017 Select Select Pairs Materials Prizms Checkered Flag /1 #13
2017 Select Select Pairs Materials Prizms Checkered Flag /1 #14
2017 Select Select Pairs Materials Prizms Checkered Flag /1 #15
2017 Select Select Pairs Materials Prizms Gold /10 #13
2017 Select Select Pairs Materials Prizms Gold /10 #14
2017 Select Select Pairs Materials Prizms Gold /10 #15
2017 Select Select Pairs Materials Prizms Red /99 #13
2017 Select Select Pairs Materials Prizms Red /99 #14
2017 Select Select Pairs Materials Prizms Red /25 #15
2017 Select Select Stars #2
2017 Select Select Stars Prizms Black /3 #2
2017 Select Select Stars Prizms Checkered Flag /1 #2
2017 Select Select Stars Prizms Gold /10 #2
2017 Select Select Stars Prizms Tie Dye /24 #2
2017 Select Select Stars Prizms White /50 #2
2017 Select Select Swatches #23
2017 Select Select Swatches Prizms Blue /199 #23
2017 Select Select Swatches Prizms Checkered Flag /1 #23
2017 Select Select Swatches Prizms Gold /10 #23
2017 Select Select Swatches Prizms Red /99 #23
2017 Select Sheet Metal #12
2017 Select Sheet Metal Prizms Blue /99 #12
2017 Select Sheet Metal Prizms Checkered Flag /1 #12
2017 Select Sheet Metal Prizms Gold /10 #12
2017 Select Sheet Metal Prizms Red /49 #12
2017 Select Signature Swatches #23
2017 Select Signature Swatches Dual #17
2017 Select Signature Swatches Dual Prizms Checkered Flag /1 #17
2017 Select Signature Swatches Dual Prizms Gold /5 #17
2017 Select Signature Swatches Dual Prizms Tie Dye /7 #17
2017 Select Signature Swatches Dual Prizms White /10 #17
2017 Select Signature Swatches Prizms Checkered Flag /1 #23
2017 Select Signature Swatches Prizms Gold /5 #23
2017 Select Signature Swatches Prizms Tie Dye /7 #23
2017 Select Signature Swatches Prizms White /10 #23
2017 Select Speed Merchants #11
2017 Select Speed Merchants Prizms Black /3 #11
2017 Select Speed Merchants Prizms Checkered Flag /1 #11
2017 Select Speed Merchants Prizms Gold /10 #11
2017 Select Speed Merchants Prizms Tie Dye /24 #11
2017 Select Speed Merchants Prizms White /50 #11
2017 Select Up Close and Personal #7
2017 Select Up Close and Personal Prizms Black /3 #7
2017 Select Up Close and Personal Prizms Checkered Flag /1 #7
2017 Select Up Close and Personal Prizms Gold /10 #7
2017 Select Up Close and Personal Prizms Tie Dye /24 #7
2017 Select Up Close and Personal Prizms White /50 #7
2018 Certified #1
2018 Certified #94
2018 Certified All Certified Team /199 #5
2018 Certified All Certified Team Black /1 #5
2018 Certified All Certified Team Blue /99 #5
2018 Certified All Certified Team Gold /49 #5
2018 Certified All Certified Team Green /10 #5
2018 Certified All Certified Team Mirror Black /1 #5
2018 Certified All Certified Team Mirror Gold /25 #5
2018 Certified All Certified Team Mirror Green /5 #5
2018 Certified All Certified Team Mirror Purple /10 #5
2018 Certified All Certified Team Purple /25 #5
2018 Certified All Certified Team Red /149 #5
2018 Certified Black /1 #1
2018 Certified Black /1 #94
2018 Certified Blue /99 #1
2018 Certified Blue /99 #94
2018 Certified Complete Materials /199 #1
2018 Certified Complete Materials Black /1 #1
2018 Certified Complete Materials Blue /49 #1
2018 Certified Complete Materials Gold /25 #1
2018 Certified Complete Materials Green /5 #1
2018 Certified Complete Materials Purple /10 #1
2018 Certified Complete Materials Red /99 #1
2018 Certified Cup Swatches /499 #13
2018 Certified Cup Swatches Black /1 #13
2018 Certified Cup Swatches Blue /49 #13
2018 Certified Cup Swatches Gold /25 #13
2018 Certified Cup Swatches Green /5 #13
2018 Certified Cup Swatches Purple /10 #13
2018 Certified Cup Swatches Red /199 #13
2018 Certified Epix /199 #12
2018 Certified Epix Black /1 #12
2018 Certified Epix Blue /99 #12
2018 Certified Epix Gold /49 #12
2018 Certified Epix Green /10 #12
2018 Certified Epix Mirror Black /1 #12
2018 Certified Epix Mirror Gold /25 #12
2018 Certified Epix Mirror Green /5 #12
2018 Certified Epix Mirror Purple /10 #12
2018 Certified Epix Purple /25 #12
2018 Certified Epix Red /149 #12
2018 Certified Gold /49 #1
2018 Certified Gold /49 #94
2018 Certified Green /10 #1
2018 Certified Green /10 #94
2018 Certified Materials Signatures Black /1 #1
2018 Certified Materials Signatures Blue /15 #1
2018 Certified Materials Signatures Gold /10 #1
2018 Certified Materials Signatures Green /5 #1
2018 Certified Materials Signatures Purple /7 #1
2018 Certified Materials Signatures Red /20 #1
2018 Certified Mirror Black /1 #1
2018 Certified Mirror Black /1 #94
2018 Certified Mirror Gold /25 #1
2018 Certified Mirror Gold /25 #94
2018 Certified Mirror Green /5 #1
2018 Certified Mirror Green /5 #94
2018 Certified Mirror Purple /10 #1
2018 Certified Mirror Purple /10 #94
2018 Certified Orange /249 #1
2018 Certified Orange /249 #94
2018 Certified Piece of the Race /499 #1
2018 Certified Piece of the Race Black /1 #1
2018 Certified Piece of the Race Blue /49 #1
2018 Certified Piece of the Race Gold /25 #1
2018 Certified Piece of the Race Green /5 #1
2018 Certified Piece of the Race Purple /10 #1
2018 Certified Piece of the Race Red /199 #1
2018 Certified Purple /25 #1
2018 Certified Purple /25 #94
2018 Certified Red /199 #1
2018 Certified Red /199 #94
2018 Certified Signing Sessions Black /1 #10
2018 Certified Signing Sessions Gold /7 #10
2018 Certified Signing Sessions Green /3 #10
2018 Certified Signing Sessions Purple /5 #10
2018 Certified Skills /199 #18
2018 Certified Skills Black /1 #18
2018 Certified Skills Blue /99 #18
2018 Certified Skills Gold /49 #18
2018 Certified Skills Green /10 #18
2018 Certified Skills Mirror Black /1 #18
2018 Certified Skills Mirror Gold /25 #18
2018 Certified Skills Mirror Green /5 #18
2018 Certified Skills Mirror Purple /10 #18
2018 Certified Skills Purple /25 #18
2018 Certified Skills Red /149 #18
2018 Certified Stars /199 #18
2018 Certified Stars Black /1 #18
2018 Certified Stars Blue /99 #18
2018 Certified Stars Gold /49 #18
2018 Certified Stars Green /10 #18
2018 Certified Stars Mirror Black /1 #18
2018 Certified Stars Mirror Gold /25 #18
2018 Certified Stars Mirror Green /5 #18
2018 Certified Stars Mirror Purple /10 #18
2018 Certified Stars Purple /25 #18
2018 Certified Stars Red /149 #18
2018 Donruss #24
2018 Donruss #51A
2018 Donruss #82
2018 Donruss #141A
2018 Donruss #51B
2018 Donruss #141B
2018 Donruss Artist Proofs /25 #24
2018 Donruss Artist Proofs /25 #51A
2018 Donruss Artist Proofs /25 #82
2018 Donruss Artist Proofs /25 #141A
2018 Donruss Artist Proofs /25 #51B
2018 Donruss Artist Proofs /25 #141B
2018 Donruss Classics #5
2018 Donruss Classics Cracked Ice /999 #5
2018 Donruss Classics Xplosion /99 #5
2018 Donruss Elite Dominators /999 #2
2018 Donruss Gold Foil /499 #24
2018 Donruss Gold Foil /499 #51A
2018 Donruss Gold Foil /499 #82
2018 Donruss Gold Foil /499 #141A
2018 Donruss Gold Foil /499 #51B
2018 Donruss Gold Foil /499 #141B
2018 Donruss Gold Press Proofs /99 #24
2018 Donruss Gold Press Proofs /99 #51A
2018 Donruss Gold Press Proofs /99 #82
2018 Donruss Gold Press Proofs /99 #141A
2018 Donruss Gold Press Proofs /99 #51B
2018 Donruss Gold Press Proofs /99 #141B
2018 Donruss Green Foil /199 #24
2018 Donruss Green Foil /199 #51A
2018 Donruss Green Foil /199 #82
2018 Donruss Green Foil /199 #141A
2018 Donruss Green Foil /199 #51B
2018 Donruss Green Foil /199 #141B
2018 Donruss Masters of the Track #1
2018 Donruss Masters of the Track Cracked Ice /999 #1
2018 Donruss Masters of the Track Xplosion /99 #1
2018 Donruss Press Proofs /49 #24
2018 Donruss Press Proofs /49 #51A
2018 Donruss Press Proofs /49 #82
2018 Donruss Press Proofs /49 #141A
2018 Donruss Press Proofs /49 #51B
2018 Donruss Press Proofs /49 #141B
2018 Donruss Printing Plates Black /1 #24
2018 Donruss Printing Plates Black /1 #51
2018 Donruss Printing Plates Black /1 #82
2018 Donruss Printing Plates Black /1 #141
2018 Donruss Printing Plates Black /1 #51B
2018 Donruss Printing Plates Black /1 #141B
2018 Donruss Printing Plates Cyan /1 #24
2018 Donruss Printing Plates Cyan /1 #51
2018 Donruss Printing Plates Cyan /1 #82
2018 Donruss Printing Plates Cyan /1 #141
2018 Donruss Printing Plates Cyan /1 #51B
2018 Donruss Printing Plates Cyan /1 #141B
2018 Donruss Printing Plates Magenta /1 #24
2018 Donruss Printing Plates Magenta /1 #51
2018 Donruss Printing Plates Magenta /1 #82
2018 Donruss Printing Plates Magenta /1 #141
2018 Donruss Printing Plates Magenta /1 #51B
2018 Donruss Printing Plates Magenta /1 #141B
2018 Donruss Printing Plates Yellow /1 #24
2018 Donruss Printing Plates Yellow /1 #51
2018 Donruss Printing Plates Yellow /1 #82
2018 Donruss Printing Plates Yellow /1 #141
2018 Donruss Printing Plates Yellow /1 #51B
2018 Donruss Printing Plates Yellow /1 #141B
2018 Donruss Racing Relics #20
2018 Donruss Racing Relics Black /10 #20
2018 Donruss Racing Relics Holo Gold /99 #20
2018 Donruss Red Foil /299 #24
2018 Donruss Red Foil /299 #51A
2018 Donruss Red Foil /299 #82
2018 Donruss Red Foil /299 #141A
2018 Donruss Red Foil /299 #51B
2018 Donruss Red Foil /299 #141B
2018 Donruss Retro Relics '85 #2
2018 Donruss Retro Relics '85 Black /10 #2
2018 Donruss Retro Relics '85 Holo Gold /99 #2
2018 Donruss Rubber Relic Signatures Black /1 #8
2018 Donruss Rubber Relic Signatures Holo Gold /2 #8
2018 Donruss Rubber Relics #15
2018 Donruss Rubber Relics Black /10 #15
2018 Donruss Rubber Relics Holo Gold /99 #15
2018 Donruss Studio #1
2018 Donruss Studio Cracked Ice /999 #1
2018 Donruss Studio Xplosion /99 #1
2018 Donruss Top Tier #1
2018 Donruss Top Tier Cracked Ice /999 #1
2018 Donruss Top Tier Xplosion /99 #1
2018 Panini Black Friday VIP Gems /5 #JJ
2018 Panini Black Friday VIP Gems Autographs /1 #JJ
2018 Panini Black Friday VIP Gems One of One /1 #JJ
2018 Panini Father's Day Panini Collection /399 #11
2018 Panini Father's Day Panini Collection Autographs #11
2018 Panini Father's Day Panini Collection Checkerboard /5 #11
2018 Panini Father's Day Panini Collection Crystal Shards /10 #11
2018 Panini Father's Day Panini Collection Escher Squares /25 #11
2018 Panini Father's Day Panini Collection Future Frames /50 #11
2018 Panini Father's Day Panini Collection Hyperplaid /1 #11
2018 Panini Father's Day Racing Memorabilia #JJ
2018 Panini Father's Day Racing Memorabilia Checkerboard /10 #JJ
2018 Panini Father's Day Racing Memorabilia Cracked Ice /25 #JJ
2018 Panini Father's Day Racing Memorabilia Escher Squares /5 #JJ
2018 Panini Father's Day Racing Memorabilia Hyperplaid /1 #JJ
2018 Panini National Convention #70
2018 Panini National Convention Black Boxes #JJ
2018 Panini National Convention Black Boxes 1/1 #JJ
2018 Panini National Convention Escher Squares /25 #70
2018 Panini National Convention Galatic Windows /5 #70
2018 Panini National Convention Hyperplaid /1 #70
2018 Panini National Convention Magnetic Fur /99 #70
2018 Panini National Convention Pyramids /10 #70
2018 Panini National Convention Rainbow Spokes /49 #70
2018 Panini Prime /50 #14
2018 Panini Prime /50 #48
2018 Panini Prime /50 #80
2018 Panini Prime Black /1 #14
2018 Panini Prime Black /1 #48
2018 Panini Prime Black /1 #80
2018 Panini Prime Dual Material Autographs /25 #14
2018 Panini Prime Dual Material Autographs Black /1 #14
2018 Panini Prime Dual Material Autographs Holo Gold /10 #14
2018 Panini Prime Dual Material Autographs Laundry Tag /1 #14
2018 Panini Prime Hats Off Button /1 #5
2018 Panini Prime Hats Off Driver Name /3 #5
2018 Panini Prime Hats Off Eyelet /4 #5
2018 Panini Prime Hats Off Headband /28 #5
2018 Panini Prime Hats Off New Era /1 #5
2018 Panini Prime Hats Off Sponsor Logo /6 #5
2018 Panini Prime Hats Off Team Logo /2 #5
2018 Panini Prime Holo Gold /25 #14
2018 Panini Prime Holo Gold /25 #48
2018 Panini Prime Holo Gold /25 #80
2018 Panini Prime Prime Jumbo Associate Sponsor 1 /1 #40
2018 Panini Prime Prime Jumbo Associate Sponsor 2 /1 #40
2018 Panini Prime Prime Jumbo Associate Sponsor 3 /1 #40
2018 Panini Prime Prime Jumbo Associate Sponsor 4 /1 #40
2018 Panini Prime Prime Jumbo Associate Sponsor 5 /1 #40
2018 Panini Prime Prime Jumbo Associate Sponsor 6 /1 #40
2018 Panini Prime Prime Jumbo Associate Sponsor 7 /1 #40
2018 Panini Prime Prime Jumbo Associate Sponsor 8 /1 #40
2018 Panini Prime Prime Jumbo Associate Sponsor 9 /1 #40
2018 Panini Prime Prime Jumbo Car Manufacturer /1 #40
2018 Panini Prime Prime Jumbo Firesuit Manufacturer /1 #40
2018 Panini Prime Prime Jumbo Glove Manufacturer Patch /1 #40
2018 Panini Prime Prime Jumbo Glove Number Patch /1 #40
2018 Panini Prime Prime Jumbo Goodyear /2 #40
2018 Panini Prime Prime Jumbo Nameplate /2 #40
2018 Panini Prime Prime Jumbo NASCAR /1 #40
2018 Panini Prime Prime Jumbo Prime Colors /21 #40
2018 Panini Prime Prime Jumbo Series Sponsor /1 #40
2018 Panini Prime Prime Jumbo Shoe Brand Logo /1 #40
2018 Panini Prime Prime Jumbo Shoe Name Patch /1 #40
2018 Panini Prime Prime Jumbo Sunoco /1 #40
2018 Panini Prime Prime Number Signatures /25 #7
2018 Panini Prime Prime Number Signatures Black /1 #7
2018 Panini Prime Prime Number Signatures Holo Gold /10 #7
2018 Panini Prime Quad Material Autographs /25 #16
2018 Panini Prime Quad Material Autographs Black /1 #16
2018 Panini Prime Quad Material Autographs Holo Gold /10 #16
2018 Panini Prime Quad Material Autographs Laundry Tag /1 #16
2018 Panini Prime Race Used Duals Firesuit Black /1 #20
2018 Panini Prime Race Used Duals Firesuit Holo Gold /25 #20
2018 Panini Prime Race Used Duals Firesuit Laundry Tag /1 #20
2018 Panini Prime Race Used Duals Sheet Metal /50 #20
2018 Panini Prime Race Used Duals Sheet Metal Black /1 #20
2018 Panini Prime Race Used Duals Sheet Metal Holo Gold /25 #20
2018 Panini Prime Race Used Duals Tire /50 #20
2018 Panini Prime Race Used Duals Tire Black /1 #20
2018 Panini Prime Race Used Duals Tire Holo Gold /25 #20
2018 Panini Prime Race Used Firesuits Black /1 #17
2018 Panini Prime Race Used Firesuits Holo Gold /25 #17
2018 Panini Prime Race Used Firesuits Laundry Tag /1 #17
2018 Panini Prime Race Used Sheet Metal /50 #17
2018 Panini Prime Race Used Sheet Metal Black /1 #17
2018 Panini Prime Race Used Sheet Metal Holo Gold /25 #17
2018 Panini Prime Race Used Tires /50 #17
2018 Panini Prime Race Used Tires Black /1 #17
2018 Panini Prime Race Used Tires Holo Gold /25 #17
2018 Panini Prime Race Used Trios Firesuit /50 #2
2018 Panini Prime Race Used Trios Firesuit Black /1 #2
2018 Panini Prime Race Used Trios Firesuit Holo Gold /25 #2
2018 Panini Prime Race Used Trios Firesuit Laundry Tag /1 #2
2018 Panini Prime Race Used Trios Sheet Metal /50 #2
2018 Panini Prime Race Used Trios Sheet Metal Black /1 #2
2018 Panini Prime Race Used Trios Sheet Metal Holo Gold /25 #2
2018 Panini Prime Race Used Trios Tire /50 #2
2018 Panini Prime Race Used Trios Tire Black /1 #2
2018 Panini Prime Race Used Trios Tire Holo Gold /25 #2
2018 Panini Prime Shadowbox Signatures /25 #19
2018 Panini Prime Shadowbox Signatures Black /1 #19
2018 Panini Prime Shadowbox Signatures Holo Gold /10 #19
2018 Panini Prime Signature Swatches /25 #8
2018 Panini Prime Signature Swatches Black /1 #8
2018 Panini Prime Signature Swatches Holo Gold /10 #8
2018 Panini Prizm #5A
2018 Panini Prizm #5B
2018 Panini Prizm #53
2018 Panini Prizm #65
2018 Panini Prizm #71
2018 Panini Prizm #89
2018 Panini Prizm Brilliance #4
2018 Panini Prizm Brilliance Prizms #4
2018 Panini Prizm Brilliance Prizms Black /1 #4
2018 Panini Prizm Brilliance Prizms Gold /10 #4
2018 Panini Prizm Fireworks #1
2018 Panini Prizm Fireworks Prizms #1
2018 Panini Prizm Fireworks Prizms Black /1 #1

2018 Panini Prizm Fireworks Prizms Gold /10 #1
2018 Panini Prizm Illumination #2
2018 Panini Prizm Illumination Prizms #2
2018 Panini Prizm Illumination Prizms Black /1 #2
2018 Panini Prizm Illumination Prizms Gold /10 #2
2018 Panini Prizm Instant Impact #1
2018 Panini Prizm Instant Impact Prizms #1
2018 Panini Prizm Instant Impact Prizms Black /1 #1
2018 Panini Prizm Instant Impact Prizms Gold /10 #1
2018 Panini Prizm National Pride #1
2018 Panini Prizm National Pride Prizms #1
2018 Panini Prizm National Pride Prizms Black /1 #1
2018 Panini Prizm National Pride Prizms Gold /10 #1
2018 Panini Prizm Patented Penmanship Prizms #11
2018 Panini Prizm Patented Penmanship Prizms Black /1 #11
2018 Panini Prizm Patented Penmanship Prizms Blue /25 #11
2018 Panini Prizm Patented Penmanship Prizms Camo #11
2018 Panini Prizm Patented Penmanship Prizms Gold /10 #11
2018 Panini Prizm Patented Penmanship Prizms Green /25 #11
2018 Panini Prizm Patented Penmanship Prizms Rainbow /24 #11
2018 Panini Prizm Patented Penmanship Prizms Red /25 #11
2018 Panini Prizm Patented Penmanship Prizms Red White and Blue /25 #11
2018 Panini Prizm Patented Penmanship Prizms White /5 #11
2018 Panini Prizm Prizms #5A
2018 Panini Prizm Prizms #5B
2018 Panini Prizm Prizms #53
2018 Panini Prizm Prizms #65
2018 Panini Prizm Prizms #71
2018 Panini Prizm Prizms #89
2018 Panini Prizm Prizms Black /1 #5A
2018 Panini Prizm Prizms Black /1 #5B
2018 Panini Prizm Prizms Black /1 #53
2018 Panini Prizm Prizms Black /1 #65
2018 Panini Prizm Prizms Black /1 #71
2018 Panini Prizm Prizms Black /1 #89
2018 Panini Prizm Prizms Blue /99 #5A
2018 Panini Prizm Prizms Blue /99 #5B
2018 Panini Prizm Prizms Blue /99 #53
2018 Panini Prizm Prizms Blue /99 #65
2018 Panini Prizm Prizms Blue /99 #71
2018 Panini Prizm Prizms Blue /99 #89
2018 Panini Prizm Prizms Camo #5A
2018 Panini Prizm Prizms Camo #5B
2018 Panini Prizm Prizms Camo #53
2018 Panini Prizm Prizms Camo #65
2018 Panini Prizm Prizms Camo #71
2018 Panini Prizm Prizms Camo #89
2018 Panini Prizm Prizms Gold /10 #5A
2018 Panini Prizm Prizms Gold /10 #5B
2018 Panini Prizm Prizms Gold /10 #53
2018 Panini Prizm Prizms Gold /10 #65
2018 Panini Prizm Prizms Gold /10 #71
2018 Panini Prizm Prizms Gold /10 #89
2018 Panini Prizm Prizms Green /149 #5A
2018 Panini Prizm Prizms Green /149 #5B
2018 Panini Prizm Prizms Green /149 #53
2018 Panini Prizm Prizms Green /149 #65
2018 Panini Prizm Prizms Green /149 #71
2018 Panini Prizm Prizms Green /149 #89
2018 Panini Prizm Prizms Purple Flash #5A
2018 Panini Prizm Prizms Purple Flash #5B
2018 Panini Prizm Prizms Purple Flash #53
2018 Panini Prizm Prizms Purple Flash #65
2018 Panini Prizm Prizms Purple Flash #71
2018 Panini Prizm Prizms Purple Flash #89
2018 Panini Prizm Prizms Rainbow /24 #5A
2018 Panini Prizm Prizms Rainbow /24 #5B
2018 Panini Prizm Prizms Rainbow /24 #53
2018 Panini Prizm Prizms Rainbow /24 #65
2018 Panini Prizm Prizms Rainbow /24 #71
2018 Panini Prizm Prizms Rainbow /24 #89
2018 Panini Prizm Prizms Red /75 #5A
2018 Panini Prizm Prizms Red /75 #5B
2018 Panini Prizm Prizms Red /75 #53
2018 Panini Prizm Prizms Red /75 #65
2018 Panini Prizm Prizms Red /75 #71
2018 Panini Prizm Prizms Red /75 #89
2018 Panini Prizm Prizms Red White and Blue #5A
2018 Panini Prizm Prizms Red White and Blue #5B
2018 Panini Prizm Prizms Red White and Blue #53
2018 Panini Prizm Prizms Red White and Blue #65
2018 Panini Prizm Prizms Red White and Blue #71
2018 Panini Prizm Prizms Red White and Blue #89
2018 Panini Prizm Prizms White /5 #5A
2018 Panini Prizm Prizms White /5 #5B
2018 Panini Prizm Prizms White /5 #53
2018 Panini Prizm Prizms White /5 #65
2018 Panini Prizm Prizms White /5 #71
2018 Panini Prizm Prizms White /5 #89
2018 Panini Prizm Stars and Stripes #15
2018 Panini Prizm Stars and Stripes Prizms #15
2018 Panini Prizm Stars and Stripes Prizms Black /1 #15
2018 Panini Prizm Stars and Stripes Prizms Gold /10 #15
2018 Panini Prizm Team Tandems #1
2018 Panini Prizm Team Tandems Prizms #1
2018 Panini Prizm Team Tandems Prizms Black /1 #1
2018 Panini Prizm Team Tandems Prizms Gold /10 #1
2018 Panini Victory Lane #25
2018 Panini Victory Lane #70
2018 Panini Victory Lane #78
2018 Panini Victory Lane #81
2018 Panini Victory Lane #84
2018 Panini Victory Lane #85
2018 Panini Victory Lane #91
2018 Panini Victory Lane #92
2018 Panini Victory Lane #99
2018 Panini Victory Lane #100
2018 Panini Victory Lane Black /1 #25
2018 Panini Victory Lane Black /1 #70
2018 Panini Victory Lane Black /1 #78
2018 Panini Victory Lane Black /1 #81
2018 Panini Victory Lane Black /1 #84
2018 Panini Victory Lane Black /1 #85
2018 Panini Victory Lane Black /1 #91
2018 Panini Victory Lane Black /1 #92
2018 Panini Victory Lane Black /1 #99
2018 Panini Victory Lane Black /1 #100
2018 Panini Victory Lane Blue /25 #25
2018 Panini Victory Lane Blue /25 #70
2018 Panini Victory Lane Blue /25 #78
2018 Panini Victory Lane Blue /25 #81
2018 Panini Victory Lane Blue /25 #84
2018 Panini Victory Lane Blue /25 #85
2018 Panini Victory Lane Blue /25 #91
2018 Panini Victory Lane Blue /25 #92
2018 Panini Victory Lane Blue /25 #99
2018 Panini Victory Lane Blue /25 #100
2018 Panini Victory Lane Celebrations #2
2018 Panini Victory Lane Celebrations Black /1 #2
2018 Panini Victory Lane Celebrations Blue /25 #2
2018 Panini Victory Lane Celebrations Gold /99 #2
2018 Panini Victory Lane Celebrations Green /5 #2
2018 Panini Victory Lane Celebrations Printing Plates Black /1 #2
2018 Panini Victory Lane Celebrations Printing Plates Cyan /1 #2
2018 Panini Victory Lane Celebrations Printing Plates Magenta /1 #2
2018 Panini Victory Lane Celebrations Printing Plates Yellow /1 #2
2018 Panini Victory Lane Celebrations Red /49 #2
2018 Panini Victory Lane Champions #1
2018 Panini Victory Lane Champions Black /1 #1
2018 Panini Victory Lane Champions Blue /25 #1
2018 Panini Victory Lane Champions Gold /99 #1
2018 Panini Victory Lane Champions Green /5 #1
2018 Panini Victory Lane Champions Printing Plates Black /1 #1
2018 Panini Victory Lane Champions Printing Plates Cyan /1 #1
2018 Panini Victory Lane Champions Printing Plates Magenta /1 #1
2018 Panini Victory Lane Champions Printing Plates Yellow /1 #1
2018 Panini Victory Lane Champions Red /49 #1
2018 Panini Victory Lane Chasing the Flag #4
2018 Panini Victory Lane Chasing the Flag Black /1 #4
2018 Panini Victory Lane Chasing the Flag Blue /25 #4
2018 Panini Victory Lane Chasing the Flag Gold /99 #4
2018 Panini Victory Lane Chasing the Flag Green /5 #4
2018 Panini Victory Lane Chasing the Flag Printing Plates Black /1 #4
2018 Panini Victory Lane Chasing the Flag Printing Plates Cyan /1 #4
2018 Panini Victory Lane Chasing the Flag Printing Plates Magenta /1 #4
2018 Panini Victory Lane Chasing the Flag Printing Plates Yellow /1 #4
2018 Panini Victory Lane Chasing the Flag Red /49 #4
2018 Panini Victory Lane Gold /99 #25
2018 Panini Victory Lane Gold /99 #70
2018 Panini Victory Lane Gold /99 #78
2018 Panini Victory Lane Gold /99 #81
2018 Panini Victory Lane Gold /99 #84
2018 Panini Victory Lane Gold /99 #85
2018 Panini Victory Lane Gold /99 #91
2018 Panini Victory Lane Gold /99 #92
2018 Panini Victory Lane Gold /99 #99
2018 Panini Victory Lane Gold /99 #100
2018 Panini Victory Lane Green /5 #25
2018 Panini Victory Lane Green /5 #70
2018 Panini Victory Lane Green /5 #78
2018 Panini Victory Lane Green /5 #81
2018 Panini Victory Lane Green /5 #84
2018 Panini Victory Lane Green /5 #85
2018 Panini Victory Lane Green /5 #91
2018 Panini Victory Lane Green /5 #92
2018 Panini Victory Lane Green /5 #99
2018 Panini Victory Lane Green /5 #100
2018 Panini Victory Lane NASCAR at 70 #9
2018 Panini Victory Lane NASCAR at 70 Black /1 #9
2018 Panini Victory Lane NASCAR at 70 Blue /25 #9
2018 Panini Victory Lane NASCAR at 70 Gold /99 #9
2018 Panini Victory Lane NASCAR at 70 Green /5 #9
2018 Panini Victory Lane NASCAR at 70 Printing Plates Black /1 #9
2018 Panini Victory Lane NASCAR at 70 Printing Plates Cyan /1 #9
2018 Panini Victory Lane NASCAR at 70 Printing Plates Magenta /1 #9
2018 Panini Victory Lane NASCAR at 70 Printing Plates Yellow /1 #9
2018 Panini Victory Lane NASCAR at 70 Red /49 #9
2018 Panini Victory Lane Pedal to the Metal #25
2018 Panini Victory Lane Pedal to the Metal #70
2018 Panini Victory Lane Pedal to the Metal Black /1 #25
2018 Panini Victory Lane Pedal to the Metal Black /1 #70
2018 Panini Victory Lane Pedal to the Metal Blue /25 #25
2018 Panini Victory Lane Pedal to the Metal Blue /25 #70
2018 Panini Victory Lane Pedal to the Metal Green /5 #25
2018 Panini Victory Lane Pedal to the Metal Green /5 #70
2018 Panini Victory Lane Printing Plates Black /1 #25
2018 Panini Victory Lane Printing Plates Black /1 #70
2018 Panini Victory Lane Printing Plates Black /1 #78
2018 Panini Victory Lane Printing Plates Black /1 #81
2018 Panini Victory Lane Printing Plates Black /1 #84
2018 Panini Victory Lane Printing Plates Black /1 #85
2018 Panini Victory Lane Printing Plates Black /1 #91
2018 Panini Victory Lane Printing Plates Black /1 #92
2018 Panini Victory Lane Printing Plates Black /1 #99
2018 Panini Victory Lane Printing Plates Black /1 #100
2018 Panini Victory Lane Printing Plates Cyan /1 #25
2018 Panini Victory Lane Printing Plates Cyan /1 #70
2018 Panini Victory Lane Printing Plates Cyan /1 #78
2018 Panini Victory Lane Printing Plates Cyan /1 #81
2018 Panini Victory Lane Printing Plates Cyan /1 #84
2018 Panini Victory Lane Printing Plates Cyan /1 #85
2018 Panini Victory Lane Printing Plates Cyan /1 #91
2018 Panini Victory Lane Printing Plates Cyan /1 #92
2018 Panini Victory Lane Printing Plates Cyan /1 #99
2018 Panini Victory Lane Printing Plates Cyan /1 #100
2018 Panini Victory Lane Printing Plates Magenta /1 #25
2018 Panini Victory Lane Printing Plates Magenta /1 #70
2018 Panini Victory Lane Printing Plates Magenta /1 #78
2018 Panini Victory Lane Printing Plates Magenta /1 #81
2018 Panini Victory Lane Printing Plates Magenta /1 #84
2018 Panini Victory Lane Printing Plates Magenta /1 #85
2018 Panini Victory Lane Printing Plates Magenta /1 #91
2018 Panini Victory Lane Printing Plates Magenta /1 #92
2018 Panini Victory Lane Printing Plates Magenta /1 #99
2018 Panini Victory Lane Printing Plates Magenta /1 #100
2018 Panini Victory Lane Printing Plates Yellow /1 #25
2018 Panini Victory Lane Printing Plates Yellow /1 #70
2018 Panini Victory Lane Printing Plates Yellow /1 #78
2018 Panini Victory Lane Printing Plates Yellow /1 #81
2018 Panini Victory Lane Printing Plates Yellow /1 #84
2018 Panini Victory Lane Printing Plates Yellow /1 #85
2018 Panini Victory Lane Printing Plates Yellow /1 #91
2018 Panini Victory Lane Printing Plates Yellow /1 #92
2018 Panini Victory Lane Printing Plates Yellow /1 #99
2018 Panini Victory Lane Printing Plates Yellow /1 #100
2018 Panini Victory Lane Race Day #1
2018 Panini Victory Lane Race Day Black /1 #1
2018 Panini Victory Lane Race Day Blue /25 #1
2018 Panini Victory Lane Race Day Gold /99 #1
2018 Panini Victory Lane Race Day Green /5 #1
2018 Panini Victory Lane Race Day Printing Plates Black /1 #1
2018 Panini Victory Lane Race Day Printing Plates Cyan /1 #1
2018 Panini Victory Lane Race Day Printing Plates Magenta /1 #1
2018 Panini Victory Lane Race Day Printing Plates Yellow /1 #1
2018 Panini Victory Lane Race Day Red /49 #1
2018 Panini Victory Lane Race Ready Materials /50 #15
2018 Panini Victory Lane Race Ready Materials Black /10 #15
2018 Panini Victory Lane Race Ready Materials Gold /48 #15
2018 Panini Victory Lane Race Ready Materials Green /25 #15
2018 Panini Victory Lane Race Ready Materials Laundry Tag /1 #15
2018 Panini Victory Lane Red /49 #25
2018 Panini Victory Lane Red /49 #70
2018 Panini Victory Lane Red /49 #78
2018 Panini Victory Lane Red /49 #81
2018 Panini Victory Lane Red /49 #84
2018 Panini Victory Lane Red /49 #85
2018 Panini Victory Lane Red /49 #91
2018 Panini Victory Lane Red /49 #92
2018 Panini Victory Lane Red /49 #99
2018 Panini Victory Lane Red /49 #100
2018 Panini Victory Lane Remarkable Remnants Material Autographs /59 #2
2018 Panini Victory Lane Remarkable Remnants Material Autographs Black /5 #2
2018 Panini Victory Lane Remarkable Remnants Material Autographs Gold /25 #2
2018 Panini Victory Lane Remarkable Remnants Material Autographs Green /10 #2
2018 Panini Victory Lane Remarkable Remnants Material Autographs Laundry Tag /1 #2
2018 Panini Victory Lane Silver #25
2018 Panini Victory Lane Silver #70
2018 Panini Victory Lane Silver #78
2018 Panini Victory Lane Silver #81
2018 Panini Victory Lane Silver #84
2018 Panini Victory Lane Silver #85
2018 Panini Victory Lane Silver #91
2018 Panini Victory Lane Silver #92
2018 Panini Victory Lane Silver #99
2018 Panini Victory Lane Silver #100
2018 Panini Victory Lane Starting Grid #22
2018 Panini Victory Lane Starting Grid Black /1 #22
2018 Panini Victory Lane Starting Grid Blue /25 #22
2018 Panini Victory Lane Starting Grid Gold /99 #22
2018 Panini Victory Lane Starting Grid Green /5 #22
2018 Panini Victory Lane Starting Grid Printing Plates Black /1 #22
2018 Panini Victory Lane Starting Grid Printing Plates Cyan /1 #22
2018 Panini Victory Lane Starting Grid Printing Plates Magenta /1 #22
2018 Panini Victory Lane Starting Grid Printing Plates Yellow /1 #22
2018 Panini Victory Lane Starting Grid Red /49 #22
2018 Panini Victory Lane Victory Lane Prime Patches Associate Sponsor 1 /1 #18
2018 Panini Victory Lane Victory Lane Prime Patches Associate Sponsor 2 /1 #18
2018 Panini Victory Lane Victory Lane Prime Patches Associate Sponsor 3 /1 #18
2018 Panini Victory Lane Victory Lane Prime Patches Associate Sponsor 4 /1 #18
2018 Panini Victory Lane Victory Lane Prime Patches Associate Sponsor 5 /1 #18
2018 Panini Victory Lane Victory Lane Prime Patches Associate Sponsor 6 /1 #18
2018 Panini Victory Lane Victory Lane Prime Patches Associate Sponsor 7 /1 #18
2018 Panini Victory Lane Victory Lane Prime Patches Associate Sponsor 8 /1 #18
2018 Panini Victory Lane Victory Lane Prime Patches Car Manufacturer /1 #18
2018 Panini Victory Lane Victory Lane Prime Patches Firesuit Manufacturer /1 #18
2018 Panini Victory Lane Victory Lane Prime Patches Goodyear /1 #18
2018 Panini Victory Lane Victory Lane Prime Patches Nameplate /2 #18
2018 Panini Victory Lane Victory Lane Prime Patches NASCAR /1 #18
2018 Panini Victory Lane Victory Lane Prime Patches Series Sponsor /1 #18
2018 Panini Victory Lane Victory Lane Prime Patches Sunoco /1 #18
2019 Donruss #1
2019 Donruss #16
2019 Donruss #48A
2019 Donruss #86
2019 Donruss #106A
2019 Donruss #48B
2019 Donruss #106B
2019 Donruss Action #12
2019 Donruss Action Cracked Ice /25 #12
2019 Donruss Action Holographic #12
2019 Donruss Action Xplosion /10 #12
2019 Donruss Artist Proofs /25 #1
2019 Donruss Artist Proofs /25 #16
2019 Donruss Artist Proofs /25 #48A
2019 Donruss Artist Proofs /25 #86
2019 Donruss Artist Proofs /25 #106A
2019 Donruss Artist Proofs /25 #48B
2019 Donruss Artist Proofs /25 #106B
2019 Donruss Black /199 #1
2019 Donruss Black /199 #16
2019 Donruss Black /199 #48A
2019 Donruss Black /199 #86
2019 Donruss Black /199 #106A
2019 Donruss Black /199 #48B
2019 Donruss Black /199 #106B
2019 Donruss Classics #4
2019 Donruss Classics Cracked Ice /25 #4
2019 Donruss Classics Holographic #4
2019 Donruss Classics Xplosion /10 #4
2019 Donruss Contenders #14
2019 Donruss Contenders Cracked Ice /25 #14
2019 Donruss Contenders Holographic #14
2019 Donruss Contenders Xplosion /10 #14
2019 Donruss Decades of Speed #1
2019 Donruss Decades of Speed Cracked Ice /25 #1
2019 Donruss Decades of Speed Holographic #1
2019 Donruss Decades of Speed Xplosion /10 #1
2019 Donruss Gold /299 #1
2019 Donruss Gold /299 #16
2019 Donruss Gold /299 #48A
2019 Donruss Gold /299 #86
2019 Donruss Gold /299 #106A
2019 Donruss Gold /299 #48B
2019 Donruss Gold /299 #106B
2019 Donruss Gold Press Proofs /99 #1
2019 Donruss Gold Press Proofs /99 #16
2019 Donruss Gold Press Proofs /99 #48A
2019 Donruss Gold Press Proofs /99 #86
2019 Donruss Gold Press Proofs /99 #106A
2019 Donruss Gold Press Proofs /99 #48B
2019 Donruss Gold Press Proofs /99 #106B
2019 Donruss Icons #2
2019 Donruss Icons Cracked Ice /25 #2
2019 Donruss Icons Holographic #2
2019 Donruss Icons Xplosion /10 #2
2019 Donruss Optic #2
2019 Donruss Optic #27
2019 Donruss Optic Blue Pulsar #2
2019 Donruss Optic Blue Pulsar #27
2019 Donruss Optic Gold /10 #2
2019 Donruss Optic Gold /10 #27
2019 Donruss Optic Gold Vinyl /1 #2
2019 Donruss Optic Gold Vinyl /1 #27
2019 Donruss Optic Holo #2
2019 Donruss Optic Holo #27
2019 Donruss Optic Illusion #1
2019 Donruss Optic Illusion Blue Pulsar #1
2019 Donruss Optic Illusion Gold /10 #1
2019 Donruss Optic Illusion Gold Vinyl /1 #1
2019 Donruss Optic Illusion Holo #1
2019 Donruss Optic Illusion Red Wave #1
2019 Donruss Optic Illusion Signatures Gold Vinyl /1 #1
2019 Donruss Optic Illusion Signatures Holo /25 #1
2019 Donruss Optic Red Wave #2
2019 Donruss Optic Red Wave #27
2019 Donruss Optic Signatures Gold Vinyl /1 #2
2019 Donruss Optic Signatures Gold Vinyl /1 #27
2019 Donruss Optic Signatures Holo /25 #2
2019 Donruss Optic Signatures Holo /25 #27
2019 Donruss Originals #1
2019 Donruss Originals Cracked Ice /25 #1
2019 Donruss Originals Holographic #1
2019 Donruss Originals Xplosion /10 #1
2019 Donruss Press Proofs /49 #16
2019 Donruss Press Proofs /49 #48A
2019 Donruss Press Proofs /49 #86
2019 Donruss Press Proofs /49 #106A
2019 Donruss Press Proofs /49 #48B
2019 Donruss Press Proofs /49 #106B
2019 Donruss Press Proofs /49 #1
2019 Donruss Printing Plates Black /1 #1
2019 Donruss Printing Plates Black /1 #16
2019 Donruss Printing Plates Black /1 #48A
2019 Donruss Printing Plates Black /1 #86
2019 Donruss Printing Plates Black /1 #106A
2019 Donruss Printing Plates Black /1 #48B
2019 Donruss Printing Plates Black /1 #106B
2019 Donruss Printing Plates Cyan /1 #1
2019 Donruss Printing Plates Cyan /1 #16
2019 Donruss Printing Plates Cyan /1 #48A
2019 Donruss Printing Plates Cyan /1 #86
2019 Donruss Printing Plates Cyan /1 #106A
2019 Donruss Printing Plates Cyan /1 #48B
2019 Donruss Printing Plates Cyan /1 #106B
2019 Donruss Printing Plates Magenta /1 #48A
2019 Donruss Printing Plates Magenta /1 #86
2019 Donruss Printing Plates Magenta /1 #106A
2019 Donruss Printing Plates Magenta /1 #48B
2019 Donruss Printing Plates Magenta /1 #106B
2019 Donruss Printing Plates Magenta /1 #1
2019 Donruss Printing Plates Magenta /1 #16
2019 Donruss Printing Plates Yellow /1 #1
2019 Donruss Printing Plates Yellow /1 #16
2019 Donruss Printing Plates Yellow /1 #48A
2019 Donruss Printing Plates Yellow /1 #86
2019 Donruss Printing Plates Yellow /1 #106A
2019 Donruss Printing Plates Yellow /1 #48B
2019 Donruss Printing Plates Yellow /1 #106B
2019 Donruss Race Day Relics #12
2019 Donruss Race Day Relics Holo Black /10 #12
2019 Donruss Race Day Relics Holo Gold /25 #12
2019 Donruss Race Day Relics Red /185 #12
2019 Donruss Retro Relics '86 #18
2019 Donruss Retro Relics '86 Holo Black /10 #18
2019 Donruss Retro Relics '86 Holo Gold /25 #18
2019 Donruss Retro Relics '86 Red /225 #18
2019 Donruss Signature Swatches #3
2019 Donruss Signature Swatches Holo Black /1 #3
2019 Donruss Signature Swatches Holo Gold /10 #3
2019 Donruss Signature Swatches Red /25 #3
2019 Donruss Silver #1
2019 Donruss Silver #16
2019 Donruss Silver #48A
2019 Donruss Silver #86
2019 Donruss Silver #106A
2019 Donruss Silver #48B
2019 Donruss Silver #106B
2019 Donruss Top Tier #1
2019 Donruss Top Tier Cracked Ice /25 #1
2019 Donruss Top Tier Holographic #1
2019 Donruss Top Tier Xplosion /10 #1
2019 Panini National Convention NASCAR #R3
2019 Panini National Convention NASCAR Galatic Windows #R3
2019 Panini National Convention NASCAR HyperPlaid /1 #R3
2019 Panini Prime /50 #30
2019 Panini Prime /50 #58
2019 Panini Prime /50 #86
2019 Panini Prime Black /10 #30
2019 Panini Prime Black /10 #58
2019 Panini Prime Black /10 #86
2019 Panini Prime Clear Silhouettes /99 #1
2019 Panini Prime Clear Silhouettes Black /10 #1
2019 Panini Prime Clear Silhouettes Holo Gold /25 #1
2019 Panini Prime Clear Silhouettes Platinum Blue /1 #1
2019 Panini Prime Emerald /5 #30
2019 Panini Prime Emerald /5 #58
2019 Panini Prime Emerald /5 #86
2019 Panini Prime Jumbo Material Signatures Firesuit /7 #14
2019 Panini Prime Jumbo Material Signatures Firesuit Platinum Blue /1 #14
2019 Panini Prime Jumbo Material Signatures Sheet Metal /10 #14
2019 Panini Prime Jumbo Material Signatures Tire /25 #14
2019 Panini Prime NASCAR Shadowbox Signatures Car Number /25 #20
2019 Panini Prime NASCAR Shadowbox Signatures Manufacturer /7 #20
2019 Panini Prime NASCAR Shadowbox Signatures Sponsor /10 #20
2019 Panini Prime NASCAR Shadowbox Signatures Team Owner /1 #20
2019 Panini Prime Platinum Blue /1 #30
2019 Panini Prime Platinum Blue /1 #58
2019 Panini Prime Platinum Blue /1 #86
2019 Panini Prime Prime Cars Die Cut Signatures /25 #9
2019 Panini Prime Prime Cars Die Cut Signatures Black /7 #9
2019 Panini Prime Prime Cars Die Cut Signatures Holo Gold /10 #9
2019 Panini Prime Prime Cars Die Cut Signatures Platinum Blue /1 #9
2019 Panini Prime Prime Jumbo Associate Sponsor 1 /1 #35
2019 Panini Prime Prime Jumbo Associate Sponsor 1 /1 #36
2019 Panini Prime Prime Jumbo Associate Sponsor 1 /1 #37
2019 Panini Prime Prime Jumbo Associate Sponsor 2 /1 #35
2019 Panini Prime Prime Jumbo Associate Sponsor 2 /1 #36
2019 Panini Prime Prime Jumbo Associate Sponsor 2 /1 #37
2019 Panini Prime Prime Jumbo Associate Sponsor 3 /1 #35
2019 Panini Prime Prime Jumbo Associate Sponsor 3 /1 #36
2019 Panini Prime Prime Jumbo Associate Sponsor 3 /1 #37
2019 Panini Prime Prime Jumbo Associate Sponsor 4 /1 #35
2019 Panini Prime Prime Jumbo Associate Sponsor 4 /1 #36
2019 Panini Prime Prime Jumbo Associate Sponsor 4 /1 #37
2019 Panini Prime Prime Jumbo Associate Sponsor 5 /1 #35
2019 Panini Prime Prime Jumbo Associate Sponsor 5 /1 #36
2019 Panini Prime Prime Jumbo Associate Sponsor 6 /1 #35
2019 Panini Prime Prime Jumbo Associate Sponsor 6 /1 #36
2019 Panini Prime Prime Jumbo Associate Sponsor 7 /1 #35
2019 Panini Prime Prime Jumbo Associate Sponsor 7 /1 #36
2019 Panini Prime Prime Jumbo Car Manufacturer /1 #35
2019 Panini Prime Prime Jumbo Car Manufacturer /1 #36
2019 Panini Prime Prime Jumbo Firesuit Manufacturer /1 #35
2019 Panini Prime Prime Jumbo Firesuit Manufacturer /1 #36
2019 Panini Prime Prime Jumbo Firesuit Manufacturer /1 #37
2019 Panini Prime Prime Jumbo Glove Manufacturer Patch /1 #35
2019 Panini Prime Prime Jumbo Glove Manufacturer Patch /1 #36
2019 Panini Prime Prime Jumbo Glove Manufacturer Patch /1 #37
2019 Panini Prime Prime Jumbo Glove Number Patch /1 #35
2019 Panini Prime Prime Jumbo Glove Number Patch /1 #36
2019 Panini Prime Prime Jumbo Glove Number Patch /1 #37
2019 Panini Prime Prime Jumbo Goodyear /1 #35
2019 Panini Prime Prime Jumbo Goodyear /2 #36
2019 Panini Prime Prime Jumbo Nameplate /3 #35
2019 Panini Prime Prime Jumbo Nameplate /2 #36
2019 Panini Prime Prime Jumbo NASCAR /1 #35
2019 Panini Prime Prime Jumbo NASCAR /1 #36
2019 Panini Prime Prime Jumbo Prime Colors /24 #35
2019 Panini Prime Prime Jumbo Prime Colors /24 #36
2019 Panini Prime Prime Jumbo Prime Colors /12 #37
2019 Panini Prime Prime Jumbo Series Sponsor /1 #35
2019 Panini Prime Prime Jumbo Series Sponsor /1 #36
2019 Panini Prime Prime Jumbo Shoe Brand Logo /1 #35
2019 Panini Prime Prime Jumbo Shoe Brand Logo /1 #36
2019 Panini Prime Prime Jumbo Shoe Brand Logo /1 #37
2019 Panini Prime Prime Jumbo Shoe Name Patch /1 #35
2019 Panini Prime Prime Jumbo Shoe Name Patch /1 #36
2019 Panini Prime Prime Jumbo Shoe Name Patch /1 #37
2019 Panini Prime Prime Jumbo Sunoco /1 #35
2019 Panini Prime Prime Jumbo Sunoco /1 #36
2019 Panini Prime Prime Names Die Cut Signatures /25 #23
2019 Panini Prime Prime Names Die Cut Signatures Black /7 #23
2019 Panini Prime Prime Names Die Cut Signatures Holo Gold /10 #23
2019 Panini Prime Prime Names Die Cut Signatures Platinum Blue /1 #23
2019 Panini Prime Prime Number Die Cut Signatures /25 #18
2019 Panini Prime Prime Number Die Cut Signatures Black /7 #18
2019 Panini Prime Prime Number Die Cut Signatures Holo Gold /10 #18
2019 Panini Prime Prime Number Die Cut Signatures Platinum Blue /1 #18
2019 Panini Prime Quad Materials Autographs /25 #13
2019 Panini Prime Quad Materials Autographs Black /7 #13
2019 Panini Prime Quad Materials Autographs Holo Gold /10 #13
2019 Panini Prime Quad Materials Autographs Laundry Tags /1 #13
2019 Panini Prime Race Used Duals Firesuits /50 #20
2019 Panini Prime Race Used Duals Firesuits Black /10 #20
2019 Panini Prime Race Used Duals Firesuits Holo Gold /25 #20
2019 Panini Prime Race Used Duals Firesuits Laundry Tags /1 #20
2019 Panini Prime Race Used Duals Sheet Metal /50 #20
2019 Panini Prime Race Used Duals Sheet Metal Black /10 #20
2019 Panini Prime Race Used Duals Sheet Metal Holo Gold /25 #20
2019 Panini Prime Race Used Duals Sheet Metal Platinum Blue /1 #20
2019 Panini Prime Race Used Duals Tires /50 #20
2019 Panini Prime Race Used Duals Tires Black /10 #20
2019 Panini Prime Race Used Duals Tires Holo Gold /25 #20
2019 Panini Prime Race Used Duals Tires Platinum Blue /1 #20
2019 Panini Prime Race Used Firesuits /50 #20
2019 Panini Prime Race Used Firesuits Black /10 #20
2019 Panini Prime Race Used Firesuits Holo Gold /25 #20
2019 Panini Prime Race Used Firesuits Laundry Tags /1 #20
2019 Panini Prime Race Used Quads Firesuits /50 #6
2019 Panini Prime Race Used Quads Firesuits Black /10 #6
2019 Panini Prime Race Used Quads Firesuits Holo Gold /25 #6
2019 Panini Prime Race Used Quads Firesuits Laundry Tags /1 #6
2019 Panini Prime Race Used Quads Sheet Metal /50 #6
2019 Panini Prime Race Used Quads Sheet Metal Black /10 #6
2019 Panini Prime Race Used Quads Sheet Metal Holo Gold /25 #6
2019 Panini Prime Race Used Quads Sheet Metal Platinum Blue /1 #6
2019 Panini Prime Race Used Quads Tires /50 #6
2019 Panini Prime Race Used Quads Tires Black /10 #6
2019 Panini Prime Race Used Quads Tires Holo Gold /25 #6
2019 Panini Prime Race Used Quads Tires Platinum Blue /1 #6
2019 Panini Prime Race Used Sheet Metal /50 #20
2019 Panini Prime Race Used Sheet Metal Black /10 #20
2019 Panini Prime Race Used Sheet Metal Holo Gold /25 #20
2019 Panini Prime Race Used Sheet Metal Platinum Blue /1 #20
2019 Panini Prime Race Used Tires /50 #20
2019 Panini Prime Race Used Tires Black /10 #20
2019 Panini Prime Race Used Tires Holo Gold /25 #20
2019 Panini Prime Race Used Tires Platinum Blue /1 #20
2019 Panini Prime Shadowbox Signatures /25 #17
2019 Panini Prime Shadowbox Signatures Black /7 #17
2019 Panini Prime Shadowbox Signatures Holo Gold /10 #17
2019 Panini Prime Shadowbox Signatures Platinum Blue /1 #17
2019 Panini Prime Timeline Signatures /25 #3
2019 Panini Prime Timeline Signatures Manufacturer /1 #3
2019 Panini Prime Timeline Signatures Name /10 #3
2019 Panini Prime Timeline Signatures Sponsor /7 #3
2019 Panini Prizm #30
2019 Panini Prizm #52
2019 Panini Prizm #61
2019 Panini Prizm #73
2019 Panini Prizm #81
2019 Panini Prizm Expert Level #1
2019 Panini Prizm Expert Level Prizms #1
2019 Panini Prizm Expert Level Prizms Black /1 #1
2019 Panini Prizm Expert Level Prizms Gold /10 #1
2019 Panini Prizm Expert Level Prizms White Sparkle #1
2019 Panini Prizm Fireworks #6
2019 Panini Prizm Fireworks Prizms #6
2019 Panini Prizm Fireworks Prizms Black /1 #6
2019 Panini Prizm Fireworks Prizms Gold /10 #6
2019 Panini Prizm Fireworks Prizms White Sparkle #6
2019 Panini Prizm In the Groove #1
2019 Panini Prizm In the Groove Prizms #1
2019 Panini Prizm In the Groove Prizms Black /1 #1
2019 Panini Prizm In the Groove Prizms Gold /10 #1
2019 Panini Prizm In the Groove Prizms White Sparkle #1
2019 Panini Prizm National Pride #9
2019 Panini Prizm National Pride Prizms #9
2019 Panini Prizm National Pride Prizms Black /1 #9
2019 Panini Prizm National Pride Prizms Gold /10 #9
2019 Panini Prizm National Pride Prizms White Sparkle #9
2019 Panini Prizm Patented Penmanship Prizms #5
2019 Panini Prizm Patented Penmanship Prizms Black /1 #5
2019 Panini Prizm Patented Penmanship Prizms Blue /25 #5
2019 Panini Prizm Patented Penmanship Prizms Camo #5
2019 Panini Prizm Patented Penmanship Prizms Gold /10 #5
2019 Panini Prizm Patented Penmanship Prizms Rainbow /24 #5
2019 Panini Prizm Patented Penmanship Prizms Red White and Blue #5
2019 Panini Prizm Patented Penmanship Prizms White /5 #5
2019 Panini Prizm Prizms #52
2019 Panini Prizm Prizms #61
2019 Panini Prizm Prizms #73
2019 Panini Prizm Prizms #81
2019 Panini Prizm Prizms #30
2019 Panini Prizm Prizms Black /1 #30
2019 Panini Prizm Prizms Black /1 #52
2019 Panini Prizm Prizms Black /1 #61
2019 Panini Prizm Prizms Black /1 #73
2019 Panini Prizm Prizms Black /1 #81
2019 Panini Prizm Prizms Blue /75 #30
2019 Panini Prizm Prizms Blue /75 #52
2019 Panini Prizm Prizms Blue /75 #61
2019 Panini Prizm Prizms Blue /75 #73
2019 Panini Prizm Prizms Blue /75 #81
2019 Panini Prizm Prizms Camo #30
2019 Panini Prizm Prizms Camo #52
2019 Panini Prizm Prizms Camo #61
2019 Panini Prizm Prizms Camo #73
2019 Panini Prizm Prizms Camo #81
2019 Panini Prizm Prizms Flash #30
2019 Panini Prizm Prizms Flash #52
2019 Panini Prizm Prizms Flash #61
2019 Panini Prizm Prizms Flash #73
2019 Panini Prizm Prizms Flash #81
2019 Panini Prizm Prizms Gold /10 #30
2019 Panini Prizm Prizms Gold /10 #52
2019 Panini Prizm Prizms Gold /10 #61
2019 Panini Prizm Prizms Gold /10 #73
2019 Panini Prizm Prizms Gold /10 #81
2019 Panini Prizm Prizms Green /99 #30
2019 Panini Prizm Prizms Green /99 #52
2019 Panini Prizm Prizms Green /99 #61
2019 Panini Prizm Prizms Green /99 #73
2019 Panini Prizm Prizms Green /99 #81
2019 Panini Prizm Prizms Rainbow /24 #30
2019 Panini Prizm Prizms Rainbow /24 #52
2019 Panini Prizm Prizms Rainbow /24 #61
2019 Panini Prizm Prizms Rainbow /24 #73
2019 Panini Prizm Prizms Rainbow /24 #81
2019 Panini Prizm Prizms Red /50 #30
2019 Panini Prizm Prizms Red /50 #52
2019 Panini Prizm Prizms Red /50 #61
2019 Panini Prizm Prizms Red /50 #73
2019 Panini Prizm Prizms Red /50 #81
2019 Panini Prizm Prizms Red White and Blue #30
2019 Panini Prizm Prizms Red White and Blue #52
2019 Panini Prizm Prizms Red White and Blue #61
2019 Panini Prizm Prizms Red White and Blue #73
2019 Panini Prizm Prizms Red White and Blue #81
2019 Panini Prizm Prizms White /5 #30
2019 Panini Prizm Prizms White /5 #52
2019 Panini Prizm Prizms White /5 #61
2019 Panini Prizm Prizms White /5 #73
2019 Panini Prizm Prizms White /5 #81
2019 Panini Prizm Prizms White Sparkle #30
2019 Panini Prizm Prizms White Sparkle #52
2019 Panini Prizm Prizms White Sparkle #61
2019 Panini Prizm Prizms White Sparkle #73
2019 Panini Prizm Prizms White Sparkle #81
2019 Panini Prizm Scripted Signatures Prizms #8
2019 Panini Prizm Scripted Signatures Prizms Black /1 #8
2019 Panini Prizm Scripted Signatures Prizms Blue /25 #8
2019 Panini Prizm Scripted Signatures Prizms Camo #8
2019 Panini Prizm Scripted Signatures Prizms Gold /10 #8
2019 Panini Prizm Scripted Signatures Prizms Rainbow /24 #8
2019 Panini Prizm Scripted Signatures Prizms Red White and Blue #8
2019 Panini Prizm Scripted Signatures Prizms White /5 #8
2019 Panini Prizm Signing Sessions Prizms #10
2019 Panini Prizm Signing Sessions Prizms Black /1 #10
2019 Panini Prizm Signing Sessions Prizms Blue /25 #10
2019 Panini Prizm Signing Sessions Prizms Camo #10
2019 Panini Prizm Signing Sessions Prizms Gold /10 #10
2019 Panini Prizm Signing Sessions Prizms Rainbow /24 #10
2019 Panini Prizm Signing Sessions Prizms Red White and Blue #10
2019 Panini Prizm Signing Sessions Prizms White /5 #10
2019 Panini Prizm Stars and Stripes #13
2019 Panini Prizm Stars and Stripes Prizms #13
2019 Panini Prizm Stars and Stripes Prizms Black /1 #13
2019 Panini Prizm Stars and Stripes Prizms Gold /10 #13
2019 Panini Prizm Stars and Stripes Prizms White Sparkle #13
2019 Panini Prizm Teammates #1
2019 Panini Prizm Teammates Prizms #1
2019 Panini Prizm Teammates Prizms Black /1 #1
2019 Panini Prizm Teammates Prizms Gold /10 #1
2019 Panini Prizm Teammates Prizms White Sparkle #1
2019 Panini Victory Lane #30
2019 Panini Victory Lane #63
2019 Panini Victory Lane #78
2019 Panini Victory Lane #84
2019 Panini Victory Lane #97
2019 Panini Victory Lane Black /1 #30
2019 Panini Victory Lane Black /1 #63
2019 Panini Victory Lane Black /1 #78
2019 Panini Victory Lane Black /1 #84
2019 Panini Victory Lane Black /1 #97
2019 Panini Victory Lane Dual Swatch Signatures #9
2019 Panini Victory Lane Dual Swatch Signatures Gold /49 #9
2019 Panini Victory Lane Dual Swatch Signatures Laundry Tag /1 #9
2019 Panini Victory Lane Dual Swatch Signatures Platinum /1 #9
2019 Panini Victory Lane Dual Swatch Signatures Red /25 #9
2019 Panini Victory Lane Dual Swatches #11
2019 Panini Victory Lane Dual Swatches Gold /99 #11
2019 Panini Victory Lane Dual Swatches Laundry Tag /1 #11
2019 Panini Victory Lane Dual Swatches Platinum /1 #11
2019 Panini Victory Lane Dual Swatches Red /25 #11
2019 Panini Victory Lane Gold /25 #30
2019 Panini Victory Lane Gold /25 #63
2019 Panini Victory Lane Gold /25 #78
2019 Panini Victory Lane Gold /25 #84
2019 Panini Victory Lane Gold /25 #97
2019 Panini Victory Lane Horsepower Heroes #1
2019 Panini Victory Lane Horsepower Heroes Black /1 #1
2019 Panini Victory Lane Horsepower Heroes Blue /99 #1
2019 Panini Victory Lane Horsepower Heroes Gold /25 #1
2019 Panini Victory Lane Horsepower Heroes Green /5 #1
2019 Panini Victory Lane Horsepower Heroes Printing Plates Black /1 #1
2019 Panini Victory Lane Horsepower Heroes Printing Plates Cyan /1 #1
2019 Panini Victory Lane Horsepower Heroes Printing Plates Magenta /1 #1
2019 Panini Victory Lane Horsepower Heroes Printing Plates Yellow /1 #1
2019 Panini Victory Lane Machines #1
2019 Panini Victory Lane Machines Black /1 #1
2019 Panini Victory Lane Machines Blue /99 #1
2019 Panini Victory Lane Machines Gold /25 #1
2019 Panini Victory Lane Machines Green /5 #1
2019 Panini Victory Lane Machines Printing Plates Black /1 #1
2019 Panini Victory Lane Machines Printing Plates Cyan /1 #1
2019 Panini Victory Lane Machines Printing Plates Magenta /1 #1
2019 Panini Victory Lane Machines Printing Plates Yellow /1 #1
2019 Panini Victory Lane Pedal to the Metal #33
2019 Panini Victory Lane Pedal to the Metal #78
2019 Panini Victory Lane Pedal to the Metal #81
2019 Panini Victory Lane Pedal to the Metal #84
2019 Panini Victory Lane Pedal to the Metal #85
2019 Panini Victory Lane Pedal to the Metal #86
2019 Panini Victory Lane Pedal to the Metal #87
2019 Panini Victory Lane Pedal to the Metal #88
2019 Panini Victory Lane Pedal to the Metal Black /1 #33
2019 Panini Victory Lane Pedal to the Metal Black /1 #78
2019 Panini Victory Lane Pedal to the Metal Black /1 #81
2019 Panini Victory Lane Pedal to the Metal Black /1 #84
2019 Panini Victory Lane Pedal to the Metal Black /1 #85
2019 Panini Victory Lane Pedal to the Metal Black /1 #86
2019 Panini Victory Lane Pedal to the Metal Black /1 #87
2019 Panini Victory Lane Pedal to the Metal Black /1 #88
2019 Panini Victory Lane Pedal to the Metal Gold /25 #33
2019 Panini Victory Lane Pedal to the Metal Gold /25 #78
2019 Panini Victory Lane Pedal to the Metal Gold /25 #81
2019 Panini Victory Lane Pedal to the Metal Gold /25 #84
2019 Panini Victory Lane Pedal to the Metal Gold /25 #85
2019 Panini Victory Lane Pedal to the Metal Gold /25 #86
2019 Panini Victory Lane Pedal to the Metal Gold /25 #87
2019 Panini Victory Lane Pedal to the Metal Gold /25 #88
2019 Panini Victory Lane Pedal to the Metal Green /5 #33
2019 Panini Victory Lane Pedal to the Metal Green /5 #78
2019 Panini Victory Lane Pedal to the Metal Green /5 #81
2019 Panini Victory Lane Pedal to the Metal Green /5 #84
2019 Panini Victory Lane Pedal to the Metal Green /5 #85
2019 Panini Victory Lane Pedal to the Metal Green /5 #86
2019 Panini Victory Lane Pedal to the Metal Green /5 #87
2019 Panini Victory Lane Pedal to the Metal Green /5 #88
2019 Panini Victory Lane Pedal to the Metal Red /3 #33
2019 Panini Victory Lane Pedal to the Metal Red /3 #78
2019 Panini Victory Lane Pedal to the Metal Red /3 #81
2019 Panini Victory Lane Pedal to the Metal Red /3 #84
2019 Panini Victory Lane Pedal to the Metal Red /3 #85
2019 Panini Victory Lane Pedal to the Metal Red /3 #86
2019 Panini Victory Lane Pedal to the Metal Red /3 #87
2019 Panini Victory Lane Pedal to the Metal Red /3 #88
2019 Panini Victory Lane Printing Plates Black /1 #30
2019 Panini Victory Lane Printing Plates Black /1 #63
2019 Panini Victory Lane Printing Plates Black /1 #78
2019 Panini Victory Lane Printing Plates Black /1 #84
2019 Panini Victory Lane Printing Plates Black /1 #97
2019 Panini Victory Lane Printing Plates Cyan /1 #30
2019 Panini Victory Lane Printing Plates Cyan /1 #63
2019 Panini Victory Lane Printing Plates Cyan /1 #78
2019 Panini Victory Lane Printing Plates Cyan /1 #84
2019 Panini Victory Lane Printing Plates Cyan /1 #97
2019 Panini Victory Lane Printing Plates Magenta /1 #30
2019 Panini Victory Lane Printing Plates Magenta /1 #63
2019 Panini Victory Lane Printing Plates Magenta /1 #78
2019 Panini Victory Lane Printing Plates Magenta /1 #84
2019 Panini Victory Lane Printing Plates Magenta /1 #97
2019 Panini Victory Lane Printing Plates Yellow /1 #30
2019 Panini Victory Lane Printing Plates Yellow /1 #63
2019 Panini Victory Lane Printing Plates Yellow /1 #78
2019 Panini Victory Lane Printing Plates Yellow /1 #84
2019 Panini Victory Lane Printing Plates Yellow /1 #97
2019 Panini Victory Lane Quad Swatches #2
2019 Panini Victory Lane Quad Swatches Gold /99 #2
2019 Panini Victory Lane Quad Swatches Laundry Tag /1 #2
2019 Panini Victory Lane Quad Swatches Platinum /1 #2
2019 Panini Victory Lane Quad Swatches Red /25 #2
2019 Panini Victory Lane Starting Grid #3
2019 Panini Victory Lane Starting Grid Black /1 #3
2019 Panini Victory Lane Starting Grid Blue /99 #3
2019 Panini Victory Lane Starting Grid Gold /25 #3
2019 Panini Victory Lane Starting Grid Green /5 #3
2019 Panini Victory Lane Starting Grid Printing Plates Black /1 #3
2019 Panini Victory Lane Starting Grid Printing Plates Cyan /1 #3
2019 Panini Victory Lane Starting Grid Printing Plates Magenta /1 #3
2019 Panini Victory Lane Starting Grid Printing Plates Yellow /1 #3

2019 Panini Victory Lane Track Stars #1
2019 Panini Victory Lane Track Stars Black /1 #1
2019 Panini Victory Lane Track Stars Blue /99 #1
2019 Panini Victory Lane Track Stars Gold /25 #1
2019 Panini Victory Lane Track Stars Green /5 #1
2019 Panini Victory Lane Track Stars Printing Plates Black /1 #1
2019 Panini Victory Lane Track Stars Printing Plates Cyan /1 #1
2019 Panini Victory Lane Track Stars Printing Plates Magenta /1 #1
2019 Panini Victory Lane Track Stars Printing Plates Yellow /1 #1
2019-20 Funko Pop Vinyl NASCAR #9
2020 Donruss #9
2020 Donruss #38
2020 Donruss #98
2020 Donruss #160
2020 Donruss #199
2020 Donruss Action Packed #6
2020 Donruss Action Packed Checkers #6
2020 Donruss Action Packed Cracked Ice /25 #6
2020 Donruss Action Packed Holographic /199 #6
2020 Donruss Action Packed Xplosion /10 #6
2020 Donruss Black Numbers /48 #9
2020 Donruss Black Numbers /48 #38
2020 Donruss Black Numbers /48 #98
2020 Donruss Black Numbers /48 #160
2020 Donruss Black Numbers /48 #199
2020 Donruss Black Trophy Club /1 #9
2020 Donruss Black Trophy Club /1 #38
2020 Donruss Black Trophy Club /1 #98
2020 Donruss Black Trophy Club /1 #160
2020 Donruss Black Trophy Club /1 #199
2020 Donruss Blue /199 #98
2020 Donruss Blue /199 #160
2020 Donruss Blue /199 #199
2020 Donruss Blue /199 #9
2020 Donruss Blue /199 #38
2020 Donruss Carolina Blue #9
2020 Donruss Carolina Blue #38
2020 Donruss Carolina Blue #98
2020 Donruss Carolina Blue #160
2020 Donruss Carolina Blue #199
2020 Donruss Classics #7
2020 Donruss Classics Checkers #7
2020 Donruss Classics Cracked Ice /25 #7
2020 Donruss Classics Holographic /199 #7
2020 Donruss Classics Xplosion /10 #7
2020 Donruss Dominators #1
2020 Donruss Dominators Checkers #1
2020 Donruss Dominators Cracked Ice /25 #1
2020 Donruss Dominators Holographic /199 #1
2020 Donruss Dominators Xplosion /10 #1
2020 Donruss Elite Series #4
2020 Donruss Elite Series Checkers #4
2020 Donruss Elite Series Cracked Ice /25 #4
2020 Donruss Elite Series Holographic /199 #4
2020 Donruss Elite Series Xplosion /10 #4
2020 Donruss Green /99 #9
2020 Donruss Green /99 #38
2020 Donruss Green /99 #98
2020 Donruss Green /99 #160
2020 Donruss Green /99 #199
2020 Donruss Optic #9
2020 Donruss Optic #18
2020 Donruss Optic #63
2020 Donruss Optic Carolina Blue Wave #18
2020 Donruss Optic Carolina Blue Wave #63
2020 Donruss Optic Carolina Blue Wave #9
2020 Donruss Optic Gold /10 #9
2020 Donruss Optic Gold /10 #18
2020 Donruss Optic Gold /10 #63
2020 Donruss Optic Gold Vinyl /1 #9
2020 Donruss Optic Gold Vinyl /1 #18
2020 Donruss Optic Gold Vinyl /1 #63
2020 Donruss Optic Holo #9
2020 Donruss Optic Holo #18
2020 Donruss Optic Holo #63
2020 Donruss Optic Illusion #2
2020 Donruss Optic Illusion Carolina Blue Wave #2
2020 Donruss Optic Illusion Gold /10 #2
2020 Donruss Optic Illusion Gold Vinyl /1 #2
2020 Donruss Optic Illusion Holo #2
2020 Donruss Optic Illusion Orange Pulsar #2
2020 Donruss Optic Illusion Red Mojo #2
2020 Donruss Optic Illusion Signatures Gold Vinyl /1 #2
2020 Donruss Optic Illusion Signatures Holo /25 #2
2020 Donruss Optic Orange Pulsar #9
2020 Donruss Optic Orange Pulsar #18
2020 Donruss Optic Orange Pulsar #63
2020 Donruss Optic Red Mojo #9
2020 Donruss Optic Red Mojo #18
2020 Donruss Optic Red Mojo #63
2020 Donruss Optic Signatures Gold Vinyl /1 #9
2020 Donruss Optic Signatures Gold Vinyl /1 #18
2020 Donruss Optic Signatures Gold Vinyl /1 #63
2020 Donruss Optic Signatures Holo /25 #9
2020 Donruss Optic Signatures Holo /25 #18
2020 Donruss Optic Signatures Holo /25 #63
2020 Donruss Orange #199
2020 Donruss Orange #9
2020 Donruss Orange #38
2020 Donruss Orange #98
2020 Donruss Orange #160
2020 Donruss Pink /25 #9
2020 Donruss Pink /25 #38
2020 Donruss Pink /25 #98
2020 Donruss Pink /25 #160
2020 Donruss Pink /25 #199
2020 Donruss Printing Plates Black /1 #9
2020 Donruss Printing Plates Black /1 #38
2020 Donruss Printing Plates Black /1 #98
2020 Donruss Printing Plates Black /1 #160
2020 Donruss Printing Plates Black /1 #199
2020 Donruss Printing Plates Cyan /1 #9
2020 Donruss Printing Plates Cyan /1 #38
2020 Donruss Printing Plates Cyan /1 #98
2020 Donruss Printing Plates Cyan /1 #160
2020 Donruss Printing Plates Cyan /1 #199
2020 Donruss Printing Plates Magenta /1 #38
2020 Donruss Printing Plates Magenta /1 #98
2020 Donruss Printing Plates Magenta /1 #160
2020 Donruss Printing Plates Magenta /1 #199
2020 Donruss Printing Plates Magenta /1 #9
2020 Donruss Printing Plates Yellow /1 #160
2020 Donruss Printing Plates Yellow /1 #199
2020 Donruss Printing Plates Yellow /1 #38
2020 Donruss Printing Plates Yellow /1 #98
2020 Donruss Purple /49 #9
2020 Donruss Purple /49 #38
2020 Donruss Purple /49 #98
2020 Donruss Purple /49 #160
2020 Donruss Purple /49 #199
2020 Donruss Race Day Relics #15
2020 Donruss Race Day Relics Holo Black /10 #15
2020 Donruss Race Day Relics Holo Gold /25 #15
2020 Donruss Race Day Relics Red /250 #15
2020 Donruss Red /299 #9
2020 Donruss Red /299 #38
2020 Donruss Red /299 #98
2020 Donruss Red /299 #160
2020 Donruss Red /299 #199
2020 Donruss Retro Relics '87 #13
2020 Donruss Retro Relics '87 Holo Black /10 #13
2020 Donruss Retro Relics '87 Holo Gold /25 #13
2020 Donruss Retro Relics '87 Red /250 #13
2020 Donruss Retro Series #3
2020 Donruss Retro Series Checkers #3
2020 Donruss Retro Series Cracked Ice /25 #3
2020 Donruss Retro Series Holographic /199 #3
2020 Donruss Retro Series Xplosion /10 #3
2020 Donruss Silver #9
2020 Donruss Silver #38
2020 Donruss Silver #98
2020 Donruss Silver #160
2020 Donruss Silver #199
2020 Donruss Timeless Treasures Material Signatures #2
2020 Donruss Timeless Treasures Material Signatures Holo Black /1 #2
2020 Donruss Timeless Treasures Material Signatures Holo Gold /7 #2
2020 Donruss Timeless Treasures Material Signatures Red /10 #2
2020 Donruss Top Tier #1
2020 Donruss Top Tier Checkers #1
2020 Donruss Top Tier Cracked Ice /25 #1
2020 Donruss Top Tier Holographic /199 #1
2020 Donruss Top Tier Xplosion /10 #1

Kasey Kahne

2003 Press Pass Optima #31
2003 Press Pass Optima Gold #G31
2003 Press Pass Optima Previews /5 #31
2003 Press Pass Optima Samples #31
2003 Press Pass Signings #36
2003 Press Pass Signings Gold /50 #36
2004 Press Pass #42
2004 Press Pass Autographs #30
2004 Press Pass Autographs #31
2004 Press Pass Eclipse #40
2004 Press Pass Eclipse Samples #40
2004 Press Pass Making the Show Collector's Series #MS6
2004 Press Pass Optima #11
2004 Press Pass Optima #49
2004 Press Pass Optima #78
2004 Press Pass Optima #87
2004 Press Pass Optima Cool Persistence #CP12
2004 Press Pass Optima Fan Favorite #FF11
2004 Press Pass Optima Gold #G11
2004 Press Pass Optima Gold #G49
2004 Press Pass Optima Gold #G78
2004 Press Pass Optima Gold #G87
2004 Press Pass Optima Previews /5 #EB11
2004 Press Pass Optima Samples #11
2004 Press Pass Optima Samples #49
2004 Press Pass Optima Samples #78
2004 Press Pass Optima Samples #87
2004 Press Pass Optima Thunder Bolts Autographs /9 #TBKK
2004 Press Pass Optima Thunder Bolts Cars /120 #TBT2
2004 Press Pass Optima Thunder Bolts Drivers /70 #TBD2
2004 Press Pass Platinum #P42
2004 Press Pass Premium #32
2004 Press Pass Premium Previews /5 #32
2004 Press Pass Premium Samples #32
2004 Press Pass Previews /5 #42
2004 Press Pass Rookie Class #RC1
2004 Press Pass Samples #42
2004 Press Pass Signings #33
2004 Press Pass Signings #34
2004 Press Pass Signings Gold /50 #30
2004 Press Pass Signings Gold /50 #31
2004 Press Pass Stealth #78
2004 Press Pass Stealth Samples #X78
2004 Press Pass Stealth X-Ray /100 #78
2004 Press Pass Top Prospects Memorabilia /100 #KKG
2004 Press Pass Top Prospects Memorabilia /150 #KKS
2004 Press Pass Top Prospects Memorabilia /200 #KKSM
2004 Press Pass Top Prospects Memorabilia /350 #KKT
2004 Press Pass Trackside #2
2004 Press Pass Trackside #54
2004 Press Pass Trackside #75
2004 Press Pass Trackside #93
2004 Press Pass Trackside Golden /100 #G2
2004 Press Pass Trackside Golden /100 #G54
2004 Press Pass Trackside Golden /100 #G75
2004 Press Pass Trackside Golden /100 #G93
2004 Press Pass Trackside Hat Giveaway #PPH14
2004 Press Pass Trackside Hot Pass #HP22
2004 Press Pass Trackside Hot Pass National #HP22
2004 Press Pass Trackside Previews /5 #EB2
2004 Press Pass Trackside Samples #2
2004 Press Pass Trackside Samples #54
2004 Press Pass Trackside Samples #75
2004 Press Pass Trackside Samples #93
2004 Super Shots CHP Sonoma #3
2004 VIP #20
2004 VIP #41
2004 VIP Head Gear #HG5
2004 VIP Head Gear Transparent #HG5
2004 VIP Lap Leaders #LL3
2004 VIP Lap Leaders Transparent #LL3
2004 VIP Making the Show #MS6
2004 VIP Previews /5 #EB20
2004 VIP Previews /5 #EB41
2004 VIP Samples #20
2004 VIP Samples #41
2004 Wheels American Thunder #11
2004 Wheels American Thunder #43
2004 Wheels American Thunder #64
2004 Wheels American Thunder #85
2004 Wheels American Thunder #90
2004 Wheels American Thunder American Muscle #AM7
2004 Wheels American Thunder Post Mark #PM27
2004 Wheels American Thunder Previews /5 #EB11
2004 Wheels American Thunder Previews /5 #EB43
2004 Wheels American Thunder Samples #11
2004 Wheels American Thunder Samples #43
2004 Wheels American Thunder Samples #64
2004 Wheels American Thunder Samples #85
2004 Wheels American Thunder Samples #90
2004 Wheels American Thunder Triple Hat /160 #TH7
2004 Wheels Autographs #34
2004 Wheels High Gear #40
2004 Wheels High Gear MPH /100 #M40
2004 Wheels High Gear Previews /5 #40
2004 Wheels High Gear Samples #40
2005 Press Pass #7
2005 Press Pass #46
2005 Press Pass #85
2005 Press Pass Autographs #29
2005 Press Pass Autographs #28
2005 Press Pass Cup Chase #CCR14
2005 Press Pass Cup Chase Prizes #CCP14
2005 Press Pass Eclipse #13
2005 Press Pass Eclipse #51
2005 Press Pass Eclipse #78
2005 Press Pass Eclipse Maxim #MX11
2005 Press Pass Eclipse Previews /5 #EB13
2005 Press Pass Eclipse Previews /5 #EB51
2005 Press Pass Eclipse Previews /1 #EB78
2005 Press Pass Eclipse Samples #13
2005 Press Pass Eclipse Samples #51
2005 Press Pass Eclipse Samples #78
2005 Press Pass Eclipse Skidmarks #SM12
2005 Press Pass Eclipse Skidmarks Holofoil /250 #SM12
2005 Press Pass Eclipse Teammates Autographs /25 #4
2005 Press Pass Hot Treads /900 #HTR6
2005 Press Pass Hot Treads Holofoil /100 #HTR6
2005 Press Pass Legends #32
2005 Press Pass Legends Autographs Black /50 #19
2005 Press Pass Legends Blue /1890 #32B
2005 Press Pass Legends Double Threads Bronze /375 #DTKV
2005 Press Pass Legends Double Threads Gold /99 #DTKV
2005 Press Pass Legends Double Threads Silver /225 #DTKV
2005 Press Pass Legends Gold /750 #32G
2005 Press Pass Legends Holofoil /100 #32H
2005 Press Pass Legends Press Plates Black /1 #32
2005 Press Pass Legends Press Plates Cyan /1 #32
2005 Press Pass Legends Press Plates Magenta /1 #32
2005 Press Pass Legends Press Plates Yellow /1 #32
2005 Press Pass Legends Previews /5 #32
2005 Press Pass Legends Solo /1 #32S
2005 Press Pass Legends Threads and Treads Bronze /375 #TTKK
2005 Press Pass Legends Threads and Treads Gold /99 #TTKK
2005 Press Pass Legends Threads and Treads Silver /225 #TTKK
2005 Press Pass Optima #14
2005 Press Pass Optima #35
2005 Press Pass Optima #51
2005 Press Pass Optima Corporate Cuts Cars /160 #CCT3
2005 Press Pass Optima Corporate Cuts Drivers /120 #CCD3
2005 Press Pass Optima Fan Favorite #FF13
2005 Press Pass Optima Gold /100 #G14
2005 Press Pass Optima Gold /100 #G35
2005 Press Pass Optima Gold /100 #G51
2005 Press Pass Optima Previews /5 #14
2005 Press Pass Optima Previews /5 #35
2005 Press Pass Optima Previews /1 #51
2005 Press Pass Optima Q & A #QA8
2005 Press Pass Optima Samples #14
2005 Press Pass Optima Samples #35
2005 Press Pass Optima Samples #51
2005 Press Pass Optima Thunder Bolts Autographs /9 #TBKK
2005 Press Pass Panorama #PPP60
2005 Press Pass Platinum /100 #P7
2005 Press Pass Platinum /100 #P46
2005 Press Pass Platinum /100 #P85
2005 Press Pass Premium #12
2005 Press Pass Premium #65
2005 Press Pass Premium Hot Threads Autographs /9 #HTKK
2005 Press Pass Premium Samples #12
2005 Press Pass Previews Green /5 #EB7
2005 Press Pass Samples #7
2005 Press Pass Samples #46
2005 Press Pass Samples #85
2005 Press Pass Signings #27
2005 Press Pass Signings #28
2005 Press Pass Signings Gold /50 #26
2005 Press Pass Signings Gold /50 #27
2005 Press Pass Signings Platinum /100 #27
2005 Press Pass Signings Platinum /100 #26
2005 Press Pass Snapshots #SN13
2005 Press Pass Stealth #2
2005 Press Pass Stealth #5
2005 Press Pass Stealth #8
2005 Press Pass Stealth #67
2005 Press Pass Stealth Previews /5 #2
2005 Press Pass Stealth Previews /5 #5
2005 Press Pass Stealth Previews /5 #8
2005 Press Pass Stealth Previews /5 #67
2005 Press Pass Stealth Samples #2
2005 Press Pass Stealth Samples #5
2005 Press Pass Stealth Samples #8
2005 Press Pass Stealth Samples #67
2005 Press Pass Stealth X-Ray /100 #X2
2005 Press Pass Stealth X-Ray /100 #X5
2005 Press Pass Stealth X-Ray /100 #X8
2005 Press Pass Stealth X-Ray /100 #X67
2005 Press Pass Trackside #14
2005 Press Pass Trackside #14B
2005 Press Pass Trackside #56
2005 Press Pass Trackside #74
2005 Press Pass Trackside Golden /100 #G14
2005 Press Pass Trackside Golden /100 #G56
2005 Press Pass Trackside Golden /100 #G74
2005 Press Pass Trackside Hat Giveaway #PPH13
2005 Press Pass Trackside Hot Pass #20
2005 Press Pass Trackside Hot Pass National #20
2005 Press Pass Trackside Previews /5 #14
2005 Press Pass Trackside Samples #14
2005 Press Pass Trackside Samples #56
2005 Press Pass Trackside Samples #74
2005 VIP #12
2005 VIP #53
2005 VIP #55
2005 VIP Head Gear #5
2005 VIP Head Gear Transparent #5
2005 VIP Lap Leaders #3
2005 VIP Lap Leaders Transparent #3
2005 VIP Making The Show #6
2005 VIP Previews /5 #EB12
2005 VIP Samples #12
2005 VIP Samples #53
2005 VIP Samples #55
2005 VIP Tradin' Paint Autographs /9 #KK
2005 VIP Tradin' Paint Cars /110 #TPT11
2005 VIP Tradin' Paint Drivers /90 #TPD11
2005 Wheels American Thunder #13
2005 Wheels American Thunder #54
2005 Wheels American Thunder #78
2005 Wheels American Thunder Medallion #MD26
2005 Wheels American Thunder Previews /5 #13
2005 Wheels American Thunder Previews /5 #78
2005 Wheels American Thunder Samples #13
2005 Wheels American Thunder Samples #54
2005 Wheels American Thunder Samples #78
2005 Wheels American Thunder Thunder Road #TR6
2005 Wheels American Thunder Triple Hat /190 #TH10
2005 Wheels Autographs #27
2005 Wheels Autographs #28
2005 Wheels High Gear #5
2005 Wheels High Gear #36
2005 Wheels High Gear #40
2005 Wheels High Gear #49
2005 Wheels High Gear #74
2005 Wheels High Gear Flag Chasers Black /55 #FC1
2005 Wheels High Gear Flag Chasers Blue-Yellow /25 #FC1
2005 Wheels High Gear Flag Chasers Checkered /10 #FC1
2005 Wheels High Gear Flag Chasers Green /55 #FC1
2005 Wheels High Gear Flag Chasers Red /55 #FC1
2005 Wheels High Gear Flag Chasers White /55 #FC1
2005 Wheels High Gear Flag Chasers Yellow /55 #FC1
2005 Wheels High Gear Flag to Flag #FF10
2005 Wheels High Gear Machine #MMB6
2005 Wheels High Gear Man #MMA6
2005 Wheels High Gear MPH /100 #M5
2005 Wheels High Gear MPH /100 #M36
2005 Wheels High Gear MPH /100 #M40
2005 Wheels High Gear MPH /100 #M49
2005 Wheels High Gear MPH /100 #M74
2005 Wheels High Gear Previews Green /5 #EB5
2005 Wheels High Gear Previews Green /5 #EB36
2005 Wheels High Gear Previews Silver /1 #EB74
2005 Wheels High Gear Samples #5
2005 Wheels High Gear Samples #36
2005 Wheels High Gear Samples #40
2005 Wheels High Gear Samples #49
2005 Wheels High Gear Samples #74
2006 Press Pass #10
2006 Press Pass #40
2006 Press Pass #89
2006 Press Pass #98
2006 Press Pass Autographs #25
2006 Press Pass Autographs #26
2006 Press Pass Blaster Kmart #KKC
2006 Press Pass Blaster Target #KKB
2006 Press Pass Blaster Wal-Mart #KKA
2006 Press Pass Blue #B10
2006 Press Pass Blue #B40
2006 Press Pass Blue #B89
2006 Press Pass Blue #B98
2006 Press Pass Burning Rubber Autographs /9 #BRKK
2006 Press Pass Burning Rubber Cars /370 #BRT9
2006 Press Pass Burning Rubber Drivers /100 #BRD9
2006 Press Pass Burning Rubber Drivers Gold /1 #BRD9
2006 Press Pass Burnouts /1050 #HT12
2006 Press Pass Burnouts Holofoil /125 #HT12
2006 Press Pass Collectors Series Making the Show #MS13
2006 Press Pass Cup Chase Prizes #CC8
2006 Press Pass Eclipse #22
2006 Press Pass Eclipse #36
2006 Press Pass Eclipse #44
2006 Press Pass Eclipse #60
2006 Press Pass Eclipse #60B
2006 Press Pass Eclipse Hyperdrive #HP6
2006 Press Pass Eclipse Previews /5 #EB22
2006 Press Pass Eclipse Previews /5 #EB36
2006 Press Pass Eclipse Previews /1 #EB60
2006 Press Pass Eclipse Racing Champions #RC6
2006 Press Pass Eclipse Racing Champions #RC21
2006 Press Pass Eclipse Skidmarks #SM12
2006 Press Pass Eclipse Skidmarks Holofoil /250 #SM12
2006 Press Pass Eclipse Teammates Autographs /25 #6
2006 Press Pass Eclipse Under Cover Cars /140 #UCT5
2006 Press Pass Eclipse Under Cover Drivers Gold /1 #UCD5
2006 Press Pass Eclipse Under Cover Drivers Holofoil /100 #UCD5
2006 Press Pass Eclipse Under Cover Drivers Red /225 #UCD5
2006 Press Pass Eclipse Under Cover Drivers Silver /400 #UCD5
2006 Press Pass Gold #G10
2006 Press Pass Gold #G40
2006 Press Pass Gold #G89
2006 Press Pass Gold #G98
2006 Press Pass Legends #43
2006 Press Pass Legends Autographs Black /50 #26
2006 Press Pass Legends Blue /1999 #B43
2006 Press Pass Legends Bronze /999 #Z43
2006 Press Pass Legends Gold /299 #G43
2006 Press Pass Legends Holofoil /99 #H43
2006 Press Pass Legends Press Plates Black /1 #PPB43
2006 Press Pass Legends Press Plates Black Backs /1 #PPB43B
2006 Press Pass Legends Press Plates Cyan /1 #PPC43
2006 Press Pass Legends Press Plates Cyan Backs /1 #PPC43B
2006 Press Pass Legends Press Plates Magenta /1 #PPM43
2006 Press Pass Legends Press Plates Magenta Backs /1 #PPM43B
2006 Press Pass Legends Press Plates Yellow /1 #PPY43
2006 Press Pass Legends Press Plates Yellow Backs /1 #PPY43B
2006 Press Pass Legends Previews /5 #EB43
2006 Press Pass Legends Solo /1 #S43
2006 Press Pass Optima #9
2006 Press Pass Optima #71
2006 Press Pass Optima #81
2006 Press Pass Optima #9B
2006 Press Pass Optima Fan Favorite #FF11
2006 Press Pass Optima Gold /100 #G9
2006 Press Pass Optima Gold /100 #G71
2006 Press Pass Optima Gold /100 #G81
2006 Press Pass Optima Pole Position #PP4
2006 Press Pass Optima Previews /5 #EB9
2006 Press Pass Optima Q & A #QA3
2006 Press Pass Optima Rookie Relics Cars /50 #RRT8
2006 Press Pass Optima Rookie Relics Drivers /50 #RRD8
2006 Press Pass Platinum /100 #P10
2006 Press Pass Platinum /100 #P40
2006 Press Pass Platinum /100 #P89
2006 Press Pass Platinum /100 #P98
2006 Press Pass Premium #13
2006 Press Pass Premium #62
2006 Press Pass Premium #82
2006 Press Pass Premium Hot Threads Autographs /9 #HTKK
2006 Press Pass Premium Hot Threads Cars /165 #HTT8
2006 Press Pass Premium Hot Threads Drivers /220 #HTD8
2006 Press Pass Premium Hot Threads Drivers Gold /1 #HTD8
2006 Press Pass Previews /5 #EB10
2006 Press Pass Previews /5 #EB40
2006 Press Pass Previews /1 #EB98
2006 Press Pass Signings #27
2006 Press Pass Signings Gold /50 #27
2006 Press Pass Signings Gold Red Ink #27
2006 Press Pass Signings Red Ink #27
2006 Press Pass Signings Silver /100 #27
2006 Press Pass Signings Silver Red Ink #27
2006 Press Pass Snapshots #SN5
2006 Press Pass Stealth #14
2006 Press Pass Stealth #64
2006 Press Pass Stealth #70
2006 Press Pass Stealth #51
2006 Press Pass Stealth Autographed Hat Entry #PPH12
2006 Press Pass Stealth Corporate Cuts /250 #CCD8
2006 Press Pass Stealth Gear Grippers Cars Retail /99 #GGT10
2006 Press Pass Stealth Gear Grippers Drivers /99 #GGD10
2006 Press Pass Stealth Hot Pass #HP15
2006 Press Pass Stealth Previews /5 #14
2006 Press Pass Stealth Profile #P4
2006 Press Pass Stealth Retail #14
2006 Press Pass Stealth Retail #51
2006 Press Pass Stealth Retail #64
2006 Press Pass Stealth Retail #70
2006 Press Pass Stealth X-Ray /100 #X14
2006 Press Pass Stealth X-Ray /100 #X51
2006 Press Pass Stealth X-Ray /100 #X64
2006 Press Pass Stealth X-Ray /100 #X70
2006 Press Pass Top 25 Drivers & Rides #C7
2006 Press Pass Top 25 Drivers & Rides #D7
2006 Sports Illustrated for Kids #69
2006 Stanley Tools Promo #2
2006 Stanley Tools Promo #5
2006 TRAKS #16
2006 TRAKS #41
2006 TRAKS Autographs #18
2006 TRAKS Autographs 25 /25 #16
2006 TRAKS Previews /1 #16
2006 TRAKS Previews /1 #41
2006 TRAKS Stickers #9
2006 VIP #12
2006 VIP #17
2006 VIP #43
2006 VIP #46
2006 VIP #51
2006 VIP #62
2006 VIP #66
2006 VIP #74
2006 VIP Head Gear #HG3
2006 VIP Head Gear Transparent #HG3
2006 VIP Lap Leader #LL4
2006 VIP Lap Leader Transparent #LL4
2006 VIP Making the Show #MS13
2006 VIP Tradin' Paint Autographs /9 #TPKK
2006 VIP Tradin' Paint Cars Bronze /145 #TPT11
2006 VIP Tradin' Paint Drivers Gold /50 #TPD11
2006 VIP Tradin' Paint Drivers Silver /80 #TPD11
2006 Wheels American Thunder #14
2006 Wheels American Thunder #52
2006 Wheels American Thunder #60
2006 Wheels American Thunder #79
2006 Wheels American Thunder #87
2006 Wheels American Thunder American Racing Idol #RI7
2006 Wheels American Thunder American Racing Idol Golden /250 #RI7
2006 Wheels American Thunder Cool Threads /329 #CT8
2006 Wheels American Thunder Double Hat /99 #DH12
2006 Wheels American Thunder Grandstand #GS11
2006 Wheels American Thunder Previews /5 #EB14
2006 Wheels American Thunder Previews /1 #EB79
2006 Wheels American Thunder Thunder Road #TR14
2006 Wheels Autographs #27
2006 Wheels Autographs #28
2006 Wheels High Gear #22
2006 Wheels High Gear #48
2006 Wheels High Gear #81
2006 Wheels High Gear #85
2006 Wheels High Gear Flag Chasers Black /110 #FC5
2006 Wheels High Gear Flag Chasers Blue-Yellow /65 #FC5
2006 Wheels High Gear Flag Chasers Checkered /3 #FC5
2006 Wheels High Gear Flag Chasers Green /110 #FC5
2006 Wheels High Gear Flag Chasers Red /110 #FC5
2006 Wheels High Gear Flag Chasers White /110 #FC5
2006 Wheels High Gear Flag Chasers Yellow /110 #FC5
2006 Wheels High Gear Flag to Flag #FF12
2006 Wheels High Gear MPH /100 #M22
2006 Wheels High Gear MPH /100 #M48
2006 Wheels High Gear MPH /100 #M81
2006 Wheels High Gear MPH /100 #M85
2006 Wheels High Gear Previews Green /5 #EB22
2006 Wheels High Gear Previews Silver /1 #EB81
2007 Press Pass #10
2007 Press Pass #84
2007 Press Pass #89
2007 Press Pass #101
2007 Press Pass #117
2007 Press Pass Autographs #21
2007 Press Pass Autographs Press Plates Magenta /1 #8
2007 Press Pass Blue #B10
2007 Press Pass Blue #B84
2007 Press Pass Blue #B89
2007 Press Pass Blue #B101
2007 Press Pass Blue #B117
2007 Press Pass Burning Rubber Drivers /75 #BRD4
2007 Press Pass Burning Rubber Drivers /75 #BRD9
2007 Press Pass Burning Rubber Drivers Gold /1 #BRD4
2007 Press Pass Burning Rubber Drivers Gold /1 #BRD9
2007 Press Pass Burning Rubber Team /325 #BRT4
2007 Press Pass Burning Rubber Team /325 #BRT9
2007 Press Pass Burnouts #BO4
2007 Press Pass Burnouts Blue /99 #BO4
2007 Press Pass Burnouts Gold /299 #BO4
2007 Press Pass Collector's Series Box Set #SB12
2007 Press Pass Cup Chase #CCR3
2007 Press Pass Double Burner Firesuit-Glove /100 #DB7
2007 Press Pass Double Burner Firesuit-Glove Exchange /100 #DB7
2007 Press Pass Double Burner Metal-Tire /100 #DBKK
2007 Press Pass Double Burner Metal-Tire Exchange /100 #DBKK
2007 Press Pass Eclipse #0
2007 Press Pass Eclipse #8
2007 Press Pass Eclipse #37
2007 Press Pass Eclipse #40
2007 Press Pass Eclipse #68
2007 Press Pass Eclipse #64
2007 Press Pass Eclipse Ecliptic #EC3
2007 Press Pass Eclipse Gold /25 #G8
2007 Press Pass Eclipse Gold /25 #G37
2007 Press Pass Eclipse Gold /25 #G40
2007 Press Pass Eclipse Gold /25 #G64
2007 Press Pass Eclipse Gold /25 #G68
2007 Press Pass Eclipse Hyperdrive #HD6
2007 Press Pass Eclipse Previews /5 #EB8
2007 Press Pass Eclipse Previews /5 #EB37
2007 Press Pass Eclipse Racing Champions #RC1
2007 Press Pass Eclipse Racing Champions #RC20
2007 Press Pass Eclipse Red /1 #R8
2007 Press Pass Eclipse Red /1 #R37
2007 Press Pass Eclipse Red /1 #R40
2007 Press Pass Eclipse Red /1 #R64
2007 Press Pass Eclipse Red /1 #R68
2007 Press Pass Eclipse Skidmarks #SM8
2007 Press Pass Eclipse Skidmarks Holofoil /250 #SM8
2007 Press Pass Eclipse Teammates Autographs /25 #2
2007 Press Pass Eclipse Under Cover Autographs /9 #UCKK
2007 Press Pass Eclipse Under Cover Drivers /450 #UCD12
2007 Press Pass Eclipse Under Cover Drivers Eclipse /1 #UCD12
2007 Press Pass Eclipse Under Cover Drivers Name /99 #UCD12
2007 Press Pass Eclipse Under Cover Drivers NASCAR /270 #UCD12
2007 Press Pass Eclipse Under Cover Teams /135 #UCT12
2007 Press Pass Eclipse Under Cover Teams NASCAR /25 #UCT12
2007 Press Pass Four Wide /50 #FWKK
2007 Press Pass Four Wide Checkered Flag /1 #FWKK
2007 Press Pass Four Wide Checkered Flag Exchange /1 #FWKK
2007 Press Pass Four Wide Exchange /50 #FWKK
2007 Press Pass Gold #G10
2007 Press Pass Gold #G84
2007 Press Pass Gold #G89
2007 Press Pass Gold #G101
2007 Press Pass Gold #G117
2007 Press Pass Hot Treads #HT1
2007 Press Pass Hot Treads Blue /99 #HT1
2007 Press Pass Hot Treads Gold /299 #HT1
2007 Press Pass K-Mart #KKC
2007 Press Pass Legends #49
2007 Press Pass Legends Autographs Blue /75 #16
2007 Press Pass Legends Blue /999 #B49
2007 Press Pass Legends Bronze /599 #Z49
2007 Press Pass Legends Gold /249 #G49
2007 Press Pass Legends Holofoil /99 #H49
2007 Press Pass Legends Press Plates Black /1 #PP49
2007 Press Pass Legends Press Plates Black Backs /1 #PP49
2007 Press Pass Legends Press Plates Cyan /1 #PP49
2007 Press Pass Legends Press Plates Cyan Backs /1 #PP49
2007 Press Pass Legends Press Plates Magenta /1 #PP49
2007 Press Pass Legends Press Plates Magenta Backs /1 #PP49
2007 Press Pass Legends Press Plates Yellow /1 #PP49
2007 Press Pass Legends Press Plates Yellow Backs /1 #PP49
2007 Press Pass Legends Previews /5 #EB49
2007 Press Pass Legends Solo /1 #S49
2007 Press Pass Legends Sunday Swatches Bronze /99 #KKSS
2007 Press Pass Legends Sunday Swatches Gold /50 #KKSS
2007 Press Pass Legends Sunday Swatches Silver /99 #KKSS
2007 Press Pass Platinum /100 #P10
2007 Press Pass Platinum /100 #P84
2007 Press Pass Platinum /100 #P89
2007 Press Pass Platinum /100 #P101
2007 Press Pass Platinum /100 #P117
2007 Press Pass Premium #8
2007 Press Pass Premium #34
2007 Press Pass Premium #58
2007 Press Pass Premium #79
2007 Press Pass Premium Hot Threads Drivers /145 #HTD1
2007 Press Pass Premium Hot Threads Drivers Gold /1 #HTD1
2007 Press Pass Premium Hot Threads Patch /10 #HTP8
2007 Press Pass Premium Hot Threads Patch /15 #HTP9
2007 Press Pass Premium Hot Threads Team /160 #HTT1
2007 Press Pass Premium Performance Driven #PD2
2007 Press Pass Premium Performance Driven Red /250 #PD2
2007 Press Pass Premium Red /15 #R8
2007 Press Pass Premium Red /15 #R34
2007 Press Pass Premium Red /15 #R58
2007 Press Pass Premium Red /5 #R79
2007 Press Pass Previews /5 #EB10
2007 Press Pass Previews /1 #EB117
2007 Press Pass Race Day #RD10
2007 Press Pass Signings #33
2007 Press Pass Signings Blue /25 #14
2007 Press Pass Signings Gold /20 #26
2007 Press Pass Signings Press Plates Black /1 #23
2007 Press Pass Signings Press Plates Cyan /1 #22
2007 Press Pass Signings Press Plates Magenta /1 #24
2007 Press Pass Signings Press Plates Yellow /1 #22
2007 Press Pass Signings Silver /100 #25
2007 Press Pass Snapshots #SN14
2007 Press Pass Stealth #13
2007 Press Pass Stealth #48
2007 Press Pass Stealth #84
2007 Press Pass Stealth Battle Armor Drivers /8 #BAD15
2007 Press Pass Stealth Battle Armor Teams /8 #BAT15
2007 Press Pass Stealth Chrome #13
2007 Press Pass Stealth Chrome #48
2007 Press Pass Stealth Chrome #84A
2007 Press Pass Stealth Chrome #84B
2007 Press Pass Stealth Chrome Exclusives /99 #X13
2007 Press Pass Stealth Chrome Exclusives /99 #X48
2007 Press Pass Stealth Chrome Exclusives /99 #X84
2007 Press Pass Stealth Chrome Platinum /25 #P13
2007 Press Pass Stealth Chrome Platinum /25 #P48
2007 Press Pass Stealth Chrome Platinum /25 #P84
2007 Press Pass Stealth Mach 07 #M7-5
2007 Press Pass Stealth Maximum Access #MA14
2007 Press Pass Stealth Maximum Access Autographs /25 #MA14
2007 Press Pass Stealth Previews /1 #EB84
2007 Press Pass Stealth Previews /5 #EB13
2007 Press Pass Target #KKB
2007 Press Pass Target Race Win Tires #RW5
2007 Press Pass Velocity #V1
2007 Press Pass Wal-Mart #KKA
2007 Press Pass Wal-Mart Autographs /45 #KK
2007 Sunoco OCC Postcards #KK
2007 Traks #13
2007 Traks #59
2007 Traks #66
2007 Traks #84
2007 Traks #97
2007 Traks Corporate Cuts Driver /99 #CCD2
2007 Traks Corporate Cuts Patch /12 #CCD2
2007 Traks Corporate Cuts Team /180 #CCT2
2007 Traks Driver's Seat #DS9B
2007 Traks Driver's Seat #DS9
2007 Traks Driver's Seat National #DS9
2007 Traks Gold #G13
2007 Traks Gold #G59
2007 Traks Gold #G66
2007 Traks Gold #G84
2007 Traks Gold #G97
2007 Traks Holofoil /50 #H13
2007 Traks Holofoil /50 #H59
2007 Traks Holofoil /50 #H66
2007 Traks Holofoil /50 #H84
2007 Traks Holofoil /50 #H97
2007 Traks Hot Pursuit #HP8
2007 Traks Previews /5 #EB13
2007 Traks Red /10 #R13
2007 Traks Red /10 #R59
2007 Traks Red /10 #R66
2007 Traks Red /10 #R84
2007 Traks Red /10 #R97
2007 Traks Target Exclusives #KKA
2007 Traks Wal-Mart Exclusives #KKB
2007 Valvoline Racing #NNO
2007 VIP #15
2007 VIP Get A Grip Autographs /9 #GGKK
2007 VIP Get A Grip Drivers /70 #GGD8
2007 VIP Get A Grip Teams /70 #GGT8
2007 VIP Pedal To The Metal /50 #PM5
2007 VIP Previews /5 #EB15
2007 VIP Sunday Best #SB12
2007 Wheels American Thunder #15
2007 Wheels American Thunder Autographed Hat Instant Winner /1 #AH16
2007 Wheels American Thunder Head to Toe /99 #HT4
2007 Wheels American Thunder Previews /5 #EB15
2007 Wheels American Thunder Thunder Road #TR15
2007 Wheels American Thunder Triple Hat /99 #TH14
2007 Wheels Autographs #18
2007 Wheels Autographs Press Plates Black /1 #17
2007 Wheels Autographs Press Plates Cyan /1 #17
2007 Wheels Autographs Press Plates Magenta /1 #17
2007 Wheels High Gear #8
2007 Wheels High Gear #55
2007 Wheels High Gear #57
2007 Wheels High Gear #61
2007 Wheels High Gear #67
2007 Wheels High Gear #75
2007 Wheels High Gear #79
2007 Wheels High Gear Driven #DR21
2007 Wheels High Gear Final Standings Gold /8 #FS8
2007 Wheels High Gear Flag Chasers Black /89 #FC9
2007 Wheels High Gear Flag Chasers Blue-Yellow /50 #FC9
2007 Wheels High Gear Flag Chasers Checkered /10 #FC9
2007 Wheels High Gear Flag Chasers Green /89 #FC9
2007 Wheels High Gear Flag Chasers Red /89 #FC9
2007 Wheels High Gear Flag Chasers White /89 #FC9
2007 Wheels High Gear Flag Chasers Yellow /89 #FC9
2007 Wheels High Gear Full Throttle #FT5
2007 Wheels High Gear Last Lap /10 #LL1
2007 Wheels High Gear MPH /100 #M8
2007 Wheels High Gear MPH /100 #M55
2007 Wheels High Gear MPH /100 #M57
2007 Wheels High Gear MPH /100 #M61
2007 Wheels High Gear MPH /100 #M67
2007 Wheels High Gear MPH /100 #M75
2007 Wheels High Gear MPH /100 #M79
2007 Wheels High Gear Previews /5 #EB8
2007 Wheels High Gear Previews /5 #EB55
2007 Wheels High Gear Previews /5 #EB57
2007 Wheels High Gear Previews /5 #EB61
2007 Wheels High Gear Top Tier #TT8
2008 Press Pass #22
2008 Press Pass Autographs #21

2008 Press Pass Autographs Press Plates Black /1 #17
2008 Press Pass Autographs Press Plates Cyan /1 #17
2008 Press Pass Autographs Press Plates Magenta /1 #17
2008 Press Pass Autographs Press Plates Yellow /1 #17
2008 Press Pass Blue #B22
2008 Press Pass Collector's Series Box Set #14
2008 Press Pass Cup Chase #CC13
2008 Press Pass Double Burner Metal-Tire /100 #DBKK
2008 Press Pass Eclipse #16
2008 Press Pass Eclipse #32
2008 Press Pass Eclipse #42
2008 Press Pass Eclipse #87
2008 Press Pass Eclipse Gold /25 #G16
2008 Press Pass Eclipse Gold /25 #G32
2008 Press Pass Eclipse Gold /25 #G42
2008 Press Pass Eclipse Gold /25 #G87
2008 Press Pass Eclipse Hyperdrive #HP6
2008 Press Pass Eclipse Previews /5 #EB16
2008 Press Pass Eclipse Previews /5 #EB32
2008 Press Pass Eclipse Red /1 #R16
2008 Press Pass Eclipse Red /1 #R32
2008 Press Pass Eclipse Red /1 #R42
2008 Press Pass Eclipse Red /1 #R87
2008 Press Pass Eclipse Star Tracks #ST8
2008 Press Pass Eclipse Star Tracks Holofoil /250 #ST8
2008 Press Pass Eclipse Stellar #ST20
2008 Press Pass Eclipse Teammates Autographs /35 #KS
2008 Press Pass Eclipse Under Cover Autographs /9 #UCKK
2008 Press Pass Four Wide /50 #FWKK
2008 Press Pass Four Wide Checkered Flag /1 #FWKK
2008 Press Pass Gillette Young Guns #5
2008 Press Pass Gold #G22
2008 Press Pass Legends #52
2008 Press Pass Legends Autographs Black /10 #KK
2008 Press Pass Legends Autographs Blue /75 #KK
2008 Press Pass Legends Autographs Press Plates Black /1 #KK
2008 Press Pass Legends Autographs Press Plates Cyan /1 #KK
2008 Press Pass Legends Autographs Press Plates Magenta /1 #KK
2008 Press Pass Legends Autographs Press Plates Yellow /1 #KK
2008 Press Pass Legends Blue /599 #52
2008 Press Pass Legends Bronze /299 #52
2008 Press Pass Legends Gold /99 #52
2008 Press Pass Legends Holo /25 #52
2008 Press Pass Legends Previews /5 #EB52
2008 Press Pass Legends Printing Plates Black /1 #52
2008 Press Pass Legends Printing Plates Cyan /1 #52
2008 Press Pass Legends Printing Plates Magenta /1 #52
2008 Press Pass Legends Printing Plates Yellow /1 #52
2008 Press Pass Legends Prominent Pieces Firesuit-Glove-Belt /25 #PP2KK
2008 Press Pass Legends Prominent Pieces Firesuit-Glove-Belt Gold /10 #PP2KK
2008 Press Pass Legends Prominent Pieces Metal-Tire Bronze /99 #PP3KK
2008 Press Pass Legends Prominent Pieces Metal-Tire Gold /25 #PP3KK
2008 Press Pass Legends Prominent Pieces Metal-Tire Silver /50 #PP3KK
2008 Press Pass Legends Solo /1 #52
2008 Press Pass Legends Victory Lane Bronze /99 #VLKK
2008 Press Pass Legends Victory Lane Gold /25 #VLKK
2008 Press Pass Legends Victory Lane Silver /50 #VLKK
2008 Press Pass Platinum /100 #P22
2008 Press Pass Premium #9
2008 Press Pass Premium #60
2008 Press Pass Premium Clean Air #CA8
2008 Press Pass Premium Previews /5 #EB9
2008 Press Pass Premium Previews /1 #EB60
2008 Press Pass Premium Red /15 #9
2008 Press Pass Premium Red /15 #60
2008 Press Pass Premium Wal-Mart #WM3
2008 Press Pass Previews /5 #EB22
2008 Press Pass Signings #32
2008 Press Pass Signings Blue /25 #14
2008 Press Pass Signings Gold /50 #28
2008 Press Pass Signings Press Plates Black /1 #22
2008 Press Pass Signings Press Plates Cyan /1 #22
2008 Press Pass Signings Press Plates Magenta /1 #22
2008 Press Pass Signings Press Plates Yellow /1 #22
2008 Press Pass Signings Silver /100 #27
2008 Press Pass Speedway #16
2008 Press Pass Speedway Gold #G16
2008 Press Pass Speedway Holofoil /50 #H16
2008 Press Pass Speedway Previews /5 #EB16
2008 Press Pass Speedway Red /10 #R16
2008 Press Pass Speedway Test Drive #TD12
2008 Press Pass Starting Grid #SG14
2008 Press Pass Stealth #17
2008 Press Pass Stealth #66
2008 Press Pass Stealth Battle Armor Autographs /9 #BASKK
2008 Press Pass Stealth Battle Armor Drivers /120 #BAD6
2008 Press Pass Stealth Battle Armor Teams /115 #BAT6
2008 Press Pass Stealth Chrome #17A
2008 Press Pass Stealth Chrome #17B
2008 Press Pass Stealth Chrome #66
2008 Press Pass Stealth Chrome Exclusives /25 #17
2008 Press Pass Stealth Chrome Exclusives /25 #66
2008 Press Pass Stealth Chrome Exclusives Gold /99 #17
2008 Press Pass Stealth Chrome Exclusives Gold /99 #66
2008 Press Pass Stealth Previews /5 #17
2008 Press Pass Stealth Target #TA9
2008 Press Pass Target #KKB
2008 Press Pass Wal-Mart #KKA
2008 VIP #17
2008 VIP #61
2008 VIP #63
2008 VIP #76
2008 VIP All Access #AA11
2008 VIP Gear Gallery #GG12
2008 VIP Gear Gallery Memorabilia /50 #GGKK
2008 VIP Gear Gallery Transparent #GG12
2008 VIP Get a Grip Autographs /9 #GGSKK
2008 VIP Get a Grip Drivers /80 #GGD4
2008 VIP Get a Grip Teams /99 #GGT4
2008 VIP Previews /5 #EB17
2008 Wheels American Thunder #16
2008 Wheels American Thunder #65
2008 Wheels American Thunder #77
2008 Wheels American Thunder #40
2008 Wheels American Thunder American Dreams #AD3
2008 Wheels American Thunder American Dreams Gold /250 #AD3
2008 Wheels American Thunder Autographed Hat Winner /1 #WHKK
2008 Wheels American Thunder Campaign Buttons #KK
2008 Wheels American Thunder Campaign Buttons Blue #KK
2008 Wheels American Thunder Campaign Buttons Gold #KK
2008 Wheels American Thunder Campaign Trail #CT16
2008 Wheels American Thunder Cool Threads /325 #CT2
2008 Wheels American Thunder Head to Toe /125 #HT15
2008 Wheels American Thunder Previews /5 #16
2008 Wheels American Thunder Previews /1 #77
2008 Wheels American Thunder Pushin' Pedal /99 #PP 15
2008 Wheels American Thunder Triple Hat /99 #TH13
2008 Wheels Autographs #17
2008 Wheels Autographs Press Plates Black /1 #17
2008 Wheels Autographs Press Plates Cyan /1 #17
2008 Wheels Autographs Press Plates Magenta /1 #17
2008 Wheels Autographs Press Plates Yellow /1 #17
2008 Wheels High Gear #17
2008 Wheels High Gear #74
2008 Wheels High Gear Driven #DR12
2008 Wheels High Gear Final Standings /19 #F17
2008 Wheels High Gear Flag Chasers Black /89 #FC8
2008 Wheels High Gear Flag Chasers Blue-Yellow /50 #FC8
2008 Wheels High Gear Flag Chasers Checkered /20 #FC8
2008 Wheels High Gear Flag Chasers Green /60 #FC8
2008 Wheels High Gear Flag Chasers Red /89 #FC8
2008 Wheels High Gear Flag Chasers White /65 #FC8
2008 Wheels High Gear Flag Chasers Yellow /89 #FC8
2008 Wheels High Gear MPH /100 #M17
2008 Wheels High Gear MPH /100 #M74
2008 Wheels High Gear Previews /5 #EB17
2009 Element #15
2009 Element #67
2009 Element Big Win /35 #BWKK
2009 Element Elements of the Race Black Flag /99 #ERBKK
2009 Element Elements of the Race Black-White Flag /50 #ERXKK
2009 Element Elements of the Race Blue-Yellow Flag /50 #ERBOKK
2009 Element Elements of the Race Checkered Flag /5 #ERCKK
2009 Element Elements of the Race Green Flag /50 #ERGKK
2009 Element Elements of the Race Red Flag /99 #ERRKK
2009 Element Elements of the Race White Flag /75 #ERWKK
2009 Element Elements of the Race Yellow Flag /99 #ERYKK
2009 Element Kinetic Energy #KE4
2009 Element Lab Report #LR15
2009 Element Previews /5 #15
2009 Element Radioactive /100 #15
2009 Element Radioactive /100 #67
2009 Element Taking the Checkers /45 #TCKK
2009 Press Pass #13
2009 Press Pass #73
2009 Press Pass #135
2009 Press Pass #184
2009 Press Pass #203
2009 Press Pass Autographs Printing Plates Black /1 #22
2009 Press Pass Autographs Printing Plates Cyan /1 #22
2009 Press Pass Autographs Printing Plates Magenta /1 #22
2009 Press Pass Autographs Printing Plates Yellow /1 #22
2009 Press Pass Autographs Silver #26
2009 Press Pass Autographs Track Edition /20 #KK
2009 Press Pass Blue #13
2009 Press Pass Blue #73
2009 Press Pass Blue #135
2009 Press Pass Blue #184
2009 Press Pass Blue #203
2009 Press Pass Burning Rubber Drivers /185 #BRD12
2009 Press Pass Burning Rubber Drivers /185 #BRD14
2009 Press Pass Burning Rubber Prime Cut /25 #BRD12
2009 Press Pass Burning Rubber Prime Cut /25 #BRD14
2009 Press Pass Burning Rubber Teams /250 #BRT12
2009 Press Pass Burning Rubber Teams /250 #BRT14
2009 Press Pass Chase for the Sprint Cup #CC5
2009 Press Pass Cup Chase #CCR14
2009 Press Pass Cup Chase Prizes #CC5
2009 Press Pass Daytona 500 Tires /25 #TTKK
2009 Press Pass Eclipse #7
2009 Press Pass Eclipse #39
2009 Press Pass Eclipse #47
2009 Press Pass Eclipse Black and White #7
2009 Press Pass Eclipse Black and White #39
2009 Press Pass Eclipse Black and White #47
2009 Press Pass Eclipse Black Hole Firesuits /50 #BH5
2009 Press Pass Eclipse Blue #7
2009 Press Pass Eclipse Blue #39
2009 Press Pass Eclipse Blue #47
2009 Press Pass Eclipse Ecliptic Path #EP16
2009 Press Pass Four Wide Checkered Flag /1 #FWKK
2009 Press Pass Four Wide Firesuit /50 #FWKK
2009 Press Pass Four Wide Sheet Metal /10 #FWKK
2009 Press Pass Four Wide Tire /25 #FWKK
2009 Press Pass Fusion #71
2009 Press Pass Fusion Bronze /150 #71
2009 Press Pass Fusion Gold /50 #71
2009 Press Pass Fusion Green /25 #71
2009 Press Pass Fusion Onyx /1 #71
2009 Press Pass Fusion Revered Relics Gold /50 #RRKK
2009 Press Pass Fusion Revered Relics Holofoil /25 #RRKK
2009 Press Pass Fusion Revered Relics Premium Swatch /10 #RRKK
2009 Press Pass Fusion Revered Relics Silver /65 #RRKK
2009 Press Pass Fusion Silver /99 #71
2009 Press Pass Game Face #GF7
2009 Press Pass Gold #13
2009 Press Pass Gold #73
2009 Press Pass Gold #135
2009 Press Pass Gold #184
2009 Press Pass Gold #203
2009 Press Pass Gold Holofoil /100 #13
2009 Press Pass Gold Holofoil /100 #73
2009 Press Pass Gold Holofoil /100 #135
2009 Press Pass Gold Holofoil /100 #184
2009 Press Pass Gold Holofoil /100 #203
2009 Press Pass Legends #49
2009 Press Pass Legends Autographs Gold #19
2009 Press Pass Legends Autographs Holofoil #18
2009 Press Pass Legends Gold /399 #49
2009 Press Pass Legends Holofoil /50 #49
2009 Press Pass Legends Previews /5 #49
2009 Press Pass Legends Printing Plates Black /1 #49
2009 Press Pass Legends Printing Plates Cyan /1 #49
2009 Press Pass Legends Printing Plates Magenta /1 #49
2009 Press Pass Legends Printing Plates Yellow /1 #49
2009 Press Pass Legends Prominent Pieces Bronze /99 #PPKK
2009 Press Pass Legends Prominent Pieces Gold /25 #PPKK
2009 Press Pass Legends Prominent Pieces Oversized /10 #PPOEKK
2009 Press Pass Legends Prominent Pieces Silver /50 #PPKK
2009 Press Pass Legends Red /199 #49
2009 Press Pass Legends Solo /1 #49
2009 Press Pass NASCAR Gallery #NG6
2009 Press Pass Pocket Portraits #P12
2009 Press Pass Pocket Portraits Checkered Flag #P12
2009 Press Pass Pocket Portraits Hometown #P12
2009 Press Pass Pocket Portraits Smoke #P12
2009 Press Pass Pocket Portraits Wal-Mart #PPW2
2009 Press Pass Premium #10
2009 Press Pass Premium #71
2009 Press Pass Premium Hot Threads /99 #HTKK1
2009 Press Pass Premium Hot Threads /299 #HTKK2
2009 Press Pass Premium Hot Threads Autographs /9 #KK
2009 Press Pass Premium Hot Threads Multi-Color /25 #HTKK
2009 Press Pass Premium Hot Threads Patches /10 #HTP-KK
2009 Press Pass Premium Hot Threads Patches /8 #HTP-KK
2009 Press Pass Premium Previews /5 #EB10
2009 Press Pass Premium Signatures #17
2009 Press Pass Premium Signatures Gold /25 #16
2009 Press Pass Premium Top Contenders #TC3
2009 Press Pass Premium Top Contenders Gold #TC3
2009 Press Pass Premium Win Streak #WS8
2009 Press Pass Premium Win Streak Victory Lane #WSVL-KK
2009 Press Pass Previews /5 #EB13
2009 Press Pass Previews /5 #EB135
2009 Press Pass Red #13
2009 Press Pass Red #73
2009 Press Pass Red #135
2009 Press Pass Red #184
2009 Press Pass Red #203
2009 Press Pass Santa Hats /50 #SH10
2009 Press Pass Showcase /499 #18
2009 Press Pass Showcase /499 #44
2009 Press Pass Showcase /499 #34
2009 Press Pass Showcase 2nd Gear /125 #18
2009 Press Pass Showcase 2nd Gear /125 #34
2009 Press Pass Showcase 2nd Gear /125 #44
2009 Press Pass Showcase 3rd Gear /50 #18
2009 Press Pass Showcase 3rd Gear /50 #34
2009 Press Pass Showcase 3rd Gear /50 #44
2009 Press Pass Showcase 4th Gear /15 #18
2009 Press Pass Showcase 4th Gear /15 #34
2009 Press Pass Showcase 4th Gear /15 #44
2009 Press Pass Showcase Classic Collections Ink /45 #8
2009 Press Pass Showcase Classic Collections Ink Gold /25 #8
2009 Press Pass Showcase Classic Collections Ink Green /5 #8
2009 Press Pass Showcase Classic Collections Ink Melting /1 #8
2009 Press Pass Showcase Elite Exhibit Ink /45 #7
2009 Press Pass Showcase Elite Exhibit Ink Gold /25 #7
2009 Press Pass Showcase Elite Exhibit Ink Green /5 #7
2009 Press Pass Showcase Elite Exhibit Ink Melting /1 #7
2009 Press Pass Showcase Elite Exhibit Triple Memorabilia /99 #EEKK
2009 Press Pass Showcase Elite Exhibit Triple Memorabilia Gold /45 #EEKK
2009 Press Pass Showcase Elite Exhibit Triple Memorabilia Green /25 #EEKK
2009 Press Pass Showcase Elite Exhibit Triple Memorabilia Melting /5 #EEKK
2009 Press Pass Showcase Printing Plates Black /1 #18
2009 Press Pass Showcase Printing Plates Black /1 #34
2009 Press Pass Showcase Printing Plates Black /1 #44
2009 Press Pass Showcase Printing Plates Cyan /1 #18
2009 Press Pass Showcase Printing Plates Cyan /1 #34
2009 Press Pass Showcase Printing Plates Cyan /1 #44
2009 Press Pass Showcase Printing Plates Magenta /1 #18
2009 Press Pass Showcase Printing Plates Magenta /1 #34
2009 Press Pass Showcase Printing Plates Magenta /1 #44
2009 Press Pass Showcase Printing Plates Yellow /1 #18
2009 Press Pass Showcase Printing Plates Yellow /1 #34
2009 Press Pass Showcase Printing Plates Yellow /1 #44
2009 Press Pass Showcase Prized Pieces Firesuit /25 #PPFKK
2009 Press Pass Showcase Prized Pieces Firesuit Patch /5 #PPFKK
2009 Press Pass Showcase Prized Pieces Ink Firesuit /5 #7
2009 Press Pass Showcase Prized Pieces Ink Firesuit Patch /1 #7
2009 Press Pass Showcase Prized Pieces Ink Sheet Metal /25 #7
2009 Press Pass Showcase Prized Pieces Ink Tire /45 #7
2009 Press Pass Showcase Prized Pieces Sheet Metal /45 #PPSKK
2009 Press Pass Showcase Prized Pieces Tire /99 #PPTKK
2009 Press Pass Signature Series Archive Edition /1 #THKK
2009 Press Pass Signings Blue /25 #20
2009 Press Pass Signings Gold #20
2009 Press Pass Signings Green /15 #20
2009 Press Pass Signings Orange /25 #20
2009 Press Pass Signings Printing Plates Cyan /1 #20
2009 Press Pass Signings Printing Plates Yellow /1 #20
2009 Press Pass Signings Purple /45 #20
2009 Press Pass Sponsor Swatches /200 #SSKK
2009 Press Pass Sponsor Swatches Select /10 #SSKK
2009 Press Pass Stealth #17
2009 Press Pass Stealth Battle Armor /210 #BAKK
2009 Press Pass Stealth Battle Armor Multi-Color /150 #BAKK
2009 Press Pass Stealth Chrome #17
2009 Press Pass Stealth Chrome Brushed Metal /25 #17
2009 Press Pass Stealth Chrome Gold /99 #17
2009 Press Pass Stealth Mach 09 #M3
2009 Press Pass Stealth Previews /5 #EB17
2009 Press Pass Target Victory Tires /50 #KKTT
2009 Press Pass Tread Marks Autographs /10 #SSKK
2009 Press Pass Unleashed #U7
2009 VIP #16
2009 VIP #80
2009 VIP Get A Grip /120 #GGKK
2009 VIP Get A Grip Autographs /9 #GGSKK
2009 VIP Get A Grip Holofoil /10 #GGKK
2009 VIP Get A Grip Logos /5 #GGLKK
2009 VIP Guest List #GG10
2009 VIP Hardware #H2
2009 VIP Leadfoot /10 #LFKK
2009 VIP Leadfoot Holofoil /10 #LFKK
2009 VIP Previews /5 #16
2009 VIP Previews /1 #80
2009 VIP Purple /25 #16
2009 VIP Purple /25 #80
2009 VIP Race Day Gear /10 #RDGKK
2009 Wheels Autographs /25 #33
2009 Wheels Autographs /25 #34
2009 Wheels Autographs #35
2009 Wheels Autographs Press Plates Black /1 #KK
2009 Wheels Autographs Press Plates Cyan /1 #KK
2009 Wheels Autographs Press Plates Magenta /1 #KK
2009 Wheels Autographs Press Plates Yellow /1 #KK
2009 Wheels Main Event #6
2009 Wheels Main Event #78
2009 Wheels Main Event #41
2009 Wheels Main Event Buyback Archive Edition /1 #TBKK
2009 Wheels Main Event Buyback Archive Edition /1 #TPKK
2009 Wheels Main Event Buyback Archive Edition /1 #HTKK
2009 Wheels Main Event Buyback Archive Edition /1 #GGKK
2009 Wheels Main Event Fast Pass Purple /25 #6
2009 Wheels Main Event Fast Pass Purple /25 #41
2009 Wheels Main Event Fast Pass Purple /25 #78
2009 Wheels Main Event Foil #6
2009 Wheels Main Event Hat Dance Patch /10 #HDKK
2009 Wheels Main Event Hat Dance Triple /99 #HDKK
2009 Wheels Main Event High Rollers #HR3
2009 Wheels Main Event Marks Clubs #29
2009 Wheels Main Event Marks Diamonds /10 #29
2009 Wheels Main Event Marks Hearts /5 #29
2009 Wheels Main Event Marks Printing Plates Black /1 #25
2009 Wheels Main Event Marks Printing Plates Cyan /1 #25
2009 Wheels Main Event Marks Printing Plates Magenta /1 #25
2009 Wheels Main Event Marks Printing Plates Yellow /1 #25
2009 Wheels Main Event Marks Spades /1 #29
2009 Wheels Main Event Playing Cards Blue #KH
2009 Wheels Main Event Playing Cards Red #KH
2009 Wheels Main Event Poker Chips #5
2009 Wheels Main Event Previews /5 #6
2009 Wheels Main Event Renegade Rounders Wanted #RR8
2009 Wheels Main Event Reward Copper /10 #RWKK
2009 Wheels Main Event Reward Holofoil /50 #RWKK
2009 Wheels Main Event Stop and Go Swatches Pit Banner /175 #SGBKK
2009 Wheels Main Event Stop and Go Swatches Pit Banner Blue All Season's Sports Cards /1 #SGBKK
2009 Wheels Main Event Stop and Go Swatches Pit Banner Blue Arena /1 #SGBKK
2009 Wheels Main Event Stop and Go Swatches Pit Banner Blue Card Stadium /1 #SGBKK
2009 Wheels Main Event Stop and Go Swatches Pit Banner Blue Chicagoland Sportscards /1 #SGBKK
2009 Wheels Main Event Stop and Go Swatches Pit Banner Blue Chris Comics /1 #SGBKK
2009 Wheels Main Event Stop and Go Swatches Pit Banner Blue Chuck's Field of Dreams /1 #SGBKK
2009 Wheels Main Event Stop and Go Swatches Pit Banner Blue Collector's Heaven /1 #SGBKK
2009 Wheels Main Event Stop and Go Swatches Pit Banner Blue D&S Racing /1 #SGBKK
2009 Wheels Main Event Stop and Go Swatches Pit Banner Blue Dave's Pitstop /1 #SGBKK
2009 Wheels Main Event Stop and Go Swatches Pit Banner Blue Diamond King Sports /1 #SGBKK
2009 Wheels Main Event Stop and Go Swatches Pit Banner Blue Georgetown Card Exchange /1 #SGBKK
2009 Wheels Main Event Stop and Go Swatches Pit Banner Blue Jaimie's Field of Dreams /1 #SGBKK
2009 Wheels Main Event Stop and Go Swatches Pit Banner Blue Juniata Cards /1 #SGBKK
2009 Wheels Main Event Stop and Go Swatches Pit Banner Blue Main Steet Sportscards /1 #SGBKK
2009 Wheels Main Event Stop and Go Swatches Pit Banner Blue Matt's Sports Cards /1 #SGBKK
2009 Wheels Main Event Stop and Go Swatches Pit Banner Blue P&T Sportscards /1 #SGBKK
2009 Wheels Main Event Stop and Go Swatches Pit Banner Blue Republic Jewelry /1 #SGBKK
2009 Wheels Main Event Stop and Go Swatches Pit Banner Blue Ron's Racing /1 #SGBKK
2009 Wheels Main Event Stop and Go Swatches Pit Banner Blue Shelby Collectibles /1 #SGBKK
2009 Wheels Main Event Stop and Go Swatches Pit Banner Blue Spectator Sportscards /1 #SGBKK
2009 Wheels Main Event Stop and Go Swatches Pit Banner Blue Squeeze Play /1 #SGBKK
2009 Wheels Main Event Stop and Go Swatches Pit Banner Blue TBJ Sports Cards /1 #SGBKK
2009 Wheels Main Event Stop and Go Swatches Pit Banner Blue TCI Sports Fan /1 #SGBKK
2009 Wheels Main Event Stop and Go Swatches Pit Banner Blue The Card Cellar /1 #SGBKK
2009 Wheels Main Event Stop and Go Swatches Pit Banner Blue TJ Warner Ballcards /1 #SGBKK
2009 Wheels Main Event Stop and Go Swatches Pit Banner Blue Trademark Sports /1 #SGBKK
2009 Wheels Main Event Stop and Go Swatches Pit Banner Blue Triple I Sportscards /1 #SGBKK
2009 Wheels Main Event Stop and Go Swatches Pit Banner Blue Triple Play /1 #SGBKK
2009 Wheels Main Event Stop and Go Swatches Pit Banner Blue West Allis /1 #SGBKK
2009 Wheels Main Event Stop and Go Swatches Pit Banner Green /10 #SGBKK
2009 Wheels Main Event Stop and Go Swatches Pit Banner Holofoil /75 #SGBKK
2009 Wheels Main Event Stop and Go Swatches Pit Banner Red /25 #SGBKK
2009 Wheels Main Event Wildcard Cuts /2 #WCCKK
2010 Element #17
2010 Element 10 in '10 #TT4
2010 Element Blue /35 #17
2010 Element Finish Line Checkered Flag /10 #FLKK
2010 Element Finish Line Green Flag /20 #FLKK
2010 Element Finish Line Tires /99 #FLKK
2010 Element Green #17
2010 Element Green-White-Checkers Blue /10 #GWCKK
2010 Element Green-White-Checkers Green /50 #GWCKK
2010 Element Previews /5 #EB17
2010 Element Purple /25 #17
2010 Element Recycled Materials Blue /25 #RMKK
2010 Element Recycled Materials Green /125 #RMKK
2010 Element Red Target #17
2010 Press Pass #6
2010 Press Pass #113
2010 Press Pass #128
2010 Press Pass #106
2010 Press Pass #88
2010 Press Pass #0
2010 Press Pass #92
2010 Press Pass Autographs #25
2010 Press Pass Autographs Chase Edition /25 #7
2010 Press Pass Autographs Printing Plates Black /1 #18
2010 Press Pass Autographs Printing Plates Cyan /1 #21
2010 Press Pass Autographs Printing Plates Cyan /1 #22
2010 Press Pass Autographs Printing Plates Magenta /1 #19
2010 Press Pass Autographs Track Edition /10 #7
2010 Press Pass Blue #6
2010 Press Pass Blue #88
2010 Press Pass Blue #92
2010 Press Pass Blue #106
2010 Press Pass Blue #113
2010 Press Pass Blue #128
2010 Press Pass Burning Rubber /250 #BR15
2010 Press Pass Burning Rubber /250 #BR21
2010 Press Pass Burning Rubber Gold /50 #BR15
2010 Press Pass Burning Rubber Gold /50 #BR21
2010 Press Pass Burning Rubber Prime Cuts /25 #BR15
2010 Press Pass Cup Chase #CCR16
2010 Press Pass Eclipse #16
2010 Press Pass Eclipse #30
2010 Press Pass Eclipse #87
2010 Press Pass Eclipse Blue #16
2010 Press Pass Eclipse Blue #30
2010 Press Pass Eclipse Blue #87
2010 Press Pass Eclipse Focus #F5
2010 Press Pass Eclipse Gold #16
2010 Press Pass Eclipse Gold #30
2010 Press Pass Eclipse Gold #87
2010 Press Pass Eclipse Previews /5 #16
2010 Press Pass Eclipse Previews /1 #30
2010 Press Pass Eclipse Purple /25 #16
2010 Press Pass Eclipse Purple /25 #30
2010 Press Pass Final Standings /120 #FS10
2010 Press Pass Five Star /35 #20
2010 Press Pass Five Star Classic Compilations Combos Firesuit Autographs /15 #CCMKKJG
2010 Press Pass Five Star Classic Compilations Combos Patches Autographs /1 #CCMKKJG
2010 Press Pass Five Star Classic Compilations Dual Memorabilia Autographs /10 #KK
2010 Press Pass Five Star Classic Compilations Firesuit Autographs /15 #KK
2010 Press Pass Five Star Classic Compilations Patch Autographs /1 #CCPKK1
2010 Press Pass Five Star Classic Compilations Patch Autographs /1 #CCPKK2
2010 Press Pass Five Star Classic Compilations Patch Autographs /1 #CCPKK3
2010 Press Pass Five Star Classic Compilations Patch Autographs /1 #CCPKK4
2010 Press Pass Five Star Classic Compilations Patch Autographs /1 #CCPKK5
2010 Press Pass Five Star Classic Compilations Patch Autographs /1 #CCPKK6
2010 Press Pass Five Star Classic Compilations Patch Autographs /1 #CCPKK7
2010 Press Pass Five Star Classic Compilations Patch Autographs /1 #CCPKK8
2010 Press Pass Five Star Classic Compilations Patch Autographs /1 #CCPKK9
2010 Press Pass Five Star Classic Compilations Patch Autographs /1 #CCPKK10
2010 Press Pass Five Star Classic Compilations Patch Autographs /1 #CCPKK11
2010 Press Pass Five Star Classic Compilations Patch Autographs /1 #CCPKK12
2010 Press Pass Five Star Classic Compilations Patch Autographs /1 #CCPKK13
2010 Press Pass Five Star Classic Compilations Patch Autographs /1 #CCPKK14
2010 Press Pass Five Star Classic Compilations Patch Autographs /1 #CCPKK15
2010 Press Pass Five Star Classic Compilations Patch Autographs /1 #CCPKK16
2010 Press Pass Five Star Classic Compilations Patch Autographs /1 #CCPKK17
2010 Press Pass Five Star Classic Compilations Sheet Metal Autographs /25 #KK
2010 Press Pass Five Star Classic Compilations Triple Memorabilia Autographs /5 #KK
2010 Press Pass Five Star Holofoil /10 #20
2010 Press Pass Five Star Melting /1 #20
2010 Press Pass Five Star Paramount Pieces Aluminum /25 #KK
2010 Press Pass Five Star Paramount Pieces Blue /20 #KK
2010 Press Pass Five Star Paramount Pieces Gold /15 #KK
2010 Press Pass Five Star Paramount Pieces Holofoil /10 #KK
2010 Press Pass Five Star Paramount Pieces Melting /1 #KK
2010 Press Pass Five Star Signature Souvenirs Aluminum /50 #SSKK
2010 Press Pass Five Star Signature Souvenirs Gold /25 #SSKK
2010 Press Pass Five Star Signature Souvenirs Holofoil /10 #SSKK
2010 Press Pass Five Star Signature Souvenirs Melting /1 #SSKK
2010 Press Pass Five Star Signatures Aluminum /35 #KK
2010 Press Pass Five Star Signatures Gold /20 #KK
2010 Press Pass Five Star Signatures Holofoil /5 #KK
2010 Press Pass Five Star Signatures Melting /1 #KK
2010 Press Pass Gold #6
2010 Press Pass Gold #88
2010 Press Pass Gold #92
2010 Press Pass Gold #106
2010 Press Pass Gold #113
2010 Press Pass Gold #128
2010 Press Pass Holofoil /100 #6
2010 Press Pass Holofoil /100 #88
2010 Press Pass Holofoil /100 #92
2010 Press Pass Holofoil /100 #106
2010 Press Pass Holofoil /100 #113
2010 Press Pass Holofoil /100 #128
2010 Press Pass Legends #49
2010 Press Pass Legends Autographs Blue /10 #33
2010 Press Pass Legends Autographs Holofoil /24 #33
2010 Press Pass Legends Autographs Printing Plates Black /1 #29
2010 Press Pass Legends Autographs Printing Plates Cyan /1 #29
2010 Press Pass Legends Autographs Printing Plates Magenta /1 #29
2010 Press Pass Legends Autographs Printing Plates Yellow /1 #29
2010 Press Pass Legends Blue /1 #49
2010 Press Pass Legends Gold /399 #49
2010 Press Pass Legends Holofoil /50 #49
2010 Press Pass Legends Legendary Links Gold /75 #LXBEKK
2010 Press Pass Legends Legendary Links Holofoil /25 #LXBEKK
2010 Press Pass Legends Motorsports Masters Autographs Printing Plates Black /1 #29
2010 Press Pass Legends Motorsports Masters Autographs Printing Plates Cyan /1 #29
2010 Press Pass Legends Motorsports Masters Autographs Printing Plates Magenta /1 #29
2010 Press Pass Legends Motorsports Masters Autographs Printing Plates Yellow /1 #29
2010 Press Pass Legends Printing Plates Black /1 #49
2010 Press Pass Legends Printing Plates Cyan /1 #49
2010 Press Pass Legends Printing Plates Magenta /1 #49
2010 Press Pass Legends Printing Plates Yellow /1 #49
2010 Press Pass Legends Prominent Pieces Copper /99 #PPKK
2010 Press Pass Legends Prominent Pieces Gold /50 #PPKK
2010 Press Pass Legends Prominent Pieces Holofoil /25 #PPKK
2010 Press Pass Legends Prominent Pieces Oversized Firesuit /25 #PPOEKK
2010 Press Pass Legends Red /199 #49
2010 Press Pass Premium #5
2010 Press Pass Premium #42
2010 Press Pass Premium #52
2010 Press Pass Premium #75
2010 Press Pass Premium Hot Threads /299 #HTKK
2010 Press Pass Premium Hot Threads Holofoil /99 #HTKK
2010 Press Pass Premium Hot Threads Two Color /125 #HTKK
2010 Press Pass Premium Pairings Firesuits /25 #PFKE
2010 Press Pass Premium Pairings Signatures /5 #PSKE
2010 Press Pass Premium Purple /25 #5
2010 Press Pass Premium Purple /25 #42
2010 Press Pass Premium Purple /25 #52
2010 Press Pass Premium Signature Series Firesuit /15 #SSFKK
2010 Press Pass Premium Signatures #PSKK
2010 Press Pass Premium Signatures Red Ink /25 #PSKK
2010 Press Pass Previews /5 #6
2010 Press Pass Previews /1 #113
2010 Press Pass Purple /25 #6
2010 Press Pass Purple /25 #88
2010 Press Pass Purple /25 #92
2010 Press Pass Purple /25 #106
2010 Press Pass Purple /25 #113
2010 Press Pass Purple /25 #128
2010 Press Pass Showcase /499 #5
2010 Press Pass Showcase /499 #44
2010 Press Pass Showcase Classic Collections Ink /15 #CCIOWN
2010 Press Pass Showcase Classic Collections Ink Gold /10 #CCIOWN
2010 Press Pass Showcase Classic Collections Ink Green /5 #CCIOWN
2010 Press Pass Showcase Classic Collections Ink Melting /1 #CCIOWN
2010 Press Pass Showcase Classic Collections Sheet Metal /75 #CCIRPM
2010 Press Pass Showcase Classic Collections Sheet Metal Gold /25 #CCIRPM
2010 Press Pass Showcase Elite Exhibit Ink /45 #EEIKK
2010 Press Pass Showcase Elite Exhibit Ink Gold /25 #EEIKK
2010 Press Pass Showcase Elite Exhibit Ink Green /5 #EEIKK
2010 Press Pass Showcase Elite Exhibit Ink Melting /1 #EEIKK
2010 Press Pass Showcase Elite Exhibit Triple Memorabilia /99 #EEMKK
2010 Press Pass Showcase Elite Exhibit Triple Memorabilia Gold /45 #EEMKK
2010 Press Pass Showcase Elite Exhibit Triple Memorabilia Green /25 #EEMKK
2010 Press Pass Showcase Elite Exhibit Triple Memorabilia Melting /5 #EEMKK
2010 Press Pass Showcase Gold /125 #5
2010 Press Pass Showcase Gold /125 #44
2010 Press Pass Showcase Green /50 #5
2010 Press Pass Showcase Green /50 #44
2010 Press Pass Showcase Melting /15 #5
2010 Press Pass Showcase Melting /15 #44
2010 Press Pass Showcase Platinum Holo /1 #5
2010 Press Pass Showcase Platinum Holo /1 #44
2010 Press Pass Showcase Prized Pieces Firesuit Green /25 #PPMKK
2010 Press Pass Showcase Prized Pieces Firesuit Ink Gold /25 #PPIKK
2010 Press Pass Showcase Prized Pieces Firesuit Ink Melting /1 #PPIKK
2010 Press Pass Showcase Prized Pieces Firesuit Patch Melting /5 #PPMKK
2010 Press Pass Showcase Prized Pieces Memorabilia Ink Green /15 #PPIKK
2010 Press Pass Showcase Prized Pieces Sheet Metal /99 #PPMKK
2010 Press Pass Showcase Prized Pieces Sheet Metal Gold /45 #PPMKK
2010 Press Pass Showcase Prized Pieces Sheet Metal Ink Silver /45 #PPIKK
2010 Press Pass Signings Blue /10 #28
2010 Press Pass Signings Gold /15 #28
2010 Press Pass Signings Red /15 #28
2010 Press Pass Signings Silver /25 #28
2010 Press Pass Stealth #16
2010 Press Pass Stealth #58
2010 Press Pass Stealth #69
2010 Press Pass Stealth Battle Armor Fast Pass /25 #BAKK
2010 Press Pass Stealth Battle Armor Holofoil /25 #BAKK
2010 Press Pass Stealth Battle Armor Silver /275 #BAKK
2010 Press Pass Stealth Black and White #16
2010 Press Pass Stealth Black and White #58
2010 Press Pass Stealth Black and White #69
2010 Press Pass Stealth Mach 10 #MT8
2010 Press Pass Stealth Previews /5 #16
2010 Press Pass Stealth Previews /5 #58
2010 Press Pass Stealth Purple /25 #16
2010 Press Pass Stealth Purple /25 #58
2010 Press Pass Stealth Signature Series Sheet Metal /15 #SSMEKK
2010 Press Pass Top 12 Tires /9 #KK
2010 Press Pass Top 12 Tires 10 /10 #KK
2010 Press Pass Unleashed #U8
2010 Wheels Autographs #24
2010 Wheels Autographs Printing Plates Black /1 #24
2010 Wheels Autographs Printing Plates Cyan /1 #24
2010 Wheels Autographs Printing Plates Magenta /1 #24
2010 Wheels Autographs Printing Plates Yellow /1 #24
2010 Wheels Autographs Special Ink /10 #9
2010 Wheels Autographs Target /10 #16
2010 Wheels Main Event #16
2010 Wheels Main Event #52
2010 Wheels Main Event Blue #16
2010 Wheels Main Event Blue #52
2010 Wheels Main Event Fight Card #FC14
2010 Wheels Main Event Fight Card Checkered Flag #FC14
2010 Wheels Main Event Fight Card Full Color Retail #FC14
2010 Wheels Main Event Fight Card Gold /25 #FC14
2010 Wheels Main Event Head to Head /150 #HHKKCE
2010 Wheels Main Event Head to Head /150 #HHKKJG
2010 Wheels Main Event Head to Head Blue /75 #HHKKCE
2010 Wheels Main Event Head to Head Blue /75 #HHKKJG
2010 Wheels Main Event Head to Head Holofoil /10 #HHKKCE
2010 Wheels Main Event Head to Head Holofoil /10 #HHKKJG
2010 Wheels Main Event Head to Head Red /25 #HHKKCE
2010 Wheels Main Event Head to Head Red /25 #HHKKJG
2010 Wheels Main Event Marks Autographs /35 #28
2010 Wheels Main Event Marks Autographs Black /1 #27
2010 Wheels Main Event Marks Autographs Blue /10 #28
2010 Wheels Main Event Marks Autographs Red /5 #28
2010 Wheels Main Event Purple /25 #16
2010 Wheels Main Event Purple /25 #52
2010 Wheels Main Event Toe to Toe /10 #TTKKCE
2010 Wheels Main Event Upper Cuts /199 #UCKK2
2010 Wheels Main Event Upper Cuts /199 #UCKK
2010 Wheels Main Event Upper Cuts Blue /75 #UCKK
2010 Wheels Main Event Upper Cuts Blue /75 #UCKK2
2010 Wheels Main Event Upper Cuts Holofoil /10 #UCKK
2010 Wheels Main Event Upper Cuts Holofoil /10 #UCKK2
2010 Wheels Main Event Upper Cuts Knock Out Patches /25 #UCKOKK
2010 Wheels Main Event Upper Cuts Red /25 #UCKK
2010 Wheels Main Event Upper Cuts Red /25 #UCKK2
2011 Element #16
2011 Element #85
2011 Element Autographs /25 #27
2011 Element Autographs Blue /5 #27
2011 Element Autographs Gold /5 #26
2011 Element Autographs Printing Plates Black /1 #27
2011 Element Autographs Printing Plates Cyan /1 #27
2011 Element Autographs Printing Plates Magenta /1 #27
2011 Element Autographs Printing Plates Yellow /1 #27
2011 Element Autographs Silver /15 #26
2011 Element Black /35 #16
2011 Element Black /35 #85
2011 Element Flagship Performers 2010 Green Flag Passes Blue-Yellow /50 #FPPKK
2011 Element Green #16
2011 Element Green #85
2011 Element Previews /5 #EB16
2011 Element Purple /25 #16
2011 Element Purple /25 #85
2011 Element Red #16
2011 Element Red #85
2011 Element Trackside Treasures Holofoil /25 #TTKK
2011 Element Trackside Treasures Silver /85 #TTKK
2011 Press Pass #17
2011 Press Pass #72
2011 Press Pass #130
2011 Press Pass #132
2011 Press Pass #127
2011 Press Pass #126
2011 Press Pass Autographs Blue /5 #27
2011 Press Pass Autographs Bronze /20 #26
2011 Press Pass Autographs Gold /5 #26
2011 Press Pass Autographs Printing Plates Black /1 #27
2011 Press Pass Autographs Printing Plates Cyan /1 #27
2011 Press Pass Autographs Printing Plates Magenta /1 #27
2011 Press Pass Autographs Printing Plates Yellow /1 #27
2011 Press Pass Autographs Silver /10 #27
2011 Press Pass Blue Holofoil /10 #17
2011 Press Pass Blue Holofoil /10 #72
2011 Press Pass Blue Holofoil /10 #126
2011 Press Pass Blue Holofoil /10 #127
2011 Press Pass Blue Holofoil /10 #130
2011 Press Pass Blue Holofoil /10 #132
2011 Press Pass Blue Retail #17
2011 Press Pass Blue Retail #72
2011 Press Pass Blue Retail #126
2011 Press Pass Blue Retail #127
2011 Press Pass Blue Retail #130
2011 Press Pass Blue Retail #132
2011 Press Pass Cup Chase #CCR17
2011 Press Pass Eclipse #15
2011 Press Pass Eclipse #85
2011 Press Pass Eclipse Blue #15
2011 Press Pass Eclipse Blue #85
2011 Press Pass Eclipse Encore #E6
2011 Press Pass Eclipse Gold /55 #15
2011 Press Pass Eclipse Gold /55 #85
2011 Press Pass Eclipse Previews /5 #EB15
2011 Press Pass Eclipse Purple /25 #15
2011 Press Pass Eclipse Spellbound Swatches /150 #SBKK2
2011 Press Pass Eclipse Spellbound Swatches /250 #SBKK1
2011 Press Pass Eclipse Spellbound Swatches /100 #SBKK3
2011 Press Pass Eclipse Spellbound Swatches /75 #SBKK4
2011 Press Pass Eclipse Spellbound Swatches /50 #SBKK5
2011 Press Pass Eclipse Spellbound Swatches Signatures /10 #NNO
2011 Press Pass FanFare #19
2011 Press Pass FanFare Autographs Blue /5 #36
2011 Press Pass FanFare Autographs Bronze /35 #36
2011 Press Pass FanFare Autographs Gold /15 #36
2011 Press Pass FanFare Autographs Printing Plates Black /1 #36
2011 Press Pass FanFare Autographs Printing Plates Cyan /1 #36
2011 Press Pass FanFare Autographs Printing Plates Magenta /1 #36
2011 Press Pass FanFare Autographs Printing Plates Yellow /1 #36
2011 Press Pass FanFare Autographs Silver /10 #36
2011 Press Pass FanFare Blue Die Cuts #19
2011 Press Pass FanFare Emerald /25 #19
2011 Press Pass FanFare Holofoil Die Cuts #19
2011 Press Pass FanFare Magnificent Materials /199 #MMKK
2011 Press Pass FanFare Magnificent Materials Dual Swatches /50 #MMDKK
2011 Press Pass FanFare Magnificent Materials Dual Swatches Holofoil /10 #MMDKK
2011 Press Pass FanFare Magnificent Materials Holofoil /50 #MMKK
2011 Press Pass FanFare Magnificent Materials Signatures /25 #MMSEKK
2011 Press Pass FanFare Magnificent Materials Signatures Holofoil /10 #MMSEKK
2011 Press Pass FanFare Rookie Standouts #RS6
2011 Press Pass FanFare Ruby Die Cuts /15 #19
2011 Press Pass FanFare Sapphire /10 #19
2011 Press Pass FanFare Silver /25 #19
2011 Press Pass Geared Up Holofoil /50 #GUKK
2011 Press Pass Gold /50 #17

2011 Press Pass Gold /50 #72
2011 Press Pass Gold /50 #126
2011 Press Pass Gold /50 #127
2011 Press Pass Gold /50 #130
2011 Press Pass Gold /50 #132
2011 Press Pass Legends #46
2011 Press Pass Legends Autographs Blue /10 #LGAKK
2011 Press Pass Legends Autographs Gold /25 #LGAKK
2011 Press Pass Legends Autographs Printing Plates Black /1 #LGAKK
2011 Press Pass Legends Autographs Printing Plates Cyan /1 #LGAKK
2011 Press Pass Legends Autographs Printing Plates Magenta /1 #LGAKK
2011 Press Pass Legends Autographs Printing Plates Yellow /1 #LGAKK
2011 Press Pass Legends Autographs Silver /99 #LGAKK
2011 Press Pass Legends Gold /250 #46
2011 Press Pass Legends Holofoil /25 #46
2011 Press Pass Legends Printing Plates Black /1 #46
2011 Press Pass Legends Printing Plates Cyan /1 #46
2011 Press Pass Legends Printing Plates Magenta /1 #46
2011 Press Pass Legends Printing Plates Yellow /1 #46
2011 Press Pass Legends Prominent Pieces Gold /50 #PPKK
2011 Press Pass Legends Prominent Pieces Holofoil /25 #PPKK
2011 Press Pass Legends Prominent Pieces Oversized Firesuit /25 #PPOEKK
2011 Press Pass Legends Prominent Pieces Purple /15 #PPKK
2011 Press Pass Legends Prominent Pieces Silver /99 #PPKK
2011 Press Pass Legends Purple /25 #46
2011 Press Pass Legends Red /99 #46
2011 Press Pass Legends Solo /1 #46
2011 Press Pass Premium #43
2011 Press Pass Premium #65
2011 Press Pass Premium #18A
2011 Press Pass Premium #18B
2011 Press Pass Premium Double Burner /25 #DBKK
2011 Press Pass Premium Hot Threads /150 #HTKK
2011 Press Pass Premium Hot Threads Fast Pass /25 #HTKK
2011 Press Pass Premium Hot Threads Multi Color /25 #HTKK
2011 Press Pass Premium Hot Threads Patches /14 #HTPKK
2011 Press Pass Premium Hot Threads Secondary Color /99 #HTKK
2011 Press Pass Premium Pairings Firesuits /25 #PPBVKK
2011 Press Pass Premium Pairings Signatures /5 #PPABVKK
2011 Press Pass Premium Purple /25 #18
2011 Press Pass Premium Purple /25 #43
2011 Press Pass Premium Purple /25 #65
2011 Press Pass Premium Signatures /37 #PSKK
2011 Press Pass Premium Signatures Red Ink /24 #PSKK
2011 Press Pass Previews /5 #EB17
2011 Press Pass Purple /25 #17
2011 Press Pass Showcase /499 #15
2011 Press Pass Showcase /499 #41
2011 Press Pass Showcase /499 #58
2011 Press Pass Showcase Classic Collections Firesuit /45 #CCMRBR
2011 Press Pass Showcase Classic Collections Firesuit Patches /5 #CCMRBR
2011 Press Pass Showcase Classic Collections Ink /25 #CCMRBR
2011 Press Pass Showcase Classic Collections Ink Gold /5 #CCMRBR
2011 Press Pass Showcase Classic Collections Ink Melting /1 #CCMRBR
2011 Press Pass Showcase Classic Collections Sheet Metal /99 #CCMRBR
2011 Press Pass Showcase Elite Exhibit Ink /50 #EEIKK
2011 Press Pass Showcase Elite Exhibit Ink Gold /25 #EEIKK
2011 Press Pass Showcase Elite Exhibit Ink Melting /1 #EEIKK
2011 Press Pass Showcase Gold /125 #15
2011 Press Pass Showcase Gold /125 #41
2011 Press Pass Showcase Gold /125 #58
2011 Press Pass Showcase Green /25 #15
2011 Press Pass Showcase Green /25 #41
2011 Press Pass Showcase Green /25 #58
2011 Press Pass Showcase Masterpieces Ink /45 #MPIKK
2011 Press Pass Showcase Masterpieces Ink Gold /25 #MPIKK
2011 Press Pass Showcase Masterpieces Ink Melting /1 #MPIKK
2011 Press Pass Showcase Masterpieces Memorabilia /99 #MPMKK
2011 Press Pass Showcase Masterpieces Memorabilia Gold /45 #MPMKK
2011 Press Pass Showcase Masterpieces Memorabilia Melting /5 #MPMKK
2011 Press Pass Showcase Melting /1 #15
2011 Press Pass Showcase Melting /1 #41
2011 Press Pass Showcase Melting /1 #58
2011 Press Pass Showcase Prized Pieces Firesuit /99 #PPMKK
2011 Press Pass Showcase Prized Pieces Firesuit Gold /45 #PPMKK
2011 Press Pass Showcase Prized Pieces Firesuit Ink /25 #PPIKK
2011 Press Pass Showcase Prized Pieces Firesuit Patches Ink /1 #PPIKK
2011 Press Pass Showcase Prized Pieces Firesuit Patches Melting /5 #PPMKK
2011 Press Pass Showcase Prized Pieces Sheet Metal Ink /45 #PPIKK
2011 Press Pass Showcase Showroom /499 #SR9
2011 Press Pass Showcase Showroom Gold /125 #SR9
2011 Press Pass Showcase Showroom Melting /1 #SR9
2011 Press Pass Showcase Showroom Memorabilia Sheet Metal /45 #SRMKK
2011 Press Pass Showcase Showroom Memorabilia Sheet Metal Gold /25 #SRMKK
2011 Press Pass Showcase Showroom Memorabilia Sheet Metal Melting /5 #SRMKK
2011 Press Pass Signature Series /11 #SSTKK
2011 Press Pass Signature Series /11 #SSBKK
2011 Press Pass Signature Series /11 #SSFKK
2011 Press Pass Signature Series /11 #SSMKK
2011 Press Pass Signings Black and White /5 #PPSKK
2011 Press Pass Signings Brushed Metal /25 #PPSKK
2011 Press Pass Signings Holofoil /10 #PPSKK
2011 Press Pass Signings Printing Plates Black /1 #PPSKK
2011 Press Pass Signings Printing Plates Cyan /1 #PPSKK
2011 Press Pass Signings Printing Plates Magenta /1 #PPSKK
2011 Press Pass Signings Printing Plates Yellow /1 #PPSKK
2011 Press Pass Stealth #19
2011 Press Pass Stealth #20
2011 Press Pass Stealth #21
2011 Press Pass Stealth #74
2011 Press Pass Stealth #92
2011 Press Pass Stealth Afterburner /99 #ABKK
2011 Press Pass Stealth Afterburner Gold /25 #ABKK
2011 Press Pass Stealth Black and White /25 #19
2011 Press Pass Stealth Black and White /25 #20
2011 Press Pass Stealth Black and White /25 #21
2011 Press Pass Stealth Black and White /25 #74
2011 Press Pass Stealth Black and White /25 #92
2011 Press Pass Stealth Holofoil /99 #19
2011 Press Pass Stealth Holofoil /99 #20
2011 Press Pass Stealth Holofoil /99 #21
2011 Press Pass Stealth Holofoil /99 #74
2011 Press Pass Stealth Holofoil /99 #92
2011 Press Pass Stealth Metal of Honor Medal of Honor /50 #BAKK
2011 Press Pass Stealth Metal of Honor Purple Heart /25 #MHKK
2011 Press Pass Stealth Metal of Honor Silver Star /99 #BAKK
2011 Press Pass Stealth Purple /25 #19
2011 Press Pass Stealth Purple /25 #20
2011 Press Pass Stealth Purple /25 #21
2011 Press Pass Stealth Supersonic #SS3
2011 Press Pass Target Winning Tickets #WTT3
2011 Wheels Main Event #18
2011 Wheels Main Event #67
2011 Wheels Main Event #79
2011 Wheels Main Event All Stars #A21
2011 Wheels Main Event All Stars Brushed Foil /199 #A21
2011 Wheels Main Event All Stars Holofoil /50 #A21
2011 Wheels Main Event Black and White #18
2011 Wheels Main Event Black and White #67
2011 Wheels Main Event Black and White #79
2011 Wheels Main Event Blue /75 #18
2011 Wheels Main Event Blue /75 #67
2011 Wheels Main Event Blue /75 #79
2011 Wheels Main Event Green /1 #18
2011 Wheels Main Event Green /1 #67
2011 Wheels Main Event Green /1 #79
2011 Wheels Main Event Headliners Holofoil /25 #HLKK
2011 Wheels Main Event Headliners Silver /99 #HLKK
2011 Wheels Main Event Lead Foot Holofoil /25 #LFKK
2011 Wheels Main Event Lead Foot Silver /99 #LFKK
2011 Wheels Main Event Marks Autographs Blue /10 #MEKK
2011 Wheels Main Event Marks Autographs Gold /25 #MEKK
2011 Wheels Main Event Marks Autographs Silver /50 #MEKK
2011 Wheels Main Event Materials Holofoil /25 #MEMKK
2011 Wheels Main Event Materials Silver /50 #MEMKK
2011 Wheels Main Event Red /20 #18
2011 Wheels Main Event Red /20 #67
2011 Wheels Main Event Red /20 #79
2012 Press Pass #18
2012 Press Pass #77
2012 Press Pass Autographs Blue /5 #PPAKK
2012 Press Pass Autographs Printing Plates Black /1 #PPAKK
2012 Press Pass Autographs Printing Plates Cyan /1 #PPAKK
2012 Press Pass Autographs Printing Plates Magenta /1 #PPAKK
2012 Press Pass Autographs Printing Plates Yellow /1 #PPAKK
2012 Press Pass Autographs Red /5 #PPAKK
2012 Press Pass Autographs Silver /15 #PPAKK
2012 Press Pass Blue #18
2012 Press Pass Blue #77
2012 Press Pass Blue Holofoil /35 #18
2012 Press Pass Blue Holofoil /35 #77
2012 Press Pass Cup Chase #CCR17
2012 Press Pass Cup Chase Prizes #CCP11
2012 Press Pass Fanfare #22
2012 Press Pass Fanfare Autographs Blue /1 #KK
2012 Press Pass Fanfare Autographs Gold /15 #KK
2012 Press Pass Fanfare Autographs Red /5 #KK
2012 Press Pass Fanfare Autographs Silver /50 #KK
2012 Press Pass Fanfare Blue Foil Die Cuts #22
2012 Press Pass Fanfare Diamond /5 #22
2012 Press Pass Fanfare Holofoil Die Cuts #22
2012 Press Pass Fanfare Magnificent Materials /125 #MMKK
2012 Press Pass Fanfare Magnificent Materials Dual Swatches /50 #MMKK
2012 Press Pass Fanfare Magnificent Materials Dual Swatches Melting /10 #MMKK
2012 Press Pass Fanfare Magnificent Materials Gold /75 #MMKK
2012 Press Pass Fanfare Magnificent Materials Signatures /25 #KK
2012 Press Pass Fanfare Magnificent Materials Signatures Blue /5 #KK
2012 Press Pass Fanfare Power Rankings #PR8
2012 Press Pass Fanfare Sapphire /20 #22
2012 Press Pass Fanfare Showtime #S4
2012 Press Pass Fanfare Silver /25 #22
2012 Press Pass Four Wide Firesuit /25 #FWKK
2012 Press Pass Four Wide Glove /1 #FWKK
2012 Press Pass Four Wide Sheet Metal /15 #FWKK
2012 Press Pass Four Wide Tire /10 #FWKK
2012 Press Pass Gold #18
2012 Press Pass Gold #77
2012 Press Pass Ignite #19
2012 Press Pass Ignite Double Burner Gun Metal /10 #DBKK
2012 Press Pass Ignite Double Burner Red /1 #DBKK
2012 Press Pass Ignite Double Burner Silver /25 #DBKK
2012 Press Pass Ignite Materials Autographs Red /5 #IMKK
2012 Press Pass Ignite Materials Autographs Silver /65 #IMKK
2012 Press Pass Ignite Materials Gun Metal /99 #IMKK
2012 Press Pass Ignite Materials Red /10 #IMKK
2012 Press Pass Ignite Materials Silver #IMKK
2012 Press Pass Ignite Proofs Black and White /50 #19
2012 Press Pass Ignite Proofs Cyan #19
2012 Press Pass Ignite Proofs Magenta #19
2012 Press Pass Ignite Proofs Yellow /10 #19
2012 Press Pass Ignite Steel Horses #SH8
2012 Press Pass Ignite Supercharged Signatures /5 #SSKK
2012 Press Pass Legends #45
2012 Press Pass Legends Blue Holofoil /1 #45
2012 Press Pass Legends Gold /275 #45
2012 Press Pass Legends Green #45
2012 Press Pass Legends Prominent Pieces Gold /50 #KK
2012 Press Pass Legends Prominent Pieces Holofoil /25 #KK
2012 Press Pass Legends Prominent Pieces Silver /99 #KK
2012 Press Pass Legends Rainbow Holofoil /50 #45
2012 Press Pass Legends Red /99 #45
2012 Press Pass Legends Silver Holofoil /25 #45
2012 Press Pass Power Picks Blue /50 #9
2012 Press Pass Power Picks Blue /50 #37
2012 Press Pass Power Picks Blue /50 #58
2012 Press Pass Power Picks Gold /50 #9
2012 Press Pass Power Picks Gold /50 #37
2012 Press Pass Power Picks Gold /50 #58
2012 Press Pass Power Picks Holofoil /10 #9
2012 Press Pass Power Picks Holofoil /10 #37
2012 Press Pass Power Picks Holofoil /10 #58
2012 Press Pass Purple /35 #18
2012 Press Pass Purple /35 #77
2012 Press Pass Redline #19
2012 Press Pass Redline Black /99 #19
2012 Press Pass Redline Cyan /50 #19
2012 Press Pass Redline Magenta /15 #19
2012 Press Pass Redline Muscle Car Sheet Metal Blue /5 #MCKK
2012 Press Pass Redline Muscle Car Sheet Metal Gold /10 #MCKK
2012 Press Pass Redline Muscle Car Sheet Metal Melting /1 #MCKK
2012 Press Pass Redline Muscle Car Sheet Metal Red /75 #MCKK
2012 Press Pass Redline Muscle Car Sheet Metal Silver /25 #MCKK
2012 Press Pass Redline Pieces of the Action Blue /5 #PAKK
2012 Press Pass Redline Pieces of the Action Gold /10 #PAKK
2012 Press Pass Redline Pieces of the Action Melting /1 #PAKK
2012 Press Pass Redline Pieces of the Action Red /25 #PAKK
2012 Press Pass Redline Pieces of the Action Silver /15 #PAKK
2012 Press Pass Redline Relic Autographs Blue /10 #RLRKK
2012 Press Pass Redline Relic Autographs Gold /25 #RLRKK
2012 Press Pass Redline Relic Autographs Melting /1 #RLRKK
2012 Press Pass Redline Relic Autographs Red /75 #RLRKK
2012 Press Pass Redline Relic Autographs Silver /50 #RLRKK
2012 Press Pass Redline Relics Blue /5 #RLKK
2012 Press Pass Redline Relics Gold /10 #RLKK
2012 Press Pass Redline Relics Melting /1 #RLKK
2012 Press Pass Redline Relics Red /25 #RLKK
2012 Press Pass Redline Relics Silver /15 #RLKK
2012 Press Pass Redline Rookie Year Relic Autographs Blue /5 #RYKK
2012 Press Pass Redline Rookie Year Relic Autographs Gold /25 #RYKK
2012 Press Pass Redline Rookie Year Relic Autographs Melting /1 #RYKK
2012 Press Pass Redline Rookie Year Relic Autographs Red /50 #RYKK
2012 Press Pass Redline RPM #RPM7
2012 Press Pass Redline Signatures Blue /5 #RSKK
2012 Press Pass Redline Signatures Gold /15 #RSKK
2012 Press Pass Redline Signatures Holofoil /10 #RSKK
2012 Press Pass Redline Signatures Melting /1 #RSKK
2012 Press Pass Redline Signatures Red /25 #RSKK
2012 Press Pass Redline V8 Relics Blue /5 #V8KK
2012 Press Pass Redline V8 Relics Gold /10 #V8KK
2012 Press Pass Redline V8 Relics Melting /1 #V8KK
2012 Press Pass Redline V8 Relics Red /25 #V8KK
2012 Press Pass Redline Yellow /1 #19
2012 Press Pass Showcase /499 #40
2012 Press Pass Showcase /499 #14
2012 Press Pass Showcase /499 #52
2012 Press Pass Showcase Classic Collections Ink /10 #CCMHMS
2012 Press Pass Showcase Classic Collections Ink Gold /5 #CCMHMS
2012 Press Pass Showcase Classic Collections Ink Melting /1 #CCMHMS
2012 Press Pass Showcase Classic Collections Memorabilia /50 #CCMHMS
2012 Press Pass Showcase Classic Collections Memorabilia Gold /25 #CCMHMS
2012 Press Pass Showcase Classic Collections Memorabilia Melting /5 #CCMHMS
2012 Press Pass Showcase Elite Exhibit Ink /50 #EEIKK
2012 Press Pass Showcase Elite Exhibit Ink Gold /25 #EEIKK
2012 Press Pass Showcase Elite Exhibit Ink Melting /1 #EEIKK
2012 Press Pass Showcase Gold /125 #14
2012 Press Pass Showcase Gold /125 #40
2012 Press Pass Showcase Gold /125 #52
2012 Press Pass Showcase Green /5 #14
2012 Press Pass Showcase Green /5 #40
2012 Press Pass Showcase Green /5 #52
2012 Press Pass Showcase Masterpieces Ink /50 #MPIKK
2012 Press Pass Showcase Masterpieces Ink Gold /25 #MPIKK
2012 Press Pass Showcase Masterpieces Ink Melting /1 #MPIKK
2012 Press Pass Showcase Masterpieces Memorabilia /99 #MPKK
2012 Press Pass Showcase Masterpieces Memorabilia Gold /50 #MPKK
2012 Press Pass Showcase Masterpieces Memorabilia Melting /5 #MPKK
2012 Press Pass Showcase Melting /1 #14
2012 Press Pass Showcase Melting /1 #40
2012 Press Pass Showcase Melting /1 #52
2012 Press Pass Showcase Prized Pieces /99 #PPKK
2012 Press Pass Showcase Prized Pieces Gold /50 #PPKK
2012 Press Pass Showcase Prized Pieces Ink /50 #PPIKK
2012 Press Pass Showcase Prized Pieces Ink Gold /25 #PPIKK
2012 Press Pass Showcase Prized Pieces Ink Melting /1 #PPIKK
2012 Press Pass Showcase Prized Pieces Melting /5 #PPKK
2012 Press Pass Showcase Purple /1 #14
2012 Press Pass Showcase Purple /1 #40
2012 Press Pass Showcase Purple /1 #52
2012 Press Pass Showcase Red /25 #14
2012 Press Pass Showcase Red /25 #40
2012 Press Pass Showcase Red /25 #52
2012 Press Pass Showcase Showroom /499 #SR10
2012 Press Pass Showcase Showroom Gold /125 #SR10
2012 Press Pass Showcase Showroom Melting /1 #SR10
2012 Press Pass Showcase Showroom Memorabilia /99 #SRKK
2012 Press Pass Showcase Showroom Memorabilia Gold /50 #SRKK
2012 Press Pass Showcase Showroom Memorabilia Melting /5 #SRKK
2012 Press Pass Showcase Signature Patches /1 #SSPKK
2012 Press Pass Signature Series Race Used /12 #PPAKK1
2012 Press Pass Signature Series Race Used /12 #PPAKK2
2012 Press Pass Snapshots #SS18
2012 Press Pass Ultimate Collection Blue Holofoil /25 #UCKK
2012 Press Pass Ultimate Collection Holofoil /50 #UCKK
2012 Total Memorabilia #15A
2012 Total Memorabilia #15B
2012 Total Memorabilia Black and White /99 #15
2012 Total Memorabilia Dual Swatch Gold /75 #TMKK
2012 Total Memorabilia Dual Swatch Holofoil /25 #TMKK
2012 Total Memorabilia Dual Swatch Melting /5 #TMKK
2012 Total Memorabilia Dual Swatch Silver /99 #TMKK
2012 Total Memorabilia Gold /275 #15
2012 Total Memorabilia Hot Rod Relics Gold /50 #HRRKK
2012 Total Memorabilia Hot Rod Relics Holofoil /10 #HRRKK
2012 Total Memorabilia Hot Rod Relics Melting /1 #HRRKK
2012 Total Memorabilia Hot Rod Relics Silver /99 #HRRKK
2012 Total Memorabilia Jumbo Swatch Gold /50 #TMKK
2012 Total Memorabilia Jumbo Swatch Holofoil /10 #TMKK
2012 Total Memorabilia Jumbo Swatch Melting /1 #TMKK
2012 Total Memorabilia Quad Swatch Gold /25 #TMKK
2012 Total Memorabilia Quad Swatch Holofoil /10 #TMKK
2012 Total Memorabilia Quad Swatch Melting /1 #TMKK
2012 Total Memorabilia Quad Swatch Silver /50 #TMKK
2012 Total Memorabilia Red Retail /250 #15
2012 Total Memorabilia Single Swatch Gold /99 #TMKK
2012 Total Memorabilia Single Swatch Holofoil /50 #TMKK
2012 Total Memorabilia Single Swatch Melting /10 #TMKK
2012 Total Memorabilia Single Swatch Silver /199 #TMKK
2012 Total Memorabilia Tandem Treasures Dual Memorabilia Gold /75 #TTJGKK
2012 Total Memorabilia Tandem Treasures Dual Memorabilia Gold /75 #TTDEKK
2012 Total Memorabilia Tandem Treasures Dual Memorabilia Holofoil /25 #TTJGKK
2012 Total Memorabilia Tandem Treasures Dual Memorabilia Holofoil /25 #TTDEKK
2012 Total Memorabilia Tandem Treasures Dual Memorabilia Melting /5 #TTJGKK
2012 Total Memorabilia Tandem Treasures Dual Memorabilia Melting /5 #TTDEKK
2012 Total Memorabilia Tandem Treasures Dual Memorabilia Silver /99 #TTDEKK
2012 Total Memorabilia Tandem Treasures Dual Memorabilia Silver /99 #TTJGKK
2012 Total Memorabilia Triple Swatch Gold /50 #TMKK
2012 Total Memorabilia Triple Swatch Holofoil /25 #TMKK
2012 Total Memorabilia Triple Swatch Melting /1 #TMKK
2012 Total Memorabilia Triple Swatch Silver /99 #TMKK
2013 Press Pass #0
2013 Press Pass #23
2013 Press Pass #72
2013 Press Pass #88
2013 Press Pass Aerodynamic Autographs Blue /1 #KK
2013 Press Pass Aerodynamic Autographs Holofoil /10 #KK
2013 Press Pass Burning Rubber Blue /50 #BRKK
2013 Press Pass Burning Rubber Blue /50 #BRKK2
2013 Press Pass Burning Rubber Gold /199 #BRKK
2013 Press Pass Burning Rubber Gold /199 #BRKK2
2013 Press Pass Burning Rubber Holofoil /75 #BRKK
2013 Press Pass Burning Rubber Holofoil /75 #BRKK2
2013 Press Pass Burning Rubber Letterman /8 #BRLKK
2013 Press Pass Burning Rubber Melting /10 #BRKK
2013 Press Pass Burning Rubber Melting /10 #BRKK2
2013 Press Pass Certified Winners Autographs Gold /10 #KK
2013 Press Pass Certified Winners Autographs Melting /5 #KK
2013 Press Pass Color Proofs Black #23
2013 Press Pass Color Proofs Black #72
2013 Press Pass Color Proofs Black #88
2013 Press Pass Color Proofs Cyan /35 #23
2013 Press Pass Color Proofs Cyan /35 #72
2013 Press Pass Color Proofs Cyan /35 #88
2013 Press Pass Color Proofs Magenta #23
2013 Press Pass Color Proofs Magenta #72
2013 Press Pass Color Proofs Magenta #88
2013 Press Pass Color Proofs Yellow /5 #23
2013 Press Pass Color Proofs Yellow /5 #72
2013 Press Pass Color Proofs Yellow /5 #88
2013 Press Pass Cup Chase #CC11
2013 Press Pass Cup Chase Prizes #CCP11
2013 Press Pass Fanfare #26
2013 Press Pass Fanfare #27
2013 Press Pass Fanfare Autographs Blue /1 #KK
2013 Press Pass Fanfare Autographs Gold /5 #KK
2013 Press Pass Fanfare Autographs Green /1 #KK
2013 Press Pass Fanfare Autographs Red /1 #KK
2013 Press Pass Fanfare Autographs Silver /5 #KK
2013 Press Pass Fanfare Diamond Die Cuts /5 #26
2013 Press Pass Fanfare Diamond Die Cuts /5 #27
2013 Press Pass Fanfare Fan Following #FF9
2013 Press Pass Fanfare Green /3 #26
2013 Press Pass Fanfare Green /3 #27
2013 Press Pass Fanfare Holofoil Die Cuts #26
2013 Press Pass Fanfare Holofoil Die Cuts #27
2013 Press Pass Fanfare Magnificent Jumbo Materials Signatures /10 #KK
2013 Press Pass Fanfare Magnificent Materials Dual Swatches /50 #KK
2013 Press Pass Fanfare Magnificent Materials Dual Swatches Melting /10 #KK
2013 Press Pass Fanfare Magnificent Materials Gold /50 #KK
2013 Press Pass Fanfare Magnificent Materials Jumbo Swatches /25 #KK
2013 Press Pass Fanfare Magnificent Materials Signatures /25 #KK
2013 Press Pass Fanfare Magnificent Materials Signatures Blue /5 #KK
2013 Press Pass Fanfare Magnificent Materials Silver /199 #KK
2013 Press Pass Fanfare Red Foil Die Cuts #26
2013 Press Pass Fanfare Red Foil Die Cuts #27
2013 Press Pass Fanfare Sapphire /20 #26
2013 Press Pass Fanfare Sapphire /20 #27
2013 Press Pass Fanfare Showtime #S1
2013 Press Pass Fanfare Silver /25 #26
2013 Press Pass Fanfare Silver /25 #27
2013 Press Pass Four Wide Gold /10 #FWKK
2013 Press Pass Four Wide Melting /1 #FWKK
2013 Press Pass Ignite #16
2013 Press Pass Ignite #56
2013 Press Pass Ignite Convoy #6
2013 Press Pass Ignite Double Burner Blue Holofoil /10 #DBKK
2013 Press Pass Ignite Double Burner Red /1 #DBKK
2013 Press Pass Ignite Double Burner Silver /25 #DBKK
2013 Press Pass Ignite Hot Threads Blue Holofoil /99 #HTKK
2013 Press Pass Ignite Hot Threads Patch Red /10 #HTKK
2013 Press Pass Ignite Hot Threads Patch Red Oversized /20 #HTPKK
2013 Press Pass Ignite Hot Threads Silver #HTKK
2013 Press Pass Ignite Ink Black /25 #IIKK
2013 Press Pass Ignite Ink Blue /10 #IIKK
2013 Press Pass Ignite Ink Red /1 #IIKK
2013 Press Pass Ignite Profile #8
2013 Press Pass Ignite Proofs Black and White /50 #16
2013 Press Pass Ignite Proofs Black and White /50 #56
2013 Press Pass Ignite Proofs Cyan #16
2013 Press Pass Ignite Proofs Cyan #56
2013 Press Pass Ignite Proofs Magenta #16
2013 Press Pass Ignite Proofs Magenta #56
2013 Press Pass Ignite Proofs Yellow /5 #16
2013 Press Pass Ignite Proofs Yellow /5 #56
2013 Press Pass Ignite Supercharged Signatures Blue Holofoil /10 #SSKK
2013 Press Pass Ignite Supercharged Signatures Red /1 #SSKK
2013 Press Pass Legends Four Wide Memorabilia Autographs Gold /25 #FWSEKK
2013 Press Pass Legends Four Wide Memorabilia Autographs Melting /5 #FWSEKK
2013 Press Pass Legends Prominent Pieces Gold /10 #PPKK
2013 Press Pass Legends Prominent Pieces Holofoil /5 #PPKK
2013 Press Pass Legends Prominent Pieces Oversized Firesuit /5 #PPKK
2013 Press Pass Legends Prominent Pieces Silver /25 #PPKK
2013 Press Pass Power Picks Blue /99 #9
2013 Press Pass Power Picks Blue /99 #39
2013 Press Pass Power Picks Gold /50 #9
2013 Press Pass Power Picks Gold /50 #39
2013 Press Pass Power Picks Holofoil /10 #9
2013 Press Pass Power Picks Holofoil /10 #39
2013 Press Pass Racing Champions #RC12
2013 Press Pass Racing Champions #RC19
2013 Press Pass Redline #25
2013 Press Pass Redline #26
2013 Press Pass Redline Black /99 #25
2013 Press Pass Redline Black /99 #26
2013 Press Pass Redline Cyan /50 #25
2013 Press Pass Redline Cyan /50 #26
2013 Press Pass Redline Dynamic Duals Dual Relic Blue /5 #DDKK
2013 Press Pass Redline Dynamic Duals Dual Relic Gold /10 #DDKK
2013 Press Pass Redline Dynamic Duals Dual Relic Melting /1 #DDKK
2013 Press Pass Redline Dynamic Duals Dual Relic Red /50 #DDKK
2013 Press Pass Redline Dynamic Duals Dual Relic Silver /25 #DDKK
2013 Press Pass Redline Intensity #6
2013 Press Pass Redline Magenta /15 #25
2013 Press Pass Redline Magenta /15 #26
2013 Press Pass Redline Muscle Car Sheet Metal Blue /5 #MCMKK
2013 Press Pass Redline Muscle Car Sheet Metal Gold /10 #MCMKK
2013 Press Pass Redline Muscle Car Sheet Metal Melting /1 #MCMKK
2013 Press Pass Redline Muscle Car Sheet Metal Red /50 #MCMKK
2013 Press Pass Redline Muscle Car Sheet Metal Silver /25 #MCMKK
2013 Press Pass Redline Pieces of the Action Blue /10 #PAKK
2013 Press Pass Redline Pieces of the Action Gold /25 #PAKK
2013 Press Pass Redline Pieces of the Action Melting /1 #PAKK
2013 Press Pass Redline Pieces of the Action Red /75 #PAKK
2013 Press Pass Redline Pieces of the Action Silver /50 #PAKK
2013 Press Pass Redline Redline Racers #8
2013 Press Pass Redline Relic Autographs Blue /10 #RRSEKK
2013 Press Pass Redline Relic Autographs Gold /25 #RRSEKK
2013 Press Pass Redline Relic Autographs Melting /1 #RRSEKK
2013 Press Pass Redline Relic Autographs Red /75 #RRSEKK
2013 Press Pass Redline Relic Autographs Silver /50 #RRSEKK
2013 Press Pass Redline Relics Blue /5 #RRKK
2013 Press Pass Redline Relics Gold /10 #RRKK
2013 Press Pass Redline Relics Melting /1 #RRKK
2013 Press Pass Redline Relics Red /50 #RRKK
2013 Press Pass Redline Relics Silver /25 #RRKK
2013 Press Pass Redline Signatures Blue /15 #RSKK1
2013 Press Pass Redline Signatures Blue /10 #RSKK2
2013 Press Pass Redline Signatures Gold /5 #RSKK1
2013 Press Pass Redline Signatures Gold /5 #RSKK2
2013 Press Pass Redline Signatures Holo /10 #RSKK1
2013 Press Pass Redline Signatures Holo /5 #RSKK2
2013 Press Pass Redline Signatures Melting /1 #RSKK1
2013 Press Pass Redline Signatures Melting /1 #RSKK2
2013 Press Pass Redline Signatures Red /10 #RSKK2
2013 Press Pass Redline Signatures Red /25 #RSKK1
2013 Press Pass Redline V8 Relics Blue /5 #V8KK
2013 Press Pass Redline V8 Relics Gold /10 #V8KK
2013 Press Pass Redline V8 Relics Melting /1 #V8KK
2013 Press Pass Redline V8 Relics Red /25 #V8KK
2013 Press Pass Redline Yellow /1 #25
2013 Press Pass Redline Yellow /1 #26
2013 Press Pass Showcase /349 #14
2013 Press Pass Showcase /349 #38
2013 Press Pass Showcase /349 #55
2013 Press Pass Showcase Black /1 #14
2013 Press Pass Showcase Black /1 #38
2013 Press Pass Showcase Black /1 #55
2013 Press Pass Showcase Blue /25 #14
2013 Press Pass Showcase Blue /25 #38
2013 Press Pass Showcase Blue /25 #55
2013 Press Pass Showcase Classic Collections Ink Gold /5 #CCIHMS
2013 Press Pass Showcase Classic Collections Ink Melting /1 #CCIHMS
2013 Press Pass Showcase Classic Collections Ink Red /1 #CCIHMS
2013 Press Pass Showcase Classic Collections Memorabilia Gold /25 #CCMHMS
2013 Press Pass Showcase Classic Collections Memorabilia Melting /5 #CCMHMS
2013 Press Pass Showcase Classic Collections Memorabilia Silver /75 #CCMHMS
2013 Press Pass Showcase Elite Exhibit Ink /25 #EEIKK
2013 Press Pass Showcase Elite Exhibit Ink Blue /30 #EEIKK
2013 Press Pass Showcase Elite Exhibit Ink Gold /10 #EEIKK
2013 Press Pass Showcase Elite Exhibit Ink Melting /1 #EEIKK
2013 Press Pass Showcase Elite Exhibit Ink Red /5 #EEIKK
2013 Press Pass Showcase Gold /99 #14
2013 Press Pass Showcase Gold /99 #38
2013 Press Pass Showcase Gold /99 #55
2013 Press Pass Showcase Green /20 #14
2013 Press Pass Showcase Green /20 #38
2013 Press Pass Showcase Green /20 #55
2013 Press Pass Showcase Masterpieces Ink /25 #MPIKK
2013 Press Pass Showcase Masterpieces Ink Gold /10 #MPIKK
2013 Press Pass Showcase Masterpieces Ink Melting /1 #MPIKK
2013 Press Pass Showcase Masterpieces Memorabilia /75 #MPKK
2013 Press Pass Showcase Masterpieces Memorabilia Gold /25 #MPKK
2013 Press Pass Showcase Masterpieces Memorabilia Melting /5 #MPKK
2013 Press Pass Showcase Prized Pieces /99 #PPMKK
2013 Press Pass Showcase Prized Pieces Blue /20 #PPMKK
2013 Press Pass Showcase Prized Pieces Gold /25 #PPMKK
2013 Press Pass Showcase Prized Pieces Ink /25 #PPIKK
2013 Press Pass Showcase Prized Pieces Ink Blue /30 #PPIKK
2013 Press Pass Showcase Prized Pieces Ink Gold /10 #PPIKK
2013 Press Pass Showcase Prized Pieces Ink Melting /1 #PPIKK
2013 Press Pass Showcase Prized Pieces Melting /5 #PPMKK
2013 Press Pass Showcase Purple /13 #14
2013 Press Pass Showcase Purple /13 #38
2013 Press Pass Showcase Purple /13 #55
2013 Press Pass Showcase Red /10 #14
2013 Press Pass Showcase Red /10 #38
2013 Press Pass Showcase Red /10 #55
2013 Press Pass Showcase Series Standouts Gold /50 #10
2013 Press Pass Showcase Showcase Patches /5 #SPKK
2013 Press Pass Showcase Showroom /299 #4
2013 Press Pass Showcase Showroom Blue /40 #4
2013 Press Pass Showcase Showroom Gold /50 #4
2013 Press Pass Showcase Showroom Green /20 #4
2013 Press Pass Showcase Showroom Melting /1 #4
2013 Press Pass Showcase Showroom Purple /13 #4
2013 Press Pass Showcase Showroom Red /10 #4
2013 Press Pass Showcase Signature Patches /14 #SSPKK
2013 Press Pass Showcase Studio Showcase /299 #10
2013 Press Pass Showcase Studio Showcase Blue /40 #10
2013 Press Pass Showcase Studio Showcase Green /25 #10
2013 Press Pass Showcase Studio Showcase Ink /25 #SSIKK
2013 Press Pass Showcase Studio Showcase Ink Gold /10 #SSIKK
2013 Press Pass Showcase Studio Showcase Ink Melting /1 #SSIKK
2013 Press Pass Showcase Studio Showcase Ink Red /5 #SSIKK
2013 Press Pass Showcase Studio Showcase Melting /1 #10
2013 Press Pass Showcase Studio Showcase Purple /13 #10
2013 Press Pass Showcase Studio Showcase Red /10 #10
2013 Press Pass Signings Blue /1 #KK
2013 Press Pass Signings Gold /5 #KK
2013 Press Pass Signings Holofoil /5 #KK
2013 Press Pass Signings Printing Plates Black /1 #KK
2013 Press Pass Signings Printing Plates Cyan /1 #KK
2013 Press Pass Signings Printing Plates Magenta /1 #KK
2013 Press Pass Signings Printing Plates Yellow /1 #KK
2013 Press Pass Signings Silver /10 #KK
2013 Total Memorabilia #21
2013 Total Memorabilia #22
2013 Total Memorabilia Black and White /99 #21
2013 Total Memorabilia Black and White /99 #22
2013 Total Memorabilia Dual Swatch Gold /199 #TMKK
2013 Total Memorabilia Gold /275 #21
2013 Total Memorabilia Gold /275 #22
2013 Total Memorabilia Hot Rod Relics Gold /50 #HRRKK
2013 Total Memorabilia Hot Rod Relics Holofoil /10 #HRRKK
2013 Total Memorabilia Hot Rod Relics Melting /1 #HRRKK
2013 Total Memorabilia Hot Rod Relics Silver /99 #HRRKK
2013 Total Memorabilia Quad Swatch Melting /10 #TMKK
2013 Total Memorabilia Red #21
2013 Total Memorabilia Red #22
2013 Total Memorabilia Signature Collection Dual Swatch Gold /10 #SCKK
2013 Total Memorabilia Signature Collection Quad Swatch Melting /1 #SCKK
2013 Total Memorabilia Signature Collection Single Swatch Silver /10 #SCKK
2013 Total Memorabilia Signature Collection Triple Swatch Holofoil /5 #SCKK
2013 Total Memorabilia Single Swatch Silver /475 #TMKK
2013 Total Memorabilia Smooth Operators #SO10
2013 Total Memorabilia Triple Swatch Holofoil /99 #TMKK
2014 Press Pass #0
2014 Press Pass #72
2014 Press Pass #18
2014 Press Pass #85
2014 Press Pass American Thunder #19
2014 Press Pass American Thunder #62
2014 Press Pass American Thunder #51
2014 Press Pass American Thunder Autographs Blue /5 #ATAKK
2014 Press Pass American Thunder Autographs Red /1 #ATAKK
2014 Press Pass American Thunder Autographs White /15 #ATAKK
2014 Press Pass American Thunder Battle Armor Blue /25 #BAKK
2014 Press Pass American Thunder Battle Armor Red /1 #BAKK
2014 Press Pass American Thunder Battle Armor Silver /99 #BAKK
2014 Press Pass American Thunder Black and White /50 #19
2014 Press Pass American Thunder Black and White /50 #51
2014 Press Pass American Thunder Black and White /50 #62
2014 Press Pass American Thunder Brothers In Arms Autographs Blue /5 #BAHMS
2014 Press Pass American Thunder Brothers In Arms Autographs Red /1 #BAHMS
2014 Press Pass American Thunder Brothers In Arms Autographs White /10 #BAHMS
2014 Press Pass American Thunder Brothers In Arms Relics Blue /25 #BAHMS
2014 Press Pass American Thunder Brothers In Arms Relics Red /5 #BAHMS
2014 Press Pass American Thunder Brothers In Arms Relics Silver /50 #BAHMS
2014 Press Pass American Thunder Class A Uniforms Blue /99 #CAUKK
2014 Press Pass American Thunder Class A Uniforms Red /10 #CAUKK
2014 Press Pass American Thunder Class A Uniforms Silver #CAUKK
2014 Press Pass American Thunder Cyan #19
2014 Press Pass American Thunder Cyan #51
2014 Press Pass American Thunder Cyan #62
2014 Press Pass American Thunder Great American Treads Autographs Blue /10 #GATKK
2014 Press Pass American Thunder Great American Treads Autographs Red /1 #GATKK
2014 Press Pass American Thunder Magenta #19
2014 Press Pass American Thunder Magenta #51
2014 Press Pass American Thunder Magenta #62
2014 Press Pass American Thunder Yellow /5 #19
2014 Press Pass American Thunder Yellow /5 #51
2014 Press Pass Burning Rubber Blue /25 #BRKK
2014 Press Pass Burning Rubber Blue /25 #BRKK2
2014 Press Pass Burning Rubber Gold /75 #BRKK
2014 Press Pass Burning Rubber Gold /75 #BRKK2
2014 Press Pass Burning Rubber Holofoil /50 #BRKK
2014 Press Pass Burning Rubber Holofoil /50 #BRKK2
2014 Press Pass Burning Rubber Letterman /8 #BRLKK
2014 Press Pass Burning Rubber Melting /10 #BRKK
2014 Press Pass Burning Rubber Melting /10 #BRKK2
2014 Press Pass Certified Winners Memorabilia Autographs Gold /5 #CWKK
2014 Press Pass Certified Winners Memorabilia Autographs Melting /1 #CWKK
2014 Press Pass Color Proofs Black /70 #18
2014 Press Pass Color Proofs Black /70 #72
2014 Press Pass Color Proofs Black /70 #85
2014 Press Pass Color Proofs Cyan /35 #18
2014 Press Pass Color Proofs Cyan /35 #72
2014 Press Pass Color Proofs Cyan /35 #85
2014 Press Pass Color Proofs Magenta #18
2014 Press Pass Color Proofs Magenta #72
2014 Press Pass Color Proofs Magenta #85
2014 Press Pass Color Proofs Yellow /5 #18
2014 Press Pass Color Proofs Yellow /5 #72
2014 Press Pass Color Proofs Yellow /5 #85
2014 Press Pass Cup Chase #9
2014 Press Pass Five Star /15 #10
2014 Press Pass Five Star Blue /5 #10
2014 Press Pass Five Star Classic Compilation Autographs Blue Triple Swatch /5 #CCKK
2014 Press Pass Five Star Classic Compilation Autographs Holofoil /10 #CCKK
2014 Press Pass Five Star Classic Compilation Autographs Holofoil Dual Swatch /10 #CCKK
2014 Press Pass Five Star Classic Compilation Autographs Melting Five Swatch /1 #CCKK
2014 Press Pass Five Star Classic Compilation Autographs Melting Quad Swatch /1 #CCKK
2014 Press Pass Five Star Classic Compilations Autographed Patch Booklet /1 #CCKK1
2014 Press Pass Five Star Classic Compilations Autographed Patch Booklet /1 #CCKK2
2014 Press Pass Five Star Classic Compilations Autographed Patch Booklet /1 #CCKK3
2014 Press Pass Five Star Classic Compilations Autographed Patch Booklet /1 #CCKK4
2014 Press Pass Five Star Classic Compilations Autographed Patch Booklet /1 #CCKK5
2014 Press Pass Five Star Classic Compilations Autographed Patch Booklet /1 #CCKK6
2014 Press Pass Five Star Classic Compilations Autographed Patch Booklet /1 #CCKK7
2014 Press Pass Five Star Classic Compilations Autographed Patch Booklet /1 #CCKK8
2014 Press Pass Five Star Classic Compilations Autographed Patch Booklet /1 #CCKK9
2014 Press Pass Five Star Classic Compilations Autographed Patch Booklet /1 #CCKK10
2014 Press Pass Five Star Classic Compilations Autographed Patch Booklet /1 #CCKK11
2014 Press Pass Five Star Classic Compilations Combo Autographs Blue /5 #CCHMS
2014 Press Pass Five Star Classic Compilations Combo Autographs Melting /1 #CCHMS
2014 Press Pass Five Star Holofoil /10 #10
2014 Press Pass Five Star Melting /1 #10
2014 Press Pass Five Star Paramount Pieces Blue /5 #PPKK
2014 Press Pass Five Star Paramount Pieces Gold /25 #PPKK
2014 Press Pass Five Star Paramount Pieces Holofoil /10 #PPKK
2014 Press Pass Five Star Paramount Pieces Melting /1 #PPKK
2014 Press Pass Five Star Paramount Pieces Melting Patch /1 #PPKK
2014 Press Pass Five Star Signature Souvenirs Blue /5 #SSKK
2014 Press Pass Five Star Signature Souvenirs Gold /50 #SSKK
2014 Press Pass Five Star Signature Souvenirs Holofoil /25 #SSKK
2014 Press Pass Five Star Signature Souvenirs Melting /1 #SSKK
2014 Press Pass Five Star Signatures Blue /5 #FSSKK
2014 Press Pass Five Star Signatures Holofoil /10 #FSSKK
2014 Press Pass Five Star Signatures Melting /1 #FSSKK
2014 Press Pass Four Wide Gold /10 #FWKK
2014 Press Pass Four Wide Melting /1 #FWKK
2014 Press Pass Gold #18
2014 Press Pass Gold #72
2014 Press Pass Gold #85
2014 Press Pass Redline #28
2014 Press Pass Redline #29
2014 Press Pass Redline Black /75 #28
2014 Press Pass Redline Black /75 #29
2014 Press Pass Redline Blue Foil #28
2014 Press Pass Redline Blue Foil #29
2014 Press Pass Redline Cyan /50 #28
2014 Press Pass Redline Cyan /50 #29
2014 Press Pass Redline Dynamic Duals Relic Autographs Blue /15 #DDKK
2014 Press Pass Redline Dynamic Duals Relic Autographs Gold /5 #DDKK
2014 Press Pass Redline Dynamic Duals Relic Autographs Melting /1 #DDKK
2014 Press Pass Redline Dynamic Duals Relic Autographs Red /25 #DDKK
2014 Press Pass Redline Green National Convention /5 #28
2014 Press Pass Redline Green National Convention /5 #29
2014 Press Pass Redline Head to Head Blue /10 #HTHDPKK
2014 Press Pass Redline Head to Head Gold /25 #HTHDPKK
2014 Press Pass Redline Head to Head Melting /1 #HTHDPKK
2014 Press Pass Redline Head to Head Red /75 #HTHDPKK
2014 Press Pass Redline Intensity #I7
2014 Press Pass Redline Magenta /10 #28
2014 Press Pass Redline Magenta /10 #29
2014 Press Pass Redline Muscle Car Sheet Metal Blue /25 #MCMKK
2014 Press Pass Redline Muscle Car Sheet Metal Gold /50 #MCMKK
2014 Press Pass Redline Muscle Car Sheet Metal Melting /1 #MCMKK
2014 Press Pass Redline Muscle Car Sheet Metal Red /75 #MCMKK
2014 Press Pass Redline Pieces of the Action Blue /10 #PAKK
2014 Press Pass Redline Pieces of the Action Gold /25 #PAKK
2014 Press Pass Redline Pieces of the Action Melting /1 #PAKK
2014 Press Pass Redline Pieces of the Action Red /75 #PAKK
2014 Press Pass Redline Redline Racers #RR10
2014 Press Pass Redline Relic Autographs Blue /5 #RRSEKK
2014 Press Pass Redline Relic Autographs Gold /15 #RRSEKK
2014 Press Pass Redline Relic Autographs Melting /1 #RRSEKK
2014 Press Pass Redline Relic Autographs Red /25 #RRSEKK
2014 Press Pass Redline Relics Blue /25 #RRKK
2014 Press Pass Redline Relics Gold /50 #RRKK
2014 Press Pass Redline Relics Melting /1 #RRKK
2014 Press Pass Redline Relics Red /75 #RRKK
2014 Press Pass Redline Signatures Blue /5 #RSKK
2014 Press Pass Redline Signatures Gold /15 #RSKK
2014 Press Pass Redline Signatures Melting /1 #RSKK
2014 Press Pass Redline Signatures Red /25 #RSKK
2014 Press Pass Redline Yellow /1 #28
2014 Press Pass Redline Yellow /1 #29
2014 Press Pass Replay #4
2014 Press Pass Replay #19
2014 Press Pass Signature Series Gold /5 #SSKK
2014 Press Pass Signings Gold /4 #PPSKK
2014 Press Pass Signings Holofoil /2 #PPSKK
2014 Press Pass Signings Melting /1 #PPSKK
2014 Press Pass Signings Printing Plates Black /1 #PPSKK
2014 Press Pass Signings Printing Plates Cyan /1 #PPSKK
2014 Press Pass Signings Printing Plates Magenta /1 #PPSKK
2014 Press Pass Signings Printing Plates Yellow /1 #PPSKK
2014 Press Pass Signings Silver /5 #PPSKK
2014 Total Memorabilia #13
2014 Total Memorabilia Autographed Memorabilia Blue /5 #SCKK
2014 Total Memorabilia Autographed Memorabilia Gold /5 #SCKK
2014 Total Memorabilia Autographed Memorabilia Melting /1 #SCKK
2014 Total Memorabilia Autographed Memorabilia Silver /10 #SC-KK
2014 Total Memorabilia Black and White /99 #13
2014 Total Memorabilia Clear Cuts Blue /175 #CCUKK
2014 Total Memorabilia Clear Cuts Melting /25 #CCUKK
2014 Total Memorabilia Dual Swatch Gold /150 #TMKK
2014 Total Memorabilia Gold /175 #13
2014 Total Memorabilia Quad Swatch Melting /25 #TMKK
2014 Total Memorabilia Red #13
2014 Total Memorabilia Single Swatch Silver /275 #TMKK
2014 Total Memorabilia Triple Swatch Blue /99 #TMKK
2015 Press Pass #19
2015 Press Pass #89
2015 Press Pass #100
2015 Press Pass Burning Rubber Blue /50 #BRKK
2015 Press Pass Burning Rubber Gold #BRKK
2015 Press Pass Burning Rubber Green /10 #BRKK
2015 Press Pass Burning Rubber Letterman /8 #BRLEKK
2015 Press Pass Burning Rubber Melting /1 #BRKK
2015 Press Pass Cup Chase #19

2015 Press Pass Cup Chase #89
2015 Press Pass Cup Chase #100
2015 Press Pass Cup Chase Blue /25 #19
2015 Press Pass Cup Chase Blue /25 #89
2015 Press Pass Cup Chase Blue /25 #100
2015 Press Pass Cup Chase Gold /75 #19
2015 Press Pass Cup Chase Gold /75 #89
2015 Press Pass Cup Chase Gold /75 #100
2015 Press Pass Cup Chase Green /10 #19
2015 Press Pass Cup Chase Green /10 #89
2015 Press Pass Cup Chase Green /10 #100
2015 Press Pass Cup Chase Melting /1 #19
2015 Press Pass Cup Chase Melting /1 #89
2015 Press Pass Cup Chase Melting /1 #100
2015 Press Pass Cup Chase Three Wide Blue /25 #3WKK
2015 Press Pass Cup Chase Three Wide Gold /50 #3WKK
2015 Press Pass Cup Chase Three Wide Green /10 #3WKK
2015 Press Pass Cup Chase Three Wide Melting /1 #3WKK
2015 Press Pass Cup Chase Upper Cuts /13 #UCKK
2015 Press Pass Cuts Blue /25 #CCCKK
2015 Press Pass Cuts Gold /50 #CCCKK
2015 Press Pass Cuts Green /10 #CCCKK
2015 Press Pass Cuts Melting /1 #CCCKK
2015 Press Pass Four Wide Signature Edition Blue /25 #4WKK
2015 Press Pass Four Wide Signature Edition Gold /50 #4WKK
2015 Press Pass Four Wide Signature Edition Green /10 #4WKK
2015 Press Pass Four Wide Signature Edition Melting /1 #4WKK
2015 Press Pass Pit Road Pieces Blue /25 #PPMKK
2015 Press Pass Pit Road Pieces Gold /50 #PPMKK
2015 Press Pass Pit Road Pieces Green /10 #PPMKK
2015 Press Pass Pit Road Pieces Melting /1 #PPMKK
2015 Press Pass Pit Road Pieces Signature Edition Blue /25 #PRPKK
2015 Press Pass Pit Road Pieces Signature Edition Gold /50 #PRPKK
2015 Press Pass Pit Road Pieces Signature Edition Green /10 #PRPKK
2015 Press Pass Pit Road Pieces Signature Edition Melting /1 #PRPKK
2015 Press Pass Purple #19
2015 Press Pass Purple #89
2015 Press Pass Purple #100
2015 Press Pass Red #19
2015 Press Pass Red #89
2015 Press Pass Red #100
2015 Press Pass Signings Blue /15 #PPSKK
2015 Press Pass Signings Gold #PPSKK
2015 Press Pass Signings Green /5 #PPSKK
2015 Press Pass Signings Melting /1 #PPSKK
2015 Press Pass Signings Red /10 #PPSKK
2016 Certified #61
2016 Certified #14
2016 Certified Complete Materials /199 #11
2016 Certified Complete Materials Mirror Black /1 #11
2016 Certified Complete Materials Mirror Blue /50 #11
2016 Certified Complete Materials Mirror Gold /25 #11
2016 Certified Complete Materials Mirror Green /5 #11
2016 Certified Complete Materials Mirror Orange /99 #11
2016 Certified Complete Materials Mirror Purple /10 #11
2016 Certified Complete Materials Mirror Red /75 #11
2016 Certified Complete Materials Mirror Silver /99 #11
2016 Certified Epix /199 #7
2016 Certified Epix Mirror Black /1 #7
2016 Certified Epix Mirror Blue /50 #7
2016 Certified Epix Mirror Gold /25 #7
2016 Certified Epix Mirror Green /5 #7
2016 Certified Epix Mirror Orange /99 #7
2016 Certified Epix Mirror Purple /10 #7
2016 Certified Epix Mirror Red /75 #7
2016 Certified Epix Mirror Silver /99 #7
2016 Certified Gold Team /199 #14
2016 Certified Gold Team Mirror Black /1 #14
2016 Certified Gold Team Mirror Blue /50 #14
2016 Certified Gold Team Mirror Gold /25 #14
2016 Certified Gold Team Mirror Green /5 #14
2016 Certified Gold Team Mirror Orange /99 #14
2016 Certified Gold Team Mirror Purple /10 #14
2016 Certified Gold Team Mirror Red /75 #14
2016 Certified Gold Team Mirror Silver /99 #14
2016 Certified Mirror Black /1 #14
2016 Certified Mirror Black /1 #61
2016 Certified Mirror Blue /50 #14
2016 Certified Mirror Blue /50 #61
2016 Certified Mirror Gold /25 #14
2016 Certified Mirror Gold /25 #61
2016 Certified Mirror Green /5 #14
2016 Certified Mirror Green /5 #61
2016 Certified Mirror Orange /99 #14
2016 Certified Mirror Orange /99 #61
2016 Certified Mirror Purple /10 #14
2016 Certified Mirror Purple /10 #61
2016 Certified Mirror Red /75 #14
2016 Certified Mirror Red /75 #61
2016 Certified Mirror Silver /99 #14
2016 Certified Mirror Silver /99 #61
2016 Certified Signatures /50 #13
2016 Certified Signatures Mirror Black /1 #13
2016 Certified Signatures Mirror Blue /25 #13
2016 Certified Signatures Mirror Gold /15 #13
2016 Certified Signatures Mirror Green /5 #13
2016 Certified Signatures Mirror Orange /5 #13
2016 Certified Signatures Mirror Purple /10 #13
2016 Certified Signatures Mirror Red /35 #13
2016 Certified Signatures Mirror Silver /4 #13
2016 Certified Skills /199 #10
2016 Certified Skills Mirror Black /1 #10
2016 Certified Skills Mirror Blue /50 #10
2016 Certified Skills Mirror Gold /25 #10
2016 Certified Skills Mirror Green /5 #10
2016 Certified Skills Mirror Orange /99 #10
2016 Certified Skills Mirror Purple /10 #10
2016 Certified Skills Mirror Red /75 #10
2016 Certified Skills Mirror Silver /99 #10
2016 Certified Sprint Cup Signature Swatches /50 #10
2016 Certified Sprint Cup Signature Swatches Mirror Black /1 #10
2016 Certified Sprint Cup Signature Swatches Mirror Blue /25 #10
2016 Certified Sprint Cup Signature Swatches Mirror Gold /15 #10
2016 Certified Sprint Cup Signature Swatches Mirror Green /5 #10
2016 Certified Sprint Cup Signature Swatches Mirror Orange /5 #10
2016 Certified Sprint Cup Signature Swatches Mirror Purple /10 #10
2016 Certified Sprint Cup Signature Swatches Mirror Red /35 #10
2016 Certified Sprint Cup Signature Swatches Mirror Silver /4 #10
2016 Certified Sprint Cup Swatches /185 #29
2016 Certified Sprint Cup Swatches Mirror Black /1 #29
2016 Certified Sprint Cup Swatches Mirror Blue /50 #29
2016 Certified Sprint Cup Swatches Mirror Gold /25 #29
2016 Certified Sprint Cup Swatches Mirror Green /5 #29
2016 Certified Sprint Cup Swatches Mirror Orange /99 #29
2016 Certified Sprint Cup Swatches Mirror Purple /10 #29
2016 Certified Sprint Cup Swatches Mirror Red /75 #29
2016 Certified Sprint Cup Swatches Mirror Silver /99 #29
2016 Panini National Treasures /25 #9
2016 Panini National Treasures Black /5 #9
2016 Panini National Treasures Blue /1 #9
2016 Panini National Treasures Dual Driver Materials /25 #7
2016 Panini National Treasures Dual Driver Materials Black /5 #7
2016 Panini National Treasures Dual Driver Materials Blue /1 #7
2016 Panini National Treasures Dual Driver Materials Gold /10 #7
2016 Panini National Treasures Dual Driver Materials Printing Plates Black /1 #7
2016 Panini National Treasures Dual Driver Materials Printing Plates Cyan /1 #7
2016 Panini National Treasures Dual Driver Materials Printing Plates Magenta /1 #7
2016 Panini National Treasures Dual Driver Materials Printing Plates Yellow /1 #7
2016 Panini National Treasures Dual Driver Materials Silver /15 #7
2016 Panini National Treasures Dual Signatures /25 #5
2016 Panini National Treasures Dual Signatures Black /10 #5
2016 Panini National Treasures Dual Signatures Blue /1 #5
2016 Panini National Treasures Dual Signatures Gold /20 #5
2016 Panini National Treasures Eight Signatures /15 #1
2016 Panini National Treasures Eight Signatures Black /5 #1
2016 Panini National Treasures Eight Signatures Blue /1 #1
2016 Panini National Treasures Eight Signatures Gold /10 #1
2016 Panini National Treasures Firesuit Materials Black /5 #10
2016 Panini National Treasures Firesuit Materials Blue /1 #10
2016 Panini National Treasures Firesuit Materials Laundry Tag /1 #10
2016 Panini National Treasures Firesuit Materials Printing Plates Black /1 #10
2016 Panini National Treasures Firesuit Materials Printing Plates Cyan /1 #10
2016 Panini National Treasures Firesuit Materials Printing Plates Magenta /1 #10
2016 Panini National Treasures Firesuit Materials Printing Plates Yellow /1 #10
2016 Panini National Treasures Gold /15 #9
2016 Panini National Treasures Jumbo Firesuit Patch Signature Booklet Alpine Stars /2 #14
2016 Panini National Treasures Jumbo Firesuit Patch Signature Booklet Associate Sponsor 1 /1 #14
2016 Panini National Treasures Jumbo Firesuit Patch Signature Booklet Associate Sponsor 10 /1 #14
2016 Panini National Treasures Jumbo Firesuit Patch Signature Booklet Associate Sponsor 11 /1 #14
2016 Panini National Treasures Jumbo Firesuit Patch Signature Booklet Associate Sponsor 12 /1 #14
2016 Panini National Treasures Jumbo Firesuit Patch Signature Booklet Associate Sponsor 13 /1 #14
2016 Panini National Treasures Jumbo Firesuit Patch Signature Booklet Associate Sponsor 14 /1 #14
2016 Panini National Treasures Jumbo Firesuit Patch Signature Booklet Associate Sponsor 2 /1 #14
2016 Panini National Treasures Jumbo Firesuit Patch Signature Booklet Associate Sponsor 3 /1 #14
2016 Panini National Treasures Jumbo Firesuit Patch Signature Booklet Associate Sponsor 4 /1 #14
2016 Panini National Treasures Jumbo Firesuit Patch Signature Booklet Associate Sponsor 5 /1 #14
2016 Panini National Treasures Jumbo Firesuit Patch Signature Booklet Associate Sponsor 6 /1 #14
2016 Panini National Treasures Jumbo Firesuit Patch Signature Booklet Associate Sponsor 7 /1 #14
2016 Panini National Treasures Jumbo Firesuit Patch Signature Booklet Associate Sponsor 8 /1 #14
2016 Panini National Treasures Jumbo Firesuit Patch Signature Booklet Associate Sponsor 9 /1 #14
2016 Panini National Treasures Jumbo Firesuit Patch Signature Booklet Goodyear /2 #14
2016 Panini National Treasures Jumbo Firesuit Patch Signature Booklet Manufacturers Logo /1 #14
2016 Panini National Treasures Jumbo Firesuit Patch Signature Booklet NASCAR /1 #14
2016 Panini National Treasures Jumbo Firesuit Patch Signature Booklet Sprint Cup Logo /1 #14
2016 Panini National Treasures Jumbo Firesuit Patch Signature Booklet Sunoco /1 #14
2016 Panini National Treasures Jumbo Firesuit Signatures Black /5 #14
2016 Panini National Treasures Jumbo Firesuit Signatures Blue /1 #14
2016 Panini National Treasures Jumbo Firesuit Signatures Printing Plates Black /1 #14
2016 Panini National Treasures Jumbo Firesuit Signatures Printing Plates Cyan /1 #14
2016 Panini National Treasures Jumbo Firesuit Signatures Printing Plates Magenta /1 #14
2016 Panini National Treasures Jumbo Firesuit Signatures Printing Plates Yellow /1 #14
2016 Panini National Treasures Jumbo Sheet Metal Signatures Black /5 #8
2016 Panini National Treasures Jumbo Sheet Metal Signatures Blue /1 #8
2016 Panini National Treasures Jumbo Sheet Metal Signatures Gold /10 #8
2016 Panini National Treasures Jumbo Sheet Metal Signatures Printing Plates Black /1 #8
2016 Panini National Treasures Jumbo Sheet Metal Signatures Printing Plates Cyan /1 #8
2016 Panini National Treasures Jumbo Sheet Metal Signatures Printing Plates Magenta /1 #8
2016 Panini National Treasures Jumbo Sheet Metal Signatures Printing Plates Yellow /1 #8
2016 Panini National Treasures Jumbo Sheet Metal Signatures Silver /15 #8
2016 Panini National Treasures Printing Plates Black /1 #9
2016 Panini National Treasures Printing Plates Cyan /1 #9
2016 Panini National Treasures Printing Plates Magenta /1 #9
2016 Panini National Treasures Printing Plates Yellow /1 #9
2016 Panini National Treasures Quad Driver Materials /25 #1
2016 Panini National Treasures Quad Driver Materials Black /5 #1
2016 Panini National Treasures Quad Driver Materials Blue /1 #1
2016 Panini National Treasures Quad Driver Materials Gold /10 #1
2016 Panini National Treasures Quad Driver Materials Printing Plates Black /1 #1
2016 Panini National Treasures Quad Driver Materials Printing Plates Cyan /1 #1
2016 Panini National Treasures Quad Driver Materials Printing Plates Magenta /1 #1
2016 Panini National Treasures Quad Driver Materials Printing Plates Yellow /1 #1
2016 Panini National Treasures Quad Driver Materials Silver /15 #1
2016 Panini National Treasures Quad Materials /25 #10
2016 Panini National Treasures Quad Materials Black /5 #10
2016 Panini National Treasures Quad Materials Blue /1 #10
2016 Panini National Treasures Quad Materials Gold /10 #10
2016 Panini National Treasures Quad Materials Printing Plates Black /1 #10
2016 Panini National Treasures Quad Materials Printing Plates Cyan /1 #10
2016 Panini National Treasures Quad Materials Printing Plates Magenta /1 #10
2016 Panini National Treasures Quad Materials Printing Plates Yellow /1 #10
2016 Panini National Treasures Quad Materials Silver /15 #10
2016 Panini National Treasures Sheet Metal Materials /25 #10
2016 Panini National Treasures Sheet Metal Materials Black /5 #10
2016 Panini National Treasures Sheet Metal Materials Blue /1 #10
2016 Panini National Treasures Sheet Metal Materials Gold /10 #10
2016 Panini National Treasures Sheet Metal Materials Printing Plates Black /1 #10
2016 Panini National Treasures Sheet Metal Materials Printing Plates Cyan /1 #10
2016 Panini National Treasures Sheet Metal Materials Printing Plates Magenta /1 #10
2016 Panini National Treasures Sheet Metal Materials Printing Plates Yellow /1 #10
2016 Panini National Treasures Sheet Metal Materials Silver /15 #10
2016 Panini National Treasures Signature Dual Materials Black /5 #14
2016 Panini National Treasures Signature Dual Materials Blue /1 #14
2016 Panini National Treasures Signature Dual Materials Gold /10 #14
2016 Panini National Treasures Signature Dual Materials Printing Plates Black /1 #14
2016 Panini National Treasures Signature Dual Materials Printing Plates Cyan /1 #14
2016 Panini National Treasures Signature Dual Materials Printing Plates Magenta /1 #14
2016 Panini National Treasures Signature Dual Materials Printing Plates Yellow /1 #14
2016 Panini National Treasures Signature Dual Materials Silver /15 #14
2016 Panini National Treasures Signature Firesuit Materials /20 #14
2016 Panini National Treasures Signature Firesuit Materials Black /5 #14
2016 Panini National Treasures Signature Firesuit Materials Blue /1 #14
2016 Panini National Treasures Signature Firesuit Materials Gold /10 #14
2016 Panini National Treasures Signature Firesuit Materials Laundry Tag /1 #14
2016 Panini National Treasures Signature Firesuit Materials Printing Plates Black /1 #14
2016 Panini National Treasures Signature Firesuit Materials Printing Plates Cyan /1 #14
2016 Panini National Treasures Signature Firesuit Materials Printing Plates Magenta /1 #14
2016 Panini National Treasures Signature Firesuit Materials Printing Plates Yellow /1 #14
2016 Panini National Treasures Signature Firesuit Materials Silver /15 #14
2016 Panini National Treasures Signature Quad Materials Black /5 #14
2016 Panini National Treasures Signature Quad Materials Blue /1 #14
2016 Panini National Treasures Signature Quad Materials Gold /10 #14
2016 Panini National Treasures Signature Quad Materials Printing Plates Black /1 #14
2016 Panini National Treasures Signature Quad Materials Printing Plates Cyan /1 #14
2016 Panini National Treasures Signature Quad Materials Printing Plates Magenta /1 #14
2016 Panini National Treasures Signature Quad Materials Printing Plates Yellow /1 #14
2016 Panini National Treasures Signature Quad Materials Silver /15 #14
2016 Panini National Treasures Signature Sheet Metal Materials Black /5 #14
2016 Panini National Treasures Signature Sheet Metal Materials Blue /1 #14
2016 Panini National Treasures Signature Sheet Metal Materials Printing Plates Black /1 #14
2016 Panini National Treasures Signature Sheet Metal Materials Printing Plates Cyan /1 #14
2016 Panini National Treasures Signature Sheet Metal Materials Printing Plates Magenta /1 #14
2016 Panini National Treasures Signature Sheet Metal Materials Printing Plates Yellow /1 #14
2016 Panini National Treasures Signatures /35 #11
2016 Panini National Treasures Signatures Black /5 #11
2016 Panini National Treasures Signatures Blue /1 #11
2016 Panini National Treasures Signatures Gold /15 #11
2016 Panini National Treasures Signatures Printing Plates Black /1 #11
2016 Panini National Treasures Signatures Printing Plates Cyan /1 #11
2016 Panini National Treasures Signatures Printing Plates Magenta /1 #11
2016 Panini National Treasures Signatures Printing Plates Yellow /1 #11
2016 Panini National Treasures Signatures Silver /25 #11
2016 Panini National Treasures Silver /20 #9
2016 Panini National Treasures Six Signatures /25 #8
2016 Panini National Treasures Six Signatures Black /10 #8
2016 Panini National Treasures Six Signatures Blue /1 #8
2016 Panini National Treasures Six Signatures Gold /15 #8
2016 Panini National Treasures Timelines /25 #8
2016 Panini National Treasures Timelines Black /5 #8
2016 Panini National Treasures Timelines Blue /1 #8
2016 Panini National Treasures Timelines Printing Plates Black /1 #8
2016 Panini National Treasures Timelines Printing Plates Cyan /1 #8
2016 Panini National Treasures Timelines Printing Plates Magenta /1 #8
2016 Panini National Treasures Timelines Printing Plates Yellow /1 #8
2016 Panini National Treasures Trio Driver Materials /25 #4
2016 Panini National Treasures Trio Driver Materials /25 #11
2016 Panini National Treasures Trio Driver Materials Black /5 #4
2016 Panini National Treasures Trio Driver Materials Black /5 #11
2016 Panini National Treasures Trio Driver Materials Blue /1 #4
2016 Panini National Treasures Trio Driver Materials Blue /1 #11
2016 Panini National Treasures Trio Driver Materials Gold /10 #4
2016 Panini National Treasures Trio Driver Materials Gold /10 #11
2016 Panini National Treasures Trio Driver Materials Printing Plates Black /1 #4
2016 Panini National Treasures Trio Driver Materials Printing Plates Black /1 #11
2016 Panini National Treasures Trio Driver Materials Printing Plates Cyan /1 #4
2016 Panini National Treasures Trio Driver Materials Printing Plates Cyan /1 #11
2016 Panini National Treasures Trio Driver Materials Printing Plates Magenta /1 #4
2016 Panini National Treasures Trio Driver Materials Printing Plates Magenta /1 #11
2016 Panini National Treasures Trio Driver Materials Printing Plates Yellow /1 #4
2016 Panini National Treasures Trio Driver Materials Printing Plates Yellow /1 #11
2016 Panini National Treasures Trio Driver Materials Silver /15 #4
2016 Panini National Treasures Trio Driver Materials Silver /15 #11
2016 Panini National Treasures Winning Signatures /25 #10
2016 Panini National Treasures Winning Signatures Black /5 #10
2016 Panini National Treasures Winning Signatures Blue /1 #10
2016 Panini National Treasures Winning Signatures Gold /15 #10
2016 Panini National Treasures Winning Signatures Printing Plates Black /1 #10
2016 Panini National Treasures Winning Signatures Printing Plates Cyan /1 #10
2016 Panini National Treasures Winning Signatures Printing Plates Magenta /1 #10
2016 Panini National Treasures Winning Signatures Printing Plates Yellow /1 #10
2016 Panini National Treasures Winning Signatures Silver /20 #10
2016 Panini Prizm #79
2016 Panini Prizm #56
2016 Panini Prizm #5A
2016 Panini Prizm Autographs Prizms #66
2016 Panini Prizm Autographs Prizms Black /3 #66
2016 Panini Prizm Autographs Prizms Blue Flag /50 #66
2016 Panini Prizm Autographs Prizms Camo /5 #66
2016 Panini Prizm Autographs Prizms Checkered Flag /1 #66
2016 Panini Prizm Autographs Prizms Gold /10 #66
2016 Panini Prizm Autographs Prizms Green Flag /75 #66
2016 Panini Prizm Autographs Prizms Rainbow /24 #66
2016 Panini Prizm Autographs Prizms Red Flag /25 #66
2016 Panini Prizm Autographs Prizms Red White and Blue /10 #66
2016 Panini Prizm Autographs Prizms White Flag /5 #66
2016 Panini Prizm Competitors #9
2016 Panini Prizm Competitors Prizms #9
2016 Panini Prizm Competitors Prizms Checkered Flag /1 #9
2016 Panini Prizm Competitors Prizms Gold /10 #9
2016 Panini Prizm Firesuit Fabrics /50 #18
2016 Panini Prizm Firesuit Fabrics Prizms Blue Flag /10 #18
2016 Panini Prizm Firesuit Fabrics Prizms Checkered Flag /1 #18
2016 Panini Prizm Firesuit Fabrics Prizms Green Flag /25 #18
2016 Panini Prizm Firesuit Fabrics Prizms Red Flag /5 #18
2016 Panini Prizm Firesuit Fabrics Team /149 #18
2016 Panini Prizm Firesuit Fabrics Team Prizms Blue Flag /10 #18
2016 Panini Prizm Firesuit Fabrics Team Prizms Checkered Flag /1 #18
2016 Panini Prizm Firesuit Fabrics Team Prizms Green Flag /25 #18
2016 Panini Prizm Firesuit Fabrics Team Prizms Red Flag /5 #18
2016 Panini Prizm Machinery #5
2016 Panini Prizm Machinery Prizms #5
2016 Panini Prizm Machinery Prizms Checkered Flag /1 #5
2016 Panini Prizm Machinery Prizms Gold /10 #5
2016 Panini Prizm Prizms #5A
2016 Panini Prizm Prizms #56
2016 Panini Prizm Prizms #79
2016 Panini Prizm Prizms Black /3 #5
2016 Panini Prizm Prizms Black /3 #56
2016 Panini Prizm Prizms Black /3 #79
2016 Panini Prizm Prizms Blue Flag /99 #5
2016 Panini Prizm Prizms Blue Flag /99 #56
2016 Panini Prizm Prizms Blue Flag /99 #79
2016 Panini Prizm Prizms Camo /5 #5
2016 Panini Prizm Prizms Camo /5 #56
2016 Panini Prizm Prizms Camo /5 #79
2016 Panini Prizm Prizms Checkered Flag /1 #5A
2016 Panini Prizm Prizms Checkered Flag /1 #56
2016 Panini Prizm Prizms Checkered Flag /1 #79
2016 Panini Prizm Prizms Gold /10 #5A
2016 Panini Prizm Prizms Gold /10 #56
2016 Panini Prizm Prizms Gold /10 #79
2016 Panini Prizm Prizms Green Flag /149 #5
2016 Panini Prizm Prizms Green Flag /149 #56
2016 Panini Prizm Prizms Green Flag /149 #79
2016 Panini Prizm Prizms Rainbow /24 #5
2016 Panini Prizm Prizms Rainbow /24 #56
2016 Panini Prizm Prizms Rainbow /24 #79
2016 Panini Prizm Prizms Red Flag /75 #5
2016 Panini Prizm Prizms Red Flag /75 #56
2016 Panini Prizm Prizms Red Flag /75 #79
2016 Panini Prizm Prizms Red White and Blue #5
2016 Panini Prizm Prizms Red White and Blue #56
2016 Panini Prizm Prizms Red White and Blue #79
2016 Panini Prizm Prizms White Flag /5 #5
2016 Panini Prizm Prizms White Flag /5 #56
2016 Panini Prizm Prizms White Flag /5 #79
2016 Panini Prizm Race Used Tire #11
2016 Panini Prizm Race Used Tire Prizms Blue Flag /49 #11
2016 Panini Prizm Race Used Tire Prizms Checkered Flag /1 #11
2016 Panini Prizm Race Used Tire Prizms Green Flag /99 #11
2016 Panini Prizm Race Used Tire Prizms Red Flag /25 #11
2016 Panini Prizm Race Used Tire Team #10
2016 Panini Prizm Race Used Tire Team Prizms Blue Flag /75 #10
2016 Panini Prizm Race Used Tire Team Prizms Checkered Flag /1 #10
2016 Panini Prizm Race Used Tire Team Prizms Green Flag /149 #10
2016 Panini Prizm Race Used Tire Team Prizms Red Flag /10 #10
2016 Panini Torque #20
2016 Panini Torque #60
2016 Panini Torque #75
2016 Panini Torque Artist Proof /50 #20
2016 Panini Torque Artist Proof /50 #60
2016 Panini Torque Artist Proof /50 #75
2016 Panini Torque Blackout /1 #20
2016 Panini Torque Blackout /1 #60
2016 Panini Torque Blackout /1 #75
2016 Panini Torque Blue /125 #20
2016 Panini Torque Blue /125 #60
2016 Panini Torque Blue /125 #75
2016 Panini Torque Clear Vision #19
2016 Panini Torque Clear Vision Blue /99 #19
2016 Panini Torque Clear Vision Gold /149 #19
2016 Panini Torque Clear Vision Green /25 #19
2016 Panini Torque Clear Vision Purple /10 #19
2016 Panini Torque Clear Vision Red /49 #19
2016 Panini Torque Gold #20
2016 Panini Torque Gold #60
2016 Panini Torque Gold #75
2016 Panini Torque Helmets #8
2016 Panini Torque Helmets Blue /99 #8
2016 Panini Torque Helmets Checkerboard /10 #8
2016 Panini Torque Helmets Green /25 #8
2016 Panini Torque Helmets Red /49 #8
2016 Panini Torque Holo Gold /5 #20
2016 Panini Torque Holo Gold /5 #60
2016 Panini Torque Holo Gold /5 #75
2016 Panini Torque Holo Silver /10 #20
2016 Panini Torque Holo Silver /10 #60
2016 Panini Torque Holo Silver /10 #75
2016 Panini Torque Horsepower Heroes #18
2016 Panini Torque Horsepower Heroes Gold /199 #18
2016 Panini Torque Horsepower Heroes Holo Silver /99 #18
2016 Panini Torque Metal Materials /249 #14
2016 Panini Torque Metal Materials Blue /99 #14
2016 Panini Torque Metal Materials Green /25 #14
2016 Panini Torque Metal Materials Purple /10 #14
2016 Panini Torque Metal Materials Red /49 #14
2016 Panini Torque Painted to Perfection #8
2016 Panini Torque Painted to Perfection Blue /99 #8
2016 Panini Torque Painted to Perfection Checkerboard /10 #8
2016 Panini Torque Painted to Perfection Green /25 #8
2016 Panini Torque Painted to Perfection Red /49 #8
2016 Panini Torque Pairings Materials /125 #3
2016 Panini Torque Pairings Materials Blue /99 #3
2016 Panini Torque Pairings Materials Green /25 #3
2016 Panini Torque Pairings Materials Purple /10 #3
2016 Panini Torque Pairings Materials Red /49 #3
2016 Panini Torque Pole Position #16
2016 Panini Torque Pole Position Blue /99 #16
2016 Panini Torque Pole Position Checkerboard /10 #16
2016 Panini Torque Pole Position Green /25 #16
2016 Panini Torque Pole Position Red /49 #16
2016 Panini Torque Printing Plates Black /1 #20
2016 Panini Torque Printing Plates Black /1 #60
2016 Panini Torque Printing Plates Black /1 #75
2016 Panini Torque Printing Plates Cyan /1 #20
2016 Panini Torque Printing Plates Cyan /1 #60
2016 Panini Torque Printing Plates Cyan /1 #75
2016 Panini Torque Printing Plates Magenta /1 #20
2016 Panini Torque Printing Plates Magenta /1 #60
2016 Panini Torque Printing Plates Magenta /1 #75
2016 Panini Torque Printing Plates Yellow /1 #20
2016 Panini Torque Printing Plates Yellow /1 #60
2016 Panini Torque Printing Plates Yellow /1 #75
2016 Panini Torque Purple /25 #20
2016 Panini Torque Purple /25 #60
2016 Panini Torque Purple /25 #75
2016 Panini Torque Quad Materials /199 #8
2016 Panini Torque Quad Materials Blue /99 #8
2016 Panini Torque Quad Materials Green /25 #8
2016 Panini Torque Quad Materials Purple /10 #8
2016 Panini Torque Quad Materials Red /49 #8
2016 Panini Torque Red /99 #20
2016 Panini Torque Red /99 #60
2016 Panini Torque Red /99 #75
2016 Panini Torque Rubber Relics /399 #14
2016 Panini Torque Rubber Relics Blue /99 #14
2016 Panini Torque Rubber Relics Green /25 #14
2016 Panini Torque Rubber Relics Purple /10 #14
2016 Panini Torque Rubber Relics Red /49 #14
2016 Panini Torque Shades #9
2016 Panini Torque Shades Gold /199 #9
2016 Panini Torque Shades Holo Silver /99 #9
2016 Panini Torque Silhouettes Firesuit Autographs /50 #13
2016 Panini Torque Silhouettes Firesuit Autographs Blue /35 #13
2016 Panini Torque Silhouettes Firesuit Autographs Green /25 #13
2016 Panini Torque Silhouettes Firesuit Autographs Purple /10 #13
2016 Panini Torque Silhouettes Firesuit Autographs Red /30 #13
2016 Panini Torque Silhouettes Sheet Metal Autographs /50 #16
2016 Panini Torque Silhouettes Sheet Metal Autographs Blue /35 #16
2016 Panini Torque Silhouettes Sheet Metal Autographs Green /25 #16
2016 Panini Torque Silhouettes Sheet Metal Autographs Purple /10 #16
2016 Panini Torque Silhouettes Sheet Metal Autographs Red /30 #16
2016 Panini Torque Superstar Vision #5
2016 Panini Torque Superstar Vision Blue /99 #5
2016 Panini Torque Superstar Vision Gold /149 #5
2016 Panini Torque Superstar Vision Green /25 #5
2016 Panini Torque Superstar Vision Purple /10 #5
2016 Panini Torque Superstar Vision Red /49 #5
2016 Panini Torque Test Proof Black /1 #20
2016 Panini Torque Test Proof Black /1 #60
2016 Panini Torque Test Proof Black /1 #75
2016 Panini Torque Test Proof Cyan /1 #20
2016 Panini Torque Test Proof Cyan /1 #60
2016 Panini Torque Test Proof Cyan /1 #75
2016 Panini Torque Test Proof Magenta /1 #20
2016 Panini Torque Test Proof Magenta /1 #60
2016 Panini Torque Test Proof Magenta /1 #75
2016 Panini Torque Test Proof Yellow /1 #20
2016 Panini Torque Test Proof Yellow /1 #60
2016 Panini Torque Test Proof Yellow /1 #75
2016 Panini Torque Victory Laps #9
2016 Panini Torque Victory Laps Gold /199 #9
2016 Panini Torque Victory Laps Holo Silver /99 #9
2016 Panini Torque Winning Vision #14
2016 Panini Torque Winning Vision Blue /99 #14
2016 Panini Torque Winning Vision Gold /149 #14
2016 Panini Torque Winning Vision Green /25 #14
2016 Panini Torque Winning Vision Purple /10 #14
2016 Panini Torque Winning Vision Red /49 #14
2017 Donruss #13
2017 Donruss #51
2017 Donruss #105
2017 Donruss #150
2017 Donruss #99
2017 Donruss Artist Proof /25 #13
2017 Donruss Artist Proof /25 #51
2017 Donruss Artist Proof /25 #99
2017 Donruss Artist Proof /25 #150
2017 Donruss Artist Proof /25 #105
2017 Donruss Blue Foil /299 #13
2017 Donruss Blue Foil /299 #99
2017 Donruss Blue Foil /299 #51
2017 Donruss Blue Foil /299 #150
2017 Donruss Blue Foil /299 #105
2017 Donruss Dual Rubber Relics #9
2017 Donruss Dual Rubber Relics Holo Black /1 #9
2017 Donruss Dual Rubber Relics Holo Gold /25 #9
2017 Donruss Gold Foil /499 #13
2017 Donruss Gold Foil /499 #99
2017 Donruss Gold Foil /499 #150
2017 Donruss Gold Foil /499 #51
2017 Donruss Gold Foil /499 #105
2017 Donruss Gold Press Proof /99 #13
2017 Donruss Gold Press Proof /99 #51
2017 Donruss Gold Press Proof /99 #99
2017 Donruss Gold Press Proof /99 #150
2017 Donruss Gold Press Proof /99 #105
2017 Donruss Green Foil /199 #13
2017 Donruss Green Foil /199 #51
2017 Donruss Green Foil /199 #99
2017 Donruss Green Foil /199 #150
2017 Donruss Green Foil /199 #105
2017 Donruss Press Proof /49 #13
2017 Donruss Press Proof /49 #51
2017 Donruss Press Proof /49 #99
2017 Donruss Press Proof /49 #150
2017 Donruss Press Proof /49 #105
2017 Donruss Printing Plates Black /1 #13
2017 Donruss Printing Plates Black /1 #51
2017 Donruss Printing Plates Black /1 #99
2017 Donruss Printing Plates Black /1 #150
2017 Donruss Printing Plates Black /1 #105
2017 Donruss Printing Plates Cyan /1 #13
2017 Donruss Printing Plates Cyan /1 #51
2017 Donruss Printing Plates Cyan /1 #99
2017 Donruss Printing Plates Cyan /1 #150
2017 Donruss Printing Plates Cyan /1 #105
2017 Donruss Printing Plates Magenta /1 #13
2017 Donruss Printing Plates Magenta /1 #99
2017 Donruss Printing Plates Magenta /1 #150
2017 Donruss Printing Plates Magenta /1 #51
2017 Donruss Printing Plates Magenta /1 #105
2017 Donruss Printing Plates Yellow /1 #13
2017 Donruss Printing Plates Yellow /1 #99
2017 Donruss Printing Plates Yellow /1 #150
2017 Donruss Printing Plates Yellow /1 #51
2017 Donruss Printing Plates Yellow /1 #105
2017 Donruss Retro Relics 1984 Holo Black /10 #25
2017 Donruss Retro Relics 1984 Holo Gold /99 #25
2017 Donruss Retro Signatures 1984 #14
2017 Donruss Retro Signatures 1984 Holo Black /1 #14
2017 Donruss Retro Signatures 1984 Holo Gold /25 #14
2017 Donruss Rubber Relics #28
2017 Donruss Rubber Relics #29
2017 Donruss Rubber Relics Holo Black /1 #28
2017 Donruss Rubber Relics Holo Black /1 #29
2017 Donruss Rubber Relics Holo Gold /25 #28
2017 Donruss Rubber Relics Holo Gold /25 #29
2017 Panini Instant Nascar #19
2017 Panini Instant Nascar Black /1 #19
2017 Panini Instant Nascar Green /10 #19
2017 Panini National Treasures /25 #14
2017 Panini National Treasures Associate Sponsor Patch Signatures 1 /1 #13
2017 Panini National Treasures Associate Sponsor Patch Signatures 10 /1 #13
2017 Panini National Treasures Associate Sponsor Patch Signatures 11 /1 #13
2017 Panini National Treasures Associate Sponsor Patch Signatures 2 /1 #13
2017 Panini National Treasures Associate Sponsor Patch Signatures 3 /1 #13
2017 Panini National Treasures Associate Sponsor Patch Signatures 4 /1 #13
2017 Panini National Treasures Associate Sponsor Patch Signatures 5 /1 #13
2017 Panini National Treasures Associate Sponsor Patch Signatures 6 /1 #13
2017 Panini National Treasures Associate Sponsor Patch Signatures 7 /1 #13
2017 Panini National Treasures Associate Sponsor Patch Signatures 8 /1 #13
2017 Panini National Treasures Associate Sponsor Patch Signatures 9 /1 #13
2017 Panini National Treasures Car Manufacturer Patch Signatures /1 #13
2017 Panini National Treasures Century Black /1 #14
2017 Panini National Treasures Century Gold /15 #14
2017 Panini National Treasures Century Green /5 #14
2017 Panini National Treasures Century Holo Gold /10 #14
2017 Panini National Treasures Century Holo Silver /20 #14
2017 Panini National Treasures Century Laundry Tags /1 #14
2017 Panini National Treasures Dual Firesuit Materials Black /1 #9
2017 Panini National Treasures Dual Firesuit Materials Green /5 #9
2017 Panini National Treasures Dual Firesuit Materials Laundry Tag /1 #9
2017 Panini National Treasures Dual Firesuit Materials Printing Plates Black /1 #9
2017 Panini National Treasures Dual Firesuit Materials Printing Plates Cyan /1 #9
2017 Panini National Treasures Dual Firesuit Materials Printing Plates Magenta /1 #9
2017 Panini National Treasures Dual Firesuit Materials Printing Plates Yellow /1 #9
2017 Panini National Treasures Dual Firesuit Signatures /25 #9
2017 Panini National Treasures Dual Firesuit Signatures Black /1 #9
2017 Panini National Treasures Dual Firesuit Signatures Gold /15 #9
2017 Panini National Treasures Dual Firesuit Signatures Green /5 #9
2017 Panini National Treasures Dual Firesuit Signatures Holo Gold /10 #9
2017 Panini National Treasures Dual Firesuit Signatures Holo Silver /20 #9
2017 Panini National Treasures Dual Firesuit Signatures Laundry Tag /1 #9
2017 Panini National Treasures Dual Firesuit Signatures Printing Plates Black /1 #9
2017 Panini National Treasures Dual Firesuit Signatures Printing Plates Cyan /1 #9
2017 Panini National Treasures Dual Firesuit Signatures Printing Plates Magenta /1 #9
2017 Panini National Treasures Dual Firesuit Signatures Printing Plates Yellow /1 #9
2017 Panini National Treasures Dual Sheet Metal Materials /25 #5
2017 Panini National Treasures Dual Sheet Metal Materials Black /1 #5
2017 Panini National Treasures Dual Sheet Metal Materials Gold /15 #5
2017 Panini National Treasures Dual Sheet Metal Materials Green /5 #5
2017 Panini National Treasures Dual Sheet Metal Materials Holo Gold /10 #5
2017 Panini National Treasures Dual Sheet Metal Materials Holo Silver /20 #5
2017 Panini National Treasures Dual Sheet Metal Materials Printing Plates Black /1 #5
2017 Panini National Treasures Dual Sheet Metal Materials Printing Plates Cyan /1 #5
2017 Panini National Treasures Dual Sheet Metal Materials Printing Plates Magenta /1 #5
2017 Panini National Treasures Dual Sheet Metal Materials Printing Plates Yellow /1 #5
2017 Panini National Treasures Dual Sheet Metal Signatures /25 #8
2017 Panini National Treasures Dual Sheet Metal Signatures Black /1 #8
2017 Panini National Treasures Dual Sheet Metal Signatures Gold /15 #8
2017 Panini National Treasures Dual Sheet Metal Signatures Green /5 #8
2017 Panini National Treasures Dual Sheet Metal Signatures Holo Gold /10 #8
2017 Panini National Treasures Dual Sheet Metal Signatures Holo Silver /20 #8
2017 Panini National Treasures Dual Sheet Metal Signatures Printing Plates Black /1 #8
2017 Panini National Treasures Dual Sheet Metal Signatures Printing Plates Cyan /1 #8
2017 Panini National Treasures Dual Sheet Metal Signatures Printing Plates Magenta /1 #8
2017 Panini National Treasures Dual Sheet Metal Signatures Printing Plates Yellow /1 #8
2017 Panini National Treasures Dual Signature Materials /50 #3
2017 Panini National Treasures Dual Signature Materials Black /1 #3
2017 Panini National Treasures Dual Signature Materials Gold /15 #3
2017 Panini National Treasures Dual Signature Materials Green /5 #3
2017 Panini National Treasures Dual Signature Materials Holo Gold /10 #3
2017 Panini National Treasures Dual Signature Materials Holo Silver /25 #3
2017 Panini National Treasures Dual Signature Materials Laundry Tag /1 #3
2017 Panini National Treasures Firesuit Manufacturer Patch Signatures /1 #13
2017 Panini National Treasures Hats Off /13 #31
2017 Panini National Treasures Hats Off Gold /2 #31
2017 Panini National Treasures Hats Off Holo Gold /5 #31
2017 Panini National Treasures Hats Off Holo Silver /1 #31
2017 Panini National Treasures Hats Off Laundry Tag /6 #31
2017 Panini National Treasures Hats Off New Era /1 #31
2017 Panini National Treasures Hats Off Printing Plates Black /1 #31
2017 Panini National Treasures Hats Off Printing Plates Cyan /1 #31
2017 Panini National Treasures Hats Off Printing Plates Magenta /1 #31
2017 Panini National Treasures Hats Off Sponsor /10 #31
2017 Panini National Treasures Jumbo Firesuit Materials Black /1 #3
2017 Panini National Treasures Jumbo Firesuit Materials Green /5 #3
2017 Panini National Treasures Jumbo Firesuit Materials Holo Gold /10 #3
2017 Panini National Treasures Jumbo Firesuit Materials Laundry Tag /1 #3
2017 Panini National Treasures Jumbo Firesuit Materials Printing Plates Black /1 #3
2017 Panini National Treasures Jumbo Firesuit Materials Printing Plates Cyan /1 #3
2017 Panini National Treasures Jumbo Firesuit Materials Printing Plates Magenta /1 #3
2017 Panini National Treasures Jumbo Firesuit Materials Printing Plates Yellow /1 #3
2017 Panini National Treasures Jumbo Firesuit Signatures Black /1 #8
2017 Panini National Treasures Jumbo Firesuit Signatures Green /5 #8
2017 Panini National Treasures Jumbo Firesuit Signatures Laundry Tag /1 #8
2017 Panini National Treasures Jumbo Firesuit Signatures Printing Plates Black /1 #8
2017 Panini National Treasures Jumbo Firesuit Signatures Printing Plates Cyan /1 #8
2017 Panini National Treasures Jumbo Firesuit Signatures Printing Plates Magenta /1 #8
2017 Panini National Treasures Jumbo Firesuit Signatures Printing Plates Yellow /1 #8
2017 Panini National Treasures Jumbo Tire Signatures /99 #10
2017 Panini National Treasures Jumbo Tire Signatures Black /1 #10
2017 Panini National Treasures Jumbo Tire Signatures Gold /25 #10
2017 Panini National Treasures Jumbo Tire Signatures Green /5 #10
2017 Panini National Treasures Jumbo Tire Signatures Holo Gold /15 #10
2017 Panini National Treasures Jumbo Tire Signatures Holo Silver /50 #10
2017 Panini National Treasures Jumbo Tire Signatures Printing Plates Black /1 #10
2017 Panini National Treasures Jumbo Tire Signatures Printing Plates Cyan /1 #10
2017 Panini National Treasures Jumbo Tire Signatures Printing Plates Magenta /1 #10
2017 Panini National Treasures Jumbo Tire Signatures Printing Plates Yellow /1 #10
2017 Panini National Treasures Nameplate Patch Signatures /1 #13
2017 Panini National Treasures NASCAR Patch Signatures /1 #13
2017 Panini National Treasures Printing Plates Black /1 #14
2017 Panini National Treasures Printing Plates Cyan /1 #14
2017 Panini National Treasures Printing Plates Magenta /1 #14
2017 Panini National Treasures Printing Plates Yellow /1 #14
2017 Panini National Treasures Quad Materials /25 #2
2017 Panini National Treasures Quad Materials Black /1 #2
2017 Panini National Treasures Quad Materials Gold /15 #2
2017 Panini National Treasures Quad Materials Green /5 #2
2017 Panini National Treasures Quad Materials Holo Gold /10 #2
2017 Panini National Treasures Quad Materials Holo Silver /20 #2
2017 Panini National Treasures Quad Materials Laundry Tag /1 #2
2017 Panini National Treasures Quad Materials Printing Plates Black /1 #2
2017 Panini National Treasures Quad Materials Printing Plates Cyan /1 #2
2017 Panini National Treasures Quad Materials Printing Plates Magenta /1 #2
2017 Panini National Treasures Quad Materials Printing Plates Yellow /1 #2
2017 Panini National Treasures Series Sponsor Patch Signatures /1 #13
2017 Panini National Treasures Six Way Swatches Black /1 #4
2017 Panini National Treasures Six Way Swatches Green /5 #4
2017 Panini National Treasures Six Way Swatches Holo Gold /10 #4
2017 Panini National Treasures Six Way Swatches Laundry Tag /1 #4
2017 Panini National Treasures Six Way Swatches Printing Plates Black /1 #4
2017 Panini National Treasures Six Way Swatches Printing Plates Cyan /1 #4
2017 Panini National Treasures Six Way Swatches Printing Plates Magenta /1 #4
2017 Panini National Treasures Six Way Swatches Printing Plates Yellow /1 #4
2017 Panini National Treasures Sunoco Patch Signatures /1 #13
2017 Panini National Treasures Teammates Dual Materials /25 #2
2017 Panini National Treasures Teammates Dual Materials Black /1 #2
2017 Panini National Treasures Teammates Dual Materials Gold /15 #2
2017 Panini National Treasures Teammates Dual Materials Green /5 #2

2017 Panini National Treasures Teammates Dual Materials Holo Gold /10 #2
2017 Panini National Treasures Teammates Dual Materials Holo Silver /20 #2
2017 Panini National Treasures Teammates Dual Materials Laundry Tag /1 #2
2017 Panini National Treasures Teammates Dual Materials Printing Plates Black /1 #2
2017 Panini National Treasures Teammates Dual Materials Printing Plates Cyan /1 #2
2017 Panini National Treasures Teammates Dual Materials Printing Plates Magenta /1 #2
2017 Panini National Treasures Teammates Dual Materials Printing Plates Yellow /1 #2
2017 Panini National Treasures Teammates Quad Materials /25 #8
2017 Panini National Treasures Teammates Quad Materials Black /1 #8
2017 Panini National Treasures Teammates Quad Materials Gold /15 #8
2017 Panini National Treasures Teammates Quad Materials Green /5 #8
2017 Panini National Treasures Teammates Quad Materials Holo Gold /10 #8
2017 Panini National Treasures Teammates Quad Materials Holo Silver /20 #8
2017 Panini National Treasures Teammates Quad Materials Laundry Tag /1 #8
2017 Panini National Treasures Teammates Quad Materials Printing Plates Black /1 #8
2017 Panini National Treasures Teammates Quad Materials Printing Plates Cyan /1 #8
2017 Panini National Treasures Teammates Quad Materials Printing Plates Magenta /1 #8
2017 Panini National Treasures Teammates Quad Materials Printing Plates Yellow /1 #8
2017 Panini National Treasures Teammates Triple Materials /25 #5
2017 Panini National Treasures Teammates Triple Materials Black /1 #5
2017 Panini National Treasures Teammates Triple Materials Gold /15 #5
2017 Panini National Treasures Teammates Triple Materials Green /5 #5
2017 Panini National Treasures Teammates Triple Materials Holo Gold /10 #5
2017 Panini National Treasures Teammates Triple Materials Holo Silver /20 #5
2017 Panini National Treasures Teammates Triple Materials Laundry Tag /1 #5
2017 Panini National Treasures Teammates Triple Materials Printing Plates Black /1 #5
2017 Panini National Treasures Teammates Triple Materials Printing Plates Cyan /1 #5
2017 Panini National Treasures Teammates Triple Materials Printing Plates Magenta /1 #5
2017 Panini National Treasures Teammates Triple Materials Printing Plates Yellow /1 #5
2017 Panini National Treasures Three Wide Signatures Black /1 #10
2017 Panini National Treasures Three Wide Signatures Gold /15 #10
2017 Panini National Treasures Three Wide Signatures Green /5 #10
2017 Panini National Treasures Three Wide Signatures Holo Gold /10 #10
2017 Panini National Treasures Three Wide Signatures Laundry Tag /1 #10
2017 Panini National Treasures Three Wide Signatures Printing Plates Black /1 #10
2017 Panini National Treasures Three Wide Signatures Printing Plates Cyan /1 #10
2017 Panini National Treasures Three Wide Signatures Printing Plates Magenta /1 #10
2017 Panini National Treasures Three Wide Signatures Printing Plates Yellow /1 #10
2017 Panini Torque #4
2017 Panini Torque #59
2017 Panini Torque #78
2017 Panini Torque Artist Proof /75 #4
2017 Panini Torque Artist Proof /75 #59
2017 Panini Torque Artist Proof /75 #78
2017 Panini Torque Blackout /1 #4
2017 Panini Torque Blackout /1 #59
2017 Panini Torque Blackout /1 #78
2017 Panini Torque Blue /150 #4
2017 Panini Torque Blue /150 #59
2017 Panini Torque Blue /150 #78
2017 Panini Torque Clear Vision #9
2017 Panini Torque Clear Vision Blue /99 #9
2017 Panini Torque Clear Vision Gold /149 #9
2017 Panini Torque Clear Vision Green /25 #9
2017 Panini Torque Clear Vision Purple /10 #9
2017 Panini Torque Clear Vision Red /49 #9
2017 Panini Torque Dual Materials /49 #15
2017 Panini Torque Dual Materials Blue /25 #15
2017 Panini Torque Dual Materials Green /5 #15
2017 Panini Torque Dual Materials Purple /1 #15
2017 Panini Torque Dual Materials Red /10 #15
2017 Panini Torque Gold #4
2017 Panini Torque Gold #59
2017 Panini Torque Gold #78
2017 Panini Torque Holo Gold /10 #4
2017 Panini Torque Holo Gold /10 #59
2017 Panini Torque Holo Gold /10 #78
2017 Panini Torque Holo Silver /25 #4
2017 Panini Torque Holo Silver /25 #59
2017 Panini Torque Holo Silver /25 #78
2017 Panini Torque Horsepower Heroes #5
2017 Panini Torque Horsepower Heroes Gold /199 #5
2017 Panini Torque Horsepower Heroes Holo Silver /99 #5
2017 Panini Torque Pairings Materials /199 #6
2017 Panini Torque Pairings Materials Blue /99 #6
2017 Panini Torque Pairings Materials Green /25 #6
2017 Panini Torque Pairings Materials Purple /10 #6
2017 Panini Torque Pairings Materials Red /49 #6
2017 Panini Torque Primary Paint #10
2017 Panini Torque Primary Paint Blue /99 #10
2017 Panini Torque Primary Paint Checkerboard /10 #10
2017 Panini Torque Primary Paint Green /25 #10
2017 Panini Torque Primary Paint Red /49 #10
2017 Panini Torque Prime Associate Sponsors Jumbo Patches /1 #11A
2017 Panini Torque Prime Associate Sponsors Jumbo Patches /1 #11B
2017 Panini Torque Prime Associate Sponsors Jumbo Patches /1 #11C
2017 Panini Torque Prime Associate Sponsors Jumbo Patches /1 #11D
2017 Panini Torque Prime Associate Sponsors Jumbo Patches /1 #11E
2017 Panini Torque Prime Associate Sponsors Jumbo Patches /1 #11F
2017 Panini Torque Prime Associate Sponsors Jumbo Patches /1 #11G
2017 Panini Torque Prime Associate Sponsors Jumbo Patches /1 #11H
2017 Panini Torque Prime Associate Sponsors Jumbo Patches /1 #11I
2017 Panini Torque Prime Associate Sponsors Jumbo Patches /1 #11J
2017 Panini Torque Prime Associate Sponsors Jumbo Patches /1 #11K
2017 Panini Torque Prime Associate Sponsors Jumbo Patches /1 #11L
2017 Panini Torque Prime Associate Sponsors Jumbo Patches /1 #11M
2017 Panini Torque Prime Associate Sponsors Jumbo Patches /1 #11N
2017 Panini Torque Prime Associate Sponsors Jumbo Patches /1 #11O
2017 Panini Torque Prime Manufacturer Jumbo Patches /1 #11
2017 Panini Torque Prime Nameplates Jumbo Patches /1 #11
2017 Panini Torque Prime NASCAR Jumbo Patches /1 #11
2017 Panini Torque Prime Series Sponsor Jumbo Patches /1 #11
2017 Panini Torque Printing Plates Black /1 #4
2017 Panini Torque Printing Plates Black /1 #59
2017 Panini Torque Printing Plates Black /1 #78
2017 Panini Torque Printing Plates Cyan /1 #4
2017 Panini Torque Printing Plates Cyan /1 #59
2017 Panini Torque Printing Plates Cyan /1 #78
2017 Panini Torque Printing Plates Magenta /1 #4
2017 Panini Torque Printing Plates Magenta /1 #59
2017 Panini Torque Printing Plates Magenta /1 #78
2017 Panini Torque Printing Plates Yellow /1 #4
2017 Panini Torque Printing Plates Yellow /1 #59
2017 Panini Torque Printing Plates Yellow /1 #78
2017 Panini Torque Purple /50 #4
2017 Panini Torque Purple /50 #59
2017 Panini Torque Purple /50 #78
2017 Panini Torque Quad Materials /25 #16
2017 Panini Torque Quad Materials Blue /15 #16
2017 Panini Torque Quad Materials Green /5 #16
2017 Panini Torque Quad Materials Purple /1 #16
2017 Panini Torque Quad Materials Red /10 #16
2017 Panini Torque Raced Relics /99 #12
2017 Panini Torque Raced Relics Blue /49 #12
2017 Panini Torque Raced Relics Green /10 #12
2017 Panini Torque Raced Relics Purple /1 #12
2017 Panini Torque Raced Relics Red /25 #12
2017 Panini Torque Red /100 #4
2017 Panini Torque Red /100 #59
2017 Panini Torque Red /100 #78
2017 Panini Torque Running Order #16
2017 Panini Torque Running Order Blue /99 #16
2017 Panini Torque Running Order Checkerboard /10 #16
2017 Panini Torque Running Order Green /25 #16
2017 Panini Torque Running Order Red /49 #16
2017 Panini Torque Silhouettes Firesuit Signatures /51 #11
2017 Panini Torque Silhouettes Firesuit Signatures Blue /49 #11
2017 Panini Torque Silhouettes Firesuit Signatures Green /15 #11
2017 Panini Torque Silhouettes Firesuit Signatures Purple /10 #11
2017 Panini Torque Silhouettes Firesuit Signatures Red /25 #11
2017 Panini Torque Silhouettes Sheet Metal Signatures /51 #22
2017 Panini Torque Silhouettes Sheet Metal Signatures Blue /33 #22
2017 Panini Torque Silhouettes Sheet Metal Signatures Green /15 #22
2017 Panini Torque Silhouettes Sheet Metal Signatures Purple /10 #22
2017 Panini Torque Silhouettes Sheet Metal Signatures Red /25 #22
2017 Panini Torque Special Paint #1
2017 Panini Torque Special Paint Gold /199 #1
2017 Panini Torque Special Paint Holo Silver /99 #1
2017 Panini Torque Superstar Vision #11
2017 Panini Torque Superstar Vision Blue /99 #11
2017 Panini Torque Superstar Vision Gold /149 #11
2017 Panini Torque Superstar Vision Green /25 #11
2017 Panini Torque Superstar Vision Purple /10 #11
2017 Panini Torque Superstar Vision Red /49 #11
2017 Panini Torque Test Proof Black /1 #4
2017 Panini Torque Test Proof Black /1 #59
2017 Panini Torque Test Proof Black /1 #78
2017 Panini Torque Test Proof Cyan /1 #4
2017 Panini Torque Test Proof Cyan /1 #59
2017 Panini Torque Test Proof Cyan /1 #78
2017 Panini Torque Test Proof Magenta /1 #4
2017 Panini Torque Test Proof Magenta /1 #59
2017 Panini Torque Test Proof Magenta /1 #78
2017 Panini Torque Test Proof Yellow /1 #4
2017 Panini Torque Test Proof Yellow /1 #59
2017 Panini Torque Test Proof Yellow /1 #78
2017 Panini Torque Track Vision #9
2017 Panini Torque Track Vision Blue /99 #9
2017 Panini Torque Track Vision Gold /149 #9
2017 Panini Torque Track Vision Green /25 #9
2017 Panini Torque Track Vision Purple /10 #9
2017 Panini Torque Track Vision Red /49 #9
2017 Panini Torque Victory Laps #13
2017 Panini Torque Victory Laps Gold /199 #13
2017 Panini Torque Victory Laps Holo Silver /99 #13
2017 Panini Torque Visions of Greatness #1
2017 Panini Torque Visions of Greatness Blue /99 #1
2017 Panini Torque Visions of Greatness Gold /149 #1
2017 Panini Torque Visions of Greatness Green /25 #1
2017 Panini Torque Visions of Greatness Purple /10 #1
2017 Panini Torque Visions of Greatness Red /49 #1
2017 Select #24
2017 Select #25
2017 Select #26
2017 Select #27
2017 Select #28
2017 Select #29
2017 Select #110
2017 Select Prizms Black /3 #24
2017 Select Prizms Black /3 #25
2017 Select Prizms Black /3 #26
2017 Select Prizms Black /3 #27
2017 Select Prizms Black /3 #28
2017 Select Prizms Black /3 #29
2017 Select Prizms Black /3 #110
2017 Select Prizms Blue /199 #24
2017 Select Prizms Blue /199 #25
2017 Select Prizms Blue /199 #26
2017 Select Prizms Blue /199 #27
2017 Select Prizms Blue /199 #28
2017 Select Prizms Blue /199 #29
2017 Select Prizms Checkered Flag /1 #24
2017 Select Prizms Checkered Flag /1 #25
2017 Select Prizms Checkered Flag /1 #26
2017 Select Prizms Checkered Flag /1 #27
2017 Select Prizms Checkered Flag /1 #28
2017 Select Prizms Checkered Flag /1 #29
2017 Select Prizms Checkered Flag /1 #110
2017 Select Prizms Gold /10 #24
2017 Select Prizms Gold /10 #25
2017 Select Prizms Gold /10 #26
2017 Select Prizms Gold /10 #27
2017 Select Prizms Gold /10 #28
2017 Select Prizms Gold /10 #29
2017 Select Prizms Gold /10 #110
2017 Select Prizms Purple Pulsar #24
2017 Select Prizms Purple Pulsar #25
2017 Select Prizms Purple Pulsar #26
2017 Select Prizms Purple Pulsar #27
2017 Select Prizms Purple Pulsar #28
2017 Select Prizms Purple Pulsar #29
2017 Select Prizms Red /99 #24
2017 Select Prizms Red /99 #25
2017 Select Prizms Red /99 #26
2017 Select Prizms Red /99 #27
2017 Select Prizms Red /99 #28
2017 Select Prizms Red /99 #29
2017 Select Prizms Red White and Blue Pulsar /299 #24
2017 Select Prizms Red White and Blue Pulsar /299 #25
2017 Select Prizms Red White and Blue Pulsar /299 #26
2017 Select Prizms Red White and Blue Pulsar /299 #27
2017 Select Prizms Red White and Blue Pulsar /299 #28
2017 Select Prizms Red White and Blue Pulsar /299 #29
2017 Select Prizms Silver #24
2017 Select Prizms Silver #25
2017 Select Prizms Silver #26
2017 Select Prizms Silver #27
2017 Select Prizms Silver #28
2017 Select Prizms Silver #29
2017 Select Prizms Tie Dye /24 #24
2017 Select Prizms Tie Dye /24 #25
2017 Select Prizms Tie Dye /24 #26
2017 Select Prizms Tie Dye /24 #27
2017 Select Prizms Tie Dye /24 #28
2017 Select Prizms Tie Dye /24 #29
2017 Select Prizms Tie Dye /24 #110
2017 Select Prizms White /50 #24
2017 Select Prizms White /50 #25
2017 Select Prizms White /50 #26
2017 Select Prizms White /50 #27
2017 Select Prizms White /50 #28
2017 Select Prizms White /50 #29
2017 Select Prizms White /50 #110
2017 Select Select Pairs Materials #14
2017 Select Select Pairs Materials #16
2017 Select Select Pairs Materials Prizms Blue /199 #14
2017 Select Select Pairs Materials Prizms Blue /199 #16
2017 Select Select Pairs Materials Prizms Blue /28 #18
2017 Select Select Pairs Materials Prizms Checkered Flag /1 #14
2017 Select Select Pairs Materials Prizms Checkered Flag /1 #16
2017 Select Select Pairs Materials Prizms Checkered Flag /1 #18
2017 Select Select Pairs Materials Prizms Gold /10 #14
2017 Select Select Pairs Materials Prizms Gold /10 #16
2017 Select Select Pairs Materials Prizms Gold /10 #18
2017 Select Select Pairs Materials Prizms Red /99 #14
2017 Select Select Pairs Materials Prizms Red /99 #16
2017 Select Select Pairs Materials Prizms Red /25 #18
2017 Select Select Stars #6
2017 Select Select Stars Prizms Black /3 #6
2017 Select Select Stars Prizms Checkered Flag /1 #6
2017 Select Select Stars Prizms Gold /10 #6
2017 Select Select Stars Prizms Tie Dye /24 #6
2017 Select Select Stars Prizms White /50 #6
2017 Select Select Swatches #26
2017 Select Select Swatches Prizms Blue /199 #26
2017 Select Select Swatches Prizms Checkered Flag /1 #26
2017 Select Select Swatches Prizms Gold /10 #26
2017 Select Select Swatches Prizms Red /99 #26
2017 Select Sheet Metal #14
2017 Select Sheet Metal Prizms Blue /75 #14
2017 Select Sheet Metal Prizms Checkered Flag /1 #14
2017 Select Sheet Metal Prizms Gold /10 #14
2017 Select Sheet Metal Prizms Red /50 #14
2017 Select Signature Paint Schemes #9
2017 Select Signature Paint Schemes Prizms Blue /50 #9
2017 Select Signature Paint Schemes Prizms Checkered Flag /1 #9
2017 Select Signature Paint Schemes Prizms Gold /10 #9
2017 Select Signature Paint Schemes Prizms Red /25 #9
2017 Select Signature Swatches #26
2017 Select Signature Swatches Prizms Checkered Flag /1 #26
2017 Select Signature Swatches Prizms Gold /10 #26
2017 Select Signature Swatches Prizms Tie Dye /24 #26
2017 Select Signature Swatches Prizms White /50 #26
2017 Select Signature Swatches Triple #15
2017 Select Signature Swatches Triple Prizms Checkered Flag /1 #15
2017 Select Signature Swatches Triple Prizms Gold /10 #15
2017 Select Signature Swatches Triple Prizms Tie Dye /24 #15
2017 Select Signature Swatches Triple Prizms White /50 #15
2017 Select Speed Merchants #4
2017 Select Speed Merchants Prizms Black /3 #4
2017 Select Speed Merchants Prizms Checkered Flag /1 #4
2017 Select Speed Merchants Prizms Gold /10 #4
2017 Select Speed Merchants Prizms Tie Dye /24 #4
2017 Select Speed Merchants Prizms White /50 #4
2018 Certified #63
2018 Certified All Certified Team /199 #16
2018 Certified All Certified Team Black /1 #16
2018 Certified All Certified Team Blue /99 #16
2018 Certified All Certified Team Gold /49 #16
2018 Certified All Certified Team Green /10 #16
2018 Certified All Certified Team Mirror Black /1 #16
2018 Certified All Certified Team Mirror Gold /25 #16
2018 Certified All Certified Team Mirror Green /5 #16
2018 Certified All Certified Team Mirror Purple /10 #16
2018 Certified All Certified Team Purple /25 #16
2018 Certified All Certified Team Red /149 #16
2018 Certified Black /1 #63
2018 Certified Blue /99 #63
2018 Certified Cup Swatches /399 #15
2018 Certified Cup Swatches Black /1 #15
2018 Certified Cup Swatches Blue /49 #15
2018 Certified Cup Swatches Gold /25 #15
2018 Certified Cup Swatches Green /5 #15
2018 Certified Cup Swatches Purple /10 #15
2018 Certified Cup Swatches Red /99 #15
2018 Certified Epix /199 #2
2018 Certified Epix Black /1 #2
2018 Certified Epix Blue /99 #2
2018 Certified Epix Gold /49 #2
2018 Certified Epix Green /10 #2
2018 Certified Epix Mirror Black /1 #2
2018 Certified Epix Mirror Gold /25 #2
2018 Certified Epix Mirror Green /5 #2
2018 Certified Epix Mirror Purple /10 #2
2018 Certified Epix Purple /25 #2
2018 Certified Epix Red /149 #2
2018 Certified Gold /49 #63
2018 Certified Green /10 #63
2018 Certified Mirror Black /1 #63
2018 Certified Mirror Gold /25 #63
2018 Certified Mirror Green /5 #63
2018 Certified Mirror Purple /10 #63
2018 Certified Orange /249 #63
2018 Certified Purple /25 #63
2018 Certified Red /199 #63
2018 Certified Signature Swatches /49 #11
2018 Certified Signature Swatches Black /1 #11
2018 Certified Signature Swatches Blue /20 #11
2018 Certified Signature Swatches Gold /15 #11
2018 Certified Signature Swatches Green /5 #11
2018 Certified Signature Swatches Purple /10 #11
2018 Certified Signature Swatches Red /25 #11
2018 Certified Signatures /25 #17
2018 Certified Signatures Black /1 #17
2018 Certified Signatures Blue /15 #17
2018 Certified Signatures Gold /10 #17
2018 Certified Signatures Green /3 #17
2018 Certified Signatures Purple /5 #17
2018 Certified Signatures Red /20 #17
2018 Certified Stars /199 #7
2018 Certified Stars Black /1 #7
2018 Certified Stars Blue /99 #7
2018 Certified Stars Gold /49 #7
2018 Certified Stars Green /10 #7
2018 Certified Stars Mirror Black /1 #7
2018 Certified Stars Mirror Gold /25 #7
2018 Certified Stars Mirror Green /5 #7
2018 Certified Stars Mirror Purple /10 #7
2018 Certified Stars Purple /25 #7
2018 Certified Stars Red /149 #7
2018 Donruss #8
2018 Donruss #35A
2018 Donruss #89
2018 Donruss #125
2018 Donruss #35B
2018 Donruss Artist Proofs /25 #8
2018 Donruss Artist Proofs /25 #35A
2018 Donruss Artist Proofs /25 #89
2018 Donruss Artist Proofs /25 #125
2018 Donruss Artist Proofs /25 #35B
2018 Donruss Gold Foil /499 #8
2018 Donruss Gold Foil /499 #35A
2018 Donruss Gold Foil /499 #89
2018 Donruss Gold Foil /499 #125
2018 Donruss Gold Foil /499 #35B
2018 Donruss Gold Press Proofs /99 #8
2018 Donruss Gold Press Proofs /99 #35A
2018 Donruss Gold Press Proofs /99 #89
2018 Donruss Gold Press Proofs /99 #125
2018 Donruss Gold Press Proofs /99 #35B
2018 Donruss Green Foil /199 #8
2018 Donruss Green Foil /199 #35A
2018 Donruss Green Foil /199 #89
2018 Donruss Green Foil /199 #125
2018 Donruss Green Foil /199 #35B
2018 Donruss Press Proofs /49 #8
2018 Donruss Press Proofs /49 #35A
2018 Donruss Press Proofs /49 #89
2018 Donruss Press Proofs /49 #125
2018 Donruss Press Proofs /49 #35B
2018 Donruss Printing Plates Black /1 #8
2018 Donruss Printing Plates Black /1 #35
2018 Donruss Printing Plates Black /1 #89
2018 Donruss Printing Plates Black /1 #125
2018 Donruss Printing Plates Black /1 #35B
2018 Donruss Printing Plates Cyan /1 #8
2018 Donruss Printing Plates Cyan /1 #35
2018 Donruss Printing Plates Cyan /1 #89
2018 Donruss Printing Plates Cyan /1 #125
2018 Donruss Printing Plates Cyan /1 #35B
2018 Donruss Printing Plates Magenta /1 #8
2018 Donruss Printing Plates Magenta /1 #35
2018 Donruss Printing Plates Magenta /1 #89
2018 Donruss Printing Plates Magenta /1 #125
2018 Donruss Printing Plates Magenta /1 #35B
2018 Donruss Printing Plates Yellow /1 #8
2018 Donruss Printing Plates Yellow /1 #35
2018 Donruss Printing Plates Yellow /1 #89
2018 Donruss Printing Plates Yellow /1 #125
2018 Donruss Printing Plates Yellow /1 #35B
2018 Donruss Red Foil /299 #8
2018 Donruss Red Foil /299 #35A
2018 Donruss Red Foil /299 #89
2018 Donruss Red Foil /299 #125
2018 Donruss Red Foil /299 #35B
2018 Donruss Retro Relics '85 #19
2018 Donruss Retro Relics '85 Black /10 #19
2018 Donruss Retro Relics '85 Holo Gold /99 #19
2018 Donruss Rubber Relics #19
2018 Donruss Rubber Relics Black /10 #19
2018 Donruss Rubber Relics Holo Gold /99 #19
2018 Donruss Studio #18
2018 Donruss Studio Cracked Ice /999 #18
2018 Donruss Studio Signatures #7
2018 Donruss Studio Signatures Black /1 #7
2018 Donruss Studio Signatures Holo Gold /25 #7
2018 Donruss Studio Xplosion /99 #18
2018 Panini Father's Day Racing Memorabilia #DD
2018 Panini Father's Day Racing Memorabilia Checkerboard /10 #DD
2018 Panini Father's Day Racing Memorabilia Cracked Ice /25 #DD
2018 Panini Father's Day Racing Memorabilia Escher Squares /5 #DD
2018 Panini Father's Day Racing Memorabilia Hyperplaid /1 #DD
2018 Panini Prime /50 #22
2018 Panini Prime /50 #55
2018 Panini Prime /50 #88
2018 Panini Prime Autograph Materials /99 #14
2018 Panini Prime Autograph Materials Black /1 #14
2018 Panini Prime Autograph Materials Holo Gold /50 #14
2018 Panini Prime Autograph Materials Laundry Tag /1 #14
2018 Panini Prime Black /1 #22
2018 Panini Prime Black /1 #55
2018 Panini Prime Black /1 #88
2018 Panini Prime Driver Signatures /99 #22
2018 Panini Prime Driver Signatures Black /1 #22
2018 Panini Prime Driver Signatures Holo Gold /50 #22
2018 Panini Prime Holo Gold /25 #22
2018 Panini Prime Holo Gold /25 #55
2018 Panini Prime Holo Gold /25 #88
2018 Panini Prime Prime Jumbo Associate Sponsor 1 /1 #48
2018 Panini Prime Prime Jumbo Associate Sponsor 2 /1 #48
2018 Panini Prime Prime Jumbo Associate Sponsor 3 /1 #48
2018 Panini Prime Prime Jumbo Associate Sponsor 4 /1 #48
2018 Panini Prime Prime Jumbo Associate Sponsor 5 /1 #48
2018 Panini Prime Prime Jumbo Associate Sponsor 6 /1 #48
2018 Panini Prime Prime Jumbo Associate Sponsor 7 /1 #48
2018 Panini Prime Prime Jumbo Associate Sponsor 8 /1 #48
2018 Panini Prime Prime Jumbo Car Manufacturer /1 #48
2018 Panini Prime Prime Jumbo Firesuit Manufacturer /1 #48
2018 Panini Prime Prime Jumbo Glove Manufacturer Patch /1 #48
2018 Panini Prime Prime Jumbo Glove Number Patch /1 #48
2018 Panini Prime Prime Jumbo Nameplate /2 #48
2018 Panini Prime Prime Jumbo NASCAR /1 #48
2018 Panini Prime Prime Jumbo Prime Colors /10 #48
2018 Panini Prime Prime Jumbo Series Sponsor /1 #48
2018 Panini Prime Prime Jumbo Shoe Brand Logo /1 #48
2018 Panini Prime Prime Jumbo Shoe Name Patch /1 #48
2018 Panini Prime Prime Jumbo Sunoco /1 #48
2018 Panini Prime Quad Material Autographs /99 #2
2018 Panini Prime Quad Material Autographs Black /1 #2
2018 Panini Prime Quad Material Autographs Holo Gold /50 #2
2018 Panini Prime Quad Material Autographs Laundry Tag /1 #2
2018 Panini Prime Race Used Duals Firesuit /50 #24
2018 Panini Prime Race Used Duals Firesuit Black /1 #24
2018 Panini Prime Race Used Duals Firesuit Laundry Tag /1 #24
2018 Panini Prime Race Used Duals Sheet Metal /50 #24
2018 Panini Prime Race Used Duals Sheet Metal Black /1 #24
2018 Panini Prime Race Used Duals Sheet Metal Holo Gold /25 #24
2018 Panini Prime Race Used Duals Tire /50 #24
2018 Panini Prime Race Used Duals Tire Black /1 #24
2018 Panini Prime Race Used Duals Tire Holo Gold /25 #24
2018 Panini Prime Race Used Firesuits /50 #21
2018 Panini Prime Race Used Firesuits Black /1 #21
2018 Panini Prime Race Used Firesuits Holo Gold /25 #21
2018 Panini Prime Race Used Firesuits Laundry Tag /1 #21
2018 Panini Prime Race Used Sheet Metal /50 #21
2018 Panini Prime Race Used Sheet Metal Black /1 #21
2018 Panini Prime Race Used Sheet Metal Holo Gold /25 #21
2018 Panini Prime Race Used Tires Black /1 #21
2018 Panini Prime Race Used Tires Holo Gold /25 #21
2018 Panini Prime Race Used Trios Firesuit /50 #20
2018 Panini Prime Race Used Trios Firesuit Black /1 #20
2018 Panini Prime Race Used Trios Firesuit Holo Gold /25 #20
2018 Panini Prime Race Used Trios Firesuit Laundry Tag /1 #20
2018 Panini Prime Race Used Trios Sheet Metal /50 #20
2018 Panini Prime Race Used Trios Sheet Metal Black /1 #20
2018 Panini Prime Race Used Trios Sheet Metal Holo Gold /25 #20
2018 Panini Prime Race Used Trios Tire /50 #20
2018 Panini Prime Race Used Trios Tire Black /1 #20
2018 Panini Prime Race Used Trios Tire Holo Gold /25 #20
2018 Panini Prime Shadowbox Signatures /99 #11
2018 Panini Prime Shadowbox Signatures Black /1 #11
2018 Panini Prime Shadowbox Signatures Holo Gold /50 #11
2018 Panini Prime Signature Tires /99 #8
2018 Panini Prime Signature Tires Black /1 #8
2018 Panini Prime Signature Tires Holo Gold /50 #8
2018 Panini Prizm #8
2018 Panini Prizm #62
2018 Panini Prizm Fireworks #15
2018 Panini Prizm Fireworks Prizms #15
2018 Panini Prizm Fireworks Prizms Black /1 #15
2018 Panini Prizm Fireworks Prizms Gold /10 #15
2018 Panini Prizm Prizms #8
2018 Panini Prizm Prizms #62
2018 Panini Prizm Prizms Black /1 #8
2018 Panini Prizm Prizms Black /1 #62
2018 Panini Prizm Prizms Blue /99 #8
2018 Panini Prizm Prizms Blue /99 #62
2018 Panini Prizm Prizms Camo #8
2018 Panini Prizm Prizms Camo #62
2018 Panini Prizm Prizms Gold /10 #8
2018 Panini Prizm Prizms Gold /10 #62
2018 Panini Prizm Prizms Green /149 #8
2018 Panini Prizm Prizms Green /149 #62
2018 Panini Prizm Prizms Purple Flash #8
2018 Panini Prizm Prizms Purple Flash #62
2018 Panini Prizm Prizms Rainbow /24 #8
2018 Panini Prizm Prizms Rainbow /24 #62
2018 Panini Prizm Prizms Red /75 #8
2018 Panini Prizm Prizms Red /75 #62
2018 Panini Prizm Prizms Red White and Blue #8
2018 Panini Prizm Prizms Red White and Blue #62
2018 Panini Prizm Prizms White /5 #8
2018 Panini Prizm Prizms White /5 #62
2018 Panini Prizm Scripted Signatures Prizms #35
2018 Panini Prizm Scripted Signatures Prizms Black /1 #35
2018 Panini Prizm Scripted Signatures Prizms Blue /35 #35
2018 Panini Prizm Scripted Signatures Prizms Camo #35
2018 Panini Prizm Scripted Signatures Prizms Gold /10 #35
2018 Panini Prizm Scripted Signatures Prizms Green /50 #35
2018 Panini Prizm Scripted Signatures Prizms Rainbow /24 #35
2018 Panini Prizm Scripted Signatures Prizms Red /25 #35
2018 Panini Prizm Scripted Signatures Prizms Red White and Blue /75 #35
2018 Panini Prizm Scripted Signatures Prizms White /5 #35
2018 Panini Victory Lane #30
2018 Panini Victory Lane Black /1 #30
2018 Panini Victory Lane Blue /25 #30
2018 Panini Victory Lane Engineered to Perfection Materials /99 #14
2018 Panini Victory Lane Engineered to Perfection Materials Black /5 #14
2018 Panini Victory Lane Engineered to Perfection Materials Gold /49 #14
2018 Panini Victory Lane Engineered to Perfection Materials Green /25 #14
2018 Panini Victory Lane Engineered to Perfection Materials Laundry Tag /1 #14
2018 Panini Victory Lane Engineered to Perfection Triple Materials /199 #10
2018 Panini Victory Lane Engineered to Perfection Triple Materials Black /25 #10
2018 Panini Victory Lane Engineered to Perfection Triple Materials Gold /99 #10
2018 Panini Victory Lane Engineered to Perfection Triple Materials Green /49 #10
2018 Panini Victory Lane Engineered to Perfection Triple Materials Laundry Tag /1 #10
2018 Panini Victory Lane Gold /99 #30
2018 Panini Victory Lane Green /5 #30
2018 Panini Victory Lane Octane Autographs /99 #21
2018 Panini Victory Lane Octane Autographs Black /1 #21
2018 Panini Victory Lane Octane Autographs Gold /25 #21
2018 Panini Victory Lane Pedal to the Metal #31
2018 Panini Victory Lane Pedal to the Metal Black /1 #31
2018 Panini Victory Lane Pedal to the Metal Blue /25 #31
2018 Panini Victory Lane Pedal to the Metal Green /5 #31
2018 Panini Victory Lane Printing Plates Black /1 #30
2018 Panini Victory Lane Printing Plates Cyan /1 #30
2018 Panini Victory Lane Printing Plates Magenta /1 #30
2018 Panini Victory Lane Printing Plates Yellow /1 #30
2018 Panini Victory Lane Race Ready Materials Black /5 #18
2018 Panini Victory Lane Race Ready Materials Laundry Tag /1 #18
2018 Panini Victory Lane Red /49 #30
2018 Panini Victory Lane Silver #30
2018 Panini Victory Lane Victory Lane Prime Patches Associate Sponsor 1 /1 #25
2018 Panini Victory Lane Victory Lane Prime Patches Associate Sponsor 2 /1 #25
2018 Panini Victory Lane Victory Lane Prime Patches Associate Sponsor 3 /1 #25
2018 Panini Victory Lane Victory Lane Prime Patches Associate Sponsor 4 /1 #25
2018 Panini Victory Lane Victory Lane Prime Patches Associate Sponsor 5 - /1 #25
2018 Panini Victory Lane Victory Lane Prime Patches Associate Sponsor 6 /1 #25
2018 Panini Victory Lane Victory Lane Prime Patches Associate Sponsor 7 /1 #25
2018 Panini Victory Lane Victory Lane Prime Patches Associate Sponsor 8 /1 #25
2018 Panini Victory Lane Victory Lane Prime Patches Associate Sponsor 9 /1 #25
2018 Panini Victory Lane Victory Lane Prime Patches Car Manufacturer /1 #25
2018 Panini Victory Lane Victory Lane Prime Patches Firesuit Manufacturer /1 #25
2018 Panini Victory Lane Victory Lane Prime Patches Nameplate /1 #25
2018 Panini Victory Lane Victory Lane Prime Patches NASCAR /1 #25
2018 Panini Victory Lane Victory Lane Prime Patches Series Sponsor /1 #25
2018 Panini Victory Lane Victory Lane Prime Patches Sunoco /1 #25
2019 Donruss #64
2019 Donruss #132
2019 Donruss Artist Proofs /25 #64
2019 Donruss Artist Proofs /25 #132
2019 Donruss Black /199 #64
2019 Donruss Black /199 #132
2019 Donruss Gold /299 #64
2019 Donruss Gold /299 #132
2019 Donruss Gold Press Proofs /99 #64
2019 Donruss Gold Press Proofs /99 #132
2019 Donruss Optic #37
2019 Donruss Optic Blue Pulsar #37
2019 Donruss Optic Gold /10 #37
2019 Donruss Optic Gold Vinyl /1 #37
2019 Donruss Optic Holo #37
2019 Donruss Optic Red Wave #37
2019 Donruss Optic Signatures Gold Vinyl /1 #37
2019 Donruss Optic Signatures Holo /75 #37
2019 Donruss Press Proofs /49 #64
2019 Donruss Press Proofs /49 #132
2019 Donruss Printing Plates Black /1 #64
2019 Donruss Printing Plates Black /1 #132
2019 Donruss Printing Plates Cyan /1 #64
2019 Donruss Printing Plates Cyan /1 #132
2019 Donruss Printing Plates Magenta /1 #64
2019 Donruss Printing Plates Magenta /1 #132
2019 Donruss Printing Plates Yellow /1 #64
2019 Donruss Printing Plates Yellow /1 #132
2019 Donruss Retro Relics '86 #6
2019 Donruss Retro Relics '86 Holo Black /10 #6
2019 Donruss Retro Relics '86 Holo Gold /25 #6
2019 Donruss Retro Relics '86 Red /250 #6
2019 Donruss Silver #64
2019 Donruss Silver #132
2019 Panini Prime Dual Material Autographs /99 #20
2019 Panini Prime Dual Material Autographs Black /10 #20
2019 Panini Prime Dual Material Autographs Holo Gold /25 #20
2019 Panini Prime Dual Material Autographs Laundry Tags /1 #20
2019 Panini Prime Jumbo Material Signatures Firesuit /10 #16
2019 Panini Prime Jumbo Material Signatures Firesuit Platinum Blue /1 #16
2019 Panini Prime Jumbo Material Signatures Sheet Metal /25 #16
2019 Panini Prime Jumbo Material Signatures Tire /99 #16
2019 Panini Prime NASCAR Shadowbox Signatures Car Number /99 #22
2019 Panini Prime NASCAR Shadowbox Signatures Manufacturer /10 #22
2019 Panini Prime NASCAR Shadowbox Signatures Sponsor /25 #22
2019 Panini Prime Prime Jumbo Associate Sponsor 1 /1 #41
2019 Panini Prime Prime Jumbo Associate Sponsor 1 /1 #42
2019 Panini Prime Prime Jumbo Associate Sponsor 1 /1 #43
2019 Panini Prime Prime Jumbo Associate Sponsor 2 /1 #41
2019 Panini Prime Prime Jumbo Associate Sponsor 2 /1 #42
2019 Panini Prime Prime Jumbo Associate Sponsor 2 /1 #43
2019 Panini Prime Prime Jumbo Associate Sponsor 3 /1 #42
2019 Panini Prime Prime Jumbo Associate Sponsor 3 /1 #43
2019 Panini Prime Prime Jumbo Associate Sponsor 4 /1 #42
2019 Panini Prime Prime Jumbo Associate Sponsor 4 /1 #43
2019 Panini Prime Prime Jumbo Associate Sponsor 5 /1 #42
2019 Panini Prime Prime Jumbo Associate Sponsor 5 /1 #43
2019 Panini Prime Prime Jumbo Associate Sponsor 6 /1 #42
2019 Panini Prime Prime Jumbo Associate Sponsor 6 /1 #43
2019 Panini Prime Prime Jumbo Associate Sponsor 7 /1 #42
2019 Panini Prime Prime Jumbo Associate Sponsor 7 /1 #43
2019 Panini Prime Prime Jumbo Associate Sponsor 8 /1 #42
2019 Panini Prime Prime Jumbo Associate Sponsor 8 /1 #43
2019 Panini Prime Prime Jumbo Associate Sponsor 9 /1 #43
2019 Panini Prime Prime Jumbo Car Manufacturer /1 #41
2019 Panini Prime Prime Jumbo Car Manufacturer /1 #42
2019 Panini Prime Prime Jumbo Car Manufacturer /1 #43
2019 Panini Prime Prime Jumbo Firesuit Manufacturer /1 #41
2019 Panini Prime Prime Jumbo Firesuit Manufacturer /1 #42
2019 Panini Prime Prime Jumbo Firesuit Manufacturer /1 #43
2019 Panini Prime Prime Jumbo Glove Manufacturer Patch /1 #41
2019 Panini Prime Prime Jumbo Glove Manufacturer Patch /1 #42
2019 Panini Prime Prime Jumbo Glove Manufacturer Patch /1 #43
2019 Panini Prime Prime Jumbo Glove Number Patch /1 #41
2019 Panini Prime Prime Jumbo Goodyear /1 #42
2019 Panini Prime Prime Jumbo Goodyear /2 #43
2019 Panini Prime Prime Jumbo Nameplate /1 #42
2019 Panini Prime Prime Jumbo Nameplate /1 #43
2019 Panini Prime Prime Jumbo NASCAR /1 #42
2019 Panini Prime Prime Jumbo NASCAR /1 #43
2019 Panini Prime Prime Jumbo Prime Colors /12 #41
2019 Panini Prime Prime Jumbo Prime Colors /21 #42
2019 Panini Prime Prime Jumbo Prime Colors /10 #43
2019 Panini Prime Prime Jumbo Series Sponsor /1 #42
2019 Panini Prime Prime Jumbo Series Sponsor /1 #43
2019 Panini Prime Prime Jumbo Shoe Brand Logo /1 #41
2019 Panini Prime Prime Jumbo Shoe Brand Logo /1 #42
2019 Panini Prime Prime Jumbo Shoe Brand Logo /1 #43
2019 Panini Prime Prime Jumbo Shoe Name Patch /1 #41
2019 Panini Prime Prime Jumbo Shoe Name Patch /1 #42
2019 Panini Prime Prime Jumbo Shoe Name Patch /1 #43
2019 Panini Prime Prime Jumbo Sunoco /1 #42
2019 Panini Prime Prime Jumbo Sunoco /1 #43
2019 Panini Prime Quad Materials Autographs /99 #14
2019 Panini Prime Quad Materials Autographs Black /10 #14
2019 Panini Prime Quad Materials Autographs Holo Gold /25 #14
2019 Panini Prime Quad Materials Autographs Laundry Tags /1 #14
2019 Panini Prime Race Used Firesuits /50 #22
2019 Panini Prime Race Used Firesuits Black /10 #22
2019 Panini Prime Race Used Firesuits Holo Gold /25 #22
2019 Panini Prime Race Used Firesuits Laundry Tags /1 #22
2019 Panini Prime Race Used Sheet Metal /50 #22
2019 Panini Prime Race Used Sheet Metal Black /10 #22
2019 Panini Prime Race Used Sheet Metal Holo Gold /25 #22
2019 Panini Prime Race Used Sheet Metal Platinum Blue /1 #22
2019 Panini Prime Race Used Tires /50 #22
2019 Panini Prime Race Used Tires Black /10 #22
2019 Panini Prime Race Used Tires Holo Gold /25 #22
2019 Panini Prime Race Used Tires Platinum Blue /1 #22
2019 Panini Prime Shadowbox Signatures /75 #11
2019 Panini Prime Shadowbox Signatures Black /10 #11
2019 Panini Prime Shadowbox Signatures Holo Gold /25 #11
2019 Panini Prime Shadowbox Signatures Platinum Blue /1 #11
2019 Panini Prizm #48
2019 Panini Prizm Endorsements Prizms #11
2019 Panini Prizm Endorsements Prizms Black /1 #11
2019 Panini Prizm Endorsements Prizms Blue /75 #11
2019 Panini Prizm Endorsements Prizms Camo #11
2019 Panini Prizm Endorsements Prizms Gold /10 #11
2019 Panini Prizm Endorsements Prizms Green /99 #11
2019 Panini Prizm Endorsements Prizms Rainbow /24 #11
2019 Panini Prizm Endorsements Prizms Red /50 #11
2019 Panini Prizm Endorsements Prizms Red White and Blue #11
2019 Panini Prizm Endorsements Prizms White /5 #11
2019 Panini Prizm Prizms #48
2019 Panini Prizm Prizms Black /1 #48
2019 Panini Prizm Prizms Blue /75 #48
2019 Panini Prizm Prizms Camo #48
2019 Panini Prizm Prizms Flash #48
2019 Panini Prizm Prizms Gold /10 #48
2019 Panini Prizm Prizms Green /99 #48
2019 Panini Prizm Prizms Rainbow /24 #48
2019 Panini Prizm Prizms Red /50 #48
2019 Panini Prizm Prizms Red White and Blue #48
2019 Panini Prizm Prizms White /5 #48
2019 Panini Prizm Prizms White Sparkle #48
2019 Panini Victory Lane #94
2019 Panini Victory Lane Black /1 #94
2019 Panini Victory Lane Dual Swatches #24
2019 Panini Victory Lane Dual Swatches Gold /99 #24
2019 Panini Victory Lane Dual Swatches Laundry Tag /1 #24
2019 Panini Victory Lane Dual Swatches Platinum /1 #24
2019 Panini Victory Lane Dual Swatches Red /25 #24
2019 Panini Victory Lane Gold /25 #94
2019 Panini Victory Lane Printing Plates Black /1 #94
2019 Panini Victory Lane Printing Plates Cyan /1 #94
2019 Panini Victory Lane Printing Plates Magenta /1 #94
2019 Panini Victory Lane Printing Plates Yellow /1 #94
2019 Panini Victory Lane Triple Swatch Signatures #9
2019 Panini Victory Lane Triple Swatch Signatures Gold /99 #9
2019 Panini Victory Lane Triple Swatch Signatures Laundry Tag /1 #9
2019 Panini Victory Lane Triple Swatch Signatures Platinum /1 #9
2019 Panini Victory Lane Triple Swatch Signatures Red /25 #9
2020 Donruss #91
2020 Donruss #120
2020 Donruss Black Numbers /9 #91
2020 Donruss Black Numbers /9 #120
2020 Donruss Black Trophy Club /1 #91
2020 Donruss Black Trophy Club /1 #120
2020 Donruss Blue /199 #91
2020 Donruss Blue /199 #120
2020 Donruss Carolina Blue #91
2020 Donruss Carolina Blue #120
2020 Donruss Green /99 #91
2020 Donruss Green /99 #120
2020 Donruss Orange #91
2020 Donruss Orange #120
2020 Donruss Pink /25 #91
2020 Donruss Pink /25 #120
2020 Donruss Printing Plates Black /1 #91
2020 Donruss Printing Plates Black /1 #120
2020 Donruss Printing Plates Cyan /1 #91
2020 Donruss Printing Plates Cyan /1 #120
2020 Donruss Printing Plates Magenta /1 #91
2020 Donruss Printing Plates Magenta /1 #120
2020 Donruss Printing Plates Yellow /1 #91
2020 Donruss Printing Plates Yellow /1 #120
2020 Donruss Purple /49 #91
2020 Donruss Purple /49 #120
2020 Donruss Red /299 #91
2020 Donruss Red /299 #120
2020 Donruss Retro Relics '87 #6
2020 Donruss Retro Relics '87 Holo Black /10 #6
2020 Donruss Retro Relics '87 Holo Gold /25 #6
2020 Donruss Retro Relics '87 Red /250 #6
2020 Donruss Silver #91
2020 Donruss Silver #120

Matt Kenseth

1991 Langenberg ARTGO #1
1999 Press Pass #38
1999 Press Pass #62
1999 Press Pass Premium #46
1999 Press Pass Premium Reflectors /1975 #R46
1999 Press Pass Signings /500 #29A
1999 Press Pass Signings /155 #29B
1999 Press Pass Signings Gold /100 #11
1999 Press Pass Skidmarks /250 #38
1999 Press Pass Skidmarks /250 #62
1999 Press Pass Stealth #43
1999 Press Pass Stealth Fusion #F43
1999 Upper Deck MVP ProSign #MKH
1999 Upper Deck MVP ProSign #MKR
1999 VIP #33
1999 VIP Explosives #X33
1999 VIP Explosives Lasers #33
1999 Wheels #46
1999 Wheels #98
1999 Wheels Golden #46
1999 Wheels Golden #98
1999 Wheels High Gear #38
1999 Wheels High Gear First Gear #38
1999 Wheels High Gear MPH #38
1999 Wheels Runnin and Gunnin #RG23
1999 Wheels Runnin and Gunnin Foils #RG23
1999 Wheels Solos #46
1999 Wheels Solos #98
2000 Maxx #17
2000 Maxx #47
2000 Maxx Collectible Covers #CCMK
2000 Maxx Drive Time #DT9
2000 Maxx Fantastic Finishes #FF4
2000 Maxx Speedway Boogie #SB2
2000 Maximum #32
2000 Maximum Cruise Control #CC6
2000 Maximum Die Cuts /250 #32
2000 Maximum MPH /17 #32
2000 Maximum Signatures #MK
2000 Maximum Signatures /100 #ROU4
2000 Maximum Signatures #MK2
2000 Maximum Young Lions #YL2
2000 Press Pass #47
2000 Press Pass #64
2000 Press Pass #72
2000 Press Pass #94
2000 Press Pass Cup Chase #CC8
2000 Press Pass Cup Chase Die Cut Prizes #CC8
2000 Press Pass Millennium #47
2000 Press Pass Millennium #64
2000 Press Pass Millennium #72
2000 Press Pass Millennium #94
2000 Press Pass Optima #10
2000 Press Pass Optima #36
2000 Press Pass Optima #46
2000 Press Pass Optima #P1
2000 Press Pass Optima G Force #GF10
2000 Press Pass Optima On the Edge #OE5
2000 Press Pass Optima Overdrive #OD10
2000 Press Pass Optima Overdrive Square Cut #OD10
2000 Press Pass Optima Platinum #10
2000 Press Pass Optima Platinum #36
2000 Press Pass Optima Platinum #46
2000 Press Pass Optima Race Used Lugnuts Cars /50 #LC18
2000 Press Pass Optima Race Used Lugnuts Drivers /55 #LD18
2000 Press Pass Pitstop #PS16
2000 Press Pass Premium #33
2000 Press Pass Premium #44
2000 Press Pass Premium #55
2000 Press Pass Premium In The Zone #IZ5
2000 Press Pass Premium Reflectors #33
2000 Press Pass Premium Reflectors #44
2000 Press Pass Premium Reflectors #55
2000 Press Pass Signings #30
2000 Press Pass Signings Gold /50 #16
2000 Press Pass Stealth #22
2000 Press Pass Stealth #23
2000 Press Pass Stealth #57
2000 Press Pass Stealth Behind the Numbers #BN1
2000 Press Pass Stealth Fusion #FS19
2000 Press Pass Stealth Fusion #FS20
2000 Press Pass Stealth Fusion #FS21
2000 Press Pass Stealth Fusion Green /1000 #FS19
2000 Press Pass Stealth Fusion Green /1000 #FS20
2000 Press Pass Stealth Fusion Green /1000 #FS21
2000 Press Pass Stealth Fusion Red #FS19
2000 Press Pass Stealth Fusion Red #FS20
2000 Press Pass Stealth Fusion Red #FS21
2000 Press Pass Stealth Profile #PR7
2000 Press Pass Stealth Race Used Gloves /100 #G9
2000 Press Pass Stealth SST #SST7
2000 Press Pass Trackside #22
2000 Press Pass Trackside Dialed In #DI7
2000 Press Pass Trackside Die Cuts #22
2000 Press Pass Trackside Generation.now #GN1
2000 Press Pass Trackside Golden #22
2000 Press Pass Trackside Panorama #P33
2000 Press Pass Trackside Pit Stoppers /200 #PS11
2000 SP Authentic #21
2000 SP Authentic /1000 #90
2000 SP Authentic Dominance #D3
2000 SP Authentic Driver's Seat #DS7
2000 SP Authentic Overdrive Gold /17 #21
2000 SP Authentic Overdrive Gold /17 #90
2000 SP Authentic Overdrive Silver /250 #21
2000 SP Authentic Overdrive Silver /250 #90
2000 SP Authentic Power Surge #PS5
2000 SP Authentic Sign of the Times #MK
2000 SP Authentic Sign of the Times Gold /25 #MK
2000 Upper Deck MVP #34
2000 Upper Deck MVP #76
2000 Upper Deck MVP #99
2000 Upper Deck MVP Gold Script /125 #34
2000 Upper Deck MVP Gold Script /125 #76
2000 Upper Deck MVP Gold Script /125 #99
2000 Upper Deck MVP Legends in the Making #LM2
2000 Upper Deck MVP Magic Numbers #MMK
2000 Upper Deck MVP Magic Numbers Autographs /17 #MAMK
2000 Upper Deck MVP NASCAR Gallery #NG6
2000 Upper Deck MVP NASCAR Stars #NS9
2000 Upper Deck MVP ProSign #PSMK
2000 Upper Deck MVP Silver Script #34
2000 Upper Deck MVP Silver Script #76
2000 Upper Deck MVP Silver Script #99
2000 Upper Deck MVP Super Script /17 #34
2000 Upper Deck MVP Super Script /17 #76
2000 Upper Deck MVP Super Script /17 #99
2000 Upper Deck Racing #32
2000 Upper Deck Racing High Groove #HG3
2000 Upper Deck Racing Record Pace #RP8
2000 Upper Deck Racing Road Signs #RSMK
2000 Upper Deck Racing Tear Aways #TAMK
2000 Upper Deck Racing Trophy Dash #TD4
2000 Upper Deck Victory Circle #31
2000 Upper Deck Victory Circle #61
2000 Upper Deck Victory Circle #83
2000 Upper Deck Victory Circle Exclusives Level 1 Silver /250 #31
2000 Upper Deck Victory Circle Exclusives Level 1 Silver /250 #61
2000 Upper Deck Victory Circle Exclusives Level 1 Silver /250 #83
2000 Upper Deck Victory Circle Exclusives Level 2 Gold /17 #31
2000 Upper Deck Victory Circle Exclusives Level 2 Gold /17 #61
2000 Upper Deck Victory Circle Exclusives Level 2 Gold /17 #83
2000 Upper Deck Victory Circle Income Statement #IS9
2000 Upper Deck Victory Circle Income Statement LTD #IS9
2000 Upper Deck Victory Circle Signature Collection #MK
2000 Upper Deck Victory Circle Victory Circle #V2
2000 Upper Deck Victory Circle Victory Circle LTD #V2
2000 Upper Deck Victory Circle Winning Material Combination /50 #CMK
2000 Upper Deck Victory Circle Winning Material Firesuit #FSMK
2000 Upper Deck Victory Circle Winning Material Tire #TMK
2000 VIP #18
2000 VIP Explosives #X18
2000 VIP Explosives Lasers #LX18
2000 VIP Making the Show #MS13
2000 Wheels High Gear #38
2000 Wheels High Gear #66
2000 Wheels High Gear Autographs #16
2000 Wheels High Gear First Gear #38
2000 Wheels High Gear First Gear #66
2000 Wheels High Gear Gear Shifters #GS13
2000 Wheels High Gear MPH #38
2000 Wheels High Gear MPH #66
2001 Press Pass #13
2001 Press Pass #45
2001 Press Pass #59
2001 Press Pass #62
2001 Press Pass Autographs #24
2001 Press Pass Cup Chase #CC15
2001 Press Pass Cup Chase Die Cut Prizes #CC15
2001 Press Pass Double Burner /100 #DB7
2001 Press Pass Gatorade Front Runner Award #2
2001 Press Pass Ground Zero #GZ1
2001 Press Pass Hot Treads /2405 #HT18
2001 Press Pass Millennium #13
2001 Press Pass Millennium #45
2001 Press Pass Millennium #59
2001 Press Pass Millennium #62
2001 Press Pass Optima #10
2001 Press Pass Optima G Force #GF9
2001 Press Pass Optima Gold #10
2001 Press Pass Optima Race Used Lugnuts Cars /115 #LNC8
2001 Press Pass Optima Race Used Lugnuts Drivers /100 #LND7
2001 Press Pass Premium #10
2001 Press Pass Premium #61
2001 Press Pass Premium Gold #10
2001 Press Pass Premium Gold #61
2001 Press Pass Premium In The Zone #IZ7
2001 Press Pass Premium Race Used Firesuit Cars /110 #FC4
2001 Press Pass Premium Race Used Firesuit Drivers /100 #FD4
2001 Press Pass Showman/Showcar #S3A
2001 Press Pass Showman/Showcar #S3B
2001 Press Pass Signings #27
2001 Press Pass Signings Gold /50 #18
2001 Press Pass Signings Transparent /100 #5
2001 Press Pass Stealth Lap Leaders #LL6
2001 Press Pass Stealth Lap Leaders #LL24
2001 Press Pass Stealth Lap Leaders Clear Cars #LL24
2001 Press Pass Stealth Lap Leaders Clear Drivers #LL6
2001 Press Pass Stealth Race Used Glove Cars /120 #RGC7
2001 Press Pass Stealth Race Used Glove Drivers /120 #RGD7
2001 Press Pass Total Memorabilia Power Pick #TM7
2001 Press Pass Trackside #22
2001 Press Pass Trackside #45
2001 Press Pass Trackside Die Cuts #22
2001 Press Pass Trackside Die Cuts #45
2001 Press Pass Trackside Golden #22
2001 Press Pass Trackside Golden #45
2001 Press Pass Trackside Pit Stoppers Cars /250 #PSC9
2001 Press Pass Trackside Pit Stoppers Drivers /100 #PSD9
2001 Press Pass Triple Burner /100 #TB7
2001 Press Pass Velocity #VL4
2001 Press Pass Vintage #VN13
2001 VIP #38
2001 VIP Explosives #38
2001 VIP Explosives Lasers /420 #LX38
2001 VIP Making the Show #8
2001 VIP Sheet Metal Cars /120 #SC12
2001 VIP Sheet Metal Drivers /75 #SD12
2001 Wheels High Gear #11
2001 Wheels High Gear #29
2001 Wheels High Gear #40
2001 Wheels High Gear #55
2001 Wheels High Gear #59
2001 Wheels High Gear Autographs #18
2001 Wheels High Gear Custom Shop #CSMK
2001 Wheels High Gear Custom Shop Prizes #MKA1
2001 Wheels High Gear Custom Shop Prizes #MKA2
2001 Wheels High Gear Custom Shop Prizes #MKA3
2001 Wheels High Gear Custom Shop Prizes #MKB1
2001 Wheels High Gear Custom Shop Prizes #MKB2
2001 Wheels High Gear Custom Shop Prizes #MKB3
2001 Wheels High Gear Custom Shop Prizes #MKC1
2001 Wheels High Gear Custom Shop Prizes #MKC2
2001 Wheels High Gear Custom Shop Prizes #MKC3
2001 Wheels High Gear First Gear #11
2001 Wheels High Gear First Gear #29
2001 Wheels High Gear First Gear #40
2001 Wheels High Gear First Gear #55
2001 Wheels High Gear First Gear #59
2001 Wheels High Gear Flag Chasers #FC4
2001 Wheels High Gear Flag Chasers Blue-Yellow /45 #FC4
2001 Wheels High Gear Flag Chasers Checkered /35 #FC4
2001 Wheels High Gear Flag Chasers Checkered Blue/Orange /45 #FC4
2001 Wheels High Gear Flag Chasers Green /75 #FC4
2001 Wheels High Gear Flag Chasers Power Pick #FCPP
2001 Wheels High Gear Flag Chasers Red /75 #FC4
2001 Wheels High Gear Flag Chasers White /75 #FC4
2001 Wheels High Gear Flag Chasers Yellow /75 #FC4
2001 Wheels High Gear Gear Shifters #GS12
2001 Wheels High Gear Hot Streaks #HS7
2001 Wheels High Gear MPH #11
2001 Wheels High Gear MPH #29
2001 Wheels High Gear MPH #40
2001 Wheels High Gear MPH #55
2001 Wheels High Gear MPH #59
2001 Wheels High Gear Sunday Sensation #SS3
2002 Press Pass #17
2002 Press Pass #79
2002 Press Pass Autographs #34
2002 Press Pass Burning Rubber Cars /120 #BRC11
2002 Press Pass Burning Rubber Drivers /90 #BRD11
2002 Press Pass Cup Chase #CC7
2002 Press Pass Cup Chase Prizes #CC7
2002 Press Pass Eclipse #12
2002 Press Pass Eclipse #37
2002 Press Pass Eclipse Samples #12
2002 Press Pass Eclipse Samples #37
2002 Press Pass Eclipse Solar Eclipse #S12
2002 Press Pass Eclipse Solar Eclipse #S37
2002 Press Pass Eclipse Supernova #SN7
2002 Press Pass Eclipse Supernova Numbered /250 #SN7
2002 Press Pass Hot Treads /2425 #HT21
2002 Press Pass Optima #15
2002 Press Pass Optima #50
2002 Press Pass Optima Cool Persistence #CP7
2002 Press Pass Optima Fan Favorite #FF12
2002 Press Pass Optima Gold #15
2002 Press Pass Optima Gold #50
2002 Press Pass Optima Promos /5 #15
2002 Press Pass Optima Promos /5 #50
2002 Press Pass Optima Q and A #QA4
2002 Press Pass Optima Race Used Lugnuts Autographs /17 #LNDA10
2002 Press Pass Optima Race Used Lugnuts Cars /100 #LNC10
2002 Press Pass Optima Race Used Lugnuts Drivers /100 #LND10
2002 Press Pass Optima Samples #15
2002 Press Pass Optima Samples #50
2002 Press Pass Platinum #17
2002 Press Pass Platinum #79
2002 Press Pass Premium #15
2002 Press Pass Premium #41
2002 Press Pass Premium #63
2002 Press Pass Premium In The Zone #IZ7
2002 Press Pass Premium Race Used Firesuit Cars /90 #FC3
2002 Press Pass Premium Race Used Firesuit Drivers /80 #FD3
2002 Press Pass Premium Red Reflectors #15
2002 Press Pass Premium Red Reflectors #41
2002 Press Pass Premium Red Reflectors #63
2002 Press Pass Premium Samples #15
2002 Press Pass Premium Samples #41
2002 Press Pass Signings #33
2002 Press Pass Signings Gold /50 #31
2002 Press Pass Signings Transparent /100 #5
2002 Press Pass Stealth #16
2002 Press Pass Stealth #17
2002 Press Pass Stealth #18
2002 Press Pass Stealth #56
2002 Press Pass Stealth Gold #16
2002 Press Pass Stealth Gold #17
2002 Press Pass Stealth Gold #18
2002 Press Pass Stealth Gold #56
2002 Press Pass Stealth Lap Leaders #LL14
2002 Press Pass Stealth Profile #P5
2002 Press Pass Stealth Race Used Glove Cars /85 #GLC6
2002 Press Pass Stealth Race Used Glove Drivers /50 #GLD6
2002 Press Pass Stealth Samples #16
2002 Press Pass Stealth Samples #17
2002 Press Pass Stealth Samples #18
2002 Press Pass Stealth Samples #56
2002 Press Pass Trackside #22
2002 Press Pass Trackside #69
2002 Press Pass Trackside #77
2002 Press Pass Trackside Generation Now #GN6
2002 Press Pass Trackside Golden /50 #G22
2002 Press Pass Trackside License to Drive #17
2002 Press Pass Trackside License to Drive Die Cuts #17
2002 Press Pass Trackside Pit Stoppers Cars /60 #PSC13
2002 Press Pass Trackside Pit Stoppers Drivers /60 #PSD13
2002 Press Pass Trackside Runnin N' Gunnin #RG5
2002 Press Pass Trackside Samples #22
2002 Press Pass Trackside Samples #69
2002 Press Pass Trackside Samples #77
2002 Press Pass Vintage #VN11
2002 VIP #7
2002 VIP #20
2002 VIP #24
2002 VIP Explosives #X7
2002 VIP Explosives #X20
2002 VIP Explosives #X24
2002 VIP Explosives Lasers #LX7
2002 VIP Explosives Lasers #LX20
2002 VIP Explosives Lasers #LX24
2002 VIP Making the Show #MS8
2002 VIP Race Used Sheet Metal Cars #SC10
2002 VIP Race Used Sheet Metal Drivers /130 #SD10
2002 VIP Samples #7
2002 VIP Samples #20
2002 VIP Samples #24
2002 Wheels High Gear #11
2002 Wheels High Gear Autographs #28
2002 Wheels High Gear First Gear #11
2002 Wheels High Gear High Groove #HG11
2002 Wheels High Gear MPH /100 #11
2003 eTopps /5000 #11
2003 Press Pass #17
2003 Press Pass #63
2003 Press Pass #74
2003 Press Pass #76
2003 Press Pass #81
2003 Press Pass #95
2003 Press Pass Autographs #30
2003 Press Pass Burning Rubber Cars /60 #BRT7
2003 Press Pass Burning Rubber Cars Autographs /17 #BRTMK
2003 Press Pass Burning Rubber Drivers /50 #BRD7
2003 Press Pass Burning Rubber Drivers Autographs /17 #BRDMK
2003 Press Pass Cup Chase #CCR8
2003 Press Pass Cup Chase Prizes #CCR8
2003 Press Pass Double Burner /100 #DB7
2003 Press Pass Double Burner Exchange /100 #DB7
2003 Press Pass Eclipse #8
2003 Press Pass Eclipse #29
2003 Press Pass Eclipse #44
2003 Press Pass Eclipse Double Hot Treads /999 #DT6
2003 Press Pass Eclipse Previews /5 #8
2003 Press Pass Eclipse Previews /5 #29
2003 Press Pass Eclipse Racing Champions #RC4
2003 Press Pass Eclipse Racing Champions #RC9
2003 Press Pass Eclipse Racing Champions #RC18
2003 Press Pass Eclipse Racing Champions #RC27
2003 Press Pass Eclipse Racing Champions #RC35
2003 Press Pass Eclipse Samples #8
2003 Press Pass Eclipse Samples #29
2003 Press Pass Eclipse Samples #44
2003 Press Pass Eclipse Skidmarks #SM9
2003 Press Pass Eclipse Solar Eclipse #P8
2003 Press Pass Eclipse Solar Eclipse #P29
2003 Press Pass Eclipse Solar Eclipse #P44
2003 Press Pass Eclipse Supernova #SN6
2003 Press Pass Eclipse Teammates Autographs /25 #MMMK
2003 Press Pass Eclipse Under Cover Cars /215 #UCT16
2003 Press Pass Eclipse Under Cover Driver Gold /260 #UCD16
2003 Press Pass Eclipse Under Cover Driver Red /100 #UCD16
2003 Press Pass Eclipse Under Cover Driver Silver /450 #UCD16
2003 Press Pass Gatorade Jumbos #2
2003 Press Pass Gold Holofoil #P17
2003 Press Pass Gold Holofoil #P63
2003 Press Pass Gold Holofoil #P74
2003 Press Pass Gold Holofoil #P76
2003 Press Pass Gold Holofoil #P81
2003 Press Pass Gold Holofoil #P95
2003 Press Pass Optima #12
2003 Press Pass Optima Cool Persistence #CP11
2003 Press Pass Optima Fan Favorite #FF3
2003 Press Pass Optima Gold #G12
2003 Press Pass Optima Previews /5 #12
2003 Press Pass Optima Samples #12
2003 Press Pass Optima Thunder Bolts Cars /95 #TBT7
2003 Press Pass Optima Thunder Bolts Cars Autographs /17 #TBTMK
2003 Press Pass Optima Thunder Bolts Drivers /60 #TBD7
2003 Press Pass Optima Thunder Bolts Drivers Autographs /17 #TBDMK
2003 Press Pass Premium #14
2003 Press Pass Premium #42
2003 Press Pass Premium #62
2003 Press Pass Premium Hot Threads Cars /160 #HTT7
2003 Press Pass Premium Hot Threads Cars Autographs /17 #HTDMK
2003 Press Pass Premium Hot Threads Drivers /285 #HTD7
2003 Press Pass Premium Hot Threads Drivers Autographs /17 #HTTMK
2003 Press Pass Premium In the Zone #IZ5
2003 Press Pass Premium Previews /5 #14
2003 Press Pass Premium Red Reflectors #14
2003 Press Pass Premium Red Reflectors #42
2003 Press Pass Premium Red Reflectors #62
2003 Press Pass Premium Samples #14
2003 Press Pass Premium Samples #42
2003 Press Pass Previews /5 #17
2003 Press Pass Samples #17
2003 Press Pass Samples #63
2003 Press Pass Samples #74
2003 Press Pass Samples #76
2003 Press Pass Samples #81
2003 Press Pass Samples #95
2003 Press Pass Signings #38
2003 Press Pass Signings Gold /50 #38
2003 Press Pass Snapshots #SN12
2003 Press Pass Stealth #16
2003 Press Pass Stealth #17
2003 Press Pass Stealth #18
2003 Press Pass Stealth Gear Grippers Cars Autographs /17 #MK
2003 Press Pass Stealth Gear Grippers Drivers Autographs /17 #MK
2003 Press Pass Stealth No Boundaries #NB15
2003 Press Pass Stealth Previews /5 #16
2003 Press Pass Stealth Previews /5 #17
2003 Press Pass Stealth Previews /5 #18
2003 Press Pass Stealth Red #P16
2003 Press Pass Stealth Red #P17
2003 Press Pass Stealth Red #P18
2003 Press Pass Stealth Samples #16
2003 Press Pass Stealth Samples #17
2003 Press Pass Stealth Samples #18
2003 Press Pass Total Memorabilia Power Pick #TM7
2003 Press Pass Trackside #5
2003 Press Pass Trackside #78
2003 Press Pass Trackside Gold Holofoil #P5
2003 Press Pass Trackside Gold Holofoil #P78
2003 Press Pass Trackside Golden /50 #G5
2003 Press Pass Trackside Hat Giveaway #PPH13
2003 Press Pass Trackside Pit Stoppers Cars /10 #PST16
2003 Press Pass Trackside Pit Stoppers Cars Autographs /17 #MK
2003 Press Pass Trackside Pit Stoppers Drivers /10 #PSD16
2003 Press Pass Trackside Pit Stoppers Drivers Autographs /17 #PSDMK
2003 Press Pass Trackside Previews /5 #5
2003 Press Pass Trackside Runnin n' Gunnin #RG12
2003 Press Pass Trackside Samples #5
2003 Press Pass Trackside Samples #78
2003 Press Pass Triple Burner /100 #TB7
2003 Press Pass Triple Burner Exchange /100 #TB7
2003 Press Pass Victory Lap #15
2003 Sports Illustrated for Kids #324
2003 VIP #9
2003 VIP #21
2003 VIP Explosives #X9
2003 VIP Explosives #X21
2003 VIP Laser Explosive #LX9
2003 VIP Laser Explosive #LX21
2003 VIP Previews /5 #9
2003 VIP Previews /5 #21
2003 VIP Samples #9
2003 VIP Samples #21
2003 VIP Tin #CT9
2003 VIP Tin #CT21
2003 VIP Tradin' Paint Car Autographs /17 #MK
2003 VIP Tradin' Paint Cars /160 #TPT7
2003 VIP Tradin' Paint Driver Autographs /17 #MK
2003 VIP Tradin' Paint Drivers /110 #TPD7
2003 Wheels American Thunder #11
2003 Wheels American Thunder #40
2003 Wheels American Thunder American Eagle #AE4
2003 Wheels American Thunder Born On /100 #BO11
2003 Wheels American Thunder Born On /100 #BO40
2003 Wheels American Thunder Golden Eagle /100 #AEG4
2003 Wheels American Thunder Head to Toe /40 #HT3
2003 Wheels American Thunder Heads Up Goodyear /90 #HUG5
2003 Wheels American Thunder Heads Up Manufacturer /90 #HUM10
2003 Wheels American Thunder Heads Up Team /90 #HUT9
2003 Wheels American Thunder Heads Up Winston /90 #HUW10
2003 Wheels American Thunder Holofoil #P11
2003 Wheels American Thunder Holofoil #P40
2003 Wheels American Thunder Post Mark #PM10
2003 Wheels American Thunder Previews /5 #11
2003 Wheels American Thunder Pushin Pedal /285 #PP4
2003 Wheels American Thunder Rookie Thunder #RT15
2003 Wheels American Thunder Samples #P11
2003 Wheels American Thunder Samples #P40
2003 Wheels American Thunder Thunder Road #TR9
2003 Wheels Autographs #28
2003 Wheels High Gear #15
2003 Wheels High Gear #35
2003 Wheels High Gear #58
2003 Wheels High Gear Blue Hawaii SCDA Promos #15
2003 Wheels High Gear Blue Hawaii SCDA Promos #35
2003 Wheels High Gear Blue Hawaii SCDA Promos #58
2003 Wheels High Gear First Gear #F15
2003 Wheels High Gear First Gear #F35
2003 Wheels High Gear First Gear #F58
2003 Wheels High Gear Flag Chasers Black /90 #FC6
2003 Wheels High Gear Flag Chasers Blue-Yellow /45 #FC6
2003 Wheels High Gear Flag Chasers Checkered /25 #FC6
2003 Wheels High Gear Flag Chasers Green /90 #FC6
2003 Wheels High Gear Flag Chasers Red /90 #FC6
2003 Wheels High Gear Flag Chasers White /90 #FC6
2003 Wheels High Gear Flag Chasers Yellow /90 #FC6
2003 Wheels High Gear Full Throttle #FT9
2003 Wheels High Gear High Groove #HG13
2003 Wheels High Gear Hot Treads /425 #HT8
2003 Wheels High Gear MPH /100 #M15
2003 Wheels High Gear MPH /100 #M35
2003 Wheels High Gear MPH /100 #M58
2003 Wheels High Gear Previews /5 #15
2003 Wheels High Gear Samples #15
2003 Wheels High Gear Samples #35
2003 Wheels High Gear Samples #58
2003 Wheels High Gear Sunday Sensation #SS1
2004 Post Cereal #5
2004 Press Pass #9C
2004 Press Pass #15
2004 Press Pass #85
2004 Press Pass #97
2004 Press Pass #100
2004 Press Pass #80
2004 Press Pass Autographs #33
2004 Press Pass Burning Rubber Autographs /17 #BRMK
2004 Press Pass Burning Rubber Cars /140 #BRT2
2004 Press Pass Burning Rubber Drivers /70 #BRD2
2004 Press Pass Cup Chase #CCR1
2004 Press Pass Cup Chase Prizes #CCR1
2004 Press Pass Cup Chase Prizes #CCR18
2004 Press Pass Double Burner /100 #DB7
2004 Press Pass Double Burner Exchange /100 #DB7
2004 Press Pass Eclipse #1
2004 Press Pass Eclipse #32
2004 Press Pass Eclipse #49
2004 Press Pass Eclipse #51
2004 Press Pass Eclipse #60
2004 Press Pass Eclipse #77
2004 Press Pass Eclipse #88
2004 Press Pass Eclipse Destination WIN #5
2004 Press Pass Eclipse Hyperdrive #HP9
2004 Press Pass Eclipse Maxim #MX1
2004 Press Pass Eclipse Previews /5 #1
2004 Press Pass Eclipse Samples #1
2004 Press Pass Eclipse Samples #32
2004 Press Pass Eclipse Samples #49
2004 Press Pass Eclipse Samples #51
2004 Press Pass Eclipse Samples #60
2004 Press Pass Eclipse Samples #77
2004 Press Pass Eclipse Samples #88
2004 Press Pass Eclipse Skidmarks #SM4
2004 Press Pass Eclipse Skidmarks Holofoil /500 #SM4
2004 Press Pass Eclipse Under Cover Cars /170 #UCD2
2004 Press Pass Eclipse Under Cover Double Cover /100 #DC9
2004 Press Pass Eclipse Under Cover Double Cover /100 #DC12
2004 Press Pass Eclipse Under Cover Double Cover /100 #DC13
2004 Press Pass Eclipse Under Cover Driver Gold /325 #UCD2
2004 Press Pass Eclipse Under Cover Driver Red /100 #UCD2
2004 Press Pass Eclipse Under Cover Driver Silver /690 #UCD2
2004 Press Pass Hot Treads /1100 #HTR4
2004 Press Pass Hot Treads Holofoil /200 #HTR4
2004 Press Pass Making the Show Collector's Series #MS11
2004 Press Pass Optima #12
2004 Press Pass Optima #39
2004 Press Pass Optima #56
2004 Press Pass Optima #80
2004 Press Pass Optima #95
2004 Press Pass Optima Cool Persistence #CP9
2004 Press Pass Optima Fan Favorite #FF12
2004 Press Pass Optima Gold #G12
2004 Press Pass Optima Gold #G39
2004 Press Pass Optima Gold #G56
2004 Press Pass Optima Gold #G80
2004 Press Pass Optima Gold #G95
2004 Press Pass Optima Previews /5 #EB12
2004 Press Pass Optima Previews /5 #EB39
2004 Press Pass Optima Q&A #QA3
2004 Press Pass Optima Samples #12
2004 Press Pass Optima Samples #39
2004 Press Pass Optima Samples #56
2004 Press Pass Optima Samples #80
2004 Press Pass Optima Samples #95
2004 Press Pass Optima Thunder Bolts Autographs /17 #TBMK
2004 Press Pass Optima Thunder Bolts Cars /120 #TBT8
2004 Press Pass Optima Thunder Bolts Drivers /70 #TBD8
2004 Press Pass Platinum #P15
2004 Press Pass Platinum #P80
2004 Press Pass Platinum #P85
2004 Press Pass Platinum #P97
2004 Press Pass Platinum #P100
2004 Press Pass Premium #8
2004 Press Pass Premium #41
2004 Press Pass Premium #57
2004 Press Pass Premium #74
2004 Press Pass Premium Hot Threads Autographs /17 #HTMK
2004 Press Pass Premium Hot Threads Drivers Bronze /125 #HTD2
2004 Press Pass Premium Hot Threads Drivers Bronze Retail /125 #HTT2
2004 Press Pass Premium Hot Threads Drivers Gold /50 #HTD2
2004 Press Pass Premium Hot Threads Drivers Silver /75 #HTD2
2004 Press Pass Premium In the Zone #IZ7
2004 Press Pass Premium In the Zone Elite Edition #IZ7
2004 Press Pass Premium Previews /5 #8
2004 Press Pass Premium Samples #8
2004 Press Pass Premium Samples #41
2004 Press Pass Previews /5 #15
2004 Press Pass Samples #15
2004 Press Pass Samples #80
2004 Press Pass Samples #85
2004 Press Pass Samples #97
2004 Press Pass Samples #100
2004 Press Pass Showcar #S3B
2004 Press Pass Showman #S3A
2004 Press Pass Signings #36
2004 Press Pass Signings #37
2004 Press Pass Signings Gold /50 #33
2004 Press Pass Signings Gold /50 #34
2004 Press Pass Signings Transparent /100 #4
2004 Press Pass Snapshots #SN12
2004 Press Pass Stealth #37
2004 Press Pass Stealth #38
2004 Press Pass Stealth #39
2004 Press Pass Stealth #85
2004 Press Pass Stealth #97
2004 Press Pass Stealth EFX #EF12
2004 Press Pass Stealth Gear Grippers Autographs /17 #HTMK
2004 Press Pass Stealth Gear Grippers Drivers /80 #GGD2
2004 Press Pass Stealth Gear Grippers Drivers Retail /120 #GGT2
2004 Press Pass Stealth No Boundaries #NB16
2004 Press Pass Stealth Profile #P5
2004 Press Pass Stealth Samples #X38
2004 Press Pass Stealth Samples #X37
2004 Press Pass Stealth Samples #X39
2004 Press Pass Stealth Samples #X85
2004 Press Pass Stealth Samples #X97
2004 Press Pass Stealth X-Ray /100 #37
2004 Press Pass Stealth X-Ray /100 #38
2004 Press Pass Stealth X-Ray /100 #39
2004 Press Pass Stealth X-Ray /100 #85
2004 Press Pass Stealth X-Ray /100 #97
2004 Press Pass Top Shelf #TS1
2004 Press Pass Total Memorabilia Power Pick #TM7
2004 Press Pass Trackside #16
2004 Press Pass Trackside #68
2004 Press Pass Trackside #117
2004 Press Pass Trackside Golden /100 #G16
2004 Press Pass Trackside Golden /100 #G68
2004 Press Pass Trackside Golden /100 #G117
2004 Press Pass Trackside Hat Giveaway #PPH38
2004 Press Pass Trackside Hot Pursuit #HP6
2004 Press Pass Trackside Pit Stoppers Autographs /17 #PSMK
2004 Press Pass Trackside Pit Stoppers Cars /20 #PST14
2004 Press Pass Trackside Pit Stoppers Drivers /20 #PSD14
2004 Press Pass Trackside Previews /5 #EB16
2004 Press Pass Trackside Runnin n' Gunnin #RG12
2004 Press Pass Trackside Samples #16
2004 Press Pass Trackside Samples #68
2004 Press Pass Trackside Samples #117
2004 Press Pass Triple Burner /100 #TB7
2004 Press Pass Triple Burner Exchange /100 #TB7
2004 Press Pass Velocity #VC5
2004 Team Caliber First Choice Beckett 1:24 #17
2004 VIP #9
2004 VIP #44
2004 VIP #45
2004 VIP Head Gear #HG6
2004 VIP Head Gear Transparent #HG6
2004 VIP Making the Show #MS11
2004 VIP Previews /5 #EB44
2004 VIP Previews /5 #EB9
2004 VIP Previews /5 #EB45
2004 VIP Samples #9
2004 VIP Samples #45
2004 VIP Samples #44
2004 VIP Tradin' Paint Bronze /130 #TPT7
2004 VIP Tradin' Paint Gold /50 #TPD7
2004 VIP Tradin' Paint Silver /70 #TPD7
2004 Wheels American Thunder #12
2004 Wheels American Thunder #37
2004 Wheels American Thunder #60
2004 Wheels American Thunder Cool Threads /525 #CT6
2004 Wheels American Thunder Head to Toe /100 #HT5
2004 Wheels American Thunder Post Mark #PM11
2004 Wheels American Thunder Previews /5 #EB12
2004 Wheels American Thunder Previews /5 #EB37
2004 Wheels American Thunder Pushin Pedal /275 #PP10
2004 Wheels American Thunder Samples #12
2004 Wheels American Thunder Samples #37
2004 Wheels American Thunder Samples #60
2004 Wheels American Thunder Thunder Road #TR8
2004 Wheels American Thunder Triple Hat /160 #TH8
2004 Wheels Autographs #36
2004 Wheels High Gear #12
2004 Wheels High Gear #46
2004 Wheels High Gear #49
2004 Wheels High Gear #60
2004 Wheels High Gear #0
2004 Wheels High Gear Flag Chasers Black /100 #FC9
2004 Wheels High Gear Flag Chasers Blue /50 #FC9
2004 Wheels High Gear Flag Chasers Checkered /35 #FC9
2004 Wheels High Gear Flag Chasers Green /100 #FC9
2004 Wheels High Gear Flag Chasers Red /100 #FC9
2004 Wheels High Gear Flag Chasers White /100 #FC9
2004 Wheels High Gear Flag Chasers Yellow /100 #FC9
2004 Wheels High Gear Full Throttle #FT5
2004 Wheels High Gear High Groove #HG11
2004 Wheels High Gear Machine #MM7B
2004 Wheels High Gear Man #MM7A
2004 Wheels High Gear MPH /100 #M12
2004 Wheels High Gear MPH /100 #M46
2004 Wheels High Gear MPH /100 #M49
2004 Wheels High Gear MPH /100 #M60
2004 Wheels High Gear Previews /5 #12
2004 Wheels High Gear Previews /5 #46
2004 Wheels High Gear Previews /5 #49
2004 Wheels High Gear Previews /5 #60
2004 Wheels High Gear Samples #12
2004 Wheels High Gear Samples #46
2004 Wheels High Gear Samples #49
2004 Wheels High Gear Samples #60
2004 Wheels High Gear Sunday Sensation #SS2
2004 Wheels High Gear Top Ten #TT1
2005 Press Pass #12
2005 Press Pass #74
2005 Press Pass Autographs #32
2005 Press Pass Autographs #31
2005 Press Pass Burning Rubber Autographs /17 #BRMK
2005 Press Pass Burning Rubber Cars /130 #BRT2
2005 Press Pass Burning Rubber Drivers /80 #BRD2
2005 Press Pass Burning Rubber Drivers Gold /1 #BRD2
2005 Press Pass Cup Chase #CCR10
2005 Press Pass Cup Chase Prizes #CCP10
2005 Press Pass Double Burner /100 #DB7
2005 Press Pass Double Burner Exchange /100 #DB7
2005 Press Pass Eclipse #8
2005 Press Pass Eclipse #34
2005 Press Pass Eclipse #60
2005 Press Pass Eclipse Destination WIN #2
2005 Press Pass Eclipse Previews /5 #EB8
2005 Press Pass Eclipse Previews /5 #EB34
2005 Press Pass Eclipse Previews /5 #EB60
2005 Press Pass Eclipse Samples #8
2005 Press Pass Eclipse Samples #34
2005 Press Pass Eclipse Samples #60
2005 Press Pass Eclipse Skidmarks #SM4
2005 Press Pass Eclipse Skidmarks Holofoil /250 #SM4
2005 Press Pass Eclipse Teammates Autographs /25 #2
2005 Press Pass Eclipse Teammates Autographs /25 #9
2005 Press Pass Eclipse Under Cover Autographs /17 #UCMK
2005 Press Pass Eclipse Under Cover Cars /120 #UCT2
2005 Press Pass Eclipse Under Cover Double Cover /340 #DC6
2005 Press Pass Eclipse Under Cover Double Cover /340 #DC7
2005 Press Pass Eclipse Under Cover Driver Red /400 #UCD2
2005 Press Pass Eclipse Under Cover Drivers Holofoil /100 #UCD2
2005 Press Pass Eclipse Under Cover Drivers Silver /690 #UCD2
2005 Press Pass Hot Treads /900 #HTR4
2005 Press Pass Hot Treads Holofoil /100 #HTR4
2005 Press Pass Legends #45
2005 Press Pass Legends Autographs Black /50 #20
2005 Press Pass Legends Blue /1890 #45B
2005 Press Pass Legends Double Threads Bronze /375 #DTMK
2005 Press Pass Legends Double Threads Bronze /375 #DTBK
2005 Press Pass Legends Double Threads Gold /99 #DTBK
2005 Press Pass Legends Double Threads Gold /99 #DTMK
2005 Press Pass Legends Double Threads Silver /225 #DTBK
2005 Press Pass Legends Double Threads Silver /225 #DTMK
2005 Press Pass Legends Gold /750 #45G
2005 Press Pass Legends Holofoil /100 #45H
2005 Press Pass Legends Press Plates Black /1 #45
2005 Press Pass Legends Press Plates Cyan /1 #45
2005 Press Pass Legends Press Plates Magenta /1 #45
2005 Press Pass Legends Press Plates Yellow /1 #45
2005 Press Pass Legends Previews /5 #45
2005 Press Pass Legends Solo /1 #45S
2005 Press Pass Optima #15
2005 Press Pass Optima #15B
2005 Press Pass Optima Corporate Cuts Cars /160 #CCT9
2005 Press Pass Optima Corporate Cuts Drivers /120 #CCD9
2005 Press Pass Optima Fan Favorite #FF14
2005 Press Pass Optima Gold /100 #G15
2005 Press Pass Optima Previews /5 #15
2005 Press Pass Optima Samples #15
2005 Press Pass Panorama #PPP6
2005 Press Pass Platinum /100 #P12
2005 Press Pass Platinum /100 #P74
2005 Press Pass Premium #13
2005 Press Pass Premium #57
2005 Press Pass Premium Hot Threads Autographs /17 #HTMK
2005 Press Pass Premium Hot Threads Cars /85 #HTT7
2005 Press Pass Premium Hot Threads Drivers /275 #HTD7
2005 Press Pass Premium Hot Threads Drivers Gold /1 #HTD7
2005 Press Pass Premium In the Zone #IZ11
2005 Press Pass Premium In the Zone Elite Edition /250 #IZ11
2005 Press Pass Premium Samples #13
2005 Press Pass Previews Green /5 #EB12
2005 Press Pass Samples #12
2005 Press Pass Samples #74
2005 Press Pass Signings #29
2005 Press Pass Signings #30
2005 Press Pass Signings Gold /50 #28
2005 Press Pass Signings Platinum /100 #28
2005 Press Pass Snapshots #SN14
2005 Press Pass Stealth #21
2005 Press Pass Stealth #24
2005 Press Pass Stealth #27
2005 Press Pass Stealth #94
2005 Press Pass Stealth EFX #EFX12
2005 Press Pass Stealth Fusion #FU8
2005 Press Pass Stealth Gear Grippers Cars /90 #GGT2
2005 Press Pass Stealth Gear Grippers Drivers /75 #GGD2
2005 Press Pass Stealth No Boundaries #NB10

2005 Press Pass Stealth Previews /5 #21
2005 Press Pass Stealth Previews /5 #24
2005 Press Pass Stealth Previews /5 #27
2005 Press Pass Stealth Samples #21
2005 Press Pass Stealth Samples #24
2005 Press Pass Stealth Samples #27
2005 Press Pass Stealth Samples #94
2005 Press Pass Stealth X-Ray /100 #X21
2005 Press Pass Stealth X-Ray /100 #X24
2005 Press Pass Stealth X-Ray /100 #X27
2005 Press Pass Stealth X-Ray /100 #X94
2005 Press Pass Top Ten #TT5
2005 Press Pass Total Memorabilia Power Pick #TM7
2005 Press Pass Trackside #30
2005 Press Pass Trackside #93
2005 Press Pass Trackside Dialed In #DI7
2005 Press Pass Trackside Golden /100 #G30
2005 Press Pass Trackside Golden /100 #G93
2005 Press Pass Trackside Hat Giveaway #PPH14
2005 Press Pass Trackside Hot Pass #9
2005 Press Pass Trackside Hot Pass National #9
2005 Press Pass Trackside Hot Pursuit #HP3
2005 Press Pass Trackside Pit Stoppers Cars /85 #PST10
2005 Press Pass Trackside Pit Stoppers Drivers /85 #PSD10
2005 Press Pass Trackside Previews /5 #30
2005 Press Pass Trackside Previews /1 #93
2005 Press Pass Trackside Runnin n' Gunnin #RG7
2005 Press Pass Trackside Samples #30
2005 Press Pass Trackside Samples #93
2005 Press Pass Triple Burner /100 #TB7
2005 Press Pass Triple Burner Exchange /100 #TB7
2005 Press Pass UMI Cup Chase #1
2005 Press Pass UMI Cup Chase #9
2005 Press Pass Velocity #V5
2005 VIP #13
2005 VIP #34
2005 VIP Head Gear #6
2005 VIP Head Gear Transparent #6
2005 VIP Lap Leaders #5
2005 VIP Lap Leaders Transparent #5
2005 VIP Making The Show #9
2005 VIP Previews /5 #EB13
2005 VIP Previews /5 #EB34
2005 VIP Samples #13
2005 VIP Samples #34
2005 VIP Tradin' Paint Autographs /17 #MK
2005 VIP Tradin' Paint Cars /110 #TPT7
2005 VIP Tradin' Paint Drivers /90 #TPD7
2005 Wheels American Thunder #14
2005 Wheels American Thunder #39
2005 Wheels American Thunder Cool Threads /475 #CT5
2005 Wheels American Thunder Head to Toe /125 #HT11
2005 Wheels American Thunder Previews /5 #14
2005 Wheels American Thunder Pushin Pedal /150 #PP14
2005 Wheels American Thunder Samples #14
2005 Wheels American Thunder Samples #39
2005 Wheels American Thunder Triple Hat /190 #TH11
2005 Wheels Autographs #31
2005 Wheels Autographs #30
2005 Wheels High Gear #10
2005 Wheels High Gear #51
2005 Wheels High Gear #56
2005 Wheels High Gear #64
2005 Wheels High Gear #90
2005 Wheels High Gear Flag to Flag #FF11
2005 Wheels High Gear MPH /100 #M10
2005 Wheels High Gear MPH /100 #M51
2005 Wheels High Gear MPH /100 #M56
2005 Wheels High Gear MPH /100 #M64
2005 Wheels High Gear MPH /100 #M90
2005 Wheels High Gear Previews Green /5 #EB10
2005 Wheels High Gear Samples #10
2005 Wheels High Gear Samples #51
2005 Wheels High Gear Samples #56
2005 Wheels High Gear Samples #64
2005 Wheels High Gear Samples #90
2005 Wheels High Gear Top Tier #TT8
2006 Press Pass #13
2006 Press Pass #95
2006 Press Pass #105
2006 Press Pass #117
2006 Press Pass Autographs #28
2006 Press Pass Blue #B13
2006 Press Pass Blue #B95
2006 Press Pass Blue #B105
2006 Press Pass Blue #B117
2006 Press Pass Burning Rubber Autographs /17 #BRMK
2006 Press Pass Burning Rubber Cars /370 #BRT10
2006 Press Pass Burning Rubber Drivers /100 #BRD10
2006 Press Pass Burning Rubber Drivers Gold /1 #BRD10
2006 Press Pass Burnouts /1050 #HT17
2006 Press Pass Burnouts Holofoil /125 #HT17
2006 Press Pass Collectors Series Making the Show #MS3
2006 Press Pass Cup Chase #CCR7
2006 Press Pass Cup Chase Prizes #CC2
2006 Press Pass Double Burner Firesuit-Glove /100 #DB3
2006 Press Pass Eclipse #7
2006 Press Pass Eclipse #65
2006 Press Pass Eclipse Previews /5 #EB7
2006 Press Pass Eclipse Racing Champions #RC10
2006 Press Pass Eclipse Racing Champions #RC22
2006 Press Pass Eclipse Skidmarks #SM4
2006 Press Pass Eclipse Skidmarks Holofoil /250 #SM4
2006 Press Pass Eclipse Supernova #SU8
2006 Press Pass Eclipse Teammates Autographs /25 #1
2006 Press Pass Eclipse Under Cover Autographs /17 #MK
2006 Press Pass Eclipse Under Cover Cars /140 #UCT1
2006 Press Pass Eclipse Under Cover Double Cover /100 #DC2
2006 Press Pass Eclipse Under Cover Double Cover /100 #DC6
2006 Press Pass Eclipse Under Cover Double Cover Holofoil /25 #DC2
2006 Press Pass Eclipse Under Cover Double Cover Holofoil /25 #DC6
2006 Press Pass Eclipse Under Cover Drivers Gold /1 #UCD1
2006 Press Pass Eclipse Under Cover Drivers Holofoil /100 #UCD1
2006 Press Pass Eclipse Under Cover Drivers Red /225 #UCD1
2006 Press Pass Eclipse Under Cover Drivers Silver /400 #UCD1
2006 Press Pass Four Wide /50 #FWMK
2006 Press Pass Four Wide Checkered Flag /1 #FWMK
2006 Press Pass Gold #G13
2006 Press Pass Gold #G95
2006 Press Pass Gold #G105
2006 Press Pass Gold #G117
2006 Press Pass Legends #38
2006 Press Pass Legends Autographs Black /50 #27
2006 Press Pass Legends Blue /1999 #B38
2006 Press Pass Legends Bronze /999 #Z38
2006 Press Pass Legends Champion Threads and Treads Bronze /399 #CTTMK
2006 Press Pass Legends Champion Threads and Treads Gold /99 #CTTMK
2006 Press Pass Legends Champion Threads and Treads Silver /299 #CTTMK
2006 Press Pass Legends Champion Threads Bronze /399 #CTMK
2006 Press Pass Legends Champion Threads Gold /50 #CTMK
2006 Press Pass Legends Champion Threads Patch /25 #CTMK
2006 Press Pass Legends Champion Threads Silver /199 #CTMK
2006 Press Pass Legends Gold /299 #G38
2006 Press Pass Legends Holofoil /99 #H38
2006 Press Pass Legends Memorable Moments Gold /199 #MM14
2006 Press Pass Legends Memorable Moments Silver /699 #MM14
2006 Press Pass Legends Press Plates Black /1 #PPB38
2006 Press Pass Legends Press Plates Black Backs /1 #PPB38B
2006 Press Pass Legends Press Plates Cyan /1 #PPC38
2006 Press Pass Legends Press Plates Cyan Backs /1 #PPC38B
2006 Press Pass Legends Press Plates Magenta /1 #PPM38
2006 Press Pass Legends Press Plates Magenta Backs /1 #PPM38B
2006 Press Pass Legends Press Plates Yellow /1 #PPY38
2006 Press Pass Legends Press Plates Yellow Backs /1 #PPY38B
2006 Press Pass Legends Previews /5 #EB38
2006 Press Pass Legends Solo /1 #S38
2006 Press Pass Legends Triple Threads /50 #TTMK
2006 Press Pass Optima #15
2006 Press Pass Optima #63
2006 Press Pass Optima #79
2006 Press Pass Optima #89
2006 Press Pass Optima #90
2006 Press Pass Optima #99
2006 Press Pass Optima #15B
2006 Press Pass Optima Gold /100 #G15
2006 Press Pass Optima Gold /100 #G63
2006 Press Pass Optima Gold /100 #G79
2006 Press Pass Optima Gold /100 #G89
2006 Press Pass Optima Gold /100 #G90
2006 Press Pass Optima Gold /100 #G99
2006 Press Pass Optima Previews /5 #EB15
2006 Press Pass Optima Rookie Relics Cars /50 #RRT12
2006 Press Pass Optima Rookie Relics Drivers /50 #RRD12
2006 Press Pass Platinum /100 #P13
2006 Press Pass Platinum /100 #P95
2006 Press Pass Platinum /100 #P105
2006 Press Pass Platinum /100 #P117
2006 Press Pass Premium #14
2006 Press Pass Premium #39
2006 Press Pass Premium #58
2006 Press Pass Premium #81
2006 Press Pass Premium Hot Threads Cars /165 #HTT2
2006 Press Pass Premium Hot Threads Drivers /220 #HTD2
2006 Press Pass Premium Hot Threads Drivers Gold /1 #HTD2
2006 Press Pass Premium In the Zone #IZ5
2006 Press Pass Premium In the Zone Red /250 #IZ5
2006 Press Pass Previews /5 #EB13
2006 Press Pass Previews /1 #EB105
2006 Press Pass Signings #28
2006 Press Pass Signings Gold /50 #28
2006 Press Pass Signings Gold Red Ink #28
2006 Press Pass Signings Silver /100 #28
2006 Press Pass Stealth #15
2006 Press Pass Stealth #41
2006 Press Pass Stealth #74
2006 Press Pass Stealth #48
2006 Press Pass Stealth Autographed Hat Entry #PPH13
2006 Press Pass Stealth Corporate Cuts /250 #CCD9
2006 Press Pass Stealth EFX #EFX11
2006 Press Pass Stealth Gear Grippers Autographs /17 #MK
2006 Press Pass Stealth Gear Grippers Cars Retail /99 #GGT7
2006 Press Pass Stealth Gear Grippers Drivers /99 #GGD7
2006 Press Pass Stealth Hot Pass #HP16
2006 Press Pass Stealth Previews /5 #15
2006 Press Pass Stealth Retail #15
2006 Press Pass Stealth Retail #41
2006 Press Pass Stealth Retail #74
2006 Press Pass Stealth Retail #48
2006 Press Pass Stealth X-Ray /100 #X15
2006 Press Pass Stealth X-Ray /100 #X41
2006 Press Pass Stealth X-Ray /100 #X48
2006 Press Pass Stealth X-Ray /100 #X74
2006 Press Pass Top 25 Drivers & Rides #C11
2006 Press Pass Top 25 Drivers & Rides #D11
2006 TRAKS #17
2006 TRAKS #45
2006 TRAKS #104
2006 TRAKS Autographs #19
2006 TRAKS Autographs 25 /25 #17
2006 TRAKS Previews /1 #17
2006 TRAKS Previews /1 #45
2006 TRAKS Previews /1 #104
2006 TRAKS Stickers #17
2006 VIP #13
2006 VIP #34
2006 VIP #41
2006 VIP Making the Show #MS3
2006 Wheels American Thunder #15
2006 Wheels American Thunder #31
2006 Wheels American Thunder #82
2006 Wheels American Thunder American Racing Idol #RI11
2006 Wheels American Thunder American Racing Idol Golden /250 #RI11
2006 Wheels American Thunder Cool Threads /329 #CT14
2006 Wheels American Thunder Double Hat /99 #DH13
2006 Wheels American Thunder Grandstand #GS12
2006 Wheels American Thunder Head to Toe /99 #HT11
2006 Wheels American Thunder Previews /5 #EB15
2006 Wheels American Thunder Thunder Road #TR17
2006 Wheels Autographs #30
2006 Wheels Autographs #31
2006 Wheels High Gear #7
2006 Wheels High Gear #49
2006 Wheels High Gear Flag to Flag #FF13
2006 Wheels High Gear MPH /100 #M7
2006 Wheels High Gear MPH /100 #M49
2006 Wheels High Gear Previews Green /5 #EB7
2006 Wheels High Gear Top Tier #TT7
2007 Press Pass #1
2007 Press Pass #75
2007 Press Pass #95
2007 Press Pass #105
2007 Press Pass #108
2007 Press Pass Autographs #22
2007 Press Pass Autographs Press Plates Black /1 #7
2007 Press Pass Autographs Press Plates Cyan /1 #7
2007 Press Pass Autographs Press Plates Magenta /1 #9
2007 Press Pass Autographs Press Plates Yellow /1 #8
2007 Press Pass Blue #B1
2007 Press Pass Blue #B75
2007 Press Pass Blue #B95
2007 Press Pass Blue #B105
2007 Press Pass Blue #B108
2007 Press Pass Burning Rubber Autographs /17 #BRSMK
2007 Press Pass Burning Rubber Drivers /75 #BRD2
2007 Press Pass Burning Rubber Drivers Gold /1 #BRD2
2007 Press Pass Burning Rubber Team /325 #BRT2
2007 Press Pass Collector's Series Box Set #SB13
2007 Press Pass Cup Chase #CCR4
2007 Press Pass Cup Chase Prizes #CC8
2007 Press Pass Double Burner Firesuit-Glove /100 #DB1
2007 Press Pass Double Burner Firesuit-Glove Exchange /100 #DB1
2007 Press Pass Double Burner Metal-Tire /100 #DBMK
2007 Press Pass Double Burner Metal-Tire Exchange /100 #DBMK
2007 Press Pass Eclipse #0
2007 Press Pass Eclipse #2
2007 Press Pass Eclipse #48
2007 Press Pass Eclipse #49
2007 Press Pass Eclipse #74
2007 Press Pass Eclipse Ecliptic #EC4
2007 Press Pass Eclipse Gold /25 #G2
2007 Press Pass Eclipse Gold /25 #G48
2007 Press Pass Eclipse Gold /25 #G49
2007 Press Pass Eclipse Gold /25 #G74
2007 Press Pass Eclipse Hyperdrive #HD2
2007 Press Pass Eclipse Previews /5 #EB2
2007 Press Pass Eclipse Racing Champions #RC5
2007 Press Pass Eclipse Racing Champions #RC15
2007 Press Pass Eclipse Red /1 #R2
2007 Press Pass Eclipse Red /1 #R48
2007 Press Pass Eclipse Red /1 #R49
2007 Press Pass Eclipse Red /1 #R74
2007 Press Pass Eclipse Skidmarks #SM4
2007 Press Pass Eclipse Skidmarks Holofoil /250 #SM4
2007 Press Pass Eclipse Teammates Autographs /25 #6
2007 Press Pass Eclipse Under Cover Autographs /17 #UCMK
2007 Press Pass Eclipse Under Cover Double Cover Name /25 #DC5
2007 Press Pass Eclipse Under Cover Double Cover NASCAR /99 #DC5
2007 Press Pass Eclipse Under Cover Drivers /450 #UCD4
2007 Press Pass Eclipse Under Cover Drivers Eclipse /1 #UCD4
2007 Press Pass Eclipse Under Cover Drivers Name /99 #UCD4
2007 Press Pass Eclipse Under Cover Drivers NASCAR /270 #UCD4
2007 Press Pass Eclipse Under Cover Teams /135 #UCT4
2007 Press Pass Eclipse Under Cover Teams NASCAR /25 #UCT4
2007 Press Pass Gold #G1
2007 Press Pass Gold #G75
2007 Press Pass Gold #G95
2007 Press Pass Gold #G105
2007 Press Pass Gold #G108
2007 Press Pass Legends #41
2007 Press Pass Legends Autographs Blue /60 #17
2007 Press Pass Legends Autographs Inscriptions Blue /9 #11
2007 Press Pass Legends Blue /999 #B41
2007 Press Pass Legends Bronze /599 #Z41
2007 Press Pass Legends Gold /249 #G41
2007 Press Pass Legends Holofoil /99 #H41
2007 Press Pass Legends Press Plates Black /1 #PP41
2007 Press Pass Legends Press Plates Black Backs /1 #PP41
2007 Press Pass Legends Press Plates Cyan /1 #PP41
2007 Press Pass Legends Press Plates Cyan Backs /1 #PP41
2007 Press Pass Legends Press Plates Magenta /1 #PP41
2007 Press Pass Legends Press Plates Magenta Backs /1 #PP41
2007 Press Pass Legends Press Plates Yellow /1 #PP41
2007 Press Pass Legends Press Plates Yellow Backs /1 #PP41
2007 Press Pass Legends Previews /5 #EB41
2007 Press Pass Legends Signature Series /25 #MK
2007 Press Pass Legends Solo /1 #S41
2007 Press Pass Platinum /100 #P1
2007 Press Pass Platinum /100 #P75
2007 Press Pass Platinum /100 #P95
2007 Press Pass Platinum /100 #P105
2007 Press Pass Platinum /100 #P108
2007 Press Pass Premium #15
2007 Press Pass Premium #42
2007 Press Pass Premium #56
2007 Press Pass Premium Hot Threads Autographs /17 #HTMK
2007 Press Pass Premium Hot Threads Drivers /145 #HTD12
2007 Press Pass Premium Hot Threads Drivers Gold /1 #HTD12
2007 Press Pass Premium Hot Threads Patch /6 #HTP23
2007 Press Pass Premium Hot Threads Patch /10 #HTP22
2007 Press Pass Premium Hot Threads Team /160 #HTT12
2007 Press Pass Premium Red /15 #R15
2007 Press Pass Premium Red /15 #R42
2007 Press Pass Premium Red /15 #R56
2007 Press Pass Previews /5 #EB1
2007 Press Pass Previews /1 #EB108
2007 Press Pass Signings #34
2007 Press Pass Signings Blue /25 #15
2007 Press Pass Signings Gold /50 #27
2007 Press Pass Signings Press Plates Black /1 #24
2007 Press Pass Signings Press Plates Cyan /1 #23
2007 Press Pass Signings Press Plates Magenta /1 #25
2007 Press Pass Signings Press Plates Yellow /1 #23
2007 Press Pass Signings Silver /100 #26
2007 Press Pass Snapshots #SN15
2007 Press Pass Stealth #14
2007 Press Pass Stealth #50
2007 Press Pass Stealth #69
2007 Press Pass Stealth #85
2007 Press Pass Stealth Battle Armor Autographs /17 #BASMK
2007 Press Pass Stealth Battle Armor Drivers /150 #BAD13
2007 Press Pass Stealth Battle Armor Teams /85 #BAT13
2007 Press Pass Stealth Chrome #14
2007 Press Pass Stealth Chrome #50
2007 Press Pass Stealth Chrome #69
2007 Press Pass Stealth Chrome #85
2007 Press Pass Stealth Chrome Exclusives /99 #X14
2007 Press Pass Stealth Chrome Exclusives /99 #X50
2007 Press Pass Stealth Chrome Exclusives /99 #X69
2007 Press Pass Stealth Chrome Exclusives /99 #X85
2007 Press Pass Stealth Chrome Platinum /25 #P14
2007 Press Pass Stealth Chrome Platinum /25 #P50
2007 Press Pass Stealth Chrome Platinum /25 #P69
2007 Press Pass Stealth Chrome Platinum /25 #P85
2007 Press Pass Stealth Maximum Access #MA15
2007 Press Pass Stealth Maximum Access Autographs /25 #MA15
2007 Press Pass Stealth Previews /1 #EB85
2007 Press Pass Stealth Previews /5 #EB14
2007 Press Pass Target Race Win Tires #RW9
2007 Press Pass Velocity #V3
2007 Press Pass Wal-Mart Autographs /50 #MK
2007 Traks #14
2007 Traks #85
2007 Traks #98
2007 Traks Corporate Cuts Driver /99 #CCD5
2007 Traks Corporate Cuts Patch /12 #CCD5
2007 Traks Corporate Cuts Team /180 #CCT5
2007 Traks Driver's Seat #DS11B
2007 Traks Driver's Seat #DS11
2007 Traks Driver's Seat National #DS11
2007 Traks Gold #G14
2007 Traks Gold #G85
2007 Traks Gold #G98
2007 Traks Holofoil /50 #H14
2007 Traks Holofoil /50 #H85
2007 Traks Holofoil /50 #H98
2007 Traks Hot Pursuit #HP11
2007 Traks Previews /5 #EB14
2007 Traks Red /10 #R14
2007 Traks Red /10 #R85
2007 Traks Red /10 #R98
2007 VIP #16
2007 VIP #65
2007 VIP #70
2007 VIP Get A Grip Autographs /17 #GGMK
2007 VIP Get A Grip Drivers /70 #GGD10
2007 VIP Get A Grip Teams /70 #GGT10
2007 VIP Previews /5 #EB16
2007 VIP Sunday Best #SB13
2007 Wheels American Thunder #16
2007 Wheels American Thunder #43
2007 Wheels American Thunder American Dreams #AD2
2007 Wheels American Thunder American Dreams Gold /250 #ADG2
2007 Wheels American Thunder American Muscle #AM3
2007 Wheels American Thunder Autographed Hat Instant Winner /1 #AH17
2007 Wheels American Thunder Cool Threads /299 #CT15
2007 Wheels American Thunder Head to Toe /99 #HT13
2007 Wheels American Thunder Previews /5 #EB16
2007 Wheels American Thunder Thunder Road #TR14
2007 Wheels American Thunder Thunder Strokes #22
2007 Wheels American Thunder Thunder Strokes Press Plates Black /1 #22
2007 Wheels American Thunder Thunder Strokes Press Plates Cyan /1 #22
2007 Wheels American Thunder Thunder Strokes Press Plates Magenta /1 #22
2007 Wheels American Thunder Thunder Strokes Press Plates Yellow /1 #22
2007 Wheels American Thunder Triple Hat /99 #TH15
2007 Wheels Autographs #19
2007 Wheels Autographs Press Plates Black /1 #18
2007 Wheels Autographs Press Plates Cyan /1 #18
2007 Wheels Autographs Press Plates Magenta /1 #18
2007 Wheels High Gear #2
2007 Wheels High Gear #58
2007 Wheels High Gear #70
2007 Wheels High Gear Driven #DR8
2007 Wheels High Gear Final Standings Gold /2 #FS2
2007 Wheels High Gear Flag Chasers Black /89 #FC10
2007 Wheels High Gear Flag Chasers Blue-Yellow /50 #FC10
2007 Wheels High Gear Flag Chasers Checkered /10 #FC10
2007 Wheels High Gear Flag Chasers Green /89 #FC10
2007 Wheels High Gear Flag Chasers Red /89 #FC10
2007 Wheels High Gear Flag Chasers White /89 #FC10
2007 Wheels High Gear Flag Chasers Yellow /89 #FC10
2007 Wheels High Gear Last Lap /10 #LL2
2007 Wheels High Gear MPH /100 #M2
2007 Wheels High Gear MPH /100 #M58
2007 Wheels High Gear MPH /100 #M70
2007 Wheels High Gear Previews /5 #EB2
2007 Wheels High Gear Previews /5 #EB58
2007 Wheels High Gear Top Tier #TT2
2008 Press Pass #0
2008 Press Pass #4
2008 Press Pass #114
2008 Press Pass Autographs #22
2008 Press Pass Autographs Press Plates Black /1 #18
2008 Press Pass Autographs Press Plates Cyan /1 #18
2008 Press Pass Autographs Press Plates Magenta /1 #18
2008 Press Pass Autographs Press Plates Yellow /1 #18
2008 Press Pass Blue #B4
2008 Press Pass Blue #B114
2008 Press Pass Burning Rubber Drivers /60 #BRD2
2008 Press Pass Burning Rubber Drivers Gold /1 #BRD2
2008 Press Pass Burning Rubber Drivers Prime Cuts /25 #BRD2
2008 Press Pass Burning Rubber Teams /175 #BRT2
2008 Press Pass Collector's Series Box Set #9
2008 Press Pass Cup Chase #CC2
2008 Press Pass Cup Chase Prizes #CC12
2008 Press Pass Double Burner Firesuit-Glove /100 #DBMK
2008 Press Pass Eclipse #4
2008 Press Pass Eclipse #61
2008 Press Pass Eclipse #75
2008 Press Pass Eclipse Gold /25 #G4
2008 Press Pass Eclipse Gold /25 #G61
2008 Press Pass Eclipse Gold /25 #G75
2008 Press Pass Eclipse Hyperdrive #HP7
2008 Press Pass Eclipse Previews /5 #EB4
2008 Press Pass Eclipse Previews /1 #EB75
2008 Press Pass Eclipse Red /1 #R4
2008 Press Pass Eclipse Red /1 #R61
2008 Press Pass Eclipse Red /1 #R75
2008 Press Pass Eclipse Star Tracks #ST13
2008 Press Pass Eclipse Star Tracks Holofoil /250 #ST13
2008 Press Pass Eclipse Stellar #ST6
2008 Press Pass Eclipse Stellar #ST21
2008 Press Pass Eclipse Under Cover Autographs /17 #UCMK
2008 Press Pass Eclipse Under Cover Double Cover Name /25 #DC3
2008 Press Pass Eclipse Under Cover Double Cover Name /25 #DC4
2008 Press Pass Eclipse Under Cover Double Cover NASCAR /99 #DC3
2008 Press Pass Eclipse Under Cover Double Cover NASCAR /99 #DC4
2008 Press Pass Eclipse Under Cover Drivers /250 #UCD9
2008 Press Pass Eclipse Under Cover Drivers Eclipse /1 #UCD9
2008 Press Pass Eclipse Under Cover Drivers Name /50 #UCD9
2008 Press Pass Eclipse Under Cover Drivers NASCAR /150 #UCD9
2008 Press Pass Eclipse Under Cover Teams /99 #UCT9
2008 Press Pass Eclipse Under Cover Teams NASCAR /25 #UCT9
2008 Press Pass Four Wide /50 #FWMK
2008 Press Pass Four Wide Checkered Flag /1 #FWMK
2008 Press Pass Gold #G4
2008 Press Pass Gold #G114
2008 Press Pass Legends #53
2008 Press Pass Legends Autographs Black Inscriptions /10 #MK
2008 Press Pass Legends Autographs Blue /75 #MK
2008 Press Pass Legends Autographs Press Plates Black /1 #MK
2008 Press Pass Legends Autographs Press Plates Cyan /1 #MK
2008 Press Pass Legends Autographs Press Plates Magenta /1 #MK
2008 Press Pass Legends Autographs Press Plates Yellow /1 #MK
2008 Press Pass Legends Blue /599 #53
2008 Press Pass Legends Bronze /299 #53
2008 Press Pass Legends Gold /99 #53
2008 Press Pass Legends Holo /25 #53
2008 Press Pass Legends Previews /5 #EB53
2008 Press Pass Legends Printing Plates Black /1 #53
2008 Press Pass Legends Printing Plates Cyan /1 #53
2008 Press Pass Legends Printing Plates Magenta /1 #53
2008 Press Pass Legends Printing Plates Yellow /1 #53
2008 Press Pass Legends Prominent Pieces Firesuit-Glove Bronze /50 #PP1MK
2008 Press Pass Legends Prominent Pieces Firesuit-Glove Gold /10 #PP1MK
2008 Press Pass Legends Prominent Pieces Firesuit-Glove Silver /25 #PP1MK
2008 Press Pass Legends Prominent Pieces Metal-Tire-Net /50 #PP4MK
2008 Press Pass Legends Prominent Pieces Metal-Tire-Net Gold /25 #PP4MK
2008 Press Pass Legends Solo /1 #53
2008 Press Pass Platinum /100 #P4
2008 Press Pass Platinum /100 #P114
2008 Press Pass Premium #14
2008 Press Pass Premium #58
2008 Press Pass Premium Clean Air #CA7
2008 Press Pass Premium Hot Threads Autographs /17 #HTMK
2008 Press Pass Premium Hot Threads Drivers /120 #HTD16
2008 Press Pass Premium Hot Threads Drivers Gold /1 #HTD16
2008 Press Pass Premium Hot Threads Patches #HTP19
2008 Press Pass Premium Hot Threads Patches /4 #HTP18
2008 Press Pass Premium Hot Threads Team /120 #HTT16
2008 Press Pass Premium Previews /5 #EB14
2008 Press Pass Premium Previews /1 #EB58
2008 Press Pass Premium Red /15 #14
2008 Press Pass Premium Red /15 #58
2008 Press Pass Premium Target #TA1
2008 Press Pass Premium Team Signed Baseballs #ROU
2008 Press Pass Premium Team Signed Baseballs #EROU
2008 Press Pass Previews /5 #EB4
2008 Press Pass Previews /1 #EB114
2008 Press Pass Race Day #RD9
2008 Press Pass Signings #33
2008 Press Pass Signings Blue /25 #15
2008 Press Pass Signings Gold /50 #29
2008 Press Pass Signings Press Plates Black /1 #23
2008 Press Pass Signings Press Plates Black /1 #MK
2008 Press Pass Signings Press Plates Cyan /1 #23
2008 Press Pass Signings Press Plates Magenta /1 #23
2008 Press Pass Signings Press Plates Yellow /1 #23
2008 Press Pass Signings Press Plates Yellow #MK
2008 Press Pass Signings Silver /100 #28
2008 Press Pass Speedway #24
2008 Press Pass Speedway Blur #B2
2008 Press Pass Speedway Cockpit #CP11
2008 Press Pass Speedway Corporate Cuts Drivers /80 #CDMK
2008 Press Pass Speedway Corporate Cuts Drivers Patches /12 #CDMK
2008 Press Pass Speedway Corporate Cuts Team /165 #CTMK
2008 Press Pass Speedway Gold #G24
2008 Press Pass Speedway Holofoil /50 #H24
2008 Press Pass Speedway Previews /5 #EB24
2008 Press Pass Speedway Red /10 #R24
2008 Press Pass Starting Grid #SG9
2008 Press Pass Stealth #18
2008 Press Pass Stealth #49
2008 Press Pass Stealth #70
2008 Press Pass Stealth #79
2008 Press Pass Stealth Battle Armor Autographs /17 #BASMK
2008 Press Pass Stealth Battle Armor Drivers /120 #BAD14
2008 Press Pass Stealth Battle Armor Teams /115 #BAT14
2008 Press Pass Stealth Chrome #18
2008 Press Pass Stealth Chrome #49
2008 Press Pass Stealth Chrome #70
2008 Press Pass Stealth Chrome #79
2008 Press Pass Stealth Chrome Exclusives /25 #18
2008 Press Pass Stealth Chrome Exclusives /25 #49
2008 Press Pass Stealth Chrome Exclusives /25 #70
2008 Press Pass Stealth Chrome Exclusives /25 #79
2008 Press Pass Stealth Chrome Exclusives Gold /99 #18
2008 Press Pass Stealth Chrome Exclusives Gold /99 #49
2008 Press Pass Stealth Chrome Exclusives Gold /99 #70
2008 Press Pass Stealth Chrome Exclusives Gold /99 #79
2008 Press Pass Stealth Maximum Access #MA15
2008 Press Pass Stealth Maximum Access Autographs /25 #MA15
2008 Press Pass Stealth Previews /5 #18
2008 Press Pass Stealth Synthesis #S5
2008 Press Pass Stealth Wal-Mart #WM7
2008 Press Pass Target Victory Tires /50 #TTMK
2008 Press Pass Wal-Mart Autographs /50 #7
2008 VIP #18
2008 VIP #80
2008 VIP All Access #AA12
2008 VIP Gear Gallery #GG9
2008 VIP Gear Gallery Memorabilia /50 #GGMK
2008 VIP Gear Gallery Transparent #GG9
2008 VIP Get a Grip Autographs /17 #GGSMK
2008 VIP Previews /5 #EB18
2008 VIP Triple Grip /25 #TG3
2008 VIP Trophy Club #TC2
2008 VIP Trophy Club Transparent #TC2
2008 Wheels American Thunder #17
2008 Wheels American Thunder #38
2008 Wheels American Thunder #80
2008 Wheels American Thunder #85
2008 Wheels American Thunder Autographed Hat Winner /1 #WHMK
2008 Wheels American Thunder Head to Toe /125 #HT13
2008 Wheels American Thunder Motorcade #M9
2008 Wheels American Thunder Previews /5 #17
2008 Wheels American Thunder Previews /1 #80
2008 Wheels American Thunder Pushin' Pedal /99 #PP 13
2008 Wheels American Thunder Trackside Treasury Autographs #MK
2008 Wheels American Thunder Trackside Treasury Autographs Gold /25 #MK
2008 Wheels American Thunder Trackside Treasury Autographs Printing Plates Black /1 #MK
2008 Wheels American Thunder Trackside Treasury Autographs Printing Plates Cyan /1 #MK
2008 Wheels American Thunder Trackside Treasury Autographs Printing Plates Magenta /1 #MK
2008 Wheels American Thunder Trackside Treasury Autographs Printing Plates Yellow /1 #MK
2008 Wheels American Thunder Triple Hat /125 #TH14
2008 Wheels Autographs #18
2008 Wheels Autographs Chase Edition /25 #7
2008 Wheels Autographs Press Plates Black /1 #18
2008 Wheels Autographs Press Plates Cyan /1 #18
2008 Wheels Autographs Press Plates Magenta /1 #18
2008 Wheels Autographs Press Plates Yellow /1 #18
2008 Wheels High Gear #4
2008 Wheels High Gear #46
2008 Wheels High Gear #59
2008 Wheels High Gear #66
2008 Wheels High Gear Driven #DR19
2008 Wheels High Gear Final Standings /4 #F4
2008 Wheels High Gear Flag Chasers Black /89 #FC9
2008 Wheels High Gear Flag Chasers Blue-Yellow /50 #FC9
2008 Wheels High Gear Flag Chasers Checkered /20 #FC9
2008 Wheels High Gear Flag Chasers Green /60 #FC9
2008 Wheels High Gear Flag Chasers Red /89 #FC9
2008 Wheels High Gear Flag Chasers White /65 #FC9
2008 Wheels High Gear Flag Chasers Yellow /89 #FC9
2008 Wheels High Gear Last Lap /10 #LL9
2008 Wheels High Gear Last Lap Holofoil /5 #LL9
2008 Wheels High Gear MPH /100 #M4
2008 Wheels High Gear MPH /100 #M46
2008 Wheels High Gear MPH /100 #M59
2008 Wheels High Gear MPH /100 #M66
2008 Wheels High Gear Previews /5 #EB4
2008 Wheels High Gear The Chase #TC4
2009 Element #16
2009 Element #64
2009 Element #88
2009 Element 1-2-3 Finish /50 #RFR
2009 Element Lab Report #LR16
2009 Element Previews /5 #16
2009 Element Radioactive /100 #16
2009 Element Radioactive /100 #64
2009 Element Radioactive /100 #88
2009 Press Pass #0
2009 Press Pass #12
2009 Press Pass #64
2009 Press Pass #118
2009 Press Pass #136
2009 Press Pass #206
2009 Press Pass Autographs Chase Edition /25 #MK
2009 Press Pass Autographs Gold #23
2009 Press Pass Autographs Printing Plates Black /1 #23
2009 Press Pass Autographs Printing Plates Cyan /1 #23
2009 Press Pass Autographs Printing Plates Magenta /1 #23
2009 Press Pass Autographs Printing Plates Yellow /1 #23
2009 Press Pass Autographs Silver #27
2009 Press Pass Autographs Track Edition /25 #MK
2009 Press Pass Blue #12
2009 Press Pass Blue #64
2009 Press Pass Blue #118
2009 Press Pass Blue #136
2009 Press Pass Blue #206
2009 Press Pass Cup Chase #CCR15
2009 Press Pass Daytona 500 Tires /25 #TTMK
2009 Press Pass Eclipse #12
2009 Press Pass Eclipse #57
2009 Press Pass Eclipse #61
2009 Press Pass Eclipse #78
2009 Press Pass Eclipse Black and White #12
2009 Press Pass Eclipse Black and White #57
2009 Press Pass Eclipse Black and White #61
2009 Press Pass Eclipse Black and White #78
2009 Press Pass Eclipse Blue #12
2009 Press Pass Eclipse Blue #57
2009 Press Pass Eclipse Blue #61
2009 Press Pass Eclipse Blue #78
2009 Press Pass Eclipse Ecliptic Path #EP1
2009 Press Pass Eclipse Under Cover Autographs /17 #UCSMK
2009 Press Pass Final Standings /160 #118
2009 Press Pass Four Wide Autographs /5 #FWMK
2009 Press Pass Four Wide Checkered Flag /1 #FWMK
2009 Press Pass Four Wide Firesuit /50 #FWMK
2009 Press Pass Four Wide Sheet Metal /10 #FWMK
2009 Press Pass Four Wide Tire /25 #FWMK
2009 Press Pass Fusion #72
2009 Press Pass Fusion Bronze /150 #72
2009 Press Pass Fusion Gold /50 #72
2009 Press Pass Fusion Green /25 #72
2009 Press Pass Fusion Onyx /1 #72
2009 Press Pass Fusion Revered Relics Gold /50 #RRGBMK
2009 Press Pass Fusion Revered Relics Holofoil /25 #RRGBMK
2009 Press Pass Fusion Revered Relics Premium Swatch /10 #RRGBMK
2009 Press Pass Fusion Revered Relics Silver /65 #RRGBMK
2009 Press Pass Fusion Silver /99 #72
2009 Press Pass Gold #12
2009 Press Pass Gold #64
2009 Press Pass Gold #118
2009 Press Pass Gold #136
2009 Press Pass Gold #206
2009 Press Pass Gold Holofoil /100 #12
2009 Press Pass Gold Holofoil /100 #64
2009 Press Pass Gold Holofoil /100 #118
2009 Press Pass Gold Holofoil /100 #136
2009 Press Pass Gold Holofoil /100 #206
2009 Press Pass Legends #50
2009 Press Pass Legends Autographs Gold /55 #20
2009 Press Pass Legends Autographs Inscriptions /25 #8
2009 Press Pass Legends Autographs Printing Plates Black /1 #15
2009 Press Pass Legends Autographs Printing Plates Cyan /1 #14
2009 Press Pass Legends Autographs Printing Plates Magenta /1 #15
2009 Press Pass Legends Autographs Printing Plates Yellow /1 #15
2009 Press Pass Legends Gold /399 #50
2009 Press Pass Legends Holofoil /50 #50
2009 Press Pass Legends Past and Present /550 #PP6
2009 Press Pass Legends Past and Present /550 #PP9
2009 Press Pass Legends Past and Present Holofoil /99 #PP6
2009 Press Pass Legends Past and Present Holofoil /99 #PP9
2009 Press Pass Legends Previews /5 #50
2009 Press Pass Legends Printing Plates Black /1 #50
2009 Press Pass Legends Printing Plates Cyan /1 #50
2009 Press Pass Legends Printing Plates Magenta /1 #50
2009 Press Pass Legends Printing Plates Yellow /1 #50
2009 Press Pass Legends Prominent Pieces Bronze /150 #PPMK
2009 Press Pass Legends Prominent Pieces Gold /25 #PPMK
2009 Press Pass Legends Prominent Pieces Oversized /25 #PPOEMK
2009 Press Pass Legends Prominent Pieces Silver /50 #PPMK
2009 Press Pass Legends Red /199 #50
2009 Press Pass Legends Solo /1 #50
2009 Press Pass NASCAR Gallery #NG4
2009 Press Pass Pieces Race Used Memorabilia #MK
2009 Press Pass Pocket Portraits #P13
2009 Press Pass Pocket Portraits Checkered Flag #P13
2009 Press Pass Pocket Portraits Hometown #P13
2009 Press Pass Pocket Portraits Smoke #P13
2009 Press Pass Pocket Portraits Wal-Mart #PPW8
2009 Press Pass Premium #0
2009 Press Pass Premium #15
2009 Press Pass Premium #40
2009 Press Pass Premium #78
2009 Press Pass Premium Hot Threads /325 #HTMK1
2009 Press Pass Premium Hot Threads /99 #HTMK2
2009 Press Pass Premium Hot Threads Autographs /17 #MK
2009 Press Pass Premium Hot Threads Multi-Color /25 #HTMK
2009 Press Pass Premium Hot Threads Patches /10 #HTP-MK
2009 Press Pass Premium Previews /5 #EB15
2009 Press Pass Premium Signatures #18
2009 Press Pass Premium Signatures Gold /25 #17
2009 Press Pass Premium Top Contenders #TC12
2009 Press Pass Premium Top Contenders Gold #TC12
2009 Press Pass Premium Win Streak #WS9
2009 Press Pass Premium Win Streak Victory Lane #WSVL-MK
2009 Press Pass Previews /5 #EB12
2009 Press Pass Previews /1 #EB118
2009 Press Pass Previews /5 #EB136
2009 Press Pass Red #12
2009 Press Pass Red #64
2009 Press Pass Red #118
2009 Press Pass Red #136
2009 Press Pass Red #206
2009 Press Pass Showcase /499 #23
2009 Press Pass Showcase /499 #46
2009 Press Pass Showcase /499 #35
2009 Press Pass Showcase 2nd Gear /125 #23
2009 Press Pass Showcase 2nd Gear /125 #35
2009 Press Pass Showcase 2nd Gear /125 #46
2009 Press Pass Showcase 3rd Gear /50 #23
2009 Press Pass Showcase 3rd Gear /50 #35
2009 Press Pass Showcase 3rd Gear /50 #46
2009 Press Pass Showcase 4th Gear /15 #23
2009 Press Pass Showcase 4th Gear /15 #35
2009 Press Pass Showcase 4th Gear /15 #46
2009 Press Pass Showcase Classic Collections Firesuit /25 #CCF8
2009 Press Pass Showcase Classic Collections Firesuit Patch /5 #CCF8
2009 Press Pass Showcase Classic Collections Ink /45 #9
2009 Press Pass Showcase Classic Collections Ink Gold /25 #9
2009 Press Pass Showcase Classic Collections Ink Green /5 #9
2009 Press Pass Showcase Classic Collections Ink Melting /1 #9
2009 Press Pass Showcase Classic Collections Sheet Metal /45 #CCS8
2009 Press Pass Showcase Classic Collections Tire /99 #CCT8
2009 Press Pass Showcase Elite Exhibit Ink /45 #8
2009 Press Pass Showcase Elite Exhibit Ink Gold /25 #8
2009 Press Pass Showcase Elite Exhibit Ink Green /5 #8
2009 Press Pass Showcase Elite Exhibit Ink Melting /1 #8
2009 Press Pass Showcase Elite Exhibit Triple Memorabilia /99 #EEMK
2009 Press Pass Showcase Elite Exhibit Triple Memorabilia Gold /45 #EEMK
2009 Press Pass Showcase Elite Exhibit Triple Memorabilia Green /25 #EEMK
2009 Press Pass Showcase Elite Exhibit Triple Memorabilia Melting /5 #EEMK
2009 Press Pass Showcase Printing Plates Black /1 #23
2009 Press Pass Showcase Printing Plates Black /1 #35
2009 Press Pass Showcase Printing Plates Black /1 #46
2009 Press Pass Showcase Printing Plates Cyan /1 #23
2009 Press Pass Showcase Printing Plates Cyan /1 #35
2009 Press Pass Showcase Printing Plates Cyan /1 #46
2009 Press Pass Showcase Printing Plates Magenta /1 #23
2009 Press Pass Showcase Printing Plates Magenta /1 #35
2009 Press Pass Showcase Printing Plates Magenta /1 #46
2009 Press Pass Showcase Printing Plates Yellow /1 #23
2009 Press Pass Showcase Printing Plates Yellow /1 #35
2009 Press Pass Showcase Printing Plates Yellow /1 #46
2009 Press Pass Showcase Prized Pieces Ink Firesuit /5 #8
2009 Press Pass Showcase Prized Pieces Ink Firesuit Patch /1 #8
2009 Press Pass Showcase Prized Pieces Ink Sheet Metal /25 #8
2009 Press Pass Showcase Prized Pieces Ink Tire /45 #8
2009 Press Pass Signature Series Archive Edition /1 #HTTMK
2009 Press Pass Signature Series Archive Edition /1 #GGMK
2009 Press Pass Signature Series Archive Edition /1 #TBMK
2009 Press Pass Signature Series Archive Edition /1 #BAMK
2009 Press Pass Signings Blue /25 #21
2009 Press Pass Signings Gold #21
2009 Press Pass Signings Green /15 #21
2009 Press Pass Signings Orange /65 #21
2009 Press Pass Signings Printing Plates Cyan /1 #21
2009 Press Pass Signings Printing Plates Yellow /1 #21
2009 Press Pass Signings Purple /45 #21
2009 Press Pass Sponsor Swatches /250 #SSMK

2009 Press Pass Sponsor Swatches Select /7 #SSMK
2009 Press Pass Stealth #18
2009 Press Pass Stealth Battle Armor /220 #BAMK2
2009 Press Pass Stealth Battle Armor /150 #BAMK1
2009 Press Pass Stealth Battle Armor Autographs /17 #BASMK
2009 Press Pass Stealth Battle Armor Multi-Color /165 #BAMK
2009 Press Pass Stealth Chrome #18
2009 Press Pass Stealth Chrome Brushed Metal /25 #18
2009 Press Pass Stealth Chrome Gold /99 #18
2009 Press Pass Stealth Confidential Classified Bronze #PC12
2009 Press Pass Stealth Confidential Secret Silver #PC12
2009 Press Pass Stealth Confidential Top Secret Gold /25 #PC12
2009 Press Pass Stealth Mach 09 #M10
2009 Press Pass Stealth Previews /5 #EB18
2009 Press Pass Tradin' Paint #TP4
2009 Press Pass Tread Marks Autographs /10 #SSMK
2009 Press Pass Wal-Mart Autographs Red #8
2009 Sportkings National Convention Memorabilia Gold /1 #SK5
2009 Sportkings National Convention Memorabilia Gold /1 #SK24
2009 Sportkings National Convention Memorabilia Silver /9 #SK5
2009 Sportkings National Convention Memorabilia Silver /9 #SK24
2009 Upper Deck Prominent Cuts Cut Signatures /4 #PCMK
2009 VIP #17
2009 VIP #55
2009 VIP #68
2009 VIP After Party #AP1
2009 VIP After Party #AP2
2009 VIP After Party Transparent #AP1
2009 VIP After Party Transparent #AP2
2009 VIP Get A Grip /100 #GGMK
2009 VIP Get A Grip Holofoil /10 #GGMK
2009 VIP Leadfoot /150 #LFMK
2009 VIP Leadfoot Holofoil /10 #LFMK
2009 VIP Previews /5 #17
2009 VIP Purple /25 #17
2009 VIP Purple /25 #55
2009 VIP Purple /25 #68
2009 Wheels Autographs #37
2009 Wheels Autographs /25 #36
2009 Wheels Autographs Press Plates Black /1 #MK
2009 Wheels Autographs Press Plates Cyan /1 #MK
2009 Wheels Autographs Press Plates Magenta /1 #MK
2009 Wheels Autographs Press Plates Yellow /1 #MK
2009 Wheels Main Event #8
2009 Wheels Main Event #56
2009 Wheels Main Event #64
2009 Wheels Main Event #38
2009 Wheels Main Event Buyback Archive Edition /1 #TBDMK
2009 Wheels Main Event Buyback Archive Edition /1 #PSMK
2009 Wheels Main Event Buyback Archive Edition /1 #HTMK
2009 Wheels Main Event Buyback Archive Edition /1 #UCMK
2009 Wheels Main Event Fast Pass Purple /25 #8
2009 Wheels Main Event Fast Pass Purple /25 #38
2009 Wheels Main Event Fast Pass Purple /25 #56
2009 Wheels Main Event Fast Pass Purple /25 #64
2009 Wheels Main Event Foil #8
2009 Wheels Main Event Hat Dance Patch /10 #HDMK
2009 Wheels Main Event Hat Dance Triple /99 #HDMK
2009 Wheels Main Event High Rollers #HR4
2009 Wheels Main Event Marks Clubs #30
2009 Wheels Main Event Marks Diamonds /10 #30
2009 Wheels Main Event Marks Hearts /5 #30
2009 Wheels Main Event Marks Printing Plates Black /1 #26
2009 Wheels Main Event Marks Printing Plates Cyan /1 #26
2009 Wheels Main Event Marks Printing Plates Magenta /1 #26
2009 Wheels Main Event Marks Printing Plates Yellow /1 #26
2009 Wheels Main Event Marks Spades /1 #30
2009 Wheels Main Event Playing Cards Blue #KC
2009 Wheels Main Event Playing Cards Red #KC
2009 Wheels Main Event Poker Chips #11
2009 Wheels Main Event Previews /5 #8
2009 Wheels Main Event Wildcard Cuts /2 #WCCMK
2010 Element #18
2010 Element #49
2010 Element Blue /35 #18
2010 Element Blue /35 #49
2010 Element Finish Line Checkered Flag /10 #FLMK
2010 Element Finish Line Green Flag /20 #FLMK
2010 Element Finish Line Tires /99 #FLMK
2010 Element Flagship Performers Championships Black /25 #FPCMK
2010 Element Flagship Performers Championships Blue-Orange /25 #FPCMK
2010 Element Flagship Performers Championships Checkered /1 #FPCMK
2010 Element Flagship Performers Championships Green /5 #FPCMK
2010 Element Flagship Performers Championships Red /25 #FPCMK
2010 Element Flagship Performers Championships White /15 #FPCMK
2010 Element Flagship Performers Championships X /25 #FPCMK
2010 Element Flagship Performers Championships Yellow /25 #FPCMK
2010 Element Flagship Performers Consecutive Starts Black /20 #FPSMK
2010 Element Flagship Performers Consecutive Starts Blue-Orange /20 #FPSMK
2010 Element Flagship Performers Consecutive Starts Checkered /1 #FPSMK
2010 Element Flagship Performers Consecutive Starts Green /5 #FPSMK
2010 Element Flagship Performers Consecutive Starts Red /20 #FPSMK
2010 Element Flagship Performers Consecutive Starts White /10 #FPSMK
2010 Element Flagship Performers Consecutive Starts X /10 #FPSMK
2010 Element Flagship Performers Consecutive Starts Yellow /20 #FPSMK
2010 Element Flagship Performers Wins Black /20 #FPWMK
2010 Element Flagship Performers Wins Blue-Orange /20 #FPWMK
2010 Element Flagship Performers Wins Checkered /1 #FPWMK
2010 Element Flagship Performers Wins Green /5 #FPWMK
2010 Element Flagship Performers Wins Red /20 #FPWMK
2010 Element Flagship Performers Wins White /15 #FPWMK
2010 Element Flagship Performers Wins X /10 #FPWMK
2010 Element Flagship Performers Wins Yellow /20 #FPWMK
2010 Element Green #18
2010 Element Green #49
2010 Element Previews /5 #EB18
2010 Element Purple /25 #18
2010 Element Purple /25 #49
2010 Element Red Target #18
2010 Element Red Target #49
2010 Press Pass #15
2010 Press Pass #87
2010 Press Pass Autographs #26
2010 Press Pass Autographs Printing Plates Black /1 #19
2010 Press Pass Autographs Printing Plates Cyan /1 #23
2010 Press Pass Autographs Printing Plates Magenta /1 #20
2010 Press Pass Autographs Printing Plates Yellow /1 #20
2010 Press Pass Autographs Track Edition /10 #8
2010 Press Pass Blue #15
2010 Press Pass Blue #87
2010 Press Pass Burning Rubber /250 #BR2
2010 Press Pass Burning Rubber /250 #BR1
2010 Press Pass Burning Rubber Autographs /17 #SSTEMK
2010 Press Pass Burning Rubber Gold /50 #BR1
2010 Press Pass Burning Rubber Gold /50 #BR2
2010 Press Pass Burning Rubber Prime Cuts /25 #BR1
2010 Press Pass By The Numbers #BN33
2010 Press Pass Cup Chase Prizes #CC11
2010 Press Pass Eclipse #22
2010 Press Pass Eclipse #90
2010 Press Pass Eclipse Blue #22
2010 Press Pass Eclipse Blue #90
2010 Press Pass Eclipse Gold #22
2010 Press Pass Eclipse Gold #90
2010 Press Pass Eclipse Previews /5 #22
2010 Press Pass Eclipse Purple /25 #22
2010 Press Pass Five Star /35 #15
2010 Press Pass Five Star Classic Compilations Combos Firesuit Autographs /15 #CCMROU
2010 Press Pass Five Star Classic Compilations Combos Patches Autographs /1 #CCMROU
2010 Press Pass Five Star Classic Compilations Dual Memorabilia Autographs /10 #MK
2010 Press Pass Five Star Classic Compilations Patch Autographs /1 #CCPMK9
2010 Press Pass Five Star Classic Compilations Patch Autographs /1 #CCPMK1
2010 Press Pass Five Star Classic Compilations Patch Autographs /1 #CCPMK2
2010 Press Pass Five Star Classic Compilations Patch Autographs /1 #CCPMK3
2010 Press Pass Five Star Classic Compilations Patch Autographs /1 #CCPMK4
2010 Press Pass Five Star Classic Compilations Patch Autographs /1 #CCPMK5
2010 Press Pass Five Star Classic Compilations Patch Autographs /1 #CCPMK6
2010 Press Pass Five Star Classic Compilations Patch Autographs /1 #CCPMK7
2010 Press Pass Five Star Classic Compilations Patch Autographs /1 #CCPMK8
2010 Press Pass Five Star Classic Compilations Triple Memorabilia Autographs /5 #MK
2010 Press Pass Five Star Holofoil /10 #15
2010 Press Pass Five Star Melting /1 #15
2010 Press Pass Five Star Paramount Pieces Aluminum /20 #MK
2010 Press Pass Five Star Paramount Pieces Blue /15 #MK
2010 Press Pass Five Star Paramount Pieces Gold /10 #MK
2010 Press Pass Five Star Paramount Pieces Holofoil /10 #MK
2010 Press Pass Five Star Paramount Pieces Melting /1 #MK
2010 Press Pass Four Wide Firesuit /25 #FWMK
2010 Press Pass Four Wide Sheet Metal /15 #FWMK
2010 Press Pass Four Wide Shoes /1 #FWMK
2010 Press Pass Four Wide Tires /10 #FWMK
2010 Press Pass Gold #15
2010 Press Pass Gold #87
2010 Press Pass Holofoil /100 #15
2010 Press Pass Holofoil /100 #87
2010 Press Pass Legends #51
2010 Press Pass Legends Autographs Blue /10 #36
2010 Press Pass Legends Autographs Holofoil /25 #36
2010 Press Pass Legends Autographs Printing Plates Black /1 #31
2010 Press Pass Legends Autographs Printing Plates Cyan /1 #31
2010 Press Pass Legends Autographs Printing Plates Magenta /1 #31
2010 Press Pass Legends Autographs Printing Plates Yellow /1 #31
2010 Press Pass Legends Blue /1 #51
2010 Press Pass Legends Gold /399 #51
2010 Press Pass Legends Holofoil /50 #51
2010 Press Pass Legends Motorsports Masters #MMMK
2010 Press Pass Legends Motorsports Masters Autographs Blue /1 #NNO
2010 Press Pass Legends Motorsports Masters Autographs Gold /25 #20
2010 Press Pass Legends Motorsports Masters Autographs Holofoil /10 #20
2010 Press Pass Legends Motorsports Masters Autographs Printing Plates Black /1 #31
2010 Press Pass Legends Motorsports Masters Autographs Printing Plates Cyan /1 #31
2010 Press Pass Legends Motorsports Masters Autographs Printing Plates Magenta /1 #31
2010 Press Pass Legends Motorsports Masters Autographs Printing Plates Yellow /1 #31
2010 Press Pass Legends Motorsports Masters Blue /10 #MMMK
2010 Press Pass Legends Motorsports Masters Gold /299 #MMMK
2010 Press Pass Legends Motorsports Masters Holofoil /149 #MMMK
2010 Press Pass Legends Printing Plates Black /1 #51
2010 Press Pass Legends Printing Plates Cyan /1 #51
2010 Press Pass Legends Printing Plates Magenta /1 #51
2010 Press Pass Legends Printing Plates Yellow /1 #51
2010 Press Pass Legends Prominent Pieces Copper /99 #PPMK
2010 Press Pass Legends Prominent Pieces Gold /50 #PPMK
2010 Press Pass Legends Prominent Pieces Holofoil /25 #PPMK
2010 Press Pass Legends Prominent Pieces Oversized Firesuit /25 #PPOEMK
2010 Press Pass Legends Red /199 #51
2010 Press Pass Premium #14
2010 Press Pass Premium #73
2010 Press Pass Premium Allies #A5
2010 Press Pass Premium Allies Signatures /5 #ASKH
2010 Press Pass Premium Purple /25 #14
2010 Press Pass Premium Rivals #R6
2010 Press Pass Premium Rivals Signatures /5 #RSGK
2010 Press Pass Premium Signatures #PSMK
2010 Press Pass Premium Signatures Red Ink /20 #PSMK
2010 Press Pass Previews /5 #15
2010 Press Pass Purple /25 #15
2010 Press Pass Purple /25 #87
2010 Press Pass Showcase /499 #14
2010 Press Pass Showcase /499 #34
2010 Press Pass Showcase /499 #46
2010 Press Pass Showcase Classic Collections Firesuit Green /25 #CCIRFR
2010 Press Pass Showcase Classic Collections Firesuit Patch Melting /5 #CCIRFR
2010 Press Pass Showcase Classic Collections Ink /15 #CCIRFR
2010 Press Pass Showcase Classic Collections Ink Gold /10 #CCIRFR
2010 Press Pass Showcase Classic Collections Ink Green /5 #CCIRFR
2010 Press Pass Showcase Classic Collections Ink Melting /1 #CCIRFR
2010 Press Pass Showcase Classic Collections Sheet Metal /99 #CCIRFR
2010 Press Pass Showcase Classic Collections Sheet Metal Gold /45 #CCIRFR
2010 Press Pass Showcase Elite Exhibit Ink /25 #EEIMK
2010 Press Pass Showcase Elite Exhibit Ink Gold /10 #EEIMK
2010 Press Pass Showcase Elite Exhibit Ink Green /5 #EEIMK
2010 Press Pass Showcase Elite Exhibit Ink Melting /1 #EEIMK
2010 Press Pass Showcase Elite Exhibit Triple Memorabilia /99 #EEMMK
2010 Press Pass Showcase Elite Exhibit Triple Memorabilia Gold /45 #EEMMK
2010 Press Pass Showcase Elite Exhibit Triple Memorabilia Green /25 #EEMMK
2010 Press Pass Showcase Elite Exhibit Triple Memorabilia Melting /5 #EEMMK
2010 Press Pass Showcase Gold /125 #14
2010 Press Pass Showcase Gold /125 #34
2010 Press Pass Showcase Gold /125 #46
2010 Press Pass Showcase Green /50 #14
2010 Press Pass Showcase Green /50 #34
2010 Press Pass Showcase Green /50 #46
2010 Press Pass Showcase Melting /15 #14
2010 Press Pass Showcase Melting /15 #34
2010 Press Pass Showcase Melting /15 #46
2010 Press Pass Showcase Platinum Holo /1 #14
2010 Press Pass Showcase Platinum Holo /1 #34
2010 Press Pass Showcase Platinum Holo /1 #46
2010 Press Pass Showcase Prized Pieces Firesuit Ink Gold /25 #PPIMK
2010 Press Pass Showcase Prized Pieces Firesuit Ink Melting /1 #PPIMK
2010 Press Pass Showcase Prized Pieces Memorabilia Ink Green /15 #PPIMK
2010 Press Pass Showcase Prized Pieces Sheet Metal Ink Silver /45 #PPIMK
2010 Press Pass Signings Blue /10 #29
2010 Press Pass Signings Gold /25 #29
2010 Press Pass Signings Red /15 #29
2010 Press Pass Signings Silver /50 #29
2010 Press Pass Stealth #17
2010 Press Pass Stealth Black and White #17
2010 Press Pass Stealth Mach 10 #MT5
2010 Press Pass Stealth Previews /5 #17
2010 Press Pass Stealth Purple /25 #17
2010 Press Pass Tradin' Paint #TP2
2010 Press Pass Tradin' Paint Sheet Metal /299 #TPMK
2010 Press Pass Tradin' Paint Sheet Metal Gold /50 #TPMK
2010 Press Pass Tradin' Paint Sheet Metal Holofoil /25 #TPMK
2010 Press Pass Unleashed #U1
2010 Wheels Autographs #25
2010 Wheels Autographs Printing Plates Black /1 #25
2010 Wheels Autographs Printing Plates Cyan /1 #25
2010 Wheels Autographs Printing Plates Magenta /1 #25
2010 Wheels Autographs Printing Plates Yellow /1 #25
2010 Wheels Autographs Special Ink /10 #10
2010 Wheels Autographs Target /10 #17
2010 Wheels Main Event #17
2010 Wheels Main Event #51
2010 Wheels Main Event American Muscle #AM4
2010 Wheels Main Event Blue #17
2010 Wheels Main Event Blue #51
2010 Wheels Main Event Fight Card #FC15
2010 Wheels Main Event Fight Card Checkered Flag #FC15
2010 Wheels Main Event Fight Card Full Color Retail #FC15
2010 Wheels Main Event Fight Card Gold /25 #FC15
2010 Wheels Main Event Head to Head /150 #HHCEMK
2010 Wheels Main Event Head to Head Blue /75 #HHCEMK
2010 Wheels Main Event Head to Head Holofoil /10 #HHCEMK
2010 Wheels Main Event Head to Head Red /25 #HHCEMK
2010 Wheels Main Event Marks Autographs /71 #29
2010 Wheels Main Event Marks Autographs Black /1 #28
2010 Wheels Main Event Marks Autographs Blue /25 #29
2010 Wheels Main Event Marks Autographs Red /5 #29
2010 Wheels Main Event Matchups Autographs /10 #MKJL
2010 Wheels Main Event Purple /25 #17
2010 Wheels Main Event Purple /25 #51
2010 Wheels Main Event Toe to Toe /10 #TTCEMK
2010 Wheels Main Event Upper Cuts /115 #UCMK
2010 Wheels Main Event Upper Cuts Blue /25 #UCMK
2010 Wheels Main Event Upper Cuts Holofoil /5 #UCMK
2010 Wheels Main Event Upper Cuts Red /10 #UCMK
2010 Wheels Main Event Wheel to Wheel /25 #WWCEMK
2010 Wheels Main Event Wheel to Wheel Holofoil /10 #WWCEMK
2011 Element #17
2011 Element #91
2011 Element #80
2011 Element Autographs /60 #28
2011 Element Autographs Blue /5 #28
2011 Element Autographs Gold /10 #27
2011 Element Autographs Printing Plates Black /1 #28
2011 Element Autographs Printing Plates Cyan /1 #28
2011 Element Autographs Printing Plates Magenta /1 #28
2011 Element Autographs Printing Plates Yellow /1 #28
2011 Element Autographs Silver /25 #27
2011 Element Black /35 #17
2011 Element Black /35 #80
2011 Element Black /35 #91
2011 Element Flagship Performers 2010 Laps Completed Yellow /50 #FPLMK
2011 Element Flagship Performers Championships Checkered /25 #FPCMK
2011 Element Flagship Performers Race Streak Without DNF Red /50 #FPDMK
2011 Element Green #17
2011 Element Green #80
2011 Element Green #91
2011 Element Previews /5 #EB17
2011 Element Purple /25 #17
2011 Element Purple /25 #80
2011 Element Purple /25 #91
2011 Element Red #17
2011 Element Red #80
2011 Element Red #91
2011 Press Pass #18
2011 Press Pass #73
2011 Press Pass #196
2011 Press Pass #0
2011 Press Pass Autographs Blue /10 #28
2011 Press Pass Autographs Bronze /99 #27
2011 Press Pass Autographs Gold /25 #27
2011 Press Pass Autographs Printing Plates Black /1 #28
2011 Press Pass Autographs Printing Plates Cyan /1 #28
2011 Press Pass Autographs Printing Plates Magenta /1 #28
2011 Press Pass Autographs Printing Plates Yellow /1 #28
2011 Press Pass Autographs Silver /50 #28
2011 Press Pass Blue Holofoil /10 #18
2011 Press Pass Blue Holofoil /10 #73
2011 Press Pass Blue Holofoil /10 #196
2011 Press Pass Blue Retail #18
2011 Press Pass Blue Retail #73
2011 Press Pass Blue Retail #196
2011 Press Pass Cup Chase #CCR11
2011 Press Pass Cup Chase Prizes #CC4
2011 Press Pass Eclipse #16
2011 Press Pass Eclipse #40
2011 Press Pass Eclipse Blue #16
2011 Press Pass Eclipse Blue #40
2011 Press Pass Eclipse Gold /55 #16
2011 Press Pass Eclipse Gold /55 #40
2011 Press Pass Eclipse Previews /5 #EB16
2011 Press Pass Eclipse Previews /1 #EB40
2011 Press Pass Eclipse Purple /25 #16
2011 Press Pass Eclipse Purple /25 #40
2011 Press Pass Eclipse Spellbound Swatches /150 #SBMK2
2011 Press Pass Eclipse Spellbound Swatches /150 #SBMK3
2011 Press Pass Eclipse Spellbound Swatches /250 #SBMK1
2011 Press Pass Eclipse Spellbound Swatches /100 #SBMK5
2011 Press Pass Eclipse Spellbound Swatches /100 #SBMK4
2011 Press Pass Eclipse Spellbound Swatches /50 #SBMK7
2011 Press Pass Eclipse Spellbound Swatches /75 #SBMK6
2011 Press Pass Eclipse Spellbound Swatches Signatures /10 #NNO
2011 Press Pass FanFare #20
2011 Press Pass FanFare Autographs Blue /5 #37
2011 Press Pass FanFare Autographs Bronze /25 #37
2011 Press Pass FanFare Autographs Gold /15 #37
2011 Press Pass FanFare Autographs Printing Plates Black /1 #37
2011 Press Pass FanFare Autographs Printing Plates Cyan /1 #37
2011 Press Pass FanFare Autographs Printing Plates Magenta /1 #37
2011 Press Pass FanFare Autographs Printing Plates Yellow /1 #37
2011 Press Pass FanFare Autographs Silver /10 #37
2011 Press Pass FanFare Blue Die Cuts #20
2011 Press Pass FanFare Championship Caliber #CC4
2011 Press Pass FanFare Dual Autographs /10 #NNO
2011 Press Pass FanFare Dual Autographs /10 #NNO
2011 Press Pass FanFare Emerald /25 #20
2011 Press Pass FanFare Holofoil Die Cuts #20
2011 Press Pass FanFare Magnificent Materials /225 #MMMK
2011 Press Pass FanFare Magnificent Materials Dual Swatches /50 #MMDMK
2011 Press Pass FanFare Magnificent Materials Dual Swatches Holofoil /10 #MMDMK
2011 Press Pass FanFare Magnificent Materials Holofoil /50 #MMMK
2011 Press Pass FanFare Magnificent Materials Signatures /50 #MMSEMK
2011 Press Pass FanFare Magnificent Materials Signatures Holofoil /25 #MMSEMK
2011 Press Pass FanFare Rookie Standouts #RS10
2011 Press Pass FanFare Ruby Die Cuts /15 #20
2011 Press Pass FanFare Sapphire /10 #20
2011 Press Pass FanFare Silver /25 #20
2011 Press Pass Flashback #FB3
2011 Press Pass Four Wide Firesuit /25 #FWMK
2011 Press Pass Four Wide Glove /1 #FWMK
2011 Press Pass Four Wide Sheet Metal /15 #FWMK
2011 Press Pass Four Wide Tire /10 #FWMK
2011 Press Pass Geared Up Gold /100 #GUMK
2011 Press Pass Geared Up Holofoil /50 #GUMK
2011 Press Pass Gold /50 #18
2011 Press Pass Gold /50 #73
2011 Press Pass Gold /50 #196
2011 Press Pass Legends #47
2011 Press Pass Legends Autographs Blue /10 #LGAMK
2011 Press Pass Legends Autographs Gold /25 #LGAMK
2011 Press Pass Legends Autographs Printing Plates Black /1 #LGAMK
2011 Press Pass Legends Autographs Printing Plates Cyan /1 #LGAMK
2011 Press Pass Legends Autographs Printing Plates Magenta /1 #LGAMK
2011 Press Pass Legends Autographs Printing Plates Yellow /1 #LGAMK
2011 Press Pass Legends Autographs Silver /99 #LGAMK
2011 Press Pass Legends Gold /250 #47
2011 Press Pass Legends Holofoil /25 #47
2011 Press Pass Legends Printing Plates Black /1 #47
2011 Press Pass Legends Printing Plates Cyan /1 #47
2011 Press Pass Legends Printing Plates Magenta /1 #47
2011 Press Pass Legends Printing Plates Yellow /1 #47
2011 Press Pass Legends Prominent Pieces Gold /50 #PPMK
2011 Press Pass Legends Prominent Pieces Holofoil /25 #PPMK
2011 Press Pass Legends Prominent Pieces Oversized Firesuit /25 #PPOEMK
2011 Press Pass Legends Prominent Pieces Purple /15 #PPMK
2011 Press Pass Legends Prominent Pieces Silver /99 #PPMK
2011 Press Pass Legends Purple /25 #47
2011 Press Pass Legends Red /99 #47
2011 Press Pass Legends Solo /1 #47
2011 Press Pass Premium #19
2011 Press Pass Premium #52
2011 Press Pass Premium #87
2011 Press Pass Premium Hot Threads /150 #HTMK
2011 Press Pass Premium Hot Threads Multi Color /25 #HTMK
2011 Press Pass Premium Hot Threads Secondary Color /25 #HTMK
2011 Press Pass Premium Purple /25 #19
2011 Press Pass Premium Purple /25 #52
2011 Press Pass Premium Purple /25 #87
2011 Press Pass Premium Signatures /189 #PSMK
2011 Press Pass Previews /5 #EB18
2011 Press Pass Previews /1 #EB196
2011 Press Pass Purple /25 #18
2011 Press Pass Purple /25 #196
2011 Press Pass Showcase /499 #16
2011 Press Pass Showcase /499 #40
2011 Press Pass Showcase /499 #55
2011 Press Pass Showcase Champions /499 #CH6
2011 Press Pass Showcase Champions Gold /125 #CH6
2011 Press Pass Showcase Champions Ink /25 #CHIMK
2011 Press Pass Showcase Champions Ink Gold /10 #CHIMK
2011 Press Pass Showcase Champions Ink Melting /1 #CHIMK
2011 Press Pass Showcase Champions Melting /1 #CH6
2011 Press Pass Showcase Champions Memorabilia Firesuit /99 #CHMMK
2011 Press Pass Showcase Champions Memorabilia Firesuit Gold /45 #CHMMK
2011 Press Pass Showcase Champions Memorabilia Firesuit Melting /5 #CHMMK
2011 Press Pass Showcase Classic Collections Firesuit /45 #CCMRFR
2011 Press Pass Showcase Classic Collections Firesuit Patches /5 #CCMRFR
2011 Press Pass Showcase Classic Collections Ink /25 #CCMRFR
2011 Press Pass Showcase Classic Collections Ink Gold /5 #CCMRFR
2011 Press Pass Showcase Classic Collections Ink Melting /1 #CCMRFR
2011 Press Pass Showcase Classic Collections Sheet Metal /99 #CCMRFR
2011 Press Pass Showcase Elite Exhibit Ink /50 #EEIMK
2011 Press Pass Showcase Elite Exhibit Ink Gold /25 #EEIMK
2011 Press Pass Showcase Elite Exhibit Ink Melting /1 #EEIMK
2011 Press Pass Showcase Gold /125 #16
2011 Press Pass Showcase Gold /125 #40
2011 Press Pass Showcase Gold /125 #55
2011 Press Pass Showcase Green /25 #16
2011 Press Pass Showcase Green /25 #40
2011 Press Pass Showcase Green /25 #55
2011 Press Pass Showcase Masterpieces Ink /45 #MPIMK
2011 Press Pass Showcase Masterpieces Ink Gold /25 #MPIMK
2011 Press Pass Showcase Masterpieces Ink Melting /1 #MPIMK
2011 Press Pass Showcase Masterpieces Memorabilia /99 #MPMMK
2011 Press Pass Showcase Masterpieces Memorabilia Gold /45 #MPMMK
2011 Press Pass Showcase Masterpieces Memorabilia Melting /5 #MPMMK
2011 Press Pass Showcase Melting /1 #16
2011 Press Pass Showcase Melting /1 #40
2011 Press Pass Showcase Melting /1 #55
2011 Press Pass Signature Series /11 #SSTMK
2011 Press Pass Signature Series /11 #SSSMK
2011 Press Pass Signature Series /11 #SSMKF
2011 Press Pass Signature Series /11 #SSMMK
2011 Press Pass Signings Black and White /10 #PPSMK
2011 Press Pass Signings Brushed Metal /50 #PPSMK
2011 Press Pass Signings Holofoil /25 #PPSMK
2011 Press Pass Stealth #44
2011 Press Pass Stealth #91
2011 Press Pass Stealth Afterburner /99 #ABMK
2011 Press Pass Stealth Afterburner Gold /25 #ABMK
2011 Press Pass Stealth Black and White /25 #44
2011 Press Pass Stealth Black and White /25 #91
2011 Press Pass Stealth Holofoil /99 #44
2011 Press Pass Stealth Holofoil /99 #91
2011 Press Pass Stealth Metal of Honor Medal of Honor /50 #BAMK
2011 Press Pass Stealth Metal of Honor Purple Heart /25 #MHMK
2011 Press Pass Stealth Metal of Honor Silver Star /99 #BAMK
2011 Press Pass Stealth Purple /25 #44
2011 Press Pass Wal-Mart Top 12 Tires /25 #T12MK
2011 Wheels Main Event #19
2011 Wheels Main Event #63
2011 Wheels Main Event #88
2011 Wheels Main Event All Stars #A6
2011 Wheels Main Event All Stars Brushed Foil /199 #A6
2011 Wheels Main Event All Stars Holofoil /50 #A6
2011 Wheels Main Event Black and White #19
2011 Wheels Main Event Black and White #63
2011 Wheels Main Event Black and White #88
2011 Wheels Main Event Blue /75 #19
2011 Wheels Main Event Blue /75 #63
2011 Wheels Main Event Blue /75 #88
2011 Wheels Main Event Gloves Off Holofoil /25 #GOMK
2011 Wheels Main Event Gloves Off Silver /99 #GOMK
2011 Wheels Main Event Green /1 #19
2011 Wheels Main Event Green /1 #63
2011 Wheels Main Event Green /1 #88
2011 Wheels Main Event Headliners Holofoil /25 #HLMK
2011 Wheels Main Event Headliners Silver /50 #HLMK
2011 Wheels Main Event Lead Foot Holofoil /25 #LFMK
2011 Wheels Main Event Lead Foot Silver /99 #LFMK
2011 Wheels Main Event Marks Autographs Blue /10 #MEMK
2011 Wheels Main Event Marks Autographs Gold /25 #MEMK
2011 Wheels Main Event Marks Autographs Silver /50 #MEMK
2011 Wheels Main Event Matchups Autographs /10 #MEMMKMM
2011 Wheels Main Event Rear View #R10
2011 Wheels Main Event Rear View Brushed Foil /199 #R10
2011 Wheels Main Event Rear View Holofoil /50 #R10
2011 Wheels Main Event Red /20 #19
2011 Wheels Main Event Red /20 #63
2011 Wheels Main Event Red /20 #88
2012 Press Pass #19
2012 Press Pass #78
2012 Press Pass Autographs Blue /5 #PPAMK
2012 Press Pass Autographs Red /5 #PPAMK
2012 Press Pass Autographs Silver /15 #PPAMK
2012 Press Pass Blue #19
2012 Press Pass Blue #78
2012 Press Pass Blue Holofoil /35 #19
2012 Press Pass Blue Holofoil /35 #78
2012 Press Pass Burning Rubber Gold /99 #BRMK2
2012 Press Pass Burning Rubber Gold /99 #BRMK
2012 Press Pass Burning Rubber Holofoil /25 #BRMK
2012 Press Pass Burning Rubber Holofoil /25 #BRMK2
2012 Press Pass Burning Rubber Prime Cuts /25 #BRMK
2012 Press Pass Burning Rubber Prime Cuts /25 #BRMK2
2012 Press Pass Burning Rubber Purple /15 #BRMK
2012 Press Pass Burning Rubber Purple /15 #BRMK2
2012 Press Pass Cup Chase #CCR11
2012 Press Pass Cup Chase Prizes #CCP8
2012 Press Pass Fanfare #23
2012 Press Pass Fanfare Autographs Blue /5 #MK
2012 Press Pass Fanfare Autographs Gold /25 #MK
2012 Press Pass Fanfare Autographs Red /10 #MK
2012 Press Pass Fanfare Autographs Silver /75 #MK
2012 Press Pass Fanfare Blue Foil Die Cuts #23
2012 Press Pass Fanfare Diamond /5 #23
2012 Press Pass Fanfare Holofoil Die Cuts #23
2012 Press Pass Fanfare Magnificent Materials /299 #MMMK
2012 Press Pass Fanfare Magnificent Materials Dual Swatches /50 #MMMK
2012 Press Pass Fanfare Magnificent Materials Dual Swatches Melting /10 #MMMK
2012 Press Pass Fanfare Magnificent Materials Gold /125 #MMMK
2012 Press Pass Fanfare Power Rankings #PR2
2012 Press Pass Fanfare Sapphire /20 #23
2012 Press Pass Fanfare Showtime #S10
2012 Press Pass Fanfare Silver /25 #23
2012 Press Pass Four Wide Firesuit /25 #FWMK
2012 Press Pass Four Wide Glove /1 #FWMK
2012 Press Pass Four Wide Sheet Metal /15 #FWMK
2012 Press Pass Four Wide Tire /10 #FWMK
2012 Press Pass Gold #19
2012 Press Pass Gold #78
2012 Press Pass Ignite #20
2012 Press Pass Ignite #66
2012 Press Pass Ignite Materials Autographs Gun Metal /45 #IMMK
2012 Press Pass Ignite Materials Autographs Red /5 #IMMK
2012 Press Pass Ignite Materials Autographs Silver /150 #IMMK
2012 Press Pass Ignite Materials Gun Metal /99 #IMMK
2012 Press Pass Ignite Materials Red /10 #IMMK
2012 Press Pass Ignite Materials Silver #IMMK
2012 Press Pass Ignite Profile #P12
2012 Press Pass Ignite Proofs Black and White /50 #20
2012 Press Pass Ignite Proofs Black and White /50 #66
2012 Press Pass Ignite Proofs Cyan #20
2012 Press Pass Ignite Proofs Cyan #66
2012 Press Pass Ignite Proofs Magenta #20
2012 Press Pass Ignite Proofs Magenta #66
2012 Press Pass Ignite Proofs Yellow /10 #20
2012 Press Pass Ignite Proofs Yellow /10 #66
2012 Press Pass Legends Prominent Pieces Gold /50 #MK
2012 Press Pass Legends Prominent Pieces Holofoil /25 #MK
2012 Press Pass Legends Prominent Pieces Oversized Firesuit /25 #MK
2012 Press Pass Legends Prominent Pieces Silver /99 #MK
2012 Press Pass Power Picks Blue /50 #10
2012 Press Pass Power Picks Blue /50 #38
2012 Press Pass Power Picks Blue /50 #67
2012 Press Pass Power Picks Gold /50 #10
2012 Press Pass Power Picks Gold /50 #38
2012 Press Pass Power Picks Gold /50 #67
2012 Press Pass Power Picks Holofoil /10 #10
2012 Press Pass Power Picks Holofoil /10 #38
2012 Press Pass Power Picks Holofoil /10 #67
2012 Press Pass Purple /35 #19
2012 Press Pass Purple /35 #78
2012 Press Pass Redline #20
2012 Press Pass Redline Black /99 #20
2012 Press Pass Redline Cyan /50 #20
2012 Press Pass Redline Full Throttle Dual Relic Blue /5 #FTMK
2012 Press Pass Redline Full Throttle Dual Relic Gold /10 #FTMK
2012 Press Pass Redline Full Throttle Dual Relic Melting /1 #FTMK
2012 Press Pass Redline Full Throttle Dual Relic Red /75 #FTMK
2012 Press Pass Redline Full Throttle Dual Relic Silver /25 #FTMK
2012 Press Pass Redline Magenta /15 #20
2012 Press Pass Redline Muscle Car Sheet Metal Blue /5 #MCMK
2012 Press Pass Redline Muscle Car Sheet Metal Gold /10 #MCMK
2012 Press Pass Redline Muscle Car Sheet Metal Melting /1 #MCMK
2012 Press Pass Redline Muscle Car Sheet Metal Red /75 #MCMK
2012 Press Pass Redline Muscle Car Sheet Metal Silver /25 #MCMK
2012 Press Pass Redline Performance Driven #PD6
2012 Press Pass Redline Relic Autographs Blue /10 #RLRMK
2012 Press Pass Redline Relic Autographs Gold /25 #RLRMK
2012 Press Pass Redline Relic Autographs Melting /1 #RLRMK
2012 Press Pass Redline Relic Autographs Red /75 #RLRMK
2012 Press Pass Redline Relic Autographs Silver /50 #RLRMK
2012 Press Pass Redline Relics Blue /5 #RLMK
2012 Press Pass Redline Relics Gold /10 #RLMK
2012 Press Pass Redline Relics Melting /1 #RLMK
2012 Press Pass Redline Relics Red /75 #RLMK
2012 Press Pass Redline Relics Silver /25 #RLMK
2012 Press Pass Redline RPM #RPM8
2012 Press Pass Redline Signatures Blue /5 #RSMK
2012 Press Pass Redline Signatures Gold /25 #RSMK
2012 Press Pass Redline Signatures Holofoil /10 #RSMK
2012 Press Pass Redline Signatures Melting /1 #RSMK
2012 Press Pass Redline Signatures Red /50 #RSMK
2012 Press Pass Redline V8 Relics Blue /5 #V8MK
2012 Press Pass Redline V8 Relics Gold /10 #V8MK
2012 Press Pass Redline V8 Relics Melting /1 #V8MK
2012 Press Pass Redline V8 Relics Red /25 #V8MK
2012 Press Pass Redline Yellow /1 #20
2012 Press Pass Showcase /499 #54
2012 Press Pass Showcase /499 #15
2012 Press Pass Showcase Classic Collections Ink /10 #CCMRFR
2012 Press Pass Showcase Classic Collections Ink Gold /5 #CCMRFR
2012 Press Pass Showcase Classic Collections Ink Melting /1 #CCMRFR
2012 Press Pass Showcase Classic Collections Memorabilia /99 #CCMRFR
2012 Press Pass Showcase Classic Collections Memorabilia Gold /50 #CCMRFR
2012 Press Pass Showcase Classic Collections Memorabilia Melting /5 #CCMRFR
2012 Press Pass Showcase Elite Exhibit Ink /50 #EEIMK
2012 Press Pass Showcase Elite Exhibit Ink Gold /25 #EEIMK
2012 Press Pass Showcase Elite Exhibit Ink Melting /1 #EEIMK
2012 Press Pass Showcase Gold /125 #15
2012 Press Pass Showcase Gold /125 #54
2012 Press Pass Showcase Green /5 #15
2012 Press Pass Showcase Green /5 #54
2012 Press Pass Showcase Masterpieces Memorabilia /99 #MPMK
2012 Press Pass Showcase Masterpieces Memorabilia Gold /50 #MPMK
2012 Press Pass Showcase Masterpieces Memorabilia Melting /5 #MPMK
2012 Press Pass Showcase Melting /1 #15
2012 Press Pass Showcase Melting /1 #54
2012 Press Pass Showcase Prized Pieces /99 #PPMK
2012 Press Pass Showcase Prized Pieces Gold /50 #PPMK
2012 Press Pass Showcase Prized Pieces Ink /50 #PPIMK
2012 Press Pass Showcase Prized Pieces Ink Gold /25 #PPIMK
2012 Press Pass Showcase Prized Pieces Ink Melting /1 #PPIMK
2012 Press Pass Showcase Prized Pieces Melting /5 #PPMK
2012 Press Pass Showcase Purple /1 #15
2012 Press Pass Showcase Purple /1 #54
2012 Press Pass Showcase Red /25 #15
2012 Press Pass Showcase Red /25 #54
2012 Press Pass Showcase Showcase Patches /5 #SSPMK
2012 Press Pass Showcase Showcase Patches Melting /1 #SSPMK
2012 Press Pass Signature Series Race Used /12 #PPAMK1
2012 Press Pass Signature Series Race Used /12 #PPAMK2
2012 Press Pass Snapshots #SS19
2012 Press Pass Target Snapshots #SSTG8
2012 Press Pass Ultimate Collection Blue Holofoil /25 #UCMK
2012 Press Pass Ultimate Collection Holofoil /50 #UCMK
2012 Total Memorabilia #16
2012 Total Memorabilia Black and White /99 #16
2012 Total Memorabilia Dual Swatch Gold /75 #TMMK
2012 Total Memorabilia Dual Swatch Holofoil /25 #TMMK
2012 Total Memorabilia Dual Swatch Melting /5 #TMMK
2012 Total Memorabilia Dual Swatch Silver /99 #TMMK
2012 Total Memorabilia Gold /275 #16
2012 Total Memorabilia Hot Rod Relics Gold /50 #HRRMK
2012 Total Memorabilia Hot Rod Relics Holofoil /10 #HRRMK
2012 Total Memorabilia Hot Rod Relics Melting /1 #HRRMK
2012 Total Memorabilia Hot Rod Relics Silver /99 #HRRMK
2012 Total Memorabilia Memory Lane #ML5
2012 Total Memorabilia Red Retail /250 #16
2012 Total Memorabilia Single Swatch Gold /99 #TMMK
2012 Total Memorabilia Single Swatch Holofoil /50 #TMMK
2012 Total Memorabilia Single Swatch Melting /10 #TMMK
2012 Total Memorabilia Single Swatch Silver /199 #TMMK
2013 Press Pass #24
2013 Press Pass #0
2013 Press Pass Burning Rubber Blue /50 #BRMK
2013 Press Pass Burning Rubber Gold /199 #BRMK
2013 Press Pass Burning Rubber Holofoil /75 #BRMK
2013 Press Pass Burning Rubber Letterman /8 #BRLMK
2013 Press Pass Burning Rubber Melting /10 #BRMK
2013 Press Pass Certified Winners Autographs Gold /10 #MK
2013 Press Pass Certified Winners Autographs Melting /5 #MK
2013 Press Pass Color Proofs Black #24
2013 Press Pass Color Proofs Cyan /35 #24
2013 Press Pass Color Proofs Magenta #24
2013 Press Pass Color Proofs Yellow /5 #24
2013 Press Pass Cup Chase #CC12
2013 Press Pass Cup Chase Prizes #CCP1
2013 Press Pass Fanfare #28
2013 Press Pass Fanfare #29
2013 Press Pass Fanfare Autographs Blue /1 #MK
2013 Press Pass Fanfare Autographs Gold /5 #MK
2013 Press Pass Fanfare Autographs Green /1 #MK
2013 Press Pass Fanfare Autographs Red /5 #MK
2013 Press Pass Fanfare Autographs Silver /10 #MK
2013 Press Pass Fanfare Diamond Die Cuts /5 #28
2013 Press Pass Fanfare Diamond Die Cuts /5 #29
2013 Press Pass Fanfare Green /3 #28
2013 Press Pass Fanfare Green /3 #29
2013 Press Pass Fanfare Holofoil Die Cuts #28
2013 Press Pass Fanfare Holofoil Die Cuts #29
2013 Press Pass Fanfare Magnificent Jumbo Materials Signatures /10 #MK
2013 Press Pass Fanfare Magnificent Materials Dual Swatches /50 #MK
2013 Press Pass Fanfare Magnificent Materials Dual Swatches Melting /10 #MK
2013 Press Pass Fanfare Magnificent Materials Gold /50 #MK
2013 Press Pass Fanfare Magnificent Materials Jumbo Swatches /25 #MK
2013 Press Pass Fanfare Magnificent Materials Signatures /50 #MK
2013 Press Pass Fanfare Magnificent Materials Signatures Blue /25 #MK
2013 Press Pass Fanfare Magnificent Materials Silver /199 #MK
2013 Press Pass Fanfare Red Foil Die Cuts #28
2013 Press Pass Fanfare Red Foil Die Cuts #29
2013 Press Pass Fanfare Sapphire /20 #28
2013 Press Pass Fanfare Sapphire /20 #29
2013 Press Pass Fanfare Showtime #S5
2013 Press Pass Fanfare Signature Ride Autographs /10 #MK
2013 Press Pass Fanfare Signature Ride Autographs Blue /1 #MK
2013 Press Pass Fanfare Signature Ride Autographs Red /5 #MK
2013 Press Pass Fanfare Silver /25 #28
2013 Press Pass Fanfare Silver /25 #29
2013 Press Pass Ignite #17
2013 Press Pass Ignite #60
2013 Press Pass Ignite Ink Black /70 #IIMK
2013 Press Pass Ignite Ink Blue /25 #IIMK
2013 Press Pass Ignite Ink Red /5 #IIMK
2013 Press Pass Ignite Profile #9
2013 Press Pass Ignite Proofs Black and White /50 #17
2013 Press Pass Ignite Proofs Black and White /50 #60
2013 Press Pass Ignite Proofs Cyan #17
2013 Press Pass Ignite Proofs Cyan #60
2013 Press Pass Ignite Proofs Magenta #17
2013 Press Pass Ignite Proofs Magenta #60
2013 Press Pass Ignite Proofs Yellow /5 #17
2013 Press Pass Ignite Proofs Yellow /5 #60
2013 Press Pass Legends Autographs Blue #LGMK
2013 Press Pass Legends Autographs Gold /4 #LGMK
2013 Press Pass Legends Autographs Holofoil /2 #LGMK
2013 Press Pass Legends Autographs Printing Plates Black /1 #LGMK
2013 Press Pass Legends Autographs Printing Plates Cyan /1 #LGMK
2013 Press Pass Legends Autographs Printing Plates Magenta /1 #LGMK
2013 Press Pass Legends Autographs Printing Plates Yellow /1 #LGMK
2013 Press Pass Legends Autographs Silver #LGMK
2013 Press Pass Legends Prominent Pieces Gold /10 #PPMK
2013 Press Pass Legends Prominent Pieces Holofoil /5 #PPMK
2013 Press Pass Legends Prominent Pieces Oversized Firesuit /5 #PPMK
2013 Press Pass Legends Prominent Pieces Silver /25 #PPMK
2013 Press Pass Power Picks Blue /99 #10
2013 Press Pass Power Picks Gold /50 #10
2013 Press Pass Power Picks Holofoil /10 #10
2013 Press Pass Racing Champions #RC29
2013 Press Pass Racing Champions #RC1
2013 Press Pass Redline #27
2013 Press Pass Redline #28
2013 Press Pass Redline Black /99 #27
2013 Press Pass Redline Black /99 #28
2013 Press Pass Redline Cyan /50 #27
2013 Press Pass Redline Cyan /50 #28
2013 Press Pass Redline Dynamic Duals Dual Relic Blue /5 #DDMK
2013 Press Pass Redline Dynamic Duals Dual Relic Gold /10 #DDMK
2013 Press Pass Redline Dynamic Duals Dual Relic Melting /1 #DDMK
2013 Press Pass Redline Dynamic Duals Dual Relic Red /75 #DDMK
2013 Press Pass Redline Dynamic Duals Dual Relic Silver /25 #DDMK
2013 Press Pass Redline Magenta /15 #27
2013 Press Pass Redline Magenta /15 #28
2013 Press Pass Redline Muscle Car Sheet Metal Blue /5 #MCMMK
2013 Press Pass Redline Muscle Car Sheet Metal Gold /10 #MCMMK
2013 Press Pass Redline Muscle Car Sheet Metal Melting /1 #MCMMK
2013 Press Pass Redline Muscle Car Sheet Metal Red /50 #MCMMK
2013 Press Pass Redline Muscle Car Sheet Metal Silver /25 #MCMMK
2013 Press Pass Redline Redline Racers #9
2013 Press Pass Redline Signatures Blue /50 #RSMK1
2013 Press Pass Redline Signatures Blue /10 #RSMK2
2013 Press Pass Redline Signatures Gold /5 #RSMK1
2013 Press Pass Redline Signatures Gold /5 #RSMK2
2013 Press Pass Redline Signatures Holo /20 #RSMK1
2013 Press Pass Redline Signatures Holo /10 #RSMK2
2013 Press Pass Redline Signatures Melting /1 #RSMK1
2013 Press Pass Redline Signatures Melting /1 #RSMK2
2013 Press Pass Redline Signatures Red /99 #RSMK1
2013 Press Pass Redline Signatures Red /25 #RSMK2
2013 Press Pass Redline V8 Relics Blue /5 #V8MK
2013 Press Pass Redline V8 Relics Gold /10 #V8MK
2013 Press Pass Redline V8 Relics Melting /1 #V8MK
2013 Press Pass Redline V8 Relics Red /25 #V8MK

2013 Press Pass Redline Yellow /1 #27
2013 Press Pass Redline Yellow /1 #28
2013 Press Pass Showcase /349 #15
2013 Press Pass Showcase /349 #39
2013 Press Pass Showcase /349 #59
2013 Press Pass Showcase Black /1 #15
2013 Press Pass Showcase Black /1 #39
2013 Press Pass Showcase Black /1 #59
2013 Press Pass Showcase Blue /25 #15
2013 Press Pass Showcase Blue /25 #39
2013 Press Pass Showcase Blue /25 #59
2013 Press Pass Showcase Classic Collections Ink Gold /5 #CCIJGR
2013 Press Pass Showcase Classic Collections Ink Melting /1 #CCIJGR
2013 Press Pass Showcase Classic Collections Ink Red /1 #CCIJGR
2013 Press Pass Showcase Classic Collections Memorabilia Gold /25 #CCMJGR
2013 Press Pass Showcase Classic Collections Memorabilia Melting /5 #CCMJGR
2013 Press Pass Showcase Classic Collections Memorabilia Silver /75 #CCMJGR
2013 Press Pass Showcase Elite Exhibit Ink /25 #EEIMK
2013 Press Pass Showcase Elite Exhibit Ink Blue /30 #EEIMK
2013 Press Pass Showcase Elite Exhibit Ink Gold /10 #EEIMK
2013 Press Pass Showcase Elite Exhibit Ink Melting /1 #EEIMK
2013 Press Pass Showcase Elite Exhibit Ink Red /5 #EEIMK
2013 Press Pass Showcase Gold /99 #15
2013 Press Pass Showcase Gold /99 #39
2013 Press Pass Showcase Gold /99 #59
2013 Press Pass Showcase Green /20 #15
2013 Press Pass Showcase Green /20 #39
2013 Press Pass Showcase Green /20 #59
2013 Press Pass Showcase Masterpieces Ink /35 #MPIMK
2013 Press Pass Showcase Masterpieces Ink Gold /10 #MPIMK
2013 Press Pass Showcase Masterpieces Ink Melting /1 #MPIMK
2013 Press Pass Showcase Masterpieces Memorabilia /75 #MPMK
2013 Press Pass Showcase Masterpieces Memorabilia Gold /25 #MPMK
2013 Press Pass Showcase Masterpieces Memorabilia Melting /5 #MPMK
2013 Press Pass Showcase Prized Pieces /99 #PPMMK
2013 Press Pass Showcase Prized Pieces Blue /20 #PPMMK
2013 Press Pass Showcase Prized Pieces Gold /25 #PPMMK
2013 Press Pass Showcase Prized Pieces Ink /50 #PPIMK
2013 Press Pass Showcase Prized Pieces Ink Gold /25 #PPIMK
2013 Press Pass Showcase Prized Pieces Ink Melting /1 #PPIMK
2013 Press Pass Showcase Prized Pieces Melting /5 #PPMMK
2013 Press Pass Showcase Purple /13 #15
2013 Press Pass Showcase Purple /13 #39
2013 Press Pass Showcase Purple /13 #59
2013 Press Pass Showcase Red /10 #15
2013 Press Pass Showcase Red /10 #39
2013 Press Pass Showcase Red /10 #59
2013 Press Pass Showcase Series Standouts Gold /50 #14
2013 Press Pass Showcase Showcase Patches /5 #SPMK
2013 Press Pass Showcase Showroom /299 #10
2013 Press Pass Showcase Showroom Blue /40 #10
2013 Press Pass Showcase Showroom Gold /50 #10
2013 Press Pass Showcase Showroom Green /20 #10
2013 Press Pass Showcase Showroom Melting /1 #10
2013 Press Pass Showcase Showroom Purple /13 #10
2013 Press Pass Showcase Showroom Red /10 #10
2013 Press Pass Showcase Signature Patches /7 #SSPMK
2013 Press Pass Showcase Studio Showcase /299 #14
2013 Press Pass Showcase Studio Showcase Blue /40 #14
2013 Press Pass Showcase Studio Showcase Green /25 #14
2013 Press Pass Showcase Studio Showcase Melting /1 #14
2013 Press Pass Showcase Studio Showcase Purple /13 #14
2013 Press Pass Showcase Studio Showcase Red /10 #14
2013 Press Pass Signings Blue /1 #MK
2013 Press Pass Signings Gold /25 #MK
2013 Press Pass Signings Holofoil /5 #MK
2013 Press Pass Signings Printing Plates Black /1 #MK
2013 Press Pass Signings Printing Plates Cyan /1 #MK
2013 Press Pass Signings Printing Plates Magenta /1 #MK
2013 Press Pass Signings Printing Plates Yellow /1 #MK
2013 Press Pass Signings Silver /50 #MK
2013 Total Memorabilia #23
2013 Total Memorabilia Black and White /99 #23
2013 Total Memorabilia Burning Rubber Chase Edition Gold /75 #BRCMK
2013 Total Memorabilia Burning Rubber Chase Edition Gold /75 #BRCMK2
2013 Total Memorabilia Burning Rubber Chase Edition Holofoil /50 #BRCMK
2013 Total Memorabilia Burning Rubber Chase Edition Holofoil /50 #BRCMK2
2013 Total Memorabilia Burning Rubber Chase Edition Melting /5 #BRCMK
2013 Total Memorabilia Burning Rubber Chase Edition Melting /5 #BRCMK2
2013 Total Memorabilia Burning Rubber Chase Edition Silver /175 #BRCMK
2013 Total Memorabilia Burning Rubber Chase Edition Silver /175 #BRCMK2
2013 Total Memorabilia Gold /275 #23
2013 Total Memorabilia Red #23
2014 Press Pass #0
2014 Press Pass #19
2014 Press Pass #66
2014 Press Pass #84
2014 Press Pass American Thunder #20
2014 Press Pass American Thunder #55
2014 Press Pass American Thunder Autographs Blue /10 #ATAMK
2014 Press Pass American Thunder Autographs Red /5 #ATAMK
2014 Press Pass American Thunder Autographs White /35 #ATAMK
2014 Press Pass American Thunder Black and White /50 #20
2014 Press Pass American Thunder Black and White /50 #55
2014 Press Pass American Thunder Brothers In Arms Autographs Blue /5 #BAJGR
2014 Press Pass American Thunder Brothers In Arms Autographs Red /1 #BAJGR
2014 Press Pass American Thunder Brothers In Arms Autographs White /10 #BAJGR
2014 Press Pass American Thunder Brothers In Arms Relics Blue /25 #BAJGR
2014 Press Pass American Thunder Brothers In Arms Relics Red /5 #BAJGR
2014 Press Pass American Thunder Brothers In Arms Relics Silver /50 #BAJGR
2014 Press Pass American Thunder Class A Uniforms Blue /99 #CAUMK
2014 Press Pass American Thunder Class A Uniforms Red /10 #CAUMK
2014 Press Pass American Thunder Class A Uniforms Silver #CAUMK
2014 Press Pass American Thunder Cyan #20
2014 Press Pass American Thunder Cyan #55
2014 Press Pass American Thunder Great American Treads Autographs Blue /25 #GATMK
2014 Press Pass American Thunder Great American Treads Autographs Red /1 #GATMK
2014 Press Pass American Thunder Magenta #20
2014 Press Pass American Thunder Magenta #55
2014 Press Pass American Thunder Yellow /5 #20
2014 Press Pass American Thunder Yellow /5 #55
2014 Press Pass Burning Rubber Blue /25 #BRMK
2014 Press Pass Burning Rubber Blue /25 #BRMK2
2014 Press Pass Burning Rubber Blue /25 #BRMK3
2014 Press Pass Burning Rubber Blue /25 #BRMK4
2014 Press Pass Burning Rubber Blue /25 #BRMK5
2014 Press Pass Burning Rubber Chase Edition Blue /25 #BRCMK
2014 Press Pass Burning Rubber Chase Edition Blue /25 #BRCMK2
2014 Press Pass Burning Rubber Chase Edition Gold /50 #BRCMK
2014 Press Pass Burning Rubber Chase Edition Gold /50 #BRCMK2
2014 Press Pass Burning Rubber Chase Edition Melting /10 #BRCMK
2014 Press Pass Burning Rubber Chase Edition Melting /10 #BRCMK2
2014 Press Pass Burning Rubber Chase Edition Silver /99 #BRCMK2
2014 Press Pass Burning Rubber Chase Edition Silver /99 #BRCMK
2014 Press Pass Burning Rubber Gold /75 #BRMK
2014 Press Pass Burning Rubber Gold /75 #BRMK3
2014 Press Pass Burning Rubber Gold /75 #BRMK4
2014 Press Pass Burning Rubber Gold /75 #BRMK5
2014 Press Pass Burning Rubber Gold /75 #BRMK2
2014 Press Pass Burning Rubber Holofoil /50 #BRMK
2014 Press Pass Burning Rubber Holofoil /50 #BRMK2
2014 Press Pass Burning Rubber Holofoil /50 #BRMK3
2014 Press Pass Burning Rubber Holofoil /50 #BRMK4
2014 Press Pass Burning Rubber Holofoil /50 #BRMK5
2014 Press Pass Burning Rubber Letterman /8 #BRLMK
2014 Press Pass Burning Rubber Melting /10 #BRMK
2014 Press Pass Burning Rubber Melting /10 #BRMK2
2014 Press Pass Burning Rubber Melting /10 #BRMK3
2014 Press Pass Burning Rubber Melting /10 #BRMK4
2014 Press Pass Burning Rubber Melting /10 #BRMK5
2014 Press Pass Certified Winners Memorabilia Autographs Gold /10 #CWMK
2014 Press Pass Certified Winners Memorabilia Autographs Melting /1 #CWMK
2014 Press Pass Color Proofs Black /70 #19
2014 Press Pass Color Proofs Black /70 #66
2014 Press Pass Color Proofs Black /70 #84
2014 Press Pass Color Proofs Cyan /35 #19
2014 Press Pass Color Proofs Cyan /35 #66
2014 Press Pass Color Proofs Cyan /35 #84
2014 Press Pass Color Proofs Magenta #19
2014 Press Pass Color Proofs Magenta #66
2014 Press Pass Color Proofs Magenta #84
2014 Press Pass Color Proofs Yellow /5 #19
2014 Press Pass Color Proofs Yellow /5 #66
2014 Press Pass Color Proofs Yellow /5 #84
2014 Press Pass Cup Chase #10
2014 Press Pass Five Star /15 #11
2014 Press Pass Five Star Blue /5 #11
2014 Press Pass Five Star Classic Compilation Autographs Blue Triple Swatch /5 #CCMK
2014 Press Pass Five Star Classic Compilation Autographs Holofoil /10 #CCMK
2014 Press Pass Five Star Classic Compilation Autographs Holofoil Dual Swatch /10 #CCMK
2014 Press Pass Five Star Classic Compilation Autographs Melting Five Swatch /1 #CCMK
2014 Press Pass Five Star Classic Compilation Autographs Melting Quad Swatch /1 #CCMK
2014 Press Pass Five Star Classic Compilations Autographed Patch Booklet /1 #CCMK1
2014 Press Pass Five Star Classic Compilations Autographed Patch Booklet /1 #CCMK2
2014 Press Pass Five Star Classic Compilations Autographed Patch Booklet /1 #CCMK3
2014 Press Pass Five Star Classic Compilations Autographed Patch Booklet /1 #CCMK4
2014 Press Pass Five Star Classic Compilations Autographed Patch Booklet /1 #CCMK5
2014 Press Pass Five Star Classic Compilations Autographed Patch Booklet /1 #CCMK6
2014 Press Pass Five Star Classic Compilations Autographed Patch Booklet /1 #CCMK7
2014 Press Pass Five Star Classic Compilations Autographed Patch Booklet /1 #CCMK8
2014 Press Pass Five Star Classic Compilations Autographed Patch Booklet /1 #CCMK9
2014 Press Pass Five Star Classic Compilations Autographed Patch Booklet /1 #CCMK10
2014 Press Pass Five Star Classic Compilations Combo Autographs Blue /5 #CCJGR
2014 Press Pass Five Star Classic Compilations Combo Autographs Melting /1 #CCJGR
2014 Press Pass Five Star Holofoil /10 #11
2014 Press Pass Five Star Melting /1 #11
2014 Press Pass Five Star Paramount Pieces Blue /5 #PPMK
2014 Press Pass Five Star Paramount Pieces Gold /25 #PPMK
2014 Press Pass Five Star Paramount Pieces Holofoil /10 #PPMK
2014 Press Pass Five Star Paramount Pieces Melting /1 #PPMK
2014 Press Pass Five Star Paramount Pieces Melting Patch /1 #PPMK
2014 Press Pass Five Star Signature Souvenirs Blue /5 #SSMK
2014 Press Pass Five Star Signature Souvenirs Gold /50 #SSMK
2014 Press Pass Five Star Signature Souvenirs Holofoil /25 #SSMK
2014 Press Pass Five Star Signature Souvenirs Melting /1 #SSMK
2014 Press Pass Five Star Signatures Blue /5 #FSSMK
2014 Press Pass Five Star Signatures Holofoil /10 #FSSMK
2014 Press Pass Five Star Signatures Melting /1 #FSSMK
2014 Press Pass Gold #19
2014 Press Pass Gold #66
2014 Press Pass Gold #84
2014 Press Pass Redline #30
2014 Press Pass Redline #31
2014 Press Pass Redline Black /75 #30
2014 Press Pass Redline Black /75 #31
2014 Press Pass Redline Blue Foil #30
2014 Press Pass Redline Blue Foil #31
2014 Press Pass Redline Cyan /50 #30
2014 Press Pass Redline Cyan /50 #31
2014 Press Pass Redline Dynamic Duals Relic Autographs Blue /25 #DDMK
2014 Press Pass Redline Dynamic Duals Relic Autographs Gold /10 #DDMK
2014 Press Pass Redline Dynamic Duals Relic Autographs Melting /1 #DDMK
2014 Press Pass Redline Dynamic Duals Relic Autographs Red /50 #DDMK
2014 Press Pass Redline Green National Convention /5 #30
2014 Press Pass Redline Green National Convention /5 #31
2014 Press Pass Redline Intensity #8
2014 Press Pass Redline Magenta /10 #30
2014 Press Pass Redline Magenta /10 #31
2014 Press Pass Redline Muscle Car Sheet Metal Blue /25 #MCMMK
2014 Press Pass Redline Muscle Car Sheet Metal Gold /50 #MCMMK
2014 Press Pass Redline Muscle Car Sheet Metal Melting /1 #MCMMK
2014 Press Pass Redline Muscle Car Sheet Metal Red /75 #MCMMK
2014 Press Pass Redline Pieces of the Action Blue /10 #PAMK
2014 Press Pass Redline Pieces of the Action Gold /25 #PAMK
2014 Press Pass Redline Pieces of the Action Melting /1 #PAMK
2014 Press Pass Redline Pieces of the Action Red /75 #PAMK
2014 Press Pass Redline Redline Racers #RR11
2014 Press Pass Redline Relic Autographs Blue /10 #RRSEMK
2014 Press Pass Redline Relic Autographs Gold /25 #RRSEMK
2014 Press Pass Redline Relic Autographs Melting /1 #RRSEMK
2014 Press Pass Redline Relic Autographs Red /50 #RRSEMK
2014 Press Pass Redline Relics Blue /25 #RRMK
2014 Press Pass Redline Relics Gold /50 #RRMK
2014 Press Pass Redline Relics Melting /1 #RRMK
2014 Press Pass Redline Relics Red /75 #RRMK
2014 Press Pass Redline Signatures Blue /10 #RSMK
2014 Press Pass Redline Signatures Gold /15 #RSMK
2014 Press Pass Redline Signatures Melting /5 #RSMK
2014 Press Pass Redline Signatures Red /30 #RSMK
2014 Press Pass Redline Yellow /1 #30
2014 Press Pass Redline Yellow /1 #31
2014 Press Pass Replay #8
2014 Press Pass Replay #11
2014 Press Pass Replay #22
2014 Press Pass Replay #17
2014 Press Pass Replay #3
2014 Press Pass Signings Gold /25 #PPSMK
2014 Press Pass Signings Holofoil /10 #PPSMK
2014 Press Pass Signings Melting /1 #PPSMK
2014 Press Pass Signings Printing Plates Black /1 #PPSMK
2014 Press Pass Signings Printing Plates Cyan /1 #PPSMK
2014 Press Pass Signings Printing Plates Magenta /1 #PPSMK
2014 Press Pass Signings Printing Plates Yellow /1 #PPSMK
2014 Press Pass Signings Silver /50 #PPSMK
2014 Press Pass Three Wide Gold /10 #TWMK
2014 Press Pass Three Wide Melting /1 #TWMK
2014 Press Pass Velocity #6
2014 Total Memorabilia #14
2014 Total Memorabilia Autographed Memorabilia Blue /5 #SCMK
2014 Total Memorabilia Autographed Memorabilia Gold /10 #SCMK
2014 Total Memorabilia Autographed Memorabilia Melting /1 #SCMK
2014 Total Memorabilia Autographed Memorabilia Silver /10 #SC-MK
2014 Total Memorabilia Black and White /99 #14
2014 Total Memorabilia Dual Swatch Gold /150 #TMMK
2014 Total Memorabilia Gold /175 #14
2014 Total Memorabilia Quad Swatch Melting /25 #TMMK
2014 Total Memorabilia Red #14
2014 Total Memorabilia Single Swatch Silver /275 #TMMK
2014 Total Memorabilia Triple Swatch Blue /99 #TMMK
2015 Press Pass #20
2015 Press Pass #96
2015 Press Pass #87
2015 Press Pass #72
2015 Press Pass #100
2015 Press Pass Championship Caliber Dual /25 #CCMMK
2015 Press Pass Championship Caliber Quad /1 #CCMMK
2015 Press Pass Championship Caliber Signature Edition Blue /25 #CCMK
2015 Press Pass Championship Caliber Signature Edition Gold /50 #CCMK
2015 Press Pass Championship Caliber Signature Edition Green /10 #CCMK
2015 Press Pass Championship Caliber Signature Edition Melting /1 #CCMK
2015 Press Pass Championship Caliber Single /50 #CCMMK
2015 Press Pass Championship Caliber Triple /10 #CCMMK
2015 Press Pass Cup Chase #20
2015 Press Pass Cup Chase #72
2015 Press Pass Cup Chase #87
2015 Press Pass Cup Chase #96
2015 Press Pass Cup Chase #100
2015 Press Pass Cup Chase Blue /25 #20
2015 Press Pass Cup Chase Blue /25 #72
2015 Press Pass Cup Chase Blue /25 #87
2015 Press Pass Cup Chase Blue /25 #96
2015 Press Pass Cup Chase Blue /25 #100
2015 Press Pass Cup Chase Gold /75 #20
2015 Press Pass Cup Chase Gold /75 #72
2015 Press Pass Cup Chase Gold /75 #87
2015 Press Pass Cup Chase Gold /75 #96
2015 Press Pass Cup Chase Gold /75 #100
2015 Press Pass Cup Chase Green /10 #20
2015 Press Pass Cup Chase Green /10 #72
2015 Press Pass Cup Chase Green /10 #87
2015 Press Pass Cup Chase Green /10 #96
2015 Press Pass Cup Chase Green /10 #100
2015 Press Pass Cup Chase Melting /1 #20
2015 Press Pass Cup Chase Melting /1 #72
2015 Press Pass Cup Chase Melting /1 #87
2015 Press Pass Cup Chase Melting /1 #96
2015 Press Pass Cup Chase Melting /1 #100
2015 Press Pass Cup Chase Three Wide Blue /25 #3WMK
2015 Press Pass Cup Chase Three Wide Gold /50 #3WMK
2015 Press Pass Cup Chase Three Wide Green /10 #3WMK
2015 Press Pass Cup Chase Three Wide Melting /1 #3WMK
2015 Press Pass Cup Chase Upper Cuts /13 #UCMK
2015 Press Pass Cuts Blue /25 #CCCMK
2015 Press Pass Cuts Gold /50 #CCCMK
2015 Press Pass Cuts Green /10 #CCCMK
2015 Press Pass Cuts Melting /1 #CCCMK
2015 Press Pass Four Wide Signature Edition Blue /10 #4WMK
2015 Press Pass Four Wide Signature Edition Gold /25 #4WMK
2015 Press Pass Four Wide Signature Edition Green /5 #4WMK
2015 Press Pass Four Wide Signature Edition Melting /1 #4WMK
2015 Press Pass Pit Road Pieces Blue /25 #PPMMK
2015 Press Pass Pit Road Pieces Gold /50 #PPMMK
2015 Press Pass Pit Road Pieces Green /10 #PPMMK
2015 Press Pass Pit Road Pieces Melting /1 #PPMMK
2015 Press Pass Pit Road Pieces Signature Edition Blue /25 #PRPMK
2015 Press Pass Pit Road Pieces Signature Edition Gold /50 #PRPMK
2015 Press Pass Pit Road Pieces Signature Edition Green /10 #PRPMK
2015 Press Pass Pit Road Pieces Signature Edition Melting /1 #PRPMK
2015 Press Pass Purple #20
2015 Press Pass Purple #72
2015 Press Pass Purple #87
2015 Press Pass Purple #96
2015 Press Pass Purple #100
2015 Press Pass Red #20
2015 Press Pass Red #72
2015 Press Pass Red #87
2015 Press Pass Red #96
2015 Press Pass Red #100
2015 Press Pass Signature Series Blue /25 #SSMK
2015 Press Pass Signature Series Gold /50 #SSMK
2015 Press Pass Signature Series Green /10 #SSMK
2015 Press Pass Signature Series Melting /1 #SSMK
2015 Press Pass Signings Blue /15 #PPSMK
2015 Press Pass Signings Gold #PPSMK
2015 Press Pass Signings Green /5 #PPSMK
2015 Press Pass Signings Red /10 #PPSMK
2016 Certified #60
2016 Certified #11
2016 Certified Complete Materials /299 #14
2016 Certified Complete Materials Mirror Black /1 #14
2016 Certified Complete Materials Mirror Blue /50 #14
2016 Certified Complete Materials Mirror Gold /25 #14
2016 Certified Complete Materials Mirror Green /5 #14
2016 Certified Complete Materials Mirror Orange /99 #14
2016 Certified Complete Materials Mirror Purple /10 #14
2016 Certified Complete Materials Mirror Red /75 #14
2016 Certified Complete Materials Mirror Silver /99 #14
2016 Certified Epix /199 #8
2016 Certified Epix Mirror Black /1 #8
2016 Certified Epix Mirror Blue /50 #8
2016 Certified Epix Mirror Gold /25 #8
2016 Certified Epix Mirror Green /5 #8
2016 Certified Epix Mirror Orange /99 #8
2016 Certified Epix Mirror Purple /10 #8
2016 Certified Epix Mirror Red /75 #8
2016 Certified Epix Mirror Silver /99 #8
2016 Certified Famed Rides /199 #12
2016 Certified Famed Rides Mirror Black /1 #12
2016 Certified Famed Rides Mirror Blue /50 #12
2016 Certified Famed Rides Mirror Gold /25 #12
2016 Certified Famed Rides Mirror Green /5 #12
2016 Certified Famed Rides Mirror Orange /99 #12
2016 Certified Famed Rides Mirror Purple /10 #12
2016 Certified Famed Rides Mirror Red /75 #12
2016 Certified Famed Rides Mirror Silver /99 #12
2016 Certified Gold Team /199 #17
2016 Certified Gold Team Mirror Black /1 #17
2016 Certified Gold Team Mirror Blue /50 #17
2016 Certified Gold Team Mirror Gold /25 #17
2016 Certified Gold Team Mirror Green /5 #17
2016 Certified Gold Team Mirror Orange /99 #17
2016 Certified Gold Team Mirror Purple /10 #17
2016 Certified Gold Team Mirror Red /75 #17
2016 Certified Gold Team Mirror Silver /99 #17
2016 Certified Mirror Black /1 #11
2016 Certified Mirror Black /1 #60
2016 Certified Mirror Blue /50 #11
2016 Certified Mirror Blue /50 #60
2016 Certified Mirror Gold /25 #11
2016 Certified Mirror Gold /25 #60
2016 Certified Mirror Green /5 #11
2016 Certified Mirror Green /5 #60
2016 Certified Mirror Orange /99 #11
2016 Certified Mirror Orange /99 #60
2016 Certified Mirror Purple /10 #11
2016 Certified Mirror Purple /10 #60
2016 Certified Mirror Red /75 #11
2016 Certified Mirror Red /75 #60
2016 Certified Mirror Silver /99 #11
2016 Certified Mirror Silver /99 #60
2016 Certified Signatures /35 #16
2016 Certified Signatures Mirror Black /1 #16
2016 Certified Signatures Mirror Blue /20 #16
2016 Certified Signatures Mirror Gold /15 #16
2016 Certified Signatures Mirror Green /5 #16
2016 Certified Signatures Mirror Orange /7 #16
2016 Certified Signatures Mirror Purple /10 #16
2016 Certified Signatures Mirror Red /25 #16
2016 Certified Signatures Mirror Silver /5 #16
2016 Certified Skills /199 #19
2016 Certified Skills Mirror Black /1 #19
2016 Certified Skills Mirror Blue /50 #19
2016 Certified Skills Mirror Gold /25 #19
2016 Certified Skills Mirror Green /5 #19
2016 Certified Skills Mirror Orange /99 #19
2016 Certified Skills Mirror Purple /10 #19
2016 Certified Skills Mirror Red /75 #19
2016 Certified Skills Mirror Silver /99 #19
2016 Certified Sprint Cup Signature Swatches /75 #13
2016 Certified Sprint Cup Signature Swatches Mirror Black /1 #13
2016 Certified Sprint Cup Signature Swatches Mirror Blue /25 #13
2016 Certified Sprint Cup Signature Swatches Mirror Gold /15 #13
2016 Certified Sprint Cup Signature Swatches Mirror Green /5 #13
2016 Certified Sprint Cup Signature Swatches Mirror Orange /6 #13
2016 Certified Sprint Cup Signature Swatches Mirror Purple /10 #13
2016 Certified Sprint Cup Signature Swatches Mirror Red /35 #13
2016 Certified Sprint Cup Signature Swatches Mirror Silver /5 #13
2016 Certified Sprint Cup Swatches /199 #4
2016 Certified Sprint Cup Swatches Mirror Black /1 #3
2016 Certified Sprint Cup Swatches Mirror Black /1 #4
2016 Certified Sprint Cup Swatches Mirror Blue /50 #3
2016 Certified Sprint Cup Swatches Mirror Blue /50 #4
2016 Certified Sprint Cup Swatches Mirror Gold /20 #3
2016 Certified Sprint Cup Swatches Mirror Gold /25 #4
2016 Certified Sprint Cup Swatches Mirror Green /5 #3
2016 Certified Sprint Cup Swatches Mirror Green /5 #4
2016 Certified Sprint Cup Swatches Mirror Orange /99 #4
2016 Certified Sprint Cup Swatches Mirror Purple /10 #3
2016 Certified Sprint Cup Swatches Mirror Purple /10 #4
2016 Certified Sprint Cup Swatches Mirror Red /60 #3
2016 Certified Sprint Cup Swatches Mirror Red /75 #4
2016 Certified Sprint Cup Swatches Mirror Silver /99 #4
2016 Panini National Treasures /25 #7
2016 Panini National Treasures /25 #32
2016 Panini National Treasures Black /5 #7
2016 Panini National Treasures Black /5 #32
2016 Panini National Treasures Blue /1 #7
2016 Panini National Treasures Blue /1 #32
2016 Panini National Treasures Championship Signature Threads /25 #2
2016 Panini National Treasures Championship Signature Threads Black /5 #2
2016 Panini National Treasures Championship Signature Threads Blue /1 #2
2016 Panini National Treasures Championship Signature Threads Gold /10 #2
2016 Panini National Treasures Championship Signature Threads Printing Plates Black /1 #2
2016 Panini National Treasures Championship Signature Threads Printing Plates Cyan /1 #2
2016 Panini National Treasures Championship Signature Threads Printing Plates Magenta /1 #2
2016 Panini National Treasures Championship Signature Threads Printing Plates Yellow /1 #2
2016 Panini National Treasures Championship Signature Threads Silver /15 #2
2016 Panini National Treasures Championship Signatures Blue /1 #7
2016 Panini National Treasures Championship Signatures Printing Plates Black /1 #7
2016 Panini National Treasures Championship Signatures Printing Plates Cyan /1 #7
2016 Panini National Treasures Championship Signatures Printing Plates Magenta /1 #7
2016 Panini National Treasures Championship Signatures Printing Plates Yellow /1 #7
2016 Panini National Treasures Dual Driver Materials /25 #6
2016 Panini National Treasures Dual Driver Materials Black /5 #6
2016 Panini National Treasures Dual Driver Materials Blue /1 #6
2016 Panini National Treasures Dual Driver Materials Gold /10 #6
2016 Panini National Treasures Dual Driver Materials Printing Plates Black /1 #6
2016 Panini National Treasures Dual Driver Materials Printing Plates Cyan /1 #6
2016 Panini National Treasures Dual Driver Materials Printing Plates Magenta /1 #6
2016 Panini National Treasures Dual Driver Materials Printing Plates Yellow /1 #6
2016 Panini National Treasures Dual Driver Materials Silver /15 #6
2016 Panini National Treasures Dual Signatures /50 #12
2016 Panini National Treasures Dual Signatures Black /10 #12
2016 Panini National Treasures Dual Signatures Blue /1 #12
2016 Panini National Treasures Dual Signatures Gold /30 #12
2016 Panini National Treasures Eight Signatures /15 #2
2016 Panini National Treasures Eight Signatures /15 #3
2016 Panini National Treasures Eight Signatures Black /5 #2
2016 Panini National Treasures Eight Signatures Black /5 #3
2016 Panini National Treasures Eight Signatures Blue /1 #2
2016 Panini National Treasures Eight Signatures Blue /1 #3
2016 Panini National Treasures Eight Signatures Gold /10 #2
2016 Panini National Treasures Eight Signatures Gold /10 #3
2016 Panini National Treasures Firesuit Materials /25 #15
2016 Panini National Treasures Firesuit Materials Black /5 #15
2016 Panini National Treasures Firesuit Materials Blue /1 #15
2016 Panini National Treasures Firesuit Materials Gold /10 #15
2016 Panini National Treasures Firesuit Materials Laundry Tag /1 #15
2016 Panini National Treasures Firesuit Materials Printing Plates Black /1 #15
2016 Panini National Treasures Firesuit Materials Printing Plates Cyan /1 #15
2016 Panini National Treasures Firesuit Materials Printing Plates Magenta /1 #15
2016 Panini National Treasures Firesuit Materials Printing Plates Yellow /1 #15
2016 Panini National Treasures Firesuit Materials Silver /15 #15
2016 Panini National Treasures Gold /15 #7
2016 Panini National Treasures Gold /15 #32
2016 Panini National Treasures Jumbo Firesuit Patch Signature Booklet Associate Sponsor 1 /1 #21
2016 Panini National Treasures Jumbo Firesuit Patch Signature Booklet Associate Sponsor 2 /1 #21
2016 Panini National Treasures Jumbo Firesuit Patch Signature Booklet Associate Sponsor 3 /1 #21
2016 Panini National Treasures Jumbo Firesuit Patch Signature Booklet Associate Sponsor 4 /1 #21
2016 Panini National Treasures Jumbo Firesuit Patch Signature Booklet Associate Sponsor 5 /1 #21
2016 Panini National Treasures Jumbo Firesuit Patch Signature Booklet Associate Sponsor 6 /1 #21
2016 Panini National Treasures Jumbo Firesuit Patch Signature Booklet Associate Sponsor 7 /1 #21
2016 Panini National Treasures Jumbo Firesuit Patch Signature Booklet Associate Sponsor 8 /1 #21
2016 Panini National Treasures Jumbo Firesuit Patch Signature Booklet Goodyear /2 #21
2016 Panini National Treasures Jumbo Firesuit Patch Signature Booklet Manufacturers Logo /3 #21
2016 Panini National Treasures Jumbo Firesuit Patch Signature Booklet Nameplate /2 #21
2016 Panini National Treasures Jumbo Firesuit Patch Signature Booklet NASCAR /1 #21
2016 Panini National Treasures Jumbo Firesuit Patch Signature Booklet Sprint Cup Logo /1 #21
2016 Panini National Treasures Jumbo Firesuit Patch Signature Booklet Sunoco /1 #21
2016 Panini National Treasures Jumbo Firesuit Signatures /25 #21
2016 Panini National Treasures Jumbo Firesuit Signatures Black /5 #21
2016 Panini National Treasures Jumbo Firesuit Signatures Blue /1 #21
2016 Panini National Treasures Jumbo Firesuit Signatures Gold /10 #21
2016 Panini National Treasures Jumbo Firesuit Signatures Printing Plates Black /1 #21
2016 Panini National Treasures Jumbo Firesuit Signatures Printing Plates Cyan /1 #21
2016 Panini National Treasures Jumbo Firesuit Signatures Printing Plates Magenta /1 #21
2016 Panini National Treasures Jumbo Firesuit Signatures Printing Plates Yellow /1 #21
2016 Panini National Treasures Jumbo Firesuit Signatures Silver /15 #21
2016 Panini National Treasures Jumbo Sheet Metal Signatures Blue /1 #15
2016 Panini National Treasures Jumbo Sheet Metal Signatures Printing Plates Black /1 #15
2016 Panini National Treasures Jumbo Sheet Metal Signatures Printing Plates Cyan /1 #15
2016 Panini National Treasures Jumbo Sheet Metal Signatures Printing Plates Magenta /1 #15
2016 Panini National Treasures Jumbo Sheet Metal Signatures Printing Plates Yellow /1 #15
2016 Panini National Treasures Printing Plates Black /1 #7
2016 Panini National Treasures Printing Plates Black /1 #32
2016 Panini National Treasures Printing Plates Cyan /1 #7
2016 Panini National Treasures Printing Plates Cyan /1 #32
2016 Panini National Treasures Printing Plates Magenta /1 #7
2016 Panini National Treasures Printing Plates Magenta /1 #32
2016 Panini National Treasures Printing Plates Yellow /1 #7
2016 Panini National Treasures Printing Plates Yellow /1 #32
2016 Panini National Treasures Quad Driver Materials /25 #2
2016 Panini National Treasures Quad Driver Materials /25 #8
2016 Panini National Treasures Quad Driver Materials Black /5 #2
2016 Panini National Treasures Quad Driver Materials Black /5 #8
2016 Panini National Treasures Quad Driver Materials Blue /1 #2
2016 Panini National Treasures Quad Driver Materials Blue /1 #8
2016 Panini National Treasures Quad Driver Materials Gold /10 #2
2016 Panini National Treasures Quad Driver Materials Gold /10 #8
2016 Panini National Treasures Quad Driver Materials Printing Plates Black /1 #2
2016 Panini National Treasures Quad Driver Materials Printing Plates Black /1 #8
2016 Panini National Treasures Quad Driver Materials Printing Plates Cyan /1 #2
2016 Panini National Treasures Quad Driver Materials Printing Plates Cyan /1 #8
2016 Panini National Treasures Quad Driver Materials Printing Plates Magenta /1 #2
2016 Panini National Treasures Quad Driver Materials Printing Plates Magenta /1 #8
2016 Panini National Treasures Quad Driver Materials Printing Plates Yellow /1 #2
2016 Panini National Treasures Quad Driver Materials Printing Plates Yellow /1 #8
2016 Panini National Treasures Quad Driver Materials Silver /15 #2
2016 Panini National Treasures Quad Driver Materials Silver /15 #8
2016 Panini National Treasures Quad Materials /25 #15
2016 Panini National Treasures Quad Materials Black /5 #15
2016 Panini National Treasures Quad Materials Blue /1 #15
2016 Panini National Treasures Quad Materials Gold /10 #15
2016 Panini National Treasures Quad Materials Printing Plates Black /1 #15
2016 Panini National Treasures Quad Materials Printing Plates Cyan /1 #15
2016 Panini National Treasures Quad Materials Printing Plates Magenta /1 #15
2016 Panini National Treasures Quad Materials Printing Plates Yellow /1 #15
2016 Panini National Treasures Quad Materials Silver /15 #15
2016 Panini National Treasures Sheet Metal Materials /25 #15
2016 Panini National Treasures Sheet Metal Materials Black /5 #15
2016 Panini National Treasures Sheet Metal Materials Blue /1 #15
2016 Panini National Treasures Sheet Metal Materials Gold /10 #15
2016 Panini National Treasures Sheet Metal Materials Printing Plates Black /1 #15
2016 Panini National Treasures Sheet Metal Materials Printing Plates Cyan /1 #15
2016 Panini National Treasures Sheet Metal Materials Printing Plates Magenta /1 #15
2016 Panini National Treasures Sheet Metal Materials Printing Plates Yellow /1 #15
2016 Panini National Treasures Sheet Metal Materials Silver /15 #15
2016 Panini National Treasures Signature Dual Materials Blue /1 #19
2016 Panini National Treasures Signature Dual Materials Printing Plates Black /1 #19
2016 Panini National Treasures Signature Dual Materials Printing Plates Cyan /1 #19
2016 Panini National Treasures Signature Dual Materials Printing Plates Magenta /1 #19
2016 Panini National Treasures Signature Dual Materials Printing Plates Yellow /1 #19
2016 Panini National Treasures Signature Firesuit Materials /25 #20
2016 Panini National Treasures Signature Firesuit Materials Black /5 #20
2016 Panini National Treasures Signature Firesuit Materials Blue /1 #20
2016 Panini National Treasures Signature Firesuit Materials Gold /10 #20
2016 Panini National Treasures Signature Firesuit Materials Laundry Tag /1 #20
2016 Panini National Treasures Signature Firesuit Materials Printing Plates Black /1 #20
2016 Panini National Treasures Signature Firesuit Materials Printing Plates Cyan /1 #20
2016 Panini National Treasures Signature Firesuit Materials Printing Plates Magenta /1 #20
2016 Panini National Treasures Signature Firesuit Materials Printing Plates Yellow /1 #20
2016 Panini National Treasures Signature Firesuit Materials Silver /15 #20
2016 Panini National Treasures Signature Quad Materials Black /5 #19
2016 Panini National Treasures Signature Quad Materials Blue /1 #19
2016 Panini National Treasures Signature Quad Materials Gold /10 #19
2016 Panini National Treasures Signature Quad Materials Printing Plates Black /1 #19
2016 Panini National Treasures Signature Quad Materials Printing Plates Cyan /1 #19
2016 Panini National Treasures Signature Quad Materials Printing Plates Magenta /1 #19
2016 Panini National Treasures Signature Quad Materials Printing Plates Yellow /1 #19
2016 Panini National Treasures Signature Quad Materials Silver /15 #19
2016 Panini National Treasures Signature Sheet Metal Materials Blue /1 #19
2016 Panini National Treasures Signature Sheet Metal Materials Printing Plates Black /1 #19
2016 Panini National Treasures Signature Sheet Metal Materials Printing Plates Cyan /1 #19
2016 Panini National Treasures Signature Sheet Metal Materials Printing Plates Magenta /1 #19
2016 Panini National Treasures Signature Sheet Metal Materials Printing Plates Yellow /1 #19
2016 Panini National Treasures Signatures Blue /1 #17
2016 Panini National Treasures Signatures Printing Plates Black /1 #17
2016 Panini National Treasures Signatures Printing Plates Cyan /1 #17
2016 Panini National Treasures Signatures Printing Plates Magenta /1 #17
2016 Panini National Treasures Signatures Printing Plates Yellow /1 #17
2016 Panini National Treasures Silver /20 #7
2016 Panini National Treasures Silver /20 #32
2016 Panini National Treasures Six Signatures /25 #1
2016 Panini National Treasures Six Signatures Black /10 #1
2016 Panini National Treasures Six Signatures Blue /1 #1
2016 Panini National Treasures Six Signatures Gold /15 #1
2016 Panini National Treasures Timelines /25 #12
2016 Panini National Treasures Timelines Black /5 #12
2016 Panini National Treasures Timelines Blue /1 #12
2016 Panini National Treasures Timelines Gold /10 #12
2016 Panini National Treasures Timelines Printing Plates Black /1 #12
2016 Panini National Treasures Timelines Printing Plates Cyan /1 #12
2016 Panini National Treasures Timelines Printing Plates Magenta /1 #12
2016 Panini National Treasures Timelines Printing Plates Yellow /1 #12
2016 Panini National Treasures Timelines Signatures Black /5 #11
2016 Panini National Treasures Timelines Signatures Blue /1 #11
2016 Panini National Treasures Timelines Signatures Gold /10 #11
2016 Panini National Treasures Timelines Signatures Printing Plates Black /1 #11
2016 Panini National Treasures Timelines Signatures Printing Plates Cyan /1 #11
2016 Panini National Treasures Timelines Signatures Printing Plates Magenta /1 #11
2016 Panini National Treasures Timelines Signatures Printing Plates Yellow /1 #11
2016 Panini National Treasures Timelines Signatures Silver /15 #11
2016 Panini National Treasures Timelines Silver /15 #12
2016 Panini National Treasures Trio Driver Materials /25 #9
2016 Panini National Treasures Trio Driver Materials Black /5 #9
2016 Panini National Treasures Trio Driver Materials Blue /1 #9
2016 Panini National Treasures Trio Driver Materials Gold /10 #9
2016 Panini National Treasures Trio Driver Materials Printing Plates Black /1 #9
2016 Panini National Treasures Trio Driver Materials Printing Plates Cyan /1 #9
2016 Panini National Treasures Trio Driver Materials Printing Plates Magenta /1 #9
2016 Panini National Treasures Trio Driver Materials Printing Plates Yellow /1 #9
2016 Panini National Treasures Trio Driver Materials Silver /15 #9
2016 Panini National Treasures Winning Signatures Black /5 #6
2016 Panini National Treasures Winning Signatures Blue /1 #6
2016 Panini National Treasures Winning Signatures Printing Plates Black /1 #6
2016 Panini National Treasures Winning Signatures Printing Plates Cyan /1 #6
2016 Panini National Treasures Winning Signatures Printing Plates Magenta /1 #6
2016 Panini National Treasures Winning Signatures Printing Plates Yellow /1 #6
2016 Panini Prizm #69
2016 Panini Prizm #51
2016 Panini Prizm #20
2016 Panini Prizm Autographs Prizms #68
2016 Panini Prizm Autographs Prizms Black /3 #68
2016 Panini Prizm Autographs Prizms Blue Flag /50 #68
2016 Panini Prizm Autographs Prizms Camo /20 #68
2016 Panini Prizm Autographs Prizms Checkered Flag /1 #68
2016 Panini Prizm Autographs Prizms Gold /10 #68
2016 Panini Prizm Autographs Prizms Green Flag /75 #68
2016 Panini Prizm Autographs Prizms Rainbow /24 #68
2016 Panini Prizm Autographs Prizms Red Flag /25 #68
2016 Panini Prizm Autographs Prizms Red White and Blue /25 #68
2016 Panini Prizm Autographs Prizms White Flag /5 #68
2016 Panini Prizm Blowing Smoke #12
2016 Panini Prizm Blowing Smoke Prizms #12
2016 Panini Prizm Blowing Smoke Prizms Checkered Flag /1 #12
2016 Panini Prizm Blowing Smoke Prizms Gold /10 #12
2016 Panini Prizm Firesuit Fabrics /149 #4
2016 Panini Prizm Firesuit Fabrics Prizms Blue Flag /75 #4
2016 Panini Prizm Firesuit Fabrics Prizms Checkered Flag /1 #4
2016 Panini Prizm Firesuit Fabrics Prizms Green Flag /99 #4
2016 Panini Prizm Firesuit Fabrics Prizms Red Flag /25 #4
2016 Panini Prizm Firesuit Fabrics Team /249 #4
2016 Panini Prizm Firesuit Fabrics Team Prizms Blue Flag /75 #4
2016 Panini Prizm Firesuit Fabrics Team Prizms Checkered Flag /1 #4
2016 Panini Prizm Firesuit Fabrics Team Prizms Green Flag /99 #4
2016 Panini Prizm Firesuit Fabrics Team Prizms Red Flag /25 #4
2016 Panini Prizm Machinery #7
2016 Panini Prizm Machinery Prizms #7
2016 Panini Prizm Machinery Prizms Checkered Flag /1 #7
2016 Panini Prizm Machinery Prizms Gold /10 #7
2016 Panini Prizm Prizms #20
2016 Panini Prizm Prizms #51
2016 Panini Prizm Prizms #69
2016 Panini Prizm Prizms Black /3 #20
2016 Panini Prizm Prizms Black /3 #51
2016 Panini Prizm Prizms Black /3 #69
2016 Panini Prizm Prizms Blue Flag /99 #20
2016 Panini Prizm Prizms Blue Flag /99 #51
2016 Panini Prizm Prizms Blue Flag /99 #69
2016 Panini Prizm Prizms Camo /20 #20
2016 Panini Prizm Prizms Camo /20 #51
2016 Panini Prizm Prizms Camo /20 #69
2016 Panini Prizm Prizms Checkered Flag /1 #20
2016 Panini Prizm Prizms Checkered Flag /1 #51
2016 Panini Prizm Prizms Checkered Flag /1 #69
2016 Panini Prizm Prizms Gold /10 #20
2016 Panini Prizm Prizms Gold /10 #51
2016 Panini Prizm Prizms Gold /10 #69
2016 Panini Prizm Prizms Green Flag /149 #20
2016 Panini Prizm Prizms Green Flag /149 #51
2016 Panini Prizm Prizms Green Flag /149 #69
2016 Panini Prizm Prizms Rainbow /24 #20
2016 Panini Prizm Prizms Rainbow /24 #51
2016 Panini Prizm Prizms Rainbow /24 #69
2016 Panini Prizm Prizms Red Flag /75 #20
2016 Panini Prizm Prizms Red Flag /75 #51
2016 Panini Prizm Prizms Red Flag /75 #69
2016 Panini Prizm Prizms Red White and Blue #20
2016 Panini Prizm Prizms Red White and Blue #51
2016 Panini Prizm Prizms Red White and Blue #69
2016 Panini Prizm Prizms White Flag /5 #20
2016 Panini Prizm Prizms White Flag /5 #51
2016 Panini Prizm Prizms White Flag /5 #69
2016 Panini Prizm Qualifying Times #5
2016 Panini Prizm Qualifying Times Prizms #5
2016 Panini Prizm Qualifying Times Prizms Checkered Flag /1 #5
2016 Panini Prizm Qualifying Times Prizms Gold /10 #5
2016 Panini Prizm Race Used Tire #4
2016 Panini Prizm Race Used Tire Prizms Blue Flag /49 #4
2016 Panini Prizm Race Used Tire Prizms Checkered Flag /1 #4
2016 Panini Prizm Race Used Tire Prizms Green Flag /99 #4
2016 Panini Prizm Race Used Tire Prizms Red Flag /25 #4
2016 Panini Prizm Raising the Flag #2
2016 Panini Prizm Raising the Flag Prizms #2
2016 Panini Prizm Raising the Flag Prizms Checkered Flag /1 #2
2016 Panini Prizm Raising the Flag Prizms Gold /10 #2
2016 Panini Prizm Winner's Circle #28

016 Panini Prizm Winner's Circle #26
016 Panini Prizm Winner's Circle #23
016 Panini Prizm Winner's Circle #21
016 Panini Prizm Winner's Circle #8
016 Panini Prizm Winner's Circle Prizms #8
016 Panini Prizm Winner's Circle Prizms #21
016 Panini Prizm Winner's Circle Prizms #23
016 Panini Prizm Winner's Circle Prizms #26
016 Panini Prizm Winner's Circle Prizms #28
016 Panini Prizm Winner's Circle Prizms Checkered Flag /1 #8
016 Panini Prizm Winner's Circle Prizms Checkered Flag /1 #21
016 Panini Prizm Winner's Circle Prizms Checkered Flag /1 #23
016 Panini Prizm Winner's Circle Prizms Checkered Flag /1 #26
016 Panini Prizm Winner's Circle Prizms Checkered Flag /1 #28
016 Panini Prizm Winner's Circle Prizms Gold /10 #8
016 Panini Prizm Winner's Circle Prizms Gold /10 #21
016 Panini Prizm Winner's Circle Prizms Gold /10 #23
016 Panini Prizm Winner's Circle Prizms Gold /10 #26
016 Panini Prizm Winner's Circle Prizms Gold /10 #28
016 Panini Torque #17
016 Panini Torque #81
016 Panini Torque Artist Proof /50 #17
016 Panini Torque Artist Proof /50 #81
016 Panini Torque Blackout /1 #17
016 Panini Torque Blackout /1 #81
016 Panini Torque Blue /125 #17
016 Panini Torque Blue /125 #81
016 Panini Torque Championship Vision #10
016 Panini Torque Championship Vision Blue /99 #10
016 Panini Torque Championship Vision Gold /149 #10
016 Panini Torque Championship Vision Green /25 #10
016 Panini Torque Championship Vision Purple /10 #10
016 Panini Torque Championship Vision Red /49 #10
016 Panini Torque Clear Vision #16
016 Panini Torque Clear Vision Blue /99 #16
016 Panini Torque Clear Vision Gold /149 #16
016 Panini Torque Clear Vision Green /25 #16
016 Panini Torque Clear Vision Purple /10 #16
016 Panini Torque Clear Vision Red /49 #16
016 Panini Torque Gas N Go #5
016 Panini Torque Gas N Go Gold /199 #5
016 Panini Torque Gas N Go Holo Silver /99 #5
016 Panini Torque Gold #17
016 Panini Torque Gold #81
016 Panini Torque Holo Gold /5 #17
016 Panini Torque Holo Gold /5 #81
016 Panini Torque Holo Silver /10 #17
016 Panini Torque Holo Silver /10 #81
016 Panini Torque Horsepower Heroes #15
016 Panini Torque Horsepower Heroes Gold /199 #15
016 Panini Torque Horsepower Heroes Holo Silver /99 #15
016 Panini Torque Jumbo Tire Autographs /30 #12
016 Panini Torque Jumbo Tire Autographs Blue /25 #12
016 Panini Torque Jumbo Tire Autographs Green /15 #12
016 Panini Torque Jumbo Tire Autographs Purple /10 #12
016 Panini Torque Jumbo Tire Autographs Red /20 #12
016 Panini Torque Metal Materials /249 #17
016 Panini Torque Metal Materials Blue /99 #17
016 Panini Torque Metal Materials Green /25 #17
016 Panini Torque Metal Materials Purple /10 #17
016 Panini Torque Metal Materials Red /49 #17
016 Panini Torque Painted to Perfection #13
016 Panini Torque Painted to Perfection Blue /99 #13
016 Panini Torque Painted to Perfection Checkerboard /10 #13
016 Panini Torque Painted to Perfection Green /25 #13
016 Panini Torque Painted to Perfection Red /49 #13
016 Panini Torque Pairings Materials /249 #14
016 Panini Torque Pairings Materials Blue /99 #14
016 Panini Torque Pairings Materials Green /25 #14
016 Panini Torque Pairings Materials Purple /10 #14
016 Panini Torque Pairings Materials Red /49 #14
016 Panini Torque Pole Position #14
016 Panini Torque Pole Position Blue /99 #14
016 Panini Torque Pole Position Checkerboard /10 #14
016 Panini Torque Pole Position Green /25 #14
016 Panini Torque Pole Position Red /49 #14
016 Panini Torque Printing Plates Black /1 #17
016 Panini Torque Printing Plates Black /1 #81
016 Panini Torque Printing Plates Cyan /1 #17
016 Panini Torque Printing Plates Cyan /1 #81
016 Panini Torque Printing Plates Magenta /1 #17
016 Panini Torque Printing Plates Magenta /1 #81
016 Panini Torque Printing Plates Yellow /1 #17
016 Panini Torque Printing Plates Yellow /1 #81
016 Panini Torque Purple /25 #17
016 Panini Torque Purple /25 #81
016 Panini Torque Red /99 #17
016 Panini Torque Red /99 #81
016 Panini Torque Rubber Relics /399 #18
016 Panini Torque Rubber Relics Blue /99 #18
016 Panini Torque Rubber Relics Green /25 #18
016 Panini Torque Rubber Relics Purple /10 #18
016 Panini Torque Rubber Relics Red /49 #18
016 Panini Torque Silhouettes Firesuit Autographs /30 #18
016 Panini Torque Silhouettes Firesuit Autographs Blue /25 #18
016 Panini Torque Silhouettes Firesuit Autographs Green /15 #18
016 Panini Torque Silhouettes Firesuit Autographs Purple /10 #18
016 Panini Torque Silhouettes Firesuit Autographs Red /20 #18
016 Panini Torque Silhouettes Sheet Metal Autographs /30 #20
016 Panini Torque Silhouettes Sheet Metal Autographs Blue /25 #20
016 Panini Torque Silhouettes Sheet Metal Autographs Green /15 #20
016 Panini Torque Silhouettes Sheet Metal Autographs Purple /10 #20
016 Panini Torque Silhouettes Sheet Metal Autographs Red /20 #20
016 Panini Torque Special Paint #5
016 Panini Torque Special Paint Gold /199 #5
016 Panini Torque Special Paint Holo Silver /99 #5
016 Panini Torque Superstar Vision #12
016 Panini Torque Superstar Vision Blue /99 #12
016 Panini Torque Superstar Vision Gold /149 #12
016 Panini Torque Superstar Vision Green /25 #12
016 Panini Torque Superstar Vision Purple /10 #12
016 Panini Torque Superstar Vision Red /49 #12
016 Panini Torque Test Proof Black /1 #17
016 Panini Torque Test Proof Black /1 #81
016 Panini Torque Test Proof Cyan /1 #17
016 Panini Torque Test Proof Cyan /1 #81
016 Panini Torque Test Proof Magenta /1 #17
016 Panini Torque Test Proof Magenta /1 #81
016 Panini Torque Test Proof Yellow /1 #17
016 Panini Torque Test Proof Yellow /1 #81
016 Panini Torque Victory Laps #6
016 Panini Torque Victory Laps Gold /199 #6
016 Panini Torque Victory Laps Holo Silver /99 #6
016 Panini Torque Winning Vision #13
016 Panini Torque Winning Vision Blue /99 #13
016 Panini Torque Winning Vision Gold /149 #13
016 Panini Torque Winning Vision Green /25 #13
016 Panini Torque Winning Vision Purple /10 #13
016 Panini Torque Winning Vision Red /49 #13
017 Donruss #10
017 Donruss #124
017 Donruss #178
017 Donruss #38A
017 Donruss #117
017 Donruss #38B
017 Donruss Artist Proof /25 #10
017 Donruss Artist Proof /25 #38A
017 Donruss Artist Proof /25 #124
2017 Donruss Artist Proof /25 #178
2017 Donruss Artist Proof /25 #38B
2017 Donruss Artist Proof /25 #117
2017 Donruss Blue Foil /299 #10
2017 Donruss Blue Foil /299 #38A
2017 Donruss Blue Foil /299 #124
2017 Donruss Blue Foil /299 #178
2017 Donruss Blue Foil /299 #38B
2017 Donruss Blue Foil /299 #117
2017 Donruss Classics #3
2017 Donruss Classics Cracked Ice /999 #3
2017 Donruss Dual Rubber Relics #13
2017 Donruss Dual Rubber Relics Holo Black /1 #13
2017 Donruss Dual Rubber Relics Holo Gold /25 #13
2017 Donruss Gold Foil /499 #10
2017 Donruss Gold Foil /499 #178
2017 Donruss Gold Foil /499 #38A
2017 Donruss Gold Foil /499 #124
2017 Donruss Gold Foil /499 #38B
2017 Donruss Gold Foil /499 #117
2017 Donruss Gold Press Proof /99 #10
2017 Donruss Gold Press Proof /99 #38A
2017 Donruss Gold Press Proof /99 #124
2017 Donruss Gold Press Proof /99 #178
2017 Donruss Gold Press Proof /99 #38B
2017 Donruss Gold Press Proof /99 #117
2017 Donruss Green Foil /199 #10
2017 Donruss Green Foil /199 #38A
2017 Donruss Green Foil /199 #124
2017 Donruss Green Foil /199 #178
2017 Donruss Green Foil /199 #38B
2017 Donruss Green Foil /199 #117
2017 Donruss Pole Position #10
2017 Donruss Pole Position Cracked Ice /999 #10
2017 Donruss Press Proof /49 #10
2017 Donruss Press Proof /49 #38A
2017 Donruss Press Proof /49 #124
2017 Donruss Press Proof /49 #178
2017 Donruss Press Proof /49 #38B
2017 Donruss Press Proof /49 #117
2017 Donruss Printing Plates Black /1 #10
2017 Donruss Printing Plates Black /1 #38A
2017 Donruss Printing Plates Black /1 #124
2017 Donruss Printing Plates Black /1 #178
2017 Donruss Printing Plates Black /1 #38B
2017 Donruss Printing Plates Black /1 #117
2017 Donruss Printing Plates Cyan /1 #10
2017 Donruss Printing Plates Cyan /1 #38A
2017 Donruss Printing Plates Cyan /1 #124
2017 Donruss Printing Plates Cyan /1 #178
2017 Donruss Printing Plates Cyan /1 #38B
2017 Donruss Printing Plates Cyan /1 #117
2017 Donruss Printing Plates Magenta /1 #10
2017 Donruss Printing Plates Magenta /1 #178
2017 Donruss Printing Plates Magenta /1 #38A
2017 Donruss Printing Plates Magenta /1 #124
2017 Donruss Printing Plates Magenta /1 #38B
2017 Donruss Printing Plates Magenta /1 #117
2017 Donruss Printing Plates Yellow /1 #10
2017 Donruss Printing Plates Yellow /1 #178
2017 Donruss Printing Plates Yellow /1 #38A
2017 Donruss Printing Plates Yellow /1 #124
2017 Donruss Printing Plates Yellow /1 #38B
2017 Donruss Printing Plates Yellow /1 #117
2017 Donruss Retro Relics 1984 Holo Black /10 #31
2017 Donruss Retro Relics 1984 Holo Gold /99 #31
2017 Donruss Rubber Relics #37
2017 Donruss Rubber Relics Holo Black /10 #37
2017 Donruss Rubber Relics Holo Gold /99 #37
2017 Donruss Significant Signatures #11
2017 Donruss Significant Signatures Holo Black /1 #11
2017 Donruss Significant Signatures Holo Gold /25 #11
2017 Donruss Track Masters #5
2017 Donruss Track Masters Cracked Ice /999 #5
2017 Panini Instant Nascar #33
2017 Panini Instant Nascar Black /1 #33
2017 Panini Instant Nascar Green /10 #33
2017 Panini National Treasures /25 #8
2017 Panini National Treasures Associate Sponsor Patch Signatures 1 /1 #7
2017 Panini National Treasures Associate Sponsor Patch Signatures 10 /1 #7
2017 Panini National Treasures Associate Sponsor Patch Signatures 2 /1 #7
2017 Panini National Treasures Associate Sponsor Patch Signatures 3 /1 #7
2017 Panini National Treasures Associate Sponsor Patch Signatures 4 /1 #7
2017 Panini National Treasures Associate Sponsor Patch Signatures 5 /1 #7
2017 Panini National Treasures Associate Sponsor Patch Signatures 6 /1 #7
2017 Panini National Treasures Associate Sponsor Patch Signatures 7 /1 #7
2017 Panini National Treasures Associate Sponsor Patch Signatures 8 /1 #7
2017 Panini National Treasures Associate Sponsor Patch Signatures 9 /1 #7
2017 Panini National Treasures Car Manufacturer Patch Signatures /1 #7
2017 Panini National Treasures Century Black /1 #8
2017 Panini National Treasures Century Gold /15 #8
2017 Panini National Treasures Century Green /5 #8
2017 Panini National Treasures Century Holo Gold /10 #8
2017 Panini National Treasures Century Holo Silver /20 #8
2017 Panini National Treasures Century Laundry Tags /1 #8
2017 Panini National Treasures Combo Material Signatures /25 #5
2017 Panini National Treasures Combo Material Signatures Black /1 #5
2017 Panini National Treasures Combo Material Signatures Gold /15 #5
2017 Panini National Treasures Combo Material Signatures Green /5 #5
2017 Panini National Treasures Combo Material Signatures Holo Gold /10 #5
2017 Panini National Treasures Combo Material Signatures Holo Silver /20 #5
2017 Panini National Treasures Dual Tire Signatures /25 #14
2017 Panini National Treasures Dual Tire Signatures Black /1 #14
2017 Panini National Treasures Dual Tire Signatures Gold /15 #14
2017 Panini National Treasures Dual Tire Signatures Green /5 #14
2017 Panini National Treasures Dual Tire Signatures Holo Gold /10 #14
2017 Panini National Treasures Dual Tire Signatures Holo Silver /20 #14
2017 Panini National Treasures Dual Tire Signatures Printing Plates Black /1 #14
2017 Panini National Treasures Dual Tire Signatures Printing Plates Cyan /1 #14
2017 Panini National Treasures Dual Tire Signatures Printing Plates Magenta /1 #14
2017 Panini National Treasures Dual Tire Signatures Printing Plates Yellow /1 #14
2017 Panini National Treasures Firesuit Manufacturer Patch Signatures /1 #7
2017 Panini National Treasures Flag Patch Signatures /1 #7
2017 Panini National Treasures Goodyear Patch Signatures /2 #7
2017 Panini National Treasures Hats Off /14 #19
2017 Panini National Treasures Hats Off Gold /1 #19
2017 Panini National Treasures Hats Off Holo Gold /5 #19
2017 Panini National Treasures Hats Off Holo Silver /1 #19
2017 Panini National Treasures Hats Off Laundry Tag /6 #19
2017 Panini National Treasures Hats Off Monster Energy Cup /14 #8
2017 Panini National Treasures Hats Off Monster Energy Cup Gold /4 #8
2017 Panini National Treasures Hats Off Monster Energy Cup Holo Gold /5 #8
2017 Panini National Treasures Hats Off Monster Energy Cup Holo Silver /1 #8
2017 Panini National Treasures Hats Off Monster Energy Cup Laundry Tag /3 #8
2017 Panini National Treasures Hats Off Monster Energy Cup New Era /1 #8
2017 Panini National Treasures Hats Off Monster Energy Cup Printing Plates Black /1 #8
2017 Panini National Treasures Hats Off Monster Energy Cup Printing Plates Cyan /1 #8
2017 Panini National Treasures Hats Off Monster Energy Cup Printing Plates Magenta /1 #8
2017 Panini National Treasures Hats Off Monster Energy Cup Printing Plates Yellow /1 #8
2017 Panini National Treasures Hats Off Monster Energy Cup Sponsor /5 #8
2017 Panini National Treasures Hats Off New Era /1 #19
2017 Panini National Treasures Hats Off Printing Plates Black /1 #19
2017 Panini National Treasures Hats Off Printing Plates Cyan /1 #19
2017 Panini National Treasures Hats Off Printing Plates Magenta /1 #19
2017 Panini National Treasures Hats Off Printing Plates Yellow /1 #19
2017 Panini National Treasures Hats Off Sponsor /10 #19
2017 Panini National Treasures Jumbo Firesuit Materials Black /1 #5
2017 Panini National Treasures Jumbo Firesuit Materials Gold /15 #5
2017 Panini National Treasures Jumbo Firesuit Materials Green /5 #5
2017 Panini National Treasures Jumbo Firesuit Materials Holo Gold /10 #5
2017 Panini National Treasures Jumbo Firesuit Materials Laundry Tag /1 #5
2017 Panini National Treasures Jumbo Firesuit Materials Printing Plates Black /1 #5
2017 Panini National Treasures Jumbo Firesuit Materials Printing Plates Cyan /1 #5
2017 Panini National Treasures Jumbo Firesuit Materials Printing Plates Magenta /1 #5
2017 Panini National Treasures Jumbo Firesuit Materials Printing Plates Yellow /1 #5
2017 Panini National Treasures Jumbo Tire Signatures /25 #14
2017 Panini National Treasures Jumbo Tire Signatures Black /1 #14
2017 Panini National Treasures Jumbo Tire Signatures Gold /15 #14
2017 Panini National Treasures Jumbo Tire Signatures Green /5 #14
2017 Panini National Treasures Jumbo Tire Signatures Holo Gold /10 #14
2017 Panini National Treasures Jumbo Tire Signatures Holo Silver /20 #14
2017 Panini National Treasures Jumbo Tire Signatures Printing Plates Black /1 #14
2017 Panini National Treasures Jumbo Tire Signatures Printing Plates Cyan /1 #14
2017 Panini National Treasures Jumbo Tire Signatures Printing Plates Magenta /1 #14
2017 Panini National Treasures Jumbo Tire Signatures Printing Plates Yellow /1 #14
2017 Panini National Treasures Nameplate Patch Signatures /2 #7
2017 Panini National Treasures NASCAR Patch Signatures /1 #7
2017 Panini National Treasures Printing Plates Black /1 #8
2017 Panini National Treasures Printing Plates Cyan /1 #8
2017 Panini National Treasures Printing Plates Magenta /1 #8
2017 Panini National Treasures Printing Plates Yellow /1 #8
2017 Panini National Treasures Quad Materials Black /1 #4
2017 Panini National Treasures Quad Materials Green /5 #4
2017 Panini National Treasures Quad Materials Laundry Tag /1 #4
2017 Panini National Treasures Quad Materials Printing Plates Black /1 #4
2017 Panini National Treasures Quad Materials Printing Plates Cyan /1 #4
2017 Panini National Treasures Quad Materials Printing Plates Magenta /1 #4
2017 Panini National Treasures Quad Materials Printing Plates Yellow /1 #4
2017 Panini National Treasures Series Sponsor Patch Signatures /1 #7
2017 Panini National Treasures Signature Sheet Metal /25 #3
2017 Panini National Treasures Signature Sheet Metal Black /1 #3
2017 Panini National Treasures Signature Sheet Metal Gold /15 #3
2017 Panini National Treasures Signature Sheet Metal Green /5 #3
2017 Panini National Treasures Signature Sheet Metal Holo Gold /10 #3
2017 Panini National Treasures Signature Sheet Metal Holo Silver /20 #3
2017 Panini National Treasures Six Way Swatches Black /1 #5
2017 Panini National Treasures Six Way Swatches Green /5 #5
2017 Panini National Treasures Six Way Swatches Laundry Tag /1 #5
2017 Panini National Treasures Six Way Swatches Printing Plates Black /1 #5
2017 Panini National Treasures Six Way Swatches Printing Plates Cyan /1 #5
2017 Panini National Treasures Six Way Swatches Printing Plates Magenta /1 #5
2017 Panini National Treasures Six Way Swatches Printing Plates Yellow /1 #5
2017 Panini National Treasures Sunoco Patch Signatures /1 #7
2017 Panini National Treasures Teammates Dual Materials /25 #6
2017 Panini National Treasures Teammates Dual Materials Black /1 #6
2017 Panini National Treasures Teammates Dual Materials Gold /15 #6
2017 Panini National Treasures Teammates Dual Materials Green /5 #6
2017 Panini National Treasures Teammates Dual Materials Holo Gold /10 #6
2017 Panini National Treasures Teammates Dual Materials Holo Silver /20 #6
2017 Panini National Treasures Teammates Dual Materials Laundry Tag /1 #6
2017 Panini National Treasures Teammates Dual Materials Printing Plates Black /1 #6
2017 Panini National Treasures Teammates Dual Materials Printing Plates Cyan /1 #6
2017 Panini National Treasures Teammates Dual Materials Printing Plates Magenta /1 #6
2017 Panini National Treasures Teammates Dual Materials Printing Plates Yellow /1 #6
2017 Panini National Treasures Teammates Triple Materials /25 #3
2017 Panini National Treasures Teammates Triple Materials Black /1 #3
2017 Panini National Treasures Teammates Triple Materials Gold /15 #3
2017 Panini National Treasures Teammates Triple Materials Green /5 #3
2017 Panini National Treasures Teammates Triple Materials Holo Gold /10 #3
2017 Panini National Treasures Teammates Triple Materials Holo Silver /20 #3
2017 Panini National Treasures Teammates Triple Materials Laundry Tag /1 #3
2017 Panini National Treasures Teammates Triple Materials Printing Plates Black /1 #3
2017 Panini National Treasures Teammates Triple Materials Printing Plates Cyan /1 #3
2017 Panini National Treasures Teammates Triple Materials Printing Plates Magenta /1 #3
2017 Panini National Treasures Teammates Triple Materials Printing Plates Yellow /1 #3
2017 Panini National Treasures Winning Material Signatures /25 #5
2017 Panini National Treasures Winning Material Signatures Black /1 #5
2017 Panini National Treasures Winning Material Signatures Gold /15 #5
2017 Panini National Treasures Winning Material Signatures Green /5 #5
2017 Panini National Treasures Winning Material Signatures Holo Gold /10 #5
2017 Panini National Treasures Winning Material Signatures Holo Silver /20 #5
2017 Panini National Treasures Winning Material Signatures Laundry Tag /1 #5
2017 Panini National Treasures Winning Material Signatures Printing Plates Black /1 #5
2017 Panini National Treasures Winning Material Signatures Printing Plates Cyan /1 #5
2017 Panini National Treasures Winning Material Signatures Printing Plates Magenta /1 #5
2017 Panini National Treasures Winning Material Signatures Printing Plates Yellow /1 #5
2017 Panini National Treasures Winning Signatures /50 #10
2017 Panini National Treasures Winning Signatures Black /1 #10
2017 Panini National Treasures Winning Signatures Gold /15 #10
2017 Panini National Treasures Winning Signatures Green /5 #10
2017 Panini National Treasures Winning Signatures Holo Gold /10 #10
2017 Panini National Treasures Winning Signatures Holo Silver /25 #10
2017 Panini National Treasures Winning Signatures Printing Plates Black /1 #10
2017 Panini National Treasures Winning Signatures Printing Plates Cyan /1 #10
2017 Panini National Treasures Winning Signatures Printing Plates Magenta /1 #10
2017 Panini National Treasures Winning Signatures Printing Plates Yellow /1 #10
2017 Panini Torque #10
2017 Panini Torque #72
2017 Panini Torque #86
2017 Panini Torque Artist Proof /75 #10
2017 Panini Torque Artist Proof /75 #72
2017 Panini Torque Artist Proof /75 #86
2017 Panini Torque Blackout /1 #10
2017 Panini Torque Blackout /1 #72
2017 Panini Torque Blackout /1 #86
2017 Panini Torque Blue /150 #10
2017 Panini Torque Blue /150 #72
2017 Panini Torque Blue /150 #86
2017 Panini Torque Claiming The Chase #8
2017 Panini Torque Claiming The Chase Gold /199 #8
2017 Panini Torque Claiming The Chase Holo Silver /99 #8
2017 Panini Torque Clear Vision #20
2017 Panini Torque Clear Vision Blue /99 #20
2017 Panini Torque Clear Vision Gold /149 #20
2017 Panini Torque Clear Vision Green /25 #20
2017 Panini Torque Clear Vision Purple /10 #20
2017 Panini Torque Clear Vision Red /49 #20
2017 Panini Torque Dual Materials /299 #18
2017 Panini Torque Dual Materials Blue /49 #18
2017 Panini Torque Dual Materials Green /10 #18
2017 Panini Torque Dual Materials Purple /1 #18
2017 Panini Torque Dual Materials Red /25 #18
2017 Panini Torque Gold #10
2017 Panini Torque Gold #72
2017 Panini Torque Gold #86
2017 Panini Torque Holo Gold /10 #10
2017 Panini Torque Holo Gold /10 #72
2017 Panini Torque Holo Gold /10 #86
2017 Panini Torque Holo Silver /25 #10
2017 Panini Torque Holo Silver /25 #72
2017 Panini Torque Holo Silver /25 #86
2017 Panini Torque Horsepower Heroes #12
2017 Panini Torque Horsepower Heroes Gold /199 #12
2017 Panini Torque Horsepower Heroes Holo Silver /99 #12
2017 Panini Torque Manufacturer Marks #5
2017 Panini Torque Manufacturer Marks Gold /199 #5
2017 Panini Torque Manufacturer Marks Holo Silver /99 #5
2017 Panini Torque Pairings Materials /99 #9
2017 Panini Torque Pairings Materials /75 #14
2017 Panini Torque Pairings Materials Blue /49 #9
2017 Panini Torque Pairings Materials Blue /49 #14
2017 Panini Torque Pairings Materials Green /10 #9
2017 Panini Torque Pairings Materials Green /10 #14
2017 Panini Torque Pairings Materials Purple /1 #9
2017 Panini Torque Pairings Materials Purple /1 #14
2017 Panini Torque Pairings Materials Red /25 #9
2017 Panini Torque Pairings Materials Red /25 #14
2017 Panini Torque Primary Paint #15
2017 Panini Torque Primary Paint Blue /99 #15
2017 Panini Torque Primary Paint Checkerboard /10 #15
2017 Panini Torque Primary Paint Green /25 #15
2017 Panini Torque Primary Paint Red /49 #15
2017 Panini Torque Prime Associate Sponsors Jumbo Patches /1 #16A
2017 Panini Torque Prime Associate Sponsors Jumbo Patches /1 #16B
2017 Panini Torque Prime Associate Sponsors Jumbo Patches /1 #16C
2017 Panini Torque Prime Associate Sponsors Jumbo Patches /1 #16D
2017 Panini Torque Prime Associate Sponsors Jumbo Patches /1 #16E
2017 Panini Torque Prime Associate Sponsors Jumbo Patches /1 #16F
2017 Panini Torque Prime Associate Sponsors Jumbo Patches /1 #16G
2017 Panini Torque Prime Associate Sponsors Jumbo Patches /1 #16H
2017 Panini Torque Prime Associate Sponsors Jumbo Patches /1 #16I
2017 Panini Torque Prime Associate Sponsors Jumbo Patches /1 #16J
2017 Panini Torque Prime Associate Sponsors Jumbo Patches /1 #16K
2017 Panini Torque Prime Associate Sponsors Jumbo Patches /1 #16L
2017 Panini Torque Prime Flag Jumbo Patches /1 #16
2017 Panini Torque Prime Goodyear Jumbo Patches /2 #16
2017 Panini Torque Prime Manufacturer Jumbo Patches /1 #16
2017 Panini Torque Prime Nameplates Jumbo Patches /2 #16
2017 Panini Torque Prime NASCAR Jumbo Patches /1 #16
2017 Panini Torque Prime Series Sponsor Jumbo Patches /1 #16
2017 Panini Torque Printing Plates Black /1 #10
2017 Panini Torque Printing Plates Black /1 #72
2017 Panini Torque Printing Plates Black /1 #86
2017 Panini Torque Printing Plates Cyan /1 #10
2017 Panini Torque Printing Plates Cyan /1 #72
2017 Panini Torque Printing Plates Cyan /1 #86
2017 Panini Torque Printing Plates Magenta /1 #10
2017 Panini Torque Printing Plates Magenta /1 #72
2017 Panini Torque Printing Plates Magenta /1 #86
2017 Panini Torque Printing Plates Yellow /1 #10
2017 Panini Torque Printing Plates Yellow /1 #72
2017 Panini Torque Printing Plates Yellow /1 #86
2017 Panini Torque Purple /50 #10
2017 Panini Torque Purple /50 #72
2017 Panini Torque Purple /50 #86
2017 Panini Torque Quad Materials /99 #22
2017 Panini Torque Quad Materials Blue /49 #22
2017 Panini Torque Quad Materials Green /10 #22
2017 Panini Torque Quad Materials Purple /1 #22
2017 Panini Torque Quad Materials Red /25 #22
2017 Panini Torque Raced Relics /499 #17
2017 Panini Torque Raced Relics Blue /99 #17
2017 Panini Torque Raced Relics Green /25 #17
2017 Panini Torque Raced Relics Purple /10 #17
2017 Panini Torque Raced Relics Red /49 #17
2017 Panini Torque Red /100 #10
2017 Panini Torque Red /100 #72
2017 Panini Torque Red /100 #86
2017 Panini Torque Running Order #5
2017 Panini Torque Running Order Blue /99 #5
2017 Panini Torque Running Order Checkerboard /10 #5
2017 Panini Torque Running Order Green /25 #5
2017 Panini Torque Running Order Red /49 #5
2017 Panini Torque Silhouettes Firesuit Signatures /141 #3
2017 Panini Torque Silhouettes Firesuit Signatures Blue /75 #3
2017 Panini Torque Silhouettes Firesuit Signatures Green /25 #3
2017 Panini Torque Silhouettes Firesuit Signatures Purple /10 #3
2017 Panini Torque Silhouettes Firesuit Signatures Red /49 #3
2017 Panini Torque Superstar Vision #7
2017 Panini Torque Superstar Vision Blue /99 #7
2017 Panini Torque Superstar Vision Gold /149 #7
2017 Panini Torque Superstar Vision Green /25 #7
2017 Panini Torque Superstar Vision Purple /10 #7
2017 Panini Torque Superstar Vision Red /49 #7
2017 Panini Torque Test Proof Black /1 #10
2017 Panini Torque Test Proof Black /1 #72
2017 Panini Torque Test Proof Black /1 #86
2017 Panini Torque Test Proof Cyan /1 #10
2017 Panini Torque Test Proof Cyan /1 #72
2017 Panini Torque Test Proof Cyan /1 #86
2017 Panini Torque Test Proof Magenta /1 #10
2017 Panini Torque Test Proof Magenta /1 #72
2017 Panini Torque Test Proof Magenta /1 #86
2017 Panini Torque Test Proof Yellow /1 #10
2017 Panini Torque Test Proof Yellow /1 #72
2017 Panini Torque Test Proof Yellow /1 #86
2017 Panini Torque Trackside #4
2017 Panini Torque Trackside Blue /99 #4
2017 Panini Torque Trackside Checkerboard /10 #4
2017 Panini Torque Trackside Green /25 #4
2017 Panini Torque Trackside Red /49 #4
2017 Panini Torque Victory Laps #9
2017 Panini Torque Victory Laps Gold /199 #9
2017 Panini Torque Victory Laps Holo Silver /99 #9
2017 Panini Torque Visions of Greatness #21
2017 Panini Torque Visions of Greatness Blue /99 #21
2017 Panini Torque Visions of Greatness Gold /149 #21
2017 Panini Torque Visions of Greatness Green /25 #21
2017 Panini Torque Visions of Greatness Purple /10 #21
2017 Panini Torque Visions of Greatness Red /49 #21
2017 Select #69
2017 Select #70
2017 Select #107
2017 Select Endorsements #25
2017 Select Endorsements Prizms Blue /50 #25
2017 Select Endorsements Prizms Checkered Flag /1 #25
2017 Select Endorsements Prizms Gold /10 #25
2017 Select Endorsements Prizms Red /25 #25
2017 Select Prizms Black /3 #69
2017 Select Prizms Black /3 #70
2017 Select Prizms Black /3 #107
2017 Select Prizms Blue /199 #69
2017 Select Prizms Blue /199 #70
2017 Select Prizms Checkered Flag /1 #69
2017 Select Prizms Checkered Flag /1 #70
2017 Select Prizms Checkered Flag /1 #107
2017 Select Prizms Gold /10 #69
2017 Select Prizms Gold /10 #70
2017 Select Prizms Gold /10 #107
2017 Select Prizms Purple Pulsar #69
2017 Select Prizms Purple Pulsar #70
2017 Select Prizms Red /99 #69
2017 Select Prizms Red /99 #70
2017 Select Prizms Red White and Blue Pulsar /299 #69
2017 Select Prizms Red White and Blue Pulsar /299 #70
2017 Select Prizms Silver #69
2017 Select Prizms Silver #70
2017 Select Prizms Tie Dye /24 #69
2017 Select Prizms Tie Dye /24 #70
2017 Select Prizms Tie Dye /24 #107
2017 Select Prizms White /50 #69
2017 Select Prizms White /50 #70
2017 Select Prizms White /50 #107
2017 Select Select Pairs Materials #22
2017 Select Select Pairs Materials #24
2017 Select Select Pairs Materials #25
2017 Select Select Pairs Materials Prizms Blue /199 #22
2017 Select Select Pairs Materials Prizms Blue /199 #24
2017 Select Select Pairs Materials Prizms Blue /199 #25
2017 Select Select Pairs Materials Prizms Checkered Flag /1 #22
2017 Select Select Pairs Materials Prizms Checkered Flag /1 #24
2017 Select Select Pairs Materials Prizms Checkered Flag /1 #25
2017 Select Select Pairs Materials Prizms Gold /10 #22
2017 Select Select Pairs Materials Prizms Gold /10 #24
2017 Select Select Pairs Materials Prizms Gold /10 #25
2017 Select Select Pairs Materials Prizms Red /99 #22
2017 Select Select Pairs Materials Prizms Red /99 #24
2017 Select Select Pairs Materials Prizms Red /99 #25
2017 Select Select Stars #10
2017 Select Select Stars Prizms Black /3 #10
2017 Select Select Stars Prizms Checkered Flag /1 #10
2017 Select Select Stars Prizms Gold /10 #10
2017 Select Select Stars Prizms Tie Dye /24 #10
2017 Select Select Stars Prizms White /50 #10
2017 Select Select Swatches #34
2017 Select Select Swatches Prizms Blue /75 #34
2017 Select Select Swatches Prizms Checkered Flag /1 #34
2017 Select Select Swatches Prizms Gold /10 #34
2017 Select Select Swatches Prizms Red /50 #34
2017 Select Sheet Metal #20
2017 Select Sheet Metal Prizms Blue /35 #20
2017 Select Sheet Metal Prizms Checkered Flag /1 #20
2017 Select Sheet Metal Prizms Gold /10 #20
2017 Select Sheet Metal Prizms Red /25 #20
2017 Select Signature Swatches #34
2017 Select Signature Swatches Prizms Checkered Flag /1 #34
2017 Select Signature Swatches Prizms Gold /10 #34
2017 Select Signature Swatches Prizms Tie Dye /24 #34
2017 Select Signature Swatches Prizms White /50 #34
2017 Select Signature Swatches Triple #21
2017 Select Signature Swatches Triple Prizms Checkered Flag /1 #21
2017 Select Signature Swatches Triple Prizms Gold /10 #21
2017 Select Signature Swatches Triple Prizms Tie Dye /24 #21
2017 Select Signature Swatches Triple Prizms White /50 #21
2017 Select Speed Merchants #6
2017 Select Speed Merchants Prizms Black /3 #6
2017 Select Speed Merchants Prizms Checkered Flag /1 #6
2017 Select Speed Merchants Prizms Gold /10 #6
2017 Select Speed Merchants Prizms Tie Dye /24 #6
2017 Select Speed Merchants Prizms White /50 #6
2018 Certified #9
2018 Certified Black /1 #9
2018 Certified Blue /99 #9
2018 Certified Gold /49 #9
2018 Certified Green /10 #9
2018 Certified Materials Signatures Black /1 #10
2018 Certified Materials Signatures Blue /25 #10
2018 Certified Materials Signatures Gold /15 #10
2018 Certified Materials Signatures Green /5 #10
2018 Certified Materials Signatures Purple /10 #10
2018 Certified Mirror Black /1 #9
2018 Certified Mirror Gold /25 #9
2018 Certified Mirror Green /5 #9
2018 Certified Mirror Purple /10 #9
2018 Certified Orange /249 #9
2018 Certified Purple /25 #9
2018 Certified Red /199 #9
2018 Certified Signature Swatches Black /1 #14
2018 Certified Signature Swatches Blue /25 #14
2018 Certified Signature Swatches Gold /15 #14
2018 Certified Signature Swatches Green /5 #14
2018 Certified Signature Swatches Purple /10 #14
2018 Certified Signatures Black /1 #23
2018 Certified Signatures Blue /25 #23
2018 Certified Signatures Gold /15 #23
2018 Certified Signatures Green /5 #23
2018 Certified Signatures Purple /10 #23
2018 Donruss #16
2018 Donruss #43A
2018 Donruss #97
2018 Donruss #133
2018 Donruss #43B
2018 Donruss Artist Proofs /25 #16
2018 Donruss Artist Proofs /25 #43A
2018 Donruss Artist Proofs /25 #97
2018 Donruss Artist Proofs /25 #133
2018 Donruss Artist Proofs /25 #43B
2018 Donruss Classics #18
2018 Donruss Classics Cracked Ice /999 #18
2018 Donruss Classics Xplosion /99 #18
2018 Donruss Gold Foil /499 #16
2018 Donruss Gold Foil /499 #43A
2018 Donruss Gold Foil /499 #97
2018 Donruss Gold Foil /499 #133
2018 Donruss Gold Foil /499 #43B
2018 Donruss Gold Press Proofs /99 #16
2018 Donruss Gold Press Proofs /99 #43A
2018 Donruss Gold Press Proofs /99 #97
2018 Donruss Gold Press Proofs /99 #133
2018 Donruss Gold Press Proofs /99 #43B
2018 Donruss Green Foil /199 #16
2018 Donruss Green Foil /199 #43A
2018 Donruss Green Foil /199 #97
2018 Donruss Green Foil /199 #133
2018 Donruss Green Foil /199 #43B
2018 Donruss Pole Position #8
2018 Donruss Pole Position Cracked Ice /999 #8
2018 Donruss Pole Position Xplosion /99 #8
2018 Donruss Press Proofs /49 #16
2018 Donruss Press Proofs /49 #43A
2018 Donruss Press Proofs /49 #97
2018 Donruss Press Proofs /49 #133
2018 Donruss Press Proofs /49 #43B
2018 Donruss Printing Plates Black /1 #16
2018 Donruss Printing Plates Black /1 #43
2018 Donruss Printing Plates Black /1 #97
2018 Donruss Printing Plates Black /1 #133
2018 Donruss Printing Plates Black /1 #43B
2018 Donruss Printing Plates Cyan /1 #16
2018 Donruss Printing Plates Cyan /1 #43
2018 Donruss Printing Plates Cyan /1 #97
2018 Donruss Printing Plates Cyan /1 #133
2018 Donruss Printing Plates Cyan /1 #43B
2018 Donruss Printing Plates Magenta /1 #16
2018 Donruss Printing Plates Magenta /1 #43
2018 Donruss Printing Plates Magenta /1 #97
2018 Donruss Printing Plates Magenta /1 #133
2018 Donruss Printing Plates Magenta /1 #43B
2018 Donruss Printing Plates Yellow /1 #16
2018 Donruss Printing Plates Yellow /1 #43
2018 Donruss Printing Plates Yellow /1 #97
2018 Donruss Printing Plates Yellow /1 #133
2018 Donruss Printing Plates Yellow /1 #43B
2018 Donruss Red Foil /299 #16
2018 Donruss Red Foil /299 #43A
2018 Donruss Red Foil /299 #97
2018 Donruss Red Foil /299 #133
2018 Donruss Red Foil /299 #43B
2018 Donruss Retro Relics '85 #14
2018 Donruss Retro Relics '85 Black /10 #14
2018 Donruss Retro Relics '85 Holo Gold /99 #14
2018 Donruss Rubber Relics #27
2018 Donruss Rubber Relics Black /10 #27
2018 Donruss Rubber Relics Holo Gold /99 #27
2018 Donruss Signature Series #28
2018 Donruss Signature Series Black /1 #28
2018 Donruss Signature Series Holo Gold /25 #28
2018 Donruss Top Tier #10
2018 Donruss Top Tier Cracked Ice /999 #10
2018 Donruss Top Tier Xplosion /99 #10
2018 Panini Prime Autograph Materials /99 #21
2018 Panini Prime Autograph Materials Black /1 #21
2018 Panini Prime Autograph Materials Holo Gold /50 #21
2018 Panini Prime Autograph Materials Laundry Tag /1 #21
2018 Panini Prime Driver Signatures /99 #13
2018 Panini Prime Driver Signatures Black /1 #13
2018 Panini Prime Driver Signatures Holo Gold /50 #13
2018 Panini Prime Prime Jumbo Associate Sponsor 1 /1 #58
2018 Panini Prime Prime Jumbo Associate Sponsor 2 /1 #58
2018 Panini Prime Prime Jumbo Car Manufacturer /1 #58
2018 Panini Prime Prime Jumbo Firesuit Manufacturer /1 #58
2018 Panini Prime Prime Jumbo Glove Manufacturer Patch /1 #58
2018 Panini Prime Prime Jumbo Glove Name Patch /1 #58
2018 Panini Prime Prime Jumbo Glove Number Patch /1 #58
2018 Panini Prime Prime Jumbo Nameplate /2 #58
2018 Panini Prime Prime Jumbo NASCAR /1 #58
2018 Panini Prime Prime Jumbo Prime Colors /18 #58
2018 Panini Prime Prime Jumbo Shoe Brand Logo /1 #58
2018 Panini Prime Prime Jumbo Shoe Name Patch /1 #58
2018 Panini Prime Prime Jumbo Sunoco /1 #58
2018 Panini Prime Prime Signatures /99 #13
2018 Panini Prime Prime Signatures Black /1 #13
2018 Panini Prime Prime Signatures Holo Gold /50 #13
2018 Panini Prime Race Used Firesuits /50 #29
2018 Panini Prime Race Used Firesuits Black /1 #29
2018 Panini Prime Race Used Firesuits Laundry Tag /1 #29
2018 Panini Prime Race Used Sheet Metal /50 #29
2018 Panini Prime Race Used Sheet Metal Black /1 #29
2018 Panini Prime Race Used Sheet Metal Holo Gold /25 #29
2018 Panini Prime Race Used Tires Black /1 #29
2018 Panini Prime Race Used Tires Holo Gold /25 #29
2018 Panini Prime Shadowbox Signatures /99 #8
2018 Panini Prime Shadowbox Signatures Black /1 #8
2018 Panini Prime Shadowbox Signatures Holo Gold /50 #8
2018 Panini Prime Signature Tires /99 #13
2018 Panini Prime Signature Tires Black /1 #13
2018 Panini Prime Signature Tires Holo Gold /50 #13
2018 Panini Prime Triple Material Autographs /99 #3
2018 Panini Prime Triple Material Autographs Black /1 #3
2018 Panini Prime Triple Material Autographs Holo Gold /50 #3
2018 Panini Prime Triple Material Autographs Laundry Tag /1 #3
2018 Panini Prizm #33
2018 Panini Prizm Patented Penmanship Prizms #9
2018 Panini Prizm Patented Penmanship Prizms Black /1 #9
2018 Panini Prizm Patented Penmanship Prizms Blue /5 #9
2018 Panini Prizm Patented Penmanship Prizms Camo #9
2018 Panini Prizm Patented Penmanship Prizms Gold /10 #9
2018 Panini Prizm Patented Penmanship Prizms Green /5 #9
2018 Panini Prizm Patented Penmanship Prizms Rainbow /24 #9
2018 Panini Prizm Patented Penmanship Prizms Red /5 #9
2018 Panini Prizm Patented Penmanship Prizms Red White and Blue /5 #9
2018 Panini Prizm Patented Penmanship Prizms White /5 #9
2018 Panini Prizm Prizms #33
2018 Panini Prizm Prizms Black /1 #33
2018 Panini Prizm Prizms Blue /99 #33
2018 Panini Prizm Prizms Camo #33
2018 Panini Prizm Prizms Gold /10 #33
2018 Panini Prizm Prizms Green /149 #33
2018 Panini Prizm Prizms Purple Flash #33
2018 Panini Prizm Prizms Rainbow /24 #33
2018 Panini Prizm Prizms Red /75 #33
2018 Panini Prizm Prizms Red White and Blue #33
2018 Panini Prizm Prizms White /5 #33
2018 Panini Victory Lane #27
2018 Panini Victory Lane #49
2018 Panini Victory Lane Black /1 #27
2018 Panini Victory Lane Black /1 #49
2018 Panini Victory Lane Blue /25 #27
2018 Panini Victory Lane Blue /25 #49
2018 Panini Victory Lane Engineered to Perfection Materials /99 #18
2018 Panini Victory Lane Engineered to Perfection Materials Black /10 #18
2018 Panini Victory Lane Engineered to Perfection Materials Gold /49 #18
2018 Panini Victory Lane Engineered to Perfection Materials Green /25 #18
2018 Panini Victory Lane Engineered to Perfection Materials Laundry Tag /1 #18
2018 Panini Victory Lane Engineered to Perfection Triple Materials /99 #13
2018 Panini Victory Lane Engineered to Perfection Triple Materials Black /10 #13
2018 Panini Victory Lane Engineered to Perfection Triple Materials Gold /49 #13
2018 Panini Victory Lane Engineered to Perfection Triple Materials Green /25 #13
2018 Panini Victory Lane Engineered to Perfection Triple Materials Laundry Tag /1 #13
2018 Panini Victory Lane Gold /99 #27
2018 Panini Victory Lane Gold /99 #49
2018 Panini Victory Lane Green /5 #27
2018 Panini Victory Lane Green /5 #49

2018 Panini Victory Lane Pedal to the Metal #40
2018 Panini Victory Lane Pedal to the Metal #71
2018 Panini Victory Lane Pedal to the Metal Black /1 #40
2018 Panini Victory Lane Pedal to the Metal Black /1 #71
2018 Panini Victory Lane Pedal to the Metal Blue /25 #40
2018 Panini Victory Lane Pedal to the Metal Blue /25 #71
2018 Panini Victory Lane Pedal to the Metal Green /5 #40
2018 Panini Victory Lane Pedal to the Metal Green /5 #71
2018 Panini Victory Lane Printing Plates Black /1 #27
2018 Panini Victory Lane Printing Plates Black /1 #49
2018 Panini Victory Lane Printing Plates Cyan /1 #27
2018 Panini Victory Lane Printing Plates Cyan /1 #49
2018 Panini Victory Lane Printing Plates Magenta /1 #27
2018 Panini Victory Lane Printing Plates Magenta /1 #49
2018 Panini Victory Lane Printing Plates Yellow /1 #27
2018 Panini Victory Lane Printing Plates Yellow /1 #49
2018 Panini Victory Lane Race Ready Materials /49 #21
2018 Panini Victory Lane Race Ready Materials Black /5 #21
2018 Panini Victory Lane Race Ready Materials Laundry Tag /1 #21
2018 Panini Victory Lane Red /49 #27
2018 Panini Victory Lane Red /49 #49
2018 Panini Victory Lane Silver #27
2018 Panini Victory Lane Silver #49
2018 Panini Victory Lane Starting Grid #23
2018 Panini Victory Lane Starting Grid Black /1 #23
2018 Panini Victory Lane Starting Grid Blue /25 #23
2018 Panini Victory Lane Starting Grid Gold /99 #23
2018 Panini Victory Lane Starting Grid Green /5 #23
2018 Panini Victory Lane Starting Grid Printing Plates Black /1 #23
2018 Panini Victory Lane Starting Grid Printing Plates Cyan /1 #23
2018 Panini Victory Lane Starting Grid Printing Plates Magenta /1 #23
2018 Panini Victory Lane Starting Grid Printing Plates Yellow /1 #23
2018 Panini Victory Lane Starting Grid Red /49 #23
2018 Panini Victory Lane Victory Marks /125 #12
2018 Panini Victory Lane Victory Marks Black /1 #12
2018 Panini Victory Lane Victory Marks Gold /99 #12
2019 Donruss #74
2019 Donruss #136
2019 Donruss Artist Proofs /25 #74
2019 Donruss Artist Proofs /25 #136
2019 Donruss Black /199 #74
2019 Donruss Black /199 #136
2019 Donruss Gold /299 #74
2019 Donruss Gold /299 #136
2019 Donruss Gold Press Proofs /99 #74
2019 Donruss Gold Press Proofs /99 #136
2019 Donruss Optic #39
2019 Donruss Optic #62
2019 Donruss Optic Blue Pulsar #39
2019 Donruss Optic Blue Pulsar /1 #62
2019 Donruss Optic Gold /10 #39
2019 Donruss Optic Gold /10 #62
2019 Donruss Optic Gold Vinyl /1 #39
2019 Donruss Optic Gold Vinyl /1 #62
2019 Donruss Optic Holo #39
2019 Donruss Optic Holo #62
2019 Donruss Optic Red Wave #39
2019 Donruss Optic Red Wave /1 #62
2019 Donruss Optic Signatures Gold Vinyl /1 #62
2019 Donruss Optic Signatures Gold Vinyl /1 #39
2019 Donruss Optic Signatures Holo /75 #39
2019 Donruss Optic Signatures Holo /75 #62
2019 Donruss Press Proofs /49 #74
2019 Donruss Press Proofs /49 #136
2019 Donruss Printing Plates Black /1 #74
2019 Donruss Printing Plates Black /1 #136
2019 Donruss Printing Plates Cyan /1 #74
2019 Donruss Printing Plates Cyan /1 #136
2019 Donruss Printing Plates Magenta /1 #74
2019 Donruss Printing Plates Magenta /1 #136
2019 Donruss Printing Plates Yellow /1 #74
2019 Donruss Printing Plates Yellow /1 #136
2019 Donruss Silver #74
2019 Donruss Silver #136
2019 Panini Prime Dual Material Autographs /99 #3
2019 Panini Prime Dual Material Autographs Black /10 #3
2019 Panini Prime Dual Material Autographs Holo Gold /25 #3
2019 Panini Prime Dual Material Autographs Laundry Tags /1 #3
2019 Panini Prime Prime Jumbo Associate Sponsor 1 /1 #55
2019 Panini Prime Prime Jumbo Car Manufacturer /1 #55
2019 Panini Prime Prime Jumbo Firesuit Manufacturer /1 #55
2019 Panini Prime Prime Jumbo Glove Manufacturer Patch /1 #55
2019 Panini Prime Prime Jumbo Glove Name Patch /1 #55
2019 Panini Prime Prime Jumbo Glove Number Patch /1 #55
2019 Panini Prime Prime Jumbo Goodyear /1 #55
2019 Panini Prime Prime Jumbo NASCAR /1 #55
2019 Panini Prime Prime Jumbo Prime Colors /12 #55
2019 Panini Prime Prime Jumbo Shoe Brand Logo /1 #55
2019 Panini Prime Prime Jumbo Shoe Name Patch /1 #55
2019 Panini Prime Prime Names Die Cut Signatures /99 #17
2019 Panini Prime Prime Names Die Cut Signatures Black /10 #17
2019 Panini Prime Prime Names Die Cut Signatures Holo Gold /25 #17
2019 Panini Prime Prime Names Die Cut Signatures Platinum Blue /1 #17
2019 Panini Prime Race Used Firesuits /39 #3
2019 Panini Prime Race Used Firesuits Black /10 #3
2019 Panini Prime Race Used Firesuits Holo Gold /25 #3
2019 Panini Prime Race Used Firesuits Laundry Tags /1 #3
2019 Panini Prime Race Used Sheet Metal /50 #3
2019 Panini Prime Race Used Sheet Metal Black /10 #3
2019 Panini Prime Race Used Sheet Metal Holo Gold /25 #3
2019 Panini Prime Race Used Sheet Metal Platinum Blue /1 #3
2019 Panini Prime Race Used Tires /50 #3
2019 Panini Prime Race Used Tires Black /10 #3
2019 Panini Prime Race Used Tires Holo Gold /25 #3
2019 Panini Prime Race Used Tires Platinum Blue /1 #3
2019 Panini Prime Shadowbox Signatures /99 #9
2019 Panini Prime Shadowbox Signatures Black /10 #9
2019 Panini Prime Shadowbox Signatures Holo Gold /25 #9
2019 Panini Prime Shadowbox Signatures Platinum Blue /1 #9
2019 Panini Prizm Endorsements Prizms #14
2019 Panini Prizm Endorsements Prizms Black /1 #14
2019 Panini Prizm Endorsements Prizms Blue /75 #14
2019 Panini Prizm Endorsements Prizms Camo #14
2019 Panini Prizm Endorsements Prizms Gold /10 #14
2019 Panini Prizm Endorsements Prizms Green /99 #14
2019 Panini Prizm Endorsements Prizms Rainbow /24 #14
2019 Panini Prizm Endorsements Prizms Red /50 #14
2019 Panini Prizm Endorsements Prizms Red White and Blue #14
2019 Panini Prizm Endorsements Prizms White /5 #14
2019 Panini Victory Lane #68
2019 Panini Victory Lane Black /1 #68
2019 Panini Victory Lane Dual Swatch Signatures #14
2019 Panini Victory Lane Dual Swatch Signatures Gold /99 #14
2019 Panini Victory Lane Dual Swatch Signatures Platinum /1 #14
2019 Panini Victory Lane Dual Swatch Signatures Red /25 #14
2019 Panini Victory Lane Gold /25 #68
2019 Panini Victory Lane Pedal to the Metal #89
2019 Panini Victory Lane Pedal to the Metal Black /1 #89
2019 Panini Victory Lane Pedal to the Metal Gold /25 #89
2019 Panini Victory Lane Pedal to the Metal Green /5 #89
2019 Panini Victory Lane Pedal to the Metal Red /3 #89
2019 Panini Victory Lane Printing Plates Black /1 #68
2019 Panini Victory Lane Printing Plates Cyan /1 #68
2019 Panini Victory Lane Printing Plates Magenta /1 #68
2019 Panini Victory Lane Printing Plates Yellow /1 #68
2020 Donruss #64
2020 Donruss #123
2020 Donruss Black Numbers /17 #64
2020 Donruss Black Numbers /17 #123
2020 Donruss Black Trophy Club /1 #84
2020 Donruss Black Trophy Club /1 #123
2020 Donruss Blue /199 #84
2020 Donruss Blue /199 #123
2020 Donruss Carolina Blue #84
2020 Donruss Carolina Blue #123
2020 Donruss Classics #12
2020 Donruss Classics Checkers #12
2020 Donruss Classics Cracked Ice /25 #12
2020 Donruss Classics Holographic /199 #12
2020 Donruss Classics Xplosion /10 #12
2020 Donruss Green /99 #84
2020 Donruss Green /99 #123
2020 Donruss Orange #84
2020 Donruss Orange #123
2020 Donruss Pink /25 #84
2020 Donruss Pink /25 #123
2020 Donruss Printing Plates Black /1 #84
2020 Donruss Printing Plates Black /1 #123
2020 Donruss Printing Plates Cyan /1 #84
2020 Donruss Printing Plates Cyan /1 #123
2020 Donruss Printing Plates Magenta /1 #84
2020 Donruss Printing Plates Magenta /1 #123
2020 Donruss Printing Plates Yellow /1 #84
2020 Donruss Printing Plates Yellow /1 #123
2020 Donruss Purple /49 #84
2020 Donruss Purple /49 #123
2020 Donruss Red /299 #84
2020 Donruss Red /299 #123
2020 Donruss Retro Relics '87 #8
2020 Donruss Retro Relics '87 Holo Black /10 #8
2020 Donruss Retro Relics '87 Holo Gold /25 #8
2020 Donruss Retro Relics '87 Red /99 #8
2020 Donruss Silver #84
2020 Donruss Silver #123

Brad Keselowski

2008 Press Pass Signings #34
2008 Press Pass Signings Gold /50 #30
2008 Press Pass Signings Press Plates Black /1 #BK
2008 Press Pass Signings Press Plates Cyan /1 #BK
2008 Press Pass Signings Press Plates Yellow /1 #BK
2008 Press Pass Signings Silver /100 #29
2008 Press Pass Speedway #39
2008 Press Pass Speedway Gold #G39
2008 Press Pass Speedway Holofoil /50 #H39
2008 Press Pass Speedway Previews /5 #EB39
2008 Press Pass Speedway Red /10 #R39
2008 Press Pass Stealth #43
2008 Press Pass Stealth Chrome #43
2008 Press Pass Stealth Chrome Exclusives /25 #43
2008 Press Pass Stealth Chrome Exclusives Gold /99 #43
2008 Press Pass Stealth Previews /5 #43
2008 Press Pass Top Prospects Gloves /175 #BKG
2008 Press Pass Top Prospects Metal-Tire /75 #BKST
2008 Press Pass Top Prospects Sheet Metal /175 #BKSM
2008 Press Pass Top Prospects Shoes /175 #BKS
2008 Press Pass Top Prospects Tires /330 #BKT
2008 Press Pass Top Prospects Tires Autographs /25 #BKAT
2008 Press Pass Top Prospects Tires Gold /100 #BKT
2009 Element #43
2009 Element Lab Report #LR17
2009 Element Radioactive /100 #43
2009 Press Pass #45
2009 Press Pass #137
2009 Press Pass #163
2009 Press Pass Autographs Gold #24
2009 Press Pass Autographs Gold #25
2009 Press Pass Autographs Printing Plates Black /1 #24
2009 Press Pass Autographs Printing Plates Cyan /1 #24
2009 Press Pass Autographs Printing Plates Magenta /1 #24
2009 Press Pass Autographs Printing Plates Yellow /1 #24
2009 Press Pass Autographs Silver #28
2009 Press Pass Blue #45
2009 Press Pass Blue #137
2009 Press Pass Blue #163
2009 Press Pass Gold #45
2009 Press Pass Gold #137
2009 Press Pass Gold #163
2009 Press Pass Gold Holofoil /100 #45
2009 Press Pass Gold Holofoil /100 #137
2009 Press Pass Gold Holofoil /100 #163
2009 Press Pass Legends Prominent Pieces Bronze /150 #PPBK
2009 Press Pass Legends Prominent Pieces Gold /25 #PPBK
2009 Press Pass Legends Prominent Pieces Oversized /25 #PPOEBK
2009 Press Pass Legends Prominent Pieces Silver /50 #PPBK
2009 Press Pass Pieces Race Used Memorabilia #BK
2009 Press Pass Pocket Portraits Wal-Mart #PPW15
2009 Press Pass Previews /5 #EB137
2009 Press Pass Prospect Pieces /100 #PPBK
2009 Press Pass Prospect Pieces Autographs /50 #PPBK
2009 Press Pass Red #45
2009 Press Pass Red #137
2009 Press Pass Red #163
2009 Press Pass Showcase /100 #53
2009 Press Pass Showcase 2nd Gear /50 #53
2009 Press Pass Showcase 3rd Gear /25 #53
2009 Press Pass Showcase 4th Gear /5 #53
2009 Press Pass Signings Blue /25 #23
2009 Press Pass Signings Blue /25 #22
2009 Press Pass Signings Gold #22
2009 Press Pass Signings Gold #23
2009 Press Pass Signings Green /15 #22
2009 Press Pass Signings Green /15 #23
2009 Press Pass Signings Orange /25 #22
2009 Press Pass Signings Orange /25 #23
2009 Press Pass Signings Printing Plates Black /1 #22
2009 Press Pass Signings Printing Plates Black /1 #23
2009 Press Pass Signings Printing Plates Cyan /1 #23
2009 Press Pass Signings Printing Plates Magenta /1 #23
2009 Press Pass Signings Printing Plates Yellow /1 #23
2009 Press Pass Signings Printing Plates Yellow /1 #22
2009 Press Pass Signings Purple /15 #22
2009 Press Pass Signings Purple /15 #23
2009 Press Pass Stealth #19
2009 Press Pass Stealth #37
2009 Press Pass Stealth Chrome #19
2009 Press Pass Stealth Chrome #37
2009 Press Pass Stealth Chrome Brushed Metal /25 #19
2009 Press Pass Stealth Chrome Brushed Metal /25 #37
2009 Press Pass Stealth Chrome Gold /99 #19
2009 Press Pass Stealth Chrome Gold /99 #37
2009 Press Pass Stealth Previews /5 #EB19
2009 VIP #18
2009 VIP After Party #AP9
2009 VIP After Party Transparent #AP9
2009 VIP Previews /5 #18
2009 VIP Purple /25 #18
2009 VIP Rookie Stripes /100 #RS3
2009 VIP Rookie Stripes Autographs /25 #RSBK
2009 Wheels Autographs #38
2009 Wheels Autographs Press Plates Black /1 #BK
2009 Wheels Autographs Press Plates Cyan /1 #BK
2009 Wheels Autographs Press Plates Magenta /1 #BK
2009 Wheels Autographs Press Plates Yellow /1 #BK
2009 Wheels Main Event #89
2009 Wheels Main Event Marks Printing Plates Black /1 #27
2009 Wheels Main Event Marks Printing Plates Cyan /1 #27
2009 Wheels Main Event Marks Printing Plates Magenta /1 #27
2009 Wheels Main Event Marks Printing Plates Yellow /1 #27
2009 Wheels Main Event Playing Cards Blue #10C
2009 Wheels Main Event Playing Cards Red #10C
2009 Wheels Main Event Poker Chips #12
2009 Wheels Main Event Rookie Marks Clubs #BK
2009 Wheels Main Event Rookie Marks Diamonds #BK
2009 Wheels Main Event Rookie Marks Hearts #BK
2009 Wheels Main Event Stop and Go Swatches Pit Banner /175 #SGBBK
2009 Wheels Main Event Stop and Go Swatches Pit Banner Green /10 #SGBBK
2009 Wheels Main Event Stop and Go Swatches Pit Banner Holofoil /75 #SGBBK
2009 Wheels Main Event Stop and Go Swatches Pit Banner Red /25 #SGBBK
2009 Wheels Main Event Stop and Go Swatches Pit Sign /175 #SGSBK
2009 Wheels Main Event Stop and Go Swatches Pit Sign Green /10 #SGSBK
2009 Wheels Main Event Stop and Go Swatches Pit Sign Holofoil /75 #SGSBK
2009 Wheels Main Event Stop and Go Swatches Pit Sign Red /25 #SGSBK
2010 Element #15
2010 Element Blue /35 #15
2010 Element Green #15
2010 Element Previews /5 #EB15
2010 Element Purple /25 #15
2010 Element Red Target #15
2010 Press Pass #36
2010 Press Pass #40
2010 Press Pass #62
2010 Press Pass #71
2010 Press Pass Autographs #27
2010 Press Pass Autographs #28
2010 Press Pass Autographs Printing Plates Black /1 #20
2010 Press Pass Autographs Printing Plates Cyan /1 #24
2010 Press Pass Autographs Printing Plates Cyan /1 #25
2010 Press Pass Autographs Printing Plates Magenta /1 #21
2010 Press Pass Autographs Printing Plates Magenta /1 #22
2010 Press Pass Autographs Printing Plates Magenta /1 #23
2010 Press Pass Autographs Printing Plates Yellow /1 #21
2010 Press Pass Autographs Printing Plates Yellow /1 #22
2010 Press Pass Blue #36
2010 Press Pass Blue #40
2010 Press Pass Blue #62
2010 Press Pass Blue #71
2010 Press Pass Burning Rubber /250 #BR8
2010 Press Pass Burning Rubber Gold /50 #BR8
2010 Press Pass Burning Rubber Prime Cuts /25 #BR8
2010 Press Pass Eclipse #1
2010 Press Pass Eclipse #86
2010 Press Pass Eclipse Blue #1
2010 Press Pass Eclipse Blue #86
2010 Press Pass Eclipse Gold #1
2010 Press Pass Eclipse Gold #86
2010 Press Pass Eclipse Previews /5 #1
2010 Press Pass Eclipse Purple /25 #1
2010 Press Pass Eclipse Spellbound Swatches /120 #SSBK1
2010 Press Pass Eclipse Spellbound Swatches /120 #SSBK2
2010 Press Pass Eclipse Spellbound Swatches /120 #SSBK3
2010 Press Pass Eclipse Spellbound Swatches /120 #SSBK4
2010 Press Pass Eclipse Spellbound Swatches /120 #SSBK5
2010 Press Pass Eclipse Spellbound Swatches /120 #SSBK6
2010 Press Pass Eclipse Spellbound Swatches /120 #SSBK7
2010 Press Pass Eclipse Spellbound Swatches /120 #SSBK8
2010 Press Pass Eclipse Spellbound Swatches /120 #SSBK9
2010 Press Pass Eclipse Spellbound Swatches /120 #SSBK10
2010 Press Pass Eclipse Spellbound Swatches Holofoil /9 #SSBK1
2010 Press Pass Eclipse Spellbound Swatches Holofoil /9 #SSBK2
2010 Press Pass Eclipse Spellbound Swatches Holofoil /9 #SSBK3
2010 Press Pass Eclipse Spellbound Swatches Holofoil /9 #SSBK4
2010 Press Pass Eclipse Spellbound Swatches Holofoil /9 #SSBK5
2010 Press Pass Eclipse Spellbound Swatches Holofoil /9 #SSBK6
2010 Press Pass Eclipse Spellbound Swatches Holofoil /9 #SSBK7
2010 Press Pass Eclipse Spellbound Swatches Holofoil /9 #SSBK8
2010 Press Pass Eclipse Spellbound Swatches Holofoil /9 #SSBK9
2010 Press Pass Eclipse Spellbound Swatches Holofoil /9 #SSBK10
2010 Press Pass Five Star Paramount Pieces Aluminum /10 #BK
2010 Press Pass Five Star Paramount Pieces Blue /20 #BK
2010 Press Pass Five Star Paramount Pieces Melting /1 #BK
2010 Press Pass Five Star Signatures Aluminum /35 #BK
2010 Press Pass Five Star Signatures Gold /20 #BK
2010 Press Pass Five Star Signatures Holofoil /5 #BK
2010 Press Pass Five Star Signatures Melting /1 #BK
2010 Press Pass Four Wide Autographs /5 #NNO
2010 Press Pass Four Wide Firesuit /25 #FWBK
2010 Press Pass Four Wide Sheet Metal /15 #FWBK
2010 Press Pass Four Wide Shoes /1 #FWBK
2010 Press Pass Four Wide Tires /10 #FWBK
2010 Press Pass Gold #36
2010 Press Pass Gold #40
2010 Press Pass Gold #62
2010 Press Pass Gold #71
2010 Press Pass Holofoil /100 #36
2010 Press Pass Holofoil /100 #40
2010 Press Pass Holofoil /100 #62
2010 Press Pass Holofoil /100 #71
2010 Press Pass Legends Autographs Blue /10 #37
2010 Press Pass Legends Autographs Holofoil /25 #37
2010 Press Pass Legends Prominent Pieces Copper /99 #PPBK
2010 Press Pass Legends Prominent Pieces Gold /50 #PPBK
2010 Press Pass Legends Prominent Pieces Holofoil /25 #PPBK
2010 Press Pass Legends Prominent Pieces Oversized Firesuit /25 #PPOEBK
2010 Press Pass Premium #33
2010 Press Pass Premium Purple /25 #33
2010 Press Pass Premium Signatures #PSBK
2010 Press Pass Premium Signatures Red Ink /24 #PSBK
2010 Press Pass Previews /5 #36
2010 Press Pass Purple /25 #36
2010 Press Pass Purple /25 #40
2010 Press Pass Purple /25 #62
2010 Press Pass Purple /25 #71
2010 Press Pass Showcase /499 #27
2010 Press Pass Showcase /499 #36
2010 Press Pass Showcase /499 #50
2010 Press Pass Showcase Classic Collections Ink /15 #CCIPEN
2010 Press Pass Showcase Classic Collections Ink Gold /10 #CCIPEN
2010 Press Pass Showcase Classic Collections Ink Green /5 #CCIPEN
2010 Press Pass Showcase Classic Collections Ink Melting /1 #CCIPEN
2010 Press Pass Showcase Elite Exhibit Ink /20 #EEIBK
2010 Press Pass Showcase Elite Exhibit Ink Gold /10 #EEIBK
2010 Press Pass Showcase Elite Exhibit Ink Green /5 #EEIBK
2010 Press Pass Showcase Elite Exhibit Ink Melting /1 #EEIBK
2010 Press Pass Showcase Gold /125 #27
2010 Press Pass Showcase Gold /125 #36
2010 Press Pass Showcase Gold /125 #50
2010 Press Pass Showcase Green /50 #27
2010 Press Pass Showcase Green /50 #36
2010 Press Pass Showcase Green /50 #50
2010 Press Pass Showcase Melting /15 #27
2010 Press Pass Showcase Melting /15 #36
2010 Press Pass Showcase Melting /15 #50
2010 Press Pass Showcase Platinum Holo /1 #27
2010 Press Pass Showcase Platinum Holo /1 #36
2010 Press Pass Showcase Platinum Holo /1 #50
2010 Press Pass Signings Blue /10 #30
2010 Press Pass Signings Gold /50 #30
2010 Press Pass Signings Red /15 #30
2010 Press Pass Signings Silver /45 #30
2010 Press Pass Stealth #18
2010 Press Pass Stealth #62
2010 Press Pass Stealth #86
2010 Press Pass Stealth Battle Armor Holofoil /25 #BABK
2010 Press Pass Stealth Battle Armor Silver /275 #BABK
2010 Press Pass Stealth Black and White #18
2010 Press Pass Stealth Black and White #62
2010 Press Pass Stealth Black and White #86
2010 Press Pass Stealth Previews /5 #18
2010 Press Pass Stealth Previews /1 #62
2010 Press Pass Stealth Purple /25 #18
2010 Press Pass Stealth Purple /25 #62
2010 Press Pass Stealth Signature Series Sheet Metal /20 #SSMEBK
2010 Press Pass Target Top Numbers Tires /50 #TNT-BK
2010 Press Pass Unleashed #U4
2010 Wheels Autographs #26
2010 Wheels Autographs #27
2010 Wheels Autographs Printing Plates Black /1 #26
2010 Wheels Autographs Printing Plates Black /1 #27
2010 Wheels Autographs Printing Plates Cyan /1 #26
2010 Wheels Autographs Printing Plates Cyan /1 #27
2010 Wheels Autographs Printing Plates Magenta /1 #26
2010 Wheels Autographs Printing Plates Magenta /1 #27
2010 Wheels Autographs Printing Plates Yellow /1 #26
2010 Wheels Autographs Printing Plates Yellow /1 #27
2010 Wheels Autographs Special Ink /10 #11
2010 Wheels Autographs Target /10 #18
2010 Wheels Main Event #18
2010 Wheels Main Event #66
2010 Wheels Main Event #67
2010 Wheels Main Event Blue #18
2010 Wheels Main Event Blue #66
2010 Wheels Main Event Blue #67
2010 Wheels Main Event Fight Card #FC16
2010 Wheels Main Event Fight Card Checkered Flag #FC16
2010 Wheels Main Event Fight Card Full Color Retail #FC16
2010 Wheels Main Event Fight Card Gold /25 #FC16
2010 Wheels Main Event Head to Head /150 #HHKBBK
2010 Wheels Main Event Head to Head Blue /75 #HHKBBK
2010 Wheels Main Event Head to Head Holofoil /10 #HHKBBK
2010 Wheels Main Event Head to Head Red /25 #HHKBBK
2010 Wheels Main Event Marks Autographs /91 #30
2010 Wheels Main Event Marks Autographs Black /1 #29
2010 Wheels Main Event Marks Autographs Blue /25 #30
2010 Wheels Main Event Marks Autographs Red /5 #30
2010 Wheels Main Event Matchups Autographs /10 #CEBK
2010 Wheels Main Event Matchups Autographs /10 #KBBK
2010 Wheels Main Event Matchups Autographs /10 #JABK
2010 Wheels Main Event Purple /25 #18
2010 Wheels Main Event Upper Cuts /199 #UCBK
2010 Wheels Main Event Upper Cuts Blue /99 #UCBK
2010 Wheels Main Event Upper Cuts Holofoil /10 #UCBK
2010 Wheels Main Event Upper Cuts Knock Out Patches /25 #UCKOBK
2010 Wheels Main Event Upper Cuts Red /25 #UCBK
2010 Wheels Main Event Wheel to Wheel /25 #WWKBBK
2010 Wheels Main Event Wheel to Wheel Holofoil /10 #WWKBBK
2011 Element #18
2011 Element #83
2011 Element Autographs /75 #29
2011 Element Autographs Blue /5 #29
2011 Element Autographs Gold /15 #28
2011 Element Autographs Printing Plates Black /1 #29
2011 Element Autographs Printing Plates Cyan /1 #29
2011 Element Autographs Printing Plates Magenta /1 #29
2011 Element Autographs Printing Plates Yellow /1 #29
2011 Element Autographs Silver /50 #28
2011 Element Black /35 #18
2011 Element Black /35 #83
2011 Element Flagship Performers 2010 Green Flag Passes Blue-Yellow /50 #FPPBK
2011 Element Green #18
2011 Element Green #83
2011 Element Previews /5 #EB18
2011 Element Purple /25 #18
2011 Element Purple /25 #83
2011 Element Red #18
2011 Element Red #83
2011 Element Trackside Treasures Holofoil /25 #TTBK
2011 Element Trackside Treasures Silver /85 #TTBK
2011 Press Pass #19
2011 Press Pass #74
2011 Press Pass #125
2011 Press Pass #127
2011 Press Pass #146
2011 Press Pass Autographs Blue /5 #29
2011 Press Pass Autographs Bronze /35 #28
2011 Press Pass Autographs Gold /10 #28
2011 Press Pass Autographs Printing Plates Black /1 #29
2011 Press Pass Autographs Printing Plates Cyan /1 #29
2011 Press Pass Autographs Printing Plates Magenta /1 #29
2011 Press Pass Autographs Printing Plates Yellow /1 #29
2011 Press Pass Autographs Silver /15 #29
2011 Press Pass Blue Holofoil /10 #19
2011 Press Pass Blue Holofoil /10 #74
2011 Press Pass Blue Holofoil /10 #125
2011 Press Pass Blue Holofoil /10 #127
2011 Press Pass Blue Holofoil /10 #146
2011 Press Pass Blue Retail #19
2011 Press Pass Blue Retail #74
2011 Press Pass Blue Retail #125
2011 Press Pass Blue Retail #127
2011 Press Pass Blue Retail #146
2011 Press Pass Cup Chase Prizes #CC11
2011 Press Pass Eclipse #17
2011 Press Pass Eclipse #56
2011 Press Pass Eclipse #60
2011 Press Pass Eclipse Blue #17
2011 Press Pass Eclipse Blue #56
2011 Press Pass Eclipse Blue #60
2011 Press Pass Eclipse Gold /55 #17
2011 Press Pass Eclipse Gold /55 #56
2011 Press Pass Eclipse Gold /55 #60
2011 Press Pass Eclipse Previews /5 #EB17
2011 Press Pass Eclipse Purple /25 #17
2011 Press Pass Eclipse Purple /25 #56
2011 Press Pass Eclipse Purple /25 #60
2011 Press Pass FanFare #21
2011 Press Pass FanFare Autographs Blue /5 #38
2011 Press Pass FanFare Autographs Bronze /70 #38
2011 Press Pass FanFare Autographs Gold /50 #38
2011 Press Pass FanFare Autographs Printing Plates Black /1 #38
2011 Press Pass FanFare Autographs Printing Plates Cyan /1 #38
2011 Press Pass FanFare Autographs Printing Plates Magenta /1 #38
2011 Press Pass FanFare Autographs Printing Plates Yellow /1 #38
2011 Press Pass FanFare Autographs Silver /25 #38
2011 Press Pass FanFare Blue Die Cuts #21
2011 Press Pass FanFare Championship Caliber #CC22
2011 Press Pass FanFare Emerald /25 #21
2011 Press Pass FanFare Holofoil Die Cuts #21
2011 Press Pass FanFare Magnificent Materials /199 #MMBK
2011 Press Pass FanFare Magnificent Materials Dual Swatches /50 #MMDBK
2011 Press Pass FanFare Magnificent Materials Dual Swatches Holofoil /10 #MMDBK
2011 Press Pass FanFare Magnificent Materials Holofoil /50 #MMBK
2011 Press Pass FanFare Ruby Die Cuts /15 #21
2011 Press Pass FanFare Sapphire /10 #21
2011 Press Pass FanFare Silver /25 #21
2011 Press Pass Four Wide Firesuit /25 #FWBK
2011 Press Pass Four Wide Glove /1 #FWBK
2011 Press Pass Four Wide Sheet Metal /15 #FWBK
2011 Press Pass Four Wide Tire /10 #FWBK
2011 Press Pass Geared Up Gold /100 #GUBK
2011 Press Pass Geared Up Holofoil /50 #GUBK
2011 Press Pass Gold /50 #19
2011 Press Pass Gold /50 #74
2011 Press Pass Gold /50 #125
2011 Press Pass Gold /50 #127
2011 Press Pass Gold /50 #146
2011 Press Pass Premium #20
2011 Press Pass Premium #79
2011 Press Pass Premium Hot Threads /150 #HTBK
2011 Press Pass Premium Hot Threads Fast Pass /25 #HTKK
2011 Press Pass Premium Hot Threads Multi Color /25 #HTBK
2011 Press Pass Premium Hot Threads Patches /13 #HTPBK
2011 Press Pass Premium Hot Threads Secondary Color /99 #HTBK
2011 Press Pass Premium Pairings Firesuits /25 #PPBKKB
2011 Press Pass Premium Pairings Signatures /5 #PPABKKB
2011 Press Pass Premium Purple /25 #20
2011 Press Pass Premium Purple /25 #79
2011 Press Pass Premium Signatures /173 #PSBK
2011 Press Pass Premium Signatures Red Ink /16 #PSBK
2011 Press Pass Previews /5 #EB19
2011 Press Pass Purple /25 #19
2011 Press Pass Showcase /499 #60
2011 Press Pass Showcase Classic Collections Firesuit /45 #CCMPEN
2011 Press Pass Showcase Classic Collections Firesuit Patches /5 #CCMPEN
2011 Press Pass Showcase Classic Collections Ink /25 #CCMPEN
2011 Press Pass Showcase Classic Collections Ink Gold /5 #CCMPEN
2011 Press Pass Showcase Classic Collections Ink Melting /1 #CCMPEN
2011 Press Pass Showcase Classic Collections Sheet Metal /99 #CCMPEN
2011 Press Pass Showcase Gold /125 #60
2011 Press Pass Showcase Green /25 #60
2011 Press Pass Showcase Masterpieces Memorabilia /99 #MPMBK
2011 Press Pass Showcase Masterpieces Memorabilia Gold /45 #MPMBK
2011 Press Pass Showcase Masterpieces Memorabilia Melting /5 #MPMBK
2011 Press Pass Showcase Melting /1 #60
2011 Press Pass Showcase Prized Pieces Firesuit /99 #PPMBK
2011 Press Pass Showcase Prized Pieces Firesuit Gold /45 #PPMBK
2011 Press Pass Showcase Prized Pieces Firesuit Patches Melting /5 #PPMBK
2011 Press Pass Signature Series /11 #SSTBK
2011 Press Pass Signature Series /11 #SSFBK
2011 Press Pass Signature Series /11 #SSFBK
2011 Press Pass Signature Series /11 #SSMBK
2011 Press Pass Signings Black and White /10 #PPSBK
2011 Press Pass Signings Brushed Metal /47 #PPSBK
2011 Press Pass Signings Holofoil /25 #PPSBK
2011 Press Pass Signings Printing Plates Cyan /1 #PPSBK
2011 Press Pass Signings Printing Plates Magenta /1 #PPSBK
2011 Press Pass Signings Printing Plates Yellow /1 #PPSBK
2011 Press Pass Stealth #45
2011 Press Pass Stealth #90
2011 Press Pass Stealth Black and White /25 #45
2011 Press Pass Stealth Black and White /25 #90
2011 Press Pass Stealth Holofoil /99 #45
2011 Press Pass Stealth Holofoil /99 #90
2011 Press Pass Stealth In Flight Report #IF8
2011 Press Pass Stealth Metal of Honor Medal of Honor /50 #BABK
2011 Press Pass Stealth Metal of Honor Purple Heart /25 #MHBK
2011 Press Pass Stealth Metal of Honor Silver Star /99 #BABK
2011 Press Pass Stealth Purple /25 #45
2011 Press Pass Wal-Mart Winning Tickets #WTW3
2011 Press Pass Wal-Mart Winning Tickets #WTW8
2011 Press Pass Winning Tickets #WT33
2011 Wheels Main Event #20
2011 Wheels Main Event #68
2011 Wheels Main Event All Stars #A18
2011 Wheels Main Event All Stars Brushed Foil /199 #A18
2011 Wheels Main Event All Stars Holofoil /50 #A18
2011 Wheels Main Event Black and White #20
2011 Wheels Main Event Black and White #68
2011 Wheels Main Event Blue /75 #20
2011 Wheels Main Event Blue /75 #68
2011 Wheels Main Event Green /1 #20
2011 Wheels Main Event Green /1 #68
2011 Wheels Main Event Lead Foot Holofoil /25 #LFBK
2011 Wheels Main Event Lead Foot Silver /99 #LFBK
2011 Wheels Main Event Marks Autographs Blue /10 #MEBK
2011 Wheels Main Event Marks Autographs Gold /25 #MEBK
2011 Wheels Main Event Marks Autographs Silver /50 #MEBK
2011 Wheels Main Event Red /20 #20
2011 Wheels Main Event Red /20 #68
2012 Press Pass #20
2012 Press Pass Autographs Blue /10 #PPABK
2012 Press Pass Autographs Printing Plates Black /1 #PPABK
2012 Press Pass Autographs Printing Plates Cyan /1 #PPABK
2012 Press Pass Autographs Printing Plates Magenta /1 #PPABK
2012 Press Pass Autographs Printing Plates Yellow /1 #PPABK
2012 Press Pass Autographs Red /25 #PPABK
2012 Press Pass Autographs Silver /175 #PPABK
2012 Press Pass Blue #20
2012 Press Pass Blue Holofoil /35 #20
2012 Press Pass Burning Rubber Gold /99 #BRBK
2012 Press Pass Burning Rubber Gold /99 #BRBK2
2012 Press Pass Burning Rubber Gold /99 #BRBK3
2012 Press Pass Burning Rubber Holofoil /25 #BRBK
2012 Press Pass Burning Rubber Holofoil /25 #BRBK2
2012 Press Pass Burning Rubber Holofoil /25 #BRBK3
2012 Press Pass Burning Rubber Prime Cuts /25 #BRBK
2012 Press Pass Burning Rubber Prime Cuts /25 #BRBK2
2012 Press Pass Burning Rubber Prime Cuts /25 #BRBK3
2012 Press Pass Burning Rubber Purple /15 #BRBK
2012 Press Pass Burning Rubber Purple /15 #BRBK2
2012 Press Pass Burning Rubber Purple /15 #BRBK3
2012 Press Pass Cup Chase #CCR12
2012 Press Pass Cup Chase Prizes #CCP4
2012 Press Pass Cup Chase Prizes #CCP
2012 Press Pass Fanfare #24
2012 Press Pass Fanfare Blue Foil Die Cuts #24
2012 Press Pass Fanfare Diamond /5 #24
2012 Press Pass Fanfare Holofoil Die Cuts #24
2012 Press Pass Fanfare Magnificent Materials /250 #MMBK
2012 Press Pass Fanfare Magnificent Materials Dual Swatches /50 #MMBK
2012 Press Pass Fanfare Magnificent Materials Dual Swatches Melting /10 #MMBK
2012 Press Pass Fanfare Magnificent Materials Gold /125 #MMBK
2012 Press Pass Fanfare Power Rankings #PR7
2012 Press Pass Fanfare Sapphire /20 #24
2012 Press Pass Fanfare Silver /25 #24
2012 Press Pass Gold #20
2012 Press Pass Ignite #21
2012 Press Pass Ignite #41
2012 Press Pass Ignite #69
2012 Press Pass Ignite Limelight #L6
2012 Press Pass Ignite Materials Autographs Gun Metal /45 #IMBK
2012 Press Pass Ignite Materials Autographs Red /5 #IMBK
2012 Press Pass Ignite Materials Autographs Silver /150 #IMBK
2012 Press Pass Ignite Materials Gun Metal /99 #IMBK
2012 Press Pass Ignite Materials Red /10 #IMBK
2012 Press Pass Ignite Materials Silver #IMBK
2012 Press Pass Ignite Proofs Black and White /50 #21
2012 Press Pass Ignite Proofs Black and White /50 #41
2012 Press Pass Ignite Proofs Black and White /50 #69
2012 Press Pass Ignite Proofs Cyan #21
2012 Press Pass Ignite Proofs Cyan #41
2012 Press Pass Ignite Proofs Cyan #69
2012 Press Pass Ignite Proofs Magenta #21
2012 Press Pass Ignite Proofs Magenta #41
2012 Press Pass Ignite Proofs Magenta #69
2012 Press Pass Ignite Proofs Yellow /10 #21
2012 Press Pass Ignite Proofs Yellow /10 #41
2012 Press Pass Ignite Proofs Yellow /10 #69
2012 Press Pass Power Picks Blue /50 #11
2012 Press Pass Power Picks Blue /50 #39
2012 Press Pass Power Picks Blue /50 #75
2012 Press Pass Power Picks Gold /50 #11
2012 Press Pass Power Picks Gold /50 #39
2012 Press Pass Power Picks Gold /50 #75
2012 Press Pass Power Picks Holofoil /10 #11
2012 Press Pass Power Picks Holofoil /10 #39
2012 Press Pass Power Picks Holofoil /10 #75
2012 Press Pass Purple /35 #20
2012 Press Pass Redline #21
2012 Press Pass Redline Black /99 #21
2012 Press Pass Redline Cyan /50 #21
2012 Press Pass Redline Magenta /15 #21
2012 Press Pass Redline Performance Driven #PD7
2012 Press Pass Redline RPM #RPM9
2012 Press Pass Redline Signatures Blue /5 #RSBK
2012 Press Pass Redline Signatures Gold /25 #RSBK
2012 Press Pass Redline Signatures Holofoil /10 #RSBK
2012 Press Pass Redline Signatures Melting /1 #RSBK
2012 Press Pass Redline Signatures Red /50 #RSBK
2012 Press Pass Redline Yellow /1 #21
2012 Press Pass Showcase /499 #58
2012 Press Pass Showcase Classic Collections Memorabilia /99 #CCMPEN
2012 Press Pass Showcase Classic Collections Memorabilia Gold /50 #CCMPEN
2012 Press Pass Showcase Classic Collections Memorabilia Melting /5 #CCMPEN
2012 Press Pass Showcase Gold /125 #58
2012 Press Pass Showcase Green /5 #58
2012 Press Pass Showcase Melting /1 #58
2012 Press Pass Showcase Purple /1 #58
2012 Press Pass Showcase Red /25 #58
2012 Press Pass Showcase Showcase Patches /5 #SSPBK
2012 Press Pass Showcase Showcase Patches Melting /1 #SSPBK
2012 Press Pass Signature Series Race Used /12 #PPABK
2012 Press Pass Snapshots #SS20
2012 Total Memorabilia #17
2012 Total Memorabilia Black and White /99 #17
2012 Total Memorabilia Dual Swatch Gold /75 #TMBK
2012 Total Memorabilia Dual Swatch Holofoil /25 #TMBK
2012 Total Memorabilia Dual Swatch Melting /5 #TMBK
2012 Total Memorabilia Dual Swatch Silver /99 #TMBK
2012 Total Memorabilia Gold /275 #17
2012 Total Memorabilia Red Retail /250 #17
2012 Total Memorabilia Single Swatch Gold /99 #TMBK
2012 Total Memorabilia Single Swatch Holofoil /50 #TMBK
2012 Total Memorabilia Single Swatch Melting /10 #TMBK
2012 Total Memorabilia Single Swatch Silver /199 #TMBK
2013 Press Pass #25
2013 Press Pass #0
2013 Press Pass Burning Rubber Blue /50 #BRBK
2013 Press Pass Burning Rubber Blue /50 #BRBK2
2013 Press Pass Burning Rubber Blue /50 #BRBK3
2013 Press Pass Burning Rubber Gold /199 #BRBK
2013 Press Pass Burning Rubber Gold /199 #BRBK2
2013 Press Pass Burning Rubber Gold /199 #BRBK3
2013 Press Pass Burning Rubber Holofoil /75 #BRBK
2013 Press Pass Burning Rubber Holofoil /75 #BRBK2
2013 Press Pass Burning Rubber Holofoil /75 #BRBK3
2013 Press Pass Burning Rubber Letterman /8 #BRLBK
2013 Press Pass Burning Rubber Melting /10 #BRBK
2013 Press Pass Burning Rubber Melting /10 #BRBK2
2013 Press Pass Burning Rubber Melting /10 #BRBK3
2013 Press Pass Color Proofs Black #25
2013 Press Pass Color Proofs Cyan /35 #25
2013 Press Pass Color Proofs Magenta #25
2013 Press Pass Color Proofs Yellow /5 #25
2013 Press Pass Cup Chase #CC13
2013 Press Pass Fanfare #30
2013 Press Pass Fanfare #31
2013 Press Pass Fanfare Diamond Die Cuts /5 #30
2013 Press Pass Fanfare Diamond Die Cuts /5 #31
2013 Press Pass Fanfare Fan Following #FF10
2013 Press Pass Fanfare Green /3 #30
2013 Press Pass Fanfare Green /3 #31
2013 Press Pass Fanfare Holofoil Die Cuts #30
2013 Press Pass Fanfare Holofoil Die Cuts #31
2013 Press Pass Fanfare Magnificent Materials Dual Swatches /50 #BK
2013 Press Pass Fanfare Magnificent Materials Dual Swatches Melting /10 #BK
2013 Press Pass Fanfare Magnificent Materials Gold /50 #BK
2013 Press Pass Fanfare Magnificent Materials Jumbo Swatches /25 #BK
2013 Press Pass Fanfare Magnificent Materials Silver /199 #BK
2013 Press Pass Fanfare Red Foil Die Cuts #30
2013 Press Pass Fanfare Red Foil Die Cuts #31
2013 Press Pass Fanfare Sapphire /20 #30
2013 Press Pass Fanfare Sapphire /20 #31
2013 Press Pass Fanfare Silver /25 #30
2013 Press Pass Fanfare Silver /25 #31
2013 Press Pass Ignite #18
2013 Press Pass Ignite Double Burner Blue Holofoil /10 #DBBK
2013 Press Pass Ignite Double Burner Red /1 #DBBK
2013 Press Pass Ignite Double Burner Silver /25 #DBBK
2013 Press Pass Ignite Hot Threads Blue Holofoil /99 #HTBK
2013 Press Pass Ignite Hot Threads Patch Red /10 #HTBK
2013 Press Pass Ignite Hot Threads Patch Red Oversized /20 #HTPBK
2013 Press Pass Ignite Hot Threads Silver #HTBK
2013 Press Pass Ignite Profile #15
2013 Press Pass Ignite Proofs Black and White /50 #18
2013 Press Pass Ignite Proofs Cyan #18
2013 Press Pass Ignite Proofs Magenta #18
2013 Press Pass Ignite Proofs Yellow /5 #18
2013 Press Pass Legends Prominent Pieces Gold /10 #PPBK
2013 Press Pass Legends Prominent Pieces Holofoil /5 #PPBK
2013 Press Pass Legends Prominent Pieces Oversized Firesuit /5 #PPBK
2013 Press Pass Legends Prominent Pieces Silver /25 #PPBK
2013 Press Pass Power Picks Blue /99 #40
2013 Press Pass Power Picks Gold /50 #40
2013 Press Pass Power Picks Holofoil /10 #40
2013 Press Pass Racing Champions #RC4
2013 Press Pass Racing Champions #RC10
2013 Press Pass Racing Champions #RC17
2013 Press Pass Racing Champions #RC33
2013 Press Pass Redline #29
2013 Press Pass Redline Black /99 #29
2013 Press Pass Redline Cyan /50 #29
2013 Press Pass Redline Magenta /15 #29
2013 Press Pass Redline Muscle Car Sheet Metal Blue /5 #MCMBK
2013 Press Pass Redline Muscle Car Sheet Metal Gold /10 #MCMBK
2013 Press Pass Redline Muscle Car Sheet Metal Melting /1 #MCMBK
2013 Press Pass Redline Muscle Car Sheet Metal Red /50 #MCMBK
2013 Press Pass Redline Muscle Car Sheet Metal Silver /25 #MCMBK
2013 Press Pass Redline Pieces of the Action Blue /10 #PABK
2013 Press Pass Redline Pieces of the Action Gold /25 #PABK
2013 Press Pass Redline Pieces of the Action Melting /1 #PABK
2013 Press Pass Redline Pieces of the Action Red /75 #PABK

2013 Press Pass Redline Pieces of the Action Silver /50 #PABK
2013 Press Pass Redline Redline Racers #15
2013 Press Pass Redline Relics Blue /5 #RRBK
2013 Press Pass Redline Relics Gold /10 #RRBK
2013 Press Pass Redline Relics Melting /1 #RRBK
2013 Press Pass Redline Relics Red /50 #RRBK
2013 Press Pass Redline Relics Silver /25 #RRBK
2013 Press Pass Redline RPM #1
2013 Press Pass Redline V8 Relics Blue /5 #V8BK
2013 Press Pass Redline V8 Relics Gold /10 #V8BK
2013 Press Pass Redline V8 Relics Melting /1 #V8BK
2013 Press Pass Redline V8 Relics Red /25 #V8BK
2013 Press Pass Redline Yellow /1 #29
2013 Press Pass Showcase /349 #16
2013 Press Pass Showcase Black /1 #16
2013 Press Pass Showcase Blue /25 #16
2013 Press Pass Showcase Gold /99 #16
2013 Press Pass Showcase Green /20 #16
2013 Press Pass Showcase Prized Pieces /99 #PPMBK
2013 Press Pass Showcase Prized Pieces Blue /20 #PPMBK
2013 Press Pass Showcase Prized Pieces Gold /25 #PPMBK
2013 Press Pass Showcase Prized Pieces Melting /5 #PPMBK
2013 Press Pass Showcase Purple /13 #16
2013 Press Pass Showcase Red /10 #16
2013 Press Pass Showcase Showroom /299 #6
2013 Press Pass Showcase Showroom Blue /40 #6
2013 Press Pass Showcase Showroom Gold /50 #6
2013 Press Pass Showcase Showroom Green /20 #6
2013 Press Pass Showcase Showroom Melting /1 #6
2013 Press Pass Showcase Showroom Purple /13 #6
2013 Press Pass Showcase Showroom Red /10 #6
2013 Sports Illustrated for Kids #244
2013 Total Memorabilia #24
2013 Total Memorabilia #50
2013 Total Memorabilia Black and White /99 #24
2013 Total Memorabilia Black and White /99 #50
2013 Total Memorabilia Burning Rubber Chase Edition Gold /75 #BRCBK
2013 Total Memorabilia Burning Rubber Chase Edition Gold /75 #BRCBK2
2013 Total Memorabilia Burning Rubber Chase Edition Holofoil /50 #BRCBK
2013 Total Memorabilia Burning Rubber Chase Edition Holofoil /50 #BRCBK2
2013 Total Memorabilia Burning Rubber Chase Edition Melting /5 #BRCBK
2013 Total Memorabilia Burning Rubber Chase Edition Melting /5 #BRCBK2
2013 Total Memorabilia Burning Rubber Chase Edition Silver /175 #BRCBK
2013 Total Memorabilia Burning Rubber Chase Edition Silver /175 #BRCBK2
2013 Total Memorabilia Gold /275 #24
2013 Total Memorabilia Gold /275 #50
2013 Total Memorabilia Red #24
2013 Total Memorabilia Red #50
2014 Press Pass #20
2014 Press Pass American Thunder #21
2014 Press Pass American Thunder #56
2014 Press Pass American Thunder Battle Armor Blue /25 #BABK
2014 Press Pass American Thunder Battle Armor Red /1 #BABK
2014 Press Pass American Thunder Battle Armor Silver /99 #BABK
2014 Press Pass American Thunder Black and White /50 #21
2014 Press Pass American Thunder Black and White /50 #56
2014 Press Pass American Thunder Brothers In Arms Relics Blue /25 #BATP
2014 Press Pass American Thunder Brothers In Arms Relics Red /5 #BATP
2014 Press Pass American Thunder Brothers In Arms Relics Silver /50 #BATP
2014 Press Pass American Thunder Class A Uniforms Blue /99 #CAUBK
2014 Press Pass American Thunder Class A Uniforms Flag /1 #CAUBK
2014 Press Pass American Thunder Class A Uniforms Red /10 #CAUBK
2014 Press Pass American Thunder Class A Uniforms Silver #CAUBK
2014 Press Pass American Thunder Cyan #21
2014 Press Pass American Thunder Cyan #56
2014 Press Pass American Thunder Magenta #21
2014 Press Pass American Thunder Magenta #56
2014 Press Pass American Thunder Top Speed #TS6
2014 Press Pass American Thunder Yellow /5 #21
2014 Press Pass American Thunder Yellow /5 #56
2014 Press Pass Burning Rubber Chase Edition Blue /25 #BRCBK
2014 Press Pass Burning Rubber Chase Edition Gold /50 #BRCBK
2014 Press Pass Burning Rubber Chase Edition Melting /10 #BRCBK
2014 Press Pass Burning Rubber Chase Edition Silver /99 #BRCBK
2014 Press Pass Color Proofs Black /70 #20
2014 Press Pass Color Proofs Cyan /35 #20
2014 Press Pass Color Proofs Magenta #20
2014 Press Pass Color Proofs Yellow /5 #20
2014 Press Pass Cup Chase #11
2014 Press Pass Five Star /15 #12
2014 Press Pass Five Star Blue /5 #12
2014 Press Pass Five Star Holofoil /10 #12
2014 Press Pass Five Star Melting /1 #12
2014 Press Pass Five Star Paramount Pieces Blue /5 #PPBK
2014 Press Pass Five Star Paramount Pieces Gold /25 #PPBK
2014 Press Pass Five Star Paramount Pieces Holofoil /10 #PPBK
2014 Press Pass Five Star Paramount Pieces Melting /1 #PPBK
2014 Press Pass Five Star Paramount Pieces Melting Patch /1 #PPBK
2014 Press Pass Gold #20
2014 Press Pass Redline #32
2014 Press Pass Redline Black /75 #32
2014 Press Pass Redline Blue Foil #32
2014 Press Pass Redline Cyan /50 #32
2014 Press Pass Redline Green National Convention /5 #32
2014 Press Pass Redline Magenta /10 #32
2014 Press Pass Redline Muscle Car Sheet Metal Blue /10 #MCMBK
2014 Press Pass Redline Muscle Car Sheet Metal Gold /25 #MCMBK
2014 Press Pass Redline Muscle Car Sheet Metal Melting /1 #MCMBK
2014 Press Pass Redline Muscle Car Sheet Metal Red /50 #MCMBK
2014 Press Pass Redline Relics Blue /25 #RRBK
2014 Press Pass Redline Relics Gold /50 #RRBK
2014 Press Pass Redline Relics Melting /1 #RRBK
2014 Press Pass Redline Relics Red /75 #RRBK
2014 Press Pass Redline RPM #RPM7
2014 Press Pass Redline Yellow /1 #32
2014 Press Pass Velocity #7
2014 Total Memorabilia #15
2014 Total Memorabilia Acceleration #AC7
2014 Total Memorabilia Black and White /99 #15
2014 Total Memorabilia Dual Swatch Gold /150 #TMBK
2014 Total Memorabilia Gold /175 #15
2014 Total Memorabilia Quad Swatch Melting /25 #TMBK
2014 Total Memorabilia Red #15
2014 Total Memorabilia Single Swatch Silver /275 #TMBK
2014 Total Memorabilia Triple Swatch Blue /99 #TMBK
2015 Press Pass #21
2015 Press Pass #71
2015 Press Pass #80
2015 Press Pass #100
2015 Press Pass Burning Rubber Blue /50 #BRBK1
2015 Press Pass Burning Rubber Blue /50 #BRBK2
2015 Press Pass Burning Rubber Blue /50 #BRBK3
2015 Press Pass Burning Rubber Blue /50 #BRBK4
2015 Press Pass Burning Rubber Gold #BRBK1
2015 Press Pass Burning Rubber Gold #BRBK2
2015 Press Pass Burning Rubber Gold #BRBK3
2015 Press Pass Burning Rubber Gold #BRBK4
2015 Press Pass Burning Rubber Green /10 #BRBK1
2015 Press Pass Burning Rubber Green /10 #BRBK2
2015 Press Pass Burning Rubber Green /10 #BRBK3
2015 Press Pass Burning Rubber Green /10 #BRBK4
2015 Press Pass Burning Rubber Letterman /8 #BRLEBK
2015 Press Pass Burning Rubber Melting /1 #BRBK1
2015 Press Pass Burning Rubber Melting /1 #BRBK2
2015 Press Pass Burning Rubber Melting /1 #BRBK3
2015 Press Pass Burning Rubber Melting /1 #BRBK4
2015 Press Pass Championship Caliber Dual /25 #CCMBK
2015 Press Pass Championship Caliber Single /50 #CCMBK
2015 Press Pass Cup Chase #21
2015 Press Pass Cup Chase #71
2015 Press Pass Cup Chase #80
2015 Press Pass Cup Chase #100
2015 Press Pass Cup Chase Blue /25 #21
2015 Press Pass Cup Chase Blue /25 #71
2015 Press Pass Cup Chase Blue /25 #80
2015 Press Pass Cup Chase Blue /25 #100
2015 Press Pass Cup Chase Gold /75 #21
2015 Press Pass Cup Chase Gold /75 #71
2015 Press Pass Cup Chase Gold /75 #80
2015 Press Pass Cup Chase Gold /75 #100
2015 Press Pass Cup Chase Green /10 #21
2015 Press Pass Cup Chase Green /10 #71
2015 Press Pass Cup Chase Green /10 #80
2015 Press Pass Cup Chase Green /10 #100
2015 Press Pass Cup Chase Melting /1 #21
2015 Press Pass Cup Chase Melting /1 #71
2015 Press Pass Cup Chase Melting /1 #80
2015 Press Pass Cup Chase Melting /1 #100
2015 Press Pass Purple #21
2015 Press Pass Purple #71
2015 Press Pass Purple #80
2015 Press Pass Purple #100
2015 Press Pass Red #21
2015 Press Pass Red #71
2015 Press Pass Red #80
2015 Press Pass Red #100
2016 Certified #6
2016 Certified #59
2016 Certified Complete Materials /299 #4
2016 Certified Complete Materials Mirror Black /1 #4
2016 Certified Complete Materials Mirror Blue /50 #4
2016 Certified Complete Materials Mirror Gold /25 #4
2016 Certified Complete Materials Mirror Green /5 #4
2016 Certified Complete Materials Mirror Orange /99 #4
2016 Certified Complete Materials Mirror Purple /10 #4
2016 Certified Complete Materials Mirror Red /75 #4
2016 Certified Complete Materials Mirror Silver /99 #4
2016 Certified Famed Rides /199 #5
2016 Certified Famed Rides Mirror Black /1 #5
2016 Certified Famed Rides Mirror Blue /50 #5
2016 Certified Famed Rides Mirror Gold /25 #5
2016 Certified Famed Rides Mirror Green /5 #5
2016 Certified Famed Rides Mirror Orange /99 #5
2016 Certified Famed Rides Mirror Purple /10 #5
2016 Certified Famed Rides Mirror Red /75 #5
2016 Certified Famed Rides Mirror Silver /99 #5
2016 Certified Gold Team /199 #15
2016 Certified Gold Team Mirror Black /1 #15
2016 Certified Gold Team Mirror Blue /50 #15
2016 Certified Gold Team Mirror Gold /25 #15
2016 Certified Gold Team Mirror Green /5 #15
2016 Certified Gold Team Mirror Orange /99 #15
2016 Certified Gold Team Mirror Purple /10 #15
2016 Certified Gold Team Mirror Red /75 #15
2016 Certified Gold Team Mirror Silver /99 #15
2016 Certified Mirror Black /1 #6
2016 Certified Mirror Black /1 #59
2016 Certified Mirror Blue /50 #6
2016 Certified Mirror Blue /50 #59
2016 Certified Mirror Gold /25 #6
2016 Certified Mirror Gold /25 #59
2016 Certified Mirror Green /5 #6
2016 Certified Mirror Green /5 #59
2016 Certified Mirror Orange /99 #6
2016 Certified Mirror Orange /99 #59
2016 Certified Mirror Purple /10 #6
2016 Certified Mirror Purple /10 #59
2016 Certified Mirror Red /75 #6
2016 Certified Mirror Red /75 #59
2016 Certified Mirror Silver /99 #6
2016 Certified Mirror Silver /99 #59
2016 Certified Signatures /199 #1
2016 Certified Signatures Mirror Black /1 #1
2016 Certified Signatures Mirror Blue /50 #1
2016 Certified Signatures Mirror Gold /25 #1
2016 Certified Signatures Mirror Green /5 #1
2016 Certified Signatures Mirror Orange /50 #1
2016 Certified Signatures Mirror Purple /10 #1
2016 Certified Signatures Mirror Red /75 #1
2016 Certified Signatures Mirror Silver /35 #1
2016 Certified Sprint Cup Swatches /299 #24
2016 Certified Sprint Cup Swatches Mirror Black /1 #24
2016 Certified Sprint Cup Swatches Mirror Blue /50 #24
2016 Certified Sprint Cup Swatches Mirror Gold /25 #24
2016 Certified Sprint Cup Swatches Mirror Green /5 #24
2016 Certified Sprint Cup Swatches Mirror Orange /99 #24
2016 Certified Sprint Cup Swatches Mirror Purple /10 #24
2016 Certified Sprint Cup Swatches Mirror Red /75 #24
2016 Certified Sprint Cup Swatches Mirror Silver /99 #24
2016 Panini Black Friday #30
2016 Panini Black Friday Autographs /25 #30
2016 Panini Black Friday Cracked Ice /25 #30
2016 Panini Black Friday Holo Plaid /1 #30
2016 Panini Black Friday Rapture /10 #30
2016 Panini Black Friday Thick Stock /50 #30
2016 Panini Black Friday Wedges /50 #30
2016 Panini National Treasures /25 #24
2016 Panini National Treasures Black /5 #24
2016 Panini National Treasures Blue /1 #24
2016 Panini National Treasures Championship Signature Threads Blue /1 #8
2016 Panini National Treasures Championship Signature Threads Printing Plates Black /1 #8
2016 Panini National Treasures Championship Signature Threads Printing Plates Cyan /1 #8
2016 Panini National Treasures Championship Signature Threads Printing Plates Magenta /1 #8
2016 Panini National Treasures Championship Signature Threads Printing Plates Yellow /1 #8
2016 Panini National Treasures Championship Signatures /49 #1
2016 Panini National Treasures Championship Signatures Black /5 #1
2016 Panini National Treasures Championship Signatures Blue /1 #1
2016 Panini National Treasures Championship Signatures Gold /15 #1
2016 Panini National Treasures Championship Signatures Printing Plates Black /1 #1
2016 Panini National Treasures Championship Signatures Printing Plates Cyan /1 #1
2016 Panini National Treasures Championship Signatures Printing Plates Magenta /1 #1
2016 Panini National Treasures Championship Signatures Printing Plates Yellow /1 #1
2016 Panini National Treasures Championship Signatures Silver /25 #1
2016 Panini National Treasures Combo Materials /25 #5
2016 Panini National Treasures Combo Materials Black /5 #5
2016 Panini National Treasures Combo Materials Blue /1 #5
2016 Panini National Treasures Combo Materials Gold /10 #5
2016 Panini National Treasures Combo Materials Printing Plates Black /1 #5
2016 Panini National Treasures Combo Materials Printing Plates Cyan /1 #5
2016 Panini National Treasures Combo Materials Printing Plates Magenta /1 #5
2016 Panini National Treasures Combo Materials Printing Plates Yellow /1 #5
2016 Panini National Treasures Combo Materials Silver /15 #5
2016 Panini National Treasures Dual Driver Materials /25 #8
2016 Panini National Treasures Dual Driver Materials Black /5 #8
2016 Panini National Treasures Dual Driver Materials Blue /1 #8
2016 Panini National Treasures Dual Driver Materials Gold /10 #8
2016 Panini National Treasures Dual Driver Materials Printing Plates Black /1 #8
2016 Panini National Treasures Dual Driver Materials Printing Plates Cyan /1 #8
2016 Panini National Treasures Dual Driver Materials Printing Plates Magenta /1 #8
2016 Panini National Treasures Dual Driver Materials Printing Plates Yellow /1 #8
2016 Panini National Treasures Dual Driver Materials Silver /15 #8
2016 Panini National Treasures Dual Signatures /99 #1
2016 Panini National Treasures Dual Signatures /50 #24
2016 Panini National Treasures Dual Signatures Black /25 #1
2016 Panini National Treasures Dual Signatures Black /10 #24
2016 Panini National Treasures Dual Signatures Blue /1 #1
2016 Panini National Treasures Dual Signatures Blue /1 #24
2016 Panini National Treasures Dual Signatures Gold /49 #ss,
2016 Panini National Treasures Dual Signatures Gold /15 #24
2016 Panini National Treasures Gold /15 #24
2016 Panini National Treasures Printing Plates Black /1 #24
2016 Panini National Treasures Printing Plates Cyan /1 #24
2016 Panini National Treasures Printing Plates Magenta /1 #24
2016 Panini National Treasures Printing Plates Yellow /1 #24
2016 Panini National Treasures Signatures /99 #1
2016 Panini National Treasures Signatures Black /5 #1
2016 Panini National Treasures Signatures Blue /1 #1
2016 Panini National Treasures Signatures Gold /15 #1
2016 Panini National Treasures Signatures Printing Plates Black /1 #1
2016 Panini National Treasures Signatures Printing Plates Cyan /1 #1
2016 Panini National Treasures Signatures Printing Plates Magenta /1 #1
2016 Panini National Treasures Signatures Printing Plates Yellow /1 #1
2016 Panini National Treasures Signatures Silver /25 #1
2016 Panini National Treasures Silver /20 #24
2016 Panini National Treasures Six Signatures Black /10 #7
2016 Panini National Treasures Six Signatures Blue /1 #7
2016 Panini National Treasures Trio Driver Materials /25 #5
2016 Panini National Treasures Trio Driver Materials Black /5 #5
2016 Panini National Treasures Trio Driver Materials Blue /1 #5
2016 Panini National Treasures Trio Driver Materials Gold /10 #5
2016 Panini National Treasures Trio Driver Materials Printing Plates Black /1 #5
2016 Panini National Treasures Trio Driver Materials Printing Plates Cyan /1 #5
2016 Panini National Treasures Trio Driver Materials Printing Plates Magenta /1 #5
2016 Panini National Treasures Trio Driver Materials Printing Plates Yellow /1 #5
2016 Panini National Treasures Trio Driver Materials Silver /15 #5
2016 Panini National Treasures Winning Signatures /99 #1
2016 Panini National Treasures Winning Signatures Black /5 #1
2016 Panini National Treasures Winning Signatures Blue /1 #1
2016 Panini National Treasures Winning Signatures Gold /15 #1
2016 Panini National Treasures Winning Signatures Printing Plates Black /1 #1
2016 Panini National Treasures Winning Signatures Printing Plates Cyan /1 #1
2016 Panini National Treasures Winning Signatures Printing Plates Magenta /1 #1
2016 Panini National Treasures Winning Signatures Printing Plates Yellow /1 #1
2016 Panini National Treasures Winning Signatures Silver /25 #1
2016 Panini Prizm #2A
2016 Panini Prizm #48
2016 Panini Prizm #70
2016 Panini Prizm #82
2016 Panini Prizm Blowing Smoke #11
2016 Panini Prizm Blowing Smoke Prizms #11
2016 Panini Prizm Blowing Smoke Prizms Checkered Flag /1 #11
2016 Panini Prizm Blowing Smoke Prizms Gold /10 #11
2016 Panini Prizm Prizms #2A
2016 Panini Prizm Prizms #48
2016 Panini Prizm Prizms #70
2016 Panini Prizm Prizms #82
2016 Panini Prizm Prizms Black /3 #2
2016 Panini Prizm Prizms Black /3 #48
2016 Panini Prizm Prizms Black /3 #70
2016 Panini Prizm Prizms Black /3 #82
2016 Panini Prizm Prizms Blue Flag /99 #2
2016 Panini Prizm Prizms Blue Flag /99 #48
2016 Panini Prizm Prizms Blue Flag /99 #70
2016 Panini Prizm Prizms Blue Flag /99 #82
2016 Panini Prizm Prizms Camo /2 #2
2016 Panini Prizm Prizms Camo /2 #48
2016 Panini Prizm Prizms Camo /2 #70
2016 Panini Prizm Prizms Camo /2 #82
2016 Panini Prizm Prizms Checkered Flag /1 #2A
2016 Panini Prizm Prizms Checkered Flag /1 #48
2016 Panini Prizm Prizms Checkered Flag /1 #70
2016 Panini Prizm Prizms Checkered Flag /1 #82
2016 Panini Prizm Prizms Gold /10 #2A
2016 Panini Prizm Prizms Gold /10 #48
2016 Panini Prizm Prizms Gold /10 #70
2016 Panini Prizm Prizms Gold /10 #82
2016 Panini Prizm Prizms Green Flag /149 #2
2016 Panini Prizm Prizms Green Flag /149 #48
2016 Panini Prizm Prizms Green Flag /149 #70
2016 Panini Prizm Prizms Green Flag /149 #82
2016 Panini Prizm Prizms Rainbow /24 #2
2016 Panini Prizm Prizms Rainbow /24 #48
2016 Panini Prizm Prizms Rainbow /24 #70
2016 Panini Prizm Prizms Rainbow /24 #82
2016 Panini Prizm Prizms Red Flag /75 #2
2016 Panini Prizm Prizms Red Flag /75 #48
2016 Panini Prizm Prizms Red Flag /75 #70
2016 Panini Prizm Prizms Red Flag /75 #82
2016 Panini Prizm Prizms Red White and Blue #2
2016 Panini Prizm Prizms Red White and Blue #48
2016 Panini Prizm Prizms Red White and Blue #70
2016 Panini Prizm Prizms Red White and Blue #82
2016 Panini Prizm Prizms White Flag /5 #2
2016 Panini Prizm Prizms White Flag /5 #48
2016 Panini Prizm Prizms White Flag /5 #70
2016 Panini Prizm Prizms White Flag /5 #82
2016 Panini Prizm Race Used Tire #8
2016 Panini Prizm Race Used Tire Prizms Blue Flag /49 #8
2016 Panini Prizm Race Used Tire Prizms Checkered Flag /1 #8
2016 Panini Prizm Race Used Tire Prizms Green Flag /99 #8
2016 Panini Prizm Race Used Tire Prizms Red Flag /25 #8
2016 Panini Prizm Race Used Tire Team #7
2016 Panini Prizm Race Used Tire Team Prizms Blue Flag /75 #7
2016 Panini Prizm Race Used Tire Team Prizms Checkered Flag /1 #7
2016 Panini Prizm Race Used Tire Team Prizms Green Flag /149 #7
2016 Panini Prizm Race Used Tire Team Prizms Red Flag /10 #7
2016 Panini Prizm Winner's Circle #5
2016 Panini Prizm Winner's Circle Prizms #5
2016 Panini Prizm Winner's Circle Prizms Checkered Flag /1 #5
2016 Panini Prizm Winner's Circle Prizms Gold /10 #5
2016 Panini Torque #11
2016 Panini Torque #61
2016 Panini Torque #87
2016 Panini Torque Artist Proof /50 #11
2016 Panini Torque Artist Proof /50 #61
2016 Panini Torque Artist Proof /50 #87
2016 Panini Torque Blackout /1 #11
2016 Panini Torque Blackout /1 #61
2016 Panini Torque Blackout /1 #87
2016 Panini Torque Blue /125 #11
2016 Panini Torque Blue /125 #61
2016 Panini Torque Blue /125 #87
2016 Panini Torque Championship Vision #8
2016 Panini Torque Championship Vision Blue /99 #8
2016 Panini Torque Championship Vision Gold /149 #8
2016 Panini Torque Championship Vision Green /25 #8
2016 Panini Torque Championship Vision Purple /10 #8
2016 Panini Torque Championship Vision Red /49 #8
2016 Panini Torque Clear Vision #11
2016 Panini Torque Clear Vision Blue /99 #11
2016 Panini Torque Clear Vision Gold /149 #11
2016 Panini Torque Clear Vision Green /25 #11
2016 Panini Torque Clear Vision Purple /10 #11
2016 Panini Torque Clear Vision Red /49 #11
2016 Panini Torque Gas N Go #1
2016 Panini Torque Gas N Go Gold /199 #1
2016 Panini Torque Gas N Go Holo Silver /99 #1
2016 Panini Torque Gold #11
2016 Panini Torque Gold #61
2016 Panini Torque Gold #87
2016 Panini Torque Helmets #6
2016 Panini Torque Helmets Blue /99 #6
2016 Panini Torque Helmets Checkerboard /10 #6
2016 Panini Torque Helmets Green /25 #6
2016 Panini Torque Helmets Red /49 #6
2016 Panini Torque Holo Gold /5 #11
2016 Panini Torque Holo Gold /5 #61
2016 Panini Torque Holo Gold /5 #87
2016 Panini Torque Holo Silver /10 #11
2016 Panini Torque Holo Silver /10 #61
2016 Panini Torque Holo Silver /10 #87
2016 Panini Torque Horsepower Heroes #7
2016 Panini Torque Horsepower Heroes Gold /199 #7
2016 Panini Torque Horsepower Heroes Holo Silver /99 #7
2016 Panini Torque Jumbo Firesuit Autographs /35 #2
2016 Panini Torque Jumbo Firesuit Autographs Blue /25 #2
2016 Panini Torque Jumbo Firesuit Autographs Green /2 #2
2016 Panini Torque Jumbo Firesuit Autographs Purple /1 #2
2016 Panini Torque Jumbo Firesuit Autographs Red /10 #2
2016 Panini Torque Jumbo Tire Autographs /35 #8
2016 Panini Torque Jumbo Tire Autographs Blue /25 #8
2016 Panini Torque Jumbo Tire Autographs Green /2 #8
2016 Panini Torque Jumbo Tire Autographs Purple /1 #8
2016 Panini Torque Jumbo Tire Autographs Red /10 #8
2016 Panini Torque Metal Materials /249 #4
2016 Panini Torque Metal Materials Blue /99 #4
2016 Panini Torque Metal Materials Green /25 #4
2016 Panini Torque Metal Materials Purple /10 #4
2016 Panini Torque Metal Materials Red /49 #4
2016 Panini Torque Painted to Perfection #12
2016 Panini Torque Painted to Perfection Blue /99 #12
2016 Panini Torque Painted to Perfection Checkerboard /10 #12
2016 Panini Torque Painted to Perfection Green /25 #12
2016 Panini Torque Painted to Perfection Red /49 #12
2016 Panini Torque Pairings Materials /125 #18
2016 Panini Torque Pairings Materials Blue /99 #18
2016 Panini Torque Pairings Materials Green /25 #18
2016 Panini Torque Pairings Materials Purple /10 #18
2016 Panini Torque Pairings Materials Red /49 #18
2016 Panini Torque Pole Position #11
2016 Panini Torque Pole Position Blue /99 #11
2016 Panini Torque Pole Position Checkerboard /10 #11
2016 Panini Torque Pole Position Green /25 #11
2016 Panini Torque Pole Position Red /49 #11
2016 Panini Torque Printing Plates Black /1 #11
2016 Panini Torque Printing Plates Black /1 #61
2016 Panini Torque Printing Plates Black /1 #87
2016 Panini Torque Printing Plates Cyan /1 #11
2016 Panini Torque Printing Plates Cyan /1 #61
2016 Panini Torque Printing Plates Cyan /1 #87
2016 Panini Torque Printing Plates Magenta /1 #11
2016 Panini Torque Printing Plates Magenta /1 #61
2016 Panini Torque Printing Plates Magenta /1 #87
2016 Panini Torque Printing Plates Yellow /1 #11
2016 Panini Torque Printing Plates Yellow /1 #61
2016 Panini Torque Printing Plates Yellow /1 #87
2016 Panini Torque Purple /25 #11
2016 Panini Torque Purple /25 #61
2016 Panini Torque Purple /25 #87
2016 Panini Torque Red /99 #11
2016 Panini Torque Red /99 #61
2016 Panini Torque Red /99 #87
2016 Panini Torque Rubber Relics /399 #3
2016 Panini Torque Rubber Relics Blue /99 #3
2016 Panini Torque Rubber Relics Green /25 #3
2016 Panini Torque Rubber Relics Purple /10 #3
2016 Panini Torque Rubber Relics Red /49 #3
2016 Panini Torque Shades #6
2016 Panini Torque Shades Gold /199 #6
2016 Panini Torque Shades Holo Silver /99 #6
2016 Panini Torque Silhouettes Firesuit Autographs /35 #2
2016 Panini Torque Silhouettes Firesuit Autographs Blue /25 #2
2016 Panini Torque Silhouettes Firesuit Autographs Green /5 #2
2016 Panini Torque Silhouettes Firesuit Autographs Purple /1 #2
2016 Panini Torque Silhouettes Firesuit Autographs Red /10 #2
2016 Panini Torque Silhouettes Sheet Metal Autographs /35 #2
2016 Panini Torque Silhouettes Sheet Metal Autographs Blue /25 #2
2016 Panini Torque Silhouettes Sheet Metal Autographs Green /5 #2
2016 Panini Torque Silhouettes Sheet Metal Autographs Purple /1 #2
2016 Panini Torque Silhouettes Sheet Metal Autographs Red /10 #2
2016 Panini Torque Superstar Vision #11
2016 Panini Torque Superstar Vision Blue /99 #11
2016 Panini Torque Superstar Vision Gold /149 #11
2016 Panini Torque Superstar Vision Green /25 #11
2016 Panini Torque Superstar Vision Purple /10 #11
2016 Panini Torque Superstar Vision Red /49 #11
2016 Panini Torque Test Proof Black /1 #11
2016 Panini Torque Test Proof Black /1 #61
2016 Panini Torque Test Proof Black /1 #87
2016 Panini Torque Test Proof Cyan /1 #11
2016 Panini Torque Test Proof Cyan /1 #61
2016 Panini Torque Test Proof Cyan /1 #87
2016 Panini Torque Test Proof Magenta /1 #11
2016 Panini Torque Test Proof Magenta /1 #61
2016 Panini Torque Test Proof Magenta /1 #87
2016 Panini Torque Test Proof Yellow /1 #11
2016 Panini Torque Test Proof Yellow /1 #61
2016 Panini Torque Test Proof Yellow /1 #87
2016 Panini Torque Victory Laps #10
2016 Panini Torque Victory Laps Gold /199 #10
2016 Panini Torque Victory Laps Holo Silver /99 #10
2016 Panini Torque Winning Vision #11
2016 Panini Torque Winning Vision Blue /99 #11
2016 Panini Torque Winning Vision Gold /149 #11
2016 Panini Torque Winning Vision Green /25 #11
2016 Panini Torque Winning Vision Purple /10 #11
2016 Panini Torque Winning Vision Red /49 #11
2017 Donruss #39
2017 Donruss #98
2017 Donruss #127
2017 Donruss #149
2017 Donruss #104
2017 Donruss Artist Proof /25 #9
2017 Donruss Artist Proof /25 #39
2017 Donruss Artist Proof /25 #98
2017 Donruss Artist Proof /25 #127
2017 Donruss Artist Proof /25 #149
2017 Donruss Artist Proof /25 #104
2017 Donruss Blue Foil /299 #9
2017 Donruss Blue Foil /299 #98
2017 Donruss Blue Foil /299 #127
2017 Donruss Blue Foil /299 #39
2017 Donruss Blue Foil /299 #149
2017 Donruss Blue Foil /299 #104
2017 Donruss Classics #8
2017 Donruss Classics Cracked Ice /999 #8
2017 Donruss Dual Rubber Relics #1
2017 Donruss Dual Rubber Relics Holo Black /10 #1
2017 Donruss Dual Rubber Relics Holo Gold /25 #1
2017 Donruss Elite Dominators /999 #4
2017 Donruss Gold Foil /499 #9
2017 Donruss Gold Foil /499 #98
2017 Donruss Gold Foil /499 #127
2017 Donruss Gold Foil /499 #149
2017 Donruss Gold Foil /499 #39
2017 Donruss Gold Foil /499 #104
2017 Donruss Gold Press Proof /99 #9
2017 Donruss Gold Press Proof /99 #39
2017 Donruss Gold Press Proof /99 #98
2017 Donruss Gold Press Proof /99 #127
2017 Donruss Gold Press Proof /99 #149
2017 Donruss Gold Press Proof /99 #104
2017 Donruss Green Foil /199 #9
2017 Donruss Green Foil /199 #39
2017 Donruss Green Foil /199 #98
2017 Donruss Green Foil /199 #127
2017 Donruss Green Foil /199 #149
2017 Donruss Green Foil /199 #104
2017 Donruss Pole Position #7
2017 Donruss Pole Position Cracked Ice /999 #7
2017 Donruss Press Proof /49 #9
2017 Donruss Press Proof /49 #39
2017 Donruss Press Proof /49 #98
2017 Donruss Press Proof /49 #127
2017 Donruss Press Proof /49 #149
2017 Donruss Press Proof /49 #104
2017 Donruss Printing Plates Black /1 #9
2017 Donruss Printing Plates Black /1 #39
2017 Donruss Printing Plates Black /1 #98
2017 Donruss Printing Plates Black /1 #127
2017 Donruss Printing Plates Black /1 #149
2017 Donruss Printing Plates Black /1 #104
2017 Donruss Printing Plates Cyan /1 #9
2017 Donruss Printing Plates Cyan /1 #39
2017 Donruss Printing Plates Cyan /1 #98
2017 Donruss Printing Plates Cyan /1 #127
2017 Donruss Printing Plates Cyan /1 #149
2017 Donruss Printing Plates Cyan /1 #104
2017 Donruss Printing Plates Magenta /1 #9
2017 Donruss Printing Plates Magenta /1 #98
2017 Donruss Printing Plates Magenta /1 #127
2017 Donruss Printing Plates Magenta /1 #149
2017 Donruss Printing Plates Magenta /1 #39
2017 Donruss Printing Plates Magenta /1 #104
2017 Donruss Printing Plates Yellow /1 #9
2017 Donruss Printing Plates Yellow /1 #98
2017 Donruss Printing Plates Yellow /1 #127
2017 Donruss Printing Plates Yellow /1 #149
2017 Donruss Printing Plates Yellow /1 #39
2017 Donruss Printing Plates Yellow /1 #104
2017 Donruss Retro Relics 1984 #4
2017 Donruss Retro Relics 1984 Holo Black /10 #4
2017 Donruss Retro Relics 1984 Holo Gold /99 #4
2017 Donruss Rubber Relics #3
2017 Donruss Rubber Relics Holo Black /10 #3
2017 Donruss Rubber Relics Holo Gold /50 #3
2017 Donruss Significant Signatures #3
2017 Donruss Significant Signatures Holo Black /1 #3
2017 Donruss Significant Signatures Holo Gold /25 #3
2017 Donruss Top Tier #3
2017 Donruss Top Tier Cracked Ice /999 #3
2017 Donruss Track Masters #8
2017 Donruss Track Masters Cracked Ice /999 #8
2017 Panini Day #59
2017 Panini Day Cracked Ice /25 #59
2017 Panini Day Decoy /50 #59
2017 Panini Day Hyperplaid /1 #59
2017 Panini Day Rapture /10 #59
2017 Panini Day Wedges /50 #59
2017 Panini Instant Nascar /64 #2
2017 Panini Instant Nascar /64 #6
2017 Panini Instant Nascar #29
2017 Panini Instant Nascar Black /1 #2
2017 Panini Instant Nascar Black /1 #6
2017 Panini Instant Nascar Black /1 #29
2017 Panini Instant Nascar Green /10 #2
2017 Panini Instant Nascar Green /10 #6
2017 Panini Instant Nascar Green /10 #29
2017 Panini National Convention #R7
2017 Panini National Convention Autographs #R7
2017 Panini National Convention Autographs Hyperplaid /1 #R7
2017 Panini National Convention Escher Squares /25 #R7
2017 Panini National Convention Escher Squares Thick Stock /10 #R7
2017 Panini National Convention Galatic Windows /5 #R7
2017 Panini National Convention Hyperplaid /1 #R7
2017 Panini National Convention Pyramids /10 #R7
2017 Panini National Convention Rainbow Spokes /49 #R7
2017 Panini National Convention Rainbow Spokes Thick Stock /25 #R7
2017 Panini National Convention Rapture /99 #R7
2017 Panini National Treasures /25 #4
2017 Panini National Treasures Century Black /1 #4
2017 Panini National Treasures Century Gold /15 #4
2017 Panini National Treasures Century Green /5 #4
2017 Panini National Treasures Century Holo Gold /10 #4
2017 Panini National Treasures Century Holo Silver /20 #4
2017 Panini National Treasures Century Laundry Tags /1 #4
2017 Panini National Treasures Championship Signatures /50 #7
2017 Panini National Treasures Championship Signatures Black /1 #7
2017 Panini National Treasures Championship Signatures Gold /20 #7
2017 Panini National Treasures Championship Signatures Green /2 #7
2017 Panini National Treasures Championship Signatures Holo Gold /15 #7
2017 Panini National Treasures Championship Signatures Holo Silver /25 #7
2017 Panini National Treasures Championship Signatures Printing Plates Black /1 #7
2017 Panini National Treasures Championship Signatures Printing Plates Cyan /1 #7
2017 Panini National Treasures Championship Signatures Printing Plates Magenta /1 #7
2017 Panini National Treasures Championship Signatures Printing Plates Yellow /1 #7
2017 Panini National Treasures Championship Swatches /25 #1
2017 Panini National Treasures Championship Swatches Black /1 #1
2017 Panini National Treasures Championship Swatches Gold /15 #1
2017 Panini National Treasures Championship Swatches Green /5 #1
2017 Panini National Treasures Championship Swatches Holo Gold /10 #1
2017 Panini National Treasures Championship Swatches Holo Silver /20 #1
2017 Panini National Treasures Championship Swatches Laundry Tag /1 #1
2017 Panini National Treasures Championship Swatches Printing Plates Black /1 #1
2017 Panini National Treasures Championship Swatches Printing Plates Cyan /1 #1
2017 Panini National Treasures Championship Swatches Printing Plates Magenta /1 #1
2017 Panini National Treasures Championship Swatches Printing Plates Yellow /1 #1
2017 Panini National Treasures Dual Sheet Metal Signatures /25 #3
2017 Panini National Treasures Dual Sheet Metal Signatures Black /1 #3
2017 Panini National Treasures Dual Sheet Metal Signatures Gold /15 #3
2017 Panini National Treasures Dual Sheet Metal Signatures Green /5 #3
2017 Panini National Treasures Dual Sheet Metal Signatures Holo Gold /10 #3
2017 Panini National Treasures Dual Sheet Metal Signatures Holo Silver /20 #3
2017 Panini National Treasures Dual Sheet Metal Signatures Printing Plates Black /1 #3
2017 Panini National Treasures Dual Sheet Metal Signatures Printing Plates Cyan /1 #3
2017 Panini National Treasures Dual Sheet Metal Signatures Printing Plates Magenta /1 #3
2017 Panini National Treasures Dual Sheet Metal Signatures Printing Plates Yellow /1 #3
2017 Panini National Treasures Dual Tire Signatures /25 #10
2017 Panini National Treasures Dual Tire Signatures Black /1 #10
2017 Panini National Treasures Dual Tire Signatures Gold /15 #10
2017 Panini National Treasures Dual Tire Signatures Green /5 #10
2017 Panini National Treasures Dual Tire Signatures Holo Gold /10 #10
2017 Panini National Treasures Dual Tire Signatures Holo Silver /20 #10
2017 Panini National Treasures Dual Tire Signatures Printing Plates Black /1 #10
2017 Panini National Treasures Dual Tire Signatures Printing Plates Cyan /1 #10
2017 Panini National Treasures Dual Tire Signatures Printing Plates Magenta /1 #10
2017 Panini National Treasures Dual Tire Signatures Printing Plates Yellow /1 #10
2017 Panini National Treasures Jumbo Tire Signatures /50 #2
2017 Panini National Treasures Jumbo Tire Signatures Black /1 #2
2017 Panini National Treasures Jumbo Tire Signatures Gold /20 #2
2017 Panini National Treasures Jumbo Tire Signatures Green /2 #2
2017 Panini National Treasures Jumbo Tire Signatures Holo Gold /15 #2
2017 Panini National Treasures Jumbo Tire Signatures Holo Silver /25 #2
2017 Panini National Treasures Jumbo Tire Signatures Printing Plates Black /1 #2
2017 Panini National Treasures Jumbo Tire Signatures Printing Plates Cyan /1 #2
2017 Panini National Treasures Jumbo Tire Signatures Printing Plates Magenta /1 #2
2017 Panini National Treasures Jumbo Tire Signatures Printing Plates Yellow /1 #2
2017 Panini National Treasures Printing Plates Black /1 #4
2017 Panini National Treasures Printing Plates Cyan /1 #4
2017 Panini National Treasures Printing Plates Magenta /1 #4
2017 Panini National Treasures Printing Plates Yellow /1 #4
2017 Panini National Treasures Quad Material Signatures /25 #4
2017 Panini National Treasures Quad Material Signatures Black /1 #4
2017 Panini National Treasures Quad Material Signatures Gold /15 #4
2017 Panini National Treasures Quad Material Signatures Green /2 #4
2017 Panini National Treasures Quad Material Signatures Holo Gold /10 #4
2017 Panini National Treasures Quad Material Signatures Holo Silver /20 #4
2017 Panini National Treasures Quad Material Signatures Laundry Tag /1 #4
2017 Panini National Treasures Quad Material Signatures Printing Plates Black /1 #4
2017 Panini National Treasures Quad Material Signatures Printing Plates Cyan /1 #4
2017 Panini National Treasures Quad Material Signatures Printing Plates Magenta /1 #4
2017 Panini National Treasures Quad Material Signatures Printing Plates Yellow /1 #4
2017 Panini National Treasures Quad Materials /25 #13
2017 Panini National Treasures Quad Materials Black /1 #13
2017 Panini National Treasures Quad Materials Gold /15 #13
2017 Panini National Treasures Quad Materials Green /5 #13
2017 Panini National Treasures Quad Materials Holo Gold /10 #13
2017 Panini National Treasures Quad Materials Holo Silver /20 #13
2017 Panini National Treasures Quad Materials Laundry Tag /1 #13
2017 Panini National Treasures Quad Materials Printing Plates Black /1 #13
2017 Panini National Treasures Quad Materials Printing Plates Cyan /1 #13
2017 Panini National Treasures Quad Materials Printing Plates Magenta /1 #13
2017 Panini National Treasures Quad Materials Printing Plates Yellow /1 #13
2017 Panini National Treasures Teammates Dual Materials /25 #5
2017 Panini National Treasures Teammates Dual Materials Black /1 #5
2017 Panini National Treasures Teammates Dual Materials Gold /15 #5
2017 Panini National Treasures Teammates Dual Materials Green /5 #5
2017 Panini National Treasures Teammates Dual Materials Holo Gold /10 #5
2017 Panini National Treasures Teammates Dual Materials Holo Silver /20 #5
2017 Panini National Treasures Teammates Dual Materials Laundry Tag /1 #5
2017 Panini National Treasures Teammates Dual Materials Printing Plates Black /1 #5
2017 Panini National Treasures Teammates Dual Materials Printing Plates Cyan /1 #5
2017 Panini National Treasures Teammates Dual Materials Printing Plates Magenta /1 #5
2017 Panini National Treasures Teammates Dual Materials Printing Plates Yellow /1 #5
2017 Panini National Treasures Teammates Quad Materials /25 #3
2017 Panini National Treasures Teammates Quad Materials Black /1 #3
2017 Panini National Treasures Teammates Quad Materials Gold /15 #3
2017 Panini National Treasures Teammates Quad Materials Green /5 #3
2017 Panini National Treasures Teammates Quad Materials Holo Gold /10 #3
2017 Panini National Treasures Teammates Quad Materials Holo Silver /20 #3
2017 Panini National Treasures Teammates Quad Materials Laundry Tag /1 #3
2017 Panini National Treasures Teammates Quad Materials Printing Plates Black /1 #3
2017 Panini National Treasures Teammates Quad Materials Printing Plates Cyan /1 #3
2017 Panini National Treasures Teammates Quad Materials Printing Plates Magenta /1 #3
2017 Panini National Treasures Teammates Quad Materials Printing Plates Yellow /1 #3
2017 Panini National Treasures Winning Material Signatures /25 #10
2017 Panini National Treasures Winning Material Signatures Black /1 #10
2017 Panini National Treasures Winning Material Signatures Gold /15 #10
2017 Panini National Treasures Winning Material Signatures Green /2 #10
2017 Panini National Treasures Winning Material Signatures Holo Gold /10 #10
2017 Panini National Treasures Winning Material Signatures Holo Silver /20 #10
2017 Panini National Treasures Winning Material Signatures Laundry Tag /1 #10
2017 Panini National Treasures Winning Material Signatures Printing Plates Black /1 #10
2017 Panini National Treasures Winning Material Signatures Printing Plates Cyan /1 #10
2017 Panini National Treasures Winning Material Signatures Printing Plates Magenta /1 #10
2017 Panini National Treasures Winning Material Signatures Printing Plates Yellow /1 #10
2017 Panini Torque #2
2017 Panini Torque #44
2017 Panini Torque #65
2017 Panini Torque Artist Proof /75 #2
2017 Panini Torque Artist Proof /75 #44

2017 Panini Torque Artist Proof /75 #65
2017 Panini Torque Blackout /1 #2
2017 Panini Torque Blackout /1 #44
2017 Panini Torque Blackout /1 #65
2017 Panini Torque Blue /150 #2
2017 Panini Torque Blue /150 #44
2017 Panini Torque Blue /150 #65
2017 Panini Torque Claiming The Chase #5
2017 Panini Torque Claiming The Chase Gold /199 #5
2017 Panini Torque Claiming The Chase Holo Silver /99 #5
2017 Panini Torque Clear Vision #2
2017 Panini Torque Clear Vision Blue /99 #2
2017 Panini Torque Clear Vision Gold /149 #2
2017 Panini Torque Clear Vision Green /25 #2
2017 Panini Torque Clear Vision Purple /10 #2
2017 Panini Torque Clear Vision Red /49 #2
2017 Panini Torque Combo Materials Signatures /50 #5
2017 Panini Torque Combo Materials Signatures Blue /25 #5
2017 Panini Torque Combo Materials Signatures Green /15 #5
2017 Panini Torque Combo Materials Signatures Purple /10 #5
2017 Panini Torque Combo Materials Signatures Red /20 #5
2017 Panini Torque Dual Materials /499 #2
2017 Panini Torque Dual Materials Blue /99 #2
2017 Panini Torque Dual Materials Green /25 #2
2017 Panini Torque Dual Materials Purple /10 #2
2017 Panini Torque Dual Materials Red /49 #2
2017 Panini Torque Gold #2
2017 Panini Torque Gold #44
2017 Panini Torque Gold #65
2017 Panini Torque Holo Gold /10 #2
2017 Panini Torque Holo Gold /10 #44
2017 Panini Torque Holo Gold /10 #65
2017 Panini Torque Holo Silver /25 #2
2017 Panini Torque Holo Silver /25 #44
2017 Panini Torque Holo Silver /25 #65
2017 Panini Torque Horsepower Heroes #2
2017 Panini Torque Horsepower Heroes Gold /199 #2
2017 Panini Torque Horsepower Heroes Holo Silver /99 #2
2017 Panini Torque Jumbo Tire Signatures /35 #3
2017 Panini Torque Jumbo Tire Signatures Blue /25 #3
2017 Panini Torque Jumbo Tire Signatures Green /15 #3
2017 Panini Torque Jumbo Tire Signatures Purple /10 #3
2017 Panini Torque Jumbo Tire Signatures Red /20 #3
2017 Panini Torque Manufacturer Marks #9
2017 Panini Torque Manufacturer Marks Gold /199 #9
2017 Panini Torque Manufacturer Marks Holo Silver /99 #9
2017 Panini Torque Pairings Materials /199 #1
2017 Panini Torque Pairings Materials Blue /99 #1
2017 Panini Torque Pairings Materials Green /25 #1
2017 Panini Torque Pairings Materials Purple /10 #1
2017 Panini Torque Pairings Materials Red /49 #1
2017 Panini Torque Primary Paint #13
2017 Panini Torque Primary Paint Blue /99 #13
2017 Panini Torque Primary Paint Checkerboard /10 #13
2017 Panini Torque Primary Paint Green /25 #13
2017 Panini Torque Primary Paint Red /49 #13
2017 Panini Torque Prime Associate Sponsors Jumbo Patches /1 #2A
2017 Panini Torque Prime Associate Sponsors Jumbo Patches /1 #2B
2017 Panini Torque Prime Associate Sponsors Jumbo Patches /1 #2C
2017 Panini Torque Prime Associate Sponsors Jumbo Patches /1 #2D
2017 Panini Torque Prime Associate Sponsors Jumbo Patches /1 #2E
2017 Panini Torque Prime Associate Sponsors Jumbo Patches /1 #2F
2017 Panini Torque Prime Associate Sponsors Jumbo Patches /1 #2G
2017 Panini Torque Prime Associate Sponsors Jumbo Patches /1 #2H
2017 Panini Torque Prime Associate Sponsors Jumbo Patches /1 #2I
2017 Panini Torque Prime Associate Sponsors Jumbo Patches /1 #2J
2017 Panini Torque Prime Associate Sponsors Jumbo Patches /1 #2K
2017 Panini Torque Prime Associate Sponsors Jumbo Patches /1 #2L
2017 Panini Torque Prime Associate Sponsors Jumbo Patches /1 #2M
2017 Panini Torque Prime Associate Sponsors Jumbo Patches /1 #2N
2017 Panini Torque Prime Flag Jumbo Patches /1 #2
2017 Panini Torque Prime Goodyear Jumbo Patches /1 #2
2017 Panini Torque Prime Manufacturer Jumbo Patches /1 #2
2017 Panini Torque Prime Nameplates Jumbo Patches /2 #2
2017 Panini Torque Prime NASCAR Jumbo Patches /1 #2
2017 Panini Torque Prime Series Sponsor Jumbo Patches /1 #2
2017 Panini Torque Printing Plates Black /1 #2
2017 Panini Torque Printing Plates Black /1 #44
2017 Panini Torque Printing Plates Black /1 #65
2017 Panini Torque Printing Plates Cyan /1 #2
2017 Panini Torque Printing Plates Cyan /1 #44
2017 Panini Torque Printing Plates Cyan /1 #65
2017 Panini Torque Printing Plates Magenta /1 #2
2017 Panini Torque Printing Plates Magenta /1 #44
2017 Panini Torque Printing Plates Magenta /1 #65
2017 Panini Torque Printing Plates Yellow /1 #2
2017 Panini Torque Printing Plates Yellow /1 #44
2017 Panini Torque Printing Plates Yellow /1 #65
2017 Panini Torque Purple /50 #2
2017 Panini Torque Purple /50 #44
2017 Panini Torque Purple /50 #65
2017 Panini Torque Quad Materials /49 #2
2017 Panini Torque Quad Materials Blue /25 #2
2017 Panini Torque Quad Materials Green /10 #2
2017 Panini Torque Quad Materials Purple /5 #2
2017 Panini Torque Quad Materials Red /15 #2
2017 Panini Torque Raced Relics /499 #2
2017 Panini Torque Raced Relics Blue /99 #2
2017 Panini Torque Raced Relics Green /25 #2
2017 Panini Torque Raced Relics Purple /10 #2
2017 Panini Torque Raced Relics Red /49 #2
2017 Panini Torque Red /100 #2
2017 Panini Torque Red /100 #44
2017 Panini Torque Red /100 #65
2017 Panini Torque Running Order #12
2017 Panini Torque Running Order Blue /99 #12
2017 Panini Torque Running Order Checkerboard /10 #12
2017 Panini Torque Running Order Green /25 #12
2017 Panini Torque Running Order Red /49 #12
2017 Panini Torque Silhouettes Sheet Metal Signatures /25 #20
2017 Panini Torque Silhouettes Sheet Metal Signatures Blue /20 #20
2017 Panini Torque Silhouettes Sheet Metal Signatures Green /10 #20
2017 Panini Torque Silhouettes Sheet Metal Signatures Purple /5 #20
2017 Panini Torque Silhouettes Sheet Metal Signatures Red /15 #20
2017 Panini Torque Test Proof Black /1 #2
2017 Panini Torque Test Proof Black /1 #44
2017 Panini Torque Test Proof Black /1 #65
2017 Panini Torque Test Proof Cyan /1 #2
2017 Panini Torque Test Proof Cyan /1 #44
2017 Panini Torque Test Proof Cyan /1 #65
2017 Panini Torque Test Proof Magenta /1 #2
2017 Panini Torque Test Proof Magenta /1 #44
2017 Panini Torque Test Proof Magenta /1 #65
2017 Panini Torque Test Proof Yellow /1 #2
2017 Panini Torque Test Proof Yellow /1 #44
2017 Panini Torque Test Proof Yellow /1 #65
2017 Panini Torque Track Vision #6
2017 Panini Torque Track Vision Blue /99 #6
2017 Panini Torque Track Vision Gold /149 #6
2017 Panini Torque Track Vision Green /25 #6
2017 Panini Torque Track Vision Purple /10 #6
2017 Panini Torque Track Vision Red /49 #6
2017 Panini Torque Victory Laps #6
2017 Panini Torque Victory Laps Gold /199 #6
2017 Panini Torque Victory Laps Holo Silver /99 #6
2017 Panini Torque Visions of Greatness #22
2017 Panini Torque Visions of Greatness Blue /99 #22
2017 Panini Torque Visions of Greatness Gold /149 #22
2017 Panini Torque Visions of Greatness Green /25 #22
2017 Panini Torque Visions of Greatness Purple /10 #22
2017 Panini Torque Visions of Greatness Red /49 #22
2017 Select #7
2017 Select #8
2017 Select #9
2017 Select #10
2017 Select #120
2017 Select Prizms Black /3 #7
2017 Select Prizms Black /3 #8
2017 Select Prizms Black /3 #9
2017 Select Prizms Black /3 #10
2017 Select Prizms Black /3 #120
2017 Select Prizms Blue /199 #7
2017 Select Prizms Blue /199 #8
2017 Select Prizms Blue /199 #9
2017 Select Prizms Blue /199 #10
2017 Select Prizms Checkered Flag /1 #7
2017 Select Prizms Checkered Flag /1 #8
2017 Select Prizms Checkered Flag /1 #9
2017 Select Prizms Checkered Flag /1 #10
2017 Select Prizms Checkered Flag /1 #120
2017 Select Prizms Gold /10 #7
2017 Select Prizms Gold /10 #8
2017 Select Prizms Gold /10 #9
2017 Select Prizms Gold /10 #10
2017 Select Prizms Gold /10 #120
2017 Select Prizms Purple Pulsar #7
2017 Select Prizms Purple Pulsar #8
2017 Select Prizms Purple Pulsar #9
2017 Select Prizms Purple Pulsar #10
2017 Select Prizms Red /99 #7
2017 Select Prizms Red /99 #8
2017 Select Prizms Red /99 #9
2017 Select Prizms Red /99 #10
2017 Select Prizms Red White and Blue Pulsar /299 #7
2017 Select Prizms Red White and Blue Pulsar /299 #8
2017 Select Prizms Red White and Blue Pulsar /299 #9
2017 Select Prizms Red White and Blue Pulsar /299 #10
2017 Select Prizms Silver #7
2017 Select Prizms Silver #8
2017 Select Prizms Silver #9
2017 Select Prizms Silver #10
2017 Select Prizms Tie Dye /24 #7
2017 Select Prizms Tie Dye /24 #8
2017 Select Prizms Tie Dye /24 #9
2017 Select Prizms Tie Dye /24 #10
2017 Select Prizms Tie Dye /24 #120
2017 Select Prizms White /50 #7
2017 Select Prizms White /50 #8
2017 Select Prizms White /50 #9
2017 Select Prizms White /50 #10
2017 Select Prizms White /50 #120
2017 Select Select Pairs Materials #2
2017 Select Select Pairs Materials #3
2017 Select Select Pairs Materials Prizms Blue /199 #2
2017 Select Select Pairs Materials Prizms Blue /199 #3
2017 Select Select Pairs Materials Prizms Checkered Flag /1 #2
2017 Select Select Pairs Materials Prizms Checkered Flag /1 #3
2017 Select Select Pairs Materials Prizms Gold /10 #2
2017 Select Select Pairs Materials Prizms Gold /10 #3
2017 Select Select Pairs Materials Prizms Red /99 #2
2017 Select Select Pairs Materials Prizms Red /99 #3
2017 Select Select Stars #14
2017 Select Select Stars Prizms Black /3 #14
2017 Select Select Stars Prizms Checkered Flag /1 #14
2017 Select Select Stars Prizms Gold /10 #14
2017 Select Select Stars Prizms Tie Dye /24 #14
2017 Select Select Stars Prizms White /50 #14
2017 Select Select Swatches #4
2017 Select Select Swatches Prizms Blue /199 #4
2017 Select Select Swatches Prizms Checkered Flag /1 #4
2017 Select Select Swatches Prizms Gold /10 #4
2017 Select Select Swatches Prizms Red /99 #4
2017 Select Sheet Metal #2
2017 Select Sheet Metal Prizms Blue /199 #2
2017 Select Sheet Metal Prizms Checkered Flag /1 #2
2017 Select Sheet Metal Prizms Gold /10 #2
2017 Select Sheet Metal Prizms Red /99 #2
2017 Select Signature Paint Schemes #1
2017 Select Signature Paint Schemes Prizms Blue /15 #1
2017 Select Signature Paint Schemes Prizms Checkered Flag /1 #1
2017 Select Signature Paint Schemes Prizms Gold /5 #1
2017 Select Signature Paint Schemes Prizms Red /10 #1
2017 Select Signature Swatches #4
2017 Select Signature Swatches Prizms Checkered Flag /1 #4
2017 Select Signature Swatches Prizms Gold /10 #4
2017 Select Signature Swatches Prizms Tie Dye /24 #4
2017 Select Signature Swatches Prizms White /50 #4
2017 Select Signature Swatches Triple #4
2017 Select Signature Swatches Triple Prizms Checkered Flag /1 #4
2017 Select Signature Swatches Triple Prizms Gold /10 #4
2017 Select Signature Swatches Triple Prizms Tie Dye /24 #4
2017 Select Signature Swatches Triple Prizms White /50 #4
2017 Select Speed Merchants #5
2017 Select Speed Merchants Prizms Black /3 #5
2017 Select Speed Merchants Prizms Checkered Flag /1 #5
2017 Select Speed Merchants Prizms Gold /10 #5
2017 Select Speed Merchants Prizms Tie Dye /24 #5
2017 Select Speed Merchants Prizms White /50 #5
2017 Select Up Close and Personal #4
2017 Select Up Close and Personal Prizms Black /3 #4
2017 Select Up Close and Personal Prizms Checkered Flag /1 #4
2017 Select Up Close and Personal Prizms Gold /10 #4
2017 Select Up Close and Personal Prizms Tie Dye /24 #4
2017 Select Up Close and Personal Prizms White /50 #4
2018 Certified #73
2018 Certified #96
2018 Certified All Certified Team /199 #19
2018 Certified All Certified Team Black /1 #19
2018 Certified All Certified Team Blue /99 #19
2018 Certified All Certified Team Gold /49 #19
2018 Certified All Certified Team Green /10 #19
2018 Certified All Certified Team Mirror Black /1 #19
2018 Certified All Certified Team Mirror Gold /25 #19
2018 Certified All Certified Team Mirror Green /5 #19
2018 Certified All Certified Team Mirror Purple /10 #19
2018 Certified All Certified Team Purple /25 #19
2018 Certified All Certified Team Red /149 #19
2018 Certified Black /1 #73
2018 Certified Black /1 #96
2018 Certified Blue /99 #73
2018 Certified Blue /99 #96
2018 Certified Cup Swatches /499 #4
2018 Certified Cup Swatches Black /1 #4
2018 Certified Cup Swatches Blue /49 #4
2018 Certified Cup Swatches Gold /25 #4
2018 Certified Cup Swatches Green /5 #4
2018 Certified Cup Swatches Purple /10 #4
2018 Certified Cup Swatches Red /199 #4
2018 Certified Epix /199 #8
2018 Certified Epix Black /1 #8
2018 Certified Epix Blue /99 #8
2018 Certified Epix Gold /49 #8
2018 Certified Epix Green /10 #8
2018 Certified Epix Mirror Black /1 #8
2018 Certified Epix Mirror Gold /25 #8
2018 Certified Epix Mirror Green /5 #8
2018 Certified Epix Mirror Purple /10 #8
2018 Certified Epix Purple /25 #8
2018 Certified Epix Red /149 #8
2018 Certified Gold /49 #73
2018 Certified Gold /49 #96
2018 Certified Green /10 #73
2018 Certified Green /10 #96
2018 Certified Mirror Black /1 #73
2018 Certified Mirror Black /1 #96
2018 Certified Mirror Gold /25 #73
2018 Certified Mirror Gold /25 #96
2018 Certified Mirror Green /5 #73
2018 Certified Mirror Green /5 #96
2018 Certified Mirror Purple /10 #73
2018 Certified Mirror Purple /10 #96
2018 Certified Orange /249 #73
2018 Certified Orange /249 #96
2018 Certified Purple /25 #73
2018 Certified Purple /25 #96
2018 Certified Red /199 #73
2018 Certified Red /199 #96
2018 Certified Signatures /99 #2
2018 Certified Signatures Black /1 #2
2018 Certified Signatures Blue /50 #2
2018 Certified Signatures Gold /25 #2
2018 Certified Signatures Green /5 #2
2018 Certified Signatures Purple /10 #2
2018 Certified Signatures Red /75 #2
2018 Certified Skills /199 #1
2018 Certified Skills Black /1 #1
2018 Certified Skills Blue /99 #1
2018 Certified Skills Gold /49 #1
2018 Certified Skills Green /10 #1
2018 Certified Skills Mirror Black /1 #1
2018 Certified Skills Mirror Gold /25 #1
2018 Certified Skills Mirror Green /5 #1
2018 Certified Skills Mirror Purple /10 #1
2018 Certified Skills Purple /25 #1
2018 Certified Skills Red /149 #1
2018 Certified Stars /199 #15
2018 Certified Stars Black /1 #15
2018 Certified Stars Blue /99 #15
2018 Certified Stars Gold /49 #15
2018 Certified Stars Green /10 #15
2018 Certified Stars Mirror Black /1 #15
2018 Certified Stars Mirror Gold /25 #15
2018 Certified Stars Mirror Green /5 #15
2018 Certified Stars Mirror Purple /10 #15
2018 Certified Stars Purple /25 #15
2018 Certified Stars Red /149 #15
2018 Donruss #5
2018 Donruss #32A
2018 Donruss #88
2018 Donruss #122
2018 Donruss #32B
2018 Donruss Artist Proofs /25 #5
2018 Donruss Artist Proofs /25 #32A
2018 Donruss Artist Proofs /25 #88
2018 Donruss Artist Proofs /25 #122
2018 Donruss Artist Proofs /25 #32B
2018 Donruss Gold Foil /499 #5
2018 Donruss Gold Foil /499 #32A
2018 Donruss Gold Foil /499 #88
2018 Donruss Gold Foil /499 #122
2018 Donruss Gold Foil /499 #32B
2018 Donruss Gold Press Proofs /99 #5
2018 Donruss Gold Press Proofs /99 #32A
2018 Donruss Gold Press Proofs /99 #88
2018 Donruss Gold Press Proofs /99 #122
2018 Donruss Gold Press Proofs /99 #32B
2018 Donruss Green Foil /199 #5
2018 Donruss Green Foil /199 #32A
2018 Donruss Green Foil /199 #88
2018 Donruss Green Foil /199 #122
2018 Donruss Green Foil /199 #32B
2018 Donruss Pole Position #6
2018 Donruss Pole Position Cracked Ice /999 #6
2018 Donruss Pole Position Xplosion /99 #6
2018 Donruss Press Proofs /49 #5
2018 Donruss Press Proofs /49 #32A
2018 Donruss Press Proofs /49 #88
2018 Donruss Press Proofs /49 #122
2018 Donruss Press Proofs /49 #32B
2018 Donruss Printing Plates Black /1 #5
2018 Donruss Printing Plates Black /1 #32
2018 Donruss Printing Plates Black /1 #88
2018 Donruss Printing Plates Black /1 #122
2018 Donruss Printing Plates Black /1 #32B
2018 Donruss Printing Plates Cyan /1 #5
2018 Donruss Printing Plates Cyan /1 #32
2018 Donruss Printing Plates Cyan /1 #88
2018 Donruss Printing Plates Cyan /1 #122
2018 Donruss Printing Plates Cyan /1 #32B
2018 Donruss Printing Plates Magenta /1 #5
2018 Donruss Printing Plates Magenta /1 #32
2018 Donruss Printing Plates Magenta /1 #88
2018 Donruss Printing Plates Magenta /1 #122
2018 Donruss Printing Plates Magenta /1 #32B
2018 Donruss Printing Plates Yellow /1 #5
2018 Donruss Printing Plates Yellow /1 #32
2018 Donruss Printing Plates Yellow /1 #88
2018 Donruss Printing Plates Yellow /1 #122
2018 Donruss Printing Plates Yellow /1 #32B
2018 Donruss Racing Relics #4
2018 Donruss Racing Relics Black /10 #4
2018 Donruss Racing Relics Holo Gold /99 #4
2018 Donruss Red Foil /299 #5
2018 Donruss Red Foil /299 #32A
2018 Donruss Red Foil /299 #88
2018 Donruss Red Foil /299 #122
2018 Donruss Red Foil /299 #32B
2018 Donruss Retro Relics '85 #13
2018 Donruss Retro Relics '85 Black /10 #13
2018 Donruss Retro Relics '85 Holo Gold /99 #13
2018 Donruss Rubber Relic Signatures #1
2018 Donruss Rubber Relic Signatures Black /1 #1
2018 Donruss Rubber Relic Signatures Holo Gold /25 #1
2018 Donruss Rubber Relics #3
2018 Donruss Rubber Relics Black /10 #3
2018 Donruss Rubber Relics Holo Gold /99 #3
2018 Donruss Studio #13
2018 Donruss Studio Cracked Ice /999 #13
2018 Donruss Studio Xplosion /99 #13
2018 Donruss Top Tier #8
2018 Donruss Top Tier Cracked Ice /999 #8
2018 Donruss Top Tier Xplosion /99 #8
2018 Panini National Convention #74
2018 Panini National Convention Escher Squares /25 #74
2018 Panini National Convention Galatic Windows /5 #74
2018 Panini National Convention Hyperplaid /1 #74
2018 Panini National Convention Magnetic Fur /99 #74
2018 Panini National Convention Pyramids /10 #74
2018 Panini National Convention Rainbow Spokes /49 #74
2018 Panini Prime /50 #6
2018 Panini Prime /50 #40
2018 Panini Prime /50 #73
2018 Panini Prime Autograph Materials /99 #5
2018 Panini Prime Autograph Materials Black /1 #5
2018 Panini Prime Autograph Materials Holo Gold /50 #5
2018 Panini Prime Autograph Materials Laundry Tag /1 #5
2018 Panini Prime Black /1 #6
2018 Panini Prime Black /1 #40
2018 Panini Prime Black /1 #73
2018 Panini Prime Clear Silhouettes /99 #3
2018 Panini Prime Clear Silhouettes Black /1 #3
2018 Panini Prime Clear Silhouettes Dual /99 #3
2018 Panini Prime Clear Silhouettes Dual Black /1 #3
2018 Panini Prime Clear Silhouettes Dual Holo Gold /50 #3
2018 Panini Prime Clear Silhouettes Holo Gold /50 #3
2018 Panini Prime Driver Signatures /99 #23
2018 Panini Prime Driver Signatures Black /1 #23
2018 Panini Prime Driver Signatures Holo Gold /23 #23
2018 Panini Prime Holo Gold /25 #6
2018 Panini Prime Holo Gold /25 #40
2018 Panini Prime Holo Gold /25 #73
2018 Panini Prime Prime Jumbo Associate Sponsor 1 /1 #7
2018 Panini Prime Prime Jumbo Associate Sponsor 1 /1 #8
2018 Panini Prime Prime Jumbo Associate Sponsor 10 /1 #7
2018 Panini Prime Prime Jumbo Associate Sponsor 10 /1 #8
2018 Panini Prime Prime Jumbo Associate Sponsor 11 /1 #7
2018 Panini Prime Prime Jumbo Associate Sponsor 12 /1 #7
2018 Panini Prime Prime Jumbo Associate Sponsor 2 /1 #7
2018 Panini Prime Prime Jumbo Associate Sponsor 2 /1 #8
2018 Panini Prime Prime Jumbo Associate Sponsor 3 /1 #7
2018 Panini Prime Prime Jumbo Associate Sponsor 3 /1 #8
2018 Panini Prime Prime Jumbo Associate Sponsor 4 /1 #7
2018 Panini Prime Prime Jumbo Associate Sponsor 4 /1 #8
2018 Panini Prime Prime Jumbo Associate Sponsor 5 /1 #7
2018 Panini Prime Prime Jumbo Associate Sponsor 5 /1 #8
2018 Panini Prime Prime Jumbo Associate Sponsor 6 /1 #7
2018 Panini Prime Prime Jumbo Associate Sponsor 6 /1 #8
2018 Panini Prime Prime Jumbo Associate Sponsor 7 /1 #7
2018 Panini Prime Prime Jumbo Associate Sponsor 7 /1 #8
2018 Panini Prime Prime Jumbo Associate Sponsor 8 /1 #7
2018 Panini Prime Prime Jumbo Associate Sponsor 8 /1 #8
2018 Panini Prime Prime Jumbo Associate Sponsor 9 /1 #7
2018 Panini Prime Prime Jumbo Associate Sponsor 9 /1 #8
2018 Panini Prime Prime Jumbo Car Manufacturer /1 #7
2018 Panini Prime Prime Jumbo Car Manufacturer /1 #8
2018 Panini Prime Prime Jumbo Firesuit Manufacturer /1 #7
2018 Panini Prime Prime Jumbo Firesuit Manufacturer /1 #8
2018 Panini Prime Prime Jumbo Flag Patch /1 #7
2018 Panini Prime Prime Jumbo Flag Patch /1 #8
2018 Panini Prime Prime Jumbo Nameplate /2 #7
2018 Panini Prime Prime Jumbo Nameplate /2 #8
2018 Panini Prime Prime Jumbo NASCAR /1 #7
2018 Panini Prime Prime Jumbo NASCAR /1 #8
2018 Panini Prime Prime Jumbo Prime Colors /12 #7
2018 Panini Prime Prime Jumbo Prime Colors /13 #8
2018 Panini Prime Prime Jumbo Series Sponsor /1 #7
2018 Panini Prime Prime Jumbo Series Sponsor /1 #8
2018 Panini Prime Prime Jumbo Sunoco /1 #7
2018 Panini Prime Prime Jumbo Sunoco /1 #8
2018 Panini Prime Prime Number Signatures /99 #2
2018 Panini Prime Prime Number Signatures Black /1 #2
2018 Panini Prime Prime Number Signatures Holo Gold /49 #2
2018 Panini Prime Quad Material Autographs /99 #6
2018 Panini Prime Quad Material Autographs Black /1 #6
2018 Panini Prime Quad Material Autographs Holo Gold /50 #6
2018 Panini Prime Quad Material Autographs Laundry Tag /1 #6
2018 Panini Prime Race Used Duals Firesuit /50 #4
2018 Panini Prime Race Used Duals Firesuit Black /1 #4
2018 Panini Prime Race Used Duals Firesuit Holo Gold /25 #4
2018 Panini Prime Race Used Duals Firesuit Laundry Tag /1 #4
2018 Panini Prime Race Used Duals Sheet Metal /50 #4
2018 Panini Prime Race Used Duals Sheet Metal Black /1 #4
2018 Panini Prime Race Used Duals Sheet Metal Holo Gold /25 #4
2018 Panini Prime Race Used Duals Tire /50 #4
2018 Panini Prime Race Used Duals Tire Black /1 #4
2018 Panini Prime Race Used Duals Tire Holo Gold /10 #4
2018 Panini Prime Race Used Firesuits /50 #3
2018 Panini Prime Race Used Firesuits Black /1 #3
2018 Panini Prime Race Used Firesuits Holo Gold /25 #3
2018 Panini Prime Race Used Firesuits Laundry Tag /1 #3
2018 Panini Prime Race Used Sheet Metal /50 #3
2018 Panini Prime Race Used Sheet Metal Black /1 #3
2018 Panini Prime Race Used Sheet Metal Holo Gold /25 #3
2018 Panini Prime Race Used Tires Black /1 #3
2018 Panini Prime Race Used Tires Holo Gold /25 #3
2018 Panini Prime Race Used Trios Firesuit /50 #9
2018 Panini Prime Race Used Trios Firesuit Black /1 #9
2018 Panini Prime Race Used Trios Firesuit Holo Gold /25 #9
2018 Panini Prime Race Used Trios Firesuit Laundry Tag /1 #9
2018 Panini Prime Race Used Trios Sheet Metal /50 #9
2018 Panini Prime Race Used Trios Sheet Metal Black /1 #9
2018 Panini Prime Race Used Trios Sheet Metal Holo Gold /25 #9
2018 Panini Prime Race Used Trios Tire Black /1 #9
2018 Panini Prime Race Used Trios Tire Holo Gold /2 #9
2018 Panini Prime Triple Material Autographs /99 #13
2018 Panini Prime Triple Material Autographs Black /1 #13
2018 Panini Prime Triple Material Autographs Holo Gold /50 #13
2018 Panini Prime Triple Material Autographs Laundry Tag /1 #13
2018 Panini Prizm #18
2018 Panini Prizm #88
2018 Panini Prizm Fireworks #7
2018 Panini Prizm Fireworks Prizms #7
2018 Panini Prizm Fireworks Prizms Black /1 #7
2018 Panini Prizm Fireworks Prizms Gold /10 #7
2018 Panini Prizm Illumination #11
2018 Panini Prizm Illumination Prizms #11
2018 Panini Prizm Illumination Prizms Black /1 #11
2018 Panini Prizm Illumination Prizms Gold /10 #11
2018 Panini Prizm Instant Impact #5
2018 Panini Prizm Instant Impact Prizms #5
2018 Panini Prizm Instant Impact Prizms Black /1 #5
2018 Panini Prizm Instant Impact Prizms Gold /10 #5
2018 Panini Prizm Prizms #18
2018 Panini Prizm Prizms #88
2018 Panini Prizm Prizms Black /1 #18
2018 Panini Prizm Prizms Black /1 #88
2018 Panini Prizm Prizms Blue /99 #18
2018 Panini Prizm Prizms Blue /99 #88
2018 Panini Prizm Prizms Camo #18
2018 Panini Prizm Prizms Camo #88
2018 Panini Prizm Prizms Gold /10 #18
2018 Panini Prizm Prizms Gold /10 #88
2018 Panini Prizm Prizms Green /149 #18
2018 Panini Prizm Prizms Green /149 #88
2018 Panini Prizm Prizms Purple Flash #18
2018 Panini Prizm Prizms Purple Flash #88
2018 Panini Prizm Prizms Rainbow /24 #18
2018 Panini Prizm Prizms Rainbow /24 #88
2018 Panini Prizm Prizms Red /75 #18
2018 Panini Prizm Prizms Red /75 #88
2018 Panini Prizm Prizms Red White and Blue #18
2018 Panini Prizm Prizms Red White and Blue #88
2018 Panini Prizm Prizms White /5 #18
2018 Panini Prizm Prizms White /5 #88
2018 Panini Prizm Scripted Signatures Prizms #25
2018 Panini Prizm Scripted Signatures Prizms Black /1 #25
2018 Panini Prizm Scripted Signatures Prizms Blue /35 #25
2018 Panini Prizm Scripted Signatures Prizms Camo #25
2018 Panini Prizm Scripted Signatures Prizms Gold /10 #25
2018 Panini Prizm Scripted Signatures Prizms Green /50 #25
2018 Panini Prizm Scripted Signatures Prizms Rainbow /24 #25
2018 Panini Prizm Scripted Signatures Prizms Red /25 #25
2018 Panini Prizm Scripted Signatures Prizms Red White and Blue /75 #25
2018 Panini Prizm Scripted Signatures Prizms White /5 #25
2018 Panini Prizm Team Tandems #6
2018 Panini Prizm Team Tandems Prizms #6
2018 Panini Prizm Team Tandems Prizms Black /1 #6
2018 Panini Prizm Team Tandems Prizms Gold /10 #6
2018 Panini Victory Lane #2
2018 Panini Victory Lane #45
2018 Panini Victory Lane #80
2018 Panini Victory Lane Black /1 #2
2018 Panini Victory Lane Black /1 #45
2018 Panini Victory Lane Black /1 #80
2018 Panini Victory Lane Blue /25 #2
2018 Panini Victory Lane Blue /25 #45
2018 Panini Victory Lane Blue /25 #80
2018 Panini Victory Lane Celebrations #5
2018 Panini Victory Lane Celebrations Black /1 #5
2018 Panini Victory Lane Celebrations Blue /25 #5
2018 Panini Victory Lane Celebrations Gold /99 #5
2018 Panini Victory Lane Celebrations Green /5 #5
2018 Panini Victory Lane Celebrations Printing Plates Black /1 #5
2018 Panini Victory Lane Celebrations Printing Plates Cyan /1 #5
2018 Panini Victory Lane Celebrations Printing Plates Magenta /1 #5
2018 Panini Victory Lane Celebrations Printing Plates Yellow /1 #5
2018 Panini Victory Lane Celebrations Red /49 #5
2018 Panini Victory Lane Champions #12
2018 Panini Victory Lane Champions Black /1 #12
2018 Panini Victory Lane Champions Blue /25 #12
2018 Panini Victory Lane Champions Gold /99 #12
2018 Panini Victory Lane Champions Green /5 #12
2018 Panini Victory Lane Champions Printing Plates Black /1 #12
2018 Panini Victory Lane Champions Printing Plates Cyan /1 #12
2018 Panini Victory Lane Champions Printing Plates Magenta /1 #12
2018 Panini Victory Lane Champions Printing Plates Yellow /1 #12
2018 Panini Victory Lane Champions Red /49 #12
2018 Panini Victory Lane Engineered to Perfection Materials /399 #2
2018 Panini Victory Lane Engineered to Perfection Materials Black /25 #2
2018 Panini Victory Lane Engineered to Perfection Materials Gold /199 #2
2018 Panini Victory Lane Engineered to Perfection Materials Green /99 #2
2018 Panini Victory Lane Engineered to Perfection Materials Laundry Tag /1 #2
2018 Panini Victory Lane Gold /99 #2
2018 Panini Victory Lane Gold /99 #45
2018 Panini Victory Lane Gold /99 #80
2018 Panini Victory Lane Green /5 #2
2018 Panini Victory Lane Green /5 #45
2018 Panini Victory Lane Green /5 #80
2018 Panini Victory Lane Pedal to the Metal #5
2018 Panini Victory Lane Pedal to the Metal #52
2018 Panini Victory Lane Pedal to the Metal Black /1 #5
2018 Panini Victory Lane Pedal to the Metal Black /1 #52
2018 Panini Victory Lane Pedal to the Metal Blue /25 #5
2018 Panini Victory Lane Pedal to the Metal Blue /25 #52
2018 Panini Victory Lane Pedal to the Metal Green /5 #5
2018 Panini Victory Lane Pedal to the Metal Green /5 #52
2018 Panini Victory Lane Printing Plates Black /1 #2
2018 Panini Victory Lane Printing Plates Black /1 #45
2018 Panini Victory Lane Printing Plates Black /1 #80
2018 Panini Victory Lane Printing Plates Cyan /1 #2
2018 Panini Victory Lane Printing Plates Cyan /1 #45
2018 Panini Victory Lane Printing Plates Cyan /1 #80
2018 Panini Victory Lane Printing Plates Magenta /1 #2
2018 Panini Victory Lane Printing Plates Magenta /1 #45
2018 Panini Victory Lane Printing Plates Magenta /1 #80
2018 Panini Victory Lane Printing Plates Yellow /1 #2
2018 Panini Victory Lane Printing Plates Yellow /1 #45
2018 Panini Victory Lane Printing Plates Yellow /1 #80
2018 Panini Victory Lane Race Day #8
2018 Panini Victory Lane Race Day Black /1 #8
2018 Panini Victory Lane Race Day Blue /25 #8
2018 Panini Victory Lane Race Day Gold /99 #8
2018 Panini Victory Lane Race Day Green /5 #8
2018 Panini Victory Lane Race Day Printing Plates Black /1 #8
2018 Panini Victory Lane Race Day Printing Plates Cyan /1 #8
2018 Panini Victory Lane Race Day Printing Plates Magenta /1 #8
2018 Panini Victory Lane Race Day Printing Plates Yellow /1 #8
2018 Panini Victory Lane Race Day Red /49 #8
2018 Panini Victory Lane Red /49 #2
2018 Panini Victory Lane Red /49 #45
2018 Panini Victory Lane Red /49 #80
2018 Panini Victory Lane Silver #2
2018 Panini Victory Lane Silver #45
2018 Panini Victory Lane Silver #80
2018 Panini Victory Lane Starting Grid #2
2018 Panini Victory Lane Starting Grid Black /1 #2
2018 Panini Victory Lane Starting Grid Blue /25 #2
2018 Panini Victory Lane Starting Grid Gold /99 #2
2018 Panini Victory Lane Starting Grid Green /5 #2
2018 Panini Victory Lane Starting Grid Printing Plates Black /1 #2
2018 Panini Victory Lane Starting Grid Printing Plates Cyan /1 #2
2018 Panini Victory Lane Starting Grid Printing Plates Magenta /1 #2
2018 Panini Victory Lane Starting Grid Printing Plates Yellow /1 #2
2018 Panini Victory Lane Starting Grid Red /49 #2
2018 Panini Victory Lane Victory Marks /125 #2
2018 Panini Victory Lane Victory Marks Black /1 #2
2018 Panini Victory Lane Victory Marks Gold /99 #2
2019 Donruss #2
2019 Donruss #56
2019 Donruss #90
2019 Donruss #113
2019 Donruss Artist Proofs /25 #2
2019 Donruss Artist Proofs /25 #56
2019 Donruss Artist Proofs /25 #90
2019 Donruss Artist Proofs /25 #113
2019 Donruss Black /199 #2
2019 Donruss Black /199 #56
2019 Donruss Black /199 #90
2019 Donruss Black /199 #113
2019 Donruss Classics #10
2019 Donruss Classics Cracked Ice /25 #10
2019 Donruss Classics Holographic #10
2019 Donruss Classics Xplosion /10 #10
2019 Donruss Contenders #4
2019 Donruss Contenders Cracked Ice /25 #4
2019 Donruss Contenders Holographic #4
2019 Donruss Contenders Xplosion /10 #4
2019 Donruss Gold /299 #2
2019 Donruss Gold /299 #56
2019 Donruss Gold /299 #90
2019 Donruss Gold /299 #113
2019 Donruss Gold Press Proofs /99 #2
2019 Donruss Gold Press Proofs /99 #56
2019 Donruss Gold Press Proofs /99 #90
2019 Donruss Gold Press Proofs /99 #113
2019 Donruss Optic #18
2019 Donruss Optic Blue Pulsar #18
2019 Donruss Optic Gold /10 #18
2019 Donruss Optic Gold Vinyl /1 #18
2019 Donruss Optic Holo #18
2019 Donruss Optic Red Wave #18
2019 Donruss Optic Signatures Gold Vinyl /1 #18
2019 Donruss Optic Signatures Holo /75 #18
2019 Donruss Originals #9
2019 Donruss Originals Cracked Ice /25 #9
2019 Donruss Originals Holographic #9
2019 Donruss Originals Xplosion /10 #9
2019 Donruss Press Proofs /49 #56
2019 Donruss Press Proofs /49 #90
2019 Donruss Press Proofs /49 #113
2019 Donruss Press Proofs /49 #2
2019 Donruss Printing Plates Black /1 #2
2019 Donruss Printing Plates Black /1 #56
2019 Donruss Printing Plates Black /1 #90
2019 Donruss Printing Plates Black /1 #113
2019 Donruss Printing Plates Cyan /1 #2
2019 Donruss Printing Plates Cyan /1 #56
2019 Donruss Printing Plates Cyan /1 #90
2019 Donruss Printing Plates Cyan /1 #113
2019 Donruss Printing Plates Magenta /1 #56
2019 Donruss Printing Plates Magenta /1 #90
2019 Donruss Printing Plates Magenta /1 #113
2019 Donruss Printing Plates Magenta /1 #2
2019 Donruss Printing Plates Yellow /1 #2
2019 Donruss Printing Plates Yellow /1 #56
2019 Donruss Printing Plates Yellow /1 #90
2019 Donruss Printing Plates Yellow /1 #113
2019 Donruss Retro Relics '86 #19
2019 Donruss Retro Relics '86 Holo Black /10 #19
2019 Donruss Retro Relics '86 Holo Gold /25 #19
2019 Donruss Retro Relics '86 Red /225 #19
2019 Donruss Signature Series #35
2019 Donruss Signature Series Holo Black /10 #35
2019 Donruss Signature Series Holo Gold /25 #35
2019 Donruss Signature Series Red /150 #35
2019 Donruss Silver #2
2019 Donruss Silver #56
2019 Donruss Silver #90
2019 Donruss Silver #113
2019 Donruss Top Tier #9
2019 Donruss Top Tier Cracked Ice /25 #9
2019 Donruss Top Tier Holographic #9
2019 Donruss Top Tier Xplosion /10 #9
2019 Panini Prime /50 #2
2019 Panini Prime /50 #36
2019 Panini Prime /50 #69
2019 Panini Prime Black /10 #2
2019 Panini Prime Black /10 #36
2019 Panini Prime Black /10 #69
2019 Panini Prime Clear Silhouettes /99 #10
2019 Panini Prime Clear Silhouettes Black /10 #10
2019 Panini Prime Clear Silhouettes Holo Gold /25 #10
2019 Panini Prime Clear Silhouettes Platinum Blue /1 #10
2019 Panini Prime Emerald /5 #2
2019 Panini Prime Emerald /5 #36
2019 Panini Prime Emerald /5 #69
2019 Panini Prime Hats Off Button /1 #15
2019 Panini Prime Hats Off Eyelets /6 #15
2019 Panini Prime Hats Off Headband /28 #15
2019 Panini Prime Hats Off Laundry Tags /2 #15
2019 Panini Prime Hats Off New Era /1 #15
2019 Panini Prime Hats Off Number /3 #15
2019 Panini Prime Hats Off Sponsor Logo /8 #15
2019 Panini Prime Hats Off Team Logo /3 #15
2019 Panini Prime Jumbo Material Signatures Firesuit /10 #4
2019 Panini Prime Jumbo Material Signatures Firesuit Platinum Blue /1 #4
2019 Panini Prime Jumbo Material Signatures Sheet Metal /25 #4
2019 Panini Prime Jumbo Material Signatures Tire /99 #4
2019 Panini Prime NASCAR Shadowbox Signatures Car Number /99 #9
2019 Panini Prime NASCAR Shadowbox Signatures Manufacturer /10 #9
2019 Panini Prime NASCAR Shadowbox Signatures Sponsor /25 #9
2019 Panini Prime NASCAR Shadowbox Signatures Team Owner /1 #9
2019 Panini Prime Platinum Blue /1 #2
2019 Panini Prime Platinum Blue /1 #36
2019 Panini Prime Platinum Blue /1 #69
2019 Panini Prime Prime Cars Die Cut Signatures /99 #2
2019 Panini Prime Prime Cars Die Cut Signatures Black /10 #2
2019 Panini Prime Prime Cars Die Cut Signatures Holo Gold /25 #2
2019 Panini Prime Prime Cars Die Cut Signatures Platinum Blue /1 #2
2019 Panini Prime Prime Jumbo Associate Sponsor 1 /1 #6
2019 Panini Prime Prime Jumbo Associate Sponsor 1 /1 #7
2019 Panini Prime Prime Jumbo Associate Sponsor 2 /1 #6
2019 Panini Prime Prime Jumbo Associate Sponsor 2 /1 #7
2019 Panini Prime Prime Jumbo Associate Sponsor 3 /1 #6
2019 Panini Prime Prime Jumbo Associate Sponsor 3 /1 #7
2019 Panini Prime Prime Jumbo Associate Sponsor 4 /1 #6
2019 Panini Prime Prime Jumbo Associate Sponsor 4 /1 #7
2019 Panini Prime Prime Jumbo Associate Sponsor 5 /1 #6
2019 Panini Prime Prime Jumbo Associate Sponsor 5 /1 #7
2019 Panini Prime Prime Jumbo Associate Sponsor 6 /1 #6
2019 Panini Prime Prime Jumbo Associate Sponsor 6 /1 #7
2019 Panini Prime Prime Jumbo Associate Sponsor 7 /1 #6
2019 Panini Prime Prime Jumbo Associate Sponsor 7 /1 #7
2019 Panini Prime Prime Jumbo Associate Sponsor 8 /1 #6
2019 Panini Prime Prime Jumbo Associate Sponsor 8 /1 #7
2019 Panini Prime Prime Jumbo Car Manufacturer /1 #6
2019 Panini Prime Prime Jumbo Car Manufacturer /1 #7
2019 Panini Prime Prime Jumbo Firesuit Manufacturer /1 #6
2019 Panini Prime Prime Jumbo Firesuit Manufacturer /1 #7
2019 Panini Prime Prime Jumbo Flag Patch /1 #6
2019 Panini Prime Prime Jumbo Goodyear /1 #7
2019 Panini Prime Prime Jumbo Nameplate /2 #6
2019 Panini Prime Prime Jumbo Nameplate /2 #7
2019 Panini Prime Prime Jumbo NASCAR /1 #6
2019 Panini Prime Prime Jumbo NASCAR /1 #7
2019 Panini Prime Prime Jumbo Prime Colors /10 #6
2019 Panini Prime Prime Jumbo Prime Colors /24 #7
2019 Panini Prime Prime Jumbo Series Sponsor /1 #6
2019 Panini Prime Prime Jumbo Series Sponsor /1 #7
2019 Panini Prime Prime Jumbo Sunoco /1 #6
2019 Panini Prime Prime Jumbo Sunoco /1 #7
2019 Panini Prime Quad Materials Autographs /99 #4
2019 Panini Prime Quad Materials Autographs Black /10 #4
2019 Panini Prime Quad Materials Autographs Holo Gold /25 #4
2019 Panini Prime Quad Materials Autographs Laundry Tags /1 #4
2019 Panini Prime Race Used Duals Firesuits /50 #9
2019 Panini Prime Race Used Duals Firesuits Black /10 #9
2019 Panini Prime Race Used Duals Firesuits Holo Gold /25 #9
2019 Panini Prime Race Used Duals Firesuits Laundry Tags /1 #9
2019 Panini Prime Race Used Duals Sheet Metal /50 #9
2019 Panini Prime Race Used Duals Sheet Metal Black /10 #9
2019 Panini Prime Race Used Duals Sheet Metal Holo Gold /25 #9
2019 Panini Prime Race Used Duals Sheet Metal Platinum Blue /1 #9
2019 Panini Prime Race Used Duals Tires /50 #9
2019 Panini Prime Race Used Duals Tires Black /10 #9
2019 Panini Prime Race Used Duals Tires Holo Gold /25 #9
2019 Panini Prime Race Used Duals Tires Platinum Blue /1 #9
2019 Panini Prime Race Used Firesuits /50 #9
2019 Panini Prime Race Used Firesuits Black /10 #9
2019 Panini Prime Race Used Firesuits Holo Gold /25 #9
2019 Panini Prime Race Used Firesuits Laundry Tags /1 #9
2019 Panini Prime Race Used Sheet Metal /50 #9
2019 Panini Prime Race Used Sheet Metal Black /10 #9
2019 Panini Prime Race Used Sheet Metal Holo Gold /25 #9
2019 Panini Prime Race Used Sheet Metal Platinum Blue /1 #9
2019 Panini Prime Race Used Tires /50 #9
2019 Panini Prime Race Used Tires Black /10 #9
2019 Panini Prime Race Used Tires Holo Gold /25 #9
2019 Panini Prime Race Used Tires Platinum Blue /1 #9
2019 Panini Prime Race Used Trios Firesuits /50 #9
2019 Panini Prime Race Used Trios Firesuits Black /10 #9
2019 Panini Prime Race Used Trios Firesuits Holo Gold /25 #9
2019 Panini Prime Race Used Trios Firesuits Laundry Tags /1 #9
2019 Panini Prime Race Used Trios Sheet Metal /50 #9
2019 Panini Prime Race Used Trios Sheet Metal Black /10 #9
2019 Panini Prime Race Used Trios Sheet Metal Holo Gold /25 #9
2019 Panini Prime Race Used Trios Sheet Metal Platinum Blue /1 #9

2019 Panini Prime Race Used Trios Tires /50 #9
2019 Panini Prime Race Used Trios Tires Black /10 #9
2019 Panini Prime Race Used Trios Tires Holo Gold /25 #9
2019 Panini Prime Race Used Trios Tires Platinum Blue /1 #9
2019 Panini Prizm #2
2019 Panini Prizm #69
2019 Panini Prizm Expert Level #9
2019 Panini Prizm Expert Level Prizms #9
2019 Panini Prizm Expert Level Prizms Black /1 #9
2019 Panini Prizm Expert Level Prizms Gold /10 #9
2019 Panini Prizm Expert Level Prizms White Sparkle #9
2019 Panini Prizm Fireworks #12
2019 Panini Prizm Fireworks Prizms #12
2019 Panini Prizm Fireworks Prizms Black /1 #12
2019 Panini Prizm Fireworks Prizms Gold /10 #12
2019 Panini Prizm Fireworks Prizms White Sparkle #12
2019 Panini Prizm In the Groove #8
2019 Panini Prizm In the Groove Prizms #8
2019 Panini Prizm In the Groove Prizms Black /1 #8
2019 Panini Prizm In the Groove Prizms Gold /10 #8
2019 Panini Prizm In the Groove Prizms White Sparkle #8
2019 Panini Prizm National Pride #6
2019 Panini Prizm National Pride Prizms #6
2019 Panini Prizm National Pride Prizms Black /1 #6
2019 Panini Prizm National Pride Prizms Gold /10 #6
2019 Panini Prizm National Pride Prizms White Sparkle #6
2019 Panini Prizm Prizms #69
2019 Panini Prizm Prizms #2
2019 Panini Prizm Prizms Black /1 #2
2019 Panini Prizm Prizms Black /1 #69
2019 Panini Prizm Prizms Blue /75 #2
2019 Panini Prizm Prizms Blue /75 #69
2019 Panini Prizm Prizms Camo #2
2019 Panini Prizm Prizms Camo #69
2019 Panini Prizm Prizms Flash #2
2019 Panini Prizm Prizms Flash #69
2019 Panini Prizm Prizms Gold /10 #2
2019 Panini Prizm Prizms Gold /10 #69
2019 Panini Prizm Prizms Green /99 #2
2019 Panini Prizm Prizms Green /99 #69
2019 Panini Prizm Prizms Rainbow /24 #2
2019 Panini Prizm Prizms Rainbow /24 #69
2019 Panini Prizm Prizms Red /50 #2
2019 Panini Prizm Prizms Red /50 #69
2019 Panini Prizm Prizms Red White and Blue #2
2019 Panini Prizm Prizms Red White and Blue #69
2019 Panini Prizm Prizms White /5 #2
2019 Panini Prizm Prizms White /5 #69
2019 Panini Prizm Prizms White Sparkle #2
2019 Panini Prizm Prizms White Sparkle #69
2019 Panini Prizm Signing Sessions Prizms #4
2019 Panini Prizm Signing Sessions Prizms Black /1 #4
2019 Panini Prizm Signing Sessions Prizms Blue /30 #4
2019 Panini Prizm Signing Sessions Prizms Camo #4
2019 Panini Prizm Signing Sessions Prizms Gold /10 #4
2019 Panini Prizm Signing Sessions Prizms Green /35 #4
2019 Panini Prizm Signing Sessions Prizms Rainbow /24 #4
2019 Panini Prizm Signing Sessions Prizms Red /25 #4
2019 Panini Prizm Signing Sessions Prizms Red White and Blue #4
2019 Panini Prizm Signing Sessions Prizms White /5 #4
2019 Panini Prizm Stars and Stripes #12
2019 Panini Prizm Stars and Stripes Prizms #12
2019 Panini Prizm Stars and Stripes Prizms Black /1 #12
2019 Panini Prizm Stars and Stripes Prizms Gold /10 #12
2019 Panini Prizm Stars and Stripes Prizms White Sparkle #12
2019 Panini Prizm Teammates #5
2019 Panini Prizm Teammates Prizms #5
2019 Panini Prizm Teammates Prizms Black /1 #5
2019 Panini Prizm Teammates Prizms Gold /10 #5
2019 Panini Prizm Teammates Prizms White Sparkle #5
2019 Panini Victory Lane #2
2019 Panini Victory Lane #51
2019 Panini Victory Lane #66
2019 Panini Victory Lane Black /1 #2
2019 Panini Victory Lane Black /1 #51
2019 Panini Victory Lane Black /1 #66
2019 Panini Victory Lane Celebrations #8
2019 Panini Victory Lane Celebrations #11
2019 Panini Victory Lane Celebrations Black /1 #8
2019 Panini Victory Lane Celebrations Black /1 #11
2019 Panini Victory Lane Celebrations Blue /99 #8
2019 Panini Victory Lane Celebrations Blue /99 #11
2019 Panini Victory Lane Celebrations Gold /25 #8
2019 Panini Victory Lane Celebrations Gold /25 #11
2019 Panini Victory Lane Celebrations Green /5 #8
2019 Panini Victory Lane Celebrations Green /5 #11
2019 Panini Victory Lane Celebrations Printing Plates Black /1 #8
2019 Panini Victory Lane Celebrations Printing Plates Black /1 #11
2019 Panini Victory Lane Celebrations Printing Plates Cyan /1 #8
2019 Panini Victory Lane Celebrations Printing Plates Cyan /1 #11
2019 Panini Victory Lane Celebrations Printing Plates Magenta /1 #8
2019 Panini Victory Lane Celebrations Printing Plates Magenta /1 #11
2019 Panini Victory Lane Celebrations Printing Plates Yellow /1 #8
2019 Panini Victory Lane Celebrations Printing Plates Yellow /1 #11
2019 Panini Victory Lane Dual Swatch Signatures #2
2019 Panini Victory Lane Dual Swatch Signatures Gold /99 #2
2019 Panini Victory Lane Dual Swatch Signatures Laundry Tag /1 #2
2019 Panini Victory Lane Dual Swatch Signatures Platinum /1 #2
2019 Panini Victory Lane Dual Swatch Signatures Red /25 #2
2019 Panini Victory Lane Dual Swatches #4
2019 Panini Victory Lane Dual Swatches Gold /99 #4
2019 Panini Victory Lane Dual Swatches Laundry Tag /1 #4
2019 Panini Victory Lane Dual Swatches Platinum /1 #4
2019 Panini Victory Lane Dual Swatches Red /25 #4
2019 Panini Victory Lane Gold /25 #2
2019 Panini Victory Lane Gold /25 #51
2019 Panini Victory Lane Gold /25 #66
2019 Panini Victory Lane Horsepower Heroes #9
2019 Panini Victory Lane Horsepower Heroes Black /1 #9
2019 Panini Victory Lane Horsepower Heroes Blue /99 #9
2019 Panini Victory Lane Horsepower Heroes Gold /25 #9
2019 Panini Victory Lane Horsepower Heroes Green /5 #9
2019 Panini Victory Lane Horsepower Heroes Printing Plates Black /1 #9
2019 Panini Victory Lane Horsepower Heroes Printing Plates Cyan /1 #9
2019 Panini Victory Lane Horsepower Heroes Printing Plates Magenta /1 #9
2019 Panini Victory Lane Horsepower Heroes Printing Plates Yellow /1 #9
2019 Panini Victory Lane Machines #11
2019 Panini Victory Lane Machines Black /1 #11
2019 Panini Victory Lane Machines Blue /99 #11
2019 Panini Victory Lane Machines Gold /25 #11
2019 Panini Victory Lane Machines Green /5 #11
2019 Panini Victory Lane Machines Printing Plates Black /1 #11
2019 Panini Victory Lane Machines Printing Plates Cyan /1 #11
2019 Panini Victory Lane Machines Printing Plates Magenta /1 #11
2019 Panini Victory Lane Machines Printing Plates Yellow /1 #11
2019 Panini Victory Lane Pedal to the Metal #14
2019 Panini Victory Lane Pedal to the Metal #53
2019 Panini Victory Lane Pedal to the Metal #82
2019 Panini Victory Lane Pedal to the Metal Black /1 #14
2019 Panini Victory Lane Pedal to the Metal Black /1 #53
2019 Panini Victory Lane Pedal to the Metal Black /1 #82
2019 Panini Victory Lane Pedal to the Metal Gold /25 #14
2019 Panini Victory Lane Pedal to the Metal Gold /25 #53
2019 Panini Victory Lane Pedal to the Metal Gold /25 #82
2019 Panini Victory Lane Pedal to the Metal Green /5 #14
2019 Panini Victory Lane Pedal to the Metal Green /5 #53
2019 Panini Victory Lane Pedal to the Metal Green /5 #82
2019 Panini Victory Lane Pedal to the Metal Red /3 #14
2019 Panini Victory Lane Pedal to the Metal Red /3 #53
2019 Panini Victory Lane Pedal to the Metal Red /3 #82
2019 Panini Victory Lane Printing Plates Black /1 #2
2019 Panini Victory Lane Printing Plates Black /1 #51
2019 Panini Victory Lane Printing Plates Black /1 #66
2019 Panini Victory Lane Printing Plates Cyan /1 #2
2019 Panini Victory Lane Printing Plates Cyan /1 #51
2019 Panini Victory Lane Printing Plates Cyan /1 #66
2019 Panini Victory Lane Printing Plates Magenta /1 #2
2019 Panini Victory Lane Printing Plates Magenta /1 #51
2019 Panini Victory Lane Printing Plates Magenta /1 #66
2019 Panini Victory Lane Printing Plates Yellow /1 #2
2019 Panini Victory Lane Printing Plates Yellow /1 #51
2019 Panini Victory Lane Printing Plates Yellow /1 #66
2019 Panini Victory Lane Starting Grid #23
2019 Panini Victory Lane Starting Grid Black /1 #23
2019 Panini Victory Lane Starting Grid Blue /99 #23
2019 Panini Victory Lane Starting Grid Gold /25 #23
2019 Panini Victory Lane Starting Grid Green /5 #23
2019 Panini Victory Lane Starting Grid Printing Plates Black /1 #23
2019 Panini Victory Lane Starting Grid Printing Plates Cyan /1 #23
2019 Panini Victory Lane Starting Grid Printing Plates Magenta /1 #23
2019 Panini Victory Lane Starting Grid Printing Plates Yellow /1 #23
2019 Panini Victory Lane Top 10 #8
2019 Panini Victory Lane Top 10 Black /1 #8
2019 Panini Victory Lane Top 10 Blue /99 #8
2019 Panini Victory Lane Top 10 Gold /25 #8
2019 Panini Victory Lane Top 10 Green /5 #8
2019 Panini Victory Lane Top 10 Printing Plates Black /1 #8
2019 Panini Victory Lane Top 10 Printing Plates Cyan /1 #8
2019 Panini Victory Lane Top 10 Printing Plates Magenta /1 #8
2019 Panini Victory Lane Top 10 Printing Plates Yellow /1 #8
2019 Panini Victory Lane Track Stars #13
2019 Panini Victory Lane Track Stars Black /1 #13
2019 Panini Victory Lane Track Stars Blue /99 #13
2019 Panini Victory Lane Track Stars Gold /25 #13
2019 Panini Victory Lane Track Stars Green /5 #13
2019 Panini Victory Lane Track Stars Printing Plates Black /1 #13
2019 Panini Victory Lane Track Stars Printing Plates Cyan /1 #13
2019 Panini Victory Lane Track Stars Printing Plates Magenta /1 #13
2019 Panini Victory Lane Track Stars Printing Plates Yellow /1 #13
2020 Donruss #2
2020 Donruss #26
2020 Donruss #105
2020 Donruss #148
2020 Donruss #190
2020 Donruss Aero Package #9
2020 Donruss Aero Package Checkers #9
2020 Donruss Aero Package Cracked Ice /25 #9
2020 Donruss Aero Package Holographic /199 #9
2020 Donruss Aero Package Xplosion /10 #9
2020 Donruss Black Numbers /2 #2
2020 Donruss Black Numbers /2 #26
2020 Donruss Black Numbers /2 #105
2020 Donruss Black Numbers /2 #148
2020 Donruss Black Numbers /2 #190
2020 Donruss Black Trophy Club /1 #2
2020 Donruss Black Trophy Club /1 #26
2020 Donruss Black Trophy Club /1 #105
2020 Donruss Black Trophy Club /1 #148
2020 Donruss Black Trophy Club /1 #190
2020 Donruss Blue /199 #105
2020 Donruss Blue /199 #148
2020 Donruss Blue /199 #190
2020 Donruss Blue /199 #2
2020 Donruss Blue /199 #26
2020 Donruss Carolina Blue #2
2020 Donruss Carolina Blue #26
2020 Donruss Carolina Blue #105
2020 Donruss Carolina Blue #148
2020 Donruss Carolina Blue #190
2020 Donruss Contenders #5
2020 Donruss Contenders Checkers #5
2020 Donruss Contenders Cracked Ice /25 #5
2020 Donruss Contenders Holographic /199 #5
2020 Donruss Contenders Xplosion /10 #5
2020 Donruss Elite Series #6
2020 Donruss Elite Series Checkers #6
2020 Donruss Elite Series Cracked Ice /25 #6
2020 Donruss Elite Series Holographic /199 #6
2020 Donruss Elite Series Xplosion /10 #6
2020 Donruss Green /99 #2
2020 Donruss Green /99 #26
2020 Donruss Green /99 #105
2020 Donruss Green /99 #148
2020 Donruss Green /99 #190
2020 Donruss Optic #2
2020 Donruss Optic Carolina Blue Wave #2
2020 Donruss Optic Gold /10 #2
2020 Donruss Optic Gold Vinyl /1 #2
2020 Donruss Optic Holo #2
2020 Donruss Optic Orange Pulsar #2
2020 Donruss Optic Red Mojo #2
2020 Donruss Optic Signatures Gold Vinyl /1 #2
2020 Donruss Optic Signatures Holo /99 #2
2020 Donruss Orange #190
2020 Donruss Orange #2
2020 Donruss Orange #26
2020 Donruss Orange #105
2020 Donruss Orange #148
2020 Donruss Pink /25 #2
2020 Donruss Pink /25 #26
2020 Donruss Pink /25 #105
2020 Donruss Pink /25 #148
2020 Donruss Pink /25 #190
2020 Donruss Printing Plates Black /1 #2
2020 Donruss Printing Plates Black /1 #26
2020 Donruss Printing Plates Black /1 #105
2020 Donruss Printing Plates Black /1 #148
2020 Donruss Printing Plates Black /1 #190
2020 Donruss Printing Plates Cyan /1 #2
2020 Donruss Printing Plates Cyan /1 #26
2020 Donruss Printing Plates Cyan /1 #105
2020 Donruss Printing Plates Cyan /1 #148
2020 Donruss Printing Plates Cyan /1 #190
2020 Donruss Printing Plates Magenta /1 #26
2020 Donruss Printing Plates Magenta /1 #105
2020 Donruss Printing Plates Magenta /1 #148
2020 Donruss Printing Plates Magenta /1 #190
2020 Donruss Printing Plates Magenta /1 #2
2020 Donruss Printing Plates Yellow /1 #148
2020 Donruss Printing Plates Yellow /1 #190
2020 Donruss Printing Plates Yellow /1 #2
2020 Donruss Printing Plates Yellow /1 #26
2020 Donruss Printing Plates Yellow /1 #105
2020 Donruss Purple /49 #2
2020 Donruss Purple /49 #26
2020 Donruss Purple /49 #105
2020 Donruss Purple /49 #148
2020 Donruss Purple /49 #190
2020 Donruss Race Day Relics #4
2020 Donruss Race Day Relics Holo Black /10 #4
2020 Donruss Race Day Relics Holo Gold /25 #4
2020 Donruss Race Day Relics Red /250 #4
2020 Donruss Red /299 #2
2020 Donruss Red /299 #26
2020 Donruss Red /299 #105
2020 Donruss Red /299 #148
2020 Donruss Red /299 #190
2020 Donruss Retro Series #9
2020 Donruss Retro Series Checkers #9
2020 Donruss Retro Series Cracked Ice /25 #9
2020 Donruss Retro Series Holographic /199 #9
2020 Donruss Retro Series Xplosion /10 #9
2020 Donruss Silver #2
2020 Donruss Silver #26
2020 Donruss Silver #105
2020 Donruss Silver #148
2020 Donruss Silver #190

Kyle Larson

2013 Press Pass Fanfare #68
2013 Press Pass Fanfare Autographs Blue /10 #KL
2013 Press Pass Fanfare Autographs Gold /125 #KL
2013 Press Pass Fanfare Autographs Green /10 #KL
2013 Press Pass Fanfare Autographs Red /99 #KL
2013 Press Pass Fanfare Autographs Silver /225 #KL
2013 Press Pass Fanfare Diamond Die Cuts /5 #68
2013 Press Pass Fanfare Green /3 #68
2013 Press Pass Fanfare Holofoil Die Cuts #68
2013 Press Pass Fanfare Magnificent Materials Gold /50 #KL
2013 Press Pass Fanfare Magnificent Materials Silver /199 #KL
2013 Press Pass Fanfare Red Foil Die Cuts #68
2013 Press Pass Fanfare Sapphire /20 #68
2013 Press Pass Fanfare Silver /25 #68
2013 Total Memorabilia #47
2013 Total Memorabilia Black and White /99 #47
2013 Total Memorabilia Gold /275 #47
2013 Total Memorabilia Red #47
2013 Total Memorabilia Rising Stars Autographs Gold /99 #RSAKL
2013 Total Memorabilia Rising Stars Autographs Holofoil /25 #RSAKL
2013 Total Memorabilia Rising Stars Autographs Melting /5 #RSAKL
2013 Total Memorabilia Rising Stars Autographs Silver /125 #RSAKL
2014 Press Pass #43
2014 Press Pass #50
2014 Press Pass American Thunder #23
2014 Press Pass American Thunder #57
2014 Press Pass American Thunder Autographs Blue /10 #ATAKL
2014 Press Pass American Thunder Autographs Red /5 #ATAKL
2014 Press Pass American Thunder Autographs White /25 #ATAKL
2014 Press Pass American Thunder Battle Armor Blue /25 #BAKL
2014 Press Pass American Thunder Battle Armor Red /1 #BAKL
2014 Press Pass American Thunder Battle Armor Silver /99 #BAKL
2014 Press Pass American Thunder Black and White /50 #23
2014 Press Pass American Thunder Black and White /50 #57
2014 Press Pass American Thunder Brothers In Arms Autographs Blue /5 #BACGRFS
2014 Press Pass American Thunder Brothers In Arms Autographs Red /1 #BACGRFS
2014 Press Pass American Thunder Brothers In Arms Autographs White /10 #BACGRFS
2014 Press Pass American Thunder Brothers In Arms Relics Blue /25 #BACGRFS
2014 Press Pass American Thunder Brothers In Arms Relics Red /5 #BACGRFS
2014 Press Pass American Thunder Brothers In Arms Relics Silver /50 #BACGRFS
2014 Press Pass American Thunder Class A Uniforms Blue /99 #CAUKL
2014 Press Pass American Thunder Class A Uniforms Flag /1 #CAUKL
2014 Press Pass American Thunder Class A Uniforms Red /10 #CAUKL
2014 Press Pass American Thunder Class A Uniforms Silver #CAUKL
2014 Press Pass American Thunder Climbing the Ranks #CR2
2014 Press Pass American Thunder Cyan #23
2014 Press Pass American Thunder Cyan #57
2014 Press Pass American Thunder Great American Treads Autographs Blue /25 #GATKL
2014 Press Pass American Thunder Great American Treads Autographs Red /1 #GATKL
2014 Press Pass American Thunder Magenta #23
2014 Press Pass American Thunder Magenta #57
2014 Press Pass American Thunder Yellow /5 #23
2014 Press Pass American Thunder Yellow /5 #57
2014 Press Pass Color Proofs Black /70 #43
2014 Press Pass Color Proofs Black /70 #50
2014 Press Pass Color Proofs Cyan /35 #43
2014 Press Pass Color Proofs Cyan /35 #50
2014 Press Pass Color Proofs Magenta #43
2014 Press Pass Color Proofs Magenta #50
2014 Press Pass Color Proofs Yellow /5 #43
2014 Press Pass Color Proofs Yellow /5 #50
2014 Press Pass Five Star /15 #18
2014 Press Pass Five Star Blue /5 #18
2014 Press Pass Five Star Holofoil /10 #18
2014 Press Pass Five Star Melting /1 #18
2014 Press Pass Gold #43
2014 Press Pass Gold #50
2014 Press Pass Redline #33
2014 Press Pass Redline Black /75 #33
2014 Press Pass Redline Blue Foil #33
2014 Press Pass Redline Cyan /50 #33
2014 Press Pass Redline Dynamic Duals Relic Autographs Blue /25 #DDKL
2014 Press Pass Redline Dynamic Duals Relic Autographs Gold /10 #DDKL
2014 Press Pass Redline Dynamic Duals Relic Autographs Melting /1 #DDKL
2014 Press Pass Redline Dynamic Duals Relic Autographs Red /50 #DDKL
2014 Press Pass Redline Full Throttle Relics Blue /10 #FTKL
2014 Press Pass Redline Full Throttle Relics Gold /25 #FTKL
2014 Press Pass Redline Full Throttle Relics Melting /1 #FTKL
2014 Press Pass Redline Full Throttle Relics Red /50 #FTKL
2014 Press Pass Redline Green National Convention /5 #33
2014 Press Pass Redline Head to Head Blue /10 #HTHKBKL
2014 Press Pass Redline Head to Head Gold /25 #HTHKBKL
2014 Press Pass Redline Head to Head Melting /1 #HTHKBKL
2014 Press Pass Redline Head to Head Red /75 #HTHKBKL
2014 Press Pass Redline Magenta /10 #33
2014 Press Pass Redline Redline Racers #RR12
2014 Press Pass Redline RPM #RPM8
2014 Press Pass Redline Signatures Blue /15 #RSKL
2014 Press Pass Redline Signatures Gold /25 #RSKL
2014 Press Pass Redline Signatures Melting /10 #RSKL
2014 Press Pass Redline Signatures Red /50 #RSKL
2014 Press Pass Redline Yellow /1 #33
2014 Total Memorabilia #33
2014 Total Memorabilia Black and White /99 #33
2014 Total Memorabilia Dirt Track Treads Blue /25 #DTTKL
2014 Total Memorabilia Dirt Track Treads Gold /50 #DTTKL
2014 Total Memorabilia Dirt Track Treads Melting /10 #DTTKL
2014 Total Memorabilia Dirt Track Treads Silver /99 #DTTKL
2014 Total Memorabilia Dual Swatch Gold /65 #TMKL
2014 Total Memorabilia Gold /175 #33
2014 Total Memorabilia Red #33
2014 Total Memorabilia Single Swatch Silver /275 #TMKL
2015 Press Pass #22
2015 Press Pass #73
2015 Press Pass #97
2015 Press Pass Championship Caliber Dual /25 #CCMKL
2015 Press Pass Championship Caliber Quad /1 #CCMKL
2015 Press Pass Championship Caliber Signature Edition Blue /10 #CCKL
2015 Press Pass Championship Caliber Signature Edition Gold /25 #CCKL
2015 Press Pass Championship Caliber Signature Edition Green /5 #CCKL
2015 Press Pass Championship Caliber Signature Edition Melting /1 #CCKL
2015 Press Pass Championship Caliber Single /50 #CCMKL
2015 Press Pass Championship Caliber Triple /10 #CCMKL
2015 Press Pass Cup Chase #22
2015 Press Pass Cup Chase #73
2015 Press Pass Cup Chase #97
2015 Press Pass Cup Chase Blue /25 #22
2015 Press Pass Cup Chase Blue /25 #73
2015 Press Pass Cup Chase Blue /25 #97
2015 Press Pass Cup Chase Gold /75 #22
2015 Press Pass Cup Chase Gold /75 #73
2015 Press Pass Cup Chase Gold /75 #97
2015 Press Pass Cup Chase Green /10 #22
2015 Press Pass Cup Chase Green /10 #73
2015 Press Pass Cup Chase Green /10 #97
2015 Press Pass Cup Chase Melting /1 #22
2015 Press Pass Cup Chase Melting /1 #73
2015 Press Pass Cup Chase Melting /1 #97
2015 Press Pass Cup Chase Upper Cuts /13 #UCKL
2015 Press Pass Cuts Blue /25 #CCCKL
2015 Press Pass Cuts Gold /50 #CCCKL
2015 Press Pass Cuts Green /10 #CCCKL
2015 Press Pass Cuts Melting /1 #CCCKL
2015 Press Pass Pit Road Pieces Blue /25 #PPMKL
2015 Press Pass Pit Road Pieces Gold /50 #PPMKL
2015 Press Pass Pit Road Pieces Green /10 #PPMKL
2015 Press Pass Pit Road Pieces Melting /1 #PPMKL
2015 Press Pass Pit Road Pieces Signature Edition Blue /10 #PRPKL
2015 Press Pass Pit Road Pieces Signature Edition Gold /25 #PRPKL
2015 Press Pass Pit Road Pieces Signature Edition Green /5 #PRPKL
2015 Press Pass Pit Road Pieces Signature Edition Melting /1 #PRPKL
2015 Press Pass Purple #22
2015 Press Pass Purple #73
2015 Press Pass Purple #97
2015 Press Pass Red #22
2015 Press Pass Red #73
2015 Press Pass Red #97
2015 Press Pass Signature Series Blue /10 #SSKL
2015 Press Pass Signature Series Gold /25 #SSKL
2015 Press Pass Signature Series Green /5 #SSKL
2015 Press Pass Signature Series Melting /1 #SSKL
2015 Press Pass Signings Blue /15 #PPSKL
2015 Press Pass Signings Gold #PPSKL
2015 Press Pass Signings Green /5 #PPSKL
2015 Press Pass Signings Melting /1 #PPSKL
2015 Press Pass Signings Red /10 #PPSKL
2016 Certified #19
2016 Certified Complete Materials /199 #16
2016 Certified Complete Materials Mirror Blue /50 #16
2016 Certified Complete Materials Mirror Green /5 #16
2016 Certified Complete Materials Mirror Purple /10 #16
2016 Certified Complete Materials Mirror Silver /99 #16
2016 Certified Mirror Black /1 #19
2016 Certified Mirror Blue /50 #19
2016 Certified Mirror Gold /25 #19
2016 Certified Mirror Green /5 #19
2016 Certified Mirror Orange /99 #19
2016 Certified Mirror Purple /10 #19
2016 Certified Mirror Red /75 #19
2016 Certified Mirror Silver /99 #19
2016 Certified Signatures /75 #39
2016 Certified Signatures Mirror Black /1 #39
2016 Certified Signatures Mirror Blue /35 #39
2016 Certified Signatures Mirror Gold /25 #39
2016 Certified Signatures Mirror Green /5 #39
2016 Certified Signatures Mirror Orange /50 #39
2016 Certified Signatures Mirror Purple /10 #39
2016 Certified Signatures Mirror Red /49 #39
2016 Certified Signatures Mirror Silver /50 #39
2016 Certified Sprint Cup Swatches /199 #18
2016 Certified Sprint Cup Swatches Mirror Black /1 #18
2016 Certified Sprint Cup Swatches Mirror Blue /50 #18
2016 Certified Sprint Cup Swatches Mirror Gold /25 #18
2016 Certified Sprint Cup Swatches Mirror Green /5 #18
2016 Certified Sprint Cup Swatches Mirror Orange /50 #18
2016 Certified Sprint Cup Swatches Mirror Purple /10 #18
2016 Certified Sprint Cup Swatches Mirror Red /75 #18
2016 Certified Sprint Cup Swatches Mirror Silver /50 #18
2016 Panini National Treasures Combo Materials /25 #11
2016 Panini National Treasures Combo Materials Black /5 #11
2016 Panini National Treasures Combo Materials Blue /1 #11
2016 Panini National Treasures Combo Materials Gold /10 #11
2016 Panini National Treasures Combo Materials Printing Plates Black /1 #11
2016 Panini National Treasures Combo Materials Printing Plates Cyan /1 #11
2016 Panini National Treasures Combo Materials Printing Plates Magenta /1 #11
2016 Panini National Treasures Combo Materials Printing Plates Yellow /1 #11
2016 Panini National Treasures Combo Materials Silver /15 #11
2016 Panini National Treasures Dual Driver Materials /25 #13
2016 Panini National Treasures Dual Driver Materials Black /5 #13
2016 Panini National Treasures Dual Driver Materials Blue /1 #13
2016 Panini National Treasures Dual Driver Materials Gold /10 #13
2016 Panini National Treasures Dual Driver Materials Printing Plates Black /1 #13
2016 Panini National Treasures Dual Driver Materials Printing Plates Cyan /1 #13
2016 Panini National Treasures Dual Driver Materials Printing Plates Magenta /1 #13
2016 Panini National Treasures Dual Driver Materials Printing Plates Yellow /1 #13
2016 Panini National Treasures Dual Driver Materials Silver /15 #13
2016 Panini National Treasures Dual Signatures /25 #2
2016 Panini National Treasures Dual Signatures Black /10 #2
2016 Panini National Treasures Dual Signatures Blue /1 #2
2016 Panini National Treasures Dual Signatures Gold /15 #2
2016 Panini National Treasures Jumbo Firesuit Patch Signature Booklet Associate Sponsor 1 /1 #18
2016 Panini National Treasures Jumbo Firesuit Patch Signature Booklet Associate Sponsor 10 /1 #18
2016 Panini National Treasures Jumbo Firesuit Patch Signature Booklet Associate Sponsor 11 /1 #18
2016 Panini National Treasures Jumbo Firesuit Patch Signature Booklet Associate Sponsor 12 /1 #18
2016 Panini National Treasures Jumbo Firesuit Patch Signature Booklet Associate Sponsor 13 /1 #18
2016 Panini National Treasures Jumbo Firesuit Patch Signature Booklet Associate Sponsor 14 /1 #18
2016 Panini National Treasures Jumbo Firesuit Patch Signature Booklet Associate Sponsor 15 /1 #18
2016 Panini National Treasures Jumbo Firesuit Patch Signature Booklet Associate Sponsor 16 /1 #18
2016 Panini National Treasures Jumbo Firesuit Patch Signature Booklet Associate Sponsor 17 /1 #18
2016 Panini National Treasures Jumbo Firesuit Patch Signature Booklet Associate Sponsor 18 /1 #18
2016 Panini National Treasures Jumbo Firesuit Patch Signature Booklet Associate Sponsor 19 /1 #18
2016 Panini National Treasures Jumbo Firesuit Patch Signature Booklet Associate Sponsor 2 /1 #18
2016 Panini National Treasures Jumbo Firesuit Patch Signature Booklet Associate Sponsor 20 /1 #18
2016 Panini National Treasures Jumbo Firesuit Patch Signature Booklet Associate Sponsor 3 /1 #18
2016 Panini National Treasures Jumbo Firesuit Patch Signature Booklet Associate Sponsor 4 /1 #18
2016 Panini National Treasures Jumbo Firesuit Patch Signature Booklet Associate Sponsor 5 /1 #18
2016 Panini National Treasures Jumbo Firesuit Patch Signature Booklet Associate Sponsor 6 /1 #18
2016 Panini National Treasures Jumbo Firesuit Patch Signature Booklet Associate Sponsor 7 /1 #18
2016 Panini National Treasures Jumbo Firesuit Patch Signature Booklet Associate Sponsor 8 /1 #18
2016 Panini National Treasures Jumbo Firesuit Patch Signature Booklet Associate Sponsor 9 /1 #18
2016 Panini National Treasures Jumbo Firesuit Patch Signature Booklet Flag /1 #18
2016 Panini National Treasures Jumbo Firesuit Patch Signature Booklet Manufacturers Logo /2 #18
2016 Panini National Treasures Jumbo Firesuit Patch Signature Booklet Nameplate /2 #18
2016 Panini National Treasures Jumbo Firesuit Patch Signature Booklet NASCAR /1 #18
2016 Panini National Treasures Jumbo Firesuit Patch Signature Booklet Sprint Cup Logo /1 #18
2016 Panini National Treasures Jumbo Firesuit Patch Signature Booklet Sunoco /1 #18
2016 Panini National Treasures Jumbo Firesuit Signatures Black /5 #18
2016 Panini National Treasures Jumbo Firesuit Signatures Blue /1 #18
2016 Panini National Treasures Jumbo Firesuit Signatures Gold /10 #18
2016 Panini National Treasures Jumbo Firesuit Signatures Printing Plates Black /1 #18
2016 Panini National Treasures Jumbo Firesuit Signatures Printing Plates Cyan /1 #18
2016 Panini National Treasures Jumbo Firesuit Signatures Printing Plates Magenta /1 #18
2016 Panini National Treasures Jumbo Firesuit Signatures Printing Plates Yellow /1 #18
2016 Panini National Treasures Signature Dual Materials /25 #18
2016 Panini National Treasures Signature Dual Materials Black /5 #18
2016 Panini National Treasures Signature Dual Materials Blue /1 #18
2016 Panini National Treasures Signature Dual Materials Gold /10 #18
2016 Panini National Treasures Signature Dual Materials Printing Plates Black /1 #18
2016 Panini National Treasures Signature Dual Materials Printing Plates Cyan /1 #18
2016 Panini National Treasures Signature Dual Materials Printing Plates Magenta /1 #18
2016 Panini National Treasures Signature Dual Materials Printing Plates Yellow /1 #18
2016 Panini National Treasures Signature Dual Materials Silver /15 #18
2016 Panini National Treasures Signature Firesuit Materials /25 #18
2016 Panini National Treasures Signature Firesuit Materials Black /5 #18
2016 Panini National Treasures Signature Firesuit Materials Blue /1 #18
2016 Panini National Treasures Signature Firesuit Materials Laundry Tag /1 #18
2016 Panini National Treasures Signature Firesuit Materials Printing Plates Black /1 #18
2016 Panini National Treasures Signature Firesuit Materials Printing Plates Cyan /1 #18
2016 Panini National Treasures Signature Firesuit Materials Printing Plates Magenta /1 #18
2016 Panini National Treasures Signature Firesuit Materials Printing Plates Yellow /1 #18
2016 Panini National Treasures Signature Firesuit Materials Silver /15 #18
2016 Panini National Treasures Signature Quad Materials /25 #18
2016 Panini National Treasures Signature Quad Materials Black /5 #18
2016 Panini National Treasures Signature Quad Materials Blue /1 #18
2016 Panini National Treasures Signature Quad Materials Gold /10 #18
2016 Panini National Treasures Signature Quad Materials Printing Plates Black /1 #18
2016 Panini National Treasures Signature Quad Materials Printing Plates Cyan /1 #18
2016 Panini National Treasures Signature Quad Materials Printing Plates Magenta /1 #18
2016 Panini National Treasures Signature Quad Materials Printing Plates Yellow /1 #18
2016 Panini National Treasures Signature Quad Materials Silver /15 #18
2016 Panini National Treasures Signature Sheet Metal Materials /25 #18
2016 Panini National Treasures Signature Sheet Metal Materials Black /5 #18
2016 Panini National Treasures Signature Sheet Metal Materials Blue /1 #18
2016 Panini National Treasures Signature Sheet Metal Materials Gold /10 #18
2016 Panini National Treasures Signature Sheet Metal Materials Printing Plates Black /1 #18
2016 Panini National Treasures Signature Sheet Metal Materials Printing Plates Cyan /1 #18
2016 Panini National Treasures Signature Sheet Metal Materials Printing Plates Magenta /1 #18
2016 Panini National Treasures Signature Sheet Metal Materials Printing Plates Yellow /1 #18
2016 Panini National Treasures Signature Sheet Metal Materials Silver /15 #18
2016 Panini National Treasures Signatures /25 #14
2016 Panini National Treasures Signatures Black /5 #14
2016 Panini National Treasures Signatures Blue /1 #14
2016 Panini National Treasures Signatures Gold /15 #14
2016 Panini National Treasures Signatures Printing Plates Black /1 #14
2016 Panini National Treasures Signatures Printing Plates Cyan /1 #14
2016 Panini National Treasures Signatures Printing Plates Magenta /1 #14
2016 Panini National Treasures Signatures Printing Plates Yellow /1 #14
2016 Panini National Treasures Signatures Silver /20 #14
2016 Panini National Treasures Timelines Blue /1 #10
2016 Panini National Treasures Timelines Printing Plates Black /1 #10
2016 Panini National Treasures Timelines Printing Plates Cyan /1 #10
2016 Panini National Treasures Timelines Printing Plates Magenta /1 #10
2016 Panini National Treasures Timelines Printing Plates Yellow /1 #10
2016 Panini National Treasures Timelines Signatures Black /5 #8
2016 Panini National Treasures Timelines Signatures Blue /1 #8
2016 Panini National Treasures Timelines Signatures Gold /10 #8
2016 Panini National Treasures Timelines Signatures Printing Plates Black /1 #8
2016 Panini National Treasures Timelines Signatures Printing Plates Cyan /1 #8
2016 Panini National Treasures Timelines Signatures Printing Plates Magenta /1 #8
2016 Panini National Treasures Timelines Signatures Printing Plates Yellow /1 #8
2016 Panini Prizm #36
2016 Panini Prizm #85
2016 Panini Prizm Autographs Prizms #41
2016 Panini Prizm Autographs Prizms Black /3 #41
2016 Panini Prizm Autographs Prizms Blue Flag /35 #41
2016 Panini Prizm Autographs Prizms Camo /42 #41
2016 Panini Prizm Autographs Prizms Checkered Flag /1 #41
2016 Panini Prizm Autographs Prizms Gold /10 #41
2016 Panini Prizm Autographs Prizms Green Flag /50 #41
2016 Panini Prizm Autographs Prizms Rainbow /24 #41
2016 Panini Prizm Autographs Prizms Red Flag /25 #41
2016 Panini Prizm Autographs Prizms Red White and Blue /25 #41
2016 Panini Prizm Autographs Prizms White Flag /5 #41
2016 Panini Prizm Firesuit Fabrics /149 #19
2016 Panini Prizm Firesuit Fabrics Prizms Blue Flag /75 #19
2016 Panini Prizm Firesuit Fabrics Prizms Checkered Flag /1 #19
2016 Panini Prizm Firesuit Fabrics Prizms Green Flag /99 #19
2016 Panini Prizm Firesuit Fabrics Prizms Red Flag /25 #19
2016 Panini Prizm Firesuit Fabrics Team /249 #19
2016 Panini Prizm Firesuit Fabrics Team Prizms Blue Flag /75 #19
2016 Panini Prizm Firesuit Fabrics Team Prizms Checkered Flag /1 #19
2016 Panini Prizm Firesuit Fabrics Team Prizms Green Flag /99 #19
2016 Panini Prizm Firesuit Fabrics Team Prizms Red Flag /5 #19
2016 Panini Prizm Prizms #36
2016 Panini Prizm Prizms #85
2016 Panini Prizm Prizms Black /3 #36
2016 Panini Prizm Prizms Black /3 #85
2016 Panini Prizm Prizms Blue Flag /99 #36
2016 Panini Prizm Prizms Blue Flag /99 #85
2016 Panini Prizm Prizms Camo /42 #36
2016 Panini Prizm Prizms Camo /42 #85
2016 Panini Prizm Prizms Checkered Flag /1 #36
2016 Panini Prizm Prizms Checkered Flag /1 #85
2016 Panini Prizm Prizms Gold /10 #36
2016 Panini Prizm Prizms Gold /10 #85
2016 Panini Prizm Prizms Green Flag /149 #36
2016 Panini Prizm Prizms Green Flag /149 #85
2016 Panini Prizm Prizms Rainbow /24 #36
2016 Panini Prizm Prizms Rainbow /24 #85
2016 Panini Prizm Prizms Red Flag /75 #36
2016 Panini Prizm Prizms Red Flag /75 #85
2016 Panini Prizm Prizms Red White and Blue #36
2016 Panini Prizm Prizms Red White and Blue #85
2016 Panini Prizm Prizms White Flag /5 #36
2016 Panini Prizm Prizms White Flag /5 #85
2016 Panini Torque #26
2016 Panini Torque Artist Proof /50 #26
2016 Panini Torque Blackout /1 #26
2016 Panini Torque Blue /125 #26
2016 Panini Torque Clear Vision #22
2016 Panini Torque Clear Vision Blue /99 #22
2016 Panini Torque Clear Vision Gold /149 #22
2016 Panini Torque Clear Vision Green /25 #22
2016 Panini Torque Clear Vision Purple /10 #22
2016 Panini Torque Clear Vision Red /49 #22
2016 Panini Torque Dual Materials /149 #15
2016 Panini Torque Dual Materials Blue /99 #15
2016 Panini Torque Dual Materials Green /25 #15
2016 Panini Torque Dual Materials Purple /10 #15
2016 Panini Torque Dual Materials Red /49 #15
2016 Panini Torque Gold #26
2016 Panini Torque Holo Gold /5 #26
2016 Panini Torque Holo Silver /10 #26
2016 Panini Torque Horsepower Heroes #19
2016 Panini Torque Horsepower Heroes Gold /199 #19
2016 Panini Torque Horsepower Heroes Holo Silver /99 #19
2016 Panini Torque Jumbo Firesuit Autographs /145 #6
2016 Panini Torque Jumbo Firesuit Autographs Blue /75 #6
2016 Panini Torque Jumbo Firesuit Autographs Green /25 #6
2016 Panini Torque Jumbo Firesuit Autographs Purple /10 #6
2016 Panini Torque Jumbo Firesuit Autographs Red /45 #6
2016 Panini Torque Pairings Materials /249 #20
2016 Panini Torque Pairings Materials Blue /99 #20
2016 Panini Torque Pairings Materials Green /25 #20
2016 Panini Torque Pairings Materials Purple /10 #20
2016 Panini Torque Pairings Materials Red /49 #20
2016 Panini Torque Printing Plates Black /1 #26
2016 Panini Torque Printing Plates Cyan /1 #26
2016 Panini Torque Printing Plates Magenta /1 #26
2016 Panini Torque Printing Plates Yellow /1 #26
2016 Panini Torque Purple /25 #26
2016 Panini Torque Red /99 #26
2016 Panini Torque Test Proof Black /1 #26
2016 Panini Torque Test Proof Cyan /1 #26
2016 Panini Torque Test Proof Magenta /1 #26
2016 Panini Torque Test Proof Yellow /1 #26
2016 Topps First Pitch #FP10
2017 Donruss #133
2017 Donruss #159
2017 Donruss #111
2017 Donruss Artist Proof /25 #133
2017 Donruss Artist Proof /25 #159
2017 Donruss Artist Proof /25 #111
2017 Donruss Blue Foil /299 #133
2017 Donruss Blue Foil /299 #159
2017 Donruss Blue Foil /299 #111
2017 Donruss Gold Foil /499 #133
2017 Donruss Gold Foil /499 #159
2017 Donruss Gold Foil /499 #111
2017 Donruss Gold Press Proof /99 #133
2017 Donruss Gold Press Proof /99 #159
2017 Donruss Gold Press Proof /99 #111
2017 Donruss Green Foil /199 #133
2017 Donruss Green Foil /199 #159
2017 Donruss Green Foil /199 #111
2017 Donruss Press Proof /49 #133
2017 Donruss Press Proof /49 #159
2017 Donruss Press Proof /49 #111
2017 Donruss Printing Plates Black /1 #133
2017 Donruss Printing Plates Black /1 #159
2017 Donruss Printing Plates Black /1 #111
2017 Donruss Printing Plates Cyan /1 #133
2017 Donruss Printing Plates Cyan /1 #159
2017 Donruss Printing Plates Cyan /1 #111
2017 Donruss Printing Plates Magenta /1 #133
2017 Donruss Printing Plates Magenta /1 #159
2017 Donruss Printing Plates Magenta /1 #111
2017 Donruss Printing Plates Yellow /1 #133
2017 Donruss Printing Plates Yellow /1 #159
2017 Donruss Printing Plates Yellow /1 #111
2017 Donruss Rubber Relics #35
2017 Donruss Rubber Relics Holo Black /1 #35
2017 Donruss Rubber Relics Holo Gold /25 #35
2017 Donruss Studio Signatures #9
2017 Donruss Studio Signatures Holo Black /1 #9
2017 Donruss Studio Signatures Holo Gold /25 #9
2017 Panini Day Memorabilia #45
2017 Panini Day Memorabilia Galactic Window /25 #45
2017 Panini Day Memorabilia Hyperplaid /1 #45
2017 Panini Instant Nascar /80 #5
2017 Panini Instant Nascar #22
2017 Panini Instant Nascar #24
2017 Panini Instant Nascar Black /1 #5
2017 Panini Instant Nascar Black /1 #22
2017 Panini Instant Nascar Black /1 #24
2017 Panini Instant Nascar Green /10 #5
2017 Panini Instant Nascar Green /10 #22
2017 Panini Instant Nascar Green /10 #24
2017 Panini National Convention #R10
2017 Panini National Convention Autographs #R10
2017 Panini National Convention Autographs Hyperplaid /1 #R10
2017 Panini National Convention Escher Squares /25 #R10
2017 Panini National Convention Escher Squares Thick Stock /10 #R10
2017 Panini National Convention Galatic Windows /5 #R10
2017 Panini National Convention Hyperplaid /1 #R10
2017 Panini National Convention Pyramids /10 #R10
2017 Panini National Convention Rainbow Spokes /49 #R10
2017 Panini National Convention Rainbow Spokes Thick Stock /25 #R10
2017 Panini National Convention Rapture /99 #R10
2017 Panini National Treasures Associate Sponsor Patch Signatures 1 /1 #23
2017 Panini National Treasures Associate Sponsor Patch Signatures 10 /1 #23
2017 Panini National Treasures Associate Sponsor Patch Signatures 11 /1 #23
2017 Panini National Treasures Associate Sponsor Patch Signatures 12 /1 #23
2017 Panini National Treasures Associate Sponsor Patch Signatures 13 /1 #23
2017 Panini National Treasures Associate Sponsor Patch Signatures 14 /1 #23
2017 Panini National Treasures Associate Sponsor Patch Signatures 15 /1 #23
2017 Panini National Treasures Associate Sponsor Patch Signatures 16 /1 #23

2017 Panini National Treasures Associate Sponsor Patch Signatures 17 /1 #23
2017 Panini National Treasures Associate Sponsor Patch Signatures 18 /1 #23
2017 Panini National Treasures Associate Sponsor Patch Signatures 19 /1 #23
2017 Panini National Treasures Associate Sponsor Patch Signatures 2 /1 #23
2017 Panini National Treasures Associate Sponsor Patch Signatures 20 /1 #23
2017 Panini National Treasures Associate Sponsor Patch Signatures 3 /1 #23
2017 Panini National Treasures Associate Sponsor Patch Signatures 4 /1 #23
2017 Panini National Treasures Associate Sponsor Patch Signatures 5 /1 #23
2017 Panini National Treasures Associate Sponsor Patch Signatures 6 /1 #23
2017 Panini National Treasures Associate Sponsor Patch Signatures 7 /1 #23
2017 Panini National Treasures Associate Sponsor Patch Signatures 8 /1 #23
2017 Panini National Treasures Associate Sponsor Patch Signatures 9 /1 #23
2017 Panini National Treasures Car Manufacturer Patch Signatures /1 #23
2017 Panini National Treasures Dual Firesuit Materials Black /1 #10
2017 Panini National Treasures Dual Firesuit Materials Green /5 #10
2017 Panini National Treasures Dual Firesuit Materials Holo Gold /10 #10
2017 Panini National Treasures Dual Firesuit Materials Laundry Tag /1 #10
2017 Panini National Treasures Dual Firesuit Materials Printing Plates Black /1 #10
2017 Panini National Treasures Dual Firesuit Materials Printing Plates Cyan /1 #10
2017 Panini National Treasures Dual Firesuit Materials Printing Plates Magenta /1 #10
2017 Panini National Treasures Dual Firesuit Materials Printing Plates Yellow /1 #10
2017 Panini National Treasures Dual Firesuit Signatures /25 #10
2017 Panini National Treasures Dual Firesuit Signatures Black /1 #10
2017 Panini National Treasures Dual Firesuit Signatures Gold /15 #10
2017 Panini National Treasures Dual Firesuit Signatures Green /5 #10
2017 Panini National Treasures Dual Firesuit Signatures Holo Silver /20 #10
2017 Panini National Treasures Dual Firesuit Signatures Laundry Tag /1 #10
2017 Panini National Treasures Dual Firesuit Signatures Printing Plates Black /1 #10
2017 Panini National Treasures Dual Firesuit Signatures Printing Plates Cyan /1 #10
2017 Panini National Treasures Dual Firesuit Signatures Printing Plates Magenta /1 #10
2017 Panini National Treasures Dual Firesuit Signatures Printing Plates Yellow /1 #10
2017 Panini National Treasures Dual Sheet Metal Materials Black /1 #9
2017 Panini National Treasures Dual Sheet Metal Materials Gold /15 #9
2017 Panini National Treasures Dual Sheet Metal Materials Green /5 #9
2017 Panini National Treasures Dual Sheet Metal Materials Holo Gold /10 #9
2017 Panini National Treasures Dual Sheet Metal Materials Printing Plates Black /1 #9
2017 Panini National Treasures Dual Sheet Metal Materials Printing Plates Cyan /1 #9
2017 Panini National Treasures Dual Sheet Metal Materials Printing Plates Magenta /1 #9
2017 Panini National Treasures Dual Sheet Metal Materials Printing Plates Yellow /1 #9
2017 Panini National Treasures Firesuit Manufacturer Patch Signatures /1 #23
2017 Panini National Treasures Flag Patch Signatures /1 #23
2017 Panini National Treasures Goodyear Patch Signatures /1 #23
2017 Panini National Treasures Hats Off /13 #26
2017 Panini National Treasures Hats Off Gold /2 #26
2017 Panini National Treasures Hats Off Holo Gold /5 #26
2017 Panini National Treasures Hats Off Holo Silver /1 #26
2017 Panini National Treasures Hats Off Laundry Tag /6 #26
2017 Panini National Treasures Hats Off Monster Energy Cup /15 #14
2017 Panini National Treasures Hats Off Monster Energy Cup Gold /4 #14
2017 Panini National Treasures Hats Off Monster Energy Cup Holo Gold /5 #14
2017 Panini National Treasures Hats Off Monster Energy Cup Holo Silver /1 #14
2017 Panini National Treasures Hats Off Monster Energy Cup Laundry Tag /6 #14
2017 Panini National Treasures Hats Off Monster Energy Cup New Era /1 #14
2017 Panini National Treasures Hats Off Monster Energy Cup Printing Plates Black /1 #14
2017 Panini National Treasures Hats Off Monster Energy Cup Printing Plates Cyan /1 #14
2017 Panini National Treasures Hats Off Monster Energy Cup Printing Plates Magenta /1 #14
2017 Panini National Treasures Hats Off Monster Energy Cup Printing Plates Yellow /1 #14
2017 Panini National Treasures Hats Off Monster Energy Cup Sponsor /5 #14
2017 Panini National Treasures Hats Off New Era /1 #26
2017 Panini National Treasures Hats Off Printing Plates Black /1 #26
2017 Panini National Treasures Hats Off Printing Plates Cyan /1 #26
2017 Panini National Treasures Hats Off Printing Plates Magenta /1 #26
2017 Panini National Treasures Hats Off Printing Plates Yellow /1 #26
2017 Panini National Treasures Hats Off Sponsor /5 #26
2017 Panini National Treasures Nameplate Patch Signatures /2 #23
2017 Panini National Treasures NASCAR Patch Signatures /1 #23
2017 Panini National Treasures Quad Materials Black /1 #5
2017 Panini National Treasures Quad Materials Green /5 #5
2017 Panini National Treasures Quad Materials Laundry Tag /1 #5
2017 Panini National Treasures Quad Materials Printing Plates Black /1 #5
2017 Panini National Treasures Quad Materials Printing Plates Cyan /1 #5
2017 Panini National Treasures Quad Materials Printing Plates Magenta /1 #5
2017 Panini National Treasures Quad Materials Printing Plates Yellow /1 #5
2017 Panini National Treasures Series Sponsor Patch Signatures /1 #23
2017 Panini National Treasures Sunoco Patch Signatures /1 #23
2017 Panini National Treasures Teammates Dual Materials /25 #9
2017 Panini National Treasures Teammates Dual Materials Black /1 #9
2017 Panini National Treasures Teammates Dual Materials Gold /15 #9
2017 Panini National Treasures Teammates Dual Materials Green /5 #9
2017 Panini National Treasures Teammates Dual Materials Holo Gold /10 #9
2017 Panini National Treasures Teammates Dual Materials Holo Silver /20 #9
2017 Panini National Treasures Teammates Dual Materials Laundry Tag /1 #9
2017 Panini National Treasures Teammates Dual Materials Printing Plates Black /1 #9
2017 Panini National Treasures Teammates Dual Materials Printing Plates Cyan /1 #9
2017 Panini National Treasures Teammates Dual Materials Printing Plates Magenta /1 #9
2017 Panini National Treasures Teammates Dual Materials Printing Plates Yellow /1 #9
2017 Panini National Treasures Teammates Quad Materials /25 #9
2017 Panini National Treasures Teammates Quad Materials Black /1 #9
2017 Panini National Treasures Teammates Quad Materials Gold /15 #9
2017 Panini National Treasures Teammates Quad Materials Green /5 #9
2017 Panini National Treasures Teammates Quad Materials Holo Gold /10 #9
2017 Panini National Treasures Teammates Quad Materials Holo Silver /20 #9
2017 Panini National Treasures Teammates Quad Materials Laundry Tag /1 #9
2017 Panini National Treasures Teammates Quad Materials Printing Plates Black /1 #9
2017 Panini National Treasures Teammates Quad Materials Printing Plates Cyan /1 #9
2017 Panini National Treasures Teammates Quad Materials Printing Plates Magenta /1 #9
2017 Panini National Treasures Teammates Quad Materials Printing Plates Yellow /1 #9
2017 Panini National Treasures Three Wide Black /1 #15
2017 Panini National Treasures Three Wide Gold /15 #15
2017 Panini National Treasures Three Wide Green /5 #15
2017 Panini National Treasures Three Wide Holo Gold /10 #15
2017 Panini National Treasures Three Wide Laundry Tag /1 #15
2017 Panini National Treasures Three Wide Printing Plates Black /1 #15
2017 Panini National Treasures Three Wide Printing Plates Cyan /1 #15
2017 Panini National Treasures Three Wide Printing Plates Magenta /1 #15
2017 Panini National Treasures Three Wide Printing Plates Yellow /1 #15
2017 Panini Torque #17
2017 Panini Torque Artist Proof /75 #17
2017 Panini Torque Blackout /1 #17
2017 Panini Torque Blue /150 #17
2017 Panini Torque Clear Vision #17
2017 Panini Torque Clear Vision Blue /99 #17
2017 Panini Torque Clear Vision Gold /149 #17
2017 Panini Torque Clear Vision Green /25 #17
2017 Panini Torque Clear Vision Purple /10 #17
2017 Panini Torque Clear Vision Red /49 #17
2017 Panini Torque Combo Materials Signatures /30 #8
2017 Panini Torque Combo Materials Signatures Blue /25 #8
2017 Panini Torque Combo Materials Signatures Green /15 #8
2017 Panini Torque Combo Materials Signatures Purple /10 #8
2017 Panini Torque Combo Materials Signatures Red /20 #8
2017 Panini Torque Gold #17
2017 Panini Torque Holo Gold /10 #17
2017 Panini Torque Holo Silver /25 #17
2017 Panini Torque Horsepower Heroes #23
2017 Panini Torque Horsepower Heroes Gold /199 #23
2017 Panini Torque Horsepower Heroes Holo Silver /99 #23
2017 Panini Torque Jumbo Tire Signatures /30 #13
2017 Panini Torque Jumbo Tire Signatures Blue /25 #13
2017 Panini Torque Jumbo Tire Signatures Green /15 #13
2017 Panini Torque Jumbo Tire Signatures Purple /10 #13
2017 Panini Torque Jumbo Tire Signatures Red /20 #13
2017 Panini Torque Metal Materials /99 #11
2017 Panini Torque Metal Materials Blue /49 #11
2017 Panini Torque Metal Materials Green /10 #11
2017 Panini Torque Metal Materials Purple /1 #11
2017 Panini Torque Metal Materials Red /25 #11
2017 Panini Torque Pairings Materials /199 #2
2017 Panini Torque Pairings Materials Blue /99 #2
2017 Panini Torque Pairings Materials Green /25 #2
2017 Panini Torque Pairings Materials Purple /10 #2
2017 Panini Torque Pairings Materials Red /49 #2
2017 Panini Torque Printing Plates Black /1 #17
2017 Panini Torque Printing Plates Cyan /1 #17
2017 Panini Torque Printing Plates Magenta /1 #17
2017 Panini Torque Printing Plates Yellow /1 #17
2017 Panini Torque Purple /50 #17
2017 Panini Torque Quad Materials /99 #20
2017 Panini Torque Quad Materials Blue /49 #20
2017 Panini Torque Quad Materials Green /10 #20
2017 Panini Torque Quad Materials Purple /1 #20
2017 Panini Torque Quad Materials Red /25 #20
2017 Panini Torque Red /100 #17
2017 Panini Torque Running Order #9
2017 Panini Torque Running Order Blue /99 #9
2017 Panini Torque Running Order Checkerboard /10 #9
2017 Panini Torque Running Order Green /25 #9
2017 Panini Torque Running Order Red /49 #9
2017 Panini Torque Silhouettes Sheet Metal Signatures /30 #21
2017 Panini Torque Silhouettes Sheet Metal Signatures Blue /25 #21
2017 Panini Torque Silhouettes Sheet Metal Signatures Green /15 #21
2017 Panini Torque Silhouettes Sheet Metal Signatures Purple /10 #21
2017 Panini Torque Silhouettes Sheet Metal Signatures Red /20 #21
2017 Panini Torque Test Proof Black /1 #17
2017 Panini Torque Test Proof Cyan /1 #17
2017 Panini Torque Test Proof Magenta /1 #17
2017 Panini Torque Test Proof Yellow /1 #17
2017 Panini Torque Victory Laps #12
2017 Panini Torque Victory Laps Gold /199 #12
2017 Panini Torque Victory Laps Holo Silver /99 #12
2017 Select #95
2017 Select #96
2017 Select #97
2017 Select #130
2017 Select Prizms Black /3 #95
2017 Select Prizms Black /3 #96
2017 Select Prizms Black /3 #97
2017 Select Prizms Black /3 #130
2017 Select Prizms Blue /199 #95
2017 Select Prizms Blue /199 #96
2017 Select Prizms Blue /199 #97
2017 Select Prizms Checkered Flag /1 #95
2017 Select Prizms Checkered Flag /1 #96
2017 Select Prizms Checkered Flag /1 #97
2017 Select Prizms Checkered Flag /1 #130
2017 Select Prizms Gold /10 #95
2017 Select Prizms Gold /10 #96
2017 Select Prizms Gold /10 #97
2017 Select Prizms Gold /10 #130
2017 Select Prizms Purple Pulsar #95
2017 Select Prizms Purple Pulsar #96
2017 Select Prizms Purple Pulsar #97
2017 Select Prizms Red /99 #95
2017 Select Prizms Red /99 #96
2017 Select Prizms Red /99 #97
2017 Select Prizms Red White and Blue Pulsar /299 #95
2017 Select Prizms Red White and Blue Pulsar /299 #96
2017 Select Prizms Red White and Blue Pulsar /299 #97
2017 Select Prizms Silver #95
2017 Select Prizms Silver #96
2017 Select Prizms Silver #97
2017 Select Prizms Tie Dye /24 #95
2017 Select Prizms Tie Dye /24 #96
2017 Select Prizms Tie Dye /24 #97
2017 Select Prizms Tie Dye /24 #130
2017 Select Prizms White /50 #95
2017 Select Prizms White /50 #96
2017 Select Prizms White /50 #97
2017 Select Prizms White /50 #130
2017 Select Select Pairs Materials #1
2017 Select Select Pairs Materials Prizms Blue /199 #1
2017 Select Select Pairs Materials Prizms Checkered Flag /1 #1
2017 Select Select Pairs Materials Prizms Gold /10 #1
2017 Select Select Pairs Materials Prizms Red /99 #1
2017 Select Select Swatches #30
2017 Select Select Swatches Prizms Blue /199 #30
2017 Select Select Swatches Prizms Checkered Flag /1 #30
2017 Select Select Swatches Prizms Gold /10 #30
2017 Select Select Swatches Prizms Red /99 #30
2017 Select Sheet Metal #18
2017 Select Sheet Metal Prizms Blue /99 #18
2017 Select Sheet Metal Prizms Checkered Flag /1 #18
2017 Select Sheet Metal Prizms Gold /10 #18
2017 Select Sheet Metal Prizms Red /49 #18
2017 Select Signature Paint Schemes #11
2017 Select Signature Paint Schemes Prizms Blue /50 #11
2017 Select Signature Paint Schemes Prizms Checkered Flag /1 #11
2017 Select Signature Paint Schemes Prizms Gold /10 #11
2017 Select Signature Paint Schemes Prizms Red /25 #11
2017 Select Signature Swatches #30
2017 Select Signature Swatches Prizms Checkered Flag /1 #30
2017 Select Signature Swatches Prizms Gold /10 #30
2017 Select Signature Swatches Prizms Tie Dye /24 #30
2017 Select Signature Swatches Prizms White /50 #30
2017 Select Signature Swatches Triple #19
2017 Select Signature Swatches Triple Prizms Checkered Flag /1 #19
2017 Select Signature Swatches Triple Prizms Gold /10 #19
2017 Select Signature Swatches Triple Prizms Tie Dye /24 #19
2017 Select Signature Swatches Triple Prizms White /50 #19
2017 Select Speed Merchants #9
2017 Select Speed Merchants Prizms Black /3 #9
2017 Select Speed Merchants Prizms Checkered Flag /1 #9
2017 Select Speed Merchants Prizms Gold /10 #9
2017 Select Speed Merchants Prizms Tie Dye /24 #9
2017 Select Speed Merchants Prizms White /50 #9
2018 Certified #77
2018 Certified All Certified Team /199 #12
2018 Certified All Certified Team Black /1 #12
2018 Certified All Certified Team Blue /99 #12
2018 Certified All Certified Team Gold /49 #12
2018 Certified All Certified Team Green /10 #12
2018 Certified All Certified Team Mirror Black /1 #12
2018 Certified All Certified Team Mirror Gold /25 #12
2018 Certified All Certified Team Mirror Green /5 #12
2018 Certified All Certified Team Mirror Purple /10 #12
2018 Certified All Certified Team Purple /25 #12
2018 Certified All Certified Team Red /149 #12
2018 Certified Black /1 #77
2018 Certified Blue /99 #77
2018 Certified Cup Swatches /499 #19
2018 Certified Cup Swatches Black /1 #19
2018 Certified Cup Swatches Blue /49 #19
2018 Certified Cup Swatches Gold /25 #19
2018 Certified Cup Swatches Green /5 #19
2018 Certified Cup Swatches Purple /10 #19
2018 Certified Cup Swatches Red /199 #19
2018 Certified Epix /199 #13
2018 Certified Epix Black /1 #13
2018 Certified Epix Blue /99 #13
2018 Certified Epix Gold /49 #13
2018 Certified Epix Green /10 #13
2018 Certified Epix Mirror Black /1 #13
2018 Certified Epix Mirror Gold /25 #13
2018 Certified Epix Mirror Green /5 #13
2018 Certified Epix Mirror Purple /10 #13
2018 Certified Epix Purple /25 #13
2018 Certified Epix Red /149 #13
2018 Certified Fresh Faces Signatures /25 #16
2018 Certified Fresh Faces Signatures Black /1 #16
2018 Certified Fresh Faces Signatures Blue /15 #16
2018 Certified Fresh Faces Signatures Gold /10 #16
2018 Certified Fresh Faces Signatures Green /5 #16
2018 Certified Fresh Faces Signatures Purple /8 #16
2018 Certified Fresh Faces Signatures Red /20 #16
2018 Certified Gold /49 #77
2018 Certified Green /10 #77
2018 Certified Materials Signatures /99 #13
2018 Certified Materials Signatures Black /1 #13
2018 Certified Materials Signatures Blue /42 #13
2018 Certified Materials Signatures Gold /25 #13
2018 Certified Materials Signatures Green /5 #13
2018 Certified Materials Signatures Purple /10 #13
2018 Certified Materials Signatures Red /50 #13
2018 Certified Mirror Black /1 #77
2018 Certified Mirror Gold /25 #77
2018 Certified Mirror Green /5 #77
2018 Certified Mirror Purple /10 #77
2018 Certified Orange /249 #77
2018 Certified Piece of the Race /199 #14
2018 Certified Piece of the Race Black /1 #14
2018 Certified Piece of the Race Blue /49 #14
2018 Certified Piece of the Race Gold /25 #14
2018 Certified Piece of the Race Green /5 #14
2018 Certified Piece of the Race Purple /10 #14
2018 Certified Piece of the Race Red /99 #14
2018 Certified Purple /25 #77
2018 Certified Red /199 #77
2018 Certified Signatures Black /1 #39
2018 Certified Signatures Blue /42 #39
2018 Certified Signatures Gold /25 #39
2018 Certified Signatures Green /5 #39
2018 Certified Signatures Purple /10 #39
2018 Certified Signatures Red /50 #39
2018 Certified Skills /199 #15
2018 Certified Skills Black /1 #15
2018 Certified Skills Blue /99 #15
2018 Certified Skills Gold /49 #15
2018 Certified Skills Green /10 #15
2018 Certified Skills Mirror Black /1 #15
2018 Certified Skills Mirror Gold /25 #15
2018 Certified Skills Mirror Green /5 #15
2018 Certified Skills Mirror Purple /10 #15
2018 Certified Skills Purple /25 #15
2018 Certified Skills Red /149 #15
2018 Certified Stars /199 #19
2018 Certified Stars Black /1 #19
2018 Certified Stars Blue /99 #19
2018 Certified Stars Gold /49 #19
2018 Certified Stars Green /10 #19
2018 Certified Stars Mirror Black /1 #19
2018 Certified Stars Mirror Gold /25 #19
2018 Certified Stars Mirror Green /5 #19
2018 Certified Stars Mirror Purple /10 #19
2018 Certified Stars Purple /25 #19
2018 Certified Stars Red /149 #19
2018 Donruss #20
2018 Donruss #47A
2018 Donruss #85
2018 Donruss #137
2018 Donruss #47B
2018 Donruss Artist Proofs /25 #20
2018 Donruss Artist Proofs /25 #47A
2018 Donruss Artist Proofs /25 #85
2018 Donruss Artist Proofs /25 #137
2018 Donruss Artist Proofs /25 #47B
2018 Donruss Classics #9
2018 Donruss Classics Cracked Ice /999 #9
2018 Donruss Classics Xplosion /99 #9
2018 Donruss Elite Dominators /999 #5
2018 Donruss Gold Foil /499 #20
2018 Donruss Gold Foil /499 #47A
2018 Donruss Gold Foil /499 #85
2018 Donruss Gold Foil /499 #137
2018 Donruss Gold Foil /499 #47B
2018 Donruss Gold Press Proofs /99 #20
2018 Donruss Gold Press Proofs /99 #47A
2018 Donruss Gold Press Proofs /99 #85
2018 Donruss Gold Press Proofs /99 #137
2018 Donruss Gold Press Proofs /99 #47B
2018 Donruss Green Foil /199 #20
2018 Donruss Green Foil /199 #47A
2018 Donruss Green Foil /199 #85
2018 Donruss Green Foil /199 #137
2018 Donruss Green Foil /199 #47B
2018 Donruss Pole Position #4
2018 Donruss Pole Position Cracked Ice /999 #4
2018 Donruss Pole Position Xplosion /99 #4
2018 Donruss Press Proofs /49 #20
2018 Donruss Press Proofs /49 #47
2018 Donruss Press Proofs /49 #85
2018 Donruss Press Proofs /49 #137
2018 Donruss Press Proofs /49 #47B
2018 Donruss Printing Plates Black /1 #20
2018 Donruss Printing Plates Black /1 #47
2018 Donruss Printing Plates Black /1 #85
2018 Donruss Printing Plates Black /1 #137
2018 Donruss Printing Plates Black /1 #47B
2018 Donruss Printing Plates Cyan /1 #20
2018 Donruss Printing Plates Cyan /1 #47
2018 Donruss Printing Plates Cyan /1 #85
2018 Donruss Printing Plates Cyan /1 #137
2018 Donruss Printing Plates Cyan /1 #47B
2018 Donruss Printing Plates Magenta /1 #20
2018 Donruss Printing Plates Magenta /1 #47
2018 Donruss Printing Plates Magenta /1 #85
2018 Donruss Printing Plates Magenta /1 #137
2018 Donruss Printing Plates Magenta /1 #47B
2018 Donruss Printing Plates Yellow /1 #20
2018 Donruss Printing Plates Yellow /1 #47
2018 Donruss Printing Plates Yellow /1 #85
2018 Donruss Printing Plates Yellow /1 #137
2018 Donruss Printing Plates Yellow /1 #47B
2018 Donruss Racing Relics #14
2018 Donruss Racing Relics Black /10 #14
2018 Donruss Racing Relics Holo Gold /99 #14
2018 Donruss Red Foil /299 #20
2018 Donruss Red Foil /299 #47A
2018 Donruss Red Foil /299 #85
2018 Donruss Red Foil /299 #137
2018 Donruss Red Foil /299 #47B
2018 Donruss Rubber Relic Signatures #13
2018 Donruss Rubber Relic Signatures Black /1 #13
2018 Donruss Rubber Relic Signatures Holo Gold /25 #13
2018 Donruss Rubber Relics #24
2018 Donruss Rubber Relics Black /10 #24
2018 Donruss Rubber Relics Holo Gold /99 #24
2018 Donruss Studio #9
2018 Donruss Studio Cracked Ice /999 #9
2018 Donruss Studio Xplosion /99 #9
2018 Donruss Top Tier #9
2018 Donruss Top Tier Cracked Ice /999 #9
2018 Donruss Top Tier Xplosion /99 #9
2018 Panini Father's Day Racing Memorabilia #KL
2018 Panini Father's Day Racing Memorabilia Checkerboard /10 #KL
2018 Panini Father's Day Racing Memorabilia Cracked Ice /25 #KL
2018 Panini Father's Day Racing Memorabilia Escher Squares /5 #KL
2018 Panini Father's Day Racing Memorabilia Hyperplaid /1 #KL
2018 Panini Prime /50 #10
2018 Panini Prime /50 #44
2018 Panini Prime /50 #77
2018 Panini Prime Autograph Materials /50 #18
2018 Panini Prime Autograph Materials Black /1 #18
2018 Panini Prime Autograph Materials Holo Gold /25 #18
2018 Panini Prime Autograph Materials Laundry Tag /1 #18
2018 Panini Prime Black /1 #10
2018 Panini Prime Black /1 #44
2018 Panini Prime Black /1 #77
2018 Panini Prime Clear Silhouettes /99 #21
2018 Panini Prime Clear Silhouettes Black /1 #21
2018 Panini Prime Clear Silhouettes Dual /99 #23
2018 Panini Prime Clear Silhouettes Dual Black /1 #23
2018 Panini Prime Clear Silhouettes Dual Holo Gold /50 #23
2018 Panini Prime Clear Silhouettes Holo Gold /50 #21
2018 Panini Prime Dual Material Autographs /50 #7
2018 Panini Prime Dual Material Autographs Black /1 #7
2018 Panini Prime Dual Material Autographs Holo Gold /42 #7
2018 Panini Prime Dual Material Autographs Laundry Tag /1 #7
2018 Panini Prime Dual Signatures /50 #10
2018 Panini Prime Dual Signatures Black /1 #10
2018 Panini Prime Dual Signatures Holo Gold /25 #10
2018 Panini Prime Holo Gold /25 #10
2018 Panini Prime Holo Gold /25 #44
2018 Panini Prime Holo Gold /25 #77
2018 Panini Prime Prime Jumbo Associate Sponsor 1 /1 #52
2018 Panini Prime Prime Jumbo Associate Sponsor 1 /1 #53
2018 Panini Prime Prime Jumbo Associate Sponsor 1 /1 #54
2018 Panini Prime Prime Jumbo Associate Sponsor 10 /1 #53
2018 Panini Prime Prime Jumbo Associate Sponsor 10 /1 #54
2018 Panini Prime Prime Jumbo Associate Sponsor 11 /1 #54
2018 Panini Prime Prime Jumbo Associate Sponsor 12 /1 #54
2018 Panini Prime Prime Jumbo Associate Sponsor 13 /1 #54
2018 Panini Prime Prime Jumbo Associate Sponsor 14 /1 #54
2018 Panini Prime Prime Jumbo Associate Sponsor 15 /1 #54
2018 Panini Prime Prime Jumbo Associate Sponsor 2 /1 #52
2018 Panini Prime Prime Jumbo Associate Sponsor 2 /1 #53
2018 Panini Prime Prime Jumbo Associate Sponsor 2 /1 #54
2018 Panini Prime Prime Jumbo Associate Sponsor 3 /1 #52
2018 Panini Prime Prime Jumbo Associate Sponsor 3 /1 #53
2018 Panini Prime Prime Jumbo Associate Sponsor 3 /1 #54
2018 Panini Prime Prime Jumbo Associate Sponsor 4 /1 #52
2018 Panini Prime Prime Jumbo Associate Sponsor 4 /1 #53
2018 Panini Prime Prime Jumbo Associate Sponsor 4 /1 #54
2018 Panini Prime Prime Jumbo Associate Sponsor 5 /1 #52
2018 Panini Prime Prime Jumbo Associate Sponsor 5 /1 #53
2018 Panini Prime Prime Jumbo Associate Sponsor 5 /1 #54
2018 Panini Prime Prime Jumbo Associate Sponsor 6 /1 #52
2018 Panini Prime Prime Jumbo Associate Sponsor 6 /1 #53
2018 Panini Prime Prime Jumbo Associate Sponsor 6 /1 #54
2018 Panini Prime Prime Jumbo Associate Sponsor 7 /1 #52
2018 Panini Prime Prime Jumbo Associate Sponsor 7 /1 #53
2018 Panini Prime Prime Jumbo Associate Sponsor 7 /1 #54
2018 Panini Prime Prime Jumbo Associate Sponsor 8 /1 #52
2018 Panini Prime Prime Jumbo Associate Sponsor 8 /1 #53
2018 Panini Prime Prime Jumbo Associate Sponsor 8 /1 #54
2018 Panini Prime Prime Jumbo Associate Sponsor 9 /1 #53
2018 Panini Prime Prime Jumbo Associate Sponsor 9 /1 #54
2018 Panini Prime Prime Jumbo Car Manufacturer /1 #52
2018 Panini Prime Prime Jumbo Car Manufacturer /1 #53
2018 Panini Prime Prime Jumbo Car Manufacturer /1 #54
2018 Panini Prime Prime Jumbo Firesuit Manufacturer /1 #52
2018 Panini Prime Prime Jumbo Firesuit Manufacturer /1 #53
2018 Panini Prime Prime Jumbo Firesuit Manufacturer /1 #54
2018 Panini Prime Prime Jumbo Glove Manufacturer Patch /1 #52
2018 Panini Prime Prime Jumbo Glove Manufacturer Patch /1 #53
2018 Panini Prime Prime Jumbo Glove Manufacturer Patch /1 #54
2018 Panini Prime Prime Jumbo Glove Number Patch /1 #52
2018 Panini Prime Prime Jumbo Glove Number Patch /1 #53
2018 Panini Prime Prime Jumbo Glove Number Patch /1 #54
2018 Panini Prime Prime Jumbo Goodyear /2 #52
2018 Panini Prime Prime Jumbo Goodyear /2 #54
2018 Panini Prime Prime Jumbo Nameplate /2 #52
2018 Panini Prime Prime Jumbo Nameplate /2 #53
2018 Panini Prime Prime Jumbo Nameplate /1 #54
2018 Panini Prime Prime Jumbo NASCAR /1 #52
2018 Panini Prime Prime Jumbo NASCAR /1 #53
2018 Panini Prime Prime Jumbo NASCAR /1 #54
2018 Panini Prime Prime Jumbo Prime Colors /17 #52
2018 Panini Prime Prime Jumbo Prime Colors /12 #53
2018 Panini Prime Prime Jumbo Prime Colors /12 #54
2018 Panini Prime Prime Jumbo Series Sponsor /1 #53
2018 Panini Prime Prime Jumbo Series Sponsor /1 #54
2018 Panini Prime Prime Jumbo Shoe Brand Logo /1 #52
2018 Panini Prime Prime Jumbo Shoe Brand Logo /1 #53
2018 Panini Prime Prime Jumbo Shoe Brand Logo /1 #54
2018 Panini Prime Prime Jumbo Sunoco /1 #52
2018 Panini Prime Prime Jumbo Sunoco /1 #53
2018 Panini Prime Prime Jumbo Sunoco /1 #54
2018 Panini Prime Prime Number Signatures /99 #12
2018 Panini Prime Prime Number Signatures Black /1 #12
2018 Panini Prime Prime Number Signatures Holo Gold /25 #12
2018 Panini Prime Quad Material Autographs /50 #9
2018 Panini Prime Quad Material Autographs Black /1 #9
2018 Panini Prime Quad Material Autographs Holo Gold /49 #9
2018 Panini Prime Quad Material Autographs Laundry Tag /1 #9
2018 Panini Prime Race Used Firesuits Black /1 #26
2018 Panini Prime Race Used Firesuits Holo Gold /25 #26
2018 Panini Prime Race Used Firesuits Laundry Tag /1 #26
2018 Panini Prime Race Used Sheet Metal /50 #26
2018 Panini Prime Race Used Sheet Metal Black /1 #26
2018 Panini Prime Race Used Sheet Metal Holo Gold /25 #26
2018 Panini Prime Race Used Tires Black /1 #26
2018 Panini Prime Race Used Tires Holo Gold /25 #26
2018 Panini Prime Signature Swatches /99 #14
2018 Panini Prime Signature Swatches Black /1 #14
2018 Panini Prime Signature Swatches Holo Gold /25 #14
2018 Panini Prime Triple Material Autographs /50 #14
2018 Panini Prime Triple Material Autographs Black /1 #14
2018 Panini Prime Triple Material Autographs Holo Gold /49 #14
2018 Panini Prime Triple Material Autographs Laundry Tag /1 #14
2018 Panini Prizm #34
2018 Panini Prizm Autographs Prizms #35
2018 Panini Prizm Autographs Prizms Black /1 #35
2018 Panini Prizm Autographs Prizms Blue /35 #35
2018 Panini Prizm Autographs Prizms Camo #35
2018 Panini Prizm Autographs Prizms Gold /10 #35
2018 Panini Prizm Autographs Prizms Green /50 #35
2018 Panini Prizm Autographs Prizms Rainbow /24 #35
2018 Panini Prizm Autographs Prizms Red /25 #35
2018 Panini Prizm Autographs Prizms Red White and Blue /75 #35
2018 Panini Prizm Autographs Prizms White /5 #35
2018 Panini Prizm Instant Impact #3
2018 Panini Prizm Instant Impact Prizms #3
2018 Panini Prizm Instant Impact Prizms Black /1 #3
2018 Panini Prizm Instant Impact Prizms Gold /10 #3
2018 Panini Prizm Prizms #34
2018 Panini Prizm Prizms Black /1 #34
2018 Panini Prizm Prizms Blue /99 #34
2018 Panini Prizm Prizms Camo #34
2018 Panini Prizm Prizms Gold /10 #34
2018 Panini Prizm Prizms Green /149 #34
2018 Panini Prizm Prizms Purple Flash #34
2018 Panini Prizm Prizms Rainbow /24 #34
2018 Panini Prizm Prizms Red /75 #34
2018 Panini Prizm Prizms Red White and Blue #34
2018 Panini Prizm Prizms White /5 #34
2018 Panini Prizm Team Tandems #5
2018 Panini Prizm Team Tandems Prizms #5
2018 Panini Prizm Team Tandems Prizms Black /1 #5
2018 Panini Prizm Team Tandems Prizms Gold /10 #5
2018 Panini Victory Lane #23
2018 Panini Victory Lane Black /1 #23
2018 Panini Victory Lane Blue /25 #23
2018 Panini Victory Lane Celebrations #15
2018 Panini Victory Lane Celebrations Black /1 #15
2018 Panini Victory Lane Celebrations Blue /25 #15
2018 Panini Victory Lane Celebrations Gold /99 #15
2018 Panini Victory Lane Celebrations Green /5 #15
2018 Panini Victory Lane Celebrations Printing Plates Black /1 #15
2018 Panini Victory Lane Celebrations Printing Plates Cyan /1 #15
2018 Panini Victory Lane Celebrations Printing Plates Magenta /1 #15
2018 Panini Victory Lane Celebrations Printing Plates Yellow /1 #15
2018 Panini Victory Lane Celebrations Red /49 #15
2018 Panini Victory Lane Gold /99 #23
2018 Panini Victory Lane Green /5 #23
2018 Panini Victory Lane Octane Autographs Black /1 #24
2018 Panini Victory Lane Octane Autographs Gold /99 #24
2018 Panini Victory Lane Pedal to the Metal #36
2018 Panini Victory Lane Pedal to the Metal #68
2018 Panini Victory Lane Pedal to the Metal Black /1 #36
2018 Panini Victory Lane Pedal to the Metal Black /1 #68
2018 Panini Victory Lane Pedal to the Metal Blue /25 #36
2018 Panini Victory Lane Pedal to the Metal Blue /25 #68
2018 Panini Victory Lane Pedal to the Metal Green /5 #36
2018 Panini Victory Lane Pedal to the Metal Green /5 #68
2018 Panini Victory Lane Printing Plates Black /1 #23
2018 Panini Victory Lane Printing Plates Cyan /1 #23
2018 Panini Victory Lane Printing Plates Magenta /1 #23
2018 Panini Victory Lane Printing Plates Yellow /1 #23
2018 Panini Victory Lane Red /49 #23
2018 Panini Victory Lane Silver #23
2018 Panini Victory Lane Starting Grid #19
2018 Panini Victory Lane Starting Grid Black /1 #19
2018 Panini Victory Lane Starting Grid Blue /25 #19
2018 Panini Victory Lane Starting Grid Gold /99 #19
2018 Panini Victory Lane Starting Grid Green /5 #19
2018 Panini Victory Lane Starting Grid Printing Plates Black /1 #19
2018 Panini Victory Lane Starting Grid Printing Plates Cyan /1 #19
2018 Panini Victory Lane Starting Grid Printing Plates Magenta /1 #19
2018 Panini Victory Lane Starting Grid Printing Plates Yellow /1 #19
2018 Panini Victory Lane Starting Grid Red /49 #19
2018 Panini Victory Lane Victory Lane Prime Patches Associate Sponsor 1 /1 #4
2018 Panini Victory Lane Victory Lane Prime Patches Associate Sponsor 10 /1 #4
2018 Panini Victory Lane Victory Lane Prime Patches Associate Sponsor 2 /1 #4
2018 Panini Victory Lane Victory Lane Prime Patches Associate Sponsor 3 /1 #4
2018 Panini Victory Lane Victory Lane Prime Patches Associate Sponsor 4 /1 #4
2018 Panini Victory Lane Victory Lane Prime Patches Associate Sponsor 5 /1 #4
2018 Panini Victory Lane Victory Lane Prime Patches Associate Sponsor 6 /1 #4
2018 Panini Victory Lane Victory Lane Prime Patches Associate Sponsor 7 /1 #4
2018 Panini Victory Lane Victory Lane Prime Patches Associate Sponsor 8 /1 #4
2018 Panini Victory Lane Victory Lane Prime Patches Associate Sponsor 9 /1 #4
2018 Panini Victory Lane Victory Lane Prime Patches Car Manufacturer /1 #4
2018 Panini Victory Lane Victory Lane Prime Patches Firesuit Manufacturer /1 #4
2018 Panini Victory Lane Victory Lane Prime Patches Goodyear /2 #4
2018 Panini Victory Lane Victory Lane Prime Patches Nameplate /2 #4
2018 Panini Victory Lane Victory Lane Prime Patches NASCAR /1 #4
2018 Panini Victory Lane Victory Lane Prime Patches Series Sponsor /1 #4
2018 Panini Victory Lane Victory Lane Prime Patches Sunoco /1 #4
2019 Donruss #70
2019 Donruss #93
2019 Donruss #116
2019 Donruss Action #10
2019 Donruss Action Cracked Ice /25 #10
2019 Donruss Action Holographic #10
2019 Donruss Action Xplosion /10 #10
2019 Donruss Artist Proofs /25 #70
2019 Donruss Artist Proofs /25 #93
2019 Donruss Artist Proofs /25 #116
2019 Donruss Black /199 #70
2019 Donruss Black /199 #93
2019 Donruss Black /199 #116
2019 Donruss Classics #14
2019 Donruss Classics Cracked Ice /25 #14
2019 Donruss Classics Holographic #14
2019 Donruss Classics Xplosion /10 #14
2019 Donruss Contenders #7
2019 Donruss Contenders Cracked Ice /25 #7
2019 Donruss Contenders Holographic #7
2019 Donruss Contenders Xplosion /10 #7
2019 Donruss Gold /299 #70
2019 Donruss Gold /299 #93
2019 Donruss Gold /299 #116
2019 Donruss Gold Press Proofs /99 #70
2019 Donruss Gold Press Proofs /99 #93
2019 Donruss Gold Press Proofs /99 #116
2019 Donruss Limited Spotlight Signatures #4
2019 Donruss Limited Spotlight Signatures Holo Black /10 #4
2019 Donruss Limited Spotlight Signatures Holo Gold /25 #4
2019 Donruss Limited Spotlight Signatures Red /99 #4
2019 Donruss Optic #20
2019 Donruss Optic #80
2019 Donruss Optic Blue Pulsar #20
2019 Donruss Optic Blue Pulsar /1 #80
2019 Donruss Optic Gold /10 #20
2019 Donruss Optic Gold /10 #80
2019 Donruss Optic Gold Vinyl /1 #20
2019 Donruss Optic Gold Vinyl /1 #80
2019 Donruss Optic Holo #20
2019 Donruss Optic Holo #80
2019 Donruss Optic Red Wave #20
2019 Donruss Optic Red Wave /1 #80
2019 Donruss Optic Signatures Gold Vinyl /1 #80
2019 Donruss Optic Signatures Gold Vinyl /1 #20
2019 Donruss Optic Signatures Holo /75 #20
2019 Donruss Optic Signatures Holo /75 #80
2019 Donruss Originals #10
2019 Donruss Originals Cracked Ice /25 #10
2019 Donruss Originals Holographic #10
2019 Donruss Originals Xplosion /10 #10
2019 Donruss Press Proofs /49 #70
2019 Donruss Press Proofs /49 #93
2019 Donruss Press Proofs /49 #116
2019 Donruss Printing Plates Black /1 #70
2019 Donruss Printing Plates Black /1 #93
2019 Donruss Printing Plates Black /1 #116
2019 Donruss Printing Plates Cyan /1 #70
2019 Donruss Printing Plates Cyan /1 #93
2019 Donruss Printing Plates Cyan /1 #116
2019 Donruss Printing Plates Magenta /1 #70
2019 Donruss Printing Plates Magenta /1 #93
2019 Donruss Printing Plates Magenta /1 #116
2019 Donruss Printing Plates Yellow /1 #70
2019 Donruss Printing Plates Yellow /1 #93
2019 Donruss Printing Plates Yellow /1 #116
2019 Donruss Retro Relics '86 #8
2019 Donruss Retro Relics '86 Holo Black /10 #8
2019 Donruss Retro Relics '86 Holo Gold /25 #8
2019 Donruss Retro Relics '86 Red /250 #8
2019 Donruss Silver #70
2019 Donruss Silver #93
2019 Donruss Silver #116
2019 Panini National Convention NASCAR #R10
2019 Panini National Convention NASCAR Galatic Windows /25 #R10
2019 Panini National Convention NASCAR HyperPlaid /1 #R10
2019 Panini Prime /50 #27
2019 Panini Prime /50 #55
2019 Panini Prime /50 #84
2019 Panini Prime Black /10 #27
2019 Panini Prime Black /10 #55
2019 Panini Prime Black /10 #84
2019 Panini Prime Clear Silhouettes /99 #9
2019 Panini Prime Clear Silhouettes Black /10 #9
2019 Panini Prime Clear Silhouettes Holo Gold /25 #9
2019 Panini Prime Clear Silhouettes Platinum Blue /1 #9
2019 Panini Prime Clear Vision Signatures Black /10 #9
2019 Panini Prime Clear Vision Signatures Holo Gold /25 #9
2019 Panini Prime Clear Vision Signatures Platinum Blue /1 #9
2019 Panini Prime Dual Material Autographs Black /10 #24
2019 Panini Prime Dual Material Autographs Holo Gold /25 #24
2019 Panini Prime Dual Material Autographs Laundry Tags /1 #24
2019 Panini Prime Emerald /5 #27
2019 Panini Prime Emerald /5 #55
2019 Panini Prime Emerald /5 #84
2019 Panini Prime Hats Off Button /1 #5
2019 Panini Prime Hats Off Eyelets /6 #5
2019 Panini Prime Hats Off Headband /36 #5
2019 Panini Prime Hats Off Laundry Tags /2 #5
2019 Panini Prime Hats Off New Era /1 #5
2019 Panini Prime Hats Off Number /2 #5
2019 Panini Prime Hats Off Sponsor Logo /6 #5
2019 Panini Prime Hats Off Team Logo /3 #5
2019 Panini Prime Jumbo Material Signatures Firesuit /10 #20
2019 Panini Prime Jumbo Material Signatures Firesuit Platinum Blue /1 #20
2019 Panini Prime Jumbo Material Signatures Sheet Metal /25 #20
2019 Panini Prime NASCAR Shadowbox Signatures Car Number /42 #27
2019 Panini Prime NASCAR Shadowbox Signatures Manufacturer /10 #27
2019 Panini Prime NASCAR Shadowbox Signatures Sponsor /25 #27
2019 Panini Prime NASCAR Shadowbox Signatures Team Owner /1 #27
2019 Panini Prime Platinum Blue /1 #27
2019 Panini Prime Platinum Blue /1 #55
2019 Panini Prime Platinum Blue /1 #84
2019 Panini Prime Prime Cars Die Cut Signatures Black /10 #19
2019 Panini Prime Prime Cars Die Cut Signatures Holo Gold /25 #19
2019 Panini Prime Prime Cars Die Cut Signatures Platinum Blue /1 #19
2019 Panini Prime Prime Jumbo Associate Sponsor 1 /1 #48
2019 Panini Prime Prime Jumbo Associate Sponsor 2 /1 #48
2019 Panini Prime Prime Jumbo Associate Sponsor 3 /1 #48
2019 Panini Prime Prime Jumbo Associate Sponsor 4 /1 #48
2019 Panini Prime Prime Jumbo Associate Sponsor 5 /1 #48
2019 Panini Prime Prime Jumbo Associate Sponsor 6 /1 #48
2019 Panini Prime Prime Jumbo Associate Sponsor 7 /1 #48
2019 Panini Prime Prime Jumbo Associate Sponsor 8 /1 #48
2019 Panini Prime Prime Jumbo Car Manufacturer /1 #48
2019 Panini Prime Prime Jumbo Firesuit Manufacturer /1 #48
2019 Panini Prime Prime Jumbo Glove Manufacturer Patch /1 #48
2019 Panini Prime Prime Jumbo Glove Name Patch /1 #48
2019 Panini Prime Prime Jumbo Glove Number Patch /1 #48
2019 Panini Prime Prime Jumbo NASCAR /1 #48
2019 Panini Prime Prime Jumbo Prime Colors /11 #48
2019 Panini Prime Prime Jumbo Series Sponsor /1 #48
2019 Panini Prime Prime Jumbo Shoe Brand Logo /1 #48
2019 Panini Prime Prime Jumbo Shoe Name Patch /1 #48
2019 Panini Prime Prime Number Die Cut Signatures /42 #15
2019 Panini Prime Prime Number Die Cut Signatures Black /10 #15
2019 Panini Prime Prime Number Die Cut Signatures Holo Gold /25 #15
2019 Panini Prime Prime Number Die Cut Signatures Platinum Blue /1 #15
2019 Panini Prime Quad Materials Autographs Black /10 #17
2019 Panini Prime Quad Materials Autographs Holo Gold /25 #17
2019 Panini Prime Quad Materials Autographs Laundry Tags /1 #17
2019 Panini Prime Race Used Duals Firesuits Black /10 #27
2019 Panini Prime Race Used Duals Firesuits Holo Gold /25 #27
2019 Panini Prime Race Used Duals Firesuits Laundry Tags /1 #27
2019 Panini Prime Race Used Duals Sheet Metal Black /10 #27
2019 Panini Prime Race Used Duals Sheet Metal Platinum Blue /1 #27
2019 Panini Prime Race Used Duals Tires Black /10 #27
2019 Panini Prime Race Used Duals Tires Platinum Blue /1 #27
2019 Panini Prime Race Used Firesuits Black /10 #27
2019 Panini Prime Race Used Firesuits Holo Gold /25 #27

nini Prime Race Used Firesuits Laundry Tags /1 #27
nini Prime Race Used Sheet Metal Black /10 #27
nini Prime Race Used Sheet Metal Platinum Blue /1 #27
nini Prime Race Used Tires Black /10 #27
nini Prime Race Used Tires Platinum Blue /1 #27
nini Prime Race Used Trios Firesuits Black /10 #5
nini Prime Race Used Trios Firesuits Holo Gold /25 #5
nini Prime Race Used Trios Firesuits Laundry Tags /1 #5
nini Prime Race Used Trios Sheet Metal Black /10 #5
nini Prime Race Used Trios Sheet Metal Platinum Blue /1 #5
nini Prime Race Used Trios Tires Black /10 #5
nini Prime Race Used Trios Tires Platinum Blue /1 #5
nini Prizm #27
nini Prizm #80
nini Prizm Fireworks #10
nini Prizm Fireworks Prizms #10
nini Prizm Fireworks Prizms Black /1 #10
nini Prizm Fireworks Prizms Gold /10 #10
nini Prizm Fireworks Prizms White Sparkle #10
nini Prizm In the Groove #11
nini Prizm In the Groove Prizms #11
nini Prizm In the Groove Prizms Black /1 #11
nini Prizm In the Groove Prizms Gold /10 #11
nini Prizm In the Groove Prizms White Sparkle #11
nini Prizm Patented Penmanship Prizms #9
nini Prizm Patented Penmanship Prizms Black /1 #9
nini Prizm Patented Penmanship Prizms Blue /30 #9
nini Prizm Patented Penmanship Prizms Camo #9
nini Prizm Patented Penmanship Prizms Gold /10 #9
nini Prizm Patented Penmanship Prizms Green /35 #9
nini Prizm Patented Penmanship Prizms Rainbow /24 #9
nini Prizm Patented Penmanship Prizms Red /25 #9
nini Prizm Patented Penmanship Prizms Red White and Blue #9
nini Prizm Patented Penmanship Prizms White /5 #9
nini Prizm Prizms #80
nini Prizm Prizms #27
nini Prizm Prizms Black /1 #27
nini Prizm Prizms Black /1 #80
nini Prizm Prizms Blue /75 #27
nini Prizm Prizms Blue /75 #80
nini Prizm Prizms Camo #27
nini Prizm Prizms Camo #80
nini Prizm Prizms Flash #27
nini Prizm Prizms Flash #80
anini Prizm Prizms Gold /10 #27
anini Prizm Prizms Gold /10 #80
anini Prizm Prizms Green /99 #27
anini Prizm Prizms Green /99 #80
anini Prizm Prizms Rainbow /24 #27
anini Prizm Prizms Rainbow /24 #80
anini Prizm Prizms Red /50 #27
anini Prizm Prizms Red /50 #80
anini Prizm Prizms Red White and Blue #27
anini Prizm Prizms Red White and Blue #80
anini Prizm Prizms White /5 #27
anini Prizm Prizms White /5 #80
anini Prizm Prizms White Sparkle #27
anini Prizm Prizms White Sparkle #80
anini Prizm Signing Sessions Prizms #16
anini Prizm Signing Sessions Prizms Black /1 #16
anini Prizm Signing Sessions Prizms Blue /30 #16
anini Prizm Signing Sessions Prizms Camo #16
anini Prizm Signing Sessions Prizms Gold /10 #16
anini Prizm Signing Sessions Prizms Green /35 #16
anini Prizm Signing Sessions Prizms Rainbow /24 #16
anini Prizm Signing Sessions Prizms Red /25 #16
anini Prizm Signing Sessions Prizms Red White and Blue #16
anini Prizm Signing Sessions Prizms White /5 #16
anini Prizm Teammates #8
anini Prizm Teammates Prizms #8
anini Prizm Teammates Prizms Black /1 #8
anini Prizm Teammates Prizms Gold /10 #8
anini Prizm Teammates Prizms White Sparkle #8
anini Victory Lane #27
anini Victory Lane #93
anini Victory Lane Black /1 #27
anini Victory Lane Black /1 #93
anini Victory Lane Dual Swatch Signatures #13
anini Victory Lane Dual Swatch Signatures Gold /99 #13
anini Victory Lane Dual Swatch Signatures Laundry Tag /1 #13
anini Victory Lane Dual Swatch Signatures Platinum /1 #13
anini Victory Lane Dual Swatch Signatures Red /25 #13
anini Victory Lane Dual Swatches #17
anini Victory Lane Dual Swatches Gold /99 #17
anini Victory Lane Dual Swatches Laundry Tag /1 #17
anini Victory Lane Dual Swatches Platinum /1 #17
anini Victory Lane Dual Swatches Red /25 #17
anini Victory Lane Gold /25 #27
anini Victory Lane Gold /25 #93
anini Victory Lane Machines #13
anini Victory Lane Machines Black /1 #13
anini Victory Lane Machines Blue /99 #13
anini Victory Lane Machines Gold /25 #13
anini Victory Lane Machines Green /5 #13
Panini Victory Lane Machines Printing Plates Black /1 #13
Panini Victory Lane Machines Printing Plates Cyan /1 #13
Panini Victory Lane Machines Printing Plates Magenta /1 #13
Panini Victory Lane Machines Printing Plates Yellow /1 #13
Panini Victory Lane Pedal to the Metal #17
Panini Victory Lane Pedal to the Metal #54
Panini Victory Lane Pedal to the Metal Black /1 #17
Panini Victory Lane Pedal to the Metal Black /1 #54
Panini Victory Lane Pedal to the Metal Gold /25 #17
Panini Victory Lane Pedal to the Metal Gold /25 #54
Panini Victory Lane Pedal to the Metal Green /5 #17
Panini Victory Lane Pedal to the Metal Green /5 #54
Panini Victory Lane Pedal to the Metal Red /3 #17
Panini Victory Lane Pedal to the Metal Red /3 #54
Panini Victory Lane Printing Plates Black /1 #27
Panini Victory Lane Printing Plates Black /1 #93
Panini Victory Lane Printing Plates Cyan /1 #27
Panini Victory Lane Printing Plates Cyan /1 #93
Panini Victory Lane Printing Plates Magenta /1 #27
Panini Victory Lane Printing Plates Magenta /1 #93
Panini Victory Lane Printing Plates Yellow /1 #27
Panini Victory Lane Printing Plates Yellow /1 #93
Panini Victory Lane Starting Grid #16
Panini Victory Lane Starting Grid Black /1 #16
Panini Victory Lane Starting Grid Blue /99 #16
Panini Victory Lane Starting Grid Gold /25 #16
Panini Victory Lane Starting Grid Green /5 #16
Panini Victory Lane Starting Grid Printing Plates Black /1 #16
Panini Victory Lane Starting Grid Printing Plates Cyan /1 #16
Panini Victory Lane Starting Grid Printing Plates Magenta /1 #16
Panini Victory Lane Starting Grid Printing Plates Yellow /1 #16
Panini Victory Lane Top 10 #9
Panini Victory Lane Top 10 Black /1 #9
Panini Victory Lane Top 10 Blue /99 #9
Panini Victory Lane Top 10 Gold /25 #9
Panini Victory Lane Top 10 Green /5 #9
Panini Victory Lane Top 10 Printing Plates Black /1 #9
Panini Victory Lane Top 10 Printing Plates Cyan /1 #9
Panini Victory Lane Top 10 Printing Plates Magenta /1 #9
Panini Victory Lane Top 10 Printing Plates Yellow /1 #9
Panini Victory Lane Track Stars #15
Panini Victory Lane Track Stars Black /1 #15
Panini Victory Lane Track Stars Blue /99 #15
Panini Victory Lane Track Stars Gold /25 #15
2019 Panini Victory Lane Track Stars Green /5 #15
2019 Panini Victory Lane Track Stars Printing Plates Black /1 #15
2019 Panini Victory Lane Track Stars Printing Plates Cyan /1 #15
2019 Panini Victory Lane Track Stars Printing Plates Magenta /1 #15
2019 Panini Victory Lane Track Stars Printing Plates Yellow /1 #15
2020 Donruss #13
2020 Donruss #43
2020 Donruss #110
2020 Donruss #162
2020 Donruss Aero Package #5
2020 Donruss Aero Package Checkers #5
2020 Donruss Aero Package Cracked Ice /25 #5
2020 Donruss Aero Package Holographic /199 #5
2020 Donruss Aero Package Xplosion /10 #5
2020 Donruss Black Numbers /42 #13
2020 Donruss Black Numbers /42 #43
2020 Donruss Black Numbers /42 #110
2020 Donruss Black Numbers /42 #162
2020 Donruss Black Trophy Club /1 #13
2020 Donruss Black Trophy Club /1 #43
2020 Donruss Black Trophy Club /1 #110
2020 Donruss Black Trophy Club /1 #162
2020 Donruss Blue /199 #110
2020 Donruss Blue /199 #162
2020 Donruss Blue /199 #13
2020 Donruss Blue /199 #43
2020 Donruss Carolina Blue #13
2020 Donruss Carolina Blue #43
2020 Donruss Carolina Blue #110
2020 Donruss Carolina Blue #162
2020 Donruss Contenders #8
2020 Donruss Contenders Checkers #8
2020 Donruss Contenders Cracked Ice /25 #8
2020 Donruss Contenders Holographic /199 #8
2020 Donruss Contenders Xplosion /10 #8
2020 Donruss Green /99 #13
2020 Donruss Green /99 #43
2020 Donruss Green /99 #110
2020 Donruss Green /99 #162
2020 Donruss Optic #25
2020 Donruss Optic #70
2020 Donruss Optic Carolina Blue Wave #25
2020 Donruss Optic Carolina Blue Wave #70
2020 Donruss Optic Gold /10 #25
2020 Donruss Optic Gold /10 #70
2020 Donruss Optic Gold Vinyl /1 #25
2020 Donruss Optic Gold Vinyl /1 #70
2020 Donruss Optic Holo #25
2020 Donruss Optic Holo #70
2020 Donruss Optic Orange Pulsar #25
2020 Donruss Optic Orange Pulsar #70
2020 Donruss Optic Red Mojo #25
2020 Donruss Optic Red Mojo #70
2020 Donruss Optic Signatures Gold Vinyl /1 #25
2020 Donruss Optic Signatures Gold Vinyl /1 #70
2020 Donruss Optic Signatures Holo /99 #25
2020 Donruss Optic Signatures Holo /99 #70
2020 Donruss Orange #13
2020 Donruss Orange #43
2020 Donruss Orange #110
2020 Donruss Orange #162
2020 Donruss Pink /25 #13
2020 Donruss Pink /25 #43
2020 Donruss Pink /25 #110
2020 Donruss Pink /25 #162
2020 Donruss Printing Plates Black /1 #13
2020 Donruss Printing Plates Black /1 #43
2020 Donruss Printing Plates Black /1 #110
2020 Donruss Printing Plates Black /1 #162
2020 Donruss Printing Plates Cyan /1 #13
2020 Donruss Printing Plates Cyan /1 #43
2020 Donruss Printing Plates Cyan /1 #110
2020 Donruss Printing Plates Cyan /1 #162
2020 Donruss Printing Plates Magenta /1 #43
2020 Donruss Printing Plates Magenta /1 #110
2020 Donruss Printing Plates Magenta /1 #162
2020 Donruss Printing Plates Magenta /1 #13
2020 Donruss Printing Plates Yellow /1 #162
2020 Donruss Printing Plates Yellow /1 #13
2020 Donruss Printing Plates Yellow /1 #43
2020 Donruss Printing Plates Yellow /1 #110
2020 Donruss Purple /49 #13
2020 Donruss Purple /49 #43
2020 Donruss Purple /49 #110
2020 Donruss Purple /49 #162
2020 Donruss Race Day Relics #20
2020 Donruss Race Day Relics Holo Black /10 #20
2020 Donruss Race Day Relics Holo Gold /25 #20
2020 Donruss Race Day Relics Red /250 #20
2020 Donruss Red /299 #13
2020 Donruss Red /299 #43
2020 Donruss Red /299 #110
2020 Donruss Red /299 #162
2020 Donruss Signature Series Holo Black /1 #24
2020 Donruss Signature Series Holo Gold /25 #24
2020 Donruss Signature Series Red /42 #24
2020 Donruss Silver #13
2020 Donruss Silver #43
2020 Donruss Silver #110
2020 Donruss Silver #162

Joey Logano

2008 Press Pass Legends Autographs Blue /126 #JL
2008 Press Pass Legends Autographs Blue Inscriptions /10 #JL
2008 Press Pass Legends Autographs Press Plates Black /1 #JL
2008 Press Pass Legends Autographs Press Plates Cyan /1 #JL
2008 Press Pass Legends Autographs Press Plates Magenta /1 #JL
2008 Press Pass Legends Autographs Press Plates Yellow /1 #JL
2008 Press Pass Signings #37
2008 Press Pass Signings Gold /50 #33
2008 Press Pass Signings Press Plates Black #JL
2008 Press Pass Signings Press Plates Magenta #JL
2008 Press Pass Signings Press Plates Yellow #JL
2008 Press Pass Signings Silver /100 #32
2008 VIP /499 #0
2008 Wheels American Thunder Campaign Trail #CT18
2008 Wheels American Thunder Delegates #D20
2008 Wheels American Thunder Trackside Treasury Autographs #JL
2008 Wheels American Thunder Trackside Treasury Autographs Gold /25 #JL
2008 Wheels American Thunder Trackside Treasury Autographs Printing Plates Black /1 #JL
2008 Wheels American Thunder Trackside Treasury Autographs Printing Plates Cyan /1 #JL
2008 Wheels American Thunder Trackside Treasury Autographs Printing Plates Yellow /1 #JL
2009 Element #19
2009 Element #44
2009 Element #49
2009 Element #78
2009 Element #81
2009 Element Kinetic Energy #KE7
2009 Element Lab Report #LR19
2009 Element Nobel Prize #NP5
2009 Element Previews /5 #19
2009 Element Previews /1 #49
2009 Element Radioactive /100 #19
2009 Element Radioactive /100 #44
2009 Element Radioactive /100 #49
2009 Element Radioactive /100 #78
2009 Element Radioactive /100 #81
2009 Element Taking the Checkers /45 #TCJL
2009 Press Pass #36
2009 Press Pass #98
2009 Press Pass #99
2009 Press Pass #100
2009 Press Pass #101
2009 Press Pass #102
2009 Press Pass #103
2009 Press Pass #104
2009 Press Pass #105
2009 Press Pass #106
2009 Press Pass #139
2009 Press Pass #208
2009 Press Pass #214
2009 Press Pass Autographs Gold #29
2009 Press Pass Autographs Printing Plates Black /1 #27
2009 Press Pass Autographs Printing Plates Cyan /1 #27
2009 Press Pass Autographs Printing Plates Magenta /1 #27
2009 Press Pass Autographs Printing Plates Yellow /1 #27
2009 Press Pass Autographs Silver #31
2009 Press Pass Autographs Track Edition /25 #JL
2009 Press Pass Blue #36
2009 Press Pass Blue #98
2009 Press Pass Blue #99
2009 Press Pass Blue #100
2009 Press Pass Blue #101
2009 Press Pass Blue #102
2009 Press Pass Blue #103
2009 Press Pass Blue #104
2009 Press Pass Blue #105
2009 Press Pass Blue #106
2009 Press Pass Blue #139
2009 Press Pass Blue #208
2009 Press Pass Blue #214
2009 Press Pass Burning Rubber Drivers /185 #BRDJL
2009 Press Pass Burning Rubber Prime Cut /25 #BRDJL
2009 Press Pass Burning Rubber Teams /250 #BRTJL
2009 Press Pass Cup Chase #CCR8
2009 Press Pass Daytona 500 Tires /25 #TTJL
2009 Press Pass Eclipse #14
2009 Press Pass Eclipse Black and White #14
2009 Press Pass Eclipse Blue #14
2009 Press Pass Eclipse Ecliptic Path #EP15
2009 Press Pass Four Wide Firesuit /50 #FWJL
2009 Press Pass Four Wide Tire /25 #FWJL
2009 Press Pass Freeze Frame #FF12
2009 Press Pass Fusion #73
2009 Press Pass Fusion Bronze /150 #73
2009 Press Pass Fusion Gold /50 #73
2009 Press Pass Fusion Green /25 #73
2009 Press Pass Fusion Onyx /1 #73
2009 Press Pass Fusion Revered Relics Gold /50 #RRJL
2009 Press Pass Fusion Revered Relics Holofoil /25 #RRJL
2009 Press Pass Fusion Revered Relics Premium Swatch /10 #RRJL
2009 Press Pass Fusion Revered Relics Silver /65 #RRJL
2009 Press Pass Fusion Silver /99 #73
2009 Press Pass Gold #36
2009 Press Pass Gold #98
2009 Press Pass Gold #99
2009 Press Pass Gold #100
2009 Press Pass Gold #101
2009 Press Pass Gold #102
2009 Press Pass Gold #103
2009 Press Pass Gold #104
2009 Press Pass Gold #105
2009 Press Pass Gold #106
2009 Press Pass Gold #139
2009 Press Pass Gold #208
2009 Press Pass Gold #214
2009 Press Pass Gold Holofoil /100 #36
2009 Press Pass Gold Holofoil /100 #98
2009 Press Pass Gold Holofoil /100 #99
2009 Press Pass Gold Holofoil /100 #100
2009 Press Pass Gold Holofoil /100 #101
2009 Press Pass Gold Holofoil /100 #102
2009 Press Pass Gold Holofoil /100 #103
2009 Press Pass Gold Holofoil /100 #104
2009 Press Pass Gold Holofoil /100 #105
2009 Press Pass Gold Holofoil /100 #106
2009 Press Pass Gold Holofoil /100 #139
2009 Press Pass Gold Holofoil /100 #208
2009 Press Pass Gold Holofoil /100 #214
2009 Press Pass Legends #52
2009 Press Pass Legends Autographs Gold /30 #22
2009 Press Pass Legends Autographs Inscriptions /15 #9
2009 Press Pass Legends Autographs Printing Plates Black /1 #17
2009 Press Pass Legends Autographs Printing Plates Cyan /1 #16
2009 Press Pass Legends Autographs Printing Plates Magenta /1 #17
2009 Press Pass Legends Autographs Printing Plates Yellow /1 #17
2009 Press Pass Legends Gold /399 #52
2009 Press Pass Legends Holofoil /50 #52
2009 Press Pass Legends Previews /5 #52
2009 Press Pass Legends Printing Plates Black /1 #52
2009 Press Pass Legends Printing Plates Cyan /1 #52
2009 Press Pass Legends Printing Plates Magenta /1 #52
2009 Press Pass Legends Printing Plates Yellow /1 #52
2009 Press Pass Legends Prominent Pieces Bronze /99 #PPJL
2009 Press Pass Legends Prominent Pieces Gold /25 #PPJL
2009 Press Pass Legends Prominent Pieces Oversized /25 #PPOEJL
2009 Press Pass Legends Prominent Pieces Silver /50 #PPJL
2009 Press Pass Legends Red /199 #52
2009 Press Pass Legends Solo /1 #52
2009 Press Pass NASCAR Gallery #NG12
2009 Press Pass Pocket Portraits #P15
2009 Press Pass Pocket Portraits Checkered Flag #P15
2009 Press Pass Pocket Portraits Hometown #P15
2009 Press Pass Pocket Portraits Smoke #P15
2009 Press Pass Pocket Portraits Target #PPT7
2009 Press Pass Premium #88
2009 Press Pass Premium Hot Threads /325 #HTJL2
2009 Press Pass Premium Hot Threads /99 #HTJL1
2009 Press Pass Premium Hot Threads Multi-Color /25 #HTJL
2009 Press Pass Premium Hot Threads Patches /10 #HTP-JL
2009 Press Pass Premium Signatures #21
2009 Press Pass Premium Signatures Gold /25 #20
2009 Press Pass Premium Win Streak #WS12
2009 Press Pass Premium Win Streak Victory Lane #WSVL-JL
2009 Press Pass Previews /5 #EB36
2009 Press Pass Previews /5 #EB98
2009 Press Pass Previews /5 #EB99
2009 Press Pass Previews /5 #EB100
2009 Press Pass Previews /5 #EB101
2009 Press Pass Previews /5 #EB102
2009 Press Pass Previews /5 #EB103
2009 Press Pass Previews /5 #EB104
2009 Press Pass Previews /5 #EB105
2009 Press Pass Previews /5 #EB106
2009 Press Pass Previews /5 #EB139
2009 Press Pass Red #36
2009 Press Pass Red #98
2009 Press Pass Red #99
2009 Press Pass Red #100
2009 Press Pass Red #101
2009 Press Pass Red #102
2009 Press Pass Red #103
2009 Press Pass Red #104
2009 Press Pass Red #105
2009 Press Pass Red #106
2009 Press Pass Red #139
2009 Press Pass Red #208
2009 Press Pass Red #214
2009 Press Pass Showcase /499 #30
2009 Press Pass Showcase /100 #51
2009 Press Pass Showcase 2nd Gear /125 #30
2009 Press Pass Showcase 2nd Gear /50 #51
2009 Press Pass Showcase 3rd Gear /50 #30
2009 Press Pass Showcase 3rd Gear /25 #51
2009 Press Pass Showcase 4th Gear /15 #30
2009 Press Pass Showcase 4th Gear /5 #51
2009 Press Pass Showcase Classic Collections Firesuit /25 #CCF5
2009 Press Pass Showcase Classic Collections Firesuit Patch /5 #CCF5
2009 Press Pass Showcase Classic Collections Ink /45 #3
2009 Press Pass Showcase Classic Collections Ink Gold /25 #3
2009 Press Pass Showcase Classic Collections Ink Green /5 #3
2009 Press Pass Showcase Classic Collections Ink Melting /1 #3
2009 Press Pass Showcase Classic Collections Sheet Metal /45 #CCS5
2009 Press Pass Showcase Classic Collections Tire /99 #CCT5
2009 Press Pass Showcase Elite Exhibit Ink /45 #9
2009 Press Pass Showcase Elite Exhibit Ink Gold /25 #9
2009 Press Pass Showcase Elite Exhibit Ink Green /5 #9
2009 Press Pass Showcase Elite Exhibit Ink Melting /1 #9
2009 Press Pass Showcase Elite Exhibit Triple Memorabilia /99 #EEJL
2009 Press Pass Showcase Elite Exhibit Triple Memorabilia Gold /45 #EEJL
2009 Press Pass Showcase Elite Exhibit Triple Memorabilia Green /25 #EEJL
2009 Press Pass Showcase Elite Exhibit Triple Memorabilia Melting /5 #EEJL
2009 Press Pass Showcase Printing Plates Black /1 #30
2009 Press Pass Showcase Printing Plates Cyan /1 #30
2009 Press Pass Showcase Printing Plates Magenta /1 #30
2009 Press Pass Showcase Printing Plates Yellow /1 #30
2009 Press Pass Showcase Prized Pieces Firesuit /25 #PPFJL
2009 Press Pass Showcase Prized Pieces Firesuit Patch /5 #PPFJL
2009 Press Pass Showcase Prized Pieces Sheet Metal /45 #PPSJL
2009 Press Pass Showcase Prized Pieces Tire /99 #PPTJL
2009 Press Pass Signings Blue /25 #26
2009 Press Pass Signings Gold #26
2009 Press Pass Signings Green /15 #26
2009 Press Pass Signings Orange /25 #26
2009 Press Pass Signings Printing Plates Cyan /1 #26
2009 Press Pass Signings Printing Plates Magenta /1 #26
2009 Press Pass Signings Purple /45 #26
2009 Press Pass Sponsor Swatches /250 #SSJL
2009 Press Pass Sponsor Swatches Select /8 #SSJL
2009 Press Pass Stealth #20
2009 Press Pass Stealth #47
2009 Press Pass Stealth #58A
2009 Press Pass Stealth #68
2009 Press Pass Stealth #58B
2009 Press Pass Stealth Battle Armor /240 #BAJL1
2009 Press Pass Stealth Battle Armor /70 #BAJL2
2009 Press Pass Stealth Battle Armor /4 #BAJL3
2009 Press Pass Stealth Battle Armor Multi-Color /130 #BAJL
2009 Press Pass Stealth Chrome #20
2009 Press Pass Stealth Chrome #47
2009 Press Pass Stealth Chrome #58A
2009 Press Pass Stealth Chrome #68
2009 Press Pass Stealth Chrome #58B
2009 Press Pass Stealth Chrome Brushed Metal /25 #20
2009 Press Pass Stealth Chrome Brushed Metal /25 #47
2009 Press Pass Stealth Chrome Brushed Metal /25 #58
2009 Press Pass Stealth Chrome Brushed Metal /25 #68
2009 Press Pass Stealth Chrome Gold /99 #20
2009 Press Pass Stealth Chrome Gold /99 #47
2009 Press Pass Stealth Chrome Gold /99 #58
2009 Press Pass Stealth Chrome Gold /99 #68
2009 Press Pass Stealth Confidential Classified Bronze #PC13
2009 Press Pass Stealth Confidential Secret Silver #PC13
2009 Press Pass Stealth Confidential Top Secret Gold /25 #PC13
2009 Press Pass Stealth Mach 09 #M4
2009 Press Pass Stealth Previews /5 #EB20
2009 Press Pass Target Victory Tires /50 #JLTT
2009 Press Pass Total Tire /25 #TT4
2009 Press Pass Tread Marks Autographs /10 #SSJL
2009 Press Pass Unleashed #U12
2009 Press Pass Wal-Mart Autographs Red #9
2009 Press Pass Wal-Mart Signature Edition /50 #JL
2009 VIP #20
2009 VIP #40
2009 VIP #59
2009 VIP #63
2009 VIP Get A Grip /100 #GGJL
2009 VIP Get A Grip Autographs /20 #GGSJL
2009 VIP Get A Grip Holofoil /10 #GGJL
2009 VIP Guest List #GG23
2009 VIP Leadfoot /150 #LFJL
2009 VIP Leadfoot Holofoil /10 #LFJL
2009 VIP Leadfoot Logos /5 #LFLJL
2009 VIP National Promos #4
2009 VIP Previews /5 #20
2009 VIP Purple /25 #20
2009 VIP Purple /25 #40
2009 VIP Purple /25 #59
2009 VIP Purple /25 #63
2009 VIP Rookie Stripes /100 #RS1
2009 VIP Rookie Stripes Autographs /25 #RSJL
2009 Wheels Autographs /25 #41
2009 Wheels Autographs /25 #42
2009 Wheels Autographs #43
2009 Wheels Autographs Press Plates Black /1 #JL
2009 Wheels Autographs Press Plates Cyan /1 #JL
2009 Wheels Autographs Press Plates Magenta /1 #JL
2009 Wheels Autographs Press Plates Yellow /1 #JL
2009 Wheels Main Event #40
2009 Wheels Main Event #54
2009 Wheels Main Event #87
2009 Wheels Main Event Fast Pass Purple /25 #40
2009 Wheels Main Event Fast Pass Purple /25 #54
2009 Wheels Main Event Hat Dance Patch /10 #HDJL
2009 Wheels Main Event Hat Dance Triple /99 #HDJL
2009 Wheels Main Event Playing Cards Blue #JH
2009 Wheels Main Event Playing Cards Red #JH
2009 Wheels Main Event Reward Copper /10 #RWJL
2009 Wheels Main Event Reward Holofoil /50 #RWJL
2009 Wheels Main Event Rookie Marks Clubs #JL
2009 Wheels Main Event Rookie Marks Diamonds #JL
2009 Wheels Main Event Rookie Marks Hearts #JL
2009 Wheels Main Event Wildcard Cuts /2 #WCCJL
2010 Element #21
2010 Element #51
2010 Element #76
2010 Element #93
2010 Element Blue /35 #21
2010 Element Blue /35 #51
2010 Element Blue /35 #76
2010 Element Blue /35 #93
2010 Element Finish Line Checkered Flag /10 #FLJL
2010 Element Finish Line Green Flag /20 #FLJL
2010 Element Finish Line Tires /99 #FLJL
2010 Element Green #21
2010 Element Green #51
2010 Element Green #76
2010 Element Green #93
2010 Element Previews /5 #EB21
2010 Element Purple /25 #21
2010 Element Purple /25 #51
2010 Element Recycled Materials Blue /25 #RMJL
2010 Element Recycled Materials Green /125 #RMJL
2010 Element Red Target #21
2010 Element Red Target #51
2010 Element Red Target #76
2010 Element Red Target #93
2010 Press Pass #20
2010 Press Pass #39
2010 Press Pass #60
2010 Press Pass #72
2010 Press Pass #92
2010 Press Pass #95
2010 Press Pass Autographs #32
2010 Press Pass Autographs Printing Plates Black /1 #24
2010 Press Pass Autographs Printing Plates Cyan /1 #29
2010 Press Pass Autographs Printing Plates Magenta /1 #27
2010 Press Pass Autographs Printing Plates Yellow /1 #26
2010 Press Pass Autographs Track Edition /10 #9
2010 Press Pass Blue #20
2010 Press Pass Blue #39
2010 Press Pass Blue #60
2010 Press Pass Blue #72
2010 Press Pass Blue #92
2010 Press Pass Blue #95
2010 Press Pass Burning Rubber /250 #BR16
2010 Press Pass Burning Rubber Autographs /20 #SSTEJL
2010 Press Pass Burning Rubber Gold /50 #BR16
2010 Press Pass Burning Rubber Prime Cuts /25 #BR16
2010 Press Pass Cup Chase #CCR5
2010 Press Pass Eclipse #14
2010 Press Pass Eclipse #36
2010 Press Pass Eclipse #70
2010 Press Pass Eclipse #80
2010 Press Pass Eclipse Blue #14
2010 Press Pass Eclipse Blue #36
2010 Press Pass Eclipse Blue #70
2010 Press Pass Eclipse Blue #80
2010 Press Pass Eclipse Cars #C4
2010 Press Pass Eclipse Gold #14
2010 Press Pass Eclipse Gold #36
2010 Press Pass Eclipse Gold #70
2010 Press Pass Eclipse Gold #80
2010 Press Pass Eclipse Previews /5 #14
2010 Press Pass Eclipse Previews /1 #36
2010 Press Pass Eclipse Purple /25 #14
2010 Press Pass Eclipse Purple /25 #36
2010 Press Pass Eclipse Signature Series Shoes Autographs /20 #SSSEJL
2010 Press Pass Eclipse Spellbound Swatches /299 #SSJL1
2010 Press Pass Eclipse Spellbound Swatches /299 #SSJL2
2010 Press Pass Eclipse Spellbound Swatches /299 #SSJL3
2010 Press Pass Eclipse Spellbound Swatches /299 #SSJL4
2010 Press Pass Eclipse Spellbound Swatches /299 #SSJL5
2010 Press Pass Eclipse Spellbound Swatches /299 #SSJL6
2010 Press Pass Eclipse Spellbound Swatches Holofoil /20 #SSJL1
2010 Press Pass Eclipse Spellbound Swatches Holofoil /20 #SSJL2
2010 Press Pass Eclipse Spellbound Swatches Holofoil /20 #SSJL3
2010 Press Pass Eclipse Spellbound Swatches Holofoil /20 #SSJL4
2010 Press Pass Eclipse Spellbound Swatches Holofoil /20 #SSJL5
2010 Press Pass Eclipse Spellbound Swatches Holofoil /20 #SSJL6
2010 Press Pass Five Star /35 #21
2010 Press Pass Five Star Classic Compilations Combos Firesuit Autographs /15 #CCMJGR
2010 Press Pass Five Star Classic Compilations Combos Patches Autographs /1 #CCMJGR
2010 Press Pass Five Star Classic Compilations Dual Memorabilia Autographs /10 #JL
2010 Press Pass Five Star Classic Compilations Firesuit Autographs /15 #JL
2010 Press Pass Five Star Classic Compilations Patch Autographs /1 #CCPJL15
2010 Press Pass Five Star Classic Compilations Patch Autographs /1 #CCPJL1
2010 Press Pass Five Star Classic Compilations Patch Autographs /1 #CCPJL2
2010 Press Pass Five Star Classic Compilations Patch Autographs /1 #CCPJL3
2010 Press Pass Five Star Classic Compilations Patch Autographs /1 #CCPJL4
2010 Press Pass Five Star Classic Compilations Patch Autographs /1 #CCPJL5
2010 Press Pass Five Star Classic Compilations Patch Autographs /1 #CCPJL6
2010 Press Pass Five Star Classic Compilations Patch Autographs /1 #CCPJL7
2010 Press Pass Five Star Classic Compilations Patch Autographs /1 #CCPJL8
2010 Press Pass Five Star Classic Compilations Patch Autographs /1 #CCPJL9
2010 Press Pass Five Star Classic Compilations Patch Autographs /1 #CCPJL10
2010 Press Pass Five Star Classic Compilations Patch Autographs /1 #CCPJL11
2010 Press Pass Five Star Classic Compilations Patch Autographs /1 #CCPJL12
2010 Press Pass Five Star Classic Compilations Patch Autographs /1 #CCPJL13
2010 Press Pass Five Star Classic Compilations Patch Autographs /1 #CCPJL14
2010 Press Pass Five Star Classic Compilations Sheet Metal Autographs /25 #JL
2010 Press Pass Five Star Classic Compilations Triple Memorabilia Autographs /5 #JL
2010 Press Pass Five Star Holofoil /10 #21
2010 Press Pass Five Star Melting /1 #21
2010 Press Pass Five Star Paramount Pieces Aluminum /20 #JL
2010 Press Pass Five Star Paramount Pieces Blue /15 #JL
2010 Press Pass Five Star Paramount Pieces Gold /10 #JL
2010 Press Pass Five Star Paramount Pieces Holofoil /5 #JL
2010 Press Pass Five Star Paramount Pieces Melting /1 #JL
2010 Press Pass Five Star Signature Souvenirs Aluminum /50 #SSJL
2010 Press Pass Five Star Signature Souvenirs Gold /25 #SSJL
2010 Press Pass Five Star Signature Souvenirs Holofoil /10 #SSJL
2010 Press Pass Five Star Signature Souvenirs Melting /1 #SSJL
2010 Press Pass Five Star Signatures Aluminum /35 #JL
2010 Press Pass Five Star Signatures Gold /20 #JL
2010 Press Pass Five Star Signatures Holofoil /5 #JL
2010 Press Pass Five Star Signatures Melting /1 #JL
2010 Press Pass Four Wide Autographs /5 #NNO
2010 Press Pass Four Wide Firesuit /25 #FWJL
2010 Press Pass Four Wide Sheet Metal /15 #FWJL
2010 Press Pass Four Wide Shoes /1 #FWJL
2010 Press Pass Four Wide Tires /10 #FWJL
2010 Press Pass Gold #20
2010 Press Pass Gold #39
2010 Press Pass Gold #60
2010 Press Pass Gold #72
2010 Press Pass Gold #92
2010 Press Pass Gold #95
2010 Press Pass Holofoil /100 #20
2010 Press Pass Holofoil /100 #39
2010 Press Pass Holofoil /100 #60
2010 Press Pass Holofoil /100 #72
2010 Press Pass Holofoil /100 #92
2010 Press Pass Holofoil /100 #95
2010 Press Pass Legends Autographs Blue /10 #39
2010 Press Pass Legends Autographs Holofoil /25 #39
2010 Press Pass Legends Autographs Printing Plates Black /1 #33
2010 Press Pass Legends Autographs Printing Plates Cyan /1 #33
2010 Press Pass Legends Autographs Printing Plates Magenta /1 #33
2010 Press Pass Legends Autographs Printing Plates Yellow /1 #33
2010 Press Pass Legends Motorsports Masters Autographs Printing Plates Black /1 #33
2010 Press Pass Legends Motorsports Masters Autographs Printing Plates Cyan /1 #33
2010 Press Pass Legends Motorsports Masters Autographs Printing Plates Magenta /1 #33
2010 Press Pass Legends Motorsports Masters Autographs Printing Plates Yellow /1 #33
2010 Press Pass Premium #19
2010 Press Pass Premium #46
2010 Press Pass Premium #59
2010 Press Pass Premium Hot Threads /299 #HTJL
2010 Press Pass Premium Hot Threads Holofoil /99 #HTJL
2010 Press Pass Premium Hot Threads Multi Color /25 #HTJL
2010 Press Pass Premium Hot Threads Two Color /125 #HTJL
2010 Press Pass Premium Pairings Firesuits /25 #PFBL
2010 Press Pass Premium Pairings Signatures /5 #PSBL
2010 Press Pass Premium Purple /25 #19
2010 Press Pass Premium Purple /25 #46
2010 Press Pass Premium Purple /25 #59
2010 Press Pass Premium Signature Series Firesuit /15 #SSFJL
2010 Press Pass Premium Signatures #PSJL
2010 Press Pass Premium Signatures Red Ink /24 #PSJL
2010 Press Pass Previews /5 #20
2010 Press Pass Purple /25 #20
2010 Press Pass Purple /25 #39
2010 Press Pass Purple /25 #60
2010 Press Pass Purple /25 #72
2010 Press Pass Purple /25 #92
2010 Press Pass Purple /25 #95
2010 Press Pass Showcase /499 #19
2010 Press Pass Showcase /499 #35
2010 Press Pass Showcase /499 #49
2010 Press Pass Showcase Classic Collections Firesuit Green /25 #CCIJGR
2010 Press Pass Showcase Classic Collections Firesuit Patch Melting /5 #CCIJGR
2010 Press Pass Showcase Classic Collections Ink /15 #CCIJGR
2010 Press Pass Showcase Classic Collections Ink Gold /10 #CCIJGR
2010 Press Pass Showcase Classic Collections Ink Green /5 #CCIJGR
2010 Press Pass Showcase Classic Collections Ink Melting /1 #CCIJGR
2010 Press Pass Showcase Classic Collections Sheet Metal /99 #CCIJGR
2010 Press Pass Showcase Classic Collections Sheet Metal Gold /45 #CCIJGR
2010 Press Pass Showcase Elite Exhibit Ink /45 #EEIJL
2010 Press Pass Showcase Elite Exhibit Ink Gold /25 #EEIJL
2010 Press Pass Showcase Elite Exhibit Ink Green /5 #EEIJL
2010 Press Pass Showcase Elite Exhibit Ink Melting /1 #EEIJL
2010 Press Pass Showcase Elite Exhibit Triple Memorabilia /99 #EEMJL
2010 Press Pass Showcase Elite Exhibit Triple Memorabilia Gold /45 #EEMJL
2010 Press Pass Showcase Elite Exhibit Triple Memorabilia Green /25 #EEMJL
2010 Press Pass Showcase Elite Exhibit Triple Memorabilia Melting /5 #EEMJL
2010 Press Pass Showcase Gold /125 #19
2010 Press Pass Showcase Gold /125 #35
2010 Press Pass Showcase Gold /125 #49
2010 Press Pass Showcase Green /50 #19
2010 Press Pass Showcase Green /50 #35
2010 Press Pass Showcase Green /50 #49
2010 Press Pass Showcase Melting /15 #19
2010 Press Pass Showcase Melting /15 #35
2010 Press Pass Showcase Melting /15 #49
2010 Press Pass Showcase Platinum Holo /1 #19
2010 Press Pass Showcase Platinum Holo /1 #35
2010 Press Pass Showcase Platinum Holo /1 #49
2010 Press Pass Showcase Prized Pieces Firesuit Green /25 #PPMJL
2010 Press Pass Showcase Prized Pieces Firesuit Ink Gold /25 #PPIJL
2010 Press Pass Showcase Prized Pieces Firesuit Ink Melting /1 #PPIJL
2010 Press Pass Showcase Prized Pieces Firesuit Patch Melting /5 #PPMJL
2010 Press Pass Showcase Prized Pieces Memorabilia Ink Green /15 #PPIJL
2010 Press Pass Showcase Prized Pieces Sheet Metal /99 #PPMJL
2010 Press Pass Showcase Prized Pieces Sheet Metal Gold /45 #PPMJL
2010 Press Pass Showcase Prized Pieces Sheet Metal Ink Silver /45 #PPIJL
2010 Press Pass Signings Blue /10 #35
2010 Press Pass Signings Gold /25 #35
2010 Press Pass Signings Red /15 #35
2010 Press Pass Signings Silver /99 #35
2010 Press Pass Stealth #21
2010 Press Pass Stealth #64
2010 Press Pass Stealth #79
2010 Press Pass Stealth #84
2010 Press Pass Stealth Battle Armor Holofoil /25 #BAJL
2010 Press Pass Stealth Battle Armor Silver /225 #BAJL
2010 Press Pass Stealth Black and White #21
2010 Press Pass Stealth Black and White #64
2010 Press Pass Stealth Black and White #79
2010 Press Pass Stealth Black and White #84
2010 Press Pass Stealth Previews /5 #21
2010 Press Pass Stealth Previews /1 #64
2010 Press Pass Stealth Purple /25 #21
2010 Press Pass Stealth Purple /25 #64
2010 Press Pass Stealth Signature Series Sheet Metal /15 #SSMEJL
2010 Press Pass Stealth Weekend Warriors Holofoil /25 #WWJL
2010 Press Pass Stealth Weekend Warriors Silver /199 #WWJL
2010 Press Pass Target By The Numbers #BNT3
2010 Press Pass Unleashed #U9
2010 Press Pass Wal-Mart By The Numbers #BNW3
2010 Press Pass Wal-Mart Top Numbers Tires /50 #TNW-JL
2010 Wheels Autographs #31
2010 Wheels Autographs Printing Plates Black /1 #31
2010 Wheels Autographs Printing Plates Cyan /1 #31
2010 Wheels Autographs Printing Plates Magenta /1 #31
2010 Wheels Autographs Printing Plates Yellow /1 #31
2010 Wheels Autographs Special Ink /10 #12
2010 Wheels Autographs Target /10 #20
2010 Wheels Main Event #21
2010 Wheels Main Event Blue #21
2010 Wheels Main Event Fight Card #FC17
2010 Wheels Main Event Fight Card Checkered Flag #FC17
2010 Wheels Main Event Fight Card Full Color Retail #FC17
2010 Wheels Main Event Fight Card Gold /25 #FC17
2010 Wheels Main Event Head to Head /150 #HHKHJL
2010 Wheels Main Event Head to Head /150 #HHKBJL
2010 Wheels Main Event Head to Head Blue /75 #HHKHJL
2010 Wheels Main Event Head to Head Blue /75 #HHKBJL
2010 Wheels Main Event Head to Head Holofoil /10 #HHKHJL
2010 Wheels Main Event Head to Head Holofoil /10 #HHKBJL
2010 Wheels Main Event Head to Head Red /25 #HHKHJL
2010 Wheels Main Event Head to Head Red /25 #HHKBJL
2010 Wheels Main Event Marks Autographs /49 #35
2010 Wheels Main Event Marks Autographs Black /1 #34
2010 Wheels Main Event Marks Autographs Blue /20 #35
2010 Wheels Main Event Marks Autographs Red /5 #35
2010 Wheels Main Event Matchups Autographs /10 #MKJL
2010 Wheels Main Event Purple /25 #21
2010 Wheels Main Event Tale of the Tape #TT1
2010 Wheels Main Event Toe to Toe /10 #TTKBJL
2010 Wheels Main Event Upper Cuts Knock Out Patches /25 #UCKOJL
2010 Wheels Main Event Wheel to Wheel /25 #WWKBJL

2010 Wheels Main Event Wheel to Wheel Holofoil /10 #WWKBJL
2011 Element #21
2011 Element #81
2011 Element Autographs /25 #34
2011 Element Autographs Blue /5 #34
2011 Element Autographs Gold /5 #33
2011 Element Autographs Printing Plates Black /1 #34
2011 Element Autographs Printing Plates Cyan /1 #34
2011 Element Autographs Printing Plates Magenta /1 #34
2011 Element Autographs Printing Plates Yellow /1 #34
2011 Element Autographs Silver /15 #33
2011 Element Black /35 #21
2011 Element Black /35 #81
2011 Element Flagship Performers 2010 Green Flag Passes Blue-Yellow /50 #FPPJL
2011 Element Flagship Performers 2010 Laps Completed Yellow /50 #FPLJL
2011 Element Green #21
2011 Element Green #81
2011 Element Previews /5 #EB21
2011 Element Purple /25 #21
2011 Element Purple /25 #81
2011 Element Red #21
2011 Element Red #81
2011 Press Pass #22
2011 Press Pass #77
2011 Press Pass #120
2011 Press Pass #163
2011 Press Pass #165
2011 Press Pass #185
2011 Press Pass Autographs Blue /10 #34
2011 Press Pass Autographs Bronze /99 #33
2011 Press Pass Autographs Gold /25 #33
2011 Press Pass Autographs Printing Plates Black /1 #34
2011 Press Pass Autographs Printing Plates Cyan /1 #34
2011 Press Pass Autographs Printing Plates Magenta /1 #34
2011 Press Pass Autographs Printing Plates Yellow /1 #34
2011 Press Pass Autographs Silver /50 #34
2011 Press Pass Blue Holofoil /10 #22
2011 Press Pass Blue Holofoil /10 #77
2011 Press Pass Blue Holofoil /10 #120
2011 Press Pass Blue Holofoil /10 #163
2011 Press Pass Blue Holofoil /10 #165
2011 Press Pass Blue Holofoil /10 #185
2011 Press Pass Blue Retail #22
2011 Press Pass Blue Retail #77
2011 Press Pass Blue Retail #120
2011 Press Pass Blue Retail #163
2011 Press Pass Blue Retail #165
2011 Press Pass Blue Retail #185
2011 Press Pass Eclipse #20
2011 Press Pass Eclipse #42
2011 Press Pass Eclipse #79
2011 Press Pass Eclipse Blue #20
2011 Press Pass Eclipse Blue #42
2011 Press Pass Eclipse Blue #79
2011 Press Pass Eclipse Encore #E8
2011 Press Pass Eclipse Gold /55 #20
2011 Press Pass Eclipse Gold /55 #42
2011 Press Pass Eclipse Gold /55 #79
2011 Press Pass Eclipse In Focus #IF5
2011 Press Pass Eclipse Previews /5 #EB20
2011 Press Pass Eclipse Previews /1 #EB42
2011 Press Pass Eclipse Purple /25 #20
2011 Press Pass Eclipse Purple /25 #42
2011 Press Pass Eclipse Rides #R4
2011 Press Pass Eclipse Spellbound Swatches /250 #SBJL1
2011 Press Pass Eclipse Spellbound Swatches /150 #SBJL2
2011 Press Pass Eclipse Spellbound Swatches /150 #SBJL3
2011 Press Pass Eclipse Spellbound Swatches /100 #SBJL4
2011 Press Pass Eclipse Spellbound Swatches /75 #SBJL5
2011 Press Pass Eclipse Spellbound Swatches /50 #SBJL6
2011 Press Pass Eclipse Spellbound Swatches Signatures /10 #NNO
2011 Press Pass FanFare #24
2011 Press Pass FanFare Autographs Blue /5 #44
2011 Press Pass FanFare Autographs Bronze /50 #44
2011 Press Pass FanFare Autographs Gold /25 #44
2011 Press Pass FanFare Autographs Printing Plates Black /1 #44
2011 Press Pass FanFare Autographs Printing Plates Cyan /1 #44
2011 Press Pass FanFare Autographs Printing Plates Magenta /1 #44
2011 Press Pass FanFare Autographs Printing Plates Yellow /1 #44
2011 Press Pass FanFare Autographs Silver /15 #44
2011 Press Pass FanFare Blue Die Cuts #24
2011 Press Pass FanFare Emerald /25 #24
2011 Press Pass FanFare Holofoil Die Cuts #24
2011 Press Pass FanFare Magnificent Materials /199 #MMJL
2011 Press Pass FanFare Magnificent Materials Dual Swatches /50 #MMDJL
2011 Press Pass FanFare Magnificent Materials Dual Swatches Holofoil /10 #MMDJL
2011 Press Pass FanFare Magnificent Materials Holofoil /50 #MMJL
2011 Press Pass FanFare Rookie Standouts #RS2
2011 Press Pass FanFare Ruby Die Cuts /15 #24
2011 Press Pass FanFare Sapphire /10 #24
2011 Press Pass FanFare Silver /25 #24
2011 Press Pass Four Wide Firesuit /25 #FWJL
2011 Press Pass Four Wide Glove /1 #FWJL
2011 Press Pass Four Wide Sheet Metal /15 #FWJL
2011 Press Pass Four Wide Shoes /1 #FWJL
2011 Press Pass Four Wide Tire /10 #FWJL
2011 Press Pass Geared Up Holofoil /20 #GUJL
2011 Press Pass Gold /50 #22
2011 Press Pass Gold /50 #77
2011 Press Pass Gold /50 #120
2011 Press Pass Gold /50 #163
2011 Press Pass Gold /50 #165
2011 Press Pass Gold /50 #185
2011 Press Pass Legends Autographs Printing Plates Black /1 #LGAJL
2011 Press Pass Legends Autographs Printing Plates Cyan /1 #LGAJL
2011 Press Pass Legends Autographs Printing Plates Magenta /1 #LGAJL
2011 Press Pass Legends Autographs Printing Plates Yellow /1 #LGAJL
2011 Press Pass Premium #23
2011 Press Pass Premium #90
2011 Press Pass Premium Hot Threads /150 #HTJL
2011 Press Pass Premium Hot Threads Fast Pass /25 #HTJL
2011 Press Pass Premium Hot Threads Multi Color /25 #HTJL
2011 Press Pass Premium Hot Threads Secondary Color /99 #HTJL
2011 Press Pass Premium Purple /25 #23
2011 Press Pass Premium Purple /25 #90
2011 Press Pass Premium Signatures /146 #PSJL
2011 Press Pass Premium Signatures Red Ink /43 #PSJL
2011 Press Pass Previews /5 #EB22
2011 Press Pass Purple /25 #22
2011 Press Pass Showcase /499 #20
2011 Press Pass Showcase /499 #54
2011 Press Pass Showcase Classic Collections Firesuit /45 #CCMJGR
2011 Press Pass Showcase Classic Collections Firesuit Patches /5 #CCMJGR
2011 Press Pass Showcase Classic Collections Ink /25 #CCMJGR
2011 Press Pass Showcase Classic Collections Ink Gold /5 #CCMJGR
2011 Press Pass Showcase Classic Collections Ink Melting /1 #CCMJGR
2011 Press Pass Showcase Classic Collections Sheet Metal /99 #CCMJGR
2011 Press Pass Showcase Elite Exhibit Ink /50 #EEIJL
2011 Press Pass Showcase Elite Exhibit Ink Gold /25 #EEIJL
2011 Press Pass Showcase Elite Exhibit Ink Melting /1 #EEIJL
2011 Press Pass Showcase Gold /125 #20
2011 Press Pass Showcase Gold /125 #54
2011 Press Pass Showcase Green /25 #20
2011 Press Pass Showcase Green /25 #54
2011 Press Pass Showcase Masterpieces Ink /45 #MPIJL
2011 Press Pass Showcase Masterpieces Ink Gold /25 #MPIJL
2011 Press Pass Showcase Masterpieces Ink Melting /1 #MPIJL
2011 Press Pass Showcase Masterpieces Memorabilia /99 #MPMJL
2011 Press Pass Showcase Masterpieces Memorabilia Gold /45 #MPMJL
2011 Press Pass Showcase Masterpieces Memorabilia Melting /5 #MPMJL
2011 Press Pass Showcase Melting /1 #20
2011 Press Pass Showcase Melting /1 #54
2011 Press Pass Showcase Prized Pieces Firesuit /99 #PPMJL
2011 Press Pass Showcase Prized Pieces Firesuit Gold /45 #PPMJL
2011 Press Pass Showcase Prized Pieces Firesuit Ink /25 #PPIJL
2011 Press Pass Showcase Prized Pieces Firesuit Patches Ink /1 #PPIJL
2011 Press Pass Showcase Prized Pieces Firesuit Patches Melting /5 #PPMJL
2011 Press Pass Showcase Prized Pieces Sheet Metal Ink /45 #PPIJL
2011 Press Pass Signature Series /11 #SSTJL
2011 Press Pass Signature Series /11 #SSSJL
2011 Press Pass Signature Series /11 #SSFJL
2011 Press Pass Signature Series /11 #SSMJL
2011 Press Pass Signings Black and White /10 #PPSJL1
2011 Press Pass Signings Brushed Metal /48 #PPSJL1
2011 Press Pass Signings Holofoil /24 #PPSJL1
2011 Press Pass Signings Printing Plates Black /1 #PPSJL1
2011 Press Pass Signings Printing Plates Magenta /1 #PPSJL1
2011 Press Pass Signings Printing Plates Yellow /1 #PPSJL1
2011 Press Pass Stealth #47
2011 Press Pass Stealth #84
2011 Press Pass Stealth Afterburner /99 #ABJL
2011 Press Pass Stealth Afterburner Gold /25 #ABJL
2011 Press Pass Stealth Black and White /25 #47
2011 Press Pass Stealth Black and White /25 #84
2011 Press Pass Stealth Holofoil /99 #47
2011 Press Pass Stealth Holofoil /99 #84
2011 Press Pass Stealth Metal of Honor Medal of Honor /50 #BAJL
2011 Press Pass Stealth Metal of Honor Purple Heart /25 #MHJL
2011 Press Pass Stealth Metal of Honor Silver Star /99 #BAJL
2011 Press Pass Stealth Purple /25 #47
2011 Press Pass Stealth Supersonic #SS8
2011 Press Pass Target Winning Tickets #WTT8
2011 Press Pass Winning Tickets #WT35
2011 Wheels Main Event #23
2011 Wheels Main Event #90
2011 Wheels Main Event Black and White #23
2011 Wheels Main Event Black and White #90
2011 Wheels Main Event Blue /75 #23
2011 Wheels Main Event Blue /75 #90
2011 Wheels Main Event Gloves Off Holofoil /25 #GOJL
2011 Wheels Main Event Gloves Off Silver /99 #GOJL
2011 Wheels Main Event Green /1 #23
2011 Wheels Main Event Green /1 #90
2011 Wheels Main Event Headliners Holofoil /25 #HLJL
2011 Wheels Main Event Headliners Silver /99 #HLJL
2011 Wheels Main Event Joe Gibbs Racing 20th Anniversary #JGR5
2011 Wheels Main Event Joe Gibbs Racing 20th Anniversary Brushed Foil /199 #JGR5
2011 Wheels Main Event Joe Gibbs Racing 20th Anniversary Holofoil /50 #JGR5
2011 Wheels Main Event Marks Autographs Blue /5 #MEJL
2011 Wheels Main Event Marks Autographs Gold /15 #MEJL
2011 Wheels Main Event Marks Autographs Silver /30 #MEJL
2011 Wheels Main Event Materials Holofoil /25 #MEMJL
2011 Wheels Main Event Materials Silver /99 #MEMJL
2011 Wheels Main Event Red /20 #23
2011 Wheels Main Event Red /20 #90
2012 Press Pass #23
2012 Press Pass #79
2012 Press Pass Autographs Blue /5 #PPAJL1
2012 Press Pass Autographs Printing Plates Black /1 #PPAJL1
2012 Press Pass Autographs Printing Plates Cyan /1 #PPAJL1
2012 Press Pass Autographs Printing Plates Magenta /1 #PPAJL1
2012 Press Pass Autographs Printing Plates Yellow /1 #PPAJL1
2012 Press Pass Autographs Red /5 #PPAJL1
2012 Press Pass Autographs Silver /15 #PPAJL1
2012 Press Pass Blue #23
2012 Press Pass Blue #79
2012 Press Pass Blue Holofoil /35 #23
2012 Press Pass Blue Holofoil /35 #79
2012 Press Pass Fanfare #26
2012 Press Pass Fanfare Autographs Blue /1 #JL1
2012 Press Pass Fanfare Autographs Gold /5 #JL1
2012 Press Pass Fanfare Autographs Red /1 #JL1
2012 Press Pass Fanfare Autographs Silver /5 #JL1
2012 Press Pass Fanfare Blue Foil Die Cuts #26
2012 Press Pass Fanfare Diamond /5 #26
2012 Press Pass Fanfare Holofoil Die Cuts #26
2012 Press Pass Fanfare Magnificent Materials /125 #MMJL
2012 Press Pass Fanfare Magnificent Materials Dual Swatches /50 #MMJL
2012 Press Pass Fanfare Magnificent Materials Dual Swatches Melting /10 #MMJL
2012 Press Pass Fanfare Magnificent Materials Gold /75 #MMJL
2012 Press Pass Fanfare Magnificent Materials Signatures /95 #JL2
2012 Press Pass Fanfare Magnificent Materials Signatures Blue /25 #JL2
2012 Press Pass Fanfare Sapphire /20 #26
2012 Press Pass Fanfare Silver /25 #26
2012 Press Pass Four Wide Firesuit /25 #FWJL
2012 Press Pass Four Wide Glove /1 #FWJL
2012 Press Pass Four Wide Sheet Metal /15 #FWJL
2012 Press Pass Four Wide Tire /10 #FWJL
2012 Press Pass Gold #23
2012 Press Pass Gold #79
2012 Press Pass Ignite #23
2012 Press Pass Ignite #42
2012 Press Pass Ignite #70
2012 Press Pass Ignite Materials Autographs Gun Metal /45 #IMJL
2012 Press Pass Ignite Materials Autographs Red /5 #IMJL
2012 Press Pass Ignite Materials Autographs Silver /150 #IMJL
2012 Press Pass Ignite Materials Gun Metal /99 #IMJL
2012 Press Pass Ignite Materials Red /10 #IMJL
2012 Press Pass Ignite Materials Silver #IMJL
2012 Press Pass Ignite Proofs Black and White /50 #23
2012 Press Pass Ignite Proofs Black and White /50 #42
2012 Press Pass Ignite Proofs Black and White /50 #70
2012 Press Pass Ignite Proofs Cyan #23
2012 Press Pass Ignite Proofs Cyan #42
2012 Press Pass Ignite Proofs Cyan #70
2012 Press Pass Ignite Proofs Magenta #23
2012 Press Pass Ignite Proofs Magenta #42
2012 Press Pass Ignite Proofs Magenta #70
2012 Press Pass Ignite Proofs Yellow /10 #23
2012 Press Pass Ignite Proofs Yellow /10 #42
2012 Press Pass Ignite Proofs Yellow /10 #70
2012 Press Pass Power Picks Blue /50 #12
2012 Press Pass Power Picks Blue /50 #41
2012 Press Pass Power Picks Blue /50 #64
2012 Press Pass Power Picks Gold /50 #12
2012 Press Pass Power Picks Gold /50 #41
2012 Press Pass Power Picks Gold /50 #64
2012 Press Pass Power Picks Holofoil /10 #12
2012 Press Pass Power Picks Holofoil /10 #41
2012 Press Pass Power Picks Holofoil /10 #64
2012 Press Pass Preferred Line #PL1
2012 Press Pass Purple /35 #23
2012 Press Pass Purple /35 #79
2012 Press Pass Redline #24
2012 Press Pass Redline Black /99 #24
2012 Press Pass Redline Cyan /50 #24
2012 Press Pass Redline Full Throttle Dual Relic Blue /5 #FTJL
2012 Press Pass Redline Full Throttle Dual Relic Gold /10 #FTJL
2012 Press Pass Redline Full Throttle Dual Relic Melting /1 #FTJL
2012 Press Pass Redline Full Throttle Dual Relic Red /75 #FTJL
2012 Press Pass Redline Full Throttle Dual Relic Silver /25 #FTJL
2012 Press Pass Redline Magenta /15 #24
2012 Press Pass Redline Muscle Car Sheet Metal Blue /5 #MCJL
2012 Press Pass Redline Muscle Car Sheet Metal Gold /10 #MCJL
2012 Press Pass Redline Muscle Car Sheet Metal Melting /1 #MCJL
2012 Press Pass Redline Muscle Car Sheet Metal Red /75 #MCJL
2012 Press Pass Redline Muscle Car Sheet Metal Silver /25 #MCJL
2012 Press Pass Redline Relic Autographs Blue /10 #RLRJL
2012 Press Pass Redline Relic Autographs Gold /25 #RLRJL
2012 Press Pass Redline Relic Autographs Melting /1 #RLRJL
2012 Press Pass Redline Relic Autographs Red /75 #RLRJL
2012 Press Pass Redline Relic Autographs Silver /50 #RLRJL
2012 Press Pass Redline Relics Blue /5 #RLJL
2012 Press Pass Redline Relics Gold /10 #RLJL
2012 Press Pass Redline Relics Melting /1 #RLJL
2012 Press Pass Redline Relics Red /75 #RLJL
2012 Press Pass Redline Relics Silver /25 #RLJL
2012 Press Pass Redline Rookie Year Relic Autographs Blue /5 #RYJL
2012 Press Pass Redline Rookie Year Relic Autographs Gold /25 #RYJL
2012 Press Pass Redline Rookie Year Relic Autographs Melting /1 #RYJL
2012 Press Pass Redline Rookie Year Relic Autographs Red /49 #RYJL
2012 Press Pass Redline Signatures Blue /5 #RSJL1
2012 Press Pass Redline Signatures Blue /5 #RSJL2
2012 Press Pass Redline Signatures Gold /25 #RSJL1
2012 Press Pass Redline Signatures Gold /15 #RSJL2
2012 Press Pass Redline Signatures Holofoil /10 #RSJL1
2012 Press Pass Redline Signatures Holofoil /10 #RSJL2
2012 Press Pass Redline Signatures Melting /1 #RSJL1
2012 Press Pass Redline Signatures Melting /1 #RSJL2
2012 Press Pass Redline Signatures Red /50 #RSJL1
2012 Press Pass Redline Signatures Red /25 #RSJL2
2012 Press Pass Redline Yellow /1 #24
2012 Press Pass Showcase /499 #17
2012 Press Pass Showcase /499 #56
2012 Press Pass Showcase Classic Collections Ink /10 #CCMJGR
2012 Press Pass Showcase Classic Collections Ink Gold /5 #CCMJGR
2012 Press Pass Showcase Classic Collections Ink Melting /1 #CCMJGR
2012 Press Pass Showcase Classic Collections Memorabilia /99 #CCMJGR
2012 Press Pass Showcase Classic Collections Memorabilia Gold /50 #CCMJGR
2012 Press Pass Showcase Classic Collections Memorabilia Melting /5 #CCMJGR
2012 Press Pass Showcase Elite Exhibit Ink /50 #EEIJL
2012 Press Pass Showcase Elite Exhibit Ink Gold /25 #EEIJL
2012 Press Pass Showcase Elite Exhibit Ink Melting /1 #EEIJL
2012 Press Pass Showcase Gold /125 #17
2012 Press Pass Showcase Gold /125 #56
2012 Press Pass Showcase Green /5 #17
2012 Press Pass Showcase Green /5 #56
2012 Press Pass Showcase Masterpieces Ink /50 #MPIJL
2012 Press Pass Showcase Masterpieces Ink Gold /25 #MPIJL
2012 Press Pass Showcase Masterpieces Ink Melting /1 #MPIJL
2012 Press Pass Showcase Masterpieces Memorabilia /99 #MPJL
2012 Press Pass Showcase Masterpieces Memorabilia Gold /50 #MPJL
2012 Press Pass Showcase Masterpieces Memorabilia Melting /5 #MPJL
2012 Press Pass Showcase Melting /1 #17
2012 Press Pass Showcase Melting /1 #56
2012 Press Pass Showcase Prized Pieces /20 #PPJL
2012 Press Pass Showcase Prized Pieces Gold /10 #PPJL
2012 Press Pass Showcase Prized Pieces Melting /5 #PPJL
2012 Press Pass Showcase Purple /1 #17
2012 Press Pass Showcase Purple /1 #56
2012 Press Pass Showcase Red /25 #17
2012 Press Pass Showcase Red /25 #56
2012 Press Pass Showcase Showcase Patches /5 #SSPJL
2012 Press Pass Showcase Showcase Patches Melting /1 #SSPJL
2012 Press Pass Showcase Signature Patches /1 #SSPJL
2012 Press Pass Signature Series Race Used /12 #PPAJL1
2012 Press Pass Signature Series Race Used /12 #PPAJL2
2012 Press Pass Snapshots #SS23
2012 Press Pass Target Snapshots #SSTG9
2012 Total Memorabilia #20
2012 Total Memorabilia Black and White /99 #20
2012 Total Memorabilia Dual Swatch Gold /75 #TMJL
2012 Total Memorabilia Dual Swatch Holofoil /25 #TMJL
2012 Total Memorabilia Dual Swatch Melting /5 #TMJL
2012 Total Memorabilia Dual Swatch Silver /99 #TMJL
2012 Total Memorabilia Gold /275 #20
2012 Total Memorabilia Jumbo Swatch Gold /50 #TMJL
2012 Total Memorabilia Jumbo Swatch Holofoil /10 #TMJL
2012 Total Memorabilia Jumbo Swatch Melting /1 #TMJL
2012 Total Memorabilia Red Retail /250 #20
2012 Total Memorabilia Signature Collection Dual Swatch Silver /10 #SCJL
2012 Total Memorabilia Signature Collection Quad Swatch Holofoil /5 #SCJL
2012 Total Memorabilia Signature Collection Single Swatch Melting /1 #SCJL
2012 Total Memorabilia Signature Collection Triple Swatch Gold /10 #SCJL
2012 Total Memorabilia Single Swatch Gold /99 #TMJL
2012 Total Memorabilia Single Swatch Holofoil /50 #TMJL
2012 Total Memorabilia Single Swatch Melting /10 #TMJL
2012 Total Memorabilia Single Swatch Silver /299 #TMJL
2012 Total Memorabilia Triple Swatch Gold /50 #TMJL
2012 Total Memorabilia Triple Swatch Holofoil /25 #TMJL
2012 Total Memorabilia Triple Swatch Melting /1 #TMJL
2012 Total Memorabilia Triple Swatch Silver /99 #TMJL
2013 Press Pass #27
2013 Press Pass Burning Rubber Blue /50 #BRJL
2013 Press Pass Burning Rubber Gold /199 #BRJL
2013 Press Pass Burning Rubber Holofoil /75 #BRJL
2013 Press Pass Burning Rubber Melting /10 #BRJL
2013 Press Pass Certified Winners Autographs Gold /10 #JL
2013 Press Pass Certified Winners Autographs Melting /5 #JL
2013 Press Pass Color Proofs Black #27
2013 Press Pass Color Proofs Cyan /35 #27
2013 Press Pass Color Proofs Magenta #27
2013 Press Pass Color Proofs Yellow /5 #27
2013 Press Pass Cup Chase Prizes #CCP6
2013 Press Pass Fanfare #34
2013 Press Pass Fanfare #35
2013 Press Pass Fanfare Autographs Blue /1 #JL
2013 Press Pass Fanfare Autographs Gold /10 #JL
2013 Press Pass Fanfare Autographs Green /2 #JL
2013 Press Pass Fanfare Autographs Red /5 #JL
2013 Press Pass Fanfare Autographs Silver /50 #JL
2013 Press Pass Fanfare Diamond Die Cuts /5 #34
2013 Press Pass Fanfare Diamond Die Cuts /5 #35
2013 Press Pass Fanfare Fan Following #FF12
2013 Press Pass Fanfare Green /3 #34
2013 Press Pass Fanfare Green /3 #35
2013 Press Pass Fanfare Holofoil Die Cuts #34
2013 Press Pass Fanfare Holofoil Die Cuts #35
2013 Press Pass Fanfare Magnificent Materials Dual Swatches /50 #JL
2013 Press Pass Fanfare Magnificent Materials Dual Swatches Melting /10 #JL
2013 Press Pass Fanfare Magnificent Materials Gold /50 #JL
2013 Press Pass Fanfare Magnificent Materials Jumbo Swatches /25 #JL
2013 Press Pass Fanfare Magnificent Materials Silver /199 #JL
2013 Press Pass Fanfare Red Foil Die Cuts #34
2013 Press Pass Fanfare Red Foil Die Cuts #35
2013 Press Pass Fanfare Sapphire /20 #34
2013 Press Pass Fanfare Sapphire /20 #35
2013 Press Pass Fanfare Silver /25 #34
2013 Press Pass Fanfare Silver /25 #35
2013 Press Pass Ignite #21
2013 Press Pass Ignite #59
2013 Press Pass Ignite Great American Treads Autographs Blue Holofoil /20 #GATJL
2013 Press Pass Ignite Great American Treads Autographs Red /1 #GATJL
2013 Press Pass Ignite Hot Threads Blue Holofoil /99 #HTJL
2013 Press Pass Ignite Hot Threads Patch Red /10 #HTJL
2013 Press Pass Ignite Hot Threads Silver #HTJL
2013 Press Pass Ignite Ink Black /50 #IIJL
2013 Press Pass Ignite Ink Blue /25 #IIJL
2013 Press Pass Ignite Ink Red /5 #IIJL
2013 Press Pass Ignite Proofs Black and White /50 #21
2013 Press Pass Ignite Proofs Black and White /50 #59
2013 Press Pass Ignite Proofs Cyan #21
2013 Press Pass Ignite Proofs Cyan #59
2013 Press Pass Ignite Proofs Magenta #21
2013 Press Pass Ignite Proofs Magenta #59
2013 Press Pass Ignite Proofs Yellow /5 #21
2013 Press Pass Ignite Proofs Yellow /5 #59
2013 Press Pass Power Picks Blue /99 #12
2013 Press Pass Power Picks Blue /99 #42
2013 Press Pass Power Picks Gold /50 #12
2013 Press Pass Power Picks Gold /50 #42
2013 Press Pass Power Picks Holofoil /10 #12
2013 Press Pass Power Picks Holofoil /10 #42
2013 Press Pass Racing Champions #RC14
2013 Press Pass Racing Champions #RC36
2013 Press Pass Redline #31
2013 Press Pass Redline #32
2013 Press Pass Redline Black /99 #31
2013 Press Pass Redline Black /99 #32
2013 Press Pass Redline Cyan /50 #31
2013 Press Pass Redline Cyan /50 #32
2013 Press Pass Redline Magenta /15 #31
2013 Press Pass Redline Magenta /15 #32
2013 Press Pass Redline Relics Blue /5 #RRJL
2013 Press Pass Redline Relics Gold /10 #RRJL
2013 Press Pass Redline Relics Melting /1 #RRJL
2013 Press Pass Redline Relics Red /50 #RRJL
2013 Press Pass Redline Relics Silver /25 #RRJL
2013 Press Pass Redline V8 Relics Blue /5 #V8JL
2013 Press Pass Redline V8 Relics Gold /10 #V8JL
2013 Press Pass Redline V8 Relics Melting /1 #V8JL
2013 Press Pass Redline V8 Relics Red /25 #V8JL
2013 Press Pass Redline Yellow /1 #31
2013 Press Pass Redline Yellow /1 #32
2013 Press Pass Showcase /349 #18
2013 Press Pass Showcase /349 #40
2013 Press Pass Showcase Black /1 #18
2013 Press Pass Showcase Black /1 #40
2013 Press Pass Showcase Blue /25 #18
2013 Press Pass Showcase Blue /25 #40
2013 Press Pass Showcase Elite Exhibit Ink /25 #EEIJL
2013 Press Pass Showcase Elite Exhibit Ink Blue /30 #EEIJL
2013 Press Pass Showcase Elite Exhibit Ink Gold /10 #EEIJL
2013 Press Pass Showcase Elite Exhibit Ink Melting /1 #EEIJL
2013 Press Pass Showcase Elite Exhibit Ink Red /5 #EEIJL
2013 Press Pass Showcase Gold /99 #18
2013 Press Pass Showcase Gold /99 #40
2013 Press Pass Showcase Green /20 #18
2013 Press Pass Showcase Green /20 #40
2013 Press Pass Showcase Masterpieces Ink /35 #MPIJL
2013 Press Pass Showcase Masterpieces Ink Gold /10 #MPIJL
2013 Press Pass Showcase Prized Pieces /99 #PPMJL
2013 Press Pass Showcase Prized Pieces Blue /20 #PPMJL
2013 Press Pass Showcase Prized Pieces Gold /25 #PPMJL
2013 Press Pass Showcase Prized Pieces Ink /50 #PPIJL
2013 Press Pass Showcase Prized Pieces Ink Gold /25 #PPIJL
2013 Press Pass Showcase Prized Pieces Ink Melting /1 #PPIJL
2013 Press Pass Showcase Prized Pieces Melting /5 #PPMJL
2013 Press Pass Showcase Purple /13 #18
2013 Press Pass Showcase Purple /13 #40
2013 Press Pass Showcase Red /10 #18
2013 Press Pass Showcase Red /10 #40
2013 Press Pass Showcase Series Standouts Gold /50 #11
2013 Press Pass Showcase Showcase Patches /5 #SPJL
2013 Press Pass Showcase Studio Showcase /299 #11
2013 Press Pass Showcase Studio Showcase Blue /40 #11
2013 Press Pass Showcase Studio Showcase Green /25 #11
2013 Press Pass Showcase Studio Showcase Ink /25 #SSIJL
2013 Press Pass Showcase Studio Showcase Ink Gold /10 #SSIJL
2013 Press Pass Showcase Studio Showcase Ink Melting /1 #SSIJL
2013 Press Pass Showcase Studio Showcase Ink Red /5 #SSIJL
2013 Press Pass Showcase Studio Showcase Melting /1 #11
2013 Press Pass Showcase Studio Showcase Purple /13 #11
2013 Press Pass Showcase Studio Showcase Red /10 #11
2013 Press Pass Signings Blue /1 #JL
2013 Press Pass Signings Gold /25 #JL
2013 Press Pass Signings Holofoil /10 #JL
2013 Press Pass Signings Printing Plates Black /1 #JL
2013 Press Pass Signings Printing Plates Cyan /1 #JL
2013 Press Pass Signings Printing Plates Magenta /1 #JL
2013 Press Pass Signings Printing Plates Yellow /1 #JL
2013 Press Pass Signings Silver /50 #JL
2013 Total Memorabilia #26
2013 Total Memorabilia Black and White /99 #26
2013 Total Memorabilia Gold /275 #26
2013 Total Memorabilia Red #26
2014 Press Pass #23
2014 Press Pass American Thunder #24
2014 Press Pass American Thunder #56
2014 Press Pass American Thunder Autographs Blue /10 #ATAJL
2014 Press Pass American Thunder Autographs Red /5 #ATAJL
2014 Press Pass American Thunder Autographs White /35 #ATAJL
2014 Press Pass American Thunder Black and White /50 #24
2014 Press Pass American Thunder Black and White /50 #56
2014 Press Pass American Thunder Brothers In Arms Relics Blue /25 #BATP
2014 Press Pass American Thunder Brothers In Arms Relics Red /5 #BATP
2014 Press Pass American Thunder Brothers In Arms Relics Silver /50 #BATP
2014 Press Pass American Thunder Class A Uniforms Blue /99 #CAUJL
2014 Press Pass American Thunder Class A Uniforms Flag /1 #CAUJL
2014 Press Pass American Thunder Class A Uniforms Red /10 #CAUJL
2014 Press Pass American Thunder Class A Uniforms Silver #CAUJL
2014 Press Pass American Thunder Cyan #24
2014 Press Pass American Thunder Cyan #56
2014 Press Pass American Thunder Great American Treads Autographs Blue /25 #GATJL
2014 Press Pass American Thunder Great American Treads Autographs Red /1 #GATJL
2014 Press Pass American Thunder Magenta #24
2014 Press Pass American Thunder Magenta #56
2014 Press Pass American Thunder Yellow /5 #24
2014 Press Pass American Thunder Yellow /5 #56
2014 Press Pass Burning Rubber Blue /25 #BRJL
2014 Press Pass Burning Rubber Gold /75 #BRJL
2014 Press Pass Burning Rubber Holofoil /50 #BRJL
2014 Press Pass Burning Rubber Melting /10 #BRJL
2014 Press Pass Color Proofs Black /70 #23
2014 Press Pass Color Proofs Cyan /35 #23
2014 Press Pass Color Proofs Magenta #23
2014 Press Pass Color Proofs Yellow /5 #23
2014 Press Pass Cup Chase #12
2014 Press Pass Five Star Signatures Blue /5 #FSSJL
2014 Press Pass Five Star Signatures Holofoil /10 #FSSJL
2014 Press Pass Five Star Signatures Melting /1 #FSSJL
2014 Press Pass Gold #23
2014 Press Pass Redline #34
2014 Press Pass Redline #35
2014 Press Pass Redline Black /75 #34
2014 Press Pass Redline Black /75 #35
2014 Press Pass Redline Blue Foil #34
2014 Press Pass Redline Blue Foil #35
2014 Press Pass Redline Cyan /50 #34
2014 Press Pass Redline Cyan /50 #35
2014 Press Pass Redline Dynamic Duals Relic Autographs Blue /10 #DDJL
2014 Press Pass Redline Dynamic Duals Relic Autographs Gold /5 #DDJL
2014 Press Pass Redline Dynamic Duals Relic Autographs Melting /1 #DDJL
2014 Press Pass Redline Dynamic Duals Relic Autographs Red /15 #DDJL
2014 Press Pass Redline Green National Convention /5 #34
2014 Press Pass Redline Green National Convention /5 #35
2014 Press Pass Redline Magenta /10 #34
2014 Press Pass Redline Magenta /10 #35
2014 Press Pass Redline Muscle Car Sheet Metal Blue /10 #MCMJL
2014 Press Pass Redline Muscle Car Sheet Metal Gold /25 #MCMJL
2014 Press Pass Redline Muscle Car Sheet Metal Melting /1 #MCMJL
2014 Press Pass Redline Muscle Car Sheet Metal Red /50 #MCMJL
2014 Press Pass Redline Pieces of the Action Blue /10 #PAJL
2014 Press Pass Redline Pieces of the Action Gold /25 #PAJL
2014 Press Pass Redline Pieces of the Action Melting /1 #PAJL
2014 Press Pass Redline Pieces of the Action Red /75 #PAJL
2014 Press Pass Redline Redline Racers #RR13
2014 Press Pass Redline Relic Autographs Blue /5 #RRSEJL
2014 Press Pass Redline Relic Autographs Gold /10 #RRSEJL
2014 Press Pass Redline Relic Autographs Melting /1 #RRSEJL
2014 Press Pass Redline Relic Autographs Red /15 #RRSEJL
2014 Press Pass Redline Relics Blue /25 #RRJL
2014 Press Pass Redline Relics Gold /50 #RRJL
2014 Press Pass Redline Relics Melting /1 #RRJL
2014 Press Pass Redline Relics Red /75 #RRJL
2014 Press Pass Redline Signatures Blue /5 #RSJL
2014 Press Pass Redline Signatures Gold /10 #RSJL
2014 Press Pass Redline Signatures Melting /1 #RSJL
2014 Press Pass Redline Signatures Red /15 #RSJL
2014 Press Pass Redline Yellow /1 #34
2014 Press Pass Redline Yellow /1 #35
2014 Press Pass Replay #21
2014 Press Pass Signings Gold /10 #PPSJL
2014 Press Pass Signings Holofoil /5 #PPSJL
2014 Press Pass Signings Melting /1 #PPSJL
2014 Press Pass Signings Printing Plates Black /1 #PPSJL
2014 Press Pass Signings Printing Plates Cyan /1 #PPSJL
2014 Press Pass Signings Printing Plates Magenta /1 #PPSJL
2014 Press Pass Signings Printing Plates Yellow /1 #PPSJL
2014 Press Pass Signings Silver /50 #PPSJL
2014 Total Memorabilia #17
2014 Total Memorabilia Autographed Memorabilia Blue /5 #SCJL
2014 Total Memorabilia Autographed Memorabilia Gold /9 #SCJL
2014 Total Memorabilia Autographed Memorabilia Melting /1 #SCJL
2014 Total Memorabilia Autographed Memorabilia Silver /10 #SC-JL
2014 Total Memorabilia Black and White /99 #17
2014 Total Memorabilia Dual Swatch Gold /150 #TMJL
2014 Total Memorabilia Gold /175 #17
2014 Total Memorabilia Quad Swatch Melting /25 #TMJL
2014 Total Memorabilia Red #17
2014 Total Memorabilia Single Swatch Silver /275 #TMJL
2014 Total Memorabilia Triple Swatch Blue /99 #TMJL
2015 Press Pass #23
2015 Press Pass #74
2015 Press Pass #83
2015 Press Pass #100
2015 Press Pass Burning Rubber Blue /50 #BRJL1
2015 Press Pass Burning Rubber Blue /50 #BRJL2
2015 Press Pass Burning Rubber Blue /50 #BRJL3
2015 Press Pass Burning Rubber Gold #BRJL1
2015 Press Pass Burning Rubber Gold #BRJL2
2015 Press Pass Burning Rubber Gold #BRJL3
2015 Press Pass Burning Rubber Green /10 #BRJL1
2015 Press Pass Burning Rubber Green /10 #BRJL2
2015 Press Pass Burning Rubber Green /10 #BRJL3
2015 Press Pass Burning Rubber Letterman /8 #BRLEJL
2015 Press Pass Burning Rubber Melting /1 #BRJL1
2015 Press Pass Burning Rubber Melting /1 #BRJL2
2015 Press Pass Burning Rubber Melting /1 #BRJL3
2015 Press Pass Championship Caliber Dual /25 #CCMJL
2015 Press Pass Championship Caliber Quad /1 #CCMJL
2015 Press Pass Championship Caliber Signature Edition Blue /25 #CCJL
2015 Press Pass Championship Caliber Signature Edition Gold /50 #CCJL
2015 Press Pass Championship Caliber Signature Edition Green /10 #CCJL
2015 Press Pass Championship Caliber Signature Edition Melting /1 #CCJL
2015 Press Pass Championship Caliber Single /50 #CCMJL
2015 Press Pass Championship Caliber Triple /10 #CCMJL
2015 Press Pass Cup Chase #23
2015 Press Pass Cup Chase #74
2015 Press Pass Cup Chase #83
2015 Press Pass Cup Chase #100
2015 Press Pass Cup Chase Blue /25 #23
2015 Press Pass Cup Chase Blue /25 #74
2015 Press Pass Cup Chase Blue /25 #83
2015 Press Pass Cup Chase Blue /25 #100
2015 Press Pass Cup Chase Gold /75 #23
2015 Press Pass Cup Chase Gold /75 #74
2015 Press Pass Cup Chase Gold /75 #83
2015 Press Pass Cup Chase Gold /75 #100
2015 Press Pass Cup Chase Green /10 #23
2015 Press Pass Cup Chase Green /10 #74
2015 Press Pass Cup Chase Green /10 #83
2015 Press Pass Cup Chase Green /10 #100
2015 Press Pass Cup Chase Melting /1 #23
2015 Press Pass Cup Chase Melting /1 #74
2015 Press Pass Cup Chase Melting /1 #83
2015 Press Pass Cup Chase Melting /1 #100
2015 Press Pass Cup Chase Three Wide Blue /25 #3WJL
2015 Press Pass Cup Chase Three Wide Gold /50 #3WJL
2015 Press Pass Cup Chase Three Wide Green /10 #3WJL
2015 Press Pass Cup Chase Three Wide Melting /1 #3WJL
2015 Press Pass Cup Chase Upper Cuts /13 #UCJL
2015 Press Pass Cuts Blue /25 #CCCJL
2015 Press Pass Cuts Gold /50 #CCCJL
2015 Press Pass Cuts Green /10 #CCCJL
2015 Press Pass Cuts Melting /1 #CCCJL
2015 Press Pass Four Wide Signature Edition Blue /15 #4WJL
2015 Press Pass Four Wide Signature Edition Gold /25 #4WJL
2015 Press Pass Four Wide Signature Edition Green /10 #4WJL
2015 Press Pass Four Wide Signature Edition Melting /1 #4WJL
2015 Press Pass Pit Road Pieces Blue /25 #PPMJL
2015 Press Pass Pit Road Pieces Gold /50 #PPMJL
2015 Press Pass Pit Road Pieces Green /10 #PPMJL
2015 Press Pass Pit Road Pieces Melting /1 #PPMJL
2015 Press Pass Pit Road Pieces Signature Edition Blue /25 #PRPJL
2015 Press Pass Pit Road Pieces Signature Edition Gold /50 #PRPJL
2015 Press Pass Pit Road Pieces Signature Edition Green /10 #PRPJL
2015 Press Pass Pit Road Pieces Signature Edition Melting /1 #PRPJL
2015 Press Pass Purple #23
2015 Press Pass Purple #74
2015 Press Pass Purple #83
2015 Press Pass Purple #100
2015 Press Pass Red #23
2015 Press Pass Red #74
2015 Press Pass Red #83
2015 Press Pass Red #100
2015 Press Pass Signings Blue /15 #PPSJL
2015 Press Pass Signings Gold #PPSJL
2015 Press Pass Signings Green /5 #PPSJL
2015 Press Pass Signings Melting /1 #PPSJL
2015 Press Pass Signings Red /10 #PPSJL
2016 Certified #7
2016 Certified #57
2016 Certified Complete Materials /299 #10
2016 Certified Complete Materials Mirror Black /1 #10
2016 Certified Complete Materials Mirror Blue /50 #10
2016 Certified Complete Materials Mirror Gold /25 #10
2016 Certified Complete Materials Mirror Green /5 #10
2016 Certified Complete Materials Mirror Orange /99 #10
2016 Certified Complete Materials Mirror Purple /10 #10
2016 Certified Complete Materials Mirror Red /75 #10
2016 Certified Complete Materials Mirror Silver /99 #10
2016 Certified Epix /199 #11
2016 Certified Epix Mirror Black /1 #11
2016 Certified Epix Mirror Blue /50 #11
2016 Certified Epix Mirror Gold /25 #11
2016 Certified Epix Mirror Green /5 #11
2016 Certified Epix Mirror Orange /99 #11
2016 Certified Epix Mirror Purple /10 #11
2016 Certified Epix Mirror Red /75 #11
2016 Certified Epix Mirror Silver /99 #11
2016 Certified Famed Rides /199 #13
2016 Certified Famed Rides Mirror Black /1 #13
2016 Certified Famed Rides Mirror Blue /50 #13
2016 Certified Famed Rides Mirror Gold /25 #13
2016 Certified Famed Rides Mirror Green /5 #13
2016 Certified Famed Rides Mirror Orange /99 #13
2016 Certified Famed Rides Mirror Purple /10 #13
2016 Certified Famed Rides Mirror Red /75 #13
2016 Certified Famed Rides Mirror Silver /99 #13
2016 Certified Gold Team /199 #13
2016 Certified Gold Team Mirror Black /1 #13
2016 Certified Gold Team Mirror Blue /50 #13
2016 Certified Gold Team Mirror Gold /25 #13
2016 Certified Gold Team Mirror Green /5 #13
2016 Certified Gold Team Mirror Orange /99 #13
2016 Certified Gold Team Mirror Purple /10 #13
2016 Certified Gold Team Mirror Red /75 #13
2016 Certified Gold Team Mirror Silver /99 #13
2016 Certified Mirror Black /1 #7
2016 Certified Mirror Black /1 #57
2016 Certified Mirror Blue /50 #7
2016 Certified Mirror Blue /50 #57
2016 Certified Mirror Gold /25 #7
2016 Certified Mirror Gold /25 #57
2016 Certified Mirror Green /5 #7
2016 Certified Mirror Green /5 #57
2016 Certified Mirror Orange /99 #7
2016 Certified Mirror Orange /99 #57
2016 Certified Mirror Purple /10 #7
2016 Certified Mirror Purple /10 #57
2016 Certified Mirror Red /75 #7
2016 Certified Mirror Red /75 #57
2016 Certified Mirror Silver /99 #7
2016 Certified Mirror Silver /99 #57
2016 Certified Signatures /35 #11
2016 Certified Signatures Mirror Black /1 #11
2016 Certified Signatures Mirror Blue /20 #11
2016 Certified Signatures Mirror Gold /15 #11
2016 Certified Signatures Mirror Green /5 #11
2016 Certified Signatures Mirror Orange /5 #11
2016 Certified Signatures Mirror Purple /10 #11
2016 Certified Signatures Mirror Red /25 #11
2016 Certified Signatures Mirror Silver /5 #11
2016 Certified Skills /199 #7
2016 Certified Skills Mirror Black /1 #7
2016 Certified Skills Mirror Blue /50 #7
2016 Certified Skills Mirror Gold /25 #7
2016 Certified Skills Mirror Green /5 #7
2016 Certified Skills Mirror Orange /99 #7
2016 Certified Skills Mirror Purple /10 #7
2016 Certified Skills Mirror Red /75 #7
2016 Certified Skills Mirror Silver /99 #7
2016 Certified Sprint Cup Signature Swatches /60 #9
2016 Certified Sprint Cup Signature Swatches Mirror Black /1 #9
2016 Certified Sprint Cup Signature Swatches Mirror Blue /25 #9
2016 Certified Sprint Cup Signature Swatches Mirror Gold /15 #9
2016 Certified Sprint Cup Signature Swatches Mirror Green /5 #9
2016 Certified Sprint Cup Signature Swatches Mirror Orange /10 #9
2016 Certified Sprint Cup Signature Swatches Mirror Purple /10 #9
2016 Certified Sprint Cup Signature Swatches Mirror Red /50 #9
2016 Certified Sprint Cup Signature Swatches Mirror Silver /3 #9
2016 Panini Black Friday #31
2016 Panini Black Friday Autographs /25 #31
2016 Panini Black Friday Cracked Ice /25 #31
2016 Panini Black Friday Holo Plaid /1 #31
2016 Panini Black Friday Rapture /10 #31
2016 Panini Black Friday Thick Stock /50 #31
2016 Panini Black Friday Wedges /50 #31
2016 Panini Instant #6
2016 Panini Instant #9
2016 Panini Instant #13
2016 Panini Instant Black /1 #6
2016 Panini Instant Black /1 #9
2016 Panini Instant Black /1 #13
2016 Panini Instant Blue /25 #6
2016 Panini Instant Blue /25 #9
2016 Panini Instant Blue /25 #13
2016 Panini Instant Green /5 #6
2016 Panini Instant Green /5 #9
2016 Panini Instant Green /5 #13
2016 Panini Instant Orange /50 #6
2016 Panini Instant Orange /50 #9
2016 Panini Instant Orange /50 #13
2016 Panini Instant Purple /10 #6
2016 Panini Instant Purple /10 #9
2016 Panini Instant Purple /10 #13
2016 Panini National Convention #39
2016 Panini National Convention Autographs /25 #39
2016 Panini National Convention Cracked Ice /25 #39
2016 Panini National Convention Decoy Cracked Ice /25 #39
2016 Panini National Convention Decoy Escher Squares /10 #39
2016 Panini National Convention Decoy Rapture /1 #39
2016 Panini National Convention Decoy Wedges /99 #39
2016 Panini National Convention Diamond Awe /49 #39
2016 Panini National Convention Escher Squares /10 #39
2016 Panini National Convention Rapture /1 #39
2016 Panini National Convention Wedges /99 #39
2016 Panini National Treasures /25 #8
2016 Panini National Treasures Black /5 #8
2016 Panini National Treasures Blue /1 #8
2016 Panini National Treasures Dual Driver Materials /25 #8
2016 Panini National Treasures Dual Driver Materials Black /5 #8
2016 Panini National Treasures Dual Driver Materials Blue /1 #8
2016 Panini National Treasures Dual Driver Materials Gold /10 #8
2016 Panini National Treasures Dual Driver Materials Printing Plates B /1 #8
2016 Panini National Treasures Dual Driver Materials Printing Plates C /1 #8
2016 Panini National Treasures Dual Driver Materials Printing Plates Magenta /1 #8
2016 Panini National Treasures Dual Driver Materials Printing Plates Y /1 #8
2016 Panini National Treasures Dual Driver Materials Silver /15 #8
2016 Panini National Treasures Dual Signatures /99 #1
2016 Panini National Treasures Dual Signatures Black /25 #1
2016 Panini National Treasures Dual Signatures Blue /1 #1
2016 Panini National Treasures Dual Signatures Gold /49 #ss,
2016 Panini National Treasures Firesuit Materials /25 #9

nini National Treasures Firesuit Materials Black /5 #9
nini National Treasures Firesuit Materials Blue /1 #9
nini National Treasures Firesuit Materials Gold /10 #9
nini National Treasures Firesuit Materials Laundry Tag /1 #9
nini National Treasures Firesuit Materials Printing Plates Black /1
nini National Treasures Firesuit Materials Printing Plates Cyan /1 #9
nini National Treasures Firesuit Materials Printing Plates Magenta #9
nini National Treasures Firesuit Materials Printing Plates Yellow /1
nini National Treasures Firesuit Materials Silver /15 #9
nini National Treasures Gold /15 #8
nini National Treasures Jumbo Firesuit Patch Signature Booklet sociate Sponsor 1 /1 #13
nini National Treasures Jumbo Firesuit Patch Signature Booklet ssociate Sponsor 10 /1 #13
nini National Treasures Jumbo Firesuit Patch Signature Booklet ssociate Sponsor 2 /1 #13
nini National Treasures Jumbo Firesuit Patch Signature Booklet ssociate Sponsor 3 /1 #13
nini National Treasures Jumbo Firesuit Patch Signature Booklet ssociate Sponsor 4 /1 #13
nini National Treasures Jumbo Firesuit Patch Signature Booklet ssociate Sponsor 5 /1 #13
nini National Treasures Jumbo Firesuit Patch Signature Booklet ssociate Sponsor 6 /1 #13
nini National Treasures Jumbo Firesuit Patch Signature Booklet ssociate Sponsor 7 /1 #13
nini National Treasures Jumbo Firesuit Patch Signature Booklet ssociate Sponsor 8 /1 #13
nini National Treasures Jumbo Firesuit Patch Signature Booklet ssociate Sponsor 9 /1 #13
nini National Treasures Jumbo Firesuit Patch Signature Booklet Flag #13
nini National Treasures Jumbo Firesuit Patch Signature Booklet oodyear /2 #13
nini National Treasures Jumbo Firesuit Patch Signature Booklet Manufacturers Logo /2 #13
nini National Treasures Jumbo Firesuit Patch Signature Booklet ameplate /2 #13
nini National Treasures Jumbo Firesuit Patch Signature Booklet ASCAR /1 #13
nini National Treasures Jumbo Firesuit Patch Signature Booklet unoco /1 #13
nini National Treasures Jumbo Firesuit Signatures /25 #13
nini National Treasures Jumbo Firesuit Signatures Black /5 #13
nini National Treasures Jumbo Firesuit Signatures Gold /10 #13
nini National Treasures Jumbo Firesuit Signatures Printing Plates lack /1 #13
nini National Treasures Jumbo Firesuit Signatures Printing Plates yan /1 #13
nini National Treasures Jumbo Firesuit Signatures Printing Plates Magenta /1 #13
nini National Treasures Jumbo Firesuit Signatures Printing Plates ellow /1 #13
nini National Treasures Jumbo Firesuit Signatures Silver /15 #13
nini National Treasures Jumbo Sheet Metal Signature Booklet /50 4
nini National Treasures Jumbo Sheet Metal Signature Booklet Black 35 #4
nini National Treasures Jumbo Sheet Metal Signature Booklet Blue 1 #4
nini National Treasures Jumbo Sheet Metal Signature Booklet Gold 20 #4
nini National Treasures Jumbo Sheet Metal Signatures Blue /1 #7
nini National Treasures Jumbo Sheet Metal Signatures Gold /10 #7
nini National Treasures Jumbo Sheet Metal Signatures Printing Plates Black /1 #7
nini National Treasures Jumbo Sheet Metal Signatures Printing Plates Cyan /1 #7
nini National Treasures Jumbo Sheet Metal Signatures Printing Plates Magenta /1 #7
nini National Treasures Jumbo Sheet Metal Signatures Printing Plates Yellow /1 #7
nini National Treasures Jumbo Sheet Metal Signatures Silver /15 #7
nini National Treasures Printing Plates Black /1 #8
nini National Treasures Printing Plates Cyan /1 #8
nini National Treasures Printing Plates Magenta /1 #8
nini National Treasures Printing Plates Yellow /1 #8
nini National Treasures Quad Materials /25 #9
nini National Treasures Quad Materials Black /5 #9
nini National Treasures Quad Materials Blue /1 #9
nini National Treasures Quad Materials Gold /10 #9
nini National Treasures Quad Materials Printing Plates Black /1 #9
nini National Treasures Quad Materials Printing Plates Cyan /1 #9
nini National Treasures Quad Materials Printing Plates Magenta /1 #9
anini National Treasures Quad Materials Printing Plates Yellow /1 #9
anini National Treasures Quad Materials Silver /15 #9
anini National Treasures Sheet Metal Materials /25 #9
anini National Treasures Sheet Metal Materials Black /5 #9
anini National Treasures Sheet Metal Materials Blue /1 #9
anini National Treasures Sheet Metal Materials Gold /10 #9
anini National Treasures Sheet Metal Materials Printing Plates Black /1 #9
anini National Treasures Sheet Metal Materials Printing Plates Cyan /1 #9
anini National Treasures Sheet Metal Materials Printing Plates Magenta /1 #9
anini National Treasures Sheet Metal Materials Printing Plates Yellow /1 #9
anini National Treasures Sheet Metal Materials Silver /15 #9
anini National Treasures Signature Dual Materials Black /5 #13
anini National Treasures Signature Dual Materials Blue /1 #13
anini National Treasures Signature Dual Materials Printing Plates Black /1 #13
anini National Treasures Signature Dual Materials Printing Plates Cyan /1 #13
anini National Treasures Signature Dual Materials Printing Plates Magenta /1 #13
anini National Treasures Signature Dual Materials Printing Plates Yellow /1 #13
anini National Treasures Signature Firesuit Materials Black /5 #13
anini National Treasures Signature Firesuit Materials Gold /10 #13
anini National Treasures Signature Firesuit Materials Laundry Tag /1 #13
anini National Treasures Signature Firesuit Materials Printing Plates Black /1 #13
anini National Treasures Signature Firesuit Materials Printing Plates Cyan /1 #13
anini National Treasures Signature Firesuit Materials Printing Plates Magenta /1 #13
anini National Treasures Signature Firesuit Materials Printing Plates Yellow /1 #13
anini National Treasures Signature Firesuit Materials Silver /15 #13
anini National Treasures Signature Quad Materials Blue /1 #13
anini National Treasures Signature Quad Materials Printing Plates Black /1 #13
anini National Treasures Signature Quad Materials Printing Plates Cyan /1 #13
anini National Treasures Signature Quad Materials Printing Plates Magenta /1 #13
anini National Treasures Signature Quad Materials Printing Plates Yellow /1 #13
anini National Treasures Signature Sheet Metal Materials Black /5 #13
anini National Treasures Signature Sheet Metal Materials Blue /1 #13
2016 Panini National Treasures Signature Sheet Metal Materials Printing Plates Black /1 #13
2016 Panini National Treasures Signature Sheet Metal Materials Printing Plates Cyan /1 #13
2016 Panini National Treasures Signature Sheet Metal Materials Printing Plates Magenta /1 #13
2016 Panini National Treasures Signature Sheet Metal Materials Printing Plates Yellow /1 #13
2016 Panini National Treasures Signatures Blue /1 #10
2016 Panini National Treasures Signatures Printing Plates Black /1 #10
2016 Panini National Treasures Signatures Printing Plates Cyan /1 #10
2016 Panini National Treasures Signatures Printing Plates Magenta /1 #10
2016 Panini National Treasures Signatures Printing Plates Yellow /1 #10
2016 Panini National Treasures Silver /20 #8
2016 Panini National Treasures Six Signatures Black /10 #7
2016 Panini National Treasures Six Signatures Blue /1 #7
2016 Panini National Treasures Timelines /25 #7
2016 Panini National Treasures Timelines Black /5 #7
2016 Panini National Treasures Timelines Blue /1 #7
2016 Panini National Treasures Timelines Gold /10 #7
2016 Panini National Treasures Timelines Printing Plates Black /1 #7
2016 Panini National Treasures Timelines Printing Plates Cyan /1 #7
2016 Panini National Treasures Timelines Printing Plates Magenta /1 #7
2016 Panini National Treasures Timelines Printing Plates Yellow /1 #7
2016 Panini National Treasures Timelines Silver /15 #7
2016 Panini National Treasures Trio Driver Materials /25 #5
2016 Panini National Treasures Trio Driver Materials Black /5 #5
2016 Panini National Treasures Trio Driver Materials Blue /1 #5
2016 Panini National Treasures Trio Driver Materials Gold /10 #5
2016 Panini National Treasures Trio Driver Materials Printing Plates Black /1 #5
2016 Panini National Treasures Trio Driver Materials Printing Plates Cyan /1 #5
2016 Panini National Treasures Trio Driver Materials Printing Plates Magenta /1 #5
2016 Panini National Treasures Trio Driver Materials Printing Plates Yellow /1 #5
2016 Panini National Treasures Trio Driver Materials Silver /15 #5
2016 Panini National Treasures Winning Signatures Blue /1 #4
2016 Panini National Treasures Winning Signatures Printing Plates Black /1 #4
2016 Panini National Treasures Winning Signatures Printing Plates Cyan /1 #4
2016 Panini National Treasures Winning Signatures Printing Plates Magenta /1 #4
2016 Panini National Treasures Winning Signatures Printing Plates Yellow /1 #4
2016 Panini Prizm #22A
2016 Panini Prizm #60
2016 Panini Prizm #77
2016 Panini Prizm Autographs Prizms #65
2016 Panini Prizm Autographs Prizms Black /3 #65
2016 Panini Prizm Autographs Prizms Blue Flag /50 #65
2016 Panini Prizm Autographs Prizms Camo /22 #65
2016 Panini Prizm Autographs Prizms Checkered Flag /1 #65
2016 Panini Prizm Autographs Prizms Gold /10 #65
2016 Panini Prizm Autographs Prizms Green Flag /75 #65
2016 Panini Prizm Autographs Prizms Rainbow /24 #65
2016 Panini Prizm Autographs Prizms Red Flag /25 #65
2016 Panini Prizm Autographs Prizms Red White and Blue /25 #65
2016 Panini Prizm Autographs Prizms White Flag /5 #65
2016 Panini Prizm Blowing Smoke #10
2016 Panini Prizm Blowing Smoke Prizms #10
2016 Panini Prizm Blowing Smoke Prizms Checkered Flag /1 #10
2016 Panini Prizm Blowing Smoke Prizms Gold /10 #10
2016 Panini Prizm Competitors #7
2016 Panini Prizm Competitors Prizms #7
2016 Panini Prizm Competitors Prizms Checkered Flag /1 #7
2016 Panini Prizm Competitors Prizms Gold /10 #7
2016 Panini Prizm Prizms #22A
2016 Panini Prizm Prizms #60
2016 Panini Prizm Prizms #77
2016 Panini Prizm Prizms Black /3 #22
2016 Panini Prizm Prizms Black /3 #60
2016 Panini Prizm Prizms Black /3 #77
2016 Panini Prizm Prizms Blue Flag /99 #22
2016 Panini Prizm Prizms Blue Flag /99 #60
2016 Panini Prizm Prizms Blue Flag /99 #77
2016 Panini Prizm Prizms Camo /22 #22
2016 Panini Prizm Prizms Camo /22 #60
2016 Panini Prizm Prizms Camo /22 #77
2016 Panini Prizm Prizms Checkered Flag /1 #22A
2016 Panini Prizm Prizms Checkered Flag /1 #60
2016 Panini Prizm Prizms Checkered Flag /1 #77
2016 Panini Prizm Prizms Gold /10 #22A
2016 Panini Prizm Prizms Gold /10 #60
2016 Panini Prizm Prizms Gold /10 #77
2016 Panini Prizm Prizms Green Flag /149 #22
2016 Panini Prizm Prizms Green Flag /149 #60
2016 Panini Prizm Prizms Green Flag /149 #77
2016 Panini Prizm Prizms Rainbow /24 #22
2016 Panini Prizm Prizms Rainbow /24 #60
2016 Panini Prizm Prizms Rainbow /24 #77
2016 Panini Prizm Prizms Red Flag /75 #22
2016 Panini Prizm Prizms Red Flag /75 #60
2016 Panini Prizm Prizms Red Flag /75 #77
2016 Panini Prizm Prizms Red White and Blue #22
2016 Panini Prizm Prizms Red White and Blue #60
2016 Panini Prizm Prizms Red White and Blue #77
2016 Panini Prizm Prizms White Flag /5 #22
2016 Panini Prizm Prizms White Flag /5 #60
2016 Panini Prizm Prizms White Flag /5 #77
2016 Panini Prizm Race Used Tire #5
2016 Panini Prizm Race Used Tire Prizms Blue Flag /49 #5
2016 Panini Prizm Race Used Tire Prizms Checkered Flag /1 #5
2016 Panini Prizm Race Used Tire Prizms Green Flag /99 #5
2016 Panini Prizm Race Used Tire Prizms Red Flag /25 #5
2016 Panini Prizm Race Used Tire Team #4
2016 Panini Prizm Race Used Tire Team Prizms Blue Flag /75 #4
2016 Panini Prizm Race Used Tire Team Prizms Checkered Flag /1 #4
2016 Panini Prizm Race Used Tire Team Prizms Green Flag /149 #4
2016 Panini Prizm Race Used Tire Team Prizms Red Flag /10 #4
2016 Panini Prizm Raising the Flag #4
2016 Panini Prizm Raising the Flag Prizms #4
2016 Panini Prizm Raising the Flag Prizms Checkered Flag /1 #4
2016 Panini Prizm Raising the Flag Prizms Gold /10 #4
2016 Panini Prizm Winner's Circle #1
2016 Panini Prizm Winner's Circle #22
2016 Panini Prizm Winner's Circle #24
2016 Panini Prizm Winner's Circle #30
2016 Panini Prizm Winner's Circle #31
2016 Panini Prizm Winner's Circle #32
2016 Panini Prizm Winner's Circle Prizms #1
2016 Panini Prizm Winner's Circle Prizms #22
2016 Panini Prizm Winner's Circle Prizms #24
2016 Panini Prizm Winner's Circle Prizms #30
2016 Panini Prizm Winner's Circle Prizms #31
2016 Panini Prizm Winner's Circle Prizms #32
2016 Panini Prizm Winner's Circle Prizms Checkered Flag /1 #1
2016 Panini Prizm Winner's Circle Prizms Checkered Flag /1 #22
2016 Panini Prizm Winner's Circle Prizms Checkered Flag /1 #24
2016 Panini Prizm Winner's Circle Prizms Checkered Flag /1 #30
2016 Panini Prizm Winner's Circle Prizms Checkered Flag /1 #31
2016 Panini Prizm Winner's Circle Prizms Checkered Flag /1 #32
2016 Panini Prizm Winner's Circle Prizms Gold /10 #1
2016 Panini Prizm Winner's Circle Prizms Gold /10 #22
2016 Panini Prizm Winner's Circle Prizms Gold /10 #24
2016 Panini Prizm Winner's Circle Prizms Gold /10 #30
2016 Panini Prizm Winner's Circle Prizms Gold /10 #31
2016 Panini Prizm Winner's Circle Prizms Gold /10 #32
2016 Panini Torque #8
2016 Panini Torque #59
2016 Panini Torque #86
2016 Panini Torque Artist Proof /50 #8
2016 Panini Torque Artist Proof /50 #59
2016 Panini Torque Artist Proof /50 #86
2016 Panini Torque Blackout /1 #8
2016 Panini Torque Blackout /1 #59
2016 Panini Torque Blackout /1 #86
2016 Panini Torque Blue /125 #8
2016 Panini Torque Blue /125 #59
2016 Panini Torque Blue /125 #86
2016 Panini Torque Clear Vision #8
2016 Panini Torque Clear Vision Blue /99 #8
2016 Panini Torque Clear Vision Gold /149 #8
2016 Panini Torque Clear Vision Green /25 #8
2016 Panini Torque Clear Vision Purple /10 #8
2016 Panini Torque Clear Vision Red /49 #8
2016 Panini Torque Gas N Go #2
2016 Panini Torque Gas N Go Gold /199 #2
2016 Panini Torque Gas N Go Holo Silver /99 #2
2016 Panini Torque Gold #8
2016 Panini Torque Gold #59
2016 Panini Torque Gold #86
2016 Panini Torque Holo Gold /5 #8
2016 Panini Torque Holo Gold /5 #59
2016 Panini Torque Holo Gold /5 #86
2016 Panini Torque Holo Silver /10 #8
2016 Panini Torque Holo Silver /10 #59
2016 Panini Torque Holo Silver /10 #86
2016 Panini Torque Horsepower Heroes #6
2016 Panini Torque Horsepower Heroes Gold /199 #6
2016 Panini Torque Horsepower Heroes Holo Silver /99 #6
2016 Panini Torque Jumbo Tire Autographs /49 #17
2016 Panini Torque Jumbo Tire Autographs Blue /25 #17
2016 Panini Torque Jumbo Tire Autographs Green /10 #17
2016 Panini Torque Jumbo Tire Autographs Purple /1 #17
2016 Panini Torque Jumbo Tire Autographs Red /15 #17
2016 Panini Torque Metal Materials /249 #12
2016 Panini Torque Metal Materials Blue /99 #12
2016 Panini Torque Metal Materials Green /25 #12
2016 Panini Torque Metal Materials Purple /10 #12
2016 Panini Torque Metal Materials Red /49 #12
2016 Panini Torque Painted to Perfection #10
2016 Panini Torque Painted to Perfection Blue /99 #10
2016 Panini Torque Painted to Perfection Checkerboard /10 #10
2016 Panini Torque Painted to Perfection Green /25 #10
2016 Panini Torque Painted to Perfection Red /49 #10
2016 Panini Torque Pairings Materials /125 #18
2016 Panini Torque Pairings Materials Blue /99 #18
2016 Panini Torque Pairings Materials Green /25 #18
2016 Panini Torque Pairings Materials Purple /10 #18
2016 Panini Torque Pairings Materials Red /49 #18
2016 Panini Torque Pole Position #8
2016 Panini Torque Pole Position Blue /99 #8
2016 Panini Torque Pole Position Checkerboard /10 #8
2016 Panini Torque Pole Position Green /25 #8
2016 Panini Torque Pole Position Red /49 #8
2016 Panini Torque Printing Plates Black /1 #8
2016 Panini Torque Printing Plates Black /1 #59
2016 Panini Torque Printing Plates Black /1 #86
2016 Panini Torque Printing Plates Cyan /1 #8
2016 Panini Torque Printing Plates Cyan /1 #59
2016 Panini Torque Printing Plates Cyan /1 #86
2016 Panini Torque Printing Plates Magenta /1 #8
2016 Panini Torque Printing Plates Magenta /1 #59
2016 Panini Torque Printing Plates Magenta /1 #86
2016 Panini Torque Printing Plates Yellow /1 #8
2016 Panini Torque Printing Plates Yellow /1 #59
2016 Panini Torque Printing Plates Yellow /1 #86
2016 Panini Torque Purple /25 #8
2016 Panini Torque Purple /25 #59
2016 Panini Torque Purple /25 #86
2016 Panini Torque Red /99 #8
2016 Panini Torque Red /99 #59
2016 Panini Torque Red /99 #86
2016 Panini Torque Rubber Relics /399 #13
2016 Panini Torque Rubber Relics Blue /99 #13
2016 Panini Torque Rubber Relics Green /25 #13
2016 Panini Torque Rubber Relics Purple /10 #13
2016 Panini Torque Rubber Relics Red /49 #13
2016 Panini Torque Shades #14
2016 Panini Torque Shades Gold /199 #14
2016 Panini Torque Shades Holo Silver /99 #14
2016 Panini Torque Silhouettes Firesuit Autographs /49 #12
2016 Panini Torque Silhouettes Firesuit Autographs Blue /25 #12
2016 Panini Torque Silhouettes Firesuit Autographs Green /10 #12
2016 Panini Torque Silhouettes Firesuit Autographs Purple /1 #12
2016 Panini Torque Silhouettes Firesuit Autographs Red /15 #12
2016 Panini Torque Silhouettes Sheet Metal Autographs /49 #15
2016 Panini Torque Silhouettes Sheet Metal Autographs Blue /25 #15
2016 Panini Torque Silhouettes Sheet Metal Autographs Green /10 #15
2016 Panini Torque Silhouettes Sheet Metal Autographs Purple /1 #15
2016 Panini Torque Silhouettes Sheet Metal Autographs Red /15 #15
2016 Panini Torque Special Paint #6
2016 Panini Torque Special Paint Gold /199 #6
2016 Panini Torque Special Paint Holo Silver /99 #6
2016 Panini Torque Superstar Vision #18
2016 Panini Torque Superstar Vision Blue /99 #18
2016 Panini Torque Superstar Vision Gold /149 #18
2016 Panini Torque Superstar Vision Green /25 #18
2016 Panini Torque Superstar Vision Purple /10 #18
2016 Panini Torque Superstar Vision Red /49 #18
2016 Panini Torque Test Proof Black /1 #8
2016 Panini Torque Test Proof Black /1 #59
2016 Panini Torque Test Proof Black /1 #86
2016 Panini Torque Test Proof Cyan /1 #8
2016 Panini Torque Test Proof Cyan /1 #59
2016 Panini Torque Test Proof Cyan /1 #86
2016 Panini Torque Test Proof Magenta /1 #8
2016 Panini Torque Test Proof Magenta /1 #59
2016 Panini Torque Test Proof Magenta /1 #86
2016 Panini Torque Test Proof Yellow /1 #8
2016 Panini Torque Test Proof Yellow /1 #59
2016 Panini Torque Test Proof Yellow /1 #86
2016 Panini Torque Victory Laps #7
2016 Panini Torque Victory Laps Gold /199 #7
2016 Panini Torque Victory Laps Holo Silver /99 #7
2016 Panini Torque Winning Vision #8
2016 Panini Torque Winning Vision Blue /99 #8
2016 Panini Torque Winning Vision Gold /149 #8
2016 Panini Torque Winning Vision Green /25 #8
2016 Panini Torque Winning Vision Purple /10 #8
2016 Panini Torque Winning Vision Red /49 #8
2017 Donruss #8
2017 Donruss #43
2017 Donruss #97
2017 Donruss #125
2017 Donruss #142
2017 Donruss #116
2017 Donruss Artist Proof /25 #8
2017 Donruss Artist Proof /25 #43
2017 Donruss Artist Proof /25 #97
2017 Donruss Artist Proof /25 #125
2017 Donruss Artist Proof /25 #142
2017 Donruss Artist Proof /25 #116
2017 Donruss Blue Foil /299 #8
2017 Donruss Blue Foil /299 #97
2017 Donruss Blue Foil /299 #125
2017 Donruss Blue Foil /299 #43
2017 Donruss Blue Foil /299 #142
2017 Donruss Blue Foil /299 #116
2017 Donruss Cut to The Chase #6
2017 Donruss Cut to The Chase #9
2017 Donruss Cut to The Chase Cracked Ice /999 #6
2017 Donruss Cut to The Chase Cracked Ice /999 #9
2017 Donruss Dual Rubber Relics #8
2017 Donruss Dual Rubber Relics Holo Black /1 #8
2017 Donruss Dual Rubber Relics Holo Gold /25 #8
2017 Donruss Gold Foil /499 #8
2017 Donruss Gold Foil /499 #97
2017 Donruss Gold Foil /499 #125
2017 Donruss Gold Foil /499 #142
2017 Donruss Gold Foil /499 #43
2017 Donruss Gold Foil /499 #116
2017 Donruss Gold Press Proof /99 #8
2017 Donruss Gold Press Proof /99 #43
2017 Donruss Gold Press Proof /99 #97
2017 Donruss Gold Press Proof /99 #125
2017 Donruss Gold Press Proof /99 #142
2017 Donruss Gold Press Proof /99 #116
2017 Donruss Green Foil /199 #8
2017 Donruss Green Foil /199 #43
2017 Donruss Green Foil /199 #97
2017 Donruss Green Foil /199 #125
2017 Donruss Green Foil /199 #142
2017 Donruss Green Foil /199 #116
2017 Donruss Pole Position #3
2017 Donruss Pole Position Cracked Ice /999 #3
2017 Donruss Press Proof /49 #8
2017 Donruss Press Proof /49 #43
2017 Donruss Press Proof /49 #97
2017 Donruss Press Proof /49 #125
2017 Donruss Press Proof /49 #142
2017 Donruss Press Proof /49 #116
2017 Donruss Printing Plates Black /1 #8
2017 Donruss Printing Plates Black /1 #43
2017 Donruss Printing Plates Black /1 #97
2017 Donruss Printing Plates Black /1 #125
2017 Donruss Printing Plates Black /1 #142
2017 Donruss Printing Plates Black /1 #116
2017 Donruss Printing Plates Cyan /1 #8
2017 Donruss Printing Plates Cyan /1 #43
2017 Donruss Printing Plates Cyan /1 #97
2017 Donruss Printing Plates Cyan /1 #125
2017 Donruss Printing Plates Cyan /1 #142
2017 Donruss Printing Plates Cyan /1 #116
2017 Donruss Printing Plates Magenta /1 #8
2017 Donruss Printing Plates Magenta /1 #97
2017 Donruss Printing Plates Magenta /1 #125
2017 Donruss Printing Plates Magenta /1 #142
2017 Donruss Printing Plates Magenta /1 #43
2017 Donruss Printing Plates Magenta /1 #116
2017 Donruss Printing Plates Yellow /1 #8
2017 Donruss Printing Plates Yellow /1 #97
2017 Donruss Printing Plates Yellow /1 #125
2017 Donruss Printing Plates Yellow /1 #142
2017 Donruss Printing Plates Yellow /1 #43
2017 Donruss Printing Plates Yellow /1 #116
2017 Donruss Retro Relics 1984 #22
2017 Donruss Retro Relics 1984 Holo Black /5 #22
2017 Donruss Retro Relics 1984 Holo Gold /99 #22
2017 Donruss Retro Signatures 1984 #13
2017 Donruss Retro Signatures 1984 Holo Black /1 #13
2017 Donruss Retro Signatures 1984 Holo Gold /25 #13
2017 Donruss Rubber Relics #26
2017 Donruss Rubber Relics #27
2017 Donruss Rubber Relics Holo Black /1 #26
2017 Donruss Rubber Relics Holo Black /1 #27
2017 Donruss Rubber Relics Holo Gold /25 #26
2017 Donruss Rubber Relics Holo Gold /25 #27
2017 Donruss Track Masters #7
2017 Donruss Track Masters Cracked Ice /999 #7
2017 Panini Black Friday Happy Holiday Memorabilia #HHJL
2017 Panini Black Friday Happy Holiday Memorabilia Cracked Ice /25 #HHJL
2017 Panini Black Friday Happy Holiday Memorabilia Galactic Windows /10 #HHJL
2017 Panini Black Friday Happy Holiday Memorabilia Hyperplaid /1 #HHJL
2017 Panini Day #55
2017 Panini Day Cracked Ice /25 #55
2017 Panini Day Decoy /50 #55
2017 Panini Day Hyperplaid /1 #55
2017 Panini Day Memorabilia #44
2017 Panini Day Memorabilia Galactic Window /25 #44
2017 Panini Day Memorabilia Hyperplaid /1 #44
2017 Panini Day Rapture /10 #55
2017 Panini Day Wedges /50 #55
2017 Panini National Convention #R12
2017 Panini National Convention Autographs #R12
2017 Panini National Convention Autographs Hyperplaid /1 #R12
2017 Panini National Convention Escher Squares /25 #R12
2017 Panini National Convention Escher Squares Thick Stock /10 #R12
2017 Panini National Convention Galatic Windows /5 #R12
2017 Panini National Convention Hyperplaid /1 #R12
2017 Panini National Convention Pyramids /10 #R12
2017 Panini National Convention Rainbow Spokes /49 #R12
2017 Panini National Convention Rainbow Spokes Thick Stock /25 #R12
2017 Panini National Convention Rapture /99 #R12
2017 Panini National Treasures /25 #11
2017 Panini National Treasures Associate Sponsor Patch Signatures 1 /1 #10
2017 Panini National Treasures Associate Sponsor Patch Signatures 10 /1 #10
2017 Panini National Treasures Associate Sponsor Patch Signatures 2 /1 #10
2017 Panini National Treasures Associate Sponsor Patch Signatures 3 /1 #10
2017 Panini National Treasures Associate Sponsor Patch Signatures 4 /1 #10
2017 Panini National Treasures Associate Sponsor Patch Signatures 5 /1 #10
2017 Panini National Treasures Associate Sponsor Patch Signatures 6 /1 #10
2017 Panini National Treasures Associate Sponsor Patch Signatures 7 /1 #10
2017 Panini National Treasures Associate Sponsor Patch Signatures 8 /1 #10
2017 Panini National Treasures Associate Sponsor Patch Signatures 9 /1 #10
2017 Panini National Treasures Car Manufacturer Patch Signatures /1 #10
2017 Panini National Treasures Century Black /1 #11
2017 Panini National Treasures Century Gold /15 #11
2017 Panini National Treasures Century Green /5 #11
2017 Panini National Treasures Century Holo Gold /10 #11
2017 Panini National Treasures Century Holo Silver /20 #11
2017 Panini National Treasures Century Laundry Tags /1 #11
2017 Panini National Treasures Dual Firesuit Materials Black /1 #8
2017 Panini National Treasures Dual Firesuit Materials Green /5 #8
2017 Panini National Treasures Dual Firesuit Materials Holo Gold /10 #8
2017 Panini National Treasures Dual Firesuit Materials Laundry Tag /1 #8
2017 Panini National Treasures Dual Firesuit Materials Printing Plates Black /1 #8
2017 Panini National Treasures Dual Firesuit Materials Printing Plates Cyan /1 #8
2017 Panini National Treasures Dual Firesuit Materials Printing Plates Magenta /1 #8
2017 Panini National Treasures Dual Firesuit Materials Printing Plates Yellow /1 #8
2017 Panini National Treasures Dual Firesuit Signatures /25 #8
2017 Panini National Treasures Dual Firesuit Signatures Black /1 #8
2017 Panini National Treasures Dual Firesuit Signatures Gold /15 #8
2017 Panini National Treasures Dual Firesuit Signatures Green /5 #8
2017 Panini National Treasures Dual Firesuit Signatures Holo Gold /10 #8
2017 Panini National Treasures Dual Firesuit Signatures Holo Silver /20 #8
2017 Panini National Treasures Dual Firesuit Signatures Laundry Tag /1 #8
2017 Panini National Treasures Dual Firesuit Signatures Printing Plates Black /1 #8
2017 Panini National Treasures Dual Firesuit Signatures Printing Plates Cyan /1 #8
2017 Panini National Treasures Dual Firesuit Signatures Printing Plates Magenta /1 #8
2017 Panini National Treasures Dual Firesuit Signatures Printing Plates Yellow /1 #8
2017 Panini National Treasures Dual Sheet Metal Signatures Black /1 #7
2017 Panini National Treasures Dual Sheet Metal Signatures Gold /15 #7
2017 Panini National Treasures Dual Sheet Metal Signatures Green /5 #7
2017 Panini National Treasures Dual Sheet Metal Signatures Holo Gold /10 #7
2017 Panini National Treasures Dual Sheet Metal Signatures Printing Plates Black /1 #7
2017 Panini National Treasures Dual Sheet Metal Signatures Printing Plates Cyan /1 #7
2017 Panini National Treasures Dual Sheet Metal Signatures Printing Plates Magenta /1 #7
2017 Panini National Treasures Dual Sheet Metal Signatures Printing Plates Yellow /1 #7
2017 Panini National Treasures Firesuit Manufacturer Patch Signatures /1 #10
2017 Panini National Treasures Flag Patch Signatures /1 #10
2017 Panini National Treasures Hats Off /14 #27
2017 Panini National Treasures Hats Off /14 #28
2017 Panini National Treasures Hats Off Gold /4 #27
2017 Panini National Treasures Hats Off Gold /4 #28
2017 Panini National Treasures Hats Off Holo Gold /5 #27
2017 Panini National Treasures Hats Off Holo Gold /5 #28
2017 Panini National Treasures Hats Off Holo Silver /1 #27
2017 Panini National Treasures Hats Off Holo Silver /1 #28
2017 Panini National Treasures Hats Off Laundry Tag /6 #27
2017 Panini National Treasures Hats Off Laundry Tag /6 #28
2017 Panini National Treasures Hats Off New Era /1 #27
2017 Panini National Treasures Hats Off New Era /1 #28
2017 Panini National Treasures Hats Off Printing Plates Black /1 #27
2017 Panini National Treasures Hats Off Printing Plates Black /1 #28
2017 Panini National Treasures Hats Off Printing Plates Cyan /1 #27
2017 Panini National Treasures Hats Off Printing Plates Cyan /1 #28
2017 Panini National Treasures Hats Off Printing Plates Magenta /1 #27
2017 Panini National Treasures Hats Off Printing Plates Magenta /1 #28
2017 Panini National Treasures Hats Off Printing Plates Yellow /1 #27
2017 Panini National Treasures Hats Off Printing Plates Yellow /1 #28
2017 Panini National Treasures Hats Off Sponsor /5 #27
2017 Panini National Treasures Hats Off Sponsor /5 #28
2017 Panini National Treasures Jumbo Firesuit Materials Black /1 #2
2017 Panini National Treasures Jumbo Firesuit Materials Green /5 #2
2017 Panini National Treasures Jumbo Firesuit Materials Laundry Tag /1 #2
2017 Panini National Treasures Jumbo Firesuit Materials Printing Plates Black /1 #2
2017 Panini National Treasures Jumbo Firesuit Materials Printing Plates Cyan /1 #2
2017 Panini National Treasures Jumbo Firesuit Materials Printing Plates Magenta /1 #2
2017 Panini National Treasures Jumbo Firesuit Materials Printing Plates Yellow /1 #2
2017 Panini National Treasures Jumbo Tire Signatures /99 #9
2017 Panini National Treasures Jumbo Tire Signatures Black /1 #9
2017 Panini National Treasures Jumbo Tire Signatures Gold /25 #9
2017 Panini National Treasures Jumbo Tire Signatures Green /5 #9
2017 Panini National Treasures Jumbo Tire Signatures Holo Gold /15 #9
2017 Panini National Treasures Jumbo Tire Signatures Holo Silver /50 #9
2017 Panini National Treasures Jumbo Tire Signatures Printing Plates Black /1 #9
2017 Panini National Treasures Jumbo Tire Signatures Printing Plates Cyan /1 #9
2017 Panini National Treasures Jumbo Tire Signatures Printing Plates Magenta /1 #9
2017 Panini National Treasures Jumbo Tire Signatures Printing Plates Yellow /1 #9
2017 Panini National Treasures Nameplate Patch Signatures /2 #10
2017 Panini National Treasures NASCAR Patch Signatures /1 #10
2017 Panini National Treasures Printing Plates Black /1 #11
2017 Panini National Treasures Printing Plates Cyan /1 #11
2017 Panini National Treasures Printing Plates Magenta /1 #11
2017 Panini National Treasures Printing Plates Yellow /1 #11
2017 Panini National Treasures Quad Material Signatures Black /1 #7
2017 Panini National Treasures Quad Material Signatures Gold /15 #7
2017 Panini National Treasures Quad Material Signatures Green /5 #7
2017 Panini National Treasures Quad Material Signatures Holo Gold /10 #7
2017 Panini National Treasures Quad Material Signatures Laundry Tag /1 #7
2017 Panini National Treasures Quad Material Signatures Printing Plates Black /1 #7
2017 Panini National Treasures Quad Material Signatures Printing Plates Cyan /1 #7
2017 Panini National Treasures Quad Material Signatures Printing Plates Magenta /1 #7
2017 Panini National Treasures Quad Material Signatures Printing Plates Yellow /1 #7
2017 Panini National Treasures Signature Six Way Swatches /25 #7
2017 Panini National Treasures Signature Six Way Swatches Black /1 #7
2017 Panini National Treasures Signature Six Way Swatches Gold /15 #7
2017 Panini National Treasures Signature Six Way Swatches Green /5 #7
2017 Panini National Treasures Signature Six Way Swatches Holo Gold /10 #7
2017 Panini National Treasures Signature Six Way Swatches Holo Silver /20 #7
2017 Panini National Treasures Signature Six Way Swatches Laundry Tag /1 #7
2017 Panini National Treasures Sunoco Patch Signatures /1 #10
2017 Panini National Treasures Teammates Dual Materials /25 #5
2017 Panini National Treasures Teammates Dual Materials Black /1 #5
2017 Panini National Treasures Teammates Dual Materials Gold /15 #5
2017 Panini National Treasures Teammates Dual Materials Green /5 #5
2017 Panini National Treasures Teammates Dual Materials Holo Gold /10 #5
2017 Panini National Treasures Teammates Dual Materials Holo Silver /20 #5
2017 Panini National Treasures Teammates Dual Materials Laundry Tag /1 #5
2017 Panini National Treasures Teammates Dual Materials Printing Plates Black /1 #5
2017 Panini National Treasures Teammates Dual Materials Printing Plates Cyan /1 #5
2017 Panini National Treasures Teammates Dual Materials Printing Plates Magenta /1 #5
2017 Panini National Treasures Teammates Dual Materials Printing Plates Yellow /1 #5
2017 Panini National Treasures Teammates Quad Materials /25 #3
2017 Panini National Treasures Teammates Quad Materials Black /1 #3
2017 Panini National Treasures Teammates Quad Materials Gold /15 #3
2017 Panini National Treasures Teammates Quad Materials Green /5 #3
2017 Panini National Treasures Teammates Quad Materials Holo Gold /10 #3
2017 Panini National Treasures Teammates Quad Materials Holo Silver /20 #3
2017 Panini National Treasures Teammates Quad Materials Laundry Tag /1 #3
2017 Panini National Treasures Teammates Quad Materials Printing Plates Black /1 #3
2017 Panini National Treasures Teammates Quad Materials Printing Plates Cyan /1 #3
2017 Panini National Treasures Teammates Quad Materials Printing Plates Magenta /1 #3
2017 Panini National Treasures Teammates Quad Materials Printing Plates Yellow /1 #3
2017 Panini National Treasures Three Wide Signatures Black /1 #13
2017 Panini National Treasures Three Wide Signatures Gold /15 #13
2017 Panini National Treasures Three Wide Signatures Green /5 #13
2017 Panini National Treasures Three Wide Signatures Holo Gold /10 #13
2017 Panini National Treasures Three Wide Signatures Holo Silver /20 #13
2017 Panini National Treasures Three Wide Signatures Laundry Tag /1 #13
2017 Panini National Treasures Three Wide Signatures Printing Plates Black /1 #13
2017 Panini National Treasures Three Wide Signatures Printing Plates Cyan /1 #13
2017 Panini National Treasures Three Wide Signatures Printing Plates Magenta /1 #13
2017 Panini National Treasures Three Wide Signatures Printing Plates Yellow /1 #13
2017 Panini Torque #12
2017 Panini Torque #45
2017 Panini Torque #69
2017 Panini Torque #81
2017 Panini Torque #92
2017 Panini Torque Artist Proof /75 #12
2017 Panini Torque Artist Proof /75 #45
2017 Panini Torque Artist Proof /75 #69
2017 Panini Torque Artist Proof /75 #81
2017 Panini Torque Artist Proof /75 #92
2017 Panini Torque Blackout /1 #12
2017 Panini Torque Blackout /1 #45
2017 Panini Torque Blackout /1 #69
2017 Panini Torque Blackout /1 #81
2017 Panini Torque Blackout /1 #92
2017 Panini Torque Blue /150 #12
2017 Panini Torque Blue /150 #45
2017 Panini Torque Blue /150 #69
2017 Panini Torque Blue /150 #81
2017 Panini Torque Blue /150 #92
2017 Panini Torque Claiming The Chase #4
2017 Panini Torque Claiming The Chase Gold /199 #4
2017 Panini Torque Claiming The Chase Holo Silver /99 #4
2017 Panini Torque Clear Vision #12
2017 Panini Torque Clear Vision Blue /99 #12
2017 Panini Torque Clear Vision Gold /149 #12
2017 Panini Torque Clear Vision Green /25 #12
2017 Panini Torque Clear Vision Purple /10 #12
2017 Panini Torque Clear Vision Red /49 #12
2017 Panini Torque Dual Materials /199 #14
2017 Panini Torque Dual Materials Blue /99 #14
2017 Panini Torque Dual Materials Green /25 #14
2017 Panini Torque Dual Materials Purple /10 #14
2017 Panini Torque Dual Materials Red /49 #14
2017 Panini Torque Gold #12
2017 Panini Torque Gold #45
2017 Panini Torque Gold #69
2017 Panini Torque Gold #81
2017 Panini Torque Gold #92
2017 Panini Torque Holo Gold /10 #12
2017 Panini Torque Holo Gold /10 #45
2017 Panini Torque Holo Gold /10 #69
2017 Panini Torque Holo Gold /10 #81
2017 Panini Torque Holo Gold /10 #92
2017 Panini Torque Holo Silver /25 #12
2017 Panini Torque Holo Silver /25 #45
2017 Panini Torque Holo Silver /25 #69
2017 Panini Torque Holo Silver /25 #81
2017 Panini Torque Holo Silver /25 #92
2017 Panini Torque Horsepower Heroes #14
2017 Panini Torque Horsepower Heroes Gold /199 #14
2017 Panini Torque Horsepower Heroes Holo Silver /99 #14
2017 Panini Torque Jumbo Firesuit Signatures /51 #13
2017 Panini Torque Jumbo Firesuit Signatures Blue /49 #13
2017 Panini Torque Jumbo Firesuit Signatures Green /15 #13
2017 Panini Torque Jumbo Firesuit Signatures Purple /10 #13
2017 Panini Torque Jumbo Firesuit Signatures Red /25 #13
2017 Panini Torque Manufacturer Marks #10
2017 Panini Torque Manufacturer Marks Gold /199 #10
2017 Panini Torque Manufacturer Marks Holo Silver /99 #10
2017 Panini Torque Metal Materials /199 #9
2017 Panini Torque Metal Materials Blue /99 #9
2017 Panini Torque Metal Materials Green /25 #9
2017 Panini Torque Metal Materials Purple /10 #9
2017 Panini Torque Metal Materials Red /49 #9
2017 Panini Torque Pairings Materials /199 #1
2017 Panini Torque Pairings Materials Blue /99 #1
2017 Panini Torque Pairings Materials Green /25 #1
2017 Panini Torque Pairings Materials Purple /10 #1
2017 Panini Torque Pairings Materials Red /49 #1
2017 Panini Torque Primary Paint #12
2017 Panini Torque Primary Paint Blue /99 #12
2017 Panini Torque Primary Paint Checkerboard /10 #12
2017 Panini Torque Primary Paint Green /25 #12
2017 Panini Torque Primary Paint Red /49 #12
2017 Panini Torque Prime Associate Sponsors Jumbo Patches /1 #10A
2017 Panini Torque Prime Associate Sponsors Jumbo Patches /1 #10B
2017 Panini Torque Prime Associate Sponsors Jumbo Patches /1 #10C
2017 Panini Torque Prime Associate Sponsors Jumbo Patches /1 #10D
2017 Panini Torque Prime Associate Sponsors Jumbo Patches /1 #10E
2017 Panini Torque Prime Associate Sponsors Jumbo Patches /1 #10F
2017 Panini Torque Prime Associate Sponsors Jumbo Patches /1 #10G
2017 Panini Torque Prime Associate Sponsors Jumbo Patches /1 #10H
2017 Panini Torque Prime Associate Sponsors Jumbo Patches /1 #10I
2017 Panini Torque Prime Associate Sponsors Jumbo Patches /1 #10J
2017 Panini Torque Prime Associate Sponsors Jumbo Patches /1 #10K
2017 Panini Torque Prime Associate Sponsors Jumbo Patches /1 #10L
2017 Panini Torque Prime Associate Sponsors Jumbo Patches /1 #10M
2017 Panini Torque Prime Associate Sponsors Jumbo Patches /1 #10N
2017 Panini Torque Prime Flag Jumbo Patches /1 #10
2017 Panini Torque Prime Manufacturer Jumbo Patches /1 #10
2017 Panini Torque Prime Nameplates Jumbo Patches /2 #10
2017 Panini Torque Prime NASCAR Jumbo Patches /1 #10
2017 Panini Torque Prime Series Sponsor Jumbo Patches /1 #10
2017 Panini Torque Printing Plates Black /1 #12
2017 Panini Torque Printing Plates Black /1 #45
2017 Panini Torque Printing Plates Black /1 #69
2017 Panini Torque Printing Plates Black /1 #81
2017 Panini Torque Printing Plates Black /1 #92
2017 Panini Torque Printing Plates Cyan /1 #12
2017 Panini Torque Printing Plates Cyan /1 #45
2017 Panini Torque Printing Plates Cyan /1 #69
2017 Panini Torque Printing Plates Cyan /1 #81
2017 Panini Torque Printing Plates Cyan /1 #92
2017 Panini Torque Printing Plates Magenta /1 #12
2017 Panini Torque Printing Plates Magenta /1 #45
2017 Panini Torque Printing Plates Magenta /1 #69
2017 Panini Torque Printing Plates Magenta /1 #81
2017 Panini Torque Printing Plates Magenta /1 #92
2017 Panini Torque Printing Plates Yellow /1 #12
2017 Panini Torque Printing Plates Yellow /1 #45
2017 Panini Torque Printing Plates Yellow /1 #69

2017 Panini Torque Printing Plates Yellow /1 #81
2017 Panini Torque Printing Plates Yellow /1 #92
2017 Panini Torque Purple /50 #12
2017 Panini Torque Purple /50 #45
2017 Panini Torque Purple /50 #69
2017 Panini Torque Purple /50 #81
2017 Panini Torque Purple /50 #92
2017 Panini Torque Quad Materials /99 #15
2017 Panini Torque Quad Materials Blue /49 #15
2017 Panini Torque Quad Materials Green /10 #15
2017 Panini Torque Quad Materials Purple /1 #15
2017 Panini Torque Quad Materials Red /25 #15
2017 Panini Torque Raced Relics /499 #11
2017 Panini Torque Raced Relics Blue /99 #11
2017 Panini Torque Raced Relics Green /25 #11
2017 Panini Torque Raced Relics Purple /10 #11
2017 Panini Torque Raced Relics Red /49 #11
2017 Panini Torque Red /100 #12
2017 Panini Torque Red /100 #45
2017 Panini Torque Red /100 #69
2017 Panini Torque Red /100 #81
2017 Panini Torque Red /100 #92
2017 Panini Torque Running Order #2
2017 Panini Torque Running Order Blue /99 #2
2017 Panini Torque Running Order Checkerboard /10 #2
2017 Panini Torque Running Order Green /25 #2
2017 Panini Torque Running Order Red /49 #2
2017 Panini Torque Silhouettes Sheet Metal Signatures /51 #23
2017 Panini Torque Silhouettes Sheet Metal Signatures Blue /49 #23
2017 Panini Torque Silhouettes Sheet Metal Signatures Green /15 #23
2017 Panini Torque Silhouettes Sheet Metal Signatures Purple /10 #23
2017 Panini Torque Silhouettes Sheet Metal Signatures Red /25 #23
2017 Panini Torque Special Paint #4
2017 Panini Torque Special Paint Gold /199 #4
2017 Panini Torque Special Paint Holo Silver /99 #4
2017 Panini Torque Superstar Vision #5
2017 Panini Torque Superstar Vision Blue /99 #5
2017 Panini Torque Superstar Vision Gold /149 #5
2017 Panini Torque Superstar Vision Green /25 #5
2017 Panini Torque Superstar Vision Purple /10 #5
2017 Panini Torque Superstar Vision Red /49 #5
2017 Panini Torque Test Proof Black /1 #12
2017 Panini Torque Test Proof Black /1 #45
2017 Panini Torque Test Proof Black /1 #69
2017 Panini Torque Test Proof Black /1 #81
2017 Panini Torque Test Proof Black /1 #92
2017 Panini Torque Test Proof Cyan /1 #12
2017 Panini Torque Test Proof Cyan /1 #45
2017 Panini Torque Test Proof Cyan /1 #69
2017 Panini Torque Test Proof Cyan /1 #81
2017 Panini Torque Test Proof Cyan /1 #92
2017 Panini Torque Test Proof Magenta /1 #12
2017 Panini Torque Test Proof Magenta /1 #45
2017 Panini Torque Test Proof Magenta /1 #69
2017 Panini Torque Test Proof Magenta /1 #81
2017 Panini Torque Test Proof Magenta /1 #92
2017 Panini Torque Test Proof Yellow /1 #12
2017 Panini Torque Test Proof Yellow /1 #45
2017 Panini Torque Test Proof Yellow /1 #69
2017 Panini Torque Test Proof Yellow /1 #81
2017 Panini Torque Test Proof Yellow /1 #92
2017 Panini Torque Victory Laps #4
2017 Panini Torque Victory Laps Gold /199 #4
2017 Panini Torque Victory Laps Holo Silver /99 #4
2017 Select #37
2017 Select #38
2017 Select #39
2017 Select #127
2017 Select Prizms Black /3 #37
2017 Select Prizms Black /3 #38
2017 Select Prizms Black /3 #39
2017 Select Prizms Black /3 #127
2017 Select Prizms Blue /199 #37
2017 Select Prizms Blue /199 #38
2017 Select Prizms Blue /199 #39
2017 Select Prizms Checkered Flag /1 #37
2017 Select Prizms Checkered Flag /1 #38
2017 Select Prizms Checkered Flag /1 #39
2017 Select Prizms Checkered Flag /1 #127
2017 Select Prizms Gold /10 #37
2017 Select Prizms Gold /10 #38
2017 Select Prizms Gold /10 #39
2017 Select Prizms Gold /10 #127
2017 Select Prizms Purple Pulsar #37
2017 Select Prizms Purple Pulsar #38
2017 Select Prizms Purple Pulsar #39
2017 Select Prizms Red /99 #37
2017 Select Prizms Red /99 #38
2017 Select Prizms Red /99 #39
2017 Select Prizms Red White and Blue Pulsar /299 #37
2017 Select Prizms Red White and Blue Pulsar /299 #38
2017 Select Prizms Red White and Blue Pulsar /299 #39
2017 Select Prizms Silver #37
2017 Select Prizms Silver #38
2017 Select Prizms Silver #39
2017 Select Prizms Tie Dye /24 #37
2017 Select Prizms Tie Dye /24 #38
2017 Select Prizms Tie Dye /24 #39
2017 Select Prizms Tie Dye /24 #127
2017 Select Prizms White /50 #37
2017 Select Prizms White /50 #38
2017 Select Prizms White /50 #39
2017 Select Prizms White /50 #127
2017 Select Select Pairs Materials #3
2017 Select Select Pairs Materials #4
2017 Select Select Pairs Materials Prizms Blue /199 #3
2017 Select Select Pairs Materials Prizms Blue /199 #4
2017 Select Select Pairs Materials Prizms Checkered Flag /1 #3
2017 Select Select Pairs Materials Prizms Checkered Flag /1 #4
2017 Select Select Pairs Materials Prizms Gold /10 #3
2017 Select Select Pairs Materials Prizms Gold /10 #4
2017 Select Select Pairs Materials Prizms Red /99 #3
2017 Select Select Pairs Materials Prizms Red /99 #4
2017 Select Select Swatches #24
2017 Select Select Swatches Prizms Blue /199 #24
2017 Select Select Swatches Prizms Checkered Flag /1 #24
2017 Select Select Swatches Prizms Gold /10 #24
2017 Select Select Swatches Prizms Red /99 #24
2017 Select Sheet Metal #13
2017 Select Sheet Metal Prizms Blue /50 #13
2017 Select Sheet Metal Prizms Checkered Flag /1 #13
2017 Select Sheet Metal Prizms Gold /10 #13
2017 Select Sheet Metal Prizms Red /25 #13
2017 Select Signature Paint Schemes #8
2017 Select Signature Paint Schemes Prizms Blue /50 #8
2017 Select Signature Paint Schemes Prizms Checkered Flag /1 #8
2017 Select Signature Paint Schemes Prizms Gold /10 #8
2017 Select Signature Paint Schemes Prizms Red /25 #8
2017 Select Signature Swatches #24
2017 Select Signature Swatches Prizms Checkered Flag /1 #24
2017 Select Signature Swatches Prizms Gold /10 #24
2017 Select Signature Swatches Prizms Tie Dye /24 #24
2017 Select Signature Swatches Prizms White /50 #24
2017 Select Signature Swatches Triple #14
2017 Select Signature Swatches Triple Prizms Checkered Flag /1 #14
2017 Select Signature Swatches Triple Prizms Gold /10 #14
2017 Select Signature Swatches Triple Prizms Tie Dye /24 #14
2017 Select Signature Swatches Triple Prizms White /50 #14
2017 Select Speed Merchants #7
2017 Select Speed Merchants Prizms Black /3 #7
2017 Select Speed Merchants Prizms Checkered Flag /1 #7
2017 Select Speed Merchants Prizms Gold /10 #7
2017 Select Speed Merchants Prizms Tie Dye /24 #7
2017 Select Speed Merchants Prizms White /50 #7
2017 Select Up Close and Personal #1
2017 Select Up Close and Personal Prizms Black /3 #1
2017 Select Up Close and Personal Prizms Checkered Flag /1 #1
2017 Select Up Close and Personal Prizms Gold /10 #1
2017 Select Up Close and Personal Prizms Tie Dye /24 #1
2017 Select Up Close and Personal Prizms White /50 #1
2018 Certified #75
2018 Certified #99
2018 Certified All Certified Team /199 #15
2018 Certified All Certified Team Black /1 #15
2018 Certified All Certified Team Blue /99 #15
2018 Certified All Certified Team Gold /49 #15
2018 Certified All Certified Team Green /10 #15
2018 Certified All Certified Team Mirror Black /1 #15
2018 Certified All Certified Team Mirror Gold /25 #15
2018 Certified All Certified Team Mirror Green /5 #15
2018 Certified All Certified Team Mirror Purple /10 #15
2018 Certified All Certified Team Purple /25 #15
2018 Certified All Certified Team Red /149 #15
2018 Certified Black /1 #75
2018 Certified Black /1 #99
2018 Certified Blue /99 #75
2018 Certified Blue /99 #99
2018 Certified Complete Materials /299 #10
2018 Certified Complete Materials Black /1 #10
2018 Certified Complete Materials Blue /49 #10
2018 Certified Complete Materials Gold /25 #10
2018 Certified Complete Materials Green /5 #10
2018 Certified Complete Materials Purple /10 #10
2018 Certified Complete Materials Red /199 #10
2018 Certified Cup Swatches /399 #14
2018 Certified Cup Swatches Black /1 #14
2018 Certified Cup Swatches Blue /49 #14
2018 Certified Cup Swatches Gold /25 #14
2018 Certified Cup Swatches Green /5 #14
2018 Certified Cup Swatches Purple /10 #14
2018 Certified Cup Swatches Red /199 #14
2018 Certified Epix /199 #15
2018 Certified Epix Black /1 #15
2018 Certified Epix Blue /99 #15
2018 Certified Epix Gold /49 #15
2018 Certified Epix Green /10 #15
2018 Certified Epix Mirror Black /1 #15
2018 Certified Epix Mirror Gold /25 #15
2018 Certified Epix Mirror Green /5 #15
2018 Certified Epix Mirror Purple /10 #15
2018 Certified Epix Purple /25 #15
2018 Certified Epix Red /149 #15
2018 Certified Gold /49 #75
2018 Certified Gold /49 #99
2018 Certified Green /10 #75
2018 Certified Green /10 #99
2018 Certified Materials Signatures Black /1 #11
2018 Certified Materials Signatures Blue /25 #11
2018 Certified Materials Signatures Gold /15 #11
2018 Certified Materials Signatures Green /5 #11
2018 Certified Materials Signatures Purple /10 #11
2018 Certified Materials Signatures Red /50 #11
2018 Certified Mirror Black /1 #75
2018 Certified Mirror Black /1 #99
2018 Certified Mirror Gold /25 #75
2018 Certified Mirror Gold /25 #99
2018 Certified Mirror Green /5 #75
2018 Certified Mirror Green /5 #99
2018 Certified Mirror Purple /10 #75
2018 Certified Mirror Purple /10 #99
2018 Certified Orange /249 #75
2018 Certified Orange /249 #99
2018 Certified Piece of the Race /499 #10
2018 Certified Piece of the Race Black /1 #10
2018 Certified Piece of the Race Blue /49 #10
2018 Certified Piece of the Race Gold /25 #10
2018 Certified Piece of the Race Green /5 #10
2018 Certified Piece of the Race Purple /10 #10
2018 Certified Piece of the Race Red /199 #10
2018 Certified Purple /25 #75
2018 Certified Purple /25 #99
2018 Certified Red /199 #75
2018 Certified Red /199 #99
2018 Certified Signature Swatches Black /1 #10
2018 Certified Signature Swatches Blue /25 #10
2018 Certified Signature Swatches Gold /15 #10
2018 Certified Signature Swatches Green /5 #10
2018 Certified Signature Swatches Purple /10 #10
2018 Certified Signature Swatches Red /50 #10
2018 Certified Signing Sessions Black /1 #11
2018 Certified Signing Sessions Gold /22 #11
2018 Certified Signing Sessions Green /5 #11
2018 Certified Signing Sessions Purple /10 #11
2018 Certified Skills /199 #11
2018 Certified Skills Black /1 #11
2018 Certified Skills Blue /99 #11
2018 Certified Skills Gold /49 #11
2018 Certified Skills Green /10 #11
2018 Certified Skills Mirror Black /1 #11
2018 Certified Skills Mirror Gold /25 #11
2018 Certified Skills Mirror Green /5 #11
2018 Certified Skills Mirror Purple /10 #11
2018 Certified Skills Purple /25 #11
2018 Certified Skills Red /149 #11
2018 Certified Stars /199 #3
2018 Certified Stars Black /1 #3
2018 Certified Stars Blue /99 #3
2018 Certified Stars Gold /49 #3
2018 Certified Stars Green /10 #3
2018 Certified Stars Mirror Black /1 #3
2018 Certified Stars Mirror Gold /25 #3
2018 Certified Stars Mirror Green /5 #3
2018 Certified Stars Mirror Purple /10 #3
2018 Certified Stars Purple /25 #3
2018 Certified Stars Red /149 #3
2018 Donruss #17
2018 Donruss #44A
2018 Donruss #96
2018 Donruss #134
2018 Donruss #44B
2018 Donruss Artist Proofs /25 #17
2018 Donruss Artist Proofs /25 #44A
2018 Donruss Artist Proofs /25 #96
2018 Donruss Artist Proofs /25 #134
2018 Donruss Artist Proofs /25 #44B
2018 Donruss Elite Dominators /999 #4
2018 Donruss Gold Foil /499 #17
2018 Donruss Gold Foil /499 #44A
2018 Donruss Gold Foil /499 #96
2018 Donruss Gold Foil /499 #134
2018 Donruss Gold Foil /499 #44B
2018 Donruss Gold Press Proofs /99 #17
2018 Donruss Gold Press Proofs /99 #44A
2018 Donruss Gold Press Proofs /99 #96
2018 Donruss Gold Press Proofs /99 #134
2018 Donruss Gold Press Proofs /99 #44B
2018 Donruss Green Foil /199 #17
2018 Donruss Green Foil /199 #44A
2018 Donruss Green Foil /199 #96
2018 Donruss Green Foil /199 #134
2018 Donruss Green Foil /199 #44B
2018 Donruss Pole Position #3
2018 Donruss Pole Position Cracked Ice /999 #3
2018 Donruss Pole Position Xplosion /99 #3
2018 Donruss Press Proofs /49 #17
2018 Donruss Press Proofs /49 #44A
2018 Donruss Press Proofs /49 #96
2018 Donruss Press Proofs /49 #134
2018 Donruss Press Proofs /49 #44B
2018 Donruss Printing Plates Black /1 #17
2018 Donruss Printing Plates Black /1 #44
2018 Donruss Printing Plates Black /1 #96
2018 Donruss Printing Plates Black /1 #134
2018 Donruss Printing Plates Black /1 #44B
2018 Donruss Printing Plates Cyan /1 #17
2018 Donruss Printing Plates Cyan /1 #44
2018 Donruss Printing Plates Cyan /1 #96
2018 Donruss Printing Plates Cyan /1 #134
2018 Donruss Printing Plates Cyan /1 #44B
2018 Donruss Printing Plates Magenta /1 #17
2018 Donruss Printing Plates Magenta /1 #44
2018 Donruss Printing Plates Magenta /1 #96
2018 Donruss Printing Plates Magenta /1 #134
2018 Donruss Printing Plates Magenta /1 #44B
2018 Donruss Printing Plates Yellow /1 #17
2018 Donruss Printing Plates Yellow /1 #44
2018 Donruss Printing Plates Yellow /1 #96
2018 Donruss Printing Plates Yellow /1 #134
2018 Donruss Printing Plates Yellow /1 #44B
2018 Donruss Red Foil /299 #17
2018 Donruss Red Foil /299 #44A
2018 Donruss Red Foil /299 #96
2018 Donruss Red Foil /299 #134
2018 Donruss Red Foil /299 #44B
2018 Donruss Rubber Relic Signatures #9
2018 Donruss Rubber Relic Signatures Black /1 #9
2018 Donruss Rubber Relic Signatures Holo Gold /25 #9
2018 Donruss Rubber Relics #16
2018 Donruss Rubber Relics Black /10 #16
2018 Donruss Rubber Relics Holo Gold /99 #16
2018 Panini Father's Day Racing Memorabilia #JL
2018 Panini Father's Day Racing Memorabilia Checkerboard /10 #JL
2018 Panini Father's Day Racing Memorabilia Cracked Ice /25 #JL
2018 Panini Father's Day Racing Memorabilia Escher Squares /5 #JL
2018 Panini Father's Day Racing Memorabilia Hyperplaid /1 #JL
2018 Panini Prime /50 #2
2018 Panini Prime /50 #36
2018 Panini Prime /50 #69
2018 Panini Prime Black /1 #2
2018 Panini Prime Black /1 #36
2018 Panini Prime Black /1 #69
2018 Panini Prime Clear Silhouettes /99 #15
2018 Panini Prime Clear Silhouettes Black /1 #15
2018 Panini Prime Clear Silhouettes Dual /99 #15
2018 Panini Prime Clear Silhouettes Dual Black /1 #15
2018 Panini Prime Clear Silhouettes Dual Holo Gold /50 #15
2018 Panini Prime Clear Silhouettes Holo Gold /50 #15
2018 Panini Prime Driver Signatures /60 #24
2018 Panini Prime Driver Signatures Black /1 #24
2018 Panini Prime Driver Signatures Holo Gold /25 #24
2018 Panini Prime Dual Signatures /50 #11
2018 Panini Prime Dual Signatures Black /1 #11
2018 Panini Prime Dual Signatures Holo Gold /25 #11
2018 Panini Prime Hats Off Button /1 #6
2018 Panini Prime Hats Off Eyelet /6 #6
2018 Panini Prime Hats Off Headband /36 #6
2018 Panini Prime Hats Off Laundry Tag /1 #6
2018 Panini Prime Hats Off New Era /1 #6
2018 Panini Prime Hats Off Number /2 #6
2018 Panini Prime Hats Off Sponsor Logo /3 #6
2018 Panini Prime Holo Gold /25 #2
2018 Panini Prime Holo Gold /25 #36
2018 Panini Prime Holo Gold /25 #69
2018 Panini Prime Prime Jumbo Associate Sponsor 1 /1 #44
2018 Panini Prime Prime Jumbo Associate Sponsor 10 /1 #44
2018 Panini Prime Prime Jumbo Associate Sponsor 11 /1 #44
2018 Panini Prime Prime Jumbo Associate Sponsor 12 /1 #44
2018 Panini Prime Prime Jumbo Associate Sponsor 13 /1 #44
2018 Panini Prime Prime Jumbo Associate Sponsor 14 /1 #44
2018 Panini Prime Prime Jumbo Associate Sponsor 15 /1 #44
2018 Panini Prime Prime Jumbo Associate Sponsor 2 /1 #44
2018 Panini Prime Prime Jumbo Associate Sponsor 3 /1 #44
2018 Panini Prime Prime Jumbo Associate Sponsor 4 /1 #44
2018 Panini Prime Prime Jumbo Associate Sponsor 5 /1 #44
2018 Panini Prime Prime Jumbo Associate Sponsor 6 /1 #44
2018 Panini Prime Prime Jumbo Associate Sponsor 7 /1 #44
2018 Panini Prime Prime Jumbo Associate Sponsor 8 /1 #44
2018 Panini Prime Prime Jumbo Associate Sponsor 9 /1 #44
2018 Panini Prime Prime Jumbo Car Manufacturer /1 #44
2018 Panini Prime Prime Jumbo Firesuit Manufacturer /1 #44
2018 Panini Prime Prime Jumbo Flag Patch /1 #44
2018 Panini Prime Prime Jumbo Glove Manufacturer Patch /1 #44
2018 Panini Prime Prime Jumbo Glove Name Patch /1 #44
2018 Panini Prime Prime Jumbo Nameplate /2 #44
2018 Panini Prime Prime Jumbo NASCAR /1 #44
2018 Panini Prime Prime Jumbo Prime Colors /14 #44
2018 Panini Prime Prime Jumbo Series Sponsor /1 #44
2018 Panini Prime Prime Jumbo Shoe Brand Logo /1 #44
2018 Panini Prime Prime Jumbo Shoe Name Patch /1 #44
2018 Panini Prime Prime Jumbo Sunoco /1 #44
2018 Panini Prime Prime Number Signatures /50 #8
2018 Panini Prime Prime Number Signatures Black /1 #8
2018 Panini Prime Prime Number Signatures Holo Gold /25 #8
2018 Panini Prime Quad Material Autographs /75 #10
2018 Panini Prime Quad Material Autographs Black /1 #10
2018 Panini Prime Quad Material Autographs Holo Gold /25 #10
2018 Panini Prime Quad Material Autographs Laundry Tag /1 #10
2018 Panini Prime Race Used Duals Firesuit /50 #21
2018 Panini Prime Race Used Duals Firesuit Black /1 #21
2018 Panini Prime Race Used Duals Firesuit Holo Gold /25 #21
2018 Panini Prime Race Used Duals Firesuit Laundry Tag /1 #21
2018 Panini Prime Race Used Duals Sheet Metal /50 #21
2018 Panini Prime Race Used Duals Sheet Metal Black /1 #21
2018 Panini Prime Race Used Duals Sheet Metal Holo Gold /25 #21
2018 Panini Prime Race Used Duals Tire /50 #21
2018 Panini Prime Race Used Duals Tire Black /1 #21
2018 Panini Prime Race Used Duals Tire Holo Gold /25 #21
2018 Panini Prime Race Used Firesuits Black /1 #18
2018 Panini Prime Race Used Firesuits Holo Gold /25 #18
2018 Panini Prime Race Used Firesuits Laundry Tag /1 #18
2018 Panini Prime Race Used Sheet Metal /50 #18
2018 Panini Prime Race Used Sheet Metal Black /1 #18
2018 Panini Prime Race Used Sheet Metal Holo Gold /25 #18
2018 Panini Prime Race Used Tires Black /1 #18
2018 Panini Prime Race Used Tires Holo Gold /25 #18
2018 Panini Prime Race Used Trios Firesuit /50 #10
2018 Panini Prime Race Used Trios Firesuit Black /1 #10
2018 Panini Prime Race Used Trios Firesuit Holo Gold /25 #10
2018 Panini Prime Race Used Trios Firesuit Laundry Tag /1 #10
2018 Panini Prime Race Used Trios Sheet Metal /50 #ROTJL
2018 Panini Prime Race Used Trios Sheet Metal Black /1 #10
2018 Panini Prime Race Used Trios Sheet Metal Holo Gold /25 #10
2018 Panini Prime Race Used Trios Tire /50 #10
2018 Panini Prime Race Used Trios Tire Black /1 #10
2018 Panini Prime Race Used Trios Tire Holo Gold /25 #10
2018 Panini Prime Shadowbox Signatures /99 #4
2018 Panini Prime Shadowbox Signatures Black /1 #4
2018 Panini Prime Shadowbox Signatures Holo Gold /50 #4
2018 Panini Prime Signature Swatches /60 #7
2018 Panini Prime Signature Swatches Black /1 #7
2018 Panini Prime Signature Swatches Holo Gold /22 #7
2018 Panini Prime Triple Material Autographs /50 #15
2018 Panini Prime Triple Material Autographs Black /1 #15
2018 Panini Prime Triple Material Autographs Holo Gold /25 #15
2018 Panini Prime Triple Material Autographs Laundry Tag /1 #15
2018 Panini Prizm #45
2018 Panini Prizm #73
2018 Panini Prizm Brilliance #3
2018 Panini Prizm Brilliance Prizms #3
2018 Panini Prizm Brilliance Prizms Black /1 #3
2018 Panini Prizm Brilliance Prizms Gold /10 #3
2018 Panini Prizm Illumination #12
2018 Panini Prizm Illumination Prizms #12
2018 Panini Prizm Illumination Prizms Black /1 #12
2018 Panini Prizm Illumination Prizms Gold /10 #12
2018 Panini Prizm Instant Impact #8
2018 Panini Prizm Instant Impact Prizms #8
2018 Panini Prizm Instant Impact Prizms Black /1 #8
2018 Panini Prizm Instant Impact Prizms Gold /10 #8
2018 Panini Prizm National Pride #11
2018 Panini Prizm National Pride Prizms #11
2018 Panini Prizm National Pride Prizms Black /1 #11
2018 Panini Prizm National Pride Prizms Gold /10 #11
2018 Panini Prizm Prizms #45
2018 Panini Prizm Prizms #73
2018 Panini Prizm Prizms Black /1 #45
2018 Panini Prizm Prizms Black /1 #73
2018 Panini Prizm Prizms Blue /99 #45
2018 Panini Prizm Prizms Blue /99 #73
2018 Panini Prizm Prizms Camo #45
2018 Panini Prizm Prizms Camo #73
2018 Panini Prizm Prizms Gold /10 #45
2018 Panini Prizm Prizms Gold /10 #73
2018 Panini Prizm Prizms Green /149 #45
2018 Panini Prizm Prizms Green /149 #73
2018 Panini Prizm Prizms Purple Flash #45
2018 Panini Prizm Prizms Purple Flash #73
2018 Panini Prizm Prizms Rainbow /24 #45
2018 Panini Prizm Prizms Rainbow /24 #73
2018 Panini Prizm Prizms Red /75 #45
2018 Panini Prizm Prizms Red /75 #73
2018 Panini Prizm Prizms Red White and Blue #45
2018 Panini Prizm Prizms Red White and Blue #73
2018 Panini Prizm Prizms White /5 #45
2018 Panini Prizm Prizms White /5 #73
2018 Panini Prizm Scripted Signatures Prizms #34
2018 Panini Prizm Scripted Signatures Prizms Black /1 #34
2018 Panini Prizm Scripted Signatures Prizms Blue /35 #34
2018 Panini Prizm Scripted Signatures Prizms Camo #34
2018 Panini Prizm Scripted Signatures Prizms Gold /10 #34
2018 Panini Prizm Scripted Signatures Prizms Green /50 #34
2018 Panini Prizm Scripted Signatures Prizms Rainbow /24 #34
2018 Panini Prizm Scripted Signatures Prizms Red /25 #34
2018 Panini Prizm Scripted Signatures Prizms Red White and Blue /75 #34
2018 Panini Prizm Scripted Signatures Prizms White /5 #34
2018 Panini Prizm Stars and Stripes #13
2018 Panini Prizm Stars and Stripes Prizms #13
2018 Panini Prizm Stars and Stripes Prizms Black /1 #13
2018 Panini Prizm Stars and Stripes Prizms Gold /10 #13
2018 Panini Prizm Team Tandems #6
2018 Panini Prizm Team Tandems Prizms #6
2018 Panini Prizm Team Tandems Prizms Black /1 #6
2018 Panini Prizm Team Tandems Prizms Gold /10 #6
2018 Panini Victory Lane #16
2018 Panini Victory Lane #66
2018 Panini Victory Lane #87
2018 Panini Victory Lane Black /1 #16
2018 Panini Victory Lane Black /1 #66
2018 Panini Victory Lane Black /1 #87
2018 Panini Victory Lane Blue /25 #16
2018 Panini Victory Lane Blue /25 #66
2018 Panini Victory Lane Blue /25 #87
2018 Panini Victory Lane Celebrations #8
2018 Panini Victory Lane Celebrations Black /1 #8
2018 Panini Victory Lane Celebrations Blue /25 #8
2018 Panini Victory Lane Celebrations Gold /99 #8
2018 Panini Victory Lane Celebrations Green /5 #8
2018 Panini Victory Lane Celebrations Printing Plates Black /1 #8
2018 Panini Victory Lane Celebrations Printing Plates Cyan /1 #8
2018 Panini Victory Lane Celebrations Printing Plates Magenta /1 #8
2018 Panini Victory Lane Celebrations Printing Plates Yellow /1 #8
2018 Panini Victory Lane Celebrations Red /49 #8
2018 Panini Victory Lane Engineered to Perfection Materials /399 #13
2018 Panini Victory Lane Engineered to Perfection Materials Black /25 #13
2018 Panini Victory Lane Engineered to Perfection Materials Gold /199 #13
2018 Panini Victory Lane Engineered to Perfection Materials Green /99 #13
2018 Panini Victory Lane Engineered to Perfection Materials Laundry Tag /1 #13
2018 Panini Victory Lane Gold /99 #16
2018 Panini Victory Lane Gold /99 #66
2018 Panini Victory Lane Gold /99 #87
2018 Panini Victory Lane Green /5 #16
2018 Panini Victory Lane Green /5 #66
2018 Panini Victory Lane Green /5 #87
2018 Panini Victory Lane Octane Autographs /76 #19
2018 Panini Victory Lane Octane Autographs Black /1 #19
2018 Panini Victory Lane Octane Autographs Gold /49 #19
2018 Panini Victory Lane Pedal to the Metal #27
2018 Panini Victory Lane Pedal to the Metal #65
2018 Panini Victory Lane Pedal to the Metal Black /1 #27
2018 Panini Victory Lane Pedal to the Metal Black /1 #65
2018 Panini Victory Lane Pedal to the Metal Blue /25 #27
2018 Panini Victory Lane Pedal to the Metal Blue /25 #65
2018 Panini Victory Lane Pedal to the Metal Green /5 #27
2018 Panini Victory Lane Pedal to the Metal Green /5 #65
2018 Panini Victory Lane Printing Plates Black /1 #16
2018 Panini Victory Lane Printing Plates Black /1 #66
2018 Panini Victory Lane Printing Plates Black /1 #87
2018 Panini Victory Lane Printing Plates Cyan /1 #16
2018 Panini Victory Lane Printing Plates Cyan /1 #66
2018 Panini Victory Lane Printing Plates Cyan /1 #87
2018 Panini Victory Lane Printing Plates Magenta /1 #16
2018 Panini Victory Lane Printing Plates Magenta /1 #66
2018 Panini Victory Lane Printing Plates Magenta /1 #87
2018 Panini Victory Lane Printing Plates Yellow /1 #16
2018 Panini Victory Lane Printing Plates Yellow /1 #66
2018 Panini Victory Lane Printing Plates Yellow /1 #87
2018 Panini Victory Lane Race Ready Dual Materials /399 #9
2018 Panini Victory Lane Race Ready Dual Materials Black /25 #9
2018 Panini Victory Lane Race Ready Dual Materials Gold /199 #9
2018 Panini Victory Lane Race Ready Dual Materials Green /99 #9
2018 Panini Victory Lane Race Ready Dual Materials Laundry Tag /1 #9
2018 Panini Victory Lane Race Ready Materials Black /14 #16
2018 Panini Victory Lane Race Ready Materials Laundry Tag /1 #16
2018 Panini Victory Lane Red /49 #16
2018 Panini Victory Lane Red /49 #66
2018 Panini Victory Lane Red /49 #87
2018 Panini Victory Lane Remarkable Remnants Material Autographs /100 #7
2018 Panini Victory Lane Remarkable Remnants Material Autographs Black /25 #7
2018 Panini Victory Lane Remarkable Remnants Material Autographs Gold /99 #7
2018 Panini Victory Lane Remarkable Remnants Material Autographs Green /49 #7
2018 Panini Victory Lane Remarkable Remnants Material Autographs Laundry Tag /1 #7
2018 Panini Victory Lane Silver #16
2018 Panini Victory Lane Silver #66
2018 Panini Victory Lane Silver #87
2018 Panini Victory Lane Starting Grid #16
2018 Panini Victory Lane Starting Grid Black /1 #16
2018 Panini Victory Lane Starting Grid Blue /25 #16
2018 Panini Victory Lane Starting Grid Gold /99 #16
2018 Panini Victory Lane Starting Grid Green /5 #16
2018 Panini Victory Lane Starting Grid Printing Plates Black /1 #16
2018 Panini Victory Lane Starting Grid Printing Plates Cyan /1 #16
2018 Panini Victory Lane Starting Grid Printing Plates Magenta /1 #16
2018 Panini Victory Lane Starting Grid Printing Plates Yellow /1 #16
2018 Panini Victory Lane Starting Grid Red /49 #16
2018 Panini Victory Lane Victory Lane Prime Patches Associate Sponsor 1 /1 #39
2018 Panini Victory Lane Victory Lane Prime Patches Associate Sponsor 10 /1 #39
2018 Panini Victory Lane Victory Lane Prime Patches Associate Sponsor 2 /1 #39
2018 Panini Victory Lane Victory Lane Prime Patches Associate Sponsor 3 /1 #39
2018 Panini Victory Lane Victory Lane Prime Patches Associate Sponsor 4 /1 #39
2018 Panini Victory Lane Victory Lane Prime Patches Associate Sponsor 5 /1 #39
2018 Panini Victory Lane Victory Lane Prime Patches Associate Sponsor 6 /1 #39
2018 Panini Victory Lane Victory Lane Prime Patches Associate Sponsor 7 /1 #39
2018 Panini Victory Lane Victory Lane Prime Patches Associate Sponsor 8 /1 #39
2018 Panini Victory Lane Victory Lane Prime Patches Associate Sponsor 9 /1 #39
2018 Panini Victory Lane Victory Lane Prime Patches Car Manufacturer /1 #39
2018 Panini Victory Lane Victory Lane Prime Patches Firesuit Manufacturer /1 #39
2018 Panini Victory Lane Victory Lane Prime Patches Goodyear /1 #39
2018 Panini Victory Lane Victory Lane Prime Patches Nameplate /2 #39
2018 Panini Victory Lane Victory Lane Prime Patches NASCAR /1 #39
2018 Panini Victory Lane Victory Lane Prime Patches Series Sponsor /1 #39
2018 Panini Victory Lane Victory Lane Prime Patches Sunoco /1 #39
2019 Donruss #12
2019 Donruss #49A
2019 Donruss #91
2019 Donruss #114
2019 Donruss #49B
2019 Donruss Action #4
2019 Donruss Action Cracked Ice /25 #4
2019 Donruss Action Holographic #4
2019 Donruss Action Xplosion /10 #4
2019 Donruss Artist Proofs /25 #12
2019 Donruss Artist Proofs /25 #49A
2019 Donruss Artist Proofs /25 #91
2019 Donruss Artist Proofs /25 #114
2019 Donruss Artist Proofs /25 #49B
2019 Donruss Black /199 #12
2019 Donruss Black /199 #49A
2019 Donruss Black /199 #91
2019 Donruss Black /199 #114
2019 Donruss Black /199 #49B
2019 Donruss Champion #1
2019 Donruss Champion Cracked Ice /25 #1
2019 Donruss Champion Holographic #1
2019 Donruss Champion Xplosion /10 #1
2019 Donruss Classics #11
2019 Donruss Classics Cracked Ice /25 #11
2019 Donruss Classics Holographic #11
2019 Donruss Classics Xplosion /10 #11
2019 Donruss Contenders #5
2019 Donruss Contenders Cracked Ice /25 #5
2019 Donruss Contenders Holographic #5
2019 Donruss Contenders Xplosion /10 #5
2019 Donruss Gold /299 #12
2019 Donruss Gold /299 #49A
2019 Donruss Gold /299 #91
2019 Donruss Gold /299 #114
2019 Donruss Gold /299 #49B
2019 Donruss Gold Press Proofs /99 #12
2019 Donruss Gold Press Proofs /99 #49A
2019 Donruss Gold Press Proofs /99 #91
2019 Donruss Gold Press Proofs /99 #114
2019 Donruss Gold Press Proofs /99 #49B
2019 Donruss Optic #19
2019 Donruss Optic #71
2019 Donruss Optic Blue Pulsar #19
2019 Donruss Optic Blue Pulsar /1 #71
2019 Donruss Optic Gold /10 #19
2019 Donruss Optic Gold /10 #71
2019 Donruss Optic Gold Vinyl /1 #19
2019 Donruss Optic Gold Vinyl /1 #71
2019 Donruss Optic Holo #19
2019 Donruss Optic Holo #71
2019 Donruss Optic Red Wave #19
2019 Donruss Optic Red Wave /1 #71
2019 Donruss Optic Signatures Gold Vinyl /1 #71
2019 Donruss Optic Signatures Gold Vinyl /1 #19
2019 Donruss Optic Signatures Holo /75 #19
2019 Donruss Optic Signatures Holo /75 #71
2019 Donruss Originals #8
2019 Donruss Originals Cracked Ice /25 #8
2019 Donruss Originals Holographic #8
2019 Donruss Originals Xplosion /10 #8
2019 Donruss Press Proofs /49 #12
2019 Donruss Press Proofs /49 #49A
2019 Donruss Press Proofs /49 #91
2019 Donruss Press Proofs /49 #114
2019 Donruss Press Proofs /49 #49B
2019 Donruss Printing Plates Black /1 #12
2019 Donruss Printing Plates Black /1 #49A
2019 Donruss Printing Plates Black /1 #91
2019 Donruss Printing Plates Black /1 #114
2019 Donruss Printing Plates Black /1 #49B
2019 Donruss Printing Plates Cyan /1 #12
2019 Donruss Printing Plates Cyan /1 #49A
2019 Donruss Printing Plates Cyan /1 #91
2019 Donruss Printing Plates Cyan /1 #114
2019 Donruss Printing Plates Cyan /1 #49B
2019 Donruss Printing Plates Magenta /1 #49A
2019 Donruss Printing Plates Magenta /1 #91
2019 Donruss Printing Plates Magenta /1 #114
2019 Donruss Printing Plates Magenta /1 #49B
2019 Donruss Printing Plates Magenta /1 #12
2019 Donruss Printing Plates Yellow /1 #12
2019 Donruss Printing Plates Yellow /1 #49A
2019 Donruss Printing Plates Yellow /1 #91
2019 Donruss Printing Plates Yellow /1 #114
2019 Donruss Printing Plates Yellow /1 #49B
2019 Donruss Race Day Relics #15
2019 Donruss Race Day Relics Holo Black /10 #15
2019 Donruss Race Day Relics Holo Gold /25 #15
2019 Donruss Race Day Relics Red /185 #15
2019 Donruss Silver #12
2019 Donruss Silver #49A
2019 Donruss Silver #91
2019 Donruss Silver #114
2019 Donruss Silver #49B
2019 Panini National Convention NASCAR #R9
2019 Panini National Convention NASCAR Galatic Windows /25 #R9
2019 Panini National Convention NASCAR HyperPlaid /1 #R9
2019 Panini Prime /50 #19
2019 Panini Prime /50 #51
2019 Panini Prime /50 #81
2019 Panini Prime Black /10 #19
2019 Panini Prime Black /10 #51
2019 Panini Prime Black /10 #81
2019 Panini Prime Clear Silhouettes /99 #13
2019 Panini Prime Clear Silhouettes Black /10 #13
2019 Panini Prime Clear Silhouettes Holo Gold /25 #13
2019 Panini Prime Clear Silhouettes Platinum Blue /1 #13
2019 Panini Prime Dual Material Autographs /75 #2
2019 Panini Prime Dual Material Autographs Black /10 #2
2019 Panini Prime Dual Material Autographs Holo Gold /25 #2
2019 Panini Prime Dual Material Autographs Laundry Tags /1 #2
2019 Panini Prime Emerald /5 #19
2019 Panini Prime Emerald /5 #51
2019 Panini Prime Emerald /5 #81
2019 Panini Prime Jumbo Material Signatures Firesuit /10 #15
2019 Panini Prime Jumbo Material Signatures Firesuit Platinum Blue
2019 Panini Prime Jumbo Material Signatures Sheet Metal /25 #15
2019 Panini Prime Jumbo Material Signatures Tire /75 #15
2019 Panini Prime NASCAR Shadowbox Signatures Car Number /75
2019 Panini Prime NASCAR Shadowbox Signatures Manufacturer /10
2019 Panini Prime NASCAR Shadowbox Signatures Sponsor /25 #21
2019 Panini Prime NASCAR Shadowbox Signatures Team Owner /1 #
2019 Panini Prime Platinum Blue /1 #19
2019 Panini Prime Platinum Blue /1 #51
2019 Panini Prime Platinum Blue /1 #81
2019 Panini Prime Prime Cars Die Cut Signatures /50 #17
2019 Panini Prime Prime Cars Die Cut Signatures Black /10 #17
2019 Panini Prime Prime Cars Die Cut Signatures Holo Gold /25 #17
2019 Panini Prime Prime Cars Die Cut Signatures Platinum Blue /1 #
2019 Panini Prime Prime Jumbo Associate Sponsor 1 /1 #38
2019 Panini Prime Prime Jumbo Associate Sponsor 10 /1 #38
2019 Panini Prime Prime Jumbo Associate Sponsor 2 /1 #38
2019 Panini Prime Prime Jumbo Associate Sponsor 3 /1 #38
2019 Panini Prime Prime Jumbo Associate Sponsor 4 /1 #38
2019 Panini Prime Prime Jumbo Associate Sponsor 5 /1 #38
2019 Panini Prime Prime Jumbo Associate Sponsor 6 /1 #38
2019 Panini Prime Prime Jumbo Associate Sponsor 7 /1 #38
2019 Panini Prime Prime Jumbo Associate Sponsor 8 /1 #38
2019 Panini Prime Prime Jumbo Associate Sponsor 9 /1 #38
2019 Panini Prime Prime Jumbo Car Manufacturer /1 #38
2019 Panini Prime Prime Jumbo Flag Patch /1 #38
2019 Panini Prime Prime Jumbo Glove Manufacturer Patch /1 #38
2019 Panini Prime Prime Jumbo Glove Name Patch /1 #38
2019 Panini Prime Prime Jumbo Nameplate /2 #38
2019 Panini Prime Prime Jumbo NASCAR /1 #38
2019 Panini Prime Prime Jumbo Prime Colors /14 #38
2019 Panini Prime Prime Jumbo Shoe Brand Logo /1 #38
2019 Panini Prime Prime Jumbo Shoe Name Patch /1 #38
2019 Panini Prime Prime Jumbo Sunoco /1 #38
2019 Panini Prime Prime Number Die Cut Signatures /50 #11
2019 Panini Prime Prime Number Die Cut Signatures Black /10 #11
2019 Panini Prime Prime Number Die Cut Signatures Holo Gold /25 #
2019 Panini Prime Prime Number Die Cut Signatures Platinum Blue /
2019 Panini Prime Race Used Duals Firesuits Black /10 #21
2019 Panini Prime Race Used Duals Firesuits Laundry Tags /1 #21
2019 Panini Prime Race Used Duals Sheet Metal Black /10 #21
2019 Panini Prime Race Used Duals Sheet Metal Platinum Blue /1 #2
2019 Panini Prime Race Used Duals Tires Black /10 #21
2019 Panini Prime Race Used Duals Tires Platinum Blue /1 #21
2019 Panini Prime Race Used Firesuits Black /10 #21
2019 Panini Prime Race Used Firesuits Laundry Tags /1 #21
2019 Panini Prime Race Used Quads Firesuits /50 #7
2019 Panini Prime Race Used Quads Firesuits Black /10 #7
2019 Panini Prime Race Used Quads Firesuits Holo Gold /25 #7
2019 Panini Prime Race Used Quads Firesuits Laundry Tags /1 #7
2019 Panini Prime Race Used Quads Sheet Metal /50 #7
2019 Panini Prime Race Used Quads Sheet Metal Black /10 #7
2019 Panini Prime Race Used Quads Sheet Metal Holo Gold /25 #7
2019 Panini Prime Race Used Quads Sheet Metal Platinum Blue /1 #7
2019 Panini Prime Race Used Quads Tires /50 #7
2019 Panini Prime Race Used Quads Tires Black /10 #7
2019 Panini Prime Race Used Quads Tires Holo Gold /25 #7
2019 Panini Prime Race Used Quads Tires Platinum Blue /1 #7
2019 Panini Prime Race Used Sheet Metal Black /10 #21
2019 Panini Prime Race Used Sheet Metal Platinum Blue /1 #21
2019 Panini Prime Race Used Tires Black /10 #21
2019 Panini Prime Race Used Tires Platinum Blue /1 #21
2019 Panini Prime Race Used Trios Firesuits Black /10 #20
2019 Panini Prime Race Used Trios Firesuits Laundry Tags /1 #20
2019 Panini Prime Race Used Trios Sheet Metal Black /10 #20
2019 Panini Prime Race Used Trios Sheet Metal Platinum Blue /1 #20
2019 Panini Prime Race Used Trios Tires Black /10 #20
2019 Panini Prime Race Used Trios Tires Platinum Blue /1 #20
2019 Panini Prime Timeline Signatures /50 #9
2019 Panini Prime Timeline Signatures Manufacturer /1 #9
2019 Panini Prime Timeline Signatures Name /25 #9
2019 Panini Prime Timeline Signatures Sponsor /10 #9
2019 Panini Prizm #19A
2019 Panini Prizm #54
2019 Panini Prizm #62
2019 Panini Prizm #74
2019 Panini Prizm #19B
2019 Panini Prizm Apex #12
2019 Panini Prizm Apex Prizms #12
2019 Panini Prizm Apex Prizms Black /1 #12
2019 Panini Prizm Apex Prizms Gold /10 #12
2019 Panini Prizm Apex Prizms White Sparkle #12
2019 Panini Prizm Expert Level #2
2019 Panini Prizm Expert Level Prizms #2
2019 Panini Prizm Expert Level Prizms Black /1 #2
2019 Panini Prizm Expert Level Prizms Gold /10 #2
2019 Panini Prizm Expert Level Prizms White Sparkle #2
2019 Panini Prizm In the Groove #6
2019 Panini Prizm In the Groove Prizms #6
2019 Panini Prizm In the Groove Prizms Black /1 #6
2019 Panini Prizm In the Groove Prizms Gold /10 #6
2019 Panini Prizm In the Groove Prizms White Sparkle #6
2019 Panini Prizm Prizms #54
2019 Panini Prizm Prizms #62
2019 Panini Prizm Prizms #74
2019 Panini Prizm Prizms #19B
2019 Panini Prizm Prizms #19A
2019 Panini Prizm Prizms Black /1 #19A
2019 Panini Prizm Prizms Black /1 #54
2019 Panini Prizm Prizms Black /1 #62
2019 Panini Prizm Prizms Black /1 #74
2019 Panini Prizm Prizms Black /1 #19B
2019 Panini Prizm Prizms Blue /75 #19A
2019 Panini Prizm Prizms Blue /75 #54
2019 Panini Prizm Prizms Blue /75 #62
2019 Panini Prizm Prizms Blue /75 #74
2019 Panini Prizm Prizms Blue /75 #19B
2019 Panini Prizm Prizms Camo #19A
2019 Panini Prizm Prizms Camo #54
2019 Panini Prizm Prizms Camo #62
2019 Panini Prizm Prizms Camo #74
2019 Panini Prizm Prizms Camo #19B

2019 Panini Prizm Prizms Flash #19A
2019 Panini Prizm Prizms Flash #54
2019 Panini Prizm Prizms Flash #62
2019 Panini Prizm Prizms Flash #74
2019 Panini Prizm Prizms Flash #19B
2019 Panini Prizm Prizms Gold /10 #19A
2019 Panini Prizm Prizms Gold /10 #54
2019 Panini Prizm Prizms Gold /10 #62
2019 Panini Prizm Prizms Gold /10 #74
2019 Panini Prizm Prizms Gold /10 #19B
2019 Panini Prizm Prizms Green /99 #19A
2019 Panini Prizm Prizms Green /99 #54
2019 Panini Prizm Prizms Green /99 #62
2019 Panini Prizm Prizms Green /99 #74
2019 Panini Prizm Prizms Green /99 #19B
2019 Panini Prizm Prizms Rainbow /24 #19A
2019 Panini Prizm Prizms Rainbow /24 #54
2019 Panini Prizm Prizms Rainbow /24 #62
2019 Panini Prizm Prizms Rainbow /24 #74
2019 Panini Prizm Prizms Rainbow /24 #19B
2019 Panini Prizm Prizms Red /50 #19A
2019 Panini Prizm Prizms Red /50 #54
2019 Panini Prizm Prizms Red /50 #62
2019 Panini Prizm Prizms Red /50 #74
2019 Panini Prizm Prizms Red /50 #19B
2019 Panini Prizm Prizms Red White and Blue #19A
2019 Panini Prizm Prizms Red White and Blue #54
2019 Panini Prizm Prizms Red White and Blue #62
2019 Panini Prizm Prizms Red White and Blue #74
2019 Panini Prizm Prizms Red White and Blue #19B
2019 Panini Prizm Prizms White /5 #19A
2019 Panini Prizm Prizms White /5 #54
2019 Panini Prizm Prizms White /5 #62
2019 Panini Prizm Prizms White /5 #74
2019 Panini Prizm Prizms White /5 #19B
2019 Panini Prizm Prizms White Sparkle #19A
2019 Panini Prizm Prizms White Sparkle #54
2019 Panini Prizm Prizms White Sparkle #62
2019 Panini Prizm Prizms White Sparkle #74
2019 Panini Prizm Prizms White Sparkle #19B
2019 Panini Prizm Signing Sessions Prizms #11
2019 Panini Prizm Signing Sessions Prizms Black /1 #11
2019 Panini Prizm Signing Sessions Prizms Blue /75 #11
2019 Panini Prizm Signing Sessions Prizms Camo #11
2019 Panini Prizm Signing Sessions Prizms Gold /10 #11
2019 Panini Prizm Signing Sessions Prizms Green /99 #11
2019 Panini Prizm Signing Sessions Prizms Rainbow /24 #11
2019 Panini Prizm Signing Sessions Prizms Red /50 #11
2019 Panini Prizm Signing Sessions Prizms Red White and Blue #11
2019 Panini Prizm Signing Sessions Prizms White /5 #11
2019 Panini Prizm Teammates #5
2019 Panini Prizm Teammates Prizms #5
2019 Panini Prizm Teammates Prizms Black /1 #5
2019 Panini Prizm Teammates Prizms Gold /10 #5
2019 Panini Prizm Teammates Prizms White Sparkle #5
2019 Panini Victory Lane #19
2019 Panini Victory Lane #57
2019 Panini Victory Lane #60
2019 Panini Victory Lane #61
2019 Panini Victory Lane Black /1 #19
2019 Panini Victory Lane Black /1 #57
2019 Panini Victory Lane Black /1 #60
2019 Panini Victory Lane Black /1 #61
2019 Panini Victory Lane Celebrations #13
2019 Panini Victory Lane Celebrations #14
2019 Panini Victory Lane Celebrations #15
2019 Panini Victory Lane Celebrations Black /1 #13
2019 Panini Victory Lane Celebrations Black /1 #14
2019 Panini Victory Lane Celebrations Black /1 #15
2019 Panini Victory Lane Celebrations Blue /99 #13
2019 Panini Victory Lane Celebrations Blue /99 #14
2019 Panini Victory Lane Celebrations Blue /99 #15
2019 Panini Victory Lane Celebrations Gold /25 #13
2019 Panini Victory Lane Celebrations Gold /25 #14
2019 Panini Victory Lane Celebrations Gold /25 #15
2019 Panini Victory Lane Celebrations Green /5 #13
2019 Panini Victory Lane Celebrations Green /5 #14
2019 Panini Victory Lane Celebrations Green /5 #15
2019 Panini Victory Lane Celebrations Printing Plates Black /1 #13
2019 Panini Victory Lane Celebrations Printing Plates Black /1 #14
2019 Panini Victory Lane Celebrations Printing Plates Black /1 #15
2019 Panini Victory Lane Celebrations Printing Plates Cyan /1 #13
2019 Panini Victory Lane Celebrations Printing Plates Cyan /1 #14
2019 Panini Victory Lane Celebrations Printing Plates Cyan /1 #15
2019 Panini Victory Lane Celebrations Printing Plates Magenta /1 #13
2019 Panini Victory Lane Celebrations Printing Plates Magenta /1 #14
2019 Panini Victory Lane Celebrations Printing Plates Magenta /1 #15
2019 Panini Victory Lane Celebrations Printing Plates Yellow /1 #13
2019 Panini Victory Lane Celebrations Printing Plates Yellow /1 #14
2019 Panini Victory Lane Celebrations Printing Plates Yellow /1 #15
2019 Panini Victory Lane Dual Swatches #12
2019 Panini Victory Lane Dual Swatches Gold /99 #12
2019 Panini Victory Lane Dual Swatches Laundry Tag /1 #12
2019 Panini Victory Lane Dual Swatches Platinum /1 #12
2019 Panini Victory Lane Dual Swatches Red /25 #12
2019 Panini Victory Lane Gold /25 #19
2019 Panini Victory Lane Gold /25 #57
2019 Panini Victory Lane Gold /25 #60
2019 Panini Victory Lane Gold /25 #61
2019 Panini Victory Lane Horsepower Heroes #4
2019 Panini Victory Lane Horsepower Heroes Black /1 #4
2019 Panini Victory Lane Horsepower Heroes Blue /99 #4
2019 Panini Victory Lane Horsepower Heroes Gold /25 #4
2019 Panini Victory Lane Horsepower Heroes Green /5 #4
2019 Panini Victory Lane Horsepower Heroes Printing Plates Black /1 #4
2019 Panini Victory Lane Horsepower Heroes Printing Plates Cyan /1 #4
2019 Panini Victory Lane Horsepower Heroes Printing Plates Magenta /1 #4
2019 Panini Victory Lane Horsepower Heroes Printing Plates Yellow /1 #4
2019 Panini Victory Lane Machines #7
2019 Panini Victory Lane Machines Black /1 #7
2019 Panini Victory Lane Machines Blue /99 #7
2019 Panini Victory Lane Machines Gold /25 #7
2019 Panini Victory Lane Machines Green /5 #7
2019 Panini Victory Lane Machines Printing Plates Black /1 #7
2019 Panini Victory Lane Machines Printing Plates Cyan /1 #7
2019 Panini Victory Lane Machines Printing Plates Magenta /1 #7
2019 Panini Victory Lane Machines Printing Plates Yellow /1 #7
2019 Panini Victory Lane Pedal to the Metal #39
2019 Panini Victory Lane Pedal to the Metal #64
2019 Panini Victory Lane Pedal to the Metal #76
2019 Panini Victory Lane Pedal to the Metal Black /1 #39
2019 Panini Victory Lane Pedal to the Metal Black /1 #64
2019 Panini Victory Lane Pedal to the Metal Black /1 #76
2019 Panini Victory Lane Pedal to the Metal Gold /25 #39
2019 Panini Victory Lane Pedal to the Metal Gold /25 #64
2019 Panini Victory Lane Pedal to the Metal Gold /25 #76
2019 Panini Victory Lane Pedal to the Metal Green /5 #39
2019 Panini Victory Lane Pedal to the Metal Green /5 #64
2019 Panini Victory Lane Pedal to the Metal Green /5 #76
2019 Panini Victory Lane Pedal to the Metal Red /3 #39
2019 Panini Victory Lane Pedal to the Metal Red /3 #64
2019 Panini Victory Lane Pedal to the Metal Red /3 #76
2019 Panini Victory Lane Printing Plates Black /1 #19
2019 Panini Victory Lane Printing Plates Black /1 #57
2019 Panini Victory Lane Printing Plates Black /1 #60
2019 Panini Victory Lane Printing Plates Black /1 #61
2019 Panini Victory Lane Printing Plates Cyan /1 #19
2019 Panini Victory Lane Printing Plates Cyan /1 #57
2019 Panini Victory Lane Printing Plates Cyan /1 #60
2019 Panini Victory Lane Printing Plates Cyan /1 #61
2019 Panini Victory Lane Printing Plates Magenta /1 #19
2019 Panini Victory Lane Printing Plates Magenta /1 #57
2019 Panini Victory Lane Printing Plates Magenta /1 #60
2019 Panini Victory Lane Printing Plates Magenta /1 #61
2019 Panini Victory Lane Printing Plates Yellow /1 #19
2019 Panini Victory Lane Printing Plates Yellow /1 #57
2019 Panini Victory Lane Printing Plates Yellow /1 #60
2019 Panini Victory Lane Printing Plates Yellow /1 #61
2019 Panini Victory Lane Quad Swatches #5
2019 Panini Victory Lane Quad Swatches Gold /99 #5
2019 Panini Victory Lane Quad Swatches Laundry Tag /1 #5
2019 Panini Victory Lane Quad Swatches Platinum /1 #5
2019 Panini Victory Lane Quad Swatches Red /25 #5
2019 Panini Victory Lane Signature Swatches #11
2019 Panini Victory Lane Signature Swatches Gold /99 #11
2019 Panini Victory Lane Signature Swatches Platinum /1 #11
2019 Panini Victory Lane Signature Swatches Red /25 #11
2019 Panini Victory Lane Starting Grid #12
2019 Panini Victory Lane Starting Grid Black /1 #12
2019 Panini Victory Lane Starting Grid Blue /99 #12
2019 Panini Victory Lane Starting Grid Gold /25 #12
2019 Panini Victory Lane Starting Grid Green /5 #12
2019 Panini Victory Lane Starting Grid Printing Plates Black /1 #12
2019 Panini Victory Lane Starting Grid Printing Plates Cyan /1 #12
2019 Panini Victory Lane Starting Grid Printing Plates Magenta /1 #12
2019 Panini Victory Lane Starting Grid Printing Plates Yellow /1 #12
2019 Panini Victory Lane Top 10 #1
2019 Panini Victory Lane Top 10 Black /1 #1
2019 Panini Victory Lane Top 10 Blue /99 #1
2019 Panini Victory Lane Top 10 Gold /25 #1
2019 Panini Victory Lane Top 10 Green /5 #1
2019 Panini Victory Lane Top 10 Printing Plates Black /1 #1
2019 Panini Victory Lane Top 10 Printing Plates Cyan /1 #1
2019 Panini Victory Lane Top 10 Printing Plates Magenta /1 #1
2019 Panini Victory Lane Top 10 Printing Plates Yellow /1 #1
2019 Panini Victory Lane Track Stars #7
2019 Panini Victory Lane Track Stars Black /1 #7
2019 Panini Victory Lane Track Stars Blue /99 #7
2019 Panini Victory Lane Track Stars Gold /25 #7
2019 Panini Victory Lane Track Stars Green /5 #7
2019 Panini Victory Lane Track Stars Printing Plates Black /1 #7
2019 Panini Victory Lane Track Stars Printing Plates Cyan /1 #7
2019 Panini Victory Lane Track Stars Printing Plates Magenta /1 #7
2019 Panini Victory Lane Track Stars Printing Plates Yellow /1 #7
2020 Donruss #6
2020 Donruss #39
2020 Donruss #106
2020 Donruss #172
2020 Donruss Action Packed #3
2020 Donruss Action Packed Checkers #3
2020 Donruss Action Packed Cracked Ice /25 #3
2020 Donruss Action Packed Holographic /199 #3
2020 Donruss Action Packed Xplosion /10 #3
2020 Donruss Aero Package #10
2020 Donruss Aero Package Checkers #10
2020 Donruss Aero Package Cracked Ice /25 #10
2020 Donruss Aero Package Holographic /199 #10
2020 Donruss Aero Package Xplosion /10 #10
2020 Donruss Black Numbers /22 #6
2020 Donruss Black Numbers /22 #39
2020 Donruss Black Numbers /22 #106
2020 Donruss Black Numbers /22 #172
2020 Donruss Black Trophy Club /1 #6
2020 Donruss Black Trophy Club /1 #39
2020 Donruss Black Trophy Club /1 #106
2020 Donruss Black Trophy Club /1 #172
2020 Donruss Blue /199 #106
2020 Donruss Blue /199 #172
2020 Donruss Blue /199 #6
2020 Donruss Blue /199 #39
2020 Donruss Carolina Blue #6
2020 Donruss Carolina Blue #39
2020 Donruss Carolina Blue #106
2020 Donruss Carolina Blue #172
2020 Donruss Contenders #3
2020 Donruss Contenders Checkers #3
2020 Donruss Contenders Cracked Ice /25 #3
2020 Donruss Contenders Holographic /199 #3
2020 Donruss Contenders Xplosion /10 #3
2020 Donruss Green /99 #6
2020 Donruss Green /99 #39
2020 Donruss Green /99 #106
2020 Donruss Green /99 #172
2020 Donruss Optic #6
2020 Donruss Optic #22
2020 Donruss Optic #67
2020 Donruss Optic Carolina Blue Wave #22
2020 Donruss Optic Carolina Blue Wave #67
2020 Donruss Optic Carolina Blue Wave #6
2020 Donruss Optic Gold /10 #6
2020 Donruss Optic Gold /10 #22
2020 Donruss Optic Gold /10 #67
2020 Donruss Optic Gold Vinyl /1 #6
2020 Donruss Optic Gold Vinyl /1 #22
2020 Donruss Optic Gold Vinyl /1 #67
2020 Donruss Optic Holo #6
2020 Donruss Optic Holo #22
2020 Donruss Optic Holo #67
2020 Donruss Optic Orange Pulsar #6
2020 Donruss Optic Orange Pulsar #22
2020 Donruss Optic Orange Pulsar #67
2020 Donruss Optic Red Mojo #6
2020 Donruss Optic Red Mojo #22
2020 Donruss Optic Red Mojo #67
2020 Donruss Optic Signatures Gold Vinyl /1 #6
2020 Donruss Optic Signatures Gold Vinyl /1 #22
2020 Donruss Optic Signatures Gold Vinyl /1 #67
2020 Donruss Optic Signatures Holo /99 #6
2020 Donruss Optic Signatures Holo /99 #22
2020 Donruss Optic Signatures Holo /99 #67
2020 Donruss Orange #6
2020 Donruss Orange #39
2020 Donruss Orange #106
2020 Donruss Orange #172
2020 Donruss Pink /25 #6
2020 Donruss Pink /25 #39
2020 Donruss Pink /25 #106
2020 Donruss Pink /25 #172
2020 Donruss Printing Plates Black /1 #6
2020 Donruss Printing Plates Black /1 #39
2020 Donruss Printing Plates Black /1 #106
2020 Donruss Printing Plates Black /1 #172
2020 Donruss Printing Plates Cyan /1 #6
2020 Donruss Printing Plates Cyan /1 #39
2020 Donruss Printing Plates Cyan /1 #106
2020 Donruss Printing Plates Cyan /1 #172
2020 Donruss Printing Plates Magenta /1 #39
2020 Donruss Printing Plates Magenta /1 #106
2020 Donruss Printing Plates Magenta /1 #172
2020 Donruss Printing Plates Magenta /1 #6
2020 Donruss Printing Plates Yellow /1 #172
2020 Donruss Printing Plates Yellow /1 #6
2020 Donruss Printing Plates Yellow /1 #39
2020 Donruss Printing Plates Yellow /1 #106
2020 Donruss Purple /49 #6
2020 Donruss Purple /49 #39
2020 Donruss Purple /49 #106
2020 Donruss Purple /49 #172
2020 Donruss Race Day Relics #16
2020 Donruss Race Day Relics Holo Black /10 #16
2020 Donruss Race Day Relics Holo Gold /25 #16
2020 Donruss Race Day Relics Red /250 #16
2020 Donruss Red /299 #6
2020 Donruss Red /299 #39
2020 Donruss Red /299 #106
2020 Donruss Red /299 #172
2020 Donruss Retro Relics '87 #19
2020 Donruss Retro Relics '87 Holo Black /10 #19
2020 Donruss Retro Relics '87 Holo Gold /25 #19
2020 Donruss Retro Relics '87 Red /250 #19
2020 Donruss Retro Series #2
2020 Donruss Retro Series Checkers #2
2020 Donruss Retro Series Cracked Ice /25 #2
2020 Donruss Retro Series Holographic /199 #2
2020 Donruss Retro Series Xplosion /10 #2
2020 Donruss Silver #6
2020 Donruss Silver #39
2020 Donruss Silver #106
2020 Donruss Silver #172

Jamie McMurray

2002 Press Pass #49
2002 Press Pass Autographs #44
2002 Press Pass Hot Treads /2425 #HT18
2002 Press Pass Optima #37
2002 Press Pass Optima Gold #37
2002 Press Pass Optima Promos /5 #37
2002 Press Pass Optima Samples #37
2002 Press Pass Platinum #49
2002 Press Pass Signings #44
2002 Press Pass Signings Gold /50 #41
2002 Press Pass Stealth #51
2002 Press Pass Stealth Gold #51
2002 Press Pass Stealth Samples #51
2002 Wheels High Gear #42
2002 Wheels High Gear Autographs #37
2002 Wheels High Gear First Gear #42
2002 Wheels High Gear MPH /100 #42
2003 eTopps /3000 #3
2003 Press Pass #44
2003 Press Pass #0
2003 Press Pass Autographs #39
2003 Press Pass Eclipse #27
2003 Press Pass Eclipse Double Hot Treads /999 #DT5
2003 Press Pass Eclipse Previews /5 #27
2003 Press Pass Eclipse Racing Champions #RC32
2003 Press Pass Eclipse Samples #27
2003 Press Pass Eclipse Skidmarks #SM10
2003 Press Pass Eclipse Solar Eclipse #P27
2003 Press Pass Eclipse Teammates Autographs /25 #SMJM
2003 Press Pass Gold Holofoil #P44
2003 Press Pass Optima #17
2003 Press Pass Optima Fan Favorite #FF5
2003 Press Pass Optima Gold #G17
2003 Press Pass Optima Previews /5 #17
2003 Press Pass Optima Samples #17
2003 Press Pass Optima Young Guns #YG3
2003 Press Pass Premium #32
2003 Press Pass Premium Previews /5 #32
2003 Press Pass Premium Red Reflectors #32
2003 Press Pass Premium Samples #32
2003 Press Pass Samples #44
2003 Press Pass Signings #48
2003 Press Pass Signings Gold /50 #48
2003 Press Pass Stealth Fusion #FU6
2003 Press Pass Stealth No Boundaries #NB20
2003 Press Pass Trackside #14
2003 Press Pass Trackside Gold Holofoil #P14
2003 Press Pass Trackside Golden /50 #G14
2003 Press Pass Trackside Hat Giveaway #PPH18
2003 Press Pass Trackside Pit Stoppers Cars /175 #PST15
2003 Press Pass Trackside Pit Stoppers Drivers /100 #PSD15
2003 Press Pass Trackside Previews /5 #14
2003 Press Pass Trackside Samples #14
2003 VIP Making the Show #MS18
2003 Wheels American Thunder #16
2003 Wheels American Thunder Born On /100 #BO16
2003 Wheels American Thunder Cool Threads /285 #CT8
2003 Wheels American Thunder Heads Up Manufacturer /90 #HUM12
2003 Wheels American Thunder Heads Up Team /60 #HUT11
2003 Wheels American Thunder Heads Up Winston /90 #HUW12
2003 Wheels American Thunder Holofoil #P16
2003 Wheels American Thunder Post Mark #PM12
2003 Wheels American Thunder Previews /5 #16
2003 Wheels American Thunder Rookie Class #RC3
2003 Wheels American Thunder Rookie Class Prizes #RC3
2003 Wheels American Thunder Rookie Class Prizes /600 #NNO
2003 Wheels American Thunder Rookie Thunder #RT21
2003 Wheels American Thunder Samples #P16
2003 Wheels American Thunder Thunder Road #TR12
2003 Wheels American Thunder Triple Hat /25 #TH4
2003 Wheels Autographs #38
2003 Wheels Autographs #39
2003 Wheels High Gear #46
2003 Wheels High Gear Blue Hawaii SCDA Promos #46
2003 Wheels High Gear First Gear #F46
2003 Wheels High Gear Flag Chasers Black /90 #FC7
2003 Wheels High Gear Flag Chasers Blue-Yellow /45 #FC7
2003 Wheels High Gear Flag Chasers Checkered /25 #FC7
2003 Wheels High Gear Flag Chasers Green /90 #FC7
2003 Wheels High Gear Flag Chasers Red /90 #FC7
2003 Wheels High Gear Flag Chasers White /90 #FC7
2003 Wheels High Gear Flag Chasers Yellow /90 #FC7
2003 Wheels High Gear Hot Treads /425 #HT12
2003 Wheels High Gear MPH /100 #M46
2003 Wheels High Gear Samples #46
2004 Press Pass #21
2004 Press Pass #21B
2004 Press Pass #73
2004 Press Pass #88
2004 Press Pass #92
2004 Press Pass Autographs #42
2004 Press Pass Burning Rubber Cars /140 #BRT12
2004 Press Pass Burning Rubber Drivers /70 #BRD12
2004 Press Pass Eclipse #12
2004 Press Pass Eclipse #86
2004 Press Pass Eclipse Previews /5 #12
2004 Press Pass Eclipse Samples #12
2004 Press Pass Eclipse Samples #86
2004 Press Pass Eclipse Skidmarks #SM18
2004 Press Pass Eclipse Skidmarks Holofoil /500 #SM18
2004 Press Pass Eclipse Teammates Autographs /25 #6
2004 Press Pass Hot Treads /1250 #HTR17
2004 Press Pass Hot Treads Holofoil /200 #HTR17
2004 Press Pass Making the Show Collector's Series #MS21
2004 Press Pass Optima #17
2004 Press Pass Optima Gold #G17
2004 Press Pass Optima Previews /5 #EB17
2004 Press Pass Optima Samples #17
2004 Press Pass Optima Thunder Bolts Cars /120 #TBT15
2004 Press Pass Optima Thunder Bolts Drivers /70 #TBD15
2004 Press Pass Platinum #P21
2004 Press Pass Platinum #P73
2004 Press Pass Platinum #P88
2004 Press Pass Platinum #P92
2004 Press Pass Premium #24
2004 Press Pass Premium #63
2004 Press Pass Premium Previews /5 #24
2004 Press Pass Premium Samples #24
2004 Press Pass Previews /5 #21
2004 Press Pass Samples #21
2004 Press Pass Samples #73
2004 Press Pass Samples #88
2004 Press Pass Samples #92
2004 Press Pass Signings #43
2004 Press Pass Signings Gold /50 #40
2004 Press Pass Snapshots #SN17
2004 Press Pass Stealth #10
2004 Press Pass Stealth #11
2004 Press Pass Stealth #12
2004 Press Pass Stealth #92
2004 Press Pass Stealth Previews /5 #EB10
2004 Press Pass Stealth Previews /5 #EB11
2004 Press Pass Stealth Previews /5 #EB12
2004 Press Pass Stealth Profile #P6
2004 Press Pass Stealth Samples #X10
2004 Press Pass Stealth Samples #X11
2004 Press Pass Stealth Samples #X12
2004 Press Pass Stealth Samples #X92
2004 Press Pass Stealth X-Ray /100 #10
2004 Press Pass Stealth X-Ray /100 #11
2004 Press Pass Stealth X-Ray /100 #12
2004 Press Pass Stealth X-Ray /100 #92
2004 Press Pass Trackside #4
2004 Press Pass Trackside #70
2004 Press Pass Trackside #70B
2004 Press Pass Trackside Dialed In #DI5
2004 Press Pass Trackside Golden /100 #G4
2004 Press Pass Trackside Golden /100 #G70
2004 Press Pass Trackside Hat Giveaway #PPH21
2004 Press Pass Trackside Pit Stoppers Cars /150 #PST13
2004 Press Pass Trackside Pit Stoppers Drivers /95 #PSD13
2004 Press Pass Trackside Previews /5 #EB4
2004 Press Pass Trackside Runnin n' Gunnin #RG11
2004 Press Pass Trackside Samples #4
2004 Press Pass Trackside Samples #70
2004 Super Shots CHP Sonoma #5
2004 VIP #26
2004 VIP #33
2004 VIP Making the Show #MS21
2004 VIP Previews /5 #EB26
2004 VIP Previews /5 #EB33
2004 VIP Samples #26
2004 VIP Samples #33
2004 Wheels American Thunder #18
2004 Wheels American Thunder #66
2004 Wheels American Thunder #90
2004 Wheels American Thunder American Eagle #AE8
2004 Wheels American Thunder Cool Threads /525 #CT9
2004 Wheels American Thunder Golden Eagle /250 #AE8
2004 Wheels American Thunder Post Mark #PM21
2004 Wheels American Thunder Previews /5 #EB18
2004 Wheels American Thunder Samples #18
2004 Wheels American Thunder Samples #66
2004 Wheels American Thunder Samples #90
2004 Wheels American Thunder Thunder Road #TR15
2004 Wheels American Thunder Triple Hat /160 #TH13
2004 Wheels Autographs #45
2004 Wheels High Gear #17
2004 Wheels High Gear #47
2004 Wheels High Gear #67
2004 Wheels High Gear High Groove #HG16
2004 Wheels High Gear MPH /100 #M17
2004 Wheels High Gear MPH /100 #M47
2004 Wheels High Gear MPH /100 #M67
2004 Wheels High Gear Previews /5 #17
2004 Wheels High Gear Previews /5 #47
2004 Wheels High Gear Samples #17
2004 Wheels High Gear Samples #47
2004 Wheels High Gear Samples #67
2005 Press Pass #29
2005 Press Pass Autographs #40
2005 Press Pass Burning Rubber Cars /130 #BRT9
2005 Press Pass Burning Rubber Drivers /80 #BRD9
2005 Press Pass Burning Rubber Drivers Gold /1 #BRD9
2005 Press Pass Cup Chase #CCR4
2005 Press Pass Cup Chase Prizes #CCP4
2005 Press Pass Eclipse #11
2005 Press Pass Eclipse #36
2005 Press Pass Eclipse #86
2005 Press Pass Eclipse Maxim #MX5
2005 Press Pass Eclipse Previews /5 #EB11
2005 Press Pass Eclipse Previews /5 #EB36
2005 Press Pass Eclipse Previews /1 #EB86
2005 Press Pass Eclipse Samples #11
2005 Press Pass Eclipse Samples #36
2005 Press Pass Eclipse Samples #86
2005 Press Pass Eclipse Skidmarks #SM18
2005 Press Pass Eclipse Skidmarks Holofoil /250 #SM18
2005 Press Pass Hot Treads /900 #HTR17
2005 Press Pass Hot Treads Holofoil /100 #HTR17
2005 Press Pass Optima #20
2005 Press Pass Optima #78
2005 Press Pass Optima Fan Favorite #FF18
2005 Press Pass Optima Gold /100 #G20
2005 Press Pass Optima Gold /100 #G78
2005 Press Pass Optima Previews /5 #20
2005 Press Pass Optima Samples #20
2005 Press Pass Optima Samples #78
2005 Press Pass Platinum /100 #P29
2005 Press Pass Premium #21
2005 Press Pass Premium #64
2005 Press Pass Premium Samples #21
2005 Press Pass Previews Green /5 #EB29
2005 Press Pass Samples #29
2005 Press Pass Signings #40
2005 Press Pass Signings Gold /50 #38
2005 Press Pass Signings Platinum /100 #37
2005 Press Pass Stealth #3
2005 Press Pass Stealth #6
2005 Press Pass Stealth #9
2005 Press Pass Stealth Gear Grippers Cars /90 #GGT1
2005 Press Pass Stealth Gear Grippers Drivers /75 #GGD1
2005 Press Pass Stealth Previews /5 #3
2005 Press Pass Stealth Previews /5 #6
2005 Press Pass Stealth Previews /5 #9
2005 Press Pass Stealth Samples #3
2005 Press Pass Stealth Samples #6
2005 Press Pass Stealth Samples #9
2005 Press Pass Stealth X-Ray /100 #X3
2005 Press Pass Stealth X-Ray /100 #X6
2005 Press Pass Stealth X-Ray /100 #X9
2005 Press Pass Trackside #18
2005 Press Pass Trackside #71
2005 Press Pass Trackside Golden /100 #G18
2005 Press Pass Trackside Golden /100 #G71
2005 Press Pass Trackside Hat Giveaway #PPH21
2005 Press Pass Trackside Pit Stoppers Cars /85 #PST9
2005 Press Pass Trackside Pit Stoppers Drivers /85 #PSD9
2005 Press Pass Trackside Previews /5 #18
2005 Press Pass Trackside Samples #18
2005 Press Pass Trackside Samples #71
2005 VIP #20
2005 VIP #32
2005 VIP Making The Show #21
2005 VIP Previews /5 #EB20
2005 VIP Previews /5 #EB32
2005 VIP Samples #20
2005 VIP Samples #32
2005 Wheels American Thunder #22
2005 Wheels American Thunder #76
2005 Wheels American Thunder Cool Threads /475 #CT10
2005 Wheels American Thunder Previews /5 #22
2005 Wheels American Thunder Previews /5 #76
2005 Wheels American Thunder Samples #22
2005 Wheels American Thunder Samples #76
2005 Wheels American Thunder Triple Hat /190 #TH16
2005 Wheels Autographs #39
2005 Wheels High Gear #22
2005 Wheels High Gear #62
2005 Wheels High Gear #68
2005 Wheels High Gear Flag to Flag #FF16
2005 Wheels High Gear Machine #MMB3
2005 Wheels High Gear Man #MMA3
2005 Wheels High Gear MPH /100 #M22
2005 Wheels High Gear MPH /100 #M62
2005 Wheels High Gear MPH /100 #M68
2005 Wheels High Gear Previews Green /5 #EB22
2005 Wheels High Gear Samples #22
2005 Wheels High Gear Samples #62
2005 Wheels High Gear Samples #68
2006 Press Pass #24
2006 Press Pass Autographs #38
2006 Press Pass Blue #B24
2006 Press Pass Burning Rubber Cars /370 #BRT14
2006 Press Pass Burning Rubber Drivers /100 #BRD14
2006 Press Pass Burning Rubber Drivers Gold /1 #BRD14
2006 Press Pass Collectors Series Making the Show #MS9
2006 Press Pass Cup Chase #CCR8
2006 Press Pass Eclipse #11
2006 Press Pass Eclipse Previews /5 #EB11
2006 Press Pass Gold #G24
2006 Press Pass Optima #21
2006 Press Pass Optima #54
2006 Press Pass Optima Fan Favorite #FF15
2006 Press Pass Optima Gold /100 #G21
2006 Press Pass Optima Gold /100 #G54
2006 Press Pass Optima Previews /5 #EB21
2006 Press Pass Optima Q & A #QA9
2006 Press Pass Optima Rookie Relics Cars /50 #RRT9
2006 Press Pass Optima Rookie Relics Drivers /50 #RRD9
2006 Press Pass Platinum /100 #P24
2006 Press Pass Previews /5 #EB24
2006 Press Pass Signings #38
2006 Press Pass Signings Silver /100 #38
2006 Press Pass Stealth #20
2006 Press Pass Stealth #48
2006 Press Pass Stealth Autographed Hat Entry #PPH17
2006 Press Pass Stealth Previews /5 #20
2006 Press Pass Stealth Retail #20
2006 Press Pass Stealth Retail #48
2006 Press Pass Stealth X-Ray /100 #X20
2006 Press Pass Stealth X-Ray /100 #X48
2006 TRAKS Stickers #26
2006 VIP #18
2006 VIP #61
2006 VIP Making the Show #MS9
2006 Wheels American Thunder #21
2006 Wheels American Thunder #40
2006 Wheels American Thunder #55
2006 Wheels American Thunder Double Hat /99 #DH16
2006 Wheels American Thunder Grandstand #GS18
2006 Wheels American Thunder Previews /5 #EB21
2006 Wheels American Thunder Thunder Road #TR1
2006 Wheels Autographs #41
2006 Wheels High Gear #11
2006 Wheels High Gear Flag to Flag #FF18
2006 Wheels High Gear MPH /100 #M11
2006 Wheels High Gear Previews Green /5 #EB11
2007 Press Pass #19
2007 Press Pass Autographs #30
2007 Press Pass Blue #B19
2007 Press Pass Collector's Series Box Set #SB17
2007 Press Pass Cup Chase #CCR7
2007 Press Pass Eclipse #23
2007 Press Pass Eclipse Ecliptic #EC10
2007 Press Pass Eclipse Gold /25 #G23
2007 Press Pass Eclipse Previews /5 #EB23
2007 Press Pass Eclipse Red /1 #R23
2007 Press Pass Gold #G19
2007 Press Pass Platinum /100 #P19
2007 Press Pass Previews /5 #EB19
2007 Press Pass Signings #44
2007 Press Pass Signings Blue /25 #19
2007 Press Pass Signings Gold /50 #35
2007 Press Pass Signings Silver /100 #34
2007 Press Pass Snapshots #SN20
2007 Press Pass Stealth #17
2007 Press Pass Stealth #69
2007 Press Pass Stealth Chrome #17
2007 Press Pass Stealth Chrome #69
2007 Press Pass Stealth Chrome Exclusives /99 #X17
2007 Press Pass Stealth Chrome Exclusives /99 #X69
2007 Press Pass Stealth Chrome Platinum /25 #P17
2007 Press Pass Stealth Chrome Platinum /25 #P69
2007 Press Pass Stealth Previews /5 #EB17
2007 Press Pass Velocity #V7
2007 Traks #17
2007 Traks Gold #G17
2007 Traks Holofoil /50 #H17
2007 Traks Previews /5 #EB17
2007 Traks Red /10 #R17
2007 VIP #20
2007 VIP #54
2007 VIP Get A Grip Drivers /70 #GGD4
2007 VIP Get A Grip Teams /70 #GGT4
2007 VIP Pedal To The Metal /50 #PM7
2007 VIP Previews /5 #EB20
2007 VIP Sunday Best #SB17
2007 Wheels American Thunder #20
2007 Wheels American Thunder #46
2007 Wheels American Thunder #72
2007 Wheels American Thunder Double Hat /99 #DH5
2007 Wheels American Thunder Previews /5 #EB20
2007 Wheels American Thunder Pushin' Pedal /99 #PP6
2007 Wheels American Thunder Starting Grid #SG7
2007 Wheels American Thunder Thunder Road #TR4
2007 Wheels Autographs #26
2007 Wheels Autographs Press Plates Black /1 #25
2007 Wheels Autographs Press Plates Cyan /1 #25
2007 Wheels Autographs Press Plates Magenta /1 #25
2007 Wheels High Gear #23
2007 Wheels High Gear Driven #DR15
2007 Wheels High Gear Final Standings Gold /25 #FS23
2007 Wheels High Gear MPH /100 #M23
2007 Wheels High Gear Previews /5 #EB23
2008 Press Pass #19
2008 Press Pass #69
2008 Press Pass #91
2008 Press Pass Blue #B19
2008 Press Pass Blue #B69
2008 Press Pass Blue #B91
2008 Press Pass Burning Rubber Drivers /60 #BRD17
2008 Press Pass Burning Rubber Drivers Gold /1 #BRD17
2008 Press Pass Burning Rubber Drivers Prime Cuts /25 #BRD17
2008 Press Pass Burning Rubber Teams /175 #BRT17
2008 Press Pass Cup Chase #CC10
2008 Press Pass Eclipse #14
2008 Press Pass Eclipse #56
2008 Press Pass Eclipse Escape Velocity #EV5
2008 Press Pass Eclipse Gold /25 #G14
2008 Press Pass Eclipse Gold /25 #G56
2008 Press Pass Eclipse Previews /5 #EB14
2008 Press Pass Eclipse Red /1 #R14
2008 Press Pass Eclipse Red /1 #R56
2008 Press Pass Eclipse Star Tracks #ST16
2008 Press Pass Eclipse Star Tracks Holofoil /250 #ST16
2008 Press Pass Eclipse Stellar #ST13
2008 Press Pass Gold #G19
2008 Press Pass Gold #G69
2008 Press Pass Gold #G91
2008 Press Pass Legends Prominent Pieces Metal-Tire-Net /50 #PP4JM
2008 Press Pass Legends Prominent Pieces Metal-Tire-Net Gold /25 #PP4JM
2008 Press Pass Platinum /100 #P19
2008 Press Pass Platinum /100 #P69
2008 Press Pass Platinum /100 #P91
2008 Press Pass Premium #20
2008 Press Pass Premium Previews /5 #EB20
2008 Press Pass Premium Red /15 #20
2008 Press Pass Premium Team Signed Baseballs #ROU
2008 Press Pass Premium Team Signed Baseballs #EROU
2008 Press Pass Previews /5 #EB19
2008 Press Pass Signings #41
2008 Press Pass Signings Blue /25 #19
2008 Press Pass Signings Gold /50 #36
2008 Press Pass Signings Press Plates Black /1 #27
2008 Press Pass Signings Press Plates Black /1 #JM
2008 Press Pass Signings Press Plates Cyan /1 #27
2008 Press Pass Signings Press Plates Cyan #JM
2008 Press Pass Signings Press Plates Magenta /1 #27
2008 Press Pass Signings Press Plates Yellow /1 #27
2008 Press Pass Signings Press Plates Yellow #JM
2008 Press Pass Signings Silver /100 #35
2008 Press Pass Slideshow #SS20
2008 Press Pass Speedway #26
2008 Press Pass Speedway #86
2008 Press Pass Speedway Cockpit #CP14
2008 Press Pass Speedway Corporate Cuts Drivers /80 #CDJM
2008 Press Pass Speedway Corporate Cuts Drivers Patches /14 #CDJM
2008 Press Pass Speedway Corporate Cuts Team /165 #CTJM
2008 Press Pass Speedway Gold #G26
2008 Press Pass Speedway Gold #G86
2008 Press Pass Speedway Holofoil /50 #H26
2008 Press Pass Speedway Holofoil /50 #H86
2008 Press Pass Speedway Previews /5 #EB26
2008 Press Pass Speedway Red /10 #R26
2008 Press Pass Speedway Red /10 #R86
2008 Press Pass Stealth #23
2008 Press Pass Stealth #70
2008 Press Pass Stealth Chrome #23
2008 Press Pass Stealth Chrome #70
2008 Press Pass Stealth Chrome Exclusives /25 #23
2008 Press Pass Stealth Chrome Exclusives /25 #70
2008 Press Pass Stealth Chrome Exclusives Gold /99 #23
2008 Press Pass Stealth Chrome Exclusives Gold /99 #70
2008 Press Pass Stealth Maximum Access #MA18
2008 Press Pass Stealth Maximum Access Autographs /25 #MA18
2008 Press Pass Stealth Previews /5 #23
2008 Press Pass Weekend Warriors #WW3
2008 VIP #22
2008 VIP All Access #AA16
2008 VIP Get a Grip Drivers /80 #GGD9
2008 VIP Get a Grip Teams /99 #GGT9
2008 VIP Previews /5 #EB22
2008 Wheels American Thunder #21
2008 Wheels American Thunder #38
2008 Wheels American Thunder Cool Threads /285 #CT1
2008 Wheels American Thunder Double Hat /99 #DH7
2008 Wheels American Thunder Head to Toe /99 #HT2
2008 Wheels American Thunder Previews /5 #21
2008 Wheels American Thunder Pushin' Pedal /99 #PP 2
2008 Wheels American Thunder Trackside Treasury Autographs #JM
2008 Wheels American Thunder Trackside Treasury Autographs Gold /25 #JM
2008 Wheels American Thunder Trackside Treasury Autographs Printing Plates Black /1 #JM
2008 Wheels American Thunder Trackside Treasury Autographs Printing Plates Cyan /1 #JM
2008 Wheels American Thunder Trackside Treasury Autographs Printing Plates Magenta /1 #JM
2008 Wheels American Thunder Trackside Treasury Autographs Printing Plates Yellow /1 #JM
2008 Wheels High Gear #15
2008 Wheels High Gear Driven #DR24
2008 Wheels High Gear Final Standings /17 #F15
2008 Wheels High Gear Last Lap /10 #LL11
2008 Wheels High Gear Last Lap Holofoil /5 #LL11
2008 Wheels High Gear MPH /100 #M15
2008 Wheels High Gear Previews /5 #EB15
2009 Element #21
2009 Element Previews /5 #21
2009 Element Radioactive /100 #21
2009 Press Pass #18
2009 Press Pass #141
2009 Press Pass Autographs Gold #33
2009 Press Pass Autographs Printing Plates Black /1 #29
2009 Press Pass Autographs Printing Plates Cyan /1 #29
2009 Press Pass Autographs Printing Plates Magenta /1 #29
2009 Press Pass Autographs Printing Plates Yellow /1 #29
2009 Press Pass Autographs Silver #33
2009 Press Pass Blue #18
2009 Press Pass Blue #141
2009 Press Pass Eclipse #16
2009 Press Pass Eclipse #52
2009 Press Pass Eclipse #79
2009 Press Pass Eclipse Black and White #16
2009 Press Pass Eclipse Black and White #52
2009 Press Pass Eclipse Black and White #79
2009 Press Pass Eclipse Blue #16
2009 Press Pass Eclipse Blue #52
2009 Press Pass Eclipse Blue #79
2009 Press Pass Eclipse Ecliptic Path #EP14
2009 Press Pass Gold #18
2009 Press Pass Gold #141
2009 Press Pass Gold Holofoil /100 #18
2009 Press Pass Gold Holofoil /100 #141
2009 Press Pass Pieces Race Used Memorabilia #JM
2009 Press Pass Pocket Portraits #P17
2009 Press Pass Pocket Portraits Hometown #P17
2009 Press Pass Pocket Portraits Smoke #P17
2009 Press Pass Premium #19
2009 Press Pass Premium Hot Threads /299 #HTJaM1
2009 Press Pass Premium Hot Threads /99 #HTJaM2
2009 Press Pass Premium Hot Threads Multi-Color /25 #HTJaM
2009 Press Pass Premium Hot Threads Patches /10 #HTP-JaM

2009 Press Pass Premium Previews /5 #EB19
2009 Press Pass Premium Signatures #23
2009 Press Pass Premium Signatures Gold /25 #22
2009 Press Pass Previews /5 #EB18
2009 Press Pass Previews /5 #EB141
2009 Press Pass Red #18
2009 Press Pass Red #141
2009 Press Pass Showcase /499 #24
2009 Press Pass Showcase /499 #35
2009 Press Pass Showcase 2nd Gear /125 #24
2009 Press Pass Showcase 2nd Gear /125 #35
2009 Press Pass Showcase 3rd Gear /50 #24
2009 Press Pass Showcase 3rd Gear /50 #35
2009 Press Pass Showcase 4th Gear /15 #24
2009 Press Pass Showcase 4th Gear /15 #35
2009 Press Pass Showcase Classic Collections Firesuit /25 #CCF8
2009 Press Pass Showcase Classic Collections Firesuit Patch /5 #CCF8
2009 Press Pass Showcase Classic Collections Ink /45 #9
2009 Press Pass Showcase Classic Collections Ink Gold /25 #9
2009 Press Pass Showcase Classic Collections Ink Green /5 #9
2009 Press Pass Showcase Classic Collections Ink Melting /1 #9
2009 Press Pass Showcase Classic Collections Sheet Metal /45 #CCS8
2009 Press Pass Showcase Classic Collections Tire /99 #CCT8
2009 Press Pass Showcase Printing Plates Black /1 #24
2009 Press Pass Showcase Printing Plates Black /1 #35
2009 Press Pass Showcase Printing Plates Cyan /1 #24
2009 Press Pass Showcase Printing Plates Cyan /1 #35
2009 Press Pass Showcase Printing Plates Magenta /1 #24
2009 Press Pass Showcase Printing Plates Magenta /1 #35
2009 Press Pass Showcase Printing Plates Yellow /1 #24
2009 Press Pass Showcase Printing Plates Yellow /1 #35
2009 Press Pass Signings Blue /25 #30
2009 Press Pass Signings Gold #30
2009 Press Pass Signings Orange /65 #30
2009 Press Pass Sponsor Swatches /200 #SSJM
2009 Press Pass Sponsor Swatches Select /6 #SSJM
2009 Press Pass Stealth #22
2009 Press Pass Stealth Battle Armor /290 #BAJM1
2009 Press Pass Stealth Battle Armor /75 #BAJM2
2009 Press Pass Stealth Battle Armor Multi-Color /160 #BAJM
2009 Press Pass Stealth Chrome #22
2009 Press Pass Stealth Chrome Brushed Metal /25 #22
2009 Press Pass Stealth Chrome Gold /99 #22
2009 Press Pass Stealth Confidential Classified Bronze #PC8
2009 Press Pass Stealth Confidential Secret Silver #PC8
2009 Press Pass Stealth Confidential Top Secret Gold /25 #PC8
2009 Press Pass Stealth Previews /5 #EB22
2009 VIP Leadfoot /150 #LFJM
2009 VIP Leadfoot Holofoil /10 #LFJM
2009 Wheels Autographs #45
2009 Wheels Autographs Press Plates Black /1 #JM
2009 Wheels Autographs Press Plates Cyan /1 #JM
2009 Wheels Autographs Press Plates Yellow /1 #JM
2009 Wheels Main Event #23
2009 Wheels Main Event #38
2009 Wheels Main Event Fast Pass Purple /25 #23
2009 Wheels Main Event Fast Pass Purple /25 #38
2009 Wheels Main Event Foil #23
2009 Wheels Main Event Hat Dance Double /99 #HDJM
2009 Wheels Main Event Hat Dance Patch /10 #HDJM
2009 Wheels Main Event Marks Clubs #38
2009 Wheels Main Event Marks Diamonds /50 #38
2009 Wheels Main Event Marks Hearts /10 #38
2009 Wheels Main Event Marks Printing Plates Black /1 #34
2009 Wheels Main Event Marks Printing Plates Cyan /1 #34
2009 Wheels Main Event Marks Printing Plates Magenta /1 #34
2009 Wheels Main Event Marks Printing Plates Yellow /1 #34
2009 Wheels Main Event Marks Spades /1 #38
2009 Wheels Main Event Playing Cards Blue #9D
2009 Wheels Main Event Playing Cards Red #9D
2009 Wheels Main Event Previews /5 #23
2010 Action Racing Collectables Platinum 1:24 /106 #1
2010 Action Racing Collectables Platinum 1:24 /206 #1
2010 Element #20
2010 Element Blue /35 #20
2010 Element Green #20
2010 Element Green-White-Checkers Blue /10 #GWCJM
2010 Element Green-White-Checkers Green /50 #GWCJM
2010 Element Previews /5 #EB20
2010 Element Purple /25 #20
2010 Element Red Target #20
2010 Press Pass #24
2010 Press Pass Autographs #34
2010 Press Pass Autographs Printing Plates Cyan /1 #31
2010 Press Pass Autographs Printing Plates Magenta /1 #29
2010 Press Pass Autographs Printing Plates Yellow /1 #28
2010 Press Pass Blue #24
2010 Press Pass Burning Rubber /250 #BR29
2010 Press Pass Burning Rubber Gold /99 #BR29
2010 Press Pass Burning Rubber Prime Cuts /25 #BRD29
2010 Press Pass Gold #24
2010 Press Pass Holofoil /100 #24
2010 Press Pass Premium #22
2010 Press Pass Premium #100
2010 Press Pass Premium Purple /25 #22
2010 Press Pass Premium Signatures #PSJM
2010 Press Pass Premium Signatures Red Ink /25 #PSJM
2010 Press Pass Previews /5 #24
2010 Press Pass Purple /25 #24
2010 Press Pass Showcase /499 #22
2010 Press Pass Showcase Gold /125 #22
2010 Press Pass Showcase Green /50 #22
2010 Press Pass Showcase Melting /15 #22
2010 Press Pass Showcase Platinum Holo /1 #22
2010 Press Pass Signings Blue /10 #38
2010 Press Pass Signings Gold /50 #38
2010 Press Pass Signings Red /15 #38
2010 Press Pass Signings Silver /90 #37
2010 Press Pass Stealth #23
2010 Press Pass Stealth #90
2010 Press Pass Stealth Battle Armor Holofoil /25 #BAJM
2010 Press Pass Stealth Battle Armor Silver /225 #BAJM
2010 Press Pass Stealth Black and White #23
2010 Press Pass Stealth Black and White #90
2010 Press Pass Stealth Previews /5 #23
2010 Press Pass Stealth Purple /25 #23
2010 Wheels Autographs #34
2010 Wheels Autographs Printing Plates Black /1 #34
2010 Wheels Autographs Printing Plates Cyan /1 #34
2010 Wheels Autographs Printing Plates Magenta /1 #34
2010 Wheels Autographs Printing Plates Yellow /1 #34
2010 Wheels Autographs Target /10 #22
2010 Wheels Main Event #23
2010 Wheels Main Event #55
2010 Wheels Main Event #64
2010 Wheels Main Event #69
2010 Wheels Main Event #70
2010 Wheels Main Event Blue #23
2010 Wheels Main Event Blue #55
2010 Wheels Main Event Blue #64
2010 Wheels Main Event Blue #69
2010 Wheels Main Event Blue #70
2010 Wheels Main Event Fight Card #FC19
2010 Wheels Main Event Fight Card Checkered Flag #FC19
2010 Wheels Main Event Fight Card Full Color Retail #FC19
2010 Wheels Main Event Fight Card Gold /25 #FC19
2010 Wheels Main Event Head to Head /150 #HHJMJP
2010 Wheels Main Event Head to Head Blue /75 #HHJMJP
2010 Wheels Main Event Head to Head Holofoil /10 #HHJMJP
2010 Wheels Main Event Head to Head Red /25 #HHJMJP
2010 Wheels Main Event Marks Autographs /61 #39
2010 Wheels Main Event Marks Autographs Black /1 #38
2010 Wheels Main Event Marks Autographs Blue /25 #39
2010 Wheels Main Event Marks Autographs Red /15 #39
2010 Wheels Main Event Matchups Autographs /10 #JMJR
2010 Wheels Main Event Matchups Autographs /10 #KHJM
2010 Wheels Main Event Purple /25 #23
2010 Wheels Main Event Toe to Toe /10 #TTJMJP
2010 Wheels Main Event Upper Cuts /150 #UCJM
2010 Wheels Main Event Upper Cuts /199 #UCJM2
2010 Wheels Main Event Upper Cuts Blue /75 #UCJM
2010 Wheels Main Event Upper Cuts Blue /75 #UCJM2
2010 Wheels Main Event Upper Cuts Holofoil /10 #UCJM
2010 Wheels Main Event Upper Cuts Holofoil /10 #UCJM2
2010 Wheels Main Event Upper Cuts Knock Out Patches /25 #UCKOJM
2010 Wheels Main Event Upper Cuts Red /25 #UCJM
2010 Wheels Main Event Upper Cuts Red /25 #UCJM2
2010 Wheels Main Event Wheel to Wheel /25 #WWJMJP
2010 Wheels Main Event Wheel to Wheel Holofoil /10 #WWJMJP
2011 Element #23
2011 Element #63
2011 Element #82
2011 Element #88
2011 Element Autographs /60 #37
2011 Element Autographs Blue /5 #37
2011 Element Autographs Gold /10 #36
2011 Element Autographs Printing Plates Black /1 #37
2011 Element Autographs Printing Plates Cyan /1 #37
2011 Element Autographs Printing Plates Magenta /1 #37
2011 Element Autographs Printing Plates Yellow /1 #37
2011 Element Autographs Silver /25 #36
2011 Element Black /35 #23
2011 Element Black /35 #63
2011 Element Black /35 #82
2011 Element Black /35 #88
2011 Element Finish Line Checkered Flag /10 #FLJM
2011 Element Finish Line Green Flag /25 #FLJM
2011 Element Finish Line Tires /99 #FLJM
2011 Element Flagship Performers 2010 Laps Completed Yellow /50 #FPLJM
2011 Element Flagship Performers Race Streak Without DNF Red /50 #FPDJM
2011 Element Green #23
2011 Element Green #63
2011 Element Green #82
2011 Element Green #88
2011 Element Previews /5 #EB23
2011 Element Purple /25 #23
2011 Element Purple /25 #63
2011 Element Purple /25 #82
2011 Element Purple /25 #88
2011 Element Red #23
2011 Element Red #63
2011 Element Red #82
2011 Element Red #88
2011 Element Trackside Treasures Holofoil /25 #TTJM
2011 Element Trackside Treasures Silver /85 #TTJM
2011 Press Pass #24
2011 Press Pass #79
2011 Press Pass #121
2011 Press Pass #137
2011 Press Pass #154
2011 Press Pass #157
2011 Press Pass Autographs Blue /10 #37
2011 Press Pass Autographs Bronze /99 #37
2011 Press Pass Autographs Gold /25 #36
2011 Press Pass Autographs Printing Plates Black /1 #38
2011 Press Pass Autographs Printing Plates Cyan /1 #38
2011 Press Pass Autographs Printing Plates Magenta /1 #38
2011 Press Pass Autographs Printing Plates Yellow /1 #38
2011 Press Pass Autographs Silver /50 #38
2011 Press Pass Blue Holofoil /10 #24
2011 Press Pass Blue Holofoil /10 #79
2011 Press Pass Blue Holofoil /10 #121
2011 Press Pass Blue Holofoil /10 #137
2011 Press Pass Blue Holofoil /10 #154
2011 Press Pass Blue Holofoil /10 #157
2011 Press Pass Blue Retail #24
2011 Press Pass Blue Retail #79
2011 Press Pass Blue Retail #121
2011 Press Pass Blue Retail #137
2011 Press Pass Blue Retail #154
2011 Press Pass Blue Retail #157
2011 Press Pass Burning Rubber Autographs /10 #BRJM
2011 Press Pass Burning Rubber Fast Pass /10 #BRJM
2011 Press Pass Burning Rubber Fast Pass /10 #BRJM2
2011 Press Pass Burning Rubber Gold /150 #BRJM
2011 Press Pass Burning Rubber Gold /150 #BRJM2
2011 Press Pass Burning Rubber Gold /150 #BRCJM
2011 Press Pass Burning Rubber Holofoil /50 #BRJM
2011 Press Pass Burning Rubber Holofoil /50 #BRJM2
2011 Press Pass Burning Rubber Holofoil /50 #BRCJM
2011 Press Pass Burning Rubber Prime Cuts /25 #BRJM
2011 Press Pass Burning Rubber Prime Cuts /25 #BRCJM
2011 Press Pass Cup Chase #CCR16
2011 Press Pass Eclipse #22
2011 Press Pass Eclipse #34
2011 Press Pass Eclipse #54
2011 Press Pass Eclipse Blue #22
2011 Press Pass Eclipse Blue #34
2011 Press Pass Eclipse Blue #54
2011 Press Pass Eclipse Gold /55 #22
2011 Press Pass Eclipse Gold /55 #34
2011 Press Pass Eclipse Gold /55 #54
2011 Press Pass Eclipse In Focus #IF2
2011 Press Pass Eclipse Previews /5 #EB22
2011 Press Pass Eclipse Previews /1 #EB34
2011 Press Pass Eclipse Purple /25 #22
2011 Press Pass Eclipse Purple /25 #34
2011 Press Pass Eclipse Purple /25 #54
2011 Press Pass Eclipse Rides #R7
2011 Press Pass FanFare #26
2011 Press Pass FanFare Autographs Blue /5 #49
2011 Press Pass FanFare Autographs Bronze /65 #49
2011 Press Pass FanFare Autographs Gold /50 #49
2011 Press Pass FanFare Autographs Printing Plates Black /1 #49
2011 Press Pass FanFare Autographs Printing Plates Cyan /1 #49
2011 Press Pass FanFare Autographs Printing Plates Magenta /1 #49
2011 Press Pass FanFare Autographs Printing Plates Yellow /1 #49
2011 Press Pass FanFare Autographs Silver /25 #49
2011 Press Pass FanFare Blue Die Cuts #26
2011 Press Pass FanFare Emerald /25 #26
2011 Press Pass FanFare Holofoil Die Cuts #26
2011 Press Pass FanFare Magnificent Materials /199 #MMJM
2011 Press Pass FanFare Magnificent Materials Dual Swatches /50 #MMDJM
2011 Press Pass FanFare Magnificent Materials Dual Swatches Holofoil /10 #MMDJM
2011 Press Pass FanFare Magnificent Materials Holofoil /50 #MMJM
2011 Press Pass FanFare Rookie Standouts #RS7
2011 Press Pass FanFare Ruby Die Cuts /15 #26
2011 Press Pass FanFare Sapphire /10 #26
2011 Press Pass FanFare Silver /25 #26
2011 Press Pass Four Wide Firesuit /25 #FWJM
2011 Press Pass Four Wide Glove /1 #FWJM
2011 Press Pass Four Wide Sheet Metal /15 #FWJM
2011 Press Pass Four Wide Shoes /1 #FWJM
2011 Press Pass Four Wide Tire /10 #FWJM
2011 Press Pass Geared Up Gold /100 #GUJM
2011 Press Pass Geared Up Holofoil /50 #GUJM
2011 Press Pass Gold /50 #24
2011 Press Pass Gold /50 #79
2011 Press Pass Gold /50 #121
2011 Press Pass Gold /50 #137
2011 Press Pass Gold /50 #154
2011 Press Pass Gold /50 #157
2011 Press Pass Premium #25
2011 Press Pass Premium #53
2011 Press Pass Premium #69
2011 Press Pass Premium Crystal Ball #CB1
2011 Press Pass Premium Crystal Ball Autographs /10 #CBAJM
2011 Press Pass Premium Hot Threads /150 #HTJM
2011 Press Pass Premium Hot Threads Multi Color /25 #HTJM
2011 Press Pass Premium Hot Threads Secondary Color /99 #HTJM
2011 Press Pass Premium Purple /25 #25
2011 Press Pass Premium Purple /25 #53
2011 Press Pass Premium Purple /25 #69
2011 Press Pass Premium Signatures /90 #PSJM
2011 Press Pass Premium Signatures Red Ink /100 #PSJM
2011 Press Pass Previews /5 #EB24
2011 Press Pass Purple /25 #24
2011 Press Pass Showcase /499 #21
2011 Press Pass Showcase /499 #56
2011 Press Pass Showcase Classic Collections Firesuit /45 #CCMEGR
2011 Press Pass Showcase Classic Collections Firesuit Patches /5 #CCMEGR
2011 Press Pass Showcase Classic Collections Ink /25 #CCMEGR
2011 Press Pass Showcase Classic Collections Ink Gold /5 #CCMEGR
2011 Press Pass Showcase Classic Collections Ink Melting /1 #CCMEGR
2011 Press Pass Showcase Classic Collections Sheet Metal /99 #CCMEGR
2011 Press Pass Showcase Gold /125 #21
2011 Press Pass Showcase Gold /125 #56
2011 Press Pass Showcase Green /25 #21
2011 Press Pass Showcase Green /25 #56
2011 Press Pass Showcase Melting /1 #21
2011 Press Pass Showcase Melting /1 #56
2011 Press Pass Showcase Prized Pieces Firesuit Ink /25 #PPIJM
2011 Press Pass Showcase Prized Pieces Firesuit Patches Ink /1 #PPIJM
2011 Press Pass Showcase Prized Pieces Sheet Metal Ink /45 #PPIJM
2011 Press Pass Signings Black and White /10 #PPSJM
2011 Press Pass Signings Brushed Metal /60 #PPSJM
2011 Press Pass Signings Holofoil /25 #PPSJM
2011 Press Pass Signings Printing Plates Black /1 #PPSJM
2011 Press Pass Signings Printing Plates Cyan /1 #PPSJM
2011 Press Pass Signings Printing Plates Magenta /1 #PPSJM
2011 Press Pass Signings Printing Plates Yellow /1 #PPSJM
2011 Press Pass Stealth #48
2011 Press Pass Stealth #97
2011 Press Pass Stealth Black and White /25 #48
2011 Press Pass Stealth Black and White /25 #97
2011 Press Pass Stealth Holofoil /99 #48
2011 Press Pass Stealth Holofoil /99 #97
2011 Press Pass Stealth Metal of Honor Medal of Honor /50 #BAJM
2011 Press Pass Stealth Metal of Honor Purple Heart /25 #MHJM
2011 Press Pass Stealth Metal of Honor Silver Star /99 #BAJM
2011 Press Pass Stealth Purple /25 #48
2011 Press Pass Stealth Supersonic #SS9
2011 Press Pass Target Winning Tickets #WTT5
2011 Press Pass Winning Tickets #WT1
2011 Press Pass Winning Tickets #WT20
2011 Wheels Main Event #25
2011 Wheels Main Event All Stars #A17
2011 Wheels Main Event All Stars Brushed Foil /199 #A17
2011 Wheels Main Event All Stars Holofoil /50 #A17
2011 Wheels Main Event Black and White #25
2011 Wheels Main Event Blue /75 #25
2011 Wheels Main Event Green /1 #25
2011 Wheels Main Event Marks Autographs Blue /10 #MEJM
2011 Wheels Main Event Marks Autographs Gold /25 #MEJM
2011 Wheels Main Event Marks Autographs Silver /50 #MEJM
2011 Wheels Main Event Materials Holofoil /25 #MEMJM
2011 Wheels Main Event Materials Silver /50 #MEMJM
2011 Wheels Main Event Red /20 #25
2012 Press Pass #25
2012 Press Pass Autographs Blue /5 #PPAJM
2012 Press Pass Autographs Printing Plates Black /1 #PPAJM
2012 Press Pass Autographs Printing Plates Cyan /1 #PPAJM
2012 Press Pass Autographs Printing Plates Magenta /1 #PPAJM
2012 Press Pass Autographs Printing Plates Yellow /1 #PPAJM
2012 Press Pass Autographs Red /5 #PPAJM
2012 Press Pass Autographs Silver /10 #PPAJM
2012 Press Pass Blue #25
2012 Press Pass Blue Holofoil /35 #25
2012 Press Pass Cup Chase #CCR16
2012 Press Pass Fanfare #29
2012 Press Pass Fanfare Autographs Blue /5 #JM
2012 Press Pass Fanfare Autographs Gold /75 #JM
2012 Press Pass Fanfare Autographs Red /25 #JM
2012 Press Pass Fanfare Autographs Silver /99 #JM
2012 Press Pass Fanfare Blue Foil Die Cuts #29
2012 Press Pass Fanfare Diamond /5 #29
2012 Press Pass Fanfare Holofoil Die Cuts #29
2012 Press Pass Fanfare Magnificent Materials /250 #MMJM
2012 Press Pass Fanfare Magnificent Materials Dual Swatches /50 #MMJM
2012 Press Pass Fanfare Magnificent Materials Dual Swatches Melting /10 #MMJM
2012 Press Pass Fanfare Magnificent Materials Gold /99 #MMJM
2012 Press Pass Fanfare Sapphire /20 #29
2012 Press Pass Fanfare Silver /25 #29
2012 Press Pass Gold #25
2012 Press Pass Ignite #25
2012 Press Pass Ignite Materials Autographs Gun Metal /45 #IMJM
2012 Press Pass Ignite Materials Autographs Red /5 #IMJM
2012 Press Pass Ignite Materials Autographs Silver /150 #IMJM
2012 Press Pass Ignite Materials Gun Metal /99 #IMJM
2012 Press Pass Ignite Materials Red /10 #IMJM
2012 Press Pass Ignite Materials Silver #IMJM
2012 Press Pass Ignite Proofs Black and White /50 #25
2012 Press Pass Ignite Proofs Cyan #25
2012 Press Pass Ignite Proofs Magenta #25
2012 Press Pass Ignite Proofs Yellow /10 #25
2012 Press Pass Power Picks Blue /50 #43
2012 Press Pass Power Picks Gold /50 #43
2012 Press Pass Power Picks Holofoil /10 #43
2012 Press Pass Purple /35 #25
2012 Press Pass Redline #27
2012 Press Pass Redline Black /99 #27
2012 Press Pass Redline Cyan /50 #27
2012 Press Pass Redline Magenta /15 #27
2012 Press Pass Redline Signatures Blue /5 #RSJM
2012 Press Pass Redline Signatures Gold /23 #RSJM
2012 Press Pass Redline Signatures Holofoil /10 #RSJM
2012 Press Pass Redline Signatures Melting /1 #RSJM
2012 Press Pass Redline Signatures Red /50 #RSJM
2012 Press Pass Redline Yellow /1 #27
2012 Press Pass Showcase /499 #57
2012 Press Pass Showcase Classic Collections Ink /10 #CCMEGR
2012 Press Pass Showcase Classic Collections Ink Gold /5 #CCMEGR
2012 Press Pass Showcase Classic Collections Ink Melting /1 #CCMEGR
2012 Press Pass Showcase Classic Collections Memorabilia /99 #CCMEGR
2012 Press Pass Showcase Classic Collections Memorabilia Gold /50 #CCMEGR
2012 Press Pass Showcase Classic Collections Memorabilia Melting /5 #CCMEGR
2012 Press Pass Showcase Gold /125 #57
2012 Press Pass Showcase Green /5 #57
2012 Press Pass Showcase Melting /1 #57
2012 Press Pass Showcase Purple /1 #57
2012 Press Pass Showcase Red /25 #57
2012 Press Pass Signature Series Race Used /12 #PPAJM
2012 Press Pass Snapshots #SS25
2012 Total Memorabilia #22
2012 Total Memorabilia Black and White /99 #22
2012 Total Memorabilia Dual Swatch Gold /75 #TMJM
2012 Total Memorabilia Dual Swatch Holofoil /25 #TMJM
2012 Total Memorabilia Dual Swatch Melting /5 #TMJM
2012 Total Memorabilia Dual Swatch Silver /99 #TMJM
2012 Total Memorabilia Gold /275 #22
2012 Total Memorabilia Jumbo Swatch Gold /50 #TMJM
2012 Total Memorabilia Jumbo Swatch Holofoil /10 #TMJM
2012 Total Memorabilia Jumbo Swatch Melting /1 #TMJM
2012 Total Memorabilia Quad Swatch Gold /25 #TMJM
2012 Total Memorabilia Quad Swatch Holofoil /10 #TMJM
2012 Total Memorabilia Quad Swatch Melting /1 #TMJM
2012 Total Memorabilia Quad Swatch Silver /50 #TMJM
2012 Total Memorabilia Red Retail /250 #22
2012 Total Memorabilia Signature Collection Dual Swatch Silver /10 #SCJM
2012 Total Memorabilia Signature Collection Quad Swatch Holofoil /5 #SCJM
2012 Total Memorabilia Signature Collection Single Swatch Melting /1 #SCJM
2012 Total Memorabilia Signature Collection Triple Swatch Gold /10 #SCJM
2012 Total Memorabilia Single Swatch Gold /99 #TMJM
2012 Total Memorabilia Single Swatch Holofoil /50 #TMJM
2012 Total Memorabilia Single Swatch Melting /10 #TMJM
2012 Total Memorabilia Single Swatch Silver /299 #TMJM
2012 Total Memorabilia Triple Swatch Gold /50 #TMJM
2012 Total Memorabilia Triple Swatch Holofoil /25 #TMJM
2012 Total Memorabilia Triple Swatch Melting /1 #TMJM
2012 Total Memorabilia Triple Swatch Silver /99 #TMJM
2013 Press Pass #30
2013 Press Pass Color Proofs Black #30
2013 Press Pass Color Proofs Cyan /35 #30
2013 Press Pass Color Proofs Magenta #30
2013 Press Pass Color Proofs Yellow /5 #30
2013 Press Pass Fanfare #39
2013 Press Pass Fanfare Autographs Blue /1 #JM
2013 Press Pass Fanfare Autographs Gold /5 #JM
2013 Press Pass Fanfare Autographs Green /2 #JM
2013 Press Pass Fanfare Autographs Red /5 #JM
2013 Press Pass Fanfare Autographs Silver /10 #JM
2013 Press Pass Fanfare Diamond Die Cuts /5 #39
2013 Press Pass Fanfare Green /3 #39
2013 Press Pass Fanfare Holofoil Die Cuts #39
2013 Press Pass Fanfare Magnificent Jumbo Materials Signatures /10 #JM
2013 Press Pass Fanfare Magnificent Materials Dual Swatches /50 #JM
2013 Press Pass Fanfare Magnificent Materials Dual Swatches Melting /10 #JM
2013 Press Pass Fanfare Magnificent Materials Gold /50 #JM
2013 Press Pass Fanfare Magnificent Materials Jumbo Swatches /25 #JM
2013 Press Pass Fanfare Magnificent Materials Signatures /99 #JM
2013 Press Pass Fanfare Magnificent Materials Signatures Blue /25 #JM
2013 Press Pass Fanfare Magnificent Materials Silver /199 #JM
2013 Press Pass Fanfare Red Foil Die Cuts #39
2013 Press Pass Fanfare Sapphire /20 #39
2013 Press Pass Fanfare Signature Ride Autographs /10 #JM
2013 Press Pass Fanfare Signature Ride Autographs Blue /1 #JM
2013 Press Pass Fanfare Signature Ride Autographs Red /5 #JM
2013 Press Pass Fanfare Silver /25 #39
2013 Press Pass Ignite #24
2013 Press Pass Ignite Hot Threads Blue Holofoil /99 #HTJM
2013 Press Pass Ignite Hot Threads Patch Red /10 #HTJM
2013 Press Pass Ignite Hot Threads Silver #HTJM
2013 Press Pass Ignite Ink Black /75 #IIJM
2013 Press Pass Ignite Ink Blue /20 #IIJM
2013 Press Pass Ignite Ink Red /5 #IIJM
2013 Press Pass Ignite Proofs Black and White /50 #24
2013 Press Pass Ignite Proofs Cyan #24
2013 Press Pass Ignite Proofs Magenta #24
2013 Press Pass Ignite Proofs Yellow /5 #24
2013 Press Pass Power Picks Blue /99 #44
2013 Press Pass Power Picks Gold /50 #44
2013 Press Pass Power Picks Holofoil /10 #44
2013 Press Pass Redline #34
2013 Press Pass Redline #35
2013 Press Pass Redline Black /99 #34
2013 Press Pass Redline Black /99 #35
2013 Press Pass Redline Cyan /50 #34
2013 Press Pass Redline Cyan /50 #35
2013 Press Pass Redline Dark Horse Relic Autographs Blue /5 #DHJM
2013 Press Pass Redline Dark Horse Relic Autographs Gold /25 #DHJM
2013 Press Pass Redline Dark Horse Relic Autographs Melting /1 #DHJM
2013 Press Pass Redline Dark Horse Relic Autographs Red /50 #DHJM
2013 Press Pass Redline Magenta /15 #34
2013 Press Pass Redline Magenta /15 #35
2013 Press Pass Redline Relics Blue /5 #RRJM
2013 Press Pass Redline Relics Gold /10 #RRJM
2013 Press Pass Redline Relics Melting /1 #RRJM
2013 Press Pass Redline Relics Red /50 #RRJM
2013 Press Pass Redline Relics Silver /25 #RRJM
2013 Press Pass Redline Signatures Blue /10 #RSJMCM1
2013 Press Pass Redline Signatures Blue /10 #RSJMCM2
2013 Press Pass Redline Signatures Gold /1 #RSJMCM1
2013 Press Pass Redline Signatures Gold /5 #RSJMCM2
2013 Press Pass Redline Signatures Holo /5 #RSJMCM1
2013 Press Pass Redline Signatures Holo /5 #RSJMCM2
2013 Press Pass Redline Signatures Melting /1 #RSJMCM1
2013 Press Pass Redline Signatures Melting /1 #RSJMCM2
2013 Press Pass Redline Signatures Red /25 #RSJMCM1
2013 Press Pass Redline Signatures Red /10 #RSJMCM2
2013 Press Pass Redline Yellow /1 #34
2013 Press Pass Redline Yellow /1 #35
2013 Press Pass Showcase /349 #20
2013 Press Pass Showcase Black /1 #20
2013 Press Pass Showcase Blue /25 #20
2013 Press Pass Showcase Classic Collections Memorabilia Gold /25 #CCMEGR
2013 Press Pass Showcase Classic Collections Memorabilia Melting /5 #CCMEGR
2013 Press Pass Showcase Classic Collections Memorabilia Silver /75 #CCMEGR
2013 Press Pass Showcase Gold /99 #20
2013 Press Pass Showcase Green /20 #20
2013 Press Pass Showcase Purple /13 #20
2013 Press Pass Showcase Red /10 #20
2013 Press Pass Showcase Showcase Patches /5 #SPJM
2013 Press Pass Signings Blue /1 #JM
2013 Press Pass Signings Gold /25 #JM
2013 Press Pass Signings Holofoil /10 #JM
2013 Press Pass Signings Printing Plates Black /1 #JM
2013 Press Pass Signings Printing Plates Cyan /1 #JM
2013 Press Pass Signings Printing Plates Magenta /1 #JM
2013 Press Pass Signings Printing Plates Yellow /1 #JM
2013 Press Pass Signings Silver /50 #JM
2013 Total Memorabilia #28
2013 Total Memorabilia Black and White /99 #28
2013 Total Memorabilia Dual Swatch Gold /199 #TMJM
2013 Total Memorabilia Gold /275 #28
2013 Total Memorabilia Quad Swatch Melting /10 #TMJM
2013 Total Memorabilia Red #28
2013 Total Memorabilia Single Swatch Silver /475 #TMJM
2013 Total Memorabilia Triple Swatch Holofoil /99 #TMJM
2014 Press Pass #26
2014 Press Pass American Thunder #26
2014 Press Pass American Thunder #57
2014 Press Pass American Thunder Autographs Blue /10 #ATAJM
2014 Press Pass American Thunder Autographs Red /5 #ATAJM
2014 Press Pass American Thunder Autographs White /25 #ATAJM
2014 Press Pass American Thunder Black and White /50 #26
2014 Press Pass American Thunder Black and White /50 #57
2014 Press Pass American Thunder Brothers In Arms Autographs Blue /5 #BACGRFS
2014 Press Pass American Thunder Brothers In Arms Autographs Red /1 #BACGRFS
2014 Press Pass American Thunder Brothers In Arms Autographs White /10 #BACGRFS
2014 Press Pass American Thunder Brothers In Arms Relics Blue /25 #BACGRFS
2014 Press Pass American Thunder Brothers In Arms Relics Red /5 #BACGRFS
2014 Press Pass American Thunder Brothers In Arms Relics Silver /50 #BACGRFS
2014 Press Pass American Thunder Class A Uniforms Blue /99 #CAUJM
2014 Press Pass American Thunder Class A Uniforms Flag /1 #CAUJM
2014 Press Pass American Thunder Class A Uniforms Red /10 #CAUJM
2014 Press Pass American Thunder Class A Uniforms Silver #CAUJM
2014 Press Pass American Thunder Cyan #26
2014 Press Pass American Thunder Cyan #57
2014 Press Pass American Thunder Magenta #26
2014 Press Pass American Thunder Magenta #57
2014 Press Pass American Thunder Yellow /5 #26
2014 Press Pass American Thunder Yellow /5 #57
2014 Press Pass Burning Rubber Chase Edition Blue /25 #BRCJM
2014 Press Pass Burning Rubber Chase Edition Gold /50 #BRCJM
2014 Press Pass Burning Rubber Chase Edition Melting /10 #BRCJM
2014 Press Pass Burning Rubber Chase Edition Silver /99 #BRCJM
2014 Press Pass Color Proofs Black /70 #26
2014 Press Pass Color Proofs Cyan /35 #26
2014 Press Pass Color Proofs Magenta #26
2014 Press Pass Color Proofs Yellow /5 #26
2014 Press Pass Five Star Classic Compilations Autographed Patch Booklet /1 #CCJM1
2014 Press Pass Five Star Classic Compilations Autographed Patch Booklet /1 #CCJM2
2014 Press Pass Five Star Classic Compilations Autographed Patch Booklet /1 #CCJM3
2014 Press Pass Five Star Classic Compilations Autographed Patch Booklet /1 #CCJM4
2014 Press Pass Five Star Classic Compilations Autographed Patch Booklet /1 #CCJM5
2014 Press Pass Five Star Classic Compilations Autographed Patch Booklet /1 #CCJM6
2014 Press Pass Five Star Classic Compilations Autographed Patch Booklet /1 #CCJM7
2014 Press Pass Five Star Classic Compilations Autographed Patch Booklet /1 #CCJM8
2014 Press Pass Five Star Classic Compilations Autographed Patch Booklet /1 #CCJM9
2014 Press Pass Five Star Classic Compilations Autographed Patch Booklet /1 #CCJM10
2014 Press Pass Five Star Classic Compilations Combo Autographs Blue /5 #CCEGR
2014 Press Pass Five Star Classic Compilations Combo Autographs Melting /1 #CCEGR
2014 Press Pass Gold #26
2014 Press Pass Redline #37
2014 Press Pass Redline #38
2014 Press Pass Redline Black /75 #37
2014 Press Pass Redline Black /75 #38
2014 Press Pass Redline Blue Foil #37
2014 Press Pass Redline Blue Foil #38
2014 Press Pass Redline Cyan /50 #37
2014 Press Pass Redline Cyan /50 #38
2014 Press Pass Redline Green National Convention /5 #37
2014 Press Pass Redline Green National Convention /5 #38
2014 Press Pass Redline Magenta /10 #37
2014 Press Pass Redline Magenta /10 #38
2014 Press Pass Redline Relic Autographs Blue /10 #RRSEJM
2014 Press Pass Redline Relic Autographs Gold /15 #RRSEJM
2014 Press Pass Redline Relic Autographs Melting /1 #RRSEJM
2014 Press Pass Redline Relic Autographs Red /25 #RRSEJM
2014 Press Pass Redline Relics Blue /25 #RRJM
2014 Press Pass Redline Relics Gold /50 #RRJM
2014 Press Pass Redline Relics Melting /1 #RRJM
2014 Press Pass Redline Relics Red /75 #RRJM
2014 Press Pass Redline Signatures Blue /10 #RSJM
2014 Press Pass Redline Signatures Gold /25 #RSJM
2014 Press Pass Redline Signatures Melting /1 #RSJM
2014 Press Pass Redline Signatures Red /50 #RSJM
2014 Press Pass Redline Yellow /1 #37
2014 Press Pass Redline Yellow /1 #38
2014 Press Pass Signings Gold /25 #PPSJM
2014 Press Pass Signings Holofoil /10 #PPSJM
2014 Press Pass Signings Melting /1 #PPSJM
2014 Press Pass Signings Printing Plates Black /1 #PPSJM
2014 Press Pass Signings Printing Plates Cyan /1 #PPSJM
2014 Press Pass Signings Printing Plates Magenta /1 #PPSJM
2014 Press Pass Signings Printing Plates Yellow /1 #PPSJM
2014 Press Pass Signings Silver /50 #PPSJM
2014 Total Memorabilia #19
2014 Total Memorabilia Black and White /99 #19
2014 Total Memorabilia Dual Swatch Gold /150 #TMJM
2014 Total Memorabilia Gold /175 #19
2014 Total Memorabilia Quad Swatch Melting /25 #TMJM
2014 Total Memorabilia Red #19
2014 Total Memorabilia Single Swatch Silver /275 #TMJM
2014 Total Memorabilia Triple Swatch Blue /99 #TMJM
2015 Press Pass #25
2015 Press Pass Cup Chase #25
2015 Press Pass Cup Chase Blue /25 #25
2015 Press Pass Cup Chase Gold /75 #25
2015 Press Pass Cup Chase Green /10 #25
2015 Press Pass Cup Chase Melting /1 #25
2015 Press Pass Purple #25
2015 Press Pass Red #25
2015 Press Pass Signings Blue /99 #PPSJM
2015 Press Pass Signings Gold #PPSJM
2015 Press Pass Signings Green /50 #PPSJM
2015 Press Pass Signings Melting /10 #PPSJM
2015 Press Pass Signings Red /75 #PPSJM
2016 Certified #13
2016 Certified Complete Materials /249 #9
2016 Certified Complete Materials Mirror Black /1 #9
2016 Certified Complete Materials Mirror Blue /50 #9
2016 Certified Complete Materials Mirror Gold /25 #9
2016 Certified Complete Materials Mirror Green /5 #9
2016 Certified Complete Materials Mirror Orange /99 #9
2016 Certified Complete Materials Mirror Purple /10 #9
2016 Certified Complete Materials Mirror Red /75 #9
2016 Certified Complete Materials Mirror Silver /99 #9
2016 Certified Famed Rides /199 #15
2016 Certified Famed Rides Mirror Black /1 #15
2016 Certified Famed Rides Mirror Blue /50 #15
2016 Certified Famed Rides Mirror Gold /25 #15
2016 Certified Famed Rides Mirror Green /5 #15
2016 Certified Famed Rides Mirror Orange /99 #15
2016 Certified Famed Rides Mirror Purple /10 #15
2016 Certified Famed Rides Mirror Red /75 #15
2016 Certified Famed Rides Mirror Silver /99 #15
2016 Certified Mirror Black /1 #13
2016 Certified Mirror Blue /50 #13
2016 Certified Mirror Gold /25 #13
2016 Certified Mirror Green /5 #13
2016 Certified Mirror Orange /99 #13
2016 Certified Mirror Purple /10 #13
2016 Certified Mirror Red /75 #13
2016 Certified Mirror Silver /99 #13
2016 Certified Signatures /54 #10
2016 Certified Signatures Mirror Black /1 #10
2016 Certified Signatures Mirror Blue /25 #10
2016 Certified Signatures Mirror Gold /15 #10
2016 Certified Signatures Mirror Green /5 #10
2016 Certified Signatures Mirror Orange /15 #10
2016 Certified Signatures Mirror Purple /10 #10
2016 Certified Signatures Mirror Red /30 #10
2016 Certified Signatures Mirror Silver /10 #10
2016 Certified Sprint Cup Signature Swatches /99 #7
2016 Certified Sprint Cup Signature Swatches Mirror Black /1 #7
2016 Certified Sprint Cup Signature Swatches Mirror Blue /25 #7
2016 Certified Sprint Cup Signature Swatches Mirror Gold /15 #7
2016 Certified Sprint Cup Signature Swatches Mirror Green /5 #7
2016 Certified Sprint Cup Signature Swatches Mirror Orange /15 #7
2016 Certified Sprint Cup Signature Swatches Mirror Purple /10 #7
2016 Certified Sprint Cup Signature Swatches Mirror Red /30 #7
2016 Certified Sprint Cup Signature Swatches Mirror Silver /10 #7
2016 Certified Sprint Cup Swatches /199 #17
2016 Certified Sprint Cup Swatches Mirror Black /1 #17
2016 Certified Sprint Cup Swatches Mirror Blue /50 #17
2016 Certified Sprint Cup Swatches Mirror Gold /25 #17
2016 Certified Sprint Cup Swatches Mirror Green /5 #17
2016 Certified Sprint Cup Swatches Mirror Orange /99 #17
2016 Certified Sprint Cup Swatches Mirror Purple /10 #17
2016 Certified Sprint Cup Swatches Mirror Red /75 #17
2016 Certified Sprint Cup Swatches Mirror Silver /99 #17
2016 Panini National Treasures /25 #13
2016 Panini National Treasures Black /5 #13
2016 Panini National Treasures Blue /1 #13
2016 Panini National Treasures Combo Materials /25 #9
2016 Panini National Treasures Combo Materials Black /5 #9
2016 Panini National Treasures Combo Materials Blue /1 #9
2016 Panini National Treasures Combo Materials Gold /10 #9
2016 Panini National Treasures Combo Materials Printing Plates Black /1 #9
2016 Panini National Treasures Combo Materials Printing Plates Cyan /1 #9
2016 Panini National Treasures Combo Materials Printing Plates Magenta /1 #9
2016 Panini National Treasures Combo Materials Printing Plates Yellow /1 #9
2016 Panini National Treasures Combo Materials Silver /15 #9
2016 Panini National Treasures Dual Driver Materials /25 #13
2016 Panini National Treasures Dual Driver Materials Black /5 #13
2016 Panini National Treasures Dual Driver Materials Blue /1 #13
2016 Panini National Treasures Dual Driver Materials Gold /10 #13
2016 Panini National Treasures Dual Driver Materials Printing Plates Black /1 #13
2016 Panini National Treasures Dual Driver Materials Printing Plates Cyan /1 #13
2016 Panini National Treasures Dual Driver Materials Printing Plates Magenta /1 #13
2016 Panini National Treasures Dual Driver Materials Printing Plates Yellow /1 #13
2016 Panini National Treasures Dual Driver Materials Silver /15 #13
2016 Panini National Treasures Dual Signatures /25 #2
2016 Panini National Treasures Dual Signatures /48 #23
2016 Panini National Treasures Dual Signatures Black /10 #2
2016 Panini National Treasures Dual Signatures Black /10 #23
2016 Panini National Treasures Dual Signatures Blue /1 #2
2016 Panini National Treasures Dual Signatures Blue /1 #23
2016 Panini National Treasures Dual Signatures Gold /15 #2
2016 Panini National Treasures Dual Signatures Gold /15 #23
2016 Panini National Treasures Gold /15 #13
2016 Panini National Treasures Jumbo Firesuit Patch Signature Booklet Associate Sponsor 1 /1 #11
2016 Panini National Treasures Jumbo Firesuit Patch Signature Booklet Associate Sponsor 10 /1 #11
2016 Panini National Treasures Jumbo Firesuit Patch Signature Booklet Associate Sponsor 11 /1 #11
2016 Panini National Treasures Jumbo Firesuit Patch Signature Booklet Associate Sponsor 12 /1 #11
2016 Panini National Treasures Jumbo Firesuit Patch Signature Booklet Associate Sponsor 13 /1 #11
2016 Panini National Treasures Jumbo Firesuit Patch Signature Booklet Associate Sponsor 14 /1 #11
2016 Panini National Treasures Jumbo Firesuit Patch Signature Booklet Associate Sponsor 15 /1 #11
2016 Panini National Treasures Jumbo Firesuit Patch Signature Booklet Associate Sponsor 16 /1 #11
2016 Panini National Treasures Jumbo Firesuit Patch Signature Booklet Associate Sponsor 2 /1 #11
2016 Panini National Treasures Jumbo Firesuit Patch Signature Booklet Associate Sponsor 3 /1 #11
2016 Panini National Treasures Jumbo Firesuit Patch Signature Booklet Associate Sponsor 4 /1 #11
2016 Panini National Treasures Jumbo Firesuit Patch Signature Booklet Associate Sponsor 5 /1 #11
2016 Panini National Treasures Jumbo Firesuit Patch Signature Booklet Associate Sponsor 6 /1 #11
2016 Panini National Treasures Jumbo Firesuit Patch Signature Booklet Associate Sponsor 7 /1 #11
2016 Panini National Treasures Jumbo Firesuit Patch Signature Booklet Associate Sponsor 8 /1 #11
2016 Panini National Treasures Jumbo Firesuit Patch Signature Booklet Associate Sponsor 9 /1 #11
2016 Panini National Treasures Jumbo Firesuit Patch Signature Booklet Flag /1 #11
2016 Panini National Treasures Jumbo Firesuit Patch Signature Booklet Goodyear /2 #11
2016 Panini National Treasures Jumbo Firesuit Patch Signature Booklet Manufacturers Logo /2 #11
2016 Panini National Treasures Jumbo Firesuit Patch Signature Booklet Nameplate /2 #11
2016 Panini National Treasures Jumbo Firesuit Patch Signature Booklet NASCAR /1 #11
2016 Panini National Treasures Jumbo Firesuit Signatures Black /5 #11
2016 Panini National Treasures Jumbo Firesuit Signatures Blue /1 #11
2016 Panini National Treasures Jumbo Firesuit Signatures Printing Plates Black /1 #11
2016 Panini National Treasures Jumbo Firesuit Signatures Printing Plates Cyan /1 #11
2016 Panini National Treasures Jumbo Firesuit Signatures Printing Plates Magenta /1 #11
2016 Panini National Treasures Jumbo Firesuit Signatures Printing Plates Yellow /1 #11
2016 Panini National Treasures Jumbo Sheet Metal Signatures /25 #12
2016 Panini National Treasures Jumbo Sheet Metal Signatures Black /5 #12
2016 Panini National Treasures Jumbo Sheet Metal Signatures Blue /1 #12
2016 Panini National Treasures Jumbo Sheet Metal Signatures Gold /10 #12
2016 Panini National Treasures Jumbo Sheet Metal Signatures Printing Plates Black /1 #12
2016 Panini National Treasures Jumbo Sheet Metal Signatures Printing Plates Cyan /1 #12
2016 Panini National Treasures Jumbo Sheet Metal Signatures Printing Plates Magenta /1 #12
2016 Panini National Treasures Jumbo Sheet Metal Signatures Printing Plates Yellow /1 #12
2016 Panini National Treasures Jumbo Sheet Metal Signatures Silver /15 #12
2016 Panini National Treasures Printing Plates Black /1 #13

2016 Panini National Treasures Printing Plates Cyan /1 #13
2016 Panini National Treasures Printing Plates Magenta /1 #13
2016 Panini National Treasures Printing Plates Yellow /1 #13
2016 Panini National Treasures Signature Dual Materials Black /5 #11
2016 Panini National Treasures Signature Dual Materials Blue /1 #11
2016 Panini National Treasures Signature Dual Materials Printing Plates Black /1 #11
2016 Panini National Treasures Signature Dual Materials Printing Plates Cyan /1 #11
2016 Panini National Treasures Signature Dual Materials Printing Plates Magenta /1 #11
2016 Panini National Treasures Signature Dual Materials Printing Plates Yellow /1 #11
2016 Panini National Treasures Signature Firesuit Materials Blue /1 #11
2016 Panini National Treasures Signature Firesuit Materials Laundry Tag /1 #11
2016 Panini National Treasures Signature Firesuit Materials Printing Plates Black /1 #11
2016 Panini National Treasures Signature Firesuit Materials Printing Plates Cyan /1 #11
2016 Panini National Treasures Signature Firesuit Materials Printing Plates Magenta /1 #11
2016 Panini National Treasures Signature Firesuit Materials Printing Plates Yellow /1 #11
2016 Panini National Treasures Signature Quad Materials Black /5 #11
2016 Panini National Treasures Signature Quad Materials Blue /1 #11
2016 Panini National Treasures Signature Quad Materials Printing Plates Black /1 #11
2016 Panini National Treasures Signature Quad Materials Printing Plates Cyan /1 #11
2016 Panini National Treasures Signature Quad Materials Printing Plates Magenta /1 #11
2016 Panini National Treasures Signature Quad Materials Printing Plates Yellow /1 #11
2016 Panini National Treasures Signature Sheet Metal Materials Black /5 #11
2016 Panini National Treasures Signature Sheet Metal Materials Blue /1 #11
2016 Panini National Treasures Signature Sheet Metal Materials Gold /10 #11
2016 Panini National Treasures Signature Sheet Metal Materials Printing Plates Black /1 #11
2016 Panini National Treasures Signature Sheet Metal Materials Printing Plates Cyan /1 #11
2016 Panini National Treasures Signature Sheet Metal Materials Printing Plates Magenta /1 #11
2016 Panini National Treasures Signature Sheet Metal Materials Printing Plates Yellow /1 #11
2016 Panini National Treasures Signatures Blue /1 #8
2016 Panini National Treasures Signatures Printing Plates Black /1 #8
2016 Panini National Treasures Signatures Printing Plates Cyan /1 #8
2016 Panini National Treasures Signatures Printing Plates Magenta /1 #8
2016 Panini National Treasures Signatures Printing Plates Yellow /1 #8
2016 Panini National Treasures Silver /20 #13
2016 Panini National Treasures Timelines /25 #6
2016 Panini National Treasures Timelines Blue /1 #6
2016 Panini National Treasures Timelines Printing Plates Black /1 #6
2016 Panini National Treasures Timelines Printing Plates Cyan /1 #6
2016 Panini National Treasures Timelines Printing Plates Magenta /1 #6
2016 Panini National Treasures Timelines Printing Plates Yellow /1 #6
2016 Panini National Treasures Timelines Signatures Blue /1 #6
2016 Panini National Treasures Timelines Signatures Printing Plates Black /1 #6
2016 Panini National Treasures Timelines Signatures Printing Plates Cyan /1 #6
2016 Panini National Treasures Timelines Signatures Printing Plates Magenta /1 #6
2016 Panini National Treasures Timelines Signatures Printing Plates Yellow /1 #6
2016 Panini National Treasures Timelines Silver /15 #6
2016 Panini Prizm #1A
2016 Panini Prizm #53
2016 Panini Prizm #89
2016 Panini Prizm #100
2016 Panini Prizm Autographs Prizms #30
2016 Panini Prizm Autographs Prizms Black /3 #30
2016 Panini Prizm Autographs Prizms Blue Flag /75 #30
2016 Panini Prizm Autographs Prizms Camo /1 #30
2016 Panini Prizm Autographs Prizms Checkered Flag /1 #30
2016 Panini Prizm Autographs Prizms Gold /10 #30
2016 Panini Prizm Autographs Prizms Green Flag /99 #30
2016 Panini Prizm Autographs Prizms Rainbow /24 #30
2016 Panini Prizm Autographs Prizms Red Flag /50 #30
2016 Panini Prizm Autographs Prizms Red White and Blue /49 #30
2016 Panini Prizm Autographs Prizms White Flag /5 #30
2016 Panini Prizm Firesuit Fabrics /149 #12
2016 Panini Prizm Firesuit Fabrics Prizms Blue Flag /75 #12
2016 Panini Prizm Firesuit Fabrics Prizms Checkered Flag /1 #12
2016 Panini Prizm Firesuit Fabrics Prizms Green Flag /99 #12
2016 Panini Prizm Firesuit Fabrics Prizms Red Flag /25 #12
2016 Panini Prizm Firesuit Fabrics Team /249 #12
2016 Panini Prizm Firesuit Fabrics Team Prizms Blue Flag /75 #12
2016 Panini Prizm Firesuit Fabrics Team Prizms Checkered Flag /1 #12
2016 Panini Prizm Firesuit Fabrics Team Prizms Green Flag /99 #12
2016 Panini Prizm Firesuit Fabrics Team Prizms Red Flag /25 #12
2016 Panini Prizm Prizms #1A
2016 Panini Prizm Prizms #53
2016 Panini Prizm Prizms #89
2016 Panini Prizm Prizms #100
2016 Panini Prizm Prizms Black /3 #1
2016 Panini Prizm Prizms Black /3 #53
2016 Panini Prizm Prizms Black /3 #89
2016 Panini Prizm Prizms Black /3 #100
2016 Panini Prizm Prizms Blue Flag /99 #1
2016 Panini Prizm Prizms Blue Flag /99 #53
2016 Panini Prizm Prizms Blue Flag /99 #89
2016 Panini Prizm Prizms Blue Flag /99 #100
2016 Panini Prizm Prizms Camo /1 #1
2016 Panini Prizm Prizms Camo /1 #53
2016 Panini Prizm Prizms Camo /1 #89
2016 Panini Prizm Prizms Camo /18 #100
2016 Panini Prizm Prizms Checkered Flag /1 #53
2016 Panini Prizm Prizms Checkered Flag /1 #89
2016 Panini Prizm Prizms Checkered Flag /1 #100
2016 Panini Prizm Prizms Gold /10 #1A
2016 Panini Prizm Prizms Gold /10 #53
2016 Panini Prizm Prizms Gold /10 #89
2016 Panini Prizm Prizms Gold /10 #100
2016 Panini Prizm Prizms Green Flag /149 #1
2016 Panini Prizm Prizms Green Flag /149 #53
2016 Panini Prizm Prizms Green Flag /149 #89
2016 Panini Prizm Prizms Green Flag /149 #100
2016 Panini Prizm Prizms Rainbow /24 #1
2016 Panini Prizm Prizms Rainbow /24 #53
2016 Panini Prizm Prizms Rainbow /24 #89
2016 Panini Prizm Prizms Rainbow /24 #100
2016 Panini Prizm Prizms Red Flag /75 #1
2016 Panini Prizm Prizms Red Flag /75 #53
2016 Panini Prizm Prizms Red Flag /75 #89
2016 Panini Prizm Prizms Red Flag /75 #100
2016 Panini Prizm Prizms Red White and Blue #1
2016 Panini Prizm Prizms Red White and Blue #53
2016 Panini Prizm Prizms Red White and Blue #89
2016 Panini Prizm Prizms Red White and Blue #100
2016 Panini Prizm Prizms White Flag /5 #1
2016 Panini Prizm Prizms White Flag /5 #53
2016 Panini Prizm Prizms White Flag /5 #89
2016 Panini Prizm Prizms White Flag /5 #100
2016 Panini Prizm Race Used Tire Team #9
2016 Panini Prizm Race Used Tire Team Prizms Blue Flag /75 #9
2016 Panini Prizm Race Used Tire Team Prizms Checkered Flag /1 #9
2016 Panini Prizm Race Used Tire Team Prizms Green Flag /149 #9
2016 Panini Prizm Race Used Tire Team Prizms Red Flag /10 #9
2016 Panini Torque #14
2016 Panini Torque #79
2016 Panini Torque Artist Proof /50 #14
2016 Panini Torque Artist Proof /50 #79
2016 Panini Torque Blackout /1 #14
2016 Panini Torque Blackout /1 #79
2016 Panini Torque Blue /125 #14
2016 Panini Torque Blue /125 #79
2016 Panini Torque Clear Vision #14
2016 Panini Torque Clear Vision Blue /99 #14
2016 Panini Torque Clear Vision Gold /149 #14
2016 Panini Torque Clear Vision Green /25 #14
2016 Panini Torque Clear Vision Purple /10 #14
2016 Panini Torque Clear Vision Red /49 #14
2016 Panini Torque Combo Materials Autographs /50 #1
2016 Panini Torque Combo Materials Autographs Blue /25 #1
2016 Panini Torque Combo Materials Autographs Green /15 #1
2016 Panini Torque Combo Materials Autographs Purple /5 #1
2016 Panini Torque Combo Materials Autographs Red /20 #1
2016 Panini Torque Gold #14
2016 Panini Torque Gold #79
2016 Panini Torque Holo Gold /5 #14
2016 Panini Torque Holo Gold /5 #79
2016 Panini Torque Holo Silver /10 #14
2016 Panini Torque Holo Silver /10 #79
2016 Panini Torque Horsepower Heroes #13
2016 Panini Torque Horsepower Heroes Gold /199 #13
2016 Panini Torque Horsepower Heroes Holo Silver /99 #13
2016 Panini Torque Jumbo Tire Autographs /50 #20
2016 Panini Torque Jumbo Tire Autographs Blue /25 #20
2016 Panini Torque Jumbo Tire Autographs Green /15 #20
2016 Panini Torque Jumbo Tire Autographs Purple /5 #20
2016 Panini Torque Jumbo Tire Autographs Red /20 #20
2016 Panini Torque Painted to Perfection #20
2016 Panini Torque Painted to Perfection Blue /99 #20
2016 Panini Torque Painted to Perfection Checkerboard /10 #20
2016 Panini Torque Painted to Perfection Green /25 #20
2016 Panini Torque Painted to Perfection Red /49 #20
2016 Panini Torque Pairings Materials /249 #20
2016 Panini Torque Pairings Materials /249 #27
2016 Panini Torque Pairings Materials Blue /99 #20
2016 Panini Torque Pairings Materials Blue /99 #27
2016 Panini Torque Pairings Materials Green /25 #20
2016 Panini Torque Pairings Materials Green /25 #27
2016 Panini Torque Pairings Materials Purple /10 #20
2016 Panini Torque Pairings Materials Purple /10 #27
2016 Panini Torque Pairings Materials Red /49 #20
2016 Panini Torque Pairings Materials Red /49 #27
2016 Panini Torque Printing Plates Black /1 #14
2016 Panini Torque Printing Plates Black /1 #79
2016 Panini Torque Printing Plates Cyan /1 #14
2016 Panini Torque Printing Plates Cyan /1 #79
2016 Panini Torque Printing Plates Magenta /1 #14
2016 Panini Torque Printing Plates Magenta /1 #79
2016 Panini Torque Printing Plates Yellow /1 #14
2016 Panini Torque Printing Plates Yellow /1 #79
2016 Panini Torque Purple /25 #14
2016 Panini Torque Purple /25 #79
2016 Panini Torque Red /99 #14
2016 Panini Torque Red /99 #79
2016 Panini Torque Shades #10
2016 Panini Torque Shades Gold /199 #10
2016 Panini Torque Shades Holo Silver /99 #10
2016 Panini Torque Silhouettes Firesuit Autographs /50 #10
2016 Panini Torque Silhouettes Firesuit Autographs Blue /25 #10
2016 Panini Torque Silhouettes Firesuit Autographs Green /15 #10
2016 Panini Torque Silhouettes Firesuit Autographs Purple /10 #10
2016 Panini Torque Silhouettes Firesuit Autographs Red /20 #10
2016 Panini Torque Test Proof Black /1 #14
2016 Panini Torque Test Proof Black /1 #79
2016 Panini Torque Test Proof Cyan /1 #14
2016 Panini Torque Test Proof Cyan /1 #79
2016 Panini Torque Test Proof Magenta /1 #14
2016 Panini Torque Test Proof Magenta /1 #79
2016 Panini Torque Test Proof Yellow /1 #14
2016 Panini Torque Test Proof Yellow /1 #79
2016 Panini Torque Winning Vision #18
2016 Panini Torque Winning Vision Blue /99 #18
2016 Panini Torque Winning Vision Gold /149 #18
2016 Panini Torque Winning Vision Green /25 #18
2016 Panini Torque Winning Vision Purple /10 #18
2016 Panini Torque Winning Vision Red /49 #18
2017 Donruss #17
2017 Donruss #50A
2017 Donruss #134
2017 Donruss #170
2017 Donruss #50B
2017 Donruss Artist Proof /25 #17
2017 Donruss Artist Proof /25 #50A
2017 Donruss Artist Proof /25 #134
2017 Donruss Artist Proof /25 #170
2017 Donruss Artist Proof /25 #50B
2017 Donruss Blue Foil /299 #17
2017 Donruss Blue Foil /299 #134
2017 Donruss Blue Foil /299 #50A
2017 Donruss Blue Foil /299 #170
2017 Donruss Blue Foil /299 #50B
2017 Donruss Gold Foil /499 #17
2017 Donruss Gold Foil /499 #134
2017 Donruss Gold Foil /499 #170
2017 Donruss Gold Foil /499 #50A
2017 Donruss Gold Foil /499 #50B
2017 Donruss Gold Press Proof /99 #17
2017 Donruss Gold Press Proof /99 #50A
2017 Donruss Gold Press Proof /99 #134
2017 Donruss Gold Press Proof /99 #170
2017 Donruss Gold Press Proof /99 #50B
2017 Donruss Green Foil /199 #17
2017 Donruss Green Foil /199 #50A
2017 Donruss Green Foil /199 #134
2017 Donruss Green Foil /199 #170
2017 Donruss Green Foil /199 #50B
2017 Donruss Press Proof /49 #17
2017 Donruss Press Proof /49 #50A
2017 Donruss Press Proof /49 #134
2017 Donruss Press Proof /49 #170
2017 Donruss Press Proof /49 #50B
2017 Donruss Printing Plates Black /1 #17
2017 Donruss Printing Plates Black /1 #50A
2017 Donruss Printing Plates Black /1 #134
2017 Donruss Printing Plates Black /1 #170
2017 Donruss Printing Plates Black /1 #50B
2017 Donruss Printing Plates Cyan /1 #17
2017 Donruss Printing Plates Cyan /1 #50A
2017 Donruss Printing Plates Cyan /1 #134
2017 Donruss Printing Plates Cyan /1 #170
2017 Donruss Printing Plates Cyan /1 #50B
2017 Donruss Printing Plates Magenta /1 #17
2017 Donruss Printing Plates Magenta /1 #134
2017 Donruss Printing Plates Magenta /1 #170
2017 Donruss Printing Plates Magenta /1 #50A
2017 Donruss Printing Plates Magenta /1 #50B
2017 Donruss Printing Plates Yellow /1 #17
2017 Donruss Printing Plates Yellow /1 #134
2017 Donruss Printing Plates Yellow /1 #170
2017 Donruss Printing Plates Yellow /1 #50A
2017 Donruss Printing Plates Yellow /1 #50B
2017 Donruss Rubber Relics #21
2017 Donruss Rubber Relics Holo Black /1 #21
2017 Donruss Rubber Relics Holo Gold /25 #21
2017 Panini Father's Day Racing Memorabilia /100 #3
2017 Panini Father's Day Racing Memorabilia Cracked Ice /25 #3
2017 Panini Father's Day Racing Memorabilia Hyperplaid /1 #3
2017 Panini Father's Day Racing Memorabilia Shimmer /10 #3
2017 Panini National Treasures Associate Sponsor Patch Signatures 1 /1 #29
2017 Panini National Treasures Associate Sponsor Patch Signatures 10 /1 #29
2017 Panini National Treasures Associate Sponsor Patch Signatures 11 /1 #29
2017 Panini National Treasures Associate Sponsor Patch Signatures 12 /1 #29
2017 Panini National Treasures Associate Sponsor Patch Signatures 13 /1 #29
2017 Panini National Treasures Associate Sponsor Patch Signatures 14 /1 #29
2017 Panini National Treasures Associate Sponsor Patch Signatures 15 /1 #29
2017 Panini National Treasures Associate Sponsor Patch Signatures 2 /1 #29
2017 Panini National Treasures Associate Sponsor Patch Signatures 3 /1 #29
2017 Panini National Treasures Associate Sponsor Patch Signatures 4 /1 #29
2017 Panini National Treasures Associate Sponsor Patch Signatures 5 /1 #29
2017 Panini National Treasures Associate Sponsor Patch Signatures 6 /1 #29
2017 Panini National Treasures Associate Sponsor Patch Signatures 7 /1 #29
2017 Panini National Treasures Associate Sponsor Patch Signatures 8 /1 #29
2017 Panini National Treasures Associate Sponsor Patch Signatures 9 /1 #29
2017 Panini National Treasures Car Manufacturer Patch Signatures /1 #29
2017 Panini National Treasures Dual Firesuit Materials Black /1 #7
2017 Panini National Treasures Dual Firesuit Materials Green /5 #7
2017 Panini National Treasures Dual Firesuit Materials Laundry Tag /1 #7
2017 Panini National Treasures Dual Firesuit Materials Printing Plates Black /1 #7
2017 Panini National Treasures Dual Firesuit Materials Printing Plates Cyan /1 #7
2017 Panini National Treasures Dual Firesuit Materials Printing Plates Magenta /1 #7
2017 Panini National Treasures Dual Firesuit Materials Printing Plates Yellow /1 #7
2017 Panini National Treasures Dual Firesuit Signatures Black /1 #7
2017 Panini National Treasures Dual Firesuit Signatures Green /5 #7
2017 Panini National Treasures Dual Firesuit Signatures Holo Gold /10 #7
2017 Panini National Treasures Dual Firesuit Signatures Laundry Tag /1 #7
2017 Panini National Treasures Dual Firesuit Signatures Printing Plates Black /1 #7
2017 Panini National Treasures Dual Firesuit Signatures Printing Plates Cyan /1 #7
2017 Panini National Treasures Dual Firesuit Signatures Printing Plates Magenta /1 #7
2017 Panini National Treasures Dual Firesuit Signatures Printing Plates Yellow /1 #7
2017 Panini National Treasures Dual Tire Signatures /25 #6
2017 Panini National Treasures Dual Tire Signatures Black /1 #6
2017 Panini National Treasures Dual Tire Signatures Gold /15 #6
2017 Panini National Treasures Dual Tire Signatures Green /5 #6
2017 Panini National Treasures Dual Tire Signatures Holo Gold /10 #6
2017 Panini National Treasures Dual Tire Signatures Holo Silver /20 #6
2017 Panini National Treasures Dual Tire Signatures Printing Plates Black /1 #6
2017 Panini National Treasures Dual Tire Signatures Printing Plates Cyan /1 #6
2017 Panini National Treasures Dual Tire Signatures Printing Plates Magenta /1 #6
2017 Panini National Treasures Dual Tire Signatures Printing Plates Yellow /1 #6
2017 Panini National Treasures Flag Patch Signatures /1 #29
2017 Panini National Treasures Hats Off /14 #3
2017 Panini National Treasures Hats Off /14 #4
2017 Panini National Treasures Hats Off Gold /2 #3
2017 Panini National Treasures Hats Off Gold /2 #4
2017 Panini National Treasures Hats Off Holo Gold /5 #3
2017 Panini National Treasures Hats Off Holo Gold /5 #4
2017 Panini National Treasures Hats Off Holo Silver /1 #3
2017 Panini National Treasures Hats Off Holo Silver /1 #4
2017 Panini National Treasures Hats Off Laundry Tag /6 #3
2017 Panini National Treasures Hats Off Laundry Tag /6 #4
2017 Panini National Treasures Hats Off Monster Energy Cup /16 #3
2017 Panini National Treasures Hats Off Monster Energy Cup Gold /4 #3
2017 Panini National Treasures Hats Off Monster Energy Cup Holo Gold /5 #3
2017 Panini National Treasures Hats Off Monster Energy Cup Holo Silver /1 #3
2017 Panini National Treasures Hats Off Monster Energy Cup Laundry Tag /3 #3
2017 Panini National Treasures Hats Off Monster Energy Cup New Era /1 #3
2017 Panini National Treasures Hats Off Monster Energy Cup Printing Plates Black /1 #3
2017 Panini National Treasures Hats Off Monster Energy Cup Printing Plates Cyan /1 #3
2017 Panini National Treasures Hats Off Monster Energy Cup Printing Plates Magenta /1 #3
2017 Panini National Treasures Hats Off Monster Energy Cup Printing Plates Yellow /1 #3
2017 Panini National Treasures Hats Off Monster Energy Cup Sponsor /5 #3
2017 Panini National Treasures Hats Off New Era /1 #3
2017 Panini National Treasures Hats Off New Era /1 #4
2017 Panini National Treasures Hats Off Printing Plates Black /1 #3
2017 Panini National Treasures Hats Off Printing Plates Black /1 #4
2017 Panini National Treasures Hats Off Printing Plates Cyan /1 #3
2017 Panini National Treasures Hats Off Printing Plates Cyan /1 #4
2017 Panini National Treasures Hats Off Printing Plates Magenta /1 #4
2017 Panini National Treasures Hats Off Printing Plates Yellow /1 #3
2017 Panini National Treasures Hats Off Printing Plates Yellow /1 #4
2017 Panini National Treasures Hats Off Sponsor /5 #3
2017 Panini National Treasures Hats Off Sponsor /5 #4
2017 Panini National Treasures Jumbo Firesuit Materials Black /1 #7
2017 Panini National Treasures Jumbo Firesuit Materials Gold /15 #7
2017 Panini National Treasures Jumbo Firesuit Materials Green /5 #7
2017 Panini National Treasures Jumbo Firesuit Materials Holo Gold /10 #7
2017 Panini National Treasures Jumbo Firesuit Materials Holo Silver /20 #7
2017 Panini National Treasures Jumbo Firesuit Materials Laundry Tag /1 #7
2017 Panini National Treasures Jumbo Firesuit Materials Printing Plates Black /1 #7
2017 Panini National Treasures Jumbo Firesuit Materials Printing Plates Cyan /1 #7
2017 Panini National Treasures Jumbo Firesuit Materials Printing Plates Magenta /1 #7
2017 Panini National Treasures Jumbo Firesuit Materials Printing Plates Yellow /1 #7
2017 Panini National Treasures Jumbo Firesuit Signatures Black /1 #12
2017 Panini National Treasures Jumbo Firesuit Signatures Green /5 #12
2017 Panini National Treasures Jumbo Firesuit Signatures Holo Gold /10 #12
2017 Panini National Treasures Jumbo Firesuit Signatures Laundry Tag /1 #12
2017 Panini National Treasures Jumbo Firesuit Signatures Printing Plates Black /1 #12
2017 Panini National Treasures Jumbo Firesuit Signatures Printing Plates Cyan /1 #12
2017 Panini National Treasures Jumbo Firesuit Signatures Printing Plates Magenta /1 #12
2017 Panini National Treasures Jumbo Firesuit Signatures Printing Plates Yellow /1 #12
2017 Panini National Treasures Jumbo Sheet Metal Materials Black /1 #7
2017 Panini National Treasures Jumbo Sheet Metal Materials Green /5 #7
2017 Panini National Treasures Jumbo Sheet Metal Materials Holo Gold /10 #7
2017 Panini National Treasures Jumbo Sheet Metal Materials Printing Plates Black /1 #7
2017 Panini National Treasures Jumbo Sheet Metal Materials Printing Plates Cyan /1 #7
2017 Panini National Treasures Jumbo Sheet Metal Materials Printing Plates Magenta /1 #7
2017 Panini National Treasures Jumbo Sheet Metal Materials Printing Plates Yellow /1 #7
2017 Panini National Treasures Nameplate Patch Signatures /2 #29
2017 Panini National Treasures NASCAR Patch Signatures /1 #29
2017 Panini National Treasures Quad Material Signatures Black /1 #6
2017 Panini National Treasures Quad Material Signatures Gold /15 #6
2017 Panini National Treasures Quad Material Signatures Green /5 #6
2017 Panini National Treasures Quad Material Signatures Holo Gold /10 #6
2017 Panini National Treasures Quad Material Signatures Laundry Tag /1 #6
2017 Panini National Treasures Quad Material Signatures Printing Plates Black /1 #6
2017 Panini National Treasures Quad Material Signatures Printing Plates Cyan /1 #6
2017 Panini National Treasures Quad Material Signatures Printing Plates Magenta /1 #6
2017 Panini National Treasures Quad Material Signatures Printing Plates Yellow /1 #6
2017 Panini National Treasures Quad Materials /25 #11
2017 Panini National Treasures Quad Materials Black /1 #11
2017 Panini National Treasures Quad Materials Gold /15 #11
2017 Panini National Treasures Quad Materials Green /5 #11
2017 Panini National Treasures Quad Materials Holo Gold /10 #11
2017 Panini National Treasures Quad Materials Holo Silver /20 #11
2017 Panini National Treasures Quad Materials Laundry Tag /1 #11
2017 Panini National Treasures Quad Materials Printing Plates Black /1 #11
2017 Panini National Treasures Quad Materials Printing Plates Cyan /1 #11
2017 Panini National Treasures Quad Materials Printing Plates Magenta /1 #11
2017 Panini National Treasures Quad Materials Printing Plates Yellow /1 #11
2017 Panini National Treasures Series Sponsor Patch Signatures /1 #29
2017 Panini National Treasures Sunoco Patch Signatures /1 #29
2017 Panini National Treasures Teammates Dual Materials /25 #9
2017 Panini National Treasures Teammates Dual Materials Black /1 #9
2017 Panini National Treasures Teammates Dual Materials Gold /15 #9
2017 Panini National Treasures Teammates Dual Materials Green /5 #9
2017 Panini National Treasures Teammates Dual Materials Holo Gold /10 #9
2017 Panini National Treasures Teammates Dual Materials Holo Silver /20 #9
2017 Panini National Treasures Teammates Dual Materials Laundry Tag /1 #9
2017 Panini National Treasures Teammates Dual Materials Printing Plates Black /1 #9
2017 Panini National Treasures Teammates Dual Materials Printing Plates Cyan /1 #9
2017 Panini National Treasures Teammates Dual Materials Printing Plates Magenta /1 #9
2017 Panini National Treasures Teammates Dual Materials Printing Plates Yellow /1 #9
2017 Panini National Treasures Teammates Quad Materials /25 #9
2017 Panini National Treasures Teammates Quad Materials Black /1 #9
2017 Panini National Treasures Teammates Quad Materials Gold /15 #9
2017 Panini National Treasures Teammates Quad Materials Green /5 #9
2017 Panini National Treasures Teammates Quad Materials Holo Gold /10 #9
2017 Panini National Treasures Teammates Quad Materials Holo Silver /20 #9
2017 Panini National Treasures Teammates Quad Materials Laundry Tag /1 #9
2017 Panini National Treasures Teammates Quad Materials Printing Plates Black /1 #9
2017 Panini National Treasures Teammates Quad Materials Printing Plates Cyan /1 #9
2017 Panini National Treasures Teammates Quad Materials Printing Plates Magenta /1 #9
2017 Panini National Treasures Teammates Quad Materials Printing Plates Yellow /1 #9
2017 Panini National Treasures Three Wide Black /1 #10
2017 Panini National Treasures Three Wide Gold /15 #10
2017 Panini National Treasures Three Wide Green /5 #10
2017 Panini National Treasures Three Wide Holo Gold /10 #10
2017 Panini National Treasures Three Wide Holo Silver /20 #10
2017 Panini National Treasures Three Wide Laundry Tag /1 #10
2017 Panini National Treasures Three Wide Printing Plates Black /1 #10
2017 Panini National Treasures Three Wide Printing Plates Cyan /1 #10
2017 Panini National Treasures Three Wide Printing Plates Magenta /1 #10
2017 Panini National Treasures Three Wide Printing Plates Yellow /1 #10
2017 Panini Torque #1
2017 Panini Torque #68
2017 Panini Torque Artist Proof /75 #1
2017 Panini Torque Artist Proof /75 #68
2017 Panini Torque Blackout /1 #1
2017 Panini Torque Blackout /1 #68
2017 Panini Torque Blue /150 #1
2017 Panini Torque Blue /150 #68
2017 Panini Torque Clear Vision #1
2017 Panini Torque Clear Vision Blue /99 #1
2017 Panini Torque Clear Vision Gold /149 #1
2017 Panini Torque Clear Vision Green /25 #1
2017 Panini Torque Clear Vision Purple /10 #1
2017 Panini Torque Clear Vision Red /49 #1
2017 Panini Torque Combo Materials Signatures /51 #2
2017 Panini Torque Combo Materials Signatures Blue /49 #2
2017 Panini Torque Combo Materials Signatures Green /15 #2
2017 Panini Torque Combo Materials Signatures Purple /10 #2
2017 Panini Torque Combo Materials Signatures Red /25 #2
2017 Panini Torque Gold #1
2017 Panini Torque Gold #68
2017 Panini Torque Holo Gold /10 #1
2017 Panini Torque Holo Gold /10 #68
2017 Panini Torque Holo Silver /25 #1
2017 Panini Torque Holo Silver /25 #68
2017 Panini Torque Horsepower Heroes #1
2017 Panini Torque Horsepower Heroes Gold /199 #1
2017 Panini Torque Horsepower Heroes Holo Silver /99 #1
2017 Panini Torque Jumbo Firesuit Signatures /51 #11
2017 Panini Torque Jumbo Firesuit Signatures Blue /49 #11
2017 Panini Torque Jumbo Firesuit Signatures Green /15 #11
2017 Panini Torque Jumbo Firesuit Signatures Purple /10 #11
2017 Panini Torque Jumbo Firesuit Signatures Red /25 #11
2017 Panini Torque Manufacturer Marks #11
2017 Panini Torque Manufacturer Marks Gold /199 #11
2017 Panini Torque Manufacturer Marks Holo Silver /99 #11
2017 Panini Torque Metal Materials /199 #8
2017 Panini Torque Metal Materials Blue /99 #8
2017 Panini Torque Metal Materials Green /25 #8
2017 Panini Torque Metal Materials Purple /10 #8
2017 Panini Torque Metal Materials Red /49 #8
2017 Panini Torque Pairings Materials /199 #2
2017 Panini Torque Pairings Materials Blue /99 #2
2017 Panini Torque Pairings Materials Green /25 #2
2017 Panini Torque Pairings Materials Purple /10 #2
2017 Panini Torque Pairings Materials Red /49 #2
2017 Panini Torque Primary Paint #18
2017 Panini Torque Primary Paint Blue /99 #18
2017 Panini Torque Primary Paint Checkerboard /10 #18
2017 Panini Torque Primary Paint Green /25 #18
2017 Panini Torque Primary Paint Red /49 #18
2017 Panini Torque Printing Plates Black /1 #1
2017 Panini Torque Printing Plates Black /1 #68
2017 Panini Torque Printing Plates Cyan /1 #1
2017 Panini Torque Printing Plates Cyan /1 #68
2017 Panini Torque Printing Plates Magenta /1 #1
2017 Panini Torque Printing Plates Magenta /1 #68
2017 Panini Torque Printing Plates Yellow /1 #1
2017 Panini Torque Printing Plates Yellow /1 #68
2017 Panini Torque Purple /50 #1
2017 Panini Torque Purple /50 #68
2017 Panini Torque Quad Materials /99 #12
2017 Panini Torque Quad Materials Blue /49 #12
2017 Panini Torque Quad Materials Green /10 #12
2017 Panini Torque Quad Materials Purple /1 #12
2017 Panini Torque Quad Materials Red /25 #12
2017 Panini Torque Raced Relics /499 #9
2017 Panini Torque Raced Relics Blue /99 #9
2017 Panini Torque Raced Relics Green /25 #9
2017 Panini Torque Raced Relics Purple /10 #9
2017 Panini Torque Raced Relics Red /49 #9
2017 Panini Torque Red /100 #1
2017 Panini Torque Red /100 #68
2017 Panini Torque Running Order #13
2017 Panini Torque Running Order Blue /99 #13
2017 Panini Torque Running Order Checkerboard /10 #13
2017 Panini Torque Running Order Green /25 #13
2017 Panini Torque Running Order Red /49 #13
2017 Panini Torque Test Proof Black /1 #1
2017 Panini Torque Test Proof Black /1 #68
2017 Panini Torque Test Proof Cyan /1 #1
2017 Panini Torque Test Proof Cyan /1 #68
2017 Panini Torque Test Proof Magenta /1 #1
2017 Panini Torque Test Proof Magenta /1 #68
2017 Panini Torque Test Proof Yellow /1 #1
2017 Panini Torque Test Proof Yellow /1 #68
2017 Panini Torque Visions of Greatness #3
2017 Panini Torque Visions of Greatness Blue /99 #3
2017 Panini Torque Visions of Greatness Gold /149 #3
2017 Panini Torque Visions of Greatness Green /25 #3
2017 Panini Torque Visions of Greatness Purple /10 #3
2017 Panini Torque Visions of Greatness Red /49 #3
2017 Select #56
2017 Select #57
2017 Select #58
2017 Select #106
2017 Select Prizms Black /3 #56
2017 Select Prizms Black /3 #57
2017 Select Prizms Black /3 #58
2017 Select Prizms Black /3 #106
2017 Select Prizms Blue /199 #56
2017 Select Prizms Blue /199 #57
2017 Select Prizms Blue /199 #58
2017 Select Prizms Checkered Flag /1 #56
2017 Select Prizms Checkered Flag /1 #57
2017 Select Prizms Checkered Flag /1 #58
2017 Select Prizms Checkered Flag /1 #106
2017 Select Prizms Gold /10 #56
2017 Select Prizms Gold /10 #57
2017 Select Prizms Gold /10 #58
2017 Select Prizms Gold /10 #106
2017 Select Prizms Purple Pulsar #56
2017 Select Prizms Purple Pulsar #57
2017 Select Prizms Purple Pulsar #58
2017 Select Prizms Red /99 #56
2017 Select Prizms Red /99 #57
2017 Select Prizms Red /99 #58
2017 Select Prizms Red White and Blue Pulsar /299 #56
2017 Select Prizms Red White and Blue Pulsar /299 #57
2017 Select Prizms Red White and Blue Pulsar /299 #58
2017 Select Prizms Silver #56
2017 Select Prizms Silver #57
2017 Select Prizms Silver #58
2017 Select Prizms Tie Dye /24 #56
2017 Select Prizms Tie Dye /24 #57
2017 Select Prizms Tie Dye /24 #58
2017 Select Prizms Tie Dye /24 #106
2017 Select Prizms White /50 #56
2017 Select Prizms White /50 #57
2017 Select Prizms White /50 #58
2017 Select Prizms White /50 #106
2017 Select Select Pairs Materials #1
2017 Select Select Pairs Materials Prizms Blue /199 #1
2017 Select Select Pairs Materials Prizms Checkered Flag /1 #1
2017 Select Select Pairs Materials Prizms Gold /10 #1
2017 Select Select Pairs Materials Prizms Red /99 #1
2017 Select Select Stars #24
2017 Select Select Stars Prizms Black /3 #24
2017 Select Select Stars Prizms Checkered Flag /1 #24
2017 Select Select Stars Prizms Gold /10 #24
2017 Select Select Stars Prizms Tie Dye /24 #24
2017 Select Select Stars Prizms White /50 #24
2017 Select Select Swatches #21
2017 Select Select Swatches Prizms Blue /199 #21
2017 Select Select Swatches Prizms Checkered Flag /1 #21
2017 Select Select Swatches Prizms Gold /10 #21
2017 Select Select Swatches Prizms Red /99 #21
2017 Select Sheet Metal #11
2017 Select Sheet Metal Prizms Blue /199 #11
2017 Select Sheet Metal Prizms Checkered Flag /1 #11
2017 Select Sheet Metal Prizms Gold /10 #11
2017 Select Sheet Metal Prizms Red /50 #11
2017 Select Signature Paint Schemes #5
2017 Select Signature Paint Schemes Prizms Blue /50 #5
2017 Select Signature Paint Schemes Prizms Checkered Flag /1 #5
2017 Select Signature Paint Schemes Prizms Gold /10 #5
2017 Select Signature Paint Schemes Prizms Red /25 #5
2017 Select Signature Swatches #21
2017 Select Signature Swatches Prizms Checkered Flag /1 #21
2017 Select Signature Swatches Prizms Gold /10 #21
2017 Select Signature Swatches Prizms Tie Dye /24 #21
2017 Select Signature Swatches Prizms White /50 #21
2017 Select Signature Swatches Triple #12
2017 Select Signature Swatches Triple Prizms Checkered Flag /1 #12
2017 Select Signature Swatches Triple Prizms Gold /10 #12
2017 Select Signature Swatches Triple Prizms Tie Dye /24 #12
2017 Select Signature Swatches Triple Prizms White /50 #12
2017 Select Speed Merchants #17
2017 Select Speed Merchants Prizms Black /3 #17
2017 Select Speed Merchants Prizms Checkered Flag /1 #17
2017 Select Speed Merchants Prizms Gold /10 #17
2017 Select Speed Merchants Prizms Tie Dye /24 #17
2017 Select Speed Merchants Prizms White /50 #17
2018 Certified #55
2018 Certified Black /1 #55
2018 Certified Blue /99 #55
2018 Certified Cup Swatches /499 #12
2018 Certified Cup Swatches Black /1 #12
2018 Certified Cup Swatches Blue /49 #12
2018 Certified Cup Swatches Gold /25 #12
2018 Certified Cup Swatches Green /5 #12
2018 Certified Cup Swatches Purple /10 #12
2018 Certified Cup Swatches Red /199 #12
2018 Certified Gold /49 #55
2018 Certified Green /10 #55
2018 Certified Mirror Black /1 #55
2018 Certified Mirror Gold /25 #55
2018 Certified Mirror Green /5 #55
2018 Certified Mirror Purple /10 #55
2018 Certified Orange /249 #55
2018 Certified Purple /25 #55
2018 Certified Red /199 #55
2018 Certified Signature Swatches /149 #9
2018 Certified Signature Swatches Black /1 #9
2018 Certified Signature Swatches Blue /49 #9
2018 Certified Signature Swatches Gold /25 #9
2018 Certified Signature Swatches Green /5 #9
2018 Certified Signature Swatches Purple /10 #9
2018 Certified Signature Swatches Red /99 #9
2018 Certified Signing Sessions /50 #9
2018 Certified Signing Sessions Black /1 #9
2018 Certified Signing Sessions Blue /25 #9
2018 Certified Signing Sessions Gold /20 #9
2018 Certified Signing Sessions Green /5 #9
2018 Certified Signing Sessions Purple /10 #9
2018 Certified Signing Sessions Red /35 #9
2018 Certified Stars /199 #21
2018 Certified Stars Black /1 #21
2018 Certified Stars Blue /99 #21
2018 Certified Stars Gold /49 #21
2018 Certified Stars Green /10 #21
2018 Certified Stars Mirror Black /1 #21
2018 Certified Stars Mirror Gold /25 #21
2018 Certified Stars Mirror Green /5 #21
2018 Certified Stars Mirror Purple /10 #21
2018 Certified Stars Purple /25 #21
2018 Certified Stars Red /149 #21
2018 Donruss #4
2018 Donruss #31
2018 Donruss #84
2018 Donruss #121
2018 Donruss Artist Proofs /25 #4
2018 Donruss Artist Proofs /25 #31
2018 Donruss Artist Proofs /25 #84
2018 Donruss Artist Proofs /25 #121
2018 Donruss Gold Foil /499 #4
2018 Donruss Gold Foil /499 #31
2018 Donruss Gold Foil /499 #84
2018 Donruss Gold Foil /499 #121
2018 Donruss Gold Press Proofs /99 #4
2018 Donruss Gold Press Proofs /99 #31
2018 Donruss Gold Press Proofs /99 #84
2018 Donruss Gold Press Proofs /99 #121
2018 Donruss Green Foil /199 #4
2018 Donruss Green Foil /199 #31
2018 Donruss Green Foil /199 #84
2018 Donruss Green Foil /199 #121
2018 Donruss Press Proofs /49 #4
2018 Donruss Press Proofs /49 #31
2018 Donruss Press Proofs /49 #84
2018 Donruss Press Proofs /49 #121
2018 Donruss Printing Plates Black /1 #4
2018 Donruss Printing Plates Black /1 #31
2018 Donruss Printing Plates Black /1 #84
2018 Donruss Printing Plates Black /1 #121
2018 Donruss Printing Plates Cyan /1 #4
2018 Donruss Printing Plates Cyan /1 #31
2018 Donruss Printing Plates Cyan /1 #84
2018 Donruss Printing Plates Cyan /1 #121
2018 Donruss Printing Plates Magenta /1 #4
2018 Donruss Printing Plates Magenta /1 #31
2018 Donruss Printing Plates Magenta /1 #84
2018 Donruss Printing Plates Magenta /1 #121
2018 Donruss Printing Plates Yellow /1 #4
2018 Donruss Printing Plates Yellow /1 #31
2018 Donruss Printing Plates Yellow /1 #84
2018 Donruss Printing Plates Yellow /1 #121
2018 Donruss Red Foil /299 #4
2018 Donruss Red Foil /299 #31
2018 Donruss Red Foil /299 #84
2018 Donruss Red Foil /299 #121
2018 Donruss Studio Signatures #9
2018 Donruss Studio Signatures Black /1 #9
2018 Donruss Studio Signatures Holo Gold /25 #9
2018 Panini Prime Autograph Materials /50 #13
2018 Panini Prime Autograph Materials Black /1 #13
2018 Panini Prime Autograph Materials Holo Gold /25 #13
2018 Panini Prime Autograph Materials Laundry Tag /1 #13
2018 Panini Prime Clear Silhouettes /99 #13
2018 Panini Prime Clear Silhouettes Dual /99 #13
2018 Panini Prime Clear Silhouettes Dual Black /1 #13
2018 Panini Prime Clear Silhouettes Dual Holo Gold /50 #13
2018 Panini Prime Clear Silhouettes Holo Gold /50 #13
2018 Panini Prime Dual Material Autographs /50 #5
2018 Panini Prime Dual Material Autographs Black /1 #5
2018 Panini Prime Dual Material Autographs Holo Gold /34 #5
2018 Panini Prime Dual Material Autographs Laundry Tag /1 #5
2018 Panini Prime Dual Signatures /50 #10
2018 Panini Prime Dual Signatures Black /1 #10
2018 Panini Prime Dual Signatures Holo Gold /25 #10
2018 Panini Prime Hats Off Button /1 #4
2018 Panini Prime Hats Off Eyelet /6 #4
2018 Panini Prime Hats Off Headband /14 #4
2018 Panini Prime Hats Off Laundry Tag /1 #4
2018 Panini Prime Hats Off New Era /1 #4
2018 Panini Prime Hats Off Number /1 #4
2018 Panini Prime Hats Off Sponsor Logo /4 #4
2018 Panini Prime Hats Off Team Logo /2 #4
2018 Panini Prime Prime Jumbo Associate Sponsor 1 /1 #35
2018 Panini Prime Prime Jumbo Associate Sponsor 1 /1 #36
2018 Panini Prime Prime Jumbo Associate Sponsor 1 /1 #37
2018 Panini Prime Prime Jumbo Associate Sponsor 10 /1 #36
2018 Panini Prime Prime Jumbo Associate Sponsor 10 /1 #37
2018 Panini Prime Prime Jumbo Associate Sponsor 11 /1 #36
2018 Panini Prime Prime Jumbo Associate Sponsor 11 /1 #37
2018 Panini Prime Prime Jumbo Associate Sponsor 12 /1 #36
2018 Panini Prime Prime Jumbo Associate Sponsor 12 /1 #37
2018 Panini Prime Prime Jumbo Associate Sponsor 13 /1 #36
2018 Panini Prime Prime Jumbo Associate Sponsor 13 /1 #37
2018 Panini Prime Prime Jumbo Associate Sponsor 14 /1 #36
2018 Panini Prime Prime Jumbo Associate Sponsor 14 /1 #37
2018 Panini Prime Prime Jumbo Associate Sponsor 15 /1 #37
2018 Panini Prime Prime Jumbo Associate Sponsor 2 /1 #35
2018 Panini Prime Prime Jumbo Associate Sponsor 2 /1 #36
2018 Panini Prime Prime Jumbo Associate Sponsor 2 /1 #37
2018 Panini Prime Prime Jumbo Associate Sponsor 3 /1 #35
2018 Panini Prime Prime Jumbo Associate Sponsor 3 /1 #36
2018 Panini Prime Prime Jumbo Associate Sponsor 3 /1 #37
2018 Panini Prime Prime Jumbo Associate Sponsor 4 /1 #35
2018 Panini Prime Prime Jumbo Associate Sponsor 4 /1 #36
2018 Panini Prime Prime Jumbo Associate Sponsor 4 /1 #37
2018 Panini Prime Prime Jumbo Associate Sponsor 5 /1 #35
2018 Panini Prime Prime Jumbo Associate Sponsor 5 /1 #36
2018 Panini Prime Prime Jumbo Associate Sponsor 5 /1 #37
2018 Panini Prime Prime Jumbo Associate Sponsor 6 /1 #35
2018 Panini Prime Prime Jumbo Associate Sponsor 6 /1 #36
2018 Panini Prime Prime Jumbo Associate Sponsor 6 /1 #37
2018 Panini Prime Prime Jumbo Associate Sponsor 7 /1 #35
2018 Panini Prime Prime Jumbo Associate Sponsor 7 /1 #36

2018 Panini Prime Prime Jumbo Associate Sponsor 7 /1 #37
2018 Panini Prime Prime Jumbo Associate Sponsor 8 /1 #35
2018 Panini Prime Prime Jumbo Associate Sponsor 8 /1 #36
2018 Panini Prime Prime Jumbo Associate Sponsor 8 /1 #37
2018 Panini Prime Prime Jumbo Associate Sponsor 9 /1 #36
2018 Panini Prime Prime Jumbo Associate Sponsor 9 /1 #37
2018 Panini Prime Prime Jumbo Car Manufacturer /1 #36
2018 Panini Prime Prime Jumbo Car Manufacturer /1 #37
2018 Panini Prime Prime Jumbo Firesuit Manufacturer /1 #35
2018 Panini Prime Prime Jumbo Firesuit Manufacturer /1 #36
2018 Panini Prime Prime Jumbo Firesuit Manufacturer /1 #37
2018 Panini Prime Prime Jumbo Flag Patch /1 #36
2018 Panini Prime Prime Jumbo Flag Patch /1 #37
2018 Panini Prime Prime Jumbo Glove Manufacturer Patch /1 #35
2018 Panini Prime Prime Jumbo Glove Manufacturer Patch /1 #36
2018 Panini Prime Prime Jumbo Glove Manufacturer Patch /1 #37
2018 Panini Prime Prime Jumbo Glove Name Patch /1 #35
2018 Panini Prime Prime Jumbo Glove Name Patch /1 #36
2018 Panini Prime Prime Jumbo Glove Name Patch /1 #37
2018 Panini Prime Prime Jumbo Goodyear /1 #37
2018 Panini Prime Prime Jumbo Nameplate /1 #36
2018 Panini Prime Prime Jumbo Nameplate /1 #37
2018 Panini Prime Prime Jumbo NASCAR /1 #37
2018 Panini Prime Prime Jumbo Prime Colors /20 #35
2018 Panini Prime Prime Jumbo Prime Colors /12 #36
2018 Panini Prime Prime Jumbo Prime Colors /16 #37
2018 Panini Prime Prime Jumbo Series Sponsor /1 #36
2018 Panini Prime Prime Jumbo Series Sponsor /1 #37
2018 Panini Prime Prime Jumbo Shoe Brand Logo /1 #35
2018 Panini Prime Prime Jumbo Shoe Brand Logo /1 #36
2018 Panini Prime Prime Jumbo Shoe Name Patch /1 #37
2018 Panini Prime Prime Jumbo Shoe Number Patch /1 #35
2018 Panini Prime Prime Jumbo Sunoco /1 #36
2018 Panini Prime Prime Jumbo Sunoco /1 #37
2018 Panini Prime Prime Number Signatures /99 #6
2018 Panini Prime Prime Number Signatures Black /1 #6
2018 Panini Prime Prime Number Signatures Holo Gold /25 #6
2018 Panini Prime Quad Material Autographs /50 #7
2018 Panini Prime Quad Material Autographs Black /1 #7
2018 Panini Prime Quad Material Autographs Holo Gold /49 #7
2018 Panini Prime Quad Material Autographs Laundry Tag /1 #7
2018 Panini Prime Race Used Duals Firesuit /50 #19
2018 Panini Prime Race Used Duals Firesuit Black /1 #19
2018 Panini Prime Race Used Duals Firesuit Holo Gold /25 #19
2018 Panini Prime Race Used Duals Firesuit Laundry Tag /1 #19
2018 Panini Prime Race Used Duals Sheet Metal /50 #19
2018 Panini Prime Race Used Duals Sheet Metal Black /1 #19
2018 Panini Prime Race Used Duals Sheet Metal Holo Gold /25 #19
2018 Panini Prime Race Used Duals Tire /50 #19
2018 Panini Prime Race Used Duals Tire Black /1 #19
2018 Panini Prime Race Used Duals Tire Holo Gold /25 #19
2018 Panini Prime Race Used Firesuits /50 #16
2018 Panini Prime Race Used Firesuits Black /1 #16
2018 Panini Prime Race Used Firesuits Holo Gold /25 #16
2018 Panini Prime Race Used Firesuits Laundry Tag /1 #16
2018 Panini Prime Race Used Sheet Metal /50 #16
2018 Panini Prime Race Used Sheet Metal Black /1 #16
2018 Panini Prime Race Used Sheet Metal Holo Gold /25 #16
2018 Panini Prime Race Used Tires Black /1 #16
2018 Panini Prime Race Used Tires Holo Gold /25 #16
2018 Panini Prime Race Used Trios Firesuit /50 #16
2018 Panini Prime Race Used Trios Firesuit Black /1 #16
2018 Panini Prime Race Used Trios Firesuit Holo Gold /25 #16
2018 Panini Prime Race Used Trios Firesuit Laundry Tag /1 #16
2018 Panini Prime Race Used Trios Sheet Metal /50 #16
2018 Panini Prime Race Used Trios Sheet Metal Black /1 #16
2018 Panini Prime Race Used Trios Sheet Metal Holo Gold /25 #16
2018 Panini Prime Race Used Trios Tire /50 #16
2018 Panini Prime Race Used Trios Tire Black /1 #16
2018 Panini Prime Race Used Trios Tire Holo Gold /25 #16
2018 Panini Prime Signature Swatches /99 #12
2018 Panini Prime Signature Swatches Black /1 #12
2018 Panini Prime Signature Swatches Holo Gold /25 #12
2018 Panini Prime Signature Tires /99 #7
2018 Panini Prime Signature Tires Black /1 #7
2018 Panini Prime Signature Tires Holo Gold /25 #7
2018 Panini Prizm #44
2018 Panini Prizm Patented Pennmanship Prizms Black /1 #7
2018 Panini Prizm Patented Pennmanship Prizms Blue /10 #7
2018 Panini Prizm Patented Pennmanship Prizms Camo #7
2018 Panini Prizm Patented Pennmanship Prizms Gold /10 #7
2018 Panini Prizm Patented Pennmanship Prizms Green /10 #7
2018 Panini Prizm Patented Pennmanship Prizms Rainbow /24 #7
2018 Panini Prizm Patented Pennmanship Prizms Red /10 #7
2018 Panini Prizm Patented Pennmanship Prizms Red White and Blue /10 #7
2018 Panini Prizm Patented Pennmanship Prizms White /5 #7
2018 Panini Prizm Prizms #44
2018 Panini Prizm Prizms Black /1 #44
2018 Panini Prizm Prizms Blue /99 #44
2018 Panini Prizm Prizms Camo #44
2018 Panini Prizm Prizms Gold /10 #44
2018 Panini Prizm Prizms Green /149 #44
2018 Panini Prizm Prizms Purple Flash #44
2018 Panini Prizm Prizms Rainbow /24 #44
2018 Panini Prizm Prizms Red /75 #44
2018 Panini Prizm Prizms Red White and Blue #44
2018 Panini Prizm Prizms White /5 #44
2018 Panini Prizm Stars and Stripes #1
2018 Panini Prizm Stars and Stripes Prizms #1
2018 Panini Prizm Stars and Stripes Prizms Black /1 #1
2018 Panini Prizm Stars and Stripes Prizms Gold /10 #1
2018 Panini Prizm Team Tandems #5
2018 Panini Prizm Team Tandems Prizms #5
2018 Panini Prizm Team Tandems Prizms Black /1 #5
2018 Panini Prizm Team Tandems Prizms Gold /10 #5
2018 Panini Victory Lane #1
2018 Panini Victory Lane Black /1 #1
2018 Panini Victory Lane Blue /25 #1
2018 Panini Victory Lane Engineered to Perfection Materials Black /25 #12
2018 Panini Victory Lane Engineered to Perfection Materials Gold /199 #12
2018 Panini Victory Lane Engineered to Perfection Materials Green /99 #12
2018 Panini Victory Lane Engineered to Perfection Materials Laundry Tag /1 #12
2018 Panini Victory Lane Gold /99 #1
2018 Panini Victory Lane Green /5 #1
2018 Panini Victory Lane Octane Autographs /125 #17
2018 Panini Victory Lane Octane Autographs Black /1 #17
2018 Panini Victory Lane Octane Autographs Gold /99 #17
2018 Panini Victory Lane Pedal to the Metal #23
2018 Panini Victory Lane Pedal to the Metal #51
2018 Panini Victory Lane Pedal to the Metal Black /1 #23
2018 Panini Victory Lane Pedal to the Metal Black /1 #51
2018 Panini Victory Lane Pedal to the Metal Blue /25 #23
2018 Panini Victory Lane Pedal to the Metal Blue /25 #51
2018 Panini Victory Lane Pedal to the Metal Green /5 #23
2018 Panini Victory Lane Pedal to the Metal Green /5 #51
2018 Panini Victory Lane Printing Plates Black /1 #1
2018 Panini Victory Lane Printing Plates Cyan /1 #1
2018 Panini Victory Lane Printing Plates Magenta /1 #1
2018 Panini Victory Lane Printing Plates Yellow /1 #1
2018 Panini Victory Lane Race Ready Materials Black /5 #14
2018 Panini Victory Lane Red /49 #1
2018 Panini Victory Lane Signatures /125 #36
2018 Panini Victory Lane Signatures Black /1 #36
2018 Panini Victory Lane Signatures Gold /99 #36
2018 Panini Victory Lane Silver #1
2018 Panini Victory Lane Starting Grid #1
2018 Panini Victory Lane Starting Grid Black /1 #1
2018 Panini Victory Lane Starting Grid Blue /25 #1
2018 Panini Victory Lane Starting Grid Gold /99 #1
2018 Panini Victory Lane Starting Grid Green /5 #1
2018 Panini Victory Lane Starting Grid Printing Plates Black /1 #1
2018 Panini Victory Lane Starting Grid Printing Plates Cyan /1 #1
2018 Panini Victory Lane Starting Grid Printing Plates Magenta /1 #1
2018 Panini Victory Lane Starting Grid Printing Plates Yellow /1 #1
2018 Panini Victory Lane Starting Grid Red /49 #1
2018 Panini Victory Lane Victory Lane Prime Patches Associate Sponsor 1 /1 #24
2018 Panini Victory Lane Victory Lane Prime Patches Associate Sponsor 10 /1 #24
2018 Panini Victory Lane Victory Lane Prime Patches Associate Sponsor 2 /1 #24
2018 Panini Victory Lane Victory Lane Prime Patches Associate Sponsor 3 /1 #24
2018 Panini Victory Lane Victory Lane Prime Patches Associate Sponsor 4 /1 #24
2018 Panini Victory Lane Victory Lane Prime Patches Associate Sponsor 5 /1 #24
2018 Panini Victory Lane Victory Lane Prime Patches Associate Sponsor 6 /1 #24
2018 Panini Victory Lane Victory Lane Prime Patches Associate Sponsor 7 /1 #24
2018 Panini Victory Lane Victory Lane Prime Patches Associate Sponsor 8 /1 #24
2018 Panini Victory Lane Victory Lane Prime Patches Associate Sponsor 9 /1 #24
2018 Panini Victory Lane Victory Lane Prime Patches Car Manufacturer /1 #24
2018 Panini Victory Lane Victory Lane Prime Patches Firesuit Manufacturer /1 #24
2018 Panini Victory Lane Victory Lane Prime Patches Goodyear /2 #24
2018 Panini Victory Lane Victory Lane Prime Patches Nameplate /2 #24
2018 Panini Victory Lane Victory Lane Prime Patches NASCAR /1 #24
2018 Panini Victory Lane Victory Lane Prime Patches Series Sponsor /1 #24
2018 Panini Victory Lane Victory Lane Prime Patches Sunoco /1 #24
2019 Donruss #62
2019 Donruss #127A
2019 Donruss #127B
2019 Donruss Artist Proofs /25 #62
2019 Donruss Artist Proofs /25 #127A
2019 Donruss Artist Proofs /25 #127B
2019 Donruss Black /199 #62
2019 Donruss Black /199 #127A
2019 Donruss Black /199 #127B
2019 Donruss Gold /299 #62
2019 Donruss Gold /299 #127A
2019 Donruss Gold /299 #127B
2019 Donruss Gold Press Proofs /99 #62
2019 Donruss Gold Press Proofs /99 #127A
2019 Donruss Gold Press Proofs /99 #127B
2019 Donruss Optic #32
2019 Donruss Optic Blue Pulsar #32
2019 Donruss Optic Gold /10 #32
2019 Donruss Optic Gold Vinyl /1 #32
2019 Donruss Optic Holo #32
2019 Donruss Optic Red Wave #32
2019 Donruss Optic Signatures Gold Vinyl /1 #32
2019 Donruss Optic Signatures Holo /75 #32
2019 Donruss Press Proofs /49 #62
2019 Donruss Press Proofs /49 #127A
2019 Donruss Press Proofs /49 #127B
2019 Donruss Printing Plates Black /1 #62
2019 Donruss Printing Plates Black /1 #127A
2019 Donruss Printing Plates Black /1 #127B
2019 Donruss Printing Plates Cyan /1 #62
2019 Donruss Printing Plates Cyan /1 #127A
2019 Donruss Printing Plates Cyan /1 #127B
2019 Donruss Printing Plates Magenta /1 #62
2019 Donruss Printing Plates Magenta /1 #127A
2019 Donruss Printing Plates Magenta /1 #127B
2019 Donruss Printing Plates Yellow /1 #62
2019 Donruss Printing Plates Yellow /1 #127A
2019 Donruss Printing Plates Yellow /1 #127B
2019 Donruss Retro Relics '86 #10
2019 Donruss Retro Relics '86 Holo Black /10 #10
2019 Donruss Retro Relics '86 Holo Gold /25 #10
2019 Donruss Retro Relics '86 Red /225 #10
2019 Donruss Signature Series #38
2019 Donruss Signature Series Holo Black /10 #38
2019 Donruss Signature Series Holo Gold /25 #38
2019 Donruss Signature Series Red /99 #38
2019 Donruss Silver #62
2019 Donruss Silver #127A
2019 Donruss Silver #127B
2019 Panini Prime Clear Vision Signatures /25 #7
2019 Panini Prime Clear Vision Signatures Black /5 #7
2019 Panini Prime Clear Vision Signatures Holo Gold /10 #7
2019 Panini Prime Clear Vision Signatures Platinum Blue /1 #7
2019 Panini Prime Dual Material Autographs /25 #21
2019 Panini Prime Dual Material Autographs Black /5 #21
2019 Panini Prime Dual Material Autographs Holo Gold /10 #21
2019 Panini Prime Dual Material Autographs Laundry Tags /1 #21
2019 Panini Prime Jumbo Material Signatures Firesuit /5 #13
2019 Panini Prime Jumbo Material Signatures Firesuit Platinum Blue /1 #13
2019 Panini Prime Jumbo Material Signatures Sheet Metal /10 #13
2019 Panini Prime Jumbo Material Signatures Tire /25 #13
2019 Panini Prime NASCAR Shadowbox Signatures Car Number /10 #19
2019 Panini Prime NASCAR Shadowbox Signatures Manufacturer /1 #19
2019 Panini Prime NASCAR Shadowbox Signatures Sponsor /5 #19
2019 Panini Prime Prime Cars Die Cut Signatures Black /5 #14
2019 Panini Prime Prime Cars Die Cut Signatures Holo Gold /10 #14
2019 Panini Prime Prime Cars Die Cut Signatures Platinum Blue /1 #14
2019 Panini Prime Quad Materials Autographs /25 #12
2019 Panini Prime Quad Materials Autographs Black /5 #12
2019 Panini Prime Quad Materials Autographs Holo Gold /10 #12
2019 Panini Prime Quad Materials Autographs Laundry Tags /1 #12
2019 Panini Prime Race Used Duals Firesuits /50 #19
2019 Panini Prime Race Used Duals Firesuits Black /10 #19
2019 Panini Prime Race Used Duals Firesuits Holo Gold /25 #19
2019 Panini Prime Race Used Duals Firesuits Laundry Tags /1 #19
2019 Panini Prime Race Used Duals Sheet Metal Black /10 #19
2019 Panini Prime Race Used Duals Sheet Metal Platinum Blue /1 #19
2019 Panini Prime Race Used Duals Tires Black /10 #19
2019 Panini Prime Race Used Duals Tires Platinum Blue /1 #19
2019 Panini Prime Race Used Firesuits /50 #19
2019 Panini Prime Race Used Firesuits Black /10 #19
2019 Panini Prime Race Used Firesuits Holo Gold /25 #19
2019 Panini Prime Race Used Firesuits Laundry Tags /1 #19
2019 Panini Prime Race Used Sheet Metal Black /10 #19
2019 Panini Prime Race Used Sheet Metal Platinum Blue /1 #19
2019 Panini Prime Race Used Tires Black /10 #19
2019 Panini Prime Race Used Tires Platinum Blue /1 #19
2019 Panini Prime Shadowbox Signatures /25 #10
2019 Panini Prime Shadowbox Signatures Black /5 #10
2019 Panini Prime Shadowbox Signatures Holo Gold /10 #10
2019 Panini Prime Shadowbox Signatures Platinum Blue /1 #10
2019 Panini Prizm Endorsements Prizms #9
2019 Panini Prizm Endorsements Prizms Black /1 #9
2019 Panini Prizm Endorsements Prizms Blue /75 #9
2019 Panini Prizm Endorsements Prizms Camo #9
2019 Panini Prizm Endorsements Prizms Gold /10 #9
2019 Panini Prizm Endorsements Prizms Green /99 #9
2019 Panini Prizm Endorsements Prizms Rainbow /24 #9
2019 Panini Prizm Endorsements Prizms Red /50 #9
2019 Panini Prizm Endorsements Prizms Red White and Blue #9
2019 Panini Prizm Endorsements Prizms White /5 #9
2019 Panini Victory Lane Dual Swatch Signatures #8
2019 Panini Victory Lane Dual Swatch Signatures Gold /99 #8
2019 Panini Victory Lane Dual Swatch Signatures Laundry Tag /1 #8
2019 Panini Victory Lane Dual Swatch Signatures Platinum /1 #8
2019 Panini Victory Lane Dual Swatch Signatures Red /25 #8
2019 Panini Victory Lane Triple Swatches #6
2019 Panini Victory Lane Triple Swatches Gold /99 #6
2019 Panini Victory Lane Triple Swatches Laundry Tag /1 #6
2019 Panini Victory Lane Triple Swatches Platinum /1 #6
2019 Panini Victory Lane Triple Swatches Red /25 #6
2020 Donruss #37
2020 Donruss #178
2020 Donruss Black Numbers /1 #37
2020 Donruss Black Numbers /1 #178
2020 Donruss Black Trophy Club /1 #37
2020 Donruss Black Trophy Club /1 #178
2020 Donruss Blue /199 #178
2020 Donruss Blue /199 #37
2020 Donruss Carolina Blue #37
2020 Donruss Carolina Blue #178
2020 Donruss Green /99 #37
2020 Donruss Green /99 #178
2020 Donruss Optic #46
2020 Donruss Optic #83
2020 Donruss Optic Carolina Blue Wave #46
2020 Donruss Optic Carolina Blue Wave #83
2020 Donruss Optic Gold /10 #46
2020 Donruss Optic Gold /10 #83
2020 Donruss Optic Gold Vinyl /1 #46
2020 Donruss Optic Gold Vinyl /1 #83
2020 Donruss Optic Holo #46
2020 Donruss Optic Holo #83
2020 Donruss Optic Orange Pulsar #46
2020 Donruss Optic Orange Pulsar #83
2020 Donruss Optic Red Mojo #46
2020 Donruss Optic Red Mojo #83
2020 Donruss Optic Signatures Gold Vinyl /1 #46
2020 Donruss Optic Signatures Gold Vinyl /1 #83
2020 Donruss Optic Signatures Holo /99 #46
2020 Donruss Optic Signatures Holo /99 #83
2020 Donruss Orange #178
2020 Donruss Orange #37
2020 Donruss Pink /25 #37
2020 Donruss Pink /25 #178
2020 Donruss Printing Plates Black /1 #37
2020 Donruss Printing Plates Black /1 #178
2020 Donruss Printing Plates Cyan /1 #37
2020 Donruss Printing Plates Cyan /1 #178
2020 Donruss Printing Plates Magenta /1 #37
2020 Donruss Printing Plates Magenta /1 #178
2020 Donruss Printing Plates Yellow /1 #178
2020 Donruss Printing Plates Yellow /1 #37
2020 Donruss Purple /49 #37
2020 Donruss Purple /49 #178
2020 Donruss Race Day Relics #14
2020 Donruss Race Day Relics Holo Black /10 #14
2020 Donruss Race Day Relics Holo Gold /25 #14
2020 Donruss Race Day Relics Red /150 #14
2020 Donruss Red /299 #37
2020 Donruss Red /299 #178
2020 Donruss Signature Series Holo Black /1 #10
2020 Donruss Signature Series Holo Gold /25 #10
2020 Donruss Silver #37
2020 Donruss Silver #178

Paul Menard

2004 Press Pass Signings #45
2004 Press Pass Signings Gold /50 #42
2004 Press Pass Stealth #68
2004 Press Pass Stealth No Boundaries #NB6
2004 Press Pass Stealth Samples #X68
2004 Press Pass Stealth X-Ray /100 #68
2004 Press Pass Top Prospects Memorabilia /100 #PMG
2004 Press Pass Top Prospects Memorabilia /150 #PMS
2004 Press Pass Top Prospects Memorabilia /350 #PMT
2004 Press Pass Top Prospects Memorabilia /200 #PMSM
2004 Press Pass Trackside #34
2004 Press Pass Trackside Golden /100 #G34
2004 Press Pass Trackside Previews /5 #EB34
2004 Press Pass Trackside Samples #34
2006 Press Pass Optima #36
2006 Press Pass Optima Fan Favorite #FF22
2006 Press Pass Optima Gold /100 #G36
2006 Press Pass Signings #40
2006 Press Pass Signings Gold /50 #40
2006 Press Pass Signings Gold Red Ink #40
2006 Press Pass Stealth #34
2006 Press Pass Stealth Retail #34
2006 Press Pass Stealth X-Ray /100 #X34
2006 TRAKS #59
2006 TRAKS Previews /1 #59
2007 Press Pass #39
2007 Press Pass Autographs #32
2007 Press Pass Autographs Press Plates Cyan /1 #16
2007 Press Pass Blue #B39
2007 Press Pass Eclipse #86
2007 Press Pass Eclipse Gold /25 #G86
2007 Press Pass Eclipse Previews /1 #EB86
2007 Press Pass Eclipse Racing Champions #RC25
2007 Press Pass Eclipse Red /1 #R86
2007 Press Pass Eclipse Teammates Autographs /25 #1
2007 Press Pass Gold #G39
2007 Press Pass Legends Signature Series /25 #PM
2007 Press Pass Legends Sunday Swatches Bronze /199 #PMSS
2007 Press Pass Legends Sunday Swatches Gold /50 #PMSS
2007 Press Pass Legends Sunday Swatches Silver /99 #PMSS
2007 Press Pass Platinum /100 #P39
2007 Press Pass Premium #85
2007 Press Pass Premium Red /5 #R85
2007 Press Pass Previews /5 #EB39
2007 Press Pass Signings #46
2007 Press Pass Signings Blue /25 #20
2007 Press Pass Signings Gold /50 #37
2007 Press Pass Signings Press Plates Black /1 #30
2007 Press Pass Signings Press Plates Cyan /1 #29
2007 Press Pass Signings Press Plates Magenta /1 #31
2007 Press Pass Signings Press Plates Yellow /1 #30
2007 Press Pass Signings Silver /100 #36
2007 Press Pass Snapshots #SN29
2007 Press Pass Stealth #31
2007 Press Pass Stealth #71
2007 Press Pass Stealth Chrome #31
2007 Press Pass Stealth Chrome #71
2007 Press Pass Stealth Chrome Exclusives /99 #X31
2007 Press Pass Stealth Chrome Exclusives /99 #X71
2007 Press Pass Stealth Chrome Platinum /25 #P31
2007 Press Pass Stealth Chrome Platinum /25 #P71
2007 Press Pass Stealth Maximum Access #MA19
2007 Press Pass Stealth Maximum Access Autographs /25 #MA19
2007 Press Pass Stealth Previews /5 #EB31
2007 Traks #33
2007 Traks Gold #G33
2007 Traks Holofoil /50 #H33
2007 Traks Previews /5 #EB33
2007 Traks Red /10 #R33
2007 VIP #86
2007 VIP Previews /1 #EB86
2007 VIP Rookie Stripes /100 #RS2
2007 VIP Rookie Stripes Autographs /25 #RSPM
2007 Wheels American Thunder /365 #86A
2007 Wheels American Thunder /1 #86B
2007 Wheels American Thunder Autographed Hat Instant Winner /1 #AH22
2007 Wheels American Thunder Head to Toe /99 #HT10
2007 Wheels American Thunder Triple Hat /99 #TH19
2007 Wheels Autographs #28
2007 Wheels Autographs Press Plates Black /1 #27
2007 Wheels Autographs Press Plates Cyan /1 #27
2007 Wheels Autographs Press Plates Magenta /1 #27
2007 Wheels High Gear #35
2007 Wheels High Gear #87
2007 Wheels High Gear MPH /100 #M35
2007 Wheels High Gear MPH /100 #M87
2007 Wheels High Gear Previews /5 #EB35
2007 Wheels High Gear Previews /1 #EB87
2008 Press Pass #30
2008 Press Pass #84
2008 Press Pass Autographs #28
2008 Press Pass Autographs Press Plates Black /1 #23
2008 Press Pass Autographs Press Plates Cyan /1 #23
2008 Press Pass Autographs Press Plates Magenta /1 #23
2008 Press Pass Autographs Press Plates Yellow /1 #23
2008 Press Pass Blue #B30
2008 Press Pass Blue #B84
2008 Press Pass Eclipse #23
2008 Press Pass Eclipse Gold /25 #G23
2008 Press Pass Eclipse Previews /5 #EB23
2008 Press Pass Eclipse Red /1 #R23
2008 Press Pass Gold #G30
2008 Press Pass Gold #G84
2008 Press Pass Platinum /100 #P30
2008 Press Pass Platinum /100 #P84
2008 Press Pass Premium #12
2008 Press Pass Premium Hot Threads Drivers /120 #HTD14
2008 Press Pass Premium Hot Threads Drivers Gold /1 #HTD14
2008 Press Pass Premium Hot Threads Patches #HTP27
2008 Press Pass Premium Hot Threads Patches /22 #HTP28
2008 Press Pass Premium Hot Threads Patches /5 #HTP29
2008 Press Pass Premium Hot Threads Team /120 #HTT14
2008 Press Pass Premium Previews /5 #EB12
2008 Press Pass Premium Red /15 #12
2008 Press Pass Previews /5 #EB30
2008 Press Pass Signings #43
2008 Press Pass Signings Blue /25 #20
2008 Press Pass Signings Gold /50 #38
2008 Press Pass Signings Press Plates Black /1 #28
2008 Press Pass Signings Press Plates Black #PM
2008 Press Pass Signings Press Plates Cyan /1 #28
2008 Press Pass Signings Press Plates Cyan /1 #PM
2008 Press Pass Signings Press Plates Magenta /1 #28
2008 Press Pass Signings Press Plates Magenta #PM
2008 Press Pass Signings Press Plates Yellow /1 #28
2008 Press Pass Signings Silver /100 #37
2008 Press Pass Speedway #9
2008 Press Pass Speedway Cockpit #CP16
2008 Press Pass Speedway Gold #G9
2008 Press Pass Speedway Holofoil /50 #H9
2008 Press Pass Speedway Previews /5 #EB9
2008 Press Pass Speedway Red /10 #R9
2008 Press Pass Stealth #25
2008 Press Pass Stealth #65
2008 Press Pass Stealth Chrome #25
2008 Press Pass Stealth Chrome #65
2008 Press Pass Stealth Chrome Exclusives /25 #25
2008 Press Pass Stealth Chrome Exclusives /25 #65
2008 Press Pass Stealth Chrome Exclusives Gold /99 #25
2008 Press Pass Stealth Chrome Exclusives Gold /99 #65
2008 Press Pass Stealth Previews /5 #25
2008 Wheels American Thunder #23
2008 Wheels American Thunder #37
2008 Wheels American Thunder #69
2008 Wheels American Thunder Autographed Hat Winner /1 #WHPM
2008 Wheels American Thunder Previews /5 #23
2008 Wheels American Thunder Trackside Treasury Autographs #PM
2008 Wheels American Thunder Trackside Treasury Autographs Gold /25 #PM
2008 Wheels American Thunder Trackside Treasury Autographs Printing Plates Black /1 #PM
2008 Wheels American Thunder Trackside Treasury Autographs Printing Plates Cyan /1 #PM
2008 Wheels American Thunder Trackside Treasury Autographs Printing Plates Magenta /1 #PM
2008 Wheels American Thunder Trackside Treasury Autographs Printing Plates Yellow /1 #PM
2008 Wheels American Thunder Triple Hat /99 #TH18
2008 Wheels High Gear #23
2008 Wheels High Gear Final Standings /34 #F23
2008 Wheels High Gear MPH /100 #M23
2008 Wheels High Gear Previews /5 #EB23
2009 Element #23
2009 Element Previews /5 #23
2009 Element Radioactive /100 #23
2009 Press Pass #143
2009 Press Pass #174
2009 Press Pass Autographs Gold #34
2009 Press Pass Autographs Printing Plates Black /1 #31
2009 Press Pass Autographs Printing Plates Cyan /1 #31
2009 Press Pass Autographs Printing Plates Magenta /1 #31
2009 Press Pass Autographs Printing Plates Yellow /1 #31
2009 Press Pass Autographs Silver #35
2009 Press Pass Blue #143
2009 Press Pass Blue #174
2009 Press Pass Gold #143
2009 Press Pass Gold #174
2009 Press Pass Gold Holofoil /100 #143
2009 Press Pass Gold Holofoil /100 #174
2009 Press Pass Premium #34
2009 Press Pass Premium Hot Threads /299 #HTPM1
2009 Press Pass Premium Hot Threads /99 #HTPM2
2009 Press Pass Premium Hot Threads Multi-Color /25 #HTPM
2009 Press Pass Premium Hot Threads Patches /6 #HTP-PM
2009 Press Pass Premium Previews /5 #EB34
2009 Press Pass Premium Signatures #25
2009 Press Pass Premium Signatures Gold /25 #24
2009 Press Pass Previews /5 #EB143
2009 Press Pass Red #143
2009 Press Pass Red #174
2009 Press Pass Signings Blue /25 #32
2009 Press Pass Signings Gold #32
2009 Press Pass Signings Green /10 #32
2009 Press Pass Signings Orange /65 #32
2009 Press Pass Signings Printing Plates Black /1 #32
2009 Press Pass Signings Printing Plates Cyan /1 #32
2009 Press Pass Signings Purple /45 #32
2009 Press Pass Stealth #24
2009 Press Pass Stealth Chrome #24
2009 Press Pass Stealth Chrome Brushed Metal /25 #24
2009 Press Pass Stealth Chrome Gold /99 #24
2009 Press Pass Stealth Confidential Classified Bronze #PC15
2009 Press Pass Stealth Confidential Secret Silver #PC15
2009 Press Pass Stealth Confidential Top Secret Gold /25 #PC15
2009 Press Pass Stealth Previews /5 #EB24
2009 VIP #23
2009 VIP Get A Grip /120 #GGPM
2009 VIP Get A Grip Holofoil /10 #GGPM
2009 VIP Guest List #GG18
2009 VIP Leadfoot /150 #LFPM
2009 VIP Leadfoot Holofoil /10 #LFPM
2009 VIP Previews /5 #23
2009 VIP Purple /25 #23
2009 Wheels Autographs #47
2009 Wheels Autographs Press Plates Black /1 #PM
2009 Wheels Autographs Press Plates Cyan /1 #PM
2009 Wheels Autographs Press Plates Magenta /1 #PM
2009 Wheels Autographs Press Plates Yellow /1 #PM
2009 Wheels Main Event #32
2009 Wheels Main Event Fast Pass Purple /25 #32
2009 Wheels Main Event Hat Dance Double /99 #HDPM
2009 Wheels Main Event Hat Dance Patch /10 #HDPM
2009 Wheels Main Event Marks Clubs #40
2009 Wheels Main Event Marks Diamonds /50 #40
2009 Wheels Main Event Marks Hearts /10 #40
2009 Wheels Main Event Marks Printing Plates Black /1 #36
2009 Wheels Main Event Marks Printing Plates Cyan /1 #36
2009 Wheels Main Event Marks Printing Plates Magenta /1 #36
2009 Wheels Main Event Marks Printing Plates Yellow /1 #36
2009 Wheels Main Event Marks Spades /1 #40
2009 Wheels Main Event Playing Cards Blue #6S
2009 Wheels Main Event Playing Cards Red #6S
2009 Wheels Main Event Previews /5 #32
2010 Element #32
2010 Element Blue /35 #32
2010 Element Green #32
2010 Element Previews /5 #EB32
2010 Element Purple /25 #32
2010 Element Red Target #32
2010 Press Pass #31
2010 Press Pass Autographs #36
2010 Press Pass Autographs Printing Plates Black /1 #27
2010 Press Pass Autographs Printing Plates Cyan /1 #33
2010 Press Pass Autographs Printing Plates Magenta /1 #31
2010 Press Pass Autographs Printing Plates Yellow /1 #30
2010 Press Pass Blue #31
2010 Press Pass By The Numbers #BN28
2010 Press Pass Gold #31
2010 Press Pass Holofoil /100 #31
2010 Press Pass Premium #29
2010 Press Pass Premium Purple /25 #29
2010 Press Pass Premium Signatures #PSPM
2010 Press Pass Premium Signatures Red Ink /24 #PSPM
2010 Press Pass Previews /5 #31
2010 Press Pass Purple /25 #31
2010 Press Pass Showcase Classic Collections Ink /15 #CCIOWN
2010 Press Pass Showcase Classic Collections Ink Gold /10 #CCIOWN
2010 Press Pass Signings Blue /10 #39
2010 Press Pass Signings Gold /50 #39
2010 Press Pass Signings Red /15 #39
2010 Press Pass Signings Silver /90 #38
2010 Press Pass Stealth #24
2010 Press Pass Stealth Black and White #24
2010 Press Pass Stealth Previews /5 #24
2010 Press Pass Stealth Purple /25 #24
2010 Wheels Autographs #36
2010 Wheels Autographs Printing Plates Black /1 #36
2010 Wheels Autographs Printing Plates Cyan /1 #36
2010 Wheels Autographs Printing Plates Magenta /1 #36
2010 Wheels Autographs Printing Plates Yellow /1 #36
2010 Wheels Autographs Target /10 #24
2010 Wheels Main Event #24
2010 Wheels Main Event Blue #24
2010 Wheels Main Event Marks Autographs /35 #40
2010 Wheels Main Event Marks Autographs Black /1 #39
2010 Wheels Main Event Marks Autographs Blue /15 #40
2010 Wheels Main Event Marks Autographs Red /25 #40
2010 Wheels Main Event Purple /25 #24
2011 Element Autographs /125 #38
2011 Element Autographs Blue /10 #38
2011 Element Autographs Gold /25 #37
2011 Element Autographs Printing Plates Black /1 #38
2011 Element Autographs Printing Plates Cyan /1 #38
2011 Element Autographs Printing Plates Magenta /1 #38
2011 Element Autographs Printing Plates Yellow /1 #38
2011 Element Autographs Silver /50 #37
2011 Press Pass #25
2011 Press Pass #80
2011 Press Pass Autographs Blue /9 #38
2011 Press Pass Autographs Bronze /78 #38
2011 Press Pass Autographs Gold /21 #37
2011 Press Pass Autographs Printing Plates Black /1 #39
2011 Press Pass Autographs Printing Plates Cyan /1 #39
2011 Press Pass Autographs Printing Plates Magenta /1 #39
2011 Press Pass Autographs Printing Plates Yellow /1 #39
2011 Press Pass Autographs Silver /52 #39
2011 Press Pass Blue Holofoil /10 #25
2011 Press Pass Blue Holofoil /10 #80
2011 Press Pass Blue Retail #25
2011 Press Pass Blue Retail #80
2011 Press Pass Eclipse #23
2011 Press Pass Eclipse #89
2011 Press Pass Eclipse Blue #23
2011 Press Pass Eclipse Blue #89
2011 Press Pass Eclipse Gold /55 #23
2011 Press Pass Eclipse Gold /55 #89
2011 Press Pass Eclipse Previews /5 #EB23
2011 Press Pass Eclipse Purple /25 #23
2011 Press Pass FanFare #28
2011 Press Pass FanFare Autographs Blue /5 #51
2011 Press Pass FanFare Autographs Bronze /65 #51
2011 Press Pass FanFare Autographs Gold /50 #51
2011 Press Pass FanFare Autographs Printing Plates Black /1 #51
2011 Press Pass FanFare Autographs Printing Plates Cyan /1 #51
2011 Press Pass FanFare Autographs Printing Plates Magenta /1 #51
2011 Press Pass FanFare Autographs Printing Plates Yellow /1 #51
2011 Press Pass FanFare Autographs Silver /25 #51
2011 Press Pass FanFare Blue Die Cuts #28
2011 Press Pass FanFare Emerald /25 #28
2011 Press Pass FanFare Holofoil Die Cuts #28
2011 Press Pass FanFare Magnificent Materials /199 #MMPM
2011 Press Pass FanFare Magnificent Materials Holofoil /50 #MMPM
2011 Press Pass FanFare Ruby Die Cuts /15 #28
2011 Press Pass FanFare Sapphire /10 #28
2011 Press Pass FanFare Silver /25 #28
2011 Press Pass Geared Up Holofoil /50 #GUPM
2011 Press Pass Gold /50 #25
2011 Press Pass Gold /50 #80
2011 Press Pass Premium #27
2011 Press Pass Premium Hot Threads /150 #HTPM
2011 Press Pass Premium Hot Threads Multi Color /25 #HTPM
2011 Press Pass Premium Hot Threads Secondary Color /99 #HTPM
2011 Press Pass Premium Purple /25 #27
2011 Press Pass Premium Signatures /200 #PSPM
2011 Press Pass Previews /5 #EB25
2011 Press Pass Purple /25 #25
2011 Press Pass Showcase /499 #57
2011 Press Pass Showcase Classic Collections Firesuit /45 #CCMRCR
2011 Press Pass Showcase Classic Collections Firesuit Patches /5 #CCMRCR
2011 Press Pass Showcase Classic Collections Ink /25 #CCMRCR
2011 Press Pass Showcase Classic Collections Ink Gold /5 #CCMRCR
2011 Press Pass Showcase Classic Collections Ink Melting /1 #CCMRCR
2011 Press Pass Showcase Classic Collections Sheet Metal /99 #CCMRCR
2011 Press Pass Showcase Gold /125 #57
2011 Press Pass Showcase Green /25 #57
2011 Press Pass Showcase Melting /1 #57
2011 Press Pass Signings Black and White /10 #PPSPM
2011 Press Pass Signings Brushed Metal /60 #PPSPM
2011 Press Pass Signings Holofoil /25 #PPSPM
2011 Press Pass Signings Printing Plates Black /1 #PPSPM
2011 Press Pass Signings Printing Plates Cyan /1 #PPSPM
2011 Press Pass Signings Printing Plates Magenta /1 #PPSPM
2011 Press Pass Signings Printing Plates Yellow /1 #PPSPM
2011 Press Pass Stealth #49
2011 Press Pass Stealth #78
2011 Press Pass Stealth Black and White /25 #49
2011 Press Pass Stealth Black and White /25 #78
2011 Press Pass Stealth Holofoil /99 #49
2011 Press Pass Stealth Holofoil /99 #78
2011 Press Pass Stealth Metal of Honor Medal of Honor /50 #BAPM
2011 Press Pass Stealth Metal of Honor Purple Heart /25 #MHPM
2011 Press Pass Stealth Metal of Honor Silver Star /99 #BAPM
2011 Press Pass Stealth Purple /25 #49
2011 Wheels Main Event #27
2011 Wheels Main Event Black and White #27
2011 Wheels Main Event Blue /75 #27
2011 Wheels Main Event Green /1 #27
2011 Wheels Main Event Marks Autographs Blue /10 #MEPM
2011 Wheels Main Event Marks Autographs Gold /25 #MEPM
2011 Wheels Main Event Marks Autographs Silver /65 #MEPM
2011 Wheels Main Event Red /20 #27
2012 Press Pass #27
2012 Press Pass #88
2012 Press Pass #92
2012 Press Pass Autographs Blue /10 #PPAPM
2012 Press Pass Autographs Printing Plates Black /1 #PPAPM
2012 Press Pass Autographs Printing Plates Cyan /1 #PPAPM
2012 Press Pass Autographs Printing Plates Magenta /1 #PPAPM
2012 Press Pass Autographs Printing Plates Yellow /1 #PPAPM
2012 Press Pass Autographs Red /35 #PPAPM
2012 Press Pass Autographs Silver /199 #PPAPM
2012 Press Pass Blue #27
2012 Press Pass Blue #88
2012 Press Pass Blue #92
2012 Press Pass Blue Holofoil /35 #27
2012 Press Pass Blue Holofoil /35 #88
2012 Press Pass Blue Holofoil /35 #92
2012 Press Pass Burning Rubber Gold /99 #BRPM
2012 Press Pass Burning Rubber Holofoil /25 #BRPM
2012 Press Pass Burning Rubber Prime Cuts /25 #BRPM
2012 Press Pass Burning Rubber Purple /15 #BRPM
2012 Press Pass Fanfare #31
2012 Press Pass Fanfare Autographs Blue /25 #PM
2012 Press Pass Fanfare Autographs Gold /99 #PM
2012 Press Pass Fanfare Autographs Red /75 #PM
2012 Press Pass Fanfare Autographs Silver /199 #PM
2012 Press Pass Fanfare Blue Foil Die Cuts #31
2012 Press Pass Fanfare Diamond /5 #31
2012 Press Pass Fanfare Holofoil Die Cuts #31
2012 Press Pass Fanfare Magnificent Materials /250 #MMPM
2012 Press Pass Fanfare Magnificent Materials Dual Swatches /50 #MMPM
2012 Press Pass Fanfare Magnificent Materials Dual Swatches Melting /10 #MMPM
2012 Press Pass Fanfare Magnificent Materials Gold /125 #MMPM
2012 Press Pass Fanfare Magnificent Materials Signatures /99 #PM
2012 Press Pass Fanfare Magnificent Materials Signatures Blue /25 #PM
2012 Press Pass Fanfare Power Rankings #PR15
2012 Press Pass Fanfare Sapphire /20 #31
2012 Press Pass Fanfare Silver /25 #31
2012 Press Pass Gold #27
2012 Press Pass Gold #88
2012 Press Pass Gold #92
2012 Press Pass Ignite #27
2012 Press Pass Ignite #64
2012 Press Pass Ignite Materials Autographs Gun Metal /20 #IMPM
2012 Press Pass Ignite Materials Autographs Red /5 #IMPM
2012 Press Pass Ignite Materials Autographs Silver /125 #IMPM
2012 Press Pass Ignite Materials Gun Metal /99 #IMPM
2012 Press Pass Ignite Materials Red /10 #IMPM
2012 Press Pass Ignite Materials Silver #IMPM
2012 Press Pass Ignite Profile #P3
2012 Press Pass Ignite Proofs Black and White /50 #27
2012 Press Pass Ignite Proofs Black and White /50 #64
2012 Press Pass Ignite Proofs Cyan #27
2012 Press Pass Ignite Proofs Cyan #64
2012 Press Pass Ignite Proofs Magenta #27
2012 Press Pass Ignite Proofs Magenta #64
2012 Press Pass Ignite Proofs Yellow /10 #27
2012 Press Pass Ignite Proofs Yellow /10 #64
2012 Press Pass Power Picks Blue /50 #44
2012 Press Pass Power Picks Gold /50 #44
2012 Press Pass Power Picks Holofoil /10 #44
2012 Press Pass Purple /35 #27
2012 Press Pass Purple /35 #88
2012 Press Pass Purple /35 #92
2012 Press Pass Redline #29
2012 Press Pass Redline Black /99 #29
2012 Press Pass Redline Cyan /50 #29
2012 Press Pass Redline Magenta /15 #29
2012 Press Pass Redline Signatures Blue /5 #RSPM
2012 Press Pass Redline Signatures Gold /25 #RSPM
2012 Press Pass Redline Signatures Holofoil /10 #RSPM
2012 Press Pass Redline Signatures Melting /1 #RSPM
2012 Press Pass Redline Signatures Red /50 #RSPM
2012 Press Pass Redline Yellow /1 #29
2012 Press Pass Showcase /499 #55
2012 Press Pass Showcase Classic Collections Ink /10 #CCMRCR
2012 Press Pass Showcase Classic Collections Ink Gold /5 #CCMRCR
2012 Press Pass Showcase Classic Collections Ink Melting /1 #CCMRCR
2012 Press Pass Showcase Classic Collections Memorabilia /99 #CCMRCR
2012 Press Pass Showcase Classic Collections Memorabilia Gold /50 #CCMRCR
2012 Press Pass Showcase Classic Collections Memorabilia Melting /5 #CCMRCR
2012 Press Pass Showcase Gold /125 #55
2012 Press Pass Showcase Green /5 #55
2012 Press Pass Showcase Melting /1 #55
2012 Press Pass Showcase Purple /1 #55
2012 Press Pass Showcase Red /25 #55
2012 Press Pass Snapshots #SS27
2012 Total Memorabilia #24
2012 Total Memorabilia Black and White /99 #24
2012 Total Memorabilia Dual Swatch Gold /75 #TMPM
2012 Total Memorabilia Dual Swatch Holofoil /25 #TMPM
2012 Total Memorabilia Dual Swatch Melting /5 #TMPM
2012 Total Memorabilia Dual Swatch Silver /99 #TMPM
2012 Total Memorabilia Gold /275 #24
2012 Total Memorabilia Jumbo Swatch Gold /50 #TMPM
2012 Total Memorabilia Jumbo Swatch Holofoil /10 #TMPM
2012 Total Memorabilia Jumbo Swatch Melting /1 #TMPM
2012 Total Memorabilia Quad Swatch Gold /25 #TMPM
2012 Total Memorabilia Quad Swatch Holofoil /10 #TMPM
2012 Total Memorabilia Quad Swatch Melting /1 #TMPM
2012 Total Memorabilia Quad Swatch Silver /50 #TMPM
2012 Total Memorabilia Red Retail /250 #24
2012 Total Memorabilia Single Swatch Gold /99 #TMPM
2012 Total Memorabilia Single Swatch Holofoil /50 #TMPM
2012 Total Memorabilia Single Swatch Melting /10 #TMPM
2012 Total Memorabilia Single Swatch Silver /199 #TMPM
2012 Total Memorabilia Triple Swatch Gold /50 #TMPM
2012 Total Memorabilia Triple Swatch Holofoil /25 #TMPM
2012 Total Memorabilia Triple Swatch Melting /1 #TMPM

tal Memorabilia Triple Swatch Silver /99 #TMPM
ess Pass #32
ess Pass Color Proofs Black #32
ess Pass Color Proofs Cyan /35 #32
ess Pass Color Proofs Magenta #32
ess Pass Color Proofs Yellow /5 #32
ress Pass Fanfare #41
ess Pass Fanfare #42
ess Pass Fanfare Autographs Blue /1 #PM
ess Pass Fanfare Autographs Gold /5 #PM
ress Pass Fanfare Autographs Green /6 #PM
ress Pass Fanfare Autographs Red /1 #PM
ress Pass Fanfare Autographs Silver /10 #PM
ress Pass Fanfare Diamond Die Cuts /5 #41
ress Pass Fanfare Diamond Die Cuts /5 #42
ress Pass Fanfare Green /3 #41
ress Pass Fanfare Green /3 #42
ress Pass Fanfare Holofoil Die Cuts #41
ress Pass Fanfare Holofoil Die Cuts #42
ress Pass Fanfare Magnificent Jumbo Materials Signatures /10 #PM
ress Pass Fanfare Magnificent Materials Dual Swatches /50 #PM
ress Pass Fanfare Magnificent Materials Dual Swatches Melting /10 #PM
ress Pass Fanfare Magnificent Materials Gold /50 #PM
ress Pass Fanfare Magnificent Materials Jumbo Swatches /25 #PM
ress Pass Fanfare Magnificent Materials Signatures /99 #PM
ress Pass Fanfare Magnificent Materials Signatures Blue /25 #PM
ress Pass Fanfare Magnificent Materials Silver /199 #PM
ress Pass Fanfare Red Foil Die Cuts #41
ress Pass Fanfare Red Foil Die Cuts #42
ress Pass Fanfare Sapphire /20 #41
ress Pass Fanfare Sapphire /20 #42
ress Pass Fanfare Signature Ride Autographs /10 #PM
ress Pass Fanfare Signature Ride Autographs Blue /1 #PM
ress Pass Fanfare Signature Ride Autographs Red /5 #PM
ress Pass Fanfare Silver /25 #41
ress Pass Fanfare Silver /25 #42
ress Pass Ignite #26
ress Pass Ignite #64
ress Pass Ignite Great American Treads Autographs Blue Holofoil /20 #GATPM
ress Pass Ignite Great American Treads Autographs Red /1 #GATPM
ress Pass Ignite Hot Threads Blue Holofoil /99 #HTPM
ress Pass Ignite Hot Threads Patch Red /10 #HTPM
ress Pass Ignite Hot Threads Silver #HTPM
ress Pass Ignite Ink Black /75 #IIPM
ress Pass Ignite Ink Blue /25 #IIPM
ress Pass Ignite Ink Red /5 #IIPM
Press Pass Ignite Proofs Black and White /50 #26
Press Pass Ignite Proofs Black and White /50 #64
Press Pass Ignite Proofs Cyan #26
Press Pass Ignite Proofs Cyan #64
Press Pass Ignite Proofs Magenta #26
Press Pass Ignite Proofs Magenta #64
Press Pass Ignite Proofs Yellow /5 #26
Press Pass Ignite Proofs Yellow /5 #64
Press Pass Power Picks Blue /99 #45
Press Pass Power Picks Gold /50 #45
Press Pass Power Picks Holofoil /10 #45
Press Pass Redline #36
Press Pass Redline Black /99 #36
Press Pass Redline Cyan /50 #36
Press Pass Redline Magenta /15 #36
Press Pass Redline Relics Blue /5 #RRPM
Press Pass Redline Relics Gold /10 #RRPM
Press Pass Redline Relics Melting /1 #RRPM
Press Pass Redline Relics Red /50 #RRPM
Press Pass Redline Relics Silver /25 #RRPM
Press Pass Redline Signatures Blue /50 #RSPM
3 Press Pass Redline Signatures Gold /5 #RSPM
3 Press Pass Redline Signatures Holo /27 #RSPM
3 Press Pass Redline Signatures Melting /1 #RSPM
3 Press Pass Redline Signatures Red /95 #RSPM
3 Press Pass Redline Yellow /1 #36
3 Press Pass Showcase /349 #21
3 Press Pass Showcase /349 #58
3 Press Pass Showcase Black /1 #21
3 Press Pass Showcase Black /1 #58
3 Press Pass Showcase Blue /25 #21
3 Press Pass Showcase Blue /25 #58
3 Press Pass Showcase Classic Collections Ink Gold /5 #CCIRCR
3 Press Pass Showcase Classic Collections Ink Melting /1 #CCIRCR
3 Press Pass Showcase Classic Collections Ink Red /1 #CCIRCR
3 Press Pass Showcase Classic Collections Memorabilia Gold /25 #CCMRCR
3 Press Pass Showcase Classic Collections Memorabilia Melting /5 #CCMRCR
3 Press Pass Showcase Classic Collections Memorabilia Silver /75 #CCMRCR
13 Press Pass Showcase Gold /99 #21
3 Press Pass Showcase Gold /99 #58
3 Press Pass Showcase Green /20 #21
3 Press Pass Showcase Green /20 #58
3 Press Pass Showcase Purple /13 #21
3 Press Pass Showcase Purple /13 #58
3 Press Pass Showcase Red /10 #21
3 Press Pass Showcase Red /10 #58
3 Press Pass Signings Blue /1 #PM
13 Press Pass Signings Gold /25 #PM
13 Press Pass Signings Holofoil /10 #PM
13 Press Pass Signings Printing Plates Black /1 #PM
13 Press Pass Signings Printing Plates Cyan /1 #PM
13 Press Pass Signings Printing Plates Magenta /1 #PM
13 Press Pass Signings Printing Plates Yellow /1 #PM
13 Press Pass Signings Silver /65 #PM
13 Total Memorabilia #29
13 Total Memorabilia Black and White /99 #29
13 Total Memorabilia Dual Swatch Gold /199 #TMPM
13 Total Memorabilia Gold /275 #29
13 Total Memorabilia Red #29
13 Total Memorabilia Single Swatch Silver /385 #TMPM
13 Total Memorabilia Triple Swatch Holofoil /99 #TMPM
14 Press Pass #28
14 Press Pass American Thunder #28
14 Press Pass American Thunder #54
14 Press Pass American Thunder Autographs Blue /10 #ATAPM
14 Press Pass American Thunder Autographs Red /5 #ATAPM
14 Press Pass American Thunder Autographs White /25 #ATAPM
14 Press Pass American Thunder Black and White /50 #28
14 Press Pass American Thunder Black and White /50 #54
14 Press Pass American Thunder Brothers In Arms Autographs Blue /5 #BARCR
14 Press Pass American Thunder Brothers In Arms Autographs Red /1 #BARCR
014 Press Pass American Thunder Brothers In Arms Autographs White /10 #BARCR
014 Press Pass American Thunder Brothers In Arms Relics Blue /25 #BARCR
014 Press Pass American Thunder Brothers In Arms Relics Red /5 #BARCR
014 Press Pass American Thunder Brothers In Arms Relics Silver /50 #BARCR
014 Press Pass American Thunder Class A Uniforms Blue /99 #CAUPM
014 Press Pass American Thunder Class A Uniforms Flag /1 #CAUPM
014 Press Pass American Thunder Class A Uniforms Red /10 #CAUPM
014 Press Pass American Thunder Class A Uniforms Silver #CAUPM
014 Press Pass American Thunder Cyan #28
014 Press Pass American Thunder Cyan #54
014 Press Pass American Thunder Magenta #28

2014 Press Pass American Thunder Magenta #54
2014 Press Pass American Thunder Top Speed #TS10
2014 Press Pass American Thunder With Honors #WH1
2014 Press Pass American Thunder Yellow /5 #28
2014 Press Pass American Thunder Yellow /5 #54
2014 Press Pass Color Proofs Black /70 #28
2014 Press Pass Color Proofs Cyan /35 #28
2014 Press Pass Color Proofs Magenta #28
2014 Press Pass Color Proofs Yellow /5 #28
2014 Press Pass Five Star Classic Compilations Autographed Patch Booklet /1 #CCPM1
2014 Press Pass Five Star Classic Compilations Autographed Patch Booklet /1 #CCPM2
2014 Press Pass Five Star Classic Compilations Autographed Patch Booklet /1 #CCPM3
2014 Press Pass Five Star Classic Compilations Autographed Patch Booklet /1 #CCPM4
2014 Press Pass Five Star Classic Compilations Autographed Patch Booklet /1 #CCPM5
2014 Press Pass Five Star Classic Compilations Autographed Patch Booklet /1 #CCPM6
2014 Press Pass Five Star Classic Compilations Autographed Patch Booklet /1 #CCPM7
2014 Press Pass Five Star Classic Compilations Autographed Patch Booklet /1 #CCPM8
2014 Press Pass Five Star Classic Compilations Autographed Patch Booklet /1 #CCPM9
2014 Press Pass Five Star Classic Compilations Autographed Patch Booklet /1 #CCPM10
2014 Press Pass Five Star Classic Compilations Autographed Patch Booklet /1 #CCPM11
2014 Press Pass Five Star Classic Compilations Autographed Patch Booklet /1 #CCPM12
2014 Press Pass Five Star Classic Compilations Combo Autographs Blue /5 #CCRCR
2014 Press Pass Five Star Classic Compilations Combo Autographs Melting /1 #CCRCR
2014 Press Pass Gold #28
2014 Press Pass Redline #40
2014 Press Pass Redline Black /75 #40
2014 Press Pass Redline Blue Foil #40
2014 Press Pass Redline Cyan /50 #40
2014 Press Pass Redline Green National Convention /5 #40
2014 Press Pass Redline Magenta /10 #40
2014 Press Pass Redline Relic Autographs Blue /10 #RRSEPM
2014 Press Pass Redline Relic Autographs Gold /25 #RRSEPM
2014 Press Pass Redline Relic Autographs Melting /1 #RRSEPM
2014 Press Pass Redline Relic Autographs Red /50 #RRSEPM
2014 Press Pass Redline Relics Blue /25 #RRPM
2014 Press Pass Redline Relics Gold /50 #RRPM
2014 Press Pass Redline Relics Melting /1 #RRPM
2014 Press Pass Redline Relics Red /75 #RRPM
2014 Press Pass Redline Signatures Blue /25 #RSPM
2014 Press Pass Redline Signatures Gold /50 #RSPM
2014 Press Pass Redline Signatures Melting /10 #RSPM
2014 Press Pass Redline Signatures Red /65 #RSPM
2014 Press Pass Redline Yellow /1 #40
2014 Press Pass Signings Gold /50 #PPSPM
2014 Press Pass Signings Holofoil /10 #PPSPM
2014 Press Pass Signings Melting /1 #PPSPM
2014 Press Pass Signings Printing Plates Black /1 #PPSPM
2014 Press Pass Signings Printing Plates Cyan /1 #PPSPM
2014 Press Pass Signings Printing Plates Magenta /1 #PPSPM
2014 Press Pass Signings Printing Plates Yellow /1 #PPSPM
2014 Press Pass Signings Silver /100 #PPSPM
2014 Total Memorabilia #21
2014 Total Memorabilia Black and White /99 #21
2014 Total Memorabilia Dual Swatch Gold /150 #TMPM
2014 Total Memorabilia Gold /175 #21
2014 Total Memorabilia Quad Swatch Melting /25 #TMPM
2014 Total Memorabilia Red #21
2014 Total Memorabilia Single Swatch Silver /275 #TMPM
2014 Total Memorabilia Triple Swatch Blue /99 #TMPM
2015 Press Pass #27
2015 Press Pass Cup Chase #27
2015 Press Pass Cup Chase Blue /25 #27
2015 Press Pass Cup Chase Gold /75 #27
2015 Press Pass Cup Chase Green /10 #27
2015 Press Pass Cup Chase Melting /1 #27
2015 Press Pass Purple #27
2015 Press Pass Red #27
2015 Press Pass Signature Series Blue /25 #SSPM
2015 Press Pass Signature Series Gold /50 #SSPM
2015 Press Pass Signature Series Green /10 #SSPM
2015 Press Pass Signature Series Melting /1 #SSPM
2015 Press Pass Signings Blue /110 #PPSPM
2015 Press Pass Signings Gold #PPSPM
2015 Press Pass Signings Melting /10 #PPSPM
2015 Press Pass Signings Red /75 #PPSPM
2016 Certified #20
2016 Certified Mirror Black /1 #20
2016 Certified Mirror Blue /50 #20
2016 Certified Mirror Gold /25 #20
2016 Certified Mirror Green /5 #20
2016 Certified Mirror Orange /99 #20
2016 Certified Mirror Purple /10 #20
2016 Certified Mirror Red /75 #20
2016 Certified Mirror Silver /99 #20
2016 Certified Potential Signatures /30 #34
2016 Certified Potential Signatures Mirror Black /1 #34
2016 Certified Potential Signatures Mirror Blue /20 #34
2016 Certified Potential Signatures Mirror Gold /15 #34
2016 Certified Potential Signatures Mirror Green /5 #34
2016 Certified Potential Signatures Mirror Orange /95 #34
2016 Certified Potential Signatures Mirror Purple /10 #34
2016 Certified Potential Signatures Mirror Red /25 #34
2016 Certified Potential Signatures Mirror Silver /95 #34
2016 Certified Signatures /30 #48
2016 Certified Signatures Mirror Black /1 #48
2016 Certified Signatures Mirror Blue /20 #48
2016 Certified Signatures Mirror Gold /15 #48
2016 Certified Signatures Mirror Green /5 #48
2016 Certified Signatures Mirror Orange /49 #48
2016 Certified Signatures Mirror Purple /10 #48
2016 Certified Signatures Mirror Red /25 #48
2016 Certified Signatures Mirror Silver /49 #48
2016 Certified Sprint Cup Swatches /199 #33
2016 Certified Sprint Cup Swatches Mirror Black /1 #33
2016 Certified Sprint Cup Swatches Mirror Blue /50 #33
2016 Certified Sprint Cup Swatches Mirror Gold /25 #33
2016 Certified Sprint Cup Swatches Mirror Green /5 #33
2016 Certified Sprint Cup Swatches Mirror Orange /85 #33
2016 Certified Sprint Cup Swatches Mirror Purple /10 #33
2016 Certified Sprint Cup Swatches Mirror Red /75 #33
2016 Certified Sprint Cup Swatches Mirror Silver /80 #33
2016 Panini National Treasures Combo Materials /25 #12
2016 Panini National Treasures Combo Materials Black /5 #12
2016 Panini National Treasures Combo Materials Blue /1 #12
2016 Panini National Treasures Combo Materials Gold /10 #12
2016 Panini National Treasures Combo Materials Printing Plates Black /1 #12
2016 Panini National Treasures Combo Materials Printing Plates Cyan /1 #12
2016 Panini National Treasures Combo Materials Printing Plates Magenta /1 #12
2016 Panini National Treasures Combo Materials Printing Plates Yellow /1 #12
2016 Panini National Treasures Combo Materials Silver /15 #12

2016 Panini National Treasures Dual Driver Materials /25 #3
2016 Panini National Treasures Dual Driver Materials /25 #11
2016 Panini National Treasures Dual Driver Materials Black /5 #3
2016 Panini National Treasures Dual Driver Materials Black /5 #11
2016 Panini National Treasures Dual Driver Materials Blue /1 #3
2016 Panini National Treasures Dual Driver Materials Blue /1 #11
2016 Panini National Treasures Dual Driver Materials Gold /10 #3
2016 Panini National Treasures Dual Driver Materials Gold /10 #11
2016 Panini National Treasures Dual Driver Materials Printing Plates Black /1 #3
2016 Panini National Treasures Dual Driver Materials Printing Plates Black /1 #11
2016 Panini National Treasures Dual Driver Materials Printing Plates Cyan /1 #3
2016 Panini National Treasures Dual Driver Materials Printing Plates Cyan /1 #11
2016 Panini National Treasures Dual Driver Materials Printing Plates Magenta /1 #3
2016 Panini National Treasures Dual Driver Materials Printing Plates Magenta /1 #11
2016 Panini National Treasures Dual Driver Materials Printing Plates Yellow /1 #3
2016 Panini National Treasures Dual Driver Materials Printing Plates Yellow /1 #11
2016 Panini National Treasures Dual Driver Materials Silver /15 #3
2016 Panini National Treasures Dual Driver Materials Silver /15 #11
2016 Panini National Treasures Dual Signatures /25 #4
2016 Panini National Treasures Dual Signatures Black /10 #4
2016 Panini National Treasures Dual Signatures Blue /1 #4
2016 Panini National Treasures Dual Signatures Gold /15 #4
2016 Panini National Treasures Jumbo Firesuit Patch Signature Booklet Associate Sponsor 1 /1 #22
2016 Panini National Treasures Jumbo Firesuit Patch Signature Booklet Associate Sponsor 10 /1 #22
2016 Panini National Treasures Jumbo Firesuit Patch Signature Booklet Associate Sponsor 11 /1 #22
2016 Panini National Treasures Jumbo Firesuit Patch Signature Booklet Associate Sponsor 12 /1 #22
2016 Panini National Treasures Jumbo Firesuit Patch Signature Booklet Associate Sponsor 13 /1 #22
2016 Panini National Treasures Jumbo Firesuit Patch Signature Booklet Associate Sponsor 14 /1 #22
2016 Panini National Treasures Jumbo Firesuit Patch Signature Booklet Associate Sponsor 15 /1 #22
2016 Panini National Treasures Jumbo Firesuit Patch Signature Booklet Associate Sponsor 16 /1 #22
2016 Panini National Treasures Jumbo Firesuit Patch Signature Booklet Associate Sponsor 17 /1 #22
2016 Panini National Treasures Jumbo Firesuit Patch Signature Booklet Associate Sponsor 18 /1 #22
2016 Panini National Treasures Jumbo Firesuit Patch Signature Booklet Associate Sponsor 19 /1 #22
2016 Panini National Treasures Jumbo Firesuit Patch Signature Booklet Associate Sponsor 2 /1 #22
2016 Panini National Treasures Jumbo Firesuit Patch Signature Booklet Associate Sponsor 20 /1 #22
2016 Panini National Treasures Jumbo Firesuit Patch Signature Booklet Associate Sponsor 3 /1 #22
2016 Panini National Treasures Jumbo Firesuit Patch Signature Booklet Associate Sponsor 4 /1 #22
2016 Panini National Treasures Jumbo Firesuit Patch Signature Booklet Associate Sponsor 5 /1 #22
2016 Panini National Treasures Jumbo Firesuit Patch Signature Booklet Associate Sponsor 6 /1 #22
2016 Panini National Treasures Jumbo Firesuit Patch Signature Booklet Associate Sponsor 7 /1 #22
2016 Panini National Treasures Jumbo Firesuit Patch Signature Booklet Associate Sponsor 8 /1 #22
2016 Panini National Treasures Jumbo Firesuit Patch Signature Booklet Associate Sponsor 9 /1 #22
2016 Panini National Treasures Jumbo Firesuit Patch Signature Booklet Flag /1 #22
2016 Panini National Treasures Jumbo Firesuit Patch Signature Booklet Goodyear /2 #22
2016 Panini National Treasures Jumbo Firesuit Patch Signature Booklet Manufacturers Logo /2 #22
2016 Panini National Treasures Jumbo Firesuit Patch Signature Booklet Nameplate /2 #22
2016 Panini National Treasures Jumbo Firesuit Patch Signature Booklet NASCAR /1 #22
2016 Panini National Treasures Jumbo Firesuit Patch Signature Booklet Sprint Cup Logo /1 #22
2016 Panini National Treasures Jumbo Firesuit Patch Signature Booklet Sunoco /1 #22
2016 Panini National Treasures Jumbo Firesuit Signatures Black /5 #22
2016 Panini National Treasures Jumbo Firesuit Signatures Blue /1 #22
2016 Panini National Treasures Jumbo Firesuit Signatures Gold /10 #22
2016 Panini National Treasures Jumbo Firesuit Signatures Printing Plates Black /1 #22
2016 Panini National Treasures Jumbo Firesuit Signatures Printing Plates Cyan /1 #22
2016 Panini National Treasures Jumbo Firesuit Signatures Printing Plates Magenta /1 #22
2016 Panini National Treasures Jumbo Firesuit Signatures Printing Plates Yellow /1 #22
2016 Panini National Treasures Jumbo Firesuit Signatures Silver /15 #22
2016 Panini National Treasures Signature Dual Materials Black /5 #20
2016 Panini National Treasures Signature Dual Materials Blue /1 #20
2016 Panini National Treasures Signature Dual Materials Gold /10 #20
2016 Panini National Treasures Signature Dual Materials Printing Plates Black /1 #20
2016 Panini National Treasures Signature Dual Materials Printing Plates Cyan /1 #20
2016 Panini National Treasures Signature Dual Materials Printing Plates Magenta /1 #20
2016 Panini National Treasures Signature Dual Materials Printing Plates Yellow /1 #20
2016 Panini National Treasures Signature Firesuit Materials Black /5 #21
2016 Panini National Treasures Signature Firesuit Materials Blue /1 #21
2016 Panini National Treasures Signature Firesuit Materials Gold /10 #21
2016 Panini National Treasures Signature Firesuit Materials Laundry Tag /1 #21
2016 Panini National Treasures Signature Firesuit Materials Printing Plates Black /1 #21
2016 Panini National Treasures Signature Firesuit Materials Printing Plates Cyan /1 #21
2016 Panini National Treasures Signature Firesuit Materials Printing Plates Magenta /1 #21
2016 Panini National Treasures Signature Firesuit Materials Printing Plates Yellow /1 #21
2016 Panini National Treasures Signature Sheet Metal Materials Black /5 #20
2016 Panini National Treasures Signature Sheet Metal Materials Blue /1 #20
2016 Panini National Treasures Signature Sheet Metal Materials Gold /10 #20
2016 Panini National Treasures Signature Sheet Metal Materials Printing Plates Black /1 #20
2016 Panini National Treasures Signature Sheet Metal Materials Printing Plates Cyan /1 #20
2016 Panini National Treasures Signature Sheet Metal Materials Printing Plates Magenta /1 #20
2016 Panini National Treasures Signature Sheet Metal Materials Printing Plates Yellow /1 #20
2016 Panini National Treasures Signatures Blue /1 #18
2016 Panini National Treasures Signatures Printing Plates Black /1 #18
2016 Panini National Treasures Signatures Printing Plates Cyan /1 #18
2016 Panini National Treasures Signatures Printing Plates Magenta /1 #18
2016 Panini National Treasures Signatures Printing Plates Yellow /1 #18

2016 Panini National Treasures Six Signatures /25 #3
2016 Panini National Treasures Six Signatures Black /10 #3
2016 Panini National Treasures Six Signatures Blue /1 #3
2016 Panini National Treasures Six Signatures Gold /15 #3
2016 Panini National Treasures Timelines Black /5 #13
2016 Panini National Treasures Timelines Blue /1 #13
2016 Panini National Treasures Timelines Printing Plates Black /1 #13
2016 Panini National Treasures Timelines Printing Plates Cyan /1 #13
2016 Panini National Treasures Timelines Printing Plates Magenta /1 #13
2016 Panini National Treasures Timelines Printing Plates Yellow /1 #13
2016 Panini National Treasures Timelines Signatures Black /5 #12
2016 Panini National Treasures Timelines Signatures Blue /1 #12
2016 Panini National Treasures Timelines Signatures Gold /10 #12
2016 Panini National Treasures Timelines Signatures Printing Plates Black /1 #12
2016 Panini National Treasures Timelines Signatures Printing Plates Cyan /1 #12
2016 Panini National Treasures Timelines Signatures Printing Plates Magenta /1 #12
2016 Panini National Treasures Timelines Signatures Printing Plates Yellow /1 #12
2016 Panini National Treasures Trio Driver Materials /25 #6
2016 Panini National Treasures Trio Driver Materials Black /5 #6
2016 Panini National Treasures Trio Driver Materials Blue /1 #6
2016 Panini National Treasures Trio Driver Materials Gold /10 #6
2016 Panini National Treasures Trio Driver Materials Printing Plates Black /1 #6
2016 Panini National Treasures Trio Driver Materials Printing Plates Cyan /1 #6
2016 Panini National Treasures Trio Driver Materials Printing Plates Magenta /1 #6
2016 Panini National Treasures Trio Driver Materials Printing Plates Yellow /1 #6
2016 Panini National Treasures Trio Driver Materials Silver /15 #6
2016 Panini Prizm #27
2016 Panini Prizm #90
2016 Panini Prizm Autographs Prizms #48
2016 Panini Prizm Autographs Prizms Black /3 #48
2016 Panini Prizm Autographs Prizms Blue Flag /75 #48
2016 Panini Prizm Autographs Prizms Camo /27 #48
2016 Panini Prizm Autographs Prizms Checkered Flag /1 #48
2016 Panini Prizm Autographs Prizms Gold /10 #48
2016 Panini Prizm Autographs Prizms Green Flag /99 #48
2016 Panini Prizm Autographs Prizms Rainbow /24 #48
2016 Panini Prizm Autographs Prizms Red Flag /50 #48
2016 Panini Prizm Autographs Prizms Red White and Blue /25 #48
2016 Panini Prizm Autographs Prizms White Flag /5 #48
2016 Panini Prizm Firesuit Fabrics /149 #15
2016 Panini Prizm Firesuit Fabrics Prizms Blue Flag /75 #15
2016 Panini Prizm Firesuit Fabrics Prizms Checkered Flag /1 #15
2016 Panini Prizm Firesuit Fabrics Prizms Green Flag /99 #15
2016 Panini Prizm Firesuit Fabrics Prizms Red Flag /25 #15
2016 Panini Prizm Firesuit Fabrics Team /249 #15
2016 Panini Prizm Firesuit Fabrics Team Prizms Blue Flag /75 #15
2016 Panini Prizm Firesuit Fabrics Team Prizms Checkered Flag /1 #15
2016 Panini Prizm Firesuit Fabrics Team Prizms Green Flag /99 #15
2016 Panini Prizm Firesuit Fabrics Team Prizms Red Flag /25 #15
2016 Panini Prizm Prizms #27
2016 Panini Prizm Prizms #90
2016 Panini Prizm Prizms Black /3 #27
2016 Panini Prizm Prizms Black /3 #90
2016 Panini Prizm Prizms Blue Flag /99 #27
2016 Panini Prizm Prizms Blue Flag /99 #90
2016 Panini Prizm Prizms Camo /27 #27
2016 Panini Prizm Prizms Camo /27 #90
2016 Panini Prizm Prizms Checkered Flag /1 #27
2016 Panini Prizm Prizms Checkered Flag /1 #90
2016 Panini Prizm Prizms Gold /10 #27
2016 Panini Prizm Prizms Gold /10 #90
2016 Panini Prizm Prizms Green Flag /149 #27
2016 Panini Prizm Prizms Green Flag /149 #90
2016 Panini Prizm Prizms Rainbow /24 #27
2016 Panini Prizm Prizms Rainbow /24 #90
2016 Panini Prizm Prizms Red Flag /75 #27
2016 Panini Prizm Prizms Red Flag /75 #90
2016 Panini Prizm Prizms Red White and Blue #27
2016 Panini Prizm Prizms Red White and Blue #90
2016 Panini Prizm Prizms White Flag /5 #27
2016 Panini Prizm Prizms White Flag /5 #90
2016 Panini Torque #24
2016 Panini Torque Artist Proof /50 #24
2016 Panini Torque Blackout /1 #24
2016 Panini Torque Blue /125 #24
2016 Panini Torque Gold #24
2016 Panini Torque Holo Gold /5 #24
2016 Panini Torque Holo Silver /10 #24
2016 Panini Torque Horsepower Heroes #14
2016 Panini Torque Horsepower Heroes Gold /199 #14
2016 Panini Torque Horsepower Heroes Holo Silver /99 #14
2016 Panini Torque Jumbo Firesuit Autographs /100 #14
2016 Panini Torque Jumbo Firesuit Autographs Blue /75 #14
2016 Panini Torque Jumbo Firesuit Autographs Green /25 #14
2016 Panini Torque Jumbo Firesuit Autographs Purple /10 #14
2016 Panini Torque Jumbo Firesuit Autographs Red /40 #14
2016 Panini Torque Pairings Materials /249 #19
2016 Panini Torque Pairings Materials /125 #28
2016 Panini Torque Pairings Materials Blue /99 #19
2016 Panini Torque Pairings Materials Blue /99 #28
2016 Panini Torque Pairings Materials Green /25 #19
2016 Panini Torque Pairings Materials Green /25 #28
2016 Panini Torque Pairings Materials Purple /10 #19
2016 Panini Torque Pairings Materials Purple /10 #28
2016 Panini Torque Pairings Materials Red /49 #19
2016 Panini Torque Pairings Materials Red /49 #28
2016 Panini Torque Printing Plates Black /1 #24
2016 Panini Torque Printing Plates Cyan /1 #24
2016 Panini Torque Printing Plates Magenta /1 #24
2016 Panini Torque Printing Plates Yellow /1 #24
2016 Panini Torque Purple /25 #24
2016 Panini Torque Quad Materials /199 #5
2016 Panini Torque Quad Materials Blue /99 #5
2016 Panini Torque Quad Materials Green /25 #5
2016 Panini Torque Quad Materials Purple /10 #5
2016 Panini Torque Quad Materials Red /49 #5
2016 Panini Torque Red /99 #24
2016 Panini Torque Special Paint #9
2016 Panini Torque Special Paint Gold /199 #9
2016 Panini Torque Special Paint Holo Silver /99 #9
2016 Panini Torque Test Proof Black /1 #24
2016 Panini Torque Test Proof Cyan /1 #24
2016 Panini Torque Test Proof Magenta /1 #24
2016 Panini Torque Test Proof Yellow /1 #24
2017 Donruss #20
2017 Donruss #56
2017 Donruss #115
2017 Donruss Artist Proof /25 #20
2017 Donruss Artist Proof /25 #56
2017 Donruss Artist Proof /25 #115
2017 Donruss Blue Foil /299 #20
2017 Donruss Blue Foil /299 #56
2017 Donruss Blue Foil /299 #115
2017 Donruss Gold Foil /499 #20
2017 Donruss Gold Foil /499 #56
2017 Donruss Gold Foil /499 #115
2017 Donruss Gold Press Proof /99 #20
2017 Donruss Gold Press Proof /99 #56
2017 Donruss Gold Press Proof /99 #115
2017 Donruss Green Foil /199 #20

2017 Donruss Green Foil /199 #56
2017 Donruss Green Foil /199 #115
2017 Donruss Press Proof /49 #20
2017 Donruss Press Proof /49 #56
2017 Donruss Press Proof /49 #115
2017 Donruss Printing Plates Black /1 #20
2017 Donruss Printing Plates Black /1 #56
2017 Donruss Printing Plates Black /1 #115
2017 Donruss Printing Plates Cyan /1 #20
2017 Donruss Printing Plates Cyan /1 #56
2017 Donruss Printing Plates Cyan /1 #115
2017 Donruss Printing Plates Magenta /1 #20
2017 Donruss Printing Plates Magenta /1 #56
2017 Donruss Printing Plates Magenta /1 #115
2017 Donruss Printing Plates Yellow /1 #20
2017 Donruss Printing Plates Yellow /1 #56
2017 Donruss Printing Plates Yellow /1 #115
2017 Donruss Rubber Relics #38
2017 Donruss Rubber Relics Holo Black /10 #38
2017 Donruss Rubber Relics Holo Gold /17 #38
2017 Donruss Studio Signatures #10
2017 Donruss Studio Signatures Holo Black /1 #10
2017 Donruss Studio Signatures Holo Gold /25 #10
2018 Panini Prime Autograph Materials /10 #22
2018 Panini Prime Autograph Materials Black /1 #22
2018 Panini Prime Autograph Materials Holo Gold /5 #22
2018 Panini Prime Autograph Materials Laundry Tag /1 #22
2018 Panini Prime Clear Silhouettes /99 #24
2018 Panini Prime Clear Silhouettes Black /1 #24
2018 Panini Prime Clear Silhouettes Dual /99 #26
2018 Panini Prime Clear Silhouettes Dual Black /1 #26
2018 Panini Prime Clear Silhouettes Dual Holo Gold /50 #26
2018 Panini Prime Clear Silhouettes Holo Gold /50 #24
2018 Panini Prime Dual Material Autographs /10 #18
2018 Panini Prime Dual Material Autographs Black /1 #18
2018 Panini Prime Dual Material Autographs Holo Gold /5 #18
2018 Panini Prime Dual Material Autographs Laundry Tag /1 #18
2018 Panini Prime Hats Off Button /1 #14
2018 Panini Prime Hats Off Eyelet /6 #14
2018 Panini Prime Hats Off Headband /36 #14
2018 Panini Prime Hats Off Laundry Tag /1 #14
2018 Panini Prime Hats Off New Era /1 #14
2018 Panini Prime Hats Off Number /2 #14
2018 Panini Prime Hats Off Sponsor Logo /5 #14
2018 Panini Prime Hats Off Team Logo /2 #14
2018 Panini Prime Prime Jumbo Associate Sponsor 1 /1 #60
2018 Panini Prime Prime Jumbo Associate Sponsor 10 /1 #60
2018 Panini Prime Prime Jumbo Associate Sponsor 11 /1 #60
2018 Panini Prime Prime Jumbo Associate Sponsor 12 /1 #60
2018 Panini Prime Prime Jumbo Associate Sponsor 13 /1 #60
2018 Panini Prime Prime Jumbo Associate Sponsor 14 /1 #60
2018 Panini Prime Prime Jumbo Associate Sponsor 15 /1 #60
2018 Panini Prime Prime Jumbo Associate Sponsor 2 /1 #60
2018 Panini Prime Prime Jumbo Associate Sponsor 3 /1 #60
2018 Panini Prime Prime Jumbo Associate Sponsor 4 /1 #60
2018 Panini Prime Prime Jumbo Associate Sponsor 5 /1 #60
2018 Panini Prime Prime Jumbo Associate Sponsor 6 /1 #60
2018 Panini Prime Prime Jumbo Associate Sponsor 7 /1 #60
2018 Panini Prime Prime Jumbo Associate Sponsor 8 /1 #60
2018 Panini Prime Prime Jumbo Associate Sponsor 9 /1 #60
2018 Panini Prime Prime Jumbo Car Manufacturer /1 #60
2018 Panini Prime Prime Jumbo Firesuit Manufacturer /1 #60
2018 Panini Prime Prime Jumbo Flag Patch /1 #60
2018 Panini Prime Prime Jumbo Glove Manufacturer Patch /1 #60
2018 Panini Prime Prime Jumbo Glove Name Patch /1 #60
2018 Panini Prime Prime Jumbo Glove Number Patch /1 #60
2018 Panini Prime Prime Jumbo Nameplate /1 #60
2018 Panini Prime Prime Jumbo NASCAR /1 #60
2018 Panini Prime Prime Jumbo Prime Colors /4 #60
2018 Panini Prime Prime Jumbo Shoe Brand Logo /1 #60
2018 Panini Prime Prime Jumbo Shoe Name Patch /1 #60
2018 Panini Prime Prime Jumbo Shoe Number Patch /1 #60
2018 Panini Prime Prime Jumbo Sunoco /1 #60
2018 Panini Prime Prime Number Signatures /50 #14
2018 Panini Prime Prime Number Signatures Black /1 #14
2018 Panini Prime Prime Number Signatures Holo Gold /25 #14
2018 Panini Prime Quad Material Autographs /50 #20
2018 Panini Prime Quad Material Autographs Black /1 #20
2018 Panini Prime Quad Material Autographs Holo Gold /25 #20
2018 Panini Prime Quad Material Autographs Laundry Tag /1 #20
2018 Panini Prime Race Used Duals Firesuit /50 #27
2018 Panini Prime Race Used Duals Firesuit Black /1 #27
2018 Panini Prime Race Used Duals Firesuit Holo Gold /25 #27
2018 Panini Prime Race Used Duals Firesuit Laundry Tag /1 #27
2018 Panini Prime Race Used Duals Sheet Metal /50 #27
2018 Panini Prime Race Used Duals Sheet Metal Black /1 #27
2018 Panini Prime Race Used Duals Sheet Metal Holo Gold /25 #27
2018 Panini Prime Race Used Duals Tire /50 #27
2018 Panini Prime Race Used Duals Tire Black /1 #27
2018 Panini Prime Race Used Duals Tire Holo Gold /25 #27
2018 Panini Prime Race Used Firesuits Black /1 #31
2018 Panini Prime Race Used Firesuits Holo Gold /25 #31
2018 Panini Prime Race Used Firesuits Laundry Tag /1 #31
2018 Panini Prime Race Used Sheet Metal /50 #31
2018 Panini Prime Race Used Sheet Metal Black /1 #31
2018 Panini Prime Race Used Sheet Metal Holo Gold /25 #31
2018 Panini Prime Race Used Tires Black /1 #31
2018 Panini Prime Race Used Tires Holo Gold /25 #31
2018 Panini Prime Race Used Trios Firesuit /50 #13
2018 Panini Prime Race Used Trios Firesuit Black /1 #13
2018 Panini Prime Race Used Trios Firesuit Holo Gold /25 #13
2018 Panini Prime Race Used Trios Firesuit Laundry Tag /1 #13
2018 Panini Prime Race Used Trios Sheet Metal /50 #13
2018 Panini Prime Race Used Trios Sheet Metal Black /1 #13
2018 Panini Prime Race Used Trios Sheet Metal Holo Gold /25 #13
2018 Panini Prime Race Used Trios Tire /50 #13
2018 Panini Prime Race Used Trios Tire Black /1 #13
2018 Panini Prime Race Used Trios Tire Holo Gold /25 #13
2018 Panini Prime Signature Tires /10 #14
2018 Panini Prime Signature Tires Black /1 #14
2018 Panini Prime Signature Tires Holo Gold /5 #14
2018 Panini Prime Triple Material Autographs /35 #23
2018 Panini Prime Triple Material Autographs Black /1 #23
2018 Panini Prime Triple Material Autographs Holo Gold /10 #23
2018 Panini Prime Triple Material Autographs Laundry Tag /1 #23
2018 Panini Prizm #14
2018 Panini Prizm Autographs Prizms #11
2018 Panini Prizm Autographs Prizms Black /1 #11
2018 Panini Prizm Autographs Prizms Blue /75 #11
2018 Panini Prizm Autographs Prizms Camo #11
2018 Panini Prizm Autographs Prizms Gold /10 #11
2018 Panini Prizm Autographs Prizms Green /99 #11
2018 Panini Prizm Autographs Prizms Rainbow /24 #11
2018 Panini Prizm Autographs Prizms Red /50 #11
2018 Panini Prizm Autographs Prizms Red White and Blue /125 #11
2018 Panini Prizm Autographs Prizms White /5 #11
2018 Panini Prizm Prizms #14
2018 Panini Prizm Prizms Black /1 #14
2018 Panini Prizm Prizms Blue /99 #14
2018 Panini Prizm Prizms Camo #14
2018 Panini Prizm Prizms Gold /10 #14
2018 Panini Prizm Prizms Green /149 #14
2018 Panini Prizm Prizms Purple Flash #14
2018 Panini Prizm Prizms Rainbow /24 #14
2018 Panini Prizm Prizms Red /75 #14
2018 Panini Prizm Prizms Red White and Blue #14
2018 Panini Prizm Prizms White /5 #14
2018 Panini Prizm Team Tandems #7

2018 Panini Prizm Team Tandems Prizms #7
2018 Panini Prizm Team Tandems Prizms Black /1 #7
2018 Panini Prizm Team Tandems Prizms Gold /10 #7
2018 Panini Victory Lane #15
2018 Panini Victory Lane Black /1 #15
2018 Panini Victory Lane Blue /25 #15
2018 Panini Victory Lane Engineered to Perfection Materials Black /25 #20
2018 Panini Victory Lane Engineered to Perfection Materials Green /99 #20
2018 Panini Victory Lane Gold /99 #15
2018 Panini Victory Lane Green /5 #15
2018 Panini Victory Lane Octane Autographs /125 #31
2018 Panini Victory Lane Octane Autographs Black /1 #31
2018 Panini Victory Lane Octane Autographs Gold /99 #31
2018 Panini Victory Lane Pedal to the Metal #43
2018 Panini Victory Lane Pedal to the Metal Black /1 #43
2018 Panini Victory Lane Pedal to the Metal Blue /25 #43
2018 Panini Victory Lane Pedal to the Metal Green /5 #43
2018 Panini Victory Lane Printing Plates Black /1 #15
2018 Panini Victory Lane Printing Plates Cyan /1 #15
2018 Panini Victory Lane Printing Plates Magenta /1 #15
2018 Panini Victory Lane Printing Plates Yellow /1 #15
2018 Panini Victory Lane Race Ready Dual Materials Black /25 #17
2018 Panini Victory Lane Race Ready Dual Materials Green /99 #17
2018 Panini Victory Lane Red /49 #15
2018 Panini Victory Lane Silver #15
2018 Panini Victory Lane Starting Grid #15
2018 Panini Victory Lane Starting Grid Black /1 #15
2018 Panini Victory Lane Starting Grid Blue /25 #15
2018 Panini Victory Lane Starting Grid Gold /99 #15
2018 Panini Victory Lane Starting Grid Green /5 #15
2018 Panini Victory Lane Starting Grid Printing Plates Black /1 #15
2018 Panini Victory Lane Starting Grid Printing Plates Cyan /1 #15
2018 Panini Victory Lane Starting Grid Printing Plates Magenta /1 #15
2018 Panini Victory Lane Starting Grid Printing Plates Yellow /1 #15
2018 Panini Victory Lane Starting Grid Red /49 #15
2018 Panini Victory Lane Victory Lane Prime Patches Associate Sponsor 1 /1 #6
2018 Panini Victory Lane Victory Lane Prime Patches Associate Sponsor 10 /1 #6
2018 Panini Victory Lane Victory Lane Prime Patches Associate Sponsor 2 /1 #6
2018 Panini Victory Lane Victory Lane Prime Patches Associate Sponsor 3 /1 #6
2018 Panini Victory Lane Victory Lane Prime Patches Associate Sponsor 4 /1 #6
2018 Panini Victory Lane Victory Lane Prime Patches Associate Sponsor 5 /1 #6
2018 Panini Victory Lane Victory Lane Prime Patches Associate Sponsor 6 /1 #6
2018 Panini Victory Lane Victory Lane Prime Patches Associate Sponsor 7 /1 #6
2018 Panini Victory Lane Victory Lane Prime Patches Associate Sponsor 8 /1 #6
2018 Panini Victory Lane Victory Lane Prime Patches Associate Sponsor 9 /1 #6
2018 Panini Victory Lane Victory Lane Prime Patches Car Manufacturer /1 #6
2018 Panini Victory Lane Victory Lane Prime Patches Firesuit Manufacturer /1 #6
2018 Panini Victory Lane Victory Lane Prime Patches Nameplate /2 #6
2018 Panini Victory Lane Victory Lane Prime Patches NASCAR /1 #6
2018 Panini Victory Lane Victory Lane Prime Patches Series Sponsor /1 #6
2018 Panini Victory Lane Victory Lane Prime Patches Sunoco /1 #6
2019 Donruss #77
2019 Donruss #124
2019 Donruss Artist Proofs /25 #77
2019 Donruss Artist Proofs /25 #124
2019 Donruss Black /199 #77
2019 Donruss Black /199 #124
2019 Donruss Gold /299 #77
2019 Donruss Gold /299 #124
2019 Donruss Gold Press Proofs /99 #77
2019 Donruss Gold Press Proofs /99 #124
2019 Donruss Optic #29
2019 Donruss Optic #81
2019 Donruss Optic Blue Pulsar #29
2019 Donruss Optic Blue Pulsar /1 #81
2019 Donruss Optic Gold /10 #29
2019 Donruss Optic Gold /10 #81
2019 Donruss Optic Gold Vinyl /1 #29
2019 Donruss Optic Gold Vinyl /1 #81
2019 Donruss Optic Holo #29
2019 Donruss Optic Holo #81
2019 Donruss Optic Red Wave #29
2019 Donruss Optic Red Wave /1 #81
2019 Donruss Optic Signatures Gold Vinyl /1 #81
2019 Donruss Optic Signatures Gold Vinyl /1 #29
2019 Donruss Optic Signatures Holo /75 #29
2019 Donruss Optic Signatures Holo /75 #81
2019 Donruss Press Proofs /49 #77
2019 Donruss Press Proofs /49 #124
2019 Donruss Printing Plates Black /1 #77
2019 Donruss Printing Plates Black /1 #124
2019 Donruss Printing Plates Cyan /1 #77
2019 Donruss Printing Plates Cyan /1 #124
2019 Donruss Printing Plates Magenta /1 #77
2019 Donruss Printing Plates Magenta /1 #124
2019 Donruss Printing Plates Yellow /1 #77
2019 Donruss Printing Plates Yellow /1 #124
2019 Donruss Race Day Relics #21
2019 Donruss Race Day Relics Holo Black /10 #21
2019 Donruss Race Day Relics Holo Gold /25 #21
2019 Donruss Race Day Relics Red /185 #21
2019 Donruss Signature Series #30
2019 Donruss Signature Series Holo Black /10 #30
2019 Donruss Signature Series Holo Gold /25 #30
2019 Donruss Signature Series Red /49 #30
2019 Donruss Silver #77
2019 Donruss Silver #124
2019 Panini Prime /50 #18
2019 Panini Prime /50 #50
2019 Panini Prime Black /10 #18
2019 Panini Prime Black /10 #50
2019 Panini Prime Emerald /5 #18
2019 Panini Prime Emerald /5 #50
2019 Panini Prime Jumbo Material Signatures Firesuit /2 #22
2019 Panini Prime Jumbo Material Signatures Firesuit Platinum Blue /1 #22
2019 Panini Prime Jumbo Material Signatures Sheet Metal /5 #22
2019 Panini Prime Platinum Blue /1 #18
2019 Panini Prime Platinum Blue /1 #50
2019 Panini Prime Prime Jumbo Associate Sponsor 1 /1 #60
2019 Panini Prime Prime Jumbo Associate Sponsor 1 /1 #61
2019 Panini Prime Prime Jumbo Associate Sponsor 10 /1 #60
2019 Panini Prime Prime Jumbo Associate Sponsor 11 /1 #60
2019 Panini Prime Prime Jumbo Associate Sponsor 12 /1 #60
2019 Panini Prime Prime Jumbo Associate Sponsor 13 /1 #60
2019 Panini Prime Prime Jumbo Associate Sponsor 2 /1 #60
2019 Panini Prime Prime Jumbo Associate Sponsor 2 /1 #61
2019 Panini Prime Prime Jumbo Associate Sponsor 3 /1 #60
2019 Panini Prime Prime Jumbo Associate Sponsor 3 /1 #61
2019 Panini Prime Prime Jumbo Associate Sponsor 4 /1 #60
2019 Panini Prime Prime Jumbo Associate Sponsor 4 /1 #61
2019 Panini Prime Prime Jumbo Associate Sponsor 5 /1 #60
2019 Panini Prime Prime Jumbo Associate Sponsor 5 /1 #61
2019 Panini Prime Prime Jumbo Associate Sponsor 6 /1 #60
2019 Panini Prime Prime Jumbo Associate Sponsor 6 /1 #61
2019 Panini Prime Prime Jumbo Associate Sponsor 7 /1 #60
2019 Panini Prime Prime Jumbo Associate Sponsor 8 /1 #60

2019 Panini Prime Prime Jumbo Associate Sponsor 9 /1 #60
2019 Panini Prime Prime Jumbo Car Manufacturer /1 #60
2019 Panini Prime Prime Jumbo Car Manufacturer /1 #61
2019 Panini Prime Prime Jumbo Firesuit Manufacturer /1 #60
2019 Panini Prime Prime Jumbo Firesuit Manufacturer /1 #61
2019 Panini Prime Prime Jumbo Flag Patch /1 #60
2019 Panini Prime Prime Jumbo Flag Patch /1 #61
2019 Panini Prime Prime Jumbo Glove Manufacturer Patch /1 #60
2019 Panini Prime Prime Jumbo Glove Manufacturer Patch /1 #61
2019 Panini Prime Prime Jumbo Glove Name Patch /1 #60
2019 Panini Prime Prime Jumbo Glove Number Patch /1 #60
2019 Panini Prime Prime Jumbo Glove Number Patch /1 #61
2019 Panini Prime Prime Jumbo Goodyear /1 #60
2019 Panini Prime Prime Jumbo Goodyear /2 #61
2019 Panini Prime Prime Jumbo Nameplate /1 #60
2019 Panini Prime Prime Jumbo Nameplate /1 #61
2019 Panini Prime Prime Jumbo NASCAR /1 #60
2019 Panini Prime Prime Jumbo NASCAR /1 #61
2019 Panini Prime Prime Jumbo Prime Colors /7 #60
2019 Panini Prime Prime Jumbo Prime Colors /13 #61
2019 Panini Prime Prime Jumbo Series Sponsor /1 #61
2019 Panini Prime Prime Jumbo Shoe Brand Logo /1 #60
2019 Panini Prime Prime Jumbo Shoe Brand Logo /1 #61
2019 Panini Prime Prime Jumbo Shoe Name Patch /1 #60
2019 Panini Prime Prime Jumbo Shoe Name Patch /1 #61
2019 Panini Prime Prime Jumbo Shoe Number Patch /1 #60
2019 Panini Prime Prime Jumbo Sunoco /1 #60
2019 Panini Prime Prime Jumbo Sunoco /1 #61
2019 Panini Prime Prime Number Die Cut Signatures Black /2 #10
2019 Panini Prime Prime Number Die Cut Signatures Holo Gold /3 #10
2019 Panini Prime Prime Number Die Cut Signatures Platinum Blue /1 #10
2019 Panini Prizm #18
2019 Panini Prizm Prizms #18
2019 Panini Prizm Prizms Black /1 #18
2019 Panini Prizm Prizms Blue /75 #18
2019 Panini Prizm Prizms Camo #18
2019 Panini Prizm Prizms Flash #18
2019 Panini Prizm Prizms Gold /10 #18
2019 Panini Prizm Prizms Green /99 #18
2019 Panini Prizm Prizms Rainbow /24 #18
2019 Panini Prizm Prizms Red /50 #18
2019 Panini Prizm Prizms Red White and Blue #18
2019 Panini Prizm Prizms White /5 #18
2019 Panini Prizm Prizms White Sparkle #18
2019 Panini Victory Lane #18
2019 Panini Victory Lane Black /1 #18
2019 Panini Victory Lane Gold /25 #18
2019 Panini Victory Lane Pedal to the Metal #15
2019 Panini Victory Lane Pedal to the Metal Black /1 #15
2019 Panini Victory Lane Pedal to the Metal Gold /25 #15
2019 Panini Victory Lane Pedal to the Metal Green /5 #15
2019 Panini Victory Lane Pedal to the Metal Red /3 #15
2019 Panini Victory Lane Printing Plates Black /1 #18
2019 Panini Victory Lane Printing Plates Cyan /1 #18
2019 Panini Victory Lane Printing Plates Magenta /1 #18
2019 Panini Victory Lane Printing Plates Yellow /1 #18
2019 Panini Victory Lane Signature Swatches #16
2019 Panini Victory Lane Signature Swatches Gold /99 #16
2019 Panini Victory Lane Signature Swatches Laundry Tag /1 #16
2019 Panini Victory Lane Signature Swatches Platinum /1 #16
2019 Panini Victory Lane Signature Swatches Red /25 #16
2019 Panini Victory Lane Triple Swatches #12
2019 Panini Victory Lane Triple Swatches Gold /99 #12
2019 Panini Victory Lane Triple Swatches Laundry Tag /1 #12
2019 Panini Victory Lane Triple Swatches Platinum /1 #12
2019 Panini Victory Lane Triple Swatches Red /25 #12
2020 Donruss #48
2020 Donruss #134
2020 Donruss Black Numbers /21 #48
2020 Donruss Black Numbers /21 #134
2020 Donruss Black Trophy Club /1 #48
2020 Donruss Black Trophy Club /1 #134
2020 Donruss Blue /199 #134
2020 Donruss Blue /199 #48
2020 Donruss Carolina Blue #48
2020 Donruss Carolina Blue #134
2020 Donruss Green /99 #48
2020 Donruss Green /99 #134
2020 Donruss Optic #35
2020 Donruss Optic #80
2020 Donruss Optic Carolina Blue Wave #35
2020 Donruss Optic Carolina Blue Wave #80
2020 Donruss Optic Gold /10 #35
2020 Donruss Optic Gold /10 #80
2020 Donruss Optic Gold Vinyl /1 #35
2020 Donruss Optic Gold Vinyl /1 #80
2020 Donruss Optic Holo #35
2020 Donruss Optic Holo #80
2020 Donruss Optic Orange Pulsar #35
2020 Donruss Optic Orange Pulsar #80
2020 Donruss Optic Red Mojo #35
2020 Donruss Optic Red Mojo #80
2020 Donruss Optic Signatures Gold Vinyl /1 #35
2020 Donruss Optic Signatures Gold Vinyl /1 #80
2020 Donruss Optic Signatures Holo /99 #35
2020 Donruss Optic Signatures Holo /99 #80
2020 Donruss Orange #48
2020 Donruss Orange #134
2020 Donruss Pink /25 #48
2020 Donruss Pink /25 #134
2020 Donruss Printing Plates Black /1 #48
2020 Donruss Printing Plates Black /1 #134
2020 Donruss Printing Plates Cyan /1 #48
2020 Donruss Printing Plates Cyan /1 #134
2020 Donruss Printing Plates Magenta /1 #48
2020 Donruss Printing Plates Magenta /1 #134
2020 Donruss Printing Plates Yellow /1 #134
2020 Donruss Printing Plates Yellow /1 #48
2020 Donruss Purple /49 #48
2020 Donruss Purple /49 #134
2020 Donruss Race Day Relics #25
2020 Donruss Race Day Relics Holo Black /10 #25
2020 Donruss Race Day Relics Holo Gold /25 #25
2020 Donruss Race Day Relics Red /250 #25
2020 Donruss Red /299 #48
2020 Donruss Red /299 #134
2020 Donruss Silver #48
2020 Donruss Silver #134

Ryan Newman

2001 Press Pass #96
2001 Press Pass Millennium #96
2001 Press Pass Optima #37
2001 Press Pass Optima Gold #37
2001 Press Pass Signings #39
2001 Wheels High Gear #66
2001 Wheels High Gear First Gear #66
2001 Wheels High Gear MPH #66
2002 Press Pass #26
2002 Press Pass #50
2002 Press Pass #71
2002 Press Pass Autographs #48
2002 Press Pass Eclipse #28
2002 Press Pass Eclipse #43
2002 Press Pass Eclipse Samples #28
2002 Press Pass Eclipse Samples #43
2002 Press Pass Eclipse Solar Eclipse #S28
2002 Press Pass Eclipse Solar Eclipse #S43
2002 Press Pass Eclipse Under Cover Drivers #CD9
2002 Press Pass Eclipse Under Cover Gold Cars /300 #CD9
2002 Press Pass Eclipse Under Cover Gold Drivers /400 #CD9
2002 Press Pass Eclipse Under Cover Holofoil Drivers /100 #CD9
2002 Press Pass Hot Treads /2375 #HT31
2002 Press Pass Optima #21
2002 Press Pass Optima #46
2002 Press Pass Optima Fan Favorite #FF18
2002 Press Pass Optima Gold #21
2002 Press Pass Optima Gold #46
2002 Press Pass Optima Promos /5 #21
2002 Press Pass Optima Promos /5 #46
2002 Press Pass Optima Race Used Lugnuts Autographs /12 #LNDA14
2002 Press Pass Optima Race Used Lugnuts Cars /100 #LNC14
2002 Press Pass Optima Race Used Lugnuts Drivers /100 #LND14
2002 Press Pass Optima Samples #21
2002 Press Pass Optima Samples #46
2002 Press Pass Optima Up Close #UC3
2002 Press Pass Platinum #26
2002 Press Pass Platinum #50
2002 Press Pass Platinum #71
2002 Press Pass Premium #23
2002 Press Pass Premium #35
2002 Press Pass Premium #66
2002 Press Pass Premium Red Reflectors #23
2002 Press Pass Premium Red Reflectors #35
2002 Press Pass Premium Red Reflectors #66
2002 Press Pass Premium Samples #23
2002 Press Pass Premium Samples #35
2002 Press Pass Signings #48
2002 Press Pass Signings Gold /50 #45
2002 Press Pass Signings Transparent /100 #7
2002 Press Pass Stealth #13
2002 Press Pass Stealth #14
2002 Press Pass Stealth #15
2002 Press Pass Stealth #72
2002 Press Pass Stealth EFX #FX10
2002 Press Pass Stealth Fusion #F10
2002 Press Pass Stealth Gold #13
2002 Press Pass Stealth Gold #14
2002 Press Pass Stealth Gold #15
2002 Press Pass Stealth Gold #72
2002 Press Pass Stealth Lap Leaders #LL20
2002 Press Pass Stealth Profile #P7
2002 Press Pass Stealth Race Used Glove Cars /85 #GLC12
2002 Press Pass Stealth Race Used Glove Drivers /50 #GLD12
2002 Press Pass Stealth Samples #13
2002 Press Pass Stealth Samples #14
2002 Press Pass Stealth Samples #15
2002 Press Pass Stealth Samples #72
2002 Press Pass Trackside #24
2002 Press Pass Trackside #57
2002 Press Pass Trackside #89
2002 Press Pass Trackside Generation Now #GN5
2002 Press Pass Trackside Golden /50 #G24
2002 Press Pass Trackside License to Drive #24
2002 Press Pass Trackside License to Drive Die Cuts #24
2002 Press Pass Trackside Pit Stoppers Cars /350 #PSC6
2002 Press Pass Trackside Pit Stoppers Drivers /175 #PSD6
2002 Press Pass Trackside Samples #24
2002 Press Pass Trackside Samples #57
2002 Press Pass Trackside Samples #89
2002 VIP #6
2002 VIP #30
2002 VIP Explosives #X6
2002 VIP Explosives #X30
2002 VIP Explosives Lasers #LX6
2002 VIP Explosives Lasers #LX30
2002 VIP Making the Show #MS7
2002 VIP Mile Masters #MM7
2002 VIP Mile Masters Transparent #MM7
2002 VIP Mile Masters Transparent LTD #MM7
2002 VIP Race Used Sheet Metal Cars #SC5
2002 VIP Race Used Sheet Metal Drivers /130 #SD5
2002 VIP Samples #6
2002 VIP Samples #30
2002 Wheels High Gear #43
2002 Wheels High Gear #67
2002 Wheels High Gear Autographs #41
2002 Wheels High Gear Custom Shop #CSRN
2002 Wheels High Gear Custom Shop Prizes #RNA1
2002 Wheels High Gear Custom Shop Prizes #RNA2
2002 Wheels High Gear Custom Shop Prizes #RNA3
2002 Wheels High Gear Custom Shop Prizes #RNB1
2002 Wheels High Gear Custom Shop Prizes #RNB2
2002 Wheels High Gear Custom Shop Prizes #RNB3
2002 Wheels High Gear Custom Shop Prizes #RNC1
2002 Wheels High Gear Custom Shop Prizes #RNC2
2002 Wheels High Gear Custom Shop Prizes #RNC3
2002 Wheels High Gear First Gear #43
2002 Wheels High Gear First Gear #67
2002 Wheels High Gear MPH /100 #43
2002 Wheels High Gear MPH /100 #67
2003 eTopps /4000 #6
2003 Press Pass #23
2003 Press Pass #62
2003 Press Pass #63
2003 Press Pass #68
2003 Press Pass #69
2003 Press Pass #94
2003 Press Pass Autographs #42
2003 Press Pass Burning Rubber Cars /60 #BRT2
2003 Press Pass Burning Rubber Cars Autographs /12 #BRTRN
2003 Press Pass Burning Rubber Drivers /50 #BRD2
2003 Press Pass Burning Rubber Drivers Autographs /12 #BRDRN
2003 Press Pass Cup Chase #CCR12
2003 Press Pass Cup Chase Prizes #CCR12
2003 Press Pass Double Burner /100 #DB2
2003 Press Pass Double Burner Exchange /100 #DB2
2003 Press Pass Eclipse #6
2003 Press Pass Eclipse #28
2003 Press Pass Eclipse #34
2003 Press Pass Eclipse #43
2003 Press Pass Eclipse #47
2003 Press Pass Eclipse Double Hot Treads /999 #DT9
2003 Press Pass Eclipse Previews /5 #6
2003 Press Pass Eclipse Previews /5 #28
2003 Press Pass Eclipse Previews /5 #34
2003 Press Pass Eclipse Racing Champions #RC14
2003 Press Pass Eclipse Racing Champions #RC28
2003 Press Pass Eclipse Samples #6
2003 Press Pass Eclipse Samples #28
2003 Press Pass Eclipse Samples #34
2003 Press Pass Eclipse Samples #43
2003 Press Pass Eclipse Samples #47
2003 Press Pass Eclipse Skidmarks #SM5
2003 Press Pass Eclipse Solar Eclipse #P6
2003 Press Pass Eclipse Solar Eclipse #P28
2003 Press Pass Eclipse Solar Eclipse #P34
2003 Press Pass Eclipse Solar Eclipse #P43
2003 Press Pass Eclipse Solar Eclipse #P47
2003 Press Pass Eclipse Teammates Autographs /25 #RNRW
2003 Press Pass Eclipse Under Cover Cars /215 #UCT2
2003 Press Pass Eclipse Under Cover Cars Autographs /12 #UCTRN
2003 Press Pass Eclipse Under Cover Driver Autographs /12 #UCDRN
2003 Press Pass Eclipse Under Cover Driver Gold /260 #UCD2
2003 Press Pass Eclipse Under Cover Driver Red /100 #UCD2
2003 Press Pass Eclipse Under Cover Driver Silver /450 #UCD2
2003 Press Pass Gatorade Jumbos #4
2003 Press Pass Gold Holofoil #P23
2003 Press Pass Gold Holofoil #P62
2003 Press Pass Gold Holofoil #P63
2003 Press Pass Gold Holofoil #P68
2003 Press Pass Gold Holofoil #P69
2003 Press Pass Gold Holofoil #P94
2003 Press Pass Optima #19
2003 Press Pass Optima #50
2003 Press Pass Optima Fan Favorite #FF18
2003 Press Pass Optima Gold #G19
2003 Press Pass Optima Gold #G50
2003 Press Pass Optima Previews /5 #19
2003 Press Pass Optima Q and A #QA6
2003 Press Pass Optima Samples #19
2003 Press Pass Optima Samples #50
2003 Press Pass Optima Thunder Bolts Cars /95 #TBT2
2003 Press Pass Optima Thunder Bolts Cars Autographs /12 #TBTRN
2003 Press Pass Optima Thunder Bolts Drivers /60 #TBD2
2003 Press Pass Optima Thunder Bolts Drivers Autographs /12 #TBDRN
2003 Press Pass Premium #21
2003 Press Pass Premium #65
2003 Press Pass Premium #76
2003 Press Pass Premium Hot Threads Cars /160 #HTT2
2003 Press Pass Premium Hot Threads Cars Autographs /12 #HTDRN
2003 Press Pass Premium Hot Threads Drivers /285 #HTD2
2003 Press Pass Premium Hot Threads Drivers Autographs /12 #HTTRN
2003 Press Pass Premium In the Zone #IZ7
2003 Press Pass Premium Previews /5 #21
2003 Press Pass Premium Red Reflectors #21
2003 Press Pass Premium Red Reflectors #65
2003 Press Pass Premium Red Reflectors #76
2003 Press Pass Premium Samples #21
2003 Press Pass Previews /5 #23
2003 Press Pass Samples #23
2003 Press Pass Samples #62
2003 Press Pass Samples #63
2003 Press Pass Samples #68
2003 Press Pass Samples #69
2003 Press Pass Samples #94
2003 Press Pass Showcar #S2B
2003 Press Pass Showman #S2A
2003 Press Pass Signings #53
2003 Press Pass Signings Gold /50 #53
2003 Press Pass Signings Transparent /100 #7
2003 Press Pass Snapshots #SN17
2003 Press Pass Stealth EFX #FX5
2003 Press Pass Stealth Gear Grippers Cars /150 #GGT2
2003 Press Pass Stealth Gear Grippers Cars Autographs /12 #RN
2003 Press Pass Stealth Gear Grippers Drivers /75 #GGD2
2003 Press Pass Stealth Gear Grippers Drivers Autographs /12 #RN
2003 Press Pass Stealth Profile #PR7
2003 Press Pass Top Shelf #TS7
2003 Press Pass Total Memorabilia Power Pick #TM2
2003 Press Pass Trackside #16
2003 Press Pass Trackside #63
2003 Press Pass Trackside #76
2003 Press Pass Trackside Dialed In #DI9
2003 Press Pass Trackside Gold Holofoil #P16
2003 Press Pass Trackside Gold Holofoil #P63
2003 Press Pass Trackside Gold Holofoil #P76
2003 Press Pass Trackside Golden /50 #G16
2003 Press Pass Trackside Hat Giveaway #PPH21
2003 Press Pass Trackside Hot Pursuit #HP5
2003 Press Pass Trackside License to Drive #LD13
2003 Press Pass Trackside Pit Stoppers Cars /175 #PST8
2003 Press Pass Trackside Pit Stoppers Cars Autographs /12 #RN
2003 Press Pass Trackside Pit Stoppers Drivers /100 #PSD8
2003 Press Pass Trackside Pit Stoppers Drivers Autographs /12 #PSDRN
2003 Press Pass Trackside Previews /5 #16
2003 Press Pass Trackside Runnin n' Gunnin #RG10
2003 Press Pass Trackside Samples #16
2003 Press Pass Trackside Samples #63
2003 Press Pass Trackside Samples #76
2003 Press Pass Triple Burner /100 #TB2
2003 Press Pass Triple Burner Exchange /100 #TB2
2003 VIP #14
2003 VIP #25
2003 VIP #29
2003 VIP #46
2003 VIP Explosives #X14
2003 VIP Explosives #X25
2003 VIP Explosives #X29
2003 VIP Explosives #X46
2003 VIP Laser Explosive #LX14
2003 VIP Laser Explosive #LX25
2003 VIP Laser Explosive #LX29
2003 VIP Laser Explosive #LX46
2003 VIP Previews /5 #14
2003 VIP Previews /5 #25
2003 VIP Previews /5 #29
2003 VIP Samples #14
2003 VIP Samples #25
2003 VIP Samples #29
2003 VIP Samples #46
2003 VIP Tin #CT14
2003 VIP Tin #CT25
2003 VIP Tin #CT29
2003 VIP Tin #CT46
2003 VIP Tradin' Paint Car Autographs /12 #RN
2003 VIP Tradin' Paint Cars /160 #TPT2
2003 VIP Tradin' Paint Driver Autographs /12 #RN
2003 VIP Tradin' Paint Drivers /110 #TPD2
2003 Wheels American Thunder #17
2003 Wheels American Thunder #30
2003 Wheels American Thunder #42
2003 Wheels American Thunder American Eagle #AE3
2003 Wheels American Thunder American Muscle #AM7
2003 Wheels American Thunder Born On /100 #BO17
2003 Wheels American Thunder Born On /100 #BO30
2003 Wheels American Thunder Born On /100 #BO42
2003 Wheels American Thunder Cool Threads /285 #CT3
2003 Wheels American Thunder Golden Eagle /100 #AEG3
2003 Wheels American Thunder Heads Up Goodyear /90 #HUG6
2003 Wheels American Thunder Heads Up Manufacturer /90 #HUM15
2003 Wheels American Thunder Heads Up Team /90 #HUT13
2003 Wheels American Thunder Heads Up Winston /90 #HUW15
2003 Wheels American Thunder Holofoil #P17
2003 Wheels American Thunder Holofoil #P30
2003 Wheels American Thunder Holofoil #P42
2003 Wheels American Thunder Post Mark #PM14
2003 Wheels American Thunder Previews /5 #17
2003 Wheels American Thunder Previews /5 #30
2003 Wheels American Thunder Rookie Class #RC1
2003 Wheels American Thunder Rookie Class Prizes #RC1
2003 Wheels American Thunder Rookie Thunder #RT24
2003 Wheels American Thunder Samples #P17
2003 Wheels American Thunder Samples #P30
2003 Wheels American Thunder Samples #P42
2003 Wheels American Thunder Thunder Road #TR5
2003 Wheels Autographs #45
2003 Wheels High Gear #20
2003 Wheels High Gear #31
2003 Wheels High Gear #59
2003 Wheels High Gear #63
2003 Wheels High Gear #65
2003 Wheels High Gear #68
2003 Wheels High Gear Blue Hawaii SCDA Promos #20
2003 Wheels High Gear Blue Hawaii SCDA Promos #31
2003 Wheels High Gear Blue Hawaii SCDA Promos #59
2003 Wheels High Gear Blue Hawaii SCDA Promos #63
2003 Wheels High Gear Blue Hawaii SCDA Promos #65
2003 Wheels High Gear Blue Hawaii SCDA Promos #68
2003 Wheels High Gear Custom Shop #CSRN
2003 Wheels High Gear Custom Shop Autograph Redemption #CSRN
2003 Wheels High Gear Custom Shop Prizes #RNA1
2003 Wheels High Gear Custom Shop Prizes #RNA2
2003 Wheels High Gear Custom Shop Prizes #RNA3
2003 Wheels High Gear Custom Shop Prizes #RNB1
2003 Wheels High Gear Custom Shop Prizes #RNB2
2003 Wheels High Gear Custom Shop Prizes #RNB3
2003 Wheels High Gear Custom Shop Prizes #RNC1
2003 Wheels High Gear Custom Shop Prizes #RNC2
2003 Wheels High Gear Custom Shop Prizes #RNC3
2003 Wheels High Gear First Gear #F20
2003 Wheels High Gear First Gear #F31
2003 Wheels High Gear First Gear #F59
2003 Wheels High Gear First Gear #F63
2003 Wheels High Gear First Gear #F65
2003 Wheels High Gear First Gear #F68
2003 Wheels High Gear Flag Chasers Black /90 #FC4
2003 Wheels High Gear Flag Chasers Blue-Yellow /45 #FC4
2003 Wheels High Gear Flag Chasers Checkered /25 #FC4
2003 Wheels High Gear Flag Chasers Green /90 #FC4
2003 Wheels High Gear Flag Chasers Red /90 #FC4
2003 Wheels High Gear Flag Chasers White /90 #FC4
2003 Wheels High Gear Flag Chasers Yellow /90 #FC4
2003 Wheels High Gear Full Throttle #FT3
2003 Wheels High Gear High Groove #HG18
2003 Wheels High Gear Hot Treads /425 #HT13
2003 Wheels High Gear Machine #MM5B
2003 Wheels High Gear Man #MM5A
2003 Wheels High Gear MPH /100 #M20
2003 Wheels High Gear MPH /100 #M31
2003 Wheels High Gear MPH /100 #M59
2003 Wheels High Gear MPH /100 #M63
2003 Wheels High Gear MPH /100 #M65
2003 Wheels High Gear MPH /100 #M68
2003 Wheels High Gear Previews /5 #20
2003 Wheels High Gear Samples #20
2003 Wheels High Gear Samples #31
2003 Wheels High Gear Samples #59
2003 Wheels High Gear Samples #63
2003 Wheels High Gear Samples #65
2003 Wheels High Gear Samples #68
2003 Wheels High Gear Sunday Sensation #SS6
2003 Wheels High Gear Top Tier #TT6
2004 Press Pass /600 #0
2004 Press Pass #24
2004 Press Pass #67
2004 Press Pass #98
2004 Press Pass #76
2004 Press Pass Autographs #45
2004 Press Pass Burning Rubber Autographs /12 #BRRN
2004 Press Pass Burning Rubber Cars /140 #BRT7
2004 Press Pass Burning Rubber Drivers /70 #BRD7
2004 Press Pass Cup Chase #CCR15
2004 Press Pass Cup Chase Prizes #CCR15
2004 Press Pass Double Burner /100 #DB2
2004 Press Pass Double Burner Exchange /100 #DB2
2004 Press Pass Eclipse #6
2004 Press Pass Eclipse #46
2004 Press Pass Eclipse #50
2004 Press Pass Eclipse #54
2004 Press Pass Eclipse #65
2004 Press Pass Eclipse #69
2004 Press Pass Eclipse #70
2004 Press Pass Eclipse #83
2004 Press Pass Eclipse Destination WIN #9
2004 Press Pass Eclipse Destination WIN #15
2004 Press Pass Eclipse Destination WIN #20
2004 Press Pass Eclipse Destination WIN #23
2004 Press Pass Eclipse Hyperdrive #HP4
2004 Press Pass Eclipse Previews /5 #6
2004 Press Pass Eclipse Samples #6
2004 Press Pass Eclipse Samples #46
2004 Press Pass Eclipse Samples #50
2004 Press Pass Eclipse Samples #54
2004 Press Pass Eclipse Samples #65
2004 Press Pass Eclipse Samples #69
2004 Press Pass Eclipse Samples #70
2004 Press Pass Eclipse Samples #83
2004 Press Pass Eclipse Skidmarks #SM11
2004 Press Pass Eclipse Skidmarks Holofoil /500 #SM11
2004 Press Pass Eclipse Teammates Autographs /25 #7
2004 Press Pass Eclipse Under Cover Autographs /12 #UCRN
2004 Press Pass Eclipse Under Cover Cars /170 #UCD7
2004 Press Pass Eclipse Under Cover Double Cover /100 #DC2
2004 Press Pass Eclipse Under Cover Driver Gold /325 #UCD7
2004 Press Pass Eclipse Under Cover Driver Red /100 #UCD7
2004 Press Pass Eclipse Under Cover Driver Silver /690 #UCD7
2004 Press Pass Hot Treads /1100 #HTR5
2004 Press Pass Hot Treads Holofoil /200 #HTR5
2004 Press Pass Making the Show Collector's Series #MS8
2004 Press Pass Optima #19
2004 Press Pass Optima #57
2004 Press Pass Optima Cool Persistence #CP7
2004 Press Pass Optima Fan Favorite #FF18
2004 Press Pass Optima Gold #G19
2004 Press Pass Optima Gold #G57
2004 Press Pass Optima Previews /5 #EB19
2004 Press Pass Optima Samples #19
2004 Press Pass Optima Samples #57
2004 Press Pass Optima Thunder Bolts Autographs /12 #TBRN
2004 Press Pass Optima Thunder Bolts Cars /120 #TBT5
2004 Press Pass Optima Thunder Bolts Drivers /70 #TBD5
2004 Press Pass Platinum #P24
2004 Press Pass Platinum #P67
2004 Press Pass Platinum #P76
2004 Press Pass Platinum #P98
2004 Press Pass Premium #21
2004 Press Pass Premium #61
2004 Press Pass Premium Asphalt Jungle #A3
2004 Press Pass Premium Hot Threads Autographs /12 #HTRN
2004 Press Pass Premium Hot Threads Drivers Bronze /125 #HTD7
2004 Press Pass Premium Hot Threads Drivers Bronze Retail /125 #HTT7
2004 Press Pass Premium Hot Threads Drivers Gold /50 #HTD7
2004 Press Pass Premium Hot Threads Drivers Silver /75 #HTD7
2004 Press Pass Premium In the Zone #IZ11
2004 Press Pass Premium In the Zone Elite Edition #IZ11
2004 Press Pass Premium Performance Driven #PD2
2004 Press Pass Premium Previews /5 #21
2004 Press Pass Premium Samples #21
2004 Press Pass Previews /5 #24
2004 Press Pass Samples #24
2004 Press Pass Samples #67
2004 Press Pass Samples #76
2004 Press Pass Samples #98
2004 Press Pass Signings #47
2004 Press Pass Signings Gold /20 #43
2004 Press Pass Signings Transparent /100 #6
2004 Press Pass Snapshots #SN20
2004 Press Pass Stealth #46
2004 Press Pass Stealth #47
2004 Press Pass Stealth #48
2004 Press Pass Stealth EFX #EF5
2004 Press Pass Stealth Fusion #FU5
2004 Press Pass Stealth Gear Grippers Autographs /12 #HTRN
2004 Press Pass Stealth Gear Grippers Drivers /80 #GGD6
2004 Press Pass Stealth Gear Grippers Drivers Retail /120 #GGT6
2004 Press Pass Stealth No Boundaries #NB22
2004 Press Pass Stealth Samples #X48
2004 Press Pass Stealth Samples #X46
2004 Press Pass Stealth Samples #X47
2004 Press Pass Stealth X-Ray /100 #46
2004 Press Pass Stealth X-Ray /100 #47
2004 Press Pass Stealth X-Ray /100 #48
2004 Press Pass Top Shelf #TS4
2004 Press Pass Total Memorabilia Power Pick #TM2
2004 Press Pass Trackside #6
2004 Press Pass Trackside #55
2004 Press Pass Trackside #67
2004 Press Pass Trackside #103
2004 Press Pass Trackside #118
2004 Press Pass Trackside Golden /100 #G6
2004 Press Pass Trackside Golden /100 #G55
2004 Press Pass Trackside Golden /100 #G67
2004 Press Pass Trackside Golden /100 #G103
2004 Press Pass Trackside Golden /100 #G118
2004 Press Pass Trackside Hat Giveaway #PPH24
2004 Press Pass Trackside Hot Pass #HP12
2004 Press Pass Trackside Hot Pass National #HP12
2004 Press Pass Trackside Pit Stoppers Autographs /12 #PSRN
2004 Press Pass Trackside Pit Stoppers Cars /150 #PST8
2004 Press Pass Trackside Pit Stoppers Drivers /95 #PSD8
2004 Press Pass Trackside Previews /5 #EB6
2004 Press Pass Trackside Samples #6
2004 Press Pass Trackside Samples #55
2004 Press Pass Trackside Samples #67
2004 Press Pass Trackside Samples #103
2004 Press Pass Trackside Samples #118
2004 Press Pass Triple Burner /100 #TB2
2004 Press Pass Triple Burner Exchange /100 #TB2
2004 Team Caliber First Choice Beckett 1:24 #12
2004 VIP #14
2004 VIP #34
2004 VIP #63
2004 VIP #79
2004 VIP Lap Leaders #LL4
2004 VIP Lap Leaders Transparent #LL4
2004 VIP Making the Show #MS8
2004 VIP Previews /5 #EB14
2004 VIP Previews /5 #EB34
2004 VIP Samples #14
2004 VIP Samples #34
2004 VIP Samples #63
2004 VIP Samples #79
2004 VIP Tradin' Paint Bronze /130 #TPT5
2004 VIP Tradin' Paint Gold /50 #TPD5
2004 VIP Tradin' Paint Silver /70 #TPD5
2004 Wheels American Thunder #21
2004 Wheels American Thunder #38
2004 Wheels American Thunder Cool Threads /525 #CT12
2004 Wheels American Thunder Cup Quest #CQ6
2004 Wheels American Thunder Post Mark #PM8
2004 Wheels American Thunder Previews /5 #EB21
2004 Wheels American Thunder Previews /5 #EB38
2004 Wheels American Thunder Samples #21
2004 Wheels American Thunder Samples #38
2004 Wheels American Thunder Thunder Road #TR5
2004 Wheels American Thunder Triple Hat /160 #TH35
2004 Wheels Autographs #48
2004 Wheels High Gear #20
2004 Wheels High Gear #48
2004 Wheels High Gear #63
2004 Wheels High Gear Flag Chasers Black /100 #FC8
2004 Wheels High Gear Flag Chasers Blue /50 #FC8
2004 Wheels High Gear Flag Chasers Checkered /35 #FC8
2004 Wheels High Gear Flag Chasers Green /100 #FC8
2004 Wheels High Gear Flag Chasers Red /100 #FC8
2004 Wheels High Gear Flag Chasers White /100 #FC8
2004 Wheels High Gear Flag Chasers Yellow /100 #FC8
2004 Wheels High Gear Full Throttle #FT3
2004 Wheels High Gear High Groove #HG19
2004 Wheels High Gear MPH /100 #M20
2004 Wheels High Gear MPH /100 #M48
2004 Wheels High Gear MPH /100 #M63
2004 Wheels High Gear Previews /5 #20
2004 Wheels High Gear Previews /5 #48
2004 Wheels High Gear Samples #20
2004 Wheels High Gear Samples #48
2004 Wheels High Gear Samples #63
2004 Wheels High Gear Sunday Sensation #SS6
2004 Wheels High Gear Sunday Sensation #SS8
2004 Wheels High Gear Top Ten #TT6
2005 Press Pass #9
2005 Press Pass #64
2005 Press Pass #116
2005 Press Pass Autographs #43
2005 Press Pass Burning Rubber Autographs /12 #BRRN
2005 Press Pass Cup Chase #CCR13
2005 Press Pass Cup Chase Prizes #CCP13
2005 Press Pass Double Burner /100 #DB2
2005 Press Pass Double Burner Exchange /100 #DB2
2005 Press Pass Eclipse #7
2005 Press Pass Eclipse #32
2005 Press Pass Eclipse #47
2005 Press Pass Eclipse #64
2005 Press Pass Eclipse Destination WIN #14
2005 Press Pass Eclipse Maxim #MX1
2005 Press Pass Eclipse Previews /5 #EB7
2005 Press Pass Eclipse Previews /5 #EB32
2005 Press Pass Eclipse Previews /5 #EB47
2005 Press Pass Eclipse Previews /5 #EB64
2005 Press Pass Eclipse Samples #7
2005 Press Pass Eclipse Samples #32
2005 Press Pass Eclipse Samples #47
2005 Press Pass Eclipse Samples #64
2005 Press Pass Eclipse Skidmarks #SM11
2005 Press Pass Eclipse Skidmarks Holofoil /250 #SM11
2005 Press Pass Eclipse Teammates Autographs /25 #3
2005 Press Pass Eclipse Under Cover Autographs /12 #UCRN
2005 Press Pass Eclipse Under Cover Cars /120 #UCT7
2005 Press Pass Eclipse Under Cover Double Cover /340 #DC2
2005 Press Pass Eclipse Under Cover Driver Red /400 #UCD7
2005 Press Pass Eclipse Under Cover Drivers Holofoil /100 #UCD7
2005 Press Pass Eclipse Under Cover Drivers Silver /690 #UCD7
2005 Press Pass Hot Treads /900 #HTR3
2005 Press Pass Hot Treads Holofoil /100 #HTR3
2005 Press Pass Legends Autographs Black /50 #24
2005 Press Pass Legends Double Threads Bronze /375 #DTNW
2005 Press Pass Legends Double Threads Gold /99 #DTNW
2005 Press Pass Legends Double Threads Silver /225 #DTNW
2005 Press Pass Legends Threads and Treads Bronze /375 #TTRN
2005 Press Pass Legends Threads and Treads Gold /99 #TTRN
2005 Press Pass Legends Threads and Treads Silver /225 #TTRN
2005 Press Pass Optima #23
2005 Press Pass Optima #23B
2005 Press Pass Optima #69
2005 Press Pass Optima Gold /100 #G23
2005 Press Pass Optima Gold /100 #G69
2005 Press Pass Optima Previews /5 #23
2005 Press Pass Optima Samples #23
2005 Press Pass Optima Samples #69
2005 Press Pass Optima Thunder Bolts Autographs /12 #TBRN
2005 Press Pass Platinum /100 #P9
2005 Press Pass Platinum /100 #P64
2005 Press Pass Platinum /100 #P116
2005 Press Pass Premium #24
2005 Press Pass Premium #62
2005 Press Pass Premium #73
2005 Press Pass Premium Hot Threads Cars /85 #HTT6
2005 Press Pass Premium Hot Threads Drivers /275 #HTD6
2005 Press Pass Premium Hot Threads Drivers Gold /1 #HTD6
2005 Press Pass Premium In the Zone #IZ4
2005 Press Pass Premium In the Zone Elite Edition /250 #IZ4
2005 Press Pass Premium Samples #24
2005 Press Pass Previews Green /5 #EB9
2005 Press Pass Samples #9
2005 Press Pass Samples #64
2005 Press Pass Samples #116
2005 Press Pass Signings #43
2005 Press Pass Signings Gold /50 #41
2005 Press Pass Signings Platinum /100 #39
2005 Press Pass Stealth #10
2005 Press Pass Stealth #13
2005 Press Pass Stealth #16
2005 Press Pass Stealth Fusion #FU3
2005 Press Pass Stealth Gear Grippers Cars /90 #GGT6
2005 Press Pass Stealth Gear Grippers Drivers /75 #GGD6
2005 Press Pass Stealth No Boundaries #NB7
2005 Press Pass Stealth Previews /5 #10
2005 Press Pass Stealth Previews /5 #13
2005 Press Pass Stealth Previews /5 #16
2005 Press Pass Stealth Samples #10
2005 Press Pass Stealth Samples #13
2005 Press Pass Stealth Samples #16
2005 Press Pass Stealth X-Ray /100 #X10
2005 Press Pass Stealth X-Ray /100 #X13
2005 Press Pass Stealth X-Ray /100 #X16
2005 Press Pass Top Ten #TT10
2005 Press Pass Total Memorabilia Power Pick #TM2
2005 Press Pass Trackside #20
2005 Press Pass Trackside #57
2005 Press Pass Trackside Golden /100 #G20
2005 Press Pass Trackside Golden /100 #G57
2005 Press Pass Trackside Hat Giveaway #PPH24
2005 Press Pass Trackside Hot Pass #12
2005 Press Pass Trackside Hot Pass National #12
2005 Press Pass Trackside Hot Pursuit #HP6
2005 Press Pass Trackside Pit Stoppers Autographs /12 #PSRN
2005 Press Pass Trackside Pit Stoppers Cars /85 #PST6
2005 Press Pass Trackside Pit Stoppers Drivers /85 #PSD6
2005 Press Pass Trackside Previews /5 #20
2005 Press Pass Trackside Runnin n' Gunnin #RG4
2005 Press Pass Trackside Samples #20
2005 Press Pass Trackside Samples #57
2005 Press Pass Triple Burner /100 #TB2
2005 Press Pass Triple Burner Exchange /100 #TB2
2005 Press Pass UMI Cup Chase #1
2005 Press Pass UMI Cup Chase #11
2005 VIP #23
2005 VIP #56
2005 VIP #59
2005 VIP Making The Show #8
2005 VIP Previews /5 #EB23
2005 VIP Samples #23
2005 VIP Samples #56
2005 VIP Samples #59
2005 Wheels American Thunder Cool Threads /475 #CT13
2005 Wheels American Thunder Double Hat /190 #DH8
2005 Wheels Autographs #42
2005 Wheels High Gear #7
2005 Wheels High Gear #44
2005 Wheels High Gear #50
2005 Wheels High Gear #57
2005 Wheels High Gear #82
2005 Wheels High Gear Flag Chasers Black /55 #FC5
2005 Wheels High Gear Flag Chasers Blue-Yellow /25 #FC5
2005 Wheels High Gear Flag Chasers Checkered /10 #FC5
2005 Wheels High Gear Flag Chasers Green /55 #FC5
2005 Wheels High Gear Flag Chasers Red /55 #FC5
2005 Wheels High Gear Flag Chasers White /55 #FC5
2005 Wheels High Gear Flag Chasers Yellow /55 #FC5
2005 Wheels High Gear Flag to Flag #FF19
2005 Wheels High Gear MPH /100 #M7
2005 Wheels High Gear MPH /100 #M44
2005 Wheels High Gear MPH /100 #M50
2005 Wheels High Gear MPH /100 #M57
2005 Wheels High Gear MPH /100 #M82
2005 Wheels High Gear Previews Green /5 #EB7
2005 Wheels High Gear Samples #7
2005 Wheels High Gear Samples #50
2005 Wheels High Gear Samples #57
2005 Wheels High Gear Samples #82
2005 Wheels High Gear Top Tier #TT7
2006 Press Pass #11
2006 Press Pass #99
2006 Press Pass #118
2006 Press Pass Autographs #41
2006 Press Pass Blue #B11
2006 Press Pass Blue #B99
2006 Press Pass Blue #B118
2006 Press Pass Burning Rubber Autographs /12 #BRRN
2006 Press Pass Burnouts /1050 #HT18
2006 Press Pass Burnouts Holofoil /125 #HT18
2006 Press Pass Collectors Series Making the Show #MS4
2006 Press Pass Cup Chase #CCR9
2006 Press Pass Double Burner Firesuit-Glove /100 #DB8
2006 Press Pass Eclipse #6
2006 Press Pass Eclipse #39
2006 Press Pass Eclipse #52
2006 Press Pass Eclipse #67
2006 Press Pass Eclipse #65
2006 Press Pass Eclipse #69
2006 Press Pass Eclipse Previews /5 #EB6
2006 Press Pass Eclipse Racing Champions #RC12
2006 Press Pass Eclipse Racing Champions #RC26
2006 Press Pass Eclipse Skidmarks #SM6
2006 Press Pass Eclipse Skidmarks Holofoil /250 #SM6
2006 Press Pass Eclipse Supernova #SU1
2006 Press Pass Eclipse Teammates Autographs /25 #7
2006 Press Pass Eclipse Under Cover Autographs /12 #RN
2006 Press Pass Eclipse Under Cover Cars /140 #UCT2
2006 Press Pass Eclipse Under Cover Double Cover /100 #DC4
2006 Press Pass Eclipse Under Cover Double Cover Holofoil /25 #DC4
2006 Press Pass Eclipse Under Cover Drivers Gold /1 #UCD2
2006 Press Pass Eclipse Under Cover Drivers Holofoil /100 #UCD2
2006 Press Pass Eclipse Under Cover Drivers Red /225 #UCD2
2006 Press Pass Eclipse Under Cover Drivers Silver /400 #UCD2
2006 Press Pass Four Wide /50 #FWRN
2006 Press Pass Four Wide Checkered Flag /1 #FWRN
2006 Press Pass Gold #G11
2006 Press Pass Gold #G99
2006 Press Pass Gold #G118
2006 Press Pass Legends #42
2006 Press Pass Legends Autographs Black /50 #31
2006 Press Pass Legends Blue /1999 #B42
2006 Press Pass Legends Bronze /999 #Z42
2006 Press Pass Legends Gold /299 #G42

ress Pass Legends Holofoil /99 #H42
ress Pass Legends Press Plates Black /1 #PPB42
ress Pass Legends Press Plates Black Backs /1 #PPB42B
ress Pass Legends Press Plates Cyan /1 #PPC42
ress Pass Legends Press Plates Cyan Backs /1 #PPC42B
ress Pass Legends Press Plates Magenta /1 #PPM42
ress Pass Legends Press Plates Magenta Backs /1 #PPM42B
ress Pass Legends Press Plates Yellow /1 #PPY42
ress Pass Legends Press Plates Yellow Backs /1 #PPY42B
ress Pass Legends Previews /5 #EB42
ress Pass Legends Solo /1 #S42
ress Pass Legends Triple Threads /50 #TTRN
ress Pass Optima #12
ress Pass Optima Fan Favorite #FF17
ress Pass Optima Gold /100 #G12
ress Pass Optima Pole Position #PP7
ress Pass Optima Previews /5 #EB12
ress Pass Optima Rookie Relics Cars /50 #RRT10
ress Pass Optima Rookie Relics Drivers /50 #RRD10
ress Pass Platinum /100 #P11
ress Pass Platinum /100 #P99
ress Pass Platinum /100 #P118
ress Pass Premium #22
ress Pass Premium #78
ress Pass Premium Hot Threads Cars /165 #HTT10
ress Pass Premium Hot Threads Drivers /220 #HTD10
ress Pass Premium Hot Threads Drivers Gold /1 #HTD10
ress Pass Previews /5 #EB11
ress Pass Previews /1 #EB99
ress Pass Signings #42
ress Pass Signings Gold /50 #42
ress Pass Signings Gold Red Ink #42
ress Pass Signings Silver /100 #42
ress Pass Signings Silver Red Ink #42
ress Pass Stealth #23
ress Pass Stealth #55
Press Pass Stealth Autographed Hat Entry #PPH19
Press Pass Stealth Corporate Cuts /250 #CCD13
Press Pass Stealth Gear Grippers Autographs /12 #RN
Press Pass Stealth Gear Grippers Cars Retail /99 #GGT2
Press Pass Stealth Gear Grippers Drivers /99 #GGD2
Press Pass Stealth Hot Pass #HP21
Press Pass Stealth Previews /5 #23
Press Pass Stealth Retail #55
Press Pass Stealth Retail #23
Press Pass Stealth X-Ray /100 #X23
Press Pass Stealth X-Ray /100 #X55
Press Pass Top 25 Drivers & Rides #C9
Press Pass Top 25 Drivers & Rides #D9
TRAKS #25
TRAKS #43
TRAKS Autographs #28
TRAKS Autographs 25 /25 #26
TRAKS Previews /1 #25
TRAKS Previews /1 #43
TRAKS Stickers #12
VIP #21
VIP #65
VIP Making the Show #MS4
VIP Tradin' Paint Cars Bronze /145 #TPT15
VIP Tradin' Paint Drivers Gold /50 #TPD15
VIP Tradin' Paint Drivers Silver /80 #TPD15
Wheels American Thunder #24
Wheels American Thunder #80
Wheels American Thunder Cool Threads /329 #CT10
6 Wheels American Thunder Double Hat /99 #DH18
6 Wheels American Thunder Grandstand #GS19
6 Wheels American Thunder Head to Toe /99 #HT2
6 Wheels American Thunder Previews /5 #EB24
6 Wheels American Thunder Previews /1 #EB80
6 Wheels American Thunder Pushin' Pedal /199 #PP5
6 Wheels Autographs #44
6 Wheels High Gear #6
6 Wheels High Gear #59
6 Wheels High Gear #63
6 Wheels High Gear #87
6 Wheels High Gear Flag Chasers Black /110 #FC6
6 Wheels High Gear Flag Chasers Blue-Yellow /65 #FC6
6 Wheels High Gear Flag Chasers Checkered /3 #FC6
6 Wheels High Gear Flag Chasers Green /110 #FC6
6 Wheels High Gear Flag Chasers Red /110 #FC6
06 Wheels High Gear Flag Chasers White /110 #FC6
06 Wheels High Gear Flag Chasers Yellow /110 #FC6
6 Wheels High Gear Flag to Flag #FF19
6 Wheels High Gear MPH /100 #M6
6 Wheels High Gear MPH /100 #M59
6 Wheels High Gear MPH /100 #M63
6 Wheels High Gear MPH /100 #M87
06 Wheels High Gear Previews Green /5 #EB6
06 Wheels High Gear Top Tier #TT6
07 Press Pass #17
07 Press Pass Autographs #34
07 Press Pass Blue #B17
07 Press Pass Collector's Series Box Set #SB19
07 Press Pass Cup Chase #CCR6
07 Press Pass Eclipse #17
07 Press Pass Eclipse #36
07 Press Pass Eclipse Ecliptic #EC6
07 Press Pass Eclipse Gold /25 #G17
07 Press Pass Eclipse Gold /25 #G36
07 Press Pass Eclipse Previews /5 #EB17
07 Press Pass Eclipse Previews /5 #EB36
07 Press Pass Eclipse Red /1 #R17
07 Press Pass Eclipse Red /1 #R36
07 Press Pass Eclipse Skidmarks #SM17
07 Press Pass Eclipse Skidmarks Holofoil /250 #SM17
07 Press Pass Eclipse Teammates Autographs /25 #5
07 Press Pass Eclipse Under Cover Autographs /12 #UCRN
07 Press Pass Eclipse Under Cover Double Cover Name /25 #DC4
07 Press Pass Eclipse Under Cover Double Cover NASCAR /99 #DC4
07 Press Pass Eclipse Under Cover Drivers /450 #UCD8
07 Press Pass Eclipse Under Cover Drivers Eclipse /1 #UCD8
07 Press Pass Eclipse Under Cover Drivers Name /99 #UCD8
007 Press Pass Eclipse Under Cover Drivers NASCAR /270 #UCD8
07 Press Pass Eclipse Under Cover Teams /135 #UCT8
007 Press Pass Eclipse Under Cover Teams NASCAR /25 #UCT8
007 Press Pass Four Wide /50 #FWRN
007 Press Pass Four Wide Checkered Flag /1 #FWRN
007 Press Pass Four Wide Checkered Flag Exchange /1 #FWRN
007 Press Pass Four Wide Exchange /50 #FWRN
007 Press Pass Gold #G17
007 Press Pass Legends #46
007 Press Pass Legends Blue /999 #B46
007 Press Pass Legends Bronze /599 #Z46
007 Press Pass Legends Gold /249 #G46
007 Press Pass Legends Holofoil /99 #H46
2007 Press Pass Legends Press Plates Black /1 #PP46
2007 Press Pass Legends Press Plates Black Backs /1 #PP46
2007 Press Pass Legends Press Plates Cyan /1 #PP46
2007 Press Pass Legends Press Plates Cyan Backs /1 #PP46
2007 Press Pass Legends Press Plates Magenta /1 #PP46
2007 Press Pass Legends Press Plates Magenta Backs /1 #PP46
2007 Press Pass Legends Press Plates Yellow /1 #PP46
2007 Press Pass Legends Press Plates Yellow Backs /1 #PP46
2007 Press Pass Legends Previews /5 #EB46
2007 Press Pass Legends Signature Series /25 #RN
2007 Press Pass Legends Solo /1 #S46
2007 Press Pass Platinum /100 #P17

2007 Press Pass Premium #11
2007 Press Pass Premium Hot Threads Drivers /145 #HTD3
2007 Press Pass Premium Hot Threads Drivers Gold /1 #HTD3
2007 Press Pass Premium Hot Threads Patch /10 #HTP27
2007 Press Pass Premium Hot Threads Team /160 #HTT3
2007 Press Pass Premium Red /15 #R11
2007 Press Pass Previews /5 #EB17
2007 Press Pass Signings #51
2007 Press Pass Signings Blue /25 #23
2007 Press Pass Signings Gold /50 #41
2007 Press Pass Signings Silver /100 #40
2007 Press Pass Stealth #19
2007 Press Pass Stealth #67
2007 Press Pass Stealth Battle Armor Autographs /12 #BASRN
2007 Press Pass Stealth Battle Armor Drivers /150 #BAD5
2007 Press Pass Stealth Battle Armor Teams /85 #BAT5
2007 Press Pass Stealth Chrome #19
2007 Press Pass Stealth Chrome #67
2007 Press Pass Stealth Chrome Exclusives /99 #X19
2007 Press Pass Stealth Chrome Exclusives /99 #X67
2007 Press Pass Stealth Chrome Platinum /25 #P19
2007 Press Pass Stealth Chrome Platinum /25 #P67
2007 Press Pass Stealth Maximum Access #MA21
2007 Press Pass Stealth Maximum Access Autographs /25 #MA21
2007 Press Pass Stealth Previews /5 #EB19
2007 Traks #20
2007 Traks #60
2007 Traks Corporate Cuts Driver /99 #CCD9
2007 Traks Corporate Cuts Patch /15 #CCD9
2007 Traks Corporate Cuts Team /180 #CCT9
2007 Traks Driver's Seat #DS5B
2007 Traks Driver's Seat #DS5
2007 Traks Driver's Seat National #DS5
2007 Traks Gold #G20
2007 Traks Gold #G60
2007 Traks Holofoil /50 #H20
2007 Traks Holofoil /50 #H60
2007 Traks Previews /5 #EB20
2007 Traks Red /10 #R20
2007 Traks Red /10 #R60
2007 VIP #66
2007 VIP Gear Gallery #GG1
2007 VIP Gear Gallery Transparent #GG1
2007 VIP Get A Grip Drivers /70 #GGD6
2007 VIP Get A Grip Teams /70 #GGT6
2007 VIP Sunday Best #SB19
2007 VIP Trophy Club #TC8
2007 VIP Trophy Club Transparent #TC8
2007 Wheels American Thunder #23
2007 Wheels American Thunder #62
2007 Wheels American Thunder #40
2007 Wheels American Thunder Autographed Hat Instant Winner /1 #AH25
2007 Wheels American Thunder Cool Threads /299 #CT9
2007 Wheels American Thunder Previews /5 #EB23
2007 Wheels American Thunder Thunder Road #TR5
2007 Wheels American Thunder Thunder Strokes #31
2007 Wheels American Thunder Thunder Strokes Press Plates Black /1 #31
2007 Wheels American Thunder Thunder Strokes Press Plates Cyan /1 #31
2007 Wheels American Thunder Thunder Strokes Press Plates Magenta /1 #31
2007 Wheels American Thunder Thunder Strokes Press Plates Yellow /1 #31
2007 Wheels American Thunder Triple Hat /99 #TH21
2007 Wheels Autographs #30
2007 Wheels Autographs Press Plates Black /1 #29
2007 Wheels Autographs Press Plates Cyan /1 #29
2007 Wheels Autographs Press Plates Magenta /1 #29
2007 Wheels High Gear #17
2007 Wheels High Gear #68
2007 Wheels High Gear #80
2007 Wheels High Gear Driven #DR11
2007 Wheels High Gear Final Standings Gold /18 #FS17
2007 Wheels High Gear MPH /100 #M17
2007 Wheels High Gear MPH /100 #M68
2007 Wheels High Gear MPH /100 #M80
2007 Wheels High Gear Previews /5 #EB17
2008 Press Pass #14
2008 Press Pass #72
2008 Press Pass Autographs #29
2008 Press Pass Autographs Press Plates Black /1 #24
2008 Press Pass Autographs Press Plates Cyan /1 #24
2008 Press Pass Autographs Press Plates Magenta /1 #24
2008 Press Pass Autographs Press Plates Yellow /1 #24
2008 Press Pass Blue #B14
2008 Press Pass Blue #B72
2008 Press Pass Collector's Series Box Set #16
2008 Press Pass Cup Chase #CC1
2008 Press Pass Eclipse #12
2008 Press Pass Eclipse #29
2008 Press Pass Eclipse #41
2008 Press Pass Eclipse #57
2008 Press Pass Eclipse #66
2008 Press Pass Eclipse Escape Velocity #EV8
2008 Press Pass Eclipse Gold /25 #G12
2008 Press Pass Eclipse Gold /25 #G29
2008 Press Pass Eclipse Gold /25 #G41
2008 Press Pass Eclipse Gold /25 #G57
2008 Press Pass Eclipse Gold /25 #G66
2008 Press Pass Eclipse Previews /5 #EB12
2008 Press Pass Eclipse Previews /5 #EB29
2008 Press Pass Eclipse Red /1 #R12
2008 Press Pass Eclipse Red /1 #R29
2008 Press Pass Eclipse Red /1 #R41
2008 Press Pass Eclipse Red /1 #R57
2008 Press Pass Eclipse Red /1 #R66
2008 Press Pass Eclipse Star Tracks #ST6
2008 Press Pass Eclipse Star Tracks Holofoil /250 #ST6
2008 Press Pass Eclipse Teammates Autographs /35 #BN
2008 Press Pass Eclipse Under Cover Autographs /12 #UCRN
2008 Press Pass Eclipse Under Cover Double Cover Name /25 #DC5
2008 Press Pass Eclipse Under Cover Double Cover NASCAR /99 #DC5
2008 Press Pass Eclipse Under Cover Drivers /250 #UCD7
2008 Press Pass Eclipse Under Cover Drivers Eclipse /1 #UCD7
2008 Press Pass Eclipse Under Cover Drivers Name /50 #UCD7
2008 Press Pass Eclipse Under Cover Drivers NASCAR /150 #UCD7
2008 Press Pass Eclipse Under Cover Teams /99 #UCT7
2008 Press Pass Eclipse Under Cover Teams NASCAR /25 #UCT7
2008 Press Pass Gillette Young Guns #6
2008 Press Pass Gold #G14
2008 Press Pass Gold #G72
2008 Press Pass Legends Autographs Black /10 #RN
2008 Press Pass Legends Autographs Blue /75 #RN
2008 Press Pass Legends Autographs Press Plates Black /1 #RN
2008 Press Pass Legends Autographs Press Plates Cyan /1 #RN
2008 Press Pass Legends Autographs Press Plates Magenta /1 #RN
2008 Press Pass Legends Autographs Press Plates Yellow /1 #RN
2008 Press Pass Legends Prominent Pieces Firesuit-Glove-Belt /25 #PP2RN
2008 Press Pass Legends Prominent Pieces Firesuit-Glove-Belt Gold /10 #PP2RN
2008 Press Pass Legends Prominent Pieces Metal-Tire Bronze /99 #PP3RN
2008 Press Pass Legends Prominent Pieces Metal-Tire Gold /25 #PP3RN
2008 Press Pass Legends Prominent Pieces Metal-Tire Silver /50 #PP3RN
2008 Press Pass Legends Victory Lane Bronze /99 #VLRN
2008 Press Pass Legends Victory Lane Gold /25 #VLRN
2008 Press Pass Legends Victory Lane Silver /50 #VLRN
2008 Press Pass Platinum /100 #P14
2008 Press Pass Platinum /100 #P72
2008 Press Pass Premium #0

2008 Press Pass Premium #11
2008 Press Pass Premium Hot Threads Drivers /120 #HTD10
2008 Press Pass Premium Hot Threads Drivers Gold /1 #HTD10
2008 Press Pass Premium Hot Threads Patches #HTP37
2008 Press Pass Premium Hot Threads Patches #HTP36
2008 Press Pass Premium Hot Threads Patches /7 #HTP35
2008 Press Pass Premium Hot Threads Patches /5 #HTP34
2008 Press Pass Premium Hot Threads Team /120 #HTT10
2008 Press Pass Premium Previews /5 #EB11
2008 Press Pass Premium Red /15 #11
2008 Press Pass Previews /5 #EB14
2008 Press Pass Race Day #RD2
2008 Press Pass Signings #46
2008 Press Pass Signings Blue /25 #22
2008 Press Pass Signings Gold /50 #42
2008 Press Pass Signings Press Plates Black /1 #29
2008 Press Pass Signings Press Plates Black /1 #RN
2008 Press Pass Signings Press Plates Cyan /1 #29
2008 Press Pass Signings Press Plates Magenta /1 #29
2008 Press Pass Signings Press Plates Yellow /1 #29
2008 Press Pass Signings Press Plates Yellow #RN
2008 Press Pass Signings Silver /100 #41
2008 Press Pass Slideshow #SS25
2008 Press Pass Speedway #19
2008 Press Pass Speedway #60
2008 Press Pass Speedway #72
2008 Press Pass Speedway #98
2008 Press Pass Speedway #93
2008 Press Pass Speedway Blur #B4
2008 Press Pass Speedway Cockpit #CP17
2008 Press Pass Speedway Corporate Cuts Drivers /80 #CDRN
2008 Press Pass Speedway Corporate Cuts Drivers Patches /15 #CDRN
2008 Press Pass Speedway Corporate Cuts Team /165 #CTRN
2008 Press Pass Speedway Gold #G19
2008 Press Pass Speedway Gold #G60
2008 Press Pass Speedway Gold #G72
2008 Press Pass Speedway Gold #G93
2008 Press Pass Speedway Gold #G98
2008 Press Pass Speedway Holofoil /50 #H19
2008 Press Pass Speedway Holofoil /50 #H60
2008 Press Pass Speedway Holofoil /50 #H72
2008 Press Pass Speedway Holofoil /50 #H93
2008 Press Pass Speedway Holofoil /50 #H98
2008 Press Pass Speedway Previews /5 #EB19
2008 Press Pass Speedway Previews /1 #EB93
2008 Press Pass Speedway Previews /1 #EB98
2008 Press Pass Speedway Red /10 #R19
2008 Press Pass Speedway Red /10 #R60
2008 Press Pass Speedway Red /10 #R72
2008 Press Pass Speedway Red /10 #R93
2008 Press Pass Speedway Red /10 #R98
2008 Press Pass Speedway Test Drive #TD6
2008 Press Pass Starting Grid #SG16
2008 Press Pass Stealth #27
2008 Press Pass Stealth #48
2008 Press Pass Stealth #87
2008 Press Pass Stealth Battle Armor Drivers /120 #BAD8
2008 Press Pass Stealth Battle Armor Teams /115 #BAT8
2008 Press Pass Stealth Chrome #27
2008 Press Pass Stealth Chrome #48
2008 Press Pass Stealth Chrome #87
2008 Press Pass Stealth Chrome Exclusives /25 #27
2008 Press Pass Stealth Chrome Exclusives /25 #48
2008 Press Pass Stealth Chrome Exclusives /25 #87
2008 Press Pass Stealth Chrome Exclusives Gold /99 #27
2008 Press Pass Stealth Chrome Exclusives Gold /99 #48
2008 Press Pass Stealth Chrome Exclusives Gold /99 #87
2008 Press Pass Stealth Mach 08 #M8-9
2008 Press Pass Stealth Maximum Access #MA21
2008 Press Pass Stealth Maximum Access Autographs /25 #MA21
2008 Press Pass Stealth Previews /5 #27
2008 Press Pass Stealth Previews /1 #87
2008 VIP #26
2008 VIP #65
2008 VIP #78
2008 VIP #88
2008 VIP All Access #AA18
2008 VIP Gear Gallery #GG3
2008 VIP Gear Gallery Memorabilia /50 #GGRN
2008 VIP Gear Gallery Transparent #GG3
2008 VIP Get a Grip Autographs /12 #GGSRN
2008 VIP Previews /5 #EB26
2008 VIP Previews /1 #EB88
2008 VIP Trophy Club #TC5
2008 VIP Trophy Club Transparent #TC5
2008 Wheels American Thunder #26
2008 Wheels American Thunder #44
2008 Wheels American Thunder Autographed Hat Winner /1 #IWHRN
2008 Wheels American Thunder Double Hat /99 #DH8
2008 Wheels American Thunder Motorcade #M5
2008 Wheels American Thunder Previews /5 #26
2008 Wheels American Thunder Trackside Treasury Autographs #RN
2008 Wheels American Thunder Trackside Treasury Autographs Gold /25 #RN
2008 Wheels American Thunder Trackside Treasury Autographs Printing Plates Black /1 #RN
2008 Wheels American Thunder Trackside Treasury Autographs Printing Plates Cyan /1 #RN
2008 Wheels American Thunder Trackside Treasury Autographs Printing Plates Magenta /1 #RN
2008 Wheels American Thunder Trackside Treasury Autographs Printing Plates Yellow /1 #RN
2008 Wheels Autographs #22
2008 Wheels Autographs Press Plates Black /1 #22
2008 Wheels Autographs Press Plates Cyan /1 #22
2008 Wheels Autographs Press Plates Magenta /1 #22
2008 Wheels Autographs Press Plates Yellow /1 #22
2008 Wheels High Gear #13
2008 Wheels High Gear Driven #DR21
2008 Wheels High Gear Final Standings /13 #F13
2008 Wheels High Gear MPH /100 #M13
2008 Wheels High Gear Previews /5 #EB13
2009 Element #26
2009 Element #83
2009 Element Big Win /35 #BWRN
2009 Element Previews /5 #26
2009 Element Radioactive /100 #26
2009 Element Radioactive /100 #83
2009 Press Pass #16
2009 Press Pass #68
2009 Press Pass #82
2009 Press Pass #145
2009 Press Pass #217
2009 Press Pass Autographs Gold #38
2009 Press Pass Autographs Printing Plates Black /1 #35
2009 Press Pass Autographs Printing Plates Cyan /1 #35
2009 Press Pass Autographs Printing Plates Magenta /1 #35
2009 Press Pass Autographs Printing Plates Yellow /1 #35
2009 Press Pass Autographs Silver #39
2009 Press Pass Blue #16
2009 Press Pass Blue #68
2009 Press Pass Blue #82
2009 Press Pass Blue #145
2009 Press Pass Blue #217
2009 Press Pass Burning Rubber Drivers /185 #BRD1
2009 Press Pass Burning Rubber Prime Cut /25 #BRD1
2009 Press Pass Burning Rubber Teams /180 #BRT1
2009 Press Pass Chase for the Sprint Cup #CC10

2009 Press Pass Cup Chase Prizes #CC10
2009 Press Pass Daytona 500 Tires /25 #TTRN
2009 Press Pass Eclipse #20
2009 Press Pass Eclipse #37
2009 Press Pass Eclipse Black and White #20
2009 Press Pass Eclipse Black and White #37
2009 Press Pass Eclipse Blue #20
2009 Press Pass Eclipse Blue #37
2009 Press Pass Four Wide Firesuit /50 #FWRN
2009 Press Pass Four Wide Tire /25 #FWRN
2009 Press Pass Gold #16
2009 Press Pass Gold #68
2009 Press Pass Gold #82
2009 Press Pass Gold #145
2009 Press Pass Gold #217
2009 Press Pass Gold Holofoil /100 #16
2009 Press Pass Gold Holofoil /100 #68
2009 Press Pass Gold Holofoil /100 #82
2009 Press Pass Gold Holofoil /100 #145
2009 Press Pass Gold Holofoil /100 #217
2009 Press Pass Legends Autographs Gold /40 #25
2009 Press Pass Legends Autographs Holofoil /20 #22
2009 Press Pass Legends Autographs Printing Plates Black /1 #20
2009 Press Pass Legends Autographs Printing Plates Cyan /1 #19
2009 Press Pass Legends Autographs Printing Plates Magenta /1 #20
2009 Press Pass Legends Autographs Printing Plates Yellow /1 #20
2009 Press Pass Legends Prominent Pieces Gold /25 #PPRN
2009 Press Pass Legends Prominent Pieces Silver /50 #PPRN
2009 Press Pass Pocket Portraits #P19
2009 Press Pass Pocket Portraits Hometown #P19
2009 Press Pass Pocket Portraits Smoke #P19
2009 Press Pass Pocket Portraits Target #PPT12
2009 Press Pass Premium #24
2009 Press Pass Premium #46
2009 Press Pass Premium #57
2009 Press Pass Premium #72
2009 Press Pass Premium Previews /5 #EB24
2009 Press Pass Premium Signatures #26
2009 Press Pass Premium Signatures Gold /25 #25
2009 Press Pass Previews /5 #EB16
2009 Press Pass Previews /5 #EB145
2009 Press Pass Red #16
2009 Press Pass Red #68
2009 Press Pass Red #82
2009 Press Pass Red #145
2009 Press Pass Red #217
2009 Press Pass Showcase /499 #26
2009 Press Pass Showcase /499 #36
2009 Press Pass Showcase 2nd Gear /125 #26
2009 Press Pass Showcase 2nd Gear /125 #36
2009 Press Pass Showcase 3rd Gear /50 #26
2009 Press Pass Showcase 3rd Gear /50 #36
2009 Press Pass Showcase 4th Gear /15 #26
2009 Press Pass Showcase 4th Gear /15 #36
2009 Press Pass Showcase Classic Collections Firesuit /25 #CCF9
2009 Press Pass Showcase Classic Collections Firesuit Patch /5 #CCF9
2009 Press Pass Showcase Classic Collections Ink /45 #10
2009 Press Pass Showcase Classic Collections Ink Gold /25 #10
2009 Press Pass Showcase Classic Collections Ink Green /5 #10
2009 Press Pass Showcase Classic Collections Ink Melting /1 #10
2009 Press Pass Showcase Classic Collections Sheet Metal /45 #CCS9
2009 Press Pass Showcase Classic Collections Tire /99 #CCT9
2009 Press Pass Showcase Printing Plates Black /1 #26
2009 Press Pass Showcase Printing Plates Black /1 #36
2009 Press Pass Showcase Printing Plates Cyan /1 #26
2009 Press Pass Showcase Printing Plates Cyan /1 #36
2009 Press Pass Showcase Printing Plates Magenta /1 #26
2009 Press Pass Showcase Printing Plates Magenta /1 #36
2009 Press Pass Showcase Printing Plates Yellow /1 #26
2009 Press Pass Showcase Printing Plates Yellow /1 #36
2009 Press Pass Signature Series Archive Edition /1 #BRDRN
2009 Press Pass Signature Series Archive Edition /1 #PSRN
2009 Press Pass Signings Blue /25 #35
2009 Press Pass Signings Gold #35
2009 Press Pass Signings Green /15 #35
2009 Press Pass Signings Orange /65 #35
2009 Press Pass Signings Printing Plates Magenta /1 #35
2009 Press Pass Signings Printing Plates Yellow /1 #35
2009 Press Pass Signings Purple /45 #35
2009 Press Pass Sponsor Swatches /200 #SSRN
2009 Press Pass Sponsor Swatches Select /8 #SSRN
2009 Press Pass Stealth Confidential Classified Bronze #PC10
2009 Press Pass Stealth Confidential Secret Silver #PC10
2009 Press Pass Stealth Confidential Top Secret Gold /25 #PC10
2009 Press Pass Tread Marks Autographs /10 #SSRN
2009 Press Pass Unleashed #U2
2009 VIP #25
2009 VIP #43
2009 VIP #67
2009 VIP Get A Grip /120 #GGRN
2009 VIP Get A Grip Autographs /39 #GGSRN
2009 VIP Get A Grip Holofoil /10 #GGRN
2009 VIP Guest List #GG25
2009 VIP Leadfoot /150 #LFRN
2009 VIP Leadfoot Holofoil /10 #LFRN
2009 VIP Previews /5 #25
2009 VIP Purple /25 #25
2009 VIP Purple /25 #43
2009 VIP Purple /25 #67
2009 Wheels Main Event #9
2009 Wheels Main Event Buyback Archive Edition /1 #GGRN
2009 Wheels Main Event Fast Pass Purple /25 #9
2009 Wheels Main Event Foil #9
2009 Wheels Main Event Hat Dance Patch /10 #HDRN
2009 Wheels Main Event Hat Dance Triple /99 #HDRN
2009 Wheels Main Event High Rollers #HR12
2009 Wheels Main Event Marks Clubs #43
2009 Wheels Main Event Marks Diamonds /10 #43
2009 Wheels Main Event Marks Hearts /5 #43
2009 Wheels Main Event Marks Printing Plates Black /1 #39
2009 Wheels Main Event Marks Printing Plates Cyan /1 #39
2009 Wheels Main Event Marks Printing Plates Magenta /1 #39
2009 Wheels Main Event Marks Printing Plates Yellow /1 #39
2009 Wheels Main Event Marks Spades /1 #43
2009 Wheels Main Event Playing Cards Blue #QS
2009 Wheels Main Event Playing Cards Red #QS
2009 Wheels Main Event Previews /5 #9
2009 Wheels Main Event Renegade Rounders Wanted #RR7
2009 Wheels Main Event Reward Copper /10 #RWRN
2009 Wheels Main Event Reward Holofoil /50 #RWRN
2009 Wheels Main Event Stop and Go Swatches Pit Banner /125 #SGBRN
2009 Wheels Main Event Stop and Go Swatches Pit Banner Blue All Season's Sports Cards /1 #SGBRN
2009 Wheels Main Event Stop and Go Swatches Pit Banner Blue Arena /1 #SGBRN
2009 Wheels Main Event Stop and Go Swatches Pit Banner Blue Card Stadium /1 #SGBRN
2009 Wheels Main Event Stop and Go Swatches Pit Banner Blue Chicagoland Sportscards /1 #SGBRN
2009 Wheels Main Event Stop and Go Swatches Pit Banner Blue Chris Comics /1 #SGBRN
2009 Wheels Main Event Stop and Go Swatches Pit Banner Blue Chuck's Field of Dreams /1 #SGBRN
2009 Wheels Main Event Stop and Go Swatches Pit Banner Blue Collector's Heaven /1 #SGBRN
2009 Wheels Main Event Stop and Go Swatches Pit Banner Blue D&S Racing /1 #SGBRN

2009 Wheels Main Event Stop and Go Swatches Pit Banner Blue Dave's Pitstop /1 #SGBRN
2009 Wheels Main Event Stop and Go Swatches Pit Banner Blue Diamond King Sports /1 #SGBRN
2009 Wheels Main Event Stop and Go Swatches Pit Banner Blue Georgetown Card Exchange /1 #SGBRN
2009 Wheels Main Event Stop and Go Swatches Pit Banner Blue Jaimie's Field of Dreams /1 #SGBRN
2009 Wheels Main Event Stop and Go Swatches Pit Banner Blue Juniata Cards /1 #SGBRN
2009 Wheels Main Event Stop and Go Swatches Pit Banner Blue Main Steet Sportscards /1 #SGBRN
2009 Wheels Main Event Stop and Go Swatches Pit Banner Blue Matt's Sports Cards /1 #SGBRN
2009 Wheels Main Event Stop and Go Swatches Pit Banner Blue P&T Sportscards /1 #SGBRN
2009 Wheels Main Event Stop and Go Swatches Pit Banner Blue Republic Jewelry /1 #SGBRN
2009 Wheels Main Event Stop and Go Swatches Pit Banner Blue Ron's Racing /1 #SGBRN
2009 Wheels Main Event Stop and Go Swatches Pit Banner Blue Shelby Collectibles /1 #SGBRN
2009 Wheels Main Event Stop and Go Swatches Pit Banner Blue Spectator Sportscards /1 #SGBRN
2009 Wheels Main Event Stop and Go Swatches Pit Banner Blue Squeeze Play /1 #SGBRN
2009 Wheels Main Event Stop and Go Swatches Pit Banner Blue TBJ Sports Cards /1 #SGBRN
2009 Wheels Main Event Stop and Go Swatches Pit Banner Blue TCI Sports Fan /1 #SGBRN
2009 Wheels Main Event Stop and Go Swatches Pit Banner Blue The Card Cellar /1 #SGBRN
2009 Wheels Main Event Stop and Go Swatches Pit Banner Blue TJ Warner Ballcards /1 #SGBRN
2009 Wheels Main Event Stop and Go Swatches Pit Banner Blue Trademark Sports /1 #SGBRN
2009 Wheels Main Event Stop and Go Swatches Pit Banner Blue Triple I Sportscards /1 #SGBRN
2009 Wheels Main Event Stop and Go Swatches Pit Banner Blue Triple Play /1 #SGBRN
2009 Wheels Main Event Stop and Go Swatches Pit Banner Blue West Allis /1 #SGBRN
2009 Wheels Main Event Stop and Go Swatches Pit Banner Green /10 #SGBRN
2009 Wheels Main Event Stop and Go Swatches Pit Banner Holofoil /75 #SGBRN
2009 Wheels Main Event Stop and Go Swatches Pit Banner Red /25 #SGBRN
2009 Wheels Main Event Wildcard Cuts /2 #WCCRN
2010 Action Racing Collectables Platinum 1:24 /252 #39
2010 Element #11
2010 Element #45
2010 Element #94
2010 Element Blue /35 #11
2010 Element Blue /35 #45
2010 Element Blue /35 #94
2010 Element Flagship Performers Consecutive Starts Black /20 #FPSRN
2010 Element Flagship Performers Consecutive Starts Blue-Orange /20 #FPSRN
2010 Element Flagship Performers Consecutive Starts Checkered /1 #FPSRN
2010 Element Flagship Performers Consecutive Starts Green /5 #FPSRN
2010 Element Flagship Performers Consecutive Starts Red /20 #FPSRN
2010 Element Flagship Performers Consecutive Starts White /10 #FPSRN
2010 Element Flagship Performers Consecutive Starts X /10 #FPSRN
2010 Element Flagship Performers Consecutive Starts Yellow /20 #FPSRN
2010 Element Green #11
2010 Element Green #45
2010 Element Green #94
2010 Element Previews /5 #EB11
2010 Element Purple /25 #11
2010 Element Purple /25 #45
2010 Element Recycled Materials Blue /25 #RMRN
2010 Element Recycled Materials Green /125 #RMRN
2010 Element Red Target #11
2010 Element Red Target #45
2010 Element Red Target #94
2010 Press Pass #11
2010 Press Pass #118
2010 Press Pass #129
2010 Press Pass #0
2010 Press Pass #92
2010 Press Pass Autographs #39
2010 Press Pass Autographs Chase Edition /25 #10
2010 Press Pass Autographs Printing Plates Black /1 #30
2010 Press Pass Autographs Printing Plates Cyan /1 #36
2010 Press Pass Autographs Printing Plates Magenta /1 #34
2010 Press Pass Autographs Printing Plates Yellow /1 #33
2010 Press Pass Blue #11
2010 Press Pass Blue #92
2010 Press Pass Blue #118
2010 Press Pass Blue #127
2010 Press Pass Cup Chase #CCR7
2010 Press Pass Eclipse #25
2010 Press Pass Eclipse #40
2010 Press Pass Eclipse #75
2010 Press Pass Eclipse Blue #25
2010 Press Pass Eclipse Blue #40
2010 Press Pass Eclipse Blue #75
2010 Press Pass Eclipse Gold #25
2010 Press Pass Eclipse Gold #40
2010 Press Pass Eclipse Gold #75
2010 Press Pass Eclipse Previews /5 #25
2010 Press Pass Eclipse Previews /1 #40
2010 Press Pass Eclipse Purple /25 #25
2010 Press Pass Eclipse Purple /25 #40
2010 Press Pass Final Standings /110 #FS9
2010 Press Pass Five Star /35 #19
2010 Press Pass Five Star Classic Compilations Patch Autographs /1 #CCPRN1
2010 Press Pass Five Star Classic Compilations Patch Autographs /1 #CCPRN2
2010 Press Pass Five Star Classic Compilations Patch Autographs /1 #CCPRN3
2010 Press Pass Five Star Classic Compilations Patch Autographs /1 #CCPRN4
2010 Press Pass Five Star Classic Compilations Patch Autographs /1 #CCPRN5
2010 Press Pass Five Star Classic Compilations Patch Autographs /1 #CCPRN6
2010 Press Pass Five Star Classic Compilations Patch Autographs /1 #CCPRN7
2010 Press Pass Five Star Classic Compilations Patch Autographs /1 #CCPRN8
2010 Press Pass Five Star Holofoil /10 #19
2010 Press Pass Five Star Melting /1 #19
2010 Press Pass Four Wide Firesuit /25 #FWRN
2010 Press Pass Four Wide Sheet Metal /15 #FWRN
2010 Press Pass Four Wide Shoes /1 #FWRN
2010 Press Pass Four Wide Tires /10 #FWRN
2010 Press Pass Gold #11
2010 Press Pass Gold #92
2010 Press Pass Gold #118
2010 Press Pass Gold #127
2010 Press Pass Holofoil /100 #11
2010 Press Pass Holofoil /100 #92
2010 Press Pass Holofoil /100 #118
2010 Press Pass Holofoil /100 #127

2010 Press Pass Legends Autographs Blue /10 #44
2010 Press Pass Legends Autographs Holofoil /25 #44
2010 Press Pass Legends Autographs Printing Plates Black /1 #36
2010 Press Pass Legends Autographs Printing Plates Cyan /1 #36
2010 Press Pass Legends Autographs Printing Plates Magenta /1 #36
2010 Press Pass Legends Autographs Printing Plates Yellow /1 #36
2010 Press Pass Legends Motorsports Masters Autographs Printing Plates Black /1 #36
2010 Press Pass Legends Motorsports Masters Autographs Printing Plates Cyan /1 #36
2010 Press Pass Legends Motorsports Masters Autographs Printing Plates Magenta /1 #36
2010 Press Pass Legends Motorsports Masters Autographs Printing Plates Yellow /1 #36
2010 Press Pass Premium #10
2010 Press Pass Premium #62
2010 Press Pass Premium Allies #A7
2010 Press Pass Premium Allies Signatures /5 #ASSN
2010 Press Pass Premium Hot Threads /299 #HTRN
2010 Press Pass Premium Hot Threads Holofoil /99 #HTRN
2010 Press Pass Premium Hot Threads Multi Color /25 #HTRN
2010 Press Pass Premium Hot Threads Patches /35 #HTPRN
2010 Press Pass Premium Hot Threads Two Color /125 #HTRN
2010 Press Pass Premium Purple /25 #10
2010 Press Pass Premium Purple /25 #62
2010 Press Pass Premium Signature Series Firesuit /15 #SSFRN
2010 Press Pass Premium Signatures #PSRN
2010 Press Pass Premium Signatures Red Ink /25 #PSRN
2010 Press Pass Previews /5 #11
2010 Press Pass Previews /1 #118
2010 Press Pass Purple /25 #11
2010 Press Pass Purple /25 #92
2010 Press Pass Purple /25 #118
2010 Press Pass Purple /25 #127
2010 Press Pass Showcase /499 #10
2010 Press Pass Showcase Elite Exhibit Ink /20 #EEIRN
2010 Press Pass Showcase Elite Exhibit Ink Gold /10 #EEIRN
2010 Press Pass Showcase Elite Exhibit Ink Green /5 #EEIRN
2010 Press Pass Showcase Elite Exhibit Ink Melting /1 #EEIRN
2010 Press Pass Showcase Elite Exhibit Triple Memorabilia /99 #EEMRN
2010 Press Pass Showcase Elite Exhibit Triple Memorabilia Gold /45 #EEMRN
2010 Press Pass Showcase Elite Exhibit Triple Memorabilia Green /25 #EEMRN
2010 Press Pass Showcase Elite Exhibit Triple Memorabilia Melting /5 #EEMRN
2010 Press Pass Showcase Gold /125 #10
2010 Press Pass Showcase Green /50 #10
2010 Press Pass Showcase Melting /15 #10
2010 Press Pass Showcase Platinum Holo /1 #10
2010 Press Pass Showcase Prized Pieces Firesuit Ink Gold /25 #PPIRN
2010 Press Pass Showcase Prized Pieces Firesuit Ink Melting /1 #PPIRN
2010 Press Pass Showcase Prized Pieces Memorabilia Ink Green /15 #PPIRN
2010 Press Pass Showcase Prized Pieces Sheet Metal Ink Silver /45 #PPIRN
2010 Press Pass Signings Blue /10 #42
2010 Press Pass Signings Gold /15 #42
2010 Press Pass Signings Red /15 #42
2010 Press Pass Signings Silver /44 #41
2010 Press Pass Stealth #27
2010 Press Pass Stealth #78
2010 Press Pass Stealth Battle Armor Holofoil /25 #BARN
2010 Press Pass Stealth Battle Armor Silver /225 #BARN
2010 Press Pass Stealth Black and White #27
2010 Press Pass Stealth Black and White #78
2010 Press Pass Stealth Mach 10 #MT4
2010 Press Pass Stealth Previews /5 #27
2010 Press Pass Stealth Purple /25 #27
2010 Press Pass Stealth Signature Series Sheet Metal /15 #SSMERN
2010 Press Pass Top 12 Tires /39 #RN
2010 Press Pass Top 12 Tires 10 /10 #RN
2010 Press Pass Tradin' Paint Sheet Metal /299 #TPRN
2010 Press Pass Tradin' Paint Sheet Metal Gold /50 #TPRN
2010 Press Pass Tradin' Paint Sheet Metal Holofoil /25 #TPRN
2010 Wheels Autographs #39
2010 Wheels Autographs Printing Plates Black /1 #39
2010 Wheels Autographs Printing Plates Cyan /1 #39
2010 Wheels Autographs Printing Plates Magenta /1 #39
2010 Wheels Autographs Printing Plates Yellow /1 #39
2010 Wheels Autographs Target /10 #27
2010 Wheels Main Event #27
2010 Wheels Main Event #74
2010 Wheels Main Event Blue #27
2010 Wheels Main Event Blue #74
2010 Wheels Main Event Fight Card #FC21
2010 Wheels Main Event Fight Card Checkered Flag #FC21
2010 Wheels Main Event Fight Card Full Color Retail #FC21
2010 Wheels Main Event Fight Card Gold /25 #FC21
2010 Wheels Main Event Head to Head /150 #HHTSRN
2010 Wheels Main Event Head to Head Blue /75 #HHTSRN
2010 Wheels Main Event Head to Head Holofoil /10 #HHTSRN
2010 Wheels Main Event Head to Head Red /25 #HHTSRN
2010 Wheels Main Event Marks Autographs /50 #43
2010 Wheels Main Event Marks Autographs Black /1 #42
2010 Wheels Main Event Marks Autographs Blue /20 #43
2010 Wheels Main Event Marks Autographs Red /5 #43
2010 Wheels Main Event Purple /25 #27
2010 Wheels Main Event Toe to Toe /10 #TTTSRN
2010 Wheels Main Event Upper Cuts Knock Out Patches /25 #UCKORN
2010 Wheels Main Event Wheel to Wheel /25 #WWTSRN
2010 Wheels Main Event Wheel to Wheel Holofoil /10 #WWTSRN
2011 Element #26
2011 Element #69
2011 Element #86
2011 Element Autographs /70 #41
2011 Element Autographs Blue /5 #41
2011 Element Autographs Gold /15 #40
2011 Element Autographs Printing Plates Black /1 #41
2011 Element Autographs Printing Plates Cyan /1 #41
2011 Element Autographs Printing Plates Magenta /1 #41
2011 Element Autographs Printing Plates Yellow /1 #41
2011 Element Autographs Silver /35 #40
2011 Element Black /35 #26
2011 Element Black /35 #69
2011 Element Black /35 #86
2011 Element Finish Line Checkered Flag /10 #FLRN
2011 Element Finish Line Green Flag /25 #FLRN
2011 Element Finish Line Tires /99 #FLRN
2011 Element Flagship Performers Race Streak Without DNF Red /50 #FPDRN
2011 Element Green #26
2011 Element Green #69
2011 Element Green #86
2011 Element Previews /5 #EB26
2011 Element Purple /25 #26
2011 Element Purple /25 #69
2011 Element Purple /25 #86
2011 Element Red #26
2011 Element Red #69
2011 Element Red #86
2011 Element Trackside Treasures Holofoil /25 #TTRN
2011 Element Trackside Treasures Silver /85 #TTRN
2011 Press Pass #28
2011 Press Pass #83
2011 Press Pass #140
2011 Press Pass #188
2011 Press Pass #165
2011 Press Pass #127

2011 Press Pass Autographs Blue /10 #41
2011 Press Pass Autographs Bronze /99 #42
2011 Press Pass Autographs Bronze /44 #43
2011 Press Pass Autographs Gold /25 #40
2011 Press Pass Autographs Printing Plates Black /1 #42
2011 Press Pass Autographs Printing Plates Cyan /1 #42
2011 Press Pass Autographs Printing Plates Magenta /1 #42
2011 Press Pass Autographs Printing Plates Yellow /1 #42
2011 Press Pass Autographs Silver /50 #42
2011 Press Pass Blue Holofoil /10 #28
2011 Press Pass Blue Holofoil /10 #83
2011 Press Pass Blue Holofoil /10 #127
2011 Press Pass Blue Holofoil /10 #140
2011 Press Pass Blue Holofoil /10 #165
2011 Press Pass Blue Holofoil /10 #188
2011 Press Pass Blue Retail #28
2011 Press Pass Blue Retail #83
2011 Press Pass Blue Retail #127
2011 Press Pass Blue Retail #140
2011 Press Pass Blue Retail #165
2011 Press Pass Blue Retail #188
2011 Press Pass Burning Rubber Autographs /10 #BRRN
2011 Press Pass Burning Rubber Fast Pass /10 #BRRN
2011 Press Pass Burning Rubber Gold /150 #BRRN
2011 Press Pass Burning Rubber Holofoil /50 #BRRN
2011 Press Pass Burning Rubber Prime Cuts /25 #BRRN
2011 Press Pass Cup Chase #CCR15
2011 Press Pass Cup Chase Prizes #CC8
2011 Press Pass Eclipse #25
2011 Press Pass Eclipse #46
2011 Press Pass Eclipse Blue #25
2011 Press Pass Eclipse Blue #46
2011 Press Pass Eclipse Gold /55 #25
2011 Press Pass Eclipse Gold /55 #46
2011 Press Pass Eclipse Previews /5 #EB25
2011 Press Pass Eclipse Previews /1 #EB46
2011 Press Pass Eclipse Purple /25 #25
2011 Press Pass Eclipse Purple /25 #46
2011 Press Pass FanFare #31
2011 Press Pass FanFare Autographs Blue /5 #54
2011 Press Pass FanFare Autographs Bronze /50 #54
2011 Press Pass FanFare Autographs Gold /25 #54
2011 Press Pass FanFare Autographs Printing Plates Black /1 #54
2011 Press Pass FanFare Autographs Printing Plates Cyan /1 #54
2011 Press Pass FanFare Autographs Printing Plates Magenta /1 #54
2011 Press Pass FanFare Autographs Printing Plates Yellow /1 #54
2011 Press Pass FanFare Autographs Silver /15 #54
2011 Press Pass FanFare Blue Die Cuts #31
2011 Press Pass FanFare Emerald /25 #31
2011 Press Pass FanFare Holofoil Die Cuts #31
2011 Press Pass FanFare Magnificent Materials /225 #MMRN
2011 Press Pass FanFare Magnificent Materials Dual Swatches /50 #MMDRN
2011 Press Pass FanFare Magnificent Materials Dual Swatches Holofoil /10 #MMDRN
2011 Press Pass FanFare Magnificent Materials Holofoil /50 #MMRN
2011 Press Pass FanFare Rookie Standouts #RS8
2011 Press Pass FanFare Ruby Die Cuts /15 #31
2011 Press Pass FanFare Sapphire /10 #31
2011 Press Pass FanFare Silver /25 #31
2011 Press Pass Four Wide Firesuit /25 #FWRN
2011 Press Pass Four Wide Glove /1 #FWRN
2011 Press Pass Four Wide Sheet Metal /15 #FWRN
2011 Press Pass Four Wide Tire /10 #FWRN
2011 Press Pass Gold /50 #28
2011 Press Pass Gold /50 #83
2011 Press Pass Gold /50 #127
2011 Press Pass Gold /50 #140
2011 Press Pass Gold /50 #165
2011 Press Pass Gold /50 #188
2011 Press Pass Legends #52
2011 Press Pass Legends Gold /250 #52
2011 Press Pass Legends Holofoil /25 #52
2011 Press Pass Legends Printing Plates Black /1 #52
2011 Press Pass Legends Printing Plates Cyan /1 #52
2011 Press Pass Legends Printing Plates Magenta /1 #52
2011 Press Pass Legends Printing Plates Yellow /1 #52
2011 Press Pass Legends Purple /25 #52
2011 Press Pass Legends Red /99 #52
2011 Press Pass Legends Solo /1 #52
2011 Press Pass Premium #29
2011 Press Pass Premium Hot Threads /150 #HTRN
2011 Press Pass Premium Hot Threads Multi Color /25 #HTRN
2011 Press Pass Premium Hot Threads Secondary Color /99 #HTRN
2011 Press Pass Premium Purple /25 #29
2011 Press Pass Premium Signatures /149 #PSRN
2011 Press Pass Premium Signatures Red Ink /11 #PSRN
2011 Press Pass Previews /5 #EB28
2011 Press Pass Purple /25 #28
2011 Press Pass Showcase /499 #8
2011 Press Pass Showcase /499 #59
2011 Press Pass Showcase Classic Collections Firesuit /45 #CCMSHR
2011 Press Pass Showcase Classic Collections Firesuit Patches /5 #CCMSHR
2011 Press Pass Showcase Classic Collections Ink /25 #CCMSHR
2011 Press Pass Showcase Classic Collections Ink Gold /5 #CCMSHR
2011 Press Pass Showcase Classic Collections Ink Melting /1 #CCMSHR
2011 Press Pass Showcase Classic Collections Sheet Metal /99 #CCMSHR
2011 Press Pass Showcase Gold /125 #8
2011 Press Pass Showcase Gold /125 #59
2011 Press Pass Showcase Green /25 #8
2011 Press Pass Showcase Green /25 #59
2011 Press Pass Showcase Masterpieces Ink /45 #MPIRN
2011 Press Pass Showcase Masterpieces Ink Gold /25 #MPIRN
2011 Press Pass Showcase Masterpieces Ink Melting /1 #MPIRN
2011 Press Pass Showcase Masterpieces Memorabilia /99 #MPMRN
2011 Press Pass Showcase Masterpieces Memorabilia Gold /45 #MPMRN
2011 Press Pass Showcase Masterpieces Memorabilia Melting /5 #MPMRN
2011 Press Pass Showcase Melting /1 #8
2011 Press Pass Showcase Melting /1 #59
2011 Press Pass Signature Series /11 #SSTRN
2011 Press Pass Signature Series /11 #SSBRN
2011 Press Pass Signature Series /11 #SSFRN
2011 Press Pass Signature Series /11 #SSMRN
2011 Press Pass Signings Black and White /10 #PPSRN
2011 Press Pass Signings Brushed Metal /50 #PPSRN
2011 Press Pass Signings Holofoil /25 #PPSRN
2011 Press Pass Signings Printing Plates Cyan /1 #PPSRN
2011 Press Pass Signings Printing Plates Magenta /1 #PPSRN
2011 Press Pass Signings Printing Plates Yellow /1 #PPSRN
2011 Press Pass Stealth #34
2011 Press Pass Stealth #35
2011 Press Pass Stealth #36
2011 Press Pass Stealth #89
2011 Press Pass Stealth Black and White /25 #34
2011 Press Pass Stealth Black and White /25 #35
2011 Press Pass Stealth Black and White /25 #36
2011 Press Pass Stealth Black and White /25 #89
2011 Press Pass Stealth Holofoil /99 #34
2011 Press Pass Stealth Holofoil /99 #35
2011 Press Pass Stealth Holofoil /99 #36
2011 Press Pass Stealth Holofoil /99 #89
2011 Press Pass Stealth In Flight Report #IF7
2011 Press Pass Stealth Metal of Honor Medal of Honor /50 #BARN
2011 Press Pass Stealth Metal of Honor Purple Heart /25 #MHRN
2011 Press Pass Stealth Metal of Honor Silver Star /99 #BARN
2011 Press Pass Stealth Purple /25 #34
2011 Press Pass Stealth Purple /25 #35
2011 Press Pass Stealth Purple /25 #36
2011 Press Pass Tradin' Paint #TP1
2011 Press Pass Tradin' Paint Sheet Metal Blue /25 #TPRN
2011 Press Pass Tradin' Paint Sheet Metal Holofoil /50 #TPRN
2011 Press Pass Winning Tickets #WT7
2011 Wheels Main Event #29
2011 Wheels Main Event #84
2011 Wheels Main Event All Stars #A10
2011 Wheels Main Event All Stars Brushed Foil /199 #A10
2011 Wheels Main Event All Stars Holofoil /50 #A10
2011 Wheels Main Event Black and White #29
2011 Wheels Main Event Black and White #84
2011 Wheels Main Event Blue /75 #29
2011 Wheels Main Event Blue /75 #84
2011 Wheels Main Event Green /1 #29
2011 Wheels Main Event Green /1 #84
2011 Wheels Main Event Headliners Holofoil /25 #HLRN
2011 Wheels Main Event Headliners Silver /50 #HLRN
2011 Wheels Main Event Marks Autographs Blue /10 #MERN
2011 Wheels Main Event Marks Autographs Gold /25 #MERN
2011 Wheels Main Event Marks Autographs Silver /50 #MERN
2011 Wheels Main Event Red /20 #29
2011 Wheels Main Event Red /20 #84
2012 Press Pass #87
2012 Press Pass #29
2012 Press Pass #66
2012 Press Pass Autographs Blue /5 #PPARN
2012 Press Pass Autographs Printing Plates Black /1 #PPARN
2012 Press Pass Autographs Printing Plates Cyan /1 #PPARN
2012 Press Pass Autographs Printing Plates Magenta /1 #PPARN
2012 Press Pass Autographs Printing Plates Yellow /1 #PPARN
2012 Press Pass Autographs Red /25 #PPARN
2012 Press Pass Autographs Silver /99 #PPARN
2012 Press Pass Blue #29
2012 Press Pass Blue #66
2012 Press Pass Blue #87
2012 Press Pass Blue Holofoil /35 #29
2012 Press Pass Blue Holofoil /35 #66
2012 Press Pass Blue Holofoil /35 #87
2012 Press Pass Burning Rubber Gold /99 #BRRN
2012 Press Pass Burning Rubber Holofoil /25 #BRRN
2012 Press Pass Burning Rubber Prime Cuts /25 #BRRN
2012 Press Pass Burning Rubber Purple /15 #BRRN
2012 Press Pass Cup Chase #CCR15
2012 Press Pass Fanfare #34
2012 Press Pass Fanfare Autographs Blue /5 #RN
2012 Press Pass Fanfare Autographs Gold /50 #RN
2012 Press Pass Fanfare Autographs Red /25 #RN
2012 Press Pass Fanfare Autographs Silver /99 #RN
2012 Press Pass Fanfare Blue Foil Die Cuts #34
2012 Press Pass Fanfare Diamond /5 #34
2012 Press Pass Fanfare Holofoil Die Cuts #34
2012 Press Pass Fanfare Magnificent Materials /250 #MMRN
2012 Press Pass Fanfare Magnificent Materials Dual Swatches /50 #MMRN
2012 Press Pass Fanfare Magnificent Materials Dual Swatches Melting /10 #MMRN
2012 Press Pass Fanfare Magnificent Materials Gold /99 #MMRN
2012 Press Pass Fanfare Magnificent Materials Signatures /99 #RN
2012 Press Pass Fanfare Magnificent Materials Signatures Blue /25 #RN
2012 Press Pass Fanfare Power Rankings #PR14
2012 Press Pass Fanfare Sapphire /20 #34
2012 Press Pass Fanfare Silver /25 #34
2012 Press Pass Gold #29
2012 Press Pass Gold #66
2012 Press Pass Gold #87
2012 Press Pass Ignite #29
2012 Press Pass Ignite #67
2012 Press Pass Ignite Materials Autographs Gun Metal /20 #IMRN
2012 Press Pass Ignite Materials Autographs Red /5 #IMRN
2012 Press Pass Ignite Materials Autographs Silver /125 #IMRN
2012 Press Pass Ignite Materials Gun Metal /99 #IMRN
2012 Press Pass Ignite Materials Red /10 #IMRN
2012 Press Pass Ignite Materials Silver #IMRN
2012 Press Pass Ignite Profile #P1
2012 Press Pass Ignite Proofs Black and White /50 #29
2012 Press Pass Ignite Proofs Black and White /50 #67
2012 Press Pass Ignite Proofs Cyan #29
2012 Press Pass Ignite Proofs Cyan #67
2012 Press Pass Ignite Proofs Magenta #29
2012 Press Pass Ignite Proofs Magenta #67
2012 Press Pass Ignite Proofs Yellow /10 #29
2012 Press Pass Ignite Proofs Yellow /10 #67
2012 Press Pass Power Picks Blue /50 #14
2012 Press Pass Power Picks Blue /50 #69
2012 Press Pass Power Picks Blue /50 #46
2012 Press Pass Power Picks Gold /50 #14
2012 Press Pass Power Picks Gold /50 #46
2012 Press Pass Power Picks Gold /50 #69
2012 Press Pass Power Picks Holofoil /10 #14
2012 Press Pass Power Picks Holofoil /10 #69
2012 Press Pass Power Picks Holofoil /10 #46
2012 Press Pass Preferred Line #PL3
2012 Press Pass Purple /35 #29
2012 Press Pass Purple /35 #66
2012 Press Pass Purple /35 #87
2012 Press Pass Redline #31
2012 Press Pass Redline Black /99 #31
2012 Press Pass Redline Cyan /50 #31
2012 Press Pass Redline Full Throttle Dual Relic Blue /5 #FTRN
2012 Press Pass Redline Full Throttle Dual Relic Gold /10 #FTRN
2012 Press Pass Redline Full Throttle Dual Relic Melting /1 #FTRN
2012 Press Pass Redline Full Throttle Dual Relic Red /75 #FTRN
2012 Press Pass Redline Full Throttle Dual Relic Silver /25 #FTRN
2012 Press Pass Redline Magenta /15 #31
2012 Press Pass Redline Signatures Blue /5 #RSRN
2012 Press Pass Redline Signatures Gold /25 #RSRN
2012 Press Pass Redline Signatures Holofoil /10 #RSRN
2012 Press Pass Redline Signatures Melting /1 #RSRN
2012 Press Pass Redline Signatures Red /50 #RSRN
2012 Press Pass Redline Yellow /1 #31
2012 Press Pass Showcase /499 #19
2012 Press Pass Showcase /499 #53
2012 Press Pass Showcase Classic Collections Ink /10 #CCMSHR
2012 Press Pass Showcase Classic Collections Ink Gold /5 #CCMSHR
2012 Press Pass Showcase Classic Collections Ink Melting /1 #CCMSHR
2012 Press Pass Showcase Classic Collections Memorabilia /99 #CCMSHR
2012 Press Pass Showcase Classic Collections Memorabilia Gold /50 #CCMSHR
2012 Press Pass Showcase Classic Collections Memorabilia Melting /5 #CCMSHR
2012 Press Pass Showcase Gold /125 #19
2012 Press Pass Showcase Gold /125 #53
2012 Press Pass Showcase Green /5 #19
2012 Press Pass Showcase Green /5 #53
2012 Press Pass Showcase Masterpieces Memorabilia /99 #MPRN
2012 Press Pass Showcase Masterpieces Memorabilia Gold /50 #MPRN
2012 Press Pass Showcase Masterpieces Memorabilia Melting /5 #MPRN
2012 Press Pass Showcase Melting /1 #19
2012 Press Pass Showcase Melting /1 #53
2012 Press Pass Showcase Prized Pieces /99 #PPRN
2012 Press Pass Showcase Prized Pieces Gold /50 #PPRN
2012 Press Pass Showcase Prized Pieces Ink /50 #PPIRN
2012 Press Pass Showcase Prized Pieces Ink Gold /25 #PPIRN
2012 Press Pass Showcase Prized Pieces Ink Melting /1 #PPIRN
2012 Press Pass Showcase Prized Pieces Melting /5 #PPRN
2012 Press Pass Showcase Purple /1 #19
2012 Press Pass Showcase Purple /1 #53
2012 Press Pass Showcase Red /25 #19
2012 Press Pass Showcase Red /25 #53
2012 Press Pass Signature Series Race Used /12 #PPARN1
2012 Press Pass Signature Series Race Used /12 #PPARN2
2012 Press Pass Snapshots #SS29
2012 Press Pass Wal-Mart Snapshots #SSWM8
2012 Total Memorabilia #27A
2012 Total Memorabilia #27B
2012 Total Memorabilia Black and White /99 #27
2012 Total Memorabilia Dual Swatch Gold /75 #TMRN
2012 Total Memorabilia Dual Swatch Holofoil /25 #TMRN
2012 Total Memorabilia Dual Swatch Melting /5 #TMRN
2012 Total Memorabilia Dual Swatch Silver /99 #TMRN
2012 Total Memorabilia Gold /275 #27
2012 Total Memorabilia Jumbo Swatch Gold /50 #TMRN
2012 Total Memorabilia Jumbo Swatch Holofoil /10 #TMRN
2012 Total Memorabilia Jumbo Swatch Melting /1 #TMRN
2012 Total Memorabilia Memory Lane #ML2
2012 Total Memorabilia Red Retail /250 #27
2012 Total Memorabilia Signature Collection Dual Swatch Silver /10 #SCRN
2012 Total Memorabilia Signature Collection Quad Swatch Holofoil /5 #SCRN
2012 Total Memorabilia Signature Collection Single Swatch Melting /1 #SCRN
2012 Total Memorabilia Signature Collection Triple Swatch Gold /10 #SCRN
2012 Total Memorabilia Single Swatch Gold /99 #TMRN
2012 Total Memorabilia Single Swatch Holofoil /50 #TMRN
2012 Total Memorabilia Single Swatch Melting /10 #TMRN
2012 Total Memorabilia Single Swatch Silver /299 #TMRN
2012 Total Memorabilia Triple Swatch Gold /50 #TMRN
2012 Total Memorabilia Triple Swatch Holofoil /25 #TMRN
2012 Total Memorabilia Triple Swatch Melting /1 #TMRN
2012 Total Memorabilia Triple Swatch Silver /99 #TMRN
2013 Press Pass #35
2013 Press Pass #98
2013 Press Pass Burning Rubber Blue /50 #BRRN
2013 Press Pass Burning Rubber Gold /199 #BRRN
2013 Press Pass Burning Rubber Holofoil /75 #BRRN
2013 Press Pass Burning Rubber Melting /10 #BRRN
2013 Press Pass Certified Winners Autographs Gold /10 #RN
2013 Press Pass Certified Winners Autographs Melting /5 #RN
2013 Press Pass Color Proofs Black #35
2013 Press Pass Color Proofs Black #98
2013 Press Pass Color Proofs Cyan /35 #35
2013 Press Pass Color Proofs Cyan /35 #98
2013 Press Pass Color Proofs Magenta #35
2013 Press Pass Color Proofs Magenta #98
2013 Press Pass Color Proofs Yellow /5 #35
2013 Press Pass Color Proofs Yellow /5 #98
2013 Press Pass Cup Chase #CC15
2013 Press Pass Cup Chase Prizes #CCE12
2013 Press Pass Fanfare #45
2013 Press Pass Fanfare #44
2013 Press Pass Fanfare Autographs Blue /1 #RN
2013 Press Pass Fanfare Autographs Gold /10 #RN
2013 Press Pass Fanfare Autographs Green /2 #RN
2013 Press Pass Fanfare Autographs Red /5 #RN
2013 Press Pass Fanfare Autographs Silver /30 #RN
2013 Press Pass Fanfare Diamond Die Cuts /5 #44
2013 Press Pass Fanfare Diamond Die Cuts /5 #45
2013 Press Pass Fanfare Green /3 #44
2013 Press Pass Fanfare Green /3 #45
2013 Press Pass Fanfare Holofoil Die Cuts #44
2013 Press Pass Fanfare Holofoil Die Cuts #45
2013 Press Pass Fanfare Magnificent Jumbo Materials Signatures /10 #RN
2013 Press Pass Fanfare Magnificent Materials Dual Swatches /50 #RN
2013 Press Pass Fanfare Magnificent Materials Dual Swatches Melting /10 #RN
2013 Press Pass Fanfare Magnificent Materials Gold /50 #RN
2013 Press Pass Fanfare Magnificent Materials Jumbo Swatches /25 #RN
2013 Press Pass Fanfare Magnificent Materials Signatures /99 #RN
2013 Press Pass Fanfare Magnificent Materials Signatures Blue /25 #RN
2013 Press Pass Fanfare Magnificent Materials Silver /199 #RN
2013 Press Pass Fanfare Red Foil Die Cuts #44
2013 Press Pass Fanfare Red Foil Die Cuts #45
2013 Press Pass Fanfare Sapphire /20 #44
2013 Press Pass Fanfare Sapphire /20 #45
2013 Press Pass Fanfare Signature Ride Autographs /10 #RN
2013 Press Pass Fanfare Signature Ride Autographs Blue /1 #RN
2013 Press Pass Fanfare Signature Ride Autographs Red /5 #RN
2013 Press Pass Fanfare Silver /25 #44
2013 Press Pass Fanfare Silver /25 #45
2013 Press Pass Ignite #28
2013 Press Pass Ignite #54
2013 Press Pass Ignite Convoy #7
2013 Press Pass Ignite Great American Treads Autographs Blue Holofoil /20 #GATRN
2013 Press Pass Ignite Great American Treads Autographs Red /1 #GATRN
2013 Press Pass Ignite Hot Threads Blue Holofoil /99 #HTRN
2013 Press Pass Ignite Hot Threads Patch Red /10 #HTRN
2013 Press Pass Ignite Hot Threads Silver #HTRN
2013 Press Pass Ignite Ink Black /50 #IIRN
2013 Press Pass Ignite Ink Blue /20 #IIRN
2013 Press Pass Ignite Ink Red /5 #IIRN
2013 Press Pass Ignite Proofs Black and White /50 #28
2013 Press Pass Ignite Proofs Black and White /50 #54
2013 Press Pass Ignite Proofs Cyan #28
2013 Press Pass Ignite Proofs Cyan #54
2013 Press Pass Ignite Proofs Magenta #28
2013 Press Pass Ignite Proofs Magenta #54
2013 Press Pass Ignite Proofs Yellow /5 #28
2013 Press Pass Ignite Proofs Yellow /5 #54
2013 Press Pass Power Picks Blue /99 #14
2013 Press Pass Power Picks Blue /99 #47
2013 Press Pass Power Picks Gold /50 #14
2013 Press Pass Power Picks Gold /50 #47
2013 Press Pass Power Picks Holofoil /10 #14
2013 Press Pass Power Picks Holofoil /10 #47
2013 Press Pass Racing Champions #RC6
2013 Press Pass Redline #38
2013 Press Pass Redline #39
2013 Press Pass Redline Black /99 #38
2013 Press Pass Redline Black /99 #39
2013 Press Pass Redline Cyan /50 #38
2013 Press Pass Redline Cyan /50 #39
2013 Press Pass Redline Dynamic Duals Dual Relic Blue /5 #DDRN
2013 Press Pass Redline Dynamic Duals Dual Relic Gold /10 #DDRN
2013 Press Pass Redline Dynamic Duals Dual Relic Melting /1 #DDRN
2013 Press Pass Redline Dynamic Duals Dual Relic Red /75 #DDRN
2013 Press Pass Redline Dynamic Duals Dual Relic Silver /25 #DDRN
2013 Press Pass Redline Intensity #7
2013 Press Pass Redline Magenta /15 #38
2013 Press Pass Redline Magenta /15 #39
2013 Press Pass Redline Muscle Car Sheet Metal Blue /5 #MCMRN
2013 Press Pass Redline Muscle Car Sheet Metal Gold /10 #MCMRN
2013 Press Pass Redline Muscle Car Sheet Metal Melting /1 #MCMRN
2013 Press Pass Redline Muscle Car Sheet Metal Red /50 #MCMRN
2013 Press Pass Redline Muscle Car Sheet Metal Silver /25 #MCMRN
2013 Press Pass Redline Relic Autographs Blue /10 #RRSERN
2013 Press Pass Redline Relic Autographs Gold /25 #RRSERN
2013 Press Pass Redline Relic Autographs Melting /1 #RRSERN
2013 Press Pass Redline Relic Autographs Red /95 #RRSERN
2013 Press Pass Redline Relic Autographs Silver /39 #RRSERN
2013 Press Pass Redline Relics Blue /5 #RRRN
2013 Press Pass Redline Relics Gold /10 #RRRN
2013 Press Pass Redline Relics Melting /1 #RRRN
2013 Press Pass Redline Relics Red /50 #RRRN
2013 Press Pass Redline Relics Silver /25 #RRRN
2013 Press Pass Redline Signatures Blue /10 #RSRN1
2013 Press Pass Redline Signatures Blue /10 #RSRN2
2013 Press Pass Redline Signatures Gold /5 #RSRN1
2013 Press Pass Redline Signatures Gold /5 #RSRN2
2013 Press Pass Redline Signatures Holo /5 #RSRN1
2013 Press Pass Redline Signatures Holo /5 #RSRN2
2013 Press Pass Redline Signatures Melting /1 #RSRN1
2013 Press Pass Redline Signatures Melting /1 #RSRN2
2013 Press Pass Redline Signatures Red /10 #RSRN2
2013 Press Pass Redline Signatures Red /20 #RSRN1
2013 Press Pass Redline Yellow /1 #38
2013 Press Pass Redline Yellow /1 #39
2013 Press Pass Showcase /349 #23
2013 Press Pass Showcase /349 #48
2013 Press Pass Showcase /349 #56
2013 Press Pass Showcase Black /1 #23
2013 Press Pass Showcase Black /1 #48
2013 Press Pass Showcase Black /1 #56
2013 Press Pass Showcase Blue /25 #23
2013 Press Pass Showcase Blue /25 #48
2013 Press Pass Showcase Blue /25 #56
2013 Press Pass Showcase Classic Collections Ink Gold /5 #CCISHR
2013 Press Pass Showcase Classic Collections Ink Melting /1 #CCISHR
2013 Press Pass Showcase Classic Collections Ink Red /1 #CCISHR
2013 Press Pass Showcase Classic Collections Memorabilia Gold /25 #CCMSHR
2013 Press Pass Showcase Classic Collections Memorabilia Melting /5 #CCMSHR
2013 Press Pass Showcase Classic Collections Memorabilia Silver /75 #CCMSHR
2013 Press Pass Showcase Gold /99 #23
2013 Press Pass Showcase Gold /99 #48
2013 Press Pass Showcase Gold /99 #56
2013 Press Pass Showcase Green /20 #23
2013 Press Pass Showcase Green /20 #48
2013 Press Pass Showcase Green /20 #56
2013 Press Pass Showcase Masterpieces Ink /35 #MPIRN
2013 Press Pass Showcase Masterpieces Ink Gold /10 #MPIRN
2013 Press Pass Showcase Masterpieces Ink Melting /1 #MPIRN
2013 Press Pass Showcase Masterpieces Memorabilia /75 #MPRN
2013 Press Pass Showcase Masterpieces Memorabilia Gold /25 #MPRN
2013 Press Pass Showcase Masterpieces Memorabilia Melting /5 #MPRN
2013 Press Pass Showcase Prized Pieces /99 #PPMRN
2013 Press Pass Showcase Prized Pieces Blue /20 #PPMRN
2013 Press Pass Showcase Prized Pieces Gold /25 #PPMRN
2013 Press Pass Showcase Prized Pieces Ink /25 #PPIRN
2013 Press Pass Showcase Prized Pieces Ink Gold /10 #PPIRN
2013 Press Pass Showcase Prized Pieces Ink Melting /1 #PPIRN
2013 Press Pass Showcase Prized Pieces Melting /5 #PPMRN
2013 Press Pass Showcase Purple /13 #23
2013 Press Pass Showcase Purple /13 #48
2013 Press Pass Showcase Purple /13 #56
2013 Press Pass Showcase Red /10 #23
2013 Press Pass Showcase Red /10 #48
2013 Press Pass Showcase Red /10 #56
2013 Press Pass Showcase Series Standouts Memorabilia /75 #SSMRN
2013 Press Pass Showcase Series Standouts Memorabilia Blue /20 #SSMRN
2013 Press Pass Showcase Series Standouts Memorabilia Gold /25 #SSMRN
2013 Press Pass Showcase Series Standouts Memorabilia Melting /5 #SSMRN
2013 Press Pass Showcase Showcase Patches /5 #SPRN
2013 Press Pass Signings Blue /1 #RN
2013 Press Pass Signings Gold /25 #RN
2013 Press Pass Signings Holofoil /10 #RN
2013 Press Pass Signings Printing Plates Black /1 #RN
2013 Press Pass Signings Printing Plates Cyan /1 #RN
2013 Press Pass Signings Printing Plates Magenta /1 #RN
2013 Press Pass Signings Printing Plates Yellow /1 #RN
2013 Press Pass Signings Silver /50 #RN
2013 Total Memorabilia #32
2013 Total Memorabilia Black and White /99 #32
2013 Total Memorabilia Dual Swatch Gold /179 #TMRN
2013 Total Memorabilia Gold /275 #32
2013 Total Memorabilia Quad Swatch Melting /10 #TMRN
2013 Total Memorabilia Red #32
2013 Total Memorabilia Signature Collection Dual Swatch Gold /10 #SCRN
2013 Total Memorabilia Signature Collection Quad Swatch Melting /1 #SCRN
2013 Total Memorabilia Signature Collection Single Swatch Silver /10 #SCRN
2013 Total Memorabilia Signature Collection Triple Swatch Holofoil /5 #SCRN
2013 Total Memorabilia Single Swatch Silver /475 #TMRN
2013 Total Memorabilia Triple Swatch Holofoil /99 #TMRN
2014 Press Pass American Thunder #29
2014 Press Pass American Thunder #54
2014 Press Pass American Thunder Autographs Blue /10 #ATARN
2014 Press Pass American Thunder Autographs Red /5 #ATARN
2014 Press Pass American Thunder Autographs White /35 #ATARN
2014 Press Pass American Thunder Black and White /50 #29
2014 Press Pass American Thunder Black and White /50 #54
2014 Press Pass American Thunder Brothers In Arms Autographs Blue /5 #BARCR
2014 Press Pass American Thunder Brothers In Arms Autographs Red /1 #BARCR
2014 Press Pass American Thunder Brothers In Arms Autographs White /10 #BARCR
2014 Press Pass American Thunder Brothers In Arms Relics Blue /25 #BARCR
2014 Press Pass American Thunder Brothers In Arms Relics Red /5 #BARCR
2014 Press Pass American Thunder Brothers In Arms Relics Silver /50 #BARCR
2014 Press Pass American Thunder Class A Uniforms Blue /99 #CAURN
2014 Press Pass American Thunder Class A Uniforms Flag /1 #CAURN
2014 Press Pass American Thunder Class A Uniforms Red /10 #CAURN
2014 Press Pass American Thunder Class A Uniforms Silver #CAURN
2014 Press Pass American Thunder Cyan #29
2014 Press Pass American Thunder Cyan #54
2014 Press Pass American Thunder Great American Treads Autographs Blue /25 #GATRN
2014 Press Pass American Thunder Great American Treads Autographs Red /1 #GATRN
2014 Press Pass American Thunder Magenta #29
2014 Press Pass American Thunder Magenta #54
2014 Press Pass American Thunder Top Speed #TS5
2014 Press Pass American Thunder Yellow /5 #29
2014 Press Pass American Thunder Yellow /5 #54
2014 Press Pass Redline #42
2014 Press Pass Redline #41
2014 Press Pass Redline Black /75 #41
2014 Press Pass Redline Black /75 #42
2014 Press Pass Redline Blue Foil #41
2014 Press Pass Redline Blue Foil #42
2014 Press Pass Redline Cyan /50 #41
2014 Press Pass Redline Cyan /50 #42
2014 Press Pass Redline Green National Convention /5 #41
2014 Press Pass Redline Green National Convention /5 #42
2014 Press Pass Redline Magenta /10 #41
2014 Press Pass Redline Magenta /10 #42
2014 Press Pass Redline Relic Autographs Blue /5 #RRSERN
2014 Press Pass Redline Relic Autographs Gold /15 #RRSERN
2014 Press Pass Redline Relic Autographs Melting /1 #RRSERN
2014 Press Pass Redline Relic Autographs Red /25 #RRSERN
2014 Press Pass Redline Relics Blue /25 #RRRN
2014 Press Pass Redline Relics Gold /50 #RRRN
2014 Press Pass Redline Relics Melting /1 #RRRN
2014 Press Pass Redline Relics Red /75 #RRRN
2014 Press Pass Redline Signatures Blue /5 #RSRN
2014 Press Pass Redline Signatures Gold /15 #RSRN
2014 Press Pass Redline Signatures Melting /1 #RSRN
2014 Press Pass Redline Signatures Red /25 #RSRN
2014 Press Pass Redline Yellow /1 #41
2014 Press Pass Redline Yellow /1 #42
2014 Total Memorabilia #22
2014 Total Memorabilia Black and White /99 #22
2014 Total Memorabilia Gold /175 #22
2014 Total Memorabilia Red #22
2015 Press Pass #28
2015 Press Pass #88
2015 Press Pass #75
2015 Press Pass #100
2015 Press Pass Championship Caliber Dual /25 #CCMRN
2015 Press Pass Championship Caliber Quad /1 #CCMRN
2015 Press Pass Championship Caliber Signature Edition Blue /25 #CCRN
2015 Press Pass Championship Caliber Signature Edition Gold /50 #CCRN
2015 Press Pass Championship Caliber Signature Edition Green /10 #CCRN
2015 Press Pass Championship Caliber Signature Edition Melting /1 #CCRN
2015 Press Pass Championship Caliber Single /50 #CCMRN
2015 Press Pass Championship Caliber Triple /10 #CCMRN
2015 Press Pass Cup Chase #28
2015 Press Pass Cup Chase #75
2015 Press Pass Cup Chase #88
2015 Press Pass Cup Chase #100
2015 Press Pass Cup Chase Blue /25 #28
2015 Press Pass Cup Chase Blue /25 #75
2015 Press Pass Cup Chase Blue /25 #88
2015 Press Pass Cup Chase Blue /25 #100
2015 Press Pass Cup Chase Gold /75 #28
2015 Press Pass Cup Chase Gold /75 #75
2015 Press Pass Cup Chase Gold /75 #88
2015 Press Pass Cup Chase Gold /75 #100
2015 Press Pass Cup Chase Green /10 #28
2015 Press Pass Cup Chase Green /10 #75
2015 Press Pass Cup Chase Green /10 #88
2015 Press Pass Cup Chase Green /10 #100
2015 Press Pass Cup Chase Melting /1 #28
2015 Press Pass Cup Chase Melting /1 #75
2015 Press Pass Cup Chase Melting /1 #88
2015 Press Pass Cup Chase Melting /1 #100
2015 Press Pass Cup Chase Upper Cuts /13 #UCRN
2015 Press Pass Pit Road Pieces Blue /25 #PPMRN
2015 Press Pass Pit Road Pieces Gold /50 #PPMRN
2015 Press Pass Pit Road Pieces Green /10 #PPMRN
2015 Press Pass Pit Road Pieces Melting /1 #PPMRN
2015 Press Pass Pit Road Pieces Signature Edition Blue /25 #PRPRN
2015 Press Pass Pit Road Pieces Signature Edition Gold /50 #PRPRN
2015 Press Pass Pit Road Pieces Signature Edition Green /10 #PRPRN
2015 Press Pass Pit Road Pieces Signature Edition Melting /1 #PRPRN
2015 Press Pass Purple #28
2015 Press Pass Purple #75
2015 Press Pass Purple #88
2015 Press Pass Purple #100
2015 Press Pass Red #28
2015 Press Pass Red #75
2015 Press Pass Red #88
2015 Press Pass Red #100
2015 Press Pass Signature Series Blue /15 #SSRN
2015 Press Pass Signature Series Gold /20 #SSRN
2015 Press Pass Signature Series Green /10 #SSRN
2015 Press Pass Signature Series Melting /1 #SSRN
2015 Press Pass Signings Blue /15 #PPSRN
2015 Press Pass Signings Gold #PPSRN
2015 Press Pass Signings Green /5 #PPSRN
2015 Press Pass Signings Melting /1 #PPSRN
2015 Press Pass Signings Red /10 #PPSRN
2016 Certified #16
2016 Certified Complete Materials /199 #24
2016 Certified Complete Materials Mirror Black /1 #24
2016 Certified Complete Materials Mirror Blue /50 #24
2016 Certified Complete Materials Mirror Gold /25 #24
2016 Certified Complete Materials Mirror Green /5 #24
2016 Certified Complete Materials Mirror Orange /99 #24
2016 Certified Complete Materials Mirror Purple /10 #24
2016 Certified Complete Materials Mirror Red /75 #24
2016 Certified Complete Materials Mirror Silver /99 #24
2016 Certified Mirror Black /1 #16
2016 Certified Mirror Blue /50 #16
2016 Certified Mirror Gold /25 #16
2016 Certified Mirror Green /5 #16
2016 Certified Mirror Orange /99 #16
2016 Certified Mirror Purple /10 #16
2016 Certified Mirror Red /75 #16
2016 Certified Mirror Silver /99 #16
2016 Certified Signatures /35 #17
2016 Certified Signatures Mirror Black /1 #17
2016 Certified Signatures Mirror Blue /20 #17
2016 Certified Signatures Mirror Gold /15 #17
2016 Certified Signatures Mirror Green /5 #17
2016 Certified Signatures Mirror Orange /5 #17
2016 Certified Signatures Mirror Purple /10 #17
2016 Certified Signatures Mirror Red /25 #17
2016 Certified Signatures Mirror Silver /5 #17
2016 Certified Skills /199 #1
2016 Certified Skills Mirror Black /1 #1
2016 Certified Skills Mirror Blue /50 #1
2016 Certified Skills Mirror Gold /25 #1
2016 Certified Skills Mirror Green /5 #1
2016 Certified Skills Mirror Orange /99 #1
2016 Certified Skills Mirror Purple /10 #1
2016 Certified Skills Mirror Red /75 #1
2016 Certified Skills Mirror Silver /99 #1
2016 Certified Sprint Cup Signature Swatches /75 #14
2016 Certified Sprint Cup Signature Swatches Mirror Black /1 #14
2016 Certified Sprint Cup Signature Swatches Mirror Blue /25 #14
2016 Certified Sprint Cup Signature Swatches Mirror Gold /15 #14
2016 Certified Sprint Cup Signature Swatches Mirror Green /5 #14
2016 Certified Sprint Cup Signature Swatches Mirror Orange /8 #14
2016 Certified Sprint Cup Signature Swatches Mirror Purple /10 #14
2016 Certified Sprint Cup Signature Swatches Mirror Red /35 #14
2016 Certified Sprint Cup Signature Swatches Mirror Silver /5 #14
2016 Certified Sprint Cup Swatches Mirror Black /1 #34
2016 Certified Sprint Cup Swatches Mirror Blue /50 #34
2016 Certified Sprint Cup Swatches Mirror Gold /25 #34
2016 Certified Sprint Cup Swatches Mirror Green /5 #34
2016 Certified Sprint Cup Swatches Mirror Orange /5 #34
2016 Certified Sprint Cup Swatches Mirror Purple /10 #34
2016 Certified Sprint Cup Swatches Mirror Red /75 #34
2016 Certified Sprint Cup Swatches Mirror Silver /5 #34
2016 Panini Black Friday Racing Memorabilia #R4
2016 Panini Black Friday Racing Memorabilia Cracked Ice /25 #R4
2016 Panini Black Friday Racing Memorabilia Galactic Window /10 #R4
2016 Panini Black Friday Racing Memorabilia Holo Plaid /1 #R4
2016 Panini National Treasures /25 #18
2016 Panini National Treasures Black /5 #18
2016 Panini National Treasures Blue /1 #18
2016 Panini National Treasures Combo Materials /25 #13
2016 Panini National Treasures Combo Materials Black /5 #13
2016 Panini National Treasures Combo Materials Blue /1 #13
2016 Panini National Treasures Combo Materials Gold /10 #13
2016 Panini National Treasures Combo Materials Printing Plates Black /1 #13
2016 Panini National Treasures Combo Materials Printing Plates Cyan /1 #13
2016 Panini National Treasures Combo Materials Printing Plates Mag #13
2016 Panini National Treasures Combo Materials Printing Plates Yell #13
2016 Panini National Treasures Combo Materials Silver /15 #13
2016 Panini National Treasures Dual Driver Materials /25 #11
2016 Panini National Treasures Dual Driver Materials Black /5 #11
2016 Panini National Treasures Dual Driver Materials Blue /1 #11
2016 Panini National Treasures Dual Driver Materials Gold /10 #11
2016 Panini National Treasures Dual Driver Materials Printing Plates B /1 #11
2016 Panini National Treasures Dual Driver Materials Printing Plates C /1 #11
2016 Panini National Treasures Dual Driver Materials Printing Plates Magenta /1 #11
2016 Panini National Treasures Dual Driver Materials Printing Plates Y /1 #11
2016 Panini National Treasures Dual Driver Materials Silver /15 #11
2016 Panini National Treasures Dual Signatures /25 #4
2016 Panini National Treasures Dual Signatures Black /10 #4
2016 Panini National Treasures Dual Signatures Blue /1 #4
2016 Panini National Treasures Dual Signatures Gold /15 #4
2016 Panini National Treasures Gold /15 #18
2016 Panini National Treasures Jumbo Firesuit Patch Signature Booklet Associate Sponsor 1 /1 #24
2016 Panini National Treasures Jumbo Firesuit Patch Signature Booklet Associate Sponsor 10 /1 #24
2016 Panini National Treasures Jumbo Firesuit Patch Signature Booklet Associate Sponsor 11 /1 #24
2016 Panini National Treasures Jumbo Firesuit Patch Signature Booklet Associate Sponsor 12 /1 #24
2016 Panini National Treasures Jumbo Firesuit Patch Signature Booklet Associate Sponsor 13 /1 #24
2016 Panini National Treasures Jumbo Firesuit Patch Signature Booklet Associate Sponsor 14 /1 #24
2016 Panini National Treasures Jumbo Firesuit Patch Signature Booklet Associate Sponsor 15 /1 #24
2016 Panini National Treasures Jumbo Firesuit Patch Signature Booklet Associate Sponsor 16 /1 #24
2016 Panini National Treasures Jumbo Firesuit Patch Signature Booklet Associate Sponsor 17 /1 #24
2016 Panini National Treasures Jumbo Firesuit Patch Signature Booklet Associate Sponsor 2 /1 #24
2016 Panini National Treasures Jumbo Firesuit Patch Signature Booklet Associate Sponsor 3 /1 #24
2016 Panini National Treasures Jumbo Firesuit Patch Signature Booklet Associate Sponsor 4 /1 #24
2016 Panini National Treasures Jumbo Firesuit Patch Signature Booklet Associate Sponsor 5 /1 #24
2016 Panini National Treasures Jumbo Firesuit Patch Signature Booklet Associate Sponsor 6 /1 #24
2016 Panini National Treasures Jumbo Firesuit Patch Signature Booklet Associate Sponsor 7 /1 #24
2016 Panini National Treasures Jumbo Firesuit Patch Signature Booklet Associate Sponsor 8 /1 #24
2016 Panini National Treasures Jumbo Firesuit Patch Signature Booklet Associate Sponsor 9 /1 #24
2016 Panini National Treasures Jumbo Firesuit Patch Signature Booklet /1 #24
2016 Panini National Treasures Jumbo Firesuit Patch Signature Booklet Manufacturers Logo /2 #24
2016 Panini National Treasures Jumbo Firesuit Patch Signature Booklet Nameplate /2 #24
2016 Panini National Treasures Jumbo Firesuit Patch Signature Booklet NASCAR /1 #24
2016 Panini National Treasures Jumbo Firesuit Patch Signature Booklet Sprint Cup Logo /1 #24
2016 Panini National Treasures Jumbo Firesuit Patch Signature Booklet Sunoco /1 #24
2016 Panini National Treasures Jumbo Firesuit Signatures /25 #24
2016 Panini National Treasures Jumbo Firesuit Signatures Black /5 #24
2016 Panini National Treasures Jumbo Firesuit Signatures Blue /1 #24
2016 Panini National Treasures Jumbo Firesuit Signatures Gold /10 #24
2016 Panini National Treasures Jumbo Firesuit Signatures Printing Plates Black /1 #24
2016 Panini National Treasures Jumbo Firesuit Signatures Printing Plates Cyan /1 #24
2016 Panini National Treasures Jumbo Firesuit Signatures Printing Plates Magenta /1 #24
2016 Panini National Treasures Jumbo Firesuit Signatures Printing Plates Yellow /1 #24
2016 Panini National Treasures Jumbo Firesuit Signatures Silver /15 #24
2016 Panini National Treasures Printing Plates Black /1 #18
2016 Panini National Treasures Printing Plates Cyan /1 #18
2016 Panini National Treasures Printing Plates Magenta /1 #18
2016 Panini National Treasures Printing Plates Yellow /1 #18
2016 Panini National Treasures Sheet Metal Materials /25 #1
2016 Panini National Treasures Sheet Metal Materials Black /5 #1
2016 Panini National Treasures Sheet Metal Materials Blue /1 #1
2016 Panini National Treasures Sheet Metal Materials Gold /10 #1
2016 Panini National Treasures Sheet Metal Materials Printing Plates Blac /1 #1
2016 Panini National Treasures Sheet Metal Materials Printing Plates Cyan /1 #1
2016 Panini National Treasures Sheet Metal Materials Printing Plates Magenta /1 #1
2016 Panini National Treasures Sheet Metal Materials Printing Plates Yell /1 #1
2016 Panini National Treasures Sheet Metal Materials Silver /15 #1
2016 Panini National Treasures Signature Dual Materials /25 #21
2016 Panini National Treasures Signature Dual Materials Black /5 #21
2016 Panini National Treasures Signature Dual Materials Blue /1 #21
2016 Panini National Treasures Signature Dual Materials Gold /10 #21
2016 Panini National Treasures Signature Dual Materials Printing Plates Black /1 #21
2016 Panini National Treasures Signature Dual Materials Printing Plates Cyan /1 #21
2016 Panini National Treasures Signature Dual Materials Printing Plates Magenta /1 #21
2016 Panini National Treasures Signature Dual Materials Printing Plates Yellow /1 #21
2016 Panini National Treasures Signature Dual Materials Silver /15 #21
2016 Panini National Treasures Signature Firesuit Materials /25 #23
2016 Panini National Treasures Signature Firesuit Materials Black /5 #23
2016 Panini National Treasures Signature Firesuit Materials Blue /1 #23
2016 Panini National Treasures Signature Firesuit Materials Gold /10 #23
2016 Panini National Treasures Signature Firesuit Materials Laundry Tag /1 #23
2016 Panini National Treasures Signature Firesuit Materials Printing Plates Black /1 #23
2016 Panini National Treasures Signature Firesuit Materials Printing Plates Cyan /1 #23
2016 Panini National Treasures Signature Firesuit Materials Printing Plates Magenta /1 #23
2016 Panini National Treasures Signature Firesuit Materials Printing Plates Yellow /1 #23
2016 Panini National Treasures Signature Firesuit Materials Silver /15 #23
2016 Panini National Treasures Signature Quad Materials /25 #21
2016 Panini National Treasures Signature Quad Materials Black /5 #21
2016 Panini National Treasures Signature Quad Materials Blue /1 #21
2016 Panini National Treasures Signature Quad Materials Gold /10 #21
2016 Panini National Treasures Signature Quad Materials Printing Plates Black /1 #21
2016 Panini National Treasures Signature Quad Materials Printing Plates Cyan /1 #21
2016 Panini National Treasures Signature Quad Materials Printing Plates Magenta /1 #21

2016 Panini National Treasures Signature Quad Materials Printing Plates Yellow /1 #21
2016 Panini National Treasures Signature Quad Materials Silver /15 #21
2016 Panini National Treasures Signature Sheet Metal Materials /25 #21
2016 Panini National Treasures Signature Sheet Metal Materials Black /5 #21
2016 Panini National Treasures Signature Sheet Metal Materials Blue /1 #21
2016 Panini National Treasures Signature Sheet Metal Materials Gold /10 #21
2016 Panini National Treasures Signature Sheet Metal Materials Printing Plates Black /1 #21
2016 Panini National Treasures Signature Sheet Metal Materials Printing Plates Cyan /1 #21
2016 Panini National Treasures Signature Sheet Metal Materials Printing Plates Magenta /1 #21
2016 Panini National Treasures Signature Sheet Metal Materials Printing Plates Yellow /1 #21
2016 Panini National Treasures Signature Sheet Metal Materials Silver /15 #21
2016 Panini National Treasures Signatures Black /5 #20
2016 Panini National Treasures Signatures Blue /1 #20
2016 Panini National Treasures Signatures Printing Plates Black /1 #20
2016 Panini National Treasures Signatures Printing Plates Cyan /1 #20
2016 Panini National Treasures Signatures Printing Plates Magenta /1 #20
2016 Panini National Treasures Signatures Printing Plates Yellow /1 #20
2016 Panini National Treasures Silver /20 #18
2016 Panini National Treasures Six Signatures /25 #3
2016 Panini National Treasures Six Signatures Black /10 #3
2016 Panini National Treasures Six Signatures Blue /1 #3
2016 Panini National Treasures Six Signatures Gold /15 #3
2016 Panini National Treasures Timelines /25 #15
2016 Panini National Treasures Timelines Black /5 #15
2016 Panini National Treasures Timelines Blue /1 #15
2016 Panini National Treasures Timelines Gold /10 #15
2016 Panini National Treasures Timelines Printing Plates Black /1 #15
2016 Panini National Treasures Timelines Printing Plates Cyan /1 #15
2016 Panini National Treasures Timelines Printing Plates Magenta /1 #15
2016 Panini National Treasures Timelines Printing Plates Yellow /1 #15
2016 Panini National Treasures Timelines Signatures /25 #14
2016 Panini National Treasures Timelines Signatures Black /5 #14
2016 Panini National Treasures Timelines Signatures Blue /1 #14
2016 Panini National Treasures Timelines Signatures Gold /10 #14
2016 Panini National Treasures Timelines Signatures Printing Plates Black /1 #14
2016 Panini National Treasures Timelines Signatures Printing Plates Cyan /1 #14
2016 Panini National Treasures Timelines Signatures Printing Plates Magenta /1 #14
2016 Panini National Treasures Timelines Signatures Printing Plates Yellow /1 #14
2016 Panini National Treasures Timelines Signatures Silver /15 #14
2016 Panini National Treasures Timelines Silver /15 #15
2016 Panini National Treasures Trio Driver Materials /25 #6
2016 Panini National Treasures Trio Driver Materials /25 #15
2016 Panini National Treasures Trio Driver Materials Black /5 #6
2016 Panini National Treasures Trio Driver Materials Black /5 #15
2016 Panini National Treasures Trio Driver Materials Blue /1 #6
2016 Panini National Treasures Trio Driver Materials Blue /1 #15
2016 Panini National Treasures Trio Driver Materials Gold /10 #6
2016 Panini National Treasures Trio Driver Materials Gold /10 #15
2016 Panini National Treasures Trio Driver Materials Printing Plates Black /1 #6
2016 Panini National Treasures Trio Driver Materials Printing Plates Black /1 #15
2016 Panini National Treasures Trio Driver Materials Printing Plates Cyan /1 #6
2016 Panini National Treasures Trio Driver Materials Printing Plates Cyan /1 #15
2016 Panini National Treasures Trio Driver Materials Printing Plates Magenta /1 #6
2016 Panini National Treasures Trio Driver Materials Printing Plates Magenta /1 #15
2016 Panini National Treasures Trio Driver Materials Printing Plates Yellow /1 #6
2016 Panini National Treasures Trio Driver Materials Printing Plates Yellow /1 #15
2016 Panini National Treasures Trio Driver Materials Silver /15 #6
2016 Panini National Treasures Trio Driver Materials Silver /15 #15
2016 Panini Prizm #83
2016 Panini Prizm #54
2016 Panini Prizm #31
2016 Panini Prizm Autographs Prizms #54
2016 Panini Prizm Autographs Prizms Black /3 #54
2016 Panini Prizm Autographs Prizms Blue Flag /50 #54
2016 Panini Prizm Autographs Prizms Camo /31 #54
2016 Panini Prizm Autographs Prizms Checkered Flag /1 #54
2016 Panini Prizm Autographs Prizms Gold /10 #54
2016 Panini Prizm Autographs Prizms Green Flag /75 #54
2016 Panini Prizm Autographs Prizms Rainbow /24 #54
2016 Panini Prizm Autographs Prizms Red Flag /25 #54
2016 Panini Prizm Autographs Prizms Red White and Blue /25 #54
2016 Panini Prizm Autographs Prizms White Flag /5 #54
2016 Panini Prizm Firesuit Fabrics /149 #14
2016 Panini Prizm Firesuit Fabrics Prizms Blue Flag /75 #14
2016 Panini Prizm Firesuit Fabrics Prizms Checkered Flag /1 #14
2016 Panini Prizm Firesuit Fabrics Prizms Green Flag /99 #14
2016 Panini Prizm Firesuit Fabrics Prizms Red Flag /25 #14
2016 Panini Prizm Firesuit Fabrics Team /249 #14
2016 Panini Prizm Firesuit Fabrics Team Prizms Blue Flag /75 #14
2016 Panini Prizm Firesuit Fabrics Team Prizms Checkered Flag /1 #14
2016 Panini Prizm Firesuit Fabrics Team Prizms Green Flag /99 #14
2016 Panini Prizm Firesuit Fabrics Team Prizms Red Flag /25 #14
2016 Panini Prizm Prizms #31
2016 Panini Prizm Prizms #54
2016 Panini Prizm Prizms #83
2016 Panini Prizm Prizms Black /3 #31
2016 Panini Prizm Prizms Black /3 #54
2016 Panini Prizm Prizms Black /3 #83
2016 Panini Prizm Prizms Blue Flag /99 #31
2016 Panini Prizm Prizms Blue Flag /99 #54
2016 Panini Prizm Prizms Blue Flag /99 #83
2016 Panini Prizm Prizms Camo /31 #31
2016 Panini Prizm Prizms Camo /31 #54
2016 Panini Prizm Prizms Camo /31 #83
2016 Panini Prizm Prizms Checkered Flag /1 #31
2016 Panini Prizm Prizms Checkered Flag /1 #54
2016 Panini Prizm Prizms Checkered Flag /1 #83
2016 Panini Prizm Prizms Gold /10 #31
2016 Panini Prizm Prizms Gold /10 #54
2016 Panini Prizm Prizms Gold /10 #83
2016 Panini Prizm Prizms Green Flag /149 #31
2016 Panini Prizm Prizms Green Flag /149 #54
2016 Panini Prizm Prizms Green Flag /149 #83
2016 Panini Prizm Prizms Rainbow /24 #31
2016 Panini Prizm Prizms Rainbow /24 #54
2016 Panini Prizm Prizms Rainbow /24 #83
2016 Panini Prizm Prizms Red Flag /75 #31
2016 Panini Prizm Prizms Red Flag /75 #54
2016 Panini Prizm Prizms Red Flag /75 #83
2016 Panini Prizm Prizms Red White and Blue #31
2016 Panini Prizm Prizms Red White and Blue #54
2016 Panini Prizm Prizms Red White and Blue #83
2016 Panini Prizm Prizms White Flag /5 #31
2016 Panini Prizm Prizms White Flag /5 #54
2016 Panini Prizm Prizms White Flag /5 #83
2016 Panini Prizm Race Used Tire #10
2016 Panini Prizm Race Used Tire Prizms Blue Flag /49 #10
2016 Panini Prizm Race Used Tire Prizms Checkered Flag /1 #10
2016 Panini Prizm Race Used Tire Prizms Green Flag /99 #10
2016 Panini Prizm Race Used Tire Prizms Red Flag /25 #10
2016 Panini Torque #22
2016 Panini Torque Artist Proof /50 #22
2016 Panini Torque Blackout /1 #22
2016 Panini Torque Blue /125 #22
2016 Panini Torque Clear Vision #21
2016 Panini Torque Clear Vision Blue /99 #21
2016 Panini Torque Clear Vision Gold /149 #21
2016 Panini Torque Clear Vision Green /25 #21
2016 Panini Torque Clear Vision Purple /10 #21
2016 Panini Torque Clear Vision Red /49 #21
2016 Panini Torque Dual Materials /299 #9
2016 Panini Torque Dual Materials Blue /99 #9
2016 Panini Torque Dual Materials Green /25 #9
2016 Panini Torque Dual Materials Purple /10 #9
2016 Panini Torque Dual Materials Red /49 #9
2016 Panini Torque Gas N Go #3
2016 Panini Torque Gas N Go Gold /199 #3
2016 Panini Torque Gas N Go Holo Silver /99 #3
2016 Panini Torque Gold #22
2016 Panini Torque Holo Gold /5 #22
2016 Panini Torque Holo Silver /10 #22
2016 Panini Torque Horsepower Heroes #11
2016 Panini Torque Horsepower Heroes Gold /199 #11
2016 Panini Torque Horsepower Heroes Holo Silver /99 #11
2016 Panini Torque Jumbo Tire Autographs /30 #13
2016 Panini Torque Jumbo Tire Autographs Blue /25 #13
2016 Panini Torque Jumbo Tire Autographs Green /15 #13
2016 Panini Torque Jumbo Tire Autographs Purple /10 #13
2016 Panini Torque Jumbo Tire Autographs Red /20 #13
2016 Panini Torque Metal Materials /249 #19
2016 Panini Torque Metal Materials Blue /99 #19
2016 Panini Torque Metal Materials Green /25 #19
2016 Panini Torque Metal Materials Purple /10 #19
2016 Panini Torque Metal Materials Red /49 #19
2016 Panini Torque Painted to Perfection #15
2016 Panini Torque Painted to Perfection Blue /99 #15
2016 Panini Torque Painted to Perfection Checkerboard /10 #15
2016 Panini Torque Painted to Perfection Green /25 #15
2016 Panini Torque Painted to Perfection Red /49 #15
2016 Panini Torque Pairings Materials /249 #19
2016 Panini Torque Pairings Materials /125 #29
2016 Panini Torque Pairings Materials Blue /99 #19
2016 Panini Torque Pairings Materials Blue /99 #29
2016 Panini Torque Pairings Materials Green /25 #19
2016 Panini Torque Pairings Materials Green /25 #29
2016 Panini Torque Pairings Materials Purple /10 #19
2016 Panini Torque Pairings Materials Purple /10 #29
2016 Panini Torque Pairings Materials Red /49 #19
2016 Panini Torque Pairings Materials Red /49 #29
2016 Panini Torque Pole Position #17
2016 Panini Torque Pole Position Blue /99 #17
2016 Panini Torque Pole Position Checkerboard /10 #17
2016 Panini Torque Pole Position Green /25 #17
2016 Panini Torque Pole Position Red /49 #17
2016 Panini Torque Printing Plates Black /1 #22
2016 Panini Torque Printing Plates Cyan /1 #22
2016 Panini Torque Printing Plates Magenta /1 #22
2016 Panini Torque Printing Plates Yellow /1 #22
2016 Panini Torque Purple /25 #22
2016 Panini Torque Red /99 #22
2016 Panini Torque Silhouettes Firesuit Autographs /30 #22
2016 Panini Torque Silhouettes Firesuit Autographs Blue /25 #22
2016 Panini Torque Silhouettes Firesuit Autographs Green /15 #22
2016 Panini Torque Silhouettes Firesuit Autographs Purple /10 #22
2016 Panini Torque Silhouettes Firesuit Autographs Red /20 #22
2016 Panini Torque Silhouettes Sheet Metal Autographs /30 #23
2016 Panini Torque Silhouettes Sheet Metal Autographs Blue /25 #23
2016 Panini Torque Silhouettes Sheet Metal Autographs Green /15 #23
2016 Panini Torque Silhouettes Sheet Metal Autographs Purple /10 #23
2016 Panini Torque Silhouettes Sheet Metal Autographs Red /20 #23
2016 Panini Torque Superstar Vision #13
2016 Panini Torque Superstar Vision Blue /99 #13
2016 Panini Torque Superstar Vision Gold /149 #13
2016 Panini Torque Superstar Vision Green /25 #13
2016 Panini Torque Superstar Vision Purple /10 #13
2016 Panini Torque Superstar Vision Red /49 #13
2016 Panini Torque Test Proof Black /1 #22
2016 Panini Torque Test Proof Cyan /1 #22
2016 Panini Torque Test Proof Magenta /1 #22
2016 Panini Torque Test Proof Yellow /1 #22
2016 Panini Torque Winning Vision #16
2016 Panini Torque Winning Vision Blue /99 #16
2016 Panini Torque Winning Vision Gold /149 #16
2016 Panini Torque Winning Vision Green /25 #16
2016 Panini Torque Winning Vision Purple /10 #16
2016 Panini Torque Winning Vision Red /49 #16
2017 Donruss #19
2017 Donruss #114
2017 Donruss #180
2017 Donruss #60A
2017 Donruss #60B
2017 Donruss Artist Proof /25 #19
2017 Donruss Artist Proof /25 #60A
2017 Donruss Artist Proof /25 #180
2017 Donruss Artist Proof /25 #60B
2017 Donruss Artist Proof /25 #114
2017 Donruss Blue Foil /299 #19
2017 Donruss Blue Foil /299 #60A
2017 Donruss Blue Foil /299 #180
2017 Donruss Blue Foil /299 #60B
2017 Donruss Blue Foil /299 #114
2017 Donruss Dual Rubber Relics #14
2017 Donruss Dual Rubber Relics Holo Black /10 #14
2017 Donruss Dual Rubber Relics Holo Gold /25 #14
2017 Donruss Gold Foil /499 #19
2017 Donruss Gold Foil /499 #180
2017 Donruss Gold Foil /499 #60A
2017 Donruss Gold Foil /499 #60B
2017 Donruss Gold Foil /499 #114
2017 Donruss Gold Press Proof /99 #19
2017 Donruss Gold Press Proof /99 #60A
2017 Donruss Gold Press Proof /99 #180
2017 Donruss Gold Press Proof /99 #60B
2017 Donruss Gold Press Proof /99 #114
2017 Donruss Green Foil /199 #19
2017 Donruss Green Foil /199 #60A
2017 Donruss Green Foil /199 #180
2017 Donruss Green Foil /199 #60B
2017 Donruss Green Foil /199 #114
2017 Donruss Press Proof /49 #19
2017 Donruss Press Proof /49 #60A
2017 Donruss Press Proof /49 #180
2017 Donruss Press Proof /49 #60B
2017 Donruss Press Proof /49 #114
2017 Donruss Printing Plates Black /1 #19
2017 Donruss Printing Plates Black /1 #60A
2017 Donruss Printing Plates Black /1 #180
2017 Donruss Printing Plates Black /1 #60B
2017 Donruss Printing Plates Black /1 #114
2017 Donruss Printing Plates Cyan /1 #19
2017 Donruss Printing Plates Cyan /1 #60A
2017 Donruss Printing Plates Cyan /1 #180
2017 Donruss Printing Plates Cyan /1 #60B
2017 Donruss Printing Plates Cyan /1 #114
2017 Donruss Printing Plates Magenta /1 #19
2017 Donruss Printing Plates Magenta /1 #180
2017 Donruss Printing Plates Magenta /1 #60A
2017 Donruss Printing Plates Magenta /1 #60B
2017 Donruss Printing Plates Magenta /1 #114
2017 Donruss Printing Plates Yellow /1 #19
2017 Donruss Printing Plates Yellow /1 #180
2017 Donruss Printing Plates Yellow /1 #60A
2017 Donruss Printing Plates Yellow /1 #60B
2017 Donruss Printing Plates Yellow /1 #114
2017 Donruss Rubber Relics #40
2017 Donruss Rubber Relics Holo Black /10 #40
2017 Donruss Rubber Relics Holo Gold /25 #40
2017 Donruss Speed #6
2017 Donruss Speed Cracked Ice /999 #6
2017 Donruss Studio Signatures #13
2017 Donruss Studio Signatures Holo Black /1 #13
2017 Donruss Studio Signatures Holo Gold /25 #13
2017 Panini Father's Day Racing Memorabilia /100 #4
2017 Panini Father's Day Racing Memorabilia Cracked Ice /25 #4
2017 Panini Father's Day Racing Memorabilia Hyperplaid /1 #4
2017 Panini Father's Day Racing Memorabilia Shimmer /10 #4
2017 Panini Instant Nascar #4
2017 Panini Instant Nascar Black /1 #4
2017 Panini Instant Nascar Green /10 #4
2017 Panini National Treasures /25 #13
2017 Panini National Treasures Associate Sponsor Patch Signatures 1 /1 #12
2017 Panini National Treasures Associate Sponsor Patch Signatures 10 /1 #12
2017 Panini National Treasures Associate Sponsor Patch Signatures 11 /1 #12
2017 Panini National Treasures Associate Sponsor Patch Signatures 12 /1 #12
2017 Panini National Treasures Associate Sponsor Patch Signatures 2 /1 #12
2017 Panini National Treasures Associate Sponsor Patch Signatures 3 /1 #12
2017 Panini National Treasures Associate Sponsor Patch Signatures 4 /1 #12
2017 Panini National Treasures Associate Sponsor Patch Signatures 5 /1 #12
2017 Panini National Treasures Associate Sponsor Patch Signatures 6 /1 #12
2017 Panini National Treasures Associate Sponsor Patch Signatures 7 /1 #12
2017 Panini National Treasures Associate Sponsor Patch Signatures 8 /1 #12
2017 Panini National Treasures Associate Sponsor Patch Signatures 9 /1 #12
2017 Panini National Treasures Car Manufacturer Patch Signatures /1 #12
2017 Panini National Treasures Century Black /1 #13
2017 Panini National Treasures Century Gold /15 #13
2017 Panini National Treasures Century Green /5 #13
2017 Panini National Treasures Century Holo Gold /10 #13
2017 Panini National Treasures Century Holo Silver /20 #13
2017 Panini National Treasures Century Laundry Tags /1 #13
2017 Panini National Treasures Dual Firesuit Materials /25 #15
2017 Panini National Treasures Dual Firesuit Materials Black /1 #15
2017 Panini National Treasures Dual Firesuit Materials Gold /15 #15
2017 Panini National Treasures Dual Firesuit Materials Green /5 #15
2017 Panini National Treasures Dual Firesuit Materials Holo Gold /10 #15
2017 Panini National Treasures Dual Firesuit Materials Holo Silver /20 #15
2017 Panini National Treasures Dual Firesuit Materials Laundry Tag /1 #15
2017 Panini National Treasures Dual Firesuit Materials Printing Plates Black /1 #15
2017 Panini National Treasures Dual Firesuit Materials Printing Plates Cyan /1 #15
2017 Panini National Treasures Dual Firesuit Materials Printing Plates Magenta /1 #15
2017 Panini National Treasures Dual Firesuit Materials Printing Plates Yellow /1 #15
2017 Panini National Treasures Dual Firesuit Signatures /25 #15
2017 Panini National Treasures Dual Firesuit Signatures Black /1 #15
2017 Panini National Treasures Dual Firesuit Signatures Gold /15 #15
2017 Panini National Treasures Dual Firesuit Signatures Green /5 #15
2017 Panini National Treasures Dual Firesuit Signatures Holo Gold /10 #15
2017 Panini National Treasures Dual Firesuit Signatures Holo Silver /20 #15
2017 Panini National Treasures Dual Firesuit Signatures Laundry Tag /1 #15
2017 Panini National Treasures Dual Firesuit Signatures Printing Plates Black /1 #15
2017 Panini National Treasures Dual Firesuit Signatures Printing Plates Cyan /1 #15
2017 Panini National Treasures Dual Firesuit Signatures Printing Plates Magenta /1 #15
2017 Panini National Treasures Dual Firesuit Signatures Printing Plates Yellow /1 #15
2017 Panini National Treasures Dual Sheet Metal Signatures /25 #11
2017 Panini National Treasures Dual Sheet Metal Signatures Black /1 #11
2017 Panini National Treasures Dual Sheet Metal Signatures Gold /15 #11
2017 Panini National Treasures Dual Sheet Metal Signatures Green /5 #11
2017 Panini National Treasures Dual Sheet Metal Signatures Holo Gold /10 #11
2017 Panini National Treasures Dual Sheet Metal Signatures Holo Silver /20 #11
2017 Panini National Treasures Dual Sheet Metal Signatures Printing Plates Black /1 #11
2017 Panini National Treasures Dual Sheet Metal Signatures Printing Plates Cyan /1 #11
2017 Panini National Treasures Dual Sheet Metal Signatures Printing Plates Magenta /1 #11
2017 Panini National Treasures Dual Sheet Metal Signatures Printing Plates Yellow /1 #11
2017 Panini National Treasures Firesuit Manufacturer Patch Signatures /1 #12
2017 Panini National Treasures Flag Patch Signatures /1 #12
2017 Panini National Treasures Goodyear Patch Signatures /1 #12
2017 Panini National Treasures Hats Off /13 #6
2017 Panini National Treasures Hats Off Gold /2 #6
2017 Panini National Treasures Hats Off Holo Gold /5 #6
2017 Panini National Treasures Hats Off Laundry Tag /6 #6
2017 Panini National Treasures Hats Off New Era /1 #6
2017 Panini National Treasures Hats Off Printing Plates Black /1 #6
2017 Panini National Treasures Hats Off Printing Plates Cyan /1 #6
2017 Panini National Treasures Hats Off Printing Plates Magenta /1 #6
2017 Panini National Treasures Hats Off Sponsor /5 #6
2017 Panini National Treasures Jumbo Firesuit Signatures /25 #10
2017 Panini National Treasures Jumbo Firesuit Signatures Black /1 #10
2017 Panini National Treasures Jumbo Firesuit Signatures Gold /15 #10
2017 Panini National Treasures Jumbo Firesuit Signatures Green /5 #10
2017 Panini National Treasures Jumbo Firesuit Signatures Holo Gold /10 #10
2017 Panini National Treasures Jumbo Firesuit Signatures Holo Silver /20 #10
2017 Panini National Treasures Jumbo Firesuit Signatures Laundry Tag /1 #10
2017 Panini National Treasures Jumbo Firesuit Signatures Printing Plates Black /1 #10
2017 Panini National Treasures Jumbo Firesuit Signatures Printing Plates Cyan /1 #10
2017 Panini National Treasures Jumbo Firesuit Signatures Printing Plates Magenta /1 #10
2017 Panini National Treasures Jumbo Firesuit Signatures Printing Plates Yellow /1 #10
2017 Panini National Treasures Nameplate Patch Signatures /2 #12
2017 Panini National Treasures NASCAR Patch Signatures /1 #12
2017 Panini National Treasures Printing Plates Black /1 #13
2017 Panini National Treasures Printing Plates Cyan /1 #13
2017 Panini National Treasures Printing Plates Magenta /1 #13
2017 Panini National Treasures Printing Plates Yellow /1 #13
2017 Panini National Treasures Quad Materials /25 #7
2017 Panini National Treasures Quad Materials Gold /15 #7
2017 Panini National Treasures Quad Materials Green /5 #7
2017 Panini National Treasures Quad Materials Holo Gold /10 #7
2017 Panini National Treasures Quad Materials Holo Silver /20 #7
2017 Panini National Treasures Quad Materials Printing Plates Black /1 #7
2017 Panini National Treasures Quad Materials Printing Plates Cyan /1 #7
2017 Panini National Treasures Quad Materials Printing Plates Magenta /1 #7
2017 Panini National Treasures Quad Materials Printing Plates Yellow /1 #7
2017 Panini National Treasures Series Sponsor Patch Signatures /1 #12
2017 Panini National Treasures Signature Sheet Metal /25 #4
2017 Panini National Treasures Signature Sheet Metal Black /1 #4
2017 Panini National Treasures Signature Sheet Metal Gold /15 #4
2017 Panini National Treasures Signature Sheet Metal Green /5 #4
2017 Panini National Treasures Signature Sheet Metal Holo Gold /10 #4
2017 Panini National Treasures Signature Sheet Metal Holo Silver /20 #4
2017 Panini National Treasures Sunoco Patch Signatures /1 #12
2017 Panini National Treasures Teammates Dual Materials /25 #8
2017 Panini National Treasures Teammates Dual Materials Black /1 #8
2017 Panini National Treasures Teammates Dual Materials Gold /15 #8
2017 Panini National Treasures Teammates Dual Materials Green /5 #8
2017 Panini National Treasures Teammates Dual Materials Holo Gold /10 #8
2017 Panini National Treasures Teammates Dual Materials Holo Silver /20 #8
2017 Panini National Treasures Teammates Dual Materials Laundry Tag /1 #8
2017 Panini National Treasures Teammates Dual Materials Printing Plates Black /1 #8
2017 Panini National Treasures Teammates Dual Materials Printing Plates Cyan /1 #8
2017 Panini National Treasures Teammates Dual Materials Printing Plates Magenta /1 #8
2017 Panini National Treasures Teammates Dual Materials Printing Plates Yellow /1 #8
2017 Panini National Treasures Teammates Quad Materials /25 #10
2017 Panini National Treasures Teammates Quad Materials Black /1 #10
2017 Panini National Treasures Teammates Quad Materials Gold /15 #10
2017 Panini National Treasures Teammates Quad Materials Green /5 #10
2017 Panini National Treasures Teammates Quad Materials Holo Gold /10 #10
2017 Panini National Treasures Teammates Quad Materials Holo Silver /20 #10
2017 Panini National Treasures Teammates Quad Materials Laundry Tag /1 #10
2017 Panini National Treasures Teammates Quad Materials Printing Plates Black /1 #10
2017 Panini National Treasures Teammates Quad Materials Printing Plates Cyan /1 #10
2017 Panini National Treasures Teammates Quad Materials Printing Plates Magenta /1 #10
2017 Panini National Treasures Teammates Quad Materials Printing Plates Yellow /1 #10
2017 Panini National Treasures Teammates Triple Materials /25 #4
2017 Panini National Treasures Teammates Triple Materials Black /1 #4
2017 Panini National Treasures Teammates Triple Materials Gold /15 #4
2017 Panini National Treasures Teammates Triple Materials Green /5 #4
2017 Panini National Treasures Teammates Triple Materials Holo Gold /10 #4
2017 Panini National Treasures Teammates Triple Materials Holo Silver /20 #4
2017 Panini National Treasures Teammates Triple Materials Laundry Tag /1 #4
2017 Panini National Treasures Teammates Triple Materials Printing Plates Black /1 #4
2017 Panini National Treasures Teammates Triple Materials Printing Plates Cyan /1 #4
2017 Panini National Treasures Teammates Triple Materials Printing Plates Magenta /1 #4
2017 Panini National Treasures Teammates Triple Materials Printing Plates Yellow /1 #4
2017 Panini National Treasures Three Wide Signatures /25 #12
2017 Panini National Treasures Three Wide Signatures Black /1 #12
2017 Panini National Treasures Three Wide Signatures Gold /15 #12
2017 Panini National Treasures Three Wide Signatures Green /5 #12
2017 Panini National Treasures Three Wide Signatures Holo Gold /10 #12
2017 Panini National Treasures Three Wide Signatures Holo Silver /20 #12
2017 Panini National Treasures Three Wide Signatures Laundry Tag /1 #12
2017 Panini National Treasures Three Wide Signatures Printing Plates Black /1 #12
2017 Panini National Treasures Three Wide Signatures Printing Plates Cyan /1 #12
2017 Panini National Treasures Three Wide Signatures Printing Plates Magenta /1 #12
2017 Panini National Treasures Three Wide Signatures Printing Plates Yellow /1 #12
2017 Panini Torque #15
2017 Panini Torque #71
2017 Panini Torque #77
2017 Panini Torque #87
2017 Panini Torque #100
2017 Panini Torque Artist Proof /75 #15
2017 Panini Torque Artist Proof /75 #71
2017 Panini Torque Artist Proof /75 #77
2017 Panini Torque Artist Proof /75 #87
2017 Panini Torque Artist Proof /75 #100
2017 Panini Torque Blackout /1 #15
2017 Panini Torque Blackout /1 #71
2017 Panini Torque Blackout /1 #77
2017 Panini Torque Blackout /1 #87
2017 Panini Torque Blackout /1 #100
2017 Panini Torque Blue /150 #15
2017 Panini Torque Blue /150 #71
2017 Panini Torque Blue /150 #77
2017 Panini Torque Blue /150 #87
2017 Panini Torque Blue /150 #100
2017 Panini Torque Clear Vision #15
2017 Panini Torque Clear Vision Blue /99 #15
2017 Panini Torque Clear Vision Gold /149 #15
2017 Panini Torque Clear Vision Green /25 #15
2017 Panini Torque Clear Vision Purple /10 #15
2017 Panini Torque Clear Vision Red /49 #15
2017 Panini Torque Combo Materials Signatures /51 #4
2017 Panini Torque Combo Materials Signatures Blue /49 #4
2017 Panini Torque Combo Materials Signatures Green /15 #4
2017 Panini Torque Combo Materials Signatures Purple /10 #4
2017 Panini Torque Combo Materials Signatures Red /25 #4
2017 Panini Torque Dual Materials /399 #19
2017 Panini Torque Dual Materials Blue /99 #19
2017 Panini Torque Dual Materials Green /25 #19
2017 Panini Torque Dual Materials Purple /10 #19
2017 Panini Torque Dual Materials Red /49 #19
2017 Panini Torque Gold #15
2017 Panini Torque Gold #71
2017 Panini Torque Gold #77
2017 Panini Torque Gold #87
2017 Panini Torque Gold #100
2017 Panini Torque Holo Gold /10 #15
2017 Panini Torque Holo Gold /10 #71
2017 Panini Torque Holo Gold /10 #77
2017 Panini Torque Holo Gold /10 #87
2017 Panini Torque Holo Gold /10 #100
2017 Panini Torque Holo Silver /25 #15
2017 Panini Torque Holo Silver /25 #71
2017 Panini Torque Holo Silver /25 #77
2017 Panini Torque Holo Silver /25 #87
2017 Panini Torque Holo Silver /25 #100
2017 Panini Torque Manufacturer Marks #15
2017 Panini Torque Manufacturer Marks Gold /199 #15
2017 Panini Torque Manufacturer Marks Holo Silver /99 #15
2017 Panini Torque Pairings Materials /199 #3
2017 Panini Torque Pairings Materials Blue /99 #3
2017 Panini Torque Pairings Materials Green /25 #3
2017 Panini Torque Pairings Materials Purple /10 #3
2017 Panini Torque Pairings Materials Red /49 #3
2017 Panini Torque Prime Associate Sponsors Jumbo Patches /1 #17A
2017 Panini Torque Prime Associate Sponsors Jumbo Patches /1 #17B
2017 Panini Torque Prime Associate Sponsors Jumbo Patches /1 #17C
2017 Panini Torque Prime Associate Sponsors Jumbo Patches /1 #17D
2017 Panini Torque Prime Associate Sponsors Jumbo Patches /1 #17E
2017 Panini Torque Prime Associate Sponsors Jumbo Patches /1 #17F
2017 Panini Torque Prime Associate Sponsors Jumbo Patches /1 #17G
2017 Panini Torque Prime Associate Sponsors Jumbo Patches /1 #17H
2017 Panini Torque Prime Associate Sponsors Jumbo Patches /1 #17I
2017 Panini Torque Prime Associate Sponsors Jumbo Patches /1 #17J
2017 Panini Torque Prime Associate Sponsors Jumbo Patches /1 #17K
2017 Panini Torque Prime Associate Sponsors Jumbo Patches /1 #17L
2017 Panini Torque Prime Associate Sponsors Jumbo Patches /1 #17M
2017 Panini Torque Prime Associate Sponsors Jumbo Patches /1 #17N
2017 Panini Torque Prime Associate Sponsors Jumbo Patches /1 #17O
2017 Panini Torque Prime Flag Jumbo Patches /1 #17
2017 Panini Torque Prime Goodyear Jumbo Patches /1 #17
2017 Panini Torque Prime Manufacturer Jumbo Patches /1 #17
2017 Panini Torque Prime Nameplates Jumbo Patches /2 #17
2017 Panini Torque Prime NASCAR Jumbo Patches /1 #17
2017 Panini Torque Prime Series Sponsor Jumbo Patches /1 #17
2017 Panini Torque Printing Plates Black /1 #15
2017 Panini Torque Printing Plates Black /1 #71
2017 Panini Torque Printing Plates Black /1 #77
2017 Panini Torque Printing Plates Black /1 #87
2017 Panini Torque Printing Plates Black /1 #100
2017 Panini Torque Printing Plates Cyan /1 #15
2017 Panini Torque Printing Plates Cyan /1 #71
2017 Panini Torque Printing Plates Cyan /1 #77
2017 Panini Torque Printing Plates Cyan /1 #87
2017 Panini Torque Printing Plates Cyan /1 #100
2017 Panini Torque Printing Plates Magenta /1 #15
2017 Panini Torque Printing Plates Magenta /1 #71
2017 Panini Torque Printing Plates Magenta /1 #77
2017 Panini Torque Printing Plates Magenta /1 #87
2017 Panini Torque Printing Plates Magenta /1 #100
2017 Panini Torque Printing Plates Yellow /1 #15
2017 Panini Torque Printing Plates Yellow /1 #71
2017 Panini Torque Printing Plates Yellow /1 #77
2017 Panini Torque Printing Plates Yellow /1 #87
2017 Panini Torque Printing Plates Yellow /1 #100
2017 Panini Torque Purple /50 #15
2017 Panini Torque Purple /50 #71
2017 Panini Torque Purple /50 #77
2017 Panini Torque Purple /50 #87
2017 Panini Torque Purple /50 #100
2017 Panini Torque Quad Materials /199 #24
2017 Panini Torque Quad Materials Blue /99 #24
2017 Panini Torque Quad Materials Green /25 #24
2017 Panini Torque Quad Materials Purple /10 #24
2017 Panini Torque Quad Materials Red /49 #24
2017 Panini Torque Raced Relics /499 #19
2017 Panini Torque Raced Relics Blue /99 #19
2017 Panini Torque Raced Relics Green /25 #19
2017 Panini Torque Raced Relics Purple /10 #19
2017 Panini Torque Raced Relics Red /49 #19
2017 Panini Torque Red /100 #15
2017 Panini Torque Red /100 #71
2017 Panini Torque Red /100 #77
2017 Panini Torque Red /100 #87
2017 Panini Torque Red /100 #100
2017 Panini Torque Running Order #17
2017 Panini Torque Running Order Blue /99 #17
2017 Panini Torque Running Order Checkerboard /10 #17
2017 Panini Torque Running Order Green /25 #17
2017 Panini Torque Running Order Red /49 #17
2017 Panini Torque Silhouettes Firesuit Signatures /51 #7
2017 Panini Torque Silhouettes Firesuit Signatures Blue /49 #7
2017 Panini Torque Silhouettes Firesuit Signatures Green /15 #7
2017 Panini Torque Silhouettes Firesuit Signatures Purple /10 #7
2017 Panini Torque Silhouettes Firesuit Signatures Red /25 #7
2017 Panini Torque Special Paint #6
2017 Panini Torque Special Paint Gold /199 #6
2017 Panini Torque Special Paint Holo Silver /99 #6
2017 Panini Torque Superstar Vision #14
2017 Panini Torque Superstar Vision Blue /99 #14
2017 Panini Torque Superstar Vision Gold /149 #14
2017 Panini Torque Superstar Vision Green /25 #14
2017 Panini Torque Superstar Vision Purple /10 #14
2017 Panini Torque Superstar Vision Red /49 #14
2017 Panini Torque Test Proof Black /1 #15
2017 Panini Torque Test Proof Black /1 #71
2017 Panini Torque Test Proof Black /1 #77
2017 Panini Torque Test Proof Black /1 #87
2017 Panini Torque Test Proof Black /1 #100
2017 Panini Torque Test Proof Cyan /1 #15
2017 Panini Torque Test Proof Cyan /1 #71
2017 Panini Torque Test Proof Cyan /1 #77
2017 Panini Torque Test Proof Cyan /1 #87
2017 Panini Torque Test Proof Cyan /1 #100
2017 Panini Torque Test Proof Magenta /1 #15
2017 Panini Torque Test Proof Magenta /1 #71
2017 Panini Torque Test Proof Magenta /1 #77
2017 Panini Torque Test Proof Magenta /1 #87
2017 Panini Torque Test Proof Magenta /1 #100
2017 Panini Torque Test Proof Yellow /1 #15
2017 Panini Torque Test Proof Yellow /1 #71
2017 Panini Torque Test Proof Yellow /1 #77
2017 Panini Torque Test Proof Yellow /1 #87
2017 Panini Torque Test Proof Yellow /1 #100
2017 Panini Torque Visions of Greatness #25
2017 Panini Torque Visions of Greatness Blue /99 #25
2017 Panini Torque Visions of Greatness Gold /149 #25
2017 Panini Torque Visions of Greatness Green /25 #25
2017 Panini Torque Visions of Greatness Purple /10 #25
2017 Panini Torque Visions of Greatness Red /49 #25
2017 Select #59
2017 Select #60
2017 Select #105
2017 Select Prizms Black /3 #59
2017 Select Prizms Black /3 #60
2017 Select Prizms Black /3 #105
2017 Select Prizms Blue /199 #59
2017 Select Prizms Blue /199 #60
2017 Select Prizms Checkered Flag /1 #59
2017 Select Prizms Checkered Flag /1 #60
2017 Select Prizms Checkered Flag /1 #105
2017 Select Prizms Gold /10 #59
2017 Select Prizms Gold /10 #60
2017 Select Prizms Gold /10 #105
2017 Select Prizms Purple Pulsar #59
2017 Select Prizms Purple Pulsar #60
2017 Select Prizms Red /99 #59
2017 Select Prizms Red /99 #60
2017 Select Prizms Red White and Blue Pulsar /299 #59
2017 Select Prizms Red White and Blue Pulsar /299 #60
2017 Select Prizms Silver #59
2017 Select Prizms Silver #60
2017 Select Prizms Tie Dye /24 #59
2017 Select Prizms Tie Dye /24 #60
2017 Select Prizms Tie Dye /24 #105
2017 Select Prizms White /50 #59
2017 Select Prizms White /50 #60
2017 Select Prizms White /50 #105
2017 Select Select Pairs Materials #5
2017 Select Select Pairs Materials Prizms Blue /199 #5
2017 Select Select Pairs Materials Prizms Checkered Flag /1 #5
2017 Select Select Pairs Materials Prizms Gold /10 #5
2017 Select Select Pairs Materials Prizms Red /99 #5
2017 Select Select Swatches #41
2017 Select Select Swatches Prizms Blue /199 #41
2017 Select Select Swatches Prizms Checkered Flag /1 #41
2017 Select Select Swatches Prizms Gold /10 #41
2017 Select Select Swatches Prizms Red /99 #41
2017 Select Sheet Metal #23
2017 Select Sheet Metal Prizms Blue /199 #23
2017 Select Sheet Metal Prizms Checkered Flag /1 #23
2017 Select Sheet Metal Prizms Gold /10 #23
2017 Select Sheet Metal Prizms Red /99 #23
2017 Select Signature Paint Schemes Prizms Blue /50 #15
2017 Select Signature Paint Schemes Prizms Checkered Flag /1 #15
2017 Select Signature Swatches #41
2017 Select Signature Swatches Prizms Checkered Flag /1 #41
2017 Select Signature Swatches Prizms Gold /10 #41
2017 Select Signature Swatches Prizms Tie Dye /24 #41
2017 Select Signature Swatches Prizms White /50 #41
2017 Select Signature Swatches Triple #24
2017 Select Signature Swatches Triple Prizms Checkered Flag /1 #24
2017 Select Signature Swatches Triple Prizms Gold /10 #24
2017 Select Signature Swatches Triple Prizms Tie Dye /24 #24
2017 Select Signature Swatches Triple Prizms White /50 #24
2017 Select Speed Merchants #18
2017 Select Speed Merchants Prizms Black /3 #18
2017 Select Speed Merchants Prizms Checkered Flag /1 #18
2017 Select Speed Merchants Prizms Gold /10 #18
2017 Select Speed Merchants Prizms Tie Dye /24 #18
2017 Select Speed Merchants Prizms White /50 #18
2017 Select Up Close and Personal #8
2017 Select Up Close and Personal Prizms Black /3 #8
2017 Select Up Close and Personal Prizms Checkered Flag /1 #8
2017 Select Up Close and Personal Prizms Gold /10 #8
2017 Select Up Close and Personal Prizms Tie Dye /24 #8
2017 Select Up Close and Personal Prizms White /50 #8
2018 Certified #54
2018 Certified Black /1 #54
2018 Certified Blue /99 #54
2018 Certified Cup Swatches /499 #24
2018 Certified Cup Swatches Black /1 #24
2018 Certified Cup Swatches Blue /49 #24
2018 Certified Cup Swatches Gold /25 #24
2018 Certified Cup Swatches Green /5 #24
2018 Certified Cup Swatches Purple /10 #24
2018 Certified Cup Swatches Red /199 #24
2018 Certified Gold /49 #54
2018 Certified Green /10 #54
2018 Certified Materials Signatures /75 #15
2018 Certified Materials Signatures Black /1 #15
2018 Certified Materials Signatures Blue /25 #15
2018 Certified Materials Signatures Gold /15 #15
2018 Certified Materials Signatures Green /5 #15
2018 Certified Materials Signatures Purple /10 #15
2018 Certified Materials Signatures Red /31 #15
2018 Certified Mirror Black /1 #54
2018 Certified Mirror Gold /25 #54
2018 Certified Mirror Green /5 #54
2018 Certified Mirror Purple /10 #54
2018 Certified Orange /249 #54
2018 Certified Piece of the Race /499 #17
2018 Certified Piece of the Race Black /1 #17
2018 Certified Piece of the Race Blue /49 #17
2018 Certified Piece of the Race Gold /25 #17
2018 Certified Piece of the Race Green /5 #17
2018 Certified Piece of the Race Purple /10 #17
2018 Certified Piece of the Race Red /199 #17
2018 Certified Purple /25 #54
2018 Certified Red /199 #54
2018 Certified Signature Swatches /75 #17
2018 Certified Signature Swatches Black /1 #17
2018 Certified Signature Swatches Blue /25 #17
2018 Certified Signature Swatches Gold /15 #17
2018 Certified Signature Swatches Green /5 #17
2018 Certified Signature Swatches Purple /10 #17
2018 Certified Signature Swatches Red /31 #17
2018 Certified Signing Sessions /31 #23
2018 Certified Signing Sessions Black /1 #23
2018 Certified Signing Sessions Blue /20 #23
2018 Certified Signing Sessions Gold /15 #23
2018 Certified Signing Sessions Green /5 #23
2018 Certified Signing Sessions Purple /10 #23
2018 Certified Signing Sessions Red /25 #23
2018 Certified Skills /199 #13
2018 Certified Skills Black /1 #13
2018 Certified Skills Blue /99 #13
2018 Certified Skills Gold /49 #13
2018 Certified Skills Green /10 #13
2018 Certified Skills Mirror Black /1 #13
2018 Certified Skills Mirror Gold /25 #13
2018 Certified Skills Mirror Green /5 #13
2018 Certified Skills Mirror Purple /10 #13
2018 Certified Skills Purple /25 #13
2018 Certified Skills Red /149 #13
2018 Certified Stars /199 #8
2018 Certified Stars Black /1 #8
2018 Certified Stars Blue /99 #8
2018 Certified Stars Gold /49 #8
2018 Certified Stars Green /10 #8
2018 Certified Stars Mirror Black /1 #8
2018 Certified Stars Mirror Gold /25 #8
2018 Certified Stars Mirror Green /5 #8
2018 Certified Stars Mirror Purple /10 #8
2018 Certified Stars Purple /25 #8
2018 Certified Stars Red /149 #8
2018 Donruss #19
2018 Donruss #46A
2018 Donruss #136
2018 Donruss #46B
2018 Donruss Artist Proofs /25 #19
2018 Donruss Artist Proofs /25 #46A
2018 Donruss Artist Proofs /25 #136
2018 Donruss Artist Proofs /25 #46B
2018 Donruss Classics #16
2018 Donruss Classics Cracked Ice /999 #16
2018 Donruss Classics Xplosion /99 #16
2018 Donruss Gold Foil /499 #19
2018 Donruss Gold Foil /499 #46A
2018 Donruss Gold Foil /499 #136
2018 Donruss Gold Foil /499 #46B
2018 Donruss Gold Press Proofs /99 #19
2018 Donruss Gold Press Proofs /99 #46A
2018 Donruss Gold Press Proofs /99 #136
2018 Donruss Gold Press Proofs /99 #46B
2018 Donruss Green Foil /199 #19
2018 Donruss Green Foil /199 #46A
2018 Donruss Green Foil /199 #136
2018 Donruss Green Foil /199 #46B
2018 Donruss Press Proofs /49 #19
2018 Donruss Press Proofs /49 #46
2018 Donruss Press Proofs /49 #136
2018 Donruss Press Proofs /49 #46B

2018 Donruss Printing Plates Black /1 #19
2018 Donruss Printing Plates Black /1 #46
2018 Donruss Printing Plates Black /1 #136
2018 Donruss Printing Plates Black /1 #46B
2018 Donruss Printing Plates Cyan /1 #19
2018 Donruss Printing Plates Cyan /1 #46
2018 Donruss Printing Plates Cyan /1 #136
2018 Donruss Printing Plates Cyan /1 #46B
2018 Donruss Printing Plates Magenta /1 #19
2018 Donruss Printing Plates Magenta /1 #46
2018 Donruss Printing Plates Magenta /1 #136
2018 Donruss Printing Plates Magenta /1 #46B
2018 Donruss Printing Plates Yellow /1 #19
2018 Donruss Printing Plates Yellow /1 #46
2018 Donruss Printing Plates Yellow /1 #136
2018 Donruss Printing Plates Yellow /1 #46B
2018 Donruss Racing Relics #17
2018 Donruss Racing Relics Black /10 #17
2018 Donruss Racing Relics Holo Gold /99 #17
2018 Donruss Red Foil /299 #19
2018 Donruss Red Foil /299 #46A
2018 Donruss Red Foil /299 #136
2018 Donruss Red Foil /299 #46B
2018 Donruss Rubber Relic Signatures #15
2018 Donruss Rubber Relic Signatures Black /1 #15
2018 Donruss Rubber Relic Signatures Holo Gold /25 #15
2018 Donruss Rubber Relics #35
2018 Donruss Rubber Relics Black /10 #35
2018 Donruss Rubber Relics Holo Gold /99 #35
2018 Donruss Signature Series #12
2018 Donruss Signature Series Black /1 #12
2018 Donruss Signature Series Holo Gold /25 #12
2018 Donruss Studio #19
2018 Donruss Studio Cracked Ice /999 #19
2018 Donruss Studio Xplosion /99 #19
2018 Panini Prime /50 #16
2018 Panini Prime /50 #49
2018 Panini Prime /50 #82
2018 Panini Prime Black /1 #16
2018 Panini Prime Black /1 #49
2018 Panini Prime Black /1 #82
2018 Panini Prime Clear Silhouettes /99 #26
2018 Panini Prime Clear Silhouettes Black /1 #26
2018 Panini Prime Clear Silhouettes Dual /99 #28
2018 Panini Prime Clear Silhouettes Dual Black /1 #28
2018 Panini Prime Clear Silhouettes Dual Holo Gold /50 #28
2018 Panini Prime Clear Silhouettes Holo Gold /50 #26
2018 Panini Prime Dual Material Autographs /50 #9
2018 Panini Prime Dual Material Autographs Black /1 #9
2018 Panini Prime Dual Material Autographs Holo Gold /25 #9
2018 Panini Prime Dual Material Autographs Laundry Tag /1 #9
2018 Panini Prime Dual Signatures /50 #15
2018 Panini Prime Dual Signatures Black /1 #15
2018 Panini Prime Dual Signatures Holo Gold /25 #15
2018 Panini Prime Hats Off Button /1 #15
2018 Panini Prime Hats Off Eyelet /6 #15
2018 Panini Prime Hats Off Headband /20 #15
2018 Panini Prime Hats Off Laundry Tag /1 #15
2018 Panini Prime Hats Off New Era /1 #15
2018 Panini Prime Hats Off Number /4 #15
2018 Panini Prime Hats Off Sponsor Logo /6 #15
2018 Panini Prime Hats Off Team Logo /2 #15
2018 Panini Prime Holo Gold /25 #16
2018 Panini Prime Holo Gold /25 #49
2018 Panini Prime Holo Gold /25 #82
2018 Panini Prime Prime Jumbo Associate Sponsor 1 /1 #65
2018 Panini Prime Prime Jumbo Associate Sponsor 10 /1 #65
2018 Panini Prime Prime Jumbo Associate Sponsor 11 /1 #65
2018 Panini Prime Prime Jumbo Associate Sponsor 12 /1 #65
2018 Panini Prime Prime Jumbo Associate Sponsor 13 /1 #65
2018 Panini Prime Prime Jumbo Associate Sponsor 14 /1 #65
2018 Panini Prime Prime Jumbo Associate Sponsor 15 /1 #65
2018 Panini Prime Prime Jumbo Associate Sponsor 2 /1 #65
2018 Panini Prime Prime Jumbo Associate Sponsor 3 /1 #65
2018 Panini Prime Prime Jumbo Associate Sponsor 4 /1 #65
2018 Panini Prime Prime Jumbo Associate Sponsor 5 /1 #65
2018 Panini Prime Prime Jumbo Associate Sponsor 6 /1 #65
2018 Panini Prime Prime Jumbo Associate Sponsor 7 /1 #65
2018 Panini Prime Prime Jumbo Associate Sponsor 8 /1 #65
2018 Panini Prime Prime Jumbo Associate Sponsor 9 /1 #65
2018 Panini Prime Prime Jumbo Car Manufacturer /1 #65
2018 Panini Prime Prime Jumbo Firesuit Manufacturer /1 #65
2018 Panini Prime Prime Jumbo Flag Patch /1 #65
2018 Panini Prime Prime Jumbo Glove Manufacturer Patch /1 #65
2018 Panini Prime Prime Jumbo Glove Name Patch /1 #65
2018 Panini Prime Prime Jumbo Goodyear /1 #65
2018 Panini Prime Prime Jumbo Nameplate /2 #65
2018 Panini Prime Prime Jumbo NASCAR /1 #65
2018 Panini Prime Prime Jumbo Prime Colors /17 #65
2018 Panini Prime Prime Jumbo Series Sponsor /1 #65
2018 Panini Prime Prime Jumbo Shoe Brand Logo /1 #65
2018 Panini Prime Prime Jumbo Sunoco /1 #65
2018 Panini Prime Prime Number Signatures /99 #17
2018 Panini Prime Prime Number Signatures Black /1 #17
2018 Panini Prime Prime Number Signatures Holo Gold /25 #17
2018 Panini Prime Quad Material Autographs /50 #13
2018 Panini Prime Quad Material Autographs Black /1 #13
2018 Panini Prime Quad Material Autographs Holo Gold /49 #13
2018 Panini Prime Quad Material Autographs Laundry Tag /1 #13
2018 Panini Prime Race Used Duals Firesuit /50 #28
2018 Panini Prime Race Used Duals Firesuit Black /1 #28
2018 Panini Prime Race Used Duals Firesuit Holo Gold /25 #28
2018 Panini Prime Race Used Duals Firesuit Laundry Tag /1 #28
2018 Panini Prime Race Used Duals Sheet Metal /50 #28
2018 Panini Prime Race Used Duals Sheet Metal Black /1 #28
2018 Panini Prime Race Used Duals Sheet Metal Holo Gold /25 #28
2018 Panini Prime Race Used Duals Tire /50 #28
2018 Panini Prime Race Used Duals Tire Black /1 #28
2018 Panini Prime Race Used Duals Tire Holo Gold /25 #28
2018 Panini Prime Race Used Firesuits Black /1 #34
2018 Panini Prime Race Used Firesuits Holo Gold /25 #34
2018 Panini Prime Race Used Firesuits Laundry Tag /1 #34
2018 Panini Prime Race Used Sheet Metal /50 #34
2018 Panini Prime Race Used Sheet Metal Black /1 #34
2018 Panini Prime Race Used Sheet Metal Holo Gold /25 #34
2018 Panini Prime Race Used Tires Black /1 #34
2018 Panini Prime Race Used Tires Holo Gold /25 #34
2018 Panini Prime Race Used Trios Firesuit /50 #15
2018 Panini Prime Race Used Trios Firesuit Black /1 #15
2018 Panini Prime Race Used Trios Firesuit Holo Gold /25 #15
2018 Panini Prime Race Used Trios Firesuit Laundry Tag /1 #15
2018 Panini Prime Race Used Trios Sheet Metal /50 #15
2018 Panini Prime Race Used Trios Sheet Metal Black /1 #15
2018 Panini Prime Race Used Trios Sheet Metal Holo Gold /25 #15
2018 Panini Prime Race Used Trios Tire /50 #15
2018 Panini Prime Race Used Trios Tire Black /1 #15
2018 Panini Prime Race Used Trios Tire Holo Gold /25 #15
2018 Panini Prime Signature Tires /99 #16
2018 Panini Prime Signature Tires Black /1 #16
2018 Panini Prime Signature Tires Holo Gold /25 #16
2018 Panini Prime Triple Material Autographs /50 #18
2018 Panini Prime Triple Material Autographs Black /1 #18
2018 Panini Prime Triple Material Autographs Holo Gold /37 #18
2018 Panini Prime Triple Material Autographs Laundry Tag /1 #18
2018 Panini Prizm #10
2018 Panini Prizm #76
2018 Panini Prizm Fireworks #16
2018 Panini Prizm Fireworks Prizms #16
2018 Panini Prizm Fireworks Prizms Black /1 #16
2018 Panini Prizm Fireworks Prizms Gold /10 #16
2018 Panini Prizm Instant Impact #4
2018 Panini Prizm Instant Impact Prizms #4
2018 Panini Prizm Instant Impact Prizms Black /1 #4
2018 Panini Prizm Instant Impact Prizms Gold /10 #4
2018 Panini Prizm National Pride #12
2018 Panini Prizm National Pride Prizms #12
2018 Panini Prizm National Pride Prizms Black /1 #12
2018 Panini Prizm National Pride Prizms Gold /10 #12
2018 Panini Prizm Prizms #10
2018 Panini Prizm Prizms #76
2018 Panini Prizm Prizms Black /1 #10
2018 Panini Prizm Prizms Black /1 #76
2018 Panini Prizm Prizms Blue /99 #10
2018 Panini Prizm Prizms Blue /99 #76
2018 Panini Prizm Prizms Camo #10
2018 Panini Prizm Prizms Camo #76
2018 Panini Prizm Prizms Gold /10 #10
2018 Panini Prizm Prizms Gold /10 #76
2018 Panini Prizm Prizms Green /149 #10
2018 Panini Prizm Prizms Green /149 #76
2018 Panini Prizm Prizms Purple Flash #10
2018 Panini Prizm Prizms Purple Flash #76
2018 Panini Prizm Prizms Rainbow /24 #10
2018 Panini Prizm Prizms Rainbow /24 #76
2018 Panini Prizm Prizms Red /75 #10
2018 Panini Prizm Prizms Red /75 #76
2018 Panini Prizm Prizms Red White and Blue #10
2018 Panini Prizm Prizms Red White and Blue #76
2018 Panini Prizm Prizms White /5 #10
2018 Panini Prizm Prizms White /5 #76
2018 Panini Prizm Scripted Signatures Prizms #22
2018 Panini Prizm Scripted Signatures Prizms Black /1 #22
2018 Panini Prizm Scripted Signatures Prizms Blue /60 #22
2018 Panini Prizm Scripted Signatures Prizms Camo #22
2018 Panini Prizm Scripted Signatures Prizms Gold /10 #22
2018 Panini Prizm Scripted Signatures Prizms Green /75 #22
2018 Panini Prizm Scripted Signatures Prizms Rainbow /24 #22
2018 Panini Prizm Scripted Signatures Prizms Red /50 #22
2018 Panini Prizm Scripted Signatures Prizms Red White and Blue /99 #22
2018 Panini Prizm Scripted Signatures Prizms White /5 #22
2018 Panini Prizm Stars and Stripes #14
2018 Panini Prizm Stars and Stripes Prizms #14
2018 Panini Prizm Stars and Stripes Prizms Black /1 #14
2018 Panini Prizm Stars and Stripes Prizms Gold /10 #14
2018 Panini Victory Lane #17
2018 Panini Victory Lane Black /1 #17
2018 Panini Victory Lane Blue /25 #17
2018 Panini Victory Lane Celebrations #11
2018 Panini Victory Lane Celebrations Black /1 #11
2018 Panini Victory Lane Celebrations Blue /25 #11
2018 Panini Victory Lane Celebrations Gold /99 #11
2018 Panini Victory Lane Celebrations Green /5 #11
2018 Panini Victory Lane Celebrations Printing Plates Black /1 #11
2018 Panini Victory Lane Celebrations Printing Plates Cyan /1 #11
2018 Panini Victory Lane Celebrations Printing Plates Magenta /1 #11
2018 Panini Victory Lane Celebrations Printing Plates Yellow /1 #11
2018 Panini Victory Lane Celebrations Red /49 #11
2018 Panini Victory Lane Engineered to Perfection Materials /399 #22
2018 Panini Victory Lane Engineered to Perfection Materials Black /25 #22
2018 Panini Victory Lane Engineered to Perfection Materials Gold /199 #22
2018 Panini Victory Lane Engineered to Perfection Materials Green /99 #22
2018 Panini Victory Lane Engineered to Perfection Triple Materials /49 #17
2018 Panini Victory Lane Engineered to Perfection Triple Materials Black /5 #17
2018 Panini Victory Lane Engineered to Perfection Triple Materials Gold /25 #17
2018 Panini Victory Lane Engineered to Perfection Triple Materials Green /10 #17
2018 Panini Victory Lane Engineered to Perfection Triple Materials Laundry Tag /1 #17
2018 Panini Victory Lane Gold /99 #17
2018 Panini Victory Lane Green /5 #17
2018 Panini Victory Lane Pedal to the Metal #46
2018 Panini Victory Lane Pedal to the Metal #66
2018 Panini Victory Lane Pedal to the Metal Black /1 #46
2018 Panini Victory Lane Pedal to the Metal Black /1 #66
2018 Panini Victory Lane Pedal to the Metal Blue /25 #46
2018 Panini Victory Lane Pedal to the Metal Blue /25 #66
2018 Panini Victory Lane Pedal to the Metal Green /5 #46
2018 Panini Victory Lane Pedal to the Metal Green /5 #66
2018 Panini Victory Lane Printing Plates Black /1 #17
2018 Panini Victory Lane Printing Plates Cyan /1 #17
2018 Panini Victory Lane Printing Plates Magenta /1 #17
2018 Panini Victory Lane Printing Plates Yellow /1 #17
2018 Panini Victory Lane Race Ready Materials Black /25 #23
2018 Panini Victory Lane Red /49 #17
2018 Panini Victory Lane Silver #17
2018 Panini Victory Lane Starting Grid #17
2018 Panini Victory Lane Starting Grid Black /1 #17
2018 Panini Victory Lane Starting Grid Blue /25 #17
2018 Panini Victory Lane Starting Grid Gold /99 #17
2018 Panini Victory Lane Starting Grid Green /5 #17
2018 Panini Victory Lane Starting Grid Printing Plates Black /1 #17
2018 Panini Victory Lane Starting Grid Printing Plates Cyan /1 #17
2018 Panini Victory Lane Starting Grid Printing Plates Magenta /1 #17
2018 Panini Victory Lane Starting Grid Printing Plates Yellow /1 #17
2018 Panini Victory Lane Starting Grid Red /49 #17
2018 Panini Victory Lane Victory Lane Prime Patches Associate Sponsor 1 /1 #16
2018 Panini Victory Lane Victory Lane Prime Patches Associate Sponsor 10 /1 #16
2018 Panini Victory Lane Victory Lane Prime Patches Associate Sponsor 2 /1 #16
2018 Panini Victory Lane Victory Lane Prime Patches Associate Sponsor 3 /1 #16
2018 Panini Victory Lane Victory Lane Prime Patches Associate Sponsor 4 /1 #16
2018 Panini Victory Lane Victory Lane Prime Patches Associate Sponsor 5 /1 #16
2018 Panini Victory Lane Victory Lane Prime Patches Associate Sponsor 6 /1 #16
2018 Panini Victory Lane Victory Lane Prime Patches Associate Sponsor 7 /1 #16
2018 Panini Victory Lane Victory Lane Prime Patches Associate Sponsor 8 /1 #16
2018 Panini Victory Lane Victory Lane Prime Patches Associate Sponsor 9 /1 #16
2018 Panini Victory Lane Victory Lane Prime Patches Car Manufacturer /1 #16
2018 Panini Victory Lane Victory Lane Prime Patches Firesuit Manufacturer /1 #16
2018 Panini Victory Lane Victory Lane Prime Patches Goodyear /1 #16
2018 Panini Victory Lane Victory Lane Prime Patches Nameplate /2 #16
2018 Panini Victory Lane Victory Lane Prime Patches NASCAR /1 #16
2018 Panini Victory Lane Victory Lane Prime Patches Series Sponsor /1 #16
2018 Panini Victory Lane Victory Lane Prime Patches Sunoco /1 #16
2018 Panini Victory Lane Victory Marks /100 #20
2018 Panini Victory Lane Victory Marks Black /1 #20
2018 Panini Victory Lane Victory Marks Gold /25 #20
2019 Donruss #81A
2019 Donruss #123
2019 Donruss #81B
2019 Donruss Artist Proofs /25 #81A
2019 Donruss Artist Proofs /25 #123
2019 Donruss Artist Proofs /25 #81B
2019 Donruss Black /199 #81A
2019 Donruss Black /199 #123
2019 Donruss Black /199 #81B
2019 Donruss Classics #20
2019 Donruss Classics Cracked Ice /25 #20
2019 Donruss Classics Holographic #20
2019 Donruss Classics Xplosion /10 #20
2019 Donruss Gold /299 #81A
2019 Donruss Gold /299 #123
2019 Donruss Gold /299 #81B
2019 Donruss Gold Press Proofs /99 #81A
2019 Donruss Gold Press Proofs /99 #123
2019 Donruss Gold Press Proofs /99 #81B
2019 Donruss Limited Spotlight Signatures #5
2019 Donruss Limited Spotlight Signatures Holo Black /10 #5
2019 Donruss Limited Spotlight Signatures Holo Gold /25 #5
2019 Donruss Limited Spotlight Signatures Red /99 #5
2019 Donruss Optic #28
2019 Donruss Optic Blue Pulsar #28
2019 Donruss Optic Gold /10 #28
2019 Donruss Optic Gold Vinyl /1 #28
2019 Donruss Optic Holo #28
2019 Donruss Optic Red Wave #28
2019 Donruss Optic Signatures Gold Vinyl /1 #28
2019 Donruss Optic Signatures Holo /75 #28
2019 Donruss Press Proofs /49 #81A
2019 Donruss Press Proofs /49 #123
2019 Donruss Press Proofs /49 #81B
2019 Donruss Printing Plates Black /1 #81A
2019 Donruss Printing Plates Black /1 #123
2019 Donruss Printing Plates Black /1 #81B
2019 Donruss Printing Plates Cyan /1 #81A
2019 Donruss Printing Plates Cyan /1 #123
2019 Donruss Printing Plates Cyan /1 #81B
2019 Donruss Printing Plates Magenta /1 #81A
2019 Donruss Printing Plates Magenta /1 #123
2019 Donruss Printing Plates Magenta /1 #81B
2019 Donruss Printing Plates Yellow /1 #81A
2019 Donruss Printing Plates Yellow /1 #123
2019 Donruss Printing Plates Yellow /1 #81B
2019 Donruss Race Day Relics #23
2019 Donruss Race Day Relics Holo Black /10 #23
2019 Donruss Race Day Relics Holo Gold /25 #23
2019 Donruss Race Day Relics Red /185 #23
2019 Donruss Silver #81A
2019 Donruss Silver #123
2019 Donruss Silver #81B
2019 Panini Prime /50 #5
2019 Panini Prime /50 #39
2019 Panini Prime /50 #72
2019 Panini Prime Black /10 #5
2019 Panini Prime Black /10 #39
2019 Panini Prime Black /10 #72
2019 Panini Prime Clear Silhouettes /99 #15
2019 Panini Prime Clear Silhouettes Black /10 #15
2019 Panini Prime Clear Silhouettes Holo Gold /25 #15
2019 Panini Prime Clear Silhouettes Platinum Blue /1 #15
2019 Panini Prime Dual Material Autographs /49 #11
2019 Panini Prime Dual Material Autographs Black /10 #11
2019 Panini Prime Dual Material Autographs Holo Gold /25 #11
2019 Panini Prime Dual Material Autographs Laundry Tags /1 #11
2019 Panini Prime Emerald /5 #5
2019 Panini Prime Emerald /5 #39
2019 Panini Prime Emerald /5 #72
2019 Panini Prime Jumbo Material Signatures Firesuit /10 #24
2019 Panini Prime Jumbo Material Signatures Firesuit Platinum Blue /1 #24
2019 Panini Prime Jumbo Material Signatures Sheet Metal /25 #24
2019 Panini Prime Jumbo Material Signatures Tire /99 #24
2019 Panini Prime NASCAR Shadowbox Signatures Car Number /49 #5
2019 Panini Prime NASCAR Shadowbox Signatures Manufacturer /10 #5
2019 Panini Prime NASCAR Shadowbox Signatures Sponsor /25 #5
2019 Panini Prime NASCAR Shadowbox Signatures Team Owner /1 #5
2019 Panini Prime Platinum Blue /1 #5
2019 Panini Prime Platinum Blue /1 #39
2019 Panini Prime Platinum Blue /1 #72
2019 Panini Prime Prime Cars Die Cut Signatures /49 #5
2019 Panini Prime Prime Cars Die Cut Signatures Black /10 #5
2019 Panini Prime Prime Cars Die Cut Signatures Holo Gold /25 #5
2019 Panini Prime Prime Cars Die Cut Signatures Platinum Blue /1 #5
2019 Panini Prime Prime Jumbo Associate Sponsor 1 /1 #70
2019 Panini Prime Prime Jumbo Associate Sponsor 1 /1 #71
2019 Panini Prime Prime Jumbo Associate Sponsor 1 /1 #72
2019 Panini Prime Prime Jumbo Associate Sponsor 10 /1 #71
2019 Panini Prime Prime Jumbo Associate Sponsor 11 /1 #71
2019 Panini Prime Prime Jumbo Associate Sponsor 2 /1 #70
2019 Panini Prime Prime Jumbo Associate Sponsor 2 /1 #71
2019 Panini Prime Prime Jumbo Associate Sponsor 2 /1 #72
2019 Panini Prime Prime Jumbo Associate Sponsor 3 /1 #70
2019 Panini Prime Prime Jumbo Associate Sponsor 3 /1 #71
2019 Panini Prime Prime Jumbo Associate Sponsor 3 /1 #72
2019 Panini Prime Prime Jumbo Associate Sponsor 4 /1 #70
2019 Panini Prime Prime Jumbo Associate Sponsor 4 /1 #71
2019 Panini Prime Prime Jumbo Associate Sponsor 4 /1 #72
2019 Panini Prime Prime Jumbo Associate Sponsor 5 /1 #70
2019 Panini Prime Prime Jumbo Associate Sponsor 5 /1 #71
2019 Panini Prime Prime Jumbo Associate Sponsor 5 /1 #72
2019 Panini Prime Prime Jumbo Associate Sponsor 6 /1 #70
2019 Panini Prime Prime Jumbo Associate Sponsor 6 /1 #71
2019 Panini Prime Prime Jumbo Associate Sponsor 6 /1 #72
2019 Panini Prime Prime Jumbo Associate Sponsor 7 /1 #70
2019 Panini Prime Prime Jumbo Associate Sponsor 7 /1 #71
2019 Panini Prime Prime Jumbo Associate Sponsor 7 /1 #72
2019 Panini Prime Prime Jumbo Associate Sponsor 8 /1 #70
2019 Panini Prime Prime Jumbo Associate Sponsor 8 /1 #71
2019 Panini Prime Prime Jumbo Associate Sponsor 9 /1 #70
2019 Panini Prime Prime Jumbo Associate Sponsor 9 /1 #71
2019 Panini Prime Prime Jumbo Car Manufacturer /1 #70
2019 Panini Prime Prime Jumbo Car Manufacturer /1 #71
2019 Panini Prime Prime Jumbo Car Manufacturer /1 #72
2019 Panini Prime Prime Jumbo Firesuit Manufacturer /1 #70
2019 Panini Prime Prime Jumbo Firesuit Manufacturer /1 #71
2019 Panini Prime Prime Jumbo Firesuit Manufacturer /1 #72
2019 Panini Prime Prime Jumbo Flag Patch /1 #70
2019 Panini Prime Prime Jumbo Flag Patch /1 #71
2019 Panini Prime Prime Jumbo Flag Patch /1 #72
2019 Panini Prime Prime Jumbo Glove Manufacturer Patch /1 #70
2019 Panini Prime Prime Jumbo Glove Manufacturer Patch /1 #71
2019 Panini Prime Prime Jumbo Glove Manufacturer Patch /1 #72
2019 Panini Prime Prime Jumbo Goodyear /1 #71
2019 Panini Prime Prime Jumbo Goodyear /2 #72
2019 Panini Prime Prime Jumbo Nameplate /2 #70
2019 Panini Prime Prime Jumbo Nameplate /2 #71
2019 Panini Prime Prime Jumbo Nameplate /2 #72
2019 Panini Prime Prime Jumbo NASCAR /1 #70
2019 Panini Prime Prime Jumbo NASCAR /1 #71
2019 Panini Prime Prime Jumbo NASCAR /1 #72
2019 Panini Prime Prime Jumbo Prime Colors /17 #70
2019 Panini Prime Prime Jumbo Prime Colors /8 #71
2019 Panini Prime Prime Jumbo Prime Colors /17 #72
2019 Panini Prime Prime Jumbo Series Sponsor /1 #71
2019 Panini Prime Prime Jumbo Series Sponsor /1 #72
2019 Panini Prime Prime Jumbo Shoe Brand Logo /1 #70
2019 Panini Prime Prime Jumbo Shoe Brand Logo /1 #71
2019 Panini Prime Prime Jumbo Shoe Brand Logo /1 #72
2019 Panini Prime Prime Jumbo Sunoco /1 #70
2019 Panini Prime Prime Jumbo Sunoco /1 #71
2019 Panini Prime Prime Jumbo Sunoco /1 #72
2019 Panini Prime Quad Materials Autographs /49 #22
2019 Panini Prime Quad Materials Autographs Black /10 #22
2019 Panini Prime Quad Materials Autographs Holo Gold /25 #22
2019 Panini Prime Quad Materials Autographs Laundry Tags /1 #22
2019 Panini Prime Race Used Duals Firesuits Black /10 #13
2019 Panini Prime Race Used Duals Firesuits Laundry Tags /1 #13
2019 Panini Prime Race Used Duals Sheet Metal Black /10 #13
2019 Panini Prime Race Used Duals Sheet Metal Platinum Blue /1 #13
2019 Panini Prime Race Used Duals Tires Black /10 #13
2019 Panini Prime Race Used Duals Tires Platinum Blue /1 #13
2019 Panini Prime Race Used Firesuits Black /10 #32
2019 Panini Prime Race Used Firesuits Laundry Tags /1 #32
2019 Panini Prime Race Used Sheet Metal Black /10 #32
2019 Panini Prime Race Used Sheet Metal Platinum Blue /1 #32
2019 Panini Prime Race Used Tires Black /10 #32
2019 Panini Prime Race Used Tires Platinum Blue /1 #32
2019 Panini Prime Race Used Trios Firesuits Black /10 #13
2019 Panini Prime Race Used Trios Firesuits Laundry Tags /1 #13
2019 Panini Prime Race Used Trios Sheet Metal Black /10 #13
2019 Panini Prime Race Used Trios Sheet Metal Platinum Blue /1 #13
2019 Panini Prime Race Used Trios Tires Black /10 #13
2019 Panini Prime Race Used Trios Tires Platinum Blue /1 #13
2019 Panini Prizm #5
2019 Panini Prizm #60
2019 Panini Prizm #88
2019 Panini Prizm Expert Level #7
2019 Panini Prizm Expert Level Prizms #7
2019 Panini Prizm Expert Level Prizms Black /1 #7
2019 Panini Prizm Expert Level Prizms Gold /10 #7
2019 Panini Prizm Expert Level Prizms White Sparkle #7
2019 Panini Prizm Fireworks #14
2019 Panini Prizm Fireworks Prizms #14
2019 Panini Prizm Fireworks Prizms Black /1 #14
2019 Panini Prizm Fireworks Prizms Gold /10 #14
2019 Panini Prizm Fireworks Prizms White Sparkle #14
2019 Panini Prizm In the Groove #14
2019 Panini Prizm In the Groove Prizms #14
2019 Panini Prizm In the Groove Prizms Black /1 #14
2019 Panini Prizm In the Groove Prizms Gold /10 #14
2019 Panini Prizm In the Groove Prizms White Sparkle #14
2019 Panini Prizm Patented Penmanship Prizms #17
2019 Panini Prizm Patented Penmanship Prizms Black /1 #17
2019 Panini Prizm Patented Penmanship Prizms Blue /30 #17
2019 Panini Prizm Patented Penmanship Prizms Camo #17
2019 Panini Prizm Patented Penmanship Prizms Gold /10 #17
2019 Panini Prizm Patented Penmanship Prizms Green /35 #17
2019 Panini Prizm Patented Penmanship Prizms Rainbow /24 #17
2019 Panini Prizm Patented Penmanship Prizms Red /25 #17
2019 Panini Prizm Patented Penmanship Prizms Red White and Blue #17
2019 Panini Prizm Patented Penmanship Prizms White /5 #17
2019 Panini Prizm Prizms #60
2019 Panini Prizm Prizms #88
2019 Panini Prizm Prizms #5
2019 Panini Prizm Prizms Black /1 #5
2019 Panini Prizm Prizms Black /1 #60
2019 Panini Prizm Prizms Black /1 #88
2019 Panini Prizm Prizms Blue /75 #5
2019 Panini Prizm Prizms Blue /75 #60
2019 Panini Prizm Prizms Blue /75 #88
2019 Panini Prizm Prizms Camo #5
2019 Panini Prizm Prizms Camo #60
2019 Panini Prizm Prizms Camo #88
2019 Panini Prizm Prizms Flash #5
2019 Panini Prizm Prizms Flash #60
2019 Panini Prizm Prizms Flash #88
2019 Panini Prizm Prizms Gold /10 #5
2019 Panini Prizm Prizms Gold /10 #60
2019 Panini Prizm Prizms Gold /10 #88
2019 Panini Prizm Prizms Green /99 #5
2019 Panini Prizm Prizms Green /99 #60
2019 Panini Prizm Prizms Green /99 #88
2019 Panini Prizm Prizms Rainbow /24 #5
2019 Panini Prizm Prizms Rainbow /24 #60
2019 Panini Prizm Prizms Rainbow /24 #88
2019 Panini Prizm Prizms Red /50 #5
2019 Panini Prizm Prizms Red /50 #60
2019 Panini Prizm Prizms Red /50 #88
2019 Panini Prizm Prizms Red White and Blue #5
2019 Panini Prizm Prizms Red White and Blue #60
2019 Panini Prizm Prizms Red White and Blue #88
2019 Panini Prizm Prizms White /5 #5
2019 Panini Prizm Prizms White /5 #60
2019 Panini Prizm Prizms White /5 #88
2019 Panini Prizm Prizms White Sparkle #5
2019 Panini Prizm Prizms White Sparkle #60
2019 Panini Prizm Prizms White Sparkle #88
2019 Panini Prizm Signing Sessions Prizms #19
2019 Panini Prizm Signing Sessions Prizms Black /1 #19
2019 Panini Prizm Signing Sessions Prizms Blue /30 #19
2019 Panini Prizm Signing Sessions Prizms Camo #19
2019 Panini Prizm Signing Sessions Prizms Gold /10 #19
2019 Panini Prizm Signing Sessions Prizms Green /35 #19
2019 Panini Prizm Signing Sessions Prizms Rainbow /24 #19
2019 Panini Prizm Signing Sessions Prizms Red /25 #19
2019 Panini Prizm Signing Sessions Prizms Red White and Blue #19
2019 Panini Prizm Signing Sessions Prizms White /5 #19
2019 Panini Victory Lane #5
2019 Panini Victory Lane #88
2019 Panini Victory Lane Black /1 #5
2019 Panini Victory Lane Black /1 #88
2019 Panini Victory Lane Dual Swatches #20
2019 Panini Victory Lane Dual Swatches Gold /99 #20
2019 Panini Victory Lane Dual Swatches Laundry Tag /1 #20
2019 Panini Victory Lane Dual Swatches Platinum /1 #20
2019 Panini Victory Lane Dual Swatches Red /25 #20
2019 Panini Victory Lane Gold /25 #5
2019 Panini Victory Lane Gold /25 #88
2019 Panini Victory Lane Machines #16
2019 Panini Victory Lane Machines Black /1 #16
2019 Panini Victory Lane Machines Blue /99 #16
2019 Panini Victory Lane Machines Gold /25 #16
2019 Panini Victory Lane Machines Green /5 #16
2019 Panini Victory Lane Machines Printing Plates Black /1 #16
2019 Panini Victory Lane Machines Printing Plates Cyan /1 #16
2019 Panini Victory Lane Machines Printing Plates Magenta /1 #16
2019 Panini Victory Lane Machines Printing Plates Yellow /1 #16
2019 Panini Victory Lane Pedal to the Metal #47
2019 Panini Victory Lane Pedal to the Metal Black /1 #47
2019 Panini Victory Lane Pedal to the Metal Gold /25 #47
2019 Panini Victory Lane Pedal to the Metal Green /5 #47
2019 Panini Victory Lane Pedal to the Metal Red /3 #47
2019 Panini Victory Lane Printing Plates Black /1 #5
2019 Panini Victory Lane Printing Plates Black /1 #88
2019 Panini Victory Lane Printing Plates Cyan /1 #5
2019 Panini Victory Lane Printing Plates Cyan /1 #88
2019 Panini Victory Lane Printing Plates Magenta /1 #5
2019 Panini Victory Lane Printing Plates Magenta /1 #88
2019 Panini Victory Lane Printing Plates Yellow /1 #5
2019 Panini Victory Lane Printing Plates Yellow /1 #88
2019 Panini Victory Lane Signature Swatches #22
2019 Panini Victory Lane Signature Swatches Gold /99 #22
2019 Panini Victory Lane Signature Swatches Laundry Tag /1 #22
2019 Panini Victory Lane Signature Swatches Platinum /1 #22
2019 Panini Victory Lane Signature Swatches Red /25 #22
2019 Panini Victory Lane Starting Grid #25
2019 Panini Victory Lane Starting Grid Black /1 #25
2019 Panini Victory Lane Starting Grid Blue /99 #25
2019 Panini Victory Lane Starting Grid Gold /25 #25
2019 Panini Victory Lane Starting Grid Green /5 #25
2019 Panini Victory Lane Starting Grid Printing Plates Black /1 #25
2019 Panini Victory Lane Starting Grid Printing Plates Cyan /1 #25
2019 Panini Victory Lane Starting Grid Printing Plates Magenta /1 #25
2019 Panini Victory Lane Starting Grid Printing Plates Yellow /1 #25
2019 Panini Victory Lane Triple Swatches #11
2019 Panini Victory Lane Triple Swatches Gold /99 #11
2019 Panini Victory Lane Triple Swatches Laundry Tag /1 #11
2019 Panini Victory Lane Triple Swatches Platinum /1 #11
2019 Panini Victory Lane Triple Swatches Red /25 #11
2020 Donruss #4
2020 Donruss #52
2020 Donruss #115
2020 Donruss #187
2020 Donruss #192
2020 Donruss Black Numbers /6 #4
2020 Donruss Black Numbers /6 #52
2020 Donruss Black Numbers /6 #115
2020 Donruss Black Numbers /6 #187
2020 Donruss Black Numbers /6 #192
2020 Donruss Black Trophy Club /1 #4
2020 Donruss Black Trophy Club /1 #52
2020 Donruss Black Trophy Club /1 #115
2020 Donruss Black Trophy Club /1 #187
2020 Donruss Black Trophy Club /1 #192
2020 Donruss Blue /199 #115
2020 Donruss Blue /199 #187
2020 Donruss Blue /199 #192
2020 Donruss Blue /199 #4
2020 Donruss Blue /199 #52
2020 Donruss Carolina Blue #4
2020 Donruss Carolina Blue #52
2020 Donruss Carolina Blue #115
2020 Donruss Carolina Blue #187
2020 Donruss Carolina Blue #192
2020 Donruss Contenders #13
2020 Donruss Contenders Checkers #13
2020 Donruss Contenders Cracked Ice /25 #13
2020 Donruss Contenders Holographic /199 #13
2020 Donruss Contenders Xplosion /10 #13
2020 Donruss Elite Series #3
2020 Donruss Elite Series Checkers #3
2020 Donruss Elite Series Cracked Ice /25 #3
2020 Donruss Elite Series Holographic /199 #3
2020 Donruss Elite Series Xplosion /10 #3
2020 Donruss Green /99 #4
2020 Donruss Green /99 #52
2020 Donruss Green /99 #115
2020 Donruss Green /99 #187
2020 Donruss Green /99 #192
2020 Donruss Optic #4
2020 Donruss Optic #30
2020 Donruss Optic #75
2020 Donruss Optic Carolina Blue Wave #30
2020 Donruss Optic Carolina Blue Wave #75
2020 Donruss Optic Carolina Blue Wave #4
2020 Donruss Optic Gold /10 #4
2020 Donruss Optic Gold /10 #30
2020 Donruss Optic Gold /10 #75
2020 Donruss Optic Gold Vinyl /1 #4
2020 Donruss Optic Gold Vinyl /1 #30
2020 Donruss Optic Gold Vinyl /1 #75
2020 Donruss Optic Holo #4
2020 Donruss Optic Holo #30
2020 Donruss Optic Holo #75
2020 Donruss Optic Illusion #9
2020 Donruss Optic Illusion Carolina Blue Wave #9
2020 Donruss Optic Illusion Gold /10 #9
2020 Donruss Optic Illusion Gold Vinyl /1 #9
2020 Donruss Optic Illusion Holo #9
2020 Donruss Optic Illusion Orange Pulsar #9
2020 Donruss Optic Illusion Red Mojo #9
2020 Donruss Optic Illusion Signatures Gold Vinyl /1 #9
2020 Donruss Optic Illusion Signatures Holo /99 #9
2020 Donruss Optic Orange Pulsar #4
2020 Donruss Optic Orange Pulsar #30
2020 Donruss Optic Orange Pulsar #75
2020 Donruss Optic Red Mojo #4
2020 Donruss Optic Red Mojo #30
2020 Donruss Optic Red Mojo #75
2020 Donruss Optic Signatures Gold Vinyl /1 #4
2020 Donruss Optic Signatures Gold Vinyl /1 #30
2020 Donruss Optic Signatures Gold Vinyl /1 #75
2020 Donruss Optic Signatures Holo /99 #4
2020 Donruss Optic Signatures Holo /99 #30
2020 Donruss Optic Signatures Holo /99 #75
2020 Donruss Orange #187
2020 Donruss Orange #192
2020 Donruss Orange #4
2020 Donruss Orange #52
2020 Donruss Orange #115
2020 Donruss Pink /25 #4
2020 Donruss Pink /25 #52
2020 Donruss Pink /25 #115
2020 Donruss Pink /25 #187
2020 Donruss Pink /25 #192
2020 Donruss Printing Plates Black /1 #4
2020 Donruss Printing Plates Black /1 #52
2020 Donruss Printing Plates Black /1 #115
2020 Donruss Printing Plates Black /1 #187
2020 Donruss Printing Plates Black /1 #192
2020 Donruss Printing Plates Cyan /1 #4
2020 Donruss Printing Plates Cyan /1 #52
2020 Donruss Printing Plates Cyan /1 #115
2020 Donruss Printing Plates Cyan /1 #187
2020 Donruss Printing Plates Cyan /1 #192
2020 Donruss Printing Plates Magenta /1 #52
2020 Donruss Printing Plates Magenta /1 #115
2020 Donruss Printing Plates Magenta /1 #187
2020 Donruss Printing Plates Magenta /1 #192
2020 Donruss Printing Plates Magenta /1 #4
2020 Donruss Printing Plates Yellow /1 #187
2020 Donruss Printing Plates Yellow /1 #192
2020 Donruss Printing Plates Yellow /1 #4
2020 Donruss Printing Plates Yellow /1 #52
2020 Donruss Printing Plates Yellow /1 #115
2020 Donruss Purple /49 #4
2020 Donruss Purple /49 #52
2020 Donruss Purple /49 #115
2020 Donruss Purple /49 #187
2020 Donruss Purple /49 #192
2020 Donruss Race Day Relics /0 #29
2020 Donruss Race Day Relics Holo Black /10 #29
2020 Donruss Race Day Relics Holo Gold /25 #29
2020 Donruss Race Day Relics Red /250 #29
2020 Donruss Red /299 #4
2020 Donruss Red /299 #52
2020 Donruss Red /299 #115
2020 Donruss Red /299 #187
2020 Donruss Red /299 #192
2020 Donruss Silver #4
2020 Donruss Silver #52
2020 Donruss Silver #115
2020 Donruss Silver #187
2020 Donruss Silver #192
2020 Donruss Timeless Treasures Signatures #9
2020 Donruss Timeless Treasures Signatures Holo Black /1 #9
2020 Donruss Timeless Treasures Signatures Holo Gold /6 #9
2020 Donruss Timeless Treasures Signatures Red /12 #9

Danica Patrick

2006 Topps Allen and Ginter #305
2006 Topps Allen and Ginter Autographs /100 #DP
2006 Topps Allen and Ginter Mini #305
2006 Topps Allen and Ginter Mini A and G Back #305
2006 Topps Allen and Ginter Mini Bazooka /25 #305
2006 Topps Allen and Ginter Mini Black #305
2006 Topps Allen and Ginter Mini No Card Number /50 #305
2006 Topps Allen and Ginter Mini Printing Plates Black /1 #305
2006 Topps Allen and Ginter Mini Printing Plates Cyan /1 #305
2006 Topps Allen and Ginter Mini Printing Plates Magenta /1 #305
2006 Topps Allen and Ginter Mini Printing Plates Yellow /1 #305
2006 Topps Allen and Ginter Mini Wood /1 #305
2006 Topps Allen and Ginter Postcards Personalized /1 #DP
2007 Rittenhouse IRL #P1
2007 Rittenhouse IRL #1
2007 Rittenhouse IRL #2
2007 Rittenhouse IRL #3
2007 Rittenhouse IRL Autographs #12
2007 Rittenhouse IRL Shades of Victory #R1
2008 Sports Illustrated Swimsuit Danica Patrick #DP10
2008 Sports Illustrated Swimsuit Danica Patrick #DP9
2008 Sports Illustrated Swimsuit Danica Patrick #DP8
2008 Sports Illustrated Swimsuit Danica Patrick #DP7
2008 Sports Illustrated Swimsuit Danica Patrick #DP6
2008 Sports Illustrated Swimsuit Danica Patrick #DP5
2008 Sports Illustrated Swimsuit Danica Patrick #DP4
2008 Sports Illustrated Swimsuit Danica Patrick #DP3
2008 Sports Illustrated Swimsuit Danica Patrick #DP2
2008 Sports Illustrated Swimsuit Danica Patrick #DP1
2008 Sports Illustrated Swimsuit Editor's Choice #EC5
2008 Sports Illustrated Swimsuit Material #DPM
2008 Sports Illustrated Swimsuit Printing Plates /1 #DP1
2008 Sports Illustrated Swimsuit Printing Plates /1 #DP2
2008 Sports Illustrated Swimsuit Printing Plates /1 #DP3
2008 Sports Illustrated Swimsuit Printing Plates /1 #DP4
2008 Sports Illustrated Swimsuit Printing Plates /1 #DP5
2008 Sports Illustrated Swimsuit Printing Plates /1 #DP6
2008 Sports Illustrated Swimsuit Printing Plates /1 #DP7
2008 Sports Illustrated Swimsuit Printing Plates /1 #DP8
2008 Sports Illustrated Swimsuit Printing Plates /1 #DP9
2008 Sports Illustrated Swimsuit Printing Plates /1 #DP10
2008 Sports Illustrated Swimsuit Printing Plates /1 #EC5
2009 Hot Wheels #NNO
2009 Sports Illustrated for Kids #402
2009 Sports Illustrated Swimsuit Danica Patrick #D10
2009 Sports Illustrated Swimsuit Danica Patrick #D9
2009 Sports Illustrated Swimsuit Danica Patrick #D8
2009 Sports Illustrated Swimsuit Danica Patrick #D7
2009 Sports Illustrated Swimsuit Danica Patrick #D6
2009 Sports Illustrated Swimsuit Danica Patrick #D5
2009 Sports Illustrated Swimsuit Danica Patrick #D4
2009 Sports Illustrated Swimsuit Danica Patrick #D3
2009 Sports Illustrated Swimsuit Danica Patrick #D2
2009 Sports Illustrated Swimsuit Danica Patrick #D1
2009 Sports Illustrated Swimsuit Danica Patrick Printing Plates Black /1 #D1
2009 Sports Illustrated Swimsuit Danica Patrick Printing Plates Black /1 #D2
2009 Sports Illustrated Swimsuit Danica Patrick Printing Plates Black /1 #D3
2009 Sports Illustrated Swimsuit Danica Patrick Printing Plates Black /1 #D4
2009 Sports Illustrated Swimsuit Danica Patrick Printing Plates Black /1 #D5
2009 Sports Illustrated Swimsuit Danica Patrick Printing Plates Black /1 #D6
2009 Sports Illustrated Swimsuit Danica Patrick Printing Plates Black /1 #D7
2009 Sports Illustrated Swimsuit Danica Patrick Printing Plates Black /1 #D8
2009 Sports Illustrated Swimsuit Danica Patrick Printing Plates Black /1 #D9
2009 Sports Illustrated Swimsuit Danica Patrick Printing Plates Black /1 #D10
2009 Sports Illustrated Swimsuit Danica Patrick Printing Plates Cyan /1 #D1
2009 Sports Illustrated Swimsuit Danica Patrick Printing Plates Cyan /1 #D2
2009 Sports Illustrated Swimsuit Danica Patrick Printing Plates Cyan /1 #D3
2009 Sports Illustrated Swimsuit Danica Patrick Printing Plates Cyan /1 #D4
2009 Sports Illustrated Swimsuit Danica Patrick Printing Plates Cyan /1 #D5
2009 Sports Illustrated Swimsuit Danica Patrick Printing Plates Cyan /1 #D6
2009 Sports Illustrated Swimsuit Danica Patrick Printing Plates Cyan /1 #D7
2009 Sports Illustrated Swimsuit Danica Patrick Printing Plates Cyan /1 #D8
2009 Sports Illustrated Swimsuit Danica Patrick Printing Plates Cyan /1 #D9
2009 Sports Illustrated Swimsuit Danica Patrick Printing Plates Cyan /1 #D10
2009 Sports Illustrated Swimsuit Danica Patrick Printing Plates Magenta /1 #D1
2009 Sports Illustrated Swimsuit Danica Patrick Printing Plates Magenta /1 #D2
2009 Sports Illustrated Swimsuit Danica Patrick Printing Plates Magenta /1 #D3
2009 Sports Illustrated Swimsuit Danica Patrick Printing Plates Magenta /1 #D4
2009 Sports Illustrated Swimsuit Danica Patrick Printing Plates Magenta /1 #D5
2009 Sports Illustrated Swimsuit Danica Patrick Printing Plates Magenta /1 #D6
2009 Sports Illustrated Swimsuit Danica Patrick Printing Plates Magenta /1 #D7
2009 Sports Illustrated Swimsuit Danica Patrick Printing Plates Magenta /1 #D8
2009 Sports Illustrated Swimsuit Danica Patrick Printing Plates Magenta /1 #D9
2009 Sports Illustrated Swimsuit Danica Patrick Printing Plates Magenta /1 #D10
2009 Sports Illustrated Swimsuit Danica Patrick Printing Plates Yellow /1 #D1
2009 Sports Illustrated Swimsuit Danica Patrick Printing Plates Yellow /1 #D2
2009 Sports Illustrated Swimsuit Danica Patrick Printing Plates Yellow /1 #D3
2009 Sports Illustrated Swimsuit Danica Patrick Printing Plates Yellow /1 #D4
2009 Sports Illustrated Swimsuit Danica Patrick Printing Plates Yellow /1 #D5
2009 Sports Illustrated Swimsuit Danica Patrick Printing Plates Yellow /1 #D6
2009 Sports Illustrated Swimsuit Danica Patrick Printing Plates Yellow /1 #D7
2009 Sports Illustrated Swimsuit Danica Patrick Printing Plates Yellow /1 #D8
2009 Sports Illustrated Swimsuit Danica Patrick Printing Plates Yellow /1 #D9
2009 Sports Illustrated Swimsuit Danica Patrick Printing Plates Yellow /1 #D10
2009 Sports Illustrated Swimsuit Materials #DP1M
2009 Sports Illustrated Swimsuit Materials #DP2M
2009 Sports Illustrated Swimsuit Materials Printing Plates Black /1 #DP1M
2009 Sports Illustrated Swimsuit Materials Printing Plates Black /1 #DP2M
2009 Sports Illustrated Swimsuit Materials Printing Plates Cyan /1 #DP1M
2009 Sports Illustrated Swimsuit Materials Printing Plates Cyan /1 #DP2M
2009 Sports Illustrated Swimsuit Materials Printing Plates Magenta /1 #DP1M
2009 Sports Illustrated Swimsuit Materials Printing Plates Magenta /1 #DP2M
2009 Sports Illustrated Swimsuit Materials Printing Plates Yellow /1 #DP1M
2009 Sports Illustrated Swimsuit Materials Printing Plates Yellow /1 #DP2M
2010 Element #59
2010 Element 10 in '10 #TT10
2010 Element Blue /35 #59
2010 Element Green #59
2010 Element Previews /1 #EB59
2010 Element Purple /25 #59
2010 Element Red Target #59

2010 Press Pass Eclipse #27
2010 Press Pass Eclipse Blue #27
2010 Press Pass Eclipse Danica #DP2
2010 Press Pass Eclipse Danica #DP1
2010 Press Pass Eclipse Gold #27
2010 Press Pass Eclipse Previews /5 #27
2010 Press Pass Eclipse Purple /25 #27
2010 Press Pass Five Star /35 #22
2010 Press Pass Five Star Classic Compilations Combos Firesuit Autographs /15 #CCMDPDE
2010 Press Pass Five Star Classic Compilations Combos Patches Autographs /1 #CCMDPDE
2010 Press Pass Five Star Classic Compilations Dual Memorabilia Autographs /10 #DP
2010 Press Pass Five Star Classic Compilations Firesuit Autographs /15 #DP
2010 Press Pass Five Star Classic Compilations Patch Autographs /1 #CCPDP16
2010 Press Pass Five Star Classic Compilations Patch Autographs /1 #CCPDP1
2010 Press Pass Five Star Classic Compilations Patch Autographs /1 #CCPDP2
2010 Press Pass Five Star Classic Compilations Patch Autographs /1 #CCPDP3
2010 Press Pass Five Star Classic Compilations Patch Autographs /1 #CCPDP4
2010 Press Pass Five Star Classic Compilations Patch Autographs /1 #CCPDP5
2010 Press Pass Five Star Classic Compilations Patch Autographs /1 #CCPDP6
2010 Press Pass Five Star Classic Compilations Patch Autographs /1 #CCPDP7
2010 Press Pass Five Star Classic Compilations Patch Autographs /1 #CCPDP8
2010 Press Pass Five Star Classic Compilations Patch Autographs /1 #CCPDP9
2010 Press Pass Five Star Classic Compilations Patch Autographs /1 #CCPDP10
2010 Press Pass Five Star Classic Compilations Patch Autographs /1 #CCPDP11
2010 Press Pass Five Star Classic Compilations Patch Autographs /1 #CCPDP12
2010 Press Pass Five Star Classic Compilations Patch Autographs /1 #CCPDP13
2010 Press Pass Five Star Classic Compilations Patch Autographs /1 #CCPDP14
2010 Press Pass Five Star Classic Compilations Patch Autographs /1 #CCPDP15
2010 Press Pass Five Star Classic Compilations Sheet Metal Autographs /25 #DP
2010 Press Pass Five Star Classic Compilations Triple Memorabilia Autographs /5 #DP
2010 Press Pass Five Star Holofoil /10 #22
2010 Press Pass Five Star Melting /1 #22
2010 Press Pass Five Star Paramount Pieces Aluminum /25 #DP
2010 Press Pass Five Star Paramount Pieces Blue /20 #DP
2010 Press Pass Five Star Paramount Pieces Gold /15 #DP
2010 Press Pass Five Star Paramount Pieces Holofoil /10 #DP
2010 Press Pass Five Star Paramount Pieces Melting /1 #DP
2010 Press Pass Five Star Signature Souvenirs Aluminum /50 #SSDP
2010 Press Pass Five Star Signature Souvenirs Gold /25 #SSDP
2010 Press Pass Five Star Signature Souvenirs Holofoil /10 #SSDP
2010 Press Pass Five Star Signature Souvenirs Melting /1 #SSDP
2010 Press Pass Five Star Signatures Aluminum /35 #DP
2010 Press Pass Five Star Signatures Gold /20 #DP
2010 Press Pass Five Star Signatures Holofoil /5 #DP
2010 Press Pass Five Star Signatures Melting /1 #DP
2010 Press Pass Four Wide Autographs /5 #NNO
2010 Press Pass Legends Autographs Blue /10 #45
2010 Press Pass Legends Autographs Holofoil /25 #45
2010 Press Pass Legends Autographs Printing Plates Black /1 #37
2010 Press Pass Legends Autographs Printing Plates Cyan /1 #37
2010 Press Pass Legends Autographs Printing Plates Magenta /1 #37
2010 Press Pass Legends Autographs Printing Plates Yellow /1 #37
2010 Press Pass Legends Motorsports Masters Autographs Printing Plates Black /1 #37
2010 Press Pass Legends Motorsports Masters Autographs Printing Plates Cyan /1 #37
2010 Press Pass Legends Motorsports Masters Autographs Printing Plates Magenta /1 #37
2010 Press Pass Legends Motorsports Masters Autographs Printing Plates Yellow /1 #37
2010 Press Pass Legends Prominent Pieces Copper /99 #PPDP
2010 Press Pass Legends Prominent Pieces Gold /50 #PPDP
2010 Press Pass Legends Prominent Pieces Holofoil /25 #PPDP
2010 Press Pass Legends Prominent Pieces Oversized Firesuit /25 #PPOEDP
2010 Press Pass Premium #91
2010 Press Pass Premium #99
2010 Press Pass Premium Danica Patrick #DP1
2010 Press Pass Premium Danica Patrick #DP2
2010 Press Pass Premium Danica Patrick #DP4
2010 Press Pass Premium Danica Patrick #DP3
2010 Press Pass Premium Hot Threads /299 #HTDP
2010 Press Pass Premium Hot Threads Holofoil /99 #HTDP
2010 Press Pass Premium Hot Threads Multi Color /25 #HTDP
2010 Press Pass Premium Hot Threads Patches /25 #HTPDP
2010 Press Pass Premium Hot Threads Two Color /125 #HTDP
2010 Press Pass Premium Iron On Patch #4
2010 Press Pass Premium Pairings Firesuits /25 #PFMP
2010 Press Pass Premium Pairings Firesuits /25 #PFPE
2010 Press Pass Premium Pairings Signatures /5 #PSMP
2010 Press Pass Premium Pairings Signatures /5 #PSPE
2010 Press Pass Premium Signatures #PSDP
2010 Press Pass Premium Signatures Red Ink /25 #PSDP
2010 Press Pass Showcase /75 #51
2010 Press Pass Showcase /499 #30
2010 Press Pass Showcase /499 #31
2010 Press Pass Showcase Classic Collections Firesuit Green /25 #CCIFAN
2010 Press Pass Showcase Classic Collections Firesuit Green /25 #CCIJRM
2010 Press Pass Showcase Classic Collections Firesuit Patch Melting /5 #CCIFAN
2010 Press Pass Showcase Classic Collections Firesuit Patch Melting /5 #CCIJRM
2010 Press Pass Showcase Classic Collections Ink /15 #CCIJRM
2010 Press Pass Showcase Classic Collections Ink /15 #CCIFAN
2010 Press Pass Showcase Classic Collections Ink Gold /10 #CCIFAN
2010 Press Pass Showcase Classic Collections Ink Gold /10 #CCIJRM
2010 Press Pass Showcase Classic Collections Ink Green /5 #CCIFAN
2010 Press Pass Showcase Classic Collections Ink Green /5 #CCIJRM
2010 Press Pass Showcase Classic Collections Ink Melting /1 #CCIFAN
2010 Press Pass Showcase Classic Collections Ink Melting /1 #CCIJRM
2010 Press Pass Showcase Classic Collections Sheet Metal /99 #CCIFAN
2010 Press Pass Showcase Classic Collections Sheet Metal /99 #CCIJRM
2010 Press Pass Showcase Classic Collections Sheet Metal Gold /45 #CCIFAN
2010 Press Pass Showcase Classic Collections Sheet Metal Gold /45 #CCIJRM
2010 Press Pass Showcase Elite Exhibit Ink /45 #EEIDP
2010 Press Pass Showcase Elite Exhibit Ink Gold /25 #EEIDP
2010 Press Pass Showcase Elite Exhibit Ink Green /5 #EEIDP
2010 Press Pass Showcase Elite Exhibit Ink Melting /1 #EEIDP
2010 Press Pass Showcase Elite Exhibit Triple Memorabilia /99 #EEMDP
2010 Press Pass Showcase Elite Exhibit Triple Memorabilia Gold /45 #EEMDP
2010 Press Pass Showcase Elite Exhibit Triple Memorabilia Green /25 #EEMDP
2010 Press Pass Showcase Elite Exhibit Triple Memorabilia Melting /5 #EEMDP
2010 Press Pass Showcase Gold /125 #30
2010 Press Pass Showcase Gold /125 #31
2010 Press Pass Showcase Gold /25 #51
2010 Press Pass Showcase Green /50 #30
2010 Press Pass Showcase Green /50 #31
2010 Press Pass Showcase Green /10 #51
2010 Press Pass Showcase Melting /15 #30
2010 Press Pass Showcase Melting /15 #31
2010 Press Pass Showcase Melting /1 #51
2010 Press Pass Showcase Platinum Holo /1 #30
2010 Press Pass Showcase Platinum Holo /1 #31
2010 Press Pass Showcase Prized Pieces Firesuit Green /25 #PPMDP
2010 Press Pass Showcase Prized Pieces Firesuit Ink Gold /25 #PPIDP
2010 Press Pass Showcase Prized Pieces Firesuit Ink Melting /1 #PPIDP
2010 Press Pass Showcase Prized Pieces Firesuit Patch Melting /5 #PPMDP
2010 Press Pass Showcase Prized Pieces Memorabilia Ink Green /15 #PPIDP
2010 Press Pass Showcase Prized Pieces Sheet Metal /99 #PPMDP
2010 Press Pass Showcase Prized Pieces Sheet Metal Gold /45 #PPMDP
2010 Press Pass Showcase Prized Pieces Sheet Metal Ink Silver /50 #PPIDP
2010 Press Pass Signings Blue /10 #43
2010 Press Pass Signings Gold /15 #43
2010 Press Pass Signings Red /15 #43
2010 Press Pass Signings Silver /25 #42
2010 Press Pass Stealth #41
2010 Press Pass Stealth #54
2010 Press Pass Stealth Battle Armor Fast Pass /25 #BADP
2010 Press Pass Stealth Battle Armor Holofoil /25 #BADP
2010 Press Pass Stealth Battle Armor Silver /225 #BADP
2010 Press Pass Stealth Black and White #41
2010 Press Pass Stealth Black and White #54
2010 Press Pass Stealth Mach 10 #MT9
2010 Press Pass Stealth National Convention #VIP6
2010 Press Pass Stealth Power Players #PP7
2010 Press Pass Stealth Previews /1 #41
2010 Press Pass Stealth Previews /5 #54
2010 Press Pass Stealth Purple /25 #54
2010 Press Pass Stealth Purple /25 #41
2010 Wheels Main Event #91
2010 Wheels Main Event Blue #91
2010 Wheels Main Event Fight Card #FC25
2010 Wheels Main Event Fight Card Checkered Flag #FC25
2010 Wheels Main Event Fight Card Full Color Retail #FC25
2010 Wheels Main Event Fight Card Gold /25 #FC25
2010 Wheels Main Event Head to Head /150 #HHDEDP
2010 Wheels Main Event Head to Head Blue /75 #HHDEDP
2010 Wheels Main Event Head to Head Holofoil /10 #HHDEDP
2010 Wheels Main Event Head to Head Red /25 #HHDEDP
2010 Wheels Main Event Marks Autographs /25 #45
2010 Wheels Main Event Marks Autographs Black /1 #44
2010 Wheels Main Event Marks Autographs Blue /10 #45
2010 Wheels Main Event Marks Autographs Red /5 #45
2010 Wheels Main Event Upper Cuts Knock Out Patches /25 #UCKODP
2011 Element #47
2011 Element Autographs /10 #43
2011 Element Autographs Blue /5 #43
2011 Element Autographs Gold /5 #41
2011 Element Autographs Printing Plates Black /1 #43
2011 Element Autographs Printing Plates Cyan /1 #43
2011 Element Autographs Printing Plates Magenta /1 #43
2011 Element Autographs Printing Plates Yellow /1 #43
2011 Element Autographs Silver /5 #41
2011 Element Black /35 #47
2011 Element Cut and Collect Exclusives #NNO
2011 Element Green #47
2011 Element Previews /1 #EB47
2011 Element Purple /25 #47
2011 Element Red #47
2011 Element Trackside Treasures Holofoil /25 #TTDP
2011 Element Trackside Treasures Silver /85 #TTDP
2011 Press Pass #94
2011 Press Pass #117
2011 Press Pass #39
2011 Press Pass #155
2011 Press Pass Autographs Blue /10 #43
2011 Press Pass Autographs Bronze /50 #44
2011 Press Pass Autographs Gold /15 #41
2011 Press Pass Autographs Printing Plates Black /1 #44
2011 Press Pass Autographs Printing Plates Cyan /1 #44
2011 Press Pass Autographs Printing Plates Magenta /1 #44
2011 Press Pass Autographs Printing Plates Yellow /1 #44
2011 Press Pass Autographs Silver /25 #44
2011 Press Pass Blue Holofoil /10 #39
2011 Press Pass Blue Holofoil /10 #94
2011 Press Pass Blue Holofoil /10 #117
2011 Press Pass Blue Holofoil /10 #155
2011 Press Pass Blue Retail #39
2011 Press Pass Blue Retail #94
2011 Press Pass Blue Retail #117
2011 Press Pass Blue Retail #155
2011 Press Pass Eclipse #80
2011 Press Pass Eclipse Blue #80
2011 Press Pass Eclipse Gold /55 #80
2011 Press Pass Eclipse Rides #R9
2011 Press Pass Eclipse Spellbound Swatches /150 #SBDP2
2011 Press Pass Eclipse Spellbound Swatches /150 #SBDP3
2011 Press Pass Eclipse Spellbound Swatches /250 #SBDP1
2011 Press Pass Eclipse Spellbound Swatches /100 #SBDP4
2011 Press Pass Eclipse Spellbound Swatches /100 #SBDP5
2011 Press Pass Eclipse Spellbound Swatches /75 #SBDP6
2011 Press Pass Eclipse Spellbound Swatches /50 #SBDP7
2011 Press Pass Eclipse Spellbound Swatches Signatures /10 #NNO
2011 Press Pass FanFare #45
2011 Press Pass FanFare Autographs Blue /5 #58
2011 Press Pass FanFare Autographs Bronze /70 #58
2011 Press Pass FanFare Autographs Gold /50 #58
2011 Press Pass FanFare Autographs Printing Plates Black /1 #58
2011 Press Pass FanFare Autographs Printing Plates Cyan /1 #58
2011 Press Pass FanFare Autographs Printing Plates Magenta /1 #58
2011 Press Pass FanFare Autographs Printing Plates Yellow /1 #58
2011 Press Pass FanFare Autographs Silver /15 #58
2011 Press Pass FanFare Blue Die Cuts #45
2011 Press Pass FanFare Dual Autographs /10 #NNO
2011 Press Pass FanFare Emerald /25 #45
2011 Press Pass FanFare Holofoil Die Cuts #45
2011 Press Pass FanFare Magnificent Materials /199 #MMDP
2011 Press Pass FanFare Magnificent Materials Dual Swatches /50 #MMDDP
2011 Press Pass FanFare Magnificent Materials Dual Swatches Holofoil /10 #MMDDP
2011 Press Pass FanFare Magnificent Materials Holofoil /50 #MMDP
2011 Press Pass FanFare Magnificent Materials Signatures /25 #MMSEDP
2011 Press Pass FanFare Magnificent Materials Signatures Holofoil /10 #MMSEDP
2011 Press Pass FanFare Ruby Die Cuts /15 #45
2011 Press Pass FanFare Sapphire /10 #45
2011 Press Pass FanFare Silver /25 #45
2011 Press Pass Four Wide Autographs /5 #FWADP
2011 Press Pass Four Wide Firesuit /25 #FWDP
2011 Press Pass Four Wide Glove /1 #FWDP
2011 Press Pass Four Wide Sheet Metal /15 #FWDP
2011 Press Pass Four Wide Tire /10 #FWDP
2011 Press Pass Geared Up Holofoil /50 #GUDP
2011 Press Pass Gold /50 #39
2011 Press Pass Gold /50 #94
2011 Press Pass Gold /50 #117
2011 Press Pass Gold /50 #155
2011 Press Pass Legends #49
2011 Press Pass Legends Autographs Blue /5 #LGADP2
2011 Press Pass Legends Autographs Gold /20 #LGADP2
2011 Press Pass Legends Autographs Printing Plates Black /1 #LGADP2
2011 Press Pass Legends Autographs Printing Plates Cyan /1 #LGADP2
2011 Press Pass Legends Autographs Printing Plates Magenta /1 #LGADP2
2011 Press Pass Legends Autographs Printing Plates Yellow /1 #LGADP2
2011 Press Pass Legends Autographs Silver /35 #LGADP2
2011 Press Pass Legends Gold /250 #49
2011 Press Pass Legends Holofoil /25 #49
2011 Press Pass Legends Printing Plates Black /1 #49
2011 Press Pass Legends Printing Plates Cyan /1 #49
2011 Press Pass Legends Printing Plates Magenta /1 #49
2011 Press Pass Legends Printing Plates Yellow /1 #49
2011 Press Pass Legends Prominent Pieces Gold /50 #PPDP
2011 Press Pass Legends Prominent Pieces Holofoil /25 #PPDP
2011 Press Pass Legends Prominent Pieces Oversized Firesuit /25 #PPOEDP
2011 Press Pass Legends Prominent Pieces Purple /15 #PPDP
2011 Press Pass Legends Prominent Pieces Silver /99 #PPDP
2011 Press Pass Legends Purple /25 #49
2011 Press Pass Legends Red /99 #49
2011 Press Pass Legends Solo /1 #49
2011 Press Pass Premium #89
2011 Press Pass Premium Crystal Ball #CB6
2011 Press Pass Premium Crystal Ball Autographs /10 #CBADP
2011 Press Pass Premium Double Burner /25 #DBDP
2011 Press Pass Premium Hot Pursuit 3D #HP6
2011 Press Pass Premium Hot Pursuit Autographs /10 #HPADP
2011 Press Pass Premium Hot Pursuit National Convention #HP6
2011 Press Pass Premium Hot Threads /150 #HTDP
2011 Press Pass Premium Hot Threads Fast Pass /25 #HTDP
2011 Press Pass Premium Hot Threads Multi Color /25 #HTDP
2011 Press Pass Premium Hot Threads Patches /15 #HTPDP
2011 Press Pass Premium Hot Threads Secondary Color /99 #HTDP
2011 Press Pass Premium Purple /25 #89
2011 Press Pass Premium Signatures /17 #PSDP
2011 Press Pass Purple /25 #39
2011 Press Pass Showcase /499 #52
2011 Press Pass Showcase Elite Exhibit Ink /50 #EEIDP
2011 Press Pass Showcase Elite Exhibit Ink Gold /25 #EEIDP
2011 Press Pass Showcase Elite Exhibit Ink Melting /1 #EEIDP
2011 Press Pass Showcase Gold /125 #52
2011 Press Pass Showcase Green /25 #52
2011 Press Pass Showcase Masterpieces Ink /45 #MPIDP
2011 Press Pass Showcase Masterpieces Ink Gold /25 #MPIDP
2011 Press Pass Showcase Masterpieces Ink Melting /1 #MPIDP
2011 Press Pass Showcase Masterpieces Memorabilia /99 #MPMDP
2011 Press Pass Showcase Masterpieces Memorabilia Gold /45 #MPMDP
2011 Press Pass Showcase Masterpieces Memorabilia Melting /5 #MPMDP
2011 Press Pass Showcase Melting /1 #52
2011 Press Pass Showcase Prized Pieces Firesuit /99 #PPMDP
2011 Press Pass Showcase Prized Pieces Firesuit Gold /45 #PPMDP
2011 Press Pass Showcase Prized Pieces Firesuit Ink /25 #PPIDP
2011 Press Pass Showcase Prized Pieces Firesuit Patches Ink /1 #PPIDP
2011 Press Pass Showcase Prized Pieces Firesuit Patches Melting /5 #PPMDP
2011 Press Pass Showcase Prized Pieces Sheet Metal Ink /45 #PPIDP
2011 Press Pass Showcase Showroom /499 #SR8
2011 Press Pass Showcase Showroom Gold /125 #SR8
2011 Press Pass Showcase Showroom Melting /1 #SR8
2011 Press Pass Showcase Showroom Memorabilia Sheet Metal /45 #SRMDP
2011 Press Pass Showcase Showroom Memorabilia Sheet Metal Gold /25 #SRMDP
2011 Press Pass Showcase Showroom Memorabilia Sheet Metal Melting /5 #SRMDP
2011 Press Pass Signature Series /11 #SSTDP
2011 Press Pass Signature Series /11 #SSRDP
2011 Press Pass Signature Series /11 #SSFDP
2011 Press Pass Signature Series /11 #SSMDP
2011 Press Pass Signings Black and White /5 #PPSDP
2011 Press Pass Signings Brushed Metal /15 #PPSDP
2011 Press Pass Signings Holofoil /10 #PPSDP
2011 Press Pass Stealth #60
2011 Press Pass Stealth Afterburner /99 #ABDP
2011 Press Pass Stealth Afterburner Gold /25 #ABDP
2011 Press Pass Stealth Black and White /25 #60
2011 Press Pass Stealth Holofoil /99 #60
2011 Press Pass Stealth In Flight Report #IF9
2011 Press Pass Stealth Metal of Honor Medal of Honor /50 #BADP
2011 Press Pass Stealth Metal of Honor Purple Heart /25 #MHDP
2011 Press Pass Stealth Metal of Honor Silver Star /99 #BADP
2011 Press Pass Stealth Purple /25 #60
2011 Wheels Main Event #42
2011 Wheels Main Event Black and White #42
2011 Wheels Main Event Blue /75 #42
2011 Wheels Main Event Gloves Off Holofoil /25 #GODP
2011 Wheels Main Event Gloves Off Silver /99 #GODP
2011 Wheels Main Event Green /1 #42
2011 Wheels Main Event Headliners Holofoil /25 #HLDP
2011 Wheels Main Event Headliners Silver /99 #HLDP
2011 Wheels Main Event Marks Autographs Blue /10 #MEDP
2011 Wheels Main Event Marks Autographs Gold /25 #MEDP
2011 Wheels Main Event Marks Autographs Silver /35 #MEDP
2011 Wheels Main Event Red /20 #42
2012 Press Pass #42
2012 Press Pass #94
2012 Press Pass Autographs Blue /5 #PPADP
2012 Press Pass Autographs Printing Plates Black /1 #PPADP
2012 Press Pass Autographs Printing Plates Cyan /1 #PPADP
2012 Press Pass Autographs Printing Plates Magenta /1 #PPADP
2012 Press Pass Autographs Printing Plates Yellow /1 #PPADP
2012 Press Pass Autographs Red /10 #PPADP
2012 Press Pass Autographs Silver /150 #PPADP
2012 Press Pass Blue #42
2012 Press Pass Blue #94
2012 Press Pass Blue Holofoil /35 #42
2012 Press Pass Blue Holofoil /35 #94
2012 Press Pass Fanfare #55
2012 Press Pass Fanfare #35
2012 Press Pass Fanfare Autographs Blue /1 #DP
2012 Press Pass Fanfare Autographs Gold /1 #DP
2012 Press Pass Fanfare Autographs Red /1 #DP
2012 Press Pass Fanfare Autographs Silver /1 #DP
2012 Press Pass Fanfare Blue Foil Die Cuts #35
2012 Press Pass Fanfare Blue Foil Die Cuts #55
2012 Press Pass Fanfare Diamond /5 #35
2012 Press Pass Fanfare Diamond /5 #55
2012 Press Pass Fanfare Holofoil Die Cuts #35
2012 Press Pass Fanfare Holofoil Die Cuts #55
2012 Press Pass Fanfare Magnificent Materials /250 #MMDP
2012 Press Pass Fanfare Magnificent Materials /250 #MMDP2
2012 Press Pass Fanfare Magnificent Materials Dual Swatches /50 #MMDP
2012 Press Pass Fanfare Magnificent Materials Dual Swatches /50 #MMDP2
2012 Press Pass Fanfare Magnificent Materials Dual Swatches Melting /10 #MMDP
2012 Press Pass Fanfare Magnificent Materials Dual Swatches Melting /10 #MMDP2
2012 Press Pass Fanfare Magnificent Materials Gold /99 #MMDP
2012 Press Pass Fanfare Magnificent Materials Gold /99 #MMDP2
2012 Press Pass Fanfare Magnificent Materials Signatures /10 #DP
2012 Press Pass Fanfare Magnificent Materials Signatures Blue /5 #DP
2012 Press Pass Fanfare Sapphire /20 #55
2012 Press Pass Fanfare Sapphire /20 #35
2012 Press Pass Fanfare Showtime #S6
2012 Press Pass Fanfare Silver /25 #55
2012 Press Pass Fanfare Silver /25 #35
2012 Press Pass Four Wide Firesuit /25 #FWDP
2012 Press Pass Four Wide Glove /1 #FWDP
2012 Press Pass Four Wide Sheet Metal /15 #FWDP
2012 Press Pass Four Wide Tire /10 #FWDP
2012 Press Pass Gold #42
2012 Press Pass Gold #94
2012 Press Pass Ignite #45
2012 Press Pass Ignite #30
2012 Press Pass Ignite Double Burner Gun Metal /10 #DBDP
2012 Press Pass Ignite Double Burner Red /1 #DBDP
2012 Press Pass Ignite Double Burner Silver /25 #DBDP
2012 Press Pass Ignite Limelight #L1
2012 Press Pass Ignite Materials Autographs Gun Metal /5 #IMDP2
2012 Press Pass Ignite Materials Autographs Red /5 #IMDP
2012 Press Pass Ignite Materials Autographs Red /5 #IMDP2
2012 Press Pass Ignite Materials Autographs Silver /65 #IMDP
2012 Press Pass Ignite Materials Autographs Silver /65 #IMDP2
2012 Press Pass Ignite Materials Gun Metal /99 #IMDP
2012 Press Pass Ignite Materials Gun Metal /99 #IMDP2
2012 Press Pass Ignite Materials Red /10 #IMDP
2012 Press Pass Ignite Materials Red /10 #IMDP2
2012 Press Pass Ignite Materials Silver #IMDP
2012 Press Pass Ignite Materials Silver #IMDP2
2012 Press Pass Ignite Profile #P4
2012 Press Pass Ignite Proofs Black and White /50 #45
2012 Press Pass Ignite Proofs Black and White /50 #30
2012 Press Pass Ignite Proofs Cyan #45
2012 Press Pass Ignite Proofs Cyan #30
2012 Press Pass Ignite Proofs Magenta #45
2012 Press Pass Ignite Proofs Magenta #30
2012 Press Pass Ignite Proofs Yellow /10 #30
2012 Press Pass Ignite Proofs Yellow /10 #45
2012 Press Pass Ignite Steel Horses #SH3
2012 Press Pass Ignite Supercharged Signatures /5 #SSDP
2012 Press Pass Legends #49
2012 Press Pass Legends Blue Holofoil /1 #49
2012 Press Pass Legends Gold /275 #49
2012 Press Pass Legends Green #49
2012 Press Pass Legends Prominent Pieces Gold /50 #DP
2012 Press Pass Legends Prominent Pieces Holofoil /25 #DP
2012 Press Pass Legends Prominent Pieces Oversized Firesuit /25 #DP
2012 Press Pass Legends Prominent Pieces Silver /99 #DP
2012 Press Pass Legends Rainbow Holofoil /50 #49
2012 Press Pass Legends Red /99 #49
2012 Press Pass Legends Silver Holofoil /25 #49
2012 Press Pass Legends Trailblazers #TB15
2012 Press Pass Power Picks Blue /50 #47
2012 Press Pass Power Picks Blue /50 #54
2012 Press Pass Power Picks Blue /50 #60
2012 Press Pass Power Picks Blue /50 #61
2012 Press Pass Power Picks Gold /50 #47
2012 Press Pass Power Picks Gold /50 #54
2012 Press Pass Power Picks Gold /50 #61
2012 Press Pass Power Picks Gold /50 #60
2012 Press Pass Power Picks Holofoil /10 #47
2012 Press Pass Power Picks Holofoil /10 #54
2012 Press Pass Power Picks Holofoil /10 #60
2012 Press Pass Power Picks Holofoil /10 #61
2012 Press Pass Preferred Line #PL6
2012 Press Pass Purple /35 #42
2012 Press Pass Purple /35 #94
2012 Press Pass Redline #32
2012 Press Pass Redline #44
2012 Press Pass Redline Black /99 #32
2012 Press Pass Redline Black /99 #44
2012 Press Pass Redline Cyan /50 #32
2012 Press Pass Redline Cyan /50 #44
2012 Press Pass Redline Full Throttle Dual Relic Blue /5 #FTDP
2012 Press Pass Redline Full Throttle Dual Relic Gold /10 #FTDP
2012 Press Pass Redline Full Throttle Dual Relic Melting /1 #FTDP
2012 Press Pass Redline Full Throttle Dual Relic Red /50 #FTDP
2012 Press Pass Redline Full Throttle Dual Relic Silver /25 #FTDP
2012 Press Pass Redline Intensity #I8
2012 Press Pass Redline Magenta /15 #32
2012 Press Pass Redline Magenta /15 #44
2012 Press Pass Redline Muscle Car Sheet Metal Blue /5 #MCDP1
2012 Press Pass Redline Muscle Car Sheet Metal Blue /5 #MCDP2
2012 Press Pass Redline Muscle Car Sheet Metal Gold /10 #MCDP1
2012 Press Pass Redline Muscle Car Sheet Metal Gold /10 #MCDP2
2012 Press Pass Redline Muscle Car Sheet Metal Melting /1 #MCDP1
2012 Press Pass Redline Muscle Car Sheet Metal Melting /1 #MCDP2
2012 Press Pass Redline Muscle Car Sheet Metal Red /75 #MCDP2
2012 Press Pass Redline Muscle Car Sheet Metal Red /75 #MCDP1
2012 Press Pass Redline Muscle Car Sheet Metal Silver /25 #MCDP1
2012 Press Pass Redline Muscle Car Sheet Metal Silver /25 #MCDP2
2012 Press Pass Redline Performance Driven #PD8
2012 Press Pass Redline Pieces of the Action Blue /10 #PADP
2012 Press Pass Redline Pieces of the Action Gold /25 #PADP
2012 Press Pass Redline Pieces of the Action Melting /1 #PADP
2012 Press Pass Redline Pieces of the Action Red /75 #PADP
2012 Press Pass Redline Pieces of the Action Silver /50 #PADP
2012 Press Pass Redline Relic Autographs Blue /1 #RLRDP1
2012 Press Pass Redline Relic Autographs Blue /5 #RLRDP2
2012 Press Pass Redline Relic Autographs Gold /5 #RLRDP1
2012 Press Pass Redline Relic Autographs Gold /15 #RLRDP2
2012 Press Pass Redline Relic Autographs Melting /1 #RLRDP1
2012 Press Pass Redline Relic Autographs Melting /1 #RLRDP2
2012 Press Pass Redline Relic Autographs Red /25 #RLRDP2
2012 Press Pass Redline Relic Autographs Red /19 #RLRDP1
2012 Press Pass Redline Relic Autographs Silver /10 #RLRDP1
2012 Press Pass Redline Relic Autographs Silver /14 #RLRDP2
2012 Press Pass Redline Relics Blue /5 #RLDP1
2012 Press Pass Redline Relics Blue /5 #RLDP2
2012 Press Pass Redline Relics Gold /10 #RLDP1
2012 Press Pass Redline Relics Gold /10 #RLDP2
2012 Press Pass Redline Relics Melting /1 #RLDP1
2012 Press Pass Redline Relics Melting /1 #RLDP2
2012 Press Pass Redline Relics Red /75 #RLDP2
2012 Press Pass Redline Relics Red /25 #RLDP1
2012 Press Pass Redline Relics Silver /15 #RLDP1
2012 Press Pass Redline Relics Silver /25 #RLDP2
2012 Press Pass Redline Rookie Year Relic Autographs Blue /5 #RYDP1
2012 Press Pass Redline Rookie Year Relic Autographs Gold /9 #RYDP1
2012 Press Pass Redline Rookie Year Relic Autographs Melting /1 #RYDP1
2012 Press Pass Redline Rookie Year Relic Autographs Red /19 #RYDP1
2012 Press Pass Redline RPM #RPM11
2012 Press Pass Redline Signatures Blue /5 #RSDP1
2012 Press Pass Redline Signatures Blue /1 #RSDP2
2012 Press Pass Redline Signatures Gold /20 #RSDP1
2012 Press Pass Redline Signatures Gold /5 #RSDP2
2012 Press Pass Redline Signatures Holofoil /10 #RSDP1
2012 Press Pass Redline Signatures Holofoil /1 #RSDP2
2012 Press Pass Redline Signatures Melting /1 #RSDP1
2012 Press Pass Redline Signatures Melting /1 #RSDP2
2012 Press Pass Redline Signatures Red /10 #RSDP2
2012 Press Pass Redline Signatures Red /25 #RSDP1
2012 Press Pass Redline V8 Relics Blue /5 #V8DP
2012 Press Pass Redline V8 Relics Gold /10 #V8DP
2012 Press Pass Redline V8 Relics Melting /1 #V8DP
2012 Press Pass Redline V8 Relics Red /25 #V8DP
2012 Press Pass Redline Yellow /1 #32
2012 Press Pass Redline Yellow /1 #44
2012 Press Pass Showcase /499 #48
2012 Press Pass Showcase /499 #41
2012 Press Pass Showcase /499 #23
2012 Press Pass Showcase /50 #61
2012 Press Pass Showcase /499 #53
2012 Press Pass Showcase Classic Collections Ink /10 #CCMSHR
2012 Press Pass Showcase Classic Collections Ink Gold /5 #CCMSHR
2012 Press Pass Showcase Classic Collections Ink Melting /1 #CCMSHR
2012 Press Pass Showcase Classic Collections Memorabilia /99 #CCMSHR
2012 Press Pass Showcase Classic Collections Memorabilia Gold /50 #CCMSHR
2012 Press Pass Showcase Classic Collections Memorabilia Melting /5 #CCMSHR
2012 Press Pass Showcase Elite Exhibit Ink /23 #EEIDP
2012 Press Pass Showcase Elite Exhibit Ink Gold /10 #EEIDP
2012 Press Pass Showcase Elite Exhibit Ink Melting /1 #EEIDP
2012 Press Pass Showcase Gold /125 #23
2012 Press Pass Showcase Gold /125 #41
2012 Press Pass Showcase Gold /125 #48
2012 Press Pass Showcase Gold /125 #53
2012 Press Pass Showcase Gold /25 #61
2012 Press Pass Showcase Green /5 #23
2012 Press Pass Showcase Green /5 #41
2012 Press Pass Showcase Green /5 #48
2012 Press Pass Showcase Green /5 #53
2012 Press Pass Showcase Green /5 #61
2012 Press Pass Showcase Masterpieces Ink /50 #MPIDP
2012 Press Pass Showcase Masterpieces Ink Gold /25 #MPIDP
2012 Press Pass Showcase Masterpieces Ink Melting /1 #MPIDP
2012 Press Pass Showcase Masterpieces Memorabilia /99 #MPDP
2012 Press Pass Showcase Masterpieces Memorabilia Gold /50 #MPDP
2012 Press Pass Showcase Masterpieces Memorabilia Melting /5 #MPDP
2012 Press Pass Showcase Melting /1 #23
2012 Press Pass Showcase Melting /1 #41
2012 Press Pass Showcase Melting /1 #48
2012 Press Pass Showcase Melting /1 #53
2012 Press Pass Showcase Melting /1 #61
2012 Press Pass Showcase Prized Pieces /99 #PPDP
2012 Press Pass Showcase Prized Pieces Gold /50 #PPDP
2012 Press Pass Showcase Prized Pieces Ink /25 #PPIDP
2012 Press Pass Showcase Prized Pieces Ink Gold /10 #PPIDP
2012 Press Pass Showcase Prized Pieces Ink Melting /1 #PPIDP
2012 Press Pass Showcase Prized Pieces Melting /5 #PPDP
2012 Press Pass Showcase Purple /1 #23
2012 Press Pass Showcase Purple /1 #41
2012 Press Pass Showcase Purple /1 #48
2012 Press Pass Showcase Purple /1 #53
2012 Press Pass Showcase Purple /1 #61
2012 Press Pass Showcase Red /25 #23
2012 Press Pass Showcase Red /25 #41
2012 Press Pass Showcase Red /25 #48
2012 Press Pass Showcase Red /25 #53
2012 Press Pass Showcase Richard Petty 75th Birthday Tribute /10 #RPDP2
2012 Press Pass Showcase Richard Petty 75th Birthday Tribute Melting /1 #RPDP2
2012 Press Pass Showcase Showcase Patches /5 #SSPDP
2012 Press Pass Showcase Showcase Patches Melting /1 #SSPDP
2012 Press Pass Showcase Showroom /499 #SR5
2012 Press Pass Showcase Showroom Gold /125 #SR5
2012 Press Pass Showcase Showroom Melting /1 #SR5
2012 Press Pass Showcase Showroom Memorabilia /99 #SRDP
2012 Press Pass Showcase Showroom Memorabilia Gold /50 #SRDP
2012 Press Pass Showcase Showroom Memorabilia Melting /5 #SRDP
2012 Press Pass Showcase Signature Patches /1 #SSPDP
2012 Press Pass Signature Series Race Used /12 #PPADP1
2012 Press Pass Signature Series Race Used /12 #PPADP2
2012 Press Pass Snapshots #SS44
2012 Press Pass Triple Gear 3 in 1 /5 #TGDP
2012 Press Pass Triple Gear Firesuit and Sheet Metal /15 #TGDP
2012 Press Pass Triple Gear Tire /25 #TGDP
2012 Sports Illustrated Swimsuit Decade of Supermodels #18
2012 Sports Illustrated Swimsuit Decade of Supermodels Celebrities #C4
2012 Sports Illustrated Swimsuit Decade of Supermodels Celebrities Printing Plates Black /1 #C4
2012 Sports Illustrated Swimsuit Decade of Supermodels Celebrities Printing Plates Cyan /1 #C4
2012 Sports Illustrated Swimsuit Decade of Supermodels Celebrities Printing Plates Magenta /1 #C4
2012 Sports Illustrated Swimsuit Decade of Supermodels Celebrities Printing Plates Yellow /1 #C4
2012 Sports Illustrated Swimsuit Decade of Supermodels Danica Patrick Memorabilia #DP10
2012 Sports Illustrated Swimsuit Decade of Supermodels Danica Patrick Memorabilia #DP9
2012 Sports Illustrated Swimsuit Decade of Supermodels Danica Patrick Memorabilia #DP8
2012 Sports Illustrated Swimsuit Decade of Supermodels Danica Patrick Memorabilia #DP7
2012 Sports Illustrated Swimsuit Decade of Supermodels Danica Patrick Memorabilia #DP6
2012 Sports Illustrated Swimsuit Decade of Supermodels Danica Patrick Memorabilia #DP5
2012 Sports Illustrated Swimsuit Decade of Supermodels Danica Patrick Memorabilia #DP4
2012 Sports Illustrated Swimsuit Decade of Supermodels Danica Patrick Memorabilia #DP3
2012 Sports Illustrated Swimsuit Decade of Supermodels Danica Patrick Memorabilia #DP2
2012 Sports Illustrated Swimsuit Decade of Supermodels Danica Patrick Memorabilia #DP1
2012 Sports Illustrated Swimsuit Decade of Supermodels Danica Patrick Memorabilia Printing Plates Black /1 #DP1
2012 Sports Illustrated Swimsuit Decade of Supermodels Danica Patrick Memorabilia Printing Plates Black /1 #DP2
2012 Sports Illustrated Swimsuit Decade of Supermodels Danica Patrick Memorabilia Printing Plates Black /1 #DP3
2012 Sports Illustrated Swimsuit Decade of Supermodels Danica Patrick Memorabilia Printing Plates Black /1 #DP4
2012 Sports Illustrated Swimsuit Decade of Supermodels Danica Patrick Memorabilia Printing Plates Black /1 #DP5
2012 Sports Illustrated Swimsuit Decade of Supermodels Danica Patrick Memorabilia Printing Plates Black /1 #DP6
2012 Sports Illustrated Swimsuit Decade of Supermodels Danica Patrick Memorabilia Printing Plates Black /1 #DP7
2012 Sports Illustrated Swimsuit Decade of Supermodels Danica Patrick Memorabilia Printing Plates Black /1 #DP8
2012 Sports Illustrated Swimsuit Decade of Supermodels Danica Patrick Memorabilia Printing Plates Black /1 #DP9
2012 Sports Illustrated Swimsuit Decade of Supermodels Danica Patrick Memorabilia Printing Plates Black /1 #DP10
2012 Sports Illustrated Swimsuit Decade of Supermodels Danica Patrick Memorabilia Printing Plates Cyan /1 #DP1
2012 Sports Illustrated Swimsuit Decade of Supermodels Danica Patrick Memorabilia Printing Plates Cyan /1 #DP2
2012 Sports Illustrated Swimsuit Decade of Supermodels Danica Patrick Memorabilia Printing Plates Cyan /1 #DP3
2012 Sports Illustrated Swimsuit Decade of Supermodels Danica Patrick Memorabilia Printing Plates Cyan /1 #DP4
2012 Sports Illustrated Swimsuit Decade of Supermodels Danica Patrick Memorabilia Printing Plates Cyan /1 #DP5
2012 Sports Illustrated Swimsuit Decade of Supermodels Danica Patrick Memorabilia Printing Plates Cyan /1 #DP6
2012 Sports Illustrated Swimsuit Decade of Supermodels Danica Patrick Memorabilia Printing Plates Cyan /1 #DP7
2012 Sports Illustrated Swimsuit Decade of Supermodels Danica Patrick Memorabilia Printing Plates Cyan /1 #DP8
2012 Sports Illustrated Swimsuit Decade of Supermodels Danica Patrick Memorabilia Printing Plates Cyan /1 #DP9
2012 Sports Illustrated Swimsuit Decade of Supermodels Danica Patrick Memorabilia Printing Plates Cyan /1 #DP10
2012 Sports Illustrated Swimsuit Decade of Supermodels Danica Patrick Memorabilia Printing Plates Magenta /1 #DP1
2012 Sports Illustrated Swimsuit Decade of Supermodels Danica Patrick Memorabilia Printing Plates Magenta /1 #DP2
2012 Sports Illustrated Swimsuit Decade of Supermodels Danica Patrick Memorabilia Printing Plates Magenta /1 #DP3
2012 Sports Illustrated Swimsuit Decade of Supermodels Danica Patrick Memorabilia Printing Plates Magenta /1 #DP4
2012 Sports Illustrated Swimsuit Decade of Supermodels Danica Patrick Memorabilia Printing Plates Magenta /1 #DP5
2012 Sports Illustrated Swimsuit Decade of Supermodels Danica Patrick Memorabilia Printing Plates Magenta /1 #DP6
2012 Sports Illustrated Swimsuit Decade of Supermodels Danica Patrick Memorabilia Printing Plates Magenta /1 #DP7
2012 Sports Illustrated Swimsuit Decade of Supermodels Danica Patrick Memorabilia Printing Plates Magenta /1 #DP8
2012 Sports Illustrated Swimsuit Decade of Supermodels Danica Patrick Memorabilia Printing Plates Magenta /1 #DP9
2012 Sports Illustrated Swimsuit Decade of Supermodels Danica Patrick Memorabilia Printing Plates Magenta /1 #DP10
2012 Sports Illustrated Swimsuit Decade of Supermodels Danica Patrick Memorabilia Printing Plates Yellow /1 #DP1
2012 Sports Illustrated Swimsuit Decade of Supermodels Danica Patrick Memorabilia Printing Plates Yellow /1 #DP2
2012 Sports Illustrated Swimsuit Decade of Supermodels Danica Patrick Memorabilia Printing Plates Yellow /1 #DP3
2012 Sports Illustrated Swimsuit Decade of Supermodels Danica Patrick Memorabilia Printing Plates Yellow /1 #DP4
2012 Sports Illustrated Swimsuit Decade of Supermodels Danica Patrick Memorabilia Printing Plates Yellow /1 #DP5
2012 Sports Illustrated Swimsuit Decade of Supermodels Danica Patrick Memorabilia Printing Plates Yellow /1 #DP6
2012 Sports Illustrated Swimsuit Decade of Supermodels Danica Patrick Memorabilia Printing Plates Yellow /1 #DP7
2012 Sports Illustrated Swimsuit Decade of Supermodels Danica Patrick Memorabilia Printing Plates Yellow /1 #DP8
2012 Sports Illustrated Swimsuit Decade of Supermodels Danica Patrick Memorabilia Printing Plates Yellow /1 #DP9
2012 Sports Illustrated Swimsuit Decade of Supermodels Danica Patrick Memorabilia Printing Plates Yellow /1 #DP10
2012 Sports Illustrated Swimsuit Decade of Supermodels Printing Plates Black /1 #18
2012 Sports Illustrated Swimsuit Decade of Supermodels Printing Plates Cyan /1 #18
2012 Sports Illustrated Swimsuit Decade of Supermodels Printing Plates Magenta /1 #18
2012 Sports Illustrated Swimsuit Decade of Supermodels Printing Plates Yellow /1 #18
2012 Total Memorabilia #34A
2012 Total Memorabilia #34B
2012 Total Memorabilia Black and White /99 #34
2012 Total Memorabilia Dual Swatch Gold /75 #TMDP
2012 Total Memorabilia Dual Swatch Holofoil /25 #TMDP
2012 Total Memorabilia Dual Swatch Melting /5 #TMDP
2012 Total Memorabilia Dual Swatch Silver /99 #TMDP
2012 Total Memorabilia Gold /275 #34
2012 Total Memorabilia Hot Rod Relics Gold /50 #HRRDP
2012 Total Memorabilia Hot Rod Relics Holofoil /10 #HRRDP
2012 Total Memorabilia Hot Rod Relics Melting /1 #HRRDP
2012 Total Memorabilia Hot Rod Relics Silver /99 #HRRDP
2012 Total Memorabilia Jumbo Swatch Gold /50 #TMDP
2012 Total Memorabilia Jumbo Swatch Holofoil /10 #TMDP
2012 Total Memorabilia Jumbo Swatch Melting /1 #TMDP
2012 Total Memorabilia Quad Swatch Gold /25 #TMDP
2012 Total Memorabilia Quad Swatch Holofoil /10 #TMDP
2012 Total Memorabilia Quad Swatch Melting /1 #TMDP
2012 Total Memorabilia Quad Swatch Silver /50 #TMDP
2012 Total Memorabilia Red Retail /250 #34
2012 Total Memorabilia Signature Collection Dual Swatch Silver /10 #SCDP
2012 Total Memorabilia Signature Collection Quad Swatch Holofoil /5 #SCDP
2012 Total Memorabilia Signature Collection Single Swatch Melting /1 #SCDP
2012 Total Memorabilia Signature Collection Triple Swatch Gold /10 #SCDP
2012 Total Memorabilia Single Swatch Gold /99 #TMDP
2012 Total Memorabilia Single Swatch Holofoil /50 #TMDP
2012 Total Memorabilia Single Swatch Melting /10 #TMDP
2012 Total Memorabilia Single Swatch Silver /199 #TMDP
2012 Total Memorabilia Tandem Treasures Dual Memorabilia Gold /75 #TTTSDP
2012 Total Memorabilia Tandem Treasures Dual Memorabilia Holofoil /25 #TTTSDP
2012 Total Memorabilia Tandem Treasures Dual Memorabilia Melting /5 #TTTSDP
2012 Total Memorabilia Tandem Treasures Dual Memorabilia Silver /99 #TTTSDP
2012 Total Memorabilia Triple Swatch Gold /50 #TMDP
2012 Total Memorabilia Triple Swatch Holofoil /25 #TMDP
2012 Total Memorabilia Triple Swatch Melting /1 #TMDP
2012 Total Memorabilia Triple Swatch Silver /99 #TMDP
2012-13 Exquisite Collection Sports Autographs /10 #DP
2012-13 Exquisite Collection Sports Autographs Gold Spectrum /1 #DP
2012-13 The Cup Sidney Crosby Tribute /10 #180DP
2013 Press Pass #36
2013 Press Pass #54
2013 Press Pass #91
2013 Press Pass Aerodynamic Autographs Blue /1 #DP
2013 Press Pass Aerodynamic Autographs Holofoil /10 #DP
2013 Press Pass Color Proofs Black #36
2013 Press Pass Color Proofs Black #54
2013 Press Pass Color Proofs Black #91
2013 Press Pass Color Proofs Cyan /35 #36
2013 Press Pass Color Proofs Cyan /35 #54
2013 Press Pass Color Proofs Cyan /35 #91
2013 Press Pass Color Proofs Magenta #36
2013 Press Pass Color Proofs Magenta #54
2013 Press Pass Color Proofs Magenta #91
2013 Press Pass Color Proofs Yellow /5 #36
2013 Press Pass Color Proofs Yellow /5 #54
2013 Press Pass Color Proofs Yellow /5 #91
2013 Press Pass Cool Persistence #CP2
2013 Press Pass Cup Chase #CC16
2013 Press Pass Fanfare #46
2013 Press Pass Fanfare #100
2013 Press Pass Fanfare #47
2013 Press Pass Fanfare Autographs Blue /1 #DP
2013 Press Pass Fanfare Autographs Gold /1 #DP
2013 Press Pass Fanfare Autographs Green /1 #DP
2013 Press Pass Fanfare Autographs Red /1 #DP
2013 Press Pass Fanfare Autographs Silver /1 #DP
2013 Press Pass Fanfare Diamond Die Cuts /5 #46
2013 Press Pass Fanfare Diamond Die Cuts /5 #47
2013 Press Pass Fanfare Diamond Die Cuts /5 #100
2013 Press Pass Fanfare Fan Following #FF5
2013 Press Pass Fanfare Fan Following National Convention VIP #FFN5
2013 Press Pass Fanfare Green /3 #46
2013 Press Pass Fanfare Green /3 #47
2013 Press Pass Fanfare Green /3 #100
2013 Press Pass Fanfare Holofoil Die Cuts #46
2013 Press Pass Fanfare Holofoil Die Cuts #47
2013 Press Pass Fanfare Holofoil Die Cuts #100
2013 Press Pass Fanfare Magnificent Jumbo Materials Signatures /5 #DP
2013 Press Pass Fanfare Magnificent Materials Dual Swatches /50 #DP
2013 Press Pass Fanfare Magnificent Materials Dual Swatches Melting /10 #DP
2013 Press Pass Fanfare Magnificent Materials Gold /50 #DP
2013 Press Pass Fanfare Magnificent Materials Jumbo Swatches /25 #DP
2013 Press Pass Fanfare Magnificent Materials Signatures /5 #DP

2013 Press Pass Fanfare Magnificent Materials Signatures Blue /1 #DP
2013 Press Pass Fanfare Magnificent Materials Silver /199 #DP
2013 Press Pass Fanfare Red Foil Die Cuts #46
2013 Press Pass Fanfare Red Foil Die Cuts #47
2013 Press Pass Fanfare Red Foil Die Cuts #100
2013 Press Pass Fanfare Rookie Stripes Memorabilia /25 #DP
2013 Press Pass Fanfare Rookie Stripes Memorabilia Autographs /10 #DP
2013 Press Pass Fanfare Sapphire /20 #46
2013 Press Pass Fanfare Sapphire /20 #47
2013 Press Pass Fanfare Sapphire /20 #100
2013 Press Pass Fanfare Showtime #S2
2013 Press Pass Fanfare Silver /25 #46
2013 Press Pass Fanfare Silver /25 #47
2013 Press Pass Fanfare Silver /25 #100
2013 Press Pass Ignite #0
2013 Press Pass Ignite #29
2013 Press Pass Ignite #51
2013 Press Pass Ignite Convoy #8
2013 Press Pass Ignite Double Burner Blue Holofoil /10 #DBDP
2013 Press Pass Ignite Double Burner Red /1 #DBDP
2013 Press Pass Ignite Double Burner Silver /25 #DBDP
2013 Press Pass Ignite Great American Treads Autographs Blue Holofoil /5 #GATDP
2013 Press Pass Ignite Great American Treads Autographs Red /1 #GATDP
2013 Press Pass Ignite Hot Threads Blue Holofoil /99 #HTDP
2013 Press Pass Ignite Hot Threads Patch Red /10 #HTDP
2013 Press Pass Ignite Hot Threads Patch Red Oversized /20 #HTPDP
2013 Press Pass Ignite Hot Threads Silver #HTDP
2013 Press Pass Ignite Ink Black /10 #IIDP
2013 Press Pass Ignite Ink Blue /5 #IIDP
2013 Press Pass Ignite Ink Red /1 #IIDP
2013 Press Pass Ignite Profile #12
2013 Press Pass Ignite Proofs Black and White /50 #29
2013 Press Pass Ignite Proofs Black and White /50 #51
2013 Press Pass Ignite Proofs Cyan #29
2013 Press Pass Ignite Proofs Cyan #51
2013 Press Pass Ignite Proofs Magenta #29
2013 Press Pass Ignite Proofs Magenta #51
2013 Press Pass Ignite Proofs Yellow /5 #29
2013 Press Pass Ignite Proofs Yellow /5 #51
2013 Press Pass Ignite Supercharged Signatures Blue Holofoil /5 #SSDP
2013 Press Pass Ignite Supercharged Signatures Red /1 #SSDP
2013 Press Pass Ignite Turning Point #7
2013 Press Pass Legends #47
2013 Press Pass Legends Autographs Blue #LGDP3
2013 Press Pass Legends Autographs Gold /4 #LGDP3
2013 Press Pass Legends Autographs Holofoil /2 #LGDP3
2013 Press Pass Legends Autographs Printing Plates Black /1 #LGDP3
2013 Press Pass Legends Autographs Printing Plates Cyan /1 #LGDP3
2013 Press Pass Legends Autographs Printing Plates Magenta /1 #LGDP3
2013 Press Pass Legends Autographs Printing Plates Yellow /1 #LGDP3
2013 Press Pass Legends Autographs Silver #LGDP3
2013 Press Pass Legends Blue #47
2013 Press Pass Legends Blue Holofoil /1 #47
2013 Press Pass Legends Four Wide Memorabilia Autographs Gold /25 #FWSEDP
2013 Press Pass Legends Four Wide Memorabilia Autographs Melting /4 #FWSEDP
2013 Press Pass Legends Gold /149 #47
2013 Press Pass Legends Holofoil /10 #47
2013 Press Pass Legends Printing Plates Black /1 #47
2013 Press Pass Legends Printing Plates Cyan /1 #47
2013 Press Pass Legends Printing Plates Magenta /1 #47
2013 Press Pass Legends Printing Plates Yellow /1 #47
2013 Press Pass Legends Prominent Pieces Gold /10 #PPDP
2013 Press Pass Legends Prominent Pieces Holofoil /5 #PPDP
2013 Press Pass Legends Prominent Pieces Oversized Firesuit /5 #PPDP
2013 Press Pass Legends Prominent Pieces Silver /25 #PPDP
2013 Press Pass Legends Red /99 #47
2013 Press Pass Power Picks Blue /99 #18
2013 Press Pass Power Picks Blue /99 #48
2013 Press Pass Power Picks Gold /50 #18
2013 Press Pass Power Picks Gold /50 #48
2013 Press Pass Power Picks Holofoil /10 #18
2013 Press Pass Power Picks Holofoil /10 #48
2013 Press Pass Redline #40
2013 Press Pass Redline Black /99 #40
2013 Press Pass Redline Cyan /50 #40
2013 Press Pass Redline Dark Horse Relic Autographs Blue /5 #DHDP
2013 Press Pass Redline Dark Horse Relic Autographs Gold /10 #DHDP
2013 Press Pass Redline Dark Horse Relic Autographs Melting /1 #DHDP
2013 Press Pass Redline Dark Horse Relic Autographs Red /25 #DHDP
2013 Press Pass Redline Dynamic Duals Dual Relic Blue /5 #DDDP
2013 Press Pass Redline Dynamic Duals Dual Relic Gold /10 #DDDP
2013 Press Pass Redline Dynamic Duals Dual Relic Melting /1 #DDDP
2013 Press Pass Redline Dynamic Duals Dual Relic Red /50 #DDDP
2013 Press Pass Redline Dynamic Duals Dual Relic Silver /25 #DDDP
2013 Press Pass Redline Intensity #8
2013 Press Pass Redline Magenta /15 #40
2013 Press Pass Redline Muscle Car Sheet Metal Blue /5 #MCMDP
2013 Press Pass Redline Muscle Car Sheet Metal Gold /10 #MCMDP
2013 Press Pass Redline Muscle Car Sheet Metal Melting /1 #MCMDP
2013 Press Pass Redline Muscle Car Sheet Metal Red /50 #MCMDP
2013 Press Pass Redline Muscle Car Sheet Metal Silver /25 #MCMDP
2013 Press Pass Redline Pieces of the Action Blue /10 #PADP
2013 Press Pass Redline Pieces of the Action Gold /25 #PADP
2013 Press Pass Redline Pieces of the Action Melting /1 #PADP
2013 Press Pass Redline Pieces of the Action Red /75 #PADP
2013 Press Pass Redline Pieces of the Action Silver /50 #PADP
2013 Press Pass Redline Redline Racers #12
2013 Press Pass Redline Relic Autographs Blue /5 #RRSEDP
2013 Press Pass Redline Relic Autographs Gold /5 #RRSEDP
2013 Press Pass Redline Relic Autographs Melting /1 #RRSEDP
2013 Press Pass Redline Relic Autographs Red /10 #RRSEDP
2013 Press Pass Redline Relic Autographs Silver /10 #RRSEDP
2013 Press Pass Redline Relics Blue /5 #RRDP
2013 Press Pass Redline Relics Gold /10 #RRDP
2013 Press Pass Redline Relics Melting /1 #RRDP
2013 Press Pass Redline Relics Red /50 #RRDP
2013 Press Pass Redline Relics Silver /25 #RRDP
2013 Press Pass Redline RPM #7
2013 Press Pass Redline Signatures Blue /10 #RSDP
2013 Press Pass Redline Signatures Gold /5 #RSDP
2013 Press Pass Redline Signatures Holo /5 #RSDP
2013 Press Pass Redline Signatures Melting /1 #RSDP
2013 Press Pass Redline Signatures Red /10 #RSDP
2013 Press Pass Redline Yellow /1 #40
2013 Press Pass Showcase /349 #25
2013 Press Pass Showcase /349 #42
2013 Press Pass Showcase /349 #53
2013 Press Pass Showcase /349 #56
2013 Press Pass Showcase Black /1 #25
2013 Press Pass Showcase Black /1 #42
2013 Press Pass Showcase Black /1 #53
2013 Press Pass Showcase Black /1 #56
2013 Press Pass Showcase Blue /25 #25
2013 Press Pass Showcase Blue /25 #42
2013 Press Pass Showcase Blue /25 #53
2013 Press Pass Showcase Blue /25 #56
2013 Press Pass Showcase Classic Collections Ink Gold /5 #CCISHR
2013 Press Pass Showcase Classic Collections Ink Melting /1 #CCISHR
2013 Press Pass Showcase Classic Collections Ink Red /1 #CCISHR
2013 Press Pass Showcase Classic Collections Memorabilia Gold /25 #CCMSHR
2013 Press Pass Showcase Classic Collections Memorabilia Melting /5 #CCMSHR
2013 Press Pass Showcase Classic Collections Memorabilia Silver /75 #CCMSHR
2013 Press Pass Showcase Elite Exhibit Ink /25 #EEIDP
2013 Press Pass Showcase Elite Exhibit Ink Blue /30 #EEIDP
2013 Press Pass Showcase Elite Exhibit Ink Gold /10 #EEIDP
2013 Press Pass Showcase Elite Exhibit Ink Melting /1 #EEIDP
2013 Press Pass Showcase Elite Exhibit Ink Red /5 #EEIDP
2013 Press Pass Showcase Gold /99 #25
2013 Press Pass Showcase Gold /99 #42
2013 Press Pass Showcase Gold /99 #53
2013 Press Pass Showcase Gold /99 #56
2013 Press Pass Showcase Green /20 #25
2013 Press Pass Showcase Green /20 #42
2013 Press Pass Showcase Green /20 #53
2013 Press Pass Showcase Green /20 #56
2013 Press Pass Showcase Masterpieces Ink /25 #MPIDP
2013 Press Pass Showcase Masterpieces Ink Gold /10 #MPIDP
2013 Press Pass Showcase Masterpieces Ink Melting /1 #MPIDP
2013 Press Pass Showcase Masterpieces Memorabilia /75 #MPDP
2013 Press Pass Showcase Masterpieces Memorabilia Gold /25 #MPDP
2013 Press Pass Showcase Masterpieces Memorabilia Melting /5 #MPDP
2013 Press Pass Showcase Purple /13 #25
2013 Press Pass Showcase Purple /13 #42
2013 Press Pass Showcase Purple /13 #53
2013 Press Pass Showcase Purple /13 #56
2013 Press Pass Showcase Red /10 #25
2013 Press Pass Showcase Red /10 #42
2013 Press Pass Showcase Red /10 #53
2013 Press Pass Showcase Red /10 #56
2013 Press Pass Showcase Rookie Contenders /299 #1
2013 Press Pass Showcase Rookie Contenders Autographs Melting /13 #RCADP
2013 Press Pass Showcase Rookie Contenders Gold /50 #1
2013 Press Pass Showcase Rookie Contenders Green /25 #1
2013 Press Pass Showcase Rookie Contenders Melting /1 #1
2013 Press Pass Showcase Rookie Contenders Memorabilia Gold /20 #RCMDP
2013 Press Pass Showcase Rookie Contenders Memorabilia Melting /13 #RCMDP
2013 Press Pass Showcase Rookie Contenders Purple /13 #1
2013 Press Pass Showcase Rookie Contenders Red /10 #1
2013 Press Pass Showcase Series Standouts Gold /50 #15
2013 Press Pass Showcase Series Standouts Memorabilia /75 #SSMDP
2013 Press Pass Showcase Series Standouts Memorabilia Blue /50 #SSMDP
2013 Press Pass Showcase Series Standouts Memorabilia Gold /25 #SSMDP
2013 Press Pass Showcase Series Standouts Memorabilia Melting /5 #SSMDP
2013 Press Pass Showcase Showcase Patches /5 #SPDP
2013 Press Pass Showcase Showroom /299 #9
2013 Press Pass Showcase Showroom Blue /40 #9
2013 Press Pass Showcase Showroom Gold /50 #9
2013 Press Pass Showcase Showroom Green /20 #9
2013 Press Pass Showcase Showroom Melting /1 #9
2013 Press Pass Showcase Showroom Purple /13 #9
2013 Press Pass Showcase Showroom Red /10 #9
2013 Press Pass Showcase Signature Patches /10 #SSPDP
2013 Press Pass Showcase Studio Showcase /299 #15
2013 Press Pass Showcase Studio Showcase Blue /40 #15
2013 Press Pass Showcase Studio Showcase Green /25 #15
2013 Press Pass Showcase Studio Showcase Melting /1 #15
2013 Press Pass Showcase Studio Showcase Purple /13 #15
2013 Press Pass Showcase Studio Showcase Red /10 #15
2013 Press Pass Signings Blue /1 #DP1
2013 Press Pass Signings Blue /1 #DP2
2013 Press Pass Signings Gold /15 #DP1
2013 Press Pass Signings Gold /5 #DP2
2013 Press Pass Signings Holofoil /10 #DP1
2013 Press Pass Signings Holofoil /1 #DP2
2013 Press Pass Signings Printing Plates Black /1 #DP1
2013 Press Pass Signings Printing Plates Black /1 #DP2
2013 Press Pass Signings Printing Plates Cyan /1 #DP1
2013 Press Pass Signings Printing Plates Cyan /1 #DP2
2013 Press Pass Signings Printing Plates Magenta /1 #DP1
2013 Press Pass Signings Printing Plates Magenta /1 #DP2
2013 Press Pass Signings Printing Plates Yellow /1 #DP1
2013 Press Pass Signings Printing Plates Yellow /1 #DP2
2013 Press Pass Signings Silver /5 #DP2
2013 Press Pass Signings Silver /25 #DP1
2013 Sports Illustrated for Kids #233
2013 Total Memorabilia #33
2013 Total Memorabilia #41
2013 Total Memorabilia Black and White /99 #33
2013 Total Memorabilia Black and White /99 #41
2013 Total Memorabilia Dual Swatch Gold /199 #TMDP
2013 Total Memorabilia Dual Swatch Gold /199 #TMDP2
2013 Total Memorabilia Gold /275 #33
2013 Total Memorabilia Gold /275 #41
2013 Total Memorabilia Hot Rod Relics Gold /50 #HRRDP
2013 Total Memorabilia Hot Rod Relics Holofoil /10 #HRRDP
2013 Total Memorabilia Hot Rod Relics Melting /1 #HRRDP
2013 Total Memorabilia Hot Rod Relics Silver /99 #HRRDP
2013 Total Memorabilia Quad Swatch Melting /10 #TMDP
2013 Total Memorabilia Quad Swatch Melting /10 #TMDP2
2013 Total Memorabilia Red #33
2013 Total Memorabilia Red #41
2013 Total Memorabilia Signature Collection Dual Swatch Gold /7 #SCDP1
2013 Total Memorabilia Signature Collection Dual Swatch Gold /10 #SCDP2
2013 Total Memorabilia Signature Collection Quad Swatch Melting /1 #SCDP1
2013 Total Memorabilia Signature Collection Quad Swatch Melting /1 #SCDP2
2013 Total Memorabilia Signature Collection Single Swatch Silver /10 #SCDP1
2013 Total Memorabilia Signature Collection Single Swatch Silver /10 #SCDP2
2013 Total Memorabilia Signature Collection Triple Swatch Holofoil /5 #SCDP1
2013 Total Memorabilia Signature Collection Triple Swatch Holofoil /5 #SCDP2
2013 Total Memorabilia Single Swatch Silver /475 #TMDP
2013 Total Memorabilia Single Swatch Silver /475 #TMDP2
2013 Total Memorabilia Triple Swatch Holofoil /99 #TMDP
2013 Total Memorabilia Triple Swatch Holofoil /99 #TMDP2
2013 Upper Deck Goodwin Champions #131
2013 Upper Deck Goodwin Champions Autographs #ADP
2013 Upper Deck Goodwin Champions Memorabilia #MDP
2013 Upper Deck Goodwin Champions Memorabilia Dual #M2DP
2013 Upper Deck Goodwin Champions Mini #131
2013 Upper Deck Goodwin Champions Mini Canvas /99 #131
2013 Upper Deck Goodwin Champions Mini Foil Magician Red /13 #131
2013 Upper Deck Goodwin Champions Mini Foil Presidential Gold /1 #131
2013 Upper Deck Goodwin Champions Mini Green #131
2013 Upper Deck Goodwin Champions Mini Green Blank Back #131
2013 Upper Deck Goodwin Champions Mini Printing Plates Black /1 #131
2013 Upper Deck Goodwin Champions Mini Printing Plates Cyan /1 #131
2013 Upper Deck Goodwin Champions Mini Printing Plates Magenta /1 #131
2013 Upper Deck Goodwin Champions Mini Printing Plates Yellow /1 #131
2014 Press Pass #30
2014 Press Pass #31
2014 Press Pass #74
2014 Press Pass #97
2014 Press Pass #88
2014 Press Pass Aerodynamic Autographs Blue /1 #AADP
2014 Press Pass Aerodynamic Autographs Holofoil /5 #AADP
2014 Press Pass Aerodynamic Autographs Printing Plates Black /1 #AADP
2014 Press Pass Aerodynamic Autographs Printing Plates Cyan /1 #AADP
2014 Press Pass Aerodynamic Autographs Printing Plates Magenta /1 #AADP
2014 Press Pass Aerodynamic Autographs Printing Plates Yellow /1 #AADP
2014 Press Pass American Thunder #30
2014 Press Pass American Thunder #63
2014 Press Pass American Thunder #50
2014 Press Pass American Thunder Autographs Blue /5 #ATADP
2014 Press Pass American Thunder Autographs Red /1 #ATADP
2014 Press Pass American Thunder Autographs White /15 #ATADP
2014 Press Pass American Thunder Battle Armor Blue /25 #BADP
2014 Press Pass American Thunder Battle Armor Red /1 #BADP
2014 Press Pass American Thunder Battle Armor Silver /99 #BADP
2014 Press Pass American Thunder Black and White /50 #30
2014 Press Pass American Thunder Black and White /50 #50
2014 Press Pass American Thunder Black and White /50 #63
2014 Press Pass American Thunder Brothers In Arms Autographs Blue /5 #BASHR
2014 Press Pass American Thunder Brothers In Arms Autographs Red /1 #BASHR
2014 Press Pass American Thunder Brothers In Arms Autographs White /10 #BASHR
2014 Press Pass American Thunder Brothers In Arms Relics Blue /25 #BASHR
2014 Press Pass American Thunder Brothers In Arms Relics Red /5 #BASHR
2014 Press Pass American Thunder Brothers In Arms Relics Silver /50 #BASHR
2014 Press Pass American Thunder Class A Uniforms Blue /99 #CAUDP
2014 Press Pass American Thunder Class A Uniforms Flag /1 #CAUDP
2014 Press Pass American Thunder Class A Uniforms Red /10 #CAUDP
2014 Press Pass American Thunder Class A Uniforms Silver #CAUDP
2014 Press Pass American Thunder Climbing the Ranks #CR9
2014 Press Pass American Thunder Cyan #30
2014 Press Pass American Thunder Cyan #50
2014 Press Pass American Thunder Cyan #63
2014 Press Pass American Thunder Great American Treads Autographs Blue /10 #GATDP
2014 Press Pass American Thunder Great American Treads Autographs Red /1 #GATDP
2014 Press Pass American Thunder Magenta #30
2014 Press Pass American Thunder Magenta #50
2014 Press Pass American Thunder Magenta #63
2014 Press Pass American Thunder With Honors #WH7
2014 Press Pass American Thunder Yellow /5 #30
2014 Press Pass American Thunder Yellow /5 #50
2014 Press Pass Color Proofs Black /70 #30
2014 Press Pass Color Proofs Black /70 #31
2014 Press Pass Color Proofs Black /70 #74
2014 Press Pass Color Proofs Black /70 #88
2014 Press Pass Color Proofs Black /70 #97
2014 Press Pass Color Proofs Cyan /35 #30
2014 Press Pass Color Proofs Cyan /35 #31
2014 Press Pass Color Proofs Cyan /35 #74
2014 Press Pass Color Proofs Cyan /35 #88
2014 Press Pass Color Proofs Cyan /35 #97
2014 Press Pass Color Proofs Magenta #30
2014 Press Pass Color Proofs Magenta #31
2014 Press Pass Color Proofs Magenta #74
2014 Press Pass Color Proofs Magenta #88
2014 Press Pass Color Proofs Magenta #97
2014 Press Pass Color Proofs Yellow /5 #30
2014 Press Pass Color Proofs Yellow /5 #31
2014 Press Pass Color Proofs Yellow /5 #74
2014 Press Pass Color Proofs Yellow /5 #88
2014 Press Pass Color Proofs Yellow /5 #97
2014 Press Pass Cup Chase #13
2014 Press Pass Five Star /15 #14
2014 Press Pass Five Star Blue /5 #14
2014 Press Pass Five Star Classic Compilation Autographs Blue Triple Swatch /5 #CCDP
2014 Press Pass Five Star Classic Compilation Autographs Holofoil /10 #CCDP
2014 Press Pass Five Star Classic Compilation Autographs Holofoil Dual Swatch /10 #CCDP
2014 Press Pass Five Star Classic Compilation Autographs Melting Five Swatch /1 #CCDP
2014 Press Pass Five Star Classic Compilation Autographs Melting Quad Swatch /1 #CCDP
2014 Press Pass Five Star Classic Compilations Autographed Patch Booklet /1 #CCDP1
2014 Press Pass Five Star Classic Compilations Autographed Patch Booklet /1 #CCDP2
2014 Press Pass Five Star Classic Compilations Autographed Patch Booklet /1 #CCDP3
2014 Press Pass Five Star Classic Compilations Autographed Patch Booklet /1 #CCDP4
2014 Press Pass Five Star Classic Compilations Autographed Patch Booklet /1 #CCDP5
2014 Press Pass Five Star Classic Compilations Autographed Patch Booklet /1 #CCDP6
2014 Press Pass Five Star Classic Compilations Autographed Patch Booklet /1 #CCDP7
2014 Press Pass Five Star Classic Compilations Autographed Patch Booklet /1 #CCDP8
2014 Press Pass Five Star Classic Compilations Autographed Patch Booklet /1 #CCDP9
2014 Press Pass Five Star Classic Compilations Autographed Patch Booklet /1 #CCDP10
2014 Press Pass Five Star Classic Compilations Autographed Patch Booklet /1 #CCDP11
2014 Press Pass Five Star Classic Compilations Autographed Patch Booklet /1 #CCDP12
2014 Press Pass Five Star Classic Compilations Autographed Patch Booklet /1 #CCDP13
2014 Press Pass Five Star Classic Compilations Autographed Patch Booklet /1 #CCDP14
2014 Press Pass Five Star Classic Compilations Combo Autographs Blue /5 #CCSHR
2014 Press Pass Five Star Classic Compilations Combo Autographs Melting /1 #CCSHR
2014 Press Pass Five Star Holofoil /10 #14
2014 Press Pass Five Star Melting /1 #14
2014 Press Pass Five Star Paramount Pieces Blue /5 #PPDP
2014 Press Pass Five Star Paramount Pieces Gold /25 #PPDP
2014 Press Pass Five Star Paramount Pieces Holofoil /10 #PPDP
2014 Press Pass Five Star Paramount Pieces Melting /1 #PPDP
2014 Press Pass Five Star Paramount Pieces Melting Patch /1 #PPDP
2014 Press Pass Five Star Signature Souvenirs Blue /1 #SSDP
2014 Press Pass Five Star Signature Souvenirs Gold /50 #SSDP
2014 Press Pass Five Star Signature Souvenirs Holofoil /25 #SSDP
2014 Press Pass Five Star Signature Souvenirs Melting /1 #SSDP
2014 Press Pass Five Star Signatures Blue /5 #FSSDP
2014 Press Pass Five Star Signatures Holofoil /10 #FSSDP
2014 Press Pass Five Star Signatures Melting /1 #FSSDP
2014 Press Pass Four Wide Gold /10 #FWDP
2014 Press Pass Four Wide Melting /1 #FWDP
2014 Press Pass Gold #30
2014 Press Pass Gold #31
2014 Press Pass Gold #74
2014 Press Pass Gold #88
2014 Press Pass Gold #97
2014 Press Pass Intensity National Convention VIP #NE4
2014 Press Pass Redline #43
2014 Press Pass Redline #44
2014 Press Pass Redline Black /75 #43
2014 Press Pass Redline Black /75 #44
2014 Press Pass Redline Blue Foil #43
2014 Press Pass Redline Blue Foil #44
2014 Press Pass Redline Cyan /50 #43
2014 Press Pass Redline Cyan /50 #44
2014 Press Pass Redline Dynamic Duals Relic Autographs Blue /10 #DDDP
2014 Press Pass Redline Dynamic Duals Relic Autographs Gold /5 #DDDP
2014 Press Pass Redline Dynamic Duals Relic Autographs Melting /1 #DDDP
2014 Press Pass Redline Dynamic Duals Relic Autographs Red /15 #DDDP
2014 Press Pass Redline Green National Convention /5 #43
2014 Press Pass Redline Green National Convention /5 #44
2014 Press Pass Redline Head to Head Blue /10 #HTHDPKK
2014 Press Pass Redline Head to Head Gold /25 #HTHDPKK
2014 Press Pass Redline Head to Head Melting /1 #HTHDPKK
2014 Press Pass Redline Head to Head Red /75 #HTHDPKK
2014 Press Pass Redline Intensity #I9
2014 Press Pass Redline Magenta /10 #43
2014 Press Pass Redline Magenta /10 #44
2014 Press Pass Redline Muscle Car Sheet Metal Blue /25 #MCMDP
2014 Press Pass Redline Muscle Car Sheet Metal Gold /50 #MCMDP
2014 Press Pass Redline Muscle Car Sheet Metal Melting /1 #MCMDP
2014 Press Pass Redline Muscle Car Sheet Metal Red /75 #MCMDP
2014 Press Pass Redline Pieces of the Action Blue /10 #PADP
2014 Press Pass Redline Pieces of the Action Gold /25 #PADP
2014 Press Pass Redline Pieces of the Action Melting /1 #PADP
2014 Press Pass Redline Pieces of the Action Red /75 #PADP
2014 Press Pass Redline Redline Racers #RR14
2014 Press Pass Redline Relic Autographs Blue /5 #RRSEDP
2014 Press Pass Redline Relic Autographs Gold /10 #RRSEDP
2014 Press Pass Redline Relic Autographs Melting /1 #RRSEDP
2014 Press Pass Redline Relic Autographs Red /15 #RRSEDP
2014 Press Pass Redline Relics Blue /25 #RRDP
2014 Press Pass Redline Relics Gold /50 #RRDP
2014 Press Pass Redline Relics Melting /1 #RRDP
2014 Press Pass Redline Relics Red /75 #RRDP
2014 Press Pass Redline RPM #RPM9
2014 Press Pass Redline Signatures Blue /5 #RSDP
2014 Press Pass Redline Signatures Gold /10 #RSDP
2014 Press Pass Redline Signatures Melting /1 #RSDP
2014 Press Pass Redline Signatures Red /15 #RSDP
2014 Press Pass Redline Yellow /1 #43
2014 Press Pass Redline Yellow /1 #44
2014 Press Pass Signature Series Gold /5 #SSDP
2014 Press Pass Signature Series Melting /1 #SSDP
2014 Press Pass Signings Gold /1 #PPSDP
2014 Press Pass Signings Holofoil /1 #PPSDP
2014 Press Pass Signings Melting /1 #PPSDP
2014 Press Pass Signings Printing Plates Black /1 #PPSDP
2014 Press Pass Signings Printing Plates Cyan /1 #PPSDP
2014 Press Pass Signings Printing Plates Magenta /1 #PPSDP
2014 Press Pass Signings Printing Plates Yellow /1 #PPSDP
2014 Press Pass Signings Silver /2 #PPSDP
2014 SP Authentic Tiger Woods '01 Tribute /10 #TWDP
2014 Total Memorabilia #23
2014 Total Memorabilia Acceleration #AC9
2014 Total Memorabilia Autographed Memorabilia Blue /5 #SCDP
2014 Total Memorabilia Autographed Memorabilia Gold /5 #SCDP
2014 Total Memorabilia Autographed Memorabilia Melting /1 #SCDP
2014 Total Memorabilia Autographed Memorabilia Silver /5 #SC-DP
2014 Total Memorabilia Black and White /99 #23
2014 Total Memorabilia Clear Cuts Blue /175 #CCUDP
2014 Total Memorabilia Clear Cuts Melting /25 #CCUDP
2014 Total Memorabilia Dual Swatch Gold /150 #TMDP
2014 Total Memorabilia Gold /175 #23
2014 Total Memorabilia Quad Swatch Melting /25 #TMDP
2014 Total Memorabilia Red #23
2014 Total Memorabilia Single Swatch Silver /275 #TMDP
2014 Total Memorabilia Triple Swatch Blue /99 #TMDP
2014 Upper Deck 25th Anniversary #27
2014 Upper Deck 25th Anniversary Autographs /25 #27
2014 Upper Deck 25th Anniversary Printing Plates Black /1 #27
2014 Upper Deck 25th Anniversary Printing Plates Cyan /1 #27
2014 Upper Deck 25th Anniversary Printing Plates Magenta /1 #27
2014 Upper Deck 25th Anniversary Printing Plates Yellow /1 #27
2014 Upper Deck 25th Anniversary Silver /250 #27
2014 Upper Deck Industry Summit 25th Anniversary Autographs #LVDP
2014-15 SP Authentic LeBron James '03 Tribute Autographs /10 #LJDP
2015 Press Pass #29
2015 Press Pass Cup Chase #29
2015 Press Pass Cup Chase Blue /25 #29
2015 Press Pass Cup Chase Gold /75 #29
2015 Press Pass Cup Chase Green /10 #29
2015 Press Pass Cup Chase Melting /1 #29
2015 Press Pass Cup Chase Three Wide Blue /25 #3WDP
2015 Press Pass Cup Chase Three Wide Gold /50 #3WDP
2015 Press Pass Cup Chase Three Wide Green /10 #3WDP
2015 Press Pass Cup Chase Three Wide Melting /1 #3WDP
2015 Press Pass Cup Chase Upper Cuts /13 #UCDP
2015 Press Pass Cuts Blue /25 #CCCDP
2015 Press Pass Cuts Gold /50 #CCCDP
2015 Press Pass Cuts Green /10 #CCCDP
2015 Press Pass Cuts Melting /1 #CCCDP
2015 Press Pass Four Wide Signature Edition Blue /10 #4WDP
2015 Press Pass Four Wide Signature Edition Gold /15 #4WDP
2015 Press Pass Four Wide Signature Edition Green /5 #4WDP
2015 Press Pass Four Wide Signature Edition Melting /1 #4WDP
2015 Press Pass Pit Road Pieces Blue /25 #PPMDP
2015 Press Pass Pit Road Pieces Gold /50 #PPMDP
2015 Press Pass Pit Road Pieces Green /10 #PPMDP
2015 Press Pass Pit Road Pieces Melting /1 #PPMDP
2015 Press Pass Pit Road Pieces Signature Edition Blue /10 #PRPDP
2015 Press Pass Pit Road Pieces Signature Edition Gold /20 #PRPDP
2015 Press Pass Pit Road Pieces Signature Edition Green /5 #PRPDP
2015 Press Pass Pit Road Pieces Signature Edition Melting /1 #PRPDP
2015 Press Pass Purple #29
2015 Press Pass Red #29
2015 Press Pass Signature Series Blue /10 #SSDP
2015 Press Pass Signature Series Gold /15 #SSDP
2015 Press Pass Signature Series Green /5 #SSDP
2015 Press Pass Signature Series Melting /1 #SSDP
2015 Press Pass Signings Blue /15 #PPSDP
2015 Press Pass Signings Gold #PPSDP
2015 Press Pass Signings Green /5 #PPSDP
2015 Press Pass Signings Melting /1 #PPSDP
2015 Press Pass Signings Red /10 #PPSDP
2015 Topps Allen and Ginter Mini 10th Anniversary '06 Autographs /10 #AGA06DP
2015 Topps Allen and Ginter Mini 10th Anniversary '07 Autographs /10 #AGA07DP
2015 Topps Allen and Ginter Mini 10th Anniversary '08 Autographs /10 #AGA08DP
2015 Topps Allen and Ginter Mini 10th Anniversary '09 Autographs /10 #AGA09DP
2015 Topps Allen and Ginter Mini 10th Anniversary '10 Autographs /10 #AGA10DP
2015 Topps Allen and Ginter Mini 10th Anniversary '11 Autographs /10 #AGA11DP
2015 Topps Allen and Ginter Mini 10th Anniversary '12 Autographs /10 #AGA12DP
2015 Topps Allen and Ginter Mini 10th Anniversary '13 Autographs /10 #AGA13DP
2015 Topps Allen and Ginter Mini 10th Anniversary '14 Autographs /10 #AGA14DP
2015 Topps Allen and Ginter Mini 10th Anniversary '15 Autographs /10 #AGA15DP
2015 Upper Deck Goodwin Champions Goudey #26
2015 Upper Deck Goodwin Champions Goudey Memorabilia #GMDP
2015 Upper Deck Goodwin Champions Goudey Memorabilia Premium Series /50 #GMDP
2015 Upper Deck National Convention #NSCC12
2016 Certified #54
2016 Certified #21
2016 Certified Complete Materials Mirror Black /1 #12
2016 Certified Complete Materials Mirror Blue /20 #12
2016 Certified Complete Materials Mirror Gold /15 #12
2016 Certified Complete Materials Mirror Green /5 #12
2016 Certified Complete Materials Mirror Orange /5 #12
2016 Certified Complete Materials Mirror Purple /10 #12
2016 Certified Complete Materials Mirror Red /25 #12
2016 Certified Complete Materials Mirror Silver /5 #12
2016 Certified Epix /199 #5
2016 Certified Epix Mirror Black /1 #5
2016 Certified Epix Mirror Blue /50 #5
2016 Certified Epix Mirror Gold /25 #5
2016 Certified Epix Mirror Green /5 #5
2016 Certified Epix Mirror Orange /99 #5
2016 Certified Epix Mirror Purple /10 #5
2016 Certified Epix Mirror Red /75 #5
2016 Certified Epix Mirror Silver /99 #5
2016 Certified Gold Team /199 #19
2016 Certified Gold Team Mirror Black /1 #19
2016 Certified Gold Team Mirror Blue /50 #19
2016 Certified Gold Team Mirror Gold /25 #19
2016 Certified Gold Team Mirror Green /5 #19
2016 Certified Gold Team Mirror Orange /99 #19
2016 Certified Gold Team Mirror Purple /10 #19
2016 Certified Gold Team Mirror Red /75 #19
2016 Certified Gold Team Mirror Silver /99 #19
2016 Certified Mirror Black /1 #21
2016 Certified Mirror Black /1 #54
2016 Certified Mirror Blue /50 #21
2016 Certified Mirror Blue /50 #54
2016 Certified Mirror Gold /25 #21
2016 Certified Mirror Gold /25 #54
2016 Certified Mirror Green /5 #21
2016 Certified Mirror Green /5 #54
2016 Certified Mirror Orange /99 #21
2016 Certified Mirror Orange /99 #54
2016 Certified Mirror Purple /10 #21
2016 Certified Mirror Purple /10 #54
2016 Certified Mirror Red /75 #21
2016 Certified Mirror Red /75 #54
2016 Certified Mirror Silver /99 #21
2016 Certified Mirror Silver /99 #54
2016 Certified Signatures /65 #7
2016 Certified Signatures Mirror Black /1 #7
2016 Certified Signatures Mirror Blue /35 #7
2016 Certified Signatures Mirror Gold /25 #7
2016 Certified Signatures Mirror Green /5 #7
2016 Certified Signatures Mirror Orange /15 #7
2016 Certified Signatures Mirror Purple /10 #7
2016 Certified Signatures Mirror Red /50 #7
2016 Certified Signatures Mirror Silver /20 #7
2016 Certified Skills /199 #16
2016 Certified Skills Mirror Black /1 #16
2016 Certified Skills Mirror Blue /50 #16
2016 Certified Skills Mirror Gold /25 #16
2016 Certified Skills Mirror Green /5 #16
2016 Certified Skills Mirror Orange /99 #16
2016 Certified Skills Mirror Purple /10 #16
2016 Certified Skills Mirror Red /75 #16
2016 Certified Skills Mirror Silver /99 #16
2016 Certified Sprint Cup Signature Swatches #5
2016 Certified Sprint Cup Signature Swatches Mirror Black /1 #5
2016 Certified Sprint Cup Signature Swatches Mirror Blue #5
2016 Certified Sprint Cup Signature Swatches Mirror Gold #5
2016 Certified Sprint Cup Signature Swatches Mirror Green #5
2016 Certified Sprint Cup Signature Swatches Mirror Orange #5
2016 Certified Sprint Cup Signature Swatches Mirror Purple #5
2016 Certified Sprint Cup Signature Swatches Mirror Red #5
2016 Certified Sprint Cup Signature Swatches Mirror Silver #5
2016 Certified Sprint Cup Swatches Mirror Black /1 #25
2016 Certified Sprint Cup Swatches Mirror Blue /20 #25
2016 Certified Sprint Cup Swatches Mirror Gold /15 #25
2016 Certified Sprint Cup Swatches Mirror Green /5 #25
2016 Certified Sprint Cup Swatches Mirror Orange /5 #25
2016 Certified Sprint Cup Swatches Mirror Purple /10 #25
2016 Certified Sprint Cup Swatches Mirror Red /25 #25
2016 Certified Sprint Cup Swatches Mirror Silver /5 #25
2016 Panini Black Friday #29
2016 Panini Black Friday Autographs /25 #29
2016 Panini Black Friday Cracked Ice /25 #29
2016 Panini Black Friday Holo Plaid /1 #29
2016 Panini Black Friday Manufactured Patches #8
2016 Panini Black Friday Manufactured Patches Cracked Ice /25 #8
2016 Panini Black Friday Manufactured Patches Galactic Window /10 #8
2016 Panini Black Friday Manufactured Patches Holo Plaid /1 #8
2016 Panini Black Friday Rapture /10 #29
2016 Panini Black Friday Thick Stock /50 #29
2016 Panini Black Friday Wedges /50 #29
2016 Panini Cyber Monday #28
2016 Panini National Convention #37
2016 Panini National Convention Autographs /25 #37
2016 Panini National Convention Cracked Ice /25 #37
2016 Panini National Convention Decoy Cracked Ice /25 #37
2016 Panini National Convention Decoy Escher Squares /10 #37
2016 Panini National Convention Decoy Rapture /1 #37
2016 Panini National Convention Decoy Wedges /99 #37
2016 Panini National Convention Diamond Awe /49 #37
2016 Panini National Convention Escher Squares /10 #37
2016 Panini National Convention Rapture /1 #37
2016 Panini National Convention VIP #92
2016 Panini National Convention VIP Autographs Gold Vinyl /1 #92
2016 Panini National Convention VIP Autographs Kaleidoscope Red /25 #92
2016 Panini National Convention VIP Blue Wave Gold /10 #92
2016 Panini National Convention VIP Cracked Ice /25 #92
2016 Panini National Convention VIP Flash Green /5 #92
2016 Panini National Convention VIP Gold Vinyl /1 #92
2016 Panini National Convention VIP Memorabilia Gold Vinyl /1 #92
2016 Panini National Convention VIP Memorabilia Kaleidoscope Blue /25 #92
2016 Panini National Convention VIP Prizm /99 #92
2016 Panini National Convention VIP Purple Pulsar /50 #92
2016 Panini National Convention Wedges /99 #37
2016 Panini National Treasures /25 #5
2016 Panini National Treasures /25 #30
2016 Panini National Treasures Black /5 #5
2016 Panini National Treasures Black /5 #30
2016 Panini National Treasures Blue /1 #5
2016 Panini National Treasures Blue /1 #30
2016 Panini National Treasures Dual Signatures /26 #9
2016 Panini National Treasures Dual Signatures Black /10 #9
2016 Panini National Treasures Dual Signatures Blue /1 #9
2016 Panini National Treasures Dual Signatures Gold /15 #9
2016 Panini National Treasures Eight Signatures /15 #1
2016 Panini National Treasures Eight Signatures Black /5 #1
2016 Panini National Treasures Eight Signatures Blue /1 #1
2016 Panini National Treasures Eight Signatures Gold /10 #1
2016 Panini National Treasures Firesuit Materials Black /5 #6
2016 Panini National Treasures Firesuit Materials Blue /1 #6
2016 Panini National Treasures Firesuit Materials Laundry Tag /1 #6
2016 Panini National Treasures Firesuit Materials Printing Plates Black /1 #6
2016 Panini National Treasures Firesuit Materials Printing Plates Cyan /1 #6
2016 Panini National Treasures Firesuit Materials Printing Plates Magenta /1 #6
2016 Panini National Treasures Firesuit Materials Printing Plates Yellow /1 #6
2016 Panini National Treasures Gold /15 #5
2016 Panini National Treasures Gold /15 #30
2016 Panini National Treasures Jumbo Firesuit Patch Signature Booklet Alpine Stars /2 #8
2016 Panini National Treasures Jumbo Firesuit Patch Signature Booklet Associate Sponsor 1 /1 #8
2016 Panini National Treasures Jumbo Firesuit Patch Signature Booklet Associate Sponsor 10 /1 #8
2016 Panini National Treasures Jumbo Firesuit Patch Signature Booklet Associate Sponsor 2 /1 #8
2016 Panini National Treasures Jumbo Firesuit Patch Signature Booklet Associate Sponsor 3 /1 #8
2016 Panini National Treasures Jumbo Firesuit Patch Signature Booklet Associate Sponsor 4 /1 #8
2016 Panini National Treasures Jumbo Firesuit Patch Signature Booklet Associate Sponsor 5 /1 #8
2016 Panini National Treasures Jumbo Firesuit Patch Signature Booklet Associate Sponsor 6 /1 #8
2016 Panini National Treasures Jumbo Firesuit Patch Signature Booklet Associate Sponsor 7 /1 #8
2016 Panini National Treasures Jumbo Firesuit Patch Signature Booklet Associate Sponsor 8 /1 #8
2016 Panini National Treasures Jumbo Firesuit Patch Signature Booklet Associate Sponsor 9 /1 #8
2016 Panini National Treasures Jumbo Firesuit Patch Signature Booklet Goodyear /2 #8
2016 Panini National Treasures Jumbo Firesuit Patch Signature Booklet Manufacturers Logo /2 #8
2016 Panini National Treasures Jumbo Firesuit Patch Signature Booklet Nameplate /1 #8
2016 Panini National Treasures Jumbo Firesuit Patch Signature Booklet NASCAR /1 #8
2016 Panini National Treasures Jumbo Firesuit Patch Signature Booklet Sunoco /1 #8
2016 Panini National Treasures Jumbo Firesuit Signatures Blue /1 #8
2016 Panini National Treasures Jumbo Firesuit Signatures Printing Plates Black /1 #8
2016 Panini National Treasures Jumbo Firesuit Signatures Printing Plates Cyan /1 #8
2016 Panini National Treasures Jumbo Firesuit Signatures Printing Plates Magenta /1 #8
2016 Panini National Treasures Jumbo Firesuit Signatures Printing Plates Yellow /1 #8
2016 Panini National Treasures Jumbo Sheet Metal Signature Booklet /50 #2
2016 Panini National Treasures Jumbo Sheet Metal Signature Booklet Black /10 #2
2016 Panini National Treasures Jumbo Sheet Metal Signature Booklet Blue /1 #2
2016 Panini National Treasures Jumbo Sheet Metal Signature Booklet Gold /25 #2
2016 Panini National Treasures Jumbo Sheet Metal Signatures /25 #4
2016 Panini National Treasures Jumbo Sheet Metal Signatures Black /5 #4
2016 Panini National Treasures Jumbo Sheet Metal Signatures Blue /1 #4
2016 Panini National Treasures Jumbo Sheet Metal Signatures Gold /10 #4
2016 Panini National Treasures Jumbo Sheet Metal Signatures Printing Plates Black /1 #4
2016 Panini National Treasures Jumbo Sheet Metal Signatures Printing Plates Cyan /1 #4
2016 Panini National Treasures Jumbo Sheet Metal Signatures Printing Plates Magenta /1 #4
2016 Panini National Treasures Jumbo Sheet Metal Signatures Printing Plates Yellow /1 #4
2016 Panini National Treasures Jumbo Sheet Metal Signatures Silver /15 #4
2016 Panini National Treasures Printing Plates Black /1 #5
2016 Panini National Treasures Printing Plates Black /1 #30
2016 Panini National Treasures Printing Plates Cyan /1 #5
2016 Panini National Treasures Printing Plates Cyan /1 #30
2016 Panini National Treasures Printing Plates Magenta /1 #5
2016 Panini National Treasures Printing Plates Magenta /1 #30
2016 Panini National Treasures Printing Plates Yellow /1 #5
2016 Panini National Treasures Printing Plates Yellow /1 #30
2016 Panini National Treasures Quad Driver Materials /25 #10
2016 Panini National Treasures Quad Driver Materials Black /5 #10
2016 Panini National Treasures Quad Driver Materials Blue /1 #10
2016 Panini National Treasures Quad Driver Materials Gold /10 #10
2016 Panini National Treasures Quad Driver Materials Printing Plates Black /1 #10
2016 Panini National Treasures Quad Driver Materials Printing Plates Cyan /1 #10
2016 Panini National Treasures Quad Driver Materials Printing Plates Magenta /1 #10
2016 Panini National Treasures Quad Driver Materials Printing Plates Yellow /1 #10
2016 Panini National Treasures Quad Driver Materials Silver /15 #10
2016 Panini National Treasures Quad Materials /25 #6
2016 Panini National Treasures Quad Materials Black /5 #6
2016 Panini National Treasures Quad Materials Blue /1 #6
2016 Panini National Treasures Quad Materials Gold /10 #6
2016 Panini National Treasures Quad Materials Printing Plates Black /1 #6
2016 Panini National Treasures Quad Materials Printing Plates Cyan /1 #6
2016 Panini National Treasures Quad Materials Printing Plates Magenta /1 #6
2016 Panini National Treasures Quad Materials Printing Plates Yellow /1 #6
2016 Panini National Treasures Quad Materials Silver /15 #6
2016 Panini National Treasures Sheet Metal Materials Black /5 #6
2016 Panini National Treasures Sheet Metal Materials Blue /1 #6
2016 Panini National Treasures Sheet Metal Materials Printing Plates Black /1 #6
2016 Panini National Treasures Sheet Metal Materials Printing Plates Cyan /1 #6
2016 Panini National Treasures Sheet Metal Materials Printing Plates Magenta /1 #6
2016 Panini National Treasures Sheet Metal Materials Printing Plates Yellow /1 #6
2016 Panini National Treasures Signature Dual Materials Black /5 #8
2016 Panini National Treasures Signature Dual Materials Blue /1 #8
2016 Panini National Treasures Signature Dual Materials Gold /10 #8
2016 Panini National Treasures Signature Dual Materials Printing Plates Black /1 #8
2016 Panini National Treasures Signature Dual Materials Printing Plates Cyan /1 #8
2016 Panini National Treasures Signature Dual Materials Printing Plates Magenta /1 #8
2016 Panini National Treasures Signature Dual Materials Printing Plates Yellow /1 #8
2016 Panini National Treasures Signature Firesuit Materials Blue /1 #8
2016 Panini National Treasures Signature Firesuit Materials Laundry Tag /1 #8
2016 Panini National Treasures Signature Firesuit Materials Printing Plates Black /1 #8
2016 Panini National Treasures Signature Firesuit Materials Printing Plates Cyan /1 #8
2016 Panini National Treasures Signature Firesuit Materials Printing Plates Magenta /1 #8
2016 Panini National Treasures Signature Firesuit Materials Printing Plates Yellow /1 #8
2016 Panini National Treasures Signature Quad Materials /25 #8
2016 Panini National Treasures Signature Quad Materials Black /5 #8
2016 Panini National Treasures Signature Quad Materials Blue /1 #8
2016 Panini National Treasures Signature Quad Materials Gold /10 #8
2016 Panini National Treasures Signature Quad Materials Printing Plates Black /1 #8
2016 Panini National Treasures Signature Quad Materials Printing Plates Cyan /1 #8
2016 Panini National Treasures Signature Quad Materials Printing Plates Magenta /1 #8
2016 Panini National Treasures Signature Quad Materials Printing Plates Yellow /1 #8

2016 Panini National Treasures Signature Quad Materials Silver /15 #8
2016 Panini National Treasures Signature Sheet Metal Materials Black /5 #8
2016 Panini National Treasures Signature Sheet Metal Materials Printing Plates Black /1 #8
2016 Panini National Treasures Signature Sheet Metal Materials Printing Plates Cyan /1 #8
2016 Panini National Treasures Signature Sheet Metal Materials Printing Plates Magenta /1 #8
2016 Panini National Treasures Signature Sheet Metal Materials Printing Plates Yellow /1 #8
2016 Panini National Treasures Silver /20 #5
2016 Panini National Treasures Silver /20 #30
2016 Panini National Treasures Six Signatures /25 #8
2016 Panini National Treasures Six Signatures Black /10 #8
2016 Panini National Treasures Six Signatures Blue /1 #8
2016 Panini National Treasures Six Signatures Gold /15 #8
2016 Panini National Treasures Trio Driver Materials /25 #1
2016 Panini National Treasures Trio Driver Materials Black /5 #1
2016 Panini National Treasures Trio Driver Materials Blue /1 #1
2016 Panini National Treasures Trio Driver Materials Gold /10 #1
2016 Panini National Treasures Trio Driver Materials Printing Plates Black /1 #1
2016 Panini National Treasures Trio Driver Materials Printing Plates Cyan /1 #1
2016 Panini National Treasures Trio Driver Materials Printing Plates Magenta /1 #1
2016 Panini National Treasures Trio Driver Materials Printing Plates Yellow /1 #1
2016 Panini National Treasures Trio Driver Materials Silver /15 #1
2016 Panini Prizm #80
2016 Panini Prizm #57
2016 Panini Prizm #10
2016 Panini Prizm Autographs Prizms #69
2016 Panini Prizm Autographs Prizms Black /3 #69
2016 Panini Prizm Autographs Prizms Blue Flag /15 #69
2016 Panini Prizm Autographs Prizms Camo /10 #69
2016 Panini Prizm Autographs Prizms Checkered Flag /1 #69
2016 Panini Prizm Autographs Prizms Gold /10 #69
2016 Panini Prizm Autographs Prizms Rainbow /24 #69
2016 Panini Prizm Autographs Prizms Red White and Blue /5 #69
2016 Panini Prizm Autographs Prizms White Flag /5 #69
2016 Panini Prizm Competitors #3
2016 Panini Prizm Competitors Prizms #3
2016 Panini Prizm Competitors Prizms Checkered Flag /1 #3
2016 Panini Prizm Competitors Prizms Gold /10 #3
2016 Panini Prizm Firesuit Fabrics /50 #21
2016 Panini Prizm Firesuit Fabrics Prizms Blue Flag /15 #21
2016 Panini Prizm Firesuit Fabrics Prizms Checkered Flag /1 #21
2016 Panini Prizm Firesuit Fabrics Prizms Green Flag /35 #21
2016 Panini Prizm Firesuit Fabrics Prizms Red Flag /5 #21
2016 Panini Prizm Firesuit Fabrics Team /75 #16
2016 Panini Prizm Firesuit Fabrics Team Prizms Blue Flag /10 #16
2016 Panini Prizm Firesuit Fabrics Team Prizms Checkered Flag /1 #16
2016 Panini Prizm Firesuit Fabrics Team Prizms Green Flag /25 #16
2016 Panini Prizm Firesuit Fabrics Team Prizms Red Flag /5 #16
2016 Panini Prizm Machinery #2
2016 Panini Prizm Machinery Prizms #2
2016 Panini Prizm Machinery Prizms Checkered Flag /1 #2
2016 Panini Prizm Machinery Prizms Gold /10 #2
2016 Panini Prizm Patented Penmanship Prizms #11
2016 Panini Prizm Patented Penmanship Prizms Black /3 #11
2016 Panini Prizm Patented Penmanship Prizms Blue Flag /15 #11
2016 Panini Prizm Patented Penmanship Prizms Camo /10 #11
2016 Panini Prizm Patented Penmanship Prizms Checkered Flag /1 #11
2016 Panini Prizm Patented Penmanship Prizms Gold /10 #11
2016 Panini Prizm Patented Penmanship Prizms Rainbow /24 #11
2016 Panini Prizm Patented Penmanship Prizms Red White and Blue /5 #11
2016 Panini Prizm Patented Penmanship Prizms White Flag /5 #11
2016 Panini Prizm Prizms #10
2016 Panini Prizm Prizms #57
2016 Panini Prizm Prizms #80
2016 Panini Prizm Prizms Black /3 #10
2016 Panini Prizm Prizms Black /3 #57
2016 Panini Prizm Prizms Black /3 #80
2016 Panini Prizm Prizms Blue Flag /99 #10
2016 Panini Prizm Prizms Blue Flag /99 #57
2016 Panini Prizm Prizms Blue Flag /99 #80
2016 Panini Prizm Prizms Camo /10 #10
2016 Panini Prizm Prizms Camo /10 #57
2016 Panini Prizm Prizms Camo /10 #80
2016 Panini Prizm Prizms Checkered Flag /1 #10
2016 Panini Prizm Prizms Checkered Flag /1 #57
2016 Panini Prizm Prizms Checkered Flag /1 #80
2016 Panini Prizm Prizms Gold /10 #10
2016 Panini Prizm Prizms Gold /10 #57
2016 Panini Prizm Prizms Gold /10 #80
2016 Panini Prizm Prizms Green Flag /149 #10
2016 Panini Prizm Prizms Green Flag /149 #57
2016 Panini Prizm Prizms Green Flag /149 #80
2016 Panini Prizm Prizms Rainbow /24 #10
2016 Panini Prizm Prizms Rainbow /24 #80
2016 Panini Prizm Prizms Rainbow /24 #57
2016 Panini Prizm Prizms Red Flag /75 #10
2016 Panini Prizm Prizms Red Flag /75 #57
2016 Panini Prizm Prizms Red Flag /75 #80
2016 Panini Prizm Prizms Red White and Blue #10
2016 Panini Prizm Prizms Red White and Blue #57
2016 Panini Prizm Prizms Red White and Blue #80
2016 Panini Prizm Prizms White Flag /5 #10
2016 Panini Prizm Prizms White Flag /5 #57
2016 Panini Prizm Prizms White Flag /5 #80
2016 Panini Prizm Qualifying Times #9
2016 Panini Prizm Qualifying Times Prizms #9
2016 Panini Prizm Qualifying Times Prizms Checkered Flag /1 #9
2016 Panini Prizm Qualifying Times Prizms Gold /10 #9
2016 Panini Prizm Race Used Tire #12
2016 Panini Prizm Race Used Tire Prizms Blue Flag /49 #12
2016 Panini Prizm Race Used Tire Prizms Checkered Flag /1 #12
2016 Panini Prizm Race Used Tire Prizms Green Flag /99 #12
2016 Panini Prizm Race Used Tire Prizms Red Flag /25 #12
2016 Panini Prizm Race Used Tire Team #11
2016 Panini Prizm Race Used Tire Team Prizms Blue Flag /75 #11
2016 Panini Prizm Race Used Tire Team Prizms Green Flag /149 #11
2016 Panini Prizm Race Used Tire Team Prizms Red Flag /10 #11
2016 Panini Torque #31
2016 Panini Torque #76
2016 Panini Torque Artist Proof /50 #31
2016 Panini Torque Artist Proof /50 #76
2016 Panini Torque Blackout /1 #31
2016 Panini Torque Blackout /1 #76
2016 Panini Torque Blue /125 #31
2016 Panini Torque Blue /125 #76
2016 Panini Torque Clear Vision #24
2016 Panini Torque Clear Vision Blue /99 #24
2016 Panini Torque Clear Vision Gold /149 #24
2016 Panini Torque Clear Vision Green /25 #24
2016 Panini Torque Clear Vision Purple /10 #24
2016 Panini Torque Clear Vision Red /49 #24
2016 Panini Torque Combo Materials Autographs /20 #9
2016 Panini Torque Combo Materials Autographs Blue /15 #9
2016 Panini Torque Combo Materials Autographs Green /5 #9
2016 Panini Torque Combo Materials Autographs Purple /1 #9
2016 Panini Torque Combo Materials Autographs Red /10 #9
2016 Panini Torque Gas N Go #9
2016 Panini Torque Gas N Go Gold /199 #9
2016 Panini Torque Gas N Go Holo Silver /99 #9
2016 Panini Torque Gold #31
2016 Panini Torque Gold #76
2016 Panini Torque Helmets #4
2016 Panini Torque Helmets Blue /99 #4
2016 Panini Torque Helmets Checkerboard /10 #4
2016 Panini Torque Helmets Green /25 #4
2016 Panini Torque Helmets Red /49 #4
2016 Panini Torque Holo Gold /5 #31
2016 Panini Torque Holo Gold /5 #76
2016 Panini Torque Holo Silver /10 #31
2016 Panini Torque Holo Silver /10 #76
2016 Panini Torque Horsepower Heroes #24
2016 Panini Torque Horsepower Heroes Gold /199 #24
2016 Panini Torque Horsepower Heroes Holo Silver /99 #24
2016 Panini Torque Jumbo Firesuit Autographs /20 #4
2016 Panini Torque Jumbo Firesuit Autographs Blue /10 #4
2016 Panini Torque Jumbo Firesuit Autographs Green /2 #4
2016 Panini Torque Jumbo Firesuit Autographs Purple /1 #4
2016 Panini Torque Jumbo Firesuit Autographs Red /5 #4
2016 Panini Torque Jumbo Tire Autographs /15 #15
2016 Panini Torque Jumbo Tire Autographs Blue /10 #15
2016 Panini Torque Jumbo Tire Autographs Green /2 #15
2016 Panini Torque Jumbo Tire Autographs Purple /1 #15
2016 Panini Torque Jumbo Tire Autographs Red /5 #15
2016 Panini Torque Metal Materials /249 #10
2016 Panini Torque Metal Materials Blue /99 #10
2016 Panini Torque Metal Materials Green /25 #10
2016 Panini Torque Metal Materials Purple /10 #10
2016 Panini Torque Metal Materials Red /49 #10
2016 Panini Torque Painted to Perfection #14
2016 Panini Torque Painted to Perfection Blue /99 #14
2016 Panini Torque Painted to Perfection Checkerboard /10 #14
2016 Panini Torque Painted to Perfection Green /25 #14
2016 Panini Torque Painted to Perfection Red /49 #14
2016 Panini Torque Pairings Materials /249 #9
2016 Panini Torque Pairings Materials /249 #30
2016 Panini Torque Pairings Materials Blue /99 #9
2016 Panini Torque Pairings Materials Blue /99 #30
2016 Panini Torque Pairings Materials Green /25 #9
2016 Panini Torque Pairings Materials Green /25 #30
2016 Panini Torque Pairings Materials Purple /10 #9
2016 Panini Torque Pairings Materials Purple /10 #30
2016 Panini Torque Pairings Materials Red /49 #9
2016 Panini Torque Pairings Materials Red /49 #30
2016 Panini Torque Pole Position #19
2016 Panini Torque Pole Position Blue /99 #19
2016 Panini Torque Pole Position Checkerboard /10 #19
2016 Panini Torque Pole Position Green /25 #19
2016 Panini Torque Pole Position Red /49 #19
2016 Panini Torque Printing Plates Black /1 #31
2016 Panini Torque Printing Plates Black /1 #76
2016 Panini Torque Printing Plates Cyan /1 #31
2016 Panini Torque Printing Plates Cyan /1 #76
2016 Panini Torque Printing Plates Magenta /1 #31
2016 Panini Torque Printing Plates Magenta /1 #76
2016 Panini Torque Printing Plates Yellow /1 #31
2016 Panini Torque Printing Plates Yellow /1 #76
2016 Panini Torque Purple /25 #31
2016 Panini Torque Purple /25 #76
2016 Panini Torque Quad Materials /149 #10
2016 Panini Torque Quad Materials Blue /99 #10
2016 Panini Torque Quad Materials Green /25 #10
2016 Panini Torque Quad Materials Purple /10 #10
2016 Panini Torque Quad Materials Red /49 #10
2016 Panini Torque Red /99 #31
2016 Panini Torque Red /99 #76
2016 Panini Torque Rubber Relics /399 #8
2016 Panini Torque Rubber Relics Blue /99 #8
2016 Panini Torque Rubber Relics Green /25 #8
2016 Panini Torque Rubber Relics Purple /10 #8
2016 Panini Torque Rubber Relics Red /49 #8
2016 Panini Torque Shades #4
2016 Panini Torque Shades Gold /199 #4
2016 Panini Torque Shades Holo Silver /99 #4
2016 Panini Torque Silhouettes Firesuit Autographs /20 #7
2016 Panini Torque Silhouettes Firesuit Autographs Blue /15 #7
2016 Panini Torque Silhouettes Firesuit Autographs Green /5 #7
2016 Panini Torque Silhouettes Firesuit Autographs Purple /1 #7
2016 Panini Torque Silhouettes Firesuit Autographs Red /10 #7
2016 Panini Torque Silhouettes Sheet Metal Autographs /20 #7
2016 Panini Torque Silhouettes Sheet Metal Autographs Blue /15 #7
2016 Panini Torque Silhouettes Sheet Metal Autographs Green /5 #7
2016 Panini Torque Silhouettes Sheet Metal Autographs Purple /1 #7
2016 Panini Torque Silhouettes Sheet Metal Autographs Red /10 #7
2016 Panini Torque Superstar Vision #4
2016 Panini Torque Superstar Vision Blue /99 #4
2016 Panini Torque Superstar Vision Gold /149 #4
2016 Panini Torque Superstar Vision Green /25 #4
2016 Panini Torque Superstar Vision Purple /10 #4
2016 Panini Torque Superstar Vision Red /49 #4
2016 Panini Torque Test Proof Black /1 #31
2016 Panini Torque Test Proof Black /1 #76
2016 Panini Torque Test Proof Cyan /1 #31
2016 Panini Torque Test Proof Cyan /1 #76
2016 Panini Torque Test Proof Magenta /1 #31
2016 Panini Torque Test Proof Magenta /1 #76
2016 Panini Torque Test Proof Yellow /1 #31
2016 Panini Torque Test Proof Yellow /1 #76
2016 Upper Deck All-Time Greats Master Collection Autographs Silver /20 #MCDP
2016 Upper Deck All-Time Greats Master Collection Box Topper Autographs /10 #BTDP
2016 Upper Deck All-Time Greats Master Collection Logo Collection Puzzle /125 #LC13
2016 Upper Deck All-Time Greats Master Collection Logo Collection Puzzle Gold /25 #LC13
2016 Upper Deck All-Time Greats Master Collection Logo Collection Puzzle Silver /50 #LC13
2016 Upper Deck All-Time Greats Master Collection Masterful Paintings Autographs /1 #DP
2017 Donruss #7
2017 Donruss #52
2017 Donruss #94
2017 Donruss #110
2017 Donruss #152
2017 Donruss Artist Proof /25 #7
2017 Donruss Artist Proof /25 #52
2017 Donruss Artist Proof /25 #94
2017 Donruss Artist Proof /25 #152
2017 Donruss Artist Proof /25 #110
2017 Donruss Blue Foil /299 #7
2017 Donruss Blue Foil /299 #94
2017 Donruss Blue Foil /299 #52
2017 Donruss Blue Foil /299 #152
2017 Donruss Blue Foil /299 #110
2017 Donruss Classics #16
2017 Donruss Classics Cracked Ice /999 #16
2017 Donruss Dual Rubber Relics #5
2017 Donruss Dual Rubber Relics Holo Black /1 #5
2017 Donruss Dual Rubber Relics Holo Gold /25 #5
2017 Donruss Gold Foil /499 #7
2017 Donruss Gold Foil /499 #94
2017 Donruss Gold Foil /499 #152
2017 Donruss Gold Foil /499 #52
2017 Donruss Gold Foil /499 #110
2017 Donruss Gold Press Proof /99 #7
2017 Donruss Gold Press Proof /99 #52
2017 Donruss Gold Press Proof /99 #94
2017 Donruss Gold Press Proof /99 #152
2017 Donruss Gold Press Proof /99 #110
2017 Donruss Green Foil /199 #7
2017 Donruss Green Foil /199 #52
2017 Donruss Green Foil /199 #94
2017 Donruss Green Foil /199 #152
2017 Donruss Green Foil /199 #110
2017 Donruss Press Proof /49 #7
2017 Donruss Press Proof /49 #52
2017 Donruss Press Proof /49 #94
2017 Donruss Press Proof /49 #152
2017 Donruss Press Proof /49 #110
2017 Donruss Printing Plates Black /1 #7
2017 Donruss Printing Plates Black /1 #52
2017 Donruss Printing Plates Black /1 #94
2017 Donruss Printing Plates Black /1 #152
2017 Donruss Printing Plates Black /1 #110
2017 Donruss Printing Plates Cyan /1 #7
2017 Donruss Printing Plates Cyan /1 #52
2017 Donruss Printing Plates Cyan /1 #94
2017 Donruss Printing Plates Cyan /1 #152
2017 Donruss Printing Plates Cyan /1 #110
2017 Donruss Printing Plates Magenta /1 #7
2017 Donruss Printing Plates Magenta /1 #94
2017 Donruss Printing Plates Magenta /1 #152
2017 Donruss Printing Plates Magenta /1 #52
2017 Donruss Printing Plates Magenta /1 #110
2017 Donruss Printing Plates Yellow /1 #7
2017 Donruss Printing Plates Yellow /1 #94
2017 Donruss Printing Plates Yellow /1 #152
2017 Donruss Printing Plates Yellow /1 #52
2017 Donruss Printing Plates Yellow /1 #110
2017 Donruss Retro Signatures 1984 #7
2017 Donruss Retro Signatures 1984 Holo Black /1 #7
2017 Donruss Retro Signatures 1984 Holo Gold /25 #7
2017 Donruss Rubber Relics #15
2017 Donruss Rubber Relics Holo Black /1 #15
2017 Donruss Rubber Relics Holo Gold /25 #15
2017 Donruss Rubber Relics Signatures /99 #2
2017 Donruss Rubber Relics Signatures Holo Black /1 #2
2017 Donruss Rubber Relics Signatures Holo Gold /25 #2
2017 Donruss Speed #8
2017 Donruss Speed Cracked Ice /999 #8
2017 Donruss Studio Signatures #6
2017 Donruss Studio Signatures Holo Black /1 #6
2017 Donruss Studio Signatures Holo Gold /25 #6
2017 Donruss Top Tier #5
2017 Donruss Top Tier Cracked Ice /999 #5
2017 Panini Black Friday Happy Holiday Memorabilia #HHDP
2017 Panini Black Friday Happy Holiday Memorabilia Cracked Ice /25 #HHDP
2017 Panini Black Friday Happy Holiday Memorabilia Galactic Windows /10 #HHDP
2017 Panini Black Friday Happy Holiday Memorabilia Hyperplaid /1 #HHDP
2017 Panini Day #54
2017 Panini Day Cracked Ice /25 #54
2017 Panini Day Decoy /50 #54
2017 Panini Day Hyperplaid /1 #54
2017 Panini Day Memorabilia #37
2017 Panini Day Memorabilia Galactic Window /25 #37
2017 Panini Day Memorabilia Hyperplaid /1 #37
2017 Panini Day Rapture /10 #54
2017 Panini Day Wedges /50 #54
2017 Panini National Convention #R2
2017 Panini National Convention Autographs #R2
2017 Panini National Convention Autographs Hyperplaid /1 #R2
2017 Panini National Convention Escher Squares /25 #R2
2017 Panini National Convention Escher Squares Thick Stock /10 #R2
2017 Panini National Convention Galatic Windows /5 #R2
2017 Panini National Convention Hyperplaid /1 #R2
2017 Panini National Convention Memorabilia #DP
2017 Panini National Convention Memorabilia Escher Squares /10 #DP
2017 Panini National Convention Memorabilia Hyperplaid /1 #DP
2017 Panini National Convention Memorabilia Pyramids /5 #DP
2017 Panini National Convention Memorabilia Rainbow Spokes /25 #DP
2017 Panini National Convention Memorabilia Rapture /49 #DP
2017 Panini National Convention Pyramids /10 #R2
2017 Panini National Convention Rainbow Spokes /49 #R2
2017 Panini National Convention Rainbow Spokes Thick Stock /25 #R2
2017 Panini National Convention Rapture /99 #R2
2017 Panini National Convention VIP #79
2017 Panini National Convention VIP Gems #DP
2017 Panini National Convention VIP Gems Autographs /1 #DP
2017 Panini National Convention VIP Gems Gold /1 #DP
2017 Panini National Convention VIP Prizm #79
2017 Panini National Convention VIP Prizm Black /1 #79
2017 Panini National Convention VIP Prizm Cracked Ice /25 #79
2017 Panini National Convention VIP Prizm Gold /15 #79
2017 Panini National Convention VIP Prizm Green /5 #79
2017 Panini National Treasures /25 #7
2017 Panini National Treasures /25 #19
2017 Panini National Treasures Associate Sponsor Patch Signatures 1 /1 #6
2017 Panini National Treasures Associate Sponsor Patch Signatures 10 /1 #6
2017 Panini National Treasures Associate Sponsor Patch Signatures 2 /1 #6
2017 Panini National Treasures Associate Sponsor Patch Signatures 3 /1 #6
2017 Panini National Treasures Associate Sponsor Patch Signatures 4 /1 #6
2017 Panini National Treasures Associate Sponsor Patch Signatures 5 /1 #6
2017 Panini National Treasures Associate Sponsor Patch Signatures 6 /1 #6
2017 Panini National Treasures Associate Sponsor Patch Signatures 7 /1 #6
2017 Panini National Treasures Associate Sponsor Patch Signatures 8 /1 #6
2017 Panini National Treasures Associate Sponsor Patch Signatures 9 /1 #6
2017 Panini National Treasures Car Manufacturer Patch Signatures /1 #6
2017 Panini National Treasures Century Black /1 #7
2017 Panini National Treasures Century Black /1 #19
2017 Panini National Treasures Century Gold /15 #7
2017 Panini National Treasures Century Gold /15 #19
2017 Panini National Treasures Century Green /5 #7
2017 Panini National Treasures Century Green /5 #19
2017 Panini National Treasures Century Holo Gold /10 #7
2017 Panini National Treasures Century Holo Gold /10 #19
2017 Panini National Treasures Century Holo Silver /20 #7
2017 Panini National Treasures Century Holo Silver /20 #19
2017 Panini National Treasures Century Laundry Tags /1 #7
2017 Panini National Treasures Combo Material Signatures /25 #2
2017 Panini National Treasures Combo Material Signatures Black /1 #2
2017 Panini National Treasures Combo Material Signatures Gold /15 #2
2017 Panini National Treasures Combo Material Signatures Green /5 #2
2017 Panini National Treasures Combo Material Signatures Holo Gold /10 #2
2017 Panini National Treasures Combo Material Signatures Holo Silver /20 #2
2017 Panini National Treasures Dual Firesuit Materials Black /1 #1
2017 Panini National Treasures Dual Firesuit Materials Gold /15 #1
2017 Panini National Treasures Dual Firesuit Materials Green /5 #1
2017 Panini National Treasures Dual Firesuit Materials Holo Gold /10 #1
2017 Panini National Treasures Dual Firesuit Materials Laundry Tag /1 #1
2017 Panini National Treasures Dual Firesuit Materials Printing Plates Black /1 #1
2017 Panini National Treasures Dual Firesuit Materials Printing Plates Cyan /1 #1
2017 Panini National Treasures Dual Firesuit Materials Printing Plates Magenta /1 #1
2017 Panini National Treasures Dual Firesuit Materials Printing Plates Yellow /1 #1
2017 Panini National Treasures Dual Firesuit Signatures /25 #1
2017 Panini National Treasures Dual Firesuit Signatures Black /1 #1
2017 Panini National Treasures Dual Firesuit Signatures Gold /15 #1
2017 Panini National Treasures Dual Firesuit Signatures Green /5 #1
2017 Panini National Treasures Dual Firesuit Signatures Holo Gold /10 #1
2017 Panini National Treasures Dual Firesuit Signatures Holo Silver /20 #1
2017 Panini National Treasures Dual Firesuit Signatures Laundry Tag /1 #1
2017 Panini National Treasures Dual Firesuit Signatures Printing Plates Black /1 #1
2017 Panini National Treasures Dual Firesuit Signatures Printing Plates Cyan /1 #1
2017 Panini National Treasures Dual Firesuit Signatures Printing Plates Magenta /1 #1
2017 Panini National Treasures Dual Firesuit Signatures Printing Plates Yellow /1 #1
2017 Panini National Treasures Dual Sheet Metal Materials Black /1 #15
2017 Panini National Treasures Dual Sheet Metal Materials Green /5 #15
2017 Panini National Treasures Dual Sheet Metal Materials Printing Plates Black /1 #15
2017 Panini National Treasures Dual Sheet Metal Materials Printing Plates Cyan /1 #15
2017 Panini National Treasures Dual Sheet Metal Materials Printing Plates Magenta /1 #15
2017 Panini National Treasures Dual Sheet Metal Materials Printing Plates Yellow /1 #15
2017 Panini National Treasures Dual Tire Signatures Black /1 #4
2017 Panini National Treasures Dual Tire Signatures Gold /15 #4
2017 Panini National Treasures Dual Tire Signatures Green /5 #4
2017 Panini National Treasures Dual Tire Signatures Holo Gold /10 #4
2017 Panini National Treasures Dual Tire Signatures Printing Plates Black /1 #4
2017 Panini National Treasures Dual Tire Signatures Printing Plates Cyan /1 #4
2017 Panini National Treasures Dual Tire Signatures Printing Plates Magenta /1 #4
2017 Panini National Treasures Dual Tire Signatures Printing Plates Yellow /1 #4
2017 Panini National Treasures Firesuit Manufacturer Patch Signatures /1 #6
2017 Panini National Treasures Goodyear Patch Signatures /1 #6
2017 Panini National Treasures Hats Off Monster Energy Cup /15 #2
2017 Panini National Treasures Hats Off Monster Energy Cup Gold /4 #2
2017 Panini National Treasures Hats Off Monster Energy Cup Holo Gold /5 #2
2017 Panini National Treasures Hats Off Monster Energy Cup Holo Silver /1 #2
2017 Panini National Treasures Hats Off Monster Energy Cup Laundry Tag /6 #2
2017 Panini National Treasures Hats Off Monster Energy Cup New Era /1 #2
2017 Panini National Treasures Hats Off Monster Energy Cup Printing Plates Black /1 #2
2017 Panini National Treasures Hats Off Monster Energy Cup Printing Plates Cyan /1 #2
2017 Panini National Treasures Hats Off Monster Energy Cup Printing Plates Magenta /1 #2
2017 Panini National Treasures Hats Off Monster Energy Cup Printing Plates Yellow /1 #2
2017 Panini National Treasures Hats Off Monster Energy Cup Sponsor /5 #2
2017 Panini National Treasures Jumbo Sheet Metal Materials Black /1 #4
2017 Panini National Treasures Jumbo Sheet Metal Materials Printing Plates Black /1 #4
2017 Panini National Treasures Jumbo Sheet Metal Materials Printing Plates Cyan /1 #4
2017 Panini National Treasures Jumbo Sheet Metal Materials Printing Plates Magenta /1 #4
2017 Panini National Treasures Jumbo Sheet Metal Materials Printing Plates Yellow /1 #4
2017 Panini National Treasures Magnificent Marks /25 #2
2017 Panini National Treasures Magnificent Marks Black /1 #2
2017 Panini National Treasures Magnificent Marks Gold /15 #2
2017 Panini National Treasures Magnificent Marks Green /5 #2
2017 Panini National Treasures Magnificent Marks Holo Gold /10 #2
2017 Panini National Treasures Magnificent Marks Holo Silver /20 #2
2017 Panini National Treasures Magnificent Marks Printing Plates Black /1 #2
2017 Panini National Treasures Magnificent Marks Printing Plates Cyan /1 #2
2017 Panini National Treasures Magnificent Marks Printing Plates Magenta /1 #2
2017 Panini National Treasures Magnificent Marks Printing Plates Yellow /1 #2
2017 Panini National Treasures Nameplate Patch Signatures /1 #6
2017 Panini National Treasures Printing Plates Black /1 #7
2017 Panini National Treasures Printing Plates Black /1 #19
2017 Panini National Treasures Printing Plates Cyan /1 #7
2017 Panini National Treasures Printing Plates Cyan /1 #19
2017 Panini National Treasures Printing Plates Magenta /1 #7
2017 Panini National Treasures Printing Plates Magenta /1 #19
2017 Panini National Treasures Printing Plates Yellow /1 #7
2017 Panini National Treasures Printing Plates Yellow /1 #19
2017 Panini National Treasures Series Sponsor Patch Signatures /1 #6
2017 Panini National Treasures Signature Sheet Metal /25 #5
2017 Panini National Treasures Signature Sheet Metal Black /1 #5
2017 Panini National Treasures Signature Sheet Metal Gold /15 #5
2017 Panini National Treasures Signature Sheet Metal Green /5 #5
2017 Panini National Treasures Signature Sheet Metal Holo Gold /10 #5
2017 Panini National Treasures Signature Sheet Metal Holo Silver /20 #5
2017 Panini National Treasures Signature Six Way Swatches /25 #3
2017 Panini National Treasures Signature Six Way Swatches Black /1 #3
2017 Panini National Treasures Signature Six Way Swatches Gold /15 #3
2017 Panini National Treasures Signature Six Way Swatches Green /5 #3
2017 Panini National Treasures Signature Six Way Swatches Holo Gold /10 #3
2017 Panini National Treasures Signature Six Way Swatches Holo Silver /20 #3
2017 Panini National Treasures Signature Six Way Swatches Laundry Tag /1 #3
2017 Panini National Treasures Sunoco Patch Signatures /1 #6
2017 Panini National Treasures Teammates Dual Materials /25 #3
2017 Panini National Treasures Teammates Dual Materials Black /1 #3
2017 Panini National Treasures Teammates Dual Materials Gold /15 #3
2017 Panini National Treasures Teammates Dual Materials Green /5 #3
2017 Panini National Treasures Teammates Dual Materials Holo Gold /10 #3
2017 Panini National Treasures Teammates Dual Materials Holo Silver /20 #3
2017 Panini National Treasures Teammates Dual Materials Laundry Tag /1 #3
2017 Panini National Treasures Teammates Dual Materials Printing Plates Black /1 #3
2017 Panini National Treasures Teammates Dual Materials Printing Plates Cyan /1 #3
2017 Panini National Treasures Teammates Dual Materials Printing Plates Magenta /1 #3
2017 Panini National Treasures Teammates Dual Materials Printing Plates Yellow /1 #3
2017 Panini National Treasures Teammates Quad Materials /25 #5
2017 Panini National Treasures Teammates Quad Materials Black /1 #5
2017 Panini National Treasures Teammates Quad Materials Gold /15 #5
2017 Panini National Treasures Teammates Quad Materials Green /5 #5
2017 Panini National Treasures Teammates Quad Materials Holo Gold /10 #5
2017 Panini National Treasures Teammates Quad Materials Holo Silver /20 #5
2017 Panini National Treasures Teammates Quad Materials Laundry Tag /1 #5
2017 Panini National Treasures Teammates Quad Materials Printing Plates Black /1 #5
2017 Panini National Treasures Teammates Quad Materials Printing Plates Cyan /1 #5
2017 Panini National Treasures Teammates Quad Materials Printing Plates Magenta /1 #5
2017 Panini National Treasures Teammates Quad Materials Printing Plates Yellow /1 #5
2017 Panini National Treasures Teammates Triple Materials /25 #2
2017 Panini National Treasures Teammates Triple Materials Black /1 #2
2017 Panini National Treasures Teammates Triple Materials Gold /15 #2
2017 Panini National Treasures Teammates Triple Materials Green /5 #2
2017 Panini National Treasures Teammates Triple Materials Holo Gold /10 #2
2017 Panini National Treasures Teammates Triple Materials Holo Silver /20 #2
2017 Panini National Treasures Teammates Triple Materials Laundry Tag /1 #2
2017 Panini National Treasures Teammates Triple Materials Printing Plates Black /1 #2
2017 Panini National Treasures Teammates Triple Materials Printing Plates Cyan /1 #2
2017 Panini National Treasures Teammates Triple Materials Printing Plates Magenta /1 #2
2017 Panini National Treasures Teammates Triple Materials Printing Plates Yellow /1 #2
2017 Panini Torque #22
2017 Panini Torque #56
2017 Panini Torque #75
2017 Panini Torque #95
2017 Panini Torque Artist Proof /75 #22
2017 Panini Torque Artist Proof /75 #56
2017 Panini Torque Artist Proof /75 #75
2017 Panini Torque Artist Proof /75 #95
2017 Panini Torque Blackout /1 #22
2017 Panini Torque Blackout /1 #56
2017 Panini Torque Blackout /1 #75
2017 Panini Torque Blackout /1 #95
2017 Panini Torque Blue /150 #22
2017 Panini Torque Blue /150 #56
2017 Panini Torque Blue /150 #75
2017 Panini Torque Blue /150 #95
2017 Panini Torque Clear Vision #10
2017 Panini Torque Clear Vision Blue /99 #10
2017 Panini Torque Clear Vision Gold /149 #10
2017 Panini Torque Clear Vision Green /25 #10
2017 Panini Torque Clear Vision Purple /10 #10
2017 Panini Torque Clear Vision Red /49 #10
2017 Panini Torque Dual Materials /199 #8
2017 Panini Torque Dual Materials Blue /99 #8
2017 Panini Torque Dual Materials Green /25 #8
2017 Panini Torque Dual Materials Purple /10 #8
2017 Panini Torque Dual Materials Red /49 #8
2017 Panini Torque Gold #22
2017 Panini Torque Gold #56
2017 Panini Torque Gold #75
2017 Panini Torque Gold #95
2017 Panini Torque Holo Gold /10 #22
2017 Panini Torque Holo Gold /10 #56
2017 Panini Torque Holo Gold /10 #75
2017 Panini Torque Holo Gold /10 #95
2017 Panini Torque Holo Silver /25 #22
2017 Panini Torque Holo Silver /25 #56
2017 Panini Torque Holo Silver /25 #75
2017 Panini Torque Holo Silver /25 #95
2017 Panini Torque Horsepower Heroes #8
2017 Panini Torque Horsepower Heroes Gold /199 #8
2017 Panini Torque Horsepower Heroes Holo Silver /99 #8
2017 Panini Torque Jumbo Tire Signatures /75 #9
2017 Panini Torque Jumbo Tire Signatures Blue /50 #9
2017 Panini Torque Jumbo Tire Signatures Green /15 #9
2017 Panini Torque Jumbo Tire Signatures Purple /10 #9
2017 Panini Torque Jumbo Tire Signatures Red /25 #9
2017 Panini Torque Manufacturer Marks #6
2017 Panini Torque Manufacturer Marks Gold /199 #6
2017 Panini Torque Manufacturer Marks Holo Silver /99 #6
2017 Panini Torque Metal Materials /49 #16
2017 Panini Torque Metal Materials Blue /25 #16
2017 Panini Torque Metal Materials Green /5 #16
2017 Panini Torque Metal Materials Purple /1 #16
2017 Panini Torque Metal Materials Red /10 #16
2017 Panini Torque Pairings Materials /199 #5
2017 Panini Torque Pairings Materials Blue /99 #5
2017 Panini Torque Pairings Materials Green /25 #5
2017 Panini Torque Pairings Materials Purple /10 #5
2017 Panini Torque Pairings Materials Red /49 #5
2017 Panini Torque Primary Paint #7
2017 Panini Torque Primary Paint Blue /99 #7
2017 Panini Torque Primary Paint Checkerboard /10 #7
2017 Panini Torque Primary Paint Green /25 #7
2017 Panini Torque Primary Paint Red /49 #7
2017 Panini Torque Prime Associate Sponsors Jumbo Patches /1 #6A
2017 Panini Torque Prime Associate Sponsors Jumbo Patches /1 #6B
2017 Panini Torque Printing Plates Black /1 #22
2017 Panini Torque Printing Plates Black /1 #56
2017 Panini Torque Printing Plates Black /1 #75
2017 Panini Torque Printing Plates Black /1 #95
2017 Panini Torque Printing Plates Cyan /1 #22
2017 Panini Torque Printing Plates Cyan /1 #56
2017 Panini Torque Printing Plates Cyan /1 #75
2017 Panini Torque Printing Plates Cyan /1 #95
2017 Panini Torque Printing Plates Magenta /1 #22
2017 Panini Torque Printing Plates Magenta /1 #56
2017 Panini Torque Printing Plates Magenta /1 #75
2017 Panini Torque Printing Plates Magenta /1 #95
2017 Panini Torque Printing Plates Yellow /1 #22
2017 Panini Torque Printing Plates Yellow /1 #56
2017 Panini Torque Printing Plates Yellow /1 #75
2017 Panini Torque Printing Plates Yellow /1 #95
2017 Panini Torque Purple /50 #22
2017 Panini Torque Purple /50 #56
2017 Panini Torque Purple /50 #75
2017 Panini Torque Purple /50 #95
2017 Panini Torque Quad Materials /20 #7
2017 Panini Torque Quad Materials Blue /15 #7
2017 Panini Torque Quad Materials Green /5 #7
2017 Panini Torque Quad Materials Purple /1 #7
2017 Panini Torque Quad Materials Red /10 #7
2017 Panini Torque Raced Relics /99 #6
2017 Panini Torque Raced Relics Blue /49 #6
2017 Panini Torque Raced Relics Green /20 #6
2017 Panini Torque Raced Relics Purple /10 #6
2017 Panini Torque Raced Relics Red /25 #6
2017 Panini Torque Red /100 #22
2017 Panini Torque Red /100 #56
2017 Panini Torque Red /100 #75
2017 Panini Torque Red /100 #95
2017 Panini Torque Running Order #20
2017 Panini Torque Running Order Blue /99 #20
2017 Panini Torque Running Order Checkerboard /10 #20
2017 Panini Torque Running Order Green /25 #20
2017 Panini Torque Running Order Red /49 #20
2017 Panini Torque Silhouettes Sheet Metal Signatures /50 #7
2017 Panini Torque Silhouettes Sheet Metal Signatures Blue /35 #7
2017 Panini Torque Silhouettes Sheet Metal Signatures Green /10 #7
2017 Panini Torque Silhouettes Sheet Metal Signatures Purple /5 #7
2017 Panini Torque Silhouettes Sheet Metal Signatures Red /25 #7
2017 Panini Torque Special Paint #2
2017 Panini Torque Special Paint Gold /199 #2
2017 Panini Torque Special Paint Holo Silver /99 #2
2017 Panini Torque Superstar Vision #3
2017 Panini Torque Superstar Vision Blue /99 #3
2017 Panini Torque Superstar Vision Gold /149 #3
2017 Panini Torque Superstar Vision Green /25 #3
2017 Panini Torque Superstar Vision Purple /10 #3
2017 Panini Torque Superstar Vision Red /49 #3
2017 Panini Torque Test Proof Black /1 #22
2017 Panini Torque Test Proof Black /1 #56
2017 Panini Torque Test Proof Black /1 #75
2017 Panini Torque Test Proof Black /1 #95
2017 Panini Torque Test Proof Cyan /1 #22
2017 Panini Torque Test Proof Cyan /1 #56
2017 Panini Torque Test Proof Cyan /1 #75
2017 Panini Torque Test Proof Cyan /1 #95
2017 Panini Torque Test Proof Magenta /1 #22
2017 Panini Torque Test Proof Magenta /1 #56
2017 Panini Torque Test Proof Magenta /1 #75
2017 Panini Torque Test Proof Magenta /1 #95
2017 Panini Torque Test Proof Yellow /1 #22
2017 Panini Torque Test Proof Yellow /1 #56
2017 Panini Torque Test Proof Yellow /1 #75
2017 Panini Torque Test Proof Yellow /1 #95
2017 Panini Torque Track Vision #4
2017 Panini Torque Track Vision Blue /99 #4
2017 Panini Torque Track Vision Gold /149 #4
2017 Panini Torque Track Vision Green /25 #4
2017 Panini Torque Track Vision Purple /10 #4
2017 Panini Torque Track Vision Red /49 #4
2017 Select #40
2017 Select #41
2017 Select #42
2017 Select #43
2017 Select #125
2017 Select Endorsements #22
2017 Select Endorsements Prizms Blue /50 #22
2017 Select Endorsements Prizms Checkered Flag /1 #22
2017 Select Endorsements Prizms Gold /10 #22
2017 Select Endorsements Prizms Red /25 #22
2017 Select Prizms Black /3 #40
2017 Select Prizms Black /3 #41
2017 Select Prizms Black /3 #42
2017 Select Prizms Black /3 #43
2017 Select Prizms Black /3 #125
2017 Select Prizms Blue /199 #40
2017 Select Prizms Blue /199 #41
2017 Select Prizms Blue /199 #42
2017 Select Prizms Blue /199 #43
2017 Select Prizms Checkered Flag /1 #40
2017 Select Prizms Checkered Flag /1 #41
2017 Select Prizms Checkered Flag /1 #42
2017 Select Prizms Checkered Flag /1 #43
2017 Select Prizms Checkered Flag /1 #125
2017 Select Prizms Gold /10 #40
2017 Select Prizms Gold /10 #41
2017 Select Prizms Gold /10 #42
2017 Select Prizms Gold /10 #43
2017 Select Prizms Gold /10 #125
2017 Select Prizms Purple Pulsar #40
2017 Select Prizms Purple Pulsar #41
2017 Select Prizms Purple Pulsar #42
2017 Select Prizms Purple Pulsar #43
2017 Select Prizms Red /99 #40
2017 Select Prizms Red /99 #41
2017 Select Prizms Red /99 #42
2017 Select Prizms Red /99 #43
2017 Select Prizms Red White and Blue Pulsar /299 #40
2017 Select Prizms Red White and Blue Pulsar /299 #41
2017 Select Prizms Red White and Blue Pulsar /299 #42
2017 Select Prizms Red White and Blue Pulsar /299 #43
2017 Select Prizms Silver #40
2017 Select Prizms Silver #41
2017 Select Prizms Silver #42
2017 Select Prizms Silver #43
2017 Select Prizms Tie Dye /24 #40
2017 Select Prizms Tie Dye /24 #41
2017 Select Prizms Tie Dye /24 #42
2017 Select Prizms Tie Dye /24 #43
2017 Select Prizms Tie Dye /24 #125
2017 Select Prizms White /50 #40
2017 Select Prizms White /50 #41
2017 Select Prizms White /50 #42
2017 Select Prizms White /50 #43
2017 Select Prizms White /50 #125
2017 Select Select Pairs Materials #8
2017 Select Select Pairs Materials #10
2017 Select Select Pairs Materials #12
2017 Select Select Pairs Materials Prizms Blue /199 #8
2017 Select Select Pairs Materials Prizms Blue /199 #10
2017 Select Select Pairs Materials Prizms Blue /199 #12
2017 Select Select Pairs Materials Prizms Checkered Flag /1 #8
2017 Select Select Pairs Materials Prizms Checkered Flag /1 #10
2017 Select Select Pairs Materials Prizms Checkered Flag /1 #12
2017 Select Select Pairs Materials Prizms Gold /10 #8
2017 Select Select Pairs Materials Prizms Gold /10 #10
2017 Select Select Pairs Materials Prizms Gold /10 #12
2017 Select Select Pairs Materials Prizms Red /99 #8
2017 Select Select Pairs Materials Prizms Red /99 #10
2017 Select Select Pairs Materials Prizms Red /99 #12
2017 Select Select Stars #11
2017 Select Select Stars Prizms Black /3 #11
2017 Select Select Stars Prizms Checkered Flag /1 #11
2017 Select Select Stars Prizms Gold /10 #11
2017 Select Select Stars Prizms Tie Dye /24 #11
2017 Select Select Stars Prizms White /50 #11
2017 Select Select Swatches #13
2017 Select Select Swatches Prizms Blue /50 #13
2017 Select Select Swatches Prizms Checkered Flag /1 #13
2017 Select Select Swatches Prizms Gold /10 #13
2017 Select Select Swatches Prizms Red /25 #13
2017 Select Sheet Metal #6
2017 Select Sheet Metal Prizms Blue /50 #6
2017 Select Sheet Metal Prizms Checkered Flag /1 #6
2017 Select Sheet Metal Prizms Gold /10 #6
2017 Select Sheet Metal Prizms Red /25 #6
2017 Select Signature Swatches #13
2017 Select Signature Swatches Dual #13
2017 Select Signature Swatches Dual Prizms Checkered Flag /1 #13
2017 Select Signature Swatches Dual Prizms Gold /10 #13
2017 Select Signature Swatches Dual Prizms Tie Dye /24 #13
2017 Select Signature Swatches Dual Prizms White /50 #13
2017 Select Signature Swatches Prizms Checkered Flag /1 #13
2017 Select Signature Swatches Prizms Gold /10 #13
2017 Select Signature Swatches Prizms Tie Dye /24 #13
2017 Select Signature Swatches Prizms White /50 #13
2017 Select Speed Merchants #21
2017 Select Speed Merchants Prizms Black /3 #21
2017 Select Speed Merchants Prizms Checkered Flag /1 #21
2017 Select Speed Merchants Prizms Gold /10 #21
2017 Select Speed Merchants Prizms Tie Dye /24 #21
2017 Select Speed Merchants Prizms White /50 #21
2018 Certified #72
2018 Certified #95
2018 Certified All Certified Team /199 #9
2018 Certified All Certified Team Black /1 #9
2018 Certified All Certified Team Blue /99 #9
2018 Certified All Certified Team Gold /49 #9
2018 Certified All Certified Team Green /10 #9
2018 Certified All Certified Team Mirror Black /1 #9
2018 Certified All Certified Team Mirror Gold /25 #9
2018 Certified All Certified Team Mirror Green /5 #9
2018 Certified All Certified Team Mirror Purple /10 #9
2018 Certified All Certified Team Purple /25 #9

2018 Certified All Certified Team Red /149 #9
2018 Certified Black /1 #72
2018 Certified Black /1 #95
2018 Certified Blue /99 #72
2018 Certified Blue /99 #95
2018 Certified Epix /199 #3
2018 Certified Epix Black /1 #3
2018 Certified Epix Blue /99 #3
2018 Certified Epix Gold /49 #3
2018 Certified Epix Green /10 #3
2018 Certified Epix Mirror Black /1 #3
2018 Certified Epix Mirror Gold /25 #3
2018 Certified Epix Mirror Green /5 #3
2018 Certified Epix Mirror Purple /10 #3
2018 Certified Epix Purple /25 #3
2018 Certified Epix Red /149 #3
2018 Certified Gold /49 #72
2018 Certified Gold /49 #95
2018 Certified Green /10 #72
2018 Certified Green /10 #95
2018 Certified Materials Signatures /45 #5
2018 Certified Materials Signatures Black /1 #5
2018 Certified Materials Signatures Blue /20 #5
2018 Certified Materials Signatures Gold /15 #5
2018 Certified Materials Signatures Green /5 #5
2018 Certified Materials Signatures Purple /10 #5
2018 Certified Materials Signatures Red /25 #5
2018 Certified Mirror Black /1 #72
2018 Certified Mirror Black /1 #95
2018 Certified Mirror Gold /25 #72
2018 Certified Mirror Gold /25 #95
2018 Certified Mirror Green /5 #72
2018 Certified Mirror Green /5 #95
2018 Certified Mirror Purple /10 #72
2018 Certified Mirror Purple /10 #95
2018 Certified Orange /249 #72
2018 Certified Orange /249 #95
2018 Certified Piece of the Race /499 #13
2018 Certified Piece of the Race Black /1 #13
2018 Certified Piece of the Race Blue /49 #13
2018 Certified Piece of the Race Gold /25 #13
2018 Certified Piece of the Race Green /5 #13
2018 Certified Piece of the Race Purple /10 #13
2018 Certified Piece of the Race Red /199 #13
2018 Certified Purple /25 #72
2018 Certified Purple /25 #95
2018 Certified Red /199 #72
2018 Certified Red /199 #95
2018 Certified Signing Sessions /25 #5
2018 Certified Signing Sessions Black /1 #5
2018 Certified Signing Sessions Blue /15 #5
2018 Certified Signing Sessions Gold /10 #5
2018 Certified Signing Sessions Green /3 #5
2018 Certified Signing Sessions Purple /5 #5
2018 Certified Signing Sessions Red /20 #5
2018 Certified Stars /199 #6
2018 Certified Stars Black /1 #6
2018 Certified Stars Blue /99 #6
2018 Certified Stars Gold /49 #6
2018 Certified Stars Green /10 #6
2018 Certified Stars Mirror Black /1 #6
2018 Certified Stars Mirror Gold /25 #6
2018 Certified Stars Mirror Green /5 #6
2018 Certified Stars Mirror Purple /10 #6
2018 Certified Stars Purple /25 #6
2018 Certified Stars Red /149 #6
2018 Donruss #25
2018 Donruss #52A
2018 Donruss #142A
2018 Donruss #52B
2018 Donruss #142B
2018 Donruss Artist Proofs /25 #25
2018 Donruss Artist Proofs /25 #52A
2018 Donruss Artist Proofs /25 #142A
2018 Donruss Artist Proofs /25 #52B
2018 Donruss Artist Proofs /25 #142B
2018 Donruss Classics #19
2018 Donruss Classics Cracked Ice /999 #19
2018 Donruss Classics Xplosion /99 #19
2018 Donruss Elite Series /999 #3
2018 Donruss Gold Foil /499 #25
2018 Donruss Gold Foil /499 #52A
2018 Donruss Gold Foil /499 #142A
2018 Donruss Gold Foil /499 #52B
2018 Donruss Gold Foil /499 #142B
2018 Donruss Gold Press Proofs /99 #25
2018 Donruss Gold Press Proofs /99 #52A
2018 Donruss Gold Press Proofs /99 #142A
2018 Donruss Gold Press Proofs /99 #52B
2018 Donruss Gold Press Proofs /99 #142B
2018 Donruss Green Foil /199 #25
2018 Donruss Green Foil /199 #52A
2018 Donruss Green Foil /199 #142A
2018 Donruss Green Foil /199 #52B
2018 Donruss Green Foil /199 #142B
2018 Donruss Press Proofs /49 #25
2018 Donruss Press Proofs /49 #52A
2018 Donruss Press Proofs /49 #142A
2018 Donruss Press Proofs /49 #52B
2018 Donruss Press Proofs /49 #142B
2018 Donruss Printing Plates Black /1 #25
2018 Donruss Printing Plates Black /1 #52
2018 Donruss Printing Plates Black /1 #142
2018 Donruss Printing Plates Black /1 #52B
2018 Donruss Printing Plates Black /1 #142B
2018 Donruss Printing Plates Cyan /1 #25
2018 Donruss Printing Plates Cyan /1 #52
2018 Donruss Printing Plates Cyan /1 #142
2018 Donruss Printing Plates Cyan /1 #52B
2018 Donruss Printing Plates Cyan /1 #142B
2018 Donruss Printing Plates Magenta /1 #25
2018 Donruss Printing Plates Magenta /1 #52
2018 Donruss Printing Plates Magenta /1 #142
2018 Donruss Printing Plates Magenta /1 #52B
2018 Donruss Printing Plates Magenta /1 #142B
2018 Donruss Printing Plates Yellow /1 #25
2018 Donruss Printing Plates Yellow /1 #52
2018 Donruss Printing Plates Yellow /1 #142
2018 Donruss Printing Plates Yellow /1 #52B
2018 Donruss Printing Plates Yellow /1 #142B
2018 Donruss Racing Relics Black /5 #10
2018 Donruss Racing Relics Holo Gold /99 #10
2018 Donruss Red Foil /299 #25
2018 Donruss Red Foil /299 #52A
2018 Donruss Red Foil /299 #142A
2018 Donruss Red Foil /299 #52B
2018 Donruss Red Foil /299 #142B
2018 Donruss Retro Relics '85 Black /5 #3
2018 Donruss Retro Relics '85 Holo Gold /99 #3
2018 Donruss Rubber Relic Signatures #6
2018 Donruss Rubber Relic Signatures Black /1 #6
2018 Donruss Rubber Relic Signatures Holo Gold /25 #6
2018 Donruss Rubber Relics #10
2018 Donruss Rubber Relics Black /10 #10
2018 Donruss Rubber Relics Holo Gold /99 #10
2018 Donruss Studio #3
2018 Donruss Studio Cracked Ice /999 #3
2018 Donruss Studio Xplosion /99 #3

2018 Panini Prime /50 #24
2018 Panini Prime /50 #57
2018 Panini Prime /50 #90
2018 Panini Prime Autograph Materials /25 #1
2018 Panini Prime Autograph Materials Black /1 #1
2018 Panini Prime Autograph Materials Holo Gold /10 #1
2018 Panini Prime Autograph Materials Laundry Tag /1 #1
2018 Panini Prime Black /1 #24
2018 Panini Prime Black /1 #57
2018 Panini Prime Black /1 #90
2018 Panini Prime Driver Signatures /25 #6
2018 Panini Prime Driver Signatures Black /1 #6
2018 Panini Prime Driver Signatures Holo Gold /10 #6
2018 Panini Prime Dual Material Autographs /25 #1
2018 Panini Prime Dual Material Autographs Black /1 #1
2018 Panini Prime Dual Material Autographs Holo Gold /10 #1
2018 Panini Prime Dual Material Autographs Laundry Tag /1 #1
2018 Panini Prime Dual Signatures /10 #7
2018 Panini Prime Dual Signatures Black /1 #7
2018 Panini Prime Dual Signatures Holo Gold /5 #7
2018 Panini Prime Holo Gold /25 #24
2018 Panini Prime Holo Gold /25 #57
2018 Panini Prime Holo Gold /25 #90
2018 Panini Prime Prime Signatures /25 #6
2018 Panini Prime Prime Signatures Black /1 #6
2018 Panini Prime Prime Signatures Holo Gold /10 #6
2018 Panini Prime Shadowbox Signatures /25 #1
2018 Panini Prime Shadowbox Signatures Black /1 #1
2018 Panini Prime Shadowbox Signatures Holo Gold /10 #1
2018 Panini Prime Signature Swatches /25 #18
2018 Panini Prime Signature Swatches Black /1 #18
2018 Panini Prime Signature Swatches Holo Gold /10 #18
2018 Panini Prime Signature Tires /25 #4
2018 Panini Prime Signature Tires Black /1 #4
2018 Panini Prime Signature Tires Holo Gold /10 #4
2018 Panini Prizm #15
2018 Panini Prizm #52
2018 Panini Prizm #67
2018 Panini Prizm #75
2018 Panini Prizm #85
2018 Panini Prizm Brilliance #7
2018 Panini Prizm Brilliance Prizms #7
2018 Panini Prizm Brilliance Prizms Black /1 #7
2018 Panini Prizm Brilliance Prizms Gold /10 #7
2018 Panini Prizm Fireworks #4
2018 Panini Prizm Fireworks Prizms #4
2018 Panini Prizm Fireworks Prizms Black /1 #4
2018 Panini Prizm Fireworks Prizms Gold /10 #4
2018 Panini Prizm Illumination #4
2018 Panini Prizm Illumination Prizms #4
2018 Panini Prizm Illumination Prizms Black /1 #4
2018 Panini Prizm Illumination Prizms Gold /10 #4
2018 Panini Prizm Instant Impact #13
2018 Panini Prizm Instant Impact Prizms #13
2018 Panini Prizm Instant Impact Prizms Black /1 #13
2018 Panini Prizm Instant Impact Prizms Gold /10 #13
2018 Panini Prizm Patented Penmanship Prizms #18
2018 Panini Prizm Patented Penmanship Prizms Black /1 #18
2018 Panini Prizm Patented Penmanship Prizms Blue /10 #18
2018 Panini Prizm Patented Penmanship Prizms Camo #18
2018 Panini Prizm Patented Penmanship Prizms Gold /10 #18
2018 Panini Prizm Patented Penmanship Prizms Green /10 #18
2018 Panini Prizm Patented Penmanship Prizms Rainbow /24 #18
2018 Panini Prizm Patented Penmanship Prizms Red /10 #18
2018 Panini Prizm Patented Penmanship Prizms Red White and Blue /20 #18
2018 Panini Prizm Patented Penmanship Prizms White /5 #18
2018 Panini Prizm Prizms #15
2018 Panini Prizm Prizms #52
2018 Panini Prizm Prizms #67
2018 Panini Prizm Prizms #75
2018 Panini Prizm Prizms #85
2018 Panini Prizm Prizms Black /1 #15
2018 Panini Prizm Prizms Black /1 #52
2018 Panini Prizm Prizms Black /1 #67
2018 Panini Prizm Prizms Black /1 #75
2018 Panini Prizm Prizms Black /1 #85
2018 Panini Prizm Prizms Blue /99 #15
2018 Panini Prizm Prizms Blue /99 #52
2018 Panini Prizm Prizms Blue /99 #67
2018 Panini Prizm Prizms Blue /99 #75
2018 Panini Prizm Prizms Blue /99 #85
2018 Panini Prizm Prizms Camo #15
2018 Panini Prizm Prizms Camo #52
2018 Panini Prizm Prizms Camo #67
2018 Panini Prizm Prizms Camo #75
2018 Panini Prizm Prizms Camo #85
2018 Panini Prizm Prizms Gold /10 #15
2018 Panini Prizm Prizms Gold /10 #52
2018 Panini Prizm Prizms Gold /10 #67
2018 Panini Prizm Prizms Gold /10 #75
2018 Panini Prizm Prizms Gold /10 #85
2018 Panini Prizm Prizms Green /149 #15
2018 Panini Prizm Prizms Green /149 #52
2018 Panini Prizm Prizms Green /149 #67
2018 Panini Prizm Prizms Green /149 #75
2018 Panini Prizm Prizms Green /149 #85
2018 Panini Prizm Prizms Purple Flash #15
2018 Panini Prizm Prizms Purple Flash #52
2018 Panini Prizm Prizms Purple Flash #67
2018 Panini Prizm Prizms Purple Flash #75
2018 Panini Prizm Prizms Purple Flash #85
2018 Panini Prizm Prizms Rainbow /24 #15
2018 Panini Prizm Prizms Rainbow /24 #52
2018 Panini Prizm Prizms Rainbow /24 #67
2018 Panini Prizm Prizms Rainbow /24 #75
2018 Panini Prizm Prizms Rainbow /24 #85
2018 Panini Prizm Prizms Red /75 #15
2018 Panini Prizm Prizms Red /75 #52
2018 Panini Prizm Prizms Red /75 #67
2018 Panini Prizm Prizms Red /75 #75
2018 Panini Prizm Prizms Red /75 #85
2018 Panini Prizm Prizms Red White and Blue #15
2018 Panini Prizm Prizms Red White and Blue #52
2018 Panini Prizm Prizms Red White and Blue #67
2018 Panini Prizm Prizms Red White and Blue #75
2018 Panini Prizm Prizms Red White and Blue #85
2018 Panini Prizm Prizms White /5 #15
2018 Panini Prizm Prizms White /5 #52
2018 Panini Prizm Prizms White /5 #67
2018 Panini Prizm Prizms White /5 #75
2018 Panini Prizm Prizms White /5 #85
2018 Panini Prizm Scripted Signatures Prizms #20
2018 Panini Prizm Scripted Signatures Prizms Black /1 #20
2018 Panini Prizm Scripted Signatures Prizms Blue /10 #20
2018 Panini Prizm Scripted Signatures Prizms Camo #20
2018 Panini Prizm Scripted Signatures Prizms Gold /10 #20
2018 Panini Prizm Scripted Signatures Prizms Green /10 #20
2018 Panini Prizm Scripted Signatures Prizms Rainbow /24 #20
2018 Panini Prizm Scripted Signatures Prizms Red /10 #20
2018 Panini Prizm Scripted Signatures Prizms Red White and Blue /20 #20
2018 Panini Prizm Scripted Signatures Prizms White /5 #20
2018 Panini Prizm Stars and Stripes #9
2018 Panini Prizm Stars and Stripes Prizms #9
2018 Panini Prizm Stars and Stripes Prizms Black /1 #9
2018 Panini Prizm Stars and Stripes Prizms Gold /10 #9
2018 Panini Victory Lane Chasing the Flag #1
2018 Panini Victory Lane Chasing the Flag Black /1 #1

2018 Panini Victory Lane Chasing the Flag Blue /25 #1
2018 Panini Victory Lane Chasing the Flag Gold /99 #1
2018 Panini Victory Lane Chasing the Flag Green /5 #1
2018 Panini Victory Lane Chasing the Flag Printing Plates Black /1 #1
2018 Panini Victory Lane Chasing the Flag Printing Plates Cyan /1 #1
2018 Panini Victory Lane Chasing the Flag Printing Plates Magenta /1 #1
2018 Panini Victory Lane Chasing the Flag Printing Plates Yellow /1 #1
2018 Panini Victory Lane Chasing the Flag Red /49 #1
2018 Panini Victory Lane Foundations #5
2018 Panini Victory Lane Foundations Black /1 #5
2018 Panini Victory Lane Foundations Blue /25 #5
2018 Panini Victory Lane Foundations Gold /99 #5
2018 Panini Victory Lane Foundations Green /5 #5
2018 Panini Victory Lane Foundations Printing Plates Black /1 #5
2018 Panini Victory Lane Foundations Printing Plates Cyan /1 #5
2018 Panini Victory Lane Foundations Printing Plates Magenta /1 #5
2018 Panini Victory Lane Foundations Printing Plates Yellow /1 #5
2018 Panini Victory Lane Foundations Red /49 #5
2018 Panini Victory Lane Octane Autographs /49 #10
2018 Panini Victory Lane Octane Autographs Black /1 #10
2018 Panini Victory Lane Octane Autographs Gold /25 #10
2018 Panini Victory Lane Pedal to the Metal #15
2018 Panini Victory Lane Pedal to the Metal #74
2018 Panini Victory Lane Pedal to the Metal Black /1 #15
2018 Panini Victory Lane Pedal to the Metal Black /1 #74
2018 Panini Victory Lane Pedal to the Metal Blue /25 #15
2018 Panini Victory Lane Pedal to the Metal Blue /25 #74
2018 Panini Victory Lane Pedal to the Metal Green /5 #15
2018 Panini Victory Lane Pedal to the Metal Green /5 #74
2018 Panini Victory Lane Race Day #9
2018 Panini Victory Lane Race Day Black /1 #9
2018 Panini Victory Lane Race Day Blue /25 #9
2018 Panini Victory Lane Race Day Gold /99 #9
2018 Panini Victory Lane Race Day Green /5 #9
2018 Panini Victory Lane Race Day Printing Plates Black /1 #9
2018 Panini Victory Lane Race Day Printing Plates Cyan /1 #9
2018 Panini Victory Lane Race Day Printing Plates Magenta /1 #9
2018 Panini Victory Lane Race Day Printing Plates Yellow /1 #9
2018 Panini Victory Lane Race Day Red /49 #9
2018 Panini Victory Lane Race Ready Materials /399 #9
2018 Panini Victory Lane Race Ready Materials Black /25 #9
2018 Panini Victory Lane Race Ready Materials Gold /199 #9
2018 Panini Victory Lane Race Ready Materials Green /99 #9
2019 Donruss #18
2019 Donruss #39A
2019 Donruss #100
2019 Donruss #101
2019 Donruss #39B
2019 Donruss Artist Proofs /25 #18
2019 Donruss Artist Proofs /25 #39A
2019 Donruss Artist Proofs /25 #100
2019 Donruss Artist Proofs /25 #101
2019 Donruss Artist Proofs /25 #39B
2019 Donruss Black /199 #18
2019 Donruss Black /199 #39A
2019 Donruss Black /199 #100
2019 Donruss Black /199 #101
2019 Donruss Black /199 #39B
2019 Donruss Classics #5
2019 Donruss Classics Cracked Ice /25 #5
2019 Donruss Classics Holographic #5
2019 Donruss Classics Xplosion /10 #5
2019 Donruss Gold /299 #18
2019 Donruss Gold /299 #39A
2019 Donruss Gold /299 #100
2019 Donruss Gold /299 #101
2019 Donruss Gold /299 #39B
2019 Donruss Gold Press Proofs /99 #18
2019 Donruss Gold Press Proofs /99 #39A
2019 Donruss Gold Press Proofs /99 #100
2019 Donruss Gold Press Proofs /99 #101
2019 Donruss Gold Press Proofs /99 #39B
2019 Donruss Optic #7
2019 Donruss Optic #40
2019 Donruss Optic Blue Pulsar #7
2019 Donruss Optic Blue Pulsar #40
2019 Donruss Optic Gold /10 #7
2019 Donruss Optic Gold /10 #40
2019 Donruss Optic Gold Vinyl /1 #7
2019 Donruss Optic Gold Vinyl /1 #40
2019 Donruss Optic Holo #7
2019 Donruss Optic Holo #40
2019 Donruss Optic Illusion #4
2019 Donruss Optic Illusion Blue Pulsar #4
2019 Donruss Optic Illusion Gold /10 #4
2019 Donruss Optic Illusion Gold Vinyl /1 #4
2019 Donruss Optic Illusion Holo #4
2019 Donruss Optic Illusion Red Wave #4
2019 Donruss Optic Illusion Signatures Gold Vinyl /1 #4
2019 Donruss Optic Illusion Signatures Holo /25 #4
2019 Donruss Optic Red Wave #7
2019 Donruss Optic Red Wave #40
2019 Donruss Optic Signatures Gold Vinyl /1 #40
2019 Donruss Optic Signatures Gold Vinyl /1 #7
2019 Donruss Optic Signatures Holo /75 #7
2019 Donruss Optic Signatures Holo /49 #40
2019 Donruss Press Proofs /49 #18
2019 Donruss Press Proofs /49 #39A
2019 Donruss Press Proofs /49 #100
2019 Donruss Press Proofs /49 #101
2019 Donruss Press Proofs /49 #39B
2019 Donruss Printing Plates Black /1 #18
2019 Donruss Printing Plates Black /1 #39A
2019 Donruss Printing Plates Black /1 #100
2019 Donruss Printing Plates Black /1 #101
2019 Donruss Printing Plates Black /1 #39B
2019 Donruss Printing Plates Cyan /1 #18
2019 Donruss Printing Plates Cyan /1 #39A
2019 Donruss Printing Plates Cyan /1 #100
2019 Donruss Printing Plates Cyan /1 #101
2019 Donruss Printing Plates Cyan /1 #39B
2019 Donruss Printing Plates Magenta /1 #39A
2019 Donruss Printing Plates Magenta /1 #100
2019 Donruss Printing Plates Magenta /1 #101
2019 Donruss Printing Plates Magenta /1 #39B
2019 Donruss Printing Plates Magenta /1 #18
2019 Donruss Printing Plates Yellow /1 #18
2019 Donruss Printing Plates Yellow /1 #39A
2019 Donruss Printing Plates Yellow /1 #100
2019 Donruss Printing Plates Yellow /1 #101
2019 Donruss Printing Plates Yellow /1 #39B
2019 Donruss Signature Swatches #4
2019 Donruss Signature Swatches Holo Black /10 #4
2019 Donruss Signature Swatches Holo Gold /25 #4
2019 Donruss Signature Swatches Red /50 #4
2019 Donruss Silver #18
2019 Donruss Silver #39A
2019 Donruss Silver #100
2019 Donruss Silver #101
2019 Donruss Silver #39B
2019 Panini National Convention NASCAR #R2
2019 Panini National Convention NASCAR Galatic Windows /25 #R2
2019 Panini National Convention NASCAR HyperPlaid /1 #R2
2019 Panini Prime /50 #63
2019 Panini Prime /50 #91
2019 Panini Prime Autograph Materials /25 #3
2019 Panini Prime Autograph Materials Black /10 #3
2019 Panini Prime Autograph Materials Holo Gold /15 #3

2019 Panini Prime Autograph Materials Platinum Blue /1 #3
2019 Panini Prime Black /10 #63
2019 Panini Prime Black /10 #91
2019 Panini Prime Emerald /5 #63
2019 Panini Prime Emerald /5 #91
2019 Panini Prime Platinum Blue /1 #63
2019 Panini Prime Platinum Blue /1 #91
2019 Panini Prime Prime Names Die Cut Signatures /25 #15
2019 Panini Prime Prime Names Die Cut Signatures Black /10 #15
2019 Panini Prime Prime Names Die Cut Signatures Holo Gold /15 #15
2019 Panini Prime Prime Names Die Cut Signatures Platinum Blue /1 #15
2019 Panini Prime Race Used Firesuits Black /10 #40
2019 Panini Prime Race Used Firesuits Laundry Tags /1 #40
2019 Panini Prime Race Used Sheet Metal /50 #40
2019 Panini Prime Race Used Sheet Metal Black /10 #40
2019 Panini Prime Race Used Sheet Metal Holo Gold /25 #40
2019 Panini Prime Race Used Sheet Metal Platinum Blue /1 #40
2019 Panini Prime Race Used Tires /50 #40
2019 Panini Prime Race Used Tires Black /10 #40
2019 Panini Prime Race Used Tires Holo Gold /25 #40
2019 Panini Prime Race Used Tires Platinum Blue /1 #40
2019 Panini Prime Shadowbox Signatures /50 #1
2019 Panini Prime Shadowbox Signatures Black /10 #1
2019 Panini Prime Shadowbox Signatures Holo Gold /25 #1
2019 Panini Prime Shadowbox Signatures Platinum Blue /1 #1
2019 Panini Prizm #42A
2019 Panini Prizm #42B
2019 Panini Prizm Apex #4
2019 Panini Prizm Apex Prizms #4
2019 Panini Prizm Apex Prizms Black /1 #4
2019 Panini Prizm Apex Prizms Gold /10 #4
2019 Panini Prizm Apex Prizms White Sparkle #4
2019 Panini Prizm Endorsements Prizms #5
2019 Panini Prizm Endorsements Prizms Black /1 #5
2019 Panini Prizm Endorsements Prizms Blue /5 #5
2019 Panini Prizm Endorsements Prizms Camo #5
2019 Panini Prizm Endorsements Prizms Gold /10 #5
2019 Panini Prizm Endorsements Prizms Green /5 #5
2019 Panini Prizm Endorsements Prizms Rainbow /5 #5
2019 Panini Prizm Endorsements Prizms Red /50 #5
2019 Panini Prizm Endorsements Prizms Red White and Blue #5
2019 Panini Prizm Endorsements Prizms White /5 #5
2019 Panini Prizm Fireworks #2
2019 Panini Prizm Fireworks Prizms #2
2019 Panini Prizm Fireworks Prizms Black /1 #2
2019 Panini Prizm Fireworks Prizms Gold /10 #2
2019 Panini Prizm Fireworks Prizms White Sparkle #2
2019 Panini Prizm National Pride #5
2019 Panini Prizm National Pride Prizms #5
2019 Panini Prizm National Pride Prizms Black /1 #5
2019 Panini Prizm National Pride Prizms Gold /10 #5
2019 Panini Prizm National Pride Prizms White Sparkle #5
2019 Panini Prizm Patented Penmanship Prizms #3
2019 Panini Prizm Patented Penmanship Prizms Black /1 #3
2019 Panini Prizm Patented Penmanship Prizms Blue /5 #3
2019 Panini Prizm Patented Penmanship Prizms Camo #3
2019 Panini Prizm Patented Penmanship Prizms Gold /10 #3
2019 Panini Prizm Patented Penmanship Prizms Green /5 #3
2019 Panini Prizm Patented Penmanship Prizms Rainbow /5 #3
2019 Panini Prizm Patented Penmanship Prizms Red /5 #3
2019 Panini Prizm Patented Penmanship Prizms Red White and Blue #3
2019 Panini Prizm Patented Penmanship Prizms White /5 #3
2019 Panini Prizm Prizms #42A
2019 Panini Prizm Prizms #42B
2019 Panini Prizm Prizms Black /1 #42A
2019 Panini Prizm Prizms Black /1 #42B
2019 Panini Prizm Prizms Blue /75 #42A
2019 Panini Prizm Prizms Blue /75 #42B
2019 Panini Prizm Prizms Camo #42A
2019 Panini Prizm Prizms Camo #42B
2019 Panini Prizm Prizms Flash #42A
2019 Panini Prizm Prizms Flash #42B
2019 Panini Prizm Prizms Gold /10 #42A
2019 Panini Prizm Prizms Gold /10 #42B
2019 Panini Prizm Prizms Green /99 #42A
2019 Panini Prizm Prizms Green /99 #42B
2019 Panini Prizm Prizms Rainbow /24 #42A
2019 Panini Prizm Prizms Rainbow /24 #42B
2019 Panini Prizm Prizms Red /50 #42A
2019 Panini Prizm Prizms Red /50 #42B
2019 Panini Prizm Prizms Red White and Blue #42A
2019 Panini Prizm Prizms Red White and Blue #42B
2019 Panini Prizm Prizms White /5 #42A
2019 Panini Prizm Prizms White /5 #42B
2019 Panini Prizm Prizms White Sparkle #42A
2019 Panini Prizm Prizms White Sparkle #42B
2019 Panini Prizm Stars and Stripes #9
2019 Panini Prizm Stars and Stripes Prizms #9
2019 Panini Prizm Stars and Stripes Prizms Black /1 #9
2019 Panini Prizm Stars and Stripes Prizms Gold /10 #9
2019 Panini Prizm Stars and Stripes Prizms White Sparkle #9
2019 Panini Victory Lane #47
2019 Panini Victory Lane Black /1 #47
2019 Panini Victory Lane Gold /25 #47
2019 Panini Victory Lane Horsepower Heroes #12
2019 Panini Victory Lane Horsepower Heroes Black /1 #12
2019 Panini Victory Lane Horsepower Heroes Blue /99 #12
2019 Panini Victory Lane Horsepower Heroes Gold /25 #12
2019 Panini Victory Lane Horsepower Heroes Green /5 #12
2019 Panini Victory Lane Horsepower Heroes Printing Plates Black /1 #12
2019 Panini Victory Lane Horsepower Heroes Printing Plates Cyan /1 #12
2019 Panini Victory Lane Horsepower Heroes Printing Plates Magenta /1 #12
2019 Panini Victory Lane Horsepower Heroes Printing Plates Yellow /1 #12
2019 Panini Victory Lane Printing Plates Black /1 #47
2019 Panini Victory Lane Printing Plates Cyan /1 #47
2019 Panini Victory Lane Printing Plates Magenta /1 #47
2019 Panini Victory Lane Printing Plates Yellow /1 #47
2019 Panini Victory Lane Signature Swatches #5
2019 Panini Victory Lane Signature Swatches Gold /99 #5
2019 Panini Victory Lane Signature Swatches Laundry Tag /1 #5
2019 Panini Victory Lane Signature Swatches Platinum /1 #5
2019 Panini Victory Lane Signature Swatches Red /25 #5
2019 Panini Victory Lane Track Stars #11
2019 Panini Victory Lane Track Stars Black /1 #11
2019 Panini Victory Lane Track Stars Blue /99 #11
2019 Panini Victory Lane Track Stars Gold /25 #11
2019 Panini Victory Lane Track Stars Green /5 #11
2019 Panini Victory Lane Track Stars Printing Plates Black /1 #11
2019 Panini Victory Lane Track Stars Printing Plates Cyan /1 #11
2019 Panini Victory Lane Track Stars Printing Plates Magenta /1 #11
2019 Panini Victory Lane Track Stars Printing Plates Yellow /1 #11
2019 The Bar Pieces of the Past /1 #NNO
2019 The Bar Pieces of the Past /1 #NNO
2020 Donruss #86
2020 Donruss #141
2020 Donruss Black Numbers /9 #86
2020 Donruss Black Numbers /9 #141
2020 Donruss Black Trophy Club /1 #86
2020 Donruss Black Trophy Club /1 #141
2020 Donruss Blue /199 #86
2020 Donruss Blue /199 #141
2020 Donruss Carolina Blue #86
2020 Donruss Carolina Blue #141
2020 Donruss Classics #2
2020 Donruss Classics Checkers #2
2020 Donruss Classics Cracked Ice /25 #2
2020 Donruss Classics Holographic /199 #2

2020 Donruss Classics Xplosion /10 #2
2020 Donruss Green /99 #86
2020 Donruss Green /99 #141
2020 Donruss Optic #60
2020 Donruss Optic #87
2020 Donruss Optic Carolina Blue Wave #60
2020 Donruss Optic Carolina Blue Wave #87
2020 Donruss Optic Gold /10 #60
2020 Donruss Optic Gold /10 #87
2020 Donruss Optic Gold Vinyl /1 #60
2020 Donruss Optic Gold Vinyl /1 #87
2020 Donruss Optic Holo #60
2020 Donruss Optic Holo #87
2020 Donruss Optic Orange Pulsar #60
2020 Donruss Optic Orange Pulsar #87
2020 Donruss Optic Red Mojo #60
2020 Donruss Optic Red Mojo #87
2020 Donruss Optic Signatures Gold Vinyl /1 #60
2020 Donruss Optic Signatures Gold Vinyl /1 #87
2020 Donruss Optic Signatures Holo /99 #60
2020 Donruss Optic Signatures Holo /99 #87
2020 Donruss Orange #86
2020 Donruss Orange #141
2020 Donruss Pink /25 #86
2020 Donruss Pink /25 #141
2020 Donruss Printing Plates Black /1 #86
2020 Donruss Printing Plates Black /1 #141
2020 Donruss Printing Plates Cyan /1 #86
2020 Donruss Printing Plates Cyan /1 #141
2020 Donruss Printing Plates Magenta /1 #86
2020 Donruss Printing Plates Magenta /1 #141
2020 Donruss Printing Plates Yellow /1 #141
2020 Donruss Printing Plates Yellow /1 #86
2020 Donruss Purple /49 #86
2020 Donruss Purple /49 #141
2020 Donruss Red /299 #86
2020 Donruss Red /299 #141
2020 Donruss Retro Relics '87 /0 #4
2020 Donruss Retro Relics '87 Holo Black #4
2020 Donruss Retro Relics '87 Holo Gold /25 #4
2020 Donruss Retro Relics '87 Red /149 #4
2020 Donruss Silver #86
2020 Donruss Silver #141
2020 Donruss Timeless Treasures Signatures #1
2020 Donruss Timeless Treasures Signatures Holo Black /1 #1
2020 Donruss Timeless Treasures Signatures Holo Gold /5 #1
2020 Donruss Timeless Treasures Signatures Red /10 #1
2020 Donruss Top Tier #5
2020 Donruss Top Tier Checkers #5
2020 Donruss Top Tier Cracked Ice /25 #5
2020 Donruss Top Tier Holographic /199 #5
2020 Donruss Top Tier Xplosion /10 #5

Richard Petty

1972 STP #11
1977-79 Sportscaster Series 11 #1115
1983 UNO Racing #23
1985 SportStars Photo-Graphics Stickers #NNO
1986 SportStars Photo-Graphics #10
1988 Maxx Charlotte #2
1988 Maxx Charlotte #15
1988 Maxx Charlotte #31
1988 Maxx Charlotte #60
1988 Maxx Charlotte #82
1988 Maxx Charlotte #84
1988 Maxx Charlotte #43
1989 Maxx #101
1989 Maxx #181
1989 Maxx #193
1989 Maxx #220
1989 Maxx #43
1989 Maxx Crisco #17
1989 Maxx Previews #6
1989-90 TG Racing Masters of Racing #59
1989-90 TG Racing Masters of Racing #237
1990 Maxx #43
1990 Maxx #192
1990 Maxx Glossy #43
1990 Maxx Glossy #192
1990 Maxx Holly Farms #HF6
1991 Maxx #43
1991 Maxx #122
1991 Maxx McDonald's #26
1991 Maxx Racing for Kids #3
1991 Maxx Update #43
1991 Maxx Winston 20th Anniversary Foils #1
1991 Maxx Winston 20th Anniversary Foils #2
1991 Maxx Winston 20th Anniversary Foils #4
1991 Maxx Winston 20th Anniversary Foils #5
1991 Maxx Winston 20th Anniversary Foils #9
1991 Pro Set #65
1991 Pro Set #68
1991 Pro Set #130
1991 Pro Set Petty Family #2
1991 Pro Set Petty Family #13
1991 Pro Set Petty Family #16
1991 Pro Set Petty Family #17
1991 Pro Set Petty Family #19
1991 Pro Set Petty Family #20
1991 Pro Set Petty Family #21
1991 Pro Set Petty Family #22
1991 Pro Set Petty Family #23
1991 Pro Set Petty Family #24
1991 Pro Set Petty Family #27
1991 Pro Set Petty Family #28
1991 Pro Set Petty Family #30
1991 Pro Set Petty Family #31
1991 Pro Set Petty Family #32
1991 Pro Set Petty Family #33
1991 Pro Set Petty Family #37
1991 Pro Set Petty Family #38
1991 Pro Set Petty Family #41
1991 Pro Set Petty Family #42
1991 Pro Set Petty Family #43
1991 Pro Set Petty Family #44
1991 Pro Set Petty Family #47
1991 Pro Set Petty Family #50
1991 Pro Set Petty Family #1
1991 Pro Set Petty Family #9
1991 Pro Set Petty Family #15
1991 Pro Set Petty Family #18
1991 Pro Set Petty Family #34
1991 Pro Set Petty Family #35
1991 Pro Set Petty Family #36
1991 Pro Set Petty Family #49
1991 Pro Set Petty Family Prototypes #P3
1991 STP Richard Petty #1
1991 STP Richard Petty #2
1991 STP Richard Petty #3
1991 STP Richard Petty #5
1991 STP Richard Petty #6
1991 STP Richard Petty #7
1991 STP Richard Petty #8
1991 STP Richard Petty #9
1991 STP Richard Petty #4
1991 Sunbelt Racing Legends #1

1991 Superior Racing Metals #10
1991 Texas World Speedway #5
1991 Texas World Speedway #7
1991 TG Racing David Pearson #5
1991 Tiger Tom Pistone #13
1991 Traks #43
1991 Traks #85
1991 Traks #200
1991 Traks Promos #P4
1991 Traks Promos #P6
1991 Traks Promos #P5
1991 Traks Richard Petty #1
1991 Traks Richard Petty #2
1991 Traks Richard Petty #3
1991 Traks Richard Petty #4
1991 Traks Richard Petty #5
1991 Traks Richard Petty #6
1991 Traks Richard Petty #7
1991 Traks Richard Petty #8
1991 Traks Richard Petty #9
1991 Traks Richard Petty #10
1991 Traks Richard Petty #11
1991 Traks Richard Petty #12
1991 Traks Richard Petty #13
1991 Traks Richard Petty #14
1991 Traks Richard Petty #15
1991 Traks Richard Petty #16
1991 Traks Richard Petty #17
1991 Traks Richard Petty #18
1991 Traks Richard Petty #19
1991 Traks Richard Petty #20
1991 Traks Richard Petty #21
1991 Traks Richard Petty #23
1991 Traks Richard Petty #24
1991 Traks Richard Petty #25
1991 Traks Richard Petty #26
1991 Traks Richard Petty #27
1991 Traks Richard Petty #28
1991 Traks Richard Petty #29
1991 Traks Richard Petty #30
1991 Traks Richard Petty #31
1991 Traks Richard Petty #32
1991 Traks Richard Petty #33
1991 Traks Richard Petty #34
1991 Traks Richard Petty #35
1991 Traks Richard Petty #36
1991 Traks Richard Petty #37
1991 Traks Richard Petty #38
1991 Traks Richard Petty #39
1991 Traks Richard Petty #40
1991 Traks Richard Petty #41
1991 Traks Richard Petty #42
1991 Traks Richard Petty #43
1991 Traks Richard Petty #44
1991 Traks Richard Petty #45
1991 Traks Richard Petty #46
1991 Traks Richard Petty #47
1991 Traks Richard Petty #48
1991 Traks Richard Petty #49
1991 Traks Richard Petty #50
1991 Traks Richard Petty #22
1991 Winner's Choice Ricky Craven #17
1991-92 TG Racing Masters of Racing Update #59
1992 Action Packed Richard Petty /100000 #RP1
1992 Action Packed Richard Petty /100000 #RP2
1992 Action Packed Richard Petty /50000 #RP3
1992 Bikers of the Racing Scene #1
1992 Food Lion Richard Petty #2
1992 Food Lion Richard Petty #3
1992 Food Lion Richard Petty #4
1992 Food Lion Richard Petty #6
1992 Food Lion Richard Petty #7
1992 Food Lion Richard Petty #8
1992 Food Lion Richard Petty #10
1992 Food Lion Richard Petty #11
1992 Food Lion Richard Petty #12
1992 Food Lion Richard Petty #14
1992 Food Lion Richard Petty #15
1992 Food Lion Richard Petty #16
1992 Food Lion Richard Petty #18
1992 Food Lion Richard Petty #19
1992 Food Lion Richard Petty #20
1992 Food Lion Richard Petty #22
1992 Food Lion Richard Petty #23
1992 Food Lion Richard Petty #24
1992 Food Lion Richard Petty #26
1992 Food Lion Richard Petty #27
1992 Food Lion Richard Petty #28
1992 Food Lion Richard Petty #30
1992 Food Lion Richard Petty #31
1992 Food Lion Richard Petty #32
1992 Food Lion Richard Petty #34
1992 Food Lion Richard Petty #35
1992 Food Lion Richard Petty #36
1992 Food Lion Richard Petty #38
1992 Food Lion Richard Petty #39
1992 Food Lion Richard Petty #40
1992 Food Lion Richard Petty #42
1992 Food Lion Richard Petty #43
1992 Food Lion Richard Petty #44
1992 Food Lion Richard Petty #46
1992 Food Lion Richard Petty #47
1992 Food Lion Richard Petty #48
1992 Food Lion Richard Petty #50
1992 Food Lion Richard Petty #51
1992 Food Lion Richard Petty #52
1992 Food Lion Richard Petty #54
1992 Food Lion Richard Petty #55
1992 Food Lion Richard Petty #56
1992 Food Lion Richard Petty #58
1992 Food Lion Richard Petty #59
1992 Food Lion Richard Petty #60
1992 Food Lion Richard Petty #62
1992 Food Lion Richard Petty #63
1992 Food Lion Richard Petty #64
1992 Food Lion Richard Petty #66
1992 Food Lion Richard Petty #67
1992 Food Lion Richard Petty #68
1992 Food Lion Richard Petty #70
1992 Food Lion Richard Petty #71
1992 Food Lion Richard Petty #72
1992 Food Lion Richard Petty #74
1992 Food Lion Richard Petty #75
1992 Food Lion Richard Petty #76
1992 Food Lion Richard Petty #78
1992 Food Lion Richard Petty #79
1992 Food Lion Richard Petty #80
1992 Food Lion Richard Petty #82
1992 Food Lion Richard Petty #83
1992 Food Lion Richard Petty #84
1992 Food Lion Richard Petty #86
1992 Food Lion Richard Petty #87
1992 Food Lion Richard Petty #88
1992 Food Lion Richard Petty #90
1992 Food Lion Richard Petty #91
1992 Food Lion Richard Petty #92
1992 Food Lion Richard Petty #94
1992 Food Lion Richard Petty #95

1992 Food Lion Richard Petty #96
1992 Food Lion Richard Petty #98
1992 Food Lion Richard Petty #99
1992 Food Lion Richard Petty #100
1992 Food Lion Richard Petty #102
1992 Food Lion Richard Petty #103
1992 Food Lion Richard Petty #104
1992 Food Lion Richard Petty #106
1992 Food Lion Richard Petty #107
1992 Food Lion Richard Petty #108
1992 Food Lion Richard Petty #110
1992 Food Lion Richard Petty #111
1992 Food Lion Richard Petty #112
1992 Food Lion Richard Petty #114
1992 Food Lion Richard Petty #115
1992 Food Lion Richard Petty #116
1992 Food Lion Richard Petty #NNO
1992 Mac Tools Winner's Cup #17
1992 Maxx Black #43
1992 Maxx IMHOF #35
1992 Maxx McDonald's #30
1992 Maxx Red #43
1992 Maxx Sam Bass #1
1992 Maxx The Winston #9
1992 Maxx The Winston #29
1992 Pepsi Richard Petty #1
1992 Pepsi Richard Petty #2
1992 Pepsi Richard Petty #3
1992 Pepsi Richard Petty #4
1992 Pepsi Richard Petty #5
1992 Pro Set #43
1992 Pro Set #45
1992 Pro Set #114
1992 Pro Set #124
1992 Pro Set Maxwell House #25
1992 Pro Set Racing Club #6
1992 Pro Set Rudy Farms #15
1992 Redline Standups #3
1992 Sports Illustrated for Kids II #66
1992 STP Daytona 500 #1
1992 STP Daytona 500 #2
1992 STP Daytona 500 #4
1992 STP Daytona 500 #5
1992 STP Daytona 500 #7
1992 STP Daytona 500 #9
1992 Traks #43
1992 Traks #85
1992 Traks #200
1992 Traks #P3
1992 Traks Autographs #A1
1992 Traks Benny Parsons #28
1992 Traks Benny Parsons #31
1992 Traks Benny Parsons #39
1992 Traks Goody's #25
1992 Traks Kodak Ernie Irvan #1A
1992 Traks Kodak Ernie Irvan #1B
1992 Traks Racing Machines #18
1992 Traks Racing Machines #19
1992 Traks Racing Machines #43
1992 Traks Racing Machines #55
1992 Traks Racing Machines #80
1992 Traks Racing Machines #97
1992 Traks Racing Machines #100
1992 Traks Team Sets #176
1992 Traks Team Sets #184
1992 Traks Team Sets #185
1992 Traks Team Sets #195
1992 Traks Team Sets #200
1993 Action Packed #10
1993 Action Packed #31
1993 Action Packed #50
1993 Action Packed #51
1993 Action Packed #52
1993 Action Packed #53
1993 Action Packed #54
1993 Action Packed #70
1993 Action Packed #71
1993 Action Packed #72
1993 Action Packed #75
1993 Action Packed #76
1993 Action Packed #81
1993 Action Packed #82
1993 Action Packed #92
1993 Action Packed #160
1993 Action Packed 24K Gold #15G
1993 Action Packed 24K Gold #16G
1993 Action Packed 24K Gold #17G
1993 Action Packed 24K Gold #13G
1993 Action Packed 24K Gold #14G
1993 Action Packed 24K Gold #35G
1993 Action Packed Alan Kulwicki #AK3
1993 Card Dynamics Gant Oil /6000 #1
1993 Card Dynamics Quik Chek /5000 #3
1993 Finish Line #61
1993 Finish Line #85
1993 Finish Line #114
1993 Finish Line Commemorative Sheets #12
1993 Finish Line Commemorative Sheets #27
1993 Finish Line Commemorative Sheets #29
1993 Finish Line Silver #61
1993 Finish Line Silver #85
1993 Finish Line Silver #114
1993 Maxwell House #15
1993 Maxwell House #18
1993 Maxx #43
1993 Maxx #156
1993 Maxx #199
1993 Maxx #245
1993 Maxx Premier Plus #43
1993 Maxx Premier Plus #48
1993 Maxx Premier Plus #57
1993 Maxx Premier Plus #74
1993 Maxx Premier Series #43
1993 Maxx Premier Series #156
1993 Maxx Premier Series #199
1993 Maxx Premier Series #245
1993 Traks Preferred Collector #15
1993 Traks Preferred Collector #16
1993 Wheels Rookie Thunder #2
1993 Wheels Rookie Thunder #61
1993 Wheels Rookie Thunder #79
1993 Wheels Rookie Thunder #80
1993 Wheels Rookie Thunder #95
1993 Wheels Rookie Thunder #96
1993 Wheels Rookie Thunder #99
1993 Wheels Rookie Thunder Platinum #2
1993 Wheels Rookie Thunder Platinum #61
1993 Wheels Rookie Thunder Platinum #79
1993 Wheels Rookie Thunder Platinum #80
1993 Wheels Rookie Thunder Platinum #95
1993 Wheels Rookie Thunder Platinum #96
1993 Wheels Rookie Thunder Platinum #99
1993 Wheels Rookie Thunder Promos #P1
1993 Wheels Rookie Thunder SPs #SP6
1993 Wheels Rookie Thunder SPs #SP7
1993-95 Miscellaneous Phone Cards #15
1994 Action Packed #178
1994 Action Packed Mint #178
1994 Finish Line #58
1994 Finish Line #64
1994 Finish Line Gold #83
1994 Finish Line Silver #58
1994 Finish Line Silver #64
1994 Hi-Tech Brickyard 400 Prototypes #1
1994 Hi-Tech Brickyard 400 Richard Petty #1
1994 Hi-Tech Brickyard 400 Richard Petty #2
1994 Hi-Tech Brickyard 400 Richard Petty #3
1994 Hi-Tech Brickyard 400 Richard Petty #4
1994 Hi-Tech Brickyard 400 Richard Petty #5
1994 Hi-Tech Brickyard 400 Richard Petty #6
1994 Maxx #43
1994 Maxx Premier Plus #43
1994 Maxx Premier Series #43
1994 Maxx Premier Series Jumbos #6
1994 Pepsi 400 Victory Lane #1
1994 Power #PO64
1994 Power #110
1994 Power Gold #PO64
1994 Power Gold #110
1994 Wheels High Gear #28
1994 Wheels High Gear Gold #28
1994 Wheels High Gear Legends #LS4
1994 Wheels High Gear Promos #P3
1994 Wheels High Gear Promos Gold #P3
1994-96 John Deere #4
1995 Action Packed Country #20
1995 Action Packed Country Silver Speed #20
1995 Action Packed Preview #73
1995 Action Packed Preview 24K Gold #5G
1995 Assets $100 Phone Cards #4
1995 Assets $25 Phone Cards #8
1995 Assets $5 Phone Cards #8
1995 Finish Line #43
1995 Finish Line #104
1995 Finish Line Printer's Proof /398 #43
1995 Finish Line Printer's Proof /398 #104
1995 Finish Line Silver #43
1995 Finish Line Silver #104
1995 Matchbook Winston Cup Champions #1
1995 Matchbook Winston Cup Champions #2
1995 Matchbook Winston Cup Champions #4
1995 Matchbook Winston Cup Champions #5
1995 Matchbook Winston Cup Champions #9
1995 Maxx #43
1995 Maxx Premier Plus #43
1995 Maxx Premier Plus Crown Chrome #43
1995 Maxx Premier Series #43
1995 Maxx Stand Ups #6
1995 Metallic Impressions Richard Petty #1
1995 Metallic Impressions Richard Petty #2
1995 Metallic Impressions Richard Petty #3
1995 Metallic Impressions Richard Petty #4
1995 Metallic Impressions Richard Petty #5
1995 Metallic Impressions Winston Cup Champions 10-Card Tin #1
1995 Press Pass #86
1995 Press Pass #126
1995 Press Pass #132
1995 Press Pass Premium #20
1995 Press Pass Premium Holofoil #20
1995 Press Pass Premium Red Hot #20
1995 Press Pass Red Hot #86
1995 Press Pass Red Hot #126
1995 Press Pass Red Hot #132
1995 Select #73
1995 Select #109
1995 Select #129
1995 Select Flat Out #73
1995 Select Flat Out #109
1995 Select Flat Out #129
1995 SP #127
1995 SP Back-To-Back #BB1
1995 SP Die Cuts #127
1995 Traks #NNO
1995 Traks 5th Anniversary Retrospective #R15
1995 Traks Valvoline #73
1995 Traks Valvoline #85
1995 Upper Deck #151
1995 Upper Deck Gold Signature/Electric Gold #151
1995 Upper Deck Silver Signature/Electric Silver #151
1995 VIP #49
1995 VIP Cool Blue #49
1995 VIP Emerald Proofs #49
1995 VIP Helmets #H7
1995 VIP Helmets #H8
1995 VIP Helmets #H9
1995 VIP Helmets Gold #H7
1995 VIP Helmets Gold #H8
1995 VIP Helmets Gold #H9
1995 VIP Red Hot #49
1996 Action Packed Credentials #78
1996 Assets Racing #47
1996 Autographed Racing #10
1996 Autographed Racing Front Runners #15
1996 Autographed Racing Front Runners #22
1996 Autographed Racing Front Runners #29
1996 Autographed Racing Front Runners #30
1996 Autographed Racing Front Runners #78
1996 Classic #12
1996 Classic Printer's Proof #12
1996 Classic Silver #12
1996 Flair #51
1996 Maxx #43
1996 Maxx Made in America #43
1996 Maxx Odyssey #43
1996 Maxx Premier Series #43
1996 Maxx Premier Series #52
1996 Metallic Impressions 25th Anniversary Winston Cup Champions #1
1996 Metallic Impressions 25th Anniversary Winston Cup Champions #2
1996 Metallic Impressions 25th Anniversary Winston Cup Champions #4
1996 Metallic Impressions 25th Anniversary Winston Cup Champions #5
1996 Metallic Impressions 25th Anniversary Winston Cup Champions #9
1996 M-Force #14
1996 M-Force Silvers #S8
1996 Press Pass #80
1996 Press Pass #89
1996 Press Pass Scorchers #80
1996 Press Pass Scorchers #89
1996 Press Pass Torquers #80
1996 Press Pass Torquers #89
1996 SP Richard Petty/STP 25th Anniversary #RP1
1996 SP Richard Petty/STP 25th Anniversary #RP2
1996 SP Richard Petty/STP 25th Anniversary #RP3
1996 SP Richard Petty/STP 25th Anniversary #RP4
1996 SP Richard Petty/STP 25th Anniversary #RP5
1996 SP Richard Petty/STP 25th Anniversary #RP6
1996 SP Richard Petty/STP 25th Anniversary #RP7
1996 SP Richard Petty/STP 25th Anniversary #RP8
1996 SP Richard Petty/STP 25th Anniversary #RP9
1996 UDA Commemorative Cards /5140 #1
1996 Ultra #146
1996 Ultra Autographs #28
1996 Upper Deck #127
1996 Upper Deck #139
1996 Upper Deck Racing Legends #RLC1
1996 Zenith Champion Salute #17
1996 Zenith Champion Salute #21
1996 Zenith Champion Salute #22
1996 Zenith Champion Salute #24
1996 Zenith Champion Salute #25
1997 Action Packed #67
1997 Action Packed Fifth Anniversary #1
1997 Action Packed Fifth Anniversary Autographs #1
1997 Action Packed First Impressions #67
1997 Collector's Choice #126
1997 Collector's Choice Upper Deck 500 #UD29
1997 Press Pass #97
1997 Press Pass #108
1997 Press Pass Lasers Silver #97
1997 Press Pass Lasers Silver #108
1997 Press Pass Oil Slicks /100 #97
1997 Press Pass Oil Slicks /100 #108
1997 Press Pass Torquers Blue #97
1997 Press Pass Torquers Blue #108
1997 Racer's Choice #86
1997 Racer's Choice Showcase Series #86
1997 SB Motorsports #8
1997 SB Motorsports #30
1997 Score Board IQ #32
1997 Score Board IQ Remarques #SB7
1997 Score Board IQ Remarques Sam Bass Finished #SB7
1997 SkyBox Profile #33
1997 SportsCom FanScan #10
1997 SPx Tag Team #TT5
1997 SPx Tag Team Autographs #TA5
1997 Ultra #62
1997 Ultra Shoney's #15
1997 Ultra Update #47
1997 Ultra Winn Dixie #WD5
1998 Maxx 10th Anniversary #39
1998 Maxx 10th Anniversary #84
1998 Maxx 10th Anniversary #94
1998 Maxx 10th Anniversary #108
1998 Maxx 10th Anniversary Buy Back Autographs /12 #40
1998 Maxx 10th Anniversary Buy Back Autographs #41
1998 Maxx 10th Anniversary Buy Back Autographs /250 #42
1998 Maxx 10th Anniversary Card of the Year #CY2
1998 Maxx 10th Anniversary Card of the Year #CY6
1998 Maxx 10th Anniversary Champions Past #CP9
1998 Maxx 10th Anniversary Champions Past Die Cuts /1000 #CP9
1998 Maxx Signed, Sealed, and Delivered /250 #S4
1998 Press Pass #134
1998 Press Pass Premium Rivalries #2B
1998 SP Authentic Mark of a Legend /220 #M1
1998 SP Authentic Traditions #T1
1998 Upper Deck Road To The Cup 50th Anniversary #AN10
1998 Upper Deck Road To The Cup 50th Anniversary #AN14
1998 Upper Deck Road To The Cup 50th Anniversary #AN17
1998 Upper Deck Road To The Cup 50th Anniversary #AN21
1998 Upper Deck Road To The Cup 50th Anniversary #AN27
1998 Upper Deck Road To The Cup 50th Anniversary #AN36
1998 Upper Deck Road To The Cup 50th Anniversary #AN41
1998 Upper Deck Road To The Cup 50th Anniversary Autographs /50 #AN14
1998 Wheels #90
1998 Wheels Golden #90
1998 Wheels High Gear Pure Gold #PG2
1999 Press Pass #132
2000 Press Pass Techno-Retro #TR34
2001 Press Pass Signings #43
2002 Press Pass Autographs #54
2002 Press Pass Eclipse Father and Son Autographs /100 #FS5
2002 Press Pass Eclipse Racing Champions #RC36
2002 Press Pass Signings #53
2002 Press Pass Signings Gold /50 #50
2002 Press Pass Vintage #VN27
2002 VIP #49
2002 VIP Explosives #X49
2002 VIP Explosives Lasers #LX49
2002 VIP Samples #49
2002 Wheels High Gear Autographs #45
2003 eTopps /3065 #25
2003 Press Pass Autographs #47
2003 Press Pass Signings #59
2003 Press Pass Signings Gold /50 #59
2003 Press Pass Snapshots #SN27
2003 Press Pass Trackside #60
2003 Press Pass Trackside #NNO
2003 Press Pass Trackside Gold Holofoil #P60
2003 Press Pass Trackside Samples #60
2003 Press Pass Victory Lap #2
2003 VIP #42
2003 VIP Explosives #X42
2003 VIP Laser Explosive #LX42
2003 VIP Previews /5 #42
2003 VIP Samples #42
2003 VIP Tin #CT42
2004 Press Pass Autographs #49
2004 Press Pass Signings #52
2004 Press Pass Signings Gold /50 #48
2004 Press Pass Signings Transparent /100 #7
2004 Press Pass Snapshots #SN27
2004 VIP #72
2004 VIP #82
2004 VIP Samples #72
2004 VIP Samples #82
2004 Wheels Autographs #53
2004 Wheels High Gear Winston Victory Lap Tribute #WVL3
2004 Wheels High Gear Winston Victory Lap Tribute Gold #WVL3
2005 Press Pass #81
2005 Press Pass #91
2005 Press Pass Autographs #48
2005 Press Pass Legends #10
2005 Press Pass Legends #34
2005 Press Pass Legends #47
2005 Press Pass Legends #50
2005 Press Pass Legends Autographs Black /50 #9
2005 Press Pass Legends Autographs Blue /100 #9
2005 Press Pass Legends Blue /1890 #10B
2005 Press Pass Legends Blue /1890 #34B
2005 Press Pass Legends Blue /1890 #47B
2005 Press Pass Legends Blue /1890 #50B
2005 Press Pass Legends Gold /750 #10G
2005 Press Pass Legends Gold /750 #34G
2005 Press Pass Legends Gold /750 #47G
2005 Press Pass Legends Gold /750 #50G
2005 Press Pass Legends Greatest Moments /640 #GM4
2005 Press Pass Legends Greatest Moments /640 #GM6
2005 Press Pass Legends Heritage /480 #HE8
2005 Press Pass Legends Holofoil /100 #10H
2005 Press Pass Legends Holofoil /100 #34H
2005 Press Pass Legends Holofoil /100 #47H
2005 Press Pass Legends Holofoil /100 #50H
2005 Press Pass Legends Press Plates Black /1 #10
2005 Press Pass Legends Press Plates Black /1 #34
2005 Press Pass Legends Press Plates Black /1 #47
2005 Press Pass Legends Press Plates Black /1 #50
2005 Press Pass Legends Press Plates Cyan /1 #10
2005 Press Pass Legends Press Plates Cyan /1 #34
2005 Press Pass Legends Press Plates Cyan /1 #47
2005 Press Pass Legends Press Plates Cyan /1 #50
2005 Press Pass Legends Press Plates Magenta /1 #10
2005 Press Pass Legends Press Plates Magenta /1 #34
2005 Press Pass Legends Press Plates Magenta /1 #47
2005 Press Pass Legends Press Plates Magenta /1 #50
2005 Press Pass Legends Press Plates Yellow /1 #10
2005 Press Pass Legends Press Plates Yellow /1 #34
2005 Press Pass Legends Press Plates Yellow /1 #47
2005 Press Pass Legends Press Plates Yellow /1 #50
2005 Press Pass Legends Previews /5 #10
2005 Press Pass Legends Previews /5 #34
2005 Press Pass Legends Previews /5 #47
2005 Press Pass Legends Previews /5 #50
2005 Press Pass Legends Solo /1 #10S
2005 Press Pass Legends Solo /1 #34S
2005 Press Pass Legends Solo /1 #47S
2005 Press Pass Legends Solo /1 #50S
2005 Press Pass Platinum /100 #P81
2005 Press Pass Platinum /100 #P91
2005 Press Pass Samples #81
2005 Press Pass Samples #91
2005 Press Pass Signings #46
2005 Press Pass Signings Gold /50 #44
2005 Press Pass Signings Platinum /100 #42
2005 Press Pass Snapshots #SN34
2005 Press Pass Trackside #79
2005 Press Pass Trackside Golden /100 #G79
2005 Press Pass Trackside Samples #79
2005 Wheels Autographs #47
2006 Press Pass Autographs #45
2006 Press Pass Goody's #GCC1
2006 Press Pass Goody's #GCC2
2006 Press Pass Goody's #GCC4
2006 Press Pass Legends #14
2006 Press Pass Legends #46
2006 Press Pass Legends #48
2006 Press Pass Legends #49
2006 Press Pass Legends Autographs Black /50 #12
2006 Press Pass Legends Autographs Blue /100 #14
2006 Press Pass Legends Blue /1999 #B14
2006 Press Pass Legends Blue /1999 #B46
2006 Press Pass Legends Blue /1999 #B48
2006 Press Pass Legends Blue /1999 #B49
2006 Press Pass Legends Bronze /999 #Z14
2006 Press Pass Legends Bronze /999 #Z46
2006 Press Pass Legends Bronze /999 #Z48
2006 Press Pass Legends Bronze /999 #Z49
2006 Press Pass Legends Gold /299 #G14
2006 Press Pass Legends Gold /299 #G46
2006 Press Pass Legends Gold /299 #G48
2006 Press Pass Legends Gold /299 #G49
2006 Press Pass Legends Heritage Gold /99 #HE1
2006 Press Pass Legends Heritage Gold /99 #HE13
2006 Press Pass Legends Heritage Silver /549 #HE1
2006 Press Pass Legends Heritage Silver /549 #HE13
2006 Press Pass Legends Holofoil /99 #H14
2006 Press Pass Legends Holofoil /99 #H46
2006 Press Pass Legends Holofoil /99 #H48
2006 Press Pass Legends Holofoil /99 #H49
2006 Press Pass Legends Memorable Moments Gold /199 #MM9
2006 Press Pass Legends Memorable Moments Gold /199 #MM10
2006 Press Pass Legends Memorable Moments Gold /199 #MM15
2006 Press Pass Legends Memorable Moments Silver /699 #MM9
2006 Press Pass Legends Memorable Moments Silver /699 #MM10
2006 Press Pass Legends Memorable Moments Silver /699 #MM15
2006 Press Pass Legends Press Plates Black /1 #PPB14
2006 Press Pass Legends Press Plates Black /1 #PPB46
2006 Press Pass Legends Press Plates Black /1 #PPB48
2006 Press Pass Legends Press Plates Black /1 #PPB49
2006 Press Pass Legends Press Plates Black Backs /1 #PPB14B
2006 Press Pass Legends Press Plates Black Backs /1 #PPB46B
2006 Press Pass Legends Press Plates Black Backs /1 #PPB48B
2006 Press Pass Legends Press Plates Black Backs /1 #PPB49B
2006 Press Pass Legends Press Plates Cyan /1 #PPC14
2006 Press Pass Legends Press Plates Cyan /1 #PPC46
2006 Press Pass Legends Press Plates Cyan /1 #PPC48
2006 Press Pass Legends Press Plates Cyan /1 #PPC49
2006 Press Pass Legends Press Plates Cyan Backs /1 #PPC14B
2006 Press Pass Legends Press Plates Cyan Backs /1 #PPC46B
2006 Press Pass Legends Press Plates Cyan Backs /1 #PPC48B
2006 Press Pass Legends Press Plates Cyan Backs /1 #PPC49B
2006 Press Pass Legends Press Plates Magenta /1 #PPM14
2006 Press Pass Legends Press Plates Magenta /1 #PPM46
2006 Press Pass Legends Press Plates Magenta /1 #PPM48
2006 Press Pass Legends Press Plates Magenta /1 #PPM49
2006 Press Pass Legends Press Plates Magenta Backs /1 #PPM14B
2006 Press Pass Legends Press Plates Magenta Backs /1 #PPM46B
2006 Press Pass Legends Press Plates Magenta Backs /1 #PPM48B
2006 Press Pass Legends Press Plates Magenta Backs /1 #PPM49B
2006 Press Pass Legends Press Plates Yellow /1 #PPY14
2006 Press Pass Legends Press Plates Yellow /1 #PPY46
2006 Press Pass Legends Press Plates Yellow /1 #PPY48
2006 Press Pass Legends Press Plates Yellow /1 #PPY49
2006 Press Pass Legends Press Plates Yellow Backs /1 #PPY14B
2006 Press Pass Legends Press Plates Yellow Backs /1 #PPY46B
2006 Press Pass Legends Press Plates Yellow Backs /1 #PPY48B
2006 Press Pass Legends Press Plates Yellow Backs /1 #PPY49B
2006 Press Pass Legends Previews /5 #EB14
2006 Press Pass Legends Previews /1 #EB46
2006 Press Pass Legends Previews /1 #EB48
2006 Press Pass Legends Previews /1 #EB49
2006 Press Pass Legends Racing Artifacts Hat /99 #RPH
2006 Press Pass Legends Solo /1 #S14
2006 Press Pass Legends Solo /1 #S46
2006 Press Pass Legends Solo /1 #S48
2006 Press Pass Legends Solo /1 #S49
2006 Press Pass Optima #65
2006 Press Pass Optima Gold /100 #G65
2006 Press Pass Signings #47
2006 Press Pass Signings Gold /50 #47
2006 Press Pass Signings Gold Red Ink #47
2006 Press Pass Signings Silver /100 #47
2006 TRAKS #83
2006 TRAKS Previews /1 #83
2006 Wheels Autographs #48
2007 Press Pass Legends #18
2007 Press Pass Legends #55
2007 Press Pass Legends #66
2007 Press Pass Legends #69
2007 Press Pass Legends Autographs Black /48 #12
2007 Press Pass Legends Autographs Blue /570 #24
2007 Press Pass Legends Autographs Inscriptions Blue /19 #15
2007 Press Pass Legends Blue /999 #B18
2007 Press Pass Legends Blue /999 #B55
2007 Press Pass Legends Blue /999 #B66
2007 Press Pass Legends Blue /999 #B69
2007 Press Pass Legends Bronze /599 #Z18
2007 Press Pass Legends Bronze /599 #Z55
2007 Press Pass Legends Bronze /599 #Z66
2007 Press Pass Legends Bronze /599 #Z69
2007 Press Pass Legends Gold /249 #G18
2007 Press Pass Legends Gold /249 #G55
2007 Press Pass Legends Gold /249 #G66
2007 Press Pass Legends Gold /249 #G69
2007 Press Pass Legends Holofoil /99 #H18
2007 Press Pass Legends Holofoil /99 #H55
2007 Press Pass Legends Holofoil /99 #H66
2007 Press Pass Legends Holofoil /99 #H69
2007 Press Pass Legends Memorable Moments Gold /169 #MM6
2007 Press Pass Legends Memorable Moments Gold /169 #MM11
2007 Press Pass Legends Memorable Moments Silver /499 #MM6
2007 Press Pass Legends Memorable Moments Silver /499 #MM11
2007 Press Pass Legends Press Plates Black /1 #PP18
2007 Press Pass Legends Press Plates Black /1 #PP55
2007 Press Pass Legends Press Plates Black /1 #PP66
2007 Press Pass Legends Press Plates Black /1 #PP69
2007 Press Pass Legends Press Plates Black Backs /1 #PP18
2007 Press Pass Legends Press Plates Black Backs /1 #PP55
2007 Press Pass Legends Press Plates Black Backs /1 #PP66
2007 Press Pass Legends Press Plates Black Backs /1 #PP69
2007 Press Pass Legends Press Plates Cyan /1 #PP18
2007 Press Pass Legends Press Plates Cyan /1 #PP55
2007 Press Pass Legends Press Plates Cyan /1 #PP66
2007 Press Pass Legends Press Plates Cyan /1 #PP69
2007 Press Pass Legends Press Plates Cyan Backs /1 #PP18
2007 Press Pass Legends Press Plates Cyan Backs /1 #PP55
2007 Press Pass Legends Press Plates Cyan Backs /1 #PP66
2007 Press Pass Legends Press Plates Cyan Backs /1 #PP69
2007 Press Pass Legends Press Plates Magenta /1 #PP18
2007 Press Pass Legends Press Plates Magenta /1 #PP55
2007 Press Pass Legends Press Plates Magenta /1 #PP66
2007 Press Pass Legends Press Plates Magenta /1 #PP69
2007 Press Pass Legends Press Plates Magenta Backs /1 #PP18
2007 Press Pass Legends Press Plates Magenta Backs /1 #PP55
2007 Press Pass Legends Press Plates Magenta Backs /1 #PP66
2007 Press Pass Legends Press Plates Magenta Backs /1 #PP69
2007 Press Pass Legends Press Plates Yellow /1 #PP18
2007 Press Pass Legends Press Plates Yellow /1 #PP55
2007 Press Pass Legends Press Plates Yellow /1 #PP66
2007 Press Pass Legends Press Plates Yellow /1 #PP69
2007 Press Pass Legends Press Plates Yellow Backs /1 #PP18
2007 Press Pass Legends Press Plates Yellow Backs /1 #PP55
2007 Press Pass Legends Press Plates Yellow Backs /1 #PP66
2007 Press Pass Legends Press Plates Yellow Backs /1 #PP69
2007 Press Pass Legends Previews /5 #EB18
2007 Press Pass Legends Previews /1 #EB66
2007 Press Pass Legends Previews /1 #EB69
2007 Press Pass Legends Racing Artifacts Hat /50 #RPH
2007 Press Pass Legends Solo /1 #S18
2007 Press Pass Legends Solo /1 #S55
2007 Press Pass Legends Solo /1 #S66
2007 Press Pass Legends Solo /1 #S69
2007 Press Pass Signings #57
2007 Press Pass Signings Blue Daytona /150 #6
2007 Press Pass Signings Press Plates Black /1 #35
2007 Press Pass Signings Press Plates Cyan /1 #34
2007 Press Pass Signings Press Plates Magenta /1 #36
2007 Press Pass Signings Press Plates Yellow /1 #35
2008 Americana Celebrity Cuts /499 #73
2008 Americana Celebrity Cuts Century Gold /25 #73
2008 Americana Celebrity Cuts Century Material /100 #73
2008 Americana Celebrity Cuts Century Material Combo /50 #73
2008 Americana Celebrity Cuts Century Platinum /1 #73
2008 Americana Celebrity Cuts Century Signature Gold /200 #73
2008 Americana Celebrity Cuts Century Signature Material /50 #73
2008 Americana Celebrity Cuts Century Signature Material Combo /10 #73
2008 Americana Celebrity Cuts Century Signature Platinum /1 #73
2008 Americana Celebrity Cuts Century Silver /50 #73
2008 Americana II Sports Legends /500 #12
2008 Americana II Sports Legends Material /100 #12
2008 Americana II Sports Legends Signature /50 #12
2008 Americana II Sports Legends Signature Material /100 #12
2008 Donruss Sports Legends #137
2008 Donruss Sports Legends Certified Cuts /20 #20
2008 Donruss Sports Legends Materials Mirror Black /1 #137
2008 Donruss Sports Legends Materials Mirror Blue /250 #137
2008 Donruss Sports Legends Materials Mirror Emerald /5 #137
2008 Donruss Sports Legends Materials Mirror Gold /25 #137
2008 Donruss Sports Legends Materials Mirror Red /400 #137
2008 Donruss Sports Legends Mirror Black /1 #137
2008 Donruss Sports Legends Mirror Blue /100 #137
2008 Donruss Sports Legends Mirror Emerald /5 #137
2008 Donruss Sports Legends Mirror Gold /25 #137
2008 Donruss Sports Legends Mirror Red /250 #137
2008 Donruss Sports Legends Signature Connection Combos /100 #16
2008 Donruss Sports Legends Signatures Mirror Black /1 #137
2008 Donruss Sports Legends Signatures Mirror Blue /65 #137
2008 Donruss Sports Legends Signatures Mirror Emerald /5 #137
2008 Donruss Sports Legends Signatures Mirror Gold /10 #137
2008 Press Pass Daytona 500 50th Anniversary #5
2008 Press Pass Daytona 500 50th Anniversary #7
2008 Press Pass Daytona 500 50th Anniversary #11
2008 Press Pass Daytona 500 50th Anniversary #12
2008 Press Pass Daytona 500 50th Anniversary #13
2008 Press Pass Daytona 500 50th Anniversary #18
2008 Press Pass Daytona 500 50th Anniversary #20
2008 Press Pass Daytona 500 50th Anniversary #46
2008 Press Pass Legends #30
2008 Press Pass Legends #62
2008 Press Pass Legends 500 Club /560 #5C1
2008 Press Pass Legends 500 Club Cut Autographs /2 #5CCRP
2008 Press Pass Legends 500 Club Gold /99 #5C1
2008 Press Pass Legends Autographs Blue /717 #RP
2008 Press Pass Legends Autographs Blue Inscriptions /52 #RP
2008 Press Pass Legends Autographs Press Plates Black /1 #RP
2008 Press Pass Legends Autographs Press Plates Cyan /1 #RP
2008 Press Pass Legends Autographs Press Plates Magenta /1 #RP
2008 Press Pass Legends Autographs Press Plates Yellow /1 #RP
2008 Press Pass Legends Blue /599 #30
2008 Press Pass Legends Blue /599 #62
2008 Press Pass Legends Bronze /299 #30
2008 Press Pass Legends Bronze /299 #62
2008 Press Pass Legends Gold /99 #30
2008 Press Pass Legends Gold /99 #62
2008 Press Pass Legends Holo /25 #30
2008 Press Pass Legends Holo /25 #62
2008 Press Pass Legends Previews /5 #EB30
2008 Press Pass Legends Previews /1 #EB62
2008 Press Pass Legends Printing Plates Black /1 #30
2008 Press Pass Legends Printing Plates Black /1 #62
2008 Press Pass Legends Printing Plates Cyan /1 #30
2008 Press Pass Legends Printing Plates Cyan /1 #62
2008 Press Pass Legends Printing Plates Magenta /1 #30
2008 Press Pass Legends Printing Plates Magenta /1 #62
2008 Press Pass Legends Printing Plates Yellow /1 #30
2008 Press Pass Legends Printing Plates Yellow /1 #62
2008 Press Pass Legends Racing Artifacts Firesuit Bronze /180 #RPF
2008 Press Pass Legends Racing Artifacts Firesuit Gold /25 #RPF
2008 Press Pass Legends Racing Artifacts Firesuit Patch /10 #RPF
2008 Press Pass Legends Racing Artifacts Firesuit Silver /50 #RPF
2008 Press Pass Legends Racing Artifacts Hat /50 #RPH
2008 Press Pass Legends Solo /1 #30
2008 Press Pass Legends Solo /1 #62
2008 Press Pass Signings #49
2008 Press Pass Signings Blue /100 #24
2008 Press Pass Signings Press Plates Black /1 #32
2008 Press Pass Signings Press Plates Black /1 #RP
2008 Press Pass Signings Press Plates Cyan /1 #32
2008 Press Pass Signings Press Plates Magenta /1 #32
2008 Press Pass Signings Press Plates Magenta /1 #RP
2008 Press Pass Signings Press Plates Yellow /1 #32
2008 Wheels American Thunder #53
2009 Press Pass Autographs Track Edition /25 #RP
2009 Press Pass Four Wide Autographs /5 #FWRP
2009 Press Pass Fusion #76
2009 Press Pass Fusion Bronze /150 #76
2009 Press Pass Fusion Cross Training #CT8
2009 Press Pass Fusion Gold /50 #76
2009 Press Pass Fusion Green /25 #76
2009 Press Pass Fusion Onyx /1 #76
2009 Press Pass Fusion Revered Relics Gold /15 #RRRP
2009 Press Pass Fusion Revered Relics Holofoil /25 #RRRP
2009 Press Pass Fusion Revered Relics Premium Swatch /10 #RRRP
2009 Press Pass Fusion Silver /99 #76
2009 Press Pass Legends #27
2009 Press Pass Legends #63
2009 Press Pass Legends #66
2009 Press Pass Legends #67
2009 Press Pass Legends #68
2009 Press Pass Legends #69
2009 Press Pass Legends Artifacts Autographs /10 #SERP
2009 Press Pass Legends Artifacts Firesuits Bronze /199 #RPF
2009 Press Pass Legends Artifacts Firesuits Gold /25 #RPF
2009 Press Pass Legends Artifacts Firesuits Silver /50 #RPF
2009 Press Pass Legends Artifacts Sheet Metal Bronze /199 #RPS
2009 Press Pass Legends Artifacts Sheet Metal Gold /25 #RPS
2009 Press Pass Legends Artifacts Sheet Metal Silver /50 #RPS
2009 Press Pass Legends Autographs #12
2009 Press Pass Legends Autographs Gold /105 #27
2009 Press Pass Legends Autographs Holofoil /25 #24
2009 Press Pass Legends Autographs Printing Plates Black /1 #21
2009 Press Pass Legends Autographs Printing Plates Cyan /1 #20
2009 Press Pass Legends Autographs Printing Plates Magenta /1 #21
2009 Press Pass Legends Autographs Printing Plates Yellow /1 #21
2009 Press Pass Legends Autographs Red /55 #7
2009 Press Pass Legends Family Cuts /1 #3
2009 Press Pass Legends Family Portraits /550 #FP20
2009 Press Pass Legends Family Portraits /550 #FP21
2009 Press Pass Legends Family Portraits /550 #FP22
2009 Press Pass Legends Family Portraits /550 #FP23
2009 Press Pass Legends Family Portraits Holofoil /99 #FP20
2009 Press Pass Legends Family Portraits Holofoil /99 #FP21
2009 Press Pass Legends Family Portraits Holofoil /99 #FP22
2009 Press Pass Legends Family Portraits Holofoil /99 #FP23
2009 Press Pass Legends Gold /399 #27
2009 Press Pass Legends Gold /399 #63
2009 Press Pass Legends Gold /399 #66
2009 Press Pass Legends Gold /399 #67
2009 Press Pass Legends Gold /399 #68
2009 Press Pass Legends Gold /399 #69
2009 Press Pass Legends Holofoil /50 #27
2009 Press Pass Legends Holofoil /50 #63
2009 Press Pass Legends Holofoil /50 #66
2009 Press Pass Legends Holofoil /50 #67
2009 Press Pass Legends Holofoil /50 #68
2009 Press Pass Legends Holofoil /50 #69
2009 Press Pass Legends Past and Present /550 #PP1
2009 Press Pass Legends Past and Present /550 #PP9
2009 Press Pass Legends Past and Present Holofoil /99 #PP1
2009 Press Pass Legends Past and Present Holofoil /99 #PP9
2009 Press Pass Legends Petty 200th Win Autographs /25 #RP1
2009 Press Pass Legends Petty 200th Win Autographs /25 #RP2
2009 Press Pass Legends Petty 200th Win Autographs /25 #RP3
2009 Press Pass Legends Petty 200th Win Autographs /25 #RP4
2009 Press Pass Legends Petty 200th Win Cut /1 #1
2009 Press Pass Legends Previews /5 #27
2009 Press Pass Legends Previews /1 #63
2009 Press Pass Legends Previews /1 #66
2009 Press Pass Legends Previews /1 #67
2009 Press Pass Legends Previews /1 #68
2009 Press Pass Legends Previews /1 #69
2009 Press Pass Legends Printing Plates Black /1 #27
2009 Press Pass Legends Printing Plates Black /1 #63
2009 Press Pass Legends Printing Plates Black /1 #66
2009 Press Pass Legends Printing Plates Black /1 #67
2009 Press Pass Legends Printing Plates Black /1 #68
2009 Press Pass Legends Printing Plates Black /1 #69
2009 Press Pass Legends Printing Plates Cyan /1 #27
2009 Press Pass Legends Printing Plates Cyan /1 #63
2009 Press Pass Legends Printing Plates Cyan /1 #66
2009 Press Pass Legends Printing Plates Cyan /1 #67
2009 Press Pass Legends Printing Plates Cyan /1 #68
2009 Press Pass Legends Printing Plates Cyan /1 #69
2009 Press Pass Legends Printing Plates Magenta /1 #27
2009 Press Pass Legends Printing Plates Magenta /1 #63
2009 Press Pass Legends Printing Plates Magenta /1 #66
2009 Press Pass Legends Printing Plates Magenta /1 #67
2009 Press Pass Legends Printing Plates Magenta /1 #68
2009 Press Pass Legends Printing Plates Magenta /1 #69
2009 Press Pass Legends Printing Plates Yellow /1 #27
2009 Press Pass Legends Printing Plates Yellow /1 #63
2009 Press Pass Legends Printing Plates Yellow /1 #66
2009 Press Pass Legends Printing Plates Yellow /1 #67
2009 Press Pass Legends Printing Plates Yellow /1 #68
2009 Press Pass Legends Printing Plates Yellow /1 #69
2009 Press Pass Legends Red /199 #27
2009 Press Pass Legends Red /199 #63
2009 Press Pass Legends Red /199 #66
2009 Press Pass Legends Red /199 #67
2009 Press Pass Legends Red /199 #68
2009 Press Pass Legends Red /199 #69
2009 Press Pass Legends Rivalries Autographs /10 #1
2009 Press Pass Legends Solo /1 #27
2009 Press Pass Legends Solo /1 #63
2009 Press Pass Legends Solo /1 #66
2009 Press Pass Legends Solo /1 #67
2009 Press Pass Legends Solo /1 #68
2009 Press Pass Legends Solo /1 #69
2009 Press Pass Pocket Portraits #P30
2009 Press Pass Pocket Portraits Checkered Flag #P30
2009 Press Pass Pocket Portraits Hometown #P30
2009 Press Pass Pocket Portraits Smoke #P30
2009 Press Pass Pocket Portraits Wal-Mart #PPW6
2009 Press Pass Showcase /499 #49
2009 Press Pass Showcase 2nd Gear /125 #49
2009 Press Pass Showcase 3rd Gear /50 #49
2009 Press Pass Showcase 4th Gear /15 #49
2009 Press Pass Showcase Elite Exhibit Ink /45 #10
2009 Press Pass Showcase Elite Exhibit Ink Gold /25 #10
2009 Press Pass Showcase Elite Exhibit Ink Green /5 #10
2009 Press Pass Showcase Elite Exhibit Ink Melting /1 #10
2009 Press Pass Showcase Printing Plates Black /1 #49
2009 Press Pass Showcase Printing Plates Cyan /1 #49
2009 Press Pass Showcase Printing Plates Magenta /1 #49
2009 Press Pass Showcase Printing Plates Yellow /1 #49
2009 Press Pass Showcase Prized Pieces Ink Firesuit /5 #9
2009 Press Pass Showcase Prized Pieces Ink Firesuit Patch /1 #9
2009 Sportkings National Convention Memorabilia Gold /1 #SK6
2009 Sportkings National Convention Memorabilia Silver /9 #SK6
2009 Topps American Heritage Heroes Presidential Medal of Freedom #MOF16
2010 Press Pass #106
2010 Press Pass Blue #106
2010 Press Pass By The Numbers #BN5
2010 Press Pass By The Numbers #BN25
2010 Press Pass By The Numbers #BN42
2010 Press Pass By The Numbers #BN7
2010 Press Pass Eclipse #46
2010 Press Pass Eclipse Blue #46
2010 Press Pass Eclipse Gold #46
2010 Press Pass Eclipse Previews /1 #46
2010 Press Pass Eclipse Purple /25 #46
2010 Press Pass Eclipse Spellbound Swatches Holofoil /7 #SSRP2
2010 Press Pass Eclipse Spellbound Swatches Holofoil /7 #SSRP3
2010 Press Pass Eclipse Spellbound Swatches Holofoil /7 #SSRP4
2010 Press Pass Eclipse Spellbound Swatches Holofoil /7 #SSRP5
2010 Press Pass Eclipse Spellbound Swatches Holofoil /43 #SSRP1
2010 Press Pass Five Star /35 #1
2010 Press Pass Five Star Classic Compilations Combos Firesuit Autographs /15 #CCMLEG

2010 Press Pass Five Star Classic Compilations Combos Patches Autographs /1 #CCMLEG
2010 Press Pass Five Star Classic Compilations Dual Memorabilia Autographs /10 #RP
2010 Press Pass Five Star Classic Compilations Firesuit Autographs /2 #RP
2010 Press Pass Five Star Classic Compilations Patch Autographs /1 #CCPRP1
2010 Press Pass Five Star Classic Compilations Patch Autographs /1 #CCPRP2
2010 Press Pass Five Star Classic Compilations Patch Autographs /1 #CCPRP3
2010 Press Pass Five Star Classic Compilations Patch Autographs /1 #CCPRP4
2010 Press Pass Five Star Classic Compilations Patch Autographs /1 #CCPRP5
2010 Press Pass Five Star Classic Compilations Patch Autographs /1 #CCPRP6
2010 Press Pass Five Star Classic Compilations Patch Autographs /1 #CCPRP7
2010 Press Pass Five Star Classic Compilations Sheet Metal Autographs /25 #RP
2010 Press Pass Five Star Classic Compilations Triple Memorabilia Autographs /5 #RP
2010 Press Pass Five Star Holofoil /10 #1
2010 Press Pass Five Star Melting /1 #1
2010 Press Pass Five Star Paramount Pieces Aluminum /25 #RP
2010 Press Pass Five Star Paramount Pieces Blue /20 #RP
2010 Press Pass Five Star Paramount Pieces Gold /15 #RP
2010 Press Pass Five Star Paramount Pieces Holofoil /10 #RP
2010 Press Pass Five Star Paramount Pieces Melting /1 #RP
2010 Press Pass Five Star Signature Souvenirs Aluminum /50 #SSRP
2010 Press Pass Five Star Signature Souvenirs Gold /25 #SSRP
2010 Press Pass Five Star Signature Souvenirs Holofoil /10 #SSRP
2010 Press Pass Five Star Signature Souvenirs Melting /1 #SSRP
2010 Press Pass Five Star Signatures Aluminum /35 #RP
2010 Press Pass Five Star Signatures Gold /20 #RP
2010 Press Pass Five Star Signatures Holofoil /5 #RP
2010 Press Pass Four Wide Autographs /5 #NNO
2010 Press Pass Gold #106
2010 Press Pass Holofoil /100 #106
2010 Press Pass Legends #30
2010 Press Pass Legends #72
2010 Press Pass Legends #61
2010 Press Pass Legends #59
2010 Press Pass Legends #57
2010 Press Pass Legends 50 Win Club Memorabilia Gold /75 #50RP
2010 Press Pass Legends 50 Win Club Memorabilia Holofoil /25 #50RP
2010 Press Pass Legends Autographs Blue /10 #47
2010 Press Pass Legends Autographs Copper /125 #29
2010 Press Pass Legends Autographs Gold /50 #31
2010 Press Pass Legends Autographs Holofoil /25 #47
2010 Press Pass Legends Autographs Printing Plates Black /1 #39
2010 Press Pass Legends Autographs Printing Plates Cyan /1 #39
2010 Press Pass Legends Autographs Printing Plates Magenta /1 #39
2010 Press Pass Legends Autographs Printing Plates Yellow /1 #39
2010 Press Pass Legends Blue /1 #57
2010 Press Pass Legends Blue /1 #59
2010 Press Pass Legends Blue /1 #61
2010 Press Pass Legends Blue /1 #72
2010 Press Pass Legends Gold /399 #30
2010 Press Pass Legends Gold /399 #57
2010 Press Pass Legends Gold /399 #59
2010 Press Pass Legends Gold /399 #61
2010 Press Pass Legends Gold /399 #72
2010 Press Pass Legends Holofoil /50 #30
2010 Press Pass Legends Holofoil /50 #57
2010 Press Pass Legends Holofoil /50 #59
2010 Press Pass Legends Holofoil /50 #61
2010 Press Pass Legends Holofoil /50 #72
2010 Press Pass Legends Lasting Legacies Autographs /25 #LLRP
2010 Press Pass Legends Lasting Legacies Copper /175 #LLRP3
2010 Press Pass Legends Lasting Legacies Copper /175 #LLRP2
2010 Press Pass Legends Lasting Legacies Copper /150 #LLRP1
2010 Press Pass Legends Lasting Legacies Gold /75 #LLRP4
2010 Press Pass Legends Lasting Legacies Gold /75 #LLRP1
2010 Press Pass Legends Lasting Legacies Gold /75 #LLRP2
2010 Press Pass Legends Lasting Legacies Gold /75 #LLRP3
2010 Press Pass Legends Lasting Legacies Holofoil /25 #LLRP1
2010 Press Pass Legends Lasting Legacies Holofoil /25 #LLRP3
2010 Press Pass Legends Lasting Legacies Holofoil /25 #LLRP2
2010 Press Pass Legends Lasting Legacies Holofoil /25 #LLRP4
2010 Press Pass Legends Make and Model Blue /99 #4
2010 Press Pass Legends Make and Model Blue /99 #5
2010 Press Pass Legends Make and Model Gold /299 #5
2010 Press Pass Legends Make and Model Gold /299 #4
2010 Press Pass Legends Make and Model Holofoil /199 #4
2010 Press Pass Legends Make and Model Holofoil /199 #5
2010 Press Pass Legends Memorable Matchups /25 #MMRPCY
2010 Press Pass Legends Memorable Matchups /25 #MMRPDP
2010 Press Pass Legends Memorable Matchups Autographs /25 #NNO
2010 Press Pass Legends Memorable Matchups Autographs /21 #NNO
2010 Press Pass Legends Motorsports Masters #MMRP
2010 Press Pass Legends Motorsports Masters Autographs Blue /1 #NNO
2010 Press Pass Legends Motorsports Masters Autographs Gold /50 #24
2010 Press Pass Legends Motorsports Masters Autographs Holofoil /25 #24
2010 Press Pass Legends Motorsports Masters Autographs Printing Plates Black /1 #39
2010 Press Pass Legends Motorsports Masters Autographs Printing Plates Cyan /1 #39
2010 Press Pass Legends Motorsports Masters Autographs Printing Plates Magenta /1 #39
2010 Press Pass Legends Motorsports Masters Autographs Printing Plates Yellow /1 #39
2010 Press Pass Legends Motorsports Masters Autographs Silver /99 #20
2010 Press Pass Legends Motorsports Masters Blue /10 #MMRP
2010 Press Pass Legends Motorsports Masters Gold /299 #MMRP
2010 Press Pass Legends Motorsports Masters Holofoil /149 #MMRP
2010 Press Pass Legends Printing Plates Black /1 #30
2010 Press Pass Legends Printing Plates Black /1 #57
2010 Press Pass Legends Printing Plates Black /1 #59
2010 Press Pass Legends Printing Plates Black /1 #61
2010 Press Pass Legends Printing Plates Black /1 #72
2010 Press Pass Legends Printing Plates Cyan /1 #30
2010 Press Pass Legends Printing Plates Cyan /1 #57
2010 Press Pass Legends Printing Plates Cyan /1 #59
2010 Press Pass Legends Printing Plates Cyan /1 #61
2010 Press Pass Legends Printing Plates Cyan /1 #72
2010 Press Pass Legends Printing Plates Magenta /1 #30
2010 Press Pass Legends Printing Plates Magenta /1 #57
2010 Press Pass Legends Printing Plates Magenta /1 #59
2010 Press Pass Legends Printing Plates Magenta /1 #61
2010 Press Pass Legends Printing Plates Magenta /1 #72
2010 Press Pass Legends Printing Plates Yellow /1 #30
2010 Press Pass Legends Printing Plates Yellow /1 #57
2010 Press Pass Legends Printing Plates Yellow /1 #59
2010 Press Pass Legends Printing Plates Yellow /1 #61
2010 Press Pass Legends Printing Plates Yellow /1 #72
2010 Press Pass Legends Red /199 #30
2010 Press Pass Legends Red /199 #57
2010 Press Pass Legends Red /199 #59
2010 Press Pass Legends Red /199 #61
2010 Press Pass Legends Red /199 #72
2010 Press Pass NASCAR Hall of Fame #NHOF16
2010 Press Pass NASCAR Hall of Fame #NHOF29
2010 Press Pass NASCAR Hall of Fame #NHOF40
2010 Press Pass NASCAR Hall of Fame #NHOF61
2010 Press Pass NASCAR Hall of Fame #NHOF62
2010 Press Pass NASCAR Hall of Fame #NHOF63
2010 Press Pass NASCAR Hall of Fame #NHOF64
2010 Press Pass NASCAR Hall of Fame #NHOF65
2010 Press Pass NASCAR Hall of Fame #NHOF66
2010 Press Pass NASCAR Hall of Fame #NHOF67
2010 Press Pass NASCAR Hall of Fame #NHOF68
2010 Press Pass NASCAR Hall of Fame #NHOF69
2010 Press Pass NASCAR Hall of Fame #NHOF70
2010 Press Pass NASCAR Hall of Fame #NHOF27
2010 Press Pass NASCAR Hall of Fame Blue #NHOF27
2010 Press Pass NASCAR Hall of Fame Blue #NHOF29
2010 Press Pass NASCAR Hall of Fame Blue #NHOF16
2010 Press Pass NASCAR Hall of Fame Blue #NHOF40
2010 Press Pass NASCAR Hall of Fame Blue #NHOF61
2010 Press Pass NASCAR Hall of Fame Blue #NHOF62
2010 Press Pass NASCAR Hall of Fame Blue #NHOF63
2010 Press Pass NASCAR Hall of Fame Blue #NHOF64
2010 Press Pass NASCAR Hall of Fame Blue #NHOF65
2010 Press Pass NASCAR Hall of Fame Blue #NHOF66
2010 Press Pass NASCAR Hall of Fame Blue #NHOF67
2010 Press Pass NASCAR Hall of Fame Blue #NHOF68
2010 Press Pass NASCAR Hall of Fame Blue #NHOF69
2010 Press Pass NASCAR Hall of Fame Blue #NHOF70
2010 Press Pass NASCAR Hall of Fame Holofoil /50 #NHOF27
2010 Press Pass NASCAR Hall of Fame Holofoil /50 #NHOF29
2010 Press Pass NASCAR Hall of Fame Holofoil /50 #NHOF40
2010 Press Pass NASCAR Hall of Fame Holofoil /50 #NHOF61
2010 Press Pass NASCAR Hall of Fame Holofoil /50 #NHOF62
2010 Press Pass NASCAR Hall of Fame Holofoil /50 #NHOF63
2010 Press Pass NASCAR Hall of Fame Holofoil /50 #NHOF64
2010 Press Pass NASCAR Hall of Fame Holofoil /50 #NHOF65
2010 Press Pass NASCAR Hall of Fame Holofoil /50 #NHOF66
2010 Press Pass NASCAR Hall of Fame Holofoil /50 #NHOF67
2010 Press Pass NASCAR Hall of Fame Holofoil /50 #NHOF68
2010 Press Pass NASCAR Hall of Fame Holofoil /50 #NHOF69
2010 Press Pass NASCAR Hall of Fame Holofoil /50 #NHOF70
2010 Press Pass NASCAR Hall of Fame Holofoil /50 #NHOF16
2010 Press Pass Premium Rivals #R8
2010 Press Pass Premium Signature Series Firesuit /10 #SSFRP
2010 Press Pass Purple /25 #106
2010 Press Pass Showcase /499 #29
2010 Press Pass Showcase Classic Collections Firesuit Green /25 #CCI500
2010 Press Pass Showcase Classic Collections Firesuit Patch Melting /5 #CCI500
2010 Press Pass Showcase Classic Collections Ink /15 #CCI500
2010 Press Pass Showcase Classic Collections Ink Gold /10 #CCI500
2010 Press Pass Showcase Classic Collections Ink Green /5 #CCI500
2010 Press Pass Showcase Classic Collections Ink Melting /1 #CCI500
2010 Press Pass Showcase Elite Exhibit Triple Memorabilia Gold /15 #EEMRP
2010 Press Pass Showcase Elite Exhibit Triple Memorabilia Green /10 #EEMRP
2010 Press Pass Showcase Elite Exhibit Triple Memorabilia Melting /5 #EEMRP
2010 Press Pass Showcase Gold /125 #29
2010 Press Pass Showcase Green /50 #29
2010 Press Pass Showcase Melting /15 #29
2010 Press Pass Showcase Platinum Holo /1 #29
2010 Press Pass Showcase Prized Pieces Firesuit Green /10 #PPMJL
2010 Press Pass Showcase Prized Pieces Firesuit Ink Gold /25 #PPIRP
2010 Press Pass Showcase Prized Pieces Firesuit Ink Melting /1 #PPIRP
2010 Press Pass Showcase Prized Pieces Firesuit Patch Melting /5 #PPMJL
2010 Press Pass Showcase Prized Pieces Memorabilia Ink Green /15 #PPIRP
2010 Press Pass Showcase Prized Pieces Sheet Metal /45 #PPMJL
2010 Press Pass Showcase Prized Pieces Sheet Metal Gold /15 #PPMJL
2010 Press Pass Showcase Prized Pieces Sheet Metal Ink Silver /45 #PPIRP
2010 Press Pass Showcase Racing's Finest /499 #RF2
2010 Press Pass Showcase Racing's Finest Gold /125 #RF2
2010 Press Pass Showcase Racing's Finest Green /50 #RF2
2010 Press Pass Showcase Racing's Finest Ink /25 #RFIRP
2010 Press Pass Showcase Racing's Finest Ink Gold /10 #RFIRP
2010 Press Pass Showcase Racing's Finest Ink Green /5 #RFIRP
2010 Press Pass Showcase Racing's Finest Ink Melting /1 #RFIRP
2010 Press Pass Showcase Racing's Finest Melting /15 #RF2
2011 Element Tales from the Track #TT3
2011 Element Tales from the Track #TT4
2011 Element Tales from the Track #TT7
2011 Leaf Cut Signature Edition /9 #591
2011 Leaf Legends of Sport Cut Signatures #RP5
2011 Press Pass FanFare #92
2011 Press Pass FanFare Blue Die Cuts #92
2011 Press Pass FanFare Championship Caliber #CC15
2011 Press Pass FanFare Emerald /25 #92
2011 Press Pass FanFare Holofoil Die Cuts #92
2011 Press Pass FanFare Rookie Standouts #RS15
2011 Press Pass FanFare Ruby Die Cuts /15 #92
2011 Press Pass FanFare Sapphire /10 #92
2011 Press Pass FanFare Silver /25 #92
2011 Press Pass Legends #30
2011 Press Pass Legends #55
2011 Press Pass Legends #75
2011 Press Pass Legends #76
2011 Press Pass Legends Autographs Blue /5 #LGARP
2011 Press Pass Legends Autographs Gold /10 #LGARP
2011 Press Pass Legends Autographs Printing Plates Black /1 #LGARP
2011 Press Pass Legends Autographs Printing Plates Cyan /1 #LGARP
2011 Press Pass Legends Autographs Printing Plates Magenta /1 #LGARP
2011 Press Pass Legends Autographs Printing Plates Yellow /1 #LGARP
2011 Press Pass Legends Autographs Silver /25 #LGARP
2011 Press Pass Legends Famed Fabrics Gold /50 #HOFRP
2011 Press Pass Legends Famed Fabrics Holofoil /25 #HOFRP
2011 Press Pass Legends Famed Fabrics Purple /15 #HOFRP
2011 Press Pass Legends Gold /250 #30
2011 Press Pass Legends Gold /250 #55
2011 Press Pass Legends Gold /250 #75
2011 Press Pass Legends Gold /250 #76
2011 Press Pass Legends Holofoil /25 #30
2011 Press Pass Legends Holofoil /25 #55
2011 Press Pass Legends Holofoil /25 #75
2011 Press Pass Legends Holofoil /25 #76
2011 Press Pass Legends Lasting Legacies Autographs /25 #LLSERP
2011 Press Pass Legends Lasting Legacies Memorabilia Gold /50 #LLRP
2011 Press Pass Legends Lasting Legacies Memorabilia Holofoil /25 #LLRP
2011 Press Pass Legends Lasting Legacies Memorabilia Purple /15 #LLRP
2011 Press Pass Legends Lasting Legacies Memorabilia Silver /175 #LLRP
2011 Press Pass Legends Motorsports Masters #MM13
2011 Press Pass Legends Motorsports Masters Autographs Blue /1 #MMAERP
2011 Press Pass Legends Motorsports Masters Autographs Gold /5 #MMAERP
2011 Press Pass Legends Motorsports Masters Autographs Printing Plates Black /1 #MMAERP
2011 Press Pass Legends Motorsports Masters Autographs Printing Plates Cyan /1 #MMAERP
2011 Press Pass Legends Motorsports Masters Autographs Printing Plates Magenta /1 #MMAERP
2011 Press Pass Legends Motorsports Masters Autographs Printing Plates Yellow /1 #MMAERP
2011 Press Pass Legends Motorsports Masters Autographs Silver /25 #MMAERP
2011 Press Pass Legends Motorsports Masters Brushed Foil /199 #MM13
2011 Press Pass Legends Motorsports Masters Holofoil /50 #MM13
2011 Press Pass Legends Pacing The Field #PF2
2011 Press Pass Legends Pacing The Field Autographs Blue /10 #PFARP
2011 Press Pass Legends Pacing The Field Autographs Printing Plates Black /1 #PFARP
2011 Press Pass Legends Pacing The Field Autographs Printing Plates Cyan /1 #PFARP
2011 Press Pass Legends Pacing The Field Autographs Printing Plates Magenta /1 #PFARP
2011 Press Pass Legends Pacing The Field Autographs Printing Plates Yellow /1 #PFARP
2011 Press Pass Legends Pacing The Field Autographs Silver /15 #PFARP
2011 Press Pass Legends Pacing The Field Brushed Foil /199 #PF2
2011 Press Pass Legends Pacing The Field Holofoil /50 #PF2
2011 Press Pass Legends Printing Plates Black /1 #30
2011 Press Pass Legends Printing Plates Black /1 #55
2011 Press Pass Legends Printing Plates Black /1 #75
2011 Press Pass Legends Printing Plates Black /1 #76
2011 Press Pass Legends Printing Plates Cyan /1 #30
2011 Press Pass Legends Printing Plates Cyan /1 #55
2011 Press Pass Legends Printing Plates Cyan /1 #75
2011 Press Pass Legends Printing Plates Cyan /1 #76
2011 Press Pass Legends Printing Plates Magenta /1 #30
2011 Press Pass Legends Printing Plates Magenta /1 #55
2011 Press Pass Legends Printing Plates Magenta /1 #75
2011 Press Pass Legends Printing Plates Magenta /1 #76
2011 Press Pass Legends Printing Plates Yellow /1 #30
2011 Press Pass Legends Printing Plates Yellow /1 #55
2011 Press Pass Legends Printing Plates Yellow /1 #75
2011 Press Pass Legends Printing Plates Yellow /1 #76
2011 Press Pass Legends Purple /25 #30
2011 Press Pass Legends Purple /25 #55
2011 Press Pass Legends Purple /25 #75
2011 Press Pass Legends Purple /25 #76
2011 Press Pass Legends Red /99 #30
2011 Press Pass Legends Red /99 #55
2011 Press Pass Legends Red /99 #75
2011 Press Pass Legends Red /99 #76
2011 Press Pass Legends Solo /1 #30
2011 Press Pass Legends Solo /1 #55
2011 Press Pass Legends Solo /1 #75
2011 Press Pass Legends Solo /1 #76
2011 Press Pass Legends Trophy Room Gold /50 #TRRP
2011 Press Pass Legends Trophy Room Holofoil /25 #TRRP
2011 Press Pass Legends Trophy Room Purple /15 #TRRP
2011 Press Pass Showcase /499 #28
2011 Press Pass Showcase Champions /499 #CH2
2011 Press Pass Showcase Champions Gold /125 #CH2
2011 Press Pass Showcase Champions Ink /25 #CHIRP
2011 Press Pass Showcase Champions Ink Gold /10 #CHIRP
2011 Press Pass Showcase Champions Ink Melting /1 #CHIRP
2011 Press Pass Showcase Champions Melting /1 #CH2
2011 Press Pass Showcase Champions Memorabilia Firesuit /99 #CHMRP
2011 Press Pass Showcase Champions Memorabilia Firesuit Gold /45 #CHMRP
2011 Press Pass Showcase Champions Memorabilia Firesuit Melting /5 #CHMRP
2011 Press Pass Showcase Gold /125 #28
2011 Press Pass Showcase Green /25 #28
2011 Press Pass Showcase Melting /1 #28
2011 Press Pass Showcase Prized Pieces Firesuit /99 #PPMRP
2011 Press Pass Showcase Prized Pieces Firesuit Gold /45 #PPMRP
2011 Press Pass Showcase Prized Pieces Firesuit Ink /25 #PPIRP
2011 Press Pass Showcase Prized Pieces Firesuit Patches Ink /1 #PPIRP
2011 Press Pass Showcase Prized Pieces Firesuit Patches Melting /5 #PPMRP
2011 Press Pass Showcase Prized Pieces Sheet Metal Ink /45 #PPIRP
2011 Press Pass Winning Tickets #WT49
2012 Historic Autographs Peerless /14 #125
2012 Leaf Cut Signature Edition /11 #727
2012 Leaf Sports Icons Cut Signatures /35 #381
2012 Leaf Sports Icons Cut Signatures Dual Cuts /2 #193
2012 Leaf Sports Icons Cut Signatures Dual Cuts /2 #318
2012 Leaf Sports Icons Cut Signatures Dual Cuts /2 #518
2012 Leaf Sports Icons Cut Signatures Dual Cuts /5 #536
2012 Leaf Sports Icons Cut Signatures Dual Cuts /4 #602
2012 Leaf Sports Icons Cut Signatures Dual Cuts /1 #708
2012 Panini Golden Age #93
2012 Panini Golden Age Black /1 #93
2012 Panini Golden Age Ferguson Bakery Pennants Blue #41
2012 Panini Golden Age Ferguson Bakery Pennants Yellow #41
2012 Panini Golden Age Historic Signatures #49
2012 Panini Golden Age Mini Black /1 #93
2012 Panini Golden Age Mini Broadleaf Blue Ink #93
2012 Panini Golden Age Mini Broadleaf Brown Ink #93
2012 Panini Golden Age Mini Crofts Candy Blue Ink #93
2012 Panini Golden Age Mini Crofts Candy Red Ink #93
2012 Panini Golden Age Mini Ty Cobb Tobacco #93
2012 Panini Golden Age Museum Age Memorabilia #18
2012 Press Pass Fanfare #95
2012 Press Pass Fanfare Blue Foil Die Cuts #95
2012 Press Pass Fanfare Diamond /5 #95
2012 Press Pass Fanfare Holofoil Die Cuts #95
2012 Press Pass Fanfare Sapphire /20 #95
2012 Press Pass Fanfare Silver /25 #95
2012 Press Pass Ignite Materials Gun Metal /50 #IMRP
2012 Press Pass Ignite Materials Red /10 #IMRP
2012 Press Pass Ignite Materials Silver #IMRP
2012 Press Pass Legends #31
2012 Press Pass Legends Autographs Blue /1 #RP
2012 Press Pass Legends Autographs Gold /5 #RP
2012 Press Pass Legends Autographs Holofoil /1 #RP
2012 Press Pass Legends Autographs Printing Plates Black /1 #RP
2012 Press Pass Legends Autographs Printing Plates Cyan /1 #RP
2012 Press Pass Legends Autographs Printing Plates Magenta /1 #RP
2012 Press Pass Legends Autographs Printing Plates Yellow /1 #RP
2012 Press Pass Legends Autographs Silver /5 #RP
2012 Press Pass Legends Blue Holofoil /1 #31
2012 Press Pass Legends Gold /275 #31
2012 Press Pass Legends Green #31
2012 Press Pass Legends Memorable Moments #MM2
2012 Press Pass Legends Memorable Moments #MM7
2012 Press Pass Legends Memorable Moments #MM10
2012 Press Pass Legends Memorable Moments Holofoil /99 #MM2
2012 Press Pass Legends Memorable Moments Holofoil /99 #MM7
2012 Press Pass Legends Memorable Moments Holofoil /99 #MM10
2012 Press Pass Legends Memorable Moments Melting /10 #MM2
2012 Press Pass Legends Memorable Moments Melting /10 #MM7
2012 Press Pass Legends Memorable Moments Melting /10 #MM10
2012 Press Pass Legends Pieces of History Memorabilia Autographs Gold /25 #PHSRP
2012 Press Pass Legends Pieces of History Memorabilia Autographs Melting /5 #PHSRP
2012 Press Pass Legends Pieces of History Memorabilia Gold /50 #RP2
2012 Press Pass Legends Pieces of History Memorabilia Gold /50 #RP3
2012 Press Pass Legends Pieces of History Memorabilia Gold /99 #RP1
2012 Press Pass Legends Pieces of History Memorabilia Holofoil /25 #RP1
2012 Press Pass Legends Pieces of History Memorabilia Holofoil /25 #RP2
2012 Press Pass Legends Pieces of History Memorabilia Holofoil /25 #RP3
2012 Press Pass Legends Pieces of History Memorabilia Silver /199 #RP1
2012 Press Pass Legends Pieces of History Memorabilia Silver /99 #RP2
2012 Press Pass Legends Pieces of History Memorabilia Silver /99 #RP3
2012 Press Pass Legends Rainbow Holofoil /50 #31
2012 Press Pass Legends Red /99 #31
2012 Press Pass Legends Silver Holofoil /25 #31
2012 Press Pass Legends Trailblazers #TB1
2012 Press Pass Legends Trailblazers Autographs Blue /1 #TBRP
2012 Press Pass Legends Trailblazers Autographs Gold /5 #TBRP
2012 Press Pass Legends Trailblazers Autographs Holofoil /1 #TBRP
2012 Press Pass Legends Trailblazers Autographs Printing Plates Black /1 #TBRP
2012 Press Pass Legends Trailblazers Autographs Printing Plates Cyan /1 #TBRP
2012 Press Pass Legends Trailblazers Autographs Printing Plates Magenta /1 #TBRP
2012 Press Pass Legends Trailblazers Autographs Printing Plates Yellow /1 #TBRP
2012 Press Pass Legends Trailblazers Autographs Silver /5 #TBRP
2012 Press Pass Power Picks Blue /50 #16
2012 Press Pass Power Picks Blue /50 #73
2012 Press Pass Power Picks Gold /50 #16
2012 Press Pass Power Picks Gold /50 #73
2012 Press Pass Power Picks Holofoil /10 #16
2012 Press Pass Power Picks Holofoil /10 #73
2012 Press Pass Redline #49
2012 Press Pass Redline Black /99 #49
2012 Press Pass Redline Cyan /50 #49
2012 Press Pass Redline Hall of Fame Relic Autographs Blue /5 #HOFRP
2012 Press Pass Redline Hall of Fame Relic Autographs Gold /25 #HOFRP
2012 Press Pass Redline Hall of Fame Relic Autographs Melting /1 #HOFRP
2012 Press Pass Redline Hall of Fame Relic Autographs Red /47 #HOFRP
2012 Press Pass Redline Magenta /15 #49
2012 Press Pass Redline Rookie Year Relic Autographs Blue /5 #RYRP
2012 Press Pass Redline Rookie Year Relic Autographs Gold /25 #RYRP
2012 Press Pass Redline Rookie Year Relic Autographs Melting /1 #RYRP
2012 Press Pass Redline Rookie Year Relic Autographs Red /50 #RYRP
2012 Press Pass Redline Yellow /1 #49
2012 Press Pass Showcase /499 #44
2012 Press Pass Showcase /499 #30
2012 Press Pass Showcase Champions Memorabilia /99 #CHRP
2012 Press Pass Showcase Champions Memorabilia Gold /50 #CHRP
2012 Press Pass Showcase Champions Memorabilia Melting /5 #CHRP
2012 Press Pass Showcase Champions Showcase /499 #CH1
2012 Press Pass Showcase Champions Showcase Gold /125 #CH1
2012 Press Pass Showcase Champions Showcase Ink /50 #CHSRP
2012 Press Pass Showcase Champions Showcase Ink Gold /25 #CHSRP
2012 Press Pass Showcase Champions Showcase Ink Melting /1 #CHSRP
2012 Press Pass Showcase Champions Showcase Melting /1 #CH1
2012 Press Pass Showcase Gold /125 #30
2012 Press Pass Showcase Gold /125 #44
2012 Press Pass Showcase Green /5 #30
2012 Press Pass Showcase Green /5 #44
2012 Press Pass Showcase Masterpieces Ink /50 #MPIRP
2012 Press Pass Showcase Masterpieces Ink Gold /25 #MPIRP
2012 Press Pass Showcase Masterpieces Ink Melting /1 #MPIRP
2012 Press Pass Showcase Masterpieces Memorabilia /99 #MPRP
2012 Press Pass Showcase Masterpieces Memorabilia Gold /50 #MPRP
2012 Press Pass Showcase Masterpieces Memorabilia Melting /5 #MPRP
2012 Press Pass Showcase Melting /1 #30
2012 Press Pass Showcase Melting /1 #44
2012 Press Pass Showcase Purple /1 #30
2012 Press Pass Showcase Purple /1 #44
2012 Press Pass Showcase Red /25 #30
2012 Press Pass Showcase Red /25 #44
2012 Press Pass Showcase Showroom /499 #SR8
2012 Press Pass Showcase Showroom Gold /125 #SR8
2012 Press Pass Showcase Showroom Melting /1 #SR8
2012 Press Pass Showcase Showroom Memorabilia /99 #SRRP
2012 Press Pass Showcase Showroom Memorabilia Gold /50 #SRRP
2012 Press Pass Showcase Showroom Memorabilia Melting /5 #SRRP
2012 Press Pass Snapshots #SS65
2012 Sportkings Premium Back Redemption Paintings /1 #44
2012 Topps Allen and Ginter #61
2012 Topps Allen and Ginter Autographs #RPT
2012 Topps Allen and Ginter Autographs Codebreakers #RPT
2012 Topps Allen and Ginter Autographs Red Ink /10 #RPT
2012 Topps Allen and Ginter Mini #61
2012 Topps Allen and Ginter Mini A and G Back #61
2012 Topps Allen and Ginter Mini A and G Red Back /25 #61
2012 Topps Allen and Ginter Mini Black #61
2012 Topps Allen and Ginter Mini Framed Printing Plates Black /1 #61
2012 Topps Allen and Ginter Mini Framed Printing Plates Cyan /1 #61
2012 Topps Allen and Ginter Mini Framed Printing Plates Magenta /1 #61
2012 Topps Allen and Ginter Mini Framed Printing Plates Yellow /1 #61
2012 Topps Allen and Ginter Mini Gold Border #61
2012 Topps Allen and Ginter Mini No Card Number #61
2012 Topps Allen and Ginter Mini Wood /1 #61
2012 Topps Allen and Ginter Relics #RPE
2012 Total Memorabilia #39
2012 Total Memorabilia Black and White /99 #39
2012 Total Memorabilia Gold /275 #39
2012 Total Memorabilia Red Retail /250 #39
2012 Upper Deck All-Time Greats /99 #54
2012 Upper Deck All-Time Greats /99 #55
2012 Upper Deck All-Time Greats /99 #56
2012 Upper Deck All-Time Greats /99 #57
2012 Upper Deck All-Time Greats /99 #58
2012 Upper Deck All-Time Greats Athletes of the Century Booklet Autographs /30 #ACRP
2012 Upper Deck All-Time Greats Blue /10 #54
2012 Upper Deck All-Time Greats Blue /10 #55
2012 Upper Deck All-Time Greats Blue /10 #56
2012 Upper Deck All-Time Greats Blue /10 #57
2012 Upper Deck All-Time Greats Blue /10 #58
2012 Upper Deck All-Time Greats Bronze /65 #54
2012 Upper Deck All-Time Greats Bronze /65 #55
2012 Upper Deck All-Time Greats Bronze /65 #56
2012 Upper Deck All-Time Greats Bronze /65 #57
2012 Upper Deck All-Time Greats Bronze /65 #58
2012 Upper Deck All-Time Greats Gold /1 #54
2012 Upper Deck All-Time Greats Gold /1 #55
2012 Upper Deck All-Time Greats Gold /1 #56
2012 Upper Deck All-Time Greats Gold /1 #57
2012 Upper Deck All-Time Greats Gold /1 #58
2012 Upper Deck All-Time Greats Legacy Cuts /2 #LPM
2012 Upper Deck All-Time Greats Letterman Autographs /25 #LRP
2012 Upper Deck All-Time Greats Personal Touch Autographs /10 #PTRP1
2012 Upper Deck All-Time Greats Personal Touch Autographs /10 #PTRP2
2012 Upper Deck All-Time Greats Personal Touch Autographs /10 #PTRP3
2012 Upper Deck All-Time Greats Personal Touch Autographs /10 #PTRP4
2012 Upper Deck All-Time Greats Personal Touch Autographs /10 #PTRP5
2012 Upper Deck All-Time Greats Personal Touch Autographs /10 #PTRP6
2012 Upper Deck All-Time Greats Shining Moments Autographs /20 #SMRP2
2012 Upper Deck All-Time Greats Shining Moments Autographs /20 #SMRP3
2012 Upper Deck All-Time Greats Shining Moments Autographs /20 #SMRP4
2012 Upper Deck All-Time Greats Shining Moments Autographs /20 #SMRP5
2012 Upper Deck All-Time Greats Shining Moments Autographs /20 #SMRP1
2012 Upper Deck All-Time Greats Shining Moments Autographs Gold /1 #SMRP1
2012 Upper Deck All-Time Greats Shining Moments Autographs Gold /1 #SMRP2
2012 Upper Deck All-Time Greats Shining Moments Autographs Gold /1 #SMRP3
2012 Upper Deck All-Time Greats Shining Moments Autographs Gold /1 #SMRP4
2012 Upper Deck All-Time Greats Shining Moments Autographs Gold /1 #SMRP5
2012 Upper Deck All-Time Greats Signatures /20 #GARP1
2012 Upper Deck All-Time Greats Signatures /20 #GARP2
2012 Upper Deck All-Time Greats Signatures /20 #GARP3
2012 Upper Deck All-Time Greats Signatures /20 #GARP4
2012 Upper Deck All-Time Greats Signatures /20 #GARP5
2012 Upper Deck All-Time Greats Signatures Gold /1 #GARP1
2012 Upper Deck All-Time Greats Signatures Gold /1 #GARP2
2012 Upper Deck All-Time Greats Signatures Gold /1 #GARP3
2012 Upper Deck All-Time Greats Signatures Gold /1 #GARP4
2012 Upper Deck All-Time Greats Signatures Gold /1 #GARP5
2012 Upper Deck All-Time Greats Signatures Silver /10 #GARP1
2012 Upper Deck All-Time Greats Signatures Silver /10 #GARP2
2012 Upper Deck All-Time Greats Signatures Silver /10 #GARP3
2012 Upper Deck All-Time Greats Signatures Silver /10 #GARP4
2012 Upper Deck All-Time Greats Signatures Silver /10 #GARP5
2012 Upper Deck All-Time Greats Silver /35 #54
2012 Upper Deck All-Time Greats Silver /35 #55
2012 Upper Deck All-Time Greats Silver /35 #56
2012 Upper Deck All-Time Greats Silver /35 #57
2012 Upper Deck All-Time Greats Silver /35 #58
2012 Upper Deck All-Time Greats SPx All-Time Forces Autographs /30 #ATFRP
2012 Upper Deck Goodwin Champions #62
2012 Upper Deck Goodwin Champions Autographs #ARP
2012 Upper Deck Goodwin Champions Mini #62
2012 Upper Deck Goodwin Champions Mini Foil /99 #62
2012 Upper Deck Goodwin Champions Mini Foil Magician Red /12 #62
2012 Upper Deck Goodwin Champions Mini Foil Presidential Gold /1 #62
2012 Upper Deck Goodwin Champions Mini Green #62
2012 Upper Deck Goodwin Champions Mini Green Blank Back #62
2012 Upper Deck Goodwin Champions Mini Printing Plates Black /1 #62
2012 Upper Deck Goodwin Champions Mini Printing Plates Cyan /1 #62
2012 Upper Deck Goodwin Champions Mini Printing Plates Magenta /1 #62
2012 Upper Deck Goodwin Champions Mini Printing Plates Yellow /1 #62
2013 Panini Golden Age Playing Cards #32
2013 Press Pass Fanfare #92
2013 Press Pass Fanfare Diamond Die Cuts /5 #92
2013 Press Pass Fanfare Green /3 #92
2013 Press Pass Fanfare Holofoil Die Cuts #92
2013 Press Pass Fanfare Red Foil Die Cuts #92
2013 Press Pass Fanfare Sapphire /20 #92
2013 Press Pass Fanfare Silver /25 #92
2013 Press Pass Legends #30
2013 Press Pass Legends Autographs Blue #LGRP
2013 Press Pass Legends Autographs Gold /10 #LGRP
2013 Press Pass Legends Autographs Holofoil /5 #LGRP
2013 Press Pass Legends Autographs Printing Plates Black /1 #LGRP
2013 Press Pass Legends Autographs Printing Plates Cyan /1 #LGRP
2013 Press Pass Legends Autographs Printing Plates Magenta /1 #LGRP
2013 Press Pass Legends Autographs Printing Plates Yellow /1 #LGRP
2013 Press Pass Legends Autographs Silver #LGRP
2013 Press Pass Legends Blue #30
2013 Press Pass Legends Blue Holofoil /1 #30
2013 Press Pass Legends Famous Feats #FF4
2013 Press Pass Legends Famous Feats Autographs Blue /1 #FFRP
2013 Press Pass Legends Famous Feats Autographs Gold /10 #FFRP
2013 Press Pass Legends Famous Feats Autographs Holofoil /4 #FFRP
2013 Press Pass Legends Famous Feats Autographs Printing Plates Black /1 #FFRP
2013 Press Pass Legends Famous Feats Autographs Printing Plates Cyan /1 #FFRP
2013 Press Pass Legends Famous Feats Autographs Printing Plates Magenta /1 #FFRP
2013 Press Pass Legends Famous Feats Autographs Printing Plates Yellow /1 #FFRP
2013 Press Pass Legends Famous Feats Autographs Silver #FFRP
2013 Press Pass Legends Famous Feats Blue /5 #FF4
2013 Press Pass Legends Famous Feats Holofoil /99 #FF4
2013 Press Pass Legends Famous Feats Melting /10 #FF4
2013 Press Pass Legends Gold /149 #30
2013 Press Pass Legends Holofoil /10 #30
2013 Press Pass Legends Pieces of History Memorabilia Autographs Gold /25 #PHSERP
2013 Press Pass Legends Pieces of History Memorabilia Autographs Melting /5 #PHSERP
2013 Press Pass Legends Pieces of History Memorabilia Gold /50 #PHRP
2013 Press Pass Legends Pieces of History Memorabilia Holofoil /25 #PHRP
2013 Press Pass Legends Pieces of History Memorabilia Silver /75 #PHRP
2013 Press Pass Legends Printing Plates Black /1 #30
2013 Press Pass Legends Printing Plates Cyan /1 #30
2013 Press Pass Legends Printing Plates Magenta /1 #30
2013 Press Pass Legends Printing Plates Yellow /1 #30
2013 Press Pass Legends Red /99 #30
2013 Press Pass Legends Signature Style #SS1
2013 Press Pass Legends Signature Style Autographs Blue /1 #SSRP
2013 Press Pass Legends Signature Style Autographs Gold /10 #SSRP
2013 Press Pass Legends Signature Style Autographs Holofoil #SSRP
2013 Press Pass Legends Signature Style Autographs Printing Plates Black /1 #SSRP
2013 Press Pass Legends Signature Style Autographs Printing Plates Cyan /1 #SSRP
2013 Press Pass Legends Signature Style Autographs Printing Plates Magenta /1 #SSRP
2013 Press Pass Legends Signature Style Autographs Printing Plates Yellow /1 #SSRP
2013 Press Pass Legends Signature Style Autographs Silver #SSRP
2013 Press Pass Legends Signature Style Blue /5 #SS1
2013 Press Pass Legends Signature Style Holofoil /99 #SS1
2013 Press Pass Legends Signature Style Melting /10 #SS1
2013 Press Pass Power Picks Blue /99 #16
2013 Press Pass Power Picks Gold /50 #16
2013 Press Pass Power Picks Holofoil /10 #16
2013 Press Pass Redline Career Wins Relic Autographs Blue /5 #CWRP
2013 Press Pass Redline Career Wins Relic Autographs Gold /25 #CWRP
2013 Press Pass Redline Career Wins Relic Autographs Melting /1 #CWRP
2013 Press Pass Redline Career Wins Relic Autographs Red /43 #CWRP
2013 Press Pass Redline Remarkable Relic Autographs Blue /5 #RMRRP
2013 Press Pass Redline Remarkable Relic Autographs Gold /25 #RMRRP
2013 Press Pass Redline Remarkable Relic Autographs Melting /1 #RMRRP
2013 Press Pass Redline Remarkable Relic Autographs Red /43 #RMRRP
2013 Press Pass Showcase Classic Collections Memorabilia Melting /5 #CCMRPM
2013 Press Pass Showcase Classic Collections Memorabilia Silver /75 #CCMRPM
2013 Total Memorabilia Memory Lane #ML8
2013 Upper Deck Goodwin Champions #88B
2013 Upper Deck Goodwin Champions #88A
2013 Upper Deck Goodwin Champions Mini #88
2013 Upper Deck Goodwin Champions Mini Canvas /99 #88
2013 Upper Deck Goodwin Champions Mini Foil Magician Red /13 #88
2013 Upper Deck Goodwin Champions Mini Foil Presidential Gold /1 #88
2013 Upper Deck Goodwin Champions Mini Green #88
2013 Upper Deck Goodwin Champions Mini Green Blank Back #88
2013 Upper Deck Goodwin Champions Mini Printing Plates Black /1 #88
2013 Upper Deck Goodwin Champions Mini Printing Plates Cyan /1 #88
2013 Upper Deck Goodwin Champions Mini Printing Plates Magenta /1 #88
2013 Upper Deck Goodwin Champions Mini Printing Plates Yellow /1 #88
2013 Upper Deck Goodwin Champions Sport Royalty Autographs #SRARP
2014 Press Pass American Thunder Great American Legend #GAL2
2014 Press Pass American Thunder Great American Legend #GAL3
2014 Press Pass American Thunder Great American Legend #GAL4
2014 Press Pass American Thunder Great American Legend #GAL5
2014 Press Pass American Thunder Great American Legend #GAL6
2014 Press Pass American Thunder Great American Legend #GAL7
2014 Press Pass American Thunder Great American Legend #GAL8
2014 Press Pass American Thunder Great American Legend #GAL9
2014 Press Pass American Thunder Great American Legend #GAL10
2014 Press Pass American Thunder Great American Legend #GAL1
2014 Press Pass American Thunder Great American Legend Autographs /50 #GLARP
2014 Press Pass American Thunder Great American Legend Relics Blue /50 #GLMRP
2014 Press Pass American Thunder Great American Legend Relics Red /50 #GLMRP
2014 Press Pass Five Star /15 #23
2014 Press Pass Five Star Blue /5 #23
2014 Press Pass Five Star Classic Compilations Autographed Patch Booklet /1 #CCRP1
2014 Press Pass Five Star Classic Compilations Autographed Patch Booklet /1 #CCRP2
2014 Press Pass Five Star Classic Compilations Autographed Patch Booklet /1 #CCRP3
2014 Press Pass Five Star Classic Compilations Autographed Patch Booklet /1 #CCRP4
2014 Press Pass Five Star Classic Compilations Autographed Patch Booklet /1 #CCRP5
2014 Press Pass Five Star Classic Compilations Combo Autographs Blue /5 #CCRPM
2014 Press Pass Five Star Classic Compilations Combo Autographs Blue /5 #CCRPJF
2014 Press Pass Five Star Classic Compilations Combo Autographs Blue /5 #CCWINS
2014 Press Pass Five Star Classic Compilations Combo Autographs Melting /1 #CCRPM
2014 Press Pass Five Star Classic Compilations Combo Autographs Melting /1 #CCRPJF
2014 Press Pass Five Star Classic Compilations Combo Autographs Melting /1 #CCWINS
2014 Press Pass Five Star Classic Compilations Cut Autograph Booklet /5 #CCLPRP
2014 Press Pass Five Star Holofoil /10 #23
2014 Press Pass Five Star Melting /1 #23
2014 Press Pass Five Star Paramount Pieces Blue /5 #PPRP
2014 Press Pass Five Star Paramount Pieces Gold /25 #PPRP
2014 Press Pass Five Star Paramount Pieces Holofoil /10 #PPRP
2014 Press Pass Five Star Paramount Pieces Melting /1 #PPRP
2014 Press Pass Five Star Signature Souvenirs Blue /1 #SSRP
2014 Press Pass Five Star Signature Souvenirs Gold /10 #SSRP
2014 Press Pass Five Star Signature Souvenirs Holofoil /5 #SSRP
2014 Press Pass Five Star Signature Souvenirs Melting /1 #SSRP
2014 Press Pass Five Star Signatures Blue /5 #FSSRP
2014 Press Pass Five Star Signatures Holofoil /10 #FSSRP
2014 Press Pass Five Star Signatures Melting /1 #FSSRP
2014 Press Pass Redline #78
2014 Press Pass Redline Black /75 #78
2014 Press Pass Redline Blue Foil #78
2014 Press Pass Redline Cyan /50 #78
2014 Press Pass Redline Green National Convention /5 #78
2014 Press Pass Redline Magenta /10 #78
2014 Press Pass Redline Remarkable Relic Autographs Blue /10 #RMRRP
2014 Press Pass Redline Remarkable Relic Autographs Gold /25 #RMRRP
2014 Press Pass Redline Remarkable Relic Autographs Melting /1 #RMRRP
2014 Press Pass Redline Remarkable Relic Autographs Red /50 #RMRRP
2014 Press Pass Redline Signatures Blue /10 #RSRP
2014 Press Pass Redline Signatures Gold /15 #RSRP
2014 Press Pass Redline Signatures Melting /1 #RSRP
2014 Press Pass Redline Signatures Red /25 #RSRP
2014 Press Pass Redline Yellow /1 #78
2014 Total Memorabilia Hall of Fame Plaques #HI2
2015 Topps Heritage Celebrity Cut Signatures /1 #66CCSRPE
2016 Certified #81
2016 Certified Epix /199 #18
2016 Certified Epix Mirror Black /1 #18
2016 Certified Epix Mirror Blue /50 #18
2016 Certified Epix Mirror Gold /25 #18
2016 Certified Epix Mirror Green /5 #18
2016 Certified Epix Mirror Orange /99 #18
2016 Certified Epix Mirror Purple /10 #18
2016 Certified Epix Mirror Red /75 #18
2016 Certified Epix Mirror Silver /99 #18
2016 Certified Famed Rides /199 #2
2016 Certified Famed Rides Mirror Black /1 #2
2016 Certified Famed Rides Mirror Blue /50 #2
2016 Certified Famed Rides Mirror Gold /25 #2
2016 Certified Famed Rides Mirror Green /5 #2
2016 Certified Famed Rides Mirror Orange /99 #2
2016 Certified Famed Rides Mirror Purple /10 #2
2016 Certified Famed Rides Mirror Red /75 #2
2016 Certified Famed Rides Mirror Silver /99 #2
2016 Certified Gold Team /199 #7
2016 Certified Gold Team Mirror Black /1 #7
2016 Certified Gold Team Mirror Blue /50 #7
2016 Certified Gold Team Mirror Gold /25 #7
2016 Certified Gold Team Mirror Green /5 #7
2016 Certified Gold Team Mirror Orange /99 #7
2016 Certified Gold Team Mirror Purple /10 #7
2016 Certified Gold Team Mirror Red /75 #7
2016 Certified Gold Team Mirror Silver /99 #7
2016 Certified Gold Team Signatures /50 #3
2016 Certified Gold Team Signatures Mirror Black /1 #3
2016 Certified Gold Team Signatures Mirror Gold /25 #3
2016 Certified Legends /199 #2
2016 Certified Legends Mirror Black /1 #2
2016 Certified Legends Mirror Blue /50 #2
2016 Certified Legends Mirror Gold /25 #2
2016 Certified Legends Mirror Green /5 #2
2016 Certified Legends Mirror Orange /99 #2
2016 Certified Legends Mirror Purple /10 #2
2016 Certified Legends Mirror Red /75 #2
2016 Certified Legends Mirror Silver /99 #2
2016 Certified Mirror Black /1 #81
2016 Certified Mirror Blue /50 #81
2016 Certified Mirror Gold /25 #81
2016 Certified Mirror Green /5 #81
2016 Certified Mirror Orange /99 #81
2016 Certified Mirror Purple /10 #81
2016 Certified Mirror Red /75 #81
2016 Certified Mirror Silver /99 #81
2016 Panini Black Friday #47
2016 Panini Black Friday Autographs /25 #47
2016 Panini Black Friday Cracked Ice /25 #47
2016 Panini Black Friday Holo Plaid /1 #47
2016 Panini Black Friday Rapture /10 #47
2016 Panini Black Friday Thick Stock /50 #47
2016 Panini Black Friday Wedges /50 #47
2016 Panini National Convention Legends #LEG9
2016 Panini National Convention Legends Autographs #LEG9
2016 Panini National Convention Legends Cracked Ice /25 #LEG9
2016 Panini National Convention Legends Decoy Cracked Ice /25 #LEG9
2016 Panini National Convention Legends Decoy Escher Squares /10 #LEG9
2016 Panini National Convention Legends Decoy Rapture /1 #LEG9
2016 Panini National Convention Legends Decoy Wedges /99 #LEG9
2016 Panini National Convention Legends Diamond Awe /49 #LEG9
2016 Panini National Convention Legends Escher Squares /10 #LEG9
2016 Panini National Convention Legends Rapture /1 #LEG9
2016 Panini National Convention Legends Wedges /99 #LEG9
2016 Panini National Convention VIP #93
2016 Panini National Convention VIP Autographs Gold Vinyl /1 #93
2016 Panini National Convention VIP Autographs Kaleidoscope Red /25 #93
2016 Panini National Convention VIP Blue Wave Gold /10 #93
2016 Panini National Convention VIP Cracked Ice /25 #93
2016 Panini National Convention VIP Flash Green /5 #93
2016 Panini National Convention VIP Gold Vinyl /1 #93
2016 Panini National Convention VIP Memorabilia Gold Vinyl /1 #93
2016 Panini National Convention VIP Memorabilia Kaleidoscope Blue /25 #93
2016 Panini National Convention VIP Prizm /99 #93
2016 Panini National Convention VIP Purple Pulsar /50 #93
2016 Panini National Treasures /25 #34
2016 Panini National Treasures /25 #37
2016 Panini National Treasures Black /5 #34
2016 Panini National Treasures Black /5 #37
2016 Panini National Treasures Blue /1 #34
2016 Panini National Treasures Blue /1 #37
2016 Panini National Treasures Championship Signatures /99 #8
2016 Panini National Treasures Championship Signatures Black /10 #8

2016 Panini National Treasures Championship Signatures Blue /1 #8
2016 Panini National Treasures Championship Signatures Gold /25 #8
2016 Panini National Treasures Championship Signatures Printing Plates Cyan /1 #8
2016 Panini National Treasures Championship Signatures Printing Plates Magenta /1 #8
2016 Panini National Treasures Championship Signatures Printing Plates Yellow /1 #8
2016 Panini National Treasures Championship Signatures Silver /50 #8
2016 Panini National Treasures Eight Signatures /15 #3
2016 Panini National Treasures Eight Signatures Black /5 #3
2016 Panini National Treasures Eight Signatures Blue /1 #3
2016 Panini National Treasures Eight Signatures Gold /10 #3
2016 Panini National Treasures Gold /15 #34
2016 Panini National Treasures Gold /15 #37
2016 Panini National Treasures Printing Plates Black /1 #34
2016 Panini National Treasures Printing Plates Black /1 #37
2016 Panini National Treasures Printing Plates Cyan /1 #34
2016 Panini National Treasures Printing Plates Cyan /1 #37
2016 Panini National Treasures Printing Plates Magenta /1 #34
2016 Panini National Treasures Printing Plates Magenta /1 #37
2016 Panini National Treasures Printing Plates Yellow /1 #34
2016 Panini National Treasures Printing Plates Yellow /1 #37
2016 Panini National Treasures Silver /20 #34
2016 Panini National Treasures Silver /20 #37
2016 Panini National Treasures Six Signatures /25 #6
2016 Panini National Treasures Six Signatures Black /10 #6
2016 Panini National Treasures Six Signatures Blue /1 #6
2016 Panini National Treasures Six Signatures Gold /15 #6
2016 Panini Prizm #43B
2016 Panini Prizm #91
2016 Panini Prizm #72
2016 Panini Prizm #92
2016 Panini Prizm Blowing Smoke #8
2016 Panini Prizm Blowing Smoke Prizms #8
2016 Panini Prizm Blowing Smoke Prizms Checkered Flag /1 #8
2016 Panini Prizm Blowing Smoke Prizms Gold /10 #8
2016 Panini Prizm Champions #1
2016 Panini Prizm Champions Prizms #1
2016 Panini Prizm Champions Prizms Checkered Flag /1 #1
2016 Panini Prizm Champions Prizms Gold /10 #1
2016 Panini Prizm Patented Penmanship Prizms #9
2016 Panini Prizm Patented Penmanship Prizms Black /3 #9
2016 Panini Prizm Patented Penmanship Prizms Blue Flag #9
2016 Panini Prizm Patented Penmanship Prizms Camo #9
2016 Panini Prizm Patented Penmanship Prizms Checkered Flag /1 #9
2016 Panini Prizm Patented Penmanship Prizms Gold /10 #9
2016 Panini Prizm Patented Penmanship Prizms Green Flag #9
2016 Panini Prizm Patented Penmanship Prizms Rainbow /24 #9
2016 Panini Prizm Patented Penmanship Prizms Red Flag #9
2016 Panini Prizm Patented Penmanship Prizms Red White and Blue #9
2016 Panini Prizm Patented Penmanship Prizms White Flag /5 #9
2016 Panini Prizm Prizms #72
2016 Panini Prizm Prizms #91
2016 Panini Prizm Prizms #92
2016 Panini Prizm Prizms #43B
2016 Panini Prizm Prizms Black /3 #72
2016 Panini Prizm Prizms Black /3 #91
2016 Panini Prizm Prizms Black /3 #92
2016 Panini Prizm Prizms Blue Flag /99 #72
2016 Panini Prizm Prizms Blue Flag /99 #91
2016 Panini Prizm Prizms Blue Flag /99 #92
2016 Panini Prizm Prizms Camo /43 #72
2016 Panini Prizm Prizms Camo /43 #91
2016 Panini Prizm Prizms Camo /43 #92
2016 Panini Prizm Prizms Checkered Flag /1 #72
2016 Panini Prizm Prizms Checkered Flag /1 #91
2016 Panini Prizm Prizms Checkered Flag /1 #92
2016 Panini Prizm Prizms Checkered Flag /1 #43B
2016 Panini Prizm Prizms Gold /10 #72
2016 Panini Prizm Prizms Gold /10 #91
2016 Panini Prizm Prizms Gold /10 #92
2016 Panini Prizm Prizms Gold /10 #43B
2016 Panini Prizm Prizms Green Flag /149 #72
2016 Panini Prizm Prizms Green Flag /149 #91
2016 Panini Prizm Prizms Green Flag /149 #92
2016 Panini Prizm Prizms Rainbow /24 #72
2016 Panini Prizm Prizms Rainbow /24 #91
2016 Panini Prizm Prizms Rainbow /24 #92
2016 Panini Prizm Prizms Red Flag /75 #72
2016 Panini Prizm Prizms Red Flag /75 #91
2016 Panini Prizm Prizms Red Flag /75 #92
2016 Panini Prizm Prizms Red White and Blue #72
2016 Panini Prizm Prizms Red White and Blue #91
2016 Panini Prizm Prizms Red White and Blue #92
2016 Panini Prizm Prizms White Flag /5 #72
2016 Panini Prizm Prizms White Flag /5 #91
2016 Panini Prizm Prizms White Flag /5 #92
2016 Panini Torque #90
2016 Panini Torque #96
2016 Panini Torque Artist Proof /50 #90
2016 Panini Torque Artist Proof /50 #96
2016 Panini Torque Blackout /1 #90
2016 Panini Torque Blackout /1 #96
2016 Panini Torque Blue /125 #90
2016 Panini Torque Blue /125 #96
2016 Panini Torque Championship Vision #1
2016 Panini Torque Championship Vision Blue /99 #1
2016 Panini Torque Championship Vision Gold /149 #1
2016 Panini Torque Championship Vision Green /25 #1
2016 Panini Torque Championship Vision Purple /10 #1
2016 Panini Torque Championship Vision Red /49 #1
2016 Panini Torque Clear Vision #36
2016 Panini Torque Clear Vision Blue /99 #36
2016 Panini Torque Clear Vision Gold /149 #36
2016 Panini Torque Clear Vision Green /25 #36
2016 Panini Torque Clear Vision Purple /10 #36
2016 Panini Torque Clear Vision Red /49 #36
2016 Panini Torque Gold #90
2016 Panini Torque Gold #96
2016 Panini Torque Holo Gold /5 #90
2016 Panini Torque Holo Gold /5 #96
2016 Panini Torque Holo Silver /10 #90
2016 Panini Torque Holo Silver /10 #96
2016 Panini Torque Legends Autographs #12
2016 Panini Torque Legends Autographs Blue /20 #12
2016 Panini Torque Legends Autographs Checkerboard /5 #12
2016 Panini Torque Legends Autographs Green /10 #12
2016 Panini Torque Legends Autographs Red /15 #12
2016 Panini Torque Nicknames #6
2016 Panini Torque Nicknames Gold /199 #6
2016 Panini Torque Nicknames Holo Silver /99 #6
2016 Panini Torque Painted to Perfection #3
2016 Panini Torque Painted to Perfection Blue /99 #3
2016 Panini Torque Painted to Perfection Checkerboard /10 #3
2016 Panini Torque Painted to Perfection Green /25 #3
2016 Panini Torque Painted to Perfection Red /49 #3
2016 Panini Torque Pairings Materials /125 #7
2016 Panini Torque Pairings Materials Blue /99 #7
2016 Panini Torque Pairings Materials Green /10 #7
2016 Panini Torque Pairings Materials Red /25 #7
2016 Panini Torque Printing Plates Black /1 #90
2016 Panini Torque Printing Plates Black /1 #96
2016 Panini Torque Printing Plates Cyan /1 #90
2016 Panini Torque Printing Plates Cyan /1 #96
2016 Panini Torque Printing Plates Magenta /1 #90
2016 Panini Torque Printing Plates Magenta /1 #96
2016 Panini Torque Printing Plates Yellow /1 #90
2016 Panini Torque Printing Plates Yellow /1 #96
2016 Panini Torque Purple /25 #90
2016 Panini Torque Purple /25 #96
2016 Panini Torque Race Kings #2
2016 Panini Torque Race Kings Gold /199 #2
2016 Panini Torque Race Kings Holo Silver /99 #2
2016 Panini Torque Red /99 #90
2016 Panini Torque Red /99 #96
2016 Panini Torque Rubber Relics /49 #19
2016 Panini Torque Rubber Relics Blue /25 #19
2016 Panini Torque Rubber Relics Green /5 #19
2016 Panini Torque Rubber Relics Red /10 #19
2016 Panini Torque Superstar Vision #24
2016 Panini Torque Superstar Vision Blue /99 #24
2016 Panini Torque Superstar Vision Gold /149 #24
2016 Panini Torque Superstar Vision Green /25 #24
2016 Panini Torque Superstar Vision Purple /10 #24
2016 Panini Torque Superstar Vision Red /49 #24
2016 Panini Torque Test Proof Black /1 #90
2016 Panini Torque Test Proof Black /1 #96
2016 Panini Torque Test Proof Cyan /1 #90
2016 Panini Torque Test Proof Cyan /1 #96
2016 Panini Torque Test Proof Magenta /1 #90
2016 Panini Torque Test Proof Magenta /1 #96
2016 Panini Torque Test Proof Yellow /1 #90
2016 Panini Torque Test Proof Yellow /1 #96
2016 Panini Torque Victory Laps #8
2016 Panini Torque Victory Laps Gold /199 #8
2016 Panini Torque Victory Laps Holo Silver /99 #8
2016 Panini Torque Winning Vision #24
2016 Panini Torque Winning Vision Blue /99 #24
2016 Panini Torque Winning Vision Gold /149 #24
2016 Panini Torque Winning Vision Green /25 #24
2016 Panini Torque Winning Vision Purple /10 #24
2016 Panini Torque Winning Vision Red /49 #24
2017 Donruss #177
2017 Donruss #183
2017 Donruss Artist Proof /25 #177
2017 Donruss Artist Proof /25 #183
2017 Donruss Blue Foil /299 #177
2017 Donruss Blue Foil /299 #183
2017 Donruss Call to the Hall #11
2017 Donruss Call to the Hall Cracked Ice /999 #11
2017 Donruss Classics #5
2017 Donruss Classics Cracked Ice /999 #5
2017 Donruss Elite Series /999 #4
2017 Donruss Gold Foil /499 #177
2017 Donruss Gold Foil /499 #183
2017 Donruss Gold Press Proof /99 #177
2017 Donruss Gold Press Proof /99 #183
2017 Donruss Green Foil /199 #177
2017 Donruss Green Foil /199 #183
2017 Donruss Press Proof /49 #177
2017 Donruss Press Proof /49 #183
2017 Donruss Printing Plates Black /1 #177
2017 Donruss Printing Plates Black /1 #183
2017 Donruss Printing Plates Cyan /1 #177
2017 Donruss Printing Plates Cyan /1 #183
2017 Donruss Printing Plates Magenta /1 #177
2017 Donruss Printing Plates Magenta /1 #183
2017 Donruss Printing Plates Yellow /1 #177
2017 Donruss Printing Plates Yellow /1 #183
2017 Donruss Retro Signatures 1984 #19
2017 Donruss Retro Signatures 1984 Holo Black /1 #19
2017 Donruss Retro Signatures 1984 Holo Gold /25 #19
2017 Panini National Convention Legends /299 #LEG28
2017 Panini National Convention Legends Escher Squares /25 #LEG28
2017 Panini National Convention Legends Escher Squares Thick Stock /10 #LEG28
2017 Panini National Convention Legends Galatic Windows /5 #LEG28
2017 Panini National Convention Legends Hyperplaid /1 #LEG28
2017 Panini National Convention Legends Pyramids /10 #LEG28
2017 Panini National Convention Legends Rainbow Spokes /49 #LEG28
2017 Panini National Convention Legends Rainbow Spokes Thick Stock /25 #LEG28
2017 Panini National Convention Legends Rapture /99 #LEG28
2017 Panini National Convention VIP #84
2017 Panini National Convention VIP Prizm #84
2017 Panini National Convention VIP Prizm Black /1 #84
2017 Panini National Convention VIP Prizm Cracked Ice /25 #84
2017 Panini National Convention VIP Prizm Gold /15 #84
2017 Panini National Convention VIP Prizm Green /5 #84
2017 Panini National Treasures /25 #29
2017 Panini National Treasures Century Black /1 #29
2017 Panini National Treasures Century Gold /15 #29
2017 Panini National Treasures Century Green /5 #29
2017 Panini National Treasures Century Holo Gold /10 #29
2017 Panini National Treasures Century Holo Silver /20 #29
2017 Panini National Treasures Championship Signatures Black /1 #3
2017 Panini National Treasures Championship Signatures Gold /10 #3
2017 Panini National Treasures Championship Signatures Green /5 #3
2017 Panini National Treasures Championship Signatures Holo Gold /7 #3
2017 Panini National Treasures Championship Signatures Holo Silver /15 #3
2017 Panini National Treasures Championship Signatures Printing Plates Black /1 #3
2017 Panini National Treasures Championship Signatures Printing Plates Cyan /1 #3
2017 Panini National Treasures Championship Signatures Printing Plates Magenta /1 #3
2017 Panini National Treasures Championship Signatures Printing Plates Yellow /1 #3
2017 Panini National Treasures Dual Signature Materials /25 #10
2017 Panini National Treasures Dual Signature Materials Black /1 #10
2017 Panini National Treasures Dual Signature Materials Gold /15 #10
2017 Panini National Treasures Dual Signature Materials Green /5 #10
2017 Panini National Treasures Dual Signature Materials Holo Gold /7 #10
2017 Panini National Treasures Dual Signature Materials Holo Silver /20 #10
2017 Panini National Treasures Dual Signature Materials Laundry Tag /1 #10
2017 Panini National Treasures Dual Tire Signatures Black /1 #8
2017 Panini National Treasures Dual Tire Signatures Gold /10 #8
2017 Panini National Treasures Dual Tire Signatures Green /5 #8
2017 Panini National Treasures Dual Tire Signatures Holo Gold /7 #8
2017 Panini National Treasures Dual Tire Signatures Printing Plates Black /1 #8
2017 Panini National Treasures Dual Tire Signatures Printing Plates Cyan /1 #8
2017 Panini National Treasures Dual Tire Signatures Printing Plates Magenta /1 #8
2017 Panini National Treasures Dual Tire Signatures Printing Plates Yellow /1 #8
2017 Panini National Treasures Legendary Material Signatures Black /1 #5
2017 Panini National Treasures Legendary Material Signatures Gold /10 #5
2017 Panini National Treasures Legendary Material Signatures Green /5 #5
2017 Panini National Treasures Legendary Material Signatures Holo Gold /7 #5
2017 Panini National Treasures Legendary Material Signatures Printing Plates Black /1 #5
2017 Panini National Treasures Legendary Material Signatures Printing Plates Cyan /1 #5
2017 Panini National Treasures Legendary Material Signatures Printing Plates Magenta /1 #5
2017 Panini National Treasures Legendary Material Signatures Printing Plates Yellow /1 #5
2017 Panini National Treasures Legendary Signatures Black /1 #10
2017 Panini National Treasures Legendary Signatures Gold /10 #10
2017 Panini National Treasures Legendary Signatures Green /5 #10
2017 Panini National Treasures Legendary Signatures Holo Gold /7 #10
2017 Panini National Treasures Legendary Signatures Printing Plates Black /1 #10
2017 Panini National Treasures Legendary Signatures Printing Plates Cyan /1 #10
2017 Panini National Treasures Legendary Signatures Printing Plates Magenta /1 #10
2017 Panini National Treasures Legendary Signatures Printing Plates Yellow /1 #10
2017 Panini National Treasures Printing Plates Black /1 #29
2017 Panini National Treasures Printing Plates Cyan /1 #29
2017 Panini National Treasures Printing Plates Magenta /1 #29
2017 Panini National Treasures Printing Plates Yellow /1 #29
2017 Panini National Treasures Winning Signatures Black /1 #1
2017 Panini National Treasures Winning Signatures Gold /10 #1
2017 Panini National Treasures Winning Signatures Green /5 #1
2017 Panini National Treasures Winning Signatures Holo Gold /7 #1
2017 Panini National Treasures Winning Signatures Printing Plates Black /1 #1
2017 Panini National Treasures Winning Signatures Printing Plates Cyan /1 #1
2017 Panini National Treasures Winning Signatures Printing Plates Magenta /1 #1
2017 Panini National Treasures Winning Signatures Printing Plates Yellow /1 #1
2017 Panini Torque #30
2017 Panini Torque Artist Proof /75 #30
2017 Panini Torque Blackout /1 #30
2017 Panini Torque Blue /150 #30
2017 Panini Torque Clear Vision #36
2017 Panini Torque Clear Vision Blue /99 #36
2017 Panini Torque Clear Vision Gold /149 #36
2017 Panini Torque Clear Vision Green /25 #36
2017 Panini Torque Clear Vision Purple /10 #36
2017 Panini Torque Clear Vision Red /49 #36
2017 Panini Torque Driver Scripts #28
2017 Panini Torque Driver Scripts Blue /50 #28
2017 Panini Torque Driver Scripts Checkerboard /10 #28
2017 Panini Torque Driver Scripts Green /15 #28
2017 Panini Torque Driver Scripts Red /25 #28
2017 Panini Torque Gold #30
2017 Panini Torque Holo Gold /10 #30
2017 Panini Torque Holo Silver /25 #30
2017 Panini Torque Primary Paint #16
2017 Panini Torque Primary Paint Blue /99 #16
2017 Panini Torque Primary Paint Checkerboard /10 #16
2017 Panini Torque Primary Paint Green /25 #16
2017 Panini Torque Primary Paint Red /49 #16
2017 Panini Torque Printing Plates Black /1 #30
2017 Panini Torque Printing Plates Cyan /1 #30
2017 Panini Torque Printing Plates Magenta /1 #30
2017 Panini Torque Printing Plates Yellow /1 #30
2017 Panini Torque Purple /50 #30
2017 Panini Torque Red /100 #30
2017 Panini Torque Test Proof Black /1 #30
2017 Panini Torque Test Proof Cyan /1 #30
2017 Panini Torque Test Proof Magenta /1 #30
2017 Panini Torque Test Proof Yellow /1 #30
2017 Panini Torque Trackside #10
2017 Panini Torque Trackside Blue /99 #10
2017 Panini Torque Trackside Checkerboard /10 #10
2017 Panini Torque Trackside Green /25 #10
2017 Panini Torque Trackside Red /49 #10
2017 Panini Torque Victory Laps #15
2017 Panini Torque Victory Laps Gold /199 #15
2017 Panini Torque Victory Laps Holo Silver /99 #15
2017 Panini Torque Visions of Greatness #4
2017 Panini Torque Visions of Greatness Blue /99 #4
2017 Panini Torque Visions of Greatness Gold /149 #4
2017 Panini Torque Visions of Greatness Green /25 #4
2017 Panini Torque Visions of Greatness Purple /10 #4
2017 Panini Torque Visions of Greatness Red /49 #4
2017 Select #138
2017 Select Endorsements #14
2017 Select Endorsements Prizms Blue /43 #14
2017 Select Endorsements Prizms Checkered Flag /1 #14
2017 Select Endorsements Prizms Gold /10 #14
2017 Select Endorsements Prizms Red /25 #14
2017 Select Prizms Black /3 #138
2017 Select Prizms Checkered Flag /1 #138
2017 Select Prizms Gold /10 #138
2017 Select Prizms Tie Dye /24 #138
2017 Select Prizms White /50 #138
2017 Select Select Stars #1
2017 Select Select Stars Prizms Black /3 #1
2017 Select Select Stars Prizms Checkered Flag /1 #1
2017 Select Select Stars Prizms Gold /10 #1
2017 Select Select Stars Prizms Tie Dye /24 #1
2017 Select Select Stars Prizms White /50 #1
2018 Certified #88
2018 Certified All Certified Team /199 #1
2018 Certified All Certified Team Black /1 #1
2018 Certified All Certified Team Blue /99 #1
2018 Certified All Certified Team Gold /49 #1
2018 Certified All Certified Team Green /10 #1
2018 Certified All Certified Team Mirror Black /1 #1
2018 Certified All Certified Team Mirror Gold /25 #1
2018 Certified All Certified Team Mirror Green /5 #1
2018 Certified All Certified Team Mirror Purple /10 #1
2018 Certified All Certified Team Purple /25 #1
2018 Certified All Certified Team Red /149 #1
2018 Certified Black /1 #88
2018 Certified Blue /99 #88
2018 Certified Epix /199 #9
2018 Certified Epix Black /1 #9
2018 Certified Epix Blue /99 #9
2018 Certified Epix Gold /49 #9
2018 Certified Epix Green /10 #9
2018 Certified Epix Mirror Black /1 #9
2018 Certified Epix Mirror Gold /25 #9
2018 Certified Epix Mirror Green /5 #9
2018 Certified Epix Mirror Purple /10 #9
2018 Certified Epix Purple /25 #9
2018 Certified Epix Red /149 #9
2018 Certified Gold /49 #88
2018 Certified Green /10 #88
2018 Certified Materials Signatures Black /1 #7
2018 Certified Materials Signatures Blue /10 #7
2018 Certified Materials Signatures Gold /7 #7
2018 Certified Materials Signatures Green /3 #7
2018 Certified Materials Signatures Purple /5 #7
2018 Certified Materials Signatures Red /15 #7
2018 Certified Mirror Black /1 #88
2018 Certified Mirror Gold /25 #88
2018 Certified Mirror Green /5 #88
2018 Certified Mirror Purple /10 #88
2018 Certified Orange /249 #88
2018 Certified Purple /25 #88
2018 Certified Red /199 #88
2018 Certified Signing Sessions Black /1 #20
2018 Certified Signing Sessions Blue /10 #20
2018 Certified Signing Sessions Gold /7 #20
2018 Certified Signing Sessions Green /3 #20
2018 Certified Signing Sessions Purple /5 #20
2018 Certified Signing Sessions Red /15 #20
2018 Certified Stars /199 #25
2018 Certified Stars Black /1 #25
2018 Certified Stars Blue /99 #25
2018 Certified Stars Gold /49 #25
2018 Certified Stars Green /10 #25
2018 Certified Stars Mirror Black /1 #25
2018 Certified Stars Mirror Gold /25 #25
2018 Certified Stars Mirror Green /5 #25
2018 Certified Stars Mirror Purple /10 #25
2018 Certified Stars Purple /25 #25
2018 Certified Stars Red /149 #25
2018 Donruss #104
2018 Donruss #151
2018 Donruss Artist Proofs /25 #104
2018 Donruss Artist Proofs /25 #151
2018 Donruss Classics #3
2018 Donruss Classics Cracked Ice /999 #3
2018 Donruss Classics Xplosion /99 #3
2018 Donruss Gold Foil /499 #104
2018 Donruss Gold Foil /499 #151
2018 Donruss Gold Press Proofs /99 #104
2018 Donruss Gold Press Proofs /99 #151
2018 Donruss Green Foil /199 #104
2018 Donruss Green Foil /199 #151
2018 Donruss Masters of the Track #2
2018 Donruss Masters of the Track Cracked Ice /999 #2
2018 Donruss Masters of the Track Xplosion /99 #2
2018 Donruss Press Proofs /49 #104
2018 Donruss Press Proofs /49 #151
2018 Donruss Printing Plates Black /1 #104
2018 Donruss Printing Plates Black /1 #151
2018 Donruss Printing Plates Cyan /1 #104
2018 Donruss Printing Plates Cyan /1 #151
2018 Donruss Printing Plates Magenta /1 #104
2018 Donruss Printing Plates Magenta /1 #151
2018 Donruss Printing Plates Yellow /1 #104
2018 Donruss Printing Plates Yellow /1 #151
2018 Donruss Red Foil /299 #104
2018 Donruss Red Foil /299 #151
2018 Donruss Significant Signatures #18
2018 Donruss Significant Signatures Black /1 #18
2018 Donruss Significant Signatures Holo Gold /10 #18
2018 Donruss Slingshot #SS1
2018 Panini Black Friday Panini Collection /199 #KING
2018 Panini Black Friday Panini Collection Autographs /10 #KING
2018 Panini Black Friday Panini Collection Autographs HyperPlaid /1 #KING
2018 Panini Black Friday Panini Collection Checkboard /1 #KING
2018 Panini Black Friday Panini Collection Cracked Ice /10 #KING
2018 Panini Black Friday Panini Collection Rapture /25 #KING
2018 Panini Prime /50 #94
2018 Panini Prime /50 #61
2018 Panini Prime /50 #28
2018 Panini Prime Black /1 #28
2018 Panini Prime Black /1 #61
2018 Panini Prime Black /1 #94
2018 Panini Prime Driver Signatures /25 #16
2018 Panini Prime Driver Signatures Black /1 #16
2018 Panini Prime Driver Signatures Holo Gold /10 #16
2018 Panini Prime Dual Signatures /7 #5
2018 Panini Prime Dual Signatures Black /1 #5
2018 Panini Prime Dual Signatures Holo Gold /3 #5
2018 Panini Prime Holo Gold /25 #28
2018 Panini Prime Holo Gold /25 #61
2018 Panini Prime Holo Gold /25 #94
2018 Panini Prime Prime Signatures /25 #16
2018 Panini Prime Prime Signatures Black /1 #16
2018 Panini Prime Prime Signatures Holo Gold /10 #16
2018 Panini Prime Shadowbox Signatures /25 #18
2018 Panini Prime Shadowbox Signatures Black /1 #18
2018 Panini Prime Shadowbox Signatures Holo Gold /10 #18
2018 Panini Prizm #47A
2018 Panini Prizm #47B
2018 Panini Prizm Fireworks #2
2018 Panini Prizm Fireworks Prizms #2
2018 Panini Prizm Fireworks Prizms Black /1 #2
2018 Panini Prizm Fireworks Prizms Gold /10 #2
2018 Panini Prizm Illumination #13
2018 Panini Prizm Illumination Prizms #13
2018 Panini Prizm Illumination Prizms Black /1 #13
2018 Panini Prizm Illumination Prizms Gold /10 #13
2018 Panini Prizm Patented Penmanship Prizms #10
2018 Panini Prizm Patented Penmanship Prizms Black /1 #10
2018 Panini Prizm Patented Penmanship Prizms Blue /10 #10
2018 Panini Prizm Patented Penmanship Prizms Camo #10
2018 Panini Prizm Patented Penmanship Prizms Gold /10 #10
2018 Panini Prizm Patented Penmanship Prizms Green /10 #10
2018 Panini Prizm Patented Penmanship Prizms Rainbow /24 #10
2018 Panini Prizm Patented Penmanship Prizms Red /10 #10
2018 Panini Prizm Patented Penmanship Prizms Red White and Blue /10 #10
2018 Panini Prizm Patented Penmanship Prizms White /5 #10
2018 Panini Prizm Prizms #47A
2018 Panini Prizm Prizms #47B
2018 Panini Prizm Prizms Black /1 #47A
2018 Panini Prizm Prizms Black /1 #47B
2018 Panini Prizm Prizms Blue /99 #47A
2018 Panini Prizm Prizms Blue /99 #47B
2018 Panini Prizm Prizms Camo #47A
2018 Panini Prizm Prizms Camo #47B
2018 Panini Prizm Prizms Gold /10 #47A
2018 Panini Prizm Prizms Gold /10 #47B
2018 Panini Prizm Prizms Green /149 #47A
2018 Panini Prizm Prizms Green /149 #47B
2018 Panini Prizm Prizms Purple Flash #47A
2018 Panini Prizm Prizms Purple Flash #47B
2018 Panini Prizm Prizms Rainbow /24 #47A
2018 Panini Prizm Prizms Rainbow /24 #47B
2018 Panini Prizm Prizms Red /75 #47A
2018 Panini Prizm Prizms Red /75 #47B
2018 Panini Prizm Prizms Red White and Blue #47A
2018 Panini Prizm Prizms Red White and Blue #47B
2018 Panini Prizm Prizms White /5 #47A
2018 Panini Prizm Prizms White /5 #47B
2018 Panini Victory Lane #51
2018 Panini Victory Lane #54
2018 Panini Victory Lane #55
2018 Panini Victory Lane #59
2018 Panini Victory Lane #62
2018 Panini Victory Lane #71
2018 Panini Victory Lane Black /1 #51
2018 Panini Victory Lane Black /1 #54
2018 Panini Victory Lane Black /1 #55
2018 Panini Victory Lane Black /1 #59
2018 Panini Victory Lane Black /1 #62
2018 Panini Victory Lane Black /1 #71
2018 Panini Victory Lane Blue /25 #51
2018 Panini Victory Lane Blue /25 #54
2018 Panini Victory Lane Blue /25 #55
2018 Panini Victory Lane Blue /25 #59
2018 Panini Victory Lane Blue /25 #62
2018 Panini Victory Lane Blue /25 #71
2018 Panini Victory Lane Champions #2
2018 Panini Victory Lane Champions Black /1 #2
2018 Panini Victory Lane Champions Blue /25 #2
2018 Panini Victory Lane Champions Gold /99 #2
2018 Panini Victory Lane Champions Green /5 #2
2018 Panini Victory Lane Champions Printing Plates Black /1 #2
2018 Panini Victory Lane Champions Printing Plates Cyan /1 #2
2018 Panini Victory Lane Champions Printing Plates Magenta /1 #2
2018 Panini Victory Lane Champions Printing Plates Yellow /1 #2
2018 Panini Victory Lane Champions Red /49 #2
2018 Panini Victory Lane Chasing the Flag #7
2018 Panini Victory Lane Chasing the Flag Black /1 #7
2018 Panini Victory Lane Chasing the Flag Blue /25 #7
2018 Panini Victory Lane Chasing the Flag Gold /99 #7
2018 Panini Victory Lane Chasing the Flag Green /5 #7
2018 Panini Victory Lane Chasing the Flag Printing Plates Black /1 #7
2018 Panini Victory Lane Chasing the Flag Printing Plates Cyan /1 #7
2018 Panini Victory Lane Chasing the Flag Printing Plates Magenta /1 #7
2018 Panini Victory Lane Chasing the Flag Printing Plates Yellow /1 #7
2018 Panini Victory Lane Chasing the Flag Red /49 #7
2018 Panini Victory Lane Foundations #6
2018 Panini Victory Lane Foundations Black /1 #6
2018 Panini Victory Lane Foundations Blue /25 #6
2018 Panini Victory Lane Foundations Gold /99 #6
2018 Panini Victory Lane Foundations Green /5 #6
2018 Panini Victory Lane Foundations Printing Plates Black /1 #6
2018 Panini Victory Lane Foundations Printing Plates Cyan /1 #6
2018 Panini Victory Lane Foundations Printing Plates Magenta /1 #6
2018 Panini Victory Lane Foundations Printing Plates Yellow /1 #6
2018 Panini Victory Lane Foundations Red /49 #6
2018 Panini Victory Lane Gold /99 #51
2018 Panini Victory Lane Gold /99 #54
2018 Panini Victory Lane Gold /99 #55
2018 Panini Victory Lane Gold /99 #59
2018 Panini Victory Lane Gold /99 #62
2018 Panini Victory Lane Gold /99 #71
2018 Panini Victory Lane Green /5 #51
2018 Panini Victory Lane Green /5 #54
2018 Panini Victory Lane Green /5 #55
2018 Panini Victory Lane Green /5 #59
2018 Panini Victory Lane Green /5 #62
2018 Panini Victory Lane Green /5 #71
2018 Panini Victory Lane NASCAR at 70 #1
2018 Panini Victory Lane NASCAR at 70 Black /1 #1
2018 Panini Victory Lane NASCAR at 70 Blue /25 #1
2018 Panini Victory Lane NASCAR at 70 Gold /99 #1
2018 Panini Victory Lane NASCAR at 70 Green /5 #1
2018 Panini Victory Lane NASCAR at 70 Printing Plates Black /1 #1
2018 Panini Victory Lane NASCAR at 70 Printing Plates Cyan /1 #1
2018 Panini Victory Lane NASCAR at 70 Printing Plates Magenta /1 #1
2018 Panini Victory Lane NASCAR at 70 Printing Plates Yellow /1 #1
2018 Panini Victory Lane NASCAR at 70 Red /49 #1
2018 Panini Victory Lane Pedal to the Metal #76
2018 Panini Victory Lane Pedal to the Metal Black /1 #76
2018 Panini Victory Lane Pedal to the Metal Blue /25 #76
2018 Panini Victory Lane Pedal to the Metal Green /5 #76
2018 Panini Victory Lane Printing Plates Black /1 #51
2018 Panini Victory Lane Printing Plates Black /1 #54
2018 Panini Victory Lane Printing Plates Black /1 #55
2018 Panini Victory Lane Printing Plates Black /1 #59
2018 Panini Victory Lane Printing Plates Black /1 #62
2018 Panini Victory Lane Printing Plates Black /1 #71
2018 Panini Victory Lane Printing Plates Cyan /1 #51
2018 Panini Victory Lane Printing Plates Cyan /1 #54
2018 Panini Victory Lane Printing Plates Cyan /1 #55
2018 Panini Victory Lane Printing Plates Cyan /1 #59
2018 Panini Victory Lane Printing Plates Cyan /1 #62
2018 Panini Victory Lane Printing Plates Cyan /1 #71
2018 Panini Victory Lane Printing Plates Magenta /1 #51
2018 Panini Victory Lane Printing Plates Magenta /1 #54
2018 Panini Victory Lane Printing Plates Magenta /1 #55
2018 Panini Victory Lane Printing Plates Magenta /1 #59
2018 Panini Victory Lane Printing Plates Magenta /1 #62
2018 Panini Victory Lane Printing Plates Magenta /1 #71
2018 Panini Victory Lane Printing Plates Yellow /1 #51
2018 Panini Victory Lane Printing Plates Yellow /1 #54
2018 Panini Victory Lane Printing Plates Yellow /1 #55
2018 Panini Victory Lane Printing Plates Yellow /1 #59
2018 Panini Victory Lane Printing Plates Yellow /1 #62
2018 Panini Victory Lane Printing Plates Yellow /1 #71
2018 Panini Victory Lane Red /49 #51
2018 Panini Victory Lane Red /49 #54
2018 Panini Victory Lane Red /49 #55
2018 Panini Victory Lane Red /49 #59
2018 Panini Victory Lane Red /49 #62
2018 Panini Victory Lane Red /49 #71
2018 Panini Victory Lane Silver #51
2018 Panini Victory Lane Silver #54
2018 Panini Victory Lane Silver #55
2018 Panini Victory Lane Silver #59
2018 Panini Victory Lane Silver #62
2018 Panini Victory Lane Silver #71
2018 Panini Victory Lane Victory Marks Black /1 #13
2018 Panini Victory Lane Victory Marks Gold /43 #13
2019 Donruss #7
2019 Donruss #17
2019 Donruss #34A
2019 Donruss #104A
2019 Donruss #169
2019 Donruss #34B
2019 Donruss #104B
2019 Donruss Artist Proofs /25 #7
2019 Donruss Artist Proofs /25 #17
2019 Donruss Artist Proofs /25 #34A
2019 Donruss Artist Proofs /25 #104A
2019 Donruss Artist Proofs /25 #169
2019 Donruss Artist Proofs /25 #34B
2019 Donruss Artist Proofs /25 #104B
2019 Donruss Black /199 #7
2019 Donruss Black /199 #17
2019 Donruss Black /199 #34A
2019 Donruss Black /199 #104A
2019 Donruss Black /199 #169
2019 Donruss Black /199 #34B
2019 Donruss Black /199 #104B
2019 Donruss Classics #13
2019 Donruss Classics Cracked Ice /25 #13
2019 Donruss Classics Holographic #13
2019 Donruss Classics Xplosion /10 #13
2019 Donruss Decades of Speed #5
2019 Donruss Decades of Speed #6
2019 Donruss Decades of Speed #7
2019 Donruss Decades of Speed Cracked Ice /25 #5
2019 Donruss Decades of Speed Cracked Ice /25 #6
2019 Donruss Decades of Speed Cracked Ice /25 #7
2019 Donruss Decades of Speed Holographic #5
2019 Donruss Decades of Speed Holographic #6
2019 Donruss Decades of Speed Holographic #7
2019 Donruss Decades of Speed Xplosion /10 #5
2019 Donruss Decades of Speed Xplosion /10 #6
2019 Donruss Decades of Speed Xplosion /10 #7
2019 Donruss Gold /299 #7
2019 Donruss Gold /299 #17
2019 Donruss Gold /299 #34A
2019 Donruss Gold /299 #104A
2019 Donruss Gold /299 #169
2019 Donruss Gold /299 #34B
2019 Donruss Gold /299 #104B
2019 Donruss Gold Press Proofs /99 #7
2019 Donruss Gold Press Proofs /99 #17
2019 Donruss Gold Press Proofs /99 #34A
2019 Donruss Gold Press Proofs /99 #104A
2019 Donruss Gold Press Proofs /99 #169
2019 Donruss Gold Press Proofs /99 #34B
2019 Donruss Gold Press Proofs /99 #104B
2019 Donruss Icons Cracked Ice /25 #1
2019 Donruss Icons Holographic #1
2019 Donruss Icons Xplosion /10 #1
2019 Donruss Optic #1
2019 Donruss Optic #6
2019 Donruss Optic #90
2019 Donruss Optic Blue Pulsar #1
2019 Donruss Optic Blue Pulsar #6
2019 Donruss Optic Blue Pulsar #90
2019 Donruss Optic Gold /10 #1
2019 Donruss Optic Gold /10 #6
2019 Donruss Optic Gold /10 #90
2019 Donruss Optic Gold Vinyl /1 #1
2019 Donruss Optic Gold Vinyl /1 #6
2019 Donruss Optic Gold Vinyl /1 #90
2019 Donruss Optic Holo #1
2019 Donruss Optic Holo #6
2019 Donruss Optic Holo #90
2019 Donruss Optic Red Wave #1
2019 Donruss Optic Red Wave #6
2019 Donruss Optic Red Wave #90
2019 Donruss Optic Signatures Gold Vinyl /1 #90
2019 Donruss Optic Signatures Gold Vinyl /1 #1
2019 Donruss Optic Signatures Gold Vinyl /1 #6
2019 Donruss Optic Signatures Holo /25 #1
2019 Donruss Optic Signatures Holo /25 #6
2019 Donruss Optic Signatures Holo /25 #90
2019 Donruss Press Proofs /49 #17
2019 Donruss Press Proofs /49 #34A
2019 Donruss Press Proofs /49 #104A
2019 Donruss Press Proofs /49 #169
2019 Donruss Press Proofs /49 #34B
2019 Donruss Press Proofs /49 #104B
2019 Donruss Press Proofs /49 #7
2019 Donruss Printing Plates Black /1 #7
2019 Donruss Printing Plates Black /1 #17
2019 Donruss Printing Plates Black /1 #34A
2019 Donruss Printing Plates Black /1 #104A
2019 Donruss Printing Plates Black /1 #169
2019 Donruss Printing Plates Black #34B
2019 Donruss Printing Plates Black /1 #104B
2019 Donruss Printing Plates Cyan /1 #7
2019 Donruss Printing Plates Cyan /1 #17
2019 Donruss Printing Plates Cyan /1 #34A
2019 Donruss Printing Plates Cyan /1 #104A
2019 Donruss Printing Plates Cyan /1 #169
2019 Donruss Printing Plates Cyan #34B
2019 Donruss Printing Plates Cyan /1 #104B
2019 Donruss Printing Plates Magenta /1 #34A
2019 Donruss Printing Plates Magenta /1 #104A
2019 Donruss Printing Plates Magenta /1 #169
2019 Donruss Printing Plates Magenta #34B
2019 Donruss Printing Plates Magenta /1 #104B
2019 Donruss Printing Plates Magenta /1 #7
2019 Donruss Printing Plates Magenta /1 #17
2019 Donruss Printing Plates Yellow /1 #7
2019 Donruss Printing Plates Yellow /1 #17
2019 Donruss Printing Plates Yellow /1 #34A
2019 Donruss Printing Plates Yellow /1 #104A
2019 Donruss Printing Plates Yellow /1 #169
2019 Donruss Printing Plates Yellow #34B
2019 Donruss Printing Plates Yellow /1 #104B
2019 Donruss Signature Swatches #1
2019 Donruss Signature Swatches Holo Black /5 #1
2019 Donruss Signature Swatches Holo Gold /10 #1
2019 Donruss Signature Swatches Red /25 #1
2019 Donruss Silver #7
2019 Donruss Silver #17
2019 Donruss Silver #34A
2019 Donruss Silver #104A
2019 Donruss Silver #169
2019 Donruss Silver #34B
2019 Donruss Silver #104B
2019 Panini Prime /50 #66
2019 Panini Prime /50 #89
2019 Panini Prime Autograph Materials /43 #2
2019 Panini Prime Autograph Materials Black /10 #2
2019 Panini Prime Autograph Materials Holo Gold /25 #2
2019 Panini Prime Autograph Materials Platinum Blue /1 #2
2019 Panini Prime Black /10 #66
2019 Panini Prime Black /10 #89
2019 Panini Prime Emerald /5 #66
2019 Panini Prime Emerald /5 #89
2019 Panini Prime Legacy Signatures /43 #8
2019 Panini Prime Legacy Signatures Black /10 #8
2019 Panini Prime Legacy Signatures Holo Gold /25 #8
2019 Panini Prime Legacy Signatures Platinum Blue /1 #8
2019 Panini Prime Platinum Blue /1 #66
2019 Panini Prime Platinum Blue /1 #89
2019 Panini Prime Prime Names Die Cut Signatures /43 #20
2019 Panini Prime Prime Names Die Cut Signatures Black /10 #20
2019 Panini Prime Prime Names Die Cut Signatures Holo Gold /25 #20
2019 Panini Prime Prime Names Die Cut Signatures Platinum Blue /1 #20
2019 Panini Prime Race Used Firesuits /50 #5
2019 Panini Prime Race Used Firesuits Black /10 #5
2019 Panini Prime Race Used Firesuits Holo Gold /25 #5
2019 Panini Prime Race Used Firesuits Laundry Tags /1 #5
2019 Panini Prime Race Used Sheet Metal Black /2 #5
2019 Panini Prime Race Used Sheet Metal Platinum Blue /1 #5
2019 Panini Prime Race Used Tires /25 #5
2019 Panini Prime Race Used Tires Black /2 #5
2019 Panini Prime Race Used Tires Holo Gold /10 #5
2019 Panini Prime Race Used Tires Platinum Blue /1 #5
2019 Panini Prime Shadowbox Signatures /43 #14
2019 Panini Prime Shadowbox Signatures Black /10 #14
2019 Panini Prime Shadowbox Signatures Holo Gold /25 #14
2019 Panini Prime Shadowbox Signatures Platinum Blue /1 #14
2019 Panini Prizm #40A
2019 Panini Prizm #40B
2019 Panini Prizm Apex #6
2019 Panini Prizm Apex Prizms #6
2019 Panini Prizm Apex Prizms Black /1 #6
2019 Panini Prizm Apex Prizms Gold /10 #6
2019 Panini Prizm Apex Prizms White Sparkle #6
2019 Panini Prizm Endorsements Prizms #17
2019 Panini Prizm Endorsements Prizms Black /1 #17
2019 Panini Prizm Endorsements Prizms Blue /5 #17
2019 Panini Prizm Endorsements Prizms Camo #17
2019 Panini Prizm Endorsements Prizms Gold /10 #17
2019 Panini Prizm Endorsements Prizms Green /5 #17
2019 Panini Prizm Endorsements Prizms Rainbow /5 #17
2019 Panini Prizm Endorsements Prizms Red /5 #17
2019 Panini Prizm Endorsements Prizms Red White and Blue #17
2019 Panini Prizm Endorsements Prizms White /5 #17
2019 Panini Prizm Expert Level #5
2019 Panini Prizm Expert Level Prizms #5
2019 Panini Prizm Expert Level Prizms Black /1 #5
2019 Panini Prizm Expert Level Prizms Gold /10 #5
2019 Panini Prizm Expert Level Prizms White Sparkle #5
2019 Panini Prizm Fireworks #18
2019 Panini Prizm Fireworks Prizms #18
2019 Panini Prizm Fireworks Prizms Black /1 #18
2019 Panini Prizm Fireworks Prizms Gold /10 #18
2019 Panini Prizm Fireworks Prizms White Sparkle #18
2019 Panini Prizm National Pride #10
2019 Panini Prizm National Pride Prizms #10
2019 Panini Prizm National Pride Prizms Black /1 #10
2019 Panini Prizm National Pride Prizms Gold /10 #10
2019 Panini Prizm National Pride Prizms White Sparkle #10

2019 Panini Prizm Patented Penmanship Prizms #14
2019 Panini Prizm Patented Penmanship Prizms Black /1 #14
2019 Panini Prizm Patented Penmanship Prizms Blue /5 #14
2019 Panini Prizm Patented Penmanship Prizms Camo #14
2019 Panini Prizm Patented Penmanship Prizms Gold /10 #14
2019 Panini Prizm Patented Penmanship Prizms Green /5 #14
2019 Panini Prizm Patented Penmanship Prizms Rainbow /5 #14
2019 Panini Prizm Patented Penmanship Prizms Red /5 #14
2019 Panini Prizm Patented Penmanship Prizms Red White and Blue #14
2019 Panini Prizm Patented Penmanship Prizms White /5 #14
2019 Panini Prizm Prizms #40B
2019 Panini Prizm Prizms #40A
2019 Panini Prizm Prizms Black /1 #40A
2019 Panini Prizm Prizms Black /1 #40B
2019 Panini Prizm Prizms Blue /75 #40A
2019 Panini Prizm Prizms Blue /75 #40B
2019 Panini Prizm Prizms Camo #40A
2019 Panini Prizm Prizms Camo #40B
2019 Panini Prizm Prizms Flash #40A
2019 Panini Prizm Prizms Flash #40B
2019 Panini Prizm Prizms Gold /10 #40A
2019 Panini Prizm Prizms Gold /10 #40B
2019 Panini Prizm Prizms Green /99 #40A
2019 Panini Prizm Prizms Green /99 #40B
2019 Panini Prizm Prizms Rainbow /24 #40A
2019 Panini Prizm Prizms Rainbow /24 #40B
2019 Panini Prizm Prizms Red /50 #40A
2019 Panini Prizm Prizms Red /50 #40B
2019 Panini Prizm Prizms Red White and Blue #40A
2019 Panini Prizm Prizms Red White and Blue #40B
2019 Panini Prizm Prizms White /5 #40A
2019 Panini Prizm Prizms White /5 #40B
2019 Panini Prizm Prizms White Sparkle #40A
2019 Panini Prizm Prizms White Sparkle #40B
2019 Panini Prizm Stars and Stripes #2
2019 Panini Prizm Stars and Stripes Prizms #2
2019 Panini Prizm Stars and Stripes Prizms Black /1 #2
2019 Panini Prizm Stars and Stripes Prizms Gold /10 #2
2019 Panini Prizm Stars and Stripes Prizms White Sparkle #2
2019 Panini Prizm Teammates #9
2019 Panini Prizm Teammates Prizms #9
2019 Panini Prizm Teammates Prizms Black /1 #9
2019 Panini Prizm Teammates Prizms Gold /10 #9
2019 Panini Prizm Teammates Prizms White Sparkle #9
2019 Panini Victory Lane #45
2019 Panini Victory Lane #75
2019 Panini Victory Lane #79
2019 Panini Victory Lane #90
2019 Panini Victory Lane #95
2019 Panini Victory Lane #99
2019 Panini Victory Lane Black /1 #45
2019 Panini Victory Lane Black /1 #75
2019 Panini Victory Lane Black /1 #79
2019 Panini Victory Lane Black /1 #90
2019 Panini Victory Lane Black /1 #95
2019 Panini Victory Lane Black /1 #99
2019 Panini Victory Lane Dual Swatches #18
2019 Panini Victory Lane Dual Swatches Gold /99 #18
2019 Panini Victory Lane Dual Swatches Laundry Tag /1 #18
2019 Panini Victory Lane Dual Swatches Platinum /1 #18
2019 Panini Victory Lane Dual Swatches Red /25 #18
2019 Panini Victory Lane Gold /25 #45
2019 Panini Victory Lane Gold /25 #75
2019 Panini Victory Lane Gold /25 #79
2019 Panini Victory Lane Gold /25 #90
2019 Panini Victory Lane Gold /25 #95
2019 Panini Victory Lane Gold /25 #99
2019 Panini Victory Lane Horsepower Heroes #6
2019 Panini Victory Lane Horsepower Heroes Black /1 #6
2019 Panini Victory Lane Horsepower Heroes Blue /99 #6
2019 Panini Victory Lane Horsepower Heroes Gold /25 #6
2019 Panini Victory Lane Horsepower Heroes Green /5 #6
2019 Panini Victory Lane Horsepower Heroes Printing Plates Black /1 #6
2019 Panini Victory Lane Horsepower Heroes Printing Plates Cyan /1 #6
2019 Panini Victory Lane Horsepower Heroes Printing Plates Magenta /1 #6
2019 Panini Victory Lane Horsepower Heroes Printing Plates Yellow /1 #6
2019 Panini Victory Lane Pedal to the Metal #66
2019 Panini Victory Lane Pedal to the Metal #97
2019 Panini Victory Lane Pedal to the Metal #98
2019 Panini Victory Lane Pedal to the Metal #99
2019 Panini Victory Lane Pedal to the Metal #100
2019 Panini Victory Lane Pedal to the Metal Black /1 #66
2019 Panini Victory Lane Pedal to the Metal Black /1 #97
2019 Panini Victory Lane Pedal to the Metal Black /1 #98
2019 Panini Victory Lane Pedal to the Metal Black /1 #99
2019 Panini Victory Lane Pedal to the Metal Black /1 #100
2019 Panini Victory Lane Pedal to the Metal Gold /25 #97
2019 Panini Victory Lane Pedal to the Metal Gold /25 #98
2019 Panini Victory Lane Pedal to the Metal Gold /25 #99
2019 Panini Victory Lane Pedal to the Metal Gold /25 #100
2019 Panini Victory Lane Pedal to the Metal Gold /25 #66
2019 Panini Victory Lane Pedal to the Metal Green /5 #66
2019 Panini Victory Lane Pedal to the Metal Green /5 #97
2019 Panini Victory Lane Pedal to the Metal Green /5 #98
2019 Panini Victory Lane Pedal to the Metal Green /5 #99
2019 Panini Victory Lane Pedal to the Metal Green /5 #100
2019 Panini Victory Lane Pedal to the Metal Red /3 #66
2019 Panini Victory Lane Pedal to the Metal Red /3 #97
2019 Panini Victory Lane Pedal to the Metal Red /3 #98
2019 Panini Victory Lane Pedal to the Metal Red /3 #99
2019 Panini Victory Lane Pedal to the Metal Red /3 #100
2019 Panini Victory Lane Printing Plates Black /1 #45
2019 Panini Victory Lane Printing Plates Black /1 #75
2019 Panini Victory Lane Printing Plates Black /1 #79
2019 Panini Victory Lane Printing Plates Black /1 #90
2019 Panini Victory Lane Printing Plates Black /1 #95
2019 Panini Victory Lane Printing Plates Black /1 #99
2019 Panini Victory Lane Printing Plates Cyan /1 #45
2019 Panini Victory Lane Printing Plates Cyan /1 #75
2019 Panini Victory Lane Printing Plates Cyan /1 #79
2019 Panini Victory Lane Printing Plates Cyan /1 #90
2019 Panini Victory Lane Printing Plates Cyan /1 #95
2019 Panini Victory Lane Printing Plates Cyan /1 #99
2019 Panini Victory Lane Printing Plates Magenta /1 #45
2019 Panini Victory Lane Printing Plates Magenta /1 #75
2019 Panini Victory Lane Printing Plates Magenta /1 #79
2019 Panini Victory Lane Printing Plates Magenta /1 #90
2019 Panini Victory Lane Printing Plates Magenta /1 #95
2019 Panini Victory Lane Printing Plates Magenta /1 #99
2019 Panini Victory Lane Printing Plates Yellow /1 #45
2019 Panini Victory Lane Printing Plates Yellow /1 #75
2019 Panini Victory Lane Printing Plates Yellow /1 #79
2019 Panini Victory Lane Printing Plates Yellow /1 #90
2019 Panini Victory Lane Printing Plates Yellow /1 #95
2019 Panini Victory Lane Printing Plates Yellow /1 #99
2019 Panini Victory Lane Signature Swatches #17
2019 Panini Victory Lane Signature Swatches Gold /25 #17
2019 Panini Victory Lane Signature Swatches Laundry Tag /1 #17
2019 Panini Victory Lane Signature Swatches Platinum /1 #17
2019 Panini Victory Lane Signature Swatches Red /10 #17
2019 The Bar Pieces of the Past /1 #NNO
2019-20 Funko Pop Vinyl NASCAR #2
2020 Donruss #7
2020 Donruss #97
2020 Donruss #129
2020 Donruss Black Numbers /43 #7
2020 Donruss Black Numbers /43 #97
2020 Donruss Black Numbers /43 #129
2020 Donruss Black Trophy Club /1 #7
2020 Donruss Black Trophy Club /1 #97
2020 Donruss Black Trophy Club /1 #129
2020 Donruss Blue /199 #97
2020 Donruss Blue /199 #129
2020 Donruss Blue /199 #7
2020 Donruss Carolina Blue #7
2020 Donruss Carolina Blue #97
2020 Donruss Carolina Blue #129
2020 Donruss Classics #4
2020 Donruss Classics Checkers #4
2020 Donruss Classics Cracked Ice /25 #4
2020 Donruss Classics Holographic /199 #4
2020 Donruss Classics Xplosion /10 #4
2020 Donruss Dominators #5
2020 Donruss Dominators Checkers #5
2020 Donruss Dominators Cracked Ice /25 #5
2020 Donruss Dominators Holographic /199 #5
2020 Donruss Dominators Xplosion /10 #5
2020 Donruss Downtown #2
2020 Donruss Green /99 #7
2020 Donruss Green /99 #97
2020 Donruss Green /99 #129
2020 Donruss Optic #7
2020 Donruss Optic #90
2020 Donruss Optic Carolina Blue Wave #90
2020 Donruss Optic Carolina Blue Wave #7
2020 Donruss Optic Gold /10 #7
2020 Donruss Optic Gold /10 #90
2020 Donruss Optic Gold Vinyl /1 #7
2020 Donruss Optic Gold Vinyl /1 #90
2020 Donruss Optic Holo #7
2020 Donruss Optic Holo #90
2020 Donruss Optic Orange Pulsar #7
2020 Donruss Optic Orange Pulsar #90
2020 Donruss Optic Red Mojo #7
2020 Donruss Optic Red Mojo #90
2020 Donruss Optic Signatures Gold Vinyl /1 #7
2020 Donruss Optic Signatures Gold Vinyl /1 #90
2020 Donruss Optic Signatures Holo /99 #7
2020 Donruss Optic Signatures Holo /99 #90
2020 Donruss Orange #7
2020 Donruss Orange #97
2020 Donruss Orange #129
2020 Donruss Pink /25 #7
2020 Donruss Pink /25 #97
2020 Donruss Pink /25 #129
2020 Donruss Printing Plates Black /1 #7
2020 Donruss Printing Plates Black /1 #97
2020 Donruss Printing Plates Black /1 #129
2020 Donruss Printing Plates Cyan /1 #7
2020 Donruss Printing Plates Cyan /1 #97
2020 Donruss Printing Plates Cyan /1 #129
2020 Donruss Printing Plates Magenta /1 #97
2020 Donruss Printing Plates Magenta /1 #129
2020 Donruss Printing Plates Magenta /1 #7
2020 Donruss Printing Plates Yellow /1 #129
2020 Donruss Printing Plates Yellow /1 #7
2020 Donruss Printing Plates Yellow /1 #97
2020 Donruss Purple /49 #7
2020 Donruss Purple /49 #97
2020 Donruss Purple /49 #129
2020 Donruss Red /299 #7
2020 Donruss Red /299 #97
2020 Donruss Red /299 #129
2020 Donruss Retro Relics '87 #10
2020 Donruss Retro Relics '87 Holo Black /1 #10
2020 Donruss Retro Relics '87 Holo Gold /7 #10
2020 Donruss Retro Relics '87 Red /43 #10
2020 Donruss Silver #7
2020 Donruss Silver #97
2020 Donruss Silver #129
2020 Donruss Timeless Treasures Signatures #8
2020 Donruss Timeless Treasures Signatures Holo Black /1 #8
2020 Donruss Timeless Treasures Signatures Holo Gold /10 #8
2020 Donruss Timeless Treasures Signatures Red /25 #8
2020 Donruss Top Tier #8
2020 Donruss Top Tier Checkers #8
2020 Donruss Top Tier Cracked Ice /25 #8
2020 Donruss Top Tier Holographic /199 #8
2020 Donruss Top Tier Xplosion /10 #8

David Ragan

2006 Press Pass Optima #47
2006 Press Pass Optima Fan Favorite #FF27
2006 Press Pass Optima Gold /100 #G47
2007 AAA Limited Edition /5000 #1
2007 AAA Limited Edition /5000 #2
2007 AAA Limited Edition /5000 #3
2007 AAA Limited Edition /5000 #4
2007 AAA Limited Edition /5000 #5
2007 AAA Limited Edition /5000 #6
2007 AAA Limited Edition /5000 #7
2007 AAA Limited Edition /5000 #8
2007 AAA Limited Edition /5000 #9
2007 AAA Limited Edition /5000 #10
2007 AAA Limited Edition /5000 #11
2007 AAA Limited Edition /5000 #12
2007 AAA Limited Edition /5000 #13
2007 AAA Limited Edition /5000 #14
2007 AAA Limited Edition /5000 #15
2007 AAA Limited Edition /5000 #16
2007 AAA Limited Edition /5000 #17
2007 AAA Limited Edition /5000 #18
2007 AAA Limited Edition /5000 #19
2007 AAA Limited Edition /5000 #20
2007 AAA Limited Edition /5000 #21
2007 AAA Limited Edition /5000 #22
2007 AAA Limited Edition /5000 #23
2007 AAA Limited Edition /5000 #24
2007 AAA Limited Edition /5000 #25
2007 AAA Limited Edition /5000 #26
2007 AAA Limited Edition /5000 #27
2007 AAA Limited Edition /5000 #28
2007 AAA Limited Edition /5000 #29
2007 AAA Limited Edition /5000 #30
2007 AAA Limited Edition /5000 #31
2007 AAA Limited Edition /5000 #32
2007 AAA Limited Edition /5000 #33
2007 AAA Limited Edition /5000 #34
2007 AAA Limited Edition /5000 #35
2007 AAA Limited Edition /5000 #36
2007 AAA Limited Edition /5000 #37
2007 AAA Limited Edition /5000 #38
2007 Press Pass #51
2007 Press Pass Autographs #36
2007 Press Pass Blue #B51
2007 Press Pass Gold #G51
2007 Press Pass Platinum /100 #P51
2007 Press Pass Premium #87
2007 Press Pass Premium Red /5 #R87
2007 Press Pass Signings #58
2007 Press Pass Signings Blue /25 #24
2007 Press Pass Signings Gold /50 #44
2007 Press Pass Signings Press Plates Black /1 #36
2007 Press Pass Signings Press Plates Cyan /1 #35
2007 Press Pass Signings Press Plates Magenta /1 #37
2007 Press Pass Signings Press Plates Yellow /1 #36
2007 Press Pass Signings Silver /100 #42
2007 Press Pass Stealth #33
2007 Press Pass Stealth #42
2007 Press Pass Stealth #69
2007 Press Pass Stealth #74
2007 Press Pass Stealth Battle Armor Drivers /150 #BAD4
2007 Press Pass Stealth Battle Armor Teams /85 #BAT4
2007 Press Pass Stealth Chrome #33
2007 Press Pass Stealth Chrome #42
2007 Press Pass Stealth Chrome #69
2007 Press Pass Stealth Chrome #74
2007 Press Pass Stealth Chrome Exclusives /99 #X33
2007 Press Pass Stealth Chrome Exclusives /99 #X42
2007 Press Pass Stealth Chrome Exclusives /99 #X69
2007 Press Pass Stealth Chrome Exclusives /99 #X74
2007 Press Pass Stealth Chrome Platinum /25 #P33
2007 Press Pass Stealth Chrome Platinum /25 #P42
2007 Press Pass Stealth Chrome Platinum /25 #P69
2007 Press Pass Stealth Chrome Platinum /25 #P74
2007 Press Pass Stealth Maximum Access #MA22
2007 Press Pass Stealth Maximum Access Autographs /25 #MA22
2007 Press Pass Stealth Previews /5 #EB33
2007 Press Pass Stealth Previews /5 #EB42
2007 Press Pass Top Prospects Sheet Metal /350 #DRASM
2007 Press Pass Top Prospects Sheet Metal-Tire /75 #DRAST
2007 Press Pass Top Prospects Shoes /200 #DRAS
2007 Press Pass Top Prospects Tire Autographs /25 #DRAA
2007 Press Pass Top Prospects Tires Gold /99 #DRaT
2007 Press Pass Top Prospects Tires Silver /250 #DRaT
2007 Traks #35
2007 Traks Corporate Cuts Driver /99 #CCD3
2007 Traks Corporate Cuts Patch /15 #CCD3
2007 Traks Corporate Cuts Team /180 #CCT3
2007 Traks Gold #G35
2007 Traks Holofoil /50 #H35
2007 Traks Previews /5 #EB35
2007 Traks Red /10 #R35
2007 VIP #88
2007 VIP Get A Grip Drivers /70 #GGD24
2007 VIP Get A Grip Teams /70 #GGT24
2007 VIP Previews /1 #EB88
2007 VIP Rookie Stripes /100 #RS4
2007 VIP Rookie Stripes Autographs /25 #RSDRA
2007 Wheels American Thunder /305 #88
2007 Wheels American Thunder Autographed Hat Instant Winner /1 #AH28
2007 Wheels American Thunder Head to Toe /99 #HT7
2007 Wheels American Thunder Triple Hat /99 #TH23
2007 Wheels Autographs #33
2007 Wheels Autographs Press Plates Black /1 #32
2007 Wheels Autographs Press Plates Cyan /1 #32
2007 Wheels Autographs Press Plates Magenta /1 #32
2007 Wheels High Gear #45
2007 Wheels High Gear MPH /100 #M45
2008 Press Pass #23
2008 Press Pass #83
2008 Press Pass #86
2008 Press Pass Autographs #30
2008 Press Pass Autographs Press Plates Black /1 #25
2008 Press Pass Autographs Press Plates Cyan /1 #25
2008 Press Pass Autographs Press Plates Magenta /1 #25
2008 Press Pass Autographs Press Plates Yellow /1 #25
2008 Press Pass Blue #B23
2008 Press Pass Blue #B83
2008 Press Pass Blue #B86
2008 Press Pass Collector's Series Box Set #13
2008 Press Pass Eclipse #19
2008 Press Pass Eclipse #60
2008 Press Pass Eclipse Gold /25 #G19
2008 Press Pass Eclipse Gold /25 #G60
2008 Press Pass Eclipse Previews /5 #EB19
2008 Press Pass Eclipse Red /1 #R19
2008 Press Pass Eclipse Red /1 #R60
2008 Press Pass Eclipse Under Cover Double Cover Name /25 #DC4
2008 Press Pass Eclipse Under Cover Double Cover Name /25 #DC7
2008 Press Pass Eclipse Under Cover Double Cover NASCAR /99 #DC4
2008 Press Pass Eclipse Under Cover Double Cover NASCAR /99 #DC7
2008 Press Pass Eclipse Under Cover Drivers /250 #UCD10
2008 Press Pass Eclipse Under Cover Drivers Eclipse /1 #UCD10
2008 Press Pass Eclipse Under Cover Drivers Name /50 #UCD10
2008 Press Pass Eclipse Under Cover Drivers NASCAR /150 #UCD10
2008 Press Pass Eclipse Under Cover Teams /99 #UCT10
2008 Press Pass Eclipse Under Cover Teams NASCAR /25 #UCT10
2008 Press Pass Gold #G23
2008 Press Pass Gold #G83
2008 Press Pass Gold #G86
2008 Press Pass Legends Prominent Pieces Firesuit-Glove-Belt /25 #PP2DR
2008 Press Pass Legends Prominent Pieces Firesuit-Glove-Belt Gold /10 #PP2DR
2008 Press Pass Legends Prominent Pieces Metal-Tire-Net /50 #PP4DR
2008 Press Pass Legends Prominent Pieces Metal-Tire-Net Gold /25 #PP4DR
2008 Press Pass Platinum /100 #P23
2008 Press Pass Platinum /100 #P83
2008 Press Pass Platinum /100 #P86
2008 Press Pass Premium #7
2008 Press Pass Premium Previews /5 #EB7
2008 Press Pass Premium Red /15 #7
2008 Press Pass Premium Team Signed Baseballs #ROU
2008 Press Pass Premium Team Signed Baseballs #EROU
2008 Press Pass Previews /5 #EB23
2008 Press Pass Signings #50
2008 Press Pass Signings Blue /25 #25
2008 Press Pass Signings Gold /50 #43
2008 Press Pass Signings Press Plates Black /1 #33
2008 Press Pass Signings Press Plates Cyan /1 #33
2008 Press Pass Signings Press Plates Cyan /1 #DR
2008 Press Pass Signings Press Plates Magenta /1 #33
2008 Press Pass Signings Press Plates Magenta #DR
2008 Press Pass Signings Press Plates Yellow /1 #33
2008 Press Pass Signings Press Plates Yellow #DR
2008 Press Pass Signings Silver /100 #42
2008 Press Pass Speedway #27
2008 Press Pass Speedway #46
2008 Press Pass Speedway Corporate Cuts Drivers /80 #CDDR
2008 Press Pass Speedway Corporate Cuts Drivers Patches /11 #CDDR
2008 Press Pass Speedway Corporate Cuts Team /165 #CTDR
2008 Press Pass Speedway Gold #G27
2008 Press Pass Speedway Gold #G46
2008 Press Pass Speedway Holofoil /50 #H27
2008 Press Pass Speedway Holofoil /50 #H46
2008 Press Pass Speedway Previews /5 #EB27
2008 Press Pass Speedway Previews /5 #EB46
2008 Press Pass Speedway Red /10 #R27
2008 Press Pass Speedway Red /10 #R46
2008 Press Pass Starting Grid #SG13
2008 Press Pass Stealth #29
2008 Press Pass Stealth #70
2008 Press Pass Stealth #80
2008 Press Pass Stealth Chrome #29
2008 Press Pass Stealth Chrome #70
2008 Press Pass Stealth Chrome #80
2008 Press Pass Stealth Chrome Exclusives /25 #29
2008 Press Pass Stealth Chrome Exclusives /25 #70
2008 Press Pass Stealth Chrome Exclusives /25 #80
2008 Press Pass Stealth Chrome Exclusives Gold /99 #29
2008 Press Pass Stealth Chrome Exclusives Gold /99 #70
2008 Press Pass Stealth Chrome Exclusives Gold /99 #80
2008 Press Pass Stealth Maximum Access #MA22
2008 Press Pass Stealth Maximum Access Autographs /25 #MA22
2008 Press Pass Stealth Previews /5 #29
2008 VIP #28
2008 VIP Previews /5 #EB28
2008 Wheels American Thunder #28
2008 Wheels American Thunder #38
2008 Wheels American Thunder #62
2008 Wheels American Thunder #68
2008 Wheels American Thunder Autographed Hat Winner /1 #IWHDR
2008 Wheels American Thunder Cool Threads /325 #CT12
2008 Wheels American Thunder Head to Toe /99 #HT4
2008 Wheels American Thunder Previews /5 #28
2008 Wheels American Thunder Pushin' Pedal /99 #PP 4
2008 Wheels American Thunder Trackside Treasury Autographs #DR
2008 Wheels American Thunder Trackside Treasury Autographs Gold /25 #DR
2008 Wheels American Thunder Trackside Treasury Autographs Printing Plates Black /1 #DR
2008 Wheels American Thunder Trackside Treasury Autographs Printing Plates Cyan /1 #DR
2008 Wheels American Thunder Trackside Treasury Autographs Printing Plates Magenta /1 #DR
2008 Wheels American Thunder Trackside Treasury Autographs Printing Plates Yellow /1 #DR
2008 Wheels American Thunder Triple Hat /99 #TH21
2008 Wheels Autographs #23
2008 Wheels Autographs Press Plates Black /1 #23
2008 Wheels Autographs Press Plates Cyan /1 #23
2008 Wheels Autographs Press Plates Magenta /1 #23
2008 Wheels Autographs Press Plates Yellow /1 #23
2008 Wheels High Gear #20
2008 Wheels High Gear Driven #DR5
2008 Wheels High Gear Final Standings /23 #F20
2008 Wheels High Gear MPH /100 #M20
2008 Wheels High Gear Previews /5 #EB20
2009 Element #28
2009 Element #71
2009 Element Lab Report #LR22
2009 Element Previews /5 #28
2009 Element Radioactive /100 #28
2009 Element Radioactive /100 #71
2009 Press Pass #14
2009 Press Pass #47
2009 Press Pass #79
2009 Press Pass #146
2009 Press Pass #177
2009 Press Pass Autographs Gold #39
2009 Press Pass Autographs Printing Plates Black /1 #36
2009 Press Pass Autographs Printing Plates Cyan /1 #36
2009 Press Pass Autographs Printing Plates Magenta /1 #36
2009 Press Pass Autographs Printing Plates Yellow /1 #36
2009 Press Pass Autographs Silver #40
2009 Press Pass Blue #14
2009 Press Pass Blue #47
2009 Press Pass Blue #79
2009 Press Pass Blue #146
2009 Press Pass Blue #177
2009 Press Pass Eclipse #5
2009 Press Pass Eclipse #83
2009 Press Pass Eclipse Black and White #5
2009 Press Pass Eclipse Black and White #83
2009 Press Pass Eclipse Blue #5
2009 Press Pass Eclipse Blue #83
2009 Press Pass Eclipse Ecliptic Path #EP8
2009 Press Pass Four Wide Checkered Flag /1 #FWDR
2009 Press Pass Four Wide Firesuit /50 #FWDR
2009 Press Pass Four Wide Sheet Metal /10 #FWDR
2009 Press Pass Four Wide Tire /25 #FWDR
2009 Press Pass Four Wide Tire /25 #FWDR2
2009 Press Pass Gold #14
2009 Press Pass Gold #47
2009 Press Pass Gold #79
2009 Press Pass Gold #146
2009 Press Pass Gold #177
2009 Press Pass Gold Holofoil /100 #14
2009 Press Pass Gold Holofoil /100 #47
2009 Press Pass Gold Holofoil /100 #79
2009 Press Pass Gold Holofoil /100 #146
2009 Press Pass Gold Holofoil /100 #177
2009 Press Pass Legends Prominent Pieces Bronze /99 #PPDR
2009 Press Pass Legends Prominent Pieces Gold /25 #PPDR
2009 Press Pass Legends Prominent Pieces Silver /50 #PPDR
2009 Press Pass Pocket Portraits #P20
2009 Press Pass Pocket Portraits Hometown #P20
2009 Press Pass Pocket Portraits Smoke #P20
2009 Press Pass Pocket Portraits Wal-Mart #PPW10
2009 Press Pass Premium #7
2009 Press Pass Premium #37
2009 Press Pass Premium #59
2009 Press Pass Premium Hot Threads /299 #HTDR1
2009 Press Pass Premium Hot Threads /99 #HTDR2
2009 Press Pass Premium Hot Threads Multi-Color /25 #HTDR
2009 Press Pass Premium Previews /5 #EB7
2009 Press Pass Premium Signatures #27
2009 Press Pass Premium Signatures Gold /25 #26
2009 Press Pass Premium Win Streak #WS13
2009 Press Pass Premium Win Streak Victory Lane #WSVL-DR
2009 Press Pass Previews /5 #EB14
2009 Press Pass Previews /5 #EB146
2009 Press Pass Red #14
2009 Press Pass Red #47
2009 Press Pass Red #79
2009 Press Pass Red #146
2009 Press Pass Red #177
2009 Press Pass Santa Hats /50 #SH15
2009 Press Pass Showcase /499 #25
2009 Press Pass Showcase /499 #35
2009 Press Pass Showcase 2nd Gear /125 #25
2009 Press Pass Showcase 2nd Gear /125 #35
2009 Press Pass Showcase 3rd Gear /50 #25
2009 Press Pass Showcase 3rd Gear /50 #35
2009 Press Pass Showcase 4th Gear /15 #25
2009 Press Pass Showcase 4th Gear /15 #35
2009 Press Pass Showcase Classic Collections Firesuit /25 #CCF8
2009 Press Pass Showcase Classic Collections Firesuit Patch /5 #CCF8
2009 Press Pass Showcase Classic Collections Ink /45 #9
2009 Press Pass Showcase Classic Collections Ink Gold /25 #9
2009 Press Pass Showcase Classic Collections Ink Green /5 #9
2009 Press Pass Showcase Classic Collections Ink Melting /1 #9
2009 Press Pass Showcase Classic Collections Sheet Metal /45 #CCS8
2009 Press Pass Showcase Classic Collections Tire /99 #CCT8
2009 Press Pass Showcase Printing Plates Black /1 #25
2009 Press Pass Showcase Printing Plates Black /1 #35
2009 Press Pass Showcase Printing Plates Cyan /1 #25
2009 Press Pass Showcase Printing Plates Cyan /1 #35
2009 Press Pass Showcase Printing Plates Magenta /1 #25
2009 Press Pass Showcase Printing Plates Magenta /1 #35
2009 Press Pass Showcase Printing Plates Yellow /1 #25
2009 Press Pass Showcase Printing Plates Yellow /1 #35
2009 Press Pass Signings Blue /25 #36
2009 Press Pass Signings Gold #36
2009 Press Pass Signings Green /15 #36
2009 Press Pass Signings Orange /65 #36
2009 Press Pass Signings Printing Plates Black /1 #36
2009 Press Pass Signings Printing Plates Cyan /1 #36
2009 Press Pass Signings Printing Plates Magenta /1 #36
2009 Press Pass Signings Printing Plates Yellow /1 #36
2009 Press Pass Signings Purple /45 #36
2009 Press Pass Sponsor Swatches /200 #SSDR
2009 Press Pass Sponsor Swatches Select /10 #SSDR
2009 Press Pass Stealth #26
2009 Press Pass Stealth #45
2009 Press Pass Stealth #65
2009 Press Pass Stealth Battle Armor /320 #BADR
2009 Press Pass Stealth Battle Armor Multi-Color /160 #BADR
2009 Press Pass Stealth Chrome #26
2009 Press Pass Stealth Chrome #45
2009 Press Pass Stealth Chrome #65
2009 Press Pass Stealth Chrome Brushed Metal /25 #26
2009 Press Pass Stealth Chrome Brushed Metal /25 #45
2009 Press Pass Stealth Chrome Brushed Metal /25 #65
2009 Press Pass Stealth Chrome Gold /99 #26
2009 Press Pass Stealth Chrome Gold /99 #45
2009 Press Pass Stealth Chrome Gold /99 #65
2009 Press Pass Stealth Confidential Classified Bronze #PC24
2009 Press Pass Stealth Confidential Secret Silver #PC24
2009 Press Pass Stealth Confidential Top Secret Gold /25 #PC24
2009 Press Pass Stealth Mach 09 #M12
2009 Press Pass Stealth Previews /5 #EB26
2009 Press Pass Tradin' Paint #TP5
2009 Press Pass Tread Marks Autographs /15 #SSDR
2009 VIP #26
2009 VIP #37
2009 VIP #49
2009 VIP Get A Grip /120 #GGDR
2009 VIP Get A Grip Autographs /6 #GGSDR
2009 VIP Get A Grip Holofoil /10 #GGDR
2009 VIP Leadfoot /150 #LFDRa
2009 VIP Leadfoot Holofoil /10 #LFDRa
2009 VIP Previews /5 #26
2009 VIP Purple /25 #26
2009 VIP Purple /25 #37
2009 VIP Purple /25 #49
2009 Wheels Autographs #51
2009 Wheels Autographs /25 #52
2009 Wheels Autographs Press Plates Black /1 #DR
2009 Wheels Autographs Press Plates Cyan /1 #DR
2009 Wheels Autographs Press Plates Magenta /1 #DR
2009 Wheels Autographs Press Plates Yellow /1 #DR
2009 Wheels Main Event #24
2009 Wheels Main Event #38
2009 Wheels Main Event Fast Pass Purple /25 #24
2009 Wheels Main Event Fast Pass Purple /25 #38
2009 Wheels Main Event Foil #24
2009 Wheels Main Event Hat Dance Patch /10 #HDDR
2009 Wheels Main Event Hat Dance Triple /99 #HDDR
2009 Wheels Main Event Marks Clubs #46
2009 Wheels Main Event Marks Diamonds /50 #46
2009 Wheels Main Event Marks Hearts /10 #46
2009 Wheels Main Event Marks Printing Plates Black /1 #40
2009 Wheels Main Event Marks Printing Plates Cyan /1 #40
2009 Wheels Main Event Marks Printing Plates Magenta /1 #40
2009 Wheels Main Event Marks Printing Plates Yellow /1 #40
2009 Wheels Main Event Marks Spades /1 #46
2009 Wheels Main Event Playing Cards Blue #9C
2009 Wheels Main Event Playing Cards Red #9C
2009 Wheels Main Event Previews /5 #24
2009 Wheels Main Event Renegade Rounders Wanted #RR9
2009 Wheels Main Event Reward Copper /10 #RWDR
2009 Wheels Main Event Reward Holofoil /50 #RWDR
2009 Wheels Main Event Stop and Go Swatches Pit Banner /125 #SGBDR
2009 Wheels Main Event Stop and Go Swatches Pit Banner Green /10 #SGBDR
2009 Wheels Main Event Stop and Go Swatches Pit Banner Holofoil /75 #SGBDR
2009 Wheels Main Event Stop and Go Swatches Pit Banner Red /25 #SGBDR
2009 Wheels Main Event Wildcard Cuts /2 #WCCDR
2010 Element #24
2010 Element Blue /35 #24
2010 Element Green #24
2010 Element Previews /5 #EB24
2010 Element Purple /25 #24
2010 Element Red Target #24
2010 Press Pass #30
2010 Press Pass Autographs #40
2010 Press Pass Autographs Printing Plates Cyan /1 #37
2010 Press Pass Autographs Printing Plates Magenta /1 #35
2010 Press Pass Autographs Printing Plates Magenta /1 #36
2010 Press Pass Autographs Printing Plates Yellow /1 #34
2010 Press Pass Blue #30
2010 Press Pass Eclipse #7
2010 Press Pass Eclipse Blue #7
2010 Press Pass Eclipse Gold #7
2010 Press Pass Eclipse Previews /5 #7
2010 Press Pass Eclipse Purple /25 #7
2010 Press Pass Eclipse Signature Series Shoes Autographs /6 #SSSEDR
2010 Press Pass Five Star Classic Compilations Combos Firesuit Autographs /15 #CCMROU
2010 Press Pass Five Star Classic Compilations Combos Patches Autographs /1 #CCMROU
2010 Press Pass Gold #30
2010 Press Pass Holofoil /100 #30
2010 Press Pass Premium #27
2010 Press Pass Premium #63
2010 Press Pass Premium Purple /25 #27
2010 Press Pass Premium Purple /25 #63
2010 Press Pass Premium Signatures #PSDR
2010 Press Pass Premium Signatures Red Ink /24 #PSDR
2010 Press Pass Previews /5 #30
2010 Press Pass Purple /25 #30
2010 Press Pass Showcase /499 #25
2010 Press Pass Showcase /499 #34
2010 Press Pass Showcase Classic Collections Firesuit Green /25 #CCIRFR
2010 Press Pass Showcase Classic Collections Firesuit Patch Melting /5 #CCIRFR
2010 Press Pass Showcase Classic Collections Ink /15 #CCIRFR
2010 Press Pass Showcase Classic Collections Ink Gold /10 #CCIRFR
2010 Press Pass Showcase Classic Collections Ink Green /5 #CCIRFR
2010 Press Pass Showcase Classic Collections Ink Melting /1 #CCIRFR
2010 Press Pass Showcase Classic Collections Sheet Metal /99 #CCIRFR
2010 Press Pass Showcase Classic Collections Sheet Metal Gold /45 #CCIRFR
2010 Press Pass Showcase Gold /125 #25
2010 Press Pass Showcase Gold /125 #34
2010 Press Pass Showcase Green /50 #25
2010 Press Pass Showcase Green /50 #34
2010 Press Pass Showcase Melting /15 #25
2010 Press Pass Showcase Melting /15 #34
2010 Press Pass Showcase Platinum Holo /1 #25
2010 Press Pass Showcase Platinum Holo /1 #34
2010 Press Pass Signings Blue /10 #44
2010 Press Pass Signings Gold /50 #44
2010 Press Pass Signings Red /15 #44
2010 Press Pass Signings Silver /75 #43
2010 Press Pass Stealth #28
2010 Press Pass Stealth Battle Armor Holofoil /25 #BADR1
2010 Press Pass Stealth Battle Armor Silver /275 #BADR1
2010 Press Pass Stealth Black and White #28
2010 Press Pass Stealth Previews /5 #28
2010 Press Pass Stealth Purple /25 #28
2010 Press Pass Stealth Signature Series Sheet Metal /15 #SSMEDR
2010 Wheels Autographs #40
2010 Wheels Autographs Printing Plates Black /1 #40
2010 Wheels Autographs Printing Plates Cyan /1 #40
2010 Wheels Autographs Printing Plates Magenta /1 #40
2010 Wheels Autographs Printing Plates Yellow /1 #40
2010 Wheels Autographs Special Ink /10 #13
2010 Wheels Autographs Target /10 #28
2010 Wheels Main Event #28
2010 Wheels Main Event Blue #28
2010 Wheels Main Event Fight Card #FC22
2010 Wheels Main Event Fight Card Checkered Flag #FC22
2010 Wheels Main Event Fight Card Full Color Retail #FC22
2010 Wheels Main Event Fight Card Gold /25 #FC22
2010 Wheels Main Event Marks Autographs /76 #46
2010 Wheels Main Event Marks Autographs Black /1 #45
2010 Wheels Main Event Marks Autographs Blue /50 #46
2010 Wheels Main Event Marks Autographs Red /25 #46
2010 Wheels Main Event Purple /25 #28
2011 Element #27
2011 Element #80
2011 Element Autographs /85 #44
2011 Element Autographs Blue /10 #44
2011 Element Autographs Gold /25 #42
2011 Element Autographs Printing Plates Black /1 #44
2011 Element Autographs Printing Plates Cyan /1 #44
2011 Element Autographs Printing Plates Magenta /1 #44
2011 Element Autographs Printing Plates Yellow /1 #44
2011 Element Autographs Silver /50 #42
2011 Element Black /35 #27
2011 Element Black /35 #80
2011 Element Flagship Performers 2010 Green Flag Passes Blue-Yellow /50 #FPPDR
2011 Element Green #27
2011 Element Green #80
2011 Element Previews /5 #EB27
2011 Element Purple /25 #27
2011 Element Purple /25 #80
2011 Element Red #27
2011 Element Red #80
2011 Element Trackside Treasures Holofoil /25 #TTDR
2011 Element Trackside Treasures Silver /85 #TTDR
2011 Press Pass #29
2011 Press Pass #84
2011 Press Pass #131
2011 Press Pass #163
2011 Press Pass Autographs Blue /10 #44
2011 Press Pass Autographs Bronze /75 #45
2011 Press Pass Autographs Gold /25 #42
2011 Press Pass Autographs Printing Plates Black /1 #45
2011 Press Pass Autographs Printing Plates Cyan /1 #45
2011 Press Pass Autographs Printing Plates Magenta /1 #45
2011 Press Pass Autographs Printing Plates Yellow /1 #45
2011 Press Pass Autographs Silver /50 #45
2011 Press Pass Blue Holofoil /10 #29
2011 Press Pass Blue Holofoil /10 #84
2011 Press Pass Blue Holofoil /10 #131
2011 Press Pass Blue Holofoil /10 #163
2011 Press Pass Blue Retail #29
2011 Press Pass Blue Retail #84
2011 Press Pass Blue Retail #131
2011 Press Pass Blue Retail #163
2011 Press Pass Eclipse #26
2011 Press Pass Eclipse #36
2011 Press Pass Eclipse Blue #26
2011 Press Pass Eclipse Blue #36
2011 Press Pass Eclipse Gold /55 #26
2011 Press Pass Eclipse Gold /55 #36
2011 Press Pass Eclipse Previews /5 #EB26
2011 Press Pass Eclipse Previews /1 #EB36
2011 Press Pass Eclipse Purple /25 #26
2011 Press Pass Eclipse Purple /25 #36
2011 Press Pass FanFare #32
2011 Press Pass FanFare Autographs Blue /5 #61
2011 Press Pass FanFare Autographs Bronze /65 #61
2011 Press Pass FanFare Autographs Gold /50 #61
2011 Press Pass FanFare Autographs Printing Plates Black /1 #61
2011 Press Pass FanFare Autographs Printing Plates Cyan /1 #61
2011 Press Pass FanFare Autographs Printing Plates Magenta /1 #61
2011 Press Pass FanFare Autographs Printing Plates Yellow /1 #61
2011 Press Pass FanFare Autographs Silver /25 #61
2011 Press Pass FanFare Blue Die Cuts #32
2011 Press Pass FanFare Emerald /25 #32
2011 Press Pass FanFare Holofoil Die Cuts #32
2011 Press Pass FanFare Magnificent Materials /199 #MMDR
2011 Press Pass FanFare Magnificent Materials Dual Swatches /50 #MMDDR
2011 Press Pass FanFare Magnificent Materials Dual Swatches Holofoil /10 #MMDDR
2011 Press Pass FanFare Magnificent Materials Holofoil /50 #MMDR
2011 Press Pass FanFare Ruby Die Cuts /15 #32
2011 Press Pass FanFare Sapphire /10 #32
2011 Press Pass FanFare Silver /25 #32
2011 Press Pass Geared Up Gold /100 #GUDRA
2011 Press Pass Geared Up Holofoil /50 #GUDRA
2011 Press Pass Gold /50 #29
2011 Press Pass Gold /50 #84
2011 Press Pass Gold /50 #131
2011 Press Pass Gold /50 #163
2011 Press Pass Premium #30
2011 Press Pass Premium Hot Threads /150 #HTDR
2011 Press Pass Premium Hot Threads Multi Color /25 #HTDR
2011 Press Pass Premium Hot Threads Secondary Color /99 #HTDR
2011 Press Pass Premium Purple /25 #30
2011 Press Pass Premium Signatures /200 #PSDR1
2011 Press Pass Previews /5 #EB29
2011 Press Pass Purple /25 #29
2011 Press Pass Showcase /499 #23
2011 Press Pass Showcase /499 #55
2011 Press Pass Showcase Classic Collections Firesuit /45 #CCMRFR
2011 Press Pass Showcase Classic Collections Firesuit Patches /5 #CCMRFR
2011 Press Pass Showcase Classic Collections Ink /25 #CCMRFR
2011 Press Pass Showcase Classic Collections Ink Gold /5 #CCMRFR
2011 Press Pass Showcase Classic Collections Ink Melting /1 #CCMRFR
2011 Press Pass Showcase Classic Collections Sheet Metal /99 #CCMRFR
2011 Press Pass Showcase Gold /125 #23
2011 Press Pass Showcase Gold /125 #55
2011 Press Pass Showcase Green /25 #23
2011 Press Pass Showcase Green /25 #55
2011 Press Pass Showcase Melting /1 #23
2011 Press Pass Showcase Melting /1 #55
2011 Press Pass Signings Black and White /10 #PPSDR1
2011 Press Pass Signings Brushed Metal /60 #PPSDR1
2011 Press Pass Signings Holofoil /25 #PPSDR1
2011 Press Pass Signings Printing Plates Black /1 #PPSDR1
2011 Press Pass Signings Printing Plates Cyan /1 #PPSDR1
2011 Press Pass Signings Printing Plates Magenta /1 #PPSDR1
2011 Press Pass Signings Printing Plates Yellow /1 #PPSDR1
2011 Press Pass Stealth #51
2011 Press Pass Stealth Black and White /25 #51
2011 Press Pass Stealth Holofoil /99 #51
2011 Press Pass Stealth Metal of Honor Medal of Honor /50 #BADR
2011 Press Pass Stealth Metal of Honor Purple Heart /25 #MHDR
2011 Press Pass Stealth Metal of Honor Silver Star /99 #BADR
2011 Press Pass Stealth Purple /25 #51
2011 Wheels Main Event #30
2011 Wheels Main Event #65
2011 Wheels Main Event All Stars #A8
2011 Wheels Main Event All Stars Brushed Foil /199 #A8

2011 Wheels Main Event All Stars Holofoil /50 #A8
2011 Wheels Main Event Black and White #30
2011 Wheels Main Event Black and White #65
2011 Wheels Main Event Blue /75 #30
2011 Wheels Main Event Blue /75 #65
2011 Wheels Main Event Green /1 #30
2011 Wheels Main Event Green /1 #65
2011 Wheels Main Event Lead Foot Holofoil /25 #LFDR
2011 Wheels Main Event Lead Foot Silver /99 #LFDR
2011 Wheels Main Event Marks Autographs Blue /10 #MEDR
2011 Wheels Main Event Marks Autographs Gold /25 #MEDR
2011 Wheels Main Event Marks Autographs Silver /65 #MEDR
2011 Wheels Main Event Red /20 #30
2011 Wheels Main Event Red /20 #65
2012 Press Pass #30
2012 Press Pass #74
2012 Press Pass #92
2012 Press Pass Autographs Blue /10 #PPADR1
2012 Press Pass Autographs Printing Plates Black /1 #PPADR1
2012 Press Pass Autographs Printing Plates Cyan /1 #PPADR1
2012 Press Pass Autographs Printing Plates Magenta /1 #PPADR1
2012 Press Pass Autographs Printing Plates Yellow /1 #PPADR1
2012 Press Pass Autographs Red /35 #PPADR1
2012 Press Pass Autographs Silver /199 #PPADR1
2012 Press Pass Blue #30
2012 Press Pass Blue #74
2012 Press Pass Blue #92
2012 Press Pass Blue Holofoil /35 #30
2012 Press Pass Blue Holofoil /35 #74
2012 Press Pass Blue Holofoil /35 #92
2012 Press Pass Burning Rubber Gold /99 #BRDR
2012 Press Pass Burning Rubber Holofoil /25 #BRDR
2012 Press Pass Burning Rubber Prime Cuts /25 #BRDR
2012 Press Pass Burning Rubber Purple /15 #BRDR
2012 Press Pass Fanfare #36
2012 Press Pass Fanfare Autographs Blue /25 #DR
2012 Press Pass Fanfare Autographs Gold /99 #DR
2012 Press Pass Fanfare Autographs Red /75 #DR
2012 Press Pass Fanfare Autographs Silver /299 #DR
2012 Press Pass Fanfare Blue Foil Die Cuts #36
2012 Press Pass Fanfare Diamond /5 #36
2012 Press Pass Fanfare Holofoil Die Cuts #36
2012 Press Pass Fanfare Magnificent Materials /75 #MMDR
2012 Press Pass Fanfare Magnificent Materials Dual Swatches /50 #MMDR
2012 Press Pass Fanfare Magnificent Materials Dual Swatches Melting /10 #MMDR
2012 Press Pass Fanfare Magnificent Materials Gold /50 #MMDR
2012 Press Pass Fanfare Sapphire /20 #36
2012 Press Pass Fanfare Silver /25 #36
2012 Press Pass Gold #30
2012 Press Pass Gold #74
2012 Press Pass Gold #92
2012 Press Pass Ignite #31
2012 Press Pass Ignite #65
2012 Press Pass Ignite Materials Gun Metal /99 #IMDR
2012 Press Pass Ignite Materials Red /10 #IMDR
2012 Press Pass Ignite Materials Silver #IMDR1
2012 Press Pass Ignite Proofs Black and White /50 #31
2012 Press Pass Ignite Proofs Black and White /50 #65
2012 Press Pass Ignite Proofs Cyan #31
2012 Press Pass Ignite Proofs Cyan #65
2012 Press Pass Ignite Proofs Magenta #31
2012 Press Pass Ignite Proofs Magenta #65
2012 Press Pass Ignite Proofs Yellow /10 #31
2012 Press Pass Ignite Proofs Yellow /10 #65
2012 Press Pass Power Picks Blue /50 #48
2012 Press Pass Power Picks Gold /50 #48
2012 Press Pass Power Picks Holofoil /10 #48
2012 Press Pass Purple /35 #30
2012 Press Pass Purple /35 #74
2012 Press Pass Purple /35 #92
2012 Press Pass Redline #33
2012 Press Pass Redline Black /99 #33
2012 Press Pass Redline Cyan /50 #33
2012 Press Pass Redline Magenta /15 #33
2012 Press Pass Redline Yellow /1 #33
2012 Press Pass Snapshots #SS30
2012 Total Memorabilia Dual Swatch Gold /75 #TMDR2
2012 Total Memorabilia Dual Swatch Holofoil /25 #TMDR2
2012 Total Memorabilia Dual Swatch Melting /5 #TMDR2
2012 Total Memorabilia Dual Swatch Silver /99 #TMDR2
2012 Total Memorabilia Quad Swatch Gold /25 #TMDR2
2012 Total Memorabilia Quad Swatch Holofoil /10 #TMDR2
2012 Total Memorabilia Quad Swatch Melting /1 #TMDR2
2012 Total Memorabilia Quad Swatch Silver /50 #TMDR2
2012 Total Memorabilia Single Swatch Gold /99 #TMDR2
2012 Total Memorabilia Single Swatch Holofoil /50 #TMDR2
2012 Total Memorabilia Single Swatch Melting /10 #TMDR2
2012 Total Memorabilia Single Swatch Silver /299 #TMDR2
2012 Total Memorabilia Triple Swatch Gold /50 #TMDR2
2012 Total Memorabilia Triple Swatch Holofoil /25 #TMDR2
2012 Total Memorabilia Triple Swatch Melting /1 #TMDR2
2012 Total Memorabilia Triple Swatch Silver /99 #TMDR2
2013 Press Pass #37
2013 Press Pass Color Proofs Black #37
2013 Press Pass Color Proofs Cyan /35 #37
2013 Press Pass Color Proofs Magenta #37
2013 Press Pass Color Proofs Yellow /5 #37
2013 Press Pass Fanfare #48
2013 Press Pass Fanfare Autographs Blue /10 #DR
2013 Press Pass Fanfare Autographs Gold /99 #DR
2013 Press Pass Fanfare Autographs Green /6 #DR
2013 Press Pass Fanfare Autographs Red /25 #DR
2013 Press Pass Fanfare Autographs Silver /149 #DR
2013 Press Pass Fanfare Diamond Die Cuts /5 #48
2013 Press Pass Fanfare Green /3 #48
2013 Press Pass Fanfare Holofoil Die Cuts #48
2013 Press Pass Fanfare Magnificent Materials Gold /50 #DR
2013 Press Pass Fanfare Magnificent Materials Silver /199 #DR
2013 Press Pass Fanfare Red Foil Die Cuts #48
2013 Press Pass Fanfare Sapphire /20 #48
2013 Press Pass Fanfare Silver /25 #48
2013 Press Pass Ignite #30
2013 Press Pass Ignite Hot Threads Blue Holofoil /99 #HTDR
2013 Press Pass Ignite Hot Threads Patch Red /10 #HTDR
2013 Press Pass Ignite Hot Threads Silver #HTDR
2013 Press Pass Ignite Ink Black /75 #IIDR
2013 Press Pass Ignite Ink Blue /20 #IIDR
2013 Press Pass Ignite Ink Red /5 #IIDR
2013 Press Pass Ignite Proofs Black and White /50 #30
2013 Press Pass Ignite Proofs Cyan #30
2013 Press Pass Ignite Proofs Magenta #30
2013 Press Pass Ignite Proofs Yellow /5 #30
2013 Total Memorabilia Dual Swatch Gold /199 #TMDR
2013 Total Memorabilia Single Swatch Silver /312 #TMDR
2014 Press Pass #32
2014 Press Pass American Thunder #31
2014 Press Pass American Thunder Autographs Blue /10 #ATADR
2014 Press Pass American Thunder Autographs Red /5 #ATADR
2014 Press Pass American Thunder Autographs White /25 #ATADR
2014 Press Pass American Thunder Black and White /50 #31
2014 Press Pass American Thunder Class A Uniforms Blue /99 #CAUDR
2014 Press Pass American Thunder Class A Uniforms Flag /1 #CAUDR
2014 Press Pass American Thunder Class A Uniforms Red /10 #CAUDR
2014 Press Pass American Thunder Class A Uniforms Silver #CAUDR
2014 Press Pass American Thunder Cyan #31
2014 Press Pass American Thunder Magenta #31
2014 Press Pass American Thunder Yellow /5 #31
2014 Press Pass Burning Rubber Blue /25 #BRDR
2014 Press Pass Burning Rubber Gold /75 #BRDR
2014 Press Pass Burning Rubber Holofoil /50 #BRDR
2014 Press Pass Burning Rubber Melting /10 #BRDR
2014 Press Pass Certified Winners Memorabilia Autographs Gold /10 #CWDR
2014 Press Pass Certified Winners Memorabilia Autographs Melting /1 #CWDR
2014 Press Pass Color Proofs Black /70 #32
2014 Press Pass Color Proofs Cyan /35 #32
2014 Press Pass Color Proofs Magenta #32
2014 Press Pass Color Proofs Yellow /5 #32
2014 Press Pass Gold #32
2014 Press Pass Redline #45
2014 Press Pass Redline Black /75 #45
2014 Press Pass Redline Blue Foil #45
2014 Press Pass Redline Cyan /50 #45
2014 Press Pass Redline Green National Convention /5 #45
2014 Press Pass Redline Magenta /10 #45
2014 Press Pass Redline Relics Blue /25 #RRDR
2014 Press Pass Redline Relics Gold /50 #RRDR
2014 Press Pass Redline Relics Melting /1 #RRDR
2014 Press Pass Redline Relics Red /75 #RRDR
2014 Press Pass Redline Signatures Blue /25 #RSDR
2014 Press Pass Redline Signatures Gold /50 #RSDR
2014 Press Pass Redline Signatures Melting /10 #RSDR
2014 Press Pass Redline Signatures Red /60 #RSDR
2014 Press Pass Redline Yellow /1 #45
2014 Press Pass Replay #10
2014 Press Pass Signings Gold /25 #PPSDR1
2014 Press Pass Signings Holofoil /10 #PPSDR1
2014 Press Pass Signings Melting /1 #PPSDR1
2014 Press Pass Signings Printing Plates Black /1 #PPSDR1
2014 Press Pass Signings Printing Plates Cyan /1 #PPSDR1
2014 Press Pass Signings Printing Plates Magenta /1 #PPSDR1
2014 Press Pass Signings Printing Plates Yellow /1 #PPSDR1
2014 Press Pass Signings Silver /50 #PPSDR1
2014 Total Memorabilia #24
2014 Total Memorabilia Black and White /99 #24
2014 Total Memorabilia Gold /175 #24
2014 Total Memorabilia Red #24
2015 Press Pass #30
2015 Press Pass Cup Chase #30
2015 Press Pass Cup Chase Blue /25 #30
2015 Press Pass Cup Chase Gold /75 #30
2015 Press Pass Cup Chase Green /10 #30
2015 Press Pass Cup Chase Melting /1 #30
2015 Press Pass Purple #30
2015 Press Pass Red #30
2015 Press Pass Signings Blue /99 #PPSDR
2015 Press Pass Signings Gold #PPSDR
2015 Press Pass Signings Green /25 #PPSDR
2015 Press Pass Signings Melting /10 #PPSDR
2015 Press Pass Signings Red /50 #PPSDR
2016 Certified #27
2016 Certified Mirror Black /1 #27
2016 Certified Mirror Blue /50 #27
2016 Certified Mirror Gold /25 #27
2016 Certified Mirror Green /5 #27
2016 Certified Mirror Orange /99 #27
2016 Certified Mirror Purple /10 #27
2016 Certified Mirror Red /75 #27
2016 Certified Mirror Silver /99 #27
2016 Certified Signatures /261 #46
2016 Certified Signatures Mirror Black /1 #46
2016 Certified Signatures Mirror Blue /50 #46
2016 Certified Signatures Mirror Gold /25 #46
2016 Certified Signatures Mirror Green /5 #46
2016 Certified Signatures Mirror Orange /149 #46
2016 Certified Signatures Mirror Purple /10 #46
2016 Certified Signatures Mirror Red /75 #46
2016 Certified Signatures Mirror Silver /99 #46
2016 Certified Sprint Cup Swatches /299 #16
2016 Certified Sprint Cup Swatches Mirror Black /1 #16
2016 Certified Sprint Cup Swatches Mirror Blue /50 #16
2016 Certified Sprint Cup Swatches Mirror Gold /25 #16
2016 Certified Sprint Cup Swatches Mirror Green /5 #16
2016 Certified Sprint Cup Swatches Mirror Orange /99 #16
2016 Certified Sprint Cup Swatches Mirror Purple /10 #16
2016 Certified Sprint Cup Swatches Mirror Red /75 #16
2016 Certified Sprint Cup Swatches Mirror Silver /99 #16
2016 Panini National Treasures /25 #17
2016 Panini National Treasures Black /5 #17
2016 Panini National Treasures Blue /1 #17
2016 Panini National Treasures Gold /15 #17
2016 Panini National Treasures Printing Plates Black /1 #17
2016 Panini National Treasures Printing Plates Cyan /1 #17
2016 Panini National Treasures Printing Plates Magenta /1 #17
2016 Panini National Treasures Printing Plates Yellow /1 #17
2016 Panini National Treasures Quad Driver Materials /25 #6
2016 Panini National Treasures Quad Driver Materials Black /5 #6
2016 Panini National Treasures Quad Driver Materials Blue /1 #6
2016 Panini National Treasures Quad Driver Materials Gold /10 #6
2016 Panini National Treasures Quad Driver Materials Printing Plates Black /1 #6
2016 Panini National Treasures Quad Driver Materials Printing Plates Cyan /1 #6
2016 Panini National Treasures Quad Driver Materials Printing Plates Magenta /1 #6
2016 Panini National Treasures Quad Driver Materials Printing Plates Yellow /1 #6
2016 Panini National Treasures Quad Driver Materials Silver /15 #6
2016 Panini National Treasures Silver /20 #17
2016 Panini Prizm #12
2016 Panini Prizm Autographs Prizms #80
2016 Panini Prizm Autographs Prizms Black /3 #80
2016 Panini Prizm Autographs Prizms Blue Flag /75 #80
2016 Panini Prizm Autographs Prizms Camo /23 #80
2016 Panini Prizm Autographs Prizms Checkered Flag /1 #80
2016 Panini Prizm Autographs Prizms Gold /10 #80
2016 Panini Prizm Autographs Prizms Green Flag /99 #80
2016 Panini Prizm Autographs Prizms Rainbow /24 #80
2016 Panini Prizm Autographs Prizms Red Flag /50 #80
2016 Panini Prizm Autographs Prizms Red White and Blue /49 #80
2016 Panini Prizm Autographs Prizms White Flag /5 #80
2016 Panini Prizm Prizms #12
2016 Panini Prizm Prizms Black /3 #12
2016 Panini Prizm Prizms Blue Flag /99 #12
2016 Panini Prizm Prizms Camo /23 #12
2016 Panini Prizm Prizms Checkered Flag /1 #12
2016 Panini Prizm Prizms Gold /10 #12
2016 Panini Prizm Prizms Green Flag /149 #12
2016 Panini Prizm Prizms Rainbow /24 #12
2016 Panini Prizm Prizms Red Flag /75 #12
2016 Panini Prizm Prizms Red White and Blue #12
2016 Panini Prizm Prizms White Flag /5 #12
2016 Panini Torque #32
2016 Panini Torque Artist Proof /50 #32
2016 Panini Torque Blackout /1 #32
2016 Panini Torque Blue /125 #32
2016 Panini Torque Dual Materials /199 #2
2016 Panini Torque Dual Materials Blue /99 #2
2016 Panini Torque Dual Materials Green /25 #2
2016 Panini Torque Dual Materials Purple /10 #2
2016 Panini Torque Dual Materials Red /49 #2
2016 Panini Torque Gold #32
2016 Panini Torque Holo Gold /5 #32
2016 Panini Torque Holo Silver /10 #32
2016 Panini Torque Jumbo Tire Autographs /91 #11
2016 Panini Torque Jumbo Tire Autographs Blue /75 #11
2016 Panini Torque Jumbo Tire Autographs Green /25 #11
2016 Panini Torque Jumbo Tire Autographs Purple /10 #11
2016 Panini Torque Jumbo Tire Autographs Red /49 #11
2016 Panini Torque Painted to Perfection #19
2016 Panini Torque Painted to Perfection Blue /99 #19
2016 Panini Torque Painted to Perfection Checkerboard /10 #19
2016 Panini Torque Painted to Perfection Green /25 #19
2016 Panini Torque Painted to Perfection Red /49 #19
2016 Panini Torque Pairings Materials /149 #24
2016 Panini Torque Pairings Materials Blue /99 #24
2016 Panini Torque Pairings Materials Green /25 #24
2016 Panini Torque Pairings Materials Purple /10 #24
2016 Panini Torque Pairings Materials Red /49 #24
2016 Panini Torque Printing Plates Black /1 #32
2016 Panini Torque Printing Plates Cyan /1 #32
2016 Panini Torque Printing Plates Magenta /1 #32
2016 Panini Torque Printing Plates Yellow /1 #32
2016 Panini Torque Purple /25 #32
2016 Panini Torque Red /99 #32
2016 Panini Torque Test Proof Black /1 #32
2016 Panini Torque Test Proof Cyan /1 #32
2016 Panini Torque Test Proof Magenta /1 #32
2016 Panini Torque Test Proof Yellow /1 #32
2016 Panini Torque Winning Vision #20
2016 Panini Torque Winning Vision Blue /99 #20
2016 Panini Torque Winning Vision Gold /149 #20
2016 Panini Torque Winning Vision Green /25 #20
2016 Panini Torque Winning Vision Purple /10 #20
2016 Panini Torque Winning Vision Red /49 #20
2017 Donruss #72
2017 Donruss #168
2017 Donruss Artist Proof /25 #72
2017 Donruss Artist Proof /25 #168
2017 Donruss Blue Foil /299 #72
2017 Donruss Blue Foil /299 #168
2017 Donruss Gold Foil /499 #168
2017 Donruss Gold Foil /499 #72
2017 Donruss Gold Press Proof /99 #72
2017 Donruss Gold Press Proof /99 #168
2017 Donruss Green Foil /199 #72
2017 Donruss Green Foil /199 #168
2017 Donruss Press Proof /49 #72
2017 Donruss Press Proof /49 #168
2017 Donruss Printing Plates Black /1 #72
2017 Donruss Printing Plates Black /1 #168
2017 Donruss Printing Plates Cyan /1 #72
2017 Donruss Printing Plates Cyan /1 #168
2017 Donruss Printing Plates Magenta /1 #168
2017 Donruss Printing Plates Magenta /1 #72
2017 Donruss Printing Plates Yellow /1 #168
2017 Donruss Printing Plates Yellow /1 #72
2017 Donruss Rubber Relics #17
2017 Donruss Rubber Relics Holo Black /10 #17
2017 Donruss Rubber Relics Holo Gold /25 #17
2017 Donruss Signature Series #19
2017 Donruss Signature Series Holo Black /1 #SSDR
2017 Donruss Signature Series Holo Gold /25 #SSDR
2017 Panini National Treasures Associate Sponsor Patch Signatures 1 /1 #28
2017 Panini National Treasures Associate Sponsor Patch Signatures 2 /1 #28
2017 Panini National Treasures Associate Sponsor Patch Signatures 3 /1 #28
2017 Panini National Treasures Associate Sponsor Patch Signatures 4 /1 #28
2017 Panini National Treasures Associate Sponsor Patch Signatures 5 /1 #28
2017 Panini National Treasures Associate Sponsor Patch Signatures 6 /1 #28
2017 Panini National Treasures Associate Sponsor Patch Signatures 7 /1 #28
2017 Panini National Treasures Car Manufacturer Patch Signatures /1 #28
2017 Panini National Treasures Firesuit Manufacturer Patch Signatures /1 #28
2017 Panini National Treasures Nameplate Patch Signatures /2 #28
2017 Panini National Treasures Quad Material Signatures /25 #1
2017 Panini National Treasures Quad Material Signatures Black /1 #1
2017 Panini National Treasures Quad Material Signatures Gold /15 #1
2017 Panini National Treasures Quad Material Signatures Green /5 #1
2017 Panini National Treasures Quad Material Signatures Holo Gold /10 #1
2017 Panini National Treasures Quad Material Signatures Holo Silver /20 #1
2017 Panini National Treasures Quad Material Signatures Laundry Tag /1 #1
2017 Panini National Treasures Quad Material Signatures Printing Plates Black /1 #1
2017 Panini National Treasures Quad Material Signatures Printing Plates Cyan /1 #1
2017 Panini National Treasures Quad Material Signatures Printing Plates Magenta /1 #1
2017 Panini National Treasures Quad Material Signatures Printing Plates Yellow /1 #1
2017 Panini National Treasures Quad Materials /25 #15
2017 Panini National Treasures Quad Materials Black /1 #15
2017 Panini National Treasures Quad Materials Gold /15 #15
2017 Panini National Treasures Quad Materials Green /5 #15
2017 Panini National Treasures Quad Materials Holo Gold /10 #15
2017 Panini National Treasures Quad Materials Holo Silver /20 #15
2017 Panini National Treasures Quad Materials Laundry Tag /1 #15
2017 Panini National Treasures Quad Materials Printing Plates Black /1 #15
2017 Panini National Treasures Quad Materials Printing Plates Cyan /1 #15
2017 Panini National Treasures Quad Materials Printing Plates Magenta /1 #15
2017 Panini National Treasures Quad Materials Printing Plates Yellow /1 #15
2017 Panini National Treasures Series Sponsor Patch Signatures /1 #28
2017 Panini National Treasures Sunoco Patch Signatures /1 #28
2017 Panini National Treasures Three Wide /25 #14
2017 Panini National Treasures Three Wide Black /1 #14
2017 Panini National Treasures Three Wide Gold /15 #14
2017 Panini National Treasures Three Wide Green /5 #14
2017 Panini National Treasures Three Wide Holo Gold /10 #14
2017 Panini National Treasures Three Wide Holo Silver /20 #14
2017 Panini National Treasures Three Wide Laundry Tag /1 #14
2017 Panini National Treasures Three Wide Printing Plates Black /1 #14
2017 Panini National Treasures Three Wide Printing Plates Cyan /1 #14
2017 Panini National Treasures Three Wide Printing Plates Magenta /1 #14
2017 Panini National Treasures Three Wide Printing Plates Yellow /1 #14
2017 Panini Torque Dual Materials /199 #10
2017 Panini Torque Dual Materials Blue /49 #10
2017 Panini Torque Dual Materials Green /10 #10
2017 Panini Torque Dual Materials Purple /1 #10
2017 Panini Torque Dual Materials Red /25 #10
2017 Panini Torque Jumbo Tire Signatures /60 #11
2017 Panini Torque Jumbo Tire Signatures Blue /50 #11
2017 Panini Torque Jumbo Tire Signatures Green /25 #11
2017 Panini Torque Jumbo Tire Signatures Purple /10 #11
2017 Panini Torque Jumbo Tire Signatures Red /25 #11
2017 Panini Torque Pairings Materials /199 #11
2017 Panini Torque Pairings Materials Blue /99 #11
2017 Panini Torque Pairings Materials Green /25 #11
2017 Panini Torque Pairings Materials Purple /10 #11
2017 Panini Torque Pairings Materials Red /49 #11
2017 Panini Torque Primary Paint #5
2017 Panini Torque Primary Paint Blue /99 #5
2017 Panini Torque Primary Paint Checkerboard /10 #5
2017 Panini Torque Primary Paint Green /25 #5
2017 Panini Torque Primary Paint Red /49 #5
2017 Panini Torque Quad Materials /49 #9
2017 Panini Torque Quad Materials Blue /25 #9
2017 Panini Torque Quad Materials Green /15 #9
2017 Panini Torque Quad Materials Purple /10 #9
2017 Panini Torque Quad Materials Red /20 #9
2017 Panini Torque Silhouettes Sheet Metal Signatures /35 #10
2017 Panini Torque Silhouettes Sheet Metal Signatures Blue /25 #10
2017 Panini Torque Silhouettes Sheet Metal Signatures Green /10 #10
2017 Panini Torque Silhouettes Sheet Metal Signatures Purple /5 #10
2017 Panini Torque Silhouettes Sheet Metal Signatures Red /15 #10
2017 Select #13
2017 Select #129
2017 Select Prizms Black /3 #13
2017 Select Prizms Black /3 #129
2017 Select Prizms Blue /199 #13
2017 Select Prizms Checkered Flag /1 #13
2017 Select Prizms Checkered Flag /1 #129
2017 Select Prizms Gold /10 #13
2017 Select Prizms Gold /10 #129
2017 Select Prizms Purple Pulsar #13
2017 Select Prizms Red /99 #13
2017 Select Prizms Red White and Blue Pulsar /299 #13
2017 Select Prizms Silver #13
2017 Select Prizms Tie Dye /24 #13
2017 Select Prizms Tie Dye /24 #129
2017 Select Prizms White /50 #13
2017 Select Prizms White /50 #129
2017 Select Select Swatches #16
2017 Select Select Swatches Prizms Blue /99 #16
2017 Select Select Swatches Prizms Checkered Flag /1 #16
2017 Select Select Swatches Prizms Gold /10 #16
2017 Select Select Swatches Prizms Red /50 #16
2017 Select Signature Swatches #16
2017 Select Signature Swatches Prizms Checkered Flag /1 #16
2017 Select Signature Swatches Prizms Gold /10 #16
2017 Select Signature Swatches Prizms Tie Dye /24 #16
2017 Select Signature Swatches Prizms White /40 #16
2017 Select Signature Swatches Triple #9
2017 Select Signature Swatches Triple Prizms Checkered Flag /1 #9
2017 Select Signature Swatches Triple Prizms Gold /10 #9
2017 Select Signature Swatches Triple Prizms Tie Dye /24 #9
2017 Select Signature Swatches Triple Prizms White /40 #9
2018 Certified #48
2018 Certified Black /1 #48
2018 Certified Blue /99 #48
2018 Certified Gold /49 #48
2018 Certified Green /10 #48
2018 Certified Mirror Black /1 #48
2018 Certified Mirror Gold /25 #48
2018 Certified Mirror Green /5 #48
2018 Certified Mirror Purple /10 #48
2018 Certified Orange /249 #48
2018 Certified Purple /25 #48
2018 Certified Red /199 #48
2018 Certified Signatures /149 #8
2018 Certified Signatures Black /1 #8
2018 Certified Signatures Blue /49 #8
2018 Certified Signatures Gold /25 #8
2018 Certified Signatures Green /5 #8
2018 Certified Signatures Purple /10 #8
2018 Certified Signatures Red /99 #8
2018 Donruss #63
2018 Donruss #101A
2018 Donruss Artist Proofs /25 #63
2018 Donruss Artist Proofs /25 #101
2018 Donruss Gold Foil /499 #63
2018 Donruss Gold Foil /499 #101
2018 Donruss Gold Press Proofs /99 #63
2018 Donruss Gold Press Proofs /99 #101
2018 Donruss Green Foil /199 #63
2018 Donruss Green Foil /199 #101
2018 Donruss Press Proofs /49 #63
2018 Donruss Press Proofs /49 #101A
2018 Donruss Printing Plates Black /1 #63
2018 Donruss Printing Plates Black /1 #101
2018 Donruss Printing Plates Cyan /1 #63
2018 Donruss Printing Plates Cyan /1 #101
2018 Donruss Printing Plates Magenta /1 #63
2018 Donruss Printing Plates Magenta /1 #101
2018 Donruss Printing Plates Yellow /1 #63
2018 Donruss Printing Plates Yellow /1 #101
2018 Donruss Red Foil /299 #63
2018 Donruss Red Foil /299 #101A
2018 Donruss Retro Relics '85 #7
2018 Donruss Retro Relics '85 Black /10 #7
2018 Donruss Retro Relics '85 Holo Gold /99 #7
2018 Donruss Retro Signatures '85 #8
2018 Donruss Retro Signatures '85 Black /1 #8
2018 Donruss Retro Signatures '85 Holo Gold /25 #8
2018 Panini Prime Clear Silhouettes /99 #9
2018 Panini Prime Clear Silhouettes Black /1 #9
2018 Panini Prime Clear Silhouettes Dual /99 #9
2018 Panini Prime Clear Silhouettes Dual Black /1 #9
2018 Panini Prime Clear Silhouettes Dual Holo Gold /50 #9
2018 Panini Prime Clear Silhouettes Holo Gold /50 #9
2018 Panini Prime Prime Jumbo Associate Sponsor 1 /1 #27
2018 Panini Prime Prime Jumbo Associate Sponsor 10 /1 #27
2018 Panini Prime Prime Jumbo Associate Sponsor 11 /1 #27
2018 Panini Prime Prime Jumbo Associate Sponsor 2 /1 #27
2018 Panini Prime Prime Jumbo Associate Sponsor 3 /1 #27
2018 Panini Prime Prime Jumbo Associate Sponsor 4 /1 #27
2018 Panini Prime Prime Jumbo Associate Sponsor 5 /1 #27
2018 Panini Prime Prime Jumbo Associate Sponsor 6 /1 #27
2018 Panini Prime Prime Jumbo Associate Sponsor 7 /1 #27
2018 Panini Prime Prime Jumbo Associate Sponsor 8 /1 #27
2018 Panini Prime Prime Jumbo Associate Sponsor 9 /1 #27
2018 Panini Prime Prime Jumbo Car Manufacturer /1 #27
2018 Panini Prime Prime Jumbo Firesuit Manufacturer /1 #27
2018 Panini Prime Prime Jumbo Glove Manufacturer Patch /1 #27
2018 Panini Prime Prime Jumbo Glove Name Patch /1 #27
2018 Panini Prime Prime Jumbo Nameplate /2 #27
2018 Panini Prime Prime Jumbo NASCAR /1 #27
2018 Panini Prime Prime Jumbo Prime Colors /15 #27
2018 Panini Prime Prime Jumbo Series Sponsor /1 #27
2018 Panini Prime Prime Jumbo Shoe Brand Logo /1 #27
2018 Panini Prime Prime Jumbo Shoe Name Patch /1 #27
2018 Panini Prime Prime Jumbo Sunoco /1 #27
2018 Panini Prime Race Used Duals Firesuit /50 #15
2018 Panini Prime Race Used Duals Firesuit Black /1 #15
2018 Panini Prime Race Used Duals Firesuit Holo Gold /25 #15
2018 Panini Prime Race Used Duals Firesuit Laundry Tag /1 #15
2018 Panini Prime Race Used Duals Sheet Metal /50 #15
2018 Panini Prime Race Used Duals Sheet Metal Black /1 #15
2018 Panini Prime Race Used Duals Sheet Metal Holo Gold /25 #15
2018 Panini Prime Race Used Duals Tire /50 #15
2018 Panini Prime Race Used Duals Tire Black /1 #15
2018 Panini Prime Race Used Duals Tire Holo Gold /25 #15
2018 Panini Prime Race Used Firesuits /50 #12
2018 Panini Prime Race Used Firesuits Black /1 #12
2018 Panini Prime Race Used Firesuits Holo Gold /25 #12
2018 Panini Prime Race Used Firesuits Laundry Tag /1 #12
2018 Panini Prime Race Used Sheet Metal /50 #12
2018 Panini Prime Race Used Sheet Metal Black /1 #12
2018 Panini Prime Race Used Sheet Metal Holo Gold /25 #12
2018 Panini Prime Race Used Tires Black /1 #12
2018 Panini Prime Race Used Tires Holo Gold /25 #12
2018 Panini Prizm Scripted Signatures Prizms #5
2018 Panini Prizm Scripted Signatures Prizms Black /1 #5
2018 Panini Prizm Scripted Signatures Prizms Blue /75 #5
2018 Panini Prizm Scripted Signatures Prizms Camo #5
2018 Panini Prizm Scripted Signatures Prizms Gold /10 #5
2018 Panini Prizm Scripted Signatures Prizms Green /99 #5
2018 Panini Prizm Scripted Signatures Prizms Rainbow /24 #5
2018 Panini Prizm Scripted Signatures Prizms Red /50 #5
2018 Panini Prizm Scripted Signatures Prizms Red White and Blue /125 #5
2018 Panini Prizm Scripted Signatures Prizms White /5 #5
2018 Panini Victory Lane Octane Autographs /299 #12
2018 Panini Victory Lane Octane Autographs Black /1 #12
2018 Panini Victory Lane Octane Autographs Gold /99 #12
2018 Panini Victory Lane Pedal to the Metal #18
2018 Panini Victory Lane Pedal to the Metal Black /1 #18
2018 Panini Victory Lane Pedal to the Metal Blue /25 #18
2018 Panini Victory Lane Pedal to the Metal Green /5 #18
2018 Panini Victory Lane Signatures /40 #18
2018 Panini Victory Lane Signatures Black /1 #18
2018 Panini Victory Lane Signatures Gold /10 #18
2018 Panini Victory Lane Victory Lane Prime Patches Associate Sponsor 1 /1 #33
2018 Panini Victory Lane Victory Lane Prime Patches Associate Sponsor 2 /1 #33
2018 Panini Victory Lane Victory Lane Prime Patches Associate Sponsor 3 /1 #33
2018 Panini Victory Lane Victory Lane Prime Patches Associate Sponsor 4 /1 #33
2018 Panini Victory Lane Victory Lane Prime Patches Associate Sponsor 5 /1 #33
2018 Panini Victory Lane Victory Lane Prime Patches Associate Sponsor 6 /1 #33
2018 Panini Victory Lane Victory Lane Prime Patches Associate Sponsor 7 /1 #33
2018 Panini Victory Lane Victory Lane Prime Patches Associate Sponsor 8 /1 #33
2018 Panini Victory Lane Victory Lane Prime Patches Associate Sponsor 9 /1 #33
2018 Panini Victory Lane Victory Lane Prime Patches Car Manufacturer /1 #33
2018 Panini Victory Lane Victory Lane Prime Patches Firesuit Manufacturer /1 #33
2018 Panini Victory Lane Victory Lane Prime Patches Nameplate /2 #33
2018 Panini Victory Lane Victory Lane Prime Patches NASCAR /1 #33
2018 Panini Victory Lane Victory Lane Prime Patches Series Sponsor /1 #33
2018 Panini Victory Lane Victory Lane Prime Patches Sunoco /1 #33
2019 Donruss #37
2019 Donruss #130
2019 Donruss Artist Proofs /25 #37
2019 Donruss Artist Proofs /25 #130
2019 Donruss Black /199 #37
2019 Donruss Black /199 #130
2019 Donruss Gold /299 #37
2019 Donruss Gold /299 #130
2019 Donruss Gold Press Proofs /99 #37
2019 Donruss Gold Press Proofs /99 #130
2019 Donruss Optic #35
2019 Donruss Optic #56
2019 Donruss Optic Blue Pulsar #35
2019 Donruss Optic Blue Pulsar /1 #56
2019 Donruss Optic Gold /10 #35
2019 Donruss Optic Gold /10 #56
2019 Donruss Optic Gold Vinyl /1 #35
2019 Donruss Optic Gold Vinyl /1 #56
2019 Donruss Optic Holo #35
2019 Donruss Optic Holo #56
2019 Donruss Optic Red Wave #35
2019 Donruss Optic Red Wave /1 #56
2019 Donruss Optic Signatures Gold Vinyl /1 #56
2019 Donruss Optic Signatures Gold Vinyl /1 #35
2019 Donruss Optic Signatures Holo /75 #35
2019 Donruss Optic Signatures Holo /75 #56
2019 Donruss Press Proofs /49 #37
2019 Donruss Press Proofs /49 #130
2019 Donruss Printing Plates Black /1 #37
2019 Donruss Printing Plates Black /1 #130
2019 Donruss Printing Plates Cyan /1 #37
2019 Donruss Printing Plates Cyan /1 #130
2019 Donruss Printing Plates Magenta /1 #37
2019 Donruss Printing Plates Magenta /1 #130
2019 Donruss Printing Plates Yellow /1 #37
2019 Donruss Printing Plates Yellow /1 #130
2019 Donruss Retro Relics '86 #7
2019 Donruss Retro Relics '86 Holo Black /10 #7
2019 Donruss Retro Relics '86 Holo Gold /25 #7
2019 Donruss Retro Relics '86 Red /250 #7
2019 Donruss Signature Series #13
2019 Donruss Signature Series Holo Black /10 #13
2019 Donruss Signature Series Holo Gold /25 #13
2019 Donruss Signature Series Red /99 #13
2019 Donruss Silver #37
2019 Donruss Silver #130
2019 Panini Prime /50 #25
2019 Panini Prime Black /10 #25
2019 Panini Prime Emerald /5 #25
2019 Panini Prime Platinum Blue /1 #25
2019 Panini Prime Prime Jumbo Associate Sponsor 1 /1 #24
2019 Panini Prime Prime Jumbo Associate Sponsor 1 /1 #25
2019 Panini Prime Prime Jumbo Associate Sponsor 1 /1 #26
2019 Panini Prime Prime Jumbo Associate Sponsor 2 /1 #24
2019 Panini Prime Prime Jumbo Associate Sponsor 2 /1 #26
2019 Panini Prime Prime Jumbo Associate Sponsor 3 /1 #24
2019 Panini Prime Prime Jumbo Associate Sponsor 3 /1 #26
2019 Panini Prime Prime Jumbo Associate Sponsor 4 /1 #24
2019 Panini Prime Prime Jumbo Associate Sponsor 4 /1 #26
2019 Panini Prime Prime Jumbo Associate Sponsor 5 /1 #24
2019 Panini Prime Prime Jumbo Associate Sponsor 6 /1 #24
2019 Panini Prime Prime Jumbo Associate Sponsor 7 /1 #24
2019 Panini Prime Prime Jumbo Associate Sponsor 8 /1 #24
2019 Panini Prime Prime Jumbo Associate Sponsor 9 /1 #24
2019 Panini Prime Prime Jumbo Car Manufacturer /1 #24
2019 Panini Prime Prime Jumbo Car Manufacturer /1 #25
2019 Panini Prime Prime Jumbo Car Manufacturer /1 #26
2019 Panini Prime Prime Jumbo Firesuit Manufacturer /1 #24
2019 Panini Prime Prime Jumbo Firesuit Manufacturer /1 #25
2019 Panini Prime Prime Jumbo Firesuit Manufacturer /1 #26
2019 Panini Prime Prime Jumbo Glove Manufacturer Patch /1 #24
2019 Panini Prime Prime Jumbo Glove Manufacturer Patch /1 #25
2019 Panini Prime Prime Jumbo Glove Manufacturer Patch /1 #26
2019 Panini Prime Prime Jumbo Glove Name Patch /1 #24
2019 Panini Prime Prime Jumbo Glove Name Patch /1 #25
2019 Panini Prime Prime Jumbo Glove Name Patch /1 #26
2019 Panini Prime Prime Jumbo Goodyear /2 #24
2019 Panini Prime Prime Jumbo Goodyear /2 #26
2019 Panini Prime Prime Jumbo Nameplate /1 #24
2019 Panini Prime Prime Jumbo Nameplate /2 #26
2019 Panini Prime Prime Jumbo NASCAR /1 #24
2019 Panini Prime Prime Jumbo NASCAR /1 #26
2019 Panini Prime Prime Jumbo Prime Colors /16 #24
2019 Panini Prime Prime Jumbo Prime Colors /12 #25
2019 Panini Prime Prime Jumbo Prime Colors /6 #26
2019 Panini Prime Prime Jumbo Series Sponsor /1 #24
2019 Panini Prime Prime Jumbo Series Sponsor /1 #26
2019 Panini Prime Prime Jumbo Shoe Brand Logo /1 #24
2019 Panini Prime Prime Jumbo Shoe Brand Logo /1 #26
2019 Panini Prime Prime Jumbo Shoe Name Patch /1 #24
2019 Panini Prime Prime Jumbo Shoe Name Patch /1 #25
2019 Panini Prime Prime Jumbo Shoe Name Patch /1 #26
2019 Panini Prime Prime Jumbo Sunoco /1 #24
2019 Panini Prime Prime Jumbo Sunoco /1 #26
2019 Panini Prizm #25
2019 Panini Prizm Prizms #25
2019 Panini Prizm Prizms Black /1 #25
2019 Panini Prizm Prizms Blue /75 #25
2019 Panini Prizm Prizms Camo #25
2019 Panini Prizm Prizms Flash #25
2019 Panini Prizm Prizms Gold /10 #25
2019 Panini Prizm Prizms Green /99 #25
2019 Panini Prizm Prizms Rainbow /24 #25
2019 Panini Prizm Prizms Red /50 #25
2019 Panini Prizm Prizms Red White and Blue #25
2019 Panini Prizm Prizms White /5 #25
2019 Panini Prizm Prizms White Sparkle #25
2019 Panini Victory Lane #25
2019 Panini Victory Lane Black /1 #25
2019 Panini Victory Lane Gold /25 #25
2019 Panini Victory Lane Pedal to the Metal #43
2019 Panini Victory Lane Pedal to the Metal Black /1 #43
2019 Panini Victory Lane Pedal to the Metal Gold /25 #43
2019 Panini Victory Lane Pedal to the Metal Green /5 #43
2019 Panini Victory Lane Pedal to the Metal Red /3 #43
2019 Panini Victory Lane Printing Plates Black /1 #25
2019 Panini Victory Lane Printing Plates Cyan /1 #25
2019 Panini Victory Lane Printing Plates Magenta /1 #25
2019 Panini Victory Lane Printing Plates Yellow /1 #25
2019 Panini Victory Lane Triple Swatch Signatures #6
2019 Panini Victory Lane Triple Swatch Signatures Gold /40 #6
2019 Panini Victory Lane Triple Swatch Signatures Laundry Tag /1 #6
2019 Panini Victory Lane Triple Swatch Signatures Platinum /1 #6
2019 Panini Victory Lane Triple Swatch Signatures Red /25 #6
2019 Panini Victory Lane Triple Swatches #15
2019 Panini Victory Lane Triple Swatches Gold /99 #15
2019 Panini Victory Lane Triple Swatches Laundry Tag /1 #15
2019 Panini Victory Lane Triple Swatches Platinum /1 #15
2019 Panini Victory Lane Triple Swatches Red /25 #15
2020 Donruss #34
2020 Donruss #132
2020 Donruss Black Numbers /38 #34
2020 Donruss Black Numbers /38 #132
2020 Donruss Black Trophy Club /1 #34
2020 Donruss Black Trophy Club /1 #132
2020 Donruss Blue /199 #132
2020 Donruss Blue /199 #34
2020 Donruss Carolina Blue #34
2020 Donruss Carolina Blue #132
2020 Donruss Green /99 #34
2020 Donruss Green /99 #132
2020 Donruss Orange #34
2020 Donruss Orange #132
2020 Donruss Pink /25 #34
2020 Donruss Pink /25 #132
2020 Donruss Printing Plates Black /1 #34
2020 Donruss Printing Plates Black /1 #132
2020 Donruss Printing Plates Cyan /1 #34
2020 Donruss Printing Plates Cyan /1 #132
2020 Donruss Printing Plates Magenta /1 #34
2020 Donruss Printing Plates Magenta /1 #132
2020 Donruss Printing Plates Yellow /1 #132
2020 Donruss Printing Plates Yellow /1 #34
2020 Donruss Purple /49 #34
2020 Donruss Purple /49 #132
2020 Donruss Red /299 #34
2020 Donruss Red /299 #132
2020 Donruss Signature Series #4
2020 Donruss Signature Series Holo Black /1 #4
2020 Donruss Signature Series Holo Gold /25 #4
2020 Donruss Signature Series Red /200 #4
2020 Donruss Silver #34
2020 Donruss Silver #132

Ricky Stenhouse Jr.

2009 Element #99
2009 Element Radioactive /100 #99
2009 Element Undiscovered Elements Autographs /130 #UERS
2009 Element Undiscovered Elements Autographs Red Ink /25 #UERS
2009 Press Pass Autographs Gold #49
2009 Wheels Main Event Marks Clubs #53
2009 Wheels Main Event Marks Diamonds /50 #53
2009 Wheels Main Event Marks Hearts /10 #53
2009 Wheels Main Event Marks Printing Plates Black /1 #47
2009 Wheels Main Event Marks Printing Plates Cyan /1 #47
2009 Wheels Main Event Marks Printing Plates Magenta /1 #47
2009 Wheels Main Event Marks Printing Plates Yellow /1 #47
2009 Wheels Main Event Marks Spades /1 #53
2010 Element #60
2010 Element Blue /35 #60
2010 Element Green #60
2010 Element Purple /25 #60
2010 Element Red Target #60
2010 Press Pass #47
2010 Press Pass Autographs #49
2010 Press Pass Autographs Printing Plates Black /1 #36
2010 Press Pass Autographs Printing Plates Cyan /1 #44
2010 Press Pass Autographs Printing Plates Magenta /1 #43
2010 Press Pass Autographs Printing Plates Yellow /1 #41
2010 Press Pass Blue #47
2010 Press Pass Gold #47
2010 Press Pass Holofoil /100 #47
2010 Press Pass Purple /25 #47
2010 Press Pass Signings Blue /10 #52
2010 Press Pass Signings Gold /40 #52
2010 Press Pass Signings Red /15 #52
2010 Press Pass Signings Silver /99 #51
2010 Press Pass Stealth #43
2010 Press Pass Stealth Black and White #43
2010 Press Pass Stealth Purple /25 #43
2010 Wheels Autographs #47
2010 Wheels Autographs Printing Plates Black /1 #47
2010 Wheels Autographs Printing Plates Cyan /1 #47
2010 Wheels Autographs Printing Plates Magenta /1 #47
2010 Wheels Autographs Printing Plates Yellow /1 #47
2010 Wheels Main Event Marks Autographs /71 #54
2010 Wheels Main Event Marks Autographs Black /1 #53
2010 Wheels Main Event Marks Autographs Blue /30 #54
2010 Wheels Main Event Marks Autographs Red /25 #54
2011 Element #49
2011 Element Autographs /45 #52
2011 Element Autographs Blue /5 #52
2011 Element Autographs Gold /10 #50
2011 Element Autographs Printing Plates Black /1 #52
2011 Element Autographs Printing Plates Cyan /1 #52
2011 Element Autographs Printing Plates Magenta /1 #52
2011 Element Autographs Printing Plates Yellow /1 #52
2011 Element Autographs Silver /15 #50
2011 Element Black /35 #49
2011 Element Green #49
2011 Element Previews /1 #EB49
2011 Element Purple /25 #49
2011 Element Red #49
2011 Press Pass Autographs Blue /10 #52
2011 Press Pass Autographs Bronze /72 #53
2011 Press Pass Autographs Gold /15 #50
2011 Press Pass Autographs Printing Plates Black /1 #53
2011 Press Pass Autographs Printing Plates Cyan /1 #53
2011 Press Pass Autographs Printing Plates Magenta /1 #53

2011 Press Pass Autographs Printing Plates Yellow /1 #53
2011 Press Pass Autographs Silver /50 #53
2011 Press Pass Eclipse #57
2011 Press Pass Eclipse Blue #57
2011 Press Pass Eclipse Gold /55 #57
2011 Press Pass Eclipse Purple /25 #57
2011 Press Pass FanFare #50
2011 Press Pass FanFare Autographs Blue /5 #70
2011 Press Pass FanFare Autographs Bronze /120 #70
2011 Press Pass FanFare Autographs Gold /99 #70
2011 Press Pass FanFare Autographs Printing Plates Black /1 #70
2011 Press Pass FanFare Autographs Printing Plates Cyan /1 #70
2011 Press Pass FanFare Autographs Printing Plates Magenta /1 #70
2011 Press Pass FanFare Autographs Printing Plates Yellow /1 #70
2011 Press Pass FanFare Autographs Silver /50 #70
2011 Press Pass FanFare Blue Die Cuts #50
2011 Press Pass FanFare Dual Autographs /10 #NNO
2011 Press Pass FanFare Emerald /25 #50
2011 Press Pass FanFare Holofoil Die Cuts #50
2011 Press Pass FanFare Magnificent Materials /199 #MMRS
2011 Press Pass FanFare Magnificent Materials Dual Swatches /50 #MMSRS
2011 Press Pass FanFare Magnificent Materials Dual Swatches Holofoil /10 #MMSRS
2011 Press Pass FanFare Magnificent Materials Holofoil /50 #MMRS
2011 Press Pass FanFare Magnificent Materials Signatures /99 #MMSERS2
2011 Press Pass FanFare Magnificent Materials Signatures Holofoil /25 #MMSERS2
2011 Press Pass FanFare Ruby Die Cuts /15 #50
2011 Press Pass FanFare Sapphire /10 #50
2011 Press Pass FanFare Silver /25 #50
2011 Press Pass Signings Black and White /10 #PPSRS3
2011 Press Pass Signings Brushed Metal /50 #PPSRS3
2011 Press Pass Signings Holofoil /24 #PPSRS3
2011 Press Pass Signings Printing Plates Black /1 #PPSRS3
2011 Press Pass Signings Printing Plates Cyan /1 #PPSRS3
2011 Press Pass Signings Printing Plates Magenta /1 #PPSRS3
2011 Press Pass Stealth #65
2011 Press Pass Stealth Black and White /25 #65
2011 Press Pass Stealth Holofoil /99 #65
2011 Press Pass Stealth Purple /25 #65
2011 Wheels Main Event #44
2011 Wheels Main Event Black and White #44
2011 Wheels Main Event Blue /75 #44
2011 Wheels Main Event Green /1 #44
2011 Wheels Main Event Marks Autographs Blue /10 #MERS
2011 Wheels Main Event Marks Autographs Gold /25 #MERS
2011 Wheels Main Event Marks Autographs Silver /65 #MERS
2011 Wheels Main Event Red /20 #44
2012 Press Pass #45
2012 Press Pass #89
2012 Press Pass Blue #45
2012 Press Pass Blue #89
2012 Press Pass Blue Holofoil /35 #45
2012 Press Pass Blue Holofoil /35 #89
2012 Press Pass Fanfare #58
2012 Press Pass Fanfare Autographs Blue /25 #RS2
2012 Press Pass Fanfare Autographs Gold /99 #RS2
2012 Press Pass Fanfare Autographs Red /75 #RS2
2012 Press Pass Fanfare Autographs Silver /175 #RS2
2012 Press Pass Fanfare Blue Foil Die Cuts #58
2012 Press Pass Fanfare Diamond /5 #58
2012 Press Pass Fanfare Holofoil Die Cuts #58
2012 Press Pass Fanfare Magnificent Materials /250 #MMRS2
2012 Press Pass Fanfare Magnificent Materials Dual Swatches /50 #MMRS2
2012 Press Pass Fanfare Magnificent Materials Dual Swatches Melting /10 #MMRS2
2012 Press Pass Fanfare Magnificent Materials Gold /99 #MMRS2
2012 Press Pass Fanfare Magnificent Materials Signatures /99 #RS2
2012 Press Pass Fanfare Magnificent Materials Signatures Blue /25 #RS2
2012 Press Pass Fanfare Sapphire /20 #58
2012 Press Pass Fanfare Silver /25 #58
2012 Press Pass Gold #45
2012 Press Pass Gold #89
2012 Press Pass Ignite #47
2012 Press Pass Ignite #58
2012 Press Pass Ignite Proofs Black and White /50 #47
2012 Press Pass Ignite Proofs Black and White /50 #58
2012 Press Pass Ignite Proofs Cyan #47
2012 Press Pass Ignite Proofs Cyan #58
2012 Press Pass Ignite Proofs Magenta #47
2012 Press Pass Ignite Proofs Magenta #58
2012 Press Pass Ignite Proofs Yellow /10 #47
2012 Press Pass Ignite Proofs Yellow /10 #58
2012 Press Pass Purple /35 #45
2012 Press Pass Purple /35 #89
2012 Press Pass Snapshots #SS48
2012 Total Memorabilia #35
2012 Total Memorabilia Black and White /99 #35
2012 Total Memorabilia Gold /275 #35
2012 Total Memorabilia Red Retail /250 #35
2012 Total Memorabilia Single Swatch Gold /99 #TMRS2
2012 Total Memorabilia Single Swatch Holofoil /50 #TMRS2
2012 Total Memorabilia Single Swatch Melting /10 #TMRS2
2012 Total Memorabilia Single Swatch Silver /199 #TMRS2
2013 Press Pass #56
2013 Press Pass Color Proofs Black #56
2013 Press Pass Color Proofs Cyan /35 #56
2013 Press Pass Color Proofs Magenta #56
2013 Press Pass Color Proofs Yellow /5 #56
2013 Press Pass Fanfare #52
2013 Press Pass Fanfare #53
2013 Press Pass Fanfare #100
2013 Press Pass Fanfare Autographs Blue /1 #RSJ
2013 Press Pass Fanfare Autographs Gold /10 #RSJ
2013 Press Pass Fanfare Autographs Green /5 #RSJ
2013 Press Pass Fanfare Autographs Red /5 #RSJ
2013 Press Pass Fanfare Autographs Silver /25 #RSJ
2013 Press Pass Fanfare Diamond Die Cuts /5 #52
2013 Press Pass Fanfare Diamond Die Cuts /5 #53
2013 Press Pass Fanfare Diamond Die Cuts /5 #100
2013 Press Pass Fanfare Fan Following #FF14
2013 Press Pass Fanfare Green /3 #52
2013 Press Pass Fanfare Green /3 #53
2013 Press Pass Fanfare Green /3 #100
2013 Press Pass Fanfare Holofoil Die Cuts #52
2013 Press Pass Fanfare Holofoil Die Cuts #53
2013 Press Pass Fanfare Holofoil Die Cuts #100
2013 Press Pass Fanfare Magnificent Materials Dual Swatches /50 #RS
2013 Press Pass Fanfare Magnificent Materials Dual Swatches Melting /10 #RS
2013 Press Pass Fanfare Magnificent Materials Gold /50 #RS
2013 Press Pass Fanfare Magnificent Materials Jumbo Swatches /25 #RS
2013 Press Pass Fanfare Magnificent Materials Silver /199 #RS
2013 Press Pass Fanfare Red Foil Die Cuts #52
2013 Press Pass Fanfare Red Foil Die Cuts #53
2013 Press Pass Fanfare Red Foil Die Cuts #100
2013 Press Pass Fanfare Rookie Stripes Memorabilia /25 #RS
2013 Press Pass Fanfare Rookie Stripes Memorabilia Autographs /17 #RS
2013 Press Pass Fanfare Sapphire /20 #52
2013 Press Pass Fanfare Sapphire /20 #53
2013 Press Pass Fanfare Sapphire /20 #100
2013 Press Pass Fanfare Signature Ride Autographs /75 #RSJ
2013 Press Pass Fanfare Signature Ride Autographs Blue /10 #RSJ
2013 Press Pass Fanfare Signature Ride Autographs Red /50 #RSJ
2013 Press Pass Fanfare Silver /25 #52
2013 Press Pass Fanfare Silver /25 #53
2013 Press Pass Fanfare Silver /25 #100
2013 Press Pass Ignite #34
2013 Press Pass Ignite #62
2013 Press Pass Ignite Great American Treads Autographs Blue Holofoil /20 #GATRS
2013 Press Pass Ignite Great American Treads Autographs Red /1 #GATRS
2013 Press Pass Ignite Hot Threads Blue Holofoil /99 #HTRS
2013 Press Pass Ignite Hot Threads Patch Red /10 #HTRS
2013 Press Pass Ignite Hot Threads Silver #HTRS
2013 Press Pass Ignite Ink Black /75 #IIRSJ
2013 Press Pass Ignite Ink Blue /25 #IIRSJ
2013 Press Pass Ignite Ink Red /5 #IIRSJ
2013 Press Pass Ignite Profile #13
2013 Press Pass Ignite Proofs Black and White /50 #34
2013 Press Pass Ignite Proofs Black and White /50 #62
2013 Press Pass Ignite Proofs Cyan #34
2013 Press Pass Ignite Proofs Cyan #62
2013 Press Pass Ignite Proofs Magenta #34
2013 Press Pass Ignite Proofs Magenta #62
2013 Press Pass Ignite Proofs Yellow /5 #34
2013 Press Pass Ignite Proofs Yellow /5 #62
2013 Press Pass Power Picks Blue /99 #49
2013 Press Pass Power Picks Gold /50 #49
2013 Press Pass Power Picks Holofoil /10 #49
2013 Press Pass Redline #42
2013 Press Pass Redline Black /99 #42
2013 Press Pass Redline Cyan /50 #42
2013 Press Pass Redline Dark Horse Relic Autographs Blue /8 #DHRS
2013 Press Pass Redline Dark Horse Relic Autographs Gold /20 #DHRS
2013 Press Pass Redline Dark Horse Relic Autographs Melting /1 #DHRS
2013 Press Pass Redline Dark Horse Relic Autographs Red /40 #DHRS
2013 Press Pass Redline Magenta /15 #42
2013 Press Pass Redline Redline Racers #13
2013 Press Pass Redline Relic Autographs Blue /5 #RRSERS
2013 Press Pass Redline Relic Autographs Gold /10 #RRSERS
2013 Press Pass Redline Relic Autographs Melting /1 #RRSERS
2013 Press Pass Redline Relic Autographs Red /45 #RRSERS
2013 Press Pass Redline Relic Autographs Silver /17 #RRSERS
2013 Press Pass Redline Relics Blue /5 #RRRS
2013 Press Pass Redline Relics Gold /10 #RRRS
2013 Press Pass Redline Relics Melting /1 #RRRS
2013 Press Pass Redline Relics Red /50 #RRRS
2013 Press Pass Redline Relics Silver /25 #RRRS
2013 Press Pass Redline Signatures Blue /10 #RSRSJR
2013 Press Pass Redline Signatures Gold /5 #RSRSJR
2013 Press Pass Redline Signatures Holo /10 #RSRSJR
2013 Press Pass Redline Signatures Melting /1 #RSRSJR
2013 Press Pass Redline Signatures Red /35 #RSRSJR
2013 Press Pass Redline Yellow /1 #42
2013 Press Pass Showcase /349 #57
2013 Press Pass Showcase /75 #61
2013 Press Pass Showcase Black /1 #57
2013 Press Pass Showcase Black /1 #61
2013 Press Pass Showcase Blue /25 #57
2013 Press Pass Showcase Classic Collections Ink Gold /5 #CCIRFR
2013 Press Pass Showcase Classic Collections Ink Melting /1 #CCIRFR
2013 Press Pass Showcase Classic Collections Ink Red /1 #CCIRFR
2013 Press Pass Showcase Classic Collections Memorabilia Gold /25 #CCMRFR
2013 Press Pass Showcase Classic Collections Memorabilia Melting /5 #CCMRFR
2013 Press Pass Showcase Classic Collections Memorabilia Silver /75 #CCMRFR
2013 Press Pass Showcase Gold /99 #57
2013 Press Pass Showcase Gold /50 #61
2013 Press Pass Showcase Green /20 #57
2013 Press Pass Showcase Purple /13 #57
2013 Press Pass Showcase Red /10 #57
2013 Press Pass Showcase Rookie Contenders /299 #2
2013 Press Pass Showcase Rookie Contenders Autographs Melting /13 #RCARS
2013 Press Pass Showcase Rookie Contenders Gold /50 #2
2013 Press Pass Showcase Rookie Contenders Green /25 #2
2013 Press Pass Showcase Rookie Contenders Melting /1 #2
2013 Press Pass Showcase Rookie Contenders Memorabilia Gold /20 #RCMRS
2013 Press Pass Showcase Rookie Contenders Memorabilia Melting /13 #RCMRS
2013 Press Pass Showcase Rookie Contenders Purple /13 #2
2013 Press Pass Showcase Rookie Contenders Red /10 #2
2013 Press Pass Signings Blue /1 #RSJ
2013 Press Pass Signings Gold /25 #RSJ
2013 Press Pass Signings Holofoil /10 #RSJ
2013 Press Pass Signings Printing Plates Black /1 #RSJ
2013 Press Pass Signings Printing Plates Cyan /1 #RSJ
2013 Press Pass Signings Printing Plates Magenta /1 #RSJ
2013 Press Pass Signings Printing Plates Yellow /1 #RSJ
2013 Press Pass Signings Silver /65 #RSJ
2013 Total Memorabilia #43
2013 Total Memorabilia Black and White /99 #43
2013 Total Memorabilia Gold /275 #43
2013 Total Memorabilia Red #43
2014 Press Pass #36
2014 Press Pass Aerodynamic Autographs Blue /1 #AARS
2014 Press Pass Aerodynamic Autographs Holofoil /10 #AARS
2014 Press Pass Aerodynamic Autographs Printing Plates Black /1 #AARS
2014 Press Pass Aerodynamic Autographs Printing Plates Cyan /1 #AARS
2014 Press Pass Aerodynamic Autographs Printing Plates Magenta /1 #AARS
2014 Press Pass Aerodynamic Autographs Printing Plates Yellow /1 #AARS
2014 Press Pass American Thunder #32
2014 Press Pass American Thunder #53
2014 Press Pass American Thunder Autographs Blue /10 #ATARS
2014 Press Pass American Thunder Autographs Red /5 #ATARS
2014 Press Pass American Thunder Autographs White /25 #ATARS
2014 Press Pass American Thunder Black and White /50 #32
2014 Press Pass American Thunder Black and White /50 #53
2014 Press Pass American Thunder Brothers In Arms Autographs Blue /5 #BARFR
2014 Press Pass American Thunder Brothers In Arms Autographs Red /1 #BARFR
2014 Press Pass American Thunder Brothers In Arms Autographs White /10 #BARFR
2014 Press Pass American Thunder Brothers In Arms Relics Blue /25 #BARFR
2014 Press Pass American Thunder Brothers In Arms Relics Red /5 #BARFR
2014 Press Pass American Thunder Brothers In Arms Relics Silver /50 #BARFR
2014 Press Pass American Thunder Class A Uniforms Blue /99 #CAURS
2014 Press Pass American Thunder Class A Uniforms Flag /1 #CAURS
2014 Press Pass American Thunder Class A Uniforms Red /10 #CAURS
2014 Press Pass American Thunder Class A Uniforms Silver #CAURS
2014 Press Pass American Thunder Climbing the Ranks #CR10
2014 Press Pass American Thunder Cyan #32
2014 Press Pass American Thunder Cyan #53
2014 Press Pass American Thunder Great American Treads Autographs Blue /25 #GATRS
2014 Press Pass American Thunder Great American Treads Autographs Red /1 #GATRS
2014 Press Pass American Thunder Magenta #32
2014 Press Pass American Thunder Magenta #53
2014 Press Pass American Thunder Top Speed #TS9
2014 Press Pass American Thunder Yellow /5 #32
2014 Press Pass American Thunder Yellow /5 #53
2014 Press Pass Color Proofs Black /70 #36
2014 Press Pass Color Proofs Cyan /35 #36
2014 Press Pass Color Proofs Magenta #36
2014 Press Pass Color Proofs Yellow /5 #36
2014 Press Pass Cup Chase #14
2014 Press Pass Five Star Classic Compilations Autographed Patch Booklet /1 #CCRS1
2014 Press Pass Five Star Classic Compilations Autographed Patch Booklet /1 #CCRS2
2014 Press Pass Five Star Classic Compilations Autographed Patch Booklet /1 #CCRS3
2014 Press Pass Five Star Classic Compilations Autographed Patch Booklet /1 #CCRS4
2014 Press Pass Five Star Classic Compilations Autographed Patch Booklet /1 #CCRS5
2014 Press Pass Five Star Classic Compilations Autographed Patch Booklet /1 #CCRS6
2014 Press Pass Five Star Classic Compilations Autographed Patch Booklet /1 #CCRS7
2014 Press Pass Five Star Classic Compilations Autographed Patch Booklet /1 #CCRS8
2014 Press Pass Five Star Classic Compilations Autographed Patch Booklet /1 #CCRS9
2014 Press Pass Five Star Classic Compilations Autographed Patch Booklet /1 #CCRS10
2014 Press Pass Five Star Classic Compilations Autographed Patch Booklet /1 #CCRS11
2014 Press Pass Five Star Classic Compilations Autographed Patch Booklet /1 #CCRS12
2014 Press Pass Five Star Classic Compilations Combo Autographs Blue /5 #CCRFR
2014 Press Pass Five Star Classic Compilations Combo Autographs Melting /1 #CCRFR
2014 Press Pass Five Star Signatures Blue /5 #FSSRS
2014 Press Pass Five Star Signatures Holofoil /10 #FSSRS
2014 Press Pass Five Star Signatures Melting /1 #FSSRS
2014 Press Pass Gold #36
2014 Press Pass Redline #46
2014 Press Pass Redline #47
2014 Press Pass Redline Black /75 #46
2014 Press Pass Redline Black /75 #47
2014 Press Pass Redline Blue Foil #46
2014 Press Pass Redline Blue Foil #47
2014 Press Pass Redline Cyan /50 #46
2014 Press Pass Redline Cyan /50 #47
2014 Press Pass Redline Green National Convention /5 #46
2014 Press Pass Redline Green National Convention /5 #47
2014 Press Pass Redline Magenta /10 #46
2014 Press Pass Redline Magenta /10 #47
2014 Press Pass Redline Relic Autographs Blue /10 #RRSERSJ
2014 Press Pass Redline Relic Autographs Gold /25 #RRSERSJ
2014 Press Pass Redline Relic Autographs Melting /1 #RRSERSJ
2014 Press Pass Redline Relic Autographs Red /50 #RRSERSJ
2014 Press Pass Redline Relics Blue /25 #RRRSJ
2014 Press Pass Redline Relics Gold /50 #RRRSJ
2014 Press Pass Redline Relics Melting /1 #RRRSJ
2014 Press Pass Redline Relics Red /75 #RRRSJ
2014 Press Pass Redline Signatures Blue /25 #RSRSJ
2014 Press Pass Redline Signatures Gold /50 #RSRSJ
2014 Press Pass Redline Signatures Melting /10 #RSRSJ
2014 Press Pass Redline Signatures Red /65 #RSRSJ
2014 Press Pass Redline Yellow /1 #46
2014 Press Pass Redline Yellow /1 #47
2014 Press Pass Signings Gold /50 #PPSRSJ
2014 Press Pass Signings Holofoil /10 #PPSRSJ
2014 Press Pass Signings Melting /1 #PPSRSJ
2014 Press Pass Signings Printing Plates Black /1 #PPSRSJ
2014 Press Pass Signings Printing Plates Cyan /1 #PPSRSJ
2014 Press Pass Signings Printing Plates Magenta /1 #PPSRSJ
2014 Press Pass Signings Printing Plates Yellow /1 #PPSRSJ
2014 Press Pass Signings Silver /80 #PPSRSJ
2014 Press Pass Three Wide Gold /10 #TWRSJ
2014 Press Pass Three Wide Melting /1 #TWRSJ
2014 Total Memorabilia #25
2014 Total Memorabilia #49
2014 Total Memorabilia Black and White /99 #25
2014 Total Memorabilia Black and White /99 #49
2014 Total Memorabilia Dual Swatch Gold /150 #TMRSJ
2014 Total Memorabilia Gold /175 #25
2014 Total Memorabilia Gold /175 #49
2014 Total Memorabilia Quad Swatch Melting /25 #TMRSJ
2014 Total Memorabilia Red #25
2014 Total Memorabilia Red #49
2014 Total Memorabilia Single Swatch Silver /275 #TMRSJ
2014 Total Memorabilia Triple Swatch Blue /99 #TMRSJ
2015 Press Pass #31
2015 Press Pass Cup Chase #31
2015 Press Pass Cup Chase Blue /25 #31
2015 Press Pass Cup Chase Gold /75 #31
2015 Press Pass Cup Chase Green /10 #31
2015 Press Pass Cup Chase Melting /1 #31
2015 Press Pass Purple #31
2015 Press Pass Red #31
2015 Press Pass Signings Blue /99 #PPSRST
2015 Press Pass Signings Gold #PPSRST
2015 Press Pass Signings Green /50 #PPSRST
2015 Press Pass Signings Melting /10 #PPSRS
2015 Press Pass Signings Red /75 #PPSRST
2016 Certified #18
2016 Certified Mirror Black /1 #18
2016 Certified Mirror Blue /50 #18
2016 Certified Mirror Gold /25 #18
2016 Certified Mirror Green /5 #18
2016 Certified Mirror Orange /99 #18
2016 Certified Mirror Purple /10 #18
2016 Certified Mirror Red /75 #18
2016 Certified Mirror Silver /99 #18
2016 Certified Potential Signatures /99 #22
2016 Certified Potential Signatures Mirror Black /1 #22
2016 Certified Potential Signatures Mirror Blue /50 #22
2016 Certified Potential Signatures Mirror Gold /25 #22
2016 Certified Potential Signatures Mirror Green /5 #22
2016 Certified Potential Signatures Mirror Orange /80 #22
2016 Certified Potential Signatures Mirror Purple /10 #22
2016 Certified Potential Signatures Mirror Red /75 #22
2016 Certified Potential Signatures Mirror Silver /80 #22
2016 Certified Skills /199 #12
2016 Certified Skills Mirror Black /1 #12
2016 Certified Skills Mirror Blue /50 #12
2016 Certified Skills Mirror Gold /25 #12
2016 Certified Skills Mirror Green /5 #12
2016 Certified Skills Mirror Orange /99 #12
2016 Certified Skills Mirror Purple /10 #12
2016 Certified Skills Mirror Red /75 #12
2016 Certified Skills Mirror Silver /99 #12
2016 Certified Sprint Cup Swatches /299 #5
2016 Certified Sprint Cup Swatches Mirror Black /1 #5
2016 Certified Sprint Cup Swatches Mirror Blue /50 #5
2016 Certified Sprint Cup Swatches Mirror Gold /25 #5
2016 Certified Sprint Cup Swatches Mirror Green /5 #5
2016 Certified Sprint Cup Swatches Mirror Orange /199 #5
2016 Certified Sprint Cup Swatches Mirror Purple /10 #5
2016 Certified Sprint Cup Swatches Mirror Red /75 #5
2016 Certified Sprint Cup Swatches Mirror Silver /199 #5
2016 Panini National Treasures /25 #11
2016 Panini National Treasures Black /5 #11
2016 Panini National Treasures Blue /1 #11
2016 Panini National Treasures Dual Signatures Black /5 #7
2016 Panini National Treasures Dual Signatures Blue /1 #7
2016 Panini National Treasures Gold /15 #11
2016 Panini National Treasures Printing Plates Black /1 #11
2016 Panini National Treasures Printing Plates Cyan /1 #11
2016 Panini National Treasures Printing Plates Magenta /1 #11
2016 Panini National Treasures Printing Plates Yellow /1 #11
2016 Panini National Treasures Quad Driver Materials /25 #3
2016 Panini National Treasures Quad Driver Materials /25 #7
2016 Panini National Treasures Quad Driver Materials /25 #9
2016 Panini National Treasures Quad Driver Materials Black /5 #3
2016 Panini National Treasures Quad Driver Materials Black /5 #7
2016 Panini National Treasures Quad Driver Materials Black /5 #9
2016 Panini National Treasures Quad Driver Materials Blue /1 #3
2016 Panini National Treasures Quad Driver Materials Blue /1 #7
2016 Panini National Treasures Quad Driver Materials Blue /1 #9
2016 Panini National Treasures Quad Driver Materials Gold /10 #3
2016 Panini National Treasures Quad Driver Materials Gold /10 #7
2016 Panini National Treasures Quad Driver Materials Gold /10 #9
2016 Panini National Treasures Quad Driver Materials Printing Plates Black /1 #3
2016 Panini National Treasures Quad Driver Materials Printing Plates Black /1 #7
2016 Panini National Treasures Quad Driver Materials Printing Plates Black /1 #9
2016 Panini National Treasures Quad Driver Materials Printing Plates Cyan /1 #3
2016 Panini National Treasures Quad Driver Materials Printing Plates Cyan /1 #7
2016 Panini National Treasures Quad Driver Materials Printing Plates Cyan /1 #9
2016 Panini National Treasures Quad Driver Materials Printing Plates Magenta /1 #3
2016 Panini National Treasures Quad Driver Materials Printing Plates Magenta /1 #7
2016 Panini National Treasures Quad Driver Materials Printing Plates Magenta /1 #9
2016 Panini National Treasures Quad Driver Materials Printing Plates Yellow /1 #3
2016 Panini National Treasures Quad Driver Materials Printing Plates Yellow /1 #7
2016 Panini National Treasures Quad Driver Materials Printing Plates Yellow /1 #9
2016 Panini National Treasures Quad Driver Materials Silver /15 #3
2016 Panini National Treasures Quad Driver Materials Silver /15 #7
2016 Panini National Treasures Quad Driver Materials Silver /15 #9
2016 Panini National Treasures Signature Firesuit Materials Black /5 #25
2016 Panini National Treasures Signature Firesuit Materials Blue /1 #25
2016 Panini National Treasures Signature Firesuit Materials Gold /7 #25
2016 Panini National Treasures Signature Firesuit Materials Laundry Tag /1 #25
2016 Panini National Treasures Signature Firesuit Materials Printing Plates Black /1 #25
2016 Panini National Treasures Signature Firesuit Materials Printing Plates Cyan /1 #25
2016 Panini National Treasures Signature Firesuit Materials Printing Plates Magenta /1 #25
2016 Panini National Treasures Signature Firesuit Materials Printing Plates Yellow /1 #25
2016 Panini National Treasures Silver /20 #11
2016 Panini National Treasures Six Signatures /25 #2
2016 Panini National Treasures Six Signatures Black /10 #2
2016 Panini National Treasures Six Signatures Blue /1 #2
2016 Panini National Treasures Six Signatures Gold /15 #2
2016 Panini National Treasures Trio Driver Materials /25 #7
2016 Panini National Treasures Trio Driver Materials Black /5 #7
2016 Panini National Treasures Trio Driver Materials Blue /1 #7
2016 Panini National Treasures Trio Driver Materials Gold /10 #7
2016 Panini National Treasures Trio Driver Materials Printing Plates Black /1 #7
2016 Panini National Treasures Trio Driver Materials Printing Plates Cyan /1 #7
2016 Panini National Treasures Trio Driver Materials Printing Plates Magenta /1 #7
2016 Panini National Treasures Trio Driver Materials Printing Plates Yellow /1 #7
2016 Panini National Treasures Trio Driver Materials Silver /15 #7
2016 Panini Prizm #17A
2016 Panini Prizm #84
2016 Panini Prizm Autographs Prizms #50
2016 Panini Prizm Autographs Prizms Black /3 #50
2016 Panini Prizm Autographs Prizms Blue Flag /75 #50
2016 Panini Prizm Autographs Prizms Camo /17 #50
2016 Panini Prizm Autographs Prizms Checkered Flag /1 #50
2016 Panini Prizm Autographs Prizms Gold /10 #50
2016 Panini Prizm Autographs Prizms Green Flag /99 #50
2016 Panini Prizm Autographs Prizms Rainbow /24 #50
2016 Panini Prizm Autographs Prizms Red Flag /50 #50
2016 Panini Prizm Autographs Prizms Red White and Blue /49 #50
2016 Panini Prizm Autographs Prizms White Flag /5 #50
2016 Panini Prizm Firesuit Fabrics /149 #7
2016 Panini Prizm Firesuit Fabrics Prizms Blue Flag /75 #7
2016 Panini Prizm Firesuit Fabrics Prizms Checkered Flag /1 #7
2016 Panini Prizm Firesuit Fabrics Prizms Green Flag /99 #7
2016 Panini Prizm Firesuit Fabrics Prizms Red Flag /25 #7
2016 Panini Prizm Prizms #17A
2016 Panini Prizm Prizms #84
2016 Panini Prizm Prizms Black /3 #17
2016 Panini Prizm Prizms Black /3 #84
2016 Panini Prizm Prizms Blue Flag /99 #17
2016 Panini Prizm Prizms Blue Flag /99 #84
2016 Panini Prizm Prizms Camo /17 #17
2016 Panini Prizm Prizms Camo /17 #84
2016 Panini Prizm Prizms Checkered Flag /1 #17A
2016 Panini Prizm Prizms Checkered Flag /1 #84
2016 Panini Prizm Prizms Gold /10 #17A
2016 Panini Prizm Prizms Gold /10 #84
2016 Panini Prizm Prizms Green Flag /149 #17
2016 Panini Prizm Prizms Green Flag /149 #84
2016 Panini Prizm Prizms Rainbow /24 #17
2016 Panini Prizm Prizms Rainbow /24 #84
2016 Panini Prizm Prizms Red Flag /75 #17
2016 Panini Prizm Prizms Red Flag /75 #84
2016 Panini Prizm Prizms Red White and Blue #17
2016 Panini Prizm Prizms Red White and Blue #84
2016 Panini Prizm Prizms White Flag /5 #17
2016 Panini Prizm Prizms White Flag /5 #84
2016 Panini Torque #16
2016 Panini Torque Artist Proof /50 #16
2016 Panini Torque Blackout /1 #16
2016 Panini Torque Blue /125 #16
2016 Panini Torque Clear Vision #15
2016 Panini Torque Clear Vision Blue /99 #15
2016 Panini Torque Clear Vision Gold /149 #15
2016 Panini Torque Clear Vision Green /25 #15
2016 Panini Torque Clear Vision Purple /10 #15
2016 Panini Torque Clear Vision Red /49 #15
2016 Panini Torque Dual Materials /149 #8
2016 Panini Torque Dual Materials Blue /99 #8
2016 Panini Torque Dual Materials Green /25 #8
2016 Panini Torque Dual Materials Purple /10 #8
2016 Panini Torque Dual Materials Red /49 #8
2016 Panini Torque Gold #16
2016 Panini Torque Holo Gold /5 #16
2016 Panini Torque Holo Silver /10 #16
2016 Panini Torque Jumbo Tire Autographs /75 #18
2016 Panini Torque Jumbo Tire Autographs Blue /50 #18
2016 Panini Torque Jumbo Tire Autographs Green /10 #18
2016 Panini Torque Jumbo Tire Autographs Purple /5 #18
2016 Panini Torque Jumbo Tire Autographs Red /15 #18
2016 Panini Torque Pairings Materials /125 #22
2016 Panini Torque Pairings Materials Blue /99 #22
2016 Panini Torque Pairings Materials Green /25 #22
2016 Panini Torque Pairings Materials Purple /10 #22
2016 Panini Torque Pairings Materials Red /49 #22
2016 Panini Torque Pole Position #13
2016 Panini Torque Pole Position Blue /99 #13
2016 Panini Torque Pole Position Checkerboard /10 #13
2016 Panini Torque Pole Position Green /25 #13
2016 Panini Torque Pole Position Red /49 #13
2016 Panini Torque Printing Plates Black /1 #16
2016 Panini Torque Printing Plates Cyan /1 #16
2016 Panini Torque Printing Plates Magenta /1 #16
2016 Panini Torque Printing Plates Yellow /1 #16
2016 Panini Torque Purple /25 #16
2016 Panini Torque Red /99 #16
2016 Panini Torque Silhouettes Firesuit Autographs /75 #20
2016 Panini Torque Silhouettes Firesuit Autographs Blue /25 #20
2016 Panini Torque Silhouettes Firesuit Autographs Green /10 #20
2016 Panini Torque Silhouettes Firesuit Autographs Purple /5 #20
2016 Panini Torque Silhouettes Firesuit Autographs Red /20 #20
2016 Panini Torque Silhouettes Sheet Metal Autographs /50 #21
2016 Panini Torque Silhouettes Sheet Metal Autographs Blue /25 #21
2016 Panini Torque Silhouettes Sheet Metal Autographs Green /10 #21
2016 Panini Torque Silhouettes Sheet Metal Autographs Purple /5 #21
2016 Panini Torque Silhouettes Sheet Metal Autographs Red /20 #21
2016 Panini Torque Test Proof Black /1 #16
2016 Panini Torque Test Proof Cyan /1 #16
2016 Panini Torque Test Proof Magenta /1 #16
2016 Panini Torque Test Proof Yellow /1 #16
2017 Donruss #58
2017 Donruss #156
2017 Donruss Artist Proof /25 #58
2017 Donruss Artist Proof /25 #156
2017 Donruss Blue Foil /299 #58
2017 Donruss Blue Foil /299 #156
2017 Donruss Gold Foil /499 #156
2017 Donruss Gold Foil /499 #58
2017 Donruss Gold Press Proof /99 #58
2017 Donruss Gold Press Proof /99 #156
2017 Donruss Green Foil /199 #58
2017 Donruss Green Foil /199 #156
2017 Donruss Press Proof /49 #58
2017 Donruss Press Proof /49 #156
2017 Donruss Printing Plates Black /1 #58
2017 Donruss Printing Plates Black /1 #156
2017 Donruss Printing Plates Cyan /1 #58
2017 Donruss Printing Plates Cyan /1 #156
2017 Donruss Printing Plates Magenta /1 #156
2017 Donruss Printing Plates Magenta /1 #58
2017 Donruss Printing Plates Yellow /1 #156
2017 Donruss Printing Plates Yellow /1 #58
2017 Donruss Retro Relics 1984 #32
2017 Donruss Retro Relics 1984 Holo Black /10 #32
2017 Donruss Retro Relics 1984 Holo Gold /99 #32
2017 Donruss Rubber Relics #39
2017 Donruss Rubber Relics Holo Black /10 #39
2017 Donruss Rubber Relics Holo Gold /50 #39
2017 Donruss Studio Signatures #11
2017 Donruss Studio Signatures Holo Black /1 #11
2017 Donruss Studio Signatures Holo Gold /25 #11
2017 Panini National Treasures Associate Sponsor Patch Signatures 1 /1 #28
2017 Panini National Treasures Associate Sponsor Patch Signatures 2 /1 #28
2017 Panini National Treasures Associate Sponsor Patch Signatures 3 /1 #28
2017 Panini National Treasures Associate Sponsor Patch Signatures 4 /1 #28
2017 Panini National Treasures Associate Sponsor Patch Signatures 5 /1 #28
2017 Panini National Treasures Associate Sponsor Patch Signatures 6 /1 #28
2017 Panini National Treasures Associate Sponsor Patch Signatures 7 /1 #28
2017 Panini National Treasures Car Manufacturer Patch Signatures /1 #28
2017 Panini National Treasures Firesuit Manufacturer Patch Signatures /1 #28
2017 Panini National Treasures Nameplate Patch Signatures /2 #28
2017 Panini National Treasures Quad Material Signatures /25 #1
2017 Panini National Treasures Quad Material Signatures Black /1 #1
2017 Panini National Treasures Quad Material Signatures Gold /15 #1
2017 Panini National Treasures Quad Material Signatures Green /5 #1
2017 Panini National Treasures Quad Material Signatures Holo Gold /10 #1
2017 Panini National Treasures Quad Material Signatures Holo Silver /20 #1
2017 Panini National Treasures Quad Material Signatures Laundry Tag /1 #1
2017 Panini National Treasures Quad Material Signatures Printing Plates Black /1 #1
2017 Panini National Treasures Quad Material Signatures Printing Plates Cyan /1 #1
2017 Panini National Treasures Quad Material Signatures Printing Plates Magenta /1 #1
2017 Panini National Treasures Quad Material Signatures Printing Plates Yellow /1 #1
2017 Panini National Treasures Quad Materials /25 #15
2017 Panini National Treasures Quad Materials Black /1 #15
2017 Panini National Treasures Quad Materials Gold /15 #15
2017 Panini National Treasures Quad Materials Green /5 #15
2017 Panini National Treasures Quad Materials Holo Gold /10 #15
2017 Panini National Treasures Quad Materials Holo Silver /20 #15
2017 Panini National Treasures Quad Materials Laundry Tag /1 #15
2017 Panini National Treasures Quad Materials Printing Plates Black /1 #15
2017 Panini National Treasures Quad Materials Printing Plates Cyan /1 #15
2017 Panini National Treasures Quad Materials Printing Plates Magenta /1 #15
2017 Panini National Treasures Quad Materials Printing Plates Yellow /1 #15
2017 Panini National Treasures Series Sponsor Patch Signatures /1 #28
2017 Panini National Treasures Sunoco Patch Signatures /1 #28
2017 Panini National Treasures Three Wide /25 #14
2017 Panini National Treasures Three Wide Black /1 #14
2017 Panini National Treasures Three Wide Gold /15 #14
2017 Panini National Treasures Three Wide Green /5 #14
2017 Panini National Treasures Three Wide Holo Gold /10 #14
2017 Panini National Treasures Three Wide Holo Silver /20 #14
2017 Panini National Treasures Three Wide Laundry Tag /1 #14
2017 Panini National Treasures Three Wide Printing Plates Black /1 #14
2017 Panini National Treasures Three Wide Printing Plates Cyan /1 #14
2017 Panini National Treasures Three Wide Printing Plates Magenta /1 #14
2017 Panini National Treasures Three Wide Printing Plates Yellow /1 #14
2017 Panini Torque Dual Materials /199 #10
2017 Panini Torque Dual Materials Blue /49 #10
2017 Panini Torque Dual Materials Green /10 #10
2017 Panini Torque Dual Materials Purple /1 #10
2017 Panini Torque Dual Materials Red /25 #10
2017 Panini Torque Jumbo Tire Signatures /60 #11
2017 Panini Torque Jumbo Tire Signatures Blue /50 #11
2017 Panini Torque Jumbo Tire Signatures Green /15 #11
2017 Panini Torque Jumbo Tire Signatures Purple /10 #11
2017 Panini Torque Jumbo Tire Signatures Red /25 #11
2017 Panini Torque Pairings Materials /199 #11
2017 Panini Torque Pairings Materials Blue /99 #11
2017 Panini Torque Pairings Materials Green /25 #11
2017 Panini Torque Pairings Materials Purple /10 #11
2017 Panini Torque Pairings Materials Red /49 #11
2017 Panini Torque Primary Paint #5
2017 Panini Torque Primary Paint Blue /99 #5
2017 Panini Torque Primary Paint Checkerboard /10 #5
2017 Panini Torque Primary Paint Green /25 #5
2017 Panini Torque Primary Paint Red /49 #5
2017 Panini Torque Quad Materials /49 #9
2017 Panini Torque Quad Materials Blue /25 #9
2017 Panini Torque Quad Materials Green /15 #9
2017 Panini Torque Quad Materials Purple /10 #9
2017 Panini Torque Quad Materials Red /20 #9
2017 Panini Torque Silhouettes Sheet Metal Signatures /35 #10
2017 Panini Torque Silhouettes Sheet Metal Signatures Blue /25 #10
2017 Panini Torque Silhouettes Sheet Metal Signatures Green /10 #10
2017 Panini Torque Silhouettes Sheet Metal Signatures Purple /5 #10
2017 Panini Torque Silhouettes Sheet Metal Signatures Red /15 #10
2017 Select #13
2017 Select #129
2017 Select Prizms Black /3 #13
2017 Select Prizms Black /3 #129
2017 Select Prizms Blue /199 #13
2017 Select Prizms Checkered Flag /1 #13
2017 Select Prizms Checkered Flag /1 #129
2017 Select Prizms Gold /10 #13
2017 Select Prizms Gold /10 #129
2017 Select Prizms Purple Pulsar #13
2017 Select Prizms Red /99 #13
2017 Select Prizms Red White and Blue Pulsar /299 #13
2017 Select Prizms Silver #13
2017 Select Prizms Tie Dye /24 #13
2017 Select Prizms Tie Dye /24 #129
2017 Select Prizms White /50 #13
2017 Select Prizms White /50 #129
2017 Select Select Swatches #16
2017 Select Select Swatches Prizms Blue /99 #16
2017 Select Select Swatches Prizms Checkered Flag /1 #16
2017 Select Select Swatches Prizms Gold /10 #16
2017 Select Select Swatches Prizms Red /50 #16
2017 Select Signature Swatches #16
2017 Select Signature Swatches Prizms Checkered Flag /1 #16
2017 Select Signature Swatches Prizms Gold /10 #16
2017 Select Signature Swatches Prizms Tie Dye /24 #16
2017 Select Signature Swatches Prizms White /40 #16
2017 Select Signature Swatches Triple #9
2017 Select Signature Swatches Triple Prizms Checkered Flag /1 #9
2017 Select Signature Swatches Triple Prizms Gold /10 #9
2017 Select Signature Swatches Triple Prizms Tie Dye /24 #9
2017 Select Signature Swatches Triple Prizms White /40 #9
2018 Certified #48
2018 Certified Black /1 #48
2018 Certified Blue /99 #48
2018 Certified Gold /49 #48
2018 Certified Green /10 #48
2018 Certified Mirror Black /1 #48
2018 Certified Mirror Gold /25 #48
2018 Certified Mirror Green /5 #48
2018 Certified Mirror Purple /10 #48
2018 Certified Orange /249 #48
2018 Certified Purple /25 #48
2018 Certified Red /199 #48
2018 Certified Signatures /149 #8
2018 Certified Signatures Black /1 #8
2018 Certified Signatures Blue /49 #8
2018 Certified Signatures Gold /25 #8
2018 Certified Signatures Green /5 #8
2018 Certified Signatures Purple /10 #8
2018 Certified Signatures Red /99 #8
2018 Donruss #63
2018 Donruss #101A
2018 Donruss Artist Proofs /25 #63
2018 Donruss Artist Proofs /25 #101
2018 Donruss Gold Foil /499 #63
2018 Donruss Gold Foil /499 #101
2018 Donruss Gold Press Proofs /99 #63
2018 Donruss Gold Press Proofs /99 #101
2018 Donruss Green Foil /199 #63
2018 Donruss Green Foil /199 #101
2018 Donruss Press Proofs /49 #63
2018 Donruss Press Proofs /49 #101A
2018 Donruss Printing Plates Black /1 #63
2018 Donruss Printing Plates Black /1 #101
2018 Donruss Printing Plates Cyan /1 #63
2018 Donruss Printing Plates Cyan /1 #101
2018 Donruss Printing Plates Magenta /1 #63
2018 Donruss Printing Plates Magenta /1 #101
2018 Donruss Printing Plates Yellow /1 #63
2018 Donruss Printing Plates Yellow /1 #101
2018 Donruss Red Foil /299 #63
2018 Donruss Red Foil /299 #101A
2018 Donruss Retro Relics '85 #7
2018 Donruss Retro Relics '85 Black /10 #7
2018 Donruss Retro Relics '85 Holo Gold /99 #7
2018 Donruss Retro Signatures '85 #8
2018 Donruss Retro Signatures '85 Black /1 #8
2018 Donruss Retro Signatures '85 Holo Gold /25 #8
2018 Panini Prime Clear Silhouettes /99 #9
2018 Panini Prime Clear Silhouettes Black /1 #9
2018 Panini Prime Clear Silhouettes Dual /99 #9
2018 Panini Prime Clear Silhouettes Dual Black /1 #9
2018 Panini Prime Clear Silhouettes Dual Holo Gold /50 #9
2018 Panini Prime Clear Silhouettes Holo Gold /50 #9
2018 Panini Prime Prime Jumbo Associate Sponsor 1 /1 #27
2018 Panini Prime Prime Jumbo Associate Sponsor 10 /1 #27
2018 Panini Prime Prime Jumbo Associate Sponsor 11 /1 #27
2018 Panini Prime Prime Jumbo Associate Sponsor 2 /1 #27
2018 Panini Prime Prime Jumbo Associate Sponsor 3 /1 #27
2018 Panini Prime Prime Jumbo Associate Sponsor 4 /1 #27
2018 Panini Prime Prime Jumbo Associate Sponsor 5 /1 #27
2018 Panini Prime Prime Jumbo Associate Sponsor 6 /1 #27
2018 Panini Prime Prime Jumbo Associate Sponsor 7 /1 #27
2018 Panini Prime Prime Jumbo Associate Sponsor 8 /1 #27
2018 Panini Prime Prime Jumbo Associate Sponsor 9 /1 #27
2018 Panini Prime Prime Jumbo Car Manufacturer /1 #27
2018 Panini Prime Prime Jumbo Firesuit Manufacturer /1 #27
2018 Panini Prime Prime Jumbo Glove Manufacturer Patch /1 #27
2018 Panini Prime Prime Jumbo Glove Name Patch /1 #27
2018 Panini Prime Prime Jumbo Nameplate /2 #27
2018 Panini Prime Prime Jumbo NASCAR /1 #27
2018 Panini Prime Prime Jumbo Prime Colors /15 #27
2018 Panini Prime Prime Jumbo Series Sponsor /1 #27
2018 Panini Prime Prime Jumbo Shoe Brand Logo /1 #27
2018 Panini Prime Prime Jumbo Shoe Name Patch /1 #27
2018 Panini Prime Prime Jumbo Sunoco /1 #27
2018 Panini Prime Race Used Duals Firesuit /50 #15
2018 Panini Prime Race Used Duals Firesuit Black /1 #15
2018 Panini Prime Race Used Duals Firesuit Holo Gold /25 #15
2018 Panini Prime Race Used Duals Firesuit Laundry Tag /1 #15
2018 Panini Prime Race Used Duals Sheet Metal /50 #15
2018 Panini Prime Race Used Duals Sheet Metal Black /1 #15
2018 Panini Prime Race Used Duals Sheet Metal Holo Gold /25 #15
2018 Panini Prime Race Used Duals Tire /50 #15
2018 Panini Prime Race Used Duals Tire Black /1 #15
2018 Panini Prime Race Used Duals Tire Holo Gold /25 #15
2018 Panini Prime Race Used Firesuits /50 #12
2018 Panini Prime Race Used Firesuits Black /1 #12
2018 Panini Prime Race Used Firesuits Holo Gold /25 #12
2018 Panini Prime Race Used Firesuits Laundry Tag /1 #12
2018 Panini Prime Race Used Sheet Metal /50 #12
2018 Panini Prime Race Used Sheet Metal Black /1 #12
2018 Panini Prime Race Used Sheet Metal Holo Gold /25 #12
2018 Panini Prime Race Used Tires Black /1 #12
2018 Panini Prime Race Used Tires Holo Gold /25 #12
2018 Panini Prizm Scripted Signatures Prizms #5
2018 Panini Prizm Scripted Signatures Prizms Black /1 #5
2018 Panini Prizm Scripted Signatures Prizms Blue /75 #5
2018 Panini Prizm Scripted Signatures Prizms Camo #5

2018 Panini Prizm Scripted Signatures Prizms Gold /10 #5
2018 Panini Prizm Scripted Signatures Prizms Green /99 #5
2018 Panini Prizm Scripted Signatures Prizms Rainbow /24 #5
2018 Panini Prizm Scripted Signatures Prizms Red /50 #5
2018 Panini Prizm Scripted Signatures Prizms Red White and Blue /125 #5
2018 Panini Prizm Scripted Signatures Prizms White /5 #5
2018 Panini Victory Lane Octane Autographs /299 #12
2018 Panini Victory Lane Octane Autographs Black /1 #12
2018 Panini Victory Lane Octane Autographs Gold /99 #12
2018 Panini Victory Lane Pedal to the Metal #18
2018 Panini Victory Lane Pedal to the Metal Black /1 #18
2018 Panini Victory Lane Pedal to the Metal Blue /25 #18
2018 Panini Victory Lane Pedal to the Metal Green /5 #18
2018 Panini Victory Lane Signatures /40 #18
2018 Panini Victory Lane Signatures Black /1 #18
2018 Panini Victory Lane Signatures Gold /10 #18
2018 Panini Victory Lane Victory Lane Prime Patches Associate Sponsor 1 /1 #33
2018 Panini Victory Lane Victory Lane Prime Patches Associate Sponsor 2 /1 #33
2018 Panini Victory Lane Victory Lane Prime Patches Associate Sponsor 3 /1 #33
2018 Panini Victory Lane Victory Lane Prime Patches Associate Sponsor 4 /1 #33
2018 Panini Victory Lane Victory Lane Prime Patches Associate Sponsor 5 /1 #33
2018 Panini Victory Lane Victory Lane Prime Patches Associate Sponsor 6 /1 #33
2018 Panini Victory Lane Victory Lane Prime Patches Associate Sponsor 7 /1 #33
2018 Panini Victory Lane Victory Lane Prime Patches Associate Sponsor 8 /1 #33
2018 Panini Victory Lane Victory Lane Prime Patches Associate Sponsor 9 /1 #33
2018 Panini Victory Lane Victory Lane Prime Patches Car Manufacturer /1 #33
2018 Panini Victory Lane Victory Lane Prime Patches Firesuit Manufacturer /1 #33
2018 Panini Victory Lane Victory Lane Prime Patches Nameplate /2 #33
2018 Panini Victory Lane Victory Lane Prime Patches NASCAR /1 #33
2018 Panini Victory Lane Victory Lane Prime Patches Series Sponsor /1 #33
2018 Panini Victory Lane Victory Lane Prime Patches Sunoco /1 #33
2019 Donruss #37
2019 Donruss #130
2019 Donruss Artist Proofs /25 #37
2019 Donruss Artist Proofs /25 #130
2019 Donruss Black /199 #37
2019 Donruss Black /199 #130
2019 Donruss Gold /299 #37
2019 Donruss Gold /299 #130
2019 Donruss Gold Press Proofs /99 #37
2019 Donruss Gold Press Proofs /99 #130
2019 Donruss Optic #35
2019 Donruss Optic #56
2019 Donruss Optic Blue Pulsar #35
2019 Donruss Optic Blue Pulsar /1 #56
2019 Donruss Optic Gold /10 #35
2019 Donruss Optic Gold /10 #56
2019 Donruss Optic Gold Vinyl /1 #35
2019 Donruss Optic Gold Vinyl /1 #56
2019 Donruss Optic Holo #35
2019 Donruss Optic Holo #56
2019 Donruss Optic Red Wave #35
2019 Donruss Optic Red Wave /1 #56
2019 Donruss Optic Signatures Gold Vinyl /1 #56
2019 Donruss Optic Signatures Gold Vinyl /1 #35
2019 Donruss Optic Signatures Holo /75 #35
2019 Donruss Optic Signatures Holo /75 #56
2019 Donruss Press Proofs /49 #37
2019 Donruss Press Proofs /49 #130
2019 Donruss Printing Plates Black /1 #37
2019 Donruss Printing Plates Black /1 #130
2019 Donruss Printing Plates Cyan /1 #37
2019 Donruss Printing Plates Cyan /1 #130
2019 Donruss Printing Plates Magenta /1 #37
2019 Donruss Printing Plates Magenta /1 #130
2019 Donruss Printing Plates Yellow /1 #37
2019 Donruss Printing Plates Yellow /1 #130
2019 Donruss Retro Relics '86 #7
2019 Donruss Retro Relics '86 Holo Black /10 #7
2019 Donruss Retro Relics '86 Holo Gold /25 #7
2019 Donruss Retro Relics '86 Red /250 #7
2019 Donruss Signature Series #13
2019 Donruss Signature Series Holo Black /10 #13
2019 Donruss Signature Series Holo Gold /25 #13
2019 Donruss Signature Series Red /99 #13
2019 Donruss Silver #37
2019 Donruss Silver #130
2019 Panini Prime /50 #14
2019 Panini Prime /50 #46
2019 Panini Prime Black /10 #14
2019 Panini Prime Black /10 #46
2019 Panini Prime Emerald /5 #14
2019 Panini Prime Emerald /5 #46
2019 Panini Prime Platinum Blue /1 #14
2019 Panini Prime Platinum Blue /1 #46
2019 Panini Prime Prime Jumbo Associate Sponsor 1 /1 #63
2019 Panini Prime Prime Jumbo Associate Sponsor 1 /1 #64
2019 Panini Prime Prime Jumbo Associate Sponsor 1 /1 #65
2019 Panini Prime Prime Jumbo Associate Sponsor 2 /1 #65
2019 Panini Prime Prime Jumbo Associate Sponsor 3 /1 #65
2019 Panini Prime Prime Jumbo Associate Sponsor 4 /1 #65
2019 Panini Prime Prime Jumbo Associate Sponsor 5 /1 #65
2019 Panini Prime Prime Jumbo Car Manufacturer /1 #63
2019 Panini Prime Prime Jumbo Car Manufacturer /1 #64
2019 Panini Prime Prime Jumbo Car Manufacturer /1 #65
2019 Panini Prime Prime Jumbo Firesuit Manufacturer /1 #63
2019 Panini Prime Prime Jumbo Firesuit Manufacturer /1 #64
2019 Panini Prime Prime Jumbo Firesuit Manufacturer /1 #65
2019 Panini Prime Prime Jumbo Glove Manufacturer Patch /1 #63
2019 Panini Prime Prime Jumbo Glove Manufacturer Patch /1 #64
2019 Panini Prime Prime Jumbo Glove Manufacturer Patch /1 #65
2019 Panini Prime Prime Jumbo Glove Name Patch /1 #63
2019 Panini Prime Prime Jumbo Glove Name Patch /1 #64
2019 Panini Prime Prime Jumbo Glove Name Patch /1 #65
2019 Panini Prime Prime Jumbo Glove Number Patch /1 #63
2019 Panini Prime Prime Jumbo Glove Number Patch /1 #64
2019 Panini Prime Prime Jumbo Glove Number Patch /1 #65
2019 Panini Prime Prime Jumbo Laundry Tag /1 #63
2019 Panini Prime Prime Jumbo Nameplate /2 #63
2019 Panini Prime Prime Jumbo Nameplate /2 #64
2019 Panini Prime Prime Jumbo NASCAR /1 #65
2019 Panini Prime Prime Jumbo Prime Colors /4 #63
2019 Panini Prime Prime Jumbo Prime Colors /8 #64
2019 Panini Prime Prime Jumbo Prime Colors /11 #65
2019 Panini Prime Prime Jumbo Series Sponsor /1 #65
2019 Panini Prime Prime Jumbo Shoe Brand Logo /1 #63
2019 Panini Prime Prime Jumbo Shoe Brand Logo /1 #64
2019 Panini Prime Prime Jumbo Shoe Brand Logo /1 #65
2019 Panini Prime Prime Jumbo Shoe Name Patch /1 #63
2019 Panini Prime Prime Jumbo Shoe Name Patch /1 #64
2019 Panini Prime Prime Jumbo Shoe Name Patch /1 #65
2019 Panini Prime Prime Jumbo Sunoco /1 #65
2019 Panini Prizm #14
2019 Panini Prizm Patented Penmanship Prizms #15
2019 Panini Prizm Patented Penmanship Prizms Black /1 #15
2019 Panini Prizm Patented Penmanship Prizms Blue /25 #15
2019 Panini Prizm Patented Penmanship Prizms Camo #15
2019 Panini Prizm Patented Penmanship Prizms Gold /10 #15
2019 Panini Prizm Patented Penmanship Prizms Rainbow /24 #15
2019 Panini Prizm Patented Penmanship Prizms Red /25 #15
2019 Panini Prizm Patented Penmanship Prizms Red White and Blue #15
2019 Panini Prizm Patented Penmanship Prizms White /5 #15
2019 Panini Prizm Prizms #14
2019 Panini Prizm Prizms Black /1 #14
2019 Panini Prizm Prizms Blue /75 #14
2019 Panini Prizm Prizms Camo #14
2019 Panini Prizm Prizms Flash #14
2019 Panini Prizm Prizms Gold /10 #14
2019 Panini Prizm Prizms Green /99 #14
2019 Panini Prizm Prizms Rainbow /24 #14
2019 Panini Prizm Prizms Red /50 #14
2019 Panini Prizm Prizms Red White and Blue #14
2019 Panini Prizm Prizms White /5 #14
2019 Panini Prizm Prizms White Sparkle #14
2019 Panini Victory Lane #14
2019 Panini Victory Lane #86
2019 Panini Victory Lane Black /1 #14
2019 Panini Victory Lane Black /1 #86
2019 Panini Victory Lane Gold /25 #14
2019 Panini Victory Lane Gold /25 #86
2019 Panini Victory Lane Pedal to the Metal #36
2019 Panini Victory Lane Pedal to the Metal Black /1 #36
2019 Panini Victory Lane Pedal to the Metal Gold /25 #36
2019 Panini Victory Lane Pedal to the Metal Green /5 #36
2019 Panini Victory Lane Pedal to the Metal Red /3 #36
2019 Panini Victory Lane Printing Plates Black /1 #14
2019 Panini Victory Lane Printing Plates Black /1 #86
2019 Panini Victory Lane Printing Plates Cyan /1 #14
2019 Panini Victory Lane Printing Plates Cyan /1 #86
2019 Panini Victory Lane Printing Plates Magenta /1 #14
2019 Panini Victory Lane Printing Plates Magenta /1 #86
2019 Panini Victory Lane Printing Plates Yellow /1 #14
2019 Panini Victory Lane Printing Plates Yellow /1 #86
2019 Panini Victory Lane Signature Swatches #18
2019 Panini Victory Lane Signature Swatches Gold /49 #18
2019 Panini Victory Lane Signature Swatches Laundry Tag /1 #18
2019 Panini Victory Lane Signature Swatches Platinum /1 #18
2019 Panini Victory Lane Signature Swatches Red /25 #18
2019 Panini Victory Lane Starting Grid #2
2019 Panini Victory Lane Starting Grid Black /1 #2
2019 Panini Victory Lane Starting Grid Blue /99 #2
2019 Panini Victory Lane Starting Grid Gold /25 #2
2019 Panini Victory Lane Starting Grid Green /5 #2
2019 Panini Victory Lane Starting Grid Printing Plates Black /1 #2
2019 Panini Victory Lane Starting Grid Printing Plates Cyan /1 #2
2019 Panini Victory Lane Starting Grid Printing Plates Magenta /1 #2
2019 Panini Victory Lane Starting Grid Printing Plates Yellow /1 #2
2020 Donruss #50
2020 Donruss #133
2020 Donruss Black Numbers /17 #50
2020 Donruss Black Numbers /17 #133
2020 Donruss Black Trophy Club /1 #50
2020 Donruss Black Trophy Club /1 #133
2020 Donruss Blue /199 #133
2020 Donruss Blue /199 #50
2020 Donruss Carolina Blue #50
2020 Donruss Carolina Blue #133
2020 Donruss Green /99 #50
2020 Donruss Green /99 #133
2020 Donruss Optic #38
2020 Donruss Optic Carolina Blue Wave #38
2020 Donruss Optic Gold /10 #38
2020 Donruss Optic Gold Vinyl /1 #38
2020 Donruss Optic Holo #38
2020 Donruss Optic Orange Pulsar #38
2020 Donruss Optic Red Mojo #38
2020 Donruss Optic Signatures Gold Vinyl /1 #38
2020 Donruss Optic Signatures Holo /99 #38
2020 Donruss Orange #50
2020 Donruss Orange #133
2020 Donruss Pink /25 #50
2020 Donruss Pink /25 #133
2020 Donruss Printing Plates Black /1 #50
2020 Donruss Printing Plates Black /1 #133
2020 Donruss Printing Plates Cyan /1 #50
2020 Donruss Printing Plates Cyan /1 #133
2020 Donruss Printing Plates Magenta /1 #50
2020 Donruss Printing Plates Magenta /1 #133
2020 Donruss Printing Plates Yellow /1 #133
2020 Donruss Printing Plates Yellow /1 #50
2020 Donruss Purple /49 #50
2020 Donruss Purple /49 #133
2020 Donruss Race Day Relics #27
2020 Donruss Race Day Relics Holo Black /10 #27
2020 Donruss Race Day Relics Holo Gold /25 #27
2020 Donruss Race Day Relics Red /250 #27
2020 Donruss Red /299 #50
2020 Donruss Red /299 #133
2020 Donruss Silver #50
2020 Donruss Silver #133

Tony Stewart

1991 DK IMCA Dirt Track #20
1997 Hi-Tech IRL #9
1997 Hi-Tech IRL Disney 200 #D3
1997 Hi-Tech IRL Phoenix #P7
1998 Press Pass Premium #5
1998 Press Pass Premium Reflectors #5
1998 Press Pass Signings #21
1998 Press Pass Stealth #44
1998 Press Pass Stealth Fusion #44
1998 Upper Deck Road To The Cup #115
1998 VIP #36
1998 VIP Explosives #36
1998 VIP Solos #36
1998 Wheels #58
1998 Wheels #63
1998 Wheels Golden #58
1998 Wheels Golden #63
1999 Maxx #70
1999 Maxx #71
1999 Maxx #72
1999 Maxx FANtastic Finishes #F28
1999 Maxx Race Ticket #RT18
1999 Maxx Racing Images #RI15
1999 Press Pass #61
1999 Press Pass #94
1999 Press Pass Autographs /500 #19
1999 Press Pass Premium #23
1999 Press Pass Premium Burning Desire #FD6B
1999 Press Pass Premium Reflectors /1975 #R23
1999 Press Pass Signings /500 #55
1999 Press Pass Signings Gold /100 #26
1999 Press Pass Skidmarks /250 #61
1999 Press Pass Skidmarks /250 #94
1999 Press Pass Stealth #31
1999 Press Pass Stealth #32
1999 Press Pass Stealth #54
1999 Press Pass Stealth #P1
1999 Press Pass Stealth Big Numbers #BN16
1999 Press Pass Stealth Big Numbers Die Cuts #BN16
1999 Press Pass Stealth Fusion #F31
1999 Press Pass Stealth Fusion #F32
1999 Press Pass Stealth Fusion #F54
1999 Press Pass Stealth Headlines #SH6
1999 Press Pass Stealth Octane SLX #O21
1999 Press Pass Stealth Octane SLX #O29
1999 Press Pass Stealth Octane SLX Die Cuts #O21
1999 Press Pass Stealth Octane SLX Die Cuts #O29
1999 Press Pass Stealth Race Used Gloves /150 #G8
1999 Press Pass Stealth SST Cars #SS8
1999 Press Pass Stealth SST Drivers #SS8
1999 Press Pass Tony Stewart Fan Club #NNO
1999 SP Authentic #3
1999 SP Authentic #36
1999 SP Authentic #81
1999 SP Authentic Cup Challengers #CC9
1999 SP Authentic Driving Force #DF11
1999 SP Authentic In the Driver's Seat #DS4
1999 SP Authentic Overdrive #3
1999 SP Authentic Overdrive #36
1999 SP Authentic Overdrive /20 #81
1999 SP Authentic Sign of the Times #TS
1999 Upper Deck MVP ProSign #TSH
1999 Upper Deck MVP ProSign #TSR
1999 Upper Deck Road to the Cup #6
1999 Upper Deck Road to the Cup #58
1999 Upper Deck Road to the Cup #66
1999 Upper Deck Road to the Cup #84
1999 Upper Deck Road to the Cup NASCAR Chronicles #NC19
1999 Upper Deck Road to the Cup Signature Collection #TS
1999 Upper Deck Road to the Cup Signature Collection Checkered Flag #TS
1999 Upper Deck Road to the Cup Upper Deck Profiles #P11
1999 Upper Deck Victory Circle #88
1999 Upper Deck Victory Circle UD Exclusives #88
1999 VIP #25
1999 VIP #48
1999 VIP Double Take #DT3
1999 VIP Explosives #X25
1999 VIP Explosives #X48
1999 VIP Explosives Lasers #25
1999 VIP Explosives Lasers #48
1999 VIP Head Gear #HG3
1999 VIP Head Gear Plastic #HG3
1999 VIP Out of the Box #OB11
1999 VIP Rear View Mirror #RM9
1999 VIP Sheet Metal #SM6
1999 Wheels #33
1999 Wheels #68
1999 Wheels #95
1999 Wheels Autographs /350 #22
1999 Wheels Golden #33
1999 Wheels Golden #68
1999 Wheels Golden #95
1999 Wheels High Gear #45
1999 Wheels High Gear #61
1999 Wheels High Gear First Gear #45
1999 Wheels High Gear First Gear #61
1999 Wheels High Gear MPH #45
1999 Wheels High Gear MPH #61
1999 Wheels Runnin and Gunnin #RG18
1999 Wheels Runnin and Gunnin Foils #RG18
1999 Wheels Solos #33
1999 Wheels Solos #68
1999 Wheels Solos #95
2000 Coca-Cola Racing Family #14
2000 Coca-Cola Racing Family #15
2000 Coca-Cola Racing Family #16
2000 Maxx #20
2000 Maxx #40
2000 Maxx #80
2000 Maxx Collectible Covers #CCTS
2000 Maxx Drive Time #DT1
2000 Maxx Fantastic Finishes #FF5
2000 Maxx Focus On A Champion #FC2
2000 Maxx Racer's Ink #TS
2000 Maxx Speedway Boogie #SB10
2000 Maximum #4
2000 Maximum Dialed In #DI2
2000 Maximum Die Cuts /250 #4
2000 Maximum MPH /20 #4
2000 Maximum Pure Adrenaline #PA1
2000 Maximum Roots of Racing #R3
2000 Maximum Signatures #SL2
2000 Maximum Signatures #TS
2000 Maximum Signatures /100 #GIB4
2000 Maximum Signatures #BTJ3
2000 Press Pass #4
2000 Press Pass #42
2000 Press Pass #44
2000 Press Pass #55
2000 Press Pass #67
2000 Press Pass Burning Rubber /200 #BR4
2000 Press Pass Chef Boyardee #2
2000 Press Pass Chef Boyardee #4
2000 Press Pass Chef Boyardee #6
2000 Press Pass Cup Chase #CC15
2000 Press Pass Cup Chase Die Cut Prizes #CC15
2000 Press Pass Gatorade Front Runner Award #4
2000 Press Pass Millennium #4
2000 Press Pass Millennium #42
2000 Press Pass Millennium #44
2000 Press Pass Millennium #55
2000 Press Pass Millennium #67
2000 Press Pass Oil Cans #OC1
2000 Press Pass Optima #24
2000 Press Pass Optima #48
2000 Press Pass Optima Encore #EN7
2000 Press Pass Optima G Force #GF23
2000 Press Pass Optima On the Edge #OE6
2000 Press Pass Optima Overdrive #OD8
2000 Press Pass Optima Overdrive Square Cut #OD8
2000 Press Pass Optima Platinum #24
2000 Press Pass Optima Platinum #48
2000 Press Pass Optima Race Used Lugnuts Cars /50 #LC20
2000 Press Pass Optima Race Used Lugnuts Drivers /55 #LD20
2000 Press Pass Pitstop #PS13
2000 Press Pass Premium #10
2000 Press Pass Premium #35
2000 Press Pass Premium #57
2000 Press Pass Premium #67
2000 Press Pass Premium In The Zone #IZ1
2000 Press Pass Premium Performance Driven #PD3
2000 Press Pass Premium Race Used Firesuit /130 #F7
2000 Press Pass Premium Reflectors #10
2000 Press Pass Premium Reflectors #35
2000 Press Pass Premium Reflectors #57
2000 Press Pass Premium Reflectors #67
2000 Press Pass Showcar #SC17
2000 Press Pass Showcar Die Cuts #SC17
2000 Press Pass Showman #SM17
2000 Press Pass Showman Die Cuts #SM17
2000 Press Pass Signings #57
2000 Press Pass Signings Gold /100 #30
2000 Press Pass Skidmarks #SK4
2000 Press Pass Stealth #28
2000 Press Pass Stealth #29
2000 Press Pass Stealth #66
2000 Press Pass Stealth Behind the Numbers #BN6
2000 Press Pass Stealth Fusion #FS22
2000 Press Pass Stealth Fusion #FS23
2000 Press Pass Stealth Fusion #FS24
2000 Press Pass Stealth Fusion #FS34
2000 Press Pass Stealth Fusion #FS35
2000 Press Pass Stealth Fusion #FS36
2000 Press Pass Stealth Fusion Green /1000 #FS22
2000 Press Pass Stealth Fusion Green /1000 #FS23
2000 Press Pass Stealth Fusion Green /1000 #FS24
2000 Press Pass Stealth Fusion Green /1000 #FS34
2000 Press Pass Stealth Fusion Green /1000 #FS35
2000 Press Pass Stealth Fusion Green /1000 #FS36
2000 Press Pass Stealth Fusion Red #FS22
2000 Press Pass Stealth Fusion Red #FS23
2000 Press Pass Stealth Fusion Red #FS24
2000 Press Pass Stealth Fusion Red #FS34
2000 Press Pass Stealth Fusion Red #FS35
2000 Press Pass Stealth Fusion Red #FS36
2000 Press Pass Stealth Intensity #IN4
2000 Press Pass Stealth Profile #PR3
2000 Press Pass Stealth Race Used Gloves /100 #G12
2000 Press Pass Stealth SST #SST5
2000 Press Pass Techno-Retro #TR24
2000 Press Pass Trackside #14
2000 Press Pass Trackside #35
2000 Press Pass Trackside Dialed In #DI5
2000 Press Pass Trackside Die Cuts #14
2000 Press Pass Trackside Die Cuts #35
2000 Press Pass Trackside Generation.now #GN5
2000 Press Pass Trackside Golden #14
2000 Press Pass Trackside Golden #35
2000 Press Pass Trackside Panorama #P36
2000 Press Pass Trackside Pit Stoppers /200 #PS7
2000 Press Pass Trackside Runnin N' Gunnin #RG1
2000 Press Pass Trackside Too Tough To Tame #TT4
2000 SLU Racing Winner's Circle #40
2000 SP Authentic #10
2000 SP Authentic /1000 #85
2000 SP Authentic Dominance #D1
2000 SP Authentic Driver's Seat #DS4
2000 SP Authentic Overdrive Gold /20 #10
2000 SP Authentic Overdrive Gold /20 #85
2000 SP Authentic Overdrive Silver /250 #10
2000 SP Authentic Overdrive Silver /250 #85
2000 SP Authentic Power Surge #PS3
2000 SP Authentic Race for the Cup #R7
2000 Upper Deck MVP #20
2000 Upper Deck MVP #48
2000 Upper Deck MVP #78
2000 Upper Deck MVP #101
2000 Upper Deck MVP Cup Quest 2000 #CQ5
2000 Upper Deck MVP Gold Script /125 #20
2000 Upper Deck MVP Gold Script /125 #48
2000 Upper Deck MVP Gold Script /125 #78
2000 Upper Deck MVP Gold Script /125 #101
2000 Upper Deck MVP Legends in the Making #LM10
2000 Upper Deck MVP Magic Numbers #MTS
2000 Upper Deck MVP Magic Numbers Autographs /20 #MATS
2000 Upper Deck MVP NASCAR Gallery #NG2
2000 Upper Deck MVP NASCAR Stars #NS1
2000 Upper Deck MVP ProSign #PSTS
2000 Upper Deck MVP Silver Script #20
2000 Upper Deck MVP Silver Script #48
2000 Upper Deck MVP Silver Script #78
2000 Upper Deck MVP Silver Script #101
2000 Upper Deck MVP Super Script /20 #20
2000 Upper Deck MVP Super Script /20 #48
2000 Upper Deck MVP Super Script /20 #78
2000 Upper Deck MVP Super Script /20 #101
2000 Upper Deck Racing #4
2000 Upper Deck Racing #45
2000 Upper Deck Racing High Groove #HG4
2000 Upper Deck Racing Record Pace #RP9
2000 Upper Deck Racing Road Signs #RSTS
2000 Upper Deck Racing Speeding Ticket #ST4
2000 Upper Deck Racing Thunder Road #TR6
2000 Upper Deck Racing Tony Stewart Tribute #TS1
2000 Upper Deck Racing Tony Stewart Tribute #TS2
2000 Upper Deck Racing Tony Stewart Tribute #TS3
2000 Upper Deck Racing Tony Stewart Tribute #TS4
2000 Upper Deck Racing Tony Stewart Tribute #TS5
2000 Upper Deck Racing Tony Stewart Tribute #TS6
2000 Upper Deck Racing Tony Stewart Tribute #TS7
2000 Upper Deck Racing Tony Stewart Tribute #TS8
2000 Upper Deck Racing Tony Stewart Tribute #TS9
2000 Upper Deck Racing Tony Stewart Tribute #TS10
2000 Upper Deck Racing Tony Stewart Tribute #TS11
2000 Upper Deck Racing Tony Stewart Tribute #TS12
2000 Upper Deck Racing Tony Stewart Tribute #TS13
2000 Upper Deck Racing Tony Stewart Tribute #TS14
2000 Upper Deck Racing Tony Stewart Tribute #TS15
2000 Upper Deck Racing Tony Stewart Tribute #TS16
2000 Upper Deck Racing Tony Stewart Tribute #TS17
2000 Upper Deck Racing Tony Stewart Tribute #TS18
2000 Upper Deck Racing Tony Stewart Tribute #TS19
2000 Upper Deck Racing Tony Stewart Tribute #TS20
2000 Upper Deck Racing Tony Stewart Tribute #TS21
2000 Upper Deck Racing Tony Stewart Tribute #TS22
2000 Upper Deck Racing Tony Stewart Tribute #TS23
2000 Upper Deck Racing Tony Stewart Tribute #TS24
2000 Upper Deck Racing Tony Stewart Tribute #TS25
2000 Upper Deck Racing Trophy Dash #TD9
2000 Upper Deck Racing Winning Formula #WF5
2000 Upper Deck Victory Circle #22
2000 Upper Deck Victory Circle #64
2000 Upper Deck Victory Circle #67
2000 Upper Deck Victory Circle #80
2000 Upper Deck Victory Circle #85
2000 Upper Deck Victory Circle Exclusives Level 1 Silver /250 #22
2000 Upper Deck Victory Circle Exclusives Level 1 Silver /250 #64
2000 Upper Deck Victory Circle Exclusives Level 1 Silver /250 #67
2000 Upper Deck Victory Circle Exclusives Level 1 Silver /250 #80
2000 Upper Deck Victory Circle Exclusives Level 1 Silver /250 #85
2000 Upper Deck Victory Circle Exclusives Level 2 Gold /20 #22
2000 Upper Deck Victory Circle Exclusives Level 2 Gold /20 #64
2000 Upper Deck Victory Circle Exclusives Level 2 Gold /20 #67
2000 Upper Deck Victory Circle Exclusives Level 2 Gold /20 #80
2000 Upper Deck Victory Circle Exclusives Level 2 Gold /20 #85
2000 Upper Deck Victory Circle Income Statement #IS5
2000 Upper Deck Victory Circle Income Statement LTD #IS5
2000 Upper Deck Victory Circle PowerDeck #PD4
2000 Upper Deck Victory Circle Signature Collection #TS
2000 Upper Deck Victory Circle Signature Collection Gold /20 #5
2000 Upper Deck Victory Circle Winning Material Tire #TTS
2000 VIP #11
2000 VIP #27
2000 VIP #36
2000 VIP Explosives #X11
2000 VIP Explosives #X27
2000 VIP Explosives #X36
2000 VIP Explosives Lasers #LX11
2000 VIP Explosives Lasers #LX27
2000 VIP Explosives Lasers #LX36
2000 VIP Head Gear #HG3
2000 VIP Head Gear Explosives #HG3
2000 VIP Head Gear Explosives Laser Die Cuts #HG3
2000 VIP Lap Leaders #LL2
2000 VIP Lap Leaders Explosives #LL2
2000 VIP Lap Leaders Explosives Lasers #LL2
2000 VIP Making the Show #MS21
2000 VIP Rear View Mirror #RM6
2000 VIP Rear View Mirror Explosives #RM6
2000 VIP Rear View Mirror Explosives Laser Die Cuts #RM6
2000 VIP Sheet Metal #SM6
2000 VIP Under the Lights #UL5
2000 VIP Under the Lights Explosives #UL5
2000 VIP Under the Lights Explosives Lasers #UL5
2000 Wheels High Gear #5
2000 Wheels High Gear #32
2000 Wheels High Gear #47
2000 Wheels High Gear #61
2000 Wheels High Gear #2000
2000 Wheels High Gear Autographs #26
2000 Wheels High Gear Custom Shop #CSTS
2000 Wheels High Gear Custom Shop Prizes #TSA1
2000 Wheels High Gear Custom Shop Prizes #TSA2
2000 Wheels High Gear Custom Shop Prizes #TSA3
2000 Wheels High Gear Custom Shop Prizes #TSB1
2000 Wheels High Gear Custom Shop Prizes #TSB2
2000 Wheels High Gear Custom Shop Prizes #TSB3
2000 Wheels High Gear Custom Shop Prizes #TSC1
2000 Wheels High Gear Custom Shop Prizes #TSC2
2000 Wheels High Gear Custom Shop Prizes #TSC3
2000 Wheels High Gear First Gear #5
2000 Wheels High Gear First Gear #32
2000 Wheels High Gear First Gear #47
2000 Wheels High Gear First Gear #61
2000 Wheels High Gear Flag Chasers #FC5
2000 Wheels High Gear Flag Chasers Blue-Yellow #FC5
2000 Wheels High Gear Flag Chasers Checkered #FC5
2000 Wheels High Gear Flag Chasers Checkered Blue/Orange #FC5
2000 Wheels High Gear Flag Chasers Green #FC5
2000 Wheels High Gear Flag Chasers Red #FC5
2000 Wheels High Gear Flag Chasers White #FC5
2000 Wheels High Gear Flag Chasers Yellow #FC5
2000 Wheels High Gear Gear Shifters #GS4
2000 Wheels High Gear Man and Machine Cars #MM1B
2000 Wheels High Gear Man and Machine Drivers #MM1A
2000 Wheels High Gear MPH #5
2000 Wheels High Gear MPH #32
2000 Wheels High Gear MPH #47
2000 Wheels High Gear MPH #61
2000 Wheels High Gear Sunday Sensation #OC1
2000 Wheels High Gear Top Tier #TT5
2000 Wheels High Gear Vintage #V3
2000 Wheels High Gear Winning Edge #WE4
2001 Press Pass #6
2001 Press Pass #53
2001 Press Pass #68
2001 Press Pass #92
2001 Press Pass Autographs #43
2001 Press Pass Burning Rubber Cars /105 #BRC9
2001 Press Pass Burning Rubber Drivers /90 #BRD9
2001 Press Pass Coca-Cola Racing Family #2
2001 Press Pass Cup Chase #CC9
2001 Press Pass Cup Chase Die Cut Prizes #CC9
2001 Press Pass Double Burner /100 #DB5
2001 Press Pass Ground Zero #GZ5
2001 Press Pass Hot Treads /2405 #HT2
2001 Press Pass Millennium #6
2001 Press Pass Millennium #53
2001 Press Pass Millennium #68
2001 Press Pass Millennium #92
2001 Press Pass Optima #25
2001 Press Pass Optima #48
2001 Press Pass Optima G Force #GF25
2001 Press Pass Optima Gold #25
2001 Press Pass Optima Gold #48
2001 Press Pass Optima On the Edge #OE8
2001 Press Pass Optima Race Used Lugnuts Cars /115 #LNC15
2001 Press Pass Optima Race Used Lugnuts Drivers /100 #LND14
2001 Press Pass Premium #25
2001 Press Pass Premium #35
2001 Press Pass Premium #68
2001 Press Pass Premium #80
2001 Press Pass Premium Gold #25
2001 Press Pass Premium Gold #35
2001 Press Pass Premium Gold #68
2001 Press Pass Premium Gold #80
2001 Press Pass Premium Performance Driven #PD8
2001 Press Pass Premium Race Used Firesuit Cars /110 #FC7
2001 Press Pass Premium Race Used Firesuit Drivers /100 #FD7
2001 Press Pass Showman/Showcar #S10A
2001 Press Pass Showman/Showcar #S10B
2001 Press Pass Signings #51
2001 Press Pass Signings Gold /50 #33
2001 Press Pass Signings Transparent /100 #11
2001 Press Pass Stealth #22
2001 Press Pass Stealth #23
2001 Press Pass Stealth #24
2001 Press Pass Stealth #70
2001 Press Pass Stealth Behind The Numbers #BN5
2001 Press Pass Stealth Fusion #F8
2001 Press Pass Stealth Holofoils #22
2001 Press Pass Stealth Holofoils #23
2001 Press Pass Stealth Holofoils #24
2001 Press Pass Stealth Holofoils #70
2001 Press Pass Stealth Lap Leaders #LL8
2001 Press Pass Stealth Lap Leaders #LL26
2001 Press Pass Stealth Lap Leaders Clear Cars #LL26
2001 Press Pass Stealth Lap Leaders Clear Drivers #LL8
2001 Press Pass Stealth Profile #PR3
2001 Press Pass Stealth Race Used Glove Cars /120 #RGC4
2001 Press Pass Stealth Race Used Glove Drivers /120 #RGD4
2001 Press Pass Total Memorabilia Power Pick #TM5
2001 Press Pass Trackside #15
2001 Press Pass Trackside #47
2001 Press Pass Trackside #67
2001 Press Pass Trackside #88
2001 Press Pass Trackside Die Cuts #15
2001 Press Pass Trackside Die Cuts #47
2001 Press Pass Trackside Die Cuts #67
2001 Press Pass Trackside Die Cuts #88
2001 Press Pass Trackside Golden #15
2001 Press Pass Trackside Golden #47
2001 Press Pass Trackside Mirror Image #MI4
2001 Press Pass Trackside Pit Stoppers Cars /250 #PSC2
2001 Press Pass Trackside Pit Stoppers Drivers /100 #PSD2
2001 Press Pass Trackside Runnin N' Gunnin #RG7
2001 Press Pass Triple Burner /100 #TB5
2001 Press Pass Velocity #VL5
2001 Press Pass Vintage #VN6
2001 Super Shots Sears Point CHP #SP3
2001 VIP #11
2001 VIP #27
2001 VIP #37
2001 VIP #48
2001 VIP Driver's Choice #DC5
2001 VIP Driver's Choice Precious Metal /100 #DC5
2001 VIP Driver's Choice Transparent #DC5
2001 VIP Explosives #11
2001 VIP Explosives #27
2001 VIP Explosives #37
2001 VIP Explosives #48
2001 VIP Explosives Lasers /420 #LX11
2001 VIP Explosives Lasers /420 #LX27
2001 VIP Explosives Lasers /420 #LX37
2001 VIP Explosives Lasers /420 #LX48
2001 VIP Making the Show #10
2001 VIP Mile Masters #MM2
2001 VIP Mile Masters Precious Metal /325 #MM2
2001 VIP Mile Masters Transparent #MM2
2001 VIP Rear View Mirror #RV6
2001 VIP Rear View Mirror Die Cuts #RV6
2001 VIP Sheet Metal Cars /120 #SC4
2001 VIP Sheet Metal Drivers /75 #SD4
2001 Wheels High Gear #5
2001 Wheels High Gear #27
2001 Wheels High Gear Autographs #31
2001 Wheels High Gear Custom Shop #CSTS
2001 Wheels High Gear Custom Shop Prizes #TSA1
2001 Wheels High Gear Custom Shop Prizes #TSA2
2001 Wheels High Gear Custom Shop Prizes #TSA3
2001 Wheels High Gear Custom Shop Prizes #TSB1
2001 Wheels High Gear Custom Shop Prizes #TSB2
2001 Wheels High Gear Custom Shop Prizes #TSB3
2001 Wheels High Gear Custom Shop Prizes #TSC1
2001 Wheels High Gear Custom Shop Prizes #TSC2
2001 Wheels High Gear Custom Shop Prizes #TSC3
2001 Wheels High Gear First Gear #5
2001 Wheels High Gear First Gear #27
2001 Wheels High Gear Flag Chasers #FC2
2001 Wheels High Gear Flag Chasers Blue-Yellow /45 #FC2
2001 Wheels High Gear Flag Chasers Checkered /35 #FC2
2001 Wheels High Gear Flag Chasers Checkered Blue/Orange /45 #FC2
2001 Wheels High Gear Flag Chasers Green /75 #FC2
2001 Wheels High Gear Flag Chasers Power Pick #FCPP
2001 Wheels High Gear Flag Chasers Red /75 #FC2
2001 Wheels High Gear Flag Chasers White /75 #FC2
2001 Wheels High Gear Flag Chasers Yellow /75 #FC2
2001 Wheels High Gear Gear Shifters #GS5
2001 Wheels High Gear Hot Streaks #HS1
2001 Wheels High Gear Man and Machine Cars #MM1B
2001 Wheels High Gear Man and Machine Drivers #MM1A
2001 Wheels High Gear MPH #5
2001 Wheels High Gear MPH #27
2001 Wheels High Gear Sunday Sensation #SS5
2001 Wheels High Gear Top Tier #TT6
2001 Wheels High Gear Top Tier Holofoils #TT6
2002 Press Pass #34
2002 Press Pass #70
2002 Press Pass #81
2002 Press Pass Autographs #66
2002 Press Pass Burning Rubber Cars /120 #BRC10
2002 Press Pass Burning Rubber Drivers /90 #BRD10
2002 Press Pass Cup Chase #CC15
2002 Press Pass Cup Chase Prizes #NNO
2002 Press Pass Cup Chase Prizes #CC15
2002 Press Pass Double Burner /100 #DB8
2002 Press Pass Eclipse #2
2002 Press Pass Eclipse Racing Champions #RC11
2002 Press Pass Eclipse Racing Champions #RC16
2002 Press Pass Eclipse Racing Champions #RC24
2002 Press Pass Eclipse Samples #2
2002 Press Pass Eclipse Skidmarks #SK8
2002 Press Pass Eclipse Solar Eclipse #S2
2002 Press Pass Eclipse Supernova #SN9
2002 Press Pass Eclipse Supernova Numbered /250 #SN9
2002 Press Pass Eclipse Under Cover Double Cover /625 #DC7
2002 Press Pass Eclipse Under Cover Drivers #CD6
2002 Press Pass Eclipse Under Cover Gold Cars /300 #CD6
2002 Press Pass Eclipse Under Cover Gold Drivers /400 #CD6
2002 Press Pass Eclipse Under Cover Holofoil Drivers /100 #CD6
2002 Press Pass Eclipse Warp Speed #WS5
2002 Press Pass Hot Treads /900 #HT36
2002 Press Pass Hot Treads /2300 #HT5
2002 Press Pass Optima #28
2002 Press Pass Optima Cool Persistence #CP11
2002 Press Pass Optima Fan Favorite #FF25
2002 Press Pass Optima Gold #28
2002 Press Pass Optima Promos /5 #28
2002 Press Pass Optima Q and A #QA9
2002 Press Pass Optima Race Used Lugnuts Autographs /20 #LNDA17
2002 Press Pass Optima Race Used Lugnuts Cars /100 #LNC17
2002 Press Pass Optima Race Used Lugnuts Drivers /100 #LND17
2002 Press Pass Optima Samples #28
2002 Press Pass Platinum #34
2002 Press Pass Platinum #70
2002 Press Pass Platinum #81
2002 Press Pass Premium #30
2002 Press Pass Premium #44
2002 Press Pass Premium #48
2002 Press Pass Premium #50
2002 Press Pass Premium #68
2002 Press Pass Premium #80
2002 Press Pass Premium In The Zone #IZ11
2002 Press Pass Premium Performance Driven #PD8
2002 Press Pass Premium Race Used Firesuit Cars /90 #FC6
2002 Press Pass Premium Race Used Firesuit Drivers /80 #FD6
2002 Press Pass Premium Red Reflectors #30
2002 Press Pass Premium Red Reflectors #44
2002 Press Pass Premium Red Reflectors #48
2002 Press Pass Premium Red Reflectors #50
2002 Press Pass Premium Red Reflectors #68
2002 Press Pass Premium Red Reflectors #80
2002 Press Pass Premium Samples #30
2002 Press Pass Premium Samples #44
2002 Press Pass Premium Samples #48
2002 Press Pass Premium Samples #50
2002 Press Pass Showcar #S11B
2002 Press Pass Showman #S11A
2002 Press Pass Signings #65
2002 Press Pass Signings Transparent /100 #9
2002 Press Pass Stealth #22
2002 Press Pass Stealth #23
2002 Press Pass Stealth #24
2002 Press Pass Stealth #61
2002 Press Pass Stealth #70
2002 Press Pass Stealth Behind the Numbers #BN5
2002 Press Pass Stealth EFX #FX7
2002 Press Pass Stealth Fusion #F11
2002 Press Pass Stealth Gold #22
2002 Press Pass Stealth Gold #23
2002 Press Pass Stealth Gold #24

2002 Press Pass Stealth Gold #61
2002 Press Pass Stealth Gold #70
2002 Press Pass Stealth Lap Leaders #LL26
2002 Press Pass Stealth Profile #P3
2002 Press Pass Stealth Race Used Glove Cars /85 #GLC3
2002 Press Pass Stealth Race Used Glove Drivers /50 #GLD3
2002 Press Pass Stealth Samples #22
2002 Press Pass Stealth Samples #23
2002 Press Pass Stealth Samples #24
2002 Press Pass Stealth Samples #61
2002 Press Pass Stealth Samples #70
2002 Press Pass Tony Stewart Fan Club #NNO
2002 Press Pass Top Shelf #TS8
2002 Press Pass Total Memorabilia Power Pick #TM8
2002 Press Pass Trackside #15
2002 Press Pass Trackside #58
2002 Press Pass Trackside #71
2002 Press Pass Trackside #80
2002 Press Pass Trackside Dialed In #DI11
2002 Press Pass Trackside Generation Now #GN2
2002 Press Pass Trackside Golden /50 #G15
2002 Press Pass Trackside License to Drive #32
2002 Press Pass Trackside License to Drive Die Cuts #32
2002 Press Pass Trackside Mirror Image #MI8
2002 Press Pass Trackside Pit Stoppers Cars /350 #PSC2
2002 Press Pass Trackside Pit Stoppers Drivers /150 #PSD2
2002 Press Pass Trackside Runnin N' Gunnin #RG8
2002 Press Pass Trackside Samples #15
2002 Press Pass Trackside Samples #58
2002 Press Pass Trackside Samples #71
2002 Press Pass Trackside Samples #80
2002 Press Pass Triple Burner /100 #TB8
2002 Press Pass Vintage #VN24
2002 Super Shots California Speedway #CS4
2002 VIP #9
2002 VIP #21
2002 VIP #27
2002 VIP #32
2002 VIP Driver's Choice #DC5
2002 VIP Driver's Choice Transparent #DC5
2002 VIP Driver's Choice Transparent LTD #DC5
2002 VIP Explosives #X9
2002 VIP Explosives #X21
2002 VIP Explosives #X27
2002 VIP Explosives #X32
2002 VIP Explosives Lasers #LX9
2002 VIP Explosives Lasers #LX21
2002 VIP Explosives Lasers #LX27
2002 VIP Explosives Lasers #LX32
2002 VIP Head Gear #HG7
2002 VIP Head Gear Die Cuts #HG7
2002 VIP Making the Show #MS11
2002 VIP Mile Masters #MM2
2002 VIP Mile Masters Transparent #MM2
2002 VIP Mile Masters Transparent LTD #MM2
2002 VIP Race Used Sheet Metal Cars #SC8
2002 VIP Race Used Sheet Metal Drivers /130 #SD8
2002 VIP Rear View Mirror #RM6
2002 VIP Rear View Mirror Die Cuts #RM6
2002 VIP Samples #9
2002 VIP Samples #21
2002 VIP Samples #27
2002 VIP Samples #32
2002 Wheels High Gear #25
2002 Wheels High Gear #32
2002 Wheels High Gear #54
2002 Wheels High Gear Autographs #55
2002 Wheels High Gear Custom Shop #CSTS
2002 Wheels High Gear Custom Shop Prizes #TSA1
2002 Wheels High Gear Custom Shop Prizes #TSA2
2002 Wheels High Gear Custom Shop Prizes #TSA3
2002 Wheels High Gear Custom Shop Prizes #TSB1
2002 Wheels High Gear Custom Shop Prizes #TSB2
2002 Wheels High Gear Custom Shop Prizes #TSB3
2002 Wheels High Gear Custom Shop Prizes #TSC1
2002 Wheels High Gear Custom Shop Prizes #TSC2
2002 Wheels High Gear Custom Shop Prizes #TSC3
2002 Wheels High Gear First Gear #25
2002 Wheels High Gear First Gear #32
2002 Wheels High Gear First Gear #54
2002 Wheels High Gear Flag Chasers /130 #FC5
2002 Wheels High Gear Flag Chasers Black /90 #FC5
2002 Wheels High Gear Flag Chasers Blue-Yellow /40 #FC5
2002 Wheels High Gear Flag Chasers Checkered /35 #FC5
2002 Wheels High Gear Flag Chasers Checkered Blue/Orange /10 #FC5
2002 Wheels High Gear Flag Chasers Green /90 #FC5
2002 Wheels High Gear Flag Chasers Red /90 #FC5
2002 Wheels High Gear Flag Chasers Yellow /110 #FC5
2002 Wheels High Gear High Groove #HG25
2002 Wheels High Gear Hot Streaks #HS8
2002 Wheels High Gear Man and Machine Cars #MM8B
2002 Wheels High Gear Man and Machine Drivers #MM8A
2002 Wheels High Gear MPH /100 #25
2002 Wheels High Gear MPH /100 #32
2002 Wheels High Gear MPH /100 #54
2002 Wheels High Gear Sunday Sensation #SS8
2002 Wheels High Gear Top Tier #TT2
2002 Wheels High Gear Top Tier Numbered /250 #TT2
2003 eTopps /3194 #1
2003 Press Pass #31
2003 Press Pass #61
2003 Press Pass #72
2003 Press Pass #84
2003 Press Pass #96
2003 Press Pass Burning Rubber Cars /60 #BRT9
2003 Press Pass Burning Rubber Drivers /50 #BRD9
2003 Press Pass Burning Rubber Drivers Autographs /20 #BRDTS
2003 Press Pass Coca-Cola Racing Family #11
2003 Press Pass Coca-Cola Racing Family Regional #3
2003 Press Pass Cup Chase #CCR15
2003 Press Pass Cup Chase Prizes #CCR18
2003 Press Pass Cup Chase Prizes #CCR15
2003 Press Pass Double Burner /100 #DB9
2003 Press Pass Double Burner Exchange /100 #DB9
2003 Press Pass Eclipse #1
2003 Press Pass Eclipse #32
2003 Press Pass Eclipse #41
2003 Press Pass Eclipse #45
2003 Press Pass Eclipse #50
2003 Press Pass Eclipse Double Hot Treads /999 #DT1
2003 Press Pass Eclipse Previews /5 #1
2003 Press Pass Eclipse Previews /5 #32
2003 Press Pass Eclipse Racing Champions #RC1
2003 Press Pass Eclipse Racing Champions #RC6
2003 Press Pass Eclipse Racing Champions #RC13
2003 Press Pass Eclipse Racing Champions #RC23
2003 Press Pass Eclipse Samples #1
2003 Press Pass Eclipse Samples #32
2003 Press Pass Eclipse Samples #41
2003 Press Pass Eclipse Samples #45
2003 Press Pass Eclipse Samples #50
2003 Press Pass Eclipse Skidmarks #SM3
2003 Press Pass Eclipse Solar Eclipse #P1
2003 Press Pass Eclipse Solar Eclipse #P32
2003 Press Pass Eclipse Solar Eclipse #P41
2003 Press Pass Eclipse Solar Eclipse #P45
2003 Press Pass Eclipse Solar Eclipse #P50
2003 Press Pass Eclipse Supernova #SN11
2003 Press Pass Eclipse Under Cover Cars /215 #UCT5
2003 Press Pass Eclipse Under Cover Double Cover /530 #DC7
2003 Press Pass Eclipse Under Cover Driver Gold /260 #UCD5
2003 Press Pass Eclipse Under Cover Driver Red /100 #UCD5
2003 Press Pass Eclipse Under Cover Driver Silver /450 #UCD5
2003 Press Pass Eclipse Warp Speed #WS5
2003 Press Pass Gold Holofoil #P31
2003 Press Pass Gold Holofoil #P61
2003 Press Pass Gold Holofoil #P72
2003 Press Pass Gold Holofoil #P84
2003 Press Pass Gold Holofoil #P96
2003 Press Pass Optima #24
2003 Press Pass Optima #44
2003 Press Pass Optima Cool Persistence #CP9
2003 Press Pass Optima Fan Favorite #FF23
2003 Press Pass Optima Gold #G24
2003 Press Pass Optima Gold #G44
2003 Press Pass Optima Previews /5 #24
2003 Press Pass Optima Q and A #QA1
2003 Press Pass Optima Samples #24
2003 Press Pass Optima Samples #44
2003 Press Pass Optima Thunder Bolts Cars /95 #TBT16
2003 Press Pass Optima Thunder Bolts Drivers /65 #TBD16
2003 Press Pass Premium #27
2003 Press Pass Premium #56
2003 Press Pass Premium #78
2003 Press Pass Premium Hot Threads Cars /160 #HTT9
2003 Press Pass Premium Hot Threads Drivers /285 #HTD9
2003 Press Pass Premium In the Zone #IZ10
2003 Press Pass Premium Performance Driven #PD7
2003 Press Pass Premium Previews /5 #27
2003 Press Pass Premium Red Reflectors #27
2003 Press Pass Premium Red Reflectors #56
2003 Press Pass Premium Red Reflectors #78
2003 Press Pass Premium Samples #27
2003 Press Pass Previews /5 #31
2003 Press Pass Samples #31
2003 Press Pass Samples #61
2003 Press Pass Samples #72
2003 Press Pass Samples #84
2003 Press Pass Samples #96
2003 Press Pass Showcar #S11B
2003 Press Pass Showman #S11A
2003 Press Pass Signings #70
2003 Press Pass Signings Gold /50 #71
2003 Press Pass Signings Transparent /100 #8
2003 Press Pass Snapshots #SN24
2003 Press Pass Stealth #22
2003 Press Pass Stealth #23
2003 Press Pass Stealth #24
2003 Press Pass Stealth #70
2003 Press Pass Stealth EFX #FX10
2003 Press Pass Stealth Gear Grippers Cars /150 #GGT8
2003 Press Pass Stealth Gear Grippers Drivers /75 #GGD8
2003 Press Pass Stealth Previews /5 #22
2003 Press Pass Stealth Previews /5 #23
2003 Press Pass Stealth Previews /5 #24
2003 Press Pass Stealth Red #P22
2003 Press Pass Stealth Red #P23
2003 Press Pass Stealth Red #P24
2003 Press Pass Stealth Red #P70
2003 Press Pass Stealth Samples #22
2003 Press Pass Stealth Samples #23
2003 Press Pass Stealth Samples #24
2003 Press Pass Stealth Samples #70
2003 Press Pass Top Shelf #TS8
2003 Press Pass Total Memorabilia Power Pick #TM9
2003 Press Pass Trackside #29
2003 Press Pass Trackside #74
2003 Press Pass Trackside Dialed In #DI10
2003 Press Pass Trackside Gold Holofoil #P29
2003 Press Pass Trackside Gold Holofoil #P74
2003 Press Pass Trackside Golden /50 #G29
2003 Press Pass Trackside Hat Giveaway #PPH27
2003 Press Pass Trackside Hot Pursuit #HP6
2003 Press Pass Trackside License to Drive #LD18
2003 Press Pass Trackside Mirror Image #MI7
2003 Press Pass Trackside Pit Stoppers Cars /175 #PST7
2003 Press Pass Trackside Pit Stoppers Drivers /100 #PSD7
2003 Press Pass Trackside Previews /5 #29
2003 Press Pass Trackside Samples #29
2003 Press Pass Trackside Samples #74
2003 Press Pass Triple Burner /100 #TB9
2003 Press Pass Triple Burner Exchange /100 #TB9
2003 Press Pass Velocity #VC8
2003 Press Pass Victory Lap #14
2003 VIP #16
2003 VIP Explosives #X16
2003 VIP Laser Explosive #LX16
2003 VIP Making the Show #MS10
2003 VIP Mile Masters #MM10
2003 VIP Mile Masters National #MM10
2003 VIP Mile Masters Transparent #MM10
2003 VIP Mile Masters Transparent LTD #MM10
2003 VIP Previews /5 #16
2003 VIP Samples #16
2003 VIP Tin #CT16
2003 VIP Tradin' Paint Cars /160 #TPT9
2003 VIP Tradin' Paint Drivers /110 #TPD9
2003 Wheels American Thunder #19
2003 Wheels American Thunder #26
2003 Wheels American Thunder #32
2003 Wheels American Thunder American Eagle #AE2
2003 Wheels American Thunder American Muscle #AM9
2003 Wheels American Thunder Born On /100 #BO19
2003 Wheels American Thunder Born On /100 #BO26
2003 Wheels American Thunder Born On /100 #BO32
2003 Wheels American Thunder Golden Eagle /100 #AEG2
2003 Wheels American Thunder Head to Toe /40 #HT7
2003 Wheels American Thunder Heads Up Manufacturer /90 #HUM21
2003 Wheels American Thunder Heads Up Team /60 #HUT19
2003 Wheels American Thunder Heads Up Winston /90 #HUW21
2003 Wheels American Thunder Holofoil #P19
2003 Wheels American Thunder Holofoil #P26
2003 Wheels American Thunder Holofoil #P32
2003 Wheels American Thunder Post Mark #PM16
2003 Wheels American Thunder Previews /5 #19
2003 Wheels American Thunder Previews /5 #26
2003 Wheels American Thunder Previews /5 #32
2003 Wheels American Thunder Pushin Pedal /285 #PP7
2003 Wheels American Thunder Rookie Thunder #RT32
2003 Wheels American Thunder Samples #P19
2003 Wheels American Thunder Samples #P26
2003 Wheels American Thunder Samples #P32
2003 Wheels American Thunder Thunder Road #TR3
2003 Wheels American Thunder Triple Hat /25 #TH12
2003 Wheels High Gear #28
2003 Wheels High Gear #34
2003 Wheels High Gear #54
2003 Wheels High Gear #64
2003 Wheels High Gear #72
2003 Wheels High Gear #0
2003 Wheels High Gear Blue Hawaii SCDA Promos #28
2003 Wheels High Gear Blue Hawaii SCDA Promos #34
2003 Wheels High Gear Blue Hawaii SCDA Promos #54
2003 Wheels High Gear Blue Hawaii SCDA Promos #64
2003 Wheels High Gear Blue Hawaii SCDA Promos #72
2003 Wheels High Gear Custom Shop #CSTS
2003 Wheels High Gear Custom Shop Autograph Redemption #CSTS
2003 Wheels High Gear Custom Shop Autographs /10 #TSB2
2003 Wheels High Gear Custom Shop Prizes #TSA1
2003 Wheels High Gear Custom Shop Prizes #TSA2
2003 Wheels High Gear Custom Shop Prizes #TSA3
2003 Wheels High Gear Custom Shop Prizes #TSB1
2003 Wheels High Gear Custom Shop Prizes #TSB2
2003 Wheels High Gear Custom Shop Prizes #TSB3
2003 Wheels High Gear Custom Shop Prizes #TSC1
2003 Wheels High Gear Custom Shop Prizes #TSC2
2003 Wheels High Gear Custom Shop Prizes #TSC3
2003 Wheels High Gear First Gear #F28
2003 Wheels High Gear First Gear #F34
2003 Wheels High Gear First Gear #F54
2003 Wheels High Gear First Gear #F64
2003 Wheels High Gear First Gear #F72
2003 Wheels High Gear Flag Chasers Black /90 #FC5
2003 Wheels High Gear Flag Chasers Blue-Yellow /45 #FC5
2003 Wheels High Gear Flag Chasers Checkered /25 #FC5
2003 Wheels High Gear Flag Chasers Green /90 #FC5
2003 Wheels High Gear Flag Chasers Red /90 #FC5
2003 Wheels High Gear Flag Chasers White /90 #FC5
2003 Wheels High Gear Flag Chasers Yellow /90 #FC5
2003 Wheels High Gear Full Throttle #FT8
2003 Wheels High Gear High Groove #HG25
2003 Wheels High Gear Hot Treads /425 #HT16
2003 Wheels High Gear Machine #MM4B
2003 Wheels High Gear Man #MM4A
2003 Wheels High Gear MPH /100 #M28
2003 Wheels High Gear MPH /100 #M34
2003 Wheels High Gear MPH /100 #M54
2003 Wheels High Gear MPH /100 #M64
2003 Wheels High Gear MPH /100 #M72
2003 Wheels High Gear Previews /5 #28
2003 Wheels High Gear Samples #28
2003 Wheels High Gear Samples #34
2003 Wheels High Gear Samples #54
2003 Wheels High Gear Samples #64
2003 Wheels High Gear Samples #72
2003 Wheels High Gear Sunday Sensation #SS7
2003 Wheels High Gear Top Tier #TT1
2004 National Trading Card Day #PP5
2004 Press Pass #31B
2004 Press Pass #31
2004 Press Pass #69
2004 Press Pass Burning Rubber Cars /140 #BRT13
2004 Press Pass Burning Rubber Drivers /70 #BRD13
2004 Press Pass Cup Chase #CCR11
2004 Press Pass Cup Chase Prizes #CCR11
2004 Press Pass Double Burner /100 #DB9
2004 Press Pass Double Burner Exchange /100 #DB9
2004 Press Pass Eclipse #7
2004 Press Pass Eclipse #7B
2004 Press Pass Eclipse #34
2004 Press Pass Eclipse #63
2004 Press Pass Eclipse #64
2004 Press Pass Eclipse #84
2004 Press Pass Eclipse Destination WIN #16
2004 Press Pass Eclipse Destination WIN #25
2004 Press Pass Eclipse Hyperdrive #HP3
2004 Press Pass Eclipse Maxim #MX6
2004 Press Pass Eclipse Previews /5 #7
2004 Press Pass Eclipse Samples #7
2004 Press Pass Eclipse Samples #34
2004 Press Pass Eclipse Samples #63
2004 Press Pass Eclipse Samples #64
2004 Press Pass Eclipse Samples #84
2004 Press Pass Eclipse Skidmarks #SM13
2004 Press Pass Eclipse Skidmarks Holofoil /500 #SM13
2004 Press Pass Eclipse Teammates Autographs /25 #4
2004 Press Pass Eclipse Under Cover Cars /170 #UCD14
2004 Press Pass Eclipse Under Cover Double Cover /100 #DC10
2004 Press Pass Eclipse Under Cover Driver Gold /325 #UCD14
2004 Press Pass Eclipse Under Cover Driver Red /100 #UCD14
2004 Press Pass Eclipse Under Cover Driver Silver /690 #UCD14
2004 Press Pass Hot Treads /1250 #HTR12
2004 Press Pass Hot Treads Holofoil /200 #HTR12
2004 Press Pass Making the Show Collector's Series #MS14
2004 Press Pass Making the Show Collector's Series Tins #NNO
2004 Press Pass Optima #24
2004 Press Pass Optima #79
2004 Press Pass Optima #86
2004 Press Pass Optima Cool Persistence #CP8
2004 Press Pass Optima Fan Favorite #FF22
2004 Press Pass Optima G Force #GF3
2004 Press Pass Optima Gold #G24
2004 Press Pass Optima Gold #G79
2004 Press Pass Optima Gold #G86
2004 Press Pass Optima Previews /5 #EB24
2004 Press Pass Optima Q&A #QA4
2004 Press Pass Optima Samples #24
2004 Press Pass Optima Samples #79
2004 Press Pass Optima Samples #86
2004 Press Pass Optima Thunder Bolts Cars /120 #TBT3
2004 Press Pass Optima Thunder Bolts Drivers /70 #TBD3
2004 Press Pass Platinum #P31
2004 Press Pass Platinum #P69
2004 Press Pass Premium #2
2004 Press Pass Premium #50
2004 Press Pass Premium #56
2004 Press Pass Premium #72
2004 Press Pass Premium Asphalt Jungle #A1
2004 Press Pass Premium Hot Threads Autographs /20 #HTTS
2004 Press Pass Premium Hot Threads Drivers Bronze /125 #HTD10
2004 Press Pass Premium Hot Threads Drivers Bronze Retail /125 #HTT10
2004 Press Pass Premium Hot Threads Drivers Gold /50 #HTD10
2004 Press Pass Premium Hot Threads Drivers Silver /75 #HTD10
2004 Press Pass Premium In the Zone #IZ12
2004 Press Pass Premium In the Zone Elite Edition #IZ12
2004 Press Pass Premium Performance Driven #PD1
2004 Press Pass Premium Previews /5 #2
2004 Press Pass Premium Samples #2
2004 Press Pass Premium Samples #50
2004 Press Pass Previews /5 #31
2004 Press Pass Samples #31
2004 Press Pass Samples #69
2004 Press Pass Schedule #4
2004 Press Pass Showcar #S11B
2004 Press Pass Showman #S11A
2004 Press Pass Signings #59
2004 Press Pass Signings Gold /50 #55
2004 Press Pass Signings Transparent /100 #9
2004 Press Pass Snapshots #SN25
2004 Press Pass Stealth #31
2004 Press Pass Stealth #32
2004 Press Pass Stealth #33
2004 Press Pass Stealth #96
2004 Press Pass Stealth EFX #EF4
2004 Press Pass Stealth Gear Grippers Drivers /80 #GGD16
2004 Press Pass Stealth Gear Grippers Drivers Retail /120 #GGT16
2004 Press Pass Stealth Previews /5 #EB31
2004 Press Pass Stealth Previews /5 #EB32
2004 Press Pass Stealth Previews /5 #EB33
2004 Press Pass Stealth Profile #P7
2004 Press Pass Stealth Samples #X32
2004 Press Pass Stealth Samples #X96
2004 Press Pass Stealth Samples #X33
2004 Press Pass Stealth Samples #X31
2004 Press Pass Stealth X-Ray /100 #31
2004 Press Pass Stealth X-Ray /100 #32
2004 Press Pass Stealth X-Ray /100 #33
2004 Press Pass Stealth X-Ray /100 #96
2004 Press Pass Top Shelf #TS7
2004 Press Pass Total Memorabilia Power Pick #TM9
2004 Press Pass Trackside #28
2004 Press Pass Trackside #65
2004 Press Pass Trackside #105
2004 Press Pass Trackside #116
2004 Press Pass Trackside Dialed In #DI6
2004 Press Pass Trackside Golden /100 #G28
2004 Press Pass Trackside Golden /100 #G65
2004 Press Pass Trackside Golden /100 #G105
2004 Press Pass Trackside Golden /100 #G116
2004 Press Pass Trackside Hat Giveaway #PPH30
2004 Press Pass Trackside Hot Pass #HP16
2004 Press Pass Trackside Hot Pass National #HP16
2004 Press Pass Trackside Pit Stoppers Autographs /20 #PSTS
2004 Press Pass Trackside Pit Stoppers Cars /150 #PST7
2004 Press Pass Trackside Pit Stoppers Drivers /95 #PSD7
2004 Press Pass Trackside Previews /5 #EB28
2004 Press Pass Trackside Runnin n' Gunnin #RG6
2004 Press Pass Trackside Samples #28
2004 Press Pass Trackside Samples #65
2004 Press Pass Trackside Samples #105
2004 Press Pass Trackside Samples #116
2004 Press Pass Triple Burner /100 #TB9
2004 Press Pass Triple Burner Exchange /100 #TB9
2004 VIP #16
2004 VIP #36
2004 VIP #60
2004 VIP #75
2004 VIP Head Gear #HG10
2004 VIP Head Gear Transparent #HG10
2004 VIP Lap Leaders #LL6
2004 VIP Lap Leaders Transparent #LL6
2004 VIP Making the Show #MS14
2004 VIP Previews /5 #EB16
2004 VIP Previews /5 #EB36
2004 VIP Samples #16
2004 VIP Samples #36
2004 VIP Samples #60
2004 VIP Samples #75
2004 VIP Tradin' Paint Autographs /20 #TPTS
2004 VIP Tradin' Paint Bronze /130 #TPT4
2004 VIP Tradin' Paint Gold /50 #TPD4
2004 VIP Tradin' Paint Silver /70 #TPD4
2004 Wheels American Thunder #24
2004 Wheels American Thunder #39
2004 Wheels American Thunder #78
2004 Wheels American Thunder American Muscle #AM6
2004 Wheels American Thunder Cup Quest #CQ4
2004 Wheels American Thunder Post Mark #PM13
2004 Wheels American Thunder Previews /5 #EB24
2004 Wheels American Thunder Previews /5 #EB39
2004 Wheels American Thunder Pushin Pedal /275 #PP15
2004 Wheels American Thunder Samples #24
2004 Wheels American Thunder Samples #39
2004 Wheels American Thunder Samples #78
2004 Wheels American Thunder Thunder Road #TR10
2004 Wheels American Thunder Triple Hat /160 #TH21
2004 Wheels Autographs #63
2004 Wheels High Gear #25
2004 Wheels High Gear Custom Shop #CSTS
2004 Wheels High Gear Flag Chasers Black /100 #FC5
2004 Wheels High Gear Flag Chasers Blue /50 #FC5
2004 Wheels High Gear Flag Chasers Checkered /35 #FC5
2004 Wheels High Gear Flag Chasers Green /100 #FC5
2004 Wheels High Gear Flag Chasers Red /100 #FC5
2004 Wheels High Gear Flag Chasers White /100 #FC5
2004 Wheels High Gear Flag Chasers Yellow /100 #FC5
2004 Wheels High Gear Full Throttle #FT4
2004 Wheels High Gear High Groove #HG25
2004 Wheels High Gear Machine #MM1B
2004 Wheels High Gear Man #MM1A
2004 Wheels High Gear MPH /100 #M25
2004 Wheels High Gear Previews /5 #25
2004 Wheels High Gear Samples #25
2004 Wheels High Gear Sunday Sensation #SS5
2004 Wheels High Gear Top Ten #TT7
2005 Coca-Cola Racing Family AutoZone #8
2005 Press Pass #15
2005 Press Pass #83
2005 Press Pass Autographs #56
2005 Press Pass Burning Rubber Autographs /20 #BRTS
2005 Press Pass Burning Rubber Cars /130 #BRT10
2005 Press Pass Burning Rubber Drivers /80 #BRD10
2005 Press Pass Burning Rubber Drivers Gold /1 #BRD10
2005 Press Pass Cup Chase #CCR8
2005 Press Pass Cup Chase Prizes /500 #NNO
2005 Press Pass Cup Chase Prizes #CCP8
2005 Press Pass Double Burner /100 #DB9
2005 Press Pass Double Burner Exchange /100 #DB9
2005 Press Pass Eclipse #6
2005 Press Pass Eclipse #63
2005 Press Pass Eclipse #66
2005 Press Pass Eclipse #69
2005 Press Pass Eclipse #84
2005 Press Pass Eclipse Destination WIN #16
2005 Press Pass Eclipse Destination WIN #19
2005 Press Pass Eclipse Maxim #MX6
2005 Press Pass Eclipse Previews /5 #EB6
2005 Press Pass Eclipse Previews /5 #EB63
2005 Press Pass Eclipse Previews /5 #EB66
2005 Press Pass Eclipse Previews /5 #EB69
2005 Press Pass Eclipse Previews /1 #EB84
2005 Press Pass Eclipse Samples #6
2005 Press Pass Eclipse Samples #63
2005 Press Pass Eclipse Samples #66
2005 Press Pass Eclipse Samples #69
2005 Press Pass Eclipse Samples #84
2005 Press Pass Eclipse Skidmarks #SM13
2005 Press Pass Eclipse Skidmarks Holofoil /250 #SM13
2005 Press Pass Eclipse Teammates Autographs /25 #1
2005 Press Pass Eclipse Under Cover Autographs /20 #UCTS
2005 Press Pass Eclipse Under Cover Cars /120 #UCT13
2005 Press Pass Eclipse Under Cover Double Cover /340 #DC5
2005 Press Pass Eclipse Under Cover Driver Red /400 #UCD13
2005 Press Pass Eclipse Under Cover Drivers Holofoil /100 #UCD13
2005 Press Pass Eclipse Under Cover Drivers Silver /690 #UCD13
2005 Press Pass Game Face #GF7
2005 Press Pass Hot Treads /900 #HTR11
2005 Press Pass Hot Treads Holofoil /100 #HTR11
2005 Press Pass Legends #29
2005 Press Pass Legends #44
2005 Press Pass Legends Autographs Black /50 #26
2005 Press Pass Legends Blue /1890 #29B
2005 Press Pass Legends Blue /1890 #44B
2005 Press Pass Legends Double Threads Bronze /375 #DTSL
2005 Press Pass Legends Double Threads Gold /99 #DTSL
2005 Press Pass Legends Double Threads Silver /225 #DTSL
2005 Press Pass Legends Gold /750 #29G
2005 Press Pass Legends Gold /750 #44G
2005 Press Pass Legends Holofoil /100 #29H
2005 Press Pass Legends Holofoil /100 #44H
2005 Press Pass Legends Press Plates Black /1 #29
2005 Press Pass Legends Press Plates Black /1 #44
2005 Press Pass Legends Press Plates Cyan /1 #29
2005 Press Pass Legends Press Plates Cyan /1 #44
2005 Press Pass Legends Press Plates Magenta /1 #29
2005 Press Pass Legends Press Plates Magenta /1 #44
2005 Press Pass Legends Press Plates Yellow /1 #29
2005 Press Pass Legends Press Plates Yellow /1 #44
2005 Press Pass Legends Previews /5 #29
2005 Press Pass Legends Previews /5 #44
2005 Press Pass Legends Solo /1 #29S
2005 Press Pass Legends Solo /1 #44S
2005 Press Pass Legends Threads and Treads Bronze /375 #TTTS
2005 Press Pass Legends Threads and Treads Gold /99 #TTTS
2005 Press Pass Legends Threads and Treads Silver /225 #TTTS
2005 Press Pass Optima #27
2005 Press Pass Optima #27B
2005 Press Pass Optima #66
2005 Press Pass Optima #89
2005 Press Pass Optima #100
2005 Press Pass Optima Cool Persistence #CP12
2005 Press Pass Optima Corporate Cuts Cars /160 #CCT1
2005 Press Pass Optima Corporate Cuts Drivers /120 #CCD1
2005 Press Pass Optima Fan Favorite #FF24
2005 Press Pass Optima Gold /100 #G27
2005 Press Pass Optima Gold /100 #G66
2005 Press Pass Optima Gold /100 #G89
2005 Press Pass Optima Gold /100 #G100
2005 Press Pass Optima Previews /5 #27
2005 Press Pass Optima Q & A #QA7
2005 Press Pass Optima Samples #27
2005 Press Pass Optima Samples #66
2005 Press Pass Optima Samples #89
2005 Press Pass Optima Samples #100
2005 Press Pass Optima Thunder Bolts Autographs /20 #TBTS
2005 Press Pass Panorama #PPP14
2005 Press Pass Panorama #PPP32
2005 Press Pass Panorama #PPP46
2005 Press Pass Panorama #PPP47
2005 Press Pass Panorama #PPP62
2005 Press Pass Platinum /100 #P15
2005 Press Pass Platinum /100 #P83
2005 Press Pass Premium #30
2005 Press Pass Premium #41
2005 Press Pass Premium #46
2005 Press Pass Premium #50
2005 Press Pass Premium #56
2005 Press Pass Premium #79
2005 Press Pass Premium Asphalt Jungle #AJ5
2005 Press Pass Premium Hot Threads Autographs /20 #HTTS
2005 Press Pass Premium Hot Threads Cars /85 #HTT5
2005 Press Pass Premium Hot Threads Drivers /275 #HTD5
2005 Press Pass Premium Hot Threads Drivers Gold /1 #HTD5
2005 Press Pass Premium In the Zone #IZ3
2005 Press Pass Premium In the Zone Elite Edition /250 #IZ3
2005 Press Pass Premium Performance Driven #PD9
2005 Press Pass Premium Samples #30
2005 Press Pass Premium Samples #41
2005 Press Pass Premium Samples #46
2005 Press Pass Premium Samples #50
2005 Press Pass Previews Green /5 #EB15
2005 Press Pass Samples #15
2005 Press Pass Samples #83
2005 Press Pass Showcar #SC10
2005 Press Pass Showman #SM10
2005 Press Pass Signings #55
2005 Press Pass Signings Gold /50 #52
2005 Press Pass Signings Platinum /100 #50
2005 Press Pass Snapshots #SN24
2005 Press Pass Stealth #55
2005 Press Pass Stealth #58
2005 Press Pass Stealth #61
2005 Press Pass Stealth #86
2005 Press Pass Stealth #91
2005 Press Pass Stealth EFX #EFX5
2005 Press Pass Stealth Fusion #FU7
2005 Press Pass Stealth Gear Grippers Autographs /20 #GGTS
2005 Press Pass Stealth Gear Grippers Cars /90 #GGT13
2005 Press Pass Stealth Gear Grippers Drivers /75 #GGD13
2005 Press Pass Stealth No Boundaries #NB3
2005 Press Pass Stealth Previews /5 #55
2005 Press Pass Stealth Previews /5 #58
2005 Press Pass Stealth Previews /5 #61
2005 Press Pass Stealth Profile #PR9
2005 Press Pass Stealth Samples #55
2005 Press Pass Stealth Samples #58
2005 Press Pass Stealth Samples #61
2005 Press Pass Stealth Samples #86
2005 Press Pass Stealth Samples #91
2005 Press Pass Stealth X-Ray /100 #X55
2005 Press Pass Stealth X-Ray /100 #X58
2005 Press Pass Stealth X-Ray /100 #X61
2005 Press Pass Stealth X-Ray /100 #X86
2005 Press Pass Stealth X-Ray /100 #X91
2005 Press Pass Top Ten #TT4
2005 Press Pass Total Memorabilia Power Pick #TM9
2005 Press Pass Trackside #10
2005 Press Pass Trackside #60
2005 Press Pass Trackside #68
2005 Press Pass Trackside #88
2005 Press Pass Trackside #97
2005 Press Pass Trackside Dialed In #DI5
2005 Press Pass Trackside Golden /100 #G10
2005 Press Pass Trackside Golden /100 #G60
2005 Press Pass Trackside Golden /100 #G68
2005 Press Pass Trackside Golden /100 #G88
2005 Press Pass Trackside Golden /100 #G97
2005 Press Pass Trackside Hat Giveaway #PPH31
2005 Press Pass Trackside Hot Pass #16
2005 Press Pass Trackside Hot Pass National #16
2005 Press Pass Trackside Hot Pursuit #HP8
2005 Press Pass Trackside Pit Stoppers Autographs /20 #PSTS
2005 Press Pass Trackside Pit Stoppers Cars /85 #PST5
2005 Press Pass Trackside Pit Stoppers Drivers /85 #PSD5
2005 Press Pass Trackside Previews /5 #10
2005 Press Pass Trackside Previews /1 #88
2005 Press Pass Trackside Runnin n' Gunnin #RG6
2005 Press Pass Trackside Samples #10
2005 Press Pass Trackside Samples #60
2005 Press Pass Trackside Samples #68
2005 Press Pass Trackside Samples #88
2005 Press Pass Trackside Samples #97
2005 Press Pass Triple Burner /100 #TB9
2005 Press Pass Triple Burner Exchange /100 #TB9
2005 Press Pass UMI Cup Chase #1
2005 Press Pass UMI Cup Chase #2
2005 VIP #27
2005 VIP #39
2005 VIP #78
2005 VIP #86
2005 VIP Driver's Choice #DC6
2005 VIP Driver's Choice Die Cuts #DC6
2005 VIP Head Gear #10
2005 VIP Head Gear Transparent #10
2005 VIP Lap Leaders #6
2005 VIP Lap Leaders Transparent #6
2005 VIP Making The Show #14
2005 VIP Previews /5 #EB27
2005 VIP Previews /5 #EB39
2005 VIP Samples #27
2005 VIP Samples #39
2005 VIP Samples #78
2005 VIP Samples #86
2005 VIP Tradin' Paint Autographs /20 #TS
2005 VIP Tradin' Paint Cars /110 #TPT4
2005 VIP Tradin' Paint Drivers /90 #TPD4
2005 Wheels American Thunder #27
2005 Wheels American Thunder #43
2005 Wheels American Thunder #50
2005 Wheels American Thunder #58
2005 Wheels American Thunder #73
2005 Wheels American Thunder Head to Toe /125 #HT6
2005 Wheels American Thunder Medallion #MD11
2005 Wheels American Thunder Previews /5 #27
2005 Wheels American Thunder Pushin Pedal /150 #PP8
2005 Wheels American Thunder Samples #27
2005 Wheels American Thunder Samples #43
2005 Wheels American Thunder Samples #50
2005 Wheels American Thunder Samples #58
2005 Wheels American Thunder Samples #73
2005 Wheels American Thunder Thunder Road #TR10
2005 Wheels American Thunder Triple Hat /190 #TH23
2005 Wheels Autographs #56
2005 Wheels High Gear #13
2005 Wheels High Gear #37
2005 Wheels High Gear #48
2005 Wheels High Gear #58
2005 Wheels High Gear #69
2005 Wheels High Gear #78
2005 Wheels High Gear Flag Chasers Black /55 #FC3
2005 Wheels High Gear Flag Chasers Blue-Yellow /25 #FC3
2005 Wheels High Gear Flag Chasers Checkered /10 #FC3
2005 Wheels High Gear Flag Chasers Green /55 #FC3
2005 Wheels High Gear Flag Chasers Red /55 #FC3
2005 Wheels High Gear Flag Chasers White /55 #FC3
2005 Wheels High Gear Flag Chasers Yellow /55 #FC3
2005 Wheels High Gear Flag to Flag #FF24
2005 Wheels High Gear Full Throttle #FT2
2005 Wheels High Gear Machine #MMB8
2005 Wheels High Gear Man #MMA8
2005 Wheels High Gear MPH /100 #M13
2005 Wheels High Gear MPH /100 #M37
2005 Wheels High Gear MPH /100 #M48
2005 Wheels High Gear MPH /100 #M58
2005 Wheels High Gear MPH /100 #M69
2005 Wheels High Gear MPH /100 #M78
2005 Wheels High Gear Previews Green /5 #EB13
2005 Wheels High Gear Previews Silver /1 #EB78
2005 Wheels High Gear Samples #13
2005 Wheels High Gear Samples #37
2005 Wheels High Gear Samples #48
2005 Wheels High Gear Samples #58
2005 Wheels High Gear Samples #69
2005 Wheels High Gear Samples #78
2005 Wheels High Gear Top Tier #TT6
2006 Press Pass #16
2006 Press Pass #93
2006 Press Pass #94
2006 Press Pass #100
2006 Press Pass #109
2006 Press Pass #120
2006 Press Pass Autographs #53
2006 Press Pass Blaster Kmart #TSC
2006 Press Pass Blaster Target #TSB
2006 Press Pass Blaster Wal-Mart #TSA
2006 Press Pass Blue #B16
2006 Press Pass Blue #B93
2006 Press Pass Blue #B94
2006 Press Pass Blue #B100
2006 Press Pass Blue #B109
2006 Press Pass Blue #B120
2006 Press Pass Burning Rubber Autographs /20 #BRTS
2006 Press Pass Burning Rubber Cars /370 #BRT16
2006 Press Pass Burning Rubber Drivers /100 #BRD16
2006 Press Pass Burning Rubber Drivers Gold /1 #BRD16
2006 Press Pass Coca Cola AutoZone #TS
2006 Press Pass Collectors Series Making the Show #MS17
2006 Press Pass Cup Chase #CCR1
2006 Press Pass Double Burner Firesuit-Glove /100 #DB9
2006 Press Pass Double Burner Metal-Tire /100 #DB8
2006 Press Pass Eclipse #0
2006 Press Pass Eclipse #1
2006 Press Pass Eclipse #45
2006 Press Pass Eclipse #50
2006 Press Pass Eclipse #62
2006 Press Pass Eclipse #70
2006 Press Pass Eclipse #71
2006 Press Pass Eclipse #72
2006 Press Pass Eclipse #78
2006 Press Pass Eclipse #85
2006 Press Pass Eclipse #70
2006 Press Pass Eclipse #65
2006 Press Pass Eclipse #69
2006 Press Pass Eclipse Hyperdrive #HP2
2006 Press Pass Eclipse Previews /5 #EB1
2006 Press Pass Eclipse Previews /1 #EB62
2006 Press Pass Eclipse Racing Champions #RC7
2006 Press Pass Eclipse Racing Champions #RC15
2006 Press Pass Eclipse Skidmarks #SM16
2006 Press Pass Eclipse Skidmarks Holofoil /250 #SM16
2006 Press Pass Eclipse Supernova #SU5
2006 Press Pass Eclipse Under Cover Autographs /20 #TS
2006 Press Pass Eclipse Under Cover Cars /140 #UCT9
2006 Press Pass Eclipse Under Cover Drivers Gold /1 #UCD9
2006 Press Pass Eclipse Under Cover Drivers Holofoil /100 #UCD9
2006 Press Pass Eclipse Under Cover Drivers Red /225 #UCD9
2006 Press Pass Eclipse Under Cover Drivers Silver /400 #UCD9
2006 Press Pass Four Wide /50 #FWTS

2006 Press Pass Four Wide Checkered Flag /1 #FWTS
2006 Press Pass Gold #G16
2006 Press Pass Gold #G93
2006 Press Pass Gold #G94
2006 Press Pass Gold #G100
2006 Press Pass Gold #G109
2006 Press Pass Gold #G120
2006 Press Pass Legends #36
2006 Press Pass Legends Autographs Black /50 #32
2006 Press Pass Legends Blue /1999 #B36
2006 Press Pass Legends Bronze /999 #Z36
2006 Press Pass Legends Champion Threads and Treads Bronze /399 #CTTTS
2006 Press Pass Legends Champion Threads and Treads Gold /99 #CTTTS
2006 Press Pass Legends Champion Threads and Treads Silver /299 #CTTTS
2006 Press Pass Legends Champion Threads Bronze /399 #CTTS
2006 Press Pass Legends Champion Threads Gold /50 #CTTS
2006 Press Pass Legends Champion Threads Patch /25 #CTTS
2006 Press Pass Legends Champion Threads Silver /199 #CTTS
2006 Press Pass Legends Gold /299 #G36
2006 Press Pass Legends Heritage Gold /99 #HE10
2006 Press Pass Legends Heritage Silver /549 #HE10
2006 Press Pass Legends Holofoil /99 #H36
2006 Press Pass Legends Press Plates Black /1 #PPB36
2006 Press Pass Legends Press Plates Black Backs /1 #PPB36B
2006 Press Pass Legends Press Plates Cyan /1 #PPC36
2006 Press Pass Legends Press Plates Cyan Backs /1 #PPC36B
2006 Press Pass Legends Press Plates Magenta /1 #PPM36
2006 Press Pass Legends Press Plates Magenta Backs /1 #PPM36B
2006 Press Pass Legends Press Plates Yellow /1 #PPY36
2006 Press Pass Legends Press Plates Yellow Backs /1 #PPY36B
2006 Press Pass Legends Previews /5 #EB36
2006 Press Pass Legends Solo /1 #S36
2006 Press Pass Legends Triple Threads /50 #TTTS
2006 Press Pass Optima #17
2006 Press Pass Optima #55
2006 Press Pass Optima #70
2006 Press Pass Optima #83
2006 Press Pass Optima Fan Favorite #FF21
2006 Press Pass Optima Gold /100 #G17
2006 Press Pass Optima Gold /100 #G55
2006 Press Pass Optima Gold /100 #G70
2006 Press Pass Optima Gold /100 #G83
2006 Press Pass Optima Previews /5 #EB17
2006 Press Pass Optima Q & A #QA12
2006 Press Pass Optima Rookie Relics Cars /50 #RRT13
2006 Press Pass Optima Rookie Relics Drivers /50 #RRD13
2006 Press Pass Platinum /100 #P16
2006 Press Pass Platinum /100 #P93
2006 Press Pass Platinum /100 #P94
2006 Press Pass Platinum /100 #P100
2006 Press Pass Platinum /100 #P109
2006 Press Pass Platinum /100 #P120
2006 Press Pass Premium #28
2006 Press Pass Premium #47
2006 Press Pass Premium #55
2006 Press Pass Premium #75
2006 Press Pass Premium Asphalt Jungle #AJ4
2006 Press Pass Premium Hot Threads Autographs /20 #HTTS
2006 Press Pass Premium Hot Threads Cars /165 #HTT1
2006 Press Pass Premium Hot Threads Drivers /220 #HTD1
2006 Press Pass Premium Hot Threads Drivers Gold /1 #HTD1
2006 Press Pass Premium In the Zone #IZ4
2006 Press Pass Premium In the Zone Red /250 #IZ4
2006 Press Pass Previews /5 #EB16
2006 Press Pass Previews /1 #EB100
2006 Press Pass Signings #58
2006 Press Pass Signings Gold /50 #58
2006 Press Pass Signings Gold Red Ink #58
2006 Press Pass Signings Red Ink #58
2006 Press Pass Signings Silver /100 #58
2006 Press Pass Signings Silver Red Ink #58
2006 Press Pass Stealth #28
2006 Press Pass Stealth #49
2006 Press Pass Stealth #60
2006 Press Pass Stealth #79
2006 Press Pass Stealth Autographed Hat Entry #PPH22
2006 Press Pass Stealth Corporate Cuts /250 #CCD10
2006 Press Pass Stealth EFX #EFX1
2006 Press Pass Stealth Gear Grippers Autographs /20 #TS
2006 Press Pass Stealth Gear Grippers Cars Retail /99 #GGT5
2006 Press Pass Stealth Gear Grippers Drivers /99 #GGD5
2006 Press Pass Stealth Hot Pass #HP25
2006 Press Pass Stealth Previews /5 #28
2006 Press Pass Stealth Profile #P7
2006 Press Pass Stealth Retail #49
2006 Press Pass Stealth Retail #79
2006 Press Pass Stealth Retail #60
2006 Press Pass Stealth Retail #28
2006 Press Pass Stealth X-Ray /100 #X28
2006 Press Pass Stealth X-Ray /100 #X49
2006 Press Pass Stealth X-Ray /100 #X60
2006 Press Pass Stealth X-Ray /100 #X79
2006 Press Pass Top 25 Drivers & Rides #C13
2006 Press Pass Top 25 Drivers & Rides #D13
2006 Press Pass Velocity #VE6
2006 Sports Illustrated for Kids #9
2006 TRAKS #32
2006 TRAKS #46
2006 TRAKS Autographs #36
2006 TRAKS Autographs 25 /25 #34
2006 TRAKS Previews /1 #32
2006 TRAKS Previews /1 #46
2006 TRAKS Stickers #20
2006 VIP #26
2006 VIP #39
2006 VIP #45
2006 VIP #55
2006 VIP #72
2006 VIP Head Gear #HG8
2006 VIP Head Gear Transparent #HG8
2006 VIP Lap Leader #LL1
2006 VIP Lap Leader Transparent #LL1
2006 VIP Making the Show #MS17
2006 VIP Tradin' Paint Autographs /20 #TPTS
2006 VIP Tradin' Paint Cars Bronze /145 #TPT17
2006 VIP Tradin' Paint Drivers Gold /50 #TPD17
2006 VIP Tradin' Paint Drivers Silver /80 #TPD17
2006 Wheels American Thunder #30
2006 Wheels American Thunder #35
2006 Wheels American Thunder #50
2006 Wheels American Thunder #61
2006 Wheels American Thunder #71
2006 Wheels American Thunder #75
2006 Wheels American Thunder #88
2006 Wheels American Thunder American Muscle #AM3
2006 Wheels American Thunder American Racing Idol #RI10
2006 Wheels American Thunder American Racing Idol Golden /250 #RI10
2006 Wheels American Thunder Double Hat /99 #DH23
2006 Wheels American Thunder Grandstand #GS21
2006 Wheels American Thunder Head to Toe /99 #HT4
2006 Wheels American Thunder Previews /5 #EB30
2006 Wheels American Thunder Previews /1 #EB75
2006 Wheels American Thunder Pushin' Pedal /199 #PP4
2006 Wheels American Thunder Thunder Road #TR6
2006 Wheels Autographs #58
2006 Wheels High Gear #1
2006 Wheels High Gear #51
2006 Wheels High Gear #55
2006 Wheels High Gear #60
2006 Wheels High Gear #61
2006 Wheels High Gear #62
2006 Wheels High Gear #65
2006 Wheels High Gear #82
2006 Wheels High Gear #88
2006 Wheels High Gear #0
2006 Wheels High Gear Flag Chasers Black /110 #FC4
2006 Wheels High Gear Flag Chasers Blue-Yellow /65 #FC4
2006 Wheels High Gear Flag Chasers Checkered /3 #FC4
2006 Wheels High Gear Flag Chasers Green /110 #FC4
2006 Wheels High Gear Flag Chasers Red /110 #FC4
2006 Wheels High Gear Flag Chasers White /110 #FC4
2006 Wheels High Gear Flag Chasers Yellow /110 #FC4
2006 Wheels High Gear Flag to Flag #FF24
2006 Wheels High Gear Full Throttle #FT6
2006 Wheels High Gear Man & Machine Cars #MMB1
2006 Wheels High Gear Man & Machine Drivers #MMA1
2006 Wheels High Gear MPH /100 #M1
2006 Wheels High Gear MPH /100 #M51
2006 Wheels High Gear MPH /100 #M55
2006 Wheels High Gear MPH /100 #M60
2006 Wheels High Gear MPH /100 #M61
2006 Wheels High Gear MPH /100 #M62
2006 Wheels High Gear MPH /100 #M65
2006 Wheels High Gear MPH /100 #M82
2006 Wheels High Gear MPH /100 #M88
2006 Wheels High Gear Previews Green /5 #EB1
2006 Wheels High Gear Previews Silver /1 #EB82
2006 Wheels High Gear Top Tier #TT1
2007 Press Pass #11
2007 Press Pass #79
2007 Press Pass #91
2007 Press Pass #103
2007 Press Pass Autographs #43
2007 Press Pass Autographs Press Plates Black /1 #23
2007 Press Pass Autographs Press Plates Cyan /1 #24
2007 Press Pass Autographs Press Plates Magenta /1 #25
2007 Press Pass Autographs Press Plates Yellow /1 #24
2007 Press Pass Blue #B11
2007 Press Pass Blue #B79
2007 Press Pass Blue #B91
2007 Press Pass Blue #B103
2007 Press Pass Burning Rubber Autographs /20 #BRSTS
2007 Press Pass Burning Rubber Drivers /75 #BRD3
2007 Press Pass Burning Rubber Drivers /75 #BRD12
2007 Press Pass Burning Rubber Drivers Gold /1 #BRD3
2007 Press Pass Burning Rubber Drivers Gold /1 #BRD12
2007 Press Pass Burning Rubber Team /325 #BRT3
2007 Press Pass Burning Rubber Team /325 #BRT12
2007 Press Pass Burnouts #BO5
2007 Press Pass Burnouts Blue /99 #BO5
2007 Press Pass Burnouts Gold /299 #BO5
2007 Press Pass Collector's Series Box Set #SB21
2007 Press Pass Cup Chase #CCR5
2007 Press Pass Cup Chase Prizes #CC3
2007 Press Pass Double Burner Metal-Tire /100 #DBTS
2007 Press Pass Double Burner Metal-Tire Exchange /100 #DBTS
2007 Press Pass Eclipse #11
2007 Press Pass Eclipse #78
2007 Press Pass Eclipse #59B
2007 Press Pass Eclipse #59A
2007 Press Pass Eclipse #67
2007 Press Pass Eclipse #70
2007 Press Pass Eclipse Ecliptic #EC7
2007 Press Pass Eclipse Gold /25 #G11
2007 Press Pass Eclipse Gold /25 #G59
2007 Press Pass Eclipse Gold /25 #G67
2007 Press Pass Eclipse Gold /25 #G70
2007 Press Pass Eclipse Gold /25 #G78
2007 Press Pass Eclipse Hyperdrive #HD1
2007 Press Pass Eclipse Previews /5 #EB11
2007 Press Pass Eclipse Racing Champions #RC4
2007 Press Pass Eclipse Racing Champions #RC26
2007 Press Pass Eclipse Red /1 #R11
2007 Press Pass Eclipse Red /1 #R59
2007 Press Pass Eclipse Red /1 #R67
2007 Press Pass Eclipse Red /1 #R70
2007 Press Pass Eclipse Red /1 #R78
2007 Press Pass Eclipse Skidmarks #SM10
2007 Press Pass Eclipse Skidmarks Holofoil /250 #SM10
2007 Press Pass Eclipse Teammates Autographs /25 #4
2007 Press Pass Eclipse Under Cover Autographs /20 #UCTS
2007 Press Pass Eclipse Under Cover Drivers /450 #UCD9
2007 Press Pass Eclipse Under Cover Drivers Eclipse /1 #UCD9
2007 Press Pass Eclipse Under Cover Drivers Name /99 #UCD9
2007 Press Pass Eclipse Under Cover Drivers NASCAR /270 #UCD9
2007 Press Pass Eclipse Under Cover Teams /135 #UCT9
2007 Press Pass Eclipse Under Cover Teams NASCAR /25 #UCT9
2007 Press Pass Four Wide /50 #FWTS
2007 Press Pass Four Wide Checkered Flag /1 #FWTS
2007 Press Pass Four Wide Checkered Flag Exchange /1 #FWTS
2007 Press Pass Four Wide Exchange /50 #FWTS
2007 Press Pass Gold #G11
2007 Press Pass Gold #G79
2007 Press Pass Gold #G91
2007 Press Pass Gold #G103
2007 Press Pass Hot Treads #HT2
2007 Press Pass Hot Treads Blue /99 #HT2
2007 Press Pass Hot Treads Gold /299 #HT2
2007 Press Pass K-Mart #TSC
2007 Press Pass Legends #39
2007 Press Pass Legends Blue /999 #B39
2007 Press Pass Legends Bronze /599 #Z39
2007 Press Pass Legends Gold /249 #G39
2007 Press Pass Legends Holofoil /99 #H39
2007 Press Pass Legends Press Plates Black /1 #PP39
2007 Press Pass Legends Press Plates Black Backs /1 #PP39
2007 Press Pass Legends Press Plates Cyan /1 #PP39
2007 Press Pass Legends Press Plates Cyan Backs /1 #PP39
2007 Press Pass Legends Press Plates Magenta /1 #PP39
2007 Press Pass Legends Press Plates Magenta Backs /1 #PP39
2007 Press Pass Legends Press Plates Yellow /1 #PP39
2007 Press Pass Legends Press Plates Yellow Backs /1 #PP39
2007 Press Pass Legends Previews /5 #EB39
2007 Press Pass Legends Signature Series /25 #TS
2007 Press Pass Legends Solo /1 #S39
2007 Press Pass Legends Sunday Swatches Bronze /199 #TSSS
2007 Press Pass Legends Sunday Swatches Gold /50 #TSSS
2007 Press Pass Legends Sunday Swatches Silver /99 #TSSS
2007 Press Pass Legends Victory Lane Bronze /199 #VL8
2007 Press Pass Legends Victory Lane Gold /25 #VL8
2007 Press Pass Legends Victory Lane Silver /99 #VL8
2007 Press Pass Platinum /100 #P11
2007 Press Pass Platinum /100 #P79
2007 Press Pass Platinum /100 #P91
2007 Press Pass Platinum /100 #P103
2007 Press Pass Premium #18
2007 Press Pass Premium #67
2007 Press Pass Premium #80
2007 Press Pass Premium #76
2007 Press Pass Premium #46
2007 Press Pass Premium #48
2007 Press Pass Premium #54
2007 Press Pass Premium #37
2007 Press Pass Premium Concrete Chaos #CC4
2007 Press Pass Premium Hot Threads Autographs /20 #HTTS
2007 Press Pass Premium Hot Threads Drivers /145 #HTD5
2007 Press Pass Premium Hot Threads Drivers Gold /1 #HTD5
2007 Press Pass Premium Hot Threads Patch /8 #HTP16
2007 Press Pass Premium Hot Threads Patch /15 #HTP17
2007 Press Pass Premium Hot Threads Team /160 #HTT5
2007 Press Pass Premium Performance Driven #PD8
2007 Press Pass Premium Performance Driven Red /250 #PD8
2007 Press Pass Premium Red /15 #R18
2007 Press Pass Premium Red /15 #R37
2007 Press Pass Premium Red /15 #R46
2007 Press Pass Premium Red /15 #R48
2007 Press Pass Premium Red /15 #R54
2007 Press Pass Premium Red /15 #R67
2007 Press Pass Premium Red /5 #R76
2007 Press Pass Premium Red /5 #R80
2007 Press Pass Previews /5 #EB11
2007 Press Pass Race Day #RD3
2007 Press Pass Signings #69
2007 Press Pass Signings Blue /25 #31
2007 Press Pass Signings Gold /50 #52
2007 Press Pass Signings Press Plates Black /1 #40
2007 Press Pass Signings Press Plates Cyan /1 #39
2007 Press Pass Signings Press Plates Magenta /1 #42
2007 Press Pass Signings Press Plates Yellow /1 #40
2007 Press Pass Signings Silver /100 #51
2007 Press Pass Snapshots #SN26
2007 Press Pass Stealth #24
2007 Press Pass Stealth #87
2007 Press Pass Stealth #51
2007 Press Pass Stealth #59
2007 Press Pass Stealth #65
2007 Press Pass Stealth Battle Armor Autographs /20 #BASTS
2007 Press Pass Stealth Battle Armor Drivers /150 #BAD10
2007 Press Pass Stealth Battle Armor Teams /85 #BAT10
2007 Press Pass Stealth Chrome #24
2007 Press Pass Stealth Chrome #87
2007 Press Pass Stealth Chrome #51
2007 Press Pass Stealth Chrome #59
2007 Press Pass Stealth Chrome #65
2007 Press Pass Stealth Chrome Exclusives /99 #X24
2007 Press Pass Stealth Chrome Exclusives /99 #X51
2007 Press Pass Stealth Chrome Exclusives /99 #X59
2007 Press Pass Stealth Chrome Exclusives /99 #X65
2007 Press Pass Stealth Chrome Exclusives /99 #X87
2007 Press Pass Stealth Chrome Platinum /25 #P24
2007 Press Pass Stealth Chrome Platinum /25 #P51
2007 Press Pass Stealth Chrome Platinum /25 #P59
2007 Press Pass Stealth Chrome Platinum /25 #P65
2007 Press Pass Stealth Chrome Platinum /25 #P87
2007 Press Pass Stealth Fusion #F3
2007 Press Pass Stealth Mach 07 #M7-3
2007 Press Pass Stealth Maximum Access #MA25
2007 Press Pass Stealth Maximum Access Autographs /25 #MA25
2007 Press Pass Stealth Previews /1 #EB87
2007 Press Pass Stealth Previews /5 #EB24
2007 Press Pass Target #TSB
2007 Press Pass Target Race Win Tires #RW7
2007 Press Pass Velocity #V8
2007 Press Pass Wal-Mart #TSA
2007 Press Pass Wal-Mart Autographs /50 #TS
2007 Sunoco OCC Postcards #TS
2007 Traks #28
2007 Traks #75
2007 Traks #99
2007 Traks #61
2007 Traks #86
2007 Traks Corporate Cuts Driver /99 #CCD13
2007 Traks Corporate Cuts Patch /4 #CCD13
2007 Traks Corporate Cuts Team /180 #CCT13
2007 Traks Driver's Seat #DS4B
2007 Traks Driver's Seat #DS4
2007 Traks Driver's Seat National #DS4
2007 Traks Gold #G28
2007 Traks Gold #G61
2007 Traks Gold #G75
2007 Traks Gold #G86
2007 Traks Gold #G99
2007 Traks Holofoil /50 #H28
2007 Traks Holofoil /50 #H61
2007 Traks Holofoil /50 #H75
2007 Traks Holofoil /50 #H86
2007 Traks Holofoil /50 #H99
2007 Traks Hot Pursuit #HP3
2007 Traks Previews /5 #EB28
2007 Traks Previews /1 #EB75
2007 Traks Red /10 #R28
2007 Traks Red /10 #R61
2007 Traks Red /10 #R75
2007 Traks Red /10 #R86
2007 Traks Red /10 #R99
2007 Traks Target Exclusives #TSA
2007 Traks Track Time #TT8
2007 Traks Wal-Mart Exclusives #TSB
2007 VIP #27
2007 VIP #63
2007 VIP #52
2007 VIP #41
2007 VIP Gear Gallery #GG9
2007 VIP Gear Gallery Transparent #GG9
2007 VIP Get A Grip Drivers /70 #GGD12
2007 VIP Get A Grip Teams /70 #GGT12
2007 VIP Pedal To The Metal /50 #PM1
2007 VIP Previews /5 #EB27
2007 VIP Sunday Best #SB21
2007 VIP Trophy Club #TC1
2007 VIP Trophy Club Transparent #TC1
2007 Wheels American Thunder #33
2007 Wheels American Thunder #74
2007 Wheels American Thunder #68
2007 Wheels American Thunder #61
2007 Wheels American Thunder #52
2007 Wheels American Thunder #44
2007 Wheels American Thunder American Dreams #AD12
2007 Wheels American Thunder American Dreams Gold /250 #ADG12
2007 Wheels American Thunder American Muscle #AM2
2007 Wheels American Thunder Autographed Hat Instant Winner /1 #AH38
2007 Wheels American Thunder Double Hat /99 #DH7
2007 Wheels American Thunder Head to Toe /99 #HT2
2007 Wheels American Thunder Previews /5 #EB33
2007 Wheels American Thunder Previews /1 #EB52
2007 Wheels American Thunder Pushin' Pedal /99 #PP2
2007 Wheels American Thunder Thunder Road #TR17
2007 Wheels American Thunder Thunder Strokes #37
2007 Wheels American Thunder Thunder Strokes Press Plates Black /1 #37
2007 Wheels American Thunder Thunder Strokes Press Plates Cyan /1 #37
2007 Wheels American Thunder Thunder Strokes Press Plates Magenta /1 #37
2007 Wheels American Thunder Thunder Strokes Press Plates Yellow /1 #37
2007 Wheels Autographs #38
2007 Wheels Autographs Press Plates Black /1 #37
2007 Wheels Autographs Press Plates Cyan /1 #37
2007 Wheels Autographs Press Plates Magenta /1 #37
2007 Wheels High Gear #11
2007 Wheels High Gear #54
2007 Wheels High Gear #62
2007 Wheels High Gear #63
2007 Wheels High Gear #81
2007 Wheels High Gear Driven #DR12
2007 Wheels High Gear Final Standings Gold /11 #FS11
2007 Wheels High Gear Flag Chasers Black /89 #FC4
2007 Wheels High Gear Flag Chasers Blue-Yellow /50 #FC4
2007 Wheels High Gear Flag Chasers Checkered /10 #FC4
2007 Wheels High Gear Flag Chasers Green /89 #FC4
2007 Wheels High Gear Flag Chasers Red /89 #FC4
2007 Wheels High Gear Flag Chasers White /89 #FC4
2007 Wheels High Gear Flag Chasers Yellow /89 #FC4
2007 Wheels High Gear Full Throttle #FT8
2007 Wheels High Gear Last Lap /10 #LL5
2007 Wheels High Gear MPH /100 #M11
2007 Wheels High Gear MPH /100 #M54
2007 Wheels High Gear MPH /100 #M62
2007 Wheels High Gear MPH /100 #M63
2007 Wheels High Gear MPH /100 #M81
2007 Wheels High Gear Previews /5 #EB11
2007 Wheels High Gear Previews /5 #EB54
2007 Wheels High Gear Previews /5 #EB62
2007 Wheels High Gear Previews /5 #EB63
2008 Indianapolis Motor Speedway #6
2008 Press Pass #0
2008 Press Pass #2
2008 Press Pass #95
2008 Press Pass #109
2008 Press Pass Autographs #40
2008 Press Pass Autographs Press Plates Black /1 #32
2008 Press Pass Autographs Press Plates Cyan /1 #33
2008 Press Pass Autographs Press Plates Magenta /1 #33
2008 Press Pass Autographs Press Plates Yellow /1 #32
2008 Press Pass Blue #B2
2008 Press Pass Blue #B95
2008 Press Pass Blue #B109
2008 Press Pass Burning Rubber Drivers /60 #BRD18
2008 Press Pass Burning Rubber Drivers /60 #BRD19
2008 Press Pass Burning Rubber Drivers /60 #BRD21
2008 Press Pass Burning Rubber Drivers Gold /1 #BRD18
2008 Press Pass Burning Rubber Drivers Gold /1 #BRD19
2008 Press Pass Burning Rubber Drivers Gold /1 #BRD21
2008 Press Pass Burning Rubber Drivers Prime Cuts /25 #BRD18
2008 Press Pass Burning Rubber Drivers Prime Cuts /25 #BRD19
2008 Press Pass Burning Rubber Drivers Prime Cuts /25 #BRD21
2008 Press Pass Burning Rubber Teams /175 #BRT18
2008 Press Pass Burning Rubber Teams /175 #BRT19
2008 Press Pass Burning Rubber Teams /175 #BRT21
2008 Press Pass Burnouts #BO5
2008 Press Pass Burnouts Blue /99 #BO5
2008 Press Pass Burnouts Gold /299 #BO5
2008 Press Pass Collector's Series Box Set #8
2008 Press Pass Cup Chase #CC11
2008 Press Pass Cup Chase Prizes #CC8
2008 Press Pass Double Burner Firesuit-Glove /100 #DBTS
2008 Press Pass Eclipse #5A
2008 Press Pass Eclipse #78
2008 Press Pass Eclipse #5B
2008 Press Pass Eclipse #74
2008 Press Pass Eclipse #75
2008 Press Pass Eclipse Escape Velocity #EV4
2008 Press Pass Eclipse Gold /25 #G5
2008 Press Pass Eclipse Gold /25 #G74
2008 Press Pass Eclipse Gold /25 #G75
2008 Press Pass Eclipse Gold /25 #G78
2008 Press Pass Eclipse Hyperdrive #HP1
2008 Press Pass Eclipse Previews /5 #EB5
2008 Press Pass Eclipse Previews /1 #EB74
2008 Press Pass Eclipse Previews /1 #EB75
2008 Press Pass Eclipse Previews /1 #EB78
2008 Press Pass Eclipse Red /1 #R5
2008 Press Pass Eclipse Red /1 #R74
2008 Press Pass Eclipse Red /1 #R75
2008 Press Pass Eclipse Red /1 #R78
2008 Press Pass Eclipse Star Tracks #ST2
2008 Press Pass Eclipse Star Tracks Holofoil /250 #ST2
2008 Press Pass Eclipse Stellar #ST4
2008 Press Pass Eclipse Teammates Autographs /35 #BHS
2008 Press Pass Eclipse Under Cover Drivers /250 #UCD2
2008 Press Pass Eclipse Under Cover Drivers Eclipse /1 #UCD2
2008 Press Pass Eclipse Under Cover Drivers Name /50 #UCD2
2008 Press Pass Eclipse Under Cover Drivers NASCAR /150 #UCD2
2008 Press Pass Eclipse Under Cover Teams /99 #UCT2
2008 Press Pass Eclipse Under Cover Teams NASCAR /25 #UCT2
2008 Press Pass Four Wide /50 #FWTS
2008 Press Pass Four Wide Checkered Flag /1 #FWTS
2008 Press Pass Gold #G2
2008 Press Pass Gold #G95
2008 Press Pass Gold #G109
2008 Press Pass Hot Treads #HT8
2008 Press Pass Hot Treads Blue /99 #HT8
2008 Press Pass Hot Treads Gold /299 #HT8
2008 Press Pass Legends #55
2008 Press Pass Legends Autographs Black #TS
2008 Press Pass Legends Autographs Blue /74 #TS
2008 Press Pass Legends Autographs Press Plates Black /1 #TS
2008 Press Pass Legends Autographs Press Plates Cyan /1 #TS
2008 Press Pass Legends Autographs Press Plates Magenta /1 #TS
2008 Press Pass Legends Autographs Press Plates Yellow /1 #TS
2008 Press Pass Legends Blue /599 #55
2008 Press Pass Legends Bronze /299 #55
2008 Press Pass Legends Gold /99 #55
2008 Press Pass Legends Holo /25 #55
2008 Press Pass Legends IROC Champions /380 #I25
2008 Press Pass Legends IROC Champions Gold /99 #I25
2008 Press Pass Legends Previews /5 #EB55
2008 Press Pass Legends Printing Plates Black /1 #55
2008 Press Pass Legends Printing Plates Cyan /1 #55
2008 Press Pass Legends Printing Plates Magenta /1 #55
2008 Press Pass Legends Printing Plates Yellow /1 #55
2008 Press Pass Legends Prominent Pieces Firesuit-Glove Bronze /99 #PP1TS
2008 Press Pass Legends Prominent Pieces Firesuit-Glove Gold /10 #PP1TS
2008 Press Pass Legends Prominent Pieces Firesuit-Glove Silver /30 #PP1TS
2008 Press Pass Legends Prominent Pieces Metal-Tire Bronze /99 #PP3TS
2008 Press Pass Legends Prominent Pieces Metal-Tire Gold /25 #PP3TS
2008 Press Pass Legends Prominent Pieces Metal-Tire Silver /50 #PP3TS
2008 Press Pass Legends Solo /1 #55
2008 Press Pass Legends Victory Lane Bronze /99 #VLTS
2008 Press Pass Legends Victory Lane Gold /25 #VLTS
2008 Press Pass Legends Victory Lane Silver /50 #VLTS
2008 Press Pass Platinum /100 #P2
2008 Press Pass Platinum /100 #P95
2008 Press Pass Platinum /100 #P109
2008 Press Pass Premium #17
2008 Press Pass Premium #47
2008 Press Pass Premium #61
2008 Press Pass Premium #68
2008 Press Pass Premium #85
2008 Press Pass Premium #53
2008 Press Pass Premium Clean Air #CA12
2008 Press Pass Premium Going Global #GG3
2008 Press Pass Premium Going Global Red /250 #GG3
2008 Press Pass Premium Hot Threads Drivers /120 #HTD17
2008 Press Pass Premium Hot Threads Drivers Gold /1 #HTD17
2008 Press Pass Premium Hot Threads Patches /8 #HTP43
2008 Press Pass Premium Hot Threads Patches #HTP42
2008 Press Pass Premium Hot Threads Patches #HTP41
2008 Press Pass Premium Hot Threads Patches #HTP40
2008 Press Pass Premium Hot Threads Team /120 #HTT17
2008 Press Pass Premium Previews /5 #EB17
2008 Press Pass Premium Previews /1 #EB61
2008 Press Pass Premium Red /15 #17
2008 Press Pass Premium Red /15 #47
2008 Press Pass Premium Red /15 #53
2008 Press Pass Premium Red /15 #61
2008 Press Pass Premium Red /15 #68
2008 Press Pass Premium Red /5 #85
2008 Press Pass Premium Target #TA4
2008 Press Pass Premium Team Signed Baseballs #GIB
2008 Press Pass Premium Team Signed Baseballs #EGIB
2008 Press Pass Previews /5 #EB2
2008 Press Pass Previews /1 #EB109
2008 Press Pass Race Day #RD1
2008 Press Pass Signings #57
2008 Press Pass Signings Blue /25 #30
2008 Press Pass Signings Gold /50 #50
2008 Press Pass Signings Press Plates Black /1 #38
2008 Press Pass Signings Press Plates Cyan /1 #38
2008 Press Pass Signings Press Plates Magenta /1 #38
2008 Press Pass Signings Press Plates Yellow /1 #38
2008 Press Pass Signings Press Plates Yellow /1 #TS
2008 Press Pass Signings Silver /100 #49
2008 Press Pass Slideshow #SS17
2008 Press Pass Speedway #33
2008 Press Pass Speedway #75
2008 Press Pass Speedway #81
2008 Press Pass Speedway #84
2008 Press Pass Speedway Blur #B8
2008 Press Pass Speedway Cockpit #CP23
2008 Press Pass Speedway Corporate Cuts Drivers /80 #CDTS
2008 Press Pass Speedway Corporate Cuts Drivers Patches #CDTS
2008 Press Pass Speedway Corporate Cuts Team /165 #CTTS
2008 Press Pass Speedway Garage Graphs Duals /50 #SZ
2008 Press Pass Speedway Gold #G33
2008 Press Pass Speedway Gold #G75
2008 Press Pass Speedway Gold #G81
2008 Press Pass Speedway Gold #G84
2008 Press Pass Speedway Holofoil /50 #H33
2008 Press Pass Speedway Holofoil /50 #H75
2008 Press Pass Speedway Holofoil /50 #H81
2008 Press Pass Speedway Holofoil /50 #H84
2008 Press Pass Speedway Previews /5 #EB33
2008 Press Pass Speedway Red /10 #R33
2008 Press Pass Speedway Red /10 #R75
2008 Press Pass Speedway Red /10 #R81
2008 Press Pass Speedway Red /10 #R84
2008 Press Pass Speedway Test Drive #TD4
2008 Press Pass Starting Grid #SG8
2008 Press Pass Stealth #32
2008 Press Pass Stealth #44
2008 Press Pass Stealth #50
2008 Press Pass Stealth #59
2008 Press Pass Stealth #81
2008 Press Pass Stealth #88
2008 Press Pass Stealth #68
2008 Press Pass Stealth Battle Armor Autographs /20 #BASTS
2008 Press Pass Stealth Battle Armor Drivers /120 #BAD20
2008 Press Pass Stealth Battle Armor Teams /115 #BAT20
2008 Press Pass Stealth Chrome #32
2008 Press Pass Stealth Chrome #44
2008 Press Pass Stealth Chrome #50
2008 Press Pass Stealth Chrome #59
2008 Press Pass Stealth Chrome #81A
2008 Press Pass Stealth Chrome #88
2008 Press Pass Stealth Chrome #81B
2008 Press Pass Stealth Chrome #68
2008 Press Pass Stealth Chrome Exclusives /25 #32
2008 Press Pass Stealth Chrome Exclusives /25 #44
2008 Press Pass Stealth Chrome Exclusives /25 #50
2008 Press Pass Stealth Chrome Exclusives /25 #59
2008 Press Pass Stealth Chrome Exclusives /25 #68
2008 Press Pass Stealth Chrome Exclusives /25 #81
2008 Press Pass Stealth Chrome Exclusives /25 #88
2008 Press Pass Stealth Chrome Exclusives Gold /99 #32
2008 Press Pass Stealth Chrome Exclusives Gold /99 #44
2008 Press Pass Stealth Chrome Exclusives Gold /99 #50
2008 Press Pass Stealth Chrome Exclusives Gold /99 #59
2008 Press Pass Stealth Chrome Exclusives Gold /99 #68
2008 Press Pass Stealth Chrome Exclusives Gold /99 #81
2008 Press Pass Stealth Chrome Exclusives Gold /99 #88
2008 Press Pass Stealth Mach 08 #M8-3
2008 Press Pass Stealth Maximum Access #MA24
2008 Press Pass Stealth Maximum Access Autographs /25 #MA24
2008 Press Pass Stealth Previews /5 #32
2008 Press Pass Stealth Previews /5 #44
2008 Press Pass Stealth Previews /1 #88
2008 Press Pass Stealth Synthesis #S4
2008 Press Pass Stealth Wal-Mart #WM10
2008 Press Pass Target #TSB
2008 Press Pass Target Victory Tires /50 #TTTS
2008 Press Pass VIP National Convention Promo #2
2008 Press Pass Wal-Mart #TSA
2008 Press Pass Wal-Mart Autographs /50 #9
2008 Press Pass Weekend Warriors #WW2
2008 VIP #33
2008 VIP #54
2008 VIP #81
2008 VIP #86
2008 VIP #90
2008 VIP All Access #AA22
2008 VIP Gear Gallery #GG7
2008 VIP Gear Gallery Memorabilia /50 #GGTS
2008 VIP Gear Gallery Transparent #GG7
2008 VIP National Promos #2
2008 VIP Previews /5 #EB33
2008 VIP Previews /1 #EB86
2008 Wheels American Thunder #33
2008 Wheels American Thunder #78
2008 Wheels American Thunder #84
2008 Wheels American Thunder #42
2008 Wheels American Thunder American Dreams #AD2
2008 Wheels American Thunder American Dreams Gold /250 #AD2
2008 Wheels American Thunder Autographed Hat Winner /1 #WHTS
2008 Wheels American Thunder Campaign Buttons #TS
2008 Wheels American Thunder Campaign Buttons Blue #TS
2008 Wheels American Thunder Campaign Buttons Gold #TS
2008 Wheels American Thunder Campaign Trail #CT10
2008 Wheels American Thunder Delegates #D16
2008 Wheels American Thunder Head to Toe /150 #HT1
2008 Wheels American Thunder Motorcade #M7
2008 Wheels American Thunder Previews /5 #33
2008 Wheels American Thunder Previews /1 #78
2008 Wheels American Thunder Pushin' Pedal /150 #PP 1
2008 Wheels American Thunder Trackside Treasury Autographs #TS
2008 Wheels American Thunder Trackside Treasury Autographs Gold /25 #TS
2008 Wheels American Thunder Trackside Treasury Autographs Printing Plates Black /1 #TS
2008 Wheels American Thunder Trackside Treasury Autographs Printing Plates Cyan /1 #TS
2008 Wheels American Thunder Trackside Treasury Autographs Printing Plates Magenta /1 #TS
2008 Wheels American Thunder Trackside Treasury Autographs Printing Plates Yellow /1 #TS
2008 Wheels American Thunder Triple Hat /125 #TH24
2008 Wheels Autographs #31
2008 Wheels Autographs Chase Edition /25 #8
2008 Wheels Autographs Press Plates Black /1 #31
2008 Wheels Autographs Press Plates Cyan /1 #31
2008 Wheels Autographs Press Plates Magenta /1 #31
2008 Wheels Autographs Press Plates Yellow /1 #31
2008 Wheels High Gear #6
2008 Wheels High Gear #47A
2008 Wheels High Gear #75
2008 Wheels High Gear #47B
2008 Wheels High Gear Driven #DR2
2008 Wheels High Gear Final Standings /6 #F6
2008 Wheels High Gear Flag Chasers Black /89 #FC2
2008 Wheels High Gear Flag Chasers Blue-Yellow /50 #FC2
2008 Wheels High Gear Flag Chasers Checkered /20 #FC2
2008 Wheels High Gear Flag Chasers Green /60 #FC2
2008 Wheels High Gear Flag Chasers Red /89 #FC2
2008 Wheels High Gear Flag Chasers White /65 #FC2
2008 Wheels High Gear Flag Chasers Yellow /89 #FC2
2008 Wheels High Gear Full Throttle #FT9
2008 Wheels High Gear Last Lap /10 #LL1
2008 Wheels High Gear Last Lap Holofoil /5 #LL1
2008 Wheels High Gear MPH /100 #M6
2008 Wheels High Gear MPH /100 #M47
2008 Wheels High Gear MPH /100 #M75
2008 Wheels High Gear Previews /5 #EB6
2008 Wheels High Gear The Chase #TC6
2009 Element #32
2009 Element #53
2009 Element #61
2009 Element #84
2009 Element #87
2009 Element Big Win /35 #BWTS
2009 Element Elements of the Race Black Flag /99 #ERBTS
2009 Element Elements of the Race Black-White Flag /50 #ERXTS
2009 Element Elements of the Race Blue-Yellow Flag /50 #ERBOTS
2009 Element Elements of the Race Checkered Flag /5 #ERCTS
2009 Element Elements of the Race Green Flag /50 #ERGTS
2009 Element Elements of the Race Red Flag /99 #ERRTS
2009 Element Elements of the Race White Flag /75 #ERWTS
2009 Element Elements of the Race Yellow Flag /99 #ERYTS
2009 Element Lab Report #LR25
2009 Element Previews /5 #32
2009 Element Previews /1 #53
2009 Element Radioactive /100 #32
2009 Element Radioactive /100 #53
2009 Element Radioactive /100 #61
2009 Element Radioactive /100 #84
2009 Element Radioactive /100 #87
2009 Press Pass #0
2009 Press Pass #8
2009 Press Pass #80
2009 Press Pass #87
2009 Press Pass #88
2009 Press Pass #89
2009 Press Pass #90
2009 Press Pass #91
2009 Press Pass #92
2009 Press Pass #93
2009 Press Pass #94
2009 Press Pass #95
2009 Press Pass #96
2009 Press Pass #97
2009 Press Pass #114
2009 Press Pass #152
2009 Press Pass #165
2009 Press Pass #182
2009 Press Pass #205
2009 Press Pass #213
2009 Press Pass Autographs Chase Edition /25 #TS
2009 Press Pass Autographs Gold #50
2009 Press Pass Blue #8
2009 Press Pass Blue #80
2009 Press Pass Blue #87
2009 Press Pass Blue #88
2009 Press Pass Blue #89
2009 Press Pass Blue #90
2009 Press Pass Blue #91
2009 Press Pass Blue #92
2009 Press Pass Blue #93
2009 Press Pass Blue #94
2009 Press Pass Blue #95
2009 Press Pass Blue #96
2009 Press Pass Blue #97
2009 Press Pass Blue #114
2009 Press Pass Blue #152
2009 Press Pass Blue #165
2009 Press Pass Blue #182
2009 Press Pass Blue #205
2009 Press Pass Blue #213
2009 Press Pass Burning Rubber Drivers /320 #BRD30
2009 Press Pass Burning Rubber Prime Cut /25 #BRD30
2009 Press Pass Burning Rubber Teams /85 #BRT30
2009 Press Pass Chase for the Sprint Cup #CC2
2009 Press Pass Cup Chase #CCR17
2009 Press Pass Cup Chase Prizes #CC2
2009 Press Pass Daytona 500 Tires /25 #TTTS
2009 Press Pass Eclipse #10
2009 Press Pass Eclipse #33
2009 Press Pass Eclipse #56
2009 Press Pass Eclipse #62
2009 Press Pass Eclipse #73
2009 Press Pass Eclipse Black and White #10
2009 Press Pass Eclipse Black and White #33
2009 Press Pass Eclipse Black and White #56
2009 Press Pass Eclipse Black and White #62
2009 Press Pass Eclipse Black and White #73
2009 Press Pass Eclipse Blue #10
2009 Press Pass Eclipse Blue #33

2009 Press Pass Eclipse Blue #56
2009 Press Pass Eclipse Blue #62
2009 Press Pass Eclipse Blue #73
2009 Press Pass Eclipse Ecliptic Path #EP18
2009 Press Pass Eclipse Solar Swatches /250 #SSTS5
2009 Press Pass Eclipse Solar Swatches /250 #SSTS7
2009 Press Pass Eclipse Solar Swatches /250 #SSTS3
2009 Press Pass Eclipse Solar Swatches /299 #SSTS6
2009 Press Pass Eclipse Solar Swatches /299 #SSTS2
2009 Press Pass Eclipse Solar Swatches /50 #SSTS4
2009 Press Pass Eclipse Solar Swatches /99 #SSTS1
2009 Press Pass Eclipse Solar System #SS9
2009 Press Pass Eclipse Under Cover Autographs /20 #UCSTS
2009 Press Pass Final Standings /140 #114
2009 Press Pass Four Wide Autographs /5 #FWTS2
2009 Press Pass Four Wide Checkered Flag /1 #FWTS
2009 Press Pass Four Wide Firesuit /50 #FWTS2
2009 Press Pass Four Wide Firesuit /50 #FWTS
2009 Press Pass Four Wide Sheet Metal /10 #FWTS
2009 Press Pass Four Wide Tire /25 #FWTS
2009 Press Pass Four Wide Tire /25 #FWTS2
2009 Press Pass Freeze Frame #FF19
2009 Press Pass Freeze Frame #FF32
2009 Press Pass Fusion #75
2009 Press Pass Fusion Bronze /150 #75
2009 Press Pass Fusion Gold /50 #75
2009 Press Pass Fusion Green /25 #75
2009 Press Pass Fusion Onyx /1 #75
2009 Press Pass Fusion Revered Relics Gold /50 #RRTS
2009 Press Pass Fusion Revered Relics Holofoil /25 #RRTS
2009 Press Pass Fusion Revered Relics Premium Swatch /10 #RRTS
2009 Press Pass Fusion Revered Relics Silver /65 #RRTS
2009 Press Pass Fusion Silver /99 #75
2009 Press Pass Game Face #GF9
2009 Press Pass Gold #8
2009 Press Pass Gold #80
2009 Press Pass Gold #87
2009 Press Pass Gold #88
2009 Press Pass Gold #89
2009 Press Pass Gold #90
2009 Press Pass Gold #91
2009 Press Pass Gold #92
2009 Press Pass Gold #93
2009 Press Pass Gold #94
2009 Press Pass Gold #95
2009 Press Pass Gold #96
2009 Press Pass Gold #97
2009 Press Pass Gold #114
2009 Press Pass Gold #152
2009 Press Pass Gold #165
2009 Press Pass Gold #182
2009 Press Pass Gold #205
2009 Press Pass Gold #213
2009 Press Pass Gold Holofoil /100 #8
2009 Press Pass Gold Holofoil /100 #80
2009 Press Pass Gold Holofoil /100 #87
2009 Press Pass Gold Holofoil /100 #88
2009 Press Pass Gold Holofoil /100 #89
2009 Press Pass Gold Holofoil /100 #90
2009 Press Pass Gold Holofoil /100 #91
2009 Press Pass Gold Holofoil /100 #92
2009 Press Pass Gold Holofoil /100 #93
2009 Press Pass Gold Holofoil /100 #94
2009 Press Pass Gold Holofoil /100 #95
2009 Press Pass Gold Holofoil /100 #96
2009 Press Pass Gold Holofoil /100 #97
2009 Press Pass Gold Holofoil /100 #114
2009 Press Pass Gold Holofoil /100 #152
2009 Press Pass Gold Holofoil /100 #165
2009 Press Pass Gold Holofoil /100 #182
2009 Press Pass Gold Holofoil /100 #205
2009 Press Pass Gold Holofoil /100 #213
2009 Press Pass Legends #55
2009 Press Pass Legends Autographs Gold /40 #30
2009 Press Pass Legends Autographs Printing Plates Black /1 #24
2009 Press Pass Legends Autographs Printing Plates Cyan /1 #23
2009 Press Pass Legends Autographs Printing Plates Magenta /1 #24
2009 Press Pass Legends Autographs Printing Plates Yellow /1 #24
2009 Press Pass Legends Gold /399 #55
2009 Press Pass Legends Holofoil /50 #55
2009 Press Pass Legends Past and Present /550 #PP12
2009 Press Pass Legends Past and Present Holofoil /99 #PP12
2009 Press Pass Legends Previews /5 #55
2009 Press Pass Legends Printing Plates Black /1 #55
2009 Press Pass Legends Printing Plates Cyan /1 #55
2009 Press Pass Legends Printing Plates Magenta /1 #55
2009 Press Pass Legends Printing Plates Yellow /1 #55
2009 Press Pass Legends Prominent Pieces Bronze /99 #PPTS
2009 Press Pass Legends Prominent Pieces Gold /25 #PPTS
2009 Press Pass Legends Prominent Pieces Oversized /25 #PPOETS
2009 Press Pass Legends Prominent Pieces Silver /50 #PPTS
2009 Press Pass Legends Red /199 #55
2009 Press Pass Legends Solo /1 #55
2009 Press Pass NASCAR Gallery #NG3
2009 Press Pass Pieces Race Used Memorabilia #TS
2009 Press Pass Pocket Portraits #P24
2009 Press Pass Pocket Portraits Checkered Flag #P24
2009 Press Pass Pocket Portraits Hometown #P24
2009 Press Pass Pocket Portraits Smoke #P24
2009 Press Pass Pocket Portraits Target #PPT4
2009 Press Pass Premium #13
2009 Press Pass Premium #39
2009 Press Pass Premium #56
2009 Press Pass Premium #58
2009 Press Pass Premium #65
2009 Press Pass Premium #76
2009 Press Pass Premium #84
2009 Press Pass Premium Gold #84
2009 Press Pass Premium Hot Threads /99 #HTTS1
2009 Press Pass Premium Hot Threads /325 #HTTS2
2009 Press Pass Premium Hot Threads Multi-Color /25 #HTTS
2009 Press Pass Premium Previews /5 #EB13
2009 Press Pass Premium Previews /1 #EB55
2009 Press Pass Premium Signatures #34
2009 Press Pass Premium Signatures Gold /25 #33
2009 Press Pass Premium Top Contenders #TC4
2009 Press Pass Premium Top Contenders Gold #TC4
2009 Press Pass Premium Win Streak #WS6
2009 Press Pass Premium Win Streak Victory Lane #WSVL-TS
2009 Press Pass Previews /5 #EB8
2009 Press Pass Previews /1 #EB114
2009 Press Pass Previews /5 #EB152
2009 Press Pass Red #8
2009 Press Pass Red #80
2009 Press Pass Red #87
2009 Press Pass Red #88
2009 Press Pass Red #89
2009 Press Pass Red #90
2009 Press Pass Red #91
2009 Press Pass Red #92
2009 Press Pass Red #93
2009 Press Pass Red #94
2009 Press Pass Red #95
2009 Press Pass Red #96
2009 Press Pass Red #97
2009 Press Pass Red #114
2009 Press Pass Red #152
2009 Press Pass Red #165
2009 Press Pass Red #182
2009 Press Pass Red #205
2009 Press Pass Red #213
2009 Press Pass Showcase /499 #27
2009 Press Pass Showcase /499 #43
2009 Press Pass Showcase /499 #36
2009 Press Pass Showcase 2nd Gear /125 #27
2009 Press Pass Showcase 2nd Gear /125 #36
2009 Press Pass Showcase 2nd Gear /125 #43
2009 Press Pass Showcase 3rd Gear /50 #27
2009 Press Pass Showcase 3rd Gear /50 #36
2009 Press Pass Showcase 3rd Gear /50 #43
2009 Press Pass Showcase 4th Gear /15 #27
2009 Press Pass Showcase 4th Gear /15 #36
2009 Press Pass Showcase 4th Gear /15 #43
2009 Press Pass Showcase Classic Collections Firesuit /25 #CCF9
2009 Press Pass Showcase Classic Collections Firesuit Patch /5 #CCF9
2009 Press Pass Showcase Classic Collections Ink /45 #10
2009 Press Pass Showcase Classic Collections Ink Gold /25 #10
2009 Press Pass Showcase Classic Collections Ink Green /5 #10
2009 Press Pass Showcase Classic Collections Ink Melting /1 #10
2009 Press Pass Showcase Classic Collections Sheet Metal /45 #CCS9
2009 Press Pass Showcase Classic Collections Tire /99 #CCT9
2009 Press Pass Showcase Elite Exhibit Ink /45 #11
2009 Press Pass Showcase Elite Exhibit Ink Gold /25 #11
2009 Press Pass Showcase Elite Exhibit Ink Green /5 #11
2009 Press Pass Showcase Elite Exhibit Ink Melting /1 #11
2009 Press Pass Showcase Elite Exhibit Triple Memorabilia /99 #EETS
2009 Press Pass Showcase Elite Exhibit Triple Memorabilia Gold /45 #EETS
2009 Press Pass Showcase Elite Exhibit Triple Memorabilia Green /25 #EETS
2009 Press Pass Showcase Elite Exhibit Triple Memorabilia Melting /5 #EETS
2009 Press Pass Showcase Printing Plates Black /1 #27
2009 Press Pass Showcase Printing Plates Black /1 #36
2009 Press Pass Showcase Printing Plates Black /1 #43
2009 Press Pass Showcase Printing Plates Cyan /1 #27
2009 Press Pass Showcase Printing Plates Cyan /1 #36
2009 Press Pass Showcase Printing Plates Cyan /1 #43
2009 Press Pass Showcase Printing Plates Magenta /1 #27
2009 Press Pass Showcase Printing Plates Magenta /1 #36
2009 Press Pass Showcase Printing Plates Magenta /1 #43
2009 Press Pass Showcase Printing Plates Yellow /1 #27
2009 Press Pass Showcase Printing Plates Yellow /1 #36
2009 Press Pass Showcase Printing Plates Yellow /1 #43
2009 Press Pass Showcase Prized Pieces Firesuit /25 #PPFTS
2009 Press Pass Showcase Prized Pieces Firesuit Patch /5 #PPFTS
2009 Press Pass Showcase Prized Pieces Ink Firesuit /5 #10
2009 Press Pass Showcase Prized Pieces Ink Firesuit Patch /1 #10
2009 Press Pass Showcase Prized Pieces Ink Sheet Metal /25 #9
2009 Press Pass Showcase Prized Pieces Ink Tire /45 #9
2009 Press Pass Showcase Prized Pieces Sheet Metal /45 #PPSTS
2009 Press Pass Showcase Prized Pieces Tire /99 #PPTTS
2009 Press Pass Signature Series Archive Edition /1 #BRDTS
2009 Press Pass Signature Series Archive Edition /1 #PSTS
2009 Press Pass Signature Series Archive Edition /1 #PSTS
2009 Press Pass Signature Series Archive Edition /1 #TPTS
2009 Press Pass Signature Series Archive Edition /1 #HTTS
2009 Press Pass Signature Series Archive Edition /1 #BATS
2009 Press Pass Signings Blue /25 #45
2009 Press Pass Signings Gold #45
2009 Press Pass Signings Green /15 #45
2009 Press Pass Signings Orange /25 #45
2009 Press Pass Signings Printing Plates Black /1 #45
2009 Press Pass Signings Printing Plates Magenta /1 #45
2009 Press Pass Signings Purple /15 #45
2009 Press Pass Sponsor Swatches /250 #SSTS
2009 Press Pass Sponsor Swatches Select /10 #SSTS
2009 Press Pass Stealth #32A
2009 Press Pass Stealth #49
2009 Press Pass Stealth #89
2009 Press Pass Stealth #32B
2009 Press Pass Stealth Battle Armor /210 #BATS1
2009 Press Pass Stealth Battle Armor /170 #BATS2
2009 Press Pass Stealth Battle Armor Multi-Color /160 #BATS
2009 Press Pass Stealth Chrome #32A
2009 Press Pass Stealth Chrome #49
2009 Press Pass Stealth Chrome #89
2009 Press Pass Stealth Chrome #32B
2009 Press Pass Stealth Chrome Brushed Metal /25 #32
2009 Press Pass Stealth Chrome Brushed Metal /25 #49
2009 Press Pass Stealth Chrome Brushed Metal /25 #89
2009 Press Pass Stealth Chrome Gold /99 #32
2009 Press Pass Stealth Chrome Gold /99 #49
2009 Press Pass Stealth Chrome Gold /99 #89
2009 Press Pass Stealth Confidential Classified Bronze #PC19
2009 Press Pass Stealth Confidential Secret Silver #PC19
2009 Press Pass Stealth Confidential Top Secret Gold /25 #PC19
2009 Press Pass Stealth Mach 09 #M1
2009 Press Pass Stealth Previews /5 #EB32
2009 Press Pass Target #TSB
2009 Press Pass Tony Stewart 10 Years Firesuit /300 #TS1
2009 Press Pass Tony Stewart 10 Years Firesuit /300 #TS2
2009 Press Pass Tony Stewart 10 Years Firesuit /300 #TS3
2009 Press Pass Total Tire /25 #TT6
2009 Press Pass Tradin' Paint #TP3
2009 Press Pass Tread Marks Autographs /10 #SSTS
2009 Press Pass Wal-Mart #TSA
2009 Press Pass Wal-Mart Autographs Red #11
2009 VIP #32
2009 VIP #69
2009 VIP #81
2009 VIP Get A Grip /120 #GGTS
2009 VIP Get A Grip Holofoil /10 #GGTS
2009 VIP Guest List #GG4
2009 VIP Hardware #H7
2009 VIP Hardware Transparent #H7
2009 VIP Leadfoot /150 #LFTS
2009 VIP Leadfoot Holofoil /10 #LFTS
2009 VIP Leadfoot Logos /5 #LFLTS
2009 VIP National Promos #5
2009 VIP Previews /5 #32
2009 VIP Previews /1 #81
2009 VIP Purple /25 #32
2009 VIP Purple /25 #69
2009 VIP Purple /25 #81
2009 VIP Race Day Gear /25 #RDGTS
2009 Wheels Main Event #3
2009 Wheels Main Event #20
2009 Wheels Main Event #44
2009 Wheels Main Event #62
2009 Wheels Main Event #69
2009 Wheels Main Event #75
2009 Wheels Main Event Buyback Archive Edition /1 #TPTS
2009 Wheels Main Event Buyback Archive Edition /1 #BRTS
2009 Wheels Main Event Buyback Archive Edition /1 #GGTS
2009 Wheels Main Event Buyback Archive Edition /1 #HTTS
2009 Wheels Main Event Buyback Archive Edition /1 #UCTS
2009 Wheels Main Event Fast Pass Purple /25 #3
2009 Wheels Main Event Fast Pass Purple /25 #20
2009 Wheels Main Event Fast Pass Purple /25 #44
2009 Wheels Main Event Fast Pass Purple /25 #62
2009 Wheels Main Event Fast Pass Purple /25 #69
2009 Wheels Main Event Fast Pass Purple /25 #75
2009 Wheels Main Event Foil #3
2009 Wheels Main Event Foil #20
2009 Wheels Main Event Hat Dance Patch /10 #HDTS
2009 Wheels Main Event Hat Dance Triple /99 #HDTS
2009 Wheels Main Event High Rollers #HR2
2009 Wheels Main Event Marks Clubs #54
2009 Wheels Main Event Marks Diamonds /10 #54
2009 Wheels Main Event Marks Hearts /5 #54
2009 Wheels Main Event Marks Printing Plates Black /1 #48
2009 Wheels Main Event Marks Printing Plates Cyan /1 #48
2009 Wheels Main Event Marks Printing Plates Magenta /1 #48
2009 Wheels Main Event Marks Printing Plates Yellow /1 #48
2009 Wheels Main Event Marks Spades /1 #54
2009 Wheels Main Event Playing Cards Blue #AD
2009 Wheels Main Event Playing Cards Blue #4S
2009 Wheels Main Event Playing Cards Red #AD
2009 Wheels Main Event Playing Cards Red #4S
2009 Wheels Main Event Poker Chips #4
2009 Wheels Main Event Previews /5 #3
2009 Wheels Main Event Previews /5 #20
2009 Wheels Main Event Stop and Go Swatches Pit Banner /175 #SGBTS1
2009 Wheels Main Event Stop and Go Swatches Pit Banner /175 #SGBTS2
2009 Wheels Main Event Stop and Go Swatches Pit Banner Blue All Season's Sports Cards /1 #SGBTS1
2009 Wheels Main Event Stop and Go Swatches Pit Banner Blue Arena /1 #SGBTS1
2009 Wheels Main Event Stop and Go Swatches Pit Banner Blue Card Stadium /1 #SGBTS1
2009 Wheels Main Event Stop and Go Swatches Pit Banner Blue Chicagoland Sportscards /1 #SGBTS1
2009 Wheels Main Event Stop and Go Swatches Pit Banner Blue Chris Comics /1 #SGBTS1
2009 Wheels Main Event Stop and Go Swatches Pit Banner Blue Chuck's Field of Dreams /1 #SGBTS1
2009 Wheels Main Event Stop and Go Swatches Pit Banner Blue Collector's Heaven /1 #SGBTS1
2009 Wheels Main Event Stop and Go Swatches Pit Banner Blue D&S Racing /1 #SGBTS1
2009 Wheels Main Event Stop and Go Swatches Pit Banner Blue Dave's Pitstop /1 #SGBTS1
2009 Wheels Main Event Stop and Go Swatches Pit Banner Blue Diamond King Sports /1 #SGBTS1
2009 Wheels Main Event Stop and Go Swatches Pit Banner Blue Georgetown Card Exchange /1 #SGBTS1
2009 Wheels Main Event Stop and Go Swatches Pit Banner Blue Jaimie's Field of Dreams /1 #SGBTS1
2009 Wheels Main Event Stop and Go Swatches Pit Banner Blue Juniata Cards /1 #SGBTS1
2009 Wheels Main Event Stop and Go Swatches Pit Banner Blue Main Steet Sportscards /1 #SGBTS1
2009 Wheels Main Event Stop and Go Swatches Pit Banner Blue Matt's Sports Cards /1 #SGBTS1
2009 Wheels Main Event Stop and Go Swatches Pit Banner Blue P&T Sportscards /1 #SGBTS1
2009 Wheels Main Event Stop and Go Swatches Pit Banner Blue Republic Jewelry /1 #SGBTS1
2009 Wheels Main Event Stop and Go Swatches Pit Banner Blue Ron's Racing /1 #SGBTS1
2009 Wheels Main Event Stop and Go Swatches Pit Banner Blue Shelby Collectibles /1 #SGBTS1
2009 Wheels Main Event Stop and Go Swatches Pit Banner Blue Spectator Sportscards /1 #SGBTS1
2009 Wheels Main Event Stop and Go Swatches Pit Banner Blue Squeeze Play /1 #SGBTS1
2009 Wheels Main Event Stop and Go Swatches Pit Banner Blue TBJ Sports Cards /1 #SGBTS1
2009 Wheels Main Event Stop and Go Swatches Pit Banner Blue TCI Sports Fan /1 #SGBTS1
2009 Wheels Main Event Stop and Go Swatches Pit Banner Blue The Card Cellar /1 #SGBTS1
2009 Wheels Main Event Stop and Go Swatches Pit Banner Blue TJ Warner Ballcards /1 #SGBTS1
2009 Wheels Main Event Stop and Go Swatches Pit Banner Blue Trademark Sports /1 #SGBTS1
2009 Wheels Main Event Stop and Go Swatches Pit Banner Blue Triple I Sportscards /1 #SGBTS1
2009 Wheels Main Event Stop and Go Swatches Pit Banner Blue Triple Play /1 #SGBTS1
2009 Wheels Main Event Stop and Go Swatches Pit Banner Blue West Allis /1 #SGBTS1
2009 Wheels Main Event Stop and Go Swatches Pit Banner Green /10 #SGBTS1
2009 Wheels Main Event Stop and Go Swatches Pit Banner Green /10 #SGBTS2
2009 Wheels Main Event Stop and Go Swatches Pit Banner Holofoil /75 #SGBTS1
2009 Wheels Main Event Stop and Go Swatches Pit Banner Holofoil /75 #SGBTS2
2009 Wheels Main Event Stop and Go Swatches Pit Banner Red /25 #SGBTS1
2009 Wheels Main Event Stop and Go Swatches Pit Banner Red /25 #SGBTS2
2009 Wheels Main Event Wildcard Cuts /2 #WCCTS
2010 Element #3
2010 Element #38
2010 Element #72
2010 Element #75
2010 Element #81
2010 Element #97
2010 Element 10 in '10 #TT2
2010 Element Blue /35 #3
2010 Element Blue /35 #38
2010 Element Blue /35 #72
2010 Element Blue /35 #75
2010 Element Blue /35 #81
2010 Element Blue /35 #97
2010 Element Finish Line Checkered Flag /10 #FLTS
2010 Element Finish Line Green Flag /20 #FLTS
2010 Element Finish Line Tires /99 #FLTS
2010 Element Flagship Performers Championships Black /25 #FPCTS
2010 Element Flagship Performers Championships Blue-Orange /25 #FPCTS
2010 Element Flagship Performers Championships Checkered /1 #FPCTS
2010 Element Flagship Performers Championships Green /5 #FPCTS
2010 Element Flagship Performers Championships Red /25 #FPCTS
2010 Element Flagship Performers Championships White /15 #FPCTS
2010 Element Flagship Performers Championships X /25 #FPCTS
2010 Element Flagship Performers Championships Yellow /25 #FPCTS
2010 Element Flagship Performers Consecutive Starts Black /20 #FPSTS
2010 Element Flagship Performers Consecutive Starts Blue-Orange /20 #FPSTS
2010 Element Flagship Performers Consecutive Starts Checkered /1 #FPSTS
2010 Element Flagship Performers Consecutive Starts Green /5 #FPSTS
2010 Element Flagship Performers Consecutive Starts Red /20 #FPSTS
2010 Element Flagship Performers Consecutive Starts White /10 #FPSTS
2010 Element Flagship Performers Consecutive Starts X /10 #FPSTS
2010 Element Flagship Performers Consecutive Starts Yellow /20 #FPSTS
2010 Element Flagship Performers Wins Black /20 #FPWTS
2010 Element Flagship Performers Wins Blue-Orange /20 #FPWTS
2010 Element Flagship Performers Wins Checkered /1 #FPWTS
2010 Element Flagship Performers Wins Green /5 #FPWTS
2010 Element Flagship Performers Wins Red /20 #FPWTS
2010 Element Flagship Performers Wins White /15 #FPWTS
2010 Element Flagship Performers Wins X /10 #FPWTS
2010 Element Flagship Performers Wins Yellow /20 #FPWTS
2010 Element Green #3
2010 Element Green #38
2010 Element Green #72
2010 Element Green #75
2010 Element Green #81
2010 Element Green #97
2010 Element Previews /5 #EB3
2010 Element Previews /1 #EB81
2010 Element Purple /25 #3
2010 Element Purple /25 #38
2010 Element Recycled Materials Blue /25 #RMTS
2010 Element Recycled Materials Green /125 #RMTS
2010 Element Red Target #3
2010 Element Red Target #38
2010 Element Red Target #72
2010 Element Red Target #75
2010 Element Red Target #81
2010 Element Red Target #97
2010 Press Pass #3
2010 Press Pass #110
2010 Press Pass #126
2010 Press Pass #1
2010 Press Pass #91
2010 Press Pass #98
2010 Press Pass #99
2010 Press Pass #100
2010 Press Pass #0
2010 Press Pass #93
2010 Press Pass Autographs Chase Edition /25 #11
2010 Press Pass Autographs Track Edition /10 #10
2010 Press Pass Blue #1
2010 Press Pass Blue #3
2010 Press Pass Blue #91
2010 Press Pass Blue #93
2010 Press Pass Blue #98
2010 Press Pass Blue #99
2010 Press Pass Blue #100
2010 Press Pass Blue #110
2010 Press Pass Blue #124
2010 Press Pass Burning Rubber /250 #BR11
2010 Press Pass Burning Rubber /250 #BR13
2010 Press Pass Burning Rubber /250 #BR25
2010 Press Pass Burning Rubber Gold /50 #BR11
2010 Press Pass Burning Rubber Gold /50 #BR13
2010 Press Pass Burning Rubber Gold /99 #BR25
2010 Press Pass Burning Rubber Prime Cuts /25 #BR13
2010 Press Pass Burning Rubber Prime Cuts /25 #BRD25
2010 Press Pass By The Numbers #BN11
2010 Press Pass By The Numbers #BN31
2010 Press Pass Cup Chase #CCR1
2010 Press Pass Cup Chase Prizes #CC6
2010 Press Pass Eclipse #26
2010 Press Pass Eclipse #32
2010 Press Pass Eclipse #64
2010 Press Pass Eclipse #73
2010 Press Pass Eclipse #84
2010 Press Pass Eclipse Blue #26
2010 Press Pass Eclipse Blue #32
2010 Press Pass Eclipse Blue #64
2010 Press Pass Eclipse Blue #73
2010 Press Pass Eclipse Blue #84
2010 Press Pass Eclipse Cars #C2
2010 Press Pass Eclipse Decade #D3
2010 Press Pass Eclipse Element Inserts #4
2010 Press Pass Eclipse Focus #F2
2010 Press Pass Eclipse Gold #26
2010 Press Pass Eclipse Gold #32
2010 Press Pass Eclipse Gold #64
2010 Press Pass Eclipse Gold #73
2010 Press Pass Eclipse Gold #84
2010 Press Pass Eclipse Previews /5 #26
2010 Press Pass Eclipse Previews /1 #32
2010 Press Pass Eclipse Purple /25 #26
2010 Press Pass Eclipse Purple /25 #32
2010 Press Pass Eclipse Purple /25 #64
2010 Press Pass Eclipse Signature Series Shoes Autographs /14 #SSSETS
2010 Press Pass Eclipse Spellbound Swatches /99 #SSTS2
2010 Press Pass Eclipse Spellbound Swatches /99 #SSTS3
2010 Press Pass Eclipse Spellbound Swatches /99 #SSTS4
2010 Press Pass Eclipse Spellbound Swatches /99 #SSTS5
2010 Press Pass Eclipse Spellbound Swatches /99 #SSTS6
2010 Press Pass Eclipse Spellbound Swatches /99 #SSTS7
2010 Press Pass Eclipse Spellbound Swatches /99 #SSTS1
2010 Press Pass Eclipse Spellbound Swatches Holofoil /14 #SSTS2
2010 Press Pass Eclipse Spellbound Swatches Holofoil /14 #SSTS3
2010 Press Pass Eclipse Spellbound Swatches Holofoil /14 #SSTS4
2010 Press Pass Eclipse Spellbound Swatches Holofoil /14 #SSTS5
2010 Press Pass Eclipse Spellbound Swatches Holofoil /14 #SSTS6
2010 Press Pass Eclipse Spellbound Swatches Holofoil /14 #SSTS7
2010 Press Pass Eclipse Spellbound Swatches Holofoil /14 #SSTS1
2010 Press Pass Final Standings /80 #FS6
2010 Press Pass Five Star /35 #9
2010 Press Pass Five Star Classic Compilations Combos Firesuit Autographs /15 #CCMTSDE
2010 Press Pass Five Star Classic Compilations Combos Patches Autographs /1 #CCMTSDE
2010 Press Pass Five Star Classic Compilations Dual Memorabilia Autographs /10 #TS
2010 Press Pass Five Star Classic Compilations Firesuit Autographs /15 #TS
2010 Press Pass Five Star Classic Compilations Patch Autographs /1 #CCPTS17
2010 Press Pass Five Star Classic Compilations Patch Autographs /1 #CCPTS1
2010 Press Pass Five Star Classic Compilations Patch Autographs /1 #CCPTS2
2010 Press Pass Five Star Classic Compilations Patch Autographs /1 #CCPTS3
2010 Press Pass Five Star Classic Compilations Patch Autographs /1 #CCPTS4
2010 Press Pass Five Star Classic Compilations Patch Autographs /1 #CCPTS5
2010 Press Pass Five Star Classic Compilations Patch Autographs /1 #CCPTS6
2010 Press Pass Five Star Classic Compilations Patch Autographs /1 #CCPTS7
2010 Press Pass Five Star Classic Compilations Patch Autographs /1 #CCPTS8
2010 Press Pass Five Star Classic Compilations Patch Autographs /1 #CCPTS9
2010 Press Pass Five Star Classic Compilations Patch Autographs /1 #CCPTS10
2010 Press Pass Five Star Classic Compilations Patch Autographs /1 #CCPTS11
2010 Press Pass Five Star Classic Compilations Patch Autographs /1 #CCPTS12
2010 Press Pass Five Star Classic Compilations Patch Autographs /1 #CCPTS13
2010 Press Pass Five Star Classic Compilations Patch Autographs /1 #CCPTS14
2010 Press Pass Five Star Classic Compilations Patch Autographs /1 #CCPTS15
2010 Press Pass Five Star Classic Compilations Patch Autographs /1 #CCPTS16
2010 Press Pass Five Star Classic Compilations Sheet Metal Autographs /25 #TS
2010 Press Pass Five Star Classic Compilations Triple Memorabilia Autographs /5 #TS
2010 Press Pass Five Star Holofoil /10 #9
2010 Press Pass Five Star Melting /1 #9
2010 Press Pass Five Star Paramount Pieces Aluminum /25 #TS
2010 Press Pass Five Star Paramount Pieces Blue /20 #TS
2010 Press Pass Five Star Paramount Pieces Gold /15 #TS
2010 Press Pass Five Star Paramount Pieces Holofoil /10 #TS
2010 Press Pass Five Star Paramount Pieces Melting /1 #TS
2010 Press Pass Five Star Signature Souvenirs Aluminum /50 #SSTS
2010 Press Pass Five Star Signature Souvenirs Gold /25 #SSTS
2010 Press Pass Five Star Signature Souvenirs Holofoil /10 #SSTS
2010 Press Pass Five Star Signature Souvenirs Melting /1 #SSTS
2010 Press Pass Five Star Signatures Aluminum /35 #TST
2010 Press Pass Five Star Signatures Gold /20 #TST
2010 Press Pass Five Star Signatures Holofoil /5 #TST
2010 Press Pass Five Star Signatures Melting /1 #TST
2010 Press Pass Four Wide Autographs /5 #NNO
2010 Press Pass Four Wide Firesuit /25 #FWTS
2010 Press Pass Four Wide Sheet Metal /15 #FWTS
2010 Press Pass Four Wide Shoes /1 #FWTS
2010 Press Pass Four Wide Tires /10 #FWTS
2010 Press Pass Gold #1
2010 Press Pass Gold #3
2010 Press Pass Gold #91
2010 Press Pass Gold #93
2010 Press Pass Gold #98
2010 Press Pass Gold #99
2010 Press Pass Gold #100
2010 Press Pass Gold #110
2010 Press Pass Gold #124
2010 Press Pass Holofoil /100 #1
2010 Press Pass Holofoil /100 #3
2010 Press Pass Holofoil /100 #91
2010 Press Pass Holofoil /100 #93
2010 Press Pass Holofoil /100 #98
2010 Press Pass Holofoil /100 #99
2010 Press Pass Holofoil /100 #100
2010 Press Pass Holofoil /100 #110
2010 Press Pass Holofoil /100 #124
2010 Press Pass Legends #54
2010 Press Pass Legends Autographs Blue /10 #50
2010 Press Pass Legends Autographs Holofoil /25 #50
2010 Press Pass Legends Autographs Printing Plates Black /1 #40
2010 Press Pass Legends Autographs Printing Plates Cyan /1 #40
2010 Press Pass Legends Autographs Printing Plates Magenta /1 #40
2010 Press Pass Legends Autographs Printing Plates Yellow /1 #40
2010 Press Pass Legends Blue /1 #54
2010 Press Pass Legends Gold /399 #54
2010 Press Pass Legends Holofoil /50 #54
2010 Press Pass Legends Legendary Links Gold /75 #LXTSMA
2010 Press Pass Legends Legendary Links Holofoil /25 #LXTSMA
2010 Press Pass Legends Motorsports Masters #MMTS
2010 Press Pass Legends Motorsports Masters Autographs Blue /1 #NNO
2010 Press Pass Legends Motorsports Masters Autographs Gold /25 #27
2010 Press Pass Legends Motorsports Masters Autographs Holofoil /10 #27
2010 Press Pass Legends Motorsports Masters Autographs Printing Plates Black /1 #40
2010 Press Pass Legends Motorsports Masters Autographs Printing Plates Cyan /1 #40
2010 Press Pass Legends Motorsports Masters Autographs Printing Plates Magenta /1 #40
2010 Press Pass Legends Motorsports Masters Autographs Printing Plates Yellow /1 #40
2010 Press Pass Legends Motorsports Masters Blue /10 #MMTS
2010 Press Pass Legends Motorsports Masters Gold /299 #MMTS
2010 Press Pass Legends Motorsports Masters Holofoil /149 #MMTS
2010 Press Pass Legends Printing Plates Black /1 #54
2010 Press Pass Legends Printing Plates Cyan /1 #54
2010 Press Pass Legends Printing Plates Magenta /1 #54
2010 Press Pass Legends Printing Plates Yellow /1 #54
2010 Press Pass Legends Prominent Pieces Copper /99 #PPTS
2010 Press Pass Legends Prominent Pieces Gold /50 #PPTS
2010 Press Pass Legends Prominent Pieces Holofoil /25 #PPTS
2010 Press Pass Legends Prominent Pieces Oversized Firesuit /25 #PPOETS
2010 Press Pass Legends Red /199 #54
2010 Press Pass Premium #2
2010 Press Pass Premium #41
2010 Press Pass Premium #50
2010 Press Pass Premium #55
2010 Press Pass Premium #70
2010 Press Pass Premium #76
2010 Press Pass Premium #83
2010 Press Pass Premium #92
2010 Press Pass Premium Allies #A2
2010 Press Pass Premium Allies #A7
2010 Press Pass Premium Allies #A9
2010 Press Pass Premium Allies Signatures /5 #ASSE
2010 Press Pass Premium Allies Signatures /5 #ASSN
2010 Press Pass Premium Hot Threads /299 #HTTS1
2010 Press Pass Premium Hot Threads /299 #HTTS2
2010 Press Pass Premium Hot Threads Holofoil /99 #HTTS1
2010 Press Pass Premium Hot Threads Holofoil /99 #HTTS2
2010 Press Pass Premium Hot Threads Multi Color /25 #HTTS1
2010 Press Pass Premium Hot Threads Multi Color /25 #HTTS2
2010 Press Pass Premium Hot Threads Patches /36 #HTPTS1
2010 Press Pass Premium Hot Threads Patches /35 #HTPTS2
2010 Press Pass Premium Hot Threads Two Color /125 #HTTS1
2010 Press Pass Premium Hot Threads Two Color /125 #HTTS2
2010 Press Pass Premium Iron On Patch #3
2010 Press Pass Premium Purple /25 #2
2010 Press Pass Premium Purple /25 #41
2010 Press Pass Premium Purple /25 #50
2010 Press Pass Premium Purple /25 #55
2010 Press Pass Premium Rivals #R3
2010 Press Pass Premium Rivals Signatures /5 #RSSM
2010 Press Pass Premium Signature Series Firesuit /10 #SSFTS2
2010 Press Pass Premium Signature Series Firesuit /10 #SSFTS1
2010 Press Pass Premium Signatures #PSTS
2010 Press Pass Premium Signatures Red Ink /50 #PSTS
2010 Press Pass Previews /5 #3
2010 Press Pass Previews /1 #110
2010 Press Pass Purple /25 #1
2010 Press Pass Purple /25 #3
2010 Press Pass Purple /25 #91
2010 Press Pass Purple /25 #93
2010 Press Pass Purple /25 #98
2010 Press Pass Purple /25 #99
2010 Press Pass Purple /25 #100
2010 Press Pass Purple /25 #110
2010 Press Pass Purple /25 #124
2010 Press Pass Showcase /499 #2
2010 Press Pass Showcase /499 #43
2010 Press Pass Showcase /499 #30
2010 Press Pass Showcase /499 #28
2010 Press Pass Showcase Classic Collections Firesuit Green /25 #CCIFAN
2010 Press Pass Showcase Classic Collections Firesuit Green /25 #CCIWIN
2010 Press Pass Showcase Classic Collections Firesuit Patch Melting /5 #CCIWIN
2010 Press Pass Showcase Classic Collections Firesuit Patch Melting /5 #CCIFAN
2010 Press Pass Showcase Classic Collections Ink /15 #CCIWIN
2010 Press Pass Showcase Classic Collections Ink /15 #CCIFAN
2010 Press Pass Showcase Classic Collections Ink Gold /10 #CCIWIN
2010 Press Pass Showcase Classic Collections Ink Gold /10 #CCIFAN
2010 Press Pass Showcase Classic Collections Ink Green /5 #CCIWIN
2010 Press Pass Showcase Classic Collections Ink Green /5 #CCIFAN
2010 Press Pass Showcase Classic Collections Ink Melting /1 #CCIWIN
2010 Press Pass Showcase Classic Collections Ink Melting /1 #CCIFAN
2010 Press Pass Showcase Classic Collections Sheet Metal /99 #CCIFAN
2010 Press Pass Showcase Classic Collections Sheet Metal /99 #CCIWIN
2010 Press Pass Showcase Classic Collections Sheet Metal Gold /45 #CCIWIN
2010 Press Pass Showcase Classic Collections Sheet Metal Gold /45 #CCIFAN
2010 Press Pass Showcase Elite Exhibit Ink /45 #EEITS
2010 Press Pass Showcase Elite Exhibit Ink Gold /25 #EEITS
2010 Press Pass Showcase Elite Exhibit Ink Green /5 #EEITS
2010 Press Pass Showcase Elite Exhibit Ink Melting /1 #EEITS
2010 Press Pass Showcase Elite Exhibit Triple Memorabilia /99 #EEMTS
2010 Press Pass Showcase Elite Exhibit Triple Memorabilia Gold /45 #EEMTS
2010 Press Pass Showcase Elite Exhibit Triple Memorabilia Green /25 #EEMTS
2010 Press Pass Showcase Elite Exhibit Triple Memorabilia Melting /5 #EEMTS
2010 Press Pass Showcase Gold /125 #2
2010 Press Pass Showcase Gold /125 #28
2010 Press Pass Showcase Gold /125 #30
2010 Press Pass Showcase Gold /125 #43
2010 Press Pass Showcase Green /50 #2
2010 Press Pass Showcase Green /50 #28
2010 Press Pass Showcase Green /50 #30
2010 Press Pass Showcase Green /50 #43
2010 Press Pass Showcase Melting /15 #2
2010 Press Pass Showcase Melting /15 #28
2010 Press Pass Showcase Melting /15 #30
2010 Press Pass Showcase Melting /15 #43
2010 Press Pass Showcase Platinum Holo /1 #2
2010 Press Pass Showcase Platinum Holo /1 #28
2010 Press Pass Showcase Platinum Holo /1 #30
2010 Press Pass Showcase Platinum Holo /1 #43
2010 Press Pass Showcase Prized Pieces Firesuit Green /25 #PPMTS
2010 Press Pass Showcase Prized Pieces Firesuit Ink Gold /25 #PPITS
2010 Press Pass Showcase Prized Pieces Firesuit Ink Melting /1 #PPITS
2010 Press Pass Showcase Prized Pieces Firesuit Patch Melting /5 #PPMTS
2010 Press Pass Showcase Prized Pieces Memorabilia Ink Green /15 #PPITS
2010 Press Pass Showcase Prized Pieces Sheet Metal /99 #PPMTS
2010 Press Pass Showcase Prized Pieces Sheet Metal Gold /45 #PPMTS
2010 Press Pass Showcase Prized Pieces Sheet Metal Ink Silver /45 #PPITS
2010 Press Pass Showcase Racing's Finest /499 #RF11
2010 Press Pass Showcase Racing's Finest Gold /125 #RF11
2010 Press Pass Showcase Racing's Finest Green /50 #RF11
2010 Press Pass Showcase Racing's Finest Melting /15 #RF11
2010 Press Pass Signings Blue /10 #53
2010 Press Pass Signings Gold /50 #53
2010 Press Pass Signings Red /15 #53
2010 Press Pass Signings Silver /20 #52
2010 Press Pass Stealth #66
2010 Press Pass Stealth #33
2010 Press Pass Stealth Battle Armor Fast Pass /25 #BATS1
2010 Press Pass Stealth Battle Armor Fast Pass /25 #BATS2
2010 Press Pass Stealth Battle Armor Holofoil /25 #BATS1
2010 Press Pass Stealth Battle Armor Holofoil /25 #BATS2
2010 Press Pass Stealth Battle Armor Silver /225 #BATS1
2010 Press Pass Stealth Battle Armor Silver /225 #BATS2
2010 Press Pass Stealth Black and White #33
2010 Press Pass Stealth Black and White #66
2010 Press Pass Stealth Mach 10 #MT1
2010 Press Pass Stealth National Convention #VIP3
2010 Press Pass Stealth Previews /5 #33
2010 Press Pass Stealth Previews /1 #66
2010 Press Pass Stealth Purple /25 #33
2010 Press Pass Stealth Purple /25 #66
2010 Press Pass Stealth Signature Series Sheet Metal /15 #SSMETS
2010 Press Pass Stealth Weekend Warriors Holofoil /25 #WWTS
2010 Press Pass Stealth Weekend Warriors Silver /199 #WWTS
2010 Press Pass Target By The Numbers #BNT5
2010 Press Pass Top 12 Tires /14 #TS
2010 Press Pass Top 12 Tires 10 /10 #TS
2010 Press Pass Tradin' Paint #TP4
2010 Press Pass Tradin' Paint Sheet Metal /299 #TPTS
2010 Press Pass Tradin' Paint Sheet Metal Gold /50 #TPTS
2010 Press Pass Tradin' Paint Sheet Metal Holofoil /25 #TPTS
2010 Press Pass Unleashed #U7
2010 Press Pass Wal-Mart By The Numbers #BNW5
2010 Wheels Autographs #48
2010 Wheels Autographs Printing Plates Black /1 #48
2010 Wheels Autographs Printing Plates Cyan /1 #48
2010 Wheels Autographs Printing Plates Magenta /1 #48
2010 Wheels Autographs Printing Plates Yellow /1 #48
2010 Wheels Autographs Special Ink /10 #14
2010 Wheels Autographs Target /10 #34
2010 Wheels Main Event #33
2010 Wheels Main Event #43
2010 Wheels Main Event #49
2010 Wheels Main Event #62
2010 Wheels Main Event #93
2010 Wheels Main Event American Muscle #AM3
2010 Wheels Main Event Blue #33
2010 Wheels Main Event Blue #43
2010 Wheels Main Event Blue #49
2010 Wheels Main Event Blue #62
2010 Wheels Main Event Blue #93
2010 Wheels Main Event Fight Card #FC24
2010 Wheels Main Event Fight Card Checkered Flag #FC24
2010 Wheels Main Event Fight Card Full Color Retail #FC24
2010 Wheels Main Event Fight Card Gold /25 #FC24
2010 Wheels Main Event Head to Head /150 #HHTSRN
2010 Wheels Main Event Head to Head /150 #HHTSDE
2010 Wheels Main Event Head to Head Blue /75 #HHTSDE
2010 Wheels Main Event Head to Head Blue /75 #HHTSRN
2010 Wheels Main Event Head to Head Holofoil /10 #HHTSDE
2010 Wheels Main Event Head to Head Holofoil /10 #HHTSRN
2010 Wheels Main Event Head to Head Red /25 #HHTSDE
2010 Wheels Main Event Head to Head Red /25 #HHTSRN
2010 Wheels Main Event Marks Autographs /29 #55
2010 Wheels Main Event Marks Autographs Black /1 #54
2010 Wheels Main Event Marks Autographs Blue /15 #55
2010 Wheels Main Event Marks Autographs Red /5 #55
2010 Wheels Main Event Purple /25 #33
2010 Wheels Main Event Purple /25 #43
2010 Wheels Main Event Purple /25 #49

2010 Wheels Main Event Tale of the Tape #TT7
2010 Wheels Main Event Toe to Toe /10 #TTTSRN
2010 Wheels Main Event Upper Cuts /150 #UCTS
2010 Wheels Main Event Upper Cuts Blue /75 #UCTS
2010 Wheels Main Event Upper Cuts Holofoil /10 #UCTS
2010 Wheels Main Event Upper Cuts Knock Out Patches /25 #UCKOTS
2010 Wheels Main Event Upper Cuts Red /25 #UCTS
2010 Wheels Main Event Wheel to Wheel /25 #WWDETS
2010 Wheels Main Event Wheel to Wheel /25 #WWTSRN
2010 Wheels Main Event Wheel to Wheel Holofoil /10 #WWTSRN
2010 Wheels Main Event Wheel to Wheel Holofoil /10 #WWDETS
2011 Element #31
2011 Element #40
2011 Element #78
2011 Element #86
2011 Element Autographs /25 #53
2011 Element Autographs Blue /5 #53
2011 Element Autographs Gold /5 #51
2011 Element Autographs Printing Plates Black /1 #53
2011 Element Autographs Printing Plates Cyan /1 #53
2011 Element Autographs Printing Plates Magenta /1 #53
2011 Element Autographs Printing Plates Yellow /1 #53
2011 Element Autographs Silver /15 #51
2011 Element Black /35 #31
2011 Element Black /35 #40
2011 Element Black /35 #78
2011 Element Black /35 #86
2011 Element Finish Line Checkered Flag /10 #FLTS
2011 Element Finish Line Green Flag /25 #FLTS
2011 Element Finish Line Tires /99 #FLTS
2011 Element Finish Line Tires Purple Fast Pass /30 #FLTS
2011 Element Flagship Performers 2010 Laps Completed Yellow /50 #FPLTS
2011 Element Flagship Performers Career Wins White /50 #FPWTS
2011 Element Flagship Performers Championships Checkered /25 #FPCTS
2011 Element Flagship Performers Race Streak Without DNF Red /50 #FPDTS
2011 Element Flagstand Swatches /25 #FSSTS
2011 Element Green #31
2011 Element Green #40
2011 Element Green #78
2011 Element Green #86
2011 Element Previews /5 #EB31
2011 Element Purple /25 #31
2011 Element Purple /25 #40
2011 Element Purple /25 #78
2011 Element Purple /25 #86
2011 Element Red #31
2011 Element Red #40
2011 Element Red #78
2011 Element Red #86
2011 Press Pass #34
2011 Press Pass #89
2011 Press Pass #112
2011 Press Pass #153
2011 Press Pass #186
2011 Press Pass #194
2011 Press Pass #123
2011 Press Pass #132
2011 Press Pass #0
2011 Press Pass Autographs Blue /5 #53
2011 Press Pass Autographs Bronze /20 #54
2011 Press Pass Autographs Gold /5 #51
2011 Press Pass Autographs Printing Plates Black /1 #54
2011 Press Pass Autographs Printing Plates Cyan /1 #54
2011 Press Pass Autographs Printing Plates Magenta /1 #54
2011 Press Pass Autographs Printing Plates Yellow /1 #54
2011 Press Pass Autographs Silver /10 #54
2011 Press Pass Blue Holofoil /10 #34
2011 Press Pass Blue Holofoil /10 #89
2011 Press Pass Blue Holofoil /10 #112
2011 Press Pass Blue Holofoil /10 #123
2011 Press Pass Blue Holofoil /10 #132
2011 Press Pass Blue Holofoil /10 #153
2011 Press Pass Blue Holofoil /10 #186
2011 Press Pass Blue Holofoil /10 #194
2011 Press Pass Blue Retail #34
2011 Press Pass Blue Retail #89
2011 Press Pass Blue Retail #112
2011 Press Pass Blue Retail #123
2011 Press Pass Blue Retail #132
2011 Press Pass Blue Retail #153
2011 Press Pass Blue Retail #186
2011 Press Pass Blue Retail #194
2011 Press Pass Burning Rubber Fast Pass /10 #BRTS
2011 Press Pass Burning Rubber Gold /150 #BRTS
2011 Press Pass Burning Rubber Gold /150 #BRCTS
2011 Press Pass Burning Rubber Holofoil /50 #BRTS
2011 Press Pass Burning Rubber Holofoil /50 #BRCTS
2011 Press Pass Burning Rubber Prime Cuts /25 #BRCTS
2011 Press Pass Cup Chase #CCR6
2011 Press Pass Cup Chase Prizes #CC9
2011 Press Pass Cup Chase Prizes #CCP
2011 Press Pass Eclipse #29
2011 Press Pass Eclipse #38
2011 Press Pass Eclipse #59
2011 Press Pass Eclipse #61
2011 Press Pass Eclipse #75
2011 Press Pass Eclipse Blue #29
2011 Press Pass Eclipse Blue #38
2011 Press Pass Eclipse Blue #59
2011 Press Pass Eclipse Blue #61
2011 Press Pass Eclipse Blue #75
2011 Press Pass Eclipse Encore #E3
2011 Press Pass Eclipse Gold /55 #29
2011 Press Pass Eclipse Gold /55 #38
2011 Press Pass Eclipse Gold /55 #59
2011 Press Pass Eclipse Gold /55 #61
2011 Press Pass Eclipse Gold /55 #75
2011 Press Pass Eclipse In Focus #IF3
2011 Press Pass Eclipse Previews /5 #EB29
2011 Press Pass Eclipse Previews /1 #EB38
2011 Press Pass Eclipse Purple /25 #29
2011 Press Pass Eclipse Purple /25 #38
2011 Press Pass Eclipse Purple /25 #59
2011 Press Pass Eclipse Purple /25 #61
2011 Press Pass Eclipse Spellbound Swatches /150 #SBTS2
2011 Press Pass Eclipse Spellbound Swatches /150 #SBTS3
2011 Press Pass Eclipse Spellbound Swatches /200 #SBTS1
2011 Press Pass Eclipse Spellbound Swatches /100 #SBTS5
2011 Press Pass Eclipse Spellbound Swatches /100 #SBTS4
2011 Press Pass Eclipse Spellbound Swatches /75 #SBTS6
2011 Press Pass Eclipse Spellbound Swatches /50 #SBTS7
2011 Press Pass Eclipse Spellbound Swatches Signatures /10 #NNO
2011 Press Pass FanFare #35
2011 Press Pass FanFare Autographs Blue /5 #71
2011 Press Pass FanFare Autographs Bronze /35 #71
2011 Press Pass FanFare Autographs Gold /15 #71
2011 Press Pass FanFare Autographs Printing Plates Black /1 #71
2011 Press Pass FanFare Autographs Printing Plates Cyan /1 #71
2011 Press Pass FanFare Autographs Printing Plates Magenta /1 #71
2011 Press Pass FanFare Autographs Printing Plates Yellow /1 #71
2011 Press Pass FanFare Autographs Silver /10 #71
2011 Press Pass FanFare Blue Die Cuts #35
2011 Press Pass FanFare Championship Caliber #CC2
2011 Press Pass FanFare Emerald /25 #35
2011 Press Pass FanFare Holofoil Die Cuts #35
2011 Press Pass FanFare Magnificent Materials /199 #MMTS
2011 Press Pass FanFare Magnificent Materials Dual Swatches /50 #MMDTS
2011 Press Pass FanFare Magnificent Materials Dual Swatches Holofoil /10 #MMDTS
2011 Press Pass FanFare Magnificent Materials Holofoil /50 #MMTS
2011 Press Pass FanFare Magnificent Materials Signatures /25 #MMSETS
2011 Press Pass FanFare Magnificent Materials Signatures Holofoil /10 #MMSETS
2011 Press Pass FanFare Rookie Standouts #RS11
2011 Press Pass FanFare Ruby Die Cuts /15 #35
2011 Press Pass FanFare Sapphire /10 #35
2011 Press Pass FanFare Silver /25 #35
2011 Press Pass Flashback #FB9
2011 Press Pass Four Wide Firesuit /25 #FWTS
2011 Press Pass Four Wide Glove /1 #FWTS
2011 Press Pass Four Wide Sheet Metal /15 #FWTS
2011 Press Pass Four Wide Tire /10 #FWTS
2011 Press Pass Geared Up Gold /100 #GUTS
2011 Press Pass Geared Up Holofoil /50 #GUTS
2011 Press Pass Gold /50 #34
2011 Press Pass Gold /50 #89
2011 Press Pass Gold /50 #112
2011 Press Pass Gold /50 #123
2011 Press Pass Gold /50 #132
2011 Press Pass Gold /50 #153
2011 Press Pass Gold /50 #186
2011 Press Pass Gold /50 #194
2011 Press Pass Legends #50
2011 Press Pass Legends Autographs Blue /5 #LGATS
2011 Press Pass Legends Autographs Gold /25 #LGATS
2011 Press Pass Legends Autographs Printing Plates Black /1 #LGATS
2011 Press Pass Legends Autographs Printing Plates Cyan /1 #LGATS
2011 Press Pass Legends Autographs Printing Plates Magenta /1 #LGATS
2011 Press Pass Legends Autographs Printing Plates Yellow /1 #LGATS
2011 Press Pass Legends Gold /250 #50
2011 Press Pass Legends Holofoil /25 #50
2011 Press Pass Legends Motorsports Masters #MM20
2011 Press Pass Legends Motorsports Masters Brushed Foil /199 #MM20
2011 Press Pass Legends Motorsports Masters Holofoil /50 #MM20
2011 Press Pass Legends Pacing The Field #PF9
2011 Press Pass Legends Pacing The Field Autographs Silver /25 #PFATS
2011 Press Pass Legends Pacing The Field Brushed Foil /199 #PF9
2011 Press Pass Legends Pacing The Field Holofoil /50 #PF9
2011 Press Pass Legends Printing Plates Black /1 #50
2011 Press Pass Legends Printing Plates Cyan /1 #50
2011 Press Pass Legends Printing Plates Magenta /1 #50
2011 Press Pass Legends Printing Plates Yellow /1 #50
2011 Press Pass Legends Prominent Pieces Gold /50 #PPTS
2011 Press Pass Legends Prominent Pieces Holofoil /25 #PPTS
2011 Press Pass Legends Prominent Pieces Oversized Firesuit /25 #PPOETS
2011 Press Pass Legends Prominent Pieces Purple /15 #PPTS
2011 Press Pass Legends Prominent Pieces Silver /99 #PPTS
2011 Press Pass Legends Purple /25 #50
2011 Press Pass Legends Red /99 #50
2011 Press Pass Legends Solo /1 #50
2011 Press Pass Premium #42
2011 Press Pass Premium #66
2011 Press Pass Premium #84
2011 Press Pass Premium #33A
2011 Press Pass Premium #33B
2011 Press Pass Premium Crystal Ball #CB7
2011 Press Pass Premium Crystal Ball Autographs /10 #CBATS
2011 Press Pass Premium Double Burner /25 #DBTS
2011 Press Pass Premium Hot Pursuit 3D #HP8
2011 Press Pass Premium Hot Pursuit Autographs /10 #HPATS
2011 Press Pass Premium Hot Pursuit National Convention #HP8
2011 Press Pass Premium Hot Threads /150 #HTTS
2011 Press Pass Premium Hot Threads Fast Pass /25 #HTTS
2011 Press Pass Premium Hot Threads Multi Color /25 #HTTS
2011 Press Pass Premium Hot Threads Patches /10 #HTPTS
2011 Press Pass Premium Hot Threads Secondary Color /99 #HTTS
2011 Press Pass Premium Purple /25 #33
2011 Press Pass Premium Purple /25 #42
2011 Press Pass Premium Purple /25 #66
2011 Press Pass Premium Purple /25 #84
2011 Press Pass Premium Signatures /36 #PSTS
2011 Press Pass Premium Signatures Red Ink /30 #PSTS
2011 Press Pass Previews /5 #EB34
2011 Press Pass Previews /1 #EB194
2011 Press Pass Purple /25 #34
2011 Press Pass Purple /25 #194
2011 Press Pass Showcase /499 #4
2011 Press Pass Showcase /499 #35
2011 Press Pass Showcase /499 #47
2011 Press Pass Showcase /499 #59
2011 Press Pass Showcase Champions /499 #CH3
2011 Press Pass Showcase Champions Gold /125 #CH3
2011 Press Pass Showcase Champions Ink /25 #CHITS
2011 Press Pass Showcase Champions Ink Gold /10 #CHITS
2011 Press Pass Showcase Champions Ink Melting /1 #CHITS
2011 Press Pass Showcase Champions Melting /1 #CH3
2011 Press Pass Showcase Champions Memorabilia Firesuit /99 #CHMTS
2011 Press Pass Showcase Champions Memorabilia Firesuit Gold /45 #CHMTS
2011 Press Pass Showcase Champions Memorabilia Firesuit Melting /5 #CHMTS
2011 Press Pass Showcase Classic Collections Firesuit /45 #CCMSHR
2011 Press Pass Showcase Classic Collections Firesuit Patches /5 #CCMSHR
2011 Press Pass Showcase Classic Collections Ink /25 #CCMSHR
2011 Press Pass Showcase Classic Collections Ink Gold /5 #CCMSHR
2011 Press Pass Showcase Classic Collections Ink Melting /1 #CCMSHR
2011 Press Pass Showcase Classic Collections Sheet Metal /99 #CCMSHR
2011 Press Pass Showcase Elite Exhibit Ink /50 #EEITS
2011 Press Pass Showcase Elite Exhibit Ink Gold /25 #EEITS
2011 Press Pass Showcase Elite Exhibit Ink Melting /1 #EEITS
2011 Press Pass Showcase Gold /125 #4
2011 Press Pass Showcase Gold /125 #35
2011 Press Pass Showcase Gold /125 #47
2011 Press Pass Showcase Gold /125 #59
2011 Press Pass Showcase Green /25 #4
2011 Press Pass Showcase Green /25 #35
2011 Press Pass Showcase Green /25 #47
2011 Press Pass Showcase Green /25 #59
2011 Press Pass Showcase Masterpieces Ink /45 #MPITS
2011 Press Pass Showcase Masterpieces Ink Gold /25 #MPITS
2011 Press Pass Showcase Masterpieces Ink Melting /1 #MPITS
2011 Press Pass Showcase Masterpieces Memorabilia /99 #MPMTS
2011 Press Pass Showcase Masterpieces Memorabilia Gold /45 #MPMTS
2011 Press Pass Showcase Masterpieces Memorabilia Melting /5 #MPMTS
2011 Press Pass Showcase Melting /1 #4
2011 Press Pass Showcase Melting /1 #35
2011 Press Pass Showcase Melting /1 #47
2011 Press Pass Showcase Melting /1 #59
2011 Press Pass Showcase Prized Pieces Firesuit /99 #PPMTS
2011 Press Pass Showcase Prized Pieces Firesuit Gold /45 #PPMTS
2011 Press Pass Showcase Prized Pieces Firesuit Ink /25 #PPITS
2011 Press Pass Showcase Prized Pieces Firesuit Patches Ink /1 #PPITS
2011 Press Pass Showcase Prized Pieces Firesuit Patches Melting /5 #PPMTS
2011 Press Pass Showcase Prized Pieces Sheet Metal Ink /45 #PPITS
2011 Press Pass Showcase Showroom /499 #SR5
2011 Press Pass Showcase Showroom Gold /125 #SR5
2011 Press Pass Showcase Showroom Melting /1 #SR5
2011 Press Pass Showcase Showroom Memorabilia Sheet Metal /45 #SRMTS
2011 Press Pass Showcase Showroom Memorabilia Sheet Metal Gold /25 #SRMTS
2011 Press Pass Showcase Showroom Memorabilia Sheet Metal Melting /5 #SRMTS
2011 Press Pass Signature Series /11 #SSTST
2011 Press Pass Signature Series /11 #SSBTS
2011 Press Pass Signature Series /11 #SSFTS
2011 Press Pass Signature Series /11 #SSMTS
2011 Press Pass Signings Black and White /5 #PPSTS
2011 Press Pass Signings Brushed Metal /25 #PPSTS
2011 Press Pass Signings Holofoil /10 #PPSTS
2011 Press Pass Signings Printing Plates Black /1 #PPSTS
2011 Press Pass Signings Printing Plates Cyan /1 #PPSTS
2011 Press Pass Signings Printing Plates Magenta /1 #PPSTS
2011 Press Pass Signings Printing Plates Yellow /1 #PPSTS
2011 Press Pass Stealth #10
2011 Press Pass Stealth #11
2011 Press Pass Stealth #12
2011 Press Pass Stealth #86
2011 Press Pass Stealth #94
2011 Press Pass Stealth #89
2011 Press Pass Stealth Afterburner /99 #ABTS
2011 Press Pass Stealth Afterburner Gold /25 #ABTS
2011 Press Pass Stealth Black and White /25 #10
2011 Press Pass Stealth Black and White /25 #11
2011 Press Pass Stealth Black and White /25 #12
2011 Press Pass Stealth Black and White /25 #86
2011 Press Pass Stealth Black and White /25 #89
2011 Press Pass Stealth Black and White /25 #94
2011 Press Pass Stealth Holofoil /99 #10
2011 Press Pass Stealth Holofoil /99 #11
2011 Press Pass Stealth Holofoil /99 #12
2011 Press Pass Stealth Holofoil /99 #86
2011 Press Pass Stealth Holofoil /99 #89
2011 Press Pass Stealth Holofoil /99 #94
2011 Press Pass Stealth Metal of Honor Medal of Honor /50 #BATS
2011 Press Pass Stealth Metal of Honor Purple Heart /25 #MHTS
2011 Press Pass Stealth Metal of Honor Silver Star /99 #BATS
2011 Press Pass Stealth Purple /25 #10
2011 Press Pass Stealth Purple /25 #11
2011 Press Pass Stealth Purple /25 #12
2011 Press Pass Stealth Supersonic #SS2
2011 Press Pass Tradin' Paint #TP8
2011 Press Pass Tradin' Paint Sheet Metal Blue /25 #TPTS
2011 Press Pass Tradin' Paint Sheet Metal Holofoil /50 #TPTS
2011 Press Pass Wal-Mart Top 12 Tires /25 #T12TS
2011 Press Pass Winning Tickets #WT25
2011 Wheels Main Event #33
2011 Wheels Main Event #73
2011 Wheels Main Event #81
2011 Wheels Main Event All Stars #A4
2011 Wheels Main Event All Stars Brushed Foil /199 #A4
2011 Wheels Main Event All Stars Holofoil /50 #A4
2011 Wheels Main Event Black and White #33
2011 Wheels Main Event Black and White #73
2011 Wheels Main Event Black and White #81
2011 Wheels Main Event Blue /75 #33
2011 Wheels Main Event Blue /75 #73
2011 Wheels Main Event Blue /75 #81
2011 Wheels Main Event Green /1 #33
2011 Wheels Main Event Green /1 #73
2011 Wheels Main Event Green /1 #81
2011 Wheels Main Event Headliners Holofoil /25 #HLTS
2011 Wheels Main Event Headliners Silver /99 #HLTS
2011 Wheels Main Event Joe Gibbs Racing 20th Anniversary #JGR3
2011 Wheels Main Event Joe Gibbs Racing 20th Anniversary Brushed Foil /199 #JGR3
2011 Wheels Main Event Joe Gibbs Racing 20th Anniversary Holofoil /50 #JGR3
2011 Wheels Main Event Marks Autographs Blue /10 #METS
2011 Wheels Main Event Marks Autographs Gold /25 #METS
2011 Wheels Main Event Marks Autographs Silver /50 #METS
2011 Wheels Main Event Rear View #R4
2011 Wheels Main Event Rear View Brushed Foil /199 #R4
2011 Wheels Main Event Rear View Holofoil /50 #R4
2011 Wheels Main Event Red /20 #33
2011 Wheels Main Event Red /20 #73
2011 Wheels Main Event Red /20 #81
2012 Press Pass #33
2012 Press Pass Autographs Blue /10 #PPATS
2012 Press Pass Autographs Printing Plates Black /1 #PPATS
2012 Press Pass Autographs Printing Plates Cyan /1 #PPATS
2012 Press Pass Autographs Printing Plates Magenta /1 #PPATS
2012 Press Pass Autographs Printing Plates Yellow /1 #PPATS
2012 Press Pass Autographs Red /25 #PPATS
2012 Press Pass Autographs Silver /75 #PPATS
2012 Press Pass Blue #33
2012 Press Pass Blue Holofoil /35 #33
2012 Press Pass Cup Chase #CCR6
2012 Press Pass Cup Chase Prizes #CCP3
2012 Press Pass Fanfare #39
2012 Press Pass Fanfare #40
2012 Press Pass Fanfare Autographs Blue /1 #TS
2012 Press Pass Fanfare Autographs Gold /5 #TS
2012 Press Pass Fanfare Autographs Red /1 #TS
2012 Press Pass Fanfare Autographs Silver /10 #TS
2012 Press Pass Fanfare Blue Foil Die Cuts #39
2012 Press Pass Fanfare Blue Foil Die Cuts #40
2012 Press Pass Fanfare Diamond /5 #39
2012 Press Pass Fanfare Diamond /5 #40
2012 Press Pass Fanfare Holofoil Die Cuts #39
2012 Press Pass Fanfare Holofoil Die Cuts #40
2012 Press Pass Fanfare Magnificent Materials /250 #MMTS
2012 Press Pass Fanfare Magnificent Materials /250 #MMTS2
2012 Press Pass Fanfare Magnificent Materials Dual Swatches /50 #MMTS
2012 Press Pass Fanfare Magnificent Materials Dual Swatches /50 #MMTS2
2012 Press Pass Fanfare Magnificent Materials Dual Swatches Melting /10 #MMTS
2012 Press Pass Fanfare Magnificent Materials Dual Swatches Melting /10 #MMTS2
2012 Press Pass Fanfare Magnificent Materials Gold /99 #MMTS
2012 Press Pass Fanfare Magnificent Materials Gold /99 #MMTS2
2012 Press Pass Fanfare Magnificent Materials Signatures /25 #TS
2012 Press Pass Fanfare Magnificent Materials Signatures Blue /5 #TS
2012 Press Pass Fanfare Power Rankings #PR11
2012 Press Pass Fanfare Sapphire /20 #39
2012 Press Pass Fanfare Sapphire /20 #40
2012 Press Pass Fanfare Showtime #S5
2012 Press Pass Fanfare Silver /25 #39
2012 Press Pass Fanfare Silver /25 #40
2012 Press Pass Four Wide Autographs /5 #TS
2012 Press Pass Four Wide Firesuit /25 #FWTS
2012 Press Pass Four Wide Glove /1 #FWTS
2012 Press Pass Four Wide Sheet Metal /15 #FWTS
2012 Press Pass Four Wide Tire /10 #FWTS
2012 Press Pass Gold #33
2012 Press Pass Ignite #33
2012 Press Pass Ignite #60
2012 Press Pass Ignite Double Burner Gun Metal /10 #DBTS
2012 Press Pass Ignite Double Burner Red /1 #DBTS
2012 Press Pass Ignite Double Burner Silver /25 #DBTS
2012 Press Pass Ignite Limelight #L2
2012 Press Pass Ignite Materials Autographs Gun Metal /20 #IMTS
2012 Press Pass Ignite Materials Autographs Red /5 #IMTS
2012 Press Pass Ignite Materials Autographs Silver /75 #IMTS
2012 Press Pass Ignite Materials Gun Metal /99 #IMTS1
2012 Press Pass Ignite Materials Gun Metal /99 #IMTS2
2012 Press Pass Ignite Materials Red /10 #IMTS1
2012 Press Pass Ignite Materials Red /10 #IMTS2
2012 Press Pass Ignite Materials Silver #IMTS1
2012 Press Pass Ignite Materials Silver #IMTS2
2012 Press Pass Ignite Profile #P9
2012 Press Pass Ignite Proofs Black and White /50 #33
2012 Press Pass Ignite Proofs Black and White /50 #60
2012 Press Pass Ignite Proofs Cyan #33
2012 Press Pass Ignite Proofs Cyan #60
2012 Press Pass Ignite Proofs Magenta #33
2012 Press Pass Ignite Proofs Magenta #60
2012 Press Pass Ignite Proofs Yellow /10 #33
2012 Press Pass Ignite Proofs Yellow /10 #60
2012 Press Pass Ignite Steel Horses #SH4
2012 Press Pass Ignite Supercharged Signatures /5 #SSTS
2012 Press Pass Legends #50
2012 Press Pass Legends Blue Holofoil /1 #50
2012 Press Pass Legends Gold /275 #50
2012 Press Pass Legends Green #50
2012 Press Pass Legends Prominent Pieces Gold /50 #TS
2012 Press Pass Legends Prominent Pieces Holofoil /25 #TS
2012 Press Pass Legends Prominent Pieces Oversized Firesuit /25 #TS
2012 Press Pass Legends Prominent Pieces Silver /99 #TS
2012 Press Pass Legends Rainbow Holofoil /50 #50
2012 Press Pass Legends Red /99 #50
2012 Press Pass Legends Silver Holofoil /25 #50
2012 Press Pass Legends Trailblazers #TB11
2012 Press Pass Legends Trailblazers Holofoil /99 #TB11
2012 Press Pass Legends Trailblazers Melting /10 #TB11
2012 Press Pass Power Picks Blue /50 #15
2012 Press Pass Power Picks Blue /50 #49
2012 Press Pass Power Picks Blue /50 #59
2012 Press Pass Power Picks Gold /50 #15
2012 Press Pass Power Picks Gold /50 #49
2012 Press Pass Power Picks Gold /50 #59
2012 Press Pass Power Picks Holofoil /10 #15
2012 Press Pass Power Picks Holofoil /10 #49
2012 Press Pass Power Picks Holofoil /10 #59
2012 Press Pass Preferred Line #PL7
2012 Press Pass Purple /35 #33
2012 Press Pass Redline #35
2012 Press Pass Redline Black /99 #35
2012 Press Pass Redline Cyan /50 #35
2012 Press Pass Redline Full Throttle Dual Relic Blue /5 #FTTS
2012 Press Pass Redline Full Throttle Dual Relic Gold /10 #FTTS
2012 Press Pass Redline Full Throttle Dual Relic Melting /1 #FTTS
2012 Press Pass Redline Full Throttle Dual Relic Red /75 #FTTS
2012 Press Pass Redline Full Throttle Dual Relic Silver /25 #FTTS
2012 Press Pass Redline Intensity #I9
2012 Press Pass Redline Magenta /15 #35
2012 Press Pass Redline Muscle Car Sheet Metal Blue /5 #MCTS1
2012 Press Pass Redline Muscle Car Sheet Metal Blue /5 #MCTS2
2012 Press Pass Redline Muscle Car Sheet Metal Gold /10 #MCTS1
2012 Press Pass Redline Muscle Car Sheet Metal Gold /10 #MCTS2
2012 Press Pass Redline Muscle Car Sheet Metal Melting /1 #MCTS1
2012 Press Pass Redline Muscle Car Sheet Metal Melting /1 #MCTS2
2012 Press Pass Redline Muscle Car Sheet Metal Red /75 #MCTS1
2012 Press Pass Redline Muscle Car Sheet Metal Red /75 #MCTS2
2012 Press Pass Redline Muscle Car Sheet Metal Silver /25 #MCTS1
2012 Press Pass Redline Muscle Car Sheet Metal Silver /25 #MCTS2
2012 Press Pass Redline Performance Driven #PD9
2012 Press Pass Redline Pieces of the Action Blue /10 #PATS
2012 Press Pass Redline Pieces of the Action Gold /25 #PATS
2012 Press Pass Redline Pieces of the Action Melting /1 #PATS
2012 Press Pass Redline Pieces of the Action Red /75 #PATS
2012 Press Pass Redline Pieces of the Action Silver /50 #PATS
2012 Press Pass Redline Relic Autographs Blue /10 #RLRTS
2012 Press Pass Redline Relic Autographs Gold /25 #RLRTS
2012 Press Pass Redline Relic Autographs Melting /1 #RLRTS
2012 Press Pass Redline Relic Autographs Red /75 #RLRTS
2012 Press Pass Redline Relic Autographs Silver /50 #RLRTS
2012 Press Pass Redline Relics Blue /5 #RLTS
2012 Press Pass Redline Relics Gold /10 #RLTS
2012 Press Pass Redline Relics Melting /1 #RLTS
2012 Press Pass Redline Relics Red /75 #RLTS
2012 Press Pass Redline Relics Silver /25 #RLTS
2012 Press Pass Redline Rookie Year Relic Autographs Blue /5 #RYTS
2012 Press Pass Redline Rookie Year Relic Autographs Gold /25 #RYTS
2012 Press Pass Redline Rookie Year Relic Autographs Melting /1 #RYTS
2012 Press Pass Redline Rookie Year Relic Autographs Red /50 #RYTS
2012 Press Pass Redline RPM #RPM12
2012 Press Pass Redline Signatures Blue /5 #RSTS1
2012 Press Pass Redline Signatures Blue /5 #RSTS2
2012 Press Pass Redline Signatures Gold /25 #RSTS1
2012 Press Pass Redline Signatures Gold /15 #RSTS2
2012 Press Pass Redline Signatures Holofoil /10 #RSTS1
2012 Press Pass Redline Signatures Holofoil /10 #RSTS2
2012 Press Pass Redline Signatures Melting /1 #RSTS1
2012 Press Pass Redline Signatures Melting /1 #RSTS2
2012 Press Pass Redline Signatures Red /50 #RSTS1
2012 Press Pass Redline Signatures Red /25 #RSTS2
2012 Press Pass Redline V8 Relics Blue /5 #V8TS
2012 Press Pass Redline V8 Relics Gold /10 #V8TS
2012 Press Pass Redline V8 Relics Melting /1 #V8TS
2012 Press Pass Redline V8 Relics Red /25 #V8TS
2012 Press Pass Redline Yellow /1 #35
2012 Press Pass Showcar #SC3
2012 Press Pass Showcase /499 #20
2012 Press Pass Showcase /499 #42
2012 Press Pass Showcase /499 #51
2012 Press Pass Showcase /499 #53
2012 Press Pass Showcase Champions Memorabilia /99 #CHTS
2012 Press Pass Showcase Champions Memorabilia Gold /50 #CHTS
2012 Press Pass Showcase Champions Memorabilia Melting /5 #CHTS
2012 Press Pass Showcase Champions Showcase /499 #CH3
2012 Press Pass Showcase Champions Showcase Gold /125 #CH3
2012 Press Pass Showcase Champions Showcase Ink /50 #CHSTS
2012 Press Pass Showcase Champions Showcase Ink Gold /25 #CHSTS
2012 Press Pass Showcase Champions Showcase Ink Melting /1 #CHSTS
2012 Press Pass Showcase Champions Showcase Melting /1 #CH3
2012 Press Pass Showcase Classic Collections Ink /10 #CCMSHR
2012 Press Pass Showcase Classic Collections Ink Gold /5 #CCMSHR
2012 Press Pass Showcase Classic Collections Ink Melting /1 #CCMSHR
2012 Press Pass Showcase Classic Collections Memorabilia /99 #CCMSHR
2012 Press Pass Showcase Classic Collections Memorabilia Gold /50 #CCMSHR
2012 Press Pass Showcase Classic Collections Memorabilia Melting /5 #CCMSHR
2012 Press Pass Showcase Elite Exhibit Ink /25 #EEITS
2012 Press Pass Showcase Elite Exhibit Ink Gold /10 #EEITS
2012 Press Pass Showcase Elite Exhibit Ink Melting /1 #EEITS
2012 Press Pass Showcase Gold /125 #20
2012 Press Pass Showcase Gold /125 #42
2012 Press Pass Showcase Gold /125 #51
2012 Press Pass Showcase Gold /125 #53
2012 Press Pass Showcase Green /5 #20
2012 Press Pass Showcase Green /5 #42
2012 Press Pass Showcase Green /5 #51
2012 Press Pass Showcase Green /5 #53
2012 Press Pass Showcase Masterpieces Ink /50 #MPITS
2012 Press Pass Showcase Masterpieces Ink Gold /25 #MPITS
2012 Press Pass Showcase Masterpieces Ink Melting /1 #MPITS
2012 Press Pass Showcase Masterpieces Memorabilia /99 #MPTS
2012 Press Pass Showcase Masterpieces Memorabilia Gold /50 #MPTS
2012 Press Pass Showcase Masterpieces Memorabilia Melting /5 #MPTS
2012 Press Pass Showcase Melting /1 #20
2012 Press Pass Showcase Melting /1 #42
2012 Press Pass Showcase Melting /1 #51
2012 Press Pass Showcase Melting /1 #53
2012 Press Pass Showcase Prized Pieces /14 #PPTS
2012 Press Pass Showcase Prized Pieces Gold /10 #PPTS
2012 Press Pass Showcase Prized Pieces Melting /5 #PPTS
2012 Press Pass Showcase Purple /1 #20
2012 Press Pass Showcase Purple /1 #42
2012 Press Pass Showcase Purple /1 #51
2012 Press Pass Showcase Purple /1 #53
2012 Press Pass Showcase Red /25 #20
2012 Press Pass Showcase Red /25 #42
2012 Press Pass Showcase Red /25 #51
2012 Press Pass Showcase Red /25 #53
2012 Press Pass Showcase Richard Petty 75th Birthday Tribute /10 #RPTS
2012 Press Pass Showcase Richard Petty 75th Birthday Tribute Melting /1 #RPTS
2012 Press Pass Showcase Showcase Patches /5 #SSPTS
2012 Press Pass Showcase Showcase Patches Melting /1 #SSPTS
2012 Press Pass Showcase Showroom /499 #SR3
2012 Press Pass Showcase Showroom Gold /125 #SR3
2012 Press Pass Showcase Showroom Melting /1 #SR3
2012 Press Pass Showcase Showroom Memorabilia /99 #SRTS
2012 Press Pass Showcase Showroom Memorabilia Gold /50 #SRTS
2012 Press Pass Showcase Showroom Memorabilia Melting /5 #SRTS
2012 Press Pass Showcase Signature Patches /1 #SSPTS
2012 Press Pass Showman #SM3
2012 Press Pass Signature Series Race Used /12 #PPATS1
2012 Press Pass Signature Series Race Used /12 #PPATS2
2012 Press Pass Snapshots #SS33
2012 Press Pass Snapshots #SS75
2012 Press Pass Triple Gear 3 in 1 /5 #TGTS
2012 Press Pass Triple Gear Firesuit and Sheet Metal /15 #TGTS
2012 Press Pass Triple Gear Tire /25 #TGTS
2012 Press Pass Wal-Mart Snapshots #SSWM1
2012 Sports Illustrated for Kids #117
2012 Total Memorabilia #29A
2012 Total Memorabilia #0
2012 Total Memorabilia #29B
2012 Total Memorabilia Black and White /99 #29
2012 Total Memorabilia Dual Swatch Gold /75 #TMTS
2012 Total Memorabilia Dual Swatch Holofoil /25 #TMTS
2012 Total Memorabilia Dual Swatch Melting /5 #TMTS
2012 Total Memorabilia Dual Swatch Silver /99 #TMTS
2012 Total Memorabilia Gold /275 #29
2012 Total Memorabilia Hot Rod Relics Gold /50 #HRRTS
2012 Total Memorabilia Hot Rod Relics Holofoil /10 #HRRTS
2012 Total Memorabilia Hot Rod Relics Melting /1 #HRRTS
2012 Total Memorabilia Hot Rod Relics Silver /99 #HRRTS
2012 Total Memorabilia Jumbo Swatch Gold /50 #TMTS
2012 Total Memorabilia Jumbo Swatch Holofoil /10 #TMTS
2012 Total Memorabilia Jumbo Swatch Melting /1 #TMTS
2012 Total Memorabilia Memory Lane #ML1
2012 Total Memorabilia Quad Swatch Gold /25 #TMTS
2012 Total Memorabilia Quad Swatch Holofoil /10 #TMTS
2012 Total Memorabilia Quad Swatch Melting /1 #TMTS
2012 Total Memorabilia Quad Swatch Silver /50 #TMTS
2012 Total Memorabilia Red Retail /250 #29
2012 Total Memorabilia Signature Collection Dual Swatch Silver /10 #SCTS
2012 Total Memorabilia Signature Collection Quad Swatch Holofoil /5 #SCTS
2012 Total Memorabilia Signature Collection Single Swatch Melting /1 #SCTS
2012 Total Memorabilia Signature Collection Triple Swatch Gold /10 #SCTS
2012 Total Memorabilia Single Swatch Gold /99 #TMTS
2012 Total Memorabilia Single Swatch Holofoil /50 #TMTS
2012 Total Memorabilia Single Swatch Melting /10 #TMTS
2012 Total Memorabilia Single Swatch Silver /199 #TMTS
2012 Total Memorabilia Tandem Treasures Dual Memorabilia Gold /75 #TTTSDP
2012 Total Memorabilia Tandem Treasures Dual Memorabilia Gold /75 #TTTSSA
2012 Total Memorabilia Tandem Treasures Dual Memorabilia Holofoil /25 #TTTSDP
2012 Total Memorabilia Tandem Treasures Dual Memorabilia Holofoil /25 #TTTSSA
2012 Total Memorabilia Tandem Treasures Dual Memorabilia Melting /5 #TTTSDP
2012 Total Memorabilia Tandem Treasures Dual Memorabilia Melting /5 #TTTSSA
2012 Total Memorabilia Tandem Treasures Dual Memorabilia Silver /99 #TTTSSA
2012 Total Memorabilia Tandem Treasures Dual Memorabilia Silver /99 #TTTSDP
2012 Total Memorabilia Triple Swatch Gold /50 #TMTS
2012 Total Memorabilia Triple Swatch Holofoil /25 #TMTS
2012 Total Memorabilia Triple Swatch Melting /1 #TMTS
2012 Total Memorabilia Triple Swatch Silver /99 #TMTS
2013 Press Pass #40
2013 Press Pass #41
2013 Press Pass #100
2013 Press Pass #90
2013 Press Pass #66
2013 Press Pass #0
2013 Press Pass Aerodynamic Autographs Blue /1 #TS
2013 Press Pass Aerodynamic Autographs Holofoil /5 #TS
2013 Press Pass Burning Rubber Blue /50 #BRTS
2013 Press Pass Burning Rubber Blue /50 #BRTS2
2013 Press Pass Burning Rubber Blue /50 #BRTS3
2013 Press Pass Burning Rubber Gold /199 #BRTS2
2013 Press Pass Burning Rubber Gold /199 #BRTS3
2013 Press Pass Burning Rubber Gold /199 #BRTS
2013 Press Pass Burning Rubber Holofoil /75 #BRTS
2013 Press Pass Burning Rubber Holofoil /75 #BRTS2
2013 Press Pass Burning Rubber Holofoil /75 #BRTS3
2013 Press Pass Burning Rubber Letterman /8 #BRLTS
2013 Press Pass Burning Rubber Melting /10 #BRTS
2013 Press Pass Burning Rubber Melting /10 #BRTS2
2013 Press Pass Burning Rubber Melting /10 #BRTS3
2013 Press Pass Certified Winners Autographs Gold /10 #TS
2013 Press Pass Certified Winners Autographs Melting /5 #TS
2013 Press Pass Color Proofs Black #40
2013 Press Pass Color Proofs Black #41
2013 Press Pass Color Proofs Black #66
2013 Press Pass Color Proofs Black #90
2013 Press Pass Color Proofs Black #100
2013 Press Pass Color Proofs Cyan /35 #40
2013 Press Pass Color Proofs Cyan /35 #41
2013 Press Pass Color Proofs Cyan /35 #66
2013 Press Pass Color Proofs Cyan /35 #90
2013 Press Pass Color Proofs Cyan /35 #100
2013 Press Pass Color Proofs Magenta #40
2013 Press Pass Color Proofs Magenta #41
2013 Press Pass Color Proofs Magenta #66
2013 Press Pass Color Proofs Magenta #90
2013 Press Pass Color Proofs Magenta #100
2013 Press Pass Color Proofs Yellow /5 #40
2013 Press Pass Color Proofs Yellow /5 #41
2013 Press Pass Color Proofs Yellow /5 #66
2013 Press Pass Color Proofs Yellow /5 #90
2013 Press Pass Color Proofs Yellow /5 #100
2013 Press Pass Cup Chase #CC17
2013 Press Pass Fanfare #54
2013 Press Pass Fanfare #55
2013 Press Pass Fanfare Autographs Blue /1 #TS
2013 Press Pass Fanfare Autographs Gold /1 #TS
2013 Press Pass Fanfare Autographs Green /1 #TS
2013 Press Pass Fanfare Autographs Red /1 #TS
2013 Press Pass Fanfare Autographs Silver /1 #TS
2013 Press Pass Fanfare Diamond Die Cuts /5 #54
2013 Press Pass Fanfare Diamond Die Cuts /5 #55
2013 Press Pass Fanfare Fan Following #FF4
2013 Press Pass Fanfare Fan Following National Convention VIP #FFN4
2013 Press Pass Fanfare Green /3 #54
2013 Press Pass Fanfare Green /3 #55
2013 Press Pass Fanfare Holofoil Die Cuts #54
2013 Press Pass Fanfare Holofoil Die Cuts #55
2013 Press Pass Fanfare Magnificent Jumbo Materials Signatures /10 #TS
2013 Press Pass Fanfare Magnificent Materials Dual Swatches /50 #TS
2013 Press Pass Fanfare Magnificent Materials Dual Swatches Melting /10 #TS
2013 Press Pass Fanfare Magnificent Materials Gold /50 #TS
2013 Press Pass Fanfare Magnificent Materials Jumbo Swatches /25 #TS
2013 Press Pass Fanfare Magnificent Materials Signatures /25 #TS
2013 Press Pass Fanfare Magnificent Materials Signatures Blue /10 #TS
2013 Press Pass Fanfare Magnificent Materials Silver /199 #TS
2013 Press Pass Fanfare Red Foil Die Cuts #54
2013 Press Pass Fanfare Red Foil Die Cuts #55
2013 Press Pass Fanfare Sapphire /20 #54
2013 Press Pass Fanfare Sapphire /20 #55
2013 Press Pass Fanfare Showtime #S3
2013 Press Pass Fanfare Signature Ride Autographs /5 #TS
2013 Press Pass Fanfare Signature Ride Autographs Blue /1 #TS
2013 Press Pass Fanfare Signature Ride Autographs Red /1 #TS
2013 Press Pass Fanfare Silver /25 #54
2013 Press Pass Fanfare Silver /25 #55
2013 Press Pass Four Wide Gold /10 #FWTS
2013 Press Pass Four Wide Melting /1 #FWTS
2013 Press Pass Ignite #35
2013 Press Pass Ignite #55
2013 Press Pass Ignite Convoy #9
2013 Press Pass Ignite Double Burner Blue Holofoil /10 #DBTS
2013 Press Pass Ignite Double Burner Red /1 #DBTS
2013 Press Pass Ignite Double Burner Silver /25 #DBTS
2013 Press Pass Ignite Hot Threads Blue Holofoil /99 #HTTS
2013 Press Pass Ignite Hot Threads Patch Red /10 #HTTS
2013 Press Pass Ignite Hot Threads Patch Red Oversized /20 #HTPTS
2013 Press Pass Ignite Hot Threads Silver #HTTS
2013 Press Pass Ignite Ink Black /35 #IITS
2013 Press Pass Ignite Ink Blue /10 #IITS
2013 Press Pass Ignite Ink Red /5 #IITS
2013 Press Pass Ignite Profile #14
2013 Press Pass Ignite Proofs Black and White /50 #35
2013 Press Pass Ignite Proofs Black and White /50 #55
2013 Press Pass Ignite Proofs Cyan #35
2013 Press Pass Ignite Proofs Cyan #55
2013 Press Pass Ignite Proofs Magenta #35
2013 Press Pass Ignite Proofs Magenta #55
2013 Press Pass Ignite Proofs Yellow /5 #35
2013 Press Pass Ignite Proofs Yellow /5 #55
2013 Press Pass Ignite Supercharged Signatures Blue Holofoil /10 #SSTS
2013 Press Pass Ignite Supercharged Signatures Red /1 #SSTS
2013 Press Pass Ignite Turning Point #6
2013 Press Pass Legends #48
2013 Press Pass Legends Autographs Blue #LGTS
2013 Press Pass Legends Autographs Gold /4 #LGTS
2013 Press Pass Legends Autographs Holofoil #LGTS
2013 Press Pass Legends Autographs Printing Plates Black /1 #LGTS
2013 Press Pass Legends Autographs Printing Plates Cyan /1 #LGTS
2013 Press Pass Legends Autographs Printing Plates Magenta /1 #LGTS
2013 Press Pass Legends Autographs Printing Plates Yellow /1 #LGTS
2013 Press Pass Legends Autographs Silver #LGTS
2013 Press Pass Legends Blue #48
2013 Press Pass Legends Blue Holofoil /1 #48
2013 Press Pass Legends Four Wide Memorabilia Autographs Gold /25 #FWSETS
2013 Press Pass Legends Four Wide Memorabilia Autographs Melting /5 #FWSETS
2013 Press Pass Legends Gold /149 #48
2013 Press Pass Legends Holofoil /10 #48
2013 Press Pass Legends Printing Plates Black /1 #48
2013 Press Pass Legends Printing Plates Cyan /1 #48
2013 Press Pass Legends Printing Plates Magenta /1 #48
2013 Press Pass Legends Printing Plates Yellow /1 #48
2013 Press Pass Legends Prominent Pieces Gold /10 #PPTS
2013 Press Pass Legends Prominent Pieces Holofoil /5 #PPTS
2013 Press Pass Legends Prominent Pieces Oversized Firesuit /5 #PPTS
2013 Press Pass Legends Prominent Pieces Silver /25 #PPTS
2013 Press Pass Legends Red /99 #48
2013 Press Pass Power Picks Blue /99 #15
2013 Press Pass Power Picks Blue /99 #50
2013 Press Pass Power Picks Gold /50 #15
2013 Press Pass Power Picks Gold /50 #50
2013 Press Pass Power Picks Holofoil /10 #15
2013 Press Pass Power Picks Holofoil /10 #50
2013 Press Pass Racing Champions #RC18
2013 Press Pass Racing Champions #RC3
2013 Press Pass Racing Champions #RC5
2013 Press Pass Racing Champions #RC28
2013 Press Pass Redline #43
2013 Press Pass Redline #44
2013 Press Pass Redline Black /99 #43
2013 Press Pass Redline Black /99 #44
2013 Press Pass Redline Career Wins Relic Autographs Blue /5 #CWTS
2013 Press Pass Redline Career Wins Relic Autographs Gold /25 #CWTS
2013 Press Pass Redline Career Wins Relic Autographs Melting /1 #CWTS
2013 Press Pass Redline Career Wins Relic Autographs Red /50 #CWTS
2013 Press Pass Redline Cyan /50 #43
2013 Press Pass Redline Cyan /50 #44
2013 Press Pass Redline Dynamic Duals Dual Relic Blue /5 #DDTS
2013 Press Pass Redline Dynamic Duals Dual Relic Gold /10 #DDTS
2013 Press Pass Redline Dynamic Duals Dual Relic Melting /1 #DDTS
2013 Press Pass Redline Dynamic Duals Dual Relic Red /50 #DDTS
2013 Press Pass Redline Dynamic Duals Dual Relic Silver /25 #DDTS
2013 Press Pass Redline Intensity #9
2013 Press Pass Redline Magenta /15 #43
2013 Press Pass Redline Magenta /15 #44
2013 Press Pass Redline Muscle Car Sheet Metal Blue /5 #MCMTS
2013 Press Pass Redline Muscle Car Sheet Metal Gold /10 #MCMTS
2013 Press Pass Redline Muscle Car Sheet Metal Melting /1 #MCMTS

2013 Press Pass Redline Muscle Car Sheet Metal Red /50 #MCMTS
2013 Press Pass Redline Muscle Car Sheet Metal Silver /25 #MCMTS
2013 Press Pass Redline Pieces of the Action Blue /10 #PATS
2013 Press Pass Redline Pieces of the Action Gold /25 #PATS
2013 Press Pass Redline Pieces of the Action Melting /1 #PATS
2013 Press Pass Redline Pieces of the Action Red /75 #PATS
2013 Press Pass Redline Pieces of the Action Silver /50 #PATS
2013 Press Pass Redline Redline Racers #14
2013 Press Pass Redline Relic Autographs Blue /5 #RRSETS
2013 Press Pass Redline Relic Autographs Gold /14 #RRSETS
2013 Press Pass Redline Relic Autographs Melting /1 #RRSETS
2013 Press Pass Redline Relic Autographs Red /50 #RRSETS
2013 Press Pass Redline Relic Autographs Silver /25 #RRSETS
2013 Press Pass Redline Relics Blue /5 #RRTS
2013 Press Pass Redline Relics Gold /10 #RRTS
2013 Press Pass Redline Relics Melting /1 #RRTS
2013 Press Pass Redline Relics Red /50 #RRTS
2013 Press Pass Redline Relics Silver /25 #RRTS
2013 Press Pass Redline RPM #6
2013 Press Pass Redline Signatures Blue /14 #RSTS1
2013 Press Pass Redline Signatures Blue /5 #RSTS2
2013 Press Pass Redline Signatures Gold /5 #RSTS1
2013 Press Pass Redline Signatures Gold /1 #RSTS2
2013 Press Pass Redline Signatures Holo /10 #RSTS1
2013 Press Pass Redline Signatures Holo /5 #RSTS2
2013 Press Pass Redline Signatures Melting /1 #RSTS2
2013 Press Pass Redline Signatures Red /20 #RSTS1
2013 Press Pass Redline V8 Relics Blue /5 #V8TS
2013 Press Pass Redline V8 Relics Gold /10 #V8TS
2013 Press Pass Redline V8 Relics Melting /1 #V8TS
2013 Press Pass Redline V8 Relics Red /25 #V8TS
2013 Press Pass Redline Yellow /1 #43
2013 Press Pass Redline Yellow /1 #44
2013 Press Pass Showcase /349 #26
2013 Press Pass Showcase /349 #43
2013 Press Pass Showcase /349 #47
2013 Press Pass Showcase /349 #56
2013 Press Pass Showcase Black /1 #26
2013 Press Pass Showcase Black /1 #43
2013 Press Pass Showcase Black /1 #47
2013 Press Pass Showcase Black /1 #56
2013 Press Pass Showcase Blue /25 #26
2013 Press Pass Showcase Blue /25 #43
2013 Press Pass Showcase Blue /25 #47
2013 Press Pass Showcase Blue /25 #56
2013 Press Pass Showcase Classic Collections Ink Gold /5 #CCISHR
2013 Press Pass Showcase Classic Collections Ink Melting /1 #CCISHR
2013 Press Pass Showcase Classic Collections Ink Red /1 #CCISHR
2013 Press Pass Showcase Classic Collections Memorabilia Gold /25 #CCMSHR
2013 Press Pass Showcase Classic Collections Memorabilia Melting /5 #CCMSHR
2013 Press Pass Showcase Classic Collections Memorabilia Silver /75 #CCMSHR
2013 Press Pass Showcase Elite Exhibit Ink /20 #EEITS
2013 Press Pass Showcase Elite Exhibit Ink Blue /30 #EEITP1
2013 Press Pass Showcase Elite Exhibit Ink Blue /20 #EEITP2
2013 Press Pass Showcase Elite Exhibit Ink Gold /10 #EEITS
2013 Press Pass Showcase Elite Exhibit Ink Melting /1 #EEITS
2013 Press Pass Showcase Elite Exhibit Ink Red /5 #EEITS
2013 Press Pass Showcase Gold /99 #26
2013 Press Pass Showcase Gold /99 #43
2013 Press Pass Showcase Gold /99 #47
2013 Press Pass Showcase Gold /99 #56
2013 Press Pass Showcase Green /20 #26
2013 Press Pass Showcase Green /20 #43
2013 Press Pass Showcase Green /20 #47
2013 Press Pass Showcase Green /20 #56
2013 Press Pass Showcase Masterpieces Ink /25 #MPITS
2013 Press Pass Showcase Masterpieces Ink Gold /10 #MPITS
2013 Press Pass Showcase Masterpieces Ink Melting /1 #MPITS
2013 Press Pass Showcase Masterpieces Memorabilia /75 #MPTS
2013 Press Pass Showcase Masterpieces Memorabilia Gold /25 #MPTS
2013 Press Pass Showcase Masterpieces Memorabilia Melting /5 #MPTS
2013 Press Pass Showcase Prized Pieces /99 #PPMTS
2013 Press Pass Showcase Prized Pieces Blue /20 #PPMTS
2013 Press Pass Showcase Prized Pieces Gold /25 #PPMTS
2013 Press Pass Showcase Prized Pieces Ink /25 #PPITS
2013 Press Pass Showcase Prized Pieces Ink Gold /10 #PPITS
2013 Press Pass Showcase Prized Pieces Ink Melting /1 #PPITS
2013 Press Pass Showcase Prized Pieces Melting /5 #PPMTS
2013 Press Pass Showcase Purple /13 #26
2013 Press Pass Showcase Purple /13 #43
2013 Press Pass Showcase Purple /13 #47
2013 Press Pass Showcase Purple /13 #56
2013 Press Pass Showcase Red /10 #26
2013 Press Pass Showcase Red /10 #43
2013 Press Pass Showcase Red /10 #47
2013 Press Pass Showcase Red /10 #56
2013 Press Pass Showcase Series Standouts Gold /50 #12
2013 Press Pass Showcase Series Standouts Memorabilia /75 #SSMTS
2013 Press Pass Showcase Series Standouts Memorabilia Blue /80 #SSMTS
2013 Press Pass Showcase Series Standouts Memorabilia Gold /25 #SSMTS
2013 Press Pass Showcase Series Standouts Memorabilia Melting /5 #SSMTS
2013 Press Pass Showcase Showcase Patches /5 #SPTS
2013 Press Pass Showcase Signature Patches /9 #SSPTS
2013 Press Pass Showcase Studio Showcase /299 #12
2013 Press Pass Showcase Studio Showcase Blue /40 #12
2013 Press Pass Showcase Studio Showcase Green /25 #12
2013 Press Pass Showcase Studio Showcase Ink /25 #SSITS
2013 Press Pass Showcase Studio Showcase Ink Gold /10 #SSITS
2013 Press Pass Showcase Studio Showcase Ink Melting /1 #SSITS
2013 Press Pass Showcase Studio Showcase Ink Red /5 #SSITS
2013 Press Pass Showcase Studio Showcase Melting /1 #12
2013 Press Pass Showcase Studio Showcase Purple /13 #12
2013 Press Pass Showcase Studio Showcase Red /10 #12
2013 Press Pass Signature Series Gold /10 #TS
2013 Press Pass Signature Series Melting /5 #TS
2013 Press Pass Signings Blue /1 #TS
2013 Press Pass Signings Gold /5 #TS
2013 Press Pass Signings Holofoil /1 #TS
2013 Press Pass Signings Printing Plates Black /1 #TS
2013 Press Pass Signings Printing Plates Cyan /1 #TS
2013 Press Pass Signings Printing Plates Magenta /1 #TS
2013 Press Pass Signings Printing Plates Yellow /1 #TS
2013 Press Pass Signings Silver /5 #TS
2013 Press Pass Three Wide Gold /10 #TWTS
2013 Press Pass Three Wide Melting /1 #TWTS
2013 Total Memorabilia #34
2013 Total Memorabilia Black and White /99 #34
2013 Total Memorabilia Dual Swatch Gold /199 #TMTS
2013 Total Memorabilia Gold /275 #34
2013 Total Memorabilia Hot Rod Relics Gold /50 #HRRTS
2013 Total Memorabilia Hot Rod Relics Holofoil /10 #HRRTS
2013 Total Memorabilia Hot Rod Relics Melting /1 #HRRTS
2013 Total Memorabilia Hot Rod Relics Silver /99 #HRRTS
2013 Total Memorabilia Quad Swatch Melting /10 #TMTS
2013 Total Memorabilia Red #34
2013 Total Memorabilia Signature Collection Dual Swatch Gold /10 #SCTS
2013 Total Memorabilia Signature Collection Quad Swatch Melting /1 #SCTS
2013 Total Memorabilia Signature Collection Single Swatch Silver /10 #SCTS
2013 Total Memorabilia Signature Collection Triple Swatch Holofoil /5 #SCTS
2013 Total Memorabilia Single Swatch Silver /475 #TMTS
2013 Total Memorabilia Smooth Operators #SO1
2013 Total Memorabilia Triple Swatch Holofoil /99 #TMTS
2014 Press Pass #37
2014 Press Pass #38
2014 Press Pass #87
2014 Press Pass American Thunder #64
2014 Press Pass American Thunder #50
2014 Press Pass American Thunder #33
2014 Press Pass American Thunder Autographs Blue /5 #ATATS
2014 Press Pass American Thunder Autographs Red /1 #ATATS
2014 Press Pass American Thunder Autographs White /15 #ATATS
2014 Press Pass American Thunder Battle Armor Blue /25 #BATS
2014 Press Pass American Thunder Battle Armor Red /1 #BATS
2014 Press Pass American Thunder Battle Armor Silver /99 #BATS
2014 Press Pass American Thunder Black and White /50 #33
2014 Press Pass American Thunder Black and White /50 #50
2014 Press Pass American Thunder Black and White /50 #64
2014 Press Pass American Thunder Brothers In Arms Autographs Blue /5 #BASHR
2014 Press Pass American Thunder Brothers In Arms Autographs Red /1 #BASHR
2014 Press Pass American Thunder Brothers In Arms Autographs White /10 #BASHR
2014 Press Pass American Thunder Brothers In Arms Relics Blue /25 #BASHR
2014 Press Pass American Thunder Brothers In Arms Relics Red /5 #BASHR
2014 Press Pass American Thunder Brothers In Arms Relics Silver /50 #BASHR
2014 Press Pass American Thunder Class A Uniforms Blue /99 #CAUTS
2014 Press Pass American Thunder Class A Uniforms Red /10 #CAUTS
2014 Press Pass American Thunder Class A Uniforms Silver #CAUTS
2014 Press Pass American Thunder Cyan #33
2014 Press Pass American Thunder Cyan #50
2014 Press Pass American Thunder Cyan #64
2014 Press Pass American Thunder Great American Treads Autographs Blue /10 #GATTS
2014 Press Pass American Thunder Great American Treads Autographs Red /1 #GATTS
2014 Press Pass American Thunder Magenta #33
2014 Press Pass American Thunder Magenta #50
2014 Press Pass American Thunder Magenta #64
2014 Press Pass American Thunder Yellow /5 #33
2014 Press Pass American Thunder Yellow /5 #50
2014 Press Pass Burning Rubber Blue /25 #BRTS
2014 Press Pass Burning Rubber Gold /75 #BRTS
2014 Press Pass Burning Rubber Holofoil /50 #BRTS
2014 Press Pass Burning Rubber Letterman /8 #BRLTS
2014 Press Pass Burning Rubber Melting /10 #BRTS
2014 Press Pass Color Proofs Black /70 #37
2014 Press Pass Color Proofs Black /70 #38
2014 Press Pass Color Proofs Black /70 #87
2014 Press Pass Color Proofs Cyan /35 #37
2014 Press Pass Color Proofs Cyan /35 #38
2014 Press Pass Color Proofs Cyan /35 #87
2014 Press Pass Color Proofs Magenta #37
2014 Press Pass Color Proofs Magenta #38
2014 Press Pass Color Proofs Magenta #87
2014 Press Pass Color Proofs Yellow /5 #37
2014 Press Pass Color Proofs Yellow /5 #38
2014 Press Pass Color Proofs Yellow /5 #87
2014 Press Pass Cup Chase #15
2014 Press Pass Five Star /15 #15
2014 Press Pass Five Star Blue /5 #15
2014 Press Pass Five Star Classic Compilation Autographs Blue Triple Swatch /5 #CCTS
2014 Press Pass Five Star Classic Compilation Autographs Holofoil /10 #CCTS
2014 Press Pass Five Star Classic Compilation Autographs Holofoil Dual Swatch /10 #CCTS
2014 Press Pass Five Star Classic Compilation Autographs Melting Five Swatch /1 #CCTS
2014 Press Pass Five Star Classic Compilation Autographs Melting Quad Swatch /1 #CCTS
2014 Press Pass Five Star Classic Compilations Autographed Patch Booklet /1 #CCTS1
2014 Press Pass Five Star Classic Compilations Autographed Patch Booklet /1 #CCTS2
2014 Press Pass Five Star Classic Compilations Autographed Patch Booklet /1 #CCTS3
2014 Press Pass Five Star Classic Compilations Autographed Patch Booklet /1 #CCTS4
2014 Press Pass Five Star Classic Compilations Autographed Patch Booklet /1 #CCTS5
2014 Press Pass Five Star Classic Compilations Autographed Patch Booklet /1 #CCTS6
2014 Press Pass Five Star Classic Compilations Autographed Patch Booklet /1 #CCTS7
2014 Press Pass Five Star Classic Compilations Autographed Patch Booklet /1 #CCTS8
2014 Press Pass Five Star Classic Compilations Autographed Patch Booklet /1 #CCTS9
2014 Press Pass Five Star Classic Compilations Autographed Patch Booklet /1 #CCTS10
2014 Press Pass Five Star Classic Compilations Autographed Patch Booklet /1 #CCTS11
2014 Press Pass Five Star Classic Compilations Autographed Patch Booklet /1 #CCTS12
2014 Press Pass Five Star Classic Compilations Autographed Patch Booklet /1 #CCTS13
2014 Press Pass Five Star Classic Compilations Autographed Patch Booklet /1 #CCTS14
2014 Press Pass Five Star Classic Compilations Autographed Patch Booklet /1 #CCTS15
2014 Press Pass Five Star Classic Compilations Combo Autographs Blue /5 #CCSHR
2014 Press Pass Five Star Classic Compilations Combo Autographs Blue /5 #CCTSDE
2014 Press Pass Five Star Classic Compilations Combo Autographs Melting /1 #CCSHR
2014 Press Pass Five Star Classic Compilations Combo Autographs Melting /1 #CCTSDE
2014 Press Pass Five Star Holofoil /10 #15
2014 Press Pass Five Star Melting /1 #15
2014 Press Pass Five Star Paramount Pieces Blue /5 #PPTS
2014 Press Pass Five Star Paramount Pieces Gold /25 #PPTS
2014 Press Pass Five Star Paramount Pieces Holofoil /10 #PPTS
2014 Press Pass Five Star Paramount Pieces Melting /1 #PPTS
2014 Press Pass Five Star Paramount Pieces Melting Patch /1 #PPTS
2014 Press Pass Five Star Signature Souvenirs Blue /5 #SSTS
2014 Press Pass Five Star Signature Souvenirs Gold /50 #SSTS
2014 Press Pass Five Star Signature Souvenirs Holofoil /25 #SSTS
2014 Press Pass Five Star Signature Souvenirs Melting /1 #SSTS
2014 Press Pass Five Star Signatures Blue /5 #FSSTS
2014 Press Pass Five Star Signatures Holofoil /10 #FSSTS
2014 Press Pass Five Star Signatures Melting /1 #FSSTS
2014 Press Pass Four Wide Gold /10 #FWTS
2014 Press Pass Four Wide Melting /1 #FWTS
2014 Press Pass Gold #37
2014 Press Pass Gold #38
2014 Press Pass Gold #87
2014 Press Pass Intensity National Convention VIP #NE5
2014 Press Pass Redline #48
2014 Press Pass Redline #49
2014 Press Pass Redline Black /75 #48
2014 Press Pass Redline Black /75 #49
2014 Press Pass Redline Blue Foil #48
2014 Press Pass Redline Blue Foil #49
2014 Press Pass Redline Cyan /50 #48
2014 Press Pass Redline Cyan /50 #49
2014 Press Pass Redline Green National Convention /5 #48
2014 Press Pass Redline Green National Convention /5 #49
2014 Press Pass Redline Head to Head Blue /10 #HTHJJTS
2014 Press Pass Redline Head to Head Gold /25 #HTHJJTS
2014 Press Pass Redline Head to Head Melting /1 #HTHJJTS
2014 Press Pass Redline Head to Head Red /75 #HTHJJTS
2014 Press Pass Redline Intensity #I10
2014 Press Pass Redline Magenta /10 #48
2014 Press Pass Redline Magenta /10 #49
2014 Press Pass Redline Muscle Car Sheet Metal Blue /25 #MCMTS
2014 Press Pass Redline Muscle Car Sheet Metal Gold /50 #MCMTS
2014 Press Pass Redline Muscle Car Sheet Metal Melting /1 #MCMTS
2014 Press Pass Redline Muscle Car Sheet Metal Red /75 #MCMTS
2014 Press Pass Redline Pieces of the Action Blue /10 #PATS
2014 Press Pass Redline Pieces of the Action Gold /25 #PATS
2014 Press Pass Redline Pieces of the Action Melting /1 #PATS
2014 Press Pass Redline Pieces of the Action Red /75 #PATS
2014 Press Pass Redline Redline Racers #RR15
2014 Press Pass Redline Relics Blue /25 #RRTS
2014 Press Pass Redline Relics Gold /50 #RRTS
2014 Press Pass Redline Relics Melting /1 #RRTS
2014 Press Pass Redline Relics Red /75 #RRTS
2014 Press Pass Redline RPM #RPM10
2014 Press Pass Redline Yellow /1 #48
2014 Press Pass Redline Yellow /1 #49
2014 Press Pass Replay #13
2014 Total Memorabilia #26
2014 Total Memorabilia Acceleration #AC1
2014 Total Memorabilia Autographed Memorabilia Blue /5 #SCTS
2014 Total Memorabilia Autographed Memorabilia Gold /5 #SCTS
2014 Total Memorabilia Autographed Memorabilia Melting /1 #SCTS
2014 Total Memorabilia Autographed Memorabilia Silver /10 #SC-TS
2014 Total Memorabilia Black and White /99 #26
2014 Total Memorabilia Dual Swatch Gold /150 #TMTS
2014 Total Memorabilia Gold /175 #26
2014 Total Memorabilia Quad Swatch Melting /25 #TMTS
2014 Total Memorabilia Red #26
2014 Total Memorabilia Single Swatch Silver /275 #TMTS
2014 Total Memorabilia Triple Swatch Blue /99 #TMTS
2015 Press Pass #32
2015 Press Pass #98
2015 Press Pass Cup Chase #32
2015 Press Pass Cup Chase #98
2015 Press Pass Cup Chase Blue /25 #32
2015 Press Pass Cup Chase Blue /25 #98
2015 Press Pass Cup Chase Gold /75 #32
2015 Press Pass Cup Chase Gold /75 #98
2015 Press Pass Cup Chase Green /10 #32
2015 Press Pass Cup Chase Green /10 #98
2015 Press Pass Cup Chase Melting /1 #32
2015 Press Pass Cup Chase Melting /1 #98
2015 Press Pass Cup Chase Three Wide Blue /25 #3WTS
2015 Press Pass Cup Chase Three Wide Gold /50 #3WTS
2015 Press Pass Cup Chase Three Wide Green /10 #3WTS
2015 Press Pass Cup Chase Three Wide Melting /1 #3WTS
2015 Press Pass Cuts Blue /25 #CCCTS
2015 Press Pass Cuts Gold /50 #CCCTS
2015 Press Pass Cuts Green /10 #CCCTS
2015 Press Pass Cuts Melting /1 #CCCTS
2015 Press Pass Pit Road Pieces Blue /25 #PPMTS
2015 Press Pass Pit Road Pieces Gold /50 #PPMTS
2015 Press Pass Pit Road Pieces Green /10 #PPMTS
2015 Press Pass Pit Road Pieces Melting /1 #PPMTS
2015 Press Pass Purple #32
2015 Press Pass Purple #98
2015 Press Pass Red #32
2015 Press Pass Red #98
2016 Certified #53
2016 Certified #33
2016 Certified Epix /199 #3
2016 Certified Epix Mirror Black /1 #3
2016 Certified Epix Mirror Blue /50 #3
2016 Certified Epix Mirror Gold /25 #3
2016 Certified Epix Mirror Green /5 #3
2016 Certified Epix Mirror Orange /99 #3
2016 Certified Epix Mirror Purple /10 #3
2016 Certified Epix Mirror Red /75 #3
2016 Certified Epix Mirror Silver /99 #3
2016 Certified Famed Fabrics /299 #3
2016 Certified Famed Fabrics Mirror Black /1 #3
2016 Certified Famed Fabrics Mirror Blue /50 #3
2016 Certified Famed Fabrics Mirror Gold /25 #3
2016 Certified Famed Fabrics Mirror Green /5 #3
2016 Certified Famed Fabrics Mirror Orange /199 #3
2016 Certified Famed Fabrics Mirror Purple /10 #3
2016 Certified Famed Fabrics Mirror Red /75 #3
2016 Certified Famed Fabrics Mirror Silver /199 #3
2016 Certified Gold Team /199 #1
2016 Certified Gold Team Mirror Black /1 #1
2016 Certified Gold Team Mirror Blue /50 #1
2016 Certified Gold Team Mirror Gold /25 #1
2016 Certified Gold Team Mirror Green /5 #1
2016 Certified Gold Team Mirror Orange /99 #1
2016 Certified Gold Team Mirror Purple /10 #1
2016 Certified Gold Team Mirror Red /75 #1
2016 Certified Gold Team Mirror Silver /99 #1
2016 Certified Legends /199 #3
2016 Certified Legends Mirror Black /1 #3
2016 Certified Legends Mirror Blue /50 #3
2016 Certified Legends Mirror Gold /25 #3
2016 Certified Legends Mirror Green /5 #3
2016 Certified Legends Mirror Orange /99 #3
2016 Certified Legends Mirror Purple /10 #3
2016 Certified Legends Mirror Red /75 #3
2016 Certified Legends Mirror Silver /99 #3
2016 Certified Mirror Black /1 #33
2016 Certified Mirror Black /1 #53
2016 Certified Mirror Blue /50 #33
2016 Certified Mirror Blue /50 #53
2016 Certified Mirror Gold /25 #33
2016 Certified Mirror Gold /25 #53
2016 Certified Mirror Green /5 #33
2016 Certified Mirror Green /5 #53
2016 Certified Mirror Orange /99 #33
2016 Certified Mirror Orange /99 #53
2016 Certified Mirror Purple /10 #33
2016 Certified Mirror Purple /10 #53
2016 Certified Mirror Red /75 #33
2016 Certified Mirror Red /75 #53
2016 Certified Mirror Silver /99 #33
2016 Certified Mirror Silver /99 #53
2016 Certified Skills /199 #3
2016 Certified Skills Mirror Black /1 #3
2016 Certified Skills Mirror Blue /50 #3
2016 Certified Skills Mirror Gold /25 #3
2016 Certified Skills Mirror Green /5 #3
2016 Certified Skills Mirror Orange /99 #3
2016 Certified Skills Mirror Purple /10 #3
2016 Certified Skills Mirror Red /75 #3
2016 Certified Skills Mirror Silver /99 #3
2016 Panini Instant #14
2016 Panini Instant Black /1 #14
2016 Panini Instant Blue /25 #14
2016 Panini Instant Green /5 #14
2016 Panini Instant Orange /50 #14
2016 Panini Instant Purple /10 #14
2016 Panini National Convention VIP #95
2016 Panini National Convention VIP Autographs Gold Vinyl /1 #95
2016 Panini National Convention VIP Autographs Kaleidoscope Red /25 #95
2016 Panini National Convention VIP Blue Wave Gold /10 #95
2016 Panini National Convention VIP Cracked Ice /25 #95
2016 Panini National Convention VIP Flash Green /5 #95
2016 Panini National Convention VIP Gold Vinyl /1 #95
2016 Panini National Convention VIP Memorabilia Gold Vinyl /1 #95
2016 Panini National Convention VIP Memorabilia Kaleidoscope Blue /25 #95
2016 Panini National Convention VIP Prizm /99 #95
2016 Panini National Convention VIP Purple Pulsar /50 #95
2016 Panini National Treasures /25 #4
2016 Panini National Treasures /25 #29
2016 Panini National Treasures Black /5 #4
2016 Panini National Treasures Black /5 #29
2016 Panini National Treasures Blue /1 #4
2016 Panini National Treasures Blue /1 #29
2016 Panini National Treasures Dual Driver Materials /25 #4
2016 Panini National Treasures Dual Driver Materials Black /5 #4
2016 Panini National Treasures Dual Driver Materials Blue /1 #4
2016 Panini National Treasures Dual Driver Materials Gold /10 #4
2016 Panini National Treasures Dual Driver Materials Printing Plates Black /1 #4
2016 Panini National Treasures Dual Driver Materials Printing Plates Cyan /1 #4
2016 Panini National Treasures Dual Driver Materials Printing Plates Magenta /1 #4
2016 Panini National Treasures Dual Driver Materials Printing Plates Yellow /1 #4
2016 Panini National Treasures Dual Driver Materials Silver /15 #4
2016 Panini National Treasures Gold /15 #4
2016 Panini National Treasures Gold /15 #29
2016 Panini National Treasures Printing Plates Black /1 #4
2016 Panini National Treasures Printing Plates Black /1 #29
2016 Panini National Treasures Printing Plates Cyan /1 #4
2016 Panini National Treasures Printing Plates Cyan /1 #29
2016 Panini National Treasures Printing Plates Magenta /1 #4
2016 Panini National Treasures Printing Plates Magenta /1 #29
2016 Panini National Treasures Printing Plates Yellow /1 #4
2016 Panini National Treasures Printing Plates Yellow /1 #29
2016 Panini National Treasures Quad Driver Materials /25 #10
2016 Panini National Treasures Quad Driver Materials Black /5 #10
2016 Panini National Treasures Quad Driver Materials Blue /1 #10
2016 Panini National Treasures Quad Driver Materials Gold /10 #10
2016 Panini National Treasures Quad Driver Materials Printing Plates Black /1 #10
2016 Panini National Treasures Quad Driver Materials Printing Plates Cyan /1 #10
2016 Panini National Treasures Quad Driver Materials Printing Plates Magenta /1 #10
2016 Panini National Treasures Quad Driver Materials Printing Plates Yellow /1 #10
2016 Panini National Treasures Quad Driver Materials Silver /15 #10
2016 Panini National Treasures Silver /20 #4
2016 Panini National Treasures Silver /20 #29
2016 Panini National Treasures Timelines /25 #14
2016 Panini National Treasures Timelines Black /5 #14
2016 Panini National Treasures Timelines Blue /1 #14
2016 Panini National Treasures Timelines Gold /10 #14
2016 Panini National Treasures Timelines Printing Plates Black /1 #14
2016 Panini National Treasures Timelines Printing Plates Cyan /1 #14
2016 Panini National Treasures Timelines Printing Plates Magenta /1 #14
2016 Panini National Treasures Timelines Printing Plates Yellow /1 #14
2016 Panini National Treasures Timelines Silver /15 #14
2016 Panini National Treasures Trio Driver Materials /25 #1
2016 Panini National Treasures Trio Driver Materials Black /5 #1
2016 Panini National Treasures Trio Driver Materials Blue /1 #1
2016 Panini National Treasures Trio Driver Materials Gold /10 #1
2016 Panini National Treasures Trio Driver Materials Printing Plates Black /1 #1
2016 Panini National Treasures Trio Driver Materials Printing Plates Cyan /1 #1
2016 Panini National Treasures Trio Driver Materials Printing Plates Magenta /1 #1
2016 Panini National Treasures Trio Driver Materials Printing Plates Yellow /1 #1
2016 Panini National Treasures Trio Driver Materials Silver /15 #1
2016 Panini Prizm #75
2016 Panini Prizm #67
2016 Panini Prizm #58
2016 Panini Prizm #14
2016 Panini Prizm Blowing Smoke #6
2016 Panini Prizm Blowing Smoke Prizms #6
2016 Panini Prizm Blowing Smoke Prizms Checkered Flag /1 #6
2016 Panini Prizm Blowing Smoke Prizms Gold /10 #6
2016 Panini Prizm Champions #5
2016 Panini Prizm Champions Prizms #5
2016 Panini Prizm Champions Prizms Checkered Flag /1 #5
2016 Panini Prizm Champions Prizms Gold /10 #5
2016 Panini Prizm Competitors #5
2016 Panini Prizm Competitors Prizms #5
2016 Panini Prizm Competitors Prizms Checkered Flag /1 #5
2016 Panini Prizm Competitors Prizms Gold /10 #5
2016 Panini Prizm Machinery #4
2016 Panini Prizm Machinery Prizms #4
2016 Panini Prizm Machinery Prizms Checkered Flag /1 #4
2016 Panini Prizm Machinery Prizms Gold /10 #4
2016 Panini Prizm Prizms #14
2016 Panini Prizm Prizms #58
2016 Panini Prizm Prizms #67
2016 Panini Prizm Prizms #75
2016 Panini Prizm Prizms Black /3 #14
2016 Panini Prizm Prizms Black /3 #58
2016 Panini Prizm Prizms Black /3 #67
2016 Panini Prizm Prizms Black /3 #75
2016 Panini Prizm Prizms Blue Flag /99 #14
2016 Panini Prizm Prizms Blue Flag /99 #58
2016 Panini Prizm Prizms Blue Flag /99 #67
2016 Panini Prizm Prizms Blue Flag /99 #75
2016 Panini Prizm Prizms Camo /14 #14
2016 Panini Prizm Prizms Camo /14 #58
2016 Panini Prizm Prizms Camo /14 #67
2016 Panini Prizm Prizms Camo /14 #75
2016 Panini Prizm Prizms Checkered Flag /1 #14
2016 Panini Prizm Prizms Checkered Flag /1 #58
2016 Panini Prizm Prizms Checkered Flag /1 #67
2016 Panini Prizm Prizms Checkered Flag /1 #75
2016 Panini Prizm Prizms Gold /10 #14
2016 Panini Prizm Prizms Gold /10 #58
2016 Panini Prizm Prizms Gold /10 #67
2016 Panini Prizm Prizms Gold /10 #75
2016 Panini Prizm Prizms Green Flag /149 #14
2016 Panini Prizm Prizms Green Flag /149 #58
2016 Panini Prizm Prizms Green Flag /149 #67
2016 Panini Prizm Prizms Green Flag /149 #75
2016 Panini Prizm Prizms Rainbow /24 #14
2016 Panini Prizm Prizms Rainbow /24 #58
2016 Panini Prizm Prizms Rainbow /24 #67
2016 Panini Prizm Prizms Rainbow /24 #75
2016 Panini Prizm Prizms Red Flag /75 #14
2016 Panini Prizm Prizms Red Flag /75 #58
2016 Panini Prizm Prizms Red Flag /75 #67
2016 Panini Prizm Prizms Red Flag /75 #75
2016 Panini Prizm Prizms Red White and Blue #14
2016 Panini Prizm Prizms Red White and Blue #58
2016 Panini Prizm Prizms Red White and Blue #67
2016 Panini Prizm Prizms Red White and Blue #75
2016 Panini Prizm Prizms White Flag /5 #14
2016 Panini Prizm Prizms White Flag /5 #58
2016 Panini Prizm Prizms White Flag /5 #67
2016 Panini Prizm Prizms White Flag /5 #75
2016 Panini Prizm Qualifying Times #8
2016 Panini Prizm Qualifying Times Prizms #8
2016 Panini Prizm Qualifying Times Prizms Checkered Flag /1 #8
2016 Panini Prizm Qualifying Times Prizms Gold /10 #8
2016 Panini Prizm Race Used Tire #13
2016 Panini Prizm Race Used Tire Prizms Blue Flag /49 #13
2016 Panini Prizm Race Used Tire Prizms Checkered Flag /1 #13
2016 Panini Prizm Race Used Tire Prizms Green Flag /99 #13
2016 Panini Prizm Race Used Tire Prizms Red Flag /25 #13
2016 Panini Prizm Race Used Tire Team #12
2016 Panini Prizm Race Used Tire Team Prizms Blue Flag /75 #12
2016 Panini Prizm Race Used Tire Team Prizms Green Flag /149 #12
2016 Panini Prizm Race Used Tire Team Prizms Red Flag /10 #12
2016 Panini Prizm Raising the Flag #9
2016 Panini Prizm Raising the Flag Prizms #9
2016 Panini Prizm Raising the Flag Prizms Checkered Flag /1 #9
2016 Panini Prizm Raising the Flag Prizms Gold /10 #9
2016 Panini Torque #2
2016 Panini Torque #78
2016 Panini Torque Artist Proof /50 #2
2016 Panini Torque Artist Proof /50 #78
2016 Panini Torque Blackout /1 #2
2016 Panini Torque Blackout /1 #78
2016 Panini Torque Blue /125 #2
2016 Panini Torque Blue /125 #78
2016 Panini Torque Championship Vision #5
2016 Panini Torque Championship Vision Blue /99 #5
2016 Panini Torque Championship Vision Gold /149 #5
2016 Panini Torque Championship Vision Green /25 #5
2016 Panini Torque Championship Vision Purple /10 #5
2016 Panini Torque Championship Vision Red /49 #5
2016 Panini Torque Clear Vision #2
2016 Panini Torque Clear Vision Blue /99 #2
2016 Panini Torque Clear Vision Gold /149 #2
2016 Panini Torque Clear Vision Green /25 #2
2016 Panini Torque Clear Vision Purple /10 #2
2016 Panini Torque Clear Vision Red /49 #2
2016 Panini Torque Gas N Go #10
2016 Panini Torque Gas N Go Gold /199 #10
2016 Panini Torque Gas N Go Holo Silver /99 #10
2016 Panini Torque Gold #2
2016 Panini Torque Gold #78
2016 Panini Torque Helmets #5
2016 Panini Torque Helmets Blue /99 #5
2016 Panini Torque Helmets Checkerboard /10 #5
2016 Panini Torque Helmets Green /25 #5
2016 Panini Torque Helmets Red /49 #5
2016 Panini Torque Holo Gold /5 #2
2016 Panini Torque Holo Gold /5 #78
2016 Panini Torque Holo Silver /10 #2
2016 Panini Torque Holo Silver /10 #78
2016 Panini Torque Horsepower Heroes #25
2016 Panini Torque Horsepower Heroes Gold /199 #25
2016 Panini Torque Horsepower Heroes Holo Silver /99 #25
2016 Panini Torque Nicknames #4
2016 Panini Torque Nicknames Gold /199 #4
2016 Panini Torque Nicknames Holo Silver /99 #4
2016 Panini Torque Painted to Perfection #4
2016 Panini Torque Painted to Perfection Blue /99 #4
2016 Panini Torque Painted to Perfection Checkerboard /10 #4
2016 Panini Torque Painted to Perfection Green /25 #4
2016 Panini Torque Painted to Perfection Red /49 #4
2016 Panini Torque Pairings Materials /249 #9
2016 Panini Torque Pairings Materials /125 #17
2016 Panini Torque Pairings Materials Blue /99 #9
2016 Panini Torque Pairings Materials Blue /99 #17
2016 Panini Torque Pairings Materials Green /25 #9
2016 Panini Torque Pairings Materials Green /25 #17
2016 Panini Torque Pairings Materials Purple /10 #9
2016 Panini Torque Pairings Materials Purple /10 #17
2016 Panini Torque Pairings Materials Red /49 #9
2016 Panini Torque Pairings Materials Red /49 #17
2016 Panini Torque Pole Position #2
2016 Panini Torque Pole Position Blue /99 #2
2016 Panini Torque Pole Position Checkerboard /10 #2
2016 Panini Torque Pole Position Green /25 #2
2016 Panini Torque Pole Position Red /49 #2
2016 Panini Torque Printing Plates Black /1 #2
2016 Panini Torque Printing Plates Black /1 #78
2016 Panini Torque Printing Plates Cyan /1 #2
2016 Panini Torque Printing Plates Cyan /1 #78
2016 Panini Torque Printing Plates Magenta /1 #2
2016 Panini Torque Printing Plates Magenta /1 #78
2016 Panini Torque Printing Plates Yellow /1 #2
2016 Panini Torque Printing Plates Yellow /1 #78
2016 Panini Torque Purple /25 #2
2016 Panini Torque Purple /25 #78
2016 Panini Torque Race Kings #12
2016 Panini Torque Race Kings Gold /199 #12
2016 Panini Torque Race Kings Holo Silver /99 #12
2016 Panini Torque Red /99 #2
2016 Panini Torque Red /99 #78
2016 Panini Torque Rubber Relics /399 #20
2016 Panini Torque Rubber Relics Blue /99 #20
2016 Panini Torque Rubber Relics Green /25 #20
2016 Panini Torque Rubber Relics Purple /10 #20
2016 Panini Torque Rubber Relics Red /49 #20
2016 Panini Torque Shades #5
2016 Panini Torque Shades Gold /199 #5
2016 Panini Torque Shades Holo Silver /99 #5
2016 Panini Torque Superstar Vision #1
2016 Panini Torque Superstar Vision Blue /99 #1
2016 Panini Torque Superstar Vision Gold /149 #1
2016 Panini Torque Superstar Vision Green /25 #1
2016 Panini Torque Superstar Vision Purple /10 #1
2016 Panini Torque Superstar Vision Red /49 #1
2016 Panini Torque Test Proof Black /1 #2
2016 Panini Torque Test Proof Black /1 #78
2016 Panini Torque Test Proof Cyan /1 #2
2016 Panini Torque Test Proof Cyan /1 #78
2016 Panini Torque Test Proof Magenta /1 #2
2016 Panini Torque Test Proof Magenta /1 #78
2016 Panini Torque Test Proof Yellow /1 #2
2016 Panini Torque Test Proof Yellow /1 #78
2016 Panini Torque Winning Vision #2
2016 Panini Torque Winning Vision Blue /99 #2
2016 Panini Torque Winning Vision Gold /149 #2
2016 Panini Torque Winning Vision Green /25 #2
2016 Panini Torque Winning Vision Purple /10 #2
2016 Panini Torque Winning Vision Red /49 #2
2017 Donruss #27
2017 Donruss #136
2017 Donruss #188
2017 Donruss Artist Proof /25 #27
2017 Donruss Artist Proof /25 #136
2017 Donruss Artist Proof /25 #188
2017 Donruss Blue Foil /299 #27
2017 Donruss Blue Foil /299 #136
2017 Donruss Blue Foil /299 #188
2017 Donruss Classics #15
2017 Donruss Classics Cracked Ice /999 #15
2017 Donruss Gold Foil /499 #27
2017 Donruss Gold Foil /499 #136
2017 Donruss Gold Foil /499 #188
2017 Donruss Gold Press Proof /99 #27
2017 Donruss Gold Press Proof /99 #136
2017 Donruss Gold Press Proof /99 #188
2017 Donruss Green Foil /199 #27
2017 Donruss Green Foil /199 #136
2017 Donruss Green Foil /199 #188
2017 Donruss Press Proof /49 #27
2017 Donruss Press Proof /49 #136
2017 Donruss Press Proof /49 #188
2017 Donruss Printing Plates Black /1 #27
2017 Donruss Printing Plates Black /1 #136
2017 Donruss Printing Plates Black /1 #188
2017 Donruss Printing Plates Cyan /1 #27
2017 Donruss Printing Plates Cyan /1 #136
2017 Donruss Printing Plates Cyan /1 #188
2017 Donruss Printing Plates Magenta /1 #27
2017 Donruss Printing Plates Magenta /1 #136
2017 Donruss Printing Plates Magenta /1 #188
2017 Donruss Printing Plates Yellow /1 #27
2017 Donruss Printing Plates Yellow /1 #136
2017 Donruss Printing Plates Yellow /1 #188
2017 Donruss Rubber Relics #42
2017 Donruss Rubber Relics Holo Black /10 #42
2017 Donruss Rubber Relics Holo Gold /99 #42
2017 Panini National Treasures /25 #31
2017 Panini National Treasures Century Black /1 #31
2017 Panini National Treasures Century Gold /15 #31
2017 Panini National Treasures Century Green /5 #31
2017 Panini National Treasures Century Holo Gold /10 #31
2017 Panini National Treasures Century Holo Silver /20 #31
2017 Panini National Treasures Century Laundry Tags /1 #31
2017 Panini National Treasures Championship Signatures /25 #11
2017 Panini National Treasures Championship Signatures Black /1 #11
2017 Panini National Treasures Championship Signatures Gold /15 #11
2017 Panini National Treasures Championship Signatures Green /5 #11
2017 Panini National Treasures Championship Signatures Holo Gold /10 #11
2017 Panini National Treasures Championship Signatures Holo Silver /20 #11
2017 Panini National Treasures Championship Signatures Printing Plates Black /1 #11
2017 Panini National Treasures Championship Signatures Printing Plates Cyan /1 #11
2017 Panini National Treasures Championship Signatures Printing Plates Magenta /1 #11
2017 Panini National Treasures Championship Signatures Printing Plates Yellow /1 #11
2017 Panini National Treasures Dual Firesuit Signatures /25 #21
2017 Panini National Treasures Dual Firesuit Signatures Black /1 #21
2017 Panini National Treasures Dual Firesuit Signatures Gold /15 #21
2017 Panini National Treasures Dual Firesuit Signatures Green /5 #21
2017 Panini National Treasures Dual Firesuit Signatures Holo Gold /10 #21
2017 Panini National Treasures Dual Firesuit Signatures Holo Silver /20 #21
2017 Panini National Treasures Dual Firesuit Signatures Laundry Tag /1 #21
2017 Panini National Treasures Dual Firesuit Signatures Printing Plates Black /1 #21
2017 Panini National Treasures Dual Firesuit Signatures Printing Plates Cyan /1 #21
2017 Panini National Treasures Dual Firesuit Signatures Printing Plates Magenta /1 #21
2017 Panini National Treasures Dual Firesuit Signatures Printing Plates Yellow /1 #21
2017 Panini National Treasures Dual Tire Signatures /25 #16
2017 Panini National Treasures Dual Tire Signatures Black /1 #16
2017 Panini National Treasures Dual Tire Signatures Gold /15 #16
2017 Panini National Treasures Dual Tire Signatures Green /5 #16
2017 Panini National Treasures Dual Tire Signatures Holo Gold /10 #16
2017 Panini National Treasures Dual Tire Signatures Holo Silver /20 #16
2017 Panini National Treasures Dual Tire Signatures Printing Plates Black /1 #16
2017 Panini National Treasures Dual Tire Signatures Printing Plates Cyan /1 #16
2017 Panini National Treasures Dual Tire Signatures Printing Plates Magenta /1 #16
2017 Panini National Treasures Dual Tire Signatures Printing Plates Yellow /1 #16
2017 Panini National Treasures Jumbo Firesuit Signatures /25 #16
2017 Panini National Treasures Jumbo Firesuit Signatures Black /1 #16
2017 Panini National Treasures Jumbo Firesuit Signatures Gold /15 #16
2017 Panini National Treasures Jumbo Firesuit Signatures Green /5 #16
2017 Panini National Treasures Jumbo Firesuit Signatures Holo Gold /10 #16
2017 Panini National Treasures Jumbo Firesuit Signatures Holo Silver /20 #16
2017 Panini National Treasures Jumbo Firesuit Signatures Laundry Tag /1 #16
2017 Panini National Treasures Jumbo Firesuit Signatures Printing Plates Black /1 #16
2017 Panini National Treasures Jumbo Firesuit Signatures Printing Plates Cyan /1 #16
2017 Panini National Treasures Jumbo Firesuit Signatures Printing Plates Magenta /1 #16
2017 Panini National Treasures Jumbo Firesuit Signatures Printing Plates Yellow /1 #16
2017 Panini National Treasures Printing Plates Black /1 #31
2017 Panini National Treasures Printing Plates Cyan /1 #31
2017 Panini National Treasures Printing Plates Magenta /1 #31
2017 Panini National Treasures Printing Plates Yellow /1 #31
2018 Certified #34
2018 Certified #81
2018 Certified All Certified Team /199 #3
2018 Certified All Certified Team Black /1 #3
2018 Certified All Certified Team Blue /99 #3
2018 Certified All Certified Team Gold /49 #3
2018 Certified All Certified Team Green /10 #3
2018 Certified All Certified Team Mirror Black /1 #3
2018 Certified All Certified Team Mirror Gold /25 #3
2018 Certified All Certified Team Mirror Green /5 #3

2018 Certified All Certified Team Mirror Purple /10 #3
2018 Certified All Certified Team Purple /25 #3
2018 Certified All Certified Team Red /149 #3
2018 Certified Black /1 #34
2018 Certified Black /1 #81
2018 Certified Blue /99 #34
2018 Certified Blue /99 #81
2018 Certified Epix /199 #20
2018 Certified Epix Black /1 #20
2018 Certified Epix Blue /99 #20
2018 Certified Epix Gold /49 #20
2018 Certified Epix Green /10 #20
2018 Certified Epix Mirror Black /1 #20
2018 Certified Epix Mirror Gold /25 #20
2018 Certified Epix Mirror Green /5 #20
2018 Certified Epix Mirror Purple /10 #20
2018 Certified Epix Purple /25 #20
2018 Certified Epix Red /149 #20
2018 Certified Gold /49 #34
2018 Certified Gold /49 #81
2018 Certified Green /10 #34
2018 Certified Green /10 #81
2018 Certified Materials Signatures Black /1 #8
2018 Certified Materials Signatures Gold /14 #8
2018 Certified Materials Signatures Green /5 #8
2018 Certified Materials Signatures Purple /10 #8
2018 Certified Mirror Black /1 #34
2018 Certified Mirror Black /1 #81
2018 Certified Mirror Gold /25 #34
2018 Certified Mirror Gold /25 #81
2018 Certified Mirror Green /5 #34
2018 Certified Mirror Green /5 #81
2018 Certified Mirror Purple /10 #34
2018 Certified Mirror Purple /10 #81
2018 Certified Orange /249 #34
2018 Certified Orange /249 #81
2018 Certified Piece of the Race /499 #12
2018 Certified Piece of the Race Black /1 #12
2018 Certified Piece of the Race Blue /49 #12
2018 Certified Piece of the Race Gold /25 #12
2018 Certified Piece of the Race Green /5 #12
2018 Certified Piece of the Race Purple /10 #12
2018 Certified Piece of the Race Red /199 #12
2018 Certified Purple /25 #34
2018 Certified Purple /25 #81
2018 Certified Red /199 #34
2018 Certified Red /199 #81
2018 Certified Signature Swatches Black /1 #18
2018 Certified Signature Swatches Blue /25 #18
2018 Certified Signature Swatches Gold /14 #18
2018 Certified Signature Swatches Green /5 #18
2018 Certified Signature Swatches Purple /10 #18
2018 Certified Signing Sessions Black /1 #25
2018 Certified Signing Sessions Green /5 #25
2018 Certified Signing Sessions Purple /10 #25
2018 Certified Stars /199 #23
2018 Certified Stars Black /1 #23
2018 Certified Stars Blue /99 #23
2018 Certified Stars Gold /49 #23
2018 Certified Stars Green /10 #23
2018 Certified Stars Mirror Black /1 #23
2018 Certified Stars Mirror Gold /25 #23
2018 Certified Stars Mirror Green /5 #23
2018 Certified Stars Mirror Purple /10 #23
2018 Certified Stars Purple /25 #23
2018 Certified Stars Red /149 #23
2018 Donruss #1
2018 Donruss #102A
2018 Donruss #102B
2018 Donruss Artist Proofs /25 #1
2018 Donruss Artist Proofs /25 #102
2018 Donruss Artist Proofs /25 #102B
2018 Donruss Classics #2
2018 Donruss Classics #20
2018 Donruss Classics Cracked Ice /999 #2
2018 Donruss Classics Cracked Ice /999 #20
2018 Donruss Classics Xplosion /99 #2
2018 Donruss Classics Xplosion /99 #20
2018 Donruss Elite Dominators /999 #1
2018 Donruss Elite Series /999 #1
2018 Donruss Gold Foil /499 #1
2018 Donruss Gold Foil /499 #102
2018 Donruss Gold Foil /499 #102B
2018 Donruss Gold Press Proofs /99 #1
2018 Donruss Gold Press Proofs /99 #102
2018 Donruss Gold Press Proofs /99 #102B
2018 Donruss Green Foil /199 #1
2018 Donruss Green Foil /199 #102
2018 Donruss Green Foil /199 #102B
2018 Donruss Masters of the Track #3
2018 Donruss Masters of the Track Cracked Ice /999 #3
2018 Donruss Masters of the Track Xplosion /99 #3
2018 Donruss Press Proofs /49 #1
2018 Donruss Press Proofs /49 #102A
2018 Donruss Press Proofs /49 #102B
2018 Donruss Printing Plates Black /1 #1
2018 Donruss Printing Plates Black /1 #102
2018 Donruss Printing Plates Black /1 #102B
2018 Donruss Printing Plates Cyan /1 #1
2018 Donruss Printing Plates Cyan /1 #102
2018 Donruss Printing Plates Cyan /1 #102B
2018 Donruss Printing Plates Magenta /1 #1
2018 Donruss Printing Plates Magenta /1 #102
2018 Donruss Printing Plates Magenta /1 #102B
2018 Donruss Printing Plates Yellow /1 #1
2018 Donruss Printing Plates Yellow /1 #102
2018 Donruss Printing Plates Yellow /1 #102B
2018 Donruss Racing Relics #19
2018 Donruss Racing Relics Black /10 #19
2018 Donruss Racing Relics Holo Gold /99 #19
2018 Donruss Red Foil /299 #1
2018 Donruss Red Foil /299 #102A
2018 Donruss Red Foil /299 #102B
2018 Donruss Retro Relics '85 #17
2018 Donruss Retro Relics '85 Black /10 #17
2018 Donruss Retro Relics '85 Holo Gold /99 #17
2018 Donruss Rubber Relic Signatures #10
2018 Donruss Rubber Relic Signatures Black /1 #10
2018 Donruss Rubber Relic Signatures Holo Gold /25 #10
2018 Donruss Rubber Relics #37
2018 Donruss Rubber Relics Black /10 #37
2018 Donruss Rubber Relics Holo Gold /99 #37
2018 Donruss Slingshot #SS3
2018 Donruss Studio #20
2018 Donruss Studio Cracked Ice /999 #20
2018 Donruss Studio Xplosion /99 #20
2018 Panini Prime /50 #26
2018 Panini Prime /50 #59
2018 Panini Prime /50 #92
2018 Panini Prime Autograph Materials /10 #24
2018 Panini Prime Autograph Materials Black /1 #24
2018 Panini Prime Autograph Materials Holo Gold /5 #24
2018 Panini Prime Autograph Materials Laundry Tag /1 #24
2018 Panini Prime Black /1 #26
2018 Panini Prime Black /1 #59
2018 Panini Prime Black /1 #92
2018 Panini Prime Clear Silhouettes Dual /99 #30
2018 Panini Prime Clear Silhouettes Dual Black /1 #30
2018 Panini Prime Clear Silhouettes Dual Holo Gold /50 #30
2018 Panini Prime Driver Signatures /5 #19
2018 Panini Prime Driver Signatures Black /1 #19
2018 Panini Prime Driver Signatures Holo Gold /3 #19
2018 Panini Prime Dual Signatures /10 #6
2018 Panini Prime Dual Signatures Black /1 #6
2018 Panini Prime Dual Signatures Holo Gold /5 #6
2018 Panini Prime Holo Gold /25 #26
2018 Panini Prime Holo Gold /25 #59
2018 Panini Prime Holo Gold /25 #92
2018 Panini Prime Prime Jumbo Associate Sponsor 1 /1 #70
2018 Panini Prime Prime Jumbo Associate Sponsor 1 /1 #71
2018 Panini Prime Prime Jumbo Associate Sponsor 1 /1 #72
2018 Panini Prime Prime Jumbo Associate Sponsor 10 /1 #71
2018 Panini Prime Prime Jumbo Associate Sponsor 10 /1 #72
2018 Panini Prime Prime Jumbo Associate Sponsor 11 /1 #71
2018 Panini Prime Prime Jumbo Associate Sponsor 12 /1 #71
2018 Panini Prime Prime Jumbo Associate Sponsor 2 /1 #70
2018 Panini Prime Prime Jumbo Associate Sponsor 2 /1 #71
2018 Panini Prime Prime Jumbo Associate Sponsor 2 /1 #72
2018 Panini Prime Prime Jumbo Associate Sponsor 3 /1 #70
2018 Panini Prime Prime Jumbo Associate Sponsor 3 /1 #71
2018 Panini Prime Prime Jumbo Associate Sponsor 3 /1 #72
2018 Panini Prime Prime Jumbo Associate Sponsor 4 /1 #70
2018 Panini Prime Prime Jumbo Associate Sponsor 4 /1 #71
2018 Panini Prime Prime Jumbo Associate Sponsor 4 /1 #72
2018 Panini Prime Prime Jumbo Associate Sponsor 5 /1 #70
2018 Panini Prime Prime Jumbo Associate Sponsor 5 /1 #71
2018 Panini Prime Prime Jumbo Associate Sponsor 5 /1 #72
2018 Panini Prime Prime Jumbo Associate Sponsor 6 /1 #70
2018 Panini Prime Prime Jumbo Associate Sponsor 6 /1 #71
2018 Panini Prime Prime Jumbo Associate Sponsor 6 /1 #72
2018 Panini Prime Prime Jumbo Associate Sponsor 7 /1 #70
2018 Panini Prime Prime Jumbo Associate Sponsor 7 /1 #71
2018 Panini Prime Prime Jumbo Associate Sponsor 7 /1 #72
2018 Panini Prime Prime Jumbo Associate Sponsor 8 /1 #71
2018 Panini Prime Prime Jumbo Associate Sponsor 8 /1 #72
2018 Panini Prime Prime Jumbo Associate Sponsor 9 /1 #71
2018 Panini Prime Prime Jumbo Associate Sponsor 9 /1 #72
2018 Panini Prime Prime Jumbo Firesuit Manufacturer /1 #70
2018 Panini Prime Prime Jumbo Firesuit Manufacturer /1 #71
2018 Panini Prime Prime Jumbo Firesuit Manufacturer /1 #72
2018 Panini Prime Prime Jumbo Goodyear /2 #70
2018 Panini Prime Prime Jumbo Goodyear /2 #71
2018 Panini Prime Prime Jumbo Nameplate /1 #70
2018 Panini Prime Prime Jumbo Nameplate /1 #72
2018 Panini Prime Prime Jumbo NASCAR /1 #70
2018 Panini Prime Prime Jumbo NASCAR /1 #71
2018 Panini Prime Prime Jumbo NASCAR /1 #72
2018 Panini Prime Prime Jumbo Prime Colors /16 #72
2018 Panini Prime Prime Jumbo Series Sponsor /1 #70
2018 Panini Prime Prime Jumbo Series Sponsor /1 #71
2018 Panini Prime Prime Jumbo Series Sponsor /1 #72
2018 Panini Prime Prime Jumbo Shoe Brand Logo /1 #70
2018 Panini Prime Prime Jumbo Shoe Brand Logo /1 #72
2018 Panini Prime Prime Jumbo Shoe Name Patch /1 #70
2018 Panini Prime Prime Jumbo Shoe Name Patch /1 #72
2018 Panini Prime Prime Jumbo Sunoco /1 #70
2018 Panini Prime Prime Jumbo Sunoco /1 #71
2018 Panini Prime Prime Jumbo Sunoco /1 #72
2018 Panini Prime Prime Signatures /5 #19
2018 Panini Prime Prime Signatures Black /1 #19
2018 Panini Prime Prime Signatures Holo Gold /3 #19
2018 Panini Prime Race Used Duals Firesuit Black /1 #30
2018 Panini Prime Race Used Duals Firesuit Holo Gold /25 #30
2018 Panini Prime Race Used Duals Firesuit Laundry Tag /1 #30
2018 Panini Prime Race Used Duals Sheet Metal /50 #30
2018 Panini Prime Race Used Duals Sheet Metal Black /1 #30
2018 Panini Prime Race Used Duals Sheet Metal Holo Gold /25 #30
2018 Panini Prime Race Used Duals Tire /50 #30
2018 Panini Prime Race Used Duals Tire Black /1 #30
2018 Panini Prime Race Used Duals Tire Holo Gold /25 #30
2018 Panini Prime Race Used Firesuits Black /1 #37
2018 Panini Prime Race Used Firesuits Holo Gold /25 #37
2018 Panini Prime Race Used Firesuits Laundry Tag /1 #37
2018 Panini Prime Race Used Sheet Metal /50 #37
2018 Panini Prime Race Used Sheet Metal Black /1 #37
2018 Panini Prime Race Used Sheet Metal Holo Gold /25 #37
2018 Panini Prime Race Used Tires /50 #37
2018 Panini Prime Race Used Tires Black /1 #37
2018 Panini Prime Race Used Tires Holo Gold /25 #37
2018 Panini Prime Race Used Trios Firesuit /50 #4
2018 Panini Prime Race Used Trios Firesuit Black /1 #4
2018 Panini Prime Race Used Trios Firesuit Holo Gold /25 #4
2018 Panini Prime Race Used Trios Firesuit Laundry Tag /1 #4
2018 Panini Prime Race Used Trios Sheet Metal /50 #4
2018 Panini Prime Race Used Trios Sheet Metal Black /1 #4
2018 Panini Prime Race Used Trios Sheet Metal Holo Gold /25 #4
2018 Panini Prime Race Used Trios Tire /50 #4
2018 Panini Prime Race Used Trios Tire Black /1 #4
2018 Panini Prime Race Used Trios Tire Holo Gold /25 #4
2018 Panini Prime Shadowbox Signatures /10 #6
2018 Panini Prime Shadowbox Signatures Black /1 #6
2018 Panini Prime Shadowbox Signatures Holo Gold /5 #6
2018 Panini Prime Signature Swatches /10 #19
2018 Panini Prime Signature Swatches Black /1 #19
2018 Panini Prime Signature Swatches Holo Gold /5 #19
2018 Panini Prime Signature Tires /10 #17
2018 Panini Prime Signature Tires Black /1 #17
2018 Panini Prime Signature Tires Holo Gold /5 #17
2018 Panini Prime Triple Material Autographs /10 #2
2018 Panini Prime Triple Material Autographs Black /1 #2
2018 Panini Prime Triple Material Autographs Holo Gold /5 #2
2018 Panini Prime Triple Material Autographs Laundry Tag /1 #2
2018 Panini Prizm #2A
2018 Panini Prizm #2B
2018 Panini Prizm #55
2018 Panini Prizm #61
2018 Panini Prizm #79
2018 Panini Prizm #86
2018 Panini Prizm Brilliance #8
2018 Panini Prizm Brilliance Prizms #8
2018 Panini Prizm Brilliance Prizms Black /1 #8
2018 Panini Prizm Brilliance Prizms Gold /10 #8
2018 Panini Prizm Illumination #3
2018 Panini Prizm Illumination Prizms #3
2018 Panini Prizm Illumination Prizms Black /1 #3
2018 Panini Prizm Illumination Prizms Gold /10 #3
2018 Panini Prizm Patented Penmanship Prizms #14
2018 Panini Prizm Patented Penmanship Prizms Black /1 #14
2018 Panini Prizm Patented Penmanship Prizms Blue /25 #14
2018 Panini Prizm Patented Penmanship Prizms Camo #14
2018 Panini Prizm Patented Penmanship Prizms Gold /10 #14
2018 Panini Prizm Patented Penmanship Prizms Green /25 #14
2018 Panini Prizm Patented Penmanship Prizms Rainbow /24 #14
2018 Panini Prizm Patented Penmanship Prizms Red /25 #14
2018 Panini Prizm Patented Penmanship Prizms Red White and Blue /25 #14
2018 Panini Prizm Patented Penmanship Prizms White /5 #14
2018 Panini Prizm Prizms #2A
2018 Panini Prizm Prizms #2B
2018 Panini Prizm Prizms #55
2018 Panini Prizm Prizms #61
2018 Panini Prizm Prizms #79
2018 Panini Prizm Prizms #86
2018 Panini Prizm Prizms Black /1 #2A
2018 Panini Prizm Prizms Black /1 #2B
2018 Panini Prizm Prizms Black /1 #55
2018 Panini Prizm Prizms Black /1 #61
2018 Panini Prizm Prizms Black /1 #79
2018 Panini Prizm Prizms Black /1 #86
2018 Panini Prizm Prizms Blue /99 #2A
2018 Panini Prizm Prizms Blue /99 #2B
2018 Panini Prizm Prizms Blue /99 #55
2018 Panini Prizm Prizms Blue /99 #61
2018 Panini Prizm Prizms Blue /99 #79
2018 Panini Prizm Prizms Blue /99 #86
2018 Panini Prizm Prizms Camo #2A
2018 Panini Prizm Prizms Camo #2B
2018 Panini Prizm Prizms Camo #55
2018 Panini Prizm Prizms Camo #61
2018 Panini Prizm Prizms Camo #79
2018 Panini Prizm Prizms Camo #86
2018 Panini Prizm Prizms Gold /10 #2A
2018 Panini Prizm Prizms Gold /10 #2B
2018 Panini Prizm Prizms Gold /10 #55
2018 Panini Prizm Prizms Gold /10 #61
2018 Panini Prizm Prizms Gold /10 #79
2018 Panini Prizm Prizms Gold /10 #86
2018 Panini Prizm Prizms Green /149 #2A
2018 Panini Prizm Prizms Green /149 #2B
2018 Panini Prizm Prizms Green /149 #55
2018 Panini Prizm Prizms Green /149 #61
2018 Panini Prizm Prizms Green /149 #79
2018 Panini Prizm Prizms Green /149 #86
2018 Panini Prizm Prizms Purple Flash #2A
2018 Panini Prizm Prizms Purple Flash #2B
2018 Panini Prizm Prizms Purple Flash #55
2018 Panini Prizm Prizms Purple Flash #61
2018 Panini Prizm Prizms Purple Flash #79
2018 Panini Prizm Prizms Purple Flash #86
2018 Panini Prizm Prizms Rainbow /24 #2A
2018 Panini Prizm Prizms Rainbow /24 #2B
2018 Panini Prizm Prizms Rainbow /24 #55
2018 Panini Prizm Prizms Rainbow /24 #61
2018 Panini Prizm Prizms Rainbow /24 #79
2018 Panini Prizm Prizms Rainbow /24 #86
2018 Panini Prizm Prizms Red /75 #2A
2018 Panini Prizm Prizms Red /75 #2B
2018 Panini Prizm Prizms Red /75 #55
2018 Panini Prizm Prizms Red /75 #61
2018 Panini Prizm Prizms Red /75 #79
2018 Panini Prizm Prizms Red /75 #86
2018 Panini Prizm Prizms Red White and Blue #2A
2018 Panini Prizm Prizms Red White and Blue #2B
2018 Panini Prizm Prizms Red White and Blue #55
2018 Panini Prizm Prizms Red White and Blue #61
2018 Panini Prizm Prizms Red White and Blue #79
2018 Panini Prizm Prizms Red White and Blue #86
2018 Panini Prizm Prizms White /5 #2A
2018 Panini Prizm Prizms White /5 #2B
2018 Panini Prizm Prizms White /5 #55
2018 Panini Prizm Prizms White /5 #61
2018 Panini Prizm Prizms White /5 #79
2018 Panini Prizm Prizms White /5 #86
2018 Panini Victory Lane #52
2018 Panini Victory Lane #61
2018 Panini Victory Lane #77
2018 Panini Victory Lane #82
2018 Panini Victory Lane #89
2018 Panini Victory Lane Black /1 #52
2018 Panini Victory Lane Black /1 #61
2018 Panini Victory Lane Black /1 #77
2018 Panini Victory Lane Black /1 #82
2018 Panini Victory Lane Black /1 #89
2018 Panini Victory Lane Blue /25 #52
2018 Panini Victory Lane Blue /25 #61
2018 Panini Victory Lane Blue /25 #77
2018 Panini Victory Lane Blue /25 #82
2018 Panini Victory Lane Blue /25 #89
2018 Panini Victory Lane Celebrations #7
2018 Panini Victory Lane Celebrations Black /1 #7
2018 Panini Victory Lane Celebrations Blue /25 #7
2018 Panini Victory Lane Celebrations Gold /99 #7
2018 Panini Victory Lane Celebrations Green /5 #7
2018 Panini Victory Lane Celebrations Printing Plates Black /1 #7
2018 Panini Victory Lane Celebrations Printing Plates Cyan /1 #7
2018 Panini Victory Lane Celebrations Printing Plates Magenta /1 #7
2018 Panini Victory Lane Celebrations Printing Plates Yellow /1 #7
2018 Panini Victory Lane Celebrations Red /49 #7
2018 Panini Victory Lane Champions #5
2018 Panini Victory Lane Champions Black /1 #5
2018 Panini Victory Lane Champions Blue /25 #5
2018 Panini Victory Lane Champions Gold /99 #5
2018 Panini Victory Lane Champions Green /5 #5
2018 Panini Victory Lane Champions Printing Plates Black /1 #5
2018 Panini Victory Lane Champions Printing Plates Cyan /1 #5
2018 Panini Victory Lane Champions Printing Plates Magenta /1 #5
2018 Panini Victory Lane Champions Printing Plates Yellow /1 #5
2018 Panini Victory Lane Champions Red /49 #5
2018 Panini Victory Lane Chasing the Flag #5
2018 Panini Victory Lane Chasing the Flag Black /1 #5
2018 Panini Victory Lane Chasing the Flag Blue /25 #5
2018 Panini Victory Lane Chasing the Flag Gold /99 #5
2018 Panini Victory Lane Chasing the Flag Green /5 #5
2018 Panini Victory Lane Chasing the Flag Printing Plates Black /1 #5
2018 Panini Victory Lane Chasing the Flag Printing Plates Cyan /1 #5
2018 Panini Victory Lane Chasing the Flag Printing Plates Magenta /1 #5
2018 Panini Victory Lane Chasing the Flag Printing Plates Yellow /1 #5
2018 Panini Victory Lane Chasing the Flag Red /49 #5
2018 Panini Victory Lane Engineered to Perfection Materials /399 #23
2018 Panini Victory Lane Engineered to Perfection Materials Black /25 #23
2018 Panini Victory Lane Engineered to Perfection Materials Gold /199 #23
2018 Panini Victory Lane Engineered to Perfection Materials Green /99 #23
2018 Panini Victory Lane Engineered to Perfection Materials Laundry Tag /1 #23
2018 Panini Victory Lane Foundations #2
2018 Panini Victory Lane Foundations Black /1 #2
2018 Panini Victory Lane Foundations Blue /25 #2
2018 Panini Victory Lane Foundations Gold /99 #2
2018 Panini Victory Lane Foundations Green /5 #2
2018 Panini Victory Lane Foundations Printing Plates Black /1 #2
2018 Panini Victory Lane Foundations Printing Plates Cyan /1 #2
2018 Panini Victory Lane Foundations Printing Plates Magenta /1 #2
2018 Panini Victory Lane Foundations Printing Plates Yellow /1 #2
2018 Panini Victory Lane Foundations Red /49 #2
2018 Panini Victory Lane Gold /99 #52
2018 Panini Victory Lane Gold /99 #61
2018 Panini Victory Lane Gold /99 #77
2018 Panini Victory Lane Gold /99 #82
2018 Panini Victory Lane Gold /99 #89
2018 Panini Victory Lane Green /5 #52
2018 Panini Victory Lane Green /5 #61
2018 Panini Victory Lane Green /5 #77
2018 Panini Victory Lane Green /5 #82
2018 Panini Victory Lane Green /5 #89
2018 Panini Victory Lane Pedal to the Metal #100
2018 Panini Victory Lane Pedal to the Metal Black /1 #100
2018 Panini Victory Lane Pedal to the Metal Blue /25 #100
2018 Panini Victory Lane Pedal to the Metal Green /5 #100
2018 Panini Victory Lane Printing Plates Black /1 #52
2018 Panini Victory Lane Printing Plates Black /1 #61
2018 Panini Victory Lane Printing Plates Black /1 #77
2018 Panini Victory Lane Printing Plates Black /1 #82
2018 Panini Victory Lane Printing Plates Black /1 #89
2018 Panini Victory Lane Printing Plates Cyan /1 #52
2018 Panini Victory Lane Printing Plates Cyan /1 #61
2018 Panini Victory Lane Printing Plates Cyan /1 #77
2018 Panini Victory Lane Printing Plates Cyan /1 #82
2018 Panini Victory Lane Printing Plates Cyan /1 #89
2018 Panini Victory Lane Printing Plates Magenta /1 #52
2018 Panini Victory Lane Printing Plates Magenta /1 #61
2018 Panini Victory Lane Printing Plates Magenta /1 #77
2018 Panini Victory Lane Printing Plates Magenta /1 #82
2018 Panini Victory Lane Printing Plates Magenta /1 #89
2018 Panini Victory Lane Printing Plates Yellow /1 #52
2018 Panini Victory Lane Printing Plates Yellow /1 #61
2018 Panini Victory Lane Printing Plates Yellow /1 #77
2018 Panini Victory Lane Printing Plates Yellow /1 #82
2018 Panini Victory Lane Printing Plates Yellow /1 #89
2018 Panini Victory Lane Race Ready Dual Materials /399 #8
2018 Panini Victory Lane Race Ready Dual Materials Black /25 #8
2018 Panini Victory Lane Race Ready Dual Materials Gold /199 #8
2018 Panini Victory Lane Race Ready Dual Materials Green /99 #8
2018 Panini Victory Lane Race Ready Dual Materials Laundry Tag /1 #8
2018 Panini Victory Lane Race Ready Materials /399 #24
2018 Panini Victory Lane Race Ready Materials Black /25 #24
2018 Panini Victory Lane Race Ready Materials Gold /199 #24
2018 Panini Victory Lane Race Ready Materials Green /99 #24
2018 Panini Victory Lane Race Ready Materials Laundry Tag /1 #24
2018 Panini Victory Lane Red /49 #52
2018 Panini Victory Lane Red /49 #61
2018 Panini Victory Lane Red /49 #77
2018 Panini Victory Lane Red /49 #82
2018 Panini Victory Lane Red /49 #89
2018 Panini Victory Lane Remarkable Remnants Material Autographs /145 #5
2018 Panini Victory Lane Remarkable Remnants Material Autographs Black /14 #5
2018 Panini Victory Lane Remarkable Remnants Material Autographs Gold /50 #5
2018 Panini Victory Lane Remarkable Remnants Material Autographs Green /25 #5
2018 Panini Victory Lane Remarkable Remnants Material Autographs Laundry Tag /1 #5
2018 Panini Victory Lane Silver #52
2018 Panini Victory Lane Silver #61
2018 Panini Victory Lane Silver #77
2018 Panini Victory Lane Silver #82
2018 Panini Victory Lane Silver #89
2018 Panini Victory Lane Victory Marks /25 #16
2018 Panini Victory Lane Victory Marks Black /1 #16
2018 Panini Victory Lane Victory Marks Gold /14 #16
2019 Donruss #14
2019 Donruss #65A
2019 Donruss #105
2019 Donruss #171
2019 Donruss #65B
2019 Donruss Artist Proofs /25 #14
2019 Donruss Artist Proofs /25 #65A
2019 Donruss Artist Proofs /25 #105
2019 Donruss Artist Proofs /25 #171
2019 Donruss Artist Proofs /25 #65B
2019 Donruss Black /199 #14
2019 Donruss Black /199 #65A
2019 Donruss Black /199 #105
2019 Donruss Black /199 #171
2019 Donruss Black /199 #65B
2019 Donruss Gold /299 #14
2019 Donruss Gold /299 #65A
2019 Donruss Gold /299 #105
2019 Donruss Gold /299 #171
2019 Donruss Gold /299 #65B
2019 Donruss Gold Press Proofs /99 #14
2019 Donruss Gold Press Proofs /99 #65A
2019 Donruss Gold Press Proofs /99 #105
2019 Donruss Gold Press Proofs /99 #171
2019 Donruss Gold Press Proofs /99 #65B
2019 Donruss Icons #8
2019 Donruss Icons Cracked Ice /25 #8
2019 Donruss Icons Holographic #8
2019 Donruss Icons Xplosion /10 #8
2019 Donruss Optic Illusion #8
2019 Donruss Optic Illusion Blue Pulsar #8
2019 Donruss Optic Illusion Gold /10 #8
2019 Donruss Optic Illusion Gold Vinyl /1 #8
2019 Donruss Optic Illusion Holo #8
2019 Donruss Optic Illusion Red Wave #8
2019 Donruss Optic Illusion Signatures Gold Vinyl /1 #8
2019 Donruss Optic Illusion Signatures Holo /75 #8
2019 Donruss Press Proofs /49 #14
2019 Donruss Press Proofs /49 #65A
2019 Donruss Press Proofs /49 #105
2019 Donruss Press Proofs /49 #171
2019 Donruss Press Proofs /49 #65B
2019 Donruss Printing Plates Black /1 #14
2019 Donruss Printing Plates Black /1 #65A
2019 Donruss Printing Plates Black /1 #105
2019 Donruss Printing Plates Black /1 #171
2019 Donruss Printing Plates Black /1 #65B
2019 Donruss Printing Plates Cyan /1 #14
2019 Donruss Printing Plates Cyan /1 #65A
2019 Donruss Printing Plates Cyan /1 #105
2019 Donruss Printing Plates Cyan /1 #171
2019 Donruss Printing Plates Cyan /1 #65B
2019 Donruss Printing Plates Magenta /1 #65A
2019 Donruss Printing Plates Magenta /1 #105
2019 Donruss Printing Plates Magenta /1 #171
2019 Donruss Printing Plates Magenta /1 #65B
2019 Donruss Printing Plates Magenta /1 #14
2019 Donruss Printing Plates Yellow /1 #14
2019 Donruss Printing Plates Yellow /1 #65A
2019 Donruss Printing Plates Yellow /1 #105
2019 Donruss Printing Plates Yellow /1 #171
2019 Donruss Printing Plates Yellow /1 #65B
2019 Donruss Race Day Relics #13
2019 Donruss Race Day Relics Holo Black /10 #13
2019 Donruss Race Day Relics Holo Gold /25 #13
2019 Donruss Race Day Relics Red /185 #13
2019 Donruss Retro Relics '86 #11
2019 Donruss Retro Relics '86 Holo Black /10 #11
2019 Donruss Retro Relics '86 Holo Gold /25 #11
2019 Donruss Retro Relics '86 Red /225 #11
2019 Donruss Signature Swatches #8
2019 Donruss Signature Swatches Holo Black /10 #8
2019 Donruss Signature Swatches Holo Gold /25 #8
2019 Donruss Signature Swatches Red /49 #8
2019 Donruss Silver #14
2019 Donruss Silver #65A
2019 Donruss Silver #105
2019 Donruss Silver #171
2019 Donruss Silver #65B
2019 Panini Prime /50 #64
2019 Panini Prime /50 #93
2019 Panini Prime Black /10 #64
2019 Panini Prime Black /10 #93
2019 Panini Prime Clear Silhouettes /25 #5
2019 Panini Prime Clear Silhouettes Black /3 #5
2019 Panini Prime Clear Silhouettes Holo Gold /7 #5
2019 Panini Prime Clear Silhouettes Platinum Blue /1 #5
2019 Panini Prime Dual Material Autographs /25 #9
2019 Panini Prime Dual Material Autographs Black /5 #9
2019 Panini Prime Dual Material Autographs Holo Gold /14 #9
2019 Panini Prime Dual Material Autographs Laundry Tags /1 #9
2019 Panini Prime Emerald /5 #64
2019 Panini Prime Emerald /5 #93
2019 Panini Prime Platinum Blue /1 #64
2019 Panini Prime Platinum Blue /1 #93
2019 Panini Prime Prime Jumbo Associate Sponsor 1 /1 #75
2019 Panini Prime Prime Jumbo Associate Sponsor 1 /1 #76
2019 Panini Prime Prime Jumbo Associate Sponsor 1 /1 #77
2019 Panini Prime Prime Jumbo Associate Sponsor 2 /1 #75
2019 Panini Prime Prime Jumbo Associate Sponsor 2 /1 #76
2019 Panini Prime Prime Jumbo Associate Sponsor 2 /1 #77
2019 Panini Prime Prime Jumbo Associate Sponsor 3 /1 #75
2019 Panini Prime Prime Jumbo Associate Sponsor 3 /1 #76
2019 Panini Prime Prime Jumbo Car Manufacturer /1 #75
2019 Panini Prime Prime Jumbo Car Manufacturer /1 #77
2019 Panini Prime Prime Jumbo Firesuit Manufacturer /1 #75
2019 Panini Prime Prime Jumbo Firesuit Manufacturer /1 #76
2019 Panini Prime Prime Jumbo Firesuit Manufacturer /1 #77
2019 Panini Prime Prime Jumbo Goodyear /2 #76
2019 Panini Prime Prime Jumbo Nameplate /1 #76
2019 Panini Prime Prime Jumbo NASCAR /1 #77
2019 Panini Prime Prime Jumbo Prime Colors /15 #75
2019 Panini Prime Prime Jumbo Prime Colors /20 #76
2019 Panini Prime Prime Jumbo Prime Colors /10 #77
2019 Panini Prime Prime Jumbo Shoe Brand Logo /1 #75
2019 Panini Prime Prime Jumbo Shoe Brand Logo /1 #76
2019 Panini Prime Prime Jumbo Shoe Brand Logo /1 #77
2019 Panini Prime Prime Names Die Cut Signatures /25 #22
2019 Panini Prime Prime Names Die Cut Signatures Black /5 #22
2019 Panini Prime Prime Names Die Cut Signatures Holo Gold /14 #22
2019 Panini Prime Prime Names Die Cut Signatures Platinum Blue /1 #22
2019 Panini Prime Race Used Duals Firesuits Laundry Tags /1 #4
2019 Panini Prime Race Used Duals Sheet Metal Black /10 #4
2019 Panini Prime Race Used Duals Sheet Metal Platinum Blue /1 #4
2019 Panini Prime Race Used Duals Tires Platinum Blue /1 #4
2019 Panini Prime Race Used Firesuits Laundry Tags /1 #35
2019 Panini Prime Race Used Sheet Metal /50 #35
2019 Panini Prime Race Used Sheet Metal Black /10 #35
2019 Panini Prime Race Used Sheet Metal Holo Gold /25 #35
2019 Panini Prime Race Used Sheet Metal Platinum Blue /1 #35
2019 Panini Prime Race Used Tires /27 #35
2019 Panini Prime Race Used Tires Black /10 #35
2019 Panini Prime Race Used Tires Holo Gold /25 #35
2019 Panini Prime Race Used Tires Platinum Blue /1 #35
2019 Panini Prime Race Used Trios Firesuits Laundry Tags /1 #4
2019 Panini Prime Race Used Trios Sheet Metal Black /10 #4
2019 Panini Prime Race Used Trios Sheet Metal Platinum Blue /1 #4
2019 Panini Prime Race Used Trios Tires Platinum Blue /1 #4
2019 Panini Prime Shadowbox Signatures /25 #19
2019 Panini Prime Shadowbox Signatures Black /5 #19
2019 Panini Prime Shadowbox Signatures Holo Gold /14 #19
2019 Panini Prime Shadowbox Signatures Platinum Blue /1 #19
2019 Panini Prizm #43A
2019 Panini Prizm #43B
2019 Panini Prizm Apex #14
2019 Panini Prizm Apex Prizms #14
2019 Panini Prizm Apex Prizms Black /1 #14
2019 Panini Prizm Apex Prizms Gold /10 #14
2019 Panini Prizm Apex Prizms White Sparkle #14
2019 Panini Prizm Endorsements Prizms #20
2019 Panini Prizm Endorsements Prizms Black /1 #20
2019 Panini Prizm Endorsements Prizms Blue /5 #20
2019 Panini Prizm Endorsements Prizms Camo #20
2019 Panini Prizm Endorsements Prizms Gold /5 #20
2019 Panini Prizm Endorsements Prizms Rainbow /5 #20
2019 Panini Prizm Endorsements Prizms Red /5 #20
2019 Panini Prizm Endorsements Prizms Red White and Blue #20
2019 Panini Prizm Endorsements Prizms White /5 #20
2019 Panini Prizm Fireworks #20
2019 Panini Prizm Fireworks Prizms #20
2019 Panini Prizm Fireworks Prizms Black /1 #20
2019 Panini Prizm Fireworks Prizms Gold /10 #20
2019 Panini Prizm Fireworks Prizms White Sparkle #20
2019 Panini Prizm National Pride #1
2019 Panini Prizm National Pride Prizms #1
2019 Panini Prizm National Pride Prizms Black /1 #1
2019 Panini Prizm National Pride Prizms Gold /10 #1
2019 Panini Prizm National Pride Prizms White Sparkle #1
2019 Panini Prizm Prizms #43A
2019 Panini Prizm Prizms #43B
2019 Panini Prizm Prizms Black /1 #43A
2019 Panini Prizm Prizms Black /1 #43B
2019 Panini Prizm Prizms Blue /75 #43A
2019 Panini Prizm Prizms Blue /75 #43B
2019 Panini Prizm Prizms Camo #43A
2019 Panini Prizm Prizms Camo #43B
2019 Panini Prizm Prizms Flash #43A
2019 Panini Prizm Prizms Flash #43B
2019 Panini Prizm Prizms Gold /10 #43A
2019 Panini Prizm Prizms Gold /10 #43B
2019 Panini Prizm Prizms Green /99 #43A
2019 Panini Prizm Prizms Green /99 #43B
2019 Panini Prizm Prizms Rainbow /24 #43A
2019 Panini Prizm Prizms Rainbow /24 #43B
2019 Panini Prizm Prizms Red /50 #43A
2019 Panini Prizm Prizms Red /50 #43B
2019 Panini Prizm Prizms Red White and Blue #43A
2019 Panini Prizm Prizms Red White and Blue #43B
2019 Panini Prizm Prizms White /5 #43A
2019 Panini Prizm Prizms White /5 #43B
2019 Panini Prizm Prizms White Sparkle #43A
2019 Panini Prizm Prizms White Sparkle #43B
2019 Panini Prizm Scripted Signatures Prizms #16
2019 Panini Prizm Scripted Signatures Prizms Black /1 #16
2019 Panini Prizm Scripted Signatures Prizms Blue /5 #16
2019 Panini Prizm Scripted Signatures Prizms Camo #16
2019 Panini Prizm Scripted Signatures Prizms Gold /5 #16
2019 Panini Prizm Scripted Signatures Prizms Rainbow /5 #16
2019 Panini Prizm Scripted Signatures Prizms Red /5 #16
2019 Panini Prizm Scripted Signatures Prizms Red White and Blue #16
2019 Panini Prizm Scripted Signatures Prizms White /5 #16
2019 Panini Prizm Stars and Stripes #7
2019 Panini Prizm Stars and Stripes Prizms #7
2019 Panini Prizm Stars and Stripes Prizms Black /1 #7
2019 Panini Prizm Stars and Stripes Prizms Gold /10 #7
2019 Panini Prizm Stars and Stripes Prizms White Sparkle #7
2019 Panini Victory Lane #67
2019 Panini Victory Lane #96
2019 Panini Victory Lane Black /1 #67
2019 Panini Victory Lane Black /1 #96
2019 Panini Victory Lane Dual Swatches Gold /25 #9
2019 Panini Victory Lane Dual Swatches Laundry Tag /1 #9
2019 Panini Victory Lane Dual Swatches Platinum /1 #9
2019 Panini Victory Lane Dual Swatches Red /5 #9
2019 Panini Victory Lane Gold /25 #67
2019 Panini Victory Lane Gold /25 #96
2019 Panini Victory Lane Pedal to the Metal #72
2019 Panini Victory Lane Pedal to the Metal #83
2019 Panini Victory Lane Pedal to the Metal Black /1 #72
2019 Panini Victory Lane Pedal to the Metal Black /1 #83
2019 Panini Victory Lane Pedal to the Metal Gold /25 #72
2019 Panini Victory Lane Pedal to the Metal Gold /25 #83
2019 Panini Victory Lane Pedal to the Metal Green /5 #72
2019 Panini Victory Lane Pedal to the Metal Green /5 #83
2019 Panini Victory Lane Pedal to the Metal Red /3 #72
2019 Panini Victory Lane Pedal to the Metal Red /3 #83
2019 Panini Victory Lane Printing Plates Black /1 #67
2019 Panini Victory Lane Printing Plates Black /1 #96
2019 Panini Victory Lane Printing Plates Cyan /1 #67
2019 Panini Victory Lane Printing Plates Cyan /1 #96
2019 Panini Victory Lane Printing Plates Magenta /1 #67
2019 Panini Victory Lane Printing Plates Magenta /1 #96
2019 Panini Victory Lane Printing Plates Yellow /1 #67
2019 Panini Victory Lane Printing Plates Yellow /1 #96
2019 Panini Victory Lane Quad Swatches Gold /25 #9
2019 Panini Victory Lane Quad Swatches Laundry Tag /1 #9
2019 Panini Victory Lane Quad Swatches Platinum /1 #9
2019 Panini Victory Lane Quad Swatches Red /10 #9
2019 Panini Victory Lane Signature Swatches #24
2019 Panini Victory Lane Signature Swatches Gold /25 #24
2019 Panini Victory Lane Signature Swatches Laundry Tag /1 #24
2019 Panini Victory Lane Signature Swatches Platinum /1 #24
2019 Panini Victory Lane Signature Swatches Red /10 #24
2020 Donruss #11
2020 Donruss #89
2020 Donruss #156
2020 Donruss Black Numbers /14 #11
2020 Donruss Black Numbers /14 #89
2020 Donruss Black Numbers /14 #156
2020 Donruss Black Trophy Club /1 #11
2020 Donruss Black Trophy Club /1 #89
2020 Donruss Black Trophy Club /1 #156
2020 Donruss Blue /199 #89
2020 Donruss Blue /199 #156
2020 Donruss Blue /199 #11
2020 Donruss Carolina Blue #11
2020 Donruss Carolina Blue #89
2020 Donruss Carolina Blue #156
2020 Donruss Dominators #2
2020 Donruss Dominators Checkers #2
2020 Donruss Dominators Cracked Ice /25 #2
2020 Donruss Dominators Holographic /199 #2
2020 Donruss Dominators Xplosion /10 #2
2020 Donruss Downtown #1
2020 Donruss Green /99 #11
2020 Donruss Green /99 #89
2020 Donruss Green /99 #156
2020 Donruss Orange #11
2020 Donruss Orange #89
2020 Donruss Orange #156
2020 Donruss Pink /25 #11
2020 Donruss Pink /25 #89
2020 Donruss Pink /25 #156
2020 Donruss Printing Plates Black /1 #11
2020 Donruss Printing Plates Black /1 #89
2020 Donruss Printing Plates Black /1 #156
2020 Donruss Printing Plates Cyan /1 #11
2020 Donruss Printing Plates Cyan /1 #89
2020 Donruss Printing Plates Cyan /1 #156
2020 Donruss Printing Plates Magenta /1 #89
2020 Donruss Printing Plates Magenta /1 #156
2020 Donruss Printing Plates Magenta /1 #11
2020 Donruss Printing Plates Yellow /1 #156
2020 Donruss Printing Plates Yellow /1 #11
2020 Donruss Printing Plates Yellow /1 #89
2020 Donruss Purple /49 #11
2020 Donruss Purple /49 #89
2020 Donruss Purple /49 #156
2020 Donruss Red /299 #11
2020 Donruss Red /299 #89
2020 Donruss Red /299 #156
2020 Donruss Retro Relics '87 #7
2020 Donruss Retro Relics '87 Holo Black /10 #7
2020 Donruss Retro Relics '87 Holo Gold /25 #7
2020 Donruss Retro Relics '87 Red /99 #7
2020 Donruss Silver #11
2020 Donruss Silver #89
2020 Donruss Silver #156
2020 Donruss Timeless Treasures Material Signatures #5
2020 Donruss Timeless Treasures Material Signatures Holo Black /1 #5
2020 Donruss Timeless Treasures Material Signatures Holo Gold /10 #5
2020 Donruss Timeless Treasures Material Signatures Red /14 #5

Martin Truex Jr.

2004 Bass Pro Shops Racing #2
2004 Bass Pro Shops Racing #3
2004 Press Pass Dale Earnhardt Jr. #44
2004 Press Pass Dale Earnhardt Jr. #45
2004 Press Pass Dale Earnhardt Jr. #59
2004 Press Pass Dale Earnhardt Jr. #60
2004 Press Pass Dale Earnhardt Jr. #61
2004 Press Pass Dale Earnhardt Jr. Blue #C44
2004 Press Pass Dale Earnhardt Jr. Blue #C45
2004 Press Pass Dale Earnhardt Jr. Blue #C59
2004 Press Pass Dale Earnhardt Jr. Blue #C60
2004 Press Pass Dale Earnhardt Jr. Blue #C61
2004 Press Pass Dale Earnhardt Jr. Bronze #B44
2004 Press Pass Dale Earnhardt Jr. Bronze #B45
2004 Press Pass Dale Earnhardt Jr. Bronze #B59
2004 Press Pass Dale Earnhardt Jr. Bronze #B60
2004 Press Pass Dale Earnhardt Jr. Bronze #B61
2004 Press Pass Dale Earnhardt Jr. Gold #D44
2004 Press Pass Dale Earnhardt Jr. Gold #D45
2004 Press Pass Dale Earnhardt Jr. Gold #D59
2004 Press Pass Dale Earnhardt Jr. Gold #D60
2004 Press Pass Dale Earnhardt Jr. Gold #D61
2004 Press Pass Optima #37
2004 Press Pass Optima Gold #G37
2004 Press Pass Optima Previews /5 #EB37
2004 Press Pass Optima Samples #37
2004 Press Pass Signings #61
2004 Press Pass Signings Gold /50 #57
2004 Press Pass Stealth #71
2004 Press Pass Stealth No Boundaries #NB8
2004 Press Pass Stealth Samples #X71

2004 Press Pass Stealth X-Ray /100 #71
2004 Press Pass Top Prospects Memorabilia /350 #MTT
2004 Press Pass Top Prospects Memorabilia /200 #MTSM
2004 Press Pass Trackside #39
2004 Press Pass Trackside #39B
2004 Press Pass Trackside #99
2004 Press Pass Trackside Golden /100 #G39
2004 Press Pass Trackside Golden /100 #G99
2004 Press Pass Trackside Hat Giveaway #PPH35
2004 Press Pass Trackside Previews /5 #EB39
2004 Press Pass Trackside Samples #39
2004 Press Pass Trackside Samples #99
2004 Wheels Autographs #64
2005 McFarlane NASCAR Series 5 #110
2005 Press Pass #41
2005 Press Pass #90
2005 Press Pass Autographs #57
2005 Press Pass Eclipse #37
2005 Press Pass Eclipse #89
2005 Press Pass Eclipse Previews /5 #EB37
2005 Press Pass Eclipse Previews /5 #EB89
2005 Press Pass Eclipse Samples #37
2005 Press Pass Eclipse Samples #89
2005 Press Pass Hot Treads /900 #HTR14
2005 Press Pass Hot Treads Holofoil /100 #HTR14
2005 Press Pass Optima #38
2005 Press Pass Optima #49
2005 Press Pass Optima #60
2005 Press Pass Optima Fan Favorite #FF25
2005 Press Pass Optima G Force #GF1
2005 Press Pass Optima Gold /100 #G38
2005 Press Pass Optima Gold /100 #G49
2005 Press Pass Optima Gold /100 #G60
2005 Press Pass Optima Previews /5 #38
2005 Press Pass Optima Previews /1 #49
2005 Press Pass Optima Samples #38
2005 Press Pass Optima Samples #49
2005 Press Pass Optima Samples #60
2005 Press Pass Panorama #PPP15
2005 Press Pass Panorama #PPP55
2005 Press Pass Panorama #PPP65
2005 Press Pass Panorama #PPP80
2005 Press Pass Platinum /100 #P41
2005 Press Pass Platinum /100 #P90
2005 Press Pass Previews Green /5 #EB41
2005 Press Pass Samples #41
2005 Press Pass Samples #90
2005 Press Pass Signings Gold /50 #54
2005 Press Pass Stealth EFX #EFX6
2005 Press Pass Stealth No Boundaries #NB22
2005 Press Pass Top Prospects Memorabilia /100 #MTG
2005 Press Pass Top Prospects Memorabilia /200 #MTS
2005 Press Pass Top Prospects Memorabilia /50 #MTSM
2005 Press Pass Top Prospects Memorabilia /350 #MTT
2005 Press Pass Trackside #43
2005 Press Pass Trackside Golden /100 #G43
2005 Press Pass Trackside Hat Giveaway #PPH36
2005 Press Pass Trackside Hot Pass #24
2005 Press Pass Trackside Hot Pass National #24
2005 Press Pass Trackside Previews /5 #43
2005 Press Pass Trackside Samples #43
2005 VIP #57
2005 VIP Making The Show #4
2005 VIP Samples #57
2005 Wheels American Thunder #41
2005 Wheels American Thunder #75
2005 Wheels American Thunder #80
2005 Wheels American Thunder American Eagle #AE6
2005 Wheels American Thunder Golden Eagle /250 #GE6
2005 Wheels American Thunder License to Drive #5
2005 Wheels American Thunder Previews /5 #80
2005 Wheels American Thunder Samples #41
2005 Wheels American Thunder Samples #75
2005 Wheels American Thunder Samples #80
2005 Wheels American Thunder Single Hat /190 #SH2
2005 Wheels American Thunder Thunder Road #TR15
2005 Wheels Autographs #57
2005 Wheels High Gear #28
2005 Wheels High Gear #47
2005 Wheels High Gear #79
2005 Wheels High Gear MPH /100 #M28
2005 Wheels High Gear MPH /100 #M47
2005 Wheels High Gear MPH /100 #M79
2005 Wheels High Gear Previews Green /5 #EB28
2005 Wheels High Gear Samples #28
2005 Wheels High Gear Samples #47
2005 Wheels High Gear Samples #79
2006 Press Pass #3
2006 Press Pass #33
2006 Press Pass #102
2006 Press Pass Autographs #54
2006 Press Pass Blue #B3
2006 Press Pass Blue #B33
2006 Press Pass Blue #B102
2006 Press Pass Burning Rubber Cars /370 #BRT17
2006 Press Pass Burning Rubber Drivers /100 #BRD17
2006 Press Pass Burning Rubber Drivers Gold /1 #BRD17
2006 Press Pass Burnouts /900 #HT3
2006 Press Pass Burnouts Holofoil /100 #HT3
2006 Press Pass Collectors Series Making the Show #MS14
2006 Press Pass Double Burner Metal-Tire /100 #DB9
2006 Press Pass Eclipse #28
2006 Press Pass Eclipse #41
2006 Press Pass Eclipse #59
2006 Press Pass Eclipse #79
2006 Press Pass Eclipse #86
2006 Press Pass Eclipse Hyperdrive #HP8
2006 Press Pass Eclipse Previews /5 #EB28
2006 Press Pass Eclipse Previews /1 #EB59
2006 Press Pass Eclipse Racing Champions #RC17
2006 Press Pass Eclipse Skidmarks #SM11
2006 Press Pass Eclipse Skidmarks Holofoil /250 #SM11
2006 Press Pass Eclipse Supernova #SU4
2006 Press Pass Game Face #GF8
2006 Press Pass Gold #G3
2006 Press Pass Gold #G33
2006 Press Pass Gold #G102
2006 Press Pass Legends Triple Threads /50 #TTMT
2006 Press Pass Optima #3
2006 Press Pass Optima #77
2006 Press Pass Optima Gold /100 #G3
2006 Press Pass Optima Gold /100 #G77
2006 Press Pass Optima Previews /5 #EB3
2006 Press Pass Optima Previews /1 #EB77
2006 Press Pass Optima Q & A #QA2
2006 Press Pass Optima Rookie Relics Cars /50 #RRT5
2006 Press Pass Optima Rookie Relics Drivers /50 #RRD5
2006 Press Pass Platinum /100 #P3
2006 Press Pass Platinum /100 #P33
2006 Press Pass Platinum /100 #P102
2006 Press Pass Premium #35
2006 Press Pass Premium #52
2006 Press Pass Premium #74
2006 Press Pass Premium In the Zone #IZ9
2006 Press Pass Premium In the Zone Red /250 #IZ9
2006 Press Pass Previews /5 #EB3
2006 Press Pass Previews /5 #EB33
2006 Press Pass Previews /1 #EB102
2006 Press Pass Signings #59
2006 Press Pass Signings Gold /50 #59
2006 Press Pass Signings Red Ink #59
2006 Press Pass Signings Silver /100 #59
2006 Press Pass Snapshots #SN19
2006 Press Pass Snapshots #SN35
2006 Press Pass Stealth #43
2006 Press Pass Stealth #52
2006 Press Pass Stealth #61
2006 Press Pass Stealth #96
2006 Press Pass Stealth Autographed Hat Entry #PPH24
2006 Press Pass Stealth EFX #EFX5
2006 Press Pass Stealth Gear Grippers Cars Retail /99 #GGT16
2006 Press Pass Stealth Gear Grippers Drivers /99 #GGD16
2006 Press Pass Stealth Hot Pass #HP26
2006 Press Pass Stealth Previews /1 #96
2006 Press Pass Stealth Profile #P8
2006 Press Pass Stealth Retail #43
2006 Press Pass Stealth Retail #52
2006 Press Pass Stealth Retail #61
2006 Press Pass Stealth Retail #96
2006 Press Pass Stealth X-Ray /100 #X43
2006 Press Pass Stealth X-Ray /100 #X52
2006 Press Pass Stealth X-Ray /100 #X61
2006 Press Pass Stealth X-Ray /100 #X96
2006 Press Pass Top 25 Drivers & Rides #C1
2006 Press Pass Top 25 Drivers & Rides #D1
2006 Press Pass Velocity #VE7
2006 TRAKS #34
2006 TRAKS #37
2006 TRAKS #100
2006 TRAKS Autographs #37
2006 TRAKS Autographs 100 /100 #19
2006 TRAKS Autographs 25 /25 #35
2006 TRAKS Previews /1 #34
2006 TRAKS Previews /1 #37
2006 TRAKS Previews /1 #100
2006 TRAKS Stickers #1
2006 VIP #33
2006 VIP #73
2006 VIP #94
2006 VIP Making the Show #MS14
2006 VIP Rookie Stripes /100 #RS5
2006 Wheels American Thunder #53
2006 Wheels American Thunder /350 #94
2006 Wheels American Thunder American Muscle #AM5
2006 Wheels American Thunder American Racing Idol #RI12
2006 Wheels American Thunder American Racing Idol Golden /250 #RI12
2006 Wheels American Thunder Cool Threads /329 #CT3
2006 Wheels American Thunder Double Hat /99 #DH25
2006 Wheels American Thunder Grandstand #GS22
2006 Wheels American Thunder Head to Toe /99 #HT7
2006 Wheels American Thunder Pushin' Pedal /199 #PP10
2006 Wheels American Thunder Thunder Road #TR7
2006 Wheels American Thunder Thunder Strokes /400 #11
2006 Wheels High Gear #28
2006 Wheels High Gear #57
2006 Wheels High Gear #83
2006 Wheels High Gear Flag to Flag #FF25
2006 Wheels High Gear Full Throttle #FT1
2006 Wheels High Gear Man & Machine Cars #MMB7
2006 Wheels High Gear Man & Machine Drivers #MMA7
2006 Wheels High Gear MPH /100 #M28
2006 Wheels High Gear MPH /100 #M57
2006 Wheels High Gear MPH /100 #M83
2006 Wheels High Gear Previews Green /5 #EB28
2006 Wheels High Gear Previews Silver /1 #EB83
2007 Press Pass #22
2007 Press Pass #68
2007 Press Pass Autographs #45
2007 Press Pass Autographs Press Plates Black /1 #24
2007 Press Pass Autographs Press Plates Cyan /1 #25
2007 Press Pass Autographs Press Plates Magenta /1 #26
2007 Press Pass Autographs Press Plates Yellow /1 #25
2007 Press Pass Blue #B22
2007 Press Pass Blue #B68
2007 Press Pass Collector's Series Box Set #SB23
2007 Press Pass Cup Chase #CCR11
2007 Press Pass Cup Chase Prizes #CC7
2007 Press Pass Double Burner Firesuit-Glove /100 #DB5
2007 Press Pass Double Burner Firesuit-Glove Exchange /100 #DB5
2007 Press Pass Eclipse #18
2007 Press Pass Eclipse Gold /25 #G18
2007 Press Pass Eclipse Previews /5 #EB18
2007 Press Pass Eclipse Racing Champions #RC27
2007 Press Pass Eclipse Red /1 #R18
2007 Press Pass Eclipse Skidmarks #SM18
2007 Press Pass Eclipse Skidmarks Holofoil /250 #SM18
2007 Press Pass Eclipse Teammates Autographs /25 #1
2007 Press Pass Eclipse Under Cover Double Cover Name /25 #DC6
2007 Press Pass Eclipse Under Cover Double Cover NASCAR /99 #DC6
2007 Press Pass Eclipse Under Cover Drivers /450 #UCD10
2007 Press Pass Eclipse Under Cover Drivers Eclipse /1 #UCD10
2007 Press Pass Eclipse Under Cover Drivers Name /99 #UCD10
2007 Press Pass Eclipse Under Cover Drivers NASCAR /270 #UCD10
2007 Press Pass Eclipse Under Cover Teams /135 #UCT10
2007 Press Pass Eclipse Under Cover Teams NASCAR /25 #UCT10
2007 Press Pass Four Wide /50 #FWMT
2007 Press Pass Four Wide Checkered Flag /1 #FWMT
2007 Press Pass Four Wide Checkered Flag Exchange /1 #FWMT
2007 Press Pass Four Wide Exchange /50 #FWMT
2007 Press Pass Gold #G22
2007 Press Pass Gold #G68
2007 Press Pass Legends Signature Series /25 #MT
2007 Press Pass Legends Sunday Swatches Bronze /199 #MTSS
2007 Press Pass Legends Sunday Swatches Gold /50 #MTSS
2007 Press Pass Legends Sunday Swatches Silver /99 #MTSS
2007 Press Pass Legends Victory Lane Bronze /199 #VL9
2007 Press Pass Legends Victory Lane Gold /25 #VL9
2007 Press Pass Legends Victory Lane Silver /99 #VL9
2007 Press Pass Platinum /100 #P22
2007 Press Pass Platinum /100 #P68
2007 Press Pass Premium #4
2007 Press Pass Premium #43
2007 Press Pass Premium Hot Threads Drivers /145 #HTD2
2007 Press Pass Premium Hot Threads Drivers Gold /1 #HTD2
2007 Press Pass Premium Hot Threads Patch /15 #HTP4
2007 Press Pass Premium Hot Threads Team /160 #HTT2
2007 Press Pass Premium Red /15 #R4
2007 Press Pass Premium Red /15 #R43
2007 Press Pass Previews /5 #EB22
2007 Press Pass Race Day #RD11
2007 Press Pass Signings #71
2007 Press Pass Signings Blue /25 #32
2007 Press Pass Signings Gold /50 #54
2007 Press Pass Signings Press Plates Black /1 #41
2007 Press Pass Signings Press Plates Cyan /1 #40
2007 Press Pass Signings Press Plates Magenta /1 #43
2007 Press Pass Signings Press Plates Yellow /1 #41
2007 Press Pass Signings Silver /100 #53
2007 Press Pass Snapshots #SN27
2007 Press Pass Stealth #25
2007 Press Pass Stealth #55
2007 Press Pass Stealth #71
2007 Press Pass Stealth Battle Armor Drivers /150 #BAD17
2007 Press Pass Stealth Battle Armor Teams /85 #BAT17
2007 Press Pass Stealth Chrome #25
2007 Press Pass Stealth Chrome #55
2007 Press Pass Stealth Chrome #71
2007 Press Pass Stealth Chrome Exclusives /99 #X25
2007 Press Pass Stealth Chrome Exclusives /99 #X55
2007 Press Pass Stealth Chrome Exclusives /99 #X71
2007 Press Pass Stealth Chrome Platinum /25 #P25
2007 Press Pass Stealth Chrome Platinum /25 #P55
2007 Press Pass Stealth Chrome Platinum /25 #P71
2007 Press Pass Stealth Maximum Access #MA26
2007 Press Pass Stealth Maximum Access Autographs /25 #MA26
2007 Press Pass Stealth Previews /5 #EB25
2007 Press Pass Wal-Mart Autographs /50 #MT
2007 Traks #29
2007 Traks #77
2007 Traks #82
2007 Traks Driver's Seat #DS3
2007 Traks Driver's Seat #DS3B
2007 Traks Driver's Seat National #DS3
2007 Traks Gold #G29
2007 Traks Gold #G77
2007 Traks Gold #G82
2007 Traks Holofoil /50 #H29
2007 Traks Holofoil /50 #H77
2007 Traks Holofoil /50 #H82
2007 Traks Hot Pursuit #HP4
2007 Traks Previews /5 #EB29
2007 Traks Previews /1 #EB77
2007 Traks Red /10 #R29
2007 Traks Red /10 #R77
2007 Traks Red /10 #R82
2007 Traks Track Time #TT9
2007 VIP #1
2007 VIP #29
2007 VIP #49
2007 VIP #68
2007 VIP #81
2007 VIP Get A Grip Drivers /70 #GGD28
2007 VIP Get A Grip Teams /70 #GGT28
2007 VIP Previews /5 #EB1
2007 VIP Previews /5 #EB29
2007 VIP Sunday Best #SB23
2007 Wheels American Thunder #34
2007 Wheels American Thunder #38
2007 Wheels American Thunder #51
2007 Wheels American Thunder American Dreams #AD8
2007 Wheels American Thunder American Dreams Gold /250 #ADG8
2007 Wheels American Thunder American Muscle #AM6
2007 Wheels American Thunder Autographed Hat Instant Winner /1 #AH39
2007 Wheels American Thunder Cool Threads /299 #CT7
2007 Wheels American Thunder Head to Toe /99 #HT3
2007 Wheels American Thunder Previews /5 #EB34
2007 Wheels American Thunder Previews /1 #EB51
2007 Wheels American Thunder Pushin' Pedal /99 #PP9
2007 Wheels American Thunder Starting Grid #SG8
2007 Wheels American Thunder Thunder Road #TR3
2007 Wheels American Thunder Thunder Strokes #39
2007 Wheels American Thunder Thunder Strokes Press Plates Black /1 #39
2007 Wheels American Thunder Thunder Strokes Press Plates Cyan /1 #39
2007 Wheels American Thunder Thunder Strokes Press Plates Magenta /1 #39
2007 Wheels American Thunder Thunder Strokes Press Plates Yellow /1 #39
2007 Wheels American Thunder Triple Hat /99 #TH30
2007 Wheels Autographs #39
2007 Wheels Autographs Press Plates Black /1 #38
2007 Wheels Autographs Press Plates Cyan /1 #38
2007 Wheels Autographs Press Plates Magenta /1 #38
2007 Wheels High Gear #18
2007 Wheels High Gear Driven #DR6
2007 Wheels High Gear Final Standings Gold /19 #FS18
2007 Wheels High Gear Full Throttle #FT9
2007 Wheels High Gear MPH /100 #M18
2007 Wheels High Gear Previews /5 #EB18
2008 Press Pass #11
2008 Press Pass #65
2008 Press Pass #79
2008 Press Pass #90
2008 Press Pass #113
2008 Press Pass Autographs #41
2008 Press Pass Autographs Press Plates Black /1 #33
2008 Press Pass Autographs Press Plates Cyan /1 #34
2008 Press Pass Autographs Press Plates Magenta /1 #34
2008 Press Pass Autographs Press Plates Yellow /1 #33
2008 Press Pass Blue #B11
2008 Press Pass Blue #B65
2008 Press Pass Blue #B79
2008 Press Pass Blue #B90
2008 Press Pass Blue #B113
2008 Press Pass Burning Rubber Drivers /60 #BRD12
2008 Press Pass Burning Rubber Drivers Gold /1 #BRD12
2008 Press Pass Burning Rubber Drivers Prime Cuts /25 #BRD12
2008 Press Pass Burning Rubber Teams /175 #BRT12
2008 Press Pass Burnouts #BO8
2008 Press Pass Burnouts Blue /99 #BO8
2008 Press Pass Burnouts Gold /299 #BO8
2008 Press Pass Collector's Series Box Set #17
2008 Press Pass Cup Chase #CC8
2008 Press Pass Double Burner Firesuit-Glove /100 #DBMT
2008 Press Pass Double Burner Metal-Tire /100 #DBMT
2008 Press Pass Eclipse #10
2008 Press Pass Eclipse #43
2008 Press Pass Eclipse #59
2008 Press Pass Eclipse Escape Velocity #EV6
2008 Press Pass Eclipse Gold /25 #G10
2008 Press Pass Eclipse Gold /25 #G43
2008 Press Pass Eclipse Gold /25 #G59
2008 Press Pass Eclipse Hyperdrive #HP4
2008 Press Pass Eclipse Previews /5 #EB10
2008 Press Pass Eclipse Red /1 #R10
2008 Press Pass Eclipse Red /1 #R43
2008 Press Pass Eclipse Red /1 #R59
2008 Press Pass Eclipse Star Tracks #ST12
2008 Press Pass Eclipse Star Tracks Holofoil /250 #ST12
2008 Press Pass Eclipse Stellar #ST11
2008 Press Pass Eclipse Under Cover Autographs /1 #UCMT
2008 Press Pass Eclipse Under Cover Double Cover Name /25 #DC1
2008 Press Pass Eclipse Under Cover Double Gover NASCAR /99 #DC1
2008 Press Pass Eclipse Under Cover Drivers /250 #UCD1
2008 Press Pass Eclipse Under Cover Drivers Eclipse /1 #UCD1
2008 Press Pass Eclipse Under Cover Drivers Name /50 #UCD1
2008 Press Pass Eclipse Under Cover Drivers NASCAR /150 #UCD1
2008 Press Pass Eclipse Under Cover Teams /99 #UCT1
2008 Press Pass Eclipse Under Cover Teams NASCAR /25 #UCT1
2008 Press Pass Four Wide /50 #FWMT
2008 Press Pass Four Wide Checkered Flag /1 #FWMT
2008 Press Pass Gold #G11
2008 Press Pass Gold #G65
2008 Press Pass Gold #G79
2008 Press Pass Gold #G90
2008 Press Pass Gold #G113
2008 Press Pass Hot Treads #HT4
2008 Press Pass Hot Treads Blue /99 #HT4
2008 Press Pass Hot Treads Gold /299 #HT4
2008 Press Pass Legends #56
2008 Press Pass Legends Autographs Black /85 #MT
2008 Press Pass Legends Autographs Press Plates Black /1 #MT
2008 Press Pass Legends Autographs Press Plates Cyan /1 #MT
2008 Press Pass Legends Autographs Press Plates Magenta /1 #MT
2008 Press Pass Legends Autographs Press Plates Yellow /1 #MT
2008 Press Pass Legends Blue /599 #56
2008 Press Pass Legends Bronze /299 #56
2008 Press Pass Legends Gold /99 #56
2008 Press Pass Legends Holo /25 #56
2008 Press Pass Legends Previews /5 #EB56
2008 Press Pass Legends Printing Plates Black /1 #56
2008 Press Pass Legends Printing Plates Cyan /1 #56
2008 Press Pass Legends Printing Plates Magenta /1 #56
2008 Press Pass Legends Printing Plates Yellow /1 #56
2008 Press Pass Legends Prominent Pieces Metal-Tire-Net /50 #PP4MT
2008 Press Pass Legends Prominent Pieces Metal-Tire-Net Gold /25 #PP4MT
2008 Press Pass Legends Solo /1 #56
2008 Press Pass Platinum /100 #P11
2008 Press Pass Platinum /100 #P65
2008 Press Pass Platinum /100 #P79
2008 Press Pass Platinum /100 #P90
2008 Press Pass Platinum /100 #P113
2008 Press Pass Premium #4
2008 Press Pass Premium #40
2008 Press Pass Premium #62
2008 Press Pass Premium Clean Air #CA2
2008 Press Pass Premium Hot Threads Autographs /1 #HTMT
2008 Press Pass Premium Hot Threads Drivers /120 #HTD2
2008 Press Pass Premium Hot Threads Drivers Gold /1 #HTD2
2008 Press Pass Premium Hot Threads Patches /3 #HTP44
2008 Press Pass Premium Hot Threads Patches #HTP45
2008 Press Pass Premium Hot Threads Team /120 #HTT2
2008 Press Pass Premium Previews /5 #EB4
2008 Press Pass Premium Previews /1 #EB62
2008 Press Pass Premium Red /15 #4
2008 Press Pass Premium Red /15 #40
2008 Press Pass Premium Red /15 #62
2008 Press Pass Premium Wal-Mart #WM6
2008 Press Pass Previews /5 #EB11
2008 Press Pass Previews /1 #EB113
2008 Press Pass Race Day #RD3
2008 Press Pass Signings #58
2008 Press Pass Signings Gold /50 #51
2008 Press Pass Signings Press Plates Cyan #MT
2008 Press Pass Signings Press Plates Magenta #MT
2008 Press Pass Signings Press Plates Yellow #MT
2008 Press Pass Signings Silver /100 #50
2008 Press Pass Slideshow #SS22
2008 Press Pass Speedway #11
2008 Press Pass Speedway #66
2008 Press Pass Speedway #74
2008 Press Pass Speedway #80
2008 Press Pass Speedway #82
2008 Press Pass Speedway Blur #B6
2008 Press Pass Speedway Cockpit #CP24
2008 Press Pass Speedway Corporate Cuts Drivers /80 #CDMT
2008 Press Pass Speedway Corporate Cuts Drivers Patches /17 #CDMT
2008 Press Pass Speedway Corporate Cuts Team /165 #CTMT
2008 Press Pass Speedway Gold #G11
2008 Press Pass Speedway Gold #G66
2008 Press Pass Speedway Gold #G74
2008 Press Pass Speedway Gold #G80
2008 Press Pass Speedway Gold #G82
2008 Press Pass Speedway Holofoil /50 #H11
2008 Press Pass Speedway Holofoil /50 #H66
2008 Press Pass Speedway Holofoil /50 #H74
2008 Press Pass Speedway Holofoil /50 #H80
2008 Press Pass Speedway Holofoil /50 #H82
2008 Press Pass Speedway Previews /5 #EB11
2008 Press Pass Speedway Red /10 #R11
2008 Press Pass Speedway Red /10 #R66
2008 Press Pass Speedway Red /10 #R74
2008 Press Pass Speedway Red /10 #R80
2008 Press Pass Speedway Red /10 #R82
2008 Press Pass Speedway Test Drive #TD5
2008 Press Pass Starting Grid #SG17
2008 Press Pass Stealth #33
2008 Press Pass Stealth #46
2008 Press Pass Stealth #65
2008 Press Pass Stealth #89
2008 Press Pass Stealth Battle Armor Drivers /120 #BAD13
2008 Press Pass Stealth Battle Armor Teams /115 #BAT13
2008 Press Pass Stealth Chrome #33
2008 Press Pass Stealth Chrome #46
2008 Press Pass Stealth Chrome #65
2008 Press Pass Stealth Chrome #89
2008 Press Pass Stealth Chrome Exclusives /25 #33
2008 Press Pass Stealth Chrome Exclusives /25 #46
2008 Press Pass Stealth Chrome Exclusives /25 #65
2008 Press Pass Stealth Chrome Exclusives /25 #89
2008 Press Pass Stealth Chrome Exclusives Gold /99 #33
2008 Press Pass Stealth Chrome Exclusives Gold /99 #46
2008 Press Pass Stealth Chrome Exclusives Gold /99 #65
2008 Press Pass Stealth Chrome Exclusives Gold /99 #89
2008 Press Pass Stealth Mach 08 #M8-6
2008 Press Pass Stealth Maximum Access #MA25
2008 Press Pass Stealth Maximum Access Autographs /25 #MA25
2008 Press Pass Stealth Previews /5 #33
2008 Press Pass Stealth Previews /1 #89
2008 Press Pass Stealth Target #TA12
2008 Press Pass Target Victory Tires /50 #TTMT
2008 Press Pass Wal-Mart Autographs /50 #10
2008 Press Pass Weekend Warriors #WW7
2008 VIP #34
2008 VIP #53
2008 VIP All Access #AA23
2008 VIP Gear Gallery #GG4
2008 VIP Gear Gallery Memorabilia /50 #GGMT
2008 VIP Gear Gallery Transparent #GG4
2008 VIP Get a Grip Autographs /1 #GGSMT
2008 VIP Get a Grip Drivers /80 #GGD1
2008 VIP Get a Grip Teams /99 #GGT1
2008 VIP Previews /5 #EB34
2008 VIP Trophy Club #TC4
2008 VIP Trophy Club Transparent #TC4
2008 Wheels American Thunder #34
2008 Wheels American Thunder #37
2008 Wheels American Thunder American Dreams #AD6
2008 Wheels American Thunder American Dreams Gold /250 #AD6
2008 Wheels American Thunder Autographed Hat Winner /1 #WHMT
2008 Wheels American Thunder Campaign Trail #CT2
2008 Wheels American Thunder Cool Threads /325 #CT9
2008 Wheels American Thunder Head to Toe /99 #HT12
2008 Wheels American Thunder Previews /5 #34
2008 Wheels American Thunder Pushin' Pedal /99 #PP 12
2008 Wheels American Thunder Trackside Treasury Autographs #MT
2008 Wheels American Thunder Trackside Treasury Autographs Gold /25 #MT
2008 Wheels American Thunder Trackside Treasury Autographs Printing Plates Black /1 #MT
2008 Wheels American Thunder Trackside Treasury Autographs Printing Plates Cyan /1 #MT
2008 Wheels American Thunder Trackside Treasury Autographs Printing Plates Magenta /1 #MT
2008 Wheels American Thunder Trackside Treasury Autographs Printing Plates Yellow /1 #MT
2008 Wheels American Thunder Triple Hat /125 #TH25
2008 Wheels Autographs #33
2008 Wheels Autographs Chase Edition /25 #9
2008 Wheels Autographs Press Plates Black /1 #33
2008 Wheels Autographs Press Plates Cyan /1 #33
2008 Wheels Autographs Press Plates Magenta /1 #33
2008 Wheels Autographs Press Plates Yellow /1 #33
2008 Wheels High Gear #11
2008 Wheels High Gear #64
2008 Wheels High Gear Driven #DR15
2008 Wheels High Gear Final Standings /11 #F11
2008 Wheels High Gear Full Throttle #FT8
2008 Wheels High Gear Last Lap /10 #LL5
2008 Wheels High Gear Last Lap Holofoil /5 #LL5
2008 Wheels High Gear MPH /100 #M11
2008 Wheels High Gear MPH /100 #M64
2008 Wheels High Gear Previews /5 #EB11
2008 Wheels High Gear The Chase #TC11
2009 Element #33
2009 Element #70
2009 Element #85
2009 Element Lab Report #LR26
2009 Element Previews /5 #33
2009 Element Radioactive /100 #33
2009 Element Radioactive /100 #70
2009 Element Radioactive /100 #85
2009 Press Pass #17
2009 Press Pass #63
2009 Press Pass #153
2009 Press Pass Autographs Gold #52
2009 Press Pass Autographs Silver #47
2009 Press Pass Blue #17
2009 Press Pass Blue #63
2009 Press Pass Blue #153
2009 Press Pass Cup Chase #CCR4
2009 Press Pass Eclipse #2
2009 Press Pass Eclipse Black and White #2
2009 Press Pass Eclipse Blue #2
2009 Press Pass Four Wide Firesuit /50 #FWMT
2009 Press Pass Four Wide Tire /25 #FWMT
2009 Press Pass Gold #17
2009 Press Pass Gold #63
2009 Press Pass Gold #153
2009 Press Pass Gold Holofoil /100 #17
2009 Press Pass Gold Holofoil /100 #63
2009 Press Pass Gold Holofoil /100 #153
2009 Press Pass Legends Autographs Gold /55 #32
2009 Press Pass Legends Autographs Holofoil /30 #27
2009 Press Pass Legends Autographs Printing Plates Black /1 #26
2009 Press Pass Legends Autographs Printing Plates Cyan /1 #25
2009 Press Pass Legends Autographs Printing Plates Magenta /1 #26
2009 Press Pass Legends Autographs Printing Plates Yellow /1 #26
2009 Press Pass Legends Prominent Pieces Bronze /150 #PPMT
2009 Press Pass Legends Prominent Pieces Gold /25 #PPMT
2009 Press Pass Legends Prominent Pieces Oversized /10 #PPOEMT
2009 Press Pass Legends Prominent Pieces Silver /50 #PPMT
2009 Press Pass Pieces Race Used Memorabilia #MT
2009 Press Pass Pocket Portraits Wal-Mart #PPW11
2009 Press Pass Premium #4
2009 Press Pass Premium #53
2009 Press Pass Premium Hot Threads /299 #HTMT1
2009 Press Pass Premium Hot Threads /99 #HTMT2
2009 Press Pass Premium Hot Threads Multi-Color /25 #HTMT
2009 Press Pass Premium Hot Threads Patches /6 #HTP-MT
2009 Press Pass Premium Previews /5 #EB4
2009 Press Pass Premium Previews /1 #EB52
2009 Press Pass Premium Signatures #36
2009 Press Pass Premium Signatures Gold /25 #34
2009 Press Pass Previews /5 #EB17
2009 Press Pass Previews /5 #EB153
2009 Press Pass Red #17
2009 Press Pass Red #63
2009 Press Pass Red #153
2009 Press Pass Showcase /499 #2
2009 Press Pass Showcase /499 #28
2009 Press Pass Showcase 2nd Gear /125 #2
2009 Press Pass Showcase 2nd Gear /125 #28
2009 Press Pass Showcase 3rd Gear /50 #2
2009 Press Pass Showcase 3rd Gear /50 #28
2009 Press Pass Showcase 4th Gear /15 #2
2009 Press Pass Showcase 4th Gear /15 #28
2009 Press Pass Showcase Classic Collections Ink /45 #1
2009 Press Pass Showcase Classic Collections Ink Gold /25 #1
2009 Press Pass Showcase Classic Collections Ink Green /5 #1
2009 Press Pass Showcase Classic Collections Ink Melting /1 #1
2009 Press Pass Showcase Printing Plates Black /1 #2
2009 Press Pass Showcase Printing Plates Black /1 #28
2009 Press Pass Showcase Printing Plates Cyan /1 #2
2009 Press Pass Showcase Printing Plates Cyan /1 #28
2009 Press Pass Showcase Printing Plates Magenta /1 #2
2009 Press Pass Showcase Printing Plates Magenta /1 #28
2009 Press Pass Showcase Printing Plates Yellow /1 #2
2009 Press Pass Showcase Printing Plates Yellow /1 #28
2009 Press Pass Signings Blue /25 #46
2009 Press Pass Signings Gold #46
2009 Press Pass Signings Green /15 #46
2009 Press Pass Signings Orange /65 #46
2009 Press Pass Signings Printing Plates Cyan /1 #46
2009 Press Pass Signings Printing Plates Yellow /1 #46
2009 Press Pass Signings Purple /45 #46
2009 Press Pass Sponsor Swatches /200 #SSMT
2009 Press Pass Sponsor Swatches Select /10 #SSMT
2009 Press Pass Stealth #34
2009 Press Pass Stealth #55
2009 Press Pass Stealth Battle Armor /25 #BAMT1
2009 Press Pass Stealth Battle Armor /20 #BAMT2
2009 Press Pass Stealth Battle Armor /10 #BAMT3
2009 Press Pass Stealth Battle Armor Multi-Color /170 #BAMT
2009 Press Pass Stealth Chrome #34
2009 Press Pass Stealth Chrome #55
2009 Press Pass Stealth Chrome Brushed Metal /25 #34
2009 Press Pass Stealth Chrome Brushed Metal /25 #55
2009 Press Pass Stealth Chrome Gold /99 #34
2009 Press Pass Stealth Chrome Gold /99 #55
2009 Press Pass Stealth Confidential Classified Bronze #PC18
2009 Press Pass Stealth Confidential Secret Silver #PC18
2009 Press Pass Stealth Confidential Top Secret Gold /25 #PC18
2009 Press Pass Stealth Mach 09 #M9
2009 Press Pass Stealth Previews /5 #EB34
2009 VIP #34
2009 VIP #82
2009 VIP Get A Grip /120 #GGMT
2009 VIP Get A Grip Holofoil /10 #GGMT
2009 VIP Guest List #GG6
2009 VIP Leadfoot /150 #LFMT
2009 VIP Leadfoot Holofoil /10 #LFMT
2009 VIP Previews /5 #34
2009 VIP Purple /25 #34
2009 VIP Purple /25 #82
2009 Wheels Autographs #59
2009 Wheels Autographs Press Plates Black /1 #MT
2009 Wheels Autographs Press Plates Cyan /1 #MT
2009 Wheels Autographs Press Plates Magenta /1 #MT
2009 Wheels Autographs Press Plates Yellow /1 #MT
2009 Wheels Main Event #21
2009 Wheels Main Event Fast Pass Purple /25 #21
2009 Wheels Main Event Foil #21
2009 Wheels Main Event Hat Dance Patch /10 #HDMT
2009 Wheels Main Event Hat Dance Triple /99 #HDMT
2009 Wheels Main Event Marks Clubs #55
2009 Wheels Main Event Marks Diamonds /10 #55
2009 Wheels Main Event Marks Hearts /5 #55
2009 Wheels Main Event Marks Printing Plates Black /1 #49
2009 Wheels Main Event Marks Printing Plates Cyan /1 #49
2009 Wheels Main Event Marks Printing Plates Magenta /1 #49
2009 Wheels Main Event Marks Printing Plates Yellow /1 #49
2009 Wheels Main Event Marks Spades /1 #55
2009 Wheels Main Event Playing Cards Blue #9S
2009 Wheels Main Event Playing Cards Red #9S
2009 Wheels Main Event Previews /5 #21
2009 Wheels Main Event Renegade Rounders Wanted #RR3
2009 Wheels Main Event Reward Copper /10 #RWMT
2009 Wheels Main Event Reward Holofoil /50 #RWMT
2009 Wheels Main Event Stop and Go Swatches Pit Sign /125 #SGSMT
2009 Wheels Main Event Stop and Go Swatches Pit Sign Green /10 #SGSMT
2009 Wheels Main Event Stop and Go Swatches Pit Sign Holofoil /75 #SGSMT
2009 Wheels Main Event Stop and Go Swatches Pit Sign Red /25 #SGSMT
2009 Wheels Main Event Stop and Go Swatches Pit Stackers /120 #SGWMT
2009 Wheels Main Event Stop and Go Swatches Pit Stackers Green /5 #SGWMT
2009 Wheels Main Event Stop and Go Swatches Pit Stackers Holofoil /75 #SGWMT
2009 Wheels Main Event Stop and Go Swatches Pit Stackers Red /25 #SGWMT
2009 Wheels Main Event Wildcard Cuts /2 #WCCMT
2010 Element #30
2010 Element Blue /35 #30
2010 Element Green #30
2010 Element Previews /5 #EB30
2010 Element Purple /25 #30
2010 Element Red Target #30
2010 Press Pass #26
2010 Press Pass Autographs #50
2010 Press Pass Autographs Printing Plates Black /1 #37
2010 Press Pass Autographs Printing Plates Cyan /1 #45
2010 Press Pass Autographs Printing Plates Magenta /1 #44
2010 Press Pass Autographs Printing Plates Yellow /1 #42
2010 Press Pass Blue #26
2010 Press Pass Eclipse #89
2010 Press Pass Eclipse Blue #89
2010 Press Pass Eclipse Gold #89
2010 Press Pass Four Wide Firesuit /25 #FWMT
2010 Press Pass Four Wide Sheet Metal /15 #FWMT
2010 Press Pass Four Wide Shoes /1 #FWMT
2010 Press Pass Four Wide Tires /10 #FWMT
2010 Press Pass Gold #26
2010 Press Pass Holofoil /100 #26
2010 Press Pass Premium #24
2010 Press Pass Premium Purple /25 #24
2010 Press Pass Premium Rivals #R7
2010 Press Pass Premium Rivals Signatures /5 #RSBT
2010 Press Pass Premium Signatures #PSMT
2010 Press Pass Premium Signatures Red Ink /24 #PSMT
2010 Press Pass Previews /5 #26
2010 Press Pass Purple /25 #26
2010 Press Pass Showcase /499 #24
2010 Press Pass Showcase Gold /125 #24
2010 Press Pass Showcase Green /50 #24
2010 Press Pass Showcase Melting /15 #24
2010 Press Pass Showcase Platinum Holo /1 #24
2010 Press Pass Signings Blue /10 #54
2010 Press Pass Signings Gold /50 #54
2010 Press Pass Signings Red /15 #54
2010 Press Pass Signings Silver /90 #53
2010 Press Pass Stealth #34
2010 Press Pass Stealth #87
2010 Press Pass Stealth Battle Armor Holofoil /25 #BAMT
2010 Press Pass Stealth Battle Armor Silver /225 #BAMT
2010 Press Pass Stealth Black and White #34
2010 Press Pass Stealth Black and White #87
2010 Press Pass Stealth Previews /5 #34
2010 Press Pass Stealth Purple /25 #34
2010 Wheels Autographs #49
2010 Wheels Autographs Printing Plates Black /1 #49
2010 Wheels Autographs Printing Plates Cyan /1 #49
2010 Wheels Autographs Printing Plates Magenta /1 #49
2010 Wheels Autographs Printing Plates Yellow /1 #49
2010 Wheels Autographs Target /10 #35
2010 Wheels Main Event #34
2010 Wheels Main Event #50
2010 Wheels Main Event American Muscle #AM10
2010 Wheels Main Event Blue #34
2010 Wheels Main Event Blue #50
2010 Wheels Main Event Head to Head /150 #HHDRMT
2010 Wheels Main Event Head to Head /150 #HHMTMA
2010 Wheels Main Event Head to Head Blue /75 #HHDRMT
2010 Wheels Main Event Head to Head Blue /75 #HHMTMA
2010 Wheels Main Event Head to Head Holofoil /10 #HHDRMT
2010 Wheels Main Event Head to Head Holofoil /10 #HHMTMA
2010 Wheels Main Event Head to Head Red /25 #HHDRMT
2010 Wheels Main Event Head to Head Red /25 #HHMTMA
2010 Wheels Main Event Marks Autographs /50 #56
2010 Wheels Main Event Marks Autographs Black /1 #55
2010 Wheels Main Event Marks Autographs Blue /25 #56
2010 Wheels Main Event Marks Autographs Red /25 #56
2010 Wheels Main Event Purple /25 #34
2010 Wheels Main Event Purple /25 #50
2010 Wheels Main Event Toe to Toe /10 #TTMTMW
2010 Wheels Main Event Upper Cuts /150 #UCMT
2010 Wheels Main Event Upper Cuts Blue /75 #UCMT
2010 Wheels Main Event Upper Cuts Holofoil /10 #UCMT
2010 Wheels Main Event Upper Cuts Knock Out Patches /25 #UCKOMT
2010 Wheels Main Event Upper Cuts Red /25 #UCMT
2011 Element #32
2011 Element #84
2011 Element Autographs /75 #54
2011 Element Autographs Blue /10 #54
2011 Element Autographs Gold /25 #52
2011 Element Autographs Printing Plates Black /1 #54
2011 Element Autographs Printing Plates Cyan /1 #54
2011 Element Autographs Printing Plates Magenta /1 #54

2011 Element Autographs Printing Plates Yellow /1 #54
2011 Element Autographs Silver /50 #52
2011 Element Black /35 #32
2011 Element Black /35 #84
2011 Element Flagship Performers 2010 Green Flag Passes Blue-Yellow /50 #FPPMT
2011 Element Green #32
2011 Element Green #84
2011 Element Previews /5 #EB32
2011 Element Purple /25 #32
2011 Element Purple /25 #84
2011 Element Red #32
2011 Element Red #84
2011 Element Trackside Treasures Holofoil /25 #TTMT
2011 Element Trackside Treasures Silver /85 #TTMT
2011 Press Pass #35
2011 Press Pass #90
2011 Press Pass #187
2011 Press Pass Autographs Blue /10 #54
2011 Press Pass Autographs Bronze /99 #55
2011 Press Pass Autographs Gold /25 #52
2011 Press Pass Autographs Printing Plates Black /1 #55
2011 Press Pass Autographs Printing Plates Cyan /1 #55
2011 Press Pass Autographs Printing Plates Magenta /1 #55
2011 Press Pass Autographs Printing Plates Yellow /1 #55
2011 Press Pass Autographs Silver /50 #55
2011 Press Pass Blue Holofoil /10 #35
2011 Press Pass Blue Holofoil /10 #90
2011 Press Pass Blue Holofoil /10 #187
2011 Press Pass Blue Retail #35
2011 Press Pass Blue Retail #90
2011 Press Pass Blue Retail #187
2011 Press Pass Eclipse #30
2011 Press Pass Eclipse #48
2011 Press Pass Eclipse Blue #30
2011 Press Pass Eclipse Blue #48
2011 Press Pass Eclipse Gold /55 #30
2011 Press Pass Eclipse Gold /55 #48
2011 Press Pass Eclipse Previews /5 #EB30
2011 Press Pass Eclipse Purple /25 #30
2011 Press Pass Eclipse Purple /25 #48
2011 Press Pass Eclipse Spellbound Swatches /250 #SBMT1
2011 Press Pass Eclipse Spellbound Swatches /150 #SBMT2
2011 Press Pass Eclipse Spellbound Swatches /150 #SBMT3
2011 Press Pass Eclipse Spellbound Swatches /75 #SBMT4
2011 Press Pass Eclipse Spellbound Swatches /75 #SBMT5
2011 Press Pass Eclipse Spellbound Swatches /50 #SBMT6
2011 Press Pass Eclipse Spellbound Swatches /25 #SBMT7
2011 Press Pass Eclipse Spellbound Swatches Signatures /10 #NNO
2011 Press Pass FanFare #36
2011 Press Pass FanFare Autographs Blue /5 #73
2011 Press Pass FanFare Autographs Bronze /55 #73
2011 Press Pass FanFare Autographs Gold /35 #73
2011 Press Pass FanFare Autographs Printing Plates Black /1 #73
2011 Press Pass FanFare Autographs Printing Plates Cyan /1 #73
2011 Press Pass FanFare Autographs Printing Plates Magenta /1 #73
2011 Press Pass FanFare Autographs Printing Plates Yellow /1 #73
2011 Press Pass FanFare Autographs Silver /25 #73
2011 Press Pass FanFare Blue Die Cuts #36
2011 Press Pass FanFare Championship Caliber #CC27
2011 Press Pass FanFare Emerald /25 #36
2011 Press Pass FanFare Holofoil Die Cuts #36
2011 Press Pass FanFare Magnificent Materials /199 #MMMT
2011 Press Pass FanFare Magnificent Materials Dual Swatches /50 #MMDMT
2011 Press Pass FanFare Magnificent Materials Dual Swatches Holofoil /10 #MMDMT
2011 Press Pass FanFare Magnificent Materials Holofoil /50 #MMMT
2011 Press Pass FanFare Ruby Die Cuts /15 #36
2011 Press Pass FanFare Sapphire /10 #36
2011 Press Pass FanFare Silver /25 #36
2011 Press Pass Geared Up Gold /100 #GUMT
2011 Press Pass Geared Up Holofoil /50 #GUMT
2011 Press Pass Gold /50 #35
2011 Press Pass Gold /50 #90
2011 Press Pass Gold /50 #187
2011 Press Pass Premium #34
2011 Press Pass Premium #86
2011 Press Pass Premium Purple /25 #34
2011 Press Pass Premium Purple /25 #86
2011 Press Pass Premium Signatures /200 #PSMTJ
2011 Press Pass Previews /5 #EB35
2011 Press Pass Purple /25 #35
2011 Press Pass Showcase /499 #17
2011 Press Pass Showcase Classic Collections Firesuit /45 #CCMMWR
2011 Press Pass Showcase Classic Collections Firesuit Patches /5 #CCMMWR
2011 Press Pass Showcase Classic Collections Ink /25 #CCMMWR
2011 Press Pass Showcase Classic Collections Ink Gold /5 #CCMMWR
2011 Press Pass Showcase Classic Collections Ink Melting /1 #CCMMWR
2011 Press Pass Showcase Classic Collections Sheet Metal /99 #CCMMWR
2011 Press Pass Showcase Gold /125 #17
2011 Press Pass Showcase Green /25 #17
2011 Press Pass Showcase Melting /1 #17
2011 Press Pass Signings Black and White /10 #PPSMT
2011 Press Pass Signings Brushed Metal /60 #PPSMT
2011 Press Pass Signings Holofoil /25 #PPSMT
2011 Press Pass Signings Printing Plates Cyan /1 #PPSMT
2011 Press Pass Signings Printing Plates Magenta /1 #PPSMT
2011 Press Pass Signings Printing Plates Yellow /1 #PPSMT
2011 Press Pass Stealth #53
2011 Press Pass Stealth #79
2011 Press Pass Stealth Black and White /25 #53
2011 Press Pass Stealth Black and White /25 #79
2011 Press Pass Stealth Holofoil /99 #53
2011 Press Pass Stealth Holofoil /99 #79
2011 Press Pass Stealth Metal of Honor Medal of Honor /50 #BAMT
2011 Press Pass Stealth Metal of Honor Purple Heart /25 #MHMT
2011 Press Pass Stealth Metal of Honor Silver Star /99 #BAMT
2011 Press Pass Stealth Purple /25 #53
2011 Press Pass Wal-Mart Winning Tickets #WTW5
2011 Wheels Main Event #34
2011 Wheels Main Event Black and White #34
2011 Wheels Main Event Blue /75 #34
2011 Wheels Main Event Green /1 #34
2011 Wheels Main Event Marks Autographs Blue /10 #MEMT
2011 Wheels Main Event Marks Autographs Gold /25 #MEMT
2011 Wheels Main Event Marks Autographs Silver /50 #MEMT
2011 Wheels Main Event Materials Holofoil /25 #MEMMT
2011 Wheels Main Event Materials Silver /99 #MEMMT
2011 Wheels Main Event Red /20 #34
2012 Press Pass #34
2012 Press Pass Blue #34
2012 Press Pass Blue Holofoil /35 #34
2012 Press Pass Cup Chase Prizes #CCP10
2012 Press Pass Fanfare #41
2012 Press Pass Fanfare Blue Foil Die Cuts #41
2012 Press Pass Fanfare Diamond /5 #41
2012 Press Pass Fanfare Dual Autographs /10 #TT
2012 Press Pass Fanfare Holofoil Die Cuts #41
2012 Press Pass Fanfare Magnificent Materials /250 #MMMT
2012 Press Pass Fanfare Magnificent Materials Dual Swatches /50 #MMMT
2012 Press Pass Fanfare Magnificent Materials Dual Swatches Melting /10 #MMMT
2012 Press Pass Fanfare Magnificent Materials Gold /99 #MMMT
2012 Press Pass Fanfare Magnificent Materials Signatures /99 #MT
2012 Press Pass Fanfare Magnificent Materials Signatures Blue /25 #MT
2012 Press Pass Fanfare Power Rankings #PR9
2012 Press Pass Fanfare Sapphire /20 #41
2012 Press Pass Fanfare Silver /25 #41
2012 Press Pass Gold #34
2012 Press Pass Ignite #34
2012 Press Pass Ignite #57
2012 Press Pass Ignite Materials Autographs Gun Metal /45 #IMMT
2012 Press Pass Ignite Materials Autographs Red /5 #IMMT
2012 Press Pass Ignite Materials Autographs Silver /150 #IMMT
2012 Press Pass Ignite Materials Gun Metal /99 #IMMT
2012 Press Pass Ignite Materials Red /10 #IMMT
2012 Press Pass Ignite Materials Silver #IMMT
2012 Press Pass Ignite Proofs Black and White /50 #34
2012 Press Pass Ignite Proofs Black and White /50 #57
2012 Press Pass Ignite Proofs Cyan #34
2012 Press Pass Ignite Proofs Cyan #57
2012 Press Pass Ignite Proofs Magenta #34
2012 Press Pass Ignite Proofs Magenta #57
2012 Press Pass Ignite Proofs Yellow /10 #34
2012 Press Pass Ignite Proofs Yellow /10 #57
2012 Press Pass Power Picks Blue /50 #50
2012 Press Pass Power Picks Blue /50 #70
2012 Press Pass Power Picks Gold /50 #50
2012 Press Pass Power Picks Gold /50 #70
2012 Press Pass Power Picks Holofoil /10 #50
2012 Press Pass Power Picks Holofoil /10 #70
2012 Press Pass Purple /35 #34
2012 Press Pass Redline #36
2012 Press Pass Redline Black /99 #36
2012 Press Pass Redline Cyan /50 #36
2012 Press Pass Redline Magenta /15 #36
2012 Press Pass Redline Signatures Blue /5 #RSMT
2012 Press Pass Redline Signatures Gold /22 #RSMT
2012 Press Pass Redline Signatures Holofoil /10 #RSMT
2012 Press Pass Redline Signatures Melting /1 #RSMT
2012 Press Pass Redline Signatures Red /50 #RSMT
2012 Press Pass Redline Yellow /1 #36
2012 Press Pass Showcase /499 #21
2012 Press Pass Showcase /499 #60
2012 Press Pass Showcase Classic Collections Ink /10 #CCMMWR
2012 Press Pass Showcase Classic Collections Ink Gold /5 #CCMMWR
2012 Press Pass Showcase Classic Collections Ink Melting /1 #CCMMWR
2012 Press Pass Showcase Classic Collections Memorabilia /99 #CCMMWR
2012 Press Pass Showcase Classic Collections Memorabilia Gold /50 #CCMMWR
2012 Press Pass Showcase Classic Collections Memorabilia Melting /5 #CCMMWR
2012 Press Pass Showcase Gold /125 #21
2012 Press Pass Showcase Gold /125 #60
2012 Press Pass Showcase Green /5 #21
2012 Press Pass Showcase Green /5 #60
2012 Press Pass Showcase Melting /1 #21
2012 Press Pass Showcase Melting /1 #60
2012 Press Pass Showcase Purple /1 #21
2012 Press Pass Showcase Purple /1 #60
2012 Press Pass Showcase Red /25 #21
2012 Press Pass Showcase Red /25 #60
2012 Press Pass Snapshots #SS34
2012 Total Memorabilia #30
2012 Total Memorabilia Black and White /99 #30
2012 Total Memorabilia Dual Swatch Gold /75 #TMMT
2012 Total Memorabilia Dual Swatch Holofoil /25 #TMMT
2012 Total Memorabilia Dual Swatch Melting /5 #TMMT
2012 Total Memorabilia Dual Swatch Silver /99 #TMMT
2012 Total Memorabilia Gold /275 #30
2012 Total Memorabilia Jumbo Swatch Gold /50 #TMMT
2012 Total Memorabilia Jumbo Swatch Holofoil /10 #TMMT
2012 Total Memorabilia Jumbo Swatch Melting /1 #TMMT
2012 Total Memorabilia Memory Lane #ML4
2012 Total Memorabilia Red Retail /250 #30
2012 Total Memorabilia Single Swatch Gold /99 #TMMT
2012 Total Memorabilia Single Swatch Holofoil /50 #TMMT
2012 Total Memorabilia Single Swatch Melting /10 #TMMT
2012 Total Memorabilia Single Swatch Silver /199 #TMMT
2013 Press Pass #42
2013 Press Pass #83
2013 Press Pass #94
2013 Press Pass #0
2013 Press Pass Color Proofs Black #42
2013 Press Pass Color Proofs Black #83
2013 Press Pass Color Proofs Black #94
2013 Press Pass Color Proofs Cyan /35 #42
2013 Press Pass Color Proofs Cyan /35 #83
2013 Press Pass Color Proofs Cyan /35 #94
2013 Press Pass Color Proofs Magenta #42
2013 Press Pass Color Proofs Magenta #83
2013 Press Pass Color Proofs Magenta #94
2013 Press Pass Color Proofs Yellow /5 #42
2013 Press Pass Color Proofs Yellow /5 #83
2013 Press Pass Color Proofs Yellow /5 #94
2013 Press Pass Fanfare #57
2013 Press Pass Fanfare #58
2013 Press Pass Fanfare Autographs Blue /1 #MTJ
2013 Press Pass Fanfare Autographs Gold /5 #MTJ
2013 Press Pass Fanfare Autographs Green /6 #MTJ
2013 Press Pass Fanfare Autographs Red /1 #MTJ
2013 Press Pass Fanfare Autographs Silver /10 #MTJ
2013 Press Pass Fanfare Diamond Die Cuts /5 #57
2013 Press Pass Fanfare Diamond Die Cuts /5 #58
2013 Press Pass Fanfare Green /3 #57
2013 Press Pass Fanfare Green /3 #58
2013 Press Pass Fanfare Holofoil Die Cuts #57
2013 Press Pass Fanfare Holofoil Die Cuts #58
2013 Press Pass Fanfare Magnificent Jumbo Materials Signatures /10 #MTJ
2013 Press Pass Fanfare Magnificent Materials Dual Swatches /50 #MTJ
2013 Press Pass Fanfare Magnificent Materials Dual Swatches Melting /10 #MTJ
2013 Press Pass Fanfare Magnificent Materials Gold /50 #MTJ
2013 Press Pass Fanfare Magnificent Materials Jumbo Swatches /25 #MTJ
2013 Press Pass Fanfare Magnificent Materials Signatures /99 #MTJ
2013 Press Pass Fanfare Magnificent Materials Signatures Blue /25 #MTJ
2013 Press Pass Fanfare Magnificent Materials Silver /199 #MTJ
2013 Press Pass Fanfare Red Foil Die Cuts #57
2013 Press Pass Fanfare Red Foil Die Cuts #58
2013 Press Pass Fanfare Sapphire /20 #57
2013 Press Pass Fanfare Sapphire /20 #58
2013 Press Pass Fanfare Signature Ride Autographs /10 #MTJ
2013 Press Pass Fanfare Signature Ride Autographs Blue /1 #MTJ
2013 Press Pass Fanfare Signature Ride Autographs Red /5 #MTJ
2013 Press Pass Fanfare Silver /25 #57
2013 Press Pass Fanfare Silver /25 #58
2013 Press Pass Ignite #37
2013 Press Pass Ignite #69
2013 Press Pass Ignite Hot Threads Blue Holofoil /99 #HTMT
2013 Press Pass Ignite Hot Threads Patch Red /10 #HTMT
2013 Press Pass Ignite Hot Threads Silver #HTMT
2013 Press Pass Ignite Ink Black /99 #IIMT
2013 Press Pass Ignite Ink Blue /25 #IIMT
2013 Press Pass Ignite Ink Red /5 #IIMT
2013 Press Pass Ignite Proofs Black and White /50 #37
2013 Press Pass Ignite Proofs Black and White /50 #69
2013 Press Pass Ignite Proofs Cyan #37
2013 Press Pass Ignite Proofs Cyan #69
2013 Press Pass Ignite Proofs Magenta #37
2013 Press Pass Ignite Proofs Magenta #69
2013 Press Pass Ignite Proofs Yellow /5 #37
2013 Press Pass Ignite Proofs Yellow /5 #69
2013 Press Pass Redline #45
2013 Press Pass Redline Black /99 #45
2013 Press Pass Redline Cyan /50 #45
2013 Press Pass Redline Dark Horse Relic Autographs Blue /5 #DHMT
2013 Press Pass Redline Dark Horse Relic Autographs Gold /25 #DHMT
2013 Press Pass Redline Dark Horse Relic Autographs Melting /1 #DHMT
2013 Press Pass Redline Dark Horse Relic Autographs Red /50 #DHMT
2013 Press Pass Redline Magenta /15 #45
2013 Press Pass Redline Relics Blue /5 #RRMT
2013 Press Pass Redline Relics Gold /10 #RRMT
2013 Press Pass Redline Relics Melting /1 #RRMT
2013 Press Pass Redline Relics Red /50 #RRMT
2013 Press Pass Redline Relics Silver /25 #RRMT
2013 Press Pass Redline Signatures Blue /55 #RSMT
2013 Press Pass Redline Signatures Gold /5 #RSMT
2013 Press Pass Redline Signatures Holo /10 #RSMT
2013 Press Pass Redline Signatures Melting /1 #RSMT
2013 Press Pass Redline Signatures Red /75 #RSMT
2013 Press Pass Redline Yellow /1 #45
2013 Press Pass Showcase /349 #27
2013 Press Pass Showcase /349 #60
2013 Press Pass Showcase Black /1 #27
2013 Press Pass Showcase Black /1 #60
2013 Press Pass Showcase Blue /25 #27
2013 Press Pass Showcase Blue /25 #60
2013 Press Pass Showcase Classic Collections Ink Gold /5 #CCIMWR
2013 Press Pass Showcase Classic Collections Ink Melting /1 #CCIMWR
2013 Press Pass Showcase Classic Collections Ink Red /1 #CCIMWR
2013 Press Pass Showcase Classic Collections Memorabilia Gold /25 #CCMMWR
2013 Press Pass Showcase Classic Collections Memorabilia Melting /5 #CCMMWR
2013 Press Pass Showcase Classic Collections Memorabilia Silver /75 #CCMMWR
2013 Press Pass Showcase Gold /99 #27
2013 Press Pass Showcase Gold /99 #60
2013 Press Pass Showcase Green /20 #27
2013 Press Pass Showcase Green /20 #60
2013 Press Pass Showcase Purple /13 #27
2013 Press Pass Showcase Purple /13 #60
2013 Press Pass Showcase Red /10 #27
2013 Press Pass Showcase Red /10 #60
2013 Press Pass Signings Blue /1 #MT
2013 Press Pass Signings Gold /50 #MT
2013 Press Pass Signings Holofoil /10 #MT
2013 Press Pass Signings Printing Plates Black /1 #MT
2013 Press Pass Signings Printing Plates Cyan /1 #MT
2013 Press Pass Signings Printing Plates Magenta /1 #MT
2013 Press Pass Signings Printing Plates Yellow /1 #MT
2013 Press Pass Signings Silver /100 #MT
2013 Total Memorabilia #35
2013 Total Memorabilia Black and White /99 #35
2013 Total Memorabilia Dual Swatch Gold /199 #TMMT
2013 Total Memorabilia Gold /275 #35
2013 Total Memorabilia Quad Swatch Melting /10 #TMMT
2013 Total Memorabilia Red #35
2013 Total Memorabilia Signature Collection Dual Swatch Gold /10 #SCMT
2013 Total Memorabilia Signature Collection Quad Swatch Melting /1 #SCMT
2013 Total Memorabilia Signature Collection Single Swatch Silver /10 #SCMT
2013 Total Memorabilia Signature Collection Triple Swatch Holofoil /5 #SCMT
2013 Total Memorabilia Single Swatch Silver /466 #TMMT
2013 Total Memorabilia Smooth Operators #S03
2013 Total Memorabilia Triple Swatch Holofoil /99 #TMMT
2014 Press Pass #39
2014 Press Pass American Thunder #35
2014 Press Pass American Thunder Autographs Blue /10 #ATAMTJ
2014 Press Pass American Thunder Autographs Red /5 #ATAMTJ
2014 Press Pass American Thunder Autographs White /25 #ATAMTJ
2014 Press Pass American Thunder Black and White /50 #35
2014 Press Pass American Thunder Class A Uniforms Blue /99 #CAUMTJ
2014 Press Pass American Thunder Class A Uniforms Red /10 #CAUMTJ
2014 Press Pass American Thunder Class A Uniforms Silver #CAUMTJ
2014 Press Pass American Thunder Cyan #35
2014 Press Pass American Thunder Magenta #35
2014 Press Pass American Thunder Top Speed #TS2
2014 Press Pass American Thunder Yellow /5 #35
2014 Press Pass Burning Rubber Blue /25 #BRMTJ
2014 Press Pass Burning Rubber Gold /75 #BRMTJ
2014 Press Pass Burning Rubber Holofoil /50 #BRMTJ
2014 Press Pass Burning Rubber Letterman /8 #BRLMTJ
2014 Press Pass Burning Rubber Melting /10 #BRMTJ
2014 Press Pass Color Proofs Black /70 #39
2014 Press Pass Color Proofs Cyan /35 #39
2014 Press Pass Color Proofs Magenta #39
2014 Press Pass Color Proofs Yellow /5 #39
2014 Press Pass Gold #39
2014 Press Pass Redline #51
2014 Press Pass Redline Black /75 #51
2014 Press Pass Redline Blue Foil #51
2014 Press Pass Redline Cyan /50 #51
2014 Press Pass Redline Green National Convention /5 #51
2014 Press Pass Redline Magenta /10 #51
2014 Press Pass Redline Relic Autographs Blue /10 #RRSEMTJ
2014 Press Pass Redline Relic Autographs Gold /25 #RRSEMTJ
2014 Press Pass Redline Relic Autographs Melting /1 #RRSEMTJ
2014 Press Pass Redline Relic Autographs Red /50 #RRSEMTJ
2014 Press Pass Redline Relics Blue /25 #RRMTJ
2014 Press Pass Redline Relics Gold /50 #RRMTJ
2014 Press Pass Redline Relics Melting /1 #RRMTJ
2014 Press Pass Redline Relics Red /75 #RRMTJ
2014 Press Pass Redline Signatures Blue /25 #RSMTJ
2014 Press Pass Redline Signatures Gold /50 #RSMTJ
2014 Press Pass Redline Signatures Melting /10 #RSMTJ
2014 Press Pass Redline Signatures Red /65 #RSMTJ
2014 Press Pass Redline Yellow /1 #51
2014 Press Pass Replay #16
2014 Press Pass Three Wide Gold /10 #TWMTJ
2014 Press Pass Three Wide Melting /1 #TWMTJ
2014 Total Memorabilia #27
2014 Total Memorabilia Acceleration #AC4
2014 Total Memorabilia Black and White /99 #27
2014 Total Memorabilia Dual Swatch Gold /150 #TMMT
2014 Total Memorabilia Gold /175 #27
2014 Total Memorabilia Quad Swatch Melting /25 #TMMT
2014 Total Memorabilia Red #27
2014 Total Memorabilia Single Swatch Silver /275 #TMMT
2014 Total Memorabilia Triple Swatch Blue /99 #TMMT
2015 Press Pass #34
2015 Press Pass Cup Chase #34
2015 Press Pass Cup Chase Blue /25 #34
2015 Press Pass Cup Chase Gold /75 #34
2015 Press Pass Cup Chase Green /10 #34
2015 Press Pass Cup Chase Melting /1 #34
2015 Press Pass Purple #34
2015 Press Pass Red #34
2015 Press Pass Signings Blue /99 #PPSMT
2015 Press Pass Signings Gold #PPSMT
2015 Press Pass Signings Green /50 #PPSMT
2015 Press Pass Signings Melting /10 #PPSMT
2015 Press Pass Signings Red /75 #PPSMT
2016 Certified #8
2016 Certified #58
2016 Certified Complete Materials /299 #13
2016 Certified Complete Materials Mirror Black /1 #13
2016 Certified Complete Materials Mirror Blue /50 #13
2016 Certified Complete Materials Mirror Gold /25 #13
2016 Certified Complete Materials Mirror Green /5 #13
2016 Certified Complete Materials Mirror Orange /99 #13
2016 Certified Complete Materials Mirror Purple /10 #13
2016 Certified Complete Materials Mirror Red /75 #13
2016 Certified Complete Materials Mirror Silver /99 #13
2016 Certified Epix /199 #12
2016 Certified Epix Mirror Black /1 #12
2016 Certified Epix Mirror Blue /50 #12
2016 Certified Epix Mirror Gold /25 #12
2016 Certified Epix Mirror Green /5 #12
2016 Certified Epix Mirror Orange /99 #12
2016 Certified Epix Mirror Purple /10 #12
2016 Certified Epix Mirror Red /75 #12
2016 Certified Epix Mirror Silver /99 #12
2016 Certified Mirror Black /1 #8
2016 Certified Mirror Black /1 #58
2016 Certified Mirror Blue /50 #8
2016 Certified Mirror Blue /50 #58
2016 Certified Mirror Gold /25 #8
2016 Certified Mirror Gold /25 #58
2016 Certified Mirror Green /5 #8
2016 Certified Mirror Green /5 #58
2016 Certified Mirror Orange /99 #8
2016 Certified Mirror Orange /99 #58
2016 Certified Mirror Purple /10 #8
2016 Certified Mirror Purple /10 #58
2016 Certified Mirror Red /75 #8
2016 Certified Mirror Red /75 #58
2016 Certified Mirror Silver /99 #8
2016 Certified Mirror Silver /99 #58
2016 Certified Signatures /165 #15
2016 Certified Signatures Mirror Black /1 #15
2016 Certified Signatures Mirror Blue /35 #15
2016 Certified Signatures Mirror Gold /25 #15
2016 Certified Signatures Mirror Green /5 #15
2016 Certified Signatures Mirror Orange /5 #15
2016 Certified Signatures Mirror Purple /10 #15
2016 Certified Signatures Mirror Red /49 #15
2016 Certified Signatures Mirror Silver /5 #15
2016 Certified Sprint Cup Swatches /200 #21
2016 Certified Sprint Cup Swatches Mirror Black /1 #21
2016 Certified Sprint Cup Swatches Mirror Blue /50 #21
2016 Certified Sprint Cup Swatches Mirror Gold /25 #21
2016 Certified Sprint Cup Swatches Mirror Green /5 #21
2016 Certified Sprint Cup Swatches Mirror Orange /99 #21
2016 Certified Sprint Cup Swatches Mirror Purple /10 #21
2016 Certified Sprint Cup Swatches Mirror Red /75 #21
2016 Certified Sprint Cup Swatches Mirror Silver /99 #21
2016 Panini Black Friday #34
2016 Panini Black Friday Autographs /25 #34
2016 Panini Black Friday Cracked Ice /25 #34
2016 Panini Black Friday Holo Plaid /1 #34
2016 Panini Black Friday Rapture /10 #34
2016 Panini Black Friday Thick Stock /50 #34
2016 Panini Black Friday Wedges /50 #34
2016 Panini Instant #1
2016 Panini Instant #3
2016 Panini Instant Black /1 #1
2016 Panini Instant Black /1 #3
2016 Panini Instant Blue /25 #1
2016 Panini Instant Blue /25 #3
2016 Panini Instant Green /5 #1
2016 Panini Instant Green /5 #3
2016 Panini Instant Orange /50 #1
2016 Panini Instant Orange /50 #3
2016 Panini Instant Purple /10 #1
2016 Panini Instant Purple /10 #3
2016 Panini National Treasures /25 #10
2016 Panini National Treasures Black /5 #10
2016 Panini National Treasures Blue /1 #10
2016 Panini National Treasures Eight Signatures /15 #2
2016 Panini National Treasures Eight Signatures Black /5 #2
2016 Panini National Treasures Eight Signatures Blue /1 #2
2016 Panini National Treasures Eight Signatures Gold /10 #2
2016 Panini National Treasures Firesuit Materials /25 #14
2016 Panini National Treasures Firesuit Materials Black /5 #14
2016 Panini National Treasures Firesuit Materials Blue /1 #14
2016 Panini National Treasures Firesuit Materials Gold /10 #14
2016 Panini National Treasures Firesuit Materials Laundry Tag /1 #14
2016 Panini National Treasures Firesuit Materials Printing Plates Black /1 #14
2016 Panini National Treasures Firesuit Materials Printing Plates Cyan /1 #14
2016 Panini National Treasures Firesuit Materials Printing Plates Magenta /1 #14
2016 Panini National Treasures Firesuit Materials Printing Plates Yellow /1 #14
2016 Panini National Treasures Firesuit Materials Silver /15 #14
2016 Panini National Treasures Gold /15 #10
2016 Panini National Treasures Jumbo Firesuit Patch Signature Booklet Associate Sponsor 1 /1 #20
2016 Panini National Treasures Jumbo Firesuit Patch Signature Booklet Associate Sponsor 2 /1 #20
2016 Panini National Treasures Jumbo Firesuit Patch Signature Booklet Associate Sponsor 3 /1 #20
2016 Panini National Treasures Jumbo Firesuit Patch Signature Booklet Associate Sponsor 4 /1 #20
2016 Panini National Treasures Jumbo Firesuit Patch Signature Booklet Associate Sponsor 5 /1 #20
2016 Panini National Treasures Jumbo Firesuit Patch Signature Booklet Flag /1 #20
2016 Panini National Treasures Jumbo Firesuit Patch Signature Booklet Goodyear /2 #20
2016 Panini National Treasures Jumbo Firesuit Patch Signature Booklet Manufacturers Logo /3 #20
2016 Panini National Treasures Jumbo Firesuit Patch Signature Booklet Nameplate /2 #20
2016 Panini National Treasures Jumbo Firesuit Patch Signature Booklet NASCAR /1 #20
2016 Panini National Treasures Jumbo Firesuit Patch Signature Booklet Sprint Cup Logo /1 #20
2016 Panini National Treasures Jumbo Firesuit Patch Signature Booklet Sunoco /1 #20
2016 Panini National Treasures Jumbo Firesuit Signatures /25 #20
2016 Panini National Treasures Jumbo Firesuit Signatures Black /5 #20
2016 Panini National Treasures Jumbo Firesuit Signatures Blue /1 #20
2016 Panini National Treasures Jumbo Firesuit Signatures Gold /10 #20
2016 Panini National Treasures Jumbo Firesuit Signatures Printing Plates Black /1 #20
2016 Panini National Treasures Jumbo Firesuit Signatures Printing Plates Cyan /1 #20
2016 Panini National Treasures Jumbo Firesuit Signatures Printing Plates Magenta /1 #20
2016 Panini National Treasures Jumbo Firesuit Signatures Printing Plates Yellow /1 #20
2016 Panini National Treasures Jumbo Firesuit Signatures Silver /15 #20
2016 Panini National Treasures Printing Plates Black /1 #10
2016 Panini National Treasures Printing Plates Cyan /1 #10
2016 Panini National Treasures Printing Plates Magenta /1 #10
2016 Panini National Treasures Printing Plates Yellow /1 #10
2016 Panini National Treasures Quad Driver Materials /25 #6
2016 Panini National Treasures Quad Driver Materials Black /5 #6
2016 Panini National Treasures Quad Driver Materials Blue /1 #6
2016 Panini National Treasures Quad Driver Materials Gold /10 #6
2016 Panini National Treasures Quad Driver Materials Printing Plates Black /1 #6
2016 Panini National Treasures Quad Driver Materials Printing Plates Cyan /1 #6
2016 Panini National Treasures Quad Driver Materials Printing Plates Magenta /1 #6
2016 Panini National Treasures Quad Driver Materials Printing Plates Yellow /1 #6
2016 Panini National Treasures Quad Driver Materials Silver /15 #6
2016 Panini National Treasures Quad Materials /25 #14
2016 Panini National Treasures Quad Materials Black /5 #14
2016 Panini National Treasures Quad Materials Blue /1 #14
2016 Panini National Treasures Quad Materials Gold /10 #14
2016 Panini National Treasures Quad Materials Printing Plates Black /1 #14
2016 Panini National Treasures Quad Materials Printing Plates Cyan /1 #14
2016 Panini National Treasures Quad Materials Printing Plates Magenta /1 #14
2016 Panini National Treasures Quad Materials Printing Plates Yellow /1 #14
2016 Panini National Treasures Quad Materials Silver /15 #14
2016 Panini National Treasures Sheet Metal Materials /25 #14
2016 Panini National Treasures Sheet Metal Materials Black /5 #14
2016 Panini National Treasures Sheet Metal Materials Blue /1 #14
2016 Panini National Treasures Sheet Metal Materials Gold /10 #14
2016 Panini National Treasures Sheet Metal Materials Printing Plates Black /1 #14
2016 Panini National Treasures Sheet Metal Materials Printing Plates Cyan /1 #14
2016 Panini National Treasures Sheet Metal Materials Printing Plates Magenta /1 #14
2016 Panini National Treasures Sheet Metal Materials Printing Plates Yellow /1 #14
2016 Panini National Treasures Sheet Metal Materials Silver /15 #14
2016 Panini National Treasures Signature Firesuit Materials /25 #19
2016 Panini National Treasures Signature Firesuit Materials Black /5 #19
2016 Panini National Treasures Signature Firesuit Materials Blue /1 #19
2016 Panini National Treasures Signature Firesuit Materials Gold /10 #19
2016 Panini National Treasures Signature Firesuit Materials Laundry Tag /1 #19
2016 Panini National Treasures Signature Firesuit Materials Printing Plates Black /1 #19
2016 Panini National Treasures Signature Firesuit Materials Printing Plates Cyan /1 #19
2016 Panini National Treasures Signature Firesuit Materials Printing Plates Magenta /1 #19
2016 Panini National Treasures Signature Firesuit Materials Printing Plates Yellow /1 #19
2016 Panini National Treasures Signature Firesuit Materials Silver /15 #19
2016 Panini National Treasures Signatures /49 #16
2016 Panini National Treasures Signatures Black /5 #16
2016 Panini National Treasures Signatures Blue /1 #16
2016 Panini National Treasures Signatures Gold /15 #16
2016 Panini National Treasures Signatures Printing Plates Black /1 #16
2016 Panini National Treasures Signatures Printing Plates Cyan /1 #16
2016 Panini National Treasures Signatures Printing Plates Magenta /1 #16
2016 Panini National Treasures Signatures Printing Plates Yellow /1 #16
2016 Panini National Treasures Signatures Silver /25 #16
2016 Panini National Treasures Silver /20 #10
2016 Panini National Treasures Timelines /25 #11
2016 Panini National Treasures Timelines Black /5 #11
2016 Panini National Treasures Timelines Blue /1 #11
2016 Panini National Treasures Timelines Gold /10 #11
2016 Panini National Treasures Timelines Printing Plates Black /1 #11
2016 Panini National Treasures Timelines Printing Plates Cyan /1 #11
2016 Panini National Treasures Timelines Printing Plates Magenta /1 #11
2016 Panini National Treasures Timelines Printing Plates Yellow /1 #11
2016 Panini National Treasures Timelines Signatures /25 #10
2016 Panini National Treasures Timelines Signatures Black /5 #10
2016 Panini National Treasures Timelines Signatures Blue /1 #10
2016 Panini National Treasures Timelines Signatures Gold /10 #10
2016 Panini National Treasures Timelines Signatures Printing Plates Black /1 #10
2016 Panini National Treasures Timelines Signatures Printing Plates Cyan /1 #10
2016 Panini National Treasures Timelines Signatures Printing Plates Magenta /1 #10
2016 Panini National Treasures Timelines Signatures Printing Plates Yellow /1 #10
2016 Panini National Treasures Timelines Signatures Silver /15 #10
2016 Panini National Treasures Timelines Silver /15 #11
2016 Panini National Treasures Winning Signatures Black /10 #8
2016 Panini National Treasures Winning Signatures Blue /1 #8
2016 Panini National Treasures Winning Signatures Gold /25 #8
2016 Panini National Treasures Winning Signatures Printing Plates Black /1 #8
2016 Panini National Treasures Winning Signatures Printing Plates Cyan /1 #8
2016 Panini National Treasures Winning Signatures Printing Plates Magenta /1 #8
2016 Panini National Treasures Winning Signatures Printing Plates Yellow /1 #8
2016 Panini National Treasures Winning Signatures Silver /50 #8
2016 Panini Prizm #25
2016 Panini Prizm #62
2016 Panini Prizm Autographs Prizms #43
2016 Panini Prizm Autographs Prizms Black /3 #43
2016 Panini Prizm Autographs Prizms Blue Flag /35 #43
2016 Panini Prizm Autographs Prizms Camo /78 #43
2016 Panini Prizm Autographs Prizms Checkered Flag /1 #43
2016 Panini Prizm Autographs Prizms Gold /10 #43
2016 Panini Prizm Autographs Prizms Green Flag /50 #43
2016 Panini Prizm Autographs Prizms Rainbow /24 #43
2016 Panini Prizm Autographs Prizms Red Flag /25 #43
2016 Panini Prizm Autographs Prizms Red White and Blue /25 #43
2016 Panini Prizm Autographs Prizms White Flag /5 #43
2016 Panini Prizm Machinery #8
2016 Panini Prizm Machinery Prizms #8
2016 Panini Prizm Machinery Prizms Checkered Flag /1 #8
2016 Panini Prizm Machinery Prizms Gold /10 #8
2016 Panini Prizm Prizms #25
2016 Panini Prizm Prizms #62
2016 Panini Prizm Prizms Black /3 #25
2016 Panini Prizm Prizms Black /3 #62
2016 Panini Prizm Prizms Blue Flag /99 #25
2016 Panini Prizm Prizms Blue Flag /99 #62
2016 Panini Prizm Prizms Camo /78 #25
2016 Panini Prizm Prizms Camo /78 #62
2016 Panini Prizm Prizms Checkered Flag /1 #25
2016 Panini Prizm Prizms Checkered Flag /1 #62
2016 Panini Prizm Prizms Gold /10 #25
2016 Panini Prizm Prizms Gold /10 #62
2016 Panini Prizm Prizms Green Flag /149 #25
2016 Panini Prizm Prizms Green Flag /149 #62
2016 Panini Prizm Prizms Rainbow /24 #25
2016 Panini Prizm Prizms Rainbow /24 #62
2016 Panini Prizm Prizms Red Flag /75 #25
2016 Panini Prizm Prizms Red Flag /75 #62
2016 Panini Prizm Prizms Red White and Blue #25
2016 Panini Prizm Prizms Red White and Blue #62
2016 Panini Prizm Prizms White Flag /5 #25
2016 Panini Prizm Prizms White Flag /5 #62
2016 Panini Prizm Race Used Tire #9
2016 Panini Prizm Race Used Tire Prizms Blue Flag /49 #9
2016 Panini Prizm Race Used Tire Prizms Green Flag /99 #9
2016 Panini Prizm Race Used Tire Prizms Red Flag /25 #9
2016 Panini Prizm Race Used Tire Team #8
2016 Panini Prizm Race Used Tire Team Prizms Blue Flag /75 #8
2016 Panini Prizm Race Used Tire Team Prizms Green Flag /149 #8
2016 Panini Prizm Race Used Tire Team Prizms Red Flag /10 #8
2016 Panini Prizm Winner's Circle #14
2016 Panini Prizm Winner's Circle Prizms #14
2016 Panini Prizm Winner's Circle Prizms Checkered Flag /1 #14
2016 Panini Prizm Winner's Circle Prizms Gold /10 #14
2016 Panini Torque #13
2016 Panini Torque #89
2016 Panini Torque Artist Proof /50 #13
2016 Panini Torque Artist Proof /50 #89
2016 Panini Torque Blackout /1 #13
2016 Panini Torque Blackout /1 #89
2016 Panini Torque Blue /125 #13
2016 Panini Torque Blue /125 #89
2016 Panini Torque Clear Vision #13
2016 Panini Torque Clear Vision Blue /99 #13
2016 Panini Torque Clear Vision Gold /149 #13
2016 Panini Torque Clear Vision Green /25 #13
2016 Panini Torque Clear Vision Purple /10 #13
2016 Panini Torque Clear Vision Red /49 #13
2016 Panini Torque Gold #13
2016 Panini Torque Gold #89
2016 Panini Torque Holo Gold /5 #13
2016 Panini Torque Holo Gold /5 #89
2016 Panini Torque Holo Silver /10 #13
2016 Panini Torque Holo Silver /10 #89
2016 Panini Torque Horsepower Heroes #4
2016 Panini Torque Horsepower Heroes Gold /199 #4
2016 Panini Torque Horsepower Heroes Holo Silver /99 #4
2016 Panini Torque Pole Position #1
2016 Panini Torque Pole Position Blue /99 #1
2016 Panini Torque Pole Position Checkerboard /10 #1
2016 Panini Torque Pole Position Green /25 #1
2016 Panini Torque Pole Position Red /49 #1
2016 Panini Torque Printing Plates Black /1 #13
2016 Panini Torque Printing Plates Black /1 #89
2016 Panini Torque Printing Plates Cyan /1 #13
2016 Panini Torque Printing Plates Cyan /1 #89
2016 Panini Torque Printing Plates Magenta /1 #13
2016 Panini Torque Printing Plates Magenta /1 #89
2016 Panini Torque Printing Plates Yellow /1 #13
2016 Panini Torque Printing Plates Yellow /1 #89
2016 Panini Torque Purple /25 #13
2016 Panini Torque Purple /25 #89
2016 Panini Torque Red /99 #13
2016 Panini Torque Red /99 #89
2016 Panini Torque Shades #11
2016 Panini Torque Shades Gold /199 #11
2016 Panini Torque Shades Holo Silver /99 #11
2016 Panini Torque Silhouettes Firesuit Autographs /150 #17
2016 Panini Torque Silhouettes Firesuit Autographs Blue /75 #17
2016 Panini Torque Silhouettes Firesuit Autographs Green /25 #17
2016 Panini Torque Silhouettes Firesuit Autographs Purple /10 #17
2016 Panini Torque Silhouettes Firesuit Autographs Red /40 #17
2016 Panini Torque Special Paint #10
2016 Panini Torque Special Paint Gold /199 #10
2016 Panini Torque Special Paint Holo Silver /99 #10
2016 Panini Torque Test Proof Black /1 #13
2016 Panini Torque Test Proof Black /1 #89
2016 Panini Torque Test Proof Cyan /1 #13
2016 Panini Torque Test Proof Cyan /1 #89
2016 Panini Torque Test Proof Magenta /1 #13
2016 Panini Torque Test Proof Magenta /1 #89
2016 Panini Torque Test Proof Yellow /1 #13
2016 Panini Torque Test Proof Yellow /1 #89
2016 Panini Torque Victory Laps #13
2016 Panini Torque Victory Laps Gold /199 #13
2016 Panini Torque Victory Laps Holo Silver /99 #13
2016 Panini Torque Winning Vision #12
2016 Panini Torque Winning Vision Blue /99 #12
2016 Panini Torque Winning Vision Gold /149 #12
2016 Panini Torque Winning Vision Green /25 #12
2016 Panini Torque Winning Vision Purple /10 #12
2016 Panini Torque Winning Vision Red /49 #12
2017 Donruss #16
2017 Donruss #49
2017 Donruss #96
2017 Donruss #121
2017 Donruss #172
2017 Donruss #106
2017 Donruss Artist Proof /25 #16
2017 Donruss Artist Proof /25 #49
2017 Donruss Artist Proof /25 #96
2017 Donruss Artist Proof /25 #121
2017 Donruss Artist Proof /25 #172
2017 Donruss Artist Proof /25 #106
2017 Donruss Blue Foil /299 #16
2017 Donruss Blue Foil /299 #96
2017 Donruss Blue Foil /299 #121
2017 Donruss Blue Foil /299 #49
2017 Donruss Blue Foil /299 #172
2017 Donruss Blue Foil /299 #106
2017 Donruss Cut to The Chase #1
2017 Donruss Cut to The Chase #3
2017 Donruss Cut to The Chase Cracked Ice /999 #1
2017 Donruss Cut to The Chase Cracked Ice /999 #3
2017 Donruss Gold Foil /499 #16
2017 Donruss Gold Foil /499 #96
2017 Donruss Gold Foil /499 #121
2017 Donruss Gold Foil /499 #172
2017 Donruss Gold Foil /499 #49
2017 Donruss Gold Foil /499 #106
2017 Donruss Gold Press Proof /99 #16
2017 Donruss Gold Press Proof /99 #49
2017 Donruss Gold Press Proof /99 #96
2017 Donruss Gold Press Proof /99 #121
2017 Donruss Gold Press Proof /99 #172
2017 Donruss Gold Press Proof /99 #106
2017 Donruss Green Foil /199 #16
2017 Donruss Green Foil /199 #49
2017 Donruss Green Foil /199 #96
2017 Donruss Green Foil /199 #121
2017 Donruss Green Foil /199 #172

2017 Donruss Green Foil /199 #106
2017 Donruss Pole Position #2
2017 Donruss Pole Position Cracked Ice /999 #2
2017 Donruss Press Proof /49 #16
2017 Donruss Press Proof /49 #49
2017 Donruss Press Proof /49 #96
2017 Donruss Press Proof /49 #121
2017 Donruss Press Proof /49 #172
2017 Donruss Press Proof /49 #106
2017 Donruss Printing Plates Black /1 #16
2017 Donruss Printing Plates Black /1 #49
2017 Donruss Printing Plates Black /1 #96
2017 Donruss Printing Plates Black /1 #121
2017 Donruss Printing Plates Black /1 #172
2017 Donruss Printing Plates Black /1 #106
2017 Donruss Printing Plates Cyan /1 #16
2017 Donruss Printing Plates Cyan /1 #49
2017 Donruss Printing Plates Cyan /1 #96
2017 Donruss Printing Plates Cyan /1 #121
2017 Donruss Printing Plates Cyan /1 #172
2017 Donruss Printing Plates Cyan /1 #106
2017 Donruss Printing Plates Magenta /1 #16
2017 Donruss Printing Plates Magenta /1 #96
2017 Donruss Printing Plates Magenta /1 #121
2017 Donruss Printing Plates Magenta /1 #172
2017 Donruss Printing Plates Magenta /1 #49
2017 Donruss Printing Plates Magenta /1 #106
2017 Donruss Printing Plates Yellow /1 #16
2017 Donruss Printing Plates Yellow /1 #96
2017 Donruss Printing Plates Yellow /1 #121
2017 Donruss Printing Plates Yellow /1 #172
2017 Donruss Printing Plates Yellow /1 #49
2017 Donruss Printing Plates Yellow /1 #106
2017 Donruss Retro Relics 1984 #30
2017 Donruss Retro Relics 1984 Holo Black /10 #30
2017 Donruss Retro Relics 1984 Holo Gold /99 #30
2017 Donruss Retro Signatures 1984 #17
2017 Donruss Retro Signatures 1984 Holo Black /1 #17
2017 Donruss Retro Signatures 1984 Holo Gold /25 #17
2017 Donruss Speed #4
2017 Donruss Speed Cracked Ice /999 #4
2017 Donruss Top Tier #1
2017 Donruss Top Tier Cracked Ice /999 #1
2017 Donruss Track Masters #6
2017 Donruss Track Masters Cracked Ice /999 #6
2017 Panini Father's Day Racing Memorabilia /100 #9
2017 Panini Father's Day Racing Memorabilia Cracked Ice /25 #9
2017 Panini Father's Day Racing Memorabilia Hyperplaid /1 #9
2017 Panini Father's Day Racing Memorabilia Shimmer /10 #9
2017 Panini Instant Nascar /60 #3
2017 Panini Instant Nascar #10
2017 Panini Instant Nascar #17
2017 Panini Instant Nascar #21
2017 Panini Instant Nascar #25
2017 Panini Instant Nascar #26
2017 Panini Instant Nascar #28
2017 Panini Instant Nascar #30
2017 Panini Instant Nascar #34
2017 Panini Instant Nascar Black /1 #3
2017 Panini Instant Nascar Black /1 #10
2017 Panini Instant Nascar Black /1 #17
2017 Panini Instant Nascar Black /1 #21
2017 Panini Instant Nascar Black /1 #25
2017 Panini Instant Nascar Black /1 #28
2017 Panini Instant Nascar Black /1 #30
2017 Panini Instant Nascar Black /1 #26
2017 Panini Instant Nascar Black /1 #34
2017 Panini Instant Nascar Green /10 #3
2017 Panini Instant Nascar Green /10 #10
2017 Panini Instant Nascar Green /10 #17
2017 Panini Instant Nascar Green /10 #21
2017 Panini Instant Nascar Green /10 #25
2017 Panini Instant Nascar Green /10 #26
2017 Panini Instant Nascar Green /10 #28
2017 Panini Instant Nascar Green /10 #30
2017 Panini Instant Nascar Green /10 #34
2017 Panini National Convention #R9
2017 Panini National Convention Autographs #R9
2017 Panini National Convention Autographs Hyperplaid /1 #R9
2017 Panini National Convention Escher Squares /25 #R9
2017 Panini National Convention Escher Squares Thick Stock /10 #R9
2017 Panini National Convention Galatic Windows /5 #R9
2017 Panini National Convention Hyperplaid /1 #R9
2017 Panini National Convention Pyramids /10 #R9
2017 Panini National Convention Rainbow Spokes /49 #R9
2017 Panini National Convention Rainbow Spokes Thick Stock /25 #R9
2017 Panini National Convention Rapture /99 #R9
2017 Panini National Treasures /25 #15
2017 Panini National Treasures Associate Sponsor Patch Signatures 1 /1 #14
2017 Panini National Treasures Associate Sponsor Patch Signatures 2 /1 #14
2017 Panini National Treasures Associate Sponsor Patch Signatures 3 /1 #14
2017 Panini National Treasures Associate Sponsor Patch Signatures 4 /1 #14
2017 Panini National Treasures Associate Sponsor Patch Signatures 5 /1 #14
2017 Panini National Treasures Car Manufacturer Patch Signatures /1 #14
2017 Panini National Treasures Century Black /1 #15
2017 Panini National Treasures Century Gold /15 #15
2017 Panini National Treasures Century Green /5 #15
2017 Panini National Treasures Century Holo Gold /10 #15
2017 Panini National Treasures Century Holo Silver /20 #15
2017 Panini National Treasures Century Laundry Tags /1 #15
2017 Panini National Treasures Dual Firesuit Materials /25 #11
2017 Panini National Treasures Dual Firesuit Materials Black /1 #11
2017 Panini National Treasures Dual Firesuit Materials Gold /15 #11
2017 Panini National Treasures Dual Firesuit Materials Green /5 #11
2017 Panini National Treasures Dual Firesuit Materials Holo Gold /10 #11
2017 Panini National Treasures Dual Firesuit Materials Holo Silver /20 #11
2017 Panini National Treasures Dual Firesuit Materials Laundry Tag /1 #11
2017 Panini National Treasures Dual Firesuit Materials Printing Plates Black /1 #11
2017 Panini National Treasures Dual Firesuit Materials Printing Plates Cyan /1 #11
2017 Panini National Treasures Dual Firesuit Materials Printing Plates Magenta /1 #11
2017 Panini National Treasures Dual Firesuit Materials Printing Plates Yellow /1 #11
2017 Panini National Treasures Dual Firesuit Signatures /25 #11
2017 Panini National Treasures Dual Firesuit Signatures Black /1 #11
2017 Panini National Treasures Dual Firesuit Signatures Gold /15 #11
2017 Panini National Treasures Dual Firesuit Signatures Green /5 #11
2017 Panini National Treasures Dual Firesuit Signatures Holo Gold /10 #11
2017 Panini National Treasures Dual Firesuit Signatures Holo Silver /20 #11
2017 Panini National Treasures Dual Firesuit Signatures Laundry Tag /1 #11
2017 Panini National Treasures Dual Firesuit Signatures Printing Plates Black /1 #11
2017 Panini National Treasures Dual Firesuit Signatures Printing Plates Cyan /1 #11
2017 Panini National Treasures Dual Firesuit Signatures Printing Plates Magenta /1 #11
2017 Panini National Treasures Dual Firesuit Signatures Printing Plates Yellow /1 #11
2017 Panini National Treasures Dual Sheet Metal Signatures /25 #10
2017 Panini National Treasures Dual Sheet Metal Signatures Black /1 #10
2017 Panini National Treasures Dual Sheet Metal Signatures Gold /15 #10
2017 Panini National Treasures Dual Sheet Metal Signatures Green /5 #10
2017 Panini National Treasures Dual Sheet Metal Signatures Holo Gold /10 #10
2017 Panini National Treasures Dual Sheet Metal Signatures Holo Silver /20 #10
2017 Panini National Treasures Dual Sheet Metal Signatures Printing Plates Black /1 #10
2017 Panini National Treasures Dual Sheet Metal Signatures Printing Plates Cyan /1 #10
2017 Panini National Treasures Dual Sheet Metal Signatures Printing Plates Magenta /1 #10
2017 Panini National Treasures Dual Sheet Metal Signatures Printing Plates Yellow /1 #10
2017 Panini National Treasures Dual Tire Signatures /25 #11
2017 Panini National Treasures Dual Tire Signatures Black /1 #11
2017 Panini National Treasures Dual Tire Signatures Gold /15 #11
2017 Panini National Treasures Dual Tire Signatures Green /5 #11
2017 Panini National Treasures Dual Tire Signatures Holo Gold /10 #11
2017 Panini National Treasures Dual Tire Signatures Holo Silver /20 #11
2017 Panini National Treasures Dual Tire Signatures Printing Plates Black /1 #11
2017 Panini National Treasures Dual Tire Signatures Printing Plates Cyan /1 #11
2017 Panini National Treasures Dual Tire Signatures Printing Plates Magenta /1 #11
2017 Panini National Treasures Dual Tire Signatures Printing Plates Yellow /1 #11
2017 Panini National Treasures Flag Patch Signatures /1 #14
2017 Panini National Treasures Goodyear Patch Signatures /2 #14
2017 Panini National Treasures Hats Off /16 #17
2017 Panini National Treasures Hats Off /16 #18
2017 Panini National Treasures Hats Off Gold /5 #17
2017 Panini National Treasures Hats Off Gold /6 #18
2017 Panini National Treasures Hats Off Holo Gold /5 #17
2017 Panini National Treasures Hats Off Holo Gold /5 #18
2017 Panini National Treasures Hats Off Holo Silver /1 #17
2017 Panini National Treasures Hats Off Holo Silver /1 #18
2017 Panini National Treasures Hats Off Laundry Tag /3 #17
2017 Panini National Treasures Hats Off Laundry Tag /3 #18
2017 Panini National Treasures Hats Off Printing Plates Black /1 #17
2017 Panini National Treasures Hats Off Printing Plates Black /1 #18
2017 Panini National Treasures Hats Off Printing Plates Cyan /1 #17
2017 Panini National Treasures Hats Off Printing Plates Cyan /1 #18
2017 Panini National Treasures Hats Off Printing Plates Magenta /1 #17
2017 Panini National Treasures Hats Off Printing Plates Magenta /1 #18
2017 Panini National Treasures Hats Off Printing Plates Yellow /1 #17
2017 Panini National Treasures Hats Off Printing Plates Yellow /1 #18
2017 Panini National Treasures Hats Off Sponsor /5 #17
2017 Panini National Treasures Hats Off Sponsor /5 #18
2017 Panini National Treasures Jumbo Firesuit Signatures /25 #9
2017 Panini National Treasures Jumbo Firesuit Signatures Black /1 #9
2017 Panini National Treasures Jumbo Firesuit Signatures Gold /15 #9
2017 Panini National Treasures Jumbo Firesuit Signatures Green /5 #9
2017 Panini National Treasures Jumbo Firesuit Signatures Holo Gold /10 #9
2017 Panini National Treasures Jumbo Firesuit Signatures Holo Silver /20 #9
2017 Panini National Treasures Jumbo Firesuit Signatures Laundry Tag /1 #9
2017 Panini National Treasures Jumbo Firesuit Signatures Printing Plates Black /1 #9
2017 Panini National Treasures Jumbo Firesuit Signatures Printing Plates Cyan /1 #9
2017 Panini National Treasures Jumbo Firesuit Signatures Printing Plates Magenta /1 #9
2017 Panini National Treasures Jumbo Firesuit Signatures Printing Plates Yellow /1 #9
2017 Panini National Treasures Jumbo Tire Signatures /45 #13
2017 Panini National Treasures Jumbo Tire Signatures Black /1 #13
2017 Panini National Treasures Jumbo Tire Signatures Gold /25 #13
2017 Panini National Treasures Jumbo Tire Signatures Green /5 #13
2017 Panini National Treasures Jumbo Tire Signatures Holo Gold /15 #13
2017 Panini National Treasures Jumbo Tire Signatures Holo Silver /35 #13
2017 Panini National Treasures Jumbo Tire Signatures Printing Plates Black /1 #13
2017 Panini National Treasures Jumbo Tire Signatures Printing Plates Cyan /1 #13
2017 Panini National Treasures Jumbo Tire Signatures Printing Plates Magenta /1 #13
2017 Panini National Treasures Jumbo Tire Signatures Printing Plates Yellow /1 #13
2017 Panini National Treasures Nameplate Patch Signatures /2 #14
2017 Panini National Treasures NASCAR Patch Signatures /1 #14
2017 Panini National Treasures Printing Plates Black /1 #15
2017 Panini National Treasures Printing Plates Cyan /1 #15
2017 Panini National Treasures Printing Plates Magenta /1 #15
2017 Panini National Treasures Printing Plates Yellow /1 #15
2017 Panini National Treasures Quad Materials /25 #8
2017 Panini National Treasures Quad Materials Black /1 #8
2017 Panini National Treasures Quad Materials Gold /15 #8
2017 Panini National Treasures Quad Materials Green /5 #8
2017 Panini National Treasures Quad Materials Holo Gold /10 #8
2017 Panini National Treasures Quad Materials Holo Silver /20 #8
2017 Panini National Treasures Quad Materials Laundry Tag /1 #8
2017 Panini National Treasures Quad Materials Printing Plates Black /1 #8
2017 Panini National Treasures Quad Materials Printing Plates Cyan /1 #8
2017 Panini National Treasures Quad Materials Printing Plates Magenta /1 #8
2017 Panini National Treasures Quad Materials Printing Plates Yellow /1 #8
2017 Panini National Treasures Series Sponsor Patch Signatures /1 #14
2017 Panini National Treasures Sunoco Patch Signatures /1 #14
2017 Panini National Treasures Teammates Quad Materials /25 #1
2017 Panini National Treasures Teammates Quad Materials Black /1 #1
2017 Panini National Treasures Teammates Quad Materials Gold /15 #1
2017 Panini National Treasures Teammates Quad Materials Green /5 #1
2017 Panini National Treasures Teammates Quad Materials Holo Gold /10 #1
2017 Panini National Treasures Teammates Quad Materials Holo Silver /20 #1
2017 Panini National Treasures Teammates Quad Materials Laundry Tag /1 #1
2017 Panini National Treasures Teammates Quad Materials Printing Plates Black /1 #1
2017 Panini National Treasures Teammates Quad Materials Printing Plates Cyan /1 #1
2017 Panini National Treasures Teammates Quad Materials Printing Plates Magenta /1 #1
2017 Panini National Treasures Teammates Quad Materials Printing Plates Yellow /1 #1
2017 Panini National Treasures Three Wide Signatures /25 #11
2017 Panini National Treasures Three Wide Signatures Black /1 #11
2017 Panini National Treasures Three Wide Signatures Gold /15 #11
2017 Panini National Treasures Three Wide Signatures Green /5 #11
2017 Panini National Treasures Three Wide Signatures Holo Gold /10 #11
2017 Panini National Treasures Three Wide Signatures Holo Silver /20 #11
2017 Panini National Treasures Three Wide Signatures Laundry Tag /1 #11
2017 Panini National Treasures Three Wide Signatures Printing Plates Black /1 #11
2017 Panini National Treasures Three Wide Signatures Printing Plates Cyan /1 #11
2017 Panini National Treasures Three Wide Signatures Printing Plates Magenta /1 #11
2017 Panini National Treasures Three Wide Signatures Printing Plates Yellow /1 #11
2017 Panini Torque #25
2017 Panini Torque #70
2017 Panini Torque Artist Proof /75 #25
2017 Panini Torque Artist Proof /75 #70
2017 Panini Torque Blackout /1 #25
2017 Panini Torque Blackout /1 #70
2017 Panini Torque Blue /150 #25
2017 Panini Torque Blue /150 #70
2017 Panini Torque Claiming The Chase #9
2017 Panini Torque Claiming The Chase Gold /199 #9
2017 Panini Torque Claiming The Chase Holo Silver /99 #9
2017 Panini Torque Clear Vision #25
2017 Panini Torque Clear Vision Blue /99 #25
2017 Panini Torque Clear Vision Gold /149 #25
2017 Panini Torque Clear Vision Green /25 #25
2017 Panini Torque Clear Vision Purple /10 #25
2017 Panini Torque Clear Vision Red /49 #25
2017 Panini Torque Combo Materials Signatures /75 #6
2017 Panini Torque Combo Materials Signatures Blue /50 #6
2017 Panini Torque Combo Materials Signatures Green /15 #6
2017 Panini Torque Combo Materials Signatures Purple /10 #6
2017 Panini Torque Combo Materials Signatures Red /25 #6
2017 Panini Torque Gold #25
2017 Panini Torque Gold #70
2017 Panini Torque Holo Gold /10 #25
2017 Panini Torque Holo Gold /10 #70
2017 Panini Torque Holo Silver /25 #25
2017 Panini Torque Holo Silver /25 #70
2017 Panini Torque Horsepower Heroes #22
2017 Panini Torque Horsepower Heroes Gold /199 #22
2017 Panini Torque Horsepower Heroes Holo Silver /99 #22
2017 Panini Torque Manufacturer Marks #14
2017 Panini Torque Manufacturer Marks Gold /199 #14
2017 Panini Torque Manufacturer Marks Holo Silver /99 #14
2017 Panini Torque Pairings Materials /199 #13
2017 Panini Torque Pairings Materials Blue /99 #13
2017 Panini Torque Pairings Materials Green /25 #13
2017 Panini Torque Pairings Materials Purple /10 #13
2017 Panini Torque Pairings Materials Red /49 #13
2017 Panini Torque Prime Associate Sponsors Jumbo Patches /1 #15A
2017 Panini Torque Prime Associate Sponsors Jumbo Patches /1 #15B
2017 Panini Torque Prime Associate Sponsors Jumbo Patches /1 #15C
2017 Panini Torque Prime Associate Sponsors Jumbo Patches /1 #15D
2017 Panini Torque Prime Associate Sponsors Jumbo Patches /1 #15E
2017 Panini Torque Prime Associate Sponsors Jumbo Patches /1 #15F
2017 Panini Torque Prime Associate Sponsors Jumbo Patches /1 #15G
2017 Panini Torque Prime Associate Sponsors Jumbo Patches /1 #15H
2017 Panini Torque Prime Flag Jumbo Patches /1 #15
2017 Panini Torque Prime Goodyear Jumbo Patches /2 #15
2017 Panini Torque Prime Manufacturer Jumbo Patches /1 #15
2017 Panini Torque Prime Nameplates Jumbo Patches /2 #15
2017 Panini Torque Prime NASCAR Jumbo Patches /1 #15
2017 Panini Torque Prime Series Sponsor Jumbo Patches /1 #15
2017 Panini Torque Printing Plates Black /1 #25
2017 Panini Torque Printing Plates Black /1 #70
2017 Panini Torque Printing Plates Cyan /1 #25
2017 Panini Torque Printing Plates Cyan /1 #70
2017 Panini Torque Printing Plates Magenta /1 #25
2017 Panini Torque Printing Plates Magenta /1 #70
2017 Panini Torque Printing Plates Yellow /1 #25
2017 Panini Torque Printing Plates Yellow /1 #70
2017 Panini Torque Purple /50 #25
2017 Panini Torque Purple /50 #70
2017 Panini Torque Quad Materials /299 #21
2017 Panini Torque Quad Materials Blue /99 #21
2017 Panini Torque Quad Materials Green /25 #21
2017 Panini Torque Quad Materials Purple /10 #21
2017 Panini Torque Quad Materials Red /49 #21
2017 Panini Torque Raced Relics /499 #16
2017 Panini Torque Raced Relics Blue /99 #16
2017 Panini Torque Raced Relics Green /25 #16
2017 Panini Torque Raced Relics Purple /10 #16
2017 Panini Torque Raced Relics Red /49 #16
2017 Panini Torque Red /100 #25
2017 Panini Torque Red /100 #70
2017 Panini Torque Running Order #11
2017 Panini Torque Running Order Blue /99 #11
2017 Panini Torque Running Order Checkerboard /10 #11
2017 Panini Torque Running Order Green /25 #11
2017 Panini Torque Running Order Red /49 #11
2017 Panini Torque Silhouettes Firesuit Signatures /75 #2
2017 Panini Torque Silhouettes Firesuit Signatures Blue /50 #2
2017 Panini Torque Silhouettes Firesuit Signatures Green /15 #2
2017 Panini Torque Silhouettes Firesuit Signatures Purple /10 #2
2017 Panini Torque Silhouettes Firesuit Signatures Red /25 #2
2017 Panini Torque Superstar Vision #13
2017 Panini Torque Superstar Vision Blue /99 #13
2017 Panini Torque Superstar Vision Gold /149 #13
2017 Panini Torque Superstar Vision Green /25 #13
2017 Panini Torque Superstar Vision Purple /10 #13
2017 Panini Torque Superstar Vision Red /49 #13
2017 Panini Torque Test Proof Black /1 #25
2017 Panini Torque Test Proof Black /1 #70
2017 Panini Torque Test Proof Cyan /1 #25
2017 Panini Torque Test Proof Cyan /1 #70
2017 Panini Torque Test Proof Magenta /1 #25
2017 Panini Torque Test Proof Magenta /1 #70
2017 Panini Torque Test Proof Yellow /1 #25
2017 Panini Torque Test Proof Yellow /1 #70
2017 Panini Torque Track Vision #10
2017 Panini Torque Track Vision Blue /99 #10
2017 Panini Torque Track Vision Gold /149 #10
2017 Panini Torque Track Vision Green /25 #10
2017 Panini Torque Track Vision Purple /10 #10
2017 Panini Torque Track Vision Red /49 #10
2017 Panini Torque Trackside #6
2017 Panini Torque Trackside Blue /99 #6
2017 Panini Torque Trackside Checkerboard /10 #6
2017 Panini Torque Trackside Green /25 #6
2017 Panini Torque Trackside Red /49 #6
2017 Panini Torque Victory Laps #5
2017 Panini Torque Victory Laps Gold /199 #5
2017 Panini Torque Victory Laps Holo Silver /99 #5
2017 Select #31
2017 Select #32
2017 Select #33
2017 Select #103
2017 Select Prizms Black /3 #31
2017 Select Prizms Black /3 #32
2017 Select Prizms Black /3 #33
2017 Select Prizms Black /3 #103
2017 Select Prizms Blue /199 #31
2017 Select Prizms Blue /199 #32
2017 Select Prizms Blue /199 #33
2017 Select Prizms Checkered Flag /1 #31
2017 Select Prizms Checkered Flag /1 #32
2017 Select Prizms Checkered Flag /1 #33
2017 Select Prizms Checkered Flag /1 #103
2017 Select Prizms Gold /10 #31
2017 Select Prizms Gold /10 #32
2017 Select Prizms Gold /10 #33
2017 Select Prizms Gold /10 #103
2017 Select Prizms Purple Pulsar #31
2017 Select Prizms Purple Pulsar #32
2017 Select Prizms Purple Pulsar #33
2017 Select Prizms Red /99 #31
2017 Select Prizms Red /99 #32
2017 Select Prizms Red /99 #33
2017 Select Prizms Red White and Blue Pulsar /299 #31
2017 Select Prizms Red White and Blue Pulsar /299 #32
2017 Select Prizms Red White and Blue Pulsar /299 #33
2017 Select Prizms Silver #31
2017 Select Prizms Silver #32
2017 Select Prizms Silver #33
2017 Select Prizms Tie Dye /24 #31
2017 Select Prizms Tie Dye /24 #32
2017 Select Prizms Tie Dye /24 #33
2017 Select Prizms Tie Dye /24 #103
2017 Select Prizms White /50 #31
2017 Select Prizms White /50 #32
2017 Select Prizms White /50 #33
2017 Select Prizms White /50 #103
2017 Select Select Stars #25
2017 Select Select Stars Prizms Black /3 #25
2017 Select Select Stars Prizms Checkered Flag /1 #25
2017 Select Select Stars Prizms Gold /10 #25
2017 Select Select Stars Prizms Tie Dye /24 #25
2017 Select Select Stars Prizms White /50 #25
2017 Select Select Swatches #32
2017 Select Select Swatches Prizms Blue /199 #32
2017 Select Select Swatches Prizms Checkered Flag /1 #32
2017 Select Select Swatches Prizms Gold /10 #32
2017 Select Select Swatches Prizms Red /99 #32
2017 Select Sheet Metal #19
2017 Select Sheet Metal Prizms Blue /199 #19
2017 Select Sheet Metal Prizms Checkered Flag /1 #19
2017 Select Sheet Metal Prizms Gold /10 #19
2017 Select Sheet Metal Prizms Red /99 #19
2017 Select Signature Paint Schemes #12
2017 Select Signature Paint Schemes Prizms Blue /50 #12
2017 Select Signature Paint Schemes Prizms Checkered Flag /1 #12
2017 Select Signature Paint Schemes Prizms Gold /10 #12
2017 Select Signature Paint Schemes Prizms Red /25 #12
2017 Select Signature Swatches #32
2017 Select Signature Swatches Prizms Checkered Flag /1 #32
2017 Select Signature Swatches Prizms Gold /10 #32
2017 Select Signature Swatches Prizms Tie Dye /24 #32
2017 Select Signature Swatches Prizms White /50 #32
2017 Select Signature Swatches Triple #20
2017 Select Signature Swatches Triple Prizms Checkered Flag /1 #20
2017 Select Signature Swatches Triple Prizms Gold /10 #20
2017 Select Signature Swatches Triple Prizms Tie Dye /24 #20
2017 Select Signature Swatches Triple Prizms White /50 #20
2017 Select Speed Merchants #1
2017 Select Speed Merchants Prizms Black /3 #1
2017 Select Speed Merchants Prizms Checkered Flag /1 #1
2017 Select Speed Merchants Prizms Gold /10 #1
2017 Select Speed Merchants Prizms Tie Dye /24 #1
2017 Select Speed Merchants Prizms White /50 #1
2018 Certified #26
2018 Certified #92
2018 Certified All Certified Team /199 #10
2018 Certified All Certified Team Black /1 #10
2018 Certified All Certified Team Blue /99 #10
2018 Certified All Certified Team Gold /49 #10
2018 Certified All Certified Team Green /10 #10
2018 Certified All Certified Team Mirror Black /1 #10
2018 Certified All Certified Team Mirror Gold /25 #10
2018 Certified All Certified Team Mirror Green /5 #10
2018 Certified All Certified Team Mirror Purple /10 #10
2018 Certified All Certified Team Purple /25 #10
2018 Certified All Certified Team Red /149 #10
2018 Certified Black /1 #26
2018 Certified Black /1 #92
2018 Certified Blue /99 #26
2018 Certified Blue /99 #92
2018 Certified Complete Materials /199 #8
2018 Certified Complete Materials Black /1 #8
2018 Certified Complete Materials Blue /49 #8
2018 Certified Complete Materials Gold /25 #8
2018 Certified Complete Materials Green /5 #8
2018 Certified Complete Materials Purple /10 #8
2018 Certified Complete Materials Red /99 #8
2018 Certified Cup Swatches /499 #20
2018 Certified Cup Swatches Black /1 #20
2018 Certified Cup Swatches Blue /49 #20
2018 Certified Cup Swatches Gold /25 #20
2018 Certified Cup Swatches Green /5 #20
2018 Certified Cup Swatches Purple /10 #20
2018 Certified Cup Swatches Red /199 #20
2018 Certified Epix /199 #16
2018 Certified Epix Black /1 #16
2018 Certified Epix Blue /99 #16
2018 Certified Epix Gold /49 #16
2018 Certified Epix Green /10 #16
2018 Certified Epix Mirror Black /1 #16
2018 Certified Epix Mirror Gold /25 #16
2018 Certified Epix Mirror Green /5 #16
2018 Certified Epix Mirror Purple /10 #16
2018 Certified Epix Purple /25 #16
2018 Certified Epix Red /149 #16
2018 Certified Gold /49 #26
2018 Certified Gold /49 #92
2018 Certified Green /10 #26
2018 Certified Green /10 #92
2018 Certified Mirror Black /1 #26
2018 Certified Mirror Black /1 #92
2018 Certified Mirror Gold /25 #26
2018 Certified Mirror Gold /25 #92
2018 Certified Mirror Green /5 #26
2018 Certified Mirror Green /5 #92
2018 Certified Mirror Purple /10 #26
2018 Certified Mirror Purple /10 #92
2018 Certified Orange /249 #26
2018 Certified Orange /249 #92
2018 Certified Piece of the Race /499 #8
2018 Certified Piece of the Race Black /1 #8
2018 Certified Piece of the Race Blue /49 #8
2018 Certified Piece of the Race Gold /25 #8
2018 Certified Piece of the Race Green /5 #8
2018 Certified Piece of the Race Purple /10 #8
2018 Certified Piece of the Race Red /199 #8
2018 Certified Purple /25 #26
2018 Certified Purple /25 #92
2018 Certified Red /199 #26
2018 Certified Red /199 #92
2018 Certified Signature Swatches /78 #13
2018 Certified Signature Swatches Black /1 #13
2018 Certified Signature Swatches Blue /30 #13
2018 Certified Signature Swatches Gold /25 #13
2018 Certified Signature Swatches Green /5 #13
2018 Certified Signature Swatches Purple /10 #13
2018 Certified Signature Swatches Red /49 #13
2018 Certified Signing Sessions Black /1 #19
2018 Certified Signing Sessions Blue /15 #19
2018 Certified Signing Sessions Gold /10 #19
2018 Certified Signing Sessions Green /2 #19
2018 Certified Signing Sessions Purple /5 #19
2018 Certified Signing Sessions Red /25 #19
2018 Certified Skills /199 #19
2018 Certified Skills Black /1 #19
2018 Certified Skills Blue /99 #19
2018 Certified Skills Gold /49 #19
2018 Certified Skills Green /10 #19
2018 Certified Skills Mirror Black /1 #19
2018 Certified Skills Mirror Gold /25 #19
2018 Certified Skills Mirror Green /5 #19
2018 Certified Skills Mirror Purple /10 #19
2018 Certified Skills Purple /25 #19
2018 Certified Skills Red /149 #19
2018 Certified Stars /199 #17
2018 Certified Stars Black /1 #17
2018 Certified Stars Blue /99 #17
2018 Certified Stars Gold /49 #17
2018 Certified Stars Green /10 #17
2018 Certified Stars Mirror Black /1 #17
2018 Certified Stars Mirror Gold /25 #17
2018 Certified Stars Mirror Green /5 #17
2018 Certified Stars Mirror Purple /10 #17
2018 Certified Stars Purple /25 #17
2018 Certified Stars Red /149 #17
2018 Donruss #22
2018 Donruss #49A
2018 Donruss #83
2018 Donruss #139
2018 Donruss #49B
2018 Donruss Artist Proofs /25 #22
2018 Donruss Artist Proofs /25 #49A
2018 Donruss Artist Proofs /25 #83
2018 Donruss Artist Proofs /25 #139
2018 Donruss Artist Proofs /25 #49B
2018 Donruss Elite Dominators /999 #3
2018 Donruss Gold Foil /499 #22
2018 Donruss Gold Foil /499 #49A
2018 Donruss Gold Foil /499 #83
2018 Donruss Gold Foil /499 #139
2018 Donruss Gold Foil /499 #49B
2018 Donruss Gold Press Proofs /99 #22
2018 Donruss Gold Press Proofs /99 #49A
2018 Donruss Gold Press Proofs /99 #83
2018 Donruss Gold Press Proofs /99 #139
2018 Donruss Gold Press Proofs /99 #49B
2018 Donruss Green Foil /199 #22
2018 Donruss Green Foil /199 #49A
2018 Donruss Green Foil /199 #83
2018 Donruss Green Foil /199 #139
2018 Donruss Green Foil /199 #49B
2018 Donruss Pole Position #12
2018 Donruss Pole Position Cracked Ice /999 #12
2018 Donruss Pole Position Xplosion /99 #12
2018 Donruss Press Proofs /49 #22
2018 Donruss Press Proofs /49 #49
2018 Donruss Press Proofs /49 #83
2018 Donruss Press Proofs /49 #139
2018 Donruss Press Proofs /49 #49B
2018 Donruss Printing Plates Black /1 #22
2018 Donruss Printing Plates Black /1 #49
2018 Donruss Printing Plates Black /1 #83
2018 Donruss Printing Plates Black /1 #139
2018 Donruss Printing Plates Black /1 #49B
2018 Donruss Printing Plates Cyan /1 #22
2018 Donruss Printing Plates Cyan /1 #49
2018 Donruss Printing Plates Cyan /1 #83
2018 Donruss Printing Plates Cyan /1 #139
2018 Donruss Printing Plates Cyan /1 #49B
2018 Donruss Printing Plates Magenta /1 #22
2018 Donruss Printing Plates Magenta /1 #49
2018 Donruss Printing Plates Magenta /1 #83
2018 Donruss Printing Plates Magenta /1 #139
2018 Donruss Printing Plates Magenta /1 #49B
2018 Donruss Printing Plates Yellow /1 #22
2018 Donruss Printing Plates Yellow /1 #49
2018 Donruss Printing Plates Yellow /1 #83
2018 Donruss Printing Plates Yellow /1 #139
2018 Donruss Printing Plates Yellow /1 #49B
2018 Donruss Racing Relics #15
2018 Donruss Racing Relics Black /10 #15
2018 Donruss Racing Relics Holo Gold /99 #15
2018 Donruss Red Foil /299 #22
2018 Donruss Red Foil /299 #49A
2018 Donruss Red Foil /299 #83
2018 Donruss Red Foil /299 #139
2018 Donruss Red Foil /299 #49B
2018 Donruss Retro Relics '85 #9
2018 Donruss Retro Relics '85 Black /10 #9
2018 Donruss Retro Relics '85 Holo Gold /99 #9
2018 Donruss Rubber Relic Signatures #14
2018 Donruss Rubber Relic Signatures Black /1 #14
2018 Donruss Rubber Relic Signatures Holo Gold /25 #14
2018 Donruss Rubber Relics #25
2018 Donruss Rubber Relics Black /10 #25
2018 Donruss Rubber Relics Holo Gold /99 #25
2018 Donruss Studio #11
2018 Donruss Studio Cracked Ice /999 #11
2018 Donruss Studio Xplosion /99 #11
2018 Donruss Top Tier #6
2018 Donruss Top Tier Cracked Ice /999 #6
2018 Donruss Top Tier Xplosion /99 #6
2018 Panini National Convention #75
2018 Panini National Convention Escher Squares /25 #75
2018 Panini National Convention Galatic Windows /5 #75
2018 Panini National Convention Hyperplaid /1 #75
2018 Panini National Convention Magnetic Fur /99 #75
2018 Panini National Convention Pyramids /10 #75
2018 Panini National Convention Rainbow Spokes /49 #75
2018 Panini Prime /50 #9
2018 Panini Prime /50 #43
2018 Panini Prime /50 #76
2018 Panini Prime Autograph Materials /99 #20
2018 Panini Prime Autograph Materials Black /1 #20
2018 Panini Prime Autograph Materials Holo Gold /25 #20
2018 Panini Prime Autograph Materials Laundry Tag /1 #20
2018 Panini Prime Black /1 #9
2018 Panini Prime Black /1 #43
2018 Panini Prime Black /1 #76
2018 Panini Prime Clear Silhouettes /99 #22
2018 Panini Prime Clear Silhouettes Black /1 #22
2018 Panini Prime Clear Silhouettes Dual /99 #24
2018 Panini Prime Clear Silhouettes Dual Black /1 #24
2018 Panini Prime Clear Silhouettes Dual Holo Gold /50 #24
2018 Panini Prime Clear Silhouettes Holo Gold /50 #22
2018 Panini Prime Hats Off Button /1 #12
2018 Panini Prime Hats Off Button /1 #13
2018 Panini Prime Hats Off Eyelet /6 #12
2018 Panini Prime Hats Off Eyelet /6 #13
2018 Panini Prime Hats Off Headband /36 #12
2018 Panini Prime Hats Off Headband /34 #13
2018 Panini Prime Hats Off Laundry Tag /1 #12
2018 Panini Prime Hats Off Laundry Tag /1 #13
2018 Panini Prime Hats Off New Era /1 #12
2018 Panini Prime Hats Off New Era /1 #13
2018 Panini Prime Hats Off Number /2 #12
2018 Panini Prime Hats Off Number /2 #13
2018 Panini Prime Hats Off Sponsor Logo /4 #12
2018 Panini Prime Hats Off Sponsor Logo /6 #13
2018 Panini Prime Hats Off Team Logo /2 #12
2018 Panini Prime Hats Off Team Logo /2 #13
2018 Panini Prime Holo Gold /25 #9
2018 Panini Prime Holo Gold /25 #43
2018 Panini Prime Holo Gold /25 #76
2018 Panini Prime Prime Jumbo Associate Sponsor 1 /1 #56
2018 Panini Prime Prime Jumbo Associate Sponsor 2 /1 #56
2018 Panini Prime Prime Jumbo Associate Sponsor 3 /1 #56
2018 Panini Prime Prime Jumbo Associate Sponsor 4 /1 #56
2018 Panini Prime Prime Jumbo Associate Sponsor 5 /1 #56
2018 Panini Prime Prime Jumbo Associate Sponsor 6 /1 #56
2018 Panini Prime Prime Jumbo Car Manufacturer /1 #56
2018 Panini Prime Prime Jumbo Firesuit Manufacturer /1 #56
2018 Panini Prime Prime Jumbo Flag Patch /1 #56
2018 Panini Prime Prime Jumbo Glove Manufacturer Patch /1 #56
2018 Panini Prime Prime Jumbo Glove Name Patch /1 #56
2018 Panini Prime Prime Jumbo Glove Number Patch /1 #56
2018 Panini Prime Prime Jumbo Goodyear /2 #56
2018 Panini Prime Prime Jumbo Nameplate /2 #56
2018 Panini Prime Prime Jumbo Prime Colors /21 #56
2018 Panini Prime Prime Jumbo Series Sponsor /1 #56
2018 Panini Prime Prime Jumbo Shoe Brand Logo /1 #56
2018 Panini Prime Prime Jumbo Shoe Name Patch /1 #56
2018 Panini Prime Prime Jumbo Sunoco /1 #56
2018 Panini Prime Prime Number Signatures /25 #13
2018 Panini Prime Prime Number Signatures Black /1 #13
2018 Panini Prime Prime Number Signatures Holo Gold /10 #13
2018 Panini Prime Quad Material Autographs /99 #11
2018 Panini Prime Quad Material Autographs Black /1 #11
2018 Panini Prime Quad Material Autographs Holo Gold /50 #11
2018 Panini Prime Quad Material Autographs Laundry Tag /1 #11
2018 Panini Prime Race Used Firesuits /50 #27
2018 Panini Prime Race Used Firesuits Black /1 #27
2018 Panini Prime Race Used Firesuits Holo Gold /25 #27
2018 Panini Prime Race Used Firesuits Laundry Tag /1 #27
2018 Panini Prime Race Used Sheet Metal Black /1 #27
2018 Panini Prime Race Used Sheet Metal Holo Gold /25 #27
2018 Panini Prime Race Used Tires /50 #27
2018 Panini Prime Race Used Tires Black /1 #27
2018 Panini Prime Race Used Tires Holo Gold /25 #27
2018 Panini Prime Race Used Trios Firesuit /50 #17
2018 Panini Prime Race Used Trios Firesuit Black /1 #17
2018 Panini Prime Race Used Trios Firesuit Holo Gold /25 #17
2018 Panini Prime Race Used Trios Firesuit Laundry Tag /1 #17
2018 Panini Prime Race Used Trios Sheet Metal /50 #17
2018 Panini Prime Race Used Trios Sheet Metal Black /1 #17
2018 Panini Prime Race Used Trios Sheet Metal Holo Gold /25 #17
2018 Panini Prime Race Used Trios Tire /50 #17
2018 Panini Prime Race Used Trios Tire Black /1 #17
2018 Panini Prime Race Used Trios Tire Holo Gold /25 #17
2018 Panini Prime Signature Swatches /99 #15
2018 Panini Prime Signature Swatches Black /1 #15
2018 Panini Prime Signature Swatches Holo Gold /50 #15
2018 Panini Prime Signature Tires /25 #12
2018 Panini Prime Signature Tires Black /1 #12
2018 Panini Prime Signature Tires Holo Gold /10 #12
2018 Panini Prime Triple Material Autographs /99 #16
2018 Panini Prime Triple Material Autographs Black /1 #16
2018 Panini Prime Triple Material Autographs Holo Gold /50 #16
2018 Panini Prime Triple Material Autographs Laundry Tag /1 #16
2018 Panini Prizm #40
2018 Panini Prizm #60
2018 Panini Prizm #90
2018 Panini Prizm Autographs Prizms #40
2018 Panini Prizm Autographs Prizms Black /1 #40
2018 Panini Prizm Autographs Prizms Blue /10 #40
2018 Panini Prizm Autographs Prizms Camo #40
2018 Panini Prizm Autographs Prizms Gold /10 #40
2018 Panini Prizm Autographs Prizms Green /10 #40
2018 Panini Prizm Autographs Prizms Rainbow /24 #40
2018 Panini Prizm Autographs Prizms Red /10 #40
2018 Panini Prizm Autographs Prizms Red White and Blue /10 #40
2018 Panini Prizm Autographs Prizms White /5 #40
2018 Panini Prizm Fireworks #9
2018 Panini Prizm Fireworks Prizms #9
2018 Panini Prizm Fireworks Prizms Black /1 #9
2018 Panini Prizm Fireworks Prizms Gold /10 #9
2018 Panini Prizm Illumination #14
2018 Panini Prizm Illumination Prizms #14
2018 Panini Prizm Illumination Prizms Black /1 #14
2018 Panini Prizm Illumination Prizms Gold /10 #14
2018 Panini Prizm Instant Impact #2
2018 Panini Prizm Instant Impact Prizms #2
2018 Panini Prizm Instant Impact Prizms Black /1 #2
2018 Panini Prizm Instant Impact Prizms Gold /10 #2
2018 Panini Prizm National Pride #8
2018 Panini Prizm National Pride Prizms #8
2018 Panini Prizm National Pride Prizms Black /1 #8
2018 Panini Prizm National Pride Prizms Gold /10 #8
2018 Panini Prizm Prizms #40
2018 Panini Prizm Prizms #60
2018 Panini Prizm Prizms #90
2018 Panini Prizm Prizms Black /1 #40
2018 Panini Prizm Prizms Black /1 #60
2018 Panini Prizm Prizms Black /1 #90
2018 Panini Prizm Prizms Blue /99 #40
2018 Panini Prizm Prizms Blue /99 #60
2018 Panini Prizm Prizms Blue /99 #90
2018 Panini Prizm Prizms Camo #40
2018 Panini Prizm Prizms Camo #60
2018 Panini Prizm Prizms Camo #90
2018 Panini Prizm Prizms Gold /10 #40
2018 Panini Prizm Prizms Gold /10 #60
2018 Panini Prizm Prizms Gold /10 #90
2018 Panini Prizm Prizms Green /149 #40
2018 Panini Prizm Prizms Green /149 #60
2018 Panini Prizm Prizms Green /149 #90
2018 Panini Prizm Prizms Purple Flash #40
2018 Panini Prizm Prizms Purple Flash #60
2018 Panini Prizm Prizms Purple Flash #90
2018 Panini Prizm Prizms Rainbow /24 #40
2018 Panini Prizm Prizms Rainbow /24 #60
2018 Panini Prizm Prizms Rainbow /24 #90
2018 Panini Prizm Prizms Red /75 #40
2018 Panini Prizm Prizms Red /75 #60
2018 Panini Prizm Prizms Red /75 #90
2018 Panini Prizm Prizms Red White and Blue #40
2018 Panini Prizm Prizms Red White and Blue #60
2018 Panini Prizm Prizms Red White and Blue #90
2018 Panini Prizm Prizms White /5 #40
2018 Panini Prizm Prizms White /5 #60
2018 Panini Prizm Prizms White /5 #90

2018 Panini Prizm Scripted Signatures Prizms #38
2018 Panini Prizm Scripted Signatures Prizms Black /1 #38
2018 Panini Prizm Scripted Signatures Prizms Blue /10 #38
2018 Panini Prizm Scripted Signatures Prizms Camo #38
2018 Panini Prizm Scripted Signatures Prizms Gold /10 #38
2018 Panini Prizm Scripted Signatures Prizms Green /10 #38
2018 Panini Prizm Scripted Signatures Prizms Rainbow /24 #38
2018 Panini Prizm Scripted Signatures Prizms Red /10 #38
2018 Panini Prizm Scripted Signatures Prizms Red White and Blue /10 #38
2018 Panini Prizm Scripted Signatures Prizms White /5 #38
2018 Panini Victory Lane #28
2018 Panini Victory Lane #41
2018 Panini Victory Lane #44
2018 Panini Victory Lane #46
2018 Panini Victory Lane #50
2018 Panini Victory Lane Black /1 #28
2018 Panini Victory Lane Black /1 #41
2018 Panini Victory Lane Black /1 #44
2018 Panini Victory Lane Black /1 #46
2018 Panini Victory Lane Black /1 #50
2018 Panini Victory Lane Blue /25 #28
2018 Panini Victory Lane Blue /25 #41
2018 Panini Victory Lane Blue /25 #44
2018 Panini Victory Lane Blue /25 #46
2018 Panini Victory Lane Blue /25 #50
2018 Panini Victory Lane Celebrations #9
2018 Panini Victory Lane Celebrations Black /1 #9
2018 Panini Victory Lane Celebrations Blue /25 #9
2018 Panini Victory Lane Celebrations Gold /99 #9
2018 Panini Victory Lane Celebrations Green /5 #9
2018 Panini Victory Lane Celebrations Printing Plates Black /1 #9
2018 Panini Victory Lane Celebrations Printing Plates Cyan /1 #9
2018 Panini Victory Lane Celebrations Printing Plates Magenta /1 #9
2018 Panini Victory Lane Celebrations Printing Plates Yellow /1 #9
2018 Panini Victory Lane Celebrations Red /49 #9
2018 Panini Victory Lane Champions #15
2018 Panini Victory Lane Champions Black /1 #15
2018 Panini Victory Lane Champions Blue /25 #15
2018 Panini Victory Lane Champions Gold /99 #15
2018 Panini Victory Lane Champions Green /5 #15
2018 Panini Victory Lane Champions Printing Plates Black /1 #15
2018 Panini Victory Lane Champions Printing Plates Cyan /1 #15
2018 Panini Victory Lane Champions Printing Plates Magenta /1 #15
2018 Panini Victory Lane Champions Printing Plates Yellow /1 #15
2018 Panini Victory Lane Champions Red /49 #15
2018 Panini Victory Lane Engineered to Perfection Materials /399 #16
2018 Panini Victory Lane Engineered to Perfection Materials Black /25 #16
2018 Panini Victory Lane Engineered to Perfection Materials Gold /199 #16
2018 Panini Victory Lane Engineered to Perfection Materials Green /99 #16
2018 Panini Victory Lane Engineered to Perfection Materials Laundry Tag /1 #16
2018 Panini Victory Lane Engineered to Perfection Triple Materials /399 #11
2018 Panini Victory Lane Engineered to Perfection Triple Materials Black /25 #11
2018 Panini Victory Lane Engineered to Perfection Triple Materials Gold /199 #11
2018 Panini Victory Lane Engineered to Perfection Triple Materials Green /99 #11
2018 Panini Victory Lane Engineered to Perfection Triple Materials Laundry Tag /1 #11
2018 Panini Victory Lane Gold /99 #28
2018 Panini Victory Lane Gold /99 #41
2018 Panini Victory Lane Gold /99 #44
2018 Panini Victory Lane Gold /99 #46
2018 Panini Victory Lane Gold /99 #50
2018 Panini Victory Lane Green /5 #28
2018 Panini Victory Lane Green /5 #41
2018 Panini Victory Lane Green /5 #44
2018 Panini Victory Lane Green /5 #46
2018 Panini Victory Lane Green /5 #50
2018 Panini Victory Lane Pedal to the Metal #38
2018 Panini Victory Lane Pedal to the Metal #72
2018 Panini Victory Lane Pedal to the Metal Black /1 #38
2018 Panini Victory Lane Pedal to the Metal Black /1 #72
2018 Panini Victory Lane Pedal to the Metal Blue /25 #38
2018 Panini Victory Lane Pedal to the Metal Blue /25 #72
2018 Panini Victory Lane Pedal to the Metal Green /5 #38
2018 Panini Victory Lane Pedal to the Metal Green /5 #72
2018 Panini Victory Lane Printing Plates Black /1 #28
2018 Panini Victory Lane Printing Plates Black /1 #41
2018 Panini Victory Lane Printing Plates Black /1 #44
2018 Panini Victory Lane Printing Plates Black /1 #46
2018 Panini Victory Lane Printing Plates Black /1 #50
2018 Panini Victory Lane Printing Plates Cyan /1 #28
2018 Panini Victory Lane Printing Plates Cyan /1 #41
2018 Panini Victory Lane Printing Plates Cyan /1 #44
2018 Panini Victory Lane Printing Plates Cyan /1 #46
2018 Panini Victory Lane Printing Plates Cyan /1 #50
2018 Panini Victory Lane Printing Plates Magenta /1 #28
2018 Panini Victory Lane Printing Plates Magenta /1 #41
2018 Panini Victory Lane Printing Plates Magenta /1 #44
2018 Panini Victory Lane Printing Plates Magenta /1 #46
2018 Panini Victory Lane Printing Plates Magenta /1 #50
2018 Panini Victory Lane Printing Plates Yellow /1 #28
2018 Panini Victory Lane Printing Plates Yellow /1 #41
2018 Panini Victory Lane Printing Plates Yellow /1 #44
2018 Panini Victory Lane Printing Plates Yellow /1 #46
2018 Panini Victory Lane Printing Plates Yellow /1 #50
2018 Panini Victory Lane Race Day #7
2018 Panini Victory Lane Race Day Black /1 #7
2018 Panini Victory Lane Race Day Blue /25 #7
2018 Panini Victory Lane Race Day Gold /99 #7
2018 Panini Victory Lane Race Day Green /5 #7
2018 Panini Victory Lane Race Day Printing Plates Black /1 #7
2018 Panini Victory Lane Race Day Printing Plates Cyan /1 #7
2018 Panini Victory Lane Race Day Printing Plates Magenta /1 #7
2018 Panini Victory Lane Race Day Printing Plates Yellow /1 #7
2018 Panini Victory Lane Race Day Red /49 #7
2018 Panini Victory Lane Red /49 #28
2018 Panini Victory Lane Red /49 #41
2018 Panini Victory Lane Red /49 #44
2018 Panini Victory Lane Red /49 #46
2018 Panini Victory Lane Red /49 #50
2018 Panini Victory Lane Remarkable Remnants Material Autographs /100 #9
2018 Panini Victory Lane Remarkable Remnants Material Autographs Black /25 #9
2018 Panini Victory Lane Remarkable Remnants Material Autographs Gold /99 #9
2018 Panini Victory Lane Remarkable Remnants Material Autographs Green /49 #9
2018 Panini Victory Lane Remarkable Remnants Material Autographs Laundry Tag /1 #9
2018 Panini Victory Lane Signatures /37 #35
2018 Panini Victory Lane Signatures Black /1 #35
2018 Panini Victory Lane Signatures Gold /25 #35
2018 Panini Victory Lane Silver #28
2018 Panini Victory Lane Silver #41
2018 Panini Victory Lane Silver #44
2018 Panini Victory Lane Silver #46
2018 Panini Victory Lane Silver #50
2018 Panini Victory Lane Starting Grid #24
2018 Panini Victory Lane Starting Grid Black /1 #24
2018 Panini Victory Lane Starting Grid Blue /25 #24
2018 Panini Victory Lane Starting Grid Gold /99 #24
2018 Panini Victory Lane Starting Grid Green /5 #24
2018 Panini Victory Lane Starting Grid Printing Plates Black /1 #24
2018 Panini Victory Lane Starting Grid Printing Plates Cyan /1 #24
2018 Panini Victory Lane Starting Grid Printing Plates Magenta /1 #24
2018 Panini Victory Lane Starting Grid Printing Plates Yellow /1 #24
2018 Panini Victory Lane Starting Grid Red /49 #24
2018 Panini Victory Lane Victory Lane Prime Patches Associate Sponsor 1 /1 #42
2018 Panini Victory Lane Victory Lane Prime Patches Associate Sponsor 2 /1 #42
2018 Panini Victory Lane Victory Lane Prime Patches Associate Sponsor 3 /1 #42
2018 Panini Victory Lane Victory Lane Prime Patches Associate Sponsor 4 /1 #42
2018 Panini Victory Lane Victory Lane Prime Patches Associate Sponsor 5 /1 #42
2018 Panini Victory Lane Victory Lane Prime Patches Associate Sponsor 6 /1 #42
2018 Panini Victory Lane Victory Lane Prime Patches Car Manufacturer /1 #42
2018 Panini Victory Lane Victory Lane Prime Patches Firesuit Manufacturer /1 #42
2018 Panini Victory Lane Victory Lane Prime Patches Goodyear /2 #42
2018 Panini Victory Lane Victory Lane Prime Patches Nameplate /2 #42
2018 Panini Victory Lane Victory Lane Prime Patches NASCAR /1 #42
2018 Panini Victory Lane Victory Lane Prime Patches Series Sponsor /1 #42
2018 Panini Victory Lane Victory Lane Prime Patches Sunoco /1 #42
2018 Panini Victory Lane Victory Marks /37 #11
2018 Panini Victory Lane Victory Marks Black /1 #11
2018 Panini Victory Lane Victory Marks Gold /25 #11
2019 Donruss #3
2019 Donruss #30
2019 Donruss #87
2019 Donruss #111
2019 Donruss Artist Proofs /25 #3
2019 Donruss Artist Proofs /25 #30
2019 Donruss Artist Proofs /25 #87
2019 Donruss Artist Proofs /25 #111
2019 Donruss Black /199 #3
2019 Donruss Black /199 #30
2019 Donruss Black /199 #87
2019 Donruss Black /199 #111
2019 Donruss Classics #3
2019 Donruss Classics Cracked Ice /25 #3
2019 Donruss Classics Holographic #3
2019 Donruss Classics Xplosion /10 #3
2019 Donruss Contenders #1
2019 Donruss Contenders Cracked Ice /25 #1
2019 Donruss Contenders Holographic #1
2019 Donruss Contenders Xplosion /10 #1
2019 Donruss Gold /299 #3
2019 Donruss Gold /299 #30
2019 Donruss Gold /299 #87
2019 Donruss Gold /299 #111
2019 Donruss Gold Press Proofs /99 #3
2019 Donruss Gold Press Proofs /99 #30
2019 Donruss Gold Press Proofs /99 #87
2019 Donruss Gold Press Proofs /99 #111
2019 Donruss Optic #13
2019 Donruss Optic Blue Pulsar #13
2019 Donruss Optic Gold /10 #13
2019 Donruss Optic Gold Vinyl /1 #13
2019 Donruss Optic Holo #13
2019 Donruss Optic Illusion #3
2019 Donruss Optic Illusion Blue Pulsar #3
2019 Donruss Optic Illusion Gold /10 #3
2019 Donruss Optic Illusion Gold Vinyl /1 #3
2019 Donruss Optic Illusion Holo #3
2019 Donruss Optic Illusion Red Wave #3
2019 Donruss Optic Illusion Signatures Gold Vinyl /1 #3
2019 Donruss Optic Illusion Signatures Holo /25 #3
2019 Donruss Optic Red Wave #13
2019 Donruss Optic Signatures Gold Vinyl /1 #13
2019 Donruss Optic Signatures Holo /75 #13
2019 Donruss Press Proofs /49 #30
2019 Donruss Press Proofs /49 #87
2019 Donruss Press Proofs /49 #111
2019 Donruss Press Proofs /49 #3
2019 Donruss Printing Plates Black /1 #3
2019 Donruss Printing Plates Black /1 #30
2019 Donruss Printing Plates Black /1 #87
2019 Donruss Printing Plates Black /1 #111
2019 Donruss Printing Plates Cyan /1 #3
2019 Donruss Printing Plates Cyan /1 #30
2019 Donruss Printing Plates Cyan /1 #87
2019 Donruss Printing Plates Cyan /1 #111
2019 Donruss Printing Plates Magenta /1 #87
2019 Donruss Printing Plates Magenta /1 #111
2019 Donruss Printing Plates Magenta /1 #3
2019 Donruss Printing Plates Magenta /1 #30
2019 Donruss Printing Plates Yellow /1 #3
2019 Donruss Printing Plates Yellow /1 #30
2019 Donruss Printing Plates Yellow /1 #87
2019 Donruss Printing Plates Yellow /1 #111
2019 Donruss Race Day Relics #20
2019 Donruss Race Day Relics Holo Black /10 #20
2019 Donruss Race Day Relics Holo Gold /25 #20
2019 Donruss Race Day Relics Red /185 #20
2019 Donruss Signature Swatches #10
2019 Donruss Signature Swatches Holo Black /10 #10
2019 Donruss Signature Swatches Holo Gold /25 #10
2019 Donruss Signature Swatches Red /50 #10
2019 Donruss Silver #3
2019 Donruss Silver #30
2019 Donruss Silver #87
2019 Donruss Silver #111
2019 Donruss Top Tier #6
2019 Donruss Top Tier Cracked Ice /25 #6
2019 Donruss Top Tier Holographic #6
2019 Donruss Top Tier Xplosion /10 #6
2019 Panini Prime /50 #16
2019 Panini Prime /50 #48
2019 Panini Prime /50 #80
2019 Panini Prime Black /10 #16
2019 Panini Prime Black /10 #48
2019 Panini Prime Black /10 #80
2019 Panini Prime Clear Silhouettes /99 #14
2019 Panini Prime Clear Silhouettes Black /10 #14
2019 Panini Prime Clear Silhouettes Dual /99 #9
2019 Panini Prime Clear Silhouettes Dual Black /10 #9
2019 Panini Prime Clear Silhouettes Dual Holo Gold /25 #9
2019 Panini Prime Clear Silhouettes Dual Platinum Blue /1 #9
2019 Panini Prime Clear Silhouettes Holo Gold /25 #14
2019 Panini Prime Clear Silhouettes Platinum Blue /1 #14
2019 Panini Prime Clear Vision Signatures /49 #5
2019 Panini Prime Clear Vision Signatures Black /10 #5
2019 Panini Prime Clear Vision Signatures Holo Gold /19 #5
2019 Panini Prime Clear Vision Signatures Platinum Blue /1 #5
2019 Panini Prime Emerald /5 #16
2019 Panini Prime Emerald /5 #48
2019 Panini Prime Emerald /5 #80
2019 Panini Prime Jumbo Material Signatures Firesuit /10 #21
2019 Panini Prime Jumbo Material Signatures Firesuit Platinum Blue /1 #21
2019 Panini Prime Jumbo Material Signatures Sheet Metal /19 #21
2019 Panini Prime Jumbo Material Signatures Tire /25 #21
2019 Panini Prime NASCAR Shadowbox Signatures Car Number /49 #28
2019 Panini Prime NASCAR Shadowbox Signatures Manufacturer /10 #28
2019 Panini Prime NASCAR Shadowbox Signatures Sponsor /19 #28
2019 Panini Prime NASCAR Shadowbox Signatures Team Owner /1 #28
2019 Panini Prime Platinum Blue /1 #16
2019 Panini Prime Platinum Blue /1 #48
2019 Panini Prime Platinum Blue /1 #80
2019 Panini Prime Prime Cars Die Cut Signatures /25 #20
2019 Panini Prime Prime Cars Die Cut Signatures Black /10 #20
2019 Panini Prime Prime Cars Die Cut Signatures Holo Gold /19 #20
2019 Panini Prime Prime Cars Die Cut Signatures Platinum Blue /1 #20
2019 Panini Prime Prime Jumbo Associate Sponsor 1 /1 #50
2019 Panini Prime Prime Jumbo Associate Sponsor 1 /1 #51
2019 Panini Prime Prime Jumbo Associate Sponsor 2 /1 #50
2019 Panini Prime Prime Jumbo Associate Sponsor 2 /1 #51
2019 Panini Prime Prime Jumbo Associate Sponsor 3 /1 #50
2019 Panini Prime Prime Jumbo Associate Sponsor 4 /1 #50
2019 Panini Prime Prime Jumbo Associate Sponsor 5 /1 #50
2019 Panini Prime Prime Jumbo Associate Sponsor 6 /1 #50
2019 Panini Prime Prime Jumbo Associate Sponsor 7 /1 #50
2019 Panini Prime Prime Jumbo Associate Sponsor 8 /1 #50
2019 Panini Prime Prime Jumbo Associate Sponsor 9 /1 #50
2019 Panini Prime Prime Jumbo Car Manufacturer /1 #50
2019 Panini Prime Prime Jumbo Car Manufacturer /1 #51
2019 Panini Prime Prime Jumbo Firesuit Manufacturer /1 #50
2019 Panini Prime Prime Jumbo Firesuit Manufacturer /1 #51
2019 Panini Prime Prime Jumbo Flag Patch /1 #50
2019 Panini Prime Prime Jumbo Glove Manufacturer Patch /1 #50
2019 Panini Prime Prime Jumbo Glove Manufacturer Patch /1 #51
2019 Panini Prime Prime Jumbo Glove Name Patch /1 #50
2019 Panini Prime Prime Jumbo Glove Name Patch /1 #51
2019 Panini Prime Prime Jumbo Glove Number Patch /1 #50
2019 Panini Prime Prime Jumbo Glove Number Patch /1 #51
2019 Panini Prime Prime Jumbo Goodyear /1 #50
2019 Panini Prime Prime Jumbo Nameplate /1 #50
2019 Panini Prime Prime Jumbo Nameplate /2 #51
2019 Panini Prime Prime Jumbo NASCAR /1 #50
2019 Panini Prime Prime Jumbo NASCAR /1 #51
2019 Panini Prime Prime Jumbo Prime Colors /15 #50
2019 Panini Prime Prime Jumbo Prime Colors /15 #51
2019 Panini Prime Prime Jumbo Series Sponsor /1 #51
2019 Panini Prime Prime Jumbo Shoe Brand Logo /1 #50
2019 Panini Prime Prime Jumbo Shoe Brand Logo /1 #51
2019 Panini Prime Prime Jumbo Shoe Name Patch /1 #50
2019 Panini Prime Prime Jumbo Shoe Name Patch /1 #51
2019 Panini Prime Prime Jumbo Sunoco /1 #50
2019 Panini Prime Prime Jumbo Sunoco /1 #51
2019 Panini Prime Prime Number Die Cut Signatures /25 #8
2019 Panini Prime Prime Number Die Cut Signatures Black /10 #8
2019 Panini Prime Prime Number Die Cut Signatures Holo Gold /19 #8
2019 Panini Prime Prime Number Die Cut Signatures Platinum Blue /1 #8
2019 Panini Prime Quad Materials Autographs /49 #18
2019 Panini Prime Quad Materials Autographs Black /10 #18
2019 Panini Prime Quad Materials Autographs Holo Gold /19 #18
2019 Panini Prime Quad Materials Autographs Laundry Tags /1 #18
2019 Panini Prime Race Used Duals Firesuits Black /10 #28
2019 Panini Prime Race Used Duals Firesuits Holo Gold /25 #28
2019 Panini Prime Race Used Duals Firesuits Laundry Tags /1 #28
2019 Panini Prime Race Used Duals Sheet Metal Black /10 #28
2019 Panini Prime Race Used Duals Sheet Metal Platinum Blue /1 #28
2019 Panini Prime Race Used Duals Tires Black /10 #28
2019 Panini Prime Race Used Duals Tires Platinum Blue /1 #28
2019 Panini Prime Race Used Firesuits Black /10 #28
2019 Panini Prime Race Used Firesuits Holo Gold /25 #28
2019 Panini Prime Race Used Firesuits Laundry Tags /1 #28
2019 Panini Prime Race Used Sheet Metal Black /10 #28
2019 Panini Prime Race Used Sheet Metal Platinum Blue /1 #28
2019 Panini Prime Race Used Tires Black /10 #28
2019 Panini Prime Race Used Tires Platinum Blue /1 #28
2019 Panini Prime Timeline Signatures /25 #10
2019 Panini Prime Timeline Signatures Manufacturer /1 #10
2019 Panini Prime Timeline Signatures Name /19 #10
2019 Panini Prime Timeline Signatures Sponsor /10 #10
2019 Panini Prizm #16
2019 Panini Prizm #56
2019 Panini Prizm #63
2019 Panini Prizm #77
2019 Panini Prizm #85
2019 Panini Prizm Apex #11
2019 Panini Prizm Apex Prizms #11
2019 Panini Prizm Apex Prizms Black /1 #11
2019 Panini Prizm Apex Prizms Gold /10 #11
2019 Panini Prizm Apex Prizms White Sparkle #11
2019 Panini Prizm Expert Level #3
2019 Panini Prizm Expert Level Prizms #3
2019 Panini Prizm Expert Level Prizms Black /1 #3
2019 Panini Prizm Expert Level Prizms Gold /10 #3
2019 Panini Prizm Expert Level Prizms White Sparkle #3
2019 Panini Prizm Fireworks #17
2019 Panini Prizm Fireworks Prizms #17
2019 Panini Prizm Fireworks Prizms Black /1 #17
2019 Panini Prizm Fireworks Prizms Gold /10 #17
2019 Panini Prizm Fireworks Prizms White Sparkle #17
2019 Panini Prizm In the Groove #5
2019 Panini Prizm In the Groove Prizms #5
2019 Panini Prizm In the Groove Prizms Black /1 #5
2019 Panini Prizm In the Groove Prizms Gold /10 #5
2019 Panini Prizm In the Groove Prizms White Sparkle #5
2019 Panini Prizm National Pride #14
2019 Panini Prizm National Pride Prizms #14
2019 Panini Prizm National Pride Prizms Black /1 #14
2019 Panini Prizm National Pride Prizms Gold /10 #14
2019 Panini Prizm National Pride Prizms White Sparkle #14
2019 Panini Prizm Patented Penmanship Prizms #13
2019 Panini Prizm Patented Penmanship Prizms Black /1 #13
2019 Panini Prizm Patented Penmanship Prizms Blue /75 #13
2019 Panini Prizm Patented Penmanship Prizms Camo #13
2019 Panini Prizm Patented Penmanship Prizms Gold /10 #13
2019 Panini Prizm Patented Penmanship Prizms Green /99 #13
2019 Panini Prizm Patented Penmanship Prizms Rainbow /24 #13
2019 Panini Prizm Patented Penmanship Prizms Red /50 #13
2019 Panini Prizm Patented Penmanship Prizms Red White and Blue #13
2019 Panini Prizm Patented Penmanship Prizms White /5 #13
2019 Panini Prizm Prizms #56
2019 Panini Prizm Prizms #63
2019 Panini Prizm Prizms #77
2019 Panini Prizm Prizms #85
2019 Panini Prizm Prizms #16
2019 Panini Prizm Prizms Black /1 #16
2019 Panini Prizm Prizms Black /1 #56
2019 Panini Prizm Prizms Black /1 #63
2019 Panini Prizm Prizms Black /1 #77
2019 Panini Prizm Prizms Black /1 #85
2019 Panini Prizm Prizms Blue /75 #16
2019 Panini Prizm Prizms Blue /75 #56
2019 Panini Prizm Prizms Blue /75 #63
2019 Panini Prizm Prizms Blue /75 #77
2019 Panini Prizm Prizms Blue /75 #85
2019 Panini Prizm Prizms Camo #16
2019 Panini Prizm Prizms Camo #56
2019 Panini Prizm Prizms Camo #63
2019 Panini Prizm Prizms Camo #77
2019 Panini Prizm Prizms Camo #85
2019 Panini Prizm Prizms Flash #16
2019 Panini Prizm Prizms Flash #56
2019 Panini Prizm Prizms Flash #63
2019 Panini Prizm Prizms Flash #77
2019 Panini Prizm Prizms Flash #85
2019 Panini Prizm Prizms Gold /10 #16
2019 Panini Prizm Prizms Gold /10 #56
2019 Panini Prizm Prizms Gold /10 #63
2019 Panini Prizm Prizms Gold /10 #77
2019 Panini Prizm Prizms Gold /10 #85
2019 Panini Prizm Prizms Green /99 #16
2019 Panini Prizm Prizms Green /99 #56
2019 Panini Prizm Prizms Green /99 #63
2019 Panini Prizm Prizms Green /99 #77
2019 Panini Prizm Prizms Green /99 #85
2019 Panini Prizm Prizms Rainbow /24 #16
2019 Panini Prizm Prizms Rainbow /24 #56
2019 Panini Prizm Prizms Rainbow /24 #63
2019 Panini Prizm Prizms Rainbow /24 #77
2019 Panini Prizm Prizms Rainbow /24 #85
2019 Panini Prizm Prizms Red /50 #16
2019 Panini Prizm Prizms Red /50 #56
2019 Panini Prizm Prizms Red /50 #63
2019 Panini Prizm Prizms Red /50 #77
2019 Panini Prizm Prizms Red /50 #85
2019 Panini Prizm Prizms Red White and Blue #16
2019 Panini Prizm Prizms Red White and Blue #56
2019 Panini Prizm Prizms Red White and Blue #63
2019 Panini Prizm Prizms Red White and Blue #77
2019 Panini Prizm Prizms Red White and Blue #85
2019 Panini Prizm Prizms White /5 #16
2019 Panini Prizm Prizms White /5 #56
2019 Panini Prizm Prizms White /5 #63
2019 Panini Prizm Prizms White /5 #77
2019 Panini Prizm Prizms White /5 #85
2019 Panini Prizm Prizms White Sparkle #16
2019 Panini Prizm Prizms White Sparkle #56
2019 Panini Prizm Prizms White Sparkle #63
2019 Panini Prizm Prizms White Sparkle #77
2019 Panini Prizm Prizms White Sparkle #85
2019 Panini Prizm Signing Sessions Prizms #17
2019 Panini Prizm Signing Sessions Prizms Black /1 #17
2019 Panini Prizm Signing Sessions Prizms Blue /75 #17
2019 Panini Prizm Signing Sessions Prizms Camo #17
2019 Panini Prizm Signing Sessions Prizms Gold /10 #17
2019 Panini Prizm Signing Sessions Prizms Green /99 #17
2019 Panini Prizm Signing Sessions Prizms Rainbow /24 #17
2019 Panini Prizm Signing Sessions Prizms Red /50 #17
2019 Panini Prizm Signing Sessions Prizms Red White and Blue #17
2019 Panini Prizm Signing Sessions Prizms White /5 #17
2019 Panini Prizm Stars and Stripes #3
2019 Panini Prizm Stars and Stripes Prizms #3
2019 Panini Prizm Stars and Stripes Prizms Black /1 #3
2019 Panini Prizm Stars and Stripes Prizms Gold /10 #3
2019 Panini Prizm Stars and Stripes Prizms White Sparkle #3
2019 Panini Prizm Teammates #3
2019 Panini Prizm Teammates #4
2019 Panini Prizm Teammates Prizms #3
2019 Panini Prizm Teammates Prizms #4
2019 Panini Prizm Teammates Prizms Black /1 #3
2019 Panini Prizm Teammates Prizms Black /1 #4
2019 Panini Prizm Teammates Prizms Gold /10 #3
2019 Panini Prizm Teammates Prizms Gold /10 #4
2019 Panini Prizm Teammates Prizms White Sparkle #3
2019 Panini Prizm Teammates Prizms White Sparkle #4
2019 Panini Victory Lane #16
2019 Panini Victory Lane #62
2019 Panini Victory Lane Black /1 #16
2019 Panini Victory Lane Black /1 #62
2019 Panini Victory Lane Celebrations #4
2019 Panini Victory Lane Celebrations Black /1 #4
2019 Panini Victory Lane Celebrations Blue /99 #4
2019 Panini Victory Lane Celebrations Gold /25 #4
2019 Panini Victory Lane Celebrations Green /5 #4
2019 Panini Victory Lane Celebrations Printing Plates Black /1 #4
2019 Panini Victory Lane Celebrations Printing Plates Cyan /1 #4
2019 Panini Victory Lane Celebrations Printing Plates Magenta /1 #4
2019 Panini Victory Lane Celebrations Printing Plates Yellow /1 #4
2019 Panini Victory Lane Dual Swatches #25
2019 Panini Victory Lane Dual Swatches Gold /99 #25
2019 Panini Victory Lane Dual Swatches Platinum /1 #25
2019 Panini Victory Lane Dual Swatches Red /25 #25
2019 Panini Victory Lane Gold /25 #16
2019 Panini Victory Lane Gold /25 #62
2019 Panini Victory Lane Horsepower Heroes #3
2019 Panini Victory Lane Horsepower Heroes Black /1 #3
2019 Panini Victory Lane Horsepower Heroes Blue /99 #3
2019 Panini Victory Lane Horsepower Heroes Gold /25 #3
2019 Panini Victory Lane Horsepower Heroes Green /5 #3
2019 Panini Victory Lane Horsepower Heroes Printing Plates Black /1 #3
2019 Panini Victory Lane Horsepower Heroes Printing Plates Cyan /1 #3
2019 Panini Victory Lane Horsepower Heroes Printing Plates Magenta /1 #3
2019 Panini Victory Lane Horsepower Heroes Printing Plates Yellow /1 #3
2019 Panini Victory Lane Machines #5
2019 Panini Victory Lane Machines Black /1 #5
2019 Panini Victory Lane Machines Blue /99 #5
2019 Panini Victory Lane Machines Gold /25 #5
2019 Panini Victory Lane Machines Green /5 #5
2019 Panini Victory Lane Machines Printing Plates Black /1 #5
2019 Panini Victory Lane Machines Printing Plates Cyan /1 #5
2019 Panini Victory Lane Machines Printing Plates Magenta /1 #5
2019 Panini Victory Lane Machines Printing Plates Yellow /1 #5
2019 Panini Victory Lane Pedal to the Metal #27
2019 Panini Victory Lane Pedal to the Metal #65
2019 Panini Victory Lane Pedal to the Metal #77
2019 Panini Victory Lane Pedal to the Metal Black /1 #27
2019 Panini Victory Lane Pedal to the Metal Black /1 #65
2019 Panini Victory Lane Pedal to the Metal Black /1 #77
2019 Panini Victory Lane Pedal to the Metal Gold /25 #27
2019 Panini Victory Lane Pedal to the Metal Gold /25 #65
2019 Panini Victory Lane Pedal to the Metal Gold /25 #77
2019 Panini Victory Lane Pedal to the Metal Green /5 #27
2019 Panini Victory Lane Pedal to the Metal Green /5 #65
2019 Panini Victory Lane Pedal to the Metal Green /5 #77
2019 Panini Victory Lane Pedal to the Metal Red /3 #27
2019 Panini Victory Lane Pedal to the Metal Red /3 #65
2019 Panini Victory Lane Pedal to the Metal Red /3 #77
2019 Panini Victory Lane Printing Plates Black /1 #16
2019 Panini Victory Lane Printing Plates Black /1 #62
2019 Panini Victory Lane Printing Plates Cyan /1 #16
2019 Panini Victory Lane Printing Plates Cyan /1 #62
2019 Panini Victory Lane Printing Plates Magenta /1 #16
2019 Panini Victory Lane Printing Plates Magenta /1 #62
2019 Panini Victory Lane Printing Plates Yellow /1 #16
2019 Panini Victory Lane Printing Plates Yellow /1 #62
2019 Panini Victory Lane Quad Swatches #6
2019 Panini Victory Lane Quad Swatches Gold /99 #6
2019 Panini Victory Lane Quad Swatches Laundry Tag /1 #6
2019 Panini Victory Lane Quad Swatches Platinum /1 #6
2019 Panini Victory Lane Quad Swatches Red /25 #6
2019 Panini Victory Lane Signature Swatches #14
2019 Panini Victory Lane Signature Swatches Gold /99 #14
2019 Panini Victory Lane Signature Swatches Laundry Tag /1 #14
2019 Panini Victory Lane Signature Swatches Platinum /1 #14
2019 Panini Victory Lane Signature Swatches Red /25 #14
2019 Panini Victory Lane Starting Grid #11
2019 Panini Victory Lane Starting Grid Black /1 #11
2019 Panini Victory Lane Starting Grid Blue /99 #11
2019 Panini Victory Lane Starting Grid Gold /25 #11
2019 Panini Victory Lane Starting Grid Green /5 #11
2019 Panini Victory Lane Starting Grid Printing Plates Black /1 #11
2019 Panini Victory Lane Starting Grid Printing Plates Cyan /1 #11
2019 Panini Victory Lane Starting Grid Printing Plates Magenta /1 #11
2019 Panini Victory Lane Starting Grid Printing Plates Yellow /1 #11
2019 Panini Victory Lane Top 10 #2
2019 Panini Victory Lane Top 10 Black /1 #2
2019 Panini Victory Lane Top 10 Blue /99 #2
2019 Panini Victory Lane Top 10 Gold /25 #2
2019 Panini Victory Lane Top 10 Green /5 #2
2019 Panini Victory Lane Top 10 Printing Plates Black /1 #2
2019 Panini Victory Lane Top 10 Printing Plates Cyan /1 #2
2019 Panini Victory Lane Top 10 Printing Plates Magenta /1 #2
2019 Panini Victory Lane Top 10 Printing Plates Yellow /1 #2
2019 Panini Victory Lane Track Stars #5
2019 Panini Victory Lane Track Stars Black /1 #5
2019 Panini Victory Lane Track Stars Blue /99 #5
2019 Panini Victory Lane Track Stars Gold /25 #5
2019 Panini Victory Lane Track Stars Green /5 #5
2019 Panini Victory Lane Track Stars Printing Plates Black /1 #5
2019 Panini Victory Lane Track Stars Printing Plates Cyan /1 #5
2019 Panini Victory Lane Track Stars Printing Plates Magenta /1 #5
2019 Panini Victory Lane Track Stars Printing Plates Yellow /1 #5
2019-20 Funko Pop Vinyl NASCAR #10
2020 Donruss #10
2020 Donruss #44
2020 Donruss #103
2020 Donruss #180
2020 Donruss Action Packed #2
2020 Donruss Action Packed Checkers #2
2020 Donruss Action Packed Cracked Ice /25 #2
2020 Donruss Action Packed Holographic /199 #2
2020 Donruss Action Packed Xplosion /10 #2
2020 Donruss Aero Package #8
2020 Donruss Aero Package Checkers #8
2020 Donruss Aero Package Cracked Ice /25 #8
2020 Donruss Aero Package Holographic /199 #8
2020 Donruss Aero Package Xplosion /10 #8
2020 Donruss Black Numbers /19 #10
2020 Donruss Black Numbers /19 #44
2020 Donruss Black Numbers /19 #103
2020 Donruss Black Numbers /19 #180
2020 Donruss Black Trophy Club /1 #10
2020 Donruss Black Trophy Club /1 #44
2020 Donruss Black Trophy Club /1 #103
2020 Donruss Black Trophy Club /1 #180
2020 Donruss Blue /199 #103
2020 Donruss Blue /199 #180
2020 Donruss Blue /199 #10
2020 Donruss Blue /199 #44
2020 Donruss Carolina Blue #10
2020 Donruss Carolina Blue #44
2020 Donruss Carolina Blue #103
2020 Donruss Carolina Blue #180
2020 Donruss Contenders #1
2020 Donruss Contenders Checkers #1
2020 Donruss Contenders Cracked Ice /25 #1
2020 Donruss Contenders Holographic /199 #1
2020 Donruss Contenders Xplosion /10 #1
2020 Donruss Green /99 #10
2020 Donruss Green /99 #44
2020 Donruss Green /99 #103
2020 Donruss Green /99 #180
2020 Donruss Optic #10
2020 Donruss Optic #19
2020 Donruss Optic #64
2020 Donruss Optic Carolina Blue Wave #19
2020 Donruss Optic Carolina Blue Wave #64
2020 Donruss Optic Carolina Blue Wave #10
2020 Donruss Optic Gold /10 #10
2020 Donruss Optic Gold /10 #19
2020 Donruss Optic Gold /10 #64
2020 Donruss Optic Gold Vinyl /1 #10
2020 Donruss Optic Gold Vinyl /1 #19
2020 Donruss Optic Gold Vinyl /1 #64
2020 Donruss Optic Holo #10
2020 Donruss Optic Holo #19
2020 Donruss Optic Holo #64
2020 Donruss Optic Orange Pulsar #10
2020 Donruss Optic Orange Pulsar #19
2020 Donruss Optic Orange Pulsar #64
2020 Donruss Optic Red Mojo #10
2020 Donruss Optic Red Mojo #19
2020 Donruss Optic Red Mojo #64
2020 Donruss Optic Signatures Gold Vinyl /1 #10
2020 Donruss Optic Signatures Gold Vinyl /1 #19
2020 Donruss Optic Signatures Gold Vinyl /1 #64
2020 Donruss Optic Signatures Holo /99 #10
2020 Donruss Optic Signatures Holo /99 #19
2020 Donruss Optic Signatures Holo /99 #64
2020 Donruss Orange #180
2020 Donruss Orange #10
2020 Donruss Orange #44
2020 Donruss Orange #103
2020 Donruss Pink /25 #10
2020 Donruss Pink /25 #44
2020 Donruss Pink /25 #103
2020 Donruss Pink /25 #180
2020 Donruss Printing Plates Black /1 #10
2020 Donruss Printing Plates Black /1 #44
2020 Donruss Printing Plates Black /1 #103
2020 Donruss Printing Plates Black /1 #180
2020 Donruss Printing Plates Cyan /1 #10
2020 Donruss Printing Plates Cyan /1 #44
2020 Donruss Printing Plates Cyan /1 #103
2020 Donruss Printing Plates Cyan /1 #180
2020 Donruss Printing Plates Magenta /1 #44
2020 Donruss Printing Plates Magenta /1 #103
2020 Donruss Printing Plates Magenta /1 #180
2020 Donruss Printing Plates Magenta /1 #10
2020 Donruss Printing Plates Yellow /1 #180
2020 Donruss Printing Plates Yellow /1 #10
2020 Donruss Printing Plates Yellow /1 #44
2020 Donruss Printing Plates Yellow /1 #103
2020 Donruss Purple /49 #10
2020 Donruss Purple /49 #44
2020 Donruss Purple /49 #103
2020 Donruss Purple /49 #180
2020 Donruss Race Day Relics #21
2020 Donruss Race Day Relics Holo Black /10 #21
2020 Donruss Race Day Relics Holo Gold /25 #21
2020 Donruss Race Day Relics Red /250 #21
2020 Donruss Red /299 #10
2020 Donruss Red /299 #44
2020 Donruss Red /299 #103
2020 Donruss Red /299 #180
2020 Donruss Retro Relics '87 #20
2020 Donruss Retro Relics '87 Holo Black /10 #20
2020 Donruss Retro Relics '87 Holo Gold /25 #20
2020 Donruss Retro Relics '87 Red /250 #20
2020 Donruss Retro Series #1
2020 Donruss Retro Series Checkers #1
2020 Donruss Retro Series Cracked Ice /25 #1
2020 Donruss Retro Series Holographic /199 #1
2020 Donruss Retro Series Xplosion /10 #1
2020 Donruss Signature Series Holo Black /1 #29
2020 Donruss Signature Series Holo Gold /18 #29
2020 Donruss Signature Series Red /25 #29
2020 Donruss Silver #10
2020 Donruss Silver #44
2020 Donruss Silver #103
2020 Donruss Silver #180

Darrell Waltrip

1983 UNO Racing #28
1985 SportStars Photo-Graphics Stickers #NNO
1986 SportStars Photo-Graphics #12
1988 Maxx Charlotte #10
1988 Maxx Charlotte #27
1988 Maxx Charlotte #75
1989 Maxx #17
1989 Maxx #125
1989 Maxx #140
1989 Maxx #150
1989 Maxx #164
1989 Maxx Crisco #2
1990 AC Racing Proven Winners #2
1990 Maxx #17
1990 Maxx #50
1990 Maxx #100
1990 Maxx #167
1990 Maxx #168
1990 Maxx #174
1990 Maxx #177
1990 Maxx #178
1990 Maxx #185
1990 Maxx Glossy #17
1990 Maxx Glossy #50
1990 Maxx Glossy #100
1990 Maxx Glossy #167
1990 Maxx Glossy #168
1990 Maxx Glossy #174
1990 Maxx Glossy #177
1990 Maxx Glossy #178
1990 Maxx Glossy #185
1990 Maxx Holly Farms #HF3
1991 AC Racing #3
1991 Maxx #17
1991 Maxx #150
1991 Maxx McDonald's #20
1991 Maxx Racing for Kids #3
1991 Maxx The Winston Acrylics #20
1991 Maxx Update #17
1991 Maxx Update #150
1991 Maxx Winston 20th Anniversary Foils #12
1991 Maxx Winston 20th Anniversary Foils #12
1991 Maxx Winston 20th Anniversary Foils #15
1991 Pro Set #117
1991 Pro Set #118
1991 Pro Set #119
1991 Sunbelt Racing Legends #7
1991 Superior Racing Metals #12
1991 Texas World Speedway #9
1991 Traks Richard Petty #22
1991-92 Pioneers of Stock Car Racing #4
1992 AC Racing Postcards #8
1992 AC-Delco #4
1992 Card Dynamics Darrell Waltrip /4000 #1
1992 Card Dynamics Darrell Waltrip /4000 #2
1992 Card Dynamics Darrell Waltrip /4000 #3
1992 Card Dynamics Darrell Waltrip /4000 #4
1992 Card Dynamics Darrell Waltrip /4000 #5
1992 Card Dynamics Gant Oil /4000 #1
1992 Maxx Black #17
1992 Maxx Black #190
1992 Maxx Black #195
1992 Maxx Black #270
1992 Maxx Black #277
1992 Maxx Craftsman #7
1992 Maxx IMHOF #36
1992 Maxx McDonald's #16
1992 Maxx Red #17
1992 Maxx Red #190
1992 Maxx Red #195
1992 Maxx Red #270
1992 Maxx Red #277
1992 Maxx The Winston #11
1992 Maxx The Winston #31
1992 Pro Set #93
1992 Pro Set #97
1992 Pro Set #209
1992 Pro Set #245
1992 Pro Set Maxwell House #14
1992 Pro Set Rudy Farms #7
1992 Redline Standups #17
1992 Sports Illustrated for Kids II #48
1992 Traks #17
1992 Traks #56
1992 Traks #191
1992 Traks #198
1992 Traks ASA #42
1992 Traks Racing Machines #17
1992 Traks Racing Machines #23
1992 Traks Racing Machines #37
1992 Traks Team Sets #127
1992 Traks Team Sets #130
1992 Traks Team Sets #138
1992 Traks Team Sets #142
1992 Traks Team Sets #150
1993 AC Racing Foldouts #17
1993 Action Packed #3
1993 Action Packed #16
1993 Action Packed #17
1993 Action Packed #24
1993 Action Packed #41
1993 Action Packed #103
1993 Action Packed #104
1993 Action Packed #164
1993 Action Packed #190
1993 Action Packed 24K Gold #2G
1993 Action Packed 24K Gold #72G
1993 Finish Line #4
1993 Finish Line #51
1993 Finish Line #95

1993 Finish Line #107
1993 Finish Line Commemorative Sheets #8
1993 Finish Line Commemorative Sheets #18
1993 Finish Line Commemorative Sheets #30
1993 Finish Line Silver #4
1993 Finish Line Silver #51
1993 Finish Line Silver #95
1993 Finish Line Silver #107
1993 Hi-Tech Tire Test #2
1993 Maxwell House #8
1993 Maxwell House #21
1993 Maxx #17
1993 Maxx #226
1993 Maxx #280
1993 Maxx #284
1993 Maxx #285
1993 Maxx Lowes Foods Stickers #2
1993 Maxx Premier Plus #17
1993 Maxx Premier Plus #65
1993 Maxx Premier Plus #195
1993 Maxx Premier Plus #199
1993 Maxx Premier Plus #200
1993 Maxx Premier Series #17
1993 Maxx Premier Series #226
1993 Maxx Premier Series #280
1993 Maxx Premier Series #284
1993 Maxx Premier Series #285
1993 Maxx Retail Jumbos #1
1993 Maxx The Winston #6
1993 Maxx The Winston #26
1993 Traks Preferred Collector #9
1994 Action Packed #13
1994 Action Packed #70
1994 Action Packed #100
1994 Action Packed #127
1994 Action Packed #166
1994 Action Packed 24K Gold #24G
1994 Action Packed Coastars #17
1994 Action Packed Mint #13
1994 Action Packed Mint #70
1994 Action Packed Mint #100
1994 Action Packed Mint #127
1994 Action Packed Mint #166
1994 Action Packed Select 24K Gold #W1
1994 Card Dynamics Gant Oil /6000 #6
1994 Finish Line #40
1994 Finish Line #102
1994 Finish Line #129
1994 Finish Line Gold #13
1994 Finish Line Gold #30
1994 Finish Line Gold #31
1994 Finish Line Gold #64
1994 Finish Line Gold #66
1994 Finish Line Gold Phone Cards /3000 #9
1994 Finish Line Gold Teamwork #TG10
1994 Finish Line Phone Cards #15
1994 Finish Line Silver #40
1994 Finish Line Silver #102
1994 Finish Line Silver #129
1994 Hi-Tech Brickyard 400 #18
1994 Hi-Tech Brickyard 400 #48
1994 Hi-Tech Brickyard 400 Artist Proofs #18
1994 Hi-Tech Brickyard 400 Artist Proofs #48
1994 Maxx #17
1994 Maxx #64
1994 Maxx Medallion #5
1994 Maxx Premier Plus #17
1994 Maxx Premier Plus #64
1994 Maxx Premier Series #17
1994 Maxx Premier Series #64
1994 Maxx Premier Series Jumbos #5
1994 Maxx The Select 25 #13
1994 Power #SL46
1994 Power #PR60
1994 Power #PO69
1994 Power #125
1994 Power #150
1994 Power Gold #SL46
1994 Power Gold #PR60
1994 Power Gold #PO69
1994 Power Gold #125
1994 Power Gold #150
1994 Power Preview #9
1994 Press Pass #29
1994 Press Pass #33
1994 Press Pass #87
1994 Press Pass Cup Chase #CC29
1994 Press Pass Optima XL #23
1994 Press Pass Optima XL #36
1994 Press Pass Optima XL Red Hot #23
1994 Press Pass Optima XL Red Hot #36
1994 SkyBox #2
1994 SkyBox #25
1994 VIP #35
1994 VIP #54
1994 Wheels High Gear #117
1994 Wheels High Gear Day One #117
1994 Wheels High Gear Day One Gold #117
1994 Wheels High Gear Gold #117
1994 Wheels High Gear Mega Gold #MG11
1995 Action Packed Country #4
1995 Action Packed Country #18
1995 Action Packed Country #21
1995 Action Packed Country #32
1995 Action Packed Country #33
1995 Action Packed Country #34
1995 Action Packed Country #35
1995 Action Packed Country #36
1995 Action Packed Country #37
1995 Action Packed Country Silver Speed #4
1995 Action Packed Country Silver Speed #18
1995 Action Packed Country Silver Speed #21
1995 Action Packed Country Silver Speed #32
1995 Action Packed Country Silver Speed #33
1995 Action Packed Country Silver Speed #34
1995 Action Packed Country Silver Speed #35
1995 Action Packed Country Silver Speed #36
1995 Action Packed Country Silver Speed #37
1995 Action Packed Preview #24
1995 Action Packed Preview #67
1995 Action Packed Preview #78
1995 Action Packed Preview 24K Gold #10G
1995 Action Packed Stars #10
1995 Action Packed Stars #39
1995 Action Packed Stars Silver Speed #10
1995 Action Packed Stars Silver Speed #39
1995 Assets #7
1995 Assets #35
1995 Assets $2 Phone Cards #6
1995 Assets $2 Phone Cards Gold Signature #6
1995 Assets $25 Phone Cards #3
1995 Assets $5 Phone Cards #3
1995 Assets 1-Minute Phone Cards #6
1995 Assets 1-Minute Phone Cards Gold Signature #6
1995 Assets Gold Signature #7
1995 Assets Gold Signature #35
1995 Classic Five Sport #176
1995 Classic Five Sport Autographs Numbered /225 #176
1995 Classic Five Sport Printer's Proofs /795 #176
1995 Classic Five Sport Red Die Cuts #176
1995 Classic Five Sport Silver Die Cuts #176
1995 Classic Five Sport Strive For Five #RC6
1995 Crown Jewels #10
1995 Crown Jewels #33
1995 Crown Jewels #51
1995 Crown Jewels #64
1995 Crown Jewels Diamond /599 #10
1995 Crown Jewels Diamond /599 #33
1995 Crown Jewels Diamond /599 #51
1995 Crown Jewels Diamond /599 #64
1995 Crown Jewels Emerald /1199 #10
1995 Crown Jewels Emerald /1199 #33
1995 Crown Jewels Emerald /1199 #51
1995 Crown Jewels Emerald /1199 #64
1995 Crown Jewels Sapphire /2500 #10
1995 Crown Jewels Sapphire /2500 #33
1995 Crown Jewels Sapphire /2500 #51
1995 Crown Jewels Sapphire /2500 #64
1995 Finish Line #3
1995 Finish Line #17
1995 Finish Line #58
1995 Finish Line Coca-Cola 600 #7
1995 Finish Line Coca-Cola 600 #35
1995 Finish Line Coca-Cola 600 Winners #CC1
1995 Finish Line Coca-Cola 600 Winners #CC4
1995 Finish Line Coca-Cola 600 Winners #CC5
1995 Finish Line Gold Signature #GS12
1995 Finish Line Printer's Proof /398 #3
1995 Finish Line Printer's Proof /398 #17
1995 Finish Line Printer's Proof /398 #58
1995 Finish Line Silver #3
1995 Finish Line Silver #17
1995 Finish Line Silver #58
1995 Finish Line Standout Cars #SC8
1995 Finish Line Standout Drivers #SD8
1995 Hi-Tech Brickyard 400 #25
1995 Hi-Tech Brickyard 400 #78
1995 Hi-Tech Brickyard 400 Top Ten #BY6
1995 Images #17
1995 Images #47
1995 Images Driven #D15
1995 Images Gold #17
1995 Images Gold #47
1995 Matchbook Winston Cup Champions #11
1995 Matchbook Winston Cup Champions #12
1995 Matchbook Winston Cup Champions #15
1995 Maxx #17
1995 Maxx #174
1995 Maxx #206
1995 Maxx #207
1995 Maxx License to Drive #12
1995 Maxx Medallion #13
1995 Maxx Medallion #43
1995 Maxx Medallion Blue #13
1995 Maxx Medallion Blue #43
1995 Maxx Over the Wall #5
1995 Maxx Premier Plus #17
1995 Maxx Premier Plus #63
1995 Maxx Premier Plus #P1
1995 Maxx Premier Plus Crown Chrome #17
1995 Maxx Premier Plus Crown Chrome #63
1995 Maxx Premier Plus PaceSetters #PS8
1995 Maxx Premier Plus PaceSetters Crown Chrome #PS8
1995 Maxx Premier Series #17
1995 Maxx Premier Series #63
1995 Metallic Impressions Winston Cup Champions 10-Card Tin #5
1995 Press Pass #35
1995 Press Pass #54
1995 Press Pass #108
1995 Press Pass Cup Chase #35
1995 Press Pass Optima XL #23
1995 Press Pass Optima XL Cool Blue #23
1995 Press Pass Optima XL Die Cut #23
1995 Press Pass Optima XL Prototypes #XL2
1995 Press Pass Optima XL Red Hot #23
1995 Press Pass Optima XL Stealth #XLS17
1995 Press Pass Premium #9
1995 Press Pass Premium Holofoil #9
1995 Press Pass Premium Red Hot #9
1995 Press Pass Red Hot #35
1995 Press Pass Red Hot #54
1995 Press Pass Red Hot #108
1995 Select #35
1995 Select #54
1995 Select #88
1995 Select #113
1995 Select #133
1995 Select Dream Machines #DM10
1995 Select Flat Out #35
1995 Select Flat Out #54
1995 Select Flat Out #88
1995 Select Flat Out #113
1995 Select Flat Out #133
1995 Select Skills #SS16
1995 SP #14
1995 SP #48
1995 SP #90
1995 SP #130
1995 SP Die Cuts #14
1995 SP Die Cuts #48
1995 SP Die Cuts #90
1995 SP Die Cuts #130
1995 SP Speed Merchants #SM17
1995 SP Speed Merchants Die Cuts #SM17
1995 Upper Deck #5
1995 Upper Deck #48
1995 Upper Deck #73
1995 Upper Deck #141
1995 Upper Deck #170
1995 Upper Deck #197
1995 Upper Deck #241
1995 Upper Deck #278
1995 Upper Deck Autographs #197
1995 Upper Deck Gold Signature/Electric Gold #5
1995 Upper Deck Gold Signature/Electric Gold #48
1995 Upper Deck Gold Signature/Electric Gold #73
1995 Upper Deck Gold Signature/Electric Gold #141
1995 Upper Deck Gold Signature/Electric Gold #170
1995 Upper Deck Gold Signature/Electric Gold #197
1995 Upper Deck Gold Signature/Electric Gold #241
1995 Upper Deck Gold Signature/Electric Gold #278
1995 Upper Deck Silver Signature/Electric Silver #5
1995 Upper Deck Silver Signature/Electric Silver #48
1995 Upper Deck Silver Signature/Electric Silver #73
1995 Upper Deck Silver Signature/Electric Silver #141
1995 Upper Deck Silver Signature/Electric Silver #170
1995 Upper Deck Silver Signature/Electric Silver #197
1995 Upper Deck Silver Signature/Electric Silver #241
1995 Upper Deck Silver Signature/Electric Silver #278
1995 VIP #29
1995 VIP #54
1995 VIP Cool Blue #29
1995 VIP Cool Blue #54
1995 VIP Emerald Proofs #29
1995 VIP Emerald Proofs #54
1995 VIP Red Hot #29
1995 VIP Red Hot #54
1995 Wheels High Gear #7
1995 Wheels High Gear #79
1995 Wheels High Gear Day One #7
1995 Wheels High Gear Day One #79
1995 Wheels High Gear Day One Gold #7
1995 Wheels High Gear Day One Gold #79
1995 Wheels High Gear Gold #7
1995 Wheels High Gear Gold #79
1995 Zenith #17
1995 Zenith #47
1995-96 Classic Five Sport Signings #89
1995-96 Classic Five Sport Signings Blue Signature #89
1995-96 Classic Five Sport Signings Die Cuts #89
1995-96 Classic Five Sport Signings Red Signature #89
1996 Action Packed Credentials #38
1996 Action Packed Credentials #61
1996 Action Packed Credentials #79
1996 Action Packed Credentials #90
1996 Action Packed Credentials #94
1996 Action Packed Credentials Silver Speed #38
1996 Assets Racing #8
1996 Assets Racing #43
1996 Assets Racing $100 Cup Champion Interactive Phone Cards #6
1996 Assets Racing $1000 Cup Champion Interactive Phone Cards #11
1996 Assets Racing $2 Phone Cards #11
1996 Assets Racing $5 Phone Cards #4
1996 Assets Racing Competitor's License #CL10
1996 Autographed Racing #35
1996 Autographed Racing Autographs #59
1996 Autographed Racing Autographs Certified Golds #59
1996 Autographed Racing Front Runners #81
1996 Autographed Racing Front Runners #82
1996 Autographed Racing Front Runners #83
1996 Autographed Racing Front Runners #84
1996 Autographed Racing Front Runners #85
1996 Autographed Racing High Performance #HP17
1996 Classic #24
1996 Classic #60
1996 Classic Printer's Proof #24
1996 Classic Race Chase #RC15
1996 Classic Silver #24
1996 Crown Jewels Elite #12
1996 Crown Jewels Elite Birthstones of the Champions #BC4
1996 Crown Jewels Elite Birthstones of the Champions Diamond Tribute #BC4
1996 Crown Jewels Elite Birthstones of the Champions Treasure Chest #BC4
1996 Crown Jewels Elite Diamond Tribute /2500 #12
1996 Crown Jewels Elite Diamond Tribute Citrine /999 #12
1996 Crown Jewels Elite Dual Jewels Amethyst #DJ5
1996 Crown Jewels Elite Dual Jewels Amethyst Diamond Tribute #DJ5
1996 Crown Jewels Elite Dual Jewels Amethyst Treasure Chest #DJ5
1996 Crown Jewels Elite Dual Jewels Garnet #DJ5
1996 Crown Jewels Elite Dual Jewels Garnet Diamond Tribute #DJ5
1996 Crown Jewels Elite Dual Jewels Garnet Treasure Chest #DJ5
1996 Crown Jewels Elite Dual Jewels Sapphire #DJ5
1996 Crown Jewels Elite Dual Jewels Sapphire Treasure Chest #DJ5
1996 Crown Jewels Elite Emerald /599 #12
1996 Crown Jewels Elite Emerald Treasure Chest #12
1996 Crown Jewels Elite Retail Blue #12
1996 Crown Jewels Elite Sapphire #12
1996 Crown Jewels Elite Sapphire Treasure Chest /1099 #12
1996 Crown Jewels Elite Treasure Chest #12
1996 Finish Line #11
1996 Finish Line #56
1996 Finish Line #67
1996 Finish Line #68
1996 Finish Line Black Gold #C12
1996 Finish Line Black Gold #D13
1996 Finish Line Gold Signature #GS11
1996 Finish Line Phone Pak #39
1996 Finish Line Phone Pak #40
1996 Finish Line Phone Pak $10 #12
1996 Finish Line Phone Pak $2 Signature #39
1996 Finish Line Phone Pak $2 Signature #40
1996 Finish Line Phone Pak $5 #24
1996 Finish Line Printer's Proof #11
1996 Finish Line Printer's Proof #56
1996 Finish Line Printer's Proof #67
1996 Finish Line Printer's Proof #68
1996 Finish Line Silver #11
1996 Finish Line Silver #56
1996 Finish Line Silver #67
1996 Finish Line Silver #68
1996 KnightQuest #17
1996 KnightQuest Black Knights #17
1996 KnightQuest Knights of the Round Table #KT3
1996 KnightQuest Protectors of the Crown /899 #PC1
1996 KnightQuest Red Knight Preview #17
1996 KnightQuest Royalty #17
1996 KnightQuest White Knights #17
1996 Maxx #17
1996 Maxx #27
1996 Maxx Family Ties #FT5
1996 Maxx Made in America #17
1996 Maxx Made in America #27
1996 Maxx Made in America Blue Ribbon #BR11
1996 Maxx Odyssey #17
1996 Maxx Odyssey #27
1996 Maxx Odyssey Radio Active #RA11
1996 Maxx On The Road Again #OTRA4
1996 Maxx Pepsi 500 #3
1996 Maxx Premier Series #17
1996 Maxx Premier Series #60
1996 Maxx SuperTrucks #ST8
1996 Metallic Impressions 25th Anniversary Winston Cup Champions #11
1996 Metallic Impressions 25th Anniversary Winston Cup Champions #12
1996 Metallic Impressions 25th Anniversary Winston Cup Champions #15
1996 Metallic Impressions Avon All-Time Racing Greatest #2
1996 M-Force #15
1996 Pinnacle #17
1996 Pinnacle #46
1996 Pinnacle Artist Proofs #17
1996 Pinnacle Artist Proofs #46
1996 Pinnacle Checkered Flag #15
1996 Pinnacle Foil #17
1996 Pinnacle Foil #46
1996 Pinnacle Pole Position #17
1996 Pinnacle Pole Position #35
1996 Pinnacle Pole Position #81
1996 Pinnacle Pole Position Lightning Fast #17
1996 Pinnacle Pole Position Lightning Fast #35
1996 Pinnacle Pole Position Lightning Fast #81
1996 Pinnacle Pole Position No Limit #12
1996 Pinnacle Pole Position No Limit Gold #12
1996 Pinnacle Winston Cup Collection Dufex #17
1996 Pinnacle Winston Cup Collection Dufex #46
1996 Press Pass #35
1996 Press Pass #54
1996 Press Pass #90
1996 Press Pass Cup Chase #35
1996 Press Pass Cup Chase Foil Prizes #35
1996 Press Pass Premium #19
1996 Press Pass Premium Emerald Proofs /380 #19
1996 Press Pass Premium Holofoil #19
1996 Press Pass R and N China #35
1996 Press Pass Scorchers #35
1996 Press Pass Scorchers #54
1996 Press Pass Scorchers #90
1996 Press Pass Torquers #35
1996 Press Pass Torquers #54
1996 Press Pass Torquers #90
1996 Racer's Choice #21
1996 Racer's Choice #37
1996 Racer's Choice #105
1996 Racer's Choice Speedway Collection #21
1996 Racer's Choice Speedway Collection #37
1996 Racer's Choice Speedway Collection #105
1996 Racer's Choice Speedway Collection Artist's Proofs #21
1996 Racer's Choice Speedway Collection Artist's Proofs #37
1996 Racer's Choice Speedway Collection Artist's Proofs #105
1996 SP #17
1996 SP #60
1996 SP Holoview Maximum Effects #ME17
1996 SP Holoview Maximum Effects Die Cuts #ME17
1996 Speedflix #7
1996 Speedflix #22
1996 Speedflix Artist Proof's #7
1996 Speedflix Artist Proof's #22
1996 Speedflix In Motion #7
1996 Speedflix ProMotion #10
1996 SPx #17
1996 SPx Gold #17
1996 Tide #1
1996 Tide #2
1996 Tide #3
1996 Tide #4
1996 Tide #5
1996 Tide #6
1996 Tide #7
1996 Upper Deck #15
1996 Upper Deck #55
1996 Upper Deck #95
1996 Upper Deck #130
1996 Upper Deck Racing Legends #RLC9
1996 Upper Deck Road To The Cup #RC18
1996 Upper Deck Road To The Cup #RC67
1996 Upper Deck Road To The Cup #RC101
1996 Upper Deck Road To The Cup #RC141
1996 Upper Deck Road To The Cup Autographs #H18
1996 Upper Deck Road To The Cup Predictor Top 3 #T4
1996 Upper Deck Road To The Cup Predictor Top 3 Prizes #R7
1996 Upper Deck Virtual Velocity #VV8
1996 Upper Deck Virtual Velocity Gold #VV8
1996 VIP #28
1996 VIP Emerald Proofs #28
1996 VIP Head Gear #HG8
1996 VIP Head Gear Die Cuts #HG8
1996 VIP Torquers #28
1996 VIP War Paint #WP8
1996 VIP War Paint Gold #WP8
1996 Viper #13
1996 Viper Black Mamba #13
1996 Viper Black Mamba First Strike #13
1996 Viper Busch Clash #B6
1996 Viper Busch Clash First Strike #B6
1996 Viper Copperhead Die Cuts #13
1996 Viper Copperhead Die Cuts First Strike #13
1996 Viper First Strike #13
1996 Viper Green Mamba #13
1996 Viper Red Cobra /1799 #13
1996 Visions #119
1996 Visions Signings #96
1996 Zenith #18
1996 Zenith #41
1996 Zenith Artist Proofs #18
1996 Zenith Artist Proofs #41
1996 Zenith Champion Salute #11
1996 Zenith Champion Salute #14
1996 Zenith Champion Salute #15
1996 Zenith Highlights #6
1997 Action Packed #17
1997 Action Packed #38
1997 Action Packed #85
1997 Action Packed Chevy Madness #2
1997 Action Packed First Impressions #17
1997 Action Packed First Impressions #38
1997 Action Packed First Impressions #85
1997 Action Packed Rolling Thunder #7
1997 Autographed Racing #15
1997 Autographed Racing #48
1997 Autographed Racing Autographs #54
1997 Autographed Racing Mayne Street #KM15
1997 Collector's Choice #17
1997 Collector's Choice #67
1997 Collector's Choice #119
1997 Collector's Choice #151
1997 Collector's Choice Speedecals #S33
1997 Collector's Choice Speedecals #S34
1997 Collector's Choice Upper Deck 500 #UD34
1997 Collector's Choice Upper Deck 500 #UD35
1997 Collector's Choice Victory Circle #VC1
1997 Finish Line Phone Pak II #10
1997 Finish Line Phone Pak II #48
1997 Finish Line Phone Pak II #75
1997 Jurassic Park #17
1997 Jurassic Park Triceratops #17
1997 Maxx #17
1997 Maxx #62
1997 Maxx #119
1997 Maxx Flag Firsts #FF17
1997 Pinnacle #17
1997 Pinnacle #46
1997 Pinnacle #94
1997 Pinnacle Artist Proofs #17
1997 Pinnacle Artist Proofs #46
1997 Pinnacle Artist Proofs #94
1997 Pinnacle Certified #17
1997 Pinnacle Certified #51
1997 Pinnacle Certified #69
1997 Pinnacle Certified #70
1997 Pinnacle Certified #71
1997 Pinnacle Certified Epix #E8
1997 Pinnacle Certified Epix Emerald #E8
1997 Pinnacle Certified Epix Purple #E8
1997 Pinnacle Certified Mirror Blue #17
1997 Pinnacle Certified Mirror Blue #51
1997 Pinnacle Certified Mirror Blue #69
1997 Pinnacle Certified Mirror Blue #70
1997 Pinnacle Certified Mirror Blue #71
1997 Pinnacle Certified Mirror Gold #17
1997 Pinnacle Certified Mirror Gold #51
1997 Pinnacle Certified Mirror Gold #69
1997 Pinnacle Certified Mirror Gold #70
1997 Pinnacle Certified Mirror Gold #71
1997 Pinnacle Certified Mirror Red #17
1997 Pinnacle Certified Mirror Red #51
1997 Pinnacle Certified Mirror Red #69
1997 Pinnacle Certified Mirror Red #70
1997 Pinnacle Certified Mirror Red #71
1997 Pinnacle Certified Red #17
1997 Pinnacle Certified Red #51
1997 Pinnacle Certified Red #69
1997 Pinnacle Certified Red #70
1997 Pinnacle Certified Red #71
1997 Pinnacle Mint #4
1997 Pinnacle Mint Bronze #4
1997 Pinnacle Mint Coins #4
1997 Pinnacle Mint Coins 24K Gold Plated #4
1997 Pinnacle Mint Coins Nickel-Silver #4
1997 Pinnacle Mint Gold #4
1997 Pinnacle Mint Silver #4
1997 Pinnacle Press Plates #17
1997 Pinnacle Press Plates #46
1997 Pinnacle Press Plates #94
1997 Pinnacle Press Plates #TP4A
1997 Pinnacle Team Pinnacle #4
1997 Pinnacle Team Pinnacle Red #4
1997 Pinnacle Totally Certified Platinum Blue #17
1997 Pinnacle Totally Certified Platinum Blue #51
1997 Pinnacle Totally Certified Platinum Blue #69
1997 Pinnacle Totally Certified Platinum Blue #70
1997 Pinnacle Totally Certified Platinum Blue #71
1997 Pinnacle Totally Certified Platinum Gold #17
1997 Pinnacle Totally Certified Platinum Gold #51
1997 Pinnacle Totally Certified Platinum Gold #69
1997 Pinnacle Totally Certified Platinum Gold #70
1997 Pinnacle Totally Certified Platinum Gold #71
1997 Pinnacle Totally Certified Platinum Red #17
1997 Pinnacle Totally Certified Platinum Red #51
1997 Pinnacle Totally Certified Platinum Red #69
1997 Pinnacle Totally Certified Platinum Red #70
1997 Pinnacle Totally Certified Platinum Red #71
1997 Pinnacle Trophy Collection #17
1997 Pinnacle Trophy Collection #46
1997 Pinnacle Trophy Collection #94
1997 Predator #18
1997 Predator American Eagle #AE10
1997 Predator American Eagle First Slash #AE10
1997 Predator Black Wolf #18
1997 Predator Black Wolf First Slash /3750 #18
1997 Predator First Slash #18
1997 Predator Gatorback #GB9
1997 Predator Gatorback Authentic #GBA9
1997 Predator Gatorback Authentic First Slash #GBA9
1997 Predator Gatorback First Slash #GB9
1997 Predator Golden Eagle #GE10
1997 Predator Golden Eagle First Slash #GE10
1997 Predator Grizzly #18
1997 Predator Grizzly First Slash #18
1997 Predator Red Wolf #18
1997 Predator Red Wolf First Slash #18
1997 Press Pass #25
1997 Press Pass #54
1997 Press Pass Autographs #38
1997 Press Pass Lasers Silver #25
1997 Press Pass Lasers Silver #54
1997 Press Pass Oil Slicks /100 #25
1997 Press Pass Oil Slicks /100 #54
1997 Press Pass Premium #25
1997 Press Pass Premium Emerald Proofs /380 #25
1997 Press Pass Premium Mirrors #25
1997 Press Pass Premium Oil Slicks /100 #25
1997 Press Pass Torquers Blue #25
1997 Press Pass Torquers Blue #54
1997 Race Sharks #11
1997 Race Sharks First Bite #11
1997 Race Sharks Great White #11
1997 Race Sharks Hammerhead #11
1997 Race Sharks Hammerhead First Bite #11
1997 Race Sharks Shark Attack First Bite Previews #7
1997 Race Sharks Tiger Shark #11
1997 Race Sharks Tiger Shark First Bite #11
1997 Racer's Choice #17
1997 Racer's Choice #52
1997 Racer's Choice Showcase Series #17
1997 Racer's Choice Showcase Series #52
1997 SB Motorsports #28
1997 SB Motorsports #54
1997 Score Board IQ #15
1997 Score Board IQ Remarques #SB6
1997 Score Board IQ Remarques Sam Bass Finished #SB6
1997 SP #17
1997 SP #59
1997 SP #97
1997 SP Super Series #17
1997 SP Super Series #59
1997 SP Super Series #97
1997 SPx #17
1997 SPx Blue #17
1997 SPx Gold #17
1997 SPx Silver #17
1997 Upper Deck Road To The Cup #30
1997 Upper Deck Road To The Cup #72
1997 Upper Deck Road To The Cup #103
1997 Upper Deck Road To The Cup #117
1997 Upper Deck Road To The Cup #139
1997 Upper Deck Road To The Cup Predictor Plus #20
1997 Upper Deck Road To The Cup Predictor Plus Cel Die Cuts #20
1997 Upper Deck Road To The Cup Predictor Plus Cels #20
1997 Upper Deck Victory Circle #17
1997 Upper Deck Victory Circle #67
1997 Upper Deck Victory Circle #117
1997 VIP #24
1997 VIP Explosives #24
1997 VIP Oil Slicks #24
1997 Viper #17
1997 Viper Anaconda Jumbos #A7
1997 Viper Black Racer #17
1997 Viper Black Racer First Strike #17
1997 Viper First Strike #17
1998 Big League Cards Creative Images #7
1998 Collector's Choice #17
1998 Collector's Choice #53
1998 Collector's Choice #112
1998 Collector's Choice CC600 #CC21
1998 Collector's Choice CC600 #CC54
1998 Collector's Choice CC600 #CC87
1998 Collector's Choice Star Quest #SQ35
1998 Maxx #17
1998 Maxx #47
1998 Maxx #63
1998 Maxx 10th Anniversary #16
1998 Maxx 10th Anniversary #61
1998 Maxx 10th Anniversary #98
1998 Maxx 10th Anniversary #118
1998 Maxx 10th Anniversary Buy Back Autographs /179 #48
1998 Maxx 10th Anniversary Card of the Year #CY4
1998 Maxx 10th Anniversary Champions Past #CP7
1998 Maxx 10th Anniversary Champions Past Die Cuts /1000 #CP7
1998 Maxx 10th Anniversary Maxximum Preview #P1
1998 Maxx 1997 Year In Review #23
1998 Maxx 1997 Year In Review #30
1998 Maxx 1997 Year In Review #48
1998 Maxx 1997 Year In Review #55
1998 Maxx 1997 Year In Review #95
1998 Maxx 1997 Year In Review #140
1998 Maxx 1997 Year In Review #155
1998 Maxximum #1
1998 Maxximum #26
1998 Maxximum #51
1998 Maxximum #76
1998 Maxximum Battle Proven #B1
1998 Maxximum Field Generals Four Star Autographs /1 #9
1998 Maxximum Field Generals One Star /2000 #9
1998 Maxximum Field Generals Three Star Autographs /100 #9
1998 Maxximum Field Generals Two Star /1000 #9
1998 Maxximum First Class #F19
1998 Press Pass #22
1998 Press Pass #113
1998 Press Pass Autographs /158 #13
1998 Press Pass Oil Slicks /100 #22
1998 Press Pass Pit Stop #PS8
1998 SP Authentic #17
1998 SP Authentic #51
1998 SP Authentic #69
1998 SP Authentic Sign of the Times #S7
1998 SportsCom FanScan #9
1998 Upper Deck Road To The Cup #17
1998 Upper Deck Road To The Cup 50th Anniversary #AN30
1998 Upper Deck Road To The Cup 50th Anniversary #AN35
1998 Upper Deck Road To The Cup 50th Anniversary Autographs /50 #AN35
1998 Upper Deck Road To The Cup Cover Story #CS3
1998 Upper Deck Road To The Cup Cover Story #CS16
1998 Upper Deck Victory Circle #17
1998 Upper Deck Victory Circle #62
1998 Upper Deck Victory Circle #141
1998 Upper Deck Victory Circle Piece of the Engine #PE1
1998 Upper Deck Victory Circle Piece of the Engine #PE6
1998 Wheels High Gear #23
1998 Wheels High Gear #70
1998 Wheels High Gear Autographs /250 #22
1998 Wheels High Gear First Gear #21
1998 Wheels High Gear Gear Jammers #GJ8
1998 Wheels High Gear MPH /100 #21
1998 Wheels High Gear Pure Gold #PG6
1999 Maxx #46
1999 Maxx #47
1999 Maxx #48
1999 Maxx FANtastic Finishes #F20
1999 Maxx Race Ticket #RT26
1999 Maxx Racing Images #RI1
1999 Press Pass #21
1999 Press Pass #121
1999 Press Pass Bryan #10
1999 Press Pass Signings /175 #57
1999 Press Pass Signings Gold /100 #29
1999 Press Pass Skidmarks /250 #21
1999 SP Authentic #26
1999 SP Authentic #47
1999 SP Authentic #63
1999 SP Authentic Overdrive #26
1999 SP Authentic Overdrive #47
1999 SP Authentic Overdrive #63
1999 SportsCom FanScan #9
1999 Upper Deck MVP ProSign #DWH
1999 Upper Deck MVP ProSign #DWR
1999 Upper Deck Road to the Cup #10
1999 Upper Deck Road to the Cup #35
1999 Upper Deck Road to the Cup #64
1999 Upper Deck Victory Circle #19
1999 Upper Deck Victory Circle #47
1999 Upper Deck Victory Circle Signature Collection #DW
1999 Upper Deck Victory Circle Track Masters #TM13
1999 Upper Deck Victory Circle UD Exclusives #19
1999 Upper Deck Victory Circle UD Exclusives #47
1999 Wheels #35
1999 Wheels Golden #35
1999 Wheels High Gear #57
1999 Wheels High Gear First Gear #57
1999 Wheels High Gear Gear Shifters #GS21
1999 Wheels High Gear MPH #21
1999 Wheels High Gear MPH #57
1999 Wheels Runnin and Gunnin #RG31
1999 Wheels Runnin and Gunnin Foils #RG31
1999 Wheels Solos #35
2000 Maxx #35
2000 Maxximum #30
2000 Maxximum Cruise Control #CC10
2000 Maxximum Die Cuts /250 #30
2000 Maxximum MPH /66 #30
2000 Maxximum Signatures #MD2
2000 Press Pass #27
2000 Press Pass Millennium #27
2000 Press Pass Optima #26
2000 Press Pass Optima G Force #GF26
2000 Press Pass Optima Platinum #26
2000 Press Pass Premium #24
2000 Press Pass Premium #51
2000 Press Pass Premium Reflectors #24
2000 Press Pass Premium Reflectors #51
2000 Press Pass Showcar #SC1
2000 Press Pass Showcar Die Cuts #SC1
2000 Press Pass Showman #SM1
2000 Press Pass Showman Die Cuts #SM1
2000 Press Pass Signings #61
2000 Press Pass Signings Gold /100 #32
2000 Press Pass Techno-Retro #TR26
2000 Press Pass Trackside #25
2000 Press Pass Trackside Die Cuts #25
2000 Press Pass Trackside Golden #25
2000 Press Pass Trackside Panorama #P24
2000 SP Authentic #34
2000 SP Authentic /2500 #70
2000 SP Authentic High Velocity #HV3
2000 SP Authentic Overdrive Gold /66 #34
2000 SP Authentic Overdrive Gold /66 #70
2000 SP Authentic Overdrive Silver /250 #34
2000 SP Authentic Overdrive Silver /250 #70
2000 Upper Deck MVP #35
2000 Upper Deck MVP #69

2000 Upper Deck MVP #96
2000 Upper Deck MVP Gold Script /125 #35
2000 Upper Deck MVP Gold Script /125 #69
2000 Upper Deck MVP Gold Script /125 #96
2000 Upper Deck MVP ProSign #PSDW
2000 Upper Deck MVP Silver Script #35
2000 Upper Deck MVP Silver Script #69
2000 Upper Deck MVP Silver Script #96
2000 Upper Deck MVP Super Script /66 #35
2000 Upper Deck MVP Super Script /66 #69
2000 Upper Deck MVP Super Script /66 #96
2000 Upper Deck Racing #30
2000 Upper Deck Racing Brickyard's Best #BB4
2000 Upper Deck Victory Circle #24
2000 Upper Deck Victory Circle #79
2000 Upper Deck Victory Circle Exclusives Level 1 Silver /250 #24
2000 Upper Deck Victory Circle Exclusives Level 1 Silver /250 #79
2000 Upper Deck Victory Circle Exclusives Level 2 Gold /66 #24
2000 Upper Deck Victory Circle Exclusives Level 2 Gold /66 #79
2000 Upper Deck Victory Circle Signature Collection #DW
2000 Upper Deck Victory Circle Signature Collection Gold /66 #6
2000 VIP #38
2000 VIP #47
2000 VIP Explosives #X38
2000 VIP Explosives #X47
2000 VIP Explosives Lasers #LX38
2000 VIP Explosives Lasers #LX47
2000 Wheels High Gear #26
2000 Wheels High Gear First Gear #26
2000 Wheels High Gear Gear Shifters #GS21
2000 Wheels High Gear MPH #26
2001 Press Pass #31
2001 Press Pass Excedrin Racing #3
2001 Press Pass Millennium #31
2001 Press Pass Signings #53
2001 Press Pass Signings Gold /50 #35
2001 Press Pass Signings Transparent /100 #13
2001 Super Shots Hendrick Motorsports #H3
2001 Super Shots Hendrick Motorsports #H5
2001 Super Shots Hendrick Motorsports Autographs /71 #HSA4
2001 Super Shots Hendrick Motorsports Gold /100 #HG3
2001 Super Shots Hendrick Motorsports Gold /100 #HG5
2001 Super Shots Hendrick Motorsports Silver /500 #HS3
2001 Super Shots Hendrick Motorsports Silver /500 #HS5
2001 Super Shots Hendrick Motorsports Victory Banners /775 #HRB5
2002 Press Pass Autographs #68
2002 Press Pass Signings Gold /50 #65
2002 Press Pass Vintage #VN34
2002 Wheels High Gear Autographs #57
2003 Press Pass Victory Lap #6
2004 Press Pass Trackside #79
2004 Press Pass Trackside Golden /100 #G79
2004 Press Pass Trackside Samples #79
2004 VIP #85
2004 VIP Samples #85
2004 Wheels High Gear Winston Victory Lap Tribute #WVL5
2004 Wheels High Gear Winston Victory Lap Tribute Gold #WVL5
2006 Press Pass Legends #21
2006 Press Pass Legends Autographs Black /25 #14
2006 Press Pass Legends Autographs Blue /45 #16
2006 Press Pass Legends Blue /1999 #B21
2006 Press Pass Legends Bronze /999 #Z21
2006 Press Pass Legends Gold /299 #G21
2006 Press Pass Legends Heritage Gold /99 #HE4
2006 Press Pass Legends Heritage Silver /549 #HE4
2006 Press Pass Legends Holofoil /99 #H21
2006 Press Pass Legends Press Plates Black /1 #PPB21
2006 Press Pass Legends Press Plates Black Backs /1 #PPB21B
2006 Press Pass Legends Press Plates Cyan /1 #PPC21
2006 Press Pass Legends Press Plates Cyan Backs /1 #PPC21B
2006 Press Pass Legends Press Plates Magenta /1 #PPM21
2006 Press Pass Legends Press Plates Magenta Backs /1 #PPM21B
2006 Press Pass Legends Press Plates Yellow /1 #PPY21
2006 Press Pass Legends Press Plates Yellow Backs /1 #PPY21B
2006 Press Pass Legends Previews /5 #EB21
2006 Press Pass Legends Solo /1 #S21
2007 Press Pass Dale The Movie #7
2007 Press Pass Dale The Movie #22
2007 Press Pass Legends #28
2007 Press Pass Legends #56
2007 Press Pass Legends #65
2007 Press Pass Legends #67
2007 Press Pass Legends Autographs Black /48 #13
2007 Press Pass Legends Autographs Blue /182 #25
2007 Press Pass Legends Autographs Inscriptions Blue /15 #16
2007 Press Pass Legends Blue /999 #B28
2007 Press Pass Legends Blue /999 #B56
2007 Press Pass Legends Blue /999 #B65
2007 Press Pass Legends Blue /999 #B67
2007 Press Pass Legends Bronze /599 #Z28
2007 Press Pass Legends Bronze /599 #Z56
2007 Press Pass Legends Bronze /599 #Z65
2007 Press Pass Legends Bronze /599 #Z67
2007 Press Pass Legends Gold /249 #G28
2007 Press Pass Legends Gold /249 #G56
2007 Press Pass Legends Gold /249 #G65
2007 Press Pass Legends Gold /249 #G67
2007 Press Pass Legends Holofoil /99 #H28
2007 Press Pass Legends Holofoil /99 #H56
2007 Press Pass Legends Holofoil /99 #H65
2007 Press Pass Legends Holofoil /99 #H67
2007 Press Pass Legends Memorable Moments Gold /169 #MM1
2007 Press Pass Legends Memorable Moments Gold /169 #MM9
2007 Press Pass Legends Memorable Moments Silver /499 #MM1
2007 Press Pass Legends Memorable Moments Silver /499 #MM9
2007 Press Pass Legends Press Plates Black /1 #PP28
2007 Press Pass Legends Press Plates Black /1 #PP56
2007 Press Pass Legends Press Plates Black /1 #PP65
2007 Press Pass Legends Press Plates Black /1 #PP67
2007 Press Pass Legends Press Plates Black Backs /1 #PP28
2007 Press Pass Legends Press Plates Black Backs /1 #PP56
2007 Press Pass Legends Press Plates Black Backs /1 #PP65
2007 Press Pass Legends Press Plates Black Backs /1 #PP67
2007 Press Pass Legends Press Plates Cyan /1 #PP28
2007 Press Pass Legends Press Plates Cyan /1 #PP56
2007 Press Pass Legends Press Plates Cyan /1 #PP65
2007 Press Pass Legends Press Plates Cyan /1 #PP67
2007 Press Pass Legends Press Plates Cyan Backs /1 #PP28
2007 Press Pass Legends Press Plates Cyan Backs /1 #PP56
2007 Press Pass Legends Press Plates Cyan Backs /1 #PP65
2007 Press Pass Legends Press Plates Cyan Backs /1 #PP67
2007 Press Pass Legends Press Plates Magenta /1 #PP28
2007 Press Pass Legends Press Plates Magenta /1 #PP56
2007 Press Pass Legends Press Plates Magenta /1 #PP65
2007 Press Pass Legends Press Plates Magenta /1 #PP67
2007 Press Pass Legends Press Plates Magenta Backs /1 #PP28
2007 Press Pass Legends Press Plates Magenta Backs /1 #PP56
2007 Press Pass Legends Press Plates Magenta Backs /1 #PP65
2007 Press Pass Legends Press Plates Magenta Backs /1 #PP67
2007 Press Pass Legends Press Plates Yellow /1 #PP28
2007 Press Pass Legends Press Plates Yellow /1 #PP56
2007 Press Pass Legends Press Plates Yellow /1 #PP65
2007 Press Pass Legends Press Plates Yellow /1 #PP67
2007 Press Pass Legends Press Plates Yellow Backs /1 #PP28
2007 Press Pass Legends Press Plates Yellow Backs /1 #PP56
2007 Press Pass Legends Press Plates Yellow Backs /1 #PP65
2007 Press Pass Legends Press Plates Yellow Backs /1 #PP67
2007 Press Pass Legends Previews /5 #EB28
2007 Press Pass Legends Previews /1 #EB65
2007 Press Pass Legends Previews /1 #EB67
2007 Press Pass Legends Racing Artifacts Firesuit Bronze /199 #DWF
2007 Press Pass Legends Racing Artifacts Firesuit Gold /50 #DWF
2007 Press Pass Legends Racing Artifacts Firesuit Patch /25 #DWF
2007 Press Pass Legends Racing Artifacts Firesuit Silver /99 #DWF
2007 Press Pass Legends Solo /1 #S28
2007 Press Pass Legends Solo /1 #S56
2007 Press Pass Legends Solo /1 #S65
2007 Press Pass Legends Solo /1 #S67
2007 Traks #63
2007 Traks Gold #G63
2007 Traks Holofoil /50 #H63
2007 Traks Red /10 #R63
2008 Press Pass Daytona 500 50th Anniversary #26
2008 Press Pass Legends #40
2008 Press Pass Legends Autographs Black /15 #DW
2008 Press Pass Legends Autographs Black Inscriptions /21 #DW
2008 Press Pass Legends Autographs Black Inscriptions /30 #DW
2008 Press Pass Legends Autographs Blue /36 #DW
2008 Press Pass Legends Autographs Press Plates Black /1 #DW
2008 Press Pass Legends Autographs Press Plates Cyan /1 #DW
2008 Press Pass Legends Autographs Press Plates Magenta /1 #DW
2008 Press Pass Legends Autographs Press Plates Yellow /1 #DW
2008 Press Pass Legends Blue /599 #40
2008 Press Pass Legends Bronze /299 #40
2008 Press Pass Legends Gold /99 #40
2008 Press Pass Legends Holo /25 #40
2008 Press Pass Legends Previews /5 #EB40
2008 Press Pass Legends Printing Plates Black /1 #40
2008 Press Pass Legends Printing Plates Cyan /1 #40
2008 Press Pass Legends Printing Plates Magenta /1 #40
2008 Press Pass Legends Printing Plates Yellow /1 #40
2008 Press Pass Legends Racing Artifacts Firesuit Bronze /180 #DWF
2008 Press Pass Legends Racing Artifacts Firesuit Gold /25 #DWF
2008 Press Pass Legends Racing Artifacts Firesuit Patch /10 #DWF
2008 Press Pass Legends Racing Artifacts Firesuit Silver /50 #DWF
2008 Press Pass Legends Solo /1 #40
2009 Press Pass Legends #35
2009 Press Pass Legends #65
2009 Press Pass Legends Artifacts Autographs /10 #SEDW
2009 Press Pass Legends Artifacts Firesuits Bronze /250 #DWF
2009 Press Pass Legends Artifacts Firesuits Gold /25 #DWF
2009 Press Pass Legends Artifacts Firesuits Silver /50 #DWF
2009 Press Pass Legends Artifacts Sheet Metal Bronze /199 #DWS
2009 Press Pass Legends Artifacts Sheet Metal Gold /25 #DWS
2009 Press Pass Legends Artifacts Sheet Metal Silver /50 #DWS
2009 Press Pass Legends Autographs #20
2009 Press Pass Legends Autographs Gold /105 #37
2009 Press Pass Legends Autographs Holofoil /30 #32
2009 Press Pass Legends Autographs Inscriptions /1 #17
2009 Press Pass Legends Autographs Inscriptions /5 #16
2009 Press Pass Legends Autographs Inscriptions /5 #15
2009 Press Pass Legends Autographs Inscriptions /50 #14
2009 Press Pass Legends Autographs Printing Plates Black /1 #30
2009 Press Pass Legends Autographs Printing Plates Cyan /1 #29
2009 Press Pass Legends Autographs Printing Plates Magenta /1 #30
2009 Press Pass Legends Autographs Printing Plates Yellow /1 #30
2009 Press Pass Legends Family Autographs /25 #8
2009 Press Pass Legends Family Portraits /550 #FP25
2009 Press Pass Legends Family Portraits Holofoil /99 #FP25
2009 Press Pass Legends Family Relics Bronze /99 #FRWa
2009 Press Pass Legends Family Relics Bronze /75 #FRWa2
2009 Press Pass Legends Family Relics Gold /25 #FRWa
2009 Press Pass Legends Family Relics Gold /25 #FRWa2
2009 Press Pass Legends Family Relics Silver /50 #FRWa
2009 Press Pass Legends Family Relics Silver /50 #FRWa2
2009 Press Pass Legends Gold /399 #35
2009 Press Pass Legends Gold /399 #65
2009 Press Pass Legends Holofoil /50 #35
2009 Press Pass Legends Holofoil /50 #65
2009 Press Pass Legends Past and Present /550 #PP7
2009 Press Pass Legends Past and Present Holofoil /99 #PP7
2009 Press Pass Legends Previews /5 #35
2009 Press Pass Legends Previews /1 #65
2009 Press Pass Legends Printing Plates Black /1 #35
2009 Press Pass Legends Printing Plates Black /1 #65
2009 Press Pass Legends Printing Plates Cyan /1 #35
2009 Press Pass Legends Printing Plates Cyan /1 #65
2009 Press Pass Legends Printing Plates Magenta /1 #35
2009 Press Pass Legends Printing Plates Magenta /1 #65
2009 Press Pass Legends Printing Plates Yellow /1 #35
2009 Press Pass Legends Printing Plates Yellow /1 #65
2009 Press Pass Legends Red /199 #35
2009 Press Pass Legends Red /199 #65
2009 Press Pass Legends Rivalries Autographs /10 #2
2009 Press Pass Legends Solo /1 #35
2009 Press Pass Legends Solo /1 #65
2009 Press Pass Showcase Elite Exhibit Ink /45 #12
2009 Press Pass Showcase Elite Exhibit Ink Gold /25 #12
2009 Press Pass Showcase Elite Exhibit Ink Green /5 #12
2009 Press Pass Showcase Elite Exhibit Ink Melting /1 #12
2009 Press Pass Showcase Prized Pieces Ink Firesuit /5 #11
2009 Press Pass Showcase Prized Pieces Ink Firesuit Patch /1 #11
2009 VIP #70
2009 VIP Previews /1 #70
2009 VIP Purple /25 #70
2010 Press Pass By The Numbers #BN17
2010 Press Pass By The Numbers #BN29
2010 Press Pass Five Star Classic Compilations Combos Firesuit Autographs /15 #CCMLEG
2010 Press Pass Five Star Classic Compilations Combos Patches Autographs /1 #CCMLEG
2010 Press Pass Legends #34
2010 Press Pass Legends #60
2010 Press Pass Legends #64
2010 Press Pass Legends #74
2010 Press Pass Legends 50 Win Club Memorabilia Gold /75 #50DW
2010 Press Pass Legends 50 Win Club Memorabilia Holofoil /25 #50DW
2010 Press Pass Legends Autographs Blue /10 #52
2010 Press Pass Legends Autographs Copper /125 #33
2010 Press Pass Legends Autographs Gold /50 #35
2010 Press Pass Legends Autographs Holofoil /24 #52
2010 Press Pass Legends Autographs Printing Plates Black /1 #42
2010 Press Pass Legends Autographs Printing Plates Cyan /1 #42
2010 Press Pass Legends Autographs Printing Plates Magenta /1 #42
2010 Press Pass Legends Autographs Printing Plates Yellow /1 #42
2010 Press Pass Legends Blue /1 #34
2010 Press Pass Legends Blue /1 #60
2010 Press Pass Legends Blue /1 #64
2010 Press Pass Legends Blue /1 #74
2010 Press Pass Legends Family Autographs /25 #8
2010 Press Pass Legends Gold /399 #34
2010 Press Pass Legends Gold /399 #60
2010 Press Pass Legends Gold /399 #64
2010 Press Pass Legends Gold /399 #74
2010 Press Pass Legends Holofoil /50 #34
2010 Press Pass Legends Holofoil /50 #60
2010 Press Pass Legends Holofoil /50 #64
2010 Press Pass Legends Holofoil /50 #74
2010 Press Pass Legends Lasting Legacies Autographs /25 #LLDW
2010 Press Pass Legends Lasting Legacies Copper /175 #LLDW
2010 Press Pass Legends Lasting Legacies Gold /75 #LLDW1
2010 Press Pass Legends Lasting Legacies Gold /75 #LLDW2
2010 Press Pass Legends Lasting Legacies Holofoil /25 #LLDW1
2010 Press Pass Legends Lasting Legacies Holofoil /25 #LLDW2
2010 Press Pass Legends Legendary Links Gold /75 #LXBEDW
2010 Press Pass Legends Legendary Links Holofoil /25 #LXBEDW
2010 Press Pass Legends Make and Model Blue /99 #7
2010 Press Pass Legends Make and Model Gold /299 #7
2010 Press Pass Legends Make and Model Holofoil /199 #7
2010 Press Pass Legends Memorable Matchups /25 #MMDWBA
2010 Press Pass Legends Memorable Matchups /25 #MMRWDW
2010 Press Pass Legends Memorable Matchups Autographs /25 #NNO
2010 Press Pass Legends Memorable Matchups Autographs /25 #NNO
2010 Press Pass Legends Motorsports Masters #MMDW
2010 Press Pass Legends Motorsports Masters Autographs Blue /1 #NNO
2010 Press Pass Legends Motorsports Masters Autographs Gold /50 #29
2010 Press Pass Legends Motorsports Masters Autographs Holofoil /24 #29
2010 Press Pass Legends Motorsports Masters Autographs Printing Plates Black /1 #42
2010 Press Pass Legends Motorsports Masters Autographs Printing Plates Cyan /1 #42
2010 Press Pass Legends Motorsports Masters Autographs Printing Plates Magenta /1 #42
2010 Press Pass Legends Motorsports Masters Autographs Printing Plates Yellow /1 #42
2010 Press Pass Legends Motorsports Masters Autographs Silver /99 #23
2010 Press Pass Legends Motorsports Masters Blue /10 #MMDW
2010 Press Pass Legends Motorsports Masters Gold /299 #MMDW
2010 Press Pass Legends Motorsports Masters Holofoil /149 #MMDW
2010 Press Pass Legends Printing Plates Black /1 #34
2010 Press Pass Legends Printing Plates Black /1 #60
2010 Press Pass Legends Printing Plates Black /1 #64
2010 Press Pass Legends Printing Plates Black /1 #74
2010 Press Pass Legends Printing Plates Cyan /1 #34
2010 Press Pass Legends Printing Plates Cyan /1 #60
2010 Press Pass Legends Printing Plates Cyan /1 #64
2010 Press Pass Legends Printing Plates Cyan /1 #74
2010 Press Pass Legends Printing Plates Magenta /1 #34
2010 Press Pass Legends Printing Plates Magenta /1 #60
2010 Press Pass Legends Printing Plates Magenta /1 #64
2010 Press Pass Legends Printing Plates Magenta /1 #74
2010 Press Pass Legends Printing Plates Yellow /1 #34
2010 Press Pass Legends Printing Plates Yellow /1 #60
2010 Press Pass Legends Printing Plates Yellow /1 #64
2010 Press Pass Legends Printing Plates Yellow /1 #74
2010 Press Pass Legends Red /199 #34
2010 Press Pass Legends Red /199 #60
2010 Press Pass Legends Red /199 #64
2010 Press Pass Legends Red /199 #74
2010 Press Pass NASCAR Hall of Fame #NHOF25
2010 Press Pass NASCAR Hall of Fame #NHOF44
2010 Press Pass NASCAR Hall of Fame Blue #NHOF25
2010 Press Pass NASCAR Hall of Fame Blue #NHOF44
2010 Press Pass NASCAR Hall of Fame Holofoil /50 #NHOF25
2010 Press Pass NASCAR Hall of Fame Holofoil /50 #NHOF44
2010 Press Pass Premium Signature Series Firesuit /10 #SSFDW
2010 Press Pass Showcase /499 #29
2010 Press Pass Showcase Classic Collections Firesuit Green /25 #CCI500
2010 Press Pass Showcase Classic Collections Firesuit Patch Melting /5 #CCI500
2010 Press Pass Showcase Classic Collections Ink /15 #CCI500
2010 Press Pass Showcase Classic Collections Ink Gold /10 #CCI500
2010 Press Pass Showcase Classic Collections Ink Green /5 #CCI500
2010 Press Pass Showcase Classic Collections Ink Melting /1 #CCI500
2010 Press Pass Showcase Gold /125 #29
2010 Press Pass Showcase Green /50 #29
2010 Press Pass Showcase Melting /15 #29
2010 Press Pass Showcase Platinum Holo /1 #29
2010 Press Pass Showcase Prized Pieces Firesuit Ink Gold /25 #PPIDW
2010 Press Pass Showcase Prized Pieces Firesuit Ink Melting /1 #PPIDW
2010 Press Pass Showcase Prized Pieces Memorabilia Ink Green /15 #PPIDW
2010 Press Pass Showcase Prized Pieces Sheet Metal Ink Silver /45 #PPIDW
2010 Press Pass Showcase Racing's Finest /499 #RF7
2010 Press Pass Showcase Racing's Finest Gold /125 #RF7
2010 Press Pass Showcase Racing's Finest Green /50 #RF7
2010 Press Pass Showcase Racing's Finest Ink /15 #RFIDW
2010 Press Pass Showcase Racing's Finest Ink Gold /10 #RFIDW
2010 Press Pass Showcase Racing's Finest Ink Green /5 #RFIDW
2010 Press Pass Showcase Racing's Finest Ink Melting /1 #RFIDW
2010 Press Pass Showcase Racing's Finest Melting /15 #RF7
2011 Press Pass FanFare #94
2011 Press Pass FanFare Blue Die Cuts #94
2011 Press Pass FanFare Championship Caliber #CC13
2011 Press Pass FanFare Emerald /25 #94
2011 Press Pass FanFare Holofoil Die Cuts #94
2011 Press Pass FanFare Ruby Die Cuts /15 #94
2011 Press Pass FanFare Sapphire /10 #94
2011 Press Pass FanFare Silver /25 #94
2011 Press Pass Legends #35
2011 Press Pass Legends #62
2011 Press Pass Legends #78
2011 Press Pass Legends Autographs Blue /10 #LGADW
2011 Press Pass Legends Autographs Blue /5 #LGADW2
2011 Press Pass Legends Autographs Gold /50 #LGADW
2011 Press Pass Legends Autographs Gold /25 #LGADW2
2011 Press Pass Legends Autographs Printing Plates Black /1 #LGADW
2011 Press Pass Legends Autographs Printing Plates Black /1 #LGADW2
2011 Press Pass Legends Autographs Printing Plates Cyan /1 #LGADW
2011 Press Pass Legends Autographs Printing Plates Cyan /1 #LGADW2
2011 Press Pass Legends Autographs Printing Plates Magenta /1 #LGADW
2011 Press Pass Legends Autographs Printing Plates Magenta /1 #LGADW2
2011 Press Pass Legends Autographs Printing Plates Yellow /1 #LGADW
2011 Press Pass Legends Autographs Printing Plates Yellow /1 #LGADW2
2011 Press Pass Legends Autographs Silver /99 #LGADW
2011 Press Pass Legends Autographs Silver /50 #LGADW2
2011 Press Pass Legends Famed Fabrics Gold /50 #HOFDW
2011 Press Pass Legends Famed Fabrics Holofoil /25 #HOFDW
2011 Press Pass Legends Famed Fabrics Purple /15 #HOFDW
2011 Press Pass Legends Gold /250 #35
2011 Press Pass Legends Gold /250 #62
2011 Press Pass Legends Gold /250 #78
2011 Press Pass Legends Holofoil /25 #35
2011 Press Pass Legends Holofoil /25 #62
2011 Press Pass Legends Holofoil /25 #78
2011 Press Pass Legends Lasting Legacies Autographs /25 #LLSEDW
2011 Press Pass Legends Lasting Legacies Memorabilia Gold /50 #LLDW
2011 Press Pass Legends Lasting Legacies Memorabilia Holofoil /25 #LLDW
2011 Press Pass Legends Lasting Legacies Memorabilia Purple /15 #LLDW
2011 Press Pass Legends Lasting Legacies Memorabilia Silver /175 #LLDW
2011 Press Pass Legends Motorsports Masters #MM16
2011 Press Pass Legends Motorsports Masters Autographs Blue /1 #MMAEDW
2011 Press Pass Legends Motorsports Masters Autographs Gold /25 #MMAEDW
2011 Press Pass Legends Motorsports Masters Autographs Printing Plates Black /1 #MMAEDW
2011 Press Pass Legends Motorsports Masters Autographs Printing Plates Cyan /1 #MMAEDW
2011 Press Pass Legends Motorsports Masters Autographs Printing Plates Magenta /1 #MMAEDW
2011 Press Pass Legends Motorsports Masters Autographs Printing Plates Yellow /1 #MMAEDW
2011 Press Pass Legends Motorsports Masters Autographs Silver /50 #MMAEDW
2011 Press Pass Legends Motorsports Masters Brushed Foil /199 #MM16
2011 Press Pass Legends Motorsports Masters Holofoil /50 #MM16
2011 Press Pass Legends Printing Plates Black /1 #35
2011 Press Pass Legends Printing Plates Black /1 #62
2011 Press Pass Legends Printing Plates Black /1 #78
2011 Press Pass Legends Printing Plates Cyan /1 #35
2011 Press Pass Legends Printing Plates Cyan /1 #62
2011 Press Pass Legends Printing Plates Cyan /1 #78
2011 Press Pass Legends Printing Plates Magenta /1 #35
2011 Press Pass Legends Printing Plates Magenta /1 #62
2011 Press Pass Legends Printing Plates Magenta /1 #78
2011 Press Pass Legends Printing Plates Yellow /1 #35
2011 Press Pass Legends Printing Plates Yellow /1 #62
2011 Press Pass Legends Printing Plates Yellow /1 #78
2011 Press Pass Legends Purple /25 #35
2011 Press Pass Legends Purple /25 #62
2011 Press Pass Legends Purple /25 #78
2011 Press Pass Legends Red /99 #35
2011 Press Pass Legends Red /99 #62
2011 Press Pass Legends Red /99 #78
2011 Press Pass Legends Solo /1 #35
2011 Press Pass Legends Solo /1 #62
2011 Press Pass Legends Solo /1 #78
2011 Press Pass Legends Trophy Room Gold /50 #TRDW
2011 Press Pass Legends Trophy Room Holofoil /25 #TRDW
2011 Press Pass Legends Trophy Room Purple /15 #TRDW
2011 Press Pass Winning Tickets #WT54
2012 Historic Autographs Peerless /4 #174
2012 Press Pass Fanfare #98
2012 Press Pass Fanfare Blue Foil Die Cuts #98
2012 Press Pass Fanfare Diamond /5 #98
2012 Press Pass Fanfare Holofoil Die Cuts #98
2012 Press Pass Fanfare Sapphire /20 #98
2012 Press Pass Fanfare Silver /25 #98
2012 Press Pass Legends #35
2012 Press Pass Legends Autographs Blue /1 #DW
2012 Press Pass Legends Autographs Gold /25 #DW
2012 Press Pass Legends Autographs Holofoil /5 #DW
2012 Press Pass Legends Autographs Printing Plates Black /1 #DW
2012 Press Pass Legends Autographs Printing Plates Cyan /1 #DW
2012 Press Pass Legends Autographs Printing Plates Magenta /1 #DW
2012 Press Pass Legends Autographs Printing Plates Yellow /1 #DW
2012 Press Pass Legends Autographs Silver /50 #DW
2012 Press Pass Legends Blue Holofoil /1 #35
2012 Press Pass Legends Gold /275 #35
2012 Press Pass Legends Green #35
2012 Press Pass Legends Memorable Moments #MM2
2012 Press Pass Legends Memorable Moments Holofoil /99 #MM2
2012 Press Pass Legends Memorable Moments Melting /10 #MM2
2012 Press Pass Legends Pieces of History Memorabilia Autographs Gold /25 #PHSDW
2012 Press Pass Legends Pieces of History Memorabilia Autographs Melting /5 #PHSDW
2012 Press Pass Legends Pieces of History Memorabilia Gold /50 #DW2
2012 Press Pass Legends Pieces of History Memorabilia Gold /99 #DW1
2012 Press Pass Legends Pieces of History Memorabilia Holofoil /25 #DW2
2012 Press Pass Legends Pieces of History Memorabilia Holofoil /25 #DW1
2012 Press Pass Legends Pieces of History Memorabilia Silver /99 #DW2
2012 Press Pass Legends Pieces of History Memorabilia Silver /199 #DW1
2012 Press Pass Legends Rainbow Holofoil /50 #35
2012 Press Pass Legends Red /99 #35
2012 Press Pass Legends Silver Holofoil /25 #35
2012 Press Pass Legends Trailblazers #TB2
2012 Press Pass Legends Trailblazers Autographs Blue /1 #TBDW
2012 Press Pass Legends Trailblazers Autographs Gold /5 #TBDW
2012 Press Pass Legends Trailblazers Autographs Holofoil /1 #TBDW
2012 Press Pass Legends Trailblazers Autographs Printing Plates Black /1 #TBDW
2012 Press Pass Legends Trailblazers Autographs Printing Plates Cyan /1 #TBDW
2012 Press Pass Legends Trailblazers Autographs Printing Plates Magenta /1 #TBDW
2012 Press Pass Legends Trailblazers Autographs Printing Plates Yellow /1 #TBDW
2012 Press Pass Legends Trailblazers Autographs Silver /5 #TBDW
2012 Press Pass Legends Trailblazers Holofoil /99 #TB2
2012 Press Pass Legends Trailblazers Melting /10 #TB2
2012 Press Pass NASCAR Hall of Fame #NHOF131
2012 Press Pass NASCAR Hall of Fame #NHOF132
2012 Press Pass NASCAR Hall of Fame #NHOF133
2012 Press Pass NASCAR Hall of Fame #NHOF134
2012 Press Pass NASCAR Hall of Fame #NHOF135
2012 Press Pass NASCAR Hall of Fame Blue #NHOF131
2012 Press Pass NASCAR Hall of Fame Blue #NHOF132
2012 Press Pass NASCAR Hall of Fame Blue #NHOF133
2012 Press Pass NASCAR Hall of Fame Blue #NHOF134
2012 Press Pass NASCAR Hall of Fame Blue #NHOF135
2012 Press Pass NASCAR Hall of Fame Holofoil /50 #NHOF131
2012 Press Pass NASCAR Hall of Fame Holofoil /50 #NHOF132
2012 Press Pass NASCAR Hall of Fame Holofoil /50 #NHOF133
2012 Press Pass NASCAR Hall of Fame Holofoil /50 #NHOF134
2012 Press Pass NASCAR Hall of Fame Holofoil /50 #NHOF135
2012 Press Pass Power Picks Blue /50 #21
2012 Press Pass Power Picks Gold /50 #21
2012 Press Pass Power Picks Holofoil /10 #21
2012 Press Pass Redline Hall of Fame Relic Autographs Blue /5 #HOFDW
2012 Press Pass Redline Hall of Fame Relic Autographs Gold /25 #HOFDW
2012 Press Pass Redline Hall of Fame Relic Autographs Melting /1 #HOFDW
2012 Press Pass Redline Hall of Fame Relic Autographs Red /50 #HOFDW
2012 Press Pass Showcase /499 #32
2012 Press Pass Showcase Champions Showcase /499 #CH7
2012 Press Pass Showcase Champions Showcase Gold /125 #CH7
2012 Press Pass Showcase Champions Showcase Melting /1 #CH7
2012 Press Pass Showcase Gold /125 #32
2012 Press Pass Showcase Green /5 #32
2012 Press Pass Showcase Melting /1 #32
2012 Press Pass Showcase Purple /1 #32
2012 Press Pass Showcase Red /25 #32
2012 Press Pass Showcase Richard Petty 75th Birthday Tribute /10 #RPDW
2012 Press Pass Showcase Richard Petty 75th Birthday Tribute Melting /1 #RPDW
2012 Press Pass Snapshots #SS36
2013 Panini Golden Age #122
2013 Panini Golden Age Black /1 #122
2013 Panini Golden Age Delong Gum #9
2013 Panini Golden Age Historic Signatures #DW
2013 Panini Golden Age Mini American Caramel Blue Back #122
2013 Panini Golden Age Mini American Caramel Red Back #122
2013 Panini Golden Age Mini Carolina Brights Green Back #122
2013 Panini Golden Age Mini Carolina Brights Purple Back #122
2013 Panini Golden Age Mini Nadja Caramels Back #122
2013 Panini Golden Age Mini Panini Logo Black Back /1 #122
2013 Panini Golden Age National Convention /5 #122
2013 Panini Golden Age White #122
2013 Press Pass Fanfare #93
2013 Press Pass Fanfare Diamond Die Cuts /5 #93
2013 Press Pass Fanfare Green /3 #93
2013 Press Pass Fanfare Holofoil Die Cuts #93
2013 Press Pass Fanfare Red Foil Die Cuts #93
2013 Press Pass Fanfare Sapphire /20 #93
2013 Press Pass Fanfare Silver /25 #93
2013 Press Pass Legends #38
2013 Press Pass Legends Autographs Blue #LGDW
2013 Press Pass Legends Autographs Gold /10 #LGDW
2013 Press Pass Legends Autographs Holofoil #LGDW
2013 Press Pass Legends Autographs Printing Plates Black /1 #LGDW
2013 Press Pass Legends Autographs Printing Plates Cyan /1 #LGDW
2013 Press Pass Legends Autographs Printing Plates Magenta /1 #LGDW
2013 Press Pass Legends Autographs Printing Plates Yellow /1 #LGDW
2013 Press Pass Legends Autographs Silver /50 #LGDW
2013 Press Pass Legends Blue #38
2013 Press Pass Legends Blue Holofoil /1 #38
2013 Press Pass Legends Gold /149 #38
2013 Press Pass Legends Holofoil /10 #38
2013 Press Pass Legends Pieces of History Memorabilia Autographs Gold /25 #PHSEDW
2013 Press Pass Legends Pieces of History Memorabilia Autographs Melting /5 #PHSEDW
2013 Press Pass Legends Pieces of History Memorabilia Gold /50 #PHDW
2013 Press Pass Legends Pieces of History Memorabilia Holofoil /25 #PHDW
2013 Press Pass Legends Pieces of History Memorabilia Silver /75 #PHDW
2013 Press Pass Legends Printing Plates Black /1 #38
2013 Press Pass Legends Printing Plates Cyan /1 #38
2013 Press Pass Legends Printing Plates Magenta /1 #38
2013 Press Pass Legends Printing Plates Yellow /1 #38
2013 Press Pass Legends Red /99 #38
2013 Press Pass Legends Signature Style #SS8
2013 Press Pass Legends Signature Style Autographs Blue /1 #SSDW
2013 Press Pass Legends Signature Style Autographs Gold /10 #SSDW
2013 Press Pass Legends Signature Style Autographs Holofoil /5 #SSDW
2013 Press Pass Legends Signature Style Autographs Printing Plates Black /1 #SSDW
2013 Press Pass Legends Signature Style Autographs Printing Plates Cyan /1 #SSDW
2013 Press Pass Legends Signature Style Autographs Printing Plates Magenta /1 #SSDW
2013 Press Pass Legends Signature Style Autographs Printing Plates Yellow /1 #SSDW
2013 Press Pass Legends Signature Style Autographs Silver /25 #SSDW
2013 Press Pass Legends Signature Style Blue /5 #SS8
2013 Press Pass Legends Signature Style Holofoil /99 #SS8
2013 Press Pass Legends Signature Style Melting /10 #SS8
2013 Press Pass Redline Career Wins Relic Autographs Blue /5 #CWDW
2013 Press Pass Redline Career Wins Relic Autographs Gold /17 #CWDW
2013 Press Pass Redline Career Wins Relic Autographs Melting /1 #CWDW
2013 Press Pass Redline Career Wins Relic Autographs Red /25 #CWDW
2013 Press Pass Redline Remarkable Relic Autographs Blue /5 #RMRDW
2013 Press Pass Redline Remarkable Relic Autographs Gold /11 #RMRDW
2013 Press Pass Redline Remarkable Relic Autographs Melting /1 #RMRDW
2013 Press Pass Redline Remarkable Relic Autographs Red /25 #RMRDW
2014 Press Pass Five Star /15 #25
2014 Press Pass Five Star Blue /5 #25
2014 Press Pass Five Star Holofoil /10 #25
2014 Press Pass Five Star Melting /1 #25
2014 Press Pass Five Star Signatures Blue /5 #FSSDW
2014 Press Pass Five Star Signatures Holofoil /10 #FSSDW
2014 Press Pass Five Star Signatures Melting /1 #FSSDW
2014 Press Pass Redline #80
2014 Press Pass Redline Black /75 #80
2014 Press Pass Redline Blue Foil #80
2014 Press Pass Redline Cyan /50 #80
2014 Press Pass Redline Green National Convention /5 #80
2014 Press Pass Redline Magenta /10 #80
2014 Press Pass Redline Remarkable Relic Autographs Blue /10 #RMRDW
2014 Press Pass Redline Remarkable Relic Autographs Gold /25 #RMRDW
2014 Press Pass Redline Remarkable Relic Autographs Melting /1 #RMRDW
2014 Press Pass Redline Remarkable Relic Autographs Red /50 #RMRDW
2014 Press Pass Redline Signatures Blue /10 #RSDW
2014 Press Pass Redline Signatures Gold /15 #RSDW
2014 Press Pass Redline Signatures Melting /1 #RSDW
2014 Press Pass Redline Signatures Red /25 #RSDW
2014 Press Pass Redline Yellow /1 #80
2014 Total Memorabilia Hall of Fame Plaques #HI12
2016 Certified #66
2016 Certified Famed Rides /199 #9
2016 Certified Famed Rides Mirror Black /1 #9
2016 Certified Famed Rides Mirror Blue /50 #9
2016 Certified Famed Rides Mirror Gold /25 #9
2016 Certified Famed Rides Mirror Green /5 #9
2016 Certified Famed Rides Mirror Orange /99 #9
2016 Certified Famed Rides Mirror Purple /10 #9
2016 Certified Famed Rides Mirror Red /75 #9
2016 Certified Famed Rides Mirror Silver /99 #9
2016 Certified Gold Team /199 #16
2016 Certified Gold Team Mirror Black /1 #16
2016 Certified Gold Team Mirror Blue /50 #16
2016 Certified Gold Team Mirror Gold /25 #16
2016 Certified Gold Team Mirror Green /5 #16
2016 Certified Gold Team Mirror Orange /99 #16
2016 Certified Gold Team Mirror Purple /10 #16
2016 Certified Gold Team Mirror Red /75 #16
2016 Certified Gold Team Mirror Silver /99 #16
2016 Certified Gold Team Signatures /49 #8
2016 Certified Gold Team Signatures Mirror Black /1 #8
2016 Certified Gold Team Signatures Mirror Gold /25 #8
2016 Certified Legends /199 #11
2016 Certified Legends Mirror Black /1 #11
2016 Certified Legends Mirror Blue /50 #11
2016 Certified Legends Mirror Gold /25 #11
2016 Certified Legends Mirror Green /5 #11
2016 Certified Legends Mirror Orange /99 #11
2016 Certified Legends Mirror Purple /10 #11
2016 Certified Legends Mirror Red /75 #11
2016 Certified Legends Mirror Silver /99 #11
2016 Certified Mirror Black /1 #66
2016 Certified Mirror Blue /50 #66
2016 Certified Mirror Gold /25 #66
2016 Certified Mirror Green /5 #66
2016 Certified Mirror Orange /99 #66
2016 Certified Mirror Purple /10 #66
2016 Certified Mirror Red /75 #66
2016 Certified Mirror Silver /99 #66
2016 Certified Signatures /29 #25
2016 Certified Signatures Mirror Black /1 #25
2016 Certified Signatures Mirror Blue /20 #25
2016 Certified Signatures Mirror Gold /15 #25
2016 Certified Signatures Mirror Green /5 #25
2016 Certified Signatures Mirror Orange /10 #25
2016 Certified Signatures Mirror Purple /10 #25
2016 Certified Signatures Mirror Red /25 #25
2016 Certified Signatures Mirror Silver /10 #25
2016 Panini National Treasures /25 #40
2016 Panini National Treasures Black /5 #40
2016 Panini National Treasures Blue /1 #40
2016 Panini National Treasures Championship Signatures /25 #2
2016 Panini National Treasures Championship Signatures Black /5 #2
2016 Panini National Treasures Championship Signatures Blue /1 #2
2016 Panini National Treasures Championship Signatures Gold /10 #2
2016 Panini National Treasures Championship Signatures Printing Plates Black /1 #2
2016 Panini National Treasures Championship Signatures Printing Plates Cyan /1 #2
2016 Panini National Treasures Championship Signatures Printing Plates Magenta /1 #2
2016 Panini National Treasures Championship Signatures Printing Plates Yellow /1 #2
2016 Panini National Treasures Championship Signatures Silver /20 #2
2016 Panini National Treasures Dual Signatures /25 #22
2016 Panini National Treasures Dual Signatures /25 #26
2016 Panini National Treasures Dual Signatures Black /10 #22
2016 Panini National Treasures Dual Signatures Black /10 #26
2016 Panini National Treasures Dual Signatures Blue /1 #22
2016 Panini National Treasures Dual Signatures Blue /1 #26
2016 Panini National Treasures Dual Signatures Gold /15 #22
2016 Panini National Treasures Dual Signatures Gold /15 #26
2016 Panini National Treasures Eight Signatures /15 #3
2016 Panini National Treasures Eight Signatures Black /5 #3
2016 Panini National Treasures Eight Signatures Blue /1 #3
2016 Panini National Treasures Eight Signatures Gold /10 #3
2016 Panini National Treasures Gold /15 #40
2016 Panini National Treasures Printing Plates Black /1 #40
2016 Panini National Treasures Printing Plates Cyan /1 #40
2016 Panini National Treasures Printing Plates Magenta /1 #40
2016 Panini National Treasures Printing Plates Yellow /1 #40
2016 Panini National Treasures Silver /20 #40
2016 Panini National Treasures Six Signatures /25 #4
2016 Panini National Treasures Six Signatures /25 #5
2016 Panini National Treasures Six Signatures Black /10 #4
2016 Panini National Treasures Six Signatures Black /10 #5
2016 Panini National Treasures Six Signatures Blue /1 #4
2016 Panini National Treasures Six Signatures Blue /1 #5
2016 Panini National Treasures Six Signatures Gold /15 #4
2016 Panini National Treasures Six Signatures Gold /15 #5
2016 Panini Prizm #93
2016 Panini Prizm #17B
2016 Panini Prizm Champions #4
2016 Panini Prizm Champions Prizms #4
2016 Panini Prizm Champions Prizms Checkered Flag /1 #4
2016 Panini Prizm Champions Prizms Gold /10 #4
2016 Panini Prizm Patented Penmanship Prizms #13
2016 Panini Prizm Patented Penmanship Prizms Black /3 #13
2016 Panini Prizm Patented Penmanship Prizms Blue Flag /50 #13
2016 Panini Prizm Patented Penmanship Prizms Camo /17 #13
2016 Panini Prizm Patented Penmanship Prizms Checkered Flag /1 #13
2016 Panini Prizm Patented Penmanship Prizms Gold /10 #13
2016 Panini Prizm Patented Penmanship Prizms Green Flag /75 #13
2016 Panini Prizm Patented Penmanship Prizms Rainbow /24 #13
2016 Panini Prizm Patented Penmanship Prizms Red Flag /25 #13
2016 Panini Prizm Patented Penmanship Prizms Red White and Blue /25 #13
2016 Panini Prizm Patented Penmanship Prizms White Flag /5 #13
2016 Panini Prizm Prizms #93
2016 Panini Prizm Prizms #17B
2016 Panini Prizm Prizms Black /3 #93
2016 Panini Prizm Prizms Blue Flag /99 #93
2016 Panini Prizm Prizms Camo /88 #93
2016 Panini Prizm Prizms Checkered Flag /1 #93
2016 Panini Prizm Prizms Checkered Flag /1 #17B
2016 Panini Prizm Prizms Gold /10 #93
2016 Panini Prizm Prizms Gold /10 #17B
2016 Panini Prizm Prizms Green Flag /149 #93
2016 Panini Prizm Prizms Rainbow /24 #93
2016 Panini Prizm Prizms Red Flag /75 #93
2016 Panini Prizm Prizms Red White and Blue #93
2016 Panini Prizm Prizms White Flag /5 #93
2016 Panini Torque #94
2016 Panini Torque Artist Proof /50 #94
2016 Panini Torque Blackout /1 #94
2016 Panini Torque Blue /125 #94
2016 Panini Torque Clear Vision #34
2016 Panini Torque Clear Vision Blue /99 #34
2016 Panini Torque Clear Vision Gold /149 #34
2016 Panini Torque Clear Vision Green /25 #34
2016 Panini Torque Clear Vision Purple /10 #34
2016 Panini Torque Clear Vision Red /49 #34
2016 Panini Torque Gold #94
2016 Panini Torque Holo Gold /5 #94
2016 Panini Torque Holo Silver /10 #94
2016 Panini Torque Legends Autographs #4
2016 Panini Torque Legends Autographs Blue /50 #4
2016 Panini Torque Legends Autographs Checkerboard /10 #4
2016 Panini Torque Legends Autographs Green /15 #4
2016 Panini Torque Legends Autographs Red /25 #4
2016 Panini Torque Nicknames #7
2016 Panini Torque Nicknames Gold /199 #7
2016 Panini Torque Nicknames Holo Silver /99 #7
2016 Panini Torque Printing Plates Black /1 #94
2016 Panini Torque Printing Plates Cyan /1 #94
2016 Panini Torque Printing Plates Magenta /1 #94
2016 Panini Torque Printing Plates Yellow /1 #94
2016 Panini Torque Purple /25 #94
2016 Panini Torque Race Kings #7
2016 Panini Torque Race Kings Gold /199 #7
2016 Panini Torque Race Kings Holo Silver /99 #7
2016 Panini Torque Red /99 #94
2016 Panini Torque Superstar Vision #22
2016 Panini Torque Superstar Vision Blue /99 #22
2016 Panini Torque Superstar Vision Gold /149 #22
2016 Panini Torque Superstar Vision Green /25 #22
2016 Panini Torque Superstar Vision Purple /10 #22
2016 Panini Torque Superstar Vision Red /49 #22
2016 Panini Torque Test Proof Black /1 #94
2016 Panini Torque Test Proof Cyan /1 #94
2016 Panini Torque Test Proof Magenta /1 #94
2016 Panini Torque Test Proof Yellow /1 #94
2017 Donruss #165
2017 Donruss Artist Proof /25 #165
2017 Donruss Blue Foil /299 #165
2017 Donruss Classics #12
2017 Donruss Classics Cracked Ice /999 #12
2017 Donruss Elite Series /999 #3
2017 Donruss Gold Foil /499 #165
2017 Donruss Gold Press Proof /99 #165
2017 Donruss Green Foil /199 #165
2017 Donruss Press Proof /49 #165
2017 Donruss Printing Plates Black /1 #165
2017 Donruss Printing Plates Cyan /1 #165
2017 Donruss Printing Plates Magenta /1 #165
2017 Donruss Printing Plates Yellow /1 #165
2017 Panini National Convention Legends /299 #LEG29
2017 Panini National Convention Legends Autographs #LEG29
2017 Panini National Convention Legends Autographs Hyperplaid /1 #LEG29
2017 Panini National Convention Legends Escher Squares /25 #LEG29
2017 Panini National Convention Legends Escher Squares Thick Stock /10 #LEG29
2017 Panini National Convention Legends Galatic Windows /5 #LEG29
2017 Panini National Convention Legends Hyperplaid /1 #LEG29
2017 Panini National Convention Legends Pyramids /10 #LEG29

2017 Panini National Convention Legends Rainbow Spokes /49 #LEG29
2017 Panini National Convention Legends Rainbow Spokes Thick Stock /25 #LEG29
2017 Panini National Convention Legends Rapture /99 #LEG29
2017 Panini National Treasures /25 #25
2017 Panini National Treasures Century Black /1 #25
2017 Panini National Treasures Century Gold /15 #25
2017 Panini National Treasures Century Green /5 #25
2017 Panini National Treasures Century Holo Gold /10 #25
2017 Panini National Treasures Century Holo Silver /20 #25
2017 Panini National Treasures Championship Signatures /25 #9
2017 Panini National Treasures Championship Signatures Black /1 #9
2017 Panini National Treasures Championship Signatures Gold /15 #9
2017 Panini National Treasures Championship Signatures Green /5 #9
2017 Panini National Treasures Championship Signatures Holo Gold /10 #9
2017 Panini National Treasures Championship Signatures Holo Silver /20 #9
2017 Panini National Treasures Championship Signatures Printing Plates Black /1 #9
2017 Panini National Treasures Championship Signatures Printing Plates Cyan /1 #9
2017 Panini National Treasures Championship Signatures Printing Plates Magenta /1 #9
2017 Panini National Treasures Championship Signatures Printing Plates Yellow /1 #9
2017 Panini National Treasures Dual Signature Materials /25 #8
2017 Panini National Treasures Dual Signature Materials Black /1 #8
2017 Panini National Treasures Dual Signature Materials Gold /15 #8
2017 Panini National Treasures Dual Signature Materials Green /5 #8
2017 Panini National Treasures Dual Signature Materials Holo Gold /10 #8
2017 Panini National Treasures Dual Signature Materials Holo Silver /20 #8
2017 Panini National Treasures Dual Signature Materials Laundry Tag /1 #8
2017 Panini National Treasures Legendary Material Signatures Black /1 #3
2017 Panini National Treasures Legendary Material Signatures Green /5 #3
2017 Panini National Treasures Legendary Material Signatures Printing Plates Black /1 #3
2017 Panini National Treasures Legendary Material Signatures Printing Plates Cyan /1 #3
2017 Panini National Treasures Legendary Material Signatures Printing Plates Magenta /1 #3
2017 Panini National Treasures Legendary Material Signatures Printing Plates Yellow /1 #3
2017 Panini National Treasures Legendary Signatures Black /1 #9
2017 Panini National Treasures Legendary Signatures Gold /15 #9
2017 Panini National Treasures Legendary Signatures Green /5 #9
2017 Panini National Treasures Legendary Signatures Holo Gold /10 #9
2017 Panini National Treasures Legendary Signatures Printing Plates Black /1 #9
2017 Panini National Treasures Legendary Signatures Printing Plates Cyan /1 #9
2017 Panini National Treasures Legendary Signatures Printing Plates Magenta /1 #9
2017 Panini National Treasures Legendary Signatures Printing Plates Yellow /1 #9
2017 Panini National Treasures Printing Plates Black /1 #25
2017 Panini National Treasures Printing Plates Cyan /1 #25
2017 Panini National Treasures Printing Plates Magenta /1 #25
2017 Panini National Treasures Printing Plates Yellow /1 #25
2017 Panini National Treasures Winning Signatures Black /1 #2
2017 Panini National Treasures Winning Signatures Gold /15 #2
2017 Panini National Treasures Winning Signatures Green /5 #2
2017 Panini National Treasures Winning Signatures Holo Gold /10 #2
2017 Panini National Treasures Winning Signatures Printing Plates Black /1 #2
2017 Panini National Treasures Winning Signatures Printing Plates Cyan /1 #2
2017 Panini National Treasures Winning Signatures Printing Plates Magenta /1 #2
2017 Panini National Treasures Winning Signatures Printing Plates Yellow /1 #2
2017 Panini Torque Driver Scripts #11
2017 Panini Torque Driver Scripts Blue /75 #11
2017 Panini Torque Driver Scripts Checkerboard /10 #11
2017 Panini Torque Driver Scripts Green /25 #11
2017 Panini Torque Driver Scripts Red /49 #11
2017 Panini Torque Visions of Greatness #8
2017 Panini Torque Visions of Greatness Blue /99 #8
2017 Panini Torque Visions of Greatness Gold /149 #8
2017 Panini Torque Visions of Greatness Green /25 #8
2017 Panini Torque Visions of Greatness Purple /10 #8
2017 Panini Torque Visions of Greatness Red /49 #8
2017 Select #132
2017 Select Endorsements #17
2017 Select Endorsements Prizms Blue /50 #17
2017 Select Endorsements Prizms Checkered Flag /1 #17
2017 Select Endorsements Prizms Gold /10 #17
2017 Select Endorsements Prizms Red /25 #17
2017 Select Prizms Black /3 #132
2017 Select Prizms Checkered Flag /1 #132
2017 Select Prizms Gold /10 #132
2017 Select Prizms Tie Dye /24 #132
2017 Select Prizms White /50 #132
2017 Select Select Stars #23
2017 Select Select Stars Prizms Black /3 #23
2017 Select Select Stars Prizms Checkered Flag /1 #23
2017 Select Select Stars Prizms Gold /10 #23
2017 Select Select Stars Prizms Tie Dye /24 #23
2017 Select Select Stars Prizms White /50 #23
2018 Certified #83
2018 Certified Black /1 #83
2018 Certified Blue /99 #83
2018 Certified Gold /49 #83
2018 Certified Green /10 #83
2018 Certified Mirror Black /1 #83
2018 Certified Mirror Gold /25 #83
2018 Certified Mirror Green /5 #83
2018 Certified Mirror Purple /10 #83
2018 Certified Orange /249 #83
2018 Certified Purple /25 #83
2018 Certified Red /199 #83
2018 Donruss #162
2018 Donruss Artist Proofs /25 #162
2018 Donruss Classics #4
2018 Donruss Classics Cracked Ice /999 #4
2018 Donruss Classics Xplosion /99 #4
2018 Donruss Gold Foil /499 #162
2018 Donruss Gold Press Proofs /99 #162
2018 Donruss Green Foil /199 #162
2018 Donruss Masters of the Track #8
2018 Donruss Masters of the Track Cracked Ice /999 #8
2018 Donruss Masters of the Track Xplosion /99 #8
2018 Donruss Press Proofs /49 #162
2018 Donruss Printing Plates Black /1 #162
2018 Donruss Printing Plates Cyan /1 #162
2018 Donruss Printing Plates Magenta /1 #162
2018 Donruss Printing Plates Yellow /1 #162
2018 Donruss Red Foil /299 #162
2018 Donruss Significant Signatures #3
2018 Donruss Significant Signatures Black /1 #3
2018 Donruss Significant Signatures Holo Gold /25 #3
2018 Panini Prime /50 #32
2018 Panini Prime /50 #65
2018 Panini Prime /50 #98
2018 Panini Prime Black /1 #32
2018 Panini Prime Black /1 #65
2018 Panini Prime Black /1 #98
2018 Panini Prime Driver Signatures /99 #7
2018 Panini Prime Driver Signatures Black /1 #7
2018 Panini Prime Driver Signatures Holo Gold /50 #7
2018 Panini Prime Dual Signatures /10 #1
2018 Panini Prime Dual Signatures Black /1 #1
2018 Panini Prime Dual Signatures Holo Gold /5 #1
2018 Panini Prime Holo Gold /25 #32
2018 Panini Prime Holo Gold /25 #65
2018 Panini Prime Holo Gold /25 #98
2018 Panini Prime Prime Signatures /99 #7
2018 Panini Prime Prime Signatures Black /1 #7
2018 Panini Prime Prime Signatures Holo Gold /50 #7
2018 Panini Prime Shadowbox Signatures /99 #9
2018 Panini Prime Shadowbox Signatures Black /1 #9
2018 Panini Prime Shadowbox Signatures Holo Gold /50 #9
2018 Panini Prizm #12
2018 Panini Prizm Prizms #12
2018 Panini Prizm Prizms Black /1 #12
2018 Panini Prizm Prizms Blue /99 #12
2018 Panini Prizm Prizms Camo #12
2018 Panini Prizm Prizms Gold /10 #12
2018 Panini Prizm Prizms Green /149 #12
2018 Panini Prizm Prizms Purple Flash #12
2018 Panini Prizm Prizms Rainbow /24 #12
2018 Panini Prizm Prizms Red /75 #12
2018 Panini Prizm Prizms Red White and Blue #12
2018 Panini Prizm Prizms White /5 #12
2018 Panini Victory Lane #72
2018 Panini Victory Lane Black /1 #72
2018 Panini Victory Lane Blue /25 #72
2018 Panini Victory Lane Champions #4
2018 Panini Victory Lane Champions Black /1 #4
2018 Panini Victory Lane Champions Blue /25 #4
2018 Panini Victory Lane Champions Gold /99 #4
2018 Panini Victory Lane Champions Green /5 #4
2018 Panini Victory Lane Champions Printing Plates Black /1 #4
2018 Panini Victory Lane Champions Printing Plates Cyan /1 #4
2018 Panini Victory Lane Champions Printing Plates Magenta /1 #4
2018 Panini Victory Lane Champions Printing Plates Yellow /1 #4
2018 Panini Victory Lane Champions Red /49 #4
2018 Panini Victory Lane Foundations #7
2018 Panini Victory Lane Foundations Black /1 #7
2018 Panini Victory Lane Foundations Blue /25 #7
2018 Panini Victory Lane Foundations Gold /99 #7
2018 Panini Victory Lane Foundations Green /5 #7
2018 Panini Victory Lane Foundations Printing Plates Black /1 #7
2018 Panini Victory Lane Foundations Printing Plates Cyan /1 #7
2018 Panini Victory Lane Foundations Printing Plates Magenta /1 #7
2018 Panini Victory Lane Foundations Printing Plates Yellow /1 #7
2018 Panini Victory Lane Foundations Red /49 #7
2018 Panini Victory Lane Gold /99 #72
2018 Panini Victory Lane Green /5 #72
2018 Panini Victory Lane NASCAR at 70 #7
2018 Panini Victory Lane NASCAR at 70 Black /1 #7
2018 Panini Victory Lane NASCAR at 70 Blue /25 #7
2018 Panini Victory Lane NASCAR at 70 Gold /99 #7
2018 Panini Victory Lane NASCAR at 70 Green /5 #7
2018 Panini Victory Lane NASCAR at 70 Printing Plates Black /1 #7
2018 Panini Victory Lane NASCAR at 70 Printing Plates Cyan /1 #7
2018 Panini Victory Lane NASCAR at 70 Printing Plates Magenta /1 #7
2018 Panini Victory Lane NASCAR at 70 Printing Plates Yellow /1 #7
2018 Panini Victory Lane NASCAR at 70 Red /49 #7
2018 Panini Victory Lane Pedal to the Metal #77
2018 Panini Victory Lane Pedal to the Metal Black /1 #77
2018 Panini Victory Lane Pedal to the Metal Blue /25 #77
2018 Panini Victory Lane Pedal to the Metal Green /5 #77
2018 Panini Victory Lane Printing Plates Black /1 #72
2018 Panini Victory Lane Printing Plates Cyan /1 #72
2018 Panini Victory Lane Printing Plates Magenta /1 #72
2018 Panini Victory Lane Printing Plates Yellow /1 #72
2018 Panini Victory Lane Red /49 #72
2018 Panini Victory Lane Silver #72
2018 Panini Victory Lane Victory Marks /100 #5
2018 Panini Victory Lane Victory Marks Black /1 #5
2018 Panini Victory Lane Victory Marks Gold /49 #5
2019 Donruss #11
2019 Donruss #25
2019 Donruss #55A
2019 Donruss #158
2019 Donruss #170
2019 Donruss #55B
2019 Donruss Artist Proofs /25 #11
2019 Donruss Artist Proofs /25 #25
2019 Donruss Artist Proofs /25 #55A
2019 Donruss Artist Proofs /25 #158
2019 Donruss Artist Proofs /25 #170
2019 Donruss Artist Proofs /25 #55B
2019 Donruss Black /199 #11
2019 Donruss Black /199 #25
2019 Donruss Black /199 #55A
2019 Donruss Black /199 #158
2019 Donruss Black /199 #170
2019 Donruss Black /199 #55B
2019 Donruss Gold /299 #11
2019 Donruss Gold /299 #25
2019 Donruss Gold /299 #55A
2019 Donruss Gold /299 #158
2019 Donruss Gold /299 #170
2019 Donruss Gold /299 #55B
2019 Donruss Gold Press Proofs /99 #11
2019 Donruss Gold Press Proofs /99 #25
2019 Donruss Gold Press Proofs /99 #55A
2019 Donruss Gold Press Proofs /99 #158
2019 Donruss Gold Press Proofs /99 #170
2019 Donruss Gold Press Proofs /99 #55B
2019 Donruss Icons #4
2019 Donruss Icons Cracked Ice /25 #4
2019 Donruss Icons Holographic #4
2019 Donruss Icons Xplosion /10 #4
2019 Donruss Optic #88
2019 Donruss Optic Blue Pulsar #88
2019 Donruss Optic Gold /10 #88
2019 Donruss Optic Gold Vinyl /1 #88
2019 Donruss Optic Holo #88
2019 Donruss Optic Red Wave #88
2019 Donruss Optic Signatures Gold Vinyl /1 #88
2019 Donruss Optic Signatures Holo /75 #88
2019 Donruss Press Proofs /49 #11
2019 Donruss Press Proofs /49 #25
2019 Donruss Press Proofs /49 #55A
2019 Donruss Press Proofs /49 #158
2019 Donruss Press Proofs /49 #170
2019 Donruss Press Proofs /49 #55B
2019 Donruss Printing Plates Black /1 #11
2019 Donruss Printing Plates Black /1 #25
2019 Donruss Printing Plates Black /1 #55A
2019 Donruss Printing Plates Black /1 #158
2019 Donruss Printing Plates Black /1 #170
2019 Donruss Printing Plates Black /1 #55B
2019 Donruss Printing Plates Cyan /1 #11
2019 Donruss Printing Plates Cyan /1 #25
2019 Donruss Printing Plates Cyan /1 #55A
2019 Donruss Printing Plates Cyan /1 #158
2019 Donruss Printing Plates Cyan /1 #170
2019 Donruss Printing Plates Cyan /1 #55B
2019 Donruss Printing Plates Magenta /1 #55A
2019 Donruss Printing Plates Magenta /1 #158
2019 Donruss Printing Plates Magenta /1 #170
2019 Donruss Printing Plates Magenta /1 #55B
2019 Donruss Printing Plates Magenta /1 #11
2019 Donruss Printing Plates Magenta /1 #25
2019 Donruss Printing Plates Yellow /1 #11
2019 Donruss Printing Plates Yellow /1 #25
2019 Donruss Printing Plates Yellow /1 #55A
2019 Donruss Printing Plates Yellow /1 #158
2019 Donruss Printing Plates Yellow /1 #170
2019 Donruss Printing Plates Yellow /1 #55B
2019 Donruss Silver #11
2019 Donruss Silver #25
2019 Donruss Silver #55A
2019 Donruss Silver #158
2019 Donruss Silver #170
2019 Donruss Silver #55B
2019 Panini Prime /50 #97
2019 Panini Prime Black /10 #97
2019 Panini Prime Emerald /5 #97
2019 Panini Prime Legacy Signatures /99 #6
2019 Panini Prime Legacy Signatures Black /10 #6
2019 Panini Prime Legacy Signatures Holo Gold /25 #6
2019 Panini Prime Legacy Signatures Platinum Blue /1 #6
2019 Panini Prime Platinum Blue /1 #97
2019 Panini Prime Prime Names Die Cut Signatures /99 #4
2019 Panini Prime Prime Names Die Cut Signatures Black /10 #4
2019 Panini Prime Prime Names Die Cut Signatures Holo Gold /25 #4
2019 Panini Prime Prime Names Die Cut Signatures Platinum Blue /1 #4
2019 Panini Prime Shadowbox Signatures /99 #7
2019 Panini Prime Shadowbox Signatures Black /10 #7
2019 Panini Prime Shadowbox Signatures Holo Gold /25 #7
2019 Panini Prime Shadowbox Signatures Platinum Blue /1 #7
2019 Panini Prizm Endorsements Prizms #6
2019 Panini Prizm Endorsements Prizms Black /1 #6
2019 Panini Prizm Endorsements Prizms Blue /50 #6
2019 Panini Prizm Endorsements Prizms Camo #6
2019 Panini Prizm Endorsements Prizms Gold /10 #6
2019 Panini Prizm Endorsements Prizms Green /75 #6
2019 Panini Prizm Endorsements Prizms Rainbow /24 #6
2019 Panini Prizm Endorsements Prizms Red /50 #6
2019 Panini Prizm Endorsements Prizms Red White and Blue #6
2019 Panini Prizm Endorsements Prizms White /5 #6
2019 Panini Victory Lane #50
2019 Panini Victory Lane #74
2019 Panini Victory Lane #83
2019 Panini Victory Lane #100
2019 Panini Victory Lane Black /1 #50
2019 Panini Victory Lane Black /1 #74
2019 Panini Victory Lane Black /1 #83
2019 Panini Victory Lane Black /1 #100
2019 Panini Victory Lane Gold /25 #50
2019 Panini Victory Lane Gold /25 #74
2019 Panini Victory Lane Gold /25 #83
2019 Panini Victory Lane Gold /25 #100
2019 Panini Victory Lane Pedal to the Metal #67
2019 Panini Victory Lane Pedal to the Metal #95
2019 Panini Victory Lane Pedal to the Metal Black /1 #67
2019 Panini Victory Lane Pedal to the Metal Black /1 #95
2019 Panini Victory Lane Pedal to the Metal Gold /25 #95
2019 Panini Victory Lane Pedal to the Metal Gold /25 #67
2019 Panini Victory Lane Pedal to the Metal Green /5 #67
2019 Panini Victory Lane Pedal to the Metal Green /5 #95
2019 Panini Victory Lane Pedal to the Metal Red /3 #67
2019 Panini Victory Lane Pedal to the Metal Red /3 #95
2019 Panini Victory Lane Printing Plates Black /1 #50
2019 Panini Victory Lane Printing Plates Black /1 #74
2019 Panini Victory Lane Printing Plates Black /1 #83
2019 Panini Victory Lane Printing Plates Black /1 #100
2019 Panini Victory Lane Printing Plates Cyan /1 #50
2019 Panini Victory Lane Printing Plates Cyan /1 #74
2019 Panini Victory Lane Printing Plates Cyan /1 #83
2019 Panini Victory Lane Printing Plates Cyan /1 #100
2019 Panini Victory Lane Printing Plates Magenta /1 #50
2019 Panini Victory Lane Printing Plates Magenta /1 #74
2019 Panini Victory Lane Printing Plates Magenta /1 #83
2019 Panini Victory Lane Printing Plates Magenta /1 #100
2019 Panini Victory Lane Printing Plates Yellow /1 #50
2019 Panini Victory Lane Printing Plates Yellow /1 #74
2019 Panini Victory Lane Printing Plates Yellow /1 #83
2019 Panini Victory Lane Printing Plates Yellow /1 #100
2020 Donruss #80
2020 Donruss #155
2020 Donruss Black Numbers /11 #80
2020 Donruss Black Numbers /11 #155
2020 Donruss Black Trophy Club /1 #80
2020 Donruss Black Trophy Club /1 #155
2020 Donruss Blue /199 #155
2020 Donruss Blue /199 #80
2020 Donruss Carolina Blue #80
2020 Donruss Carolina Blue #155
2020 Donruss Classics #8
2020 Donruss Classics Checkers #8
2020 Donruss Classics Cracked Ice /25 #8
2020 Donruss Classics Holographic /199 #8
2020 Donruss Classics Xplosion /10 #8
2020 Donruss Dominators #7
2020 Donruss Dominators Checkers #7
2020 Donruss Dominators Cracked Ice /25 #7
2020 Donruss Dominators Holographic /199 #7
2020 Donruss Dominators Xplosion /10 #7
2020 Donruss Green /99 #80
2020 Donruss Green /99 #155
2020 Donruss Orange #80
2020 Donruss Orange #155
2020 Donruss Pink /25 #80
2020 Donruss Pink /25 #155
2020 Donruss Printing Plates Black /1 #80
2020 Donruss Printing Plates Black /1 #155
2020 Donruss Printing Plates Cyan /1 #80
2020 Donruss Printing Plates Cyan /1 #155
2020 Donruss Printing Plates Magenta /1 #80
2020 Donruss Printing Plates Magenta /1 #155
2020 Donruss Printing Plates Yellow /1 #155
2020 Donruss Printing Plates Yellow /1 #80
2020 Donruss Purple /49 #80
2020 Donruss Purple /49 #155
2020 Donruss Red /299 #80
2020 Donruss Red /299 #155
2020 Donruss Silver #80
2020 Donruss Silver #155

Michael Waltrip

1988 Maxx Charlotte #23
1988 Maxx Charlotte #98
1989 Maxx #30
1989 Maxx #140
1989 Maxx Crisco #21
1989 Maxx Previews #8
1990 Maxx #30
1990 Maxx #194
1990 Maxx Glossy #30
1990 Maxx Glossy #194
1990 Maxx Holly Farms #HF18
1991 Maxx #30
1991 Maxx #118
1991 Maxx #127
1991 Maxx McDonald's #16
1991 Maxx Racing for Kids #1
1991 Maxx Update #30
1991 Pro Set #60
1991 Traks #30
1991 Traks #75
1992 Bikers of the Racing Scene #30
1992 Bikers of the Racing Scene #31
1992 Card Dynamics Michael Waltrip /2000 #1
1992 Card Dynamics Michael Waltrip /2000 #2
1992 Card Dynamics Michael Waltrip /2000 #3
1992 Card Dynamics Michael Waltrip /2000 #4
1992 Card Dynamics Michael Waltrip /2000 #5
1992 Maxx Black #30
1992 Maxx McDonald's #22
1992 Maxx Red #30
1992 Maxx The Winston #15
1992 Maxx The Winston #35
1992 Maxx The Winston #43
1992 Pro Set #23
1992 Pro Set #92
1992 Pro Set #102
1992 Pro Set #111
1992 Pro Set #178
1992 Pro Set Maxwell House #20
1992 Pro Set Rudy Farms #13
1992 Traks #30
1992 Traks #75
1992 Traks Goody's #23
1992 Traks Racing Machines #30
1992 Traks Racing Machines #36
1992 Traks Racing Machines #65
1992 Traks Racing Machines #72
1992 Traks Racing Machines #83
1992 Traks Team Sets #76
1992 Traks Team Sets #77
1992 Traks Team Sets #79
1992 Traks Team Sets #82
1992 Traks Team Sets #84
1992 Traks Team Sets #90
1992 Traks Team Sets #95
1992 Traks Team Sets #99
1992 Traks Team Sets #100
1993 Action Packed #67
1993 Action Packed #68
1993 Action Packed #136
1993 Action Packed #137
1993 Action Packed #164
1993 Action Packed #179
1993 Action Packed #206
1993 Action Packed 24K Gold #61G
1993 Finish Line #15
1993 Finish Line #109
1993 Finish Line #123
1993 Finish Line Commemorative Sheets #13
1993 Finish Line Commemorative Sheets #23
1993 Finish Line Silver #15
1993 Finish Line Silver #109
1993 Finish Line Silver #123
1993 Maxwell House #21
1993 Maxx #30
1993 Maxx Premier Plus #30
1993 Maxx Premier Series #30
1993 Maxx The Winston #18
1993 Maxx The Winston #38
1993 Stove Top #6
1993 Traks #30
1993 Traks #125
1993 Traks #186
1993 Traks First Run #30
1993 Traks First Run #125
1993 Traks First Run #186
1993 Traks Preferred Collector #1
1993 Traks Trivia #30
1994 Action Packed #17
1994 Action Packed #88
1994 Action Packed #97
1994 Action Packed #133
1994 Action Packed #167
1994 Action Packed 24K Gold #42G
1994 Action Packed Coastars #18
1994 Action Packed Mint #17
1994 Action Packed Mint #88
1994 Action Packed Mint #97
1994 Action Packed Mint #133
1994 Action Packed Mint #167
1994 Finish Line #32
1994 Finish Line #43
1994 Finish Line #134
1994 Finish Line Gold #12
1994 Finish Line Gold #62
1994 Finish Line Gold #74
1994 Finish Line Gold #84
1994 Finish Line Gold Autographs #84
1994 Finish Line Silver #32
1994 Finish Line Silver #43
1994 Finish Line Silver #134
1994 Hi-Tech Brickyard 400 #56
1994 Hi-Tech Brickyard 400 Artist Proofs #56
1994 Maxx #30
1994 Maxx #70
1994 Maxx #260
1994 Maxx #261
1994 Maxx Medallion #7
1994 Maxx Premier Plus #30
1994 Maxx Premier Plus #70
1994 Maxx Premier Series #30
1994 Maxx Premier Series #70
1994 Maxx The Select 25 #17
1994 Power #SL58
1994 Power #126
1994 Power #143
1994 Power Gold #SL58
1994 Power Gold #126
1994 Power Gold #143
1994 Power Preview #6
1994 Power Preview #27
1994 Press Pass #30
1994 Press Pass #33
1994 Press Pass #49
1994 Press Pass Cup Chase #CC30
1994 Press Pass Optima XL #24
1994 Press Pass Optima XL Red Hot #24
1994 SkyBox #25
1994 Traks #30
1994 Traks #49
1994 Traks #154
1994 Traks Auto Value #7
1994 Traks First Run #30
1994 Traks First Run #49
1994 Traks First Run #154
1994 VIP #36
1994 VIP #49
1994 Wheels High Gear #11
1994 Wheels High Gear Gold #11
1994 Wheels High Gear Mega Gold #MG12
1995 Action Packed Country #69
1995 Action Packed Country Silver Speed #69
1995 Action Packed Preview #25
1995 Action Packed Stars #17
1995 Action Packed Stars Silver Speed #17
1995 Assets #19
1995 Assets $2 Phone Cards #14
1995 Assets $2 Phone Cards Gold Signature #14
1995 Assets 1-Minute Phone Cards #14
1995 Assets 1-Minute Phone Cards Gold Signature #14
1995 Assets Gold Signature #19
1995 Classic Five Sport #168
1995 Classic Five Sport Printer's Proofs /795 #168
1995 Classic Five Sport Red Die Cuts #168
1995 Classic Five Sport Silver Die Cuts #168
1995 Crown Jewels #17
1995 Crown Jewels Diamond /599 #17
1995 Crown Jewels Emerald /1199 #17
1995 Crown Jewels Sapphire /2500 #17
1995 Finish Line #30
1995 Finish Line #61
1995 Finish Line #95
1995 Finish Line Coca-Cola 600 #19
1995 Finish Line Gold Signature #GS11
1995 Finish Line Printer's Proof /398 #30
1995 Finish Line Printer's Proof /398 #61
1995 Finish Line Printer's Proof /398 #95
1995 Finish Line Silver #30
1995 Finish Line Silver #61
1995 Finish Line Silver #95
1995 Finish Line Standout Cars #SC10
1995 Finish Line Standout Drivers #SD10
1995 Hi-Tech Brickyard 400 #14
1995 Hi-Tech Brickyard 400 #59
1995 Hi-Tech Brickyard 400 Top Ten #BY8
1995 Images #30
1995 Images #70
1995 Images Driven #D11
1995 Images Gold #30
1995 Images Gold #70
1995 Images Hard Chargers #HC7
1995 Maxx #30
1995 Maxx #167
1995 Maxx #244
1995 Maxx #245
1995 Maxx #246
1995 Maxx #247
1995 Maxx Autographs #30
1995 Maxx License to Drive #11
1995 Maxx Medallion #21
1995 Maxx Medallion #51
1995 Maxx Medallion Blue #21
1995 Maxx Medallion Blue #51
1995 Maxx Premier Plus #30
1995 Maxx Premier Plus #47
1995 Maxx Premier Plus Crown Chrome #30
1995 Maxx Premier Plus Crown Chrome #47
1995 Maxx Premier Series #30
1995 Maxx Premier Series #69
1995 MW Windows #4
1995 MW Windows #5
1995 Press Pass #36
1995 Press Pass #48
1995 Press Pass #117
1995 Press Pass Cup Chase #36
1995 Press Pass Optima XL #24
1995 Press Pass Optima XL Cool Blue #24
1995 Press Pass Optima XL Die Cut #24
1995 Press Pass Optima XL Red Hot #24
1995 Press Pass Optima XL Stealth #XLS18
1995 Press Pass Premium #10
1995 Press Pass Premium Holofoil #10
1995 Press Pass Premium Phone Cards $5 #9
1995 Press Pass Premium Phone Cards $50 #9
1995 Press Pass Premium Red Hot #10
1995 Press Pass Red Hot #36
1995 Press Pass Red Hot #48
1995 Press Pass Red Hot #117
1995 Select #36
1995 Select #48
1995 Select #113
1995 Select Dream Machines #DM9
1995 Select Flat Out #36
1995 Select Flat Out #48
1995 Select Flat Out #113
1995 Select Skills #SS12
1995 SP #23
1995 SP #62
1995 SP #103
1995 SP Die Cuts #23
1995 SP Die Cuts #62
1995 SP Die Cuts #103
1995 SP Speed Merchants #SM30
1995 SP Speed Merchants Die Cuts #SM30
1995 Traks #49
1995 Traks #69
1995 Traks 5th Anniversary #31
1995 Traks 5th Anniversary #53
1995 Traks 5th Anniversary Clear Contenders #C8
1995 Traks 5th Anniversary Gold #31
1995 Traks 5th Anniversary Gold #53
1995 Traks 5th Anniversary Jumbos #E8
1995 Traks 5th Anniversary Jumbos Gold /100 #E8
1995 Traks 5th Anniversary Red #31
1995 Traks 5th Anniversary Red #53
1995 Traks Auto Value #32
1995 Traks First Run #49
1995 Traks First Run #69
1995 Traks Racing Machines #RM15
1995 Traks Racing Machines First Run #RM15
1995 Traks Series Stars #SS13
1995 Traks Series Stars First Run #SS13
1995 Upper Deck #9
1995 Upper Deck #52
1995 Upper Deck #77
1995 Upper Deck #145
1995 Upper Deck #209
1995 Upper Deck #252
1995 Upper Deck Autographs #209
1995 Upper Deck Gold Signature/Electric Gold #9
1995 Upper Deck Gold Signature/Electric Gold #52
1995 Upper Deck Gold Signature/Electric Gold #77
1995 Upper Deck Gold Signature/Electric Gold #145
1995 Upper Deck Gold Signature/Electric Gold #209
1995 Upper Deck Gold Signature/Electric Gold #252
1995 Upper Deck Silver Signature/Electric Silver #9
1995 Upper Deck Silver Signature/Electric Silver #52
1995 Upper Deck Silver Signature/Electric Silver #77
1995 Upper Deck Silver Signature/Electric Silver #145
1995 Upper Deck Silver Signature/Electric Silver #209
1995 Upper Deck Silver Signature/Electric Silver #252
1995 VIP #30
1995 VIP Cool Blue #30
1995 VIP Emerald Proofs #30
1995 VIP Promos #3G
1995 VIP Promos #3R
1995 VIP Red Hot #30
1995 Wheels High Gear #9
1995 Wheels High Gear #84
1995 Wheels High Gear Day One #9
1995 Wheels High Gear Day One #84
1995 Wheels High Gear Day One Gold #9
1995 Wheels High Gear Day One Gold #84
1995 Wheels High Gear Gold #9
1995 Wheels High Gear Gold #84
1995 Zenith #29
1995 Zenith #54
1995 Zenith Z-Team #7
1995-96 Classic Five Sport Signings #83
1995-96 Classic Five Sport Signings Blue Signature #83
1995-96 Classic Five Sport Signings Die Cuts #83
1995-96 Classic Five Sport Signings Red Signature #83
1996 Action Packed Credentials #31
1996 Action Packed Credentials #58
1996 Action Packed Credentials #96
1996 Action Packed Credentials Silver Speed #31
1996 Assets Racing #28
1996 Assets Racing $100 Cup Champion Interactive Phone Cards #14
1996 Assets Racing $1000 Cup Champion Interactive Phone Cards #7
1996 Assets Racing $2 Phone Cards #18
1996 Assets Racing $5 Phone Cards #9
1996 Assets Racing Competitor's License #CL14
1996 Assets Racing Race Day #RD9
1996 Autographed Racing #34
1996 Autographed Racing Autographs #60
1996 Autographed Racing Autographs Certified Golds /265 #60
1996 Autographed Racing Front Runners #82
1996 Autographed Racing Front Runners #83
1996 Autographed Racing Front Runners #84
1996 Autographed Racing Front Runners #85
1996 Autographed Racing Front Runners #86
1996 Autographed Racing Front Runners #87
1996 Autographed Racing Front Runners #88
1996 Autographed Racing Front Runners #89
1996 Autographed Racing High Performance #HP9
1996 Classic #26
1996 Classic #35
1996 Classic #41
1996 Classic #54
1996 Classic Innerview #IV15
1996 Classic Mark Martin's Challengers #MC2
1996 Classic Printer's Proof #26
1996 Classic Printer's Proof #35
1996 Classic Printer's Proof #41
1996 Classic Race Chase #RC1
1996 Classic Race Chase #RC11
1996 Classic Silver #26
1996 Classic Silver #35
1996 Classic Silver #41
1996 Crown Jewels Elite #15
1996 Crown Jewels Elite Diamond Tribute /2500 #15
1996 Crown Jewels Elite Diamond Tribute Citrine /999 #15
1996 Crown Jewels Elite Dual Jewels Amethyst #DJ5
1996 Crown Jewels Elite Dual Jewels Amethyst Diamond Tribute #DJ5
1996 Crown Jewels Elite Dual Jewels Amethyst Treasure Chest #DJ5
1996 Crown Jewels Elite Dual Jewels Garnet #DJ5
1996 Crown Jewels Elite Dual Jewels Garnet Diamond Tribute #DJ5
1996 Crown Jewels Elite Dual Jewels Garnet Treasure Chest #DJ5
1996 Crown Jewels Elite Dual Jewels Sapphire #DJ5
1996 Crown Jewels Elite Dual Jewels Sapphire Treasure Chest #DJ5
1996 Crown Jewels Elite Emerald /599 #15
1996 Crown Jewels Elite Emerald Treasure Chest #15
1996 Crown Jewels Elite Retail Blue #15
1996 Crown Jewels Elite Sapphire #15
1996 Crown Jewels Elite Sapphire Treasure Chest /1099 #15
1996 Crown Jewels Elite Treasure Chest #15
1996 Finish Line #15
1996 Finish Line #34
1996 Finish Line #61
1996 Finish Line Black Gold #C14
1996 Finish Line Black Gold #D16
1996 Finish Line Gold Signature #GS12
1996 Finish Line Phone Pak #38
1996 Finish Line Phone Pak $2 Signature #38
1996 Finish Line Phone Pak $5 #23
1996 Finish Line Printer's Proof #15
1996 Finish Line Printer's Proof #34
1996 Finish Line Printer's Proof #61
1996 Finish Line Silver #15
1996 Finish Line Silver #34
1996 Finish Line Silver #61
1996 Flair #36
1996 Flair #92
1996 KnightQuest #19
1996 KnightQuest Black Knights #19
1996 KnightQuest Knights of the Round Table #KT9
1996 KnightQuest Red Knight Preview #19
1996 KnightQuest Royalty #19
1996 KnightQuest White Knights #19
1996 Maxx #30
1996 Maxx #39
1996 Maxx Family Ties #FT5
1996 Maxx Made in America #21
1996 Maxx Made in America #51
1996 Maxx Made in America #80
1996 Maxx Made in America #81
1996 Maxx Made in America Blue Ribbon #BR5
1996 Maxx Odyssey #21
1996 Maxx Odyssey #51
1996 Maxx Odyssey #80
1996 Maxx Odyssey #81
1996 Maxx Odyssey On The Road Again #OTRA2
1996 Maxx Odyssey Radio Active #RA5
1996 Maxx Premier Series #30
1996 Maxx Premier Series #65
1996 Maxx Premier Series #190
1996 Maxx Premier Series #191
1996 M-Force #18
1996 Pinnacle #21
1996 Pinnacle #48
1996 Pinnacle Artist Proofs #21

1996 Pinnacle Artist Proofs #48
1996 Pinnacle Checkered Flag #11
1996 Pinnacle Foil #21
1996 Pinnacle Foil #48
1996 Pinnacle Pole Position #21
1996 Pinnacle Pole Position #37
1996 Pinnacle Pole Position #66
1996 Pinnacle Pole Position Lightning Fast #21
1996 Pinnacle Pole Position Lightning Fast #37
1996 Pinnacle Pole Position Lightning Fast #66
1996 Pinnacle Winston Cup Collection Dufex #21
1996 Pinnacle Winston Cup Collection Dufex #48
1996 Press Pass #36
1996 Press Pass #48
1996 Press Pass #118
1996 Press Pass Cup Chase #36
1996 Press Pass Cup Chase Foil Prizes #36
1996 Press Pass Premium #12
1996 Press Pass Premium #33
1996 Press Pass Premium $10 Phone Cards #9
1996 Press Pass Premium $20 Phone Cards #9
1996 Press Pass Premium $5 Phone Cards #9
1996 Press Pass Premium Emerald Proofs /380 #12
1996 Press Pass Premium Emerald Proofs /380 #33
1996 Press Pass Premium Holofoil #12
1996 Press Pass Premium Holofoil #33
1996 Press Pass Premium Hot Pursuit #HP9
1996 Press Pass R and N China #36
1996 Press Pass Scorchers #36
1996 Press Pass Scorchers #48
1996 Press Pass Scorchers #118
1996 Press Pass Torquers #36
1996 Press Pass Torquers #48
1996 Press Pass Torquers #118
1996 Racer's Choice #11
1996 Racer's Choice #39
1996 Racer's Choice #78
1996 Racer's Choice Speedway Collection #11
1996 Racer's Choice Speedway Collection #39
1996 Racer's Choice Speedway Collection #78
1996 Racer's Choice Speedway Collection Artist's Proofs #11
1996 Racer's Choice Speedway Collection Artist's Proofs #39
1996 Racer's Choice Speedway Collection Artist's Proofs #78
1996 SP #21
1996 SP #53
1996 SP #75
1996 Speedflix #8
1996 Speedflix #48
1996 Speedflix Artist Proof's #8
1996 Speedflix Artist Proof's #48
1996 Speedflix ProMotion #5
1996 SPx #21
1996 SPx Gold #21
1996 Traks Review and Preview #28
1996 Traks Review and Preview First Run #28
1996 Traks Review and Preview Magnets #28
1996 Traks Review and Preview Triple-Chase #TC5
1996 Traks Review and Preview Triple-Chase Gold #TC5
1996 Traks Review and Preview Triple-Chase Holofoil #TC5
1996 Ultra #44
1996 Ultra #45
1996 Ultra #46
1996 Ultra Autographs #37
1996 Ultra Boxed Set #12
1996 Ultra Update #33
1996 Ultra Update #79
1996 Ultra Update #88
1996 Upper Deck #28
1996 Upper Deck #68
1996 Upper Deck #100
1996 Upper Deck #108
1996 Upper Deck Road To The Cup #RC11
1996 Upper Deck Road To The Cup #RC60
1996 Upper Deck Road To The Cup #RC96
1996 Upper Deck Road To The Cup Autographs #H11
1996 Upper Deck Virtual Velocity #VV14
1996 Upper Deck Virtual Velocity Gold #VV14
1996 VIP #29
1996 VIP Autographs #26
1996 VIP Emerald Proofs #29
1996 VIP Head Gear #HG9
1996 VIP Head Gear Die Cuts #HG9
1996 VIP Torquers #29
1996 VIP War Paint #WP10
1996 VIP War Paint Gold #WP10
1996 Viper #16
1996 Viper #59
1996 Viper Black Mamba #16
1996 Viper Black Mamba #59
1996 Viper Black Mamba First Strike #16
1996 Viper Black Mamba First Strike #59
1996 Viper Copperhead Die Cuts #16
1996 Viper Copperhead Die Cuts #59
1996 Viper Copperhead Die Cuts First Strike #16
1996 Viper Copperhead Die Cuts First Strike #59
1996 Viper First Strike #16
1996 Viper First Strike #59
1996 Viper Green Mamba #16
1996 Viper Green Mamba #59
1996 Viper Red Cobra /1799 #16
1996 Viper Red Cobra /1799 #59
1996 Visions #115
1996 Visions Signings #93
1996 Visions Signings Autographs Silver /285 #78
1996 Zenith #13
1996 Zenith #49
1996 Zenith #62
1996 Zenith Artist Proofs #13
1996 Zenith Artist Proofs #49
1996 Zenith Artist Proofs #62
1996 Zenith Highlights #10
1997 Action Packed #15
1997 Action Packed #36
1997 Action Packed #59
1997 Action Packed #71
1997 Action Packed #74
1997 Action Packed 24K Gold #10
1997 Action Packed First Impressions #15
1997 Action Packed First Impressions #36
1997 Action Packed First Impressions #59
1997 Action Packed First Impressions #71
1997 Action Packed First Impressions #74
1997 Autographed Racing #5
1997 Autographed Racing #40
1997 Autographed Racing #41
1997 Autographed Racing #45
1997 Autographed Racing Autographs #55
1997 Autographed Racing Mayne Street #KM5
1997 Collector's Choice #21
1997 Collector's Choice #71
1997 Collector's Choice #108
1997 Collector's Choice Speedecals #S41
1997 Collector's Choice Speedecals #S42
1997 Collector's Choice Triple Force #E3
1997 Collector's Choice Upper Deck 500 #UD42
1997 Collector's Choice Upper Deck 500 #UD43
1997 Finish Line Phone Pak II #16
1997 Finish Line Phone Pak II #36
1997 Finish Line Phone Pak II #54
1997 Finish Line Phone Pak II #77
1997 Jurassic Park #10
1997 Jurassic Park #36
1997 Jurassic Park Raptors #R7
1997 Jurassic Park Triceratops #10
1997 Jurassic Park Triceratops #36
1997 Maxx #21
1997 Maxx #66
1997 Maxx #113
1997 Maxx Chase the Champion #C8
1997 Maxx Chase the Champion Gold Die Cuts #C8
1997 Pinnacle #21
1997 Pinnacle #50
1997 Pinnacle #83
1997 Pinnacle Artist Proofs #21
1997 Pinnacle Artist Proofs #50
1997 Pinnacle Artist Proofs #83
1997 Pinnacle Certified #21
1997 Pinnacle Certified #55
1997 Pinnacle Certified #78
1997 Pinnacle Certified Mirror Blue #21
1997 Pinnacle Certified Mirror Blue #55
1997 Pinnacle Certified Mirror Blue #78
1997 Pinnacle Certified Mirror Gold #21
1997 Pinnacle Certified Mirror Gold #55
1997 Pinnacle Certified Mirror Gold #78
1997 Pinnacle Certified Mirror Red #21
1997 Pinnacle Certified Mirror Red #55
1997 Pinnacle Certified Mirror Red #78
1997 Pinnacle Certified Red #21
1997 Pinnacle Certified Red #55
1997 Pinnacle Certified Red #78
1997 Pinnacle Mint #13
1997 Pinnacle Mint Bronze #13
1997 Pinnacle Mint Coins #13
1997 Pinnacle Mint Coins 24K Gold Plated #13
1997 Pinnacle Mint Coins Nickel-Silver #13
1997 Pinnacle Mint Gold #13
1997 Pinnacle Mint Silver #13
1997 Pinnacle Portraits #13
1997 Pinnacle Portraits #33
1997 Pinnacle Portraits #48
1997 Pinnacle Press Plates #21
1997 Pinnacle Press Plates #50
1997 Pinnacle Press Plates #83
1997 Pinnacle Totally Certified Platinum Blue #21
1997 Pinnacle Totally Certified Platinum Blue #55
1997 Pinnacle Totally Certified Platinum Blue #78
1997 Pinnacle Totally Certified Platinum Gold #21
1997 Pinnacle Totally Certified Platinum Gold #55
1997 Pinnacle Totally Certified Platinum Gold #78
1997 Pinnacle Totally Certified Platinum Red #21
1997 Pinnacle Totally Certified Platinum Red #55
1997 Pinnacle Totally Certified Platinum Red #78
1997 Pinnacle Trophy Collection #21
1997 Pinnacle Trophy Collection #50
1997 Pinnacle Trophy Collection #83
1997 Predator #11
1997 Predator #40
1997 Predator Black Wolf #11
1997 Predator Black Wolf #40
1997 Predator Black Wolf First Slash /3750 #11
1997 Predator Black Wolf First Slash /3750 #40
1997 Predator First Slash #11
1997 Predator First Slash #40
1997 Predator Grizzly #11
1997 Predator Grizzly #40
1997 Predator Grizzly First Slash #11
1997 Predator Grizzly First Slash #40
1997 Predator Red Wolf #11
1997 Predator Red Wolf #40
1997 Predator Red Wolf First Slash #11
1997 Predator Red Wolf First Slash #40
1997 Press Pass #14
1997 Press Pass #38
1997 Press Pass #63
1997 Press Pass #78
1997 Press Pass #79
1997 Press Pass #93
1997 Press Pass #100
1997 Press Pass #123
1997 Press Pass Autographs #13
1997 Press Pass Burning Rubber /400 #BR4
1997 Press Pass Clear Cut #C10
1997 Press Pass Cup Chase #CC19
1997 Press Pass Cup Chase Gold Die Cuts #CC19
1997 Press Pass Lasers Silver #14
1997 Press Pass Lasers Silver #38
1997 Press Pass Lasers Silver #63
1997 Press Pass Lasers Silver #78
1997 Press Pass Lasers Silver #79
1997 Press Pass Lasers Silver #93
1997 Press Pass Lasers Silver #100
1997 Press Pass Lasers Silver #123
1997 Press Pass Oil Slicks /100 #14
1997 Press Pass Oil Slicks /100 #38
1997 Press Pass Oil Slicks /100 #63
1997 Press Pass Oil Slicks /100 #78
1997 Press Pass Oil Slicks /100 #79
1997 Press Pass Oil Slicks /100 #93
1997 Press Pass Oil Slicks /100 #100
1997 Press Pass Oil Slicks /100 #123
1997 Press Pass Premium #14
1997 Press Pass Premium Double Burners /350 #DB5
1997 Press Pass Premium Emerald Proofs /380 #14
1997 Press Pass Premium Lap Leaders #LL12
1997 Press Pass Premium Mirrors #14
1997 Press Pass Premium Oil Slicks /100 #14
1997 Press Pass Torquers Blue #14
1997 Press Pass Torquers Blue #38
1997 Press Pass Torquers Blue #63
1997 Press Pass Torquers Blue #78
1997 Press Pass Torquers Blue #79
1997 Press Pass Torquers Blue #93
1997 Press Pass Torquers Blue #100
1997 Press Pass Torquers Blue #123
1997 Press Pass Victory Lane #VL9A
1997 Press Pass Victory Lane #VL9B
1997 Race Sharks #12
1997 Race Sharks First Bite #12
1997 Race Sharks Great White #12
1997 Race Sharks Hammerhead #12
1997 Race Sharks Hammerhead First Bite #12
1997 Race Sharks Shark Attack #SA7
1997 Race Sharks Shark Attack First Bite #SA7
1997 Race Sharks Tiger Shark #12
1997 Race Sharks Tiger Shark First Bite #12
1997 Racer's Choice #21
1997 Racer's Choice #56
1997 Racer's Choice #100
1997 Racer's Choice Showcase Series #21
1997 Racer's Choice Showcase Series #56
1997 Racer's Choice Showcase Series #100
1997 SB Motorsports #16
1997 SB Motorsports #52
1997 SB Motorsports #90
1997 Score Board IQ #5
1997 Score Board IQ #44
1997 Score Board Seven-Eleven Phone Cards #4
1997 SkyBox Profile #31
1997 SkyBox Profile #69
1997 SkyBox Profile Autographs /200 #31
1997 SkyBox Profile Pace Setters #E7
1997 SP #21
1997 SP #63
1997 SP #99
1997 SP Super Series #21
1997 SP Super Series #63
1997 SP Super Series #99
1997 SPx #21
1997 SPx Blue #21
1997 SPx Gold #21
1997 SPx Silver #21
1997 Ultra #37
1997 Ultra #55
1997 Ultra Inside Out #DC15
1997 Ultra Shoney's #13
1997 Ultra Update #15
1997 Ultra Update #85
1997 Ultra Update Autographs #15
1997 Ultra Update Double Trouble #DT5
1997 Upper Deck Road To The Cup #16
1997 Upper Deck Road To The Cup #58
1997 Upper Deck Road To The Cup #113
1997 Upper Deck Team Hot Wheels Pro Racing #M16
1997 Upper Deck Victory Circle #21
1997 Upper Deck Victory Circle #71
1997 VIP #25
1997 VIP Explosives #25
1997 VIP Head Gear #HG9
1997 VIP Head Gear Die Cuts #HG9
1997 VIP Oil Slicks #25
1997 Viper #10
1997 Viper #39
1997 Viper Black Racer #10
1997 Viper Black Racer #39
1997 Viper Black Racer First Strike #10
1997 Viper Black Racer First Strike #39
1997 Viper First Strike #10
1997 Viper First Strike #39
1997 Viper Sidewinder #S7
1997 Viper Sidewinder First Strike #S7
1998 Collector's Choice #21
1998 Collector's Choice #57
1998 Collector's Choice #106
1998 Collector's Choice CC600 #CC25
1998 Collector's Choice CC600 #CC58
1998 Collector's Choice Star Quest #SQ22
1998 Maxx #21
1998 Maxx #51
1998 Maxx 10th Anniversary #19
1998 Maxx 10th Anniversary #64
1998 Maxx 10th Anniversary #99
1998 Maxx 10th Anniversary Buy Back Autographs /149 #49
1998 Maxx 10th Anniversary Maxximum Preview #P21
1998 Maxx 1997 Year In Review #24
1998 Maxx 1997 Year In Review #94
1998 Maxximum #21
1998 Maxximum #46
1998 Maxximum #71
1998 Maxximum #96
1998 Maxximum First Class #F4
1998 Pinnacle Mint #12
1998 Pinnacle Mint #24
1998 Pinnacle Mint Coins #12
1998 Pinnacle Mint Coins #24
1998 Pinnacle Mint Coins Bronze Proof #12
1998 Pinnacle Mint Coins Bronze Proof #24
1998 Pinnacle Mint Coins Gold Plated #12
1998 Pinnacle Mint Coins Gold Plated #24
1998 Pinnacle Mint Coins Gold Plated Proofs #12
1998 Pinnacle Mint Coins Gold Plated Proofs #24
1998 Pinnacle Mint Coins Nickel-Silver #12
1998 Pinnacle Mint Coins Nickel-Silver #24
1998 Pinnacle Mint Coins Silver Plated Proofs #12
1998 Pinnacle Mint Coins Silver Plated Proofs #24
1998 Pinnacle Mint Coins Solid Gold #12
1998 Pinnacle Mint Coins Solid Gold #24
1998 Pinnacle Mint Coins Solid Silver #12
1998 Pinnacle Mint Coins Solid Silver #24
1998 Pinnacle Mint Die Cuts #12
1998 Pinnacle Mint Die Cuts #24
1998 Pinnacle Mint Gold Team #12
1998 Pinnacle Mint Gold Team #24
1998 Pinnacle Mint Silver Team #12
1998 Pinnacle Mint Silver Team #24
1998 Press Pass #14
1998 Press Pass Autographs /285 #9
1998 Press Pass Cup Chase #CC19
1998 Press Pass Cup Chase Die Cut Prizes #CC19
1998 Press Pass Oil Slicks /100 #14
1998 Press Pass Pit Stop #PS10
1998 Press Pass Premium #7
1998 Press Pass Premium #45
1998 Press Pass Premium Flag Chasers #FC12
1998 Press Pass Premium Flag Chasers Reflectors #FC12
1998 Press Pass Premium Reflectors #7
1998 Press Pass Premium Reflectors #45
1998 Press Pass Shockers #ST12A
1998 Press Pass Signings #13
1998 Press Pass Signings Gold /100 #13
1998 Press Pass Stealth #34
1998 Press Pass Stealth #35
1998 Press Pass Stealth Fusion #34
1998 Press Pass Stealth Fusion #35
1998 Press Pass Stealth Stars #18
1998 Press Pass Stealth Stars Die Cuts #18
1998 Press Pass Torpedoes #ST12B
1998 SP Authentic #21
1998 SP Authentic #55
1998 SP Authentic Behind the Wheel #BW17
1998 SP Authentic Behind the Wheel Die Cuts #BW17
1998 SP Authentic Behind the Wheel Gold #BW17
1998 SP Authentic Sign of the Times #S6
1998 Upper Deck Road To The Cup #21
1998 Upper Deck Road To The Cup #53
1998 Upper Deck Road To The Cup #106
1998 Upper Deck Victory Circle #21
1998 Upper Deck Victory Circle #66
1998 Upper Deck Victory Circle #133
1998 Upper Deck Victory Circle Point Leaders #PL18
1998 VIP #27
1998 VIP Explosives #27
1998 VIP Solos #27
1998 Wheels #30
1998 Wheels #59
1998 Wheels 50th Anniversary #A15
1998 Wheels Autographs /200 #9
1998 Wheels Golden #30
1998 Wheels Golden #59
1998 Wheels Green Flags #GF18
1998 Wheels High Gear #18
1998 Wheels High Gear #68
1998 Wheels High Gear Autographs /250 #23
1998 Wheels High Gear First Gear #14
1998 Wheels High Gear First Gear #68
1998 Wheels High Gear Gear Jammers #GJ10
1998 Wheels High Gear MPH /100 #14
1998 Wheels High Gear MPH /100 #68
1999 Maxx FANtastic Finishes #F30
1999 Maxx Race Ticket #RT29
1999 Maxx Racing Images #RI20
1999 Press Pass #15
1999 Press Pass #51
1999 Press Pass #115
1999 Press Pass Autographs /250 #21
1999 Press Pass Bryan #11
1999 Press Pass Chase Cars #10B
1999 Press Pass Pit Stop #11
1999 Press Pass Premium #27
1999 Press Pass Premium #50
1999 Press Pass Premium Badge of Honor #BH3A
1999 Press Pass Premium Badge of Honor Reflectors #BH3A
1999 Press Pass Premium Reflectors /1975 #R27
1999 Press Pass Premium Reflectors /1975 #R50
1999 Press Pass Showman #10A
1999 Press Pass Signings /500 #58
1999 Press Pass Skidmarks /250 #15
1999 Press Pass Skidmarks /250 #51
1999 Press Pass Stealth #48
1999 Press Pass Stealth Big Numbers #BN18
1999 Press Pass Stealth Big Numbers Die Cuts #BN18
1999 Press Pass Stealth Fusion #F48
1999 Press Pass Stealth Octane SLX #O23
1999 Press Pass Stealth Octane SLX Die Cuts #O23
1999 SP Authentic #21
1999 SP Authentic #59
1999 SP Authentic Overdrive #21
1999 SP Authentic Overdrive #59
1999 Upper Deck Victory Circle #28
1999 Upper Deck Victory Circle #69
1999 Upper Deck Victory Circle Signature Collection #MW
1999 Upper Deck Victory Circle UD Exclusives #28
1999 Upper Deck Victory Circle UD Exclusives #69
1999 VIP #27
1999 VIP Explosives #X27
1999 VIP Explosives Lasers #27
1999 Wheels #36
1999 Wheels Autographs /200 #24
1999 Wheels Golden #36
1999 Wheels High Gear #17
1999 Wheels High Gear #43
1999 Wheels High Gear Autographs /350 #26
1999 Wheels High Gear First Gear #17
1999 Wheels High Gear First Gear #43
1999 Wheels High Gear MPH #15
1999 Wheels Runnin and Gunnin #RG10
1999 Wheels Runnin and Gunnin Foils #RG10
1999 Wheels Solos #36
2000 Maxx #7
2000 Maxximum #27
2000 Maxximum Die Cuts /250 #27
2000 Maxximum MPH /7 #27
2000 Maxximum Signatures #MD2
2000 Press Pass #25
2000 Press Pass #51
2000 Press Pass #98
2000 Press Pass Millennium #25
2000 Press Pass Millennium #51
2000 Press Pass Millennium #98
2000 Press Pass Optima #27
2000 Press Pass Optima Platinum #27
2000 Press Pass Premium #6
2000 Press Pass Premium Reflectors #6
2000 Press Pass Signings #62
2000 Press Pass Signings Gold /100 #33
2000 Press Pass Techno-Retro #TR27
2000 Press Pass Trackside #5
2000 Press Pass Trackside Die Cuts #5
2000 Press Pass Trackside Golden #5
2000 Press Pass Trackside Panorama #P5
2000 SP Authentic #26
2000 SP Authentic /2500 #53
2000 SP Authentic Overdrive Gold /7 #26
2000 SP Authentic Overdrive Gold /7 #53
2000 SP Authentic Overdrive Silver /250 #26
2000 SP Authentic Overdrive Silver /250 #53
2000 Upper Deck MVP #27
2000 Upper Deck MVP #37
2000 Upper Deck MVP #80
2000 Upper Deck MVP Gold Script /125 #27
2000 Upper Deck MVP Gold Script /125 #37
2000 Upper Deck MVP Gold Script /125 #80
2000 Upper Deck MVP Silver Script #27
2000 Upper Deck MVP Silver Script #37
2000 Upper Deck MVP Silver Script #80
2000 Upper Deck MVP Super Script /7 #27
2000 Upper Deck MVP Super Script /7 #37
2000 Upper Deck MVP Super Script /7 #80
2000 Upper Deck Racing #27
2000 Upper Deck Victory Circle #6
2000 Upper Deck Victory Circle Exclusives Level 1 Silver /250 #6
2000 Upper Deck Victory Circle Exclusives Level 2 Gold /7 #6
2000 VIP Making the Show #MS22
2000 Wheels High Gear #27
2000 Wheels High Gear #68
2000 Wheels High Gear Autographs #28
2000 Wheels High Gear First Gear #27
2000 Wheels High Gear First Gear #68
2000 Wheels High Gear Gear Shifters #GS25
2000 Wheels High Gear MPH #27
2000 Wheels High Gear MPH #68
2001 Press Pass Optima #27
2001 Press Pass Optima G Force #GF27
2001 Press Pass Optima Gold #27
2001 Press Pass Premium #27
2001 Press Pass Premium #33
2001 Press Pass Premium #69
2001 Press Pass Premium #0
2001 Press Pass Premium Gold #27
2001 Press Pass Premium Gold #33
2001 Press Pass Premium Gold #69
2001 Press Pass Signings #54
2001 Press Pass Signings Gold /50 #36
2001 Press Pass Stealth #16
2001 Press Pass Stealth #17
2001 Press Pass Stealth #18
2001 Press Pass Stealth #72
2001 Press Pass Stealth Holofoils #16
2001 Press Pass Stealth Holofoils #17
2001 Press Pass Stealth Holofoils #18
2001 Press Pass Stealth Holofoils #72
2001 Press Pass Stealth Lap Leaders #LL5
2001 Press Pass Stealth Lap Leaders #LL23
2001 Press Pass Stealth Lap Leaders Clear Cars #LL23
2001 Press Pass Stealth Lap Leaders Clear Drivers #LL5
2001 Press Pass Stealth Race Used Glove Cars /170 #RGC3
2001 Press Pass Stealth Race Used Glove Drivers /170 #RGD3
2001 Press Pass Trackside #11
2001 Press Pass Trackside #44
2001 Press Pass Trackside Dialed In #D12
2001 Press Pass Trackside Die Cuts #11
2001 Press Pass Trackside Die Cuts #44
2001 Press Pass Trackside Golden #11
2001 Press Pass Trackside Golden #44
2001 Press Pass Trackside Pit Stoppers Cars /200 #PSC11
2001 Press Pass Trackside Pit Stoppers Drivers /75 #PSD11
2001 Super Shots Hendrick Motorsports #H3
2001 Super Shots Hendrick Motorsports Gold /100 #HG3
2001 Super Shots Hendrick Motorsports Silver /500 #HS3
2001 VIP #13
2001 VIP #19
2001 VIP #42
2001 VIP Driver's Choice #DC8
2001 VIP Driver's Choice Precious Metal /100 #DC8
2001 VIP Driver's Choice Transparent #DC8
2001 VIP Explosives #13
2001 VIP Explosives #19
2001 VIP Explosives #42
2001 VIP Explosives Lasers /420 #LX13
2001 VIP Explosives Lasers /420 #LX19
2001 VIP Explosives Lasers /420 #LX42
2001 VIP Making the Show #7
2001 VIP Mile Masters #MM3
2001 VIP Mile Masters Precious Metal /325 #MM3
2001 VIP Mile Masters Transparent #MM3
2001 VIP Sheet Metal Cars /120 #SC10
2001 VIP Sheet Metal Drivers /75 #SD10
2002 Press Pass #36
2002 Press Pass #64
2002 Press Pass #78
2002 Press Pass Autographs #69
2002 Press Pass Burning Rubber Cars /120 #BRC12
2002 Press Pass Burning Rubber Drivers /90 #BRD12
2002 Press Pass Cup Chase #CC17
2002 Press Pass Cup Chase Prizes #CC17
2002 Press Pass Eclipse #20
2002 Press Pass Eclipse Racing Champions #RC1
2002 Press Pass Eclipse Samples #20
2002 Press Pass Eclipse Solar Eclipse #S20
2002 Press Pass Eclipse Under Cover Double Cover /625 #DC8
2002 Press Pass Eclipse Under Cover Drivers #CD11
2002 Press Pass Eclipse Under Cover Gold Cars /300 #CD11
2002 Press Pass Eclipse Under Cover Gold Drivers /400 #CD11
2002 Press Pass Eclipse Under Cover Holofoil Drivers /100 #CD11
2002 Press Pass Hot Treads /2300 #HT7
2002 Press Pass Hot Treads /900 #HT34
2002 Press Pass Nabisco Albertsons #4
2002 Press Pass Optima #30
2002 Press Pass Optima Gold #30
2002 Press Pass Optima Promos /5 #30
2002 Press Pass Optima Samples #30
2002 Press Pass Platinum #36
2002 Press Pass Platinum #64
2002 Press Pass Platinum #78
2002 Press Pass Premium #33
2002 Press Pass Premium #47
2002 Press Pass Premium #69
2002 Press Pass Premium Red Reflectors #33
2002 Press Pass Premium Red Reflectors #47
2002 Press Pass Premium Red Reflectors #69
2002 Press Pass Premium Samples #33
2002 Press Pass Premium Samples #47
2002 Press Pass Showcar #S9B
2002 Press Pass Showman #S9A
2002 Press Pass Signings #69
2002 Press Pass Signings Gold /50 #66
2002 Press Pass Trackside #12
2002 Press Pass Trackside #68
2002 Press Pass Trackside #74
2002 Press Pass Trackside Golden /50 #G12
2002 Press Pass Trackside License to Drive #35
2002 Press Pass Trackside License to Drive Die Cuts #35
2002 Press Pass Trackside Samples #12
2002 Press Pass Trackside Samples #68
2002 Press Pass Trackside Samples #74
2002 Press Pass Vintage #VN26
2002 Wheels High Gear #27
2002 Wheels High Gear #60
2002 Wheels High Gear Autographs #58
2002 Wheels High Gear First Gear #27
2002 Wheels High Gear First Gear #60
2002 Wheels High Gear High Groove #HG27
2002 Wheels High Gear MPH /100 #27
2002 Wheels High Gear MPH /100 #60
2003 Nilla Wafers Team Nabisco #3
2003 Nilla Wafers Team Nabisco #4
2003 Press Pass #33
2003 Press Pass Autographs #60
2003 Press Pass Coca-Cola Racing Family #12
2003 Press Pass Coca-Cola Racing Family Scratch-off #6
2003 Press Pass Eclipse #13
2003 Press Pass Eclipse Double Hot Treads /999 #DT11
2003 Press Pass Eclipse Previews /5 #13
2003 Press Pass Eclipse Racing Champions #RC20
2003 Press Pass Eclipse Samples #13
2003 Press Pass Eclipse Solar Eclipse #P13
2003 Press Pass Eclipse Supernova #SN10
2003 Press Pass Eclipse Under Cover Cars /215 #UCT11
2003 Press Pass Eclipse Under Cover Driver Gold /260 #UCD11
2003 Press Pass Eclipse Under Cover Driver Red /100 #UCD11
2003 Press Pass Eclipse Under Cover Driver Silver /450 #UCD11
2003 Press Pass Eclipse Warp Speed #WS8
2003 Press Pass Gold Holofoil #P33
2003 Press Pass Nabisco Albertsons #5
2003 Press Pass Optima #27
2003 Press Pass Optima Fan Favorite #FF24
2003 Press Pass Optima Gold #27
2003 Press Pass Optima Previews /5 #27
2003 Press Pass Optima Samples #27
2003 Press Pass Optima Thunder Bolts Cars /95 #TBT18
2003 Press Pass Optima Thunder Bolts Drivers /65 #TBD18
2003 Press Pass Premium #30
2003 Press Pass Premium #44
2003 Press Pass Premium #50
2003 Press Pass Premium #68
2003 Press Pass Premium #80
2003 Press Pass Premium #0
2003 Press Pass Premium In the Zone #IZ12
2003 Press Pass Premium Performance Driven #PD9
2003 Press Pass Premium Previews /5 #30
2003 Press Pass Premium Red Reflectors #30
2003 Press Pass Premium Red Reflectors #44
2003 Press Pass Premium Red Reflectors #68
2003 Press Pass Premium Red Reflectors #80
2003 Press Pass Premium Samples #30
2003 Press Pass Premium Samples #44
2003 Press Pass Previews /5 #33
2003 Press Pass Race Exclusives #1
2003 Press Pass Samples #33
2003 Press Pass Signings #74
2003 Press Pass Signings Gold /50 #75
2003 Press Pass Stealth #13
2003 Press Pass Stealth #14
2003 Press Pass Stealth #15
2003 Press Pass Stealth #59
2003 Press Pass Stealth EFX #FX12
2003 Press Pass Stealth Fusion #FU12
2003 Press Pass Stealth Gear Grippers Cars /30 #GGT12
2003 Press Pass Stealth Gear Grippers Drivers /30 #GGD12
2003 Press Pass Stealth No Boundaries #NB25
2003 Press Pass Stealth Previews /5 #13
2003 Press Pass Stealth Previews /5 #14
2003 Press Pass Stealth Previews /5 #15
2003 Press Pass Stealth Red #P13
2003 Press Pass Stealth Red #P14
2003 Press Pass Stealth Red #P15
2003 Press Pass Stealth Red #P59
2003 Press Pass Stealth Samples #13
2003 Press Pass Stealth Samples #14
2003 Press Pass Stealth Samples #15
2003 Press Pass Stealth Samples #59
2003 Press Pass Stealth Supercharged #SC5
2003 Press Pass Trackside #30
2003 Press Pass Trackside #65
2003 Press Pass Trackside Dialed In #DI12
2003 Press Pass Trackside Gold Holofoil #P30
2003 Press Pass Trackside Gold Holofoil #P65
2003 Press Pass Trackside Golden /50 #G30
2003 Press Pass Trackside Hat Giveaway #PPH30
2003 Press Pass Trackside Hot Pursuit #HP7
2003 Press Pass Trackside License to Drive #LD20
2003 Press Pass Trackside Mirror Image #MI9
2003 Press Pass Trackside Pit Stoppers Cars /175 #PST12
2003 Press Pass Trackside Pit Stoppers Drivers /100 #PSD12
2003 Press Pass Trackside Previews /5 #30
2003 Press Pass Trackside Runnin n' Gunnin #RG9
2003 Press Pass Trackside Samples #30
2003 Press Pass Trackside Samples #65
2003 VIP #18
2003 VIP #19
2003 VIP #35
2003 VIP Driver's Choice #DC9
2003 VIP Driver's Choice Die Cuts #DC9
2003 VIP Driver's Choice National #DC9
2003 VIP Explosives #X18
2003 VIP Explosives #X19
2003 VIP Explosives #X35
2003 VIP Lap Leaders #LL7
2003 VIP Lap Leaders National #LL7
2003 VIP Lap Leaders Transparent #LL7
2003 VIP Lap Leaders Transparent LTD #LL7
2003 VIP Laser Explosive #LX18
2003 VIP Laser Explosive #LX19
2003 VIP Laser Explosive #LX35
2003 VIP Making the Show #MS6
2003 VIP Mile Masters #MM12
2003 VIP Mile Masters National #MM12
2003 VIP Mile Masters Transparent #MM12
2003 VIP Mile Masters Transparent LTD #MM12
2003 VIP Previews /5 #18
2003 VIP Previews /5 #19
2003 VIP Previews /5 #35
2003 VIP Samples #18
2003 VIP Samples #19
2003 VIP Samples #35
2003 VIP Tin #CT18
2003 VIP Tin #CT19
2003 VIP Tin #CT35
2003 VIP Tradin' Paint Cars /160 #TPT15
2003 VIP Tradin' Paint Drivers /110 #TPD15
2003 Wheels American Thunder #21
2003 Wheels American Thunder #33
2003 Wheels American Thunder #39
2003 Wheels American Thunder #47
2003 Wheels American Thunder American Muscle #AM11
2003 Wheels American Thunder Born On /100 #BO21
2003 Wheels American Thunder Born On /100 #BO33
2003 Wheels American Thunder Born On /100 #BO39
2003 Wheels American Thunder Born On /100 #BO47
2003 Wheels American Thunder Head to Toe /40 #HT9
2003 Wheels American Thunder Heads Up Manufacturer /90 #HUM23
2003 Wheels American Thunder Heads Up Team /60 #HUT21
2003 Wheels American Thunder Heads Up Winston /90 #HUW23
2003 Wheels American Thunder Holofoil #P21
2003 Wheels American Thunder Holofoil #P33
2003 Wheels American Thunder Holofoil #P39
2003 Wheels American Thunder Holofoil #P47
2003 Wheels American Thunder Post Mark #PM18
2003 Wheels American Thunder Previews /5 #21
2003 Wheels American Thunder Previews /5 #33
2003 Wheels American Thunder Pushin Pedal /285 #PP9
2003 Wheels American Thunder Rookie Thunder #RT35
2003 Wheels American Thunder Samples #P21
2003 Wheels American Thunder Samples #P33
2003 Wheels American Thunder Samples #P39
2003 Wheels American Thunder Samples #P47
2003 Wheels American Thunder Thunder Road #TR10
2003 Wheels American Thunder Triple Hat /25 #TH5
2003 Wheels Autographs #60
2003 Wheels High Gear #30
2003 Wheels High Gear Blue Hawaii SCDA Promos #30
2003 Wheels High Gear First Gear #F30
2003 Wheels High Gear High Groove #HG27
2003 Wheels High Gear Hot Treads /425 #HT0
2003 Wheels High Gear MPH /100 #M30
2003 Wheels High Gear Previews /5 #30
2003 Wheels High Gear Samples #30
2004 Post Cereal #7
2004 Press Pass #33
2004 Press Pass Burning Rubber Cars /140 #BRT11
2004 Press Pass Burning Rubber Drivers /70 #BRD11
2004 Press Pass Cup Chase #CCR5

2004 Press Pass Cup Chase Prizes #CCR5
2004 Press Pass Dale Earnhardt Jr. #42
2004 Press Pass Dale Earnhardt Jr. Blue #C42
2004 Press Pass Dale Earnhardt Jr. Bronze #B42
2004 Press Pass Dale Earnhardt Jr. Gold #D42
2004 Press Pass Eclipse #14
2004 Press Pass Eclipse #31
2004 Press Pass Eclipse #61
2004 Press Pass Eclipse #80
2004 Press Pass Eclipse #80B
2004 Press Pass Eclipse Destination WIN #3
2004 Press Pass Eclipse Destination WIN #24
2004 Press Pass Eclipse Hyperdrive #HP1
2004 Press Pass Eclipse Maxim #MX9
2004 Press Pass Eclipse Previews /5 #14
2004 Press Pass Eclipse Samples #14
2004 Press Pass Eclipse Samples #31
2004 Press Pass Eclipse Samples #61
2004 Press Pass Eclipse Samples #80
2004 Press Pass Eclipse Skidmarks #SM17
2004 Press Pass Eclipse Skidmarks Holofoil /500 #SM17
2004 Press Pass Eclipse Under Cover Cars /170 #UCD10
2004 Press Pass Eclipse Under Cover Double Cover /100 #DC1
2004 Press Pass Eclipse Under Cover Driver Gold /325 #UCD10
2004 Press Pass Eclipse Under Cover Driver Red /100 #UCD10
2004 Press Pass Eclipse Under Cover Driver Silver /690 #UCD10
2004 Press Pass Hot Treads /1250 #HTR16
2004 Press Pass Hot Treads Holofoil /200 #HTR16
2004 Press Pass Making the Show Collector's Series #MS9
2004 Press Pass Nilla Wafers #4
2004 Press Pass Optima #27
2004 Press Pass Optima #92
2004 Press Pass Optima Fan Favorite #FF25
2004 Press Pass Optima G Force #GF4
2004 Press Pass Optima Gold #G27
2004 Press Pass Optima Gold #G92
2004 Press Pass Optima Previews /5 #EB27
2004 Press Pass Optima Q&A #QA8
2004 Press Pass Optima Samples #27
2004 Press Pass Optima Samples #92
2004 Press Pass Optima Thunder Bolts Cars /120 #TBT4
2004 Press Pass Optima Thunder Bolts Drivers /70 #TBD4
2004 Press Pass Platinum #P33
2004 Press Pass Premium #26
2004 Press Pass Premium #40
2004 Press Pass Premium #64
2004 Press Pass Premium #70
2004 Press Pass Premium Hot Threads Drivers Bronze /125 #HTD15
2004 Press Pass Premium Hot Threads Drivers Bronze Retail /125 #HTT15
2004 Press Pass Premium Hot Threads Drivers Gold /50 #HTD15
2004 Press Pass Premium Hot Threads Drivers Silver /75 #HTD15
2004 Press Pass Premium In the Zone #IZ8
2004 Press Pass Premium In the Zone Elite Edition #IZ8
2004 Press Pass Premium Previews /5 #26
2004 Press Pass Premium Samples #26
2004 Press Pass Premium Samples #40
2004 Press Pass Previews /5 #33
2004 Press Pass Samples #33
2004 Press Pass Showcar #S12B
2004 Press Pass Showman #S12A
2004 Press Pass Signings #64
2004 Press Pass Signings Gold /50 #60
2004 Press Pass Signings Transparent /100 #11
2004 Press Pass Snapshots #SN23
2004 Press Pass Stealth #34
2004 Press Pass Stealth #35
2004 Press Pass Stealth #36
2004 Press Pass Stealth #84
2004 Press Pass Stealth #98
2004 Press Pass Stealth EFX #EF9
2004 Press Pass Stealth Fusion #FU4
2004 Press Pass Stealth Gear Grippers Drivers /80 #GGD10
2004 Press Pass Stealth Gear Grippers Drivers Retail /120 #GGT10
2004 Press Pass Stealth No Boundaries #NB26
2004 Press Pass Stealth Previews /5 #EB34
2004 Press Pass Stealth Previews /5 #EB35
2004 Press Pass Stealth Previews /5 #EB36
2004 Press Pass Stealth Profile #P11
2004 Press Pass Stealth Samples #X34
2004 Press Pass Stealth Samples #X35
2004 Press Pass Stealth Samples #X36
2004 Press Pass Stealth Samples #X84
2004 Press Pass Stealth Samples #X98
2004 Press Pass Stealth X-Ray /100 #34
2004 Press Pass Stealth X-Ray /100 #35
2004 Press Pass Stealth X-Ray /100 #36
2004 Press Pass Stealth X-Ray /100 #84
2004 Press Pass Stealth X-Ray /100 #98
2004 Press Pass Trackside #30
2004 Press Pass Trackside #56
2004 Press Pass Trackside #72
2004 Press Pass Trackside #110
2004 Press Pass Trackside Dialed In #DI4
2004 Press Pass Trackside Golden /100 #G30
2004 Press Pass Trackside Golden /100 #G56
2004 Press Pass Trackside Golden /100 #G72
2004 Press Pass Trackside Golden /100 #G110
2004 Press Pass Trackside Hat Giveaway #PPH33
2004 Press Pass Trackside Hot Pass #HP18
2004 Press Pass Trackside Hot Pass National #HP18
2004 Press Pass Trackside Hot Pursuit #HP3
2004 Press Pass Trackside Pit Stoppers Cars /150 #PST12
2004 Press Pass Trackside Pit Stoppers Drivers /95 #PSD12
2004 Press Pass Trackside Previews /5 #EB30
2004 Press Pass Trackside Runnin n' Gunnin #RG4
2004 Press Pass Trackside Samples #30
2004 Press Pass Trackside Samples #56
2004 Press Pass Trackside Samples #72
2004 Press Pass Trackside Samples #110
2004 Press Pass Velocity #VC1
2004 VIP #18
2004 VIP #29
2004 VIP Driver's Choice #DC6
2004 VIP Driver's Choice Die Cuts #DC6
2004 VIP Head Gear #HG12
2004 VIP Head Gear Transparent #HG12
2004 VIP Lap Leaders #LL5
2004 VIP Lap Leaders Transparent #LL5
2004 VIP Making the Show #MS9
2004 VIP Previews /5 #EB18
2004 VIP Previews /5 #EB29
2004 VIP Samples #18
2004 VIP Samples #29
2004 VIP Tradin' Paint Bronze /130 #TPT18
2004 VIP Tradin' Paint Gold /50 #TPD18
2004 VIP Tradin' Paint Silver /70 #TPD18
2004 Wheels American Thunder #27
2004 Wheels American Thunder #36
2004 Wheels American Thunder #40
2004 Wheels American Thunder #49
2004 Wheels American Thunder #55
2004 Wheels American Thunder #67
2004 Wheels American Thunder #81
2004 Wheels American Thunder American Eagle #AE12
2004 Wheels American Thunder Cool Threads /525 #CT15
2004 Wheels American Thunder Cup Quest #CQ9
2004 Wheels American Thunder Golden Eagle /250 #AE12
2004 Wheels American Thunder Post Mark #PM9
2004 Wheels American Thunder Previews /5 #EB27
2004 Wheels American Thunder Previews /5 #EB36
2004 Wheels American Thunder Previews /5 #EB40
2004 Wheels American Thunder Samples #27
2004 Wheels American Thunder Samples #36
2004 Wheels American Thunder Samples #40
2004 Wheels American Thunder Samples #49
2004 Wheels American Thunder Samples #55
2004 Wheels American Thunder Samples #67
2004 Wheels American Thunder Samples #81
2004 Wheels American Thunder Thunder Road #TR6
2004 Wheels American Thunder Triple Hat /160 #TH24
2004 Wheels Autographs #68
2004 Wheels High Gear #27
2004 Wheels High Gear #66
2004 Wheels High Gear Flag Chasers Black /100 #FC4
2004 Wheels High Gear Flag Chasers Blue /50 #FC4
2004 Wheels High Gear Flag Chasers Checkered /35 #FC4
2004 Wheels High Gear Flag Chasers Green /100 #FC4
2004 Wheels High Gear Flag Chasers Red /100 #FC4
2004 Wheels High Gear Flag Chasers White /100 #FC4
2004 Wheels High Gear Flag Chasers Yellow /100 #FC4
2004 Wheels High Gear High Groove #HG27
2004 Wheels High Gear Machine #MM4B
2004 Wheels High Gear Man #MM4A
2004 Wheels High Gear MPH /100 #M27
2004 Wheels High Gear MPH /100 #M66
2004 Wheels High Gear Previews /5 #27
2004 Wheels High Gear Samples #27
2004 Wheels High Gear Samples #66
2004 Wheels High Gear Sunday Sensation #SS1
2005 NAPA #NNO
2005 Press Pass #10
2005 Press Pass #99
2005 Press Pass #103
2005 Press Pass Autographs #61
2005 Press Pass Burning Rubber Cars /130 #BRT8
2005 Press Pass Burning Rubber Drivers /80 #BRD8
2005 Press Pass Burning Rubber Drivers Gold /1 #BRD8
2005 Press Pass Cup Chase #CCR12
2005 Press Pass Cup Chase Prizes #CCP12
2005 Press Pass Eclipse #19
2005 Press Pass Eclipse #33
2005 Press Pass Eclipse #61
2005 Press Pass Eclipse #80
2005 Press Pass Eclipse Hyperdrive #HD1
2005 Press Pass Eclipse Maxim #MX9
2005 Press Pass Eclipse Previews /5 #EB19
2005 Press Pass Eclipse Previews /5 #EB33
2005 Press Pass Eclipse Previews /5 #EB61
2005 Press Pass Eclipse Previews /1 #EB80
2005 Press Pass Eclipse Samples #19
2005 Press Pass Eclipse Samples #33
2005 Press Pass Eclipse Samples #61
2005 Press Pass Eclipse Samples #80
2005 Press Pass Eclipse Skidmarks #SM17
2005 Press Pass Eclipse Skidmarks Holofoil /250 #SM17
2005 Press Pass Eclipse Under Cover Cars /120 #UCT10
2005 Press Pass Eclipse Under Cover Double Cover /340 #DC1
2005 Press Pass Eclipse Under Cover Driver Red /400 #UCD10
2005 Press Pass Eclipse Under Cover Drivers Holofoil /100 #UCD10
2005 Press Pass Eclipse Under Cover Drivers Silver /690 #UCD10
2005 Press Pass Game Face #GF8
2005 Press Pass Hot Treads /900 #HTR15
2005 Press Pass Hot Treads Holofoil /100 #HTR15
2005 Press Pass Legends Double Threads Bronze /375 #DTEW
2005 Press Pass Legends Double Threads Gold /99 #DTEW
2005 Press Pass Legends Double Threads Silver /225 #DTEW
2005 Press Pass Legends Heritage /480 #HE11
2005 Press Pass Panorama #PPP17
2005 Press Pass Panorama #PPP24
2005 Press Pass Platinum /100 #P10
2005 Press Pass Platinum /100 #P99
2005 Press Pass Platinum /100 #P103
2005 Press Pass Premium #33
2005 Press Pass Premium #42
2005 Press Pass Premium #47
2005 Press Pass Premium Hot Threads Cars /85 #HTT13
2005 Press Pass Premium Hot Threads Drivers /275 #HTD13
2005 Press Pass Premium Hot Threads Drivers Gold /1 #HTD13
2005 Press Pass Premium In the Zone #IZ1
2005 Press Pass Premium In the Zone Elite Edition /250 #IZ1
2005 Press Pass Premium Samples #33
2005 Press Pass Premium Samples #42
2005 Press Pass Premium Samples #47
2005 Press Pass Previews Green /5 #EB10
2005 Press Pass Previews Silver /1 #EB103
2005 Press Pass Samples #10
2005 Press Pass Samples #99
2005 Press Pass Samples #103
2005 Press Pass Showcar #SC9
2005 Press Pass Showman #SM9
2005 Press Pass Signings #59
2005 Press Pass Signings Gold /50 #58
2005 Press Pass Signings Platinum /100 #53
2005 Press Pass Snapshots #SN26
2005 Press Pass Stealth #56
2005 Press Pass Stealth #59
2005 Press Pass Stealth #62
2005 Press Pass Stealth #84
2005 Press Pass Stealth #98
2005 Press Pass Stealth EFX #EFX4
2005 Press Pass Stealth Fusion #FU4
2005 Press Pass Stealth Gear Grippers Autographs /15 #GGMW
2005 Press Pass Stealth Gear Grippers Cars /90 #GGT9
2005 Press Pass Stealth Gear Grippers Drivers /75 #GGD9
2005 Press Pass Stealth No Boundaries #NB1
2005 Press Pass Stealth Previews /5 #56
2005 Press Pass Stealth Previews /5 #59
2005 Press Pass Stealth Previews /5 #62
2005 Press Pass Stealth Samples #56
2005 Press Pass Stealth Samples #59
2005 Press Pass Stealth Samples #62
2005 Press Pass Stealth Samples #84
2005 Press Pass Stealth Samples #98
2005 Press Pass Stealth X-Ray /100 #X56
2005 Press Pass Stealth X-Ray /100 #X59
2005 Press Pass Stealth X-Ray /100 #X62
2005 Press Pass Stealth X-Ray /100 #X84
2005 Press Pass Stealth X-Ray /100 #X98
2005 Press Pass Trackside #58
2005 Press Pass Trackside #89
2005 Press Pass Trackside Dialed In #DI4
2005 Press Pass Trackside Golden /100 #G58
2005 Press Pass Trackside Golden /100 #G89
2005 Press Pass Trackside Hat Giveaway #PPH34
2005 Press Pass Trackside Hot Pass #18
2005 Press Pass Trackside Hot Pass National #18
2005 Press Pass Trackside Pit Stoppers Cars /85 #PST8
2005 Press Pass Trackside Pit Stoppers Drivers /85 #PSD8
2005 Press Pass Trackside Previews /1 #89
2005 Press Pass Trackside Samples #58
2005 Press Pass Trackside Samples #89
2005 Press Pass Velocity #V6
2005 Wheels Autographs #61
2005 Wheels High Gear #8
2005 Wheels High Gear #60
2005 Wheels High Gear #76
2005 Wheels High Gear Flag to Flag #FF27
2005 Wheels High Gear Machine #MMB1
2005 Wheels High Gear Man #MMA1
2005 Wheels High Gear MPH /100 #M8
2005 Wheels High Gear MPH /100 #M60
2005 Wheels High Gear MPH /100 #M76
2005 Wheels High Gear Previews Green /5 #EB8
2005 Wheels High Gear Previews Silver /1 #EB76
2005 Wheels High Gear Samples #8
2005 Wheels High Gear Samples #60
2005 Wheels High Gear Samples #76
2007 Press Pass Collector's Series Box Set #SB25
2007 Press Pass Dale The Movie #46
2007 Press Pass Legends Sunday Swatches Bronze /199 #MWSS
2007 Press Pass Legends Sunday Swatches Gold /50 #MWSS
2007 Press Pass Legends Sunday Swatches Silver /99 #MWSS
2007 Press Pass Premium #75
2007 Press Pass Premium Performance Driven #PD5
2007 Press Pass Premium Performance Driven Red /250 #PD5
2007 Press Pass Premium Red /5 #R75
2007 Press Pass Signings #75
2007 Press Pass Signings Blue /25 #34
2007 Press Pass Signings Gold /50 #56
2007 Press Pass Signings Press Plates Black /1 #43
2007 Press Pass Signings Press Plates Cyan /1 #42
2007 Press Pass Signings Press Plates Magenta /1 #45
2007 Press Pass Signings Press Plates Yellow /1 #43
2007 Press Pass Signings Silver /100 #54
2007 Press Pass Stealth #28
2007 Press Pass Stealth Chrome #28
2007 Press Pass Stealth Chrome Exclusives /99 #X28
2007 Press Pass Stealth Chrome Platinum /25 #P28
2007 Press Pass Stealth Fusion #F4
2007 Press Pass Stealth Previews /5 #EB28
2007 Traks #31
2007 Traks Corporate Cuts Driver /99 #CCD14
2007 Traks Corporate Cuts Patch /12 #CCD14
2007 Traks Corporate Cuts Team /180 #CCT14
2007 Traks Driver's Seat #DS19
2007 Traks Driver's Seat #DS19B
2007 Traks Driver's Seat National #DS19
2007 Traks Gold #G31
2007 Traks Holofoil /50 #H31
2007 Traks Previews /5 #EB31
2007 Traks Red /10 #R31
2007 VIP #31
2007 VIP #44
2007 VIP Gear Gallery #GG8
2007 VIP Gear Gallery Transparent #GG8
2007 VIP Get A Grip Drivers /70 #GGD3
2007 VIP Get A Grip Teams /70 #GGT3
2007 VIP Pedal To The Metal /50 #PM4
2007 VIP Previews /5 #EB31
2007 VIP Sunday Best #SB25
2007 Wheels American Thunder #36
2007 Wheels American Thunder #69
2007 Wheels American Thunder Autographed Hat Instant Winner /1 #AH41
2007 Wheels American Thunder Cool Threads /299 #CT2
2007 Wheels American Thunder Head to Toe /99 #HT1
2007 Wheels American Thunder Previews /5 #EB36
2007 Wheels American Thunder Pushin' Pedal /99 #PP5
2007 Wheels American Thunder Starting Grid #SG10
2007 Wheels American Thunder Thunder Road #TR2
2007 Wheels American Thunder Thunder Strokes #42
2007 Wheels American Thunder Thunder Strokes Press Plates Black /1 #42
2007 Wheels American Thunder Thunder Strokes Press Plates Cyan /1 #42
2007 Wheels American Thunder Thunder Strokes Press Plates Magenta /1 #42
2007 Wheels American Thunder Thunder Strokes Press Plates Yellow /1 #42
2007 Wheels American Thunder Triple Hat /99 #TH31
2008 Press Pass #36
2008 Press Pass #120
2008 Press Pass Autographs #43
2008 Press Pass Autographs Press Plates Black /1 #35
2008 Press Pass Autographs Press Plates Cyan /1 #36
2008 Press Pass Autographs Press Plates Magenta /1 #36
2008 Press Pass Autographs Press Plates Yellow /1 #35
2008 Press Pass Blue #B36
2008 Press Pass Blue #B120
2008 Press Pass Daytona 500 50th Anniversary #38
2008 Press Pass Daytona 500 50th Anniversary #40
2008 Press Pass Eclipse #27
2008 Press Pass Eclipse #36
2008 Press Pass Eclipse #71
2008 Press Pass Eclipse Escape Velocity #EV2
2008 Press Pass Eclipse Gold /25 #G27
2008 Press Pass Eclipse Gold /25 #G36
2008 Press Pass Eclipse Gold /25 #G71
2008 Press Pass Eclipse Previews /5 #EB27
2008 Press Pass Eclipse Previews /5 #EB36
2008 Press Pass Eclipse Red /1 #R27
2008 Press Pass Eclipse Red /1 #R36
2008 Press Pass Eclipse Red /1 #R71
2008 Press Pass Eclipse Star Tracks #ST18
2008 Press Pass Eclipse Star Tracks Holofoil /250 #ST18
2008 Press Pass Eclipse Under Cover Drivers /250 #UCD13
2008 Press Pass Eclipse Under Cover Drivers Eclipse /1 #UCD13
2008 Press Pass Eclipse Under Cover Drivers Name /50 #UCD13
2008 Press Pass Eclipse Under Cover Drivers NASCAR /150 #UCD13
2008 Press Pass Eclipse Under Cover Teams /99 #UCT13
2008 Press Pass Eclipse Under Cover Teams NASCAR /25 #UCT13
2008 Press Pass Gold #G36
2008 Press Pass Gold #G120
2008 Press Pass Legends Prominent Pieces Firesuit-Glove-Belt /25 #PP2MW
2008 Press Pass Legends Prominent Pieces Firesuit-Glove-Belt Gold /10 #PP2MW
2008 Press Pass Platinum /100 #P36
2008 Press Pass Platinum /100 #P120
2008 Press Pass Premium #30
2008 Press Pass Premium #39
2008 Press Pass Premium Clean Air #CA3
2008 Press Pass Premium Hot Threads Autographs /55 #HTMW
2008 Press Pass Premium Hot Threads Patches /14 #HTP50
2008 Press Pass Premium Hot Threads Patches /14 #HTP51
2008 Press Pass Premium Hot Threads Patches /6 #HTP52
2008 Press Pass Premium Previews /5 #EB30
2008 Press Pass Premium Red /15 #30
2008 Press Pass Premium Red /15 #39
2008 Press Pass Previews /5 #EB36
2008 Press Pass Race Day #RD12
2008 Press Pass Signings #60
2008 Press Pass Signings Blue /25 #32
2008 Press Pass Signings Gold /50 #53
2008 Press Pass Signings Press Plates Cyan #MW
2008 Press Pass Signings Press Plates Magenta /1 #MW
2008 Press Pass Signings Press Plates Yellow #MW
2008 Press Pass Signings Silver /100 #52
2008 Press Pass Slideshow #SS10
2008 Press Pass Slideshow #SS34
2008 Press Pass Speedway #35
2008 Press Pass Speedway Cockpit #CP26
2008 Press Pass Speedway Corporate Cuts Drivers /80 #CDMW
2008 Press Pass Speedway Corporate Cuts Drivers Patches /13 #CDMW
2008 Press Pass Speedway Corporate Cuts Team /165 #CTMW
2008 Press Pass Speedway Gold #G35
2008 Press Pass Speedway Holofoil /50 #H35
2008 Press Pass Speedway Previews /5 #EB35
2008 Press Pass Speedway Red /10 #R35
2008 Press Pass Speedway Test Drive #TD9
2008 Press Pass Stealth #35
2008 Press Pass Stealth Battle Armor Drivers /120 #BAD2
2008 Press Pass Stealth Battle Armor Teams /115 #BAT2
2008 Press Pass Stealth Chrome #35
2008 Press Pass Stealth Chrome Exclusives /25 #35
2008 Press Pass Stealth Chrome Exclusives Gold /99 #35
2008 Press Pass Stealth Maximum Access #MA27
2008 Press Pass Stealth Maximum Access Autographs /25 #MA27
2008 Press Pass Stealth Previews /5 #35
2008 Press Pass Stealth Synthesis #S8
2008 VIP #35
2008 VIP #43
2008 VIP #87
2008 VIP All Access #AA24
2008 VIP Get a Grip Drivers /80 #GGD10
2008 VIP Get a Grip Teams /99 #GGT10
2008 VIP Previews /5 #EB35
2008 VIP Previews /1 #EB87
2008 Wheels American Thunder #36
2008 Wheels American Thunder #43
2008 Wheels American Thunder #51
2008 Wheels American Thunder #76
2008 Wheels American Thunder Autographed Hat Winner /1 #WHMW
2008 Wheels American Thunder Campaign Trail #CT17
2008 Wheels American Thunder Cool Threads /285 #CT3
2008 Wheels American Thunder Head to Toe /99 #HT5
2008 Wheels American Thunder Motorcade #M2
2008 Wheels American Thunder Previews /5 #36
2008 Wheels American Thunder Previews /1 #76
2008 Wheels American Thunder Pushin' Pedal /99 #PP 5
2008 Wheels American Thunder Trackside Treasury Autographs #MW
2008 Wheels American Thunder Trackside Treasury Autographs Gold /25 #MW
2008 Wheels American Thunder Trackside Treasury Autographs Printing Plates Black /1 #MW
2008 Wheels American Thunder Trackside Treasury Autographs Printing Plates Cyan /1 #MW
2008 Wheels American Thunder Trackside Treasury Autographs Printing Plates Magenta /1 #MW
2008 Wheels American Thunder Trackside Treasury Autographs Printing Plates Yellow /1 #MW
2008 Wheels American Thunder Triple Hat /125 #TH26
2008 Wheels Autographs #35
2008 Wheels Autographs Press Plates Black /1 #35
2008 Wheels Autographs Press Plates Cyan /1 #35
2008 Wheels Autographs Press Plates Magenta /1 #35
2008 Wheels Autographs Press Plates Yellow /1 #35
2008 Wheels High Gear #27
2008 Wheels High Gear Driven #DR16
2008 Wheels High Gear Final Standings /44 #F27
2008 Wheels High Gear MPH /100 #M27
2008 Wheels High Gear Previews /5 #EB27
2009 Element #35
2009 Element Previews /5 #35
2009 Element Radioactive /100 #35
2009 Press Pass #155
2009 Press Pass #178
2009 Press Pass Autographs Gold #55
2009 Press Pass Autographs Printing Plates Black /1 #44
2009 Press Pass Autographs Printing Plates Cyan /1 #44
2009 Press Pass Autographs Printing Plates Magenta /1 #44
2009 Press Pass Autographs Printing Plates Yellow /1 #44
2009 Press Pass Autographs Silver #49
2009 Press Pass Blue #155
2009 Press Pass Blue #178
2009 Press Pass Eclipse #23
2009 Press Pass Eclipse Black and White #23
2009 Press Pass Eclipse Blue #23
2009 Press Pass Eclipse Solar Swatches /299 #SSMW1
2009 Press Pass Eclipse Solar Swatches /250 #SSMW2
2009 Press Pass Eclipse Solar Swatches /299 #SSMW3
2009 Press Pass Eclipse Solar Swatches /99 #SSMW4
2009 Press Pass Eclipse Solar Swatches /299 #SSMW5
2009 Press Pass Eclipse Solar Swatches /50 #SSMW6
2009 Press Pass Eclipse Solar Swatches /299 #SSMW7
2009 Press Pass Eclipse Under Cover Autographs /55 #UCSMW
2009 Press Pass Four Wide Firesuit /50 #FWMW
2009 Press Pass Four Wide Tire /25 #FWMW
2009 Press Pass Gold #155
2009 Press Pass Gold #178
2009 Press Pass Gold Holofoil /100 #155
2009 Press Pass Gold Holofoil /100 #178
2009 Press Pass Legends #65
2009 Press Pass Legends Family Autographs /25 #8
2009 Press Pass Legends Family Portraits /550 #FP25
2009 Press Pass Legends Family Portraits Holofoil /99 #FP25
2009 Press Pass Legends Family Relics Bronze /99 #FRWa
2009 Press Pass Legends Family Relics Bronze /75 #FRWa2
2009 Press Pass Legends Family Relics Gold /25 #FRWa
2009 Press Pass Legends Family Relics Gold /25 #FRWa2
2009 Press Pass Legends Family Relics Silver /50 #FRWa
2009 Press Pass Legends Family Relics Silver /50 #FRWa2
2009 Press Pass Legends Gold /399 #65
2009 Press Pass Legends Holofoil /50 #65
2009 Press Pass Legends Previews /1 #65
2009 Press Pass Legends Printing Plates Black /1 #65
2009 Press Pass Legends Printing Plates Cyan /1 #65
2009 Press Pass Legends Printing Plates Magenta /1 #65
2009 Press Pass Legends Printing Plates Yellow /1 #65
2009 Press Pass Legends Prominent Pieces Bronze /150 #PPMW
2009 Press Pass Legends Prominent Pieces Gold /25 #PPMW
2009 Press Pass Legends Prominent Pieces Silver /50 #PPMW
2009 Press Pass Legends Red /199 #65
2009 Press Pass Legends Solo /1 #65
2009 Press Pass Pieces Race Used Memorabilia #MW
2009 Press Pass Pocket Portraits #P26
2009 Press Pass Pocket Portraits Hometown #P26
2009 Press Pass Pocket Portraits Smoke #P26
2009 Press Pass Pocket Portraits Wal-Mart #PPW12
2009 Press Pass Premium #29
2009 Press Pass Premium Hot Threads /299 #HTMW
2009 Press Pass Premium Hot Threads Autographs /55 #MW
2009 Press Pass Premium Hot Threads Multi-Color /25 #HTMW
2009 Press Pass Premium Hot Threads Patches /10 #HTP-MW
2009 Press Pass Premium Previews /5 #EB29
2009 Press Pass Premium Signatures #38
2009 Press Pass Premium Signatures Gold /25 #36
2009 Press Pass Previews /5 #EB155
2009 Press Pass Red #155
2009 Press Pass Red #178
2009 Press Pass Santa Hats /50 #SH18
2009 Press Pass Showcase Classic Collections Firesuit /25 #CCF10
2009 Press Pass Showcase Classic Collections Firesuit Patch /5 #CCF10
2009 Press Pass Showcase Classic Collections Ink /45 #4
2009 Press Pass Showcase Classic Collections Ink Gold /25 #4
2009 Press Pass Showcase Classic Collections Ink Green /5 #4
2009 Press Pass Showcase Classic Collections Ink Melting /1 #4
2009 Press Pass Showcase Classic Collections Sheet Metal /45 #CCS10
2009 Press Pass Showcase Classic Collections Tire /99 #CCT10
2009 Press Pass Signings Blue /25 #48
2009 Press Pass Signings Gold #48
2009 Press Pass Signings Green /5 #48
2009 Press Pass Signings Orange /65 #48
2009 Press Pass Signings Printing Plates Black /1 #48
2009 Press Pass Signings Printing Plates Yellow /1 #48
2009 Press Pass Signings Purple /15 #48
2009 Press Pass Sponsor Swatches /250 #SSMW
2009 Press Pass Sponsor Swatches Select /7 #SSMW
2009 Press Pass Stealth #36
2009 Press Pass Stealth #72
2009 Press Pass Stealth Chrome #36
2009 Press Pass Stealth Chrome #72
2009 Press Pass Stealth Chrome Brushed Metal /25 #36
2009 Press Pass Stealth Chrome Brushed Metal /25 #72
2009 Press Pass Stealth Chrome Gold /99 #36
2009 Press Pass Stealth Chrome Gold /99 #72
2009 Press Pass Stealth Previews /5 #EB36
2009 VIP #36
2009 VIP #46
2009 VIP #60
2009 VIP Guest List #GG9
2009 VIP Leadfoot /150 #LFMW
2009 VIP Leadfoot Holofoil /10 #LFMW
2009 VIP Previews /5 #36
2009 VIP Purple /25 #36
2009 VIP Purple /25 #46
2009 VIP Purple /25 #60
2009 Wheels Autographs #61
2009 Wheels Autographs Press Plates Black /1 #MW
2009 Wheels Autographs Press Plates Cyan /1 #MW
2009 Wheels Autographs Press Plates Magenta /1 #MW
2009 Wheels Autographs Press Plates Yellow /1 #MW
2009 Wheels Main Event #30
2009 Wheels Main Event Fast Pass Purple /25 #30
2009 Wheels Main Event Foil #30
2009 Wheels Main Event Hat Dance Patch /10 #HDMW
2009 Wheels Main Event Hat Dance Triple /99 #HDMW
2009 Wheels Main Event Marks Clubs #58
2009 Wheels Main Event Marks Diamonds /10 #58
2009 Wheels Main Event Marks Hearts /5 #58
2009 Wheels Main Event Marks Printing Plates Black /1 #52
2009 Wheels Main Event Marks Printing Plates Cyan /1 #52
2009 Wheels Main Event Marks Printing Plates Magenta /1 #52
2009 Wheels Main Event Marks Printing Plates Yellow /1 #52
2009 Wheels Main Event Marks Spades /1 #58
2009 Wheels Main Event Playing Cards Blue #7H
2009 Wheels Main Event Playing Cards Red #7H
2009 Wheels Main Event Previews /5 #30
2009 Wheels Main Event Stop and Go Swatches Pit Banner /125 #SGBMW
2009 Wheels Main Event Stop and Go Swatches Pit Banner Green /10 #SGBMW
2009 Wheels Main Event Stop and Go Swatches Pit Banner Holofoil /75 #SGBMW
2009 Wheels Main Event Stop and Go Swatches Pit Banner Red /25 #SGBMW
2009 Wheels Main Event Stop and Go Swatches Pit Sign /125 #SGSMW
2009 Wheels Main Event Stop and Go Swatches Pit Sign Green /10 #SGSMW
2009 Wheels Main Event Stop and Go Swatches Pit Sign Holofoil /75 #SGSMW
2009 Wheels Main Event Stop and Go Swatches Pit Sign Red /25 #SGSMW
2009 Wheels Main Event Stop and Go Swatches Pit Stackers /120 #SGWMW
2009 Wheels Main Event Stop and Go Swatches Pit Stackers Green /5 #SGWMW
2009 Wheels Main Event Stop and Go Swatches Pit Stackers Holofoil /75 #SGWMW
2009 Wheels Main Event Stop and Go Swatches Pit Stackers Red /25 #SGWMW
2009 Wheels Main Event Wildcard Cuts /2 #WCCMW
2010 Element #31
2010 Element Blue /35 #31
2010 Element Green #31
2010 Element Previews /5 #EB31
2010 Element Purple /25 #31
2010 Element Red Target #31
2010 Press Pass #32
2010 Press Pass Autographs #53
2010 Press Pass Autographs Printing Plates Black /1 #40
2010 Press Pass Autographs Printing Plates Cyan /1 #48
2010 Press Pass Autographs Printing Plates Magenta /1 #47
2010 Press Pass Autographs Printing Plates Yellow /1 #45
2010 Press Pass Blue #32
2010 Press Pass By The Numbers #BN24
2010 Press Pass Eclipse #23
2010 Press Pass Eclipse Blue #23
2010 Press Pass Eclipse Gold #23
2010 Press Pass Eclipse Previews /5 #23
2010 Press Pass Eclipse Purple /25 #23
2010 Press Pass Gold #32
2010 Press Pass Holofoil /100 #32
2010 Press Pass Legends Family Autographs /25 #8
2010 Press Pass Premium #30
2010 Press Pass Premium Allies #A8
2010 Press Pass Premium Purple /25 #30
2010 Press Pass Premium Signatures #PSMW
2010 Press Pass Premium Signatures Red Ink /24 #PSMW
2010 Press Pass Previews /5 #32
2010 Press Pass Purple /25 #32
2010 Press Pass Signings Blue /10 #57
2010 Press Pass Signings Gold /10 #57
2010 Press Pass Signings Red /15 #57
2010 Press Pass Signings Silver /99 #56
2010 Press Pass Stealth #36
2010 Press Pass Stealth Battle Armor Holofoil /25 #BAMW
2010 Press Pass Stealth Battle Armor Silver /225 #BAMW
2010 Press Pass Stealth Black and White #36
2010 Press Pass Stealth Previews /5 #36
2010 Press Pass Stealth Purple /25 #36
2010 Wheels Autographs #52
2010 Wheels Autographs Printing Plates Black /1 #52
2010 Wheels Autographs Printing Plates Cyan /1 #52
2010 Wheels Autographs Printing Plates Magenta /1 #52
2010 Wheels Autographs Printing Plates Yellow /1 #52
2010 Wheels Autographs Target /10 #37
2010 Wheels Main Event #36
2010 Wheels Main Event Blue #36
2010 Wheels Main Event Marks Autographs /19 #59
2010 Wheels Main Event Marks Autographs Black /1 #58
2010 Wheels Main Event Marks Autographs Blue /5 #59
2010 Wheels Main Event Marks Autographs Red /25 #59
2010 Wheels Main Event Purple /25 #36
2010 Wheels Main Event Toe to Toe /10 #TTMTMW
2011 Element #34
2011 Element #84
2011 Element Autographs /10 #57
2011 Element Autographs Blue /5 #57
2011 Element Autographs Gold /5 #55
2011 Element Autographs Printing Plates Black /1 #57
2011 Element Autographs Printing Plates Cyan /1 #57
2011 Element Autographs Printing Plates Magenta /1 #57
2011 Element Autographs Printing Plates Yellow /1 #57
2011 Element Autographs Silver /5 #55
2011 Element Black /35 #34
2011 Element Black /35 #84
2011 Element Flagship Performers Career Starts Green /25 #FPSMW
2011 Element Green #34
2011 Element Green #84
2011 Element High Octane Vehicle #HOV9
2011 Element Previews /5 #EB34
2011 Element Purple /25 #34
2011 Element Purple /25 #84
2011 Element Red #34
2011 Element Red #84
2011 Element Trackside Treasures Holofoil /25 #TTMW
2011 Element Trackside Treasures Silver /85 #TTMW
2011 Press Pass #123
2011 Press Pass #163
2011 Press Pass Autographs Blue /10 #57
2011 Press Pass Autographs Bronze /99 #58
2011 Press Pass Autographs Gold /25 #55
2011 Press Pass Autographs Printing Plates Black /1 #58
2011 Press Pass Autographs Printing Plates Cyan /1 #58
2011 Press Pass Autographs Printing Plates Magenta /1 #58
2011 Press Pass Autographs Printing Plates Yellow /1 #58
2011 Press Pass Autographs Silver /50 #58
2011 Press Pass Blue Holofoil /10 #123
2011 Press Pass Blue Holofoil /10 #163
2011 Press Pass Blue Retail #123
2011 Press Pass Blue Retail #163
2011 Press Pass Eclipse #32
2011 Press Pass Eclipse Blue #32
2011 Press Pass Eclipse Gold /55 #32
2011 Press Pass Eclipse Previews /5 #EB32
2011 Press Pass Eclipse Purple /25 #32
2011 Press Pass FanFare #38
2011 Press Pass FanFare Autographs Blue /5 #79
2011 Press Pass FanFare Autographs Bronze /10 #79
2011 Press Pass FanFare Autographs Gold /5 #79
2011 Press Pass FanFare Autographs Printing Plates Black /1 #79
2011 Press Pass FanFare Autographs Printing Plates Cyan /1 #79
2011 Press Pass FanFare Autographs Printing Plates Magenta /1 #79
2011 Press Pass FanFare Autographs Printing Plates Yellow /1 #79
2011 Press Pass FanFare Autographs Silver /5 #79
2011 Press Pass FanFare Blue Die Cuts #38
2011 Press Pass FanFare Emerald /25 #38
2011 Press Pass FanFare Holofoil Die Cuts #38
2011 Press Pass FanFare Magnificent Materials /199 #MMMW
2011 Press Pass FanFare Magnificent Materials Dual Swatches /50 #MMDMW
2011 Press Pass FanFare Magnificent Materials Dual Swatches Holofoil /10 #MMDMW
2011 Press Pass FanFare Magnificent Materials Holofoil /50 #MMMW
2011 Press Pass FanFare Ruby Die Cuts /15 #38
2011 Press Pass FanFare Sapphire /10 #38
2011 Press Pass FanFare Silver /25 #38
2011 Press Pass Flashback #FB12
2011 Press Pass Geared Up Gold /100 #GUMW
2011 Press Pass Geared Up Holofoil /50 #GUMW
2011 Press Pass Gold /50 #123
2011 Press Pass Gold /50 #163
2011 Press Pass Legends #51
2011 Press Pass Legends Autographs Gold /20 #LGAMW
2011 Press Pass Legends Autographs Printing Plates Black /1 #LGAMW
2011 Press Pass Legends Autographs Printing Plates Cyan /1 #LGAMW
2011 Press Pass Legends Autographs Printing Plates Magenta /1 #LGAMW
2011 Press Pass Legends Autographs Printing Plates Yellow /1 #LGAMW
2011 Press Pass Legends Gold /250 #51
2011 Press Pass Legends Holofoil /25 #51
2011 Press Pass Legends Printing Plates Black /1 #51
2011 Press Pass Legends Printing Plates Cyan /1 #51
2011 Press Pass Legends Printing Plates Magenta /1 #51
2011 Press Pass Legends Printing Plates Yellow /1 #51
2011 Press Pass Legends Purple /25 #51
2011 Press Pass Legends Red /99 #51
2011 Press Pass Legends Solo /1 #51
2011 Press Pass Premium #83
2011 Press Pass Premium Purple /25 #83
2011 Press Pass Premium Signatures /100 #PSMW
2011 Press Pass Showcase Classic Collections Firesuit /45 #CCMMWR
2011 Press Pass Showcase Classic Collections Firesuit Patches /5 #CCMMWR
2011 Press Pass Showcase Classic Collections Ink /25 #CCMMWR
2011 Press Pass Showcase Classic Collections Ink Gold /5 #CCMMWR
2011 Press Pass Showcase Classic Collections Ink Melting /1 #CCMMWR
2011 Press Pass Showcase Classic Collections Sheet Metal /99 #CCMMWR
2011 Press Pass Signings Black and White /5 #PPSMW
2011 Press Pass Signings Brushed Metal /30 #PPSMW
2011 Press Pass Signings Holofoil /10 #PPSMW
2011 Press Pass Signings Printing Plates Black /1 #PPSMW
2011 Press Pass Signings Printing Plates Cyan /1 #PPSMW
2011 Press Pass Signings Printing Plates Magenta /1 #PPSMW
2011 Press Pass Signings Printing Plates Yellow /1 #PPSMW
2011 Press Pass Winning Tickets #WT58
2011 Wheels Main Event #36
2011 Wheels Main Event Black and White #36
2011 Wheels Main Event Blue /75 #36
2011 Wheels Main Event Green /1 #36
2011 Wheels Main Event Marks Autographs Blue /5 #MEMW
2011 Wheels Main Event Marks Autographs Gold /10 #MEMW
2011 Wheels Main Event Marks Autographs Silver /15 #MEMW
2011 Wheels Main Event Materials Holofoil /25 #MEMMW
2011 Wheels Main Event Materials Silver /99 #MEMMW
2011 Wheels Main Event Red /20 #36
2012 Press Pass #36
2012 Press Pass Blue #36
2012 Press Pass Blue Holofoil /35 #36
2012 Press Pass Fanfare #42
2012 Press Pass Fanfare Autographs Blue /1 #MW
2012 Press Pass Fanfare Autographs Gold /10 #MW
2012 Press Pass Fanfare Autographs Red /5 #MW
2012 Press Pass Fanfare Autographs Silver /15 #MW
2012 Press Pass Fanfare Blue Foil Die Cuts #42
2012 Press Pass Fanfare Diamond /5 #42
2012 Press Pass Fanfare Holofoil Die Cuts #42
2012 Press Pass Fanfare Magnificent Materials /299 #MMMW

2012 Press Pass Fanfare Magnificent Materials Dual Swatches /50 #MMMW
2012 Press Pass Fanfare Magnificent Materials Dual Swatches Melting /10 #MMMW
2012 Press Pass Fanfare Magnificent Materials Gold /125 #MMMW
2012 Press Pass Fanfare Sapphire /20 #42
2012 Press Pass Fanfare Silver /25 #42
2012 Press Pass Gold #36
2012 Press Pass Ignite #35
2012 Press Pass Ignite Materials Autographs Red /5 #IMMW
2012 Press Pass Ignite Materials Autographs Silver /20 #IMMW
2012 Press Pass Ignite Materials Gun Metal /99 #IMMW
2012 Press Pass Ignite Materials Red /10 #IMMW
2012 Press Pass Ignite Materials Silver #IMMW
2012 Press Pass Ignite Proofs Black and White /50 #35
2012 Press Pass Ignite Proofs Cyan #35
2012 Press Pass Ignite Proofs Magenta #35
2012 Press Pass Ignite Proofs Yellow /10 #35
2012 Press Pass Power Picks Blue /50 #51
2012 Press Pass Power Picks Gold /50 #51
2012 Press Pass Power Picks Holofoil /10 #51
2012 Press Pass Purple /35 #36
2012 Press Pass Redline #37
2012 Press Pass Redline Black /99 #37
2012 Press Pass Redline Cyan /50 #37
2012 Press Pass Redline Magenta /15 #37
2012 Press Pass Redline Signatures Blue /5 #RSMW
2012 Press Pass Redline Signatures Gold /25 #RSMW
2012 Press Pass Redline Signatures Holofoil /10 #RSMW
2012 Press Pass Redline Signatures Melting /1 #RSMW
2012 Press Pass Redline Signatures Red /50 #RSMW
2012 Press Pass Redline Yellow /1 #37
2012 Press Pass Showcase /499 #60
2012 Press Pass Showcase Classic Collections Ink /10 #CCMMWR
2012 Press Pass Showcase Classic Collections Ink Gold /5 #CCMMWR
2012 Press Pass Showcase Classic Collections Ink Melting /1 #CCMMWR
2012 Press Pass Showcase Classic Collections Memorabilia /99 #CCMMWR
2012 Press Pass Showcase Classic Collections Memorabilia Gold /50 #CCMMWR
2012 Press Pass Showcase Classic Collections Memorabilia Melting /5 #CCMMWR
2012 Press Pass Showcase Gold /125 #60
2012 Press Pass Showcase Green /5 #60
2012 Press Pass Showcase Melting /1 #60
2012 Press Pass Showcase Purple /1 #60
2012 Press Pass Showcase Red /25 #60
2012 Press Pass Showcase Richard Petty 75th Birthday Tribute /10 #RPMW
2012 Press Pass Showcase Richard Petty 75th Birthday Tribute Melting /1 #RPMW
2012 Press Pass Snapshots #SS37
2012 Sportkings Spectacular Patch /1 #SP4
2012 Total Memorabilia #32
2012 Total Memorabilia Black and White /99 #32
2012 Total Memorabilia Gold /275 #32
2012 Total Memorabilia Memory Lane #ML8
2012 Total Memorabilia Red Retail /250 #32
2013 Press Pass #43
2013 Press Pass Color Proofs Black #43
2013 Press Pass Color Proofs Cyan /35 #43
2013 Press Pass Color Proofs Magenta #43
2013 Press Pass Color Proofs Yellow /5 #43
2013 Press Pass Fanfare #59
2013 Press Pass Fanfare Autographs Blue /1 #MW
2013 Press Pass Fanfare Autographs Gold /10 #MW
2013 Press Pass Fanfare Autographs Green /2 #MW
2013 Press Pass Fanfare Autographs Red /5 #MW
2013 Press Pass Fanfare Autographs Silver /10 #MW
2013 Press Pass Fanfare Diamond Die Cuts /5 #59
2013 Press Pass Fanfare Green /3 #59
2013 Press Pass Fanfare Holofoil Die Cuts #59
2013 Press Pass Fanfare Magnificent Materials Dual Swatches /50 #MW
2013 Press Pass Fanfare Magnificent Materials Dual Swatches Melting /10 #MW
2013 Press Pass Fanfare Magnificent Materials Gold /50 #MW
2013 Press Pass Fanfare Magnificent Materials Jumbo Swatches /25 #MW
2013 Press Pass Fanfare Magnificent Materials Silver /199 #MW
2013 Press Pass Fanfare Red Foil Die Cuts #59
2013 Press Pass Fanfare Sapphire /20 #59
2013 Press Pass Fanfare Silver /25 #59
2013 Press Pass Ignite #38
2013 Press Pass Ignite Hot Threads Blue Holofoil /99 #HTMW
2013 Press Pass Ignite Hot Threads Patch Red /10 #HTMW
2013 Press Pass Ignite Hot Threads Silver #HTMW
2013 Press Pass Ignite Ink Black /20 #IIMW
2013 Press Pass Ignite Ink Blue /5 #IIMW
2013 Press Pass Ignite Ink Red /1 #IIMW
2013 Press Pass Ignite Proofs Black and White /50 #38
2013 Press Pass Ignite Proofs Cyan #38
2013 Press Pass Ignite Proofs Magenta #38
2013 Press Pass Ignite Proofs Yellow /5 #38
2013 Press Pass Redline #46
2013 Press Pass Redline Black /99 #46
2013 Press Pass Redline Cyan /50 #46
2013 Press Pass Redline Magenta /15 #46
2013 Press Pass Redline Signatures Blue /55 #RSMW
2013 Press Pass Redline Signatures Gold /5 #RSMW
2013 Press Pass Redline Signatures Holo /10 #RSMW
2013 Press Pass Redline Signatures Melting /1 #RSMW
2013 Press Pass Redline Signatures Red /70 #RSMW
2013 Press Pass Redline Yellow /1 #46
2013 Press Pass Showcase /349 #60
2013 Press Pass Showcase Black /1 #60
2013 Press Pass Showcase Classic Collections Ink Gold /5 #CCIMWR
2013 Press Pass Showcase Classic Collections Ink Melting /1 #CCIMWR
2013 Press Pass Showcase Classic Collections Ink Red /1 #CCIMWR
2013 Press Pass Showcase Classic Collections Memorabilia Gold /25 #CCMMWR
2013 Press Pass Showcase Classic Collections Memorabilia Melting /5 #CCMMWR
2013 Press Pass Showcase Classic Collections Memorabilia Silver /75 #CCMMWR
2013 Press Pass Showcase Gold /99 #60
2013 Press Pass Showcase Green /20 #60
2013 Press Pass Showcase Prized Pieces /99 #PPMMW
2013 Press Pass Showcase Prized Pieces Blue /20 #PPMMW
2013 Press Pass Showcase Prized Pieces Gold /25 #PPMMW
2013 Press Pass Showcase Prized Pieces Melting /5 #PPMMW
2013 Press Pass Showcase Purple /13 #60
2013 Press Pass Showcase Red /10 #60
2013 Press Pass Signings Blue /1 #MW
2013 Press Pass Signings Gold /5 #MW
2013 Press Pass Signings Holofoil /5 #MW
2013 Press Pass Signings Printing Plates Black /1 #MW
2013 Press Pass Signings Printing Plates Cyan /1 #MW
2013 Press Pass Signings Printing Plates Magenta /1 #MW
2013 Press Pass Signings Printing Plates Yellow /1 #MW
2013 Press Pass Signings Silver /5 #MW
2013 Sportkings National Convention Spectacular Patch /1 #SKFR38
2013 Total Memorabilia #36
2013 Total Memorabilia Black and White /99 #36
2013 Total Memorabilia Dual Swatch Gold /199 #TMMW
2013 Total Memorabilia Gold /275 #36
2013 Total Memorabilia Quad Swatch Melting /10 #TMMW
2013 Total Memorabilia Red #36
2013 Total Memorabilia Single Swatch Silver /475 #TMMW
2013 Total Memorabilia Triple Swatch Holofoil /99 #TMMW
2014 Press Pass #92
2014 Press Pass American Thunder #37
2014 Press Pass American Thunder #52
2014 Press Pass American Thunder Autographs Blue /10 #ATAMW
2014 Press Pass American Thunder Autographs Red /5 #ATAMW
2014 Press Pass American Thunder Autographs White /25 #ATAMW
2014 Press Pass American Thunder Black and White /50 #37
2014 Press Pass American Thunder Black and White /50 #52
2014 Press Pass American Thunder Brothers In Arms Autographs Blue /5 #BAMWR
2014 Press Pass American Thunder Brothers In Arms Autographs Red /1 #BAMWR
2014 Press Pass American Thunder Brothers In Arms Autographs White /10 #BAMWR
2014 Press Pass American Thunder Brothers In Arms Relics Blue /25 #BAMWR
2014 Press Pass American Thunder Brothers In Arms Relics Red /5 #BAMWR
2014 Press Pass American Thunder Brothers In Arms Relics Silver /50 #BAMWR
2014 Press Pass American Thunder Class A Uniforms Blue /99 #CAUMW
2014 Press Pass American Thunder Class A Uniforms Red /10 #CAUMW
2014 Press Pass American Thunder Class A Uniforms Silver #CAUMW
2014 Press Pass American Thunder Cyan #37
2014 Press Pass American Thunder Cyan #52
2014 Press Pass American Thunder Magenta #37
2014 Press Pass American Thunder Magenta #52
2014 Press Pass American Thunder Yellow /5 #37
2014 Press Pass American Thunder Yellow /5 #52
2014 Press Pass Color Proofs Black /70 #92
2014 Press Pass Color Proofs Cyan /35 #92
2014 Press Pass Color Proofs Magenta #92
2014 Press Pass Color Proofs Yellow /5 #92
2014 Press Pass Five Star Classic Compilations Autographed Patch Booklet /1 #CCMW1
2014 Press Pass Five Star Classic Compilations Autographed Patch Booklet /1 #CCMW2
2014 Press Pass Five Star Classic Compilations Autographed Patch Booklet /1 #CCMW3
2014 Press Pass Five Star Classic Compilations Autographed Patch Booklet /1 #CCMW4
2014 Press Pass Five Star Classic Compilations Autographed Patch Booklet /1 #CCMW5
2014 Press Pass Five Star Classic Compilations Autographed Patch Booklet /1 #CCMW6
2014 Press Pass Five Star Classic Compilations Autographed Patch Booklet /1 #CCMW7
2014 Press Pass Five Star Classic Compilations Autographed Patch Booklet /1 #CCMW8
2014 Press Pass Five Star Classic Compilations Autographed Patch Booklet /1 #CCMW9
2014 Press Pass Five Star Classic Compilations Autographed Patch Booklet /1 #CCMW10
2014 Press Pass Five Star Classic Compilations Autographed Patch Booklet /1 #CCMW11
2014 Press Pass Gold #92
2014 Press Pass Redline #53
2014 Press Pass Redline Black /75 #53
2014 Press Pass Redline Blue Foil #53
2014 Press Pass Redline Cyan /50 #53
2014 Press Pass Redline Green National Convention /5 #53
2014 Press Pass Redline Magenta /10 #53
2014 Press Pass Redline Relics Blue /25 #RRMW
2014 Press Pass Redline Relics Gold /50 #RRMW
2014 Press Pass Redline Relics Melting /1 #RRMW
2014 Press Pass Redline Relics Red /75 #RRMW
2014 Press Pass Redline Signatures Blue /15 #RSMW
2014 Press Pass Redline Signatures Gold /25 #RSMW
2014 Press Pass Redline Signatures Melting /5 #RSMW
2014 Press Pass Redline Signatures Red /50 #RSMW
2014 Press Pass Redline Yellow /1 #53
2014 Press Pass Signings Gold /5 #PPSMW
2014 Press Pass Signings Holofoil /1 #PPSMW
2014 Press Pass Signings Melting /1 #PPSMW
2014 Press Pass Signings Printing Plates Black /1 #PPSMW
2014 Press Pass Signings Printing Plates Cyan /1 #PPSMW
2014 Press Pass Signings Printing Plates Magenta /1 #PPSMW
2014 Press Pass Signings Printing Plates Yellow /1 #PPSMW
2014 Press Pass Signings Silver /10 #PPSMW
2014 Total Memorabilia #29
2014 Total Memorabilia Black and White /99 #29
2014 Total Memorabilia Dual Swatch Gold /150 #TMMW
2014 Total Memorabilia Gold /175 #29
2014 Total Memorabilia Quad Swatch Melting /25 #TMMW
2014 Total Memorabilia Red #29
2014 Total Memorabilia Single Swatch Silver /275 #TMMW
2014 Total Memorabilia Triple Swatch Blue /99 #TMMW
2015 Press Pass #36
2015 Press Pass Cup Chase #36
2015 Press Pass Cup Chase Blue /25 #36
2015 Press Pass Cup Chase Gold /75 #36
2015 Press Pass Cup Chase Green /10 #36
2015 Press Pass Cup Chase Melting /1 #36
2015 Press Pass Purple #36
2015 Press Pass Red #36
2015 Press Pass Signings Blue /15 #PPSMW
2015 Press Pass Signings Gold #PPSMW
2015 Press Pass Signings Green /5 #PPSMW
2015 Press Pass Signings Melting /1 #PPSMW
2015 Press Pass Signings Red /10 #PPSMW
2016 Certified Famed Rides /199 #18
2016 Certified Famed Rides Mirror Black /1 #18
2016 Certified Famed Rides Mirror Blue /50 #18
2016 Certified Famed Rides Mirror Gold /25 #18
2016 Certified Famed Rides Mirror Green /5 #18
2016 Certified Famed Rides Mirror Orange /99 #18
2016 Certified Famed Rides Mirror Purple /10 #18
2016 Certified Famed Rides Mirror Red /75 #18
2016 Certified Famed Rides Mirror Silver /99 #18
2016 Certified Legends /199 #20
2016 Certified Legends Mirror Black /1 #20
2016 Certified Legends Mirror Blue /50 #20
2016 Certified Legends Mirror Gold /25 #20
2016 Certified Legends Mirror Green /5 #20
2016 Certified Legends Mirror Orange /99 #20
2016 Certified Legends Mirror Purple /10 #20
2016 Certified Legends Mirror Red /75 #20
2016 Certified Legends Mirror Silver /99 #20
2016 Panini National Treasures Six Signatures /25 #5
2016 Panini National Treasures Six Signatures Black /10 #5
2016 Panini National Treasures Six Signatures Blue /1 #5
2016 Panini National Treasures Six Signatures Gold /15 #5
2017 Donruss #140
2017 Donruss Artist Proof /25 #140
2017 Donruss Blue Foil /299 #140
2017 Donruss Classics #13
2017 Donruss Classics Cracked Ice /999 #13
2017 Donruss Gold Foil /499 #140
2017 Donruss Gold Press Proof /99 #140
2017 Donruss Green Foil /199 #140
2017 Donruss Press Proof /49 #140
2017 Donruss Printing Plates Black /1 #140
2017 Donruss Printing Plates Cyan /1 #140
2017 Donruss Printing Plates Magenta /1 #140
2017 Donruss Printing Plates Yellow /1 #140
2017 Donruss Retro Signatures 1984 #18
2017 Donruss Retro Signatures 1984 Holo Black /1 #18
2017 Donruss Retro Signatures 1984 Holo Gold /25 #18
2017 Panini National Treasures /25 #28
2017 Panini National Treasures Century Black /1 #28
2017 Panini National Treasures Century Gold /15 #28
2017 Panini National Treasures Century Green /5 #28
2017 Panini National Treasures Century Holo Gold /10 #28
2017 Panini National Treasures Century Holo Silver /20 #28
2017 Panini National Treasures Dual Signature Materials /25 #8
2017 Panini National Treasures Dual Signature Materials Black /1 #8
2017 Panini National Treasures Dual Signature Materials Gold /15 #8
2017 Panini National Treasures Dual Signature Materials Green /5 #8
2017 Panini National Treasures Dual Signature Materials Holo Gold /10 #8
2017 Panini National Treasures Dual Signature Materials Holo Silver /20 #8
2017 Panini National Treasures Dual Signature Materials Laundry Tag /1 #8
2017 Panini National Treasures Legendary Material Signatures Black /1 #9
2017 Panini National Treasures Legendary Material Signatures Gold /15 #9
2017 Panini National Treasures Legendary Material Signatures Green /5 #9
2017 Panini National Treasures Legendary Material Signatures Holo Gold /10 #9
2017 Panini National Treasures Legendary Material Signatures Holo Silver /19 #9
2017 Panini National Treasures Legendary Material Signatures Printing Plates Black /1 #9
2017 Panini National Treasures Legendary Material Signatures Printing Plates Cyan /1 #9
2017 Panini National Treasures Legendary Material Signatures Printing Plates Yellow /1 #9
2017 Panini National Treasures Legendary Signatures /30 #8
2017 Panini National Treasures Legendary Signatures Black /1 #8
2017 Panini National Treasures Legendary Signatures Gold /15 #8
2017 Panini National Treasures Legendary Signatures Green /5 #8
2017 Panini National Treasures Legendary Signatures Holo Gold /10 #8
2017 Panini National Treasures Legendary Signatures Holo Silver /25 #8
2017 Panini National Treasures Legendary Signatures Printing Plates Black /1 #8
2017 Panini National Treasures Legendary Signatures Printing Plates Cyan /1 #8
2017 Panini National Treasures Legendary Signatures Printing Plates Magenta /1 #8
2017 Panini National Treasures Legendary Signatures Printing Plates Yellow /1 #8
2017 Panini National Treasures Magnificent Marks /25 #4
2017 Panini National Treasures Magnificent Marks Black /1 #4
2017 Panini National Treasures Magnificent Marks Gold /15 #4
2017 Panini National Treasures Magnificent Marks Green /5 #4
2017 Panini National Treasures Magnificent Marks Holo Gold /10 #4
2017 Panini National Treasures Magnificent Marks Holo Silver /20 #4
2017 Panini National Treasures Magnificent Marks Printing Plates Black /1 #4
2017 Panini National Treasures Magnificent Marks Printing Plates Cyan /1 #4
2017 Panini National Treasures Magnificent Marks Printing Plates Magenta /1 #4
2017 Panini National Treasures Magnificent Marks Printing Plates Yellow /1 #4
2017 Panini National Treasures Printing Plates Black /1 #28
2017 Panini National Treasures Printing Plates Cyan /1 #28
2017 Panini National Treasures Printing Plates Magenta /1 #28
2017 Panini National Treasures Printing Plates Yellow /1 #28
2017 Panini Torque Clear Vision #19
2017 Panini Torque Clear Vision Blue /99 #19
2017 Panini Torque Clear Vision Gold /149 #19
2017 Panini Torque Clear Vision Green /25 #19
2017 Panini Torque Clear Vision Purple /10 #19
2017 Panini Torque Clear Vision Red /49 #19
2017 Panini Torque Driver Scripts #22
2017 Panini Torque Driver Scripts Blue /50 #22
2017 Panini Torque Driver Scripts Checkerboard /10 #22
2017 Panini Torque Driver Scripts Green /25 #22
2017 Panini Torque Driver Scripts Red /35 #22
2017 Panini Torque Visions of Greatness #13
2017 Panini Torque Visions of Greatness Blue /99 #13
2017 Panini Torque Visions of Greatness Gold /149 #13
2017 Panini Torque Visions of Greatness Green /25 #13
2017 Panini Torque Visions of Greatness Purple /10 #13
2017 Panini Torque Visions of Greatness Red /49 #13
2017 Select Signatures #33
2017 Select Signatures Prizms Blue /99 #33
2017 Select Signatures Prizms Checkered Flag /1 #33
2017 Select Signatures Prizms Gold /10 #33
2017 Select Signatures Prizms Red /50 #33
2018 Donruss #117
2018 Donruss #173
2018 Donruss Artist Proofs /25 #117
2018 Donruss Artist Proofs /25 #173
2018 Donruss Classics #17
2018 Donruss Classics Cracked Ice /999 #17
2018 Donruss Classics Xplosion /99 #17
2018 Donruss Gold Foil /499 #117
2018 Donruss Gold Foil /499 #173
2018 Donruss Gold Press Proofs /99 #117
2018 Donruss Gold Press Proofs /99 #173
2018 Donruss Green Foil /199 #117
2018 Donruss Green Foil /199 #173
2018 Donruss Press Proofs /49 #117
2018 Donruss Press Proofs /49 #173
2018 Donruss Printing Plates Black /1 #117
2018 Donruss Printing Plates Black /1 #173
2018 Donruss Printing Plates Cyan /1 #117
2018 Donruss Printing Plates Cyan /1 #173
2018 Donruss Printing Plates Magenta /1 #117
2018 Donruss Printing Plates Magenta /1 #173
2018 Donruss Printing Plates Yellow /1 #117
2018 Donruss Printing Plates Yellow /1 #173
2018 Donruss Red Foil /299 #117
2018 Donruss Red Foil /299 #173
2018 Donruss Significant Signatures #15
2018 Donruss Significant Signatures Black /1 #15
2018 Donruss Significant Signatures Holo Gold /25 #15
2018 Panini Prime Driver Signatures /99 #14
2018 Panini Prime Driver Signatures Black /1 #14
2018 Panini Prime Driver Signatures Holo Gold /50 #14
2018 Panini Prime Dual Signatures /10 #1
2018 Panini Prime Dual Signatures Black /1 #1
2018 Panini Prime Dual Signatures Holo Gold /5 #1
2018 Panini Prime Prime Signatures /99 #14
2018 Panini Prime Prime Signatures Black /1 #14
2018 Panini Prime Prime Signatures Holo Gold /50 #14
2018 Panini Victory Lane #74
2018 Panini Victory Lane Black /1 #74
2018 Panini Victory Lane Blue /25 #74
2018 Panini Victory Lane Gold /99 #74
2018 Panini Victory Lane Green /5 #74
2018 Panini Victory Lane Octane Autographs /99 #29
2018 Panini Victory Lane Octane Autographs Black /1 #29
2018 Panini Victory Lane Octane Autographs Gold /25 #29
2018 Panini Victory Lane Pedal to the Metal #96
2018 Panini Victory Lane Pedal to the Metal Black /1 #96
2018 Panini Victory Lane Pedal to the Metal Blue /25 #96
2018 Panini Victory Lane Pedal to the Metal Green /5 #96
2018 Panini Victory Lane Printing Plates Black /1 #74
2018 Panini Victory Lane Printing Plates Cyan /1 #74
2018 Panini Victory Lane Printing Plates Magenta /1 #74
2018 Panini Victory Lane Printing Plates Yellow /1 #74
2018 Panini Victory Lane Red /49 #74
2018 Panini Victory Lane Silver #74
2019 Donruss #23
2019 Donruss Artist Proofs /25 #23
2019 Donruss Black /199 #23
2019 Donruss Gold /299 #23
2019 Donruss Gold Press Proofs /99 #23
2019 Donruss Press Proofs /49 #23
2019 Donruss Printing Plates Black /1 #23
2019 Donruss Printing Plates Cyan /1 #23
2019 Donruss Printing Plates Magenta /1 #23
2019 Donruss Printing Plates Yellow /1 #23
2019 Donruss Signature Series #27
2019 Donruss Signature Series Holo Black /10 #27
2019 Donruss Signature Series Holo Gold /25 #27
2019 Donruss Signature Series Red /149 #27
2019 Donruss Silver #23
2019 Panini Prime /50 #99
2019 Panini Prime Black /10 #99
2019 Panini Prime Emerald /5 #99
2019 Panini Prime Platinum Blue /1 #99
2019 Panini Prime Prime Names Die Cut Signatures /99 #10
2019 Panini Prime Prime Names Die Cut Signatures Black /10 #10
2019 Panini Prime Prime Names Die Cut Signatures Holo Gold /25 #10
2019 Panini Prime Prime Names Die Cut Signatures Platinum Blue /1 #10
2019 Panini Prime Shadowbox Signatures /99 #13
2019 Panini Prime Shadowbox Signatures Black /10 #13
2019 Panini Prime Shadowbox Signatures Holo Gold /25 #13
2019 Panini Prime Shadowbox Signatures Platinum Blue /1 #13
2019 Panini Prizm Endorsements Prizms #15
2019 Panini Prizm Endorsements Prizms Black /1 #15
2019 Panini Prizm Endorsements Prizms Blue /75 #15
2019 Panini Prizm Endorsements Prizms Camo #15
2019 Panini Prizm Endorsements Prizms Gold /10 #15
2019 Panini Prizm Endorsements Prizms Green /99 #15
2019 Panini Prizm Endorsements Prizms Rainbow /24 #15
2019 Panini Prizm Endorsements Prizms Red /50 #15
2019 Panini Prizm Endorsements Prizms Red White and Blue #15
2019 Panini Prizm Endorsements Prizms White /5 #15
2019 Panini Prizm Scripted Signatures Prizms #12
2019 Panini Prizm Scripted Signatures Prizms Black /1 #12
2019 Panini Prizm Scripted Signatures Prizms Blue /75 #12
2019 Panini Prizm Scripted Signatures Prizms Camo #12
2019 Panini Prizm Scripted Signatures Prizms Gold /10 #12
2019 Panini Prizm Scripted Signatures Prizms Green /99 #12
2019 Panini Prizm Scripted Signatures Prizms Rainbow /24 #12
2019 Panini Prizm Scripted Signatures Prizms Red /50 #12
2019 Panini Prizm Scripted Signatures Prizms Red White and Blue #12
2019 Panini Prizm Scripted Signatures Prizms White /5 #12
2020 Donruss #95
2020 Donruss #128
2020 Donruss Black Numbers /55 #95
2020 Donruss Black Numbers /55 #128
2020 Donruss Black Trophy Club /1 #95
2020 Donruss Black Trophy Club /1 #128
2020 Donruss Blue /199 #95
2020 Donruss Blue /199 #128
2020 Donruss Carolina Blue #95
2020 Donruss Carolina Blue #128
2020 Donruss Green /99 #95
2020 Donruss Green /99 #128
2020 Donruss Orange #95
2020 Donruss Orange #128
2020 Donruss Pink /25 #95
2020 Donruss Pink /25 #128
2020 Donruss Printing Plates Black /1 #95
2020 Donruss Printing Plates Black /1 #128
2020 Donruss Printing Plates Cyan /1 #95
2020 Donruss Printing Plates Cyan /1 #128
2020 Donruss Printing Plates Magenta /1 #95
2020 Donruss Printing Plates Magenta /1 #128
2020 Donruss Printing Plates Yellow /1 #128
2020 Donruss Printing Plates Yellow /1 #95
2020 Donruss Purple /49 #95
2020 Donruss Purple /49 #128
2020 Donruss Red /299 #95
2020 Donruss Red /299 #128
2020 Donruss Retro Relics '87 Holo Black /1 #9
2020 Donruss Retro Relics '87 Holo Gold /4 #9
2020 Donruss Silver #95
2020 Donruss Silver #128
2020 Donruss Timeless Treasures Signatures Holo Black /1 #7
2020 Donruss Timeless Treasures Signatures Holo Gold /15 #7
2020 Donruss Timeless Treasures Signatures Red /55 #7

Cole Whitt

2011 Element #98
2011 Element Black /35 #98
2011 Element Green #98
2011 Element Purple /25 #98
2011 Element Red #98
2011 Elements Undiscovered Elements Autographs /225 #5
2011 Elements Undiscovered Elements Autographs Red Ink /25 #5
2011 Press Pass FanFare #74
2011 Press Pass FanFare Autographs Blue /5 #80
2011 Press Pass FanFare Autographs Bronze /250 #80
2011 Press Pass FanFare Autographs Gold /150 #80
2011 Press Pass FanFare Autographs Printing Plates Black /1 #80
2011 Press Pass FanFare Autographs Printing Plates Cyan /1 #80
2011 Press Pass FanFare Autographs Printing Plates Magenta /1 #80
2011 Press Pass FanFare Autographs Printing Plates Yellow /1 #80
2011 Press Pass FanFare Autographs Silver /75 #80
2011 Press Pass FanFare Blue Die Cuts #74
2011 Press Pass FanFare Emerald /25 #74
2011 Press Pass FanFare Holofoil Die Cuts #74
2011 Press Pass FanFare Magnificent Materials /145 #MMCW
2011 Press Pass FanFare Magnificent Materials Dual Swatches /50 #MMDCW
2011 Press Pass FanFare Magnificent Materials Dual Swatches Holofoil /10 #MMDCW
2011 Press Pass FanFare Magnificent Materials Holofoil /50 #MMCW
2011 Press Pass FanFare Ruby Die Cuts /15 #74
2011 Press Pass FanFare Sapphire /10 #74
2011 Press Pass FanFare Silver /25 #74
2012 Press Pass Fanfare #61
2012 Press Pass Fanfare Autographs Blue /25 #CW
2012 Press Pass Fanfare Autographs Gold /99 #CW
2012 Press Pass Fanfare Autographs Red /75 #CW
2012 Press Pass Fanfare Autographs Silver /175 #CW
2012 Press Pass Fanfare Blue Foil Die Cuts #61
2012 Press Pass Fanfare Diamond /5 #61
2012 Press Pass Fanfare Holofoil Die Cuts #61
2012 Press Pass Fanfare Magnificent Materials /299 #MMCW
2012 Press Pass Fanfare Magnificent Materials Dual Swatches /50 #MMCW
2012 Press Pass Fanfare Magnificent Materials Dual Swatches Melting /10 #MMCW
2012 Press Pass Fanfare Magnificent Materials Gold /125 #MMCW
2012 Press Pass Fanfare Magnificent Materials Signatures /99 #CW
2012 Press Pass Fanfare Magnificent Materials Signatures Blue /25 #CW
2012 Press Pass Fanfare Sapphire /20 #61
2012 Press Pass Fanfare Silver /25 #61
2012 Press Pass Ignite #49
2012 Press Pass Ignite Proofs Black and White /50 #49
2012 Press Pass Ignite Proofs Cyan #49
2012 Press Pass Ignite Proofs Magenta #49
2012 Press Pass Ignite Proofs Yellow /10 #49
2013 Press Pass #58
2013 Press Pass Color Proofs Black #58
2013 Press Pass Color Proofs Cyan /35 #58
2013 Press Pass Color Proofs Magenta #58
2013 Press Pass Color Proofs Yellow /5 #58
2013 Press Pass Signings Blue /1 #CW
2013 Press Pass Signings Gold /25 #CW
2013 Press Pass Signings Holofoil /10 #CW
2013 Press Pass Signings Printing Plates Black /1 #CW
2013 Press Pass Signings Printing Plates Cyan /1 #CW
2013 Press Pass Signings Printing Plates Magenta /1 #CW
2013 Press Pass Signings Printing Plates Yellow /1 #CW
2013 Press Pass Signings Silver /65 #CW
2013 Total Memorabilia Dual Swatch Gold /199 #TMCW
2013 Total Memorabilia Single Swatch Silver /475 #TMCW
2013 Total Memorabilia Triple Swatch Holofoil /99 #TMCW
2014 Press Pass American Thunder #38
2014 Press Pass American Thunder #60
2014 Press Pass American Thunder Autographs Blue /10 #ATACW
2014 Press Pass American Thunder Autographs Red /5 #ATACW
2014 Press Pass American Thunder Autographs White /25 #ATACW
2014 Press Pass American Thunder Black and White /50 #38
2014 Press Pass American Thunder Black and White /50 #60
2014 Press Pass American Thunder Brothers In Arms Autographs Blue /5 #BASR
2014 Press Pass American Thunder Brothers In Arms Autographs Red /1 #BASR
2014 Press Pass American Thunder Brothers In Arms Autographs White /10 #BASR
2014 Press Pass American Thunder Cyan #38
2014 Press Pass American Thunder Cyan #60
2014 Press Pass American Thunder Magenta #38
2014 Press Pass American Thunder Magenta #60
2014 Press Pass American Thunder Yellow /5 #38
2014 Press Pass American Thunder Yellow /5 #60
2014 Press Pass Redline #54
2014 Press Pass Redline Black /75 #54
2014 Press Pass Redline Blue Foil #54
2014 Press Pass Redline Cyan /50 #54
2014 Press Pass Redline Full Throttle Relics Blue /10 #FTCW
2014 Press Pass Redline Full Throttle Relics Gold /25 #FTCW
2014 Press Pass Redline Full Throttle Relics Melting /1 #FTCW
2014 Press Pass Redline Full Throttle Relics Red /50 #FTCW
2014 Press Pass Redline Green National Convention /5 #54
2014 Press Pass Redline Magenta /10 #54
2014 Press Pass Redline Signatures Blue /25 #RSCW
2014 Press Pass Redline Signatures Gold /50 #RSCW
2014 Press Pass Redline Signatures Melting /10 #RSCW
2014 Press Pass Redline Signatures Red /60 #RSCW
2014 Press Pass Redline Yellow /1 #54
2015 Press Pass #37
2015 Press Pass Cup Chase #37
2015 Press Pass Cup Chase Blue /25 #37
2015 Press Pass Cup Chase Gold /75 #37
2015 Press Pass Cup Chase Green /10 #37
2015 Press Pass Cup Chase Melting /1 #37
2015 Press Pass Purple #37
2015 Press Pass Red #37
2015 Press Pass Signings Blue /99 #PPSCW
2015 Press Pass Signings Gold #PPSCW
2015 Press Pass Signings Green /50 #PPSCW
2015 Press Pass Signings Melting /10 #PPSCW
2015 Press Pass Signings Red /75 #PPSCW
2016 Certified #32
2016 Certified Mirror Black /1 #32
2016 Certified Mirror Blue /50 #32
2016 Certified Mirror Gold /25 #32
2016 Certified Mirror Green /5 #32
2016 Certified Mirror Orange /99 #32
2016 Certified Mirror Purple /10 #32
2016 Certified Mirror Red /75 #32
2016 Certified Mirror Silver /99 #32
2016 Certified Sprint Cup Signature Swatches /199 #3
2016 Certified Sprint Cup Signature Swatches Mirror Black /1 #3
2016 Certified Sprint Cup Signature Swatches Mirror Blue /50 #3
2016 Certified Sprint Cup Signature Swatches Mirror Gold /25 #3
2016 Certified Sprint Cup Signature Swatches Mirror Green /5 #3
2016 Certified Sprint Cup Signature Swatches Mirror Orange /99 #3
2016 Certified Sprint Cup Signature Swatches Mirror Purple /10 #3
2016 Certified Sprint Cup Signature Swatches Mirror Red /75 #3
2016 Certified Sprint Cup Signature Swatches Mirror Silver /99 #3
2016 Panini National Treasures Eight Signatures /15 #2
2016 Panini National Treasures Eight Signatures Black /5 #2
2016 Panini National Treasures Eight Signatures Blue /1 #2
2016 Panini National Treasures Eight Signatures Gold /10 #2
2016 Panini Torque #39
2016 Panini Torque Artist Proof /50 #39
2016 Panini Torque Blackout /1 #39
2016 Panini Torque Blue /125 #39
2016 Panini Torque Clear Vision #26
2016 Panini Torque Clear Vision Blue /99 #26
2016 Panini Torque Clear Vision Gold /149 #26
2016 Panini Torque Clear Vision Green /25 #26
2016 Panini Torque Clear Vision Purple /10 #26
2016 Panini Torque Clear Vision Red /49 #26
2016 Panini Torque Gold #39
2016 Panini Torque Holo Gold /5 #39
2016 Panini Torque Holo Silver /10 #39
2016 Panini Torque Printing Plates Black /1 #39
2016 Panini Torque Printing Plates Cyan /1 #39
2016 Panini Torque Printing Plates Magenta /1 #39
2016 Panini Torque Printing Plates Yellow /1 #39
2016 Panini Torque Purple /25 #39
2016 Panini Torque Red /99 #39
2016 Panini Torque Test Proof Black /1 #39
2016 Panini Torque Test Proof Cyan /1 #39
2016 Panini Torque Test Proof Magenta /1 #39
2016 Panini Torque Test Proof Yellow /1 #39
2017 Donruss Retro Relics 1984 #12
2017 Donruss Retro Relics 1984 Holo Black /10 #12
2017 Donruss Retro Relics 1984 Holo Gold /99 #12
2017 Donruss Signature Series #13
2017 Donruss Signature Series Holo Black /1 #SSCW
2017 Donruss Signature Series Holo Gold /25 #SSCW
2018 Panini Prime Autograph Materials /99 #7
2018 Panini Prime Autograph Materials Black /1 #7
2018 Panini Prime Autograph Materials Holo Gold /50 #7
2018 Panini Prime Autograph Materials Laundry Tag /1 #7
2018 Panini Prime Dual Material Autographs /99 #10
2018 Panini Prime Dual Material Autographs Black /1 #10
2018 Panini Prime Dual Material Autographs Holo Gold /50 #10
2018 Panini Prime Dual Material Autographs Laundry Tag /1 #10
2018 Panini Prime Prime Jumbo Associate Sponsor 1 /1 #21
2018 Panini Prime Prime Jumbo Associate Sponsor 2 /1 #21
2018 Panini Prime Prime Jumbo Associate Sponsor 3 /1 #21
2018 Panini Prime Prime Jumbo Associate Sponsor 4 /1 #21
2018 Panini Prime Prime Jumbo Associate Sponsor 5 /1 #21
2018 Panini Prime Prime Jumbo Car Manufacturer /1 #21
2018 Panini Prime Prime Jumbo Firesuit Manufacturer /1 #21
2018 Panini Prime Prime Jumbo Glove Manufacturer Patch /1 #21
2018 Panini Prime Prime Jumbo Glove Name Patch /1 #21
2018 Panini Prime Prime Jumbo Glove Number Patch /1 #21
2018 Panini Prime Prime Jumbo Nameplate /1 #21
2018 Panini Prime Prime Jumbo NASCAR /1 #21
2018 Panini Prime Prime Jumbo Series Sponsor /1 #21
2018 Panini Prime Prime Jumbo Shoe Brand Logo /1 #21
2018 Panini Prime Prime Jumbo Shoe Name Patch /1 #21
2018 Panini Prime Prime Jumbo Sunoco /1 #21
2018 Panini Prime Quad Material Autographs /99 #14
2018 Panini Prime Quad Material Autographs Black /1 #14
2018 Panini Prime Quad Material Autographs Holo Gold /50 #14
2018 Panini Prime Quad Material Autographs Laundry Tag /1 #14
2018 Panini Prime Race Used Duals Firesuit /50 #11
2018 Panini Prime Race Used Duals Firesuit Black /1 #11
2018 Panini Prime Race Used Duals Firesuit Holo Gold /25 #11
2018 Panini Prime Race Used Duals Firesuit Laundry Tag /1 #11
2018 Panini Prime Race Used Duals Sheet Metal /50 #11
2018 Panini Prime Race Used Duals Sheet Metal Black /1 #11
2018 Panini Prime Race Used Duals Sheet Metal Holo Gold /25 #11
2018 Panini Prime Race Used Quads Firesuit /50 #6
2018 Panini Prime Race Used Quads Firesuit Black /1 #6
2018 Panini Prime Race Used Quads Firesuit Holo Gold /25 #6
2018 Panini Prime Race Used Quads Firesuit Laundry Tag /1 #6
2018 Panini Prime Race Used Quads Sheet Metal /50 #6
2018 Panini Prime Race Used Quads Sheet Metal Black /1 #6
2018 Panini Prime Race Used Quads Sheet Metal Holo Gold /25 #6
2018 Panini Prime Signature Swatches /99 #2
2018 Panini Prime Signature Swatches Black /1 #2
2018 Panini Prime Signature Swatches Holo Gold /34 #2
2018 Panini Prizm Autographs Prizms #32
2018 Panini Prizm Autographs Prizms Black /1 #32
2018 Panini Prizm Autographs Prizms Blue /75 #32
2018 Panini Prizm Autographs Prizms Camo #32
2018 Panini Prizm Autographs Prizms Gold /10 #32
2018 Panini Prizm Autographs Prizms Green /99 #32
2018 Panini Prizm Autographs Prizms Rainbow /24 #32
2018 Panini Prizm Autographs Prizms Red /50 #32
2018 Panini Prizm Autographs Prizms Red White and Blue /199 #32
2018 Panini Prizm Autographs Prizms White /5 #32
2018 Panini Victory Lane #26
2018 Panini Victory Lane Black /1 #26
2018 Panini Victory Lane Blue /25 #26
2018 Panini Victory Lane Engineered to Perfection Materials Black /25 #10
2018 Panini Victory Lane Engineered to Perfection Materials Green /99 #10
2018 Panini Victory Lane Engineered to Perfection Materials Laundry Tag /1 #10
2018 Panini Victory Lane Gold /99 #26
2018 Panini Victory Lane Green /5 #26
2018 Panini Victory Lane Pedal to the Metal #12
2018 Panini Victory Lane Pedal to the Metal Black /1 #12
2018 Panini Victory Lane Pedal to the Metal Blue /25 #12
2018 Panini Victory Lane Pedal to the Metal Green /5 #12
2018 Panini Victory Lane Printing Plates Black /1 #26
2018 Panini Victory Lane Printing Plates Cyan /1 #26
2018 Panini Victory Lane Printing Plates Magenta /1 #26
2018 Panini Victory Lane Printing Plates Yellow /1 #26
2018 Panini Victory Lane Red /49 #26
2018 Panini Victory Lane Signatures /125 #11
2018 Panini Victory Lane Signatures Black /1 #11
2018 Panini Victory Lane Signatures Gold /99 #11
2018 Panini Victory Lane Silver #26
2018 Panini Victory Lane Victory Lane Prime Patches Associate Sponsor 1 /1 #3
2018 Panini Victory Lane Victory Lane Prime Patches Associate Sponsor 10 /1 #3
2018 Panini Victory Lane Victory Lane Prime Patches Associate Sponsor 2 /1 #3
2018 Panini Victory Lane Victory Lane Prime Patches Associate Sponsor 3 /1 #3
2018 Panini Victory Lane Victory Lane Prime Patches Associate Sponsor 4 /1 #3
2018 Panini Victory Lane Victory Lane Prime Patches Associate Sponsor 5 /1 #3
2018 Panini Victory Lane Victory Lane Prime Patches Associate Sponsor 6 /1 #3
2018 Panini Victory Lane Victory Lane Prime Patches Associate Sponsor 7 /1 #3
2018 Panini Victory Lane Victory Lane Prime Patches Associate Sponsor 8 /1 #3
2018 Panini Victory Lane Victory Lane Prime Patches Associate Sponsor 9 /1 #3
2018 Panini Victory Lane Victory Lane Prime Patches Car Manufacturer /1 #3
2018 Panini Victory Lane Victory Lane Prime Patches Firesuit Manufacturer /1 #3
2018 Panini Victory Lane Victory Lane Prime Patches Goodyear /2 #3
2018 Panini Victory Lane Victory Lane Prime Patches Nameplate /1 #3
2018 Panini Victory Lane Victory Lane Prime Patches NASCAR /1 #3
2018 Panini Victory Lane Victory Lane Prime Patches Series Sponsor /1 #3
2018 Panini Victory Lane Victory Lane Prime Patches Sunoco /1 #3
2019 Donruss #78
2019 Donruss #138
2019 Donruss Artist Proofs /25 #78
2019 Donruss Artist Proofs /25 #138
2019 Donruss Black /199 #78
2019 Donruss Black /199 #138
2019 Donruss Gold /299 #78
2019 Donruss Gold /299 #138
2019 Donruss Gold Press Proofs /99 #78
2019 Donruss Gold Press Proofs /99 #138
2019 Donruss Press Proofs /49 #78
2019 Donruss Press Proofs /49 #138
2019 Donruss Printing Plates Black /1 #78
2019 Donruss Printing Plates Black /1 #138
2019 Donruss Printing Plates Cyan /1 #78
2019 Donruss Printing Plates Cyan /1 #138
2019 Donruss Printing Plates Magenta /1 #78
2019 Donruss Printing Plates Magenta /1 #138
2019 Donruss Printing Plates Yellow /1 #78
2019 Donruss Printing Plates Yellow /1 #138
2019 Donruss Race Day Relics #7
2019 Donruss Race Day Relics Holo Black /10 #7
2019 Donruss Race Day Relics Holo Gold /25 #7
2019 Donruss Race Day Relics Red /185 #7
2019 Donruss Silver #78
2019 Donruss Silver #138

Acknowledgments

Those who worked closely with us on this edition and past versions of this book have proven themselves invaluable. We would like to thank the following manufacturers for their contributions to checklist data over the years — Action Performance (Fred & Lisa Wagenhals), Brookfield Collector's Guild and RCCA (Terry Rubritz), Checkered Flag Sports (Butch Hamlet), Ertl Collectibles (Terri Rehkop), GreenLight Toys (Katie Roland & Kevin Davies), Hot Wheels, Peachstate/GMP, Lionel, Motorsports Authentics (Howard Hitchcock, Michael Kirchgessner,Tara Larson), Press Pass (Tom Farrell, Bob Bove and Miles Atkins), Racing Champions (Mary Stevens and Leah Giarritano), SportCoins (Gregg Yetter), Team Caliber (Mike Brown), TRG Motorsports (Adriana Wells). The success of the Beckett Price Guides has always been a result of a team effort and, to that end, we'll always be grateful to the original leader and founder of the company - Dr. Jim Beckett.

It is very difficult to be "accurate" when it comes to secondary market pricing — one can only do one's best. But this job is especially difficult since we're shooting at a moving target. Prices are fluctuating all the time. Having several full-time pricing experts and expert software working together to provide you, our readers, with the most accurate prices possible, is our approach.

In addition, many other people have provided price input, illustrative material, checklist verifications, errata, and/or background information for this year's book and past editions. We should like to individually thank Red Barnes (Baseline Sports), Russ Dickey (GoMotorBids), Mark Dorsey (Hamps Supply), Ed & Lynn Gaffney (North Coast Racing), Dave Gaumer (Dave's Pit Stop Race Cards), David Giffert (Victory Lane Race Cards), Bob Harmon & Dan Talbert (North State Race Cards), Luke Krisher & Anna Schreck (A&L Racing Collectibles), Norm LaBarge, Sandy Larson (Northern Likes Racing), Tim Legee (Die-Cast Deals), Stewart Lehman (Lehman Racing Collectables), Mike Locotosh (North Coast Racing), Johnny Love (Win Racing), Buz McKim (NASCAR Hall of Fame), Dennis Morrison, Mike Otto (Bono's of Plano),Mario Raucci (Lane Automotive), John Russo (Bono's of Plano), Bono Saunders (Bono's Race Place), Richard Schultz (Racing Around), Brian Shepherd (Shepherd's Racing), Bill Spertzel (Cards Etc.), Ron Steffe (Brickel's), Danny West (Golden Legacy), and Kevin & Trish Wheeler (Sports Cards, Etc.).

Every year we actively solicit expert input. We are particularly appreciative of help (however extensive or cursory) provided for this volume. We receive many inquiries, comments and questions regarding material within this book. In fact, each and every one is read and digested. Time constraints, however, prevent us from personally replying. But keep sharing your knowledge. Your letters and input are part of the "big picture" of hobby information we can pass along to readers in our books and magazines. Even though we cannot respond to each letter, you are making significant contributions to the hobby through your interest and comments.

The effort to continually refine and improve this book also involves a growing number of people and types of expertise on our home team. Our company boasts a substantial Sports Data Publishing team, which strengthens our ability to provide comprehensive analysis of the marketplace. Sports Data Publishing capably handled numerous technical details and provided able assistance in the preparation of this edition.

Our lead racing market analyst, Justin Grunert, played a major part in compiling data for this book and his pricing analysis and careful proofreading were key contributions to the accuracy of this annual. He was ably assisted by the rest of the Price Guide Team: Matt Bible, Jeff Camay, Brian Fleischer, Eric Norton, Kristian Redulla, Sam Zimmer, Steve Dalton.

The price gathering and analytical talents of this fine group of hobbyists have helped make our Beckett team stronger, while making this guide and its companion Price Guides more widely recognized as the hobby's most reliable and relied upon sources of pricing information.

The Beckett E-Commerce Department played a critical role in technology. They spent many hours programming, testing, and implementing it to simplify the handling of thousands of prices and images that must be checked and updated.

In the Production Department, Surajpal Singh Bisht was responsible for the layout and Daniel Moscoso for the photos you see throughout the book.